2011

82ND EDITION

INTERNATIONAL MOTION PICTURE ALMANAC

Editor
JAYME KULESZ

Associate Editor
DEE QUIGLEY

Associate Editor & Operations Manager
MICHAEL QUIGLEY

Quigley Publishing Company, A Division of QP Media, Inc.
Publishers of the International Motion Picture Almanac (Annual)
& The International Television & Video Almanac (Annual)
(800) 231-8239 www.quigleypublishing.com

2011 82nd Edition
INTERNATIONAL MOTION PICTURE ALMANAC

ISSN: 0074-7084
ISBN: 978-0-900610-88-2

P.O. Box 740, Groton, MA 01450

PRINTED IN THE UNITED STATES OF AMERICA

 Quigley Publishing Company: Chairman Emeritus, Martin S. Quigley; Publisher, William J. Quigley; Editor, Jayme Kulesz; Associate Editor and Operations Manager, Michael Quigley; Associate Editor, Dee Quigley. Corporate: P.O. Box 740, Groton, MA 01450. TEL: (978) 448-0272. FAX: (978) 448-9325. Editorial & Sales: (800) 231-8239. FAX: (978) 448-9325. email: info@quigleypublishing.com www.quigleypublishing.com.

Table of Contents

DIGITAL

EXHIBITION

PROFESSIONAL ORGANIZATIONS AND GOVERNMENT OFFICES

THE WORLD MARKET

INDEX

MOTION PICTURE YEAR IN REVIEW

BY WILLIAM J. QUIGLEY

THE INDUSTRY

Box office in 2010 looks to exceed 2009's $10.6 billion, although admissions declined slightly, as has been the trend for the last several years. Box office has increased, although admissions declined, because ticket prices have been increasing at a 5% rate due to normal ticket inflation and the premium charged for 3-D films.

2010 was the year when 3D really arrived, although this is the third time it has come around to theatres. It premiered in New York City in 1922 with "Radio-Mania," then became popular in the 1950s with films like "House of Wax." "Avatar," released in 2D and 3D, became the highest grossing film of all time, a commercial and critical phenomenon that was seen as a harbinger of 3D's breakthrough to the mainstream. Then came films like "Clash of the Titans," "Piranha" and "Cats and Dogs." Roger Ebert wrote "Why I Hate 3-D (And You Should Too)" and the public debate about 3D premium pricing, especially for films shot in 2D and then converted to 3D, began. Nevertheless, the Industry is commited to 3D. Nearly 20% of boxoffice revenues in 2010 came from 3D films - up from 11% in 2009 - and the Studios need to replace DVD sales that have declined 25% from 5 years ago. Exhibitors and Distributors like the 3D average of $3.25 extra per ticket. For the time being, Exhibitors have something special to differentiate the theatrical experience from that at home, although that advantage may be short-lived. Huge consumer markets are growing around 3D in the home with over $1 billion having been spent this year by consumers on 3D televisions and DVD players, game makers have announced 3D versions and eyewear manufacturers are selling designer 3D glasses for home viewing. Almost 30 films were released in 3D during 2010 with more slated in 2011. All this has been enabled by the rapid transition to digital screens by Exhibitors this year. By year-end more than 30% of the screens in the U.S. were digital.

2010 also marked the year of the continually shrinking theatrical release window. Disney created waves with the early DVD release of "Alice in Wonderland" but debate raged over other films and dates for video-on-demand and all the other channels of distribution. This debate will continue into the foreseeable future. Studios are looking to maximize their revenues and will inevitable tinker with all release windows to that end, especially given the increasing marketing costs and difficulty in reaching a fragmented audience. Consider todays movie marketers challenge: create a nationally recognized brand in a few weeks that will impact the film's revenues forever with no chance to course-correct when the film does not open well. The only way to do this, especially with a visual product like a film, is with a TV campaign. The problem is that the Networks do not deliver the mass audience that they once did.

While overall TV viewership is at record levels, it also is increasingly fragmented across dozens of channels. Motion picture advertising on network TV actually has increased, from 35 percent of opening-weekend budgets in 2006 to 41 percent last year, in addition to an increase from 26 percent to 28 percent in cable-network spending. These increases have come largely at the expense of spot TV, down from 18 percent to 11 percent, and newspapers, down from 12 percent to 9 percent, according to Nielsen. Another huge issue for marketers about television is the use of DVRs, video-on-demand and sites that stream TV shows like Hulu, which some studies say are used by 62% of the population. Most people that "time shift" watch the shows within three days of the original airtime, but that can mean an incredible waste of marketing dollars on a film's opening weekend. Although the Internet and social media have long been touted as at least a partial solution to this problem, especially given that medium's lower ad rates, massive inventory and ability to target key demographics, television advertising is still the most effective way for a marketer to open and position his film in the marketplace.

THE STUDIOS

The September before last, Disney fired its longtime chairman, Dick Cook and replaced him with Rich Ross, a children's television executive from within Disney. Throughout 2010 Ross has made a series of changes in the personnel, culture and business models of Disney to reflect his views about a changing business model where social media and new delivery, distribution and marketing systems are changing the landscape radically. He started experimenting with unconventional advertising campaigns that raised the ire of producers such as Jerry Bruckeheimer on "Prince of Persia" and went against industry standards for a DVD release on "Alice in Wonderland" that had Exhibitors up in arms. Chuck Viane, President of Distribution for Disney, had two films this year pass the $1 billion mark during the same year for the first time in history: "Alice in Wonderland" and "Toy Story 3." The studio had a 13.3% share of the domestic boxoffice for the year. "Prince of Persia," budgeted at $200 mm, only did $90.8mm. Thanksgiving brought the animated, "Tangled" and "TRON: The Legacy" unwrapped in 3D on December 17th. "Mars Needs Moms" opens in March and Rob Marshall directs "Pirates of the Carribbean: On Stranger Tide" in theatres in May. "Cars 2," another Pixar animated film from director John Lasseter, will start its engines on June 24th. After protracted negotiations, Miramax was sold to Filmyard Holdings, owned by Ron Tutor and his partners, who bought the Miramax library from Disney for slightly more than $600 million. The deal includes the rights to more than 700 film titles at the company built by Harvey and Bob Weinstein and bought by Disney in the early 1990s.

Fox, which has been guided for many years by Bruce Snyder, President of Domestic Distribution, had a 14.8% market share through November. Fox had an extraordinary year in 2010 powered by the unprecedented success of 2009's "Avatar" which grossed over $760 million domestically and $2.78 billion worldwide. The rest of the release schedule for 2010 was just fair including titles such as: "The Lightning Thief," "Date Night," "Wall Street: Money Never Sleeps," and "Knight and Day" all grossing less than $100 million. The sole film that made it over that bar was "The A-Team" which did $110 million. The holidays brought the next film based on the C.S Lewis Narnia series, "The Chronicles of Narnia: The Voyage of the Dawn Treader" and "Gulliver's Travels," with Jack Black. 2011 will bring "X-Men: First Class" and "Caesar: Rise of the Apes" in June. Christmas of 2011 will debut "Alvin and the Chipmunks 3D" and "We Bought a Zoo," directed by Cameron Crowe.

2010 was a tumultuous year for MGM as Spyglass Entertainment's Gary Barber and Roger Birnbaum battled Lionsgate, supported by Carl Ichan, for control of the studio. Barber and Birnbaum were in advanced talks to run MGM with a plan to merge their company's assets into MGM and change the $4 billion creditors debt into equity in the merged entity, with Spyglass retaining about 4.7%. Late in the year, Ichan and Lionsgate came up with their proposal for MGM. Icahn currently owns 33% of Lionsgate and a substantial part of MGM's debt. Ironically, Icahn is backing Lionsgate on the MGM bid, but has been fighting with their management for years and still plans to replace the Lionsgate board at their next annual meeting. In late October MGM creditors voted to accept Spyglass Entertainment's plan to take over leadership of the company and take the company through a prepackaged bankruptcy.

Production and Distribution at MGM have come to a standstill and in the middle of these negotiations, Mary Parent, Chairman and Co-CEO left the company in mid-October. There are a handful of finished films in the pipeline and it looks like the two-part "The Hobbit," a co-production with Warner Bros., will be made, but the latest chapter of this storied but beleaguered studio will be determined in 2011.

Paramount finished 2010 with an impressive 16.9% mar

ket share, number 2 behind Warner Bros. Jim Tharpe, President of Domestic Distribution for Paramount, and his team released a large number of hits during the first six months of the year including: "Shutter Island," "How to Train Your Dragon," "Iron Man 2," "Shrek Forever After" and "Dinner for Schmucks." The only disappointment was M. Night Shyamalan's "The Last Airbender." Fall was sensational with "Jackass 3D," "Paranormal Activity" and "Megamind." Christmas brought Mark Wahlberg in "The Fighter" and Joel and Ethan Coen's re-make of "True Grit." 2011 will bring the animated "Rango" and a re-make of "Footloose." The summer of 2011 will be pretty Marvelous with "Thor" in May, "Captain America: The First Avenger," "Kung Fu Panda" in 3D and "Transformers 3."

Sony Pictures Releasing, headed in 2010 by Jim Amos, President, had another solid performance with a 13.3% market share. Films that performed well included: "The Karate Kid," "Grown Ups," "Salt," "The Other Guys" and Julia Roberts in "Eat Pray Love." Johnny Depp and Ms. Jolie starred in "The Tourist" which opened in December as did "How Do You Know" with Reese Witherspoon and Jack Nicholson. "The Green Hornet" with Seth Rogen buzzes into theatres in January and Adam Sandler and Jennifer Aniston open "Just Go With It" in February. The summer films will be "Zookeeper" and "The Smurfs" in 3D. Martin Scorsese's 3D "Hugo Cagret" will open for Christmas as will "The Girl With the Dragon Tattoo."

Universal had a mediocre year at the boxoffice with a 8.9% share. Adam Fogelson, who recently took over as chairman of Universal Pictures stated "on balance this was a pretty good summer for us, but that doesn't change that we've had a rough run." If there was a surprise hit this summer, it was the animated "Despicable Me," which so far has grossed more than $446 million world-wide and over $248 million in the U.S. "Despicable Me" was a major victory for Universal Pictures, which has struggled after releasing a string of box-office disappointments, a legacy of previous production executives. Nikki Rocco, President of Distribution, had "Little Fockers" to close out 2010. Next year will bring a re-make of "The Thing" and the much anticipated "Cowboys and Aliens."

Dan Fellman, President of Domestic Distribution, has presided over 11 consecutive years with over $1 billion in box office receipts. "Valentine's Day," "Clash of the Titans 3D," "Sex and the City 2" and "Inception" all performed well in the first half of the year. Clint Eastwood's, "Hereafter" looks to be an Academy Award contender. Thanksgiving brought "Harry Potter and the Deathly Hallows Part 1," but it was released in 2D, not 3D as initially planned due to quality issues and time constraints. "Yogi Bear 3D" was the Christmas family treat. 2011 starts on a light note with the Farrelly Brothers' "Hall Pass," starring Owen Wilson. The big Summer features are "Green Lantern 3D," "Harry Potter and the Deathly Hollows - Part 2 3D," "Horrible Bosses" and "Final Destination 5 3D." The 2011 holiday offerings will be Gary Marshall's "New Year's Eve" and "Sherlock Holmes 2."

MINI-MAJORS

David Spitz, Executive V.P., Distribution for Lionsgate brought Exhibitors a good first half of the year in 2010 with "Kick Ass," "Killers," "The Last Exorcism" and "The Expendables" and then kicked it into high gear in the Fall with "Saw 3D." Tyler Perry's "For Colored Girls" opened in November as did "The Next Three Days" with Russell Crowe." The holiday film was "Rabbit Hole" with Nicole Kidman. 2011 will start with Matthew McConaughey in "The Lincoln Lawyer," which will be followed by "Tyler Perry's Madea's Big Happy Family." Katherine Heigl stars as Stephanie Plum in "One For the Money" based on the extraordinary successful book series by Janet Evanovich. "The Hunger Games" and "What to Expect When You Are Expecting," both based on books, are also on the release schedule for 2011.

Three year-old Overture Films, formerly part of John Malone's Liberty Media, closed after it failed to attract enough interest from potential buyers. The company will no longer produce movies, and its marketing and distribution operations are being taken over by Relativity Media, making Ryan Kavanaugh's company an instant Mini-Major. Relativity hired 43 Overture employees, including marketing chief Peter Adee and distribution President Kyle Davies. That team remains in Overture's offices in Beverly Hills and released the three remaining Overture films: Philip Seymour Hoffman's directorial debut, "Jack Goes Boating", "Stone," starring Robert DeNiro and "Let Me In." "The Warrior's Way" opened December 3rd. On the schedule for 2011 are "Kids In America" and Robert De Niro in "The Dark Fields."

Summit Entertainment, with Distribution head Richie Fay, has really made a big impact in a few short years with a diverse slate of high performing films notably the Twilight series. "The Twilight Saga: New Moon" opened November 20, 2009 and generated a lot of its $297mm gross in 2010. "Letters to Juliet" delivered over $50mm in the Spring. "The Twilight Saga: Eclipse" opened in June and has already grossed over $300mm. "Red," with Bruce Willis, Helen Mirren, Morgan Freeman and John Malkovich had an opening weekend over $20mm. "Fair Game," based on the Valerie Plame CIA story with Naomi Watts, opened in November. Nicholas Cage will star in "Drive Angry 3D" in February and "Source Code" in April. "The Darkest Hour" will be released in 3D in August and the Fall release is "The Three Musketeers." "The Twilight Saga: Breaking Dawn" opens for Thanksgiving.

The Weinstein Company continued to struggle in 2010 as Bob and Harvey Weinstein focused on trying to acquire their old company, Miramax - from Disney, and restructuring their current business. In October 2010 Donna Gigliotti was hired as the Company's president of production. Gigliotti, who won a best picture Academy Award for "Shakespeare in Love" and was nominated last year for "The Reader," fills a post that has been vacant for a year. The Weinstein Company plans to produce eight films a year, including several from Dimension, which is working on new installments in the "Spy Kids," "Scream" and "Scary Movie" franchises. There are promising signs that the Company may be turning back to its winning ways. "The King's Speech," is considered an Oscar front-runner, and other promising pictures in the works include an adaptation of the play "August: Osage County," starring Julia Roberts and Meryl Streep. The rest of 2010 saw "The Company Men," "Miral" and two Toronto Film Festival acquisitions; "Sarah's Key" and "Dirty Girl."

STUDIO RELATED DISTRIBUTORS

Focus Features, run by President of Distribution, Jack Foley and Executive V.P. Linda Ditrinco, had a busy year in 2010 with films on limited runs and wide releases. Focus consistently distributes an interesting mix of art films and films with broad appeal. "The Kids Are All Right" was the top specialized film of the Summer and "The American," Focus' widest release to date, opened as the #1 film domestically. Sophia Coppola's "Somewhere" opened for Christmas. The first half of 2011 will bring "The Eagle," "Jane Eyre" and "Hanna." Anne Hathaway will be in "One Day" which will open in the Fall.

Fox Searchlight, run by Steve Gilula, President of Fox Searchlight Pictures, and Head of Distribution, Shelia DeLoach, delivered a nice hit from 2009 with "Crazy Heart" which played until June of 2010. "Conviction" with Hillary Swank opened on October 15th and Danny Boyles harrowing film "127 Hours" opened in November. "Black Swan" featuring Natalie Portman was the Christmas offering. George Clooney heads an impressive cast in "The Decendants" which opens in early 2011. Other interesting titles for next year include "Cedar Rapids," "Win Win" and "The Tree of Life," by director Terrence Malick.

Disney sold Miramax in 2010 to a group called Filmyard Holdings, run by Ron Tutor. It was announced in October that Mike Lang, a business-development executive from Fox, who had previously worked in corporate planning at Disney, was named CEO of the newly purchased Miramax. It remains to be seen whether or not Miramax will become a force in production and independent distribution once again or become an entity that just exploits the 700 title Miramax library.

Tom Bernard and Michael Barker continued their 25 year run at Sony Pictures Classics in 2010, with Tom Prassis as Head of Sales. Their philosophy of carefully releasing a large number of interesting films, combined with careful marketing has delivered an enviable record of longevity and profitability. Sony Classics garnered 13 Academy Award nominations this year for the previous year's films.

Pedro Almodovar's "Broken Embraces" did well and "Get Low" did north of $10mm. Woody Allen's "You Will Meet a Tall Dark Stranger" arrived in September. "Tamara Drewe," "Made in Dagenham" and "Another Year" rounded out 2010, although "Barney's Version" had Academy qualifying runs in December. Coming in 2011 are "Of Gods and Men," "In a Better World" and "Incendies."

CBS Films, established in 2007 by Les Moonves when Sumner Redstone separated Viacom from CBS, is run by Steven Friedlander, Executive Vice President, and released their first films in 2010. First up in Januay was "Extraordinary Measures," with Harrison Ford and Brendan Fraser and then "The Back-up Plan" opened in April. "Beastly" featuring Neil Patrick Harris, Vanessa Hudgens and Mary-Kate Olson will open in 2011 as will "The Mechanic.". CBS has 25 films in development, deep pockets and could become an important supplier in the years to come.

INDEPENDENTS

Anchor Bay, a subsidiary of Starz, had two high performing films in 2010: "City Island" and "Solitary Man," both grossing over $5.0mm. Raymond Zinar is the Exceutive V.P. of Sales.

Bob Berney joined Bill Pohlad to create a new distribution company called Apparition last year but Berney resigned in May, right before the Cannes Film Festival. Apparition released just over half a dozen films since its launch, including "Bright Star," "The Runaways," and "The Young Victoria." It had two films for the remainder of 2010: Terrence Malick's "Tree of Life," and "Welcome to the Rileys," a Sundance pick-up starring James Gandolfini and Kristen Stewart. Apparition's future as a Distribution company is uncertain. Berney landed at Graham King's GK Films, which was launched in 2007, where he will build a marketing and distribution team.

IFC, which is part of Rainbow Media, had a good year in 2010 with "Joan Rivers: A Piece of Work,"and "Cairo Time." "Tiny Furniture" and "Leaving" were the other two 2010 releases. Johnathan Sehring is the President and Mark Boxer is Senior V. P., Sales & Distribution. "Inhale," "White Material," starring Isabelle Huppert, "Heartless" and "Super" are on the slate for 2011.

Magnolia, owned by Mark Cuban and Todd Wagner, is noted for its policy of releasing theatrically and to video-on-demand, simultaneously. They have been releasing as many as two titles a month and are headed by Eamonn Bowles.

Music Box Films has had three big films in the last two years "Tell No One" and the two films based on the Swedish books by Stieg Larsson: "The Girl With the Dragon Tatoo" and "The Girl Who Played With Fire."

Roadside Attractions,with Gail Blumenthal, Senior V.P. Distribution had a nice arthouse hit with "Winter's Bone," and released the documentary "Cool It" in November. "I Love Phillip Morris" opened in December with Jim Carrey and Ewan McGregor,as did "Biutiful" with Javier Bardem.

IDP/Samuel Goldwyn Films, run by distribution head Michael Silberman, had good success with "To Save a Life" which opened late in 2009. John Sloss' Producers Distribution Agency did $3.3mm with "Exit Through the Gift Shop" and National Geographic had the documentary "Restrepo."

EXHIBITORS

2010 was a pretty good year for Exhibitors. Boxoffice was up from the $10.6 billion in 2009 and admissions were about flat at 1.414 billion. Average ticket prices rose to $7.50 - about a 4.5% increase - mostly due to premium ticket prices for 3D films. The trend towards more screens per location continues and the current average in the U.S. is slightly less than seven screens per site. Considering the state of the economy for the last several years, Exhibition has done quite well, especially relative to other retail businesses. However, there is concern about the flow of product in 2011 and beyond. Major studios have been actively reducing the number of films they release and still tend to cluster film releases during the Summer and holiday periods during the year, instead of spreading them across 52 weekends. In addition, the dispute between Distributors and Exhibitors over the shortening of the release windows flared up again this year with John Fithian, head of NATO, publicly decrying the Disney's early DVD release of "Alice in Wonderland." NATO tracks and publishes the DVD window for all films released theatrically and is vocal about those that take films to DVD early. With the precipitous drop in DVD revenues for the Studios and the speedy development of more sophisticated computer and television delivery technology for film, there will be increasing pressure for Studios to squeeze the theatrical window

In the first half of 2010, there were more than 10,000 digital screens in the U.S, which is up by more than 50% over the same period in 2009. By year-end more than 30% of the screens in the U.S. were digital. The tremendous increase in the number of 3D films in 2010 and the years to come - there were thirty 3D films released in 2010 - relies on the continued roll-out of digital screens. On screen advertising and the delivery of alternative content are also made more cost effective by the transition to digital screens.

However, there were two interrelated consumer issues about 3D releases that came to the forefront in 2010: premium pricing versus the quality of the film itself. Much was made in the consumer press of the perceived lack of value for the 3D upcharge on films like "Clash of the Titans," "Step Up 3D," "Cats and Dogs: The Revenge of Kitty Galore" and "Piranha 3D." There has been some evidence that approaching a $20 admission for 3D films, as AMC did last Summer in New York City, will cause patrons to vote with their pocketbooks. The idea of variable pricing for different films and changes in release windows related to perceived or demonstrated "want-to-see" or actual results are old ideas, but ones that are likely to be debated vehemently within the Industry over the next few years as all the various segments try different strategies in their own economic interest.

One thing to note about the Exhibition Industry this year is the change that has taken place among theatre circuits. Names that have been around for generations such as Kerasotes, National Amusements and Loews have shed many theatres or gone away. Many smaller theatres with two or three screens and many Independent theatres have closed. Consolidation among the largest circuits like AMC, Regal, Cinemark and Carmike continues and whether they grow by acquisition or organically, they are getting much bigger. At the same time, relative newcomers like Rave, Regency, Showplex or United Entertainment have been expanding rapidly. For an industry that seems to change very slowly - 3D was first popular in the 1950s - Exhibition demonstrates a textbook example of what Joseph Schumpeter dubbed "creative destruction" in 1942. He argued that capitalism exists in the state of ferment - "creative destruction," - with spurts of innovation destroying established enterprises and yielding new ones.

MOTION PICTURE STATISTICS

EXHIBITION

GROSSES AND ADMISSIONS

U.S and Canada grosses were reported at $10,609 million in 2009. Total U.S. and Canada theatre admissions in 2009 were 1,414.2 million.

	Gross ($ millions)	Admissions (millions)	Per week (millions)
2009	10,609.0	1,414.2	27.2
2008	9,782.1	1,363.2	26.2
2007	9,629.0	1,457.5	28.0
2006	9,487.8	1,452.9	27.9
2005	8,991.2	1,402.7	27.0
2004	9,539.2	1,536.1	29.5
2003	9,488.5	1,574.0	30.3
2002	9,519.0	1,639.3	31.5
2001	8,412.5	1,487.3	28.6
2000	7,661.0	1,420.8	27.3
1999	7,448.0	1,465.2	28.2
1998	6,949.0	1,480.7	28.5
1997	6,365.9	1,387.7	26.7
1996	5,911.5	1,338.6	25.7
1995	5,493.5	1,262.6	24.3
1994	5,396.2	1,291.7	24.8
1993	5,154.2	1,244.0	23.9
1992	4,871.0	1,173.2	22.6
1991	4,803.2	1,140.6	21.9
1990	5,021.8	1,188.6	22.9
1989	5,033.4	1,262.8	24.3
1988	4,458.4	1,084.8	20.9
1987	4,252.9	1,088.5	20.9
1986	3,778.0	1,017.2	19.6
1985	3,749.4	1,056.1	20.3
1984	4,030.6	1,199.1	23.1
1983	3,766.0	1,196.9	23.0
1982	3,452.7	1,175.4	22.6
1981	2,965.6	1,067.0	20.5
1980	2,748.5	1,021.5	19.6
1979	2,821.3	1,120.9	21.6
1978	2,643.4	1,128.2	21.7
1977	2,372.3	1,063.2	20.4
1976	2,036.4	957.1	18.4
1975	2,114.8	1,032.8	19.9
1974	1,908.5	1,010.7	19.4
1973	1,523.5	864.6	16.6
1972	1,583.1	934.1	18.0
1971	1,349.5	820.3	15.8
1970	1,429.2	920.6	17.7
1969	1,294.0	911.9	17.5
1968	1,282.0	978.6	18.8
1967	1,110.0	926.5	17.8
1966	1,067.1	975.4	18.8
1965	1,041.8	1,031.5	19.8
1964	947.6	1,024.4	19.7
1963	925.0	1,093.4	21.0
1962	874.9	1,080.1	20.8
1961	945.5	1,224.7	23.6
1960	984.4	1,304.5	25.1
1959	1,006.0	1,488.2	28.6
1958	1,010.0	1,553.8	29.9
1957	1,078.0	1,727.6	33.2
1956	1,125.0	1,893.9	36.4
1955	1,204.0	2,072.3	39.9
1954	1,251.0	2,270.4	43.7
1953	1,339.0	2,630.6	50.6
1952	1,325.0	2,777.7	53.4
1951	1,332.0	2,840.1	54.6
1950	1,379.0	3,017.5	58.0
1949	1,448.0	3,168.5	60.9
1948	1,506.0	3,422.7	65.8

Source: MPAA, NATO

ADMISSIONS PER CAPITA

	Admissions Per Capita	Yearly Change (%)	2009 Versus (%)
2009	4.3		
2008	4.5	-4.6	-4.4
2007	4.7	-4.4	-8.5
2006	4.8	-2.1	-10.4
2005	4.7	2.1	-8.5
2004	5.2	-10.6	-17.3
2003	5.4	-3.7	-20.4
2002	5.6	-3.6	-23.2
2001	5.3	5.7	-18.9
2000	5.2	1.9	-17.3
1999	5.4	-3.7	-20.4
1998	5.5	-1.8	-21.8

ADMISSION PRICES

Average admission prices increased in 2009 to $7.50, an increase of 4.5% vs. 2008. Since 1989, admission prices have risen by 88% (from $3.99, dollars not adjusted for inflation). Average admission price based on data from NATO.

	Average Admission Price ($)	Annual change (%)	2009 Versus (%)
2009	7.50	4.5	
2008	7.18	4.4	4.5
2007	6.88	5.0	9.0
2006	6.55	2.2	14.5
2005	6.41	3.2	17.0
2004	6.21	3.0	20.8
2003	6.03	3.8	24.4
2002	5.81	2.7	29.1
2001	5.66	4.9	32.5
2000	5.39	6.1	39.1
1999	5.08	8.3	47.6
1998	4.69	2.3	59.9
1997	4.59	3.9	63.4
1996	4.42	1.6	69.7
1995	4.35	4.1	72.4
1994	4.18	0.1	79.4
1993	4.14	-0.1	81.2
1992	4.15	-0.1	80.7
1991	4.21	-0.1	78.3
1990	4.23	6.0	77.3
1989	3.99	-2.9	88.0

ADMISSION DEMOGRAPHICS

The following admission demographics are compiled from the Motion Picture Association of America. These definitions apply with respect to frequency data: "Frequent" means "at least once per month," "Occasional" means "once in two to six months," "Infrequent" means "less than once in six months."

ATTENDANCE BY AGE GROUP

Age	% Resident Civilian Population as of 1/1/09	% of Total Annual Admissions		
		2009	2008	2007
12-24	19	22	25	23
25-29	8	11	10	8
30-39	13	12	15	16
40-49	15	16	16	17
50-59	14	13	11	11
60 +	18	10	10	10

% OF FREQUENT MOVIEGOERS BY AGE GROUP

Age	2009 %	2008 %	2007 %
12-24	38	40	41
25-29	11	11	10
30-39	12	17	16
40-49	14	16	17
50-59	9	8	8
60+	11	7	8

FREQUENT MOVIEGOERS BY INCOME 2006 - 2009

Income	2009 %	2008 %	2007 %	2006 %
$50k +	55	56	58	57
$35k-$49k	22	20	19	23
$25k-$34k	14	12	11	9
$15k-$24k	6	8	8	7
under $15k	3	3	4	4

FREQUENT MOVIEGOERS BY MARITAL STATUS 2006 - 2009

Marital Status	2009 %	2008 %	2007 %	2006 %
Married	19	21	17	22
Single	31	29	23	30

FREQUENT MOVIEGOERS BY HOUSEHOLD COMPOSITION 2006 - 2009

Family Type	2009 %	2008 %	2007 %	2006 %
With children, under 17	23	25	22	29
With teens, 12-17	28	26	26	32
No children	19	19	18	23

FREQUENCY OF MOVIEGOING 2002-2009

Year	Frequent %	Occasional %	Infrequent %	Never %
2009	19	38	14	29
2008	21	39	13	27
2007	22	37	12	29
2006	28	34	11	26
2005	24	34	13	29
2004	28	35	13	24
2003	25	36	11	27
2002	28	34	11	26

U.S. THEATRE AND SCREEN STATISTICS

Year	Total Screens	2010 Versus (%)	Indoor Screens	2010 Versus (%)	Drive-In Screens	2010 Versus %
2010	39,357		38,729		633	
2009	39,020	0.8	38,384	0.9	636	-0.5
2008	38,902	1.2	38,266	1.2	636	-0.5
2007	38,824	1.4	38,185	1.4	639	-0.5
2006	38,425	1.5	37,776	2.5	649	-1.0
2005	38,852	1.3	38,143	1.5	709	-11.2
2004	36,594	7.6	35,993	7.1	601	5.3
2003	35,786	10.0	35,499	9.1	647	-2.2
1994	26,586	48.0	25,701	50.7	885	-28.5
1990	23,689	66.1	22,774	70.1	915	-30.8
1984	20,200	94.8	17,368	123.0	2,832	-77.6

THE TOP 10 U.S. THEATRE CIRCUITS AS OF OCTOBER 1, 2010

The top ten circuits in the U.S. control over 50% of the screens, but generate a much higher % of the total boxoffice.

Circuit	U.S. Theatres	U.S. Screens	% of All U.S. Screens	% of Top 10
Regal Entertainment Group	543	6939	17.6	32.3
AMC Entertainment, Inc*	367	5038	12.8	23.5
Cinemark USA, Inc	296	3842	9.8	17.9
Carmike Cinemas	247	2285	5.8	10.6
Rave Motion Pictures	61	918	2.3	4.3
Marcus Theatres Corporation	56	683	1.7	3.2
Hollywood Theatres	51	555	1.4	2.6
National Amusements, Inc.	34	455	1.2	2.1
Harkins Theatres	32	443	1.1	2.0
Malco Theatres	32	320	0.8	1.5

PRODUCTION

NUMBER OF FILMS RATED & RELEASED, INCLUDING REISSUES

	Films Rated	Films Released
2009	793	558
2008	896	610
2007	839	603
2006	789	607
2005	931	549
2004	871	528
2003	940	473
2002	786	466
2001	739	483
1999	677	461
1998	661	509

HIGH GROSSING FEATURES

	Films Grossing > 10 million	Films Grossing > 20 million
2009	154	117
2008	153	119
2007	165	111
2006	169	125
2005	153	116
2004	157	111
2003	150	116
2002	151	113
2001	90	50
1999	71	42
1998	69	37
1997	66	39
1996	69	31
1995	75	36
1994	57	33
1993	64	28

AVERAGE COSTS OF NEW FEATURES: PRODUCTION, ADVERTISING AND PRINTS*

	Production costs ($ millions)	Advertising ($ millions)	Print ($ millions)	Total ($ millions)
2008	71.3	33.4	3.2	107.9
2007	70.8	32.2	3.7	106.7
2006	65.8	31.1	3.4	100.3
2005	60.0	32.3	3.8	96.1
2004	62.4	30.6	3.7	96.7
2003	63.8	39.0	4.2	107.0
2002	58.8	27.3	3.3	89.4
2001	47.7	27.2	3.7	78.6
2000	54.8	24.0	3.3	82.1
1999	51.5	21.4	3.1	76.0
1998	52.7	22.1	3.2	78.0
1997	53.4	19.2	3.0	75.6
1996	39.8	17.2	2.6	59.6
1995	36.3	15.4	2.3	54.0
1994	34.2	13.9	2.2	50.3
1993	29.9	12.1	1.9	43.9

*All figures in this table are for MPAA member companies

INDUSTRY FILM RATING SYSTEM (CARA RATINGS)

In the first three columns of the following table, "#" is the number of films released in the given year that received the corresponding rating, and "%" is the percentage of the total number of films released in the given year that received the corresponding rating. In the fourth (rightmost) column, "#" and "%" represent cumulative figures for the range 1968-2008.

	2008		2007		2006		1968-2008	
	#	%	#	%	#	%	#	%
G	42	3	18	3	48	8	1,652	7
PG	128	13	78	13	127	21	5,012	21
PG-13	73	25	154	25	79	13	2,973	12
R	359	59	353	59	352	58	13,908	59
NC-17/X	1	0	1	0	1	0	458	1
Totals	610	100.0	520	100.0	459	100.0	24,003	100.0

MPAA COMPANY ADVERTISING COST BY MEDIA

Year	Total $	Newspaper %	Network %	Spot TV %	Internet Online%	Trailers %	Other Media%	Other Non-Media%
2008	31.03	9.1	21.0	13.9	5.8	4.3	24.2	21.7
2007	32.17	10.1	21.6	13.9	4.4	4.2	24.0	21.8
2006	30.71	10.8	21.2	13.9	3.7	4.3	24.4	21.6
2005	32.36	12.7	23.2	12.9	2.6	4.4	22.3	21.9
2004	30.61	12.8	22.9	13.3	2.4	7.4	22.2	19.0
2003	34.84	13.9	23.2	15.7	1.3	4.4	21.9	19.5
2002	27.31	13.5	23.0	17.6	0.9	4.5	21.4	19.1
2001	27.28	13.1	25.4	16.9	1.3	5.1	20.2	17.9

Other media Includes: Cable TV, Network Radio, Spot Radio, Magazines and Billboards.
Other Non-Media includes: Production/ Creative Services, Exhibitor Services, Promotion and PR and Market Research

Top Grossing Films 1998-2010

The ten top-grossing films each year from 1998-2010, as selected by Quigley Publishing. Some films may have been held over from the previous year. The 2010 films are for the year as of October 31, 2010.

2010

Avatar (Fox) (opened Dec. 10, 2009) 1
Toy Story 3 (BV) 2
Alice in Wonderland (BV) 3
Iron Man 2 (Par) 4
Eclipse (Summit) 5
Inception (WB) 6
Despicable Me (Univ) 7
Shrek Forever After (Par) 8
How to Train Your Dragon (Par) 9
The Karate Kid (Sony) 10

2009

Transformers: Revenge of the Fallen (DrmWks) 1
Harry Potter and the Half-Blood Prince (WB) 2
Up (BV) 3
The Hangover (WB) 4
Star Trek (Par) 5
Monsters vs Aliens (DrmWks) 6
Ice Age: Dawn of the Dinosaurs (Fox) 7
X-Men Origins: Wolverine (Fox) 8
Night at the Museum: Battle of the Smithsonian (Fox) 9
The Proposal (BV) 10

2008

The Dark Knight (WB) 1
Iron Man (Par) 2
Indiana Jones and the Kingdom of the Cystal Skull (Par) 3
Hancock (Sony) 4
WALL-E (BV) 5
Kung Fu Panda (DrmWks) 6
Horton Hears a Who! (Fox) 7
Sex and the City (New Line) 8
The Chronicles of Narnia: Prince Caspian (BV) 9
The Incredible Hulk (Univ) 10

2007

Spider-Man 3 (Sony) 1
Shrek the Third (Par) 2
Transformers (DrmWks) 3
Pirates of the Caribbean: At the World's End (BV) 4
Harry Potter and the Order of the Phoenix (WB) 5
300 (WB) 6
The Bourne Ultimatum (Univ) 7
Ratatouille (BV) 8
The Simpsons Movie (Fox) 9
Wild Hogs (BV) 10

2006

Pirates of the Carribbean: Dead Man's Chest (BV) 1
Cars (BV) 2
X-Men: The Last Stand (Fox) 3
The Da Vinci Code (Sony) 4
Superman Returns (WB) 5
Ice Age: The Meltdown (Fox) 6
Over the Hedge (Par) 7
Talladega Nights: The Ballad of Ricky Bobby (Sony) 8
Click (Sony) 9
Mission Impossible III (Par) 10

2005

Star Wars: Episode III - Revenge of the Sith (Fox) 1
War of the Worlds (Par) 2
Wedding Crashers (NL) 3
Batman Begins (WB) 4
Charlie and the Cocolate Factory (WB) 5
Madagascar (DrmWks) 6
Mr. & Mrs. Smith (Fox) 7
Hitch (Sony) 8
The Longest Yard (Par) 9
Fantastic Four (Fox) 10

2004

Shrek 2 (DrmWks)	1
Spiderman 2 (Sony)	2
The Passion of the Christ (Newmkt)	3
Harry Potter and the Prisoner of Azbakan (WB)	4
The Day After Tomorrow (20th)	5
The Bourne Supremacy (Univ)	6
I, Robot (20th)	7
Shark Tale (DrmWks)	8
The Lord of the Rings: The Return of the King (NL)	9
Troy (WB)	10

2003

Finding Nemo (BV)	1
Pirates of the Caribbean: The Curse of the Black Pearl (BV)	2
The Matrix Reloaded (WB)	3
Bruce Almighty (Univ)	4
X2 (20th)	5
Chicago (Miramax 2002)	6
Terminator 3: Rise of the Machines (WB)	7
Bad Boys II Sony)	8
Anger Management (Sony)	9
Bringing Down the House (BV)	10

2002

Spider-Man (Sony)	1
Star Wars: Episode II–Attack of the Clones (20th)	2
Signs (BV)	3
Austin Powers in Goldmember (New Line)	4
Men in Black II (Sony)	5
My Big Fat Greek Wedding (IFC)	6
Ice Age (20th)	7
Scooby-Doo (WB)	8
Lilo & Stitch (BV)	9
XXX (Sony)	10

2001

Harry Potter and the Sorcerer's Stone (WB)	1
Shrek (DrmWks)	2
Rush Hour 2 (New Line)	3
Pearl Harbor (BV)	4
Jurassic Park III (Univ)	5
Planet of the Apes (20th)	6
American Pie 2 (Univ)	7
The Fast and the Furious (Univ)	8
Dr. Dolittle 2 (20th)	9
Legally Blonde (MGM)	10

2000

Mission Impossible 2 (Par)	1
Gladiator (DrmWks)	2
The Perfect Storm (WB)	3
X-Men (Fox)	4
Scary Movie (Mir)	5
What Lies Beneath (DrmWks)	6
Dinosaur (BV)	7
Nutty Professor II: The Klumps (Uni)	8
Big Momma's House (20th/New Regency)	9
The Patriot (Sony)	10

1999

Star Wars: Episode 1 (20th Fox)	1
The Matrix (WB)	2
The Mummy (Univ)	3
Notting Hill (Univ)	4
The Sixth Sense (BV)	5
Austin Powers: The Spy Who Shagged Me (New Line)	6
Tarzan (BV)	7
Runaway Bride (Par)	8
Wild Wild West (WB)	9
Big Daddy (Sony)	10

1998

Saving Private Ryan (DrmWks)	1
Armageddon (BV)	2
There's Something About Mary (Fox)	3
A Bug's Life (BV)	4
The Waterboy (BV)	5
Doctor Dolittle (Fox)	6
Rush Hour (New Line)	7
Deep Impact (Par)	8
Good Will Hunting (Mir)	9
Patch Adams (Uni)	10

Top 50 Grossing Films by Domestic Box Office

Movie	Year Released	Domestic B.O. (millions)	Budget (millions)	World B.O. (millions)
Avatar (Fox)	2009	760.3	237	2,787.00
Titanic (Par)	1997	600.8	200	1,835.4
The Dark Knight (WB)	2008	533.3	185	923.2
Star Wars: Episode IV - A New Hope (Fox)	1977	460.9	11	797.9
Shrek 2 (Drmwks)	2004	436.5	75	881.7
E.T. (Univ)	1982	435.3	11	757.0
Star Wars: Episode I - The Phantom Menace (Fox)	1999	431.1	110	925.5
Pirates of the Caribbean: Dead Man's Chest (BV)	2006	421.3	225	1,052.4
Spider-Man (Sony)	2002	405.8	139	806.7
Transformers:Revenge of the Fallen (DrmWks)	2009	401.5	200	831.8
Star Wars: Episode III - Revenge of the Sith	2005	380.0	115	809.0
The Lord of the Rings: The Return of the King (New Line)	2003	376.7	94	1,129.3
Spider-Man 2 (Sony)	2004	373.0	200	783.6
The Passion of the Christ (Newmkt)	2004	371.0	30	606.5
Jurassic Park (Univ)	1993	357.1	63	920.0
Finding Nemo (BV)	2003	341.2	94	866.3
The Lord of the Rings: The Two Towers (New Line)	2002	339.4	109	921.6
Spider-Man 3 (Sony)	2007	337.4	258	885.0
Forrest Gump (Par)	1994	329.7	55	680.0
The Lion King (BV)	1994	327.5	79	783.4
Shrek the Third (Par)	2007	320.8	160	756.9
Transformers (DrmWks)	2007	319.7	150	701.8
Harry Potter and the Sorcerer's Stone (WB)	2001	317.6	130	967.6
Iron Man (Par)	2008	317.0	140	570.0
Indiana Jones and the Temple of the Crystal Skull (Par)	2008	316.1	185	781.3
The Lord of the Rings: The Fellowship of the Ring (NL)	2001	313.4	93	860.3
Star Wars: Episode II - Attack of the Clones (Fox)	2002	310.7	120	648.2
Star Wars: Episode VI - Return of the Jedi (Fox)	1983	310.6	33	573.4
Pirates of the Caribbean: At the World's End (BV)	2007	309.1	300	957.7
Independence Day (Fox)	1996	309.0	75	813.1
Pirates of the Caribbean: Curse of Black Pearl (BV)	2003	306.1	140	653.2
The Sixth Sense (BV)	1999	301.0	55	661.5
Harry Potter and the Half-Blood Prince (WB)	2009	297.6	250	917.0
The Chronicles of Narnia: The Lion, the Witch & the Wardrobe (BV)	2005	293.5	180	739.8
Star Wars: Episode V - The Empire Strikes Back (Fox)	1980	292.8	18	533.9
Harry Potter and the Order of the Phoenix (WB)	2007	292.4	150	914.6
Up (BV)	2009	291.0	175	460.7
Harry Potter and the Goblet of Fire (WB)	2005	290.0	150	894.3
Home Alone (Fox)	1990	287.2	15	533.8
The Matrix Reloaded (WB)	2003	285.9	150	735.6
Meet the Fockers (Univ)	2004	279.0	80	432.7
Shrek (BV)	2001	269.0	60	465.1
The Hangover	2009	273.0	35	440.0
Harry Potter and the Chamber of Secrets (WB)	2002	267.7	100	866.3
The Incredibles (BV)	2004	261.9	92	866.3
Jaws (Univ)	1975	261.2	12	624.1
Dr. Seuss' How the Grinch Stole Christmas (Univ)	2000	260.0	123	471.0
Star Trek (Par)	2009	257.8	150	382.0
I Am Legend	2007	257.0	150	584.3
Monsters, Inc. (BV)	2001	256.2	115	340.5

Top 50 Grossing Films by Domestic Box Office, Adjusted for Inflation

Movie	Year Released	Domestic B.O. (millions)	Budget (millions)	Adjusted B.O. (millions)
Gone With the Wind	1939	198.7	3	3,078.4
Snow White and the Seven Dwarfs	1937	184.9	1	2,765.1
Star Wars: Episode IV- A New Hope	1977	460.9	11	1,637.9
Bambi	1942	102.8	2.5	1,358.2
Pinocchio	1940	84.3	3	1,296.7
Fantasia	1940	76.4	2	1,175.2
The Sound of Music	1965	163.2	8.2	1,115.7
One Hundred and One Dalmatians	1961	152.6	4	1,099.1
Jaws	1975	260.0	12	1,040.7
The Exorcist	1973	204.7	12	992.9
E.T.	1982	434.9	10.5	970.5
The Jungle Book	1967	141.8		914.3
Lady and the Tramp	1955	112.0	4	900.0
Titanic	1997	600.8	200	806.8
The Sting	1973	159.6	6	774.1
Doctor Zhivago	1965	111.7	11	763.7
Avatar	2010	760.0	237	760.0
Star Wars: Episode V - The Empire Strikes Back	1980	290.0	18	757.9
Mary Poppins	1964	102.3		710.6
Peter Pan	1953	87.4	4	704.9
The Godfather	1972	134.6	6	693.5
The Graduate	1967	104.4	3.5	673.1
Star Wars: Episode VI - Return of the Jedi	1983	309.1	33	668.3
The Ten Commandments	1956	80.0	14	633.4
Grease	1978	186.5	6	616.0
Butch Cassidy and the Sundance Kid	1969	102.3		600.3
Love Story	1970	106.4	3	590.6
Ben-Hur	1959	70.0	15	574.3
Raiders of the Lost Ark	1981	242.4	20	560.4
The Rocky Horror Picture Show	1975	140.0	1.2	557.8
Star Wars: Episode I–The Phantom Menace	1999	431.1	110	557.3
American Graffiti	1973	115.0	1	532.6
Airport	1970	100.5	10	532.2
The Dark Knight	2008	512.2	185	531.2
Jurassic Park	1993	357.1	63	522.0
Blazing Saddles	1974	119.5	2.8	518.0
Saturday Night Fever	1977	143.2		508.0
The Towering Inferno	1974	116.0	14	506.7
My Fair Lady	1964	72.0	17	500.2
Shrek 2	2004	436.5	75	497.6
Ghostbusters	1984	238.6	30	486.7
Spider-Man	2002	405.8	139	483.3
Beverly Hills Cop	1984	234.8	15	480.7
The Poseidon Adventure	1972	93.3	5	476.6
Forrest Gump	1994	329.7	55	470.9
National Lampoon's Animal House	1978	141.6	3	470.7
The Lion King	1994	328.0	79.3	470.4
Animal House	1978	142.5	3	467.7
Home Alone	1990	285.8	15	465.5
Smokey and the Bandit	1977	127.0		455.9
Close Encounters of the Third Kind	1977	128.3	20	454.2

*Adjusted using the Consumer Price Index to 2010 dollars.

Top 50 Grossing Films Worldwide

Movie	Year Released	Domestic B.O. (millions)	Budget (millions)	World B.O. (millions)
Avatar (Fox)	2009	760.3	237	2,787.00
Titanic (Par)	1997	600.8	200	1,835.4
The Lord of the Rings: The Return of the King (New Line)	2003	376.7	94	1,129.3
Pirates of the Caribbean: Dead Man's Chest (BV)	2006	421.3	225	1,052.4
Toy Story 3 (BV)	2010	412.8	200	1.061.0
Alice in Wonderland (BV)	2010	334.2	200	1,022.7
The Dark Knight (WB)	2008	533.3	185	1,002.0
Harry Potter and the Sorcerer's Stone (WB)	2001	317.6	130	967.6
Pirates of the Caribbean: At World's End (BV)	2007	309.3	300	959.2
Harry Potter and the Order of the Phoenix (WB)	2007	292.4	150	957.7
Star Wars: Episode I -- The Phantom Menace (Fox)	1999	431.1	110	937.2
The Lord of the Rings: The Two Towers (NL)	2002	339.4	109	925.5
Jurassic Park (Univ)	1993	357.1	63	921.6
Harry Potter and the Half-Blood Prince (WB)	2009	297.6	250	920.0
Harry Potter and the Goblet of Fire (WB)	2005	290.1	150	892.0
Ice Age: Dawn of the Dinosaurs (Fox)	2009	194.4	87	888.0
Spider-Man 3 (Sony)	2007	337.4	258	885.0
Shrek 2 (Dreamworks)	2004	436.5	150	881.7
Harry Potter and the Chamber of Secrets (WB)	2002	262.0	100	866.7
Finding Nemo (BV)	2003	341.2	94	866.3
The Lord of the Rings: The Fellowship of the Ring (NL)	2001	313.4	93	861.4
Star Wars: Episode III - Revenge of the Sith	2005	380.0	115	847.5
Transformers: Revenge of the Fallen (Dreamworks)	2009	401.5	200	830.6
Independence Day (Fox)	1996	309.0	75	811.0
Inception (WB)	2010	290.0	160	811.0
Spider-Man (Sony)	2002	405.8	139	807.4
Star Wars: Episode IV - A New Hope (Fox)	1977	460.9	11	798.6
Shrek the Third (Par)	2007	320.8	160	790.9
Harry Potter and the Prisoner of Azkaban (WB)	2004	250.1	130	786.7
Spider-Man 2 (Sony)	2004	373.0	200	784.2
The Lion King (BV)	1994	327.5	79	783.7
Indiana Jones and the Kingdom of the Crystal Skull (Par)	2008	316.1	185	783.0
2012 (Sony)	2009	166.1	200	767.4
The Da Vinci Code (Sony)	2006	217.5	125	757.0
E.T. (Univ)	1982	435.3	11	756.6
Narnia: The Lion, the Witch and the Wardrobe (BV)	2005	293.5	180	738.0
The Matrix Reloaded (WB)	2003	285.8	150	732.5
Up (BV)	2009	293.0	175	727.0
Transformers (DrmWks)	2007	319.7	150	700.9
New Moon (Summit)	2009	297.2	50	688.0
Eclipse (Summit)	2010	300.5	65	681.0
Star Wars: Episode V - The Empire Strikes Back (Fox)	1980	292.8	18	678.1
Forrest Gump (Par)	1994	329.7	55	677.7
The Sixth Sense (BV)	1999	295.7	55	663.0
Pirates of the Caribbean: Curse of Black Pearl (BV)	2003	306.1	140	653.1
Star Wars: Episode II -- Attack of the Clones (Fox)	2002	310.7	120	648.2
Kung Fu Panda (Dreamworks)	2008	215.4	130	633
The Incredibles (BV)	2004	261.9	92	624.1
Ice Age: The Meltdown (Fox)	2006	195.3	80	623.9
Hancock (Sony)	2008	227.4	150	622.9

QP TOP TEN MONEY-MAKERS POLL

QP TOP TEN POLL OF MONEY-MAKING STARS

In the 78th annual poll of circuit exhibitors and independent theatre owners in the United States conducted by Quigley Publishing Company, these stars were voted the top ten money-makers of 2009:

Sandra Bullock 1
Johnny Depp 2
Matt Damon 3
George Clooney 4
Robert Downey, Jr. 5
Tom Hanks 6
Meryl Streep 7
Brad Pitt 8
Shia LaBeouf 9
Denzel Washington 10

QP STARS OF TOMORROW

Major and independent exhibitors were asked to name those stars they thought would be top money-makers within the next 5-10 years. The overwhelming choices for 2009 were:

Carey Mulligan 1
Taylor Lautner 2

QP MONEY-MAKING STARS OF 1932-2008

2008 (1) Will Smith; (2) Robert Downey, Jr.; (3) Christian Bale; (4) Shia LaBeouf; (5) Harrison Ford; (6) Adam Sandler; (7) Reese Witherspoon; (8) George Clooney; (9) Angelina Jolie; (10) Daniel Craig.

2007 (1) Johnny Depp; (2) Will Smith; (3) George Clooney; (4) Matt Damon; (5) Denzel Washington; (6) Russell Crowe; (7) Tom Cruise; (8) Nicholas Cage; (9) Will Ferrell; (10) Tom Hanks.

2006 (1) Johnny Depp; (2) Leonardo DiCaprio; (3) Will Smith; (4) Denzel Washington; (5) Tom Hanks; (6) George Clooney; (7) Will Ferrell; (8) Tom Cruise; (9) Dakota Fanning; (10) Sacha Baron Cohen.

2005 (1) Tom Cruise; (2) Johnny Depp; (3) Angelina Jolie; (3) Brad Pitt; (5) Vince Vaughn; (6) George Clooney; (7) Will Smith; (8) Reese Witherspoon; (9) Adam Sandler; (10) Tom Hanks.

2004 (1) Tom Hanks; (2) Tom Cruise; (3) Leonardo Di Caprio; (4) Nicholas Cage; (5) Jim Carrey; (6) Denzel Washington; (7) Julia Roberts; (8) Will Smith; (9) Brad Pitt; (10) Adam Sandler.

2003 (1) Jim Carrey; (2) Nicole Kidman; (3) Jack Nicholson; (4) Tom Cruise; (5) Julia Roberts; (6) Johnny Depp; (7) Russell Crowe; (8) Tom Hanks; (9) Will Ferrell; (10) Renee Zellweger.

2002: (1) Tom Hanks; (2) Tom Cruise; (3) Mike Myers; (4) Reese Witherspoon; (5) Leonardo Di Caprio; (6) Nicole Kidman; (7) Catherine Zeta-Jones; (8) Denzel Washington; (9) Mel Gibson; (10) Vin Diesel.

2001:(1) Tom Cruise; (2) George Clooney; (3) Julia Roberts; (4) Russell Crowe; (5) Nicole Kidman; (6) Denzel Washington; (7) Will Smith; (8) Brad Pitt; (9) Ben Affleck; (10) Jackie Chan.

2000: (1) Tom Cruise; (2) Julia Roberts; (3) George Clooney; (4) Eddie Murphy; (5) Russell Crowe; (6) Mel Gibson; (7) Martin Lawrence; (8) Tom Hanks; (9) Jim Carrey; (10) Harrison Ford.

1999: (1) Julia Roberts; (2) Tom Hanks; (3) Adam Sandler; (4) Bruce Willis; (5) Mike Myers; (6) Tom Cruise; (7) Will Smith; (8) Mel Gibson; (9) Meg Ryan; (10) Sandra Bullock.

1998: (1) Tom Hanks; (2) Jim Carrey; (3) Leonardo DiCaprio; (4) Robin Williams; (5) Meg Ryan; (6) Mel Gibson; (7) Adam Sandler; (8) Eddie Murphy; (9) Cameron Diaz; (10) Julia Roberts.

1997: (1) Harrison Ford; (2) Julia Roberts; (3) Leonardo DiCaprio; (4) Will Smith; (5) Tom Cruise; (6) Jack Nicholson; (7) Jim Carrey; (8) John Travolta; (9) Robin Williams; (10) Tommy Lee Jones.

1996: (1) Tom Cruise & Mel Gibson; (3) John Travolta; (4) Arnold Schwarzenegger; (5) Sandra Bullock; (6) Robin Williamsl (7) Sean Connery; (8) Harrison Ford; (9) Kevin Costner; (10) Michelle Pfeiffer.

1995: (1) Tom Hanks; (2) Jim Carrey; (3) Brad Pitt; (4) Harrison Ford; (5) Robin Williams; (6) Sandra Bullock; (7) Mel Gibson; (8) Demi Moore; (9) John Travolta;

(10) Kevin Costner & Michael Douglas.

1994: (1) Tom Hanks; (2) Jim Carrey (3) Arnold Schwarzenegger; (4) Tom Cruise; (5) Harrison Ford; (6) Tim Allen; (7) Mel Gibson; (8) Jodie Foster; (9) Michael Douglas; (10) Tommy Lee Jones.

1993: (1) Clint Eastwood; (2) Tom Cruise; (3) Robin Williams; (4) Kevin Costner; (5) Harrison Ford; (6) Julia Roberts; (7) Tom Hanks; (8) Mel Gibson; (9) Whoopi Goldberg; (10) Sylvester Stallone.

1992: (1) Tom Cruise; (2) Mel Gibson; (3) Kevin Costner; (4) Jack Nicholson; (5) Macaulay Culkin; (6) Whoopi Goldberg; (7) Michael Douglas; (8) Clint Eastwood; (9) Steven Seagal; (10) Robin Williams.

1991: (1) Kevin Costner; (2) Arnold Schwarzenegger; (3) Robin Williams; (4) Julia Roberts; (5) Macaulay Culkin; (6) Jodie Foster; (7) Billy Crystal; (8) Dustin Hoffman; (9) Robert De Niro; (10) Mel Gibson.

1990: (1) Arnold Schwarzenegger; (2) Julia Roberts; (3) Bruce Willis; (4) Tom Cruise; (5) Mel Gibson; (6) Kevin Costner; (7) Patrick Swayze; (8) Sean Connery; (9) Harrison Ford; (10) Richard Gere.

1989: (1) Jack Nicholson; (2) Tom Cruise; (3) Robin Williams; (4) Michael Douglas; (5) Tom Hanks; (6) Michael J. Fox; (7) Eddie Murphy; (8) Mel Gibson; (9) Sean Connery; (10) Kathleen Turner.

1988: (1) Tom Cruise; (2) Eddie Murphy; (3) Tom Hanks; (4) Arnold Schwarzenegger; (5) Paul Hogan; (6) Danny De Vito; (7) Bette Midler; (8) Robin Williams; (9) Tom Selleck; (10) Dustin Hoffman.

1987: (1) Eddie Murphy; (2) Michael Douglas; (3) Michael J. Fox; (4) Arnold Schwarzenegger; (5) Paul Hogan; (6) Tom Cruise; (7) Glenn Close; (8) Sylvester Stallone; (9) Cher; (10) Mel Gibson.

1986: (1) Tom Cruise; (2) Eddie Murphy; (3) Paul Hogan; (4) Rodney Dangerfield; (5) Bette Midler; (6) Sylvester Stallone; (7) Clint Eastwood; (8) Whoopi Goldberg; (9) Kathleen Turner; (10) Paul Newman.

1985: (1) Sylvester Stallone; (2) Eddie Murphy; (3) Clint Eastwood; (4) Michael J. Fox; (5) Chevy Chase; (6) Arnold Schwarzenegger; (7) Chuck Norris; (8) Harrison Ford; (9) Michael Douglas; (10) Meryl Streep.

1984: (1) Clint Eastwood; (2) Bill Murray; (3) Harrison Ford; (4) Eddie Murphy; (5) Sally Field; (6) Burt Reynolds; (7) Robert Redford; (8) Prince; (9) Dan Aykroyd; (10) Meryl Streep.

1983: (1) Clint Eastwood; (2) Eddie Murphy; (3) Sylvester Stallone; (4) Burt Reynolds; (5) John Travolta; (6) Dustin Hoffman; (7) Harrison Ford; (8) Richard Gere; (9) Chevy Chase; (10) Tom Cruise.

1982: (1) Burt Reynolds; (2) Clint Eastwood; (3) Sylvester Stallone; (4) Dudley Moore; (5) Richard Pryor; (6) Dolly Parton; (7) Jane Fonda; (8) Richard Gere; (9) Paul Newman; (10) Harrison Ford.

1981: (1) Burt Reynolds; (2) Clint Eastwood; (3) Dudley Moore; (4) Dolly Parton; (5) Jane Fonda; (6) Harrison Ford; (7) Alan Alda; (8) Bo Derek; (9) Goldie Hawn; (10) Bill Murray.

1980: (1) Burt Reynolds; (2) Robert Redford; (3) Clint Eastwood; (4) Jane Fonda; (5) Dustin Hoffman; (6) John Travolta; (7) Sally Field; (8) Sissy Spacek; (9) Barbra Streisand; (10) Steve Martin.

1979: (1) Burt Reynolds; (2) Clint Eastwood; (3) Jane Fonda; (4) Woody Allen; (5) Barbra Streisand; (6) Sylvester Stallone; (7) John Travolta; (8) Jill Clayburgh; (9) Roger Moore; (10) Mel Brooks.

1978: (1) Burt Reynolds; (2) John Travolta; (3) Richard Dreyfuss; (4) Warren Beatty; (5) Clint Eastwood; (6) Woody Allen; (7) Diane Keaton; (8) Jane Fonda; (9) Peter Sellers; (10) Barbra Streisand.

1977: (1) Sylvester Stallone; (2) Barbra Streisand; (3) Clint Eastwood; (4) Burt Reynolds; (5) Robert Redford; (6) Woody Allen; (7) Mel Brooks; (8) Al Pacino; (9) Diane Keaton; (10) Robert De Niro.

1976: (1) Robert Redford; (2) Jack Nicholson; (3) Dustin Hoffman; (4) Clint Eastwood; (5) Mel Brooks; (6) Burt Reynolds; (7) Al Pacino; (8) Tatum O'Neal; (9) Woody Allen; (10) Charles Bronson.

1975: (1) Robert Redford; (2) Barbra Streisand; (3) Al Pacino; (4) Charles Bronson; (5) Paul Newman; (6) Clint Eastwood; (7) Burt Reynolds; (8) Woody Allen; (9) Steve McQueen; (10) Gene Hackman.

1974: (1) Robert Redford; (2) Clint Eastwood; (3) Paul Newman; (4) Barbra Streisand; (5) Steve McQueen; (6) Burt Reynolds; (7) Charles Bronson; (8) Jack Nicholson; (9) Al Pacino; (10) John Wayne.

1973: (1) Clint Eastwood; (2) Ryan O'Neal; (3) Steve McQueen; (4) Burt Reynolds; (5) Robert Redford; (6) Barbra Streisand; (7) Paul Newman; (8) Charles Bronson; (9) John Wayne; (10) Marlon Brando.

1972: (1) Clint Eastwood; (2) George C. Scott; (3) Gene Hackman; (4) John Wayne; (5) Barbra Streisand; (6) Marlon Brando; (7) Paul Newman; (8) Steve McQueen; (9) Dustin Hoffman;

(10) Goldie Hawn.

1971: (1) John Wayne; (2) Clint Eastwood; (3) Paul Newman; (4) Steve McQueen; (5) George C. Scott; (6) Dustin Hoffman; (7) Walter Matthau; (8) Ali MacGraw; (9) Sean Connery; (10) Lee Marvin.

1970: (1) Paul Newman; (2) Clint Eastwood; (3) Steve McQueen; (4) John Wayne; (5) Elliott Gould; (6) Dustin Hoffman; (7) Lee Marvin; (8) Jack Lemmon; (9) Barbra Streisand; (10) Walter Matthau.

1969: (1) Paul Newman; (2) John Wayne; (3) Steve McQueen; (4) Dustin Hoffman; (5) Clint Eastwood; (6) Sidney Poitier; (7) Lee Marvin; (8) Jack Lemmon; (9) Katharine Hepburn; (10) Barbra Streisand.

1968: (1) Sidney Poitier; (2) Paul Newman; (3) Julie Andrews; (4) John Wayne; (5) Clint Eastwood; (6) Dean Martin; (7) Steve McQueen; (8) Jack Lemmon; (9) Lee Marvin; (10) Elizabeth Taylor.

1967: (1) Julie Andrews; (2) Lee Marvin; (3) Paul Newman; (4) Dean Martin; (5) Sean Connery; (6) Elizabeth Taylor; (7) Sidney Poitier; (8) John Wayne; (9) Richard Burton; (10) Steve McQueen.

1966: (1) Julie Andrews; (2) Sean Connery; (3) Elizabeth Taylor; (4) Jack Lemmon; (5) Richard Burton; (6) Cary Grant; (7) John Wayne; (8) Doris Day; (9) Paul Newman; (10) Elvis Presley.

1965: (1) Sean Connery; (2) John Wayne; (3) Doris Day; (4) Julie Andrews; (5) Jack Lemmon; (6) Elvis Presley; (7) Cary Grant; (8) James Stewart; (9) Elizabeth Taylor; (10) Richard Burton.

1964: (1) Doris Day; (2) Jack Lemmon; (3) Rock Hudson; (4) John Wayne; (5) Cary Grant; (6) Elvis Presley; (7) Shirley MacLaine; (8) Ann-Margret; (9) Paul Newman; (10) Richard Burton.

1963: (1) Doris Day; (2) John Wayne; (3) Rock Hudson; (4) Jack Lemmon; (5) Cary Grant; (6) Elizabeth Taylor; (7) Elvis Presley; (8) Sandra Dee; (9) Paul Newman; (10) Jerry Lewis.

1962: (1) Doris Day; (2) Rock Hudson; (3) Cary Grant; (4) John Wayne; (5) Elvis Presley; (6) Elizabeth Taylor; (7) Jerry Lewis; (8) Frank Sinatra; (9) Sandra Dee; (10) Burt Lancaster.

1961: (1) Elizabeth Taylor; (2) Rock Hudson; (3) Doris Day; (4) John Wayne; (5) Cary Grant; (6) Sandra Dee; (7) Jerry Lewis; (8) William Holden; (9) Tony Curtis; (10) Elvis Presley.

1960: (1) Doris Day; (2) Rock Hudson; (3) Cary Grant; (4) Elizabeth Taylor; (5) Debbie Reynolds; (6) Tony Curtis; (7) Sandra Dee; (8) Frank Sinatra; (9) Jack Lemmon; (10) John Wayne.

1959: (1) Rock Hudson; (2) Cary Grant; (3) James Stewart; (4) Doris Day; (5) Debbie Reynolds; (6) Glenn Ford; (7) Frank Sinatra; (8) John Wayne; (9) Jerry Lewis; (10) Susan Hayward.

1958: (1) Glenn Ford; (2) Elizabeth Taylor; (3) Jerry Lewis; (4) Marlon Brando; (5) Rock Hudson; (6) William Holden; (7) Brigitte Bardot; (8) Yul Brynner; (9) James Stewart; (10) Frank Sinatra.

1957: (1) Rock Hudson; (2) John Wayne; (3) Pat Boone; (4) Elvis Presley; (5) Frank Sinatra; (6) Gary Cooper; (7) William Holden; (8) James Stewart; (9) Jerry Lewis; (10) Yul Brynner.

1956: (1) William Holden; (2) John Wayne; (3) James Stewart; (4) Burt Lancaster; (5) Glenn Ford; (6) Dean Martin & Jerry Lewis; (7) Gary Cooper; (8) Marilyn Monroe; (9) Kim Novak; (10) Frank Sinatra.

1955: (1) James Stewart; (2) Grace Kelly; (3) John Wayne; (4) William Holden; (5) Gary Cooper; (6) Marlon Brando; (7) Dean Martin & Jerry Lewis; (8) Humphrey Bogart; (9) June Allyson; (10) Clark Gable.

1954: (1) John Wayne; (2) Dean Martin & Jerry Lewis; (3) Gary Cooper; (4) James Stewart; (5) Marilyn Monroe; (6) Alan Ladd; (7) William Holden; (8) Bing Crosby; (9) Jane Wyman; (10) Marlon Brando.

1953: (1) Gary Cooper; (2) Martin & Lewis; (3) John Wayne; (4) Alan Ladd; (5) Bing Crosby; (6) Marilyn Monroe; (7) James Stewart; (8) Bob Hope; (9) Susan Hayward; (10) Randolph Scott.

1952: (1) Dean Martin & Jerry Lewis; (2) Gary Cooper; (3) John Wayne; (4) Bing Crosby; (5) Bob Hope; (6) James Stewart; (7) Doris Day; (8) Gregory Peck; (9) Susan Hayward; (10) Randolph Scott.

1951: (1) John Wayne; (2) Dean Martin & Jerry Lewis; (3) Betty Grable; (4) Bud Abbott & Lou Costello; (5) Bing Crosby; (6) Bob Hope; (7) Randolph Scott; (8) Gary Cooper; (9) Doris Day; (10) Spencer Tracy.

1950: (1) John Wayne; (2) Bob Hope; (3) Bing Crosby; (4) Betty Grable; (5) James Stewart; (6) Bud Abbott & Lou Costello;

(7) Clifton Webb; (8) Esther Williams; (9) Spencer Tracy; (10) Randolph Scott.

1949: (1) Bob Hope; (2) Bing Crosby; (3) Bud Abbott & Lou Costello; (4) John Wayne; (5) Gary Cooper; (6) Cary Grant; (7) Betty Grable; (8) Esther Williams; (9) Humphrey Bogart; (10) Clark Gable.

1948: (1) Bing Crosby; (2) Betty Grable; (3) Abbott & Costello; (4) Gary Cooper; (5) Bob Hope; (6) Humphrey Bogart; (7) Clark Gable; (8) Cary Grant; (9) Spencer Tracy; (10) Ingrid Bergman.

1947: (1) Bing Crosby; (2) Betty Grable; (3) Ingrid Bergman; (4) Gary Cooper; (5) Humphrey Bogart; (6) Bob Hope; (7) Clark Gable; (8) Gregory Peck; (9) Claudette Colbert; (10) Alan Ladd.

1946: (1) Bing Crosby; (2) Ingrid Bergman; (3) Van Johnson; (4) Gary Cooper; (5) Bob Hope; (6) Humphrey Bogart; (7) Greer Garson; (8) Margaret O'Brien; (9) Betty Grable; (10) Roy Rogers.

1945: (1) Bing Crosby; (2) Van Johnson; (3) Greer Garson; (4) Betty Grable; (5) Spencer Tracy; (6) Humphrey Bogart; Gary Cooper; (7) Bob Hope; (8) Judy Garland; (9) Margaret O'Brien; (10) Roy Rogers.

1944: (1) Bing Crosby; (2) Gary Cooper; (3) Bob Hope; (4) Betty Grable; (5) Spencer Tracy; (6) Greer Garson; (7) Humphrey Bogart; (8) Bud Abbott & Lou Costello; (9) Cary Grant; (10) Bette Davis.

1943: (1) Betty Grable; (2) Bob Hope; (3) Bud Abbott & Lou Costello; (4) Bing Crosby; (5) Gary Cooper; (6) Greer Garson; (7) Humphrey Bogart; (8) James Cagney; (9) Mickey Rooney; (10) Clark Gable.

1942: (1) Bud Abbott & Lou Costello; (2) Clark Gable; (3) Gary Cooper; (4) Mickey Rooney; (5) Bob Hope; (6) James Cagney; (7) Gene Autry; (8) Betty Grable; (9) Greer Garson; (10) Spencer Tracy.

1941: (1) Mickey Rooney; (2) Clark Gable; (3) Bud Abbott & Lou Costello; (4) Bob Hope; (5) Spencer Tracy; (6) Gene Autry; (7) Gary Cooper; (8) Bette Davis; (9) James Cagney; (10) Judy Garland.

1940: (1) Mickey Rooney; (2) Spencer Tracy; (3) Clark Gable; (4) Gene Autry; (5) Tyrone Power; (6) James Cagney; (7) Bing Crosby; (8) Wallace Beery; (9) Bette Davis; (10) Judy Garland.

1939: (1) Mickey Rooney; (2) Tyrone Power; (3) Spencer Tracy; (4) Clark Gable; (5) Shirley Temple; (6) Bette Davis; (7) Alice Faye; (8) Errol Flynn; (9) James Cagney; (10) Sonja Henie.

1938: (1) Shirley Temple; (2) Clark Gable; (3) Sonja Henie; (4) Mickey Rooney; (5) Spencer Tracy; (6) Robert Taylor; (7) Myrna Loy; (8) Jane Withers; (9) Alice Faye; (10) Tyrone Power.

1937: (1) Shirley Temple; (2) Clark Gable; (3) Robert Taylor; (4) Bing Crosby; (5) William Powell; (6) Jane Withers; (7) Fred Astaire and Ginger Rogers; (8) Sonja Henie; (9) Gary Cooper; (10) Myrna Loy.

1936: (1) Shirley Temple; (2) Clark Gable; (3) Fred Astaire and Ginger Rogers; (4) Robert Taylor; (5) Joe E. Brown; (6) Dick Powell; (7) Joan Crawford; (8) Claudette Colbert; (9) Jeanette MacDonald; (10) Gary Cooper.

1935: (1) Shirley Temple; (2) Will Rogers; (3) Clark Gable; (4) Fred Astaire and Ginger Rogers; (5) Joan Crawford; (6) Claudette Colbert; (7) Dick Powell; (8) Wallace Beery; (9) Joe E. Brown; (10) James Cagney.

1934: (1) Will Rogers; (2) Clark Gable; (3) Janet Gaynor; (4) Wallace Beery; (5) Mae West; (6) Joan Crawford; (7) Bing Crosby; (8) Shirley Temple; (9) Marie Dressler; (10) Norma Shearer.

1933: (1) Marie Dressler; (2) Will Rogers; (3) Janet Gaynor; (4) Eddie Cantor; (5) Wallace Beery; (6) Jean Harlow; (7) Clark Gable; (8) Mae West; (9) Norma Shearer; (10) Joan Crawford.

1932: (1) Marie Dressler; (2) Janet Gaynor; (3) Joan Crawford; (4) Charles Farrell; (5) Greta Garbo; (6) Norma Shearer; (7) Wallace Beery; (8) Clark Gable; (9) Will Rogers; (10) Joe E. Brown.

ACADEMY AWARD WINNERS 2009

The 82nd Academy Awards for outstanding film achievements were presented on March 7, 2010, by the Academy of Motion Picture Arts and Sciences at the Kodak Theatre, Los Angeles, CA.

PICTURE
The Hurt Locker. Summit Entertainment. Mark Boal, Greg Shapiro, Nicolas Chartier, Producers.
ACTOR
Jeff Bridges. Crazy Heart. Fox Searchlight Pictures.
ACTRESS
Sandra Bullock. The Blind Side. Warner Bros. Pictures.
SUPPORTING ACTOR
Christoph Waltz. Inglourious Basterds. The Weinstein Company.
SUPPORTING ACTRESS
Mo'Nique. Precious: Based on the Novel 'Push' by Sapphire. Lionsgate.
DIRECTOR
Kathryn Bigelow. The Hurt Locker. Summit Entertainment.
ANIMATED FEATURE FILM
Up. Pete Docter, Bob Peterson. Walt Disney Studios Motion Pictures.
FOREIGN LANGUAGE FILM
The Secret in Their Eyes. Argentina. Sony Pictures Classics.
ORIGINAL SCREENPLAY
Mark Boal for The Hurt Locker. Summit Entertainment.
ADAPTED SCREENPLAY
Geoffrey Fletcher for Precious: Based on the Novel 'Push' by Sapphire. Lionsgate.
CINEMATOGRAPHER
Mauro Fiore for Avatar. Twentieth Century Fox Film.
ART DIRECTION
Rick Carter and Robert Stromberg for Avatar. Twentieth Century Fox Film.
COSTUME DESIGN
Sandy Powell for The Young Victoria. Apparition.
FILM EDITING
Bob Murawski and Chris Innis for The Hurt Locker. Summit Entertainment.
ORIGINAL SCORE
Michael Giacchino for Up. Walt Disney Studios Motion Pictures.
ORIGINAL SONG
"The Weary Kind (Theme from Crazy Heart)" Music and Lyric by Ryan Bingham and T Bone Burnett. Fox Searchlight Pictures.
SHORT SUBJECT-ANIMATED
Logorama. Nicolas Schmerkin. Autour de Minuit Productions.
SHORT SUBJECT-LIVE ACTION
The New Tenants. Joachim Back and Tivi Magnusson. Park Pictures.
SOUND EDITING
Paul N.J. Ottosson for The Hurt Locker. Summit Entertainment.
SOUND MIXING
Paul N.J. Ottosson and Ray Beckett for The Hurt Locker. Summit Entertainment.
MAKEUP
Barney Burman, Mindy Hall and Joel Harlow for Star Trek. Paramount Pictures.
VISUAL EFFECTS
Joe Letteri, Stephen Rosenbaum, Richard Baneham and Andrew R. Jones for Avatar. Twentieth Century Fox Film.
DOCUMENTARY - FEATURE
The Cove. Lionsgate.
DOCUMENTARY - SHORT SUBJECT
Music by Prudence. Home Box Office (HBO).

ACADEMY AWARD WINNERS 2003-2008

Productions, players, directors and craftspersons named for superior merit by the Academy of Motion Picture Arts and Sciences, from 2003-2008. For a complete list of winners from the inception of the awards, please see Vols. 2001 and earlier.

PICTURE
Slumdog Millionaire. Fox Searchlight. A Celador Films Production, Christian Colson, Producer.
ACTOR
Sean Penn. Milk. Focus Features.
ACTRESSKate Winslet. The Reader. The Weinstein Company.
SUPPORTING ACTOR
Heath Ledger. The Dark Knight. Warner Bros.
SUPPORTING ACTRESS
Penelope Cruz. Vicky Cristina Barcelona. The Weinstein Company.
DIRECTOR
Danny Boyle. Slumdog Millionaire. Fox Searchlight.
ANIMATED FEATURE FILM
WALL-E. Andrew Stanton. Walt Disney.

FOREIGN LANGUAGE FILM
Departures. A Departures Film Partners Production, Japan. Regent Releasing.
ORIGINAL SCREENPLAY
Dustin Lance Black for Milk. Focus Features.
ADAPTED SCREENPLAY
Simon Beaufoy for Slumdog Millionaire. Fox Searchlight.
CINEMATOGRAPHER
Anthony Dod Mantle for Slumdog Millionaire. Fox Searchlight.
ART DIRECTION
Donald Graham Burt; Art direction. **Victor J. Zolfo**; Set Direction. The Curious Case of Benjamin Button. Paramount and Warner Bros.
COSTUME DESIGN
Michael O'Connor for The Duchess. Paramount Vantage, Pathé and BBC Films.
FILM EDITING
Chris Dickens for Slumdog Millionaire. Fox Searchlight.
ORIGINAL SCORE
A.R. Rahman for Slumdog Millionaire. Fox Searchlight.
ORIGINAL SONG
"Jai Ho" from Slumdog Millionaire. Music and Lyric by A.R. Rahman and Maya Arulpragasam. Fox Searchlight.
SHORT SUBJECT—ANIMATED
La Maison en Petits Cubes. A Robot Communications Production, Kunio Kato.
SHORT SUBJECT—LIVE ACTION
Spielzeugland (Toyland). A Mephisto Film Production, Jochen Alexander Freydank.
SOUND EDITING
Richard King for The Dark Knight. Warner Bros.
SOUND MIXING
Ian Tapp, Richard Pryke and Resul Pookutty for Slumdog Millionaire. Fox Searchlight.
MAKE-UP
Greg Cannom for The Curious Case of Benjamin Button. Paramount and Warner Bros.
VISUAL EFFECTS
Eric Barba, Steve Preeg, Burt Dalton and Craig Barron for The Curious Case of Benjamin Button. Paramount and Warner Bros.
DOCUMENTARY—FEATURE
Man on Wire. A Wall to Wall in association with Red Box Films Production. James Marsh and Simon Chinn. Magnolia Pictures.
DOCUMENTARY—SHORT SUBJECT
Smile Pinki. Megan Mylan. A Principe Production.
JEAN HERSHOLT HUMANITARIAN AWARD
Jerry Lewis.

2007

PICTURE
No Country for Old Men. Paramount Vantage and Miramax. A Scott Rudin/ Mike Zoss Production. Scott Rudin, Ethan Coen and Joel Coen, Producers.
ACTOR
Daniel Day-Lewis. There Will Be Blood. Paramount Vantage and Miramax.
ACTRESS
Marion Cotillard. La Vie en Rose. Picturehouse.
SUPPORTING ACTOR
Javier Bardem. No Country for Old Men. Paramount Vantage and Miramax.
SUPPORTING ACTRESS
Tilda Swinton. Michael Clayton. Warner Bros.
DIRECTOR
Joel Coen and Ethan Coen. No Country for Old Men. Paramount Vantage and Miramax.
ANIMATED FEATURE FILM
Ratatouille. Brad Bird. Walt Disney.
FOREIGN LANGUAGE FILM
The Counterfeiters. An Aichholzer Filmproduktion, Magnolia Filmproduktion Production. Austria.
ORIGINAL SCREENPLAY
Diablo Cody for Juno. Fox Searchlight.
ADAPTED SCREENPLAY
Joel Coen and Ethan Coen for No Country for Old Men. Paramount Vantage and Miramax.
CINEMATOGRAPHER
Robert Elswit for There Will Be Blood. Paramount Vantage and Miramax.

ART DIRECTION
Dante Ferretti; Art direction. **Fransesca Lo Schiavo**; Set Direction. Sweeney Todd and the Demon Barber of Fleet Street. Dreamworks/Paramount.

COSTUME DESIGN
Alexandra Bryne. Elizabeth: The Golden Age. Universal.

FILM EDITING
Chritopher Rouse for The Bourne Identity. Universal.

ORIGINAL SCORE
Dario Marianelli for Atonement. Focus Features.

ORIGINAL SONG
"Falling Slowly" from An Inconvenient Truth. Music & Lyrics by Melissa Etheridge. Paramount Classics and Participant Productions.

SHORT SUBJECT—ANIMATED
Peter & the Wolf. A Break Thru Films/Se-ma-for Studios Production. Suzie Templeton and Hugh Welchman. Break Thru Films.

SHORT SUBJECT—LIVE ACTION
Le Mozart des Pickpockets. A Kare Production, Phillipe Pollet-Villard.

SOUND EDITING
Karen Baker Landers and Per Hallberg for The Bourne Ultimatum. Universal.

SOUND MIXING
Scott Millan, David Parker and Kirk Francis for The Bourne Ultimatum. Universal.

MAKE-UP
Didier Lavergne and Jan Archibald for La Vie en Rose. Picturehouse.

VISUAL EFFECTS
John Knoll, Hal Hickel, Charles Gibson and Allen Hall The Golden Compass. New Line in association with Ingenious Film Partners.

DOCUMENTARY—FEATURE
Taxi to the Dark Side. An X-Ray Production. Alex Gibney and Eva Omer. THINKFilm.

DOCUMENTARY—SHORT SUBJECT
Freeheld. Cynthia Wade and Vanessa Roth. A Lieutenant Films Production.

2006

PICTURE
The Departed. Warner Bros, A Warner Bros. Pictures Production. Graham King, Producer.

ACTOR
Forest Whitaker. The Last King of Scotland. Fox Searchlight.

ACTRESS
Helen Mirren. The Queen. Miramax.

SUPPORTING ACTOR
Alan Arkin. Little Miss Sunshine. Fox Searchlight.

SUPPORTING ACTRESS
Jennifer Hudson. Dreamgirls. Dreamworks.

DIRECTOR
Martin Scorsese. The Departed. Warner Bros.

ANIMATED FEATURE FILM
Happy Feet. George Miller. Warner Bros.

FOREIGN LANGUAGE FILM
The Lives of Others. A Wiedemann & Berg Production. Germany.

ORIGINAL SCREENPLAY
Michael Arndt for Little Miss Sunshine. Fox Searchlight.

ADAPTED SCREENPLAY
William Monahan for The Departed. Warner Bros.

CINEMATOGRAPHER
Guillermo Navarro for Pan's Labyrinth. Picturehouse.

ART DIRECTION
Eugenio Caballero; Art direction. **Pilar Revuelta**; Set Direction. Pan's Labyrinth. Picturehouse.

COSTUME DESIGN
Milena Canonero. Marie Antoinette. Sony Pictures Releasing.

FILM EDITING
Thelma Schoonmaker for Departed. Warner Bros.

ORIGINAL SCORE
Gustavo Santaolalla for Babel. Paramount and Paramount Vantage.

ORIGINAL SONG
"I Need to Wake Up" from An Inconvenient Truth. Music & Lyrics by Melissa Etheridge. Paramount Classics and Participant Productions.

SHORT SUBJECT—ANIMATED
The Danish Poet. A Mikrofilm and National Film Board of Canada Production. Torill Kove.

SHORT SUBJECT—LIVE ACTION
West Bank Story. An Ari Sandel, Pascal Vaguelsy, Amy Kim, Ravi Malhotra and Ashley Jordan Production. Ari Sandel.

SOUND EDITING
Alan Robert Murray and Bob Asman for Letters from Iwo Jima. Warner Bros.

SOUND MIXING
Michael Minkler, Bob Beemer and Willie Burton for Dreamgirls. Dreamworks and Paramount.

MAKE-UP
David Marti and Montse Ribe for Pan's Labyrinth. Picturehouse.

VISUAL EFFECTS
John Knoll, Hal Hickel, Charles Gibson and Allen Hall for Pirates of the Caribbean: Dead Man's Chest. Buena Vista.

DOCUMENTARY—FEATURE
An Inconvenient Truth. Davis Guggenheim. A Lawrence Bender/ Laurie David Production. Paramount Classics and Participant Productions.

DOCUMENTARY—SHORT SUBJECT
The Blood of Yingzhou District. Leslie Iwerks and Mike Glad. An Iwerks/Glad Production.

HONORARY AWARD
Ennio Morricone

2005

PICTURE
Crash. Lions Gate, A Bob Yari/DEJ/Blackfriar's Bridge/ Harris Company/ApolloProscreen GmbH & Co./Bull's Eye Entertainment Production. Paul Haggis and Cathy Schulman, Producers.

ACTOR
Philip Seymour Hoffman. Capote. UA/Sony Pictures Classics.

ACTRESS
Reese Witherspoon. Walk the Line. 20th Century Fox.

SUPPORTING ACTOR
George Clooney. Syriana. Warner Bros.

SUPPORTING ACTRESS
Rachel Weisz. The Constant Gardener. Focus Features.

DIRECTOR
Ang Lee. Brokeback Mountain. Focus Features.

ANIMATED FEATURE FILM
Wallace & Gromit in the Curse of the Were-Rabbit. DreamWorks Animation SKG.

FOREIGN LANGUAGE FILM
Tsotsi. A Moviworld Production. South Africa.

ORIGINAL SCREENPLAY
Paul Haggis & Bobby Moresco for Crash. Lions Gate.

ADAPTED SCREENPLAY
Larry McMurtry & Diana Ossana for Brokeback Mountain. Focus Features.

CINEMATOGRAPHER
Dion Beebe for Memoirs of a Geisha. Sony Pictures Releasing.

ART DIRECTION
John Myhre; Art direction. **Gretchen Rau**; Set Direction. Memoirs of a Geisha. Sony Pictures Releasing.

COSTUME DESIGN
Colleen Atwood. Memoirs of a Geisha. Sony Pictures Releasing.

FILM EDITING
Hughes Winborne. for Crash. Lions Gate.

ORIGINAL SCORE
Gustavo Santaolalla. for Brokeback Mountain. Focus Features.

ORIGINAL SONG
"It's Hard Out Here for a Pimp" Music & Lyric by: Jordan Houston, Cedric Coleman and Paul Beauregard. Paramount Classics, MTV Films and New Deal Entertainment.

SHORT SUBJECT—ANIMATED
The Moon and the Son: An Imagined Conversation. A John Canemaker Production. John Canemaker and Peggy Stern.

SHORT SUBJECT—LIVE ACTION
Six Shooter. A Missing in Action Films and Funny Farm Films Production. Martin McDonagh.

SOUND EDITING
Mike Hopkins and Ethan Van der Ryn. for King Kong. Universal.

SOUND MIXING
Christopher Boyes, Michael Semanick, Michael Hedges and Hammond Peek for King Kong. Universal.

MAKE-UP
Howard Berger and Tami Lane for The Chronicles of Narnia: The Lion, the Witch and the Wardrobe. Buena Vista.

VISUAL EFFECTS
Joe Letteri, Brian Van't Hul, Christian Rivers and Richard Taylor for King Kong. Universal.

DOCUMENTARY—FEATURE
March of the Penguins. Luc Jacquet and Yves Darondeau. A Bonne Pioche Production. Warner Independent Pictures.

DOCUMENTARY—SHORT SUBJECT
A Note of Triumph: The Golden Age of Norman Corwin. Corinne Marrinan and Eric Simonson. A NomaFilms Production.

HONORARY AWARD
Robert Altman

2004

PICTURE
Million Dollar Baby. Warner Bros. A Lakeshore Entertainment/ Malpaso Productions. Clint Eastwood, Albert S. Ruddy, Tom Rosenberg and Gary Lucchesi, Producers.

ACTOR
Jamie Foxx. Ray. Universal.

ACTRESS
Hilary Swank. Million Dollar Baby. Warner Bros.

SUPPORTING ACTOR
Morgan Freeman. Million Dollar Baby. Warner Bros.

SUPPORTING ACTRESS
Cate Blanchett. The Aviator. Warner Bros.

DIRECTOR
Clint Eastwood. Million Dollar Baby. Warner Bros.

ANIMATED FEATURE FILM
The Incredibles. Brad Bird. Buena Vista.

FOREIGN LANGUAGE FILM
The Sea Inside.
Sogecine and Himenóptero Production. Spain.

ORIGINAL SCREENPLAY
Charlie Kaufman for Eternal Sunshine of the Spotless Mind. Focus Features.

ADAPTED SCREENPLAY
Alexander Payne & Jim Taylor for Sideways. Fox Searchlight.

CINEMATOGRAPHER
Robert Richardson for The Aviator. Warner Bros.

ART DIRECTION
Dante Ferretti; Art direction. **Francesca Lo Schiavo**; Set Direction. The Aviator. Warner Bros.

COSTUME DESIGN
Sandy Powell. The Aviator. Warner Bros.

FILM EDITING
Thelma Schoonmaker for The Aviator. Warner Bros.

ORIGINAL SCORE
Jan A.P. Kaczmarek for Finding Neverland. Miramax.

ORIGINAL SONG
"Al Otro Lado Del Río." The Motorcycle Diaries. Music & Lyric by Jorge Drexler. Focus Features.

SHORT SUBJECT—ANIMATED
Ryan. Chris Landreth

SHORT SUBJECT—LIVE ACTION
Wasp. Andrea Arnold.

SOUND EDITING
Michael Silvers and Randy Thom for The Incredibles. Buena Vista.

SOUND MIXING
Scott Millan, Greg Orloff, Bob Beemer and Steve Cantamessa for Ray. Universal.

MAKE-UP
Valli O'Reilly and Bill Corso for Lemony Snicket's A Series of Unfortunate Events. Paramount.

VISUAL EFFECTS
John Dykstra, Scott Stokdyk, Anthony LaMolinara and John Frazier for Spider-Man 2. Sony.

DOCUMENTARY—FEATURE
Born into Brothels. Red Light Films; Ross Kauffman and Zana Briski, producers.

DOCUMENTARY—SHORT SUBJECT
Mighty Times: The Children's March. Tell the Truth Pictures Production; Robert Hudson and Bobby Houston, producers.

JEAN HERSHOLT HUMANITARIAN AWARD
Roger Mayer.

HONORARY AWARD
Sidney Lumet.

THE GORDON E. SAWYER AWARD
Takuo Miyagishima.

2003

PICTURE
The Lord of the Rings: The Return of the King. A Wingnut Films Production. Producers: Barrie M. Osborne, Peter Jackson and Fran Walsh. New Line.

ACTOR
Sean Penn. Mystic River. Warner Bros.

ACTRESS
Charlize Theron. Monster. Newmarket Films.

SUPPORTING ACTOR
Tim Robbins. Mystic River. Warner Bros.

SUPPORTING ACTRESS
Renee Zellweger. Cold Mountain. Miramax.

DIRECTOR
Peter Jackson. The Lord of the Rings: The Return of the King. New Line.

FOREIGN LANGUAGE FILM
The Barbarian Invasions. A Cinémaginaire Inc. Production.

ORIGINAL SCREENPLAY
Sofia Coppola. Lost In Translation. Focus Features.

ADAPTED SCREENPLAY
Fran Walsh, Philippa Boyens & Peter Jackson. The Lord of the Rings: The Return of the King. New Line.

CINEMATOGRAPHER
Russell Boyd for Master and Commander: The Far Side of the World. 20th Century Fox.

ART DIRECTION
Grant Major; Set direction: **Dan Hennah and Alan Lee.** The Lord of the Rings: The Return of the King. New Line.

COSTUME DESIGN
Ngila Dickson and Richard Taylor. The Lord of the Rings: The Return of the King. New Line.

FILM EDITING
Jamie Selkirk. The Lord of the Rings: The Return of the King. New Line.

ORIGINAL SCORE
Howard Shore. The Lord of the Rings: The Return of the King. New Line.

ORIGINAL SONG
"Into the West." Music & Lyric by: Fran Walsh, Howard Shore & Annie Lennox. Lyrics for The Lord of the Rings: The Return of the King. New Line.

SHORT SUBJECT—ANIMATED
Harvie Krumpet. Adam Elliot. A Melodrama Pictures Production.

SHORT SUBJECT—LIVE ACTION
Two Soldiers. Aaron Schneider and Andrew J. Sacks. A Shoe Clerk Picture Company Production.

SOUND EDITING
Richard King for Master and Commander: The Far Side of the World. 20th Century Fox.

SOUND MIXING
Christopher Boyes, Michael Semanick, Michael Hedges and Hammond Peek for The Lord of the Rings: The Return of the King. New Line.

MAKE-UP
Richard Taylor and Peter King for The Lord of the Rings: The Return of the King. New Line.

VISUAL EFFECTS
Jim Rygiel, Joe Letteri, Randall William Cook and Alex Funke for The Lord of the Rings: Return of the King. New Line.

DOCUMENTARY—FEATURE
The Fog of War. Errol Morris and Michael Williams. A Globe Department Store Production. Sony Picture Classics

DOCUMENTARY—SHORT SUBJECT
Chernobyl Heart. Maryann DeLeo. A Downtown TV Documentaries Production.

HONORARY AWARD
Blake Edwards

AMERICAN FILM INSTITUTE AWARDS

AFI MOVIES OF THE YEAR / OFFICIAL SELECTIONS 2009

CORALINE
Principal cast: Dakota Fanning, Teri Hatcher, Jennifer Saunders

Dawn French, Keith David. *Director:* Henry Selick. *Producer:* Claire Jennings, Bill Mechanic, Mary Sandell, Henry Selick. *Screenwriter:* Henry Selick. *Cinematographer:* Pete Kozachik. *Editor:* Christopher Murrie, Ronald Sanders. *Production Design:* Henry Selick. *Art Director:* Phil Brotherton, Bo Henry, Tom Proost.

THE HANGOVER

Principal cast: Bradley Cooper, Ed Helms, Zach Galifianakis, Justin Bartha, Heather Graham. *Director:* Todd Phillips. *Producer:* Daniel Goldberg, Todd Phillips. *Screenwriter:* Jon Lucas, Scott Moore. *Composer:* Christophe Beck. *Cinematographer:* Lawrence Sher. *Editor:* Debra Neil-Fisher. *Production Design:* Bill Brzeski. *Art Director:* Andrew Max Cahn, A. Todd Holland.

THE HURT LOCKER

Principal cast: Jeremy Renner, Anthony Mackie, Brian Geraghty, Guy Pearce, Ralph Fiennes, David Morse. *Director:* Kathryn Bigelow. *Producer:* Kathryn Bigelow, Mark Boal, Nicolas Chartier, Greg Shapiro. *Screenwriter:* Mark Boal. *Composer:* Marco Beltrami, Buck Sanders. *Cinematographer:* Barry Ackroyd. *Editor:* Chris Innis, Bob Murawski. *Production Design:* Karl Júlíusson. *Art Director:* David Bryan.

THE MESSENGER

Principal cast: Ben Foster, Jena Malone, Eamonn Walker, Woody Harrelson. *Director:* Oren Moverman. *Producer:* Benjamin Goldhirsh, Mark Gordon, Lawrence Inglee, Zach Miller. *Screenwriter:* Alessandro Camon, Oren Moverman. *Composer:* Nathan Larson. *Cinematographer:* Bobby Bukowski. *Editor:* Alex Hall. *Production Design:* Stephen Beatrice. *Art Director:* Scott Anderson.

PRECIOUS: BASED ON THE NOVEL PUSH BY SAPPHIRE

Principal cast: Gabourey Sidibe, Mo'Nique, Paula Patton, Mariah Carey, Sherri Shepherd, Lenny Kravitz. *Director:* Lee Daniels. *Producer:* Lee Daniels, Gary Magness, Sarah Siegel-Magness. *Screenwriter:* Geoffrey Fletcher. *Composer:* Mario Grigorov. *Cinematographer:* Andrew Dunn. *Editor:* Joe Klotz. *Production Design:* Roshelle Berliner. *Art Director:* Matteo De Cosmo.

A SERIOUS MAN

Principal cast: Michael Stuhlbarg, Richard Kind, Fred Melamed, Sari Lennick. *Director:* Ethan Coen, Joel Coen. *Producers:* Ethan Coen, Joel Coen. *Screenwriter:* Ethan Coen, Joel Coen. *Composer:* Carter Burwell. *Cinematographer:* Roger Deakins. *Editor:* Roderick Jaynes. *Production Design:* Jess Gonchor. *Art Director:* Deborah Jensen.

A SINGLE MAN

Principal cast: Colin Firth, Julianne Moore, Nicholas Hoult, Matthew Goode. *Director:* Tom Ford. *Producers:* Tom Ford, Andrew Miano, Robert Salerno, Chris Weitz. *Screenwriter:* Tom Ford, David Scearce. *Composer:* Abel Korzeniowski. *Cinematographer:* Eduard Grau. *Editor:* Joan Sobel. *Production Design:* Dan Bishop. *Art Director:* Ian Phillips.

SUGAR

Principal cast: Algenis Perez Soto, Rayniel Rufino, Andre Holland, Ann Whitney, Ellary Porterfield. *Director:* Anna Boden, Ryan Fleck. *Producers:* Paul S. Mezey, Jamie Patricof, Jeremy Kipp Walker. *Screenwriter:* Anna Boden, Ryan Fleck. *Composer:* Michael Brook. *Editor:* Anna Boden. *Production Design:* Beth Mickle. *Art Director:* Michael Ahern.

UP

Principal cast: Ed Asner, Christopher Plummer, Jordan Nagai, Bob Peterson, Delroy Lindo, Jerome Ranft. *Director:* Pete Docter, Bob Peterson. *Producer:* Jonas Rivera. *Screenwriter:* Bob Peterson, Pete Docter. *Composer:* Michael Giacchino. *Editor:* Kevin Nolting. *Production Design:* Ricky Nierva.

UP IN THE AIR

Principal cast: George Clooney, Vera Farmiga, Anna Kendrick, Jason Bateman. *Director:* Jason Reitman. *Producers:* Jeffrey Clifford, Daniel Dubiecki, Ivan Reitman, Jason Reitman. *Screenwriter:* Jason Reitman, Sheldon Turner. *Composer:* Rolfe Kent. *Cinematographer:* Eric Steelberg. *Editor:* Dana E. Glauberman. *Production Design:* Steve Saklad. *Art Director:* Andrew Max Cahn.

LIFETIME ACHIEVEMENT

2010 RECIPIENT

Mike Nichols

PAST RECIPIENTS

Michael Douglas....2009
Warren Beatty....2008
Al Pacino....2007
Sir Sean Connery....2006
George Lucas....2005
Meryl Streep....2004
Robert De Niro....2003
Tom Hanks....2002
Barbra Streisand....2001
Harrison Ford....2000
Dustin Hoffman....1999
Robert Wise....1998
Martin Scorcese....1997
Clint Eastwood....1996
Steven Spielberg....1995
Jack Nicholson....1994
Elizabeth Taylor....1993
Sidney Poitier....1992
Kirk Douglas....1991
Sir David Lean....1990
Gregory Peck....1989
Jack Lemmon....1988
Barbara Stanwyck....1987
Billy Wilder....1986
Gene Kelly....1985
Lillian Gish....1984
John Huston....1983
Frank Capra....1982
Fred Astaire....1981
James Stewart....1980
Alfred Hitchcock....1979
Henry Fonda....1978
Bette Davis....1977
Wiliam Wyler....1976
Orson Welles....1975
James Cagney....1974
John Ford....1973

American Society of Cinematographers Awards

American Society of Cinematographers Awards were presented March 1, 2010, at the Hyatt Regency Century Plaza Hotel in Los Angeles.

OUTSTANDING ACHIEVEMENT IN CINEMATOGRAPHY/THEATRICAL RELEASES

Christian Berger, AAC for The White Ribbon.

ASC HERITAGE AWARD

Memory of Richard Moore

LIFETIME ACHIEVEMENT AWARD

Caleb Deschanel

BOARD OF GOVERNORS AWARD

Morgan Freeman

INTERNATIONAL AWARD

Chris Menges

PRESIDENT'S AWARD

Sol Negrin

British Academy of Film & Television Arts (BAFTA) Awards

The 2009 Orange British Academy Film Awards were awarded on January 21, 2010. (Orange has sponsored the film awards since 1998, and the Academy changed the name of the event to The Orange British Academy Film Awards in 2000)

BEST FILM

THE HURT LOCKER. Kathryn Bigelow, Mark Boal, Nicolas Chartier, Greg Shapiro.

THE ALEXANDER KORDA AWARD FOR OUTSTANDING BRITISH FILM OF THE YEAR

FISH TANK. Kees Kasander, Nick Laws, Andrea Arnold.

THE CARL FOREMAN AWARD FOR SPECIAL ACHIEVEMENT BY A BRITISH DIRECTOR/PRODUCER OR WRITER IN THEIR FIRST FEATURE FILM

DUNCAN JONES (Director) Moon.

THE DAVID LEAN AWARD FOR ACHIEVEMENT IN DIRECTION

Kathryn Bigelow. The Hurt Locker.

BEST ORIGINAL SCREENPLAY

Mark Boal. The Hurt Locker.

BEST ADAPTED SCREENPLAY

Jason Reitman, Sheldon Turner. Up In The Air.

BEST FILM (NOT IN THE ENGLISH LANGUAGE)

A PROPHET. Pascal Caucheteux, Marco Cherqui, Alix Raynaud,

Jacques Audiard.
BEST ACTOR
COLIN FIRTH. A Single Man.
BEST ACTRESS
CAREY MULLIGAN. An Education.
BEST SUPPORTING ACTOR
CHRISTOPH WALTZ. Inglourious Basterds.
BEST SUPPORTING ACTRESS
MO'NIQUE. Precious: Based on the Novel Push by Sapphire.
THE ANTHONY ASQUITH AWARD FOR ACHIEVEMENT IN FILM MUSIC
Michael Giacchino. UP.
BEST CINEMATOGRAPHY
Barry Ackroyd. The Hurt Locker.
BEST EDITING
Bob Murawski, Chris Innis. The Hurt Locker.
BEST PRODUCTION DESIGN
Rick Carter, Robert Stromberg, Kim Sinclair. Avatar.
BEST COSTUME DESIGN
Sandy Powell. The Young Victoria.
BEST SOUND
Ray Beckett, Paul N. J. Ottosson. The Hurt Locker.
ACHIEVEMENT IN SPECIAL VISUAL EFFECTS
Joe Letteri, Stephen Rosenbaum, Richard Baneham, Andrew R. Jones. Avatar.
BEST MAKEUP/HAIR
Jenny Shircore. The Young Victoria.
BEST SHORT ANIMATION
Sally Arthur, Emma Lazenby. Mother of Many.
BEST SHORT FILM
James Bolton, Martina Amati. I Do Air.
ACADEMY FELLOWSHIP
Vanessa Redgrave.
THE MICHAEL BALCON AWARD FOR OUTSTANDING BRITISH CONTRIBUTION TO CINEMA
Joe Dunton.
THE ORANGE RISING STAR AWARD
KRISTEN STEWART.

BROADCAST FILM CRITICS ASSOCIATION

BEST PICTURE
The Hurt Locker.
BEST ACTOR
Jeff Bridges. Crazy Heart.
BEST ACTRESS (TIE)
Meryl Streep. Julie & Julia, **Sandra Bullock.** The Blind Side.
BEST SUPPORTING ACTOR
Christoph Waltz. Inglourious Basterds.
BEST SUPPORTING ACTRESS
Mo'Nique. Precious: Based on the Novel Push by Sapphire.
BEST YOUNG ACTOR
Saoirse Ronan. The Lovely Bones.
BEST ACTING ENSEMBLE
Inglorious Basterds.
BEST DIRECTOR
Kathryn Bigelow. The Hurt Locker.
BEST ORIGINAL SCREENPLAY
Quentin Tarantino. Inglourious Basterds.
BEST ADAPTED SCREENPLAY
Jason Reitman, Sheldon Turner. Up In The Air.
BEST CINEMATOGRAPHY
Avatar.
BEST ART DIRECTION
Avatar.
BEST EDITING
Avatar.
BEST VISUAL EFFECTS
Avatar.
BEST COSTUME DESIGN
The Young Victoria.
BEST MAKEUP
District 9.
BEST FOREIGN LANGUAGE FILM
Broken Embraces.
BEST COMEDY MOVIE
The Hangover.

BEST DOCUMENTARY
The Cove.
BEST ACTION MOVIE
Avatar.
BEST ANIMATED FEATURE
Up.
BEST SONG
"The Weary Kind". Ryan Bingham and T Bone Burnett. Crazy Heart.
BEST COMPOSER
Michael Giacchino. Up.

CANNES FILM FESTIVAL AWARDS

PALME D'OR
Uncle Boonmee Who Can Recall His Past Lives. Apichatpong Weerasethakul.
PALME D'OR FOR SHORT FILM
BARKING ISLAND. Serge Avedikian.
GRAND PRIX
OF GODS AND MEN. Xavier Beauvois
BEST ACTRESS
Juliette Binoche. Certified Copy.
BEST ACTOR (TIE)
Javier Bardem. Biutiful.
Elio Germano. Our Life.
BEST DIRECTOR
Mathieu Amalric. On Tour.
BEST SCREENPLAY
Lee Chang-dong. Poetry.
JURY PRIZE
Mahamat-Saleh Haroun. A Screaming Man.
GOLDEN CAMERA
Michael Rowe. Ano Bisiesto.

DIRECTORS GUILD OF AMERICA AWARD

FILM DIRECTOR'S AWARD
KATHRYN BIGELOW. The Hurt Locker.
DOCUMENTARY AWARD
LOUIE PSIHOYOS. The Cove.
DGA HONORARY LIFE MEMBERSHIP AWARD
Norman Jewison.
FRANKLIN J. SCHAFFNER ACHIEVEMENT AWARD
Maria Jimenez Henley.
FRANK CAPRA ACHIEVEMENT AWARD
Cleve Landsberg.

GOLDEN GLOBE AWARDS

BEST PICTURE-DRAMA
Avatar.
BEST ACTOR-DRAMA
Jeff Bridges. Crazy Heart.
BEST ACTRESS-DRAMA
Sandra Bullock. The Blind Side.
BEST PICTURE-COMEDY OR MUSICAL
The Hangover.

BEST ACTOR-COMEDY OR MUSICAL
Robert Downey, Jr. Sherlock Holmes.
BEST ACTRESS-COMEDY OR MUSICAL
Meryl Streep. Julie and Julia.
BEST SUPPORTING ACTOR
Christoph Waltz. Inglourious Basterds.

BEST SUPPORTING ACTRESS
Mo'Nique. Precious: Based on the Novel Push by Sapphire.
BEST DIRECTOR
James Cameron. Avatar.
BEST SCREENPLAY
Jason Reitman, Sheldon Turner. Up in the Air.
BEST ORIGINAL SCORE
Michael Giacchino. UP.
BEST ORIGINAL SONG
"The Weary Kind" (Theme From Crazy Heart). Ryan Bingham and T Bone Burnett.
BEST FOREIGN FILM
The White Ribbon.
BEST ANIMATED FILM
UP.
CECIL B. DEMILLE AWARD
Martin Scorsese.

INDEPENDENT SPIRIT AWARDS

The 25th Independent Spirit Awards, honoring excellence in independent film, were presented March 5, 2010.

BEST FEATURE
Precious: Based on the Novel Push by Sapphire. Fox Searchlight.
BEST DIRECTOR
Lee Daniels. Precious: Based on the Novel Push by Sapphire.
BEST SCREENPLAY
Scott Neustader and Michael H. Weber. (500) Days of Summer.
BEST FIRST FEATURE
Scott Cooper, Robert Duvall, Rob Carliner, Judy Cairo, T Bone Burnett. Crazy Heart.
BEST FIRST SCREENPLAY
Geoffrey Fletcher. Precious: Based on the Novel Push by Sapphire.
BEST CINEMATOGRAPHY
Roger Deakins. A Serious Man.
BEST FOREIGN FILM
AN EDUCATION.
BEST ACTRESS
Gabourey Sidibe. Precious: Based on the Novel Push by Sapphire.
BEST ACTOR
Jeff Bridges. Crazy Heart.
BEST SUPPORTING ACTRESS
Mo'Nique. Precious: Based on the Novel Push by Sapphire.
BEST SUPPORTING ACTOR
Woody Harrelson. The Messenger.
BEST DOCUMENTARY
ANVIL! THE STORY OF ANVIL.
ROBERT ALTMAN AWARD
Ethan Coen, Joel Coen and the cast of A Serious Man.

LOS ANGELES FILM CRITICS AWARDS

BEST PICTURE
The Hurt Locker.
BEST ACTOR
Jeff Bridges. Crazy Heart.
BEST ACTRESS
Yolande Moreau. Seraphine.
BEST SUPPORTING ACTOR
Christoph Waltz. Inglourious Basterds.
BEST SUPPORTING ACTRESS
Mo'Nique. Precious: Based on the Novel Push by Sapphire.
BEST DIRECTOR
Kathryn Bigelow. The Hurt Locker.
BEST SCREENPLAY
Jason Reitman and Sheldon Turner. Up In The Air.
BEST FOREIGN LANGUAGE FILM
Summer Hours.
BEST DOCUMENTARY (TIE)
The Beaches of Agnès. The Cove.
BEST CINEMATOGRAPHY
Christian Berger. The White Ribbon.
BEST ANIMATED FILM
Fantastic Mr. Fox.
NEW GENERATION AWARD
Neill Blomkamp. District 9.

NATIONAL BOARD OF REVIEW

The National Board of Review includes teachers, actors, writers and movie-production workers. The organization publishes the magazine, Films in Review. The winners were announced Jan. 14, 2009.

BEST PICTURE
Up in the Air.
BEST DIRECTOR
Clint Eastwood. Invictus.
BEST ACTOR
Morgan Freeman. Invictus.
BEST ACTRESS
Carey Mulligan. An Education.
BEST SUPPORTING ACTOR
Woody Harrelson. The Messenger.
BEST SUPPORTING ACTRESS
Anna Kendrick. Up in the Air.
BREAKTHROUGH PERFORMANCES
Jeremy Renner. The Hurt Locker. **Gabourey Sidibe.** Precious: Based on the Novel Push by Sapphire.
BEST FOREIGN FILM
Un prophète.
BEST ENSEMBLE
It's Complicated.
BEST ORIGINAL SCREENPLAY OF THE YEAR
Joel Coen, Ethan Coen. A Serious Man.
BEST ADAPTED SCREENPLAY OF THE YEAR
Jason Reitman, Sheldon Turner. Up in the Air.
BEST ANIMATED FEATURE
UP.
WILLIAM K. EVERSON AWARD FOR FILM HISTORY
Jean Firstenberg.
SPECIAL RECOGNITION OF FILMS THAT REFLECT THE FREEDOM OF EXPRESSION (TIE)
Burma VJ: Reporter i et lukket land.
The Most Dangerous Man in America: Daniel Ellsberg and the Pentagon Papers.
Invictus.

NATIONAL SOCIETY OF FILM CRITICS AWARDS

BEST PICTURE
The Hurt Locker.
BEST ACTOR
Jeremy Renner. The Hurt Locker.
BEST ACTRESS
Yolande Moreau. Seraphine.
BEST SUPPORTING ACTOR (TIE)
Christoph Waltz. Inglourious Basterds.
PAUL SCHNEIDER. Bright Star.
BEST SUPPORTING ACTRESS
Mo'Nique. Precious: Based on the Novel Push by Sapphire.
BEST DIRECTOR
Kathryn Bigelow. The Hurt Locker.
BEST SCREENPLAY
Joel Coen and Ethan Coen. A Serious Man.
BEST CINEMATOGRAPHY
Christian Berger. The White Ribbon.

BEST FOREIGN LANGUAGE FILM
Summer Hours.
BEST NON-FICTION FILM
The Beaches of Agnes.
BEST PRODUCTION DESIGN
Nelson Lowry. Fantastic Mr. Fox.

BEST ANIMATED FILM
Fantastic Mr. Fox.
SPECIAL AWARD
Andrew Sarris.

New York Film Critics Circle Awards

The New York Film Critics Circle Awards announced its award selections December 14, 2009. The 30-member group voted for its 75th annual awards for excellence in cinema.

BEST PICTURE
The Hurt Locker.
BEST DIRECTOR
Kathryn Bigelow. The Hurt Locker.
BEST NONFICTION FILM
Of Time and the City.
BEST FOREIGN FILM
Summer Hours.
BEST FIRST FEATURE
Steve McQueen. Hunger.
BEST ACTOR
George Clooney. Up In The Air.
BEST ACTRESS
Meryl Streep. Julie & Julia.
BEST SUPPORTING ACTOR
Christoph Waltz. Inglourious Basterds.
BEST SUPPORTING ACTRESS
Mo'Nique. Precious: Based on the Novel Push by Sapphire.
BEST SCREENPLAY
Jesse Armstrong, Simon Blackwell, Armando Iannucci and Tony Roche. In the Loop.
BEST CINEMATOGRAPHER
Christian Berger. The White Ribbon.

Screen Actors Guild Awards

The Screen Actors Guild announced award winners for 2010 on Jan. 23, 2010 at the Shrine Exposition Center in Los Angeles, CA

BEST ACTOR
JEFF BRIDGES. Crazy Heart.
BEST ACTRESS
SANDRA BULLOCK. The Blind Side.
BEST SUPPORTING ACTOR
CHRISTOPH WALTZ. Inglourious Basterds.
BEST SUPPORTING ACTRESS
MO'NIQUE. Precious: Based on the Novel Push by Sapphire.
BEST ENSEMBLE CAST
INGLOURIOUS BASTERDS. Brad Pitt, Christoph Waltz, Martin Wuttke, Rod Taylor, Til Schweiger, Eli Roth, Mike Myers, Denis Menochet, Melanie Laurent, Kiane Kruger, Jacky Ido, Sylvester Groth, Michael Fassbender, Julie Dreyfus, August Diehl, Daniel Bruhl.

Writers Guild Awards

BEST ORIGINAL SCREENPLAY
Mark Boal. The Hurt Locker. Summit Entertainment.
BEST ADAPTED SCREENPLAY
Jason Reitman and Sheldon Turner. Up in the Air. Paramount Pictures
BEST DOCUMENTARY SCREENPLAY
MARK MONROE. The Cove. Lionsgate and Roadside Attractions.

INTERNATIONAL FILM & TV FESTIVALS AND MARKETS

JANUARY 2011

CINEMART
P.O. Box 21696, 3001 AR Rotterdam, The Netherlands.
TEL: (+31) 10 890 9090. FAX: (+31) 10 890 9091.
email: tiger@filmfestivalrotterdam.com
www.filmfestivalrotterdam.com

CLERMONT-FERRAND SHORT FILM FESTIVAL
La Jetée, 6, Place Michel-de-L'Hospital, 63058 Clermont-Ferrand Cedex 1, France. TEL: (04) 7391 6573.
FAX: (04) 7392 1193. email: info@clermont-filmfest.com
www.clermont-filmfest.com
CONTACT
Jean-Bernard Emery - jb.emery@cinepresscontact.com

DANCE ON CAMERA
48 W. 21st St., #907, New York, NY 10010-6989.
TEL: (212) 727-0764. email: info@dancefilms.org
www.dancefilmsassn.org www.dancefilms.org
FESTIVAL DIRECTOR
Dierdre Towers

DAYS OF EUROPEAN FILM
Eurofilmfest s.r.o., Národní 28, 110 00 Praha 1.
TEL: (+420) 604 607 477, (420) 603 844 811.
email: info@eurofilmfest.cz www.eurofilmfest.cz
CONTACTS
Magdaléna Králová, Barbora Golatová

EXPLORERS CLUB DOCUMENTARY FILM FESTIVAL
The Explorers Club, 46 E.70th St., New York, NY 10021.
TEL: (212) 628-8383. FAX: (212) 288-4449.
www.explorers.org/spec_events/filmfest/filmfest.php
OPERATIONS DIRECTOR
Matt Williams - mwilliams@explorers.org

FIPA: INTERNATIONAL FESTIVAL OF AUDIO-VISUAL PROGRAMS
14 Rue Alexandre Parodi, 75010 Paris, France.
TEL: +33 (0) (1) 4489 9999. FAX: 33 (0) (1) 4489 9960.
email: info@fipa.tm.fr www.fipa.tm.fr
Artistic Director
Teresa Cavina - delegation-generale@fipa.tm.fr

FLICKERFEST INTERNATIONAL SHORT FILM FESTIVAL
P.O. Box 7416, Bondi Beach, NSW 2026, Sydney, Australia.
TEL: +61 (0) 2 9365 6877. FAX +61 (0) 2 9365 6899.
email: coordinator@flickerfest.com.au www.flickerfest.com.au
FESTIVAL DIRECTOR
Bronwyn Kidd

FUTURE FILM FESTIVAL
In Association with Amici del Future Film Festival
Via Pietralata, 65/2, 40122 Bologna, Italy.
TEL: +39 051 2960672. FAX: +39 051 6567133.
email: ffinfo@futurefilmfestival.org www.futurefilmfestival.org
DIRECTORS
Giulietta Fara, Oscar Cosulich

GÉRARDMER FANTASY FILM FESTIVAL
40 rue Anatole, France Levallois Perret Cedex 92594, France.
TEL: +33 (0) 3 29 60 98 21. FAX: +33 (0) 3 29 60 98 14.
email: info@festival-gerardmer.com
www.gerardmer-fantasticart.com

GÖTEBORG INTERNATIONAL FILM FESTIVAL
Olof Palmes Plats, 413 04 Göteborg, Sweden.
TEL: +46 (0) 31 339 30 00. FAX: +46 (0) 31 410063.
email: info@giff.se www.filmfestival.org
ARTISTIC DIRECTOR
Marit Kapla - +46 (0) 31-339 30 03 marit.kapla@giff.se

HUNGARIAN FILM WEEK
Városligeti fasor 38, Budapest, 1068, Hungary.
TEL: +36 (1) 351 7760. FAX: +36 (1) 352 6734.
email: filmunio@filmunio.hu www.filmunio.hu
GENERAL MANAGER
Éva Vezér

KIDFILM
6116 N. Central Expwy., Ste. 105, Dallas, TX 75206.
TEL: (214) 821-6300. FAX: (214) 821-6364.
email: usafilmfestival@aol.com www.usafilmfestival.com

NATPE
5757 Wilshire Blvd., Penthouse 10, Los Angeles, CA 90036-3681. TEL: 310-453-4440. FAX: 310-453-5258. www.natpe.org
REGISTRATION & MEMBERSHIP
Eric Low - ext.. 253 eric@natpe.org

NEW YORK JEWISH FILM FESIVAL
The Jewish Museum, 1109 5th Ave., New York, NY 10128.
TEL: (212) 423-3234. FAX: (212) 423-3232.
email: filmfestival@thejm.org www.thejewishmuseum.org

PALM SPRINGS INTERNATIONAL FILM FESTIVAL
1700 E.Tahquitz Canyon Way, Ste. 3, Palm Springs, CA 92262.
TEL: (760) 322-2930. FAX: (760) 322-4087.
email: info@psfilmfest.org www.psfilmfest.org
FESTIVAL DIRECTOR
Darryl Macdonald

REEL MUSIC
Northwest Film Center, 934 SW Salmon St., Portland, OR 97205.
TEL: (503) 221-1156 ext. 10. FAX: (503) 294-0874.
email: info@nwfilm.org www.nwfilm.org
PUBLIC RELATIONS & MARKETING MANAGER
Jessica Lyness - jessica@nwfilm.org

SCIENCE FICTION + FANTASY SHORT FILM FESTIVAL
330 6th Ave. N., Ste. 200, Seattle, WA 98109.
TEL: (877) 367-7361, (206) 770-2700.
email: filmfest@empsfm.org www.empsfm.org
MEDIA CONTACT
Maggie Skinner - (206) 770-2700 pressinfo@empsfm.org

SLAMDANCE FILM FESTIVAL
5634 Melrose Ave., Los Angeles, CA 90038.
TEL: (323) 466-1786. FAX: (323) 466-1784.
email: mail@slamdance.com www.slamdance.com
PRESS INQUIRIES
Megan MacLeod - megan@slamdance.com

SOLOTHURN FILM FESTIVAL
Untere Steingrubenstrasse 19, Box Office 1564, CH-4502 Solothurn, Switzerland. TEL: 41 32 635 80 80.
FAX: 41 32 623 64 10. email: info@solothurnerfilmtage.ch
www.solothurnerfilmtage.ch
DIRECTOR
Ivo Kummer

SUNDANCE FILM FESTIVAL
8530 Wilshire Blvd., 3rd Fl., Beverly Hills, CA 90211-3114.
TEL: (310) 360-1981. FAX: (310) 360-1969.
email: Institute@sundance.org www.sundance.org
DIRECTOR
John Cooper

TRANSMEDIALE FESTIVAL FOR ART AND DIGITAL CULTURE
Klosterstraße 68 - D10179 Berlin, Germany.
TEL: +49 (0) 30 24 749 761. FAX: +49 (0) 30 24 749 763.
email: info@transmediale.de www.transmediale.de
ARTISTIC DIRECTOR
Stephen Kovats

TRIESTE FILM FESTIVAL
via Donota 1, - Trieste I, Italy 34121. TEL: +39 040 347 6076.
FAX: +39 040 662338. email: info@alpeadriacinema.it
www.triestefilmfestival.it
GENERAL MANAGEMENT
sain@alpeadriacinema.it

FEBRUARY 2011

ANIMA
Folioscope a.s.b.l., 52 Avenue de Stalingrad, B - 1000 Brussels Belgium. TEL: +32 (0) 2 534 41 25. FAX: + (0)32 2 534 22 79.
email: info@folioscope.be www.folioscope.be

ANIMATED EXETER
Exeter City Council, Civic Centre, Paris St., Exeter, EX1 1JN.
United Kingdom. TEL: 44 1392 265 208. FAX: 44 1392 265 366.
email: animatedexeter@exeter.gov.uk
www.animatedexeter.co.uk
PRESS CONTACT
Liz Harkman

BANGKOK INTERNATIONAL FILM FESTIVAL
31/9, 2nd Flr., Royal City Ave., UMG Theater, New Petchaburi Rd., Bangkapi, Huay Khwang, Bangkok 10310 Thailand.
TEL: (662) 203 0624, (662) 641 5917. FAX: (662) 6415919.
email: info@bangkokfilm.org www.bangkokfilm.org
FESTIVAL DIRECTOR
Mr. Jareuk Kaljareuk

BELGRADE INTERNATIONAL FILM FESTIVAL
20 Majke Jevrosime St., 11 000 Belgrade, Serbia and

Montenegro. TEL: 381 (11) 3346-946. email: info@fest.org.yu
www.fest.org.yu

BERLIN INTERNATIONAL FILM FESTIVAL
Potsdamer Straße 5, 10785 Berlin, Germany.
TEL: 49 30 25 9200. FAX: 49 30 259 20 299.
email: info@berlinale.de www.berlinale.de
FESTIVAL DIRECTOR
Dieter Kosslick

BIG SKY DOCUMENTARY FILM FESTIVAL
131 S. Higgins Ave., Ste. 307, Missoula, MT 59802.
TEL: (406) 541-FILM. email: info@bigskyfilmfest.org
www.bigskyfilmfest.org
FESTIVAL DIRECTOR
Mike Steinberg - steinberg@webster.edu
FESTIVAL PROGRAMMER
Doug Hawes-Davis - programming@bigskyfilmfest.org

BOULDER INTL. FILM FESTIVAL
1906 13th St., Ste. 301, Boulder, CO 80302.
TEL: (303) 449-2283. FAX: (303) 449-2274. www.biff1.com
EXECUTIVE DIRECTOR
Robin Beeck - robin@biff1.com

CINEQUEST
P.O. Box 720040, San Jose, CA 95172. TEL: (408) 295-3378.
FAX: (408) 995-5713. email: info@cinequest.org
www.cinequest.org
EXECUTIVE DIRECTOR
Halfdan Hussey

CLERMONT-FERRAND SHORT FILM FESTIVAL
La Jetée, 6 Place Michel-de-L'Hospital, 63058 Clermont-Ferrand Cedex, France. TEL: 33 (4) 7391 6573.
FAX: 33 (4) 7392 1193. email: info@clermont-filmfest.com
www.clermont-filmfest.com
CONTACT
Christian Guinot - c.guinot@clermont-filmfest.com

DAMAH FILM FESTIVAL
8033 Sunset Blvd. #1041, Hollywood, CA 90046.
TEL: (310) 237-5436. email: info@damah.com
www.damah.com
EXECUTIVE DIRECTOR
Jimmy Duke

DIY FILM FESTIVAL
7095 Hollywood Blvd., Ste. 864, Hollywood, CA 90028.
TEL: (323) 665-8080. FAX: (323) 372-3883.
email: bruce@diyconvention.com www.diyconvention.com
CONTACT
Bruce Haring

EAST LANSING CHILDREN'S FILM FESTIVAL
P.O. Box 755, 210 Abbott Road, Ste. 48, East Lansing, MI 48823. TEL: (517) 336-5802. FAX: (517) 336-2750.
email: info@elcff.com www.elcff.com
CONTACT
Susan Woods - susanwoods@elff.com

FANTASPORTO: OPORTO INTERNATIONAL FILM FESTIVAL
Rua Anibal Cunha, 84 sala 1.6, 4050-046 Porto, Portugal.
TEL: 351 22 207 6050. FAX: 351 22 207 6059.
email: info@fantasporto.online.pt www.fantasporto.com

GLASGOW FILM FESTIVAL
12 Rose St., Glasgow G3 6RB Scotland, United Kingdom.
TEL: 44 141 332 6535, 44 141 332 8128. FAX: 44 141 332 7945.
email: info@glasgowfilmfestival.org.uk
www.glasgowfilmfestival.org.uk

GOING UNDERGROUND
Rosa Luxemburg St. 2 10178 Berlin, Germany.
TEL: 49 30 256 209 10. FAX: 49 30 256 209 15.
www.going-underground.org
CONTACT
Fred Kuhaupt - fred.kuhaupt@berliner-fenster.de

HUNGARIAN FILM WEEK/MAGYAR FILMSZEMLE
Magyar Filmunió 1068 Budapest, Varosligeti fasor 38, Budapest, Hungary. TEL: 361 351 7760. FAX: 361 352 6734.
email: filmunio@filmunio.hu www.filmunio.hu

INTERNATIONAL FORUM OF NEW CINEMA
Potsdamer Straße 2, D-10785 Berlin, Germany.
TEL: 49 (30) 269 55 100. FAX: 49 (30) 269 55 111.
email: fdk@fdk-berlin.de www.fdk-berlin.de

JAMESON DUBLIN INTERNATIONAL FILM FESTIVAL
50 Upper Mount St., Dublin 2, Ireland. TEL: 353 1 662 4260.
email: info@dubliniff.com www.dubliniff.com
FESTIVAL DIRECTOR
Grainne Humphreys - grainne@jdiff.com

KESWICK FILM FESTIVAL
The Lonsdale Alhambra Cinema, St John's Street, Keswick, Cumbria CA12 5AG United Kingdom. TEL: 44 017687 74475.
FAX: 44 017687 71720.
email: info@keswickfilmclub.org
www.keswickfilmfestival.org

MONS INTL. LOVE FILM FESTIVAL
59, Rue Arthur Warocqué La Louvière 7100 Belgium.
TEL: 0032 64 31 28 00. FAX: 0032 64 31 28 01.
email: andre.ceuterick@skynet.be www.fifa-mons.be/

NEW YORK INTERNATIONAL CHILDREN'S FILM FESTIVAL
295 Greenwich St. #426, New York, NY 10007.
TEL: (212) 349-0330. FAX: (212) 966-5923.
email: info@gkids.com www.gkids.com
DIRECTORS
Eric Beckman, Emily Shapiro

NEW YORK INTL. INDEPENDENT FILM AND VIDEO FESTIVAL
505 E. Windmill Lane, Ste. 1B-102, Las Vegas, NV 89123.
TEL: (702) 263-4480. FAX: (702) 361-6309.
email: filmmfest@aol.com www.nyfilmvideo.com

PAN AFRICAN FILM FESTIVAL
3775 Santa Rosalia Dr., Los Angeles, CA 90008.
TEL: (323) 295-1706. FAX: (323) 295-1952.
email: info@paff.org www.PAFF.org
FOUNDER & EXECUTIVE DIRECTOR
AyUnited Kingdomo Babu - babu@paff.org

PORTLAND INTERNATIONAL FILM FESTIVAL
Northwest Film Center, 1219 S.W. Park Ave., Portland, OR 97205.
TEL: (503) 221-1156. FAX: (503) 294-0874.
email: info@nwfilm.org www.nwfilm.org
PUBLIC RELATIONS & MARKETING MANAGER
Jessica Lyness - jessica@nwfilm.org

SAN FRANCISCO INDEPENDENT FILM FESTIVAL
530 Divisadero St., #183 San Francisco, CA 94117.
TEL: (415) 820 3907. email: info@sfindie.com
www.sfindie.com
DIRECTOR
Jeff Ross

SCI-FI LONDON
c/o FestivalBiz, 2nd Flr., 145 - 157 St John St., London EC1V 4PY, United Kingdom. TEL: 44 020 3239 9277.
FAX: 44 20 8983 9426. email: info@sci-fi-london.com
www.sci-fi-london.com
CONTACT
Frazer Nash - 012 96 712 522

SEDONA INTL. FILM FESTIVAL
P.O. Box 162 (86339), 45 Sunset Dr., Sedona, AZ 86336.
TEL: (928) 282-1177. FAX: (928) 282-5912.
email: director@sedonafilmfestival.com
www.sedonafilmfestival.com
EXECUTIVE DIRECTOR
Patrick Schweiss

TOKYO VIDEO FESTIVAL
Victor Bldg.,1-7-1, Shinbashi, Minato-ku, Tokyo 105-0004, Japan.
TEL: 81-3-3289-2815. FAX: 81-3-3289-2819.
email: jvc-tvf1@mb.kcom.ne.jp www.jvc-victor.co.jp/english/tvf

TRANSMEDIALE FESTIVAL FOR ART AND DIGITAL CULTURE
Klosterstrasse 68-70 10179 Berlin, Germany.
TEL: 49 30 24749761. email: info@transmediale.de
www.transmediale.de

VICTORIA INDEPENDENT FILM & VIDEO FESTIVAL
1225 Blanshard St., Victoria, BC Canada V8W 3J4.
TEL: (250) 389-0444. FAX: (250) 389-0406.
email: festival@victoriafilmfestival.com
www.victoriafilmfestival.com
FESTIVAL DIRECTOR
Kathy Kay
PROGRAMMER
Donovan Aikman

THE 'WHAT THE HELL DID I JUST WATCH' COMEDY VIDEO FESTIVAL
3817 Shelby Rd., Seattle, WA 98087. TEL: (206) 888-6293.
www.whatthehelldidijustwatch.com

WORLD OF COMEDY INTERNATIONAL FILM FESTIVAL
c/o C. Nolan, 45 Balliol St., Ste. 509, Toronto, ON M4S 1C3, Canada. TEL: (416) 487-7574. email: info@worldcomedyfilmfest.com
www.worldcomedyfilmfest.com
DIRECTOR
Carla Nolan

MARCH 2011

AMNESTY INTERNATIONAL FILM FESTIVAL
P.O. Box 1968 1000 BZ, Amsterdam, Netherlands.
TEL: 31 (20) 773 3621. FAX: 31 (20) 624 0889.
email: filmfestival@amnesty.nl www.amnestyfilmfestival.nl

ANN ARBOR FILM FESTIVAL
308 1/2 S. State St., Ste. 31, Ann Arbor, MI 48104.
TEL: (734) 995-5356. FAX: (734) 995-5396.
email: info@aafilmfest.org www.aafilmfest.org
EXECUTIVE DIRECTOR
Donald Harrison - director@aafilmfest.org

BELFAST FILM FESTIVAL
3rd Fl. 23 Donegall St., Belfast, N. Ireland BT1 2FF, United Kingdom. TEL: 44 28 90 32 59 13. FAX: 44 28 90 32 93 97.
email: info@belfastfilmfestival.org www.belfastfilmfestival.org
FESTIVAL DIRECTOR
Michelle Devlin

BRADFORD FILM FESTIVAL
National Media Museum, Bradford, West Yorkshire, BD1 1NQ England. TEL: 44 1274 203 320. FAX: 44 1274 394 540.
www.bradfordfilmfestival.org.uk
FESTIVAL PROGRAMMING
Tony Earnshaw - tony.earnshaw@nmsi.ac.uk

BUFF: MALMO INTERNATIONAL CHILDREN'S AND YOUNG PEOPLE'S FILMFESTIVAL
Buff Stortorget 29, Box 4277, SE-203 14 Malmo, Sweden.
TEL: 46 40 23 92 11. FAX: 46 40 30 53 22.
email: info@buff.se www.buff.se
FESTIVAL PRODUCER
Cecilia Grubb

CANKARJEV INTL. DOCUMENTARY FILM FESTIVAL
FDF, Cankarjev dom Presernova 10 Ljubljana, Slovenia.
TEL: 386 1 24 17 150. FAX: 386 1 24 17 298.
email: simon.popek@cd-cc.si www.fdf.si
FESTIVAL PROGRAMME DIRECTOR
Simon Popek

CHERBOURG-OCTEVILLE FESTIVAL OF IRISH AND BRITISH FILM
Association Travelling 15 Passage Digard 50100 Cherbourg-Octeville, France. TEL: 33 2 3393 3894. FAX: 33 2 3393 3824.
www.festivalcherbourg.com

CINEMA DU REEL
BPI Centre Georges Pompidou 25, rue du Renard 75197 Paris cedex 04, France. TEL: 33 1 78 5 16. FAX: 33 1 44 78 12 24.
email: cinereel@bpi.fr www.cinereel.org
CONTACT
Philippe Guillaume

CINEMA NOVO FESTIVAL
Sint-Jakobsstraat 36, B-8000 Brugge, Belgium.
TEL: 32 50 34 83 54. FAX: 32 50 34 92 23.
email:info@cinemanovo.be www.cinemanovo.be

CLEVELAND INTERNATIONAL FILM FESTIVAL
2510 Market Ave., Cleveland, OH 44113-3434.
TEL: (216) 623-3456. FAX: (216) 623-0103.
email: cfs@clevelandfilm.org www.clevelandfilm.org
EXECUTIVE DIRECTOR
Marcie Goodman - mgoodman@clevelandfilm.org

CUCALORUS FILM FESTIVAL
815 Princess St., Wilmington, NC 28401. TEL: (910) 343-5995.
FAX: (910) 343-5227. email: mail@cucalorus.org
www.cucalorus.org
DIRECTOR
Dan Brawley - dan@cucalorus.org

DALLAS INTLERNATIONAL FILM FESTIVAL
1155 Broom St., Dallas, TX 75202. TEL: (214) 720-0555.
FAX: (214) 720-0551. email: info@afidallas.com
www.AFIDALLAS.com

D.C. INDEPENDENT FILM FESTIVAL
2950 Van Ness St. NW, Ste. 728, Washington, DC 20008.
TEL: (202) 333-6615. FAX: (202) 686-8867.
email: info@dciff.org www.dciff.org
EXECUTIVE DIRECTOR & FOUNDER
Carol Bidault

DOCFEST: NEW YORK INTL. DOCUMENTARY FESTIVAL
305 Degraw St., Brooklyn, NY 11231. TEL: (212) 668-1100.
FAX: (212) 943-6396. www.docfest.org

EAST LANSING FILM FESTIVAL
P.O. Box 4880, East Lansing, MI 48826. TEL: (517) 336-5802.
FAX: (517) 336-2750. www.elff.com
DIRECTOR
Susan Woods - susanwoods@elff.com

FIFI: INTERNET FILM FESTIVAL
17 rue Duperre 75009 Paris, France. TEL: 33 6 1280 4527.
www.fififestival.net
PRESIDENT
Vincy Thomas - vincythomas@fififestival.net

FILMART
38/F Office Tower, Convention Plz., 1 Harbour Rd., Wanchai, Hong Kong. TEL: 852 2584 130. www.hkfilmart.com/hkfilmart
PROJECT MANAGER
Mr. Wayne Chung - wayne.nh.chung@tdc.org.hk

FLORIDA FILM FESTIVAL
1300 S. Orlando Ave., Maitland, FL 32751.
TEL: (407) 629-1088 ext. 225. FAX: (407) 629.6870.
www.floridafilmfestival.com

FRENCH FILM FESTIVAL
P.O. Box 191, Balwyn Melbourne, VIC 3103, Australia.
TEL: 61 3 9817 6421. email: elysia@palace.net.au
www.frenchfilmfestival.org

FRIBOURG INTERNATIONAL FILM FESTIVAL
Ancienne Gare/Case postale 550, CH - 1701 Fribourg, Switzerland. TEL: 41 26 347 42 00. FAX: 41 26 347 42 01.
email: info@fiff.ch www.fiff.ch

HUMAN RIGHTS NIGHTS FILM FESTIVAL
Cineteca di Bologna, Via Riva Reno, 72-40122 Bologna, Italy.
TEL: 39 051 2194 808. FAX: 39 051 2194 821.
email: humanrightsnights@comune.bologna.it
www.humanrightsnights.org
FILM PROGRAMMING
Isabella Malaguti - isabella.malaguti@comune.bologna.it

INTL. FILM FESTIVAL ON HUMAN RIGHTS
Maison des Arts du Grutli, Premier étage, 16 Rue General Dufour, 1205 Genève, Switzerland. TEL: 41 22 809 69 04.
FAX: 41 22 329 37 47. email: contact@fifdh.ch www.fifdh.ch
CO-DIRECTORS
Leo Kaneman, Yael Reinharz Hazan

LAS PALMAS DE GRAN CANARIA INTL. FILM FESTIVAL
León y Castillo, 322, 4.ª planta, 35007 – Las Palmas de Gran Canaria, Spain. TEL: 34 928 446 833. FAX: 34 928 446 651.
email: direccion@festivalcinelaspalmas.com
www.festivalcinelaspalmas.com
DIRECTOR
Claudio Utrera

LONDON AUSTRALIAN FILM FESTIVAL
Barbican Cinema, Silk St., London EC2Y 8DS, United Kingdom. TEL: 44 20 7382 2379. FAX: 44 20 7382 7037.
email: film@barbican.org.uk www.barbican.org.uk/film

METHOD FEST INDEPENDENT FILM FESTIVAL
840 Apollo St., Ste. 314, El Segundo, CA 90245.
TEL: (310) 535-9230. FAX: (310) 535-9128.
www.methodfest.com
FESTIVAL DIRECTOR
Don Franken - don@methodfest.com

MILAN INTERNATIONAL FILM FESTIVAL
Viale Liguria, 50/A, Milano 20143, TEL: 39 02 9287 1578.
email: info@miff.it www.miff.it
DIRECTOR
Andrea Galante - agalante@miff.it

NEW DIRECTORS/NEW FILMS FESTIVAL
Film Society of Lincoln Center, 70 Lincoln Center Plaza, New York, NY 10023. TEL: (212) 875-5638. FAX: (212) 875-5636.
email: festival@filmlinc.com www.filmlinc.com
MANAGING DIRECTOR, FESTIVALS
Marian Masone

OZARK FOOTHILLS FILMFEST
195 Peel Rd., Locust Grove, AR 72550. TEL: (870) 251-1189.
FAX: (870) 251-1189. email: ozarkfilm@wildblue.net
www.ozarkfoothillsfilmfest.org

POITIERS INTERNATIONAL FILM SCHOOLS FESTIVAL
TAP - Scène Nationale, 1 bd de Verdun, 86000 Poitiers, France. TEL: 33 (5) 4903 1890. FAX: 33 (5) 4903 1899.
email: festival.rihl@tap-poitiers.com www.rihl.org
GENERAL COORDINATOR
Bertrand Lecerf - bertrand.lecerf@tap-poitiers.com

REEL WOMEN INTERNATIONAL FILM FESTIVAL
1317 N. San Fernando Blvd., # 340, Burbank, CA 91504.
TEL: (818) 749 6162. email: dmeans25@yahoo.com
www.reelwomenfest.com

RENDEZ-VOUS WITH FRENCH CINEMA
424 Madison Ave., New York, NY 10017. TEL: (212) 832-8860.
FAX: (212) 755-0629.

RIGA INTL. CHILDREN'S FILM FESTIVAL
Marstalu Str. 14, LV1050 Riga, Latvia. TEL: 371 67221620.
www.arsenals.lv
PROGRAM DEPARTMENT
Sonora Broka - sonora@arsenals.lv

ROME INDEPENDENT FILM FESTIVAL
Piazza Buenos Aires 5 00198 Rome, Italy.
TEL: 39 6 4542 5050. FAX: 39 6 2331 9206. email: info@riff.it

www.riff.it
FESTIVAL DIRECTOR
Fabrizio Ferrari - fabrizio@riff.it

SAN DIEGO LATINO FILM FESTIVAL
921 25th St., San Diego, CA 92102. TEL: (619) 230-1938.
FAX: (619) 230-1937. email: info@mediaartscenter.org
www.sdlatinofilm.com
EXECUTIVE DIRECTOR/FOUNDER
Ethan van Thillo - ethan@mediaartscenter.org

SAN LUIS OBISPO INTL. FILM FESTIVAL
P.O. Box 1449, San Luis Obispo, CA 93406.
TEL: (805) 546-3456. FAX: (805) 546-8064.
email: festivaldirector@slofilmfest.org www.slofilmfest.org
FESTIVAL DIRECTOR
Wendy Eidson

SARASOTA FILM FESTIVAL
332 Cocoanut Ave., Sarasota, FL 34236. TEL: (941) 364-9514.
FAX: (941) 364-8411. www.sarasotafilmfestival.com
FESTIVAL MANAGER
Kathy Jordan - kathy@sarasotafilmfestival.com.

SCHERMI D'AMORE: VERONA FILM FESTIVAL
Via Leoncino, 6 - 37121 Verona. TEL: 045 800 5348.
FAX: 045 593 762.
email: veronafilmfestival@comune.verona.it.
www.schermidamore.it

SILVER LAKE FILM FESTIVAL
2658 Griffith Park Blvd. #389, Los Angeles, CA 90039.
TEL: (323) 660-1935. email: info@silverlakefilmfestival.org
www.silverlakefilmfestival.org
FESTIVAL DIRECTORS
Greg Ptacek - greg@silverlakefilmfestival.org
Kate Marciniak - kate@silverlakefilmfestival.org

SOFIA INTL. FILM FESTIVAL
1, Bulgaria Sq. 1463 Sofia, Bulgaria. TEL: 359 2 9166 029.
FAX: 359 2 9166 714. email: office@sofiaiff.com
www.sofiaiff.com
DIRECTOR & PRODUCER
Stefan Kitanov

SOUTH BY SOUTHWEST FILM FESTIVAL
P.O. Box 4999, Austin, TX 78765. TEL: (512) 467-7979.
FAX: (512) 451-0754. email: sxsw@sxsw.com www.sxsw.com

TAMPERE INTERNATIONAL SHORT FILM FESTIVAL
P.O. Box 305, 33101 Tampere, Finland. TEL: 3583 223 5681.
FAX: 358 3 223 5681. email: office@tamperefilmfestival.fi
www.tamperefilmfestival.fi
FESTIVAL DIRECTOR
Juka-Pekka Laakso - festdirector@tamperefilmfestival.fi

TIBURON INTERNATIONAL FILM FESTIVAL
1680 Tiburon Blvd., Tiburon, CA 94920. TEL: (415) 381-4123.
FAX: (415) 388-4123. email: info@tiburonfilmfestival.com
www.tiburonfilmfestival.com

VCU FRENCH FILM FESTIVAL
916 W. Franklin St., Room 205, P.O. Box 843073, Richmond,
VA 23284. TEL: (804) 827-3456. FAX: (804) 828-2552.
email: frenchfilm@vcu.edu www.frenchfilm.vcu.edu
ASSOCIATE DIRECTOR
Richard W. Haselwood

VIVA! SPANISH FILM FESTIVAL
Cornerhouse, 70 Oxford St., Manchester, M1 5NH, United
Kingdom. TEL: 44 (161) 200 1510. FAX: 44 (161) 200 1506.
email: viva@cornerhouse.org www.vivafilmfestival.com
FESTIVAL COORDINATOR
Jessie Gibbs

WESTCHESTER COUNTY INTERNATIONAL FILM FESTIVAL
148 Martine Ave., Ste. 107, White Plains, NY 10601.
TEL: (914) 995-2917. FAX: (914) 995-2948.
www.westchestergov.com/filmoffice
DIRECTOR
Iris G. Stevens - iis3@westchestergov.com

WILLIAMSBURG FILM FESTIVAL
P.O. Box 524, Gloucester Point, VA 23062.
TEL: (757) 482-2490. www.williamsburgfilmfestival.org
CONTACT
Larry Floyd

WOMEN WITH VISION
Walker Art Center, 1750 Hennepin Ave., Minneapolis, MN
55403. TEL: (612) 375-7615. FAX: (612) 375-7618.
email: info@walkerart.org www.walkerart.org

APRIL 2011

168 HOUR FILM FESTIVAL
145 S. Glenoaks Blvd., Ste. #159, Burbank, CA 91502.
TEL: (818) 557-8507. FAX: (818) 953-4014.
email: info@168project.com

AMSTERDAM FANTASTIC FILM FESTIVAL
Timorplein 53, NL-1094 CC Amsterdam, The Netherlands.
TEL: 31 (20) 679 48 75. FAX: 31 (20) 470 2696.
email: info@afff.nl www.afff.nl

ASPEN SHORTSFEST
110 E. Hallam St., Ste. 102 Aspen, CO 81611.
TEL: (970) 925-6882. FAX: (970) 925-1967.
email: filmfest@aspenfilm.org www.aspenfilm.org
EXECUTIVE DIRECTOR
Laura Thielen - lthielen@aspenfilm.org

ATLANTA FILM FESTIVAL
535 Means St. NW, Ste. C Atlanta, GA 30318.
TEL: (404) 352-4225. FAX: (404) 352-0173.
email: info@atlantafilmfestival.com www.atlantafilmfestival.com
EXECUTIVE DIRECTOR
Gabe Wardell - gabe@atlantafilmfestival.com

BARCELONA ASIAN FILM FESTIVAL
Valencia, 225, 3º, 1-B 08007 Barcelona, Spain.
TEL: 34 93 511 32 52. FAX: 34 93 511 32 54.
www.baff-bcn.org

BLACK INTL. CINEMA BERLIN
Tempelhofer Damm 52, 12101 Berlin, Germany.
TEL: 49 030 782 1621. FAX: 49 030 786 3466.
email: bicdance@aol.com members.aol.com/bicdance

BRUSSELS INTERNATIONAL FESTIVAL OF FANTASTIC FILM
Rue de la Comtesse de Flandre 8, 9240 Brussels, Belgium.
TEL: 02 201 17 13. FAX: 02 201 14 69.
email: info@bifff.org www.bifff.org

BUENOS AIRES INTL. FESTIVAL OF INDEPENDENT FILM
Av. Roque Sáenz Peña 832 6th Flr., C1035AAQ, Buenos Aires,
Argentina. TEL: 0800-3337848.
email: produccion@bafici.gov.ar www.bafici.gov.ar
PRESS COORDINATION
Lola Silberman

CINARCHEA
Breiter Weg 10, D-24105 Kiel, Germany.
TEL: 49 0431 880 4941. FAX +49 (0431) 880-4940.
www.cinarchea.com
FESTIVAL MANAGEMENT
Dr. Kurt Denzer 49 0431 880-4941

CONTACT INTL. DOCUMENTARY FILM FESTIVAL
6 Saksaganskoho Str., Office 115, Kyiv, Ukraine.
TEL: 38 044 461 9803. FAX: 38 044 235 5832.
email: info@molodist.com www.molodist.com

CROSSING EUROPE: FILM FESTIVAL LINZ
Graben 30, 4020 Linz, Austria. TEL: 43 (0) 732-78 57 00-0.
FAX: 43 (0) 732-78 57 00 (-40). email: info@crossingEurope.at
www.crossingEurope.at
FESTIVAL DIRECTOR
Christine Dollhofer - dollhofer@crossingEurope.at

DEAD BY DAWN, SCOTLAND'S INTL. HORROR FILM FESTIVAL
88 Lothian Road Edinburgh, Midlothian EH39BZ United
Kingdom. TEL: 44 (0) 7980 98 77 79. FAX: 44 (0)131 229 6482.
email: info@deadbydawn.co.uk www.deadbydawn.co.uk

DOCAVIV:TEL AVIV INTL. DOCUMENTARY FILM FESTIVAL
2 Shprinzak St., P.O Box 20370, Tel Aviv 61203, Israel.
TEL: 972 3 606 0817. FAX: 972 3 62 1737.
email: info@docaviv.co.il www.docaviv.co.il

DRESDEN INTERNATIONAL FESTIVAL FOR ANIMATION & SHORT FILMS
Alaunstrasse 62 01099 Dresden, Germany.
TEL: 49 351 829470. FAX: 49 351 8294719.
email: info@filmfest-dresden.de www.filmfest-dresden.de
FESTIVAL DIRECTOR
Robin Mallick

FILMFEST DC:WASHINGTON D.C. INTL. FILM FESTIVAL
P.O. Box 21396, Washington, DC 20009. TEL: (202) 274.5782.
FAX: (202) 274-6690. email: filmfestdc@filmfestdc.org
www.filmfestdc.org
FESTIVAL DIRECTOR
Anthony Gittens

GEN ART FILM FESTIVAL
133 W. 25th St., 6th Fl., New York, NY 10001.
TEL: (212) 255-7300 ext. 505. FAX: (212) 255-7400.
email: info@genart.org www.genart.org

GOEAST FESTIVAL OF CENTRAL AND EASTERN EUROPEAN FILM
Deutsches Filminstitut, Schaumainkai 41, 60956 Frankfurt,
Germany. TEL: 49 69 96 12 20 650. FAX: 49 69 96 12 20 669.
email: info@filmfestival-goEast.de www.filmfestival-goEast.de

FESTIVAL DIRECTOR
Nadja Rademacher

HONG KONG INTL. FILM FESTIVAL
7/F., United Chinese Bank Building, 31-37 Des Voeux Road Central, Hong Kong. TEL: 852 29703300. FAX: 852 29703011.
email: info@hkiff.org.hk www.hkiff.org.hk

HOT DOCS
110 Spadina Ave., Ste. #333 Toronto, ON M5V 2K4, Canada.
TEL: (416) 203-2155. FAX: (416) 203-0446.
email: info@hotdocs.ca www.hotdocs.ca
EXECUTIVE DIRECTOR
Chris McDonald - cmcdonald@hotdocs.ca

INDIAN FILM FESTIVAL OF LOS ANGELES
5657 Wilshire Blvd, #130, Los Angeles, CA 90036-3765.
TEL: (310) 364-4403. FAX: (323) 571-8746.
email: info@indianfilmfestival.org www.indianfilmfestival.org
FESTIVAL DIRECTOR
Christina Marouda

ISTANBUL INTL. FILM FESTIVAL
Istanbul Foundation for Culture and Arts, Istiklal Caddesi 64, Beyoglu 34435 Istanbul, Turkey. TEL: 90 212 334 07 00 ext. 750.
FAX: 90 212 334 07 16. email: medya@iksv.org www.iksv.org

JCC LENORE MARWIL JEWISH FILM FESTIVAL
6600 W. Maple Rd., JCC of Metro Detroit, West Bloomfield, MI 48322. TEL: (248) 432-5577. www.jccdet.org

JEONJU INTL. FILM FESTIVAL
470-5 Jungnosong-dong, Wansan-gu, Jeonju 560-100, South Korea. TEL: 82 63 288 5433. FAX: 82 63 288 5411.
email: master@jiff.or.kr www.jiff.or.kr

KANSAS CITY FILMFEST
4741 Central, #306, Kansas City, MO 64112.
TEL/FAX: (913) 649-0244. email: kcjub@kcjubilee.org
www.kcjubilee.org
FESTIVAL COORDINATOR
Sandy Woodson

KRISTIANSAND INTL. CHILDREN'S FILM FESTIVAL
P.O.Box 356, NO-4663 Kristiansand, Norway.
TEL: 47 3810 4205. FAX: 47 3810 4201.
email: festival@krskino.no www.krskino.no

LAKE ARROWHEAD FILM FESTIVAL
P.O. Box 2143, Blue Jay, CA 92317.
TEL: (909) 337-7587.FAX: (909) 337-3753.
email: info@lakearrowheadfilmfestival.com
www.lakearrowheadfilmfestival.com

LEEDS YOUNG PEOPLE'S FILM FESTIVAL
Leeds Film Town Hall, The Headrow Leeds, LS1 3AD United Kingdom. TEL: 44 113 2478398. FAX: 44 113 2478397.
email: filmfestival@leeds.gov.uk www.leedsfilm.com

LOS ANGELES HARBOR INTL. FILM FESTIVAL
P.O. Box 5202, San Pedro, CA 90733. TEL: (310) 519-0756.
FAX: (310) 519-0756. email: stephaniemardesich@yahoo.com
www.laharborfilmfest.com

LOS ANGELES JEWISH FILM FESTIVAL
Westside Jewish Community Center, 5870 West Olympic Blvd., Los Angeles, CA 90036. TEL: (323) 938-2531.
email: info@lajfilmfest.org www.lajfilmfest.org

MALIBU FILM FESTIVAL
Malibu Film Foundation, P.O. Box 1133, Malibu, CA 90265.
TEL: (310) 699-9760. FAX: (310) 395-8895.
email: info@malibufilmfestival.org www.malibufilmfestival.org

MIAMI GAY & LESBIAN FILM FESTIVAL
7251 NE 2nd Avenue, #107, Miami, FL 33138.
TEL: (305) 534-9924. FAX: (305) 535-2377.
email: info@mglff.com www.mglff.com

MINNEAPOLIS-ST. PAUL INTL. FILM FESTIVAL
309 Oak St. SE, Minneapolis, MN 55414. TEL: (612) 331-7563.
FAX: (612) 378-7750. email: info@mnfilmarts.org
www.mnfilmarts.org
FESTIVAL PROGRAM DIRECTOR
Al Milgrom

NASHVILLE FILM FESTIVAL
P.O. Box 24330, Nashville, TN 37202. TEL: (615) 742-2500.
FAX: (615) 742-1004. email: info@nashvillefilmfestival.org
www.nashvillefilmfestival.org
EXECUTIVE DIRECTOR
Sallie Mayne - sallie@nashvillefilmfestival.org

NATFILM FESTIVAL (COPENHAGEN FILM FESTIVAL)
St. Kannikestraede 6 DK-1169 Copenhagen K, Denmark.
TEL: 45 33120 005. FAX: 45 33127 505.
email: info@natfilm.dk www.natfilm.dk
EXECUTIVE DIRECTOR
Jacob Neiiendam - jacob@cphpix.dk

NATL. SHORT FILM & VIDEO COMPETITION
6116 N. Central Expressway, Ste. 105, Dallas, TX 75206.
TEL: (214) 821-6300. FAX: (214) 821-6364.
email: usafilmfestival@aol.com www.usafilmfestival.com

NEWPORT BEACH FILM FESTIVAL
4540 Campus Dr., Newport Beach, CA 92660.
TEL: (949) 253-2880. FAX: (949) 253-2881.
email: info@NewportBeachFilmFest.com
www.NewportBeachFilmFest.com
EXECUTIVE DIRECTOR
Gregg Schwenk - gregg@NewportBeachFilmFest.com

NIPPON CONNECTION: JAPANESE FILM FESTIVAL
c/o ASTA Mertonstr. 26-28, 60316 Frankfurt, Germany.
TEL: 49 69 798 22 986. FAX: 49 69 798 22 987.
email: info@nipponconnection.de www.nipponconnection.de

PALM BEACH INTL. FILM FESTIVAL
289 Via Naranjas Royal Palm Plaza, Ste. #48, Boca Raton, FL 33432. TEL: (561) 362-0003. FAX: (561) 362-0035.
email: info@pbifilmfest.org www.pbifilmfest.org
EXECUTIVE DIRECTOR
Randi Emerman
FESTIVAL COORDINATOR
Laurie Wein - laurie@pbifilmfest.org

PHILADELPHIA FILM FESTIVAL
234 Market St., 4th Flr. Philadelphia, PA 19106.
TEL: (267) 765-9800. FAX: (215) 733-0668.
email: info@filmadelphia.org www.phillyfests.com
CONTACT
Jesse Dubus - jdubus@phillyfests.com

PHOENIX FILM FESTIVAL
1700 N. 7th Ave., #250, Phoenix, AZ 85007.
TEL: (602) 955-6444. FAX: (602) 955-0964.
email: festival@phxfilm.com www.phoenixfilmfestival.com
FESTIVAL DIRECTOR
Jason Carney - (602) 309-6848 jason@phxfilm.com

POLISH FILM FESTIVAL LOS ANGELES
7726 Ethel Ave., N. Hollywood, CA 91605.
TEL: (818) 982-8827. FAX: (818) 765-2714.
email: info@polishfilmla.org www.polishfilmla.org
FESTIVAL DIRECTOR
Vladek Juszkiewicz

RIVERRUN INTL. FILM FESTIVAL
870 West Fourth St., Winston-Salem, NC 27101.
TEL: (336) 724-1502. FAX: (336) 724-1112.
email: festival@riverrunfilm.com www.riverrunfilm.com
EXECUTIVE DIRECTOR
Andrew Rodgers - andrew@riverrunfilm.com

ROGER EBERT'S OVERLOOKED FILM FESTIVAL
Virginia Theatre, 203 W. Park Ave., Champaign, IL 61820.
www.ebertfest.com
CONTACT
Mary Susan Britt - (217) 244-0552 marsue@illinois.edu

RUSSIAN NIGHTS FESTIVAL
9 Krymsky val, Moscow 119049, Russia.
TEL: 7 495 236 27 53. FAX: 7 495 954 15 85.
email: snc@stasnamincentre.ru www.russiannightsfest.com

SAN FRANCISCO INTL. FILM FESTIVAL
39 Mesa St., Ste. 110, The Presidio, San Francisco, CA 94129.
TEL: (415) 561-5000. FAX: (415) 561-5099.
email: frontdesk@sffs.org www.sffs.org
EXECUTIVE DIRECTOR
Graham Leggat - (415) 561-5039 graham@sffs.org

SONOMA VALLEY FILM FESTIVAL
P.O. Box 1613, Sonoma, CA 95476. TEL: (707) 933-2600.
FAX: (707) 933-2612. email: info@SonomaFilmFest.org
www.sonomafilmfest.org
PROGRAM COORDINATOR
Cevin Cathell - cevin@sonomafilmfest.org

TRENTO FILM FESTIVAL
Via S.Croce, 67, Centro Santa Chiara C.P. 402 Trento Centro I-38100 Trento. TEL: 39 04 61986120. FAX: 39 04 61237832.
email: mail@trentofestival.it www.trentofestival.it

TRIBECA FILM FESTIVAL
375 Greenwich St., New York, NY 10013. TEL: (212) 941-2400.
FAX: (212) 941-3939. email: festival@tribecafilmfestival.org
www.tribecafilmfestival.org

UDINE FAR EAST FILM FESTIVAL
Centro Espressioni Cinematografiche Via Villalta, 24 - 3100 Udine/Italy. TEL: 39 0432 299545. FAX: 39 0432 229815.
email: cec@cecudine.org www.fareastfilm.com
www.cecudine.org

URUGUAY INTL. FILM FESTIVAL
Lorenzo Carnelli 1311 11200 Montevideo, Uruguay.
TEL: 5982 412-8516. FAX: 5982 419 4572.
email: cinemuy@chasque.net www.cinemateca.org.uy

USA FILM FESTIVAL
6116 N. Central Expwy., Ste. 105, Dallas, TX 75206.
TEL: (214) 821-6300. FAX: (214) 821-6364.
email: usafilmfestival@aol.com www.usafilmfestival.com

VISIONS DU REEL INTL. FILM FESTIVAL
18, rue Juste-Olivier - 1260 Nyon 1, Switzerland.
TEL: 41 22 365 44 55. FAX: 41 22 365 44 50.
email: docnyon@visionsdureel.ch www.visionsdureel.ch
DIRECTOR
Jean Perret

WORLDFEST: HOUSTON INTL. FILM FESTIVAL
9898 Bissonnet, Ste. 650, Houston, TX 77036.
TEL: (713) 965-9955. FAX: (713) 965-9960.
email: mail@worldfest.org www.worldfest.org

MAY 2011

AGON FILM FESTIVAL
10 Karitsi Sq., 102 37 Athens, Greece. TEL: 30 210 331 2990.
FAX: 30 210 331 2991. email: mpalatou@arxaiologia.gr
www.sitemaker.gr/agwn

ANIMATE THE WORLD
Barbican Cinema, Silk St., London, EC2Y 8DS, United Kingdom. TEL: 44 (020) 7382 2379. FAX: 44 (020) 7382 7037.
email: film@barbican.org.uk www.barbican.org.uk/film

BERKSHIRES FILM FESTIVAL
P.O. Box 237, Great Barrington, MA 01230.
TEL: (413) 528-8030. email: kelley@biffma.com

CANNES INTL. FILM FESTIVAL
3, rue Amelie 75007 Paris, France. TEL: 33 (1) 5359 6100.
FAX: 33 (1) 5359 6110. email: festival@festival-cannes.fr
www.festival-cannes.org

DANVILLE INTL. CHILDREN'S FILM FESTIVAL
CIFF Association, 2278 Camino Ramon, Ste. 2, San Ramon, CA 94583. TEL: (925) 558-2797. FAX: (925) 552-1490.
email: info@caindiefest.com www.dicff.org

DOK FEST: MUNICH INTL. DOCUMENTARY FILM FESTIVAL
Landwehrstr. 79, D-80336 Munich, Germany.
TEL: 49 89 51 39 97 88. FAX: 49 89 51 56 39 36.
email: press@dokfest-muenchen.de
www.dokfest-muenchen.de

FLYING BROOM INTL.WOMEN'S FILM FESTIVAL
Buyukelci Sokag 20/4 Kavakl dere Ankara 06700, Turkey.
TEL: 90 312 427 0020. FAX: 90 312 466 55 61.
email: festival@ucansupurge.org www.ucansupurge.org
GENERAL COORDINATOR
Selen Dogan

INSIDE OUT TORONTO LESBIAN AND GAY FILM AND VIDEO FESTIVAL
401 Richmond St.West, Toronto, ON M5V 3A8, Canada.
TEL: (416) 977-6847. FAX: (416) 977-8025.
email: programmer@insideout.ca www.insideout.ca
EXECUTIVE DIRECTOR
Scott Ferguson - scott@insideout.ca

INTL. WILDLIFE FILM FESTIVAL
718 S. Higgins Ave., Missoula, MT 59801.
TEL: (406) 728-9380. FAX: (406) 728-2881.
email: iwff@wildlifefilms.org www.wildlifefilms.org

JACKSONVILLE FILM FESTIVAL
128 E. Forsyth St., Ste. 300, Jacksonville, FL 32202.
TEL: (904) 633-9399. FAX: (904) 358-1874.
email: questions@jacksonvillefilmevents.com
www.jacksonvillefilmfestival.com
EXECUTIVE DIRECTOR
Jesse Rodriguez - jesse@JacksonvilleFilmFestival.com

MARYLAND FILM FESTIVAL
107 E. Read St., Baltimore, MD 21202. TEL: (410) 752-8083.
FAX: (410) 752-8273. email: information@mdfilmfest.com
www.mdfilmfest.com
DIRECTOR
Jed Dietz

OBERHAUSEN INTL. SHORT FILM FESTIVAL
Grillostr. 34 Oberhausen, 46045 Germany.
TEL: 49 208 825-2652. FAX: 49 208 825-5413.
email: info@kurzfilmtage.de www.kurzfilmtage.de
FESTIVAL DIRECTOR
Dr. Lars Henrik Gass

Q CINEMA: FORT WORTH GAY & LESBIAN INTERNATIONAL FILM FESTIVAL
9 Chase Ct., Fort Worth, TX 76110. TEL: (817) 462-3358.
FAX: (817) 390-7257. email: todd@qcinema.org
www.qcinema.org

ROSE D'OR
Sempacherstrasse 3, 6003 Lucerne, Switzerland.
TEL: 41 (0) 41 242 09 05. FAX: 41 (0) 41 242 09 06.
email: info@rosedor.com www.rosedor.com
FESTIVAL DIRECTOR
Urban Frye - urban.frye@rosedor.ch

SEATTLE INTL. FILM FESTIVAL
400 Ninth Ave., N Seattle, WA 98109. TEL: (206) 464-5830.
FAX: (206) 264-7919. email: info@siff.net
www.seattlefilm.org
MANAGING DIRECTOR
Deborah Person

SPANISH FILM FESTIVAL
P.O. Box 191, Balwyn Melbourne, VIC 3103 Australia.
TEL: 61 3 9817 6421. email: info@spanishfilmfestival.com
www.spanishfilmfestival.com
FESTIVAL DIRECTOR AND FOUNDER
Natalia Ortiz - natalia@spanishfilmfestival.com

TRENTON FILM FESTIVAL
P.O. Box 22430, Trenton, NJ 08607. TEL: (609) 396-6966.
email: info@trentonfilmfestival.org
www.trentonfilmfestival.org

VC FILMFEST: LOS ANGELES ASIAN-PACIFIC FILM FESTIVAL
120 Judge John Aiso St. Basement Level, Los Angeles, CA 90012. TEL: (213) 680-4462. FAX: (213) 687-4848.
email: info@vconline.org www.vconline.org
EXHIBITIONS & FESTIVAL CO-DIRECTOR
Abraham Ferrer

ZLIN INTL. FILM FESTIVAL FOR CHILDREN AND YOUTH
Filmova 174, CZ-761 79 Zlin, Czech Republic.
TEL: 420 577 592 275. FAX: 420 577 592 442.
email: festival@zlinfest.cz www.zlinfest.cz
PRODUCTION MANAGER
Irena Skaunicová

JUNE 2011

ANNECY INTL. ANIMATED FILM FESTIVAL
c/o Conservatoire d'Art et d'Histoire, 18 ave. du Tresum, BP 399 74013 Annecy, France. TEL: 33 (4) 5010 0900.
FAX: 33 (4) 5010 0970. email: info@annecy.org
www.annecy.org
MANAGING DIRECTOR
Tiziana Loschi

ANOTHER HOLE IN THE HEAD
530 Divisadero St., #183, San Francisco, CA 94117.
TEL: (415) 820-3907. email: info@sfindie.com
www.sfindie.com
FOUNDER/DIRECTOR
Jeff Ross

BANFF WORLD TELEVISION FESTIVAL
Achilles Media Ltd., 102 Boulder Crescent, Ste. 202, Canmore, AB T1W 1L2, Canada. TEL: (403) 678-1216.
FAX: (403) 678-3357. email: info@achillesmedia.com
www.banff2008.com

BROOKLYN INTL. FILM FESTIVAL
180 S. Fourth St., Ste. 2 S, Brooklyn, NY 11211.
TEL: (718) 388-4306. FAX: (718) 599-5039.
email: festivalwbff.org www.wbff.org
EXECUTIVE DIRECTOR
Marco Ursino

CINEMA JOVE INTL. FILM FESTIVAL
Calle La Safor 10 Despacho 5, 46015 Valencia, Spain.
TEL: 34 (96) 331 1047. FAX: 34 (96) 331 0805.
email: info@cinemajove.com www.cinemajovefilmfest.com

CONNECTICUT GAY & LESBIAN FILM FESTIVAL
P.O. Box 231191, Hartford, CT 06123. TEL: (860) 586-1136.
www.ctglff.org

DEADCENTER FILM FESTIVAL
3030 N.W. Expwy., Ste. 1200, Oklahoma City, OK 73112.
TEL: (405) 246-9233. email: info@deadcenterfilm.org
www.deadcenterfilm.org
EXECUTIVE DIRECTOR
Cacky Poarch - cacky@deadcenterfilm.org

ECOFILMS: RODOS INTL. FILMS & VISUAL ARTS FESTIVAL
23 Laskareos St., Athens 114 72 Greece.
TEL: 30 210 3636390. FAX: 30 210 3636390.
email: info@ecofilms.gr www.ecofilms.gr
ARTISTIC DIRECTOR
Lucia Rikaki - lrikaki@otenet.gr

EMDEN-AURICH-NORDERNEY INTL. FILMFEST
An der Berufsschule 3 26703 Emden, Germany.
TEL: 49 4921 915531. FAX: 49 4921 915599.
email: filmfest@vhs-emden.de www.filmfest-emden.de

FESTIVAL DIRECTOR
Silke Santjer - s.santjer@vhs-emden.de

FESTIVAL INTERNATIONAL DE CINEMA DEL MEDI AMBIENT
P.O. Box 199, 08820 El Prat de LLobregat, Barcelona, Spain. TEL: 34 93 478 93 44. email: info@ficma.com www.ficma.com
DIRECTOR
Jaume Gil i Llopart

FESTROIA
Fórum Municipal Luísa Todi, Avenida Luísa Todi, 61-65, 2900-461 Setúbal, Portugal. TEL: 351 265 525 908.
FAX: 351 265 525 681. email: info@festroia.pt www.festroia.pt

FIRSTGLANCE PHILADELPHIA FILM FEST
P.O. Box 571105, Tarzana, CA 91356. TEL: (818) 464-3544, (215) 552-8566. email: director@firstglancefilms.com www.firstglancefilms.com

FRAMELINE: SAN FRANCISCO INTL. LGBT FILM FESTIVAL
145 Ninth St., Ste. 300, San Francisco, CA 94103.
TEL: (415) 703-8650. FAX: (415) 861-1404.
email: info@frameline.org www.frameline.org
EXECUTIVE DIRECTOR
K.C. Price

HAMBURG INTL. SHORT FILM FESTIVAL
Friedensallee 7, D-22765 Hamburg, Germany.
TEL: 49 40 39 10 63 23. FAX: 49 40 39 10 62 20.
email: festival@shortfilm.com www.shortfilm.com
ARTISTIC DIRECTOR
Jürgen Kittel

HOLLYWOOD BLACK FILM FESTIVAL
8306 Wilshire Blvd., Ste. 2057, Beverly Hills, CA 90211.
TEL: (310) 407-3596. FAX: (310) 943-2326.
email: info@hbff.org www.hbff.org
FOUNDER & EXECUTIVE DIRECTOR
Tanya Kersey - tanya@hbff.org

HUESCA FILM FESTIVAL
Avda.Parque, 1 2º, 22002 Huesca, España, Spain.
TEL: 34 974 212 582. FAX: 34 974 210 065.
email: info@huesca-filmfestival.com www.huesca-filmfestival.com

INDEPENDENT TELEVISION FESTIVAL
P.O. Box 46666, Los Angeles, CA 90046. TEL: (888) 710-0899.
email: general@itvfest.org www.itvfest.org

INNSBRUCK INTL. FILM FESTIVAL
Museumstrasse 31, A-6020 Innsbruck, Austria.
TEL: 43 512 57 85 00 14. FAX: 43 512 57 85 00 13.
email: info@iffi.at www.iffi.at
GENERAL MANAGER
Evelin Stark

ISRAEL FILM FESTIVAL
6404 Wilshire Blvd, Ste. 1240, Los Angeles, CA 90048.
TEL: (323) 966-4166. FAX: 323-658-6346.
email: chelsie@israelfilmfestival.org www.israelfilmfestival.com
EXECUTIVE DIRECTOR & FOUNDER
Meir Fenigstein

KARLOVY VARY INTL. FILM FESTIVAL
Panska 1, 1100 00 Prague, 1 Czech Republic.
TEL: 420 221 411 011. FAX: 420 221 411 033.
email: festival@kviff.com www.kviff.com
EXECUTIVE DIRECTOR
Kryštof Mucha

LOS ANGELES FILM FESTIVAL
Film Independent, 9911 W. Pico Blvd., Los Angeles, CA 90035.
TEL: (310) 432-1240. FAX: (310) 432-1203.
email: LAFilmFest@FilmIndependent.org www.lafilmfest.com
FESTIVAL DIRECTOR
Richard Raddon

MAUI FILM FESTIVAL
P.O. Box 790669, Paia, HI 96779. TEL: (808) 579-9244.
FAX: (808) 579-9552. email: mauifilmfestival@mauifilmfestival.com
www.mauifilmfestival.com

MESSAGE TO MAN INTL. DOCUMENTARY, SHORT AND ANIMATED FILMS FESTIVAL
Karavannaya 12, 191011 St. Petersburg, Russia.
TEL: 7 (812) 326 8218. email: info@message-to-man.spb.ru
www.message-to-man.spb.ru

MOONDANCE INTL. FILM FESTIVAL
970 Ninth St., Boulder, CO 80302. TEL: (303) 545-0202.
email: info@moondancefilmfestival.com
www.moondancefilmfestival.com
EXECUTIVE DIRECTOR
Elizabeth English - director@moondancefilmfestival.com

MOSCOW INTL. FILM FESTIVAL
21/22, 4th Tverskaya_Yamskaya Street, 125047 Moscow, Russia. TEL: (+7495) 232-14-75/76/77/78. FAX: (+7495) 251-26-06.
email: info@moscowfilmfestival.ru www.moscowfilmfestival.ru
PRESIDENT
Nikita Mikhalkov

NANTUCKET FILM FESTIVAL
1633 Broadway, Ste. 15-310, New York, NY 10019.
TEL: (212) 708-1278. FAX: (212) 708 7490.
email: info@nantucketfilmfestival.org
www.nantucketfilmfestival.org
EXECUTIVE DIRECTOR
Colin Stanfield

NEWARK BLACK FILM FESTIVAL
The Newark Black Film Festival, c/o The Newark Museum, 49 Washington St., Newark, NJ 07102. TEL: (973) 596-6550.
email: pfaison@newarkmuseum.org

NEWFEST: THE NEW YORK LESBIAN, GAY, BISEXUAL & TRANSGENDER FILM FESTIVAL
68 Jay St, Suite 218 Brooklyn, NY 11201.
TEL: (718) 923 1950. FAX: (718) 923-1959.
email: info@newfest.org www.newfest.org

NEWPORT INTL. FILM FESTIVAL
P.O. Box 146, Newport, RI 02840. TEL: (401) 846-9100.
FAX: (401) 846-6665. email: info@newportfilmfestival.com
www.newportfilmfestival.com
PROGRAMMING DIRECTOR
Eric Bilodeau - eric@newportfilmfestival.com

PARIS CINEMA
27, Rue Saint-Antoine, 75004 Paris.
TEL: 33 1 44 78 02 41. FAX: 33 1 44 78 02 42.
www.pariscinema.org

PESARO FILM FESTIVAL
Via Villafranca, 20 - 00185 Rome, Italy. TEL: 39 06 4456643.
FAX: 39 06 491163. email: info@pesarofilmfest.it
www.pesarofilmfest.it

PROVINCETOWN INTL. FILM FESTIVAL
P.O. Box 605, Provincetown, MA 02657. TEL: (508) 487-3456.
FAX: (508) 487-2494. email: contact@ptownfilmfest.org
www.ptownfilmfest.org
EXECUTIVE DIRECTOR
Gabrielle A. Hanna

SAN FRANCISCO BLACK FILM FESTIVAL
P.O. Box 15490, San Francisco, CA 94115.
TEL: (415) 771-9271. FAX: (415) 346-9046.
email: film2fest@yahoo.com

SHANGHAI INTL. FILM FESTIVAL
11F STV Mansions 298 Wei Hai Rd., Shanghai 200041, China.
TEL: 86 21 62537115. FAX: 86 21 62552000. www.siff.com

SHORT SHORTS FILM FESTIVAL & ASIA
MBE 611, 3-28 Kioicho Chiyoda-ku, Tokyo, 102-8557, Japan.
TEL: 81-3-5214-3005. FAX: 81-3-5214-1956.
email: info@shortshortsla.org www.shortshorts.org

SHOWCOMOTION
Showroom Cinema, Paternoster Row, Sheffield, S1 2BX United Kingdom. TEL: 44 114 276 3534. FAX: 44 114 279 6522.
email: info@showcomotion.org.uk www.showcomotion.org.uk

SILVERDOCS: AFI/DISCOVERY CHANNEL DOCUMENTARY FESTIVAL
8633 Colesville Rd., Silver Spring, MD 20910.
TEL: (301) 495-6738. FAX: (301) 495-6798.
email: info@silverdocs.com www.silverdocs.com

SYDNEY FILM FESTIVAL
P.O. Box 96, Strawberry Hills Sydney, NSW 2012, Australia.
TEL: 61 2 9318 0999. FAX: 61 2 9319 0055.
email: info@sydneyfilmfestival.org www.sydneyfilmfestival.org

THUNDERBIRD INTL. FILM FESTIVAL
Southern Utah University, Communication Department, 351 W. University Blvd., Cedar City, UT 84720. TEL: (435) 586-7861.
FAX: (435) 865-8352. email: tiff@suu.edu
www.thunderbirdfilmfestival.suu.edu
FOUNDER
Mariam Arthur - ladymariam@juno.com

TRANSILVANIA INTL. FILM FESTIVAL
52 Popa Soare St., Sector 2, Bucharest, Romania.
TEL: 40 21 326 64 80. FAX: 40 21 326 02 68.
email: info@tiff.ro www.tiff.ro
FESTIVAL DIRECTOR
Mihai Chirilov - mihai@tiff.ro

WATERFRONT FILM FESTIVAL
P.O. Box 387, Saugatuck, MI 49453. TEL: (269) 857-8351.
FAX: (269) 857-8351. email: info@waterfrontfilm.org
www.waterfrontfilm.org

WORLDWIDE SHORT FILM FESTIVAL
2489 Bayview Ave., Toronto, ON M2L 1A8, Canada.
TEL: (416) 445-1446. FAX: (416) 445-9481.
email: shortfilmfest@cfccreates.com

www.worldwideshortfilmfest.com
EXECUTIVE DIRECTOR
Eileen Arandiga

JULY 2011

AUCKLAND INTL. FILM FESTIVAL

P.O. Box 9544, Marion Square, Wellington 6141, New Zealand. TEL: 64 4 385 0162. FAX: 64 4 801 7304.
email: festival@nzff.co.nz www.nzff.telecom.co.nz
FESTIVAL MANAGER
Lynn Smart - (027) 4738 230

COMIC-CON INTERNATIONAL INDEPENDENT FILM FESTIVAL

P.O. Box 128458, San Diego, CA 92112. TEL: (619) 414-1020, (619) 491-2475. FAX: (619) 414-1022.
email: cci-info@comic-con.org www.comic-con.org

ERA NEW HORIZONS FILM FESTIVAL

1 Zamenhofa, Str. 00-153 Warsaw, Poland. TEL: 48 22 530 66 40. FAX: 48 22 831 06 63. email: festival@eranowehoryzonty.pl
www.eranowehoryzonty.pl
FESTIVAL DIRECTOR
Roman Gutek - rogu@snh.org.pl

FANTASIA INTL. FILM FESTIVAL

80 Queen St., Ste. 301 Montreal, Quebec H3C 2N5, Canada. TEL: (514) 876-1760. FAX: (514) 876-1422.
email: info@fantasiafestival.com www.fantasiafestival.com

FANTASY FILMFEST GERMANY

Rosebud Entertainment, Herzog-Wilhelm-Str. 27, D-80331 München, Germany. TEL: 49 30 861 4532.
FAX: 49 30 861 4539. email: info@fantasyfilmfest.com
www.fantasyfilmfest.com
MARKETING
Andreas Bernauer - ab@rosebud-entertainment.de

GALWAY FILM FLEADH

Cluain Mhuire Monivea Rd., Galway, Ireland.
TEL: 353 91 751 655. FAX: 353 91 735 831.
email: info@galwayfilmfleadh.com www.galwayfilmfleadh.com
MANAGING DIRECTOR
Miriam Allen

HYPEFEST

5651 Wilshire Blvd., Ste. A Los Angeles, CA 90036.
TEL: (323) 938-8363. FAX: (323) 938-8757.
email: info@hypefest.com www.hypefest.com

ISCHIA GLOBAL FILM & MUSIC FEST

Ischia Intl. Arts Academy Via Messer Onofrio, 1 80076 Lacco Ameno d'Ischia, Italy. TEL: 39 081 994322.
email: info@ischiaglobal.com www.ischiaglobal.com

JERUSALEM FILM FESTIVAL

Jerusalem Cinematheque, 11 Hebron Rd., 91083 Jerusalem, Israel. TEL: 972 2 565 4333. FAX: 972 2 565 4335.
email: festival@jer-cin.org.il www.jff.org.il

LONG ISLAND INTL. FILM EXPO

Bellmore Movies, 222 Pettit Ave., Side Entrance Bellmore, NY 11710. TEL: (516) 783-3199. www.LongIslandFilm.com

MELBOURNE INTERNATIONAL FILM FESTIVAL

GPO Box 4982, Melbourne, 3001 Australia.
TEL: 613 8660 4888. FAX: 613 9654 2561.
email: miff@melbournefilmfestival.com.au
www.melbournefilmfestival.com.au

MUNICH FILMFEST

Filmwochen Sonnenstr 21, D-80331 Munich, Germany.
TEL: 49 89 381904 0. FAX: 49 89 3819 0426.
email: info@filmfest-muenchen.de www.filmfest-muenchen.de
FESTIVAL DIRECTOR
Andreas Ströhl

NAPA-SONOMA WINE COUNTRY FILM FESTIVAL

P.O. Box 303, 12000 Henno Rd., Glen Ellen, CA 95442.
TEL: (707) 935-3456. email: wcfilmfest@aol.com
www.winecountryfilmfest.com

PARNU INTL. DOCUMENTARY AND ANTHROPOLOGY FILM FESTIVAL

10, Esplanaadi St., 80010 Parnu, Estonia. TEL: 372 44 30772. FAX: 372 44 30774. email: festival@chaplin.ee
www.chaplin.ee
FESTIVAL CHIEF
Mark Soosaar - mark@chaplin.ee

PHILADELPHIA INTL. GAY & LESBIAN FILM FESTIVAL

234 Market St., 4th Flr., Philadelphia, PA 19106.
TEL: (267) 765-9700. FAX: (215) 733-0668.
www.phillyfests.com
MAMANING DIRECTOR, PHILADELPHIA FILM SOCIETY
Eric Bresler - ebresler@phillyfests.com

PIA FILM FESTIVAL

5-19 Sanban-cho, Chiyoda-ku, Tokyo, 102-0075 Japan.
TEL: 81 3 3265 1425. FAX: 81 3 3265 5659.
email: web_info@pff.jp www.pia.co.jp/pff/

PULA FILM FESTIVAL

Laginjina 5, P.O. Box 29, HR-52100 Pula, Croatia.
TEL: 385 052 393321. FAX: 385 052 393320.
email: info@pulafilmfestival.hr www.pulafilmfestival.hr
DIRECTOR
Zdenka Viskovic-Vukic - zdenka.viskovic@pulafilmfestival.hr

STONY BROOK FILM FESTIVAL

Staller Center For the Arts, Rm. 2030A, SUNY Stony Brook, Stony Brook, NY 11794. TEL: (631) 632-ARTS.
FAX: (631) 632-7354.
email: filmfestival@stonybrookfilmfestival.com
www.stonybrookfilmfestival.com

T TAURI FILM FESTIVAL

195 Peel Rd., Locust Grove, AR 72550. TEL: (870) 251-1189. FAX: (870) 251-1189. email: ttauri@wildblue.net
www.ttauri.org

UMBRIA FILM FESTIVAL

Niccone 173, 06019 Umbertide, Italy. TEL: 39 075 9410931. FAX: 39 075 9410934. email: info@umbriafilmfestival.com
www.umbriafilmfestival.com

WELLINGTON FILM FESTIVAL

P.O. Box 9544, Marion Sq., Wellington 6141 New Zealand.
TEL: 64 4 385 0162. FAX: 64 4 801 7304.
email: festival@nzff.co.nz www.nzff.co.nz

ZANZIBAR INTL. FILM FESTIVAL

P.O. Box 3032, Zanzibar, Tanzania. TEL: 255 (4) 777 411499. FAX: 255 (4) 777 419955. email: ziff@ziff.or.tz www.ziff.or.tz
CEO
Dr. Martin Mhando - martin.mhando@ziff.or.tz

AUGUST 2011

CHICHESTER FILM FESTIVAL

Chichester Cinema at New Park, New Park Rd., Chichester West Sussex, PO19 7XY. United Kingdom.
TEL: 44 1243 786650. email: info@chichestercinema.org
www.chichestercinema.org

DOUARNENEZ FILM FESTIVAL

BP 206 - 20 rue du Port Rhu 29172 Douarnenez Cedex, France. TEL: 33 02 98 92 09 21. FAX: 33 (2) 9292 2810.

EDINBURGH INTL. FILM FESTIVAL

88 Lothian Rd., Edinburgh, Scotland EH3 9BZ United Kingdom. TEL: 44 01312284051. FAX: 44 01312295501.
email: info@edfilmfest.org.uk www.edfilmfest.org.uk
MANAGING DIRECTOR
Ginnie Atkinson

ESPOO CINE INTL. FILM FESTIVAL

P.O. Box 95, FI-02101 Espoo, Finland. TEL: (358) 946-6599. FAX: (358) 946-6458. email: office@espoocine.org
www.espoocine.org
EXECUTIVE DIRECTOR
Ms. Jenni United Kingdomkonen - jenni.ukonen@espoocine.fi

HAYDENFILMS ONLINE FILM FESTIVAL

131 E. Main St., Ste. 2 Kutztown, PA 19530.
TEL: (610) 894-9639. FAX: (610) 894-9959.
email: fest@haydenfilms.com www.haydenfilms.com

JONKOPING FILM FESTIVAL

Kultur Jonkopings Kommun, Box 1029, 551 11 Jonkoping, Sweden. TEL: 46 36 10 66 94. FAX: 46 36 10 77 42.
email: britta.amft @ jonkoping.se www.filmfestival.nu

LOCARNO INTL. FILM FESTIVAL

via Ciseri 23, CH-6600 Locarno, Switzerland.
TEL: 41 91 756 21 21. FAX: 41 91 756 21 49.
email: info@pardo.ch www.pardo.ch

MONTREAL WORLD FILM FESTIVAL

1432, de Bleury St., Montreal, QC H3A 2J1, Canada.
TEL: (514) 848-3883. FAX: (514) 848-3886.
email: info@ffm-montreal.org www.ffm-montreal.org
DIRECTOR
Gilles Bériault - gberiault@ffm-montreal.org

NORWEGIAN INTERNATIONAL FILM FESTIVAL

P.O. Box 145, N-5501 Haugesund, Norway.
TEL: 47 52 74 33 75. FAX: 47 52 74 33 71.
email: info@filmfestivalen.no www.filmfestivalen.no
FESTIVAL DIRECTOR
Gunnar Johan Løvvik - gjl@filmfestivalen.no

ODENSE INTL. FILM FESTIVAL

Farvergården 7, 4. sal, Postboks 1169, 5100 Odense C, Denmark. TEL: 45 66 1313 72. FAX: 45 65 91 43 18.

email: filmfestival@odense.dk www.filmfestival.dk
FESTIVAL DIRECTOR
Cecilia Lidin - cecilia@edn.dk

OPEN AIR FILMFEST WEITERSTADT
P.O. Box 1164, D-64320 Weiterstadt, Germany.
TEL: 49 6150 12185. FAX: 49 6150 14073.
email: filmfest@weiterstadt.de www.filmfest-weiterstadt.de

RHODE ISLAND INTL. FILM FESTIVAL
P.O. Box 162, 96 Second St., Newport, RI 02840.
TEL: (401) 861-4445. FAX: (401) 490-6735.
email: info@film-festival.org www.RIFilmFest.org
EXECUTIVE DIRECTOR/CEO
George T. Marshall - georget@film-festival.org

SAO PAULO INTERNATIONAL SHORT FILM FESTIVAL
Rua Simão Álvares, 784/2, Pinheiros - 05417-020, São Paulo, SP, Brazil. TEL: 55 11 3034 5538. FAX: 55 11 3815 9474.
email: spshort@kinoforum.org www.kinoforum.org
DIRECTOR
Zita Carvalhosa

SARAJEVO FILM FESTIVAL
Zelenih beretki 12/I 71000 Sarajevo Bosnia-Herzegovina.
TEL: 387 33 209 411. FAX: 387 33 263 381.
email: press@sff.ba www.sff.ba

TELLURIDE INDIEFEST
800 Jones St., Berkeley, CA 94710. TEL: (510) 665-9494.
FAX: (510) 665-9589. email: Mail@telluridefilmfestival.org
www.telluridefilmfestival.org

SEPTEMBER 2011

ANGELUS STUDENT FILM FESTIVAL
7201 Sunset Blvd., Hollywood, CA 90046.
TEL: (800) 874-0999. FAX: (323) 874-1168.
email: info@angelus.org www.angelus.org

BIG BEAR LAKE INTL. FILM FESTIVAL
P.O. Box 1981, Big Bear Lake, CA 92315-1981.
TEL: (909) 866-3433. FAX: (909) 585-7120.
email: bigbearfilmfest@aol.com www.bigbearlakefilmfestival.com

DEAUVILLE AMERICAN FILM FESTIVAL
40, rue Anatole France - 92594 Levallois-Perret Cedex - France.
TEL: 33 1 4134 2033. FAX: 33 1 4134 2077.
email: jlasserre@lepublicsysteme.fr www.festival-deauville.com

LUND INTL. FANTASTIC FILM FESTIVAL
P.O. Box 1626, Lund, Skane SE-221 01 Sweden.
TEL: 46 (0) 46 132 135. FAX: 46 (0) 46 132 139.
email: info@fff.se www.fff.se
FESTIVAL DIRECTOR
Lars Diurlin email: lars@fff.se

MANAKI BROS. INTL. FILM CAMERA FESTIVAL
8 Mart 4 1000 Skopje, Macedonia. TEL: 389 2 32 24 334.
FAX: 389 2 32 11 811. email: office@manaki.com.mk
www.manaki.com.mk

NEW YORK FILM FESTIVAL
Film Society of Lincoln Center, 70 Lincoln Center Plaza, New York, NY 10023. TEL: (212) 875-5638. FAX: (212) 875-5636.
email: festival@filmlinc.com www.filmlinc.com
FESTIVAL DIRECTOR
Marian Masone

OLDENBURG INTL. FILM FESTIVAL
Bahnhofstr. 15, D-26122 Oldenburg, Germany.
TEL: 49 441 92508 55. FAX: 49 441 92508 56.
email:info@filmfest-oldenburg.de www.filmfest-oldenburg.de

ONE REEL FILM FESTIVAL
P.O. Box 9750, Seattle, WA 98109. TEL: (206) 281-7788.
FAX: (206) 281-7799. email: info@onereel.org
www.bumbershoot.org

PLUS CAMERIMAGE
Tumult Foundation, Rynek Nowomiejski 28, 87-100 Torun, Poland. TEL: 48 56 621 00 19. FAX: 48 56 652 21 97.
email: office@camerimage.pl www.pluscamerimage.pl
FESTIVAL DIRECTOR
Marek Zydowicz

RIGA INTL. FILM FORUM
Marstalu St. 14, LV-1050 Riga, Latvia. TEL: 371 672 10114.
FAX: 371 782 0445. email: arsenals@arsenals.lv
www.arsenals.lv
EXECUTIVE DIRECTOR
Liene Hapanioneka - liene@arsenals.lv

SAN SEBASTIÁN INTERNATIONAL FILM FESTIVAL
P.O Box 397 - 20080 Donostia-San Sebastián, Spain.
TEL: 34 943 481212. FAX: 34 943 481218.
email: ssiff@sansebastianfestival.com
www.sansebastianfestival.com

TORONTO INTL. FILM FESTIVAL
Toronto International Film Festival Group, 2 Carlton St., Ste. 1600, Toronto Ontario M5B 1J3. TEL: (416) 967-7371. www.tiffg.ca
SENIOR MANAGER, DEVELOPMENT
Sarah Bullick

VANCOUVER INTERNATIONAL FILM FESTIVAL
1181 Seymour St., Vancouver, BC V6B 3M7 Canada.
TEL: (604) 685-0260. FAX: (604) 688-8221.
email: viff@viff.org www.viff.org

OCTOBER 2011

AUSTIN FILM FESTIVAL
1145 W. 5th St., Ste. 210, Austin, TX 78703.
TEL: (512) 478-4795. FAX: (512) 478-6205.
www.austinfilmfestival.com

BEIRUT INTERNATIONAL FILM FESTIVAL
P.O. Box 175088, Beirut, Lebanon, TEL: 961 1 202411.
FAX: 961 1 585693. email: info@beirutfilmfoundation.org
www.beirutfilmfoundation.org
FESTIVAL DIRECTOR
Colette Naufal

FORT LAUDERDALE INTERNATIONAL FILM FESTIVAL
1314 E. Las Olas Blvd., Fort Lauderdale, FL 33301.
TEL: (954) 760-9898. FAX: (954) 760-9099.
email: info@fliff.com www.FLIFF.com
EXECUTIVE DIRECTOR
Hal Axler - Hal@fliff.com

GHENT INTERNATIONAL FILM FESTIVAL
Leeuwstraat 40b, 9000 Gent/Gand, Belgique.
TEL: 32 9 242 80 60. FAX: 32 9 221 90 74.
email: info@filmfestival.be www.filmfestival.be

THE HAMPTONS INTERNATIONAL FILM FESTIVAL
Hamptons Office: 3 Newtown Mews, East Hampton, NY 11937.
TEL: (631) 324-4600. FAX: (631) 324-5116.
email: info@hamptonsfilmfest.org www.hamptonsfilmfest.org
EXECUTIVE DIRECTOR
Karen Arikian

HOLLYWOOD FILM FESTIVAL
433 N. Camden Dr., Ste. 600 Los Angeles, CA 90035.
TEL: (310) 288-1882. FAX: (310) 288-0060.
email: info@hollywoodawards.com www.hollywoodfestival.com

INTERNATIONAL BUDDHIST FILM FESTIVAL
P.O. Box 3070, Oakland, CA 94609. TEL: (510) 601-5111.
FAX: (510) 985-0185. email: info@ibff.org www.ibff.org

MILL VALLEY FILM FESTIVAL
1001 Lootens Place, Ste. 220, San Rafael, CA 94901.
TEL: (415) 383-5256. FAX: (415) 383-8606.
email: info@cafilm.org

MOLODIST INTERNATIONAL FILM FESTIVAL
6 Saksahanskoho Str., Kyiv, Ukraine, 01033.
TEL: 38 044 289 2335. TEL/FAX: 38 044 289 2336.
www.molodist.com

NORTHWEST FILM & VIDEO FESTIVAL
Northwest Film Center, 1219 SW Park Ave., Portland, OR 97205. TEL: (503) 221-1156. FAX: (503) 294-0874.
email: info@nwfilm.org www.nwfilm.org

PUSAN INTERNATIONAL FILM FESTIVAL
Yachting Center, Annex 2-1, #1393, Woo 1-Dong, Haeundae-Gu, Busan 612-021 Korea. TEL: 82-51-747-3010.
FAX: 82-51-747-3012. www.piff.org

SAN FERNANDO VALLEY INTL. FILM FESTIVAL
5504 Cleon Ave., N. Hollywood, CA 91601.
TEL: (818) 623-9122. email: festival@viffi.org www.viffi.org

SITGES FESTIVAL INTERNACIONAL DE CINEMA DE CATALUNYA
Edifici Miramar, C. Davallada, 12 3º, 08870 Sitges Barcelona.
TEL: 34 93 894 9990. FAX: 34 93 894 8996.
email: festival@cinemasitges.com www.cinemasitges.com
DIRECTOR
Ángel Sala

SYRACUSE INTL. FILM AND VIDEO FESTIVAL
Hotel Syracuse, 500 S. Warren St., Syracuse, NY 13202.
TEL: (315) 443-8826. email: info@syrfilm.com
www.syrfilmfest.com
EXECUTIVE DIRECTOR
Christine Fawcett-Shapiro - christine@syrfilm.com

TAHOE/RENO INTL. FILM FESTIVAL
T-RIFF 948 Incline Way, Incline Village, NV 89451.
TEL: (775) 298-0018. FAX: (775) 298-0019.
email: tahoefilmfest@aol.com

UNITED NATIONS ASSOCIATION FILM FESTIVAL
P.O. Box 19369, Stanford, CA 94309. TEL: (650) 724-5544.
email: info@unaff.org www.unaff.org

WILLIAMSTOWN FILM FESTIVAL
145 Henderson Rd., Williamstown, MA 01267.
TEL: (413) 458-9700. FAX: (413) 458-2702.
email: contactus@williamstownfilmfest.com
www.williamstownfilmfest.com/default.asp
EXECUTIVE DIRECTOR
Steve Lawson

NOVEMBER 2011

AFI FEST
2021 N.Western Ave., Los Angeles CA 90027-1657.
TEL: (866) 234-3378. email: AFIFEST@AFI.com
www.afifest.com

AMERICAN FILM MARKET (AFM)
10850 Wilshire Blvd., 9th Flr., Los Angeles, CA 90024.
TEL: (310) 446-1000. FAX: (310) 446-1600.
email: afm@ifta-online.org www.americanfilmmarket.com
MANAGING DIRECTOR
Jonathan Wolf

BEIJING EUROPEAN FILM FESTIVAL
Asiexpo Association, 9 quater rue Montbrllant, 69003 Lyon, France. TEL: 33 (4) 7291 4373. FAX: 33 (4) 7235 9011.
email: asiexpo@asiexpo.com www.asiexpo.com/china

BOSTON JEWISH FILM FESTIVAL
1001 Watertown St., West Newton, MA 02465.
TEL: (617) 244-9899. FAX: (617) 244-9894.
email: info@bjff.org www.bjff.org
EXECUTIVE DIRECTOR
Sara L. Rubin

CAIRO INTERNATIONAL FILM FESTIVAL
17, Kasr El Nil St., Cairo-Egypt. TEL: (202) 239 23962,
(202) 239 23562. FAX: (202) 239 23562.
email: info@cairofilmfest.org www.cairofilmfest.org
PRESIDENT
Dr. Ezzat Abo Auf

THE CHICAGO LESBIAN & GAY INTERNATIONAL FILM FESTIVAL
5243 N. Clark, Chicago, IL 60640. TEL: (773) 293-1447.
FAX: (773) 293-0575. email: info@chicagofilmmakers.org
www.chicagofilmmakers.org
EXECUTIVE DIRECTOR
Brenda Webb

CINE-WORLD FILM FESTIVAL
P.O. Box 3378, Sarasota, FL 34230. TEL: (941) 364-8662.
FAX: (941) 364-8478. email: mail@filmsociety.org
www.filmsociety.org

CINEMANIA FILM FESTIVAL
1411 Stanley St., Ste. 400, Montreal, QC H3A 1P4, Canada.
TEL: (514) 878-0082. FAX: (514) 878-0092.
email: info@cinemaniafilmfestival.com
www.cinemaniafilmfestival.com

COLUMBUS INTL. FILM AND VIDEO FESTIVAL
1430 S. High St., Rm. 322 Columbus, OH 43207.
TEL: (614) 444-7460. email: info@chrisawards.org
www.chrisawards.org

FILMSTOCK INTL. FILM FESTIVAL
24 Guildford St., Luton LU1 2NR United Kingdom.
TEL: 44 (0) 1582 402 200. email: filmstock@mac.com
www.filmstock.co.uk

GIJÓN INTERNATIONAL FILM FESTIVAL
Cabrales 82, P.O. Box 76, 33201 - Gijón, Spain.
TEL: (34) 985 18 29 40. FAX: (34) 985 18 29 44.
email: info@gijonfilmfestival.com www.gijonfilmfestival.com

GLOBAL VISIONS FILM FESTIVAL
31221-10405 Jasper Ave., Standard Life Bldg., Edmonton, Alberta, T5J 3S2, Canada. TEL: (780) 414-1052.
email: info@globalvisionsfestival.com
www.globalvisionsfestival.com

INTL. LATINO FILM FESTIVAL - SAN FRANCISCO BAY AREA
984 Folsom St., San Francisco, CA 94107.
TEL: (415) 513-5308. FAX: (415) 512-7179.
email: info@latinofilmfestival.org www.latinofilmfestival.org

MAR DEL PLATA INTERNATIONAL FILM FESTIVAL
Av. de Mayo 1222, 3er 1085 Cap Fed., Argentina.
TEL: 54 11 43 835 115. FAX: 54 11 4383 5115 ext. 102.
email: info@mardelplatafilmfest.com
www.mardelplatafilmfest.com

MARGARET MEAD FILM & VIDEO FESTIVAL
American Museum of Natural History, Central Park West, 79th St., New York, NY 10024. TEL: (212) 769-5305.
FAX: (212) 769-5305. email: meadfest@amnh.org
www.amnh.org/programs/mead/index.html

NGO BLACK NIGHTS FILM FESTIVAL GONSIORI 21
10147 Tallinn, Estonia. TEL: 372 631 4640. FAX: 372 631 4644.
email: poff@poff.ee www.poff.ee

OHIO INDEPENDENT FILM FESTIVAL
1392 W. 65th St., Cleveland, OH 44102. TEL: (216) 651-7315.
FAX: (216) 651-7315. email: ohioindiefilmfest@juno.com
www.ohiofilms.com

SPOKANE GLBT FILM FESTIVAL
P.O. Box 2931, Spokane, WA 99220. TEL: (509) 216-0366.
email:spokanefilmfest@comcast.net www.spokanefilmfest.org

ST. LOUIS INTL. FILM FESTIVAL
3547 Olive St., St. Louis, MO 63103. TEL: (314) 289-4150.
email: mailroom@cinemastlouis.org www.cinemastlouis.org
EXECUTIVE DIRECTOR
Cliff Froehlich - cliff@cinemastlouis.org

TORINO FILM FESTIVAL
Via Montebello 15, 10124 Torino, Italy. TEL: 39 011 8138811.
FAX: 39 011 8138890. email: info@torinofilmfest.org
www.torinofilmfest.org

DECEMBER 2011

ANCHORAGE FILM FESTIVAL
c/o Bear Tooth Theatre
1230 W 27th Ave.Anchorage, AK 99503-2319.
TEL: (907) 276-4255. FAX: (907) 786-4981.
email: crazywind@alaska.com www.anchoragefilmfestival.com
FILM FESTIVAL COORDINATOR
Dawnell Smith

BAHAMAS INTL. FILM FESTIVAL
4th Terrace E & Collins Ave., Bldg. #10, 2nd Flr., Nassau, Bahamas. TEL: (242) 356-5939. FAX: (242) 356-2991.
email: info@bintlfilmfest.com www.bintlfilmfest.com
FOUNDER & EXECUTIVE DIRECTOR
Leslie Vanderpool

HDFEST
3208C E Colonial Dr., Ste. 292, Orlando, FL 32803.
TEL: (321) 206-5343. email: admin@hdfest.com
www.hdfest.com

NEW YORK INTL. INDEPENDENT FILM AND VIDEO FESTIVAL
505 E. Windmill Ln., Ste. 1B-102 Las Vegas, NV 89123.
TEL: (702) 263-4480. FAX: (702) 361-6309.
email:filmmfest@aol.com www.nyfilmvideo.com

WHISTLER FILM FESTIVAL
1004, 102-4369 Main St., Whistler, BC V0N 1B4, Canada.
TEL: (604) 935-8035. FAX: (604) 938-3209.
email: info@whistlerfilmfestival.com
www.whistlerfilmfestival.com
EVENTS MANAGER
Leah Primeau - events@whistlerfilmfestival.co

Biographies

WHO'S WHO

IN THE ENTERTAINMENT WORLD

A

AARON, PAUL

Director, Producer, Writer.
THEATRE: *B'way:* Salvation, Paris Is Out, '70 Girls '70, Love Me Love My Children, That's Entertainment, The Burnt Flowerbed.
PICTURES: A Different Story, A Force of One, The Octagon (co-s.p.), Imperial Navy, Deadly Force, Maxie, Morgan Stewart's Coming Home (director, as Alan Smithee) Home Front, Bill & Ted's Bogus Journey (co-prod.), In Too Deep (prod., s.p.), Looking for Sunday (prod.), Skills Like This (prod.), The Disembodied.
TELEVISION: *Movies*: The Miracle Worker (DGA nom. 1980), Thin Ice, Maid in America, When She Says No, Casebusters (exec. prod.), Save the Dog!, In Love and War, Laurel Avenue (creator, co-writer, exec. prod.), Untamed Love, Grand Avenue (creator, exec. prod.). *Series*: Under One Roof (creator, co-writer, exec. prod.).

ABERNETHY, JACK

Executive. b. Kingston, NY, 1956. e. Georgetown Univ., B.A., 1978; New York Univ., M.B.A., 1979. Abernethy began his career at NBC, where he held a variety of executive finance management positions over a 10-year period: NBC-TV Stations Division, New York, finance, 1980-84; WRC-TV Washington, director, finance & operations, 1984-90; General Electric, v.p., finance & operations, CNBC, 1990-1995, where he was instrumental in engineering the purchase and integration of the Financial News Network. In 1996, Abernethy joined FOX News as v.p. of business affairs and co-launch manager for the network in 1996. He was senior v.p. of finance & administration/CFO from 1998-2000; executive v.p., 2000-2004. In Dec. 2004, Abernethy assumed his current position as CEO of Fox Television Stations, a unit of News Corporation that includes the Fox Television Stations group and Twentieth Television and now reports to Roger Ailes, chairman & CEO of Fox News and chairman of Fox Television Stations. Abernethy has assumed an integral role in the development and fall 2006 roll out of News Corp.'s new broadcast network: My Network TV.

ABRAHAM, F. MURRAY

Actor. r.n. Fahrid Murray Abraham. b. Pittsburgh, PA, Oct. 24, 1939. e. U. of Texas, 1959-61; trained for stage at Herbert Berghof Studios with Uta Hagen. First NY acting job was as Macy's Santa Claus. Stage debut in Los Angeles in The Wonderful Ice Cream Suit, 1965. New York debut in The Fantasticks, 1966. Full professor of theatre at CUNY Brooklyn College. Honorary Doctorate, Ryder College.
THEATRE: Antigone (NYSF, 1982), Uncle Vanya (Obie, LaMamma, etc.), The Golem (NYSF), Madwoman of Chaillot, Othello, Cyrano, A Life in the Theatre, Sexual Perversity in Chicago, Duck Variations, The David Show, Adaptation/Next, Don't Drink the Water, And Miss Reardon Drinks a Little, Where Has Tommy Flowers Gone?, A Christmas Carol, The Seagull, Landscape of the Body, 6 Rms Riv Vu, Survival of St. Joan, Scuba Duba, Teibele & Her Demon, The Ritz, Legend, Bad Habits, Frankie & Johnnie in the Claire De Lune, Twelfth Night, Macbeth, A Midsummer's Night Dream, Waiting for Godot, King Lear, Angels in America: Millenium Aproaches/Perestroika, Little Murders, A Month in the Country; also 5 Children's musicals, (Theatreworks), A Christmas Carol (2002), Triumph of Love, The New Moon, L'Histoire du Soldat (narr.), The Jew of Malta, The Merchant of Venice.
PICTURES: They Might Be Giants (debut, 1971), Serpico, The Prisoner of 2nd Avenue, The Sunshine Boys, All the President's Men, The Ritz, Madman, The Big Fix, Scarface, Amadeus (Academy Award, Golden Globe Award 1985), The Name of the Rose, Slipstream, The Favorite, Russicum (The Third Solution), An Innocent Man, Beyond the Stars, Eye of the Widow, The Bonfire of the Vanities, Cadence, Mobsters, National Lampoon's Loaded Weapon 1, By the Sword, Last Action Hero, Sweet Killing, The Final Card, Surviving the Game, Nostradamus, The Case, Jamila, Quiet Flows the Dawn, Money, Dillinger and Capone, Mighty Aphrodite, Baby Face Nelson, Looking for Richard, Children of the Revolution, Eruption, Mimic, Star Trek: Insurrection, All New Adventures of Laurel and Hardy: For Love or Mummy, Muppets from Space, Excellent Cadavers, Finding Forrester, The Knights of the Quest, I Cavalieri che fecero l'impressa, 13 Ghosts, Joshua, Papa Rua Alguem 5555, The Bridge of San Luis Rey, Quiet Flows the Don, The Inquiry, A House Divided, The Stone Merchant, Come le formiche, Carnera: The Walking Mountain, Perestroika.
TELEVISION: *Movies:* Sex and the Married Woman, Galileo Galilei, Vaclav Havel's 'Largo Desolato', A Season of Giants, The First Circle, Journey to the Center of the Earth, Il Caso Dozier, Color of Justice, Esther, Noah's Ark, The Darkling, Un Dono semplice, Pompeii: The Last Day (narr. english version), Dead Lawyers, Shark Swarm. *Mini-series:* Dead Man's Walk, I Promessi sposi, Dream West, Marco Polo. *Series:* Love of Life, How to Survive a Marriage, Tikhiy Don. *Guest:* More than 61 appearances.

ABRAHAMS, JIM

Producer, Writer, Director. b. Shorewood, WI, May 10, 1944. e. U. of Wisconsin. Former private investigator. 1971, with friends David and Jerry Zucker, opened the Kentucky Fried Theatre in Madison, WI, a multimedia show specializing in live improvisational skits mixed with videotaped and film routines and sketches, with the threesome writing and appearing in most. Opened new theatre in Los Angeles in 1972 and developed large following. Co-wrote, co-dir., and co-exec. prod. TV series Police Squad!
PICTURES: With Zuckers: The Kentucky Fried Movie (co-s.p.), Airplaine! (co-dir., co-exec. prod., co-s.p. WGA Award 1981), Top Secret! (co-dir., co-s.p.,co-exec. prod.), Ruthless People (co-dir.). Also: Big Business (dir.), The Naked Gun (exec. prod., co-s.p.), Cry-Baby (co-exec. prod.), Welcome Home Roxy Carmichael (dir.), The Naked Gun 2-1/2 (co-exec. prod.), Hot Shots! (dir., co-s.p.), Hot Shots Part Deux!. (dir., co-s.p.), Naked Gun 33 1/3: The Final Insult (co-exec. prod.), Jane Austen's Mafia! (dir., s.p.), Balls of Courage, Scary Movie 4 (s.p.).
TELEVISION: *Movies:* All You Need Is Cash (soundtrack prod.), First Do No Harm (dir, exec prod, prod.). *Series:* Police Squad (s.p., Emmy nom. 1982).

ABRAMS, J.J.

Writer, Director, Producer, Composer, Actor. b. New York, June 27, 1966. e. Attended Sarah Lawrence College, Bronxville, NY. Currently chairman of Bad Robot, a production company based in Burbank, CA. Abrams is the winner of ASCAP's Film and Television Music Awards 2005 Top TV Series Award (shared with Michael Ciacchino); and in 2005 won two Emmys for the TV series Lost, Outstanding Directing for a Drama Series (2004; pilot parts 1 and 2); and Outstanding Drama Series (2004) which he shared with the show's producers.
PICTURES: *Composer:* Nightbeast. *Writer:* Taking Care of Business, Regarding Henry (also co-producer and actor), Forever Young, Gone Fishin', Armageddon, Joy Ride (also producer), Mission Impossible III (also dir.), The Good Sailor (exec. prod., dir.). *Producer:* The Pallbearer, The Suburbans (also actor), The Animated Alias: Tribunal (video short; exec. prod.), Cloverfield, Star Trek (also dir.), Morning Glory. *Actor:* Six Degrees Of Separation, Diabolique.
TELEVISION: *Movies:* The Catch (writer & exec. prod.), Six Degrees (exec. prod.), Anatomy of Hope. *Series*: Felicity (writer, creator, director, exec. prod. & composer), Alias (creator, writer, exec. prod. & composer of main theme, Emmy nom. 2002), Lost (writer, creator, dir. & exec. prod., DGA nom. 2005, 2 Emmy Awards, 2005, 3 noms., WGA Award 2006, nom. 2007), What About Brian? (exec. prod.), Fringe (writer, exec. prod. & theme composer, 2 WGA noms. 2009), Six Degrees, Undercovers.

ACKERMAN, ANDY

Director, Producer, Editor.
PICTURES: Dead and Buried (1981. second asst. dir.).
TELEVISION: *Movies:* Cheers: 200th Anniversary Special (co-prod., editor, Emmy nom. 1990), Peep Show, The Hill. *Series:* WKRP in Cincinnati (Emmy for editing, 1981, Emmy nom. 1982), Newhart (Emmy nom. edtiting 1983) *Dir.* Cheers (also co-prod., editor, Emmy Awards, 1988, 1991, Emmy Award noms. 1986, 1987), Wings, Seinfeld (also prod., DGA Awards 1997-98, Emmy Award nom. 1995-1998), Frasier, If You Love Something Leave It Alone (pilot), Almost Perfect, Everybody Loves Raymond, Suddenly Susan, Public Morals, Jenny, LateLine (also prod.), Becker (also prod.), It's Like, You Know..., The Trouble with Normal (also prod.), Curb Your Enthusiasm, Raising Dad, The Ellen Show (also prod.), Andy Richter Controls the Universe (also exec. prod.) The O'Keefes, Two and a Half Men, Come to

Papa (also exec. prod.), Center of the Universe, Life on a Stick, The New Adventures of Old Christine, Happy Hour (pilot).

ACKLAND, JOSS

Actor. b. North Kensington, London, England, Feb. 29, 1928. e. Central Sch. of Speech Training & Dramatic Art. Spent time in Central Africa as a tea planter. Over 400 TV appearances. Autobiography, I Must Be in There Somewhere. Awarded C.B.E. (Commander of the British Empire).
THEATRE: The Old Vic (3 yrs.), Mermaid Theatre (artistic dir., 3 yrs.); Hotel in Amsterdam, Jorrocks Come as You Are, The Collaborators, A Streetcar Named Desire, The Madras House, Captain Brassbound's Conversion, Never the Sinner, Henry IV Parts I & II, Peter Pan (dramatic & musical versions), A Little Night Music, Evita, The Visit, etc.
PICTURES: Seven Days to Noon, Crescendo, Trecolonne in Cronaca, The House That Dripped Blood, The Happiness Cage, Villain, England Made Me, The Black Windmill, S.P.Y.S, The Little Prince, Royal Flash, Operation Daybreak, Who Is Killing the Great Chefs of Europe, Saint Jack, The Apple, Rough Cut, Lady Jane, A Zed and Two Noughts, The Sicilian, White Mischief, To Kill a Priest, It Couldn't Happen Here, Lethal Weapon 2, The Hunt for Red October, Object of Beauty, Bill and Ted's Bogus Journey, The Palermo Connection, The Mighty Ducks, Nowhere to Run, Mother's Boys, The Princess and the Goblin (voice), Miracle on 34th Street, Giorgino, Mad Dogs and Englishmen, A Kid in the Court of King Arthur, Occhio Pinocchio, Daisies in December, To the Ends of Time, Mighty Ducks 3, Surviving Picasso, Deadly Voyage, Firelight, Milk, Passion of Mind, Mumbo Jumbo, Lounge Act (voice), Painting Faces, K-19: The Widowmaker, No Good Deed, I'll Be There, Asylum, Day of Wrath, Flawless, Moscow Zero, How About You, Prisoners of the Sun.
TELEVISION: *Movies:* Angus Slowly Sinking?, Tomorrow Just You Wait, Focus, Lord Raingo, Death of a Salesman, The Widower, On the March to the Sea, Room 13, Fall of the Goat, Before the Party, The Three Sisters, The Lie, Six Faces: True Life, Six Faces: Gallery of Faces, The Bankrupt, Access to the Children, Great Expectations, You Talk Too Much, The Love Tapes, the Barretts of Wimpole Street, The Tragedy of Coriolanus, Shadowlands, Queenie, When We Are Married, Codename: Kyril, First and Last, Jekyll & Hyde, The Secret Life of Ian Fleming, They Do It With Mirrors, A Murder of Quality, Voices in the Garden, Jacob, Citizen X, Daisies in December, Hidden in Silence, Deadly Voyage, To the Ends of Time, Gioco di specchi, Othello, Henry VIII, Icon, Hogfather, Pinocchio. *Mini-series:* Tinker, Tailor, Soldier, Spy, Bekenntnisse des Hochstaplers Felix Krull, Shroud of a Nightingale, A Killing On the Exchange, A Quiet Conspiracy, The Man Who Lived at the Ritz, A Woman Named Jackie, Ashenden, Figlio di Sandokan, II, Heat of the Sun, Above and Beyond. *Series:* The Indian Tales of Rudyard Kipling, David Copperfield, The Further Adventures of the Three Musketeers, Z Cars, Canterbury Tales, Six Faces, The Crezz, A Question of Guilt, Thicker Than Water. *Guest:* More than 125 appearances.

ADAM, KEN

Art Director, Prod. Designer. b. Berlin, Germany, Feb. 5, 1921. e. St. Pauls Sch., London, England; London U., student of architecture. 6 years war service as RAF pilot. In 1947 entered motion picture industry as draughtsman for movie, This Was a Woman. Appeared in numerous documentaries about Stanley Kubrick and also has appeared in numerous documentaries about designing various James Bond movies. Received Art Directors Guild Lifetime Achievement Award 2002.
PICTURES: The Devil's Pass, Soho Incident, Around the World in 80 Days (Academy Award nom. 1957). *Prod. Designer:* Spin a Dark Web, Night of the Demon, Gideon's Day, The Angry Hills, Beyond This Place, The Rough and the Smooth, In the Nick, Let's Get Married, Trials of Oscar Wilde, Dr. No, Sodom and Gomorrah, In the Cool of the Day, Dr. Strangelove, Goldfinger, Woman of Straw, Thunderball, The Ipcress File, Funeral in Berlin, You Only Live Twice, Chitty Chitty Bang Bang, Goodbye Mr. Chips, The Owl and the Pussycat, Diamonds Are Forever, Sleuth, The Last of Sheila, Barry Lyndon (Academy Award, 1976), Madam Kitty, The Seven Percent Solution, The Spy Who Loved Me (Academy Award nom. 1978), Moonraker, Pennies From Heaven (visual consult., assoc. prod.), King David, Agnes of God, Crimes of the Heart, The Deceivers, Dead-Bang, The Freshman, The Doctor, Company Business, Undercover Blues, Addams Family Values (Academy Award nom. 1994), The Madness of King George (Academy. Award, 1995), Boys on the Side, Bogus, In & Out, The Out of Towners, The White Hotel, Taking Sides.

ADAMS, AMY

Actress. b. Aviano, Pordenone, Italy, August 20, 1974.
PICTURES: Drop Dead Gorgeous, Psycho Beach Party, The Slaughter Rule, Pumpkin, Serving Sara, Catch Me If You Can, The Wedding Date, Junebug (Academy Award nom. 2006), Standing Still, Talladega Nights: The Ballad of Ricky Bobby, Tenacious D in The Pick of Destiny, The Ex, Underdog (voice), Enchanted (also soundtrack performer, Golden Globe nom. 2008), Charlie Wilson's War, Sunshine Cleaning, Miss Pettigrew Lives for a Day, Doubt (Golden Globe nom.; Academy Award nom. 2009), Julie & Julia, Night at the Museum 2: Battle of the Smithsonian, The Fighter Leap Year.
TELEVISION: *Series:* King of the Hill, Dr. Vegas, The Office. *Guest:* More than 50 appearances.

ADAMS, BROOKE

Actress. b. New York, NY, Feb. 8, 1949. e. H.S. of Performing Arts; Inst. of American Ballet. Studied with Lee Strasberg. Made professional debut at six in Finian's Rainbow. Worked steadily in summer stock and TV until age 18. After hiatus resumed acting career.
THEATRE: Petrified Forest, Split, Key Exchange, Linda Her, Over Mother's Dead Body, Old Neighborhood, Heidi Chronicles, Lost in Yonkers. Director: Two Faced. Helps run small summer theatre in upstate NY.
PICTURES: Shock Waves (Death Corps), Car Wash, Days of Heaven, Invasion of the Body Snatchers, Cuba, The Great Train Robbery, A Man a Woman and a Bank, Tell Me a Riddle, Utilities, The Dead Zone, Almost You, Key Exchange, The Stuff, Man on Fire, The Unborn, Gas Food Lodging, Sleepless, The Fire This Time, The Baby Sitter's Club.
TELEVISION: *Movies:* F. Scott Fitzgerald and "The Last of the Belles," The Daughters of Joshua Cabe Return, James Dean, Summer, The Innocents Abroad, Who is the Black Dahlia?, Murder on Flight 502, Lace, Haunted, Special People, Lace II, The Lion of Africa, Bridesmaids, Sometimes They Come Back, The Last Hit, Probable Cause, Gun, Song of the Succubus, Picture Windows. *Mini-series:* Picture Windows: Language of the Heart. *Series:* O.K. Crackerby. Pilot: A Girl's Life, Nero Wolfe, The Lords of Flatbush, Monk. *Documentaries as Narrator:* The Fire This Time, The Daring Project. *Guest:* More than 45 appearances.

ADAMS, CATLIN

Actress, Director, Producer. b. Los Angeles, CA, Oct. 11, 1950. Began career as actress then studied directing at American Film Institute. Made directorial debut with, Wanted: The Perfect Guy. Also directed Little Shiny Shoes (short, written and prod. with Melanie Mayron), Stolen: One Husband (TV), Toothless (TV).
THEATRE: Safe House, Scandalous Memories, Dream of a Blacklisted Actor, The Candy Store, Ruby Ruby Sam Sam, Bermuda Avenue Triangle (dir.).
PICTURES: *Actress:* The Jerk, The Jazz Singer, Sticky Fingers (also dir., co-s.p., co-prod.).
TELEVISION: *Movies:* Panic in Echo Park, Afterschool Specials: Wanted: The Perfect Guy, (dir. DGA Award 1987), Stolen: One Husband (dir.) Freaky Friday, Toothless. *Series:* Square Pegs, Beverly Hills 90210 (dir. only). *Specials:* How to Survive the 70's and Maybe Even Bump into a Little Happiness, She Loves Me She Loves Me Not.

ADAMS, JOEY LAUREN

Actress. b. Little Rock, AR, Jan. 6, 1971.
PICTURES: Exorcist II: The Heretic (as Joey Adams), Coneheads, Dazed and Confused, The Program, Sleep with Me, S.F.W., The Pros & Cons of Breathing, Mallrats, Bio-Dome (as Joey Adams), Michael, Drawing Flies (as Lauren Lyle), Chasing Amy (Golden Globe nom. 1998), A Cool Dry Place, Big Daddy, Reaching Normal,The Dress Code, Beautiful, Harvard Man, Dr. Dolittle 2 (voice), In the Shadows, Jay and Silent Bob Strike Back, Beeper, A Promise Kept, The Big Empty, Jersey Girl, Once in a Lifetime, Come Early Morning (dir., writer), The Break-Up, Endure, Apart.
TELEVISION: *Movies:* On the Edge, Remembering Charlie, Tough Trade. *Series:* Top of the Heap, Vinnie & Bobby, Second Noah.

ADAMS, JULIE

Actress. r.n. Betty May Adams. b. Waterloo, IA, Oct. 17, 1928. e. jr. coll., Little Rock, AK. Coll. dramatics. In addition to film credits, has made nearly 100 television guest appearances.
PICTURES: Red Hot and Blue (debut, 1949), The Dalton Gang, Crooked River, Hostile Country, West of the Brazos, Colorado Ranger, Fast on the Draw, Marshal of Heldorado. As Julie Adams: Hollywood Story, Finders Keepers, Bend of the River, Bright Victory, Treasure of Lost Canyon, Horizons West, Lawless Breed, Mississippi Gambler, Man From the Alamo, The Stand of Apache River, Wings of the Hawk, The Creature From the Black Lagoon, Francis Joins the WACS, The Looters, One Desire, The Private War of Major Benson, Six Bridges to Cross, Away All Boats, Four Girls in Town, Slim Carter, Slaughter on 10th Avenue, Tarawa Beachhead, Gunfight at Dodge City, Raymie, Underwater City, Tickle Me, Valley of Mystery, The Last Movie, McQ, Psychic Killer, The Wild McCullochs, Killer Inside Me, Goodbye Franklin High, The Fifth Floor, Black Roses, Catchfire, Back to the Black Lagoon, World Trade Center.
TELEVISION: *Movies*: Valley of Mystery, The Trackers, Go Ask Alice, Six Characters in Search of an Author, Code Red, Backtrack, The Conviction of Kitty Dodds. *Mini-series:* Greatest Heroes of the Bible. *Series*: Yancy Derringer, General Hospital, The Jimmy Stewart Show, Code Red, Capitol. *Guest:* More than 106 appearances.

ADAMS, MAUD

Actress. r.n. Maud Wikstrum. b. Lulea, Sweden, Feb. 12, 1945.

Formerly a model. Acting debut in The Boys in the Band. Known for work in James Bond movies and has appeared in several documentaries about the Bond films. Nearly 30 television guest appearances since 1971.
PICTURES: The Boys in the Band, The Christian Licorice Store, U-Turn, Mahoney's Estate, The Man With the Golden Gun, Rollerball, Killer Force, The Merciless Man, Tattoo, Octopussy, Target Eagle, Jane and the Lost City, The Women's Club, A Man of Passion, The Favorite, Soda Cracker, Deadly Intent, Angel III, The Kill Reflex, Forbidden Sun, Favorite, Ringer, The Seekers.
TELEVISION: *Movies:* Big Bob Johnson and His Fantastic Speed Circus, The Hostage Tower, Playing for Time, Nairobi Affair, Blacke's Magic, A Perry Mason Mystery: The Case of the Wicked Wives. *Series:* Hawaii Five-O, Chicago Story, Emerald Point N.A.S., Walker, Texas Ranger, Radioskugga, Vita lögner.

ADEFARASIN, REMI
Cinematographer.
Received best cinematography recognition for Elizabeth from BAFTA and the British Society of Cinematographers in 1999. Has more than 30 television movie cinematography/camera credits since 1973 debut.
PICTURES: Dead Lucky, Truly Madly Deeply, The Hummingbird Tree, Captives, Hollow Reed, The English Patient (dir. of photog.), Sliding Doors, Elizabeth (ASC nom., BAFTA award 1999, Academy Award nom. 1999), Onegin, The House of Mirth, Unconditional Love, The One and Only, Who Shot Victor Fox, About a Boy, Johnny English, The Haunted Mansion, In Good Company, Match Point, Amazing Grace, Scoop, Elizabeth: The Golden Age, Fred Claus, Cemetery Junction.
TELEVISION: *Movies (Assistant Camera):* Happy, An Imaginative Woman, Robinson Crusoe, Sunset Across the Bay, The Evacuees, Moll Flanders, Three Men in a Boat, Rogue Male, Arnhem: The Story of an Escape, The Price of Coal. *Cinematographer:* Grown-Ups, Home Sweet Home, The Files on Jill Hatch, Stan's Last Game, The Case of the Frightened Lady, Amy, Four Days in July, Shoot for the Sun, Sweet As You Are, Christabel, Testimony of a Child, Dream Baby, News Hounds, The Land of Dreams, Children Crossing, The Lost Language of Cranes, Memento Mori, Hot Millions, Great Moments in Aviation, Wide-Eyed and Legless, Midnight Movie, Human Bomb, Emma, Arabian Nights. *Mini-series:* Summer's Lease, Sleepers, The Buccaneers, Into the Fire, Cold Lazarus, Band of Brothers (Emmy nom. 2002), The Pacific. *Series:* The Fast Show, Love After Lunch.

ADELMAN, GARY
Executive, Producer. b. Los Angeles, CA, March 16, 1944. e. California State U., Long Beach State Coll. Assisted Winston Hock in development of 3-D process, 1975. Pres. & COO of Monarch Prods, 1976-Present. Post-prod. consultant for Jerry Gross Organization. Founder and partial owner of New Image Releasing Inc., a prod. & dist. co., 1983. Had post of secty./treas. then named v.p., chg. prod., All-American Group, 1987. Was pres. of Monarch Productions, which produces theatrical feature films, trailers, commercials and industrial films. Currently Production Supvr. for Joda Productions.
PICTURES: Incubus (1965-Restoration Consult.) The Candy Snatchers (assoc. prod.), The Severed Arm, Nobody's Perfect (assoc. prod.), Heartwood (post-prod. spvr.), The Month of August (post-prod.spvr.), Sex and the Teenage Mind (co-prod.), The Summoning (line prod.).
TELEVISION: *Movies:* Hope Ranch (line prod.), Blind Injustice.

ADELSON, GARY
Executive, Producer. b. 1954. e. UCLA, B.A. Son of Merv Adelson. Joined Lorimar Prods. 1970 as prod. asst. on TV movie Helter Skelter. In 1989, formed Adelson/Baumgarten Prods. with Craig Baumgarten. In 1993, founded Interactive Cable Systems which was acquired by MCI. Partnered with EastWest Venture Group. Currently Managing Dir. for Houlihan Lokey Howard & Zukin which represents Image Entertainment.
PICTURES: The Last Starfighter, The Boy Who Could Fly, In The Mood, Tap, Hard to Kill (also s.p.), Hook, Universal Soldier, Nowhere to Run, Blank Check, It Could Happen to You, Jade, Hidden Assassin, Rolling Thunder, The Shooter, Peter Pan.
TELEVISION: *Movies:* Helter Skelter (asst. prod.), The Blue Knight (prod.). *Exec. prod.:* Too Good To Be True, Our Family Business, Cass Malloy, The Winter of Our Discontent, Lace, Lace II, Glitz, Detective in the House, Everything to Gain, Critical Choices, The Hunchback, Love in Another Town. *Series:* Eight is Enough (supervising prod.), Sybil (assoc. prod.), Flatbush (exec. prod.), Spies, Studio 5-B (exec. prod.).

ADJANI, ISABELLE
Actress, Producer. b. Gennevilliers, France, June 27, 1955.
PICTURES: Le Petit Bougnat, Faustine and the Beautiful Summer, The Slap, The Story of Adele H. (Academy Award nom. 1976), The Tenant, Barocco, Violette and Francois, The Driver, Nosferatu—The Vampire, The Bronte Sisters, Clara et les Chics Types, Possession, L'Annee prochaine..si tout va bien, Quartet, Next Year If All Goes Well, One Deadly Summer, Antonieta, Deadly Circuit, Subway, Ishtar, Camille Claudel (also co-prod.; Academy Award nom. 1990), Toxic Affair, Queen Margot, Diabolique, Paparazzi, The Repentant, Adolphe, Bon Voyage, Monsieur Ibrahim, Mammuth.
TELEVISION: *Movies:* L' Avare, L' École des femmes, Le Secret des flamands, Ondine, Figaro. *Documentaries:* Lung Ta: The Forgotten Tibet (narr.), Claude Berri, le dernier nabab (voice).

ADLER, GILBERT
Producer, Director.
PICTURES: The Maestro (prod.as Gil Adler), Certain Fury, Basic Training, Children of the Corn: Deadly Harvest (s.p. only), Demon Knight, Bordello of Blood (also s.p.), Double Tap, House on Haunted Hall, Thir13en Ghosts, Ghost Ship, Starsky & Hutch (exec. prod.), Constantine (exec. prod.), The Fountain, Superman Returns, Valkyrie, Dead of Night.
TELEVISION: *Movies:* W.E.I.R.D. World. *Series:* Freddy's Nightmares, Tales from the Crypt, Perversions of Science, Fantasy Island, Charmed, The Strip (co-exec. prod)

ADLON, PERCY
Director, Writer, Producer. b. Munich, Germany, June 1, 1935. e. Munich Univ. m. Eleonore Adlon, with whom he has worked on several film projects. Created more than 40 tv documentaries.
PICTURES: Celeste, The Last Five Days (dir. only), The Swing, Sugarbaby, Bagdad Cafe, Rosalie Goes Shopping, Salmonberries, Younger and Younger, Eat Your Heart Out (prod. only), Forever Flirt, Hawaiian Gardens, Mahler auf der Couch (dir., s.p.).
TELEVISION: *Movies:* Herr Kischott, Herschel und die Musik der Sterne, Babycakes, Red Hot and Blue,The Guardian and His Poet (Adolf Grimme Award), Hotel Adlon. *Documentary:* Koenig's Sphere: The German Sculptor Fritz Koenig at Ground Zero.

AFFLECK, BEN
Actor, Writer, Director, Producer. b. Berkeley, CA, Aug. 15, 1972. Began acting at age 8. Brother is Casey Affleck.
PICTURES: The Dark End of the Street, School Ties, Buffy the Vampire Slayer, Dazed and Confused, I Killed My Lesbian Wife Hung Her on a Meat Hook, and Now I Have a Three-Picture Deal at Disney (dir. only), Mallrats, Glory Daze, Going All the Way, Office Killer, Chasing Amy, Good Will Hunting (also s.p., Academy Award, Golden Globe Award, WGA Award 1998), Phantoms, Armageddon, Shakespeare in Love, 200 Cigarettes, Forces of Nature, Dogma, Boiler Room, Reindeer Games, Bounce, The Third Wheel (also prod.), Daddy and Them, Pearl Harbor, Jay and Silent Bob Strike Back, Changing Lanes, Stolen Summer (prod. only) Crossing Cords (exec. prod. only), The Sum of All Fears, The Third Wheel (also exec. prod.), Speak Easy (exec. prod.) Daredevil, Gigli, Tough Love, Jersey Girl, Paycheck, The Battle of Shaker Heights (prod. & exec. prod.), Surviving Christmas, Man About Town, Feast (exec. prod. only), Hollywoodland (Golden Globe nom. 2007), Smokin' Aces, Gone, Baby, Gone (prod., writer, dir.), Extract, He's Just Not That Into You, State of Play, Extract, The Company Men, The Town (also dir., s.p.).
TELEVISION: *Movies:* Wanted: The Perfect Guy, Hands of a Stranger, Daddy, SNL Fanatic, All Grown Up (exec. prod.). *Series:* Voyage of the Mimi, Against the Grain, Lifestories: Families in Crisis (Emmy nom. 1995), Project Greenlight (Emmy nom. 2002), Project Greenlight 2 (Emmy nom. 2004), Project Greenlight 3 (Emmy nom. 2005), The Second Voyage of the Mimi, Push, Nevada (exec. prod./writer). *Specials:* A People's History of the United States (prod. only). *Guest:* More than 129 appearances.

AFFLECK, CASEY
Actor. b. Falmouth, MA, August 12, 1975. e. Columbia U., majoring in Physics. Brother is Ben Affleck. Directed series of commercials for the Sundance Channel.
THEATRE: *London:* This Is Our Youth.
PICTURES: To Die For, Race the Sun, Chasing Amy, Good Will Hunting, Desert Blue, 200 Cigarettes, Floating, Drowning Mona, Committed, Hamlet, Finding Forrester (tech. consult.), American Pie 2, Soul Survivors, Ocean's Eleven, Lonesome Jim, The Last Kiss, Ocean's Thirteen, The Assassination of Jesse James by the Coward Robert Ford (Academy Award nom., Golden Globe nom. 2008), Gone Baby Gone, The Killer Inside Me.
TELEVISION: *Movies:* Lemon Sky, All Grown Up (exec. prod.). *Mini-series:* The Kennedys of Massachusetts.

AGOGLIA, JOHN J.
Executive. Worked for 14 years for CBS Entertainment in New York, becoming v.p. business affairs. Joined NBC in 1979 as v.p., program and talent negotiations; named sr. v.p. business affairs NBC, 1980; exec. v.p. NBC Prods., 1984; exec. v.p., business affairs NBC-TV Network, 1986; in charge of foreign marketing relating to NBC Productions products, 1987; pres. of NBC Enterprises, 1990; pres. of NBC Prods., 1993-1998. After leaving NBC, formed GII Media, Inc., a consulting co. and Canan Filmworks LLC, which produces family-oriented programming. Consultant with ExperTelligence, Inc. Bd. of directors, KCET; Pres. of Bd. of Airport Commissioners. 2007 elected Chairman of the Board of Los Angeles Universal Preschool (LAUP), Los Angeles County's leader in preschool funding and quality assurance.

AGRESS, ELLEN
Executive. e. B.A. in political science from the University of Michigan, 1968. Agress has a J.D. from the Harvard Law School, 1971. She is admitted to the Bars of Massachusetts, New York and the District of Columbia. Before entering the entertainment industry in 1978, Agress worked in both private and public interest communications law practices in Washington, D.C. and New York. In 1978, Agress joined NBC and was vice president, Legal Policy and Planning, where she headed the company's in-house FCC practice Group. From NBC she joined News America Corporation, and since July 1997 she had been the senior, v.p., deputy general counsel of News America Corporation. In this position, Agress was responsible for regulatory and legislative matters affecting the various broadcast and cable businesses owned and managed by News Corporation, including the Fox Television Network, Fox Television Stations and Fox Cable Networks. Currently is senior v.p. and Deputy General Counsel of Communications, News America Incorporated.

AGUTTER, JENNY
Actress. b. Taunton, Devonshire, England, Dec. 20, 1952. e. Elmhurst Ballet Sch. Received Variety Club of Great Britain Most Promising Artiste Award, 1971.
THEATRE: School for Scandal, Rooted, Arms and the Man, The Ride Across Lake Constance, The Tempest, Spring Awakening, Hedda, Betrayal. Member, Royal Shakespeare Co.-King Lear, Arden of Taversham, The Body. Breaking the Silence, Shrew (Los Angeles), Love's Labour's Lost, Mothers and Daughters.
PICTURES: East of Sudan (debut, 1964), Ballerina (tv in U.S.), A Man Could Get Killed, Vrata raja, Star!, I Start Counting, The Railway Children, Walkabout, Shelley, Logan's Run, The Eagle Has Landed, Equus (BAFTA Award, 1977), Dominique, China 9 Liberty 37, The Riddle of the Sands, Sweet William, Amy, An American Werewolf in London, The Survivor, Miss Right, Secret Places, Amazon Women on the Moon, Dark Tower, King of the Wind, Darkman, Child's Play 2, Freddie as F.R.O. 7 (voice), Blue Juice, The Parole Officer, At Dawning, Number One Longing Number Two Regret, Heroes and Villains, In Your Dreams, Irina Palm.
TELEVISION: *Movies:* Long After Summer, The Great Mr. Dickens, The Wild Duck, The Cherry Orchard, The Snow Goose (Emmy Award, 1972), A War of Children, The Savage Curse, The Man in the Iron Mask, School Play, Mayflower: The Pilgrams' Adventure, This Office Life, Silas Marner: The Weaver of Raveloe, Love's Labour's Lost, The Grand Knockout Tournament, Not a Penny More Not a Penny Less, Romeo and Juliet, September, Bramwell: Our Brave Boys, Bramwell: Loose Women, The Railway Children, The Alan Clark Diaries, Inspector Lynley Mysteries: A Cry for Justice, Marple: What Mrs. McGillicuddy Saw, Diamond Geezer 2. *Mini-series:* Beulah Land, The Buccaneers, A Respectable Trade. *Series:* The Railway Children, TECX, The All New Alexei Sayle Show, And the Beat Goes On, Spooks, MI-5, The Alan Clark Diaries, Monday Monday, The Invisibles. *Guest:* More than 94 appearances.

AIELLO, DANNY
Actor. b. New York, NY, June 20, 1936.
THEATRE: Lampost Reunion (Theatre World Award), Wheelbarrow Closers, Gemini (Obie Award), Knockout, The Floating Light Bulb, Hurlyburly (LA Drama Critics Award), The House of Blue Leaves, Adult Entertainment.
PICTURES: Bang the Drum Slowly (debut, 1973), The Godmothers, The Godfather Part II, The Front, Hooch, Fingers, Blood Brothers, Hide in Plain Sight, Defiance, Fort Apache the Bronx, Chu Chu and the Philly Flash, Once Upon a Time in America, Old Enough, Deathmask, The Purple Rose of Cairo, Key Exchange, The Protector, The Stuff, Radio Days, Man On Fire, The Pick-Up Artist, Moonstruck, The January Man, Do the Right Thing (LA, Chicago & Boston Film Critics Awards; Academy Award nom., Golden Globe nom. 1990), Russicum (The Third Solution), Harlem Nights, Jacob's Ladder, The Closer, Once Around, Hudson Hawk, 29th Street, Shocktroop, Ruby, Mistress, The Cemetery Club, The Pickle, Me and the Kid, The Professional, Ready to Wear (Pret-a-Porter), Power of Attorney, City Hall, Two Much, 2 Days in the Valley, Mojave Moon, Bring Me The Head of Mavis Davis, A Brooklyn State of Mind, Wilbur Falls, Prince of Central Park, Off Key, Marcus Timberwolf, The Last Request, Mail Order Bride, Zeyda and the Hitman, Brooklyn Lobster, Stiffs, Lucky Number Slevin, The Last Request, 4Chosen, Anyone's Son (also dir., co-exec. prod.), Stiffs.
TELEVISION: *Movies:* The Last Tenant, Lovey: A Circle of Children Part 2, A Family of Strangers (Emmy Award, 1981), A Question of Honor, Blood Feud, Lady Blue, Daddy, Alone in the Neon Jungle, The Preppie Murder, Brothers' Destiny, The Last Laugh. *Mini-series*: The Last Don, The Last Don II. *Series:* Lady Blue, Dellaventura (also prod). *Specials:* Lieberman in Love, Harry: A Communication Breakdown (narr.). *Guest:* More than 60 appearances.

AILES, ROGER
Executive. b. May 15, 1940. e. Bachelor's degree and honorary doctorate from Ohio Univ. Longtime TV executive, earned industry recognition more than 38 years ago as exec. prod. of "The Mike Douglas Show," which was nominated for two Emmy awards and won its first Emmy in 1967 with Ailes at the helm. He also produced several TV specials. Ailes was author of You Are the Message, chosen as "one of the year's best" by The Wall Street Journal. Ailes previously was president of CNBC, guiding its growth and seeing the cable network triple its ratings and increase profits from $9 million to more than $100 million. Ailes also oversaw CNBC's 1995 worldwide expansion to Europe and Asia. At the same time, he was president of America's Talking, which later became MSNBC. In 1996, he joined Fox News and created FOX's first weekly public affairs show, FOX News Sunday, and oversaw the successful launch of FOX News Channel as the American pres. Ailes is now chairman/CEO of FOX News, overseeing all national operations for FOX News and serving as a senior advisor to Rupert Murdoch, chairman and CEO of News Corp. In Aug. 2005, Ailes was appointed to the additional position of chairman of Fox Television Stations Group, which includes Twentieth Television, producer of first-run syndicated programming and distributor of off-network programming.

AIMEE, ANOUK
Actress. r.n. Francoise Sorya Dreyfus. b. Paris, France, April 27, 1932. Studied dancing at Marseilles Opera, acting at Bauer-Therond dramatic school, Paris. Started in films as teenager billed as Anouk.
PICTURES: La Maison Sous la Mer (debut, 1946), La Fleur de l'age, Les Amants De Verone, The Golden Salamander, Noche de Tormenta, Le Rideau Cramoisi, The Man Who Watched the Trains Go By (Paris Express), Contraband Spain, Forever My Heart, Les Mauvaises Rencontres, Ich Suche Dich, Nina, Stresemann, Pot Bouille, Montparnasse 19, Tous Peuvent Me Tuer, Le Tete Contre Les Murs, The Journey, Les Dragueurs, La Dolce Vita, Le Farceur, Lola, L'Imprevu, Quai Notre-Dame, Il Giudizio Universale, Sodom and Gomorrah, Les Grand Chemins, 8 1/2, Il Terrorista, Il Successo, Liola, Le Voci Bianche, La Fuga, La Stagione del Nostro Amore, A Man and a Woman (Academy Award nom., Golden Globe Award 1967), Lo Sacandalo, Il Morbidonne, Un Soir Un Train, The Model Shop, Justine, The Appointment, Si C'Etait d Refaire, Mon Premier Amour, Salto nel Vuoto (Leap Into the Void), Tragedy of a Ridiculous Man, What Makes David Run?, Le General de l'Armee Morte, Success is the Best Revenge, Viva la Vie, A Man and A Woman: 20 Years Later, Arrivederci e Grazie, La Table Tournante, The House of the Lord, Dr. Bethune, Rabbit Face, Ready to Wear (Pret-a-Porter), A Hundred and One Nights, Ruptures, Marmottes, Men, Women: A Users Manual, LA Without a Map, Riches, Belles, One 4 All, 1999 Madeline, Festival in Cannes, The Birch-Tree Meadow, Ils se marièrent et eurent beaucoup d'enfants, De particulier à particulier, ...And They Lived Happily Ever After, là Ces amours.
TELEVISION: *Movies:* Une page d'amour, Fernanda, Voices in the Garden, Solomon, L' Île bleue, Claude Lelouch, on s'aimera (narr.). *Mini-series:* Mon dernier reve sera pour vous, Victoire, u la douleur de femmes, Napoleon.

ALBERGHETTI, ANNA MARIA
Singer, Actress. b. Pesaro, Italy, May 15, 1936. Son is Daniele Alberghetti, cellist and orchestra conductor. Concert debut in 1948 in Pesaro, then toured Italy, Scandinavia, Spain; Am. debut Carnegie Hall, 1950, sang with NY Philharmonic Society, Phila. Symphony, on television. Made B'way debut in Carnival, 1962 (Tony Award).
PICTURES: The Medium (debut, 1951), Here Comes the Groom, The Stars Are Singing, San Antonio de Bexar, Duel at Apache Wells,The Last Command, Ten Thousand Bedrooms, Cinderfella, The Whole Shebang, Friends and Family, Leadcatcher.
TELEVISION: *Movies:* Kismet. *Guest:* More than 55 appearances.

ALBRECHT, CHRIS
Executive. b.Queens, N.Y. July 24, 1952. e. B.A. degree in dramatic literature from Hofstra University in New York. From l975 to l980, Albrecht was co-owner of The Improvisation nightclub in New York City. During those years, he also served as a new talent management consultant for ABC in New York City. He then worked five years for International Creative Management (ICM), where he was instrumental in signing such talent as Jim Carrey, Keenen Ivory Wayans, Billy Crystal and Whoopi Goldberg. Albrecht joined HBO in June 1985 as senior v.p. of original programming, West Coast. He was responsible for overseeing all HBO West Coast original programming functions for HBO and Cinemax. He was pres. of HBO Independent Productions from 1990-1995. While there he managed the development and production of comedy series for distribution on HBO and the broadcast networks. Albrecht was responsible for bringing the shows Martin and Everybody Loves Raymond to television life. He was president of HBO original programming since 1995, and continues to direct all day-to-day operations of both West and East Coast original programming for HBO, Cinemax and HBO Independent Productions. With the addition of HBO Sports and HBO Film Programming, Albrecht then managed all programming for HBO and Cinemax services. In July 2002, Albrecht was promoted to chairman and CEO for HBO, Inc. and HBO original programming with overall management responsibilities for the company, which operates multiple premium networks in the United States, Europe, Asia and Latin America, as well as HBO's many other lines of business. He was fired in May 2007. In Sept. 2007 he landed at IMG, the talent agency, and headed up the agency's global media unit. He left IMG in Aug. 2008 to return to

Foresee Entertainment, the independent production and distribution company he formed before joining IMG. 2010 he joined Starz, LLC as Pres. and CEO overseeing all Starz entities such as Starz Entertainment, Overture Films, Anchor Bay Entertainment and Film Roman. Starz, LLC is a controlled subsidiary that operates Starz Media and Starz Entertainment. Starz Entertainment, LLC, is a premium movie service provider operating in the United States with 16 movie channels including the flagship Starz® and Encore® brands with approximately 17.3 million and 30.7 million subscribers respectively. Bd. member, Museum of TV & Radio, 2003-, Bd. member, American Film Institute (trustee).

ALCAINE, JOSÉ LUIS

Cinematographer. b. Tangier, Algeria, Dec. 26, 1938. e. Spanish Cinema Sch., Madrid. After graduation joined Madrid's Studio Moros doing commercials. Cinematographer on more than 115 projects.
PICTURES: El Hueso (debut 1967) More than 95 cinematography credits. Since 1994, credits include: La Pasion turca, Dile a Laura que la quiero, Two Much, Freedomfighters, In Praise of Older Women, La Pistols de mi hermano, Mas alla del jardin, Don Juan, Il Mio West, Blast from the Past, Celos, L'Amante perduto, Antonio Rapaz de Lisboa, I Know Who You Are, Sound of the Sea, Chica do Rio, The Dancer Upstairs, Don Quixote-Knight Errant, Nobody's Life, South from Granada, Bad Education, Otros días vendrán, Volver, Tu vida en 65 minutos, Theresa: The Body of Christ, Tuya siempre, Las 13 rosas, Canciones de amor en Lolita's Club, Rivales, My Life in Ruins.
TELEVISION: *Movies:* Balada del pequeño soñador, Casanova, Sur, El, Mujer de tu vida 2: Las mujeres de mi vida, Ruy Blas, Películas para no dormir: La culpa, Films to Keep You Awake: The Room Upstairs. *Mini-series:* Martes de carnaval. *Series:* Plinio, Doctor Mateo.

ALDA, ALAN

Actor, Writer, Director. r.n. Alphonso D'Abruzzo b. New York, NY, Jan. 28, 1936. e. Fordham U., 1956. Son of actor Robert Alda. Studied at Cleveland Playhouse on Ford Foundation Grant; performed with Second City, then on TV in That Was The Week That Was. Received Valentine Davies Award 2000.
THEATRE: *B'way:* Only in America, Art, The Owl and The Pussycat, Purlie Victorious, The Play What I Wrote, Glengarry Glen Ross, The Class of '55, QED, Art, Fair Game For Lovers (Theatre World Award), The Apple Tree (Tony nom. 1967), Jake's Women (Tony Award nom.). *London:* Our Town. *Author:* Never Have Your Dog Stuffed.
PICTURES: Gone Are The Days (debut, 1963), Paper Lion (Golden Globe nom. 1969), The Extraordinary Seaman, Jenny, The Moonshine War, The Mephisto Waltz, To Kill a Clown, Same Time Next Year, California Suite, The Seduction of Joe Tynan (also s.p.), The Four Seasons (also dir., s.p.), Sweet Liberty (also dir., s.p.), A New Life (also dir., s.p.), Crimes and Misdemeanors (D.W. Griffith Award, NY Film Critics Award), Betsy's Wedding (also dir., s.p.), Whispers in the Dark, Manhattan Murder Mystery, Canadian Bacon, Flirting With Disaster, Everyone Says I Love You, Murder at 1600, Mad City, The Object of My Affection, Keepers of the Frame, What Women Want, The Aviator (Academy Award nom. 2005), Resurrecting the Champ, Diminished Capacity, Nothing But the Truth, Flash of Genius.
TELEVISION: *Movies:* The Glass House, Playmates, Isn't It Shocking?, Kill Me If You Can (Emmy nom.), Free to Be...You & Me (voice), The Caryl Chessman Story, M*A*S*H: Goodbye Farewell and Amen, White Mile (Golden Globe nom. 1995), Jake's Women, Attika, Club Land (Emmy nom. 2001), The Killing Yard. *Mini-series:* And the Band Played On (Emmy nom. 1994). *Series:* Secret File USA, That Was the Week That Was, What's My Line? M*A*S*H (11 years; also wrote, dir. and creative consultant 4 Emmy Awards, 19 nom., 6 Golden Globe Awards, 9 Golden Globe noms.), Scientific American Frontiers (PBS, host), We'll Get By, The Four Seasons (creator, exec. prod.), Influences, The West Wing (Emmy Award 2006, 1 other nom.), 30 Rock (Emmy nom. 2009, guest appearance). *Pilots:* Where's Everett, Higher and Higher. *Guest:* More than 118 appearances.

ALDREDGE, THEONI V.

Costume Designer. b. Salonika, Greece, Aug. 22, 1932. m. actor Tom Aldredge. e. American School, Athens; Goodman Theatre School, Chicago, 1949-52. Costume designer on 45 pictures.
THEATRE: B'way.: Sweet Bird of Youth, That Championship Season, Sticks and Bones, Two Gentlemen of Verona, A Chorus Line, Annie (Tony Award), Ballroom, Much Ado About Nothing, Barnum (Tony Award), Dream Girls, Woman of the Year, Onward Victoria, La Cage aux Folles (Tony Award), 42nd Street, Merlin, Private Lives, The Corn is Green, The Rink, Blithe Spirit, Chess, Gypsy, Oh Kay!, The Secret Garden, High Rollers.
PICTURES: Stella (debut 1955) Since 1994 work includes: Milk Money, Pote tin Kyriaki (Academy Award nom. 1961), Phaedra (Academy Award nom. 1963), Eyes of Laura Mars (Sci Fi. Acad. Honor), Network, Ghostbusters, and Moonstruck, The First Wives Club, Mrs. Winterbourne, The Great Gatsby (Academy Award 1975), The Mirror Has Two Faces, The Rage: Carrie 2.
TELEVISION: *Movies:* After the Fall, Alice at the Palace (Emmy nom. 1982), Barnum!, A Streetcar Named Desire. *Mini-series:* Nutcracker: Money, Madness & Murder (Emmy nom. 1987).

ALEANDRO, NORMA

Actress. b. Buenos Aires, Argentina, May 2, 1936. Sister is actress Maria Vaner. As child, performed with parents in theatre troupe. In Argentina performed in every theatrical genre and epoch and also directed. Has written & published short stories (1986), poems and the screenplay for Argentinian film, Los Herederos. Was in exile in Uruguay (18 months) and Spain 1976-82 because of the military junta in Argentina. Before exile had made 12 films; after return in 1982 starred in theatre and 7 films. Industry recognition for: The Official Story (Cannes Film Festival Award, 1985, Silver Condor from Argentinian Film Critics Assn., 1986,) Gaby: A True Story (Golden Globe nom., Academy Award nom, 1988), Foolish Heart (Havana Film Festival award, 1998), Son of the Bride (won Silver Condor, Argentinian Film Critics Assn, Golden Kikito from Gramado Film Festival, 2002).
THEATRE: U.S.: About Love and Other Stories (one-woman show, toured South America, then at La Mama and later off-B'way at Public Theater 1986); The Senorita of Tacna (written for her by Mario Vargas-Llosa, 1987).
PICTURES: La Muerte en las Calles (debut 1952). Since 1994: Facundo: The Tiger's Shadow, Carlos Monzon-el segundo juicio, Autumn Sun, Foolish Heart, Prohibido, The Lighthouse, A Night with Sabrina Love, La Fuga, Son of the Bride, Every Stewardess Goes to Heaven, Desire, Cleopatra, Pura sangre, The City of Your Final Destination, Paco.
TELEVISION: *Movies:* Romeo y Julieta, Dark Holiday, One Man's War. *Series:* Casa de los Medina, La, Amor tiene cara de mujer, El, Cuatro mujeres para Adán, Alias Buen Mozo, Operación rescate.

ALEXANDER, JANE

Actress. r.n. Jane Quigley. b. Boston, MA, Oct. 28, 1939. e. Sarah Lawrence Coll., U. of Edinburgh. m. director Edwin Sherin. Mother of actor Jace Alexander. Stage career includes appearances on B'way; at Arena Stage, Washington D.C.; Kennedy Center, D.C.; Music Center, L.A.; and Shakespeare Festival at Stamford, Conn. Appointed chair of the National Endowment for the Arts, 1993.
THEATRE: NY: The Great White Hope (Tony & Theatre World Awards, 1969), 6 Rms Riv Vu, Find Your Way Home, Hamlet, The Heiress, First Monday in October, Goodbye Fidel, Losing Time, Monday After the Miracle, Old Times, Night of the Iguana, Approaching Zanzibar, Shadowlands, The Visit, The Sisters Rosensweig.
PICTURES: The Great White Hope (debut, 1970 Academy Award nom. Golden Globe nom. 1971), A Gunfight, The New Centurions, All the President's Men (Academy Award nom. 1977), The Betsy, Kramer vs. Kramer (Academy Award nom. Golden Globe nom. 1980), Brubaker, Night Crossing, Testament (Academy Award nom., Golden Globe nom. 1984), City Heat, Square Dance, Sweet Country, Glory, The Cider House Rules, Sunshine State, The Ring, Fur: An Imaginary Portrait of Diane Arbus, The Feast of Love, Gigantic, The Unborn, The Flicker's Dance, Terminator Salvation.
TELEVISION: *Movies:* Welcome Home Johnny Bristol, Miracle on 34th St., This is the West That Was, Death Be Not Proud, Eleanor and Franklin (Emmy nom. 1976), Eleanor and Franklin: The White House Years (Emmy nom. 1977), A Circle of Children, Lovey: A Circle of Children Part II, A Question of Love, Playing for Time (Emmy Award 1981), In the Custody of Strangers, When She Says No, Calamity Jane (also prod. Emmy nom. 1984), Malice in Wonderland (Emmy nom. 1985), Blood & Orchids, In Love and War, Open Admissions, A Friendship in Vienna, Daughter of the Streets, Stay the Night, Yesterday's Children, Bitter Winter, Carry Me Home (Emmy nom. 2005), Warm Springs (Emmy Award 2005), The Way. *Series:* Tell Me You Love Me. *Specials*: Mountain View, A Marriage: Georgia O'Keeffe and Alfred Stieglitz, Louisa May Alcott: The Woman Behind Little Women. *Pilot*: New Year. *Guest:* More than 77 appearances.

ALEXANDER, JASON

Actor, Producer. r.n. Jay Scott Greenspan. b. Newark, NJ, Sept. 23, 1959. e. Boston Univ. Received an honorary doctorate from Boston University.
THEATRE: NY: Merrily We Roll Along, Forbidden Broadway, The Rink, Personals, Stop the World, Light Up the Sky, Broadway Bound, Jerome Robbins' Broadway (Tony, Drama Desk & Outer Critics' Circle Awards, 1989), Accomplice. *Regional LA:* Give 'em Hell Harry.
PICTURES: The Burning (debut, 1981), Brighton Beach Memoirs, The Mosquito Coast, Pretty Woman, White Palace, Jacob's Ladder, I Don't Buy Kisses Anymore, The Return of Jafar (voice), Down on the Waterfront, Coneheads, Sexual Healing, For Goodness Sake, The Paper, North, Blankman, The Last Supper, For Better or Worse (also dir.), Dunston Checks In, The Hunchback of Notre Dame (voice), Love! Valour! Compassion!, Denial, Love and Action in Chicago, The Adventures of Rocky and Bullwinkle, Just Looking (also dir.), The Trumpet of the Swan (voice), Odessa Or Bust, On Edge, Hunchback of Notre Dame II, Shallow Hal, How to Go Out On a Date in Queens, Agent Cody Banks (exec. prod.), Madagascar, Agent Cody Banks 2: Destination London (exec. prod.), Bocce Balls, Ira and Abby, Farce of the Penguins (voice), The Grand, Rock Slyde, Hachiko: A Dog's Story, Quantum Quest: A Cassini Space Odyssey (voice).

TELEVISION: *Movies:* Senior Trip, Rockabye, Bye Bye Birdie, Cinderella, Larry David: Curb Your Enthusiasm, Jingle Bells (actor narrator), Get Into My Shorts, Stage on Screen: The Women, The Man Who Saved Christmas, The Fairly OddParents: Channel Chasers, A Christmas Carol: The Musical. *Mini-series:* Favorite Son. *Series:* E/R, Everything's Relative, Seinfeld (Emmy nom. 1992-1998, Golden Globe nom. 1993-1998), Duckman (voice), Aladdin (voice), Disney's Hercules (voice), Dilbert (voice), House of Mouse (voice), Bob Patterson, Listen Up (also prod.), Everybody Hates Chris. *Documentaries:* Dr. Seuss: Rhymes & Reasons (reader), Mississippi Rising, Broadway: The Next Generation. *Guest:* More than 134 appearances.

ALLEN, COREY

Director, Actor. r.n. Alan Cohen. b. Cleveland, OH, June 29, 1934. e. UCLA, 1951-54; UCLA law sch. 1954-55. Actor turned dir. starred in Oscar-winning UCLA student film, A Time Out of War, which also won best short film at the Cannes and Venice Film Festival. Appeared in 20 plays at Players Ring, Players Gallery and other L.A. theatres. Turned to directing in the 1970s.
PICTURES: *Actor:* Rebel Without a Cause, Shadow on the Window, The Big Caper, Juvenile Jungle, Darby's Rangers, Party Girl, Key Witness, Private Property, Sweet Bird of Youth, The Chapman Report, The Works. *Director:* The Erotic Adventures of Pinocchio (also s.p.), Thunder and Lightning, Avalanche, Lost (prod.).
TELEVISION: *Movies:* (All as dir.) See the Man Run, Cry Rape!, Yesterday's Child, Stone (pilot), Man in the Santa Claus Suit, The Return of Frank Cannon, Code Name: Foxfire (pilot), Brass, Beverly Hills Cowgirl Blues, I-Man, The Last Fling, Destination America, Star Trek: The Next Generation-Encounter at Farpoint, Ann Jillian Story, Moment of Truth:Stalking Back, The Search, Men Who Hate Women & the Women Who Love Them. *Series Dir:* More than 40 series dir. credits. Best known for Hill Street Blues (Emmy nom. 1981, Emmy Award 1984), Star Trek: The Next Generation, The Rockford Files and the Paper Chase; FBI: The Untold Stories, Star Trek: Deep Space Nine. With partner John Herman Shaner, prod. Freeway Circuit Theatre. Led Actors Workshop with actor Guy Stockwell for over 10 years.

ALLEN, DEBBIE

Actress, Choreographer, Director. b. Houston, TX, Jan. 16, 1950. e. Howard U. Sister is actress Phylicia Rashad.
THEATRE: Ti-Jean and His Brothers (debut, 1972), Purlie, Raisin, Ain't Misbehavin', West Side Story (revival), Sweet Charity (revival, Tony Award, 1986), Carrie (choreographer), Soul Possessed, Pepito's Story. *LA:* Pearl (actress).
PICTURES: The Fish That Saved Pittsburgh (1979), Fame, Ragtime, Jo Jo Dancer Your Life is Calling, Blank Check, Mona Must Die, Forget Paris (choreographer), Out of Sync (dir.), Amistad (prod. composer-song), Everything's Jake, All About You, The Painting (also exec. prod.), Tournament of Dreams, Next Day Air, A Star for Rose (also prod.), Fame.
TELEVISION: *Movies:* The Greatest Thing That Almost Happened, Ebony—Ivory and Jade, Women of San Quentin, Polly (dir., choreographer, Emmy nom. 1990), Polly-Comin' Home! (dir., choreographer), Stompin' at the Savoy (also dir.), American Hero: The Michael Jordan Story, Cool Women (dir. Emmy nom. 2001), The Old Settler (also dir., exec. prod.). *Mini-series:* Roots-The Next Generation, Celebrity. *Series*: The Jim Stafford Show, 3 Girls 3, Drawing Power, Fame (series; 3 Emmys as choreographer, 1 nom. as actress, Golden Globe Award 1983, 2 other noms., also dir., co-exec. prod.), Family Ties (dir.), A Different World (dir.,prod.), The Fresh Prince of Bel-Air (dir.), The Sinbad Show (dir.), In the House, C. Bear and Jamal (voice and voice dir.), The Jamie Foxx Show (dir.), Between Brothers (dir.), Linc's (dir.) Healthy Kids, The Twilight Zone (dir.), All of Us (dir.), Girlfriends (dir.), Everybody Hates Chris (dir.), My Parents, My Sister & Me (exec. prod., dir.). *Specials:* Ben Vereen-His Roots, Loretta Lynn in Big Apple Country, Texaco Star Theater—Opening Night, The Kids from Fame, John Schneider's Christmas Holiday, A Tribute to Martin Luther King Jr.—A Celebration of Life, Motown Returns to the Apollo, The Debbie Allen Special (also dir., chor.), Academy Awards (choreographer: 4 Emmy noms. 1992, 1993, 1995, 1999). Motown 30: What's Goin' On! (Emmy Award 1990). *Documentaries:* Disneyland's 30th Anniversary Celebration, 50 Years of Funny Females, 3 Intimate Portrait documentaries...Phylicia Rashad, Harriet Tubman and Jasmine Guy; Living Positive, Inside TV Land: African Americans in Television, Silent Crisis: Diabetes Among Us, Living Positive, Mississippi Rising, Broadway: The Next Generation, Broadway: Beyond the Golden Age. *Guest:* More than 140 appearances.

ALLEN, DEDE

Film Editor. r.n. Dorothea Carothers Allen b. Cleveland, OH, Dec. 3, 1925. Started as messenger at Columbia Pictures, moved to editing dept., then to commercials and features. Theatrical Production v.p. then pres. at Warner Brothers, 1992-1997. A.C.E. Honorary Lifetime Achievement Award, 1994.
PICTURES: Because of Eve (1948), Terror from the Year 5000, Odds Against Tomorrow, The Hustler (ACE nom. 1962), America America, Bonnie and Clyde (ACE nom. 1968), Rachel Rachel, Alice's Restaurant, Little Big Man, Slaughterhouse 5, Serpico, Night Moves, Dog Day Afternoon (Academy Award nom. 1976), The Missouri Breaks, Slap Shot, The Wiz, Reds (also exec. prod. Academy Award nom., ACE nom. 1982), Harry and Son, Mike's Murder, The Breakfast Club, Off Beat, The Milagro Beanfield War (co-ed.), Let It Ride (co-ed.), Henry and June, The Addams Family, Wonder Boys (Academy Award nom. 2001), John Q, The Final Cut, Have Dreams, Will Travel (co-ed.), Fireflies in the Garden.

ALLEN, IOAN

Executive. b. Stafford, England, Oct. 25, 1938. e. Rossall School and Dartmouth Naval College, England. Artist mgmt. and record prod., 1964-1969. Responsible for origination and devt. of Dolby Stereo film program, after joining Dolby in 1969. Currently serves as senior v.p. for Dolby. Fellow of Society of Motion Picture & Television Engineers (SMPTE), Audio Engineering Society (AES) and the British Kinematographic Sound & Television Society (BKSTS). Past Pres., Intl. Theatre Equipment Assn. U.S. correspondent on the Intl. Standards Org. cinematographic subcommittee. Adjunct Professor at the University of Southern California School of Cinema-Television and was recently awarded a prestigious honorary degree of Doctor of Science from the University of Nottingham in the UK. Engineering Director, Motion Pictures for SMPTE. Ioan has spearheaded the introduction of many of Dolby's breakthrough audio formats leading to the company's successful transition from analog audio pioneer to digital entertainment leader. Recipient: Acad. Scientific & Technical Awards, 1979 & 1987. Acad. award for work in Dolby Laboratories film program, 1989; Samuel L. Warner Award for contribution to motion picture sound, 1985. Academy Commendation for work on TASA Trailer Loudness Standard, 2001, Ken Mason Award from the Intersociety for the Enhancement of Theatrical Presentation 2002. Chairman of the Dye Track Committee which was honored in 2007 by the Academy of Motion Picture Arts and Sciences Scientific and Technical Committee for its contributions to the environmentally responsible industry conversion from silver-based to cyan dye analog soundtracks. Serves as technical chairman of the Trailer Audio Standards Assoc. (TASA).

ALLEN, JOAN

Actress. b. Rochelle, IL, Aug. 20, 1956. Founding member of Steppenwolf Theatre Co., in Chicago where she performed in over 20 shows.
THEATRE: *Chicago:* A Lesson from Aloes, Three Sisters, The Miss Firecracker Contest, Cloud 9, Balm in Gilead, Fifth of July, Reckless, Earthly Possessions. *Off B'way:* And a Nightingale Sang (Clarence Derwent, Drama Desk, Outer Critics' Circle and Theatre World Awards). *B'way:* Burn This (debut, 1987; Tony Award), The Heidi Chronicles, Impressionism.
PICTURES: Compromising Positions (debut, 1985), Manhunter, Peggy Sue Got Married, Tucker: The Man and His Dream, In Country, Ethan Frome, Searching for Bobby Fischer, Josh and S.A.M., Mad Love, Nixon (Academy Award nom. 1996), The Crucible (Academy Award nom., Golden Globe nom. 1997), The Ice Storm, Face/Off, Pleasantville, All the Rage, When the Sky Falls, The Contender (Academy Award nom., Golden Globe nom. 2001), Off the Map, The Notebook, The Bourne Supremacy, The Upside of Anger, Good Sharma, Bonneville, The Bourne Ultimatum, Good Sharma, Death Race, Hachiko: A Dog's Story, In Defiance of Gravity.
TELEVISION: *Movies:* Say Goodnight, Gracie, All My Sons,The Room Upstairs, Without Warning: The James Brady Story, Georgia O'Keeffe (also exec. prod., Golden Globe nom. 2010). *Mini-series:* Evergreen, The Mists of Avalon (Emmy nom. 2002). *Documentaries:* The Big Show, New York: A Documentary Film, War Letters. *Guest:* More than 50 appearances.

ALLEN, KAREN

Actress. b. Carrollton, IL, Oct. 5, 1951. e. George Washington U., U. of Maryland. Auditioned for theatrical company in Washington, D.C., and won a role in Saint, touring with it for 7 months. Spent several years with Washington Theatre Laboratory Co. Moved to NY, acted in student films at NYU and studied acting at Theatre Institute with Lee Strasberg.
THEATRE: NY: Monday After the Miracle (B'way debut, 1982; Theatre World Award), Extremities, The Miracle Worker, The Country Girl, Speaking in Tongues. Williamstown (MA) Theatre: Tennessee Williams–A Celebration, The Glass Menagerie.
PICTURES: National Lampoon's Animal House (debut, 1978), Manhattan, The Wanderers, Cruising, A Small Circle of Friends, Raiders of the Lost Ark, Shoot the Moon, Split Image, Until September, Starman, Terminus, The Glass Menagerie, Backfire, Scrooged, Animal Behavior, Sweet Talker, Malcolm X, The Sandlot, King of the Hill, Ghost in the Machine, The Turning, 'Til There Was You, Wind River, Falling Sky, The Basket, The Perfect Storm, In the Bedroom, World Traveler, Shallow End, The Root, When Will I Be Loved?, Poster Boy, Indiana Jones and the Kingdom of the Crystal Skull, White Irish Drinkers.
TELEVISION: *Movies:* Lovey: A Circle of Children Part II, Challenger, Secret Weapon, Voyage, Rapture, Hostile Advances: The Kerry Ellison Story, All the Winters That Have Been. My Horrible Year! *Mini-series:* East of Eden, Shaka Zulu: The Citadel. *Series:* The Road Home.

ALLEN, NANCY

Actress. b. New York, NY, June 24, 1950. e. H.S. Perf. Arts, N.Y.

PICTURES: Money in My Pocket (debut 1962), The Last Detail, The Last Entry, Carrie, I Wanna Hold Your Hand, 1941, The Maestro, Home Movies, Dressed to Kill (Golden Globe nom. 1981), Blow Out, Strange Invaders, The Buddy System, The Philadelphia Experiment, The Last Victim, Not for Publication, Terror in the Aisles, Robocop, Sweet Revenge, Poltergeist III, Limit Up, Robocop 2, Robocop 3, The Patriots, Dusting Cliff 7, Against the Law, Secret of the Andes, The Pass, Out of Sight, Children of the Corn 666: Isaac's Return, Secret of the Andes, Kiss Toledo Goodbye, For What It's Worth, Quality Time, Circuit.
TELEVISION: *Movies:* The Gladiator, Memories of Murder, Acting on Impulse, Eyes of a Stranger, The Man Who Wouldn't Die.

ALLEN, PAUL G.
Executive. e. Washington State University. Co-founder of Microsoft, Allen served as that company's executive v.p. of research and new product development, overseeing the development of its most successful products. Left Microsoft in 1983, moving on to develop other software applications, and later formed Vulcan Inc. Allen has been a private investor for more than 15 years and has interests in more than 100 enterprises and investments. His portfolio includes Vulcan Inc., Clear Blue Sky Productions, Digeo, the Portland Trail Blazers NBA and Seattle Seahawks NFL franchises, The Sporting News, and investments in Dreamworks SKG, TechTV, Vulcan Programming, Vulcan Ventures, Vulcan Cable III and numerous privately held companies. Allen has been chairman of the bd. of directors of Charter Communications, Inc. (Nasdaq: CHTR), and chairman of the bd. of directors of Charter Investment since purchasing Charter in Dec. 1998 and retains 10% ownership. Charter Communications, Inc. is a leading broadband communications company and the third-largest publicly traded cable operator in the United States. 2004 was the sole investor behind Scaled Composites' SpaceShipOne suborbital spaceship and was the first privately funded effort to successfully put a civilian in suborbital space.

ALLEN, TIM
Actor. r.n. Timothy Allen Dick. b. Denver, CO, June 13, 1953. e. W. Michigan Univ., Univ. of Detroit, studied acting. Worked as creative dir. for adv. agency before becoming stand up comedian. Made stand up tv debut on Showtime Comedy Club All-Stars, 1988. *Author:* Don't Stand Close to a Naked Man (1994).
PICTURES: Comedy's Dirtiest Dozen, The Santa Clause, Toy Story (voice), Meet Wally Sparks, Jungle2Jungle, For Richer or Poorer, Toy Story 2 (voice), Galaxy Quest, The Cat in the Hat, Who is Cletis Tout? Joe Somebody, Big Trouble, Buzz Lightyear of Star Command: The Adventure Begins, The Santa Clause 2: The Mrs. Clause, Christmas with the Kranks, The Shaggy Dog (also writer/prod.), Father Knows Best, Zoom, In the Pink, The Santa Clause 3: The Escape Clause (also exec. prod., prod.), Wild Hogs, Redbelt, The Six Wives of Henry Lefay, Crazy on the Outside (also dir.), Toy Story 3 (voice).
TELEVISION: *Movies:* Tim Allen: Men Are Pigs (also writer, exec. prod.), Tim Allen Rewires America, AFI's 100 Years,100 Laughs: America's Funniest Movies, The Beatles Revolution, Jimmy Neutron: Win, Lose and Kaboom (voice), These Guys (narr., exec. prod.). *Series:* Home Improvement (Emmy nom. 1993, 4 Golden Globe noms. Golden Globe Award 1995). *Guest:* More than 112 appearances.

ALLEN, WILLIAM
Executive. e. USC Cinema/TV Sch., Pepperdine Univ. 1979. Exec. trainee in CBS Entertainment division, eventually serving as assoc. program exec. in the Comedy Series Programming Dept.; mngr./dir. of the CBS Comedy Program Development. Dept. Joined MTM as sr. v.p., Comedy Programming, 1986-87; sr. v.p. creative affairs, 1987-88; exec. v.p. MTM Television, 1989-1991. pres., MTM Television, 1992, past pres. & ceo of non-profit, The Economic Alliance, 1994-97, pres. Starsonline Inc., Bd. mem. Top Team. Currently is the President and CEO of the Los Angeles County Economic Development Corporation. In that capacity, he also serves as the CEO of all of the subsidiary corporations of the LAEDC including the World Trade Center Association Los Angeles – Long Beach. Mr. Allen is also a Vice Chair of the Valley Economic Alliance and a member of the Board of Directors of the California Association of Local Economic Development, the Los Angeles Area Chamber of Commerce, the San Gabriel Valley Economic Partnership, Film LA, and Unite LA. In 2007, Mr. Allen was appointed by Mayor Antonio Villaraigosa to serve on the Los Angeles Economy and Jobs Committee and in 2008 he was elected to the Board of Trustees of the Weingart Foundation.

ALLEN, WOODY
Actor, Director, Writer. r.n. Allan Stewart Konigsberg. b. New York, NY, Dec. 1, 1935. e. NYU, 1953; City Coll. NY, 1953. Began writing comedy at age 17, contributing to various magazines (Playboy, New Yorker) and top TV comedy shows incl. Sid Caesar (1957), Art Carney (1958-59), Herb Shriner (1953). Appeared in nightclubs starting in 1961 as stand-up comic; later performed as a jazz musician at Michael's Pub, NY. Special Award, Berlin Film Fest., 1975. Received Lifetime Achievement Award, DGA, 1996.
AUTHOR: Getting Even, Without Feathers, Side Effects.
THEATRE: Author: Play It Again Sam (also actor), Don't Drink The Water, The Floating Lightbulb, Central Park West (from Death Defying Acts), "God", "Death" and "Sex".
PICTURES: *Actor-Screenplay:* What's New Pussycat?, What's Up Tiger Lily? (also dubbed and compiled footage; assoc. prod.), Casino Royale (actor only). *Director/Screenplay/Actor:* Take the Money and Run, Bananas, Play It Again Sam. Everything You Always Wanted to Know About Sex But Were Afraid to Ask, Sleeper, Love and Death, The Front (actor only), Annie Hall (2 Academy Awards for Best Director and Original Screenplay, 1 nom., DGA Award, 3 Golden Globe nom. 1977), Interiors (dir., s.p. only, 2 Academy Award nom., 2 Golden Globe nom. 1979), Manhattan (Academy Award nom., DGA nom. 1980), Stardust Memories, A Midsummer Night's Sex Comedy, Zelig (Golden Globe nom. 1984), Broadway Danny Rose (2 Academy Award nom. 1985), The Purple Rose of Cairo (dir., s.p. only, Academy Award, 1 nom., Golden Globe Award 1986), Hannah and Her Sisters (Academy Award for Best Original Screenplay, 1 nom., DGA nom., 2 Golden Globe noms. 1986), Radio Days (dir., s.p., narrator only, Academy Award nom. 1988), King Lear (actor only), September (dir., s.p. only), Another Woman (dir., s.p. only), New York Stories (Oedipus Wrecks segment), Crimes and Misdemeanors (2 Academy Award nom., DGA nom. 1990), Alice (dir., s.p. only, Academy Award nom. 1991), Scenes From a Mall (actor only), Shadows and Fog, Husbands and Wives (Academy Award nom. 1993), Manhattan Murder Mystery, Bullets Over Broadway (dir., s.p. only, 2 Academy Award nom. 1995), Mighty Aphrodite (Academy Award nom. 1996), Everyone Says I Love You (dir. & actor), Deconstructing Harry (Academy Award nom. 1998), The Imposters (actor only), Antz (voice), Wild Man Blues, Sweet and Lowdown,Company Man (actor only), Picking Up the Pieces (actor only),The Curse of the Jade Scorpion, Small Time Crooks, Count Mercury Goes to the Suburbs (writer only), Light Keeps Me Company (actor only), Hail Sid Caesar! The Golden Age of Comedy (actor only), Stanley Kubrick: A Life in Pictures (actor only), Hollywood Ending, Anything Else, Why Men Shouldn't Marry, Melinda and Melinda, Match Point (writer, dir., Academy Award nom., 2 Golden Globe noms. 2006), Scoop (actor, writer, dir.), Cassandra's Dream (writer, dir.), Vicky Cristina Barcelona (writer, dir., WGA nom. 2009), Whatever Works (writer, dir.), You Will Meet a Tall Dark Stranger (writer, dir.).
TELEVISION: *Movies:* Don't Drink the Water (also dir., writer), The Sunshine Boys, Woody Allen: A Life in Film, Last Laugh. *Guest:* More than 172 appearances.

ALLEY, KIRSTIE
Actress. b. Wichita, KS, Jan. 12, 1955. e. KS State U., U. of Kansas. On L.A. stage in Cat on a Hot Tin Roof.
PICTURES: Star Trek II: The Wrath of Khan (debut, 1982), Champions, Runaway, Blind Date, Summer School, Shoot to Kill, Loverboy, Look Who's Talking, Madhouse, Sibling Rivalry, Look Who's Talking Too, Look Who's Talking Now, Village of the Damned, It Takes Two, Sticks and Stones, Nevada (also co-prod.), Deconstructing Harry, For Richer or Poorer, The Mao Game, Drop Dead Gorgeous, Back by Midnight, Nailed.
TELEVISION: *Movies:* Sins of the Past, A Bunny's Tale, Stark: Mirror Image, Prince of Bel Air, Infidelity, David's Mother (Emmy Award, 1994), Radiant City, Peter and the Wolf, Toothless, Profoundly Normal (also exec. prod.), Family Sins, While I Was Gone, The Minister of Divine, Write & Wrong. *Mini-series:* North and South, North and South Book II, The Last Don, The Last Don II, Blonde, Salem Witch Trials. *Series:* Masquerade, Cheers (Emmy Award, 1991), Veronica's Closet (also prod., Emmy nom., Golden Globe nom. 1998), Fat Actress (also exec. prod., writer, creator). *Guest:* More than 89 appearances.

ALMODÓVAR, PEDRO
Director, Writer. b. La Mancha, Spain, Sept. 25, 1951. r.n.Pedro Almodovar Cabellero. Grew up in Calzada de Calatrava. At 17 moved to Madrid where worked 10 years for telephone co. while writing comic strips and articles for underground newspapers and working as actor with independent theatre co., Los Goliardos. Upon the end of Francoist repression in 1975, made Super-8 experimental films starring friends. Wrote fiction, sang with rock band and created character of porn star, Patty Diphusa, whose fictionalized confessions he published in the magazine La Luna. More than 90 International Awards and 60 noms, including Academy Award in 2003 for Talk to Her.
PICTURES: Folle...folle...Folleme Tim! (debut 1978) Pepi Lucy Bom and Other Girls on the Heap, Labyrinth of Passion (also prod.), Entre tinieblas, Dark Habits, What Have I Done to Deserve This?, The Bullfighter, Law of Desire, Women on the Verge of a Nervous Breakdown (also prod.), Tie Me Up! Tie Me Down!, Madonna:Truth or Dare (actor only), High Heels, Accion mutante, Kika, The Flower of My Secret, Mi nombre es sombra, Shampoo Horns, Live Flesh, All About My Mother (Cannes Film Fest. best dir., 1999; BAFTA best film not in Eng. and dir. award, 2000), The Devil's Backbone (prod.), The Paperboy, Talk to Her (Academy Award, best writing, and nom. for Best Achiev. in Dir., 2003. BAFTA award best film not in English and best screenplay, 2003) La Mala educacion, My Life Without Me (exec. prod.), (art dir.), Bad Education (also s.p. dir., prod., lyrics adaptor), The Secret Life of Words (exec. prod.), The Holy Girl (exec. prod.), Volver, Broken Embraces. *Guest:* More than 135 appearances.

ALONSO, MARIA CONCHITA
Actress, Singer. b. Cienfuegos, Cuba, June 29, 1957. Family moved to Venezuela when she was five. 1971, named Miss Teenager of the World. 1975, Miss Venezuela. 6th runner up, Miss World. Appeared in four feature films and 10 soap operas before coming to U.S. Recorded several albums as singer: 5 gold albums, 1 platinum, 3 Grammy noms.
THEATRE: Aurora. *B'way:* Kiss of the Spider Woman.
PICTURES 30 film appearances, including Solon (debut 1979), Scarface (singer), Fear City, Moscow on the Hudson, Extreme Prejudice, The Running Man,, Touch and Go, A Fine Mess, Colors, Vampire's Kiss, Predator 2, McBain, The House of the Spirits, Roosters, For Which He Stands, Caught, El Crito en el Cieto, Catherine's Grove, Acts of Betrayal, Knockout, Expose, Blackheart, Chain of Command, The Code Conspiracy, Blind Heat, Babylon Revisited, Homeroom, Heart of America, Chasing Papi, English as a Second Language, Smoke, I Believe in America, Richard III, Tranced, Material Girls, The Dead One, The Art of Travel, Trópico de sangre, Tranced, Spread, Dark Moon Rising (also co-prod.).
TELEVISION: *Movies:* Cuerpos clandestinos, Teamster Boss: The Jackie Presser Story, MacShayne: The Final Roll of the Dice, Texas, The Gun, Sudden Terror: Hijacking of School Bus #17, Latino Laugh Festival, Al dia con Maria Conchita, Fx, My Husband's Secret Life, A Vision of Murder: The Story of Donielle, Best Actress, High Noon, The Princess and the Barrio Boy. *Mini-series:* Kingpin, Maneater (parts 1 & 2). *Series:* Saints & Sinners. *Guest:* More than 100 appearances.

ALVARADO, TRINI
Actress. b. New York, NY, Jan. 10, 1967. e. Fordham U. m. actor Robert McNeill. Prof. acting debut at 9 in stage musical Becca.
THEATRE: Runaways, Reds, The Magic Show, Godspell.
PICTURES: Rich Kids (debut, 1989), Times Square, Mrs. Soffel, Sweet Lorraine, Satisfaction, The Chair, Stella, American Blue Note, The Babe, American Friends, Little Women, The Perez Family, The Frighteners, Paulie, Little Children, The Good Guy, All Good Things.
TELEVISION: *Movies:* A Movie Star's Daughter, Private Contentment, Dreams Don't Die, Prisoner Without a Name, Frank Nitti, Sensibility and Sense, The Christmas Tree, The Last Dance, Bitter Winter.

AMATO, LEN
Executive, Producer. b. Chicago, IL. e. B.A. degree in film/video, Columbia College in Chicago, IL, 1975. Feature film development executive and producer, whose career has spanned associations with Robert DeNiro's production co. Tribeca in New York and then Spring Creek Productions in the 1990s. In 1997, Amato made his producing debut with HBO's "First Time Felon." With a move to Los Angeles, Amato then served as co-producer on the hit comedy "Analyze This," and, in 2002, he exec. produced its sequel, "Analyze That." More recently he served as an exec. producer on the award-winning HBO drama "Iron Jawed Angels." In March 2007, Amato became senior v.p., HBO Films and in Oct. 2008 he was named to his current position, pres., HBO Films and has responsibility for creatively overseeing HBO's original films.
PICTURES: Analyze This (co-prod.), Possession (exec. prod.), Analyze That (exec. prod.), Deliver Us from Eva (prod.), Rumor Has It... (exec. prod.), The Astronaut Farmer (prod.), Blood Diamond (exec. prod.), 1906 (prod.).
TELEVISION: *Movies:* First Time Felon (prod.), Iron Jawed Angels (exec. prod.), Recount (exec. prod., Emmy Award 2008), The Defining Moment (development exec.).

AMENÁBAR, ALEJANDRO
Director, Writer. b. Santiago, Chile, March 31, 1972. Raised and educated in Madrid. Wrote, directed and produced first film short, La Cabeza, at age 19. Also composer with credits in eight pictures.
PICTURES: Himenoptero, Luna, Tesis, Open Your Eyes, Butterfly Tongues (comp.), The Others, Vanilla Sky (s.p.), The Sea Inside (also editor, composer, exec. prod.), El mal ajeno (prod.), Agora (composer, writer, dir.).
TELEVISION: *Series:* premios Goya (presenter).

AMENT, GERALD
Executive. e. Graduate of Boston University School of Law. Ament began his entertainment career at the New York law firm of Katz, Leavy, Rosensweig and Sindle. Executive positions in business affairs at the William Morris Agency and at NBC followed. He then teamed with Harry Sloan, who is now chairman & CEO of MGM, to form the law firm of Sloan, Kuppin and Ament, where, as a partner, he specialized in business matters relating to TV production including primetime series, daytime serials and Movies of the Week. From the firm he went to New World Pictures in 1983, working in various capacities. He originally joined the company as senior v.p., business affairs & production. When New World purchased the NBC series "Santa Barbara" in 1985, Ament became the company's executive in charge of production for that series, a position which made him responsible for all business and production matters relating to the series while simultaneously maintaining his business affairs and production duties at New World. When New World purchased Marvel Comics in 1987, Ament was promoted to COO of Marvel Productions and executive v.p. of new pictures while retaining "Santa Barbara" duties. He left New World Pictures in 1989 but stayed with "Santa Barbara" duties until the series was canceled in 1993. From 1993 to 2000, consultant to numerous TV production companies including Spelling Television, Inc., New World Entertainment, American Specialty Underwriters, Inc., New Line Television, and SBS as well as serving as the executive in charge of production for Spelling Television's daily serial, "Sunset Beach." In 2000 he once again teamed with Harry Sloan and joined Sloan's SBS Broadcasting S.A., one of Europe's largest broadcast groups. At SBS Ament was senior v.p., business and corporate affairs and oversaw the business affairs and production activities for each of SBS' stations and negotiated all significant acquisition deals for the SBS stations with the major studios in the U.S. Ament was integral in the acquisition of rights for SBS and the subsequent production of such major international formats as "Big Brother," "Millionaire," "Weakest Link", "Survivor," Apprentice", "Temptation Island," "Popstars," "The Bachelor," "Joe Millionaire" and many others. When Sloan came on board at MGM, Ament joined his long-time colleague and in 2006 was named executive v.p., worldwide television, business & legal affairs for MGM Studios Inc. and is the position he holds today. Ament oversees various aspects of business and legal affairs activities for MGM's reinvigorated worldwide television distribution operation.

AMIEL, JON
Director, Producer. b. London, England, May 20, 1948. e. Cambridge. Was in charge of the Oxford & Cambridge Shakespeare Co., then literary mgr. for Hamptead Theatre Club where he started directing. Became story editor for BBC, then director.
PICTURES: Silent Twins, Queen of Hearts, Tune in Tomorrow, Sommersby, Copycat, The Man Who Knew Too Little, Entrapment, Simply Irresistible (prod. only), The Core, Creation.
TELEVISION: *Movies:* Dear Janet Rosenberg-Dear Mister Kooning, A Sudden Wrench, Gates of Gold, Busted. *Mini-series:* The Singing Detective. *Series:* Tandoori Nights, Eyes (also pilot), Reunion ("1986" dir.), The Wedding Planners (dir., exec. prod.).

AMIN, MARK
Executive, Producer. b. Rafsanjan, Iran, 1950. e. M.B.A., marketing, John Anderson School of Business (UCLA), 1975. Began career in business ventures, 1975-81; co-founder, 20/20 Video, 1981-87; founder, Vidmark which then became Trimark Pictures, 1984. Chairman & CEO, Trimark Holdings, Inc., the parent company of Trimark Pictures until it merged with Lions Gate Entertainment Corporation in 2000. With the merger, Amin became vice chairman of the Lions Gate bd. of dir., a position he held from Oct. 2000 to April 2006. Since 1998, Amin has been chairman of the bd. of CinemaNow, Inc., which was a Lions Gate subsidiary company. In 2008 CinemaNow, Inc. operates as a subsidiary of Sonic Solutions Since 2001, he has been the owner and CEO of Sobini Films, a production company Amin formed to independently finance and produce specialized and maintstream motion pictures. The company maintains a first-look deal with Lions Gate Entertainment.
PICTURES: *Exec. prod.:* Demon Warp, The Sleeping Car, Whore, Servants of Twilight, Into the Sun, Interceptor, Leprechaun, Philadelphia Experiment II, Extreme Justice, Deadfall, Love and a .45, Curse of the Starving Class, Night of the Running Man, A Million to Juan, Frank and Jesse, Dangerous Touch, A Kid in King Arthur's Court, Kicking and Screaming, Separate Lives, True Crime, The Maddening, Leprechaun 3, Iron Eagle IV, Evolver, Aurora: Operation Intercept, Never Ever, The Dentist, Underworld, Sometimes They Come Back...Again, Pinocchio's Revenge, Leprechaun 4: In Space, Crossworlds, Spring, Eve's Bayou, A Kid in Aladdin's Palace, Standoff, Chairman of the Board, Carnival of Souls, Ground Control, Trance, The Dentist II, Held Up, Diplomatic Siege, Let the Devil Wear Black, Cord, Skipped Parts, The Bogus Witch Project, Attraction, Krocodylus, X Change, Fear of Flying, Pursuit, After the Storm, Frida, The Prince and Me, Gardens of the Night, Hemingway & Fuentes. *Prod.:* Peaceful Warrior, Burning Bright, Zorro Reborn, Blackwell.
TELEVISION: *Movies: Exec. prod.:* The Simple Life of Noah Dearborn, The Bogus Witch Project, After the Storm, Framed.

AMOS, JOHN
Actor. b. Newark, NJ, Dec. 27, 1941. e. East Orange H.S., Colorado State U, Long Beach City Col. Inducted as honorary Master Chief Petty Officer in U.S. Navy 1993. Worked as professional football player, social worker (heading the Vera Institute of Justice in NY), and advertising copywriter before writing television comedy material (for the Leslie Uggams Show) and performing as stand-up comedian in Greenwich Village. Has also dir. theatre with Bahamian Rep. Co. Artistic dir., John Harms Theatre, Englewood, NJ.
THEATRE: L.A.: Norman Is That You?, Master Harold...And the Boys, Split Second, The Emperor Jones. B'way: Tough to Get Help. NYSF: Twelfth Night. Off-B'way: The Past is the Past. Regional: Fences, Halley's Comet (also dir., writer). Foreign: Life and Death of a Buffalo Soldier.
PICTURES: Vanishing Point (debut, 1971), Sweet Sweetback's Baadasssss Song, The World's Greatest Athlete, Let's Do It Again,

Touched By Love, The Beastmaster, Dance of the Dwarfs, American Flyers, Coming to America, Lock Up, Die Hard 2, Ricochet, Two Evil Eyes (The Black Cat), Mac, Night Trap (Mardi Gras for the Devil), Hologram Man, For Better or Worse, A Woman Like That, The Player's Club, All Over Again, Ralph Ellison: An American Journey, My Baby's Daddy, Shadow Boxing, Ascension Day, Hauntsville, Lean Like a Cholo: The Movie.
TELEVISION: *Movies:* The President's Plane is Missing, Future Cop, Cops and Robin, Willa, Alcatraz-The Whole Shocking Story, Bonanza-the Next Generation, The Rockford Files: Murder and Misdemeanors, Something to Sing About, Disappearing Acts, The Law. *Mini-series*: Roots (Emmy nom. 1977). *Series:* Mary Tyler Moore, The Funny Side, Maude, Good Times, Hunter, South by Southwest, 704 Hauser, The Fresh Prince of Bel-Air, The West Wing, The District, All About the Andersons, Men in Trees. *Guest:* More than 80 appearances.

ANDERS, ALLISON

Director, Writer. b. Ashland, KY, Nov. 16, 1954. e. UCLA; Los Angeles. NY Film Critics Circle Award for Gas Food Lodging, (1992).
PICTURES: Border Radio (debut, 1987), Gas Food Lodging, Mi vida loca, Four Rooms (The Missing Ingredient segment), Grace of My Heart, Lover Girl (exec. prod. only), Sugar Town, Things Behind the Sun, The Pacific and Eddy, Unicorns, The Lie (actress only), Smile Now Cry Later (s.p., prod., dir.), Fireflies (exec. prod.).
TELEVISION: *Series:* Sex and the City, Grosse Pointe, Cold Case. *Documentaries:* Welcome to Hollywood, Indie Sex: Taboos, Independent View, Sundance 20, Olive Thomas: Everybody's Sweetheart, Brilliant But Cancelled: Pilot Season, In the Company of Women, Rock N Roll Mamas (exec. prod.).

ANDERSON, DAVID LEROY

Special Effects/Makeup.
PICTURES: (As Dave Anderson:The Serpent and the Rainbow, Alien Nation, Never on Tuesday, Pet Sematary) As David Leroy Anderson: Shocker, Cadence, Beyond the Law, Alien 3, Death Becomes Her (prosthetic makeup), Loaded Weapon 1, Hot Shots! Part Deux, The Three Musketeers, The Chase, Terminal Velocity, Vampire in Brooklyn, Batman Forever, Waterworld, The Arrival, The Nutty Professor, (Academy Award, Best Makeup, 1997), Men in Black (Academy Award, Best Makeup, 1998), Out of Sight, Jane Austen's Mafia, Spawn, Krippendorf's Tribe, Life, The Nutty Professor II: The Klumps, The Brightness You Keep, Dragonfly, Bruce Almighty, Dawn of the Dead, Cinderella Man (Academy Award nom. 2006), Dead Silence, Evan Almighty, Get Smart, Frost/Nixon, Angels & Demons, Cirque du Freak: The Vampire's Assistant (prosthetics superv.), The Cabin in the Woods.
TELEVISION: *Movies:* Barnum, Tuesdays With Morrie.

ANDERSON, GERRY

Hon. F.B.K.S., Producer, Director, Writer. b. London, England, April 14, 1929. Entered industry in 1946. Chmn./man. dir. Gerry Anderson Productions, Ltd. Over 320 pictures produced for TV worldwide. Co-founded Anderson Burr Pictures, 1981. Prod. Terrahawks in association with London Weekend Television, 1982; second series, Terrahawks, 1984. Space Police pilot for series in assoc. with TVS, 1985-6. Dick Spanner stop motion series for Channel Four, 1987. Entered commercials as a dir.: numerous commercials incl. Royal Bank of Scotland, Children's World, Domestos, Shout, Scotch Tape, etc. Anglo Russian Cartoon Series Astro Force and lecture tour An Evening with Garry Anderson, 1992.
PICTURES: *Producer:* Crossroads to Crime (also dir.), Thunderbirds Are Go (s.p. only), Thunderbird 6 (also s.p.), Journey to the Far Side of the Sun (also story), Invasion UFO (exec. prod., s.p. and creator, dir.) Invaders from the Deep, Thunderbirds (writer-characters), U.F.O. (writer).
TELEVISION: *Movies:* Journey Through the Black Sun, Into Infinity, Destination Moonbase Alpha (exec. prod., s.p.), Cosmic Princess (creator), Alien Attack, (also s.p. and creator), I Love Christmas. *Series:* The Adventures of Twizzle, Torchy the Battery Boy, Four Feather Falls, Supercar, Fireball XL5, Stingray, Thunderbirds 2086, Captain Scarlet vs. the Mysterons (writer/creator only), Joe 90, The Secret Service, The Protectors, UFO, Space 1999, Terrahawks, Dick Spanner, P.I., Space Precinct, Lavender Castle, Captain Scarlet. *Documentary:* Stingray: The Reunion Party (prod.).

ANDERSON, GILLIAN

Actress. b. Chicago, IL, Aug. 9, 1968. e. Cornell University, NY; DePaul University, Chicago.
THEATRE: *London:* What The Night Is For.
PICTURES: The Turning, Three at Once, A Matter of Choice, The Mighty, Chicago Cab, The X-Files: Fight the Future, Playing by Heart, The House of Mirth, The Mighty Celt, Tristram Shandy: A Cock and Bull Story, The Last King of Scotland, Straightheads, The X Files: I Want to Believe, How to Lose Friends & Alienate People, Boogie Woogie.
TELEVISION: *Movies:* The X-Files, The X-Files: The Truth. Why Planes Go Down (narr.), The Mighty Celt. *Series*: The X-Files Emmy Award, Golden Globe Award 1997, 3 Emmy nom., 3 Golden Globe nom.), Future Fantastic, Masterpiece Theatre: Bleak House (Emmy nom. 2006, Golden Globe nom. 2007), Moby Dick. *Guest:* More than 64 appearances.

ANDERSON, J. WAYNE

Executive. b. Clifton Forge, VA, Feb. 19, 1947. e. USA Signal School (1965-67); USN Service Schools (1967). USMC, 1965-69; opened and operated 1st military 35mm m.p. theatre, Freedom Hill Theatres in DaNang, Vietnam, 1967-69. R/C Theatres, dist. mgr., 1971-75; v.p., 1976-83; pres./CEO/chairman, 2005-present became Chairman of R/C Theatres. A long acknowledged leader in the technological arena, Anderson is known for building technically correct cinemas. Bd. of dirs., Maryland Permanent Bank & Trust Co., 1988-present; chmn., 1992-present. Member of NATO, bd. of dirs. for Maryland and Virginia, 1987-present; technical advancement committee, 1981-present; chmn., 1991-present. Ken Mason Inter-Society for the Enhancement of Theatrical Presentation Award (2003), member 1986-present. Huntsman bd. of dirs., 1979-83; pres., 1982-83. Member: SMPTE, NRA, 1970-life; Will Rogers Inst., 1988-present; Presidential Task Force, 1990-life. Anderson received the NATO of Ohio Distinguished Service Award, 2006; Special Award of Commendation, Scientific and Technical Academy Awards, 2007 and ShoWester of the Year— 2007, which he received together with his wife, Mary Ann Anderson, whose service to national NATO began in 1988 and extended to her retirement in 2007. Currently partnered with his wife, MaryAnn Anderson for Anderson Consulting, LLC, serving developers, lenders, investors and potential exhibitors in the evaluation of theatre sales and new construction.

ANDERSON, KEVIN

Actor. b. Gurnee, Illinois, Jan. 13, 1960. e. Goodman School. Member of Chicago's Steppenwolf Theatre where he starred in Orphans. Moved with the play to New York (1985) and later starred in the London production, as well as the film version.
THEATRE: NY: Orphans (Theatre World Award), Moonchildren, Brilliant Tracers, Red Address, Death of a Salesman, Orpheus Descending. London: Sunset Boulevard.
PICTURES: Risky Business (debut, 1983), Pink Nights, Orphans, A Walk on the Moon, Miles From Home, In Country, Sleeping With the Enemy, Liebestraum, Hoffa, The Night We Never Met, Rising Sun, A Thousand Acres, Eye of God, Firelight, A Thousand Acres, Gregory's Two Girls, Rapid Transit (stunts), Shearer's Breakfast, The Doe Boy, When Strangers Appear, Charlotte's Web.
TELEVISION: *Movies:* Orpheus Descending, Hale the Hero, The Wrong Man, The Hunt for the Unicorn Killer, Ruby's Bucket of Blood, Monday Night Mayhem, Power and Beauty, Carry Me Home. *Series:* Nothing Sacred (Golden Globe nom. 1998), Skin. *Special:* Hale the Hero, Salomaybe?.

ANDERSON, MARYANN

Executive. b. Rome, NY, Nov. 3, 1952. e. U. of Calif., Riverside, B.A. art history, 1973; U. of Oregon, Eugene, Master of Library Science, 1974. Dir., Warner Research Collection, 1975-85; Theatre Arts instructor UCLA 1980-85; mgr., CBS-TV, docudrama, 1985-88; Instructor 1980-88 UCLA Extension, American Film Institute. Amer. Film Inst., LA, 1985-88. V.P. & Executive Director National Association of Theatre Owners, 1988-2007 (retired), continues to serve as consultant. Member: Acad. Motion Picture Arts & Sciences, Foundation of the Motion Picture Pioneers, American Society of Association Executives, Phi Beta Kappa, Woman of Achievement, NATO (VP); Business and Prof'l. Women's Assoc.; Commissioner of Burbank Heritage Commission; Board of Directors Burbank Historical Society; Board member of Center of Film and Television Design. Awards include: BPOA Awarded, 1984; Friend of Tripod, 1999, for her work in promoting access to deaf and hard-of-hearing audiences; Stace Award from Dolby, 2002; the Ken Mason Award (InterSociety), 2004; Special Award of Commendation, Scientific and Technical Academy Awards, 2007; and the ShoWester of the Year—2007, which she received with her husband, J. Wayne Anderson, the president & CEO of R/C Theatres. Currently partnered with her husband, J. Wayne Anderson for Anderson Consulting, LLC, serving developers, lenders, investors and potential exhibitors in the evaluation of theatre sales and new construction.
TELEVISION: *Researcher as Mary Ann Grasso:* The Scarlet O'Hara Wars, This Year's Blonde, The Silent Lovers, A Bunnies Tale, Embassy.

ANDERSON, MELISSA SUE

Actress. b. Berkeley, CA, Sept. 26, 1962. Took up acting at suggestion of a dancing teacher. Did series of commercials; guest role in episode of Brady Bunch; episode of Shaft. Gained fame as Mary Ingalls on Little House on the Prairie series (Emmy nom.).
PICTURES: Skatetown USA, Happy Birthday to Me, Chattanooga Choo Choo, Far North, Looking Your Best, Dead Men Don't Die.
TELEVISION: *Movies:* More than 20 movies, including The Loneliest Runner, James at 15, Where Have All the Children Gone, Forbidden Nights, Earthquake in NY, 10.5: Apocalypse, Marco Polo (voice). *Series*: The Little House on the Prairie (Emmy nom. 1978). *Guest:* More than 82 appearances.

ANDERSON, MICHAEL
Director. b. London, England, Jan. 30, 1920. e. France, Germany. Ent. motion picture industry as actor, 1936. Son is actor Michael Anderson, Jr.
PICTURES: More than 35 dir. picture credits, including Private Angelo (debut, 1949; co-dir. with Peter Ustinov), Waterfront Women, Hell Is Sold Out, Night Was Our Friend, 1984, Around the World in Eighty Days (Academy Award nom., DGA nom., Golden globe nom. 1957), The Shoes of the Fisherman, Logan's Run, Murder by Phone, Millennium, Summer of the Monkeys, The New Adventures of Pinnocchio, Tenderloin.
TELEVISION: *Movies:* Sword of Gideon, Young Catherine, The Sea Wolf, Rugged Gold, Captains Courageous, 20,000 Leagues Under the Sea. *Mini-series:* The Martian Chronicles. *Series:* Scales of Justice.

ANDERSON, PAUL THOMAS
Director, Writer. b. Sudio City, CA, Jan. 1, 1970. LA Film Critics Award, New Generation, 1997. BSFC Award for Best New Filmmaker for Boogie Nights in 1997. Garnered Best Screenplay Acad. Award nominations for Boogie Nights and Magnolia. Won best picture at Berlin Int'l. Film Fest. for Magnolia (1999).
PICTURES: The Dirk Diggler Story (short), Cigarettes and Coffee(short), Sydney (aka Hard Eight), Boogie Nights (also prod., Academy Award nom., WGA nom. 1998), Flagpole Special (short), Magnolia (Academy Award nom., WGA nom. 2000), Punch Drunk Love (Cannes Golden Palm Award), A Decade Under the Influence (documentary), There Will Be Blood (dir., s.p., prod., 3 Academy Award noms.; DGA nom.; WGA nom. 2008).
TELEVISION: *Movies:* Sworn to Vengeance (prod. assistant), SNL Fanatic. *Documentaries:* Wadd: The Life and Times of John C. Holmes, That Moment: Magnolia Diary October 1998 - March 2000, In Search of Ted Demme.

ANDERSON, RICHARD DEAN
Actor. b. Minneapolis, MN. Jan. 23, 1950. Planned to become professional hockey player. Became a street mime and jester. Performed with his own rock band, Ricky Dean and Dante.
PICTURES: Young Doctors In Love, Summer Jobs, Ordinary Heroes, Fallout (voice).
TELEVISION: *Movies:* MacGyver, In the Eyes of a Stranger, Through the Eyes of a Killer, Past the Bleachers, Pandora's Clock, Stargate SG-1: Children of the Gods, Firehouse, Stargate Atlantis: Rising. *Series:* General Hospital, Seven Brides for Seven Brothers, Emerald Point N.A.S., MacGyver, Legend, Stargate SG-1.(also exec. prod.), Stargate: Atlantis, SGU Stargate Universe. *Guest:* More than 55 appearances.

ANDERSON, SYLVIA
Producer. Writer. r. n. Sylvia Thamm. b. London, England. e. London U. Entered m. p. ind. 1960. First pub. novel, Love and Hisses. Represents the American network HBO in Pinewood Studios in London, England.
PICTURES: Thunderbirds Are Go, Thunderbird Six (prod.), Journey to the Far Side of the Sun, Invaders from the Deep (prod. only), The Thunderbirds (only writing/characters).
TELEVISION: *Creator &/or Prod.:* Space 1999, UFO, Thunderbirds, Journey Through the Black Sun, Destination Moonbase Alpha, Alien Attack, I Love Christmas, Star Maidens (assoc. prod.), Captain Scarlet vs. the Mysterons.

ANDERSON, WES
Director, Writer. b. Houston, TX, May 1, 1969. e. U. of Texas, BA.
PICTURES: Bottle Rocket, Rushmore (also exec. prod.; Independent Spirit Award, best dir., New Generation Award, L.A. Film Critics), The Royal Tenenbaums (also prod.; Academy Award nom., BAFTA nom. WGA nom. for screenplay 2002), The Life Aquatic, The Squid and the Whale (prod.), The Darjeeling Limited (also prod.), Fantastic Mr. Fox (also prod., voice, soundtrack writer).

ANDERSSON, BIBI
Actress. b. Stockholm, Sweden, Nov. 11, 1935. e. Royal Dramatic Theatre School (Kungliga Dramatiska Teatern).
THEATRE: Who's Afraid of Virginia Woolf?, Long Day's Journey Into Night, The Winter's Tale, Stockholm: Peer Gynt, Goldberg Variations.
PICTURES: Featured in 70 pictures, incl. Dum-Bom (debut, 1953), Sir Arne's Treasure, Smiles of a Summer Night, The Seventh Seal, Wild Strawberries, The Magician, Brink of Life, The Face, The Devil's Eye, Square of Violence, Pleasure Garden, The Swedish Mistress, Not to Mention These Women, My Sister My Love, Persona, Duel at Diablo, A Question of Rape, The Passion of Anna, The Kremlin Letter, The Touch, I Never Promised You a Rose Garden, An Enemy of the People, The Concorde: Airport '79, Prosperous Times, The Marmalade Revolution, Black Crows, Exposed, Manika, A Passing Season, The Butterfly's Dream, Little Big Sister, Light Keeps Me Company, Anna, The Frost, Arn: The Kingdom at Road's End.
TELEVISION: *Movies:* Among 17 appearances are Rabies, Wallenberg—A Hero's Story, Till Julia, The Lost Prince, The Return of the Dancing Master. *Series:* Bror & syster.

ANDRESS, URSULA
Actress. b. Bern, Switzerland, Mar. 19, 1936. In Rome as teen where she landed roles in Italian Films.
PICTURES: Sins of Casanova (debut, 1954), An American in Rome, The Tempest Has Gone, La Catena dell'Odio, Anyone Can Play, Dr. No (Golden Globe Award 1964), Four For Texas, Fun in Acapulco, Nightmare in the Sun, She, The Tenth Victim, What's New Pussycat?, Up to His Ears, Once Before I Die, The Blue Max, Casino Royale, The Southern Star, Perfect Friday, Red Sun, Africa Express, Scaramouche, The Sensuous Nurse, Slave of the Cannibal God, Tigers in Lipstick, The Fifth Musketeer, Primitive Desires, Four Tigers in Lipstick, Clash of the Titans, Reporters, Mexico in Flames, Liberte/Egalite/Choucroute, Class Reunion, Cremaster 5, Die Vogelpredigt.
TELEVISION: *Movies:* Man Against the Mob: The Chinatown Murders, Cave of the Golden Rose III, Cave of the Golden Rose IV, In 80 Jahren um die Welt. *Mini-series:* Peter the Great. *Series*: Falcon Crest. *Guest:* More than 67 appearances.

ANDREWS, ANTHONY
Actor, Producer. b. London, England, Dec. 1, 1948. e. Royal Masonic Sch., Herts. Regional stage debut, 1967.
PICTURES: Take Me High/Hot Property (debut, 1973), Operation Daybreak, Under the Volcano, The Holcroft Covenant, The Second Victory, The Lighthorsemen, Hanna's War, Lost in Siberia, The Law Lord, Haunted (also prod.).
TELEVISION: *Movies:* A Beast With Two Backs, The Judge's Wife, A War of Children, A Day Out, French Without Tears, London Assurance, Romeo and Juliet, Much Ado About Nothing, Mistress of Paradise, Ivanhoe, The Scarlet Pimpernel, Sparkling Cyanide, Z for Zachariah, Bluegrass, Suspicion, The Woman He Loved, Columbo Goes to the Guillotine, Danielle Steel's Jewels Golden Globe nom. 1993), Strange Case of Dr. Jekyll and Mr. Hyde, Hands of a Murderer, Heartstones, Mothertime, David Copperfield, Cambridge Spies, Marple: By the Pricking of My Thumbs. *Mini-series*: QB VII, Brideshead Revisited (Golden Globe Award, Emmy nom. 1982), A.D., Love in a Cold Climate. *Series:* The Pallisers, Upstairs Downstairs, Danger UXB. *Guest:* More than 62 appearances.

ANDREWS, JULIE
Actress, Singer. r.n. Julia Wells. b. Walton-on-Thames, England. Oct. 1, 1935. m. dir./writer Blake Edwards. Debut, England Starlight Roof Revue London Hippodrome, 1948. Author of Mandy, Last of the Really Great Whangdoodles, 1973.
THEATRE: NY: The Boy Friend, My Fair Lady, Camelot, Putting It Together, Victor/Victoria. Received SAG Life Achievement Award 2007.
PICTURES: Mary Poppins (debut, 1964; Academy Award, Golden Globe Award 1965), The Americanization of Emily, The Sound of Music (Acad. Award nom. Golden Globe Award 1966), Hawaii, Torn Curtain, Thoroughly Modern Millie (Golden Globe win and nom. 1968), Star! (Golden Globe nom. 1969), Darling Lili (Golden Globe nom. 1971), The Tamarind Seed, ``10," (Golden Globe nom. 1980), S.O.B, Victor/Victoria (Acad. Award nom., Golden Globe Award, 1983) The Man Who Loved Women, That's Life (Golden Globe nom. 1987), Duet For One (Golden Globe nom, 1986), A Fine Romance, Relative Values, The Princess Diaries, Who Shot Victor Fox, Shrek 2, The Princess Diaries 2: Royal Engagement, Shrek the Third (voice), Enchanted (narr.), Tooth Fairy, Despicable Me, Shrek Forever After (voice).
TELEVISION: *Movies:* Cinderella (Emmy nom. 1958), Peter Pan (singer), Our Sons, Victor/Victoria, One Special Night, On Golden Pond, Eloise at the Plaza, Eloise at Christmastime (Emmy nom. 2004), I'm Sorry I Haven't a Clue (soundtrack per.). *Series:* The Julie Andrews Hour (Emmy Award Golden Globe nom. 1973), Julie, Broadway: The American Musical (Emmy Award, 2005). *Specials:* Appeared in more than 15 specials, incl. Julie and Carol at Carnegie Hall, The World of Walt Disney, Julie and Carol at Lincoln Center, Julie on Sesame Street, Julie Andrews' Christmas Special, Julie Andrews: My Favorite Things, Julie Andrews: The Sound of Christmas, Julie and Carol: Together Again. *Guest:* More than 183 appearances.

ANDREWS, NAVEEN
Actor. b. England, Jan. 17, 1971. e. Guildhall School of Music and Drama.
PICTURES: London Kills Me, Wild West, Kama Sutra: A Tale of Love, The English Patient, True Love and Chaos, Mighty Joe Young, A Question of Faith, Drowning on Dry Land, Blessed Art Thou, Rollerball, Easy, The Ground Beneath Her Feet, Bride and Prejudice, Provoked: A True Story, Grindhouse, The Brave One, Animals.
TELEVISION: *Movies:* Double Vision, My Own Country, The Peacock Spring, The Chippendales Murder. *Mini-series:* The Buddha of Suburbia, The Beast, The Ten Commandments. *Series:* The Beast, Lost (Emmy nom. 2005, Golden Globe nom. 2006).

ANGELOPOULOS, THEO
Director, Writer, Producer, Actor. b. Athens, Greece, April 17, 1935.
PICTURES: Reconstruction, Days of 36, The Travelling Players, The Hunters, Alexander the Great, Voyage to Kythera (Cannes Film Fest. Award, Best Screenplay, 1984), The Beekeeper, Landscape in the Mist, The Suspended Step of the Stork, The

Gaze of Odysseus (Cannes Film Fest. Award, Jury Prize, 1995), Lumiere and Company, Eternity and a Day, Trilogy: The Weeping Meadow, Port Djema (assoc. prod.), Mia aioniotita kai mia mera, The Dust of Time (dir, writer). *Documentaries:* Chorio ena, katikos enas (short), Athens, Return to the Acropolis (short).

ANISTON, JENNIFER

Actress, Producer. b. Sherman Oaks, CA, Feb. 11, 1969. e. NY High School of the Performing Arts. Daughter of actor John Aniston. Started training as a drama student in high school. In 1987, after graduation, appeared in For Dear Life and Dancing on Checker's Grave (off B'way.) Won People's Choice Awards, USA, favorite female TV performer, 2001, 2002, 2003. Co-founded movie production firm Plan B Entertainment but left in 2005. Created film company, Echo Films, with partner producer Kristin Hahn in 2008.
PICTURES: Leprechaun, Waiting for Woody, She's the One, 'Til There Was You, Picture Perfect, The Object of My Affection, Dream for an Insomniac The Thin Pink Line, Office Space, The Iron Giant (voice), Time of our Lives, Rock Star, The Good Girl, Bruce Almighty, Along Came Polly, Rumor Has It, Derailed, Running with Scissors (prod.), Friends with Money, Diary, A Million Little Pieces (prod.), Gambit, The Break-Up, Management, Marley & Me, Traveling, He's Just Not That Into You, Love Happens, The Baster (also exec. prod.), The Goree Girls (also prod.), The Bounty Hunter, Pretend Wife.
TELEVISION: *Movies:* How I Spent My Summer, Camp Cucamonga. *Series:* Molloy (debut, 1989), Ferris Bueller, The Edge, Muddling Through, Friends (Emmy Award, 2002, 4 other noms., Golden Globe Award, 2003), 30 Rock (Emmy nom. 2009 as guest). *Special:* Friends: The Stuff You've Never Seen, Bad Hair Days, Comic Relief VII, Reinventando Hollywood, Shelter from the Storm: A Concert for the Gulf Coast, Stand Up to Cancer, Comic Relief 2009, Hope for Haiti Now: A Global Benefit for Earthquake Relief. *Guest:* More than 125 appearances.

ANN-MARGRET

Actress, Singer, Dancer. r.n. Ann-Margret Olsson. b. Valsjobyn, Sweden, April 28, 1941. e. New Trier H.S., Winnetka, IL; Northwestern U. m. Roger Smith, actor, dir., prod. Radio shows, toured with band; worked with George Burns in Las Vegas. TV debut, Jack Benny Show, 1961.
PICTURES: Pocketful of Miracles (debut, 1961), State Fair, Bye Bye Birdie (Golden Globe nom. 1964), Viva Las Vegas, Kitten With a Whip, The Pleasure Seekers, Bus Riley's Back in Town, Once A Thief, The Cincinnati Kid, Made in Paris, Stagecoach, The Swinger, Murderer's Row, The Prophet, The Tiger and the Pussycat, Rebus, Criminal Affair, RPM, C. C. & Company, Carnal Knowledge (Academy Award nom., Golden Globe Award 1972), The Outside Man, The Train Robbers, Tommy (Academy Award nom., Golden Globe Award, 1976), The Last Remake of Beau Geste, The Twist, Joseph Andrews (Golden Globe nom. 1978), The Cheap Detective, Magic, The Villain, Middle Age Crazy, I Ought To Be in Pictures, Lookin' to Get Out, The Return of the Soldier, Twice in a Lifetime, 52 Pick-up, A Tiger's Tail, A New Life, Newsies, Grumpy Old Men, Grumpier Old Men, The Limey, The Last Producer, Any Given Sunday, The 10th Kingdom: The Making of an Epic, Taxi, Mem-o-re, The Santa Clause 3, The Break-Up, The Loss of a Teardrop Diamond, All's Faire in Love, Old Dogs, Legion (soundtrack performer), Lucky, A Handful of Beans.
TELEVISION: *Movies:* The Way They Were, Who Will Love My Children? (Emmy nom., Golden Globe Award 1983), A Streetcar Named Desire (Emmy nom., Golden Globe Award 1984), The Two Mrs. Grenvilles (Emmy nom., Golden Globe nom. 1987), Our Sons, Nobody's Children, Following Her Heart, Blue Rodeo, Life of the Party: The Pamela Harriman Story (Emmy nom., Golden Globe nom. 1999), Happy Face Murders, A Woman's A Helluva Thing, A Place Called Home. *Mini-series:* Queen (Emmy nom., Golden Globe nom. 1993), Scarlett, Perfect Murder, Perfect Town: JonBenét and the City of Boulder, The 10th Kingdom, Blonde. *Series:* Four Corners. *Guest:* More than 153 appearances.

ANNAUD, JEAN-JACQUES

Writer, Director. b. Draveil, France, Oct. 1, 1943. Began career as film dir. in French army, making educational pictures. Also directed 500 commercials. Received 1989 cinema prize from French Acad. for career's work. Directed IMAX film Wings of Courage.
PICTURES: Black and White in Color (winner of Best Foreign Language Film Oscar, 1978), Too Shy to Try (writer only), Coup de Tete (Hothead), Quest for Fire (Cesar Award for best dir., 1982), The Name of the Rose, The Bear (Cesar Award for best dir., 1989), The Lover, Wings of Courage, Seven Years In Tibet, Running Free (s.p. and prod.) Enemy at the Gates (also prod.), Two Brothers (also prod., exec. prod.), Kashmir (dir. only).

ANSARA, MICHAEL

Actor. b. Syria, April 15, 1922. e. Pasadena Playhouse. Served in U.S. Army; then summer stock, road shows.
PICTURES: Appeared in more than 70 pictures, incl. Soldiers Three, Only the Valiant, Julius Caesar, Mohammad Messenger of God, The Manitou, Gas, Access Code, Knights of the City, Assasination, Lethal (KGB: The Secret War), Border Shootout, Johnny Mysto: Boy Wizard, The Long Road Home.
TELEVISION: *Movies:* How I Spent My Summer Vacation, Powderkeg, Call to Danger, Ordeal, Shootout in a One-Dog Town, Barbary Coast, The Fantastic World of D.C. Collins, Batman Beyond: The Movie. *Mini-series:* Centennial. *Series:* Broken Arrow, Law of the Plainsman, I Dream of Jeannie (dir.), Buck Rogers in the 25th Century, Rambo voice), Batman: The Animated Series (voice), The New Batman/Superman Adventures (voice). *Guest:* More than 115 appearances.

ANSCHUTZ, PHILIP

Executive, Producer. b. 1939, Russell, KS. e. U. of Kansas, 1961. Entered U. of Virgina law school but returned to help with family oil wildcatting business. On first discovery of oil in 1967, Anschutz bought up surrounding oil leases on credit. When a spark ignited the entire field, threatening to bankrupt him he called in the famed firefighter, "Red" Adair, who was reluctant to cap the blazing well without assurance of compensation. Anschutz contacted Universal Studios, who were filming a story on Adair at the time, and sold them rights to film his fire, for $100,000, enough to assure payment to Adair and continued operations. In 1982, Anshutz sold land to Mobil for $500 million and 17% royalties. In 1984, he bought the small Denver & Rio Grande Western Railroad. In 1988, he took control of the Southern Pacific Railroad. Developed a fiber-optics network along the railroad right-of-way. In 1996, the Southern Pacific was sold to the Union Pacific Railroad for $5.4 billion. Anshutz retained a 5.4% stake in the combined company. In addition, he retained the telecomm company and the fiber-optics network it was based on along the railroad right-of-way. 1997, this company, now called Qwest Communications, was taken public. As a public company, Anshutz still owns 18%. Now focusing on entertainment: bought stakes in troubled United Artists, Edwards and Regal theatres comprising 20% of U.S. movie screens. Founded company Anschutz Film Group which is the parent company of Crusader, Walden Media and Bristol Bay Prductions to develop family-friendly films and partnered with Kerner Entertainment Co., and also with 20th Century Fox and will market films through Fox Walden. Trustee, Kansas University Endowment, John F. Kennedy Center for the Performing Arts; hon. board member, Museum of Natural History, New York and the National Associates Board of the Smithsonian Institute, Washington, D.C. Director, The Anschutz Foundation, Chairman of The Anschutz Film Group.
PICTURES: *Producer:* A Sound of Thunder, Swimming Upstream (US dist.), Danny Deckchair (also dist.). *Credit as Production Company:* Ray, Sahara, The Game of Their Lives, Amazing Grace, The Great Buck Howard, I Am David, Around the World in 80 Days, Because of Winn-Dixie, Aliens of the Deep (doc.), The Chronicles of Narnia: The Lion, the Witch and the Wardrobe, Hoot, How to Eat Fried Worms, Amazing Grace, Charlotte's Web, Bridge to Terabithia (also dist. worldwide, all media sales), The Seeker: The Dark Is Rising, Mr. Magorium's Wonder Emporium, The Water Horse, Nim's Island, The Chronicles of Narnia: Prince Caspian, Journey to the Center of the Earth, City of Ember, Bandslam, Tooth Fairy, Ramona and Beezus (also dist. US, 2010), The Chronicles of Narnia: The Voyage of the Dawn Treader, The Throwback.

ANSPACH, SUSAN

Actress. b. New York, NY, Nov. 23, 1945. e. Catholic U., Washington, D.C. After school returned to NY and in 3 years had performed in 11 B'way and off-B'way prods. Moved to Los Angeles and entered films.
PICTURES: The Landlord (debut, 1970), Five Easy Pieces, Play It Again Sam, Blume in Love, The Big Fix, Running, The Devil and Max Devlin, Gas, Montenegro, Misunderstood, Blue Monkey, Into the Fire, Blood Red, Back to Back, Candle Smoke, Alien X Factor, American Primitive, Dumping Grounds.
TELEVISION: *Movies:* I Want to Keep My Baby, The Secret Life of John Chapman, Rosetti & Ryan, Mad Bull, The Last Giraffe, Portrait of an Escort, The First Time, Deadly Encounter, Cagney & Lacey: The Return, Dancing at the Harvest Moon. *Mini-series:* Space. *Series:* The Yellow Rose, The Slap Maxwell Story.

ANSPAUGH, DAVID

Director, Producer. b. Decatur, IN, Sept. 24, 1946. e. Indiana U., 1965-70; USC, 1974-76. School teacher, Aspen, CO, 1970-74.
PICTURES: *Director:* Hoosiers (debut, 1986), Fresh Horses, Rudy, Moonlight and Valentino, Wise Girls, The Game of Their Lives, 4Chosen.
TELEVISION: *Movies*: Vampire (assoc. prod.), Fighting Back (assoc. prod.), Deadly Care, In the Company of Darkness, Swing Vote, LA County 187, Two Against Time. *Series*: Paris (assoc. prod.), Hill St. Blues (assoc. prod. 1980-81; prod.-dir. 1981-82; prod.-dir. 1983-84, dir. 1985. DGA Award: 1983 1 other nom., 2 Emmy Awards for producing: 1982, 1983), St. Elsewhere (dir., DGA nom. 1985), Miami Vice (dir.).

ANTHONY, LYSETTE

Actress. r.n. Lysette Chodzko. b. London, England, Sept. 26, 1963. Stage work incl. Bristol Old Vic, 1988-90.
PICTURES: Krull, Night Train to Murder, L'Etincelle, Dombey & Son, A Drop in the Ocean, Looking for Eileen, The Emperor's New Clothes, Without A Clue, Switch, The Pleasure Principle,

Husbands and Wives, The Hour of the Pig, Look Who's Talking Now, Save Me, Face the Music, The Hard Truth, A Brilliant Disguise, Affair Play, Dr. Jekyll and Ms. Hyde, Dracula: Dead and Loving It, Dead Cold, Robison Crusoe, Prince of Lies, Man of Her Dreams, Misbegotten, Tale of the Mummy, Beneath Loch Ness, Farewell to Harry.
TELEVISION: *Movies:* Ivanhoe, Oliver Twist, Frost in May, Princess Daisy, Jack the Ripper, The Lady and the Highwayman, A Ghost in Monte Carlo, Target of Suspicion, Trilogy of Terror II, Hotel!, Poirot: The Hollow. *Mini-series:* Oliver Twist, The Bretts. *Series:* Crossroads, Auf Wiedersehen Pet, Three Up Two Down (BBC), Dark Shadows, Cluedo, Night & Day, The Bill. *Guest:* More than 55 appearances.

ANTONIO, LOU
Director, Actor, Writer, Producer. b. Oklahoma City, OK, January 23, 1934. e. U. of OK. Two Emmy Noms for TV Movies.
THEATRE: *Actor:* The Buffalo Skinner (Theatre World Award), various other productions.
PICTURES: *Actor:* America America, Hawaii, Cool Hand Luke, The Phynx. *Dir.:* The Gypsy Warriors, Micki + Maude (exec. prod.).
TELEVISION: *Movies/Director:* More than 35 dir. credits, incl. Lanigan's Rabbi, Someone I Touched, Something for Joey (Emmy nom. 1978), The Critical List, Silent Victory-The Kitty O'Neil Story (Emmy nom. 1979), A Real American Hero, We're Fighting Back, Something So Right, A Good Sport, Threesome, Rearview Mirror, Face to Face, The Outside Woman (also prod.), Dark Holiday (also exec. prod.), Between Friends, Mayflower Madam, Pals, 13 at Dinner, This Gun for Hire, Lies Before Kisses, The Last Prostitute, The Rape of Dr. Willis, A Taste for Killing, Nightmare in the Daylight, The Contender, Ghost Stories (consult. prod., suprv. dir.). *Mini-series:* Rich Man, Poor Man (co-dir.), Breaking Up Is Hard to Do, The Star Maker. *Series: Dir.* for 34 series, incl. The Flying Nun (1967), Banacek, Rich Man Poor Man Book II, Party of Five, Chicago Hope (Emmy nom. 1995), American Gothic, Dark Skies, Picket Fences (DGA nom. 1994), Dawson's Creek, Vengeance Unlimited, Get Real, The West Wing, C.S.I.: Crime Scene Investigation, First Monday, The Handler, Boston Legal.

ANTONOWSKY, MARVIN
Executive. b. New York, NY, Jan. 31, 1929. e. City College of New York, B.A., M.B.A. Joined Kenyon and Eckhart in 1957 for which was media research dir. then mktg. v.p. With Norman, Craig, & Kummel as v.p., mktg. svcs. Became v.p. in charge of media research and spot buying at J. Walter Thompson, 1965. Joined ABC-TV as v.p. in charge of research, 1969. Left to become v.p. in charge of programming at NBC-TV. Became sr. v.p., Universal-TV, 1976. Joined Columbia Pictures as pres., mktg. & research, 1979. Rejoined MCA/Universal Pictures as pres, mktg., 1983. Formed Marvin Antonowsky & Assoc., mktg. consultancy firm, 1989. Rejoined Columbia Pictures in 1990 as exec. v.p. and asst. to chmn. Joined Price Entertainment as exec. v.p., 1993. Marketing consultant to movie distributors. Bd. of Dir. for LA Opera, member of Baruch College fund.

ANWAR, GABRIELLE
Actress. b. Laleham, England, Feb. 4,1970.
PICTURES: Manifesto (debut, 1989), If Looks Could Kill, Wild Hearts Can't Be Broken, Scent of a Woman, For Love or Money, The Three Musketeers, Body Snatchers, Things to Do in Denver When You're Dead, Innocent Lies, The Grave, Nevada (also co-prod.), Kimberly, The Guilty, The Manor, If You Only Knew, North Beach, Without Malice, Flying Virus, Mob Dot Com, The Marsh, Crazy Eights, iMurders, Warrior, The Family Tree.
TELEVISION: *Movies:* Prince Caspian and the Voyage of the Dawn Treader, In Pursuit of Honor, The Ripper, My Little Assassin, How to Marry a Billionaire: A Christmas Tale, Without Malice, Case of Evil, Try to Remember, Mysterious Island, Long Lost Son, The Librarian 2: Return to King Solomon's Mines, Burn Notice (pilot), Among Friends. *Mini-series:* Hideaway, First Born, Summer's Lease, Misteri della giungla nera, I. *Series:* Press Gang, Fallen Angels, John Doe, The Tudors, Burn Notice.

APATOW, JUDD
Producer, Writer. b. Syosset, NY, Dec. 6, 1967.
PICTURES: Crossing the Bridge (assoc. prod. only), Heavyweights (writer, exec. prod. and actor), Happy Gilmore (s.p. only), Celtic Pride (s.p., exec. prod.), The Cable Guy (s.p., exec. prod.), The Wedding Singer (s.p. only), The Whistlebower, Action News (prod. only), Anchorman (prod. only), Fun with Dick and Jane (s.p.), Kicking & Screaming (exec. prod.), The Shaggy Dog (writer), The 40 Year-Old Virgin (also dir.; WGA nom. 2006), Talladega Nights: The Ballad of Ricky Bobby (prod. only), Knocked Up (writer, prod., dir., WGA nom. 2008, s.p.), Super Bad (prod.), Walk Hard: The Dewey Cox Story (prod., writer, Golden Globe nom. 2008, Best Original Song), Step Brothers (prod.), Forgetting Sarah Marshall, You Don't Mess With The Zohan (s.p.), Drillbit Taylor (prod.), Pineapple Express (also writer), Year One (prod.), Funny People (prod., writer, dir.), Get Him to the Greek (prod., exec. prod.), The Zookeeper (voice).
TELEVISION: *Movies:* The TV Wheel (writer only), Life on Parole, Sick in the Head (exec. prod., writer), Night of Too Many Stars: An Overbooked Concert for Autism Education (segment dir.). *Series:* The Larry Sanders Show (dir. only, 5 Emmy nom., WGA nom. 1998), The Ben Stiller Show (actor only, Emmy Award; writer), The Critic, Freaks and Geeks (exec. prod, dir., writer), Undeclared (creator, writer, exec. prod., dir.), Help Me Help You (actor only).

APPLEGATE, CHRISTINA
Actress. b. Hollywood, CA Nov. 25, 1972.
PICTURES: Jaws of Satan (debut, 1980), Streets, Don't Tell Mom the Babysitter's Dead, Across the Moon, Wild Bill, Mars Attacks!, Nowhere, The Big Hit, Jane Austen's Mafia, The Giving Tree, Out in Fifty, Just Visiting, The Sweetest Thing, A View From the Top, Wonderland, Grand Theft Parsons, Surviving Christmas, The Rocker, Alvin and the Chipmunks: The Squeakquel (voice), Going the Distance.
TELEVISION: *Movies:* Grace Kelly, Dance 'til Dawn, Prince Charming, Suzanne's Diary for Nicholas. *Series:* Washingtoon, Heart of the City, Married...With Children, Jesse (Golden Globe nom. 1999), Samantha Who? (2 Emmy noms. 2008, 2009; 2 Golden Globe noms. 2008, 2009). *Guest:* More than 113 appearances.

APTED, MICHAEL
Director, Producer. b. Aylesbury, England, Feb. 10, 1941. e. Cambridge. Broke into industry at Granada TV in England in early 1960s as trainee, researcher and finally director. By 1965, was prod.-dir. for local programs and current affairs then staff drama dir. for TV series, plays and serials. In late 1960s left Granada to freelance. President of Directors Guild of America (DGA) 2003-2009.
PICTURES: *Director:* Triple Echo, Stardust, The Squeeze, Agatha, Coal Miner's Daughter (DGA nom. 1981), Continental Divide, Gorky Park, The River Rat (exec. prod. only), Firstborn, Critical Condition, Gorillas in the Mist: The Story of Dian Fossey, Class Action, Thunderheart, Dracula (exec. prod. only), Blink, Nell, Extreme Measures, The World Is Not Enough, Enigma, Enough, Tell No One, Black Autumn, Amazing Grace, Goal! 3, The Chronicles of Narnia: The Voyage of the Dawn Treader.
TELEVISION: *Movies/Director:* Another Sunday and Sweet F.A., The Reporters, Play for Today: Kisses at Fifty, Joy, High Kampf, Jack Point, The Collection (DGA nom. 1979), Stronger Than the Sun, P'tang Yang Kipperbang, The Long Way Home, Criminal Justice (exec. prod.), Murder Without Motive: The Edmund Perry Story, Intruders (exec. prod.), Always Outnumbered, 14 Up in America (exec. prod.), Nathan Dixon. Series: Haunted, Big Breadwinner Hog, The Dustbinmen, The Lovers, Black and Blue, My Life and Times, Crossroads (also exec. prod.), New York News, Rome (DGA Award 2006).
Documentaries: 7 Plus Seven, 21, 28 Up, 35 Up, 7-Up In America, 42: Forty Two Up, Married in America, 49 Up (dir., narr., prod.), Born in the USSR: 21 Up (consult. exec.), Married in America 2, also narr.), The Power of the Game.

ARAKI, GREGG
Director, Editor, Producer, Writer. b. Los Angeles, CA, Dec. 17, 1959.
PICTURES: Three Bewildered People in the Night (1987), The Long Weekend (O'Despair), The Living End, Totally F***ed Up, The Doom Generation, Nowhere, Splendor, Mysterious Skin, Smiley Face, Kaboom.
TELEVISION: *Movie:* Shattered Spirits (researcher), This Is How the World Ends.

ARAU, ALFONSO
Director, Actor. b. Mexico City, Mexico, Jan. 11, 1932. e. Univ. of Mexico. Studied drama there and with Saki Sano in Mexico; UCLA film school; studied pantomime in Paris.
PICTURES: *Actor:* Pedro Paramo, The Wild Bunch, Scandalous John, Run Cougar Run, Nest of Virgins, Inspector Calzonzin (also dir.), Tivoli, Posse, Used Cars, Romancing the Stone, Three Amigos!, Walker, Committed, Pickiing Up the Pieces (also dir., exec. prod.), Butterflies & Lightning. *Director:* Mojado Power (also acting, prod.), Tacos de oro (also s.p.) Como aqua para chocolate, A Walk in the Clouds, Zapata, Hijos del Topo, Los (exec. prod.), Gold on Eagle Street, El Día que me quieras (also prod.), The Dead One (voice), Dare to Love Me (also prod.).
TELEVISION: *Movies/Actor:* Stones for Ibarra, Where the Hell's That Gold?!. *Director:* Catch a Falling Star, The Magnificient Ambersons, A Painted House. *Series*: E! Show de Arau.

ARCAND, DENYS
Director. b. Deschambault, Quebec, Canada, June 25, 1941. e. U. of Montreal, 1963. While still history student, co-prod. Seul ou avec D'Autres (1962). Joined National Film Board of Canada, where he began making documentary shorts (Champlain, Les Montrealistes and La Route de l'ouest) forming a trilogy dealin with colonial Quebec. In 1970, socio-politicial doc. about Quebec textile workers, On Est au Coton, generated controversy resulting in the NFB banning film until 1976.
PICTURES: Un Maudite Galette (1st fiction feature, 1971), Dir. &/or Writer: Seoul ou Avec D'autres, Entre la Mer et L'eau Douce, Quebec: Duplessis et Apres...(doc.), Dirty Money, Rejeanne Padovani, Gina, Comfort and Indifference, Le Crime d'Ovide Plouffe, The Decline of the American Empire, Night Zoo (actor only), Jesus of Montreal (Cannes Film Fest. jury prize, 1989), Leolo (actor only), Montreal Sextet (also actor), Love and Human Remains, Poverty and other Delights, 15 moments, Joyeaux Calvaire, Stardom, The Barbarian Invasions (also actor, writer, Academy

Award nom. 2004), L' Âge des ténèbres, The Age of Ignorance (also writer, actor).
TELEVISION: *Mini-series:* Duplessis (writer), Murder in the Family, Empire, Inc.

ARCHER, ANNE
Actress. b. Los Angeles, CA, Aug. 25, 1947. Daughter of actess Marjorie Lord and actor John Archer. m. Terry Jastrow, TV network sports prod.-dir. and pres. Jack Nicklaus Prods.
THEATRE: A Coupla White Chicks Sitting Around Talking (off B'way, 1981), Les Liaison Dangereuses (Williamstown Film Fest., 1988).
PICTURES: The Honkers (debut, 1972), Cancel My Reservation, The All-American Boy, Trackdown, Lifeguard, Paradise Alley, Good Guys Wear Black, Hero at Large, Raise the Titanic, Green Ice, Waltz Across Texas (also co-story), The Naked Face, Too Scared to Scream, The Check Is in the Mail, Fatal Attraction (Academy Award nom.; Golden Globe nom. 1988), Love at Large, Narrow Margin, Eminent Domain, Patriot Games, Body of Evidence, Family Prayers, Short Cuts (Golden Globe Award 1994), Clear and Present Danger, There Goes My Baby (narrator), Mojave Moon, Nico the Unicorn, Whispers (voice), Dark Summer, Rules of Engagement, The Art of War, Uncle Nino, November, The Gray in Between, Cheer Up, Man of the House, Cut Off, End Game, Quantum Quest: A Cassini Space Odyssey (voice), Felon, The Ghosts of Girlfriends Past, Freedom for Joe.
TELEVISION: *Movies:* The Blue Knight, The Mark of Zorro, The Log of the Black Pearl, A Matter of Wife...and Death, The Dark Side of Innocence, Harold Robbins' The Pirate, The Sky's No Limit, A Different Affair, A Leap of Faith, The Last of His Tribe, Nails, Jane's House, Because Mommy Works (also co-prod.), The Man in the Attic, Jake's Women, Almost Forever, Indiscretion of an American Wife, My Husband's Secret Life, Night of the Wolf, Judicial Indiscretion, Family Practice. *Mini-series:* Seventh Avenue, Camino de Santiago. *Series:* Bob and Carol and Ted and Alice, The Family Tree, Falcon Crest, Boston Public, The L Word, Ghost Whisperer, It's Always Sunny in Philadelphia, Dennis and Dee Get a New Dad, Privileged. *Guest:* More than 76 appearances.

ARDANT, FANNY
Actress. b. Monte Carlo, March 22, 1949. Majored in political science in college. Served a 5-year apprenticeship in the French theatre acting in Polyeucte, Esther, The Mayor of Santiago, Electra and Tete d'Or. TV debut in Les Dames de la Cote.
PICTURES: Les Chiens (debut, 1979), Les uns et les Autres, The Woman Next Door, The Ins and Outs, Life Is a Novel, Confidentially Yours, Benevenuta, Desire, Swann in Love, Love Unto Death, Les Enrages, L'Ete Prochain, Family Business, Affabulazione, Melo, The Family, La Paltoquet, Three Sisters, Australia, Pleure pas My Love, Adventure of Catherine C., Afraid of the Dark, Rien Que des Mensonges, La Femme du Deserteur, Amok, Colonel Chabert, Beyond the Clouds, Sabrina, Pedale douce (France's Cesar Award, best actress, 1997), Desire, Ridicule, Elizabeth, La Cena, Augustin roi du Kung Fu, La Debandade, Le Fils du Francais, Le Libertin, Sin Noticias de Dios, Change My Life, 8 Women Callas Forever, Nathalie..., Paris, je t'aime, Emeth, Bord cadre, Ha- Sodot, Roman de gare, Divo, Il, Hello Goodbye, Face Cendres et sang (dir., writer).
TELEVISION: *Movies:* The Fall of the House of Usher, Mademoiselle Julie, Balzac: A Life of Passion. *Mini-series*: Les Mutants, Les Dames de la Cote, Le Chef de famille, Les Uns et les Autres, La Grande cabriole. *Special*: Vivement Truffaut.

ARGENTO, DARIO
Director, Writer. b. Rome, Italy, Sept. 7, 1940. Son of prod. Salvatore Argento.
PICTURES: *Writer/Co-s.p.:* Today It's Me...Tomorrow It's You, Cemetery Without Crosses, Once Upon a Time in the West, Commandos, Zero Probability, The Five Man Army, One Night at Dinner, Sexual Revoultion, Legion of the Damned, Seasons of Love (also dir./prod./co-prod.), Bird With the Crystal Plumage, Cat O'Nine Tails (also story), Four Flies on Grey Velvet, The Five Days of Milan, Deep Red, Suspiria (also music), Dawn of the Dead (prod., also music), Inferno (also story), Tenebrae Unsane (also story), Creepers, Demons, Demons 2: The Nightmare is Back, Opera (Terror at the Opera), The Church (also story), Two Evil Eyes (episode: The Black Cat), Devil's Daughter, Innocent Blood (actor only), Trauma, Stendhal's Syndrome, The Wax Mask, Phantom of the Opera, Sleepless (also dir., prod.), Il Cartaio, Mother of Tears, Martyrs (actor), Giallo (dir.), Suspiria.
TELEVISION: *Movies:* The Tram (also prod.), The Doll, La Bambola (prod.), Do You Like Hitchcock?, Masters of Horror (interviewee, dir.). *Series:* Door Into Darkness.

ARKIN, ADAM
Actor, Director. b. Brooklyn, NY, Aug. 19, 1956. Father is actor Alan Arkin. Made acting debut in short film prod. by father, People Soup.
THEATRE: I Hate Hamlet (Theatre World Award), Four Dogs and a Bone.
PICTURES: Made for Each Other, Baby Blue Marine, Improper Channels (s.p.), Under the Rainbow, Chu Chu and the Philly Flash, Full Moon High, The Doctor, With Friends Like These, Halloween: H20, With Friends Like These, Lake Placid, East of A, Hanging Up, Mission, Dropping Out, Stark Raving Mad, Marilyn Hotchkiss' Ballroom Dancing and Charm School, Hitch, Kids in America, A Serious Man, Summer Eleven.
TELEVISION: *Movies:* It Couldn't Happen to a Nicer Guy, All Together Now, In the Line of Duty: Hunt for Justice, Not in This Town, Thirst, A Slight Case of Murder, My Louisiana Sky (dir. only, Emmy Award, DGA nom. 2002), Off Season, Roughing It, Damaged Care. *Mini-series:* Pearl, Not for Ourselves Alone: The Story of Elizabeth Cady Stanton & Susan B. Anthony (voice). *Series:* Busting Loose, Teachers Only, Tough Cookies, A Year in the Life, Northern Exposure (dir., Emmy nom. 1993) Big Wave Dave's, Chicago Hope Emmy nom. 1997), Baby Bob, Monk (dir.), The West Wing, 8 Simple Rules, Boston Legal, Life, Sons of Anarchy. *Specials:* Mark Twain's America: Tom Edison, The Fourth Wise Man, Baseball (voice), The West (voice), Lewis & Clark: The Journey of the Corps of Discovery (voice), The War (reader), TV Land Moguls (mini-series, narr.), The National Parks: America's Best Idea (mini-series). *Guest:* More than 95 appearances.

ARKIN, ALAN
Actor, Director, b. New York, NY, March 26, 1934. e. Los Angeles City Col., Los Angeles State Col., Bennington (VT) Col. m. Barbara Dana, actress-author. Father of actor Adam Arkin. Was member of folk singing group The Tarriers, then one of the original members of Chicago's Second City improvisational group. Directed short films T.G.I.F., People Soup (Acad. Award nom.). Author: Tony's Hard Work Day, The Lemming Condition, Halfway Through the Door, The Clearing, Some Fine Grandpa.
THEATRE: *B'way:* Enter Laughing (Tony & Theatre World Awards, 1963), Luv. Off-B'way: Second City, Man Out Loud, From the Second City. *Director:* Eh?, Little Murders, White House Murder Case (Obie Award), Joan of Lorraine, Rubbers and Yanks Three, The Sunshine Boys, The Sorrows of Stephen, Room Service.
PICTURES: 50 credits, incl. Calypso Heat Wave (debut, 1957), The Russians Are Coming The Russians Are Coming (Golden Globe Award, Golden Globe nom. most promising newcomer, Academy Award nom. 1967), Woman Times Seven, Wait Until Dark, Inspector Clouseau, The Heart Is a Lonely Hunter (NY Film Critics Award, Academy Award nom., Golden Globe nom. 1969), Catch-22, Little murders (also dir.), Deadhead Miles, Last of the Red Hot Lovers, Freebie and the Bean, Hearts of the West (NY Film Critics Award), The 7 Per Cent Solution, Popi (Golden Globe nom. 1970), Fire Sale (also dir.), The In-Laws (also exec. prod.), Simon, Improper Channels, Chu Chu and the Philly Flash, Full Moon High, The Last Unicorn (voice), Joshua Then and Now, Bad Medicine, Big Trouble, Coupe de Ville, Edward Scissorhands, Havana, The Rocketeer, Glengarry Glen Ross, Indian Summer, So I Married an Axe Murderer, North, The Jerky Boys, Steal Big Steal Little, Mother Night, Grosse Point Blank, Gattaca, The Slums of Beverly Hills, Jakob the Liar, Arigo (also dir. & s.p.), America's Sweethearts, 13 Conversations About One Thing, Don't You Cry For Me, Counting Sheep, Firewall, The Santa Clause 3, Bee Movie (voice), Little Miss Sunshine (Academy Award 2007), Raising Flagg, Rendition, Sunshine Cleaning, Get Smart, Marley & Me, The Private Lives of Pippa Lee, Due Date.
TELEVISION: *Movies:* The Defection of Simas Kurdirka, The Other Side of Hell, A Deadly Business, Escape from Sobibor, Cooperstown, Taking the Heat, Doomsday Gun, Blood Money, Varian's War, The Pentagon Papers (Emmy nom. 2003), And Starring Pancho Villa as Himself. *Mini-series:* Escape From Sobibor (Emmy nom. Golden Globe nom. 1987). *Series:* Sesame Street, Fay (dir.), Harry, 100 Centre Street. *Specials / Documentaries:* The Love Song of Barney Kempinski, The Fourth Wise Man, A Matter of Principle, Fay (pilot; dir.), Twigs (dir.), Terror in the Aisles, The Emperor's New Clothes (Faerie Tale Theatre), The Visit (Trying Times; dir.), The Boss (Trying Times; dir.), Necessary Parties (also co-s.p., co-prod.). *Guest:* More than 60 appearances.

ARKUSH, ALLAN
Director. b. Jersey City, NJ, April 30, 1948. e. Franklin & Marshall, NYU. Film Sch. With New World Pictures as film, music and trailer editor, 1974-79. Co-dir. Hollywood Boulevard and Death Sport and was 2nd unit dir. of Grand Theft Auto before directing on own. Dir. rock videos with Bette Midler and Mick Jagger, Elvis Costello, Christine McVie.
PICTURES: Hollywood Boulevard (co-dir., co-edit.), Deathsport (co-dir.), Rock 'n' Roll High School (also story), Heartbeeps, Get Crazy, Caddyshack II.
TELEVISION: *Movies:* XXX & OOOs (co-exec. prod.), Shake Rattle and Rock,.Young at Heart, Desert Breeze (co-exec. prod.), Elvis Meets Nixon, Prince Charming. *Mini-series:* The Temptations (Emmy Award, DGA nom. 1999). *Series:* More than 30 series dir. credits, incl. Fame, St. Elsewhere, L.A. Law, Moonlighting (Emmy nom. 1987), Shannon's Deal (spv. prod.), Tattinger's, The Twilight Zone, Mann & Machine, Central Park West (co-exec. prod.), The Practice, Snoops, Ally McBeal (Emmy nom. 1998), Bull, Tucker (also prod.), Crossing Jordan (also co-exec. prod., prod.), Heroes (dir., exec. prod., Emmy nom. 2007). *Pilots:* The Bronx Zoo, Capital News (prod.), Parenthood (co-exec. prod.), Bodies of Evidence, Moon Over Miami (exec. prod.).

ARMSTRONG, BESS

Actress. b. Baltimore, MD, Dec. 11, 1953. e. Brown U m. producer John Fiedler.
PICTURES: The Four Seasons, Jekyll and Hyde—Together Again, High Road to China, Jaws 3-D, The House of God, Nothing in Common, Second Sight, Mother Mother (short), The Skateboard Kid, Serial Mom, Dream Lover, That Darn Cat, Pecker.
TELEVISION: *Movies:* Getting Married, How to Pick Up Girls, Walking Through the Fire, Lakeside Killer, Barefoot in the Park, This Girl for Hire, Lace, Take Me Home Again, She Stood Alone: The Tailhook Scandal, Mixed Blessings, Stolen Innocence, Forgotten Sins, She Cried No, Christmas Every Day, Forever Love, Her Best Friend's Husband. *Series:* On Our Own, All is Forgiven, Married People, My So-Called Life, That Was Then.

ARMSTRONG, GILLIAN

Director. b. Melbourne, Australia, Dec. 18, 1950. e. Swinburne Coll. Among 1st class in dirs. course at National Aust. Film & TV School, Sydney. Worked as art dir. on a number of films. Dir. numerous shorts (One Hundred a Day, The Singer and the Dancer) and documentaries (A Busy Kind of Bloke, Bingo Bridesmaids and Braces) before turning to features.
PICTURES: My Brilliant Career (Australian Film Inst. Award), Starstruck, Mrs. Soffel, High Tide, Little Havana, The Last Days of Chez Nous, Little Women, Not Fourteen Again, Oscar & Lucinda, Charlotte Gray, Death Defying Acts, Unfolding Florence: The Many Lives of Florence Broadhurst, Death Defying Acts.

ARMSTRONG, GORDON

Executive. b. East Orange, NJ, Nov. 26, 1937. e. Arizona State U., graduate studies at NYU. Joined 20th Century-Fox as nat. pub. dir., 1970. Was appointed dir. of adv.-pub.-promo. for Dino De Laurentiis Corp., 1975; became vice pres., worldwide marketing for the company, 1978. Named v.p., adv.-pub.-prom., Universal Pictures, 1970; exec. v.p., mktg. MCA Recreation, 1984; pres. mktg., Morgan Creek Prods., 1991. Pres., Entertainment Marketing Group, 1993. V.p., sales and mktg., ATTICA Cybernetics ,1995; v.p., sales and mktg., Doubleclick Network, 1996. Currently Senior Director of Info Technology for Washington Sports & Entertainment.

ARNOLD, TOM

Actor. b. Ottumwa, IA, June 3, 1959.
PICTURES: Has more than 25 picture credits, incl. Freddy's Dead: The Final Nightmare, Hero, Undercover Blues, True Lies, Nine Months, Big Bully, Carpool, McHale's Navy (also co-prod.), Golf Punks, Blue Ridge Fall, Ablaze, Exit Wounds, Just Sue Me, Animal Factory, We Married Margo, Lloyd, Children On Their Birthdays, True Lies 2, G-S.P.O.T, Just For Kicks, Hansel and Gretel, After School Special, Manhood, Cradle 2 the Grave, Soul Plane, Piggy Banks, Firedog, Happy Endings, The Kid & I, The Skeptic, Oranges, P.D.R, The Final Season, The 1 Second Film (exec. prod., doc.), Remarkable Power (exec. prod.), Palo Alto, Gardens of the Night, Pride, Good Dick, The Skeptic, The Jerk Theory, Hard Breakers, April Showers, Kill Speed, The Bad Penny, Last Call, Endure, Firedog.
TELEVISION: *Movies:* Backfield in Motion, Body Bags, The Woman Who Loved Elvis, Jackie's Back!, Shriek If You Know What I Did Last Friday the 13th, Romantic Comedy 101, Dennis the Menace in Cruise Control, Chasing Christmas, Three Wise Guys, Lolo's Cafe, Moonlight and Mistletoe. *Series:* Roseanne (also exec. prod., writer) The Jackie Thomas Show (also creator, exec. prod.), Tom, The Tom Show (also creator, exec. prod.), Disney's Hercules (voice), The New Gong Show (host), The Best Damn Sports Show Period (himself), Overkill. *Guest:* More than 174 appearances.

ARONOFSKY, DARREN

Director, Writer. b. Brooklyn, New York, Feb. 12, 1969. e. Harvard U.
PICTURES: Protozoa, Pi, Requiem for a Dream, Batman: Year One, Below (writer, exec. prod.), The Fountain, Death and Rebirth (doc.), The Wrestler (also prod.), RoboCop (dir.).

ARQUETTE, DAVID

Actor, Producer. b. Sept. 8, 1971. m. actress Courtney Cox. Brother of actresses Patricia and Rosanna Arquette and actors Richmond and Alexis Arquette.
PICTURES: Has appeared in 35 pictures, incl. Where the Day Takes You, Buffy the Vampire Slayer, The Killing Box, Airheads, Fall Time, Wild Bill, Beautiful Girls, Johns, Scream, Life During Wartime, Dream with the Fishes (also co-prod.), Scream 2, Ravenous, Never Been Kissed, Muppets From Space, Scream 3, Ready to Rumble, The Shrink Is In, 3000 Miles to Graceland, See Spot Run, The Grey Zone, Happy Here And Now, Eight Legged Freaks, Stealing Sinatra, A Foreign Affair, Never Die Alone, Riding the Bullet, The Adventures of Shark Boy & Lava Girl in 3-D, The OH in Ohio, Darwin Awards, The Tripper (also prod., dir., writer), Hamlet 2, The Land of the Astronauts, Scream 4.
TELEVISION: *Movies:* Cruel Doubt, Roadracers, It's a Very Merry Muppet Christmas Movie, In Case of Emergency (pilot), Talk Show Diaries (exec. prod.). *Mini-series:* Dead Man's Walk. *Series:* The Outsiders, Parenthood, Double Rush, Pelswick (voice), Mix It Up (exec. prod.), Dirt (exec. prod., prod.) In Case of Emergency, Pushing Daisies, Cougar Town (exec. prod.). *Guest:* More than 92 appearances.

ARQUETTE, PATRICIA

Actress. b. Chicago, IL, April 8, 1968. Sister of actress Rosanna Arquette and actors Richmond, Alexis and David Arquette. Prof. debut in children's version of Story Theatre. Studied acting with Milton Katselis. Won Emmy, Outstanding Lead Actress In A Drama Series for role in TV series Medium.
PICTURES: A Nightmare on Elm Street 3: Dream Warriors (debut, 1987), Pretty Smart, Time Out, Far North, Prayer of the Rollerboys, The Indian Runner, Ethan Frome, Trouble Bound, Inside Monkey Zetterland, True Romance, Holy Matrimony, Ed Wood, Beyond Rangoon, Infinity, Flirting With Disaster, The Secret Agent, Nightwatch, Lost Highway, The Hi-Lo Country, Goodbye Lover, Stigmata, Bringing Out the Dead, Little Nicky, Human Nature, Holes, Before the Devil Knows You're Dead, The Science of Sleep, Fast Food Nation.
TELEVISION: *Movies:* Daddy, Dillinger, Wildflower, Betrayed by Love, The Badge. *Series:* Medium (Emmy Award, 2005, 1 other nom. 2007, 3 Golden Globe noms.). *Special:* The Girl With the Crazy Brother. *Guest:* More than 65 appearances.

ARQUETTE, ROSANNA

Actress. b. New York, NY, Aug. 10, 1959. Granddaughter of humorist Cliff Arquette (Charlie Weaver). Daughter of actor-producer Lewis Arquette. Sister of actress Patricia Arquette and actors Richmond, Alexis and David Arquette. Prof. debut in children's version of Story Theatre. Studied acting in San Francisco. Role in LA play led to bit parts on tv then regular role as Shirley Jones' teenage daughter on series Shirley (1979).
PICTURES: 50 picture credits, incl. More American Graffiti (debut, 1979), Gorp, S.O.B., Desperately Seeking Susan (Golden Globe nom. 1986), Silverado, After Hours, 8 Million Ways To Die, Nobody's Fool, Amazon Women on the Moon, The Big Blue, The Linguini Incident, Fathers and Sons, Nowhere to Run, Pulp Fiction, Search and Destroy, Crash, Gone Fishin', Deceiver, I'm Losing You, Hell's Kitchen, Buffalo '66, The Whole Nine Yards, Lucky Numbers (music consult), Big Bad Love, Things Behind the Sun, Good Advice, Diary of a Sex Addict, Kids in America, Battle for Terra (voice), Inhale, Convincing Clooney, Exodus Fall, Scribble.
TELEVISION: *Movies:* Having Babies II, The Dark Secret of Harvest Home, Zuma Beach, The Ordeal of Patty Hearst, A Long Way Home, The Wall, The Executioner's Song (Emmy nom. 1983), Johnny Belinda, One Cooks the Other Doesn't, The Parade, Survival Guide, Promised a Miracle, Sweet Revenge, Separation, Son of the Morning Star, Black Rainbow, In the Deep Woods, The Wrong Man, Nowhere to Hide, I Know What You Did, Switched at Birth, Poison, Rush of Fear, Northern Lights. *Mini-series:* The Dark Secret of Harvest Home. *Series:* Shirley, The L Word, What About Brian (also pilot). *Guest:* More than 97 appearances.

ARTHUR, KAREN

Director, Actress. b. Omaha, NB, Aug. 24, 1941. Ballet dancer, choreographer and musical comedy singer, dancer and actress, 1950-68; actress, film, tv and theatre, 1968-75; film, tv director, 1970-.
PICTURES: *Actress:* A Guide for the Married Man, Winning, Like It Is... *Director:* Legacy (also prod.; Int'l Film Critics & Josef Von Sternberg Awards, 1975), The Mafu Cage, Lady Beware, Conditional Love.
TELEVISION: *Movies:* Charleston, Victims for Victims: The Theresa Saldana Story (Christopher Award), A Bunny's Tale, The Rape of Richard Beck, Evil in Clear River (Christopher Award), Cracked Up, Bridge to Silence, Fall from Grace, Blue Bayou, Bump in the Night, Shadow of a Doubt, The Secret, The Disappearance of Christina, Against Their Will: Women in Prison, Journey of the Heart, The Staircase, Labor of Love, The Lost Child, The Song of the Lark, Passion and Prejudice (also prod.), The Locket, The Christmas Blessing, Moonlight and Mistletoe. *Mini-series:* Love and Betrayal: The Mia Farrow Story, Crossings, Return to Eden, The Jacksons: An American Dream, Dead by Sunset, A Will of Their Own, True Women. *Series:* Hart to Hart, Rich Man Poor Man Book II, Cagney & Lacey (Emmy Award, 1985), Remington Steele, Emerald Point, New York News. *Guest:* More than 50 appearances.

ARTZ, BOB

Theatre Executive. b. Spokane, WA, Aug 21, 1946. e., B.T.A. Pasadena Playhouse College of Theatre Arts. Began in 1968 as doorman, became asst. mgr. to mgr. with National General Theatre Corporation. Joined Plitt Theatres in 1978 as dist. mgr. and ad/pub. dir., West Coast. Joined General Cinema Theatres in 1986 as reg. mktg. dir., Western region. Became dir., film mktg. in 1993. National dir., Entertainment Mktg. & Operations in 1996. Dir. client svc's., Global Cinema Network, 1998. Member: Variety Club, Film Information Council, Pasadena PlayHouse Alumni & Assoc (life mem.).

ASHER, JANE

Actress. b. London, England, April 5, 1946.
PICTURES: Mandy (Crash of Silence; debut, 1952), Third Party Risk, Dance Little Lady, Adventure in the Hopfields, Charley

Moon, Greengage Summer (Loss of Innocence), The Model Murder Case, The Masque of the Red Death, Alfie, The Winter's Tale, Deep End, The Buttercup Chain, Henry VIII and His Six Wives (from the BBC series the Six Wives of Henry VIII), Runners, Success Is the Best Revenge, Dream Child, Paris By Night, Closing Numbers, Death at a Funeral.
TELEVISION: *Movies/Specials:* The Stone Tape, East Lynne, Voyage 'Round My Father, Bright Smiler, The Volunteer, Marple: The Murder at the Vicarage, A for Andromeda. *Mini-series:* Brideshead Revisited, Wish Me Luck, The Choir. *Series:* The Mistress, Good Living (as herself), Crossroads, Holby City, The Sarah Jane Adventures (parts I &II), The Palace, The Old Guys. *Guest:* More than 84 appearances.

ASHTON, JOHN
Actor. b. Springfield, MA, Feb. 22, 1948. e. USC, BA in theatre.
THEATRE: The Last Meeting of the Knights of the White Magnolia (L.A. Drama Critics Circle Award), True West (Drama-Logue Award), A Flea in Her Ear (L.A. Drama Critics Circle Award).
PICTURES: Breaking Away, Borderline, Honky Tonk Freeway, The Adventures of Buckaroo Banzai Across the 8th Dimension, Beverly Hills Cop, The Last Resort, King Kong Lives, Some Kind of Wonderful, Beverly Hills Cop II, She's Having a Baby, Midnight Run, I Want to Go Home, Curly Sue, Little Big League, Trapped in Paradise, Hidden Assassin, Fast Money, Meet the Deedles, Instinct, Avalanche, Bill's Gun Shop, Gone, Baby, Gone.
TELEVISION: *Movies:* Elvis and the Beauty Queen, A Death in California, The Deliberate Stranger, I Know My First Name is Steven, Dirty Work, Stephen King's The Tommyknockers, Little Girls in Pretty Boxes, The Day Lincoln Was Shot, Jane Doe: Til Death Do Us Part, Reign of the Gargoyles. *Mini-series:* The Rhinemann Exchange. *Series:* Dallas, Breaking Away, Hardball. *Guest:* More than 40 appearances.

ASKIN, DICK
Executive. b. Massapequa, NY. e. Bachelor's degree in economics, Rutgers College; Master's degree in communications from Univ. of Texas, where awarded the Alcoa Graduate Fellowship; M.B.A. from Fordham Univ. Began career as an account exec. at WNBC/New York, and then relocated to Los Angeles to serve as nat'l. sales mgr. for KNBC before becoming its dir. of sales. Askin then became v.p., domestic sales, for Fries Entertainment, where he subsequently was promoted to senior v.p., distribution. From Fries, he joined Samuel Goldwyn Television, and as pres., launched American Gladiators, Tales of the Crypt Keeper's Haunted House and Flipper: The New Adventures. In 1996, Askin was named pres. and CEO of Tribune Entertainment Company, the Los Angeles-based entertainment unit of Tribune Company (NYSE: TRB), which provides programming to the TV marketplace. While at Tribune, Askin oversaw the company's entire TV program development, production and distribution activities of a wide range of programming. He successfully guided the original series Gene Roddenberry's Andromeda, Gene Roddenberry's Earth Final Conflict, and others. Askin also secured distribution rights to such hits as South Park, Family Feud and American Idol Rewind-the highest rated new syndicated series to debut in the fall of 2006. In addition, Askin oversaw the renovation of over 70,000 square feet of soundstages at the historic KTLA lot in Hollywood to create Tribune Studios, the first all-digital studio lot in the United States. Askin left Tribune in May 2006 but remains active in the industry's non-profit sector. He served two terms as chairman & CEO of the Academy of Television Arts & Sciences (ATAS) until 2008, the organization responsible for the prime time Emmy Awards. Currently he serves as President and CEO the Academy of Television Arts & Sciences AFI Bd. of Trustrees. He also sits on the bd. of the ATAS Foundation and created the Runaway Production Committee that aggressively addresses the relocation of TV production from the U.S. to other countries. Additionally, he serves as a bd. member of the Hollywood Radio & Television Society (HRTS) and a Trustee of the Entertainment Industries Council (EIC), which in 2003 presented Askin with The Larry Stewart Leadership and Inspiration Award for his role in bringing EIC's annual Prism Awards to broadcast TV. He is also a trustee of the American Film Institute (AFI.)

ASNER, EDWARD
Actor. r.n. Isaac Edward Asner. b. Kansas City, MO, Nov. 15, 1929. e. U. of Chicago, where affiliated with campus acting group. Served two years with U.S. Army in France. Returned to Chicago to join Playwright's Theatre Club. Moved to NY and joined NY Shakespeare Festival, 1960 and American Shakespeare Festival, 1961. In 1961, moved to Hollywood to become active in films and tv. National pres. Screen Actors Guild, 1981-85. Involved in more than 13 documentaries, incl. Earth and the American Dream, The Long Way Home, 187: Documented. Prod. tv & feature projects through his company, Quince. Winner of numerous humanitarian awards.
THEATRE: B'way: Face of a Hero, Born Yesterday (debut, 1989). Off-B'way: Ivanov, Threepenny Opera, Legend of Lovers, The Tempest, Venice Preserved, L.A.: Orgasms.
PICTURES:The Murder Men (debut 1961), Kid Gallahad, The Slender Thread, The Satan Bug, The Venetian Affair, El Dorado, Gunn, Change of Habit, They Call Me Mister Tibbs, Halls of Anger, Do Not Throw Cushions Into The Ring, The Todd Killings, Skin Game, The Wrestler, Gus, Fort Apache-The Bronx, O'Hara's Wife, Daniel, Pinocchio and the Emperor of the Night (voice), Moon Over Parador, JFK, Happily Ever After (voice), Cat's Don't Dance (voice), Goldilocks and the Three Bears, The Fanatics, A Christmas Carol (voice), Basil, Hard Rain, The Bachelor, Above Suspicion, Perfect Game, Mars and Beyond, Bring Him Home, The Animal, Island Prey, Donzi: The Legend, Academy Boyz, The Confidence Game, The Commission, Elf, Missing Brendan, Crab Orchard, Duplicity (also co-prod.), All In, Once in a Lifetime: Just Go for It, Channels, Christmas Is Here Again (voice), Thomas Kinkade's Home for Christmas, Trim, Up (voice).
TELEVISION: *Movies:* Nearly 50 tv movie credits, incl. The Doomsday Flight, Daughter of the Mind, The House on Greenapple Road, The Old Man Who Cried Wolf, The Last Child, They Call It Murder, The Police Story, The Imposter, Death Scream, Hey I'm Alive, Life and Assassination of the Kingfish, The Gathering, The Family Man, A Small Killing, A Case of Libel, Anatomy of an Illness, Vital Signs, Kate's Secret, The Christmas Star, Cracked Up, A Friendship in Vienna, Not a Penny More Not a Penny Less, Good Cops Bad Cops, Switched at Birth, Silent Motive, Yes Virginia There Is a Santa Claus, Cruel Doubt, Gypsy, Heads, Higher Education, Gone in the Night, The Story of Santa Claus, Payback (also prod.), Common Ground, Becoming Dick, Papa Giovanni-Ioannes XXIII, The King and Queen of Moonlight Bay, Christmas Vacation 2: Cousin Eddie's Island Adventure, Out of the Woods, Lolo's Cafe, The Christmas Card (Emmy nom. 2007), Saving Our Parents (host), Generation Gap, Christmas Dreams. *Mini-series*: Rich Man Poor Man (Emmy Award, 1976, Golden Globe Award 1977), Roots (Emmy Award, 1977), Tender Is the Night, More Tales of the City. *Series:* Has appeared in 22 series, incl. Slattery's People, The Mary Tyler Moore Show (3 Emmy Awards: 1971, 1972, 1975; 2 Golden Globe Awards 1972, 1976; 3 other nom.), Lou Grant (2 Emmy Awards: 1978, 1980; 4 other nom.; 2 Golden Globe Awards, 1978, 1980; 3 other nom.), Off the Rack, The Bronx Zoo, The Trials of Rosie O'Neill (Emmy nom. 1992), Fish Police (voice), Hearts Afire, The Magic School Bus (voice), Gargoyles (voice), Thunder Alley, Spider-Man (voice), Freakazoid (voice), Bruno the Kid (voice), Batman: Ask Harriet, The Closer, Max Steel, Studio 60 on the Sunset Strip, The Boondocks (voice), W.I.T.C.H. (voice), The Weight, The Line, CSI: NY (Emmy nom. 2009 as guest). Numerous documentaries and specials. *Guest:* More than 332 appearances.

ASSANTE, ARMAND
Actor. b. New York, NY, Oct. 4, 1949. e. American Acad. of Dramatic Arts. Appeared with regional theatre groups incl. Arena Stage, DC; Long Wharf, New Haven; Actor's Theatre of Louisville.
THEATRE: *B'way:* Boccaccio, Comedians, Romeo and Juliet, Kingdoms. *Off-B'way:* Why I Went Crazy, Rubbers, The Beauty Part, Lake of the Woods, Yankees 3 Detroit 0.
PICTURES: Paradise Alley, Prophecy, Little Darlings, Private Benjamin, Love and Money, I the Jury, Unfaithfully Yours, Belizaire the Cajun, The Penitent, Animal Behavior, Q & A (Golden Globe nom. 1991), Eternity, The Marrying Man, The Mambo Kings, 1492: Conquest of Paradise, Hoffa, Fatal Instinct, Trial by Jury, Blind Justice, Judge Dredd, Striptease, Looking for an Echo, Hunt for the Devil, The Road to El Dorado (voice), After the Storm, Last Run, Federal Protection, Partners in Action, Consequence, Citizen Verdict, Dot.Kill, Mirror Wars: Reflection One, Gilgamesh, Funny Money, Soul's Midnight, Finding Rin Tin Tin, When Nietzsche Wept, California Dreaming, The Lost, American Gangster, Killer by Nature, Order of Redemption, The Man Who Came Back, Chicago Overcoat, The Bleeding, Shadows in Paradise, Killer by Nature, The Steam Experiment, Magic Man, Paradi$e, Minkow, Goat, The Return of Joe Rich.
TELEVISION: *Movies:* Human Feelings, Lady of the House, Sophia Loren-Her Own Story, Rage of Angels, Why Me?, A Deadly Business, Stranger in My Bed, Hands of a Stranger, Jack the Ripper (Emmy nom. Golden Globe nom. 1989), Passion and Paradise, Fever, Kidnapped, Gotti (Emmy Award, Golden Globe nom.1997), The Odyssey (Golden Globe nom. 1998), C.S.S. Hunley, On The Beach, After the Storm, The Commuters, Shark Swarm, The Lost. *Mini-series:* Evergreen, Napoleon and Josephine: A Love Story. *Series:* How to Survive a Marriage, The Doctors, Push Nevada, ER, NCIS: Naval Criminal Investigative Service. *Guest:* More than 45 appearances.

ASTIN, JOHN
Actor. b. Baltimore, MD, March 30, 1930. e. Washington and Jefferson Coll., Washington Drama Sch., Johns Hopkins U., grad. BA, U. of Minnesota Graduate School. Father of actors Sean and Mackenzie Astin. Theatre debut on Off-B'way stage, Threepenny Opera. B'way debut, Major Barbara. Dir., co-prod., A Sleep of Prisoners, Phoenix Theatre. Did voices in cartoons, commercials, 1955-59. Prod. & dir. short subject Prelude (Academy Award nom. 1969.
THEATRE: The Cave Dwellers, Ulysses in Nighttown, Tall Story, Lend Me a Tenor, H.M.S. Pinafore, Once Upon a Midnight.
PICTURES: That Touch of Mink, Period Of Adjustment, Move Over Darling, The Wheeler Dealers, The Spirit is Willing, Candy, Viva Max!, Bunny O'Hare, Get to Know Your Rabbit, Every Little Crook and Nanny, The Brothers O'Toole, Freaky Friday, National Lampoon's European Vacation, Body Slam, Teen Wolf Too, Return of the Killer Tomatoes, Night Life, Gremlins 2, Killer

Tomatoes Eat France, Stepmonster, The Silence of the Hams, The Frighteners, Betaville, Starship II: Rendezvous with Ramses, What the Bleep!?: Down the Rabbit Hole (doc., voice), Starship II: Rendezvous with Ramses.
TELEVISION: *Movies:* Two on a Bench, Evil Roy Slade, Skyway to Death, Only with Married Men, The Dream Makers, Operation Petticoat (also dir.), Rossetti and Ryan: Men Who Love Women (dir. only), Operation Petticoat, Halloween with the New Addams Family, Mr. Boogedy, School of Life. *Series:* I'm Dickens He's Fenster, The Addams Family (Emmy nom. 1993), The Pruitts of Southampton, McMillan and Wife, Operation Petticoat, Mary, The Attack of the Killer Tomatoes (voice), Taz-Mania (voice), The Addams Family (voice for animated series), The Adventures of Brisco County Jr., Aladdin (voice), Twisted Adventures of Felix the Cat (voice), The New Addams Family. *Guest:* More than 140 appearances.

ASTIN, SEAN

Actor. b. Santa Monica, Feb. 25, 1971. Parents are actors John Astin and Patty Duke. Brother is actor Mackenzie Astin. First acting job at 7 opposite mother in Afterschool Special, Please Don't Hit Me Mom. Dir. short films On My Honor, Kangaroo Court (Academy Award nom. 1995). On LA stage in Lone Star.
PICTURES: The Goonies (debut, 1985), White Water Summer, Like Father Like Son, Staying Together, The War of the Roses, Memphis Belle, The Willies, Toy Soldiers, Encino Man, Where the Day Takes You, Rudy, Safe Passage, The Low Life, Courage Under Fire, The Long Way Home (voice), Bulworth, Boy Meets Girl, Kimberly, Deterrence, Icebreaker, The Last Producer, The Sky is Falling, Lord of the Rings: The Fellowship of the Ring, Lord of the Rings: The Two Towers, Lord of the Rings: The Return of the King, The Riding of the Laddie, 50 First Dates, Slipstream, Elvis Has Left the Building, Thanks to Gravity, Before the Devil Knows You're Dead, Mark Twain's Greatest Adventure: 'It's a Matter of Time', Marilyn Hotchkiss' Ballroom Dancing and Charm School, Bigger Than the Sky, What Love Is, Click, The Final Season (also exec. prod.), Spirit of the Forest (voice), Forever Strong, Stay Cool, Demoted, Alvin and the Chipmunks: The Squeakquel (voice).
TELEVISION: *Movies:* Please Don't Hit Me, Mom, The Rules of Marriage, The B.R.A.T. Patrol, Harrison Bergeron, Party Wagon (voice), Hercules, American Men, The Colour of Magic. *Pilot:* Just Our Luck. *Mini-series:* Into the West. *Series:* Perversions of Science (dir.), 100 Deeds for Eddie McDowd (dir.), Jeremiah, 24, Special Agent Oso (voice). *Guest:* More than 98 appearances.

ATHERTON, WILLIAM

Actor. r.n. William Knight. b. New Haven, CT, June 30, 1947. While in high school became youngest member of Long Wharf Theatre Co. Given scholarship to Pasadena Playhouse; then switched to Carnegie Tech Sch. of Drama in 1965. In college years toured with USO prods in Europe and in stock and industrial shows. Came to NY where first prof. job was in nat'l co. of Little Murders.
THEATRE: The House of Blue Leaves, The Basic Training of Pavlo Hummel, The Sign in Sidney Brustein's Window, Suggs (Theatre World Award, Outer Circle Critics Award, Drama Desk Award), Rich and Famous, Passing Game, Happy New Year, The American Clock, Three Acts of Recognition, The Caine Mutiny Court-Martial, Child's Play, Loco Motives.
PICTURES: The New Centurions (debut, 1972), Class of '44, The Sugarland Express, The Day of the Locust, The Hindenburg, Looking for Mr. Goodbar, Ghostbusters, Number One, No Mercy, Die Hard, Die Hard 2, Grim Prairie Tales, Oscar, The Pelican Brief, Saints and Sinners, Frank and Jesse, Bio-Dome, Hoodlum, Executive Power, Mad City, Michael Kael in Katango, The Crow: Salvation, Bread and Roses, Race to Space, Who's Your Daddy, The Last Samurai, Headspace, Work, National Lampoon's Totally Baked: A Pot-U-Mentary, Towards Darkness, The Girl Next Door, The Kane Files: Life of Trial.
TELEVISION: *Movies:* House of Mirth, Tomorrow's Child, Malibu, A Fight for Jenny, Intrigue, Buried Alive, Diagnosis Murder, Chrome Soldiers, Robin Cook's Virus, Broken Trust, Raven Hawk, Introducing Dorothy Dandridge, Strokes, Aces 'N' Eights, Ghouls. *Mini-series:* Centennial, Gone But Not Forgotten. *Series:* Life. *Guest:* More than 40 appearances.

ATKINS, CHRISTOPHER

Actor. b. Rye, NY, Feb. 21, 1961. e. Dennison U., Ohio. Early modeling jobs before being hired for theatrical film debut in The Blue Lagoon (1980).
PICTURES: The Blue Lagoon (Golden Globe nom. 1981), The Pirate Movie, A Night in Heaven, Beaks, Mortuary Academy, Listen to Me, Shakma, King's Ransom, Outrage, Dracula Rising, Die Watching, Exchange Lifeguards, A Bullet Down Under, Trigger Fast, Project Shadowchaser III, It's My Party, Mutual Needs, Breaking the Silence, Beings (writer only), Deadly Delusions, The Day October Died, Civility, Stageghost, Title to Murder, The 13th Child: Legend of the Jersey Devil, Tequila Express, The Stoneman, Mending Fences, The Employee of the Month, The Color of Water, Quigley, True Legends of the West, Payback, The Unlikely's, Chinaman's Chance, Hidden, Blind Ambition, The Hard Ride, Forget Me Not, Gathering of Heroes: Legend of the Seven Swords, Stained Glass Windows, Exodus Fall, Prism, Serpent Rising, The Hard Ride.
TELEVISION: *Movies:* Child Bride of Short Creek, Secret Weapons, Fatal Charm, Miami Killer, Bandit Goes Country, Guns of Honor, Deadman's Island, Angel Flight Down, Caved In, 100 Million BC. *Series:* Dallas, Dark Realm, 29 Minutes & Counting (writer).

ATKINSON, ROWAN

Actor, Writer. b. England, Jan. 6, 1955. e. Newcastle U., Oxford.
THEATRE: Rowan Atkinson in Revue (also writer), Not in Front of an Audience, The Nerd, Rowan Atkinson at the Atkinson (also writer; NY), Mime Gala, The Sneeze.
PICTURES: The Secret Policeman's Ball (documentary, also co-s.p.),Dead on Time, Never Say Never Again, The Appointments of Dennis Jennings, The Tall Guy, The Witches, Hot Shots Part Deux, Four Weddings and a Funeral, The Lion King (voice), Mr. Bean (also exec. prod.), Black Adder Back and Forth, Maybe Baby, Rat Race, Scooby Doo, Johnny English, Love Actually, French Bean, Hairspray, Keeping Mum, Mr. Bean's Vacation (also writer).
TELEVISION: *Movies:* Peter Cook & Co., The Grand Knockout Tournament, Blackadder's Christmas Carol, Hysteria 2!, Bernard and the Genie, Full Throttle, Reflections of Mr. Bean (himself), Comic Relief 2003: The Big Hair Do. *Series:* Not the Nine O'Clock News (also writer; BAFTA Award for acting), Black Adder (also writer), Blackadder II, Blackadder the Third, Mr Bean (also writer), Blackadder Goes Forth, The Thin Blue Line, Mr. Bean: The Animated Series (voice also co-exec. prod.). *Special:* Comic Relief 2007: The Big One. *Guest:* More than 100 appearances.

ATTENBOROUGH, LORD RICHARD (SAMUEL)

Actor, Producer, Director. b. Cambridge, England, Aug. 29, 1923. e. Wyggeston Grammar Sch., Leicester; Leverhulme Scholarship to Royal Acad. of Dramatic Art, 1941 (Bancroft Medal). m. Sheila Beryl Grant Sim, 1945. Stage debut in Ah Wilderness (Palmers Green, 1941). West End debut in Awake and Sing (1942), then The Little Foxes, Brighton Rock. Joined RAF, 1943; seconded to RAF Film Unit, and appeared in training film Journey Together, 1945; demobilized, 1946. Returned to stage, 1949, in The Way Back (Home of the Brave), To Dorothy a Son, Sweet Madness, The Mousetrap (original cast: 1952-54), Double Image, The Rape of the Belt. Formed Beaver Films with Bryan Forbes, 1959; formed Allied Film Makers, 1960. Life Peer of Richmond Upon Thames; CBE 1967; Knighted 1976.
PICTURES: *Actor:* More than 70 credits, incl. In Which We Serve (debut, 1942), The Hundred Pound Window, Journey Together, Stairway to Heaven, Secret Flight, The Smugglers, Dancing With Crime, Young Scarface, Dulcimer Street, The Guinea Pig, The Lost People, Boys in Brown, Operation Disaster, Hell Is Sold Out, The Magic Box, Glory at Sea, Father's Doing Fine, Eight O'Clock Walk, The Ship That Died of Shame, Private's Progress, The Baby and the Battleship, Strange Affection, Brothers in Law, Dunkirk, Desert Patrol, The Man Upstairs, SOS Pacific, The League of Gentlemen, Jet Storm, I'm All Right Jack, Breakout, The Angry Silence (also co-prod.), All Night Long, Only Two Can Play, Trial & Error, The Great Escape, The Third Secret, Seance on a Wet Afternoon (also prod.; San Sebastian Film Fest. & Brit. Acad. Awards for Best Actor), Guns at Batasi (Brit. Acad. Award), The Flight of the Phoenix, The Sand Pebbles (Golden Globe Award), Dr. Dolittle (Golden Globe Award), Only When I Larf, The Bliss of Mrs Blossom, The Magic Christian, The Last Grenade, A Severed Head, Loot, 10 Rillington Place, Ten Little Indians, Rosebud, Brannigan, Conduct Unbecoming, Shatranj Ke Khiladi, Magic, The Human Factor, Jurassic Park, Miracle on 34th Street, Hamlet, E=MC2, The Lost World: Jurassic Park, Elizabeth. *Producer:* Whistle Down the Wind, The L-Shaped Room, The Snow Prince. *Director:* Oh! What a Lovely War (also prod.; 16 Intl. Awards incl. Golden Globe and BAFTA UN Award), Young Winston (Golden Globe), A Bridge Too Far (Evening News Best Drama Award, 1977), Magic, Gandhi (also prod.; 8 Oscars, 5 BAFTA Awards, 5 Golden Globes, DGA Award, 1982), A Chorus Line, Cry Freedom (also prod.; Berlinale Kamera, 1987; BFI Award for Tech. Achievement; Golden Globe nom. 1988), Chaplin (also prod.), Shadowlands (also prod.; BAFTA Award for Best British Film of 1993), In Love and War (also prod.), Grey Owl (also prod.), Puckoon (also writer), Closing the Ring (also prod.), The Snow Prince.
TELEVISION: *Movies: As Actor:* David Copperfield, Joseph and the Amazing Technicolor Dreamcoat, Diana: Queen of Hearts (himself), The Railway Children, *Mini-series:* Tom and Vicky (voice), Jack and the Beanstalk: The Real Story. *Guest:* More than 83 appearances.

ATTENBOROUGH, SIR DAVID

Broadcaster. b. London, England, May 8, 1926. Brother of Lord Richard Attenborough. e. Wyggeston Sch., Leicester; Clare Coll., Cambridge. Early career, editor in educational publishing house. Ent. BBC-TV, 1952. Prod. Zoo Quest series, Travellers Tales, Eastward with Attenborough, The Tribal Eye, Life on Earth. Controller BBC-2, 1965-68; Dir. of Prog. BBC-TV, 1969-72. Received Desmond Davis Award, 1970 and a Fellowship, 1979.
PICTURES: A Zed and Two Noughts (narrator), Deep Blue (writer).
TELEVISION: Narrator &/or actor in several programs about nature &/or travel, incl. The Living Planet (Emmy nom. 1985), Wilderness Men, Ultimate Wild Paradises: The Top Ten

Destinations, The Blue Planet, Cities of the Wild (also writer), Survival Island (also writer), The Private Life of Plants (Emmy nom. 1996), The Natural World, Life in Cold Blood (doc., writer) and several others.

AUBERJONOIS, RENE

Actor. b. New York, NY, June 1, 1940. e. attended Carnegie Mellon U.
THEATRE: Dark of the Moon, Beyond the Fringe, Tartuffe, King Lear, Fire, Julius Caesar, Charley's Aunt, Coco (Tony Award, 1970), Tricks, The Ruling Class, Twelfth Night, The Good Doctor (Tony nom.), Break a Leg, The New York Idea, Every Good Boy Deserves Favor, Richard III, The Misanthrope, Flea in Her Ear, Big River (Tony nom.), Metamorphosis, City of Angels (Tony nom.).
PICTURES: Lilith (debut, 1964), Petulia, M*A*S*H*, Brewster McCloud, McCabe and Mrs. Miller, Pete 'n Tillie, Images, Hindenberg, The Big Bus, King Kong, Eyes of Laura Mars, Where the Buffalo Roam, The Last Unicorn (voice), 3:15, Walker, Police Academy 5: Assignment Miami Beach, My Best Friend is a Vampire, The Little Mermaid (voice), The Feud, The Player (himself), Little Nemo (voice), The Ballad of Little Jo, Batman Forever, Cats Don't Dance (voice), Los Locos, Inspector Gadget, The Patriot, Burning Down the House, We All Fall Down, The Princess Diaries, Snide and Prejudice, Eulogy.
TELEVISION: *Movies:* Once Upoon A Dead Man, The Birdmen, Shirts/Skins, King Lear, Panache, Kate Loves a Mystery, The Wild Wild West Revisited, Once Upon A Midnight Dreary, More Wild Wild West, The Kid from Nowhere, The Christmas Star, Longarm, Scooby Doo and the Ghoul School (voice), A Connecticut Yankee in King Arthur's Court, Absolute Strangers, Ned Blessing: The True Story of My Life, Wild Card, Sally Hemmings: An American Scandal, Gepetto, Hornswiggle. *Mini-series:* The Rhineman Exchange, Dark Secret of Harvest Home, *Series:* Work on 23 series, many featuring voice work for animated programs incl. Xyber 9: New Dawn, House of Mouse, The Legend of Tarzan, Benson (actor, Emmy nom. 1984), Star Trek: Deep Space Nine (dir.), Xiaolin Showdown, The Practice (Emmy nom. 2001), Boston Legal. *Specials*: Faerie Tale Theatre (The Frog Prince, Sleeping Beauty), King Lear, Legend of Sleepy Hollow, Fort Necessity, Incident at Vichy, The Booth, The Cask of Amontillado, Ashenden (BBC), The Lost Language of Cranes (BBC). *Guest:* More than 148 appearances.

AUDRAN, STEPHANE

Actress. b. Versailles, France, Nov. 8, 1938. r.n. Collette Suzanne Dacheville. Former wife of French star Jean-Louis Trintignant and director Claude Chabrol.
PICTURES: Has appeared in 84 pictures, incl. Les Cousins (debut under direction of Chabrol, 1959), Les Bonnes Femmes, Bluebeard, The Third Lover, Six in Paris, The Champagne Murders, Les Biches, La Femme Infidele, The Lady in the Car, Le Boucher, Without Apparent Motive, La Rupture, Just Before Nightfall, The Discreet Charm of the Bourgeoisie, Blood Wedding, The Devil's Advocate, Le Cri de Couer, Vincent Francois Paul and the Others, The Black Bird (U.S. film debut), Ten Little Indians, The Silver Bears, Eagle's Wing, The Big Red One, Coup de Torchon, La Cage aux Folles III: The Wedding, Cop au Vin, Babette's Feast, Seasons of Pleasure, Faceless, Body-To-Body, Sons, Manika: The Girl Who Lived Twice, Quiet Days in Clichy, Mass in C Minor, Betty, Poulet au Vinaigre, Au Petit Marguery, Arlette, Maximum Risk, Arlette, Madeline, Belle Maman, Lulu Kreutz's Picnic, Speaking of Bunuel, J'a Faim!!!, My Wife's Name Is Maurice, The Girl from Monaco.
TELEVISION: *Movies:* Tatort, Les Affinites electives, La Marseillaise, Poor Little Rich Girl: The Barbara Hutton Story, Champagne Charlie, Weep No More My Lady, Petit, Un printemps de chien, Sissi, l'impératrice rebelle. *Mini-series:* Orient-Express, Brideshead Revisited, The Sun also Rises, Mistral's Daughter, La Bicyclette bleu, La Battante, 3 femmes... un soir d'été. *Series:* TECX.

AUGUST, BILLE

Director. b. Brede, Denmark, Nov. 9, 1948. e. trained in advertising photography, Danish Film School, grad. 1971, cinematography. As cinematographer shot: Christiania, Homeward in the Night, Man kan inte valdtas (Men Can't Be Raped), Karleken, The Grass is Singing. Became dir. 1978 with short Kim G. and dramas for Danish TV. Won Norway's Amanda Award for Lifetime Achievement in 1993.
PICTURES: Honning Maane (also sp.), Zappa (also s.p.), Buster's World, Twist and Shout (also s.p.), Pelle the Conquerer (also s.p.), The Best Intentions (Cannes Film Festival Palm d'Or Award, 1992), The House of the Spirits (also s.p.), Jerusalem (also s.p.), Smilla's Sense of Snow, Les Miserables, A Song for Martin, Return to Sender, Without Apparent Motive, Burden of Desire, Goodbye Bafana, To Each His Cinema (segment dir.).
TELEVISION: *Movies:* Maj, Detaljer (also writer), Mördare! Mördare! (cinematographer). *Mini-series:* Den Goda viljan, Busters verden.

AUTEUIL, DANIEL

Actor. b. Algeria, Jan. 24, 1950. Parents were lyric opera singers in roving troupe. Lived in Avignon. Performed in Amer. prod. in Paris of Godspell. Then did musical comedy for 2 years. Provided voice of baby for French print of U.S. film Look Who's Talking.
PICTURES: L'Aggression, Attention Les Yeaux, La Nuit de Saint-Germain des Pres, Monsieuer Papa, L'Amour Viole (Rape of Love), Heroes Are Not Wet Behind the Ears, Us Two, Les Sous-Doues, The Woman Banker, Clara et les Chic Types, Men Prefer Fat Girls, Pour 100 Briques t'as Plus Rien Maintentant, Que les Gros Salaires Levent le Doigt!!!, L'Indic, P'tit Con, The Beast, L'Arbalete, Palace, L'Amour en Douce, Jean de Florette, Manon of the Spring, Romuald and Juliette, A Few Days With Me, My Life is Hell, L'Elegant Criminel, Un Coeur en Hiver (A Heart in Winter), Ma Saison Preferee (My Favorite Season), Queen Margot, The Separation, Un Femme Francais, According to Pereira, The Eighth Day (Best actor, Cannes 1996), Thieves, Death in Therapy, Lucie Aubrac, On Guard, The Wrong Blonde, An Interesting State, The Lost Son, The Widow of Saint-Pierre, Sade, Le Placard, Vajont, L'Adversaire, Small Cuts, Un reste, l'autre part, L'I, Peindre ou faire l'amour, Hidden, N - Napoléon, La Doublure, L' Entente cordiale, Mon meilleur ami, L' Invité, Dialogue avec mon jardinier, Le Deuxième souffle, MR 73, 15 ans et demi, Je l'aimais, A Boy and His Shoe.

AVERSANO, SCOTT

Executive, Producer. b. 1970. e. graduate, Brown Univ.; M.A. in English Literature from Univ. of Mich. Began career in ent. industry at Sid Ganis' Out of the Blue Entertainment in 1996. From 1997-1999, Aversano was dir. of development at Paramount Pictures. While there executive on 12 films and 75 development projects, including the films Wonder Boys, South Park & Runaway Bride. Aversano then spent more than seven years with Scott Rudin Productions, most recently as pres. of production. Aversano became an independent producer on Paramount Pictures lot and in Aug. 2006, Paramount named Aversano president of MTV Films and Nick Films upon elevating the production units to full film labels. He has responsibility for film development, production and acquisitions for the two film labels.
PICTURES: *Producer:* Orange County (2002), Changing Lanes (co-prod.), Lemony Snicket's A Series of Unfortunate Events (co-prod.), Failure to Launch, Five Killers, The Last Airbender. *Executive prod.:* The School of Rock, The Manchurian Candidate, Team America: World Police.
TELEVISION: *Movie:* Ghosts/Aliens.

AVERY, KELLEY

Executive. e. B.A., UCLA. Avery has more than 21 years in the entertainment industry, with 12 years at The Walt Disney Company, eight with DreamWorks and joining Paramount Worldwide Home Entertainment as its president in Feb. 2006. Her focus had been integrating the DreamWorks and Paramount Pictures two studios' homevideo operations while gearing up its high-definition disc initiatives until she resigned in May 2009.

AVILDSEN, JOHN G.

Director, Cinematographer, Editor. b. Chicago, IL, Dec. 21, 1935. e. NYU. After service in Army made film with friend, Greenwich Village Story, then joined ad agency to write, direct, photograph & edit industrial films. Entered motion picture industry as ass't cameraman on Below the Hill, followed with prod. mgr. job on two Italian filmsmade in U.S. Afterwards, made first theatrical short, Smiles. Asst. dir., Black Like Me; prod. mgr., Mickey One, Una Moglie Americana; 2nd unit dir., Hurry Sundown. Produced, photographed & edited a short, Light—Sound—Diffuse. Returned to industry to make industrial films for ad agencies before resuming theatrical career.
PICTURES: *Dir./photo./edit.:* Turn on to Love (debut), Out of It (assoc. prod., dir. of photog.), Sweet Dreams (aka Okay, Bill), Guess What We Learned in School Today?, Joe, Cry Uncle, The Stoolie, Save the Tiger, W. W. and the Dixie Dancekings, Foreplay, Rocky (Academy Award, DGA Award, Golden Globe nom. 1977), Slow Dancing in the Big City (also prod.), The Formula, Neighbors (also supv. edit.), Traveling Hopefully (documentary; Academy Award nom. 1983), A Night in Heaven, The Karate Kid, The Karate Kid: Part II, Happy New Year, For Keeps, Lean On Me (also exec. prod.), The Karate Kid Part III (also co-edit.), Rocky V (also co-edit.), The Power of One, Steal This Video Abbie Hoffman (doc.), 8 Seconds, Save The Everglades (doc.), A Fine and Private Place, Coyote Moon, Dancing Into the Future (video doc.), Stano.
TELEVISION: From No House to Options House (2 On the Town, Emmy Award) *Series:* Murder Ink.

AVIV, OREN

Executive, Writer, Producer. b. Sept. 15, 1961. e. Columbia University, B.A. in English & history. Entered entertainment industry as creative director for Grey Entertainment in New York City. Later, director of special projects for CapCities/ABC, where Aviv was responsible for TV branding spots for hit ABC series, such as "Roseanne," "Twin Peaks," and "thirtysomething." Moved to Los Angeles in 1988 and began his long-time association with The Walt Disney Company in 1991 as v.p. creative services. Promoted to senior v.p., marketing & creative advertising in 1997. Aviv's work has won such prestigious advertising awards such as Clios, Beldings and numerous Key Art Awards. Aviv was named president, Buena Vista Pictures Marketing in November 2000. He was promoted in April 2005 to president of marketing and chief creative officer of The Walt Disney Studios. He has designed and guided the marketing campaigns for such hit films as "Pirates of the Caribbean: Dead Man's Chest" (shattering all industry

records with a opening weekend box office gross of over $135 million), "The Chronicles of Narnia: The Lion, The Witch and The Wardrobe," "Chicken Little," "The Incredibles," "National Treasure," "The Village," "Pirates of the Caribbean: The Curse of the Black Pearl," "Finding Nemo," among others. On the film production side, Aviv was executive producer of Disney's "National Treasure." Based on his idea, for which he shared "Story By" credit, the film grossed nearly $350 million dollars in worldwide box office. He received the same credits for the Disney comedy "Rocket Man" in 1995. In July 2006, Aviv was promoted to his current position, president of production, Walt Disney Pictures, where he oversees live-action development and film production.
PICTURES: *Exec. prod., Writer:* RocketMan, National Treasure, National Treasure: Book of Secrets, The Sorcerer's Apprentice (exec. prod.).

AVNET, JON
Producer, Director. b. Brooklyn, NY, Nov. 17, 1949. e. U. of PA, Sarah Lawrence Coll. Began career as director of off-B'way prods. Produced and directed low-budget film, Confusion's Circle, which brought a directing fellowship at American Film Institute. Joined Weintraub/Heller Prods. as assoc. prod., where met Steve Tisch, with whom formed Tisch/Avnet Prods. Formed Avnet/Kerner Co., 1986. Currently is with Brooklyn Films.
PICTURES: Checkered Flag or Crash (assoc. prod.), Outlaw Blues (assoc. prod.). *Producer:* Coast to Coast, Risky Business, Deal of the Century (exec. prod.), Less Than Zero, Tango & Cash, Men Don't Leave, Funny About Love, Fried Green Tomatoes (also dir., co-s.p.), The Mighty Ducks, The Mighty Ducks II, The Mighty Ducks III, The Three Musketeers (co-exec. prod.), When a Man Loves a Woman, The War (also dir.), Miami Rhapsody (co-exec. prod.), Up Close and Personal (also dir.), Red Corner (also. dir.), George of the Jungle, Inspector Gadget (exec. prod.) Steal This Move (exec. prod.), Sky Captain and the World of Tomorrow, Land of the Blind, 88 Minutes (also dir.), Righteous Kill (also dir.), Red Bird (also dir.).
TELEVISION: *Movies/Producer:* No Other Love, Homeward Bound, Prime Suspect, Something So Right, Silence of the Heart, Calendar Girl Murders, Call to Glory (pilot and series), The Burning Bed (Emmy nom. 1985), In Love and War (also exec. prod.), Between Two Women (also dir., co-s.p.), My Last Love, Uprising (also writer, dir., DGA nom. 2002), Sixty Minute Man (dir. only). *Exec. Prod.:* Side By Side, My First Love, Breaking Point, Heatwave, Backfield in Motion, The Nightman, The Switch, Naomi and Wynona: Love Can Build a Bridge, Poodle Springs, Mama Flora's Family, My Last Love, A House Divided, Bunker Hill. *Mini-series:* Parting the Waters, Starter Wife (dir., Emmy nom. 2007, DGA nom. 2008). *Series:* Call to Glory, Boomtown.

AXELROD, JONATHAN
Writer, Producer. b. New York, NY, July 9, 1952. Stepson of writer George Axelrod. Started as on-set "gofer" before writing screenplays. V.p. primetime drama dev., ABC Entertainment,1978-80; v.p. exec. dir. in charge dev. ABC Ent., 1980-82. Exec. v.p., Columbia Pictures TV, 1983-85. Pres. New World Pictures, 1985-87. Co-owner, Camden Artists, 1987-. Exec. v.p. Ventura Entertainment Group, 1989. Pres. & CEO Producers Entertainment Group, 1990-93. Formed Axelrod Woddoes Productions, 1994. Formed production firm Axelrod/Edwards Company.
PICTURES: Every Little Crook and Nanny (writer).
TELEVISION: *Exec. Prod.:* Dave's World, Can't Hurry Love, A Day With, Manhattan Match, Late Bloomer, Brother's Keeper, The Price She Paid, Against the Wall (documentary), Movie Stars, Some of My Best Friends, Sex, Love & Secrets.

AYKROYD, DAN
Actor, Writer. b. Ottawa, Canada, July 1, 1952. m. actress Donna Dixon. Member of Toronto Co. of Second City Theater. Worked as mgr. of Club 505, after-hours Toronto nightclub 1970-73. Performed and recorded (Briefcase Full of Blues, Made in America) with John Belushi as the Blues Brothers. Co-owner, Hard Rock Cafe.
PICTURES: Has appeared in nearly 60 pictures since debut in 1977 with Love at First Sight (also co-s.p.). Pictures incl. Mr. Mike's Mondo Video, 1941, The Blues Brothers (also co-s.p.), Neighbors, Trading Places, Twilight Zone—The Movie, Doctor Detroit, ndiana Jones and the Temple of Doom (cameo), Ghostbusters (also co-s.p.) It Came From Hollywood, Nothing Lasts Forever, Into the Night, Spies Like Us (also co-s.p.), Dragnet (also co-s.p.), The Couch Trip, The Great Outdoors, Caddyshack II, My Stepmother Is an Alien, Ghostbusters II (also co-s.p.), Driving Miss Daisy (Academy Award nom. 1990), Loose Cannons, Nothing But Trouble (also dir., s.p.), Masters of Menace, My Girl, This Is My Life, Sneakers, Chaplin, Coneheads (also co-s.p.), My Girl 2, North, Exit to Eden, Tommy Boy, Casper (cameo), The Random Factor (voice), Rainbow, Sgt. Bilko, Getting Away With Murder, Celtic Pride, Feeling Minnesota, My Fellow Americans, Grosse Pointe Blank, Susan's Plan, Antz (voice), Blues Brothers 2000 (also prod., s.p.), The House of Mirth, Stardom, Loser, On the Nose, Hitting the Wall, Pearl Harbor, Evolution, The Curse of the Jade Scorpion, The Devil and Daniel Webster, Crossroads, Unconditional Love, Bright Young Things, 50 First Dates, Christmas with the Kranks, I Now Pronounce You Chuck and Larry, War, Inc., Yogi Bear (voice), Dorothy of OZ (voice).
TELEVISION: *Movies:* Things We Did Last Summer, All You Need Is Cash, The Arrow, Earth vs. the Spider. *Series:* Coming Up Rosie (Canada), Saturday Night Live 1975-79 (writer and performer; Emmy Award for writing: 1977, 4 other nom.). Steve Martin's Best Show Ever (performer, writer), Soul Man (also sup. prod.), Extreme Ghostbusters (writer only), According to Jim. *Guest:* More than 160 appearances.

AZARIA, HANK
Actor. b. Forest Hills, NY, April 25, 1964. e. Tufts Univ.
PICTURES: Pretty Woman, Quiz Show, Now and Then, Heat, The Birdcage (Screen Actors Guild Award, outstanding performance by a Cast, 1997), Grosse Pointe Blank, Anastasia (voice), Mystery Alaska, Homegrown, Celebrity, Godzilla, Great Expectations, The Cradle Will Rock, Mystery Men, Cyber World (voice), America's Sweethearts, Bark, Shattered Glass, Along Came Polly, Dodgeball: A True Underdog Story, Eulogy, The Simpsons Movie (voices), Run, Fat Boy, Run, Night at the Museum 2: Battle of the Smithsonian, Year One, Love and Other Drugs.
TELEVISION: *Movies:* Tuesdays With Morrie (Emmy Award 2000), Bartok the Magnificent, Cool Blue, Fail Safe, Uprising. *Series*: The Simpsons (voice, 3 Emmy Awards, 1998, 2001, 2003, 1 other nom.), Herman's Head, If Not for You, Mad About You, Stressed Eric (voice), The Hank Azaria Show, Imagine That, Friends, ! Huff (also prod., Emmy nom. 2005). *Guest:* More than 91 appearances.

B

BABENCO, HECTOR
Director. b. Buenos Aires, Argentina, Feb. 7, 1946. Early years spent in Mar del Plata. Left home at 17 and traveled throughout Europe for 8 years working as a writer, house-painter, salesman, and, in Rome, as an extra at Cinecitta. Moved to Sao Paulo, Brazil where he made several short documentaries, before turning to features in 1975.
PICTURES: Rei Da Noite (King of the Night; debut, 1975), Lucio lavio—Passageiro da Agonia, Pixote (also co-s.p.), Kiss of the pider Woman (Academy Award nom. 1986), Ironweed, Besame Mucho (prod.), At Play in the Fields of the Lord (also co-s.p.), Foolish Heart (also prod. and s.p.), The Venice Project (additional dir.), Before Night Falls (acting only), Carandiru.

BACALL, LAUREN
Actress. r.n. Betty Joan Perske. b. New York, NY, Sept. 16, 1924. e. American Acad. Dram. Arts. Was m. late Jason Robards, late Humphrey Bogart. *Autobiographies:* By Myself (1979), Now (1994). Won the B. DeMille Award 1993. Received Honorary Academy Award in recognition of her central place in the Golden Age of motion pictures, 2009.
THEATRE: *B'way:* Cactus Flower, Goodbye Charlie, Applause (Tony Award), Woman of the Year (Tony Award), Waiting in the Wings. Foreign: Sweet Bird of Youth, Woman of the Year, Waiting in the Wings. Tour: Wonderful Town.
PICTURES: To Have and Have Not (debut, 1944), Two Guys From Milwaukee (cameo), Confidential Agent, The Big Sleep, Dark Passage, Key Largo, Young Man With a Horn, Bright Leaf, How to Marry a Millionaire, A Woman's World, Cobweb, Blood Alley, Written on the Wind, Designing Woman, Gift of Love, Flame Over India, Shock Treatment, Sex and the Single Girl, Harper, Murder on the Orient Express, The Shootist, Health, The Fan, Appointment With Death, Mr. North, Innocent Victim, Misery, A Star for Two, All I Want for Christmas, Le Jour et La Nuit, Ready to Wear (Pret-a-Porter), The Mirror Has Two Faces (Academy Award nom. Golden Globe Award, 1997; Screen Actors Guild Award), My Fellow Americans, Day and Night, Madeline: Lost in Paris (voice), Diamonds, The Venice Project, Presence of Mind, Dogville, The Limit, Birth, Firedog (voice), Manderlay, The Walker, Wide Blue Yonder, Carmel, Firedog (voice).
TELEVISION: *Movies:* Blithe Spirit, Applause (Emmy nom. 1973), Perfect Gentlemen, Dinner at Eight, A Little Piece of Sunshine (BBC), The Portrait, The Parallax Garden, From the Mixed Up Files of Mrs. Basil E. Frankweiler. *Mini-series:* Too Rich: The Secret Life of Doris Duke. *Series:* Great Performances (host), The Rockford Files (Emmy nom. 1980).*Special:* Bacall on Bogart (Emmy nom. 1988). *Guest:* More than 181 appearances.

BACHARACH, BURT
Composer, Conductor, Arranger, Actor. b. Kansas City, MO, May 12, 1928. e. McGraw U., Mannes Sch. of Music, Music Acad. of the West. Studied with composers Darius Milhaud, Henry Cowell, and Bohuslav Martinu. Conducted for Marlene Dietrich, Vic Damone. As a performer albums include: Burt Bacharach; Futures, Man! His Songs. Book: The Bacharach-David Song Book (1978).
THEATRE: Promises Promises (Tony Award, 1969).
PICTURES: *Composer, Soundtrack:* Lizzie, The Sad Sack, The

Blob, Country Music Holiday, Love in a Goldfish Bowl, Wives and Lovers, Who's Been Sleeping in My Bed?, Send Me No Flowers, A House Is Not a Home, What's New Pussycat?, Alfie, Made in Paris, After the Fox, Promise Her Anything, Casino Royale, The April Fools, Butch Cassidy and the Sundance Kid (2 Acad. Awards: Best Original Score & Best Song: Raindrops Keep Fallin' on My Head; 1970), Something Big, Lost Horizon, Together?, Arthur (Academy Award for Best Song: Arthur's Theme; 1982), Night Shift, Best Defense, Tough Guys, Baby Boom, Arthur 2 on the Rocks, Love Hurts, Grace of My Heart, Austin Powers—International Man of Mystery (actor only), Austin Powers: The Spy Who Shagged Me (actor only), Isn't She Great, Bandits, Austin Powers in Goldmember, Catch Me If You Can, Two Weeks Notice, Camp, The In-Laws, In the Cut, Spider-Man 2, Bridget Jones: The Edge of Reason, A West Texas Children's Story, Alfie, MirrorMask, The Hitchhiker's Guide to the Galaxy, Imagine Me & You, Rent, Date Movie, Failure to Launch, Clerks II, Bobby, Running with Scissors, Flushed Away, I Think I Love My Wife, Grindhouse, Perfect Stranger, The Simpsons Movie, Telstar: The Joe Meek Story, Not Easily Broken.
TELEVISION: *Series:* Mont-Joye, Any Day Now. Many songs used in soundtracks. *Guest:* More than 73 appearances.

BACON, KEVIN
Actor. b. Philadelphia, PA, July 8, 1958. m. actress Kyra Sedgwick. Studied at Manning St. Actor's Theatre. Apprentice at Circle-in-the-Square in N.Y. B'way debut in Slab Boys with Sean Penn. Narrated short film, A Little Vicious.
THEATRE: *B'way:* Slab Boys. *Off-B'way:* Getting Out (debut), Album, Forty Deuce (Obie Award), Poor Little Lambs, Flux, Men Without Dates, The Author's Voice, Loot, Road, Spike Heels, An Almost Holy Picture.
PICTURES: National Lampoon's Animal House (debut, 1978), Starting Over, Hero at Large, Friday the 13th, Only When I Laugh, Forty Deuce, Diner, Enormous Changes at the Last Minute, Footloose, Quicksilver, White Water Summer, Planes Trains and Automobiles, She's Having a Baby, End of the Line, Criminal Law, The Big Picture, Tremors, Flatliners, Queens Logic, He Said/She Said, Pyrates, JFK, A Few Good Men, The Air Up There, The River Wild (Golden Globe nom. 1995), Murder in the First, Apollo 13, Balto (voice), Sleepers, Picture Perfect, Telling Lies in America, Elizabeth Jane, Digging to China, Wild Things (also exec. prod.), My Dog Skip, Stir of Echoes, Hollow Man, Novocaine, We Married Margo, Trapped, Dolan's Cadillac, Mystic River, In the Cut, Cavedweller, Loverboy, Beauty Shop, Where the Truth Lies, The Air I Breathe, The 1 Second Film (documentary, prod.), Saving Angelo, Death Sentence, Black Water Transit, Rails & Ties, Frost/Nixon, Taking Chance, My One and Only, Super.
TELEVISION: *Movies:* The Gift, The Demon Murder Case, The Tender Age (The Little Sister), Lemon Sky, Losing Chase (dir. only), Loverboy, Cavedweller, Taking Chance (Emmy nom. 2009, Golden Globe nom. 2010). *Specials:* Mr. Roberts. *Series:* Search for Tomorrow, The Guiding Light, The Closer (dir. only). *Guest:* More than 128 appearances.

BADALAMENTI, ANGELO
Composer, Orchestrator. b. New York, NY, March 22, 1937. Received Lifetime Achievement Award, 2008, from World Soundtrack Awards.
PICTURES: Gordon's War (debut 1973), Law and Disorder, Blue Velvet, Weeds, A Nightmare on Elm Street 3: Dream Warriors, Tough Guys Don't Dance, Wait Until Spring Bandini, Parents, National Lampoon's Christmas Vacation, Cousins, The Comfort of Strangers, Wild at Heart, Twin Peaks: Fire Walk with Me, Naked in New York, The City of Lost Children, The Blood Oranges, Lost Highway, Story of a Bad Boy, Arlington Road, The Straight Story (Golden Globe nom., best orig. score, 2000), Holy Smoke, Forever Mine, The Beach, A Piece of Eden, Mulholland Drive (Golden Globe nom. for best orig. score, 2002), Cet amour-la, Suspended Animation, Secretary, The Adversary Mysteries of Love, Autofocus, Cabin Fever, Rabbits, Resistance, The Company, A Very Long Engagement, Dark Water, Inland Empire, Take the Lead (soundtrack writer), The Wicker Man, The Wait, Secrets of Love, A Woman.
TELEVISION: *Movies/Specials:* Industrial Symphony No. 1: The Dream of the Broken Hearted, The Last Don, Lathe of Heaven, Undefeated, Frankenstein. *Mini-series:* Les Liaisons dangereuses. *Series:* Twin Peaks (3 Emmy nom.), On the Air, Hotel Room, Inside the Actors Studio (main theme also episodes), Cracker, Profiler (main title theme), Parashat Ha-Shavua. *Documentaries:* The Valo Man, Fortid til salg (series).

BADER, DIEDRICH
Actor. b. Alexandria, VA, Dec. 24, 1966.
PICTURES: The Beverly Hillbillies (debut 1993), Teresa's Tattoo, Office Space, Certain Guys, Couple Days...A Period Piece, Recess: School's Out (voice), Jay and Silent Bob Strike Back, Ice Age (voice), The Country Bears, Evil Alien Conquerors, Dead & Breakfast, Dinotopia: Curse of the Ruby Sunstone (voice), Miss Congeniality 2: Armed and Fabulous, Cook-Off!, Surf's Up (voice), Balls of Fury, Meet the Spartans, Bolt (voice), Calvin Marshall.
TELEVISION: *Movies:* Desert Rats, The Preppie Murder, The Assassination File, Olive the Other Reindeer (voice), Rock & Roll Back to School Special, Kim Possible: So the Drama (voice), Mr. Nice Guy, Skip Tracer. *Series:* Danger Theatre, Kim Possible, The Drew Carey Show, Disney's Hercules (voice), Baby Blues (voice), Buzz Lightyear of Star Command (voice), The Zeta Project (voice), Lloyd in Space (voice), Center of the Universe, The Grim Adventures of Billy & Mandy (voice), Mr. Nice Guy, The Secret Saturdays, Batman: The Brave and the Bold. *Guest:* More than 85 appearances.

BADER, JEFFREY D.
Executive. e. Graduated with honors, Williams College in Williamstown, MA; Master of Arts degree with distinction from the Annenberg School of Communications at the Univ. of Southern California. Bader held senior research positions at the MTM Distribution Group and at NBC before joining ABC in 1988 as supervisor, audience analysis. He became mgr., audience and program research, in 1989; mgr., program planning and scheduling, in 1991; director in 1992; executive director in 1994; v.p., current series programming, in 1995; v.p., program planning and scheduling, in 1996; and senior v.p., program planning and scheduling, in 1998. In Sept. 2000, Bader became executive v.p., ABC Entertainment. He was named to his current position in June 2009. Today, as executive v.p., planning, scheduling and distribution, ABC Entertainment Group, Bader continues as ABC Entertainment's senior executive in charge of primetime and late-night program planning and scheduling. He is also responsible for global programming, distribution and windowing strategies for all ABC Entertainment Group programs across all platforms, both domestic and international.

BADHAM, JOHN
Director, Producer. b. Luton, England, Aug. 25, 1939. Raised in Alabama. e. Yale U., B.A.; Yale Drama School, M.F.A. Sister is actress Mary Badham. Landed first job at Universal Studio mailroom; later was Universal tour guide, a casting dir. and assoc. prod. to William Sackheim. Twice nominated for Emmy Awards for TV movies. Recipient of George Pal Award.
PICTURES: The Bingo Long Traveling All-Stars and Motor Kings (debut 1976), Saturday Night Fever, Dracula (Best Horror Film award, Science Fiction/Fantasy Academy), Whose Life Is It Anyway? (San Rafael Grand Prize), Blue Thunder, War Games (Best Directing award, Science Fiction/Fantasy Academy), American Flyers, Short Circuit, Stakeout (also exec. prod.), Disorganized Crime (exec. prod. only), Bird on a Wire, The Hard Way, Point of No Return, Dragon: The Bruce Lee Story (Exec. prod. only), Another Stakeout (also exec. prod.), Drop Zone (also exec. prod.), Nick of Time (also prod.), Incognito, Floating Away, Ocean Warrior.
TELEVISION: *Movies:* Night Gallery (assoc. prod. only), Neon Ceiling (assoc. prod. only), The Impatient Heart, Isn't It Shocking?, The Law (Emmy nom. 1975), The Gun, Reflections of Murder, The Godchild, The Keegans, Relentless: Mind of a Killer (co-exec. prod. only), Rebound: The Legend of Earl "The Goat" Manigault (exec. prod. only), The Jack Bull, The Last Debate, My Brother's Keeper, Obsessed, Footsteps, Evel Knievel. *Series episodes:* The Bold Ones: The Senator (also assoc. prod., Emmy nom. 1971), Night Gallery, Streets of San Francisco, The Doctors, Owen Marshall - Counsellor at Law, Sunshine, Nichols, Cannon, Sarge, The Sixth Sense, Cool Million, Police Story, The Shield, many more.

BAER, AMY
Executive. Entered industry in 1988 as an assistant to the late Jay Moloney at talent agency CAA. She moved to become a development executive with the Guber-Peters Entertainment Co. and helped develop the films Jumanji and Single White Female. From 1992-1997, Baer worked at TriStar Pictures. Since 1998, Baer was the executive v.p. of production at Columbia Pictures, a Sony Pictures Entertainment co. During her tenure at Columbia and other Sony Pictures Entertainment companies, the movies she supervised have grossed more than $1.8 billion in worldwide box office. In Sept. 2007, Baer became the president and CEO of CBS Corporation's new film unit, CBS Films. She reports to Les Moonves, pres & CEO of CBS Corporation. CBS Films plans to develop and produce four to six movies a year, spanning all genres with production budgets up to $50 million per film. The films will be released domestically through a U.S. theatrical distribution unit to be established within CBS Films.

BAILEY, JOHN
Cinematographer. b. Moberly, MO, Aug. 10, 1942. m. film editor Carol Littleton. e. U. of Santa Clara, Loyola U., U.S.C., U. of Vienna. Lecturer, American Film Institute, 1982, 1984, 1994. Received President's Award from the Society of Camera Operators, 2001.
PICTURES: Premonition, End of August, Legacy, The Mafu Cage (visual consult.), Boulevard Nights, Winter Kills (add. photog.), American Gigolo, Ordinary People, Honky Tonk Freeway, Continental Divide, Cat People, That Championship Season, Without a Trace, The Big Chill, Racing With the Moon, The Pope of Greenwich Village, Mishima: A Life In Four Chapters (Cannes Film Fest. Award, best artistic contrib., 1985), Silverado, Crossroads, Brighton Beach Memoirs, Light of Day, Swimming to Cambodia, Tough Guys Don't Dance (visual consult.), Vibes, The Accidental Tourist, My Blue Heaven, The Search for Signs of

Intelligent Life in the Universe (also dir.), A Brief History of Time, Groundhog Day, In the Line of Fire, China Moon (dir. only), Nobody's Fool, Mariette in Ecstasy (dir. only), Extreme Measures, As Good As It Gets, Living Out Loud, Forever Mine, The Out-of-Towners, For Love of the Game, Michael Jordan to the Max, Via Dolorosa, Anti-Trust, The Anniversary Party, N'Sync: Bigger Than Life, The Kid Stays in the Picture, The Divine Secrets of the Ya-Ya Sisterhood, Naqoyqatsi, The Fig Rig, How to Lose a Guy in 10 Days, Incident at Loch Ness, The Sisterhood of the Traveling Pants, Must Love Dogs, The Producers, The Architect, The Death and Life of Bobby Z, 10 Tricks, License to Wed, Brief Interviews with Hideous Men, Over Her Dead Body, He's Just Not That Into You, Mad Money, When in Rome, Love Don't Let Me Down, Ramona and Beezus.
TELEVISION: *Movies:* Forever (camera op.), The Initiation of Sarah (camera op.), Battered, City in Fear, Time Flies When You're Alive, Passion, Always Outnumbered, Searching for Michael Cimino (documentary).

BAIO, SCOTT
Actor. b. New York, NY, Sept. 22, 1961. Started career at 9 doing commercials and voiceovers.
PICTURES: Bugsy Malone (debut 1976), Skatetown USA, Foxes, Zapped!, I Love New York, Detonator, Very Mean Men, The Bread My Sweet, Face Value, Face to Face (also s.p.), Dumb Luck, SuperBabies: Baby Geniuses 2, Life in the Fastlane, Devils Inside.
TELEVISION: *Movies:* Luke Was There, The Boy Who Drank Too Much, Senior Trip, Stoned, All the Kids Do It, Alice in Wonderland, The Truth About Alex, Perry Mason: The Case of the Fatal Fashion, Mixed Blessings, Bar Hopping, Van Stone: Tour of Duty, Redline, Finish Line. *Series:* Blansky's Beauties, Happy Days, Who's Watching the Kids?, Joanie Loves Chachi, Charles in Charge (also dir.), Baby Talk, Diagnosis Murder, Before They Were Stars (host), Arrested Development, Confessions of a Teen Idol (exec. prod., host). *Series/Director:* The New Lassie, Out of This World, First Time Out, Harry and the Hendersons, Wayans Brothers, Jamie Foxx Show, Nick Freno: Licensed Teacher, Kirk, The Parkers. *Guest:* More than 98 appearances.

BAKER, BLANCHE
Actress. r.n. Blanche Garfein. b. New York, NY, Dec. 20, 1956. Daughter of actress Carroll Baker and dir. Jack Garfein. e. Wellesley, Coll., studied acting with Uta Hagen. Acting debut, White Marriage, Yale Repertory Co. (1978), Regional Theater. B'way debut in Lolita (1981).
PICTURES: The Seduction of Joe Tynan (debut, 1979), French Postcards, Sixteen Candles, Raw Deal, Cold Feet, Nobody's Child, Shakedown, The Handmaid's Tale, Livin' Large, Bum Rap, Dead Funny, The Girl Next Door, Jackrabbit Sky, Taking Chance, Whisper Me a Lullaby, Under the Influence, Fake, An Affirmative Act.
TELEVISION: *Movies:* Mary and Joseph, The Day the Bubble Burst, The Awakening of Candra, Day the Bubble Burst, Embassy, Nobody's Child, Taking Chance. *Mini-series:* Holocaust (Emmy Award, 1978). *Specials:* Romeo & Juliet.

BAKER, CARROLL
Actress. b. Johnstown, PA, May 28, 1931. e. PA schools and St. Petersburg (FL) Junior Coll. Career started as dancer in night-clubs. Actors' Studio N.Y. Made stage debut in Escapade, then acted in All Summer Long. Autobiography: Baby Doll.
PICTURES: Easy to Love (debut, 1953), Giant, Baby Doll, The Big Country, But Not for Me, The Miracle, Bridge to the Sun, Something Wild, How the West Was Won, The Carpetbaggers, Station Six Sahara, Cheyenne Autumn, The Greatest Story Ever Told, Sylvia, Mister Moses, Harlow, Jack of Diamonds, The Sweet Body of Deborah, Paranoia, A Quiet Place to Kill, Captain Apache, The Harem, Honeymoon, My Father's Wife, Bloodbath (The Sky Is Falling), Andy Warhol's Bad, The World is Full of Married Men, Watcher in the Woods, Star 80, The Secret Diary of Sigmund Freud, Native Son, Ironweed, Red Monarch, Kindergarten Cop, Blonde Fist, Cybereden, Undercurrent, Skeletons, Just Your Luck, The Game, Nowhere to Go, Cinerama Adventure (documentary).
TELEVISION: *Movies:* Hitler's SS: Portrait in Evil, On Fire, Judgment Day: The John List Story, Men Don't Tell, A Kiss to Die For, North Shore Fish, Heart Full of Rain, Big Guns Talk: The Story of the Western, Another Woman's Husband. *Guest:* More than 66 appearances.

BAKER, DIANE
Actress. b. Hollywood, CA, Feb. 25, 1938. e. USC.
PICTURES: The Diary of Anne Frank (debut, 1959), The Best of Everything, Journey to the Center of the Earth, Tess of the Storm Country, The Wizard of Baghdad, Hemingway's Adventures of a Young Man, The Prize (Golden Globe nom. 1964), Straight Jacket, Marnie, Mirage, Sands of Beersheba, The Horse in the Grey Flannel Suit, Baker's Hawk, The Pilot, The Silence of the Lambs, The Closer, The Joy Luck Club, Twenty Bucks, Imaginary Crimes, The Net, The Cable Guy, Murder at 1600, Harrison's Flowers, On the Roof, A Mighty Wind, The Keeper: The Legend of Omar Khayyam.
TELEVISION: *Movies:* Dangerous Days of Kiowa Jones, Inherit the Wind (Emmy nom. 1966), Trial Run, The D.A.: Murder One, The Old Man Who Cried Wolf, Do You Take This Stranger?, Sarge: The Badge or the Cross, Congratulations It's a Boy!, A Little Game, Killer By Night, Police Story (pilot), A Tree Grows in Brooklyn, The Dream Makers, The Last Survivors, Fugitive Family, The Haunted, Perry Mason: The Case of the Heartbroken Bride, About Sarah, The Trouble With Marnie. *Mini-series:* The Blue and the Gray, A Woman of Substance (also prod., Emmy nom. 1985), Jackie Bouvier Kennedy Onassis. *Series:* Here We Go Again, Crazy Love, Unscripted. *Special:* The ABC Afternoon Playbreak (Emmy nom. 1975). *Guest:* More than 97 appearances.

BAKER, DYLAN
Actor. b. Syracuse, NY, Oct. 7, 1959. e. Southern Methodist Univ. (BFA), Yale Sch. of Drama (MFA).
THEATRE: B'way: Eastern Standard (Theatre World Award), La Bete (Tony nom.). Off-B'way: Not About Heroes (Obie Award). In 1999 received the Gotham Awards "Breakthrough Award."
PICTURES: Planes Trains & Automobiles (debut, 1987), The Wizard of Loneliness, The Long Walk Home, Delirious, Passed Away, Love Potion No. 9, The Last of the Mohicans, Life With Mikey, Radioland Murders, Disclosure, The Stars Fell on Henrietta, True Blue, Happiness (Ft. Lauderdale Int'l. Film Fest. Critic's Choice Award, best actor, 1998), Oxygen, Simply Irresistible, Random Hearts, Committed, Requiem for a Dream, The Cell, Thirteen Days Which Shocked the World, The Tailor of Panama, Along Came a Spider, A Gentleman's Game, The Laramie Project, Changing Lanes, Road to Perdition, Grasp (short), Head of State, How to Deal, Spider-Man 2, Kinsey, Hide and Seek, The Matador, When a Man Falls in the Forest, Fido, Let's Go to Prison, Spider-Man 3, The Story of a Mother (voice), The Hunting Party, The Stone Angel, Trick 'r Treat, Diminished Capacity, Revolutionary Road, Under New Management.
TELEVISION: *Movies:* A Case of Deadly Force, Judgment, Love Honor and Obey: The Last Mafia Marriage, Forbidden Territory: Stanley's Search for Livingstone, The Invisible Man, The Big Time, The Elizabeth Smart Story, Haskett's Chance,The Pitts. *Mini-series:* Return to Lonesome Dove, From the Earth to the Moon. *Series:* Murder One, Feds, The Pitts, The Book of Daniel, Law & Order, Drive. *Guest:* More than 50 appearances.

BAKER, GEORGE
Actor. b. Varna, Bulgaria, April 1, 1931. e. Lancing College, Sussex. Stage debut Deal Repertory Theatre, 1946. *AUTHOR:* The Fatal Spring, Imaginary Friends, Going for Broke, The Marches of Wales, The Hopkins, Just a Hunch, Sister, Dear Sister, From Doom With Death, Talking About Mira Beau, The Last Silence.
PICTURES: The Intruder (debut, 1953), The Dam Busters, The Ship That Died of Shame, Woman for Joe, The Extra Day, The Feminine Touch, A Hill in Korea, No Time for Tears, These Dangerous Years, The Moonraker, Tread Softly Stranger, Lancelot and Guinevere, Curse of the Fly, Mister Ten Per Cent, Goodbye Mr. Chips, Justine, The Executioners, On Her Majesty's Secret Service, A Warm December, The Fire Fighters, The Spy Who Loved Me, Thirty-Nine Steps, A Nightingale Sang in Berkeley Square, Hopscotch, North Sea Hijack, For Queen and Country, Back to the Secret Garden, A Married Woman.
TELEVISION: *Movies:* Has appeared in more than 35 tv movies, 23 in the role of Detective Chief Inspector Reg Wexford--Hake Hands Forever (1988), It Shouldn't Happen to a TV actor (2003). Other tv movies incl. Alice, The Bonegrinder, Fatal Spring (writer only), The Secret Adversary, The Canterville Ghost, Coast to Coast, At Bertram's Hotel. *Mini-series:* I Claudius, A Woman of Substance, Goodbye Mr. Chips, Dead Head, If Tomorrow Comes, Little Lord Fauntleroy, Ruth Rendell: The Strawberry Tree (writer only). *Series:* The Truth About Melandrinos, Nick of the River, Bowler, Triangle, No Job for a Lady, Johnny and the Dead, Coronation Street. *Guest:* More than 115 appearances.

BAKER, JOE DON
Actor. b. Groesbeck, TX, Feb. 12, 1936. e. North Texas State Coll., B.B.A., 1958. Began career on N.Y. stage, in Marathon 33 and Blues for Mr. Charlie. L.A. stage in The Caine Mutiny Court Martial.
PICTURES: Cool Hand Luke (debut, 1967), Guns of the Magnificent Seven, Adam at Six A.M., Wild Rovers, Five Days Home, Junior Bonner, Walking Tall, Charley Varrick, The Outfit, Golden Needles, Mitchell, Framed, Checkered Flag or Crash, Speedtrap, The Pack, Wacko, Joysticks, The Natural, Fletch, Getting Even, The Living Daylights, The Killing Time, Leonard Part 6, Criminal Law, The Children, Cape Fear, The Distinguished Gentleman, Reality Bites, Panther, The Underneath, Congo, Grass Harp, Goldeneye, Mars Attacks!, Tomorrow Never Dies, Vegas City of Dreams, The Commission, The Dukes of Hazzard, Strange Wilderness.
TELEVISION: *Movies:* Mongo's Back in Town, That Certain Summer, To Kill a Cop, Power, The Abduction of Kari Swenson, Edge of Darkness (BBC mini-series), Defrosting the Fridge (BBC), Citizen Cohn, Complex of Fear, Ruby Ridge: An American Tragedy, To Dance with Olivia, George Wallace, Poodle Springs, Too Rich: The Secret Life of Doris Duke. *Series:* Eischeid, In the Heat of the Night.

BAKER, KATHY

Actress. B. Midland, TX, June 8, 1950. Raised in Albuquerque, NM. e. U of C-Berkeley. Stage debut in San Francisco premiere of Fool for Love (won Obie and Theatre World Awards for New York debut in same). Also appeared in Desire Under the Elms, Aunt Dan and Lemon.
PICTURES: The Right Stuff (debut, 1983), Street Smart (Natl. Society of Film Critics Award), Permanent Record, A Killing Affair, Clean and Sober, Jacknife, Dad, Mr. Frost, Edward Scissorhands, Article 99, Jennifer Eight, Mad Dog and Glory, To Gillian on Her 37th Birthday, Inventing the Abbotts, The Cider House Rules, Things You Can Tell Just by Looking at Her, A Little Inside, Ten Tiny Love Stories, The Glass House, Assasination Tango, Cold Mountain, 13 Going on 30, Fathers and Sons, Nine Lives, All the King's Men, Shades of Ray, The Jane Austen Book Club, Miss Nobody, Last Chance Harvey, Good Day for It.
TELEVISION: *Movies:* Nobody's Child, The Image, One Special Victory, Lush Life, Not In This Town, Weapons of Mass Destruction, Oklahoma City: A Survivor's Story, A Season for Miracles, Ratz, Sanctuary, A Family's Decision, Door to Door (Emmy nom. 2003), Picking Up and Dropping Off, Sucker Free City, Spring Break Shark Attack, Fathers and Sons, Jesse Stone: Sea Change, Jesse Stone: Thin Ice, Jesse Stone: No Remorse, Unstable. *Mini-series:* Shake Rattle and Roll: An American Love Story. *Series:* Picket Fences (3 Emmy Awards: 1993, 1995, 1996, Emmy nom. 1994. Golden Globe Award 1994, Golden Globe nom. 1995, 1996), Boston Public, Murphy's Dozen, Nip/Tuck.

BAKER, RICK

Makeup Artist, Actor. b. Binghamton, NY, Dec. 8, 1950. Started as assist. to makeup artist Dick Smith before creating his own designs in 1972. Frequent film appearances in makeup, usually as gorillas. Worked on Michael Jackson's video Thriller. Winner of 6 Academy Awards.
PICTURES: *Actor:* The Thing With Two Heads, King Kong, The Kentucky Fried Movie, The Incredible Shrinking Woman, Into the Night, King Kong Dark Reel. *Makeup Design:* Shlock, Zebra Force, It's Alive, The Incredible Melting Man, Star Wars (2nd unit, also actor), It Lives Again, The Howling (consultant), Funhouse, An American Werewolf in London (Academy Award 1982), Videodrome, Greystoke: The Legend of Tarzan Lord of the Apes (also costume design; Academy Award nom. 1985), Ratboy, Harry and the Hendersons (Academy Award 1988), Coming to America (Academy Award nom. 1989), Gorillas in the Mist (also assoc. prod.), Missing Link, Wolf, Ed Wood (Academy Award 1995), Batman and Robin, Mighty Joe Young, Batman Forever (also designed monster bat), Escape From L.A. The Nutty Professor (Academy Award 1997), Men in Black (Academy Award, Best Makeup, 1998), A Thousand Acres, The Devil's Advocate, Critical Care, Psycho, Mighty Joe Young (Academy Award nom. 1999), Life (Academy Award nom. 2000), Nutty Professor II: The Klumps, How the Grinch Stole Christmas (Academy Award 2001), Planet of the Apes, Ring, Hellboy, The Hulk, The Cat in the Hat, The Haunted Mansion, Cursed, Hellboy, The Ring Two, King Kong (pilot), X-Men: The Last Stand, Click, Enchanted, Tropic Thunder, Norbit (Academy Award nom. 2008), The Wolfman. *Other:* Tanya's Island (beast design), Starman (transformation scenes), Cocoon (consultant), My Science Project (Tyrannosaurus Rex sequences consultant), Max My Love (chimpanzee consultant), Gremlins 2: The New Batch (co-prod., f/x supervisor), Baby's Day Out (baby f/x), Just Cause (special bodies), Little Panda (panda suits).
TELEVISION: *Movies:* The Autobiography of Miss Jane Pittman (Emmy Award 1974), An American Christmas Carol, Something Is Out There (Emmy nom. 1988), Body Bags, Betrayed by Love (co-prod.), Modern Vampires (sp. effects consult.) *Makeup Design: Series:* Werewolf, Beauty and the Beast (3 Emmy nom.), Harry and the Hendersons. *Guest:* More than 51 appearances.

BAKER, DR. WILLIAM F.

Executive. b. 1944. e. Case Western Reserve U., B.A., M.A., Ph.D. Recipient of honorary degrees from St. John's University, College of St. Elizabeth, Long Island University, New School University, and Seton Hall University. Began broadcasting career in Cleveland while still a student. Joined Scripps-Howard Broadcasting, 1971. Joined Group W as v.p. and general mgr., WJZ-TV, 1978; served as pres. and CEO, Group W Productions; pres. of Group W. Television, 1979; chmn., Group W Satellite Communications, 1981. Carried Explorers Club flag to top of world, becoming one of few in history to visit both North and South Poles, 1983. Since 1987 Baker has been the pres. and CEO, of Thirteen/WNET (parent company is Educational Broadcasting Corporation "EBC", NY PBS station). In Feb. 2007, he turned over the president title to 25-year news veteran Neal Shapiro (former pres. of NBC News). Baker will become president emeritus. Baker established the station's Educational Resources Center, which has become a prolific teacher trainer in multimedia techniques, and Baker helped stabilize the finances of WNET by instituting the largest endowment in public television history. He oversaw the station's transition to digital broadcasting and its historic merger with WLIW21, as well as the launch of several new digital channels. Before assuming his position at EBC, the parent company of PBS, he was pres. of Westinghouse Television and chmn. of the cable and programming companies. During his 10 years at Westinghouse, five cable networks were launched, including Discovery Channel and the Disney Channel. He was pres., NY Chapter, Nat'l. Acad. Television Arts & Sciences, 1998-2001. In 2004 Baker was inducted into the Broadcasting & Cable Hall of Fame, which honors pioneers and innovators in the field and those who have made significant contributions to the electronic arts. He has been honored by the National Academy of Television Arts & Sciences with its national Trustee's Emmy Award and Silver Circle Award, and has won seven Emmys as a TV producer. Baker has also won two Alfred I. DuPont - Columbia Awards in Television and Radio Journalism - the broadcast equivalent of the Pulitzer Prize - as well as a Gabriel Award, and many others. In Oct. 2005, Baker was inducted a Fellow into the American Academy of Arts & Sciences. Baker received a new award in Feb. 2007 from the Lincoln Center Institute; the award is named after the institute's founder, Mark A. Schubart, and recognizes those whose efforts and dedication advance the values found in art. 2008 he was appointed as a senior research fellow at the Hauser Center for Nonprofit Organizations at Harvard University. Baker serves on the boards of the Public Broadcasting Service, Rodale Press, Freedom Communications, Inc., Intrepid Sea, Air & Space Museum, Consumers Union, and Leitch Technology Corporation, and is on the advisory board of the National Park System. Currently he is Executive in Residence at Columbia U. School of Business and Journalist in Residence at Fordham U. He is also the Claudio Aquaviva Chair at the Graduate School of Education, and President Emeritus of Educational Broadcasting Corporation, parent company of WNET-TV and WLIW-TV.
AUTHOR: Down the Tube, 1998, *Co-Author:* Leading With Kindness.

BAKER, WILLIAM M.

Executive, Consultant. b. Newark, NJ, Dec. 26, 1939. e. University of Virginia, 1961. After college, Baker served as an Air Force officer. Joined FBI in 1965 and served org. for 26 years. From 1987 to 1989, took a hiatus from the FBI to serve as dir. of Public Affairs for the CIA. He retired in 1991 as FBI Assistant Director, Criminal Investigative Division. Recognition includes The President's Distinguished Executive Award, The Attorney General's Edmund Randolph Award and The Distinguished Intelligence Medal. He is a past pres. and COO of the Motion Picture Assoc. and exec. v.p., Motion Picture Assoc. of America. Currently a consultant, he sits on the boards of the J. Edgar Hoover Foundation, Aristocrat Technologies. Director, Fortress Global Investigations, Inc.
PICTURE: Once Upon a Film (exec. prod.).

BAKSHI, RALPH

Animator, Writer, Director. b. Haifa, Israel, Oct. 29, 1938. Began career at Terrytoons at age 18 as cell painter and animator, then creative dir. 1965, headed Paramount Cartoons, 1967. Pres., Bakshi Prods. Inc., 1973-.
PICTURES: *Dir./S.P./Writer:* Fritz the Cat, Heavy Traffic, Coonskin, Last Days of Coney Island (also prod.). *Prod/Co-prod.:* Wizards, The Lord of the Rings, American Pop, Hey Good Lookin', Fire and Ice, Cannonball Run II (animator), Cool World, Malcolm and Melving, Babe He Calls Me.
TELEVISION: *Movies:* Imaging America (dir. only), Cool and the Crazy. *Series*: Matty's Funday Funnies, Hector Heathcote Show (animator), The Mighty Heroes (dir. only),The Sub-Mariner, Mighty Thor, The Marvel Superheroes, Iron Man, Hulk, Captain America, The New Casper Cartoon Show, Rocket Robin Hood, Spider-Man (also prod.), Mighty Mouse: The New Adventures, Tattertown (writer and prod.), Spicy City (also exec. prod.).

BAKULA, SCOTT

Actor. b. St. Louis, MO, Oct. 9, 1955. e. Kansas Univ.
THEATRE: NY: Marilyn: An American Fable, Three Guys Naked from the Waist Down, Romance/Romance (Tony nom.). LA: Nite Club Confidential.
PICTURES: Sibling Rivalry, Necessary Roughness, Color of Night, A Passion to Kill, My Family, Lord of Illusions, Cats Don't Dance (voice), Major League: Back to the Minors, Luminarias, American Beauty, Above Suspicion, Life As A House, The Informant.
TELEVISION: *Movies:* I-Man, The Last Fling, An Eye for an Eye, Quantum Leap: Genesis, In the Shadow of a Killer, Mercy Mission: The Rescue of Flight 771, Nowhere to Hide, The Bachelor's Baby (also exec. prod.), Mean Streak, NetForce, In the Name of the People, Papa's Angels, The Trial of Old Drum, Star Trek Enterprise: Broken Bow, What Girls Learn (also exec. prod.), Quantum Leap: A Bold Leap Forward, Blue Smoke, Men of a Certain Age. *Mini-series*: The Invaders, A Girl Thing. *Series*: Gung Ho, Designing Women, Eisenhower & Lutz, Quantum Leap (4 Emmy noms., Golden Globe Award, 2 other nom., also dir.), Murphy Brown, Mr. & Mrs. Smith, Star Trek: Enterprise, State of the Union, Men of a Certain Age. *Guest:* More than 64 appearances.

BALABAN, BOB

Actor, Director. b. Chicago, IL, Aug. 16, 1945. Began studying with Second City troupe while still in high school. Attended Colgate U. and NYU while appearing on Broadway in Plaza Suite.
THEATRE: You're a Good Man Charlie Brown, The Inspector

General, Who Wants to Be the Lone Ranger?, The Basic Training of Pavlo Hummel, The Children, The White House Murder Case, Some of My Best Friends, The Three Sisters, The Boys Next Door, Speed-the-Plow, Some Americans Abroad.
PICTURES: *Actor:* Midnight Cowboy (debut, 1969), Me Natalie, The Strawberry Statement, Catch-22, Making It, Bank Shot, Report to the Commissioner, Close Encounters of the Third Kind, Girlfriends, Altered States, Prince of the City, Absence of Malice, Whose Life Is It Anyway?, 2010, In Our Hands (doc.), End of the Line, Dead-Bang, Alice, Little Man Tate, Bob Roberts, For Love or Money, Greedy, Pie in the Sky, Deconstructing Harry, Waiting For Guffman, Conversation with the Beast, The Definite Maybe (also prod.), Clockwatchers, Natural Selection, The Cradle Will Rock, Jakob the Liar, Three to Tango, Best in Show, Tex: The Passive Aggressive Gunslinger, The Mexican, Plan B, Ghost World, Gosford Park (also idea, prod., Academy Award nom. 2002), The Majestic, Voltage, The Tuxedo, A Mighty Wind, Marie and Bruce, 5-25-77, Trust the Man, Capote, Victor in December (prod. only), Dedication, Lady in the Water, For Your Consideration, Dedication, No Reservations, Jack & Addie (exec. prod.), Rage, Howl, Jack & Addie (exec. prod. only). *Director:* My Boyfriend's Back, The Last Good Time (also prod, co-s.p.), Bernard and Doris (also prod., Emmy nom. 2008, DGA npm. 2009).
TELEVISION: *Movies:* Marriage: Year One, The Face of Fear, Unnatural Pursuits, The Late Shift, Giving Up the Ghost, Swing Vote, Gerald L'Ecuyer: A Filmmaker's Journey, The Exonerated (dir. only), Recount, Georgia O'Keeffe (dir. only, DGA nom. 2010). *Series/Director:* Tales From the Darkside, Amazing Stories, Eerie Indiana, Subway Stories: Tales from the Underground, Legend, Oz, Strangers with Candy, Now and Again, Deadline, Dead Last, The Twilight Zone, Hopeless Pictures (also voice, dir.), Celebrity Charades (exec. prod. only). *Guest:* More than 67 appearances.

BALDWIN, ADAM

Actor. b. Chicago, IL, Feb. 27, 1962. While in high school in Winnetka, was chosen by dir. Tony Bill for role in My Bodyguard. Made stage debut in Album, Chicago.
PICTURES: My Bodyguard (debut, 1980), Ordinary People, D.C. Cab, Reckless, Hadley's Rebellion, Bad Guys, 3:15, Full Metal Jacket, The Chocolate War, Cohen and Tate, Next of Kin, Predator 2, Guilty By Suspicion, Radio Flyer, Where the Day Takes You, Deadbolt, Bitter Harvest, Eight Hundred Leagues Down the Amazon, Wyatt Earp, How to Make an American Quilt, Independence Day, Lover's Knot, Starquest II, The Patriot, The Right Temptaions, Pursiot of Happiness, Jackpot, The Keyman, Double Bang, Betrayal, The Crawl Space, The Freediver, Serenity, The Thirst, Little Fish, Strange Pond, Gospel Hill, Drillbit Taylor, Little Fish, Strange Pond, The Assignment.
TELEVISION: *Movies:* Off Sides, Poison Ivy, Welcome Home Bobby, Murder in High Places, Cruel Doubt, Cold Sweat, Sawbones, Smoke Jumpers, The Cape, Indiscreet, From the Earth to the Moon, Gargantua, Dr. Jekyll & Mr. Hyde, Control Factor, Monster Makers, The Poseidon Adventure, Sands of Oblivion. *Mini-series:* The Poseidon Adventure. *Series:* The Cape, Angel: The Series, Jackie Chan Adventures (voice), Firefly, The Inside, Men in Black: The Series, Day Break (also pilot), Buy More, Chuck. *Special:* The Last Shot, Sci Fi Inside: 'Serenity' (host).

BALDWIN, ALEC

Actor. r.n. Alexander Rae Baldwin III. b. Massapequa, NY, April 3, 1958. e. George Washington U., NYU. Brother of actors Stephen, William and Daniel Baldwin. Trained at Lee Strasberg Theatre Inst. and with Mira Rostova, Elaine Aiken. Started career in daytime TV on serial, The Doctors. Member, The Creative Coalition.
THEATRE: A Midsummer Night's Dream, The Wager, Summertree, A Life in the Theatre (Hartman), Study in Scarlet (Williamstown). NY: Loot (B'way debut; Theatre World Award, 1986), Serious Money, Prelude to a Kiss, A Streetcar Named Desire, Twentieth Century, Entertaining Mr. Sloane.
PICTURES: Forever Lulu (debut, 1987), She's Having a Baby, Beetlejuice, Married to the Mob, Working Girl, Talk Radio, Great Balls of Fire!, The Hunt for Red October, Miami Blues, Alice, The Marrying Man, Prelude to a Kiss, Glengarry Glen Ross, Malice, The Getaway, The Shadow, Heaven's Prisoners (also exec. prod.), The Juror, Looking For Richard, Ghosts of Mississippi, The Edge, Mercury Rising, Thick as Thieves, Notting Hill, The Confession (also prod.), Outside Providence, Thomas and the Magic Railroad, State and Main, The Acting Class, Pearl Harbor, Cats & Dogs, Final Fantasy: The Spirits Within (voice), The Royal Tenenbaums (narrator), The Devil and Daniel Webster, Broadway: The Golden Age by the Legends Who Were There, The Cooler (Academy Award nom.; Golden Globe nom. 2004), The Playmakers of New Orleans, The Cat in the Hat, Along Came Polly, The Last Shot, The SpongeBob SquarePants Movie (voice), The Aviator, Simply Halston, Elizabethtown, Mini's First Time, Fun with Dick and Jane, Nailed Right In, The Departed, The Good Shepherd, Running with Scissors, Brooklyn Rules, Suburban Girl, Brooklyn Rules, Solitary Birds (also co-prod.), My Best Friend's Girl, Madagascar: Escape 2 Africa (voice), My Sister's Keeper, It's Complicated, Cats & Dogs: The Revenge of Kitty Galore (voice).
TELEVISION: *Movies:* Sweet Revenge, Love on the Run, Dress Gray, The Alamo: 13 Days to Glory, A Streetcar Named Desire (Emmy nom.; Golden Globe nom. 1996), Path to War (Emmy nom.; Golden Globe nom. 2002), Second Nature, Nickelodeon Presents the Fairly OddParents in: Channel Chasers (voice). *Mini-series:* Nuremberg (also exec. prod., Emmy nom.; Golden globe nom. 2001). *Series:* The Doctors (1980-82), Cutter to Houston, Knots Landing, Thomas the Tank Engine & Friends (narrator), Clerks (voice), Will & Grace, 30 Rock (Golden Globe Awards 2007, 2009, 2010, 1 other nom.; Emmy Awards 2008, 2009, 1 other nom.). *Guest:* More than 184 appearances.

BALDWIN, DANIEL

Actor. b. Long Island, NY, Oct. 5, 1960. e. Nassau Comm. Col., Ball St. Univ. Brother of actors Alec, William and Stephen Baldwin.
PICTURES: Born on the Fourth of July, Harley Davidson and the Marlboro Man, Knight Moves, Car 54 Where Are You?, Bodily Harm, Yesterday's Target, Trees Lounge, Lone Justice, Mullholland Drive, The Invader, The Treat, Phoenix, The Pandora Project, On the Border, Love Kills, John Carpenter's Vampires, Water Damage, Net Worth, In Pursuit, Fall, Silver Man, Irish Eyes, Ancient Warriors., Dynamite, Water's Edge, King of the Ants, A Christmas Cop, Shut Up and Shoot!, The Blue Rose, Searching for Mickey Fish, Double Tap, The Devil's Dominoes, Nine Dead, The Truth Is Always Complicated, Double Tap, Ashley's Ashes, The Adventures of Belvis Bash, Shadowheart, The Adventures of Belvis Bash, Mission Park, Double Tap: Rewind, Death and Cremation, 1 a Minute.
TELEVISION: *Movies:* Too Good to Be True, L.A. Takedown, The Heroes of Desert Storm, Ned Blessing: The True Story of My Life, Attack of the 50 Foot Woman, Family of Cops, Twisted Desire, Wild Grizzly, Homicide: The Movie, Killing Moon, Open House, Anonymous Rex, Our Fathers, Grey Gardens. *Mini-series:* Our Fathers. *Series:* Sydney, Homicide: Life on the Street, The Sopranos, Cold Case. *Guest:* More than 54 appearances.

BALDWIN, STEPHEN

Actor. b. Long Island, NY, May 12, 1966. Brother of actors Alec, William and Daniel Baldwin. Stage debut in Off-B'way prod., Out of America.
PICTURES: The Beast of War, Born on the Fourth of July, Last Exit to Brooklyn, Crossing the Bridge, Bitter Harvest, Posse, New Eden, 8 Seconds, Threesome, A Simple Twist of Fate, Mrs. Parker and the Vicious Circle, Fall Time, The Usual Suspects, Under the Hula Moon, Bio-Dome, Fled, Sub Down, Scar City, One Tough Cop, Half Baked, The Sex Monster, The Flintstones in Viva Rock Vegas, Friends & Lovers, The Sex Monster, Mercy, Cutaway, Xchange, Table One, Dead Awake, Greenmail, Protection, Slap Shot 2: Breaking the Ice, Deadrockstar, Fly Boys, Firefight, Six: The Mark Unleashed, Shelter Island, Target, Fallacy, Six: The Mark Unleashed, Fly Boys, Robbin Hoodz (dir./writer), The Long Dark Kiss, In My Sleep, Dark Storm, The Genius Club, Midnight Clear, Let the Game Begin, Mate, To the Wall, Power & Pride, Mate, Loving the Bad Man.
TELEVISION: *Movies:* The Prodigious Mr. Hickey, Jury Duty: The Comedy, New Eden, Dead Weekend, Mr. Murder, Absence of the Good, Zebra Lounge, The Snake King, Jesse Stone: Night Passage, Earthstorm, Harpies. *Series:* The Young Riders. *Specials:* In a New Light: Sex Unplugged (co-host). *Guest:* More than 77 appearances.

BALDWIN, WILLIAM

Actor. b. Massapequa, NY, Feb. 21, 1963. e. SUNY/ Binghamton. Degree in political science; worked in Washington on staff of rep. Thomas J. Downey. Brother of actors Alec, Stephen and Daniel Baldwin. With Ford Model agency, appearing in tv ads while studying acting. Member, The Creative Coalition.
PICTURES: Born on the Fourth of July (debut, 1989), Internal Affairs, Flatliners, Backdraft, Three of Hearts, Sliver, A Pyromaniac's Love Story, Fair Game, Curdled, Shattered Image, Virus, Primary Suspect, Relative Values, One Eyed King, Double Bang, Say Nothing, You Stupid Man, Red Rover, Art Heist, The Squid and the Whale, Last Hour, Park, Lenexa, 1 Mile, Feel, 1/9, American Fork, Adrift in Manhattan, A Plumm Summer, Noise, Lymelife (co-prod.), Forgetting Sarah Marshall, 1 a Minute.
TELEVISION: *Movies:* The Preppie Murder, Brotherhood of Murder. *Series:* VH1 Legends (narrator), R.U.S./H., Waterfront (also pilot), Danny Phantom (voice), Dirty Sexy Money. *Guest:* More than 47 appearances.

BALE, CHRISTIAN

Actor. b. Pembrokeshire, Wales, Jan. 30, 1974. Acting debut at age 9 in U.S. Pac-Man commercial. London stage debut following year in The Nerd.
PICTURES: Empire of the Sun, Henry V, Newsies, Swing Kids, Royal Deceit, Little Women, Pocahontas (voice), The Secret Agent, The Portrait of a Lady, Metroland, Velvet Goldmine, All the Little Animals, A Midsummer Night's Dream, American Psycho, Shaft, Reign of Fire, Captain Corelli's Mandolin, Laurel Canyon, Reign of Fire, Equilibrium, The Machinist, Batman Begins, The New World, Harsh Times, Rescue Dawn, The Prestige, I'm Not There, 3:10 to Yuma, The Dark Knight, Terminator: Salvation, Public Enemies, The Fighter.
TELEVISION: *Specials/Movies:* Heart of the Country (BBC), Anastasia: The Mystery of Anna, Treasure Island (released the-

atrically in U.K.), A Murder of Quality, Mary Mother of Jesus. *Guest:* More than 61 appearances.

BALK, FAIRUZA

Actress. b. Point Reyes, CA, May 21, 1974.
PICTURES: Return to Oz, Discovery, The Outside Chance of Maximilian Glick, Valmont, Gas Food Lodging, Tollbooth, Imaginary Crimes, Things to Do in Denver When You're Dead, The Craft, The Island of Dr. Moreau, The Maker, American Perfekt, What Is It? (voice), American History X, The Waterboy, There's No Fish Food In Heaven, Red Letters, Almost Famous, Great Sex, Deuces Wild, Personal Velocity: Three Portraits, What Is It? (voice), Don't Come Knocking, Wild Tigers I Have Known, Humboldt County (also soundtrack performer), Thicker, Bad Lieutenant: Port of Call New Orleans.
TELEVISION: *Movies/Specials:* Best Christmas Pageant Ever, Deceptions, The Worst Witch, Poor Little Rich Girl: The Barbara Hutton Story, Deadly Intentions...Again?, Shame, The Danger of Love, Murder in the Heartland, The Witching Hour (doc. short), Shadow of a Doubt, Orpheus. *Series:* Family Guy. The Sopranos.

BALL, ALAN

Writer, Producer. b. Atlanta, GA, 1957. e. Florida State University School of Theatre.
PICTURES: American Beauty (s.p., co-prod. Academy Award, s.p., 2000, Golden Globe, s.p., 2000, WGA Award), The Parlor (exec. prod.), Towelhead (also dir.).
TELEVISION: *Series:* Grace Under Fire (writer), Cybill (exec. prod., writer), Oh Grow Up (writer/creator &prod.), Everyone's Waiting (exec. prod., writer, dir.), Six Feet Under (creator, dir. & exec. prod.; Emmy Award 2002, 5 other noms., outstanding dir./drama series, for pilot, DGA Award 2002, 2 other noms., WGA nom. 2006), True Blood (exec. prod., dir., WGA nom. 2009).

BALLARD, CARROLL

Director. b. Los Angeles, Oct. 14, 1937. e. UCLA. Prod. of 1967 film Harvest (Academy Award nom. 1968, best documentary). Camera operator on Star Wars.
PICTURES: The Black Stallion (debut, 1979), Never Cry Wolf, Nutcracker: The Motion Picture, Wind, Fly Away Home, The Cruelest Winter, How It Was with Dooms, Duma, Colter's Run.

BALLHAUS, MICHAEL

Cinematographer. b. Berlin, Germany, Aug. 5, 1935. Received ASC International Award 2007.
PICTURES: Deine Zartlichkeiten, We Two, Whity, Beware of a Holy Whore, Tschetan, The Indian Boy, The Bitter Tears of Petra von Kant, Fox and His Friends, Mother Kusters Goes to Heaven, Summer Guests, Satan's Brew, I Only Want You To Love Me, Adolf and Marlene, Chinese Roulette, Bolweiser (The Stationmaster's Wife), Willie and the Chinese Cat, Women in New York, Despair, The Marriage of Maria Braun, Germany in Autumn, German Spring, The Uprising, Big and Little, Malou, Looping, Baby It's You, Friends and Husbands, Dear Mr. Wonderful, Magic Mountain, Edith's Diary, Aus der Familie der Panzereschen, The Autograph, Heartbreakers, Old Enough, Reckless, After Hours, Under the Cherry Moon, The Color of Money, The Glass Menagerie, Broadcast News (Academy Award nom. 1988), The House on Carroll Street,The Last Temptation of Christ, Working Girl, Dirty Rotten Scoundrels, The Fabulous Baker Boys (Academy Award nom. 1990), GoodFellas, Postcards from the Edge, Guilty by Suspicion, What About Bob?, The Mambo Kings, Bram Stoker's Dracula, The Age of Innocence, Quiz Show, Outbreak, Sleepers, Air Force One, Primary Colors, Wild, Wild West, The Thirteenth Floor (exec. prod. only), What Planet Are You From?, The Legend of Bagger Vance, Gone Underground, Gangs of New York (Academy Award nom., ASC nom. 2003), Mummy, Uptown Girls, Something's Gotta Give, The Departed, The Invention of Hugo Cabret.
TELEVISION: *Movies:* More than 15 TV movie credits, incl. Martha, German Spring, Death of a Salesman, Baja Oklahoma.

BAND, CHARLES

Producer, Director. b. Los Angeles, CA, Dec. 27, 1951. e. Overseas Sch. of Rome. Son of Albert Band. Formed Media Home Ent., 1978; formed Empire Ent., 1983; formed Full Moon Ent., 1988; formed Moonbeam Productions, 1993.
PICTURES: More than 135 picture credits as prod., exec. prod. &/or dir./prod. *Producer:* Mansion of the Doomed, Cinderella, End of the World, Laserblast, Fairy Tales, Swordkill, Dungeonmaster, Puppet Master 4, Eliminators, Pet Shop, Puppet Master: Axis of Evil. *Dir./Prod.:* Crash, Parasite, Metalstorm, Trancers, Trancers II, Dr. Mordrid, Dollman vs. Demonic Toys, Hideous, The Creeps, Dead Man's Hand, Girl Talk Confidential, Evil Bong II: King Bong (dir. only). *Exec. Prod.:* Tourist Trap, Day Time Ended, Ghoulies, Zone Troopers, Troll, Terrorvision, The Caller, Spellcaster, Cellar Dweller, Ghoulies II, Enemy Territory, Deadly Weapon, Robot Jox, Prison, Buy & Cell, Ghost Town, Catacombs, Arena, Puppet Master, Shadowzone, Puppet Master II, The Pit and the Pendulum, Subspecies, Puppet Master III, Arcade, Dollman, Netherworld, Bad Channels, Trancers III, Shrunken Heads, Oblivion, Seed People, Bad Channels, Robot Wars, Subspecies II, Prehysteria, Remote, Dragonworld, Beanstalk, Prehysteria II, Curse IV: The Ultimate Sacrifice, Bloodstone: Subspecies III, Puppet Master 5, Oblivion 2: Backlash, Magic in the Mirror, Kraa! The Sea Monster, Curse of the Puppet Master, Subspecies 4: Planet Patrol, The Dead Hate the Living, Voodoo Academy, Demonicus, Groom Lake, Pulse Pounders, Subspecies 5, Deadly Stingers, The Gingerdead Man, numerous others.
TELEVISION: *Movies: As Exec. Prod.:* Alien Arsenal, Search for the Jewel of Polaris: Mysterious Museum, Puppet Master vs Demonic Toys. *Series:* Full Moon Fright Night (prod., dir.).

BANDERAS, ANTONIO

Actor, Director. r.n. Jose Antonio Dominguez Banderas. b. Malaga, Spain, Aug. 10, 1960. e. School of Dramatic Art, Malaga. m. actress Melanie Griffith. Moved to Madrid in 1981 where he made his stage debut in Los Tarantos. Other theatre incl.: The City and the Dogs, Daughter of the Air, The Tragedy of Edward II of England. *B'way:* Nine.
PICTURES: More than 50 picture credits since Labyrinth of Passion debut in 1982. Others incl. Pestanas Postizas, Y del Seguro... Libranos Senor!, El Senor Galindez, El Caso Almeria, Los Zancos, La Corte de Faraon, Requiem por un Campesino Espanol, 27 Horas, Puzzle, Matador, Asi Como Habian Sido, Law of Desire, The Pleasure of Killing, Baton Rouge, Bajarse al Moro, Women on the Verge of a Nervous Breakdown, Si te Dicen que Cai, Tie Me Up! Tie Me Down!, Contra el Viento, La Blanca Paloma, Truth or Dare, The Mambo Kings, Philadelphia, Dispara!, Of Love and Shadows, The House of the Spirits, Interview With the Vampire, Miami Rhapsody, Desperado, Four Rooms, Never Talk to Strangers, Two Much, Assassins, Evita (Golden Globe nom. 1997), The Mask of Zorro (Golden Globe nom. 1999), White River Kid (also prod.), The Thirteenth Warrior, Play it to the Bone, Original Sin, The Body, Spy Kids, Frida, Ecks vs. Sever, Spykids 2: The Island of Lost Dreams, Femme Fatale, Imagining Argentina, Spy Kids 3-D: Game Over, Once Upon a Time in Mexico, Shrek 2 (voice), Legend of Zorro, Take the Lead, Bordertown, Shrek the Third (voice), The Other Man, The Code, The Big Bang Día roto (prod. only), Shrek Forever After (voice), You Will Meet a Tall Dark Stranger, Knockout. *Director:* Crazy in Alabama (Won ALMA Award, Outstanding Dir., 2000), El Camino de los ingleses (also prod.), Tres días (prod. only).
TELEVISION: *Movies:* La Mujer de Tu Vida, La Otra historia de Rosendo Juarez, Il Giovane Mussolini, And Starring Pancho Villa as Himself (Emmy nom., Golden Globe nom. 2004), Shrek the Halls (voice). *Special:* I Love Lucy's 50th Anniversary Special. *Guest:* More than 190 appearances.

BANDY, MARY LEA

Director. b. Evanston, IL, June 16, 1943. e. Stanford U., B.A., 1965. Asst. editor, Harry Abrams and Museum of Modern Art dir., 1980-93; chief Curator 1993-. Dept. of Film, Museum of Modern Art in NY. Editor of MOMA film publications incl.: Rediscovering French Film (1983). Member: Advisory Bd., AFI's National Center for Preservation of Film and Video; Film Advisory Comm., American Federation of Arts; Advisory Comm. on Film, Japan Society; Advisory Comm., NY State Motion Picture and Television. Co-pres., National Alliance of Media Arts Center, 1986-88. Bd. mem.: Intl. Film Seminars; MacDowell Colony; Natl. Film Preservation Bd.; Library of Congress; Advisory Board, Film Foundation; Bd. of Directors, Third World Newsreel. *Documentaries:* The Race to Save 100 Years, Without Lying Down: Frances Marion and the Power of Women in Hollywood, The Old Place (exec. prod.), Budd Boetticher: A Man Can Do That (assoc. prod.).

BANERJEE, VICTOR

Actor. b. Calcutta, India, Oct. 15, 1946. Helped form the first Screen Extras Union in India. Won int'l recognition for A Passage to India. On stage in: Pirates of Penzance, An August Requiem (dir.), Desert Song, Godspell.
PICTURES: The Chess Players (debut 1977), Kalyug, Jaipur Junction (German), An August Requiem (dir. only), Arohan, A Passage to India (Won Nat'l. Board of Review Award, best actor, 1984; won Evening Standard British Film Awards, best actor, 1986), Ghare-Baire, Foreign Body, Mahaprithivi, Bitter Moon, Bhoot, Joggers' Park, It Was Raining That Night, Yatna, My Brother Nikhil, Home Delivery: Aapko... Ghar Tak, The Bong Connection, Ta Ra Rum Pum, Apne, Sarkar Raj.
TELEVISION: *Movies:* Hullabaloo Over Georgie and Bonnie's Pictures, Dadah Is Death, NY Spice, Bradford Riots. *Series:* True Adventures of Christopher Columbus.

BANNER, BOB

Producer, Director. b. Ennis, TX, Aug. 15, 1921. e. Southern Methodist U., B.A., 1939-43; Northwestern U., M.A., 1946-48. U.S. Naval Reserve 1943-46. Faculty, Northwestern U., 1948-50. Staff dir., NBC-TV in Chicago, 1949-50. Pres., Bob Banner Assocs. Visiting Prof.: Southern Methodist U.
PICTURES: Warning Shot (1967).
TELEVISION: *Movies:* Mongo's Back in Town, The Last Survivors, Journey From Darkness, My Sweet Charlie (Emmy nom. 1970), Bud and Lou, Yes Virginia There is a Santa Claus, Crash Landing, With Murder in Mind, The Sea Wolf, Angel Flight Down. *Specials:* Garroway at Large (dir.), Fred Waring Show (prod., dir.), Omnibus (dir.), Nothing But the Best (prod. dir.), Dave

Garroway Show (prod. dir), Dinah Shore Chevy Show Emmy Award 1958, 1 other nom.), Candid Camera TV Show (exec. prod.), Carnegie Hall Salutes Jack Benny (exec. prod.), Julie & Carol at Carnegie Hall, Carol & Co., Jimmy Dean Show, Calamity Jane, The Entertainers, Carol & Co., Ice Follies, Carol Burnett Show, John Davidson at Notre Dame, Here's Peggy Fleming, Peggy Fleming at Sun Valley, The American West of John Ford, Love! Love! Love!—Hallmark Hall of Fame, To Europe with Love, Peggy Fleming Visits the Soviet Union, Perry Como's Lake Tahoe Holiday, Perry Como's Christmas In Mexico, Perry Como's Hawaiian Holiday, Perry Como's Spring In New Orleans, Don Ho Show, Perry Como Las Vegas Style, Perry Como's Christmas in Austria, All-Star Anything Goes, Peggy Fleming and Holiday on Ice at Madison Square Garden, A Special Sesame Street Christmas (Emmy nom. 1979), Julie Andrews, One Step Into Spring, Leapin' Lizards, It's Liberace, Ford Motor Company's 75th Anniversary; Gift of Music, specials starring Bob Hope, Julie Andrews, Andy Williams, Los Angeles Music Center 25th Anniversay, Amazing Music Series, Happy Birthday George Gershwin. *Series:* Almost Anything Goes, Solid Gold, Star Search, It's Showtime at the Apollo, Uptown Comedy Club, Real Kids, Real Adventures (exec. prod., Emmy nom. 2001).

BARANSKI, CHRISTINE

Actress. b. Buffalo, NY, May 2, 1952. e. Juilliard Sch. of Music & Dramatic Arts.
THEATRE: NY: Private Lives, One Crack Out, Says I Says He, Shadow of a Gunman, Hide and Seek (B'way debut, 1980), Company, Coming Attractions, Operation Midnight Climax, A Midsummer Night's Dream (Obie Award, 1982), Sally and Marsha, The Real Thing (Tony Award, 1984), Hurlyburly, It's Only a Play, The House of Blue Leaves, Rumors! (Tony Award, 1989), Elliot Loves, Nick and Nora, Lips Together Teeth Apart, The Loman Family Picnic.
PICTURES: Soup for One (debut, 1982), Lovesick, Crackers, 9-1/2 Weeks, Legal Eagles, The Pick-Up Artist, Reversal of Fortune, The Night We Never Met, Life With Mikey, Addams Family Values, New Jersey Drive, The Ref, Jeffrey, The Birdcage, The Odd Couple II, Bulworth, Cruel Intentions, Bowfinger, How the Grinch Stole Christmas, Marci X, The Guru, Chicago, Marci X, Welcome to Mooseport, Falling for Grace, Relative Strangers, East Broadway, Bonneville, Mamma Mia!, The Bounty Hunter.
TELEVISION: *Movies:* Playing for Time, A Midsummer's Night Dream, House of Blue Leaves, To Dance With the White Dog, Eloise at the Plaza, Eloise at Christmastime, Recipe for a Perfect Christmas, Inseparable. *Series:* Another World, All My Children, Cybill (Emmy Award, 1995; Emmy noms.; 2 Golden Globe noms.), Welcome to New York (also exec. prod.), Frasier (Emmy nom. 1999 as guest), Happy Family, Spellbound, Ghost Whisperer, Campus Ladies, The Big Bang Theory (Emmy nom. 2009 as guest), The Good Wife. *Special:* The Addams Chronicles. *Guest:* More than 65 appearances.

BARATTA, DANA

Writer, Producer.
PICTURES: Andre (co-prod.).
TELEVISION: *Series*: Dawson's Creek, Providence, Pasadena, Kate Brasher, Cracking Up, The Studio, Life Is Wild (co-exec. prod., writer), Runaway (co-exec. prod., writer), Warehouse 13 (co-exec. prod.).

BARBEAU, ADRIENNE

Actress. b. Sacramento, CA, June 11, 1947. e. Foothill Col.
THEATRE: B'way: Fiddler on the Roof, Grease (Tony nom., Theatre World Award). L.A.: Women Behind Bars, Strange Snow, Pump Boys & Dinettes, Drop Dead. Canadian Premiere: Lost in Yonkers. Regional: Love Letters, Best Little Whorehouse in Texas.
PICTURES: The Fog, Cannonball Run, Escape From New York, Swamp Thing, Creepshow, The Next One, Back to School, Open House, Two Evil Eyes, Jungle Heat, Two Evil Eyes, Father Hood, Silk Degrees, Bimbo Movie Bash, A Wake in Providence, The Convent, Across the Line, No Place Like Home, The Reckoning, The Ocean, Unholy, The American Standard, Fly Me to the Moon 3D, The Dog Who Saved Christmas.
TELEVISION: *Movies:* The Great Houdini, Giving Birth, Red Alert, Return to Fantasy Island, Crash, Someone's Watching Me!, The Darker Side of Terror, The Top of the Hill, Valentine Magic on Love Island, Tourist, Charlie and the Great Balloon Chase, Seduced, Bridge Across Time, Blood River, Doublecrossed, The Burden of Proof, The Parsley Garden, Jailbreakers, Bram Stoker's Burial of the Rats, A Champion's Fight, Scooby Doo on Zombie Island (voice), A Champion's Fight, Spring Break Lawyer, The Santa Trap, Ring of Darkness, Christmas Do-Over, War Wolves. *Series:* Maude (Golden Globe nom. 1977), Head of the Class, Batman (voice), Gotham Girls (voice), The Drew Carey Show, Carnivàle. *Guest:* More than 136 appearances.

BARBER, FRANCES

Actress. b. Wolverhampton, England, May 13, 1957. e. Bangor U.; grad. studies in theatre, Cardiff U. Stage experience with fringe theaters including improvisational troupe Hull Truck Theatre Company, Glasgow Citizens and Tricycle Theatre (Killburn) before joining Royal Shakespeare Co. (Camille, Hamlet).
PICTURES: The Missionary (debut, 1982), A Zed and Two Noughts, White City, Castaway, Prick Up Your Ears, Sammy and Rosie Get Laid, We Think the World of You, The Grasscutter, Young Soul Rebels, Secret Friends, Soft Top Hard Shoulder, Germaine and Benjamin, Giorgino, Photographing Fairies, Still Crazy, Mauvaise passe, Esther Kahn, Toy Boys, Shiner, Superstition, La Sirene Rouge, 24 Hours in the Life of a Woman, Flyfishing, Boudica, Goal! The Dream Begins, Goal II: Living the Dream, That's for Me!.
TELEVISION: *Movies:* Clem, Jackie's Story, Home Sweet Home, Flame to the Phoenix, Those Glory Glory Days; Hard Feelings, Behaving Badly, The Leaving of Liverpool, Three Steps to Heaven, A Royal Scandal, The Ice House, Rules of Engagement, Real Women, Dalziel and Pascoe: The Wood Beyond, The Gentleman Thief, The Legend of the Tamworth Two, Trial & Retribution VIII, Marple: A Murder Is Announced. *Mini-series:* Reilly: Ace of Spies, The Nightmare Years, The Storyteller: Greek Myths, Rhodes, Plastic Man, Love in a Cold Climate. *Series:* Bremner, Bird and Fortune, Manchild, Having It Off, Monkey Dust. *Guest:* More than 84 appearances.

BARBER, GARY

Executive, Producer. Barber spent seven years at Price Waterhouse as a member of the entertainment specialty group. From Price Waterhouse, Barber served at Producers Sales Organizations. He became pres. of Vestron International Group, which was the largest independent video company in the world. During his tenure at Vestron, Barber acquired and distributed many international hits including The Princess Bride, Young Guns, Hamburger Hill, and Dirty Dancing. From Vestron, Barber became the vice chairman and COO of Morgan Creek Productions. During his eight and a half years at the company, he was in charge of all day-to-day operations for each of Morgan Creek's business entities including feature film production, foreign distribution, music, exhibition and interactive. In 1998, Barber, with partner Roger Birnbaum, founded Spyglass Entertainment, where he currently is co-chairman and co-CEO with Birnbaum. Barber has produced or executive produced over 50 feature films and TV shows including the 1994 hit that rocketed Jim Carrey to stardom, "Ace Ventura: Pet Detective," and its successful sequel, "Ace Ventura: When Nature Calls." Spyglass has enjoyed phenomenal box office success with films like The Sixth Sense, which grossed over $661 million and garnered six Academy Award® nominations. Spyglass funds three to four films a year through its partnership with J.P. Morgan Chase bank and has had distribution deals with major studios, including its current deal with Columbia Pictures.
PICTURES: Midnight Crossing (exec. prod.), Communion (exec. prod.), Young Guns II (co-exec. prod.), Pacific Heights (exec. prod.), Robin Hood: Prince of Thieves (exec. prod.), Freejack (exec. prod.), White Sands (exec. prod.), Stay Tuned (exec. prod.), The Crush (exec. prod.), True Romance, Ace Ventura: Pet Detective (exec. prod.), Chasers (exec. prod.), Major League II (exec. prod.), Silent Fall (exec. prod.), Trial by Jury (exec. prod.), Imaginary Crimes (exec. prod.), Ace Ventura: When Nature Calls (exec. prod.), Two if by Sea (exec. prod.), Big Bully (exec. prod.), Diabolique (exec. prod.), Bad Moon (exec. prod.), Wild America (exec. prod.), Incognito (exec. prod.), Major League: Back to the Minors (exec. prod.), Wrongfully Accused (exec. prod.), Keeping the Faith, Shanghai Noon, Unbreakable (exec. prod.), Out Cold (exec. prod.), The Count of Monte Cristo, Dragonfly, Abandon, The Recruit, Reign of Fire, Shanghai Knights, Bruce Almighty (exec. prod.), Seabiscuit (exec. prod.), 1 Love (exec. prod.), Mr. 3000, Connie and Carla, Four Christmases, The Pacifier, The Hitchhiker's Guide to the Galaxy, Legend of Zorro, Memoirs of a Geisha (exec. prod.), Balls of Fury, The Invisible, Stay Alive (exec. prod.), Eight Below (exec. prod.), Stick It (exec. prod.), Evan Almighty, Underdog, 27 Dresses, Wanted (exec. prod.), Welcome Home Roscoe Jenkins (exec. prod.), The Love Guru (exec. prod.), Ghost Town (exec. prod.), Flash of Genius, G.I. Joe: The Rise of Cobra (exec. prod.), Invictus (exec. prod.), Leap Year, The Tourist.
TELEVISION: *Movies:* Not a Clue, Weekends, The Ranch. *Series:* Miracles.

BARCLAY, PARIS

Director. b. June 1956. Received DGA Robert B. Aldrich Achievement Award 2007.
PICTURES: Don't Be a Menace to South Central While Drinking Your Juice in the Hood, Pedro (WGA nom. 2010 for long form s.p.).
TELEVISION: *Movies:* America's Dream, The Cherokee Kid (also actor), The Big Time (also co-exec. prod.), Hate, Prodigy/Bully (exec. prod.). *Series:* NYPD Blue (2 Emmy Awards, 2 Emmy nom. 1998, 1999, DGA Award 1999), Diagnosis: Murder, ER (DGA nom. 1997), Sliders, Clueless, Brooklyn South, The West Wing (Emmy nom. 2002, 3 DGA noms.), City of Angels (also co-exec. prod.), Fastlane, The Street Lawyer (dir. pilot), Cold Case, CSI: Crime Scene Investigation, House M.D. (DGA nom. 2006), Weeds (DGA nom. for episode 2009), In Treatment (DGA nom. for episode 2009, 2010), Glee (DGA nom. for episode 2010).

BARDEM, JAVIER

Actor. b. Las Palmas de Gran Canaria, Canary Islands, March 1,

1969. m. actress Penélope Cruz.
PICTURES: High Heels, Jamon Jamon, Live Flesh, Before Night Falls (Academy Award nom., Golden Globe nom. 2001), Don't Tempt Me, The Dancer Upstairs, Mondays in the Sun, Collateral, The Sea Inside (Golden Globe nom. 2005), Goya's Ghosts, No Country for Old Men (Academy Award, Golden Globe Award 2008), Love in the Time of Cholera, Vicky Cristina Barcelona (Golden Globe nom. 2009), Biutiful, Eat Pray Love, The Galapagos Affair, Sons of the Clouds (doc., prod.). *Guest:* More than 100 appearances.

BARDOT, BRIGITTE
Actress. b. Paris, France, Sept. 28, 1934. e. Paris Conservatory. Studied ballet, before becoming model. Studied acting with Rene Simon. On stage in L'Invitation au Chateau. Awarded French Legion of Honor, 1985. Active in the movement to preserve endangered animals. Created the Brigitte Bardot Foundation for animal protection, April 1986.
PICTURES: Le Trou Normand (debut, 1952), Nanina la Fille san Voiles, Les Dents Longues, Act of Love, Le Portrait de Son Pere, Royal Affairs in Versailles, Tradita, Le Fils de Caroline Cherie, Helen of Troy, Futures Vedettes, Les Grandes Maneuvres, Doctor at Sea, La Lumiere d'En Face, Cette Sacre Gamine, Mi Figlio Nerone, En Effeuillant la Marguerite, The Bride is Much Too Beautiful, And God Created Woman, Une Parisienne, The Night Heaven Fell, En Cas de Malheur, Le Femme et le Pantin, Babette Goes to War, Come Dance With Me, La Verite, La Bride sur le Cou, Les Amours Celebres, A Very Private Affair, Love on a Pillow, Contempt, Dear Brigitte, Viva Maria, Masculine-Feminine, Two Weeks in September, Spirits of the Dead, Shalako, Les Femmes, L'Ours et la Poupee, Les Novices, Boulevard du Rhum, Les Petroleuses, Don Juan 73, L'Historie Tres Bonne et Tres Joyeuse de Colinot Trousssechemise, Tykho Moon (singer), Laurel Canyon (singer), Rush Hour 3 (singer). Many French and International appearances.

BAREN, HARVEY M.
Executive. b. New York, NY, Nov. 25, 1931. e. State U. of New York. Served in U.S. Army, 1952-54. United Artists Corp., 1954-59 (contract dept., print dept., booker—NY branch). Asst. to general sales mgr., Magna Pictures Corp., 1959-61. Road show mgr., nat'l. sales coordinator, 20th Century-Fox, 1961-71. Asst. general sales mgr., Allied Artists Pictures, 1971-79. V.p., gen. sales mgr., Nat'l. Screen Service, 1978-79. V.p., gen. sales mgr., Cannon Pictures, 1979-80. Pres. of Summit Feature Distributors, 1980. Exec. v.p., dir., MGM/UA Classics, 1983. Joined New Century/Vista as v.p., sales admin, 1986. Pres., Sea Movies Inc., 1991-present.

BARENHOLTZ, BEN
Executive, Producer. b. Kovel, Poland, Oct. 5, 1935. A film industry veteran with a career that spans over 45 years. Entered industry as asst. theatre mgr., RKO Bushwick, Brooklyn, 1959-60. Mgr., Village Theatre, NY, 1966-68. Owner, operator, Elgin Cinema, 1968-75; originated Midnight Movie concept with El Topo. Pres., owner, Libra Film Corp., 1972-84. In 1984 Barenholtz started Circle Releasing, launching and distributing films that include Morita's The Family Game, Alain Cavalier's Therese, Ward's The Navigator, John Woo's The Killer and Joel and Ethan Coen's acclaimed first feature, Blood Simple. He went on to co-produce their following films: Raising Arizona, Miller's Crossing and Barton Fink, which won the Palme d'Or (Best Film) at the 1991 Cannes Film Festival, as well as awards for Best Director and Best Actor for John Turturro — the first time in 44 years that three top honors have gone to the same film at Cannes. In 2005, Barenholtz directed his first documentary feature, Music Inn, about the legendary jazz and folk venue of the 1950s. He is the pres. of Barenholtz Prods. Inc.
PICTURES: *Exec. Prod.:* Miller's Crossing, Barton Fink, Cheat, White Man's Burden, Georgia, Requiem for a Dream (co-exec. prod.). *Prod.:* The Naked Man, Bruiser, Rabbit, Distress, Stags. *Director:* Music Inn (doc.), And I Will (also dir., writer).
TELEVISION: *Movie:* Gourmet Club (exec. prod.).

BARIO, HOLLY
Executive. e. Emerson College, Boston, MA, 1989 graduate. Bario began her tenure at Universal in 1996, after working as an assistant to producer Marc Platt at TriStar Prods. During her 11 years as a production executive at Universal, Bario oversaw some of the studio's biggest comedies, including "Knocked Up," "I Now Pronounce You Chuck & Larry," "Bruce Almighty," "Meet the Parents" and "The 40-Year-Old Virgin." More recently, she had been overseeing such comedic projects as "Dr. Sensitive," "Coma Boy," "Baby Mama" and "The Cookie Queen." Bario worked closely with film exec. Stacey Snider during Snider's tenure at Universal. In Feb. 2008, Bario left Universal to become a senior creative executive with DreamWorks, a move that reunited her with Snider, who left Universal in 2006 to become co-chairman and CEO of DreamWorks. When DreamWorks split with Paramount Pictures in Fall 2008, Bario and colleague Mark Sourian were named co-presidents, production at the newly independent DreamWorks.

BARISH, KEITH
Producer. b. Los Angeles, CA, Nov. 11, 1944. Background in finance. Founded Keith Barish Prods., 1979. In partnership with Taft Broadcasting Co., Entertainment Div., 1984-88. Founder and chmn. of Planet Hollywood. Appeared in film Last Action Hero.
PICTURES: Sophie's Choice, Light of Day, Ironweed, Her Alibi. *Exec. prod.:* Endless Love, Prisoners, Misunderstood, Nine 1/2 Weeks, Big Trouble in Little China, The Running Man, The Monster Squad, Firebirds, The Fugitive, U.S. Marshals.
TELEVISION: *Movie:* A Streetcar Named Desire (exec. prod., Emmy nom. 1984).

BARKER, CLIVE
Writer, Producer, Director. b. Liverpool, England, Oct. 5, 1952. e. Liverpool Univ. Moved to London at twenty-one, forming theatre company. Began writing short stories which were subsequently published as Books of Blood (Vols. 1-3 & Vols. 4-6). *Author of: Novels:* The Damnation Game, Weaveworld, The Great and Secret Show, Imajica, The Thief of Always, Everville, Sacrament, Cabal, Weaveworld, The Hellbound Heart, In the Flesh, The Inhuman Condition, Abarat, Abarat: Days Of Magic, Nights Of War, Coldheart Canyon. *Books:* Clive Barker: Illustrator, The Art of Clive Barker, Incarnations. *Plays:* History of the Devil, Colossus, Frankenstein In Love, Incarnations, Forms Of Heaven. Painter with exhibitions in NY and California.
PICTURES: Underworld, Rawhead Rex (from his story), Hellraiser (dir., s.p.; from his novella The Hellbound Heart), Hellbound: Hellraiser II (co-exec. prod.; writer), Nightbreed (dir., s.p.; from his novel Cabal), Sleepwalkers (actor), Hellraiser III: Hell on Earth (exec. prod.; from his story), Candyman (exec. prod.; from his story The Forbidden), The Forbidden (short), Clive Barker's Freaks (himself), Candyman: Farewell to the Flesh (exec. prod.; from his story), Lord of Illusions (dir., s.p., co-prod.; from his story The Last Illusion), Gods and Monsters (exec. prod.), Tortured Souls: Animae Damnatae (writer from novella Tortured Souls, prod. dir.), The Plague, 2gether 4ever (exec. prod.), The Midnight Meat Train (writer, prod.), Born (s.p., exec. prod.), Hellraiser (s.p., prod), Dread (writer, prod.). *Documentary:* Mule Skinner Blues.
TELEVISION: *Movies:* Quicksilver Highway (actor, writer from The Body Politic), Saint Sinner (writer, exec. prod.). *Mini-series:* The History of the Devil (writer-play, exec. prod.).

BARKER, MICHAEL W.
Executive. b. Nuremberg, Germany, Jan. 9, 1954. e. U. of Texas at Austin, B.S. in International Communications, 1976. Joined Films Inc. 1979-80; then United Artists 1980-83, first as non-theatrical sales mgr., then as nat'l. sales mgr. of UA Classics. Co-founder and v.p., sales & mktg. for Orion Classics, a div. of Orion, 1983-1992. Co-founder and co-pres., co-chairman, Sony Pictures Classics, 1992-present. Member bd. of dirs. of BAFTA NY, and served on the Independent Features Project bd. for 14 years. Recipient of Independent Feature Project's Industry's Lifetime Achievement Award. Barker is currently on the Entertainment Media and Technology Dean's advisory bd. at the Stern School of Business, New York University and the Visiting Committee of the University of Chicago's School of the Humanities.

BARKIN, ELLEN
Actress. b. Bronx, NY, Apr. 16, 1954. e. Hunter Coll.; Actors Studio.
THEATRE: Irish Coffee (debut, Ensemble Studio Theatre), Shout Across the River, Killings Across the Last, Tobacco Road, Extremities, Eden Court.
PICTURES: Diner (debut, 1982), Tender Mercies, Daniel, Enormous Changes at the Last Minute, Eddie and the Cruisers, Harry and Son, The Adventures of Buckaroo Banzai Across the Eighth Dimension, Terminal Choice, Desert Bloom, Down by Law, The Big Easy, Siesta, Made in Heaven, Sea of Love, Johnny Handsome, Switch (Golden Globe nom. 1992), Man Trouble, Mac, This Boy's Life, Into the West, Bad Company, Wild Bill, Mad Dog Time, Fear and Loathing in Las Vegas, Drop Dead Gorgeous, The White River Kid, Crime and Punishment in Suburbia, Mercy, In the Boom Boom Room, Someone Like You, Buckaroo Banzai Declassified (video short), Palindromes, She Hate Me, Trust the Man, Ocean's Thirteen, Brooklyn's Finest, Rogue's Gallery, Happy Tears, Twelve, Shit Year, The Chameleon, Letters to Juliet (prod.).
TELEVISION: *Movies:* We're Fighting Back, Parole, Terrible Joe Moran, Act of Vengeance, Clinton and Nadine, Before Women Had Wings (Emmy Award, Golden Globe nom. 1998), Strip Search. *Series:* Search for Tomorrow.

BARNHOLTZ, BARRY
Executive, Producer. b. St. Louis, MO, Oct. 12, 1945. e. California State U., Northridge; USC; UCLA; WLAU, studied law. Concert promotions in So. CA, 1963-71. With Medallion TV as v.p., sales Barnholtz Organization, representing independent prod. cos. for feature films for cable. Founder, sr. v.p. of Vidmark Inc., and Trimark Films. Currently is pres. & CEO Barnholtz Entertainment and in 2008 created North American Motion Pictures to produce and distribute theatrical and direct-to-video productions.
PICTURES: *Associate prod.:* Leprechaun, Deadfall. *Prod.:* Cyborg 2 (co-prod.). *Executive prod.:* Trigger Fast, Jailbait, Curse

of the Starving Class (co-exec. prod.), Proteus, Sometimes They come Back 2, Crimetime, Public Enemies, Vicious Circles, Another Nine and a Half Weeks, The Lost World, The First 9 ½ Weeks, Fall: The Price of Silence, Satanic, Grad Night, The Dog Who Saved Christmas, Drifter: Henry Lee Lucas, Sam's Lake, Bob Funk, The Perfect Sleep, A Nanny for Christmas, Abandoned, Violent Blue (actor).
TELEVISION: *Movies:* The Mangler, Hostage for a Day (prod. exec.), Guns of Honor (exec. prod.), The Dog Who Saved Christmas (exec. prod, actor), Turbulent Skies (exec. prod.). *Documentary:* Mystery of the Sphinx (co-prod.). *Series:* Woke Up Dead (prod.).

BARRAULT, MARIE-CHRISTINE
Actress. b. Paris, France, March 21, 1944.
PICTURES: My Night at Maud's, Le Distrait, Lancelot of the Lake, The Aspern Papers, Les Intrus, La Famille Grossfeld, Chloe in the Afternoon, John Glueckstadt, Cousin cousine (Academy Award nom. 1977), By the Tennis Courts, Perceval, The Medusa Touch, Tout est a nous, Femme Entre Chien et Loup, Ma Cherie, Stardust Memories, Table for Five, Josephs Tochter, A Love in Germany, Les Mots Pour le Dire, Swann in Love, Grand Piano, Prisonnieres, Un Etae de orages, Savage State, Necessary Love, Next Time the Fire, Bonsoir, Obsession, C'est la tangente que je préfère, La Dilettante, Azzurro, Trivial.
TELEVISION: *Movies:* Mon pere avait raison, Les Braconniers de Belledombre, Maison de famille, Le Vieil ours et l'enfant, Le Le Don fait à Catchaires, La Deuxième vérité, Rêves en France, Saint-Germain ou La négociation, Passés troubles. *Mini-series:* Garonne, Ange de feu. *Guest:* More than 71 appearances.

BARRETT, DAVID J.
Executive. b. Chicago, IL, 1948. e. Attended Loyola Univ. in Chicago. This TV industry veteran has moved through the ranks of Hearst's media organization since he joined Hearst in 1984 as gen. mgr. of its Baltimore radio stations. He subsequently became gen. mgr. of WBAL-TV before relocating to New York to assume his corporate position in 1991. Today, as pres., CEO of Hearst-Argyle Television, Inc., Barrett oversees the 26 TV stations the company owns and the three additional stations the company manages. Its stations reach approximately 18% of U.S. TV households and the company ranks among the top national TV groups. Barrett serves on the bd. of directors of Hearst-Argyle Television, Inc., Hearst Corporation, Maximum Service Television, Inc. (MSTV), the Center for Communication, Inc., the Broadcasters' Foundation, the Television Operators Caucus (TOC), and in June 2006, he re-joined the National Association of Broadcasters (NAB) bd. of directors following prior NAB board service from 1998 to 2004. He serves as an Honorary Trustee of The Foundation of American Women in Radio and Television (AWRT), and is a member of the New England Cable News (NECN) management committee. Barrett is a past chmn. of the bd. of governors for the ABC Television Affiliates Association and the Federal Communications Commission's Media Security and Reliability Council (MSRC II), and has previously served on the bd. of directors of the International Radio and Television Society (IRTS), the Advertising Council, and Internet Broadcasting Systems, Inc. In 2004 he was named Broadcasting & Cable magazine's "Broadcaster of the Year." In October 2005 he was the recipient of The Media Institute's American Horizon Award and was also inducted into the National Academy of Television Arts and Sciences Management Hall of Fame.

BARRIE, BARBARA
Actress. b. Chicago, IL, May 23, 1931. e. U. of TX, B.F.A., 1953. Trained for stage at Herbert Berghof Studio. NY stage debut, The Wooden Dish, 1955. Author of, Lone Star (1990), Adam Zigzag (1994), Second Act (1997).
THEATRE: The Crucible, The Beaux Stratagem, The Taming of the Shrew, Conversations in the Dark, All's Well That Ends Well, Happily Never After, Horseman Pass By, Company, The Selling of the President, The Prisoner of Second Avenue, The Killdeer, California Suite, Big and Little, Isn't It Romantic, Torch Song Trilogy, Fugue, After-play.
PICTURES: Giant (debut, 1956), The Caretakers, One Potato Two Potato (best actress, Cannes Film Fest, 1964), The Bell Jar, Breaking Away (Academy Award nom. 1980), Private Benjamin, Real Men, End of the Line, Hercules (voice), $pent, Second Best, Frame of Mind, Harvest, Twelve Thirty.
TELEVISION: *Movies:* More than 20 tv movie credits, incl. Tell Me My Name, Summer of My German Soldier, To Race the Wind, The Children Nobody Wanted, Barefoot in the Park, Not Just Another Affair, Two of a Kind, The Execution, Vital Signs, Winnie, My First Love, Guess Who's Coming for Christmas?, The Odd Couple: Together Again, My Breast, A Chance of Snow, Fathers and Sons. *Mini-series:* 79 Park Avenue, Backstairs at the White House, Roots: The Next Generations, Scarlett. *Series:* Love of Life, Diana, Barney Miller, Breaking Away (Emmy nom. 1981), Tucker's Witch, Reggie, Double Trouble, Suddenly Susan, Law & Order (Emmy nom. 1992), Disney's Hercules (voice), Law & Order: Special Victims Unit (Emmy nom. 2003 as guest). *Guest:* More than 100 appearances.

BARRY, JOHN
Composer, Arranger, Conductor. r.n. John Barry Prendergast. b. York, England, Nov. 3, 1933. Started as rock 'n' roll trumpeter. Artist and prod., CBS Records.
THEATRE: London: Passion Flower Hotel, 'Brighton Rock'. NY: The Little Prince & The Aviator, Billy, Lolita My Love.
PICTURES: Composer for music in more than 100 pictures, incl. Never Let Go, The L-Shaped Room, The Amorous Mr. Prawn, From Russia With Love (Golden Globe nom. 1965), Seance on a Wet Afternoon, Zulu, Goldfinger, The Knack, King Rat, Mister Moses, Thunderball, The Chase, Born Free (2 Academy Awards: Best Music Scoring and Best Song: title song, 1967, Golden Globe nom.), The Wrong Box, The Whisperers, Deadfall, You Only Live Twice, Petulia, The Lion in Winter (Academy Award,; Golden Globe nom. 1969), Midnight Cowboy, The Appointment, On Her Majesty's Secret Service, Monte Walsh, The Last Valley, They Might Be Giants, Murphy's War, Walkabout, Diamonds Are Forever, Mary Queen of Scots (Academy Award nom.; Golden Globe nom. 1972), Alice's Adventures in Wonderland, The Public Eye, A Doll's House, The Tamarind Seed, The Dove (Golden Globe nom.1975), The Man With the Golden Gun, The Day of the Locust, Robin and Marian, King Kong, The Deep (Golden Globe nom. 1978), The Betsy, Hanover Street, Moonraker, Game of Death, Raise the Titanic, Somewhere in Time (Golden Globe nom. 1981), Inside Moves, Touched By Love, Body Heat, The Legend of the Lone Ranger, Frances, Hammett, High Road to China, Octopussy, The Golden Seal, Until September, The Cotton Club, A View to a Kill (Golden Globe nom.1986), Jagged Edge, Out of Africa (Academy Award; Golden Globe Award 1986), Howard the Duck, Peggy Sue Got Married, The Living Daylights, Hearts of Fire, Masquerade, A Killing Affair, Dances With Wolves (Academy Award; Golden Globe nom. 1991), Chaplin (Academy Award nom.; Golden Globe nom. 1993), Indecent Proposal, Deception, My Life, The Specialist, Cry the Beloved Country, The Scarlett Letter, Swept from the Sea, Playing by Heart, Mercury Rising, Enigma, The Incredibles, Madagascar (theme), Burn After Reading (soundtrack writer), Madagascar: Escape 2 Africa (soundtrack writer).
TELEVISION: *Movies:* Sophia Loren in Rome, The Glass Menagerie, Love Among the Ruins, Sporting Chance, Eleanor and Franklin, Eleanor and Franklin: The White House Years (Emmy nom. 1977), War Between the Tates, Young Joe, the Forgotten Kennedy, The Gathering, The Corn is Green, Willa, Svengali, In Search of James Bond with Jonathan Ross. *Series:* Drumbeat, Juke Box Jury, Discs a Go-Go, The Human Jungle, Impromptu, The Newcomers, Vendetta, The Persuaders!, The Adventurer, Great Mysteries, U.S.A. Today: The Television Series, Planet X, A Taste of My Life (doc.). Many credits as sountrack writer).

BARRYMORE, DREW
Actress. b. Los Angeles, CA, Feb. 22, 1975. Father is late actor John Barrymore, Jr. (John Drew Barrymore). At 11 months appeared in first commercial. Author of Little Girl Lost (1990).
PICTURES: Altered States (debut, 1980), E.T.: The Extra Terrestrial, Firestarter, Irreconcilable Differences (Golden Globe nom. 1985), Cat's Eye, See You in the Morning, Far From Home, Motorama, Poison Ivy, Waxwork II, Guncrazy (Golden Globe nom. 1993), No Place To Hide, Doppelganger, Wayne's World 2, Bad Girls, Inside the Goldmine, Boys on the Side, Mad Love, Batman Forever, Everyone Says I Love You, Scream, Best Men, Wishful Thinking, The Wedding Singer, Ever After: A Cinderella Story, Home Fries, Never Been Kissed (also exec. prod.), Titan A.E. (voice), Charlie's Angels (also prod.), Donnie Darko (also exec. prod.), Riding in Cars With Boys, Confessions of a Dangerous Mind, Duplex (also prod.), Charlie's Angels 2, So Love Returns (also prod.), 50 First Dates, A Confederacy of Dunces (also prod.), Fever Pitch (also prod.), Curious George (voice), Lucky You (also soundtrack performer), Music and Lyrics, Beverly Hills Chihuahua (voice), He's Just Not That Into You (also exec. prod.), Whip It! (also prod., dir.), Everybody's Fine, Going the Distance.
TELEVISION: *Movies:* Suddenly Love, Bogie, The Adventures of Con Sawyer and Hucklemary Finn, Babes in Toyland, Conspiracy of Love, 15 and Getting Straight, The Sketch Artist, The Amy Fisher Story, Olive-the Other Reindeer (voice, exec. prod. Emmy nom. 2000), Grey Gardens (Emmy nom. 2009, Golden Globe Award 2010). *Series:* 2000 Malibu Road, Disney's Hercules (voice), Family Guy (voice), Shoot to Kill (exec. prod.), Tough Love: Couples (exec. prod.). *Guest:* More than 161 appearances.

BART, PETER
Executive, Producer, Writer, Trade Editor. b. Martha's Vineyard, MA, July 24, 1932. e. Swarthmore College and The London School of Economics. For 10 years, Bart was a reporter for The New York Times and The Wall Street Journal before becoming a production executive at Paramount, Lorimar and MGM/UA. His work has also appeared in magazines such as Harper's, The Atlantic, Saturday Review and GQ. Bart joined Paramount Pictures in 1967, where he played a key role in developing and supervising films such as The Godfather, Paper Moon, Harold and Maude, True Grit and Rosemary's Baby. He was named exec. asst. to Robert Evans, exec. in charge of worldwide prod. He was then appointed Paramount v.p. prod. Resigned 1973 to develop and produce own films for Paramount. Appointed pres. Lorimar Films, 1977. Resigned,1979, to be inde-

pendent producer. In 1983, joined MGM/UA as sr. v.p., prod., in its motion picture div. Resigned, 1985, to be independent producer. Since 1989, he's been reporting on the entertainment industry and is the current v.p., editor-in-chief, Variety, Inc., where he also presides over Variety's sister publications, Daily Variety and Daily Variety-Gotham Edition. Received RAAM Intl. Award 2008 for contributions to the British and Irish film industry.
AUTHOR: Thy Kingdom Come (1983), Destinies (1979), Fade Out, Who Killed Hollywood? (1999), The Gross, Shoot Out: Surviving Fame and (Mis)Fortune in Hollywood (with Peter Guber, 2002), The Gross: The Hits, the Flops-the Summer That Ate Hollywood (1999), Boffo! (2006).
PICTURES: *Producer:* Fun with Dick and Jane (1977), Islands in the Stream, Youngblood, Revenge of the Nerds II: Nerds in Paradise, Fun with Dick and Jane (exec. prod., 2005), Boffo! Tinseltown's Bombs and Blockbusters (documentary, exec. prod., writer) *Writer:* Making It (1971), Reborn (creative consultant). *Actor:* An Alan Smithee Film: Burn Hollywood Burn (1997 as himself), Junket Whore (documentary, as himself), The Young and the Dead (documentary, as himself, former Paramount exec.).
TELEVISION: *Documentaries:* Marlon Brando: The Wild One, Steve McQueen: The King of Cool, Hollywood, D.C., Easy Riders Raging Bulls, Tell Them Who You Are, The Last Mogul: Life and Times of Lew Wasserman. *Series:* Showbiz Today (Daily Variety reporter), Sunday Morning Shootout (host), Storymakers (host), Square Off (exec. prod.).

BARTEK, STEVE

Composer, Orchestrator. b. Jan. 30, 1952. Co-founded musical group Oingo Boingo with composer Danny Elfman.
PICTURES: *Composer:* Guilty as Charged (1991), Past Midnight, Cabin Boy, Senior Trip, Coldblooded, Romy and Michele's High School Reunion, Meet the Deedles (also act.), Snow Day, An Extremely Goofy Movie, Coyote Ugly, Carolina, The Crew, Get Over It (also orchestrator), Novocaine, Spider-Man 2, The Break-Up, The Art of Travel. *Orchestrator:* Forbidden Zone, Pee-Wee's Big Adventure, Summer School, Beetlejuice, Midnight Run, Batman, Strike It Rich, Nightbreed, Bird on a Wire, Darkman, Edward Scissorhands, Article 99, Batman Returns (also music prod.), Sommersby, The Nightmare Before Christmas, Black Beauty, Dolores Claiborne, Dead Presidents, To Die For, The Frighteners, Extreme Measures, Good Will Hunting (also score prod.), A Simple Plan, Psycho, A Civil Action, Sleepy Hollow, Proof of Life, Men in Black II, Red Dragon, Big Fish, Hulk, Eternal Sunshine of the Spotless Mind, Chicago, Charlie and the Chocolate Factory (supr.), Corpse Bride (lead), Deep Sea 3D (doc.), Meet the Robinsons, Nacho Libre, Charlotte's Web, Wrong Turn 2 (musician), Pirates of the Caribbean: At World's End, The Simpsons Movie, The Kingdom, Wrong Turn 2: Dead End (musician), Standard Operating Procedure (doc.), Vantage Point, Forgetting Sarah Marshall, Synecdoche, New York, Wanted, Hellboy II: The Golden Army (lead), Milk, Cirque du Freak: The Vampire's Assistant, The Wolfman (supervisor). *Also songs:* Sommersby, Dolores Claiborne, Black Beauty, To Die For.
TELEVISION: *Movies:* Battlestar Galactica: Razor (musician), Empire State (musician). *Series:* Nightmare Ned, Dilbert (music producer/arranger), Desperate Housewives, Battlestar Galactica (musician), Eureka (musician), Trauma (musician).

BARTKOWIAK, ANDRZEJ

Cinematographer, Director. b. Lodz, Poland, 1950. Attended Polish Film School. Moved to U.S. in 1972, gaining experience in TV commercials and low-budget features. Protege of Sidney Lumet, for whom did several pictures.
PICTURES: Deadly Hero (1976), Prince of the City, Deathtrap, The Verdict, Daniel, Terms of Endearment, Garbo Talks, Prizzi's Honor, The Morning After, Power, Nuts, Twins, Family Business, Q&A, Hard Promises, A Stranger Among Us, Falling Down, Turkey Cake (short), Guilty As Sin, Speed, A Good Man in Africa, Losing Isaiah, Species, Jade, The Mirror Has Two Faces, Dante's Peak, The Devil's Advocate, U.S. Marshals, Lethal Weapon 4, Gossip, Thirteen Days. *Director:* Romeo Must Die (2000), Exit Wounds, Cradle 2 the Grave, Doom, Street Fighter: The Legend of Chun-Li.
TELEVISION: *Director: Movie:* The Five Forty-Eight. *Series:* HRT(pilot).

BASINGER, KIM

Actress. b. Athens, GA, Dec. 8, 1953. e. Neighborhood Playhouse. Began career as Ford model in New York.
PICTURES: Hard Country (debut, 1981), Mother Lode, Never Say Never Again, The Man Who Loved Women, The Natural (Golden Globe nom. 1985), Fool for Love, 9-1/2 Weeks, No Mercy, Blind Date, Nadine, My Stepmother is an Alien, Batman, The Marrying Man, Final Analysis, Cool World, The Real McCoy, Wayne's World 2, Prêt-à-Porter, The Getaway, L.A. Confidential (Acad. Award, Golden Globe Award, Best Supporting Actress, 1998), I Dreamed of Africa, Bless the Child, People I Know, 8 Mile, Aurora Island, The Door in the Floor, Cellular, Elvis Has Left the Building, Jump Shot, Even Money, The Sentinel, While She Was Out (also exec. prod.), The Informers, The Burning Plain, The Death and Life of Charlie St. Cloud.
TELEVISION: *Movies:* Dog and Cat (pilot), The Ghost of Flight 401, Katie: Portrait of a Centerfold, Killjoy, The Mermaid Chair. *Series:* From Here to Eternity, Dog and Cat. *Guest:* More than 78 appearances.

BASS, RONALD

Writer. b. Los Angeles, CA. 1943. e. Yale, Harvard Law School. Entered industry as entertainment lawyer, while writing novels: The Perfect Thief, Lime's Crisis, The Emerald Illusion.
PICTURES: Code Name: Emerald, Black Widow, Gardens of Stone, Rain Man (Academy Award, Golden Globe nom., WGA nom. 1989), Sleeping With the Enemy, The Joy Luck Club (also prod., WGA nom. 1994), When a Man Loves a Woman (also exec. prod), Dangerous Minds, Waiting to Exhale (exec. prod.), My Best Friend's Wedding (prod.), How Stella Got Her Groove Back (also exec. prod.), What Dreams May Come (also exec. prod.), Stepmom (also exec. prod.), Entrapment (also exec. prod.), Snow Falling on Cedars (also prod.), Passion of Mind (also prod.), The Memoirs of Elizabeth Frankenstein, The Lazarus Child (also exec. prod.), Crazy in Love, Mozart and the Whale (also prod.), The Diving Bell and the Butterfly (prod.), Amelia (also exec. prod.).
TELEVISION: *Movies:* The Enemy Within, Reunion, Border Line, Invisible Child, Swing Vote.

BASSETT, ANGELA

Actress. b. New York, NY, Aug. 16, 1958. Moved to St. Petersburg, FL, at 5 yrs. old. e. Yale.
THEATRE: B'way: Ma Rainey's Black Bottom, Joe Turner's Come and Gone, Macbeth. Off-B'way: Colored People's Time, Antigone, Black Girl, Henry IV Part 1. Regional: Beef No Chicken.
PICTURES: F/X (debut, 1986), Kindergarten Cop, Boyz N the Hood, City of Hope, Innocent Blood, Malcolm X, Passion Fish, What's Love Got to Do With It (Academy Award nom., Golden Globe Award 1994), Strange Days, Waiting to Exhale, Vampire in Brooklyn, Panther, Contact, How Stella Got Her Groove Back, Supernova, Boesman and Lena, The Score, Our America (exec. prod. only), Sunshine State, Masked & Anonymous, Mr. 3000, The Lazarus Child, Less Than Kind, Mr 3000, Mr. and Mrs. Smith (voice), Akeelah and the Bee, Time Bomb, Steppin', Meet the Robinsons (voice), Of Boys and Men, Gospel Hill, Meet the Browns, Nothing But the Truth, Notorious, Mama Black Widow, For Colored Girls Who Have Considered Suicide When the Rainbow Is Enuf.
TELEVISION: *Movies/Specials:* Liberty, Family of Spies, Challenger, Storytime (Emmy nom. 1996), Perry Mason: Case of the Silenced Singer, In the Best Interest of the Child, Line of Fire: The Morris Dees Story, The Heroes of Desert Storm, Locked Up: A Mother's Rage, One Special Victory, The Jacksons: An American Dream, Ruby's Bucket of Blood, The Rosa Parks Story (also exec. prod.; Emmy nom. 2002), Our America (Emmy nom. 2003), Time Bomb. *Mini-series:* Africans in America: America's Journey Through Slavery (narr), Unchained Memories: Readings from the Slave Narratives. *Series:* Alias, Independent Lens (host), ER. *Guest:* More than 105 appearances.

BATEMAN, JASON

Actor. b. Rye, NY, Jan. 14, 1969. Brother of actress Justine Bateman. Son of prod.-theatrical mgr. Kent Bateman. Started in commercials until cast in Little House on the Prairie at 12 (1981).
PICTURES: Teen Wolf Too, Necessary Roughness, Breaking the Rules, Love Stinks, Sol Goode, The Sweetest Thing, One Way Out, Starsky & Hutch, Dodgeball: A True Underdog Story, The Break-Up, Arthur and the Invisibles (voice), Fast Track, Smokin' Aces, Mr. Magorium's Wonder Emporium, Seven Day Itch, The Kingdom, Juno, Forgetting Sarah Marshall, The Promotion, Hancock, State of Play, Extract, Up in the Air, The Invention of Lying, Couples Retreat, The Baster, Paul, MacGruber.
TELEVISION: *Movies:* Fantastic World of D.C. Collins, The Thanksgiving Promise, Can You Feel Me Dancing, Bates Motel, Moving Target, Crossing the Mob, A Taste for Killing, Confessions: Two Faces of Evil, This Can't Be Love, Black Sheep, Hart to Hart: Secrets of the Hart. *Mini-series:* Robert Kennedy and His Times. *Series:* Little House on the Prairie, Silver Spoons, It's Your Move, Valerie, The Hogan Family, Simon, Chicago Sons, George & Leo, For Your Love (dir. only), Brother's Keeper (dir.), Some of My Best Friends, The Jake Effect, Arrested Development (Golden Globe Award, Emmy nom., 2005), Sit Down, Shut Up (also pilot). *Guest:* More than 100 appearances.

BATEMAN, JUSTINE

Actress. b. Rye, NY, Feb. 19, 1966. Brother is actor Jason Bateman.
THEATRE: Lulu, Self-Storage, The Crucible, Love Letters, Carnal Knowledge, Speed-the-Plow.
PICTURES: Satisfaction, The Closer, Primary Motive, The Night We Never Met, God's Lonely Man, Highball, Say You'll Be Mine, Kiss & Tell, The TV Set.
TELEVISION: *Movies:* First the Egg, Family Ties Vacation, Right to Kill?, Can You Feel Me Dancing?, The Fatal Image, In the Eyes of a Stranger, Deadbolt, Terror in the Night, Another Woman, Bucket of Blood, Humor Me, The Hollywood Mom's Mystery, To Have and to Hold, Hybrid. *Mini-series:* A Century of Women, Out of Order. *Series:* Family Ties (Golden Globe nom. 1987, Emmy nom. 1986, 1987), Men Behaving Badly, Arrested

Development, Men in Trees, Easy to Assemble. *Guest:* More than 53 appearances.

BATES, KATHY

Actress. b. Memphis, TN, June 28, 1948. e. S. Methodist U. Regional Theatre incl. D.C. and Actor's Theatre in Louisville. Has garnered more than 40 ent. industry wins and/or nominations for various roles throughout career, with more than eight wins and/or award nominations in 2003 for her role in About Schmidt.
THEATRE: Vanities (Off-B'way debut, 1976), Semmelweiss, Crimes of the Heart, The Art of Dining, Goodbye Fidel (B'way debut, 1980), Chocolate Cake and Final Placement, Fifth of July, Come Back to the 5 & Dime Jimmy Dean Jimmy Dean, 'night Mother (Tony nom., Outer Critics Circle Award), Two Masters: The Rain of Terror, Curse of the Starving Class, Frankie and Johnny in the Clair de Lune (Obie, L.A. Drama Critics Award), The Road to Mecca.
PICTURES: Taking Off (debut, 1971), Straight Time, Come Back to the Five & Dime Jimmy Dean Jimmy Dean, Two of a Kind, Summer Heat, My Best Friend is a Vampire, Arthur 2: On the Rocks, Signs of Life, High Stakes, Men Don't Leave, Dick Tracy, White Palace, Misery (Academy Award, Golden Globe & Chicago Film Critics Awards, Best Actress 1991), At Play in the Fields of the Lord, Fried Green Tomatoes (Golden Globe nom. 1992), Shadows and Fog, Prelude to a Kiss, Used People, Road to Mecca, A Home of Our Own, North, Curse of the Starving Class, Dolores Claiborne, Angus, Diabolique, The War at Home, Titanic, Swept from the Sea, Primary Colors (Academy Award nom.; Golden Globe nom. 1999), The Waterboy, The Dress Code, Dragonfly, American Outlaws, Love Liza, About Schmidt (Academy Award nom.; Golden Globe nom. 2003), Unconditional Love, Around the World in 80 Days, The Bridge of San Luis Rey, Little Black Book, Rumor Has It, Relative Strangers, Pushers Needed, Failure to Launch, Charlotte's Web (voice), Bonneville, Bee Movie (voice), Who Stole Santa's Sack? (voice), Charlotte's Web (voice), Fred Claus, The Golden Compass (voice), Christmas Is Here Again, P.S., I Love You, Revolutionary Road, Personal Effects, The Family That Preys, The Day the Earth Stood Still, Revolutionary Road, Cheri, The Blind Side, Earthbound.
TELEVISION: *Movies:* Johnny Bull, Murder Ordained, Hostages, The West Side Waltz, The Late Shift (Emmy nom. Golden Globe, 1997), Annie (American Comedy Award, funniest female perf., Emmy nom.; Golden Globe nom. 2000), My Sister's Keeper, Fargo (dir. only), Warm Springs (Emmy nom. 2005), Ambulance Girl (Emmy nom. 2006, also dir.). *Mini-series:* Dash and Lilly (Emmy nom. for Dir. 1999), Alice. *Series:* All My Children (1984). *Dir./episodes:* Homicide: Life on the Street, NYPD Blue, Oz, Everwood, Six Feet Under (also actress, DGA nom. 2004). *Guest:* More than 89 appearances.

BATTISTA, RICH

Executive. e. B.S. in business admin. from Georgetown Univ., cum laude; M.B.A. from Harvard Business School. Worked as a financial analyst at Morgan Stanley before he joined Fox in 1990. Within the Fox organization Battista held a variety of management roles, including executive v.p. of the Fox Networks Group. He left in 1999 to become co-founder and CEO of iFUSE, a now dissolved youth culture media company. Battista returned to Fox in 2001 as exec. v.p., Fox Television. He then became exec. v.p. of business development and strategy for the Fox Entertainment Group, which includes Fox Broadcasting Company, Fox Sports, Fox Cable networks, Twentieth Century Fox Television, Fox Television Studios and Fox International Channels. He was tapped in December 2004 to become CEO and Director, Gemstar-TV Guide International, Inc., another News Corp. company. In Sept. 2008 Battista returned to Fox as president of Fox National Cable Networks. In this role, Battista oversees a stable of networks including FX, National Geographic Channel, Fox Movie Channel, Fox Reality Channel, Fuel TV and various sports networks including the Big Ten Network co-venture with the Big Ten Conference, with the heads of all of those networks reporting to him. He also heads up cable ad sales. Battista serves on the bd. of directors of the CTAM Educational Foundation and, from 2004-2006, he served a three-year term on the Board of Directors of the National Association of Television Program Executives (NATPE). Battista is also a member of the Board of Governors of Georgetown University, a 50-person elected board which represents the school's alumni body, and is the founder and chmn. of the Georgetown Entertainment and Media Alliance, a 1,300-person nationwide alumni network of media professionals. In addition, he serves on the bd. of directors of the non-profit organization, Hands of Change, which supports at-risk young women in the U.S. and abroad.

BATTSEK, DANIEL

Executive. b. United Kingdom. e. graduate of Oxford Polytechnic, with major in Social and Political Studies. Battsek began his industry career at The Hoyts Film Corporation in Sydney, Australia, where he quickly rose to gen. mgr. in Victoria State overseeing distribution. He then became managing dir. of Palace Pictures where he was involved in all aspects of marketing, distribution and acquisitions in the UK and Ireland. Between 1985 and 1991 the company enjoyed enormous success with such films as When Harry Met Sally and The Crying Game. In 1991, The Walt Disney Co. asked Battsek to start a UK Company as part of the world-wide distribution network for Buena Vista International. In 1992, he officially joined The Walt Disney Studios. Battsek was quickly promoted to v.p./managing dir., where he handled all aspects of theatrical film distribution in the UK. He was later promoted to v.p./managing director and European acquisitions director of BVI (UK) Limited. His responsibilities also included involvement in the acquisition of distribution rights across numerous territories for such films as Muriel's Wedding, Shine, Central Station, Kolya, and Ice Storm. In 1998, Battsek was promoted to senior v.p., BVI (UK) Limited where he oversaw approximately 35 films per year from the Disney, Touchstone and Miramax labels. With his expanding role, Battsek began acquiring and developing British film projects for worldwide distribution. He created the BVI UK Comedy Label which produced four films — High Heels and Low Lifes, Hope Springs, Calendar Girls, which went on to gross over $95 million worldwide, and Kinky Boots. Battsek rose to executive v.p./managing dir. of distribution and production for BVI UK. On July 25, 2005, he was named president of Miramax Films. 2010, Battsek was announced as President of National Geographic Films.

BAUER, STEVEN

Actor. r.n. Rocky Echaveria. b. Havana, Cuba, Dec. 2, 1956. Moved with family to Miami at age 3. e. Miami Dade Jr. Coll. where studied acting. Breakthrough came with selection for role in Que Pasa U.S.A.? for Public TV. Signed by Columbia TV and moved to California.
PICTURES: Scarface (debut, Golden Globe nom. 1983), Thief of Hearts, Running Scared, The Beast, Wildfire, Gleaming the Cube, Raising Cain, Woman of Desire, Improper Conduct, Stranger by Night, Wild Side, Primal Fear, Navajo Blues, Plato's Run, Kickboxing Academy, The Versace Murder, Star Portal, Rave, Naked Lies, Forever Lulu, Traffic, Glory Glory, Rave, El Grito, The Learning Curve, Speed Limit, Masked and Anonymous, Nola, Raptor Island, Pit Fighter, The Feast of the Goat, The Lost City, A Numbers Game, Session, Charlie Valentine, The Intruders, Camouflage, Disarmed, Fast Lane (also prod.), One in the Gun, Promises, Shadows in Paradise, Bulletface, Zenitram, The Work, The Last Gamble, Sweet Lorraine, Suicide Dolls, 513, A Numbers Game, Session.
TELEVISION: *Movies:* She's in the Army Now, An Innocent Love, Sword of Gideon, Sweet Poison, False Arrest, Drive Like Lightning, Sisters and Other Strangers, Boss of Bosses, King of Texas, Raptor Island 2: Raptor Planet, Kings of South Beach. *Mini-series:* Drug Wars: The Camarena Story (Golden Globe nom. 1991). *Series:* ¿Qué pasa, U.S.A.?, From Here To Eternity, Wiseguy, UC: Undercover, South Beach. *Guest:* More than 50 appearances.

BAUMGARTEN, CRAIG

Executive, Producer. b. Aug. 27, 1949. Partner in independent prod. co., New America Cinema. Joined Paramount Pictures as prod. exec.; named v.p., prod. In 1980 went to Keith Barish Prods., of which was pres. three years. In 1983 appointed exec. v.p. & exec. asst. to the pres. & CEO, Columbia Pictures; resigned 1985. Joined Lorimar Motion Pictures as pres. Joined 20th Century Fox m.p. div. as exec. v.p. of prod., 1987; resigned. Formed Adelson/Baumgarten Prods. with Gary Adelson, 1989. Formed Baumgarten/Prophet Entertainment Inc., 1994. Partner in Baumgarten Merims Productions, 1999. Currently runs Baumgarten Management & Production.
PICTURES: *Exec. prod./prod.:* Prisoners, Misunderstood, Hook (co-prod.), Universal Soldier, Nowhere to Run, Blank Check, It Could Happen to You, Jade, The Shooter, Cold Around the Heart, Universal Soldier: The Return, Love Stinks, The Order, Shattered Glass, Peter Pan (co-prod.), Boot Camp, Never Back Down, Universal Soldier: Regeneration.
TELEVISION: *Movies(All exec. prod):* Streetcar Named Desire (Emmy nom. 1984), The Hunchback, The Devil's Child, Lathe of Heaven, Fighting the Odds: The Marilyn Gambrell Story. *Series:* Michael Hayes (exec. prod.)

BAXTER, MEREDITH

Actress. b. Los Angeles, CA, June 21, 1947. e. Interlochen Arts Academy. On stage in Guys and Dolls, Butterflies Are Free, Vanities, Country Wife, Talley's Folly, Love Letters, Diaries of Adam & Eve. Has appeared in more than 45 TV movies since 1973.
PICTURES: Ben, Stand Up and Be Counted, Bittersweet Love, All the President's Men, Jezebel's Kiss, The Mostly Unfabulous Social Life of Ethan Green.
TELEVISION: *Movies:* Cat Creature, The Stranger Who Looks Like Me, Target Risk, The Imposter, Night That Panicked America, Little Women (1978 version), The Family Man, Two Lives of Carol Letner, Take Your Best Shot, The Rape of Richard Beck, Kate's Secret, The Long Journey Home, Winnie, Diaries of Adam and Eve, She Knows Too Much, The Kissing Place, Burning Bridges, Bump in the Night, A Mother's Justice, A Woman Scorned: The Betty Broderick Story (Emmy nom. 1992), Her Final Fury: Betty Broderick—The Last Chapter, Darkness Before Dawn (also co-exec. prod.), For the Love of Aaron, One More Mountain, My Breast (also co-exec. prod.), Betrayed: A Story of Three Women (also co-exec. prod.), Inheritance, Miracle in the Woods, Let Me Call You Sweetheart, Holy Joe, Down Will Come Baby, Miracle on the 17th Green, Wednesday Woman,

Murder on the Orient Express, A Mother's Fight for Justice, Aftermath, A Christmas Visitor, Angel in the Family, Bound by a Secret. *Mini-series*: Beulah Land. *Series:* Bridget Loves Bernie, Family (2 Emmy nom. 1977, 1978), Family Ties, The Faculty, Cold Case. *Guest:* More than 100 appearances.

BAY, MICHAEL
Director, Producer. b. Los Angeles, CA, Feb. 17, 1965. e. Wesleyan U.; Pasadena's Art Center College of Design. Worked on advertisements and created music videos for artists such as Tina Turner, Meatloaf, Lionel Richie and Wilson Phillips. Recipient of the Gold Lion for The Best Beer campaign for Miller Lite; Silver Lion & Grand Prix Clio for Commercial of the Year, for the Got Milk/Aaron Burr commercial; Commercial Dir. of the Year, Directors Guild of America Award, 1995.
PICTURES: Bad Boys, The Rock, Armageddon (also prod.), Mystery Men (actor), Coyote Ugly (actor), Pearl Harbor (also prod.), Bad Boys 2, The Texas Chainsaw Massacre (prod.), The Amityville Horror (prod.), The Island (dir./prod.), The Texas Chainsaw Massacre: The Beginning (prod.), The Hitcher (prod.), Transformers (exec. prod.), The Horsemen (prod.), Friday the 13th (prod.), The Unborn (prod.), Transformers: Revenge of the Fallen (exec. prod., dir.), A Nightmare on Elm Street (prod.), Transformers 3 (exec. prod., dir.).
TELEVISION: *Movies:*Vengeance: The Story of Tony Cimo. *Series:* Night Court (prod. assist.), Cocaine Cowboys (exec. prod.).

BEACH, ADAM
Actor. b. Ashern, Manitoba, Canada, Nov. 11, 1972. Is a Saulteaux Indian from Manitoba, Canada, also Member of the Ojibwa Nation.
PICTURES: The Last Great Warrior, Dance Me Outside, Smoke Signals, Mystery, Alaska, Joe Dirt, Windtalkers, Flags of Our Fathers, Warrior, The Stranger.
TELEVISION: *Movies:* Lost in the Barrens, Spirit Rider, Harry's Case, Skinwalkers, Cowboys and Indians: The J.J. Harper Story, Coyote Waits, A Thief of Time, Johnny Tootall, Luna: Spirit of the Whale, Bury My Heart at Wounded Knee (Golden Globe nom. 2008). *Mini-series:* Comanche Moon. *Series:* North of 60, The Rez, Moose TV, Law & Order: Special Victims Unit, Big Love. *Guest:* More than 40 appearances.

BEACHAM, STEPHANIE
Actress. b. Casablanca, Morocco, Feb. 28, 1947. e. RADA. On London stage in The Basement, On Approval, London Cuckolds, etc.
PICTURES: The Games, Tam Lin, The Nightcomers, Dracula A.D., And Now the Screaming Starts!, Schizo, The Confessional, Horror Planet, The Wolves of Willoughby Chase, Troop Beverly Hills, Wedding Bell Blues, Saving Grace, Relative Values, Would I Lie to You?, The Witches Hammer, Love and Other Disasters, Plot 7.
TELEVISION: *Movies/Specials*: The Queen's Traitor, Black Exchange, Secrets, To Be the Best, Foreign Affairs, Riders, A Change of Place. When Shoulder Pads Ruled the World, A Distant Scream, *Mini-series:* Sentimental Education, Napoleon and Love, Jane Eyre, Sorrell and Son, Napoleon and Josephine: A Love Story, Lucky/Chances, No Bananas. *Series*: The Rag Trade, Marked Personal, Tenko (PBS), Connie, The Colbys, Dynasty, The Bold and the Beautiful, Sister Kate (Golden Globe nom. 1990), Cluedo, Beverly Hills 90210, SeaQuest 2032, SeaQuest DSV, Bad Girls, Having It Off, Coronation Street. *Guest:* More than 91 appearances.

BEALS, JENNIFER
Actress. b. Chicago, IL, Dec. 19, 1963. Started as fashion model before making film debut in small role in My Bodyguard, 1980.
PICTURES: My Bodyguard, Flashdance (Golden Globe nom. 1984), The Bride, Split Decisions, Vampire's Kiss, Sons, Blood and Concrete, In the Soup, The Gamble, Caro Diario, Mrs. Parker and the Vicious Circle, Arabian Knight (voice), Devil in a Blue Dress, Let It Be Me, Four Rooms, The Search for One-Eye Jimmy, Wishful Thinking, Body and Soul, Something More, Militia, Fear of Flying, Out of Line, The Anniversary Party, After the Storm, Roger Dodger, 13 Moons, Mission Without Permission, The Runaway Jury, Break a Leg, Catch That Kid, Desolation Sound, The Grudge 2, Joueuse, The Book of Eli.
TELEVISION: *Movies:* Terror Stalks the Class Reunion, Indecency, Night Owl, Twilight of the Golds, The Spree, A House Divided, Being Brewster, The Shoot Divas, Don't They?, My Name Is Sarah. *Mini-series:* Feast of All Saints. *Series:* 2000 Malibu Road, Nothing Sacred, Earthlings, The L Word. *Guest:* More than 50 appearances.

BEAN, ORSON
Actor. r.n. Dallas Frederick Burrows. b. Burlington, VT, July 22, 1928. Performed in nightclubs as comic and on Broadway (Never Too Late, Will Success Spoil Rock Hunter?, Subways Are for Sleeping, Roar of the Grease Paint, the Smell of the Crowd, Ilya Darling.) Author of Me and the Orgone. Founder, administrator, dir. 15th St. School, NY.
PICTURES: How to Be Very Very Popular (debut, 1955), Anatomy of a Murder, Lola, Forty Deuce, Innerspace, Instant Karma, Final Judgment, One of Those Nights, Being John Malkovich, Unbowed, Soccer Dog: European Cup, Waterborne, Mattie Fresno and the Holoflux Universe, Alien Autopsy, Alien Autopsy, Ashley's Ashes.
TELEVISION: *Movies/Specials:* Arsenic and Old Lace, Chance of a Lifetime, Just My Imagination, Dr. Quinn Medicine Woman: The Movie, Safe Harbor. *Series:* The Blue Angel (host), I've Got a Secret (panelist), Keep Talking, To Tell the Truth (panelist), Match Game (panelist), Mary Hartman Mary Hartman, Dr. Quinn: Medicine Woman, Normal Ohio, Knee High P.I., Desperate Housewives. *Guest:* More than 102 appearances.

BEAN, SEAN
Actor. b. Sheffield, Yorkshire, England, April 17, 1958.
THEATRE: Romeo and Juliet, Fair Maid of the West, Midsummer Night's Dream, Who Knew Mackenzie and Gone, Deathwatch, Last Days of Mankind. London: Macbeth.
PICTURES: Winter Flight, Caravaggio, Stormy Monday, War Requeim, The Field, Patriot Games. Shopping, Black Beauty, Goldeneye, When Saturday Comes, Leo Tolstoy's Anna Karenina, Ronin, Bravo Two Zero, Airborne, The Canterbury Tales (voice), The Book That Wrote Itself, Essex Boys, Don't Say a Word, Lord of the Rings: Fellowship of the Ring, Equilibrium, Tom and Thomas, Equilibrium, The Lord of the Rings: The Two Towers, The Big Empty, The Lord of the Rings:The Return of the King, Troy, National Treasure, Venetian Heat, Barry, The Dark, North Country, Flightplan, The Island, Silent Hill, The Hitcher, Ca$h!, Red Riding: 1974, Red Riding: 1983, Black Death, Percy Jackson & the Olympians: The Lightning Thief, Age of Heroes.
TELEVISION: *Movies:* Troubles, Small Zones, The Fifteen Streets, Lorna Doone, Tell Me That You Love Me, My Kingdom for a Horse, Clarissa, Fool's Gold: The Story of the Brink's-Mat Robbery, Sharpe's Rifles, Sharpe's Eagle, Lady Chatterley, A Woman's Guide to Adultery, Sharpe's Company, Sharpe's Enemy, Sharpe's Honour, Jacob, Winter Flight, Sharpe's Gold, Sharpe's Battle, Sharpe's Sword, Samson & Delilah, In Search of James Bond with Jonathan Ross, Sharpe's Regiment, The True Bride, Prince, Sharpe's Siege, Sharpe's Mission, Sharpe's Revenge, Sharpe's Justice, Sharpe's Waterloo, The Lord of the Piercing (TV short), Extremely Dangerous, Henry VIII, Pride (voice), Faceless, Sharpe's Challenge, Sharpe's Peril. *Mini-series:* Scarlett. *Series:* Game of Thrones (pilot only). *Guest:* More than 88 appearances.

BÉART, EMMANUELLE
Actress. b. Gassin, France, Aug. 14, 1965. Moved to Montreal at age 15. Returned to France and enrolled in drama school.
THEATRE: La Repetition ou l'Amour Puni, La Double Inconstance.
PICTURES: Premiers Desirs, L'Enfant Trouve, L'Amour en Douce, Manon of the Spring, Date With an Angel, A Gauche en Sortant de L'Ascenseur, Les Enfants du Desordre, Capitaine Fracasse, La Belle Noiseuse, J'Embrasse Pas, Un Coeur en Hiver, Ruptures, Divertimento, L'Enfer, Une Femme Francaise, Nelly & Mr. Arnaud, Mission: Impossible, Voleur de Vie, Le Temps Retrouve, Don Juan, Elephant Juice, Season's Beatings, Replay, Voyance et manigance, 8 femmes, Strayed, Nathalie X, The Story of Marie and Julien, À boire, Un fil à la patte, L' Enfer, A Crime, Le Héros de la famille (also soundtrack performer), Les Témoins, The Witnesses, Just the Three of Us, Ça commence par la fin.
TELEVISION: *Movies:* Zacharius, Raison Perdue, Et demain viendra le jour, Femme de sa vie, La, Marie-Antoinette, reine d'un seul amour, D'Artagnan et les trois mousquetaires.

BEATTY, NED
Actor. b. Lexington, KY, July 6, 1937. Worked at Barter Theatre in Virginia appearing in over 70 plays, 1957-66; with Arena Stage, Washington D.C. 1963-71. Made B'way debut in The Great White Hope, London: The Cat on a Hot Tin Roof.
PICTURES: Deliverance (debut, 1972), The Life and Times of Judge Roy Bean, The Thief Who Came to Dinner, The Last American Hero, White Lightning, Nashville, All the President's Men, The Big Bus, Network (nom., Academy Award, best actor in supporting role, 1977), Mikey and Nicky, Silver Streak, Exorcist II: The Heretic, Gray Lady Down, Superman, Alambrista!, Promises in the Dark, 1941, Wise Blood, American Success Company, Hopscotch, The Incredible Shrinking Woman, Superman II, The Toy, Touched, Stroker Ace, Back to School, The Big Easy, The Fourth Protocol, The Trouble With Spies, Switching Channels, Rolling Vengeance, The Unholy, Midnight Crossing, After the Rain, Physical Evidence, Time Trackers, Big Bad John, Chattahoochee, A Cry in the Wild, Repossessed, Blind Vision, Going Under, Hear My Song (Golden Globe nom. 1992), Prelude to a Kiss, Ed and His Dead Mother, Rudy, Black Water, Radioland Murders, Just Cause, The Curse of Inferno, He Got Game, Life, Cookie's Fortune, Spring Forward, Where the Red Fern Grows, Thunderpants, Sweet Land, The Walker, Shooter, Charlie Wilson's War, The Killer Inside Me, Toy Story 3 (voice).
TELEVISION: *Movies:* Has appeared in approx. 50 tv movies/mini-series, incl.: Footsteps, Marcus-Nelson Murders, Dying Room Only, The Execution of Private Slovik, Attack on Terror: The FBI vs. the Ku Klux Klan, A Question of Love, Friendly Fire (Emmy nom. 1979), Guyana Tragedy, The Violation of Sarah McDavid, Splendor in the Grass, A Woman Called Golda, Kentucky Woman, Hostage Flight, Spy, Last Train Home (Emmy nom. 1990), The Inside Story, T Bone N Weasel,

Gulliver's Travels, Crazy Horse, Homicide: The Movie, Roughing It, The Wool Cap. *Mini-series:* The Last Days of Pompeii, Robert Kennedy and His Times, Streets of Laredo, I Was a Rat. *Series:* Szysznyk, The Boys, Homicide: Life on the Street. *Documentaries:* Frederic Remington: The Truth of Other Days (voice), Lincoln (voice), Warren Oates: Across the Border (narr.), The Great War and the Shaping of the 20th Century (mini-series, voice). *Guest:* More than 115 appearances.

BEATTY, WARREN
Actor, Producer, Director, Writer. r.n. Henry Warren Beaty. b. Richmond, VA, March 30, 1937. e. Northwestern U. Sister is actress Shirley MacLaine. m. actress Annette Bening. Studied with Stella Adler. Small roles on television; on stage in Compulsion (winter stock, North Jersey Playhouse); *B'way debut:* A Loss of Roses (Theatre World Award). Received Irving G. Thalberg Memorial Award 2000. Received Cecil B. DeMille Award 2007.
PICTURES: Splendor in the Grass (debut, 1961, Golden Globe Award, 1 other nom.), The Roman Spring of Mrs. Stone, All Fall Down, Lilith, Mickey One, Promise Her Anything, Kaleidoscope, Bonnie and Clyde (also prod., 2 Academy Award nom.; Golden Globe nom. 1968), The Only Game in Town, McCabe and Mrs. Miller, $ (Dollars), The Parallax View, Shampoo (also prod., co-s.p.; Academy Award nom.; Golden Globe nom. 1976), The Fortune, Heaven Can Wait (also prod., co-dir., co-s.p.; 4 Academy Award nom. DGA nom.; Golden Globe Award 1979), Reds (also prod., dir., co-s.p.; Academy Award for Best dir., 3 other nom.; DGA Award, Golden Globe Award, 2 other nom. 1981), Ishtar (also prod.), Dick Tracy (also prod., dir.), Bugsy (also co-prod.; 2 Academy Award nom.; Golden Globe nom. 1992), Love Affair (also prod, co-s.p.), Bulworth (also prod., dir., s.p.; Academy Award nom.; 2 Golden Globe nom. 1999), Forever Hollywood, Down to Earth (s.p. 1978 s.p. Heaven Can Wait), Town and Country. *Documentary:* Arthur Penn, 1922: Themes and Variants, A Decade Under the Influence.
TELEVISION: *Movie:* Dick Tracy Special (exec. prod.). *Series:* The Many Loves of Dobie Gillis (1959-60). *Guest:* More than 97 appearances.

BECK, MICHAEL
Actor. r.n. Michael Beck Tucker. b. Memphis, TN, Feb. 4, 1949. e. Millsaps Coll. on football scholarship (quarterback). Became active in college theatre. In 1971 attended Central Sch. of Speech & Drama, London; studied 3 years, following which toured England with repertory companies for 2 years. Returned to U.S.; cast as lead in independent film, Madman (shot in Israel in 1977).
PICTURES: Madman, The Warriors, Xanadu, Megaforce, War Lords of the 21st Century, The Golden Seal, Triumphs of a Man Called Horse, Final Judgment, Forest Warrior, Jungle Book: Lost Treasure (voice), Yerba City.
TELEVISION: *Movies:* Mayflower: The Pilgrim's Adventure, Alcatraz: The Whole Shocking Story, Fly Away Home, The Last Ninja, Rearview Mirror, Chiller, Blackout, Only One Survived, Houston: Legend of Texas, Deadly Game, Stranger at My Door, Fade to Black. *Mini-series:* Holocaust, Celebrity. *Series:* Houston Knights.

BECKER, HAROLD
Director. b. New York, NY, 1950. Dir. documentaries, Eugene Atget Interview with Bruce Gordon, Blind Gary Davis, Signet, Ivanhoe Donaldson.
PICTURES: The Ragman's Daughter (debut, 1972), The Onion Field, The Black Marble, Taps, Vision Quest, The Boost, Sea of Love, Malice (also co-prod.), City Hall (also co-prod.), Mercury Rising, Domestic Disturbance (also prod.), Vengeance: A Love Story.

BECKINSALE, KATE
Actress. b. London, England, July 26, 1973.
THEATRE: London: Hayfever, Faithless, Clocks and Whistles, Sweetheart, The Seagull.
PICTURES: Prince of Jutland, Uncovered, Marie-Louise ou la permission, Haunted, Shooting Fish, The Last Days of Disco, Brokedown Palace, The Golden Bowl, Pearl Harbor, Serendipity, Laurel Canyon, Underworld, Van Helsing, The Aviator, Underworld: Evolution, Click, Snow Angels, Vacancy, Winged Creatures, Whiteout, Nothing But the Truth, Underworld: Rise of the Lycans, Everybody's Fine.
TELEVISION: *Movies:* One Against the Wind, Rachel's Dream, Cold Comfort Farm, Emma, Alice Through The Looking Glass. *Mini-series*: Devices and Desires *Series:* Hercules (voice). *Guest:* More than 70 appearances.

BEDELIA, BONNIE
Actress. r.n. Bonnie Bedelia Culkin. b. New York, NY, March 25, 1946. e. Hunter Coll. Nephew is Macaulay Culkin.
THEATRE: Enter Laughing, The Playroom, My Sweet Charlie (Theatre World Award).
PICTURES: The Gypsy Moths (debut, 1969), They Shoot Horses Don't They?, Lovers and Other Strangers, The Strange Vengeance of Rosalie, Between Friends, The Big Fix, Heart Like a Wheel (Golden Globe nom. 1984), Death of an Angel, Violets Are Blue, The Boy Who Could Fly, The Stranger, Die Hard, The Prince of Pennsylvania, Fat Man and Little Boy, Die Hard 2, Presumed Innocent, Needful Things, Speechless, Judicial Consent, Homecoming, Bad Manners, Gloria, Sordid Lives, Manhood, Berkeley.
TELEVISION: *Movies*: Then Came Bronson, Sandcastles, A Time for Love, Hawkins on Murder, Message to My Daughter, Heatwave!, Question of Love, Walking Through the Fire, Salem's Lot, Tourist, Fighting Back, Million Dollar Infield, Memorial Day, Alex: The Life of a Child, The Lady from Yesterday, Somebody Has to Shoot the Picture, Switched at Birth, A Mother's Right: The Elizabeth Morgan Story, The Fire Next Time, Legacy of Sin: The William Coit Story, Shadow of a Doubt, Her Costly Affair, Any Mother's Son, To Live Again, Locked in Silence (Emmy nom. 2000), Flowers for Algernon, Picnic. *Series:* Love of Life, The New Land, Fallen Angels (Emmy nom. 1994), Partners, Heart of the City, The Division, Big Love, Sordid Lives: The Series, Parenthood (pilot). *Guest:* More than 53 appearances.

BEEKS, STEVE
Executive. e. Bachelor of Science degree in industrial engineering from Calif. Polytechnic State Univ. in San Luis Obispo, CA. Master's degree in business admin. from Harvard Business School. From Aug. 1983 to Jan. 1985, mgt. consultant with Touche Ross & Co., now known as Deloitte Touche. From early 1986 to early 1994, he was v.p. business development for The Paragon Group, a limited partnership formed to invest in the entertainment industry; at the same time he was also executive v.p. and pres., Home Entertainment, for Republic Pictures Corporation. As part of Paragon, Beeks sought particular investment opportunities and performed financial analyses and negotiation on a number of potential deals. In August 1986 Paragon purchased a controlling interest in Republic Pictures. During his eight years at Republic Pictures, Beeks grew the home entertainment group's annual revenues from $15 million to $70 million and served as an officer of that public company. In May 1994, Republic was successfully sold to Spelling Entertainment, now a division of Paramount Pictures. Previously, Beeks started Hallmark Home Entertainment, for the Hallmark Cards company, as an independent home video distributor in October 1994, distributing filmed entertainment produced by the company as well as several other independent suppliers. HHE became one of the leading independent home video distributors with exclusive relationships with The Samuel Goldwyn Company, October Films, Showtime Original Pictures and others. He oversaw all aspects of the business, including sales, marketing, finance, accounting, and operations. Beeks was pres. of Artisan Home Entertainment, which he joined in January 1998, following the purchase of the Company by Bain Capital. He grew his division's revenue from $115 million to $300 million during his tenure. As pres. of the division, he spearheaded the marketing, advertising, sale and distribution of Artisan's theatrical films and extensive library of feature films in the videocassette and DVD market as well as overseeing the acquisition and/or production of new programming. Following the merger of Lionsgate and Artisan in 2003, Lionsgate's home entertainment division has emerged as the largest and most powerful home entertainment business in the independent marketplace, capturing nearly 6% overall market share. Lionsgate's family home entertainment division, one of the largest and fastest-growing family entertainment operations in the industry, ranks fourth among entertainment studios with approximately 10% market share in children's non-theatrical titles. Beeks moved to Lions Gate with the merger and Beeks has overseen a trend of steady growth year-over-year, with a growth rate of 13% in fiscal 2006. Beeks became pres. of Lions Gate Entertainment, Inc. in Dec. 2003. Since July 2006, he has been pres.and Co-COO since 2007 of Lions Gate Entertainment Corp. and is a member of Lionsgate's senior decision-making team with Lions Gate CEO Jon Feltheimer and Vice Chairman Michael Burns.

BEGLEY, ED, JR.
Actor. b. Los Angeles, CA, Sept. 16, 1949. Son of late actor Ed Begley. Debut in a guest appearance on My Three Sons at 17. On NY stage in The Cryptogram.
PICTURES: Now You See Him Now You Don't (debut, 1972), Showdown, Superdad, Cockfighter, Stay Hungry, Blue Collar, The One and Only, Goin' South, Hardcore, The In-Laws, The Concorde: Airport '79, Private Lessons, Cat People, Eating Raoul, This Is Spinal Tap, Streets of Fire, Protocol, Transylvania 6-5000, Waiting to Act, Amazon Women on the Moon, The Accidental Tourist, Scenes From the Class Struggle in Beverly Hills, She-Devil, Meet the Applegates, Dark Horse, Greedy, Even Cowgirls Get the Blues, Renaissance Man, The Pagemaster, Sensation, Batman Forever, Rave Review, Storybook Hourglass, The Crazysitter, Santa With Muscles, Lay of the Land, Ms. Bear, Joey, I'm Losing You, Best In Show, Get Over It, Anthrax, Diary of a Sex Addict, Bug, Auto Focus, Back By Midnight, Net Games, Bathroom Boy, A Mighty Wind, Going Down, Stateside, Relative Strangers, Desolation Sound, Francis Hamper, The Optimist, Making Change, The Legend of William Tell, Tripping Forward, For Your Consideration, The Elder Son, One Long Night, He's Such a Girl, Fly Me to the Moon 3D (voice), Whatever Works, 21 and a Wake-Up, Around the World in 50 Years 3D (voice), Making Change, The Penthouse.
TELEVISION: *Movies:* Family Flight, Amateur Night at the Dixie

Bar and Grill, Elvis, Hot Rod, A Shining Season, Rascals and Robbers - Secret Adventures of Tom Sawyer and Huck Finn, Tales of the Apple Dumpling Gang, Not Just Another Affair, Still the Beaver, An Uncommon Love, Roman Holiday, Spies Lies & Naked Thighs, Not a Penny More Not a Penny Less, In the Best Interest of the Child, Chance of a Lifetime, The Story Lady, In the Line of Duty: Siege at Marion, Exclusive, Running Mates,. Cooperstown, Columbo: Undercover, Incident at Deception Ridge, The Shaggy Dog, Murder She Purred: A Mrs. Murphy Mystery, Homicide The Movie, Hounded, Life on Liberty Street, Spirit Bear: The Simon Jackson Story, Recount. *Mini-series:* Kingdom Hospital. *Series:* Roll Out, Battlestar Galactica, Scooby and Scrappy-Doo (voice), The Smurfs (voice), St. Elsewhere (6 Emmy nom.; Golden Globe nom. 1986), The All-New Scooby and Scrappy-Doo Show (actor/voice), Parenthood, Captain Planet and the Planeteers (voice), Earth Aid, NYPD Blue, Winnetka Road, Meego, Providence, Pigs Next Door, Jack & Bobby, Six Feet Under, Arrested Development, My Adventures in Television, Boston Legal, Veronica Mars, Gary Unmarried. *Guest:* More than 231 appearances.

BEHRING, JOHN

Director.
TELEVISION: *Movies:* My Indian Summer. *Series:* Touched by an Angel, The Cape, The Lazarus Man, Dawson's Creek, Charmed, Roswell, Resurrection Blvd., L.A. Dragnet, One Tree Hill, Numb3rs (also supr. prod., prod.).

BEINEIX, JEAN-JACQUES

Director, Writer, Producer. b. Paris France, October, 8, 1946. Various films as second unit director or assistant director.
PICTURES:Diva (also writer), Moon in the Gutter (also writer), Betty Blue (also writer, prod.), Roselyne et les lions (also writer), IP5: Island of the Pachyderms (also writer, prod.), Mortal Transfer (also writer), Requiem for Billy the Kid (exec. prod.), Allez, yallah! (documentary).
TELEVISION: *Documentaries:* Loft Paradoxe, CosmicConnexion.

BELAFONTE, HARRY

Actor, Singer, Producer. r.n. Harold George Belafonte, b. New York, NY, March 1, 1927. d. is Shari Belafonte. Trained for stage at the Actors Studio, New Sch. for Social Research and American Negro Theatre. Professional debut, Royal Roost nightclub, N.Y., Village Vanguard, 1950. Broadway debut: John Murray Anderson's Almanac, 1953. Recording, concert artist. Emmy Award for Tonight With Harry Belafonte, 1961.
THEATRE: Juno and the Paycock, John Murray Anderson's Almanac. (Tony Award, 1953), Three for Tonight, A Night With Belafonte, To Be Young Gifted and Black (prod.), Asinamali (co-prod.).
PICTURES: Bright Road (debut, 1953), Carmen Jones, Island in the Sun, Odds Against Tomorrow, The World the Flesh and the Devil, Angel Levine, Buck and the Preacher, Uptown Saturday Night, Beat Street (prod., composer), The Player, Prêt-à-Porter, White Man's Burden, Kansas City (NY Society of Film Critics Award, 1997), Jazz '34 (narr.),Life and Debt (sountrack writer, performer), Beyond the Sea (soundtrack writer), No Direction Home: Bob Dylan (doc. soundtrack performer), Bobby.
TELEVISION: *Movies:* Grambling's White Tiger, Swing Vote, The Nightclub Years, Kansas City, No Direction Home: Bob Dylan (soundtrack). Many variety specials and more than 12 documentaries. *Mini-series:* Parting the Waters (exec. prod.). *Series:* Sugar Hill Times. *Guest:* More than 133 appearances.

BELAFONTE, SHARI

Actress. b. New York, NY, Sept. 22, 1954. e. Carnegie-Mellon U., BFA, 1976. Daughter of actor-singer Harry Belafonte. Worked as publicist's asst. at Hanna Barbera Prods. before becoming successful model (appearing on more than 200 magazine covers and in numerous TV commercials).
PICTURES: If You Could See What I Hear, Time Walker, Speed Zone!, Feuer Eis & Dynamit, Murder by Numbers, The Player, Mars, Loving Evangeline.
TELEVISION: *Movies:* Hotel, The Midnight Hour, Kate's Secret, Perry Mason: The Case of the All-Star Assassin, French Silk, Heidi Chronicles, Thirdspace. *Host:* Big Hex of Little Lulu, AM Los Angeles, Living the Dream: a Tribute to Dr. Martin Luther King Jr., Lifestyles with Robin Leach and Shari Belafonte, First Edition, The Caribbean with Shari Belafonte, Intimate Portrait: Diahann Carroll (narr.). *Series:* Hotel, *Pilot:* Velvet, Beyond Reality. *Guest:* More than 52 appearances.

BELGRAD, DOUG

Executive. Belgrad is a film production executive who's been running production for Columbia Pictures with colleague Matt Tolmach since 2003. In March 2008, the pair were promoted to co-presidents of Columbia Pictures, A Sony Pictures Entertainment Company, and extended their contracts with the studio through 2011. They reported to Amy Pascal and Michael Lynton, co-chairmen of the studio. Since Belgrad and Tolmach became Columbia's presidents of production in 2003, films under their guidance have grossed approximately $7.6 billion. Twenty-five titles developed and produced by them and their team opened #1. During their tenure, they have overseen one of the most lucrative and successful eras in Columbia Pictures history. Belgrad became president of Columbia Pictures in 2010. Hits with Tolmach include the "Spider-Man" franchise, "Casino Royale," "Superbad," "Hitch," "The DaVinci Code," "Talladega Nights: The Ballad of Ricky Bobby," "Ghost Rider," "The Pursuit of Happyness," "Click," "50 First Dates," "The Grudge," and many others. Belgrad and Tolmach jointly oversee Columbia's slate of 12 to 14 films annually. They are members of the Academy of Motion Picture Arts & Sciences and serve on the bd. of directors of the Environmental Media Association.

BELLFORT, TOM

Sound.
Sound work in over 40 pictures.
PICTURES:*Sound Editor/Suprv. Sound Editor:* Rumble Fish, The Right Stuff, Amadeus, The Terminator, The Cotton Club, The Journey of Natty Gann, Raw Deal, Seize the Day, The Bedroom Window, Gardens of Stone (ARD editor), Million Dollar Mystery (ARD artist), The Princess Bride, The Couch Trip (ADR editor), Shoot to Kill, Big, License to Drive, Tucker: The Man and His Dream, True Believer (sound effects editor), Fletch Lives (sound effect editor), Renegades (sound effects editor), Uncle Buck, Steel Magnolias, Driving Miss Daisy (ADR editor), Narrow Margin, The Godfather: Part III, Bingo!, Radioland Murders, Iron Monkey (ADR editor), The Last Supper, Mission: Impossible, One Fine Day, Volcano, Campfire Tales, Titanic (Academy Award, Best Sound Editing; Motion Picture Sound Editors, Award 1998), 54, Star Wars: Episode I-The Phantom Menace (nom. BAFTA, Academy Award nom.; Motion Picture Sound Editors 3 noms.; Best Sound Editing 2000), Fight Club (adr. editor), Frequency, Hart's War, Panic Room (ADR editor), Adventures of Pluto Nash, The Recruit, Minority Report (Motion Picture Sound Editors, nom. 2003), Radio, 13 Going On 30, Exorcist: The Beginning, The Last Shot, xXx 2: The Next Level, Serenity, Snakes on a Plane, Next, Fracture, Untraceable, Hellboy II: The Golden Army (also ADR editor, Motion Picture Sound Editors nom. 2009), G.I. Joe: The Rise of Cobra (suprv. ADR editor), Love Ranch (suprv. ADR editor).
TELEVISION: *Mini-series:* The Pacific (suprv. sound editor). *Series:* Tales from the Crypt, The Young Indiana Jones Chronicles (Emmy Award 1993).

BELLOCCHIO, MARCO

Director, Writer. b. Piacenza, Italy, Nov. 9, 1939. e. Academy of Cinematografia, Rome (studying acting, then film directing); Slade School of Fine Arts, London 1959-63.
PICTURES: Fist in His Pocket (debut, 1965), China Is Near, Amore e Rabbia (segment: Discutiamo Discutiamo), Nel Nome del Padre, Slap the Monster on the Front Page (also co-s.p.), Madmen to Be Released, Triumphal March, Il Gabbiano, The Film Machine, Leap Into the Void, The Eyes and the Mouth, Henry IV, Devil in the Flesh, The Sabba's Vision, The Conviction, The Butterfly's Dream, Broken Dreams, The Prince of Homburg, The Nanny, Another World Is Possible The Religion Hour (My Mother's Smile) (also co-prod.), Good Morning, Night, Radio West, Il Regista di matrimoni, Vincere.
TELEVISION: *Movie:* The Seagull. *Documentaries:* The Cinema Machine, ... addio del passato..., Stessa rabbia, stessa primavera (actor).

BELMONDO, JEAN-PAUL

Actor. b. Neuilly-sur-Seine, France, April 9, 1933. e. private drama school of Raymond Girard, and the Conservatoire d'Art Dramatique. Formed a theatre group with Annie Girardot and Guy Bedos.
THEATRE: (Jean Marais' production) Caesar and Cleopatra, Treasure Party, Oscar, Kean, Cyrano de Bergerac, Tailleur pour Dames, La Puce a L'Oreille.
PICTURES: A Pied a Cheval et En Voiture (By Foot Horse and Car), Look Pretty and Shut Up, Drole de Dimanche, Les Tricheurs, Les Copains du Dimanche, Charlotte et Son Jules, A Double Tour, Breathless, Classe Tous Risques, Moderato Cantabile, La Francaise et l'Amour, Les Distractions, Mademoiselle Ange, La Novice, Two Women, La Viaccia, Une Femme Est une Femme, Leon Morin Pretre, Les Amours Celebres, Un Singe en Hiver, Le Doulos, L'Aine des Ferchaux, La Mer A Boire, Banana Peel, That Man From Rio, Cent Mille Dollars au Soleil, Echappement Libre, La Chasse a l'Homme, Dieu a Choisi Paris, Weekend a Zuydcocte, Par Un Beau Matin d'Ete, Up to His Ears, Is Paris Burning?, Casino Royale, The Thief of Paris, Pierrot le Fou, The Brain, Love Is a Funny Thing, Mississippi Mermaid, Borsalino, A Man I Like, The Burglars, Tender Scoundrel, Inheritor, Stavisky, Fear Over the City, L'Animal, The Professional, Ace of Aces, The Vultures, Happy Easter, Hold Up, Le Solitaire, Itinerary of a Spoiled Child (also prod., Cesar Award), L'Inconnu dans la Maison, Les Miserables, Les Cent et une Nuits, Desire, Une chance sur deux, Peut-etre, Les Acteurs, Amazon.
TELEVISION: *Movies:* Les Trois mousquetaires, Belmondo le maqnifique, L'Aine des Ferchaux.

BELUSHI, JAMES

Actor. b. Chicago, IL, June 15, 1954. e. DuPage Coll., Southern Illinois U. Brother was late actor John Belushi. Began at Chicago's Second City Theatre.
THEATRE: Sexual Perversity in Chicago, The Pirates of

Penzance, True West, Conversations With My Father, Baal.
PICTURES: Thief (debut, 1981), Trading Places, The Man with One Red Shoe, Salvador, About Last Night, Jumpin' Jack Flash, Little Shop of Horrors, Number One With a Bullet (co-s.p. only), The Principal, Real Men, Red Heat, Who's Harry Crumb?, K-9, Homer and Eddie, Wedding Band, Taking Care of Business, Mr. Destiny, The Palermo Connection, Only the Lonely, Masters of Menace (cameo), Curly Sue, Once Upon a Crime, Diary of a Hitman (cameo), Traces of Red, Last Action Hero (cameo), Destiny Turns on the Radio, Separate Lives, Canadian Bacon, Race the Sun, Jingle All the Way, Gold in the Streets, Retroactive, Living in Peril, Gang Related, Wag the Dog, The Florentine, Angel's Dance, Made Men, Return to Me, Joe Somebody, Snow Dogs, One Way Out, K-9: P.I., Pinocchio (voice), Easy Six, Hoodwinked! (voice), The Wild (voice), Farce of the Penguins (voice), Underdog, Dorothy of OZ (voice), Mother's Little Helpers, The Ghost Writer, The Secret Lives of Dorks.
TELEVISION: *Movies:* Royce, Parallel Lives, Sahara, Who Killed Atlanta's Children?, Casper's Scare School. *Mini-series*: Wild Palms. *Series:* Who's Watching the Kids?, Working Stiffs, Saturday Night Live (Emmy nom. for outstanding writing 1984), Mighty Ducks (voice), It's Good to Be King, Total Security, According to Jim. *Guest:* More than 115 appearances.

BELZER, RICHARD
Actor, Comedian. b. Bridgeport, CT, Aug. 4, 1944.
PICTURES: The Groove Tube (debut, 1974), Fame, Author Author, Night Shift, Scarface, America, Flicks, The Wrong Guys, Freeway, Fletch Lives, The Big Picture, The Bonfire of the Vanities, Off and Running, Mad Dog and Glory, Girl 6, A Very Brady Sequel, Get on the Bus, Species II, Man on the Moon, Jump, Thira (also exec. prod.), Santorini Blue.
TELEVISION: *Movies:* The Flash, Bandit: Bandit Bandit, Hart to Hart: Crimes of the Hart, Prince for a Day, Deadly Pursuits, Homicide: The Movie. *Mini-series:* The Invaders. *Series:* The Late Show (host, 1988), When Cars Attack (host, writer), Homicide: Life on the Street, Law & Order, Crime Stories (host), Law & Order: Special Victims Unit. *Specials:* On Location: Richard Belzer in Concert (also writer), Belzer on Broadway (also writer, exec. prod.), Comic Relief, Running with Arnold (narr.). *Guest:* More than 121 appearances.

BENBEN, BRIAN
Actor. b. Winchester, VA, June 18, 1956. Raised in Marlboro, NY. m. actress Madeleine Stowe. In regional and alternative theatre before making B'way debut in Slab Boys.
PICTURES: Gangster Wars, Clean and Sober, I Come in Peace, God's Payroll, Radioland Murders.
TELEVISION: *Movies/Specials:* Family Business, Conspiracy: The Trial of the Chicago 8, Comfort Texas, The Flamingo Rising, Sister Mary Explains It All, The Mastersons of Manhattan. *Mini-series:* The Gangster Chronicles, Kingpin. *Series:* Kay O'Brien, Dream On (Cable ACE Award, 1992), The Brian Benben Show (also co-exec. prod.), Private Practice.

BENDER, LAWRENCE
Producer. b. The Bronx, NY, 1958. Together with Quentin Tarantino, founded record company called A Band Apart Records. It focuses on film soundtracks. Trademark includes small acting roles in pictures he produces.
PICTURES: Intruder (also story), Tale of Two Sisters, Reservoir Dogs, Fresh, Killing Zoe (exec. prod.), Pulp Fiction (Academy Award nom. 1995), Four Rooms, White Man's Burden, From Dusk Till Dawn (exec. prod.), Snakeland (exec. prod.), Good Will Hunting (Academy Award nom. 1998), Jackie Brown, A Price Above Rubies, Anna and the King, The Mexican, Knockaround Guys, Stark Raving Mad (exec. prod), Kill Bill: Vol. 1, Havana Nights: Dirty Dancing 2, Kill Bill: Vol. 2, The Great Raid, Casas de cartón, The Chumscrubber, Inglorious Bastards, Goal! The Dream Begins (exec. prod.), 88 Minutes (exec. prod.), An Inconvenient Truth (doc.) Killshot, Inglourious Basterds (Academy Award nom. 2010), Countdown to Zero (doc.).
TELEVISION: *Movies*: Anatomy of a Hate Crime (exec. prod.), Nancy Drew (exec. prod.), The Survivors Club, Earthsea (exec. prod.), Flirt, The Line-Up (exec. prod.), Long Island Confidential. *Mini-series:* Legend of Earthsea. *Series:* Lost in Oz, Dr. Vegas, Build or Bust (exec. prod.).

BENEDICT, DIRK
Actor. r.n. Dirk Niewoehner. b. Helena, MT, March 1, 1945. e. Whitman Coll., Walla Walla, WA. Enrolled in John Fernald Academy of Dramatic Arts, Rochester, MI, after which had season with Seattle Repertory Theatre; also in summer stock at Ann Arbor, MI. Made B'way debut in Abelard and Heloise, 1970. Author: Confessions of a Kamikaze Cowboy, And Then We Went Fishing.
PICTURES: Georgia Georgia (debut, 1972), Ssssss, W, Scavenger Hunt, Ruckus, Underground Aces, Body Slam, Blue Tornado, Shadow Force, Official Denial, The Feminine Touch, Demon Keeper, Christine's Dream (dir. only), Alaska, Steel Stomachs (host), Adventures of Young Brave, Cahoots, Strike!, Solitaire, Recon 7 Down, The A-Team.
TELEVISION: *Movies:* Journey from Darkness, Voyage Into Evil, Battlestar Gallactica, Mission Galactica: The Cylon Attack, The Georgia Peaches, Scruples, Family in Blue, Mark of the Devil, Trenchcoat in Paradise, Bejewelled, Official Denial, Abduction of Innocence, Earthstorm. *Series:* Chopper One, Battlestar Galactica, The A Team. *Guest:* More than 56 appearances.

BENIGNI, ROBERTO
Actor, Writer, Director, Producer. b. Misericordia, Arezzo, Italy, Oct. 27, 1952. Has 38 ent. industry award wins and 18 nom. Won Best Actor and Best Foreign Film Oscar for Life is Beautiful, 1999.
PICTURES: Berlinguer ti voglio bene (also s.p.), Giorni cantati, Chiedo asilo (also s.p.), Clair de femme, La Luna, In the Pope's Eye, Il Minestrone, Tu mi turbi (also s.p., dir.), F.F.S.S. cioe che mi hai portato a fare sopra Posillipo se non mi vuoi piu bene, Nothing Left to Do But Cry (also s.p., dir.), Coffee and Cigarettes, Down by Law, The Little Devil (also s.p., dir.), The Voice of the Moon, Johnny Toothpick (also s.p., dir.), Night on Earth, Son of the Pink Panther, The Monster (also s.p., dir., prod.), Life Is Beautiful (also s.p., dir.; Academy Award for Best Actor/Leading Role, 2 nom. for dir., s.p.; DGA nom.), Asterix and Obelix vs. Caesar, Fellini: Je suis un grand menteur, Pinocchio (s.p., dir.), Coffee and Cigarettes, La Tigre e la neve, (also writer, dir./prod.).
TELEVISION: *Movies:* L'Ultimo del paradiso (host), Who is Alan Smithee? (documentary).

BENING, ANNETTE
Actress. b. Topeka, KS, May 29, 1958. Raised in San Diego. e. San Francisco St. Univ. m. actor Warren Beatty. Acted with San Francisco's American Conservatory Theatre. Voted Star of the Year, 2000 at ShoWest. 2008 received ASC Bd. of Governors Award.
THEATRE: Coastal Disturbances (Tony Award nom., Theatre World & Clarence Derwent Awards), Spoils of War.
PICTURES: The Great Outdoors (debut, 1988), Valmont, Postcards from the Edge, The Grifters (Natl. Society of Film Critics Award, Academy Award nom., 1990), Guilty by Suspicion, Regarding Henry, Bugsy (Golden Globe nom. 1992), Love Affair, The American President (Golden Globe nom. 1996), Richard III, Mars Attacks!, The Seige, In Dreams, American Beauty (SAG, BAFTA awards, Academy Award nom. 2000), Forever Hollywood (documentary), What Planet Are You From?, Open Range, Being Julia (Academy Award nom.; Golden Globe Award 2005), Under My Skin, Running with Scissors (Golden Globe nom. 2007, The Women, Mother and Child, The Kids Are All Right, Hemingway & Fuentes.
TELEVISION: *Movies:* Manhunt for Claude Dallas, Hostage, Mrs. Harris (Emmy nom.; Golden Globe nom. 2006). *Guest:* More than 72 appearances.

BENJAMIN, RICHARD
Actor, Director. b. New York, NY, May 22, 1938. e. Northwestern U. m. actress Paula Prentiss.
THEATRE: (Central Park productions) The Taming of the Shrew, As You Like It; toured in Tchin Tchin, A Thousand Clowns, Barefoot in the Park, The Odd Couple. Star Spangled Girl (B'way debut; Theatre World Award, 1966). Also: The Little Black Book, The Norman Conquests, Barefoot in the Park (dir. only; London prod), Love Letters (California).
PICTURES: *Actor:* Goodbye Columbus, Catsch-22, Diary of a Mad Housewife (Golden Globe nom. 1971), The Steagle, The Marriage of a Young Stockbroker, Portnoy's Complaint, The Last of Sheila, Westworld, The Sunshine Boys (Golden Globe Award 1976), HouseCalls, Love at First Bite, Scavenger Hunt, The Last Married Couple in America, Witches' Brew, How to Beat the High Cost of Living, First Family, Saturday the 14th, Lift, Deconstructing Harry, Marci X (also dir.), Lucky 13, Keeping Up with the Steins, Henry Poole Is Here. *Director:* My Favorite Year, Racing with the Moon, City Heat, The Money Pit, Little Nikita, My Stepmother Is an Alien, Downtown, Mermaids, Made in America, Milk Money, Mrs. Winterbourne, The Shrink is In, Conditional Love.
TELEVISION: *Movies:* Fame, No Room to Run, Packin' It In, The Pentagon Wars (also dir.), Tourist Trap (dir. only), The Sports Pages (dir. only), Laughter on the 23rd Floor (dir. only), The Goodbye Girl (also dir.), A Little Thing Called Murder (dir.). *Series:* He & She (with Paula Prentiss, Emmy nom. 1968), Quark, Semi-Tough (dir. only). *Guest:* More than 48 appearances.

BENNETT, ALAN
Author, Actor. b. Leeds, England, May 9, 1934. e. Oxford U. With Jonathan Miller, Dudley Moore and Peter Cook co-authored and starred in satirical revue Beyond the Fringe in London (1961) and on B'way (special Tony Award, 1963).
THEATRE: Forty Years On (actor, author), Getting On, Habeas Corpus (actor, author), The Old Country, Enjoy, Kafka's Dick, Single Spies (also dir.), The Madness of George III.
PICTURES: *Actor:* Long Shot, Dream Child (voice), Little Dorrit, The Wind in the Willows (voice), In Love And War. *Writer:* A Private Function, Prick Up Your Ears, The Madness of King George (also actor, Academy Award nom.; WGA nom. 1995). The End of the Affair (prod. asst.), The History Boys (writer, s.p.).
TELEVISION: *Movies/Writer:* Beyond the Fringe, A Day Out, Sunset Across the Bay, Me! I'm Afraid of Virginia Woolf, Doris and Doreen, The Old Crowd, Afternoon Off (also acting), One

Fine Day, All Day on the Sands, Intensive Care (also acting), Our Winnie, A Woman of No Importance, Rolling Home, Marks, Say Something Happened, An Englishman Abroad, The Insurance Man, 102 Boulevard Haussmann, A Question of Attribution, Talking Heads (6 TV monologues). *Acting:* Alice in Wonderland, The Merry Wives of Windsor, Westminster Abbey (host), The Wind in the Willows (voice), The Willows in Winter (voice), The Young Visiters (narr.). *Mini-series:* Talking Heads (also acting, dir.), Fortunies of War (acting only), Selling Hitler (acting only), A Dance to the Music of Time (acting), Talking Heads 2 (writer), Changing Stages (as himself). *Guest:* More than 65 appearances.

BENNETT, HARVE

Producer. r.n. Harve Fischman. b. Chicago, IL, Aug. 17, 1930. e. UCLA. Quiz Kids radio show, 5 yrs.; newspaper columnist for the Chicago Sun Times, drama critic; freelance writer; Assoc. prod., CBS-TV; freelance TV writer; prod. of special events. CBS-TV; dir., Television film commercials; program exec., ABC, vice pres., programs west coast, ABC-TV. Pres., Bennett-Katleman. Productions at Columbia Studios.
PICTURES: Star Trek II: The Wrath of Khan (exec. prod., co-story), Star Trek IV: The Voyage Home (also co-s.p.), Star Trek V: The Final Frontier (also co-story).
TELEVISION: *Movies:* A Woman Called Golda (exec. prod.; Emmy Award 1982), The Jesse Owens Story (exec. prod.), Crash Landing: The Rescue of Flight 232 (writer). *Mini-series:* Rich Man Poor Man (Emmy nom. 1976). *Series:* Mod Squad (prod., writer, Emmy nom. 1970), The Young Rebels (creator-writer), Six Million Dollar Man (exec. prod.), Bionic Woman (exec. prod.). American Girls (exec. prod.). From Here to Eternity, Salvage 1, Time Trax (exec. prod.), Invasion America (also developer).

BENNETT, HYWEL

Actor, Director. b. Garnant, South Wales, Apr. 8, 1944. Early career National Youth Theatre where he played many leading Shakespearean roles followed by extensive work in British theatre. 1971-81: directed numerous stage productions.
PICTURES: The Family Way (debut, 1967), Drop Dead My Love, Twisted Nerve, The Virgin Soldiers, The Buttercup Chain, Loot, Percy, Endless Night, Alice's Adventures in Wonderland, The Love Ban, Murder Elite, Witness in the War Zone, Deadly Advice, Married 2 Malcolm, Misery Harbour, Nasty Neighbours, Vatel.
TELEVISION: *Movies:* Where The Buffalo Roam, Romeo and Juliet, Malice Aforethought, Artemis 81, The Critic, Frankie and Johnnie, Absent Friends, Trust Me, The Other Side of Paradise, Hospital!, Harper and Iles, Mary Mother of Jesus, Lloyd & Hill, The Quest, The Second Quest, The Final Quest, Casualty @ Holby City: Interactive - Something We Can Do. *Mini-series:* Pennies from Heaven, Tinker Tailor Soldier Spy, The Modern World: 10 Great Writers, NeverWhere, Karaoke. *Series:* Shelley, The Return of Shelley, EastEnders, The Bill. *Guest:* More than 54 appearances.

BENNIS, JEFFREY D.

Executive. e. Penn. State U. and U. Conn., MBA. Started with Clairol, Inc., Hair and Skin Care Divs. as marketing dir. VP Marketing/Programming of Rifkin & Assocs., 1991-94. Elected to bds. of Nat'l Cable TV Assoc. and C-SPAN in 1995. Pres. and COO, Rifkin & Assocs., 1994-2001. Principal and co-founder of 5280 Partners, L.P., in Denver, CO. 5280 is a venture capital firm investing in media & communications, software applications, outsourced business services. He represents 5280 Partners on the bd. of Alpine Access, Inc.

BENSON, ROBBY

Actor, Writer, Director. r.n. Robert Segal. b. Dallas, TX, Jan. 21, 1956. m. actress Karla DeVito. Father is Jerry Segal, novelist and screenwriter, mother is Ann Benson, veteran of Dallas stage and nat'l summer stock.. Appeared in commercials and summer stock at age 5. B'way debut at age 12 in Zelda. Made dir. debut with White Hot (a.k.a. Crack in the Mirror), 1989. Composed music for Diana Ross, Karla DeVito and soundtrack of film The Breakfast Club.
THEATRE: *NY:* Zelda, The Rothschilds, Dude, The Pirates of Penzance. Regional: Oliver!, Evita, The King and I, King of Hearts, Do Black Patent Leather Shoes Really Reflect Up?
PICTURES: Jory (debut, 1973), Susan and Jeremy(Golden Globe nom. 1974), Lucky Lady, Ode to Billy Joe, One on One (also co-s.p. with father), The End, Ice Castles, Walk Proud (also co-composer with father), Die Laughing (also prod., Tribute, National Lampoon Goes to the Movies, The Chosen, Running Brave, Harry and Son, City Limits, Rent-a-Cop, White Hot (also dir.), Modern Love (also dir., s.p., composed songs), Beauty and the Beast (voice), Billy: The Early Years (dir.).
TELEVISION: *Movies:* Remember When, All the Kind Strangers, Virginia Hill Story, Death Be Not Proud, The Last of Mrs. Lincoln, The Death of Richie, Our Town, Two of a Kind (Golden Globe nom 1983), California Girls, Invasion of Privacy, Precious Victims. *Series:* Search for Tomorrow, Tough Cookies, Sabrina The Teenage Witch, American Dreams. *Series dir.:* Dream On, Evening Shade, Good Advice, Thunder Alley, Ellen, The Naked Truth, Pearl, Life with Roger, Common Law, House Rules, Jesse, Reunited, Bob Patterson, I'm with Her, House of Mouse, American Dreams. *Pilot dir.:* Bringing Up Jack, George Wendt Show, Game Night, Family Beat, Style & Substance, Sabrina the Teenage Witch (also episodes). Director of numerous TV movies and series episodes. *Documentary:* Lincoln. *Guest:* More than 79 appearances.

BENTON, ROBERT

Writer, Director. b. Waxahachie, TX, Sept. 29, 1932. e. U. of Texas, B.A. Was art dir. and later consulting ed. at Esquire Magazine where he met David Newman, a writer-editor, and formed writing partnership. Together, wrote monthly column for Mademoiselle (10 years). Made dir. debut with Bad Company, 1972. Winner of three Academy Awards and 18 other ind. awards; 19 add'l. award nominations. 2007 received WGA Laurel Award for Screen Writing Achievement.
THEATRE: It's a Bird... It's a Plane... It's Superman (libretto), Oh! Calcutta (one sketch).
PICTURES: Bonnie and Clyde (Academy Award nom. Golden Globe nom.1968), There Was a Crooked Man, What's Up, Doc?, Oh! Calcutta (writing contrib.), Superman (with Mario Puzo and Tom Mankiewicz). *Dir./Writer:* Bad Company, The Late Show (Academy Award nom. 1978), Kramer vs. Kramer (2 Acad. Awards for Best Dir. and Adapted Screenplay, DGA Award 1980, Golden Globe, Award 1980, 1 nom.), Still of the Night, Places in the Heart (Academy Award for Best Original Screenplay, 1 Academy nom. Golden Globe nom.; DGA nom. 1985), Nadine, The House on Carroll Street (co-exec. prod. only), Billy Bathgate (dir. only), Nobody's Fool (Academy Award nom. 1995), Twilight, The Human Stain, Ice Harvest (s.p.), Feast of Love.

BERENGER, TOM

Actor. r.n. Thomas Michael Moore. b. Chicago, IL, May 31, 1950. e. U. of Missouri (drama). Studied acting at H.B. Studios. Acted in regional theatres and off-off-Broadway. Plays include Death Story, The Country Girl, National Anthems, The Rose Tattoo, Electra, Streetcar Named Desire, End as a Man (Circle Rep.).
PICTURES: Rush It, The Sentinel, Looking for Mr. Goodbar, In Praise of Older Women, Butch and Sundance: The Early Days, The Dogs of War, Beyond the Door, The Big Chill, Eddie and the Cruisers, Fear City, Rustler's Rhapsody, Platoon (Academy Award nom.; Golden Globe Award 1987), Someone to Watch Over Me, Shoot to Kill, Betrayed, Last Rites, Major League, Born on the Fourth of July, Love at Large, The Field, Shattered, At Play in the Fields of the Lord, Sniper, Sliver, Gettysburg, Major League 2, Chasers, Last of the Dogmen, The Substitute, An Occasional Hell (also exec. prod.), Shadow of a Doubt, The Gingerbread Man, Takedown, One Man's Hero (also prod.), Diplomatic Siege, Fear of Flying, Cutaway, Training Day, The Hollywood Sign, True Blue, Watchtower, D-Tox, Firedog (voice), Order of Redemption, Sinners & Saints, Last Will, Charlie Valentine, Inception, Firedog (voice).
TELEVISION: *Movies:* Johnny We Hardly Knew Ye, Flesh & Blood, The Avenging Angel, Body Language, Rough Riders (also prod.), In the Company of Spies, The Junction Boys, Sniper 2, Capital City, Detective, America's Iliad: The Siege of Charleston (narr.), Desperate Hours: An Amber Alert. *Mini-series:* If Tomorrow Comes, Johnson County War, Into the West, Nightmares and Dreamscapes: From the Stories of Stephen King. *Series:* One Life to Live (1975-76), Third Watch, Peacemakers (also prod./writer), October Road (also pilot). *Documentaries:* Dear America: Letters Home from Vietnam, Retrosexual: The 80's (mini-series), For Love of Liberty: The Story of America's Black Patriots (voice).

BERENSON, MARISA

Actress. b. New York, NY, Feb. 15, 1947. Granddaughter of haute couture fashion designer Schiaparelli. Great niece of art critic and historian Bernard Berenson. Former model.
PICTURES: Death in Venice (debut, 1971), Cabaret, Barry Lyndon, Casanova & Co., Killer Fish, S.O.B., The Secret Diary of Sigmund Freud, La Tete Dans Le Sac, L'Arbalete, Desire, Quel Treno da Vienna, Il Giardino Dei Cigliegi, Winds of the South, White Hunter Black Heart, Night of the Cyclone, The Cherry Orchard, Flagrant Desire, Tonka, Rich belles etc., The Photographer, Retour a la vie, Primetime Murder, Lonesome, Lisa, People, Colour Me Kubrick,I Am Love, Cineman, Gigola.
TELEVISION: *Movies:* Tourist, Playing for Time, Notorious, Maintenant et pour toujours, Fashion Victim: The Killing of Gianni Versace (narrator/voice), Julie, chevalier de Maupin. *Mini-series:* Sins, Hemingway, Lo Scialo, Blue Blood, Have a Nice Night, L'Enfant Des Loups, Oceano, Hollywood Detective, Bel Ami, le clan Mafiosa, Mystère. *Series:* Vénus & Apollon, Caldo criminale.

BERESFORD, BRUCE

Director, Writer. b. Sydney, Australia, Aug. 16, 1940. e. U. of Sydney, B.A. 1962. Worked as teacher in London, 1961. Film editor, East Nigerian Film Unit, 1966; sect. and head of prod., British Film Inst. Production Board, 1966-71.
PICTURES: The Adventures of Barry McKenzie (also co-s.p.), Barry McKenzie Holds His Own (also prod., co-s.p.), Don's Party, The Getting of Wisdom, Money Movers, Breaker Morant (Academy Award nom. 1981, also s.p.), The Club, Puberty Blues, Tender Mercies (Academy Award nom. Golden Globe nom. 1984), King David, The Fringe Dwellers (also s.p.), Crimes of the Heart, Aria (sequence), Her Alibi, Driving Miss Daisy, Mister

Johnson (also co-s.p.), Black Robe, Rich in Love, A Good Man in Africa, (also prod.) Silent Fall, The Last Dance, Paradise Road (also s.p.), Sydney: A Story of a City, Double Jeopardy, Bride of the Wind, Evelyn, Fever, The Contract, Canvas (co-exec. prod.), Mao's Last Dancer, Banking on Mr. Toad.
TELEVISION: *Movies:* Orpheus, Curse of the Starving Class (writer, exec. prod.), And Starring Pancho Villa as Himself.

BERG, JEFFREY
Executive. b. Los Angeles, CA, May 26, 1947. e. B.A. from U. of California, Berkeley, 1969; master's degree in liberal arts, Univ. of So. CA. Berg joined Creative Management Associates, a predecessor of International Creative Management, Inc. (ICM), in 1969 as a literary and film agent. Named pres. of the company in 1980, after its merger with the International Famous Agency, and rose to chairman of ICM in 1985. Now in his 27th year as head of the agency, Berg serves as chairman and CEO and works closely with some of Hollywood's most noted and influential artists and leads a team of more than 150 agents in Los Angeles, New York and London. Berg has represented artists and corporations in both the U.S. and international marketplace and worked extensively with global media, entertainment and telecommunications companies. Under Berg's oversight, ICM has successfully acquired and integrated 15 independent talent agencies. Berg serves on the bd. of visitors of the Anderson Graduate School of Management at UCLA and is on bd. of directors of Oracle Corporation as well as the American Film Institute. In addition, he has served as co-chair of the California Information Technology Council and was a member of the California Entertainment Commission. In 1991 Mr. Berg was awarded Italy's Cavaliere Ufficiale of the Order of Merit of the Republic, one of the country's highest honors.

BERG, PETER
Actor, Director. b. New York, NY, March 11, 1964. e. Malcalester Col., St. Paul, MN.
PICTURES: Miracle Mile, Heart of Dixie, Race for Glory, Shocker, Genuine Risk, Crooked Hearts, Late for Dinner, A Midnight Clear, Aspen Extreme, Fire in the Sky, Girl 6, The Great White Hype, Cop Land, Dill Scallion, Very Bad Things (writer, dir. only), Corky Romano, The Rundown (dir.), Collateral, Welcome to the Jungle (dir.), Friday Night Lights (dir., prod., cinematographer), Hip-Hop Cops (dir./prod.), Splinter Cell: The Movie (dir./writer/exec. prod.), The Kingdom (dir., prod.), Smokin' Aces, Lars and the Real Girl (exec. prod. only), Lions for Lambs, Hancock (dir. only), The Losers (writer), Battleship (prod., dir.).
TELEVISION: *Movies:* Rise and Walk: The Dennis Byrd Story, The Last Seduction (also released theatrically), Wonderland (dir./writer s.p., also pilot), Virtuality (also exec. prod.). *Series:* Chicago Hope, Wonderland (dir./writer/exec. prod.), Friday Night Lights (writer, exec. prod., dir., Emmy nom.; WGA nom. 2007), Trauma (exec. prod.).

BERGEN, CANDICE
Actress. b. Beverly Hills, CA, May 9, 1946. e. U. of PA. m. late dir. Louis Malle. Father was late ventriloquist Edgar Bergen. Modeled during college also freelance photo-journalist. Autobiography: Knock Wood (1984). B'way debut in Hurlyburly.
PICTURES: The Group (debut, 1966), The Sand Pebbles (Golden Globe nom. 1967), The Day the Fish Came Out, Live for Life, The Magus, The Adventurers, Getting Straight, Soldier Blue, Carnal Knowledge, The Hunting Party, T. R. Baskin, 11 Harrowhouse, The Wind and the Lion, Bite the Bullet, The Domino Principle, A Night Full of Rain, Oliver's Story, Starting Over (Academy Award nom. Golden Globe nom. 1980), Rich and Famous, Gandhi, Stick, Belly Talkers, Miss Congeniality, A View From the Top, Sweet Home Alabama, The In-Laws, Sex and the City, The Women, Bride Wars, The Romantics.
TELEVISION: *Movies:* Arthur the King, Murder: By Reason of Insanity, Mayflower Madam, Mary & Tim (also co-exec. prod.)., Footsteps. *Mini-series:* Hollywood Wives. *Series:* Murphy Brown (5 Emmy Awards: 1989, 1990, 1992, 1994, 1995, 2 Golden Globe Awards and 6 nom.), Exhale with Candice Bergen (talk show), Boston Legal (2 Emmy noms.; Golden Globe nom. 2006, Emmy nom. 2008). *Specials:* Woody Allen Special, Moving Day, A Century of Women (voice), AFI's 100 Years...100 Movies, Discovery Atlas (doc., narr.). *Guest:* More than 125 appearances.

BERGEN, POLLY
Singer, Actress. r.n. Nellie Burgin b. Bluegrass, TN, July 14, 1930. e. Compton Jr. Coll., CA. Prof. debut radio at 14; in light opera, summer stock; sang with orchestra and appeared in night clubs; Columbia recording star. Bd. chmn. Polly Bergen Co.; chmn. Culinary Co., Inc.; co-chmn. Natl. Business Council for Equal Rights Amendment. Humanitarian Award: Asthmatic Research Inst. & Hosp., 1971; Outstanding Mother's Award, 1984.
THEATRE: *B'way.:* John Murray Anderson's Almanac, Champagne Complex, First Impressions, Top Man, Plaza Suit, Love Letters.
PICTURES: At War With the Army (debut, 1950), That's My Boy, Warpath, The Stooge, Half a Hero, Cry of the Hunted, Arena, Fast Company, Escape from Fort Bravo, Belle Sommers, Cape Fear, The Caretakers (Golden Globe nom. 1964), Move Over Darling, Kisses for My President, A Guide for the Married Man, Making Mr. Right, Mother Mother, Cry-Baby, Dr. Jekyll and Ms. Hyde, Once Upon a Time..., When We Were Colored, Paradise, Texas, A Very Serious Person.
TELEVISION: *Movies:* Death Cruise, Murder on Flight 502, Telethon, How to Pick Up Girls, The Million Dollar Face, Born Beautiful, Velvet, Addicted to His Love, She Was Marked For Murder, The Haunting of Sarah Hardy, My Brother's Wife, Lightning Field, Lady Against the Odds, Perry Mason: The Case of the Skin-Deep Scandal, Leave of Absence, Hand In the Glove, In the Blink Of an Eye The Surrogate, For Hope, Candles on Bay Street (also performer). *Mini-series:* Harold Robbins' 79 Park Avenue, The Winds of War (Emmy nom.1983), War and Remembrance (Emmy nom. 1989). *Series:* Playhouse 90 (host 1954-1955, Emmy Award 1958), to tell the Truth (panelist), The Polly Bergen Show, Baby Talk, Commander in Chief, Desperate Housewives (Emmy nom. 2008). *Guest:* More than 106 appearances.

BERGER, HELMUT
Actor. r.n. Helmut Steinberger. b. Salzburg, Austria, May 29, 1943. e. Feldkirk College and U. of Perugia. First film, small role in Luchino Visconti's The Witches (Le Streghe) in 1966.
PICTURES: The Witches, I Giovani tigri, The Damned (Golden Globe nom. 1970), The Garden of the Finzi-Continis, Love Me Strangely, Dorian Gray, Ludwig, Les Voraces, Ash Wednesday, Merry-Go-Round, Conversation Piece, Order to Assassinate, The Romantic Englishwoman, Madam Kitty, The Human Beast, The Biggest Battle, Die Jäger, Heroin, Femmes, Veliki transport, Victoria! La gran aventura d'un poble, Code Name: Emerald, Faceless, The Godfather: Part III, Ludwig 1881, Under the Palms, Honey Baby, Iron Cross.
TELEVISION: *Movies:* Abgründe, Victory at Entebbe, Fantômas: Le tramway fantôme, Boomtown, L'Affaire Dreyfus, Rosa Roth-Die Abrechnung, Schneemann, sucht Schneefrau, Damals warst Du still. *Mini-series:* I Promessi sposi. *Series:* Dynasty.

BERGER, SENTA
Actress. b. Vienna, Austria, May 13, 1941. Studied ballet, then acting at Vienna's Reinhardt Seminar. Debuted in German films as a teen.
PICTURES: Die Lindenwirtin vom Donanstrand (debut 1957), The Journey, Katia, The Good Soldier Schweik, The Secret Ways, Sherlock Holmes and the Deadly Necklace, The Testament of Dr. Mabuse, The Victors, Major Dundee, The Glory Guys, Cast a Giant Shadow, Bang! Bang! You're Dead, The Poppy Is Also a Flower, The Quiller Memorandum, To Commit a Murder, The Treasure of San Gennaro, The Ambushers, Diabolically Yours, If It's Tuesday This Must Be Belgium, De Sade, When Women Had Tails, Percy, The Scarlet Letter, Merry-Go-Round, White Mafia, The Swiss Conspiracy, Cross of Iron, Nest of Nipers, The Two Lives of Mattia Pascal, The Flying Devils, Swiss Cheese, Am I Beautiful?, Satte Farben vor Schwarz, Berlin Mitte.
TELEVISION: Numerous German and Austrian television movies and series.

BERGERAC, JACQUES
Actor. b. Biarritz, France, May 26, 1927. Career includes Five Minutes With Jacques Bergerac on radio; in the theatre, on tour in Once More with Feeling; on most major network TV shows. Won the Foreign Newcomer Golden Globe award in 1957.
PICTURES: Twist of Fate, The Time is Now, Strange Intruder, Come Away With Me, Les Girls, Gigi, Man and His Past, Thunder in the Sun, Hypnotic Eye, A Sunday in Summer, Fear No More, Achille, A Global Affair, Taffy and the Jungle Hunter, The Emergency Operation: Lady Chaplin, The Unkissed Bride.

BERGIN, PATRICK
Actor. b. Ireland, Feb. 4, 1951.
PICTURES: Taffin, The Courier, Mountains of the Moon, Sleeping with the Enemy, Love Crimes, Highway to Hell, Patriot Games, The Hummingbird Tree, Map of the Human Heart, Soft Deceit, Double Cross, Lawnmower Man2: Beyond Cyberspace, Angela Mooney, The Proposition, The Island on Bird Street, Suspicious Minds, The Lost World, Escape Velocity, One Man's Hero, Eye of the Beholder, Treasure Island, Press Run, Merlin: The Return, Africa, When the Sky Falls, High Explosive, Cause of Death, The Invisible Circus, Amazons and Gladiators, Gas Station Jesus, Devil's Prey, Beneath Loch Ness, Ella Enchanted, Ghostwood, The Far Side of Jericho, The Black Pimpernel, Strength and Honour, Gallowwalker, Eva, Project Fear, Ice, Eldorado, Back2Hell.
TELEVISION: *Movies:* Act of Betrayal, Morphine and Dolly Mixtures, Robin Hood, Frankenstein, Children of the Mist, Triplecross, The Witch's Daughter, Apocalypse Watch, Stolen Women, Captured Hearts, The Ripper, Durango, St. Patrick: The Irish Legend, Jewel, King of Texas, Brush with Fate, Icon. *Mini-series:* The Real Charlotte, Dracula, The Secret World of Spying (tv documentary), Casanova's Love Letters, Driven. *Guest:* More than 40 appearances.

BERGMAN, ALAN
Executive. Bergman spent more than seven years in the entertainment practice of PricewaterhouseCoopers before joining The Walt Disney Company in 1996 as a director in the corporate controllership group with a focus on The Walt Disney Studios' (TWDS) initiatives. In 1998, he was promoted to v.p. of the com-

pany's operations planning group, where he was responsible for developing the company's annual operating plan. In 2001, Bergman was promoted to senior v.p. & CFO of TWDS and was upped to executive v.p. & CFO in 2002. Bergman was promoted to president in Dec. 2005. He reported to TWDS Chairman Dick Cook until his resignation 2010. Bergman oversaw strategy and operations for all business units including Buena Vista Motion Pictures Group, Buena Vista Pictures Distribution, Buena Vista Pictures Marketing, Buena Vista International, Miramax, Buena Vista Home Entertainment worldwide, Disney Theatrical Productions, The Buena Vista Music Group, Buena Vista Television and Buena Vista Television International. 2010 Bergman had new responsibilities as, president, TWDS, he will take on the new duties of overseeing Studio Franchises, Post Production, Disneynature and The Muppets Studio, while continuing to guide operations including Business Affairs, Legal Affairs, and Finance. He will report to studio chairman Rich Ross.

BERGMAN, ALAN

Lyricist, Composer. b. Brooklyn, NY, Sept. 11, 1925. e. U. of North Carolina, UCLA. m. Marilyn Bergman with whom he collaborates.
THEATRE: Ballroom, Something More, The Lady and the Clarinet.
PICTURES: *Lyrics:* Harlow, Harper, In the Heat of the Night, Fitzwilly, The Thomas Crown Affair (Academy Award for Best Song: The Windmills of Your Mind, Golden Globe Award 1968), John and Mary, The Happy Ending (Academy Award nom.; Golden Globe nom. 1970), Gaily Gaily, The Magic Garden of Stanley Sweetheart, Move, Pieces of Dreams (Academy Award nom.; Golden Globe nom. 1971), Wuthering Heights, The African Elephant (Golden Globe nom. 1972), Doctor's Wives, Sometimes a Great Notion (Academy Award nom. 1972), Pete 'n' Tillie, Molly and Lawless John (Golden Globe nom. 1973) The Life and Times of Judge Roy Bean (Academy Award nom.; Golden Globe nom. 1973), Breezy, 40 Carats, The Way We Were, (Academy Award for title song; Golden Globe Award 1973) Summer Wishes Winter Dreams, Harry and Walter Go To New York, Ode to Billy Joe, Breezy (Golden Globe nom. 1974) A Star Is Born, Same Time Next Year (Academy Award nom.; Golden Globe nom. 1979), From Noon Till Three (Golden Globe nom. 1977) The Promise (Academy Award nom. 1980), And Justice For All, A Change of Seasons, Back Roads, Author Author, Yes Giorgio (Academy Award nom.; Golden Globe nom. 1983), Best Friends (Academy Award nom. 1983), Tootsie (Academy Award nom. 1983), Never Say Never Again, Yentl (Academy Award for song score, 2 other nom.; 2 Golden Globe nom. 1984), The Man Who Loved Women, Micki and Maude, The January Man, The Russia House, Major League, Shirley Valentine (Academy Award nom.; Golden Globe nom. 1990), Welcome Home, Switch, The Naked Gun 2½: The Smell of Fear, For the Boys, Sabrina (Academy Award nom.; Golden Globe nom. 1996), Waiting to Exhale, Twister, Bogus, Washington Square, At First Sight, Next Friday, Austin Powers: Goldmember, The In-Laws, The School of Rock, Connie and Carla, Breakfast on Pluto, Confetti, Trying to Get Good: The Jazz Odyssey of Jack Sheldon (doc.), One True Love.
TELEVISION: Queen of the Stardust Ballroom (Emmy Award), Having Babies III, Hollow Image, Sybil (Emmy Award 1977). Themes: Bracken's World, Maude, The Sandy Duncan Show, Good Times, Alice, The Dumplings, Nancy Walker Show, The Powers That Be, Brooklyn Bridge (Emmy nom. 1992), All That Glitters, Barbra Streisand: The Concert (Emmy Award 1995), AFI's 100 Years... 100 Movies (Emmy Award 1999), AFI Life Achievement Award: A Tribute to Barbra Streisand (Emmy nom. 2001). Many more soundtracks.

BERGMAN, ANDREW

Writer, Director, Producer. b. Queens, NY, Feb. 20, 1945. e. Harpur Coll., magna cum laude; U. of Wis., Ph. D., history, 1970. Worked as publicist at United Artists. Author: We're in the Money, a study of Depression-era films, and the mysteries: The Big Kiss-Off of 1944, Hollywood and Levine, Sleepless Nights. Also wrote Broadway comedy, Social Security. Received the WGA Ian McLellan Hunter Award 2007.
PICTURES: *Writer:* Blazing Saddles (WGA Award 1975), The In Laws, So Fine (also dir.), Oh God You Devil, Fletch, The Freshman (also dir.), Soapdish, Honeymoon in Vegas (also dir.), The Scout, Striptease (also dir.), Joe's Last Chance (also dir.), The In-Laws. *Director:* It Could Happen To You, Isn't She Great. *Exec. Prod.:* Chances Are, Undercover Blues, Little Big League.

BERGMAN, MARILYN

Lyricist. b. Brooklyn, NY, Nov. 10, 1929. e. NYU. m. Alan Bergman, with whom she collaborates. Became pres. and chairman of ASCAP, 1994. 2009 Bergman retired from ASCAP.
THEATRE: Ballroom, Something More, The Lady and the Clarinet.
PICTURES: Lyrics: Harlow, Harper, In the Heat of the Night, Ten Thousand Bedrooms,The Right Approach, Fitzwilly, The Thomas Crown Affair, Charro!, A Man Called Gannon, Stiletto, John and Mary, The Happy Ending, Gaily Gaily, Pieces of Dreams, Move, The Magic Garden of Stanley Sweetheart, Doctors' Wives, Sometimes A Great Notion, The Life and Times of Judge Roy Bean, Molly and Lawless John, 40 Carats, The Way We Were (Acad. Award for title song, 1973), 99 and 44/100% Dead, Ode to Billy Joe, Harry and Walter Go to New York, From Noon Till Three, A Star Is Born, The One and Only, Same Time Next Year, ...And Justice For All, The Promise, A Change of Seasons, Bolero, Author! Author, Yes Giorgio, Tootsie, Never Say Never Again, Yentl (Academy Award for song score, 1983), The man Who Loved Women, Micki + Maude, Big, January Man, Troop Beverly Hills, Shirley Valentine, Welcome Home, The Russia House, Switch, The Naked Gun 2½: The Smell of Fear, Sabrina, Twister, Bogus, Washington Square, At First Sight, Next Friday, Austin Powers: Goldmember, The In-Laws, The School of Rock, Connie and Carla, Breakfast on Pluto, Confetti. Many more soundtrack lyrics.
TELEVISION: Queen of the Stardust Ballroom, Sybil (Emmy Award), Having Babies III, Hollow Image, Barbra Streisand: The Concert. Series/Themes: The Gale Storm Show, The Nat King Cole Show, Bracken's World, Maude, Good Times, Alice, The Nancy Walker Show, All That Glitters, Co-ed Fever, Brooklyn Bridge. Many more. *Guest:* More than 50 appearances.

BERKE, BETH

Executive. e. Berke graduated Phi Beta Kappa and summa cum laude from UCLA with a B.A; earned a Masters degree in psychology, Stanford University; and received her J.D. degree from UCLA School of Law. Berke served in Sony Pictures Entertainment legal division, rising to the post of executive v.p. & deputy general counsel. During her tenure in the legal department, she served as both chief counsel for Columbia Pictures and the head of the international and corporate legal groups for Sony Pictures. In 2006, SPE elevated Berke to lead its corporate level organization as Executive Vice President and Chief Administrative Officer. She also works with the Digital Policy Group, with the goal of addressing the challenges & opportunities arising with the digital distribution of entertainment product. Berke is a member of the American and California Bar Associations and of Women in Film.

BERKOFF, STEVEN

Actor, Director, Writer. b. London, England, Aug. 3, 1937. e. studied drama in London and Paris Founder of London Theatre Group. Author of plays; East, West, Greek Decadence, Sink the Belgrano, Kvetch (London, NY). Staged, adapted and toured with: Kafka's In the Penal Colony, The Trial and Metamorphosis; Agamemnon, the Fall of the House of Usher. Starried in Hamlet and Macbeth. *NY theatre: Dir.:* Kvetch (also writer, actor), Coriolanus, Metamorphosis (starring Baryshnikov). Also dir. Roman Polanski in Metamorphosis in Paris.
PICTURES: Nicholas and Alexandra, A Clockwork Orange, Barry Lyndon, The Passenger, Outland, McVicar, Octopussy, Beverly Hills Cop, Rambo: First Blood II, Revolution, Underworld, Absolute Beginners, Under the Cherry Moon, The Krays, Decadence (also dir., s.p.), Fair Game, Flynn, Doppelganger (voice), Love in Paris, Rancid Aluminium, Stanley Kubrick: A Life in Pictures, Riders, Bockshu the Myth, Charlie, Headrush, Head in the Clouds, Brides, The Headsman, Minotaur, PU-239, The Flying Scotsman, Drop Dead Gorgeous, The Big I Am, 44 Inch Chest, At World's End, The Rapture, Gunned Down, Dead Cert, Katherine of Alexandria.
TELEVISION: *Movies:* Beloved Enemy, Coming Out of the Ice, Metamorphosis (also writer), A Season of Giants, Intruders, Hans Christian Andersen: My Life as a Fairy Tale, NCS II, Marple: By the Pricking of My Thumbs, Umbra Mortis, Das Jüngste Gericht. *Mini-series:* Sins, War and Remembrance, In the Beginning, Changing Stages, Attila, Children of Dune. *Series:* Silent Night, NCS Manhunt. *Guest:* More than 60 appearances.

BERLINGER, WARREN

Actor. b. Brooklyn, NY, Aug. 31, 1937. e. Columbia U.
THEATRE: Annie Get Your Gun, The Happy Time, Bernardine, Take A Giant Step, Anniversary Waltz, Roomful of Roses, Blue Denim (Theatre World Award), Come Blow Your Horn, How To Succeed in Business Without Really Trying, (London) Who's Happy Now?, California Suite (1977-78 tour), Follies (Los Angeles).
PICTURES: Teenage Rebel, Three Brave Men, Blue Denim, Because They're Young, Platinum High School, The Wackiest Ship in the Army, All Hands on Deck, Billie, Spinout, Thunder Alley, Lepke, The Four Deuces, I Will I Will... for Now, Harry and Walter Go to New York, The Shaggy D.A., The Magician of Lublin, The Cannonball Run, The World According to Garp, Going Bananas, Outlaw Force, Ten Little Indians, Hero, Crime and Punishment, Feminine Touch, That Thing You Do!
TELEVISION: *Movies:* The Girl Most Likely To..., The Red Badge of Courage, Ellery Queen, Wanted: The Sundance Woman, Sex and the Single Parent, The Other Woman, Trial By Jury, Columbo: Death Hits the Jackpot, Justice, What Price Victory, Backlash, Another Pretty Face. *Series:* Secret Storm, The Joey Bishop Show, The Wonderful World of Disney, The Funny Side, A Touch of Grace, Operation Petticoat, Small & Frye, Shades of L.A. *Special:* Lily for President?. *Guest:* More than 78 appearances.

BERMAN, BRUCE

Executive, Producer. b. Manhattan, NY, April 25, 1952. e. California Inst. of the Arts Film School; UCLA, magna cum

laude, history degree 1975; Georgetown Law School and California Bar, 1978. Entered motion picture industry while in law school, as assistant to Jack Valenti, MPAA. Assistant to Peter Guber, Casablanca Filmworks, 1979. Assistant to Sean Daniel & Joel Silver, Universal Pictures, 1979; v.p. prod., Universal, 1982. V.p. prod., Warner Bros., 1984; sr. v.p., prod.,1988; pres., Theatrical Prod.,1989; pres., Worldwide Prod., 1991-96. Founded Plan B Ent., an independent motion picture prod. co., funded by Warner Bros., Inc., 1996. The company has since been acquired by Village Roadshow Pictures, where Berman now holds the post of chmn. and CEO of its U.S. operations, Village Roadshow Pictures Entertainment.
PICTURES: *(Exec. Prod.):* Practical Magic (1998), Analzye This, The Matrix, Deep Blue Sea, Three Kings, Three to Tango, Gossip, Red Planet (prod.), Miss Congeniality, Valentine, Saving Silverman, See Spot Run, Exit Wounds, Angel Eyes, Swordfish, Cats & Dogs, Training Day, Hearts in Atlantis, Don't Say a Word, Ocean's Eleven, Queen of the Damned, Showtime, Eight Legged Freaks (prod.), The Adventures of Pluto Nash, Ghost Ship, Analyze That, Two Weeks Notice, Dreamcatcher, The Matrix Reloaded, Mystic River, The Matrix Revolutions, Torque, Cats & Dogs 2, Troy, Taking Lives, Catwoman, House of Wax, Cats & Dogs 2: Tinkles' Revenge, Ocean's Twelve, Miss Congeniality 2: Armed & Fabulous, Charlie and the Chocolate Factory, The Dukes of Hazzard, Rumor Has It, Firewall, Unaccompanied Minors, The Lake House, Lucky You, The Visiting, Music and Lyrics, Ocean's Thirteen, License to Wed, No Reservations, The Invasion, The Brave One, I Am Legend, Street Kings, Speed Racer, Nights in Rodanthe, Get Smart, Yes Man, Gran Torino, Where the Wild Things Are, Sherlock Holmes.

BERMAN, GAIL
Executive. b. 1956. e. Bachelor's degree in theatre, Univ. of Maryland. Television executive whose creative savvy developing TV series has become her signature. At 23, Berman coproduced the original Broadway production of the Andrew Lloyd Webber-Tim Rice musical Joseph and the Amazing Technicolor Dreamcoat, which garnered seven Tony Award nominations. Her other Broadway productions include David Rabe's Hurlyburly (1984), Athol Fugard's Blood Knot (1985) and Larry Shue's The Nerd (1987), all of which received Tony Award nominations. In 1990, Berman transitioned into television when she joined the New York-based Comedy Channel (a precursor of Comedy Central) as the fledgling network's supervising producer. She was promoted to executive producer the following year. She next served as pres. and CEO of Sandollar Television, an offshoot of Sandy Gallin's Sandollar Entertainment, where she had both creative and bottom-line responsibility for program development and production. She remained with Sandollar six years. While president of Sandollar Television, she helped Joss Whedon develop Buffy The Vampire Slayer into a TV series for the WB Network. She then had a two-year tenure as the founding president of Regency Television, a joint venture of News Corp. and New Regency Enterprises. While at Regency, she developed the hit comedy, Malcolm in the Middle. Success at Regency led to her association with News Corp.'s Fox Broadcasting Co. as entertainment president from 2000 to March 2005. In 2003, Berman was first named to Fortune magazine's list of "50 Most Powerful Women in American Business" (No. 25). That same year she received the coveted "Lucy" award-recognizing women who have revolutionized the television industry—from Women in Film. In 2004, she was named to Forbes magazine's list of "100 Most Powerful Women in the World" (No. 49), reappeared on the Fortune list (No. 25); and received the Executive of the Year Award from the Caucus for Television Producers, Writers, and Directors. During her time at Fox, the network developed such signature series as the Emmy-winning series 24 and Arrested Development. Berman left Fox in 2005 and became pres., Paramount Motion Pictures Group. After only 18 months on the job, Berman resigned in early Jan. 2007. She opened the production company, BermanBraun, with partner Lloyd Braun, the former ABC Entertainment chmn. who recommended Berman for her Paramount job. BermanBraun focuses on TV production, the Internet and movies. 2010 BermanBraun struck a deal with Starcom Media Vest for advertising for new types of digital entertainment. The deal with Starcom is not exclusive.

BERMAN, JOEL P.
Executive. b. Forest Hills, NY, Dec. 3, 1951. e. Ohio University, BS communications, 1973. Acct. exec., Petry Television, NY, 1976-79. In radio: Dir. ad. sales, Westwood One, NY, 1979-80. East. div. mgr., Paramount Pictures Domestic Television, NY, 1981-84, VP, East. reg. mgr., 1985-87. Sr. VP/sales mgr., GTG Marketing, NY, 1987-89, where he helped launch USA Today: The TV Show. Back to Paramount Pics. Domestic TV, VP, off-network and features, 1989-90. Sr. VP/nat'l sales mgr., 1990-92, Exec. VP/sales and mktg., LA, 1992-94, pres. of distribution, 1994-97. In 2002, named president of Paramount Worldwide Television Distribution, where he added Paramount International Television & Paramount International Pay TV. Left Paramount in Oct. 2006. In 2007, Berman consulted for Discovery Communications at request of Discovery's new pres. & CEO David Zaslav.

BERMAN, RICK
Writer, Producer. r.n. Richard Keith Berman. b. Dec. 25, 1944. e. Univ. of Wisconsin-Madison, BA in speech, 1963-67. Heads the Star Trek franchise. Heads Rick Berman Productions.
PICTURES: Star Trek: Generations (also prod.), Star Trek: First Contact (also prod.), Star Trek: The Experience, Star Trek: Insurrection (also prod.), Star Trek: 3D (also story), Star Trek: Nemesis (also prod.)
TELEVISION: *Movies:* Star Trek: Deep Space Nine: Emissary (writer), Star Trek: Deep Space Nine-Behind the Scenes (writer), Caretaker (writer/creator), Star Trek Enterprise: Broken Bow (writer/creator and exec. prod.) *Series:* Star Trek: The Next Generation (writer, creator Emmy nom. 1994), Star Trek: Deep Space Nine (writer, creator), Star Trek: Voyager (writer, creator), Star Trek: Enterprise (writer, creator).

BERNARD, MARVIN A.
Executive. b. New York, NY, Oct. 1, 1934. e. NYU. Lab technician to v.p. in charge of sales, Rapid Film Technique, Inc., 1949-63; developed technological advances in film rejuvenation and preservation, responsible for public underwriting; real estate sales & investments in Bahamas, then with Tishman Realty (commercial leasing div.), 1964-69; est. B-I-G Capital Properties; v.p. and operating head of International Filmtreat 1970-1973; authored Film Damaged Control Chart, a critical analysis of film care and repair, 1971; founded Filmlife Inc. with latest chemical/mechanical and technical advancement in field of film rejuvenation and preservation. Bd. chmn. and chief executive officer of Filmlife Inc., m. p. film rejuvenation, storage and distribution company, 1973-75. Elected president in addition to remaining bd. chairman, Feb. 1975. Consultant to National Archives of U.S. on m.p. preservation, 1979. Dev. m.p. rejuvenation and preservation for 8mm and S8mm, 1981. Introduced this technology to private home movie use before and after transfer to videotape, 1986. Active member of awards comm. for tech. achievements, National Acad. TV Arts & Sciences, 1987. Recognition as leading authority and m.p. conservator from Intl. Communications Industries Assn. (ICIA), 1988. Established Film/Video Hospital, repairing broken tapes & videocassettes, 1990. His company, Filmlife,Inc., became first national film to video transfer lab in the U.S. in 1989. Bernard has been at the forefront of film transfer, restoration, preservation and repair for more than 50 years.

BERNARD, TOM
Executive. b. Long Branch, NJ. e. University of Maryland at College Park, BA in Radio/Film/TV. Held positions in theatrical sales at New Line Cinema. In 1980, established specialized distribution company, United Artists Classics; 1983, co-founded Orion Classics. Is a founding partner and co-president of Sony Pictures Classics (1992-present), with Michael Barker and Marcie Bloom. Member of A.M.P.A.S., Recipient of Independent Feature Project's Industry's Lifetime Achievement Award for consistent support of new work from filmmakers around the world. Member, Monmouth College Council for the Department of Communication, the University of Maryland Media Advisory Board, the Tribeca Film Festival Advisory Board, the AFI New York Screening Committee of the Motion Pictures Arts and Sciences. In the past Bernard has served as the chmn. of the IFP West Advisory Board and as a member of the Sundance Film Festival Advisory Board.

BERNEY, BOB
Executive. b. June 23, 1953. e. B.A. in communications from the Univ. of Texas in Austin, wher he studied film history and production. Upon graduation, Berney and a partner bought and renovated the Inwood Theatre in Dallas, which he opened as an art house venue. There he booked his favorite foreign and independent films. Later, Berney sold the theatre, which is now part of the Landmark Cinema chain. Berney has been a force in the independent film industry for more than 20 years. He began his marketing and distribution career at Film Dallas, an independent film production company in partnership with New World Pictures. He became v.p. of marketing and distribution at Triton Films, mentored by co. pres. Jonathan Dana. At Banner Entertainment, Berney was v.p. of marketing; he also served a stint as v.p., marketing with Orion Pictures. While at Orion, Berney worked on the release of Victor Nunez's Academy Award-nominated Ulee's Gold, starring Peter Fonda. Berney joined IFC Films as senior v.p., where he oversaw the distribution of the box office hit My Big Fat Greek Wedding, which grossed more than $200 million. Also, Berney oversaw the release of the critically praised hit, Y Tu Mama Tambien, directed by Alfonso Cuaron. From IFC, he co-founded and was president and partner of independent label Newmarket Films. He oversaw the release of such films as Mel Gibson's The Passion of the Christ, which earned more than $370 million at the box office and Patty Jenkins' critically acclaimed Monster, which garnered Charlize Theron a Best Actress Academy Award. Berney became president of a new theatrical distribution company, Picturehouse, in mid-2005. Picturehouse evolved from a combination of Fine Line Features and HBO Films. Picturehouse ceased operations in 2008. Berney started distribution company, Apparition, in 2009. In May 2010, Berney resigned his position at Apparition.

BERNHARD, HARVEY

Producer. b. Seattle, WA, March 5, 1924. e. Stanford U. In real estate in Seattle, 1947-50; started live lounge entertainment at the Last Frontier Hotel, Las Vegas, 1950. Partner with Sandy Howard, 1958-60; v.p. in chg. prod., David L. Wolper Prods., dividing time between TV and feature films, 1961-68; with MPC, v.p., chg. prod., 1968-70. Now pres. of Harvey Bernhard Ent., Inc.
PICTURES: The Mack (1973), Sixteen, The Omen, Damien: Omen II, Omen III: The Final Conflict, The Beast Within, Ladyhawke (exec. prod.), The Goonies, The Lost Boys, Mackin' Ain't Easy (video short, 2002).
TELEVISION: *Movies:* Omen IV: The Awakening, The Omen Legacy (TV documentary). *Special:* Movin' with Nancy.

BERNHARD, SANDRA

Actress, Comedienne, Singer. b. Flint, MI, June 6, 1955. Moved to Scottsdale, AZ at 10. Began career in Los Angeles 1974 as stand-up comedian while supporting herself as manicurist in Beverly Hills. Has written articles for Vanity Fair, Interview, Spin, recorded and written lyrics for debut album I'm Your Woman (1985) and starred in one-woman off-B'way show Without You I'm Nothing (1988). Published collection of essays, short stories and memoirs, Confessions of a Pretty Lady (1988). Frequent guest on Late Night with David Letterman and Robin Byrd Show.
PICTURES: Cheech and Chong's Nice Dreams (debut, 1981), The King of Comedy, Sesame Street Presents: Follow That Bird, The Whoopee Boys, Track 29, Heavy Petting, Without You I'm Nothing, Hudson Hawk, Inside Monkey Zetterland, Dallas Doll, Madonna: Truth or Dare, Unzipped, The Reggae Movie, Plump Fiction, Lover Girl, The Apocalypse, An Alan Smithee Film: Burn Hollywood Burn, Somewhere in the City, I Woke Up Early the Day I Died, Wrongfully Accused, Expose, Dinner Rush, Playing Mona Lisa, Zoolander, The Easter Egg Adventure, See You in September.
TELEVISION: *Movies:* Freaky Friday, The Late Shift, Hercules Zero to Hero, Sandra Bernhard: I'm Still Here Damn It!, Silver Lake, Glass Heels. *Series:* The Richard Pryor Show, Roseanne, Hercules, The Sandra Bernhard Experience, The L Word, Las Vegas. *Guest:* More than 113 appearances.

BERNSEN, CORBIN

Actor. b. North Hollywood, CA, Sept. 7, 1954. e. UCLA, B.A. theater arts; M.F.A playwriting. m. actress Amanda Pays. Son of actress Jeanne Cooper and producer, Harry Bernsen. Teaching asst. at UCLA while working on playwriting degree. 1981 studied acting in NY while supporting self as carpenter and model (Winston cigarettes). Built own theatre in loft. Formed theatre co. Theatre of the Night.
PICTURES: Three the Hard Way (debut, 1974), Eat My Dust!, King Kong, S.O.B., Hello Again, Bert Rigby You're a Fool, Major League, Disorganized Crime, Shattered, Frozen Assets, The Killing Box, Fatal Inheritance, Major League 2, Trigger Fast, A Brilliant Disguise, The New Age, Radioland Murders, Tales From the Hood, The Great White Hype, The Dentist, Menno's Mind, Circuit Breaker, Recipe for Revenge, Drop Dead, Beings, Major League: Back to the Minors, The Dentist II (also assoc. prod.), The Misadventures of Margaret, Beings, Kiss of a Stranger, Final Payback, Rubbernecking, Killer Instinct, Delicate Instruments, Borderline Normal, Quiet Kill, The Tomorrow Man, I Saw Mommy Kissing Santa Claus, Fangs, Apocalypse IV: Judgment, The Commission, Bellacam (prod. only), Big Things, Kiss, Kiss, Bang, Bang, Carpool Guy (also prod./dir.), Pirate Camp, Trapped (also assoc. prod.), Donna on Demand (also prod., dir., prod. designer), Angel's Blade: The Ascension, House of Fallen, Dead Air (also prod., dir., prod. designer), The Ascension, Since I Don't Have You, Rust (also prod., dir., writer), Billy Joel's Car, Closets, Lizzie.
TELEVISION: *Movies:* Breaking Point, Line of Fire: The Morris Dees Story, Dead on the Money, Grass Roots, Love Can Be Murder, Beyond Suspicion, I Know My Son is Alive, Where Are My Children?, Voice From Within, Dangerous Intentions, In the Heat of the Night: By Duty Bound, Bloodhounds, The Cape, Tidalwave: No Escape, Loyal Opposition: Terror in the White House, Nightworld: Riddler's Moon, Recipe for Revenge, Young Hearts Unlimited, Two of Hearts, A Place Apart, L.A. Law: Return to Justice, Atomic Twister, The Santa Trap, Gentle Ben 2: Danger on the Mountain, Love Comes Softly, They Are Among Us, Ordinary Miracles, Vipers, Confessions of a Go-Go Girl, For the Love of Grace. *Series:* Ryan's Hope, L.A. Law (2 Emmy nom. 2 Golden Globe nom. 1987, 1988), A Whole New Ballgame, The Cape, The Young and the Restless, General Hospital, Cuts, How Much Is Enough? (host), Psych. *Guest:* More than 130 appearances.

BERNSTEIN, ARMYAN

Producer, Director, Writer. Chairman of Beacon Pictures; co-founder with Marc Abraham.
PICTURES: *Prod:* One From the Heart, Satisfaction (exec. prod.), The Commitments (exec. prod.), A Midnight Clear (exec. prod.), Princess Caraboo (exec. prod.), The Road to Wellville, The Baby-Sitters Club (exec. prod.), 364 Girls a Year, Air Force One, A Thousand Acres (exec. prod.) Disturbing Behavior, For Love of the Game, The Hurricane (also s.p.), End of Days, Bring It On (exec. prod.), The Family Man (exec. prod.), Thirteen Days Which Shocked the World, Spy Game (exec. prod.), Tuck Everlasting (exec. prod.), The Emperor's Club (exec. prod.), Open Range (exec. prod.), Ladder 49 (exec. prod.), She's Gone (also s.p.), Dawn of the Dead (exec. prod. 2004), A Lot Like Love, The Wrong Element, Firewall, PU-239 (exec. prod.), Let's Go to Prison (exec. prod.), The Guardian (exec. prod.), Mardi Gras. *Writer:* Thank God It's Friday, One from the Heart, Windy City (also dir.), Cross My Heart (also dir.)

BERNSTEIN, FRED

Executive, Entertainment Attorney. e. B.A. from Univ. of Pa., cum laude, 1973. J.D. degree, UCLA School of Law, 1976, Order of the Coif. Prior to joining law firm Manatt, Phelps & Phillips in 1976, Bernstein was the head of E-Studio Network.com, an e-commerce website and communications platform for film, television, and commercial production professionals, and produced films independently through his company, Vertical Pictures. He began his career in the film industry after leaving Manatt as an associate, serving as v.p., business affairs at Casablanca FilmWorks and later Time-Life Films. In the 1980s Bernstein was sr. v.p. of business affairs and pres. of worldwide prod. for Columbia Pictures before serving as sr. v.p. of MCA Inc.'s Motion Picture Group, 1987-94. He is a former pres. of Coumbia TriStar Motion Pictures. Bernstein then returned to law as a partner with Manatt, Phelps & Phillips. In May 2006, left firm to become a partner at international law firm Proskauer Rose LLP, which expanded its entertainment practice. Bernstein, operating from the firm's Los Angeles, CA, office, focuses on the creation, financing, distribution and exploitation of content, and the leveraging of "branded entertainment" — throughout the entertainment, media and related fields for producers and distributors.

BERNSTEIN, JACK B.

Executive, Producer. b. New York, NY, May 6, 1937. e. City U. of New York, B.A., sociology. U.S. Army-Europe, 1956-58; research bacteriologist, 1959-61. Entered industry in 1962 with S.I.B. Prods., Paramount, as v.p. gen. mgr.; 1964-66, v.p. gen. mgr. C.P.I. Prods.; 1966-73, prod. mgr. asst. dir., free lance. 1973-1982, assoc. prod. exec. prod. at several studios. 1983-86, v.p. worldwide prod., Walt Disney Pictures; 1987, sr. v.p., worldwide prod., United Artists Pictures; 1988-90, sr. v.p. worldwide prod., MGM Pictures. 1994 to present Prod. Consult. to Warner Bros. Member: DGA, Friars, Academy of MP Arts & Sciences, Academy of TV Arts & Sciences, AFI.
PICTURES: *Asst. dir:* Hearts of the West. *Prod. mgr.:* Silver Streak. *Assoc. prod.:* The Other Side of Midnight, The Fury, Butch and Sundance: The Early Days, Six Pack, Unfaithfully Yours. *Exec. prod.:* North Dallas Forty, Monsignor, The Beast Within. *Co-prod.:* The Mambo Kings, Under Siege.
TELEVISION: *Series:* Deadly Games (supervising prod.), She Spies (co-exec. prod., 2002).

BERNSTEIN, WALTER

Writer, Director. b. New York, NY. Aug. 20, 1919. e. Dartmouth. Wrote for NY Magazine; in W.W.II was roving correspondent for Yank Magazine. Returned to NY after war. Wrote TV scripts; published Keep Your Head Down (collection of articles).
PICTURES: *Writer:* Kiss the Blood Off My Hands (co-s.p.), That Kind of Woman, Heller in Pink Tights, A Breath of Scandal (co-s.p.), Paris Blues, The Magnificent Seven (uncredited), Fail Safe, The Money Trap, The Train, The Molly Maguires, The Front (Academy Award nom.; WGA nom. 1977), Semi-Tough (WGA nom. 1978), The Betsy (co-s.p.), An Almost Perfect Affair, Yanks, Little Miss Marker (dir. debut), The House on Carroll Street.
TELEVISION: Women & Men 2: In Love There Are No Rules (also dir.), Doomsday Gun, The Affair (story), Miss Evers' Boys (Emmy nom. 1997), Durango, Fail Safe. *Documentaries:* American Masters: On Cukor, Marilyn Monroe: The Final Days.

BERRIDGE, ELIZABETH

Actress. b. New Rochelle, NY, May 2, 1962. Studied acting at Lee Strasberg Inst., Warren Robertson Theatre Workshop.
THEATRE: NY: The Vampires, The Incredibly Famous Willy Rivers, Outside Waco, Ground Zero Club, Cruise Control, Sorrows and Sons, Crackwalker, Coyote Ugly, Briar Patch. Regional: Tuesday's Child, Hedda Gabler, Lulu, Venus and Thumbtacks.
PICTURES: Natural Enemies (debut, 1979), The Funhouse, Amadeus, Smooth Talk, Five Corners, When the Party's Over, Payback, Broke Even, Break a Leg, Hidalgo, Please Give.
TELEVISION: *Movies:* Silence of the Heart, Home Fires Burning, Montana, When Billie Beat Bobby. *Series:* Another World: Texas, One of the Boys, The Powers That Be, The John Larroquette Show, Grounded for Life.

BERRY, HALLE

Actress. b. Cleveland, OH, Aug. 14, 1968. Named Miss Teen Ohio, Miss Teen All-American, runner up to Miss U.S.A. In 2002 Berry was first African American to win Academy Award in the Best Actress category for her role in Monster's Ball.
PICTURES: Jungle Fever, Strictly Business, The Last Boy Scout, Boomerang, Father Hood, The Program, The Flintstones, Losing Isaiah, Race the Sun, Girl 6, Executive Decision, Rich Man's Wife, B.A.P.S., Bulworth, Why Do Fools Fall in Love, X-Men, Swordfish, Monster's Ball (Academy Award for best actress, Golden Globe nom. 2002), Die Another Day, X2, Gothika, Catwoman, The Set-Up, The Guide, Robots (voice), Nappily Ever

After (also prod.), Foxy Brown (also co-exec. prod.), X-Men: The Last Stand, Perfect Stranger, Things We Lost in the Fire, Frankie and Alice, Dark Tide, For Colored Girls Who Have Considered Suicide When the Rainbow Is Enuf.
TELEVISION: *Movies:* Solomon and Sheba, The Wedding, Introducing Dorothy Dandridge (also exec. prod. Emmy Award, Emmy nom.; Golden Globe Award 2000), Lackawanna Blues (Emmy nom. 2005), Their Eyes Were Watching God (Emmy nom.; Golden Globe nom. 2006). *Mini-series:* Queen, A Century of Women. *Series:* Living Dolls, Knot's Landing. *Guest:* More than 183 appearances.

BERRY, MICHAEL P.
Executive. With a career spanning from educational institutions to topper of The Cheesecake Factory's Restaurant div., Berry's drive and enthusiasm has taken him to senior executive levels with all former employers. He's held senior positions at Harvard University, the University of California at Irvine and the University of California at Los Angeles. In 1996, he joined The Disneyland Resort and Downtown Disney as v.p. of food operations and concept development. From 1998-2001, he was senior v.p. of operations for The Disneyland Resort and Downtown Disney. He also served as pres. of Barnes & Noble, the nat'l. bookseller and in May 2002 became pres. & CEO of The Cheesecake Factory's Restaurant Div. In the fall of 2005, Berry was named COO of Pacific Theatres Entertainment Corporation, a subsidiary of Decurion, Corp. Decurion operates the historic Cinerama Dome theatre, the Grove, the ArcLight theatre complex, and theatres under the Pacific and Consolidated brands. Founder and principal/president of Michael P. Berry Consulting and Investments in Boston, MA.

BERTINELLI, VALERIE
Actress. b. Wilmington, DE, April 23, 1960. Dramatic training at Tami Lynn Academy of Artists in California. Made early TV appearances in the series, Apple's Way, in commercials, and in public service announcements. Started own prod. company to acquire properties for self.
PICTURE: C.H.O.M.P.S., Ordinary Heroes, Number One with a Bullet, Saved.
TELEVISION: *Movies:* Young Love First Love, The Promise of Love, The Princess and the Cabbie, I Was a Mail Order Bride, The Seduction of Gina, Shattered Vows, Silent Witness, Rockabye, Pancho Barnes, In a Child's Name, What She Doesn't Know, Murder of Innocence, The Haunting of Helen Walker, Two Mothers for Zachary, A Case for Life, Personally Yours, Finding John Christmas, Crazy Love, The One Day at a Time Reunion, Claire, True Confessions of a Hollywood Starlet. *Mini-series:* I'll Take Manhattan, Night Sins. *Series:* One Day at a Time (2 Emmy Awards 1981, 1982, Emmy nom. 1983), Sydney, Cafe Americain, Touched By An Angel, Hot in Cleveland. *Specials:* The Secret of Charles Dickens, The Magic of David Copperfield. *Guest:* More than 88 appearances.

BERTOLUCCI, BERNARDO
Director, Writer. b. Parma, Italy, May 16, 1940. e. Rome U. Son of Attilio Bertolucci, poet and film critic. At age 20 worked as asst. dir. to Pier Paolo Pasolini on latter's first film, Accatone. Made debut film, The Grim Reaper, from script by Pasolini, 1962; published poetry book, In Cerca del Mistero, 1962. Directed and wrote 3-part TV documentary, La vie del Petrolio for Ital. Oil co. in Iran, 1965-66. Collaborated on s.p. for Ballata de un Milliardo, Sergio Leone's Once Upon a Time in the West, L'inchiesta. Prod.: Sconcerto Rock, Lo Con Te Non Ci Sto Piu, Lost and Found.
PICTURES: The Grim Reaper, Before the Revolution, Love and Rage (episode: Agony), Partner, The Spider's Strategem, The Conformist (Academy Award nom. 1972), Last Tango in Paris (Academy Award nom.; Golden Globe nom.; DGA nom. 1974), 1900, Luna, Tragedy of a Ridiculous Man, The Last Emperor (2 Academy Awards for Best Dir. & Screenplay, 2 Golden Globe Awards, DGA Award, WGA nom. 1988), The Sheltering Sky (Golden Globe nom. 1991), Little Buddha, Stealing Beauty, Besieged, L'Assedio, Heaven and Hell, The Triumph of Love (also prod.), Ten Minutes Older: The Cello, The Dreamers.

BESSON, LUC
Producer, Writer, Director. b. Paris, France, March 18, 1959. Formed Les Films de Loups, which later changed name to Les Films de Dauphins.
PICTURES: Le Dernier Combat, Le Grand Carnaval (2nd unit dir.), Subway, Kamikaze (prod., s.p.), Taxi Boy (tech. advis.), The Big Blue (also lyrics, camera op.), La Femme Nikita (also song), L'Enfant lion, The Professional, The Fifth Element (dir.), Taxi (s.p., prod.), The Messenger: The Story of Joan of Arc (dir.), Nil by Mouth (prod., BAFTA Award, Outstanding Brit. Film, 1997), The Dancer (prod & writer), Taxi 2 (writer), Kiss of the Dragon (writer, prod.), Wasai (writer, prod.), The Transporter, (writer, prod.), Taxi 3 (writer, prod.), Peau d'ange (prod.), La felicita non costa niente (co-prod.), A ton image, Moi Cesar, Michel Vaillant (writer, prod.), Fanfan la tulipe (writer, prod.), Les Côtelettes, À ton image, Michel Vaillant (exec. prod, prod. & writer), Vice & Versa, Taxi (writer also), The Transporter 2, Crimson Rivers 2: Angels of the Apocalypse (co-prod. & writer), Miss June, Cheeky, Danny the Dog (prod. & writer), Flora Plum, Arthur (prod. & writer), Unleashed, Ze film, Les Yeux clairs, Le Souffleur, Colour Me Kubrick (co- prod.), The Three Burials of Melquiades Estrada (exec. prod.), Revolver (co-prod.), Le Texas n'existe pas, Spécial police, Bandidas (also writer-books), Quand j'étais chanteur (prod.), Arthur and the Invisibles (also dir., prod., writer-books), Michou d'Auber (exec. prod.), L' Invité (exec. prod.), Taxi 4 (also prod.), Un château en Espagne (exec. prod.), Frontières (co-prod.), Hitman, Taken, Ruby Tuesday, Come Like Shadows (also prod. assist.), Arthur et la guerre des deux mondes, Staten Island (co-prod.), L' Immortel, Home (doc.), Transporter 3 (also writer), I Love You Phillip Morris (exec. prod.), Arthur et la guerre des deux mondes, Un monstre à Paris, Arthur et la vengeance de Maltazard (also writer), From Paris with Love (also writer, s.p., prod.), Le Missionnaire, Banlieue 13 - Ultimatum (also writer, s.p.), Arthur et la guerre des deux mondes, 22 Bullets (prod. only), Les aventures extraordinaires d'Adèle Blanc-Sec, A Monster in Paris (prod. only).
TELEVISION: *Series:* La Femme Nikita (writer, Nikita character), Valérian et Laureline (prod./writer).

BEST, JAMES
Actor. r.n. Jules Guy. b. Corydon, IN, July 26, 1926. Magazine model; on stage in European roadshow cast of My Sister Eileen. Served as M.P. with USAAF, WWII.
PICTURES: One Way Street (debut, 1950), Commanche Territory, Winchester 73, Peggy, Kansas Raiders, Air Cadet, Cimarron Kid, Target Unknown, Apache Drums, Ma & Pa Kettle at the Fair, Steel Town, Francis Goes to West Point, Battle at Apache Pass, Flat Top, About Face, The Beast from 20000 Fathoms, Seminole, The President's Lady, City of Bad Men, Column South, Riders to the Stars, The Raid, The Caine Mutiny, Return from the Sea, They Rode West, Seven Angry Men, The Eternal Sea, A Man Called Peter, Forbidden Planet, Calling Homicide, When Gangland Strikes, Come Next Spring, Gaby, The Rack, Man on the Prowl, Hot Summer Night, Last of the Badmen, Verboten!, The Naked and the Dead, The Left Handed Gun, Cole Younger—Gunfighter, The Killer Shrews, Ride Lonesome, Cast a Long Shadow, The Mountain Road, Shock Corridor, Black Gold, The Quick Gun, Black Spurs, Shenandoah, Three on a Couch, First to Fight, Firecreek, The Brain Machine, Sounder, Ode to Billy Joe, Gator (also assoc. prod.), Nickelodeon, Rolling Thunder, The End (also assoc. prod.), Hooper, Death Mask, Moondance Alexander.
TELEVISION: *Movies:* Run Simon Run, Savages, The Runaway Barge, The Savage Bees, The Dukes of Hazzard: Reunion!, TV Road Trip. *Mini-series*: Centennial. *Series:* Dukes of Hazzard, Dukes of Hazzard 2000. *Guest:* More than 122 appearances.

BETTANY, PAUL
Actor. b. Harlesden, England, May 27, 1971. Parents are actors Thane Bettany and Anne Kettle (retired).
THEATRE: *London:* An Inspector Calls, One More Wasted Year, Love and Understanding, Romeo and Juliet, Julius Caesar, Richard III, Woyzeck.
PICTURES: Bent, The Land Girls, Gangster No. 1, A Knight's Tale, A Beautiful Mind, The Heart of Me, Dogville, The Reckoning, Master and Commander: The Far Side of the World, Wimbledon, Firewall, The Da Vinci Code, Iron Man (voice), The Secret Life of Bees, Inkheart, The Young Victoria, Creation, Legion, Iron Man 2 (voice), Priest.
TELEVISION: *Movies:* Coming Home, Sharpe's Waterloo, Killer Net, David Copperfield. *Mini-series:* Every Woman Knows a Secret. *Guest:* More than 43 appearances.

BEWKES, JEFF
Executive. e. B.A. degree from Yale University; M.B.A., Stanford Graduate School of Business. Bewkes began his career in California where he was operations director for Sonoma Vineyards, Inc., in Healdsburg. Before entering management ranks in the entertainment industry Bewkes spent two years as an account officer for Citibank, NA in New York. Bewkes joined Time Inc.'s HBO unit in 1979 as a junior finance executive. By 1995 he had risen to CEO. He helped HBO evolve from a pay-movie channel to a mini-studio — Sex and the City and The Sopranos happened on his watch — and the unit became a major profit center. In July 2002, he became Time Warner, Inc.'s chairman, entertainment & networks group. On Dec. 21, 2005, he was promoted to his current position, president and COO of Time Warner, Inc. and was elected to Time Warner, Inc.'s bd. of directors in Jan. 2007. As pres.and COO, he oversaw Time Inc., HBO, Turner Broadcasting (CNN, TNT, TBS, Cartoon Network), Warner Bros. and New Line Cinema, Time Warner Cable and AOL. January, 2008, Bewkes became CEO for Time Warner. Bewkes began serving as Chairman of the Board in January 2009. Bewkes serves on the bd. of trustees for Yale University and the Museum of the Moving Image and on the advisory boards for Stanford Graduate School of Business, the American Museum of Natural History, The Creative Coalition and the Museum of Television and Radio.

BEYMER, RICHARD
Actor. r.n. George Richard Beymer, Jr., b. Avoca, IA, Feb. 21, 1939. e. N. Hollywood H.S., Actors Studio. Performer, KTLA, Sandy Dreams, Fantastic Studios, Inc., 1949, Playhouse 90.
PICTURES: Indiscretion of an American Wife (debut, 1953), So

Big, Johnny Tremain, The Diary of Anne Frank, High Time, West Side Story, Bachelor Flat, Five Finger Exercise, Hemingway's Adventures of a Young Man, The Longest Day, The Stripper, Grass (Scream Free!), Cross Country, Silent Night Deadly Night 3: Better Watch Out, My Girl 2, The Little Death, Foxfire, The Disappearance of Kevin Johnson, Playing Patti, Home the Horror Story, West Side Memories (video documentary, 2003).
TELEVISION: *Movies:* Generation, With a Vengeance, A Face to Die For, Elvis Meets Nixon. *Series:* Paper Dolls, Twin Peaks. *Guest:* More than 42 appearances.

BIALIK, MAYIM

Actress. b. San Diego, CA, Dec. 12, 1976.
PICTURES: Beaches (debut 1988), Pumpkinhead, Kalamazoo?, The Chicago 8.
TELEVISION: *Movies:* Blossom in Paris, Don't Drink the Water. Specials: Earth Day Special, Sea World Mother Earth Celebration (host), Surviving a Break-Up, The Kingdom Chums: Original Top Ten (voice), I Hate the Way I Look, For Our Children: The Concert (host), Recess (voice). *Series:* Blossom, Hey Arnold (voice), Molloy, The Adventures of Hyperman, Recess, Katbot, Curb Your Enthusiasm, The Secret Life of the American Teenager. *Pilot:* Molloy. *Guest:* More than 51 appearances.

BIEHN, MICHAEL

Actor. b. Anniston, AL, July 31, 1956. Raised in Lincoln, NB, and Lake Havisu, AZ. At 18 years moved to Los Angeles and studied acting with Vincent Chase. First professional job in 1977 in TV pilot for Logan's Run.
PICTURES: Grease (debut, 1978), Coach, Hog Wild, The Fan, The Lords of Discipline, The Terminator, Aliens, The Seventh Sign, Rampage, In a Shallow Grave, The Abyss, Navy Seals, Time Bomb, K2, DeadFall, Tombstone, Deep Red, Jade, The Rock, Mojave Moon, The Ride, American Dragon, Dead Men Can't Dance, Susan's Plan, Wonderland, Silver Wolf, Cherry Falls, The Art of War, Meggido: The Omega Code 2, Clockstoppers, Borderline, Amerikanets, Havoc, That's Amore!, Dragon Squad, The Insatiable, You Are Here, Planet Terror, Psych 9, They Wait, Young Americans, Stiletto, Saving Grace B. Jones, Malevolence: Bereavement, Fire Bay, The Blood Bond (also dir., writer), Retractable, Kane & Lynch.
TELEVISION: *Movies:* Zuma Beach, A Fire in the Sky, China Rose, Deadly Intentions, A Taste for Killing, Strapped, Conundrum, Asteroid, Alien Evolution, When Muscles Ruled the World (tv documentary), The Legend of Butch & Sundance. *Series:* The Runaways, The Magnificent Seven, Adventure Inc., Hawaii. *Guest:* More than 50 appearances.

BIGELOW, KATHRYN

Director, Writer. b. San Carlos, CA, Nov. 27, 1951. e. SF Art Inst., Columbia. Studied to be painter before turning to film with short Set-Up, 1978. Was script supervisor on Union City; appeared in film Born in Flames. 2010 elected for a three year term to Bd. of Governors of the Academy of Motion Picture Arts and Sciences which oversees the Oscars.
PICTURES: The Loveless (feature debut as co-dir. with Monty Montgomery, 1981; also co-s.p.), Near Dark (also co-s.p.), Blue Steel (also co-s.p.), Point Break, Strange Days, Undertow (s.p.), The Weight of Water, K19 The Widowmaker (dir., prod.), Living in Darkness (doc., appearing as herself), The Hurt Locker (dir., prod., Academy Award nom.; DGA Award, Golden Globe nom. 2010).
TELEVISION: *Movie:* Undertow (writer). *Mini-series:* Wild Palms (co-dir.). *Series:* Homicide: Life on the Street, The Inside (exec. prod.).

BIGGS, JASON

Actor. b. Pompton Plains, NJ, May 12, 1978. Began acting at age 5 in national commericials.
THEATRE: Starred opposite Judd Hirsch on B'way in Conversations With My Father, toured in The Graduate.
PICTURES: Camp Stories, American Pie, Boys and Girls, The Loser, Prozac Nation, Saving Silverman, American Pie 2, Jay and Silent Bob Strike Back, American Wedding, Anything Else, Jersey Girl, Guy X, Eight Below, My Best Friend's Girl, Farce of the Penguins (voice), Lower Learning, My Best Friend's Girl.
TELEVISION: *Movie:* I'm in Hell (also prod.). *Series:* Drexel's Class, Total Security, As The World Turns (Emmy nom. 1995). *Guest:* More than 50 appearances.

BIKEL, THEODORE

Actor. b. Vienna, Austria, May 2, 1924. Moved to Israel as teen where he made stage debut in Tevye the Milkman. Studied acting at Royal Academy of Dramatic Arts in London. London stage debut in 1948. Autobiography: Theo (1995).
THEATRE: Tonight in Samarkland, The Lark, The Rope Dancers, The Sound of Music, Cafe Crown, Fiddler on the Roof.
PICTURES: The African Queen, Melba, Desperate Moment, The Divided Heart, The Little Kidnappers, The Vintage, The Pride and the Passion, The Enemy Below, Fraulein, The Defiant Ones (Academy Award nom. 1959), I Want to Live, The Angry Hills, The Blue Angel, A Dog of Flanders, My Fair Lady, Sands of the Kalahari, The Russians Are Coming the Russians Are Coming, Sweet November, My Side of the Mountain, Darker Than Amber, 200 Motels, The Little Ark, Prince Jack, Dark Tower, See You in the Morning, Shattered, Crisis in the Kremlin, My Family Treasure, Benefit of the Doubt, Shadow Conspiracy, Trickle, Second Chances, Crime and Punishment, The Lost Wooden Synagogues of Eastern Europe (narr.), The Little Traitor.
TELEVISION: *Movies:* The Eternal Light, Look Up and Live, Who Has Seen the Wind?, Noon Wine, The Diary of Anne Frank, Killer by Night, Murder on Flight 502, Victory at Entebbe, Christine Cromwell: Things That Go Bump in the Night, The Final Days, Babylon 5: In the Beginning, H.U.D. *Mini-series:* Testimony of Two Men, Loose Change, Memories of Midnight. *Series:* Another World. *Guest:* More than 132 appearances.

BILL, TONY

Director, Producer, Actor. b. San Diego, CA, Aug. 23, 1940. e. Notre Dame U. Founded Bill/Phillips Prods. with Julia and Michael Phillips, 1971-73; Tony Bill Prods. 1973-92; Barnstorm Films, producer, director 1993-. Acad. of M.P. Arts & Sciences, bd. of govs., bd of trustees, chmn. prods. branch.
PICTURES: *Director:* My Bodyguard (debut, 1980), Six Weeks, Five Corners (also co-prod.), Crazy People, Untamed Heart (also co-prod.), A Home of Our Own, Flyboys. *Prod.:* Hearts of the West (exec. prod.), Harry and Walter Go to New York, Boulevard Nights (exec. prod.), Going in Style, Little Dragons (also actor). *Co-producer:* Deadhead Miles, Steelyard Blues, The Sting (Academy Award for Best Picture, 1974), Taxi Driver. *Actor:* Come Blow Your Horn (debut, 1963), Soldier in the Rain, Marriage on the Rocks, None But the Brave, You're a Big Boy Now, Ice Station Zebra, Never a Dull Moment, Castle Keep, Flap, Shampoo, Heartbeat, Pee-wee's Big Adventure, Less Than Zero, Barb Wire, Lying In Wait, Must Love Dogs, Flyboys.
TELEVISION: *Movies/Director:* Dirty Dancing (pilot), Love Thy Neighbor, Next Door, One Christmas, Oliver Twist, Harlan County War, In the Time of the Butterflies (prod. only), Whitewash: The Clarence Brandley Story, Fitzgerald (exec. prod. only), Pictures of Hollis Woods. *Actor:* Haunts of the Very Rich, Having Babies II, The Initiation of Sarah, With This Ring, Are You in the House Alone?, Portrait of an Escort, Freedom, Washington Mistress, Running Out, The Killing Mind, Naked City: Justice with a Bullet, The Fixer (also prod.), A Chance of Snow, *Mini-series:* Washington Behind Closed Doors. *Series:* What Really Happened to the Class of '65?, Monk, Keen Eddie.

BILSON, BRUCE

Director. b. Brooklyn, NY, May 19, 1928. e. UCLA, BA, Theater Arts, 1950. m. actress Renne Jarrett. Father was prod. George Bilson, son is prod.-dir. Danny Bilson, daughter is prod. Julie Ahlberg. Asst. film ed. 1951-55; USAF photo unit 1952-53; asst. dir. 1955-65. Dir. since 1965 of more than 390 TV shows.
PICTURES: The North Avenue Irregulars, Chattanooga Choo Choo.
TELEVISION: *Movies/pilots:* The Odd Couple, The Dallas Cowboys Cheerleaders, BJ and the Bear, The Misadventures of Sheriff Lobo, Half Nelson, Finder of Lost Loves, The Girl Who Came Gift Wrapped, The Ghosts of Buxley Hall, The New Gidget, Barefoot in the Park, The Bad News Bears, Harper Valley PTA, Deadly Games. *Series:* U.S. Marshal, Bonanza, Bewitched, Gidget, Green Acres, The Sentinel, Touched by an Angel, Viper, The Flash, Dinosaurs, Barney Miller, Get Smart (Emmy Award, 1968), The Ghost & Mrs. Muir, Andy Griffith Show (asst. dir.), Route 66 (asst. dir.), The Baileys of Balboa (also assoc. prod.), Hogan's Heroes, House Calls, Alice, Private Benjamin, Life With Lucy, Spenser: For Hire, Hotel, Dallas, Hawaii Five-O, The Brady Bunch, Love, American Style, Nanny and the Professor, Arnie, The Odd Couple (DGA nom. 1972), Barefoot in the Park, Alias Smith and Jones, Emergency!, The Rookies, Temperatures Rising, The Paul Lynde Show, M*A*S*H, Dusty's Trail, The Six Million Dollar Man, Sierra, S.W.A.T., Barbary Coast, When Things Were Rotten, Wonder Woman, Hunter, Tabitha, The Love Boat, Quark, Delta House, Turnabout, The Bad News Bears, House Calls, Skag, Harper Valley P.T.A., Simon & Simon, The Powers of Matthew Star, Knight Rider, The Colbys, Sledge Hammer!, The New Munsters, Dinosaurs, Touched by an Angel, Pop-Up Brady (series doc.).

BINDER, STEVE

Producer, Director, Writer. b. Los Angeles, CA, Dec. 12. e. Univ. of Southern California. 1960-61, announcer in Austria and Germany with AFN, Europe. Prof. of Cinema, Univ. Southern CA. Mem.: DGA, Producers Guild of America, Writers Guild of America, NARAS, ATAS.
PICTURES: *Director:* The T.A.M.I. Show, Give 'Em Hell Harry!, Melissa, Father Guido Sarducci Goes to College.
TELEVISION: *Prod./Dir.:* Soupy Sales Show, Jazz Scene U.S.A., Hullaballoo, The Danny Kaye Show, Hallelujah Leslie!, TJ's, Petula, America, A Funny Thing Happened on the Way to the White House, Comedy of the 60's, Don Kirshner's Rock Concert, Olivia Newton-John, Norman Corwin Theater, Mac Davis Series, The Big Show (Emmy nom. 1980), Primetime Emmy's, Motown Revue, Peggy Fleming Special, Dorothy Hammil Special, Shields & Yarnell Series (Emmy nom. 1978, also writer) The Magic Castle Special, Star Wars Holiday Special, Father Guido Sarducci at UCSB, A Tribute to Sam Kinison, Smhatar, Jane Fonda In Search of the Missing Smhatar, Steve Allen Show (1963-65, 1973), Elvis Presley Comeback Special, Barry Manilow Special (also exec. prod., writer, Emmy Award, 2 Emmy

nom. 1977), Diana Ross '81, Ringling Bros & Barnum Bailey Circus (also writer), Pee-wee's Playhouse (exec. prod., writer), Barry Manilow Big Fun on Swing Street, Pee-wee's Playhouse Christmas Special, A Tribute to Sam Kinison, Diana Ross at Wembley, Diana Ross Sings Jazzy Blues, Diana Ross—World Tour, Diana Ross in Central Park (Cable Ace Award, also writer), Diana Ross (also writer), The International Special Olmpics, 65th Anniversary of the Grand Ole Opry, The First Annual ESPY Awards, Liza Minneli, Lucy in London, Fiesta Texas, Eddie Rabbit Special, One Night With You, Disney's First Lady of Magic (exec. prod.), The Nick at Nite Holiday Special. *Exec. Prod./Writer:* Soul Train Music Awards, Zoobilee Zoo, Disney's Greatest Hits on Ice, Disney's Aladdin on Ice, Disney's Beauty and the Beast on Ice (Emmy nom. 1997), Innocent Love (MOW), The Chevy Chase Show, SK8 TV, On the Television Series, Tales From the Whoop, The Beach Boys Summer Series, Television's Greatest Performances.

BINOCHE, JULIETTE

Actress. b. Paris, France, March 9, 1964. e. Nat'l. School of Dramatic Art, Paris. Began acting career while in school, performing on stage. In 1984, after some small roles in films and TV prods., appeared in Jean-Luc Godard's, Je Vous Salue Marie. In 1985, gained recognition at the Cannes Film Festival for her role in Andre Techine's Rendez-Vous.
PICTURES: Liberty Bell, Le Meilleur de la Vie, Adieu Blaireau, La Vie de la Familie, Je Vous Salue Marie, Les Nanas, Rendez-Vous, Mauvais Sang, Mon Beau-Frere a Tue Ma Soeur, The Unbearable Lightness of Being, Un Tour de Manege, Les Amants du Pont-Neuf, Mara, Wuthering Heights, Damage, Three Colors: Blue (Golden Globe nom. 1994), Le Hussard Sur le Toit, The English Patient (Academy Award, Golden Globe nom. 1996; BAFTA), A Couch in New York, Alice et Martin, The Widow of Saint-Pierre, Les Enfants du Siecle, La Veuve de Saint-Pierre, Code Unknown: Incomplete Tales of Several Journeys, Chocolat (Academy Award nom.; Golden Globe nom. 2001), Decolage horaire, Picasso at the Lapin Agile, Jet Lag, Country of My Skull, The Assumption, Toyer, The Monster of Longwood, Bee Season, Hidden, Paris, je t'aime, Breaking and Entering, Promise Me This, Les Disparus, Dan in Real Life, Paris, Dan in Real Life, Flight of the Red Balloon, Family Souvenirs, Disengagement, Summer Hours, Paris, Another Kind of Silence, The Certified Copy, Times to Come, Sponsoring.
TELEVISION: *Movies:* Women & Men 2: In Love There Are No Rules. *Guest:* More than 68 appearances.

BIONDI, JR. FRANK J.

Executive. b. Jan. 9, 1945. e. B.A., Princeton U., 1966; Harvard U., MBA (1968). Various investment banking positions, 1968-74. Asst. treas. Children's TV Workshop 1974-78. V.p. programming HBO 1978-82; pres. HBO 1983, then chmn. & CEO. Joined Coca-Cola Co. as exec. v.p., entertainment business arm, 1984. Resigned 1987 to join Viacom International as pres. and CEO. Pres., MCA, 1996. Resigned, 1998. Currently Senior Managing Director, WaterView Advisors, LLC, a private equity fund specializing in media. Biondi is a director of Cablevision Systems Corp., Harrahs Entertainment, Inc., Hasbro, Inc.,Director for The Bank of New York Mellon Corporation (since 1995), Seagate Technology, Amgen, Inc. and Yahoo!, Inc. Biondi is a founding member of USC's Board of Councilors of the School of Cinema-Television and is on the bd. of advisors for The Annenberg School for Comm. at USC.

BIRCH, THORA

Actress. b. Los Angeles, CA, March 11, 1982. Began acting at age 4. First appeared in commericals.
PICTURES: Paradise, All I Want for Christmas, Patriot Games, Hocus Pocus, Monkey Trouble, Clear and Present Danger, Now and Then, Alaska, American Beauty, Anywhere But Here, The Smokers, Dungeons & Dragons, Ghost World (Golden Globe nom. 2002), After The Hole, Silver City, Silence Becomes You, Vinyl (also exec. prod.), Boomerang Deal, Dark Corners, Winter of Frozen Dreams, Train, Crossmaglen, The Flicker's Dance.
TELEVISION: *Movies:* Night Ride Home, Shadow Realm, Homeless to Harvard: The Liz Murray Story (Emmy nom. 2003), Dark Avenger, Pregnancy Pact. *Series:* Day by Day, Parenthood. *Guest:* More than 60 appearances.

BIRD, ANDY

Executive. b. United Kingdom. e. B.A. degree (with honors) from the Univ. of Newcastle Upon Tyne, 1985. Began career with Piccadilly Radio in Manchester, England, as breakfast show producer. Bird then moved to London to join the Virgin Broadcasting Company working at Music Box, a Pan-European music channel. Later, Virgin asked Bird to help launch and program a satellite-delivered national radio service called Radio Radio. Bird became programming head for the service, producing radio shows for leading comedians and TV presenters. Between 1989 and 1994 Bird held a number of positions in radio and television in Europe, during which he helped start a music channel, produced and directed a popular London-based morning TV program, and produced a Saturday morning children's TV show. In 1992, Bird was tapped by Unique Broadcasting, the largest independent radio production company in the U.K., to start up and operate Unique Television. In 1994, he joined Time Warner as senior v.p. and gen. mgr. of Turner Entertainment Networks Limited, the TBS Europe arm that produced Cartoon Network. He helped grow the unit to 13 channels across Europe from one. He rose to president of TBS International in 2000, and became responsible for all TBS broadcasting outside of the continental U.S. In Jan. 2004, Bird became president of Walt Disney International. Oversaw growth opportunities for Disney outside the United States, growing and increasing penetration of existing businesses, and leading the development of business and operations in emerging markets. Currently is Chairman of Walt Disney International. He is based in Burbank, CA.

BIRKIN, JANE

Actress. b. London, England, Dec. 14, 1946. Daughter is actress Charlotte Gainsbourg. Sister of dir.-writer Andrew Birkin. Was subject of Agnes Vardas` 1988 documentary Jane B. par Agnes V.
PICTURES: The Knack...and How to Get It, Blow-Up, Kaleidoscope, Wonderwall, Les Chemins de Katmandou, La Piscine, Cannabis, Romance of a Horse Thief, Trop jolies pour etre honnetes, Dark Places, Projection Privee, La Moutarde me monte au nex, Le Mouton Enrage, 7 Morts sur Ordonnance, Catherine et Cie, La Course a l'echalote, Je T'Aime Moi Non Plus, Seriex comme let plaisir, Le Diable au Coeur, L'Animal, Death on the Nile, Au bout du bout du banc, Melancolie Baby, La Miel, La Fille Prodigue, Evil Under the Sun, L'Ami de Vincent, Circulez u'a rien a voir, Love on the Ground, le Garde du Corps, The Pirate, Beethoven's Nephew, Dust, Leave All Fair, la Femme de ma vie, Comedie!, Kung Fu Master (also story), Soigne ta droite, Daddy Nostalgia, Between the Devil and the Deep Blue Sea (voice), A Soldier's Daughter Never Cries, The Last September, This Is My Body, A Hell of a Day, Merci Docteur Rey, Le Divorce, Daltry Calhoun (soundtrack writer/performer), Boxes (also dir., writer), La Tête de maman, Sicko (doc., sountrack performer), 36 vues du Pic Saint-Loup.
TELEVISION: *Movie:* Cinderella. *Mini-series:* Red Fox. Many movies and mini-series: French TV.

BIRNBAUM, ROGER

Producer, Executive. b. Teaneck, NJ. e. Univ. of Denver. Was v.p. of both A&M Records and Arista records before becoming m.p. producer. Headed Guber/Peters Company, then named pres. of worldwide prod., United Artists; pres. of worldwide prod. and exec. v.p. of 20th Century Fox. Left Fox in 1993 to become co-founder of Caravan Pictures. Then, teamed up with Gary Barber to form Spyglass Entertainment, where both now serve as co-chairman and co-CEO. The company develops and finances all of its projects independently. Has own Production company, Roger Birnbaum Productions.
PICTURES: *Prod./Exec. Prod.:* The Sure Thing, Young Sherlock Homes, Who's That Girl, The Three Musketeers, Angie, Angels in the Outfield, A Low Down Dirty Shame, Houseguest, Tall Tale, While You Were Sleeping, Dead Presidents, Powder, Celtic Pride, The Beautician and the Beast, G.I. Jane, Gone Fishin', Grosse Pointe Blank, Washington Square, Metro, Rocket Man, A Small Miracle, Holy Man, Six Days Seven Nights, Simon Birch, Rush Hour, Stretch Armstrong, A Course in Miracles, Inspector Gadget, Shanghai Noon, The Hitchhiker's Guide to the Galaxy, Keeping the Faith, Unbreakable, Rush Hour 2, Out Cold, The Count of Monte Cristo, Dragonfly, Abandon, Reign of Fire, Shanghai Knights, Bruce Almighty, Seabiscuit, One Love, The Perfect Score, Mr. 3000, Connie and Carla, The Pacifier, Legend of Zorro, Memoirs of a Geisha, Eight Below, Stay Alive, Stick It, The Lookout, The Invisible, Balls of Fury, Evan Almighty, Underdog, Rush Hour 3, Flash of Genius, 27 Dresses, Wanted, The Love Guru, Ghost Town, Four Christmases, G.I. Joe: The Rise of Cobra, Invictus, Leap Year, The Tourist.
TELEVISION: *Movies: exec. prod.:* When Your Lover Leaves, All the Kids Do It (Daytime Emmy Award, 1985), Scandal Sheet (prod.), Bay Coven, Flash, Angels in the Endzone, Angels in the Infield, The Ranch. *Series: exec. prod.:* Miracles, Weekends.

BIRNEY, DAVID

Actor. b. Washington, DC, April 23, 1939. e. Dartmouth Coll., B.A., UCLA, M.A. Phd. Southern Utah St. (hon.). Following grad. sch. and the Army spent 2 yrs. in regional theatre, Amer. Shakespeare Festival, Lincoln Center Repertory Theatre, Great Lakes Theatre Festival, Mark Taper Forum, Shakespeare Theatre Washington DC, Hartford Stage Co., Barter Theatre, to N.Y. where appeared in Lincoln Center prod. of Summertree (Theatre World Award). Appeared for two yrs. on TV daytime series, Love Is a Many Splendored Thing, doing other stage roles in same period. Theatre panelist, Natl. Endowment for the Arts; bd. mem., Hopkins Center, Dartmouth College; bd. of Foundation for Biomedical Research.
THEATRE: Comedy of Errors (NY debut; NY Shakespeare Fest). NY & Regional: Amadeus, Benefactors, Anthony & Cleopatra, Man and Superman, Macbeth, Hamlet, Richard II, III, Romeo & Juliet, Much Ado About Nothing, King John, Titus Andronicus, Major Barbara, Biko Inquest, Playboy of the Western World, The Miser, Antigone, My Fair Lady, Camelot, Love Letters, Present Laughter, Twelfth Night, Talley's Folley, Rumors, Social Security, Enemy of the People, Mark Twain's The Diaries of Adam & Eve. *CA:* MacBeth, Open Secrets.
PICTURES: Caravan to Vaccares, Trial by Combat, Oh God Book II, Prettykill, Nightfall, Touch and Die, The Naked Truth,

Comedy of Errors.
TELEVISION: *Movies:* Murder or Mercy, Bronk, Serpico: The Deadly Game, Someone's Watching Me!, High Midnight, Only With Married Men, OHMS, Mom The Wolfman & Me, The Five of Me, The Long Journey Home (also co-exec. prod.), Love and Betrayal, Always Remember I Love You, Keeping Secrets. *Mini-series*: Night of the Fox, Seal Morning, Adam's Chronicles, Testimony of Two Men, Master of the Game, Valley of the Dolls, The Bible. Specials: Missing: Have You Seen This Person? Drop Everything and Read, 15 and Getting Straight, Mark Twain's The Diaries of Adam and Eve (co-prod.), St. Joan. *Series*: Love Is A Many Splendored Thing, A World Apart, Bridget Loves Bernie, Serpico, St. Elsewhere, Glitter, Live Shot, Beyond 2000 (host), Raising Kids (host), Great American TV Poll (host), The Perfect Pitch (tv documentary). *Guest:* More than 73 appearances.

BISHOP, LARRY
Actor. Son of late actor/comedian Joey Bishop.
PICTURES: Wild in the Street, The Savage Seven, The Devil's Eight, Angel Unchained, Chrome and Hot Leather, Shanks, How Come Nobody's on Our Side?, The Big Fix, Hey Good Lookin' (voice), The Sting II, Mad Dog Time (also dir., prod., s.p.), Underworld (also s.p.), Kill Bill: Vol. 2, Hell Ride (also s.p./dir./prod.).
TELEVISION: *Movies***:** The Third Girl from the Left, All Together Now, High Midnight, Condominium.

BISSET, JACQUELINE
Actress. r.n. Winnifred Jacqueline Fraser-Bisset, b. Weybridge, England, September 13, 1944. e. French Lycaee, London. After photographic modeling made film debut in The Knack, 1965.
PICTURES: The Knack... and How to Get It (debut, 1965), Cul de Sac, Two For The Road, Casino Royale, The Cape Town Affair, The Sweet Ride (Golden Globe nom. 1969), The Detective, Bullitt, The First Time, Secret World, Airport, The Grasshopper, The Mephisto Waltz, Believe in Me, Stand Up and Be Counted, The Life & Times of Judge Roy Bean, The Thief Who Came to Dinner, Day for Night, Le Manifique, Murder on the Orient Express, End of the Game, The Spiral Staircase, St. Ives, Sunday Woman, The Deep, The Greek Tycoon, Secrets, Who Is Killing the Great Chefs of Europe? (Golden Globe nom. 1979), Together?, When Time Ran Out, Rich and Famous, Inchon, Class, Under the Volcano (Golden Globe nom. 1985), High Season, Scenes From the Class Struggle in Beverly Hills, La Maison de Jade, Wild Orchid, The Maid, A Judgment in Stone, Dangerous Beauty, Let the Devil Wear Black, Les gens qui s'aiment, New Year's Day,The Sleepy Time Gal, Fascination, Swing, Latter Days, Joan of Arc: The Virgin Warrior, Laughing Water (Mine-Ha Ha), Domino, The Last Film Festival, Vivaldi.
TELEVISION: *Movies:* Anna Karenina, Choices, Leave of Absence, End of Summer, September, Once You Meet a Stranger, Witch Hunt, Jesus, Joan of Arc (Emmy nom.; Golden Globe nom. 1999), Britannic, Sex and Mrs X, Dancing at the Harvest Moon, America's Prince: The John F. Kennedy Jr. Story, The Survivors Club, Summer Solstice, Carolina Moon, An Old Fashioned Thanksgiving, The Eastmans. *Mini-series:* Napoleon and Josephine: A Love Story, In the Beginning. *Series:* Nip/Tuck. *Guest:* More than 79 appearances.

BLACK, JACK
Actor, Producer. Composer. b. Santa Monica, CA, August 28, 1969. E. UCLA. Member of the band Tenacious D.
PICTURES: Bob Roberts, True Romance, Airborne, Demolition Man, Bye, Bye, Love, Waterworld, Dead Man Walking, Bio-Dome, The Cable Guy, The Fan, Mars Attacks!, The Jackal, I Still Know What You Did Last Summer, Enemy of the State, Cradle Will Rock, The Love Letter, Jesus' Son, High Fidelity, Saving Silverman, Shallow Hal, Orange County, Ice Age (voice), The School of Rock (Golden Globe nom. 2004), Envy, Anchorman: The Legend of Ron Burgundy, Shark Tale (voice), King Kong, Nacho Libre (also prod.), Tenacious D in: The Pick of Destiny (also writer), The Holiday, Them (also prod.), Year of the Dog (prod.), Be Kind Rewind, Margot at the Wedding, Kung Fu Panda (voice), Tropic Thunder, Year One, Gulliver's Travels (also prod.), Kung Fu Panda: The Kaboom of Doom (voice).
TELEVISION: *Movies:* Our Shining Moment, Marked for Murder, The Innocent, Heat Vision and Jack, Awesometown, The Lewis Lectures (voice). *Series:* Tenacious D (also exec. prod., composer, writer, creator), The Animated Adventures of Computerman (also exec. prod., composer; theme), The X-Files (recurring role). Shorts: Lord of the Piercing, Jack Black: Spider-Man, The Department of Acceptable TV. *Documentary:* Tenacious D: The Complete Masterworks (video; also exec. prod., composer, writer). *Guest:* More than 142 appearances.

BLACK, KAREN
Actress. b. Park Ridge, IL, July 1, 1942. r.n. Karen Ziegler. e. Northwestern U. Left school for NY to join the Hecscher House, appearing in several Shakespearean plays. In 1965 starred in Playroom, which ran only 1 month but won her NY Drama Critic nom. as best actress.
THEATRE: Happily Never After, Keep It in the Family, Come Back to the Five and Dime Jimmy Dean Jimmy Dean.
PICTURES: Appeared in more than 115 pictures, incl.: You're a Big Boy Now (debut, 1966), Hard Contact, Easy Rider, Five Easy Pieces (Academy Award nom.; Golden Globe Award, 1971), Drive He Said, A Gunfight, Born To Win, Cisco Pike, Portnoy's Complaint, The Pyx, Little Laura and Big John, Rhinoceros, The Outfit, The Great Gatsby (Golden Globe Award 1975), Airport 1975, Law and Disorder, Day of the Locust (Golden Globe nom. 1976), Crime and Passion, Burnt Offerings, Capricorn One, In Praise of Older Women, The Squeeze, The Last Word, Chanel Solitaire, Come Back to the Five and Dime Jimmy Dean Jimmy Dean, Killing Heat, Can She Bake a Cherry Pie?, Martin's Day, Bad Manners, Cut and Run, Invaders from Mars, Hostage, Eternal Evil, The Invisible Kid, Out of the Dark, Homer and Eddie, Night Angel, Miss Right, Dixie Lanes, Twisted Justice, Over Exposure, The Children, Mirror Mirror, Haunting Fear, Quiet Fire, Children of the Night, Hotel Oklahoma, Killer's Edge, Moon Over Miami, Final Judgment, Caged Fear, Bound & Gagged: A Love Story, The Player, Rubin & Ed, The Trust, The Double O Kid, Sister Island, Plan 10 From Outer Space, Odyssey, Every Minute Is Goodbye, A Thousand Stars, I Woke Up Early the Day I Died, Felons, Fallen Arches, Bury the Evidence, Spoken in Silence, Mascara, The Underground Comedy Movie, Sugar: The Fall of the West, Karen Black: Actress At Work, The Independent, Red Dirt, Oliver Twisted, The Donor, Gypsy 83, Soulkeeper, A Light in the Darkness, Hard Luck, Don't Try This At Home, House of 1000 Corpses, Paris, Max and Grace, The Last Patient, Firecracker, America Brown, Hollywood Dreams, Go Straight to Hell, Double Duty, Katie Q, Some Guy Who Kills People, Heated Rivalry.
TELEVISION: *Movies:* Trilogy of Terror, The Strange Possession of Mrs. Oliver, Mr. Horn, Power, Where the Ladies Go, Because He's My Friend, Full Circle Again (Canadian TV), My Neighbor's Daughter, The Big Show. *Series:* The Second Hundred Years, A Force of One, Funny or Die Presents.... *Guest:* More than 78 appearances.

BLACKMAN, HONOR
Actress. b. London, England, Aug. 22, 1926. Stage debut. The Gleam 1946.
PICTURES: Fame Is the Spur (debut, 1947), Quartet, Daughter of Darkness, A Boy A Girl and a Bike, Diamond City, Conspirator, So Long at the Fair, Set a Murderer, Green Grow the Rushes, Come Die My Love, Rainbow Jacket, Outsiders, Delavine Affair, Three Musketeers, Breakaway, Homecoming, Suspended Alibi, Dangerous Drugs, A Night to Remember, The Square Peg, A Matter of Who, Present Laughter, The Recount, Serena, Jason & the Golden Fleece, Goldfinger, The Secret of My Success, Moment to Moment, Life at the Top, A Twist of Sand, Shalako, Struggle for Rome, Twinky, The Last Grenade, The Virgin and the Gypsy, Fright, Something Big, Out Damned Spot, Summer, Cat and the Canary, Russell Mulcahy's Talos the Mummy, To Walk with Lions, Color Me Kubrick, Bridget Jones's Diary, Re-Uniting the Rubins, Hotel Caledonia.
TELEVISION: *Movies:* Columbo: Dagger of the Mind, African Patrol, The Witness, Top Secret, Ghost Squad, Invisible Man, The Secret Adversary, Lace, The First Olympics: Athens 1896, Minder on the Orient Express, Voice of the Heart, The Secret Garden (voice), In Search of James Bond with Jonathan Ross, Blondes: Diana Dors, The Sight, Summer Solstice, Sound. *Mini-series:* Jack and the Beanstalk: The Real Story. *Series:* The Four Just Men, The Avengers, Probation Officer, Never the Twain, The Upper Hand, Revolver. *Guest:* More than 125 appearances.

BLADES, RUBÉN
Actor, Composer, Singer, Writer. b. Panama City, Panama, July 16, 1948. e. U. of Panama (law and political science, 1974), Harvard U., L.L.M., 1985. Has recorded more than 14 albums, winning 3 Grammy Awards (1986, 1988, 1997). With his band Seis del Solar has toured U.S., Central America and Europe. President of Panama's Papa Egoro political party.
PICTURES: Actor: The Last Fight (debut, 1982), Crossover Dreams (also co-s.p.), Critical Condition, The Milagro Beanfield War, Fatal Beauty, Homeboy, Disorganized Crime, The Lemon Sisters, Mo' Better Blues, The Two Jakes, Predator 2, Homeboy, The Super, Life With Mikey, A Million to Juan, Color of Night. Music: Beat Street, Oliver & Company, Caminos Verdes (Venezuela), Q&A (also composer), Scorpion Spring, The Devil's Own, The Chinese Box, The Cradle Will Rock, All the Pretty Horses, Assassination Tango, Empire (Composer only), Once Upon a Time in Mexico, Spin, Secuestro express, Spoken Word.
TELEVISION: *Movies:* Dead Man Out (ACE Award), One Man's War, The Josephine Baker Story (Emmy nom. 1991), Crazy from the Heart (Emmy nom. 1992), The Heart of the Deal, Miracle on I-880, The Maldonado Miracle (Emmy nom. 2004). *Series:* Gideon's Crossing.

BLAIR, LINDA
Actress. b. St. Louis, MO, Jan. 22, 1959. Model and actress on TV commercials before going into films.
PICTURES: The Sporting Club (debut, 1971), The Exorcist (Academy Award nom. Golden Globe Award and nom. 1974), Airport '75, Exorcist II: The Heretic, Roller Boogie, Wild Horse Hank, Hell Night, Ruckus, Chained Heat, Savage Streets, Savage Island, Red Heat, Night Patrol, Night Force, Silent Assassins, Grotesque (also prod.), Witchery, The Chilling, Bad Blood, Moving Target, Up Your Alley, Repossessed, Aunt Millie's Will, Zapped Again, Dead Sleep, Double Blast, Temptress, Prey

of the Jaguar, Scream, Imps* (segment).
TELEVISION: *Movies:* Born Innocent, Sarah T.: Portrait of a Teenage Alcoholic, Sweet Hostage, Victory at Entebbe, Stranger in Our House, Calendar Girl Cop Killer? The Bambi Bembenek Story, Perry Mason: The Case of the Heartbroken Bride, Fear of God: The Making of the Exorcist, Monster Makers. *Series:* Walking After Midnight, S Club 7 in L.A., The Scariest Places on Earth (Host). *Special:* Linda Blair: The E! True Hollywood Story. *Guest:* More than 110 appearances.

BLAIR, STEWART
Executive. b. Scotland. e. Glasgow Caledonian University. Was v.p. of Chase Manhattan Bank N.A. in NY, before joining Tele-Communications Inc. in 1981. Served as vice chmn. & CEO of United Artists Entertainment Co. 1992, appointed chmn. and CEO of United Artists Theatre Circuit Inc.; removed, 1996. 1997 became chief exec. for Pacific Media to lead the expansion of its international film exhibition business. Formed Spean Bridge, a London-based cinema circuit, along with several other cinema ind. players; resigned 2005. Currently he is a systems developer for NHS. Also bd. member of Foundation of Motion Picture Pioneers, exec. v.p., Will Rogers Memorial Fund.

BLAKE, JEFF
Executive. e. B.A., economics, Northwestern U. and J.D., Whittier College of Law. Began career as sales broker and mgr., Paramount Pictures, 1974-78; asst. gen. sales mgr., Buena Vista Distribution (Walt Disney Co.) 1980. mgr., Western Div., Paramount, 1981; v.p., theatrical distribution, Paramount, 1984-1987; exec. v.p. & gen. sales mgr., Columbia Pictures (Sony Pictures Entertainment-SPE); 1987-92; president, domestic distribution, SPE, 1992-94; president, Sony Pictures Releasing, 1994-99. Became a vice chmn. of SPE in Oct. 2002. Also is Chairman of Columbia TriStar Motion Picture Group, Worldwide Marketing & Distribution. Responsible for mktg. & dist. of all Columbia, TriStar, Revolution and Screen Gems releases worldwide. Member, Calif. Bar Assn., v.p. of the Motion Picture Pioneers Foundation, member of Academy of Motion Picture Arts & Sciences, member of Variety Club Children's Charities, L.A. chapter. In 2002, he was named Entertainment Marketer of the Year by Brandweek Magazine.

BLAKE, TONY
Writer, Producer.
TELEVISION: *Movies:* Magical Make-Over, Shop Like a Star: Cinema Chic (exec. prod. in charge of production). *Series:* Renegade, Lois & Clark: The New Adventures of Superman (also supervisiing prod.), Sliders (co-exec. prod.), The Pretender, Charmed (also consulting prod.), Sheena, Mutant X, She Spies, Whistler (exec. prod.), Shop Like a Star (exec./production).

BLAKELY, SUSAN
Actress. b. Frankfurt, Germany, Sept. 7, 1952, where father was stationed in Army. Studied at U. of Texas. m. prod., media consultant Steve Jaffe. Became top magazine and TV commercial model in N.Y.
PICTURES: Savages (debut, 1972), The Way We Were, The Lords of Flatbush, The Towering Inferno, Report to the Commissioner, Shampoo, Capone, Dreamer, The Concorde—Airport '79, Over the Top, Dream a Little Dream, My Mom's a Werewolf, Russian Holiday, Seven Sundays, Gut Feeling, Chain of Command, The Perfect Nanny, Crash Point Zero, Hungry Hearts, L.A. Twister, Hate Crime, Grizzly Park, The Genesis Code, Beverly Hills Chihuahua 2.
TELEVISION: *Movies:* Secrets, Make Me an Offer, A Cry For Love, The Bunker, The Oklahoma City Dolls, Will There Really Be A Morning? (Golden Globe nom. 1984), The Ted Kennedy Jr. Story, Blood & Orchids, April Morning, Fatal Confession: A Father Dowling Mystery, Broken Angel, Hiroshima Maiden, Ladykillers, Sight Unseen, The Incident, End Run, Dead Reckoning, Murder Times Seven, And the Sea Will Tell, Sight Unseen, Blackmail, Wildflower, Against Her Will: An Incident in Baltimore, Intruders, No Child of Mine, Honor Thy Father and Mother: The True Story of the Menendez Murders, Color Me Perfect, Co-ed Call Girl, Race Against Fear, Her Married Lover, A Mother's Testimony, The Perfect Neighbor, Murder 101: New Age. *Mini-series:* Rich Man Poor Man (Golden Globe Award 1977, Emmy nom. 1976). *Series:* Falcon Crest, The George Carlin Show. *Special:* Torn Between Two Fathers. *Guest:* More than 74 appearances.

BLANC, MICHEL
Actor. b. Ile-de- France, France, June 16, 1952.
PICTURES: Que la Fete Commence, The Tenant, Les Bronzes, The Adolescent, Les Bronzes font du Ski, Le Cheval d'Orgueil, Walk in the Shadow, Les Fugitives, Evening Dress, Menage, I Hate Actors!, Story of Women, Monsieur Hire, Chambre a Part, Strike It Rich, Uranus, Merci la Vie, Prospero's Books, The Favor the Watch and the Very Big Fish, Ready to Wear (Pret-a-Porter), Grosse Fatigue (also dir., s.p.), The Monster, The Grand Dukes, Embrassez qui vous voudrez (also dir., s.p.), See How They Run (also writer, dir.), Madame Edouard, Les Témoins, Je vous trouve très beau, Les Bronzés 3: amis pour la vie (also writer), Le Deuxième souffle, The Witnesses, The Second Wind, The Girl on the Train.
TELEVISION: *Movies:* Soeur Thérèse.com (writer), Les Bronzés, le père Noël, papy et les autres (tv documentary), L' Affaire Dominici, 93, rue Lauriston. *Mini-series:* Palace. Numerous French movies, mini-series and series.

BLANCHETT, CATE
Actress. b. Melbourne, Australia, May 14, 1969. e. National Institute of Dramatic Art, Australia.
THEATRE: Top Girls, Kafka Dances, Oleanna, Hamlet, Sweet Phoebe, The Tempest, The Blind Giant is Dancing.
PICTURES: Police Rescue, Parklands, Paradise Road, Thank God He Met Lizzie, Oscar and Lucinda, Pushing Tin, Elizabeth (BAFTA Award, Golden Globe Award, Academy Award nom., AFI nom.), The Talented Mr. Ripley (BAFTA nom.), An Ideal Husband, The Man Who Cried, The Gift, Bandits (AFI nom., Golden Globe nom., SAG nom.), Lord of the Rings: The Fellowship of the Ring (SAG nom.), Heaven, The Shipping News, Charlotte Gray, The Lord of the Rings: The Two Towers, The Lord of the Rings: The Return of the King, Veronica Guerin (Golden Globe nom. 2004), The Missing, The Aviator (Academy Award, Golden Globe nom. 2005), The Life Aquatic, Little Fish, Babel, Notes on a Scandal (Academy Award nom.; Golden Globe nom. 2007), The Good German, Elizabeth: The Golden Age (Academy Award nom.; Golden Globe nom. 2008), I'm Not There (Academy Award nom.; Golden Globe Award 2008), Indiana Jones and the Kingdom of the Crystal Skull, Ponyo (voice, English version), The Curious Case of Benjamin Button, The Fantastic Mr. Fox (voice), Robin Hood (2010).
TELEVISION: *Mini-series:* G.P., Heartland, Bordertown. *Guest:* More than 90 appearances

BLANK, MATTHEW
Executive. e. graduate, Univ. of Pennsylvania's Wharton School of Business; M.B.A., Baruch College. In a career spanning more than 20 years, has made an indelible mark on the cable TV industry, working for two of the industry's leading companies. Blank worked for Home Box Office Inc. for 12 years, ascending to senior v.p. of consumer marketing before departing in 1988 for Showtime Networks, Inc., now a subsidiary of the CBS Corporation. He first served as executive v.p., marketing, and oversaw all of the network's consumer marketing, creative services and public relations functions. In 1991, he became pres. and COO, followed by president and CEO, and then to his current role as Chairman and CEO in 1995. Blank is active in numerous industry associations, including the bd. of dir. and the Executive Committee of the National Cable Television Association (NCTA). Blank's service to the National Association for Multi-ethnicity in Communications (NAMIC) and Cable Positive are also among his many distinctions. He has received numerous industry and community awards and recognitions.

BLATT, DANIEL H.
Producer. e. Philips Andover Acad., Duke U., Northwestern U. Sch. of Law. Indepentent prod. since 1976; prior posts: resident counsel, ABC Pictures; exec. v.p. Palomar Pictures.
PICTURES: I Never Promised You a Rose Garden, Winter Kills, The American Success Company, The Howling, Independence Day, Cujo, Let's Get Harry, Restless, The Boost.
TELEVISION: *Movies:* Circle of Children, Zuma Beach, The Children Nobody Wanted, Sadat, V: The Final Battle, Badge of the Assassin, Raid on Entebbe (Emmy nom. 1977), Sacred Vows, A Winner Never Quits, Sworn to Silence, Common Ground, Beyond Betrayal (exec. prod.), Kissinger and Nixon (exec. prod.), It Was Him or Us (exec. prod.), Sins of Silence (exec. prod.), Childhood Sweethearts? (exec. prod.), Dead by Midnight (exec. prod.), Miracle on the 17th Green (exec. prod.), The Virginian (exec. prod.), Murder on the Orient Express (exec. prod.), A Town Without Christmas (exec. prod.), Finding John Christmas, Bad Apple (exec. prod.), Against the Law, When Angels Come to Town (exec. prod.), Saving Milly, Marlowe, Wisegal. *Mini-series:* V: The Final Battle. *Series:* V, Against the Law.

BLATTY, WILLIAM PETER
Writer, Director, Producer. b. New York, NY, Jan. 7, 1928. e. George Washington U., Seattle U. Worked as editor for U.S. Information Bureau, publicity dir. for USC and Loyola U. before becoming novelist and screenwriter. Novels include: John Goldfarb Please Come Home (filmed), Twinkle Twinkle Killer Kane, The Exorcist, Legion (filmed as Exorcist III).
PICTURES: The Man From the Diner's Club, A Shot in the Dark, Promise Her Anything, What Did You Do in the War Daddy?, Gunn, The Great Bank Robbery, Darling Lili, The Exorcist (also prod.; Academy Award for Best Adapted Screenplay, 1 other nom.; Golden Globe Award 1973), The Ninth Configuration (also dir., prod.; Golden Globe Award 1981), The Exorcist III (also dir.), Exorcist: The Beginning, Dominion: Prequel to the Exorcist (writer).
TELEVISION: Linda Blair: The E! True Hollywood Story. *Documentaries:* Mel Gibson: God's Lethal Weapon, Hollywood Ghost Stories.

BLAY, ANDRE
Executive, Producer. b. Mt. Clemens, MI. Blay is credited with bringing the home video market to life. In 1977, Detroit businessman Blay owned Magnetic Video and began offering Hollywood

movies for sale in the home-video format. Although at first feared by the movie studios as competition, home video's revenue potential was recognized by 20th Century Fox. It licensed 50 best-selling titles to Blay to start Blay's operation—including The Sound of Music and Patton. Before long direct mail sales to the public through Blay's company, Magnetic Video, reached 250,000 (through the Video Club of America). In 1979, Blay sold Magnetic Video to 20th Century Fox, and he was named pres. & CEO, 20th Century Fox Home Video; 1981, he formed The Blay Corporation; 1982, Blay joined with Norman Lear and Jerry Perenchio, founders of Embassy Communications, as chairman and CEO of Embassy Home Entertainment; 1986, when Embassy sold to Nelson Group, left to form Palisades Entertainment Group with Elliott Kastner. In 1997 Blay was chairman and CEO, Enterprise Software, Inc. His latest venture is Mackinac Media Inc., based in Farmington Hills, MI. The co. is a source of programming for home video/DVD and TV markets and distributes original productions, as well as classic and independent films, documentaries, sports programming and TV shows. Blay was inducted into the Consumer Electronics Association Hall of Fame in 2000 and is also a member of the Home Video Hall of Fame.
PICTURES: *Exec. Prod.:* Prince of Darkness, They Live, Jack's Back, Homeboy, Braindamage, The Blob, A Chorus of Disapproval, Village of the Damned (prod.), Mosquito.

BLECKNER, JEFF

Director, Producer. b. Brooklyn, NY, Aug. 12, 1943. e. Amherst College, BA., 1965; Yale Sch. of Drama, MFA 1968. Taught drama at Yale, also participated in the theatre co. 1965-68. 1968-75 theatre dir. NY Shakespeare Fest. Public Theatre (2 Drama Desk Awards, Tony nom. for Sticks and Bones); Basic Training of Pavlo Hummel (Obie Award, 1971), The Unseen Hand (Obie Award). Began TV career directing The Guiding Light, 1975.
PICTURES: *Dir.:* White Water Summer, Hostile Witness, In the Hands of the Enemy, The Beast.
TELEVISION: *Dir./Prod.* more than 25 tv movies, incl.: Henry Winkler Meets William Shakespeare (1979), On Seventh Ave., Concealed Enemies (Emmy Award, 1984), Daddy, I'm Their Momma Now (Emmy nom.), Do You Remember Love (Christopher, Humanitas, Peabody Awards, Emmy nom.; DGA nom. 1985), Serving in Silence: The Margarethe Cammermeyer Story (Emmy nom. 1995), Rear Window, Runaway Virus, Flowers for Algernon, The Music Man (DGA nom. 2004), NTSB: The Crash of Flight 323, Conspiracy (pilot), Have No Fear: The Life of Pope John Paul II, The Russell Girl, Loving Leah. *Mini-series:* The Beach Boys: An American Family (Emmy nom.; DGA Award 2000). *Series: Dir.:* Welcome Back Kotter, Knots Landing, Dynasty, Hill Street Blues (Emmy Award, DGA Award, 1983 Emmy nom. 1982), Bret Maverick, King's Crossing, Ryan's Four, Me and Mom, Mancuso FBI, The Round Table, Any Day Now, The Fugitive, 10-8: Officers on Duty, Boston Legal, Hawthorne.

BLEDEL, ALEXIS

Actress. b. Houston, Texas, Sept. 16, 1981. Began career as a model before acting in Gilmore Girls.
PICTURES: Tuck Everlasting, Bride and Prejudice, The Orphan King, Sin City, The Sisterhood of the Traveling Pants, I'm Reed Fish, The Sisterhood of the Traveling Pants 2, Post Grad, The Good Guy, The Conspirator.
TELEVISION: *Series:* Gilmore Girls.

BLETHYN, BRENDA

Actress. b. Ramsgate, Kent, England, Feb. 20, 1946.
THEATRE: Mrs. Warren's Profession (London).
PICTURES: The Witches, A River Runs Through It, Secrets & Lies (Academy Award. nom.; Golden Globe Award, 1997; L.A. Film Critics Award; BAFTA Award), Remember Me?, Girls Night, Music From Another Room, In the Winter Dark, Little Voice (Academy Award nom.; Golden Globe nom. 1999), Keeping Time, Saving Grace (Golden Globe nom. 2001), On the Nose, Daddy and Them, The Sleeping Dictionary, The Wild Thornberrys (voice), Pumpkin, Sonny, Plots With A View, Blizzard, A Way of Life, Piccadilly Jim, Beyond the Sea, Pride and Prejudice, On a Clear Day, Pooh's Heffalump Movie (voice), Clubland, Pushers Needed, Pride & Prejudice, Introducing the Dwights, Atonement, The Calling, Dead Man Running, My Angel.
TELEVISION: *Movies:* Grown-Ups, King Lear, Henry VI (Part One), Floating Off, The Bullion Boys, RKO 281, Anne Frank: The Whole Story (Emmy nom. 2001), Bob the Builder: The Knights of Fix-A-Lot (voice), Belonging, Mysterious Creatures. *Mini-series*: The Buddha of Suburbia, War and Peace. *Series:* Chance In a Million, Sunday Premiere: Claws, The Labours of Erica, Alas Smith & Jones, Outside Edge, Between the Sheets, Law & Order: Special Victims Unit (Emmy nom. 2009 as guest). *Guest:* More than 75 appearances.

BLIER, BERTRAND

Writer, Director. b. Paris, France, March 14, 1939. Son of late actor Bernard Blier. Served as asst. dir. to Georges Lautner, John Berry, Christian-Jaque, Denys de la Paatelliere and Jean Delannoy for two years before dir. debut.
PICTURES: Hitler Connais Pas (debut, 1963), If I Were A Spy, Take It Easy It's A Waltz, Going Places, Calmos, Get Out Your Handkerchiefs (Academy Award for Best Foreign-Language Film, 1978), La Femme de mon pote, Menage, Merci la vie, Un deux trois soleil, Mon Homme, Actors, Les Côtelettes, Pédale dure, Combien tu gagnes?, The Actress' Ball, Grosse fatigue, The Clink of Ice.

BLOCK, BILL H.

Executive, Producer. Began career as a talent agent at ICM, then began his own agency, InterTalent, 1988. Co. later merged with ICM. Block then served as head, West Coast operations and represented a spectrum of top-level talent in motion picture production and entertainment. President, Artisan Entertainment 1998-2001. Resigned to pursue entertainment financing and M&A. In 2004 opened prod. co., Key Creatives, with Ken Kamins and is currently its COO. In Dec. 2005, became CEO of new Beverly Hills-based financing, sales and production company, QED International, which he formed with three partners, Kimberly Fox, Paul Hanson and Elliot Ferwerda.
PICTURES: *Exec. in charge of production:* Belly (1998), Stir of Echoes, The Way of the Gun, The Center of the World, Made. *Prod.:* The Hunting Party, W. *Exec. prod.:* Vanilla Sky, Devil's Pond, Spring Break in Bosnia, Smart People, The Lucky Ones, A Perfect Getaway, District 9, Inseparable.

BLOODWORTH-THOMASON, LINDA

Producer, Writer. b. Poplar Bluff, MO, April 15, 1947. With husband Harry Thomason co-owner of Mozark Productions.
TELEVISION: *Movies:* The Man From Hope (prod.), A Place Called America (prod.), Legacy: Bill Clinton Retrospective (prod.), 12 Miles of Bad Road (writer, exec. prod.). *Series:* M*A*S*H (writer, Emmy nom. 1974), Rhoda (writer), Filthy Rich (writer, exec. prod.), Designing Women (co-exec. prod., creator, writer, 4 Emmy nom. 1988, 1989, 1990, 1991), Evening Shade (co-exec. prod., writer), Hearts Afire (writer, exec. prod.), Women of the House (prod., writer), Emeril (prod., writer), 12 Miles of Bad Road (also pilot). *Pilots:* Dribble (prod.), Over and Out (writer), London and Davis in New York (prod.).

BLOOM, CLAIRE

Actress. r.n. Patricia Claire Blume. b. London, England, Feb. 15, 1931.e. Guildhall School of Music & Drama, Central Sch. To U.S. in 1940 during London evacuation. Returned to England in 1943. Stage debut with Oxford Rep 1946 in It Depends What You Mean. Author: Limelight and After: The Education of an Actress (1982).
THEATRE: The White Devil (London debut), The Lady's Not for Burning, Ring Round the Moon, A Streetcar Named Desire; at Stratford-on-Avon, Old Vic seasons, etc. B'way: Rashomon, A Doll's House, Hedda Gabler, Vivat Vivat Regina, Cherry Orchard, Long Day's Journey Into Night, Electra.
PICTURES: The Blind Goddess (debut, 1948), Limelight, Innocents in Paris, The Man Between, Richard III, Alexander the Great, The Brothers Karamazov, The Buccaneer, Look Back in Anger, The Royal Game, The Wonderful World of the Brothers Grimm, The Chapman Report, The Haunting, 80000 Suspects, High Infidelity, The Outrage, The Spy Who Came in From the Cold, Charly, The Illustrated Man, Three Into Two Won't Go, A Red Sky at Morning, A Doll's House, Islands in the Stream, Clash of the Titans, Deja Vu, Crimes and Misdemeanors, The Ae of Innocence, The Princess and the Goblin (voice), Mighty Aphrodite, Daylight, Wrestling With Alligators, The Book of Eve, The Republic of Love, Imagining Argentina, Kalamazoo?.
TELEVISION: *Specials/Movies (U.S./UK):* Cyrano de Bergerac, Caesar and Cleopatra, Misalliance, Anna Karenina, Wuthering Heights, Ivanov, Wessex Tales, An Imaginative Woman, A Legacy, In Praise of Love, Henry VIII, Hamlet, King John, Ann and Debbie, Separate Tables, Florence Nightingale, The Ghost Writer, Time and the Conways, Shadowlands, Liberty, Promises to Keep, Hold the Dream, Anastasia, Queenie, Intimate Contact, Oedipus the King, The Lady and the Highwayman, The Mirror Crack'd, It's Nothing Personal, Remember, Imogen's Face, The Lady in Question, Love and Murder, Yesterday's Children, On Cukor, Trial & Retribution X: Sins of the Father, Marple: By the Pricking of My Thumbs, The Chatterley Affair, The Ten Commandments, Fiona's Story. *Mini-series:* Backstairs at the White House, Oresteia, Brideshead Revisited (Emmy nom. 1982), Ellis Island, The Camomile Lawn. *Series:* As The World Turns, Family Money. *Guest:* More than 93 appearances.

BLOOM, MARCIE

Executive. b. Brooklyn, NY e. B.A. degree, Cornell University, 1979. Bloom got her start in the movie business in the summer of 1978, while still a math and science student at Cornell University. Filing at the Film Society of Lincoln Center turned into a full-time job after she graduated. By 1985, Bloom was hired to do publicity for Orion Classics at the Smith & Siegal agency. By 1989 two partners at Orion Pictures, Michael Barker and Tom Bernard, asked her to join them as senior v.p., acquisitions. When its parent company's bankruptcy, Orion, disappeared, Barker, Bernard and Bloom formed Sony Pictures Classics (SPC) in 1992, with the three serving as co-presidents. The company acquires, distributes and produces art films. The trio's knack for acquiring foreign-produced films with audience appeal soon elevated them to the top of the niche art film industry, and the team's films have earned 18 Academy Awards. Bloom suffered a health setback in Nov. 1996 when she collapsed and underwent emergency brain surgery. She awoke to learn that a genetically inherited aneurysm had left her paralyzed on her left side. She is now semi-retired but still reads scripts and consults for SPC. 2008 launched The Marcie Bloom Fellowship. The New York-based initiative is a mentoring programme designed to introduce up to four students a year to the world of independent film production and distribution.

BLOOM, ORLANDO

Actor. b. Canterbury, Kent, England, Jan. 13, 1977. e. St. Edmunds School, British American Drama Academy. m. actress Miranda Kerr.
THEATRE: London: In Celebration.
PICTURES: Wilde, The Lord of the Rings: The Fellowship of the Ring, Black Hawk Down, The Lord of the Rings: The Two Towers, Ned Kelly, Pirates of the Caribbean: The Curse of the Black Pearl, The Lord of the Rings: The Return of the King, The Calcium Kid, Troy, Haven, Kingdom of Heaven, Elizabethtown, Pirates of the Caribbean: Dead Man's Chest, Pirates of the Caribbean: At World's End, New York, I Love You (segment), Sympathy for Delicious, The Good Doctor (prod. only), Main Street. *Guest:* More than 82 appearances.

BLOOM, VERNA

Actress. b. Lynn, MA, Aug. 7, 1939. e. Boston U. Studied drama at Uta Hagen-Herbert Berghof School. Performed with small theatre groups all over country; then started repertory theatre in Denver.
THEATRE: B'way: Marat/Sade, Brighton Beach Memoirs. Off B'way.: Messiah, Bits and Pieces, The Cherry Orchard.
PICTURES: Medium Cool (debut, 1969), The Hired Hand, High Plains Drifter, Badge 373, National Lampoon's Animal House, Honkytonk Man, After Hours, The Journey of Natty Gann, The Last Temptation of Christ.
TELEVISION: *Movies:* Where Have All the People Gone?, Sarah T.: Portrait of a Teenage Alcoholic, The Blue Knight, Contract on Cherry Street, Playing for Time, Rivkin–Bounty Hunter, Promises to Keep, Gibbsville, Dr. Quinn Medicine Woman.

BLOUNT, LISA

Actress. b. Fayetteville, AK, July 1, 1957. e. Univ. of AK. Auditioned for role as extra in film September 30, 1955 and was chosen as the female lead.
PICTURES: 9/30/55, Dead and Buried, An Officer and a Gentleman (Golden Globe nom. 1983), Cease Fire, What Waits Below, Radioactive Dreams, Prince of Darkness, Nightflyers, South of Reno, Out Cold, Great Balls of Fire, Blind Fury, Femme Fatale, Needful Things, Stalked, Box of Moonlight, If...Dog...Rabbit, Birdseye, Chrystal (also prod.), The Accountant (Academy Award best short film, 2002), Randy and the Mob (also prod.).
TELEVISION: *Movies:* Murder Me Murder You, Stormin' Home, The Annihilator, Unholy Matrimony, In Sickness and in Health, An American Story, Murder Between Friends, Get to the Heart: The Barbara Mandrell Story, Traffic, Trash. *Series:* Sons and Daughters, Profit. *Pilot:* Off Duty, Sons and Daughters.

BLUM, MARK

Actor. b. Newark, NJ, May 14, 1950. Studied drama at U. of Minnesota and U. of Pennsylvania. Also studied acting with Andre Gregory, Aaron Frankel and Daniel Seltzer. Extensive Off-B'way work after debut in The Cherry Orchard (1976).
THEATRE: NY: Green Julia, Say Goodnight Gracie, Table Settings, Key Exchange, Loving Reno, Messiah, It's Only a Play, Little Footsteps, Cave of Life, Gus & Al (Obie Award), Lost in Yonkers (Broadway), Thousand Clowns (Broadway). Regional: Brothers (New Brunswick, NJ), Close Ties (Long Wharf), The Cherry Orchard (Long Wharf), Iago in Othello (Dallas). Mark Taper Forum: American Clock, Wild Oats, Moby Dick Rehearsed and An American Comedy.
PICTURES: Lovesick, Desperately Seeking Susan, Just Between Friends, Crocodile Dundee, Blind Date, The Presidio, Worth Winning, Emma & Elvis, The Low Life, Miami Rhapsody, Denise Calls Up, Sudden Manhattan, Stag, You Can Thank Me Later, Getting to Know All About You, Down to You, Shattered Glass.
TELEVISION: *Movies:* Condition: Critical, Indictment: The McMartin Trial, The Judge. *Series:* Sweet Surrender, Capitol News. *Guest:* More than 28 appearances.

BLUMBERG, BARRY

Executive. e. degree in English literature from UCLA. Before Blumberg teamed with The Walt Disney Company, he spent time at Harvey Comics and in the New York advertising world. Blumberg joined Walt Disney Television Animation in 1994 as development dir. and has held a series of positions of increasing responsibility. In 2003, he became pres., Walt Disney Television Animation. During his tenure at Disney, he helped launch Disney's One Saturday Morning TV programming block on ABC in Sept. 1997. The block featured the popular Recess and Pepper Ann animated series. He was also instrumental in bringing the highly acclaimed Kim Possible series to the Disney Channel in June 2002, and Disney's The Legend of Tarzan to the UPN and international TV in Sept. 2002. With company restructuring, Blumberg resigned from Disney in Nov. 2005.

BLUNDELL, CHRISTINE

Make-Up.
PICTURES: Life is Sweet, Naked, I.D., Hackers, Secrets and Lies, Carla's Song, Career Girls, The Full Monty, Seven Years in Tibet, Martha, Meet Frank, Daniel and Laurence, Topsy-Turvey (Academy Award, 2000), Sorted, New Year's Day, Me Without You, All or Nothing, To Kill a King, Around the World in 80 Days, Finding Neverland, Vera Drake, Closer, The Constant Gardener, Doom, Basic Instinct 2, Casino Royale, When Did You Last See Your Father?, Eastern Promises, Happy-Go-Lucky, Pirate Radio, Sherlock Holmes, London Boulevard, Hippie Hippie Shake.
TELEVISION: *Movies:* Lady Chatterly, Bertie and Elizabeth. *Special:* The 72nd Annual Academy Awards (Academy Award 2001).

BLUTH, DON

Animator, Director, Producer, Writer. b. El Paso, TX, Sept. 13, 1937.e. Brigham Young U. Animator with Walt Disney Studios 1956 and 1971-79; animator with Filmation 1967; Co-founder and dir. with Gary Goldman and John Pomery, Don Bluth Productions, 1979-85; animator, Sullivan Studios, 1986. Joined Fox Animation as dir./prod., 1995.
PICTURES: *Animation director:* Robin Hood, The Rescuers, Pete's Dragon, Xanadu. *Director/Co-Producer:* The Secret of NIMH (also co-s.p.), An American Tail, The Land Before Time, All Dogs Go to Heaven (also co-story), Rock-a-Doodle, Hans Christian Andersen's Thumbelina (also s.p.), A Troll in Central Park, The Pebble and the Penguin, Anastasia, Bartok the Magnificent, Titan A.E.
TELEVISION: Banjo the Woodpile Cat (prod., dir., story, music and lyrics).

BOCHCO, STEVEN

Producer, Writer. b. New York, NY, Dec. 16, 1943. e. Carnegie Tech, MFA. Won MCA fellowship in college, joined Universal-TV as apprentice. 1978, moved to MTM Enterprises. Went on to create shows for NBC and in 1987, sealed deal with ABC to create 10 series pilots over 10 years. Awards incl. 8 Emmys, 2 Humanitas, NAACP Image, Writers Guild, George Foster Peabody, & Edgar Allen Poe Awards, DGA Diversity Award, 1999.
PICTURES: Silent Running (writer).
TELEVISION: *Movies:* More than 20, incl.: The Counterfeit Killer, Double Indemnity, Vampire, Operating Room, Name of the Game, Columbo (9 tv movies; 2 Emmy nom.), L.A. Law: The Movie, NYPD 2069, Hollis & Rae (exec. prod.). *Series:* 22 titles, incl.: Griff (prod.), The Invisible Man (prod.), Delvecchio (prod.), Paris (exec. prod.), Hill Street Blues (writer, exec. prod., Emmys 1981, 1982, 1983, 1984, 9 Emmy nom.), Bay City Blues (prod.), L.A. Law (creator, writer, exec. prod., Emmys 2 1987, 1989, 4 Emmy nom.), Hooperman (writer, prod.), Doogie Howser M.D. (writer, prod.), Cop Rock (creator, writer, prod.), Capitol Critters (prod.), NYPD Blue (creator, writer, prod., Emmy 1995, 8 Emmy nom.), The Byrds of Paradise (prod.), Murder One (writer, exec. prod.; Emmy nom.1996; WGA nom. 1997), *Exec. Prod.:* Public Morals, Brooklyn South, Total Security, City of Angels, Philly (also writer), Boston Public (co-creator), Blind Justice (pilot, exec. prod.), Over There, Commander in Chief, Raising the Bar also writer).

BOCHNER, HART

Actor, Director. b. Toronto, Canada, Oct. 3, 1956. Son of late actor Lloyd Bochner. e. U. of. San Diego. Wrote, prod., dir. short film The Buzz (1992) starring Jon Lovitz.
PICTURES: Islands in the Stream (debut, 1977), Breaking Away, Terror Train, Rich and Famous, The Wild Life, Supergirl, Making Mr. Right, Die Hard, Apartment Zero, Mr. Destiny, Mad at the Moon, The Innocent, Break Up, Anywhere But Here, Urban Legends: Final Cut, Say Nothing, Speaking of Sex, Liberty Stands Still, Company Retreat, Spread. *Dir.:* High School High, PCU, One Part Sugar (also writer, exec. prod.), Just Add Water also writer, exec. prod.).
TELEVISION: *Movies:* Having It All, Fellow Traveller, Complex of Fear, Children of the Dust, Once Around the Park, Baby for Sale. *Mini-series:* Haywire, East of Eden, The Sun Also Rises, War and Remembrance. *Series:* Callahan, The Starter Wife. *Special:* Teach 109.

BODENHEIMER, GEORGE W.

Executive. b. May 6, 1958. e. Bachelor of Arts degree in economics from Denison University, 1980. Bodenheimer, who began his ESPN career in the administration department in 1981, is a tv executive who held several executive positions in ESPN's affiliate sales and marketing area throughout the 1980s, working in the company's Bristol, New York, Chicago, Denver and Dallas offices. In 1982, became marketing representative for ESPN's South Central region. Bodenheimer was promoted to national accounts manager of the Rocky Mountain region, July 1985; and to director, affiliate sales, Eastern division, Feb. 1988. He was named vice president, affiliate sales, Eastern division in July 1989 and was promoted to vice president, national affiliate sales in June 1991. Bodenheimer was named v.p., affiliate sales and marketing in November 1992, and senior v.p., affiliate sales and marketing in Oct. 1993. He was appointed to senior v.p., sales and marketing in May 1995 and became executive v.p., sales and marketing in Sept. 1996. He was named ESPN's fifth president on Nov. 19, 1998. In May 1999, he added international responsibilities; and on March 3, 2003, he was also appointed President of ABC Sports, overseeing all the multimedia sports assets of The Walt Disney Company. He was promoted to his current role of co-chairman, Disney Media Networks on April 20, 2004, while remaining president of ESPN, Inc. and ABC Sports; and chairman of the ESPN bd. of directors. Bodenheimer serves on the boards of NCTA (The National Cable Telecommunications Association), Cable in the Classroom, The V Foundation for Cancer Research, which ESPN founded with the late Jim Valvano, and the Cable Center, a Denver-based institution that educates and informs about the power of cable television. He has been named to the "CableFax 100" list of industry leaders each year since 1998. He is a member of the Cable Programming Committee of the Museum of Television and Radio. Bodenheimer is based in New York but also works from ESPN's Bristol, Conn. headquarters.

BOGDANOVICH, PETER

Director, Producer, Writer, Actor. b. Kingston, NY, July 30, 1939. e. Collegiate Sch., Stella Adler Theatre Sch., N.Y. 1954-58. Stage debut, Amer. Shakespeare Festival, Stratford, CT, followed by N.Y. Shakespeare Festival, 1958. Off-B'way: dir./prod.: The Big Knife, Camino Real, Ten Little Indians, Rocket to the Moon, Once in a Lifetime. Film critic and feature writer, Esquire, New York Times, Village Voice, Cahiers du Cinema, Los Angeles Times, New York Magazine, Vogue, Variety, etc. 1961–. Owner: The Holly Moon Company Inc. (L.A.), 1992-present. LA Film Crits. Career Achievement Award, 1997.
PICTURES: Voyage to the Planet of the Prehistoric Women (dir., s.p., narrator; billed as Derek Thomas), The Wild Angels (2nd unit dir., co-s.p., actor). *Director:* Targets (also prod., co-s.p., actor), The Last Picture Show (also co-s.p; N.Y. Film Critics' Award, best s.p., British Academy Award, best s.p. 2 Academy Award nom.1972, DGA nom.; Golden Globe nom. 1972), Directed by John Ford (also s.p., interviewer), What's Up Doc? (also prod., co-s.p.; Writer's Guild of America Award, best s.p., 1972), Paper Moon (also prod.; Silver Shell, Mar del Plata, Spain 1973 Golden Globe nom. 1974), Daisy Miller (also prod.; Best Director, Brussels Festival, 1974), At Long Last Love (also prod., s.p.), Nickelodeon (also co-s.p.), Saint Jack (also co-s.p., actor), Pasinetti Award, Critics Prize, Venice Festival, 1979), Opening Night (actor only), They All Laughed (also co-s.p.), Mask, Illegally Yours (also prod.), Texasville (also co-prod., s.p.), Noises Off (also co-exec. prod.), The Thing Called Love, The Cat's Meow, Roman Nights, Shoot Out of Luck. *Actor:* Jean Renior, The Battle Over Citizen Kane, Ben Johnson: Third Cowboy on the Right, Mr. Jealousy, The Shore Store, Clarie Makes it Big, Rated X, The Independent, An American Dream, Festival in Cannes, John Ford Goes to War (as himself), The Definition of Insanity (as himself), The Fifth Patient, The Dukes, Dedication, Infamous, Humboldt County, The Dukes, Queen of the Lot, Abandoned.
TELEVISION: *Movies/Dir.:* To Sir with Love 2, The Price of Heaven, Rescuers; Stories of Courage/2 Women, Naked City: A Killer Christmas, A Saintly Switch, The Mystery of Natalie Wood. *Actor:* Bella Mafia, I Love New York, Hustle. *Mini-series:* Out of Order. *Series:* CBS This Morning (weekly commentary; 1987-89), The Sopranos, HDVD Extra (host). *Guest:* More than 130 appearances.

BOGOSIAN, ERIC

Actor, Writer. b. Woburn, MA, Apr. 24, 1953. e. studied 2 years at U. of Chicago, then Oberlin, theatre degree, 1976. In high school, acted in plays with Fred Zollo (now prod.) and Nick Paleologus (now MA congressman). Moved to NY and worked briefly as gofer at Chelsea Westside Theater. Then joined downtown performance space, the Kitchen, first acting in others pieces, then creating his own, incl. character Ricky Paul, a standup comedian in punk clubs. Theatre pieces include: The New World, Men Inside, Voices of America, FunHouse, Drinking in America (Drama Desk and Obie Awards), Talk Radio, Sex Drugs Rock & Roll, Pounding Nails in the Floor With My Forehead (Obie Award), Suburbia (author only).
PICTURES: Special Effects, Talk Radio (also s.p.; Silver Bear Award 1988 Berlin Film Fest.), Sex Drugs Rock & Roll (also s.p.), Naked in New York, Dolores Claiborne, Under Siege 2: Dark Territory, SubUrbia (s.p., lyricist), Deconstructing Harry, Gossip, In the Weeds, Wake Up and Smell the Coffee, Ararat, Igby Goes Down, Charlie's Angels: Full Throttle, Wonderland, The Pursuit of Happiness, King of the Corner, Blade: Trinity, Heights, Cadillac Records.
TELEVISION: *Movies:* Crime Story, Funhouse (also writer), The Caine Mutiny Court-Martial, Last Flight Out, Witch Hunt, A Bright Shining Lie, Shot in the Heart. *Mini-series:* Blonde. *Series:* High Incident (creative consult.), Love Monkey, Law & Order: Criminal Intent. *Special:* Drinking in America. *Guest:* More than 40 appearances.

BOLAM, JAMES

Actor. b. Sunderland, England, June 16, 1938. Entered industry in 1960.
PICTURES: The Kitchen, A Kind of Loving, Loneliness of the Long Distance Runner, Murder Most Foul, In Celebration, Clockwork Mice, Stella Does Tricks, Island on Bird Street, The End of the Affair, It Was an Accident, To Kill a King.
TELEVISION: *Movies:* The Four Seasons of Rosie Carr, As You Like It, Macbeth, The Maze, The Beiderbecke Tapes, Eleven Men Against Eleven, The Missing Postman, The Stalker's Apprentice, Dirty Tricks, Shipman, Dalziel and Pascoe: Sins of the Fathers, Celebration. *Mini-series:* Have Your Cake and Eat It, The Beiderbecke Connection, The Beiderbecke Affair, He Knew He Was Right. *Series:* Likely Lads, When the Boat Comes In, Only When I Laugh, Father Matthew's Daughter, Andy Capp, Second Thoughts, Close & True, Born and Bred, New Tricks. *Guest:* More than 73 appearances.

BOLOGNA, JOSEPH

Actor, Writer. b. Brooklyn, NY., Dec. 30, 1938. e. Brown U. m. actress-writer Renee Taylor. Service in Marine Corps and on discharge joined ad agency, becoming dir.-prod. of TV commercials. Collaborated with wife on short film, 2, shown at 1966 N.Y. Film Festival. Together they wrote Lovers and Other Strangers, B'way play, in which both also acted; wrote s.p. for film version. Both wrote and starred in Made for Each Other, and created and wrote TV series, Calucci's Dept.
PICTURES: Lovers and Other Strangers (co.-s.p. only Academy Award nom.; WGA nom. 1971), Made for Each Other (also co.-s.p.; WGA nom. 1972), Cops and Robbers, Mixed Company, The Big Bus , Chapter Two, My Favorite Year, Blame It on Rio, The Woman in Red, Transylvania 6-5000, It Had to Be You (also co-dir., co-s.p.), Coupe de Ville, Jersey Girl, Alligator II: The Mutation, Love Is All There Is (dir., s.p.), Heaven Before I Die, Big Daddy, Blink of an Eye, Returning Mickey Stern, Squint, Pledge of Allegiance, Boynton Beach Club, Ice Age: The Meltdown (voice), Driving Me Crazy.
TELEVISION: *Movies:* Honor Thy Father, Woman of the Year (also co-writer), Torn Between Two Lovers, One Cooks The Other Doesn't, Copacabana, A Time To Triumph, Prime Target, Thanksgiving Day, Citizen Cohn, Revenge of the Nerds IV: Nerds in Love, The Don's Analyst, Batman/Superman Adventures: World's Finest (voice), Jane Doe: Til Death Do Us Part, Fathers and Sons. *Mini-series:* Sins. *Series:* Calucci's Dept. (creator, co-writer only), Rags to Riches, Top of the Heap. *Special:* Acts of Love and Other Comedies (Emmy Award, 1974). *Guest:* More than 53 appearances.

BONHAM CARTER, HELENA

Actress. b. London, England, May 26, 1966. Great granddaughter of Liberal Prime Minister Lord Asquith. e. Westminster. Appeared on BBC in A Pattern of Roses; seen by dir. Trevor Nunn who cast her in Lady Jane, 1986, theatrical film debut. On London stage in Trelawny of the Wells.
PICTURES: Lady Jane, A Room with a View, Maurice (cameo), Francesco, La Mascheral (The Mask), Getting It Right, Hamlet, Where Angles Fear to Tread, Howards End, Mary Shelley's Frankenstein, Mighty Aphrodite, Margaret's Museum, Twelfth Night, Shadow Play, The Wings of the Dove (LA Film Crits. Award, Best Actress, 1997 Academy Award nom.; Golden Globe nom. 1998), Keep the Aspidistra Flying, The Theory of Flight, The Revengers of Comedy, Fight Club, Women Talking Dirty, Carnivale, Novcaine, Planet of the Apes, Till Human Voices Wake Us, The Heart of Me, Big Fish, The Wallace & Gromit Movie: Curse of the Wererabbit, Charlie and the Chocolate Factory, Corpse Bride (voice), Conversations with Other Women, Shantaram, Wallace & Gromit in The Curse of the Were-Rabbit (voice), Sixty Six, Harry Potter and the Order of the Phoenix, Sweeney Todd: The Demon Barber of Fleet Street (Golden Globe nom. 2008), Harry Potter and the Half-Blood Prince, Terminator Salvation, Alice in Wonderland, Harry Potter and the Deathly Hallows: Part I, Harry Potter and the Deathly Hallows: Part II, The King's Speech.
TELEVISION: *Movies:* A Hazard of Hearts (U.S.), Fatal Deception: Mrs. Lee Harvey Oswald (Golden Globe nom. 1994), Dancing Queen, Merlin (Emmy nom.; Golden Globe nom. 1998), Live From Baghdad (Emmy nom.; Golden Globe nom. 2003), Henry VIII, Magnificent 7, Enid, The Gruffalo (voice). *Guest:* More than 71 appearances.

BOOKMAN, ROBERT

Executive. b. Los Angeles, CA, Jan. 29, 1947. e. U. of California, Yale Law Sch. Motion picture literary agent, IFA 1972-74, ICM 1974-79. 1979-84, ABC Motion Pictures v.p., worldwide production; 1984-86, Columbia Pictures, exec. v.p., world-wide prod. 1986, partner Creative Artists Agency, as motion picture literary and directors' agent.

BOORMAN, JOHN

Director, Producer, Writer. b. London, England, Jan. 18, 1933. Wrote film criticism at age of 17 for British publications incl. Manchester Guardian; founder TV Mag. Day By Day; served in National Service in Army; Broadcaster and BBC radio film critic 1950-54; film editor Independent Television News; prod. documentaries for Southern Television; joined BBC, headed BBC Documentary Film Unit 1960-64, indep. doc. about D.W. Griffith; chmn. Natl. Film Studios of Ireland 1975-85; governor Brit. Film Inst. 1985-.
PICTURES: *Director:* Catch Us If You Can (debut, 1965), Point Blank, Hell in the Pacific, Leo the Last (also co-s.p., Cannes Film Fest. Award, Best Director 1970), Deliverance (also prod.; 2

Academy Award noms. 1973, Golden Globe nom.), Zardoz (also prod., s.p.), Exorcist II: The Heretic (also co-prod.), Excalibur (also exec. prod., co-s.p., Cannes Film Fest. Award, Best Art. Contribution, 1981), Danny Boy (exec. prod. only), The Emerald Forest (also prod.), Hope and Glory (also prod., s.p., actor; 3 Academy Award noms. 2 Golden Globe noms. 1988, Nat'l Film Critics Awards for dir., s.p.; L.A. Film Critics Awards for picture, s.p., dir.; U.K. Critics Awards for picture, WGA nom.), Where the Heart Is (also prod., co-s.p.), I Dreamt I Woke Up (also s.p., actor), Two Nudes Bathing (also s.p., prod.), Beyond Rangoon (also co-prod.), The General (also s.p., prod.), The Tailor of Panama (also prod., s.p.), In My Country (also prod.), The Wonderful Wizard of Oz (also prod.), Excalibur (exec. prod.).
TELEVISION: *Movies:* The Hard Way, Lee Marvin: A Personal Portrait by John Boorman. *Mini-series:* Picture Windows: Language of the Heart. *Series:* Citizen '63 (dir.), The Newcomers (dir.).

BOOTHE, POWERS
Actor. b. Snyder, TX, June 1, 1949. e. Southern Methodist U. On B'way in Lone Star.
PICTURES: The Goodbye Girl, Cruising, Southern Comfort, A Breed Apart, Red Dawn, The Emerald Forest, Extreme Prejudice, Stalingrad, Rapid Fire, Tombstone, Blue Sky, Sudden Death, Nixon, U-Turn, Men of Honor, Frailty, Sin City, The Final Season, MacGruber.
TELEVISION: *Movies:* Skag, Plutonium Incident, Guyana Tragedy—The Story of Jim Jones (Emmy Award, 1980), A Cry for Love, Into the Homeland, Family of Spies, By Dawn's Early Light, Wild Card, Marked for Murder, Web of Deception, The Spree, A Crime of Passion, Attila, Second Nature, 24: Redemption. *Mini-series:* True Women, Joan of Arc. *Series:* Skag, Philip Marlowe Private Eye, Deadwood, Justice League (voice), 24. *Guest:* More than 40 appearances.

BORGNINE, ERNEST
Actor. r.n. Ermes Effron Borgnino. b. Hamden, CT, Jan. 24, 1917. e. Randall Sch. of Dramatic Art, Hartford, CT. Joined Barter Theatre in Viginia. Served in U.S. Navy; then little theatre work, stock companies; on Broadway in Harvey, Mrs. McThing; many TV appearances. Honors: 33rd Degree of the Masonic Order, Order of the Grand Cross, from same. Named honorary Mayor of Universal City Studios.
PICTURES: Appeared in more than 100 pictures, incl.: China Corsair (debut, 1951), The Mob, Whistle at Eaton Falls, From Here to Eternity, The Stranger Wore a Gun, Demetrius & the Gladiators, Bounty Hunter, Vera Cruz, Bad Day at Black Rock, Marty (Academy Award for Best Actor, Golden Globe Award 1956), Run for Cover, Last Command, Square Jungle, Catered Affair, Best Things in Life are Free, Three Brave Men, The Vikings, Badlanders, Torpedo Run, Season of Passion, Pay or Die, Go Naked in the World, Barabbas, McHales's Navy, Flight of the Phoenix, The Oscar, The Dirty Dozen, Ice Station Zebra, The Split, The Wild Bunch, The Adventurers, Suppose They Gave a War and Nobody Came?, A Bullet for Sandoval, Willard, Rain for a Dusty Summer, Hannie Caulder, The Revengers, Ripped Off, The Poseidon Adventure, Emperor of the North Pole, The Neptune Factor, Law and Disorder, The Devil's Rain, Shoot, Love By Appointment, The Greatest, Strike Force, Diary of Madam X, The Black Hole, When Time Ran Out, High Risk, Escape from New York, Spike of Bensonhurst, The Opponent, Any Man's Death, Laser Mission, Turnaround, Captain Henkel, Moving Target, The Last Match, Mistress, McHale's Navy, Gattaca, BASEketball, An All Dogs Christmas Carol, 12 Bucks, Mel, The Last Great Ride, Abilene, Castlerock, The Long Ride Home, Crimebusters (also exec. prod.), Muraya (l'expérience secrète de Mike Blueberry), Blueberry, Strange Wilderness, Another Harvest Moon, The Lion of Judah, The Genesis Code, Snatched, Death Keeps Coming, Red.
TELEVISION: *Movies:* Sam Hill: Who Killed the Mysterious Mr. Foster?, The Trackers, Twice in a Lifetime, Future Cop, Jesus of Nazareth, Fire!, The Ghost of Flight 401, Cops and Robin, All Quiet on the Western Front (Emmy nom. 1980), Blood Feud, Carpool, Love Leads the Way, Last Days of Pompeii, The Dirty Dozen: The Next Mission, Alice in Wonderland, The Dirty Dozen: The Deadly Mission, The Dirty Dozen: The Fatal Mission, Jake Spanner-Private Eye, The Trail to Hope Rose, The Blue Light, The Trail to Hope Rose, A Grandpa for Christmas (Golden Globe nom. 2008), Aces 'N Eights, Wishing Well. *Series:* McHale's Navy (Emmy nom. 1963), Future Cop, Air Wolf, The Single Guy, All dogs Go to Heaven: the Series (voice), SpongeBob SquarePants (voice), ER (Emmy nom. 2009 as guest). *Specials:* Billy the Kid, Legend in Granite: The Vince Lombardi Story, Big Guns Talk: The Story of the Western, AFI's 100 Years 100 Thirlls: America's Most Heart Pounding Movies. *Guest:* More than 207 appearances.

BORIS, ROBERT
Writer, Director. b. NY, NY, Oct. 12, 1945. Screenwriter before also turning to direction with Oxford Blues, 1984.
PICTURES: Electra Glide in Blue, Some Kind of Hero, Doctor Detroit, Oxford Blues (also dir.), Buy and Cell (dir.), Steele Justice (dir.), Extreme Justice, Diplomatic Siege, Backyard Dogs, Deep Freeze, Run, Little Hercules in 3-D.
TELEVISION: Birds of Prey, Blood Feud (WGA Award 1984), Deadly Encounter, Izzy and Moe, Frank and Jesse (also dir.), Marilyn and Me.

BOSCO, PHILIP
Actor. b. Jersey City, NJ, Sept. 26, 1930. e. Catholic U., Washington, DC, BA. drama, 1957. Studied for stage with James Marr, Josephine Callan and Leo Brady. Consummate stage actor (in over 100 plays, 61 in NY) whose career spans the classics (with NY Shakespeare Fest. and American Shakespeare Fest, CT.), 20 plays with Arena Stage 1957-60, to modern classics as a resident actor with Lincoln Center Rep. Co. in the 1960s, winning Tony and Drama Desk Awards for the farce Lend Me a Tenor, 1988. Recipient: Clarence Derwent Award for General Excellence, Outer Critics Circle Award & Obie for Lifetime Achievement.
THEATRE: Auntie Mame (B'way debut, City Center revival, 1958), Measure for Measure, The Rape of the Belt (Tony nom.), Donnybrook, Richard III, The Alchemist, The East Wind, The Ticket of Leave Man, Galileo, Saint Joan, Tiger at the Gates, Cyrano de Bergerac, Be Happy for Me, King Lear, The Miser, The Time of Your Life, Camino Real, Operation Sidewinder, Amphitryon, In the Matter of J. Robert Oppenheimer, The Good Woman of Setzuan, The Playboy of the Western World, An Enemy of the People, Antigone, Mary Stuart, The Crucible, Enemies, Mrs. Warren's Profession, Henry V, The Threepenny Opera, Streamers, Stages, The Biko Inquest, Whose Life Is It Anyway? A Month in the Country, Don Juan in Hell, Inadmissible Evidence, Ah! Wilderness, Man and Superman, Major Barbara, The Caine Mutiny Court Martial, Heartbreak House (Tony nom.), Come Back Little Sheba, Loves of Anatol, Be Happy for Me, Master Class, You Never Can Tell, A Man for All Seasons, Devil's Disciple, Lend Me a Tenor (Tony Award, 1989), The Miser, Breaking Legs, An Inspector Calls, The Heiress, Moon Over Buffalo.
PICTURES: Requiem for a Heavyweight, A Lovely Way to Die, Trading Places, The Pope of Greenwich Village, Walls of Glass, Heaven Help Us, Flanagan, The Money Pit, Children of a Lesser God, Suspect, Three Men and a Baby, Another Woman, Working Girl, The Luckiest Man in the World, Dream Team, Blue Steel, Quick Change, True Colors, FX2, Shadows and Fog, Straight Talk, Angie, Milk Money, Nobody's Fool, Safe Passage, It Takes Two, My Best Friend's Wedding, Critical Care, Frank Lloyd Wright (voice), Wonder Boys, Shaft, Brooklyn Sonnet, Kate & Leopold, Abandon, Hitch, Freedomland, The Savages, When the Evening Comes.
TELEVISION: *Movies:* Echoes in the Darkness, Second Effort, Internal Affairs, Murder in Black and White, The Return of Eliot Ness, Against the Wall, The Forget-Me-Not Murders, Janek: A Silent Betrayal, Young at Heart, Carriers, Twelfth Night, Bonanno: A Godfather's Story, Cupid & Cate, After Amy. *Mini-series:* LIBERTY!: The American Revolution, Mark Twain (voice). *Series:* The Guiding Light, TriBeCa, As The World Turns, All My Children, Law & Order: Special Victims Unit, Damages, The American Experience (narr.). *Specials:* Prisoner of Zenda, An Enemy of the People, A Nice Place to Visit, Read Between the Lines (Emmy Award), New York: A Documentary Film (voice), The Birth of Ohio Stadium (voice), ABC Weekend Specials (Emmy Award 1988). *Guest:* More than 81 appearances.

BOSLEY, TOM
Actor. b. Chicago, IL, Oct. 1, 1927. e. DePaul U. Had roles on radio in Chicago and in stock productions before moving to New York. Appeared off-Broadway and on road before signed to play lead in Fiorello! for George Abbott on Broadway. First actor to win Tony, Drama Critics, ANTA and Newspaper Guild awards in one season for that role.
THEATRE: *B'way:* Nowhere to Go But Up, Fiorello, Cabaret, The Education of H*Y*M*A*N K*A*P*L*A*N, Show Boat, Beauty and the Beast.
PICTURES: Love with the Proper Stranger, The World of Henry Orient, Divorce American Style, Yours Mine and Ours, The Secret War of Harry Frigg, To Find a Man, Mixed Company, Gus, O'Hara's Wife, Million Dollar Mystery, Wicked Stepmother, LIttle Bigfoot II: The Journey Home, The Tangerine Bear, Returning Mickey Stern, The Chocolate Fairy, Popstar, Geppetto's Secret (voice), The Fallen Ones, Confession, The Back-up Plan.
TELEVISION: *Movies:* Thieves' Carnival, Marcus Welby M.D.: A Matter of Humanities (pilot), Night Gallery, A Step Out of Line, Vanished, Congratulations It's a Boy!, Mr. & Mrs. Bo Jo Jones, Streets of San Francisco (pilot), No Place to Run, Miracle on 34th Street, The Girl Who Came Gift Wrapped, Death Cruise, Who Is the Black Dahlia?, Last Survivors, The Night That Panicked America, Love Boat, Testimony of 2 Men, Black Market Baby, With This Ring, The Castaways on Gilligan's Island, The Rebels, For the Love of It, Jesse Owens Story, Fatal Confession: A Father Dowling Mystery, The Love Boat: A Valentine Voyage, Legend of the Candy Cane, Mary Christmas, Christmas at Water's Edge, The Fallen Ones, Hidden Places, Charlie & Me. *Mini-series:* Testimony of Two Men (actor/narrator), The Rebels. *Series:* That Was the Week That Was, The Debbie Reynolds Show, The Dean Martin Show, Sandy Duncan Show, General Mills Radio Adventure Theater (host), Wait Til Your Father Gets Home (voice), Happy Days Emmy nom. 1978), That's Hollywood (narrator), Murder She Wrote, Father Dowling Mysteries, Port Charles. *Specials:* Alice in Wonderland (1953), Arsenic and Old Lace, The Drunkard, Profiles in Courage. *Guest:* More than 167 appearances.

BOSTWICK, BARRY
Actor. b. San Mateo, CA, Feb. 24, 1946. e. USIU Sch. of Performing Arts, San Diego, BFA in acting; NYU Grad. Sch. of the Arts. Made prof. stage debut while in coll. working with Walter Pidgeon in Take Her She's Mine. Joined APA Phoenix Rep. Co. making his B'way debut in Cock-A-Doodle Dandy.
THEATRE: Salvation, House of Leather, Soon, The Screens, Colette, Grease (created role of Danny Zuko, 1972), They Knew What They Wanted, The Robber Bridegroom (Tony Award, 1977), She Loves Me, L'Historie du Soldat, Nick and Nora.
PICTURES: The Rocky Horror Picture Show, Movie Movie, Megaforce, Eight Hundred Leagues Down the Amazon, Weekend at Bernie's 2, Spy Hard, The Secret Agent Club, Swing, Chestnut: Hero of Central Park, Evening, Nancy Drew, Hannah Montana: The Movie, It's a Dog Gone Tale: Destiny's Stand, Some Guy Who Kills People, Miss Nobody, The Selling.
TELEVISION: *Movies:* The Chadwick Family, The Quinns, Murder By Natural Causes, Once Upon a Family, Moviola—The Silent Lovers, Summer Girl, An Uncommon Love, Deceptions, Betrayed by Innocence, Body of Evidence, Addicted to His Love, Parent Trap III, Challenger, Captive, Between Love and Hate, Praying Mantis, Once in a Lifetime, The Return of Hunter, The Secretary, The Trophy Wife's Secret, National Lampoon's Men in White, Love Is a Four-Letter Word. *Mini-series:* Scruples, George Washington, I'll Take Manhattan, War and Remembrance (Golden Globe Award 1989), Eating Pattern. *Series:* Foul Play, Dads, Spin City, Spellbound, Law & Order: Special Victims Unit, Phineas and Ferb, The Mountain. *Specials:* A Woman of Substance, You Can't Take It With You, Working. *Guest:* More than 123 appearances.

BOTTOMS, TIMOTHY
Actor. b. Santa Barbara, CA, Aug. 30, 1951. Early interest in acting; was member of S.B. Madrigal Society, touring Europe in 1967. Sang and danced in West Side Story local prod. With brother Sam co-prod. documentary Picture This about making of the Last Picture Show and Texasville.
PICTURES: Has appeared in more than 60 pictures, incl.: Johnny Got His Gun (debut, 1971, Golden Globe nom. 1972), The Last Picture Show, The Paper Chase, The White Dawn, Operation Daybreak, A Small Town in Texas, Rollercoaster, The Other Side of the Mountain: Part 2, Hurricane, The High Country, Tin Man, The Census Taker, In the Shadow of Kilimanjaro, The Sea Serpent, The Fantasist, Invaders from Mars, The Drifter, Return to the River Kwai, A Case of Law, Texasville, Istanbul, I'll Met By Moonlight, Uncle Sam, Ringer, Fox Hunt, Mr. Atlas, Absolute Force, Mixed Blessings, The Man in the Iron Mask, The Prince and the Surfer, X-Ray Boy, A Smaller Place, Held for Ransom, Murder Seen, The Entrepreneurs, Elephant, Paradise, Texas, The Girl Next Door, Call of the Wild, Pound of Flesh.
TELEVISION: *Movies:* The Story of David, The Gift of Love, A Shining Season, Escape, Island Sons, Mortal Challenge, DC 9/11: Time of Crisis, The Big Dance, Ike: Countdown to D-Day, Jane Doe: Now You See It, Now You Don't, Vampire Bats, Deceit, Lone Rider, Holiday in Handcuffs, The Governor's Wife, Bound by a Secret. *Mini-series:* The Money Changers, 500 Nations, East of Eden. *Series:* Land of the Lost, The Great War (voice), That's My Bush!, Dirt. *Special:* Look Homeward Angel. *Guest:* More than 50 appearances.

BOUCHEZ, ÉLODIE
Actress. b. France, April 5, 1973.
PICTURES: Stan the Flasher, The Stolen Diary, Tango, Good Old Daze, Les mots de l'amour, The Wild Reeds, Those Were the Days, Clubbed to Death, Mademoiselle Personne, Full Speed, The Proprietor, Fire in Paradise, La divine poursuite, Le ciel est a nous, The Dreamlife of Angels (Cannes Film Fest. Award, Best Actress, 1998), Louise, J'aimerais pas crever un dimanche, Zonzon, Les Kidnappeurs, Shooting Vegetarians, Lovers, Meurtre d'une petite grue, Blame it on Voltaire, Too Much Flesh, The Beat Nicks, CQ, Tom Thumb, Being Light, Le Merveilleuse odysee de l'idiot Toboggan, La guerre a Paris, Noces indiennes, Dreams of Trespass, Le Pacte du silence, Stormy Weather, America Brown, Brice de Nice, Sorry, Haters, Ma place au soleil, Je déteste les enfants des autres, Héros, Teen Spirit, Après lui, Seuls two, We're Here to Help.
TELEVISION: *Movies:* La lettre inachevée, Les brouches, Premières neiges, Douce France. *Series:* Alias.

BOUQUET, CAROLE
Actress. b. Neuilly-sur-Seine, France, Aug. 18, 1957. e. Sorbonne, Paris, Paris Conservatoire. Also model for Chanel No. 5 perfume.
PICTURES: That Obscure Object of Desire (debut, 1977), Buffet Froid, Il Cappotto di Astrakan, For Your Eyes Only, Bingo Bongo, Mystere, Nemo, Le Bon Roi Dagobert, Rive Droite Rive Gauche, Special Police, Double Messieurs, Le Mal d'aimer, Jenatsch, Bunker Palace Hotel, New York Stories, Too Beautiful for You, Against Oblivion, Tango, Women in Skirts, Grosse Fatigue, A Business Affair, Lucie Aubrac, In All Innocence, Un Pont Entre Deux Rives, Lulu Kreutz's Picnic, Speaking of Bunuel, Wasabi, Embrassez qui vous voulez, Blanche, Red Lights, Travaux, Nordeste, L' Enfer, Aurore, Un ami parfait, Les Hauts murs, Les Enfants de Timpelbach, Protéger et servir, Libre échange, Terminus des anges.
TELEVISION: *Movies:* The Red and the Black, Bérénice, Ruy Blas, Madame de, L'éloignement. *Mini-series:* Le Rouge et le Noir.

BOUTSIKARIS, DENNIS
Actor. b. Newark, NJ, Dec. 21, 1952. e. Hampshire Col.
THEATRE: *Off-B'way:* Another Language (debut, 1975), Funeral March for a One Man Band, All's Well That Ends Well, Nest of the Wood Grouse, Cheapside, Rum and Coke, The Boys Next Door, Sight Unseen, A Picasso. *B'way:* Filomena, Bent, Amadeus.
PICTURES: The Exterminator, Very Close Quarters, Batteries Not Included, Crocodile Dundee II, The Dream Team, Talent for the Game, The Boy Who Cried Bitch, Boys on the Side, Chasing the Dragon, Surviving Picasso, Blue Vision, In Dreams, Taken, Custody of the Heart, Crawlers, Cherry Crush, The Education of Charlie Banks, W., Calling It Quits, My Soul to Take.
TELEVISION: *Movies:* Rappaccini's Daughter, Internal Affairs, Thunderboat Row, The Keys, Love Lies and Murder, The Hit Man, Victim of Love: The Shannon Mohr Story, The Yarn Princess, Tonya & Nancy: The Inside Story, Beyond Betrayal, Love and Betrayal: The Mia Farrow Story, The Three Lives of Karen, Survival on the Mountain, Perfect Murder, Perfect Town: JonBenét and the City of Boulder, Custody of the Heart. *Mini-series:* The Last Don. *Series:* Nurse, Stat, The Jackie Thomas Show, Misery Loves Company, Law & Order, Six Degrees. *Guest:* More than 62 appearances.

BOWERS, MIKE
Executive. Bowers, a 14-year motion picture exhibition executive, was elevated to president & COO, of Harkins Theatres in Sept. 2006. Never before in the company's 73-year history has the role of president been held by someone outside the Harkins family. Bowers, who began his career with Mann Theatres, joined Harkins as district manager and was later promoted to vice president. Harkins is based in Scottsdale, AZ. Currently he is president and COO.

BOWIE, DAVID
Actor, Composer, Singer. r.n. David Robert Hayward - Jones. b. Brixton, South London, England, Jan. 8, 1947. m. model-actress Iman. Broadway debut: The Elephant Man (1980).
PICTURES: The Virgin Soldiers (debut, 1969), Ziggy Stardust and the Spiders from Mars (1973; U.S. release 1983), The Man Who Fell to Earth, Just a Gigolo, Radio On, Cat People (lyricist, performed song Golden Globe nom. 1983), The Hunger, Yellowbeard, Merry Christmas Mr. Lawrence, Into the Night, Absolute Beginners (also songs), Labyrinth (also songs), The Last Temptation of Christ, Linguini Incident, Twin Peaks: Fire Walk With Me, Inspirations, Mr. Rice's Secret, Il Mio West, Lou Reed: Rock and Roll Heart, Everybody Loves Sunshine, Zoolander, Mayor of Sunset Strip. Composer/Songs: Boy Meets Girl, The Falcon and the Snowman, Bad Blood, Pretty Woman, Lost Highway, The Saint, Grosse Point Blank, Almost Famous, Moulin Rouge!, The Banger Sisters, Dogville, Rugrats Go Wild!, Charlie's Angels: Full Throttle, Underworld, The School of Rock, Confessions of a Teenage Drama Queen, New York Minute, Shrek 2, Shall We Dance, The Life Aquatic with Steve Zissou (composer), Arthur and the Minimoys (voice), The Prestige, August, Bandslam. 150 credits as soundtrack performer or writer.
TELEVISION: *Series:* The Hunger. *Specials:* Christmas With Bing Crosby, The Midnight Special, Glass Spider Tour, Closure, Saturday Night Live: 25th Anniversary Special, The Beatles Revolution, Bowie at the BBC, The Old Grey Whistle Test at 30, Bad Hair Days, Hollywood Rocks the Movies: The 1970s (Emmy Award 2003), Concert for New York City, I Love Christmas, Scott Walker: 30 Century Man (exec. prod.). 70 credits as soundtrack performer or writer. *Guest:* More than 200 appearances.

BOXLEITNER, BRUCE
Actor. b. Elgin, IL, May 12, 1950. m. actress Melissa Gilbert. After high school enrolled in Chicago's Goodman Theatre, staging productions and working with lighting and set design in addition to acting.
PICTURES: Six-Pack Annie, The Baltimore Bullet, Tron, The Crystal Eye, Breakaway, Diplomatic Immunity, Kuffs, The Babe, Wyatt Earp: Return to Tombstone, Perilous, The Perfect Nanny, Life in the Balance, Contagion, Silence, Gods and Generals, Tron Legacy.
TELEVISION: *Movies:* The Chadwick Family, A Cry for Help, The Macahans, Kiss Me—Kill Me, Murder at the World Series, Happily Ever After, Wild Times, Bare Essence, I Married Wyatt Earp, Passion Flower, Angel in Green, The Gamble (I, II, III, & V), Red River, The Road Raiders, Murderous Vision, The Secret, Perfect Family, Double Jeopardy, House of Secrets, Zoya, Babylon 5: In the Beginning, Babylon 5: Thirdspace, Babylon 5: A Call to Arms, Freefall, Hope Ranch, Killer Flood: The Day the Dam Broke, They Are Among Us, Saving Emily, Detective, A Killer Upstairs, Falling in Love with the Girl Next Door, Double Cross, Mystery Woman: Wild West Mystery, Pandemic, Sharpshooter, Bone Eater, Aces 'N Eights. *Mini-series:* How the West Was Won, East of Eden, The Last Convertible, Pandemic. *Series:* How the West Was Won, Bring 'Em Back Alive, Scarecrow and Mrs. King, Babylon 5, Young Blades, She Spies, Spawn: The Animation (voice). *Guest:* More than 96 appearances.

BOYER, PHIL

TV Executive. b. Portland, OR, Dec. 13, 1940. e. Sacramento State U. Began broadcasting career as 12-year-old in Portland, establishing nation's first youth radio facility—a 5-watt facility in the basement of his home. At 16 began working at KPDQ, Portland; two years later joined KPTV, Portland, as announcer. In 1960 joined KEZI-TV, Eugene, OR, heading prod. and prog. depts. In 1965 named staff prod.-dir. for KCRA, TV, Sacramento, CA, becoming prod. mgr. in 1967 and prog. mgr. in 1969. In 1972 joined KNBC-TV, Los Angeles, as prog. dir. In 1974 named v.p., programming, of ABC Owned TV Stations; 1977, v.p.-gen. mgr., WLS-TV, Chicago; 1979, v.p.-gen. mgr. of WABC-TV, NY, 1981; v.p., gen mgr., ABC-owned TV station div.; 1984, joined ABC Video Enterprises as v.p. intl. dev.; 1986-97 sr. v.p., intl and prog. dev., CC/ABC Video Ent. Currently pres. of Aircraft Owners and Pilots Assoc. (AOPA).

BOYES, CHRISTOPHER

Sound. Has recieved BAFTA NOMS., Cinema Audio Society, USA 5 noms. and 2 Awards, Motion Picture Sound Editors, US, 9 noms. and 3 Awards.
PICTURES: Rush, Terminator 2: Judgment Day, Bingo!, Single White Female, Jurassic Park, Under Siege 2: Dark Territory, The Rock, Broken Arrow, Eraser, Titanic (Academy Award, MP Sound Editors Award 1998), Volcano, The Lost World: Jurassic Park, Con Air, Big Daddy, The 13th Warrior, Dinosaur (MP Sound Editors nom. 2001), Titan A.E.(MP Sound Editors Award 2001), Space Cowboys, Pearl Harbor (Academy Award, MP Sound Editors nom. 2002), Jurassic Park III (MP Sound Editors nom. 2002), The Lord of the Rings: Fellowship of the Ring (Academy Award nom.; C. A. S. Award 2002), Lilo & Stitch (MP Sound Editors nom. 2003), Minority Report, Blood Work, The Lord of the Rings: The Two Towers (Academy Award nom.; C. A. S. nom. 2003), Mystic River, Pirates of the Caribbean: The Curse of the Black Pearl (2 Academy nom.; C. A. S. nom.; MP Sound Editors Award, 1 other nom. 2004), The Lord of the Rings: The Return of the King (Academy Award, C. A. S. nom. 2004), Catwoman, Sky Captain and the World of Tomorrow, Million Dollar Baby, XXX 2: The Next Level, The Prize Winner of Defiance, Ohio, The Weather Man, King Kong (Academy Award,; C. A. S. nom. 2006), Pirates of the Caribbean: Dead Man's Chest (2 Academy Award noms.; C. A. S. nom. 2 MP Sound Editors noms. 2007), Charlotte's Web, Her Best Move (consult), Pirates of the Caribbean: At World's End (2 MP Sound Editors noms. 2008), Touching Home, Lions for Lambs, National Treasure: Book of Secrets, Iron Man (Academy Award nom.; C. A.S. nom.; Mp Sound Editors nom. 2009), The ESP Affair, The Taking of Pelham 123, Avatar (sound designer, re-recording mixer, supvr. sound editor 2 Academy Award noms.; C. A. S. nom. 2010).
TELEVISION: *Movie:* Young Indiana Jones and the Hollywood Follies (re-recording mixer, C. A. S. Award 1995).

BOYLE, BARBARA D.

Executive, Producer. b. New York, NY. e. U. of California, Berkeley, B.A., 1957; UCLA, J.D., 1960. Named to bar: California, 1961; New York, 1964. Attorney in business affairs dept. & corp. asst. secty., American Int'l. Pictures, Los Angeles, 1965-67; partner in entertainment law firm, Cohen & Boyle, L.A., 1967-74; exec. v.p. & gen. counsel, COO, New World Pictures, L.A., 1974-82. Sr. v.p. worldwide prod., Orion Pictures, L.A., 1982-86; exec. v.p., prod., RKO Pictures, L.A., 1986-87. Pres., Sovereign Pictures, Inc., 1988-92; Sovereign Pictures, Inc., financed and distributed internationally 25 films, with its films receiving 14 Academy Award nominations and winning four. Partner in Boyle-Taylor Prods., 1993. She then became pres., Valhalla Motion Pictures, a film and TV prod. co. Valhalla's films included The Hulk, True Whispers: the Story of the Navajo Code Talkers for ITVS; and Clockstoppers, as well as the TV show Adventure, Inc. 2003-present, Boyle is chair of UCLA's School of Theater, Film & Television. Her industry involvement includes founding member of UCLA School of Law's Entertainment Advisory Council (& co-chairperson 1979 & '80). Member: AMPAS, Women in Film (pres., 1977-78, member of bd., chairperson 1981-84), Women Entertainment Lawyers Assn., California Bar Assn., N.Y. State Bar Assn., Beverly Hills Bar Assn., Hollywood Women's Political Committee and American Film Institute. She serves on the bd. of Project: Involve and is also a past pres. of Independent Feature Projects West. Boyle has received, among others, a Vision Award from IFP, the WIF Crystal Award and the Alumni of the Year from UCLA Law.
PICTURES: *Producer:* Mrs. Munck, Phenomenon, Instinct. *Exec. prod:* Campus Man, Eight Men Out, Desperately Seeking Susan, The Terminator, Platoon, Bottle Rocket, The Hi-Line.

BOYLE, DANNY

Director, Producer. b. Manchester, UK, Oct. 20, 1956. e. Thornliegh Salesian College in Bolton, UK.
PICTURES: Shallow Grave, Trainspotting, Twin Town (exec. prod.), A Life Less Ordinary, The Beach, 28 Days Later..., Millions, Sunshine, 28 Weeks Later (exec. prod.), Slumdog Millionaire (Academy Award nom., DGA Award, Golden Globe Award 2009), 127 Hours.
TELEVISION: *Movies:* The Venus de Milo Instead, Monkeys, The Hen House, The Nightwatch (also prod.), For the Greater Good, Vacuuming Completely Nude in Paradise, Strumpet. *Mini-series:* Mr. Wroe's Virgins.

BOYLE, LARA FLYNN

Actress. b. Davenport, IA, Mar. 24, 1970. e. Chicago Academy for the Visual and Performing Arts. First studied acting at the Piven Theatre. Professional debut at age 15 in TV mini-series Amerika.
PICTURES: Poltergeist III (debut, 1988), How I Got Into College, Dead Poets Society, May Wine, The Rookie, The Dark Backward, Mobsters, Wayne's World, Where the Day Takes You, The Temp, Eye of the Storm, Equinox, Red Rock West, Threesome, Baby's Day Out, The Road to Wellville, Farmer & Chase, Cafe Society, The Big Squeeze, Afterglow, Red Meat, Susan's Plan, Happiness, Chain of Fools, Speaking of Sex, Men In Black II, Deauville, Cougar Hunting.
TELEVISION: *Movies:* Terror on Highway 91, Gang of Four, The Preppie Murder, Past Tense, Jacob, Since You've Been Gone, Shades of Black: The Conrad Black Story. *Mini-series:* Amerika. *Series:* Twin Peaks, The Practice (Emmy nom. 1999), Huff, Las Vegas, Insatiable. *Guest:* More than 48 appearances.

BRACCO, LORRAINE

Actress. b. Brooklyn, NY, Oct. 2, 1955. At 16 began modeling for Wilhelmina Agency appearing in Mademoiselle, Seventeen, Teen magazine. Moved to Paris where modeling career continued and led to TV commercials. After making her film debut in Duo sur Canape became a disc jockey on Radio Luxembourg, Paris. 1983 produced a TV special on fashion and music. In Lincoln Center workshop performance of David Rabe's Goose and Tom Tom, 1986.
PICTURES: Cormorra, The Pick-up Artist, Someone to Watch Over Me, Sing, The Dream Team, On a Moonlit Night, Good Fellas (Academy Award nom.; Golden Globe nom. 1991), Talent for the Game, Switch, Medicine Man, Radio Flyer, Traces of Red, Being Human, The Basketball Diaries, Hackers, The Liars, Ladies Room, Custody of the Heart, Riding in Cars With Boys, Death of a Dynasty, Son of Morning.
TELEVISION: *Movies:* Scam, Getting Gotti, Lifeline, The Taking of Pelham One-Two-Three, Custody of the Heart, Sex In Our Century (narr.), Snowglobe, Long Island Confidential, Women Without Men, Rizzoli & Isles, Rizzoli. *Series:* The Sopranos (4 Emmy noms.; 3 Golden Globe noms.). *Guest:* More than 43 appearances.

BRADFORD, JESSE

Actor. b. May 28, 1979. Made first appearance as infant in Q-tip commercial.
PICTURES: Falling in Love (debut, 1984), Prancer, Presmued Innocent, My Blue Heaven, The Boy Who Cried Bitch, King of the Hill, Far From Home: The Adventures of Yello Dog, Hackers, Romeo & Juliet, A Soldier's Daughter Never Cries, Speedway Junky, Cherry Falls, Bring It On, Dancing at the Blue Iguana, According to Spencer, Clockstoppers, Swimf@n, Eulogy, Heights, Happy Endings, Flags of Our Fathers, The 1 Second Film (doc., prod.), W., Son of Morning, Table for Three, I Hope They Serve Beer in Hell, The Cold.
TELEVISION: *Movies:* Classified Love, The Boys, Twenty Questions, The Eastmans. *Series:* The West Wing.

BRAEDEN, ERIC

Actor. r.n. Hans Jörg Gudegast. b. Kiel, Germany, Apr. 3, 1941. Awarded Federal Medal of Honor by pres. of Germany for promoting positive, realistic image of Germans in America.
PICTURES: Morituri, Dayton's Devils, 100 Rifles, Colossus: The Forbin Project, Escape from the Planet of the Apes, Lady Ice, The Adulteress, The Ultimate Thrill, Herbie Goes to Monte Carlo, The Ambulance, Titanic, Meet the Deedles, The Titanic Chronicles.
TELEVISION: *Movies:* Honeymoon With a Stranger, The Mask of Sheba, The Judge and Jake Wyler, Death Race, Death Scream, The New Original Wonder Woman (pilot), Code Name: Diamond Head, Happily Ever After, The Power Within, The Aliens Are Coming, A Perry Mason Mystery: The Case of the Wicked Wives. *Mini-series:* Jackie Collins' Lucky Chances. *Series:* The Rat Patrol, The Young and the Restless (People's Choice Award, Soap Opera Award, 2 Emmy noms., Emmy Award, 1998). *Guest:* More than 90 appearances.

BRAGA, SONIA

Actress. b. Maringa, Parana, Brazil, June 8, 1950. Began acting at 14 on live children's program on Brazilian TV, Gardin Encantado. Stage debut at 17 in Moliere's Jorge Dandin, then in Hair! Starred in many Brazilian soap operas including Gabriella, as well as a prod. of Sesame Street in Sao Paulo.
PICTURES: The Main Road, A Moreninha, Captain Bandeira Vs. Dr. Moura Brasil, Mestica, The Indomitable Slave, The Couple, Dona Flor and Her Two Husbands, Gabriella, I Love You, A Lady in the Bus, Kiss of the Spider Woman (Golden Globe nom. 1986), The Milagro Beanfield War, Moon Over Parador (Golden Globe nom. 1989), The Rookie, Roosters, Two Deaths, Tieta do Agreste (also co-prod.), Memorias Postumas, In the Shadow of Hollywood, Perfume, Angel Eyes, Empire, Constellation, The Bride of the Sea, Testosterone, Marilyn Hotchkiss' Ballroom Dancing and Charm School, Bordertown, The Hottest State, An Invisible Sign of My Own, Lope.

TELEVISION: *Movies:* The Man Who Broke 1000 Chains, The Last Prostitute, The Burning Season (Emmy nom.; Golden Globe nom. 1995), Money Plays, Streets of Laredo, A Will of Their Own, The Judge. *Series:* Four Corners, Forca de Um Desejo, American Family, Alias, Páginas da vida. *Guest:* More than 42 appearances.

BRANAGH, KENNETH

Actor, Director, Producer, Author. b. Belfast, Northern Ireland, Dec. 10, 1960. Moved to Reading, England at age 9. e. RADA. Went from drama school into West End hit Another Country, followed by Gamblers, The Madness, Francis. Royal Shakespeare Co.: Love Labors Lost, Hamlet, Henry V. Left Royal Shakespeare Company to form his own Renaissance Theater Co. with actor David Parfitt for which he wrote a play Public Enemy (also produced Off-B'way), wrote-directed: The Play What I Wrote, Tell Me Honestly, directed: Twelfth Night, produced-directed-starred: Romeo & Juliet, and played Hamlet, Benedick and Touchstone in a sold-out nationwide tour and London season. L.A.: King Lear, A Midsummer Night's Dream. *Author:* Beginning (1990). Received BAFTA's Michael Balcon Award for Outstanding Contribution to Cinema (1993). Made short film Swan Song (Academy Award nom.).
PICTURES: High Season (debut, 1987), A Month in the Country, Henry V (also dir., adapt.; BAFTA & Natl. Board of Review Awards for Best Dir., 2 Academy Award nom. 1989), Dead Again (also dir.), Peter's Friends (also dir., prod.), Swing Kids, Much Ado About Nothing (also dir., adapt.), Mary Shelley's Frankenstein (also dir., co-prod.), In the Bleak Mid-Winter (dir., s.p. only), Anne Frank Remembered (narrator), Othello, Looking for Richard, Hamlet (Academy Award nom. 1997, also dir, prod.), The Theory of Flight, Celebrity, The Henry V (2 Academy Award nom. 1990), Gingerbread Man, The Proposition, The Dance of Shiva, Love's Labour's Lost (also, dir., s.p.),The Betty Schimmel Story (dir. only), Wild Wild West, Galapagos: The Enchanted Voyage (voice), Love's Labourls Lost, The Road to El Dorado (voice), Conspiracy, How to Kill Your Neighbor's Dog, Alien Love Triangle, Rabbit Proof Fence, Harry Potter and the Chamber of Secrets, Five Children and It, As You Like It (exec. prod., prod., writer, dir.) The Magic Flute (actor, dir., writer), Sleuth (prod., dir.), Valkyrie, Pirate Radio, Thor (dir.).
TELEVISION: *Movies:* The Billy Plays, Maybury, To the Lighthouse, Ghosts, The Lady's Not for Burning, Strange Interlude, Twelfth Night, or What You Will (dir.), Look Back in Anger, Shadow of a Gunman, Conspiracy (Emmy Award, Golden Globe nom. 2001), Shackleton (Emmy nom. 2002), Warm Springs (Emmy nom.; Golden Globe nom. 2005), Sidetracked. *Mini-series*: Maybury, Boy in the Bush, Fortunes of War. *Series:* Wallander (also exec. prod. Emmy nom. 2009, Golden Globe nom. 2010). *Specials:* Cold War (voice), Great Composers (narr.), Walking with Dinosaurs (narr.), Galapagos: The Enchanted Voyage (narr.), Lon Chaney: A Thousand Faces (narr.), *Series*: Thompson. *Guest:* More than 87 appearances.

BRANDAUER, KLAUS MARIA

Actor, Director. r.n. Klaus Maria Steng. b. Bad Ausse, Steiermark, Austria, June 22, 1944. e. Acad. of Music and Dramatic Arts, Stuttgart, W. Germany. Was established in the German and Austrian theatre before film debut.
PICTURES: The Salzburg Connection (debut, 1972), Mephisto (Cannes Film Fest. Award, 1981). Never Say Never Again, Colonel Redl, Out of Africa (Academy Award nom., Golden Globe Award 1986), The Lightship, Streets of Gold, Burning Secret, Hanussen, Hitlerjunge Salomon, Das Spinnennetz (The Spider's Web) The French Revolution, The Russia House, White Fang, The Resurrected, Seven Minutes (also dir.), Becoming Colette, Felidae (voice), Marco and the Magician (also dir.), Die Wand (dir. only), Rembrandt, Klaus Maria Brandauer: Speer in London, Dykaren, Belief Hope and Blood, Druids, Everyman's Feast, Between Strangers, Daddy, Mein Führer - Die wirklich wahrste Wahrheit über Adolf Hitler, Tetro, The Interrogation of Harry Wind.
TELEVISION: *Movies:* Quo Vadis?, Jeremiah, Introducing Dorothy Dandridge (Emmy nom.; Golden Globe nom. 2000), Cyrano von Bergerac, Perlasca un eroe italiano, Entrusted, Kronprinz Rudolf. *Guest:* More than 60 appearances.

BRANDIS, BERNARDINE

Executive. e. B.A., (magna cum laude) UCLA, 1975. J.D., UCLA, 1978. Began career as private practice attorney. senior dist. & mktg./prod. counsel, 20th Century Fox Film Corp.; dir., business affairs, Universal Pictures, 1983-85; v.p., business affairs, Walt Disney Pictures, 1985-89; senior v.p., business and legal affairs, Hollywood Pictures, (a Disney subsidiary) 1989. Currently exec. v.p., business & legal affairs, The Walt Disney Motion Pictures Group, overseeing all aspects of business and legal affairs for the motion pictures division, studio administration, and theme park film productions. Named to Hollywood Reporter's Power 100 Women in Entertainment, 2006.

BRANDON, MICHAEL

Actor. r.n. Michael Feldman. b. Brooklyn, NY, April 20, 1945. e. AADA. Appeared on B'way in Does Tiger Wear a Necktie?
PICTURES: Lovers and Other Strangers, Jennifer on My Mind, Four Flies on Grey Velvet, Heavy Traffic (voice), FM, Promises in the Dark, A Change of Seasons, Rich and Famous, Déjà Vu, Are You Ready for Love? Me and Orson Welles, Labrats (voice).
TELEVISION: *Movies:* Appeared in 30+ tv movies, incl.: The Impatient Heart, The Strangers in 7A, The Third Girl From the Left, Hitchhike!, The Red Badge of Courage, Queen of the Stardust Ballroom, Cage Without a Key, James Dean, Scott Free, Red Alert, The Comedy Company, A Vacation in Hell, A Perfect Match, Between Two Brothers, The Seduction of Gina, Deadly Messages, Not in My Family, Moment of Truth: Murder or Memory?, The Apocalypse Watch, The Lost Battalion, Hawking, Agatha Christie Marple: The Sittaford Mystery, Trial & Retribution XI: Closure. *Series:* Emerald Point, Dempsey & Makepeace, Home Fires, Dinotopia, Dead Man Weds, Thomas the Tank Engine (narr.). *Guest:* More than 90 appearances.

BRAUGHER, ANDRE

Actor. b. Chicago, IL, July 1, 1962.
PICTURES: Glory, Striking Distance, Primal Fear, Get on the Bus, Thick as Thieves, City of Angels, All the Rage, Frequency, Duets, A Better Way to Die, Poseidon, Live!, 4: Rise of the Silver Surfer, The Mist, Passengers.
TELEVISION: *Movies:* Kojak: Fatal Flaw, Kojak: Ariana, Kojak: None So Blind, Murder in Mississippi, Somebody Has to Shoot the Picture, The Court-Martial of Jackie Robinson, Simple Justice, The Tuskegee Airmen (Emmy nom. 1996), Passing Glory, Love Songs (also dir.), 10,000 Black Men Named George, A Soldier's Girl, Salem's Lot, Thief (pilot, Emmy Award, Golden Globe nom. 2006), The Andromeda Strain, Men of a Certain Age. *Mini-series:* The Andromeda Strain. *Series:* Kojak, Homicide: Life in the Street (Emmy Award, 1998, Emmy nom. 1996), City of Angels, Gideon's Crossing (Emmy nom. Golden Globe nom. 2001), Hack, Thief, Men of a Certain Age. *Guest:* More than 60 appearances.

BRAUNSTEIN, GEORGE GREGORY

Producer. b. New York, NY, May 23, 1947. e. Culver Military Acad., U. of California, B.A., biology, chemistry, 1970. U. W.L.A. Law School, J.D. 1987. Father is Jacques Braunstein (Screen Televideo Prods. At War with the Army, Young Lions.).
PICTURES: Train Ride to Hollywood, Fade to Black, Surf II, And God Created Woman, Out Cold, Don't Tell Her It's Me, Red Scorpion 2, Uncle Sam, Expecting Mary (co-exec. prod.), Meeting Spencer.

BRAVERMAN, ALAN

Executive. b. Boston, MA. e. Brandeis Univ., B.A. degree, 1969. After completing undergrad degree, worked two years as a Vista volunteer in Gary, IN. Duquesne University, Pittsburgh, PA, J.D. summa cum laude, 1975. While at Duquesne, editor-in-chief of the Law Review. Was law clerk to the Honorable Thomas W. Pomeroy, Jr., Justice, Pennsylvania Supreme Court. In 1976, joined Washington D.C. law firm Wilmer, Cutler & Pickering. Became partner in 1983, specializing in complex commercial and administrative litigation. Braverman then joined Capital Cities/ABC, Inc. where he guided the company through numerous lawsuits regarding news reporting and news gathering practices, supervised the company's labor department, and oversaw the government relations function for Capital Cities/ABC, Inc. prior to its merger with Disney. He joined ABC, Inc. in Nov. 1993, as v.p. & deputy general counsel. In his positions with ABC, Inc. Braverman had broad responsibilities for the operation of the legal department, for government relations and for the Corporation's legal affairs. In Oct. 1994, promoted to v.p. & general counsel. In Aug. 1996, prior to Disney's acquisition of ABC, Inc., Braverman was named senior v.p. & general counsel, ABC, Inc. After the acquisition, Braverman was elevated to executive v.p. & general counsel, ABC, Inc. and deputy general counsel The Walt Disney Company. In that capacity he oversaw the legal affairs of the ABC Broadcast Group, ESPN and Disney/ABC Cable, as well as labor relations. Braverman was named executive v.p. & general counsel of The Walt Disney Company in Jan. 2003. He was promoted to his current position as senior executive v.p., general counsel & secretary, The Walt Disney Company in Oct. 2003. Today he serves as the chief legal officer of the company and oversees its team of attorneys responsible for all aspects of Disney's legal affairs around the world.

BRAVERMAN, CHARLES

Director, Producer. b. Los Angeles, CA, March 3, 1944. e. Los Angeles City Coll., USC, B.A. Child actor, 1950-57. Two-time Emmy winner.
PICTURES:Hit and Run (prod./dir.), The Best of the Big Laff Off (dir.), Peanuts to the Presidency: The Jimmy Carter Campaign (prod., documentary), Rocky and Rolanda (documentary, DGA nom. 2002), Bottom of the Ninth (documentary, DGA nom. 2003), Curtain Call (Academy Award nom for Best short subject 2001).
TELEVISION: *Movies/Dir:* The Richard Lewis "I'm In Pain" Concert (also prod.), Prince of Bel Air, Brotherhood of Justice, Final Shot: The Hank Gathers Story, *Series/Dir.:* St. Elsewhere, Crazy Like A Fox, Shadow Chasers, The Wizard, The New Mike Hammer, Sledge Hammer!, Rags to Riches, Freddy's Nightmares, Gabriel's Fire, Beverly Hills 90210 (9 episodes, 1991), Melrose Place, Hercules: The Legendary Journeys. *Documentaries:* The Making of Beatlemania, Making Marines (exec. prod/cinematographer), High School Boot Camp (DGA

Award 2001), Prison Boot Camp (exec. prod.), Debutantes.

BREGMAN, MARTIN

Producer, Writer. b. New York, NY, May 18, 1931. m. actress Cornelia Sharpe. e. Indiana U., NYU. Began career as business and personal mgr. to Barbra Streisand, Faye Dunaway, Candice Bergen, Al Pacino. Chairman NY Advisory Council for Motion Pictures, Radio and TV (co-founder, 1974).
PICTURES: Serpico, Dog Day Afternoon (Academy Award nom. 1976), The Next Man, The Seduction of Joe Tynan, Simon, The Four Seasons, Eddie Macon's Run, Venom, Scarface, Sweet Liberty, Real Men, A New Life, Sea of Love, Nesting, Betsy's Wedding, Whispers in the Dark, The Real McCoy, Carlito's Way, The Shadow, Gold Diggers: The Secret of Bear Mountain, Matilda (exec. prod.), Nothing to Lose, The Bone Collector, The Adventures of Pluto Nash, Carolina, Carlito's Way: The Beginning, Torch.
TELEVISION: S*H*E (movie). *Series:* The Four Seasons (exec. prod.).

BREMNER, EWEN

Actor. b. 1971. Edinburgh, Scotland, UK, Jan. 23, 1972.
PICTURES: The Gospel According to Vic, As You Like It, Naked, Royal Deceit, Judge Dredd, Ruffian Hearts, Dead London (short), The Name of this Film is Dogme95 (documentary), The Phoenix and the Magic Carpet, Trainspotting, Rhinoceros Hunting in Budapest, Mojo, The Life of Stuff, The Acid House, Julien Donkey-Boy, Paranoid, Snatch: Pigs and Diamonds, Pearl Harbor, Black Hawk Down, Fancy Dancing, Skagerrak, The Rundown, Welcome to the Jungle, The Reckoning, Around the World in 80 Days, AVP: Alien Vs. Predator, Letters, Therese Raquin, Match Point, Marvelous, Death at a Funeral, Mister Foe, Fool's Gold, The Last Word, You Will Meet a Tall Dark Stranger.
TELEVISION: *Movies:* A Girl Named Scooner, Love Story (tv short), Deacon Brodie, Surrealissimo: The Trial of Salvador Dali, Elizabeth I, One Night in Emergency, Dive. *Mini-series:* The Secret World of Michael Fry, The Virgin Queen, The Lost Room, The Day of the Triffids. *Series:* Harry Enfield and Chums, Coming Up, Strike Back.

BRENNAN, EILEEN

Actress. b. Los Angeles, CA, Sept. 3, 1938. e. Georgetown U., American Acad. of Dramatic Arts, N.Y. Daughter of silent film actress Jean Manahan. Big break came with lead in off-Broadway musical, Little Mary Sunshine (Obie & Theatre World Awards, 1960).
THEATRE: The Miracle Worker (tour), Hello Dolly! (Broadway), and revivals of The King and I, Guys and Dolls, Camelot, Bells Are Ringing; also An Evening with Eileen Brennan, A Couple of White Chicks Sitting Around Talking.
PICTURES: Divorce American Style (debut, 1967), The Last Picture Show (BAFTA nom.), Scarecrow, The Sting, Daisy Miller, At Long Last Love, Hustle, Murder by Death, FM, The Cheap Detective, The Last of the Cowboys (The Great Smokey Roadblock), Private Benjamin (Academy Award nom. 1981), Pandemonium, The Funny Farm, Clue, Sticky Fingers, Rented Lips, The New Adventures of Pippi Longstocking, It Had to Be You, Stella, Texasville, White Palace, I Don't Buy Kisses Anymore, Reckless, Pants on Fire, Changing Habits, Boy's Life 2, The Last Great Ride, Moonglow, Jeepers Creepers, Dumb Luck, The Hollow, The Moguls, Miss Congeniality 2: Armed & Fabulous, Mary Worth, The Kings of Appletown.
TELEVISION: *Movies:* Appeared in more than 30 tv movies, incl.: Playmates, My Father's House, The Night That Panicked America, The Death of Richie, When She Was Bad..., My Old Man, When the Circus Came to Town, Incident at Crestridge, My Name Is Kate, Take Me Home Again, Freaky Friday, Trail of Tears, Toothless. *Mini-series:* Black Beauty. *Series:* Rowan & Martin's Laugh-In, All That Glitters, 13 Queens Boulevard, A New Kind of Family, Private Benjamin (Emmy Award, 1981, 3 Emmy noms., Golden Globe Award 1982, Golden Globe nom. 1983), Off the Rack, 7th Heaven (as guest), Newhart (Emmy nom. 1989 as guest), Bonkers (voice), thirtysomething (Emmy nom. 1991 as guest), Will & Grace Emmy nom. 2004 as guest). *Specials:* Working, In Search of Dr. Seuss. *Guest:* More than 90 appearances.

BRENNEMAN, AMY

Actress. b. Glastonbury, Connecticut, June 22, 1964.
PICTURES: Bye Bye Love, Casper, Heat, Fear, Daylight, Nevada (also co-prod.), Lesser Prophets, Your Friends & Neighbors, The Suburbans, Things You Can Tell Just By Looking At Her, Off the Map, Nine Lives, 88 Minutes, The Jane Austen Book Club, Downloading Nancy.
TELEVISION: *Movies:* A.T.F., Mary Cassatt: An American Impressionist. *Series:* Middle Ages, NYPD Blue (2 Emmy nom. 1994, 1995), Judging Amy (also exec. prod, writer/creator, 3 Emmy nom., 3 Golden Globe nom. 2000, 2001, 2002), Private Practice.

BREST, MARTIN

Director, Producer. b. Bronx, NY, Aug. 8, 1951. e. NYU Sch. of Film. m. prod. Lisa Weinstein. Made award-winning short subject, Hot Dogs for Gauguin (featuring Danny DeVito). Accepted into fellowship program at American Film Institute, making first feature, Hot Tomorrows (dir., prod., s.p.), as AFI project. Appeared in Fast Times at Ridgemont High, Spies Like Us. Produced film: Josh and S.A.M.
PICTURES: Hot Tomorrows, Going in Style (also s.p.), Beverly Hills Cop, Midnight Run (also prod.), Scent of a Woman (also prod. 2 Academy Award nom. 1993), Meet Joe Black (also prod.), Gigli (also prod., writer).

BRICK, RICHARD A.

Producer. b. New York, NY, Sept. 20, 1945. e. New York University, B.A.; Columbia University, M.F.A. Chair, Columbia Univ., graduate film division, School of the Arts, 1992-94; Comm. of New York City Mayor's Office of Film, Theatre and Broadcasting, 1992-1994. Presently, ADJ Prof., Columbia Univ.; Board of Dir. for the Independent Feature Project, 1985-2001; chair 1995-96. Chairman/Founder Advisory Board for the Geri Ashur Screenwriting Award of the New York Foundation of the Arts, 1985-present. Member DGA 1981-present, Eastern AD/UPM/TC Council 2002-2004; Delegate to annual convention in 2003. PGA 1998-present. President, Silo Cinema, Inc., 1970-present.
PICTURES: Ragtime (unit mgr.), Part of the Family (prod. mgr), Andrea Doria: The Final Chapter (UPM, assoc. prod.), The Trials of Alger Hiss (UPM, assoc. prod.), Pilgrim...Farewell (prod. mgr.), Little Gloria...Happy at Last (unit prod. mgr), Silkwood (unit. prod. mgr.), Places in the Heart (unit prod. mgr.), Arizona Dream (co-prod.), Deconstructing Harry (co-prod.), Celebrity (co-prod.), Sweet and Lowdown (co-prod., UPM), Hangin' with the Homeboys (prod.), Caught (prod.), Chicago 10 (doc.), William Kunstler: Disturbing the Universe (cinematographer-archive footage).
TELEVISION: *Movies; As Prod. Mngr.:* Pilgrim, Farewell, Little Gloria... Happy at Last, Alexander Hamilton (DGA stage mngr.). *Documentaries:* Andrea Doria: The Final Chapter (assoc. prod.), Peter Jennings Reporting: The Kennedy Assassination - Beyond Conspiracy (senior prod., assoc. dir.), Peter Jennings Reporting: UFOs - Seeing Is Believing (senior prod., assoc. dir.), The American Experience (episode stage mngr.).

BRICKMAN, MARSHALL

Writer, Director. b. Rio de Janeiro, Brazil, Aug. 25, 1941. e. U. of Wisconsin. Banjoist, singer, writer with folk groups The Tarriers and The Journeymen before starting to write for TV. Appeared in films Funny and That's Adequate. Received the Ian McLellan Hunter Award 2006.
PICTURES: Co-writer (with Woody Allen): Sleeper (WGA nom. 1974), Annie Hall (Academy Award, 1978, Golden Globe nom. ; WGA Award 1978), Manhattan (Academy Award nom.; WGA nom. 1980), Manhattan Murder Mystery. *Dir./Writer:* Simon (dir. debut, 1980), Lovesick, The Manhattan Project (also prod.), For the Boys, The Cemetery Club, Manhattan Murder Mystery, Intersection, Super Size Me (doc., soundtrack performer).
TELEVISION: *Movies:* Ann in Blue (writer), The Muppet Show: Sex and Violence (writer), Sister Mary Explains It All (dir.). *Series Writer:* Candid Camera 1966, The Tonight Show 1966-70. *Specials:* Johnny Carson's Repertory Co. in an Evening of Comedy (1969), Woody Allen Special, Woody Allen Looks at 1967, A Decade Under the Influence, 50 Films to See Before You Die. *Prod.:* Dick Cavett Show (1970-72, Emmy Awards).

BRICKMAN, PAUL

Writer, Director. b. Chicago, IL, April 23, 1949. e. Claremont Men's Coll. Worked as camera asst., then story analyst at Paramount, Columbia, and Universal.
PICTURES: Handle With Care (assoc. prod., s.p.), The Bad News Bears in Breaking Training (s.p.), Risky Business (WGA nom. 1984), Deal of the Century (also co-exec. prod.), Men Don't Leave (co-s.p. only), True Crime (s.p.).
TELEVISION: *Movie:* Uprising (writer).

BRIDGES, BEAU

Actor, Director, Producer. r.n. Lloyd Vernet Bridges, III. b. Hollywood, CA, Dec. 9, 1941. e. UCLA; U. of Hawaii. Father was late actor Lloyd Bridges; brother is actor Jeff Bridges.
PICTURES: Has appeared in more than 45 pictures, incl.: Force of Evil (debut, 1948), No Minor Vices, The Red Pony, Zamba, The Explosive Generation, Village of the Giants, The Incident, For Love of Ivy (Golden Globe nom. 1969), Gaily Gaily, The Landlord, Adam's Woman, The Christian Licorice Store, Hammersmith Is Out, Child's Play, Your Three Minutes Are Up, Lovin' Molly, The Other Side of the Mountain, Dragonfly (One Summer Love), Swashbuckler, Two-Minute Warning, Greased Lightning, Norma Rae, The Fifth Musketeer, The Runner Stumbles, Silver Dream Racer, Honky Tonk Freeway, Night Crossing, Love Child, Heart Like a Wheel, The Hotel New Hampshire, The Killing Time, The Wild Pair (also dir.), Seven Hours to Judgment (also dir.), The Iron Triangle, Signs of Life, The Fabulous Baker Boys, The Wizard, Daddy's Dyin'...Who's Got the Will?, Married to It, Sidekicks, Jerry Maguire, Rocket Man, Meeting Daddy, The White River Kid, Sordid Lives, Smile, Rose and the Snake, Debating Robert Lee, The Ballad of Jack and Rose, Smile, Charlotte's Web, Americanizing Shelley, The Good German, Max Payne, Don't Fade Away, Dirty Politics, Rushlights, Columbus Circle, My Girlfriend's Boyfriend.
TELEVISION: *Movies:* Has appeared in more than 50 tv movies, incl.: The Man Without a Country, The Stranger Who Looks Like Me,

Medical Story, The Four Feathers, Shimmering Light, The President's Mistress, The Child Stealer, The Kid from Nowhere (also dir.), Outrage!, Fighting Choice, The Thanksgiving Promise (also dir., co-prod.), Everybody's Baby: The Rescue of Jessica McClure, Just Another Secret, Guess Who's Coming for Christmas?, Without Warning: The James Brady Story (Emmy Award, Golden Globe Award, 1992), Wildflower, Elvis and the Colonel, The Positively True Adventures of the Alleged Texas Cheerleader-Murdering Mom (Emmy Award, Golden Globe Award, 1994), Secret Sins of the Fathers (also dir.), Kissinger and Nixon (Emmy nom. 1996), Losing Chase (Golden Globe nom. 1997), The Defenders: Choice of Evils, The Defenders: Taking the First, Inherit the Wind (Emmy nom. 1999), Common Ground, Songs in Ordinary Time, The Christmas Secret, Sightings: Heartland Ghost, We Were the Mulvaneys (Emmy nom. 2002), Change of Heart, Out of the Ashes, Evel Knievel, 10.5: Apocalypse, Two Families, Family Practice. *Mini-series:* Benjamin Franklin, Space, The Second Civil War (Emmy Award, 1997), P.T. Barnum (Emmy nom. 2000), Voyage of the Unicorn, 10.5: Apocalypse, Into the West. *Series:* Ensign O'Toole, United States, Harts of the West, Maximum Bob, My Name Is Earl (Emmy nom. 2007), The Agency, Stargate: Atlantis, Stargate SG-1, Desperate Housewives (Emmy nom. 2009 as guest). *Specials:* 5 American Kids - 5 American Handguns (Emmy nom. 1995), Hidden in America (Emmy nom. 1997). *Guest:* More than 160 appearances.

BRIDGES, JEFF

Actor, Producer. b. Los Angeles, CA, Dec. 4, 1949. Appeared as infant in 1950 film The Company She Keeps. Made acting debut at eight in the TV series Sea Hunt starring his father, Lloyd Bridges. Studied acting at Herbert Berghof Studio, NY. Mil. service in Coast Guard reserves. Brother is actor-dir-prod. Beau Bridges. Composed and performed song for film John and Mary. Named Male Star of the Year (1990) by NATO.
PICTURES: Halls of Anger (debut, 1970), The Yin and Yang of Mr. Go, The Last Picture Show (Acad. Award nom. 1972), Fat City, Bad Company, The Iceman Cometh, The Last American Hero, Lolly-Madonna XXX, Thunderbolt and Lightfoot (Acad. Award nom. 1975), Hearts of the West, Rancho Deluxe, Stay Hungry, King Kong, Somebody Killed Her Husband, The American Success Company, Winter Kills, Heaven's Gate, Cutter's Way, Tron, Kiss Me Goodbye, Against All Odds, Starman (Acad. Award nom., Golden Globe nom. 1985), Jagged Edge, 8 Million Ways to Die, The Morning After, Nadine, Tucker: The Man and His Dream, See You in the Morning, Cold Feet, The Fabulous Baker Boys, Texasville, The Fisher King (Golden Globe nom. 1992), The Vanishing, American Heart (also co-prod.), Fearless, Blown Away, Wild Bill, White Squall, The Mirror Has Two Faces, The Big Lebowski, Arlington Road, A Soldier's Daughter Never Cries, The Muse, Simpatico, The Contender (Academy Award nom., Golden Globe nom. 2001), K-PAX, Scenes of the Crime, Masked & Anonymous, Seabiscuit, The Door in the Floor, The Moguls, Tideland, The Giver (also prod.), Stick It, Surf's Up (voice), A Dog Year, Pablo (narr.), Iron Man, How to Lose Friends & Alienate People, The Open Road, Crazy Heart (also exec. prod., Academy Award nom.; Golden Globe Award 2010), The Men Who Stare at Goats, Tron Legacy, True Grit.
TELEVISION: *Movies:* Silent Night-Lonely Night, In Search of America, Hidden in America (also exec. prod.), Raising the Mammoth (narr., tv doc.). *Special:* Faerie Tale Theatre (Rapunzel). *Guest:* More than 108 appearances.

BRIGHT, KEVIN

Producer, Director. b. 1955.
TELEVISION: *Movies:* Viva Shaf Vegas (prod.), Couples (exec. prod.). *Series:* Madame's Place (assoc. prod), In Living Color (Emmy Award 1990), Dream On (prod. only), Friends (exec. prod., dir. Emmy Award 2002, 5 Emmy nom.), Veronica's Closet (exec. prod., dir.), Jesse (exec. prod., dir.) AG, Joey (dir. pilot, co-exec. prod). *Special:* Young Comedians All-Star Reunion (prod.).

BRIGHT, RICHARD S.

Executive, Producer. b. New Rochelle, NY, Feb. 28, 1936. e. Hotchkiss Sch., 1953-54; Wharton Sch. of Finance, U. of Pennsylvania, 1954-58. With U.S. Army Finance Corp., 1959-60. Was corporate exec. prior to founding Persky-Bright Organization in 1973, private investment group to finance films. In 2004, Bright founded Sun MediaWorks, a vertically integrated film finance, development and production company based in New York, NY.
THEATRE: A History of the American Film, Album (co-prod.).
PICTURES: Last Detail, Golden Voyage of Sinbad, For Pete's Sake, California Split, The Man Who Would Be King, Funny Lady, The Front, and Equus. Financing/production services for: Hard Times, Taxi Driver, Missouri Breaks, Bound for Glory, Sinbad and the Eye of the Tiger, Hair, Body Heat, Still of the Night. *Exec. prod.:* Tribute.
TELEVISION: The President's Mistress (co-prod.).

BRIMLEY, WILFORD

Actor. b. Salt Lake City, UT, Sept. 27, 1924. Formerly a blacksmith, ranch hand and racehorse trainer; began in films as an extra and stuntman. Also acted as A. Wilford Brimley. Original member of L.A. Actors Theatre.
PICTURES: True Grit, Lawman, The China Syndrome, The Electric Horseman, Brubaker, Borderline, Absence of Malice, Death Valley, The Thing, Tender Mercies, Tough Enough, High Road to China, 10 to Midnight, Hotel New Hampshire, Harry and Son, The Stone Boy, The Natural, Country, Cocoon, Remo Williams: The Adventure Begins, American Justice, End of the Line, Cocoon: The Return, Eternity, The Firm, Hard Target, Last of the Dogmen, My Fellow Americans, In & Out, Summer of the Monkeys, All My Friends are Cowboys, Progeny, Comanche, Brigham City, The Round and Round, The Road Home, The Path of the Wind, Did You Hear About the Morgans?.
TELEVISION: *Movies:* The Oregon Trail, The Wild Wild West Revisited, Amber Waves, Roughnecks, Rodeo Girl, The Big Black Pill, Ewoks: The Battle for Endor, Murder in Space, Thompson's Last Run, Act of Vengeance, Gore Vidal's Billy the Kid, Blood River, Tom Clancy's Op Center, Crossfire Trail, The Ballad of Lucy Whipple. *Series:* Our House, Boys of Twilight.

BRISKMAN, LOUIS

Executive. e. graduate, Univ. of Pittsburgh, 1970; graduate of Georgetown Univ. Law Center, 1973. Briskman joined Westinghouse Electric Corporation in 1975, became gen. counsel of the company's broadcasting subsidiary, known as Group W, in 1983, and rose to gen. counsel of the parent corp., Westinghouse Electric Corporation, in 1993. He served in that role through the company's transformation into a pure media entity, which culminated in the acquisition of CBS in 1995 and the name change to CBS Corporation, in 1997, where he continued his service as gen. counsel and exec. v.p. Briskman was most recently senior v.p. and gen. counsel of Aetna Inc., where he has served since April of 2004. Briskman returned to CBS in Sept. 2005 as exec. v.p. and gen. counsel of CBS and currently oversees all legal activities for CBS Corporation.

BRITT, GLENN A.

Executive. B.A., economics, Dartmouth College (magna cum laude), 1971. M.B.A., Amos Tuck School of Business Administration, Dartmouth College, 1972. Also member of Phi Beta Kappa. Joined Time Inc., 1972, in controller's dept. and rose, successively, to v.p.-treasurer of Manhattan Cable Television, Inc., 1974; finance director for Time-Life Books Iran Project, 1977; v.p.-network and studio operations for Home Box Office, Inc. (HBO), and director of business development of Time Inc.'s video group, 1980. Britt was elected v.p. of Time Inc. in October 1986 and treasurer the following month. He became vice president - CFO of Time Inc. in February 1988 before the merger between Time Inc. and Warner Communications. After the merger, he became senior v.p.-treasurer of Time Warner Inc. and in 1990 became executive v.p., Time Warner Cable (then called American Television & Communications). Britt became president of Time Warner Cable (TWC) in Jan. 1999. Previously, he served as pres. and CEO of Time Warner Cable Ventures, the company's new business arm. Oversaw launch of Road Runner, the country's first high-speed Internet service, as well as the creation of Time Warner Telecom, a fast-growing provider of local telecommunications services. Britt became the cable operator's chief exec. in Aug. 2001 and was named Chairman, Pres. and CEO of TWC in Feb. 2006. TWC is the number two U.S. cable company, after Comcast. It has 14.4 million subscribers, including more than 5.4 million digital video customers. Britt serves on the bd. of the National Cable & Telecommunications Association (NCTA) and is a member of the Executive Committee. He is also a bd. member of the Walter Kaitz Foundation and a member of the bd. of directors of Xerox Corporation.

BRITTANY, MORGAN

Actress. r.n. Suzanne Cupito. b. Hollywood, CA, Dec. 5, 1951.
PICTURES: Gypsy, The Birds, Marnie, Yours Mine and Ours, Gable and Lombard, Sundown: The Vampire in Retreat, The Prodigal, Last Action Hero, The Saint, Riders in the Storm, The Protector, Legend of the Spirit Dog, The Chocolate Fairy, The Biggest Fan, Americanizing Shelley. Has acted in many videos.
TELEVISION: *Movies:* Amazing Howard Hughes, Delta County U.S.A., The Initiation of Sarah, Samurai, Fantastic Seven, Death Car on the Freeway, The Dream Merchants, Moviola: The Scarlett O'Hara War, The Wild Women of Chastity Gulch, LBJ: The Early Years, Perry Mason: The Case of the Scandalous Scoundrel, Favorite Deadly Sins. *Series:* Dallas, Glitter. *Guest:* More than 75 appearances.

BROADBENT, JIM

Actor, Writer. b. Lincolnshire, England, May 24, 1949. Member of the National Theatre and the Royal Shakespeare Company. Wrote and starred in short film, A Sense of History (Clermont-Ferrand Intl. Film Fest. Award).
THEATRE: The Recruiting Officer, A Winter's Tale, The Government Inspector, A Flea in Her Ear, Goose Pimples, Theatre of Blood (London).
PICTURES: The Shout (debut, 1978), The Passage, Breaking Glass, The Dogs of War, Time Bandits, Brazil, The Good Father, Superman IV: The Quest for Peace, Life Is Sweet, Enchanted April, The Crying Game, Widow's Peak, Princess Caraboo, Bullets Over Broadway, Rough Magic, The Secret Agent, Richard III, The Borrowers, Little Voice, The Avengers, Topsy Turvey, Bridget Jones's Diary, Moulin Rouge (BAFTA Award for best actor/supp. role, 2002), Iris (Academy Award/Golden Globe, best actor/supp. role, 2002), Gangs of New York, Nicholas Nickleby, Bright Young Things, Around the World in 80 Days, Tooth (voice),

Vanity Fair, Bridget Jones: The Edge of Reason, Valiant (voice), Tulip Fever, Robots (voice), The Magic Roundabout (voice), The Chronicles of Narnia: The Lion, the Witch & the Wardrobe, Art School Confidential, Free Jimmy (voice), The Other Side, And When Did You Last See Your Father?, The Young Victoria, Indiana Jones and the Kingdom of the Crystal Skull, Harry Potter and the Half-Blood Prince, Inkheart, Perrier's Bounty, The Young Victoria, The Damned United, Another Year, Harry Potter and the Deathly Hallows: Part II.
TELEVISION: *Movies:* Bird of Prey, Birth Of A Nation, Silas Marner: The Weaver of Raveloe, Blackadder's Christmas Carol, Work!, Wide-Eyed and Legless, The Last Englishman, The Gathering Storm (Emmy nom., Golden Globe nom. 2002), And Starring Pancho Villa as Himself, The Young Visiters (also exec. prod.), Pride (voice), Longford (Emmy nom. 2007, Golden Globe Award 2008), Einstein and Eddington. *Series:* Only Fools and Horses, Gone to Seed, The Boss, The Street. *Guest:* More than 80 appearances.

BROCKMAN, KEVIN

Executive. B.S. degree in organizational behavior, Univ. of Florida. Brockman began ent. career in theatrical publicity and then moved to Radio City Music Hall Productions (RCMHP) in New York City as its PR mgr., overseeing all aspects of media relations and corporate comm. He was responsible for the PR campaigns of more than 350 live concerts and theatricals and he also handled communication campaigns for numerous TV specials and corporate events, including the Super Bowl XXVII Half-Time Show starring Michael Jackson. Brockman began his career in TV communications as the director of PR, marketing and on-air promo for Fox Television Stations Productions (FTSP), a development division of FOX, Inc. He was part of the senior exec. team that successfully launched the UPN network in Jan. 1995 with responsibility for all corporate and ent. communications. Brockman joined The Walt Disney Company from UPN in 1997, and has served in senior exec. communication roles ever since: 2000-2004, senior v.p., ent. comm., ABC Television Network; Sept. 2004-May 2005, senior v.p., ent. comm., Disney/ABC Television Group; May 2005-March 2008, senior v.p., communications, Disney/ABC Television Group; March 2008-present, executive v.p. global communications, Disney-ABC Television Group. In his current role he oversees all corporate, news and ent. communication efforts worldwide on behalf of the Disney/ABC Television Group, which is comprised of the ABC Television Network (which includes ABC Daytime, ABC News and ABC Entertainment); Disney Channels Worldwide, cable networks ABC Family and SOAPnet; Radio Disney; Walt Disney Television Animation; Buena Vista Productions; ABC Studios; international distributor Disney-ABC-ESPN Television, the publishing unit Hyperion and ABC Corporate Initiatives. In addition Brockman is responsible for the group's photography, broadcast publicity, ratings publicity and talent relations activities, and is involved in corporate communications for ABC's 10 owned television stations.

BROCKMAN, MICHAEL

Executive. b. Brooklyn, NY, Nov. 19, 1938. e. Ithaca Coll. Became v.p., daytime programming, ABC Entertainment, 1974; later v.p., tape prod. operations and admin. Left to become v.p., daytime programs, NBC Entertainment, 1977-1980. Became v.p. programs, Lorimar Prods. 1980-82; v.p. daytime and children's prog. CBS Entertainment, 1982-89. 1986, title changed to v.p. daytime, children's and late night. Became pres. ABC daytime, children's & late night entertainment 1989-90. Joined Mark Goodson Prods. as v.p. 1991. Became sr. v.p. in 1993. Pres., M. Brockman Broadcast Inc., 1995-Present. Appointed by Ca. gov. to the Ca. Lottery Commission in 2001 for two-year term; He is a member of the National Academy of Television Arts and Sciences and the Pacific Pioneer Broadcasters.

BRODERICK, MATTHEW

Actor, Producer, Director. b. New York, NY, Mar. 21, 1962. Son of late actor James Broderick and writer-dir./artist Patricia Broderick. m. actress Sarah Jessica Parker. Acted in a workshop prod. of Horton Foote's Valentine's Day with his father (1979).
THEATRE: *NY:* Torch Song Trilogy, Brighton Beach Memoirs (Tony & Theatre World Awards, 1983), Biloxi Blues, The Widow Claire, How to Succeed in Business Without Really Trying (Tony Award, 1995), The Producers, The Odd Couple, The Philanthropist.
PICTURES: Max Dugan Returns (debut, 1983), WarGames, Ladyhawke, 1918, On Valentine's Day, Ferris Bueller's Day Off (Golden Globe nom. 1987), Project X, Biloxi Blues, Torch Song Trilogy, Glory, Family Business, The Freshman, Out on a Limb, The Night We Never Met, The Lion King (voice), The Road to Wellville, Mrs. Parker and the Vicious Circle, Infinity (also dir., co-prod.), The Cable Guy, Infinity (also dir., prod.), Addicted to Love, Lion King II: Simba's Pride (voice), Godzilla, Election, Inspector Gadget, Walking to the Waterline, You Can Count On Me, Good Boy!, Providence, The Last Shot, The Stepford Wives, Strangers with Candy, The Producers, Margaret, Bee Movie (voice), Deck the Halls, Then She Found Me, Finding Amanda, Wonderful World, Diminished Capacity, The Tale of Despereaux (voice), Margaret.
TELEVISION: *Movies:* Master Harold... and the Boys, A Life in the Theater, The Music Man, Shelley Duvall's Faerie Tale Theatre: Cinderella. *Mini-series:* Jazz (voice), The West, A Life in the Theater (Emmy nom. 1994). *Documentary:* Freedom: A History of Us. *Guest:* More than 84 appearances.

BRODY, ADRIEN

Actor. b. New York, NY, April 14, 1973 e. American Academy of Dramatic Arts and High School for the Performing Arts.
PICTURES: New York Stories, King of the Hill, Angels in the Outfield, Solo, Bullet, The Last Time I Committed Suicide, The Undertaker's Wedding, Six Ways to Sunday, Restaurant, The Thin Red Line, Summer of Sam, Oxygen, Liberty Heights, Bread and Roses, Harrison's Flowers, Love the Hard Way, The Affair of the Necklace, Dummy, The Pianist (Acad. Award, best actor/leading role, Golden Globe nom. 2003), The Singing Detective, The Village, The Jacket, King Kong, Truth, Justice, and the American Way, Hollywoodland, Manolete, The Darjeeling Limited, The Brothers Bloom, Cadillac Records, Giallo (also exec. prod.), Splice, High School, The Experiment, Fantastic Mr. Fox (voice), Wrecked (also exec. prod.), Predators.
TELEVISION: *Movies:* Home at Last, Jailbreakers. *Series:* Annie McGuire. *Guest:* More than 60 appearances.

BROKAW, CARY

Executive, Producer. b. Los Angeles, CA, June 21, 1951. e. Univ. of CA/Berkeley, UCLA Grad. School. Worked several positions at 20th Century Fox before serving as exec. v.p. for Cineplex Odeon Corp. 1983, became co-chmn., pres. of Island Alive; 1985, became co-chmn., pres. & CEO of Island Pictures. 1987, formed Avenue Pictures; In 1991, he founded and is currently Pres./CEO Avenue Entertainment Group, which includes Avenue Pictures, an independent motion picture prod. company, Avenue Pictures Television, a producer of made-for-TV movies, mini-series and movies for cable TV, and Wombat Productions, a producer of Hollywood Star profile programs.
PICTURES: *Executive prod.:* Trouble in Mind, Down by Law, Nobody's Fool, Slamdance, Pascali's Island, Signs of Life, Cold Feet, Drugstore Cowboy, After Dark My Sweet, The Object of Beauty, Sex Drugs Rock & Roll, The Player, American Heart, Normal. *Producer:* Short Cuts, Restoration, Voices From a Locked Room, Finding Graceland, Stand by Your Man, Wayward Son, Mindhunters, The Closer, The Merchant of Venice, Sex and Death 101, The Resident.
TELEVISION: *Movies: Exec. prod.:* In the Eyes of a Stranger, Amelia Earhart: The Final Flight (prod.), See Jane Run, Stranger in Town, Two Mothers for Zachary. Tell Me No Secrets, The Almost Perfect Bank Robbery, Path to Paradise: Untold Story of the WTC Bombing, Thrill Seekers, Wit (Emmy Award, 2001), Path to War (Emmy nom., 2002), Normal (Emmy nom., 2003). *Mini-series:* Angels in America (Emmy Award, 2004), The Company. *Series:* The Virgin of Akron, OH.

BROKAW, NORMAN R.

Executive. b. New York, NY, April 21, 1927. Joined William Morris Agency (WMA) as trainee in 1943; company's first junior agent, 1948; sr. agent, company exec. in m.p. and TV, 1951; He was an architect of WMA's TV dept. on the West Coast. Brokaw guided wary Hollywood into the TV business. He brought Loretta Young and other stars to TV, creating new and lucrative opportunities for these players and has been the agent of entertainment legend Bill Cosby for more than 35 years. In the 1970s, Brokaw spearheaded the agency's entry into the unexplored fields of sports, journalism and politics. The list of those represented in such areas include presidents, international leaders, cabinet members, Olympic medalists, newscasters, and sports stars. In 1974, became v.p., WMA-Worldwide. 1981, named exec. v.p. & member. of bd., WMA-Worldwide; 1986, named co-chmn. of bd., WMA-Worldwide. 1989, named pres. & CEO, William Morris Inc. Worldwide. Currently Brokaw is company chairman Emeritus of William Morris Endeavor Entertainment. Brokaw lives in Beverly Hills, CA, and makes monthly trips to WMA's New York office. He serves on the bd. of Cedars-Sinai Medical Center and St. Judes California Foundation and is pres. and founder of the Betty Ford Cancer Center. He is a longstanding member of the Academy of Motion Picture Arts and Sciences. Received Governor's Award 2010 from Creative Arts Emmy's.

BROKAW, TOM

TV Newsman, Anchorman, Host. b. Yankton, S.D., Feb. 6, 1940, e. U. of South Dakota. Newscaster, weatherman, staff announcer KTIV, Sioux City, IA, 1960-62. Joined KMTV, NBC affiliate in Omaha, in 1962; 1965, joined WSB-TV, Atlanta. Worked in L.A. bureau of NBC News, anchored local news shows for KNBC, NBC station (1966-73). In 1973 named NBC News' White House correspondent; was anchor of NBC Saturday Night News. Named host of Today Show in August, 1976. In 1982 co-anchor, NBC Nightly News; sole anchor since 1983. Anchor of "The Brokaw Report," a series of prime-time specials, 1992-1993. Co-anchor NBC newsmagazine series, "Now With Tom Brokaw & Katie Couric," 1993-94. Earned the Alfred I. DuPont-Columbia U. award for excellence in broadcast journalism for Dateline NBC Special Report examining racial separation in U.S. suburbs, 1997. WGA nom. for Dateline NBC 2000. Recipient of numerous awards, including seven Emmy awards, inducted into Broadcasting & Cable's TV Hall of Fame,

1997. He retired from anchor duties at NBC, Dec. 2004 and currently serves as a consulting prod. In Dec. 2006, Brokaw was inducted into the Academy of Television Arts & Sciences' Hall of Fame in L.A. Brokaw is also an accomplished writer; his work has appeared in The New York Times, The Washington Post, The Los Angeles Times, Newsweek, Life, among others.
AUTHOR: The Greatest Generation, The Greatest Generation Speaks.
TELEVISION: *Mini-series:* Tanner on Tanner, Brokaw Reports: 58 Days (also writer).

BROLIN, JAMES
Actor, Producer, Director. b. Los Angeles, CA, July 18, 1940. r.n. James Bruderlin. e. UCLA. Son is actor Josh Brolin. m. Barbra Streisand. Debut in Bus Stop (TV series); named most promising actor of 1970 by Fame and Photoplay magazines. Winner, Emmy and Golden Globe Awards.
PICTURES: Take Her She's Mine (debut, 1963), John Goldfarb Please Come Home, Goodbye Charlie, Dear Brigitte, Von Ryan's Express, Morituri, Fantastic Voyage, Way... Way Out, The Cape Town Affair, Our Man Flint, The Boston Strangler, Skyjacked, Westworld, Gable and Lombard, The Car, Capricorn One, The Amityville Horror, Night of the Juggler, High Risk, Pee-wee's Big Adventure, Bad Jim, Super High Score, Ted & Venus, Gas Food Lodging, Cheatin' Hearts (also exec. prod.), Back Stab, Savate, Relative Fear, Parallel Lives, Indecent Bahavior, The Expert, Tracks of a Killer, Lewis and Clark and George, Blood Money, My Brother's War, Haunted Sea, Goodbye America, Lewis & Clark & George, My Brother's War (also dir.), Haunted Sea, Traffic, Master of Disguise, Catch Me If You Can, A Guy Thing, Lies & Alibis, The Hunting Party, Mysterious, Last Chance Harvey, Escape (prod. only), The Goods: Live Hard, Sell Hard, Nailed, Last Will, A Fonder Heart, The American Standards (also prod.), Love, Wedding, Marriage, Angel Camouflaged.
TELEVISION: *Movies:* Marcus Welby M.D., Short Walk to Daylight, Class of '63, Trapped, Steel Cowboys, The Ambush Murders, Mae West, White Water Rebels, Cowboy, Beverly Hills Cowgirl Blues, Hold the Dream, Intimate Encounters, Voice of the Heart, Finish Line, Nightmare on the 13th Floor, And the Sea Will Tell, Deep Dark Secrets, The Sands of Time, Visions of Murder, Gunsmoke: The Long Ride, The Calling, Parallel Lives, A Perry Mason Mystery: The Case of the Grimacing Governor, Terminal Virus, A Marriage of Convenience, To Love Honor and Betray, Children of Fortune, The Reagans (Emmy nom., Golden Globe nom. 2004), Widow on the Hill, Category 7: The End of the World, Wedding Wars, Reinventing the Wheelers, Lost City Raiders. *Special:* City Boy (PBS), Body Human 2000: Love Sex & the Miracle of Birth. *Director:* Hotel (12 episodes), The Young Riders, Hijacked: Flight 285, Pensacola Wings of Gold (also exec. prod.), Beyond Belief, Fact or Fiction. *Series:* Marcus Welby M.D. (Emmy Award, 1970, 3 nom., Golden Globe Awards 1971, 1973, 1 nom. 1972), Hotel (2 Emmy nom. 1985), Angel Falls, Extreme, World of Discovery, Pensacola: Wings of Gold (also dir., exec. prod.), Beyond Belief: Fact or Fiction (host). *Guest:* More than 113 appearances.

BROLIN, JOSH
Actor. b. Los Angeles, CA, Feb. 12, 1968. Father is actor James Brolin. m. actress Diane Lane.
PICTURES: The Goonies, Bed of Roses, Flirting with Disaster, Nightwatch, Mimic, The Mod Squad, Best Laid Plans, All the Rage, Hollow Man, Coastlines, Milwaukee, Minnesota, Melinda and Melinda, Into the Blue, The Dead Girl, Grindhouse, No Country for Old Men, In the Valley of Elah, American Gangster, Milk (Academy Award nom. 2009), W., The People Speak (doc., also prod.), Jonah Hex, Cartel, Wall Street: Money Never Sleeps, You Will Meet a Tall Dark Stranger, True Grit.
TELEVISION: *Movies:* Private Eye (pilot), Prison for Children, Finish Line, Picnic. *Mini-series:* Into the West. *Series:* Private Eye, The Young Riders, Winnetka Road, Mister Sterling. *Guest:* More than 60 appearances.

BROMSTAD, ANGELA
Executive. b. Cardiff-by-the-Sea, CA, Aug. 26, 1961. e. B.A., theatre, Southern Methodist Univ., 1983. Bromstad began her career as an asst. at Telepictures Productions after college. She moved to Freyda Rothstein Productions (in association with Hearst Entertainment) and was its director of creative affairs from 1988-91; v.p., creative affairs from 1991-94. Bromstad joined NBC in May 1994, starting her more than two-decade association with NBC as director, mini-series and motion pictures for TV and was soon promoted to v.p., mini-series and motion pictures. Since Oct. 1996, Bromstad had held a similar position as v.p, mini-series and television, NBC Entertainment. She was v.p. mini-series and television, 1996-97; at NBC Studios she was v.p., mini-series and motion pictures, 1997-99. She shifted to v.p., primetime series for NBC Studios in 1999, and worked on audience favorites Ed, Providence and Profiler. In 2000, Bromstad served as v.p., drama development, NBC Entertainment. She rose to senior v.p., drama development for NBC Entertainment and nurtured the successful dramas such as the Peabody Award-winning Boomtown, American Dreams and Kingpin (all for NBC). In June 2003, she ascended to executive v.p., NBC Studios. Following NBC's acquisition of Universal Entertainment in May 2004, Bromstad was co-president, NBC Universal Television Studio, for one year. In March 2005, she was named sole president of NBC Universal Television Studio and held the post until May 2007. In July 2007, she was tapped to become president of international TV production at NBC Universal Media Studios, based in London. 2009 she became president, Prime Time Ent., NBC Universal Media Studios. She was named to Hollywood Reporter's Power 100 Women in Entertainment (#15) in Dec. 2006.

BRON, ELEANOR
Actress, Writer. b. Stanmore, Middlesex, England, March 14, 1934. Started career in Establishment Club, London, and on American tour. Leading lady on British TV show Not So Much a Programme—More a Way of Life. Author of Double Take, The Pillowbook of Eleanor Bron, Life and Other Punctures. Translator of Desdemona—If You Had Only Spoken, by Christine Bruckner.
THEATRE: The Doctor's Dilemma, Howards End, The Prime of Miss Jean Brodie, Hedda Gabler, The Duchess of Malfi, The Madwoman of Chaillot, Uncle Vanya, A Delicate Balance, A Perfect Ganesh, The Cherry Orchard, A Month In the Country.
PICTURES: Help!, Alfie, Two for the Road, Bedazzled, The Turtle Diary, Thank You All Very Much, Women in Love, The Millstone, Little Dorrit, Black Beauty, A Little Princess, Saint-Ex, Deadly Advice, Black Beauty, A Little Princess, Saint-Ex, The House of Mirth, Iris, The Heart of Me, Wimbledon, StreetDance 3D.
TELEVISION: *Movies:* Cucumber Castle, Pleasure at Her Majesty's, Emily (writer), The Day Christ Died, The Hound of the Baskervilles, Quartermaine's Terms, The Attic: The Hiding of Anne Frank, Intrigue, Friends in Space, Micky Love, The Blue Boy, Wyrd Sisters Ted and Alice. *Mini-series:* Ruth Rendell: The Strawberry Tree, Vanity Fair. *Series:* Not So Much a Programme, The Late Show (also writer), More a Way of Life (writer), Where Was Spring? (also co-wrote), World in Ferment, Beyond A Joke (also writer), Six Days of Justice (writer), After That, This (writer), Making Faces, Pinkerton's Progress, Fat Friends, Casualty 1909. *Guest:* More than 80 appearances.

BRONFMAN, EDGAR, JR.
Executive. b. May 16, 1955. Joined Seagram 1982 as asst. to office of the pres.; served as managing dir. of Seagram Europe until he was appointed pres. of The House of Seagram, 1984-88; became pres. & COO in 1989. June 1994 named pres. & CEO of The Seagram Company Ltd. Upon acquisition of MCA Inc. was named acting chairman, 1995. Bronfman was appointed executive vice chmn., Vivendi Universal, in December 2000. He resigned March 31, 2002, and resigned as vice chmn. of Vivendi Universal's bd. of directors on December 2, 2003. Bronfman and a group of investors purchased Warner Music Group from Time Warner in 2004, and Bronfman assumed his current position, chairman & CEO. He also serves as general partner at Accretive Technology Partners, LLC, a venture capital firm specializing in the business process outsourcing area. Before joining Warner Music Group, Bronfman was top exec. at Lexa Partners LLC, a management venture capital group based in New York City. Bronfman serves on the boards of InterActiveCorp; Fandango, the leading on-line movie ticketing company in the U.S.; New York University Medical Center; and the bd. of governors of The Joseph H. Lauder Institute of Management and International Studies at the Univ. of Pennsylvania. He is also chmn. of the bd. of Endeavor Global, a non-profit organization pioneering a new approach to international development, and is a member of JPMorgan's National Advisory Board.

BROOKS, ALBERT
Director, Writer, Actor. r.n. Albert Einstein. b. Los Angeles, CA, July 22, 1947. e. Carnegie Tech. Son of late comedian Harry Einstein (Parkyakarkus). Brother is performer Bob Einstein. Sports writer KMPC, L.A. 1962-63. Recordings: Comedy Minus One, A Star is Bought (Grammy nom.).
PICTURES: Taxi Driver, Real Life (also dir., co-s.p.), Private Benjamin, Modern Romance (also dir., co-s.p.), Twilight Zone—The Movie, Terms of Endearment (voice), Unfaithfully Yours, Lost in America (also dir., co-s.p.), Broadcast News (Academy Award nom. 1988), Defending Your Life (also dir., s.p.), I'll Do Anything, The Scout (also co-s.p.), Mother (also dir.; NY Society of Film Critics Award, Natl Society of Film Critics Award for best s.p., 1997), Doctor Dolittle (voice), Out of Sight, The Muse, My First Mister (actor), Til Death Do Us Part, Finding Nemo (voice), The In-Laws, Looking for Comedy in the Muslim World (dir., writer), The Simpsons Movie (voice).
TELEVISION: *Series:* Dean Martin Presents the Golddiggers, Saturday Night Live (writer, 1975), Hot Wheels (voices), The Associates (wrote theme song), Weeds. *Specials:* Milton Berle's Mad Mad Mad World of Comedy, General Electric's All-Star Anniversary. *Guest:* More than 43 appearances.

BROOKS, JAMES L.
Director, Producer, Writer. b. North Bergen, NJ, May 9, 1940. e. NYU. Copyboy for CBS News, N.Y.; promoted to newswriter. 1965 moved to L.A. to work for David Wolper's documentary prod. co. In 1969 conceived idea for series, Room 222; formed partnership with fellow writer Allan Burns. Together they created Mary Tyler Moore Show in 1970. 1977, established prod. co. on Paramount lot with other writers, producing and creating the series, The Associates and Taxi. Formed Gracie Films.

Directed play Brooklyn Laundry in L.A. American Cinema Editors, USA, Golden Eddie Filmmaker of the Year Award 2005. Received WGA Herb Sargent Award 2006.
PICTURES: Real Life (actor), Starting Over (s.p., co-prod.), Modern Romance (actor), Terms of Endearment (dir., prod., s.p.; 3 Academy. Awards for Best Picture, Dir. and Screenplay, Golden Globe Award, Golden Globe nom. 1984), Broadcast News (dir., prod., s.p. 2 Academy Award nom.; 2 Golden Globe nom. 1988), Big (co-prod.), Say Anything... (exec. prod.), The War of the Roses (co-prod.), I'll Do Anything (dir., prod., s.p.), Bottle Rocket, Jerry Maguire (Academy Award nom. 1997), As Good As It Gets (dir., s.p. 2 Academy Award nom.; 2 Golden Globe nom. 1998), Riding in Cars with Boys (prod.), Spanglish, (prod., writer, dir.), The Simpsons Movie (exec. prod., writer, s.p.).
TELEVISION: *Movies:* Thursday's Game (writer, prod., 1971). *Series:* The Mary Tyler Moore Show (co-creator, writer, exec. prod.; 2 Emmy Awards for writing: 1971, 1977; 10 Emmy Awards as exec. prod., 10 Emmy noms.), Rhoda (writer, prod.), The New Lorenzo Music Show (writer), Lou Grant (co-exec. prod. Emmy nom. 1978). *Series (co-creator, and/or exec. prod.):* Taxi (3 Emmy Awards as exec. prod.; 2 Emmy noms.), Cindy, The Associates, Cheers, Tracey Ullman Show (3 Emmy Awards as exec. prod., 7 Emmy noms.), The Simpsons (10 Emmy Awards as exec. prod.: 7 Emmy noms.), Phenom (exec. prod.), The Critic (exec. prod.), What About Joan (exec. prod.).

BROOKS, MEL
Writer, Director, Actor. r.n. Melvin Kaminsky. b. Brooklyn, NY, June 28, 1926. m. late actress Anne Bancroft. e. VA Military Inst. 1944. U.S. Army combat engineer 1944-46. As child, did impressions and was amateur drummer and pianist. First appearance as actor in play Separate Rooms in Red Bank, NJ. Was also social dir. of Grossinger's Resort in the Catskills. Became writer for Sid Caesar on TV's Broadway Review and Your Show of Shows. Teamed with Carl Reiner for comedy record albums: The 2000 Year Old Man, The 2000 and 13-Year-Old Man. Founded Brooksfilms Ltd., 1981. Won Academy Award for Best Short Subject (animated): The Critic (dir., s.p., narrator). Co-writer of Shinbone Alley. Received WGA Laurel Award for Screen Writing Achievement 2003.
THEATRE: *Writer:* New Faces (also prod.), Shinbone Alley (book, also prod.), All-American (book, also prod.), The Producers (Tony Award for Best Musical, Best Book of A Musical and Best Original Score, 2001).
PICTURES: New Faces (co-s.p.), The Producers (dir., s.p.; Academy Award for Best Original Screenplay, Golden Globe nom. 1968), The Twelve Chairs (dir., s.p., actor), Blazing Saddles (dir., co-s.p., actor, Academy Award nom. 1975), Young Frankenstein (dir., co-s.p.; Acad. Award nom. for s.p. 1975), Silent Movie (dir., co-s.p., actor, Golden Globe nom. 1977), Frances (exec.-prod), High Anxiety (dir., prod., co-s.p., actor, Golden Globe nom. 1978), The Muppet Movie (actor), History of the World Part 1 (dir., prod., s.p., actor, lyrics), To Be or Not To Be (exec-prod., actor), Spaceballs (dir., prod., co-s.p., actor), , Look Who's Talking Too (voice), Life Stinks (dir., prod., co-s.p., actor), Robin Hood: Men in Tights (dir., prod., co-s.p., actor), The Silence of the Hams (actor), The Little Rascals (actor), Dracula: Dead and Loving It (dir., prod., co-s.p., actor), The Prince of Egypt (voice), Svitati (actor, s.p.), Screwloose, Robots (voice), *Exec. Prod.:* The Elephant Man, My Favorite Year, The Doctor and the Devils, The Fly, 84 Charing Cross Road, Solarbabies, The Vagrant, The Fly II, Hail Sid Caesar, Robots (voice), The Producers (writer/s.p., prod., composer, lyricist, stage prod. Golden Globe nom. 2005), Get Smart (writer, creator, consult.).
TELEVISION: *Movies:* Free to Be... You & Me (voice), The Muppets Go Hollywood, The 2000 Year Old Man (voice/writer), It's a Very Merry Muppet Christmas Movie (voice). *Series:* Caesar's Hour (Emmy nom. 1956), Get Smart (co-creator, co-writer, Emmy nom. 1966), When Things Were Rotten (co-creator, co- writer, prod.), The Nutt House (prod., co-writer) Get Smart (1995, writer/characters), Jakers! The Adventures of Piggley Winks (voice, Emmy nom 2005), Spaceballs: The Animated Series (actor, writer, creator). *Specials:* The Sid Caesar-Imogene Coca-Carl Reiner-Howard Morris Special (co-writer; Emmy Award, 1967), I am Your Child, Pretty As A Picture: The Art of David Lynch, Intimate Portrait: Madeline Kahn, AFI's 100 Years 100 Laughs: America's Funniest Movies. *Guest:* More than 138 appearances.

BROSNAN, PIERCE
Actor. b. Navan, County Meath, Ireland, May 16, 1953. Left County Meath, Ireland for London at 11. Worked as commercial illustrator, then joined experimental theatre workshop and studied at the Drama Center. On London stage (Wait Until Dark, The Red Devil Battery Sign, Filumenia, etc.)
PICTURES: The Mirror Crack'd (debut, 1980), The Long Good Friday, Nomads, The Fourth Protocol, Taffin, The Deceivers, Mister Johnson, The Lawnmower Man, Entangled, Mrs. Doubtfire, Love Affair, Goldeneye, Mars Attacks, The Mirror Has Two Faces, Dante's Peak, Tomorrow Never Dies, Quest for Camelot (voice), The Nephew (also prod.), Grey Owl, The Thomas Crown Affair (also prod.), The World is Not Enough, Dolphins, The Tailor of Panama, Blood and Champagne, Die Another Day, Evelyn, (also prod.), After the Sunset, The Matador (also prod. Golden Globe nom. 2006), Instant Karma, Mexicali, The Topkapi Affair (also prod.), Seraphim Falls, Shattered (also prod.), Married Life, Mamma Mia!, The Greatest, Percy Jackson & the Olympians: The Lightning Thief, The Ghost Writer, Remember Me.
TELEVISION: *Movies/Specials:* The Heist, Murder 101, Victim of Love, Robin Hood: Myth-Man-Movie (narrator), Death Train, The Broken Chain, Don't Talk to Strangers, Night Watch. *Mini-series:* The Manions of America, Nancy Astor (Golden Globe nom.1985), Noble House, Around the World in 80 Days. *Series:* Remington Steele. *Guest:* More than 200 appearances.

BROUGHTON, BRUCE
Composer. b. Los Angeles, CA , March 8, 1945. e. U. of Southern California, B.M., 1967. Music supvr., CBS-TV, 1967-77. Since then has been freelance composer for TV and films. Member of Academy of TV Arts & Sciences Society of Composers & Lyricists (past pres.), AMPAS (governor). Nominated 17 times for Emmy. Nominated for Grammy for Young Sherlock Holmes.
PICTURES: The Prodigal, The Ice Pirates, Silverado (Academy Award nom. 1986), Young Sherlock Holmes, Sweet Liberty, The Boy Who Could Fly, Square Dance, Harry and the Hendersons, Monster Squad, Big Shots, Cross My Heart, The Rescue, The Presidio, Last Rites, Moonwalker, Jacknife, Betsy's Wedding, Narrow Margin, The Rescuers Down Under, All I Want for Christmas, Honey I Blew Up the Kid, Stay Tuned, Homeward Bound: The Incredible Journey, So I Married an Axe Murderer, For Love or Money, Tombstone (and score prod.), Holy Matrimony, Baby's Day Out, Miracle on 34th Street, Infinity, Carried Away, House Arrest, Homeward Bound II: Lost in San Francisco, The Shadow Conspiracy, A Simple Wish, One Tough Cop, Krippendorf's Tribe, Lost in Space, Fantasia 2000 (conductor Rhapsody in Blue), Last Flight Out, Bambi II.
TELEVISION: *Movies:* The Paradise Connection, Desperate Voyage, The Return of Frank Cannon, Killjoy (Emmy nom. 1982), The Master of Ballantrae, MADD, The Candy Lightner Story, The First Olympics: Athens 1896 (special, Emmy Award 1984), Two Marriages (Emmy nom. 1984), Cowboy, A Thanksgiving Promise, The Old Man and the Sea (Emmy nom. 1990), O Pioneers! (Emmy Award 1992), Night Ride Home, The Ballad of Lucy Whipple, Roughing It, Bobbie's Girl, Eloise at the Plaza (Emmy Award 2003), Lucy, Eloise at Christmastime (Emmy award 2004), Warm Springs (Emmy Award 2005), The Dive from Clausen's Pier (Emmy nom. 2006), Safe Harbor. *Mini-series:* The Blue and the Gray (Emmy nom. 1983), The First Olympics—Athens: 1896 (Emmy Award), George Washington II, Glory & Honor (Emmy Award 1998), True Women (Emmy nom. 1997). *Series:* Hawaii Five-0, Gunsmoke, Quincy (Emmy nom. 1983), How the West Was Won, Logan's Run, The Oregon Trail, Buck Rogers (Emmy Award 1981), Dallas (Emmy Awards 1978, 1984), Dinosaurs (theme), Capitol Critters (theme), Tiny Toon Adventures (Emmy Award 1991), JAG (theme Emmy nom. 1996), First Monday (Emmy nom. 2002).

BROWN, BLAIR
Actress. b. Washington, DC, April 23, 1946. e. National Theatre Sch. of Canada.
THEATRE: NY: The Threepenny Opera (NY Shakespeare Fest), Comedy of Errors, The Secret Rapture, Arcadia. Acted with Old Globe, San Diego; Stratford, Ont. Shakespeare Fest.; Guthrie Theatre MN; Arena Stage, Wash.; Long Wharf, New Haven; Shaw Festival.
PICTURES: The Paper Chase, The Choirboys, One-Trick Pony, Altered States, Continental Divide Golden Globe nom. 1982), A Flash of Green, Stealing Home, Strapless, Passed Away, The Good Policeman, The Astronaut's Wife, Random Hearts, Space Cowboys, Grasp, Dogville, Loverboy, The Sentinel, Dark Matter, The Speed of Thought.
TELEVISION: *Movies:* The 3,000 Mile Chase, And I Alone Survived, The Child Stealer, The Bad Seed, Hands of a Stranger, Eleanor and Franklin: The White House Years, Extreme Close-Up, Those Secrets, Majority Rule, Rio Shannon (pilot), The Day My Parents Ran Away, Moment of Truth: To Walk Again, The Gift of Love, The Ultimate Lie, Convictions, In His Life: The John Lennon Story, Follow the Stars Home, Hamlet, Young Dr. Freud (narrator), Copshop, The Perfect Pitch (tv doc.), Fringe. *Mini-series:* Captains and the Kings, James Michener's Space, Arthur Hailey's Wheels, Kennedy (Golden Globe nom. 1984), A Season in Purgatory, Benjamin Franklin (TV documentary). *Series:* The Days and Nights of Molly Dodd (Emmy noms. 1987-1991), Talk It Over, Feds, The American Experience, Fringe. *Specials:* School for Scandal, The Skin of Your Teeth, Lethal Innocence, Oregon Trail, The Quinns, Space. *Guest:* More than 87 appearances.

BROWN, BRYAN
Actor. b. Sydney, Australia, June 23, 1947. m. actress Rachel Ward. Began acting professionally in Sydney. Worked in repertory theatres in England with the National Theatre of Great Britain. Returned to Australia to work in films while continuing stage work with Theatre Australia.
PICTURES: Love Letters From Teralba Road (debut, 1977), The Irishman, Weekend of Shadows, Newsfront, Third Person Plural, Money Movers, Palm Beach, Cathy's Child, The Odd Angry Shot, Breaker Morant, Blood Money, Stir, Winter of Our Dreams, Far East, Give My Regards to Broad Street, Parker (Bones), The Empty Beach, F/X, Tai-Pan, Rebel, The Good Wife, Cocktail, Gorillas in the Mist, Shall We Dance, FX2 (also co-exec. prod.),

Sweet Talker (also co-wrote story), Prisoners of the Sun, Blame It on the Bellboy, The Chart of Jimmy Balcksmith, Age of Treason, Dead Heart, On the Border, Dear Claudia, Two Hands, Grizzly Falls, Risk, Mullet (voice), Styx, Dirty Deeds (also prod.), Captured (short), Along Came Polly, Cactus (also exec. prod.), Australia, Beautiful Kate (also prod.), Limbo.
TELEVISION: *Movies:* The Shiralee (Aust.), Dead in the Water, Devlin, The Last Hit, Eureka Stockade, Full Body Massage, Twisted Tales, 20,000 Leagues Under the Sea, Dogboys, Journey to the Center of the Earth, On the Beach, Footsteps, Revenge of the Middle-Aged Woman, Spring Break Shark Attack, The Poseidon Adventure, Joanne Lees: Murder in the Outback. *Mini-series:* Against the Wind, A Town Like Alice, The Thorn Birds (Emmy nom. 1983, Golden Globe nom. 1984), Eureka Stockade, The Shiralee, The Poseidon Adventure. *Series:* The Wanderer, Two Twisted (narr., prod., exec. prod.).

BROWN, CLANCY

Actor. b. Ohio, Jan. 5, 1959. e. Northwestern Univ.
PICTURES: Bad Boys (debut, 1983), The Adventures of Buckaroo Banzai, The Bride, Thunder Alley, Highlander, Extreme Prejudice, Shoot to Kill, Blue Steel, Waiting for the Light, Ambition, Past Midnight, Pet Sematary II, The Shawshank Redemption, Dead Man Walking, Female Perversions, Starship Troopers, Flubber, The Hurricane, Claire Makes it Big, Chump Change, Recess: School's Out (voice), The Laramie Project, Normal, The Making of Daniel Boone (exec. prod.), The SpongeBob SquarePants Movie (voice), Pathfinder, The Guardian, The Twenty, The Express, The Informant!, A Nightmare on Elm Street.
TELEVISION: *Movies:* Johnny Ryan, Love Lies & Murder, Cast a Deadly Spell, Desperate Rescue: The Cathy Mahone Story, Bloodlines, Last Light, The Patron Saint of Liars, The Batman/Superman Movie (voice), In the Company of Spies, Vendetta, The Night of the Headless Horseman, Boss of Bosses, Yesterday's Children, Show White, Normal. *Series:* Earth 2, ER, Voltron: The Third Dimension (voice), SpongBob SquarePants (voice), Roughnecks: The Starship Trooper Chronicles, Big Buy and Rusty the Boy Robot (voice), Jackie Chan Adventures (voice), Lloyd In Space, Breaking News, Heavy Gear: The Animated Series (voice), Carnivàle, Battle Force: Andromeda, Megas XLR (voice), The Burrowers, The Batman (voice), Super Robot Monkey Team Hyperforce Go! (voice), Justice League Unlimited, Lost, American Dragon: Jake Long, Biker Mice from Mars, The Spectacular Spider-Man, The Deep End. *Documentary:* The Moravian Massacre (narrator). *Guest:* More than 133 appearances.

BROWN, DAVID

Executive, Producer. b. New York, NY, July 28, 1916. m. writer-editor Helen Gurley Brown. e. Stanford U., A.B., 1936; Columbia U. School of Journalism, M.S., 1937. Apprentice reporter, copy-editing, San Francisco News & Wall Street Journal, 1936; night ed. asst. drama critic, Fairchild Publications, N.Y., 1937-39; edit. dir. Milk Research Council, N.Y., 1939-40; assoc. ed., Street & Smith Publ., N.Y., 1940-43; assoc. ed., exec. ed., then ed.-in-chief, Liberty Mag., N.Y., 1943-49; edit. dir., nat'l education campaign, Amer. Medical Assn., 1949; assoc. ed., mng. ed., Cosmopolitan Mag., N.Y., 1949-52; contrib. stories & articles to many nat'l mags.; man. ed., story dept., 20th-Fox, L.A., Jan., 1952; story ed. & head of scenario dept., 1953-56; appointed member of exec. staff of Darryl F. Zanuck, 1956; member of exec. staff, 20th-Fox studios, and exec. studio story editor, 1956-60; Prod. 20th-Fox Studios, Sept. 1960-62; Editorial v.p. New American Library of World Literature, Inc., 1963-64; exec. story opers., 20th Century-Fox, 1964-67; vp. dir. of story operations, 1967; exec. v.p., creative operations and member bd. of dir., 1969-71. Exec. v.p., mem. bd. of directors Warner Bros., 1971-72; partner and dir., The Zanuck/Brown Co., 1972-88. Currently, pres., Manhattan Project Ltd., a production co. based in New York. Was a former member, bd. of trustees, American Film Institute, 1972-80. Recipient with Richard D. Zanuck of the Motion Picture Academy of Arts & Sciences' Irving G. Thalberg Memorial Award. 1999 received WGA Honorary Award.
AUTHOR: Brown's Guide to Growing Gray, Delacorte, Let Me Entertain You, Morrow, The Rest of Your Life is the Best of Your Life, Barricade.
PICTURES: *Producer/Exec. prod.:* Sssssss, The Sting (Academy Award for Best Picture, 1973), Sugarland Express, Black Windmill, Willie Dynamite, The Girl from Petrovka, The Eiger Sanction, Jaws (Academy Award nom. 1976), MacArthur, Jaws 2, The Island, Neighbors, The Verdict (Academy Award nom. 1983), Cocoon, Target, Cocoon: The Return, Driving Miss Daisy, The Player, A Few Good Men (Academy award nom. 1993), The Cemetery Club, Watch It, Canadian Bacon, The Saint, Kiss the Girls, Deep Impact, Angela's Ashes, Chocolat (Academy Award nom. 2001), Enigma (co-prod.), Along Came a Spider.
TELEVISION: *Movies:* Women & Men 2: In Love There Are No Rules (prod.), A Season in Purgatory (exec. prod.), Framed (exec. prod.).
(d. February 1, 2010)

BROWN, GEORG STANFORD

Actor, Director. b. Havana, Cuba, June 24, 1943. Acted on stage with the New York Shakespeare Fest. in the 1960s. Gained fame as one of the rookie cops in the 1970s TV series, The Rookies, before turning to TV directing.
THEATRE: All's Well That Ends Well, Measure for Measure, Macbeth, Murderous Angels, Hamlet, Detective Story.
PICTURES: The Comedians, Dayton's Devils, Bullitt, Colossus: The Forbin Project, Wild in the Sky, The Man, Stir Crazy, House Party 2, Dreaming of Julia, Shackles, Imps* (segment).
TELEVISION: *Movies:* The Young Lawyers, Ritual of Evil, The Rookies (pilot), Dawn: Portrait of a Teenage Runaway, The Night the City Screamed, The Kid With the Broken Halo, In Defense of Kids, The Jesse Owens Story, Murder Without Motive, Mystery Woman: Vision of a Murder. *Dir. of movies:* Grambling's White Tiger, Kids Like These, Alone in the Neon Jungle, Stuck With Each Other (also exec. prod.), Father & Son: Dangerous Relations, The Long Shot: Believe in Courage (also co-exec. prod.), Home for Christmas, Angel in the Family, Wedding Daze, Mystery Woman: Snapshot, The Reading Room (also actor). *Series: Actor:* The Rookies (also dir.), Linc's, Freedom, Nip/Tuck. *Series/ Dir.:* Starsky and Hutch, Family, Charlie's Angels, Fantasy Island, The Paper Chase, Tenspeed and Brown Shoe, Palmerstown USA, Dynasty, Hill Street Blues (Emmy nom. 1981, 1985), The Greatest American Hero, The Fall Guy, Fame, Cagney & Lacey (Emmy Award, 1986), The Mississippi, Hotel, Miami Vice, Finder of Lost Loves, Viper. *Guest:* More than 90 appearances.

BROWN, JIM

Actor. b. St. Simons Island, GA, Feb. 17, 1936. e. Manhasset H.S., Syracuse U. For nine years played football with Cleveland Browns; in 1964 won Hickock Belt as Professional Athlete of the year. Founder, Black Economic Union.
PICTURES: Rio Conchos (debut, 1964), The Dirty Dozen, Ice Station Zebra, The Split, Riot, Dark Of The Sun, 100 Rifles, Kenner, El Condor, The Phynx, ... tick ... tick ... tick ..., The Grasshopper, Slaughter, Black Gunn, I Escaped from Devil's Island, The Slams, Slaughter's Big Rip-Off, Three the Hard Way, Take a Hard Ride, Adios Amigo, Mean Johnny Barrows, Kid Vengeance, Fingers, One Down Two to Go (also exec. prod.), Richard Pryor: Here and Now (exec. prod. only), Pacific Inferno (also exec. prod.), Abducted, The Running Man, I'm Gonna Git You Sucka, L.A. Heat, Crack House, Twisted Justice, The Divine Enforcer, Original Gangstas, Mars Attacks!, He Got Game, Small Soldiers (voice), Any Given Sunday, She Hate Me, Playmakers of New Orleans. *Documentaries:* Jim Brown: All American, Frontliners (also exec. prod.).
TELEVISION: *Movies:* Lady Blue, Hammer-Slammer & Slade, Muhammad Ali: The Whole Story (as himself), Unitas (tv documentary, as himself), Keeping the Music Alive (dir.), Sucker Free City, Sideliners. *Mini-series:* American Roots Music (dir.).*Series:* Soul Food, ESPN SportsCentury. *Guest:* More than 85 appearances.

BROWN, PETER C.

Executive. b. Kansas City, Missouri, August 7, 1958. e. University of Kansas, B.S. in business admin., 1979. Brown began his career with the Kansas City, Mo.-based AMC Entertainment Inc. in 1990 and became senior v.p. and CFO in 1991. He served as co-chairman of the board from May 1998 through July 1999 and as executive v. p. from August 1994 to January 1997. Brown was named pres. in January 1997 and became chairman, pres. and CEO in July 1999 and retired in 2009. He was only the third chairman in the company's 83-year history. In June 2005 AMC announced Loews Cineplex Entertainment Corporation would merge with AMC. Brown remained as the organization's top executive, Brown is a member of the executive committee and vice chmn. of the bd. of directors of the National Association of Theatre Owners. He is a member of the advisory bd. for the Will Rogers Motion Picture Pioneers Foundation as well as a member of Variety International's Movie Industry Advisory Council. He also is a member of the International Council of Shopping Centers (ICSC). In 2003, he received the Saleh M. Hassenein Humanitarian Award. In 2006, Brown was named "ShoWester of the Year," an honor that is given to individuals who, throughout their career, demonstrated a dedication to the betterment of the exhibition industry and its causes. Previously, Brown founded and served as chmn. of the bd. of Entertainment Properties Trust, a New York Stock Exchange-traded real estate investment trust, from 1997 to 2003. Other past corporate board memberships include LabOne, Inc., a diagnostic testing laboratory, serving from 1999 to 2001; and Protection One, Inc., a security alarm monitoring company, serving from 1999 to 2001. He's served various Kansas City-area community organizations, including the University of Kansas School of Business, Kansas City Chamber of Commerce, Kansas City Civic Council, Rockhurst High School, and the Kansas City Art Institute.

BROWNE, DON

Executive. e. graduate, Fairleigh Dickinson University. Browne also attended the Univ. of South Carolina on a football scholarship and earned three varsity letters in track and field. He served in the U.S. Coast Guard from 1967 (active) until 1973 (reserve). Browne worked for CBS News from 1967 to 1979, when he joined NBC. From 1979 to 1989, as NBC's Miami bureau chief, Browne directed news coverage of Central and South America.

From 1989 to 1991, Browne served as NBC News' executive news director. Browne helped strengthen the affiliate-network partnership in news and was instrumental in the formation of the NBC News Channel in Charlotte, NC. He was also involved in the creation and the airing of Dateline, the first successful prime-time newsmagazine in NBC's history, and he was directly involved in launching the weekend edition of the Today show. Browne was executive v.p. of NBC News in New York from 1991 - 1993. Browne then served as pres. & gen. mgr. of WTVJ, NBC's owned-and-operated station in Miami. Browne has been a long-time advocate of expanding into the Spanish-language television market, and was closely involved with NBC's purchase of the Telemundo network. While at WTVJ, he integrated the first NBC and Telemundo stations in a duopoly market; led the NBC's station efforts in creating a Southeastern Regional Hub for handling master control for multiple stations; and he spearheaded the design and construction of NBC's first fully digital TV station. Browne moved over to Telemundo as COO and was tapped to his current position, president, in May 2005. Browne oversees all aspects of programming and production, sports, network news, corporate communications, sales, marketing; human resources, research, station group, affiliate relations and distribution, operations and engineering, Telemundo Studios, and Telemundo Cable.

BROWNLOW, KEVIN
Film Historian, Writer, Director, Film Editor. b. Crowborough, England, June 2, 1938. e. University College Sch. Asst. ed./editor, World Wide Pictures, London, 1955-61; film editor, Samaritan Films, 1961-65; film editor, Woodfall Films, 1965-68. Dir., Thames Television 1975-90. Dir., Photoplay Productions 1990-present. In 2004, the American Society of Cinematographers presented Brownlow with a Special Achievement Award for historical documentation and film preservation of silent films.
PICTURES: It Happened Here (dir. with Andrew Mollo) 1964, Charge of the Light Brigade (editor), Winstanley (with Andrew Mollo), Napoleon (restoration of 1927 film, re-released 1980).
TELEVISION: Charm of Dynamite (dir., ed.), All with David Gill: Hollywood (dir., writer), Unknown Chaplin (dir., prod.; Emmy Award 1 Emmy nom. 1987), Buster Keaton: A Hard Act to Follow (prod.; 2 Emmy Awards, 1 Emmy nom. 1988), Harold Lloyd—The Third Genius (Emmy nom. 1990), D.W. Griffith: Father of Film (Emmy nom. 1993), Cinema Europe–The Other Hollywood, Universal Horror, Lon Chaney: A Thousand Faces, Cecil B. DeMille: American Epic, So Funny It Hurt: Buster Keaton & MGM, Mary Pickford (senior creative consult.), The Tramp and the Dictator (documentary, dir., writer & narration), The Cutting Edge: The Magic of Movie Editing (consultant), Garbo (documentary, dir. & writer), I'm King Kong!: The Exploits of Merian C. Cooper (doc, dir.).
AUTHOR: How It Happened Here (1968), The Parade's Gone By... (1968), Adventures with D.W. Griffith (editor, 1973), The War the West and the Wilderness (1979), Hollywood: The Pioneers (1980), Napoleon: Abel Gance's Classic Film (1983), Behind the Mask of Innocence (1990), David Lean–A Biography (1996).

BRUBAKER, JAMES D.
Producer. b. Hollywood, CA, March 30, 1937. e. Eagle Rock H.S. Transportation coordinator for 15 years before becoming unit prod. mgr., 1978-84. Then assoc. prod., exec. prod. & prod. Prod. tv movie, Runnng Mates.
PICTURES: *Assoc. Prod.:* True Confessions (also prod. mgr.), Rocky III (also prod. mgr.), Rhinestone (also prod. mgr.). Unit Prod. Mgr.: New York New York, Comes a Horseman, Uncle Joe Shannon, Rocky II, Raging Bull, Staying Alive, K-9, Problem Child, Mr. Baseball. *Prod./Exec. Prod.:* The Right Stuff, Beer, Rocky IV, Cobra, Over the Top, Problem Child (also prod. mgr.), Brain Donors (also prod. mgr.), A Walk in the Clouds, Liar Liar, The Nutty Professor (co-prod.) Life (and unit prod. mgr.), The Nutty Professor II: The Klumps, Her Majesty, Dragonfly, Bruce Almighty, A Fonder Heart, The Spanish Harlem Project.
TELEVISION: The Gifted One (Unit prod. mgr.) Running Mates, Gia (prod. and unit prod. mgr., Emmy nom.; DGA Award 1998).

BRUCKHEIMER, BONNIE
Producer. b. Brooklyn, NY. m. producer Jerry Bruckheimer. Started in advertising and public relations eventually working for treasurer of Columbia Pictures. Later worked as asst. to Arthur Penn and Ross Hunter. Became partner with Bette Midler in All Girl Productions, 1985. Currently is principle for Bonnie Bruckheimer Productions.
PICTURES: Big Business (assoc. prod.), Beaches, Stella, For the Boys, Hocus Pocus, Man of the House, That Old Feeling, Divine Secrets of the Ya-Ya Sisterhood, Kiss the Frog.
TELEVISION: *Movies:* Bette Midler in Concert: Diva Las Vegas (exec. prod. Emmy nom. 1997), Gypsy (exec. prod. Emmy nom. 1994). *Series:* Bette, Some of My Best Friends.

BRUCKHEIMER, JERRY
Producer. b. Detroit, MI, Sept. 21, 1945. e. U. of Arizona. m. producer Bonnie Bruckheimer. Was art dir./prod. of TV commercials before becoming prod. of films. 1983, formed Don Simpson/Jerry Bruckheimer Prods. with the late Don Simpson and entered into deal with Paramount Pictures to produce; company moved over to Walt Disney in early 1990s. Formed Jerry Bruckheimer Films in 1997. 2000 won PGA Award for Lifetime Achievement Award in Motion Pictures also has 1 other PGA Award for The Amazing Race. He has received 9 nominations.
PICTURES: *Assoc. Prod.:* The Culpepper Cattle Company, Rafferty and the Gold Dust Twins. *Prod.:* Farewell My Lovely, March or Die, Defiance, American Gigolo, Thief, Cat People (exec. prod.), Young Doctors in Love, Flashdance, Thief of Hearts, Beverly Hills Cop, Top Gun, Beverly Hills Cop II, Days of Thunder, The Ref, Bad Boys, Crimson Tide, Dangerous Minds, The Rock, Con Air, Enemy of the State, Armageddon, Gone in 60 Seconds, Coyote Ugly, Remember the Titans, Bad Boys II, Pearl Harbor, Black Hawk Down, Bad Company, Kangaroo Jack, Veronica Guerin, King Arthur, Pirates of the Caribbean: The Curse of the Black Pearl, National Treasure, Glory Road, Pirates of the Caribbean: Dead Man's Chest, Deja Vu, Pirates of the Caribbean: World's End, National Treasure: The Book of Secrets, G-Force, Prince of Persia: The Sands of Time, The Sorcerer's Apprentice, Confessions of a Shopaholic, Pirates of the Caribbean: On Stranger Tides.
TELEVISION: *Movies: Exec Prod:* Max Q: Emergency Landing, Swing Vote, The Legacy, Fearless, The Line. *Series/Exec. Prod.:* Soldier of Fortune, Inc., Miami Medical, CSI: Crime Scene Investigation (3 Emmy noms.), The Amazing Race (7 Emmy Awards,), Dark Blue, CSI: Miami, Without a Trace, Skin (writer/creator), Fearless (also co-prod.), Profiles from the Front Line (doc.), E-Ring, Just Legal, Modern Men, Justice, Cold Case, C.S.I.: NY, Close to Home, Eleventh Hour, Cocaine Cowboys, The Forgotten.

BRYAN, DORA
Actress. r.n. Dora Broadbent. b. Southport, Lancashire, England, Feb. 7, 1924. e. Council Sch. Stage debut 1935.
PICTURES: Once Upon a Dream, (debut, 1947), The Fallen Idol, No Room at the Inn, Blue Lamp, Cure for Love, Now Barabas, The Ringer, Women of Twilight, The Quiet Woman, The Intruder, You Know What Sailors Are, Mad About Men, See How They Run, Cockleshell Heroes, Child in the House, Green Man, Carry on Sergeant, Operation Bullshine, Desert Mice, The Night We Got the Bird, A Taste of Honey, Two a Penny, Up the Front, Screamtime, Apartment Zero, An Angel for May, MirrorMask.
TELEVISION: *Movies:* Red Peppers, Bed. *Series:* My Wife's Sister, Both Ends Meet, On the Up, Mother's Ruin, Last of the Summer Wine. *Guest:* More than 45 appearances.

BUCKLEY, BETTY
Actress. b. Fort Worth, TX, July 3, 1947. e. Texas Christian U., BA. Studied acting with Stella Adler. NY Stage debut: 1776 (1969); London debut: Promises Promises. Appeared in interactive short film Race for Your Life.
THEATRE: Johnny Pott, What's a Nice Country Like You Doing in a State Like This?, Pippin, I'm Getting My Act Together and Taking It on the Road, Cats (Tony Award, 1983), Juno's Swans, The Mystery of Edwin Drood, Song and Dance, Carrie, The Fourth Wall, The Perfectionist, Sunset Boulevard (London/B'way; Olivier Award nom.).
PICTURES: Carrie (debut, 1976), Tender Mercies, Wild Thing, Frantic, Another Woman, Rain Without Thunder, Wyatt Earp, Simply Irresistible, Last Time Out, The Keyman (co-prod. only), A Promis Kept (prod. only), Broadway: The Golden Age by the Legends Who Were There, Mummy an' the Armadillo, The Happening, Five Time Champion.
TELEVISION: *Movies:* The Ordeal of Bill Carney, Roses Are for the Rich, The Three Wishes of Billy Grier, Babycakes, Bonnie & Clyde: The True Story (Emmy nom.), Betrayal of Trust, Critical Choices, Vinegar Hill, Brothers & Sisters. *Mini-series:* Evergreen, Tribeca, The Pacific. *Series:* Eight is Enough, Oz. *Specials:* Bobby and Sarah (Emmy nom. 1989), Salute to Lady Liberty, Taking a Stand (Afterschool Special; Emmy nom 1989), Stephen Sondheim Carnegie Hall Gala, Eight is Enough: The E! True Hollywood Story, Kennedy Center Honors: A Celebration of the Performing Arts. *Guest:* More than 60 appearances.

BUCKLEY, DONALD
Executive. b. New York, NY, June 28, 1955. e. C.W. Post College, NY, School of Visual Arts. Ad. mgr., United Artists Theatres, 1975-78. Acct. exec., Grey Advertising, 1978-80. Joined Warner Bros. in 1980 as NY adv. mgr.; in 1986 promoted to east. dir. of adv./promo. for WB; 1988, named eastern dir. of adv. and publicity; 1991, promoted to v.p., East Coast Adv. & Publicity; 1996, promoted to v.p., Adv. & Publicity, v.p., WB On-Line; 1997, promoted to senior v.p., Interactive Marketing. On bd. of dir., Floss.com. Currently Exec. V.P. at Terry Hines & Assoc.. President at THA.i.

BUFF, CONRAD
Editor.
PICTURES: The Empires Strikes Back (effects ed.), Raiders of the Lost Ark (effects ed.), Poltergeist (effects ed.), E.T.: The Extra-Terrestrial (effects ed. superv.), Return of the Jedi (asst. ed.), Jagged Edge, Solarbabies, Spaceballs, Short Circuit 2, The Abyss, Side Out, Terminator 2: Judgment Day (Academy Award nom.; ACE nom. 1992), Jennifer Eight, The Getaway, True Lies (ACE nom. 1995), Species, Titanic (Academy Award, ACE Award 1998), Dante's Peak, Switchback, Arlington Road, Mystery Men, Thirteen Days, Training Day, The Antwone Fisher Story, Tears of

the Sun, King Arthur, Get Rich or Die Tryin', Seraphim Falls, Shooter, The Seeker: The Dark Is Rising, The Happening, Terminator Salvation, Pablo Escobar.

BUJOLD, GENEVIEVE

Actress. b. Montreal, Canada, July 1, 1942. e. Montreal Conservatory of Drama. Worked in a Montreal cinema as an usher; American TV debut: St. Joan.
THEATRE: The Barber of Seville, A Midsummer Night's Dream, A House...A Day.
PICTURES: La Guerre est Finie, La Fleur de L'Age, Entre La Mer et L'eau Douce, King of Hearts, The Thief of Paris, Isabel, Anne of the Thousand Days (Academy Award nom.; Golden Globe Award 1970), Act of the Heart, The Trojan Women, The Journey, Kamouraska, Earthquake, Swashbuckler, Obsession, Alex and the Gypsy, Another Man Another Chance, Coma, Murder by Decree, Final Assignment, The Last Flight of Noah's Ark, Monsignor, Tightrope, Choose Me, Trouble in Mind, The Moderns, Dead Ringers, False Identity, Secret Places of the Heart, A Paper Wedding, An Ambush of Ghosts, Mon Amie Max, Dead Innocent, The Adventures of Pinocchio, The House of Yes, You Can Thank Me Later, Last Night, Eye of the Beholder, Alex in Wonder, La Turbulence des fluides, Finding Home, Downtown: A Street Tale, Jericho Mansions, Disappearances.
TELEVISION: *Movies:* Antigone, Mistress of Paradise, Les Noces de papier, The Bookfair Murders, Children of My Heart. *Specials:* Saint Joan (Emmy nom. 1968), Antony and Cleopatra.

BULLOCK, SANDRA

Actress. b. Arlington, VA, July 26, 1964. e. East Carolina Univ., drama major. Raised in Germany; studied piano in Europe. First prof. acting job in NY in Off-B'way prod. No Time Flat.
PICTURES: Who Shot Patakango?, Love Potion No. 9, When the Party's Over, The Vanishing, The Thing Called Love, Demolition Man, Speed, Me and the Mob, While You Were Sleeping (Golden Globe nom. 1996), The Net, Two If by Sea, A Time to Kill, In Love and War, Speed 2 Cruise Control, The Prince of Egypt (voice), Making Sandwiches (also dir., s.p.), Hope Floats, Practical Magic, Forces of Nature, 28 Days, Welcome to Hollywood, Gun Shy, Famous, Miss Congeniality (Golden Globe nom. 2001), Divine Secrets of the Ya Ya Sisterhood, Murder By Numbers (also exec. prod.), Two Weeks Notice (also prod.), Exactly 3:30 (also prod.), Crash, Vapor, Prime, Miss Congeniality 2: Armed and Fabulous (also prod.), Grace (also prod.), Loverboy, Infamous, Premonition, The Lake House, All About Steve (also prod.), The Proposal (also exec. prod., soundtrack performer, Golden Globe nom. 2010), The Blind Side (Academy Award nom.; Golden Globe Award 2010).
TELEVISION: *Movies:* The Preppie Murder, Bionic Showdown: The Six Million Dollar Man and the Bionic Woman. *Mini-series:* Jackie Collins' Lucky/Chances. *Series:* Working Girl, George Lopez (also exec. prod.). *Guest:* More than 122 appearances.

BUNNELL, STEVE

Executive. b. Chicago, IL, Feb. 20, 1960. Began working in theatres in 1975 in Chicago, IL. Film buyer for Plitt Theatres (predecessor company to Cineplex) in Chicago, IL, starting in 1979 and through 1985. Film buyer for Mann Theatres in Los Angeles, CA, from 1985-1991. Became general sales mgr. at the Samuel Goldwyn Company in Los Angeles, and managed U.S. film distribution. Moved to Loews in 1993 and became v.p. in 1997. In 1999, promoted to sr. v.p. and head film buyer for Loews Cineplex Entertainment. With the Loew Cineplex-AMC Entertainment merger in June 2005, Bunnell left the company and became chairman, domestic distribution for The Weinstein Company. He was based in New York. 2009 Bunnell moved back to exhibition accepting a position as Film Buyer for Cinemark Theatres. He has been promoted to Sr. V.P. - Film Licensing.

BURGESS, R. BRANDON

Executive. Raised and educated in Germany. e. graduate of the European Business School; M.B.A., Wharton School, Univ. of Pennsylvania in Philadelphia. Burgess' early career included investment banking with Goldman Sachs in London and Frankfurt, focusing on real estate and corporate finance. Subsequently, he worked in PepsiCo's Corporate Planning group in Purchase, NY. He joined NBC, serving in various management capacities including: CFO for the NBC Television Network and its director of business development; co-head of the NBC Network Affiliate Futures Committee, a growth initiative in collaboration with NBC-affiliated stations. This initiative produced the NBCOlympics.com online multimedia venture joined by more than 200 NBC affiliate stations, as well as NBC Weather Plus, the first U.S. nationwide digital multicast broadcast network, through a joint venture he arranged between NBC and its broadcast affiliates. He played a central role in growing NBC's owned-and-operated stations group from 13 to 30 stations. Burgess also was instrumental to the May 2004 merger of NBC and Vivendi Universal and the restructuring of Rainbow Media, which gave NBC its first entertainment cable channel, Bravo. He also helped launch NBC Universal Global Networks' first free to air TV network outside the United States, Das VIERTE, in Germany, in September 2005. At NBC Universal he rose to executive v.p., business development & international channels, where he was credited with a series of strategic moves that led the U.S.-focused NBC broadcast network to evolve into an integrated global multimedia organization. NBC Universal execs called upon Burgess to look after the company's 32% stake in ION Media Networks, Inc. (formerly known as Paxson Communications) in Nov. 2005. As chairman and CEO of ION, he is spearheading efforts to turn around the financially struggling company. ION's 60 TV stations reach 83% of U.S. TV households.

BURGHOFF, GARY

Actor. b. Bristol, CT, May 24, 1943. Winner of Student Hallmark Award while in high school, 1961. Also wildlife artist, with work exhibited in many U.S. galleries.
THEATRE: NY: You're a Good Man Charlie Brown, The Nerd. Also: Finian's Rainbow, Bells Are Ringing, Sound of Music, The Boy Friend, Romanoff and Juliet, Whose Life Is It Anyway?
PICTURES: M*A*S*H*, B.S. I Love You, Small Kill (also co-dir.), Behind the Waterfall.
TELEVISION: The Man in the Santa Claus Suit, Casino. Series: The Don Knotts Show, M*A*S*H (Emmy Award, 1977 6 Emmy noms.), Pets: Part of the Family (Emmy nom. 2001). *Special:* Twigs, M*A*S*H 30th Anniversary Reunion (tv documentary, 2002).

BURKE, ALFRED

Actor. b. London, England, February 28, 1918.
PICTURES: Touch and Go, The Man Upstairs, The Angry Silence, Moment of Danger, The Man Inside, No Time To Die, Children of the Damned, The Nanny, One Day in the Life of Ivan Denisovitch, Law and Disorder, Yangtse Incident, Interpol, Bitter Victory, Guns in the Heather, One Day in the Life of Ivan Denisovich, A Midsummer Night's Dream, Harry Potter and the Chamber of Secrets.
TELEVISION: *Movies:* The Lady of the Camellias, The House on Garibaldi Street, Pope John Paul II, Kim, Bewitched (1985), Longitude. *Mini-series:* The Brontes of Haworth, The Borgias. *Series:* Public Eye, Enemy at the Door, Sophia and Constance. *Guest:* More than 67 appearances.

BURKE, DELTA

Actress. b. Orlando, FL, July 30, 1956. e. LAMDA. m. actor Gerald McRaney. Competed in Miss America contest as Miss Florida, prior to studying acting in England.
PICTURES: Maternal Instincts (also exec. prod.), Sordid Lives, What Women Want, Hansel and Gretel, Good Boy! (voice).
TELEVISION: *Movies:* Charleston, A Last Cry for Help, Mickey Spillane's Mike Hammer: Murder Me Murder You, A Bunny's Tale, Where the Hell's That Gold?!!?, Love and Curses... And All That Jazz (also co-exec. prod.), Day-O, Simon & Simon: In Trouble Again, A Promise to Carolyn, Melanie Darrow (also prod.), Dangerous Child, Going for Broke, The Year Without a Santa Claus, Bridal Fever. *Series:* The Chisholms, Filthy Rich, 1st & Ten, Designing Women 2 Emmy nom.), Delta (also co-exec. prod.), Women of the House (also exec. prod.), Any Day Now, DAG, Popular, Boston Legal. *Special:* Intimate Portrait: Dixie Carter. *Guest:* More than 84 appearances.

BURKE, STEVE

Executive. b. 1958. e Colgate University. MBA Harvard Business School, 1982. After receiving MBA, Burke worked briefly at General Foods before joining Disney in 1986. At age 29, he convinced Disney's then CEO Michael Eisner to launch a line of Disney stores which grew to 700 at their peak before becoming a financial drain on Disney's bottom line, the chain of stores was sold to Children's Place in 2004. 1996, Disney transferred Burke to New York after it entered the broadcast business by acquiring Capital Cities-ABC where he helped to oversee the integration. Served as president of ABC Broadcasting from 1996-1998 and was responsible for the 10 ABC-owned television stations; the ABC Radio Group, consisting of 27 radio stations and eight radio networks; and Buena Vista Television, the company's domestic syndication arm. Named President and CEO of Euro Disney S.A. and was responsible for major restructuring. President of Comcast Cable Communications in 1998 and Senior V.P. of Comcast Holdings Corp. Named Executive V.P. of Comcast Holdings in January 2000 and served as President of Comcast Cable Communications LLC 2002 - 2010. Comcast has become the largest cable company, largest residential internet service provider, third largest phone company in America and recently launched a wireless business. He oversees the Company's products and services, and Comcast's programming networks, advertising and Comcast Interactive Media. Burke has led Comcast to leadership in multiplatform video entertainment distribution, including the Company's industry changing video on demand platform and online video offerings. Comcast's On Demand service, which was introduced in 2003, now offers more than 17,000 choices a month and has had over 15 billion customer views since it's launch. Burke also led the integration of AT&T Broadband with Comcast. September 2010 he was named CEO of NBC Universal, and will retain his current position with Comcast Holdings during the merger between Comcast and NBC Universal, expected by year end, 2010. He has been an Independent Director of JPMorgan Chase & Co since 2003. Serves as Chairman of The Children's Hospital of Philadelphia and is a Director of Berkshire Hathaway, Inc. since December 2009. Served as Director of National Cable Satellite

Corporation and serves as Director of Banc One Corporation since February 2003. Member of the President's Council of Advisors on Science and Technology (PCAST). He earned numerous industry awards, including the 2003 Multichannel News Cable Operator of the Year Award and the National Cable & Telecommunications Association 2001 Vanguard Award for Cable Operations Management.

BURNETT, CAROL

Actress, Singer, Producer, Director. b. San Antonio, TX, April 26, 1933. e. Hollywood H.S., UCLA. Daughter was actress Carrie Hamilton (d. Jan. 20, 2002). Introduced comedy song "I Made a Fool of Myself Over John Foster Dulles," 1957; regular performer Garry Moore Show, 1959-62. Recipient outstanding commedienne award Am. Guild Variety Artists, 5 times; TV Guide award for outstanding female performer 1961, 62, 63; Peabody Award, 1963; 5 Golden Globe awards for outstanding comedienne of year; Woman of Year award Acad. TV Arts and Scis. Voted one of the world's 20 most admired women in 1977 Gallup Poll. First Annual National Television Critics Award for Outstanding Performance, 1977. Best Actress Award at San Sebastian Film Fest. for film A Wedding, 1978. Inducted Acad. of Television Arts and Sciences Hall of Fame, 1985. *Author:* Once Upon a Time (1986), Hollywood Arms (play, co-writer).
THEATRE: *NY:* Once Upon a Mattress (debut, 1959; Theatre World Award), Fade Out-Fade In, Moon Over Buffalo. Regional: Calamity Jane, Plaza Suite, I Do I Do, Same Time Next Year.
PICTURES: Who's Been Sleeping in My Bed? (debut, 1963)Pete 'n' Tillie, The Front Page, A Wedding, H.E.A.L.T.H., The Four Seasons, Chu Chu and the Philly Flash, Annie (soundtrack performer), Noises Off..., Get Bruce (documentary), The Trumpet of the Swan (voice), Broadway: The Golden Age by the Legends Who Were There (doc.), Horton Hears a Who! (voice), Post Grad.
TELEVISION: *Movies:* The Grass Is Always Greener Over the Septic Tank, Friendly Fire (Emmy nom. 1979), The Tenth Month, Life of the Party: The Story of Beatrice, Between Friends, Hostage, Seasons of the Heart, Grace, Happy Birthday Elizabeth, The Marriage Fool, Putting It Together, The Carol Burnett Show: Let's Bump Up the Lights (also exec. prod.), Once Upon a Mattress (also exec. prod.). *Mini-series:* Fresno. *Series:* Stanley, Pantomime Quiz, The Garry Moore Show (Emmy Award, 1962), The Entertainers, The Carol Burnett Show (1967-78; in syndication as Carol Burnett & Friends), Carol Burnett & Company, Carol & Company, The Carol Burnett Show (1991, 3 Emmy Awards, 4 other nom.), Mama's Family, Mad About You (Emmy Award, 1997), Law & Order: Special Victims Unit (Emmy nom. 2009 as guest). *Specials:* Julie & Carol at Carnegie Hall, Carol and Company (Emmy Award for previous 2 specials, 1963), An Evening with Carol Burnett, Calamity Jane, Once Upon a Mattress, Carol + 2, Julie & Carol at Lincoln Center, 6 Rms Riv Vu, Twigs, Sills & Burnett at the Met, Dolly & Carol in Nashville, All-Star Party for Carol Burnett, Burnett Discovers Domingo, The Laundromat, Carol Carl Whoopi & Robin, Julie & Carol—Together Again, The Carol Burnett Show: A Reunion (also co-exec. prod.), Men Movies & Carol (Emmy nom. 1995), CBS: The First 50 Years, Carol Burnett: Show Stoppers (Emmy nom. 2002), American Masters. *Guest:* More than 250 appearances.

BURNETT, CHARLES

Director, Writer, Cinematographer. b. Vicksburg, MI, April 13, 1944. e. LA Community Col., UCLA.
PICTURES: *Director:* Several Friends, Killer of Sheep (also prod., s.p., photog., edit.), My Brother's Wedding (also prod., s.p., photog.), To Sleep With Anger (also s.p.), America Becoming (also writer), The Johnny Johnson Trial (also s.p.), The Annihilation of Fish, Olivia's Story (doc., also editor), Nujoma: Where Others Wavered (also writer), Nat Turner: A Troublesome Property (also writer), Namibia: The Struggle for Liberation (also writer), Red Soil, The Glass Shield (also writer). *Cinematographer:* Bush Mama, Bless Their Little Hearts (also s.p.), Guest of Hotel Astoria.
TELEVISION: *Movies: Dir.:* Nightjohn, The Wedding, Finding Buck McHenry, Selma Lord Selma, Relative Stranger. *Mini-series:* The Blues. *Series:* American Family. *Documentaries:* The Blues (mini series, dir., writer), For Reel? (dir., writer).

BURNETT, MARK

Producer, Writer. b. London, England, July 17, 1960. Raised in London, Burnett enlisted in the British Army at 17. He later became a Section Commander of the infamous Parachute Regiment and fought in Northern Ireland and Falkland Islands. In Oct. 1982, Burnett moved to U.S. Upon his arrival, he took a live--in nanny/bodyguard job in Beverly Hills After working various jobs in several industries, Burnett began his career in unscripted drama when he created the adventure series Eco-Challenge. Eco-Challenge: British Columbia earned him a 1996 Sports Emmy Award nomination and a 1997 International Documentary Association Award nomination. In 2000, Burnett was awarded the prestigious Banff Rockie Award in the Sports Program Category by the 2000 Banff Rockie Awards Festival. In addition, he received an Emmy for Outstanding Non-Fiction Program (Special Class) for Survivor: Borneo. Burnett's legacy is the successful introduction of reality TV programming to the viewing public, and he continues to evolve the genre. Burnett has been featured in Time Magazine's "Time 100 List" of the most influential people in the world today; named to the "Top 101 Most Powerful People in Entertainment" list by Entertainment Weekly for three consecutive years; has garnered the number one position on TV Guide's "Most Valuable Players" list; and earned the Number Two position on Access Hollywood's "Top 10 in Entertainment 2000" list. Burnett was a recipient of a Special Recognition Award for Survivor from the Gay & Lesbian Alliance Against Defamation (GLAAD); was named in the Advertising Age Top 100 for 2001; and was a featured business leader in Variety's 2001 "A Tradition of Trendsetting." He also received NATPE's Brandon Tartikoff Legacy Award which recognizes individuals who have a unique passion and vision for television. Received Emmy Award for the Survivor series, 2001, also 4 Emmy noms.
TELEVISION: *Movies:* Eco Challenge: New Zealand, Global Frequency, The Contender Rematch: Mora vs. Manfredo, Live for the Moment. *Series*: Eco-Challenge: British Columbia, Eco-Challenge: Argentina, Survivor: Borneo (Emmy nom. 2001), Survivor: The Reunion, Survivor: The Australian Outback, Eco-Challenge: Borner (doc.), Survivor: Africa, Eco-Challenge: U.S. Armed Forces Championship, Combat Missions, Survivor Marquesas, Survivor: Thailand, Survivor: Men vs. Women Rumble in the Jungle, Survivor: The Amazon, Eco-Challenge: Fiji Islands, Boarding House: North Shore, The Restaurant, Survivor: Pearl Islands, Commando Nanny, The Apprentice (2 Emmy noms.), Survivor: All Stars, The Casino, Survivor: Vanuatu-Islands of Fire, Diili, Kandidaten (writer/creator only), Survivor: Palau (dir. only), The Contender (also writer), Rock Star: INXS, Survivor: Guatemala-The Maya Empire, The Apprentice: Martha Stewart (3 Emmy noms.), Rock Star: Supernova, Gold Rush, The Contender Asia, Amne$ia (writer, creator), Are You Smarter Than a 5th Grader?, Pirate Master, On the Lot, My Dad Is Better Than Your Dad, Das weiß doch jedes Kind! (writer), Our Little Genius, The Contender Australia (also writer). *Special:* 2007 MTV Movie Awards (exec. prod.), The 36th Annual People's Choice Awards (exec. prod.).

BURNS, EDWARD J.

Actor, Director, Producer. b. Valley Stream, NY, Jan. 29, 1968. Has production co. with brother Brian Burns, Irish Twins.
PICTURES: *Actor, dir. s.p.:* The Brothers McMullen (Sundance award), She's the One (also prod.), No Looking Back, Sidewalks of New York, Ash Wednesday, Flight of the Phoenix, Purple Violets (also actor), The Groomsmen (also actor), Five-Fourths (also actor). *Actor:* Saving Private Ryan (SAG nom.),15 Minutes, Life or Something Like It, Confidence, The Breakup Artist, A Sound of Thunder, Looking for Kitty, The River King, The Holiday, Purple Violets (also writer, dir., prod.), One Missed Call, 27 Dresses, Echelon Conspiracy, Loosies, American Empire.
TELEVISION: *Series:* Entertainment Tonight (prod. asst.), The Fighting Fitzgeralds (exec. prod. and writer only). New York at the Movies (tv doc.), The Lynch Pin (actor, dir., writer, prod.).

BURNS, KEN

Producer, Director, Cinematographer, Writer. b. July 29, 1953. e. Hampshire Col. Co-author: Shakers: Hands to Work Hearts to God: The History and Visions of the United Society of Believers in Christ's Second Appearance from 1774 to Present, The Civil War: An Illustrated History, Baseball: An Illustrated History.
PICTURES: Gettysburg.
TELEVISION: *Prod. and dir. Documentaries:* Brooklyn Bridge (also photog., edit.; Academy Award nom. 1982), The Shakers: Hands to Work Hearts to God (also co-writer), The Statue of Liberty (also photog.; Academy Award nom. 1986), Huey Long (also co-writer), Thomas Hart Benton (also photog.), The Congress, The Civil War (also photog., co-writer; numerous awards incl. Peabody and Emmy 1991), Lindbergh (co-prod. only), Empire of the Air: The Men Who Made Radio (also photog., music dir., Emmy nom. 1992), Baseball (co- writer, prod., dir., Emmy Award, Emmy nom. 1995), Lewis & Clark: The Journey of the Corps of Discovery (also photog.), Frank Lloyd Wright (also photog.), The West (exec. prod only), Thomas Jefferson (prod. only), Not for Ourselves Alone: The Story of Elizabeth Cady Stanton & Susan B. Anthony, Jazz (2 Emmy nom. 2001), Mark Twain, Horatio's Drive: America's First Road Trip, Unforgivable Blackness: The Rise and Fall of Jack Johnson (Emmy Award, Emmy nom. 2005), The War (series, also exec. prod., co- dir., Emmy nom., DGA nom. 2008), Medal of Honor, The National Parks: America's Best Idea (min-series, dir., exec. prod., prod., camera operator).

BURRILL, TIMOTHY

Producer, Executive. b. North Wales, June 8, 1931. e. Eton Coll., Sorbonne U., Paris. Grenadier Guards 2 yrs, then London Shipping Co. Ent. m.p. ind. as resident prod. mgr. Samaritan Films working on shorts, commercials, documentaries, 1954. Ass't. dir.: The Criminal, The Valiant Years (TV series), On The Fiddle, Reach for Glory, War Lover, Prod. mgr: The Cracksman, Night Must Fall, Lord Jim, Yellow Rolls Royce, The Heroes of Telemark, Resident prod. with World Film Services. 1970 prod. two films on pop music for Anglo-EMI. 1972 first prod. administrator National Film School in U.K. 1974 Post prod. administrator The Three Musketeers. Prod. TV Special The Canterville Ghost; assoc. prod, That Lucky Touch; UK Administrator, The Prince

and the Pauper; North American Prod. controller, Superman; 1974-1983 council member of BAFTA; mng. dir., Allied Stars (Breaking Glass, Chariots of Fire); 1979-80 V. chmn. Film BAFTA; 1980-83 chmn. BAFTA; 1981-92, Gov. National Film School, executive BFTPA mem. Cinematograph Films Council. 1982-88 Gov Royal National Theatre; 1987-93, chmn., Film Asset Developments, Formed Burrill Prods, 1979-; chmn. First Film Foundation. Exec. member PACT, 1991. Vice-chmn. (film) PACT, 1993.
PICTURES: Privilege, Oedipus the King, A Severed Head, Three Sisters, Macbeth (assoc. prod.), Alpha Beta, Tess (co-prod. Academy Award nom. 1981), Pirates of Penzance (co-prod.), Supergirl, The Fourth Protocol, To Kill a Priest (co-prod.), Return of the Musketeers (tv in U.S.), Valmont, The Rainbow Thief, The Lover, Bitter Moon, Sweet Killing, Vatel, The Pianist, Two Brothers (co-prod.), Swimming Pool (co-prod.), Double zéro (assoc. prod.), Oliver Twist (exec. prod.), Renaissance (co-prod.), La Vie en Rose (co-prod.), The Ghost Writer (co-prod.).

BURROWS, JAMES
Director, Producer. b. Los Angeles, CA, Dec. 30, 1940. e. Oberlin, B.A.; Yale, M.F.A. Son of late Abe Burrows, composer, writer, dir. Directed off-B'way. Exec. Prod./Dir. with Charles Brothers Productions.
PICTURE: Partners.
TELEVISION: *Movies:* More Than Friends, Every Stray Dog and Kid, Dexter Prep Pilot, Beverly Hills S.U.V., Traveling in Packs, The Mastersons of Manhattan. *Series:* Has dir./exec.prod. 51 series since1970, incl.: Mary Tyler Moore, Bob Newhart, Laverne and Shirley, Rhoda, Phyllis, Tony Randall Show, Betty White Show, Fay, Taxi (2 Emmy Awards: 1980, 1981, DGA nom. 1982), Lou Grant, Cheers (also prod.; 4 Emmy Awards as prod.: 1983, 1984, 1989, 1991; 2 Emmy Awards as dir.: 1983, 1991, 2 DGA Awards, 3 other nom.), Dear John, Night Court, All is Forgiven (also exec. prod.), The Fanelli Boys, Frasier (Emmy Award, DGA Award 1994), Friends, NewsRadio, Men Behaving Badly, Chicago Sons, 3rd Rock from the Sun, Pearl, Fired Up (pilot), George & Leo, Dharma & Greg (DGA nom. 1998 for pilot), Veronica's Closet, Union Square, Conrad Bloom, Jesse, The Secret Lives of Men, Ladies Man, Stark Raving Mad, Madigan Men, Cursed, Good Morning Miami, Bram and Alice (pilot), Two and a Half Men (pilot), The Stones, The Comeback (actor only), Four Kings (pilot), Courting Alex, Will & Grace (Emmy Award 2000, 10- Emmy Award nom.;DGA Award 2001, 6 other noms.), The Class, Back to You, Hank, 100 Questions, Gary Unmarried.

BURSTYN, ELLEN
Actress. r.n. Edna Rae Gilhooley. b. Detroit, MI, Dec. 7, 1932. Majored in art; was fashion model in Texas at 18. Moved to Montreal as dancer; then N.Y. to do TV commercials (under the name of Ellen McRae), appearing for a year on the Jackie Gleason show (1956-57). In 1957 turned to dramatics and won lead in B'way show, Fair Game. Then went to Hollywood to do TV and films. Returned to N.Y. to study acting with Lee Strasberg; worked in TV serial, The Doctors. Co-artistic dir. of Actor's Studio. 1982-88. Pres. Actors Equity Assn. 1982-85. On 2 panels of Natl. Endowment of the Arts and Theatre Advisory Council (NY).
THEATRE: *NY:* Fair Game, Same Time Next Year (Tony Award, 1975), 84 Charing Cross Road, Shirley Valentine, Shimada, Sacrilege. *L.A.:* Love Letters. *Regional:* The Trip to Bountiful, Oldest Living Confederate Widow Tells All.
PICTURES: As Ellen McRae: For Those Who Think Young (debut, 1964), Goodbye Charlie, Pit Stop. As Ellen Burstyn: Tropic of Cancer, Alex in Wonderland, The Last Picture Show (Academy Award nom. Golden Globe nom. 1972), The King of Marvin Gardens, The Exorcist (Academy Award nom. Golden Globe nom. 1974), Harry and Tonto, Alice Doesn't Live Here Anymore (Academy Award, Golden Globe nom. 1975), Providence, A Dream of Passion, Same Time Next Year (Academy Award nom. Golden Globe Award 1979), Resurrection (Academy Award nom. Golden Globe nom. 1981), Silence of the North, The Ambassador, In Our Hands (doc.), Twice in a Lifetime, Hanna's War, Dying Young, The Color of Evening, The Cemetery Club, When a Man Loves a Woman, Roommates, The Baby-sitters Club, How to Make an American Quilt, The Spitfire Grill, Liar, You Can Thank Me Later, Playing by Heart, The Yards, Requiem for a Dream (Academy Award nom. Golden Globe nom. 2001), Divine Secrets of the Ya-Ya Sisterhood, Cross the Line, Down in the Valley, The Fountain, 30 Days, The Wicker Man, The Stone Angel, The Loss of a Teardrop Diamond, According to Greta, W., Main Street, Chickadee, The Mighty Macs.
TELEVISION: *Movies:* The Berk, Thursday's Game, The People Vs. Jean Harris (Emmy nom. Golden Globe nom. 1981), Surviving, Act of Vengeance, Into Thin Air, Something in Common, Pack of Lies (Emmy nom. 1987), When You Remember Me, Mrs. Lambert Remembers Love, Taking Back My Life: The Nancy Ziegenmeyer Story, Grand Isle, Shattered Trust: The Shari Karney Story, Getting Out, Getting Gotti, Trick of the Eye, My Brother's Keeper, Follow the River, Our Son, the Matchmaker, Timepiece, A Deadly Vision, Flash, The Patron Saint of Liars, Night Ride Home, Mermaid (Emmy nom. 2001), Dodson's Journey, Within These Walls (also exec. prod.), Brush With Fate, The Madam's Family: The Truth About the Canal Street Brothel, The Five People You Meet in Heaven, Our Fathers, Mrs. Harris (Emmy nom. 2006), Oprah Winfrey Presents: Mitch Albom's For One More Day, Possible Side Effects. *Mini-series:* A Will of Their Own, *Series:* The Iron Horse, The Doctors, The Ellen Burstyn Show, That's Life, Big Love (Emmy nom. 2008), Law & Order: Special Victims Unit (Emmy Award 2009 as guest), The Book of Daniel. *Special:* Dear America: Letters Home From Vietnam (reader). *Guest:* More than 140 appearances.

BURTON, KATE
Actress. b. Geneva, Switzerland, Sept. 10, 1957. e. Brown Univ. (B.A.), Yale Drama Sch. Daughter of late Richard Burton. m. stage manager Michael Ritchie. Worked at Yale Repertory Theatre, Hartford, Stage Co., the Hartman, Huntington Theatre, Williamstown, Berkshire Theatre festivals, The O'Neil Playwright's Conference, Pray Street Theatre. Member of Tony Administration Committee (nominators).
THEATRE: Present Laughter (debut, 1982; Theatre World Award), Alice in Wonderland, Winners, The Accrington Pals, Doonesbury, The Playboy of the Western World, Wild Honey, Measure For Measure, Some Americans Abroad (Drama Desk nom.), Jake's Women, London Suite, Boston Marriage, The Elephant Man, Hedda Gabler, Company.
PICTURES: Big Trouble in Little China (debut, 1986), Life With Mikey, August, First Wives Club, Looking for Richard, The Ice Storm, Celebrity, The Opportunists, Unfaitfhful, Swimf@n, Stay, SherryBaby, Shall Not Want, Quid Pro Quo, Max Payne, City of Your Final Destination, Safety Point.
TELEVISION: *Movies:* Alice in Wonderland, Uncle Tom's Cabin, Journey Into Genius, Love Matters, Mistrial, Notes For My Daughter, Ellen Foster, Obsessed, The Diary of Ellen Rimbauer, Empire Falls. *Mini-series:* Ellis Island, Evergreen. *Series:* Home Fires, Monty, All My Children, The Practice, Law & Order, Grey's Anatomy (2 Emmy noms.), Rescue Me, Washingtonienne (also pilot). *Guest:* More than 50 appearances.

BURTON, LEVAR
Actor, Director. b. Landstuhl, W. Germany, Feb. 16, 1957. e. U. of Southern California. Signed to play role of Kunta Kinte in TV mini-series, Roots, while still in school. Has hosted Public TV children's shows, Rebop, and Reading Rainbow.
PICTURES: Looking for Mr. Goodbar, The Hunter, The Supernaturals, Star Trek: Generations, Star Trek: First Contact, Yesterday's Target, Star Trek: Insurrection, Dancing in September, Ali, Star Trek: Nemesis, Blizzard (dir. only), Reach for Me (also dir.).
TELEVISION: *Movies:* Billy: Portrait of a Street Kid, Battered, One in a Million: The Ron Leflore Story, Dummy, Guyana Tragedy: The Story of Jim Jones, The Acorn People, Grambling's White Tiger, Emergency Room, The Jesse Owens Story, A Special Friendship, Roots: The Gift, Firestorm: 72 Hours in Oakland, Parallel Lives, The Tiger Woods Story (dir. only), Smart House (dir. only), Taken in Broad Daylight. *Mini-series:* Roots (Emmy nom. 1977). *Series:* Rebop (host), Reading Rainbow (PBS; host, co-exec. prod.; 11 Emmy Awards, 15 other noms.), Star Trek: The Next Generation (acting and dir.), Captain Planet and the Planeteers (voice), Star Trek: Deep Space Nine (episode dir.), Star Trek: Voyager (episode dir.), Christy (acting only), Soul Food (dir. only), Star Trek: Enterprise (episodes dir.), Charmed (dir. only). *Specials:* Almos' a Man, Roots: Celebrating 25 Years. *Guest:* More than 120 appearances.

BURTON, TIM
Director, Producer. b. Burbank, CA, Aug. 25, 1958. Cartoonist since grade school in suburban Burbank. Won Disney fellowship to study animation at California Institute of the Arts. At 20 went to Burbank to work as apprentice animator on Disney lot, working on such features as The Fox and the Hound, The Black Cauldron. Made Vincent, 6-minute stop-motion animation short on his own which was released commercially in 1982 and won several film fest. awards. Also made Frankenweenie, 29 minute live-action film. Appeared in film Singles. Wrote and illustrated-children's book based on The Nightmare Before Christmas.
PICTURES: *Director:* Pee-wee's Big Adventure, Beetlejuice, Batman, Edward Scissorhands (also co-story, prod.), Batman Returns (also co-prod.), The Nightmare Before Christmas (also story, prod. design, co-prod.), Ed Wood (also co-prod.), Mars Attacks! (also prod, s.p..), Sleepy Hollow, Planet of the Apes, Big Fish, Charlie and the Chocolate Factory, Corpse Bride (also writer, Academy Award nom. 2006), 9 (prod. only), Believe It or Not (also prod.), Sweeney Todd: The Demon Barber of Fleet Street (Golden Globe nom. 2008), Frankenweenie (also prod., writer), Alice in Wonderland (also prod.). *Prod.:* 9, *Co-Prod.:* Cabin Boy, James and the Giant Peach, Batman Forever.
TELEVISION: *Movies:* Hansel and Gretel. Episode Director: Aladdin (Faerie Tale Theatre), Alfred Hitchcock Presents, Amazing Stories (Family Dog). *Exec. Prod.:* Beetlejuice, Family Dog, Lost in Oz (also creator, writer). *Writer:* Point Blank. *Guest:* More than 104 appearances.

BURWELL, LOIS
Make-Up.
PICTURES: Gregory's Girl, The Draughtsman's Contract, Legend, No Surrender, Highlander, Mona Lisa, The Princess Bride, The Lonely Passion of Judith Hearne, Without A Clue,

Dirty Rotten Scoundrels, Shirley Valentine, Air America, Hamlet, Blue Ice, The Muppet Christmas Carol, Widows' Peak, Braveheart (Academy Award 1996), Mission: Impossible, The Fifth Element, The Rainmaker, Saving Private Ryan (Academy Award nom. 1999), Hilary and Jackie, The Green Mile, Magnolia, Almost Famous, Captaon Corelli's Mandolin, Catch Me If You Can, The Last Samurai, Collateral, War of the Worlds, Lions for Lambs.
TELEVISION: *Movies:* Jack the Ripper, Charles and Diana: Unhappily Ever After, Jekyll & Hyde, The Return of the Native. *Mini-series:* Master of the Game. *Series:* Red Dwarf.

BUSCEMI, STEVE

Actor. b. Brooklyn, NY, Dec. 13, 1957. Started as standup comedian in New York City, also wrote and acted in numerous one-act plays in collaboration with Mark Boone Jr. Acted in many plays by John Jesurun and worked briefly with the Wooster Group; worked as fireman. Studied acting at Lee Strasberg Inst. in NY.
PICTURES: The Way It Is/Eurydice in the Avenue, No Picnic, Parting Glances, Sleepwalk, Heart, Kiss Daddy Good Night, Call Me, Force of Circumstance, Vibes, Heart of Midnight, Bloodhounds of Broadway, Borders, New York Stories (Life Lessons), Slaves of New York, Mystery Train, Tales from the Dark Side, Miller's Crossing, King of New York, Zandalee, Barton Fink, Billy Bathgate, Crisscross, In the Soup, Reservoir Dogs, Trusting Beatrice, Rising Sun, Twenty Bucks, Ed and His Dead Mother, The Hudsucker Proxy, Floundering, Airheads, Me and the Mob, Pulp Fiction, Billy Madison, Desperado, Somebody to Love, The Search for One-Eye Jimmy, Living in Oblivion, Things to Do in Denver When You're Dead, Pistolero, Fargo, Kansas City, Trees Lounge (also dir., s.p.), John Carpenter's Escape From L.A., Con Air, The Impostors, The Big Lebowski, The Wedding Singer, Armageddon, Louis & Frank, Big Daddy, 28 Days, Final Fantasy (voice), Ghost World (Golden Globe nom., AFI nom.), Monsters,Inc. (voice), The Grey Zone, Double Whammy, The Animal Factory (also dir.), The End of Love, Domestic Disturbance, the Laramie Project, Love in the Time of Money, Mr. Deeds, Spy Kids 2: Island of Lost Dreams, Spy Kids 3-D: Game Over, Deadrockstar, 13 Moons, The Sky Is Green, Minnesota Nice (video short, himself), Big Fish, Home on the Range (voice), The Sky Is Green, Romance & Cigarettes, Sin City, Lonesome Jim (dir. and prod.), The Island, Monster House, Delirious, je t'aime Paris, Charlotte's Web (voice), Interview (also dir., prod.), We're the Millers, The 1 Second Film (doc. assoc. prod.), I Think I Love My Wife, I Now Pronounce You Chuck and Larry, Igor (voice), John Rabe, G-Force (voice), Youth in Revolt, Saint John of Las Vegas (also exec. prod.), Handsome Harry, Rage, Pete Smalls Is Dead, Keep Coming Back, Grown Ups.
TELEVISION: *Movies:* The Last Outlaw Baseball Wives (dir.). *Mini-series:* Lonesome Dove. *Series/Dir:* Homicide: Life on the Street (DGA award nom.), The Adventures of Pete & Pete (actor), Oz, The Sopranos (also actor, DGA award nom., 2 Emmy nom.), Nurse Jackie (dir. only), 30 Rock (Emmy nom. 2008 as guest). *Guest:* More than 86 appearances.

BUSCH, H. DONALD

Exhibitor. b. Philadelphia, PA, Sept. 21, 1935. e. U. of Pennsylvania, physics, math, 1956; law school, 1959. Practiced law, anti-trust & entertainment, 1960-87. 1984, pres., Budco Theatres, Inc. 1975-87. Pres., Busch, Grafman & Von Dreusche, P.C. 1987. Pres. & CEO, AMC Philadelphia, Inc., 1986-96. NATO chmn.,1990-91; chmn. emeritus, 1992. ShowEast, gen. chmn., 1990-91. Will Rogers Memorial Fund, dir. Pres. of NATO of Pennsylvania, 1988. Motion Picture Pioneers, Inc., dir., 1995. 2007, Advisory member of Will Rogers Motion Pictures Pioneers Foundation. 2007, bd. of dir., NATO of Pa.

BUSEY, GARY

Actor, Musician. b. Goose Creek, TX, June 29, 1944. e. Coffeyville Jr. Coll. A.B., 1963; attended Kansas State Coll, Okla. State U. Played drums with the Rubber Band 1963-70. Also drummer with Leon Russell, Willie Nelson (as Teddy Jack Eddy).
PICTURES: Angels Hard as They Come (debut, 1971), Didn't You Hear?, Dirty Little Billy, The Magnificent Seven Ride, The Last American Hero, Lolly Madonna XXX, Hex, Thunderbolt and Lightfoot, The Gumball Rally, A Star Is Born, Straight Time, Big Wednesday, The Buddy Holly Story (Natl. Society of Film Critics Award; Academy Award nom.; Golden Globe nom. 1978), Foolin' Around, Carny, Barbarosa, D.C. Cab, The Bear, Insignificance, Stephen King's Silver Bullet, Let's Get Harry, Eye of the Tiger, Lethal Weapon, Bulletproof, Act of Piracy, Predator 2, My Heroes Have Always Been Cowboys, Hider in the House, Point Break, The Player, Under Siege, South Beach, The Firm, Rookie of the Year. Surviving the Game, Chasers, Breaking Point, Drop Zone, Man With a Gun, Black Sheep, Carried Away, 18 Suspicious Minds, Rough Draft, The Rage, Plato's Run, Livers Ain't Cheap, Lost Highway, Lethal Tender, Steel Sharks, Deadly Current, Warriors, Fear and Loathing in Las Vegas, Detour, Soldier, Jacob Two Two Meets the Hooded Fang, Apocalypse III: Tribulation, G-Men from Hell, Glory Glory, Down and Dirty, A Crack in the Floor, Joe Dirt, Frost: Portrait of a Vampire, Two Faced, Sam and Janet, Quigley, Skin Deep, El Padrino, Latin Dragon, The Reckoning, The Hard Easy, Chasing Ghosts, Depth, Souled Out, Shut Up and Shoot!, The Gingerdead Man, Hallettsville, Blizhny Boy: Final Fight, Depth, Crying 4 U, Lady Samurai, Blizhniy Boy: The Ultimate Fighter, Succubus: Hell Bent, Nite Tales: The Movie, Beyond the Ring, Beyond, Down and Distance, Lizzie, DaZe: Vol. Too (sic) - NonSeNse.
TELEVISION: *Movies:* Bloodsport, The Execution of Private Slovik, The Law, Wild Texas Wind, Chrome Soldiers, Universal Soldier II: Brothers in Arms, Rough Riders, The Girl Next Door, Maneater. *Mini-series:* A Dangerous Life, The Neon Empire, Into the West, Esenin. *Series:* The Texas Wheelers, Howie, Fallen Angels, A Force of One. *Guest*: More than 115 appearances.

BUSFIELD, TIMOTHY

Actor, Director. b. Lansing, MI, June 12, 1957. e. East Tennessee State U; Actor's Theatre of Louisville (as apprentice and resident). Founded Fantasy Theatre in Sacramento, 1986, a professional acting co., which performs in Northern CA schools, providing workshops on playwriting for children and sponsors annual Young Playwrights contest.
THEATRE: Richard II, Young Playwrights Festival (Circle Rep.), A Tale Told, Getting Out (European tour), Green Mountain Guilds Children Theatre, Mass Appeal, The Tempest, A Few Good Men (B'way). Founded & co-prod. The "B" Theatre, 1992, prods. Mass Appeal, Hidden in This Picture.
PICTURES: Stripes, Revenge of the Nerds, Revenge of the Nerds II, Field of Dreams, Sneakers, The Skateboard Kid, Striking Distance, Little Big League, Quiz Show, First Kid, The Souler Opposite, Erasable You, Wanted, Time at the Top, Wanted, Terminal Error, National Security.
TELEVISION: *Movies:* Strays, Calendar Girl-Cop-Killer?: The Bambi Bembenek Story, Murder Between Friends, In the Shadow of Evil, In the Line of Duty: Kidnapped, When Secrets Kill, Buffalo Soldiers, Trucks, Dreamhouse, Carson's Vertical Suburbia, The Darklings, Dead in a Heartbeat, The Lyon's Den (dir.), Summerland (dir.). *Series/Actor:* Reggie, Trapper John M.D., thirtysomething (Emmy Award, 1991; 3 other nom. also dir. 3 episodes), Byrds of Paradise, Champs, The West Wing, Without a Trace (co-exec. prod., dir.), Stuck In the Middle with You. *Dir:* Rude Awakening, Sports Night, Cover me: Based on the True Life of an FBI Family, That's Life, Ed (also co-exec. prod., supervising prod.) Lizzie McGuire, First Years, Danny, Las Vegas, Joan of Arcadia, Miss Match, Good Girls Don't... (dir. pilot), Studio 60 on the Sunset Strip (also actor, consult.), Lipstick Jungle (also episodes exec. prod.). Director of many series episodes. *Guest:* More than 77 appearances.

BUTLER, GERARD

Actor. b. Glasgow, Scotland, Nov. 13, 1969. e. Glasgow University, studied, Lawyer/Solicitor. left to become actor. He received a "Certificate of Bravery" from the Royal Humane Society for saving a drowning boy.
THEATRE: Coriolanus (stage debut), Trainspotting.
PICURES: Her Majesty, Mrs. Brown (debut, 1997), Tomorrow Never Dies, The Cherry Orchard, Harrison's Flowers, Dracula 2000, Reign of Fire, Lara Croft Tomb Raider: The Cradle of Life, Timeline, Dear Frankie, The Phantom of the Opera, The Game of Their Lives, Beowulf & Grendel, Burns, Butterfly on a Wheel, 300, Therese Raquin, Shattered, P.S. I Love You, Priest, Nim's Island, RocknRolla, Game, The Ugly Truth, Gamer, How to Train Your Dragon (voice), Law Abiding Citizen (also prod.), Coriolanus, Burns, The Bounty Hunter.
TELEVISION: *Movies:* Little White Lies, Attila. *Mini-series:* The Jury. *Series:* The Young Person's Guide to Becoming a Rock Star, Lucy Sullivan Is Getting Married. *Guest:* More than 44 appearances.

BUZZI, RUTH

Actress. b. Westerly, RI, July 24, 1936. e. Pasadena Playhouse Col. of Theatre Arts. On Country Music charts with You Oughta Hear the Song. Has received 5 Emmy nominations; Golden Globe winner, AGVA Variety Artist of the Year, 1977, Rhode Island Hall of Fame, Presidential commendation for outstanding artist in the field of entertainment, 1980, NAACP Image Award.
THEATRE: Sweet Charity (Broadway), 4 off-Broadway shows incl. A Man's A Man, Little Mary Sunshine, Cinderella, Wally's Cafe, 18 musical revues and Las Vegas club act.
PICTURES: Record City, Freaky Friday, The Apple Dumpling Gang Rides Again, The North Avenue Irregulars, The Villain, Surf Two, Skatetown USA, Chu Chu and the Philly Flash, The Being, The Bad Guys, Dixie Lanes, Up Your Alley, Diggin' Up Business, My Mom's a Werewolf, It's Your Life Michael Angelo, The Trouble Makers, Boys Will Be Boys, The Adventures of Elmo in Grouchland, Nothing But the Truth, Adventures in Home Schooling, Fallen Angels, City of Shoulders and Noses.
TELEVISION: *Movies*: In Name Only, Once Upon a Brothers Grimm, Legends of the Superheroes, Kids Incorporated: Rock In the New Year, Rockin with Judy Jetson (voice), Hollyrock-a-Bye Baby (voice). *Series*: Rowan & Martin's Laugh-In (Emmy nom. 1969, 1972 Golden Globe Award 1973), The Steve Allen Comedy Hour, Donny & Marie, The Lost Saucer, Betsy Lee's Ghost Town Jamboree, Carol Burnett's The Entertainers, Days of Our Lives, Sesame Street (Emmy nom. 1994), Cro (voice), The Savage Dragon (voice), Sheep In the Big City (voice); semi-regular on 12 other series including Flip, Tony Orlando & Dawn, That Girl, Glen Campbell's Goodtime Hour, Leslie Uggums Show, The Dean Martin Variety Hour (Emmy nom. 1974). *Guest*: More than 127 appearances.

BYRNE, DAVID
Composer, Actor, Singer, Director. b. Dumbarton, Scotland, May 14, 1952. Moved to Baltimore at 7. e. Rhode Island Sch. of Design studying photography, performance and video, and Maryland Inst. Coll. of Art 1971-72. Prod. and dir. music videos. Awarded MTV's Video Vanguard Award, 1985. Best known as the lead singer and chief songwriter of Talking Heads. Composed and performed original score for choreographer Twyla Tharp's The Catherine Wheel (B'way). Wrote music for Robert Wilson's The Knee Plays.
PICTURES: *Soundtrack Writer/Composer:* Stop Making Sense (conceived and stars in concert film), True Stories (dir., s.p., narr.), The Last Emperor (orig. score, Academy Award, Golden Globe Award 1988), Married to the Mob, Heavy Petting, Between the Teeth (also co-dir.), Young Adam, Philadelphia, Airheads, Blue in the Face (also exec. prod.), Times Square, The Animals' Film, King of Comedy, America is Waiting, Revenge of the Nerds, Down and Out in Beverly Hills, Dead End Kids, Cross My Heart, Somebody Is Waiting, The Book of Life, The Bachelor, The Family Man, Someone Like You, Dirty Pretty Things, The Banger Sisters, Young Adam, Secret Window, 13 Going On 30, In Good Company, Bewitched, Sky High, Clerks II, Open Season, Smiley Face, Lars and the Real Girl, Baby Mama, Religulous (doc.), He's Just Not That Into You, Transformers: Revenge of the Fallen, Julie & Julia.
TELEVISION: *Soundtrack/Composer:* A Family Tree, Alive From Off-Center, Survival Guides; Rolling Stone Magazine's 20 Years of Rock and Roll, The Catherine Wheel, Wired Science (theme), Big Love. *Documentaries:* Magicians of the Earth: The Giant Woman and the Lightning Man, Punk: Attitude, P.O.V. (series). *Guest:* More than 60 appearances.

BYRNE, GABRIEL
Actor. b. Dublin, Ireland, May 12, 1950. e. University Coll., Ireland. Worked as archaeologist, then taught Spanish at girls' school. Participated in amateur theatre before acting with Ireland's Focus Theatre, an experimental rep. co. and joining Dublin's Abbey Theatre Co. Cast in long-running TV series the Riordans. Also worked with National Theater in London. Author: Pictures in My Head (1994).
PICTURES: On a Paving Stone Mounted, The Outsider, Excalibur, Hanna K, The Keep, Defence of the Realm, Gothic, Lionheart, Siesta, Hello Again, Julia and Julia, A Soldier's Tale, The Courier, Miller's Crossing, Shipwrecked, Dark Obsession, Cool World, Point of No Return, Into the West (also assoc. prod.), A Dangerous Woman, In the Name of the Father (co-prod. only), Prince of Jutland, A Simple Twist of Fate, Trial by Jury, Little Women, The Usual Suspects, Frankie Starlight, Dead Man, Last of the High Kings (also co-s.p.), Mad Dog Time, Somebody Is Waiting (also prod.), The End of Violence, Toby's Story, Polish Wedding, This Is the Sea, The Man in the Iron Mask, Quest for Camelot (voice), The Brylcreem Boys (also prod.), Stigmata, End of Days, Mad About Mambo (exec. prod.), Canone inverso - Making Love, When Brendan Met Trudy, Spider, Emmett's Mark, Virginia's Run, Ghost Ship, Shade, P.S., Vanity Fair, The Bridge of San Luis Rey, Assault on Precinct 13, Played, Wah-Wah, Jindabyne, At Swim-Two-Birds.
TELEVISION: *Movies/Specials:* Wagner, The Search for Alexander the Great, Treatment, Joyce in June, Mussolini, Christopher Columbus, Lark in the Clear Air (also dir., writer), Buffalo Girls, Weapons of Mass Destruction, Patrick (doc., voice). *Series:* The Riordan's, Bracken, Madigan Men (also co-exec. prod.), In Treatment (2 Emmy noms.; Golden Globe Award 2009). *Guest:* More than 61 appearances.

BYRNE, ROSE
Actress. b. Balmain, Sydney, New South Wales, Australia, July 24, 1979.
PICTURES: Star Wars: Episode II - Attack of the Clones, City of Ghosts, I Capture the Castle, Troy, Wicker Park, The Tenants, Marie Antoinette, The Dead Girl, Sunshine, 28 Weeks Later, Just Buried, The Tender Hook, Adam, Knowing, Get Him to the Greek.
TELEVISION: *Mini-series:* Casanova. *Series:* Echo Point, Damages (2 Golden Globe noms.; Emmy nom. 2009).

C

CAAN, JAMES
Actor. b. Bronx, NY, March 26, 1939. e. Hofstra U. Studied with Sanford Meisner at the Neighborhood Playhouse. Appeared off-B'way in La Ronde, 1961. Also on B'way in Mandingo, Blood Sweat and Stanley Poole.
PICTURES: Irma La Douce (debut, 1963), Lady in a Cage, The Glory Guys (Golden Globe nom. 1966), Red Line 7000, El Dorado, Games, Countdown, Jssourney to Shiloh, Submarine X-1, The Rain People, Rabbit Run, T.R. Baskin, The Godfather (Academy Award nom.; Golden Globe nom. 1973), Slither, Cinderella Liberty, The Gambler (Golden Globe nom. 1975), Freebie and the Bean, The Godfather Part II, Funny Lady (Golden Globe nom. 1976), Rollerball, The Killer Elite, Harry and Walter Go To New York, Silent Movie, A Bridge Too Far, Another Man Another Chance, Comes a Horseman, Chapter Two, Hide in Plain Sight (also dir.), Thief, Bolero, Kiss Me Goodbye, Gardens of Stone, Alien Nation, Dick Tracy, Misery, The Dark Backward, For the Boys, Honeymoon in Vegas, The Program, Flesh & Bone, A Boy Called Hate, Bottle Rocket, Eraser, Bulletproof, This is My Father, The Yards, Mickey Blue Eyes, Luckytown, Way of the Gun, Viva Las Nowhere, In the Shadows, Night at the Golden Eagle, Dogville, City of Ghosts, This Thing of Ours, Jericho Mansions, Dallas 362, Castle of Lies, Elf, Santa's Slay, New York, I Love You, Middle Men, Mercy, Cloudy with a Chance of Meatballs (voice), The Godmother, Sweetwater, Minkow, Henry's Crime, Anyone's Son, The Last City.
TELEVISION: *Movies:* Brian's Song (Emmy nom. 1972), Poodle Springs, Warden of Red Rock, A Glimpse of Hell, Lathe of Heaven, Blood Crime, The Incredible Mrs. Ritchie (Emmy nom. 2004), Wisegal. *Mini-series:* Les Uns et les autres, Naked Hollywood (as himself). *Series:* Las Vegas. *Specials:* AFI's 100 Year 100 Stars, Playboy: The Party Continues, Las Vegas. *Guest:* More than 112 appearances.

CACOYANNIS, MICHAEL
Producer, Director, Writer. b. Limassoc, Cyprus, June 11, 1922. Aka Mihalis Kakogiannis. Studied law in London, admitted to bar at age 21. Became a producer of BBC's wartime Greek programs while attending dramatic school. After acting on the stage in England, left in 1952 for Greece, where he made his first film, Windfall in Athens, with his own script. While directing Greek classical plays, he continued making films.
PICTURES: *Director/Writer:* Windfall in Athens (Sunday Awakening; debut, 1954), Stella, Girl in Black, A Matter of Dignity (The Final Lie), Our Last Spring (Eroica), The Wastrel, Electra, Zorba the Greek (3 Academy Award noms. Golden Globe nom. 1965), The Day the Fish Came Out, The Trojan Women, Attila '74, Iphigenia, Sweet Country, Up Down and Sideways, Varya, The Cherry Orchard (also prod.).

CAGE, NICOLAS
Actor. b. Long Beach, CA, Jan. 7, 1964. r.n. Nicholas Coppola. Nephew of dir. Francis Ford Coppola. Joined San Francisco's American Conservatory Theatre at age 15. While attending Beverly Hills High School won role on tv pilot Best of Times.
PICTURES: Fast Times at Ridgemont High (debut, 1982; billed as Nicholas Coppola), Valley Girl, Rumble Fish, Racing with the Moon, The Cotton Club, Birdy, The Boy in Blue, Peggy Sue Got Married, Raising Arizona, Moonstruck (Golden Globe nom. 1988), Vampire's Kiss, Fire Birds, Wild at Heart, Tempo di Mecidere (Time to Kill), Zandalee, Honeymoon in Vegas (Golden Globe nom. 1993), Amos & Andrew, DeadFall, Red Rock West, Guarding Tess, It Could Happen to You, Trapped in Paradise, Kiss of Death, Leaving Las Vegas (Academy Award, Chicago Film Critics Award, Nat'l Society of Film Critics Award; Golden Globe Award 1996), The Rock, Con Air, Face/Off, Tom Slick: Monster Hunter, 8mm, City of Angels, Snake Eyes, Bringing Out the Dead, Gone in Sixty Seconds, Captain Corelli's Mandolin, Christmas Carol: The Movie (voice), Windtalkers, Sonny ((also prod., dir.), Adaptation (Academy Award nom., Golden Globe nom. 2003), The Life of David Gale (prod. only), Matchstick Men, Ghost Rider, National Treasure, The Weather Man, Lord of War (also prod.), Land of Destiny, Next (also prod.), World Trade Center, The Wicker Man, Ghost Rider, The Ant Bully (voice), National Treasure: The Book of Secrets, Time to Kill (also prod.), Grindhouse, Next (also prod.), Bangkok Dangerous (also prod.), G-Force (voice), The Bad Lieutenant: Port of Call - New Orleans (also prod.), Knowing, Astro Boy (voice), A Thousand Words (prod. only), The Hungry Rabbit Jumps, Kick-Ass, Season of the Witch, The Sorcerer's Apprentice (also exec. prod.), Drive Angry.
TELEVISION: *Movies:* Best of Times, Industrial Symphony No. 1: The Dream of the Broken Hearted. *Series:* The Dresden Files (exec. prod. only). *Guest:* More than 142 appearances.

CAINE, SIR MICHAEL
Actor. r.n. Maurice Micklewhite. b. London, England, March 14, 1933. Asst. stage mgr. Westminster Rep. (Sussex, UK 1953); Lowestoft Rep. 1953-55. London stage: The Room, The Dumbwaiter, Next Time I'll Sing For You (1963). Author: Michael Caine's Moving Picture Show or: Not Many People Know This Is the Movies, Acting on Film, What's It All About? (autobiography, 1993). Awarded C.B.E., 1992. Video: Michael Caine—Acting on Film.
PICTURES: Has appeared in 98 pictures, incl.: A Hill in Korea (debut, 1956; aka Hell in Korea), How to Murder A Rich Uncle, The Key, Two-Headed Spy, Blind Spot, Breakout (Danger Within), Foxhole in Cairo, Bulldog Breed, The Day the Earth Caught Fire, Solo for Sparrow, Zulu, The Ipcress File, Alfie (Academy Award nom. Golden Globe nom. 1967), The Wrong Box, Gambit (Golden Globe nom. 1967), Funeral in Berlin, Hurry Sundown, Woman Times Seven, Billion Dollar Brain, Deadfall, The Magus, Play Dirty, The Italian Job, The Battle of Britain, Too Late the Hero, The Last Valley, Get Carter, Kidnapped, X Y & Zee, Pulp, Sleuth (Academy Award nom. Golden Globe nom. 1973), The Black Windmill, The Marseille Contract, The Wilby Conspiracy, Peeper, The Romantic Englishwoman, The Man Who Would Be King, Harry and Walter Go to New York, The Eagle Has Landed, A Bridge Too Far, Ashanti, Beyond the Poseidon Adventure, The Island, Dressed to Kill, Victory, Deathtrap, Educating Rita

(Academy Award nom. Golden Globe Award 1984), Beyond the Limit, Blame It on Rio, The Jigsaw Man, The Holcroft Covenant, Hannah and Her Sisters (Academy Award for Best Supporting Actor, Golden Globe nom. 1987), Sweet Liberty, Mona Lisa, Half Moon Street, Jaws—The Revenge, The Whistle Blower, The Fourth Protocol (also exec. prod.), Surrender, Without a Clue, Dirty Rotten Scoundrels (Golden Globe nom. 1989), A Shock to the System, Mr. Destiny, Bullseye!, The Muppet Christmas Carol, On Deadly Ground, Bullet in Beijing, Blood & Wine, Shadow Run, Little Voice (Golden Globe Award 1999), Curtain Call, The Cider House Rules (Academy Award, Golden Globe nom. 2000), Quills, Shiner, Get Carter, Miss Congeniality, The Quiet American (Academy Award nom. Golden Globe nom. 2003), Last Orders, Quicksand, Austin Powers in Goldmember, The Actors, Secondhand Lions, The Statement, Around the Bend, Batman Begins, Bewitched, Miss Congeniality 2, The Weather Man, Children of Men, The Prestige, Flawless, Sleuth, The Dark Knight, Is There Anybody There?, Harry Brown, Inception.
TELEVISION: *Movies:* Jack the Ripper (Golden Globe Award 1989), Jekyll and Hyde (Emmy nom. Golden Globe nom. 1990), Blue Ice (also prod.), World War II: When Lions Roared (Emmy nom. 1994), 20,000 Leagues under the Sea, Mandela and De Klerk (Emmy nom. Golden Globe nom. 1997). *Series:* Rickles (1975). In more than 100 British teleplays 1957-63 incl. The Compartment, The Playmates, Hobson's Choice, Funny Noises with Their Mouths, The Way with Reggie, Luck of the Draw, Hamlet, The Other Man, Freedom: A History of Us (doc.). *Guest:* More than 190 appearances.

CALEMZUK, EMILIANO

Executive. TV production veteran Calemzuk's early career experiences were in Miami at Hero Productions (currently Globecast North America) where he led the start-up of the music television network HTV. He joined News Corporation in 1998 as associate director of marketing and promotions for Fox Latin America. In 2000, Calemzuk became gen. mgr. of Fox Kids Latin America where, in just one year, he successfully implemented a turnaround of the network, making it the fastest growing children's channel in Latin America. He then became v.p. and deputy managing director of FOX Latin American Channels. Based in Los Angeles, he supervised all operating divisions of the FOX channels across 19 countries. In 2002, Calemzuk took the helm of FOX International Channels Italy, leading the creation and development of the 10-channel group currently broadcasting on Sky Italia. Under Calemzuk, FOX became and remains the market leader in ratings and advertising revenues through its networks there. He was based in Rome and was responsible for day-to-day operations of the channels, in addition to supervising the FOX channels in Spain, France and Eastern Europe, and the National Geographic channel in Germany and Turkey. In Feb. 2007, after five years as pres., FOX International Channels Italy, Calemzuk was named to his current position of pres. of Fox Television Studios (FtvS). FtvS series include: Talkshow with Spike Feresten, Crowned (CW), The Shield (FX), The Riches (FX), Saving Grace (TNT), Burn Notice (USA) and The Girls Next Door (E!). 2010 he became CEO of Shine Group Americas.

CALLAN, MICHAEL

Actor, Singer, Dancer. b. Philadelphia, PA, Nov. 22, 1935. Singer, dancer, Philadelphia nightclubs; to New York in musicals including The Boy Friend and West Side Story; dancer at Copacabana nightclub; in short-run plays, Las Vegas: That Certain Girl, Love Letters. Won Golden Globe 1961, nom. 1960 for most promising newcomer.
PICTURES: They Came to Cordura (debut, 1958) The Flying Fontaines, Because They're Young, Pepe, Mysterious Island, Gidget Goes Hawaiian, 13 West Street, Bon Voyage, The Interns, The Victors, The New Interns, Cat Ballou, You Must Be Joking!, The Magnificent Seven Ride!, Frasier the Sensuous Lion, Lepke, The Photographer, The Cat and The Canary, Record City, Double Exposure (also prod.), Chained Heat, Freeway, Leprechaun III, Hello Muddah—Hello Fadduh (prod. only), Stuck On You, The Still Life.
TELEVISION: *Movies:* In Name Only, Donner Pass: The Road to Survival, Last of the Great Survivors, Young Hearts, My Wicked Wicked Ways...Legend of Errol Flynn. *Mini-series:* Blind Ambition, Scruples. *Series:* Occasional Wife, One Life To Live, The Adventures of Superboy, Murder, She Wrote. *Guest:* More than 65 appearances.

CALLEY, JOHN

Producer, Executive. b. Jersey City, NJ, June 30, 1930. Exec., Ted Bates advertising and NBC; exec. v.p., Filmways, Inc., 1961-1968; president, vice chairman, exec. v.p., Warner Bros., Inc., 1968-81; 1989-93 independent prod., president & COO, United Artists (MGM); Pres. & COO of Sony Pictures Entertainment (SPE), 1996; chairman & CEO, SPE, 1998-Oct. 2003, at which time he resigned. Currently is CEO of John Calley Productions, and Head of Prod. at Warner Bros. Pictures in Culver City, CA. 2009 received the Irving G. Thalberg Memorial Award.
PICTURES: *Assoc. prod./Prod. or Exec. Prod.:* The Wheeler Dealers, Face in the Rain, The Americanization of Emily, The Sandpiper, The Cincinnati Kid, The Loved One, Eye of the Devil, Don't Make Waves, Castle Keep, Catch-22, Fat Man & Little Boy, Postcards from the Edge, The Remains of the Day, One Night Stand (acting), The Da Vinci Code, Closer, The Jane Austen Book Club, Angels & Demons. *Documentaries:* Stanley Kubrick: A Life in Pictures, This Is Gary McFarland, A Decade Under the Influence, A Legacy of Filmmakers: The Early Years of American Zoetrope.
TELEVISION: *Mini-series: Exec. prod.:* The Company.

CALLOW, SIMON

Actor, Writer, Director. b. London, June 13, 1949. e. Queens, U. of Belfast, The Drama Centre. Originated role of Mozart in London premiere of Amadeus and Burgess/Chubb in Single Spies. Author: Being an Actor, Acting in Restoration Comedy, Charles Laughton: A Difficult Actor, Shooting the Actor, Orson Welles: The Road to Xanadu.
THEATRE: London: Plumber's Progress, The Doctor's Dilemma, Soul of the White Ant, Blood Sports, The Resistible Rise of Arturo Ui, Amadeus, Restoration, The Beastly Beatitudes of Balthazar B, Titus Andronicus (Bristol Old Vic), Faust. Shakespeare's Sonnets. Director: Loving Reno, The Infernal Machine (also translator), Jacques and His Master (also trans.; L.A.), Single Spies, Shades, My Fair Lady (Natl. tour), Shirley Valentine (London and NY), Carmen Jones, Ice.
PICTURES: Amadeus, A Room With a View, The Good Father, Maurice, Manifesto, Postcards From the Edge, Mr. and Mrs. Bridge, The Ballad of the Sad Cafe (dir. only), Howards End, Four Weddings and a Funeral, Street Fighter, Jefferson in Paris, Ace Ventura: When Nature Calls, James and the Giant Peach, The Scarlet Tunic, Bedroom and Hallways, Shakespeare in Love, Notting Hill, Junk, No Man's Land, Christmas Carol: The Movie (voice), Thunderpants, George and the Dragon, Sex & Violence, Merci Docteur Rey, Bright Young Things, The Phantom of the Opera, Cabbages & Queens, Bob the Butler, Rag Tale, Where Love Reigns, Flushed Away (voice), Surveillance 24/7 (actor), Arn: The Knight Templar (actor), Chemical Wedding Chemical Wedding (actor), No Ordinary Trifle, .
TELEVISION: *Movies:* The Crucifer of Blood, The Trials of Oz, Femme Fatale, Man of Destiny, La Ronde, All the World's a Stage, Wings of Song, The Dybbuk, Instant Enlightenment, Honour, Profit and Pleasure, Old Flames, Revolutionary Witness: Palloy, The Woman in White, Hans Christian Andersen: My Life as a Fairy Tale, Marple: The Body in the Library, The Curse of King Tut's Tomb, Anatomy of Hope (actor). *Mini-series:* Dead Head, David Copperfield, Trial & Retribution II, Angels in America, The Company (actor). *Series:* Chance in a Million, Trial & Retribution III, Deadly Appearances, Robert's Rescue, Don't Eat the Neighbours, Shoebox Zoo (voice). *Documentaries:* Judi Dench: A BAFTA Tribute, Great Composers, Alec Guinness: A Secret Man, Far Far Away Idol (short, voice). *Guest:* More than 96 appearances.

CALPETER, LYNN

Executive. Cornell Univ., B.S. degree in business mgt. and applied economics. Calpeter is a veteran General Electric (GE) executive, joining GE in 1986 through its financial mgt. program after college. After the program, Calpeter spent six years on GE's corporate audit staff, where she audited a number of GE businesses, including Aircraft Engines, Plastics and NBC. In 1993, Calpeter joined GE Plastics; by 1998, appointed manager GEP Global PSI. From 1999-2001, CFO of the NBC Television Stations Division. Moved to v.p. of GE's corporate audit staff in Fairfield, CT, during 2002. In July 2003, Calpeter became exec. v.p. & CFO of NBC. When NBC merged with Vivendi Universal in May 2004, Calpeter assumed her current post as executive v.p. & CFO of NBC Universal. She is responsible for overseeing NBC Universal's financial planning and operations and plays a key role in the company's strategic business initiatives. She reports directly to NBC Universal CEO Jeff Zucker.

CAMERON, JAMES

Director, Writer, Producer. b. Kapuskasing, Ontario, Canada, Aug. 16, 1954. e. Fullerton Junior Col. (physics). 1990, formed Lightstorm Entertainment.
PICTURES: Piranha II—The Spawning (dir.), The Terminator (dir., s.p.), Rambo: First Blood Part II (co-s.p.), Aliens (dir., s.p.), The Abyss (dir., s.p.), Terminator 2: Judgment Day (dir., co-s.p., prod.), Point Break (exec. prod.), True Lies (dir., co-s.p., prod.), Strange Days (co-prod., co-s.p., story), Titanic (dir., prod., story, Academy Award, Golden Globe Award, Best Pic., Best Dir., Best Film Edit., 1998), True Lies 2, Ghosts of the Abyss (dir. only) Solaris (prod.) Terminator 3: Rise of the Machines (writer), Battle Angel, Godspeed, Battle Angel, Aliens of the Deep (doc. also cinematographer), Fantastic Voyage, Terminator Salvation (writer), Avatar (prod., dir., writer, 3 Academy Award noms.; DGA nom.; Golden Globe Award; WGA nom. 2010), Sanctum (prod.). *Actor:* Fear City: A Family Style Comedy, Your Studio and You, Titanic, The Muse, High Heels and Low Lifes.
TELEVISION: *Movies:* Dark Angel (writer, exec. prod.), Earthship TV (dir.). *Series:* Dark Angel, Terminator: The Sarah Connor Chronicles (writer). *Actor:* Alien Evolution. *Special:* Canada for Haiti. *Documentaries:* Expedition: Bismarck (actor, prod., dir., Emmy nom. 2003), Last Mysteries of the Titanic (prod.), Titanic Adventure (prod.), The Exodus Decoded (narr., exec. prod.), The Lost Tomb of Jesus (doc., exec. prod.). *Guest:* More than 85 appearances.

CAMERON, KIRK

Actor. b. Canoga Park, CA, Oct. 12, 1970. m. actress Chelsea Noble. Sister is actress Candace Cameron. Started doing TV commercials at age 9.
PICTURES: The Best of Times, Like Father-Like Son, Listen to Me, The Willies, Left Behind: World at War, Fireproof.
TELEVISION: *Movies:* Goliath Awaits, Starflight: The Plane That Couldn't Land, A Little Piece of Heaven, Star Struck, The Computer Wore Tennis Shoes, You Lucky Dog, The Growing Pains Movie, The Miracle of the Cards, Night of Joy (host), The Magic 7 (comp.), Growing Pains II: Home Equity, Growing Pains: Return of the Seavers, Night of Joy (host), The Magic 7 (composer). *Series:* Two Marriages, Grownning Pains (2 Golden Globe nom. 1988, 1989), Kirk, The Way of the Master (himself). *Specials:* The Woman Who Willed a Miracle, Andrea's Story. Ice Capades with Kirk Cameron. *Guest:* More than 71 appearances.

CAMP, COLLEEN

Actress, Producer. b. San Francisco, CA, June 7, 1953. Spent 2 years as a bird trainer at Busch Gardens before being noticed by an agent and cast on TV. TV debut on The Dean Martin Show. Assoc. prod. on Martha Coolidge's film The City Girl. Sang several songs in They All Laughed and made Billboard charts with song One Day Since Yesterday.
PICTURES: Battle for the Planet of the Apes (debut, 1973), Swinging Cheerleaders, Death Game (The Seducers), Funny Lady, Smile, The Gumball Rally, Cats in a Cage, Game of Death, Apocalypse Now, Cloud Dancer, They All Laughed, The Seduction, Valley Girl, Smokey and the Bandit III, Rosebud Beach Hotel, The Joy of Sex, Police Academy II, Doin' Time, D.A.R.Y.L., Clue, Walk Like a Man, Illegally Yours, Track 29, Wicked Stepmother, My Blue Heaven, Wayne's World, The Vagrant, Un-Becoming Age, Sliver, Last Action Hero, Greedy, Naked in New York, Die Hard With a Vengeance, The Baby-sitter's Club, Three Wishes, Plump Fiction, House Arrest, The Ice Storm, Speed 2: Cruise Control, Jazz Night, Election, Love Stinks, Goosed, Loser, Bar Hopping, Someone Like You, An American Rhapsody, Rat Race, Second to Die, Joshua, L.A. Twister, Who's Your Daddy, War Magician, The Monster of Longwood (prod. only), In Good Company, Rumor Has It, War Magician (prod. only), 5-25-77, Material Girls, Running with Scissors, Factory Girl, Four Christmases, Hollywood & Wine, Burning Palms, Imps* (segment), Winter of Frozen Dreams, Cirque du Freak: The Vampire's Assistant, Hollywood & Wine, Burning Palms, Psych 9.
TELEVISION: *Movies:* Amelia Earhart, Lady of the House, Addicted to His Love, Backfield in Motion, For Their Own Good, The Right to Remain Silent, How to Make a Monster (also prod.), The Day the World Ended (prod. only), She Creature (prod. only), Teenage Caveman (prod. only), Mystery Woman: Mystery Weekend. *Mini-series:* Rich Man Poor Man Book II. *Series:* Dallas, The Minor Accomplishments of Jackie Woodman. *Specials:* Going Home Again, Dorothy Stratten: The E! True Hollywood Story. *Guest:* More than 47 appearances.

CAMP, JOE

Producer, Director, Writer. b. St. Louis, MO, Apr. 20, 1939. e. U. of Mississippi, B.B.A. Acct. exec. McCann-Erickson Advt., Houston 1961-62; owner Joe Camp Real Estate 1962-64; acct. exec. Norsworthy-Mercer, Dallas 1964-69; dir. TV commercials; founder and pres. Mulberry Square Prods, 1971-present. Author: Underdog.
PICTURES: *Dir./Prod./Writer:* Benji, Hawmps, For the Love of Benji, The Double McGuffin, Oh Heavenly Dog, Benji the Hunted, Benji Returns: The Promise of Christmas, Benji Returns: Rags to Riches (dir., writer, prod.), Benji: Off the Leash! (also actor).
TELEVISION: *Specials:* The Phenomenon of Benji (dir., writer, prod.), Benji's Very Own Christmas Story (dir., prod., writer, Emmy nom. 1979), Benji at Work (prod., writer, Emmy nom. 1980), Benji at Marineland (dir., writer), Benji Zax and the Alien Prince (dir.).

CAMPANELLA, TOM

Executive. b. Houston, TX, 1944. e. City U. of NY. Began career in the mail room of Paramount Pictures in 1961, which developed into an association spanning more than 40 years. From Paramount's mailroom Campanella moved through the ranks as an asst. business mgr.; then worked for corporate div. and Motion Picture Group. He was named exec. dir., nat'l adv., 1979; made v.p., nat'l. adv., 1982; appointed sr. v.p., adv., for M.P. Group. of Paramount, 1984. Exec. v.p., nat'l. adv. & promo., 1990-1997; When he stepped down at Paramount in Feb. 2004, he was exec. v.p. of worldwide marketing/advertising. Currently holds senior advisory role.

CAMPBELL, BRUCE

Actor, Producer. b. Birmingham, MI, June 22, 1958.
PICTURES: The Evil Dead (debut, 1983; also exec. prod.), Crimewave (also co-prod.), Evil Dead 2 (also co-prod.), Maniac Cop, Moontrap, Darkman, Maniac Cop 2, Sundown: The Vampire in Retreat, Mindwarp, Lunatics: A Love Story (also prod.), Waxwork II: Lost in Time, Army of Darkness (also co-prod.), The Hudsucker Proxy, The Demolitionist, Congo, Assault on Dome 4, Menno's Mind, John Carpenter's Escape From L.A., Running Time, McHale's Navy, The Ice Rink, From Dusk Till Dawn 2: Texas Blood Money, Nobody Knows, Hubert's Brain, The Majestic, Spider Man, Bubba Ho-Tep, Serving Sara, Phantasm's End, Spider-Man2, The Woods, Sky High, Depth, The Evil Dead (prod only), The Ant Bully (voice), Aqua Teen Hunger Force Colon Movie Film for Theaters (voice), My Name is Bruce (also prod., dir.), Spider-Man 3, White on Rice (voice), Cloudy with a Chance of Meatballs (voice), The Gatekeeper, Bruce Vs. Frankenstein (also dir.).
TELEVISION: *Movies:* Tornado!, Missing Links, The Love Bug, In the Line of Duty: Blaze of Glory, Goldrush: A Real Life Alaskan Adventure, Terminal Invasion, Masters of Horror (host), Man With the Screaming Brain (actor, dir. s.p., prod.), Alien Apocalypse, Touch the Top of the World, Burn Notice. *Series:* Generations, The Adventures of Brisco County Jr., Timecop, Ellen, Xena: Warrior Princess (also dir. 7 episodes), Hercules: The Legendary Journeys (also dir. 7 episodes), Jack of All Trades (also co - exec. prod.), The Replacements (voice), Burn Notice. *Guest:* More than 80 appearances.

CAMPBELL, CHRISTIAN

Actor. b. Toronto, Canada, May 12, 1972. Sister is actress Neve Campbell.
PICTURES: Next Time, Trick, Cold Hearts, Angels, Plead, Who is A.B., Thank You Good Night, The Good Things, Gargoyle, Reefer Madness: the Movie Musical, Burial at Sea, Clear Blue Tuesday, Neighbor, Casino Jack.
TELEVISION: *Movies:* School's Out, City Boy, Born to Run, Picture Perfect, Seduced by Madness, I've Been Waiting for You, The Piano Man's Daughter, Banshee, Grave Obsession, You Belong to Me. *Series:* Malibu Shores, The $treet, Max Steel, The Atwood Stories, All My Children, The Book of Daniel. *Documentary:* Queen of the Whole Wide World.

CAMPBELL, MICHAEL L.

Executive. b. Knoxville, TN, Jan. 22, 1954. Worked for White Stores, Inc. in a management position until 1982. Founded first theatre venture, Premiere Cinemas in 1982. Premiere grew to 150 screens and was sold to Cinemark in 1989. Founded Regal Cinemas in 1989. He is chairman, president and CEO of Regal Cinemas, Inc. The company is now part of Regal Entertainment Group, which includes Regal Cinemas, United Artists Theatres and Edwards Theatres. In 2005, Campbell became co-chairman, co-CEO of Regal Entertainment Group. In 2007, Regal operated 6,386 screens in 539 locations in 40 states and the District of Columbia. Regal operates approximately 18% of all indoor screens in the U.S. including theatres in 43 of the top 50 U.S. markets and growing suburban areas. Campbell was named Coopers & Lybrand regional entreprenuer of the year, 1993. Campbell is a director of NCM Inc., National CineMedia, Fandango, Inc. and the National Association of Theatre Owners ("NATO") and serves on its executive committee of the bd. of dir.

CAMPBELL, NEVE

Actress. b. Guelph, Ontario, Canada, Oct. 3, 1973. Brother is actor Christian Campbell.
PICTURES: Paint Cans, The Dark, Love Child, The Craft, Scream, Simba's Pride (voice), Scream 2, Hairshirt (also prod.), Wild Things, 54, Three to Tango, Scream 3, Investigating Sex, Panic, Drowning Mona, Lost Junction, Blind Horizon, The Remains of the Piano, The Company (also prod., writer), Churchill: The Hollywood Years, When Will I Be Loved?, Relative Strangers, Reefer Madness: the Movie Musical, The Mermaids Singing, Closing the Ring, Partition, Agent Crush (voice), Closing the Ring, Vivaldi, Scream 4, Owl Song.
TELEVISION: *Movies:* Web of Deceit, Baree, I Know My Son is Alive, The Forget-Me-Not Murders, The Canterville Ghost, Fitzgerald. *Mini-series:* Burn Up, Sea Wolf. *Series:* Catwalk, Party of Five, The Philanthropist (also pilot). *Guest:* More than 73 appearances.

CAMPION, JANE

Director, Writer. b. Wellington, New Zealand, April 30, 1954. e. Victoria Univ. of Wellington (BA, anthropology, 1975), Sydney Coll. of Arts (BA, painting, 1979). Attendend Australian Sch. of Film & TV in early 1980's, where she debuted as dir. & writer with short film Peel (1982; Palme d'Or at Cannes Film Fest., 1986). Other short films: A Girl's Own Story, Passionless Moments, After Hours, Two Friends, Mishaps of Seduction & Conquest, The Water Diary, My Sister and I, Cinema16: World Short Films.
PICTURES: *Director/Writer:* Sweetie (feature debut, 1989; Australian Film Awards for Best Director & Film; LA Film Critics New Generation Award, American Indept. Spirit Award), An Angel at My Table (Venice Film Fest. Silver Lion Award, Indept. Spirit Award), The Piano (Academy Award, WGA, LA Film Critics, NY Film Critics, & Natl. Society of Film Critics Awards for best screenplay; LA Film Critics & NY Film Critics Awards for best director; Cannes Film Fest. Award for best film 1994), The Portrait of a Lady, Holy Smoke, Soft Fruit (exec. prod.), In the Cut, Somersault (script con.), 8 (segment dir., writer), Abduction: The Megumi Yokota Story (prod., doc.), Bright Star,(dir., writer).
TELEVISION: *Movie:* Two Friends. *Series/Episode director:* Dancing Daze. *Mini-series:* Reilly: Ace of Spies, An Angel at My Table.

CANNELL, STEPHEN J.

Writer, Producer, Actor. b. Los Angeles, CA, May 2, 1941 e. U. of Oregon, B.A., 1964. After coll. worked at father's decorating firm for 4 years while writing scripts in evening. Sold 1st script for Adam 12, 1966. Was asked to serve as head writer at Universal Studios. CEO, Stephen J. Cannell Prods. TV prod. co. he formed in 1979. Also formed The Cannell Studios, parent co. 1986. Natl. chmn., Orton Dyslexia Society. Received Mystery Writers award 1975; 4 Writers Guild Awards. Acted in films: Identity Crisis, Posse. Received WGA (Laurel Award) for TV writing achievement 2006.
PICTURES: *Acting:* Identity Crisis, Posse, The Contract, Half Past Dead. *Exec. prod.:* Dead Above Ground, It Waits (also writer), *Prod.:* Bad Boy, Demon Hunter, The A-Team, Left in Darkness, The Tooth Fairy (also writer), The Poker House.
TELEVISION: *Movies/Writer/Exec. Prod.:* Toma, Chase, Columbo: Double Exposure The Rockford Files (pilot, assoc. prod.), The November Plan Scott Free, Dr. Scorpion, The Chinese Typewriter, The Night Rider (pilot), Midnight Offerings, Hunter (pilot), Brothers-in-Law, Stingray (pilot), Charley Hannah, The Last Precinct (pilot), You Ruined My Life, Scandals, The Great Pretender, Greyhounds, Two, Jake Lassiter: Justice on the Bayou, The Return of Hunter, A Child Is Missing, The Rockford Files: Friends and Foul Play, Wiseguy (pilot), The Rockford Files: Punishment and Crime (pilot), Them, Hawaii-Five O (pilot), The Rockford Files: Murder and Misdemeanors, Hunter: Return to Justice, Threshold, 24/24 Rule, Ice Spiders. *Series:* The Rockford Files (creator, writer, prod.; Emmy Award 1978, Emmy nom. 1979, 1980), The Jordan Chance, The Duke, Stone, 10 Speed and Brownshoe (Emmy nom.; WGA Award 1980), Nightside, Midnight Offerings, The Greatest American Hero (Emmy nom.; WGA nom. 1981), The Quest, Them, The Rockford Files: Crime and Punishment, The Rockford Files: Murder and Misdemeanors. *Prod.:* The A-Team, Hardcastle and McCormick, The Rousters, Riptide, Brothers-in-Law, *Creator/Prod.:* Baa Baa Black Sheep, Richie Brockelman, Hunter, Wise Guy (Emmy nom. 1989), 21 Jump Street, J.J. Starbuck, Sonny Spoon, Sirens (co-exec. prod.), Unsub (exec. prod., writer, pilot), Booker (exec. prod.), Top of the Hill (exec. prod.), Scene of the Crime (exec.-prod., creator), The Commish, The Hat Squad, Traps, Greyhounds (exec. prod., writer), Hawkeye, Marker (exec. prod., creator), Renegade (exec. prod., creator), U.S. Customs Classified (exec. prod., host), Two (exec. prod.), Profit (exec. prod.), Rockford Files: Murders and Misdemeanors, Hunter (exec. prod., 2003), The Rockford Files: If It Bleeds... It Leads, Hunter: Back in Force, Threshold.

CANNON, DANNY

Director, Producer, Writer. b. London, England, 1968.
PICTURES: Strangers (also s.p.), The Young Americans (also s.p.), Judge Dredd, Phoenix, Boston Kickout (exec prod. only), I Still Know What You Did Last Summer, Bjork: Volumen (music video), Goal! The Dream Begins (dir.).
TELEVISION: *Movies:* Capitol Law, The Line. *Series.:* C.S.I.: Crime Scene Investigation (dir. co-exec. prod.; 3 Emmy noms.), C.S.I.: Miami (co-exec. prod), C.S.I.: NY (exec. prod.), Eleventh Hour (exec. prod.), The Forgotten (exec. prod.), Dark Blue (exec. prod.).

CANNON, DYAN

Actress. r.n. Samille Diane Friesen. b. Tacoma, WA, Jan. 4, 1937. e. U. of Washington. Studied with Sanford Meisner. Modelled before becoming actress. Directed, produced and wrote short film Number One (Acad. Award nom.).
THEATRE: B'way: The Fun Couple, Ninety-Day Mistress. Tour: How to Succeed in Business Without Really Trying.
PICTURES: The Rise and Fall of Legs Diamond (debut, 1960), This Rebel Breed, Bob & Carol & Ted & Alice (Academy Award nom.; 2 Golden Globe nom. 1970), Doctors' Wives, The Anderson Tapes, The Love Machine, The Burglars, Such Good Friends (Golden Globe nom. 1972), Number One (Academy Award nom. best short film), Shamus, The Last of Sheila, Child Under a Leaf, Heaven Can Wait (Academy Award nom.; Golden Globe Award 1979), Revenge of the Pink Panther, Honeysuckle Rose, Coast To Coast, Deathtrap, Author Author, Caddyshack II, The End of Innocence (also dir., prod., s.p.), The Pickle, Out to Sea, That Darn Cat, 8 Heads in a Duffel Bag, The Sender, Allie and Me, Kiss of a Stranger, Kangaroo Jack, Boynton Beach Club.
TELEVISION: *Movies:* The Virginia Hill Story, Lady of the House, Having It All, Arthur the King, Jenny's War, Rock 'n' Roll Mom, Jailbirds, Christmas in Connecticut, Based on an Untrue Story, A Perry Mason Mystery: The Case of the Jealous Jokester, Black Jaq, Diamond Girl, My Mother the Spy, A Kiss at Midnight, Women Without Men. *Mini-series:* Master of the Game. *Series:* Ally McBeal, Three Sisters. *Guest:* More than 102 appearances.

CANTON, MARK

Executive, Producer. b. New York, NY, June 19, 1949. e. UCLA, 1978. v.p., m.p. dev., MGM; 1979, exec. v.p., JP Organization; 1980, v.p. prod., Warner Bros.; named sr. v.p., 1983 and pres. worldwide theatrical prod. div., 1985; v.p. worldwide m.p. production, 1989; appointed chmn. of Columbia Pictures, 1991. Promoted to chmn. of Columbia TriStar Motion Pictures, 1994. Resigned, 1996. 1997, Formed The Canton Co. In 2002, Canton became partner, chmn. and CEO of Artists Production Group, the moviemaking offshoot of Michael Ovitz's Artists Management Group. In Dec. 2003, chairman & CEO, Atmosphere Entertainment MM, LLC, in Los Angeles, CA. Currently president of Mark Canton Productions.
PICTURES: Caddyshack (exec./production), *As Prod.:* Jack Frost, Get Carter, Red Planet, Angel Eyes, Taking Lives, Land of the Dead, 300, Full of It, The Spiderwick Chronicles, A Perfect Getaway, Fame, Silver Cord, Piranha 3-D, Letters to Juliet, Dawn of War. *As Exec. Prod.:* Trapped, Godsend.
TELEVISION: *Series:* Jack & Jill (exec. prod.).

CAPSHAW, KATE

Actress. r.n. Kathleen Sue Nail. b. Ft. Worth, TX, Nov. 3, 1953. e. U. of Missouri. m. director Steven Spielberg. Taught school before moving to New York to try acting. m. Steven Spielberg.
PICTURES: A Little Sex (debut, 1982), Indiana Jones and the Temple of Doom, Best Defense, Dreamscape, Windy City, Power, SpaceCamp, Black Rain, Love at Large, My Heroes Have Always Been Cowboys, Love Affair, Just Cause, Duke of Groove (short), How to Make an American Quilt, The Locusts, Life During Wartime, The Love Letter (also prod.).
TELEVISION: *Movies:* Missing Children: A Mother's Story, The Quick and the Dead, Her Secret Life, Internal Affairs, Next Door, Due East. *Mini-series:* A Girl Thing. *Series:* The Edge of Night, Black Tie Affair.

CAPUS, STEVE

Executive. e. Temple University, B.A. in journalism, 1986. Capus began his journalism career in radio and print and worked at several stations and daily newspapers in the Philadelphia area. He also worked at WCAU-TV in Philadelphia in 1986. He joined KYW-TV in Philadephia in 1987 as a writer and producer. In 1990, at the age of 26, Capus became an executive producer with KYW-TV. For two years, he was responsible for the overall day-to-day management and coordination of the correspondents, production staff and the on-air production for the station. Capus first joined NBC News in 1993 as the senior producer of "NBC Nightside," the NBC News Channel's overnight news program based in Charlotte, N.C. He was the broadcast producer of "NBC News Sunrise" throughout 1994. During 1995, supervising producer for "Today." Capus had served as the senior broadcast producer for MSNBC's daytime news coverage since its launch in 1996. From 1997 to May 2001, executive producer of MSNBC's signature primetime newscast, "The News with Brian Williams." Capus was also the executive producer of numerous NBC News breaking reports and MSNBC special broadcasts. Among them were the 2000 presidential primaries and election, the "Summit in Silicon Valley" with Tom Brokaw and the political series "100 Days, 1000 Voices." Before becoming executive producer of "The News," was the executive producer of "NBC Nightly News." He was also the executive producer for much of NBC News' coverage of the terror attacks on September 11, 2001, the war in Iraq, and the "Decision 2002-2004" political coverage. Capus was named president, NBC news in November 2005. He is responsible for all aspects of NBC's network news division, as well as MSNBC and NBC News Channel. He is the arbiter of issues involving ethics, style, standards, safety and other matters that affect the division's journalistic bearing. Capus reports to Jeff Zucker, President and CEO, NBC Universal. Capus has received numerous awards, including four Emmy Awards, six Edward R. Murrow Awards, one Alfred I. duPont and six National Headliner Awards.

CARA, IRENE

Singer, Actress. b. New York, NY, March 18, 1959. Off-B'way shows include The Me Nobody Knows, Lotta. On B'way in Maggie Flynn, Ain't Misbehavin', Via Galactica. Received Academy Award for co-writing theme song from Flashdance, Golden Globe Award 1983.
THEATRE: B'way.: Maggie Flynn, The Me Nobody Knows, Via Galactica, Got to Go Disco. Off-B'way.: Ain't Misbehavin'. Regional: Lotta, The Wiz, Jesus Christ Superstar. Foreign: Mo' Magic.
PICTURES: Aaron Loves Angela, Sparkle, Fame (Golden Globe nom. 1981), D.C. Cab, City Heat, Certain Fury, Killing 'em Softly, Flashdance, Paradiso, Busted Up, Maximum Security, Happily Ever After (voice), The Magic Voyage (voice), The Full Monty (singer), Charlie's Angels: Full Throttle (singer), What Happens in Vegas (soundtrack performer).
TELEVISION: *Movies:* Guyana Tragedy: The Story of Jim Jones, Sister, Sister, For For Us the Living: The Medgar Evers Story, Gabriel's Fire. *Mini-series:* Roots—The Next Generation. *Series:* Hearts are Wild, Love of Life, The Electric Company. *Special:* Tribute to Martin Luther King, Jr., Bob Hope Thanksgiving Special, Tribute to Ray Charles, 80s (singer/archive). Many more credits for soundtracks.

CARDINALE, CLAUDIA

Actress. b. Tunis, Tunisia, April 15, 1938. Raised in Italy. Studied acting at Centro Sperimentale film school in Rome. Debuted 1956 in short French film Anneaux d'Or.
PICTURES: Goha (feature debut, 1957), Big Deal on Madonna Street, The Facts of Murder, Upstairs and Downstairs, The Battle of Austerlitz, Il Bell' Antonio, Rocco and His Brothers, Senilita, Girl With a Suitcase, The Love Makers, Cartouche, The Leopard, 8 1/2, Bebo's Girl, The Pink Panther, Circus World, Time of

Indifference, The Magnificent Cuckold, Sandra, Blindfold, Lost Command, The Professionals, Don't Make Waves, Mafia, The Queens, Day of the Owl, The Hell With Heroes, Once Upon a Time in the West, A Fine Pair, The Butterfly Affair, The Red Tent, The Legend of Frenchy King, Conversation Piece, Escape to Athena, The Salamander, Careless, Immortal Bachelor, History, The French Revolution, Hiver '54, L'abbe Pierre, Mother, 588 Rue Paradis, Women Only Have One Thing on Their Minds..., A Summer in La Goulette, Sous les pieds des Femmes, Rich Belles Etc, My Best Friend, Brigands, Luchino Visconte, And Now Ladies and Gentlemen, Le Démon de midi, Estrenando sueños, Asterix at the Olympic Games, Le Fil, Deauville, The First Man.
TELEVISION: *Movies:* Princess Daisy, History, Hit Man, Élisabeth - Ils sont tous nos enfants, Hold-up à l'italienne. *Mini-series:* Jesus of Nazareth, Mother, Nostromo, Deserto di Fuoco, Visconti (tv documentary), Mia, Liebe meines Lebens. *Series:* 10-07: L'affaire Zeus. *Guest:* More than 76 appearances.

CAREY, CHARLES (CHASE)

Executive. e. Colgate University and Harvard Business School. In early career, worked as a senior exec. for Colulmbia Pictures, 1981-1987. In 1988, began career-long association with Rupert Murdoch's News Corp., first at the Fox subsidiary in many roles including executive v.p. and COO of Fox, Inc. and CEO of Fox Television Group. Carey also served as a director, pres. and CEO of Sky Global Networks. With a focus on News Corp.'s worldwide TV businesses, Carey led operations, mgt. and strategy initiatives for FOX network, Fox TV stations, Fox's cable programming group and News Corp.'s international satellite operations. From 1996-2002, Carey was co-COO of News Corp. and also co-COO of the Fox Entertainment Group (1998-2002). During this time he also served on News Corp.'s board of directors and the board of the Fox Entertainment Group. Carey's initiatives include the launch and growth of Fox Sports, expansion of Fox TV Stations Group from seven stations to 35 (subsequently down to 27), cable channel advances at Fox News Channel, FX and at company's platforms in Europe, Asia and Latin America. In 2003, News Corp. Chairman and CEO Rupert Murdoch tapped Carey to be CEO of DirecTV. With the departure of Murdoch's number two executive, Peter Chernin, in July 2009, Carey returned to News Corp. as its deputy chairman, president and COO, with oversight responsibilities for News Corp.'s global operations. He also rejoined News Corp.'s board. He currently is a Trustee Emeritus of Colgate University. Carey is based in New York.

CAREY, DREW

Comedian, Actor. b. Cleveland, OH, May 23, 1958. First break was as contestant on TV show Star Search. Upon Bob Barker's retirement from long-running TV show The Price Is Right in 2007, Carey was named the new host.
PICTURES: Coneheads, The Big Tease, Gepetto, Hail Sid Caesar! The Golden Age of Comedy, Robots (voice).
TELEVISION: *Movies:* Freaky Friday, Geppetto (also exec. prod.). *Series:* The Good Life, The Drew Carey Show (also prod., creator), Whose Line Is It Anyway? (also exec. prod.), The Price Is Right (host), Just for Laughs, The Bob & Tom Show (exec. prod.). *Specials:* Sex, Drugs, and Freedom of Choice, Rock and Roll Back to School Special, Improv All Stars, Inside the Playboy Mansion (TV doc., interviewee) Drew Carey's Sporting Adventures: World Cup 2006. *Guest:* More than 120 appearances.

CAREY, HARRY JR.

Actor. b. Saugus, CA, May 16, 1921. e. Newhall, CA, public school, Black Fox Military Acad., Hollywood. m. Marilyn Fix. Son of silent star Harry Carey. Appeared in Railroads on Parade at 1939-40 NY World's Fair. Summer stock, Skowhegan, ME., with father; page boy, NBC, New York; U.S. Navy 1942-45. Author of Company of Heroes - My Life as an Actor in the John Ford Stock Co.
PICTURES: Rolling Home (debut, 1946), Pursued, Red River, Three Godfathers, She Wore a Yellow Ribbon, Wagonmaster, Rio Grande, Copper Canyon, Warpath, Wild Blue Yonder, Monkey Business, San Antone, Island in the Sky, Gentlemen Prefer Blondes, Beneath the 12-Mile Reef, Silver Lode, The Outcast, Long Gray Line, Mister Roberts, House of Bamboo, The Great Locomotive Chase, The Searchers, The River's Edge, Rio Bravo, The Great Imposter, Two Rode Together, Alvarez Kelly, Bandolero, The Undefeated, Dirty Dingus Magee, Big Jake, Something Big, One More Train To Rob, Cahill: U.S. Marshal, ake a Hard Ride, Nickelodeon, The Long Riders, Endangered Species, Mask, Crossroads, The Whales of August, Cherry 2000, Illegally Yours, Breaking In, Bad Jim, Back to the Future Part III, The Exorcist III, Tombstone, Wyatt Earp: Return to Tombstone, Ben Johnson: Third Cowboy on the Right, The Sunchaser, Comanche Stallion (also prod/writer).
TELEVISION: *Movies:* Flashing Spikes, Kate Bliss and the Ticker Tape Kid, The Shadow Riders, Princess Daisy, Adventures of William Tell, Wild Times, Once Upon a Texas Train, Last Stand at Saber River, Dobe and a Company of Heroes (tv doc., as himself), Horse Tales (host, writer, exec. prod). *Mini-series*: Black Beauty *Series:* Spin & Marty. *Guest*: More than 86 appearances.

CARIOU, LEN

Actor. b. Winnipeg, Manitoba, Canada, Sept. 30, 1939. e. St. Paul's College.
THEATRE: NY stage: House of Atreus, Henry V, Applause (Theatre World Award), Night Watch, A Sorrow Beyond Dreams, Up from Paradise, A Little Night Music, Cold Storage, Sweeney Todd—The Demon Barber of Fleet Street (Tony Award), Master Class, Dance a Little Closer, Teddy & Alice, Measure for Measure, Mountain, The Speed of Darkness, Papa.
PICTURES: Drying Up the Streets, A Little Night Music, One Man, The Four Seasons, There Were Times Dear, Lady in White, Getting In, Never Talk to Strangers, Executive Decision, Thirteen Days, About Schmidt, The Skulls 3 (video), Secret Window, Shall We Dance?, The Greatest Game Ever Played, The Boynton Beach Club, Flags of Our Fathers, 1408.
TELEVISION: *Movies:* Who'll Save Our Children?, Madame X, The Four Seasons, Louisiana, Surviving, Killer in the Mirror, Miracle on Interstate 880, Class of '61, The Sea Wolf, Witness to the Execution, Love on the Run, The Man in the Attic, A Dream Is a Wish Your Heart Makes: The Annette Funicello Story, Derby, The Summer of Ben Tyler, In the Company of Spies, Sex Traffic, Into the Storm. *Mini-series:* Nuremberg. *Series:* Swift Justice, Brotherhood. *Specials:* The Master Builder, Juno and the Paycock, Kurt Vonnegut's Monkey House (All the King's Men). *Guest:* More than 57 appearances.

CARLINER, MARK

Producer.
PICTURES: Viva Max!, Heaven Help Us, Crossroads.
TELEVISION: *Movies:* A Death of Innocence, Revenge, Strangers in 7A, Nightmare, The Phoenix (pilot), Disaster at Silo 7 (also story), Stalin (Emmy Award 1993), George Wallace (Emmy Award, 1998), The Diary of Ellen Rimbauer. *Mini-series:* The Shining (Emmy nom. 1997), Storm of the Century, Rose Red. *Series:* The Phoenix, Kingdom Hospital (exec. prod.).

CARLINO, LEWIS JOHN

Writer, Director. b. New York, NY, Jan. 1, 1932. e. U. of Southern California. Early interest in theatre, specializing in writing 1-act plays. Winner of Obie award (off-B'way play). Won Rockefeller Grant for Theatre, the Int'l. Playwriting Competition from British Drama League, Huntington Hartford Fellowship.
THEATRE: Cages, Telemachus Clay, The Exercise, Double Talk, Objective Case, Used Car for Sale, Junk Yard.
PICTURES: *Writer:* Seconds, The Brotherhood (WGA nom. 1969), The Fox (Golden Globe nom. 1968, co-s.p.), A Reflection of Fear, The Mechanic (also prod.), Crazy Joe, The Sailor Who Fell From Grace With the Sea (also dir.), I Never Promised You a Rose Garden (Academy Award nom.; WGA nom. 1978, co-s.p.), The Great Santini (also dir.; WGA nom. 1981), Class (dir. only), Haunted Summer.
TELEVISION: Honor Thy Father, In Search of America, Where Have All the People Gone?, Resurrection.

CARLYLE, ROBERT

Actor. b. Glasgow, Scotland, April 14, 1961.
PICTURES: Silent Scream, Riff-Raff, Safe, Being Human, Priest, Go Now, Trainspotting, Carla's Song, Face, The Full Monty (BAFTA Award, Best Actor, 1997), Ravenous, Plunkett & MacCleane, The World is Not Enough, Angela's Ashes, The Beach, There's Only One Jimmy Grimble, To End All Wars, The 51st State, Once Upon a Time in the Midlands, Black and White, Dead Fish, The Mighty Celt, Light in the Sky, Go Go Tales, Marilyn Hotchkiss' Ballroom Dancing and Charm School, Eragon, Flood, The Meat Trade, 28 Weeks Later, Stone of Destiny, Summer, The Tournament.
TELEVISION: *Movies:* Benny Lynch, Safe, Looking After Jo Jo, Hitler: The Rise of Evil (documentary), Gunpowder, Treason & Plot, Class of '76, Treason and Plot, Benny Lynch, Human Trafficking (Emmy nom. 2006), Born Equal, 24: Redemption, Zig Zag Love, The Unloved. *Mini-series:* The Last Enemy. *Series:* 99-1, Hamish Macbeth, SGU Stargate Universe. *Guest:* More than 42 appearances.

CARMEN, JULIE

Actress. b. New York, NY, Apr. 4, 1960. Studied acting at Neighborhood Playhouse. On NY stage in The Creation of the Universe, Cold Storage, Zoot Suit. Also acted with INTAR and the New Conservatory Theater. Recipient of 1992 National Council of La Raza Pioneer Award.
PICTURES: Night of the Juggler, Gloria, Man on the Wall, Comeback, Blue City, The Penitent, The Milagro Beanfield War, Fright Night 2, Kiss Me a Killer, Paint It Black, Cold Heaven, In the Mouth of Madness, Africa, Everything's George, King of the Jungle, Angels with Angles, Illegal Tender, Falling Awake, The Butcher.
TELEVISION: *Movies:* Can You Hear the Laughter?: The Story of Freddie Prinze, Three Hundred Miles for Stephanie, She's in the Army Now, Fire on the Mountain, Neon Empire, Manhunt: Search for the Night Stalker, Billy the Kid, Drug Wars: The Cocaine Cartel, Finding the Way Home, Curacao, The Omen, Gargantua, The Expendables. *Mini-series:* True Women. *Series:* Condo, Falcon Crest. *Guest:* More than 46 appearances.

CARMICHAEL, IAN

O.B.E. Actor. b. Hull, England, June 18, 1920. e. Scarborough Coll., Bromsgrove Sch. Stage debut: R.U.R. 1939. B'way debut: Boeing-Boeing (1965). One of the top ten British money making

stars Motion Picture Herald Fame Poll 1957, 1958.
PICTURES: Bond Street (debut, 1948), Trottie True (Gay Lady), Mr. Prohack, Time Gentlemen Please, Ghost Ship!, Miss Robin Hood, Meet Mr. Lucifer, Betrayed, The Colditz Story, Storm Over the Nile, Simon and Laura, Private's Progress, The Big Money, Brothers in Law, Lucky Jim, Happy Is the Bride, Left Right and Center, I'm All Right Jack, School for Scoundrels, Light Up the Sky, Double Bunk, The Amorous Prawn, Hide and Seek, Heavens Above, The Case of the 44's, Smashing Time, The Magnificent Seven Deadly Sins, From Beyond the Grave, The Lady Vanishes, Dark Obsession (Diamond Skulls).
TELEVISION: New Faces, Twice Upon a Time, Passing Show, Tell Her The Truth, Lady Luck, Give My Regards to Leicester Square, Jill Darling, Don't Look Now, Regency Room, Globe Revue, Off the Record, Here and Now, The Girl at the Next Table, Gilt and Gingerbread, The Importance of Being Earnest, Simon and Laura, 90 Years On, The World of Wooster (series), The Last of the Big Spenders, The Coward Revue, Odd Man In, Bachelor Father (series), Lord Peter Wimsey (series), Alma Mater, Comedy Tonight, Song by Song, Country Calendar, Down at the Hydro, Obituaries, Strathblair, The Great Kandinsky, Bramwell, Wives and Daughters, The Royal (series).
(d. February 5, 2010)

CARON, GLENN GORDON

Writer, Director, Producer. b. 1954. TV writer for James L. Brooks, Steve Gordon. Then formed prod. co., Picturemaker Prods., 1985.
PICTURES: Director: Clean and Sober (debut, 1988), Wilder Napalm, Love Affair, Picture Perfect (also s.p.).
TELEVISION: *Movies:* Long Time Gone, The Perfect Pitch (tv doc.), The Meant to Be's (exec. prod.). *Series:* Taxi (writer), Breaking Away (prod.), Moonlighting (2 Emmy nom. 1986, 2 Emmy nom. 1987, creator, prod., writer), Now and Again (writer, dir., exec. prod.), Fling (dir/writer), Medium (exec. prod./dir./writer).

CARON, LESLIE

Actress, Dancer. b. Paris, France, July 1, 1931. e. Convent of Assumption, Paris; Nat'l Conservatory of Dance, Paris 1947-50; joined Roland Petit's Ballet des Champs Elysees where she was spotted by Gene Kelly who chose her as his co-star in An American in Paris. Also with Ballet de Paris.
THEATRE: Orvet, Ondine, Gigi (London), 13 Rue de l'Amour, The Rehearsal, Women's Games, On Your Toes, One For the Tango.
PICTURES: An American in Paris (debut, 1951), The Man With a Cloak, Glory Alley, The Story of Three Loves, Lili (Acad. Award nom.; BFA Award 1954), The Glass Slipper, Daddy Long Legs, Gaby, Gigi, The Doctor's Dilemma, Gigi (Golden Globe nom. 1959), The Man Who Understood Women, The Subterraneans, Austerlitz, Fanny, Guns of Darkness, Three Fables of Love, The L-Shaped Room (Acad. Award nom. Golden Globe Award, BFA Award 1964), Father Goose, A Very Special Favor, Promise Her Anything, Is Paris Burning?, Head of the Family, The Beginners, Madron, Chandler, Purple Night, Valentino, The Man Who Loved Women, Golden Girl, Contract, Imperative, The Unapproachable, Dangerous Moves, Warriors and Prisoners, Courage Mountain, Damage, Funny Bones, Let It Be Me, The Reef, From Russia to Hollywood: The 100-Year Odyssey of Chekhov and Shdanoff, Chocolat, Le Divorce.
TELEVISION: *Movies:* The Man Who Lived at the Ritz, The Ring, The Last of the Blonde Bombshells, Murder on the Orient Express. *Mini-series:* QB VIII, Master of the Game, The Great War. *Series:* The Great War, Law & Order: Special Victims Unit (Emmy Award 2007). *Specials:* The Sealed Train, Jean Pierre Aumont: charme et fou rires. *Guest:* More than 63 appearances.

CARPENTER, CHARISMA

Actress. b. Las Vegas, NV, July 23, 1970. Was cheerleader for NFL's San Diego Chargers before turning to modeling, then acting.
PICTURES: Switch, The Twins, The Groomsmen, Change Up (doc., voiceover), Psychosis, The Expendables.
TELEVISION: *Movies:* Josh Kirby...Time Warrior: The Human Pets, Josh Kirby...Time Warrior: Planet of the Dino-Knights, Josh Kirby...Time Warrior: Last Battle for the Universe, See Jane Date, Like Cats and Dogs, Voodoo Moon, Flirting with Danger, Cheaters' Club, Relative Chaos, House of Bones. *Series:* Malibu Shores, Buffy the Vampire Slayer, Buffy The Animated Series (voice), Miss Match, Angel: The Series, Charmed, Veronica Mars. *Guest:* More than 45 appearances.

CARPENTER, JOHN

Director, Writer, Composer. b. Carthage, NY, Jan. 16, 1948. e. Western Kentucky U., U. of Southern California. At U.S.C. became involved in film short, Resurrection of Bronco Billy, which won Oscar as best live-action short of 1970. Also at U.S.C. began directing what ultimately became Dark Star, science fiction film that launched his career.
PICTURES: Dark Star (also co-s.p., music), Assault on Precinct 13 (also s.p., music), Halloween (also s.p., music), The Fog (also co-s.p., music), Escape from New York (also co-s.p., music), The Thing, Christine (also music), Starman, Big Trouble in Little China (also music), Prince of Darkness (also music, and s.p. as Martin Quatermass), They Live (also music, and s.p. as Frank Armitage), Memoirs of an Invisible Man, In the Mouth of Madness (also co-music), Village of the Damned (also s.p., co-music), Escape From L.A, Meltdown (also s.p.), Eyes of Laura Mars (co-sp., co-story), Halloween II (co- s.p., co-prod., co-music), Halloween III: Season of the Witch (co-prod., co-music), The Philadelphia Experiment (co-exec. prod.), Black Moon Rising (co-s.p., story), The Silence of the Hams (actor), Vampires, (also s.p. and music), Ghosts of Mars, Halloween: Ressurection (music, s.p. only), Tales From the Mist: Inside 'The Fog' (video documentary, composer), Vampires: Los Muertos (exec. prod.), Halloween (comp., writer), The Fog (s.p. 1980, prod.), Psychopath (also writer), H2: Halloween II (writer), Riot (dir. only), The Ward (dir.).
TELEVISION: *Movies/Director:* Elvis, Someone Is Watching Me (also writer), John Carpenter Presents Body Bags (also co-exec. prod., actor). *Movies/Writer:* Zuma Beach, El Diablo, Blood River, Silent Predators. *Guest:* More than 77 appearances.

CARPENTER, RUSSELL

Cinematographer, Actor. b. Van Nuys, CA, 1950.
PICTURES: The Wizard of Speed and Time (also actor), Lady in White, Critters 2: The Main Course, Cameron's Closet, Solar Crisis, Lionheart, Death Warrant, The Perfect Weapon, The Lawnmower Man, Pet Sematary II, Hard Target, True Lies, The Indian in the Cupboard, Titanic (Academy Award, ASC Award 1998), Ghosts, Money Talks, The Negotiator, Charlie's Angels, Shallow Hal, Charlie's Angels: Full Throttle, The Human Stain (dir. of photog.), Noel (comp), Monster-in-Law, Awake, Hereafter, 21, Locker 13, The Ugly Truth, Earthbound, Killers.
TELEVISION: *Movie:* Attack of the 50 Ft. Woman. *Series:* The Wonder Years, Sisters in Law, Women in Law.

CARR, CHRIS

Executive. b. Yorkshire Dales, England. e. Graduated in modern history and politics with economics, Southampton University, 1985. Carr trained with KPMG Peat Marwick and, after qualifying as a chartered accountant, joined the BBC in 1990. Carr worked on the development of the BBC's first commercial channels, BBC Prime and BBC World. In 1996, promoted to head of financial planning for BBC Worldwide Television. He was heavily involved in the negotiations that resulted in the launch of BBC America and became its CFO in March 2008. Today, Carr is COO Channels, BBC Worldwide America and is responsible for overseeing the financial, operational and commercial aspects of BBC AMERICA and future BBC Worldwide channels in the U.S.

CARR, MARTIN

Producer, Director, Writer. b. New York, NY, Jan. 20, 1932. e. Williams Coll. Recipient of: 5 Emmys, 3 Peabody awards, 2 DuPont Col. Journalism awards, Robert F. Kennedy award, Sidney Hillman award, Writers Guild Award.
PICTURES: El Efecto Mariposa (prod. mgr.), The IMAX Nutcracker (prod. mgr.) Command Approved (prod.), Vacuuming Completely Nude in Paradise (prod.), Strumpet (prod.), The Human Body (line prod.), Clubbed.
TELEVISION: PBS Smithsonian World (exec. prod.). For CBS prod., wrote and dir. CBS Reports: Hunger in America, The Search for Ulysses, Gauguin in Tahiti, Five Faces of Tokyo, Dublin Through Different Eyes. For NBC prod., wrote and dir. NBC White Paper: Migrant, NBC White Paper: This Child Is Rated X. Also directed drama, dance, music, opera specials and daytime serial for CBS-TV. ABC Close-Up. The Culture Thieves. PRS Global Paper: Waging Peace, ABC News 20/20; NBC, The Human Animal.

CARRADINE, KEITH

Actor. b. San Mateo, CA, Aug. 8, 1949. e. Colorado State U. Daughter is actress Martha Plimpton. Son of late actor John Carradine, brother of actor Robert Carradine and the late actor David Carradine. First break in rock opera Hair.
THEATRE: Wake Up It's Time to Go to Bed, Foxfire, The Will Rogers Follies. *LA:* Stuff Happens.
PICTURES: A Gunfight (debut, 1971), McCabe and Mrs. Miller, Hex, Emperor of the North Pole, Thieves Like Us, Antoine et Sebastien, Run Joe Run, Idaho Transfer, Nashville (also composed songs; Academy Award, Golden Globe Award for best song: "I'm Easy", 1976), You and Me, Lumiere, Welcome to L.A. (also composed songs), The Duellists, Pretty Baby, Sgt. Pepper's Lonely Heart Club Band (cameo), Old Boyfriends, An Almost Perfect Affair, The Long Riders, Southern Comfort, Choose Me, Maria's Lovers (also composed song), Trouble in Mind, The Inquiry (The Investigation), Backfire, The Moderns, Street of No Return, Cold Feet, Daddy's Dyin'...Who's Got the Will?, The Ballad of the Sad Cafe, Crisscross, The Bachelor, Andre, Mrs. Parker and the Vicious Circle, The Tie That Binds, Wild Bill, A Thousand Acres, Standoff, Out of the Cold, The Hunter's Moon, Cahoots, The Angel Doll, Wooly Boys, Falcons, Mending Fences, The Californians, Hair High (voice), Our Very Own, Elvis and Anabelle, The Death and Life of Bobby Z, Lake City, All Hat, Winter of Frozen Dreams, Peacock, The Absinthe Drinkers, The Family Tree.
TELEVISION: *Movies:* Man on a String, Kung Fu, The Godchild, A Rumor of War, Scorned and Swindled, A Winner Never Quits, Murder Ordained, Eye on the Sparrow, Blackout, Stones for Ibarra, My Father My Son, The Revenge of Al Capone, Judgment, Payoff, In the Best of Families: Marriage Pride & Madness, Is There Life Out There?, Trial by Fire, Hard Time: Hide and Seek, Night Ride Home, Enslavement: The True Story

of Fanny Kemble, Baby, The Diamond of Jeru, The Outsider, Monte Walsh, Coyote Waits, Where There's a Will. *Mini-series:* Chiefs (Emmy nom. 1984), Into the West. *Series:* Outreach, Metropolis, Deadwood, Complete Savages, Dexter, Dollhouse. *Guest:* More than 95 appearances.

CARRADINE, ROBERT

Actor. b. Hollywood, CA, March 24, 1954. Son of late actor John Carradine; brother of actors Keith and the late David Carradine.
PICTURES: The Cowboys (debut, 1972), Mean Streets, Aloha Bobby and Rose, Jackson County Jail, The Pom Pom Girls, Cannonball, Massacre at Central High, Joyride, Orca, Blackout, Coming Home, The Long Riders, The Big Red One, Heartaches, Tag: The Assassination Game, Wavelength, Revenge of the Nerds, Just the Way You Are, Number One With a Bullet, Revenge of the Nerds II: Nerds in Paradise, Buy and Cell, All's Fair, Rude Awakening, The Player, Bird of Prey, Escape From L.A., Scorpio One, Lycanthrope (also prod.), Stray Bullet I & II, Gunfighter, Palmer's Pick Up, The Kid With the X-Ray Eyes, The Vegas Connection, 3 Days of Rain, Ghosts of Mars, Max Keeble's Big Move, 3 Days of Rain, The Lizzie McGuire Movie, Comanche Stallion, Dreamweaver, Supercross, Deep Winter, Trick or Treat, 7-10 Split, The 1 Second Film (doc., prod.), Tooth & Nail, Deep Winter, Sex and Breakfast, Fancypants, City of Shoulders and Noses, Fight or Flight, The Summoning.
TELEVISION: *Movies:* Footsteps, Rolling Man, Go Ask Alice, The Hatfields and the McCoys, The Survival of Dana, The Sun Also Rises, Monte Carlo, The Liberators, I Saw What You Did, The Incident, Clarence, Doublecrossed, Revenge of the Nerds III: The Next Generation, Body Bags, The Disappearance of Christina, Revenge of the Nerds IV: Nerds in Love (also co-prod.), A Part of the Family, The Tommyknockers, Young Hearts Unlimited, Mom's Got A Date With A Vampire. Monte Walsh, Attack of the Sabertooth, Jane Doe: Ties That Bind. *Series:* The Cowboys, Lizzie McGuire, Express Yourself. *Specials:* Disney's Totally Minnie. *Guest:* More than 65 appearances.

CARRERA, BARBARA

Actress. b. Nicaragua, Dec. 31, 1951. Fashion model before film career; had part in film Puzzle of a Downfall Child.
PICTURES: The Master Gunfighter (Golden Globe nom. 1976), Embryo, The Island of Dr. Moreau, When Time Ran Out, Condorman, I the Jury, Lone Wolf McQuade, Never Say Never Again (Golden Globe nom. 1984), Wild Geese II, The Underachievers, Love at Stake, Wicked Stepmother, Loverboy, Spanish Rose, Night of the Archer, Tryst, Love Is All There Is, Panic.
TELEVISION: *Movies:* Sins of the Past, Murder in Paradise, Lakota Moon, Sawbones, The Rockford Files: Godfather Knows Best. *Mini-series:* Centennial, Masada, Emma: Queen of the South Seas. *Series:* Dallas.

CARRERE, TIA

Actress. r.n. Althea Janairo. b. Honolulu, HI, 1967. Was prof. model before turning to acting. Received NATO/ShoWest award for Female Star of 1994.
PICTURES: Zombie Nightmare (debut, 1987), Aloha Summer, Fatal Mission, Instant Karma, Showdown in Little Tokyo, Harley Davidson and the Marlboro Man, Wayne's World, Rising Sun, Wayne's World 2, True Lies, Jury Duty, My Generation, The Immortals, Hollow Point, Bad With Numbers, High School High, Top of the World, Dumped, Kull the Conqueror, Scar City, 20 Dates (also exec. prod), Merlin: The Return, Meet Prince Charming, Shi, Lilo & Stitch (voice), Stitch! The Movie (video, voice), Back in the Day, Beds & Breakfast, Lilo & Stitch 2, Dark Honeymoon, Wild Cherry, You May Not Kiss the Bride, Hard Breakers.
TELEVISION: *Movies:* The Road Raiders, Fine Gold, Natural Enemy, Dogboys, The Night of the Headless Horseman (voice), Leroy & Stitch (voice). *Mini-series:* James Clavell's Noble House, Supernova. *Series:* General Hospital, The Adventures of Lilo & Stitch (voice), Relic Hunter, Megas XLR, Duck Dodgers, Lilo & Stitch: The Series (voice). *Guest:* More than 72 appearances.

CARREY, JIM

Actor. b. Newmarket, Ontario, Canada, Jan. 17, 1962. Began performing act at Toronto comedy clubs while teenager. Moved to LA at 19, performing at the Comedy Store.
PICTURES: Finders Keepers (debut, 1984), Once Bitten, Peggy Sue Got Married, The Dead Pool, Earth Girls Are Easy, Pink Cadillac, High Strung, Ace Ventura: Pet Detective (also co-s.p.), The Mask (Golden Globe nom. 1995), Dumb and Dumber, Batman Forever, Ace Ventura: When Nature Calls, The Cable Guy, Liar Liar (Golden Globe nom. 1998), The Truman Show (Golden Globe Award 1999), Simon Birch, Man on the Moon (Golden Globe Award 2000), How the Grinch Stole Christmas (Golden Globe nom. 2001), The Majestic, Bruce Almighty, Eternal Sunshine of the Spotless Mind (Golden Globe nom. 2005), Lemony Snicket's A Series of Unfortunate Events, Over the Hedge (voice), Fun with Dick and Jane (also prod.), The Number 23, Horton Hears a Who (voice), Yes Man (also sound-track performer), I Love You Phillip Morris, A Christmas Carol.
TELEVISION: *Movies*: Mickey Spillane's Mike Hammer—Murder Takes All, Doin' Time on Maple Drive, In My Life. *Series:* The Duck Factory, In Living Color. *Documentaries/Specials:* Jim Carrey's Unnatural Act, Comedy Store: The E! True Hollywood Story, Concert for New York City, America: A Tribute to Heroes. Canadian TV: Introducing Janet, Copper Mountain: A Club Med Experience. *Guest:* More than 158 appearances.

CARROLL, DIAHANN

Actress, Singer. r.n. Carol Diahann Johnson. b. Bronx, NY, July 17, 1935. Started singing as teen, winning 1st place on tv's Chance of a Lifetime talent show resulting in engagement at Latin Quarter nightclub in New York. Autobiography: Diahann! (1986).
THEATRE: B'way: House of Flowers, No Strings (Tony Award, 1962), Agnes of God.
PICTURES: Carmen Jones (debut, 1954), Porgy and Bess, Goodbye Again, Paris Blues, Hurry Sundown, The Split, Claudine (Acad. Award nom. Golden Globe nom. 1975), The Five Heartbeats, Eve's Bayou, 1 a Minute.
TELEVISION: *Movies:* Death Scream, I Know Why the Caged Bird Sings, From the Dead of Night, Murder in Black and White, A Perry Mason Mystery: The Case of the Lethal Lifestyle. The Sweetest Gift (Emmy nom. 1999), Having Our Say: The Delany Sisters' First 100 Years, Jackie's Back!, The Courage to Love, Sally Hemmings: An American Scandal, Livin' for Love: The Natalie Cole Story. Inside TV Land: African Americans in Television (tv doc., as herself). TV Land Awards: A Celebration of Classic TV (tv special doc.), At Risk, The Front. *Mini-series:* Roots: The Next Generations; *Series:* Julia (Emmy nom., Golden Globe Award 1969 and Golden Globe nom. 1970), The Diahann Carroll Show, Dynasty, Sister Sister, The Court, Grey's Anatomy (Emmy nom. 2008), White Collar (also pilot). *Special:* Diahann Carroll: The Lady. The Music. The Legend. *Guest:* More than 170 appearances.

CARROLL, PAT

Actress. b. Shreveport, LA, May 5, 1927. e. Immaculate Heart Coll., L.A, Catholic U., Washington, DC. Joined U.S. Army in capacity of Civilian Actress Technician. Night club entertainer in N.Y., 1950.
THEATRE: Catch a Star (debut, 1955), Gertrude Stein Gertrude Stein (Drama Desk, Outer Critics Circle, Grammy Awards), Dancing in the End Zone, The Show Off. Shakespeare Theatre at the Folger: Romeo and Juliet (Helen Hayes Award), The Merry Wives of Windsor (Helen Hayes Award), Mother Courage (Helen Hayes Award), H.M.S. Pinafore, Volpone.
PICTURES: With Six You Get Eggroll, The Brothers O'Toole, The Last Resort, The Little Mermaid (voice), Invader, A Goofy Movie, Songcatcher, The Little Mermaid II: Return to the Sea (voice), Freedom Writers, Nancy Drew, Around the World in 50 Years 3D (voice).
TELEVISION: *Movies:* Second Chance, Just My Imagination, The Royale (Emmy nom. 1998). *Series:* Red Buttons Show, Saturday Night Revue, Caesar's Hour (Emmy Award, 1957, Emmy nom. 1958), Masquerade Party (panelist), Keep Talking, You're in the Picture (panelist), Danny Thomas Show, Getting Together, Busting Loose, The Ted Knight Show, She's the Sheriff, The Little Mermaid (voice), House of Mouse (voice), ER. *Specials:* Cinderella, Gertrude Stein. *Guest:* More than 104 appearances.

CARSEY, MARCY

Producer. b. Weymouth, MA, Nov. 21, 1944. e. degree in English, cum laude, 1966 from Univ. of New Hampshire. Was actress in TV commercials, tour guide at Rockefeller Center. Served as exec. story editor, Tomorrow Ent., 1971-74; sr. v.p. for prime time series, ABC-TV, 1978-81; founded Carsey Prods., 1981; owner, Carsey-Werner-Mandabach Co., 1982. Ran Carsey-Werner with partner Tom Werner. Her company, Carsey-Werner, has won The Emmy, the People's Choice Award, The Golden Globe, The NAACP Image Award, The Humanitas Prize, The Peabody, and humanitarian awards for Carsey and Werner's efforts to produce responsible TV. Currently is owner of Carsey-Werner-Mandabach Productions. In 1993, Carsey was named one of the top 50 women business owners in the nation and has been listed in Hollywood Reporter's Power 100 Women in Hollywood. Memberships have included: Member of USC School of Cinema-Television's Television Executive Advisory Council; co-chair of the advisory board for the UCSB Center for Film, Television, and New Media and a trustee of the UCSB Foundation (2004), bd. of dir. of Common Sense Media, an org. dedicated to improving the media and entertainment lives of kids and families (since Nov. 2005); bd. of dir. of Los Angeles' Center Theater Group (2006-07); bd. of advisors, Center for Cultural Innovation (2006).
PICTURES: Let's Go to Prison (exec. prod.), Get 'Em Wet.
TELEVISION: *Movies: Exec. prod.:* Callahan, The Mayor of Oyster Bay (producer), These guys, Are We There Yet?, Blue Aloha, Peep Show. *Series/Exec. prod.:* Oh Madeline (co-exec. prod.), The Cosby Show (Emmy Award 1985, 2 Emmy nom. 1986,1987), A Different World, Roseanne, Chicken Soup, Grand, Davis Rules, Frannie's Turn, You Bet Your Life (synd.), Grace Under Fire, Cybill, 3rd Rock from the Sun (also prod., 2 Emmy nom. 1997, 1998) Cosby (1996), Men Behaving Badly, Townies, Damon, That '70s Show, God the Devil and Bob, Normal Ohio, Grounded for Life, You Don't Know Jack, The Downer Channel, That '80s Show, Whoopi, The Tracy Morgan Show, Game Over,

Good Girls Don't..., The Scholar. *Pilots:* Callahan, I Do I Don't. *Special:* Carol, Carl, Whoopi and Robin.

CARTER, CHRIS

Producer, Composer, Writer, Director. b. Bellflower, CA, Oct. 13, 1956.
PICTURES: The X Files: Fight the Future, A Philosophical Investigation, The X Files: I Want to Believe, Flying Lessons (exec. prod.), Fencewalker.
TELEVISION: *Producer/Composer/Writer/Director:* Cameo by Night, A Brand New Life, In the Shadow of the Sun, The B.R.A.T. Patrol, Rags to Riches (co-prod. only), Millenium (also creator), The X-Files (also creator, 8 Emmy nom. 1995-1998; 3 DGA noms.; WGA nom. 1996), Harsh Realm, The Lone Gunmen, The Nanny.

CARTER, DIXIE

Actress. b. McLemoresville, TN, May 25, 1939. m. actor Hal Holbrook. e. U. of Tennessee, Knoxville, Rhodes Coll.; Memphis, Memphis State U. Off-B'way debut, A Winter's Tale with NY Shakespeare Fest (1963). London debut, Buried Inside Extra (1983). Lincoln Center musicals: The King & I, Carousel, The Merry Widow. Video: Dixie Carter's Unworkout.
THEATRE: Pal Joey (1976 revival), Jesse and the Bandit Queen (Theatre World Award), Fathers and Sons, A Winter's Tale, Taken in Marriage, Master Class, A Coupla White Chicks Sitting Around Talking, Buried Inside Extra, Sextet, That Evening Sun.
PICTURES: Going Berserk, The Big Day, That Evening Sun.
TELEVISION: *Movies:* The Killing of Randy Webster, Dazzle, Gambler V: Playing for Keeps, A Perry Mason Mystery: The Case of the Lethal Lifestyle, Gone in the Night, Comfort and Joy, Sudbury, TNA Victory Road, The Life & Adventures of Santa Claus (video), Our First Christmas. *Series:* The Edge of Night, On Our Own, Out of the Blue, Filthy Rich, Diff'rent Strokes, Designing Women, Family Law, Ladies Man, Desperate Housewives (Emmy nom. 2007 as guest). *Special:* Intimate Portrait: Dixie Carter. *Guest:* More than 55 appearances.
(d. April 10, 2010)

CARTER, JACK

Actor. r.n. Jack Chakrin. b. New York, NY, June 24, 1923. e. New Utrecht H.S., Brooklyn Coll., Feagin Sch. of Dramatic Arts. Worked as comm. artist for adv. agencies. Debut B'way in Call Me Mister, 1947; starred in TV Jack Carter Show, NBC Sat. Nite Revue. Hosted first televised Tony Awards. Seen on most major variety, dram. programs, incl. Ed Sullivan Show. Emmy nom. 1962 for Dr. Kildare seg. Played most major nightclubs. On B'way in Top Banana, Mr. Wonderful, Dir. several Lucy Shows. TV incl. specials, Top Banana, Girl Who Couldn't Lose.
PICTURES: Horizontal Lieutenant, Viva Las Vegas, The Extraordinary Seaman, Resurrection of Zachary Wheeler, Red Nights, Hustle, The Amazing Dobermans, Alligator, The Octagon, History of the World Part 1, The Arena, Deadly Embrace, In the Heat of Passion, Social Suicide, The Opposite Sex and How to Live With Them, Pastry Pain and Politics, The Modern Adventures of Tom Sawyer, Play it to the Bone, Let Me In I Hear Laughter.
TELEVISION: *Movies:* The Lonely Profession, The Family Rico, The Sex Symbol, The Great Houdinis, The Last Hurrah, Human Feelings, Rainbow, The Gossip Columnist, The Hustler of Muscle Beach, For the Love of It, Double Deception. *Series:* American Minstrels of 1949, Cavalcade of Stars, The Jack Carter Show, Make Me Laugh, Hercules (voice), ABC Matinee Today (Emmy nom. 1975), Driving Me Crazy. *Guest:* More than 102 appearances.

CARTER, LYNDA

Actress. r.n. Lynda Jean Cordoba. b. Phoenix, AZ, July 24, 1951. e. Arcadia H.S. Wrote songs and sang professionally in Ariz. from age of 15; later toured 4 yrs. with rock 'n roll band. Won beauty contests in Ariz. and became Miss World-USA 1973. Dramatic training with Milton Katselas, Greta Seacat, and Sandra Seacat.
PICTURES: Lightning in a Bottle, Broken Lizard's Super Troopers, Tattered Angel, Bloodhead, The Creature of the Sunny Side Up Trailer Park, Sky High, The Dukes of Hazzard, Between Heaven and Earth.
TELEVISION: *Movies:* The New Original Wonder Woman, A Matter of Wife...and Death, Baby Brokers, Last Song, Hotline, Rita Hayworth: The Love Goddess, Stillwatch (also exec. prod.), Mickey Spillane's Mike Hammer, Murder Takes All, Danielle Steel's Daddy, Posing: Inspired By 3 Real Stories, She Woke Up Pregnant, A Secret Between Friends, Family Blessings, A Prayer in the Dark, Someone to Love Me, Terror Peak, Slayer. *Series:* Wonder Woman, Hawkeye. *Specials:* The New Original Wonder Woman *Specials:* 5 variety specials. *Guest:* More than 106 appearances.

CARTLIDGE, WILLIAM

Director, Producer. b. England, June 16, 1942. e. Highgate Sch. Ent. m.p. ind. 1959. Early career in stills dept., Elstree Studio. Later worked as an asst. dir. on The Young Ones, Summer Holiday, The Punch & Judy Man, The Naked Edge. As 1st asst. dir. on such pictures as Born Free, Alfie, You Only Live Twice, The Adventurers, Young Winston, Friends. *As assoc. prod.,* Paul and Michelle, Seven Nights in Japan, The Spy Who Loved Me, Moonraker, An Ideal Husband. *Prod.:* Educating Rita, Not Quite Paradise, Consuming Passions, Dealers, The Playboys. Producer of Haunted, Incognito, The Scarlet Tunic (exec.), The Will to Resist (co-prod.).
TELEVISION: Dinotopia (prod. tv mini-series, Emmy nom. 2002).

CARTWRIGHT, VERONICA

Actress. b. Bristol, Eng., April 20, 1950. m. late writer-dir. Richard Compton. Sister is actress Angela Cartwright. Began career as child actress. On stage in, The Hands of Its Enemies (Mark Taper Forum, LA 1984), The Triplet Connection (off-B'way).
PICTURES: In Love and War (debut, 1958), The Children's Hour, The Birds, Spencer's Mountain, One Man's Way, Inserts, Goin' South, Invasion of the Body Snatchers, Alien, Nightmares, The Right Stuff, My Man Adam, Flight of the Navigator, Wisdom, The Witches of Eastwick, Valentino Returns, False Identity, Man Trouble, Candyman: Farewell to the Flesh, Money Talks, Sparkler, My Engagement Party, A Slipping Down Life, Trash, In the Bedroom, Scary Movie 2, Mackenheim, Straight-Jacket, Kinsey, The Visiting, Neowolf, The Invasion, Montana Amazon.
TELEVISION: *Movies:* Guyana Tragedy—The Story of Jim Jones, The Big Black Pill, Prime Suspect, Intimate Encounters, Desperate for Love, A Son's Promise, Hitler's Daughter, Dead in the Water, It's Nothing Personal, My Brother's Keeper, The Lottery, The Rat Pack, The Last Man on Planet Earth, Alien Evolution, Inside the Osmonds. *Mini-series:* Robert Kennedy and His Times. *Specials:* Who Has Seen the Wind?, Bernice Bobs Her Hair, Tell Me Not the Mournful Numbers (Emmy Award), Joe Dancer, Abby My Love, On Hope. *Series:* Daniel Boone, Invasion, Eastwick. *Guest:* More than 105 appearances.

CARUSO, DAVID

Actor. b. Queens, NY, Jan. 7, 1956.
PICTURES: Without Warning (debut, 1980), An Officer and a Gentleman, First Blood, Thief of Hearts, Blue City, China Girl, Twins, King of New York, Hudson Hawk, Mad Dog and Glory, Kiss of Death, Jade, Cold Around the Heart, Body Count, Proof of Life, Session 9, Black Point.
TELEVISION: *Movies:* Crazy Times, The First Olmypics—Athens 1896, Into the Homeland, Rainbow Drive, Mission of the Shark, Judgment Day: The John List Story, Gold Coast, Deadlocked. *Series:* N.Y.P.D. Blue (Emmy nom.; Golden Globe nom. 1994), Michael Hayes (also exec. prod.), C.S.I.: Miami.

CARVEY, DANA

Actor. b. Missoula, MT, June 2, 1955. e. San Francisco State Coll. Won San Francisco Stand-Up Comedy Competition which led to work as stand-up comedian in local S.F., then L.A. comedy clubs. TV debut as Mickey Rooney's grandson on series, One of the Boys, 1982. Received American Comedy Award (1990, 1991) as TV's Funniest Supporting Male Performer.
PICTURES: Halloween II, Racing With the Moon, This is Spinal Tap, Tough Guys, Moving, Opportunity Knocks, Wayne's World, Wayne's World 2, Clean Slate, The Road to Wellville, Trapped in Paradise, The Shot, Little Nicky, Master of Disguise (also writer), Tusker.
TELEVISION: *Series:* The Mug Root Beer Dana Carvey Show, One of the Boys, Blue Thunder, Saturday Night Live (Emmy Award, 1993, 5 Emmy noms.), The Dana Carvey Show. *Specials:* Superman's 50th Anniversary (host), Salute to Improvisation, Wayne & Garth's Saturday Night Live Music a Go-Go, Dana Carvey: Squatting Monkeys Tell No Lies (writer, exec. prod.), various Satruday Night Live specials. *Pilots:* Alone at Last, Whacked Out. *Guest:* More than 71 appearances.

CASEY, BERNIE

Actor. b. Wyco, WV, June 8, 1939. e. Bowling Green U. Played pro-football with San Francisco 49ers and L.A. Rams.
PICTURES: Guns of the Magnificent Seven (debut, 1969), Tick...Tick...Tick, Boxcar Bertha, Black Gunn, Hit Man, Cleopatra Jones, Maurie, Cornbread Earl and Me, The Man Who Fell to Earth, Dr. Black/Mr. Hyde, Brothers, Sharky's Machine, Never Say Never Again, Revenge of the Nerds, Spies Like Us, Steele Justice, Rent-a-Cop, I'm Gonna Git You Sucka, Backfire, Bill and Ted's Excellent Adventure, Another 48 HRS, Under Siege, The Cemetery Club, Street Knight, The Glass Shield, In the Mouth of Madness, Once Upon a Time...When We Were Colored, The Dinner (also prod., dir., s.p.), Tomcats, Jim Brown: All American (documentary), When I Find the Ocean.
TELEVISION: *Movies:* Brian's Song, Gargoyles, Panic on the 5:22, Mary Jane Harper Cried Last Night, It Happened at Lake Wood Manor, Ring of Passion, Love is Not Enough, Sophisticated Gents, Hear No Evil, The Fantastic World of D.C. Collins, The Simple Life of Noah Dearborn, The Last Brickmaker in America. *Mini-series*: Roots—The Next Generations, The Martian Chronicles. *Series*: Harris and Company, Bay City Blues.

CASSAVETES, NICK

Actor, Director, Writer. b. New York, NY, May 21, 1959. Son of late director/actor John Cassavetes and actress Gena Rowlands.
PICTURES: A Woman Under the Influence, Mask, The Wraith, Quiet Cool, Black Moon Rising, Assault of the Killer Bimbos, Blind Fury, Backstreet Dreams, Delta Force 3: The Killing Game, Twogether, Sins of the Night, Sins of Desire, Body of Influence,

Class of 1999 II: The Substitute, Mrs. Parker and the Vicious Circle, Just Like Dad, Black Rose of Harlem, Face/Off, Life, The Astronaut's Wife, Panic, The Independent Director: Unhook the Stars (also s.p.), She's So Lovely, John Q, Going After Cacciato, The Notebook, Five Dollars a Day, Alpha Dog (also writer), Iron Man, God Is a Bullet (also writer), Bombing Harvey (also writer). *Exec. Prod.:* The Sky Is Green. *Writer:* Blow, My Sister's Keeper (also dir.), Yellow.
TELEVISION: *Movies:* Reunion, Shooter, The Incredible Mrs. Ritchie (Emmy Award 2004), Just Like Dad.

CASSEL, SEYMOUR
Actor. b. Detroit, MI, Jan. 22, 1935. As a boy travelled with a troupe of burlesque performers including his mother. After high school appeared in summer stock in Michigan. Studied acting at American Theatre Wing and Actor's Studio. After joining a workshop taught by John Cassavetes, began a long creative association with the director-actor. On B'way in, The World of Suzy Wong, The Disenchanted.
PICTURES: Murder Inc., Shadows, Too Late Blues, Juke Box Racket, The Killers, The Sweet Ride, Coogan's Bluff, Faces (AcademyAward nom. 1969), The Revolutionary, Minnie and Moskowitz, Black Oak Conspiracy, Death Game (The Seducers), The Killing of a Chinese Bookie, The Last Tycoon, Scott Joplin, Opening Night, Valentino, Convoy, California Dreaming, Ravagers, Sunburn, The Mountain Men, King of the Mountain, I'm Almost Not Crazy..., John Cassavetes–The Man and His Work (doc.), Love Streams, Eye of the Tiger, Survival Game, Tin Men, Johnny Be Good, Plain Clothes, Colors, Track 29, Wicked Stepmother, Dick Tracy, White Fang, Cold Dog Soup, Mobsters, Diary of a Hitman, Honeymoon in Vegas, In the Soup, Trouble Bound, Indecent Proposal, Boiling Point, Chain of Desire, Chasers, There Goes My Baby, When Pigs Fly, Hand Gun, It Could Happen to You, Tollbooth, Dark Side of Genius, Imaginary Crimes, Things I Never Told You, Dead Presidents, The Last Home Run, Dream for an Insomniac, Four Rooms, Cameleone, Things I Never Told You, Seed, Motel Blue, This World Then the Fireworks, Obsession, The Treat, Snapped, Rushmore, Me and Will, Kubanisch Rauchen, Dream for an Insomniac, Relax...It's Just Sex, Black and White, Ballad of the Nightingale, Getting to Know You, Temps, The Animal Factory, The Crew, Just One Night, Women of the Night, The Cure for Boredom, The Sleepy Time Gal, Bartleby, Manna From Heaven, The Royal Tenenbaums, The Chameleon, Stealing Harvard, Sonny, Passionada, Deadrockstar, The Burial Society, Time & Again, The Biz, Wishing Time, A Good Night To Die, Stuck On You, The Bride of the Sea, The Wendell Baker Story, The Life Aquatic, The Sky Is Green, Bittersweet Place, Before It Had a Name, The Tenants, The Happiest Day of His Life, Beer League, Chasing 3000, Postal, Cosmic Radio, Beau Jest, Irene in Time, Staten Island, Reach for Me, Chasing 3000, Not Dead Yet, Now Here, Kissing Strangers, Fort McCoy, Broken Kingdom, Without Borders.
TELEVISION: *Movies:* The Hanged Man, Angel on My Shoulder, Blood Feud, I Want to Live, Beverly Hills Madame, Sweet Bird of Youth, My Shadow, Dead in the Water, Face of a Stranger, The Last Don, Emma's Wish, 61. *Series:* Good Company, Lucky, Heist. *Pilots:* Rose City, Heist. *Documentary:* Anything for John. *Special:* Partners. *Guest:* More than 60 appearances.

CASSIDY, DAVID
Actor, Singer. b. New York, NY, April 12, 1950. Son of late actor Jack Cassidy; brother of Shaun and Patrick. Composed and performed theme song for The John Larroquette Show.
THEATRE: B'way: The Fig Leaves Are Falling (debut, 1968), Joseph and the Amazing Technicolor Dreamcoat, Blood Brothers. Regional: Little Johnny Jones, Tribute. *Las Vegas:* The Rat Pack. *London:* Time.
PICTURES: Instant Karma, The Spirit of '76, Popstar.
TELEVISION: *Movies:* The Night the City Screamed, We Are Family (tv documentary, as himself), The David Cassidy Story (exec. prod.). *Series:* The Partridge Family, David Cassidy-Man Undercover, The John Larroquette Show (composer), VH1's 8-Track Flashback (host), Ask Harriet (co-prod./writer), Ruby & the Rockits. *Documentaries:* Hearthrobs of the 70s, Intimate Portrait: Shirley Jones, TV Land Awards: A Celebration of Classic TV (as himself), 70's Fever (narr.). *Guest:* More than 94 appearances.

CASSIDY, JOANNA
Actress. r.n. Joanna Virginia Caskey. b. Camden, NJ, Aug. 2, 1945. e. Syracuse U.
PICTURES: Bullitt (debut, 1968), Fools, The Laughing Policeman, The Outfit, Bank Shot, The Stepford Wives, Stay Hungry, The Late Show, Stunts, The Glove, Our Winning Season, Night Games, Blade Runner, Under Fire, Club Paradise,The Fourth Protocol, Who Framed Roger Rabbit, 1969, The Package, Where the Heart Is, Don't Tell Mom the Babysitter's Dead, All-American Murder, May Wine, Vampire in Brooklyn, Chain Reaction, Loved, Executive Power, Dangerous Beauty, Moonglow, The Right Temptation, Ghosts of Mars, Murder on the Hudson, The Virgin of Juarez, Larry the Cable Guy: Health Inspector, The Grudge 2, Anderson's Cross, Kiss the Bride, The Human Contract, For Sale by Owner, The Boy in the Box, Stay Cool, Stolen, Flying Lessons, The American Standards.
TELEVISION: *Movies:* She's Dressed to Kill, Reunion, Invitation to Hell, The Children of Times Square, Pleasures, A Father's Revenge, Nightmare at Bitter Creek, Wheels of Terror, Grass Roots, Taking Back My Life, Live! From Death Row, Perfect Family, Barbarians at the Gate, Stephen King's The Tommyknockers, The Rockford Files: I Still Love L.A, Sleep Baby Sleep, The Second Civil War, Circle of Deceit, Wildfire 7: The Inferno, Martha Inc.: The Story of Martha Stewart, Found, The Reading Room. *Mini-series:* Hollywood Wives, To Serve and Protect, Tribe. *Series*: Shields and Yarnell, The Roller Girls, 240-Robert, Family Tree, Buffalo Bill (Golden Globe Award, Emmy nom. 1984), Code Name: Foxfire, Hotel Malibu, Superman, Six Feet Under (Emmy nom. 2006), Boston Legal, Hawthorne, Call Me Fitz. *Pilot:* Second Stage. *Specials:* Roger Rabbit and the Secrets of Toontown (host), Other Mothers (Afterschool Special), Tribe. *Guest:* More than 106 appearances.

CASSIDY, PATRICK
Actor. b. Los Angeles, CA, Jan. 4, 1962. Son of late actor Jack Cassidy and actress-singer Shirley Jones. Brother is David Cassidy.
THEATRE: NY: The Pirates of Penzance, Leader of the Pack, Assassins. Regional: Conrack.
PICTURES: Off the Wall, Just the Way You Are, Fever Pitch, Nickel Mountain, Love at Stake, Longtime Companion, I'll Do Anything, Lord Protector, The Dark Mist, Man of Her Dreams, The Great Debaters (set decor.).
TELEVISION: *Movies:* Angel Dusted, Midnight Offerings, Choices of the Heart, Christmas Eve, Dress Gray, Something in Comon, Follow Your Heart, Three on a Match, How the West Was Fun, Okalhoma City: A Survivor's Story, Newton. *Mini-series:* Napoleon and Josephine: A Love Story. *Pilot:* The Six of Us. *Series:* Bay City Blues, Dirty Dancing, Smallville, Ruby & the Rockits. *Guest:* More than 46 appearances.

CASTELLANETA, DAN
Actor. b. Chicago, IL, Sept. 10, 1958.
PICTURES: Nothing in Common, The War of the Roses, K-9, Don't Tell Mom the Babysitter's Dead (voice), The Return of Jafar (voice), Super Mario Bros., The Client, Love Affair, Forget Paris, Space Jam, Plump Fiction, Rhapsody in Bloom, My Giant, The Settlement, Rugrats in Paris: The Movie (voice), Recess: School's Out (voice), Don't Try This at Home, Return to Never Land (voice), Hey Arnold! The Movie (voice), Buttleman, The Cat in the Hat (voice), Adventures in Home Schooling, I Want Someone to Eat Cheese with, I-See-You.Com, The Pursuit of Happyness, The Simpsons Movie (voice), Superhero Movie, Scratching the Surface.
TELEVISION: *Movies:* Working Tra$h, Lady Against the Odds, The Online Adventures of Ozzie the Elf (voice), The Computer Wore Tennis Shoes (1995), Olive the Other Reindeer, Laughter on the 23rd Floor, Party Wagon, The Jimmy Timmy Power Hour (voice), The Jeff Garlin Program, Sands of Oblivion, Relative Stranger. *Series:* The Tracey Ullman Show, The Simpsons (voice, 4 Emmy Awards; WGA nom. 2007), Darkwing Duck (voice), Taz-Mania (voice), Sibs, Back to the Future (voice), Eek! the Cat, Aladdin (voice), The Tick (voice), Earthworm Jim, Hey Arnold (voice), Cow and Chicken (voice), The Batman, Castle (pilot), Greek. *Guest:* More than 194 appearances.

CASTLE, NICK
Writer, Director. b. Los Angeles, CA, Sept. 21, 1947. e. Santa Monica Coll., U. of Southern California film sch. Son of late film and TV choreographer Nick Castle Sr. Appeared as child in films Anything Goes, Artists and Models. Worked with John Carpenter and other USC students on Acad. Award-winning short, The Resurrection of Bronco Billy.
PICTURES: Skatedown USA (s.p.), Tag: The Assassination Game (Kiss Me Kill Me; dir., s.p.), Escape from New York (co-s.p.), The Last Starfighter (dir.), The Boy Who Could Fly (dir.), Tap (dir., s.p.), Hook (co-story), Dennis the Menace (dir.), Major Payne (dir.), Mr. Wrong (dir.), Escape from L.A., Delivering Milo (dir.), August Rush (writer, s.p.). *Actor:* Halloween.
TELEVISION: *Movies:* Shangri-La Plaza (also exec. prod.), Twas the Night (dir.).

CATES, GILBERT
Director, Producer. r.n. Gilbert Katz. b. New York, NY, June 6, 1934. e. Syracuse U. Began TV career as guide at NBC studios in N.Y., working way up to prod. and dir. of game shows (Camouflage, Haggis Baggis, Mother's Day, etc.). Created Hootenanny and packaged and directed many TV specials. Pres. Directors Guild of America 1983-87. Awarded DGA's Robert B. Aldrich award 1989. Dir. short film The Painting. Received DGA President's Award and the Board of the Governors Award from the ASC 2005. Also received Cinema Audio Society Filmmaker Award 2007. Has 11 Emmy noms. and 1 Emmy Award for Annual Academy Awards Show.
THEATRE: *Director:* Tricks of the Trade, Voices, The Price (Long Wharf Theatre), Under the Blue Sky. *Producer:* Solitaire/Double Solitaire, The Chinese and Mr. Fish, I Never Sang for My Father, You Know I Can't Hear You When the Water's Running.
PICTURES: Rings Around the World (debut, 1966), I Never Sang for My Father (also prod.), Summer Wishes Winter Dreams, One Summer Love (Dragonfly; also prod.), The Promise, The Last Married Couple in America, Oh God!—Book II (also prod.),

Backfire, $pent (actor).
TELEVISION: *Movies:* To All My Friends on Shore, The Affair, After the Fall, Johnny, We Hardly Knew Ye, The Kid from Nowhere, Country Gold, Hobson's Choice, Burning Rage, Consenting Adult (Emmy nom. 1985), Child's Cry, Fatal Judgement, My First Love, Do You Know the Muffin Man (Emmy nom. 1990), Call Me Anna, Absolute Strangers (exec. prod.), In My Daughter's Name (co-exec. prod.), Confessions: Two Faces of Evil, Innocent Victims, Collected Stories, A Death in the Family. *Series:* Camouflage, Picture This, Reach for the Stars. *Specials: Prod. &/or Dir. unless otherwise noted:* International Showtime (1963-65 exec. prod.), Electric Showcase Specials, Academy Awards (prod. 1990-95, 1997-98), Academy Awards Show: (66th, 67th, 70th and 71st. prod., 73rd, 75th, exec. prod., 77th, prod., 78th prod., 80th exec. prod. *Specials:* To Life: America Celebrates Israel's 50th, An American Celebration at Ford's Theater (exec. prod.), A Holiday Celebration at Ford's Theatre (exec. prod.), Oscar's Red Carpet 2008 (exec. prod.).

CATES, PHOEBE
Actress. r.n. Phoebe Belle Katz. b. New York, NY, July 16, 1963. e. Juilliard. Daughter of late prod-dir. Joseph Cates. m. actor Kevin Kline. Dance prodigy and fashion model before launching acting career. NY stage debut The Nest of the Wood Grouse (1984).
THEATRE: *B'way:* The Tenth Man (debut 1989).
PICTURES: Paradise (debut, 1982), Fast Times at Ridgemont High, Private School, Gremlins, Date With an Angel, Bright Lights Big City, Shag, Heart of Dixie, I Love You to Death (unbilled), Gremlins 2: The New Batch, Drop Dead Fred, Bodies Rest & Motion, My Life's in Turnaround, Princess Caraboo, Scratch the Surface, The Anniversary Party.
TELEVISION: *Movies:* Baby Sister, Lace, Lace II. *Special:* Largo Desolato.

CATMULL, ED
Executive. b. Parkersburg, WV, March 31, 1945. B.S. degrees in computer science and physics; Ph.D. in computer science from the University of Utah. In 1979, Dr. Catmull brought his high-technology expertise to the film industry as v.p., computer division for Lucasfilm, Ltd. During that time, Dr. Catmull managed four development efforts in the areas of computer graphics, video editing, video games and digital audio. He was also a key developer of RenderMan(R), the program that creates realistic digital effects for computer graphics and animation. Catmull is a co-founder of Pixar Animation Studios and has served as a member of the executive team of Pixar since the incorporation of the company. Dr. Catmull has been honored with three Scientific and Technical Engineering Awards from The Academy of Motion Picture Arts and Sciences for his work, including an Oscar for significant advancements to the field of motion picture rendering as exemplified in Pixar's RenderMan(R). He also won the Coons Award, which is the highest achievement in computer graphics, for his lifetime contributions. Dr. Catmull is a member of the Academy of Motion Picture Arts and Sciences and the Science and Technical Awards Committee. In late Jan. 2006, Walt Disney announced the acquisition of Pixar Animation Studios for approx. $7.4 billion in stock. After the acquisition, Pixar became a wholly owned subsidiary of The Walt Disney Company. Dr. Catmull currently is president of both Pixar and Disney Animation Studios. Received Academy of Motion Picture Arts and Sciences, Gordon E. Sawyer Award for his lifetime of technical contributions and leadership in the field of computer graphics for the motion picture industry, 2009.

CATON-JONES, MICHAEL
Director. b. Broxburn, Scotland, 1958.
PICTURES: Scandal (debut, 1989), Memphis Belle, Doc Hollywood (also cameo), This Boy's Life, Rob Roy (also exec. prod.), The Jackal (also exec.), City By the Sea, Shooting Dogs, Basic Instinct 2, After the Wedding.
TELEVISION: *Movies:* Brond, Lucky Sunil. *Series*: Trinity.

CATTRALL, KIM
Actress. b. Liverpool, Eng., Aug. 21, 1956. e. American Acad. of Dramatic Arts, N.Y. Started stage career in Canada's Off-B'way in Vancouver and Toronto; later performed in L.A. in A View from the Bridge, Agnes of God, Three Sisters, etc. On B'way in Wild Honey. Chicago Goodman Theatre in the Misanthrope. Regional: Miss Julie (Princeton).
PICTURES: Rosebud (debut 1975), The Other Side of the Mountain Part II, Tribute, Ticket to Heaven, Porky's, Police Academy, Turk 182, City Limits, Hold-Up, Big Trouble in Little China, Mannequin, Masquerade, Midnight Crossing, Palais Royale, Honeymoon Academy, The Return of the Musketeers, Brown Bread Sandwiches, Bonfire of the Vanities, Star Trek VI: The Undiscovered Country, Split Second, Double Vision, Breaking Point, Unforgettable, Live Nude Girls, Where Truth Lies, Baby Geniuses, Modern Vampires, 15 Minutes, The Devil and Daniel Webster, Not a Girl, Crossroads, Ice Princess, A Tiger's Tale, Sex and the City, Miss January, The Ghost Writer, Sex and the City 2.
TELEVISION: *Movies:* Good Against Evil, The Bastard, The Night Rider, The Rebels, The Gossip Columnist, Sins of the Past, Miracle in the Wilderness, Running Delilah, Above Suspicion, The Heidi Chronicles, Two Golden Balls, Outer Limits, 36 Hours to Die, Sex and the Matrix (short), Intimate Portrait: Kim Cattrall (herself), Him and Us, My Boy Jack. *Mini-series:* Scruples, Wild Palms, Tom Clancy's Op Center, Invasion, Creature. *Series:* Angel Falls, Sex and the City (Golden Globe, 2003, also 3 noms., 5 Emmy noms. SAG Award, 2002 and 2004), Producing Parker. *Guest:* More than 125 appearances.

CAULFIELD, MAXWELL
Actor. b. Glasgow, Scotland, Nov. 23, 1959. m. actress Juliet Mills. First worked as a dancer at a London nightclub. After coming to NY in 1978, ran the concession stand at the Truck and Warehouse Theatre. Won a Theatre World Award for Class Enemy.
THEATRE: Entertaining Mr. Sloane, Salonika, Journey's End, Sleuth, The Elephant Man, An Inspector Calls, Sweet Bird of Youth, The Woman In Black.
PICTURES: Grease 2, Electric Dreams, The Boys Next Door, The Supernaturals, Sundown: The Vampire in Retreat, Mind Games, Alien Intruder, Midnight Witness, Ipi/Tombi, In a Moment of Passion, Calendar Girl, Gettysburg, Inevitable Grace, Empire Records, Prey of the Jaguar, Oblivion 2: Backlash, The Real Blonde, The Man Who Knew Too Little, Divine Lovers, Smut, More to Love, Dazzle, The Perfect Tenant, Submerged, Overnight Sensation, Facing the Enemy, The Hit, Nightmare City 2035, Dire Wolf.
TELEVISION: *Movies:* The Parade, Till We Meet Again, Blue Bayou, Dynasty: The Reunion, Missing Pieces, Dragon Storm, Cry of the Winged Serpent, Living the Quake. *Series:* Dynasty, The Colbys, All My Children, Spider Man (voice), Strip Mall, Casualty, Emmerdale Farm. *Guest:* More than 45 appearances.

CAVANI, LILIANA
Director. b. near Modena, in Emilia, Italy, Jan. 12, 1933. e. U. of Bologna, diploma in classic literature, 1960; Ph.D. in linguistics. In 1960 took courses at Centro Sperimentale di Cinematografia in Rome where made short films Incontro Notturno and L'Evento. 1961 winner of RAI sponsored contest and started working for the new second Italian TV channel, 1962-66 directing progs. of serious political and social nature incl. History of 3rd Reich, Women in the Resistance, Age of Stalin, Philippe Petain–Trial at Vichy (Golden Lion Venice Fest.), Jesus My Brother, Day of Peace, Francis of Assisi. Has also directed operas Wozzeck, Iphigenia in Tauris and Medea on stage.
PICTURES: Galileo, I Cannibali, Francesco d'Assissi, L'Ospite, Milarepa, Night Porter, Beyond Good and Evil, The Skin, Oltre la Porta, The Berlin Affair, Francesco, Where Are You I'm Here, Sans Pouvoir le Dire, Dissociated States, Ripley's Game.
TELEVISION: La Traviata, Manon Lescaut, La Cavalleria rusticana, Un Ballo in maschera, De Gasperi, l'uomo della speranza (also writer), Einstein (also writer).

CAVETT, DICK
Actor, Writer. b. Kearny, NE, Nov. 19, 1936. e. Yale U. Acted in TV dramas and Army training films. Was writer for Jack Paar and his successors on the Tonight Show. Also wrote comedy for Merv Griffin, Jerry Lewis, Johnny Carson. In 1967 began performing own comedy material in night clubs. On TV starred in specials Where It's At (ABC Stage 67) and What's In. Author of, Cavett (with Christopher Porter) 1974.
THEATRE: *B'way:* Otherwise Engaged, Into the Woods.
PICTURES: Annie Hall, Power Play, Health, Simon, A Nightmare on Elm Street 3, Beetlejuice, Moon Over Parador, After School, Funny, Year of the Gun, Forrest Gump, Frequency, Duane Hopwood, Driving Me Crazy.
TELEVISION: *Movies:* Barbarians at the Gate, Nightside, Invisible Thread, Elvis Meets Nixon (narr.). *Series:* This Morning (ABC daytime talk show, 1968), The Dick Cavett Show (ABC primetime talk show, summer 1969), The Dick Cavett Show (ABC late night talk show, 1969-72: Emmy Award, 1972), ABC Late Night (talk show, 1973-74; Emmy Award, 1974), The Dick Cavett Show (CBS primetime variety; 1975), Dick Cavett Show (talk show: PBS, 1977-82; 2 Emmy nom. 1978, 1979; USA, 1985-86; CBS, 1986), The Edge of Night (1983), The Dick Cavett Show (CNBC talk show: 1989). *Guest:* More than 122 appearances.

CAZENOVE, CHRISTOPHER
Actor. b. Winchester, Eng., Dec. 17, 1945. e. Eton, Oxford U., trained at Bristol Old Vic Theatre School.
theatrE: Hamlet (1969), The Lionel Touch, My Darling Daisy, The Winslow Boy, Joking Apart, In Praise of Rattigan, The Life and Poetry of T.S. Eliot, The Sound of Music, Goodbye Fidel (B'way debut, 1980).
PICTURES: There's a Girl in My Soup, Royal Flash, East of Elephant Rock, The Girl in Blue Velvet, Zulu Dawn, Eye of the Needle, From a Far Country, Heat and Dust, Until September, Mata Hari, The Fantastist, Hold My Hand I'm Dying, Three Men and a Little Lady, Aces: Iron Eagle III, The Proprietor, Shadow Run, The Contaminated Man, Beginner's Luck, A Knight's Tale, Young Alexander the Great.
TELEVISION: *Specials/Movies:* The Rivals of Sherlock Holmes (1971), Affairs of the Heart, Jennie: Lady Randolph Churchill, The Darkwater Hall Mystery, Ladykillers—A Smile Is Sometimes Worth a Million, The Red Signal, Lou Grant, The Letter, Jenny's War, Lace 2, Kane and Abel, Windmills of the Gods, Shades of Love, Souvenir, The Lady and the Highwayman, Tears in the Rain, Ticket to Ride (A Fine Romance), To Be the Best, The Way

to Dusty Death, Dead Man's Island, Home Song, Judge John Deed: Exacting Justice, Trance. *Mini-series:* Johnson County War, La Femme Musketeer. *Series:* The Regiment, The Duchess of Duke Street, Dynasty, A Fine Romance, Tales From the Crypt, Johnson County War, Fun at the Funeral Parlour, Judge John Deed. *Guest:* More than 50 appearances.

CELENTINO, LUCIANO
Producer, Director, Writer. b. Naples, Italy, 1940. e. Rome, Paris, London. Entered. ind. 1959. Wrote, prod., dir. many plays incl: Infamita di Questa Terra, Black Destiny, Honour, Stranger's Heart, Youth's Sin, Wanda Lontano Amore. Stage musicals such as Songs...Dots...And Fantasies, Night Club's Appointment, Filumena, Serenada, Mamma. Since 1964, film critic of Il Meridionale Italiano. From 1962, co-writer and first asst. director to Luigi Capuano and Vittorio De Sica. In 1972, formed own company, Anglo-Fortunato Films. Honorary President Accademia Di Arte Drammatica Eduardo de Filippo teaching film acting, writing, directing.
PICTURES: Blood Money, Bandito (dir. only), Toujours (dir., s.p.), Parole (dir.,s.p.), Jackpot (dir., s.p.), Panache (dir. only), Was There a Way Out? (dir. only), Hobo, Gallan (dir. only), The Pinch.

CELLAN-JONES, JAMES
Director. b. Swansea, Wales, July 13, 1931. e. St. John's Coll., Cambridge. Best known for his adaptations of classic novels for the BBC and PBS (shown on Masterpiece Theatre). Won Nymphe d'Or at Monaco Festival.
PICTURE: The Nelson Affair, Chou Chou, Une Vie de Debussy, Married 2 Malcolm.
TELEVISION: The Scarlet and the Black, The Forsythe Saga, Portrait of a Lady, The Way We Live Now, Solo, The Roads to Freedom, Eyeless In Gaza, The Golden Bowl, Jennie: Lady Randolph Churchill (Emmy nom. 1976. DGA series award), Caesar and Cleopatra, The Adams Chronicles (2 Emmy nom. 1977), The Day Christ Died, The Ambassadors, Unity Mitford, Oxbridge Blues (also prod.), Sleeps Six (also prod.), The Comedy of Errors, Fortunes of War, You Never Can Tell, Arms and the Man, A Little Piece of Sunshine, A Perfect Hero (also prod.), The Gravy Train Goes East, Maigret, Harnessing Peacocks, Brighton Belles, The Vacillations of Poppy Carew, La Musique de l'Amour, McLibel!, May and June, The Bill, Holby City.

CHABROL, CLAUDE
Director. b. Paris, France, June 24, 1930. Worked as newsman for Fox, then writer for Cahiers du Cinema. A founding director of the French New Wave.
PICTURES: Le Beau Serge, The Cousins, A Double Tour, Les Bonnes Femmes, Les Godelureaux, The Third Lover, Seven Capital Sins, Ophelia, Landru, Le Tigre Aime la Chair Fraiche, Marie-Chantal Contre le Docteur Kah, Le Tigre Se Parfume a la Dunamite, Paris vu par... Chabrol, La Ligne de Demarcation, The Champagne Murders, The Route to Corinth, Les Biches, Le Femme Infidele, This Man Must Die, Le Boucher, La Rapture, Ten Days' Wonder, Just Before Nightfall, Dr. Popaul, Les Noces Rouges, Nada, The Blood of Others, The Horse of Pride, Alouette je te plumera, Poulet au Vinaigre, Inspector Lavardin, Masques, Le Cri du Hibou, Story of Women, Clichy Days (Quiet Days in Clichy), The Lark (actor only), Doctor M (Club Extinction), Madame Bovary, Betty, Through the Eyes of Vichy, L'Enfer (Hell; also s.p.), A Judgment in Stone (also co-s.p.), Rien Ne Va Plus, The Color of Lies (also s.p.), Nightcap (also s.p.), Unfaithful (writer only), The Flower of Evil (dir., writer), La Demoiselle d'honneur, L' Ivresse du pouvoir, Lucifer et moi, The Girl Cut in Two, Bellamy.
TELEVISION: *Movies:* La Deuxième vérité. *Mini-series:* La Parure. *Series:* Les Redoutables. Many more French titles.

CHAKERES, PHILIP H.
Exhibitor. b. Springfield, OH, 1960. e. Wittenberg University, 1990, President and Chief Executive Officer of Chakeres Theatres of Ohio and Kentucky. Also president and CEO of Lobby Shoppes, Inc. Member: Rotary Club, Will Rogers Institute, Midstates NATO, National NATO, ASHA.

CHAMBERLAIN, RICHARD
Actor. r.n. George Richard Chamberlain. b. Los Angeles, CA, March 31, 1935. Studied voice, LA Conservatory of Music 1958; acting with Jeff Corey. Founding mem. City of Angels, LA Theater Company. Became TV star in Dr. Kildare series, 1961-66. Founded prod. co. Cham Enterprises. Had hit record Three Stars Will Shine Tonight (theme from Dr. Kildare) in 1962.
THEATRE: Breakfast at Tiffany's, Night of the Iguana, Fathers & Sons, Blithe Spirit, The Sound of Music, My Fair Lady.
PICTURES: The Secret of the Purple Reef (debut, 1960), A Thunder of Drums, Twilight of Honor, Joy in the Morning, Petulia, The Madwoman of Chaillot, Julius Caesar, The Music Lovers, Lady Caroline Lamb, The Three Musketeers, The Towering Inferno, The Four Musketeers, The Slipper and the Rose, The Swarm, The Last Wave, Murder by Phone (Bells), King Solomon's Mines, Alan Quartermain and the Lost City of Gold, The Return of the Musketeers (tv in U.S.), Bird of Prey, The Pavillion, Strength and Honour, I Now Pronounce You Chuck and Larry.
TELEVISION: *Movies:* F. Scott Fitzgerald and the Last of the Belles, The Count of Monte Cristo (Emmy nom. 1975), The Man in the Iron Mask, Cook and Perry: The Race to the Pole, Wallenberg: A Hero's Story (Emmy nom. Golden Globe nom. 1985), Casanova, Aftermath: A Test of Love, The Night of the Hunter, Ordeal in the Arctic, The Thorn Birds: The Missing Year, All the Winters that Have Been, Pirates: The True Story of Blackbeard. *Mini-series:* Centennial (Golden Globe nom. 1980), Shogun (Emmy nom. Golden Globe Award 1981), The Thorn Birds (Emmy nom. Golden Globe Award 1983), Dream West, The Bourne Identity (Golden Globe nom. 1989), Too Rich: The Secret Life of Doris Duke. *Series:* Dr. Kildare, Island Son (also co-exec. prod.) *Host:* The Astronomers. *Specials:* Hamlet, Portrait of a Lady, The Woman I Love, The Lady's Not for Burning, Japan: Memoirs of a Secret Empire (narr.). *Guest:* More than 102 appearances.

CHAN, JACKIE
Actor, Director, Writer. r.n. Chan Kwong-Sang. b. Hong Kong, Apr. 7, 1954. Trained in acrobatics, mime and martial arts at Peking Opera Sch. Was child actor in several films; later became stuntman before being launched as action star by prod.-dir. Lo Wei.
PICTURES: Little Tiger From Canton, New Fist of Fury, Shaolin Wooden Men, To Kill With Intrigue, Snake in the Eagle's Shadow, Snake & Crane Arts of Shaolin, Magnificent Bodyguards, Drunken Master (Drunk Monkey in the Tiger's Eyes), Spiritual Kung Fu, The Fearless Hyena, Dragon Fist, The Young Master (also dir., co-s.p.), Half a Loaf of Kung Fu, The Big Brawl, The Cannonball Run, Dragon Lord (also dir., co-s.p.), Winners and Sinners, The Fearless Hyena Part 2, Cannonball Run II, Project A (also co-dir., co-s.p.), Wheels on Meals, My Lucky Stars, The Protector, Twinkle Twinkle Lucky Stars, Heart of the Dragon (First Mission), Police Story (also dir., co-s.p.), Armour of God (also dir., co-s.p.), Project A Part 2 (also dir., co-s.p.), Dragons Forever, Police Story II (also dir., co-s.p.), Mr. Canton and Lady Rose (Miracle; also dir., co-s.p.), Armour of God II: Operation Condor (also dir., co-s.p.), Island of Fire, Twin Dragons, Police Story III: Super Cop (also dir., co-s.p.), City Hunter, Crime Story, Project S, Drunken Master II, Rumble in the Bronx, Thunderbolt, First Strike, Burn Hollywood Burn, Mr. Nice Guy, Rush Hour, Who Am I? (also dir., s.p.), Gorgeous (also exec. prod.), Shanghai Noon (also prod.), The Accidental Spy, Rush Hour 2, The Tuxedo, Shanghai Knights, Chin gei bin, The Medallion, Around the World in 80 Days (also prod.), Rush Hour 3, Rice Rhapsody (exec. prod.), Time Breaker, Joe's Last Chance, The Myth, House of Fury (exec. prod.), Rob-B-Hood (also writer and stunt coord, 90 Mins, Kung Fu Panda (voice), Rush Hour 3, The Forbidden Kingdom, Wushu (exec. prod. only), Kung Fu Panda (voice), The Shinjuku Incident (also prod.), The Spy Next Door, Little Big Soldier (also prod.), Chinese Zodiac (actor, dir.), The Karate Kid (actor only). *Guest:* More than 110 appearances.

CHANNING, CAROL
Actress. b. Seattle, WA, Jan. 31, 1921. e. Bennington Coll.
THEATRE: B'way: Gentlemen Prefer Blondes, Lend an Ear (Theatre World Award), Hello Dolly! (Tony Award, 1964), Show Girl, Lorelei. Tour: Legends.
PICTURES: Paid in Full (debut, 1950), The First Traveling Saleslady, Thoroughly Modern Millie (Academy Award nom.; Golden Globe Award 1968), Skidoo, Shinbone Alley (voice), Sgt. Pepper's Lonely Hearts Club Band (cameo), Happily Ever After (voice), Hans Christian Andersen's Thumbelina (voice), Edie & Pen, The Line King: Al Hirschfeld, Homo Heights, The Brave Little Toaster Goes to Mars (voice), Broadway: Golden Age by the Legends Who Were There.
TELEVISION: *Movies:* Free to Be...You & Me (voice), Alice in Wonderland, JFK: The Day the Nation Cried (TV documentary) *Series:* Where's Waldo? (voice), The Addams Family (voice, 1992). *Specials:* Svengali and the Blonde, Three Men on a Horse, Crescendo, The Carol Channing Special. *Guest:* More than 106 appearances.

CHANNING, STOCKARD
Actress. r.n. Susan Williams Antonia Stockard. b. New York, NY, Feb. 13, 1944. e. Radcliffe Coll., B.A., 1965. With Theatre Co. of Boston, experimental drama company, 1967.
THEATRE: Two Gentlemen of Verona, No Hard Feelings, Vanities (Mark Taper Forum, LA), They're Playing Our Song, The Lady and the Clarinet, Golden Age, The Rink, Joe Egg (Tony Award, 1985), Love Letters, Woman in Mind, House of Blue Leaves, Six Degrees of Separation, Four Baboons Adoring the Sun.
PICTURES: The Hospital (debut, 1971), Up the Sandbox, The Fortune (Golden Globe nom. 1976), The Big Bus, Sweet Revenge, Grease, The Cheap Detective, The Fish That Saved Pittsburgh, Safari 3000, Without a Trace, Heartburn, The Men's Club, A Time of Destiny, Staying Together, Meet the Applegates, Married to It, Six Degrees of Separation (Academy Award nom. Golden Globe nom. 1994), Bitter Moon, Smoke, To Wong Foo—Thanks for Everything—Julie Newmar, Up Close and Personal, Moll Flanders, Edie and Pen, The First Wives Club, Practical Magic, Baby Dance (Emmy nom., Golden Globe nom. 1999), Twilight, Lulu on the Bridge (voice), Practical Magic, Isn't She Great, The Venice Project, Where the Heart Is, The Business of Strangers, Life or Something Like It, Behind the Red Door, Le Divorce, Anything Else,

Loggerheads, Must Love Dogs, 3 Needles, Sparkle, Multiple Sarcasms, A Fonder Heart.
TELEVISION: *Movies:* The Girl Most Likely To..., Lucan, Silent Victory: The Kitty O'Neil Story, Not My Kid, The Room Upstairs, Echoes in the Darkness Emmy nom. 1988), The Perfect Witness (Emmy nom. 1990), David's Mother, An Unexpected Family (Emmy nom. 1997), Lily Dale, The Prosecutors, An Unexpected Life, The Baby Dance (Emmy nom. 1999), The Truth About Jane, The Piano Man's Daughter, The Confessions of an Ugly Stepsister, The Matthew Shepard Story (Emmy Award 2002), Hitler: The Rise of Evil, Jack (Emmy Award 2005). *Mini-series:* A Girl Thing. *Series:* Stockard Channing in Just Friends, The Stockard Channing Show, Batman Beyond (voice), Out of Practice (Emmy nom. 2006), The West Wing (Emmy Award 2002, 5 more noms.), Walking With Beasts (voice). *Special:* Tidy Endings. *Guest:* More than 98 appearances.

CHAPEK, ROBERT
Executive. e. B.S. degree, Indiana University. M.B.A., Michigan State University, 1984. Before joining The Walt Disney Company, Chapek held brand management positions in the packaged goods industry with the H.J. Heinz Company and in the advertising business with J. Walter Thompson. He joined Disney's Buena Vista Home Entertainment (BVHE) in May 1993 as director of marketing and held several titles in marketing until his promotion to president of BVHE in 2000. In a July 2006 corporate restructuring, The Walt Disney Studios named Bob Chapek president of the new division, Buena Vista Worldwide Home Entertainment. He now oversees international distribution and marketing of all the studio's films on home entertainment platforms. Additionally, Chapek oversees the development of various new technologies, including the high-definition Blu-ray Disc. He also is responsible for managing the supply chain that delivers titles to retailers, as well as the development of DVD programming and supplemental materials for Buena Vista titles. Chapek became president of the Digital Entertainment Group (formerly DVD Entertainment Group), an industry association comprised of movie studios, the music industry, and consumer electronics hardware manufacturers. The group's goal is to promote consumer awareness of the benefits of DVD-video and DVD-audio. 2007 Chapek was elected Chairman of DEG's Bd.

CHAPIN, DOUG
Producer, Executive. Began career as actor; then switched to film production, making debut with When a Stranger Calls, 1979. Currently president/manager of Doug Chapin Management.
PICTURES: Pandemonium, American Dreamer, What's Love Got to Do With It, Love! Valour! Compassion!, The Passion of Ayn Rand (co-exec.).
TELEVISION: *Movies:* All Lies End in Murder, Belle Starr, Missing Pieces, Second Sight, When A Stranger Calls Back, The Corpse Had a Familiar Face, Jackie's Back: Portrait of a Diva (exec. prod.). *Series:* Tim Conway's Funny America.

CHAPLIN, GERALDINE
Actress. b. Santa Monica, CA, July 31, 1944. e. Royal Ballet School, London. Father was late actor-director Charles Chaplin. Granddaughter of late playwright Eugene O'Neill. Starred in over 20 European productions, including seven with Spanish filmmaker, Carlos Saura. On NY stage in The Little Foxes.
PICTURES: Limelight (debut, 1952), Par un Beau Matin d'Ete, Doctor Zhivago (Golden Globe nom. 1966), Andremo in Citta, A Countess from Hong Kong, Stranger in the House (Cop-Out), I Killed Rasputin, Peppermint Frappe, Stres es Tres Tres, Honeycomb, Garden of Delights, The Hawaiians, Sur un Arbre Perche, Z.P.G. (Zero Population Growth), Innocent Bystanders, La Casa sin Fronteras, Ana and the Wolves, The Three Musketeers, Le Marriage a la Mode, The Four Musketeers, Summer of Silence, Nashville (Golden Globe nom. 1976), Elisa My Love, Noroit, Buffalo Bill and the Indians or Sitting Bull's History Lesson, Welcome to L.A., Cria, In Memorium, Une Page d'Amour, Roseland, Remember My Name, Los Ojos Vendados, The Masked Bride, L'Adoption, A Wedding, The Mirror Crack'd, Le Voyage en Douce, Bolero, Life Is a Bed of Roses, Love on the Ground, The Moderns, White Mischief, Mama Turns 100, I Want to Go Home, The Children, Buster's Bedroom, Chaplin (Golden Globe nom. 1993), The Age of Innocence, Words Upon the Window Pane, Home for the Holidays, Jane Eyre, Crimetime, The Eyes of Asia, Mother Theresa: In the Name of God's Poor, Cousin Bette, To Walk with Lions, The Last Days of Switzerland, Just Run, Faces of the Moon, The City of No Limits, Talk to Her, The Bridge of San Luis Rey, Disappearances, Bloodrayne, Heidi, Oculto, Teresa, muerte y vida, Miguel and William, Los Totenwackers, El Orfanato, Parc , Boxes, Teresa, el cuerpo de Cristo, Ramirez, Imago mortis, Diario de una ninfómana, The Making of Plus One, La Isla interior, Apóstolo, O (voice), The Wolfman, There Be Dragons, La mosquitera.
TELEVISION: *Movies:* The House of Mirth, The Corsican Brothers, Duel of Hearts, Gulliver's Travels, The Odyssey, Mary, Mother of Jesus, Winter Solstice, A Christmas Carol, Marple: Sleeping Murder, Les Aventuriers des mers du Sud. *Mini-series:* The Word, In the Beginning, Dinotopia. *Specials:* My Cousin Rachel, A Foreign Field, XVII premios Goya. *Documentaries:* Unknown Chaplin, Charlie Chaplin: The Forgotten Years, Charlie: The Life and Art of Charles Chaplin. *Guest:* More than 71 appearances.

CHAPMAN, MICHAEL
Cinematographer, Director. b. New York, NY, Nov. 21, 1935. m. writer-dir. Amy Jones. Early career in N.Y. area working on documentaries before becoming camera operator for cinematographer Gordon Willis on The Godfather, Klute, End of the Road, The Landlord. Also camera operator on Jaws. American Society of Cinematographers Lifetime Achievement Award 2004.
PICTURES: *Cinematographer:* The Last Detail, White Dawn, Taxi Driver, The Front, The Next Man, Fingers, The Last Waltz, Invasion of the Body Snatchers, Hardcore, The Wanderers, Raging Bull (Academy Award nom. 1981), Dead Men Don't Wear Plaid, Personal Best, The Man With Two Brains, Shoot to Kill, Scrooged, Ghostbusters II, Quick Change, Kindergarten Cop, Whispers in the Dark, Rising Sun, The Lost Boys, The Fugitive (Academy Award nom. 1994), Primal Fear, Space Jam, Six Days Seven Nights, The Story of Us, The White River Kid, The Watcher, Evolution, Eulogy, Suspect Zero, Hoot, Bridge to Terabithia. *Director:* All the Right Moves, The Clan of the Cave Bear, The Viking Sagas (also s.p.).
TELEVISION: Death Be Not Proud (Emmy nom. 1975), King, Gotham, Third Degree Burn (actor). *Dir.:* The Annihilator (pilot). *Mini-series:* King.

CHARBONNEAU, PATRICIA
Actress. b. Valley Stream, Long Island, NY, 1959. Stage appearances with Actors Theatre of Louisville, KY. Also in NY in My Sister in This House.
PICTURES: Desert Hearts, Manhunter, Stalking Danger, Call Me, Paranoia, Shakedown, Brain Dead, Captive, The Owl, K2, Portraits of a Killer, Kiss the Sky, She's All That, 100 Feet.
TELEVISION: *Movies:* Disaster at Silo 7, Desperado: Badlands Justice, One Special Night. *Series:* Crime Story. *Pilots:* C.A.T. Squad, Dakota's Way.

CHARLES, MARIA
Actress. b. London, England, Sept. 22, 1929. Trained at RADA. London stage debut 1946 in Pick Up Girl.
THEATRE: *London:* Women of Twilight, The Boy Friend, Divorce Me Darling!, Enter A Free Man, They Don't Grow on Trees, Winnie the Pooh, Jack the Ripper, The Matchmaker, Measure for Measure, Annie (1979-80), Fiddler on the Roof, Steaming, Peer Gynt, The Lower Depths, When We Are Married, Follies, Party Piece, School for Scandal, Driving Miss Daisy, Hay Fever, Blithe Spirit. *Dir.:* Owl and the Pussycat. *Dir./prod.:* The Boy Friend, 40, Starting Here Starting Now.
PICTURES: Folly To Be Wise, The Deadly Affair, Eye of the Devil, Great Expectations, The Return of the Pink Panther, Cuba, Victor/Victoria, Antonia and Jane, Savage Hearts, The Fool, Dear Wendy, In Your Dreams, Hot Fuzz, Sisterhood.
TELEVISION: *Movies:* Pollyanna, The Likes of 'Er, The Moon and the Yellow River, Down Our Street, Easter Passion, Nicholas Nickleby, The Voice of the Turtle, The Fourth Wall, The Good Old Days, Turn Out the Lights, Angel Pavement, The Ugliest Girl in Town, Other Peoples Houses, The Prince and the Pauper, Crown Court, Bar Mitzvah Boy, La Ronde, Shine of Harvey Moon, Sheppey, La Ronde, Brideshead Revisited, The Fallout Guy, Lovejoy, Anna, Oliver Twist, Crime and Punishment, Cor Blimey. *Mini-series:* Country Matters, A Perfect Spy, Great Expectations, The 10th Kingdom. *Series:* Crossroads, Whoops Apocalypse, Never the Twain, Thomas and Sarah, Agony, Secret Army, Seven Faces of Woman, Dream Stuffing, Agony Again, Bad Girls, Coronation Street. *Guest:* More than 63 appearances.

CHARTOFF, ROBERT
Producer. b. New York, NY., Aug. 26, 1933. e. Union College, A.B.; Columbia U., LL.B. Met Irwin Winkler through mutual client at William Morris Agency (N.M.) and established Chartoff-Winkler Prods. Currently pres., Chartoff Prods., Inc.
PICTURES: Double Trouble, Point Blank, The Split, They Shoot Horses Don't They?, The Strawberry Statement, Leo the Last, Believe in Me, The Gang That Couldn't Shoot Straight, The New Centurions, Up the Sandbox, The Mechanic, Thumb Tripping, Busting, The Gambler, S*P*Y*S, Breakout, Nickelodeon, Rocky (Academy Award 1977), New York New York, Valentino, Comes a Horseman, Uncle Joe Shannon, Rocky II, Raging Bull (Academy Award nom. 1981), True Confessions, Rocky III, The Right Stuff (Academy Award nom. 1984), Rocky IV, Beer, Rocky V, Straight Talk, In My Country, Ender's Game, Rocky Balboa (exec. prod.), The Mechanic, The Tempest.

CHASE, CHEVY
Actor. r.n. Cornelius Crane Chase. b. New York, NY, Oct. 8, 1943. e. Bard Coll.; B.A. Studied audio research at CCS Institute. Worked as writer for Mad Magazine, 1969. Teamed with Kenny Shapiro and Lane Sarasohn while still in school to collaborate on material for underground TV, which ultimately became off-off-Broadway show and later movie called Groove Tube. Co-wrote and starred in Saturday Night Live on TV, winning 2 Emmys as continuing single performance by a supporting actor and as writer for show.
PICTURES: The Groove Tube (debut, 1974), Tunnelvision, Foul Play (2 Golden Globe nom. 1979), Caddyshack, Oh Heavenly Dog, Seems Like Old Times, Under the Rainbow, Modern Problems, National Lampoon's Vacation, Deal of the Century, Fletch, National Lampoon's European Vacation, Sesame Street Presents Follow That Bird (cameo), Spies Like Us, Three

Amigos!, The Couch Trip (cameo), Funny Farm, Caddyshack II, Fletch Lives, National Lampoon's Christmas Vacation, L.A. Story (cameo), Nothing But Trouble, Memoirs of an Invisible Man, Hero (unbilled), Last Action Hero (cameo), Cops and Robbersons, Man of the House, Vegas Vacation, Dirty Work, Snow Day, Unleashed, Vacuums, Orange County, Pete's a Pizza, The Karate Dog (voice), Goose on the Loose, Doogal (voice), Bad Meat, Ellie Parker, Funny Money, Zoom, Jack and the Beanstalk, Stay Cool, Not Another Not Another Movie, Hot Tub Time Machine.
TELEVISION: *Movies:* America's Most Terrible Things, The Secret Policeman's Ball. *Mini-series:* The Hamptons. *Series:* The Smothers Brothers Show (WGA nom. 1976), Saturday Night Live 2 Emmy Awards, 2 other nom.), The Chevy Chase Show, Hjälp!, Community. *Special:* Added Attractions: The Hollywood Shorts Story (voice), The Paul Simon Special (Emmy Award for writing, 1978). *Guest:* More than 145 appearances.

CHAUDHRI, AMIN QAMAR

Executive, Director, Producer, Cinematographer, Editor. b. Punjab, India, April 18, 1942. e. Hampstead Polytechnic, London, City U. of New York. Pres., Filmart Enterprises Ltd. & Filmart Int'l Ltd., Pres./CEO, Continental Film Group Ltd. Pres./CEO, Continental Entertainment Group, Ltd., Heron Int'l. Pictures, Ltd.
PICTURES: *Director:* Kashish, Khajuraho, Eternal, Urvasi, Konarak, The Land of Buddha. *Producer:* Night Visitors, Diary of a Hit Man, The Master Mechanic. *Producer/Director:* Once Again, An Unremarkable Life, Tiger Warsaw, The Last Day of School, Gunga Din, Golden Chute, Wings of Grey, Call It Sleep, The Bookie. *Cinematography:* Right On, Sweet Vengeance, The Hopefuls, The Wicked Die Slow, Who Says I Can't Ride a Rainbow, Black Rodeo, Medium Is the Message, Death of a Dunbar Girl, Kashish, The Last Day of School. *Writer:* Seventh Veil (2000).
TELEVISION: *Movies:* Once Again. Reflections of India (prod.-dir.), Wild Wild East (camera), Nehru (edit.), Medium is the Message (photog.), America... Amerika (prod., dir.).

CHAYKIN, MAURY

Actor. b. Brooklyn, NY, July 27, 1949. e. Univ. of Buffalo. Formed theatre co. Swamp Fox; later acted with Buffalo rep. co., Public Theatre in NY. Moved to Toronto in 1980.
PICTURES: The Kidnapping of the President, Death Hunt, Soup for One, Of Unknown Origin, Harry and Son, Highpoint, Mrs. Soffel, Turk 182!, Meatballs III, The Bedroom Window, Wild Thing, Stars and Bars, Caribe, Iron Eagle II, Twins, Millenium, Breaking In, Where the Heart Is, Mr. Destiny, Dances With Wolves, George's Island, My Cousin Vinny, Leaving Normal, The Adjuster, Hero, Sommersby, Money for Nothing, Josh and S.A.M., Beethoven's 2nd, Camilla, Whale Music (Genie Award), Unstrung Heroes, Devil in a Blue Dress, Cutthroat Island, Love and Death on Long Island, Pale Saints, Strip Search, The Sweet Hereafter, A Life Less Ordinary, Mouse Hunt, Jerry & Tom, Mystery Alaska, Shegalla, Jacob Two Two Meets the Hooded Fang, Entrapment, Touched, Let the Devil Wear Black, What's Cooking, The Art of War, Bartleby, Plan B, On Their Knees, Past Perfect, Owning Mahoney, Whitecoats, Wilby Wonderful, Being Julia, Barry, Where the Truth Lies, Heavens Fall, It's a Boy Girl Thing, Bull, Production Office, Blindness.
TELEVISION: *Movies:* Riel, Jimmy B. & André, The Guardian, Hockey Night, In Like Flynn, The Suicide Murders, Act of Vengeance, Hot Paint, Split Images, Sugartime, If Looks Could Kill: The John Hawkins Story, Keeping the Promise, Northern Lights, Joan of Arc, Golden Spiders: A Nero Wolfe Mystery, Varian's War, Bleacher Bums, Tracey Ullman in the Trailer Tales, Crossed Over, Ruby Romaine Trailer Tales, Sex Traffic, The Hunt for the BTK Killer, Elijah, Glitch, Murder on Her Mind, Abroad. *Mini-series:* Race for the Bomb, Conspiracy of Silence. *Series:* Seeing Things, Oz, Emily of New Moon, A Nero Wolfe Mystery, Eureka (pilot), Entourage, Less Than Kind. *Special:* Canada's Sweetheart: The Saga of Hal Banks (Nellie Award). *Guest:* More than 68 appearances.

CHEADLE, DON

Actor. b. Kansas City, Missouri, November 29, 1964.
PICTURES: Moving Violations, Hamburger Hill, Colors, Roadside Prophets, The Meteor Man, Devil a Blue Dress, Things to Do in Denver When You're Dead, Rosewood, Volcano, Boogie Nights, Bulworth, Out of Sight, Wings Against the Wind, Mission to Mars, The Family Man, Traffic, Things Behind the Sun, Manic, Swordfish, Rush Hour 2, Ocean's Eleven, The United States of Leland, Tishomongo Blues (also dir.), After the Sunset, Ocean's Twelve, Hotel Rwanda (Academy Award nom.; Golden Globe nom. 2005), Crash (also prod.), Tishomingo Blues (also dir.), Empty City, The Dog Problem, Talk to Me, Ocean's Thirteen, Reign Over Me, Darfur Now (doc. also prod.), Traitor (also prod.), Toussaint, Hotel for Dogs, Brooklyn's Finest, Iron Man 2, The Guard.
TELEVISION: *Movies:* Rebound: The Legend of Earl "The Goat" Manigault, Lush Life, The Rat Pack (Golden Globe Award, Emmy nom. 1999), A Lesson Before Dying (Emmy nom. 1999), Things Behind the Sun (Emmy nom. 2002), Fail Safe, Make Your Own Superbowl Ad. *Series:* The Golden Palace, Picket Fences, ER (Emmy nom. 2003), Independent Lens (doc., host, narr.), Crash (co-exec. prod.), Funny or Die Presents... *Guest:* More than 107 appearances.

CHELSOM, PETER

Director, Writer. b. Blackpool, England, April 20, 1956. Studied acting at London's Central School of Drama. Acted with Royal Shakespeare Co., Royal Natl. Theatre, Royal Court Theatre. Dir. at Central School of Drama, taught acting at Actors Ints. and at Cornell Univ. Wrote and directed short film Treacle for Channel 4/British Screen. Director of many tv commercials in U.K. and U.S.
PICTURES: Hear My Song (dir., story, co-s.p.), Funny Bones (dir., co-prod., co-s.p.), The Mighty, Town and Country, Serendipity (dir.), Shall We Dance? (dir.), Tulip Fever (dir., prod.) The Food of Love, Hannah Montana: The Movie.
TELEVISION: *Movies/Actor:* Cream in My Coffee, Intensive Care, An Englishman Abroad, Star Quality. *Mini-series:* A Woman of Substance, Sorrell & Son.

CHEN, JOAN

Actress, Director. r.n. Chen Chung. b. Shanghai, China, April 26, 1961. Studied acting with actress Zhang Rei Fang at Shanghai Film Studio. Debuted as teenager in Chinese films. Moved to U.S. in 1981.
PICTURES: Little Flower, Awakening, Dim Sum: A Little Bit of Heart, Tai-Pain, The Last Emperor, Turtle Beach, When Sleeping Dogs Lie, Night Stalker, Heaven and Earth, Golden Gate, On Deadly Ground, Deadlock, The Hunted, Red Rose/White Rose, Judge Dredd, The Wild Side (also assoc. prod.), Precious Find, Purple Storm, What's Cooking, Avatar, Jasmine, Sunflower, Saving Face, Tonight at Noon, The Home Song Stories, K-Town Super Frog, Lust, Caution, The Leap Years, Mao's Last Dancer, Tonight at Noon. *Director/Writer:* Xiu Xiu: The Sent Down Girl (also exec. prod.), Autumn in New York (dir.).
TELEVISION: *Movies:* Twin Peaks, Wedlock, Steel Justice Shadow of a Stranger, In a Class of His Own. *Mini-series:* Race for the Bomb, Conspiracy of Silence. *Series:* Twin Peaks, Children of the Dragon, Journey to the West.

CHENG, ALBERT

Executive. e. B.S. degree, Massachusetts Institute of Technology; MBA , Harvard. Cheng was dir., distribution strategy, for Fox Cable Networks Group, with responsibility for bus. dev. and implementation of three digital cable channels, now known as Fox College Sports. In this role, he developed digital cable and broadband services strategies. Cheng then served as dir., bus dev. at Fox/Liberty Networks, focusing on business issues and analysis for Fox Sports Net and FX Networks. In Oct. 2000, joined ABC Cable Networks as v.p., national accounts and distribution strategy. From 2002-2004, Cheng was senior v.p., distribution strategy and operations, ABC Cable Networks Group. In this role he also oversaw development and implementation of the division's video-on-demand strategy and interactive TV applications. Next up, Cheng was senior v.p., business strategy and development for Disney and ESPN Networks Affiliate Sales and Marketing. He also oversaw the development of interactive products related to Disney-ABC Cable Networks Group's cable channels, which include ABC Family, Disney Channel, SOAPnet and Toon Disney. Work included sales forecasting and planning for Disney-ABC Cable Network Group and ESPN's finance teams for all of the company's cable TV assets. In Sept. 2005, promoted to current job as executive v.p., digital media, Disney-ABC Television Group. In addition to managing digital media, he oversees development of ancillary revenue streams for Disney-ABC Television Group's diverse portfolio of broadcast and cable networks, including ABC Entertainment, ABC News, ABC Daytime, ABC Family, Disney Channel and SOAPnet. He leads the company's digital media team that oversees product development, marketing and operations for the group's digital media content platforms, including video-on-demand, broadband, web-based and mobile platforms, as well as interactive TV technologies.

CHER

Singer, Actress. r.n. Cherilyn Sarkisian. b. El Centro, CA, May 20, 1946. Began singing as backup singer for Crystals and Ronettes, then with former husband, the late Sonny Bono in 1965; first hit record I Got You Babe, sold 3 million copies. Made two films and then debuted nightclub musical-comedy act in 1969. CBS comedy-variety series started as summer show in 1971; became regular series the following December. NY stage debut: Come Back to the Five and Dime Jimmy Dean Jimmy Dean (1982).
PICTURES: Wild on the Beach (debut, 1965), Good Times, Chastity, Come Back to the Five and Dime Jimmy Dean Jimmy Dean (Golden Globe nom. 1983), Silkwood (Academy Award nom.; Golden Globe Award 1984), Mask (Cannes Award, Golden Globe nom. 1986), The Witches of Eastwick, Suspect, Moonstruck (Academy Award, Golden Globe Award 1988), Mermaids, The Player, Ready to Wear (Prêt-à-Porter), Faithful, Tea with Mussolini, Detroit Rock City, Mayor of Sunset Strip (documentary), Stuck on You (as herself), A Walk on the Moon (singer), In the Pink, Me Without You (singer), Be Cool (singer), Lords of Dogtown (singer), The Drop-Out, The Zookeeper (voice), Burlesque.
TELEVISION: *Movies:* Sonny & Cher: Nitty Gritty Hour (co-host), If These Walls Could Talk (also dir.; Golden Globe nom. 1997), Mame, Soldier's Girl (singer), *Series:* Sonny & Cher Comedy

Hour (4 Emmy nom. 1971-74), Cher (Emmy nom.1975), The Sonny and Cher Show (1976-77). *Specials:* Cher, Cher... Special, Cher and Other Fantasies, Cher: A Celebration at Caesar's Palace, Cher: Live in Concert from Las Vegas (Emmy nom. 2000), Cher at the Mirage, The Grand Opening of Euro Disney, Comic Relief: Behind the Nose, Happy Birthday Elizabeth: A Celebration of Life, AFI's 100 Years...100 Movies, 26th Annual American Music Awards, VH1 Divas Live, AFI's 100 Years...100 Stars, I Love Lucy's 50th Anniversary Special, The Royal Variety Performance 2001, National Lottery Christmas Cracker, Judi Dench: A BAFTA Tribute, Cher: The Farewell Tour (Emmy Award 2003). Many soundtrack credits. *Guest:* More than 221 appearances.

CHERNIN, PETER

Executive. Began career as assoc. publicity director, St. Martin's Press; editor, Warner Books. v.p. of development & prod., David Gerber Co.; exec. v.p., programming & mktg., Showtime/The Movie Channel, Inc.; president & COO, Lorimar Film Entertainment; President of Fox from 1989-1992. Chmn. of Twentieth Century Fox Film Corporation from 1992-1994. Chmn. & CEO, Fox Filmed Entertainment, 1994-96. Since 1996, director, president and COO, CEO of News Corp., Rupert Murdoch's global media and entertainment organization. He left News Corp., June 30, 2009. By Sept. 2009, Chernin opened his own production company, The Chernin Entertainment, and became a producer for 20th Century Fox. He has been CEO of NAI since '96. Chernin is a director for the following organizations: Gemstar-TV Guide since April 2002; DirecTV since 2003; American Express Company since Jan. 2006; Friends of the Global Fight Against AIDS, Tuberculosis and Malaria since May 2006; Malaria No More (also nonprofit group) since 2006; Motion Picture & Television Fund Foundation in 2007. He is also a commission member of the California Commission for Jobs and Economic Growth.

CHETWYND, LIONEL

Executive, Writer, Director. b. London, England, 1940. m. actress Gloria Carlin. Emigrated to Canada, 1948. e. Sir George Williams U., Montreal, BA, economics; BCL-McGill U., Montreal. Graduate Work-Law, Trinity Coll. Oxford. Admitted to bar, Province of Quebec, 1968. C.B.C., TV-Public Affairs and Talks, 1961-1965. CTV network 1965-67. Controller commercial TV and film rights, Expo '67. Freelance writer and consultant 1961-68. Asst. managing dir. Columbia Pictures (U.K.) Ltd. London 1968-72. Asst. managing dir. Columbia-Warner UK, 1971. Story and book for musical Maybe That's Your Problem, 1971-1973. Then Bleeding Great Orchids (staged London, and Off-B'way). Also wrote The American 1776, official U.S. Bicentennial film and We the People/200 Constitutional Foundation. In 2001, appointed by President George W. Bush to serve on the President's Committee on the Arts and Humanities. Former mem. of NYU grad. film sch. faculty, lecturer on screenwriting at Frederick Douglass Ctr. Harlem. Member of Canadian Bar Association. Served on bd. of gov., Commission on Battered Children, and the Little League.
PICTURES: *Director and/or Writer:* The Apprenticeship of Duddy Kravitz (Acad. Award nom. 1975), Morning Comes, Two Solitudes (also prod., Grand Award Salonika), Quintet, The Hanoi Hilton, The Hot Touch, The Resurrection (also prod.). *Documentaries:* Darkness at High Noon: The Carl Foreman Documents, Celsius 41.11: The Temperature at Which the Brain... Begins to Die, The Resurrection.
TELEVISION: *Producer and/or Writer:* Johnny We Hardly Knew Ye (George Washington Honor Medal, Freedom Fdn.), It Happened One Christmas, Goldenrod, A Whale for the Killing, Miracle on Ice (Christopher Award), Escape From Iran: The Canadian Caper, Sadat (NAACP Image Award), Children in the Crossfire, To Heal a Nation (also exec. prod.), Evil in Clear River (exec. prod. only, Christopher Award), So Proudly We Hail (also exec. prod.), The Godfather Wars, The Heroes of Desert Storm, Reverse Angle (also exec. prod.), Doom's Day Gun, The Bible... Moses, The Bible... Jacob, The Bible... Joseph (Emmy award), Falling From the Sky: Flight 174, The Man Who Captured Eichmann, Kissinger & Nixon (also exec. prod.), Human Bomb, The Color of Justice, Ruby Ridge An American Tragedy, National Desk, Net Force, P.T. Barnum, Varian's War, DC 9/11: Time of Crisis, Ike: Countdown to D-Day (Emmy nom. 2004).

CHEUNG, MAGGIE

Actress. b. Hong Kong, Sept. 20, 1964. Extensive work in Hong Kong. Cinema.
PICTURES: Jackie Chan's Police Story, Happy Ghost 3, Kino Countdown (cameo), The Game They Call Sex, Police Story 2, Song of Exile, The Dragon from Russia, Heart Against Hearts (cameo), The Banquet, Days of Being Wild, The Actress, Dragon Inn, The Heroic Trio, Double Dragon, Police Story 3: Supercop, Family Happiness, Chasing Boys, Moon Warriors, Heroic Trio 2: Executioners, Seven Maidens, The Eagle Shooting Heroes, Green Snake, Ashes of Time, Comrades: Almost a Love Story, Irma Vep, Chinese Box, The Soong Sisters, Augustin: King of Kung-Fu, Love at First Sight, In the Mood for Love, Chin hei man bo, Hero, 2046, Clean, Hot Summer Days.

CHINICH, MICHAEL

Producer. b. New York, NY. e. Boston U. Began career as casting agent in N.Y.; moved to L.A. to join MCA-Universal Pictures as executive in casting. Named head of feature film casting; then prod. v.p.
PICTURES: *Casting dir.:* Dog Day Afternoon, Coal Miner's Daughter, Animal House, Melvin and Howard, The Blues Brothers, Mask, Midnight Run, Twins, Ghostbusters II, Kindergarten Cop, Dave, Junior, The Late Shift, Father's Day, Six Days Seven Nights. *Exec. Prod.:* Pretty in Pink, Ferris Bueller's Day Off, Some Kind of Wonderful, Planes Trains and Automobiles (co-exec. prod.), Commandments (prod.), Killing Me Softly (prod.), Deuce Bigalow: European Gigolo (development exec.), You May Not Kiss the Bride (casting dir.).

CHOMSKY, MARVIN J.

Director, Producer. b. Bronx, NY, May 23, 1929. e. Syracuse U., B.S.; Stanford U., M.A. Started in theatre business at early age as art dir. with such TV credits as U.S. Steel Hour, Playhouse 90, Studio One, etc. Later worked with Herbert Brodkin who advanced him to assoc. prod. with such TV shows as The Doctors and The Nurses. Brought to Hollywood in 1965 as assoc. prod. for Talent Associates, producing series of TV pilots. *Art dir.:* The Bubble.
PICTURES: Evel Knievel, Murph the Surf, Mackintosh and T.J., Good Luck Miss Wycoff, Tank.
TELEVISION: *Movies:* Assault on the Wayne, Mongo's Back in Town, Family Flight, Fireball Forward, Female Artillery, The Magician, The F.B.I. Story: The F.B.I. Vs. Alvin Karpas, Mrs. Sundance, Attack on Terror: The F.B.I. Vs. the Ku Klux Klan, Kate McShane, Brink's: The Great Robbery, Law and Order, A Matter of Wife and Death, Victory at Entebbe, Little Ladies of the Night, Roots (Emmy nom. 1977 co-dir.), Danger in Paradise, Holocaust (Emmy Award, DGA Award 1978), Hollow Image, King Crab, Attica (Emmy Award, 1980), Inside the Third Reich (Emmy Award, DGA Award 1982), My Body My Child, The Nairobi Affair, I Was a Mail Order Bride, Robert Kennedy and His Times, Evita Peron (Emmy nom. 1981, also prod.), Peter the Great (also prod.; Emmy Award as prod., 1986), The Deliberate Stranger (also prod.), Anastasia: The Mystery of Anna (Emmy nom. 1987, also prod.), Billionaire Boys Club (2 Emmy nom.; DGA nom. 1988, also spv. prod.), Angel in Green, I'll Be Home for Christmas (also prod.), Brotherhood of the Rose (also prod.), Telling Secrets, Strauss Dynasty (also prod.), Hurricane Andrew (also prod.), Catherine the Great (also prod.). *Series:* The Wild Wild West, Gunsmoke, Star Trek, Then Came Bronson.

CHONG, RAE DAWN

Actress, Director, Producer. b. Edmonton Alta, Canada, Feb. 28, 1961. Father is director-comedian Tommy Chong. Debut at 12 in The Whiz Kid of Riverton (TV). B'way debut 1991 in Oh Kay!
PICTURES: Stony Island (debut, 1978), Quest for Fire, Beat Street, The Corsican Brothers, Choose Me, Fear City, City Limits, American Flyers, Commando, The Color Purple, Soul Man, The Squeeze, The Principal, Walking After Midnight, Tales From the Darkside, Far Out Man, The Borrower, Amazon, Chaindance, Time Runner, When the Party's Over, In Exile, Boulevard, Boca, Hideaway, The Break, Starlight, Mask of Death, Waiting for the Man, Goodbye America, Highball, Small Time, Valentine's Day, Dangerous Attraction, The Visit, Cursed Part 3 (dir., exec. prod., writer), Max Havoc: Ring of Fire, Solitaire, Constellation, Cyrus.
TELEVISION: *Movies:* The Top of the Hill, Badge of the Assassin, Curiosity Kills, Prison Stories: Women on the Inside, Father & Son: Dangerous Relations, Thing I Forgot to Remember, The Alibi, Protector, Valentine's Day, For Hope, Deadly Skies. *Series:* Nitecap, Mysterious Ways, Zoe Busiek: Wild Card. *Guest:* More than 41 appearances.

CHONG, TOMMY

Actor, Writer, Director. b. Edmonton, Alta., Canada, May 24, 1938. Daughter is actress Rae Dawn Chong. Was guitar player with various Canadian rhythm and blues combinations, before teaming with Richard (Cheech) Marin in improvisational group. Has made comedy recordings.
PICTURES: Up in Smoke, Cheech and Chong's Next Movie (also dir., co-s.p.), Cheech and Chong's Nice Dreams (also dir., co-s.p.), Things Are Tough All Over, It Came from Hollywood, Still Smokin', Yellowbeard, The Corsican Brothers (also dir., s.p.), After Hours, Tripwire (cameo), Far Out Man (also dir., s.p.), The Spirit of 76, FernGully (voice), National Lampoon's Senior Trip, McHale's Navy, Best Buds (also s.p., exec. prod.), Half Baked (actor), Secret Agent 420, The Wash, High Times Potluck, You'll Never Wiez In This Town Again, Best Buds (also writer, exec. prod.), Secret Agent 420, Hoodwinked Too! Hood VS. Evil.
TELEVISION: Trial and Error (co-exec. prod.), That '70s Show. *Guest:* More than 56 appearances.

CHOW, RAYMOND

O.B.E. Producer. b. Hong Kong, Jan. 1, 1929. e. St. John's U., Shanghai. Worked for Hong Kong Standard; then joined the Hong Kong office of the U.S. Information Service. In 1959 joined Shaw Brothers as head of publicity, became head of production before leaving in 1970 to start Golden Harvest to produce Chinese-language films in Hong Kong. Kung-fu films featuring Bruce Lee put Harvest into int'l. market. Started English-lan-

guage films in 1977, beginning with The Amsterdam Kill and The Boys in Company C. Named Showman of the Year 1984 by NATO. Awarded O.B.E. in 1988.
PICTURES: Armour of God, The Big Boss (and subsequent Bruce Lee films), The Cannonball Run (and Part II), High Road to China, Lassiter, Miracles, Mr. Boo (a.k.a. The Private Eyes; and many subsequent Michael Hui films), Painted Faces, Police Story (and Part II), Project A (and Part II), Rouge, The Story of the Flying Fox, Love on the Rooftops, A Show of Force, China O'Brien (and Part II), Teenage Mutant Ninja Turtles (and Part II), Lord of East China Sea, The Reincarnation of Golden Lotus, Summer Snow, Rumble in the Bronx, Lost & Found, Viva Erotica, The Stunt Woman, Hold You Tight, The Soong Sisters, Kitchen, Portland Street Blues, Gorgeous, Man Called Hero, Fly Me to Polaris, Tokyo Raiders, Born to Be King, Skyline Cruisers, The Accidental Spy, You Shoot I Shoot.

CHRISTIANSEN, ROBERT W.

Producer. b. Porterville, CA. e. Bakersfield Coll. Spent 3 years in Marine Corps. Worked on Hollywood Reporter in circulation and advertising. Joined Cinema Center Films; P.A. on Monte Walsh and Hail Hero. Co-produced first feature in 1970, Adam at Six A.M., with Rick Rosenberg, with whom co-produced all credits listed. Exec. Prod. for Chris/Rose Productions.
PICTURES: Adam at Six A.M., Hide in Plain Sight, Death Benefit, Down in the Delta.
TELEVISION: *Movies:* Suddenly Single, The Glass House, Gargoyles, A Brand New Life, The Man Who Could Talk to Kids, The Autobiography of Miss Jane Pittman (Emmy Award 1974), I Love You...Goodbye, Queen of the Stardust Ballroom, Born Innocent, A Death in Canaan (Emmy nom. 1978), Strangers, Robert Kennedy and His Times (Emmy nom. 1985), Kids Don't Tell, As Summers Die, Gore Vidal's Lincoln (Emmy nom. 1988), Red Earth, White Earth, The Heist, A House of Secrets and Lies, The Last Hit, Heart of Darkness, Tad, Kingfish: A Story of Huey P. Long, Redwood Curtain, Sudden Terror: The Hijacking of Schoolbus # 17, Beyond the Call, Lost Treasure of Dos Santos, The Long Island Incident, Twice Upon a Time, Home Invasion, The Crossing, Reckless Behavior: Caught on Tape, Accidental Friendship.

CHRISTIE, JULIE

Actress. b. Chukua, Assam, India, April 14, 1941. Father had tea plantation in India. e. in Britian, at 16 studied art in France, then attended Central Sch. of Music & Drama in London. 3 yrs. with Frinton-on-Sea Rep., before TV debut in A for Andromeda. Birmingham Rep.; Royal Shakespeare Co.; East European and American tour. NY stage: Uncle Vanya. London stage: Old Times.
PICTURES: Crooks Anonymous (debut, 1962), Fast Lady, Billy Liar, Young Cassidy, Darling (Academy Award, Golden Globe nom. & BFA Award, 1965), Dr. Zhivago, Farenheit 451, Far From the Madding Crowd, Petulia, In Search of Gregory, The Go-Between, McCabe and Mrs. Miller (Academy Award nom. 1972), Don't Look Now, Shampoo (Golden Globe nom. 1976), Nashville (cameo), Demon Seed, Heaven Can Wait, Memoirs of a Survivor, The Return of the Soldier, Heat and Dust, Golddiggers, Power, Miss Mary, La Memoire tatouree (Secret Obsession), Fools of Fortune, Dragonheart, Hamlet, Afterglow (Academy Award nom. 1998), Belphegor, Hermit of Amsterdam, No Such Thing, I'm With Lucy, J. M. Barrie's Neverland, Harry Potter and the Prisoner of Azkaban, Troy, Finding Neverland, The Secret Life of Words, Away from Her, New York, I Love You.
TELEVISION: Debut: A is for Andromeda (UK series, 1962), Sins of the Fathers (Italian TV), Separate Tables, Dadah Is Death (Amer. TV debut, 1988), The Railway Station Man, The Miracle Maker. *Mini-series:* Karaoke. *Guest:* More than 50 appearances.

CHRISTOPHER, DENNIS

Actor. r.n. Dennis Carelli. b. Philadelphia, PA, Dec. 2, 1955. e. Temple U. NY stage debut, Yentl the Yeshiva Boy (1974). Other NY theater: Dr. Needle and the Infectious Laughter Epidemic, The Little Foxes, Brothers, Exmass, A Pound on Demand, Advice from a Caterpillar. Regional theater incl. Balm in Gilead, American Buffalo. Appeared in 1991 short The Disco Years.
PICTURES: Blood and Lace, Didn't You Hear?, The Young Graduates, Fellini's Roma, Salome, 3 Women, September 30, 1955, A Wedding, California Dreaming, The Last Word, Breaking Away (Golden Globe nom. 1980), Fade to Black, Chariots of Fire, Don't Cry It's Only Thunder, Alien Predator, Flight of the Spruce Goose, Jake Speed, Friends, A Sinful Life, Circuitry Man, Dead Women in Lingerie, Doppelganger, Circuitry Man II: Plughead Rewired, Skeletons, The Silencers, It's My Party, Skeletons, The Silencers, Mind Lies, Nine Lives, Queen of the Lot.
TELEVISION: *Movies:* The Oregon Trail, Stephen King's IT, False Arrest, Willing to Kill: The Texas Cheerleader Story, Curacao, Deadly Invasion: The Killer Bee Nightmare, The Ballad of Lucy Whipple, Trapped!. *Mini-series:* The Lost Room. *Series:* Profiler, Freaky Links, Deadwood. *Specials:* Bernice Bobs Her Hair, Jack and the Beanstalk (Faerie Tale Theatre), Cristabel. *Guest:* More than 52 appearances.

CHUNG, CONNIE

TV News Anchor. r.n. Constance Yu-Hwa Chung. m. anchor Maury Povich. b. Washington, D.C., Aug. 20, 1946. e. B.S., journalism, U. of Maryland. Entered field 1969 as copy person, writer then on-camera reporter for WTTG-TV, Washington; 1971, named Washington correspondent., CBS News; 1976, anchor KNXT, Los Angeles; 1983, anchor, NBC News at Sunrise; anchor, NBC Saturday Nightly News and news specials; 1989 moved to CBS as anchor, Sunday Night Evening News; anchor and reporter, Saturday Night with Connie Chung (later Face to Face With Connie Chung), 1989-90. Received Emmy Award for Shot in Hollywood (1987), Interview With Marlon Brando (1989); 2 additional Emmy Awards: 1986, 1990. Became co-anchor, with Dan Rather, of CBS Evening News, 1993-95. Prime time series: Eye to Eye With Connie Chung, 1993; Connie Chung Tonight on CNN (canceled March 2003). Emmy Award for ABC 2000: The Millennium (doc.). Returned to TV in Jan. 2006, hosting MSNBC's Weekends with Maury and Connie, with husband Maury Povich. Show was canceled in first season. Chung's many other awards include: 1 Peabody, 2 LA Emmy Awards, Golden Mike, Women in Business Award.

CHURCH, THOMAS HADEN

Actor. b. El Paso, TX, June 17, 1961.
PICTURES: Tombstone, Tales From the Crypt Presents: Demon Knight, George of the Jungle, One Night, Free Money, Scotch and Milk (prod.), The Specials, 3000 Miles To Graceland, Rolling Kansas, George of the Jungle II (video), Sideways (Academy Award nom., Golden Globe nom. 2005), Spanglish, Over the Hedge (voice), Idiocracy, Charlotte's Web (voice), Spider-Man 3, American Dog (voice), Smart People, All About Steve, Bolt (voice), Don McKay (also exec. prod.), Imagine That, Easy A, John Carter of Mars.
TELEVISION: *Movies:* Fugitive Nights: Danger in the Desert, The Badge, Mr. Murder. *Mini-series:* Broken Trail (Emmy Award, Golden Globe nom. 2007). *Series:* Wings, Ned and Stacey. *Guest:* More than 51 appearances.

CILENTO, DIANE

Actress. b. Queensland, Australia, Oct. 5, 1933. e. Toowoomba. Went to New York and finished schooling and then American Acad. of Dramatic Art. First theatre job at 16; toured U.S. with Barter Co.; returned to London and joined Royal Acad. of Dramatic Art; several small parts and later repertory at Manchester's Library Theatre.
THEATRE: London stage: Tiger at the Gates (also NY: Theatre World Award), The Third Secret, The Four Seasons, The Bonne Soup, Heartbreak House. NY: The Big Knife, Orpheus, Altona, Castle in Sweden, Naked, Marys, I've Seen You Cut Lemons.
PICTURES: Wings of Danger (Dead on Course; debut, 1952), Moulin Rouge, Meet Mr. Lucifer, All Halloween, The Angel Who Pawned Her Harp, The Passing Stranger, Passage Home, The Woman for Joe, The Admirable (Paradise Lagoon), The Truth About Women, Jet Storm, Stop Me Before I Kill! (The Full Treatment), I Thank a Fool, The Naked Edge, Tom Jones (Academy Award nom. 1964), Rattle of a Simple Man, The Third Secret, The Agony and the Ecstacy, Hombre, Negatives, Z.P.G. (Zero Population Growth), Hitler: The Last Ten Days, The Wicker Man, The Tiger Lily, The Boy Who Had Everything, Duet for Four.
TELEVISION: *Movies:* Anna Christie, Court Martial, Blackmail, Dial M for Murder, Spell of Evil, Big Toys, Rain, Lysistrata, The Kiss of Blood, For the Term of His Natural Life. *Series:* La Belle France, Rogues Gallery, Tycoon, Halfway Across the Galaxy and Turn Left.

CIMINO, MICHAEL

Writer, Director. b. New York, NY, Nov. 16, 1943. e. Yale U. BFA, MFA. Was tv commecial director before becoming screen writer.
PICTURES: Silent Running (co-s.p.), Magnum Force (co-s.p.). *Director:* Thunderbolt and Lightfoot (also s.p.), The Deer Hunter (also co-wrote story, co-prod.; 2 Academy Awards for Best Picture & DGA Award, Golden Globe Award 1979), Heaven's Gate (also s.p.), Year of the Dragon (also co-s.p.), The Sicilian (also co-prod.), Desperate Hours (also co-prod.), The Sunchaser (also co-s.p.).

CIPES, ARIANNE ULMER

Executive. b. New York, NY, July 25, 1937. e. Royal Acad. of Dramatic Art, London, U. of London. Daughter of film dir. Edgar G. Ulmer. Actress, then production and dubbing, Paris; CDC, Rome; Titra, New York; 1975-77, v.p., Best Int'l. Films (int'l. film distributor), Los Angeles; 1977 co-founder and sr. v.p./sales & services of Producers Sales Organization; 1981, named exec. v.p., American Film Marketing Assn.; 1982, founded AUC Films, consulting and intl. and domestic sales-prods. rep.; Pres. of the Edgar G. Ulmer Preservation Corp.-committed to the preservation and propagation of the work of independent, pioneering filmmakers.

CLAPP, GORDON

Actor. b. North Conway, NH, Sept. 24, 1948.
PICTURES: Running, Return of the Secaucus 7, Matewan, Eight Men Out, Termini Station, Gross Anatomy, April One, The Rage: Carrie 2, Splendor Falls, The Rules of Engagement, Skeletons in the Closet, Sunshine State, Moonlight Mile, The Sure Hand of God, Flags of Our Fathers, The Game Plan, Falling Up, The Grind.
TELEVISION: *Movies:* The Other Kingdom, Letting Go, The Right of the People, Hands of a Stranger, Small Sacrifices, Family of Spies, Blind Faith, The Secret Life of Archie's Wife, Fever, Mission of the Shark: The Saga of the U.S.S. Indianapolis, Bonds of Love, Kiss of a Killer, Family of Strangers, In the Line of Duty: Ambush in Waco, Her Hidden Truth, Abandoned and

Deceived, The Morrison Murders, Badge of Betrayal, Taking Chance. *Mini-series:* Evergreen. *Series:* Check It Out, NYPD Blue (Emmy Award, 1998, Emmy nom. 1994), The Ex List. *Guest:* More than 71 appearances.

CLARK, BILL

Producer. President of Anchor Bay Productions.
PICTURE: Fallen (as actor), Abandoned (distributor).
TELEVISION: *Movie:* Last of the Ninth (pilot, writer, exec. prod.). *Series:* NYPD Blue (WGA Award, 1997; 2 Emmy Awards, 1995, 1998; 7 other nom.), Brooklyn South, Blind Justice. *Special:* America: A Tribute to Heroes (writer, Emmy nom. 2002).

CLARK, CANDY

Actress. b. Norman, OK, June 20, 1947. Was successful model in N.Y. before landing role in Fat City, 1972. Off-B'way debut 1981: A Couple of White Chicks Sitting Around Talking; followed by It's Raining on Hope Street. Appeared in short Blind Curve.
PICTURES: Fat City (debut, 1972), American Graffiti (Academy Award nom. 1974), I Will I Will... For Now, The Man Who Fell To Earth, Citizens Band (Handle With Care), The Big Sleep, When You Comin' Back Red Ryder, More American Graffiti, National Lampoon Goes to the Movies, Q, Blue Thunder, Amityville 3-D, Hambone and Hillie, Cat's Eye, At Close Range, The Blob, Original Intent, Deuce Coupe, Cool as Ice, Buffy the Vampire Slayer, Radioland Murders, Niagara, Niagara, Zodiac, The Informant!.
TELEVISION: *Movies:* James Dean, Amateur Night at the Dixie Bar and Grill, Where the Ladies Go, Rodeo Girl, Johnny Belinda, Cocaine and Blue Eyes, The Price She Paid, Mystery Woman: Redemption. *Series:* Movie Lover's Road Trip (as herself).

CLARK, DICK

Producer, Actor, Writer. b. Mt. Vernon, NY, Nov. 30, 1929. e. Syracuse U. graduated 1951, summer announcer WRUN, Utica 1949, staff announcer WOLF, Syracuse 1950. After grad. 1951, took regular job with WOLF. Rejoined WRUN, Utica, then joined WKTV, Utica. Announcer WFIL Philadelphia 1952. Formed Dick Clark Productions, Inc., in 1956, as a TV and motion picture production company. Today company includes in-person concert division and cable TV programing dept. He serves as chairman and CEO. Clark is host of two weekly synd. radio programs: U.S. Music Survey and Rock Roll & Remember. Founder and principal owner of Unistar Communications Group. Took company public in January, 1987 (NASDAQ: DCPI), serves as chmn. & CEO. Received Emmy Lifetime Achievement Award, 1994.
PICTURES: *Actor:* Because They're Young (debut, 1960), Jamboree, The Young Doctors, Killers Three, The Phynx, Forrest Gump, The Suburbans, Spy Kids, Confessions of a Dangerous Mind (as himself). *Producer:* Psychout, The Savage Seven, Remo Williams: The Adventure Begins, Catchfire.
TELEVISION: *Movies/Prod. or Exec. Prod.:* Werewolf of Woodstock, Elvis, The Man in the Santa Claus Suit, Murder in Texas, The Demon Murder Case, The Woman Who Willed a Miracle (Emmy Award 1983, Cocacabana, A Friendly Quiet Little Town, Death Dreams, Caught in the Act, Secret Sins of the Father, The Making of a Hollywood Madam, Deep Family Secrets, ABC 50th Anniversary Blooper Celebration. *Specials:* Live Aid—An All-Star Concert for African Relief, Farm Aid III, Super Bloopers & New Practical Jokes, American Bandstand's 33 1/3 Celebration, America Picks the No. 1 Songs, You Are the Jury, Thanks for Caring, Supermodel of the World, Freedom Festival '89, What About Me I'm Only Three, 1992 USA Music Challenge, The Good Doctor, TV Censored Bloopers '98, Motown 40: The Music Is Forever. American Music Awards, Academy of Country Music Awards, Dick Clark's New Year's Rockin' Eve, ACE Awards, Daytime Emmy Awards, Golden Globe Awards, Soap Opera Awards, Superstars and Their Moms, Caught in the Act (pilot), 30th Annual American Music Awards (2003), The 15th Annual American Music Awards (Emmy nom. 1988) Golden Globe Arrivals, The 62nd Annual Golden Globe Awards, New Year's Rockin' Eve 2006, Primetime New Year's Rockin' Eve 2007, 2008, The 40th Annual Academy of Country Music Awards, 2006 American Music Awards. *Series/Himself or Host:* American Bandstand (also exec. prod.; Emmy Award as exec. prod., 1982-83), The Dick Clark Beechnut Show, Dick Clark's World of Talent, Record Years, Years of Rock. $25,000 Pyramid (3 Emmy Awards as host: 1979, 1985, 1986), $100,000 Pyramid, TV Teen Club, The Dick Clark Show, Missing Links, The Object Is, The Krypton Factor, Inside America, TV's Bloopers & Practical Jokes (also exec. prod.), The Challengers, Scattegories, Winning Lines (also exec. prod.), The Other Half. Producer: The Guns of Will Sonnett, Live Wednesday, TV Censored Bloopers 1998, Who Wants to be a Millionaire, Swinging Country, Happening, Get It Together, Shebang, Record Years, Years of Rock Has hosted and exec. prod. New Year's Rockin' Eve since 1990. *Executive Producer:* It's Happening, Where The Action Is, TV's Bloopers & Practical Jokes (also host), Rock'n'Roll Summer Action, Puttin' On the Hits, Keep On Cruisin', Trial By Jury, The Weird Al Show, Donny & Marie (1998 2 Emmy nom. 2001), Your Big Break, Greed: The Multi-Million Dollar Challenge, Winning Lines (also host), The Chamber, American Dreams. *Writer:* Your Happiest Years, 1959; Rock, Roll & Remember, 1976; To Goof or Not to Goof, 1963; Dick Clark's Easygoing Guide to Good Grooming, 1986; The History of American Bandstand, 1986, Dick Clark's American Bandstand, 1997. *Guest:* More than 288 appearances.

CLARK, DUNCAN, C.

Executive. b. Sutton, Surrey, England. Entered industry in 1972. Appointed dir. of publicity and adv., CIC, Jan. 1979, taking up similar post in 1981 for United Artists. On formation of U.I.P. in 1982, appt. dir., pub. and adv., & deputy mn. dir., 1983. 1987 appt. v.p. adv. & pub., Columbia Pictures Intl (NY). In 1987, sr. v.p. intl marketing for Columbia (Burbank); appt. sr. v.p., Columbia Tri-Star Film Distribs., Inc., (NY). Relocated to corp. headquarters in Culver City, 1991. Appointed exec. v.p. Worldwide Marketing, 1994. In 1996, appointed president Columbia TriStar Film Distributors International. The following year, Clark led CTFDI to post its first billion dollar box office year, releasing such international hits as Jerry Maguire, The Devil's Own, Men in Black and My Best Friend's Wedding. In 1998, Clark was named Distributor of the Year at Cinema Expo Intl. Clark was a key part of the executive group that spearheaded Sony's successful entry into the international film production arena. 2001, left Columbia-TriStar and became a founding member of Equity Pictures, the German-based production and financing group that went on to produce The Matador starring Pierce Brosnan. In 2005 Clark was the executive producer on the romantic comedy My Bollywood Bride. He also served as international marketing and distribution consultant on Steven Spielberg's recent films, Munich and War of the Worlds. In April 2006, Clark was appointed to newly created position of exec. v.p. International distribution for Universal Pictures International. He is based in London and reports to David Kosse, president, Universal Pictures International. Clark has overseen the marketing and distribution of over 1,000 films in more than 60 countries.

CLARK, MATT

Actor, Director. b. Washington, DC, Nov. 25, 1936.
THEATRE: NY: A Portrait of the Artist as a Young Man, The Subject Was Roses, The Trial of the Catonsville Nine; Regional: One Flew Over the Cuckoo's Nest, Tonight We Improvise.
PICTURES: Black Like Me (debut, 1964), In the Heat of the Night, Will Penny, The Bridge at Remagen, Macho Callahan, Homer (co-s.p. only), Monte Walsh, The Beguiled, The Grissom Gang, The Cowboys, The Culpepper Cattle Company, The Great Northfield Minnesota Raid, Jeremiah Johnson, The Life and Times of Judge Roy Bean, Emperor of the North Pole, The Laughing Policeman, Pat Garrett and Billy the Kid, White Lightning, The Terminal Man, Hearts of the West, Outlaw Blues,Kid Vengeance, The Driver, Dreamer, Brubaker, An Eye for an Eye, Legend of the Lone Ranger, Ruckus, Some Kind of Hero, Honkytonk Man, Love Letters, The Adventures of Buckaroo Banzai, Country, Tuff Turf, Return to Oz, Let's Get Harry, Da (dir. only), The Horror Show, Back to the Future Part III, Cadence, Class Action, Frozen Assets, Fortunes of War, The Harvest, Candyman: Farewell to the Flesh, Mother, Hacks, Claudine's Return, Homegrown, Five Aces, South of Heaven, West of Hell.
TELEVISION: *Movies*: The Execution of Private Slovik, The Great Ice Rip-Off, Melvin Purvis: G-Man, This is the West That Was, The Kansas City Massacre, Dog and Cat (pilot), Lacy and the Mississippi Queen, The Last Ride of the Dalton Gang, The Children Nobody Wanted, In the Custody of Strangers, Love Mary, Out of the Darkness, The Quick and the Dead, The Gambler III: The Legend Continues, Terror on Highway 91, Blind Witness, Deceptions, Dead Before Dawn, Barbarians at the Gate, A Season of Hope, Raven Hawk. *Mini-series*: The Winds of War, War and Remembrance, Trilogy of Special Terror II. *Pilots*: The Big Easy, Highway Honeys, Traveling Man. *Series*: Dog and Cat, The Jeff Foxworthy Show. *Specials:* Shadow of Fear, Andrea's Story. *Guest*: More than 62 appearances.

CLAYBURGH, JILL

Actress. b. New York, NY, April 30, 1944. m. playwright David Rabe. e. Sarah Lawrence Coll. 1966. Former member of Charles Playhouse, Boston.
THEATRE: The Nest (off-B'way), The Rothschilds, Jumpers, Pippin, In the Boom Boom Room, Design For Living, The Exonerated (off B'way).
PICTURES: The Wedding Party (debut, 1969), The Telephone Book, Portnoy's Complaint, The Thief Who Came to Dinner, Terminal Man, Gable and Lombard, Silver Streak, Semi-Tough, An Unmarried Woman (Academy Award nom.; Golden Globe nom.1979), Luna (Golden Globe nom. 1980), Starting Over (Academy Award nom.; Golden Globe nom. 1980), It's My Turn, First Monday in October (Golden Globe nom. 1982), I'm Dancing as Fast as I Can, Hannah K, Where Are The Children?, Shy People, Beyond the Ocean, Whispers in the Dark, Rich in Love, Day of Atonement, Naked in New York, Going All the Way, Fools Rush In, Never Again, Falling, Running with Scissors, Love and Other Drugs.
TELEVISION: *Movies:* The Snoop Sisters, Miles To Go, Hustling (Emmy nom. 1975), The Art of Crime, Griffin and Phoenix, Who Gets the Friends?, Fear Stalk, Unspeakable Acts, Reason for Living: The Jill Ireland Story, Trial: The Price of Passion, Firestorm: 72 Hours in Oakland, Honor Thy Father and Mother: The True Story of the Menedez Murders, For the Love of Nancy, The Face on the Milk Carton, Crowned & Dangerous, Sins of the Mind, My Little Assassin, Phenomenon II. *Series:* Search For

Tomorrow, Trinity, Everything's Relative, Leap of Faith, Nip/Tuck (Emmy nom. 2005), Dirty Sexy Money. *Documentaries:* In Our Hands, Lincoln (voice). *Guest:* More than 48 appearances.

CLEESE, JOHN

Actor, Writer. b. Weston-Super-Mare, England, Oct. 27, 1939. e. Clifton Coll., Cambridge U. Began acting with Cambridge University Footlights revue. With classmate Graham Chapman wrote for British TV. Co-creator of Monty Python's Flying Circus.Co-author (with psychiatrist Robin Skynner): Families and How to Survive Them (1983), Life and How to Survive It (1995).
PICTURES: Interlude (debut, 1968), The Bliss of Mrs. Blossom, The Best House in London, The Rise and Rise of Michael Rimmer (also co-s.p.), The Magic Christian (also co-s.p.), The Statue, And Now for Something Completely Different (also co-s.p.), Monty Python and the Holy Grail (also co-s.p.), The Life of Brian (also co-s.p.), The Great Muppet Caper, Time Bandits, The Secret Policeman's Other Ball, Monty Python Live at the Hollywood Bowl (also co-s.p.), Monty Python's The Meaning of Life (also co-s.p.), Yellowbeard, Privates on Parade, Silverado, Clockwise, A Fish Called Wanda (also co-s.p., exec. prod.; BAFTA Award, WGA nom.; Oscar nom. 1989), The Big Picture (cameo), Erik the Viking, An American Tail: Fievel Goes West (voice), Splitting Heirs, Mary Shelley's Frankenstein, The Swan Princess (voice), Rudyard Kipling's The Jungle Book, George of the Jungle, Fierce Creatures, Parting Shots, The Out-of-Towners, Isn't She Great, The World is Not Enough, Rat Race, Harry Potter and the Sorcerer's Stone, Taking the Wheel, Harry Potter and the Chamber of Secrets, Die Another Day, Charlie's Angels: Full Throttle, Harry Potter & the Prisoner of Azkaban, Shrek 2 (voice), Around the World in 80 Days, Valiant (voice), Bond 21, Man About Town, Complete Guide to Guys, Charlotte's Web (voice), Shrek the Third, Igor (voice), Pink Panther 2, The Day the Earth Stood Still, Planet 51 (voice), Spud, Burke and Hare.
TELEVISION: *Movies:* How to Irritate People, Pleasure at Her Majesty's, The Mermaid Frolics, Peter Cook & Co., The Taming of the Shrew, Comic Relief. *Series:* At Last the 1948 Show, Monty Python's Flying Circus (actor, writer, creator), Fawlty Towers, Look at the State We're In!, Whoops Apocalypse, My Adventures in Television, Will & Grace (Emmy nom. 2004 as guest), Just for Laughs (host, writer). *As Writer:* That Was the Week That Was, The Frost Report (also actor), Marty Broaden Your Mind, Doctor in the House, 6 Dates with Barker, Doctor at Large, The Two Ronnies, House of Mouse (narrator), Mickey Mouse Works (narr.). *Documentaries:* We Know Where You Live, Wine for the Confused, The Art of Football from A to Z. *Specials:* Taming of the Shrew, Funny Women, Laughter in the House: The Story of British Sitcom, The Human Face (Emmy nom. 2002), The Sketch Show Story. *Guest:* More than 223 appearances.

CLEMENS, BRIAN

Writer, Producer, Director. b. Croydon, England, 1931. Early career in advertising then wrote BBC TV play. Later TV filmed series as writer, script editor and features. Script editor Danger Man; Won Edgar Allen Poe Award for Best TV Thriller of 1962 (Scene of the Crime for U.S. Steel Hour). Various plays for Armchair Theatre; ATV Drama 70; Love Story. Winner two Edgar Allan Poe Awards, Cinema Fantastique Award for best s.p.
PICTURES: The Tell-Tale Heart, Station Six-Sahara, The Peking Medallion, And Soon The Darkness, The Major, When The Wind Blows, See No Evil, Dr. Jekyll and Sister Hyde, Golden Voyage of Sinbad, Watcher in the Woods, Stiff, Highlander II: The Quickening, Justine: A Private Affair (France), And Soon the Darkness (remake: writer of 1970 film).
TELEVISION: *Movies:* The Woman Hunter, Timestalkers (s.p.), Blue Blood, McBride: Fallen Idol. *Series: Writer/Prod.:* The Vise, Dial 999, Man from Interpol, The Mask of the Clown, Danger Man, The Avengers (Emmy nom. 1968), Riviera Police, The New Avengers, My Wife Next Door, The Protectors, Comedy Premiere, Wide World Mystery, Thriller, Escapade (U.S.), The Professionals, Blaues Blut, Perry Mason (numerous scripts), Loose Cannon, Father Dowling Mysteries, Bugs (writer, creator, UK), CI5: The New Professionals (writer, exec. prod), The Wrong Side of the Rainbow, McBride: Fallen Idol (writer). Writer of many more series episodes.

CLENNON, DAVID

Actor. b. Waukegan, IL, May 10, 1943. e. Univ. of Notre Dame, Yale Drama School.
THEATRE: *Off-B'way.:* The Unseen Hand, Forensic and the Navigators, As You Like It, Little Eyolf, Welcome to Andromeda, Medal of Honor Rag, The Cherry Orchard. Regional: Saved, Blood Knot, Loot, Marat/Sade, Beyond Therapy, others.
PICTURES: The Paper Chase, Bound for Glory, The Greatest, Coming Home, Gray Lady Down, Go Tell the Spartans, On the Yard, Being There, Hide in Plain Sight, Missing, The Escape Artist, The Thing, Ladies and Gentlemen the Fabulous Stains, The Right Stuff, Hannah K., Star 80, Falling in Love, Sweet Dreams, Legal Eagles, He's My Girl, The Couch Trip, Betrayed, Downtown, Man Trouble, Light Sleeper, Matinee, Two Crimes (Dos Crimenes), Grace of My Heart, Mad City, Playing by Heart, The Visit, AntiTrust, The Heart of the Possible, Silver City, Syriana, Glory Days, Flags of Our Fathers, Saving Sarah Cain, Extraordinary Measures, Callers.
TELEVISION: *Movies:* The Woman Hunter, Escapade, Timestalkers, Blue Blood, The Migrants, Crime Club, Helter Skelter, Gideon's Trumpet, Marriage is Alive and Well, Reward, Special Bulletin, Best Kept Secrets, Blood and Orchids, Conspiracy: The Trial of the Chicago 8, Nurses on the Line: The Crash of Flight 7, Black Widow Murders, Original Sins, Tecumseh: The Last Warrior, From the Earth to the Moon, The Staircase, McBride: Fallen Idol. *Series:* Rafferty, Park Place, Danger Man, Sir Francis Drake, Intrigue, The Avengers (Emmy nom. 1968), My Wife Next Door, The Protectors, Comedy Premiere, Thriller, The New Avengers (also prod.), thirtysomething, Almost Perfect, Once and Again, The Agency, The Professionals, Blaues Blut, Father Dowling Mysteries (also consult.), Bugs, Saved, CI5: The New Professionals, The Wrong Side of the Rainbow, Ghost Whisperer. *Guest:* More than 64 appearances.

CLEVELAND, HAL

Exhibitor. e. Indiana State Univ., graduated Cum Laude with degrees in political science and history. Cleveland is a 30-year cinema exhibition veteran who has moved through the ranks of several of the industry's leading cinema exhibition organizations. Between 1992 and 1997 he guided the development of more than 700 screens for United Artists. While at United Artists, Cleveland progressed through int'l. and global operations management to become executive v.p., with oversight of more than 600 locations throughout the U.S. He then became a senior v.p. with Boston-based Northeast Cinemas (previously Hoyts Cinemas Corporation), and developed over 300 screens while lowering building costs. In Jan. 2004, Cleveland became president and COO of Crown Theatres, based in South Norwalk, CT. The circuit, founded in 1991, is a 138-screen motion picture theatre circuit with theatres in CT, MD, NY, IL & MN.

CLIFFORD, GRAEME

Director. b. Sydney, New South Wales, Australia, 1942. Worked as film editor on such films as Don't Look Now, The Rocky Horror Picture Show, The Man Who Fell to Earth, F.I.S.T., The Postman Always Rings Twice, before turning to directing.
PICTURES: The Rocky Horror Picture Show, Frances, Burke & Wills, Gleaming the Cube, Deception, Ruby Cairo.
TELEVISION: *Movies:* Nightmare Classics, The Turn of the Screw, Past Tense, A Loss of Innocence. My Husband's Secret Life, The Last Witness, See You in My Dreams, Redeemer, Crossing the Line, Losing It, Profoundly Normal (also prod.), Family Sins, Write & Wrong. *Mini-series*: The Last Don, The Last Don II. *Series:* Barnaby Jones, The New Avengers, Twin Peaks, The Guardian.

CLOONEY, GEORGE

Actor, Producer, Director. b. Lexington, KY, May 6, 1961. e. Northern KY Univ. Father is TV newscaster-host Nick Clooney. Nephew of late singer Rosemary Clooney.
PICTURES: Return to Horror High, Return of the Killer Tomatoes, Red Surf, Unbecoming Age, The Harvest, One Fine Day, Full Tilt Boogie, From Dusk Till Dawn, Batman and Robin, The Peacemaker, The Thin Red Line, Out of Sight, South Park: Bigger Longer and Uncut (voice), Three Kings, The Perfect Storm, O Brother-Where Art Thou (Golden Globe Award 2001), Spy Kids, Welcome to Collinwood, Ocean's Eleven, Confessions of a Dangerous Mind, Solaris, Intolerable Cruelty, Criminal (prod.), Ocean's Twelve (also exec. prod.), The Jacket (prod./exec. prod.), Syriana (Academy Award, Golden Globe Award 2006, also prod.), Tishomingo Blues (exec. prod.), A Confederacy of Dunces (exec. prod.), Leatherheads (dir.), Rumor Has It (prod.), Goodnight, and Good Luck (2 Academy Award nom., 2 Golden Globe nom.; DGA nom.; WGA nom. 2006, actor, prod., dir., writer), PU-239, (exec. prod.), A Scanner Darkly (exec. prod.), Michael Clayton (also prod., Academy Award nom.; Golden Globe nom. 2007), The Good German, Wind Chill (exec. prod.), Ocean's Thirteen (also prod.), Leatherheads (also prod., dir., writer: s.p.), Burn After Reading, Fantastic Mr. Fox (voice), The Men Who Stare at Goats (also prod.), Up in the Air (Academy Award nom.; Golden Globe nom. 2010), The Informant! (exec. prod.), The American (also prod.), The Descendants. *Documentary:* Playground (exec. prod.).
TELEVISION: *Movies:* Playmate Pajama Party, Fail Safe. *Series:* The Facts of Life, Roseanne, Sunset Beat, Baby Talk, Sisters, Bodies of Evidence, ER (3 Golden Globe nom 1996-1998, 2 Emmy noms. 1995, 1996), K Street (exec. prod. only), Unscripted (exec. prod.,dir.), Delta Blues (exec. prod.). *Specials:* America: A Tribute to Heroes, Hope for Haiti Now: A Global Benefit for Earthquake Relief (host, exec. prod.). *Guest:* More than 225 appearances.

CLOSE, GLENN

Actress. b. Greenwich, CT, Mar. 19, 1947. e. Coll. of William and Mary. Began performing with a repertory group Fingernails, then toured country with folk-singing group Up With People. Professional debut at Phoenix Theatre, New York. Also accomplished musical performer (lyric soprano).
THEATRE: *NY:* Love for Love, Rules of the Game, Member of the Wedding, Rex, Uncommon Women and Others, The Crucifer of Blood, Wine Untouched, The Winter Dancers, Barnum, Singular Life of Albert Nobbs (Obie Award), The Real Thing (Tony Award, 1984), Childhood, Joan of Arc at the Stake,

Benefactors, Death and the Maiden (Tony Award, 1992), Sunset Boulevard (Tony Award, 1995). Regional: King Lear, Uncle Vanya, The Rose Tattoo, A Streetcar Named Desire, Brooklyn Laundry, Sunset Boulevard.
PICTURES: The World According to Garp (Academy Award nom. 1983, debut, 1982), The Big Chill (Academy Award nom. 1984), The Natural (Academy Award nom. 1985), The Stone Boy, Greystoke: The Legend of Tarzan Lord of the Apes (dubbed voice), Jagged Edge, Maxie (Golden Globe nom. 1986), Fatal Attraction (Academy Award nom., Golden Globe nom. 1988), Light Years (voice), Dangerous Liaisons (Academy Award nom. 1989), Immediate Family, Reversal of Fortune, Hamlet, Meeting Venus, Hook (cameo), The Paper, The House of the Spirits, Anne Frank Remembered (voice), Mary Reilly, Mars Attacks!, 101 Dalmatians (Golden Globe nom. 1997), Paradise Road, In the Gloaming, Airforce One, In & Out, Cookie's Fortune, Tarzan (voice), Cast and Crew, Things You Can Tell Just By Looking At Her, 102 Dalmatians, The Safety of Objects, Pinocchio (voice), Le Divorce, Anything Else, The Stepford Wives, Hoodwinked, Heights, Nine Lives, The Chumscrubber, Therese Raquin, Paint, Evening, Hoodwinked 2: Hood vs. Evil (voice), Prison Dog (doc. short, dir., exec. prod.).
TELEVISION: *Movies:* Too Far To Go, The Orphan Train, The Elephant Man, Something About Amelia (Emmy nom., Golden Globe nom. 1984), Stones for Ibarra, I'll Take Romance, Sarah: Plain and Tall (2 Emmy nom. 1991, 1993), Skylark (also co-exec. prod.), Serving in Silence: The Margarethe Cammermeyer Story (Emmy Award, Emmy nom., Golden Globe nom. 1996; also co-exec. prod.), Journey (exec. prod.), In the Gloaming (Emmy nom. 1997), Sarah (Golden globe nom. 1992), Plain and Tall: Winter's End, Baby (voice, exec. prod.), South Pacific, Brush with Fate, The Lion in Winter (Emmy nom., Golden Globe Award 2005), Strip Search. *Mini-series:* A Century of Women (voice). *Series:* Will & Grace (Emmy nom. 2002 as guest), The Shield (Emmy nom., Golden Globe nom. 2005), Damages (2 Emmy Awards 2008, 2009, 2 Golden Globe Awards 2008, 2010). *Documentaries:* Lincoln (voice), Anne Frank Remembered (voice), The Lady with the Torch, What I Want My Words to Do to You: Voices From Inside a Women's Maximum Security Prison, A Closer Walk. *Specials:* Broken Hearts Broken Homes (host, co-exec. prod.), Sondheim: A Celebration at Carnegie Hall. *Guest:* More than 158 appearances.

COATES, ANNE V.

Film Editor, Producer. b. Reigate, Surrey, Eng., 1925. e. Bartrum Gables Coll. m. late dir. Douglas Hickox. Worked as nurse at East Grinstead Plastic Surgery Hospital. Recipient of 1995 A.C.E. Career Achievement award. 2010 elected to the BD. of Governors of the Academy of Motion Picture Arts and Sciences which oversees the Oscars for a three year term.
PICTURES: Pickwick Papers, Grand National Night, Forbidden Cargo, To Paris With Love, The Truth About Women, The Horse's Mouth, Tunes of Glory, Don't Bother to Knock, Lawrence of Arabia (Academy Award, 1963; also ACE nom.), Becket (Acad. Award & ACE noms. 1965), Young Cassidy, Those Magnificent Men in Their Flying Machines (co-ed.), Hotel Paridiso, Great Catherine, The Bofors Guns, The Adventurers, Friends, The Public Eye, The Nelson Affair, 11 Harrowhouse, Murder on the Orient Express (BAFTA nom.), Man Friday, Aces High, The Eagle Has Landed, The Medusa Touch (prod. & sprv. ed.), The Legacy, The Elephant Man (Acad. Award nom., BAFTA nom. 1981), The Bushido Blade, Ragtime (co-ed.), The Pirates of Penzance, Greystoke: The Legend of Tarzan Lord of the Apes, Lady Jane, Raw Deal, Masters of the Universe, Farewell to the King (co-ed.), Listen to Me, I Love You to Death, What About Bob?, Chaplin, In the Line of Fire (Acad. Award nom., A.C.E. nom., BAFTA nom., G.B.F.E. Award, 1994), Pontiac Moon, Congo, Striptease, Out to Sea, Out of Sight (Academy Award nom. 1999), Passion of Mind, Erin Brokovich, Sweet November, Unfaithful, In and Out of Focus (documentary, as herself), Taking Lives, Catch and Release, The Golden Compass, Extraordinary Measures.
TELEVISION: *Movies:* A War of Children, Catholics, Fail Safe.

COBLENZ, WALTER

Producer.
PICTURES: The Candidate, All the President's Men (Academy Award nom. 1977), The Onion Field, The Legend of the Lone Ranger, Strange Invaders, Sister Sister, 18 Again!, For Keeps, The Babe, Money Talks, Her Majesty.
TELEVISION: *Movie:* Jack Reed: Badge of Honor, House of Secrets, Not Our Son, A Dream for Christmas. *Series:* Apples Way. *Mini-series*: The Blue Knight (Emmy nom. 1974).

COEN, ETHAN

Producer, Writer. b. St. Louis Park, MN, Sep. 21, 1957. e. Princeton U. Co-wrote s.p. with brother, Joel, XYZ Murders (renamed Crimewave).
PICTURES: *Producer/Co-Writer:* Blood Simple (also co-edited under pseudonym Roderick James), Raising Arizona, Miller's Crossing, Barton Fink, The Hudsucker Proxy, Fargo (original s.p. Academy Award, 2 other nom. 1996; Chicago Film Critics Award for s.p.; LA Film Critics Award for s.p., Golden Globe nom.; WGA Award 1997), The Naked Man, The Big Lebowski, O Brother-Where Art Thou? (Academy Award nom. 2001), The Man Who Wasn't There (Golden Globe nom.; WGA nom. 2002), Intolerable Cruelty, Bad Santa, The Ladykillers, Romance & Cigarettes, je t'aime, Paris, No Country for Old Men (also dir., editor, 4 Academy Award noms.; ACE nom.; DGA Award, Golden Globe Award, 1 other nom.; WGA nom. 2008), Seasons of Dust, Burn After Reading (also editor, WGA nom. 2009), A Serious Man (also dir., editor, Academy Award nom.; WGA nom. 2010), True Grit (also dir.).

COEN, JOEL

Director, Writer. b. St. Louis Park, MN, Nov. 29, 1954. e. Simon's Rock College, MA; studied film at NYU. m. actress Frances McDormand. Was asst. editor on Fear No Evil and Evil Dead. Co-wrote with brother, Ethan, s.p. for XYZ Murders (renamed Crime Wave.) Cameo role in film Spies Like Us, 1985.
PICTURES: *Director/Co-Writer:* Blood Simple (also co-editor, under pseudonym Roderick Jaynes), Raising Arizona, Miller's Crossing, Barton Fink (also co-editor, as Roderick Jaynes), The Hudsucker Proxy, Fargo (Best director, Cannes 1996; original s.p. Academy Award, 1997; 2 other nom.; Chicago Film Critics Award for s.p., and dir.; LA Film Critics Award for s.p.; BAFTA for achievement in dir., 2 Golden Globe nom.; DGA nom.; WGA Award 1997), The Big Lebowski, O Brother, Where Art Thou? (Academy Award nom. 2001), The Man Who Wasn't There (Golden Globe nom.; WGA nom. 2002), Intolerable Cruelty, Bad Santa (s.p. and exec. prod.), The Ladykillers, Romance & Cigarettes (prod./exec. prod.), je t'aime Paris, Seasons of Dust (exec. prod.), No Country for Old Men (also prod., editor, 4 Academy Award noms.; ACE nom.; DGA Award, Golden Globe Award, 1 other nom.; WGA nom. 2008)), Burn After Reading (also prod., editor, WGA nom. 2009), A Serious Man (also prod., editor, 2 Academy Award noms.; WGA nom. 2010), True Grit (also prod.).

COHEN, ARTHUR

Executive. President, Bloomingdale's, 1975-78. Founder & president, Lansdowne Advertising, a division of J. Walter Thompson, 1978-82, creating billings to $14 million in four years. President, Tele1st, a division of ABC Video Enterprises, 1982-85; partner with Robert Nederlander, 1985-86; exec. v.p., advertising, Revlon, 1986-89, during which time Revlon restored its consumer image to record highs. President, Worldwide Mktg., Paramount Pictures Motion Picture Group, 1989-summer 2003. In 2006, became president of ad-supported Iklipz.com a film-maker-friendly website for independents.

COHEN, BETTY

Executive. b. Racine, WI. e. B.A. in communications, graduated Phi Beta Kappa, Stanford University, 1977. Cohen began career as a broadcast producer for Public Media Center in San Francisco. She moved to New York and landed a job writing and producing on-air promotions for Cable Health Network, and later served as managing senior prod. of on-air promotion for Lifetime Television. She was director of on-air promotion and interstitial programming for Nickelodeon/Nick at Nite before joining Turner Network Television (TNT), where she rose to senior v.p. and gen. mgr. During 14 years at Turner Broadcasting Systems, Inc., she oversaw the creation and launch of the all-animation Cartoon Network. Additionally, she oversaw CartoonNetwork.com; Cartoon Network Studios, which created acclaimed series Power Puff Girls, Dexter's Lab and Samurai Jack; and programming strategies and brand marketing for Cartoon Network's Europe, Latin America, Asia Pacific and Japan entities. In Sept. 2002, she founded and was pres. of Betty Cohen Media Consulting, LLC, and advised companies on brand building, channel development and multiplatform programming. On March 31, 2005, Lifetime Entertainment Services appointed Cohen pres. and CEO. She oversaw Lifetime Television; Lifetime Movie Network; Lifetime Real Women; Lifetime Radio for Women; Lifetime Home Entertainment, and Lifetime Online. She resigned her post in April 2007 with a year left on her contract. Cohen is the recipient of many awards. In 2000 she was named one of "The 50 Most Powerful Women in Business" by Fortune Magazine and was cited by Advertising Age as one of the country's "Top 100 Marketers."

COHEN, BRUCE

Producer, Director. Owner Bruce Cohen Productions, Partner at Jinks/Cohen Productions.
PICTURES: The Color Purple (actor), *batteries not included (2nd asst. dir.), The Couch Trip (2nd asst. dir.), Satisfaction (2nd asst. dir.), Cocoon: The Return (2nd asst. dir.), The Boost (2nd asst. dir.), Always (2nd asst. dir.), Arachnophobia (1st. asst. dir.), Hook (1st. asst. dir., assoc. prod.), Alive (co-prod.), The Flintstones (prod.), To Wong Foo Thanks for Everything, Julie Newmar (exec. prod.), Mousehunt (prod.), American Beauty (prod., Academy Award 2000), The Flintstones in Viva Rock Vegas (2nd unit dir.), Down with Love (prod.), Big Fish (prod.), The Forgotten (prod.), The Nines (prod.), Milk (prod., Academy Award nom. 2009).
TELEVISION: *Movies:* Mistrial (prod.), Hate (exec. prod.), Movies Rock (exec. prod.). *Series:* Traveler (exec. prod.), Side Order of Life (exec. prod.), Pushing Daisies (exec. prod.). *Special:* Centennial Olympic Games: Torch Relay Opening Ceremonies (prod., 1996).

COHEN, LARRY

Director, Producer, Writer. b. New York, NY, July 15, 1946. e.

CCNY. Started as writer for TV series incl. Kraft Mystery Theatre, The Defenders, Arrest and Trial. Creator of series Branded, The Invaders, Cool Million, Blue Light, Cop Talk.
PICTURES: *Dir./prod./s.p.:* Daddy's Gone A-Hunting (co-s.p.), El Condor, Bone, Black Caesar, It's Alive, Demon, The Private Files of J. Edgar Hoover, It Lives Again, Success (story), Full Moon High, Q, I The Jury, Perfect Strangers, The Man Who Wasn't There (story), Special Effects, Scandalous (story), The Stuff (exec. prod.), Spies Like Us (actor), It's Alive III: Island of the Alive (exec. prod.), Return to Salem's Lot (exec. prod.), Best Seller, Deadly Illusion, Maniac Cop, Wicked Stepmother (exec. prod.), Maniac Cop II, The Ambulance, The Apparatus, Guilty As Sin, Original Gangstas, Invasion of Privacy (writer), The Ex, Misbegotten, Uncle Sam, Phone Booth, Air Force One: The Final Mission (doc., dir., prod.), Cellular (writer), Epic Proportions (writer, play), Captivity, Message Deleted, The Torture of Delva Mills (exec. prod).
TELEVISION: *Movies: Writer:* In Broad Daylight, Cool Million, Columbo: Any Old Port in a Storm, Columbo: Candidate for Crime, Man on the Outside, Shootout in a One Dog Town (co-writer, story), Columbo: An Exercise in Fatality, Momma the Detective (dir. only), Women of San Quentin, Desperado: Avalanche at Devil's Ridge, As Good as Dead (also dir., prod.), The Invaders, Ed McBain's 87th Precinct: Ice, Ed McBain's 87th Precinct: Heatwave, Defenders: Choice of Evils), The Gambler, the Girl and the Gunslinger (writer). *Series: Writer:* Kraft Television Theatre, 'Way Out, The Defenders, Sam Benedict, The Fugitive, Branded (also prod.), Never Too Young (prod. only), Blue Light, The Rat Patrol, The Invaders, (also creator), Cool Million (also creator), Griff (also creator), NYPD Blue.

COHEN, PAUL

Executive, Producer, Educator. b. New York, NY, Apr. 16, 1948. e. Hofstra U.; New School for Social Research; Jungian Inst. NY. Started in industry as exec. prod., distributor, screenwriter, producer for Masada Prods. Served as v.p. of Grand Slam Prods., exec. prod. for Moonbeam Assocs. Head of Analysis Films, 1976-84. While there, released Mephisto, which garnered the Academy Award for best foreign language film, 1982. Founded Aries Film Releasing, 1989, becoming pres. & CEO. During that time released Bad Lieutenant. Cohen was drawn to Florida in the mid 1990s and was appointed by Gov. Lawton Chiles to promote independent motion picture production in Florida. Cohen was instrumental in founding the first Florida Film Forum. In 1996, Cohen co-founded and oversaw the marketing and operation of the First Annual Palm Beach International Film Festival. Additionally, he served as a "Filmmaker in Residence" at the Graduate Film Conservatory at Florida State University, and regularly lectured at the University of Miami, Dade Community College, as well as other major Florida universities. In 1997, Cohen and Carl Icahn formed Stratosphere Entertainment, a motion picture distribution and production company based in New York. As Stratosphere pres., Cohen was responsible for the acquisition, marketing and distribution of independent motion pictures including The Thief, (1997 Academy Award nomination for Best Foreign Language Film). Cohen then became pres. & CEO of Manhattan Pictures International, a distribution co. active from 2001-2003. He then served as an advisor to the Swartz Foundation and developed pictures with scientific topics at their core until 2007 when he joined the Faculty at FSU's College of Motion Picture, Television & Recording Arts while continuing the business of acquiring theatrical projects. He currently is active on the faculty of Florida State University's Film School. He is a member of the Executive Board of Directors of the Louis B. Wolfson Film & Television Archives and serves on the Academic Advisory Committee at Miami-Dade Community College. He has served as president of the prestigious Independent Feature Project South (IFP/South), and has lectured on motion picture distribution at the American Film Institute in Los Angeles, Columbia University, New York University's Graduate Film School, and the Sundance Institute's Producers Conference in Utah where he traveled to lecture to industry members in locations such as Mexico and Jerusalem. Cohen has served as a consultant to Showtime Networks Independent Film Initiative as well as other independent production companies. He served on the jury and board of numerous film festivals including the Chicago, Bermuda, Sunfest in Puerto Rico, Ft. Lauderdale, the South Beach Independent Film Festival, and is currently on the Hamptons International Film Festival advisory board.
PICTURES: Caligula, My Brilliant Career, Maniac, Basket Case, The Chosen, Butterfly, The Innocent, Mephisto, The Thief, My Twentieth Century, Superstar: The Life and Times of Andy Warhol, Overseas, The Story of Boys and Girls, Thank You and Goodnight, Lovers, Bad Lieutenant, 12 Hours, Enigma, In Praise of Love, One Eyed King, The Secret Lives of Dentists, Off the Map.

COHEN, POLLY

Executive. e. Bachelor's degree, Univ. of Calif. at San Diego in Chinese Studies. Lived and worked in Southeast Asia before entering the entertainment industry. While still a graduate student in USC's Peter Stark Production Program, Cohen worked for Warner Bros. Pictures as a prod. mgt. trainee. Upon obtaining her MFA, she joined Jersey Films, where she spent two years, rising to the post of creative executive. Cohen joined Warner Bros. Studios in 1997 as a creative executive; named prod. executive in 1998. In 1999 she became v.p., production, and in 2003 promoted to senior v.p. In Feb. 2006, she was promoted to executive v.p., production for Warner Bros. Pictures, reporting to Jeff Robinov, pres., production, Warner Bros. Pictures. In May 2006, Cohen was named President, Warner Independent Pictures. Warner Independent Pictures ceased operations in 2008.

COHEN, ROB

Producer, Director. b. Cornwall-on-the-Hudson, NY, March 12, 1949. e. Harvard U. BA. Formerly exec. v.p. in chg of m.p. and TV for Motown. Started as dir. of m.p. for TV at 20th Century-Fox. Joined Motown at age of 24 to produce films. Headed own production co. 1985, appt. pres., Keith Barish Prods.
PICTURES: *Prod:* Mahogany, The Bingo Long Traveling All-Stars, Scott Joplin, Almost Summer, Thank God It's Friday, The Wiz, The Razor's Edge, The Legend of Billie Jean, Light of Day (co-prod.), Bird on a Wire, The Hard Way, *Co-executive prod.:* The Witches of Eastwick, The Monster Squad, Ironweed, The Running Man. *Exec. prod.:* The Serpent and the Rainbow, Disorganized Crime, xXx 2: The Next Level, Riot. *Dir.:* A Small Circle of Friends, Scandalous (also co-s.p.), The Skulls, Dragon: The Bruce Lee Story (also co-s.p., actor), Dragonheart, Daylight, The Fast and the Furious, Stealth (also s.p), The Mummy: Tomb of the Dragon Emperor.
TELEVISION: *Movies:* Amateur Night at the Dixie Bar and Grill, Knight Rider 2010, Cuba and Claude (exec. prod.), The Vanishing Son I-IV (exec. prod.), The Rat Pack (DGA nom. 1999), The Last Ride. *Series: Dir.*: Miami Vice, Hooperman, thirtysomething, The Wonder Years (writer), The Antagonists, The Guardian.

COHEN, ROBERT B.

Executive. e. George Washington U., B.A., Southern Texas Sch. of Law. 1980-84. Atty. for Pillsbury Madison's Sutro and for Greenberg, Glusker, Fields, Clamans and Machtinger (L.A.). Was asst. gen. counsel for Columbia Pictures. Joined Paramount 1985 as sr. atty. for M.P. Group. to oversee legal functions for assigned feature films; 1988 named v.p. in charge of legal affairs, Motion Picture Group of Paramount; 1990, named sr. v.p. legal affairs, motion picture group, Paramount. Currently, exec. v.p. legal affairs, 20th Century Fox Distribution.

COHEN, SACHA BARON

Actor, Writer, Producer. b. London, UK, October 13, 1971. e. Studied History at Christ's College, Cambridge. AKA: Borat Sagdiyev, Borat. Trademark characters: Ali G, Brüno, and Borat.
PICTURES: Madagascar (voice), Talladega Nights: The Ballad of Ricky Bobby, Borat: Cultural Learnings of America for Make Benefit Glorious Nation of Kazakhstan (Academy Award nom.; Golden Globe Award, WGA nom. 2007), Madagascar: Escape 2 Africa (voice), Sweeney Todd: The Demon Barber of Fleet Street, Brüno.
TELEVISION: *Movies:* Jack and Jeremy's Police 4, Live from the Lighthouse, Night of Too Many Stars: An Overbooked Event for Autism Education (as Borat Sagdiyev), Reel Comedy: Borat Moviefilms Special Preview (as Borat Sagdiyev). *Series:* Comedy Nation, The 11 O'Clock Show, Da Ali G Show (4 Emmy noms.). *Special:* Comic Relief 2007: The Big One. *Guest:* More than 83 appearances.

COHEN, SID

Executive. e. Univ. of RI Col. of Business. Served as western div. mgr. for WB TV distrib. in 1970s. 1979-84, v.p. feature planning & sales development for domestic TV distrib. div. of Paramount Pictures Corp. There he created the first satellite-delivered feature-film package for free over-the-air TV on a regularly scheduled natl. basis. 1985-91, pres. of domestic TV distrib. at King World Prods. Sept. 1991-2000 pres. of MGM Domestic TV Distribution. Now serves MGM unit in consulting role. Sits on 2006-2007 Business Advisory Council for the University of Rhode Island.

COLBERT, STEPHEN

Writer, Producer, Actor, Host. b. Washington, DC, May 13, 1964. e. Northwestern U.
Author: Wigfield: The Can-Do Town That Just May Not (with Amy Sedaris and Paul Dinello), A Citizen's Guide To Democracy Inaction (contributed material), I Am America (And So Can You!).
PICTURES: As Actor: Let It Snow, Nobody Knows Anything!, Strangers with Candy (also writer, soundtrack writer), The Great New Wonderful, Bewitched, CSNY/Déjà Vu (doc.), The Love Guru, Monsters vs Aliens (voice).
TELEVISION: *Movies:* Indecision 2000: Focus on New Hampshire (writer, correspondent also pilot), Stephen Colbert Again: A Look Back (writer), Indecision 2002: Election Night (also writer), Re-Decision 2003: The California Recall writer, host), Indecision 2008: Election Night - America's Choice (co-host, exec. prod.), A Colbert Christmas: The Greatest Gift of All! (writer, exec. prod., soundtrack performer). *Mini-series:* The Wrong Coast (voices). *Series:* Exit 57 (writer), The Dana Carvey Show (various characters, writer), Strangers with Candy (writer, co-prod.), Harvey Birdman, Attorney at Law (actor), Saturday Night Live (writer, voices), Ellen Degeneres/No Doubt (writer), The Daily Show with Jon Stewart (writer, correspondent, host,

co-host, 3 Emmy Awards), The Colbert Report (host, writer, exec. prod., 2 Emmy Awards, 10 other noms., 2 WGA noms).

COLBY, RONALD

Producer, Director, Writer. b. New York, NY. e. Hofstra U., NYU. Began career as playwright at Cafe La Mama and Caffe Cino; performed in off-B'way shows; spent year as actor-writer in residence at Pittsburgh Playhouse. Served as dialogue coach and asst. to Francis Coppola; was v.p. of Zoetrope Studios. Directed several documentaries and short films.
PICTURES: Finian's Rainbow (act. only), The Rain People (prod.), Hammett (prod.), Some Kind of Wonderful (exec. prod.), She's Having a Baby (exec. prod.), Lisa (assoc. prod., unit prod. mngr.), The Exorcist III (prod. mngr., 2nd unit), Jailbait (co-prod), Harvest of Fire, Moonbase (1st asst. dir.), Bring It On Again (video, unit production mgr.), Stop! Or My Mom Will Shoot (asst. dir. 2nd unit), Material Girls (line prod. and unit prod. mngr.).
TELEVISION: *Movies:* Margaret Bourke-White (co-prod.), Lush Life (co-prod.), Cora Unashamed (co-prod.), The Ponder Heart (sup. prod.), Almost a Woman, A Death in the Family (co-prod.). *Series:* Eye to Eye, Nightmare Cafe.

COLE, GARY

Actor. b. Park Ridge, IL, Sept. 20, 1956. e. Illinois State, theatre major. Dropped out of coll. after 3 years and moved to Chicago where he tended bar, painted houses and worked with Steppenwolf Theatre group. In 1979 helped to form Remains Theatre, left in 1986 to become ensemble member of Steppenwolf.
PICTURES: Lucas, In the Line of Fire, The Brady Bunch Movie, A Very Brady Sequel, Gang Related, Santa Fe, Cyclops Baby, A Simple Plan, I'll Be Home for Christmas, Kiss the Sky, Office Space, The Gift, The Rising Place, One Hour Photo, I Spy, Win a Date with Tad Hamilton!, Dodgeball: A True Underdog Story, Mozart & the Whale, Cry Wolf, The Ring Two, Talladega Nights: The Ballad of Ricky Bobby, Breach, Conspiracy, Forever Strong, Say Hello to Stan Talmadge, Pineapple Express, Say Hello to Stan Talmadge, The Chicago 8, Immortality Bites.
TELEVISION: *Movies:* Heart of Steel, Fatal Vision, Vital Signs, Those She Left Behind, The Old Man and the Sea, Son of the Morning Star, The Switch, When Love Kills: The Seduction of John Hearn, A Time to Heal, Fall from Grace, For My Daughter's Honor, Lies He Told, American Adventure, Cadet Kelly, Brady Bunch in the Whitehouse, Kim Possible: A Stitch in Time (voice), Pop Rocks, That Guy, Good Behavior. *Mini-series:* Echoes in the Darkness, From the Earth to the Moon. *Series:* Midnight Caller, American Gothic, Justice League, Crusade, Harvey Birdman Attorney at Law, Family Guy (voice), The West Wing, Kim Possible (voice), 12 Miles of Bad Road, Desperate Housewives. *Guest:* More than 80 appearances.

COLE, GEORGE

Actor. b. London, Eng., Apr. 22, 1925. e. secondary sch. Surrey. Stage debut in White Horse Inn, 1939; motion picture debut in Cottage to Let, 1941.PICTURES: Henry V, Quartet, My Brother's Keeper, Laughter in Paradise, Scrooge, Lady Godiva Rides Again, Who Goes There (Passionate Sentry), Morning Departure (Operation Disaster), Top Secret (Mr. Potts Goes to Moscow), Happy Family, Will Any Gentleman, Apes of the Rock, The Intruder, Happy Ever After (Tonight's the Night), Our Girl Friday (Adventures of Sadie), Belles of St. Trinian's, Prize of Gold, Where There's a Will, Constant Husband, Quentin Durward, The Weapon, It's a Wonderful Life, Green Man, Bridal Path, Too Many Crooks, Blue Murder at St. Trinians, Don't Panic Chaps, Dr. Syn, One Way Pendulum, Legend of Young Dick Turpin, The Great St. Trinian's Train Robbery, Cleopatra, The Green Shoes, Vampire Lovers, Fright, The Bluebird, Mary Reilly, The Ghost of Greville Lodge.
TELEVISION: *Movies:* The Legend of Young Dick Turpin, The Last Lonely Man, Minder on the Orient Express, Minder: An Officer and a Car Salesman, The Sleeper, Station Jim, Marple: Nemesis, A Class Apart, Diamond Geezer 2, The Dinner Party. *Mini-series:* Blott on the Landscape, Bodily Harm. *Series:* Dad, My Good Friend. A Life of Bliss, A Man of Our Times, Menace, Minder, Don't Forget To Write, The Good Life, The Bounder, Root Into Europe, An Independent Man, The Sleeper, Station Jim. *Guest:* More than 80 appearances.

COLEMAN, DABNEY

Actor. b. Austin, TX, Jan. 3, 1932. e. VA Military Inst. 1949-51; U. Texas 1951-57; Neighborhood Playhouse School Theater 1958-60.
PICTURES: The Slender Thread (debut, 1965), This Property Is Condemned, The Scalphunters, The Trouble With Girls, Downhill Racer, I Love My Wife, Cinderella Liberty, The Dove, The Towering Inferno, The Other Side of the Mountain, Bite the Bullet, The Black Streetfighter, Midway, Rolling Thunder, Viva Knievel, North Dallas Forty, Nothing Personal, How to Beat the High Cost of Living, Melvin and Howard, Nine to Five, On Golden Pond, Modern Problems, Young Doctors in Love, Tootsie, WarGames, The Muppets Take Manhattan, Cloak and Dagger, The Man with One Red Shoe, Dragnet, Hot to Trot, Where the Heart Is, Short Time, Meet the Applegates, There Goes the Neighborhood, Amos & Andrew, The Beverly Hillbillies, Clifford, You've Got Mail, Inspector Gadget, Stuart Little, Taken, Where the Red Fern Grows, Recess: School's Out (voice), The Climb, Moonlight Mile, Domino, Hard Four.
TELEVISION: *Movies:* Brotherhood of the Bell, Savage, Dying Room Only, The President's Plane is Missing, Bad Ronald, Attack on Terror: The FBI Versus the Ku Klux Klan, Returning Home, Kiss Me Kill Me, Maneaters Are Loose!, More Than Friends, Apple Pie, When She Was Bad, Murrow, Guilty of Innocence, Sworn To Silence (Golden Globe nom. 1988, Emmy Award, 1987), Baby M (Emmy nom. 1988), Maybe Baby, Never Forget, Columbo and the Murder of a Rock Star (Emmy nom. 1991), Judicial Consent, In the Line of Duty: Kidnapped, Devil's Food, Target Earth, My Date with the President's Daughter, Exiled, Must Be Santa, Kiss My Act. *Mini-series:* Fresno, Idols of the Game (host). *Series:* That Girl, Bright Promise, Mary Hartman Mary Hartman, Apple Pie, Forever Fernwood, Buffalo Bill (Golden Globe nom. 2 Emmy nom. 1984), Drexell's Class, Madman of the People, The Slap Maxwell Story (Golden Globe Award, Emmy nom. 1988), Recess (voice), The Guardian, Courting Alex, Heartland, Boardwalk Empire (also pilot). *Special:* Plaza Suite, Texan, The Perfect Pitch (TV documentary as himself). *Guest:* More than 136 appearances.

COLEMAN, GARY

Actor. b. Zion, IL, Feb. 8, 1968. Gained fame as star of TV's Diff'rent Strokes.
PICTURES: The Fish That Saved Pittsburgh, On the Right Track, Jimmy the Kid, S.F.W., Party, Dirty Work, Off the Menu: The Last Days at Chasens, Shafted!, The Flunky, Church Ball, Big Fat Important Movie, Midgets Vs. Mascots.
TELEVISION: *Movies/Actor/Producer:* The Kid from Left Field, Scout's Honor, The Kid With the Broken Halo; The Kid with the 200 I.Q., The Fantastic World of D.C. Collins, Playing With Fire, Like Father Like Santa, A Carol Christmas. *Series:* Diff'rent Strokes. *Guest:* More than 117 appearances.
(d. May 28, 2010)

COLEMAN, LEWIS

Executive. b. San Francisco, CA. e. B.A. in economics from Stanford University. Coleman worked in the banking industry for 37 years before using his financial acumen in the entertainment industry. Most recently, Coleman was a bd. director and chairman of DreamWorks Animation SKG, Inc. audit committee before being tapped in Dec. 2005 to become the company's president and CFO. The appointment has enabled CEO Jeffrey Katzenberg and COO Ann Daly to spend more time on creative responsibilities while finance veteran Coleman monitors the company's day-to-day financials. Coleman was a former vice chairman and CFO of Bank of America and also the retired founding president of the Gordon and Betty Moore Foundation, a multi-billion dollar philanthropic foundation. Alongside Katzenberg and Daly, Coleman leads the company's staff to produce two computer-generated animated movies per year and pursues company expansion into direct-to-video movies, licensing, Broadway musicals and live entertainment. Coleman also sits on the boards of directors of Chiron Corporation, Northrop Grumman Corporation and Regal Entertainment Group. He is also a member of Stanford University's Advisory Board of the Freeman Spogli Institute for International Studies and is a former Trustee for the Gordon and Betty Moore Foundation and Director of Diversified Credit Investments.

COLER, JOEL, H.

Executive, Producer. b. Bronx, NY, July 27, 1931. e. Syracuse U., B.A., journalism. Worked as adv. asst. NBC; acct. exec. Grey Advertising. Joined 20th Century-Fox in 1964 as adv. coordinator for Fox Intl.; 1967, named intl. adv./pub. mgr. 1974, named v.p. dir., intl. adv/pub. Nov. 1990, named v.p. publicity/promotions Fox Intl. 1991, v.p. Worldwide Distrib. Services. 1984, memb. L.A. Olympic Org. Comm. Left Fox in 1992 to form Joel Coler & Friends Intl. Mktg. Consultants. Member of L.A. Philharmonic Business & Professional Comm. He also has been a member of the Academy of Motion Picture Arts and Sciences since 1971 and has served on the Foreign Language Committee. He has been a member of the business and professional committee for the LA Philharmonic and in 1983 and 1984 was a key member of the Advisory Committee for the LA Olympics. In 2000, he headed up int'l. marketing for the film Mark Twain's Greatest Adventures and in 2001 he was made the film's exec. prod. and a member of the Advisory Board of Matter of Time Productions, LLC. Coler currently is PR director in the U.S. for the San Sebastian Film Festival operating from his Joel Coler & Friends headquarters in Beverly Hills, CA.
PICTURE: A Moment in Time, Mark Twain's Greatest Adventure (exec. prod.).

COLIN, MARGARET

Actress. b. Brooklyn, NY, May 26, 1957. Raised on Long Island. Studied acting at Stella Adler Conservatory, Juilliard, Hofstra U. Left Hofstra to pursue acting career in Manhattan where she was cast in daytime TV series The Edge of Night. NY Theatre incl. work at Ensemble Studio, Geva Theatre and Manhattan Theatre Club (Aristocrats, Sight Unseen).
PICTURES: Pretty in Pink, Something Wild, Like Father Like Son, Three Men and a Baby, True Believer, Martians Go Home, The Butcher's Wife, Amos & Andrew, Terminal Velocity, Independence Day, The Devil's Own, Time to Say Goodbye, Milk

and Money, The Adventures of Sebastian Cole, Blue Car, Unfaithful, First Daughter, Deception, The Missing Person, iMurders.
TELEVISION: *Movies:* Warm Hearts Cold Feet, The Return of Sherlock Holmes, The Traveling Man, Good Night Sweet Wife: A Murder in Boston, In the Shadow of Evil, Hit and Run, Swing Vote, Private Lies, The Familiar Stranger, The Wedding Dress, Remembering Charlie. *Series:* The Edge of Night, As the World Turns, Foley Square, Leg Work, Sibs, Chicago Hope, The Wright Verdicts, Now and Again, Madigan Men, Gossip Girl.

COLLETTE, TONI
Actress. b. Sydney, Australia, November 1, 1972.
THEATRE: The Wild Party (Tony Award nom.).
PICTURES: Spotswood, Muriel's Wedding (Golden Globe nom. 1996), This Marching Girl Thing, Arabian Knight, Lilian's Story, Cosi, The Pallbearer, Emma, Clockwatchers, The James Gang, Dianna & Me, The Boys, Velvet Goldmine, 8 1/2 Women, The Sixth Sense (Academy Award nom. 2000), Shaft, Hotel Splendide, The Magic Pudding, Changing Lanes, The Hours, About a Boy, Dirty Deeds, Japanese Story, Providence, Connie & Carla, The Last Shot, In Her Shoes, Like Minds, The Night Listener, Little Miss Sunshine (Golden Globe nom. 2007), The Black Balloon (also exec. prod.), Hey, Hey It's Esther Blueburger, The Dead Girl, Evening.
TELEVISION: *Movie:* Dinner with Friends, Tsunami: The Aftermath (Emmy nom.; Golden Globe nom. 2007). *Series:* United States of Tara (Emmy Award 2009, Golden Globe Award 2010). *Guest:* More than 56 appearances.

COLLINS, GARY
Actor. b. Boston, MA, Apr. 30, 1938.
PICTURES: The Pigeon That Took Rome, The Longest Day, Cleopatra, Stranded, Angel in My Pocket, Airport, Killer Fish, Hangar 18, Watchers Reborn, Jungle Book: Lost Treasure (voice), Beautiful.
TELEVISION: *Movies:* Quarantined, Getting Away from It All, Houston We've Got a Problem, The Night They Took Miss Beautiful, The Kid From Left Field, Jacqueline Susann's Valley of the Dolls, Danielle Steel's Secrets, Bandit: Bandit Bandit. *Mini-Series:* Roots. *Series:* The Wackiest Ship in the Army, The Iron Horse, Sixth Sense, Born Free, Hour Magazine (host, Emmy Award 1984), Home, Home Show. *Specials:* Hosted Miss America Pageant 1981-1990.*Guest:* More than 81 appearances.

COLLINS, JOAN
Actress. b. London, Eng., May 23, 1933. e. Francis Holland Sch., London. Sister is writer Jackie Collins. Made stage debut in A Doll's House, Arts Theatre 1946. Author: Past Imperfect (autobiography, 1978), Katy, A Fight For Life, Joan Collins Beauty Book, Prime Time, Love & Desire & Hate, My Secrets, Too Damn Famous. On London, LA and NY stage in Private Lives. Video: Secrets of Fitness and Beauty (also exec. prod.)
PICTURES: I Believe in You (debut, 1951), Lady Godiva Rides Again, Judgment Deferred, Decameron Nights, Cosh Boy, The Square Ring, Turn the Key Softly, Our Girl Friday (Adventures of Sadie), The Good Die Young, Land of the Pharaohs, Virgin Queen, Girl in the Red Velvet Swing, Opposite Sex, Sea Wife, Island in the Sun, Wayward Bus, Stopover Tokyo, The Bravados, Rally Round the Flag Boys, Seven Thieves, Esther and the King, Road to Hong Kong, Warning Shot, Can Hieronymus Merkin Ever Forget Mercy Humppe and Find True Happiness?, If It's Tuesday This Must Be Belgium, Subterfuge, The Executioner, Up in the Cellar, Quest for Love, Inn of the Frightened People, Fear in the Night, Tales from the Crypt, Tales That Witness Madness, Dark Places, Alfie Darling, The Devil Within Her, The Bawdy Adventures of Tom Jones, Empire of the Ants, The Big Sleep, The Stud, Zero to Sixty, The Bitch, Game of Vultures, Sunburn, Homework, Nutcracker, Decadence, In the Bleak Mid-Winter, Decadence, In The Bleak Midwinter, Annie: A Royal Adventure, The Line King: Al Hirschfield, The Clandestine Marriage, The Flintstones in Viva Rock Vegas, Ozzie, Ellis in Glamourland, Cowboys for Christ.
TELEVISION: *Movies*: The Cartier Affair, The Making of a Male Model, Her Life as a Man, Paper Dolls, The Wild Women of Chastity Gulch, Drive Hard Drive Fast, Dynasty: The Reunion, Annie: A Royal Adventure, Hart to Hart: Two Harts in Three Quarters Time, Sweet Deception, These Old Broads, Marple: They Do It with Mirrors. *Mini-series*: The Moneychangers, Sins, Monte Carlo (also exec. prod.) *Series:* Dynasty (Emmy nom. 1984; Golden Globe Award 1983; 5 other nom.), Pacific Palisades, Guiding Light. *Specials*: Hansel and Gretel (Faerie Tale Theater), Mama's Back, Hidden Hollywood: Treasures from the 20th Century Fox Film Vaults (Host), Star Trek: Thirty Years and Beyond, The 100 Greatest TV Ads, Elizabeth Taylor: A Musical Celebration, Cleopatra: The Film That Changed Hollywood. Intimate Portrait: Joan Collins (tv documentary). *Guest:* More than 197 appearances.

COLLINS, LARRY
Executive. A 40-year film exhibition executive, Collins' first role was student booker with Universal Pictures in 1969 in Philadelphia. He then moved to Columbia Pictures and 20th Century Fox before switching sides to exhibition and booking films for Philadelphia-based Milgram Theatres in 1973. Five years later, he moved to Pittsburgh, becoming the head film buyer for Cinemette Theatres from 1978-1994. From there, he briefly became v.p., film at Cinema World Theatres. Collins joined the Columbus, Georgia-based Carmike Cinemas circuit, as a film buyer in 1994. After supervising bookers in selecting and placing films into Carmike's competitive and non-competitive markets, Collins was promoted to his current position as v.p., film in 2005. He and his team manage the daily theatre and projects bookings and arranges the circuit's promotional film screenings. Collins received the 2008 ShowEast's "Show E Award" for his achievements, accomplishments and dedication to the movie industry.

COLLINS, PAULINE
O.B.E. Actress. b. Exmouth, Devon, Eng., Sept. 3, 1940. m. actor John Alderton (Thomas on Upstairs, Downstairs). e. Central School of Speech and Drama. Stage debut A Gazelle in Park Lane (Windsor, 1962). Best known to U.S. audiences as Sarah in Upstairs, Downstairs.
THEATRE: Passion Flower Hotel (London debut, 1965), The Erpingham Camp, The Happy Apple, The Importance of Being Earnest, The Night I Chased the Women with an Eel, Come as You Are, Judies, Engaged, Confusions, Romantic Comedy, Woman in Mind, Shirley Valentine (in London won Olivier Award as best actress, in NY won Tony, Drama Desk and Outer Critics Circle Awards)
PICTURES: Secrets of a Windmill Girl, Shirley Valentine (Academy Award nom.; Golden Globe nom. 1990), City of Joy, My Mother's Courage, Paradise Road, Mrs. Caldicot's Cabbage War, You Will Meet a Tall Dark Stranger.
TELEVISION: *Movies:* Knockback, Flowers of the Forrest, Man and Boy, Sparkling Cyanide, What We Did on Our Holiday. *Mini-series:* The Three Musketeers, The Black Tower. *Series:* Emergency-Ward 10, The Liver Birds, No, Honestly (all with husband), Whither Shall I Wander?, Upstairs Downstairs, Wodehouse Playhouse, Little Miss (voice), Thomas and Sarah, Forever Green, Forever Green, The Ambassador, Little Grey Rabbit, Bleak House. *Guest:* More than 55 appearances.

COLLINS, STEPHEN
Actor. b. Des Moines, IA, Oct. 1, 1947. Appeared off-B'way in several Joseph Papp productions before B'way debut in Moonchildren, followed by No Sex We're British, The Ritz, Loves of Anatol, Censored Scenes from King Kong. *Off-B'way:* Twelfth Night, The Play's the Thing, Beyond Therapy, One of the Guys, The Old Boy, Putting It Together. Author of play Super Sunday (Williamstown Fest.), and novel Eye Contact (1994).
PICTURES: All the President's Men, Between the Lines, The Promise, Fedora, Star Trek: The Motion Picture, Loving Couples, Brewster's Millions, Jumpin' Jack Flash, Choke Canyon, The Big Picture, Stella, My New Gun, The First Wives Club, An Unexpected Life, Drive Me Crazy, The Commission, Blood Diamond, Because I Said So.
TELEVISION: *Movies:* Brink's: The Great Robbery, The Henderson Monster, Dark Mirror, Threesome, Weekend War, A Woman Scorned: The Betty Broderick Story, Her Final Fury: Betty Broderick--The Last Chapter, The Disappearance of Nora, Barbara Taylor Bradford's Remember, A Family Divided, On Seventh Avenue, The Babysitter's Seduction, An Unexpected Family, As Time Runs Out, Every Second Counts. *Mini-series:* The Rhinemann Exchange, Hold the Dream, Inside the Third Reich, Chiefs, The Two Mrs. Grenvilles (Emmy nom. 1987), A Woman Named Jackie, Scarlett. *Series:* Tales of the Gold Monkey, Tattinger's (revamped as Nick & Hillary), Working it Out, 7th Heaven. *Guest:* More than 77 appearances.

COLTRANE, ROBBIE
Actor. b. Glasgow, Scotland, 1950. Ent. ind. 1977.
THEATRE: San Quentin theatre workshop, Oxford Theatre Group, Citizens Theatre, Traverse Theatre, Borderline Theatre, Hampstead Theatre, Bush Theatre; one man shows: Your Obedient Servant, Mistero Buffo.
PICTURES: Bad Business (dir.); Flash Gordon, Death Watch, Subway Riders, Britannia Hospital, Scrubbers, Ghost Dance, Krull, National Lampoon's European Vacation, Caravaggio, Defence of the Realm, Chinese Boxes, The Supergrass, Mona Lisa, Eat the Rich, Bert Rigby You're a Fool, Wonderland (The Fruit Machine), Let It Ride, Henry V, Slipstream, Nuns on the Run, Perfectly Normal, The Pope Must Die, Triple Bogey on a Par 5 Hole, Oh What a Night, The Adventures of Huck Finn, Goldeneye, Buddy, Montana, Frogs for Snakes, The World Is Not Enough, On the Nose, Delaney's Flutter, Harry Potter and the Sorcerer's Stone, From Hell, Harry Potter and the Chamber of Secrets, Van Helsing, Harry Potter and the Prisoner of Azkaban, Ocean's Twelve, Harry Potter and the Goblet of Fire, Provoked: A True Story, Alex Rider: Operation Stormbreaker, Harry Potter and the Order of the Phoenix, Gooby (voice), The Brothers Bloom, The Tale of Despereaux, Harry Potter and the Half-Blood Prince, Sweet Baby Jesus, Harry Potter and the Deathly Hallows: Part I, Harry Potter and the Deathly Hallows: Part II.
TELEVISION: *Movies:* Kevin Turvey: The Man Behind the Green Door, The Crystal Cube, Blackadder's Christmas Carol, Danny the Champion of the World, The Bogie Man, In Search of James Bond with Jonathan Ross, The Ebb-Tide, Alice in Wonderland, Comic Relief 2003: The Big Hair Do, The Planman (also exec. prod.), Pride, Cracker. *Mini-series:* The Lost Tribe. *Series:* Kick Up The Eighties (also writer), Laugh??? I Nearly Paid My

Licence Fee (various roles, writer), Tutti Frutti, The Comic Strip Presents..., Cracker, Murderland. *Guest:* More than 106 appearances.

COLUMBUS, CHRIS

Producer, Director, Writer. b. Spangler, PA, Sept.10, 1959. Grew up in Ohio. Started making short super 8 films in high school, studied screenwriting at New York U. Film Sch., graduated 1980. Sold first s.p., Jocks, while at college. Wrote for and developed TV cartoon series, Galaxy High School.
PICTURES: *Writer:* Reckless, Gremlins, The Goonies, Young Sherlock Holmes, Little Nemo: Adventures in Slumberland (co-s.p.). Fantastic Four (also prod.), Christmas with the Kranks. *Director:* Adventures in Babysitting (debut, 1987), Heartbreak Hotel (also s.p.), Home Alone, Only the Lonely (also s.p.), Home Alone 2: Lost in New York, Mrs. Doubtfire, Nine Months (also co-prod.), Jingle All the Way, (prod. only), Stepmom, Bicentennial Man, Monkeybone (exec. prod.), Harry Potter and the Philosopher's Stone (also exec. prod.), Harry Potter and the Sorcerer's Stone, Harry Potter and the Chamber of Secrets, Harry Potter and the Prisoner of Azkaban, Christmas with the Kranks, (also prod.), Cheaper by the Dozen, Harry Potter and the Goblet of Fire (exec. prod.), NFL Dad, Will Sebastian (prod.), Rent (also prod./writer), Sub-Mariner (also prod.), Slanted and Enchanted (also prod.), Night at the Museum (prod.), 4: Rise of the Silver Surfer (exec. prod.), I Love You, Beth Cooper (also prod.), Night at the Museum: Battle of the Smithsonian (prod. only), Percy Jackson and the Lightning Thief.
TELEVISION: *Series:* Amazing Stories, Twilight Zone, Alfred Hitchcock Presents, Galaxy High School.

COMBS, HOLLY MARIE

Actress. b. San Diego, California, December 3, 1973.
PICTURES: Walls of Glass, Sweet Hearts Dance, New York Stories, Born on the Fourth of July, Simple Men, Dr. Giggles, A Chain of Desire, A Reason to Believe.
TELEVISION: *Movies:* A Perfect Stranger, Sins of Silence, Love's Deadly Triangle : The Texas Cadet Murder, Daughters, See Jane Date, Point of Entry, Mistresses (also writer, co-prod.). *Series:* Picket Fences, Charmed.

COMSTOCK, BETH

Executive. e. undergraduate degree in biology, College of William and Mary. Comstock began her career in television in Virginia, and early in her career she held a succession of publicity positions at CBS Entertainment, Turner Broadcasting, and NBC. From 1993-1996 Comstock was v.p. NBC News Communications and from 1996-1998 was senior v.p., Communications at NBC. GE CEO Jack Welch lured Comstock to GE, and in 1998, GE made her a company officer, at which time she was named GE's vice president of Corporate Communications. Since 2003, Comstock had served as corporate vice president and chief marketing officer of General Electric. In December 2005, Comstock was tapped to lead NBC Universal's digital efforts and was named president of Digital Media and Market Development. In this role she was accountable for driving NBC Universal's digital strategy and leading the company's content and distribution efforts to capitalize on new and emerging digital platforms. In Feb. 2007, new NBC Universal CEO Jeff Zucker promoted Comstock to her current position, pres., NBC Universal Integrated Media.

CONDON, BILL

Director, Writer. b. New York, NY, Oct. 22, 1955. e. Columbia U.
PICTURES: Dead Kids (s.p. only), Strange Invaders (s.p. only), Sister Sister, F/X 2 (s.p. only), Candyman: Farewell to the Flesh (dir. only), Gods and Monsters (Academy Award for s.p. adapt.; WGA nom. 1999), The Devil and Daniel Webster (s.p. only), Chicago: The Musical (s.p. only Academy Award nom.; Golden Globe nom.; WGA nom. 2003), Kinsey (dir., s.p. WGA nom. 2005), Dreamgirls (DGA nom. 2007), Salmon Fishing in the Yemen (dir.).
TELEVISION: *Movies:* Murder 101, White Lie, Dead in the Water, Deadly Relations, The Man Who Wouldn't Die (also co-exec. prod.). *Series:* The Big C. *Special:* The 81st Annual Academy Awards (exec. prod., Emmy nom. 2009).

CONDON, CHRIS J.

Producer, Director, Motion Equipment Designer. b. Chicago, IL, Dec. 7, 1922. e. Davidson Inst., U. of Southern California. U.S. Air Force 1943-46. Founded Century Precision Optics, 1948. Designed Athenar telephoto lenses, Century Super wide-angle lenses and Duplikins. Co-founded StereoVision International, Inc. 1969 specializing in films produced in new 3-D process. Member SMPTE. Lecturer and consultant on motion picture optics and 3-D motion picture technology. CTO of Hoolywood Films (3-D division).
PICTURES: The Wild Ride, Jaws 3-D, Surfer Girls, Airline, The New Dimensions.

CONNELLY, JENNIFER

Actress. b. New York, NY, Dec. 12, 1970. e. Yale, Stamford U.
PICTURES: Once Upon a Time in America (debut, 1983), Creepers, Labyrinth, Seven Minutes in Heaven, Etoile, Some Girls, The Hot Spot, Career Opportunities, The Rocketeer, Of Love and Shadows, Higher Learning, Mulholland Falls, Far Harbor, Inventing the Abbotts, Dark City, Waking the Dead, Requiem for a Dream, Pollock, A Beautiful Mind (Academy Award, BAFTA Award, Golden Globe Award, SAG nom. 2002), Hulk, House of Sand & Fog, Dark Water, Brideshead Revisited, The Berkeley Connection, Little Children, Blood Diamond, Reservation Road, Inkheart, He's Just Not That Into You, The Day the Earth Stood Still, 9 (voice), Creation, What's Wrong with Virginia.
TELEVISION: *Movie:* The Heart of Justice. *Series:* The $treet. *Guest:* More than 64 appearances.

CONNERY, SIR SEAN

Actor. r.n. Thomas Sean Connery. b. Edinburgh, Scotland, Aug. 25, 1930. Worked as a lifeguard and a model before landing role in chorus of London prod. of South Pacific, 1953. Prod. dir., The Bowler and the Bonnet (film doc.), I've Seen You Cut Lemons (London stage). Director of Tantallon Films Ltd. (First production: Something Like the Truth). Recipient of Golden Globe Henrietta Award 1972; Cecil B. Demille Award, 1996.
PICTURES: No Road Back (debut, 1957), Time Lock, Hell Drivers, Action of the Tiger, Another Time Another Place, Darby O'Gill and the Little People, Tarzan's Greatest Adventure, Frightened City, On the Fiddle, The Longest Day, Dr. No, From Russia With Love, Marnie, Woman of Straw, Goldfinger, The Hill, Thunderball, A Fine Madness, You Only Live Twice, Shalako, The Molly Maguires, The Red Tent, The Anderson Tapes, Diamonds Are Forever, The Offence, Zardoz, Murder on the Orient Express, The Terrorists, The Wind and the Lion, The Man Who Would Be King, Robin and Marian, The Next Man, A Bridge Too Far, The Great Train Robbery, Meteor, Cuba, Outland, Time Bandits, Wrong Is Right, Five Days One Summer, Sword of the Valiant, Never Say Never Again, Highlander, The Name of the Rose, The Untouchables (Academy Award, best supporting actor, 1987), The Presidio, Memories of Me (cameo), Indiana Jones and the Last Crusade, Family Business, The Hunt for Red October, The Russia House, Robin Hood: Prince of Thieves (cameo), Highlander 2: The Quickening, Medicine Man (also exec. prod.), Rising Sun (also exec. prod.), A Good Man in Africa, Just Cause (also exec. prod.), First Knight, Dragonheart (voice), The Rock (also exec. prod.), Playing by Heart, The Avengers, Entrapment (also prod.), Finding Forrester, The League of Extraordinary Gentlemen (also exec. prod), Sir Billi (voice, prod.).
TELEVISION: *Movies:* Requiem for a Heavyweight, Anna Christie, The Square Ring, Boy with the Meataxe, Women in Love, The Crucible, Riders to the Sea, Colombe, Without the Grail, Adventure Story, Macbeth, Anna Karenina, Male of the Species. *Mini-series:* An Age of Kings. *Series:* Adventure Story. *Guest:* More than 194 appearances.

CONNICK, HARRY, JR.

Musician, Actor. b. New Orleans, LA, Sept. 11, 1967. Began performing with Bourbon Street jazz combos at age 6. Studied classical piano. Albums: Harry Connick, 20, When Harry Met Sally..., Lofty's Roach Souffle, We Are in Love (Grammy Award, 1991), Blue Light Red Light, 25, Eleven, When My Heart Finds Christmas, She, Star Turtle. Acting debut in Memphis Belle (1990). B'way debut 1990 in An Evening with Harry Connick, Jr.
PICTURES: When Harry Met Sally... (special musical performances and arrangements), Memphis Belle, The Godfather Part III (performed theme song), Little Man Tate, Sleepless in Seattle (performed song), Copycat, Independence Day, Excess Baggage, Hope Floats, The Iron Giant (voice), Wayward Son, My Dog Skip (voice), The Simian Line, Life Without Dick, Basic, Mickey, Bug, P.S. I Love You, New in Town.
TELEVISION: *Movies:* South Pacific, Living Proof. *Specials:* Swingin' Out Live, The New York Big Band Concert, The Harry Connick Jr. Christmas Special, Pistol Pete: The Life and Times of Pete Maravich, Nobel Peace Prize Concert (performer), Great Performances (Emmy nom. 1991, Emmy Award 2004). *Mini-series:* Jazz (voice). *Series:* Will and Grace. *Guest:* More than 95 appearances.

CONNORS, MIKE

Actor. r.n. Krekor Ohanian. b. Fresno, CA, Aug. 15, 1925. e. UCLA. Film debut in Sudden Fear (1952) as Touch Connors.
PICTURES: Sudden Fear (debut, 1952), Sky Commando, 49th Man, Island in the Sky, Day of Triumph, Five Guns West, The Twinkle in God's Eye, Oklahoma Woman, Swamp Woman, The Day the World Ended, The Ten Commandments, Flesh and Spur, Shake Rattle and Rock, Voodoo Woman, Live Fast Die Young, Suicide Battalion, Panic Button, Seed of Violence, Good Neighbor Sam, Where Love Has Gone, Harlow, Situation Hopeless–But Not Serious, Stagecoach, Kiss the Girls and Make Them Die, Avalanche Express, Nightkill, Too Scared to Scream, Fist Fighter, Friend to Friend, Public Enemy #2, Ciudad Baja, Wild Bill: Hollywood Maverick, Gideon.
TELEVISION: *Movies:* High Midnight, Beg Borrow or Steal, The Killer Who Wouldn't Die, Revenge for a Rape, Long Journey Back, The Death of Ocean View Park, Casino, Hart to Hart Returns, James Dean: Race With Destiny. *Mini-series*: War and Remembrance. *Series:* Tightrope, Mannix (4 Emmy noms.; Golden Globe Award 1970, 5 more noms.), Today's FBI, Crimes of the Century (host), Disney's Hercules. *Guest:* More than 101 appearances.

CONRAD, ROBERT

Actor, Director. r.n. Konrad Robert Falkowski. b. Chicago, IL, March 1, 1935. e. public schools, Northwestern U. Prof. debut, nightclub singer. Formed Robert Conrad Productions, 1966 (later A Shane Productions, then Black Sheep Productions).
PICTURES: Thundering Jets (debut, 1958), Palm Springs Weekend, Young Dillinger, The Bandits (also dir.), Murph the Surf (Live a Little Steal a Lot), The Lady in Red, Wrong Is Right, Moving Violations, Uncommon Courage, Jingle All the Way, New Jersey Turnpikes, Jingle All the Way, Garbage Day (short).
TELEVISION: *Movies*: Weekend of Terror, The D.A.: Conspiracy to Kill, Five Desperate Women, Adventures of Nick Carter, The Last Day, Smash-Up on Interstate 5, Wild Wild West Revisited, Breaking Up Is Hard To Do, More Wild Wild West, Coach of the Year, Will: G. Gordon Liddy, Confessions of a Married Man, Hard Knox, Two Fathers' Justice, Assassin, Charley Hannah, The Fifth Missile, One Police Plaza, High Mountain Rangers (also dir., co-story), Glory Days (also dir.), Anything to Survive, Mario and the Mob, Sworn to Vengeance, Two Fathers: Justice for the Innocent, Search and Rescue. *Mini-series:* Centennial. *Series*: Hawaiian Eye, Wild Wild West, The D.A., Assignment Vienna, Baa Baa Black Sheep, Black Sheep Squadron (Golden Globe nom. 1978) The Duke, A Man Called Sloane, High Mountain Rangers, Jesse Hawkes, High Sierra Search and Rescue. *Guest:* More than 94 appearances.

CONROY, KATHLEEN M.

Executive. b. Minneapolis, MN, April 20, 1956. e. B.A. in Political Science from Univ. of Minnesota, Minneapolis, MN, 1978. Studied public relations in the Master of Business Communications program at The University of St. Thomas in St.Paul, MN, 1986-1990. Graduated from the Institutes for Organization Management, Association Management, at the University of Notre Dame, South Bend, IN, June 1996. Held senior-level marketing and communications positions at a variety of trade associations and professional societies. Served as executive dir. of Color Marketing Group in Alexandria, VA, 2005-2006. Joined the National Association of Theatre Owners (NATO) in May 2007; named NATO's Executive Director in July 2007. Member of the American Society of Association Executives (ASAE), 1980 to present. Earned the Certified Association Executive (CAE) designation from ASAE in 1995.

CONSTANTINE, MICHAEL

Actor. b. Reading, PA, May 22, 1927.
PICTURES: The Hustler, Hawaii, Skidoo, Justine, If It's Tuesday This Must Be Belgium, Peeper, Voyage of the Damned, The North Avenue Irregulars, Pray for Death, In the Mood, Prancer, Dead Fall, My Life, The Juror, Stephen King's Thinner, My Big Fat Greek Wedding.
TELEVISION: *Movies:* Suddenly Single, Deadly Harvest, Say Goodbye Maggie Cole, The Bait, Death Cruise, The Night That Panicked America, Conspiracy of Terror, Wanted: The Sundance Woman, The Pirate, Crisis in Mid-Air, The Love Tapes, Evita Peron, My Palikari, Finder of Lost Loves, Leap of Faith, Because Mommy Works, WWIII. *Mini-series:* 79 Park Avenue, Roots: The Next Generations. *Series:* Hey Landlord, Room 222 (Emmy Award, 1970, 1 other nom.; Golden Globe nom. 1971), Sirota's Court (Golden Globe nom. 1977), My Big Fat Greek Life. *Guest:* More than 147 appearances.

CONTI, BILL

Composer. b. Providence, RI, April 13, 1942. Studied piano at age 7, forming first band at age 15. e. Louisiana State U., Juilliard School of Music. Moved to Italy with jazz trio where scored first film, Candidate for a Killing. Was music supvr. on Blume in Love for Paul Mazursky.
PICTURES: Harry and Tonto, Next Stop Greenwich Village, Rocky (Academy Award nom.; Golden Globe nom. 1977), Handle With Care, Slow Dancing in the Big City, An Unmarried Woman (Golden Globe nom. 1979), F.I.S.T., The Big Fix, Paradise Alley, Uncle Joe Shannon, Rocky II, A Man a Woman and A Bank, Goldengirl, The Seduction of Joe Tynan, The Formula, Gloria, Private Benjamin, Carbon Copy, Victory, For Your Eyes Only (Academy Award nom.; Golden Globe nom. 1982), I The Jury, Rocky III, Neighbors, Split Image, Bad Boys, That Championship Season, Unfaithfully Yours, The Right Stuff (Academy Award, 1984), Mass Appeal, The Karate Kid, The Bear, Big Trouble, Gotcha, Beer, Nomads, F/X, The Karate Kid II, A Prayer for the Dying, Masters of the Universe, Baby Boom, Broadcast News, For Keeps, A Night in the Life of Jimmy Reardon, Betrayed, Cohen and Tate, Big Blue, Lean On Me, The Karate Kid Part III, Lock Up, The Fourth War, Backstreet Dreams, Rocky V, Necessary Roughness, Year of the Gun, A Captive in the Land, The Adventures of Huck Finn, Bound By Honor, By the Sword, Rookie of the Year, Yellowstone, 8 Seconds, The Next Karate Kid, Bushwhacked, The Scout, Spy Hard, Wrongfully Accused, The Real Macaw, The Thomas Crown Affair, Sugihara: Conspiracy of Goodness, Tortilla Soup, Boys on the Run, G, Avenging Angelo, Soul Plane, Rocky Balboa, The King of Kong: A Fistful of Quarters (doc., soundtrack writer), Moonlight Blade, A Woman Is a Woman (music supv.), A Woman Is a Woman (music supv.), Small Town Hero, Sensual (music supv.).
TELEVISION: Kill Me If You Can, Stark, North and South, The Pirate, Smashup on Interstate 5, Papa & Me, Napoleon and Josephine, Murderers Among Us: The Simon Wiesenthal Story, American Tragedy, Judas, Coast to Coast, Letting Go, Dynasty: The Making of a Guilty Pleasure (show theme comp.). *Series themes:* Cagney and Lacy, Dynasty, Falcon Crest, The Colbys, Kenya, Heartbeat, Lifestyles of the Rich and Famous, Emerald Point N.A.S., Dolphin Cove, The Elite, Instant Recall, Inside Edition. *Specials:* Annual Academy Awards (composer: 15 shows, 3 Emmy Awards, 10 Emmy noms.).

CONTI, TOM

Actor. b. Paisley, Scotland, Nov. 22, 1941. Trained at Royal Scottish Academy of Music, Glasgow. Did repertory work in Scotland before London stage debut appearing with Paul Scofield in Savages, 1973.
THEATRE: London: Devil's Disciple, Whose Life Is It Anyway?, They're Playing Our Song, Romantic Comedy, Two Into One, Italian Straw Hat, Jeffrey Bernard is Unwell, Present Laughter. Director: Before the Party, The Housekeeper. NY: Whose Life Is It Anyway? (Tony Award, 1979), Last Licks (dir.), Present Laughter (dir.), Chapter Two.
PICTURES: Galileo (debut, 1975), Eclipse, The Duellists, The Haunting of Julia (Full Circle), Merry Christmas Mr. Lawrence, Reuben Reuben (Academy Award nom.; Golden Globe nom. 1984), American Dreamer, Miracles, Saving Grace, Beyond Therapy, The Gospel According to Vic, That Summer of White Roses, Shirley Valentine, Someone Else's America, Subdown, Something to Believe In, Out of Control, Don't Go Breaking My Heart, The Enemy, Rabbit Fever, Paid, Derailed, O Jerusalem, The Tempest, A Closed Book.
TELEVISION: *Movies:* Mother of Men (1959), Treats, The Wall, Nazi Hunter: The Beate Klarsfeld Story (Golden Globe nom. 1987), The Quick and the Dead, If It's a Man, Hang Up!, Roman Holiday, The Dumb Waiter, Faerie Tale Theater (The Princess and the Pea), Fatal Judgment, The Norman Conquests: Table Manners, The Norman Conquests: Living Together, The Norman Conquests: Round and Round the Garden, Blade on the Feather, Voices Within: The Lives of Truddi Chase, The Inheritance. *Mini-series:* The Flight of the Heron, Fall of Eagles, Madame Bovary, I Was A Rat, The Glittering Prizes. *Series:* Adam Smith, Sam, The Wright Verdicts,Deadline, Andy Pandy (narrator), DNA, Donovan, Deeply Irresponsible, Four Seasons. *Guest:* More than 81 appearances.

CONVERSE, FRANK

Actor. b. St. Louis, MO, May 22, 1938. e. Carnegie-Mellon. Early training on stage in New York. Active in repertory theatres. Two seasons with Amer. Shakespeare Fest.
THEATRE: The Seagull, Death of a Salesman, Night of the Iguana, A Man for All Seasons, The House of Blue Leaves, First One Asleep Whistle, Arturo Ui, The Philadelphia Story (1980 revival), Brothers, A Streetcar Named Desire (1988 revival), Design for Living, The Crucible, Hobson's Choice, The Ride Down Mount Morgan, etc.
PICTURES: Hurry Sundown, Hour of the Gun, The Rowdyman, The Pilot, The Bushido Blade, Spring Fever, Everybody Wins, Primary Motive.
TELEVISION: *Movies:* Dr. Cook's Garden, A Tattered Web, In Tandem, Killer on Board, Cruise Into Terror, Sgt. Matlovich vs. the U.S. Air Force, Columbo: Requiem for a Falling Star, Chelsea D.H.O., Voyage Into Evil, Steeletown, A Movie Star's Daughter, Marilyn: The Untold Story, The Miracle of Kathy Miller, Anne of Green Gables—The Sequel, Mystery at Fire Island, Momma the Detective, Uncle Tom's Cabin, Home at Last, Alone in the Neon Jungle, Voices Within: The Lives of Truddi Chase, Brother Future, Our Town. *Series:* As the World Turns, All My Children, Coronet Blue, N.Y.P.D., Movin' On, The Family Tree, Dolphin Cove, One Life to Live, Law & Order. *Guest:* More than 79 appearances.

CONWAY, KEVIN

Actor. b. New York, NY, May 29, 1942.
THEATRE: Actor: One Flew Over the Cuckoo's Nest, When You Comin' Back Red Ryder? (Obie & Drama Desk Awards), Of Mice and Men, Moonchildren, Life Class, Saved, The Elephant Man, Other Places, King John (NYSF), Other People's Money (Outer Critics Circle Award; also L.A. prod.), The Man Who Fell in Love with His Wife, Ten Below, On the Waterfront. Director: Mecca, Short Eyes (revival), One Act Play Fest (Lincoln Center), The Milk Train Doesn't Stop Here Anymore (revival), The Elephant Man (tour), Other People's Money (Chicago, L.A. & S.F.).
PICTURES: Believe in Me, Portnoy's Complaint, Slaughterhouse Five, Shamus, F.I.S.T., Paradise Alley, The Fun House, Flashpoint, Homeboy, The Sun and the Moon (dir., prod.), Funny Farm, One Good Cop, Rambling Rose, Jennifer Eight, Gettysburg, The Quick and the Dead, Lawnmower Man II, Looking for Richard, The Stupids, Mercury Rising, The Confession, Two Family House, Thirteen Days, Joan of Arc: Virgin Warrior, Black Knight, Gods and Generals, Invincible.
TELEVISION: *Movies:* Johnny We Hardly Knew Ye, The Deadliest Season, Rage of Angels, The Lathe of Heaven, Attack on Fear, Something About Amelia, Jesse, When Will I Be Loved?, Breaking the Silence, The Whipping Boy, Net Worth, Ronnie and Julie, Calm at Sunset, Sally Hemmings: An American Scandal. *Mini-series:* Streets of Laredo, Mark Twain. *Series:* One Life to Live, Oz, The Outer Limits, The Bronx Is Burning, The Black

Donnellys. *Specials:* The Scarlet Letter, The Elephant Man, Calm at Sunset. *Guest:* More than 53 appearances.

CONWAY, TIM

Actor. b. Willoughby, OH, Dec. 15, 1933. e. Bowling Green State U. After 2 yrs. Army service joined KYW-TV in Cleveland as writer-director and occasional performer. Comedienne Rose Marie discovered him and arranged audition for the Steve Allen Show on which he became regular. In 1962 signed for McHale's Navy, series. Also has done night club appearances.
PICTURES: McHale's Navy (debut, 1964), McHale's Navy Joins the Air Force, The World's Greatest Athlete, The Apple Dumpling Gang, Gus, The Shaggy D.A., Billion Dollar Hobo, The Apple Dumpling Gang Rides Again, The Prize Fighter, The Private Eyes (also co-s.p.), Cannonball Run II, The Longshot, Dear God, Speed 2: Cruise Control, Air Bud: Golden Receiver, View From the Swing.
TELEVISION: *Movies:* Roll Freddy Roll, Hermie: A Common Caterpillar, Hermie & Friends. *Series:* The Steve Allen Show, McHale's Navy (Emmy nom. 1963), Rango, The Tim Conway Show (1970), The Tim Conway Comedy Hour, The Carol Burnett Show (3 Emmy Awards as actor: 1973, 1977, 1978; Emmy Award as writer: 1976; Golden globe Award 1976; Golden Globe nom. 1977), The Tim Conway Show (1980-81), Ace Crawford: Private Eye, Tim Conway's Funny America, The College of Comedy with Alan King, Coach (Emmy Award 1996 as guest), Hercules (voice), SpongeBob SquarePants, On the Spot, Yes, Dear, 30 Rock (Emmy Award 2008 as guest). *Guest:* More than 138 appearances.

COOGAN, KEITH

Actor. b. Palm Springs, CA, Jan. 13, 1970. e. Santa Monica City Col. Grandson of late actor Jackie Coogan. Formerly acted as Keith Mitchell. Appeared in shorts All Summer in a Day and The Great O'Grady.
PICTURES: The Fox and the Hound (voice), Adventures in Babysitting, Hiding Out, Under the Boardwalk, Cousins, Cheetah, Book of Love, Toy Soldiers, Don't Tell Mom the Babysitter's Dead, Forever, In the Army Now, Life 101, Eddie (co-writer), The Power Within, A Reason to Believe, Downhill Willy, Ivory Tower, Dreamers, Python, ...Or Forever Hold Your Peace, Just a Little Harmless Sex, Soulkeeper.
TELEVISION: *Movies:* A Question of Love, Million Dollar Infield, Kid With the Broken Halo, A Town's Revenge, Over the Limit, Battered, Memorial Day, Spooner, Python. *Series:* The MacKenzies of Paradise Cove, The Waltons, Gun Shy, Crafty. *Specials:* Wrong Way Kid, The Treasure of Alpheus T. Winterborn, Rascal, Over the Limit, Spooner.

COOK, RACHAEL LEIGH

Actress. b. Minneapolis, MN, Oct. 4, 1979.
PICTURES: The Baby-Sitters Club, Tom and Huck, 26 Summer Street, Carpool, The House of Yes, The Eighteenth Angel, Strike, The Naked Man, Living Out Loud, The Hi-Line, The Bumblebee Flies Anyway, She's All That, Texas Rangers, Anti-Trust, Tangled, Josie and the Pussycats, Get Carter, Blow Dry, Texas Rangers, Sally, 29 Palms, Scorched, Tempo, Bookies, Stateside, The Big Empty, My First Wedding, Nancy Drew, The Final Season, Blonde Ambition, The Lodger, Bob Funk, Falling Up, The Family Tree, Broken Kingdom (also exec. prod.), Kerosene Cowboys.
TELEVISION: *Movies:* The Defenders: Payback, Country Justice, True Women, Fearless, Robot Chicken: Star Wars Episode II (voices). *Mini-series:* Into the West. *Series:* Batman Beyond, Las Vegas, Due to Constraints of Time and Budget (voice), Robot Chicken, Titan Maximum, Psych. *Guest:* More than 63 appearances.

COOK, RICHARD

Executive. b. Bakersfield, CA, Aug. 20, 1950.e. Degree in political science, USC. Began career as a ride operator at Disneyland, 1970. Disneyland sales rep. & manager of sales, 1971-76; manager, pay TV and non-theatrical releases, The Disney Channel, 1977-80; asst. domestic sales mgr., v.p. & general sales mgr., senior v.p., domestic dist., Buena Vista Pictures, 1980-87; president and head of dist. & mktg., Buena Vista Pictures Distribution, 1988. He established Buena Vista as a pioneer in new methods of film delivery, helped prohibit paid screen advertising in theatres exhibiting products from any of the Disney Studios' banners; promoted restoration of the classic movie palace and award-winning landmark, the El Capitan, 1989-91; and is noted for spectacular showmanship in launching new films with live stage shows, parades and gala outdoor premieres. In 1994, Cook assumed the additional responsibility of film marketing when he was promoted to president, Buena Vista Pictures Distribution and Marketing. Cook was promoted to chairman of The Walt Disney Studios Motion Picture Group in 1996, and became chairman of The Walt Disney Studios in 2002. He then oversaw the development, production, worldwide distribution and marketing for all live-action and animated films released under the Walt Disney Pictures, Touchstone Pictures and Hollywood Pictures banners. He was also responsible for Disney's worldwide home entertainment operations under Buena Vista Home Entertainment and Buena Vista Home Entertainment International, as well as the Studio's legal and business affairs departments. Under his leadership, the studio has been the leading domestic distributor for seven of the last nine years with box office receipts in excess of one billion dollars each year. Since 1990, the Studio has released 34 films that have grossed more than $100 million each domestically. In home entertainment, Cook spearheaded the highly successful launch of the "Disney DVD" brand, then consistently broke industry records with hit video and DVD releases including Toy Story, Toy Story 2, The Sixth Sense, Pearl Harbor, and Monsters, Inc. Cook has been a USC trustee since 1998 and has served as president of the USC Alumni Association. He is a member of the Academy of Motion Picture Arts & Sciences; was pres. of The Chandler School and is now president of the Flintridge Preparatory School Board of Trustees. He sits on the board of directors for Verdugo Hills Hospital, the Will Rogers Foundation, and the Foundation of Motion Picture Pioneers. The Freedoms Foundation of Valley Forge awarded him the prestigious George Washington Medal of Freedom. Cook resigned from the Walt Disney Company in September 2009.

COOLIDGE, MARTHA

Director, Writer, Producer. b. New Haven, CT, Aug. 17, 1946. e. Rhode Island Sch. of Design. NYU Inst. of Film and TV grad. sch. Dir. short films while in school. Wrote and prod. daily children's tv show Magic Tom in Canada Worked on commercials and political doc. film crews. Prod., dir. and writer of docs. which have won festival awards, including Passing Quietly Through; David: Off and On (American Film Fest.), Old Fashioned Woman (CINE Golden Eagle Award, Blue Ribbon Award, American film festival), Bimbo (short), Magic Tom in Canada. First feature film Not a Pretty Picture (won Blue Ribbon Award, Amer. Film Fest.) Helped start assn. of Indep. Video and Filmmakers, Inc. As an AFI/Academy Intern worked with Robert Wise on his film Audrey Rose, 1976. Wrote orig. story that was filmed as the The Omega Connection. DGA, member of bd. of dirs.; WIF, member bd. of dirs. Acted in film Beverly Hills Cop III. Received DGA Award: Robert B. Aldrich Achievement, 1998.
PICTURES: Not a Pretty Picture, The City Girl, Valley Girl, Joy of Sex, Real Genius, Plain Clothes, Rambling Rose (IFP Spirit Award, 1991), Lost in Yonkers, Angie, Three Wishes, Out to Sea, Aurora Island, The Prince and Me, Material Girls.
TELEVISION: *Movies:* Trenchcoat in Paradise, Bare Essentials, Crazy in Love, Introducing Dorothy Dandridge (Emmy nom.; DGA nom. 2000), If These Walls Could Talk 2 (DGA nom. 2001), The Flamingo Rising, The Ponder Heart, Infidelity (exec. prod.), The Twelve Days of Christmas Eve (dir.), Infidelity, Tribute, An American Girl: Chrissa Stands Strong (DGA nom. 2010). *Series:* The Twilight Zone, Sex and the City, Sledge Hammer (pilot), House and Home (pilot), Leap Years, Related.

COONEY, JOAN GANZ

Executive, Producer. b. Phoenix, AZ, Nov. 30, 1929. e. U. of Arizona. After working as a reporter in Phoenix, moved to NY in 1953 where she wrote soap-opera summaries at NBC. Then was publicist for U.S. Steel Hour. Became producer of live weekly political TV show Court of Reason (Emmy Award) and documentaries (Poverty, Anti-Poverty and the Poor) before founding Children's Television Workshop (renamed Sesame Workshop) and Sesame Street in 1969. She has served on the boards of Johnson & Johnson, The Metropolitan Life Ins. Co., the Museum of Television and Radio & the New York and Presbyterian Hospital, Inc. She is a Life Trustee of the National Child Labor Committee and of WNET, Channel 13. Her programs (Sesame Street, The Electric Company, 3-2-1 Contact, Square One TV, Ghostwriter, CRO, Big Bag and Dragon Tales) have achieved 79 Emmy Awards. Cooney has received numerous awards including a Daytime Emmy for Lifetime Achievement in 1989, and in 1990 was inducted into the Television Academy Hall of Fame. Additionally, she received the Founders Award from the International Council of the National Academy of Television Arts and Sciences. She was awarded the Presidential Medal of Freedom in 1995 and was inducted into the National Women's Hall of Fame in 1998. She currently is chmn. of the Exec. Committee on the Sesame Workshop Bd. of Trustees.
TELEVISION: *Series:* Sesame Street, The Electric Company, 3-2-1 Contact.

COOPER, BRADLEY

Actor. b. Philadelphia, PA, January 5, 1975. e. Georgetown U., Masters of Fine Arts, New School U.
THEATRE: *Off B'way:* Three Days of Rain.
PICTURES: Wet Hot American Summer, Wedding Crashers, Failure to Launch, The Comebacks, The Rocker, The Midnight Meat Train, Yes Man, New York, I Love You (segment), He's Just Not That Into You, The Hangover, Case 39, All About Steve, Valentine's Day, The A-Team.
TELEVISION: Movies: The Last Cowboy, I Want to Marry Ryan Banks. Series: The $treet, Touching Evil, Jack & Bobby, Alias, Kitchen Confidential, Nip/Tuck.

COOPER, HAL

Director, Performer. b. New York, NY, Feb. 22, 1923. e. U. of Michigan. m. Marta Salcido; child actor in various radio prog. starting in 1932; featured Bob Emery's Rainbow House, Mutual, 1936-46; asst. dir. Dock St. Theatre, Charleston, SC, 1946-48.
TELEVISION: Your School Reporter, TV Baby Sitter, The Magic Cottage (writer, prod.). *Director:* Valiant Lady, Search for Tomorrow, Portia Faces Life, Kitty Foyle (also assoc. prod.),

Indictment (also prod.), The Happy Time (also assoc. prod.), For Better or Worse (also prod.), The Clear Horizon, Surprise Package (also assoc. prod.), Dick Van Dyke Show, The Art Linkletter Show (also prod.), The Object Is, Death Valley Days, I Dream of Jeannie, That Girl, I Spy, Hazel, Gidget, Gilligan's Island, NYPD, Mayberry, Courtship of Eddie's Father, My World and Welcome to It, The Brady Bunch, The Odd Couple, Mary Tyler Moore, All in the Family, Pop-Up Brady (doc.). *Exec. prod./Director:* Maude (2 Emmy noms.; 3 DGA noms.), Phyl and Mikky, Love, Sidney, Gimme a Break, Empty Nest, Dear John, The Powers That Be, Too Something, Something So Right.

COOPER, JACKIE

Actor, Director, Producer. b. Los Angeles, CA, Sept. 15, 1922. Began theatrical career at age of 3 as m.p. actor; was member of Our Gang comedies (first short was Boxing Gloves in 1929). First starring role in 1931 in Skippy. Worked at every major studio, always with star billing. At 20 enlisted in Navy. After three-yr. tour of duty went to N.Y. to work in live TV. Appeared in 3 plays on B'way stage and in Mr. Roberts on natl. tour and in London. Directed as well as acted in live and filmed TV. Served as v.p. in chg. of TV prod., for Screen Gems, 1964-69, when resigned to return to acting, directing, producing. 2 Emmy Awards for directing M*A*S*H and The White Shadow.
PICTURES: Fox Movietone Follies (feature debut, 1929), Sunny Side Up, Skippy (Academy Award nom. 1931), Young Donovan's Kid, Sooky, The Champ, When a Feller Needs a Friend, Divorce in the Family, Broadway to Hollywood, The Bowery, Lone Cowboy, Treasure Island, Peck's Bad Boy, Dinky, O'Shaughnessy's Boy, Tough Guy, The Devil Is a Sissy, Boy of the Streets, White Banners, Gangster's Boy, That Certain Age, Newsboys' Home, Scouts to the Rescue (serial), Spirit of Culver, Streets of New York, What a Life, Two Bright Boys, The Big Guy, The Return of Frank James, Seventeen, Gallant Sons, Life With Henry, Ziegfeld Girl, Glamour Boy, Her First Beau, Syncopation, Men of Texas, The Navy Comes Through, Where Are Your Children?, Stork Bites Man, Kilroy Was Here, French Leave, Everything's Ducky, The Love Machine, Stand Up and Be Counted (dir. only), Chosen Survivors, Superman, Superman II, Superman III, Superman IV: The Quest for Peace, Surrender, Going Hollywood: The War Years, Hollywood Chronicles.
TELEVISION: *Movies:* Shadow on the Land, Maybe I'll Come Home in the Spring, The Astronaut, The Day the Earth Moved, The Invisible Man, Mobile Two, Operation Petticoat. *Series:* People's Choice (also directed 71 episodes), Hennesey (2 Emmy nom. 1961, 1962, also dir. 91 epsiodes), Dean Martin Comedy World (host), Mobile One. *Director:* Having Babies III, Rainbow, White Mama, M*A*S*H (Emmy Award 1974), Rodeo Girl, Sex and the Single Parent, The White Shadow (Emmy Award 1978), The Ladies, Deacon Street Deer, Perfect Gentlemen, Marathon, Leave 'Em Laughing, Rosie (also prod.), Glitter, The Night They Saved Christmas, Izzy and Moe, For Jenny with Love (actor). Has appeared in 7 tv documentaries since 1990. *Guest:* More than 153 appearances.

COOPER, JEANNE

Actress. r.n. Wilma Jean Cooper. b. Taft, CA, Oct. 25, 1928. e. College of the Pacific, Pasadena Playhouse. Son is actor Corbin Bernsen. Recipient: 3 Soap Opera Update MVP Awards, Soap Opera Digest, Pasadena Playhouse Woman of the Year and Hollywood Entertainment Museum Award.
THEATRE: The Miracle Worker, Plain and Fancy, Picnic, On the Town, The Big Knife, Tonight at 8:30, Dark Side of the Moon, Plaza Suite.
PICTURES: Man From the Alamo, The Redhead From Wyoming, The Houston Story, Red Nightmare, Plunder Road, 5 Steps to Danger, The Intruder, House of Women, 13 West Street, Let No Man Write My Epitaph, The Glory Guys, Tony Rome, The Boston Strangler, There Was a Crooked Man, Kansas City Bomber, All-American Boy, Frozen Assets, The Tomorrow Man, 3 Day Test, Carpool Guy, Donna on Demand, Dead Air.
TELEVISION: *Movies:* Sweet Hostage, The San Pedro Bums, Beyond Suspicion, Gentle Ben, Gentle Ben 2: Danger on the Mountain. *Series:* Ben Casey (Emmy nom. 1962), Bracken's World, The Young and the Restless (Emmy Award 2008, 9 Emmy noms.; Lifetime Achievemant Award 2004. 1973-). *Guest:* More than 105 apearances.

COPELAND, STEWART

Composer. b. Alexandria, Egypt, July 16, 1952. Drummer and singer for The Police. Member of pop group, Animal Logic.
PICTURES: Rumble Fish (Golden Globe nom. 1984), Out of Bounds, Wall Street, Talk Radio, She's Having a Baby, See No Evil Hear No Evil, Riff-Raff, Hidden Agenda, The First Power, Men at Work, Highlander II: The Quickening, Taking Care of Business, Wide Sargasso Sea, Bank Robber, Airborne, Raining Stones, Surviving the Game, Decadence, Fresh, Rapa Nui, Silent Fall, The Girl You Want, The Pallbearer, Boys, The Leopard Son, O Que E Isso Companheiro?, Little Boy Blue, Gridlock'd, Good Burger, Welcome to Woop-Woop, Very Bad Things, Pecker, She's All That, Made Men, Simpatico, Skipped Parts, Boys and Girls, Sunset Strip, On the Line, Deuces Wild, Me and Daphne (short), I Am David, Everyone Stares: The Police Inside Out (doc. also dir., editor, prod.), Pucked. *Actor:* Urgh! A Music War, South Park: Bigger Longer and Uncut.
TELEVISION: *Movies:* White Dwarf, Tyson The Taking of Pelham One Two Three, Futuresport, Legalese, Riding the Bus with My Sister. *Series:* The Equalizer, TV 101, Afterburn, Babylon 5, The Amanda Show, Brutally Normal, Beyond the Glory, Breaking News, Dead Like Me (Emmy nom. 2004), Beyond the Glory (doc.), The Life and Times of Juniper Lee (theme composer).

COPPOLA, FRANCIS FORD

Director, Writer, Producer. b. Detroit, MI, April 7, 1939. Raised in NYC. Son of late composer Carmine Coppola. Sister is actress Talia Shire. Nephew is Nicolas Cage. e. Hofstra U, B.A., 1958; UCLA, 1958-68, M.F.A., cinema. While at UCLA was hired as asst. to Roger Corman as dialogue dir., sound man and assoc. prod. 1969; est. American Zoetrope, (later Zoetrope Studios), a prod. center in San Francisco. Publisher, City (magazine, 1975-6). Appeared in documentary Hearts of Darkness: A Filmmaker's Apocalypse. Received Directors Guild of America Lifetime Achievement Award 1998. Awarded the Irving G. Thalberg Memorial Award 2011.
PICTURES: Tonight for Sure (dir., prod.), The Playgirls and the Bellboy (co-dir., co-s.p. of addtl. sequences for U.S. version), Premature Burial (asst. dir.), Tower of London (dialog. dir.), Battle Beyond the Sun (adapt.), The Young Races (sound, 2nd unit dir.), The Terror (assoc. prod., 2nd unit dir.), Dementia 13 (dir., s.p.), Is Paris Burning? (co-s.p.), This Property Is Condemned (co-s.p.), You're a Big Boy Now (dir., s.p.), The Wild Races (2nd unit dir.), Reflections in a Golden Eye (s.p.), Finian's Rainbow (dir.), The Rain People (dir., s.p.), Patton (co-s.p.; Academy Award, 1971), THX 1138 (exec. prod.), The Godfather (dir., co-s.p.; Academy Award for Best Screenplay, Academy Award nom. 2 Golden Globe Awards, DGA Award 1973), American Graffiti (Academy Award nom. 1974, exec. prod.), The Great Gatsby (s.p.), The Conversation (2 Academy Award nom. 2 Golden Globe nom.; DGA nom. 1975, dir., co-prod., s.p.), The Godfather Part II (dir., co-s.p., prod.; 3 Academy Awards for Best Picture, Director & Screenplay, 2 Golden Globe nom.; DGA Award 1975), Apocalypse Now (3 Academy award nom. 2 Golden Globe Awards, DGA nom. 1980, dir., prod., co-s.p., cameo), The Black Stallion (exec. prod.), Kagemusha (co-exec. prod.), One From the Heart (dir., co-s.p.), Hammett (exec. prod.), The Escape Artist (co-exec. prod.), The Black Stallion Returns (exec. prod.), The Outsiders (dir.), Rumble Fish (dir., exec. prod., co-s.p.), The Cotton Club, (Golden globe nom. 1985, dir., co-s.p.), Mishima (co-exec. prod.), Peggy Sue Got Married (dir.), Gardens of Stone (dir., co-prod.), Tough Guys Don't Dance (co-exec. prod.), Lionheart (exec. prod.), Tucker: The Man and His Dream (dir.), New York Stories (Life Without Zoe; dir., co-s.p.), The Godfather Part III (2 Academy Award nom. 2 Golden Globe nom.; DGA nom. 1991, dir., co-s.p., prod.), Wind (co-exec. prod.), Bram Stoker's Dracula (dir., co-prod.), The Secret Garden (exec. prod.), Mary Shelley's Frankenstein (prod.), Don Juan DeMarco (exec. prod.), My Family/Mi Familia (exec. prod.), Haunted (co-exec. prod.), Jack, Buddy (exec. prod.), Lanai-Loa (prod.), The Rainmaker (dir., s.p.), The Third Miracle (exec. prod.), Grapefruit Miracle (prod.), Goosed (exec. prod.), The Florentine (prod.), Sleepy Hollow (exec. prod.), Grapefruit Moon (prod.), Monster (exec. prod.), Jeepers Creepers, C.Q. (exec prod.), The Two Fridas, No Such Thing (exec prod.), Pumpkin (exec prod.), Assassination Tango (prod. only), Supernova, Megalopolis, My Dark Places: An L.A. Crime Memoir (exec. prod.), Jeepers Creepers II (exec. prod.), On the Road (prod.), Kinsey (exec. prod.), Megalopolis (dir./writer), The Good Shepherd (exec. prod.), Marie-Antoinette (exec. prod.), Youth Without Youth (prod., dir., s.p.), Tetro (prod., dir., s.p.), Somewhere (exec. prod.).
TELEVISION: *Movies:* The People (exec. prod.), White Dwarf (co-prod), Tecumseh: The Last Warrior (co-exec. prod.), Dark Angel (exec. prod.), The Odyssey (Emmy Award nom. 1997, exec. prod.), Outrage (exec. prod.), Moby Dick (Emmy Award nom. 1998, exec. prod.), The Third Miracle (exec. prod.)., Dr. Jekyll & Mr. Hyde. *Series:* The Outsiders (exec. prod.), First Wave (exec. prod.), Platinum (exec. prod.), The 4400. *Special:* Rip Van Winkle (Faerie Tale Theatre; dir.).

COPPOLA, SOFIA

Director, Screenwriter, Actor, Costume Designer, Executive Producer. b. Manhattan, NY, May 12, 1971. e. Fine arts program at the California Institute of the Arts. Born the third child and only daughter of renowned director Francis Ford Coppola and Eleanor Coppola. As infant, first appeared in film in her father's production, The Godfather. Throughout childhood and teen years, sporadically acted in minor roles. Critical reviews of on-camera work led her behind the scenes, as costume designer and ultimately to directing and screenwriting. She won the Oscar for best original screenplay for the 2003 production, Lost in Translation, and garnered nominations for best director and best picture for the film.
PICTURES: *Actress:* The Godfather (debut 1972; uncredited), The Godfather: Part II (uncredited), The Outsiders, Rumble Fish, The Cotton Club, Frankenweenie (short), Peggy Sue Got Married, Anna, The Godfather: Part III, Inside Monkey Zetterland, Star Wars: Episode I-The Phantom Menace, CQ. *Costume Designer:* New York Stories (also segment writer), The Spirit of '76. *Writer:* Lick the Star (also director, producer), The Virgin Suicides (also dir.), Lost in Translation (Academy Award, 2 other noms. Best Original Screenplay, 2003; Golden Globe

Award, 1 other nom.; DGA nom. 2004 also director & producer), Marie Antoinette (also director, producer, writer), Somewhere (also prod., dir.).
TELEVISION: *Movies: Actress:* The Princess Who Had Never Laughed. *Mini-series:* The Godfather Saga (uncredited). *Series:* Producer: Hi Octane (also host). *Executive prod.:* Platinum (also creator & writer).

CORBIN, BARRY
Actor. b. Dawson County, TX, Oct. 16, 1940. e. Texas Tech. U.
PICTURES: Urban Cowboy, Stir Crazy, Any Which Way You Can, Dead and Buried, The Night the Lights Went Out in Georgia, The Best Little Whorehouse in Texas, Six Pack, Honkytonk Man, The Ballad of Gregorio Cortez, WarGames, The Man Who Loved Women, Hard Traveling, What Comes Around, My Science Project, Nothing in Common, Under Cover, Off the Mark, Permanent Record, Critters 2: The Main Course, It Takes Two, Who is Harry Crumb?, Short Time, Ghost Dad, The Hot Spot, Career Opportunities, Solo, Kiss and Tell, Curdled, Judgment Day: The Ellie Nesler Story, Held Up, Race to Space, Nobody Knows, The Journeyman, Drive-In Movie Memories, No One Can Hear You, Dunsmore, Clover Bend, Waitin' to Live, Tin Can Shinny, Molding Clay, Beautiful Dreamer, The Dukes of Hazzard, Lake City, No Country for Old Men, In the Valley of Elah, Beer for My Horses, Not Since You, That Evening Sun, Valley of the Sun, The Next Door Neighbor, Rising Stars, NoNAMES, Minuteman.
TELEVISION: *Movies:* Rage, This House Possessed, The Killing of Randy Webster, Murder in Texas, Bitter Harvest, A Few Days in Weasel Creek, Fantasies, Prime Suspect, Travis McGee, Flight #90: Disaster on the Potomac, The Jesse Owens Story, Fatal Vision, I Know My First Name is Steven, Last Flight Out, The Chase, Conagher, Siringo, The Keys, Robin Cook's Virus, Moon Shot (Emmy nom. 1995), Deadly Family Secrets, My Son Is Easy, Columbo: A Trace of Murder, The Hired Heart, A Face to Kill For, Sealed with a Kiss, Hope Ranch, Alien Express, Monte Walsh, Hidden Places, Wyvern, Ben 10: Alien Swarm. *Mini-series:* The Thorn Birds, Lonesome Dove. *Series:* Boone, Spies, Northern Exposure (2 Emmy nom. 1993, 1994), The Big Easy, One Tree Hill, The Closer. *Guest:* More than 114 appearances.

CORD, ALEX
Actor. r.n. Alexander Viespi. b. Floral Park, NY, May 3, 1933. Early career in rodeo; left to become actor. Studied at Shakespeare Academy (Stratford, Conn.) and Actor's Studio (N.Y.). Spent two yrs. in summer stock; in 1961 went on tour with Stratford Shakespeare Co. Author of novel Sandsong. Co-founder of Chuckers for Charity polo team which has raised more than $2 million for various charities. Champion rodeo team roper and cutting horse rider.
PICTURES: Synanon (debut, 1965), Stagecoach, A Minute to Pray A Second to Die, The Brotherhood, Stiletto, The Last Grenade, The Dead Are Alive, Chosen Survivors, Inn of the Damned, Sidewinder One, Grayeagle, Jungle Warriors, Street Asylum, A Girl to Kill For, Naked Force, THe Naked Truth, CIA Code Name: Alexa, To Be the Best, Hologram Man, Fire from Below.
TELEVISION: *Movies:* The Scorpio Letters, Hunter's Man; Genesis II, Fire !, Beggerman Thief, Goliath Awaits, The Dirty Dozen: The Fatal Mission, University Blues, Dobe and a Company of Heroes (tv documentary, narrator). *Series:* W.E.B., Cassie & Company, Airwolf, Wild West Showdown (host). *Guest:* More than 60 appearances.

CORMAN, GENE
Producer. r.n. Eugene H. Corman. b. Detroit, MI, Sept. 24, 1927. e. Stanford U. Went to work for MCA as agent 1950-57; left to produce his first feature film, Hot Car Girl. Partner with brother Roger in Corman Company and New World Distributors. Vice pres. 20th Century Fox Television, 1983-87; exec. v.p. worldwide production, 21st Century Film Corp. Currently founder/owner of Gene Corman Productions.
PICTURES: Attack of the Giant Leeches, Not of This Earth, Blood and Steel, Valley of the Redwoods, Secret of the Purple Reef, Beast from Haunted Cave, Cat Burglar, The Intruder, Tobruk, You Can't Win Em All, Cool Breeze, Hit Man, The Slams, Von Richthofen and Brown, I Escaped from Devil's Island, Secret Invasion, Vigilante Force, F.I.S.T. (exec. prod.), The Big Red One, If You Could See What I Hear, Paradise, A Man Called Sarge, Harold Robbins' Body Parts.
TELEVISION: What's In It For Harry, A Woman Called Golda (Emmy and Christopher Awards as prod., 1982), Mary and Joseph, a Love Story, Blood Ties.

CORMAN, ROGER WILLIAM
Executive, Director, Producer, Writer, Distributor. b. Detroit, MI, April 5, 1921. e. Stanford U. 1947; Oxford U., England 1950. U.S. Navy 1944; 20th Century-Fox, production dept., 1948, story analyst 1948-49; Literary agent, 1951-52; story, s.p., assoc. prod., Highway Dragnet. Formed Roger Corman Prod. and Filmgroup. Prod. over 200 feature films and dir. over 60 of them. Formed production-releasing company, org., New World Pictures, Inc., 1970. Formed prod. co., Concorde, 1984; distribution co., New Horizons, 1985. On TV acted in film Body Bags. Recipient of LA Film Critics Award for Career Achievement, 1997. Has more than 400 project credits to his name. 2009 received Academy Honorary Award for his rich engendering of films and filmmakers.
AUTHOR: How I Made a Hundred Movies in Hollywood and Never Lost a Dime.
PICTURES: *Director:* Five Guns West (dir. debut, 1955), Apache Woman, Swamp Women, The Day the World Ended, The Oklahoma Woman, The Gunslinger, It Conquered the World, Not of This Earth, Naked Paradise (Thunder Over Hawaii), Attack of the Crab Monsters, Rock All Night, Teenage Doll, Carnival Rock, Sorority Girl, Saga of the Viking Women and Their Voyage to the Waters of the Great Sea Serpent, The Undead, War of the Satellites, She Gods of Shark Reef, Machine Gun Kelly, Teenage Caveman, I Mobster, A Bucket of Blood, The Wasp Woman, Ski Troop Attack, House of Usher, The Little Shop of Horrors, The Last Woman on Earth, Creature From the Haunted Sea, Atlas, The Pit and the Pendulum, The Intruder, The Premature Burial, Tales of Terror, Tower of London, The Raven, The Terror, X—The Man With the X Ray Eyes, The Haunted Palace, The Young Racers, The Secret Invasion, The Masque of the Red Death, Tomb of Ligeia, The Wild Angels, The St. Valentine's Day Massacre, The Trip, Target: Harry (credited as Henry Neill), Bloody Mama, Gas-s-s-s, Von Richtofen and Brown, Frankenstein Unbound (also s.p.). *Producer:* Boxcar Bertha, Big Bad Mama, Death Race 2000, Eat My Dust, Capone, Jackson County Jail, Fighting Mad, Thunder & Lightning, Grand Theft Auto, I Never Promised You A Rose Garden, Deathsport, Avalanche, Battle Beyond the Stars, St. Jack, Love Letters, Smokey Bites the Dust, Galaxy of Terror, Slumber Party Massacre Part II, Death Stalker, Barbarian Queen, Munchies, Stripped To Kill, Big Bad Mama II, Daddy's Boys, Lords of the Deep (also actor), The Terror Within, Two to Tango, Time Trackers, Heroes Stand Alone, Bloodfist, Silk 2, Edgar Allan Poe's The Masque of Red Death, Haunted Symphony, Midnight Tease, Death Race. *Exec. Prod.:* Black Scorpion, Black Scorpion 2, Not of This Earth, Not Like Us, Sweet Revenge (co-exec. prod.), The Drifter, Singles, Crime Zone, Watcher, The Lawless Land, Stripped to Kill 2, Hollywood Boulevard II, Rock and Roll High School Forever, Bloodfist II (prod.), One Night Stand, Haunted Sea, Future Fear, Falling fire, Eruption, Don't Sleep Alone, Detonator, Criminal Affairs, Club Vampire, Circuit Breaker, Born Bad, Alien Avengers II, Spacejacked, The Protector, Urban Justice, Stripteaser II, Termination Man, Starquest II, Shadowdancer, The Sea Wolf, Overdrive, My Brother's War, Macon County Jail, Knocking On Death's Door, Haunted Sea, Future Fear, Falling Fire, Eruption, Don't Sleep Alone, Criminal Fears, Club Vampire, Circuit Breaker, Born Bad, Black Thunder, Detonator, Watchers Reborn, A Very Unlucky Leprechaun, Vatican Air Two, Stray Bullet, Star Portal, Running Woman, Desert Thunder, The Haunting of Hell House, Shadow, The Protector, The Suicide Club, The Doorway, Avalanche Alley, The Arena, Raptor, Hard As Nails, Escape from Afghanistan (video), Sting of the Black Scorpion (video), Wolfhound (video), Slaughter Studios (video), Shakedown (video, Barbarian (video), Firefight, Rage and Discipline, Death Race. *Actor:* The Godfather Part II, Cannonball, The Howling, The State of Things, Swing Shift, The Silence of the Lambs, Philadelphia, Apollo 13, Some Nudity Required, Scream 3, The Independent, A Galaxy Far Far Away, Looney Tunes: Back in Action, The Manchurian Candidate, Rachel Getting Married, Road Raiders (exec. prod.).
TELEVISION: *Movies:* The Second Civil War, many others. *Series:* Roger Corman Presents (exec. prod.).

CORNFELD, STUART
Producer, Actor. b. Los Angeles, CA. e. U. of California, Berkeley. Entered America Film Institute's Center for Advanced Film Studies as producing fellow, 1975. Joined Brooksfilm as asst. to Mel Brooks on High Anxiety. Assoc. prod., History of the World Part I.
PICTURES: Fatso, The Elephant Man, (exec. prod.), Fast Times at Richmont High (actor only), National Lampoon's European Vacation (co-prod.), Girls Just Want to Have Fun (exec. prod.), The Fly, Moving, The Fly II (exec. prod.), Hider in the House (co-prod.), Darkman (actor only), Kafka, Wilder Napalm, Mimic (co-exec. prod.), Zoolander, Old School, Duplex, What Makes Sammy Run, Starsky & Hutch, Dodgeball: A True Underdog Story, Date School, Tenacious D in 'The Pick of Destiny', Blades of Glory, The Ruins, Tropic Thunder, Master Mind, Submarine (exec. prod.), Megamind (exec. prod.), Vamps, Help Me Spread Goodness.
TELEVISION: *Movies:* The Cover Girl and the Cop (actor), Hider in the House (co-prod.), The Station (exec. prod.). *Series:* The Animated Adventures of Computerman (actor).

CORT, BUD
Actor. r.n. Walter Edward Cox. b. New Rochelle, NY, March 29, 1950. e. NYU School of the Arts. Stage debut in Wise Child, B'way. L.A. theatre includes Forget-Me-Not Lane, August 11 1947, Endgame (Dramalogue Award), Demon Wine, The Seagull, He Who Gets Slapped. Founding member of L.A. Classical Theatre. Theatrical film debut as extra in Up the Down Staircase 1967. Television debut in The Doctors.
PICTURES: Sweet Charity, M*A*S*H, Gas-s-s-s, The Traveling Executioner, Brewster McCloud, Harold and Maude (Golden Globe nom. 1972), Die Laughing, Why Shoot the Teacher?, She Dances Alone, Hysterical, Electric Dreams (voice), Love Letters,

The Secret Diary of Sigmund Freud, Maria's Lovers, Invaders from Mars, Love at Stake, The Chocolate War, Out of the Dark, Brain Dead, Going Under, Ted and Venus (also dir., co-s.p.), Girl in the Cadillac, Heat, Theodore Rex, Sweet Jane, I Woke Up Early the Day I Died, Dogma, But I'm a Cheerleader, South of Heaven West of Hell, The Million Dollar Hotel, Coyote Ugly, Pollock, Made, The Big Empty, The Life Aquatic with Steve Zissou, The Number 23, Passion Play.
TELEVISION: *Movies:* Brave New World, The Bates Motel, And the Band Played On, Jitters. *Series:* Funny or Die Presents... *Special:* Bernice Bobs Her Hair.

CORT, ROBERT W.

Executive, Producer. e. U. of Pennsylvania (Phi Beta Kappa). Master's degree in History & MBA from Wharton. Moved into feature prod. after having worked primarily in marketing/advertising. Joined Columbia Pictures as v.p., 1976; elevated to v.p., adv./pub./promo. Named exec. v.p. of mktg. for 20th-Fox, 1980. Moved into feature prod. as senior v.p., 1981. In 1983 named exec. v.p., prod., 20th-Fox Prods. 1985, joined Interscope Comm. as pres. From 1996-2001, managing partner of Cort/Madden Prods. In 2001 formed Robert Cort Productions. In 2003 Random House published Cort's first novel, Action!, which garnered outstanding critical reviews and became a bestseller. Cort has also been a lecturer at the American Film Institute.
PICTURES: *Prod.:* Critical Condition, Outrageous Fortune, Revenge of the Nerds II, Three Men and a Baby, The Seventh Sign, Cocktail, Bill & Ted's Excellent Adventure (exec. prod.), Renegades (exec. prod.), Blind Fury (exec. prod.), An Innocent Man, The First Power (exec. prod.), Bird on a Wire, Arachnophobia, Three Man and a Little Lady, Eve of Destruction, Class Action, Bill & Ted's Bogus Journey, Paradise, The Hand That Rocks the Cradle, The Cutting Edge, FernGully, The Gun in Betty Lou's Handbag, Out on a Limb, Jersey Girl, Holy Matrimony, Imaginary Crimes, Operation Dumbo Drop, The Tie That Binds, Mr. Holland's Opus, The Associate (exec. prod.), Snow White (exec.), The Odd Couple II, The Out-Of-Towners, Runaway Bride, Save the Last Dance, The Colony, Against the Ropes, Save the Last Dance 2 (exec. prod.), Aftermath.
TELEVISION: *Movies (co-exec. prod.):* A Mother's Courage (Emmy Award 1990), A Part of the Family, Body Language, In the Company of Spies, Harlan County War, The Rats, Something the Lord Made (Emmy Award 2004).

CORWIN, BRUCE CONRAD

Exhibitor. b. Los Angeles, CA, June 11, 1940. e. Graduate, Wesleyan Univ. in CT. Recipient of honorary Doctorate of Laws. Corwin is the third generation of the Corwin family to lead Metropolitan Theatres Corporation, an 80-year-old chain of movie theatres based in Los Angeles, CA. The circuit currently operates 21 theatres with 103 screens in California, Colorado, Idaho, Utah, and British Columbia. He currently is chairman and CEO. He serves on the board of the National Association of Theatre Owners. In addition to his corporate involvements, Corwin is the chmn. and past president of Temple Emanuel of Beverly Hills, on the bd. of governors of the Cal. Community Foundation and is a trustee of the UC Santa Barbara Foundation and the National Multiple Sclerosis Society, So. California Chapter. Corwin was honored as the "ShoWester of the Year" in 1987 and as the Foundation of Motion Picture Pioneers "Pioneer of the Year" in 1997.

CORWIN, DAVID

Exhibitor. e. B.S. in business administration from Georgetown University and J.D from Univ. of Southern California. Corwin is president of Los Angeles-based Metropolitan Theatres Corporation. The privately held corporation has been owned by the Corwin family since 1923 and currently operates 21 theatres with 103 screens in California, Colorado, Idaho, Utah, and British Columbia. Corwin is a member of the bd. of directors of the National Association of Theatre Owners.

COSBY, BILL

Actor, Comedian. b. Philadelphia, PA, July 12, 1938. e. Temple U., U. of Mass., Ed.D. Served in United States Navy Medical Corps. Started as night club entertainer.
AUTHOR: The Wit and Wisdom of Fat Albert, Bill Cosby's Personal Guide to Power Tennis, Fatherhood, Time Flies.
COMEDY ALBUMS: Bill Cosby Is a Very Funny Fellow... Right! (Grammy Award, 1964), I Started Out As a Child (Grammy Award, 1965), Why Is There Air? (Grammy Award, 1966), Wonderfulness (Grammy Award, 1967), Revenge (Grammy Award, 1967), To Russell My Brother Whom I Slept With (Grammy Award, 1969), Bill Cosby Is Not Himself These Days, Rat Own Rat Own Rat Own, My Father Confused Me... What Must I Do? What Must I Do?, Disco Bill, Bill's Best Friend, Cosby and the Kids, It's True It's True, Bill Cosby - Himself, 200 MPH, Silverthroat, Hooray for the Salvation Army Band, 8:15 12:15, For Adults Only, Bill Cosby Talks to Kids About Drugs, Inside the Mind of Bill Cosby.
RADIO: The Bill Cosby Radio Program.
PICTURES: Hickey and Boggs (debut, 1972), Man and Boy, Uptown Saturday Night, Let's Do It Again, Mother Jugs and Speed, A Piece of the Action, California Suite, The Devil and Max Devlin, Bill Cosby Himself, Leonard Part VI (also co-prod., story), Ghost Dad, The Meteor Man, Jack, 4 Little Girls, Comedian (documentary), Crooklyn (comp.), Jack, Men of Honor (exec. prod.), Fat Albert (exec. prod./writer).
TELEVISION: *Movies:* To All My Friends on Shore (also exec. prod., story, music), Top Secret, I Spy Returns (also co-exec. prod.), The Cosby Show Reunion: A Look Back. *Series:* I Spy (3 Emmy Awards for Best Actor: 1966, 1967, 1968; Golden Globe nom. 1967), The Bill Cosby Show (1969-71), The New Bill Cosby Show (Golden Globe nom. 1973. 1972-73), Fat Albert and the Cosby Kids, Cos, The New Fat Albert Show (Emmy Award, 1981), The Cosby Show (3 Emmy nom. 2 Golden Globe Awards; 1 nom. 1984-92), A Different World (exec. prod. only), You Bet Your Life, Here and Now (exec. prod. only), The Cosby Mysteries, Cosby (also prod., 1996-), Kids Say the Darndest Things, Little Bill (Emmy Award 2004, Emmy nom. 2002, exec. prod./writer/creator/composer), Fatherhood (co-exec. prod./writer). *Specials:* The Bill Cosby Special, The Second Bill Cosby Special, Fat Albert Easter Special (voice), Cosby Salutes Alvin Ailey, The Kennedy Center Honors, Intimate Portrait: Phylicia Rashad, Starz 10th Anniversary. *Guest:* More than 228 appearances.

COSTA-GAVRAS (CONSTANTIN)

Director, Writer. r.n. Konstaninos Gavras. b. Athens, Greece, Feb. 13, 1933. French citizen. e. Studied at the Sorbonne; Hautes Etudes Cinematographique, (IDHEC). Was leading ballet dancer in Greece before the age of 20. Worked as second, then first assistant to Marcel Ophuls, Rene Clair, Rene Clement and Jacques Demy. Pres. of the Cinematheque Francaise, 1982-87. Appeared as actor in film Madame Rosa.
PICTURES: *Director:* The Sleeping Car Murders (also s.p.; debut, 1965), Un Homme De Trop/Shock Troops (also s.p.), Z (also co-s.p.; 2 Acad. Award noms. 1970), The Confession, State of Siege (also co- s.p.), Special Section (also co-s.p.), Clair de Femme (also s.p.), Missing (also co-s.p.; Acad. Award for Best Adapted s.p., 2 Golden Globe nom. 1983; Palm d'Or at Cannes Film Fest.), Hannah K. (also prod.), Spies Like Us (actor only), Family Business (also s.p.), Betrayed, Music Box (Golden Bear, Berlin Festival, 1989), The Little Apocalypse, Lumiere & Company, The Stupids, Mad City, Amen, Le Couperet, Mon colonel (s.p.), Eden Is West (also s.p., prod.).

COSTNER, KEVIN

Actor, Producer. b. Lynwood, CA, Jan. 18, 1955. e. CA. State U, Fullerton majored in marketing. Acted with South Coast Actors' Co-op, community theater gp. while at coll. After grad. took marketing job which lasted 30 days. Early film work in low budget exploitation film, Sizzle Beach, 1974. Then one line as Luther Adler in Frances. Role in The Big Chill was edited from final print. 1989, set up own prod. co. Tig Prods. at Raleigh Studios.
PICTURES: Sizzle Beach U.S.A., Shadows Run Black, Night Shift, Chasing Dreams, Table for Five, Testament, Stacy's Knights, The Gunrunner, Fandango, Silverado, American Flyers, The Untouchables, No Way Out, Bull Durham, Field of Dreams, Revenge (also exec. prod.), Dances With Wolves (also dir., co-prod.; 2 Academy Awards for Best Picture & Director; 1 Academy nom. Golden Globe Award and 1 nom. DGA Award 1991), Robin Hood: Prince of Thieves, JFK (Golden Globe nom. 1992), The Bodyguard (also co-prod.), A Perfect World, Wyatt Earp (also co-prod.), Rapa Nui (co-prod. only), The War, Waterworld (also co-prod.), Tin Cup (Golden Globe nom. 1997), The Postman (also dir., co-prod), For Love of the Game, Message in a Bottle (also prod.), Play it to the Bone, Thirteen Days, 3000 Miles to Graceland, Dragonfly, Open Range, The Upside of Anger, Rumor Has It, The Tortilla Curtain (also prod.), The Guardian, Mr. Brooks (also prod.), Swing Vote (also prod., soundtrack writer), The New Daughter, The Company Men, A Little War of Our Own (also dir.).
TELEVISION: *Documentaries/Specials:* 500 Nations (exec. prod., host), Rapa Nui: Legends in Stone, Spirit: A Journey in Dance, Drums & Song (narr.), Play It to the Bone, When It Was a Game 3, Thirteen Days: The Making of a Crisis, Roots of the Cuban Missile Crisis, The Heaven and Earth Show (series), Frat Boys, On Native Soil (narr.), Laffit: All About Winning (narr.), The Explorers Guild (series, voice, prod.). *Guest:* More than 129 appearances.

COTTON, RICK

Executive. e. Undergraduate degree, Harvard, 1965. Law degree, cum laude, Yale Law School, 1969. Also exec. editor of the Yale Law Journal. In between college and law school, was a correspondent in the Chicago bureau for Newsweek magazine. From 1969-1970, law clerk to Judge J. Skelly Wright of the U.S. Court of Appeals for the District of Columbia Circuit; from 1970-1971, law clerk to Justice William J. Brennan Jr. of the U.S. Supreme Court. He was appointed the deputy executive secretary of the U.S. Department of Health, Education and Welfare under Secretary Joseph A. Califano in 1977 and was named the executive secretary in 1978. In 1980 Cotton became the special counsel to Deputy Secretary John Sawhill of the U.S. Department of Energy. From 1980-1986, Cotton was in private practice. From 1987-1989, Cotton was pres. and CEO of Washington-based management company HCX Inc. From 1989-2000, Cotton served as executive v.p. and general counsel of NBC. From 2000-2004, Cotton was pres. and managing dir. of London-based CNBC Europe. Under his leadership CNBC

Europe dramatically upgraded its on-air presentation and expanded its reach across Europe to 85 million homes. Cotton assumed his current role as executive v.p. and general counsel of NBC Universal in August 2004. He supervises the NBC Universal Law Department, which provides legal advice to all NBC Universal business units for their ongoing operations and for new strategic plans and acquisitions. In addition, he oversees NBC Universal's global regulatory and legislative agenda, including the company's worldwide anti-piracy efforts.

COURIC, KATIE

Journalist. b. Arlington, VA, Jan. 7, 1957. e. Univ. of VA. Started as desk asst. at ABC News, then assignment editor for CNN, reporter for WTVJ, NBC affiliate in Miami. Moved to NBC's Washington D.C. station WRC. Became natl. correspondent for The Today Show, 1989, then co-host in 1991. Resigned from The Today Show in 2006 to take her current position, anchor the CBS Evening News. Served as co-host of Macy's Thanksgiving Day Parade, 1991-present (Emmy Award 2004, 3 other noms,). Former regular on Dateline NBC, host of XIX Winter Olympics Opening Ceremony. Appears in the film Austin Powers in Goldmember. TV series documentary host of Freedom: A History of Us.
PICTURES: Austin Powers: Goldmember, Shark Tale (voice).
TELEVISION: *Movie*: Flashpoint (host).

COURTENAY, TOM

Actor. b. Hull, England, Feb. 25, 1937 e. University Coll., London, Royal Acad. of Dramatic Art, 1960-61; Old Vic.
THEATRE: Billy Liar, Andorra, Hamlet, She Stoops to Conquer, Otherwise Engaged (N.Y. debut), The Dresser, Poison Pen, Uncle Vanya, Moscow Stations, etc.
PICTURES: The Loneliness of the Long Distance Runner (debut, 1962), Private Potter, Billy Liar, King and Country, Operation Crossbow, King Rat, Doctor Zhivago (Academy Award nom. 1966), The Night of the Generals, The Day the Fish Came Out, A Dandy in Aspic, Otley, One Day in the Life of Ivan Denisovich, Catch Me a Spy, The Dresser (Academy Award nom.; Golden Globe Award, 1984), Happy New Year, Leonard Part VI, Let Him Have It, The Last Butterfly, The Boy From Mercury, Whatever Happened to Harold Smith, Last Orders, Nicholas Nickleby, Flood, The Golden Compass.
TELEVISION: *Movies/Specials:* I Heard the Owl Call My Name, Jesus of Nazareth, Absent Friends, Chekhov in Yalta, Redemption, The Old Curiosity Shop, A Rather English Marriage, The John Thaw Story, Ready When You Are Mr. McGill. *Mini-series:* Little Dorrit (Emmy nom. 2009). *Series:* The Lads, Ghosts, Private Potter.

COUTARD, RAOUL

Cinematographer. b. Paris, France, Sept. 16, 1924. Spent 4 years in Vietnam working for French Military Info. Service, later a civilian photographer for Time and Paris-Match. During WWII worked in photo labs. After war returned to France and formed prod. co. making documentaries. Joined Jean-Luc Godard as his cinematographer on Breathless (1960). His use of hand-held camera and natural light established him as a seminal cameraman of the French New Wave, working with Godard, Truffaut and later with Costa Gavras. *Director:* Hoa Binh (1971). Received American Society of Cinematographers, International Award, 1997.
PICTURES: Breathless, Shoot the Piano Player, Lola, Jules and Jim, The Army Game, My Life to Live, Love at Twenty (segment), Les Carabiniers, Contempt, Alphaville, The Soft Skin, Male Companion, Pierrot le Fou, Made in USA, Weekend, Sailor From Gibraltar, The Bride Wore Black, Z, The Confession, Le Crabe Tambour, Passion, First Name: Carmen, Dangerous Moves, Salt on the Skin, La Garce, Max My Love, Burning Beds, Let Sleeping Cops Lie, Bethune: The Making of a Hero, Punctured Life, The Birth of Love, Happiness Is No Joke, The Phantom Heart, Wild Innocence.

COWELL, SIMON

Producer, Writer.
b. Brighton, England, October 7, 1959. He worked as a mail boy at EMI and eventually worked his way to become an A&R representative.
Author: I Don't Mean to Be Rude, But...: Backstage Gossip from American Idol & the Secrets that Can Make You a Star.
TELEVISION: *Movie:* The X Factor: Battle of the Stars (composer/theme, judge). *Series:* Cupid (exec. prod.), Celebrity Duets (exec. prod.), American Inventor (exec. prod., prod.), America's Got Talent (exec. prod., writer), X Factor (also creator, writer, composer/theme, judge), Britain's Got Talent (writer, judge), American Idol (judge, 5 Emmy noms.), The Xtra Factor (composer/theme, judge), Talent (writer), Australia's Got Talent (writer). *Guest:* More than 145 appearances.

COX, ALEX

Actor, Director, Writer. b. Liverpool, England, Dec. 15, 1954. Studied law at Oxford U. where he dir. and acted in plays for school drama society. Studied film prod. Bristol U. Received Fulbright Scholarship to study at UCLA film school, 1981.
PICTURES: Repo Man (also s.p.), Sid and Nancy (also co-s.p.), Straight to Hell (also co-s.p.), Walker (also co-editor), Highway Patrolman, Floundering (actor only), Dead Beat (actor only), The Queen of the Night (actor only), The Winner (also actor), Death and the Compass (also actor), Perdita Durango (actor only), Waldo's Hawaiian Holiday, Fear and Loathing in Las Vegas (s.p. only), Three Businessmen (also dir.), Kurosawa: The Last Emperor, Revengers Tragedy, Herod's Law, Stanley Kubrick: A Life in Pictures (documentary), A Revenger's Tragedy (acting, dir.), Waldo's Hawaiian Holiday, Searchers 2.0 (also editor), The Oxford Murders.
TELEVISION: *Movies:* Red Hot and Blue, Mike Hama-Private Detective: Mike Hama Must Die! (dir., s.p.), The Inspector Lynley Mysteries: Playing for the Ashes (location mgr.) In His Life: The John Lennon Story, A Hard Look, Bringing Godzilla Down to Size (doc. narr.).

COX, BRIAN

Actor. b. Dundee, Scotland, June 1, 1946. e. London Acad. of Music & Dramatic Art. Acted with Royal Lyceum Edinburgh and Birmingham Rep. Theatre; also season with Royal Shakespeare Company. Video: Acting and Tragedy. *Author:* The Lear Diaries, Salem in Moscow.
THEATRE: The Master Builder, King Lear, Richard III, Fashion, Rat in the Skull (Olivier Award; also B'way), Titus Andronicus (Olivier Award), Penny for a Song, St. Nicholas, Skylight.
PICTURES: Nicholas and Alexandra, In Celebration, Manhunter, Shoot for the Sun, Hidden Agenda, Prince of Jutland, Iron Will, Rob Roy, Braveheart, Chain Reaction, The Boxer, The Long Kiss Goodnight, Kiss the Girls, Rushmore, Desperate Measures, The Minus Man, The Corruptor, For Love of the Game, Longitude, The Invention of Dr. Morel, Complicity, Mad About Mambo, Whipped, A Shot at Glory, Saltwater, Super Troopers, L.I.E., Cocozza's Way, The Affair of the Necklace, The Reckoning, Murder By Numbers, Bug, The Rookie, The Bourne Identity, Adaptation, The Ring, X2, Sin, The Reckoning, Troy, The Bourne Supremacy, The Ringer, Match Point, The Chronicles of Narnia: The Lion, the Witch & the Wardrobe (voice), A Woman in Winter, Running with Scissors, Burns, The Flying Scotsman, Agent Crush (voice), The Water Horse: Legend of the Deep, Terra (voice), The Escapist (also sountrack performer), Wide Blue Yonder, Shoot on Sight, Trick 'r Treat, Tell-Tale, The Good Heart, As Good as Dead, Fantastic Mr. Fox (voice), Ironclad, Coriolanus, Wide Blue Yonder, Red. *Dir./Writer:* Scorpion Spring.
TELEVISION: *Movies:* The Year of the Sex Olympics, Changeling, King Lear, Inspector Morse, Pope John Paul II, Florence Nightingale, The Fourth Floor, Beryl Markham: A Shadow on the Sun, Murder by Moonlight, Secret Weapon, Lost Language of Cranes, The Cloning of Joanna May, Six Characters in Search of an Author, Sharpe's Rifles, Sharpe's Eagle, Grushko, Picasso, The Negotiator, Witness Against Hitler, Henry V at Shakespeare's Globe, Poodle Springs, Longitude, The Biographer, Bach, Bothwell, Churchill's People, Master of Ballantrae, Smallpox 2002: Silent Weapon (narrator), The Biographer, Blue/Orange, Lost: The Journey (narr.), The Strange Case of Sherlock Holmes & Arthur Conan Doyle, The Outsiders, The Secret of the Nutcracker, The Color of Magic. *Mini-series:* Thérèse Raquin, The Modern World: Ten Great Writers (voice), Red Fox, Shakespeare: The Animated Tales (voice), The Big Battalions, Nuremberg (Emmy Award; Golden Globe nom. 2001), The Day of the Triffids. *Series:* The Devil's Crown, Frasier (Emmy nom. 2002 as guest), Deadwood, The Take. *Guest:* More than 147 appearances.

COX ARQUETTE, COURTENEY

Actress. b. Birmingham, AL, June 15, 1964. m. actor David Arquette. Left AL to pursue modeling career in NY. Dir. Brian DePalma selected her to be the young woman who jumps out of audience and dances with Bruce Springsteen in his music video Dancing in the Dark. This break led to featured role in short-lived TV series Misfits of Science (1985-86).
PICTURES: Masters of the Universe, Down Twisted, Cocoon: The Return, Mr. Destiny, Blue Desert, Shaking the Tree, The Opposite Sex, Ace Ventura—Pet Detective, Scream, Commandments, Scream 2, The Runner, Scream 3, The Shrink is In (also exec. prod.), Alien Love Triangle, 3000 Miles to Graceland, Get Well Soon, Alien Love Triangle (short), November, Caught in the Act, The Longest Yard, Alpha Dog, The Barnyard (voice), Zoom, The Tripper, Bedtime Stories, Scream 4.
TELEVISION: *Movies:* I'll Be Home for Christmas, Roxanne: The Prize Pulitzer, Till We Meet Again, Curiosity Kills, Battling for Baby, Topper, Sketch Artist II: Hands That See, Talk Show Diaries (exec. prod.). *Series:* Misfits of Science, Family Ties, The Trouble With Larry, Friends, Mix It Up (exec. prod.), Dirt (also exec. prod.), Cougar Town (Golden Globe nom. 2010). *Guest:* More than 92 appearances.

COX, RONNY

Actor. b. Cloudcroft, NM, July 23, 1938. e. Eastern New Mexico Univ.
PICTURES: The Happiness Cage (debut, 1972), Deliverance, Hugo the Hippo (voice), Bound for Glory, The Car, Gray Lady Down, Harper Valley P.T.A., The Onion Field, Taps, The Beast Within, Some Kind of ssHero, Courage (Raw Courage), Beverly Hills Cop, Vision Quest, Hollywood Vice Squad, Steele Justice, Beverly Hills Cop II, Robocop, One Man Force, Loose Cannons, Martians Go Home!, Total Recall, Scissors, Captain America, Past Midnight, Murder at 1600, Frog and Wombat, Forces of

Nature, Deep Blue Sea, The Boys of Sunset Ridge, American Outlaws, Losing Grace, Crazy As Hell, The L.A. Riot Spectacular, Imagine That.
TELEVISION: *Movies:* The Connection, A Case of Rape, Who Is the Black Dahlia?, Having Babies, Corey: For the People, The Girl Called Hatter Fox, Lovey: A Circle of Children Part II, Transplant, When Hell Was in Session, Fugitive Family, Courage of Kavik: The Wolf Dog, The Last Song, Alcatraz—The Whole Shocking Story, Fallen Angel, Two of a Kind, The Jesse Owens Story, The Abduction of Kari Swenson, Baby Girl Scott, In the Line of Duty: The FBI Murders, The Comeback, When We Were Young, With Murder in Mind, Perry Mason: The Case of the Heartbroken Bride, A Part of the Family, Rebound: The Legend of Earl 'The Goat' Manigault, Never Give Up: The Jimmy V Story, Childhood Sweethearts, Y2K, Secret of Giving, Perfect Murder, Perfect Town: JonBenét and the City of Boulder, Love Lessons, The Agency, Point of Origin, Home for Christmas, Angel in the Family. *Mini-series:* Favorite Son, From the Earth to the Moon, Perfect Murder Perfect Town. *Series:* Apple's Way, Spencer, St. Elsewhere, Cop Rock, Sweet Justice, Spawn (voice), Invasion America (voice), The Agency, Stargate SG-1, The Starter Wife. *Specials:* Our Town, Chicago 7 Trial. *Guest:* More than 103 appearances.

COYOTE, PETER
Actor. r.n. Peter Cohon. b. New York, NY, Oct. 10, 1942. Studied with San Francisco Actors Workshop. Theatre includes The Minstrel Show (dir.), Olive Pits (also co-writer), The Red Snake, True West, The Abduction of Kari Swenson, Baby Girl Scott.
PICTURES: Die Laughing (debut, 1980), Tell Me a Riddle, Southern Comfort, The Pursuit of D.B. Cooper, E.T.: The Extra Terrestrial, Endangered Species, Timerider, Cross Creek, Slayground, Stranger's Kiss, Heartbreakers, The Legend of Billie Jean, Jagged Edge, Outrageous Fortune, A Man in Love, Stacking, Heart of Midnight, The Man Inside, Crooked Hearts, Exposure, Bitter Moon, Kika, That Eye The Sky, Moonlight and Valentino, Unforgettable, Sphere, Patch Adams, The Basket, Last Call, Random Hearts, Erin Brokovich, Red Letters, More Dogs Than Bones, A Time For Dancing, Jack the Dog, Suddenly Naked, Purpose, A Walk to Remember, Femme Fatale, Written in Blood, Northfork, The Hebrew Hammer, Bon voyage, Shadow of Fear, Deepwater, Return of the Living Dead 4: Necropolis, A Little Trip to Heaven, Return of the Living Dead 5: Rave from the Grave, End Game, Deepwater, Berkeley (narrator), Behind Enemy Lines: Axis of Evil, Resurrecting the Champ, A Single Woman, Race (dir. only), Adopt a Sailor, All Roads Lead Home, The Lena Baker Story, $5 a Day, Last Will, The Harimaya Bridge, The Gundown, Di Di Hollywood.
TELEVISION: *Movies:* Alcatraz: The Whole Shocking Story, The People vs. Jean Harris, Isabel's Choice, Best Kept Secrets, Scorned and Swindled, The Blue Yonder, Time Flyer, Child's Cry, Sworn to Silence, Echoes in the Darkness, Baja Oklahoma, Unconquered, A Seduction in Travis County, Living a Lie, Keeper of the City, Breach of Conduct, Buffalo Girls, Seduced by Madness: The Diane Borchardt Story, Dalva, Murder in My Mind, Two for Texas, Route 9, Indiscreet, A Murder On Shadow Mountain, Execution of Justice, The Wednesday Woman, Phenomenon II, Midwives, Lost: Revelation. *Series:* Commander in Chief, The 4400, The Inside, Brothers & Sisters. *Documentaries: Narrator:* National Geographic Explorer series), The Color of War, The American Frontier: Decisive Battles, Kerouac, the Movie, Contrary Warriors: A Film of the Crow Tribe, Downwind/Downstream, Waldo Salt: A Screenwriter's Journey, Orson Welles: What Went Wrong?, The Peyote Road, American Cinema (series), Cyclone!, The West (mini-series), 21st Century Jet: The Building of the 777, The Secrets of 007: The James Bond Files, Still Missing, Titanic: Breaking New Ground, Frontier: Legends of the Old Northwest (mini-series), The Pacific Century (Emmy Award 1993) National Geographic: The Battle for Midway, World's Scariest Explosions: Caught On Tape, Neighborhoods: The Hidden Cities of San Francisco - The Fillmore, Rome: Power & Glory, Founding Fathers (mini-series), Voices of the Sierra Tarahumara, Sex in the 20th Century, Founding Brothers, Unprecedented: The 2000 Presidential Election, Seth Eastman: Painting the Dakota, Hollywood's Magical Island: Catalina, Carlos Castaneda: Enigma of a Sorcerer (also actor), Oil on Ice, About Face (also actor), Kursk: A Submarine in Troubled Waters, Independent Lens, Commune, Enron: The Smartest Guys in the Room, a/k/a Tommy Chong, Destination Lost, The Sixties: The Years That Shaped a Generation, The Gospel of Judas, Nature (series), The Drug Years (mini-series), American Masters, Strange Culture, Jukebox: From Edison to Ipod, The American Experience, Fog City Mavericks, Hippies, Call of Life: Facing the Mass Extinction, Alaska Far Away: The New Deal Pioneers of the Matanuska Colony, Imagine a School... Summerhill, Stealing America: Vote by Vote, Jose Canseco: Last Shot, Spirit Riders, Save the American Wild Horse, National Geographic Explorer (narr. 3 episodes). *Guest:* More than 155 appearances.

CRAIG, DANIEL
Actor. b. Cheshire, UK, March 2, 1968. e. Guildhall School of Music and Drama at the Barbican.
THEATRE: *NY:* A Steady Rain.
PICTURES: The Power of One, A Kid in King Arthur's Court, Elizabeth, Love Is the Devil: Study for a Portrait of Francis Bacon, I Dreamed of Africa, Lara Croft: Tomb Raider, Road to Perdition, The Mother, Sylvia, Enduring Love, Layer Cake, The Jacket, Fateless, Munich, Renaissance (voice), Infamous, Casino Royale, The Golden Compass, The Invasion, Flashbacks of a Fool (also exec. prod.), Quantum of Solace, Defiance, The Adventures of Tintin: Secret of the Unicorn (voice), Dream House, Cowboys and Aliens.
TELEVISION: *Movies:* Genghis Cohn, Sharpe's Eagle, The Fortunes and Misfortunes of Moll Flanders, The Ice House, Shockers: The Visitor, Sword of Honour, Copenhagen, Archangel. *Mini-series:* Our Friends in the North. *Series:* Covington Cross (pilot). *Guest:* More than 100 appearances.

CRAIG, MICHAEL
Actor. r.n. Michael Gregson. b. Poona, India, Jan. 27, 1929. At 16 joined Merchant Navy. 1949, returned to England and made stage debut in repertory. Entered industry as extra in 1949.
PICTURES: Passport to Pimlico (debut, 1949), The Magic Box, The Cruel Sea, Malta Story, The Love Lottery, Passage Home, The Black Tent, Yield to the Night, Eye-Witness, House of Secrets, High Tide At Noon, Sea of Sand, Sapphire, Upstairs and Downstairs, The Angry Silence (Academy Award nom. 1961), Cone of Silence, Doctor In Love, Mysterious Island, Payroll, No My Darling Daughter, A Pair of Briefs, A Life for Ruth, The Iron Maiden, Captive City, Summer Flight, Stolen Flight, Of a Thousand Delights, Life at the Top, Modesty Blaise, Star!, Twinky, The Royal Hunt of the Sun, Brotherly Love (Country Dance), A Town Called Bastard, The Fourth Mrs. Anderson, Vault of Horror, Inn of the Damned, Ride a Wild Pony, The Irishman, Turkey Shoot, Stanley, Appointment With Death.
TELEVISION: *Movies:* Daddy Kiss It Better, Spoiled, St. Joan, Tartuffe, Essington, The Last Rites, Arena (writer), *Mini-series:* Husbands and Lovers, The Fourth Wish (writer), The Timeless Land, Brides of Christ, Mary Bryant. *Series:* Second Time Around, Three Men of the City, G.P., The Outsiders (writer/co-creator), The Emigrants, Triangle, Menotti (writer/creator), Grass Roots. *Guest:* More than 52 appearances.

CRAISSATI, ANDREW
Executive. b. London, UK, July 15, 1963. e. University of Durham, UK. 1983; several management positions for International Media Management. 1989; Managing Dir., Motion Picture Group, Landmark Entertainment Group. 1991-96; President-North America, Group Managing Dir. The Magna Group. 1997-99; Sp. Advisor: Office of Regional Chairman, Seagrams & Sons/Seagram (Asia Pacific). 1999 to 2004; Chairman & Chief Executive, The Virgin Group (Asia Pacific). Currently Chief Executive of investment banking firm Transpac Media Ltd.

CRAMER, DOUGLAS S.
Executive, Producer. e. Northwestern U., Sorbonne, U. of Cincinnati, B.A.; Columbia U.M.F.A. Taught at Carnegie Inst. of Tech., 1954-55; Production asst. Radio City Music Hall 1950-51; MGM Script Dept. 1952; Manag. Dir. Cincinnati Summer Playhouse 1953-54. TV supvr. Procter and Gamble 1956-59; Broadcast supvr. Ogilvy Benson and Mather adv. 1959-62; v.p. program dev. ABC-TV 1962-66; v.p. program dev. 20 Cent.-Fox TV 1966; exec. v.p. in chg. of prod., Paramount TV, 1968-71; exec. v.p. Aaron Spelling Prods. 1976-89; pres. Douglas S. Cramer Co, 1989. Now on East Coast working as theatrical producer for works such as "The Tales of the Allergist's Wife."
THEATRE: Call of Duty, Love is a Smoke, Whose Baby Are You, Last Great Dish.
PICTURES: *Exec. prod.:* Sleeping Together.
TELEVISION: *Exec. prod.:* Bridget Loves Bernie, QB VII (Emmy nom. 1975), Dawn: Portrait of a Teenage Runaway, Nightmare in Badham County, Sex Symbol, Danielle Steel's Novels; More than 19 productions, Kaleidoscope, Changes, Message from Nam, Daddy, Palamino, Once in a Lifetime, The Ring, Zoya: Trade Winds, Lake Success, Wonder Woman, Family of Cops. *Co-exec. prod.:* Love Boat (1977-86), Vegas (1978-81), Dynasty (Emmy nom. 1982), Matt Houston, Hotel, Colbys, Family of Cops III.

CRANE, DAVID
Producer, Writer. b. August 10,1957.
PICTURES: Epic Proportions (writer/play).
TELEVISION: *Movies:* Ngaio Marsh's Alleyn Mysteries: Death at the Bar (s.p. editor). *Series:* Dream On (Emmy nom. 1993, creator), Ngaio Marsh's Alleyn Mysteries (s.p. editor), Friends (Emmy Award 2002; 5 other noms., co-exec., co-creator), Veronica's Closet (exec. prod., co-creator), Jesse (exec. prod.), Joey (writer), The Class (also pilot, exec. prod., writer/creator).

CRAVEN, GEMMA
Actress. b. Dublin, Ireland, June 1, 1950. e. Loretto Coll. Studied acting at Bush Davies School. London stage debut, Fiddler on the Roof (1970).
THEATRE: *London:* Audrey, Trelawny, Dandy Dick, They're Playing Our Song, Song and Dance, Loot, A Chorus of Disapproval, Three Men on a Horse, Jacobowsky and the Colonel, The Magistrate, South Pacific, The London Vertigo, Private Lives, Present Laughter.
PICTURES: Kingdom of Gifts, Why Not Stay for Breakfast, The

Slipper and the Rose, Wagner, Double X: The Name of the Game, Words Upon the Windowpane, The Last Bus Home, After the Hole.
TELEVISION: Pennies From Heaven, Must Wear Tights, She Loves Me, Song by Song by Noel Coward, Song by Song by Alan Jay Lerner, East Lynne, Robin of Sherwood, Treasure Hunt, Gemma Girls and Gershwin, Boon, The Bill, The Marshal, The Cazelets, The Clinic, Hollyoaks Later.

CRAVEN, WES
Director, Writer. b. Cleveland, OH, Aug. 2, 1939. e. Wheaton Coll., B.A.; Johns Hopkins, M.A., philosophy. Worked as humanities prof. prior to film.
PICTURES: The Last House on the Left (also s.p., ed.), The Hills Have Eyes (also s.p., ed.), Deadly Blessing, Swamp Thing (also s.p.), A Nightmare on Elm Street (also s.p.), The Hills Have Eyes Part II (also s.p.), Deadly Friend, A Nightmare on Elm Street III: Dream Warriors (co-s.p., co-exec. prod. only), The Serpent and the Rainbow, Shocker (also exec. prod., s.p.), The People Under the Stairs (also s.p., co-exec. prod.), Wes Craven's New Nightmare (also actor, s.p.), Vampire in Brooklyn, The Fear (actor only), Scream, Wishmaster (prod. only), Scream 2, Music of the Heart, Scream 3, Jay and Silent Bob Strike Back (actor only), Carnival of Souls (exec. prod. only, Dracula 2000 (prod. only), Freddy v. Jason (writer), Cursed, Red-Eye, Feast (exec. prod.), The Hills Have Eyes (1977 s.p.), je t'aime Paris, The Breed (exec. prod.), Pulse (s.p.), Home (exec. prod.), The Hills Have Eyes II (writer, prod.), Diary of the Dead (voice), The Last House on the Left (writer of 1972 film, prod.), A Nightmare on Elm Street (writer), 25/8 (also prod.).
TELEVISION: *Movies:* A Stranger in Our House, Kent State, Invitation to Hell, Chiller, Casebusters, Night Visions (also exec. prod., co-writer), Laurel Canyon (exec. prod. only), Body Bags (actor only), Chameleon Blue, Shadow Zone: The Undead Express, Don't Look Down,They Shoot Divas, Don't They?, *Series:* Twilight Zone (1985, 7 episodes: Word Play, A Little Peace and Quiet, Shatterday, Chameleon, Dealer's Choice, The Road Less Traveled, Pilgrim Soul, The People Next Door (exec. prod.), Kamelot (exec. prod.).

CRIPPS, ANDREW
Executive. This 20-year film distribution executive joined London-based United International Pictures (UIP) in 1986 as executive assistant to the general sales manager in Japan, the country in which he was raised. UIP is the joint international distribution operation of Paramount Pictures and Universal Pictures. Fluent in Japanese, Cripps earned a v.p. of sales post for Southeast Asia and Australia. He then relocated to London in 1990, when he was named senior v.p. of international sales before moving up the ranks to UIP president & COO in 1999. When UIP announced plans to dissolve its joint Paramount and Universal distribution operations at the end of 2006, Cripps was named president, Paramount Pictures International, Paramount's new international distribution arm.

CROMWELL, JAMES
Actor. b. Los Angeles, CA, Jan. 27, 1940. e. Carnegie Mellon Univ. Father was director John Cromwell, mother was actress Kate Johnson.
PICTURES: Murder by Death, The Cheap Detective, The Man With Two Brains, House of God, Tank, Revenge of the Nerds, Oh God You Devil, Explorers, A Fine Mess, Revenge of the Nerds II: Nerds in Paradise, The Rescue, Pink Cadillac, The Runnin' Kind, The Babe, Romeo Is Bleeding, Babe (Academy Award nom. 1996), Eraser, The People vs. Larry Flynt, Star Trek: First Contact, L.A. Confidential, The Education of Little Tree, Deep Impact, Babe: Pig in the City, Species 2, Snow Falling on Cedars, The Green Mile, The General's Daughter, The Bachelor, Space Cowboys, Spirit: Stallion of the Cimarron, The Sum of All Fears, Twist of Fate, Blackball, The Snow Walker, Before the Devil Knows You're Dead, I, Robot, The Longest Yard, Dante's Inferno, The Queen, Becoming Jane, The 1 Second Film (doc. also prod.), Spider-Man 3, Tortured, W., A Lonely Place for Dying, Surrogates, Secretariat, A Year in Mooring.
TELEVISION: *Movies:* The Girl in the Empty Grave, Deadly Game, A Christmas Without Snow, The Wall, Spraggue, The Shaggy Dog, A Slight Case of Murder, Fail Safe, Enterprise: Broken Bow, Great Bear Rainforest, Door to Door, A Death in the Family, The Magnificent Ambersons, RFK, 'Salem's Lot, Avenger, Pope John Paul II, Hit Factor, The Last Days of Lehman Brothers, Under the Roman Sky. *Mini-Series:* Once an Eagle, Angels in America, RKO 281 (Emmy nom. 2000), Impact. *Series:* All in the Family, Hot L Baltimore, The Nancy Walker Show, The Last Precinct, Easy Street, Mama's Boy, Walking After Midnight, Citizen Baines, Six Feet Under (Emmy Award nom. 2003), 24, My Own Worst Enemy. *Guest:* More than 148 appearances.

CRONENBERG, DAVID
Writer, Director, Producer. b. Toronto, Ont., May 15, 1943. e. U. of Toronto. In college produced two short movies on 16mm. 1971, to Europe on a Canadian Council grant where in 1975 he shot his first feature, They Came From Within (Shivers).
PICTURES: *Director:* Transfer (also prod, s.p. and edit.), From the Drain (also s.p. and edit.), Stereo, Crimes of the Future, Jim Ritche Sculptor, They Came From Within (Shivers; also s.p.), Rabid (also s.p.), Fast Company, The Brood (also s.p.), Scanners (also s.p.), Videodrome, The Dead Zone, The Fly (also co-s.p., cameo), Dead Ringers (also co-prod., co-s.p.), Naked Lunch (also s.p.), M. Butterfly, Crash, eXistenZ (also s.p. and prod.), Camera, Spider (also prod.). Actor: Into the Night, Nightbreed, Trial by Jury, Blue, Henry & Verlin, Trial By Jury, To Die For, Blood and Donuts, The Stupids, Extreme Measures, The Grace of God, Last Night, Resurrection, The American Nightmare, Jason X, Spider, A History of Violence, London Fields, Maps to the Stars, To Each His Cinema (segment dir.), Eastern Promises.
TELEVISION: *Movies:* Moonshine Highway, The Judge.

CROSBY, MARY
Actress. b. Los Angeles, CA, Sept. 14, 1959. e. U. TX; American Conservatory Theatre. Daughter of performers Kathryn Crosby and the late Bing Crosby. Formerly acted as Mary Frances Crosby. Appeared from an early age in several TV variety specials with her parents. On stage in: Romeo & Juliet, A Gentleman of Verona (L.A.), As You Like It (L.A.), The Seagull (L.A.).
PICTURES: The Last Plane Out, The Ice Pirates, Tapeheads, Body Chemistry, Corporate Affairs, Eating, The Berlin Conspiracy, Desperate Motive (Distant Cousins), The Legend of Zorro, Queen of the Lot.
TELEVISION: *Movies:* With This Ring, A Guide for the Married Woman, Midnight Lace, Golden Gate, Confessions of a Married Man, Final Jeopardy, Stagecoach, Johnann Strauss: The King Without a Crown, Sharing the Secret, When Shoulderpads Ruled the World. *Mini-series:* Pearl, Hollywood Wives, North and South Book II. Pilot: Golden Gate, The Big Easy, Cover Up. *Series:* Brothers and Sisters, Dallas, Freddy's Nightmares, Sharing the Secret. *Specials:* Goldilocks, Bing Crosby's Christmas Show (1970-73, 1976-77), Battle of the Network Stars, The 21st Annual Academy of Country Music Awards, Crazy Dan, Tube Test Two, Best Sellers: Men Who Hate Women and the Wome Who Love Them. *Guest:* More than 65 appearances.

CROSS, BEN
Actor. r.n. Bernard Cross. b. London, England, Dec. 16, 1947. e. Royal Acad. of Dramatic Art. Worked as stagehand, prop-master, and master carpenter with Welsh Natl. Opera and as set builder, Wimbledon Theatre.
THEATRE: The Importance of Being Earnest (Lancaster, debut, 1972), I Love My Wife, Privates on Parade, Chicago, Lydie Breeze (NY debut, 1982), Caine Mutiny Court Martial.
PICTURES: A Bridge Too Far (debut, 1977), Chariots of Fire, The Unholy, The Goldsmith's Shop, Paperhouse, The House of the Lord, Eye of the Widow, Haunted Symphony, The Ascent, First Knight, Turbulence, The Corporate Ladder, The Invader, The Venice Project, Young Blades, The Order, She Me and Her, Exorcist: The Beginning, The Mechanik, The Children, Undisputed II: Last Man Standing, Behind Enemy Lines: Axis of Evil, When Nietzsche Wept, Finding Rin Tin Tin, Hero Wanted, War, Inc., Star Trek, Sweet Deceit, Ice.
TELEVISION: *Movies:* Great Expectations, Melancholy Hussar of the German Legion (1973, BBC), Coming Out of the Ice, The Assisi Underground, Arthur Hailey's Strong Medicine, Steal the Sky, Pursuit, Twist of Fate, Nightlife, Dark Shadows, She Stood Alone, Diamond Fleece, Live Wire, Deep Trouble, Cold Sweat, The House That Mary Bought, Hellfire, 20,000 Leagues Under the Sea, Solomon, The Sands of Time, The Red Phone: Manhunt, Spartacus, Icon, S.S. Doomtrooper, Hannibal, Grendel, Lost City Raiders, Hellhounds. *Mini-series:* The Flame Trees of Thika, The Citadel, The Far Pavilions, The Potato Factory. *Series:* Dark Shadows (1991), The Ark. *Documentary:* Nuremberg: Nazis on Trial. *Guest:* More than 50 appearances.

CROUSE, LINDSAY
Actress. b. New York, NY, May 12, 1948. Daughter of playwright Russel Crouse. e. Radcliffe.
THEATRE: With Circle Repertory Co. N.Y.: Hamlet, Twelfth Night, Richard II, Childe Byron, Reunion (Obie Award). NY: Serenading Louie, The Shawl, The Stick Wife, The Homecoming (B'way debut; Theatre World Award). With L.A. Matrix Theatre Co.: The Tavern, Habeus Corpus.
PICTURES: All the President's Men (debut, 1976), Slap Shot, Between the Lines, Prince of the City, The Verdict, Daniel, Iceman, Places in the Heart (Academy Award nom. 1985), House of Games, Communion, Desperate Hours, Being Human, Bye Bye Love, The Indian in the Cupboard, The Arrival, The Juror, Prefontaine, Progeny, The Insider, Stranger in My House, Almost Salinas, Imposter, Cherish, Mr. Brooks.
TELEVISION: *Movies:* Eleanor and Franklin, Chantilly Lace, Final Appeal, Out of Darkness, Parallel Lives, Between Mother and Daughter, Norma Jean and Marilyn, If These Walls Could Talk, Beyond the Prairie: The True Story of Laura Ingalls Wilder, The Warden, Beyond the Prairie, Part 2: The True Story of Laura Ingalls Wilder. *Mini-series:* The Kennedys of Massachusetts. *Specials:* Kennedy's Children, Lemon Sky, Between Mother and Daughter, If These Walls Could Talk. *Series:* American Nuclear (pilot), NYPD Blue, Traps, Millenium, Buffy the Vampire Slayer, Providence, Hack, L.A. Dragnet, Law & Order, Law & Order: Special Victims Unit. *Guest:* More than 52 appearances.

CROWE, CAMERON
Writer, Director. b. Palm Springs, CA, July 13, 1957. e. Calif. St. Univ., San Diego. Began career as journalist and editor for

Rolling Stone. Adapted his book Fast Times at Ridgemont High into Writers Guild Award-nominated screenplay for 1982 film.
PICTURES: American Hot Wax (actor). Fast Times at Ridgemont High (s.p. only), The Wild Life (s.p.,co-prod.), Say Anything..., Singles, Jerry Maguire (2 Academy Award nom.; DGA nom.; WGA nom. 1997; dir. & prod. only), Almost Famous (Academy Award, Golden Globe nom.; DGA nom.; WGA nom. 2001), Vanilla Sky (also prod), Elizabethtown (also prod., soundtrack writer).
TELEVISION: *Series:* Fast Times (creative consultant). *Documentary:* Jackson Browne: Going Home.

CROWE, RUSSELL
Actor. b. New Zealand, April 7, 1964. Raised in Australia. Worked as musician while appearing on Australian stage in Bad Boy Johnny and the Profits of Doom, Blood Brothers, Rocky Horror Show.
PICTURES: For the Moment, The Silver Brumby, Hammers Over the Anvil, Prisoners of the Sun, Love in Limbo, For the Moment, Proof (Australian Film Inst. Award), The Efficiency Expert, Romper Stomper (Australian Film Inst. Award), The Quick and the Dead, The Sum of Us, Virtuosity, Rough Magic, No Way Back, L.A. Confidential, Heaven's Burning, Breaking Up, Mystery Alaska, The Insider (Academy Award nom.; Golden Globe nom. 2000), Gladiator (Academy Award, Golden Globe nom. 2001), Proof of Life, A Beautiful Mind (Academy Award nom., Golden Globe Award 2002), Texas, Master and Commander: The Far Side of the World (Golden Globe nom. 2004), Cinderella Man (Golden Globe nom. 2006), A Good Year, Tenderness, American Gangster, 3:10 to Yuma, Body of Lies, State of Play, Robin Hood (2010), The Next Three Days.
TELEVISION: *Mini-series:* Brides of Christ. *Series:* Living with the Law. *Guest:* More than 126 appearances.

CROWN, DANIEL
Exhibitor. Crown's grandfather owned the Schine theatre chain, which flourished in the 1940s and 1950s as the largest circuit in the Northeast. Crown continued in theatre business and acquired the Cineamerica East assets, after 15 years of working with various family holdings, such as oil, coal, and real estate development. Was pres. and CEO of Crown Theatres, S. Norwalk, CT., from 1990-Jan. 2004. Became chairman in Jan. 2004 after hiring industry veteran Hal Cleveland to be the organization's pres. and CEO with day-to-day responsibilities for the 138-screen theatre circuit. In addition to numerous business interests, Crown serves on the bd. or dirs. of several prominent organizations, including Lenox Hill Hospital, Mount Sinai Children's Center Foundation and the Crohn's and Colitis Foundation of America, among others.

CRUISE, TOM
Actor, Producer. r.n. Thomas Cruise Mapother IV. b. Syracuse, NY, July 3, 1962. m. actress Katie Holmes. Acted in high school plays; secured role in dinner theatre version of Godspell. Studied acting at Neighborhood Playhouse, before landing small part in Endless Love. Received American Cinema Award for Distinguished Achievement in Film, 1991. Top winning star of all time with six number ones on Quigley's Top Ten MoneyMakers Poll, est. 1932. With producing partner Paula Wagner, took over management of United Artists in Nov. 2006, also having an ownership interest in the studio. Wagner left the studio in Aug. 2008 but remains a studio co-owner with Cruise.
PICTURES: Endless Love (debut, 1981), Taps, Losin' It, The Outsiders, Risky Business (Golden Globe nom. 1984), All the Right Moves, Legend, Top Gun, The Color of Money, Cocktail, Rain Man, Born on the 4th of July (Golden Globe Award; Academy Award nom., 1990), Days of Thunder (also co-wrote story), Far and Away, A Few Good Men (Golden Globe nom. 1993), The Firm, Interview With the Vampire, Mission: Impossible, Jerry Macguire (Academy Award nom.; Golden Globe Award, 1997), Eyes Wide Shut, Magnolia (Academy Award nom. Golden Globe Award 2000), Mission Impossible 2 (also prod.), Without Limits (prod. only) Vanilla Sky, Minority Report, Space Station (voice), Dolan's Cadillac (prod. only), Shattered Glass (exec. prod. only), The Last Samurai (Golden Globe nom. 2004, also prod.), Collateral, Mission: Impossible III (also prod.), War of the Worlds, Lions for Lambs (also exec. prod.), Lions for Lambs (also exec. prod.), Tropic Thunder (Golden Globe nom. 2009), Valkyrie (also exec. prod.), Knight and Day, Mission: Impossible IV (also writer, prod.). *Producer:* War Magician, Suspect Zero, I Married a Witch, Elizabethtown, Ghost Soldiers, The Eye, Ask the Dust, Death Race.
TELEVISION: *Director:* The Frightening Framis (episode of series Fallen Angels). *Guest:* More than 206 appearances.

CRUZ, PENÉLOPE
Actress. b. Madrid, Spain, April 28, 1974. Producer for 88 Productions. m. actor Javier Bardem.
PICTURES: The Greek Labyrinth, The Age of Beauty, Salami, Salami, The Rebel, For Love, Only For Love, Alegre ma non troppo, Life's a Bitch, Entre rojas, Brujas, La Celestina, Not Love, Just Frenzy, Love Can Seriously Damage Your Health, A Corner of Paradise, Live Flesh, Open Your Eyes, Don Juan, Twice Upon A Yesterday, Talk of Angels, The Girl of Your Dreams, The Hi-Lo Country, Nada en la Nevera, All About My Mother, Volaverunt, Blow, All the Pretty Horses, Captain Corelli's Mandolin, No News From God, Vanilla Sky, The Diary of a Young London Physician, Masked & Anonymous, Fanfan la tulipe, Gothika, Head in the Clouds, Sahara, Noel, Chromophobia, Bandidas, Volver (Academy Award nom.; Golden Globe nom. 2007), Manolete, Elegy, The Good Night, Vicky Cristina Barcelona (Academy Award, Golden Globe nom. 2009), Broken Embraces, G-Force (voice), Nine (Academy Award nom.; Golden Globe nom. 2010), Sex and the City 2, Pirates of the Caribbean: On Stranger Tides.
TELEVISION: *Movie:* Framed. *Guest:* More than 173 appearances.

CRYER, JON
Actor. b. New York, NY, Apr. 16, 1965. Son of actor David Cryer and songwriter-actress Gretchen Cryssser. On B'way stage in Brighton Beach Memoirs.
PICTURES: No Small Affair (debut, 1984), Pretty in Pink, Morgan Stewart's Coming Home, O.C. and Stiggs, Superman IV: The Quest for Peace, Hiding Out, Dudes, Penn and Teller Get Killed, Hot Shots!, The Pompatus of Love, Plan B, Went to Coney Island on a Mission from God...Back By 5, Die Wholesale, Holy Man, Unstable Fables: 3 Pigs & a Baby, Tortured, Weather Girl, Stay Cool, Shorts.
TELEVISION: *Movies:* Noon Wine, Heads. *Series:* The Famous Teddy Z, Partners, It's Good to Be King, Getting Personal, The Trouble With Normal, Hey Joel (voice), Stripperella (voice), Two and a Half Men (Emmy Award 2009, 3 Emmy noms.). *Guest:* More than 70 appearances.

CRYSTAL, BILLY
Actor, Writer, Producer, Director. b. Long Island, NY, Mar. 14, 1947. e. Marshall U., Nassau Commun. Col., NYU (BFA in tv & ilm direction). Father, Jack, produced jazz concerts; family owned Commodore jazz record label. Worked with Alumni Theatre Group at Nassau Commun. College. Later teamed with two friends (billed as We the People, Comedy Jam, 3's Company) and toured coffee houses and colleges. Became stand-up comedian on own, appearing at Catch a Rising Star, The Comedy Story and on TV. Album: Mahvelous!. Book: Absolutely Mahvelous!
PICTURES: Rabbit Test (debut, 1978), Animalympics (voice), This Is Spinal Tap, Running Scared, The Princess Bride, Throw Mama From the Train, Memories of Me (also co-prod., co-s.p.), When Harry Met Sally... (Golden Globe nom. 1990), City Slickers (Golden Globe nom. 1992, also exec. prn, od.), Mr. Saturday Night (Golden Globe nom. 1993, also dir., prod., co-s.p.), City Slickers II: The Legend of Curly's Gold (also prod., co-s.p.), Forget Paris (also dir., prod., co-s.p.), Hamlet, Father's Day, Deconstructing Harry, My Giant, Analyze This, Monsters, Inc. (voice), America's Sweethearts, Analyze That, Howl's Moving Castle (voice), Cars (voice), Tooth Fairy, Us & Them (writer), Monsters Inc. 2.
TELEVISION: *Movies:* SST—Death Flight, Human Feelings, Breaking Up Is Hard to Do, Enola Gay: The Men the Mission and the Atomic Bomb, 61 (2 Golden Globe nom.; 2 Emmy noms.; DGA nom. 2002). *Host:* Grammy Awards (Emmy Awards for hosting, 1988, 1989), Academy Awards (Emmy Award for hosting, 1991, 1997; Emmy Award for co-writing, 1992), 1999 Special Olympics World Summer Games Opening Ceremony. *Series:* Soap, The Billy Crystal Comedy Hour (also writer), Saturday Night Live (also writer), Sessions (creator, exec. prod. only), Liberty's Kids: Est. 1776 (voice). *Specials include:* Battle of the Network Stars, Billy Crystal: A Comic's Line (also writer), A Comedy Salute to Baseball (also writer), On Location: Billy Crystal - Don't Get Me Started (also dir., writer), The Three Little Pigs (Faerie Tale Theatre), The Lost Minutes of Billy Crystal, Midnight Train to Moscow (also exec. prod., co-writer; Emmy Award, 2 more nom. 1990), Comic Relief (host, writer, dir., exec. prod.; Emmy nom. 1996). *Host/Writer:* The 63rd Annual Academy Awards, The 64th Annual Academy Awards, The 65th Annual Academy Awards, The 70th Annual Academy Awards, The 76th Annual Academy Awards (writer). *Guest*: More than 214 appearances.

CUBAN, MARK
Executive. b. Pittsburgh, PA, July 31, 1958. e. graduate of Indiana Univ., 1981. Entrepreneur whose MicroSolutions, Inc. was grossing $30 million a year in 1990 before he sold the company to CompuServe and retired briefly. Cuban entered broadcasting over the Internet in 1995 with his Broadcast.com venture which enabled people to listen to radio and TV stations live on the company's website. The company went public and was sold to Yahoo.com, leaving Cuban a billionaire. With his wealth, Cuban has followed his passions and entered new industries: He acquired his hometown NBA team, the Dallas Mavericks; and he is an owner of 2929 Entertainment, which produces and finances movies through two production companies. These companies are 2929 Productions, which produces films in the $10 - $40 million budget range, and HDNet Films, which produces smaller-budget movies shot exclusively in high definition. Through its acquisition of Rysher Entertainment, 2929 Entertainment owns syndication rights to TV shows such as Hogan's Heroes, Lifestyles of the Rich and Famous and Star Search. Cuban is also a partner and chairman and pres. of HDNET, LLC, a leading high-definition national television network he co-founded with Todd Wagner.

HDNet's two 24/7 general entertainment networks are HDNet and HDNet Movies. Cuban is also a partner in Magnolia Pictures and a co-owner of Landmark Theatres, the nation's largest art-house chain.

CULBERG, PAUL S.
Executive. b. Chicago, IL, June 14, 1942. Began career in record industry, holding positions with Elektra Records & Wherehouse Records; 1977-80, v.p. sales mktg. for Cream Records' 1980-82, dir. sales for Paramount Home Video; 1982, v.p. sales mktg., Media Home Entertainment; 1984-89, New World Video; 1989, COO, RCA Columbia/TriStar Home Video. In 2000, became exec. v.p. & COO of the now defunct VM Labs. He is a former president of the DVD Entertainment Group, the industry association representing the major studios, record labels and consumer electronics companies to promote the versatile format of DVD. Culberg was inducted into the Video Business Video Hall of Fame in 2000. He is now pres. & COO of indie supplier Goldhil Entertainment, which is based in Camarillo, CA.

CULKIN, KIERAN
Actor. b. New York, NY, Sept. 30, 1982. Began working in 1990, making debut with his brother, Macauley Culkin in Home Alone.
PICTURES: Home Alone, Only the Lonely, Father of the Bride, Home Alone 2: Lost in New York, Nowhere to Run, It Runs in the Family, Father of the Bride Part II, Amanda, The Mighty, She's All That, Music of the Heart, The Cider House Rules, The Dangerous Lives of Altar Boys, Igby Goes Down (Golden Globe nom. 2003), The Other Side, Scott Pilgrim vs. the World.
TELEVISION: *Mini-series:* The Magical Legend of the Leprechauns. *Series:* Go Fish.

CULKIN, MACAULAY
Actor. b. New York, NY, Aug. 26, 1980. Brother is Kieran Culkin. Acting debut at 4 yrs. old in Bach Babies at NY's Symphony Space. Appeared in several TV commercials. Studied ballet at George Ballanchine's School of American Ballet and danced in NY productions of H.M.S. Pinafore and The Nutcracker. Received Comedy Award and Youth in Film Award for role in Home Alone. Appeared in Michael Jackson video Black and White.
THEATRE: NY: Afterschool Special, Mr. Softee, Buster B. and Olivia.
PICTURES: Rocket Gibraltar (debut, 1988), See You in the Morning, Uncle Buck, Jacob's Ladder, Home Alone (Golden Globe nom. 1991), Only the Lonely, My Girl, Home Alone 2: Lost in New York, The Good Son, George Balanchine's The Nutcracker, Getting Even With Dad, The Pagemaster, Richie Rich, Party Monster, Saved!, Sex and Breakfast.
TELEVISION: Movie:Foster Hall. *Series:* Wish Kid, Robot Chicken, Kings. *Guest:* More than 55 appearances.

CULLUM, JOHN
Actor. b. Knoxville, TN, Mar. 2, 1930. e. Univ. of TN. Son is actor John David (J.D.) Cullum.
THEATRE: NY: Camelot, On a Clear Day You Can See Forever (Theatre World Award, Tony nom.), Hamlet, Man of La Mancha, 1776, Shenandoah (Tony Award, Drama Desk & Outer Circle Critics Awards, 1975), The Trip Back Down, On the Twentieth Century (Tony Award, 1978), Deathtrap, Private Lives, Doubles, The Boys in Autumn, Aspects of Love, Showboat.
PICTURES: All the Way Home, 1776, The Prodigal, The Act, Marie, Sweet Country, The Secret Life of Algernon, Ricochet River, Held Up, The Notorious Bettie Page, The Night Listener, All Good Things.
TELEVISION: *Movies:* Androcles and the Lion, The Man Without a Country, Roll of Thunder, Hear My Cry, Summer, The Day After, Shootdown, Money, Power, Murder, With a Vengeance, Inherit the Wind. *Series:* The Edge of Night, One Life to Live, Buck James, Northern Exposure (Emmy nom. 1993), To Have and to Hold, ER, Law & Order: Special Victims Unit. *Guest:* More than 47 appearances.

CULP, ROBERT
Actor, Writer, Director. b. Berkeley, CA, Aug. 16, 1930. e. Stockton, College of the Pacific, Washington U., San Francisco State. To N.Y. to study with Herbert Berghof (played Potzo in 1st U.S. prod. of Waiting for Godot. Starred in off-B'way prod. He Who Gets Slapped. Best Actor of the Year in an off-B'way Play; motion picture debut, 1962; P.T. 109. Television guest appearances in Rawhide, Wagon Train, Bob Hope Presents the Chrysler Theatre; wrote and acted in Rifleman, Cain's Hundred, The Dick Powell Show.
THEATRE: *B'way:* The Prescott Proposals, A Clearing in the Woods, Diary of a Scoundrel.
PICTURES: PT 109 (debut, 1963), Sunday in New York, Rhino!, Bob & Carol & Ted & Alice, The Grove, Hannie Caulder, Hickey & Boggs (also dir., uncredited co-s.p.), A Name for Evil, The Castaway Cowboy, Inside Out (Golden Heist), Sky Riders, Breaking Point, The Great Scout and Cathouse Thursday, Goldengirl, National Lampoon Goes to the Movies, Turk 182!, Big Bad Mama II, Silent Night Deadly Night 3: Better Watch Out, Pucker Up and Bark Like a Dog, Timebomb, The Pelican Brief, Panther, Xtro 3: Watch the Skies, Favorite Deadly Sins, Spy Hard, Most Wanted, Wanted, Unconditional Love, Farewell My Love, Dark Summer, NewsBreak, Hunger, Santa's Slay, The Assignment.
TELEVISION: *Movies:* Sammy The Way Out Seal, The Raiders, The Hanged Man, See the Man Run, A Cold Night's Death, Outrage!, Houston We've Got a Problem, Strange Homecoming, A Cry for Help, Flood, Spectre, Last of the Good Guys, Women in White, Hot Rod, The Dream Merchants, The Night the City Screamed, Killjoy, Thou Shalt Not Kill, Her Life as a Man, The Calendar Girl Murders, Brothers-in-Law, The Blue Lightning, The Gladiator, The Key to Rebecca, Combat High, Voyage of Terror: The Achille Lauro Affair, Columbo Goes to College, I Spy Returns, Favorite Deadly Sins, Mercenary, Running Mates, Early Bird. *Series:* Trackdown, I Spy (also wrote pilot and 6 shows; 4 Emmy noms.; Golden Globe nom.1967 as writer and actor), The Greatest American Hero (also wrote 2 shows), Everybody Loves Raymond. *Guest:* More than 175 appearances.

CUMMING, ALAN
Actor. b. Perthshire, Scotland, Jan. 27, 1965.
PICTURES: Prague, Second Best, Black Beauty (voice), Circle of Friends, GoldenEye, Burn Your Phone, Emma, Spice World, For My Baby, Romy and Michele's High School Reunion, Buddy, The Flintstones in Viva Rock Vegas, Eyes Wide Shut, Plunkett & MaCleane, Titus, Urbania, Company Man, Spy Kids, Josie and the Pussycats, The Anniversary Party (also dir.), Cinemagique, Nicholas Nickleby, Zero Effect, Spy Kids 3-D: Game Over, Garfield: The Movie (voice), White on White, Son of the Mask, Gray Matters, X-Men 3, Eighteen, Every Word Is True, Neverwas, Living Neon Dreams, Coming Out, Ant Bully (voice), Gray Matters, ShowBusiness: The Road to Broadway (doc., co-exec. prod.), Jackboots on Whitehall (voice), Boogie Woogie, The Tempest, Sir Billi (voice), Jackboots on Whitehall (voice), Escape to Donegal, Burlesque.
TELEVISION: *Movies:* Bernard and the Genie, The Airzone Solution, Micky Love, That Sunday, Annie, Zero Effect, The Goodbye Girl,Reefer Madness: The Movie Musical, Riverworld. *Mini-series:* Tin Man. *Series:* Take the High Road, Shadow of the Stone, The High Life (writer/composer), God, the
Devil and Bob (voice), Shoebox Zoo (voice), The L Word, Rick & Steve the Happiest Gay Couple in All the World, Web Therapy (series short). *Guest:* More than 104 appearances.

CUNNINGHAM, SEAN S.
Producer, Director. b. New York, NY, Dec. 31 1941. e. Franklin & Marshall, B.A.; Stanford U., M.F.A. Worked briefly as actor, moving into stage-managing. Became producer of Mineola Theatre (Long Island, NY) and took several productions to B'way. Formed Sean S. Cunningham Films, Ltd., 1971. Produces commercials, industrial film, documentaries, features.
PICTURES: Together (prod., dir.), Last House on the Left (prod.), The Case of the Full Moon Murders (prod.), Here Come the Tigers (prod., dir.), Kick (prod., dir.), Friday the 13th (prod., dir.), A Stranger Is Watching (prod., dir.), Spring Break (prod., dir.), The New Kids (prod., dir.), House (prod.), House II: The Second Story (prod.), Deepstar Six (prod., dir.), The Horror Show (House III; prod.), House IV (prod.), My Boyfriend's Back (prod.), Jason Goes to Hell: The Final Friday (prod.), XCU: Extreme Close Up, Jason X, The Many Lives of Jason Voorhees (video short), Celluloid Crime of the Century (video documentary short), Freddy v. Jason (prod. only), Trapped Ashes (dir.), The Last House on the Left (prod.), Black Friday 3D (co-prod.), Friday the 13th (exec. prod.).
TELEVISION: *Movie:* Terminal Invasion (exec. prod.). *Documentary:* Reiselust (series, prod., writer).

CURLEY, JOHN J
Executive, Educator. b. Dec. 31, 1938. e. Dickinson College, BA, 1960; Columbia U., MS, 1963. Served as a lieutenant in the U.S. Army. Reporter, editor Associated Press, 1961-66. With Gannett Co., Inc., from 1969 to his retirement in early 2001. He ran Gannett News Service in Washington from 1974 to 1980 and then was publisher of the News-Journal in Wilmington, Delaware, before returning to Washington in 1982 to become the first editor of USA TODAY. In 1983 he became pres. of the Gannett Newspaper Division and a member of the Gannett bd. of dir. During 1984, he became pres.and COO, and in 1986 he became Gannett's CEO, continuing as pres. In April 1989 Curley became chairman, pres. and chief executive. He continued as pres. until Sept. 1997 when Douglas McCorkindale became pres. On June 1, 2000, Curley also turned over the CEO title to McCorkindale. After retirement from Gannett in 2001, Curley has been actively involved with journalism education at the College of Communications at Pennsylvania State Univ. In 1999 Curley was made an honorary alumnus and is on the faculty as a Distinguished Professor in Residence and is the co-director of the Center for Sports Journalism. He teaches courses in news writing, specialty reporting and issues in journalism. Curley has served on Penn State's Board of Visitors, with 10 years as the bd.'s chair. He is currently chair of the capital campaign committee.

CURRY, TIM
Actor. b. Cheshire, England, Apr. 19, 1946. e. Birmingham U. Albums: Read My Lips, Fearless, Simplicity.
THEATRE: Hair, A Midsummer Night's Dream, The Rocky Horror

Show, Travesties, Amadeus (Tony nom.), The Pirates of Penzance, Me and My Girl (U.S. tour), The Art of Success, My Favorite Year (Tony nom.).
PICTURES: The Rocky Horror Picture Show (debut, 1975), The Shout, Times Square, Annie, The Ploughman's Lunch, Blue Money, Clue, Legend, Pass the Ammo, The Hunt for Red October, Oscar, FernGully... The Last Rainforest (voice), Passed Away, Home Alone 2: Lost in New York, National Lampoon's Loaded Weapon 1, The Three Musketeers, The Shadow, Lovers' Knot, The Pebble and the Penguin (voice), Congo, The Muppet Treasure Island, Lover's Knot, McHale's Navy, The Rugrats Movie (voice), The Titanic Chronicles, Pirates of Plain, Four Dogs Playing Poker, Sorted, Charlie's Angels, Rugrats in Paris: The Movie (voice), Lion of Oz, Scary Movie 2, Ritual, The Scoundrel's Wife, The Wild Thornberrys, I Crocodile (narrator), Rescue Me (voice), Rugrats Go Wild! (voice), Kinsey, Bailey's Billion$, Valiant (voice), Christmas in Wonderland, The Chosen One, Garfield: A Tail of Two Kitties (voice), Fly Me to the Moon 3D (voice), Wolf Sheep, Burke and Hare, Around the World in 50 Years 3D (voice).
TELEVISION: *Movies:* The Duchess of Malfi, Oliver Twist, Schmoedipus, Three Men in a Boat, Oliver Twist, Lights, Camera, Annie!, Blue Money, The Worst Witch, The Wall: Live in Berlin, The Story of Santa Claus, Stephen King's IT, Doom Runners, Jackie's Back: Portrait of a Diva, The Unbelievables, Attila, Wolf Girl, Barbie in the Nutcracker (voice). Voice work—series: Peter Pan and the Pirates (Emmy Award, 1991), The Jimmy Timmy Power Hour 2: When Nerds Collide (voice), The Colour of Magic. *Mini-series:* Napoleon and Love, Life of Shakespeare, Lexx: The Dark Zone Stories, Return to Cranford. *Series:* Wiseguy (actor), *Voice:* Tale Spin, Tom and Jerry Kids Show, Gravedale High, Don Coyote and Sancho Panda, Dark Water, Prince Valiant, Darkwing Duck, Capitol Critters, Fish Police, Eek! the Cat, Wild West Cowboys from Moo Mesa (also actor), Sonic the Hedgehog (actor), Aladdin (also actor), Superhuman Samurai Syber-Squad, Gargoyles, Aaahh!!! Real Monsters, Where on Earth Is Carmen Sandiego?, The Mask, Quack Pack, Bruno the Kid, Mighty Ducks: The Animated Series, Jumanji, Over the Top (actor/prod.), Stories from My Childhood, The Net, Xyber 9: New Dawn, Mattimeo: A Tale of Redwall, Family Affair (actor), The Adventures of Jimmy Neutron: Boy Genius (voice). *Specials:* Three Men in a Boat, Rock Follies, City Sugar. *Guest:* More than 154 appearances.

CURTIN, JANE

Actress. b. Cambridge, MA, Sept. 6, 1947. e. Northeastern U. On stage in Proposition, Last of the Red Hot Lovers, Candida. Author, actress off-B'way musical revue Pretzel 1974-75.
PICTURES: Mr. Mike's Mondo Video, How to Beat the High Cost of Living, O.C. and Stiggs, Coneheads, Antz (voice), Brooklyn Lobster, The Shaggy Dog, I Love You, Man.
TELEVISION: *Movies:* What Really Happened to the Class of '65, Divorce Wars—A Love Story, Suspicion, Maybe Baby, Common Ground, Tad, Christmas in Washington, Catch a Falling Star. Our Town, The Librarian: Quest for the Spear, The Librarian: Return to King Solomon's Mines, Nice Girls Don't Get the Corner Office, The Librarian: The Curse of the Judas Chalice. *Series:* Saturday Night Live (1974-79), Kate & Allie (Emmy Awards: 1984, 1985, Emmy nom; 1987; Golden Globe nom. 1978), Working It Out, 3rd Rock from the Sun, Recess (voice), Hercules (voice), Crumbs. *Special:* Candida. *Guest:* More than 80 appearances.

CURTIS, JAMIE LEE

Actress. b. Los Angeles, CA, Nov. 22, 1958. e. Choat Rosemary Hall, CT; Univ. of the Pacific. m. actor-director Christopher Guest. Daughter of late actress Janet Leigh and Tony Curtis. While in school won contract with Universal Studios and appeared in several TV shows.
PICTURES: Halloween (debut, 1978), The Fog, Prom Night, Terror Train, Halloween II, Roadgames, Trading Places, Love Letters, Grandview USA, Perfect, Amazing Grace and Chuck, A Man in Love, Dominick and Eugene, A Fish Called Wanda (Golden Globe nom. 1989), Blue Steel, Queens Logic, My Girl, Forever Young, My Girl 2, Mother's Boys, True Lies (Golden Globe Award 1995), House Arrest, Fierce Creatures, Halloween H2O: Twenty Years Later, Homegrown, Virus, Drowning Mona, The Tailor of Panama, Daddy and Them, Marlene Dietrich: Her Own Song, Doin' the Splits, Halloween: Resurrection, Freaky Friday (Golden Globe nom. 2004), Christmas with the Kranks, South of the Border, Beverly Hills Chihuahua, You Again.
TELEVISION: *Movies:* Operation Petticoat (pilot), She's in the Army Now, Death of a Centerfold: The Dorothy Stratten Story, Money on the Side, As Summers Die, The Heidi Chronicles (Golden Globe nom. 1996), Nicholas' Gift (Emmy nom. 1998), A Home for the Holidays. *Pilot:* Callahan. *Series:* Operation Petticoat (1977-78), Anything But Love (also, dir., Golden Globe Award 1990, also 1 nom.), Pigs Next Door (voice). *Special:* Tall Tales (Annie Oakley). *Guest:* More than 130 appearances.

CURTIS, TONY

Actor. r.n. Bernard Schwartz. b. New York, NY, June 3, 1925. e. Seward Park H.S. Daughter is actress Jamie Lee Curtis. In U.S. Navy, amateur dramatics, N.Y., started Empire Players Theatre, Newark, NJ. With Dramatic Workshop, Cherry Lane Theatre, Junior Drama workshop of Walt Whitman School. First prod. work with Stanley Woolf Players. Made m.p. debut unbilled in Criss-Cross; signed with U-I. Star of Tomorrow, 1953. Author: Tony Curtis: The Autobiography (1993).
PICTURES: Criss Cross (debut, 1948), City Across the River, The Lady Gambles, Johnny Stool Pigeon, Francis, Sierra, I Was a Shoplifter, Winchester 73, Sierra, Kansas Raiders, Prince Who Was a Thief, Flesh and Fury, Son of Ali Baba, No Room for the Groom, Houdini, All American, Forbidden, Beachhead, Johnny Dark, Black Shield of Falworth, 6 Bridges to Cross, So This Is Paris, Purple Mask, Square Jungle, Rawhide Years, Trapeze, Mister Cory, Midnight Story, Sweet Smell of Success, The Vikings, Kings Go Forth, The Defiant Ones (Academy Award nom. Golden Globe nom. 1959), The Perfect Furlough, Some Like It Hot, Operation Petticoat, Who Was That Lady?, The Rat Race, Spartacus, Pepe (cameo), The Great Impostor, The Outsider, Taras Bulba, 40 Pounds of Trouble, The List of Adrian Messenger, Captain Newman, M.D., Paris When it Sizzles, Wild and Wonderful, Sex and the Single Girl, Goodbye Charlie, The Great Race, Boeing-Boeing, Chamber of Horrors (cameo), Not With My Wife You Don't!, Arrivederci Baby!, Don't Make Waves, On My Way to the Crusades I Met a Girl Who—(The Chastity Belt), The Boston Strangler (Golden Globe nom. 1969), Rosemary's Baby (voice), Those Daring Young Men in Their Jaunty Jalopies (Monte Carlo or Bust), Suppose They Gave a War and Nobody Came, You Can't Win 'Em All, Lepke, The Last Tycoon, Casanova & Co., The Manitou, The Bad News Bears Go to Japan, Sextette, Little Miss Marker, The Mirror Crack'd, Brainwaves, King of the City, Insignificance, Club Life, The Last of Philip Banter, Balboa, Midnight, Lobster Man From Mars, The High-Flying Mermaid, Prime Target, Center of the Web, Naked in New York, The Reptile Man, The Immortals, The Celluloid Closet, Hardball, Brittle Glory, Star Games, Play It to the Bone, Reflections of Evil (documentary), David & Fatima.
TELEVISION: *Movies:* The Third Girl from the Left, The Count of Monte Cristo, Vega$, The Users, Moviola: The Scarlett O'Hara War (Emmy nom. 1980), Inmates: A Love Story, Harry's Back, The Million Dollar Face, Mafia Princess, Murder in Three Acts, Portrait of a Showgirl, Tarzan in Manhattan, Thanksgiving Day, Christmas in Connecticut, A Perry Mason Mystery: The Case of the Grimacing Governor, Elvis Meets Nixon. *Series:* The Persuaders, McCoy, Vega$, Hollywood Babylon (host). *Guest:* More than 159 appearances.
(d. September 29, 2010)

CUSACK, JOAN

Actress. b. Evanston, IL, Oct. 11, 1962. Brother is actor John Cusack. e. U. of Wisconsin, Madison. Studied acting at Piven Theatre Workshop, Evanston, IL. While in coll. joined The Ark, local improvisational comedy group.
THEATRE: Road, Brilliant Traces (Theatre World Award for both), Cymbeline, The Celestial Alphabet Event, 'Tis Pity She's a Whore, A Midsummer Night's Dream.
PICTURES: My Bodyguard (debut, 1980), Class, Sixteen Candles, Grandview U.S.A., The Allnighter, Broadcast News, Stars and Bars, Married to the Mob, Working Girl (Acad. Award nom. 1988), Say Anything..., Men Don't Leave, My Blue Heaven, The Cabinet of Dr. Ramirez, Hero, Toys, Addams Family Values, Corrina Corrina, Nine Months, Mr. Wrong, Grosse Pointe Blank, A Smile Like Yours, In & Out (Academy Award nom. Golden Globe nom. 1998, NY Film Crits. Circle Award, Best Supporting Actress, 1997), Runaway Bride, The Cradle Will Rock, Arlington Road, Toy Story 2 (voice), High Fidelity, Where the Heart Is, The School of Rock, Looney Tunes: Back in Action, Raising Helen, Ice Princess, Chicken Little (voice), Friends with Money, War, Inc., The Martian Child, Kit Kittredge: An American Girl, Confessions of a Shopaholic, My Sister's Keeper, Hoodwinked 2: Hood vs. Evil (voice), Toy Story 3 (voice), Mars Needs Moms!.
TELEVISION: *Movies:* It's a Very Merry Muppet Christmas Movie, Paddy Chayefsky's The Mother, Acceptance. *Series:* Saturday Night Live (1985-86), What About Joan, Peep and the Big Wide World (Emmy nom. 2005 narr.).

CUSACK, JOHN

Actor. b. Evanston, IL, June 28, 1966. Sister is actress Joan Cusack. Member of Piven Theatre Workshop in Evanston for 10 years beginning when he was 9 years old. Appeared on several tv commercials as teen. Formed Chicago theatrical company, New Criminals.
PICTURES: Class (debut, 1983), Sixteen Candles, Grandview U.S.A., The Sure Thing, The Journey of Natty Gann, Better Off Dead, Stand By Me, One Crazy Summer, Hot Pursuit, Eight Men Out, Tapeheads, Say Anything..., Fat Man and Little Boy, The Grifters, True Colors, Shadows and Fog, Roadside Prophets, The Player, Bob Roberts, Map of the Human Heart, Money for Nothing, Bullets Over Broadway, The Road to Wellville, Floundering, City Hall, Grosse Pointe Blank (also co-prod. & s.p.), Con Air, Midnight in the Garden of Good and Evil, Anastasia (voice), This Is My Father, The Thin Red Line, Pushing Tin, Chicago Cab, Arigo (also prod.), High Fidelity (Golden Globe nom.; WGA nom. 2001, also s.p.), Cradle Will Rock, Being John Malkovich, White Jazz, Life of the Party, Arigo, Serendipity, Never Got Outta the Boat (exec prod. only), Max (assoc. prod.), 2.2 (prod. only), Adaptation, Hoffman, Identity, The Runaway Jury, The Ice Harvest, A Doll's House, Must Love Dogs, Martian Child, The Contract, Grace Is Gone (also prod.), Cosmic Banditos (also

prod.), 1408, War, Inc. (also prod., writer s.p.), Igor (voice), 2012, Shanghai, The Factory, Hot Tub Time Machine.
TELEVISION: *Movies:* The Jack Bull, Eastwood on Eastwood. *Mini-series:* Baseball (voice). Documentaries: Eastwood on Eastwood (narr.). *Guest:* More than 71 appearances.

CZERNY, HENRY
Actor. b. Toronto, Canada, Feb. 1959. Began acting career performing in musicals at Humberside collegiate in Toronto.
PICTURES: I Love a Man in Uniform, Cold Sweat, Buried on Sunday, Anchor Zone, Clear and Present Danger, Notes From Underground, The Michelle Apartments, The Interview, When Night Is Falling, Mission Impossible, Promise the Moon, Kayla, The Ice Storm, Kayla, External Affairs, Cement, After Alice, Klepto, The Limit, The Failures, The Circle, Chaos, The Pink Panther, Conversations with God (voice), Fido, The Fifth Patient, Ice Castles.
TELEVISION: Movies: The Taming of the Shrew, Deadly Matrimony, A Town Torn Apart, Lifeline to Victory, The Boys of St. Vincent, Ultimate Betrayal, Trial at Fortitude Bay, Choices of the Heart: The Margaret Sanger Story, For Hope, Glory and Honor, Promise the Moon, My Father's Shadow: The Sam Sheppard Story, P.T. Barnum, The Girl Next Door, Possessed, Range of Motion, Haven, Further Tales of the City, Come l'America, The Pact, Salem Witch Trials, The Russell Girl, Mayerthorpe, Prayers for Bobby, Christmas Dreams, The Cult. *Mini-series:* The Tudors. *Guest:* More than 47 appearances.

D

D'ABO, OLIVIA
Actress. b. England. Jan. 22, 1967. Parents, singer Michael d'Abo & actress Maggie London.
PICTURES: Conan the Destroyer, Bolero, Bullies, Into the Fire, Beyond the Stars, The Spirit of 76, Point of No Return, Wayne's World 2, Bank Robber, Greedy, Clean Slate, The Last Good Time, The Big Green, Kicking and Screaming, Live Nude Girls, Hacks, The Velocity of Gary, It Had To Be You, Texas Funeral, Seven Girlfriends, The Enemy, Jonni Nitro, Tarzan & Jane (video, voice), The Animatrix (video, voice), A Poor Kid's Guide to Success, Green Lantern: First Flight (voice).
TELEVISION: *Movies:* Not My Kid, Crash Course, Midnight's Child, Dad's Week Off, The Triangle. *Series*: The Wonder Years, The Single Guy, Mortal Kombat: The Animated Series (voice), The Legend of Tarzan (voice), Justice League Unlimited, Law & Order: Criminal Intent, Star Wars: The Clone Wars (voice).

DAFOE, WILLEM
Actor. r.n. William Dafoe. b. Appleton, WI, July 22, 1955. Worked with experimental group Theatre X on the road before coming to New York. Built sets and debuted with the Wooster Group at the Performing Garage playing (literally) a chicken heart in Elizabeth Le Compte's Nayatt School. Current member of the Wooster Group, performing with them frequently in U.S. and Europe. For them appeared in independent film The Communists Are Comfortable.
PICTURES: Heaven's Gate (debut, 1980), The Loveless, The Hunger, Streets of Fire, Roadhouse 66, To Live and Die in L.A., Platoon (Acad. Award nom. 1987), Off Limits, The Last Temptation of Christ, Mississippi Burning, Triumph of the Spirit, Born on the Fourth of July, Cry-Baby, Wild at Heart, Flight of the Intruder, White Sands, Light Sleeper, Body of Evidence, Faraway So Close!, Clear and Present Danger, Tom and Viv, The Night and the Moment, Basquiat, The English Patient, Speed 2: Cruise Control, Affliction, Lulu on the Bridge, New Rose Hotel, eXistenZ, Shadow of the Vampire (Academy Award nom.; Golden Globe nom. 2001), Bullfighter, Boondock Saints, American Psycho, The Animal Factory, Morality Play, Edges of the Lord, Bullfighter, Spider Man, Once Upon a Time in Mexico, Auto Focus, The Clearing, Spider-Man 2, The Reckoning, The Aviator, The Life Aquatic with Steve Zissou, White on White, Control, xXx 2: The Next Level, Manderlay, Before It Had a Name (also writer), American Dreamz, Inside Man, je t'aime Paris, The Walker, Anamorph, Mr. Bean's Holiday, Go Go Tales, Fireflies in the Garden, Adam Resurrected, The Dust of Time, Daybreakers, Fantastic Mr. Fox (voice), Antichrist, My Son, My Son, What Have Ye Done, Cirque du Freak: The Vampire's Assistant, The Miso Soup, Miral, A Woman, John Carter of Mars. *Guest:* More than 90 appearances.

DAHL, JOHN
Director, Writer. b. Montana, Oct. 11, 1956. e. Univ. of MT, Montana St. In collaboration with David Warfield made 30 minute rock musical, Here Come the Pugs and indept. feature, The Death Mutants. Received American Film Institute Franklin J. Schaffner Award 2003.
PICTURES: Private Investigations (co-s.p.), Kill Me Again (dir., co-s.p.), Red Rock West (dir., co-s.p.), The Last Seduction (dir.; DGA nom. 1995), Unforgettable (dir., co-s.p.), Striking Back: A Jewish Commando's War Against the Nazis (dir., prod.), Rounders (dir.), Joy Ride (dir.), The Great Raid (dir.), Ghost Soldiers (dir.), You Kill Me.
TELEVISION: *Movie:* The Line-Up. *Series:* Dexter, Californication. Director of many more series episodes.

DALE, JIM
Actor. b. Rothwell, Northhamptonshire, England, Aug. 15, 1935. Debut as solo comedian at the Savoy, 1951. Joined National Theatre Co. in 1969 playing in Love's Labour's Lost, The Merchant of Venice, The National Health, The Card. Has written songs and music for films: Twinky, Shalako, Joseph Andrews, Georgy Girl (Acad. Award nom.). Many TV appearances. Director: Asprin and Elephants. In TV movie, American Clock.
THEATRE: U.S.: Mark Taper Forum: Comedians, Scapino. N.Y.: Theater: Taming of the Shrew, Scapino, Barnum (Tony and Drama Desk Awards, 1980), Joe Egg (Tony Award nom.), Me and My Girl, Privates on Parade, Travels With My Aunt.
PICTURES: Six-Five Special (debut, 1958), Raising the Wind, Nurse on Wheels, The Iron Maiden, Carry on Cabby, Carry on Jack, Carry on Spying, Carry on Cleo, The Big Job, Carry on Cowboy, Georgy Girl (Academy Award nom. 1967), Carry on Screaming, Don't Lose Your Head, The Winter's Tale, The Plank, Follow That Camel, Carry on Doctor, Lock Up Your Daughters, Carry on Again Doctor, The National Health, Digby—The Biggest Dog in the World, Joseph Andrews, Pete's Dragon, Hot Lead Cold Feet, Unidentified Flying Oddball, Scandalous, Carry on Columbus.
TELEVISION: *Movies:* Mister Misfit, The Dancing Princesses, Adventures of Huckleberry Finn, The American Clock, Lincoln (voice), The Hunchback. *Series:* Six-Five Special (host), Rogues' Gallery, Join Jim Dale, Pushing Daisies. *Guest:* More than 50 apearances.

DALSIMER, SUSAN
Executive. Editor for E.P. Dutton before joining Lorimar Prods., as v.p. of east coast development. Left to become consultant for original programming at Home Box Office. 1987, named v.p., creative affairs, east coast, for Warner Bros. 1994, v.p., publishing for Miramax/Talk Media Books. Works for Contentville, an online magazine.

DALTON, TIMOTHY
Actor. b. Colwyn Bay, No. Wales, March 21, 1946. Started acting at Nat'l. Youth Theatre, then studied at RADA. Prof. stage debut in Richard III and As You Like It at Birmingham Rep.
THEATRE: Coriolanus, The Merchant of Venice, Richard III, The Doctor's Dilemna, St. Joan, Macbeth, Henry IV, Henry V, The Samaritan, Black Comedy, White Liars, Lunatic Lover and Poet, Love Letters (1991).
PICTURES: The Lion in Winter, Cromwell, The Voyeur, Wuthering Heights, Mary Queen of Scots, Permission to Kill, Sextette, Agatha, Flash Gordon, El Hombre Que Supo Amar, Anthony and Cleopatra, Chanel Solitaire, The Doctor and the Devils, The Living Daylights, Brenda Starr, Hawks, Licence to Kill, The King's Whore, The Rocketeer, Naked in New York, Saltwater Moose, The Reef, The Informant, The Beautician and the Beast, Made Men, Time Share, American Outlaws, Looney Tunes: Back in Action, Hot Fuzz, Toy Story 3 (voice).
TELEVISION: *Movies*: The Master of Ballantrae, Lie Down With Lions, Field of Blood, Framed, Cleopatra, The James Bond Story, Possessed, Dunkirk (narrator), Hercules, Agatha Christie Marple: The Sittaford Mystery. *Mini-series:* Centennial, Mistral's Daughter, Sins, Scarlett. *Series:* Sat'day While Sunday, Judge Dee, Hooked International, Charlie's Angels: Fallen Angel, Tales From the Crypt: Werewolf Concerto, Survival Factor Series (narr.). *Specials:* The Three Princes, Five Finger Exercise, Candida, Faerie Tale Theater: The Emperor's New Clothes (narr.), Nature: In The Company of Wolves (docu.). *Guest:* More than 80 appearances.

DALY, ANN
Executive. e. B.A. in economics from Univ. of California, Los Angeles. During a 14-year tenure at The Walt Disney Co., Daly was a video industry pioneer, heading up Buena Vista Home Video (BVHV), North America, where she ran the single largest video company in the world. While leading BVHV, she orchestrated many innovations. Beginning in 1994, Daly initiated a radically new business concept for the entertainment industry: producing high quality, family-oriented films exclusively for video and featuring some of Disney's most successful franchises. Under her leadership, the BVHV division maintained a number one market share in the industry, with over twice the revenue of its nearest competitor. In 1997, Daly became head of feature animation at DreamWorks Studios, where she guided the strategic, operational, administrative and production-oriented concerns of the animation division, as well as overseeing the worldwide video operations of DreamWorks Studios. With Dreamworks Animation SKG, Inc., public offering in Oct. 2004, Daly became COO of the new company and it is the position she holds today. Was #18 on The Hollywood Reporter's Women in Entertainment Power 100 for 2006.

DALY, ROBERT A.
Executive. b. New York, NY, Dec. 8, 1936. e. Brooklyn Coll., Hunter Coll. Joined CBS-TV in 1955; dir. of program acct.; dir. of research and cost planning; dir. of business affairs. Later named

v.p., business affairs, NY; exec. v.p. of network on April, 1976. Named president, CBS Entertainment, Oct. 1977. In Oct. 1979 became responsible for CBS Theatrical Films as well as the TV operation. In 1981, appointed chmn. of bd. and co-CEO of Warner Bros.; 1982, named chmn. of bd. and CEO; 1994, named chmn. of bd. and co-CEO, sharing office with Terry Semel; 1995, also named chmn. and co-CEO of the Warner Bros. Music Group. Former pres. and CEO, Los Angeles Dodgers baseball team. He is a former advisor to Viacom Inc. Daly served on the bd. of dir. of the American Film Institute (AFI); and is on the foundation bd. for the Motion Picture & Television Fund, member of the bd. of directors for Atom Entertainment, Inc. and a Director for Tonos Entertainment.

DALY, TIM

Actor. b. New York, NY, March 1, 1956. m. actress Amy Van Nostrand. Son of late actor James Daly, brother of actress Tyne Daly. e. Bennington Coll., B.A. Acted in summer stock while in college. Moved to NY where had own rock and roll band. Has performed in cabaret at Williamstown Theater Festival.
THEATRE: Fables for Friends, Oliver Oliver, Mass Appeal, Bus Stop, Coastal Disturbances (Theatre World Award).
PICTURES: Diner, Just the Way You Are, Made in Heaven, Spellbinder, Love or Money, Year of the Comet, Caroline at Midnight, Dr. Jekyll and Ms. Hyde, Denise Calls Up, The Associate, The Object of My Affection, Seven Girlfriends, Basic, Against the Ropes, Return to Sender, Bereft, The Mermaids Singing, Once in a Lifetime, Mr. Gibb, The Skeptic, PoliWood (doc. prod.).
TELEVISION: *Movies:* I Married a Centerfold, Mirrors, Red Earth White Earth, In the Line of Duty: Ambush in Waco, Dangerous Heart, Execution of Justice, A House Divided, The Outsider, Wilder Days, Edge of America (Emmy nom. 2006), Bereft. *Special:* The Rise and Rise of Daniel Rocket. *Mini-series:* I'll Take Manhattan, Queen, From the Earth to the Moon, Storm of the Century. *Series:* Ryan's Four, Almost Grown, Wings, Superman (voice), The New Batman/Superman Adventures (voice), Invasion America, The Sopranos (Emmy nom. 2007 as guest), The Fugitive, Eyes, The Nine, Private Practice. *Guest:* More than 71 appearances.

DALY, TYNE

Actress. r.n. Ellen Tyne Daly. b. Madison, WI, Feb. 21, 1946. Daughter of late actor James Daly and actress Hope Newell; brother is actor Timothy Daly.
THEATRE: The Butter and Egg Man, That Summer That Fall, Skirmishes, The Black Angel, Rimers of Eldritch, Ashes, Three Sisters, Come Back Little Sheba (L.A., 1987), Gypsy (Tony Award, 1990), Queen of the Stardust Ballroom, The Seagull, On the Town, Call Me Madam (in concert).
PICTURES: John and Mary, Angel Unchained, Play It As It Lays, The Adulteress, The Enforcer, Telefon, Speedtrap, Zoot Suit, The Aviator, Movers & Shakers, The Lay of the Land, Vig, Autumn Heart, The Simian Line, A Piece of Eden.
TELEVISION: *Movies:* In Search of America, A Howling in the Woods, Heat of Anger, The Man Who Could Talk to Kids, Larry, The Entertainer, Better Late Than Never, Intimate Strangers (Emmy nom. 1978), The Women's Room, A Matter of Life or Death, Your Place or Mine, Kids Like These, Stuck With Each Other, The Last to Go, Face of a Stranger, Columbo: A Bird in the Hand, Scattered Dreams: The Kathryn Messenger Story, The Forget-Me-Not Murders, Columbo: Undercover, Cagney & Lacey: The Return, Cagney & Lacey: Together Again, Bye Bye Birdie, Cagney & Lacey: True Convictions, Cagney & Lacey: The View Through the Glass Ceiling, Tricks, The Perfect Mother, Three Secrets, Execution of Justice, Absence of the Good, The Wedding Dress, Undercover Christmas, Georgia O'Keeffe. *Series:* Cagney & Lacey (4 Emmy Awards; 2 other nom.; 4 Golden Globe nom.), Wings (Emmy nom. 1992), Christy (Emmy Award, 1996; 1 other nom., Golden Globe nom.), Judging Amy (Emmy Award, 2003; 5 other noms.). *Guest:* more than 121 appearances.

DAMON, MARK

Executive, Actor. b. Chicago, IL, April 22, 1933. e. B.A. literature and MBA from UCLA. Actor: 1958 under contract to 20th Century Fox, 1960 winner Golden Globe Award-Newcomer of the Year; early career includes The Fall of The House of Usher, The Longest Day; 1961 moved to Italy, stayed 16 years appearing in leading roles in 50 films; 1974 head of foreign dept. for PAC, a leading film distributor in Italy; 1976 returned to the U.S. as exec. prod. of The Choirboys and in charge of its foreign distribution; 1979 founder and pres. of Producers Sales Organization, intl. distribution org. 1987 formed Vision Int'l.; 1993, formed MDP Worlwide Entertainment, Inc. an intl. prod. & distrib. co. was past chmn. & CEO. In 2005, Damon founded and is CEO of Foresight Unlimited, also a film production and distribution company. His first production at Foresight, Captivity, broke new ground as the first Russian-American co-production shot almost entirely at MOSFILM Studios in Moscow. He is considered one of the world's leading authorities on international distribution. Damon currently serves on the exec. committee of the Independent Film & Television Alliance and resides in California.
PICTURES: *Producer/Exec. prod.:* The Arena, The Choirboys, The Neverending Story, Das Boot, Nine 1/2 Weeks, Short Circuit, Flight of the Navigator, Lost Boys, High Spirits, Bat 21 (co-prod.), Diary of a Hit Man, Wild Orchid, Wild Orchid II: Two Shades of Blue, Stalingrad, The Jungle Book, The Jungle Book 2, The Blackout, The Winner, Orgazmo, Loved, Deceiver (also actor), Eye of the Beholder, Love & Sex, The Body, The Musketeer , FeardotCom, Extreme Ops, The United States of Leland, Monster, The I Inside, 11:14, Beyond the Sea, The Upside of Anger, O Jerusalem, Captivity, Beyond a Reasonable Doubt, Three Stories About Joan, Universal Soldier: Regeneration. *Actor:* Inside Detroit, Screaming Eagles, Between Heaven and Hell, Young and Dangerous, The Party Crashers, Life Begins at 17, House of Usher, This Rebel Breed, The Reluctant Saint, The Longest Day (uncredited), Beauty and the Beast, The Young Racers, Black Christmas, Pedro el Cruel, Son of Cleopatra, Hundred Horsemen, Ringo and His Golden Pistol, Agente segreto 777 operzione Mistero, Dio-come ti amo, One for All, Train for Durango, Death Does Not Count the Dollars, Johnny Yuma, Morti non si contano I, Kill and Pray, School Girl Killer, Anzio, Long Live Robin Hood, The Norman Swordsman, La Spada Normanna, Posate le pistole reverendo, Leoni di Petersburgo, Monta in sella figlio di...!, The Devil's Wedding Night, Little Mother, Crypt of the Living Death, Byleth, There Is No 13, Lo matas tu o lo mato yo, Do I Kill You or Do You Kill Me?, Stuck on You, Deceiver.

DAMON, MATT

Actor, Writer. b. Cambridge, MA, Oct. 8, 1970. Chicago Film Crits. Award, Most Promising New Actor, 1997.
PICTURES: *Actor:* Mystic Pizza (debut, 1988), School Ties, Geronimo: An American Legend, Courage Under Fire, Glory Daze, Chasing Amy, The Rainmaker, Good Will Hunting (also s.p., Academy Award, Golden Globe Award, WGA nom. Best Screenplay, 1997), Rounders, Saving Private Ryan, The Talented Mr. Ripley (Golden Globe nom. 2000), Dogma, All the Pretty Horses, Titan A.E. (voice), The Legend of Bagger Vance, All the Pretty Horses, Ocean's Eleven, The Majestic (voice), The Third Wheel, Spirit: Stallion of the Cimarron (voice), Gerry, The Bourne Identity, Confessions of a Dangerous Mind., Stuck On You, Eurotrip, Jersey Girl, The Bourne Supremacy, The Brothers Grimm, Ocean's Twelve, Syriana, The Good Shepherd, The Departed, The Bourne Ultimatum, Che: Part Two, Ponyo (voice), Margaret, The Informant! (Golden Globe nom. 2010), Invictus (Academy Award nom.; Golden Globe nom. 2010), Margaret, Green Zone, The Adjustment Bureau, True Grit, Hereafter, Contagion, Happy Feet 2 in 3D. *Exec. prod.:* Speakeasy, The Battle of Shaker Heights, Feast, The Departed, Ocean's Thirteen, Running the Sahara (narr., exec. prod.).
TELEVISION: *Movies:* Rising Son, The Good Old Boys, All Grown Up. *Series:* Project Greenlight Project (Emmy nom. 2002), Project Greenlight 2 (Emmy nom. 2004), Project Greenlight 3 (Emmy nom. 2005), Push, Nevada (exec. prod.). *Guest:* More than 131 appearances.

DAMSKI, MEL

Director. b. New York, NY, July 21, 1946. e. Colgate U., AFI. Worked as reporter, journalism professor. USC Cinema instructor.
PICTURES: Yellowbeard, Mischief, Happy Together, Still Kicking: The Fabulous Palm Springs Follies (doc. short, Academy Award nom. 1998), Brother's Keeper.
TELEVISION: *Movies:* The Long Journey Back, The Child Stealer, A Perfect Match, Word of Honor, American Dream (pilot, Emmy nom. 1981), For Ladies Only, The Legend of Walks Far Woman, Making the Grade, An Invasion of Privacy, Badge of the Assassin, A Winner Never Quits, Attack on Fear, Hero in the Family, Murder by the Book, The Three Kings, Everybody's Baby: The Rescue of Jessica McClure, A Connecticut Yankee in King Arthur's Court, The Girl Who Came Between Them, Blood River, Shoot First: A Cop's Vengeance, Wife Mother Murderer, Back to the Streets of San Francisco, Wild Card, The Care and Handling of Roses, Their Second Chance. *Series:* M*A*S*H, Barnaby Jones, The Bionic Woman, Lou Grant (Emmy nom. 1979), Picket Fences, Lois and Clark: The New Adventures of Superman, Harts of the West, Chicago Hope, Nowhere Man, American Gothic, Early Edition, The Practice, Ally McBeal, Any Day Now, The Love Boat: The Next Wave, Vengeance Unlimited, Charmed, Hack & Jill, Ally, Young Americans, Boston Public, The Tick, Everwood, Without a Trace, 1-800-Missing, Darcy's Wild Life, Psych (dir., co-exec. prod).

DANA, BILL

Actor, Writer. b. Quincy, MA, Oct. 5, 1924. Night clubs and TV.
PICTURES: The Busy Body, The Barefoot Executive, The Nude Bomb (also s.p.), The Right Stuff, Lena's Holiday.
TELEVISION: *Movies:* The Snoop Sisters, Rosetti & Ryan: Men Who Love Women, A Guide for the Married Woman, Murder in Texas. *Actor:* Facts of Life, Too Close for Comfort, Golden Girls, Hollywood Palace, St. Elsewhere. *Series:* The Steve Allen Show (performer, head writer, 1961), The Bill Dana Jose Jimenez Show (star, writer), Spike Jones Show (prod., writer, performer), Milton Berle Show (prod., writer, performer), No Soap Radio, Zorro and Son, All in the Family (writer), Matlock (writer), The Smothers Brothers Comedy Hour (actor). *Guest:* More than 68 appearances.

DANCE, CHARLES

Actor. b. Worcestershire, England, Oct. 10, 1946. e. Plymouth Coll. Art., Leicester Coll. of Art (graphic design degree). After first working as a West End theatre stagehand, made acting

debut in 1970 in a touring company of It's a Two-Foot-Six-Inches-above-the Ground World. Worked in provincial repertory theaters. Joined the Royal Shakespeare Company 1975-80: Hamlet, Richard III, As You Like It. Lead in Henry V (1975, N.Y.), Coriolanus (Paris, London, Stratford).
THEATRE: Plenty, McGuffin, revival of Irma La Douce (West End), Turning Over (London's Bush Theatre).
PICTURES: The Spy Who Loved Me (debut, 1977), For Your Eyes Only, Plenty, The Golden Child, Good Morning Babylon, White Mischief, The Hidden City, Pascali's Island, Alien 3, The Valley of Stone, Last Action Hero, China Moon, Century, Kabloonak, Exquisite Tenderness, Shortcut to Paradise, Undertow, Michael Collins, Space Truckers, What Rats Won't Do, Hilary & Jackie, Don't Go Breaking My Heart, Chrono-Perambulator, Dark Blue World, Gosford Park, Ali G Indahouse, Black and White, Swimming Pool, City and Crimes, Ladies in Lavender (dir./writer), Funny Farm, Scoop, Starter for 10, Intervention, There Be Dragons, Paris Connections, Your Highness.
TELEVISION: *Movies:* Very Like a Whale, The McGuffin, The Jewel in the Crown, Lightning Always Strikes Twice, Edward VII, The Fatal Spring, Little Eyolf, Frost in May, Nancy Astor, Saigon—The Last Day, Out On a Limb, BBC's The Secret Servant, Rainy Day Woman, Out of the Shadows, First Born, Goldeneye, Rebecca, Darling of the Gods, In the Presence of Mine Enemies, Justice in Wonderland, Murder Rooms, The Life and Adventures of Nicholas Nickleby, Alien Evolution, Henry VIII, Don Bosco, Fingersmith, Marple: By the Pricking of My Thumbs, Fallen Angel, Bleak House (Emmy nom. 2006). *Series:* Trinity. *Mini-series:* Phantom of the Opera, Trial & Retribution VII. *Guest:* More than 74 appearances.

D'ANGELO, BEVERLY

Actress. b. Columbus, OH, Nov. 15, 1954. Studied visual arts and was exchange student in Italy before working as cartoonist for Hanna-Barbera Studios in Hollywood. Toured Canada's coffeehouse circuit as singer and appeared with rock band called Elephant. Joined Charlotte Town Festival Company. B'way debut in rock musical, Rockabye Hamlet. *Off-B'way:* Simpatico (Theatre World Award).
PICTURES: The Sentinel (debut 1977), Annie Hall, First Love, Every Which Way But Loose, Hair, Highpoint, Coal Miner's Daughter (Golden Globe nom. 1981), Honky Tonk Freeway, Paternity, National Lampoon's Vacation, Finders Keepers, National Lampoon's European Vacation, Big Trouble, Maid to Order, In the Mood, Aria, Trading Hearts, High Spirits, National Lampoon's Christmas Vacation, Daddy's Dyin', The Miracle, The Pope Must Die, Man Trouble, Lonely Hearts, Lightning Jack, Eye for an Eye, Edie and Pen, Pterodactyl Woman from Beverly Hills, Vegas Vacation, A Ratls Take, Nowhere, Love Always, With Friends Like These, Illuminata, American History X, Sugar Town, Jazz Night, High Fidelity, Happy Birthday, Women in Film, Summer Catch, Where's Angelo?, The Pursuit of Happiness, King of the Corner, Hair High (voice), Firedog (voice), Relative Strangers, Terra (voice), Black Water Transit, I Know What Boys Like, Harold & Kumar Escape from Guantanamo Bay, The House Bunny, Black Water Transit, Popcorn Ceiling, Firedog (voice).
TELEVISION: *Movies:* A Streetcar Named Desire (Emmy nom. 1984), Doubletake, Slow Burn, Hands of a Stranger, Trial: The Price of Passion, A Child Lost Forever, The Switch, Judgment Day: The John List Story, Jonathan Stone: Threat of Innocence, Menendez: A Killing in Beverly Hills, Lansky, Talk to Me, On the Edge, Imperfect Union, Skip Tracer. *Mini-series:* Captains and the Kings. *Series:* Entourage, Law & Order: Special Victims Unit. *Special:* Sleeping Beauty (Faerie Tale Theater). *Guest:* More than 53 appearances.

DANES, CLAIRE

Actress. b. New York, NY, April 12, 1979. e. Professional Performing Arts School, NY; Lee Strasberg Studio. Acting career began with off-off-B'way appearances in Happiness, Punk Ballet and Kids on Stage.
PICTURES: Dreams of Love (debut), Thirty (short), The Pesky Suitor (short), Little Women, How to Make an American Quilt, Home for the Holidays, I Love You I Love You Not, Romeo + Juliet, To Gillian on Her 37th Birthday, Polish Wedding, U-Turn, The Rainmaker, Polish Wedding, Les Miserables, The Mod Squad, Brokedown Palace, Igby Goes Down, The Hours, It's All About Love, Terminator 3: Rise of the Machines, Stage Beauty, Shopgirl, Pushers Needed, The Family Stone, The Flock, Stardust, Evening, Me and Orson Welles.
TELEVISION: *Movies:* No Room for Opal, The Coming Out of Heidi Leiter, Temple Grandin. *Series:* Skin Deep, My So Called Life (Emmy nom. Golden Globe Award, 1995), Lifestories: Families In Crisis. *Guest:* More than 64 appearances.

DANIEL, SEAN

Executive, Producer. b. Aug. 15, 1951. e. California Inst. of Arts film school. BFA, 1973. Was journalist for Village Voice before starting m.p. career as documentary filmmaker and asst. dir. for New World Pictures. In 1976 joined Universal Pictures as prod. exec.; 1979, named v.p., then pres., production. Resigned March, 1989 to become pres., The Geffen Co., film div.; resigned from Geffen, Nov. 1989. 1990-2006, with Jim Jacks ran own prod. co. Alphaville Productions. The two split ways in 2006. Daniel still runs Alphaville from the Paramount studio and also runs the Sean Daniel Company.
PICTURES: *Prod./Exec. prod.:* Pure Luck, American Me, CB4, Hard Target, Heart and Souls, Dazed and Confused, Tombstone, Village of the Damned, Michael, Mallrats, The Jackal, The Mummy, Lucky Numbers, The Gift, Down to Earth, The Mummy Returns, Pootie Tang, Rat Race, The Scorpion King, Dark Blue, The Hunted, Intolerable Cruelty, Alfie, The Mummy: Tomb of the Dragon Emperor, The Wolf Man.
TELEVISION: *Prod./Exec. prod.:* Don't Look Back, Freedom Song, Attila, Everyday People.

DANIELS, JEFF

Actor. b. Athens, Georgia. Feb. 19, 1955. e. Central Michigan U. Apprentice with Circle Repertory Theatre, New York. Established Purple Rose Theatre Co. in Chelsea, Michigan. Playwright: The Kingdom's Coming, The Vast Difference.
THEATRE: Brontosaurus, Short-Changed Review, The Farm, Fifth of July, Johnny Got His Gun (Obie Award), Lemon Sky, The Three Sisters, The Golden Age, Redwood Curtain, God of Carnage (Tony nom. 2009).
PICTURES: Ragtime (debut, 1981), Terms of Endearment, The Purple Rose of Cairo (Golden Globe nom. 1986), Marie, Heartburn, Something Wild (Golden Globe nom. 1987), Radio Days, The House on Carroll Street, Sweet Hearts Dance, Checking Out, Arachnophobia, Welcome Home Roxy Carmichael, Love Hurts, The Butcher's Wife, There Goes the Neighborhood, Rain Without Thunder, Gettysburg, Speed, Terminal Velocity, Dumb & Dumber, 2 Days in the Valley, Fly Away Home, 101 Dalmations, Trial and Error, Pleasantville, All the Rage, My Favorite Martian, The Crossing, Cheaters, Chasing Sleep, Escanabia in da Moonlight (also dir.), Super Sucker (also dir.), Gods and Generals, Blood Work, I Witness, Imaginary Heroes, Because of Winn-Dixie, The Squid and the Whale (Golden Globe nom. 2006), Good Night, and Good Luck, Runaway Vacation, A Plumm Summer (narr.), Mama's Boy, The Lookout, Infamous, Space Chimps (voice), Traitor, Arlen Faber, State of Play, Away We Go, Paper Man, Howl.
TELEVISION: *Movies:* A Rumor of War, Invasion of Privacy, The Caine Mutiny Court Martial, No Place Like Home, Disaster in Time, Teamster Boss: The Jackie Presser Story, Redwood Curtain, The Crossing, Cheaters, The Goodbye Girl, The Five People You Meet in Heaven, Sweet Nothing in My Ear. *Specials:* Fifth of July, The Visit (Trying Times). *Guest:* More than 72 appearances.

DANIELS, WILLIAM

Actor. b. Brooklyn, NY, Mar 31, 1927. e. Northwestern U. m. actress Bonnie Bartlett. Traveled around NY as part of The Daniels Family song and dance troupe. Appeared with family on experimental TV in 1941. Stage debut in Life with Father. Brought to national attention in A Thousand Clowns in original B'way play and film version.
THEATRE: The Zoo Story, On a Clear Day You Can See Forever, 1776, Dear Me, The Sky Is Falling, A Little Night Music.
PICTURES: Ladybug Ladybug, A Thousand Clowns, Two for the Road, The Graduate, The President's Analyst, Marlowe, 1776, The Parallax View, Black Sunday, Oh God!, The One and Only, Sunburn, The Blue Lagoon, All Night Long, Reds, Blind Date, Her Alibi, Magic Kid II, Super Knight Rider, Blades of Glory.
TELEVISION: *Movies:* Rooster, Rehearsal for a Murder, Murdock's Gang, A Case of Rape, Sarah T.—Portrait of a Teenage Alcoholic, One of Our Own, Francis Gary Powers, Killer on Board, The Bastard, Big Bob Johnson and His Fantastic Speed Circus, Sgt. Matlovich Vs. the U.S. Air Force, The Rebels, City in Fear, Damien: The Leper Priest, Million Dollar Face, Drop Out Father, The Little Match Girl, Knight Rider 2000 (voice), Back to the Streets of San Francisco, The Lottery. *Mini-series:* Blind Ambition, The Adams Chronicles. *Series:* Captain Nice, The Nancy Walker Show, Freebie and the Bean, Knight Rider (voice), St. Elsewhere (Emmy Awards, 1985, 1986, 3 other noms.), Boy Meets World, The Closer. *Guest:* More than 100 appearances.

DANNER, BLYTHE

Actress. b. Philadelphia, PA, Feb. 3, 1943. e. Bard Coll. m. the late writer-prod. Bruce Paltrow. Daughter is actress Gwyneth Paltrow. Appeared in repertory cos. in U.S. before Lincoln Center productions of Cyrano de Bergerac, Summertree, and The Miser (Theatre World Award for last).
THEATRE: NY: Butterflies Are Free (Tony Award, 1971), Major Barbara, Twelfth Night, The Seagull, Ring Around The Moon, Betrayal, Blithe Spirit, A Streetcar Named Desire, Much Ado About Nothing, Sylvia. Williamstown: Picnic.
PICTURES: To Kill a Clown (debut, 1972), 1776, Lovin' Molly, Hearts of the West, Futureworld, The Great Santini, Man Woman and Child, Brighton Beach Memoirs, Another Woman, Mr. and Mrs. Bridge, Alice, The Prince of Tides, Husbands and Wives, To Wong Foo—Thanks for Everything—Julie Newmar, Homage, The Myth of Fingerprints, Mad City, The Farmhouse, The Proposition, No Looking Back, The X Files: Fight the Future, Invisible Circus, Forces of Nature, The Love Letter, Meet the Parents, 3 Days of Rain, The Invisible Circus, The Quality of Light, Sylvia, Hating Her, Howl's Moving Castle (voice), Meet the Fockers, Walk Two Moons, The Last Kiss, 'Side by Each', The Sisterhood of the

Traveling Pants 2, Waiting for Forever, The Lightkeepers, Paul, Love, Wedding, Marriage, Meet the Fockers Sequel.
TELEVISION: *Movies*: Dr. Cook's Garden, F. Scott Fitzgerald and The Last of the Belles, Sidekicks, A Love Affair: The Eleanor and Lou Gehrig Story, Too Far to Go, Eccentricities of a Nightingale, Are You in the House Alone?, Inside the Third Reich, In Defense of Kids, Helen Keller: The Miracle Continues, Guilty Conscience, Money Power Murder, Judgment, Never Forget, Cruel Doubt, Getting Up and Going Home, Oldest Living Confederate Widow Tells All, Leave of Absence, A Call to Remember, Saint Maybe, Murder She Purred: A Mrs. Murphy Mystery (voice), We Were the Mulvaneys (Emmy nom. 2002), Change of Heart, Back When We Were Grownups (Emmy nom.; Golden Globe nom. 2005), Pretty/Handsome. *Mini-series*: Mark Twain. *Series*: Adam's Rib, Tattingers (revamped as Nick & Hillary), Presidio Med, Will & Grace (2 Emmy noms. as guest), Huff (2 Emmy Awards). *Specials*: To Confuse the Angel, George M, To Be Young Gifted and Black, The Scarecrow, Kiss Kiss Dahlings. *Guest:* More than 90 appearances.

DANSON, TED

Actor, Producer. b. San Diego, CA, Dec. 29, 1947. e. Kent Sch., Stanford U., Carnegie-Mellon U, 1972. m. actress Mary Steenburgen. Studied at Actors Inst. New York stage debut, The Real Inspector Hound, 1972; mgr. and teacher, Actors Inst., L.A., 1978. Tv debut, The Doctors. Founded Amer. Oceans Campaign; bd. mem. Futures for Children.
PICTURES: The Onion Field (debut, 1979), Body Heat, Creepshow, Little Treasure, Just Between Friends, A Fine Mess, Three Men and a Baby, Cousins, Dad, Three Men and a Little Lady, Made in America, Getting Even With Dad, Pontiac Moon (also co-exec. prod.), Loch Ness, Jerry and Tom, Homegrown, Saving Private Ryan, Mumford, Scene Smoking: Cigarettes Cinema & The Myth of Cool (doc.), The Moguls, Nobel Son, Mad Money, The Open Road.
TELEVISION: *Movies:* The Women's Room, Once Upon a Spy, Our Family Business, Cowboy, Something About Amelia (Emmy nom.; 1984 Golden Globe Award 1985), When the Bough Breaks (also prod.), We Are the Children, Mercy Mission: The Rescue of Flight 771, On Promised Land, Fight For Justice, The Canterville Ghost, Gulliver's Travels, Thanks of a Grateful Nation, Surviving Love, It Must Be Love, Our Fathers, Knights of the South Bronx, Guy Walks Into a Bar, The Magic 7 (voice). *Mini-series:* Living With the Dead, Our Fathers. *Series:* Somerset, Cheers (2 Emmy Awards: 1990, 1993; 9 other nom. 2 Golden Globe Awards; 6 other nom.), Ink (also co-exec. prod.), Becker (Emmy nom.; Golden Globe nom. 2001), Help Me Help You, Damages (2 Emmy noms.; Golden Globe nom. 2008), Bored to Death. *Specials:* Monty Python's Flying Circus Live at Aspen, Intimate Portait: Christine Lahti, Cheers: The E! True Hollywood Story. *Guest:* More than 161 appearances.

DANTE, JOE

Director. b. Morristown, NJ, Nov. 28, 1946. Managing editor for Film Bulletin before going to Hollywood to work in advertising, creating campaigns for many films. Became protege of Roger Corman, co-directing Hollywood Boulevard. Edited film Grand Theft Auto; co-wrote story for Rock 'n' Roll High School.
PICTURES: *Director:* Piranha (also co-editor), The Howling (also co-editor), Twilight Zone-The Movie (dir. segment), Gremlins, Innerspace, Amazon Women on the Moon (co-dir.), The 'burbs, Gremlins II: The New Batch (also cameo), Matinee, Cat and Mouse, Small Soldiers, Haunted Lighthouse, Looney Tunes: Back in Action, The Phantom (exec. prod.), Trailers from Hell (doc.), The Hole, Thirst, Trail of Blood (exec. prod.). *Actor:* Cannonball, Slumber Party Massacre, Eating Raoul, Sleepwalkers, Beverly Hills Cop III, The Silence of the Hams, Hollywood Rated 'R', She's Alive: Creating the Bride of Frankenstein, Cinerama Adventure, The Butterfly Room.
TELEVISION: *Movies:* Runaway Daughters, The Second Civil War. Amazing Stories, Eerie Indiana, The Warlord: Battle for the Galaxy, The Greatest Show Ever. *Series:* Jeremiah (exec. prod.), Splatter (series short).

DANZA, TONY

Actor, Producer. b. Brooklyn, NY, April 21, 1951. e. U. of Dubuque, IA on a wrestling scholarship. After grad. professional boxer before tested for role in TV pilot (Fast Lane Blues) which he won. Back to New York and fighting until called to coast to appear as Tony Banta in Taxi series. On L.A. & NY Stage: Wrong Turn at Lungfish.
PICTURES: Hollywood Knights, Going Ape, Cannonball Run II, She's Out of Control, Mob Justice, Angels in the Outfield, The Jerky Boys (co-exec. prod. only), Mamamia (dir. only), The Whisper, Crash, Firedog (voice), Aftermath, The Nail: The Story of Joey Nardone, Aftermath, Firedog (voice).
TELEVISION: *Movies:* Murder Can Hurt You!, Doing Life (also exec. prod.), Single Bars Single Women, Freedom Fighter (also co-exec. prod.), The Whereabouts of Jenny (also co-exec. prod.), Dead and Alive (also co-exec. prod.), Deadly Whispers, Garbage Picking Field Goal Kicking etc., 12 Angry Men, The Girl Gets Moe, A Brooklyn State of Mind, Noah, Out of Time (exec. prod. only), Miss America, Stealing Christmas. *Series:* Taxi (Golden Globe nom. 1980), Who's the Boss (3 Golden Globe nom.), Baby Talk (voice), The Mighty Jungle (voice), George (co-exec. prod. only), Hudson Street (also co-exec. prod.), The Tony Danza Show (also prod.), The Practice, Family Law, Hollywood P.I. *Guest:* More than 127 appearances.

DARABONT, FRANK

Writer, Director. b. January 28, 1959. Director, Writer, Producer, Partner of Darkwoods Productions.
PICTURES: *Writer:* A Nightmare on Elm Street 3: Dream Warriors, The Blob, The Fly II, Frankenstein, The Shawshank Redemption (Academy Award nom.; Golden Globe nom.; DGA nom.; WGA nom. 1995), Eraser, The Fan, Saving Private Ryan, The Green Mile (also prod.; 2 Academy Award nom.; DGA nom. 2000), Collateral Damage, Minority Report, Collateral (also exec. prod.), Mission: Impossible 3. *Director:* The Woman in the Room, Frankenstein (s.p. only), The Majestic (also prod.), The Salton Sea (prod. only), Fahrenheit 451 (also dir.), Back Roads (exec. prod.), Foreign Babes in Beijing (prod.), King Kong (actor only), The Mist (also writer).
TELEVISION: *Movies:* Two-Fisted Tales (s.p.), Young Indiana Jones Travels with Father (s.p.), Buried Alive (dir.), Till Death Us Do Part (dir.), Black Cat Run (s.p. and dir.), Raines (dir., pilot). *Mini-series:* The Shining (actor). *Series:* The Young Indiana Jones Chronicles (s.p.), The Adventures of Young Indiana Jones in the Secret Service (s.p.).

D'ARBANVILLE PATTI

Actress. b. New York, NY, May 25, 1951. Grew up in Greenwich Village. Landed first job as baby in Ivory Soap commercials. In early teens worked as disc jockey where discovered by Andy Warhol and cast in small role in film Flesh. Moved to Paris at 15 where she became successful model and was featured in book Scavullo on Beauty. Made film debut in Gerard Brach's 1969 film La Maison. Fluent in French, worked in French films until 1973 when moved to Los Angeles. Won Dramalogue Award for John Patrick Shanley's Italian-American Reconciliation (L.A., 1987).
PICTURES: La Maison, La Saigne, The Crazy American Girl, Rancho DeLuxe, Bilitis, Big Wednesday, The Main Event, Time After Time, The Fifth Floor, Hog Wild, Modern Problems, Contract: Kill, The Boys Next Door, Real Genius, Call Me, Fresh Horses, Wired, Frame-Up II: The Cover Up, The Fan, Father's Day, I Know What You Did Last Summer, Celebrity, Archibald the Rainbow Painter, Celebrity, Personal Velocity: Three Portraits, A Tale of Two Pizzas, World Trade Center, You Belong to Me, The Marconi Bros., Perfect Stranger, Happy Tears, The Extra Man.
TELEVISION: *Movies:* Crossing the Mob, Blind Spot, Bad to the Bone. *Mini-series:* Once an Eagle. *Series:* New York Undercover, Another World, South Beach, The Guiding Light, Oz, The Sopranos, Third Watch, Rescue Me.

DARBY, KIM

Actress. r.n. Deborah Zerby. b. Hollywood, CA, July 8, 1948. e. Swanson's Ranch Sch., Van Nuys H.S. Studied at the Desilu Workshop in Hollywood. Professional debut on the Mr. Novak TV series; screen debut as extra in Bye Bye Birdie.
PICTURES: Bus Riley's Back in Town, The Restless Ones, True Grit, Generation (Golden Globe nom. 1970), Norwood, The Strawberry Statement, The Grissom Gang, The One and Only, Better Off Dead, Teen Wolf Too, Halloween: The Curse of Michael Myers, The Last Best Sunday, NewsBreak, Mockingbird Don't Sing, Cold Ones.
TELEVISION: *Movies:* The Karate Killers, Ironside (pilot), The People, Streets of San Francisco (pilot), Don't Be Afraid of the Dark, Story of Pretty Boy Floyd, This Was the West That Was, Flatbed Annie & Sweetiepie: Lady Truckers, Enola Gay, Embassy. *Mini-series:* Rich Man Poor Man (Emmy nom. 1976), The Last Convertible. *Specials:* Flesh and Blood, Leslie Ann Warren: A Cinderella Story. *Guest:* More than 69 appearances.

DARRIEUX, DANIELLE

Actress. b. Bordeaux, France, May 1, 1917. e. Lycee LaTour, Conservatoire de Musique.
THEATRE: Coco, The Ambassador (B'way).
PICTURES: Le Bal (debut, 1932), La Crise Est Finis, Mayerling, Tarass Boulba, Port Arthur, Un Mauvais Garcon, Club de Femmes, Abus de Confiance, Mademoiselle ma Mere, The Rage of Paris, Katia, Retour a l'Aube, Battlement de Coeur, Premier Rendezvous, Caprices, Adieu Cherie, Au Petit Bonbeur, Bethsabee, Ruy Blas, Jean de le Lune, Occupe-toi d'Amelie, La Ronde, Rich Young and Pretty, Five Fingers, Le Plaisir, La Verite sur Bebe Donge, Adorable Creatures, Le Bon Dieu sans Confession, The Earrings of Madame De, Le Rouge et le Noir, Bonnes a Tuer, Napoleon, Alexander the Great, A Friend of the Family, Loss of Innocence (Greengage Summer), Les Lions sont Laches, Les Bras de lat Nuit, Bluebeard (Landru), Patate, Le Coup de Grace, L'Or du Duc, Le Dimanche de la Vie, The Young Girls of Rochefort, La Maison de Campagne, Scene of the Crime, A Few Days With Me, Epiphany Sunday, Headstrong, Les Mamies, The Young Girls Turn 25, L'Univers de Jacques Demy, Tomorrow's Another Day, Emilie est Partie, 8 Women, Persepolis (voice), L'Heure zéro, Persepolis (voice).
TELEVISION: Marie-Marie, Miss, L'Age vermeil, La Petite fille modele, Tu crois pas si bien dire, Bonjour maitre, Le Front dans les nuages, La Misere des riches, In the Face of Truth, Jalna, Un et font six, Que reste-t-il. *Mini-series:* Dangerous Liaisons.

DARTNALL, GARY

Executive. b. Whitchurch, England, May 9, 1937. e. Kings College, Taunton. Overseas div., Associate British Pathe. European rep., 1958-60; Middle & Far East rep., Lion Intl. Films; U.S. rep., 1962; pres. Lion Intl. 1963; U.S. rep., Alliance Intl. Films Distributors Ltd., and London Indept. Prods. Ltd.; pres. Alliance Intl. Films Corp. and Dartnall Films Ltd., 1966; mng. dir., Overseas div. Walter Reade Org., 1969; pres. EMI Film Distribs., 1971; vice chmn. EMI TV Programs Inc., 1976; pres. EMI Videograms Inc., 1979; pres. VHD Programs Inc. & VHD Disc Mfg. Co, 1980; chmn. Thorn EMI Cinemas; CEO, Thorn EMI Screen Entertainment Ltd. 1987; acquired Southbrook Intl. TV and formed Palladium Inc., chmn. & CEO. 1993 formed The Douris Corporation to acquire and distribute the 700-title Rohauer Collection of classic titles. Part of Douris' operations include ClassicMovies.com, a privately held e-commerce entertainment co., with Dartnall serving as president and chairman. He is a former chairman of BAFT/LA and currently sits on the org.'s bd.

DASHWOOD, NORA

Executive, Exhibitor. For nearly 30 years, Dashwood has been involved in motion picture exhibition, serving 23 years as an executive with the AMC circuit. Most recently the senior v.p. of AMC's North American staff operations, Dashwood left AMC in May 2000 to become the COO of the Pacific Theatres circuit, which is a Decurion Corp. company led by chairman Michael Forman and CEO Chris Forman. Today, as COO, Dashwood oversees operations for the circuits 300+ movie screens in California (Los Angeles, San Diego and surrounding areas). The Forman family founded Pacific Theatres in 1946 and continues to own and operate the company through its Decurion Corp. Dashwood is based at the circuit's headquarters in Los Angeles. She currently sits on the advisory bd. of the Will Rogers Motion Picture Pioneers Foundation.

DAUMAN, PHILIPPE P.

Executive. e. B.A. from Yale, 1974; J.D. from Columbia University Law School in 1978. Began career as attorney and before entering long association with media giant Viacom, he was a partner of NY-based law firm Shearman & Sterling. While there Dauman served as principal outside counsel to Viacom and represented Sumner Redstone in acquiring Viacom in 1987. He then served in several key sr. mgt. positions through the years, including Viacom's general counsel and secretary; deputy chmn. and exec. v.p. He topped the list of highest-paid corporate lawyers in the U.S. with a salary of $3.06 million in 1996. Dauman was a director on Viacom's bd. from 1987 to 2000. Dauman left Viacom in 2000 and co-founded DND Capital Partners, a private equity firm specializing in media and telecommunication investments. In Sept. 2006, Sumner Redstone tapped Dauman to be president, CEO and Director of Viacom, replacing Tom Freston. Since his appointment, he resigned his seat on the board of Redstone's CBS Corporation, but remains an active bd. member for another of Redstone's companies, National Amusements, Inc. He is also a director for the following companies: Viacom International Inc., The Tennis Channel, Inc.; Genuity Inc.; Lafarge North America, Inc. and Lafarge Canada Inc. He also serves on the Dean's Council of Columbia University Law School. Currently is independent director for Lafarge SA.

DAVIAU, ALLEN

Cinematographer. b. New Orleans, LA, June 14, 1942. Started as still photographer and stage lighting designer. Received Gold Clio Award for Tackle (Levi's 501).Received Distinguished Career Award, Art Directors Guild 1997. Received Lifetime Achievment Award, American Society of Cinematographers, 2007.
PICTURES: Harry Tracy, E.T.: The Extra-Terrestrial (Academy Award nom. 1983), Twilight Zone: The Movie (co-photog.), Indiana Jones and the Temple of Doom (Calif. unit), The Falcon and the Snowman, The Color Purple (Academy Award nom. 1986), Harry and the Hendersons, Empire of the Sun (Academy Award nom.; BAFTA & ASC Awards 1988), Avalon (Academy Award nom.; ASC nom. 1991), Defending Your Life, Bugsy (Academy Award nom.; ASC Award 1992), Fearless, Congo, The Astronaut's Wife, Sweet, The Translator, Hearts in Atlantis, Van Helsing.
TELEVISION: *Movies:* Streets of L.A., Rage!, Legs. *Series:* Amazing Stories (pilot). *Special:* The Boy Who Drank Too Much.

DAVID, KEITH

Actor. b. New York, NY, June 4, 1954. e. Juilliard.
THEATRE: NY: The Pirates of Penzance, A Midsummer Night's Dream, Waiting for Godot, Miss Waters to You, La Boheme, Coriolanus, Titus Andronicus, A Map of the World, The Haggadah, Alec Wilder: Clues to a Life, Boesman & Lena, Jelly's Last Jam, Hedda Gabler, Seven Guitars.
PICTURES: The Thing, Platoon, Hot Pursuit, Braddock: Missing in Action III, Off Limits, Stars and Bars, Bird, They Live, Road House, Always, Men at Work, Marked for Death, Final Analysis, Article 99, Reality Bites, The Puppet Masters, The Quick and the Dead, Clockers, Dead Presidents, Johns, Dead Cold (prod.), Marked Man (prod.), Daddy's Girl (prod.), The Dentist (prod.), The Nurse (prod.), The Stranger In The House (prod.), Voodoo (exec. prod.), Serial Killer (prod./dir.), Flipping, Larger than Life, Eye for an Eye, Johns, Hercules (voice), Fallout (voice), Executive Target, Volcano, Armageddon, There's Something About Mary, Where the Heart Is., Requiem for a Dream, The Replacements, Home Invaders, G Spots, Final Fantasy: The Spirits Within (voice), Novocaine, Pretty When You Cry, 29 Palms, Barbershop, Hung-Up, Agent Cody Banks, Head of State, Kaena: The Prophecy (voice), Hollywood Homicide, Agent Cody Banks 2: Destination London, The Chronicles of Riddick, Crash, The Transporter 2, Mr. and Mrs. Smith, The OH in Ohio, Dirty, ATL, The Last Sentinel, Beautiful Loser, First Sunday, If I Had Known I Was a Genius, Behind Enemy Lines: Axis of Evil, Chasing 3000, Delta Farce, City Teacher, The Sensei, No Bad Days, Coraline, Game, All About Steve, Charlie Valentine, Between Heaven and Earth (prod. only), Don McKay, Miss January, My Place in the Horror, Now Here, Pastor Brown, Something Like a Business, The Princess and the Frog (voice), Meet Monica Velour, Chain Letter, Stomp the Yard 2: Homecoming, Spork, Song of the Knife, Now Here, No Saints for Sinners, Lottery Ticket, Death at a Funeral, The Greening of Whitney Brown.
TELEVISION: *Movies:* Ladykillers, Murder in Black and White, There Are No Children Here, Vanishing Point, Murder She Wrote: South by Southwest, Don King: Only in America, The Tiger Woods Story (Emmy nom. 1999), A.T.F, Semper Fi, The Proud Family Movie, Unforgivable Blackness: The Rise and Fall of Jack Johnson (Emmy Award 2005), The Color Purple: The Color of Success (narr.), SIS. *Mini-series:* Roots: The Next Generations, Jazz (Emmy nom. 2001), Mark Twain. *Series:* Spawn, Hercules (voice), House of Mouse (voice), The Job, The Big House, Spawn: The Animation (voice), Jazz (Emmy nom. 2001), ER. *Special:* Hallelujah, Gargoyles (Emmy nom. 1996), The War (Emmy Award 2008 episode voice over). *Guest:* More than 114 appearances.

DAVID, PIERRE

Executive, Producer. b. Montreal, Canada, May 17, 1944. e. U. of Montreal. Joined radio station CJMS 1966 as pub. rel. & spec. events dir., 1969, while running Mutual Broadcasting Network of Canada's live entertainment div., created new film dist. co. Mutual Films. 1972 added prod. unit and as prod. or exec. prod., prod. and dist. 19 French language. Canadian films. With filmmaker Roger Corman est. Mutual Pictures of Canada, Ltd to dist. films in English Canada; 1978 teamed Mutual Films with Victor Solnicki and Claude Heroux to prod. English language films. Pioneered 3-picture concept for Canadian m.p. investors. Moved to L.A. 1983 where became pres., Film Packages Int'l. where production exec. on Platoon. Then joined Larry Thompson Org. as partner involved in dev. and/or prod. of m.p., Jan., 1987, named chmn. of bd. and CEO, Image Org., Inc., an int'l. distribution co. formed by David and Rene Malo. Sold Image Org. in 1997. David is currently pres. of Lance Entertainment and also chmn. & CEO of Imagination Worldwide, LLC. He is chmn. of the Independent Film & Television Alliance (IFTA) Producers Committee.
PICTURES: *Producer (English language films):* Bingo, Hog Wild, Visiting Hours, Going Berserk, For Those I Loved, Of Unknown Origin, Breaking All the Rules, Scenes From The Goldmine (co-prod.), Hot Pursuit, Blind Fear, Martial Law, The Perfect Weapon, Scanners II: The New Order, Deep Cover, Martial Law II: Undercover (also writer), The Neighbor (co-prod.), Distant Cousins (also writer), Bounty Tracker, Marial Outlaw (also writer), Stalked (also writer), Scanner Cop (also dir. & writer), The Force, The Wrong Woman, Serial Killer (also dir.), Marked Man, Open Fire, Scanners IV: Scanner Cop, The Dentist, Daddy's Girl, Never Too Late (co-prod.), Little Men, The Nurse, Stranger in the House, Wishmaster, The Night Caller, The Dentist 2, The Landlady, Wanted, A Clean Kill, Rites of Passage, The Perfect Nanny, Alone with a Stranger, The Perfect Tenant, The Stepdaughter, Blind Obsession, Living in Fear, Facing the Enemy. *Exec. Prod.:* Platoon (prod. executive), The Brood, Quiet Cool, Scanners, Dirty Tricks, Gas, Madame Claude 2, Videodrome, Flying, The Vindicator, My Demon Lover, Pin, Internal Affairs, Scanners III: The Takeover, Dolly Dearest, Desire and Hell at Sunset Motel, The Paper Boy, Voodoo, Dead Cold, The Killing Grounds, Cupid, Man of Her Dreams, Me and Will, Outrage, Shallow Ground, Accused at Seventeen, Summer's Blood (also 2nd unit dir.), My Family's Secret, Little Deaths, Arctic Blast.
TELEVISION: *Movies:Prod./Exec. prod.:* The Perfect Bride, Deadbolt, The Secretary, Someone Is Watching, She's No Angel, The Perfect Wife, Her Perfect Spouse, Stranger at the Door, Saving Emily, A Killer Upstairs, The Perfect Neighbor, Maid of Honor, Murder in My House, The Perfect Marriage, Last Exit, The Rival, Demons from Her Past, Like Mother-Like Daughter, Framed for Murder, 'Til Lies Do Us Part, Christie's Revenge, My Daughter's Secret, The Perfect Assistant, A Teacher's Crime, Dead at 17, Her Only Child, A Sister's Secret, My Nanny's Secret, My Neighbor's Secret.

DAVIDOVICH, LOLITA

Actress. b. Ontario, Canada, July 15, 1961. Also acted under the name Lolita David.
PICTURES: Class, Adventures in Babysitting, The Big Town, Blaze, The Object of Beauty, JFK, The Inner Circle, Raising Cain, Leap of Faith, Boiling Point, Younger and Younger, Cobb, For Better or Worse, Now and Then, Jungle 2 Jungle, Touch, Gods

and Monsters, Mystery Alaska, Play It to the Bone, Forever Flirt, Dark Blue, Hollywood Homicide, September Dawn, Kill Your Darlings, Smitty.
TELEVISION: *Movies:* Two Fathers' Justice, Prison Stories: Women on the Inside (Parole Board), Keep the Change, Indictment: The McMartin Trial, McMartin Trial, Dead Silence, The Judge, Snow in August, The Kid (voice), State of Mind, Throwing Stones. *Mini-series*: I'll Take Manhattan, ZOS: Zone of Separation. *Series:* Stories from My Childhood (voice), The Agency, The L Word. *Guest:* More than 50 appearances.

DAVIDSON, MARTIN

Director, Writer. b. New York, NY, Nov. 7, 1939.
PICTURES: The Lords of Flatbush, Almost Summer, Hero at Large, Eddie and the Cruisers, Heart of Dixie (also exec. prod.), Hard Promises, Looking for an Echo.
TELEVISION: *Movies:* Long Gone, A Murderous Affair: The Carolyn Warmus Story, Follow the River, Every Woman's Dream. *Series:* Our Family Honor, Call to Glory, Law and Order, My Life and Times, Picket Fences, Chicago Hope, Judging Amy, Girls Club.

DAVIDTZ, EMBETH

Actress. b. Trenton, New Jersey, Jan. 1, 1966.
PICTURES: Sweet Murder, Mutator, Schindler's List, Army of Darkness, Murder in the First, Feast of July, Matilda, Fallen, The Gingerbread Man, Bicentennial Man, Bridget Jones's Diary, The Hole, Thir13en Ghosts, The Emperor's Club, Junebug, Fracture, Fragments, Three Backyards.
TELEVISION: *Movies:* A Private Life, 'Till Death Us Do Part, Deadly Matrimony, The Garden of Redemption, Citizen Baines (pilot), Last Rites, Shackleton. *Series:* Citizen Baines, In Treatment, Californication.

DAVIES, JOHN HOWARD

Producer, Director. b. London, England, March 9, 1939. e. Haileybory, IS.C. and Grenoble Univ. Former child actor played leading roles in Oliver Twist, The Rocking Horse Winner, Tom Brown's Schooldays.
TELEVISION: *Movies/Prod./Dir.:* A Married Man, Kim, Sleeping Murder, The Care of Time. *Mini-series:* The Edwardians, War and Peace. *Series:* Doctor Who, Monty Python's Flying Circus, Steptoe and Son, All in Good Faith, Fawlty Towers, We'll Think of Something, The Good Life, The Goodies, Good Neighbors, The Other One, No Job for a Lady, Executive Stress, Andy Capp, Mr. Bean, After Henry, Law and Disorder, Hope It Rains, The Vicar of Dibley. *Specials:* It's Black Entertainment (writer), Parrot Sketch Not Included: Twenty Years of Monty Python.

DAVIS, ANDREW

Director. b. Chicago, IL, 1947. e. Univ. of IL. Former journalist and photographer before landing job as asst. cameraman on 1969 film Medium Cool. Was dir. of photog. on several TV commercials and documentaries.
PICTURES: Lepke (dir. of photog.), Stony Island (dir., prod., co-s.p.), Over the Edge (dir. of photog.), Angel (dir. of photog.), Beat Street (co-s.p.). *Director:* The Final Terror, Code of Silence, Above the Law (also co-prod., co-story), The Package, Under Siege, The Fugitive (2 Golden Globe noms. 1994), Steal Big Steal Little (also co-prod., co-s.p., co-story), Chain Reaction, A Perfect Murder, Collateral Damage, Holes (also prod.), The Guardian.
TELEVISION: *Movies:* Hot Rod (cinematographer), Roanoak (actor). *Series:* Fraternity Life: SUNY Buffalo (editor), Just Legal (pilot). *Documentary:* Sorority Life (editor), UC Davis.

DAVIS, CARL

Composer. b. New York, NY, Oct. 28, 1936. e. Queens Coll., Bard Coll. and New England Coll. of Music. Worked as pianist with Robert Shaw Chorale and wrote music for revue Diversions (1958) and Twists (London), Moved to England 1961 writing incidental music for Joan Littlewood's Theatre Workshop Co., Royal Shakespeare Co. and National Theatre. Other theater music includes Jonathan Miller's Tempest, Forty Years On, and the musical The Vackees. Best known for composing new scores for silent classics (Napoleon, The Crowd, Greed, Intolerance, etc.) for screenings at which he conducts and for Thames TV The Silents series. Concert work: Paul McCartney's Liverpool Oratorio.
PICTURES: The Bofors Gun, Up Pompeii, Rentadick, Man Friday, The Sailor's Return, Birth of the Beatles, The French Lieutenant's Woman, Praying Mantis, The Aerodrome, Champions, Weather in the Streets, George Stevens: A Filmmaker's Journey, King David, The Rainbow, Scandal, Girl in a Swing, Fragments of Isabella, Frankenstein Unbound, Diary of a Madman, Raft of the Medusa, The Voyage, Liberation, Widow's Peak, Anne Frank Remembered, Tje Raft of Medusa, Topsey-Turvy, The Book of Eve, Head of State.
TELEVISION: *Movies:* That Was the Week That Was, Hollywood, the Pioneers, World at War, Mayor of Casterbridge, Lorna Doone, Unknown Chaplin, Buster Keaton—A Hard Act to Follow, Treasure Island, The Snow Goose (Emmy nom. 1972), Our Mutual Friend, Naked Civil Servant, Silas Marner, The Accountant, Secret Life of Ian Fleming, Why Lockerbie?, Buried Mirro, A Christmas Carol, Royal Collection, Hotel du Lac, Black Velvet Gown, Lie Down With Lions, The Return of the Native, Seesaw, Goodnight Mister Tom, Great Gatsby, Back Home, Promoted to Glory. *Mini-series:* Pride & Prejudice, Oliver's Travels, Cinema Europe: The Other Hollywood, Real Women, The Buried Mirror, A Dance to the Music of Time, The Face of Russia, Cold War, Masterpiece Theatre: Cranford, The Queen's Nose, Return to Cranford. *Series:* The Wednesday Play, Out of Bounds, Oscar, Covington Cross (Emmy nom. 1993).

DAVIS, DENNIS

Executive. e. Bachelor's degree in business admin./accounting from California State Univ.-Fresno. Davis joined Pappas Telecasting Companies in 1983 and spent nearly two decades as the company's CFO. Before being named to his current position as president and COO in Nov. 2004, he served as senior executive v.p./strategy & investments, where he played a major role in the acquisition and financing of existing and proposed Pappas ventures. He is a member of the California Society of Certified Public Accountants. Dennis served for four years in the United States Air Force, including service in Southeast Asia during the Vietnam conflict.

DAVIS, GEENA

Actress. r.n. Virginia Elizabeth Davis. b. Wareham, MA, Jan. 21, 1957. e. Boston U. Acted with Mount Washington Repertory Theatre Co., NH. Was NY model before role in Tootsie, 1982.
PICTURES: Tootsie (debut, 1982), Fletch, Transylvania 6-5000, The Fly, Beetlejuice, The Accidental Tourist (Academy Award, supporting actress, 1988), Earth Girls Are Easy, Quick Change, Thelma & Louise (Academy Award nom.; Golden Globe nom. 1989), A League of Their Own (Golden Globe nom. 1993), Hero, Angie, Speechless (also prod. Golden Globe nom. 1995), Cutthroat Island, The Long Kiss Goodnight (also prod.), Stuart Little, Stuart Little 2, Accidents Happen.
TELEVISION: *Movies:* Secret Weapons, Mistrial (exec. prod.), Exit 19. *Series:* Buffalo Bill (also wrote one episode), Sara, The Geena Davis Show, Commander in Chief (Emmy nom.; Golden Globe Award 2006). *Guest:* More than 78 appearances.

DAVIS, HOPE

Actress. b. Englewood, NJ, March 23, 1964.
THEATRE: *B'way:* God of Carnage. *Off B'way:* Spinning Into Butter. *Regional:* Camino Real.
PICTURES: Flatliners, Home Alone, Kiss of Death, The Daytrippers, Mr. Wrong, The Myth of Fingerprints, Next Stop Wonderland, The Impostors (also soundtrack per.), Arlington Road, Mumford, Joe Gould's Secret, Final (also soundtrack per.), Hearts in Atlantis, About Schmidt, The Secret Lives of Dentists, American Splendor (Golden Globe nom. 2004), The Matador, Duma, Proof, The Weather Man, Infamous, The Hoax, The Nines (also soundtrack per.), Charlie Bartlett (also soundtrack per.), Synecdoche, New York, The Lodger, The Family Tree, The Special Relationship.
TELEVISION: *Series:* Deadline, Six Degrees, In Treatment (Emmy nom. 2009).

DAVIS, JOHN

Executive, Producer. e. Bowdoin College, Harvard Bus. Sch. Served as v.p. at 20th Century Fox before forming Davis Entertainment Company, where he is chairman.
PICTURES: *Producer:* Predator, Three O'Clock High, License to Drive, Little Monsters, Enid Is Sleeping, The Last of the Finest, Predator 2, Shattered, Fortress, The Firm, The Thing Called Love, Grumpy Old Men, Gunmen, Richie Rich, The Hunted, Waterworld, The Grass Harp, Grumpier Old Men, Courage Under Fire, The Chamber, Daylight, Out to Sea, Digging to China, Doctor Dolittle, Dudley Do-Right, Labor Pains (co-prod.), Heartbreakers, Dr. Dolittle 2, Behind Enemy Lines, Life or Something Like It, Daddy Day Care, Devil's Pond, Paycheck, Garfield, I Robot, AVP: Alien vs. Predator, First Daughter, Fat Albert, Flight of the Phoenix, When a Stranger Calls, Garfield: A Tail of Two Kitties, Eragon, Norbit, Daddy Day Camp, AVPR: Aliens vs Predator - Requiem, The Express, Dr. Dolittle: Million Dollar Mutts, Reckless, Gulliver's Travels, Marmaduke, Earthbound. *Executive prod.:* Storyville, Denise Calls Up, Lewis & Clark & George, Bad Manners, The Settlement, Happy Hour, At Last.
TELEVISION: *All Executive prod. and/or producer: Movies:* Tears and Laughter: The Joan and Melissa Rivers Story, The Last Outlaw, This Can't Be Love, One Christmas, Kidnapped, Asteroid, Volcano: Fire on the Mountain, Miracle at Midnight, The Jesse Ventura Story, Little Richard, David Copperfield, Bobbie's Girl, Nadine in Date Land, Life Is Ruff, Jump In! *Mini-series:* The Old Curiosity Shop, 20,000 Leagues Under the Sea. *Series:* Criminal Behavior.

DAVIS, JUDY

Actress. b. Perth, Australia, April 23, 1955. m. actor Colin Friels. Left convent school as teenager to become a singer in a rock band. Studied at West Australia Inst. of Technology and National Inst. of Dramatic Art, Sydney. Worked with theatre companies in Adelaide and Sydney and at Royal Court Theatre, London. Los Angeles stage debut Hapgood.
PICTURES: High Rolling (debut, 1977), My Brilliant Career, Hoodwink, Heatwave, Winter of Our Dreams, The Final Option,

A Passage to India (Academy Award nom. 1985), Kangaroo, High Tide, Georgia, Alice, Impromtu, Barton Fink, Naked Lunch, Where Angels Fear to Tread, Husbands and Wives (Academy Award nom. Golden Globe nom. 1993), On My Own (Australian Film Inst. Award), The Ref, The New Age, Absolute Power, Deconstructing Harry, Blood and Wine, Celebrity, Absolute Power, Gaudi Afternoon, The Man Who Sued God, Swimming Upstream, Marie Antoinette, The Break-Up.
TELEVISION: *Movies:* Rocket to the Moon, A Woman Called Golda (Emmy nom. 1982), One Against the Wind (Emmy nom. Golden Globe Award, 1992), Serving in Silence: The Margarethe Cammermeyer Story (Emmy Award, Golden Globe nom. 1995), The Echo of Thunder (Emmy nom. 1998), Dash and Lilly (Emmy nom. Golden Globe nom. 1999), Rosamunde Pilcher - Zerrissene Herzen, A Cooler Climate (Emmy nom. 2000), Life With Judy Garland: Me & My Shadows (Emmy Award; Golden Globe Award 2001), The Reagans (Emmy nom.; Golden Globe nom. 2004), Coast to Coast, A Little Thing Called Murder (Emmy nom. 2006). *Mini-series:* The Starter Wife (Emmy Award 2007), Diamonds. *Series:* The Starter Wife.

DAVIS, PRESTON A.

Executive. b. Norfolk, VA. Served in U.S. Army. 1976, joined ABC as engineer in Washington, DC, later becoming supervisor of Electronic News Gathering; 1979, became tech. mgr. of ENG; 1983, named tech. mgr. then manager of ENG for southeast region, Atlanta; 1986, promoted to gen. mgr. ENG Operations, New York; 1988, named v.p. TV Operations, Broadcast Operations & Engineering, East Coast; In 1993, named pres. of Broadcast Operations and Engineering for ABC Television Network Group in (2007).

DAVIS, SAMMI

Actress. b. Kidderminster, Worcestershire, England, June 21, 1964. Convent-educated before taking drama course. Performed in stage prods. with local drama society in Midlands, then Birmingham Rep. and Big Brum Theatre Co. Plays include The Home Front (Golden Globe nom. 1992), The Apple Club, Nine Days, Databased, Choosey Susie. London stage debut: A Collier's Friday.
PICTURES: Mona Lisa, Lionheart, Hope and Glory, A Prayer for the Dying, Consuming Passions, The Lair of the White Worm, The Rainbow, The Horseplayer, Shadow of China, Four Rooms, Death Do Us Part, Assignment Berlin, Woundings, Soft Toilet Seats.
TELEVISION: Auf Wiedersehn Pet, The Day After the Fair, Pack of Lies, Chernobyl: The Final Warning, The Perfect Bride, Indecency, Spring Awakening. *Series:* Homefront (Golden Globe nom. 1992).

DAVIS, VIOLA

Actress. b. Saint Matthews, SC, August 11, 1965. e. Juilliard.
THEATRE: *B'way:* King Hedley (Tony Award, 2001). *Off B'way:* Everybody's Ruby (Obie Award, 1999). *LA:* Intimate Apparel.
PICTURES: The Substance of Fire, Out of Sight, Traffic, Kate & Leopold, Far from Heaven, Antwone Fisher, Solaris, Get Rich or Die Tryin', The Architect, World Trade Center, Disturbia, Nights in Rodanthe, Doubt (Academy Award nom.; Golden Globe nom. 2009), Madea Goes to Jail, State of Play, Law Abiding Citizen, Knight & Day, Eat, Pray, Love, It's Kind of a Funny Story, Trust.
TELEVISION: *Movies:* The Pentagon Wars, Grace & Glorie, Amy & Isabelle, Father Lefty, Jesse Stone: Stone Cold, Jesse Stone: Death in Paradise, Life Is Not a Fairytale: The Fantasia Barrino Story, Fort Pit, Jesse Stone: Sea Change. *Mini-series:* The Andromeda Strain. *Series:* City of Angels, Century City, Traveler, Law & Order: Special Victims Unit. *Guest:* More than 45 appearances.

DAVIS, WARWICK

Actor. b. Epsom, Surrey, England, UK, Feb. 3, 1970.
PICTURES: Star Wars: Episode VI-Return of the Jedi, Labyrinth, Willow, Leprechaun, Leprechaun 2, Leprechaun 3, Leprechaun 4: In Space, Prince Valiant, A Very Unlucky Leprechaun, The Bacchae, Star Wars: Episode I-The Phantom Menace, The New Adventures of Pinocchio, The White Pony, Harry Potter and the Sorcerer's Stone, Harry Potter and the Chamber of Secrets, Skinned Deep., Leprechaun: Back in Da Hood, Harry Potter and the Prisoner of Azkaban, Ray, The Hitchhiker's Guide to the Galaxy, Harry Potter and the Goblet of Fire, Agent One-Half (co-prod./writer), Harry Potter and the Order of the Phoenix, The Chronicles of Narnia: Prince Caspian, Harry Potter and the Half-Blood Prince, ShortFellas, Harry Potter and the Deathly Hallows: Part I.
TELEVISION: *Movies:* The Ewok Adventure, Ewoks: The Battle for Endor, Prince Caspian and the Voyage of the Dawn Treader, The Silver Chair, Gulliver's Travels, Murder Rooms: The Kingdom of Bones, Snow White: The Fairest of Them All. *Mini-series:* The 10th Kingdom. *Guest:* More than 45 appearances.

DAVISON, BRUCE

Actor. b. Philadelphia, PA, June 28, 1946. e. Pennsylvania State U., NYU. debut, Lincoln Center Repertory prod. of Tiger at the Gates, 1967.
THEATRE: NY: King Lear (Lincoln Center), The Elephant Man, Richard III (NY Shakespeare Fest.), The Glass Menagerie, The Cocktail Hour. Regional: Streamers (LA Critics Award), The Caine Mutiny Court-Martial, The Normal Heart, To Kill a Mockingbird, A Life in the Theatre, The Front Page, Downside, Breaking the Silence.
PICTURES: Last Summer (debut, 1969), The Strawberry Statement, Willard, Been Down So Long It Looks Like Up To Me, The Jerusalem File, Ulzana's Raid, Mame, Mother Jugs and Speed, Grand Jury, Short Eyes, Brass Target, French Quarter, High Risk, A Texas Legend, Lies, Crimes of Passion, Spies Like Us, The Ladies Club, The Misfit Brigade, Longtime Companion (NY Film Critics, Natl. Society of Film Critics, & Golden Globe Award, 1990; Academy Award nom. 1991), Steel and Lace, Short Cuts (Golden Globe Award 1994), An Ambush of Ghosts, Six Degrees of Separation, Far From Home: The Adventures of Yellow Dog, The Cure, The Baby-sitters Club, Homage, Grace of My Heart, The Crucible, Lovelife, Apt Pupil, Paulie, Vendetta, At First Sight, X-Men, The Other Side, Summer Catch, At Seventeen, Manfast, Mind Is A Place of Its Own, High Crimes, Dahmer, X2, Runaway Jury, Evergreen, Touched, Confession, The Dead Girl, Breach, Camp Hope, La Linea, Passengers, Christmas Angel, Arctic Blast.
TELEVISION: *Movies:* Owen Marshall: Counsellor at Law (A Pattern of Morality), The Affair, The Last Survivors, Deadman's Curve, Summer of My German Soldier, Mind Over Murder, The Gathering, Tomorrow's Child, Ghost Dancing, Poor Little Rich Girl: The Barbara Hutton Story, Lady in a Corner, Stolen: One Husband, Live! From Death Row, Desperate Choices: To Save My Child, A Mother's Revenge, Someone Else's Child, Down Out and Dangerous, The Color of Justice, Hidden in Silence, Little Girl Fly Away, A Memory in My Heart, Off Season (Emmy nom. 1998), Lathe of Heaven.(co-prod. only), Out of the Ashes, The Clinic. The Wave, Knight Rider, The Librarian: The Curse of the Judas Chalice, MegaFault. *Mini-series:* Kingdom Hospital, Mourning Becomes Electra, The Triangle. *Series:* Hunter, Harry and the Hendersons, The Practice, Knight Rider, Ghost Whisperer. *Specials:* Taming of the Shrew, Close to Home. *Guest:* More than 118 appearances.

DAVISON, DALE

Executive. b. North Hollywood, CA, March 21, 1955. e. U.C.L.A., B.A., 1978. Entered the motion picture industry in 1973 with Pacific Theatres. Employed with Great Western Theatres 1974-77 as mgr., dir. of concessions, and asst. v.p. Partner with Great Western Theatres, 1978-1984. Founder and CEO, CinemaCal Enterprises, Inc., from 1985-1999. Director of corporate development, Krikorian Premiere Theatres, 2000-01. Was v.p. of special projects, for Century Theatres, 2001-until circuit merged with Cinemark in 2006. Currently senior v.p. of operations and development for Metropolitan Theatres. NATO bd. of directors, 1994-2000. NATO of Ca. exec. comm. 1996-2000. Chief Barker, Variety Club of Northern Ca, 1997-1999.

DAVISON, JON

Producer. b. Haddonfield, NJ, July 21, 1949. e. NYU Film School. 1972, joined New World Pictures as natl. dir. of publ./adv.; 1972, named in charge of prod.; 1980, became indep. prod.
PICTURES: Hollywood Boulevard, Grand Theft Auto, Piranha, Airplane!, White Dog, Twilight Zone—The Movie (episode), Top Secret! Robocop, Robocop 2, Trapped in Paradise, Starship Troopers, The 6th Day, Starship Troopers, Searchers 2.0.
TELEVISION: *Series:* Robocop (creative consult.).

DAY, DORIS

Singer, Actress. r.n. Doris Kappelhoff. b. Cincinnati, OH, April 3, 1924. e. dancing, singing. Toured as dancer; radio and band singer; screen debut in Romance on the High Seas, 1948. Voted one of Top Ten Money-Making Stars in Motion Picture Herald-Fame poll, 1951-52. Best female vocalist. M. P. Daily radio poll, 1952. Received Cecil B. DeMille Award 1989. Recieved 2 Henrietta Awards, 1959, 1963, 2 other noms. 1955, 1966 for Favorite World Female Actress.
PICTURES: Romance on the High Seas (debut, 1948), My Dream is Yours, It's a Great Feeling, Young Man With a Horn, Tea for Two, Storm Warning, West Point Story, Lullaby of Broadway, On Moonlight Bay, I'll See You in My Dreams, Starlift, The Winning Team, April in Paris, By the Light of the Silvery Moon, Calamity Jane, Lucky Me, Young at Heart, Love Me or Leave Me, The Man Who Knew Too Much, Julie, The Pajama Game, Teacher's Pet, Tunnel of Love (Golden globe nom. nom., It Happened to Jane, Pillow Talk (Academy Award nom. 1960), Please Don't Eat the Daisies, Midnight Lace (Golden Globe nom. 1961), Lover Come Back, That Touch of Mink, Bill Rose's Jumbo (Henrietta Award, Golden Globe nom. 1963), The Thrill of It All, Move Over Darling (Golden Globe nom. 1964), Send Me No Flowers, Do Not Disturb, Glass Bottom Boat, Caprice, The Ballad of Josie, Where Were You When the Lights Went Out?, With Six You Get Eggroll, Rowan & Martin at the Movies, That's Entertainment Part II, That's Dancing, Antz (singer "High Hopes"), Girl, Interrupted (performer), Tortilla Soup (performer), Mona Lisa Smile (performer), Lady in the Water (performer), Infamous (performer), many more soundtrack credits.
TELEVISION: *Movie:* Homeward Bound. *Series:* The Doris Day Show (1968-73 Golden Globe nom. 1969), Doris Day's Best Friends (educational cable show; 1985-86).

DAY, ROBERT
Director. b. England, Sept. 11, 1922. Started as cinematographer before turning to direction.
PICTURES: The Green Man (debut, 1956), Stranger's Meeting, Grip of the Strangler (The Haunted Strangler), First Man Into Space, Bobbikins, Two-Way Stretch, Tarzan the Magnificent (also co-s.p.), The Rebel (Call Me Genius), Corridors of Blood, Operation Snatch, Tarzan's Three Challenges (also co-s.p.), She, Tarzan and the Valley of Gold, Tarzan and the Great River, Tarzan and the Jungle Boy (prod. only), The Man with Bogart's Face.
TELEVISION: *Pilots include:* Banion, Kodiak, Dan August, Sunshine, Switch, Logan's Run, Kingston, Dallas, Matlock. Movies include: The Green Man, Ritual of Evil, The House of Greenapple Road, In Broad Daylight, Having Babies, The Grass Is Always Greener Over the Septic Tank, Peter and Paul, Running Out, Scruples, Cook and Peary—The Race to the Pole, Hollywood Wives, The Lady from Yesterday, Diary of a Perfect Murder, Celebration, Higher Ground, Walking Through the Fire, Fire! Trapped on the 37th Floor.

DAY-LEWIS, DANIEL
Actor. b. London, England, April 29, 1957. Son of late C. Day-Lewis, poet laureate of Eng., and actress Jill Balcon. Grandson of late Sir Malcolm Balcon who prod. Hitchcock's Brit. films. e. Bristol Old Vic. Theatre School. First professional job at 12 as ruffian scratching cars with broken bottle in film, Sunday Bloody Sunday. Then acted with Bristol Old Vic and Royal Shakespeare Co.
THEATRE: London: Dracula, Funny Peculiar, Troilus & Cressida, A Midsummer Night's Dream, Class Enemy, Edward II, Look Back in Anger, Another Country, Romeo and Juliet The Futurists Hamlet.
PICTURES: Gandhi, The Bounty, A Room With a View, My Beautiful Laundrette, The Unbearable Lightness of Being, Stars and Bars, Nanou, Ever Smile New Jersey, My Left Foot (Academy Award, Golden Globe nom. 1990; also BAFTA, NY Film Critics, L.A. Film Critics, Natl. Society of Film Critics Awards), The Last of the Mohicans, The Age of Innocence, In the Name of the Father (Academy Award nom. Golden Globe nom. 1994), The Crucible, The Boxer (Golden Globe nom. 1998), Gangs of New York (Academy Award nom. Golden Globe nom. 2003), The Ballad of Jack and Rose (also original score prod.), There Will Be Blood (Academy Award, Golden Globe Award 2008), Nine (Golden Globe nom. 2010), Black Mass.
TELEVISION: *BBC Movies/Specials:* Eddie Shoestring, Artemis 81, The Lost Traveller, The Sugar House, Beyond the Glass, Dangerous Corner, A Frost in May, How Many Miles to Babylon?, My Brother Jonathan, The Insurance Man, History of Hamlet (host). *Guest:* More than 52 appearances.

DEAKINS, ROGER
Cinematographer. b. Devon, England, May 24, 1949. Accepted into National Film School in 1972. Working as professional film-maker from 1975 directing and photographing documentary films including Around the World With Ridgeway, Zimbabwe, Eritrea—Behind the Lines, When the World Changed, Worlds Apart S.E. Nuba, Worlds Apart Rajgonds. Photographed first feature, Another Time Another Place in 1982.
PICTURES: The Innocent, Sid & Nancy, Shadey, Defense of the Realm, White Mischief, Personal Services, Stormy Monday, Pascali's Island, The Kitchen Toto, Mountains of the Moon, Air America, The Long Walk Home, Barton Fink, Homicide, Thunderheart, Passion Fish, The Secret Garden, The Hudsucker Proxy, The Shawshank Redemption (Academy Award nom.; ASC Award 1995), Rob Roy, Dead Man Walking, Fargo (Academy Award nom.; ASC nom. 1997), Courage Under Fire, Kundun (Academy Award nom.; ASC nom. 1998), Martial Law, The Big Lebowski, The Siege, Anywhere But Here, O Brother, Where Art Thou? (Academy Award nom.; ASC nom. 2001), Thirteen Days, The Man Who Wasn't There (Academy Award nom.; ASC Award 2002), A Beautiful Mind, Levity, Intolerable Cruelty, House of Sand & Fog, The Ladykillers, The Village, Jarhead, The Assassination of Jesse James by the Coward Robert Ford (Academy Award nom.; ASC nom. 2008), In the Valley of Elah, No Country for Old Men (Academy Award nom.; ASC nom. 2008), Doubt, The Reader (Academy Award nom.; ASC nom. 2009), WALL·E (visual consult.), Revolutionary Road (ASC nom. 2009), A Serious Man (also camera operator), The Company Men, True Grit.
TELEVISION: *Movies:* The House, Dinner With Friends. *Mini-series:* Wolcott.

DEBITETTO, BOB
Executive. b. July 29, 1956. e. State Univ. of Newy York at Stony Brook, B.A., 1978; UCLA Law School, J.D., 1981. Began career as an attorney for Finley, Kumble, Wagner, Heine, Underberg, Manley, Myerson & Casey, 1981-1986. Entered entertainment industry as a studio attorney for Walt Disney Pictures, 1986-1988. became senior v.p., & v.p., business affairs, Disney Motion Picture group, 1988-1993. Promoted to senior v.p., Disney Motion Picture Group, 1993-1995. Left Disney and became senior v.p., Turner Pictures, 1995-1997. Debitetto then became the executive v.p., TNT Originals, 1997-2000. From 2000-2002, president, original programming, Turner Network Television and president/COO of TNT Originals. Was senior v.p., programming, A&E cable network from 2003-2005. In 2005 assumed his position of executive v.p. & general manager of A&E. 2008 he was promoted to president and general manager. He also oversees the Biography Channel and the Crime & Investigation Network.

DE BONT, JAN
Cinematographer, Director. b. Holland, Oct. 22, 1943.Trained at Amsterdam Film Acad. Recipient of Kodak Camera Award and Rembrandt Award.
PICTURES: *Cinematographer:* Turkish Delight, Keetje Tippel, Max Heuelaar, Soldier of Orange, Private Lessons (U.S. debut, 1981), Roar, I'm Dancing as Fast as I Can, Cujo, All the Right Moves, Bad Manners, The Fourth Man, Mischief, The Jewel of the Nile, Flesh + Blood, The Clan of the Cave Bear, Ruthless People, Who's That Girl, Leonard Part 6, Die Hard, Bert Rigby You're a Fool, Black Rain, The Hunt for Red October, Flatliners, Shining Through, Basic Instinct, Lethal Weapon 3. *Director:* Speed (debut, 1994), Twister, Speed 2: Cruise Control (also s.p., story), The Haunting (also prod.), Stopping Power, Lara Croft Tomb Raider: The Cradle of Life, Point Break Indo (also exec. prod.). *Producer:* S.L.C. Punk!, Zero Hour, Like a Hole in the Head, The Haunting, Equilibrium, Minority Report, Meg.
TELEVISION *(Photography): Movie:* The Ray Mancini Story, Parker Kane. *Episode:* Tales From the Crypt (Split Personality).

DECHERD, ROBERT W.
Executive. e. graduate of Harvard College,1973. This TV industry veteran has been a top executive with Dallas, TX-based A. H. Belo Corp. for 30+ years. Belo the Company owns 19 television stations, including nine in the top 30 markets and also owns and operates The Dallas Morning News. During the 1980s, Decherd served as v.p., executive v.p., COO, and president of Belo. On Jan. 1, 1987, Decherd became Belo's CEO. He currently serves Belo as president, chmn. & CEO (2007). Decherd has served as a director of the Newspaper Association of America, and is a past pres. of the Dallas Society of Professional Journalists and the Freedom of Information Foundation of Texas. From 2002-2006, was member of the FCC's Media Security and Reliability Council, part of President Bush's Homeland Security initiative. He received the James Madison Award from the Freedom of Information Foundation of Texas, Inc. in 1989, the Henry Cohn Humanitarian Award from the Anti-Defamation League in 1991; in 1994, became the youngest inductee to the Texas Business Hall of Fame. Decherd has been on Belo's bd. of dir. since 1976.

DECUIR, JR., JOHN F.
Art Director, Production Designer. b. Burbank, CA, Aug. 4, 1941. e. U. of Southern California, bachelor of architecture, 1965. Son of John F. De Cuir, Sr. 1966-68, U.S. Coast Guard (holds commission with rank of Lt. Commander, USCGR). 1968-72, project designer, Walt Disney World, Walt Disney Prods. 1972-74, dir. of design, Six Flags Corp. 1974-9, project designer, EPCOT, Walt Disney Prods. 1980-86, pres., John F. De Cuir, Jr. Design Consultants, Inc.; 1987-pres., Cinematix Inc.
PICTURES: *Illustrator:* Cleopatra, The Honey Pot. Design Concepts: The Agony and the Ecstasy. *Art Director:* Raise the Titanic, Ghosbusters. *Special Effects Consultant:* Dead Men Don't Wear Plaid, Monsignor. *Producer:* Jazz Club, The Baltimore Clipper, The Building Puzzle. *Prod. Designer:* Fright Night, Top Gun, Apt Pupil, Elvira Mistress of the Dark, Turner & Hooch, True Identity, Sleepwalkers, Sister Act 2: Back in the Habit, Puppies for Sale, The Land of the Free, The Nephew, Running Red, Slow Burn, Primal Scream, Krews.
TELEVISION: *Art Director:* Frank Sinatra Special—Old Blue Eyes Is Back, Annual Academy Awards Presentation 1971, Double Agent. *Production Design:* Double Switch, Earth Star Voyager, Providence, Inherit the Wind, That Championship Season, Chestnut Hill (pilot).

DEE, RUBY
Actress. b. Cleveland, OH, Oct. 27, 1924. r.n. Ruby Ann Wallace. e. Hunter Coll. m. Late actor-dir.-writer Ossie Davis. Worked as apprentice at Amer. Negro Theatre, 1941-44, studied at Actor's Workshop. Stage appearances include Jeb, Anna Lucasta, The World of Sholom Aleichem, A Raisin in the Sun, Purlie Victorious, Wedding Band, Boseman and Lena, Hamlet, Checkmates.
PICTURES: No Way Out, The Jackie Robinson Story, The Tall Target, Go Man Go!, Edge of the City, St. Louis Blues, Take a Giant Step, Virgin Island, A Raisin in the Sun, Gone Are the Days, The Balcony, The Incident, Up Tight, Buck and the Preacher, Black Girl, Countdown at Kusini, Cat People, Do the Right Thing, Love at Large, Jungle Fever, Cop and a Half, Just Cause, A Simple Wish, The Wall, A Time to Dance: The Life and Work of Norma Canner, Baby Geniuses, The Unfinished Journey, Unchained Memories: Readings from the Slave Narratives (reader), The Way Back Home, Clarksdale, American Gangster (Academy Award nom. 2008), Dream Street, Red & Blue Marbles, Video Girl, Politics of Love.
TELEVISION: *Movies:* Deadlock, The Sheriff, It's Good to Be Alive, I Know Why the Caged Bird Sings, All God's Children, The Atlanta Child Murders, Go Tell it on the Mountain, Windmills of the Gods, The Court-Martial of Jackie Robinson, Decoration Day (Emmy Award, 1991), The Ernest Green Story, Homeward Bound, Edgar Allen Poe: Terror of the Soul, Captive Heart: The

James Mink Story, Mr. & Mrs. Loving, Passing Glory, Having Our Say: The Delaney Sisters First 100 Years, Whitewash (2 Emmy noms. 1995), A Storm in Summer, Little Bill (2 Emmy noms. 2001, 2003) Finding Buck McHenry, Taking Back Our Town, Their Eyes Were Watching God, America. *Mini-series:* Roots: The Next Generation (Emmy nom. 1979), Gore Vidal's Lincoln (Emmy nom. 1988), The Stand, Christianity: The First Two Thousand Years, Feast of All Saints. *Series:* The Nurses (Emmy nom. 1964), Peyton Place, With Ossie and Ruby, Middle Ages. *Specials:* Actor's Choice, Seven Times Monday, Go Down Moses, Twin-Bit Gardens, Wedding Band, To Be Young Gifted and Black, Long Day's Journey into Night, Edgar Allan Poe: Terror of the Soul (narrator), Porgy & Bess: An American Story, The 2006 Black Movie Awards (2006). *Guest:* More than 126 appearances.

DE FINA, BARBARA

Producer. Started as prod. asst. before working at various jobs for such filmmakers as Woody Allen and Sidney Lumet. Became assoc. prod. of development for King/Hitzig Prods., working on Happy Birthday Gemini, Cattle Annie and Little Britches. Was unit mgr./assoc. prod. on Prince of the City. First worked with Martin Scorsese on The King of Comedy as unit mgr. Produced Michael Jackson music video segment Bad.
PICTURES: The Color of Money, The Last Temptation of Christ, New York Stories (segment: Life Lessons), GoodFellas (exec. prod.), The Grifters (exec. prod.), Cape Fear, Mad Dog and Glory, The Age of Innocence, Casino, Kicked in the Head, Kundun, The Hi-Lo Country, Bringing Out the Dead, Dino, You Can Count On Me, The Mesmerist, Brides, Lymelife, Little Victories, .45, No Direction Home: Bob Dylan (doc. exec. prod.), An Entire Body.

DEGENERES, ELLEN

Actress, Comedienne. b. New Orleans, LA, Jan 26, 1958.
PICTURES: Wisecracks, Coneheads, Mr. Wrong, Doctor Dolittle (voice), Edtv, Goodbye Lover, The Love Letter, Trevor, Reaching Normal, You'll Never Wiez in This Town Again, Finding Nemo (voice), Oh, God! Recipient of numerous industry awards.
TELEVISION: *Movie:* On the Edge. *Series:* Open House, Laurie Hill, Ellen (also prod., 3 Golden Globe noms.; WGA nom. 1998), Ellen: The Ellen DeGeneres Show (12 Emmy Awards, 7 other noms.; also exec. prod.), The Ellen Show (Emmy Award 1997, 2 other noms., outstanding writing/comedy show, 1997; 3 Golden Globe noms.; WGA nom. 1998), Ellen DeGeneres: Here & Now (TV doc., exec. prod.; 2 Emmy noms.), Ellen DeGeneres: The Beginning (2 Emmy noms.), American Idol (judge). *Specials:* If These Walls Could Talk 2 (Emmy nom. 2000) The 38th Annual Grammy Awards (Emmy nom. 1996 as host), Ellen DeGeneres: Here and Now (doc.), The 79th Annual Academy Awards (host, writer, Emmy nom. 2007). *Guest:* More than 147 appearances.

DE HAVILLAND, OLIVIA

Actress b. Tokyo, Japan, July 1, 1916. e. California schools and Notre Dame Convent, Belmont. Acting debut, Max Reinhardt's stage prod., A Midsummer Night's Dream; going to Warner Bros. for film debut in m.p. version, 1935. Recipient: The Snake Pit (NY Film Critics & Look Awards), The Heiress (NY Film Critics, Women's Natl. Press Club & Look Awards). Autobiography: Every Frenchman Has One (1962).
THEATRE: A Midsummer Night's Dream (Hollywood Bowl). B'way: Romeo and Juliet (1951), A Gift of Time. U.S. Tour: Candida (1951-52).
PICTURES: A Midsummer Night's Dream (debut, 1935), Alibi Ike, The Irish in Us, Captain Blood, Anthony Adverse, The Charge of the Light Brigade, Call It a Day, It's Love I'm After, The Great Garrick, Gold is Where You Find It, The Adventures of Robin Hood, Four's a Crowd, Hard to Get, Wings of the Navy, Dodge City, The Private Lives of Elizabeth and Essex, Gone With the Wind (Academy Award nom. 1940), Raffles, My Love Came Back, Santa Fe Trail, The Golden Door (Academy Award nom. 1942), Strawberry Blonde, Hold Back the Dawn, They Died With Their Boots On, The Male Animal, In This Our Life, Princess O'Rourke, Thank Your Lucky Stars, Government Girl, The Well Groomed Bride, To Each His Own (Academy Award, 1947), Devotion, Dark Mirror, The Snake Pit (Academy Award nom. 1949), The Heiress (Academy Award, Golden Globe Award 1950), My Cousin Rachel (Golden Globe nom. 1953), That Lady, Not as a Stranger, Ambassador's Daughter, Proud Rebel, Libel, Light in the Piazza, Lady in a Cage, Hush ... Hush Sweet Charlotte, The Adventurers, Pope Joan, Airport '77, The Swarm, The Fifth Musketeer.
TELEVISION: *Movies & Mini-series:* The Screaming Woman, Roots: The Next Generations, Murder is Easy, Charles & Diana: A Royal Romance, North & South Book II, Anastasia: The Mystery of Anna (Emmy nom. Golden Globe Award 1987), The Woman He Loved. *Special:* Noon Wine (Stage 67). *Guest:* More than 54 appearances.

DELANY, DANA

Actress. b. New York, NY, March 13, 1956. e. Phillips Acad., Wesleyan U.
THEATRE: B'way: Translations, A Life. Off-B'way: Blood Moon.
PICTURES: Almost You, Where the River Runs Black, Masquerade, Moon Over Parador, Patty Hearst, Housesitter, Light Sleeper, Batman: Mask of the Phantasm (voice), Tombstone, Exit to Eden, Live Nude Girls, Fly Away Home, Wide Awake, Looking for Lulu, The Curve, The Outfitters, Mother Ghost, Spin, Drunkboat, Route 30, Multiple Sarcasms, Camp Hope, A Beautiful Life.
TELEVISION: *Movies:* A Promise to Keep, Donato and Daughter, The Enemy Within, Choices of the Heart: The Margaret Sanger Story, For Hope, The Patron St. of Liars, Resurrection, Sirens, Final Jeopardy, Conviction, Open House (co-exec. prod. only), A Time to Remember, Baby for Sale. *Mini-series:* Wild Palms, True Women. *Series:* Love of Life, As the World Turns, Sweet Surrender, China Beach (2 Emmy Awards: 1989, 1992, 2 other noms; 2 Golden Globe noms.), Pasadena, Presidio Med., Justice League Unlimited, Kidnapped, Desperate Housewives. *Specials:* Texan, Fallen Angels (Good Housekeeping), The Rescuers. *Guest:* More than 104 appearances.

DE LAURENTIIS, DINO

Producer, Executive. b. Torre Annunziata, Italy, Aug. 8, 1919. Took part in Rome Experimental Film Center; dir., prod. chmn. of the bd. and CEO, De Laurentiis Entertainment Group Inc.; founded in 1984 the DEG Film Studios in Wilmington, NC. Resigned 1988. Started Dino De Laurentiis Communications, 1990. Currently operates the Dino De Laurentiis Company from Universal City, CA (2007). Also Founder/Owner of Dino de Laurentiis Cinematografica. Received Academy Award 2001: Irving G. Thalberg Memorial Award.
PICTURES: L'amore Canta, Il Bandito, La Figlia del Capitano, Riso Amaro, La Lupa, Anna, Ulysses, Mambo, La Strada, Gold of Naples, War and Peace, Nights of Cabiria, The Tempest, Great War, Five Branded Women, Everybody Go Home, Under Ten Flags, The Best of Enemies, The Unfaithfuls, Barabbas, The Bible, Operation Paradise, The Witches, The Stranger, Diabolik, Anzio, Barbarella, Waterloo, The Valachi Papers, The Stone Killer, Serpico, Death Wish, Mandingo, Three Days of the Condor, Drum, Face to Face, Buffalo Bill and the Indians, King Kong, The Shootist, Orca, White Buffalo, The Serpent's Egg, King of the Gypsies, The Brink's Job, Hurricane, Flash Gordon, Halloween II, Ragtime, Conan the Barbarian, Fighting Back, Amityville II: The Possession, Halloween III: Season of the Witch, The Dead Zone, Amityville 3-D, Firestarter, The Bounty, Conan the Destroyer, Stephen King's Cat's Eye, Red Sonja, Year of the Dragon, Marie, Stephen King's Silver Bullet, Raw Deal, Maximum Overdrive, Tai-Pan, Blue Velvet, The Bedroom Window, Crimes of the Heart, King Kong Lives, Million Dollar Mystery, Weeds, Desperate Hours, Kuffs, Once Upon a Crime, Body of Evidence, Army of Darkness, Unforgettable, Assassins, Breakdown, U-571, Hannibal, Red Dragon, Hannibal Rising, The Last Legion, Virgin Territory.
TELEVISION: Sometimes They Come Back, Slave of Dreams, Solomon & Sheba.

DE LAURENTIIS, RAFFAELLA

Producer. Daughter of Dino De Laurentiis. Began career as prod. asst. on father's film Hurricane. Independent prod.
PICTURES: Beyond the Reef, Conan the Barbarian, Conan the Destroyer, Dune, Tai-Pan, Prancer, Dragon: The Bruce Lee Story, Trading Mom, Dragonheart, Backdraft (exec. prod.), Timebomb, Daylight (exec. prod.), Krull the Conqueror, Black Dog, Prancer Returns (video, exec. prod.), Sky Captain and the World of Tomorrow (exec. prod.), The Last Legion, The Forbidden Kingdom (exec. prod.).
TELEVISION: *Movies: Exec. Prod.:* Uprising (prod.), Stealing Christmas, Vanishing Son, Vanishing Son II, Vanishing Son III, Vanishing Son IV. *Series:* The Guardian (prod.).

DEL BELSO, RICHARD

Marketing Executive. b. Albany, NY, Aug. 9, 1939. e. Fordham U, 1961, NYU, 1965. Began career in adv./research dept. at Benton & Bowles Advertising, NY. Served as research dept. group head for Kenyon and Eckhart; group head for Grudin/Appell/Haley Research Co. (now known as A/H/F/ Marketing Research, Inc.). Two years as assoc. dir. of mktg., research for Grey Advertising (N.Y.). Joined MCA/Universal in 1976 as assoc. dir., mktg. research. In 1980 named v.p. & dir. of mktg. research for Warner Bros; became worldwide v.p. of mktg. research, 1984; named sr. v.p. worldwide theatrical film market research, 1990. In 1998, promoted to sr. v.p. market strategy, Worldwide Theatrical Films. Left Warner Bros. and currently is a bd. member, Empire of Teeth, an artists collective to develop new methods in the performing arts; Del Belso also has been pres. of bd. of dir. with 18th Street Gallery.

DEL MORO, ROBERT J.

Executive. b. White Plains, NY, July 6, 1959. e. CUNY Hunter College, Seattle Central Community College. Entered industry as theatre usher in 1978. Advanced from usher to manager with General Cinema, 1978-1990; 1990-1991, mgr. with Goodrich Quality Theatres; 1991-1994, area mgr. for General Cinema. Joined Regal Entertainment in 1994 and has served as: director of concessions and purchasing; v.p. marketing and concession; v.p. entertainment centers and food service; senior v.p. food service; and in 2007 still served as Regal's senior v.p., chief purchasing officer.

DELON, ALAIN
Actor. b. Sceaux, France, Nov. 8, 1935. Discovered by Yves Allegret. Served in French Navy as a Marine.
PICTURES: When a Woman Gets Involved (debut, 1957), Be Beautiful and Keep Quiet, 3 Murderesses, Christine, Le Chemin Des Ecoliers, Plein Soleil (Purple Noon), Quelle Joie de Vivre!, Rocco and His Brothers, Famous Loves, Eclipse, The Leopard (Golden Globe nom. 1964), The Devil and the 10 Commandments, Any Number Can Win, The Black Tulip, The Felines (Joy House), L'Insoumis (also prod., co-s.p.), The Yellow Rolls Royce, Once a Thief, Lost Command, Is Paris Burning?, Texas Across the River, The Adventurers, Spirits of the Dead, Samaurai, Diabolically Yours, Girl on a Motorcycle, Goodbye Friend, The Swimming Pool, Jeff (also prod.), The Sicilian Clan, Borsalino, The Red Circle, Madly (also prod.), Doucement Les Basses, Red Sun, The Widow Cuderc, Assassination of Trotsky, Dirty Money, The Teacher, Scorpio, Shock Treatment, The Burning Barn, Big Guns, Two Men in the City, La Race des Seigneurs, Les Seins de Glace, Borsalino & Company (also prod.), Zorro, Police Story, The Gypsy, Mr. Klein (also prod.), Like a Boomerang (also prod., s.p.), The Gang (also exec. prod.), Armaggedon, L'Homme Presse, Mort d'un Pourri (also s.p.), Attention Les Enfants Regardent, The Concorde - Airport 79, The Doctor, Teheran 43, Three Men to Destroy (also prod.), For a Cop's Honor (also dir, s.p., prod.), The Shock (also s.p.), The Cache (also prod., dir., s.p.), Swann in Love, Our Story, Military Police (also exec. prod., s.p.), The Passage (also prod.), Let Sleeping Cops Lie (also prod., co-s.p.), New Wave, Dancing Machine, The Return of Casanova, Un Crime... L'Ours en Peluche, A Hundred and One Nights, Day and Night, Half a Chance, Luchino Visconti, Actors, The Death Instinct, Asterix at the Olympic Games, L' Ennemi public n° 1.
TELEVISION: *Movies:* LeChien, Belmondo Le Magnifique, Cannes...les 400 coups, Le Lion. *Mini-series:* Cinéma. *Series:* Scherzi a parte, Frank Riva, Fabio Montale.

DELPY, JULIE
Actress. b. Paris, France, Dec. 21, 1970. Made acting debut as teenager for dir. Jean-Luc Godard.
PICTURES: Detective (debut, 1985)s Bad Blood, King Lear, Beatrice, The Dark Night, Europa Europa, Voyager, The Three Musketeers, White, Killing Zoe, Younger and Younger, Before Sunrise, An American Werewolf in Paris, Tykho Moon, The Treat, LA Without a Map, The Passion of Ayn Rand, But I'm A Cheerleader, Villa des roses, Tell Me (also s.p.), Sand, Investigating Sex, Villa des roses, Cinemagique, Before Sunset (also writer s.p., dir./composer, Academy Award nom.; WGA nom. 2005), Broken Flowers, The Hoax, The Air I Breathe, 2 Days in Paris (also writer, dir., co-prod., composer, editor), The Countess (also writer, dir., prod., composer), Les passages.
TELEVISION: *Movies:* Crime and Punishment, *Mini-series:* Frankenstein. *Series:* ER.

DEL ROSSI, PAUL R.
Executive. b. Winchester, MA, Oct. 19, 1942. e. Harvard Coll, 1964; Harvard Business Sch., 1967. Sr. v.p., The Boston Co., 1977-1980; sr. consultant, Arthur D. Little, Inc.; pres. & CEO, General Cinema Theatres. 1998, chmn. General Cinema from 1998 until 2002 when the co. was acquired by AMC. Currently a director of The DeWolfe Companies, Inc. and Charlotte Russe Holdings, Inc. He is also a director of the Massachusetts Chapter of the Cystic Fibrosis Foundation.

DEL TORO, BENICIO
Actor. b. San German, Puerto Rico, February 19, 1967.
PICTURES: Big Top Pee Wee, Licence to Kill, The Indian Runner, China Moon, Christopher Columbus: The Discovery, Golden Balls, Money for Nothing, Fearless, Swimming With Sharks, The Usual Suspects, Submission (prod. & dir.), Basquiat, The Fan, The Funeral, Joyride, Cannes Man, Excess Baggage, Fear and Loathing in Las Vegas, Bread and Roses, Snatch, The Way of the Gun, The Pledge, Traffic (Academy Award; Golden Globe Award 2001), The Hunted, 21 Grams (Academy Award nom. 2004), Sin City, Che: Part One, Che: Part Two (also prod.), The Rum Diary (also dir.), Maldeamores (exec. prod.), Things We Lost in the Fire, Guerrilla, The Argentine, The Wolfman (also prod.), The Three Stooges, Somewhere, White Widow.
TELEVISION: *Mini-series:* Drug Wars: The Camarena Story. *Guest:* More than 74 appearances.

DE LUCA, MICHAEL
Executive, Writer, Producer. b. Brooklyn, Aug. 1965. Left NYU to take intern job at New Line Cinema; became story editor before becoming production exec. in 1989. 1993 named pres. of production of New Line. Resigned, 2000. Pres., production, DreamWorks SKG, 2003. Currently, De Luca runs his own prod. co., Michael De Luca Productions.
PICTURES: *Writer:* Freddy's Dead: The Final Nightmare, In the Mouth of Madness, Judge Dredd (story), *Exec. Prod.:* B.A.P.S., One Night Stand, Wag the Dog, Dark City, Lost in Space, Blade, Pleasantville, Austin Powers: The Spy Who Shagged Me, Body Shots, The Bachelor, Magnolia, Lost Souls, Little Nicky, Blow, Rush Hour 2, Life as a House, I Am Sam, Highway, Run Ronnie Run!, John Q, Blade II, Unconditional Love, S1mOne, Old School, A Man Apart. *Producer:* Zathura: A Space Adventure, Ghost Rider, 21, The Love Guru, 21, Brothers, Kashmir.
TELEVISION: *Movie:* The Way (exec. prod.). *Series/Writer:* Freddy's Nightmares, Star Trek: Voyager, The Sopranos.

DEMME, JONATHAN
Director, Writer, Producer. b. Rockville Centre, NY, Feb. 22, 1944. e. U. of Florida. First job in industry as usher; was film critic for college paper, The Florida Alligator and the Coral Gable Times. Did publicity work for United Artists, Avco Embassy; sold films for Pathe Contemporary Films; wrote for trade paper, Film Daily, 1966-68. Moved to England in 1969; musical co-ordinator on Irving Allen's EyeWitness in 1970. In 1972 co-prod and co-wrote first film, Angels Hard As They Come. Appeared in film Into the Night.
PICTURES: Hot Box (prod., co-s.p.), Black Mama White Mama (story). *Director:* Caged Heat (also s.p.), Crazy Mama (also s.p.), Fighting Mad (also s.p.), Citizen's Band (Handle With Care), Last Embrace, Melvin and Howard, Swing Shift, Stop Making Sense, Something Wild (also co-prod.), Swimming to Cambodia, Married to the Mob, Miami Blues (prod. only), The Silence of the Lambs (Academy Award; Golden Globe nom.; DGA Award 1992), Cousin Bobby, Philadelphia (also co-prod.), Devil in a Blue Dress (exec. prod. only), That Thing You Do! (prod. only), Beloved (also prod.), The Truth About Charlie (also prod., s.p.), Adaptation (prod. only), Beah: A Black Woman Speaks (documentary, prod.), The Agronomist (dir., prod., cinematographer), The Manchurian Candidate, Neil Young: Heart of Gold (doc.,dir., prod.), Jimmy Carter Man from Plains (doc., dir., prod., writer, camera op.), Rachel Getting Married, Crude Independence (exec. prod.), Marley (doc.).
TELEVISION: *Movies:* Women & Men 2: In Love There Are No Rules (prod. only), Subway Stories: Tales from the Underground, Red Hot and Blue. *Mini-series:* Right to Return: New Home Movies from the Lower 9th Ward (doc.). *Series:* Alive From Off Center, Trying Times. *Specials:* Who Am I This Time?, Accumation With Talking plus Water Motor, Survival Guides, A Family Tree (Trying Times series, PBS), Haiti: Dreams of Democracy.

DE MORNAY, REBECCA
Actress. b. Santa Rosa, CA, Aug. 29, 1962. Spent childhood in Europe, graduating from high school in Austria. Returned to America, enrolling at Lee Strasberg's Los Angeles Institute; apprenticed at Zoetrope Studios.
THEATRE: Born Yesterday (Pasadena Playhouse), Marat/Sade (Williamstown Fest.).
PICTURES: Risky Business, Testament, The Slugger's Wife, Runaway Train, The Trip to Bountiful, Beauty and the Beast, And God Created Woman, Feds, Dealers, Backdraft, The Hand That Rocks the Cradle, Guilty as Sin, The Three Musketeers, Never Talk to Strangers (also exec. prod.), The Winner (also exec. prod.), Thick As Thieves, A Table for One, The Right Temptation, Identity, Heart of Summer, Slingshot, Raise Your Voice, Lords of Dogtown, Wedding Crashers, Music Within, American Venus, Mother's Day, Flipped.
TELEVISION: *Movies:* The Murders in the Rue Morgue, By Dawn's Early Light, An Inconvenient Woman, Blindside, Getting Out, The Con, Night Ride Home, Range of Motion, Salem Witch Trials. *Mini-series:* The Shining, A Girl Thing. *Series:* The Practice, ER, John from Cincinnati. *Guest:* More than 45 appearances.

DEMPSEY, PATRICK
Actor. b. Lewiston, ME, Jan. 13, 1966. e. St. Dominic Regional h.s. in Lewiston where he became state downhill skiing champion. Juggling, magic and puppetry led to performances before Elks clubs and community orgs. Cast by Maine Acting Co. in On Golden Pond. In 1983 acted in Torch Song Trilogy in San Francisco and toured in Brighton Beach Memoirs. NY Theatre debut, 1991 in The Subject Was Roses.
PICTURES: Heaven Help Us (debut, 1985), Meatballs III, Can't Buy Me Love, In the Mood, In a Shallow Grave, Some Girls, Loverboy, Coupe de Ville, Happy Together, Run, Mobsters, For Better and For Worse, Face the Music, Bank Robber, With Honors, Outbreak, Hugo Pool, The Treat, There's No Fish Food in Heaven, Me and Will, Denial, Scream 3, Sweet Home Alabama, The Emperor's Club, Rebellion, Cattle Call, Freedom Writers, Enchanted, Made of Honor, Valentine's Day.
TELEVISION: *Movies:* A Fighting Choice, JFK: Reckless Youth, Bloodknot, Jeremiah, Crime and Punishment, 2000 Leagues Under the Sea (mini), The Escape, Blonde, Chestnut Hill, Lucky 7, Iron Jawed Angels. *Series:* Fast Times at Ridgemont High, Once and Again (Emmy nom. 2001), Rosebud, Corsairs, About a Boy, Grey's Anatomy (2 Golden Globe noms.). *Special:* Merry Christmas Baby. *Guest:* More than 88 appearances.

DE MUNN, JEFFREY
Actor. b. Buffalo, NY, April 25, 1947. e. Union Coll. Studied acting at Old Vic Theatre in Bristol, Eng.
THEATRE: NY: Comedians, A Prayer for My Daughter, Modigliani, Augusta, Hands of Its Enemy, Chekhov Sketchbook, A Midsummer Night's Dream, Total Abandon, Country Girl, Bent, K-2, Sleight of Hand, Spoils of War, One Shoe Off, Hedda Gabler, Gunshy.
PICTURES: You Better Watch Out (Christmas Evil), The First

Deadly Sin, Resurrection, Ragtime, I'm Dancing as Fast as I Can, Frances, Windy City, Enormous Changes at the Last Minute, Warning Sign, The Hitcher, The Blob, Betrayed, Blaze, Newsies, Eyes of an Angel, The Shawshank Redemption, Safe Passage, Killer, Phenomenon, Turbulence, Rocket Man, Harvest, The X-Files, Harvest, The Green Mile, The Majestic, The Lucky Ones, Hollywoodland, The Mist, Cayman Went, Burn After Reading, Shelter.
TELEVISION: *Movies:* The Last Tenant, Sanctuary of Fear, King Crab, Word of Honor, I Married Wyatt Earp, The Face of Rage, Sessions, When She Says No, Windmills of the Gods, Lincoln, Doubletake, A Time to Live, Who Is Julia?, Young Harry Houdini, Price of Justice, Switch, Elysian Fields, The Haunted, Treacherous Crossing, Jonathan: The Boy Nobody Wanted, Barbarians at the Gate, Crash: The Fate of Flight 1502, Settle the Score, Under the Influence, Betrayal of Trust, Citizen X (Emmy nom. 1995), Down Came a Blackbird, Hiroshima, Almost Golden: The Jessica Savitch Story, A Christmas Memory, Path to Paradise, Black Cat Run, Storm of the Century, Noriega: God's Favorite, Our Town, Empire Falls, Covert One: The Hades Factor. *Mini-series:* Night Sins, Liberty! The American Revolution, Storm of the Century, Covert One: The Hades Factor, *Series:* Law & Order. *Specials:* Mourning Becomes Electra, Peacemaker (Triple Play II), Sensibility and Sense, The Joy That Kills, Teacher, Pigeon Feathers, Many Mansions, Wild Jackasses, Ebbie. *Documentaries:* American Masters: Eugene O'Neill: A Glory of Ghosts, Scottsboro: An American Tragedy, The Impressionists. *Guest:* More than 73 appearances.

DENCH, DAME JUDI
Actress. b. York, England, Dec. 9, 1934. Studied for stage at Central Sch. of Speech and Drama. Theatre debut Old Vic, 1957. Created a Dame in 1988 Honours List. Recent Theatre: Cymbeline, Juno and the Paycock, A Kind of Alaska, The Cherry Orchard, The Plough and the Stars, Importance of Being Earnest, Pack of Lies, Mr. and Mrs. Nobody, Antony and Cleopatra, The Sea, Coriolanus, The Gift of the Gorgon, The Seagull. Director: Much Ado About Nothing, Look Back in Anger, Boys from Syracuse, Romeo and Juliet, Absolute Hell, A Little Night Music.
PICTURES: The Third Secret (debut, 1964), He Who Rides a Tiger, A Study in Terror, Four in the Morning, A Midsummer Night's Dream (RSC Prod.), Luther, Dead Cert, Wetherby, A Room With a View, 84 Charing Cross Road, A Handful of Dust, Henry V, Jack and Sarah, Goldeneye, Hamlet, Her Majesty, Mrs. Brown (BAFTA Award, Golden Globe Award, Chicago Film Crits. Award; Academy Award nom., Best Actress, 1998), Tomorrow Never Dies, Shakespeare in Love (Academy Award Best Supp. Actress Golden Globe nom. 1999), Tea with Mussolini, The World is Not Enough, Into the Arms of Strangers: Stories of the Kindertransport, Chocolat (Academy Award nom.; Golden Globe nom. 2001), Therese Raquin, Iris (Academy Award nom.; Golden Globe nom. 2002), The Shipping News, The Importance of Being Earnest, Die Another Day, Home on the Range (voice), Sweating Bullets, The Chronicles of Riddick, Ladies in Lavender, Bond 21, Pride and Prejudice, Mrs. Henderson Presents (Academy Award nom.; Golden Globe nom. 2006), Gnomeo and Juliet (voice), Doogal (narr.), Notes on a Scandal (Academy Award nom.; Golden Globe nom. 2007), Casino Royale, Quantum of Solace, Rage, Nine, Jane Eyre.
TELEVISION: *Movies:* Days to Come, Langrishe Go Down, The Comedy of Errors (RSC Prod.), On Giant's Shoulders, Major Barbara, Pink String and Sealing Wax, Macbeth (RSC Prod.), Going Gently, The Funambulists, Age of Kings, Jackanory, Hilda Lessways, Luther, Neighbours, Parade's End, Marching Song, On Approval, Emilie, Village Wooing, The Cherry Orchard, Saigon—Year of the Cat, Mr. and Mrs. Edgehill, The Browning Version, Ghosts, Behaving Badly, Look Back in Anger (dir.), Can You Hear Me Thinking?, Absolute Hell, The Last of the Blonde Bombshells (Emmy nom.; Golden Globe Award 2001), Richard Rodgers: Some Enchanted Evening (performer). *Mini-series:* Talking to a Stranger, Love in a Cold Climate, The Torch, Middlemarch, Masterpiece Theatre: Return to Cranford (Emmy nom. 2008, Golden Globe nom. 2009). *Series:* A Fine Romance, As Time Goes By, Angelina Ballerina (voice), As Time Goes By. *Special:* Judi Dench: A BAFTA Tribute. *Documentaries:* The Great War and the Shaping of the 20th Century (mini-series), J.R.R.T.: A Film Portrait of J.R.R. Tolkien, Into the Arms of Strangers: Stories of the Kindertransport, Bugs! (short). *Guest:* More than 136 appearances.

DENEUVE, CATHERINE
Actress. r.n. Catherine Dorleac. b. Paris, France, Oct. 22, 1943. Sister was the late Francoise Dorleac. Made screen debut as teen using adopting mother's maiden name.
PICTURES: Les Collegiennes (debut, 1956), Wild Roots of Love, L'homme a Femmes, The Doors Slam, La Parisiennes (segment: Sophie), Vice and Virtue, Satan Leads the Dance, Vacances Portugaises, Les Plus Belles Escroqueries du Monde, The Umbrellas of Cherbourg (Cannes Film Fest. Award, 1964), Male Hunt (La Chasse a l'Homme), Male Companion, La Costanza della Ragione, Repulsion, Le Chant du Monde, La Vie de Chateau (A Matter of Resistance), Who Wants to Sleep?, Les Creatures, The Young Girls of Rochefort, Belle de Jour (Venice Film Fest. Award, 1967), Benjamin, Manon 70, Mayerling, La Chamade (Heartbeat), The April Fools, Mississippi Mermaid, Don't Be Blue, Tristana, Donkey Skin, Henri Langolis, Liza, It Only Happens to Others, Dirty Money, Melampo, The Slightly Pregnant Man, Touche Pas a la Femme Blanche, La Grande Bourgeoise, Zig-Zag, La Femme aux Bottes Rouges, Hustle, Lovers Like Us, Act of Agression, The Beach Hut, Second Chance, March or Die, Ecoute voir, L'Argent des Autres, When I Was a Kid I Didn't Dare, Anima Persa, An Adventure for Two, Ils Sont Grandes ces Petits, Courage--Let's Run, The Last Metro, Je vous Aime, Choice of Arms, Hotel des Ameriques, Reporters, Daisy Chain, Le Choc, The African, The Hunger, Le Bon Plaisir, Fort Saganne, Love Songs, Let's Hope It's a Girl, Le Mauvaise Herbe, Scene of the Crime, Agent Trouble, A Strange Place to Meet (also prod.), Hotel Panique, The Man Who Loved Zoos, Frequency Murder, Helmut Newton: Frames From the Edge (doc.), The White Queen, Indochine (Academy Award nom. 1993), Ma Saison Preferee (My Favorite Season), The Chess Game, The Convent, The Child of the Night, Genealogies of a Crime, Place Vendome, Time Regained, The Last Napoleon, East-West, The Letter, Belle Maman, Pola X, Dancer in the Dark, Von Trier's 100 Eyes, Clouds: Letters to My Son, Absolument fabuleux, The Musketeer, Tom Thumb, I'm Going Home, 8 Women, Les Temps qui changent, Palais royal!, Le Héros de la famille, Persepolis (voice), Après lui, Un conte de Noël, I Want to See, The Big Picture, Potiche.
TELEVISION: *Movies:* Princesse Marie, Suddenly Gina. *Mini-series:* Les Liaisons dangereuses. *Guest:* More than 109 appearances.

DE NIRO, ROBERT
Actor, Producer. b. New York, NY, Aug. 17, 1943. Studied acting with Stella Adler and Lee Strasberg; 1988, formed Tribeca Film Center in NY.
THEATRE: One Night Stand of a Noisy Passenger (Off-B'way), Cuba and His Teddy Bear (Public Theater and B'way; Theatre World Award).
PICTURES: The Wedding Party (debut, 1969), Greetings, Sam's Song (The Swap), Bloody Mama, Hi Mom, Born to Win, Jennifer on My Mind, The Gang That Couldn't Shoot Straight, Bang the Drum Slowly, Mean Streets, The Godfather Part II (Academy Award, best supporting actor, 1975), Taxi Driver (Academy Award nom. Golden Globe nom. 1977), The Last Tycoon, New York New York (Golden Globe nom. 1978), 1900, The Deer Hunter (Academy Award nom.; Golden Globe nom. 1979), Raging Bull (Academy Award, Golden Globe Award 1981), True Confessions, The King of Comedy, Once Upon a Time in America, Falling in Love, Brazil, The Mission, Angel Heart, The Untouchables, Midnight Run (Golden Globe nom.1989), Jacknife, We're No Angels (also exec. prod.), Stanley and Iris, GoodFellas, Awakenings (Academy Award nom. 1991), Guilty by Suspicion, Backdraft, Cape Fear (Academy Award nom. Golden Globe nom. 1992; also prod.), Thunderheart (prod.), Mistress (also prod.), Night and the City, Mad Dog and Glory, This Boy's Life, A Bronx Tale (also dir., co-prod.), Mary Shelley's Frankenstein (also assoc. prod.), Casino, Heat, Marvin's Room (also exec. prod.), The Fan, Sleepers, Stolen Flower, Cop Land, Jackie Brown, Wag the Dog (also prod.), Great Expectations, Ronin, Analyze This (Golden Globe nom. 2000), Flawless (also prod.), Adventures of Rocky and Bullwinkle (also prod.), Men of Honor, Meet the Parents (Golden Globe nom. 2001; also prod.), Fifteen Minutes, The Score (also dir.), City by the Sea, Showtime, Scared Guys, Analyze That (also prod.), Godsend, The Bridge of San Luis Rey, Shark Tale (voice), Hide and Seek, Meet the Fockers (also prod.), Rent (prod.), Chaos (also prod.), The Good Shepherd (also prod., dir.), Artemis Fowl (prod.), Stardust, Bridge and Tunnel (prod.), Arthur and the Invisibles (voice), What Just Happened? (also prod.), Stardust, New Orleans, 36 (also prod.), What Just Happened?, Righteous Kill, Public Enemies (exec. prod. only), 20% Fiction (exec. prod. only), Everybody's Fine, Machete, Stone, Meet the Fockers Sequel (also prod.), The Dark Fields.
TELEVISION: *Movies:* Witness to the Mob (exec. prod. only), Holiday Heart (exec. prod. only). *Specials:* Night of 100 Stars, Dear America: Letters Home From Vietnam (reader), Lenny Bruce: Swear to Tell the Truth, America: A Tribute to Heroes, The Concert for New York City, Hello, He Lied & Other Truths From the Hollywood Trenches. *Series:* Tribeca (exec. prod. only). *Guest:* More than 162 appearances.

DENNEHY, BRIAN
Actor. b. Bridgeport, CT, July 9, 1939. e. Columbia U. In Marine Corps five years, including Vietnam. After discharge in 1965 studied with acting coaches in N.Y., while working at part time jobs as a salesman, bartender, truck driver.
THEATRE: Streamers, Galileo (Goodman Th.), The Cherry Orchard, Translations, Death of a Salesman (Tony Award, best actor, 1999)
PICTURES: Looking for Mr. Goodbar, Semi-Tough, F.I.S.T., Foul Play, 10, Butch and Sundance: The Early Days, Little Miss Marker, Split Image, First Blood, Never Cry Wolf, Gorky Park, Finders Keepers, River Rat, Cocoon, Silverado, Twice in a Lifetime, F/X, Legal Eagles, The Check Is in the Mail, Best Seller, The Belly of an Architect, Return to Snowy River Part II, Miles From Home, Cocoon: The Return, The Last of the Finest, Presumed Innocent, FX2, Gladiator, Seven Minutes, Tommy Boy, The Stars Fell on Henrietta, Midnight Movie, Romeo and Juliet, Dish Dogs, Out of the Cold, Silicon Towers, Summer Catch, Stolen Summer, She Hate Me, Assault on Precinct 13, 10th & Wolf, Everyone's Hero (voice), The Ultimate Gift, Ratatouille, Welcome to Paradise, War Eagle, Cat City, Righteous Kill, Meet Monica Velour, Every Day,

Alleged, The Next Three Days.
TELEVISION: *Movies:* Johnny We Hardly Knew Ye, It Happened at Lake Wood Manor, Ruby and Oswald, A Death in Canaan, A Real American Hero, Silent Victory: The Kitty O'Neil Story, The Jericho Mile, Dummy, The Seduction of Miss Leona, A Rumor of War, Fly Away Home, Skokie, I Take These Men, Blood Feud, Off Sides, Acceptable Risks, Private Sessions, The Lion of Africa, A Father's Revenge, Day One, Perfect Witness, Pride and Extreme Prejudice, Rising Son, A Killing in a Small Town (Emmy nom. 1990), In Broad Daylight, The Burden of Proof (Emmy nom. 1992), To Catch a Killer (Emmy nom. 1992), Diamond Fleece, Teamster: The Jackie Presser Story, Deadly Matrimony, Foreign Affairs, Murder in the Heartland (Emmy nom. 1993), Prophet of Evil: The Ervil LeBaron Story, Final Appeal, Jack Reed: Badge of Honor (also co-exec. prod.), Leave of Absence, Jack Reed: Search for Justice (also dir., co-writer), Contagious, Indefensible: The Truth About Edward Brannigan (also dir.), Voyage of Terror, Thanks of a Grateful Nation, NetForce, Sirens, Death of a Salesman (Golden Globe Award,; Emmy nom. 2000), The Warden of Redrock, Three Blind Mice, A Season on the Brink, The Roman Spring of Mrs. Stone, Behind the Camera: The Unauthorized Story of 'Three's Company', The Crooked E: The Unshredded Truth about Enron, Category 6: Day of Destruction, The Exonerated, Our Fathers (Emmy nom. 2005), Marco Polo, Bunker Hill. *Mini-series:* Pearl, The Last Place on Earth, Evergreen, Dead Man's Walk, Nostromo, A Season in Purgatory, Founding Fathers, Too Rich: The Secret Life of Doris Duke, Marco Polo. *Series:* Big Shamus Little Shamus, Star of the Family, Birdland, Arrest & Trial, The Fighting Fitzergeralds, Project Greenlight, Our Fathers (Emmy nom. 2005). *Documentaries:* Dear America: Letter Home From Vietnam (narr), Founding Fathers (mini-series, voice), Arrest & Trial (series, host), Founding Brothers (voice), Columbia: A Celebration (narr.), American Valor (narr.). *Guest:* More than 140 appearances.

DE PALMA, BRIAN

Director, Writer, Producer. b. Newark, NJ, Sept. 11, 1940. e. Columbia U.,B.A.; Sarah Lawrence, M.A. While in college made series of shorts, including Wotan's Wake, winner of Rosenthal Foundation Award for best film made by American under 25. Also judged most popular film of Midwest Film Festival (1963); later shown at San Francisco Film Festival. Dir.: The Responsive Eye (doc., 1966).
PICTURES: *Director:* Murder a La Mod (also s.p., edit.), Greetings (also co-s.p. ed.), The Wedding Party (also co-s.p., co-prod., ed.), Hi Mom (also co-story, s.p.), Dionysus in '69 (also co-prod., co-photog., co-ed.), Get To Know Your Rabbit, Sisters (also co-s.p.), Phantom of the Paradise (also co-s.p.; WGA nom. 1975), Obsession (also co-story), Carrie, The Fury, Home Movies (also s.p., co-prod.), Dressed to Kill (also s.p.), Blow Out (also s.p.), Scarface, Body Double (also prod., s.p.), Wiseguys, The Untouchables, Casualties of War, The Bonfire of the Vanities (also prod.), Raising Cain (also s.p.), Carlito's Way, Mission: Impossible, Snake Eyes (also prod., story), Mission to Mars, Femme Fatale (also s.p.), Toyer, The Black Dahlia, Redacted (also writer).

DEPARDIEU, GÉRARD

Actor. b. Chateauroux, France, Dec. 27, 1948. Studied acting at Theatre National Populaire in Paris. Made film debut at 16 in short by Roger Leenhardt (Le Beatnik et Le Minet). Acted in feature film by Agnes Varda (uncompleted).
PICTURES: Le Cri du Cormoran le Soir au-dessis des Jonques, Nathalie Granger, A Little Sun in Cold Water, Au Renedez-vous de la mort joyeuse, La Scoumone, Rude Journee our la Reine, The Holes, Going Places, Stavisky, Woman of the Granges, Vincent Francois Paul and the Others, The Wonderful Crook, 7 Morts sur ordonnance, Maitresse, Je t'Aime Moi Non Plus, The Last Woman, 1900, Barocco, Rene la Canne, Baxter Vera Baxter, The Truck, Tell Him I Love Him, At Night All Cats Are Gray, Get Out Your Handkerchiefs, The Left-Handed Woman, Bye Bye Monkey, Violanta, Le Sucre, Les Chiens, L'Ingorgo, Buffet Froid, Temporale Rosy, Mon Oncle d'Amerique, Loulou, The Last Metro, Inspector Blunder, I Love You, Choice of Arms, The Woman Next Door, Le Chevre. The Return of Martin Guerre, The Big Brother, Danton, The Moon in the Gutter, Les Comperes (also co-prod.), Fort Saganne, Le Tartuffe (also dir., co-s.p), Rive Droie Rive Gauche, Police, One Woman or Two, Menage, Ru du depart, Jean De Florette (also co-prod.), Under Satan's Sun (also co-prod.), A Strange Place for an Enounter (also co-prod.), Camille Claudel (also co-prod.), Dreux, Too Beautiful for You (also co-prod.), I Want to Go Home, Cyrano de Bergerac (Academy Award nom. 1991; also co-prod), Green Card (Golden Globe Award 1991), Uranus, Thanks for Life, Mon Pere ce Heros (My Father the Hero), 1492: Conquest of Paradise, All the Mornings of the World, Oh Woe is Me, A Pure Formality, Germinal, My Father the Hero, Colonel Chabert, La Machine, Elisa, Les Anges Gardiens, The Horseman on the Roof, Bogus, Le Garcu, She's So Lovely (exec.prod. only), Hamlet, XXL, The Man in the Iron Mask, La Parola Amore Esiste, Bimboland, Vidocq, Vatel, Mirka, Asterix and Obelix vs. Caesar, Un Pont Entre Deux Rives (also prod., dir.), All the Love There Is, Actors, Envy of the Gods, 102 Dalmatians, In the Shadow of Hollywood, The Closet, Unfair Competition, CQ, Vidocq, Streghe verso nord, Asterix & Obelix: Mission Cleopatre, I Am Dina, Blanche, Crime Spree, City of Ghosts, Between Strangers, Aime ton pere, Tais-toi, Le Pacte du silence, Ruby & Quentin, San Antonio, New France, 36, Je préfère qu'on reste amis, Boudu, Last Holiday, Knights of Manhattan, je t'aime Paris, Amici miei '400, Michou d'Auber, La Môme, Asterix at the Olympic Games, L' Invito, Last Holiday, Bastardi, Babylon A.D., L'Abbuffata, Les Enfants de Timpelbach, Disco, Vie en rose, Death Instinct, L' Ennemi public n° 1, Hello Goodbye, Diamond 13, Bellamy, Coco, Dumas, Mammuth, Vivaldi, Une femme d'affaires, La tête en friche, The Job, Potiche, Monet, la lumière blanche.
TELEVISION: *Movies:* Le Cyborg ou Le voyage vertical, Nausicaa, Balzac: A Life of Passion, Bérénice, Ruy Blas, Volpone, L'Inconnu, Vivement Truffaut, Cannes...les 400 coups, The Lady Musketeer, L' Abolition, Le grand restaurant. *Mini-series:* Un monsieur bien rangé, The Count of Monte Cristo, Les Misérables, Napoléon (Emmy nom. 2003), La Profezia dei templari, Les Rois maudits, A Cursed Monarchy. *Series:* Rendez-vous a Badenberg. *Guest:* More than 72 appearances.

DEPP, JOHNNY

Actor. b. Owensboro, KY, June 9, 1963. Raised in Miramar, FL. Played lead guitar with band The Kids, with whom he moved to L.A. in 1983. With no prior acting experience made film debut in A Nightmare on Elm Street. Johnny Depp was voted the Top Money-Making Star of 2006 and 2007 in Quigley Publishing Company's 75th and 76th Annual Top Ten Money-Making Stars Poll. Depp, who appeared in "Pirates of the Caribbean: Dead Man's Chest" in 2006, had appeared twice in the poll previously.
PICTURES: A Nightmare on Elm Street (debut, 1984), Private Resort, Platoon, Cry-Baby, Edward Scissorhands (Golden Globe nom. 1991), Freddy's Dead: The Final Nightmare (cameo), Benny & Joon (Golden Globe nom. 1994), What's Eating Gilbert Grape?, Ed Wood (Golden Globe nom.1995), Don Juan DeMarco, Dead Man, Nick of Time, Donnie Brasco, The Brave (also dir., s.p.),L.A. Without A Map, Just to Be Together, Fear and Loathing in Las Vegas, The Source, The Libertine, The Ninth Gate, The Astronauts Wife, Sleepy Hollow, The Man Who Cried, Chocolat, Blow, In Bad Taste, From Hell, Pirates of the Caribbean: The Curse of the Black Pearl (Academy Award nom.; Golden Globe nom. 2004), Charlie: The Life and Art of Charlie Chaplin, Once Upon a Time in Mexico (also theme comp.), Secret Window, Finding Neverland (Academy Award nom.; Golden Globe nom. 2005), Ils se marièrent et eurent beaucoup d'enfants, The Libertine, Charlie and the Chocolate Factory (Golden Globe nom. 2006), Corpse Bride (voice), The Diving Bell and the Butterfly, Shantaram (also prod.), Pirates of the Caribbean: Dead Man's Chest (Golden Globe nom. 2007), The Pirates of the Caribbean: At Worlds End, Sweeney Todd: The Demon Barber of Fleet Street (also soundtrack performer, Academy Award nom.; Golden Globe Award 2008), Shantaram (also prod.), Public Enemies, The Imaginarium of Doctor Parnassus, Alice in Wonderland, The Rum Diary (also exec. prod.), Rango (voice), The Tourist, Cool Water (co-prod.), Pirates of the Caribbean: On Stranger Tides.
TELEVISION: *Movie:* Slow Burn. *Series:* 21 Jump Street. *Guest:* More than 190 appearances.

DEPREZ, THÉRÈSE

Production Designer. b. 1966.
PICTURES: The Refrigerator, Swoon, The Outfit, Postcards from America, Living in Oblivion, Stonewall, The Doom Generation, I Shot Andy Warhol, Box of Moonlight, Grind, Going All the Way, No Looking Back, Happiness, Arlington Road, Summer of Sam, High Fidelity, Hedwig and the Angry Inch, Marci X, How to Lose a Guy in Ten Days, Door in the Floor, Dark Water, The Return, Mr. Magorium's Wonder Emporium, Phoebe in Wonderland, Brooklyn's Finest, Fighting, Jack Goes Boating, Howl, Black Swan.
TELEVISION: *Movies:* Dottie Gets Spanked, Path to Paradise: The Untold Story of the World Trade Center Bombing, American Splendor.

DEREK, BO

Actress. r.n. Mary Cathleen Collins. b. Torrance, CA., Nov. 20, 1956. Discovered by late actor-turned-filmmaker John Derek, whom she married.
PICTURES: Orca (debut, 1977), 10 (Golden Globe nom. 1980), A Change of Seasons, Fantasies (And Once Upon a Time), Tarzan the Ape Man (also prod.), Bolero (also prod.), Ghosts Can't Do It (also prod.), Hot Chocolate, Sognando la California (California Dreaming), Woman of Desire, Tommy Boy, Off the Menu: The Last Days of Chasens, Horror 101, Frozen With Fear, Sunstorm, Life in the Balance, The Master of Disguise, Malibu's Most Wanted, Highland Park.
TELEVISION: *Movies:* Shattered Image, Murder at the Cannes Film Festival, The Kentucky Derby, Crusader. *Series:* Hollywood Squares, Wind on Water, Fashion House. *Guest:* More than 87 appearances.

DERN, BRUCE

Actor. b. Chicago, IL, June 4, 1936. e. U. of Pennsylvania. Daughter is actress Laura Dern. Studied acting with Gordon Phillips, member, Actor's Studio, 1959 after N.Y. debut in Shadow of a Gunman. Broadway: Sweet Bird of Youth, Orpheus Descending, Strangers. Film Awards: Natl. Society of Film Critics

(Drive He Said, 1971), People's Choice (Coming Home, 1978), Genie (Middle Age Crazy, 1980), Silver Bear (That Championship Season, 1982).
PICTURES: Wild River (debut, 1960), Marnie, Hush...Hush Sweet Charlotte, The Wild Angels, The St. Valentine's Day Massacre, Waterhole No. 3, The Trip, The War Wagon, Psych-Out, Rebel Rousers, Hang 'Em High, Will Penny, Number One, Castle Keep, Support Your Local Sheriff, They Shoot Horses Don't They?, Cycle Savages, Bloody Mama, The Incredible Two-Headed Transplant, Drive He Said, Silent Running, Thumb Tripping, The Cowboys, The King of Marvin Gardens, The Laughing Policeman, The Great Gatsby (Golden Globe nom. 1975), Smile, Posse, Family Plot, Won Ton Ton the Dog Who Saved Hollywood, The Twist (Folies Bourgeoises), Black Sunday, Coming Home (Academy Award nom.; Golden Globe nom. 1979), The Driver, Middle Age Crazy, Tattoo, Harry Tracy: Desperado, That Championship Season, On the Edge, The Big Town, World Gone Wild, 1969, The 'Burbs, After Dark My Sweet, Diggstown, Wild Bill, Down Periscope, Mulholland Falls, Last Man Standing, Small Soldiers (voice), If...Dog...Rabbit, The Haunting, All the Pretty Horses, It Conquered Hollywood! The Story of American International Pictures, The Glass House, Milwaukee Minnesota, Madison, Masked & Anonymous (editor only), Monster, Down in the Valley, The Hard Easy, Believe in Me, The Astronaut Farmer, The Cake Eaters, The Golden Boys, American Cowslip, Swamp Devil, Trim, Choose.
TELEVISION: *Movies:* Sam Hill: Who Killed the Mysterious Mr. Foster?, Toughlove, Roses Are for the Rich, Uncle Tom's Cabin, Trenchcoat in Paradise, The Court-Martial of Jackie Robinson, Into the Badlands, Carolina Skeletons, It's Nothing Personal, Deadman's Revenge, Amelia Earhart: The Final Flight, A Mother's Prayer, Comfort Texas, Perfect Prey, Hard Ground. *Mini-series:* Space. *Series:* Stoney Burke, Big Love. *Guest:* More than 86 appearances.

DERN, LAURA

Actress. b. Los Angeles, CA, Feb. 10, 1967. Daughter of actors Diane Ladd and Bruce Dern. At age 5 appeared with mother on daytime serial The Secret Storm. Was an extra in several of her father's films and her mother's Alice Doesn't Live Here Anymore. Studied acting at RADA appearing on stage in Hamlet, A Midsummer Night's Dream.
THEATRE: NY: The Palace of Amateurs. LA: Brooklyn Laundry.
PICTURES: White Lightning (debut, 1973), Alice Doesn't Live Here Anymore, Foxes, Ladies and Gentlemen: The Fabulous Stains, Teachers, Mask, Smooth Talk, Blue Velvet, Haunted Summer, Fat Man and Little Boy, Wild at Heart, Rambling Rose (Academy Award nom.; Golden Globe nom. 1992), Jurassic Park, A Perfect World, Bastard Out of Carolina, Citizen Ruth, October Sky, Dr. T and the Women, Novocaine, Daddy and Them, Jurassic Park III, Focus, I Am Sam, Searching for Debra Winger, Happy Endings, We Don't Live Here Anymore, The Prize Winner of Defiance Ohio, The Girl Who Loved Tom Gordon, Lonely Hearts, Inland Empire, Tenderness, Year of the Dog, Meet the Fockers Sequel.
TELEVISION: *Movies:* Happy Endings, Three Wishes of Billy Greer, Afterburn (Golden Globe Award; Emmy nom. 1992), Down Came a Blackbird, Ruby Ridge: An American Tragedy, The Baby Dance (Golden Globe nom. 1999), Within These Walls, Damaged Care, Mysteries of Love (doc.), Recount (Emmy nom. 2008, Golden Globe Award 2009). *Series:* Fallen Angels (Emmy nom. 1994 as guest), Ellen (Emmy nom. 1997 as guest), Enlightened. *Specials:* The Gift (dir., co-story only), AFI's 100 Years 100 Stars. *Guest:* More than 82 appearances.

DESCHANEL, CALEB

Cinematographer, Director. b. Philadelphia, PA, Sept. 21, 1944. m. actress Mary Jo Deschanel. e. Johns Hopkins U., U. of Southern California Film Sch. Studied at AFI, interned under Gordon Willis then made commercials, short subjects, docs. Co-founder of Dark Light Pictures. 2010 received ASC Lifetime Achievement Award.
PICTURES: *Cinematographer:* More American Graffiti, Being There, The Black Stallion, Apocalypse Now (2nd unit photog.), The Right Stuff (Academy Award nom. 2005), Let's Spend the Night Together (co-cinematographer), The Natural (Academy Award nom. 1985), The Slugger's Wife, It Could Happen to You, Flying Wild, Fly Away Home (Academy Award nom.; ASC nom. 1997), Hope Floats, Message in a Bottle, Anna and the King, The Patriot (Academy Award nom.; ASC Award 2001), The Hunted, Timeline, The Passion of the Christ (Academy Award nom.; ASC nom. 2005), National Treasure, Ask the Dust, Killshot, The Spiderwick Chronicles, My Sister's Keeper, Dream House. *Director:* The Escape Artist, Crusoe, The Robbery of Ellie May.

DEUTCH, HOWARD

Director. b. New York, NY, September 14, 1950. e. Ohio State U. m. actress Lea Thompson. Son of music publisher Murray Deutch. Spent 10 yrs. working in various film media, including music videos and film trailer advertising, before feature debut with Pretty in Pink, 1986.
PICTURES: Pretty in Pink, Some Kind of Wonderful, The Great Outdoors, Article 99, Getting Even With Dad, Grumpier Old Men, The Odd Couple II, The Replacements, Family Affair, Electric, The Whole Ten Yards, Wounded (co-prod.), The Beginning of Wisdom, My Best Friend's Girl.
TELEVISION: *Movie:* Gleason (DGA nom. 2003). *Series*: Tales from the Crypt (2 episodes; ACE Award for Dead Right), Melrose Place, Caroline in the City, Watching Ellie.

DEUTCHMAN, IRA J.

Executive, Producer. b. Cherry Point, NC, March 24, 1953. e. Northwestern U., B.S., majoring in film. Began career with Cinema 5, Ltd. serving, 1975-79, as non-theatrical sales mgr.; dir. theatrical adv./pub./dir. acquisitions. Joined United Artists Classics, 1981, as dir. of adv./pub. 1982, left to become one of the founding partners in Cinecom Int'l. Films, where headed mktg./dist. div. from inception. In Jan. 1989 formed the Deutchman Company, Inc., a production company and marketing consultancy firm. Founded and served as pres. of Fine Line Features, a division of New Line Cinema, and sr. v.p. of parent corp, 1991-95. Became pres. of Redeemable Features, a New York-based prod. company. Currently is pres./CEO of Emerging Pictures. Adjunct prof. Columbia U. film dept. On advisory board Sundance Film Festival.
PICTURES: *Exec. Prod.:* Swimming to Cambodia, Matewan (assoc. prod.), Miles From Home (co-exec. prod.), Scenes from the Class Struggle in Beverly Hills, Straight Out of Brooklyn, Waterland, The Ballad of Little Jo, Mrs. Parker and the Vicious Circle, Lulu on the Bridge, Twelve, The Center of the World, Laura & Sal, The Lucky Ones, The Game of Their Lives (co-. prod.), Red Doors, The Brothel, For Real, Honeydripper (assoc. prod.), For Real. *Producer:* Kiss Me Guido, 54, The Hairy Bird a.k.a. Strike!, Way Past Cool, Ball in the House, Interstate 60, Beauty Remains, Superheroes.

DEUTCHMAN, LAWRENCE SCOT

Executive Writer, Producer. b. Bronx, NY, Dec. 10, 1960. e. Rutgers U. Wrote, prod. & dir. Mythbusters campaign. 1986-92, various positions: Entertainment Industries Council, Inc.; wrote, prod., co-dir. That's a Wrap campaign. 1986-88, board member, Public Interest Radio & Television Educational Society. 1987-88, wrote, exec. prod., post-prod. sprv., Buckle Up educational & music video (CINE Golden Eagle). 1989: EIC: An Industry in Action (writer, prod., dir.); Campaigns: Natl. Red Ribbon, Office for Substance Abuse Prevention (writer, dir., exec. prod.), Stop the Madness (co-writer, prod.). 1990, developed: Vince & Larry: The Amazing Crash Test Dummies (series, NBC), Drug Proofing Your Kids (TV special); Campaigns: Alcoholism Runs in Families, Texas Prevention Partnership (dir., exec. prod.), They Do as You Do (writer, exec. prod.). 1991: The Inhalant Problem in Texas docum. (co-exec. prod.), Inhalants: The Silent Epidemic award-winning drama (writer, co-exec. prod.), KBVO Fox Kids Club segments (writer, prod., set designer), The Incredible Crash Dummies toy property (co-creator), Ollie Odorfree property (creator). 1992-present: Pres., Dynamic Comm. Intl. Inc.; v.p. prod. & mktg., EIC. 1993: Hollywood Gets M.A.D.D. TV special (co-prod., TBS, TNT, synd.). 1994: Dinorock Time TV series (exec. prod., writer.); 1994-present, s.r., vp. prod. & mktg, EIC (Entertainment Industries Council, Inc.). Prod./co-writer Annual Prism Awards.

DEUTSCH, STEPHEN

Producer. b. Los Angeles, CA, June 30, 1946. e. UCLA, B.A.; Loyola Law Sch., 1974. Son of late S. Sylvan Simon. Stepson of Armand Deutsch. Private law practice before joining Rastar 1976 as asst. to Ray Stark; 1977, sr. v.p., Rastar; prod. head for SLM Inc. Film Co. entered independent prod. 1978.
PICTURES: Somewhere in Time, All the Right Moves, Russkies (co-exec. prod.), She's Out of Control, Bill & Ted's Excellent Adventure (exec. prod.), Lucky Stiff, Bill and Ted's Bogus Journey (co-exec. prod.), Body of Evidence (exec. prod.), What Dreams May Come, Quantum Project, Indigo (as Stephen Simon), Conversations with God.
TELEVISION: *Movies:* The Linda McCartney Story, Homeless to Harvard: The Liz Murray Story (Emmy nom. 2003; exec. prod. as Stephen Simon).

DEVANE, WILLIAM

Actor. b. Albany, NY, Sept. 5, 1939. Appeared in some 15 productions with N.Y. Shakespeare Festival, also B'way & off-B'way shows before heading to California for films and TV.
PICTURES: The Pursuit of Happiness (debut, 1970), The 300 Hundred Year Weekend, Lady Liberty, McCabe and Mrs. Miller, Glory Boy (My Old Man's Place), Irish Whiskey Rebellion, Report to the Commissioner, Family Plot, Marathon Man, Bad News Bears in Breaking Training, Rolling Thunder, The Dark, Yanks, Honky Tonk Freeway, Testament, Hadley's Rebellion, Vital Signs, Exception to the Rule, Payback, Poor White Trash, Space Cowboys, Hollow Man, Race to Space, Threat of Exposure, The Wind Effect (short), The Fall, Chasing the Green, The Least Among You, The River Why, The Kane Files: Life of Trial, Flag of My Father, Hell to Pay.
TELEVISION: *Movies:* Crime Club, The Bait, Fear on Trial (Emmy nom. 1976), Red Alert, Black Beauty, Red Flag: The Ultimate Game, The Other Victim, Jane Doe, With Intent to Kill, Timestalker, Murder C.O.D., Nightmare in Columbia County, Obsessed, The President's Child. Prophet of Evil: The Ervil LeBaron Story, Rubdown, For the Love of Nancy, Falling From the Sky!: Flight 174, Robin Cook's Virus, Alistair MacLean's Night Watch, Virus, Forgotten Sins, The Absolute Truth, Doomsday Rock, Miracle on the Mountain: The Kincaid Family Story, The

Man Who Used to Be Me, The Badge, A Christmas Visitor, Monte Walsh, Deceit, Jesse Stone: Death in Paradise, Jesse Stone: Sea Change, The Dealership, Jesse Stone: Thin Ice, Jesse Stone: No Remorse. *Mini-series:* A Woman Named Jackie, Knot's Landing: Back to the Cul-de-Sac. *Series:* From Here to Eternity, Knots Landing (Golden Globe nom. 1987), Phenom, The Monroes, Turks, Titans, The Michael Richards Show, Crumbs, 24, What About Brian. *Special:* The Missiles of October (Emmy nom. 1975). *Guest:* More than 100 appearances.

DE VITO, DANNY

Actor, Director, Producer. b. Asbury Park, NJ, Nov. 17, 1944. m. actress Rhea Perlman. e. Oratory Prep Sch. Studied at American Acad. of Dramatic Arts. Wilfred Acad. of Hair and Beauty Culture. At 18 worked as hair dresser for 1 yr. at his sister's shop. NY stage in The Man With a Flower in His Mouth (debut, 1969), Down the Morning Line, The Line of Least Existence, The Shrinking Bride, Call Me Charlie, Comedy of Errors, Merry Wives of Windsor (NYSF). Three By Pirandello. Performance in One Flew Over the Cuckoo's Nest led to casting in the film version. *Prod. short films:* The Sound Sleeper (1973), Minestrone (1975).
PICTURES: Lady Liberty (debut, 1971), Hurry Up or I'll Be 30, Scalawag, One Flew Over the Cuckoo's Nest, Deadly Hero, The Van, The World's Greatest Lover, Goin' South, Going Ape, Terms of Endearment, Romancing the Stone, Johnny Dangerously, The Jewel of the Nile, Head Office, Wiseguys, Ruthless People (Golden Globe nom. 1987), My Little Pony (voice), Tin Men, Throw Momma from the Train (Golden Globe nom. 1988; also dir.), Twins, The War of the Roses (also dir.), Other People's Money, Batman Returns, Hoffa (also dir., co-prod.), Jack the Bear, Last Action Hero (voice), Look Who's Talking Now (voice), Reality Bites (co-prod. only), Renaissance Man, Pulp Fiction (co-exec. prod. only), Junior, Get Shorty (also co-prod.), Sunset Park (prod.), Matilda (also dir., co-prod.), Mars Attacks, Hercules (voice), L.A. Confidential, Space Jam. (voice), The Rainmaker, Living Out Loud, Stretch Armstrong, Foolproof, Out of Sight (prod. only), Gattaca (prod. only), Man on the Moon (also prod.), The Virgin Suicides, Drowning Mona (also prod.), Erin Brockovich (Academy Award nom. 2001; prod.) Screwed, What's The Worst That Could Happen?, The Heist, Death to Smoochy, Austin Powers in Goldmember, Anything Else, Duplex (dir. only), The Marx Brothers (prod. only), Captured (prod. only), Big Fish (acting), Catching Kringle (voice), Along Came Polly (prod.), Be Cool (also prod.), Family of the Year, Marilyn Hotchkiss' Ballroom Dancing and Charm School, The Children of the Dust Bowl (prod.), I Married a Witch (dir.), A Walk Among the Tombstones (prod.), Relative Strangers (also prod.), The OH in Ohio, Jump Shot, Reno 911!: Miami (also exec. prod., dir.), One Part Sugar, Nobel Son, The Good Night, Deck the Halls, Freedom Writers (prod.), House Broken, Solitary Man, When in Rome.
TELEVISION: *Movies:* Valentine, The Ratings Game (also dir.), Happily Ever After (voice), The Pentagon Wars (exec. prod.), Other People's Business (exec. prod.), Little Spirit: Christmas in New York (narr.). *Series:* Taxi (1 Emmy Award and 3 nom.; 1 Golden Globe Award and 3 noms, 1981; also dir. episodes), Mary (dir. only), The Sport Jerks (writer, co-creator, exec. prod.), Kate Brasher (exec. prod.), The Funkhousers (exec. prod.), Reno 911! (exec. prod.), Friends (Emmy nom. 2004 as guest), The American Embassy (exec. prod.), Karen Sisco (exec. prod.), It's Always Sunny in Philadelphia. *Specials:* All the Kids Do It (Afterschool Special), A Very Special Christmas Party, Two Daddies? (voice), What a Lovely Way to Spend an Evening (dir.), The Selling of Vince DeAngelo (dir.), America: A Tribute to Heroes. *Guest:* More than 150 appearances.

DEVLIN, DEAN

Actor, Writer, Producer. b. Aug. 27, 1962. Began career as an actor, appearing in numerous film and television projects, as well as B'way production of There Must Be a Pony. Met Roland Emmerich while acting in Moon 44. Joined Emmerich as a partner at Centropolis Films. Prod. TV series, The Visitor, 1997.
PICTURES: *Actor:* My Bodyguard, The Wild Life, Real Genius, City Limits, Moon 44, Martians Go Home, Total Exposure, Predators From Beyond Nature. *Writer/Producer:* Stargate, Independence Day, Godzilla, The Mark, The Patriot, Eight Legged Freaks, Cellular, One Nation, Isobar, Flyboys (prod. only), Ghosting (prod., dir.), Northern Lights (prod. only). *Writer:* Universal Soldier, Gargoyles, Universal Soldier: Regeneration. *Documentary:* Who Killed the Electric Car? (exec. prod.).
TELEVISION: *Movies:* North Beach and Rawhide (actor), The Librarian: Quest for the Spear (exec. prod.), The Librarian 2: Return to King Solomon's Mines (exec. prod.), Blank Slate (exec. prod.), The Librarian: Curse of the Judas Chalice. *Mini-series:* The Triangle (exec. prod., writer). *Series creator:* The Visitor (exec. prod.). *Series actor:* This Is the Life, Hard Copy, Generations. *Exec. Prod. Series:* Godzilla: The Series, Talk to Me, Leverage (also writer).

DE YOUNG, CLIFF

Actor. b. Inglewood, CA, Feb. 12, 1947. e. California State Coll., Illinois State U. On stage in Hair, Sticks and Bones, Two By South, The Three Sisters, The Orphan.
PICTURES: Harry and Tonto, Blue Collar, Shock Treatment, Independence Day, The Hunger, Reckless, Protocol, Secret Admirer, F/X, Flight of the Navigator, Fear, Pulse, Rude Awakening, Glory, Flashback, Crackdown, Dr. Giggles, Carnosaur II, Final Frontier, The Craft, The Substitute, Suicide Kings, Last Flight Out, Stone & Ed, The Hunt, Solar Flare, Road to Nowhere.
TELEVISION: *Movies:* Sunshine, The 3000 Mile Chase, The Lindbergh Kidnapping Case, Scared Straight: Another Story, Invasion of Privacy, The Seeding of Sarah Burns, The Night That Panicked America, This Girl for Hire, The Awakening of Candra, Deadly Intentions, Sunshine Christmas, Fun and Games, Where Pigeons Go to Die, Fourth Story, Criminal Behavior, Love Can Be Murder, The Tommyknockers, Precious Victims, Heaven & Hell: North and South Book III, JAG, Element of Truth, The Westing Game, Nails, George Wallace, The Westing Game, The Last Man on Planet Earth, Getting Away with Murder: The JonBenet Ramsey Mystery, Deliberate Intent, The Runaway, Path to War, The Secret Life of Zoey, Love's Enduring Promise. *Mini-series:* Centennial, Master of the Game, Captains and the Kings, King, Robert Kennedy and His Times, Andersonville, Seduced By Madness, The Last Don. *Series:* Sunshine, Robocop, Relativity, The Young and the Restless. *Special:* Sticks and Bones. *Guest:* More than 98 appearances.

DIAMANT, LINCOLN

Executive, Biographer, Historian. b. New York, NY, Jan. 25, 1923. e. Columbia Coll., A.B. cum laude 1943. Cofounder, Columbia U. radio station. WKCR-FM; served in Wash. as prod., Blue Network (NBC), then in NY as CBS newswriter; 1949 joined World Pub. Co. as adv. and promo. dir.; 1952-69 worked in creative/TV dept. McCann-Erickson, Grey, then Ogilvy & Mather ad agencies (winning 6 Clio Awards). Prod. Lend Us Your Ears (Met. Museum Art broadcast series); founder, pres., Spots Alive, Inc., broadcast adv. consultants, 1969; Author, The Broadcast Communications Dictionary, Anatomy of a Television Commercial, Television's Classic Commercials, biography of Bernard Romans, Chaining the Hudson (Sons of Revolution Book Award), Stamping Our History, Yankee Doodle Days. Contrib., to Effective Advertising, to Messages and Meaning; New Routes to English; columnist Back Stage/Shoot. Member, Broadcast Pioneers, Acad. TV Arts & Sciences; v.p. Broadcast Advertising Producer's Society of America. Adjunct faculty member, Pace U., Hofstra U. Fellow, Royal Society of Arts.

DIAZ, CAMERON

Actress. b. Aug. 30, 1972. Began career as model for Elite. Feature debut was in The Mask. Received ShoWest 1996 Female Star of Tomorrow Award.
PICTURES: The Mask, The Last Supper, Keys to Tulsa, Feeling Minnesota, Head Above Water, She's the One, My Best Friend's Wedding, A Life Less Ordinary, There's Something About Mary (Golden Globe nom. 1999), Very Bad Things, Invisible Circus, Fear and Loathing in Las Vegas, Being John Malkovich (Golden Globe nom.2000), Any Given Sunday, Things You Can Tell Just By Looking At Her, Invisible Circus, Shrek, Vanilla Sky (Golden Globe nom. 2002), The Gangs of New York (Golden Globe nom. 2003), The Sweetest Thing, Charlie's Angels, Charlie's Angels: Full Throttle, Shrek 2 (voice), In Her Shoes, W.A.S.P.S., The Holiday, Shrek the Third (voice), The Box, What Happens in Vegas, Shrek Forever After (voice), My Sister's Keeper, The Box, Knight and Day, The Green Hornet, Bad Teacher.
TELEVISION: *Movie:* Shrek the Halls (voice). *Documentary:* Trippin (host, exec. prod., series). *Guest:* More than 155 appearances.

DI BONAVENTURA, LORENZO

Executive, Producer. b. New York, NY. e. B.A., intellectual history, Harvard College, M.B.A., Wharton School of Business, U. of Pennsylvania. After running a river-rafting co. following college, held numerous creative, production, and distribution positions at Columbia Pictures, including mgr. Pay Cable & Home Ent. Joined Warner Bros. Pictures as production exec., 1989; promoted to v.p., production, then named sr. v.p., production, 1993; exec. v.p., production, 1995; co-head, theatrical production, 1996. Resigned as pres., worldwide theatrical production, Warner Bros. Pictures,1998. Currently is an independent prod. for Warner Bros., also prod. for Revolution Studios.
PICTURES: Constantine, Four Brothers, Doom, Derailed, Shooter, Stardust, 1408, Transformers (also co-exec. prod.), Stardust, G.I. Joe: The Rise of Cobra, Imagine That, Transformers: Revenge of the Fallen, The Electric Slide, Salt, Red, Delivering Gen.

DICANIO, JERRY

Executive. e. Villanova University, B.A. degree, accounting. St. John's Univ., M.B.A. DiCanio joined Viacom in 1982 as a staff accountant and held a number of New York finance positions and also served as mgr. of financial planning and dir. of finance, West Coast. He eventually became v.p., finance with Viacom Productions. In 1990, named senior v.p. finance for Viacom Productions with responsibilities for all financial aspects of development and production of network and cable projects. DiCanio joined NBC Studios in May 1994. Roles there included v.p., production operations & finance and senior v.p., production operations and finance. Duties included oversight of all NBC Studios and NBC Enterprises' production and financial operations, including financial reporting and analysis, production accounting and product marketing analysis. Since June 2004, shortly after NBC and Universal combined to form one company, DiCanio has served as executive v.p. of production operations, Universal Media Studios and NBC Universal Television Distribution. He is responsible for overseeing all production for NBC Universal's TV entertainment divisions. He reports to Marc Graboff, Co-Chairman, NBC Entertainment and Universal Media Studios.

DI CAPRIO, LEONARDO

Actor. b. Hollywood, CA, Nov. 11, 1974. Started acting at age 15 in commercials and educational films. Appeared in short film The Foot Shooting Party.
PICTURES: Critters III (debut, 1991), Poison Ivy, This Boy's Life, What's Eating Gilbert Grape? (Natl. Board of Review, Chicago Film Critics & LA Film Critics Awards, Academy Award nom., Golden Globe nom. 1994), The Quick and the Dead, The Basketball Diaries, Total Eclipse, Marvin's Room, Romeo + Juliet, Titanic (Golden Globe nom. 1998), Don's Plum, Celebrity, The Man in the Iron Mask, The Beach, Don's Plum, The Gangs of New York, Catch Me if You Can (Golden Globe nom. 2003), The Assassination of Richard Nixon (exec. prod.), The Aviator (Academy Award nom.; Golden Globe Award 2005, also prod.), The Good Shepherd, Gardener of Eden (prod.), The Departed (Golden Globe nom. 2007), Blood Diamond (Academy Award nom.; Golden Globe nom. 2007), Gardener of Eden (prod.), Blink (also prod.), 11th Hour (doc., narr., prod., writer), Body of Lies, Revolutionary Road (Golden Globe nom. 2009), Orphan (prod. only), Shutter Island, Beat the Reaper (also prod.), Inception, The Beautiful and the Damned, The Low Dweller (also prod.), Prisoners.
TELEVISION: *Series:* Growing Pains, Santa Barbara, Parenthood, Greensburg (writer, exec. prod.). *Documentary:* IMAX: Hubble 3D (narr.). *Guest:* More than 123 appearances.

DICK, ANDY

Actor. b. Charleston, SC, Dec. 21, 1965.
PICTURES: Elvis Stories, Double Dragon, Reality Bites, In the Army Now, Hotel Oasis, The Cable Guy, Best Men, Ted, Bongwater, Picking up the Pieces, Inspector Gadget, Being John Malkovich, Advice From a Caterpillar, The Independent, Road Trip, Loser, Dude Where's My Car?, Scotland PA, Dr. Dolittle 2 (voice), Zoolander, Larceny, Old School, You'll Never Wiez in This Town Again, Naked Movie, The Hebrew Hammer, Scorched, Standing Still, Larceny, Love Hollywood Style, Happily N'Ever After (voice), Employee of the Month, The 1 Second Film (exec. prod.), Blonde Ambition, The Comebacks, Hoodwinked Too!: Hood vs. Evil (voice), Kissing Strangers, Rock Slyde.
TELEVISION: *Movies:* Earth Angel, The Sissy Duckling, Special Delivery, Castaway Dick, Last Laugh '04, Last Laugh '05. *Mini-series:* Pilot Season. *Series:* The Ben Stiller Show, Get Smart, NewsRadio, The Andy Dick Show, Sammy (voice), Go Fish, The Reality Show (also exec. prod.), Less Than Perfect. *Guest:* More than 152 appearances.

DICKERSON, ERNEST

(A.S.C.): Cinematographer, Director. b. Newark, NJ, 1952. e. Howard U., architecture, NYU, grad. film school. First job, filming surgical procedures for Howard U. medical school. At NYU film school shot classmate Spike Lee's student films Sarah, and Joe's Bed Stuy Barbershop: We Cut Heads. Also shot Nike commercial and several music videos including Bruce Springsteen's Born in the U.S.A., Patti LaBelle's Stir It Up and Miles Davis' Tutu; and Branford Marsalis' Royal Garden Blues directed by Spike Lee. Admitted into Amer. Soc. of Cinematographers in 1989.
PICTURES: *Cinematographer:* The Brother From Another Planet, She's Gotta Have It (also cameo), Krush Groove, School Daze, Raw, Do the Right Thing, Def By Temptation, The Laser Man, Mo' Better Blues, Jungle Fever, Sex Drugs Rock & Roll, Cousin Bobby (co-photog.), Malcolm X, Our America. *Director:* Juice (also co-s.p., story), Surviving the Game, Tales From the Crypt Presents Demon Knight, Bulletproof, Blind Faith, Ambushed, Bones, Never Die Alone, Miracle at St. Anna (2nd unit dir., dir. of photog., camera op.), Minion.
TELEVISION: *Movies: Dir:* Do it Acapella, FutureSport, Strange Justice, Monday Night Mayhem, Night Visions, Big Shot: Confessions of a Campus Bookie, Good Fences, Our America (Emmy Award 2003), For One Night. *Series:* Law & Order (cinematographer), The L Word, Weeds, The Wire, Treme.

DICKINSON, ANGIE

Actress. r.n. Angeline Brown. b. Kulm, ND, Sept. 30, 1931. e. Immaculate Heart Coll., Glendale Coll., secretarial course. Beauty contest winner.
PICTURES: Lucky Me (debut in bit part, 1954), Man With the Gun, The Return of Jack Slade, Tennessee's Partner, The Black Whip, Hidden Guns, Tension at Table Rock, Gun the Man Down, Calypso Joe, China Gate, Shoot Out at Medicine Bend, Cry Terror, I Married a Woman, Rio Bravo, The Bramble Bush, Ocean's 11, A Fever in the Blood, The Sins of Rachel Cade, Jessica, Rome Adventure, Captain Newman M.D., The Killers, The Art of Love, Cast a Giant Shadow, The Chase, The Poppy is Also a Flower, The Last Challenge, Point Blank, Sam Whiskey, Some Kind of a Nut, Young Billy Young, Pretty Maids All in a Row, The Resurrection of Zachary Wheeler, The Outside Man, Big Bad Mama, Klondike Fever, Dressed to Kill, Charlie Chan and the Curse of the Dragon Queen, Death Hunt, Big Bad Mama II, Even Cowgirls Get the Blues, The Maddening, Sabrina, The Sun The Moon and The Stars, The Last Producer, Duets, Pay it Forward, Ocean's Eleven, Scene Smoking: Cigarettes Cinema & the Myth of Cool, Big Bad Love, Elvis Has Left the Building.
TELEVISION: *Movies:* The Love War, Thief, See the Man Run, The Norliss Tapes, Pray for the Wildcats, A Sensitive Passionate Man, Overboard, The Suicide's Wife, Dial M for Murder, One Shoe Makes It Murder, Jealousy, A Touch of Scandal, Stillwatch, Police Story: The Freeway Killings, Once Upon a Texas Train, Prime Target, Treacherous Crossing, Danielle Steel's Remembrance, Deep Family Secrets, The Don's Analyst, Sealed with a Kiss, Mending Fences. *Mini-series:* Pearl, Hollywood Wives, Wild Palms. *Series:* Police Woman (3 Emmy nom., Golden Globe Award 1975; 3 other noms.), Cassie & Co. *Special:* Ira Geshwin at 100. *Guest:* More than 197 appearances.

DICKINSON, WOOD

Executive, Exhibitor. r.n. Glen Wood Dickinson III. b. Fairway, KS, Sept. 14, 1952. e. Texas Christian U (BFA Communications, MA Film). Past Chairman and CEO of Dickinson Theatres, Inc. , until 1999. Founded company called Think!, which consults in creative mgt. and is also CEO of Rolling Thunder Systems, an Int'l. software development company. In addition to Think! and Rolling Thunder Systems, Dickinson established Renegade Pictures in 2002. The company produces independent feature films using digital technologies.
PICTURES: Raising Jeffrey Dahmer (exec. prod., prod., writer, 2006).

DIESEL, VIN

Actor. b. New York, NY, July 18, 1967. e. Hunter College. Began in theatre then wrote a short film based on his experiences as an actor, called Multi-Facial (1994); shot in under three days at a cost of $3,000. Film accepted for the 1995 Cannes Film Festival.
PICTURES: Multi-Facial (also dir.), Strays (also dir.), Saving Private Ryan, The Iron Giant, Boiler Room, Pitch Black, El Diablo, The Fast and the Furious, Knockaround Guys, XxX, A Man Apart (also exec. prod.), The Chronicles of Riddick, The Pacifier, Hannibal (also prod.), Find Me Guilty (also prod.), Rockfish (voice also prod.), Hitman (exec. prod.), Babylon A.D., Fast & Furious, Fast Five (also prod.).
TELEVISION: *Movie:* Into Pitch Black. *Guest:* More than 55 appearances.

DILLER, BARRY

Executive. b. San Francisco, CA, Feb. 2, 1942. Joined ABC in April, 1966, as asst. to v.p. in chg. programming. In 1968, made exec. asst. to v.p. in chg. programming and dir. of feature films. In 1969, named v.p., feature films and program dev., east coast. In 1971, made v.p., Feature Films and Circle Entertainment, a unit of ABC Entertainment, responsible for selecting, producing and scheduling The Tuesday Movie of the Week, The Wednesday Movie of the Week, and Circle Film original features for airing on ABC-TV, as well as for acquisition and scheduling of theatrical features for telecasting on ABC Sunday Night Movie and ABC Monday Night Movie. In 1973, named v.p. in charge of prime time TV for ABC Entertainment. In 1974 joined Paramount Pictures as bd. chmn. and CEO. 1983, named pres. of Gulf & Western Entertainment and Communications Group, while retaining Paramount titles. Resigned from Paramount in 1984 to join 20th Century-Fox as bd. chmn. and CEO. Named chmn. & CEO of Fox, Inc. (comprising 20th Fox Film Corp., Fox TV Stations & Fox Broadcasting Co.), Oct. 1985. Named to bd., News Corp. Ltd., June, 1987. Received Honorary Life Member Award from DGA, 1990. Resigned from Fox in Feb., 1992. Named CEO of QVC Network Inc. Resigned QVC in 1995. CEO and bd. chair, Silver King Communications, Inc, Aug. 1995. Silver King merged with Savoy Pictures and Home Shopping Network in 1996, calling the new company HSN. In 1997 HSN bought Microsoft co-founder Paul Allen's 47% interest in Ticketmaster. Diller followed with the $4 billion purchase of USA Networks in 1998. USA Networks bought the remainder of Ticketmaster in 1998, then purchased online entertainment guide publisher CitySearch, merging it with Ticketmaster Online into a new company called Ticketmaster Online-CitySearch. USA Networks then spun off the new company to the public, retaining a 60% interest (later reduced to about 50%). In 1999 Diller failed in an attempt to merge Ticketmaster Online-CitySearch and Internet portal Lycos (now part of Terra Lycos). Diller then bought parts of PolyGram Filmed Entertainment and independent film companies Gramercy and October from Seagram, renaming them USA Films. USA Networks also bought the Hotel Reservations Network in 1999. In 2000 Diller reorganized the co. into three units: USA Electronic Retailing, USA Entertainment, and USA Information and Services. It also lost World Wrestling Federation programming to Viacom. Later in 2000, when Vivendi bought Seagram, it gained Seagram's 43% stake in USA Networks. USA Networks also agreed to sell its TV stations to Univision for $1.1 billion. Later, Diller announced that his company would buy a 65% stake in Expedia (completed in 2002) and launch a travel venture called USA Travel Group. The group eventually included Hotels.com, a cable travel channel, and USA's minority stake in cruise and vacation package provider National Leisure Group. At the end of

2001, Diller sold USA Networks' entertainment assets to Vivendi Universal for $10.3 billion. The deal was completed in May 2002 and the company changed its name to USA Interactive with Diller retaining his voting control of the firm. Diller is currently chmn, Expedia, Inc., chmn & CEO, InterActiveCorp (IAC, formerly USA Interactive Inc.). On board of directors: The Washington Post Company and The Coca-Cola Company. He also serves on the Board of the Museum of Television and Radio, Conservation International and The Educational Broadcasting Company. In addition, Diller is a member of the Board of Councilors for the University of Southern California's School of Cinema-Television, the New York University Board of Trustees, the Tisch School of the Arts Dean's Council and the Executive Board for the Medical Sciences of University of California, Los Angeles.

DILLER, PHYLLIS

Comedienne, Actress. b. Lima, OH, July 17, 1917. r.n. Phyllis Ada Driver. e. Sherwood Music Sch., 1935-37; Bluffton Coll., OH, 1938-39. Started as publicist at San Francisco radio station before becoming nightclub comic at the age of 37. Recordings: Phyllis Diller Laughs, Are You Ready for Phyllis Diller?, Great Moments of Comedy, Born to Sing. Performed with many U.S. symphonies, 1971-90.
AUTHOR: Phyllis Diller's Housekeeping Hints, Phyllis Diller's Marriage Manual, Phyllis Diller's The Complete Mother, The Joys of Aging and How to Avoid Them.
THEATRE: Hello Dolly! (B'way), Everybody Loves Opal, Happy Birthday, The Dark at the Top of the Stairs, Subject to Change, The Wizard of Oz, Nunsense, Cinderella.
PICTURES: Splendor in the Grass (debut, 1961), Boy Did I Get a Wrong Number!, The Fat Spy, Mad Monster Party (voice), Eight on the Lam, Did You Hear the One About the Traveling Saleslady?, The Private Navy of Sgt. O'Farrell, The Adding Machine, The Sunshine Boys (cameo), A Pleasure Doing Business, Pink Motel, Pucker Up and Bark Like a Dog, Dr. Hackenstein, Friend to Friend, The Nutcracker Prince (voice), The Boneyard, Wisecracks, Happily Ever After (voice), The Perfect Man, The Silence of the Hams, A Bug's Life (voice), The Debtors, Let Me In I Hear Laughter, Everything's Jake, The Last Place on Earth, Hip! Edgy! Quirky!, Forget About It, Unbeatable Harold, The Last Guy on Earth, Forget About It, Blaze of Glory.
TELEVISION: *Movie:* Casper's Scare School (voice). *Series:* Showstreet, The Pruitts of Southampton, The Bold and the Beautiful, Captain Planet and the Planeteers (voice), Blossom, Phyllis Diller Show (Golden Globe nom. 1967), Titus, Quintuplets. *Specials:* The Phyllis Diller Special, An Evening With Phyllis Diller, Phyllis Diller's 102nd Birthday Party, Titus. *Guest:* More than 198 appearances.

DILLON, KEVIN

Actor. b. Mamaroneck, NY, Aug. 19, 1965. Brother is actor Matt Dillon. Stage work includes Dark at the Top of the Stairs, The Indian Wants the Bronx.
PICTURES: No Big Deal, Heaven Help Us, Platoon, Remote Control, The Rescue, The Blob, War Party, Immediate Family, The Doors, A Midnight Clear, No Escape, True Crime, Criminal Hearts, Misbegotten, Stag, Hidden Agenda, Interstate 84, Mob Dot Com, Out for Blood, Poseidon, The Foursome, Hotel for Dogs.
TELEVISION: *Movies:* When He's Not a Stranger, Frankie's House, The Pathfinder, Gone in the Night, Medusa's Child. *Series:* That's Life, St. Michael's Crossing, Entourage (3 Emmy noms. Golden Globe nom. 2008). *Specials / Documentaries:* Dear America: Letters Home from Vietnam (voice).

DILLON, MATT

Actor. b. New Rochelle, NY, Feb. 18, 1964. Brother is actor Kevin Dillon. Discovered at age 14 in junior high school by casting dir. who cast him in Over the Edge.
THEATRE: NY: The Boys of Winter (B'way debut, 1985).
PICTURES: Over the Edge (debut, 1979), Little Darlings, My Bodyguard, Liar's Moon, Tex, The Outsiders, Rumble Fish, The Flamingo Kid, Target, Rebel, Native Son, The Big Town, Kansas, Bloodhounds of Broadway, Drugstore Cowboy, A Kiss Before Dying, Singles, Mr. Wonderful, The Saint of Fort Washington, Golden Gate, To Die For, Frankie Starlight, Beautiful Girls, Grace of My Heart, Albino Alligator, In & Out, Wild Things, There's Something About Mary, One Night At McCool's, Beyond the Banyan Trees, Deuces Wild, City of Ghosts, Employee of the Month, Crash (Academy Award nom.; Golden Globe nom. 2006), Loverboy, Herbie: Fully Loaded, Factotum, You, Me and Dupree, Nothing But the Truth, Old Dogs, Armored, Rio Sex Comedy, Takers.
TELEVISION: *Movies:* Women & Men 2: In Love There Are No Rules (Return to Kansas City), The Great American Fourth of July and Other Disasters. *Specials:/Documentaries:* Dear America: Letters Home From Vietnam (reader), Rockets Redglare!, Pitch. *Guest:* More than 83 appearances.

DILLON, MELINDA

Actress. b. Hope, AR, Oct. 13, 1939. e. Chicago Sch. of Drama, Art Inst., Goodman Theatre. Launched career on Broadway in original prod. of Who's Afraid of Virginia Woolf? (Theatre World Award, Tony Award nom., Drama Critics Award).
THEATRE: Story Theater, You Know I Can't Hear You When The Water's Running, A Way of Life, Our Town
PICTURES: The April Fools (debut, 1969), Bound for Glory (Golden Globe nom. 1977, People's Choice Award), Slap Shot, Close Encounters of the Third Kind (Academy Award nom. 1978), F.I.S.T., Absence of Malice (Academy Award nom. 1982), A Christmas Story, Songwriter, Harry and the Hendersons, Staying Together, Spontaneous Combustion, Capt. America, The Prince of Tides, Sioux City, To Fong Woo–Thanks for Everything Julie Newmar, How to Make an American Quilt, Dorothy Day, The Effects of Magic, Magnolia, Debating Robert Lee, Adam & Steve, Empty City, Reign Over Me.
TELEVISION: *Movies:* Critical List, Transplant, Marriage is Alive and Well, The Shadow Box, Fallen Angel, Hellinger's Law, Right of Way, Shattered Spirits, Shattered Innocence, Nightbreaker, Judgment Day: The John List Story, State of Emergency, Confessions: Two Faces of Evil, Naomi & Wynonna: Love Can Build a Bridge, A Painted House. *Mini-series:* Space. *Series:* Paul Sills Story Theatre.

DINDAL, MARK

Animator, Director. b. Columbus, OH.
PICTURES: The Fox and the Hound, Mickey's Christmas Carol, The Black Cauldron, The Great Mouse Detective, Oliver & Company, The Little Mermaid, The Rocketeer, Cats Don't Dance (voice, dir., writer), The Emperor's New Groove (dir., writer), Chicken Little (dir., writer), Sherlock's Secretary (dir.).

DI NOVI, DENISE

Producer. b. Canada. Started as journalist, reporter, film critic in Toronto before entering film industry as unit publicist. 1980, joined Montreal's Film Plan production co. as co-prod., assoc. prod. and exec. in charge of prod. working on such movies as Visiting Hours, Going Berserk, Videodrome. Became exec. v.p. of prod. at New World, then head of Tim Burton Prods., 1989-92.
PICTURES: Heathers, Edward Scissorhands, Meet the Applegates, Batman Returns, The Nightmare Before Christmas, Cabin Boy, Little Women, Ed Wood, James and the Giant Peach, Practical Magic, Almost Heroes, Message in a Bottle, The Second Angel, Happy Campers, Original Sin, Killing Mrs. Duke, A Walk to Remember, What a Girl Wants, New York Minute, Catwoman, Sisterhood of the Traveling Pants, Maid of Dishonor, Lucky You, Major Movie Star, Nights in Rodanthe, The Sisterhood of the Traveling Pants 2, Ramona and Beezus, Life as We Know It (exec. prod.).
TELEVISION: *Movies:* Jo (prod.). *Exec. Prod.:* Eloise at the Plaza, Eloise at Christmastime, Hotel, Sudbury. *Mini-series:* The 70s. *Series:* The District.

DIPASQUALE, SANDY

Executive. b. Buffalo, NY. DiPasquale is an experienced broadcaster and businessman who has founded and operated several successful TV broadcast groups, and has held senior positions in the TV broadcast industry for more than 25 years. Since 1994, DiPasquale was a partner with Smith Broadcasting Group, operator of four TV stations, before moving to STC Broadcasting, which he merged with LIN Broadcasting in 2002. He then founded BlueStone Television with Providence Equity Partners and operated the 13 TV station group from June 2004-May 2007, until the sale of BlueStone to Bonten Media Group. In March 2008 DiPasquale founded Newport Television with Providence Equity Partners by acquiring Clear Channel Television. Newport Television is comprised of a 50-station TV group in 22 markets across the country and Inergize Digital, a leader in fully integrated digital mgt. solutions that generate revenue for local media companies. Newport Television, based in Kansas City, MO, is the second partnership between Mr. DiPasquale and Providence Equity Partners.

DI PIETRA, ROSEMARY

Executive. Joined Paramount Pictures in 1976, rising through ranks to become director-corporate administration. 1985, promoted to exec. dir.-corporate administration. Currently is Sr. V.P. of Administration for Paramount Pictures.

DISHY, BOB

Actor. b. Brooklyn, NY. e. Syracuse U.
THEATRE: Damn Yankees, From A to Z, Second City, Flora the Red Menace, By Jupiter, Something Different, The Goodbye People, The Good Doctor, The Unknown Soldier at His Wife, The Creation of the World and Other Business, An American Millionaire, Sly Fox, Murder at Howard Johnson's, Grown Ups, Cafe Crown.
PICTURES: The Tiger Makes Out, Lovers and Other Strangers, The Big Bus, I Wonder Who's Killing Her Now?, The Last Married Couple in America, First Family, Author! Author!, Brighton Beach Memoirs, Critical Condition, Stay Tuned, Used People, My Boyfriend's Back, Don Juan DeMarco, Jungle to Jungle, A Fish in the Bathtub, Judy Berlin, Captured, Along Came Polly, The Wackness.
TELEVISION: *Movies:* Damn Yankees!, The Police, Columbo: The Greenhouse Jungle, Columbo: Now You See Him, It Couldn't Happen to a Nicer Guy, The Cafeteria, The Good Doctor, Kate Loves a Mystery, Thicker Than Blood: The Larry McLinden Story. *Series:* That Was the Week That Was. *Series:* Story Theatre, Law & Order.

DIXON, BARBARA
Executive. b. Pasadena CA. e. USC, grad. degree from Johns Hopkins U. Served as staff member of Senate Judiciary Committee and was dir. of legislation for Sen. Birch Bayh, 1974-79. Left to become dir. of Office of Government & Public Affairs of Nat'l. Transportation Safety Board. Named v.p., Fratelli Group, public relations firm in Washington; took leave of absence in 1984 to serve as deputy press secty. to Democratic V.P. candidate, Geraldine Ferraro. In 1985 joined Motion Picture Assn. of America as v.p. for public affairs. Moved to Columbia/Tristar. Currently v.p., director of the Museum of Television & Radio L.A., branch.

DIXON, WHEELER WINSTON
Educator, Writer, Filmmaker. b. New Brunswick, NJ, March 12, 1950. e. Rutgers U. In 1960s asst. writer for Time/Life publications; also writer for Interview magazine. 1976, directed TV commercials in NY. One season with TVTV, Los Angeles, as post-prod. suprv. 1978, formed Deliniator Films, Inc., serving as exec. prod./dir. Since 1988 has directed film program at Univ. of Nebraska, where holds rank of tenured full prof. and chair, Film Studies Prog.; received Rockefeller Foundation grant. Prod., dir. with Gwendolyn Audrey-Foster: Women Who Made the Movies (video). 1992, guest prog. at the Brit. Film Inst./ Natl. Film Theatre. 1993, Distinguished Teaching Award. Invited lecturer at Yale, 1995; Series ed. for SUNY Press Cultural Studies in Cinema/Video (20 vol.)
AUTHOR: The 'B' Directors, 1985; The Cinematic Vision of F. Scott Fitzgerald, 1986; PRC: A History of Producer's Releasing Corp., 1986; books on Freddie Francis, Terence Fisher, Reginald Le Borg, 1992-93; The Early Film Criticism of Francois Truffaut; Re-Viewing British Cinema, 1900-92; It Looks at You: The Returned Gaze of Cinema, 1995; The Films of Jean-Luc Godard, 1997; The Exploding Eye: A Revisionary History of 1960s American Experimental Cinema, 1997.
PICTURES: *Dir:* Quick Constant and Solid Instant, London Clouds, Serial Metaphysics, Waste Motion, Tightrope, Stargrove, Gaze, An Evening with Chris Jangaard, Dana Can Deal, Damage, Un Petit Examen, and Not So Damned Petit Either, or, The Light Shining Over the Dark, Madagascar or Caroline Kennedy's Sinful Life in London, The Diaries, Distance, What Can I Do, Squatters.

DOBSON, KEVIN
Actor. b. New York, NY, March 18, 1943.
PICTURES: Love Story, Bananas, Klute, The Anderson Tapes, The French Connection, Carnal Knowledge, Midway, All Night Long, Mom Can I Keep Her?, Nathan Grimm, Restraining Order, She's No Angel, Crash Landing, 1408, Portal, April Moon, Doesn't Texas Ever End.
TELEVISION: *Movies:* The Immigrants, Transplant, Orphan Train, Hardhat and Legs, Reunion, Mark I Love You, Mickey Splillane's Margin for Murder, Money Power Murder (also prod.), Casey's Gift: For Love of a Child, Sweet Revenge, Fatal Frienship, Dirty Work, House of Secrets and Lies, The Conviction of Kitty Dodds, If Someone Had Known, Crimes of Passion: Voice from the Grave, Nobody Lives Forever, She's No Angel, The Haunted Heart, Christmas at Cadillac Jack's. *Mini-series:* Knots Landing: Back to the Cul-de-Sac. *Series:* Kojak, Shannon, Knots Landing (also dir. 9 episodes), F/X: The Series, One Life to Live, The Bold and the Beautiful, Days of Our Lives.

DOERFLER, RONALD J.
Executive. e. Fairleigh Dickinson University, bachelor's degree in accounting & M.B.A., magna cum laude, 1972. Became CPA in 1967. Joined Capital Cities in 1969 as asst. controller. Became treas. in 1977; v.p. & CFO, 1980. 1983, named sr. v.p., then sr. v.p. & CFO. He played a major role in Capital Cities' acquisition of ABC, Inc. in 1986 and again in the 1996 Capital Cities/ABC merger with The Walt Disney Company. In Feb. 1998 became sr. v.p. & CFO of the Hearst Corporation; in 2002 Doerfler was elected to Hearst's bd. of dir. In 1986. He has served as director of Lazard Ltd. and Lazard Group since 2006. Doerfler was named one of "America's Best Chief Financial Officers," an honor awarded to 50 chief financial officers by Institutional Investor magazine. He is a former chmn. of the bd. of the Broadcast Cable Financial Management Association and is a member of the American Institute of Certified Public Accountants. He sits on the bd. of trustees of Fairleigh Dickinson University and on the bd. of dir. of the Arts & Business Council.

DOHERTY, SHANNEN
Actress. b. Memphis, TN, April 12, 1971. On stage in The Mound Builders.
PICTURES: Night Shift, The Secret of NIMH (voice), Girls Just Want to Have Fun, Heathers, Freeze Frame, Mallrats, Nowhere, Striking Poses, Jay and Silent Bob Strike Back, The Rendering, Burning Palms.
TELEVISION: *Movies:* The Other Lover, Obsessed, Blindfold, Jailbreakers, A Burning Passion: The Margaret Mitchell Story, Gone in the Night, Friends 'Til the End, Sleeping with the Devil, The Ticket, Satan's School for Girls, Another Day, Hell on Heels: The Battle of Mary Kay, View of Terror, Category 7: The End of the World, Christmas Caper, Kiss Me Deadly, Resistance, The Lost Treasure of the Grand Canyon, Encounter with Danger, Growing the Big One. *Mini-series:* Robert Kennedy and His Times. *Pilots:* His and Hers, Love, Inc. *Series:* Little House on the Prairie, Our House, Beverly Hills 90210 (1990-1994), Charmed, Scare Tactics (host), North Shore, 90210 (2008-). *Guest:* More than 110 appearances.

DOLAN, CHARLES F.
Executive. b. Cleveland, OH, Oct. 16, 1926. e. John Carroll U. Established Teleguide Inc., early 1960s. Founder of Sterling Manhattan Cable, mid 1960s. Founded Home Box Office Inc., early 1970s; after sale of HBO to Time Life Inc., organized Cablevision Systems Corp., 1973; presently, founder and Chairman of Cablevision (2007). Dolan is a trustee of Fairfield University in CT and a member of the bd. of governors of St. Francis Hospital in Port Washington, NY.

DOLAN, JAMES L.
Executive. Began working at Cablevision in the 1970s, in construction, field sales & collections depts.; named asst. gen mgr. of Cablevision of Chicago, late 1970s. Early 1980s, as Cablevision v.p., found and managed WKNR-AM, Cleveland; also oversaw weekly TV magazine Total. During the 1980s, corp. dir. adv., at Rainbow Media Holdings, Inc., & v.p. for adv. sales at Cablevision. CEO, Rainbow Media Holdings, Inc., 1993-1995. Pres. & CEO, Cablevision Systems Corp., 1995-present. Cablevision's operations also includes Rainbow Media's national and regional TV program networks owns IFC and the Sundance Channels, Madison Square Garden and its professional sports teams, and the world famous Radio City Music Hall. Dolan also serves as chmn. of Madison Square Garden where he oversees mgt. of the many Garden entities which include the arena complex, its teams—the Knicks, Rangers and Liberty, the MSG Network, Radio City Music Hall and the Hartford Civic Center. Dolan is a member of the bd. of dir. of Cablevision Systems Corporation and serves on its executive committee. He sits on the bd. of trustees of TV station WNET and is also a member of the bd. of dir. of both the Lustgarten Foundation for Pancreatic Cancer Research and The Allan Houston Foundation.

DOLGEN, JONATHAN L.
Executive. b. New York, NY, April 27, 1945. e. Cornell U., J.D. degree from NYU Sch. of Law. Began career with Wall Street law firm, Fried, Frank, Harris, Shriver & Jacobson. In 1976 joined Columbia Pictures Industries as asst. gen. counsel and deputy gen. counsel. 1979, named sr. v.p. in charge of worldwide business affairs; 1980, named exec. v.p. Joined Columbia m.p. div., 1981; named pres. of Columbia Pay-Cable & Home Entertainment Group. Also pres. Columbia Pictures domestic operations, overseeing Music Group. 1985, joined 20th-Fox in newly created position of sr. exec. v.p. for telecommunications. Became pres. of Sony Motion Picture Group, 1991. Appointed chmn. Viacom Entertainment Group, 1994, with responsibilities for the operations of Paramount Motion Picture Group (Motion Picture Production & Distribution, Famous Music Publishing, Theatrical Exhibition) and Paramount Television Group (prod. & dist. of TV product and ownership of TV stations and interests in the United Paramount Network). Dolgen resigned from Viacom July 15, 2004. In Oct. 2006, Dolgen became a sr. consultant to ARTISTdirect, Inc., to advise the co. on the development of piracy protection initiatives and new business opportunities. Since leaving Viacom, Dolgen also joined the board of directors of Charter Communications, Inc. and Expedia, Inc. and became a member of the City of Los Angeles and Los Angeles County Homeland Security Advisory Councils and the Cornell University major gifts committee. Dolgen also serves as a senior advisor to Viacom, Inc. In Sept. 2007, he invested in Veoh Networks (www.veoh.com) a leading innovator in Internet Television. Veoh develops Internet TV offerings and pursues new content partnerships to deliver high-quality online video experiences to viewers. Other Veoh investors from the ent. industry include Tom Freston and Michael Eisner (lead investor is Goldman Sachs). Facing bankruptcy 2010, Qlipso ended up buying the assets of Veoh, including its Website, filtering, recommendation, and backend technology, video library, advertising deals, and still-substantial audience. ComScore estimates that 14 million people a month still visit Veoh. Dolgen is still a Director of Expedia, Inc., Director of Live Nation Entertainment, Inc. and Director of Ticketmaster Entertainment, Inc.

DONAHUE, PHIL
Television Host. b. Cleveland, OH, Dec. 21, 1935. e. Notre Dame, BBA. m. actress Marlo Thomas. Worked as check sorter, Albuquerque Natl. Bank, 1957, then as announcer at KYW-TV & AM, Cleveland; news dir. WABJ radio, Adrian, MI; morning newscaster WHIO-TV. Interviews with Jimmy Hoffa and Billy Sol Estes picked up nationally by CBS. Host of Conversation Piece, phone-in talk show. Debuted The Phil Donahue Show, daytime talk show in Dayton, Ohio, 1967. Syndicated two years later. Moved to Chicago, 1974. Host, Donahue, in 165 outlets in U.S. In 1979 a mini-version of show became 3-times-a-week segment on NBC's Today Show, Donahue, (host 2002). Winner of 9 Emmys. Received Special Recognition Award 1993. Emmy Award, Lifetime Achievement Award, 1996. *Author:* Donahue: My Own Story (1980), The Human Animal (1985).

DONALDSON, ROGER

Director. b. Ballarat, Australia, Nov. 15, 1943. Emigrated to New Zealand at 19. Established still photography business; then began making documentaries. Directed Winners and Losers, a series of short dramas for NZ-TV.
PICTURES: Sleeping Dogs (also prod.), Smash Palace (also s.p. prod.), The Bounty, Marie, No Way Out, Cocktail, Cadillac Man (also prod.), White Sands, The Getaway, Species, Dante's Peak, Thirteen Days Which Shocked the World, The Recruit, The World's Fastest Indian, The Bank Job, The Hungry Rabbit Jumps.
TELEVISION: *Movie*: Fearless (exec. prod.). *Specials / Documentaries:* Numero Bruno, Bringing History to the Silver Screen, Spy School: Inside the CIA Training Program.

DONEN, STANLEY

Director, Producer, Choreographer. b. Columbia, SC, April 13, 1924. e. USC. Former dancer, B'way debut 1940 in chorus of Pal Joey starring Gene Kelly. Assisted Kelly as choreog. on stage prod. of Best Foot Forward; hired by MGM to repeat duties in film version. Choreographer on such films as Cover Girl, Holiday in Mexico, This Time for Keeps, A Date With Judy, Take Me Out to the Ballgame (also co-story credit). Honorary Academy Award, 1998. American Cinema Editors Award, Golden Eddie Filmmaker of the Year Award, 1999. American Society of Cinematographers, Award, Board of the Governors Award, 2002.
PICTURES: *Director:* On the Town (debut, 1949; co-dir. with Gene Kelly), Royal Wedding, Singin' in the Rain (co-dir., co-choreog. with Gene Kelly, DGA nom. 1953), Fearless Fagan, Love Is Better Than Ever, Give a Girl a Break (also co-choreog.), Seven Brides for Seven Brothers (DGA nom. 1955), Deep in My Heart (also co-choreog.), It's Always Fair Weather (co-dir., co-choreog. with Gene Kelly), Funny Face (DGA nom. 1958), The Pajama Game (co-dir., co-prod. with George Abbott), Kiss Them for Me. *Director/Producer:* Indiscreet, Damn Yankees! (co-dir., co-prod. with George Abbott, DGA nom. 1959), Once More With Feeling, Surprise Package, The Grass Is Greener, Charade, Arabesque, Two for the Road (DGA nom. 1968), Bedazzled, Staircase, The Little Prince, Lucky Lady (dir. only), Movie Movie, Saturn 3, Blame It on Rio.
TELEVISION: *Actor:* The Making of Seven Brides for Seven Brothers, The Hollywood Fashion Machine. *Dir:* Love Letters. Moonlighting. *Specials/Documentaries:* Gene Kelly: Anatomy of a Dancer.

DONNELLY, DONAL

Actor. b. Bradford, England, July 6, 1931. Studied for theatre at the Dublin Gate Theatre.
THEATRE: *NY Theatre:* Philadelphia Here I Come (B'way debut, 1966), Joe Egg, Sleuth (London, NY, U.S. tour), The Elephant Man, The Faith-Healer, The Chalk Garden, My Astonishing Self, Big Maggie, Execution of Justice, Sherlock's Last Case, Ghetto, Dancing at Lughnasa, Translations.
PICTURES: Rising of the Moon (1957), Gideon's Day, Shake Hands With the Devil, Young Cassidy, The Knack, Up Jumped a Swagman, The Mind of Mr. Soames, Waterloo, The Dead, The Godfather Part III, Squanto: A Warrior's Tale, Korea, This Is My Father, Love and Rage.
TELEVISION: Juno and the Paycock (BBC, 1958), Home Is the Hero, The Venetian Twins, The Plough and the Stars, Playboy of the Western World, Sergeant Musgrave's Dance. *Series:* Yes-Honestly. *Documentaries/Specials:* John Huston and the Dubliners. (d. January 4, 2010)

DONNER, RICHARD

Director. b. New York, NY, April 24, 1939. Began career as actor off-B'way. Worked with director Martin Ritt on TV production of Maugham's Of Human Bondage. Moved to California 1958, directing commercials, industrial films and documentaries. First TV drama: Wanted: Dead or Alive. Received American Cinema Editors Golden Eddie Filmmaker of the Year Award 2009.
PICTURES: X-15 (debut, 1961), Salt and Pepper, Twinky (Lola), The Omen, Superman, Inside Moves, The Final Conflict (exec. prod. only), The Toy (also exec. prod.), Ladyhawke (also prod.), The Goonies (also prod.), Lethal Weapon (also prod.), The Lost Boys (exec. prod. only), Scrooged (also prod.), Lethal Weapon 2 (also prod.), Delirious (exec. prod. only), Radio Flyer, Lethal Weapon 3 (also prod.), Free Willy (co-exec. prod. only), Maverick (also prod.), Tales From the Crypt Presents Demon Knight (co-exec. prod. only), Assassins (also prod.), Conspiracy Theory (also prod.), Free Willy 3: The Rescue (exec. prod.), Lethal Weapon 4, Any Given Sunday, X-Men, Timeline (also prod.), X-Men Origins: Wolverine, The 28th Amendment (prod. only).
TELEVISION: *Movies:* Lucas Tanner (pilot), Sarah T.: Portrait of a Teen-Age Alcoholic, The Six Million Dollar Man, Senior Year, A Shadow in the Streets, Tales From the Crypt (exec. prod.; also dir. episode: Dig That Cat... He's Real Gone). *As Prod/Exec. prod:* Two Fisted Tales, W.E.I.R.D. World, The Omen, Matthew Blackheart: Monster Smasher. *Series episodes:* Have Gun Will Travel, Perry Mason, Cannon, Get Smart, The Fugitive, Kojak, Petrocelli, Bronk, (also pilot), Gilligan's Island, Man From U.N.C.L.E., Wild Wild West, Tales From the Crypt, Twilight Zone, The Banana Splits, Combat, Perversions of Science.

D'ONOFRIO, VINCENT PHILLIP

Actor. b. Brooklyn, NY, June 30, 1960. Studied acting with the American Stanislavsky Theatre in NY, appearing in Of Mice and Men, The Petrified Forest, Sexual Perversity in Chicago, and The Indian Wants the Bronx.
THEATRE: *B'way:* Open Admissions.
PICTURES: The First Turn On! (debut, 1984), Full Metal Jacket, Adventures in Babysitting, Mystic Pizza, Signs of Life, The Blood of Heroes, Crooked Hearts, Dying Young, Fires Within, Naked Tango, JFK, The Player, Desire, Household Saints, Mr. Wonderful, Being Human, Ed Wood, Imaginary Crimes, Stuart Saves His Family, Strange Days, Feeling Minnesota, Men in Black, The Velocity of Gary, The Whole Wide World (also prod.), The Newton Boys, Claire Dolan, Steal This Movie (also exec. prod.), Imposter, The Thirteenth Floor, The Cell, Happy Accidents, Spanish Judges, The Dangerous Lives of Altar Boys, The Salton Sea, Bark, Imposter, Chelsea Walls, Thumbsucker, Little Victories, The Break-Up, The Narrows, Staten Island, Zaritsas: Russian Women in New York (doc., exec. prod.), The Irishman, Down and Dirty Pictures, Chlorine.
TELEVISION: *Movies:* Taking of Pelham One Two Three, That Championship Season, The Red Sneakers, Case of Evil, Sherlock. *Series:* Homicide: Life on the Street (Emmy nom. 1998), Law and Order: Criminal Intent.

DONOHOE, AMANDA

Actress. b. London, England, June 29, 1962. e. Francis Holland Sch. for Girls, Central Sch. of Speech & Drama. Member of Royal Exchange Theatre in Manchester. B'way debut 1995 in Uncle Vanya.
PICTURES: Foreign Body (debut, 1986), Castaway, The Lair of the White Worm, The Rainbow, Tank Malling, Diamond Skulls (Dark Obsession), Paper Mask, The Madness of King George, Liar Liar, Writer's Block, I'm Losing You, Stardust, The Real Howard Spitz, Circus, Starship Troopers 3: Marauder, The Calling.
TELEVISION: *Movies:* Married to Murder, Shame, It's Nothing Personal (also co-exec. prod.), The Substitute, Shame II: The Secret (also co-exec. prod.), A Knight in Camelot, In the Beginning, Rock the Boat, Lucky Day. *Series:* L.A. Law (Golden Globe Award 1992), Murder City, Bad Girls, Love Trap (narr.), Emmerdale Farm. *Special:* Game Set and Match (Mystery!). *Guest:* More than 51 appearances.

DONOVAN, TATE

Actor. b. New York, NY, Sept. 25, 1963. Raised in New Jersey. Studied acting at USC. Worked as still photographer for two Mutual of Omaha documentaries.
THEATRE: Ruffian on the Stair, The American Plan, The Rhythm of Torn Stars, Bent. B'way: Picnic.
PICTURES: SpaceCamp, Clean and Sober, Dead Bang, Memphis Belle, Love Potion No. 9, Ethan Frome, Equinox, Holy Matrimony, Murder at 1600, Hercules (voice), Waiting for Woody, The Only Thrill, October 22, Drop Back Ten, 4 a.m.: Open All Night, G-Men From Hell, The Office Party, Jesus and Hutch, Swordfish, Get Well Soon, West of Here, Exposed, The Pacifier, Good Night, and Good Luck, The Lather Effect, Shooter, Nancy Drew, Neal Cassady, American Primitive, Below the Beltway.
TELEVISION: *Movies:* Not My Kid, Into Thin Air, A Case of Deadly Force, Nutcracker: Money Madness Murder, Rising Son, Tempting Fate, Silver Bells, Painkiller Jane. *Series:* Partners, Hercules (voice), Trinity, House of Mouse (voice), Mister Sterling, The O.C., Damages. HBO *Special:* Vietnam War Stories. *Guest:* More than 55 appearances.

DOOLEY, PAUL

Actor. r.n. Paul Brown. b. Parkersburg, WV, Feb. 22, 1928. Began career on NY stage in Threepenny Opera. Later member of Second City. B'way credits include The Odd Couple, Adaptation/Next, The White House Murder Case, Hold Me. Co-creator and writer for The Electric Company on PBS.
PICTURES: What's So Bad About Feeling Good? (debut, 1968), The Out-of-Towners, Death Wish, The Gravy Train, Slap Shot, A Wedding, A Perfect Couple, Breaking Away, Rich Kids, Popeye, Health (also co-s.p.), Paternity, Endangered Species, Kiss Me Goodbye, Strange Brew, Going Berserk, Sixteen Candles, Big Trouble, O.C. and Stiggs, Monster in the Closet, Last Rites, Flashback, Shakes the Clown, The Player, My Boyfriend's Back, A Dangerous Woman, The Underneath, God's Lonely Man, Loved, Clockwatchers, Telling Lies in America, Runaway Bride, I'll Remember April, Guinevere, Happy Texas, A Woman's a Helluva Thing, The Perfect You, Madison, Insomnia, Adventures in Home Schooling, A Mighty Wind, Lake Desire, Come Away Home, For Your Consideration, Cars (voice), Hairspray, Chronic Town, Bedtime Stories, The Horsemen, Ironmen, Xander Cohen.
TELEVISION: *Movies:* Momma the Detective, The Murder of Mary Phagan, Lip Service, Guts and Glory: The Rise and Fall of Oliver North, When He's Not a Stranger, The Court Martial of Jackie Robinson, Guess Who's Coming for Christmas?, Perry Mason: The Case of the Heartbroken Bride, White Hot: The Mysterious Murder of Thelma Todd, Cooperstown, Mother of the Bride, State of Emergency, The Computer Wore Tennis Shoes, Out There, Angels in the Endzone, A Woman's a Helluva Thing, Tracey Ullman in the Trailer Tales, Comfort and Joy. *Mini-series:* Tales of the City. *Series:* The Electric Company (head writer),

The Dom DeLuise Show, Coming of Age, Mad About You, Dream On (Emmy nom. 1994), Once and Again, Grace Under Fire, Hopeless Pictures, Curb Your Enthusiasm, Desperate Housewives. *Specials:* Faerie Tale Theater, The Firm, Traveler's Rest, Sixteen Candles: The E! True Hollywood Story. *Guest:* More than 110 appearances.

DOOLEY, THOMAS

Executive. e. B.S., St. John's Univ., 1978; M.B.A., New York Univ. School of Business Administration, 1984. Dooley has spent the majority of his career working for media mogul Sumner Redstone, holding various corporate positions at Sumner's Viacom from 1980 to 2000. His positions included deputy chairman, member of its executive committee, and executive v.p. of finance, corporate development and communications; he was a Viacom bd. member from 1996 to 2000; Dooley left the company in 2000 with another Viacom management vet, Philippe Dauman, and co-founded DND, a private equity firm specializing in media and telecommunication investments. He rejoined Viacom's board in 2006 and in September 2006 Redstone created a new post for Dooley, senior executive v.p. & chief administrative officer, teaming once again with Philippe Dauman, whom Redstone named to the president and CEO post at Viacom. In Jan. 2007, Dooley assumed the additional responsibilities of Viacom's CFO. He reports to Dauman. 2010 he became COO and will continue to report to Dauman. Dooley is also a director of LaBranche & Co. Inc.

DORAN, LINDSAY

Executive, Producer. b. Los Angeles, CA. e. U. of California at Santa Cruz. Moved to London where was contributing author to The Oxford Companion to Film and the World Encyclopedia of Film. Returned to U.S. to write and produce documentaries and children's programs for Pennsylvania public affairs station WPSX-TV. Career in m.p. industry began in story dept. at Embassy Pictures which she joined in 1979; 1982 promoted to dir. of development; then v.p., creative affairs. 1985, joined Paramount Pictures as v.p., production, for MP Group. 1987, promoted to senior v.p., production. 1989. Pres., Mirage Productions. Pres. and COO, United Artists Pictures, 1996-2000. Currently producer with own company, Three Strange Angels.
PICTURES: Dead Again, Leaving Normal (exec. prod.), Sense and Sensibility (Academy Award nom.1996), Sabrina (exec. prod.), Nanny McPhee, Stranger Than Fiction, Nanny McPhee and the Big Bang.
TELEVISION: *Movie:* Miss Sherri (exec. prod.). *Series:* Fallen Angels.

DORFF, STEPHEN

Actor. b. Atlanta, GA, July 29, 1973. Started acting at age 9.
PICTURES: The Gate (debut, 1987), The Power of One, An Ambush of Ghosts, Judgment Night, Rescue Me, Backbeat, S.F.W., Reckless, Halcyon Days, Innocent Lies, I Shot Andy Warhol, The Audition, Star Truckers, City of Industry, Blade, Entropy, Blood and Wine, Earthly Possessions, Quantum Project, Cecil B. Demented, Deuces Wild, Riders, Fear Dot Com, Den of Lions, Cold Creek Manor, Alone in the Dark, Tennis, Anyone...?, Shadowboxer, World Trade Center, .45, Botched, The Passage, XIII, Black Water Transit, Felon, Public Enemies, Fallen Moon, Somewhere, Born to Be a Star.
TELEVISION: *Movies:* I Know My First Name Is Steven, Always Remember I Love You, Do You Know the Muffin Man?, A Son's Promise, Aerosmith: Cryin', Earthly Possessions, Covert One: The Hades Factor, Skip Tracer (also exec. prod.). *Mini-series:* Covert One: The Hades Factor, XIII: The Conspiracy. *Series:* What a Dummy. *Guest:* More than 53 appearances.

DORTORT, DAVID

Executive Producer. b. New York, NY, Oct. 23, 1916. e. City College of New York. Served U.S. Army, 1943-46. Novelist and short story writer, 1943-49. Also TV writer. Now pres. of Xanadu Prods., Aurora Enterprises, Inc., and Bonanza Ventures, Inc. & Pres. TV branch, WGA, West, 1954-55; TV-radio branch, 1955-57; v.p. PGA, 1967; pres. 1968. Chmn., Caucus for Producers, Writers and Directors, 1973-75. Pres., PGA, 1980-81; campaign dir., Permanent Charities Comm., 1980-81; chmn., Interguild Council 1980-81. Received WGA/West noms. for TV work on An Error in Chemistry (Climax), and The Ox-Bow Incident (20th Century Fox Hour).
AUTHOR: Novels include Burial of the Fruit, The Post of Honor.
PICTURES: The Lusty Men, Reprisal, The Big Land, Cry in the Night, Clash by Night, Going Bananas (exec. prod.).
TELEVISION: Climax Mystery Theater (Emmy nom. 1955), The 20th Century-Fox Hour (Emmy nom. 1956). *Creator and exec. prod.:* Bonanza (Emmy nom. 1966), High Chaparral, The Chisholms, Hunter's Moon, Bonanza: Legends of the Ponderosa. *Producer:* The Restless Gun, The Cowboys. *Creator, story and exec. prod.:* Bonanza: The Next Generation. *Exec. prod.:* Bonanza: The Return, Bonanza: Under Attack, Ponderosa.

DOUGLAS, ILLEANA

Actress. July 25, 1965. Grandfather was actor Melvyn Douglas. Directed short films The Perfect Woman (Aspen Film Fest. prize, 1994), Boy Crazy—Girl Crazier.
THEATRE: Takes on Women, As Sure as You Live, Black Eagles.
PICTURES: Hello Again, New York Stories, GoodFellas, Guilty By Suspicion, Cape Fear, Alive, Household Saints, Grief, Quiz Show, Search and Destroy, To Die For, Grace of My Heart, Picture Perfect, Hacks, Flypaper, Wedding Bell Blues, Stir of Echoes, Can't Stop Dancing, Message in a Bottle, Happy Texas, The Next Best Thing, Ghost World, Dummy, The Adventures of Pluto Nash, Missing Brendan, The Kiss, The Californians, Sorority Rule (dir.), Alchemy, Expired, Factory Girl, Osso Bucco, Otis, The Year of Getting to Know Us, Life Is Hot in Cracktown, April Showers, Adele.
TELEVISION: *Movies:* Weapons of Mass Distraction, Rough Riders, Bella Mafia, Lansky, Point of Origin, Not Like Everyone Else. *Series:* Action, Celebrity Garage Sale (host), Easy to Assemble. *Guest:* More than 55 appearances.

DOUGLAS, KIRK

Actor, Producer, Director. r.n. Issur Danielovitch (changed to Demsky). b. Amsterdam, NY, Dec. 9, 1916. m. Anne Buydens, pres. of Bryna Prod. Co. Father of Michael, Joel, Peter, Eric. e. St. Lawrence U, B.A, AADA. Stage debut in New York: Spring Again. U.S. Navy during W.W.II; resumed stage work. Did radio soap operas. Signed by Hal B. Wallis for film debut. *Autobiography:* The Ragman's Son (1988). *Novels:* Dance With the Devil, The Secret, Last Tango in Brooklyn. Recipient of U.S. Presidential Medal of Freedom, 1981. Career achievement award, National Board of Review, 1989. Received AFI Lifetime Achievement Award, 1991. Academy Award Honorary Award For 50 years as a creative and moral force in the motion picture community, 1996. Received Golden Globe Award, Cecil B. DeMille Award, 1968. WGA Award, Meltzer Award, 1991.
THEATRE: Spring Again, Three Sisters, Kiss and Tell, Trio, The Wind is Ninetry, Star in the Window, Man Bites Dog, One Flew Over the Cuckoo's Nest, The Boys of Autumn.
PICTURES: The Strange Love of Martha Ivers (debut, 1946), Out of the Past, I Walk Alone, Mourning Becomes Electra, The Walls of Jericho, My Dear Secretary, Letter to Three Wives, Champion (Academy Award nom. 1950), Young Man with a Horn, The Glass Menagerie, Ace in the Hole (The Big Carnival), Along the Great Divide, Detective Story (Golden Globe nom. 1952), The Big Trees, The Big Sky, Bad and the Beautiful (Academy Award nom. 1953), Story of Three Loves, The Juggler, Act of Love, 20,000 Leagues Under the Sea, Ulysses, Man Without a Star, The Racers, The Indian Fighter (also prod.), Lust for Life (Academy Award nom.; Golden Globe Award 1957), Top Secret Affair, Gunfight at the OK Corral, Paths of Glory, The Vikings (also prod.), Last Train from Gun Hill, The Devil's Disciple, Strangers When We Meet, Spartacus (also prod.), The Last Sunset, Town Without Pity, Lonely Are the Brave (also prod.), Two Weeks in Another Town, The Hook, List of Adrian Messenger (also prod.), For Love or Money, Seven Days in May (also prod.), In Harm's Way, The Heroes of Telemark, Cast a Giant Shadow, Is Paris Burning?, The Way West, The War Wagon, A Lovely Way to Die, The Brotherhood (also prod.), The Arrangement, There Was a Crooked Man, A Gunfight, Summertree (prod. only), The Light at the Edge of the World (also prod.), Catch Me a Spy, Scalawag (also dir., prod.), Master Touch, Once is Not Enough, Posse (also dir., prod.), The Chosen, The Fury, The Villain, Saturn III, Home Movies, The Final Countdown, The Man from Snowy River, Eddie Macon's Run, Tough Guys, Oscar, Welcome to Veraz, Greedy, A Century of Cinema, The Films of John Frankenheimer, Diamonds, It Runs In the Family, Illusion.
TELEVISION: *Movies:* Mousey, The Money Changers, Draw! (HBO), Victory at Entebbe, Remembrance of Love, Amos (Emmy Award nom.; Golden Globe nom. 1986), Queenie, Inherit the Wind, The Secret, Take Me Home Again. *Series:* Tales from the Crypt (Emmy Award nom.1992). *Specials:* Legend of Silent Night, Dr. Jekyll & Mr. Hyde, AFI's 100 Years, 100 Thrills: America's Most Heart-Pounding Movies, Walt:--The Man Behind the Myth. *Guest:* More than 155 appearances.

DOUGLAS, MICHAEL

Actor, Producer. b. New Brunswick, NJ, Sept 25, 1944. p. Kirk Douglas and Diana Dill. m. actress Catherine Zeta-Jones. e. Black Fox Military Acad., Choate, U. of California. Worked as asst. director on Lonely Are the Brave, Heroes of Telemark, Cast a Giant Shadow; after TV debut in The Experiment (CBS Playhouse), appeared off-Broadway in City Scene, Pinkville (Theatre World Award). Produced 1993 Off-B'way show The Best of Friends. Golden Globe Award, Cecil B. DeMille Award, 2004.
PICTURES: Hail Hero (debut, 1969, Golden Globe nom. 1970), Adam at 6 A.M., Summertree, Napoleon and Samantha, One Flew Over the Cuckoo's Nest (co-prod. only; Academy Award for Best Picture, 1976), Coma, The China Syndrome (also prod.), Running (also exec. prod.), It's My Turn, The Star Chamber, Romancing the Stone (also prod.), Starman (exec. prod. only), A Chorus Line, The Jewel of the Nile (also prod.), Fatal Attraction, Wall Street (Academy Award; Natl. Board of Review Award; Golden Globe nom. 1988), Black Rain, The War of the Roses (Golden Globe nom. 1988), Flatliners (co-exec. prod. only), Shining Through, Radio Flyer (co-exec. prod. only), Basic Instinct, Falling Down, Made in America (co-exec. prod. only), Disclosure, The American President (Golden Globe nom. 1996),

The Ghost and the Darkness, Face/Off (exec. prod. only), The Game, The Rainmaker (prod. only), A Perfect Murder, Wonder Boys (Golden Globe nom. 2001), One Night At McCool's, Traffic, Don't Say A Word, Smoke and Mirrors, It Runs in the Family, The In-Laws, The Husband I Bought (exec. prod.only), The Ride Down to Mt. Morgan (also prod.), Art Con (prod. only), The Sentinel (also prod.), Racing the Monsoon (also co-prod.), You, Me and Dupree, The King of California, The Ghosts of Girlfriends Past, Beyond a Reasonable Doubt, Solitary Man, Wall Street: Money Never Sleeps (also prod.), Knockout.
TELEVISION: *Movies:* Streets of San Francisco (pilot), When Michael Calls. *Series:* Streets of San Francisco (also dir. 1972-76; 3 Emmy nom.; Golden Globe nom. 1975), Starman (exec. prod.), Liberty's Kids: Est. 1776 (voice), Freedom: A History of Us. *Guest:* More than 176 appearances.

DOUMANIAN, JEAN

Producer. b. 1934.
PICTURES: Oxen, Bullets Over Broadway (exec. prod.), Mighty Aphrodite (exec. prod.), Everyone Says I Love You (exec. prod.), Deconstructing Harry, Story of a Bad Boy, Elements, Wild Man Blues, Deconstructing Harry, The Spanish Prisoner, Celebrity, Into My Heart, Sweet and Lowdown, Sunburn, Women Talking Dirty, Just Looking, Story of a Bad Boy, Small Time Crooks, All the Real Girls, Neal Cassady.
TELEVISION: *Movie:* Don't Drink the Water. *Series:* Saturday Night Live (talent co-ord., writer, assoc. prod.)

DOURDAN, GARY

Actor. b. Philadelphia, PA, December 11, 1966.
PICTURES: Weekend at Bernies 2, The Paper, Sunset Park, Playing God, Alien: Resurrection, Get that Number, Fool's Paradise, Thursday, Scar City, The Weekend, Trois, Dancing in September, Imposter, Black August, Perfect Stranger.
TELEVISION: *Movies:* The Good Fight, Laurel Avenue, Keys, Rendezvous, King of the World. *Series:* A Different World, The Office, Swift Justice, Lyric Cafe (host), Soul Food, CSI: Crime Scene Investigation.

DOURIF, BRAD

Actor. b. Huntington, WV, March 18, 1950. Studied with Stanford Meisner. Stage actor, three years with Circle Repertory Co., NY (When You Comin' Back Red Ryder?), before films and TV.
PICTURES: Split, One Flew Over the Cuckoo's Nest (Academy Award nom.; Golden Globe & BAFTA Awards, 1976), Group Portrait with Lady, Eyes of Laura Mars, Wise Blood, Heaven's Gate, Ragtime, Dune, Impure Thoughts, Istanbul, Blue Velvet, Fatal Beauty, Child's Play, Mississippi Burning, Medium Rare, The Exorcist: 1990, Spontaneous Combustion, Grim Prairie Tales, Sonny Boy, Graveyard Shift, Child's Play II, Hidden Agenda, Dead Certain, Jungle Fever, The Horseplayer, Body Parts, Child's Play 3, Common Bonds, Scream of Stone, Critters 4, London Kills Me, Diary of the Hurdy Gurdy Man, Murder Blues, Final Judgment, Amos & Andrew, Trauma, Color of Night, Murder in the First, Alien: Resurrection, Best Men, Brown's Requiem, Bride of Chucky (voice), Senseless, Nightwatch, Urban Legend, The Progeny, Son of Chucky (voice), Silicon Towers, Interceptors, The Hurdy Gurdy Man, Cypress Edge, Shadow Hours, The Ghost, Soul Keeper, The Calling, Lord of the Rings: The Two Towers, Child's Play 5, The Lord of the Rings: The Return of the King, Vlad, El Padrino, The Hazing, Seed of Chucky (voice), Brew, Pulse, The Wizard of Gore, The List, Humboldt County, Halloween, Touching Home, Lock and Roll Forever, Chain Letter, Blood Shot, Bad Lieutenant: Port of Call New Orleans, Junkyard Dog, The Beautiful Outsiders, My Son, My Son, What Have Ye Done, Fading of the Cries, Death and Cremation, Blood Shot, Priest, Chain Letter.
TELEVISION: *Movies:* Sgt. Matlovitch vs. the U.S. Air Force, Guyana Tragedy—The Story of Jim Jones, I Desire, Vengeance: The Story of Tony Cimo, Rage of Angels: The Story Continues, Desperado: The Outlaw Wars, Class of '61, Escape From Terror: The Teresa Stamper Story, Escape to Witch Mountain, If Looks Could Kill: The John Hawkins Story, Turbulent Skies. *Mini-series:* Studs Lonigan, Wild Palms. *Series:* Ponderosa, Deadwood (Emmy nom. 2004). *Specials:* Mound Builders, The Gardener's Son. *Guest:* More than 56 appearances.

DOWN, LESLEY-ANNE

Actress. b. London, England, March 17, 1954. At age of 10 modeled for TV and film commercials, leading to roles in features. Film debut at 14 in The Smashing Bird I Used to Know (billed as Lesley Down).
THEATRE: Great Expectations, Hamlet, etc.
PICTURES: The Smashing Bird I Used to Know (debut, 1969), All the Right Noises, Countess Dracula, Assault, Pope Joan, Scalawag, From Beyond the Grave, Brannigan, The Pink Panther Strikes Again, The Betsy, A Little Night Music, The Great Train Robbery, Hanover Street, Rough Cut, Sphinx, Nomads, Scenes from the Goldmine, Mardi Gras for the Devil, Death Wish V: The Face of Death, Munchie Stikes Back, The Unfaithful, Beastmaster III, The Secret Agent Club, Meet Wally Sparks, The King Guard, The Perfect Wife, The Meeksville Ghost, The 13th Child: Legend of the Jersey Devil, Today You Die.
TELEVISION: *Movies:* Agatha Christie's Murder is Easy, Hunchback of Notre Dame, The One and Only Phyllis Dixey, Arch of Triumph, Indiscreet, Lady Killers, Night Walk, Family of Cops, Young Hearts Unlimited, You Belong to Me, The Perfect Wife. *Mini-series:* North and South Books I & II & III (Golden Globe nom. 1986), Last Days of Pompeii. *Series:* Upstairs, Downstairs, Dallas, Sunset Beach, Days of Our Lives, The Bold & the Beautiful. *Specials:* Unity Mitford, Heartbreak House. Pilots: Shivers, 1775. *Guest:* More than 55 appearances.

DOWNEY, ROBERT, JR.

Actor. b. New York, NY, April 4, 1965. Father is indep. filmmaker Robert Downey. Film debut at age 5 in his father's film Pound.
PICTURES: Pound, Greaser's Palace, Jive, Up the Academy, Baby Its You, Firstborn, Tuff Turf, Weird Science, To Live and Die in L.A., Back to School, America, The Pick-Up Artist, Less Than Zero, Johnny B. Good, Rented Lips, 1969, True Believer, Chances Are, That's Adequate, Air America, Too Much Sun, Soapdish, Chaplin (Academy Award nom.; Golden Globe nom.; BAFTA Award 1993), Hail Caesar, Heart and Souls, The Last Party (also writer), Short Cuts (Golden Globe Award 1994), Natural Born Killers, Only You, Restoration, Danger Zone, Home for the Holidays, Richard III, Two Girls & A Guy, One Night Stand, Hugo Pool, Blue Vision, The Gingerbread Man, U.S. Marshals, Wonder Boys, In Dreams, Friends & Lovers, Bowfinger, Last Party 2000, The Singing Detective, Whatever We Do, Gothika, Eros, Kiss, Kiss, Bang, Bang, A Scanner Darkly, The Shaggy Dog, Fur: An Imaginary Portrait of Diane Arbus, A Guide to Recognizing Your Saints, Lucky You, Zodiac, Charlie Bartlett, Iron Man, The Incredible Hulk, Tropic Thunder (Academy Award nom. 2009, Golden Globe nom. 2008), The Soloist, Sherlock Holmes (Golden Globe Award 2010), Iron Man 2, Due Date.
TELEVISION: *Movie:* Mr. Willowby's Christmas Tree. *Mini-series:* Mussolini: The Untold Story. *Series:* Saturday Night Live, Ally McBeal (Emmy nom.; Golden Globe Award 2001). *Special:* Dear America (reader). *Guest:* More than 106 appearances.

DOWNS, HUGH

Broadcaster. b. Akron, OH, Feb. 14, 1921. e. Bluffton College, 1938. Wayne U., 1941. Col. U., N.Y., 1955; Supervisor of Science Programming, NBC's Science Dept. one yr.; science consultant for Westinghouse Labs., Ford Foundation, etc.; chmn. of bd., Raylin Prods., Inc. Today, Chairman, U.S. Committee for UNICEF. Chm. of bd. of governors, National Space Society. Books: Thirty Dirty Lies About Old, Rings Around Tomorrow, School of Stars, Yours Truly Hugh Downs, On Camera: My Ten Thousand Hours on Television, Perspectives, Fifty to Forever. The Hugh Downs School of Human Communication at Arizona State University is named in his honor.
TELEVISION: *Series:* Kukla Fran & Ollie (announcer), Home, Sid Caesar (announcer), The Jack Paar Show, Concentration, The Tonight Show (announcer, 1962), Today. *Host:* 20/20 (1978-1999), Over-Easy (Emmy Award, 1981), Live From Lincoln Center (Host).RADIO: NBC's Monitor, ABC's Perspectives.

DOYLE-MURRAY, BRIAN

Actor, Writer. b. Chicago, IL., Oct. 31, 1945. Brother is comedian Bill Murray. Started as member of Chicago's Second City improv. troupe, before joining the Organic Theatre of Chicago and the Boston Shakespeare Co. Appeared Off-B'way in The National Lampoon Show and on radio on weekly National Lampoon Show.
PICTURES: Caddyshack (also co-s.p.), Modern Problems, National Lampoon's Vacation, Sixteen Candles, The Razor's Edge, Legal Eagles, Club Paradise (also co-s.p.), Scrooged, The Experts, How I Got Into College, Ghostbusters II, National Lampoon's Christmas Vacation, Nothing But Trouble, JFK, Wayne's World, Groundhog Day, Cabin Boy, Jury Duty, Multiplicity, Waiting for Guffman, As Good As It Gets, Casper: A Spirited Beginning, Dennis the Menace 2, Doctor Dolittle (voice), Kill the Man, Stuart Little, Drowning Mona, Bedazzled, Getting Hal, A Gentleman's Game, Snow Dogs, Getting Hal, Nearing Grace, Daddy Day Camp, 17 Again.
TELEVISION: *Movies:* Babe Ruth, My Brother's Keeper, Frosty Returns (voice). *Series:* Saturday Night Live (also writer 3 Emmy noms.), Get a Life, Good Sports, Bakersfield P.D., The Martin Short Show, The George Wendt Show, Recess, Love & Money, The Sweet Spot, Teamo Supremo (voice), The Buzz on Maggie, Yes, Dear, The Goode Family, The Marvelous Misadventures of Flapjack, The Middle. *Special:* Texan. *Guest:* More than 80 appearances.

DRAKE, JOE

Executive. Drake spent early career as senior v.p. of international theatrical at Rysher Entertainment and also held positions at Moviestore Entertainment. He became president, Lionsgate International, and established the division as a premier supplier of theatrical feature films to the independent world. He oversaw worldwide sales and distribution of Lionsgate's international programming. He then founded and became CEO of Mandate Pictures, an independent entertainment company dedicated to the self-financing, development and production of filmed entertainment. The company, previously named Senator International, was launched in 2005 and focused on delivering broad-appeal films to studios and major independents worldwide. Upon the company's acquisition by Lionsgate, Drake returned to Lionsgate as co-COO and president of Lionsgate's motion picture group, with oversight of all areas of the company's theatrical production, distribution, marketing, acquisition and international theatrical operations. Recently, Drake greenlit Marc Forster's "Stranger Than Fiction" and launched the successful horror label Ghost House Pictures with Sam Raimi and Rob Tapert, which produced the $188 million box office worldwide hit "The Grudge" as well as its sequel "The Grudge 2" which opened # 1 in the US, along with other #1 box office titles including "Boogeyman" and "The Messengers" directed by Danny & Oxide Pang.

DRAZEN, LORI

Executive. Began career as asst. to dir. of adv. for Orion Pictures; creative dept. mgr., Kenyon & Eckhardt; gen. mgr., Seiniger Advertising; joined Warner Bros. in 1985 as v.p., world-wide adv. & pub. services. Spent two years at New Line Cinema as sr. v.p., creative marketing 1998-1999, before becoming head of marketing for Franchise Pictures in Feb. 2000. She then became pres. of worldwide marketing for Mobius/Franchise Pictures. She rejoined Warner Bros. Pictures, Inc. in March 2006 as a senior v.p., reporting to Dawn Tobin, pres. of domestic marketing.

DREYFUSS, RICHARD

Actor. b. Brooklyn, NY, Oct. 29, 1947. e. Beverly Hills H.S.; San Fernando Valley State Coll. 1965-67. Prof. career began at Gallery Theatre (L.A.) in "In Mama's House." Co-Exec. Prod. of film Quiz Show.
THEATRE: Journey to the Day, Incident at Vichy, People Need People, Enemy Line, Whose Little Boy Are You, But Seriously, Major Barbara, The Time of Your Life, The Hands of Its Enemy (L.A.), The Normal Heart, Death and the Maiden, others.
PICTURES: The Graduate, Valley of the Dolls, The Young Runaways, Hello Down There, Dillinger, American Graffiti (Golden Globe nom. 1974), The Second Coming of Suzanne, The Apprenticeship of Duddy Kravitz, Jaws, Inserts, Close Encounters of the Third Kind, The Goodbye Girl (Academy Award; Golden Globe Award 1978), The Big Fix (also co-prod.) The Competition, Whose Life Is It Anyway?, The Buddy System, Down and Out in Beverly Hills, Stand by Me, Tin Men, Stakeout, Nuts (Golden Globe nom. 1988), Moon Over Parador, Let It Ride, Always, Postcards from the Edge, Once Around, Rosencrantz and Guildenstern Are Dead, What About Bob?, Lost in Yonkers, Another Stakeout, Silent Fall, The Last Word, The American President, Mr. Holland's Opus (Academy Award nom.; Golden Globe nom. 1996), James and the Giant Peach, Night Falls on Manhattan, Mad Dog Time, The Call of the Wild (narr.), A Fine and Private Place, Krippendorf's Tribe, The Crew, The Old Man Who Read Love Stories, In Search of Peace (voice), Who Is Cletis Tout?, Manassas: End of Innocence, Johnstown Flood (documentary), Silver City, Poseidon, The Girls' Guide to Hunting & Fishing, Suburban Girl, W., My Life in Ruins, Leaves of Grass, The Lightkeepers (also exec. prod.), Lone Star Trixie, Piranha 3-D, Red.
TELEVISION: *Movies:* Two for the Money, Victory at Entebbe, Prisoner of Honor (also prod.), Lincoln (voice), The Universal Story, Frank Capra's American Dream, Oliver Twist, Lansky, Fail Safe, The Day Reagan Was Shot, Coast to Coast, Copshop (also exec. prod.), Happiness Isn't Everything. *Mini-series:* Tin Man. *Series:* Karen, The Education of Max Bickford. *Host:* American Chronicles. *Specials:* Funny You Don't Look 200 (host, co-prod., co-writer), R2-D2: Beneath the Dome, Mr. Dreyfuss Goes to Washington, TR: An American Lion (tv documentary, Theodore Roosevelt voice), Duel: Hamilton vs. Burr (doc., host, prod.). *Guest:* More than 152 appearances.

DRESCHER, FRAN

Actress. b. Queens, NY, Sept. 30, 1957. e. Queen's College.
THEATRE: *NY:* Some Girls. *Author:* Enter Whining, Cancer Schmancer.
PICTURES: Saturday Night Fever (debut), American Hot Wax, Gorp, The Hollywood Knights, Ragtime, Cadillac Man, Serious Money, UHF, This is Spinal Tap, The Big Picture, Car 54, Where Are You?, Jack, The Beautician and the Beast, Picking up the Pieces, Kid Quick, Santa's Slay, Shark Bait (voice).
TELEVISION: *Movies:* Stranger In Our House, Rock 'n' Roll Mom, Love & Betrayal, Wedding Band, Without Warning: Terror In the Towers. *Series:* Princesses, The Nanny (2 Emmy nom.; 2 Golden Globe nom., 1996,1997 also co-creator, writer. prod.), Good Morning Miami, La Niñera (writer), Moya prekrasnaya nyanya (writer only), La Nany (writer, creator), Niania (writer, creator), Living with Fran (also exec. prod.). *Guest:* More than 100 appearances.

DRIVER, MINNIE

Actress. r. n. Amelia Driver. b. England, Jan. 31, 1970. e. Bedales School, Petersfield, Hants.
PICTURES: Circle of Friends, GoldenEye, Baggage, Big Night, Sleepers, Grosse Pointe Blank, Good Will Hunting (Academy Award nom. 1998), Tarzan (voice), The Governess, Hard Rain, Slow Burn, An Ideal Husband, South Park: Bigger Longer and Uncut (voice), Return to Me, Beautiful, Slow Burn, The Upgrade, High Heels and Lowlifes, Owning Mahowny, Hope Springs, D.C. Smalls, Ella Enchanted, The Phantom of the Opera, The Virgin of Juarez, Ripple Effect (also exec. prod.), Take, Motherhood, Betty Anne Waters, Barney's Version.
TELEVISION: *Movies:* Merry Christmas George Bailey, That Sunday, Royal Celebration, Cruel Train, The Politician's Wife, Low Life. *Mini-series:* Mr. Wroe's Virgins. *Series:* God on the Rocks, My Good Friend, Will & Grace, Revisioned: Tomb Raider, The Riches (Emmy nom. 2007, Golden Globe nom. 2008), The Deep. *Guest:* More than 95 appearances.

DUBAND, WAYNE

Executive. b. Sydney, Australia, Feb. 13, 1947. Joined Warner Bros. 1969 as mgr. trainee in Australia. 1973, transferred to South Africa as mgr. dir.; 1977 gen. mgr. of CIC/Warner Bros. joint venture, also managing the CIC theatre operation there. 1980, named exec. asst. to Myron D. Karlin, pres. WB Int'l., in Burbank. 1981, mgr. dir. of Warner/Columbia joint venture in France. 1985, appt. v.p. of sales for WB Int'l. division. 1987, appt. senior v.p. for Warner Bros. Int'l. division. 1992, appt. pres. Int'l. Theatrical distribution, WB Int'l. Resigned 2000. Formed own consulting firm, Wayne Duband Consulting.

DUBOW, CRAIG A.

Executive. b. Oct. 26, 1954. e. graduate, Univ. of Texas-Austin. TV executive with 25 years experience with Gannett Co., Inc., a large diversified news and information company. Dubow joined Gannett in 1981 in advertising sales for KUSA-TV in Denver. He held various positions at KVUE-TV in Austin, TX, and was named pres. and gen. mgr. in 1990. In 1992, he became pres. and gen. mgr. of Gannett's NBC affiliate in Atlanta, WXIA-TV. Dubow was promoted and became Gannett Television's executive v.p. from 1996-2000. He was named pres. of Gannett Broadcasting in 2000, adding CEO to his title in 2001. In July 2005 he was named Gannett president and CEO. In July 2006 he added chairman to his title.

DUBUC, NANCY

Executive. b. Yonkers, NY. e. Boston University. Began her television career at the short-lived Christian Science Monitor Television as a desk assistant in 1991. By 1992, she was promoted to line producer, where she stayed until the operation folded in 1993. Production coordinator from 1993 to1995 at PBS owned WGBH-TV. Dubuc went to New York and the Discover Magazine television series as supervising producer from 1995 to1997, and then as series producer from 1997-1999. During this time, she was nominated for two Emmy awards. In 1999 through 2002, she moved to A&E Television Networks (AETN) as director of historical programming for The History Channel, and picked up another Emmy nomination for "Egypt: Beyond the Pyramids". From 2002 through 2004, Dubuc served as V.P., documentary program development at parent company A&E Network. Dubuc was named VP, non-fiction and alternative programming for A&E in 2004. In 2005 and 2006, she was named Sr. VP, non-fiction and alternative programming for A&E. Dubuc became Senior V.P., non-fiction programming and new media content for parent company AETN in 2006. Dubuc was promoted to President and General Manager of the History Channel in 2007. Under her watch, the History Channel has produced its six highest viewed series. Dubuc was promoted to President and General Manager of both Lifetime Networks and the History Channel in 2010.

DUCHOVNY, DAVID

Actor. b. New York, NY, Aug. 7, 1960. e. Yale. Was teaching asst. at Yale before landing first acting job in beer commercial. m. actress Tea Leoni.
PICTURES: Working Girl (debut, 1988), New Year's Day, Bad Influence, Julia Has Two Lovers, Don't Tell Mom the Babysitter's Dead, The Rapture, Ruby, Venice/Venice, Chaplin, Kalifornia, Playing God, The X Files: Fight the Future, Return to Me, Evolution, Zoolander, Full Frontal, My Dark Places: An L.A. Crime Memoir, Connie & Carla, House of D (also dir./writer), My Dark Places, Trust the Man, The TV Set, Things We Lost in the Fire, The X Files: I Want to Believe, The Joneses.
TELEVISION: *Movies:* Red Shoe Diaries, Red Shoe Diaries 2: Double Dare, Baby Snatcher, Red Shoe Diaries 3: Another Woman's Lipstick, Red Shoe Diaries 6: How I Met My Husband, Red Shoe Diaries 7: Burning Up, Red Shoe Diaries 8: Night of Abandon, The X-Files: The Truth. *Series:* Twin Peaks, The X Files (2 Emmy noms; Golden Globe Award, 1997, 3 other nom.), Eco-Challenge Fiji Islands (series documentary, narrator), Californication (also exec. prod., Golden Globe Award 2008, 2 other noms.). *Guest:* More than 100 appearances.

DUDLEY, ANNE

Composer. b. Chatham, Kent, England, May 7, 1956.
PICTURES: Hiding Out, Buster, The Misadventures of Mr. Wilt, The Mighty Quinn, Zwei Frauen, Say Anything..., The Pope Must Die, The Miracle, Knight Moves, The Crying Game, Felidae, When Saturday Comes, The Grotesque, Hollow Reed, The Full Monty (Academy Award, 1998), American History X, Pushing Tin, Monkeybone, Lucky Break, The Human Body, Tabloid, The Gathering, A Man Apart, Bright Young Things, Perfect Creature, Tristan & Isolde, Lake of Fire (doc.), Black Book, A Guide to Recognizing Your Saints (soundtrack writer), The Condemned, The Walker.
TELEVISION: *Movies:* Donovan Quick, The Miracle Maker, The Key, Whatever Love Means, Trial & Retribution XVII: The Rules of the Game, Trial & Retribution XVI: Conviction. Trial & Retribution XVIII: Kill the King, Trial & Retribution XV: The Box, Trial & Retribution XIX: Tracks, Commander, The: Abduction, Bill Bailey's Remarkable Guide to the Orchestra (musical dir.). *Mini-*

series: Trial & Retribution XX: Sirens. *Series:* Jeeves and Wooster, Ngaio Marsh's Alleyn Mysteries, Anna Lee, The 10th Kingdom.

DUDIKOFF, MICHAEL
Actor. b. Torrance, CA, Oct. 8, 1954.
PICTURES: Making Love, I Ought to Be in Pictures, Tron, Bachelor Party, Bloody Birthday, American Ninja, Radioactive Dreams, Avenging Force, American Ninja II: The Confrontation, Platoon Leader, River of Death, American Ninja 4: The Annihilation, Midnight Ride, Human Shield, Rescue Me, Virtual Assassin, Shooter, Executive Command, Bounty Hunters II, Crash Dive, Moving Target, Soldier Boyz, Cyberjack, Chain of Command, Strategic Command, In Her Defense, Freedom Strike, Ringmaster, Muketeers Forever, The Silencer, Ablaze, Stranded, Quicksand.
TELEVISION: *Movie:* The Woman Who Sinned. *Mini-series:* North and South Book II. *Series:* Star of the Family, Cobra. *Pilot:* Sawyer and Finn.

DUFF, HILARY
Actress. b. Houston, TX, Sept. 28, 1987.
PICTURES: Human Nature, Agent Cody Banks, The Lizzie McGuire Movie (also singer), Cheaper by the Dozen, A Cinderella Story (also singer), Raise Your Voice, The Perfect Man, Material Girls, Cheaper by the Dozen 2, Foodfight! (voice), Material Girls, Brand Hauser: Stuff Happens, Greta, (also exec. prod.), Foodfight! (voice), Stay Cool, Provinces of Night. *As Singer:* The Santa Clause 2: The Mrs. Clause, Material Girls, Her Best Move, Safety Glass, War, Inc.
TELEVISION: *Movies:* The Soul Collector, Cadet Kelly, Beauty & the Briefcase. *Series:* Lizzie McGuire, Gossip Girl. *Guest:* More than 130 appearances.

DUGAN, DENNIS
Actor, Director. b. Wheaton, IL, Sept. 5, 1946. Studied acting at Goodman Theatre School.
THEATRE: NY: A Man's Man, The House of Blue Leaves. LA: Once in a Lifetime, Rainbows for Sales, Estonia, The Dining Room, The Kitchen.
PICTURES: Night Call Nurses, The Day of the Locust, Night Moves, Smile, Harry and Walter Go to New York, Norman ... Is That You?, Unidentified Flying Oddball, The Howling, Water, Can't Buy Me Love, She's Having a Baby, The New Adventures of Pippi Longstocking, Parenthood, Problem Child (also dir.), Brain Donors (also dir.), Happy Gilmore (also dir.), Beverly Hills Ninja (dir. only), Big Daddy (also dir.), Saving Silverman, National Security (dir. only), The Benchwarmers (also dir.), I Now Pronounce You Chuck and Larry (also dir.), You Don't Mess with the Zohan (also dir.), Grown Ups (dir.), Just Go with It (dir.).
TELEVISION: *Movies:* Death Race, The Girl Most Likely To..., Last of the Good Guys, Country Gold, The Toughest Man in the World, Columbo: Butterfly in Shades of Grey, Karroll's Christmas (also dir.). *Mini-series:* Rich Man Poor Man. *Series:* Richie Brockelman: Private Eye, Empire, Moonlighting, Shadow Chasers. *Pilots:* Alice, Father O Father, Did You Hear About Josh and Kelly?, Full House, Channel 99. *Director:* Hunter, Sonny Spoon, Moonlighting, The Shaggy Dog (movie), L.A. Law, Wiseguy, Columbo, Picket Fences, NYPD Blue, The Byrds of Paradise, Traps, Chicago Hope, Ally McBeal, Shasta McNasty.

DUIGAN, JOHN
Director, Writer. b. Hartley Wintney, Hampshire, England, June 19, 1949. Lived in England and Malaysia before moving to Sydney, Australia. e. Univ. of Melbourne, philosophy, M.A. Taught for several years at Univ. of Melbourne and Latrobe U. before entering films. Directed and wrote experimental short, The Firm Man (1974). *Novels:* Badge, Players, Room to Move.
PICTURES: *Dir.-Writer:* Trespassers, Mouth to Mouth, Winter of Our Dreams (Australian Writers Guild Award), Far East, The Year My Voice Broke (Australian Acad. Award for best dir., s.p.) Romero (dir. only), Flirting, Wide Sargasso Sea, Sirens (also actor), The Journey of August King, The Leading Man, Lawn Dogs, Molly, Paranoid, The Parole Officer, Head in the Clouds.
TELEVISION: *Movies:* Room to Move, Fragments of War: The Story of Damien Parer. *Mini-series:* Vietnam (co-dir.), The Dirtwater Dynasty. *Series:* Three of a Kind (writer).

DUKAKIS, OLYMPIA
Actress. b. Lowell, MA, June 20, 1931. m. actor Louis Zorich. e. Boston U., B.A., M.F.A. Founding mem. of The Charles Playhouse, Boston, establishing summer theatre 1957-60. Taught acting at NYU: 1967-70 as instructor, 1974-83 as master teacher, and at Yale U. 1976. With husband conceived and guided artistic dev. of Whole Theatre of Monclair, NJ, 1977-90; producing artistic dir. Adapted plays for her co. and dir. theater there; also at Williamstown Theatre Fest. and Delaware Summer Fest. Appeared in more than 100 plays on B'way, Off-B'way and in regional and summer theatre.
THEATRE: Who's Who in Hell, The Aspern Papers, Night of the Iguana, The Breaking Wall, Curse of the Starving Class, Snow Orchid, The Marriage of Bette and Boo (Obie Award), Social Security.
PICTURES: Lilith, Twice a Man, John and Mary, Made for Each Other, Death Wish, Rich Kids, The Wanderers, The Idolmaker, National Lampoon Goes to the Movies, Flanagan, Moonstruck (Academy Award, best supporting actress; Golden Globe Award 1988), Working Girl, Look Who's Talking, Steel Magnolias, Dad, In the Spirit, Look Who's Talking Too, The Cemetery Club, Over the Hill, Look Who's Talking Now, Naked Gun 33 1/3: The Final Insult (cameo), I Love Trouble, Jeffrey, Mighty Aphrodite, Mr. Holland's Opus, Picture Perfect, Never Too Late, Milk and Money, Better Living, Jane Austen's Mafia, Brooklyn Sonnet, A Life for a Life, Climb Against the Odds, The Papp Project, The Event, Charlie's War, Jesus-Mary & Joey, The Great New Wonderful, The Thing About My Folks, A Confederacy of Dunces, 3 Needles, Intervention, Day on Fire, Away from Her, In the Land of Women, Poor Things, Montana Amazon (also exec. prod.), Cloudburst.
TELEVISION: *Movies:* Nicky's World, The Neighborhood, FDR-The Last Year, King of America, Lucky Day (Emmy nom. 1991), Fire in the Dark, Sinatra (Golden Globe nom. 1993), Young at Heart, A Match Made in Heaven, Scattering Heaven, The Pentagon Wars, Crimes of Honour, The Last of the Blonde Bombshells, And Never Let Her Go, Ladies and the Champ, My Beautiful Son, Babycakes, Strange Relations, Mafia Doctor, The Librarian: Quest for the Spear, The Librarian 2: Return to King Solomon's Mines. *Mini-series:* More Tales of the City (Emmy nom. 1998), More Tales of the City, Joan of Arc (Emmy nom. 1999), Further Tales of the City, Guilty Hearts. *Series:* Search for Tomorrow, One of the Boys, Center of the Universe. *Specials/Documentaries:* The Rehearsal, Sisters, Last Act is a Solo, A Century of Women, A Paralyzing Fear: The Story of Polio in America, The Papp Project, The Armenians: A Story of Survival. *Guest:* More than 71 appearances.

DUKE, BILL
Actor, Director. b. Poughkeepsie, NY, Feb. 26, 1943. e. Boston Univ., NY Univ. Sch. of the Arts. Recieved AFI Best Young Director Award for short The Hero (Gold Award, Houston Film Festival). Has written poetry, short stories for children. Member bd. of dirs. American Film Institute.
PICTURES: *Actor:* Car Wash, American Gigolo, Commando, Predator, No Man's Land, Action Jackson, Bird on a Wire, Street of No Return, Menace II Society, Payback, Foolish, The Limey, Fever, Never Again, Exit Wounds, Red Dragon, National Security, The Blackout Murders, Get Rich or Die Tryin', X-Men: The Last Stand, The Go-Getter, Acts of Charity, The Big Bang. *Director:* A Rage in Harlem, Deep Cover, The Cemetery Club, Sister Act 2: Back in the Habit, America's Dream, Hoodlum (also exec. prod.), Cover (also prod.), Prince Among Slaves (doc.), Not Easily Broken.
TELEVISION: *Actor/Movies:* Love is Not Enough, Sgt. Matlovich Vs. the U.S. Air Force, Who Killed Atlanta's Children?, Dallas: The Early Years, Always Outnumbered. *Director/Mini-series:* Miracle's Boys, Rescue at Pine Ridge. *Series:* Palmerstown U.S.A, Karen Sisco. *Director/Series:* Knots Landing, A Man Called Hawk, Cagney & Lacey, Hill Street Blues, Fame, Falcon Crest, Emerald Point N.A.S., Miami Vice, Dallas, Hell Town, Spenser: For Hire, Crime Story, Starman, Matlock, Tour of Duty, Gideon Oliver, The Outsiders, Fastlane, 1-800-Missing. *Dir. Movies:* The Killing Floor, Johnnie Mae Gibson: FBI, A Raisin in the Sun, The Golden Spiders: A Nero Wolfe Mystery, America's Dream, Deacons for Defense. *Guest:* More than 87 appearances.

DUKE, PATTY
Actress. r.n. Anna Marie Duke. b. New York, NY, Dec. 14, 1946. e. Quintano Sch. for Young Professionals. Mother of actors Sean and Mackenzie Astin. Pres., Screen Actors Guild, 1985-88. *Author:* Surviving Sexual Assault (1983), Call Me Anna (1987).
THEATRE: The Miracle Worker (Theatre World Award), Isle of Children, Oklahoma!. *CA:* Follies.
PICTURES: I'll Cry Tomorrow (debut as extra 1955), The Goddess, Happy Anniversary, The 4-D Man, The Miracle Worker (Academy Award, best supporting actress; Golden Globe nom and Award 1963), Billie, Valley of the Dolls, Me Natalie (Golden Globe Award 1970), The Swarm, By Design, Something Special, Prelude to a Kiss, Harvest of Fire, Kimberly, Caught in the Act, Bigger Than the Sky, The Four Children of Tander Welch.
TELEVISION: *Movies:* My Sweet Charlie (Emmy Award, 1970), Two on a Bench, If Tomorrow Comes, She Waits, Deadly Harvest, Nightmare, Look What's Happened to Rosemary's Baby, Fire!, Rosetti & Ryan: Men Who Love Women, Curse of the Black Widow, Killer on Board, The Storyteller, Having Babies III (Emmy nom. 1978), A Family Upside Down (Emmy nom. 1978), Women in White, Hanging by a Thread, Before and After, The Miracle Worker (Academy Award; Emmy Award, 1980), The Women's Room (Emmy nom. 1981), Mom The Wolfman and Me, The Babysitter, Violation of Sarah McDavid, Something So Right, September Gun, Best Kept Secrets, Fight for Life, Perry Mason: The Case of the Avenging Angel, A Time to Triumph, Fatal Judgment, Everybody's Baby: The Rescue of Jessica McClure, Amityville: The Evil Escapes, Call Me Anna, Always Remember I Love You, Absolute Strangers, Last Wish, Grave Secrets: The Legacy of Hilltop Drive, A Killer Among Friends, Family of Strangers, No Child of Mine, A Matter of Justice, One Woman's Courage, Cries From the Heart, When the Vows Break, Race Against Time: The Search for Sarah, The Disappearing Act, A Christmas Memory, When He Didn't Come Home, A Season for Miracle, Miracle on the Mountain: The Kincaid Family Story, Love

Lessons, Little John, Murder Without Conviction, Falling in Love with the Girl Next Door, Throwing Stones, Love Finds a Home. *Mini-series:* Captains and the Kings (Emmy Award, 1977), George Washington (Emmy nom. 1984). *Series:* The Brighter Day, The Patty Duke Show (Golden Globe nom. 1966; Emmy nom. 1964), It Takes Two, Hail to the Chief, Karen's Song, Amazing Grace. *Specials:* The Prince and the Pauper, Wuthering Heights, Swiss Family Robinson, Meet Me in St. Louis, The Power and the Glory, The Girl on the Edge of Town (Emmy nom. 1981). *Guest:* More than 183 appearances.

DULLEA, KEIR

Actor. b. Cleveland, OH, May 30, 1936. e. Rutgers Univ., San Francisco State Coll., Sanford Meisner's Neighborhood Playhouse. Acted as resident juvenile at the Totem Pole Playhouse in PA. NY theatre debut in the revue Sticks and Stones, 1956; appeared in stock co. prods. at the Berkshire Playhouse and Philadelphia's Hedgerow Theatre, 1959; off-Broadway debut in Season of Choice, 1969. Won San Francisco Film Festival Award for performance in film David and Lisa, 1963.
THEATRE: Dr. Cook's Garden, Butterflies Are Free, Cat on a Hot Tin Roof, P.S. Your Cat is Dead, The Other Side of Paradise.
PICTURES: The Hoodlum Priest (debut, 1961), David and Lisa (Golden Globe Award 1963), The Thin Red Line, Mail Order Bride, The Naked Hours, Bunny Lake Is Missing, Madame X, The Fox, 2001: A Space Odyssey, De Sade, Pope Joan, Paperback Hero, Il Diavolo nel Cervello, Paul and Michelle, Black Christmas (Silent Night Evil Night), Leopard in the Snow, Welcome to Blood City, The Haunting of Julia (Full Circle), Because He's My Friend, The Next One, Brainwaves, Blind Date, 2010, Oh What a Night, The Divine Inspiration, 3 Days of Rain, Stanley Kubrick: A Life in Pictures, Alien Hunter, Fortune, The Good Shepherd, The Accidental Husband, All Me, All the Time.
TELEVISION: *Movies:* Black Water Gold, Law and Order, Legend of the Golden Gun, Brave New World, The Hostage Tower, No Place to Hide, The Audrey Hepburn Story, Songs in Ordinary Time. *Series:* The United States Steel Hour, Alcoa Premiere, The Starlost. *Special:* Mrs. Miniver. *Guest:* More than 64 appearances.

DUNAWAY, FAYE

Actress. b. Bascom, FL, Jan. 14, 1941. e. Texas, Arkansas, Utah, Germany, U. of Florida. Awarded a Fulbright scholarship in theatre. Boston U. of Fine Applied Arts. With Lincoln Center Rep. Co. for 3 years. NY Stage: A Man for All Seasons, After the Fall, Hogan's Goat (Theatre World Award), The Curse of an Aching Heart.
PICTURES: Hurry Sundown (debut, Golden Globe nom. 1968), The Happening, Bonnie and Clyde (Academy Award nom.; Golden Globe nom. 1968), The Thomas Crown Affair, The Extraordinary Seaman, A Place for Lovers, The Arrangement, Puzzle of a Downfall Child (Golden Globe nom. 1971), Little Big Man, The Deadly Trap, Doc, Oklahoma Crude, The Three Musketeers, Chinatown (Academy Award nom.; Golden Globe nom. 1975), The Towering Inferno, The Four Musketeers, Three Days of the Condor (Golden Globe nom. 1976), Network (Academy Award, Golden Globe Award 1977), Voyage of the Damned, Eyes of Laura Mars, The Champ, The First Deadly Sin, Mommie Dearest, The Wicked Lady, Ordeal by Innocence, Supergirl, Barfly (Golden Globe nom. 1988), Midnight Crossing, Burning Secret, The Handmaid's Tale, Wait Until Spring Bandini, The Gamble, On a Moonlit Night, Scorchers, Double Edge, The Temp, Arizona Dream, Don Juan DeMarco, Drunks, Dunston Checks In, Albino Alligator, The Chamber, The Yards, The Thomas Crown Affair, The Messenger: The Story of Joan of Arc, Stanley's Gig, The Yards, Festival in Cannes, The Calling, Yellow Bird, Colored Eggs, The Rules of Attraction, Mid-Century, The Calling, El Padrino, Blind Horizon, The Last Goodbye, Kill Switch, Jennifer's Shadow, Last Goodbye, Love Hollywood Style, Ghosts Never Sleep, Say It in Russian, Cougar Club, Rain, The Gene Generation, Flick, The Seduction of Dr. Fugazzi, Master Class (prod., dir., s.p.).
TELEVISION: *Movies:* The Woman I Love, The Disappearance of Aimee, Evita, Peron, 13 at Dinner, Beverly Hills Madam, The Country Girl, Casanova, The Raspberry Ripple, Cold Sassy Tree, Silhouette, Columbo: It's All in the Game (Emmy nom. 1994), A Family Divided, Rebecca, Gia (Golden Globe Award 1999), Running Mates (Golden Globe nom. 2001), The Biographer, Back When We Were Grownups, Anonymous Rex, Pandemic, Midnight Bayou. *Mini-series:* Ellis Island (Golden Globe Award 1985), Christopher Columbus, A Will of Their Own, Pandemic. *Specials:* Hogan's Goat, After the Fall, Supergirl: The Making of the Movie (host), Inside the Dream Factory (host). *Series:* It Had to Be You. *Guest:* More than 113 appearances.

DUNCAN, LINDSAY

Actress. b. Edinburgh, Scotland, November 7, 1950. Stage actress with National Theatre, Royal Shakespeare Company.
THEATRE: Plenty, The Provok'd Wife, The Prince of Homburg, Top Girls, Progress, The Merry Wives of Windsor, Les Liaisons Dangereuses (RSC, West End, Broadway; Theatre World Award), Cat On A Hot Tin Roof, Hedda Gabler, A Midsummer Night's Dream, Cryptogram.
PICTURES: Loose Connections, Samson & Delilah, Prick Up Your Ears, Manifesto, The Reflecting Skin, Body Parts, City Hall, A Midsummer Night's Dream, An Ideal Husband, Mansfield Park, Letters to a Street Child, Under the Tuscan Sun, AfterLife, The Queen of Shebas Pearls, Starter for Ten, Burlesque Fairytales, Alice in Wonderland.
TELEVISION: *Movies:* Reilly, Ace of Spies, A Year in Provence, The Rector's Wife, Shooting the Past, Dirty Tricks, Perfect Strangers, Witness of Truth: The Railway Murders, Hamilton Mattress (voice), Longford, Frankenstein, Margaret, Margot, Marple: The Mirror Crack'd from Side to Side. *Mini-series:* Dead Head, Traffik, A Year in Provence, G.B.H., Jake's Progress, The History of Tom Jones A Foundling, Oliver Twist, Lost in Austen, The Sinking of the Laconia. *Series:* Rome. *Guest:* More than 60 appearances.

DUNCAN, MICHAEL CLARKE

Actor. b. Chicago, IL, December 10, 1957. Worked as a body-guard in Hollywood while taking bit parts.
PICTURES: Back in Business, A Night at the Roxbury, Caught Up, The Players Club, Bulworth, Armageddon, The Green Mile (Academy Award nom.; Golden Globe nom. 2000), The Underground Comedy Movie, The Whole Nine Yards, See Spot Run, The Immigrant Garden, Cats & Dogs (voice), Planet of the Apes, Hollywood Digital Diaries, The Scorpion King, Daredevil, George and the Dragon, Brother Bear (voice), Dinotopia: Curse of the Ruby Sunstone (voice), Delgo (voice), D.E.B.S, Pursued, Dinotopia: Curse of the Ruby Sunstone, Racing Stripes (voice), Delgo (voice), The Island, American Crude, Sin City, One Way, Talladega Nights: The Ballad of Ricky Bobby, Brother Bear 2 (voice), School for Scoundrels, Slipstream Dream, The Last Mimzy, Sin City 2, Transformers, One Way, Welcome Home, Roscoe Jenkins, Kung Fu Panda (voice), The Slammin' Salmon, Street Fighter: The Legend of Chun-Li, Criminal Empire for Dummy's, Black, White and Blues (also co-prod.), Cats & Dogs: The Revenge of Kitty Galore (voice).
TELEVISION: *Movies:* They Call Me Sirr, Kim Possible: A Sitch in Time (voice), Crash Nebula (voice). *Series:* The Bold and the Beautiful, Skwids, Loonatics Unleashed (voice). *Guest:* More than 103 appearances.

DUNCAN, SANDY

Actress. b. Henderson, TX, Feb. 20, 1946. m. singer-dancer Don Correia. e. Len Morris Coll.
THEATRE: The Music Man (NY debut, 1965); The Boyfriend, Ceremony of Innocence (Theatre World Award), Your Own Thing, Canterbury Tales, Peter Pan, Five Six Seven Eight Dance!, My One and Only, The Fourth Wall.
PICTURES: The Million Dollar Duck (Golden Globe nom. 1972), Star Spangled Girl (Golden Globe nom. 1972), The Cat from Outer Space, Rock a Doodle (voice), The Swan Princess (voice), Never Again.
TELEVISION: *Movies:* My Boyfriend's Back, Miracle on Interstate 880. *Mini-series:* Roots (Emmy nom. 1977). *Series:* Funny Face (Emmy nom. 1972), The Sandy Duncan Show, Valerie's Family, Ka-Ching! (host, writer, exec. prod.). *Specials:* Pinocchio, Sandy in Disneyland, The Sandy Duncan Special. *Guest:* More than 78 appearances.

DUNN, GREGORY W.

Executive. From 1991-1995, Dunn was v.p., marketing and concessions of Regal Cinemas, Inc. From 1995-2005 served as executive v.p. and COO. In May 2005 promoted to president and COO and is the position he holds today. Regal Entertainment Group (NYSE: RGC), headquartered in Knoxville, TN, is the largest motion picture exhibitor in the United States with its circuit comprised of Regal Cinemas, United Artists Theatres and Edwards Theatres. It operates 6,778 screens in 549 locations in 39 states and the District of Columbia.

DUNN, KEVIN

Actor. b. Chicago, IL, August 24, 1956.
PICTURES: Mississippi Burning, Ghostbusters II (uncredited), Taken Away, Marked for Death, Blue Steel, The Bonfire of the Vanities, Hot Shots!, Only the Lonely, Chaplin, 1492: Conquest of Paradise, Dave, Little Big League, Mad Love, Nixon, Commandments, Chain Reaction, Edwards and Hunt, The Sixth Man, Picture Perfect, Almost Heroes, Godzilla, Snake Eyes, Small Soldiers, Stir of Echoes, Out for a Kill, I Heart Huckabee's, Live Free or Die, Gridiron Gang, The Black Dahlia, All the King's Men, Gridiron Gang, Transformers, Lions for Lambs, Vicky Cristina Barcelona, Transformers: Revenge of the Fallen, Mistaken Identity, You May Not Kiss the Bride, Warrior, Unstoppable.
TELEVISION: *Movies:* Night of Courage, Blind Faith, Double Edge, Shadow of a Doubt, The Four Diamonds, Unforgivable, The Second Civil War, On the Edge of Innocence, Beach Boys: An American Family, LA County 187, NTSB: The Crash of Flight 323, Gleason, Ann Rule Presents: The Stranger Beside Me, The Path to 9/11. *Series:* Jack & Mike, Arsenio, Bette, Samantha Who?. *Guest:* More than 66 appearances.

DUNNE, GRIFFIN

Actor, Producer, Director. b. New York, NY, June 8, 1955. Son of prod.-writer Dominick Dunne. Formed Double Play Prods. with Amy Robinson. Studied at Neighborhood Playhouse and with Uta Hagen. On Stage in Album, Marie and Bruce, Coming Attractions, Hotel Play, Search and Destroy (B'way debut; Theatre World Award).
PICTURES: *Actor:* The Other Side of the Mountain (debut,

1975), Chilly Scenes of Winter (also prod.), The Fan, American Werewolf in London, Cold Feet, Almost You, Johnny Dangerously, After Hours (also co-prod., Golden Globe nom. 1986), Who's That Girl, Amazon Women on the Moon, Big Blue, Me and Him, Once Around (also co-prod.), My Girl, Straight Talk, Big Girls Don't Cry... They Get Even, The Pickle, Naked in New York, Quiz Show, I Like It Like That, Search and Destroy, Famous, Perfume, Pinero, 40 Days and 40 Nights, Cheats, Snow Angels, Broken English, The Great Buck Howard, Shrink, Last Night. *Producer only:* Baby It's You, Running on Empty, White Palace, Once Around, Joe's Apartment (exec.), Fierce People (also dir.). *Director/Writer:* Duke of Groove (short, Academy Award nom. 1996), Addicted to Love, Practical Magic, Famous, Nailed Right In, Fierce People (dir./prod.), The Accidental Husband (dir. only).
TELEVISION: *Movies:* The Wall, Secret Weapon, The Android Affair, Love Matters (Ace nom.), Partners, The Android Affair, Sounds From a Town I Love, Warning: Parental Advisory. *Specials:* Lip Service, Trying Times: Hunger Chic, Partners. Pilot: Graham. *Series:* Hotel Room, Trust Me. *Guest:* More than 55 appearances.

DUNST, KIRSTEN

Actress. b. Point Pleasant, NJ, April 30, 1982.
PICTURES: New York Stories, The Bonfire of the Vanities, Little Women, High Strung, Greedy, Interview with the Vampire: The Vampire Chronicles (Golden Globe nom. 1995), Jumanji, Mother Night, Anastasia (voice), Wag the Dog, Strike, Small Soldiers, The Virgin Suicides, Drop Dead Gorgeous, Dick, The Crow: Salvation, Luckytown Blues, Bring It On, Deeply, All Forgotten, Get Over It, Crazy/Beautiful, The Cat's Meow, Spider Man, Levity, Kaena: The Prophecy (voice), Eternal Sunshine of the Spotless Mind, Mona Lisa Smile, Spider Man 2, Wimbledon, Elizabethtown, Marie-Antoinette, Spider-Man 3, How to Lose Friends & Alienate People, All Good Things, Upside Down.
TELEVISION: *Movies:* Darkness Before Dawn, Children Remember the Holocaust (voice), Ruby Ridge: An American Tragedy, Tower of Terror, Fifteen and Pregnant, The Animated Adventures of Tom Sawyer (voice), Devil's Arithmetic, The Mummy Parody, The Death and Life of Nancy Eaton. *Series:* Stories from My Childhood. *Guest:* More than 92 appearances.

DURNING, CHARLES

Actor. b. Highland Falls, NY, Feb. 28, 1923. e. NYU. Studied acting on the G.I. Bill. Prof. stage debut, 1960. Made several appearances with Joseph Papp's NY Shakespeare Festival. 2008 received Screen Actors Guild Award for Life Achievement Award.
THEATRE: That Championship Season, Knock Knock, Au Pair Man, In the Boom Boom Room, The Happy Time, Indians, Cat on a Hot Tin Roof (Tony Award, 1990), The Tempest, Queen of the Stardust Ballroom, Inherit the Wind, The Gin Game, Glengarry Glen Ross.
PICTURES: Harvey Middleman—Fireman (debut, 1965), I Walk the Line, Hi Mom!, The Pursuit of Happiness, Dealing: or the Berkeley-to- Boston Forty-Brick Lost-Bag Blues, Deadhead Miles, Sisters, The Sting, The Front Page, Dog Day Afternoon (Golden Globe nom.1976), The Hindenburg, Breakheart Pass, Harry and Walter Go to New York, Twilight's Last Gleaming, The Choirboys, An Enemy of the People, The Fury, The Greek Tycoon, Tilt, The Muppet Movie, North Dallas Forty, Starting Over, When a Stranger Calls, Die Laughing, The Final Countdown, True Confessions, Sharky's Machine, The Best Little Whorehouse in Texas (Acad. Award nom. 1983), Tootsie, To Be or Not to Be (Academy Award nom.; Golden Globe nom. 1984), Two of a Kind, Hadley's Rebellion, Mass Appeal, Stick, The Man With One Red Shoe, Stand Alone, Big Trouble, Tough Guys, Where the River Runs Black, Solarbabies, Happy New Year, The Rosary Murders, A Tiger's Tail, Cop, Far North, Cat Chaser, Dick Tracy, V. I. Warshawski, Brenda Starr, Etolie, Fatal Sky, The Music of Chance, The Hudsucker Proxy, I.Q., Home for the Holidays, The Last Supper, The Grass Harp, Spy Hard, One Fine Day, Shelter, Secret Life of Algernon, Justice, Jerry & Tom, Hi-Life, Hunt for the Devil, O Brother Where Art Thou, Very Mean Men, The Last Producer, State and Main, Never Look Back, Lakeboat, Turn of Faith, LAPD: To Protect & to Serve, Mother Ghost, The Naked Run (short), The Last Man Club, One Last Ride, Death and Texas, Jesus-Mary-and-Joey, Duplicity, Forget About It, Murder on the Hudson, Unbeatable Harold, Resurrection: The J.R. Richard Story, Molding Clay, The Book of Joe, Dirty Deeds, Deal, Local Color, Forget About It, The Golden Boys, The Waiter, Good Dick, Polycarp, Deal, iMurders, Break, The Drum Beats Twice, A Bunch of Amateurs, Shannon's Rainbow, Three Chris's, The Waiter, An Affirmative Act.
TELEVISION: *Movies:* The Connection, The Trial of Chaplain Jensen, Queen of the Stardust Ballroom (Emmy nom. 1975), Switch, Special Olympics, Attica (Emmy nom. 1980), Perfect Match, Crisis at Central High, The Best Little Girl in the World, Dark Night of the Scarecrow, Death of a Salesman (Emmy nom. 1986), Kenny Rogers as The Gambler III—The Legend Continues, The Man Who Broke 1000 Chains, Case Closed, Unholy Matrimony, Prime Target, It Nearly Wasn't Christmas, Dinner at Eight, The Return of Eliot Ness, The Story Lady, The Water Engine, Roommates, Mrs. Santa Claus, Hard Time: Hostage Hotel, The Judge, Bleacher Bums, Mr. St. Nick, A Boyfriend for Christmas, A Very Married Christmas, Detective, Desperation. *Mini-series:* Captains and the Kings (Emmy nom.; Golden Globe nom. 1977), Studs Lonigan, The Kennedys of Massachusetts (Golden Globe Award 1991), A Woman of Independent Means, Jazz, The Detective, Desperation. *Series:* Another World (1972), The Cop and the Kid, Eye to Eye, Evening Shade (2 Emmy noms. 1991, 1992), Chicken Soup for the Soul, First Monday, First Monday, Rescue Me (Emmy nom. 2008), Family Guy. *Specials/Documentaries:* The American Revolution, Not for Ourselves Alone: The Story of Elizabeth Cady Stanton & Susan B. Anthony, The Rivalry, The Dancing Bear, Working, Mr. Roberts, Side by Side (pilot), P.O.P. (pilot), Eye to Eye, Tales from Hollywood, Normandy (narr.), Texan, Leslie's Folly. Broadway: The Golden Age, by the Legends Who Were There. *Guest:* More than 130 appearances.

DUTTON, CHARLES S.

Actor. b. Baltimore, MD, Jan. 30, 1951. e. Towson St., Yale Sch. of Drama.
THEATRE: Yale Rep: The Works, Beef No Chicken, Astopovo, Othello. NY: Ma Rainey's Black Bottom (Theatre World Award, 1983), Joe Turner's Come and Gone, The Piano Lesson.
PICTURES: No Mercy, Crocodile Dundee II, Jacknife, An Unremarkable Life, Q & A, Mississippi Masala, Alien3, The Distinguished Gentleman, Menace II Society, Rudy, Foreign Student, A Low Down Dirty Shame, Cry the Beloved Country, Nick of Time, Last Dance, A Time to Kill, Get on the Bus, Mimic, Blind Faith, Black Dog, Cookie's Fortune, Random Hearts, D-tox, Against the Ropes, Gothika, Secret Window, The L.A. Riot Spectacular, The Third Nail, Honeydripper, The Express, Fame, Legion, The Gift, The Obama Effect (also dir., writer).
TELEVISION: *Movies:* Apology, The Murder of Mary Phagan, Jack Reed: Search for Justice, The Piano Lesson (Golden Globe nom.; Emmy nom. 1995), Zooman, Aftershock: Earthquake in New York City, The Corner (Emmy Award; best dir.), Deadlocked, For Love or Country: The Arturo Sandoval Story, 10,000 Black Men Named George, Conviction, D.C. Sniper: 23 Days of Fear, Something the Lord Made, Mayday, Sleeper Cell: Home (dir. only, DGA nom. 2007), Racing for Time (also dir.), Under (dir. only). *Mini-series:* The '60s. *Series:* Roc (also prod.), The L Word, Threshold. *Guest:* More than 87 appearances.

DUVAL, JAMES

Actor. b. Detroit, MI, Sept. 10, 1973.
PICTURES: Totally F***ed Up, An Ambush of Ghosts, Mod F**k Explosion, The Doom Generation, Independence Day, River Made to Drown In, Nowhere, The Clown at Midnight, S.L.C. Punk!, How to Make the Cruelest Month, Go, The Weekend, Gone in Sixty Seconds, Donnie Darko, The Doe Boy, A Galaxy Far Away, Amerikana Comic Book Villains, May, Pledge of Allegiance, Open House, Frog-g-g, Venice Underground, Mad Cowgirl, Chasing Ghosts, Work, The Pacific and Eddy, Beyond Legend: Johnny Kakota, Toxic, The Art of Travel, The Black Waters of Echo's Pond, Cornered!, Now Here, Not Another Not Another Movie, Caller ID, 2 Dudes and a Dream, Everything Will Happen Before You Die, Noirland (also assoc. prod.), Mondo Holocausto!, Look at Me, Kaboom, Naked Angel, Sushi Girl.
TELEVISION: *Movie:* This is How the World Ends.

DUVALL, ROBERT

Actor. b. San Diego, CA, Jan. 5, 1931. e. Principia College, IL. Studied at the Neighborhood Playhouse, NY. Received American Society of Cinematographers, President's Award, 1997.
THEATRE: *Off-B'way:* The Days and Nights of Bee Bee Fenstermaker, Call Me By My Rightful Name, A View From the Bridge (Obie Award, 1965). B'way: Wait Until Dark, American Buffalo.
PICTURES: To Kill a Mockingbird (debut, 1962), Captain Newman M.D., Nightmare in the Sun, The Chase, Countdown, The Detective, Bullitt, True Grit, The Rain People, M*A*S*H, The Revolutionary, THX-1138, Lawman, The Godfather (Academy Award nom. 1973), Tomorrow, The Great Northfield Minnesota Raid, Joe Kidd, Lady Ice, Badge 373, The Outfit, The Conversation, The Godfather Part II, Breakout, The Killer Elite, The Seven Percent Solution, Network, We're Not the Jet Set (dir., co-prod. only), The Eagle Has Landed, The Greatest, The Betsy, Invasion of the Body Snatchers (cameo), Apocalypse Now (Academy Award nom.; Golden Globe Award 1980), The Great Santini (Academy Award nom. 1981), True Confessions, The Pursuit of D.B. Cooper, Tender Mercies (Academy Award; Golden Globe Award 1984; also co-prod, songwriter), Angelo My Love (dir., prod., s.p. only), The Stone Boy, The Natural, Bellizaire the Cajun (cameo; also creative consultant), The Lightship, Let's Get Harry, Hotel Colonial, Colors, The Handmaid's Tale, A Show of Force, Days of Thunder, Rambling Rose, Convicts, Newsies, Falling Down, The Plague, Geronimo: An American Legend, Wrestling Ernest Hemingway, The Paper, Something to Talk About, The Stars Fell on Henrietta, The Scarlet Letter, A Family Thing (also co-prod.), Sling Blade, Phenomenon, The Apostle (also s.p., dir., exec. prod., Academy Award nom.; Chicago Film Crits. Award, LA Film Crits. Award, Best Actor, 1998), Deep Impact, The Gingerbread Man, A Civil Action (Academy Award nom.; Golden Globe nom. 1999), Gone in Sixty Seconds, A Shot At Glory (also prod.), The 6th Day, John Q, Gods and Generals, Assassination Tango, Open Range, Secondhand Lions, The Lost City, Kicking & Screaming, A Night in Old Mexico, Thank You for Smoking, The

Berkeley Connection, Lucky You, We Own the Night, Glad All Over, The Road, Four Christmases, Get Low, Crazy Heart, The Man Who Killed Don Quixote.
TELEVISION: *Movies:* Fame Is the Name of the Game, The Terry Fox Story, Stalin (Golden Globe Award; Emmy nom. 1993), The Man Who Captured Eichmann (Emmy nom. 1997; also exec. prod.), Broken Trail (also exec. prod., 2 Emmy Awards, Golden Globe nom. 2007). *Mini-series:* Ike, Lonesome Dove (Golden Globe Award; Emmy nom. 1989), Broken Trail (also exec. prod., Emmy Award, Golden Globe nom. 2007). *Guest:* More than 141 appearances.

DUVALL, SHELLEY

Actress, Producer. b. Houston, TX, July 7, 1949. Founded Think Entertainment, TV prod. co. Appeared in 1984 short film Frankenweenie.
PICTURES: Brewster McCloud (debut, 1970), McCabe and Mrs. Miller, Thieves Like Us, Nashville, Buffalo Bill and the Indians, Three Women (Cannes Fest. Award, 1977), Annie Hall, The Shining, Popeye, Time Bandits, Roxanne, Suburban Commando, The Underneath, Portrait of a Lady, Changing Habits, Rocket Man, Russell Mulcahy's Tale of the Mummy, Home Fries, The 4th Floor, Dreams in the Attic, Stanley Kubrick: A Life in Pictures, Punch-Drunk Love (singer), Manna From Heaven, Under the Mimosa, Dark Water.
TELEVISION: *Actress:* Bernice Bobs Her Hair, Lily, Twilight Zone, Mother Goose Rock 'n' Rhyme, Faerie Tale Theatre (Rumpelstiltskin, Rapunzel), Tall Tales and Legends (Emmy nom. 1988), Alone, Casper Meets Wendy. *Exec. Producer:* Faerie Tale Theatre, Tall Tales and Legends (Emmy nom. 1988), Nightmare Classics, Dinner at Eight (movie), Mother Goose Rock 'n' Rhyme, Stories from Growing Up, Backfield in Motion (Emmy nom. 1992, movie), Shelley Duvall's Bedtime Stories (Emmy nom. 1992), Mrs. Piggle-Wiggle, Aaahh!!! Real Monsters (voice).

DYLAN, BOB

Performer, Composer, Author, Actor. r.n. Robert Allen Zimmerman. b. Duluth, MN, May 24, 1941. Raised in Hibbing, MN. Signed Recording contract with Columbia Records, 1961. *Author:* Tarantula, Lyrics: 1962-2002, Bob Dylan Chronicles: Vol.I, Bob Dylan Chronicles: Vol. II.
PICTURES: *As Composer:* Satellite, Easy Rider, Little Fauss and Big Halsy, Jud, Pat Garrett and Billy the Kid (Grammy nom. 1974), Blume in Love, Only the Wind Knows the Answer, Renaldo and Clara (also dir./editor/writer), Divine Madness!, American Pop, Band of the Hand (also singer, title song), Five Corners, Good Morning, Vietnam, The Mighty Quinn, High Stakes, Dogfight, In the Name of the Father, With Honors, Assassins, Hollow Reed, The Big Lebowski, Fear and Loathing in Las Vegas, Hope Floats, American Beauty, The Hurricane, Girl, Interrupted, Wonder Boys (Academy Award, Golden Globe, 2000, Grammy nom. Original Song), High Fidelity, Love, Money, Love, Remember the Titans, Haiku Tunnel, Honest, Me, Myself & Irene, Blow, One Night at McCool's, The Royal Tenenbaums, Bandits, Monster's Ball, Knockaround Guys, Vanilla Sky, Divine Secrets of the Ya-Ya Sisterhood, Ali, The Dancer Upstairs, Moonlight Mile, Masked and Anonymous, Gods and Generals, Dopamine, The Hunted, Identity, The Dreamers, Wonderland, I'm Not There: Suppositions on a Film Concerning Dylan, Runaway Jury, A Home at the End of the World, A Cinderella Story, Around the Bend, The Ballad of Jack and Rose, Be Cool, Walk the Line, I'm Not There, Mr. & Mrs. Smith, The King, Brokeback Mountain, Walk the Line, North Country, Lady in the Water, Lucky You, Georgia Rule, Knocked Up, 1408, Family Meeting, Young@Heart, Fred Claus, Henry Poole Is Here, Drillbit Taylor, Expelled: No Intelligence Allowed, The Brothers Bloom, W., Did You Hear About the Morgans?, Watchmen, Observe and Report, Taking Woodstock, Land of the Lost, Away We Go, Law Abiding Citizen. *As Actor:* Hearts of Fire, Paradise Cove, The Times They Are A-Changing. *Documentaries/Specials:* Dont Look Back, Jimi Hendrix, The Last Waltz, Jimi Plays Monterey, The Big One, Angel on My Shoulder, No Direction Home: Bob Dylan (Grammy Award, 1 other nom. 2006), Las Huellas de Dylan, Why We Fight, ...So Goes the Nation, Man of the Year, Guitar Man, Religulous.
TELEVISION: *Movies As Composer:* The Madhouse On Castle Street, The Times They Are A-Changing, Grandeur et décadence, The '60s. *As Actor:* The Madhouse on Castle Street, Hard Rain. *Documentaries/Specials:* The Big T.N.T. Show, Jimi Hendrix, Eat the Document (also dir./editor), Bob Dylan: 30th Anniversary Concert Celebration, Comedian, Skank: MTV Ao Vivo Ouro Preto, Golden Age of Rock'n'Roll, Sam Peckinpah's West: Legacy of a Hollywood Renegade, Bob Dylan Anthology, A Huey P. Newton Story, Jeff Buckley: Goodbye and Hello, Tarnation, Les Prisonniers de Beckett. Has more than 80 television credits. *Guest:* More than 150 appearances.

DYSART, RICHARD A.

Actor. b. Brighton, MA, March 30, 1929. e. Emerson Coll., B.S., M.S., L.L.D.(honorary). Univ. of Maine, Ph.D. (honorary). Trustee Gallaudet Univ, DC. Bd. of Dir, American Judicature Society.
THEATRE: B'way: in A Man for All Seasons, All in Good Time, The Little Foxes, A Place without Doors, That Championship Season, Another Part of the Forest. Off-B'way: in The Quare Fellow, Our Town, Epitaph for George Dillon, Six Characters in Search of an Author.
PICTURES: Petulia, The Lost Man, The Sporting Club, The Hospital, The Terminal Man, The Crazy World of Julius Vrooder, The Day of the Locust, The Hindenberg, Prophecy, Meteor, Being There, An Enemy of the People, The Thing, The Falcon and the Snowman, Mask, Warning Signs, Pale Rider, Wall Street, Back to the Future Part III, Hard Rain.
TELEVISION: *Movies:* The Autobiography of Miss Jane Pittman, Gemini Man, It Happened One Christmas, First You Cry, Bogie, The Ordeal of Dr. Mudd, Churchill and the Generals (BBC), People Vs. Jean Harris, Bitter Harvest, Missing, Last Days of Patton, Children--A Mother's Story, Malice in Wonderland, Day One, Bobby and Marilyn: Her Final Affair, Truman, A Child Is Missing, L.A. Law: Return to Justice, L.A. Law: The Movie. *Mini-series:* War and Rememberance. *Series:* L.A. Law (Emmy Award, 1992; 3 other nom.), Spawn (voice). *Specials*: Sandburg's Lincoln, Jay Leno's Family Comedy Hour, Concealed Enemies, Charlie Smith and the Fritter Tree, Moving Target. *Documentary:* Proteus (voice). *Guest:* More than 55 appearances.

DZUNDZA, GEORGE

Actor. b. Rosenheim, Germany, July 19, 1945. Spent part of childhood in displaced-persons camps before he was moved to Amsterdam in 1949. Came to NY in 1956 where he attended St. John's U. as speech and theater major.
THEATRE: King Lear (NY Shakespeare Fest., debut, 1973), That Championship Season (tour, 1973), Mert and Phil, The Ritz, Legend, A Prayer for My Daughter.
PICTURES: The Happy Hooker, The Deer Hunter, Honky Tonk Freeway, Streamers, Best Defense, No Mercy, No Way Out, The Beast, Impulse, White Hunter Black Heart, The Butcher's Wife, Basic Instinct, Crimson Tide, Dangerous Minds, That Darn Cat, Species II, Instinct, Above Suspicion, Determination of Death, City by the Sea, The Chosen One.
TELEVISION: *Movies:* The Defection of Simas Kudirka, Salem's Lot, Skokie, A Long Way Home, The Face of Rage, The Last Honor of Kathryn Beck, When She Says No, The Rape of Richard Beck, Brotherly Love, The Execution of Raymond Graham, Something is Out There, The Ryan White Story, Terror on Highway 91, What She Doesn't Know, The Enemy Within, The Babymaker: The Dr. Cecil Jacobson Story, The Limbic Region, The Batman/Superman Movie (voice), Hack (pilot). *Series:* Open All Night, Road Rovers (voice), Superman (voice), Law and Order, Batman: Gotham Knights (voice), Jesse, Hack, Grey's Anatomy. *Guest:* More than 62 appearances.

E

EADS, GEORGE

Actor. b. Fort Worth, Texas, March 1, 1967.
PICTURES: Dust to Dust.
TELEVISION: *Movies:* The Ulitmate Lie, Crowned and Dangerous, The Spring, Just A Walk in the Park, Second String, Monte Walsh, Evel Knievel. *Series:* Savannah, Grapevine, CSI: Crime Scene Investigation.

EASTWOOD, ALISON

Actress. b. May 22, 1972. Father is actor-director Clint Eastwood.
PICTURES: Bronco Billy, Tightrope, Absolute Power, Midnight in the Garden of Good and Evil, Suicide: the Comedy, Black & White, Just a Little Harmless Sex, Breakfast of Champions, Friends & Lovers, The Spring, If You Only Knew, How to Go Out on a Date in Queens, Waitin' to Live, The Storyteller, Raising the Dead (also prod.), The Drummer, One Long Night, How to Go Out on a Date in Queens, Rails & Ties (dir. only), Once Fallen.
TELEVISION: *Movies:* The Spring, They Are Among Us, I'll Be Seeing You, Lesser Evil.

EASTWOOD, CLINT

Actor, Producer, Director. b. San Francisco, CA, May 31, 1930; e. Oakland Technical H.S., Los Angeles City Coll. Daughter is actress Alison Eastwood. Worked as a lumberjack in Oregon before being drafted into the Army, Special Services 1950-54. Then contract player at Universal Studios. Starred in TV series Rawhide, 1958-65. Formed Malpaso Productions, 1969. Made a Chevalier des Lettres by French gov., 1985. Mayor, Carmel, CA, 1986-88. Best Director for Bird: Hollywood Foreign Press Assoc., Orson Award. Made Commandeur de Ordre des Arts & Lettres by French Government, 1994. Received Irving G. Thalberg Award, 1995. Received American Film Institute Life Achievement Award, 1996. Received Golden Globe Cecil B. DeMille Award 1988. 2006 Directors Guild of America, Lifetime Achievement Award.
PICTURES: Revenge of the Creature (debut, 1955), Francis in the Navy, Lady Godiva, Tarantula, Never Say Goodbye, Away All Boats, The First Traveling Saleslady, Star in the Dust, Escapade in Japan, Ambush at Cimarron Pass, Lafayette Escadrille, A Fistful of Dollars, For a Few Dollars More, The Witches, The Good The Bad and The Ugly, Hang 'Em High, Coogan's Bluff, Where Eagles Dare, Paint Your Wagon, Kelly's Heroes, Two Mules For Sister Sara, Beguiled, Play Misty For Me (also dir.),

Dirty Harry, Joe Kidd, Breezy (dir. only), High Plains Drifter (also dir.), Magnum Force, Thunderbolt & Lightfoot, The Eiger Sanction (also dir.), The Outlaw Josey Wales (also dir.), The Enforcer, The Gauntlet (also dir.), Every Which Way But Loose, Escape from Alcatraz, Bronco Billy (also dir.), Any Which Way You Can, Firefox (also dir., prod.), Honky Tonk Man (also dir., prod.), Sudden Impact (also dir., prod.), Tightrope (also prod.), City Heat, Pale Rider (also dir., prod.), Heartbreak Ridge (also dir., prod.), The Dead Pool (also prod.), Bird (Golden Globe Award 1989; dir. only), Thelonius Monk: Straight, No Chaser (exec. prod. only), Pink Cadillac, White Hunter Black Heart (also dir., prod.), The Rookie (also dir.), Unforgiven (also dir., prod.; 2 Academy Awards for Best Picture & Director; L.A. Film Critics Awards for Best Actor, Director & Picture; Natl. Society of Film Critics Awards for Best Director & Picture; Golden Globe Award for Best Director; DGA Award, 1993), In the Line of Fire, A Perfect World (also dir.), Casper (cameo), The Bridges of Madison County (also dir., prod.), The Stars Fell on Henrietta (co-prod. only), Absolute Power (also dir., prod., comp.), Midnight in the Garden of Good & Evil (also dir., prod.), True Crime (also, dir., prod.), Space Cowboys (also dir, prod.), Blood Work (also dir., prod.), Mystic River (2 Academy Award nom.; Golden Globe nom.; DGA nom. 2004, dir., prod., composer), Million Dollar Baby (also dir., composer, prod.; won 2 Academy Awards and 1 nom.;Golden Globe Award and 1 nom. DGA Award Best Dir. & Best Picture, 2004), Flags of Our Fathers (dir., prod., Golden Globe nom. 2007), Letters from Iwo Jima (dir., prod., 2 Academy Award noms.; Golden Globe nom. 2007), Grace Is Gone (soundtrack composer, 2 Golden Globe noms.), Tony Bennett: The Music Never Ends (prod.), Changeling (prod. only, Golden Globe nom. 2009), Gran Torino (also dir., prod., soundtrack writer, Golden Globe nom. 2009), Invictus (dir., prod., Golden Globe nom. 2010), Hereafter (dir., prod.).
TELEVISION: *Specials:* Fame Fortune and Romance, Happy Birthday Hollywood, Clint Eastwood: The Man From Malpaso, Don't Pave Main Street: Carmel's Heritage, Salute to Martin Scorcese, Big Guns Talk: Story of the Western, Eastwood on Eastwood, Budd Boetticher: A Man Can Do That (also exec. prod.). *Dir.:* Amazing Stories (Vanessa in the Garden). *Mini-series:* The Blues (also dir.). *Series:* Rawhide. *Guest:* More than 217 appearances.

EBERSOL, DICK

Executive. b. Torrington, CT, July 28, 1947. e. B.A. in History, Yale Univ. In 1968, while still a Yale student, was hired to become the first Olympic TV researcher. After graduation, became Roone Arledge's exec. asst. at ABC and then a producer for Wide World of Sports and the 1972 Summer Olympics. In 1974, he joined NBC as the dir. of weekend late-night programming. Hired Lorne Michaels in 1975 and helped developed NBC's long-running Saturday Night Live. Ebersol became NBC's first v.p. under the age of 30 when he was named the v.p. of late-night programming at age 28. In 1983, he formed his own production company, No Sleep Productions, and created Friday Night Videos, Later with Bob Costas and Saturday Night's Main Event. In May 1989, Ebersol became pres. of NBC Sports and was also named a sr. v.p. of NBC News. In 1992 Ebersol was awarded the Olympic Order and in 1996, the Sporting News named him the "Most Powerful Person in Sports in America." This came on the heels of the 1995-1996 season where, for the first time in history, the World Series, Super Bowl, NBA Finals and Summer Olympics were telecast by the same network. The merger between NBC and Vivendi Universal Entertainment was completed in May 2004, which formed NBC Universal. Ebersol is Chairman, NBC Universal Sports and NBC Universal Olympics and has been the driving force behind the acquisition of NBC Universal's exclusive broadcast and cable rights for summer and winter Olympics from 2000-2008. Friday Night (Emmy Award 1985), XIX Winter Olympics Opening Ceremony (Emmy nom. 2002), Athens 2004: Games of the XXVIII Olympiad (Emmy nom. 2005), Turin 2006: XX Olympic Winter Games (Emmy Award 2006). He is still an active producer, serving as exec. prod. of NBC Universal's coverage of the last three Summer Olympic Games, and is also co-exec. prod. of the NBA on NBC Universal with exec. prod. Tom Roy.

EBERTS, JOHN DAVID (JAKE)

Producer, Financier. b. Montreal, Canada, July 10, 1941. e. McGill Univ, Harvard. President Goldcrest, founder & CEO 1976-83, 1985-86; 1984 joined Embassy Communications Intl. 1985 founded and chief exec. of Allied Filmmakers. Film Prods. Award of Merit 1986; Evening Standard Special Award 1987. Publication: My Indecision Is Final (1990).
PICTURES: *Prod./Exec. Prod.:* Chariots of Fire, Gandhi, Another Country, Local Hero, The Dresser, Cal, The Emerald Forest, The Name of the Rose, Hope and Glory, Cry Freedom, The Adventures of Baron Munchausen, Driving Miss Daisy, Dances With Wolves, Black Robe, Get Back, City of Joy, A River Runs Through It, Super Mario Bros., No Escape, James and the Giant Peach, The Wind in the Willows, The Education of Little Tree, Grey Owl, Chicken Run, The Legend of Bagger Vance, K-19: Widowmaker, Open Range, Two Brothers, Emperor Zehnder, Aloft, Krakatoa, Doogal, Renaissance, The Choir, The Illusionist, Whatever Lola Wants, Confessions of a Dangerous Mind. *Documentaries:* Prisoner of Paradise, America's Heart and Soul.
TELEVISION: Snow in August (Emmy nom. 2002).

ECK, JOHN

Executive. Bachelor's degree in business, Indiana Univ. Eck started his career in GE's financial mgt. program with GE Lighting and held various financial positions with GE, including GE Capital, GE Power Generation, and GE Aircraft Engines. He joined NBC in 1993 as v.p., financial planning and analysis. In July 1998, Eck named pres., NBC Broadcast & Network Operations. In this assignment, he focused on process and digital technology improvements in NBC's news, sports, entertainment and content distribution efforts. Eck's previous assignments included serving as senior v.p. and quality leader, and CFO for NBC International and Business Development. He was instrumental in the structuring of NBC's joint venture with Microsoft, which created MSNBC and MSNBC.com, and in the combination of CNBC and Dow Jones. He also oversaw the integration efforts of NBC Universal, formed in May 2004 through the combination of NBC and Vivendi Universal Entertainment, and played a key role in NBC's due diligence efforts. In July 2005, Eck was pres., Media Works and chief information officer of NBC Universal. Eck was promoted to his current position, pres., NBC TV Network and Media Works in July 2007, which added oversight of NBC affiliate relations and NBC network operations. Eck continues to lead information technology and studio operations across NBC Universal's extensive TV networks, owned stations, and digital media properties as well as the company's film and TV production and post-production operations. In addition, Eck oversees the areas of sourcing, environmental health and safety, crisis management, and a multimillion-square-foot real estate and facilities portfolio, which includes Rockefeller Center, and Burbank and Universal City, California. Eck reports directly to Jeff Zucker, pres. and CEO of NBC Universal.

ECKERT, JOHN M.

Producer, Production Executive. b. Chatham, Ontario, Canada, e. Ryerson Poly. Inst., 1968-71 (film major). Member: DGA, DGC.
PICTURES: Power Play (assoc. prod.), Running (co-prod.), Middle Age Crazy (co-prod.), Dead Zone (unit prod. mgr.), Cats Eye (exec. in charge of prod.), Silver Bullet (assoc. prod.), The Incubus, Home Is Where the Heart Is (prod.), Millenium (suprv. prod.), Deep Sleep (prod.), Car 54 Where Are You? (s.p., prod.), Legends of the Fall (unit prod. mngr.), The Scarlet Letter (unit prod. mngr.), Flying Wild (assoc. prod.), Booty Call (co-prod.), The Big Hit (exec. prod), Three to Tango (co-prod.), Gossip (co-prod.), Loser (exec. prod.), Exit Wounds (co-prod.), Chicago (line prod).
TELEVISION: *Movies:* Terry Fox Story (assoc. prod.), Special People (prod., Christopher Award), Danger Bay (series supv. prod., 1985-87), Family Pictures (unit prod. mngr.), Getting Gotti (prod.), Brian's Song (line prod.), The Music Man (prod.), Knights of the South Bronx (unit prod. mngr.), A Raisin in the Sun. *Mini-series:* The Company (unit mangr. prod.), The Gathering. *Series:* Danger Bay.

EDELMAN, RANDY

Composer. b. Patterson, NJ, June 10, 1947.
PICTURES: Feds, Twins, Troop Beverly Hills, Ghostbusters II, Quick Change, Come See the Paradise, Kindergarten Cop, V.I. Warshawski, Drop Dead Fred, Eyes of an Angel, The Distinguished Gentleman, Beethoven, My Cousin Vinny, The Last of the Mohicans (Golden Globe nom. 1993), Gettysburg, Dragon: The Bruce Lee Story, Beethoven's 2nd, Tall Tale, Pontiac Moon, Greedy, Angels in the Outfield, The Mas, Billy Madison, While you Were Sleeping, The Indian in the Cupboard, The Big Green, Down Periscope, Diabolique, The Quest, Dragonheart, Dayllight, Anaconda, Gone Fishin', The Chipmunk Adventure, Executive Action, The Big Green, Leave It To Beaver, For Richer or Poorer, Six Days Seven Nights, EdTV, Passion of Mind, The Whole Nine Yards, The Skulls, Shanghai Noon, Head Over Heels, China: The Panda Adventure, Osmosis Jones, Who Is Cletis Tout?, Corky Romano, Black Knight, XXX, Gods and Generals, Shanghai Knights, Frank McCluskey C.I., National Security, Connie & Carla, Surviving Christmas, Stealth, Son of the Mask, Miss Congeniality 2: Armed and Fabulous, Stealth, The Last Time, Underdog, Balls of Fury (also score prod.), 27 Dresses, The Mummy: Tomb of the Dragon Emperor (also conductor, orchestrator), Paul Blart: Mall Cop (soundtrack writer), Leap Year.
TELEVISION: *Movies:* A Doctor's Story, Dennis the Menace, Citizen X, The Hunley, A Season on the Brink. *Mini-series:* The Ten Commandments. *Series:* MacGyver, The Adventures of Brisco County Jr.

EDEN, BARBARA

Actress. b. Tucson, AZ, Aug. 23, 1934. r.n. Barbara Jean Huffman. e. San Francisco Conservatory of Music. Pres. Mi-Bar Productions. Dir. Security National Bank of Chicago.
PICTURES: Back From Eternity (debut, 1956), The Wayward Girl, A Private's Affair, From the Terrace, Twelve Hours to Kill, Flaming Star, All Hands on Deck, Voyage to the Bottom of the Sea, Five Weeks in a Balloon, Swingin' Along (Double Trouble), The Wonderful World of the Brothers Grimm, The Yellow Canary, The Brass Bottle, The New Interns, Ride the Wild Surf, 7 Faces of Dr. Lao, Quick Let's Get Married, The Amazing Dobermans,

Harper Valley PTA, Chattanooga Choo Choo, A Very Brady Sequel, Mi Casa Su Casa, Carolina.
TELEVISION: *Movies:* The Feminist and the Fuzz, A Howling in the Woods, The Woman Hunter, Guess Who's Sleeping in My Bed, The Stranger Within, Let's Switch, How to Break Up a Happy Divorce, Stonestreet: Who Killed the Centerfold Model?, The Girls in the Office, Condominium, Return of the Rebels, I Dream of Jeannie: 15 Years Later, The Stepford Children, The Secret Life of Kathy McCormick (also co-prod.), Your Mother Wears Combat Boots, Opposites Attract, Her Wicked Ways, Hell Hath No Fury, I Still Dream of Jeannie, Visions of Murder I & II, Eyes of Terror, Dean Man's Island (also co-prod.), Nightclub Confidential, Gentlemen Prefer Blondes, Always and Forever. *Series:* How to Marry a Millionaire, I Dream of Jeannie (2 Golden Globe nom. 1967, 1970), Harper Valley P.T.A., A Brand New Life, Dallas, Sabrina, the Teenage Witch. *Guest:* More than 192 appearances.

EDWARDS, ANTHONY
Actor. b. Santa Barbara, CA, July 19, 1962. Grandfather designed Walt Disney Studios in the 1930s and worked for Cecil B. De Mille as conceptual artist. Joined Santa Barbara Youth Theatre; acted in 30 plays from age 12 to 17. At 16 worked professionally in TV commercials. 1980 attended Royal Acad. of Dramatic Arts, London, and studied drama at USC. On NY stage 1993 in Ten Below.
PICTURES: Fast Times at Ridgemont High (debut, 1982), Heart Like a Wheel, Revenge of the Nerds, The Sure Thing, Gotcha!, Top Gun, Summer Heat, Revenge of the Nerds II (cameo), Mr. North, Miracle Mile, How I Got Into College, Hawks, Downtown, Delta Heat, Pet Sematary II, The Client, Charlie's Ghost story, Us Begins with You (also prod.), Playing by Heart, Jackpot, Die-Die-Mommie (prod. only), Northfork, The Thunderbirds, The Forgotten, Zodiac, Motherhood, Flipped.
TELEVISION: *Movies:* The Killing of Randy Webster, High School U.S.A., Going for the Gold: The Bill Johnson Story, El Diablo, Hometown Boy Makes Good, In Cold Blood, Border Line (exec. prod.), My Louisiana Sky (Emmy Award 2002; exec. prod.), Temple Grandin (exec. prod.). *Series:* It Takes Two, Northern Exposure, ER (4 Emmy nom,; Golden Globe Award 1998; 3 other nom.), Soul Man, Rock Story. *Specials:* Unpublished Letters, Sexual Healing. *Guest:* More than 50 appearances.

EDWARDS, BLAKE
Director, Writer, Producer. r.n. William Blake McEdwards. b. Tulsa, OK, July 26, 1922. m. actress Julie Andrews. e. Beverly Hills H.S. Coast Guard during war. Film acting debut, Ten Gentlemen from West Point (1942). Honorary Academy Award 2004. Received WGA Award, Laurel Award for Screen Writing Achievement, 2002.
RADIO: Johnny Dollar, Line-up; writer-creator: Richard Diamond.
PICTURES: *Writer:* Panhandle, Stampede, Sound Off, All Ashore, Cruising Down the River, Rainbow Round My Shoulder, Drive a Crooked Road, The Atomic Kid (story), My Sister Eileen, Operation Mad Ball (WGA nom. 1958), Notorious Landlady (WGA nom. 1963), Soldier in the Rain, Pink Panther 2. *Producer:* Waterhole. *Director:* Bring Your Smile Along (also s.p.), He Laughed Last (also s.p.), Mister Cory (also s.p.), This Happy Feeling (also s.p.), The Perfect Furlough (also s.p.), Operation Petticoat, High Time, Breakfast at Tiffany's (DGA nom. 1962), Experiment in Terror, Days of Wine and Roses (Golden Globe nom. 1963), The Pink Panther (also s.p. WGA nom. 1965), A Shot in the Dark (also s.p., prod.), The Great Race (also s.p., prod.), What Did You Do in the War Daddy? (also s.p., prod.), Gunn (also prod.), The Party (also s.p., prod.), Darling Lili (also s.p., prod.), Wild Rovers (also s.p., prod.), The Carey Treatment (also s.p., prod.), The Tamarind Seed (also s.p.), The Return of the Pink Panther (also s.p., prod.; WGA nom. 1976), The Pink Panther Strikes Again (also s.p., prod.; WGA Award 1977), Revenge of the Pink Panther (also s.p., prod.), "10" (also co-prod., s.p.; WGA nom. 1980), S.O.B. (also co-prod., s.p.; WGA nom. 1982), Victor/Victoria (Academy Award nom. 1983; also co-prod., s.p.; WGA Award 1983), Trail of the Pink Panther (also co-prod., co-s.p.), The Curse of the Pink Panther (also co-prod., s.p.), The Man Who Loved Women (also prod., co-s.p.), Micki and Maude, A Fine Mess (also s.p.), That's Life (also co-prod.), Blind Date, Sunset (also s.p.), Skin Deep (also s.p.), Switch (also s.p.), Son of the Pink Panther (also s.p.), The Pink Panther 2 (writer).
TELEVISION: *Movies:* Victor/Victoria, City Detective (prod., 1953), The Dick Powell Show (dir.), Creator: Dante's Inferno, Mr. Lucky, Justin Case (exec. prod., dir., writer), Peter Gunn (2 Emmy nom.; exec. prod., dir., writer), Julie (exec. prod., dir.). *Specials:* Julie! (prod., dir.), Julie on Sesame St. (exec. prod.), Julie and Dick in Covent Garden (dir.).

EGAN, EDDIE
Executive. b. New York, NY. In 1977, just out of high school, Egan landed his first paying job as a production assistant on the New York unit of Richard Donner's worldwide blockbuster "Superman," starring Marlon Brando and Christopher Reeve. From 1978 to 1985, he held several positions in the New York and Hollywood offices of Paramount Pictures. Moved to Twentieth Century Fox Film Corporation as v.p., publicity before going over to Sony Pictures Entertainment in 1990. He became senior v.p., marketing for Sony's combined Columbia Pictures/TriStar Pictures marketing departments and later assumed the same position with TriStar Pictures. Egan joined Universal Pictures in Dec. 1994 as senior v.p. and, in March 1999 was named executive v.p., marketing for Universal Pictures. He was promoted to co-president, marketing, in May 2002. He also supervised the marketing campaign for Universal's Tony Award-winning smash Broadway musical hit "Wicked," and has launched three concurrent North American touring companies, as well as a production in London's West End. For the marketing campaign of "8 Mile," Egan and Universal Pictures President of Marketing & Distribution Adam Fogelson were named "Entertainment Marketers of the Year" by Advertising Age in 2003. Egan was named president of marketing for Universal Pictures in October 2007. In this role, Egan directs all aspects of marketing-including creative advertising, media, publicity, promotion, digital marketing and administration-for Universal's domestic feature film releases. 2010 Egan became co-president of marketing. He reports to Fogelson.

EGGAR, SAMANTHA
Actress. b. London, England,, March 5, 1939. e. student Webber-Douglas Dramatic Sch., London; Slade Sch. of Art.
PICTURES: The Wild and the Willing, Dr. Crippen, Doctor in Distress, Psyche '59, The Collector (Academy Award nom.; Golden Globe Award 1966), Return From the Ashes, Walk Don't Run, Doctor Dolittle, The Molly Maguires, The Lady in the Car With Glasses and a Gun, The Walking Stick, The Grove, The Light at the Edge of the World, The Dead Are Alive, The Seven Percent Solution, The Uncanny, Welcome to Blood City, The Brood, The Exterminator, Demonoid, Why Shoot the Teacher?, Curtains, Hot Touch, Loner, Ragin Cajun, Dark Horse, Inevitable Grace, The Phantom, Hercules, The Astronaut's Wife.
TELEVISION: *Movies:* Double Indemnity, All The Kind Strangers, The Killer Who Wouldn't Die, Ziegfeld: the Man and His Women, The Hope Diamond, Love Among Thieves, A Ghost in Monte Carlo. A Case for Murder, Barbara Taylor Bradford Trilogy: Everything to Gain, Loss of Faith. *Mini-series:* For the Term of His Natural Life, Davy Crockett, Great Escapes: Secrets of Lake Success. *Series:* Anna and the King, All My Children, Hercules (voice), Commander in Chief. *Specials:* Man of Destiny, Hemingway Play. *Guest:* More than 77 appearances.

EGOYAN, ATOM
Director, Writer, Producer, Editor, Actor, Cinematographer. b. Cairo, Egypt, July 19, 1960. Raised in Victoria, British Columbia, Canada. e. Univ. of Toronto. Made short films, one of which, Open House appeared on TV series Canadian Reflections.
PICTURES: Various credits: Howard in Particular, After Grad with Dad, Peep Show, Open House, Next of Kin, Men: A Passion Playground, Family Viewing, Speaking Parts, The Adjuster, Montreal Sextet, Calendar, Exotica, Curtis's Charm, A Portrait of Arshile, The Sweet Hereafter (2 Academy Award nom. 1998), Vinyl, Bach Cello Suite #4: Sarabande, Felicia's Journey (dir., s.p.), The Line, Ararat, Gambling-God-and LSD (documentary, exec. prod.), Foolproof (exec. prod.), Mouth to Mouth, Coldwater, Where the Truth Lies, Sabah (exec. prod.), Away from Her (exec. prod.), The 1 Second Film (prod.), Citadel (doc. dir., prod., writer, editor, cinematographer), To Each His Cinema (dir. segment), Adoration (dir., prod.), Chloe (dir.), Moving the Arts (dir., writer), Seven Wonders (dir., writer).
TELEVISION: *Movies:* In This Corner, Looking for Nothing, Gross Misconduct: The Life of Brian Spencer, Krapp's Last Tape, Escape from the Newsroom (as himself). *Series:* Alfred Hitchcock Presents, Twilight Zone, Friday the 13th, Yo-Yo Ma Inspired by Bach.

EICHHORN, LISA
Actress. b. Reading, PA, Feb. 4, 1952. e. Queen's U. Kingston, Canada and Eng. for literature studies at Oxford. Studied at Royal Acad. of Dramatic Art.
THEATRE: The Hasty Heart (debut, LA). NY: The Common Pursuit, The Summer Winds, The Speed of Darkness, Down the Road, Any Given Day.
PICTURES: Yanks (2 Golden Globe noms. 1980), The Europeans, Why Would I Lie?, Cutter and Bone, Weather in the Streets, Wild Rose; Opposing Force, Moon 44, Grim Prairie Tales, The Vanishing, King of the Hill, Sticks and Stones, First Kid, A Modern Affair, Judas Kiss, Goodbye Lover, The Talented Mr. Ripley, Boys and Girls, Defenders of Riga.
TELEVISION: *Movies:* The Wall, Blind Justice, Murder in Three Acts, Pride and Extreme Prejudice, Devlin, My Neighbor's Daughter, Kenneth Tynan: In Praise of Hardcore, Cracker. *Mini-series:* A Woman Named Jackie. *Series:* All My Children (1987), Law & Order.

EIKENBERRY, JILL
Actress. b. New Haven, CT, Jan. 21, 1947. e. Yale U. Drama Sch. m. actor Michael Tucker.
THEATRE: B'way: All Over Town, Watch on the Rhine, Onward Victoria, Summer Brave, Moonchildren. Off-B'way: Lemon Sky, Life Under Water, Uncommon Women and Others, Porch, The Primary English Class.
PICTURES: Between the Lines, The End of the World in Our Usual Bed in a Night Full of Rain, An Unmarried Woman, Butch

and Sundance: The Early Days, Rich Kids, Hide in Plain Sight, Arthur, The Manhattan Project, Manna From Heaven, The Happiest Day of His Life, Suburban Girl.
TELEVISION: *Movies:* The Deadliest Season, Orphan Train, Swan Song, Sessions, Kane & Abel, Assault and Matrimony, Family Sins, A Stoning in Fulham Country, My Boyfriend's Back, The Diane Martin Story, The Secret Life of Archie's Wife, An Inconvenient Woman, Living a Lie, A Town Torn Apart, Chantilly Lace, Parallel Lives, Without Consent, Rugged Gold, The Other Woman, Dare to Love, My Very Best Friend, Gone in a Heartbeat, Roughing It, L.A. Law: Return to Justice, L.A. Law: The Movie, Emile Norman: By His Own Design. *Series:* L.A. Law (5 Emmy noms.; Golden Globe Award 1989, 3 other noms.), The Best of Families (PBS). *Specials:* Uncommon Women & Others, Destined to Live (prod., host), A Family Again, On Hope. *Guest:* More than 51 appearances.

EISNER, MICHAEL D.

Executive. b. Mt. Kisco, NY, March 7, 1942. e. Denison U., B.A. Started career with programming dept. of CBS TV network. Joined ABC in 1966 as mgr. talent and specials. Dec., 1968 became dir. of program dev., East Coast. 1968, named v.p., daytime programming, ABC-TV. 1975 made v.p., prog. planning and dev. 1976 named sr. v.p., prime time production and dev., ABC Entertainment. 1976, left ABC to join Paramount Pictures as pres. & COO. 1984, joined The Walt Disney Company as chmn. & CEO. He hosted TV series, The Wonderful World of Disney in 1997; he is the author of: Work in Progress, (co-author with Tony Schwartz). In March 2004, the Disney announced it would split the chairman and CEO positions, with Eisner retaining the CEO title. In September, Eisner announced he would retire at the end of his contract in 2006. However, he resigned Sept. 30, 2005 and severed all ties with Disney. In 2005, Eisner founded The Tornante Company, a privately held firm which invests in media and entertainment companies. In spring 2007, Tornante unveiled a new media studio named Vuguru, which produces and distributes original content for Internet and other new media outlets. Its first production, a serialized mystery called Prom Queen, appeared online in April. Tornante also holds ownership stakes in Veoh Networks and Team Baby Entertainment. 2007 he took over Topps Co., a well known candy maker. He has also invested in an Internet video distribution network named Veoh Networks which is filming a mockumentary style show about his takeover of the Topps Co. and will air with Fox Sports and is sponsored by Skype. Eisner serves on the boards of CA. Institute of the Arts, Denison Univ., American Hospital of Paris Found., Conservation Int'l., the UCLA Exec. Bd. for Medical Sciences and the National Hockey League. He also has established and funded The Eisner Foundation.

EKBERG, ANITA

Actress. b. Malmo, Sweden, Sept. 29, 1931. Came to U.S. in 1951 as Miss Universe contestant. Worked as model before becoming actress appearing in small roles at Universal. Received Golden Globe Award 1956 for Most Promising Newcomer.
PICTURES: Mississippi Gambler, Abbott & Costello Go to Mars, Take Me to Town, The Golden Blade, Blood Alley, Artists and Models, Man in the Vault, War and Peace, Back from Eternity, Hollywood or Bust, Zarak, Pickup Alley, Valerie, Paris Holiday, The Man Inside, Screaming Mimi, Sign of the Gladiator, La Dolce Vita, The Dam on the Yellow River (Last Train to Shanghai), Little Girls and High Finance, Behind Locked Doors, The Last Judgment, The Mongols, Boccaccio '70, Call Me Bwana, 4 for Texas, L'Incastro, Who Wants to Sleep?, The Alphabet Murders, Way Way Out, How I Learned to Love Women, Woman Times Seven, The Glass Sphinx, The Cobra, Malenka the Vampire (Fangs of the Living Dead), If It's Tuesday This Must Be Belgium, The Clowns, Valley of the Widows, Killer Nun, Daisy Chain, Intervista, The Seduction of Angela, Quando ancora non c'erano i Beatles, Count Max, Cattive ragazze, Ambrogio, Bámbola, The Red Dwarf, Lost in Translation (film clip).
TELEVISION: *Movies:* Gold of the Amazon Women, S*H*E, Witness Run. *Series:* Il Bello delle donne.

ELEFANTE, TOM

Executive. Began career as usher at Loews Riviera in Coral Gables, FL; progressed through ranks to asst. mgr., mgr. & Florida division mgr. 1972, joined Wometco Theatres as gen. mgr. 1975, returned to Loews Theatres as southeast div. mgr.; 1979, named nat'l. dir. of concessions, moving to New York. 1987, appt. sr. v.p. & gen. mgr., Loews. Served as pres. and chmn. of NATO of Florida. 1990, then pres. of NATO of NY. Joined Warner Bros. Int'l Theatres as sr. v.p., 1992. Founded T.P. Consulting Co., 1997. Member Bd. of Dir.,- Advisory Member, Will Rogers Motion Pictures Pioneers Foundation.

ELFAND, MARTIN

Executive, Producer. b. Los Angeles, CA, 1937. Was talent agent for 10 yrs. with top agencies; joined Artists Ent. Complex in 1972. First film project as prod.: Kansas City Bomber, first venture of AEC, of which he was sr. v.p.; 1977, joined Warner Bros. as production chief.
PICTURES: *Prod.:* Dog Day Afternoon (Academy Award nom. 1976), It's My Turn, An Officer and a Gentleman, King David, Clara's Heart, Guarding Tess. *Exec. prod.:* Her Alibi, Talent for the Game.

ELFMAN, DANNY

Composer. b. Los Angeles, CA, May 29, 1953. Member of rock band Oingo Boingo, recorded songs for such films as The Tempest, Fast Times at Ridgemont High, 16 Candles, Beverly Hills Cop, Weird Science, Texas Chainsaw Massacre 2, Something Wild. Appeared in Hot Tomorrows, Back to School.
PICTURES: Forbidden Zone, Pee-wee's Big Adventure, Back to School, Wisdom, Summer School, Beetlejuice, Midnight Run, Big Top Pee-wee, Hot to Trot, Scrooged, Batman, Nightbreed, Dick Tracy, Darkman, Edward Scissorhands, Pure Luck, Article 99, Batman Returns, Sommersby, The Nightmare Before Christmas (Golden Globe nom. 1994; also vocalist), Black Beauty, Dolores Claiborne, To Die For, Dead Presidents, Mission: Impossible, The Frighteners, Mars Attacks!, Men in Black (Academy Award nom. 1998), Flubber, Good Will Hunting (Academy Award nom. 1998), Scream 2, A Simple Plan, A Civil Action, Modern Vampyres, My Favorite Martian, Psycho, Instinct, Anywhere But Here, Sleepy Hollow, Proof of Life, The Family Man, Spy Kids, Heartbreakers, Planet of the Apes, Novocaine, Spider Man, Red Dragon, Men In Black 2, Spy Kids: The Island of Lost Dreams, Undone, Terminator 3: Rise of the Machines, Batman: Year One, Hulk, Big Fish (Academy Award nom.; Golden Globe nom.; 2004), Sleepover, Spider Man 2, The Corpse Bride, Charlie and the Chocolate Factory, The Sixth Element, The Benchwarmers, Nacho Libre, Charlotte's Web, Spider-Man 3, A Day with Wilbur Robinson, The Visiting, Meet the Robinsons, The Simpsons Movie (main theme), The Kingdom, Wanted, Hellboy II: The Golden Army, Milk (Academy Award nom. 2009), Notorious, Terminator Salvation, The Wolfman, Alice in Wonderland, Forbidden Zone 2: The Forbidden Galaxy, Do Not Disturb, The Green Hornet.
TELEVISION: *Series:* Pee-wee's Playhouse, Sledgehammer, Fast Times, Tales from the Crypt, The Simpsons (Emmy nom. 1990), The Flash, Beetlejuice, Casper: A Spirited Beginning, Modern Vampires, The Flash (also series), The Adventures of Batman & Robin, Family Dog, Perversions of Science, Dilbert, Segments of Amazing Stories, Alfred Hitchcock Presents (The Jar), Desperate Housewives (Emmy Award 2005; main theme), Point Pleasant. *Documentary:* Deep Sea 3D, Enron: The Smartest Guys in the Room.

ELFMAN, JENNA

Actress. r. n. Jennifer Mary Butala. b. Los Angeles, CA, Sept. 30, 1971.
PICTURES: Grosse Pointe Blank, Doctor Dolittle (voice) Krippendorf's Tribe, Can't Hardly Wait, Venus, Edtv, Keeping the Faith, CyberWorld (voice), The Tangerine Bear, Town and Country, Looney Tunes: Back in Action, Clifford's Really Big Movie (voice), Touched (also exec. prod.), Love Hurts, Forbidden Zone 2: The Forbidden Galaxy.
TELEVISION: *Movies:* Her Last Chance, Obsessed, Literary Superstar. *Series:* Townies, Dharma & Greg (3 Emmy nom.; Golden Globe Award 1999; 2 other nom.), Courting Alex, Accidentally on Purpose. *Guest:* More than 63 appearances.

ELG, TAINA

Actress, Dancer. b. Helsinki, Finland, March 9, 1930. Trained and performed with Natl. Opera of Finland. Toured with Swedish Dance Theatre, then Marquis de Cuevas Ballet. Received Golden Globe Award for Foreign Newcomer, 1957.
THEATRE: Look to the Lilies, Where's Charley?, The Utter Glory of Morrissey Hall, Strider, Nine, O! Pioneers.
PICTURES: The Prodigal (debut, 1955), Diane, Gaby, Les Girls (Golden Globe nom. 1958), Watusi, Imitation General, The 39 Steps, The Bacchae, Liebestraum, The Mirror Has Two Faces.
TELEVISION: *Movie:* The Great Wallendas, Don't Drink the Water. *Mini-series:* Blood and Honor: Youth Under Hitler (narrator). *Series:* One Life to Live, Guiding Light, Loving.

ELIZONDO, HECTOR

Actor. b. New York, NY, Dec. 22, 1936. m. actress Carolee Campbell. Studied with Ballet Arts Co. of Carnegie Hall and Actors Studio. Many stage credits in N.Y. and Boston.
THEATRE: The Prisoner of Second Avenue, Dance of Death, Steambath (Obie Award), The Great White Hope, Sly Fox, The Price.
PICTURES: The Fat Black Pussycat, Valdez Is Coming, Born to Win, Pocket Money, Deadhead Miles, Stand Up and Be Counted, The Taking of Pelham One Two Three, Report to the Commissioner, Thieves, Cuba, American Gigolo, The Fan, Young Doctors in Love, The Flamingo Kid, Private Resort, Nothing in Common, Overboard, Beaches, Leviathan, Pretty Woman (Golden Globe nom. 1991), Taking Care of Business, Necessary Roughness, Frankie and Johnny, Final Approach, Samantha, There Goes the Neighborhood, Being Human, Beverly Hills Cop III, Getting Even With Dad, Exit to Eden, Perfect Alibi, Dear God, Turbulence, Entropy, Safe House, The Other Sister, Entropy, The Runaway Bride, Speak Truth to Power, Tortilla Soup, The Princess Diaries, How High, The Zoot Suit Riots (voice), Raising Helen, The Princess Diaries 2: Royal Engagement, The Celestine Prophecy, I Believe in America, Music Within, Love in the Time of Cholera, Georgia Rule, Valentine's Day, Love Is a Hurtin' Thing: The Lou Rawls Story, Deauville.
TELEVISION: *Movies:* The Impatient Heart, Wanted: The

Sundance Woman, Honeyboy, Women of San Quentin, Courage, Out of the Darkness, Addicted to His Love, Your Mother Wears Combat Boots, Forgotten Prisoners: The Amnesty Files, Finding the Way Home, Chains of Gold, The Burden of Proof, Borrowed Hearts, Safe House. *Mini-series:* The Dain Curse, Fidel. *Specials:* Medal of Honor Rag, Mrs. Cage (Emmy nom. 1992), Fidel. *Series:* Popi (1976), Casablanca, Freebie and the Bean; A.K.A. Pablo (also dir.), Foley Sq, Down and Out in Bevery Hills, Fish Police (voice), Chicago Hope (Emmy Award, 1997; 3 other noms.), Kate Brasher, Miracles, Century City, Justice League Unlimited, Cane, Monk. *Guest:* More than 114 appearances.

ELKINS, HILLARD

Producer. b. New York, NY, Oct. 18, 1929. e. NYU, B.A., 1951. Exec., William Morris Agy., 1949-51; exec. v.p., Gen. Artists Corp., 1952-53; pres., Hillard Elkins Mgmt., 1953-60; Elkins Prods. Intl. Corp., N.Y., 1960-71; Elkins Prods. Ltd., 1972-; Hillard Elkins Entertainment Corp., 1974; Media Mix Prods., Inc., 1979-82. Member of: Academy of Motion Picture Arts & Sciences, Acad. of TV Arts & Sciences, Dramatists Guild, League of New York Theatres, American Fed. of TV & Radio Artists.
THEATRE: Come On Strong, Golden Boy, Oh Calcutta!, The Rothschilds, A Doll's House, An Evening with Richard Nixon, Sizwe Banzi Is Dead, etc.
PICTURES: Alice's Restaurant, A New Leaf, Oh Calcutta!, A Doll's House, Richard Pryor Live in Concert, Sellers on Sellers, Inside, Stage Kiss, Avenue A, Stander.
TELEVISION: *Movies:* Pippin: His Life and Times,The Importance of Being Earnest, The Deadly Game, Princess Daisy, The Meeting (exec. prod.), Father & Son: Dangerous Relations, A Father for Charlie, Inside, Sex, Censorship and the Silver Screen, In His Father's Shoes (Emmy Award 1998), For Love of Liberty: The Story of America's Black Patriots (doc., exec. prod.).

ELLIOTT, CHRIS

Actor, Writer. b. New York, NY, May 31, 1960. Father is comedian Bob Elliott. Was performer in improv. theatres, summer stock; also tour guide at Rockefeller Center. Became writer/performer for David Letterman starting in 1982. *Author:* Daddy's Boy: A Son's Shocking Account of Life With a Famous Father (1989).
PICTURES: Manhunter (debut, 1986), The Abyss, Hyperspace, Groundhog Day, CB4, Cabin Boy (also co-story), Kingpin, The Sky Is Falling, There's Something About Mary, Snow Day, Nutty Professor II: The Klumps, The Sky Is Falling, The Swinger, Scary Movie 2, Osmosis Jones, First Time Caller, Scary Movie 4, I'll Believe You, Thomas Kinkade's Home for Christmas, Dance Flick, Speed-Dating, Renaissance Girl.
TELEVISION: *Movies:* Action Family, Ratbag Hero, Medusa: Dare to Be Truthful, The Barefoot Executive, Chrissy: Plain & Simple, The Fish Tank, Eagleheart. *Series*: Late Night With David Letterman (also co- writer; 4 Emmy Awards for writing:, 6 other noms.), Tattingers, Nick and Hillary, Get a Life (also creator, co-writer, prod.), The Naked Truth, Dilbert (voice), Cursed, The Weber Show, According to Jim, Everybody Loves Raymond, King of the Hill. *Specials:* Late Night With David Letterman Anniversary Specials (also co-writer; 2 Emmy Awards for writing: 1986, 1987), Chris Elliott's FDR: One-Man Show (also writer, prod.). *Guest:* More than 56 appearances.

ELLIOTT, LANG

Executive, Producer, Director. b. Los Angeles, CA, Oct. 18, 1949. Began acting in films at an early age, influenced by his uncle, the late actor William Elliott (known as Wild Bill Elliott). Elliott is a Vietnam veteran and has donated much of his time to help veterans by producing the annually televised awards production, The American Veterans Award Show, (AVA) in conjunction with The Veterans Foundation, Inc. (VFI). Early in his career he was employed by, among others, the McGowan Brothers. Turned to film production; co-founded distribution co., The International Picture Show Co., serving as exec. v.p. in charge of financing, production & distribution. In 1976 formed TriStar Pictures, Inc. to finance and distribute product. In 1980 sold TriStar to Columbia, HBO and CBS. 1982, formed Lang Elliott Productions, Inc. Co-founded Longshot Enterprises with actor Tim Conway to prod. films and home videos, 1985. Videos include Dorf on Golf (the first made-for-home-video comedy), 'Scuse Me!, Dorf and the First Olympic Games. Formed Performance Pictures, Inc., in 1989, a prod. & distrib. company. Elliott is the former CEO Of AmeriDreamEntertainment, Inc.. Currently, Elliott is president, chmn. & CEO of Sunn Classic Pictures, Inc. He received Academy Award nominations for Soldier of Orange and The Magic of Lassie. He is also a member of the Directors Guild of America(DGA).
PICTURES: *Prod:* Ride the Hot Wind, Where Time Began, The Farmer, The Billion Dollar Hobo, They Went That-a-Way & That-a-Way, The Prize Fighter. *Prod.-dir.:* The Private Eyes, Cage, Cage II.
TELEVISION: Experiment in Love (prod.), Boys Will Be Boys (writer).

ELLIOTT, SAM

Actor. b. Sacramento, CA, Aug. 9, 1944. m. actress Katharine Ross. e. U. of Oregon.
PICTURES: Butch Cassidy and the Sundance Kid (debut in bit, 1969), The Games, Frogs, Molly and Lawless John, Lifeguard, The Legacy, Mask, Fatal Beauty, Shakedown, Road House, Prancer, Sibling Rivalry, Rush, Gettysburg, Tombstone, The Desperate Trail, The Final Cut, Dog Watch, The Hi-Lo Country, The Big Lebowski, The Contender, Pretty When You Cry, We Were Soldiers, Off the Map, Hulk, Comanche Stallion, Lies & Alibis,Thank You for Smoking, The Barnyard (voice), Ghost Rider, The Golden Compass, Did You Hear About the Morgans?, Up in the Air, The Big Bang.
TELEVISION: *Movies:* The Challenge, Assault on the Wayne, The Blue Knight, I Will Fight No More Forever, The Sacketts, Wild Times, Murder in Texas, Shadow Riders, Travis McGee, A Death in California. The Blue Lightning, Houston: The Legend of Texas, The Quick and the Dead, Conagher (Golden Globe nom. 1992; also co-writer, exec. prod.), Fugitive Nights: Danger in the Desert, Buffalo Girls (Emm nom.; Golden Globe nom. 1995), The Ranger the Cook and a Hole in the Sky, Woman Undone, Blue River, Rough Riders, Texarkana, You Know My Name, Fail Safe, Avenger. *Mini-series:* Once and Eagle, Aspen (The Innocent and the Damned). *Series:* Mission: Impossible, The Yellow Rose. *Guest:* More than 63 appearances.

ELWES, CARY

Actor. b. London, England, Oct. 26, 1962. e. Harrow. Studied for stage with Julie Bovasso at Sarah Lawrence, Bronxville, NY.
PICTURES: Another Country (debut 1984), Oxford Blues, The Bride, Lady Jane, The Princess Bride, Glory, Days of Thunder, Leather Jackets, Hot Shots!, Bram Stoker's Dracula, The Crush, Robin Hood: Men in Tights, Rudyard Kipling's The Jungle Book, Twister, Kiss the Girls, The Informant, Liar Liar, Quest for Camelot (voice), The Cradle Will Rock, Shadow of the Vampire, Wish You Were Dead, Joan of Arc: The Virgin Warrior, The Cat's Meow, Comic Book Villains, American Crime, Ella Enchanted, Neo Ned, Edison, Pucked, The Trouble with Frank, Solo, Sakura: Blue-Eyed Samurai, Georgia Rule, Psych: 9, The Alphabet Killer, Sakura: Blue-Eyed Samurai, A Christmas Carol, Warrior, Flying Lessons, As Good as Dead, Shadows, Little Murder, Fallen Moon, Psych:9, Yellow Submarine, The Adventures of Tintin: The Secret of the Unicorn.
TELEVISION: *Movies:* The Pentagon Wars, Race Against Time, Uprising, The Riverman, Pope John Paul II, Haskett's Chance, Tough Trade. *Mini-series:* From the Earth to the Moon. *Series:* Hercules (voice), The X-Files.

EMMERICH, ROLAND

Director, Writer, Exec. Producer. b. Stuttgart, Germany, Nov. 10, 1955. Studied production design in film school in Munich. First film was student production, The Noah's Ark Principle, which opened the 1984 Berlin Film Festival and was sold to more than 20 countries. Formed Centropolis Film Productions. Prod. TV series, The Visitor, 1997.
PICTURES: *Co-s.p./Dir.:* Making Contact (a.k.a. Joey; dir. only), Ghost Chase, Moon 44, Universal Soldier, Stargate, Independence Day, Godzilla, The Patriot (also exec. prod.), The Day After Tomorrow (also prod.), Isobar, 10,000 B.C. (also prod.), 2012 (also prod.), Fantastic Voyage (also prod.), 2012 (dir., writer), Anonymous (dir. only). *Prod:* Eye of the Storm, The Thirteenth Floor, Eight Legged Freaks, The Day After Tomorrow, King Tut, One Nation, Soul of the Age, The Girls Next Door, Trade, The 1 Second Film, 10,000 B.C.
TELEVISION: *Movie:* Altosax (writer/actor). *Series:* The Visitor (exec. prod.), Godzilla: The Series (exec. prod.).

EMMERICH, TOBY

Executive. e. Calhoun School and Wesleyan University, graduated Phi Beta Kappa, with honors in English, concentrations in classics and film, 1985. Emmerich joined New Line Cinema in 1992 as a dual development and music executive. In his position as president of music, he oversaw the development of platinum and gold-selling soundtracks such as "Elf," "Austin Powers: The Spy Who Shagged Me," "Boogie Nights," "Love & Basketball," "The Mask," among others. In 2001, Emmerich became New Line's president, production and oversaw production during the most successful period in the company's history, which included the release of such hits as the Academy Award-winning blockbuster "The Lord of the Rings: The Return of the King," "Wedding Crashers" (2005's highest-grossing comedy), "The Texas Chainsaw Massacre," "Hairspray" and "About Schmidt," which starred Jack Nicholson in a Golden Globe-winning performance. New Line is widely credited with creating the genre of the R-rated comedy, based on the success of "Wedding Crashers" in 2005. The company is also one of the few studios that still works in the horror genre and is widely known for the iconic "Nightmare on Elm Street" franchise. On Feb. 28, 2008, Warner Bros. Pictures, A Time Warner Company, announced New Line Cinema would be absorbed into the Warner Bros. organization. With this reorganization, company co-chairmen and co-CEOs Bob Shay (who founded New Line in 1967) and Michael Lynne, departed the company. Warner Bros. tapped Emmerich in March 2008 to be president & COO of a new, scaled down New Line Cinema. Emmerich reports directly to Warner Bros. President & COO Alan Horn and works closely with President, Warner Bros. Picture Group Jeff Robinov. Emmerich's charge is to use WBPG's existing infrastructure to reduce costs and take advantage of Warner Bros.' industry-leading scale. As a unit of Warner Bros., New Line continues to maintain its own development, creative and production teams. Its marketing, publicity, distribution, business and legal affairs and physical production staff report to Emmerich, but closely coordinate with their Warner Bros. counterparts.

ENGEL, CHARLES F.

Executive, Producer. b. Los Angeles, CA, Aug. 30. e. Michigan State U., UCLA. Son of writer-prod. Samuel G. Engel. Program development, ABC-TV, 1964-68; v.p. Univ.-TV, 1972; sr. v.p., 1977; exec. v.p., 1980; pres., MCA Pay-TV Programming, 1981. ACE Award, 1988 for outstanding contribution to cable; v.p. Universal TV, exec. in charge of ABC Mystery Movie, 1989. Sr. v.p. 1992 in charge of Columbo, Murder She Wrote, SeaQuest, The Rockford Files. Founding member board of governors, the National Academy of Cable Programming. Member, Television Academy. Exec. v.p. of programming, Universal Television, 1997.
TELEVISION: Law & Order: Criminal Intent (studio exec.), The Aquarians (exec. prod.), Run a Crooked Mile (exec. prod.), Road Raiders (prod.), ABC Mystery Movie (exec. in chg. of prod.), Murder She Wrote: A Story to Die For, Murder She Wrote: The Last Free Man, Murder She Wrote: The Celtic Riddle (exec. prod.).

ENGELBERG, MORT

Producer. b. Memphis, TN. e. U. of Illinois, U. of Missouri. Taught journalism; worked as reporter for UPI, AP. Worked for U.S. government, including USIA, Peace Corps., Office of Economic Opportunity; President's Task Force on War on Poverty. Left gov. service in 1967 to become film unit publicist, working on three films in Europe: Dirty Dozen, Far From the Madding Crowd, The Comedians. Returned to U.S.; appt. pub. mgr. for United Artists. Sent to Hollywood as asst. to Herb Jaffe, UA head of west coast prod., which post he assumed when Jaffe left. Left to join now deceased indep. prod., Ray Stark.
PICTURES: Smokey and the Bandit, Hot Stuff, The Villain, The Hunter, Smokey and the Bandit II, Smokey and the Bandit III, Nobody's Perfekt, The Heavenly Kid, The Big Easy, Maid to Order, Dudes, Three For the Road, Russkies, Pass the Ammo, Trading Hearts, Fright Night Part II, Remote Control, There Goes the Neighborhood.

ENGLUND, ROBERT

Actor. b. Glendale, CA, June 6, 1949. e. UCLA, RADA. First role was in the Cleveland stage production of Godspell, 1971.
PICTURES: Buster and Billie, Hustle, Stay Hungry, Death Trap (Eaten Alive), The Last of the Cowboys, St. Ives, A Star is Born, Big Wednesday, Bloodbrothers, The Fifth Floor, Dead and Buried, Galaxy of Terror, Don't Cry It's Only Thunder, A Nightmare on Elm Street, A Nightmare on Elm Street Part 2: Freddy's Revenge, Never Too Young to Die, A Nightmare on Elm Street 3: Dream Warriors, A Nightmare on Elm Street 4: The Dream Master, 976-EVIL (dir. only), A Nightmare on Elm Street: The Dream Child, Phantom of the Opera, The Adventures of Ford Fairlane, Danse Macabre, Freddy's Dead: The Final Nightmare, Eugenie, Wes Craven's New Nightmare, The Mangler, The Paper Route, Vampyre Wars, Killer Tongue, Regeneration, Wishmaster, Meet the Deedles, Urban Legend, Strangeland, The Prince and the Surfer, Freddy vs. Jason, Python, Wish You Were Dead, Windfall, Land of Canaan, Il Ritorno di Cagliostro, 2001 Maniacs, Land of Canaan, The Demons 5, Behind the Mask: The Rise of Leslie Vernon, 2001 Maniacs, Killer Pad, The Mole Man of Belmont Avenue, Good Day for It.
TELEVISION: *Movies:* Hobson's Choice, Young Joe: The Forgotten Kennedy, The Ordeal of Patty Hearst, The Courage and the Passion, Mind Over Murder, Thou Shalt Not Kill, The Fighter, Journey's End, Starflight: The Plane That Couldn't Land, I Want to Live, Infidelity, A Perry Mason Mystery: The Case of the Lethal Lifestyle, Robin Cook's Mortal Fear, The Unspoken Truth, Black Swarm. *Mini-series:* V: The Final Battle, North and South II, V: The Second Generation. *Series:* Downtown, Freddy's Nightmares, Nightmare Cafe, The Batman (voice), Justice League Unlimited (voice), The Spectacular Spider-Man, Fear Clinic. *Host:* Horror Hall of Fame, Sci-Fi Channel, A Nightmare on Elm Street: Real Nightmares. *Guest:* More than 103 appearances.

ENGSTROM, JEWELL

Executive. e. B.A. degree in economics and businesss, Univ. of California in Los Angeles. A C.P.A. working for Price Waterhouse, Engstrom worked with clients ranging from banks to entertainment companies for first six years of career. She then joined The Walt Disney Company in 1990 and has served in financial mgt. roles there ever since, first as a mgr. of finance for the Disney Channel and working through the ranks to CFO and senior v.p. with Disney-ABC's TV units. Since Oct. 2005 Engstrom has been the CFO and executive v.p. for the Disney-ABC Cable Networks Group. Engstrom's scope of duties includes intl. finance and accounting responsibilities, overseeing all finance-related issues for Disney-ABC Cable Networks Group's international networks, including 23 Disney Channels, eight Toon Disney channels, eight Playhouse Disney channels, the wholly owned Jetix Latin America and over a dozen Jetix channels across Europe. She also is responsible for all finance-related issues concerning the division's wholly owned domestic entities, including ABC Family, Disney Channel, Toon Disney and SOAPnet. Financial issues in regard to the Walt Disney Television Animation production unit and Disney's equity interest in Lifetime Entertainment Services, A&E Television Networks and E! Networks fall under her domain, as does responsibility for formulating new financial and business opportunities for the group and overseeing long-term planning. She is a member of the Lifetime Television Board of Directors.

ENRICO, ROGER

Executive. e. Babson College. With more than 30 years as an executive responsible for building major consumer brands, Enrico joined DreamWorks Animation SKG as chairman of the bd. in Oct. 2004 shortly after the company's initial public offering. Enrico's business background: joined PepsiCo, Inc. in 1971, became president and CEO of Pepsi-Cola USA in 1983, president and CEO of PepsiCo Worldwide Beverages in 1986, chairman and CEO of Frito-Lay, Inc. in 1991, and chairman and CEO of PepsiCo Worldwide Foods in 1992. Enrico was chairman and CEO, PepsiCo Worldwide Restaurants, from 1994 to 1996. From April 1996 to April 2001, he was chairman of PepsiCo, Inc.'s board, and vice chairman from April 2001 to April 2002. He now serves as chairman on the Board of Directors of DreamWorks Animation SKG, Inc., Belo Corporation and the National Geographic Society where he also serves as chmn. of the Council of Advisors. Memberships: exec. bd. of the Dallas Symphony; a trustee of the Eisenhower Fellowship Exchange; and on bd. of the Dallas Center for the Performing Arts. Enrico is a former bd. member of PepsiCo, Prudential Financial, EDS, Target Corporation, Theravance, Dallas Opera, Lincoln Center for the Performing Arts, the New York City Opera and Babson College. Additionally, Enrico has taught leadership to high potential executives at PepsiCo, as well as to graduate students at the Yale School of Management and at the SMU Cox School of Business, and is actively involved in improving post-secondary educational opportunities for inner city students in Dallas.

EPHRON, NORA

Writer, Director. b. New York, NY, May 19, 1941. e. Wellesley Col. Daughter of writers Henry and Phoebe Ephron. m. writer Nicholas Pileggi. *Author:* Heartburn, Crazy Salad, Scribble Scribble. Appeared in Crimes and Misdemeanors, Husbands and Wives. Received WGA Award, Ian McLellan Hunter Award 2003.
PICTURES: *Writer:* Silkwood (Academy Award nom.; WGA nom. 1984), Heartburn, When Harry Met Sally... (Academy Award nom.; Golden Globe nom.; WGA nom. 1990; also assoc. prod.), Cookie (also exec. prod.), My Blue Heaven (also exec. prod.), This is My Life (also dir.), Sleepless in Seattle (Academy Award nom.; WGA nom. 1994; also dir.), Mixed Nuts (also dir.), Michael (also dir., prod., exec. prod.), You've Got Mail (also prod.), Hanging Up (also prod.), Lucky Numbers (also prod.), Bewitched, Flipped (also prod.), Julie & Julia (also prod., WGA nom. 2010).
TELEVISION: *Movies:* (writer): Perfect Gentlemen, Red Tails in Love: A Wildlife Drama in Central Park (also prod., dir.). *Series:* Adam's Rib. *Special:* The 74th Annual Academy Awards (dir., NY Tribute).

ERICE, VICTOR

Writer, Director. b. San Sebastian, Spain, June 30, 1940.
PICTURES: En la terraza, Paginas de un diario perdido, Los dias perdidos, Entre Vias, Los Desafios, The Spirit of the Beehive, Obscure August Dreams (sp. only), El Proximo otono (s.p. only), The South, The Dream of Light, Ten Minutes Older: The Trumpet.

ERICSON, JOHN

Actor. b. Detroit, MI, Sept. 25, 1926. e. American Acad. of Dramatic Arts. Appeared in stock; then Stalag 17 on Broadway.
PICTURES: Teresa (debut, 1951), Rhapsody, The Student Prince, Green Fire, Bad Day at Black Rock, The Return of Jack Slade, The Cruel Tower, Oregon Passage, Forty Guns, Day of the Bad Man, Pretty Boy Floyd, Under Ten Flags, Slave Queen of Babylon, 7 Faces of Dr. Lao, Operation Atlantis, The Money Jungle, The Destructors, Treasure of Pancho Villa, The Bamboo Saucer (Collision Course), Heads or Tails, Bedknobs and Broomsticks, Hustle Squad, Crash, Final Mission, Alien Zone, Project Saucer, Golden Triangle, Queens Are Wild, Hustler Squad, $10,000 Caper, Primary Target.
TELEVISION: *Movies:* The Bounty Man, Hog Wild, Hunter's Moon, House on the Rue Riviera, Tenafly. *Mini-series:* Robert Kennedy and His Times, Space. Specials: Saturday's Children, Heritage of Anger, The Innocent Sleep. *Series:* Honey West, General Hospital. *Guest:* More than 86 appearances.

ERMAN, JOHN

Director. b. Chicago, IL, Aug. 3, 1935. e. U. of California. Debut as TV director, Stoney Burke, 1962.
PICTURES: Making It, Ace Eli and Rodger of the Skies, Stella.
TELEVISION: *Movies:* Letters From Three Lovers, Green Eyes, Alexander the Other Side of Dawn, Just Me and You, My Old Man, Moviola (This Year's Blonde; Scarlett O'Hara War; The Silent Lovers), The Letter, Eleanor: First Lady of the World, Who Will Love My Children? (Emmy Award, 1983), Another Woman's Child, A Streetcar Named Desire, Right to Kill?, The Atlanta Child Murders, An Early Frost, The Two Mrs. Grenvilles (also sprv. prod.), When the Time Comes, The Attic: The Hiding of Anne

Frank (also prod.), David (also sprv. prod.), The Last Best Year (also sprv. prod.), The Last to Go (also prod.), Our Sons, Carolina Skeletons, Breathing Lessons (also prod.), The Sunshine Boys (also prod.), The Boys Next Door (also prod.), Ellen Foster, (also prod.), Only Love, Too Rich: The Secret Life of Doris Duke (also prod.), Victoria & Albert, The Blackwater Lightship, Candles on Bay Street (also prod.). *Mini-series:* Roots: The Next Generations (co-dir.), Queen (also co-prod.), Scarlett (also prod.).

ESPOSITO, GIANCARLO

Actor. b. Copenhagen, Denmark, April 26, 1958. Made B'way debut as child in 1968 musical Maggie Flynn.
THEATRE: B'way: Maggie Flynn, The Me Nobody Knows, Lost in the Stars, Seesaw, Merrily We Roll Along, Don't Get God Started, Sacrilege. Off-B'way: Zooman and the Sign (Theatre World Award, Obie Award), Keyboard, Who Loves the Dancer, House of Ramon Igleslas, Do Lord Remember Me, Balm in Gilead, Anchorman, Distant Fires, Trafficking in Broken Hearts.
PICTURES: Running, Taps, Trading Places, The Cotton Club, Desperately Seeking Susan, Maximum Overdrive, Sweet Lorraine, School Daze, Do the Right Thing, Mo'Better Blues, King of New York, Harley Davidson and the Marlboro Man, Night on Earth, Bob Roberts, Malcolm X, Amos & Andrew, Fresh, Smoke, The Keeper (co-prod. only), The Usual Suspects, Kla$h, Blue in the Face, The Keeper, Reckless, Loose Women, Nothing to Lose, The Maze, The People, Trouble on the Corner, Twilight, Phoenix, Stardust, Where's Marlowe?, Big City Blues, Speak Truth to Power, Josephine, Cadillac Tramps, Monkeybone, Pinero, Ali, Blind Horizon, Ash Tuesday, A Killer Within, Hate Crime, Shall Not Want, Derailed, Carlito's Way: The Beginning, I Will Avenge You, Iago!, Last Holiday, Sherrybaby, Rain, Reggaeton, The Box, Racing Daylight, Feel the Noise, Rabbit Hole, Adele.
TELEVISION: *Movies:* The Gentleman Bandit, Go Tell It on the Mountain, Relentless: Mind of a Killer, The Tomorrow Man, Five Desperate Hours, Thirst, Naked City: Justice With a Bullet, Homicide: The Movie, NYPD 2069, Chupacabra: Dark Seas, Xenophobia. *Mini-series:* 5 Days to Midnight. *Series:* Bakersfield P.D, Girls Club, South Beach, Breaking Bad. *Special:* Roanok. *Guest:* More than 74 appearances.

ESSEX, DAVID

Actor, Singer, Composer. b. Plaistow, London, England, July 23, 1947. e. Shipman Sch., Custom House. Started as a singer-drummer in East London band. 1967: Joined touring Repertory Co. in The Fantasticks, Oh, Kay, etc. 1970: West End debut in Ten Years Hard, 1972: Jesus Christ in Godspell, Che in Evita; Lord Byron in Childe Byron, 1983-84: Fletcher Christian in own musical Mutiny! on album and stage. International recording artist. Variety Club of Great Britain show business personality of 1978. Many gold & silver disc intl. awards. 1989, Royal Variety performance. World concerts since 1974.
PICTURES: Assault, All Coppers Are..., That'll Be the Day, Stardust, Silver Dream Racer (also wrote score), Shogun Mayeda, Dick (soundtrack, writer, performer "Rock On") The Devil's Rejects (soundtrack, writer, performer "Rock On".
TELEVISION: Top of the Pops, Own Specials, The River (also composed music), BBC series. U.S.: Merv Griffin, Johnny Carson, Dinah Shore, American Bandstand, Midnight Special, Grammy Awards, Salute To The Beatles, Don Kirshner's Rock Concert, A.M. America, Phil Everly in Session, Paul Ryan Show, The David Essex Showcase, The River, 10 Years of Heartbeat (tv documentary, as himself.). *Series:* Twiggs, David Essex, The River, Roy's Raiders (composer theme), many more.

ESTEVEZ, EMILIO

Actor, Director, Writer. b. New York, NY, May 12, 1962. Father is actor Martin Sheen; brother is actor Charlie Sheen. Made debut at age 20 in TV movie starring his father, In the Custody of Strangers.
PICTURES: Tex (debut, 1982), The Outsiders, Nightmares, Repo Man, The Breakfast Club, St. Elmo's Fire, That Was Then This is Now (also s.p.), Maximum Overdrive, Wisdom (also dir., s.p.), Stakeout, Young Guns. Men at Work (also dir., s.p.), Young Guns II, Freejack, The Mighty Ducks, National Lampoon's Loaded Weapon 1, Another Stakeout, Judgment Night, D2: The Mighty Ducks, The Jerky Boys (co- exec. prod. only), The War at Home (also dir. and prod.), Mighty Ducks 3, Mission: Impossible, The Bang Bang Club (dir., prod. only), Killer's Head, Rated X, Sand, The L.A. Riot Spectacular, The Mighty Ducks 4, Bobby (also writer, dir.), Arthur and the Invisibles (voice), The Way (also dir., writer, prod.).
TELEVISION: *Movies:* In the Custody of Strangers. Nightbreaker, Dollar for the Dead, Late Last Night, Rated X (also dir.). *Series: Segment Dir.:* The Guardian, Cold Case, CSI: NY, Close to Home, many more series episodes as director.

ESTEY MCLOUGHLIN, HILARY

Executive. e. Bachelor's degree, broadcasting and film, Boston Univ. Estey McLoughlin began her career as a research analyst for Seltel, Inc. in 1984. In 1986, joined the Lorimar-Telepictures research dept., holding various titles including senior research analyst, mgr. and dir. of research. In 1989, named dir., development at Lorimar-Telepictures Productions; with Telepictures Production launch in 1992, named v.p., development. Making her career at Telepictures, Estey McLoughlin has served in the following capacities: v.p., programming; exec. prod. of "The Rosie O'Donnell Show;" senior v.p., programming and development for three years; then executive v.p. & general mgr. in July 2002; promoted to current position, president, Telepictures Productions in Aug. 2006. During her tenure at Telepictures, Estey McLoughlin has developed and produced some of the biggest hits in first-run syndication, including "The Rosie O'Donnell Show" and "The Ellen DeGeneres Show." She helped build the non-scripted production division into one of the industry's top producers of first-run syndicated programming, responsible for some 17 syndicated strips. Telepictures Productions' series have received 41 Daytime Emmys.

ESTRADA, ERIK

Actor. r.n. Enrique Estrada. b. New York, NY, March 16, 1949. Began professional career in Mayor John Lindsay's Cultural Program, performing in public parks. Joined American Musical Dramatic Acad. for training. Feature film debut in The Cross and the Switchblade (1970).
PICTURES: The New Centurions, Airport '75, Midway, Trackdown, Where Is Parsifal?, Lightblast, The Repentant, Hour of the Assassin, The Lost Idol, A Show of Force, Night of the Wilding, Twisted Justice, Caged Fury, Guns, Spirits, Do or Die, The Divine Enforcer, Alien Seed, Night of the Wilding, National Lampoon's Loaded Weapon 1, The Last Riders, Gang Justice, Visions, Tom Sawyer, King Cobra, Olver Twisted, UP Michigan, Van Wilder, Code Black, Border Blues, Horrorween, Spring Break '83.
TELEVISION: *Movies:* Fire!, Honeyboy, The Dirty Dozen: The Fatal Mission, She Knows Too Much, Earth Angel, Angel Eyes, Panic in the Skies!, We're No Angels, CHiPs '99, Taylor Made, Mother Goose Parade, Husband for Hire, Dad's Funniest Moments. *Series:* CHiPS (Golden Globe nom. 1980), Walking After Midnight, The Bold and the Beautiful, Sealab 2021. *Guest:* More than 142 ap
pearances.

ESZTERHAS, JOE

Writer. b. Hungary, Nov. 23, 1944. Author of novel Charlie Simpson's Apocalypse (nom. National Book Award, 1974), Nark!, and novelization of F.I.S.T..
PICTURES: F.I.S.T., Flashdance, Jagged Edge, Big Shots, Betrayed, Checking Out, Music Box (also co-exec. prod.), Basic Instinct, Nowhere to Run (co-sp., co-exec. prod.), Sliver (also co-exec. prod.), Jade (writer, exec. prod.), Hearts of Fire, Original Sin, Showgirls, One Night Stand, Telling Lies in America, Male Pattern Baldness, An Alan Smithee Film: Burn Hollywood Burn (also actor), Jackie Chan: My Story (video documentary), Basic Instinct 2.

EVANS, HARRY KENT

Executive. b. Long Beach, CA, July 16, 1935. Int'l. representative, UAW, 1960-76. Exec. dir., International Photographers Guild, 1976-90. CEO of the ASC, 1990-94. Exec. VP, Meier Entertainment Group, Vancouver, BC, 1994-96. Exec. VP. Meier Worldwide Intermedia, 1996-.

EVANS, ROBERT

Producer. r.n. Robert J. Shapera. b. New York, NY, June 29, 1930. Son is actor Josh Evans. Radio actor at age 11; went on to appear in more than 300 radio prog. (incl. Let's Pretend, Archie Andrews, The Aldrich Family, Gangbusters) on major networks. Also appeared on early TV. At 20 joined brother, Charles, and Joseph Picone, as partner in women's clothing firm of Evan-Picone, Inc., 1952-67. In 1957 signed by Universal to play Irving Thalberg in Man of a Thousand Faces after recommendation by Norma Shearer, Thalberg's widow. Guest columnist NY Journal American, 1958. Independent prod. at 20th Century-Fox. 1966-76, with Paramount Pictures as head of prod., then exec. v.p. worldwide prod. (supervising Barefoot in the Park, Rosemary's Baby, Barbarella, Goodbye Columbus, Love Story, The Godfather I & II, The Great Gatsby, etc.). Resigned to become indep. prod. again; with exclusive contract with Paramount. *Autobiography:* The Kid Stays in the Picture (1994).
PICTURES: *Actor:* Man of a Thousand Faces, The Sun Also Rises, The Fiend Who Walked the West, The Best of Everything, Mind Games (also exec. prod.). *Producer:* Chinatown (Academy Award nom. 1975), Marathon Man, Black Sunday, Players, Urban Cowboy, Popeye, The Cotton Club, The Two Jakes, Sliver, Jade, The Phantom, The Saint, The Out of Towners, The Kid Stays in the Picture (documentary, as himself, s.p.), How to Lose a Guy in 10 Days, Triggerfish, How to Lose a Guy in 10 Days, U.F.O. (exec. prod.).
TELEVISION: *Actor:* Elizabeth and Essex (1947), Young Widow Brown, The Right to Happiness. *Prod.:* Get High on Yourself. *Series:* Kid Notorious (voice, also creator/writer, exec.prod).

EVERETT, CHAD

Actor. r.n. Raymond Lee Cramton. b. South Bend, IN, June 11, 1937. e. Wayne State U., Detroit. Signed by William T. Orr, head of TV prod. for Warner Bros. to 7-year contract. Appeared in many TV series as well as films. Next became contract player at MGM (1963-67). Received star on Hollywood Walk of Fame.
PICTURES: Claudelle Inglish (debut, 1961), The Chapman

Report, Rome Adventure, Get Yourself a College Girl, The Singing Nun, Made in Paris, Johnny Tiger, The Last Challenge, Return of the Gunfighter, First to Fight, The Impossible Years, Firechasers, Airplane II: The Sequel, Fever Pitch, Jigsaw, Heroes Stand Alone, Official Denial, Psycho, Mulholland Dr., A View From the Top, The Distance, Unspoken (narr.), Death Keeps Coming, Break.
TELEVISION: *Movies:* Intruder, The Love Boat, Police Story, Thunderboat Row, Malibu, The French Atlantic Affair, Mistress in Paradise, Journey to the Unknown, In the Glitter Palace, Hard to Forget. *Mini-series:* Centennial, McKenna, Star Command, When Time Expires. *Series:* The Dakotas, Medical Center (2 Golden Globe noms. 1971, 1973), Hagen, The Rousters, McKenna, Dark Skies, Manhattan AZ, Master's Theater (narr.). *Guest:* More than 86 appearances.

EVERETT, RUPERT

Actor. b. Norfolk, England, May 29, 1959. e. Ampleforth Central School for Speech & Drama. Apprenticed with Glasgow's Citizen's Theatre. Originated role of Guy Bennett in Another Country on London stage in 1982 and made feature film debut in screen version in 1984. Author: Are You Working Darling?
PICTURES: Another Country, Real Life, Dance with a Stranger, Duet for One, Chronicle of a Death Foretold, The Right Hand Man, Hearts of Fire, The Gold-Rimmed Glasses, Jigsaw, The Comfort of Strangers, Inside Monkey Zetterland, Ready to Wear (Pret-a-Porter), The Madness of King George, Dunston Checks In, Cemetary Man, My Best Friend's Wedding (Golden Globe nom. 1998), Shakespeare in Love, B. Monkey, A Midsummer Night's Dream, Inspector Gadget, An Ideal Husband (Golden Globe nom. 2000), The Next Best Thing, Who Shot Victor Fox, South Kensington, The Wild Thornberrys, The Importance of Being Earnest, Unconditional Love, To Kill A King, Shrek 2, Separate Lies, A Different Loyalty, People, A Way Through the Woods, ...and Quiet Flows the Don, Valiant (voice), The Chronicles of Narnia: The Lion, the Witch & the Wardrobe (voice), Shrek the Third (voice), Stardust, St. Trinian's (also exec. prod.), Wild Target, St Trinian's 2: The Legend of Fritton's Gold (also exec. prod.), Hysteria.
TELEVISION: *Movies:* Arthur the King, Soft Targets, Princess Daisy, One Night with Robbie Williams, Mr. Ambassador, Sherlock Holmes and the Case of the Silk Stocking. *Mini-series:* The Far Pavilions, Les Liasons Dangereuses. *Series:* Tikhiy Don. *Guest:* More than 73 appearances.

EVIGAN, GREG

Actor. b. South Amboy, NJ, Oct. 14, 1953. Appeared on NY stage in Jesus Christ Superstar and Grease.
PICTURES: Stripped to Kill, DeepStar Six, House of the Damned, Mel, The Pawn, Pets, Sweet Revenge, Arizona Summer, Molding Clay, Hoboken Hollow, River's End.
TELEVISION: *Movies:* B.J. and the Bear (pilot), Private Sessions, The Lady Forgets, Lies Before Kisses, TekWar, TekJustice, TekLab, TekLords, One of Her Own, Deadly Family Secrets, Nobody Lives Forever, Survivor, Murder Among Friends, Spirit, He Sees You When You're Sleeping, Straight from the Heart, Found, Cerberus, Found, Captive Hearts, Our House, My Silent Partner, Poison Ivy: The Secret Society, 100 Million BC, Mail Order Bride, Phantom Racer (also exec. prod.), Heat Wave. *Series:* A Year at the Top, B.J. and the Bear, Masquerade, My Two Dads, P.S. I Luv U, TekWar, Melrose Place, Pacific Palisades, Family Rules, Big Sound, Racin' for a Livin'. *Guest:* More than 89 appearances.

F

FAHEY, JEFF

Actor. b. Olean, NY, Nov. 29, 1956. Family moved to Buffalo when he was 10 years old. Was member of Joffrey Ballet for 3 years. Appeared on B'way in Brigadoon (1980), tour of Oklahoma!, Paris prod. of West Side Story, and London prod. of Orphans.
PICTURES: Silverado (debut, 1985), Psycho III, Riot on 42nd Street, The Serpent of Death, Wrangler, Split Decisions, Backfire, Outback, True Blood, Out of Time, Last of the Finest, Impulse, White Hunter Black Heart, Body Parts, Iron Maze, The Lawnmower Man, Woman of Desire, Freefall, Wyatt Earp, Temptation, Quick, The Sweeper (also asst. prod.), Serpent's Liar, Eye of the Wolf, Darkman III: Die Darkman Die, When Justice Fails, Waiting for the Man, Operation Delta Force, Johnny 2.0, Catherine's Grove, Lethal Tender, The Underground (also co-prod), Small Time, Detour, Spoken in Silence, Revelation, Hijack, Dazzle, The Contract, The Sculptress, Epicenter, Spin Cycle, The Newcomers, Blind Heat, Cold Heart, Close Call, Ghost Rock, Unspeakable, Outlaw, Inferno, Choosing Matthias, Out There, Fallen Angels, Darkhunters, Day of Redemption, Close Call (also prod.), Only the Brave, Scorpius Gigantus, Grindhouse, Planet Terror, Matchmaker Mary, Easy Rider: The Ride Back, Bed and Breakfast, Machete, Eldorado. *Producer:* Avenue A, Killing Cupid.
TELEVISION: *Movies:* Execution of Raymond Graham, Parker Kane, Curiosity Kills, Iran: Days of Crisis, Sketch Artist, In the Company of Darkness, The Hit List, Blindsided, Baree, Sketch Artist II: Hands That See, Virtual Seduction, Every Woman's Dream, On the Line, Johnny 2.0, Wolf Lake,Absolute Zero, Icon, Crimson Force, Locusts: The 8th Plague, Manticore, The Eden Formula. *Mini-series:* The Seventh Scroll. *Series:* One Life to Live, The Marshal, Lost.

FAIMAN, PETER

Director, Producer. b. Australia. Entered entertainment business through TV, involved early in production-direction of major variety series in Australia. Assoc. prod.-dir. of over 20 programs for The Paul Hogan Show and two Hogan specials filmed in England (1983). Developed Australia's most popular and longest-running national variety program, The Don Lane Show. Responsible for creative development of the TV Week Logie Awards on the Nine Network. For 4 years headed Special Projects Division of the Nine Network Australia. Resigned to establish own prod. co., Peter Faiman Prods. Pty Ltd. 1984. Made m.p. theatrical film debut as director of 'Crocodile' Dundee.
PICTURES: Dutch, FernGully: The Last Rainforest (prod. only).
TELEVISION: *Series:* The Graham Kennedy Show, The Paul Hogan Show, The Don Lane Show, Tonight with Bert Newton, The Pet Department (exec. prod.), Adventure Crazy (co-exec. prod.), Strictly Dancing (consulting prod.), Human Edge (exec. prod.), Spicks and Specks (consulting prod.), Rock Eisteddfod Challenge (creative consult.). *Documentary:* The Pet Show (doc. series, prod.).

FAIRCHILD, MORGAN

Actress. r.n. Patsy Ann McClenny. b. Dallas, TX, Feb. 3, 1950. e. Southern Methodist U.
PICTURES: Bullet for Pretty Boy, The Seduction, Pee-wee's Big Adventure, Red-Headed Stranger, Campus Man, Sleeping Beauty, Midnight Cop, Deadly Illusion, Phantom of the Mall, Body Chemistry 3: Point of Seduction, Freaked, Virgin Hunters, Naked Gun 33 1/3: The Final Insult, Gospa, Venus Rising, Criminal Hearts, Holy Man, Nice Guys Sleep Alone, Held For Ransom, Unshackled, Peril, Call O' The Glen, Jungle Juice, Teddy Bear's Picnic, Arizona Summer, Knuckle Sandwich, Shock to the System, The Sno Cone Stand Inc, The Steamroom, Spring Break '83, Code Enforcer, Boy Toy.
TELEVISION: *Movies:* The Initiation of Sarah, Murder in Music City, Concrete Cowboys, The Memory of Eva Ryker, Flamingo Road (pilot), The Dream Merchants, The Girl the Gold Watch and Dynamite, Honeyboy, The Zany Adventures of Robin Hood, Time Bomb, Street of Dreams, The Haunting of Sarah Harding, How to Murder a Millionare, Menu for Murder, Writer's Block. Perry Mason: The Case of the Skin-Deep Scandal, Based on an Untrue Story, Dead Man's Island, Star Command, Into the Arms of Danger, Teenage Confidential, I Was a Teenage Faust, Shock to the System, The Initiation of Sarah. *Mini-series:* 79 Park Avenue, North and South Book II. *Series:* Search for Tomorrow, Flamingo Road (Golden Globe nom. 1982), Paper Dolls, Falcon Crest, Roseanne, The City, General Hospital, Fashion House, The Bold and the Beautiful. *Guest:* More than 150 appearances.

FALK, PETER

Actor. b. New York, NY, Sept. 16, 1927. e. New Sch. for Social Research, B.A., 1951; Syracuse U. M.F.A. Studied with Eva Le Galliene and Sanford Meisner. Worked as efficiency expert for Budget Bureau State of CT. Golden Globe Award 1973 and 6 noms. for the Columbo series.
THEATRE: Off-B'way: Don Juan (debut, 1956), The Iceman Cometh, Comic Strip, Purple Dust, Bonds of Interest, The Lady's Not for Burning, Diary of a Scoundrel. On Broadway: Saint Joan, The Passion of Josef D., The Prisoner of Second Avenue. Regional: Light Up the Sky (L.A.), Glengarry Glen Ross (tour).
PICTURES: Wind Across the Everglades (debut, 1958), The Bloody Brood, Pretty Boy Floyd, The Secret of the Purple Reef, Murder Inc. (Academy Award nom. 1961), Pocketful of Miracles (Academy Award nom. 1962), Pressure Point, The Balcony, It's a Mad Mad Mad Mad World, Robin and the 7 Hoods, Italiano Brava Gente (Attack and Retreat), The Great Race, Penelope, Luv, Anzio, Castle Keep, Machine Gun McCann, Operation Snafu, Husbands, A Woman Under the Influence, Murder by Death, Mikey and Nicky, The Cheap Detective, The Brink's Job, Opening Night, The In-Laws, The Great Muppet Caper, All the Marbles, Big Trouble, Happy New Year, The Princess Bride, Wings of Desire, Vibes, Cookie, In the Spirit, Tune in Tomorrow, The Player, Faraway So Close!, Roommates, Cops and Roberts, Anything For John, Enemies of Laughter, Lakeboat, 3 Days of Rain, Hubert's Brain, Made, Corky Romano, Undisputed, Shark Tale (voice), The Thing About My Folks, Next, American Cowslip.
TELEVISION: *Movies:* Prescription: Murder, The Law and Mr. Jones (Emmy nom. 1961), A Step Out of Line, Ransom for a Dead Man, Griffin and Phoenix: A Love Story, Columbo Goes to College, Columbo: Agenda for Murder (Emmy Award 1990), Caution: Murder Can Be Hazardous to Your Health, Columbo and the Murder of a Rock Star (Emmy nom.; Golden Globe nom. 1991), Death Hits the Jackpot, Columbo: No Time to Die, Columbo: A Bird in the Hand (also exec. prod.), Columbo: It's All in the Game (also writer, exec. prod. Emmy nom.; Golden Globe nom. 1994), Columbo: Butterfly in Shades of Grey (also exec. prod.), Columbo: Undercover, Columbo: Strange Bedfellows (also exec. prod.), Pronto, Columbo: A Trace of Murder, Columbo:

Ashes to Ashes, Vig, Columbo: Murder with Too Many Notes, A Storm in Summer (Emmy nom. 2001), From Where I Sit, A Town Without Christmas, The Lost Word, Columbo: The Man Who Murdered Himself, Columbo: Columbo Likes the Nightlife, Finding John Christmas, Wilder Days, When Angels Come to Town. *Series:* The Dick Powell Theatre (Emmy Award 1962), The Trials of O'Brien, Columbo (1971-77; Emmy Awards: 1972, 1975, 1976; Golen Globe Award 1973; 8 other nom.), Columbo (1989, also co-exec. prod.; Emmy Award, 1990), The NBC Mystery Movie (4 Emmy Awards, 6 other noms.). *Specials:* The Sacco-Vanzetti Story, The Million Dollar Incident, Brigadoon, A Hatful of Rain, Clue: Movies Murder and Mystery, A Storm in Summer (Emmy nom. 2001). *Guest:* More than 195 appearances.

FANGMEIER, STEFEN

Special Visual Effects. b. El Paso, TX, Dec. 9, 1960.
PICTURES: Terminator 2: Judgment Day (comp. graph. super.), Hook (comp. graph. super.), Jurassic Park (lead comp. graph. super.), Casper (dig. char. co-super). Visual Effects Supervisor: Twister (Academy Award nom. 1997), The Trigger Effect, Speed 2: Cruise Control, Small Soldiers, Saving Private Ryan, Galaxy Quest (co-super.), Aizea: City of the Wind, The Perfect Storm (Academy Award nom. 2001), Signs, The Bourne Identity, Dreamcatcher, Master and Commander: The Far Side of the World (Academy Award nom.; VES nom. 2004), Lemony Snicket's A Series of Unfortunate Events, Eragon (dir. only), Wanted.

FANNING, DAKOTA

Actress. b. Conyers, GA, Feb. 23, 1994. Began career at age 5 for a national TV commercial. Youngest person at age 8 to be nominated for a Screen Actors Guild Award for I Am Sam. Has been nominated Young Artist Award 2002-2005. Won BFCA Award; Best Young Actor, I Am Sam.
PICTURES: Tomcats, I Am Sam, Trapped, Sweet Home Alabama, Hansel & Gretel, Uptown Girls, The Cat in the Hat, Man on Fire, Nine Lives, Hide and Seek, War of the Worlds, Dreamer: Inspired by a True Story, Charlotte's Web, Hounddog, Coraline (voice), Winged Creatures, Hurricane Mary, The Secret Life of Bees, Push, New Moon, The Runaways, The Twilight Saga: Eclipse.
TELEVISION: *Movie:* Kim Possible: A Stitch in Time (voice). *Mini-series:* Taken. *Series:* Taken. *Documentary:* In the Realms of the Unreal (narr., voices). *Specials:* Toy Mountain Christmas Special, Toy Mountain Christmas Special. *Guest:* More than 80 appearances.

FARENTINO, JAMES

Actor. b. Brooklyn, NY, Feb. 24, 1938. e. American Acad. of Dramatic Arts.
THEATRE: *B'way:* Death of a Salesman, A Streetcar Named Desire (revival, 1973; Theatre World Award). *Off-B'way:* The Days and Nights of Bebe Fenstermaker, In the Summerhouse. *Regional:* One Flew Over the Cuckoo's Nest (Jos. Jefferson, Chas. MacArthur & Chicago Drama Critics League Awards), California Suite, The Best Man, The Big Knife, Good-Bye Charlie, A Thousand Clowns, Love Letters, Boy Gets Girl.
PICTURES: Psychomania (Violent Midnight), Engine Pulver, The War Lord, The Pad... And How to Use It (Golden Globe Award, 1967), The Ride to Hangman's Tree, Banning, Rosie!, Me Natalie, The Story of a Woman, The Final Countdown, Dead and Buried, Her Alibi, Bulletproof, Termination Man, Radio Silence, The Last Producer.
TELEVISION: *Movies:* Wings of Fire, The Whole World is Watching, The Sound of Anger, Longest Night, Family Rico, Cool Million, The Elevator, Crossfire, Possessed, Silent Victory: Undercover Cop, The Kitty O'Neil Story, Son Rise: A Miracle of Love, That Secret Sunday, Something So Right, The Cradle Will Fall, License to Kill, A Summer to Remember, That Secret Sunday, Family Sins, Naked Lies, The Red Spider, Who Gets the Friends?, Picking Up the Pieces, In the Line of Duty: A Cop for the Killing, Miles From Nowhere, When No One Would Listen, One Woman's Courage, Honor Thy Father and Mother: The True Story of the Menendez Murders, Dazzle, Scandalous Me: The Jacqueline Susann Story, Murder in the Mirror, Drive/II. *Pilot:* American Nuclear. *Mini-series:* Sins, Jesus of Nazareth (Emmy nom. 1978), On Common Ground, Death of a Salesman, Vanished, Evita Peron. *Series:* The Lawyers (The Bold Ones), Cool Million, Dynasty, Blue Thunder, Mary Tyler Moore, Julie Andrews Show, Julie, ER, Melrose Place. *Guest:* More than 82 appearances.

FARGAS, ANTONIO

Actor. b. Bronx, NY, Aug. 14, 1946. Studied acting at Negro Ensemble Co. and Actor's Studio.
THEATRE: The Great White Hope, The Glass Menagerie, Mod Hamlet, Romeo and Juliet, The Slave, Toilet, The Amen Corner.
PICTURES: The Cool World (debut, 1964), Putney Swope, Pound, Believe in Me, Shaft, Cisco Pike, Across 110th Street, Cleopatra Jones, Busting, Foxy Brown, Conrack, The Gambler, Cornbread Earl and Me, Next Stop Greenwich Village, Car Wash, Pretty Baby, Up the Academy, Firestarter, Streetwalkin', Night of the Sharks, Shakedown, I'm Gonna Git You Sucka, The Borrower, Howling VI: The Freaks, The Celluloid Closet, Don't Be a Menace to South Central While Drinking Your Juice in the Hood, Gator King, Milo, The Suburbans, Unconditional Love, Three Strikes, The Riff, Osomosis Jones (voice), Extreme Honor, Sucker Punch, Jack's Law, The Caper, The Adventures of Umbweki, Abduction of Jesse Bookman, Once Fallen, Changing Hands.
TELEVISION: *Movies:* Starsky and Hutch (pilot), Huckleberry Finn, Escape, Nurse, The Ambush Murders, A Good Sport, Florida Straits, Maid for Each Other, Percy and Thunder, Soul Survivors, Ali: An American Hero. *Series:* Starsky and Hutch, All My Children, Everybody Hates Chris. *Guest:* More than 82 appearances.

FARGO, JAMES

Director. b. Republic, WA, Aug. 14, 1938. e. U. of Washington, B.A.
PICTURES: The Enforcer, Caravans, Every Which Way But Loose, A Game for Vultures, Forced Vengeance, Born to Race, Voyage of the Rock Aliens, Riding the Edge (also actor), Second Chances, Destiny.
TELEVISION: *Movies:* Gus Brown and Midnight Brewster, The Last Electric Knight, Snoops, Sky High. *Series:* Tales of the Gold Monkey, The A-Team, Scarecrow and Mrs. King, Hunter, Sidekicks, Berlin Break.

FARINA, DENNIS

Actor. b. Chicago, IL, Feb. 29, 1944. Served 18 years with Chicago police before being introduced to producer-director Michael Mann who cast him in film Thief. Celebrity Chmn. of Natl. Law Enforcement Officers Memorial in Washington, D.C.
THEATRE: A Prayer for My Daughter, Streamers, Tracers, Bleacher Bums, Some Men Need Help, The Time of Your Life.
PICTURES: Thief (debut, 1981), Jo Jo Dancer Your Life Is Calling, Manhunter, Midnight Run, Men of Respect, We're Talkin' Serious Money, Mac, Another Stakeout, Striking Distance, Romeo Is Bleeding, Little Big League, Get Shorty, Eddie, That Old Feeling, Out of Sight, Saving Private Ryan, The Mod Squad, Snatch, Sidewalks of New York, Big Trouble, The Promise, Planet of the Pitts, Stealing Harvard, Poker Night, Paparazzi, Purple Violets, National Lampoon's Bag Boy, You Kill Me, The Grand, Bottle Shock, What Happens in Vegas, The Last Rites of Joe May, Knucklehead.
TELEVISION: *Movies:* Six Against the Rock, Open Admissions, The Hillside Stranglers, People Like Us, Blind Faith, Cruel Doubt, The Disappearance of Nora, One Woman's Courage, The Corpse Had a Familiar Face, Bonanza: Under Attack, Out of Annie's Past, Bella Mafia, Empire Falls. *Mini-series*: Drug Wars: Columbia. *Series:* Crime Story, Buddy Faro (also co-exec. prod.) In-Laws, Law & Order. *Guest:* More than 53 appearances.

FARRELL, COLIN

Actor. b. Castleknock, Ireland, May 31, 1976. e. Bruce College. Studied briefly at the Gaiety School of Acting, Dublin.
PICTURES: The War Zone (debut, 1999), Ordinary Decent Criminal, Tigerland, American Outlaws, Hart's War, Minority Report, Phone Booth, The Recruit, Daredevil, Veronica Guerin, S.W.A.T., Intermission, A Home at the End of the World, Alexander, Ask the Dust, The New World, What Love Is and What's It All About, Miami Vice, Pride and Glory, Cassandra's Dream, In Bruges (Golden Globe Award 2009), Pride and Glory, The Imaginarium of Doctor Parnassus, Triage, Ondine, London Boulevard, Crazy Heart, The Way Back, London Boulevard.
TELEVISION: *Movies:* Falling for a Dancer, David Copperfield. *Series:* Ballykissangel (BBC), Love in the 21st Century. *Guest:* More than 75 appearances.

FARRELL, MIKE

Actor, Producer. b. St. Paul, MN, Feb. 6, 1939. m. actress Shelley Fabares. Currently co-chair of Human Rights Watch in CA.; pres. of Death Penalty Focus; member of the adv. bd. of the Natl Coalition to Abolish the Death Penalty; member of the adv. bd. of the Cult Awareness Network; founding bd. member of Peace Studies, ATV, at Augusta Correctional Ctr in Virginia.
PICTURES: Captain Newman M.D., The Americanization of Emily, The Graduate, Targets, The Killers Within, 187: Documented, Out at the Wedding. *Prod.:* Dominick and Eugene, Patch Adams (Golden Globe nom. 1999).
TELEVISION: *Movies:* The Longest Night, She Cried Murder!, The Questor Tapes, Live Again Die Again, McNaughton's Daughter, Battered, Sex and the Single Parent, Letters from Frank, Damien: The Leper Priest, Prime Suspect, Memorial Day (also prod.), Choices of the Heart, Private Sessions, Vanishing Act, A Deadly Silence, Price of the Bride, Incident at Dark River (also prod.), The Whereabouts of Jenny, Silent Motive (also prod.), Hart Attack, The Enemy Inside, Vows of Seduction, Twisted Path, Hart to Hart: Old Friends Never Die, Superman, Sins of the Mind, The '70s: The Decade that Changed Television (host), The Crooked E: The Unshredded Truth About Enron., Miracle Dogs, The Clinic, Locusts. *Director:* Run Till You Fall. *Series:* Days of Our Lives, The Interns, The Man and the City, M*A*S*H (Emmy nom. 1980, 1981), Providence. *Specials:* JFK: One Man Show (PBS), The Best of Natl. Geographic Specials (host/narrator), Saving the Wildlife (co-host). *Guest:* More than 106 appearances.

FARRELLY, BOBBY

Writer, Director, Producer. b. Cumberland, RI, 1958. Collaborates with brother Peter. Partner with brother, Peter in

Conundrum Entertainment.
PICTURES: Dumb & Dumber (also prod.), Bushwhacked (co-s.p. only), There's Something About Mary (also co-exec. prod.), Outside Providence (s.p., co-prod. only), Me Myself and Irene (also co-prod.), Osmosis Jones (also prod.), Say It Isn't So (prod. only), Shallow Hal, Dumb & Dumberer: When Harry Met Lloyd (writer/characters), Stuck on You (prod., writer, dir), Fever Pitch (dir.), Seven Day Itch (dir., writer), National Lampoon's Bag Boy (prod.), The Ringer (prod.), The Heartbreak Kid (dir., writer), The Three Stooges (prod., dir., s.p.), Hall Pass (prod., dir., s.p.). *Documentary:* The Lost Son of Havana (exec. prod.).
TELEVISION: *Movies:* Why Blitt? (exec. prod., dir.), I'm with Stupid (exec. prod.), *Pilot:* Unhitched. *Series:* Ozzy & Drix (exec. prod., 2 Emmy nom. 2003, 2004), Unhitched.

FARRELLY, PETER
Director, Writer, Producer. b. Cumberland, RI, 1957. Collaborates with brother Bobby. Partner with brother, Bobby in Conundrum Entertainment.
PICTURES: Dumb & Dumber, Bushwhacked (co-s.p. only), Kingpin (dir. only), There's Something About Mary (also co-exec. prod.), Outside Providence (novel, co-prod. only), Me Myself and I (also co-prod.), Say It Isn't So (prod. only), Osmosis Jones (also prod.), Shallow Hal, Dumb & Dumberer: When Harry Met Lloyd (writer/characters), Stuck on You (prod., writer, dir), Fever Pitch (dir., writer), Seven Day Itch (dir., writer), National Lampoon's Bag Boy (prod.),The Ringer (prod.), The Heartbreak Kid (dir., writer), Turkeys (prod.), The Three Stooges (prod., dir., s.p.), Hall Pass (prod., dir., s.p.).
TELEVISION: *Movies:* Why Blitt? (exec. prod., dir.), I'm with Stupid (exec. prod., dir.). *Pilot:* Unhitched. *Series:* Ozzy & Drix (exec. prod. 2 Emmy nom. 2003, 2004), Unhitched.

FARROW, MIA
Actress. b. Los Angeles, CA, Feb. 9. 1945. r.n. Maria de Lourdes Villiers Farrow. d. of actress Maureen O'Sullivan and late dir. John Farrow. e. Marymount, Los Angeles, Cygnet House, London.
THEATRE: The Importance of Being Earnest (debut, Madison Ave. Playhouse, NY, 1963); Royal Shakespeare Co. (Twelfth Night, A Midsummer Night's Dream, Ivanov, Three Sisters, The Seagull, A Doll's House), Mary Rose (London), Romantic Comedy (B'way debut, 1979).
PICTURES: Guns at Batasi (debut, 1964), A Dandy in Aspic, Rosemary's Baby (Golden Globe nom. 1969), Secret Ceremony, John and Mary (2 Golden Globe noms. 1970), See No Evil, The Public Eye, Dr. Popaul (High Heels), The Great Gatsby, Full Circle (The Haunting of Julia), Avalanche, A Wedding, Death on the Nile, Hurricane, A Midsummer Night's Sex Comedy, The Last Unicorn (voice), Zelig, Broadway Danny Rose (Golden Globe nom. 1985), Supergirl, The Purple Rose of Cairo (Golden Globe nom. 1986), Hannah and Her Sisters, Radio Days, September, Another Woman, New York Stories (Oedipus Wrecks), Crimes and Misde-meanors, Alice (Golden Globe nom. 1991; Natl. Board of Review Award, 1990), Shadows and Fog, Husbands and Wives, Widow's Peak, Miami Rhapsody, Reckless, Redux Riding Hood (voice), Private Parts, Coming Soon, Purpose, The Omen, Fast Track, Arthur and the Invisibles, The Ex, Be Kind Rewind, Arthur et la vengeance de Maltazard, Arthur et la guerre des deux mondes.
TELEVISION: *Movies:* Goodbye Raggedy Ann, Miracle at Midnight, The Secret Life of Zoey, Samantha: An American Girl Holiday. *Mini-series:* A Girl Thing, Forget Me Never (Golden Globe nom. 2000). *Series:* Peyton Place (Golden Globe nom. 1966), Third Watch. *Specials:* Johnny Belinda, Peter Pan. *Guest:* More than 75 appearances.

FAVREAU, JON
Actor, Writer, Director. b. Queens, NY, October 19, 1966. Alumnus of Chicago's Improv Olympia improvisational acting troupe.
PICTURES: Folks!, Rudy, Mrs. Parker and the Vicious Circle, PCU, Batman Forever, Notes from Underground, Swingers (also s.p.), Just Your Luck, Persons Unknown, Dogtown, Deep Impact, Very Bad Things, Love & Sex, The Replacements, Made (also dir., s.p., prod.), The First $20 Million (s.p. only), Daredevil, Elf (dir., s.p. only), The Big Empty (also exec. prod.), Something's Gotta Give, Wimbledon, Green Street Hooligans (exec. prod.), Zathura: A Space Adventure (dir.), The Break-Up, Open Season (voice), Iron Man (also exec. prod., dir.), Four Christmases, I Love You, Man, Couples Retreat (also writer), Iron Man 2 (also exec. prod., dir.), The Zookeeper (voice), Cowboys and Aliens (voice, dir.).
TELEVISION: *Movies:* Grandpa's Funeral, Smog (s.p. and dir.), Rocky Marciano, Life on Parole (dir. only). *Series:* Dinner for Five (Emmy nom. 2005), Buzz Lightyear of Star Command (voice), Undeclared (dir. only), In Case of Emergency (dir., exec. prod., also pilot), Star Wars: The Clone Wars (voice). *Guest*: More than 75 appearances.

FAWCETT, DAN
Executive. e. B.A. from Tufts, his juris doctor from the University of Pittsburgh, and his M.B.A. from Carnegie Mellon University. Early in his career, Fawcett served as a corporate and finance attorney of Reed Smith in Pittsburgh and Philadelphia. Entered ent. industry as an assistant gen. mgr. and general counsel of Fox Sports Net Pittsburgh. He joined Fox Cable Networks in Los Angeles in 1997, as senior v.p., business & legal affairs for Fox Sports Net. Became executive v.p., business & legal affairs in 1999 and oversaw all its legal and business affairs functions and matters of portfolio for more than 20 managed domestic cable and satellite sports and entertainment networks, including Fox Sports Net and FX. In 2004 became executive v.p. of programming, business and legal affairs for the DirecTV satellite television service provider. In March 2007, Fawcett was named president, digital media of Fox Entertainment Group. Fawcett is charged with growing Fox's digital media operation, with a strategy that includes exploiting Fox content across all digital platforms and with major technology players.

FAY, RICHARD M.
Exhibitor. b. New York, July 27, 1949. e. Iona College, BA in English in 1971. Industry veteran whose career spans 16 years as a v.p. with Loews Theatres; two years with Warner Bros. Distribution; three years with United Artists Distribution; three years as senior v.p. with United Artists Theatres; stint at Sony Releasing as a senior v.p.; and from 1995-2005 Fay was president of AMC Film Marketing, part of AMC Entertainment Inc. In April 2007, Fay was named president of domestic theatrical distribution for Summit Entertainment, a new production & distribution company.
Fay has received various industry and community accolades, including the Al Shapiro Distinguished Service Award in 2001, the Humanitarian Award from the Variety Boys & Girls Club of Queens in 1997, and the Kodak ShowEast Reel Award in 1995. He serves as a board member for Variety—The Children's Charity of the United States and is on exec. comm. of the Will Rogers Institute.

FEINSTEIN, ALAN
Actor. b. New York, NY, Sept. 8, 1941.
THEATRE: NY: Malcolm, Zelda, A View from the Bridge (NY Drama Desk Award), As Is, A Streetcar Named Desire.
PICTURE: Looking for Mr. Goodbar.
TELEVISION: *Movies:* Alexander: The Other Side of Dawn, Visions, The Hunted Lady, The Users, The Two Worlds of Jenny Logan, On Fire, Parallel Lives, Though None Go with Me. *Mini-series:* Masada. *Series:* Edge of Night, Love Of Life, Search for Tomorrow, Jigsaw John, The Runaways, The Family Tree, Berrenger's, General Hospital, Falcon Crest, Santa Barbara. *Guest:* More than 67 appearances.

FEITSHANS, BUZZ
Executive, Producer. b. Los Angeles, CA. e. USC. Started in film business as editor. Worked for 10 years at American-International as supervisor of prod. In 1975 formed A-Team Productions with John Milius. With Carolco Pictures: producer, 1981-6; exec. v.p. for m.p. production, member bd. dir. 1986-90. 1990-1994, v.p. for Cinergi Pictures.; is a former pres. of Cinergi.
PICTURES: *Producer:* Dillinger, Act of Vengeance, Foxy Brown, Big Wednesday, Hardcore, 1941, Extreme Prejudice (exec. prod.), Conan the Barbarian, First Blood, Uncommon Valor, Rambo II, Red Dawn, Rambo III, Total Recall, Tombstone (exec. prod.), Color of Night, Die Hard: With a Vengeance (exec. prod.), Shadow Conspiracy (exec. prod.), We Get to Win This Time (video short, himself), Afghanistan: Land in Crisis (documentary short, himself), Joe Killionaire (cinematographer).
TELEVISION: *Movie:* Supreme Courtships (cinematographer). *Series:* Las Vegas (cinematographer).

FELDMAN, COREY
Actor. b. Reseda, CA, July 16, 1971. Performing since the age of 3 in commercials, television (Love Boat, Father Murphy, Foul Play, Mork and Mindy, Eight Is Enough, Alice, Gloria) and films.
PICTURES: Time After Time, The Fox and the Hound (voice), Friday the 13th—The Final Chapter, Gremlins, Friday the 13th—A New Beginning, The Goonies, Stand by Me, Lost Boys, License to Drive, The 'burbs, Dream a Little Dream, Teenage Mutant Ninja Turtles (voice only), Rock 'n' Roll High School Forever, Edge of Honor, Meatballs 4, Round Trip to Heaven, Stepmonster, Blown Away, National Lampoon's Loaded Weapon 1, Lipstick Camera, National Lampoon's Last Resort, Maverick, Dream a Little Dream 2, A Dangerous Place, Evil Obsession, Tales From the Crypt: Bordello of Blood, Mr. Atlas, Born Bad, The Thief and the Stripper, She's Too Tall (assoc. prod.), The Million Dollar Kid, Citizen Toxie: The Toxic Avenger Part 4, My Life as a Troll, Seance, The Mayor of Sunset Strip, Dickie Roberts: Former Child Star (as himself), The Bloke Goes to Hollywood, The Adventures of Belvis Bash, Motel de Gracia, The Beautiful Outsiders.
TELEVISION: *Movies:* Willa, Father Figure, Kid with a Broken Halo, Still the Beaver, Out of the Blue, When the Whistle Blows, I'm a Big Girl Now, Exile, Legion, Puppet Master vs. Demonic Toys. *Specials:* 15 & Getting Straight, How to Eat Like a Child. *Series:* The Bad News Bears, Madame's Place, Dweebs, Super Robot Monkey Team Hyperforce Go! (voices), The Coreys (also exec. prod.), Broken Road (exec. prod.). *Guest:* More than 110 appearances.

FELDMAN, EDWARD S.
Producer. b. New York, NY, Sept. 5, 1929. e. Michigan State U. Trade press contact, newspaper and mag. contact, 20th Century

Fox, 1950; dir. info. services, Dover Air Force Base. 1954-56; publ. coordinator, The World of Suzie Wong, 1960; joined Embassy, dir. of publicity, 1969; v.p. in chg., adv. & pub, 7 Arts Prods., 1962; v.p. exec. asst. to head prod. Warner-7 Arts Studio 1967; pres., m.p. dept., Filmways, 1970; Formed Edward S. Feldman Co., 1978.
PICTURES: *Prod./exec. prod.:* What's the Matter With Helen?, Fuzz, Save the Tiger, The Other Side of the Mountain, Two-Minute Warning, The Other Side of the Mountain Part 2,The Last Married Couple in America, Six Pack, The Sender, Hot Dog... The Movie! (co-prod.), Witness (Academy Award nom. 1986), Explorers, The Golden Child, The Hitcher, Near Dark, Wired, Green Card, The Doctor, Honey I Blew Up the Kid, Forever Young, My Father the Hero, The Jungle Book, The Truman Show, 101 Dalmations, 102 Dalmations, K-19: The Widowmaker. The Hitcher-How Do These Movies Get Made? (documentary short), One More Day for Hiroshima.
TELEVISION: *Exec. Prod.:* Moon of the Wolf, My Father's House, Valentine, 300 Miles for Stephanie, Charles and Diana: A Royal Love Story, 21 Hours at Munich (Emmy nom. 1977), King (Emmy nom. 1978), Not in Front of the Children, Obsessed with a Married Woman.

FELDSHUH, TOVAH
Actress. b. New York, NY, Dec. 27, 1953. e. Sarah Lawrence Col., Univ. of MN. For humanitarian work received the Israel Peace Medal and the Eleanor Roosevelt Humanitarian Award.
THEATRE: *NY:* Cyrano, Straws in the Wind, Three Sisters, Rodgers and Hart, Yentl (Theatre World Award), Sarava, The Mistress of the Inn, Springtime for Henry, She Stoops to Conquer, Lend Me a Tenor, A Fierce Attachment, Sarah and Abraham, Six Wives, Hello Muddah! Hello Fadduh!
PICTURES: White Lies, Nunzio, The Idolmaker, Cheaper to Keep Her, Daniel, Brewster's Millions, The Blue Iguana, A Day in October, Comfortably Numb, Hudson River Blues, Montana, Charlie Hoboken, A Walk on the Moon, The Corruptor, Happy Accidents, Friends and Family, The Believer, Kissing Jessica Stein, My Angel Is a Centerfold, The 3 Little Wolfs, Broadway: The Golden Age by the Legends Who Were There, The Tollbooth, Death By Committee, Just My Luck, Alchemy (assoc. editor), Lady in the Water, Liebesleben, Old Love, O Jerusalem, Love Life, Love Comes Lately, Baker, Heterosexuals, Ten Stories Tall, Heterosexuals, Buddy Gilbert Comes Alive.
TELEVISION: *Movies:* Scream Pretty Peggy, The Amazing Howard Hughes, Terror Out of the Sky, The Triangle Factory Fire Scandal, Beggarman Thief, The Women's Room, Citizen Cohn, Sexual Considerations, Love and Betrayal: The Mia Farrow Story. *Mini-series:* Holocaust (Emmy nom. 1978), A Will of Their Own. *Series:* As the World Turns, Mariah, Law & Order, Crossing Jordan. *Specials:* Dosvedanya Mean Goodbye, Saying Kaddish. *Guest:* More than 48 appearances.

FELLMAN, DANIEL R.
Executive. b. Cleveland, OH, March 14, 1943. e. Rider Coll., B.S., 1964. Paramount Pictures, 1964-69; Loews Theatres, 1969-71; Cinema National Theatres, 1971-76; 1976-78, pres., American Theatre Mgmt. Joined Warner Bros. in 1978, named exec. v.p. Warner Bros. domestic distribution, Jan. 1993. Named pres. Warner Bros. theatrical distribution, March 1999. Currently, pres., domestic distribution, of Warner Bros. Pictures. President Variety Club Tent 35, 1977-78. Member exec. comm., Will Rogers Foundation; Past chmn., Foundation of Motion Picture Pioneers.

FELTHEIMER, JON
Executive. e. Bachelor's degree in economics with honors from Washington University. Feltheimer, a 20-year entertainment industry veteran, spent eight years at New World Entertainment, where he was promoted to president and CEO, directed the company's domestic and international distribution businesses and launched and managed its New World Television division. He also managed the company's Marvel Productions and Learning Corporation of America units. Feltheimer then joined Sony Pictures Entertainment (SPE) and engineered the creation of TriStar Television as part of SPE's acquisition of television assets from New World Entertainment Ltd. During his nine years at SPE, was named head of the Columbia TriStar Television Group and executive v.p. of SPE. Feltheimer led co. to international powerhouse status; SPE launched or partnered in nearly 30 branded channels, regional networks and co-production ventures around the world. He launched SPE's interactive TV business in 1996 and served as the architect of SPE's investment and management of the U.S.-based Spanish-language network Telemundo in conjunction with Liberty Media and Apollo Partners. Telemundo was sold to NBC in 2000 for approximately $2 billion, reflecting a threefold increase in Sony's investment in the four years since Feltheimer engineered the deal. Feltheimer then joined Lionsgate Entertainment and was named CEO in March 2000, a position he holds today. The Lionsgate film library holds more than 7,800 titles, and the company releases a feature film slate of 18 to 20 releases a year. During Feltheimer's tenure as CEO, Lionsgate has increased its revenues from approximately $150 million to nearly $1 billion annually.

FENN, SHERILYN
Actress. b. Detroit, MI, Feb. 1, 1965.
PICTURES: The Wild Life (debut, 1984), Just One of the Guys, Out of Control, Thrashin', The Wraith, Zombie High, Two Moon Junction, Crime Zone, True Blood, Meridian: Kiss of the Beast, Wild at Heart, Backstreet Dreams, Ruby, Desire and Hell at Sunset Motel, Diary of a Hit Man, Of Mice and Men, Three of Hearts, Boxing Helena, Fatal Instinct, The Shadow Men, Lovelife, Johnny Hit and Run Pauline, Just Write, Darkness Falls, Outside Ozona, Cement, The United States of Leland, Swindle, A Man Called Rage, Gin and the Rumble Within, Cavedweller, Officer Down, Cattle Call, Whitepaddy, Treasure Raiders, Novel Romance, The Scenesters.
TELEVISION: *Movies:* Silence of the Heart, Dillinger, Spring Awakening, Liz: The Elizabeth Taylor Story, Slave of Dreams, The Assassination File, The Don's Analyst, Nightmare Street, Off Season, Scent of Danger, Nightwaves, Pop Rocks, Officer Down, Deadly Isolation, Presumed Dead, The Dukes of Hazzard: The Beginning. *Mini-series*: A Season in Purgatory, Mr. Ed. *Series:* Twin Peaks (Emmy nom.; Golden Globe nom. 1990), Rude Awakening, Dawson's Creek, Birds of Prey, Three Moons Over Milford, Judging Amy, Gilmore Girls. *Specials:* Tales From the Hollywood Hills (A Table at Ciro's), Divided We Stand, A Family Again. *Guest:* More than 68 appearances.

FERRARA, ABEL
Director, Writer. b. Bronx, NY, July 11, 1952. Moved to Peekskill, NY, as teenager where he made short films with future writer Nicholas St. John. Traveled to England, worked for the BBC. Returned to U.S. to attended SUNY/Purchase, making short Could This Be Love, which received some theatrical distribution. Has used the pseudonymn Jimmy Laine.
PICTURES: Driller Killer (also actor, s.p. songs), Ms. 45 (also actor), Fear City, China Girl (also songs), Cat Chaser, King of New York, Bad Lieutenant (also co-s.p.), Dangerous Game, Body Snatchers, The Addiction, The Funeral, The Blackout, New Rose Hotel, 'R Xmas, White Boy (prod.), Mary, Exes (actor only), Go Go Tales, A Talent for Trouble (actor) Chelsea on the Rocks (doc.), Bad Lieutenant: Port of Call New Orleans (writer, adapted from film Bad Lieutenant, 1992), Uncle Bob (doc., prod.), Mulberry St. (doc., dir.), Jekyll and Hyde (dir., s.p.), Happy Life (exec. prod.).
TELEVISION: *Movies:* The Gladiator, Crime Story (pilot), SUBWAYStories: Tales from the Underground. *Series:* Miami Vice, Crime Story.

FERRARO, JOHN E.
Executive, Producer. b. Greenwich, CT, July 20, 1958. e. Emerson College, B.S. in Mass Communications, 1980. Joined Paramount Pictures Corp. in 1980. 1983-84, story analyst, Paramount TV; 1984-85 supervisor, Drama Development; 1985-87 mgr., current programs & special projects; 1987-88, dir., drama development; 1988, exec. dir., acquisitions for Paramount Pictures; 1990, v.p., acquisitions; 1997, sr. v.p., acquisitions & co-productions. Left Paramount Pictures and now works as independent producer for The Stoebner/Baumgartner Company.

FERRELL, CONCHATA
Actress. b. Charleston, WV, Mar. 28, 1943. e. Marshall Univ.
THEATRE: NY: The Three Sisters, Hot L Baltimore, Battle of Angels, The Sea Horse (Theatre World, Obie & Vernon Rice Drama Desk Awards), Wine Untouched. LA: Getting Out, Picnic.
PICTURES: Deadly Hero, Network, Heartland, Where the River Runs Black, For Keeps?, Mystic Pizza, Edward Scissorhands, Family Prayers, True Romance, Samuari Cowboy, Heaven and Earth, Freeway, My Fellow Americans, Touch, Modern Vampires, Crime and Punishment in Suburbia, Erin Brockovich, K-PAX, Mr. Deeds, Surviving Eden, Kabluey.
TELEVISION: *Movies:* The Girl Called Hatter Fox, A Death in Canaan, Who'll Save My Children?, Before and After, The Seduction of Miss Leona, Reunion, Rape and Marriage: The Rideout Case, Life of the Party: The Story of Beatrice, Emergency Room, Nadia, The Three Wishes of Billy Grier, North Beach and Rawhide, Samaritan: The Mitch Snyder Story, Eye on the Sparrow, Your Mother Wears Combat Boots, Goodbye Miss 4th of July, Opposites Attract, Deadly Intentions...Again?, Backfield in Motion, The Buccaneers, Stranger Inside, Amy & Isabelle. *Series:* Hot L Baltimore, B.J. and the Bear, McClain's Law, ER, Peaceable Kingdom, L. A. Law (Emmy nom. 1992), Hearts Afire, Townies, Teen Angel, Push Nevada, Two and a Half Men (2 Emmy noms. 2005, 2007). *Specials:* The Great Gilly Hopkins, Portrait of a White Marriage, Runaway Ralph, Picnic. *Guest:* More than 96 appearances.

FERRER, MIGUEL
Actor. b. Santa Monica, CA, Feb. 7, 1954. Son of late actor Jose Ferrer and late singer Rosemary Clooney. Began performing as a drummer. With actor Bill Mumy created comic book The Comet Man.
PICTURES: Heartbreaker (debut, 1983), Lovelines, Star Trek III: The Search for Spock, Flashpoint, Robocop, Deepstar Six, Valentino Returns, Revenge, The Guardian, Twin Peaks: Fire Walk With Me, Point of No Return, Hot Shots! Part Deux, Another Stakeout, It's All True (narrator), The Harvest, Blank Check, Death in Granada, Night Flier, Mr. Magoo, Where's Marlowe?, Mulan (voice), Traffic, Sunshine State, The Manchurian Candidate, Silver City, The Man, Noah's Ark: The

New Beginning (voice).
TELEVISION: *Movies:* Downpayment on Murder, C.A.T. Squad, Guts & Glory: The Rise and Fall of Oliver North, Murder in High Places, In the Shadow of a Killer, Cruel Doubt, Scam, Royce, Incident at Deception Ridge, Jack Reed: Search for Justice, A Promise Kept: The Oksana Baiul Story, The Return of Hunter, In the Line of Duty: Hunt for Justice, Project: ALF, Justice League of America, Brave New World, LA County 187, Sightings: Heartland Ghost, L.A. Sheriff's Homicide, Edgar Floats. *Pilot:* Badlands 2005. *Mini-series:* Drug Wars: The Camarena Story, The Stand, The Shining. *Series:* Twin Peaks, Broken Badges, On the Air, Lateline, Crossing Jordan, Bionic Woman, Jackie Chan Adventures. *Documentaries:* Boogeymen: The Killer Compilation, Brilliant But Cancelled, *Guest:* More than 84 appearances.

FERRETTI, DANTE
Production Designer. b. Macerata, Italy, February 26, 1943.
PICTURES: Medea, The Decameron, The Canterbury Tales, Io on vedo, tu non parli, lui non sente, Lulu the Tool, Bawdy Tales, Slap the Monster on Page One, Arabian Nights, How Long Can You Fall?, Salo, or the 120 Days of Sodom, Somewhere Beyond Love, The Beach Hut, La Presidentessa, Il Mostro, Bye Bye Monkey, Orchestra Rehersal, City of Women, The Skin, Il Minestrone, Tales of Ordinary Madness, That Night in Varennes, And the Ship Sails On, The Adventures of Baron von Munchausen (Academy Award nom. 1990), Ginger and Fred, The Name of the Rose, Hamlet (Academy Award nom. 1991), Dr. M, La traviata, The Age of Innocence (Academy Award nom. 1994), Interview with the Vampire: The Vampire Chronicles (Academy Award nom. 1995), Casino, Kundun (2 Academy Award noms. 1998), Meet Joe Black, Bringing Out the Dead, Titus (ADG nom. 2000), Gangs of New York (Academy Award nom.; ADG nom. 2003), Cold Mountain, The Aviator (Academy Award, ADG nom. 2005), The Black Dahlia, Sweeney Todd: The Demon Barber of Fleet Street (Academy Award, ADG nom. 2008), Shutter Island, The Invention of Hugo Cabret.
TELEVISION: Il Traviata, Cavelleria rusticana, Un ballo in maschera.

FEY, TINA
Writer, Actress, Producer. b. Upper Darby, PA, May 18, 1970. e. University of Virginia. First female head writer in SNL's history.
PICTURES: Martin & Orloff, Mean Girls (s.p., soundtrack, actor, WGA nom. 2005), Beer League, Aqua Teen Hunger Force Colon Movie Film for Theaters (voice), Baby Mama, Ponyo (voice English version), The Invention of Lying, Date Night, Megamind (voice).
TELEVISION: *Movies:* Saturday Night Live Christmas 2002 (writer), Saturday Night Live Weekend Update Halftime Special (head writer), A.S.S.S.S.C.A.T.: Improv (performer), Saturday Night Live in the '90s: Pop Culture Nation (doc., writer). *Series:* The Colin Quinn Show (writer), Saturday Night Live (writer, host, various characters, 2 Emmy Awards, 4 other noms., 2 WGA Awards 3 other noms.), 30 Rock (exec. prod., 5 Emmy Awards, 5 other noms., 2 Golden Globe Awards, 1 other nom., 3 WGA Awards, 3 other noms.). *Specials:* Saturday Night Live 25 (head writer, WGA Award 2001), NBC 75th Anniversary Special (writer, WGA nom. 2003). *Guest:* More than 100 appearances.

FIEDLER, JOHN
Executive, Producer. Launched m.p. career in 1975 working in commercials and industrial and ed. films. Joined Technicolor as sr. exec. in prod. svcs. in mktg. Joined Rastar 1980 as v.p., prod. dev. and asst. to Guy McElwaine, pres. & CEO. Joined Paramount as v.p. in prod.; then to Tri-Star Pictures in same post. Resigned to join Columbia Pictures as exec. v.p., worldwide prod., 1984, then pres. of prod. in 1986. Left in 1987 to become ind. prod. 1989 named pres. of prod., Rastar Indie Prod. Formerly worked with Polar Entertainment.
PICTURES: *Producer:* The Beast, Tune in Tomorrow, Mortal Thoughts, Serial Mom, A Good Man in Africa, Radio Inside, I Love You —I Love You Not, Pecker, Simply Irresistable, Cecil B. Demented, Ted's MBA* (*Many Brief Affairs). *Exec. prod.:* Copycat, Beneath.
TELEVISION: *Producer:* Beyond the Law.

FIELD, SALLY
Actress. b. Pasadena, CA, Nov. 6, 1946. Daughter of Paramount contract actress Maggie Field Mahoney. Stepdaughter of actor Jock Mahoney. e. Actor's Studio 1973-75. Acting classes at Columbia studios. Picked over 150 finalists to star as lead in TV series, Gidget, 1965.
PICTURES: The Way West (debut, 1967), Stay Hungry, Smokey and the Bandit (Golden Globe nom. 1978), Heroes, The End, Hooper, Norma Rae (Academy Award, Golden Globe Award 1980), Beyond the Poseidon Adventure, Smokey and the Bandit II, Back Roads, Absence of Malice (Golden Globe nom. 1982), Kiss Me Goodbye (Golden Globe nom. 1983), Places in the Heart (Academy Award, Golden Globe Award 1985), Murphy's Romance (also exec. prod. Golden Globe nom. 1986), Surrender, Punchline (also prod.), Steel Magnolias (Golden Globe nom. 1990), Not Without My Daughter, Soapdish, Dying Young (co-prod. only), Homeward Bound: The Incredible Journey (voice), Mrs. Doubtfire, Forrest Gump, Eye for an Eye, Homeward Bound II: Lost in San Francisco (voice), Beautiful (dir. only), Where the Heart Is, Say It Isn't So, Legally Blonde 2: Red White & Blonde, Two Weeks, Lincoln.
TELEVISION: *Movies:* Maybe I'll Come Home in the Spring, Marriage Year One, Mongo's Back in Town, Home for the Holidays, Hitched, Bridger, Sybil (Emmy Award, 1977), The Christmas Tree (also prod., dir., co-s.p.), Merry Christmas George Bailey, From the Earth to the Moon, A Cooler Climate (Emmy nom. 1995)., David Copperfield, Brothers & Sisters: Family Album. *Mini-series:* A Woman of Independent Means (also co-exec. prod. 2 Emmy nom. Golden Globe nom. 1995) *Series:* Gidget, The Flying Nun, Alias Smith and Jones, The Girl With Something Extra, ER, The Court, Brothers & Sisters (Emmy Award 2007, 2 other noms.; 2 Golden Globe noms.). *Special:* All the Way Home. *Host:* Barbara Stanwyck: Fire and Desire. *Guest:* More than 130 appearances.

FIELD, SHIRLEY-ANNE
Actress. b. London, Eng., June 27, 1938. Ent. films after repertory experience. Under contract to Ealing-M.G.M. 1958.
THEATRE: The Lily White Boys, Kennedy's Children, Wait Until Dark, The Life and Death of Marilyn Monroe, How the Other Half Loves.
PICTURES: It's Never Too Late, The Silken Affair, The Good Companions, Horrors of the Black Museum, Upstairs and Downstairs, Beat Girl, The Entertainer, Man in the Moon, Once More With Feeling, Peeping Tom, Saturday Night and Sunday Morning, These Are the Damned, The War Lover, Kings of the Sun, Alfie, Doctor in Clover, Hell Is Empty, With Love in Mind, House of the Living Dead (Doctor Maniac), My Beautiful Laundrette, Getting It Right, The Rachel Papers, Shag, Hear My Song, At Risk, Taking Liberty, U.F.O., Loving Deadly, Monkey's Tale, The Good Doctor, Christie Malry's Own Double-Entry, Transfer at Aachen, The Kid, The Power of Three.
TELEVISION: *Movies:* Lady Chatterly, Dalziel and Pascoe: Recalled to Life. *Series:* Bramwell, Santa Barbara, Madson, Where the Heart Is.

FIELD, TED
Producer. r.n. Frederick W. Field. e. U. of Chicago, Pomona Coll. Started career as one of owners of Field Enterprises of Chicago; transferred to west coast, concentrating on movies and records. Founded Interscope Communications, diversified co., which develops and produces theatrical films; Interscope Records, 1990; Radar Pictures, 1999.
PICTURES: Revenge of the Nerds, Turk 182!, Critical Condition, Outrageous Fortune, Revenge of the Nerds II: Nerds in Paradise, 3 Men and a Baby, The Seventh Sign, Cocktail, An Innocent Man Three Men and a Little Lady Class Action, The Cutting Edge, The Air Up There, Roommates, Mr. Holland's Opus, The Proposition Runaway Bride, The Heartbreak Kid. *Exec. Prod:* Bill & Ted's Excellent Adventure, Renegades, The First Power, Bird on a Wire, Paradise, The Hand That Rocks the Cradle, FernGully, The Gun in Betty Lou's Handbag, Out on a Limb, Jersey Girl, Holy Matrimony, Imaginary Crimes, Operation Dumbo Drop, The Tie That Binds, Jumanji, The Arrival, Kazaam, The Associate, Gridlock'd, Snow White, What Dreams May Come, Very Bad Things, Earl Watt, The 59-Story Crisis, Teaching Mrs. Tingle, They, Le Divorce, The Texas Chainsaw Massacre (2003), The Last Samurai, The Chronicles of Riddick, Son of the Mask, The Amityville Horror, Zathura: A Space Adventure, Waist Deep (exec. prod.), Waist Deep, Seven Day Itch, The Horsemen (exec. prod.), The Box (exec. prod.), All About Steve, The Heartbreak Kid, Swing Vote, The Invention of Lying (exec. rod.), Everybody's Fine, Twelve.
TELEVISION: *Movies:* The Father Clements Story (co-exec.). Everybody's Baby: The Rescue of Jessica McClure (co-exec.), My Boyfriend's Back, A Mother's Courage: The Mary Thomas Story (Emmy Award, 1990, co-exec. prod.), Crossing the Mob, Murder Ordained, Foreign Affairs (co-exec.), A Part of the Family (co-exec.), Body Language (co-exec.), Into Pitch Black (exec. prod.).

FIELD, TODD
Actor, Director, Producer. r.n. William Todd Field. b. Pomona, CA, Feb. 24, 1964. Extensive behind the scenes work in film. Dir./Writer: Too Romantic, When I Was a Boy (also cam. op.), Delivering, Nonnie & Alex (also cam. op.), If...Dog...Rabbit (s.p. only)
PICTURES: Radio Days, The Allnighter, Gross Anatomy (also comp.), Fat Man and Little Boy, Eye of the Eagle 2: Inside the Enemy, Full Fathom Five, Back to Back, Queens Logic, The End of Innocence, The Dog (also dir, comp.), Ruby in Paradise (also comp.), Sleep with Me, When I Was a Boy (dir. only), Delivering (dir. only), Nonnie & Alex (dir. only), Frank and Jesse, Twister, Walking and Talking, Farmer & Chase, Broken Vessels (also co-prod., comp.), Stranger Than Fiction, Net Worth, The Haunting, Eyes Wide Shut, New Port South, Beyond the City Limits, In the Bedroom (dir., s.p., prod., 2 Acad. Award nom., AFI nom. 2002),The Ninth Man (dir./exec. prod.), American Crude (exec. prod.), Little Children (writer, s.p., dir., prod., camera op., Academy Award nom.; Golden Globe nom.; WGA nom. 2007), Back Roads, Appearances (also writer), Open Window (exec. prod.), Little Children (dir., writer, prod., Academy Award nom.; Golden Globe nom.; WGA nom. 2007).

TELEVISION: *Movies:* Student Exchange, Lookwell, Jonathan Stone: Threat of Innocence. *Series:* Take Five, Danger Theatre, Once and Again.

FIENNES, JOSEPH

Actor. b. Salisbury, England, May 27, 1970. Brother is actor Ralph Fiennes. Worked at Young Vic Youth Theatre, and then went on to train at the Guildhall School of Music and Drama
PICTURES: Stealing Beauty, Shakespeare in Love, Elizabeth, The Very Thought of You, Forever Mine, Rancid Aluminium, Enemy at the Gates, Killing Me Softly, Dust, Leo, Sinbad: Legend of the Seven Seas (voice), Luther, The Great Raid, The Merchant of Venice, Man to Man, Therese Raquin, Darwin Awards, Running with Scissors, Goodbye Bafana, The Escapist, The Red Baron, Spring 1941, Vivaldi.
TELEVISION: *Movies:* The Vacillations of Poppy Carew, Pretty/Handsome. *Series:* FlashForward.

FIENNES, RALPH

Actor. b. Suffolk, England, Dec. 22, 1962. e. Chelsea College of Art & Design, RADA. Brother is actor Joseph Fiennes. Stage work with the Royal Shakespeare Co. includes King Lear, Troilus and Cressida, Love's Labour's Lost. B'way debut in Hamlet (Tony & Theatre World Awards, 1995).
PICTURES: Wuthering Heights (tv in U.S.), The Baby of Macon, Schindler's List (Academy Award nom.; Golden Globe nom., Natl. Society of Film Critics, NY Film Critics & BAFTA Awards 1994), Quiz Show, Strange Days, The English Patient (Academy Award nom.; Golden Globe nom. 1997), Oscar and Lucinda, The Avengers, The Prince of Egypt (voice), The Avengers, Onegin (also prod.), The Taste of Sunshine, The End of the Affair, Spider, The Good Thief, Red Dragon, Maid in Manhattan, The White Countess, The Wallace & Gromit Movie: Curse of the Wererabbit, The Constant Gardener, The Chumscrubber, Vapor, Harry Potter and the Goblet of Fire, Chromophobia, Land of the Blind, Harry Potter and the Order of the Phoenix, In Bruges, The Hurt Locker, The Duchess (Golden Globe nom. 2008), The Reader, Nanny McPhee and the Big Bang, Clash of the Titans, Coriolanus (also prod., dir.), Cemetery Junction, Harry Potter and the Deathly Hallows: Part I, Harry Potter and the Deathly Hallows: Part II.
TELEVISION: *Movies:* Prime Suspect, A Dangerous Man: Lawrence After Arabia, The Cormorant (theatrical release in U.S.), The Great War (voice), The Miracle Maker (voice), How Proust Can Change Your Life, Bernard and Doris (Emmy nom. 2008, Golden Globe nom. 2009). *Series:* Freedom: A History of Us (doc.). *Guest:* More than 70 appearances.

FIERSTEIN, HARVEY

Actor, Writer. b. New York, NY, June 6, 1954. e. Pratt Inst.
THEATRE: *Actor:* Andy Warhol's Pork, The Haunted Host, Pouf Positive, Hairspray (Seattle, WA, Tony Award 2003), Fiddler on the Roof. *Actor-Writer:* Torch Song Trilogy (NY & London; Tony Awards for best actor & play; Theatre World Award 1983), Safe Sex, A Catered Affair. *Writer:* Spookhouse, La Cage Aux Folles (Tony Award 1984), Legs Diamond. *Author:* The Sissy Duckling.
PICTURES: Garbo Talks, The Times of Harvey Milk (narrator), Torch Song Trilogy (also s.p.), The Harvest, Mrs. Doubtfire, Bullets Over Broadway, The Celluloid Closet, Dr. Jekyll & Ms. Hyde, Independence Day, Everything Relative, Kull the Conqueror, Mulan (voice), Safe Men, Hookers in a Haunted House, Jump, Playing Mona Lisa, Death to Smoochy, Duplex, Farce of the Penguins (voice), ShowBusiness: The Road to Broadway (doc., soundtrack performer), Hairspray (soundtrack performer), Foodfight!.
TELEVISION: *Movies:* The Demon Murder Case (voice), Apology, Double Platinum, The Sissy Duckling, Common Ground, The Year Without a Santa Claus. *Series:* Daddy's Girls, Cheers (Emmy nom. 1992), Happily Ever After: Fairy Tales for Every Child, Stories From My Childhood, X-Chromosome, In the Life (doc.). *Specials:* Tidy Endings, In the Shadow of Love. *Documentary:* The Times of Harvey Milk (narr.), *Guest:* More than 68 appearances.

FIGGIS, MIKE

Director, Writer, Composer. b. Kenya, Feb. 28, 1948. At age 8 family moved to Newcastle, England. Studied music before performing with band Gas Boad; joined experimental theatre group The People Show in early 70's as musician. Began making indept. films including Redheugh, Slow Fade, Animals of the City. Made 1-hr. film The House for U.K.'s Channel 4.
PICTURES: *Director:* Stormy Monday (debut, 1988; also s.p., music), Internal Affairs (also music), Liebestraum (also s.p., music), Mr. Jones, Leaving Las Vegas (also s.p., music; 2 Academy Award noms.; Golden Globe nom.; DGA nom.; WGA nom.; IFP Independent Spirit Award, 1996; Nat'l Society of Film Critics Award), One Night Stand (also s.p., comp., prod., actor), Flamenco Women, Miss Julie (also prod., music), The Loss of Sexual Innocence (also prod., music), Timecode (also. prod., music), Hotel (also prod., music), Agua Dulce (short, exec. prod.), Cold Creek Manor (dir., prod., exec. prod., writer,cinematographer, editor), je t'aime Paris, (dir. segment), Going Down, Guilty Pleasure, Love Live Long (also prod., cinematog.), Kimjongilia (doc., exec. prod.).
TELEVISION: *Movies:* Women & Men 2: In Love There Are No Rules, Canterbury's Law (dir., pilot). *Mini-series:* The Blues (documentary/episode dir.).

FINCH, JON

Actor. b. London, England, Mar. 2, 1943. Came to acting via backstage activities, working for five years as co. mgr. and dir.
PICTURES: The Vampire Lovers (debut, 1970), The Horror of Frankenstein, Sunday Bloody Sunday, L'affaire Martine Desclos, Macbeth, Frenzy, Lady Caroline Lamb, The Final Programme (The Last Days of Man on Earth), Diagnosis: Murder, Une Femme Fidele, The Man With the Green Cross, El Segundo Poder, Battle Flag, El Mister, Death on the Nile, La Sabina, Gary Cooper Which Art in Heaven, Breaking Glass, The Threat, Giro City (And Nothing But the Truth), Plaza Real, Streets of Yesterday, Game of Seduction, The Voice, Beautiful in the Kingdom, Mirror Mirror, Darklands, Lucan, Bloodlines: Legacy of a Lord, Anazapta, Kingdom of Heaven.
TELEVISION: *Movies:* Peter and Paul, The Rainbow, Unexplained Laughter, Dangerous Curves, Maigret, Beautiful Lies, Make or Break, Sherlock Homes, , Mary Queen of Scots, Riviera, White Men Are Cracking Up, A Love Renewed, Merlin of the Crystal Cave, Richard II, Henry IV, Much Ado About Nothing, South of the Border, Hammer House of Horrors, Polanski y los ojos del mal, New Tricks. *Mini-series:* The Martian Chronicles (U.S.). *Series:* Ben Hall, The Oddjob Man, Counterstrike, Tak & the Power of Juju (tech. dir.), many more series episodes as Sr. technical director.

FINCHER, DAVID

Director. b. May 10, 1963. Ent. ind. at 18, working at Lucas' Industrial Light and Magic for 4 yrs; left to make TV commercials & dir. pop videos for Madonna, Paula Abdul & Aerosmith. DGA Award 2004 for outstanding commercials.
PICTURES: *Dir.:* The Beat of the Live Drum, Alien 3, Se7en, The Game, Fight Club, Panic Room, Mission Impossible 3, Full Frontal, Zodiac, The Curious Case of Benjamin Button (Academy Award nom.; DGA nom.; Golden Globe nom. 2009), The Social Network, Pawn Sacrifice. *Exec. prod.:* Ambush, Chosen, The Follow, Star, Powder Keg, The Car Thief and the Hit Men, The Hire: Powder Keg, Lords of Dogtown, Love and Other Disasters.

FINKELSTEIN, RICK

Executive. Finkelstein practiced entertainment law with Mitchell, Silverberg and Knupp from 1978 to 1986. Moved into entertainment field as executive v.p. of De Laurentiis Entertainment Group. Then became president of Nelson Films. Joined PolyGram Filmed Entertainment (PFE) as executive v.p. Finkelstein was responsible for the integration of PFE into Universal Studios. In March 1999 Finkelstein served as senior v.p., corporate development & strategic planning for Universal Studios. Became president of Universal Pictures in Nov. 1999 and was named COO in Dec. 2000. He was promoted to vice chairman, Universal Pictures and executive v.p., Universal Studios. October, 2009 his duties included key strategic adviser to co-chairm. Donna Langley and Adam Fogelson. He is part of the Office of the Chairman for Universal Pictures and oversees special projects for Ron Meyer, president and COO, Universal Studios. Finkelstein also oversees the worldwide home entertainment and TV distribution activities of Universal Pictures. He represents Universal as a member of the bd. of directors of the Motion Picture Association of America as well as the bd. of directors of the Sundance Channel and American Cinematheque.

FINLAY, FRANK

Actor. C.B.E. b. Farnworth, Eng., Aug. 6, 1926. Rep. in Troon, 1951, Halifax and Sunderland, 1952-3, before winning Sir James Knott Scholarship to RADA. e. Studied acting at RADA. Appeared with Guildford Repertory Theatre Co. 1957. London stage debut: The Queen and the Welshman, 1957. Broadway debut, Epitaph for George Dillon, 1958.
THEATRE: Work with Royal Court, Chichester Fest., National Theatre includes: Sergeant Musgrave's Dance, Chicken Soup with Barley, Roots, Platonov, Chips with Everything, Saint Joan, Hamlet, Othello, Saturday Sunday Monday, Plunder, Watch It Come Down, Weapons of Happiness, Tribute to a Lady, Filumena (and N.Y.), Amadeus, The Cherry Orchard, Mutiny, Beyond Reasonable Doubt, Black Angel, A Slight Hangover.
PICTURES: The Loneliness of the Long Distance Runner (debut, 1962), The Longest Day, Life for Ruth (Walk in the Shadow), Private Potter, Doctor in Distress, Underworld Informers, The Comedy Man, Agent 8 3/4 (Hot Enough for June), The Wild Affair, A Study in Terror, Othello (Academy Award nom.; Golden Globe nom. 1966), The Sandwich Man, The Jokers, The Deadly Bees, Robbery, I'll Never Forget What 'is Name, The Shoes of the Fisherman, Inspector Clouseau, Twisted Nerve, The Molly Maguires, Cromwell, The Body (narrator), Assault (The Devil's Garden), Gumshoe, Danny Jones, Sitting Target, Neither the Sea Nor the Sand, Shaft in Africa, The Three Musketeers, The Four Musketeers, The Wild Geese, Murder by Decree, Enigma, The Ploughman's Lunch, The Return of the Soldier, The Key, 1919, Lifeforce, The Return of the Musketeers (tv in U.S.), King of the Wind, Cthulhu Mansion, Mountain of Diamonds, Sparrow, So This Is Romance?, Limited Edition, Stiff Upper Lips, Dreaming of Joseph Lees, Ghosthunter, For My Baby, The Martins, Silent Cry,

The Pianist, Silent Cry, Lighthouse Hill, The Statement, Oliver Twist, The Waiting Room.
TELEVISION: *Movies:* The Adventures of Don Quixote, Candide, Julius Caesar, Les Miserables, This Happy Breed, The Lie, The Death of Adolph Hitler, Voltaire, The Merchant of Venice, 84 Charing Cross Road, Saturday Sunday Monday, Count Dracula, The Last Campaign, Thief of Bagdad, Betzi, Sakharov, A Christmas Carol, Arch of Triumph, The Burning Shore, In the Secret State, Verdict of Erebus, Mountain of Diamonds, Encounter, Stalin, An Exchange of Fire, A Mind to Murder, The Magical Legend of the Leprechauns, Longitude, Station Jim, The Lost Prince, Eroica, ExxonMobil Masterpiece Theatre: Prime Suspect 6, Prime Suspect 7: The Final Act, Johnny and the Bomb, Four Seasons. *Mini-series:* Casanova, Bouquet of Barbed Wire, Charlemagne, The Sins, In the Beginning (voice), Johnny and the Bomb. *Series:* Target Luna, Common As Muck, How Do You Want Me?, Life Begins. *Guest:* More than 77 appearances.

FINNEY, ALBERT
Actor. b. Salford, England, May 9, 1936. Studied for stage at Royal Acad. Dramatic Art making his West End debut 1958 in The Party. Appeared at Stratford-Upon-Avon 1959, playing title role in Coriolanus, etc.
THEATRE: The Lily White Boys, Billy Liar, Luther (also NY), Much Ado About Nothing, Armstrong's Last Goodnight, Love for Love, Miss Julie, Black Comedy, A Flea in Her Ear, Joe Egg (NY), Alpha Beta, Krapp's Last Tape, Cromwell, Chez Nous, Hamlet, Tamburlaine, Uncle Vanya, Present Laughter. National Theatre, The Country Wife, The Cherry Orchard, Macbeth, The Biko Inquest, Sergeant Musgrave's Dance (also dir.), Orphans, Another Time (also Chicago), Reflected Glory.
PICTURES: The Entertainer (debut, 1960), Saturday Night and Sunday Morning, Tom Jones (Academy Award nom. Golden Globe nom.; Golden Globe Award 1964), The Victors, Night Must Fall (also co-prod.), Two for the Road, Charlie Bubbles (also dir.), The Picasso Summer (tv in U.K.), Scrooge (Golden Globe Award 1971), Gumshoe, Alpha Beta (tv in U.K.), Murder on the Orient Express (Academy Award nom. 1975), The Adventure of Sherlock Holmes' Smarter Brother (cameo), The Duellists, Wolfen, Looker, Loophole, Shoot the Moon (Golden Globe nom. 1983), Annie, The Dresser (Academy Award nom., Golden Globe nom. 1984), Under the Volcano (Academy Award nom., Golden Globe nom. 1985), Orphans, Miller's Crossing, The Playboys, Rich in Love, The Browning Version, A Man of No Importance, The Run of the Country, Washington Square, Breakfast of Champions, Erin Brockovich (Academy Award nom.; Golden Globe nom. 2001), Traffic, Joan of Arc: The Virgin Warrior, Delivering Milo, Hemingway: The Hunter of Death, Big Fish (Golden Globe nom. 2004), Corpse Bride (voice), The White Rose, A Good Year, Amazing Grace, The Bourne Ultimatum, Before the Devil Knows You're Dead.
TELEVISION: *Movies:* Lights, Camera, Annie!, The Claverdon Road Job, The Miser, Pope John Paul II, The Biko Inquest, Endless Game, The Image (Emmy nom. 1990), The Green Man, The Wall: Live in Berlin, A Rather English Marriage, The Gathering Storm (Emmy Award, Golden Globe Award 2002), My Uncle Silas II. *Mini-series:* Cold Lazarus, Karaoke, Nostromo. *Series:* Emergency-Ward 10, My Uncle Silas. *Documentary:* Munich the Documentary (voice). *Guest:* More than 50 appearances.

FIRTH, COLIN
Actor. b. Grayshott, Hampshire, Eng., Sept. 10, 1960. Studied acting at the Drama Centre at Chalk Farm. Author of A Month in the Country (screenplay), Making of Pride and Prejudice.
THEATRE: London: in Tartuffe, King Lear, Hamlet, Another Country, Doctor's Dilemma, The Lonely Road, Desire Under the Elms, The Caretaker, Chatsky.
PICTURES: Another Country, 1919, A Month in the Country, Apartment Zero, Valmont, Wings of Fame, The Hour of the Pig, The Pleasure Principle, Femme Fatale, Playmaker, The Advocate, Circle of Friends, The English Patient, Fever Pitch, A Thousand Acres, The World of Moss, Shakespeare in Love, The Secret Laughter of Women, My Life So Far, Blackadder Back and Forth, Relative Values, Londinium, Bridget Jones's Diary, The Importance of Being Earnest, Hope Springs, What a Girl Wants, Girl with a Pearl Earring, Love Actually, Trauma, Bridget Jones: The Edge of Reason, Nanny McPhee, Where the Truth Lies, Good, The Last Legion, London, The Meat Trade, And When Did You Last See Your Father?, Then She Found Me, St. Trinian's, The Accidental Husband, In Prison My Whole Life (doc.), Genova, Mamma Mia!, A Christmas Carol, A Single Man (Academy Award nom.; Golden Globe nom. 2010), Dorian Gray, St Trinian's 2: The Legend of Fritton's Gold, Main Street, The King's Speech, The Promised Land.
TELEVISION: *Movies:* Camille, Crown Court, Dutch Girls, Tumbledown, Hostages, Master of the Moor, The Deep Blue Sea, Pride and Prejudice, The Widowing of Mrs. Holroyd, The Turn of the Screw, Donovan Quick, Conspiracy (Emmy nom. 2001), Celebration, Born Equal. *Mini-series:* Lost Empires, Nostromo. *Specials:* Tales from the Hollywood Hills (Pat Hobby Teamed With Genius). *Guest:* More than 86 appearances.

FIRTH, PETER
Actor. b. Bradford, Yorkshire, Oct. 27, 1953. Appeared in local TV children's show where casting director spotted him and got him role in series, The Flaxton Boys. Moved to London and worked in TV, first in children's show, later on dramas for BBC. Breakthrough role in Equus at National Theatre, 1973 which he repeated in film.
THEATRE: Equus (Theatre World Award), Romeo and Juliet, Spring Awakening, Amadeus.
PICTURES: Diamonds on Wheels (debut, 1972; tv in U.S.), Brother Sun Sister Moon, Daniel and Maria, Equus (Academy Award nom.; Golden Globe nom. 1978), Joseph Andrews, Aces High, When You Comin' Back Red Ryder, Tess, Lifeforce, Letter to Brezhnev, Trouble in Paradise, White Elephant, A State of Emergency, Born of Fire, The Tree of Hands, Prisoner of Rio, Burndown, The Hunt for Red October, The Rescuers Down Under (voice), The Perfect Husband, White Angel, Shadowlands, An Awfully Big Adventure, The Garden of Redemption, Marco Polo, Amistad, Mighty Joe Young, Chill Factor, Pearl Harbor, The Greatest Game Ever Played.
TELEVISION: *Movies and Specials:* Here Comes the Doubledeckers, Castlehaven, The Sullen Sisters, The Simple Life, The Magistrate, The Protectors, Black Beauty, Arthur, Her Majesty's Pleasure, the Picture of Dorian Gray, Lady of the Camillias, Blood Royal, Northanger Abbey, The Way, The Truth: the Video, The Incident, Children Crossing, Prisoner of Honor, Married to Murder, The Laughter of God, Murder in Eden, Brighton Boy, The Broker's Man, Holding On, The Magicians, Me & Mrs. Jones, Hawking. *Mini-series:* The Battle for Rome. *Series:* The Flaxon Boys, Home and Away, Country Matters, Spooks, That's Life, MI-5. *Documentary:* Film Genre (series host). *Guest:* More than 52 appearances.

FISHBURNE, LAURENCE
Actor. b. Augusta, GA, July 30, 1961. Raised in Brooklyn. Landed role on daytime serial One Life to Live at age 11. On NY stage in Short Eyes, Two Trains Running (Tony and Theatre World Awards), Riff Raff (also wrote and directed).
PICTURES: Cornbread Earl and Me (debut, 1975), Fast Break, Apocalypse Now, Willie and Phil, Death Wish II, Rumble Fish, The Cotton Club, The Color Purple, Quicksilver, Band of the Hand, A Nightmare on Elm Street 3: Dream Warriors, Gardens of Stone, School Daze, Red Heat, King of New York, Cadence, Class Action, Boyz N the Hood, Deep Cover, What's Love Got to Do With It (Academy Award nom. 1994), Searching for Bobby Fischer, Higher Learning, Bad Company, Just Cause, Othello, Fled, Hoodlums (also exec. prod.), Event Horizon, The Matrix, Michael Jordan to the Max (voice), Osmosis Jones (voice), Once in the Life, The Matrix Reloaded, Biker Boyz, Soul of a Man (documentary, narr.), Mystic River, The Matrix Revolutions, Assault on Precinct 13, Scheherazade, Five Fingers (also prod.), The Beltway (prod. only), Akeelah and the Bee (also prod.), Mission: Impossible III, The Death and Life of Bobby Z, Bobby, 4: Rise of the Silver Surfer (voice), 21, TMNT (narr.), Tortured, Days of Wrath, Black Water Transit, Armored, 4Chosen, Predators, Contagion.
TELEVISION: *Movies:* A Rumor of War, I Take These Men, Decoration Day, The Tuskegee Airmen (Emmy nom.; Golden Globe nom. 1996), Miss Ever's Boys Emmy Award; Emmy nom. 1997), Always Outnumbered, Sex and the Matrix (short). *Series:* One Life to Live, Pee-wee's Playhouse, CSI: Crime Scene Investigation. *Documentary:* The N-Word, Tribeca (Emmy Award, 1993). *Guest:* More than 123 appearances.

FISHER, CARRIE
Actress, Writer. b. Beverly Hills, CA, Oct. 21, 1956. e. London Central Sch. of Speech & Drama. Daughter of actress Debbie Reynolds and late singer Eddie Fisher. On Broadway in the chorus of revival of Irene (1972; with mother); Author: Postcards From the Edge (1987), Surrender the Pink, Delusions of Grandma.
PICTURES: Shampoo (debut, 1975), Star Wars, Mr. Mike's Mondo Video, Star Wars: The Empire Strikes Back, The Blues Brothers, Under the Rainbow, Star Wars: Return of the Jedi, Garbo Talks, The Man with One Red Shoe, Hannah and Her Sisters, Hollywood Vice Squad, Amazon Women on the Moon, Appointment with Death, The 'Burbs, Loverboy, She's Back, When Harry Met Sally..., The Time Guardian, Postcards From the Edge (s.p. only), Sibling Rivalry, Drop Dead Fred, Soapdish, This Is My Life, George Lucas: Heroes Myths and Magic, Austin Powers: International Man of Mystery, Scream 3, Famous, Heartbreakers, Jay and Silent Bob Strike Back, A Midsummer Night's Rave, Charlie's Angels: Full Throttle, Wonderland, Stateside, Wannabe, Undiscovered, Suffering Man's Charity, Cougar Club, Fanboys, White Lightnin', The Women, Sorority Row.
TELEVISION: *Movies:* Leave Yesterday Behind, Liberty, Sunday Drive, Sweet Revenge, These Old Broads, Romancing the Bride. *Series:* Carrie on Hollywood, "Conversations From the Edge with Carrie Fisher, Homes That Made Hollywood (pilot-host), 30 Rock (Emmy nom. 2008 as guest), Family Guy (voice). *Specials:* Come Back Little Sheba, Classic Creatures: Return of the Jedi, Thumbelina (Faerie Tale Theatre), Paul Reiser: Out on a Whim, Two Daddies? (voice), Trying Times (Hunger Chic), Carrie Fisher: The Hollywood Family (also writer). *Guest:* More than 138 appearances.

FISHER, FRANCES

Actress. b. Milford-on-Sea, England, May 11, 1952. Father was intl. construction supervisor. Raised in Colombia, Canada, France, Brazil, Turkey. Made stage debut in Texas in Summer and Smoke.
THEATRE: NY: Fool for Love, Desire Under the Elms, Cat on a Hot Tin Roof, The Hitch-Hikers, Orpheus Descending, A Midsummer Night's Dream, Jammed.
PICTURES: Can She Bake a Cherry Pie? (debut, 1983), Tough Guys Don't Dance, The Principal, Patty Hearst, Bum Rap, Heavy Petting, Pink Cadillac, Lost Angels, Welcome Home Roxy Carmichael, L.A. Story, Unforgiven, Babyfever, The Stars Fell on Henrietta, Waiting for Guffman, Female Perversion, Wild America, Titanic, True Crime, The Big Tease, Gone in Sixty Seconds, The Rising Place, Blue Car, House of Sand and Fog, Laws of Attraction, Sex and Death 101, My Sexiest Year, In the Valley of Elah, A Single Woman (narr.), Jolene, The Kingdom, The Perfect Game, Janie Jones, Golf in the Kingdom, The Roommate.
TELEVISION: *Movies:* Broken Vows, Cold Sassy Tree, Matlock: The Thief, Sudie and Simpson, A Promise to Keep, Devlin, Attack of the 50 Ft. Woman, Praying Mantis, Lucy & Desi: Before the Laughter, The Other Mother, Strange Luck, Traffic, The Audrey Hepburn Story, Jackie Bouvier Kennedy Onassis, Passion and Prejudice, The Lyon's Den, Elysian Fields, Mrs. Harris, To Love and Die, Backyard Wedding. *Series:* The Edge of Night (1976-81), The Guiding Light (1985), Strange Luck, Titus, Glory Days, Becker, The Lyon's Den, Eureka, The Shield. *Guest:* More than 56 appearances.

FISHER, LUCY

Executive, Producer. b. Oct. 2, 1949. e. Harvard U., B.A. in English, cum laude. Began career as a script reader at United Artists. Moved to Samuel Goldwyn Jr. Productions as a story editor in the late '70s. Then moved to MGM where she became executive in charge of creative affairs, and later moved to 20th Century Fox where she rose to v.p., production. From 1979-1981 Fisher headed worldwide production at Francis Ford Coppola's American Zoetrope. Fisher joined Warner Bros. in 1981 and remained there until 1995, rising to executive v.p., worldwide theatrical production. Joined Columbia TriStar in March 1996 as vice chmn. Currently, producer with Red Wagon Entertainment, a prod. co. she runs with prod./husband Doug Wick. The co. has prod. deal with Sony Picturers Entertainment. The Producers Guild of America in 2007 honored Fisher and Wick with the David O. Selznick Award for outstanding achievement in theatrical motion pictures.
PICTURES: Stuart Little 2, Peter Pan, Win a Date with Tad Hamilton!, Bewitched, Jarhead, Memoirs of a Geisha, Runaway Vacation, Nailed.
TELEVISION: *Series:* Stuart Little.

FISHER, THOMAS L.

Special Effects.
PICTURES: The Devil's Rain, City on Fire, First Blood, Rambo: First Blood Part II, Legal Eagles, Extreme Prejudice, Rambo III, Total Recall, Desperate Hours, Terminator 2: Judgment Day, The Taking of Beverly Hills, The Last of the Mohicans, Under Siege, Last Action Hero, On Deadly Ground, True Lies (Academy Award nom. 1995), Batman Forever, Shadow Conspiracy, Titanic (Academy Award, Best Visual Effects, 1998), Supernova, The 13th Warrior, End of Days, Collateral Damage, Men in Black II, The Cat in the Hat, Van Helsing, Collateral, The Guardian (visual consult.).
TELEVISION: *Movies:* Fer-de-Lance, Flight of the Maiden, Louisiana, Riviera.

FISK, JACK

Director, Production Designer. b. Ipava, IL, Dec. 19, 1945. e. Cooper Union-Pa. Acad. of the Fine Arts. m. actress Sissy Spacek. Began in films as designer; turning to direction with Raggedy Man (1981).
PICTURES: *Director:* Raggedy Man, Violets Are Blue, Daddy's Dyin', ... Who's Got the Will? *Art Director:* Badlands, Phantom of the Paradise, Carrie, Days of Heaven. *Prod. Designer:* Phantom of the Paradise, Heart Beat, The Thin Red Line, The Straight Story, Mulholland Drive, The New World, There Will Be Blood (Academy Award nom.; DGA Award 2008), The Invasion, The Tree of Life.
TELEVISION: *Movie:* Final Verdict (dir.).*Series:* On the Air (dir.).

FITHIAN, JOHN

Executive. e. William and Mary, B.A.; U. of Virgina, J.D. Represented trade associations (including National Assoc. of Theatre Owners), professional athlete unions, telecomm. companies, nonprofits, publishers and advertisers with D.C.-based law firm Patton Boggs LLP. Became president and CEO of NATO, Jan. 2000, where he serves as chief public spokesperson for theatre owners before public officials and press.

FITZGERALD, TARA

Actress. b. Sept. 18, England, 1968. e. London's Drama Centre, 1990.
THEATRE: London: Our Song. NY: Hamlet.
PICTURES: Hear My Song (debut, 1991), Sirens, A Man of No Importance, The Englishman Who Went Up a Hill But Came Down a Mountain, Brassed Off!, Conquest, New World Dis Order, Childhood, Rancid Aluminium, Dark Blue World Orchestra, Secret Passage, I Capture the Castle, Five Children and It, In a Dark Place.
TELEVISION: *Movies:* The Black Candle, Anglo-Saxon Attitudes, Six Characters in Search of an Author, Fall From Grace, The Woman in White, The Student Prince, Little White Lies, Frenchman's Creek, In the Name of Love, Love Again, Marple: The Body in the Library, Like Father, Like Son, U Be Dead. *Mini-series:* The Camomile Lawn, The Tenants of Wildfell Hall,The Final Day, The Virgin Queen, Jane Eyre. *Series:* Waking the Dead. *Documentary:* Celebrity Naked Ambition.

FITZSIMONS, DENNIS J.

Executive. b. June 26, 1950. e. Bachelor's degree, political science, Fordham Univ. FitzSimons started his media career at Grey Advertising in New York. He moved into advertising sales as a director/advertising sales with Viacom International and was New York sales manager for TeleRep, Inc., a division of Cox Broadcasting. FitzSimons served as director/sales and marketing for Viacom's WVIT-TV, Hartford, CT, before joining Tribune Broadcasting in 1982 as sales dir. for WGN-TV, Chicago. In 1984 FitzSimons was appointed v.p. & gen. mgr. of WGNO-TV, New Orleans. In 1985, he returned to Chicago as Tribune Broadcasting vice president/operations, and in 1987 was appointed WGN's v.p. & gen. mgr. FitzSimons was appointed Tribune executive vice president in January 2000, with responsibility for the company's broadcasting, publishing and interactive groups, as well as the Chicago Cubs. He continued to serve as president of Tribune Broadcasting Company, which he led from 1994 to 2003. He was president of Tribune Television from 1992 to 1994. He was elected to the Tribune bd. of dir. in 2000; was named president and COO in July 2001; was named CEO in 2003 and in January 2004 was elevated to chairman of the Tribune Company. He chaired the Media Security and Reliability Council for the FCC from 2002 to 2004, and is a dir. of The Associated Press. He is also a member of The Business Council as well as the Civic Committee of The Commercial Club of Chicago. In addition, FitzSimons serves as chmn. of the McCormick Tribune Foundation, is a member of Northwestern University's board of trustees, and a dir. of United Way of Metropolitan Chicago and the Museum of Science and Industry. Additional commitments include the Big Shoulders Fund (director) and the Off The Street Club (vice president), each in Chicago. Fitzsimons retired from the Tribune Comapny in 2007. Currently he is on the Bd. of Dir. for Media General where he is a member of the Audit Committee, 2009.

FLAGG, FANNIE

Actress, Writer. b. Birmingham, AL, Sept. 21, 1944. e. Univ. of AL. Studied acting at Pittsburgh Playhouse, Town & Gown Theatre. Had her own live 90 minute tv show in Birmingham. To NY where she wrote and appeared in revues for Upstairs at the Downstairs Club. Comedy albums: Rally 'Round the Flagg, My Husband Doesn't Know I'm Making This Phone Call. *Author:* Coming Attractions: A Wonderful Novel (Daisy Fay and the Miracle Man), Fried Green Tomatoes at the Whistle Stop Cafe, A Redbird Christmas.
THEATRE: B'way: Patio Porch, Come Back to the Five and Dime Jimmy Dean Jimmy Dean, The Best Little Whorehouse in Texas. Regional: Private Lives, Gypsy, Mary Mary, Tobacco Road, Old Acquaintance, etc.
PICTURES: Five Easy Pieces (debut, 1970), Some of My Best Friends Are..., Stay Hungry, Grease, Rabbit Test, My Best Friend Is a Vampire, Fried Green Tomatoes (also co-s.p.; Academy Award nom. for s.p.; WGA nom. 1992), Crazy in Alabama, Red Bird (writer of novel A Redbird Christmas; s.p.).
TELEVISION: *Movies:* The New Original Wonder Woman, Sex and the Married Woman. *Pilots:* Comedy News, Home Cookin'. *Producer:* Morning Show. *Series:* The New Dick Van Dyke Show, Match Game P.M., Liar's Club, Harper Valley P.T.A., Dolly (writer).

FLANERY, SEAN PATRICK

Actor. b. Lake Charles, LA, Oct. 11, 1965.
PICTURES: A Tiger's Tale, Frank and Jesse, The Grass Harp, Powder, Raging Angels, Suicide Kings, Eden, Best Men, Run the Wild Fields, Girl, Simply Irresistible, The Boondock Saints, Body Shots, Run the Wild Fields, D-Tox, Con Express, Lone Hero, Kiss the Bride, Borderline, A Promise Kept, Boondock II: All Saints Day, Into the Fire, Veritas, Prince of Truth, Demon Hunter, Prisoners of the Sun, The Insatiable, Kaw, Ten Inch Hero, First Fear, To Live and Die, The Whole Truth, Sinners & Saints, Boondock Saints II: All Saints Day, Scavengers, Mongolian Death Worms.
TELEVISION: *Movies:* Guinevere, Young Indiana Jones and the Hollywood Follies, Young Indiana Jones and the Attack of the Hawkmen, Young Indiana Jones and the Treasure of the Peacock's Eye, Young Indiana Jones Travels with Father, Just Your Luck, Acceptable Risk, Diamond Hunters (mini), Borderline, Then Came Jones, Savage Planet, Into the Fire, 30 Days Until I'm Famous, Dead Lawyers, No Game (dir., exec. prod.), Citizen Jane. *Series:* The Young Indiana Jones Chronicles, The Strip, Stephen King's Dead Zone, Secrets of a Small Town (pilot).

FLEDER, GARY
Director. b. Norfolk, VA, Dec. 19, 1965.
PICTURES: Things to Do in Denver when You're Dead, Kiss the Girls, Don't Say a Word, Imposter, Runaway Jury, The Express, Protection.
TELEVISION: *Movies:* Air Time (also prod.), The Companion, Happy Town Finnegan. *Mini-series:* From the Earth to the Moon. *Series:* Homicide: Life on the Street, L.A. Doctors (pilot), Falcone, The Shield, R.U.S./H, Blind Justice, October Road (exec. prod., pilot dir.), The Evidence (dir., pilot; exec. prod.), Life Unexpected.

FLENDER, RODMAN
Director, Producer, Actor, Writer.
PICTURES: *Director:* The Unborn, In the Heat of Passion (also prod. & s.p.), Leprechaun 2, Idle Hands. *Producer:* Demon of Paradise, The Terror Within, Watchers 2, The Haunting of Morella, Body Chemistry (exec. prod.), The Unborn, In the Heat of Passion, Concealed Weapon. *Actor:* Carnosaur, Carnosaur 2, Criminal Hearts, Carnosaur 3: Primal Species, Idle Hands. *Writer:* In the Heat of Passion, Dracula Rising.
TELEVISION: *Movies: Actor:* Casper Meets Wendy, Black Scorpion, Testing Bob (dir. only), Just a Phase (dir. only). *Series dir.:* Tales from the Crypt, Party of Five, Chicago Hope, Raising Caines, Dark Skies, Millenium, Arli$$, Dawson's Creek, Tucker, Gilmore Girls, My Guide to Becoming a Rock Star, Push Nevada, Life As We Know It.

FLETCHER, LOUISE
Actress. b. Birmingham, AL, July 22, 1934. e. U. of North Carolina, B.A. Came to Hollywood at age 21; studied with Jeff Corey. Worked on TV shows (including Playhouse 90, Maverick). Gave up career to be a mother for 10 yrs.; returned to acting in 1973. Board of Directors: Deafness Research Foundation, 1980- Honorary Degrees: Doctor of Humane Letters from Gallaudet U. and West Maryland Col. Advisory board: The Caption Center, The Nat'l Institute on Deafness and Other Communication Disorders.
PICTURES: Thieves Like Us, Russian Roulette, One Flew Over the Cuckoo's Nest (Academy Award, Golden Globe Award 1976), Exorcist II: The Heretic, The Cheap Detective, Natural Enemies, The Magician of Lublin, The Lucky Star, The Lady in Red, Strange Behavior, Mamma Dracula, Brainstorm, Strange Invaders, Firestarter, Once Upon a Time in America, Overnight Sensation, Invaders from Mars, The Boy Who Could Fly, Nobody's Fool, Flowers in the Attic, Two Moon Junction, Best of the Best, Shadow Zone, Blue Steel, Blind Vision, The Player, Georgino, Tollbooth, Return to Two Moon Junction, Virtuosity, High School High, 2 Days in the Valley, Mulholland Falls, Mojave Frankenstein, Edie and Pen, Gone Fishing, High School High, Girl Gets Moe, Love Kills, Cruel Intentions, Time Served, A Map of the World, The Contract, Big Eden, Very Mean Men, More Dogs Than Bones, Silver Man, After Image, Manna From Heaven, Touched By A Killer, Finding Home, Dial 9 For Love, Finding Home, Clipping Adam, Inmates of the Heart, Aurora Borealis, Dancing in Twilight, The Last Sin Eater, The Genesis Code.
TELEVISION: *Movies:* Can Ellen Be Saved?, Thou Shalt Not Commit Adultery, A Summer to Remember, Island, Second Serve, J. Edgar Hoover, The Karen Carpenter Story, Final Notice, Nightmare on the 13th Floor, In a Child's Name, The Fire Next Time, The Haunting of Seacliff Inn, Someone Else's Child, Stepford Husbands, Twisted Path, Breastmen, Married to a Stranger, Heartless, The Devil's Arithmetic, Turning Homeward, A Time to Remember, Me and Luke, A Dad for Christmas. *Series:* Boys of Twilight, Deep Space Nine, Picket Fences, VR 5, Profiler, ER. *Guest:* More than 80 appearances.

FLOCKHART, CALISTA
Actress. b. Freeport, IL, Nov. 11, 1964. e. Rutgers College, NJ. m. actor Harrison Ford.
THEATRE: *B'way:* The Glass Menagerie. *Off B'way:* The Loop, All for One, Sophistry, Wrong Turn at Lungfish, Beside Herself, Bovver Boys. Regional: The Three Sisters, Our Town, Death Takes a Holiday, Bash: Latter Day Plays.
PICTURES: Quiz Show, Getting In, Naked in New York, Drunks, The Birdcage, Milk and Money, Telling Lies in America, A Midsummer's Night's Dream, Like A Hole in the Head, Things You Can Tell Just By Looking At Her, Providence, The Last Shot, Fragile.
TELEVISION: *Movie:* Darrow. *Series:* The Guiding Light, Ally McBeal (3 Emmy noms.; Golden Globe Award, 1998), Ally, Brothers & Sisters. *Specials:* Bash: Latterday Plays, America: A Tribute to Heroes. *Guest:* More than 71 appearances.

FLYNN, BEAU
Producer.
PICTURES: I.Q. (asst. prod.), Johns, Life During Wartime (exec. prod), The House of Yes, Dust & Stardust, Little City, Starstruck, Judas Kiss, Coming Soon, The Love Letter, Guinevere, Requiem for a Dream, Tigerland, Bubble Boy, Till Human Voices Wake Us, Slap Her She's French, 11:14, After the Sunset, Dallas 362 (exec. prod.), The Wild, The Exorcism of Emily Rose, The Wild, Dead Asleep, Boyfriend in a Box, The Guardian, Date School, Conrail, The Number 23, Choke, Our Lady of Victory (consult. prod.), Journey to the Center of the Earth 3D, The Mighty Macs (consult. prod.), Blueprint, Red Dawn, What's Your Number?, The Orphanage.
TELEVISION: *Movies: As Exec. Prod.:* Inside 'Fear', An American Town. *Series:* USA's Connonball Run 2001, Fear.

FOGARTY, JACK V.
Executive, Producer, Writer. b. Los Angeles, CA. e. UCLA. Management, MGM, 1960-62; exec. prod. mgr., Cinerama, Inc., 1962-64; assoc. prod., The Best of Cinerama, 1963; est. own p.r. firm, 1965; pres., AstroScope, Inc., 1969-74.
TELEVISION: *Writer/prod.:* The Rookies, S.W.A.T., Charlie's Angels, Most Wanted, Barnaby Jones, A Man Called Sloane, Trapper John, T.J. Hooker, Crazy Like a Fox, The Equalizer, Jake and the Fatman, Murder She Wrote, Charlie's Angels (story edit.). *Exec. Story consultant:* Most Wanted, A Man Called Sloane, Sheriff Lobo, T.J. Hooker. *Producer:* T.J. Hooker, Jessie.

FOGELSON, ADAM
Executive. e. Stanford University, B.A. in communication, 1989. Early in his career Fogelson was vice president of the AFA Company, a consulting firm focusing on production marketing and distribution, where his clients included Carolco Pictures and Nelson Entertainment. He moved to Trimark Pictures where he became snior v.p., worldwide marketing. He joined Universal Pictures as v.p., creative advertising in 1998 and rose to executive v.p., creative advertising in 2002. During that time, he worked on the campaigns for "American Pie," "American Pie 2," "The Fast and the Furious," "Erin Brockovich," "Notting Hill," "Meet the Parents," "U-571," "Bring It On" among others. From 2002 through 2007, Fogelson served as president of marketing for Universal Pictures. In that capacity, he oversaw the campaigns for such hits as "Bruce Almighty," "2 Fast 2 Furious," "Seabiscuit," "Meet The Fockers," "Ray," "The 40-Year-Old Virgin," "American Wedding," "8 Mile" and "The Break-Up." Fogelson also supervised the marketing campaign for Universal's Tony Award-winning smash-hit musical "Wicked," which continues to sell out on Broadway and has launched hugely successful engagements in Chicago and Los Angeles, as well as touring North America, London, Tokyo, Stuttgart and Melbourne. For the marketing campaign for "8 Mile," Fogelson and President of Marketing Eddie Egan were named 2003 Entertainment Marketers of the Year by Advertising Age. In 2007, a string of hits propelled Universal Pictures to its best domestic box office year ever. Fogelson was named president of marketing and distribution for Universal Pictures in Oct. 2007. In this role he was responsible for executive oversight of Universal's domestic marketing and distribution divisions. October, 2009 he was promoted to Chairman for Universal Pictures. Additionally, Fogelson supervises the marketing and distribution for Rogue Pictures, the studio's specialty genre label.

FOLEY, DAVE
Actor. b. Toronto, Canada, Jan. 4, 1963.
PICTURES: High Stakes, Three Men and a Baby, It's Pat, Kids in the Hall: Brain Candy, Hacks, A Bug's Life (voice), The Wrong Guy (also s.p.), Dick, Blast from the Past, South Park: Bigger, Longer and Uncut (voice), Toy Story 2 (voice), It's Tough to Be a Bug (voice), Cyberworld (voice), Monkeybone, Kids in the Hall: Same Guys New Dresses, The Frank Truth, On the Line, Stark Raving Mad, Run Ronnie Run!, Fancy Dancing, Swindle, Ham & Cheese, My Boss' Daughter, Whitecoats, Childstar, Sky High, Cars (voice), Out of Omaha, Netherbeast Incorporated, The Strip, Freeloaders, Last Call, 6 Month Rule.
TELEVISION: *Movies/Specials:* The Prodigious Mr. Hickey, Echoes in the Darkness, Anne of Green Gables: The Sequel, The Lawrenceville Stories, From the Earth to the Moon, It's Tough to Be a Bug (voice), Prom Queen: The Marc Hall Story, Testing Bob, Prep & Landing (voice). *Mini-series:* Death Comes to Town. *Series:* The Kids in the Hall (also dir., 3 Emmy noms.), NewsRadio (also dir.), The Andy Dick Show, Committed, The Hollow Men (exec. prod. , pilot), Sketch Pad, Celebrity Poker Showdown (host), Will & Grace, Slacker Cats, Robson Arms. *Guest:* More than 90 appearances.

FOLEY, JAMES
Director. b. Feb. 28, 1953. New York, NY. E. NYU, USC. While at USC directed two short films, Silent Night and November which brought him attention. Directed two Madonna videos.
PICTURES: Reckless, At Close Range, Who's That Girl, After Dark My Sweet, Glengarry Glen Ross, A Day to Remember, Fear, Two Bits, The Chamber, The Corruptor, Confidence, 88 Minutes, Perfect Stranger, Mary Mother of Christ.
TELEVISION: *Movie:* Hollywood Division. *Series:* Gun.

FOLSEY, GEORGE, JR.
Producer, Editor. b. Los Angeles, CA, Jan. 17, 1939. Son of late cinematographer George Folsey Sr. e. Pomona Coll., B.A., 1961. Chairman, Q Sound Labs, Canadian sound localization and Tech. Co., 1988-1992.
PICTURES: *Editor:* Glass Houses, Bone, Hammer, Black Caesar, Schlock, Trader Horn, Bucktown, J.D.'s Revenge, Norman... Is That You?, Tracks, The Chicken Chronicles, The Kentucky Fried Movie, National Lampoon's Animal House, Freedom Road, The Great Santini (addt'l editing), The Blues Brothers (also assoc. prod.), Bullet Proof, Dirty Work, Goosed, Cabin Fever, The Kings of

Brooklyn, Basic, Cheaper by the Dozen, The Ringer, The Pink Panther, Unaccompanied Minors, Hostel: Part II, The Gray Man, The Camel Wars, Sex Drive, Hot Tub Time Machine. *Producer:* An American Werewolf in London, Twilight Zone—The Movie (assoc. prod.); Trading Places (exec. prod. & 2nd unit dir.), Into the Night (co-prod.), Spies Like Us (co-prod.), Clue (co-exec. prod.), Three Amigos, Coming to America (co-prod., co-editor), Greedy (co-exec. prod.), Grumpier Old Men.
TELEVISION: *Movies:* It Happened at Lakewood Manor, Fargo. *Series:* The Monkees. *Video:* Michael Jackson's Thriller (co-prod., editor).

FONDA, BRIDGET
Actress. b. Los Angeles, CA, Jan. 27, 1964. Daughter of actor Peter Fonda. Grew up in Los Angeles and Montana. e. NYU theater prog. Studied acting at Lee Strasberg Inst., and with Harold Guskin. Starred in grad. student film PPT. Workshop stage performances include Confession and Pastels.
PICTURES: Aria (Tristan and Isolde; debut, 1987), You Can't Hurry Love, Light Years (voice), Scandal (Golden Globe nom. 1990), Shag, Strapless, Frankenstein Unbound, The Godfather Part III, Drop Dead Fred (unbilled), Doc Hollywood, Leather Jackets, Out of the Rain, Iron Maze, Single White Female, Singles, Army of Darkness, Point of No Return, Bodies Rest and Motion, Little Buddha, It Could Happen to You, The Road to Wellville, Camilla, Rough Magic, Balto (voice), City Hall, Touch, Mr. Jealousy, The Road to Graceland, Jackie Brown, The Break-Up, A Simple Plan, Lake Placid, South of Heaven West of Hell, The Whole Shebang, Delivering Milo, Monkeybone, Kiss of the Dragon.
TELEVISION: *Movies:* Jacob Have I Loved, In the Gloaming (Emmy nom. 1997), After Amy (Golden Globe nom. 2002), The Snow Queen. *Series:* The Chris Isaak Show. *Specials:* Jacob Have I Loved (Wonderworks), The Edge (The Professional Man).

FONDA, JANE
Actress. b. New York, NY, Dec. 21, 1937. e. Emma Willard Sch., Troy, NY. Active in dramatics, Vassar. Father was late actor Henry Fonda. Brother is actor Peter Fonda. Appeared with father in summer stock production, The Country Girl, Omaha, NB. Studied painting, languages, Paris. Art Students League, N.Y. Appeared in The Male Animal, Dennis, MA. Modeled, appeared on covers, Esquire, Vogue, The Ladies Home Journal, Glamour, and McCall's, 1959. Appeared in documentaries: Introduction to the Enemy, No Nukes.
THEATRE: There Was A Little Girl (Theatre World Award), Invitation to a March, The Fun Couple, Strange, 33 Variations.
PICTURES: Tall Story (debut, 1960), Walk on the Wild Side, The Chapman Report, Period of Adjustment, In the Cool of The Day, Sunday in New York, The Love Cage (Joy House), La Ronde (Circle of Love), Cat Ballou (Golden Globe nom. 1966), The Chase, La Curee (The Game is Over), Any Wednesday (Golden Globe nom. 1970), Hurry Sundown, Barefoot in the Park, Barbarella, Spirits of the Dead, They Shoot Horses Don't They? (Academy Award nom.; Golden Globe nom. 1970), Klute (Academy Award, Best Actress, Golden Globe Award 1972), F.T.A. (also prod.), Tout va Bien, Steelyard Blues, A Doll's House, The Bluebird, Fun With Dick and Jane, Julia (Academy Award nom., Golden Globe Award 1978), Coming Home (Academy Award, Best Actress, 2 Golden Globe Awards 1979), Comes a Horseman, California Suite, The China Syndrome (Academy Award nom.; Golden Globe nom. 1980), The Electric Horseman, Nine To Five, On Golden Pond (Academy Award nom.; Golden Globe nom. 1982), Rollover, Agnes of God, The Morning After (Academy Award nom. 1987), Leonard Part 6 (cameo), Old Gringo, Stanley and Iris, Bandits, A Century of Cinema, Cinéma Vérité: Defining the Moment, Searching for Debra Winger (documentary), Monster-in-Law, Georgia Rule.
TELEVISION: *Movie:* The Dollmaker (Emmy Award, Golden Globe nom. 1985). *Specials/Documentaries:* A String of Beads, Lily--Sold Out, The Helen Reddy Special, I Love Liberty, Tell Them I'm a Mermaid, Fonda on Fonda (host), A Century of Women (narrator, Emmy nom.1995), AFI's 100 Years, 100 Thrills: America's Most Heart-Pounding Movies, Complicated Women (tv documentary, narrator), A Decade Under the Influence. *Series:* 9 to 5 (exec. prod. only). *Guest:* More than 221 appearances.

FONDA, PETER
Actor, Director. b. New York, NY, Feb. 23, 1939. e. studied at U. of Omaha. Son of late actor Henry Fonda. Sister is actress Jane Fonda; daughter is actress Bridget Fonda.
PICTURES: Tammy and the Doctor (debut, 1963), The Victors (Golden Globe nom. 1964), Lilith, The Young Lovers, The Wild Angels, The Trip, Spirits of the Dead, Easy Rider (also co-s.p., prod. Academy Award nom.; WGA nom. 1970), Idaho Transfer (dir.), The Last Movie, The Hired Hand (also dir.), Two People, Dirty Mary Crazy Larry, Open Season, Race With the Devil, 92 in the Shade, Killer Force, Fighting Mad, Futureworld, Outlaw Blues, High Ballin!, Wanda Nevada (also dir.), Cannonball Run (cameo), Split Image, Certain Fury, Dance of the Dwarfs, Mercenary Fighters, Jungle Heat, Diajobu My Friend, Peppermint Frieden, Spasm, The Rose Garden, Fatal Mission, Family Spirit, Reckless, South Beach, Bodies Rest & Motion, DeadFall, Molly & Gina, Love and a .45, Painted Hero, Nadja, John Carpenter's Escape from L.A., Grace of My Heart, Ulee's Gold (NY Film Crits. Circle Award, Academy Award nom.; Golden Globe Award, Best Actor, 1998), The Limey, Thomas and the Magic Railroad, Second Skin, Wooly Boys, The Laramie Project, The Heart Is Deceitful Above All Things, Cobrador, Japan, Ghost Rider, 3:10 to Yuma, Japan, A Handful of Beans, Boondock Saints II: All Saints Day, Smitty, I Ride Alone (also prod.), A Handful of Beans.
TELEVISION: *Movies:* A Reason to Live, The Hostage Tower, A Time of Indifference, Sound, Certain Honorable Men, Montana, The Tempest (Golden Globe nom. 1999), Don't Look Back, The Passion of Ayn Rand (Emmy nom.; Golden Globe Award 2000), The Maldonado Miracle (Emmy nom. 2004), Capital City, A Thief of Time, Back When We Were Grownups, Supernova, Journey to the Center of the Earth, Revolution. *Mini-series:* American Stories: The American Dream (narr.), Dream Machines, The Gathering. *Series:* The American Dream (narr.). *Documentaries: As Narrator:* Signatures of the Soul, Hollywood Uncensored (host), Blue Water Hunting, Film Trix 2004 (short), Breaking the Rules. *Guest:* More than 116 appearances.

FONER, NAOMI
Writer, Producer. b. New York, NY. e. Barnard Col., Columbia U. Mother of actors Maggie and Jake Gyllenhaal. Was media dir. of Eugene McCarthy's 1968 political campaign, then prod. asst. & researcher at PBS. 1968 joined Children's Television Workshop on staff of Sesame Street. Later helped develop series The Electric Company, 3-2-1 Contact. Creator and co-prod. of series The Best of Families. Wrote teleplay Blackout for PBS series Visions.
PICTURES: *Writer:* Violets Are Blue, Running on Empty (Golden Globe Award, Academy Award nom.; s.p. 1989 also exec. prod.), A Dangerous Woman (also prod.), Losing Isaiah (also prod.), Homegrown, Bee Season, Grace (writer).
TELEVISION: *Mini-series:* The Best of Families (writer/creator). *Series:* The Electric Company (prod., 1971-1973).

FONTAINE, JOAN
Actress. b. Tokyo, Oct. 22, 1917. r.n. Joan de Beauvior de Havilland. e. American School in Japan. Sister is actress Olivia de Havilland. Started on stage in L.A., Santa Barbara and San Francisco in Kind Lady; then as Joan Fontaine in Call it a Day (L.A.), where she was spotted and signed to contract by prod. Jesse Lasky. Sold contract to RKO. On B'way in Tea and Sympathy (1954). Author: No Bed of Roses (1978) Appeared in The Lion in Winter at Vienna's English Speaking Theatre 1979.
PICTURES: No More Ladies (debut, 1935), Quality Street, You Can't Beat Love, Music for Madame, Maid's Night Out, A Damsel in Distress, Blonde Cheat, The Man Who Found Himself, The Duke of West Point, Sky Giant, Gunga Din, Man of Conquest, The Women, Rebecca (Academy Award nom. 1941), Suspicion (Academy Award, 1942), This Above All, The Constant Nymph (Academy Award nom. 1944), Jane Eyre, Frenchman's Creek, Affairs of Susan, From This Day Forward, Ivy, The Emperor Waltz, Letter From an Unknown Woman, Kiss the Blood Off My Hands, You Gotta Stay Happy, Born to Be Bad, September Affair, Darling How Could You?, Something to Live For, Othello (cameo), Ivanhoe, Decameron Nights, Flight to Tangier, The Bigamist, Casanova's Big Night, Serenade, Beyond a Reasonable Doubt, Island in the Sun, Until They Sail, A Certain Smile, Voyage to the Bottom of the Sea, Tender Is the Night, The Devil's Own, Busby Berkeley, All by Myself, Off the Menu: The Last Days of Chasen's.
TELEVISION: *Movies:* The Three Musketeers, Dark Mansions, Cannon, The Users, Bare Essence, Good King Wenceslas. *Mini-series*: Crossings. *Series:* Ryan's Hope. *Guest:* More than 60 appearances.

FORBES, BRYAN
Actor, Writer, Producer, Director. b. Stratford (London), July 22, 1926. m. actress Nanette Newman. Former head of prod., man. dir., Associated British Prods. (EMI). Stage debut, The Corn Is Green (London), 1942; screen debut, The Small Back Room, 1948. Pres.: National Youth Theatre of Great Britain, 1985-; Pres.: Writers Guild of Great Britain, 1988-91. Received Special BAFTA Award, 2007 for career outstanding achievement in film-making.
AUTHOR: *Short stories:* Truth Lies Sleeping. *Novels:* The Distant Laughter, Familiar Strangers (U.S.: Stranger), The Rewrite Man, The Endless Game, A Song at Twilight (U.S.: A Spy at Twlight), The Twisted Playground, Partly Cloudy, Quicksand. Novelizations: The Slipper and the Rose, International Velvet. *Non-Fiction:* Ned's Girl (bio. of Dame Edith Evans) That Despicable Race (history of the British acting tradition). *Autobiographies:* Notes for a Life, A Divided Life.
THEATRE: *Director:* Macbeth, Star Quality, Killing Jessica, The Living Room.
PICTURES: *Actor:* Tired Men, The Small Back Room All Over the Town, Dear Mr. Prohack, Green Grow The Rushes, The Million Pound Note (Man With a Million), An Inspector Calls, The Colditz Story, Passage Home, Appointment in London, Sea Devils, The Extra Day, Quatermass II, It's Great To be Young, Satellite in The Sky, The Baby and The Battleship, Yesterday's Enemy, The Guns of Navarone, A Shot in The Dark, Of Human Bondage, Restless Natives. *Writer:* The Cockleshell Heroes, The Black Tent, Danger Within, I Was Monty's Double (also actor), The League of Gentlemen (also actor), The Angry Silence (also

prod., actor, Academy Award nom. 1961), Man in the Moon, Only Two Can Play, Station Six Sahara, Of Human Bondage (also actor), Hopscotch (WGA nom. 1981), Chaplin. *Director-Writer:* Whistle Down the Wind (dir. only), The L-Shaped Room (also actor), Seance on a Wet Afternoon (also prod.), King Rat, The Wrong Box, The Whisperers, Deadfall, The Madwoman of Chaillot (dir. only), The Raging Moon (Long Ago Tomorrow; also actor), The Stepford Wives (dir., actor), The Slipper and the Rose (also actor), International Velvet (also actor), Sunday Lovers (co-dir. only), Better Late Than Never (Menage a Trois), The Naked Face, Chaplin (writer, s.p.). *Exec. Prod.:* Hoffman, Forbush and the Penguins, The Railway Children, Peter Rabbit and the Tales of Beatrix Potter, The Go-Between, And Soon The Darkness, On The Buses, Dulcima.
TELEVISION: *Actor:* Johnnie Was a Hero, The Breadwinner, French Without Tears, Journey's End, The Gift, The Road, The Heiress, December Flower, First Amongst Equals. *Writer/Dir.:* I Caught Acting Like The Measles (documentary on the life of Dame Edith Evans) Goodbye Norma Jean and Other Things (documentary on the life of Elton John) Jessie, The Endless Game.

FORD, HARRISON

Actor. b. Chicago, IL, July 13, 1942. e. Ripon Coll. m. actress Calista Flockhart. Started acting in summer stock at Williams Bay, WI, in Damn Yankees, Little Mary Sunshine. Moved to L.A. where he acted in John Brown's Body. Signed by Columbia Studios under seven-year contract. Took break from acting to undertake carpentry work which included building Sergio Mendes' recording studio. Returned to acting in American Graffiti. Received the Golden Globe Cecil B. DeMille Award 2002.
PICTURES: Dead Heat on a Merry-Go-Round (debut, 1966), Luv, A Time for Killing, Journey to Shiloh, Zabriskie Point, Getting Straight, American Graffiti, The Conversation, Star Wars, Heroes, Force 10 from Navarone, Hanover Street, The Frisco Kid, More American Graffiti (cameo), Apocalypse Now, The Empire Strikes Back, Raiders of the Lost Ark, Blade Runner, Return of the Jedi, Indiana Jones and the Temple of Doom, Witness (Academy Award nom.; Golden Globe nom. 1986), The Mosquito Coast (Golden Globe nom. 1987), Frantic, Working Girl, Indiana Jones and the Last Crusade, Presumed Innocent, Regarding Henry, Patriot Games, The Fugitive (Golden Globe nom. 1994), Jimmy Hollywood (cameo), Clear and Present Danger, Sabrina (Golden Globe nom. 1996), The Devil's Own, Air Force One, Six Days Seven Nights, Random Hearts, What Lies Beneath, Lost Worlds (voice), K-19: The Widowmaker, Hollywood Homicide, The Wrong Element, Godspeed, Firewall, Indiana Jones and the Kingdom of the Crystal Skull, Crossing Over, Extraordinary Measures (also exec. prod.), Morning Glory.
TELEVISION: *Movies:* The Intruders, James A. Michener's Dynasty, The Possessed. *Specials:* Trial of Lt. Calley, AFI's 100 Years, 100 Thrills: America's Most Heart-Pounding Movies, Concert for New York City. *Guest:* More than 210 appearances.

FORLANI, CLAIR

Actress. b. Twickenham, Middlesex, England, July 1, 1972.
PICTURES: Gypsy Eyes, Police Academy: Mission to Moscow, Mallrats, The Rock, Garage Sale, Basquiat, Basil, The Last Time I Commited Suicide, Meet Joe Black, Into My Heart, Mystery Men, Boys & Girls, Magicians, Anti-Trust, Triggermen, Johnny Domino, Going Greek, Highbinders, Trigger Men, Northfork, The Medallion, The Limit, Bobby Jones, Stroke of Genius, Mr. Ripley's Return, The Yank, Shadows in the Sun, Green Street Hooligans, Hallam Foe, For Your Consideration, In the Name of the King: A Dungeon Siege Tale, Hallam Foe, Flashbacks of a Fool, Beer for My Horses, Not Forgotten, Shannon's Rainbow, Crossmaglen, No Ordinary Trifle, Ice, Deauville.
TELEVISION: *Movies:* The Pentagon Papers (2003), Memron (also assoc. prod.), Carolina Moon. *Mini-series:* JFK: Reckless Youth, Nightmares and Dreamscapes: From the Stories of Stephen King, False Witness. *Series:* CSI: NY.

FORMAN, JEROME A.

Executive. b. Hood River, Oregon, June 20, 1934. e. U. Arizona. 1966, became gen. mgr. Forman and United Theatres of the Northwest. 1971, joined Pacific Theatres; 1972, appointed v.p. & gen. mgr.; 1978-87, exec. v.p.; became pres. in 1987. No longer active in day-to-day theatre operations. Forman is one of the original founders of the ShoWest Convention. Currently chmn. emeritus, NATO of Calif.; 1991, chmn. NATO. 1991 elected chmn. bd. of Will Rogers Memorial Fund, serves as v.p. for Will Rogers Institute, CA. Board member of the Foundation of the Motion Picture Pioneers. Also on the bd. of executive committee dir.-trustees of the Will Rogers Institute.

FORMAN, MICHAEL

Exhibitor, Executive. b. Seattle, WA. Moved to Los Angeles, CA, after attending Stanford University. Forman is the chairman and CEO of the Decurion Corporation, which is involved in land management and real estate development, mainly of its own properties. Decurion is the holding company for Pacific Theatres Corporation, a company active in motion picture exhibition. Forman is the chmn. of Pacific Theatres. The companies are active in the U.S. and Europe. Forman is active as the international v.p. of Variety International, The Children's Charity; Past activities have been as a trustee of the Los Angeles County Museum of Art, president of the Foundation of Motion Picture Pioneers, president of the Stanford Athletic Board of Stanford University; former trustee of the American Film Institute and of the American University located in Washington, D.C.and a director of the California Chamber of Commerce. Forman is still active with the Los Angeles Committee for the Weizmann Institute where he was president of the Southwest Area.

FORMAN, MILOS

Director. b. Caslav, Czechoslovakia, Feb. 18, 1932. Trained as writer at Czech Film Sch. and as director at Laterna Magika. Directed short films Audition (Competition), If There Were No Music. Won Int'l. attention with first feature length film Black Peter, 1963. Emigrated to U.S. after collapse of Dubcek govt. in Czechoslovakia, 1969. Appeared as actor in films Heartburn, New Year's Day.
PICTURES: Peter and Pavla/Black Peter (also co-s.p.; Czech Film Critics & Grand Prix Locarno Awards), Loves of a Blonde (also co- s.p.), The Firemen's Ball (also co-s.p.), Taking Off (U.S. debut, WGA nom. 1971), Visions of Eight (Decathalon segment), One Flew Over the Cuckoo's Nest (Academy Award, Golden Globe Award, DGA Award 1976), Hair, Ragtime (Golden Globe nom. 1982), Amadeus (Academy Award, Golden Globe Award, DGA Award 1985), Valmont, The People vs. Larry Flynt (Academy Award nom.; Golden Globe Award, 1997), Man on the Moon, Keeping the Faith (actor only), Milos Forman: Kinoist Wahrheit (actor only), In the Shadow of Hollywood (actor only), Way Past Cool (exec. prod.), AFI's 100 Years...100 Heroes & Villains (himself), Nomad (exec. prod.), Embers (dir., s.p.), Goya's Ghosts (also writer), Peklo s princeznou (actor).

FORREST, FREDERIC

Actor. b. Waxahachie, TX, Dec. 23, 1936. e. Texas Christian U., U. of Oklahoma, B.A. Studied with Sanford Meisner and Lee Strasberg. Began career off-off B'way at Caffe Cino in The Madness of Lady Bright then off-B'way in Futz, Massachusetts Trust and Tom Paine, all with La Mama Troupe under direction of Tom O'Horgan. Moved to Hollywood in 1970.
PICTURES: Futz (debut, 1969), When the Legends Die (Golden Globe nom. 1973), The Don Is Dead, The Conversation, The Gravy Train, Permission to Kill, The Missouri Breaks, It Lives Again!, Apocalypse Now, The Rose (Academy Award nom.; Golden Globe nom. 1980), One From the Heart, Hammett, Valley Girl, The Stone Boy, Return, Where Are the Children?, Stacking, Tucker: The Man and His Dream, Valentino Returns, Music Box, The Two Jakes, Cat Chaser, Rain Without Thunder, Falling Down, Trauma, Chasers, One Night Stand, The Brave, The End of Violence, The Boogie Boy, Point Blank, Black Thunder, Whatever, One of Our Own, Implicated, The First 9 1/2 Weeks, Shadow Hours, Militia, A Piece of Eden, The Spreading Ground, The House Next Door, The Quality of Light, All the King's Men.
TELEVISION: *Movies:* Larry, Promise Him Anything, Ruby and Oswald, Calamity Jane, Right to Kill?, The Deliberate Stranger, Quo Vadis, Little Girl Lost, Saigon: Year of the Cat (U.K.), Best Kept Secrets, Who Will Love My Children? A Shadow on the Sun, Margaret Bourke-White, Citizen Cohn, The Habitation of Dragons, Against the Wall, Double Jeopardy, Andersonville, Sweetwater, Shadow Lake, Alone, Path to War. *Mini-series*: Die Kinder.

FORREST, STEVE

Actor. r.n. William Forrest Andrews. b. Huntsville, TX, Sept. 29, 1925. Brother of late actor Dana Andrews. e. UCLA, 1950. Acted at La Jolla Playhouse; appeared on radio, TV; m.p. debut in Crash Dive billed as William Andrews.
PICTURES: Crash Dive (debut, 1942), The Ghost Ship, Geisha Girl, Sealed Cargo, Last of the Comanches, The Bad and the Beautiful (1st billing as Steve Forrest), Dream Wife, Battle Circus, The Clown, The Band Wagon, So Big (Golden Globe Award 1954), Take the High Ground, Phantom of the Rue Morgue, Prisoner of War, Rogue Cop, Bedevilled, The Living Idol, It Happened to Jane, Heller in Pink Tights, Five Branded Women, Flaming Star, The Second Time Around, The Longest Day, The Yellow Canary, Rascal, The Wild Country, The Late Liz, North Dallas Forty, Mommie Dearest, Sahara, Spies Like Us, Amazon Women on the Moon, Storyville, Killer: A Journal of Murder, S.W.A.T.
TELEVISION: *Movies:* The Hatfields and the McCoys, Wanted: The Sundance Women, The Last of the Mohicans, Testimony of Two Men, Maneaters are Loose, Hollywood Wives, Gunsmoke: Return to Dodge, Columbo: A Bird in the Hand. *Series:* The Baron, S.W.A.T., Dallas, Murder, She Wrote, Team Knight Rider. *Guest:* More than 90 appearances.

FORSTER, ROBERT

Actor. b. Rochester, NY, July 13, 1941. e. Heidelberg Coll., Alfred U., Rochester U., B.S.
THEATRE: Mrs. Dally Has a Lover, A Streetcar Named Desire, The Glass Menagerie, 12 Angry Men, The Sea Horse, One Flew Over the Cuckoo's Nest, The Big Knife, In the Moonlight Eddie.
PICTURES: Reflections in a Golden Eye (debut, 1967), The Stalking Moon, Medium Cool, Justine, Cover Me Babe, Pieces of Dreams, Journey Through Rosebud, The Don is Dead, Stunts, Avalanche, The Black Hole, Lady in Red (unbilled), Crunch, Alligator, Vigilante,

Walking the Edge, Hollywood Harry (also prod., dir.), The Delta Force, Committed, Esmeralda Bay, Heat from Another Sun, The Banker, Peacemaker, Diplomatic Immunity, 29th Street, In Between, Maniac Cop 3: Badge of Silence, South Beach, Cover Story, Body Chemistry 3: Point of Seduction, Demo University, American Perfekt, Original Gangstas, Jackie Brown (Academy Award nom. 1998), Outside Ozona, Psycho, Kiss Toledo Goodbye, Night Vision, Family Tree, Great Sex, Supernova, The Magic of Marciano, My Myself & Irene, Lakeboat, It's a Shame About Ray, Finder's Fee, Diamond Men, Mulholland Dr., Human Nature, Strange Hearts, The A-List, Lone Hero, Like Mike, Where's Angelo?, Confidence, Charlie's Angels: Full Throttle, Grand Theft Parsons, Cursed, D-War, Firewall, Lucky Number Slevin, Wild Seven, Rise, Jack and Jill vs. the World, Dragon Wars: D-War, Rise, Touching Home, Cleaner, Expecting Love, The Code, The Ghosts of Girlfriends Past, Middle Men, Kalamity, The Bannen Way, The Trial, The Descendants.
TELEVISION: *Movies:* Banyon, The Death Squad, Nakia, The City, Standing Tall, The Darker Side of Terror, Goliath Awaits, In the Shadow of a Killer, Sex Love and Cold Hard Cash, Rear Window, L.A. Sheriff's Homicide, Like Mother, Like Son: The Strange Story of Sante and Kenny Kimes, Due East, Murder in Greenwich, Undefeated, Bounty Hunters, The Hunt for the BTK Killer, 13 Graves. *Mini-series:* The Grid, Would Be Kings. *Series:* Banyon, Nakia, Once a Hero, Spawn (voice), Karen Sisco, Huff, Would Be Kings, Heroes. *Pilots:* Checkered Flag, Mickie & Frankie. *Guest:* More than 70 appearances.

FORSYTH, BILL

Director. Writer. b. Glasgow, Scotland, July 29, 1946. At 16 joined film co. For next 10 years made industrial films, then documentaries. Joined Glasgow Youth Theater.
PICTURES: *Director-Writer:* That Sinking Feeling (debut, 1979; also prod.), Gregory's Girl, Local Hero, Comfort and Joy, Housekeeping, Breaking In, Rebecca's Daughters, Being Human, Gregory's Two Girls.
TELEVISION: Andrina.

FORSYTHE, JOHN

Actor. b. Penn's Grove, NJ, Jan. 29, 1918. r.n. John Freund. Former commentator for Brooklyn Dodgers, prior to becoming actor. Debuted on tv in 1947.
THEATRE: Mr. Roberts, All My Sons, Yellow Jack, Teahouse of the August Moon and others.
PICTURES: Destination Tokyo (debut, 1943), The Captive City, It Happens Every Thursday, The Glass Web, Escape From Fort Bravo, The Trouble With Harry, The Ambassador's Daughter, Everything But the Truth, Kitten With a Whip, Madame X, In Cold Blood, The Happy Ending, Topaze, Goodbye and Amen, And Justice for All, Scrooged, Hotel de Love, Charlie's Angels (voice), Charlie's Angels: Full Throttle (voice).
TELEVISION: *Movies:* See How They Run, Shadow on the Land, Murder Once Removed, The Letters, Lisa—Bright and Dark, Cry Panic, Healers, Terror on the 40th Floor, The Deadly Tower, Amelia Earhart, Tail Gunner Joe, Never Con a Killer, Cruise Into Terror, With This Ring, The Users, A Time for Miracles, Sizzle, The Mysterious Two, On Fire, Opposites Attract, Dynasty: The Reunion. *Series:* Bachelor Father, The John Forsythe Show, To Rome With Love, Charlie's Angels (voice only), Dynasty (4 Emmy nom., 2 Golden Globe Award; 4 nom.), The Powers That Be, I Witness Video (host). *Guest:* More than 114 appearances.
(d. April 2, 2010)

FORSYTHE, WILLIAM

Actor. b. Brooklyn, NY, June 7, 1955. Studied acting at The Beverly Hills Playhouse.
THEATRE: A Streetcar Named Desire, A Hatful of Rain, Othello, Julius Caesar, 1776, Hair, Godspell, Vox Humana #3, If You Don't Like It—You Can Leave.
PICTURES: King of the Mountain, Smokey Bites the Dust, The Man Who Wasn't There, Sons, Dead Bang, Torrents of Spring, Patty Hearst, Savage Dawn, Cloak and Dagger, The Lightship, Once Upon a Time in America, Raising Arizona, Extreme Prejudice, Weeds, Dick Tracy, Career Opportunities, Out for Justice, Stone Cold, The Waterdance, American Me, The Gun in Betty Lou's Handbag, Relentless 3, Direct Hit, Beyond Desire, The Immortals, Virtuosity, Don't Ask Too Much of love, Things to Do in Denver When You're Dead, The Substitute, The Rock, Palookaville, For Which He Stands, Firestorm, Hell's Kitchen, Row Your Boat, Deuce Bigalow Male Gigalo, Sound Man, Four Days, Blue Streak, Paradise Lost, The Last Marshall, Camouflage, Big City Blues, 18 Shades of Dust, Luck of the Draw, G-Men From Hell, The Librarians, Blue Hill Avenue, Outlaw, Coastlines, City by the Sea, Destiny, The Technical Writer, Scary Movie 3, The Librarians (also writer), The Last Letter (also exec. prod.), The L.A. Riot Spectacular, The Devil's Rejects: House of 1000 Corpses 2, Freedomland, Southern Gothic, 88 Minutes, Hack!, Marble City, The Unlikely's (also prod.), Halloween, The Platform, iMurders, The Rig, The Nail: The Story of Joey Nardone, The Rig, Slip & Fall, Dear Mr. Gacy, The Way She Moves, Sweetwater, L.A., I Hate You, Devils Inside, Raging Bull II.
TELEVISION: *Movies:* The Miracle of Kathy Miller, The Long Hot Summer, Baja Oklahoma, Cruel Doubt, A Kiss to Die For, Bedroom Eyes, Willing to Kill: The Texas Cheerleader Story, Peacock Blues, Gotti, First-Time Felon, Dollar for the Dead, John Doe, Larva, Hammerhead: Shark Frenzy, Final Approach. *Mini-series:* Blind Faith, Final Approach. *Series:* The Untouchables (1993), UC: Undercover, John Doe.

FOSTER, CHRISTINE

Executive. r.n. Mary Christine Foster. b. Los Angeles, CA, March 19, 1943. e. Immaculate Heart Coll, B.A. 1967. UCLA MJ, 1968. Teacher while member of Immaculate Heart Community, 1962-65. Teacher, Pacific U., Tokyo, 1968; dir., research and dev. Metromedia Producers Corp., 1968-71; dir., dev. & prod. services, Wolper Org. 1971-76; mgr., film progs. NBC TV 1976-77; v.p. movies for TV & mini-series, Columbia Pictures TV, 1977-81; v.p. series programs, Columbia TV, 1981; v.p. prog. dev., Group W. Prods. 1981-87; v.p., The Agency, 1988-90; agent, Shapiro-Lichtman-Stein Talent Agency, 1990-. Member: exec. comm. Humanitas Awards, 1986-; exec. comm. Catholics in Media, 1993-; Activities Committee, Acad. of TV Arts & Sciences, 1989-91; L.A. Roman Catholic Archdiocesan communications Comm., 1986-89; Women in Film, bd. of dirs., 1977-78 teacher at UCLA Extension, 1987-. Foreign and domestic university and public group lecturer and speaker.

FOSTER, DAVID

Producer. b. New York, NY, Nov. 25, 1929. e. Dorsey H.S., U. of Southern California Sch. of Journalism. U.S. Army, 1952-54; entered public relations field in 1952 with Rogers, Cowan & Brenner; Jim Mahoney, 1956; Allan, Foster, Ingersoll & Weber, 1958; left field in 1968 to enter independent m.p. production. Was partner in Turman-Foster Co. Currently is partner in David Foster Productions.
PICTURES: Producer (with Mitchell Brower): McCabe and Mrs. Miller, The Getaway. Produced (with Lawrence Turman): The Nickel Ride (exec. prod.), The Drowning Pool, The Legacy, Tribute (exec. prod.), Caveman, The Thing (1982), Second Thoughts, Mass Appeal, The Mean Season, Short Circuit, Running Scared, Full Moon in Blue Water, Short Circuit II, Gleaming the Cube, The Getaway (1993), The River Wild, The Mask of Zorro, Collateral Damage, Hart's War, The Core, The Fog, The Thing (2010, exec. prod.).
TELEVISION: *Movies:* Jesse (co-exec. prod), Between Two Brothers, Surrogate Mother, The Gift of Life, News at Eleven. *Mini-series:* The Thing (exec. prod.). *Series:* Fly Into Danger.

FOSTER, JODIE

Actress. r.n. Alicia Christian Foster. b. Los Angeles, CA, Nov. 19, 1962. e. Yale U. Started acting in commercials including famous Coppertone ad. Acting debut on Mayberry, R.F.D. TV series (1968). Followed with many TV appearances, from series to movies of the week. 1996 received ASC Board of the Governors Award.
PICTURES: Napoleon and Samantha (debut, 1972), Kansas City Bomber, Tom Sawyer, One Little Indian, Alice Doesn't Live Here Anymore, Taxi Driver (Academy Award nom. 1977), Echoes of a Summer, Bugsy Malone, Freaky Friday, (Golden Globe nom. 1977), The Little Girl Who Lives Down the Lane, Il Casotto (The Beach Hut), Moi fleur bleue (Stop Calling Me Baby!), Candleshoe, Foxes, Carny, O'Hara's Wife, The Hotel New Hampshire, Mesmerized (also co-prod.), Siesta, Five Corners, Stealing Home, The Accused (Academy Award, Golden Globe Award 1989), The Silence of the Lambs (Academy Award, Golden Globe Award 1992), Little Man Tate (also dir.), Shadows and Fog, Sommersby, Maverick, Nell (Academy Award nom.; Golden Globe nom. 1995; also co-prod.), Home for the Holidays (dir., co-prod. only), Contact (Golden Globe nom. 1998), Anna and the King, The Dangerous Lives of Altar Boys, Flora Plum (dir. and prod. only), Panic Room, Tusker, A Very Long Engagement, Flightplan, Inside Man, The Brave One (also exec. prod., Golden Globe nom. 2008), Nim's Island, The Beaver (also dir.).
TELEVISION: *Movies:* Smile Jenny--You're Dead, The Blood of Others, Svengali, The Baby Dance (Emmy nom. 1999), Backtrack. *Series:* Bob & Carol & Ted & Alice, Paper Moon. *Specials:* Alexander, Rookie of the Year, Menace on the Mountain, The Secret Life of T.K. Dearing, The Fisherman's Wife, AMC: Film Preservation Classics: Film Preservation Classics with Jodie Foster (Emmy nom. 2001). *Guest:* More than 170 appearances.

FOSTER, JULIA

Actress. b. Lewes, Sussex, England, 1941. First acted with the Brighton Repertory Company, then two years with the Worthing, Harrogate and Richmond companies. 1956, TV debut as Ann Carson in Emergency Ward 10.
THEATRE: The Country Wife, What the Butler Saw.
PICTURES: Term of Trial (debut, 1962), The Loneliness of the Long Distance Runner, Two Left Feet, The Small World of Sammy Lee, The System (The Gir Getters), The Bargee, One Way Pendulum, Alfie, Half a Sixpence, All Coppers Are..., The Great McGonagall, Flick.
TELEVISION: *Movies:* A Cosy Little Arrangement, The Planemakers, Love Story, Taxi, Consequences, They Throw It at You, Crime and Punishment, The Image, Henry VI Pt. 1 of 3, Cabbage Patch, The Tragedy of Richard III. Moll Flanders. *Series:* Good Girl, The Wilde Alliance, The Cabbage Patch, Late Starter, News at Twelvse.

FOSTER, MEG
Actress. b. Reading, PA, May 14, 1948.
PICTURES: Adam at 6 A.M. (debut, 1970), Thumb Tripping, Welcome to Arrow Beach (Tender Flesh), A Different Story, Once in Paris, Carny, Ticket to Heaven, The Osterman Weekend, The Emerald Forest, Masters of the Universe, The Wind, They Live, Leviathan, Relentless, Stepfather 2, Blind Fury, Tripwire, Jezebel's Kiss, Diplomatic Immunity, Dead One: Relentless II, Project Shadowchaser, Immortal Combat, Undercover Heat, The Killers Within, Space Marines, Oblivion 2: Backlash, Spoiler, The Man in the Iron Mask, The Lost Valley, The Minus Man, The Mask of Dumas, Coming Up Easy, Go Straight to Hell, Sebastian.
TELEVISION: *Movies:* The Death of Me Yet, Sunshine, Things In Their Season, Promise Him Anything, James Dean, Sunshine Christmas, Guyana Tragedy: The Story of Jim Jones, Legend of Sleepy Hollow, Desperate Intruder, Best Kept Secrets, Betrayal of Silence, Desperate, Back Stab, To Catch a Killer, Deep Family Secrets. *Mini-series:* Washington: Behind Closed Doors. *Series:* Sunshine, Cagney & Lacey. *Special:* The Scarlet Letter. *Guest:* More than 62 appearances.

FOWKES, RICHARD O.
Executive. b. Yonkers, NY, April 15, 1946. e. NYU, Geo. Washington U. Staff attorney for The Dramatists Guild, 1973-77; joined Paramount as assoc. counsel, 1977-80; moved to UA (NYC) as prod. attorney from 1980-82; returned to Paramount as v.p., legal & bus. affairs., m.p. division (LA), 1983; promoted to sr. v.p., bus. affairs & acquisitions, 1989; promoted to sr. v.p. in charge of bus. affairs, 1994. Later, Fowkes was promoted to executive v.p. of business affairs for Paramount's Motion Picture Group. Currently a consultant for The Point Media in business affairs.

FOX, EDWARD
Actor. b. London, England, April 13, 1937. Comes from theatrical family; father was agent for leading London actors; brother is actor James Fox.
PICTURES: The Mind Benders (debut, 1962), Morgan!, The Frozen Dead, The Long Duel, The Naked Runner, The Jokers, I'll Never Forget What's 'is Name, The Battle of Britain, Oh! What a Lovely War, Skullduggery, The Go-Between, The Day of The Jackal, A Doll's House, Galileo, The Squeeze, A Bridge Too Far, The Duellists, The Big Sleep, Force 10 from Navarone, The Cat and the Canary, Soldier of Orange, The Mirror Crack'd, Gandhi, Never Say Never Again, The Dresser, The Bounty, Wild Geese II, The Shooting Party, Return From the River Kwai, A Feast at Midnight, A Month by the Lake, Prince Valiant, Lost in Space, All the Queen's Men, The Importance of Being Earnest, Nicholas Nickleby, The Republic of Love, Stage Beauty, Lassie.
TELEVISION: *Movies:* The Portrait of a Lady, The Father, A Hazard of Hearts, Anastasia: The Mystery of Anna, Quartermaine's Terms, They Never Slept, Robin Hood, The Crucifer of Blood, Forbidden Territory: Stanley's Search for Livingstone, Foyle's War, The Maitlands, Gulliver's Travels, September, Daniel Deronda, Oliver Twist, Marple: The Secret of Chimneys. *Mini-series:* Edward and Mrs. Simpson, Shaka Zulu, The Strauss Dynasty, A Dance to the Music of Time, I Was a Rat. *Guest:* More than 63 appearances.

FOX, JAMES
Actor. b. London, England, May 19, 1939. Brother is actor Edward Fox. Ent. films as child actor in 1950 as William Fox. Left acting in 1973 to follow spiritual vocation. Returned to mainstream films in 1982. B'way debut 1995 in Uncle Vanya.
PICTURES: The Miniver Story (debut, 1950; as William Fox), The Magnet, One Wild Oat, The Lavender Hill Mob, Timbuktu, The Queen's Guards, The Secret Partner, She Always Gets Their Man, What Every Woman Wants, The Loneliness of the Long-Distance Runner; Tamahine (1st film billed as James Fox), The Servant, Those Magnificent Men in Their Flying Machines or How I Flew from London to Paris in 25 hours 11 minutes (Golden Globe nom. 1966), King Rat, The Chase, Thoroughly Modern Millie, Arabella, Duffy, Isadora, Performance, No Longer Alone, Runners, Greystoke: The Legend of Tarzan, A Passage to India, Pavlova, Absolute Beginners, The Whistle Blower, Comrades, High Season, The Mighty Quinn, Farewell to the King, The Boys in the Island, The Russia House, Patriot Games, Afraid of the Dark, The Remains of the Day, Anna Karenina, Up at the Villa, Shadow Run, Mickey Blue Eyes, The Golden Bowl, Sexy Beast, All Forgotten, The Mystic Masseur, The Prince and Me, Light in the Sky, The Freediver, The Queen and I, Charlie and the Chocolate Factory, Mister Lonely, Red Riding: In the Year of Our Lord 1980, Sherlock Holmes, The Kid, Wide Blue Yonder, Cleanskin.
TELEVISION: *Movies:* Beryl Markham: A Shadow on the Sun, A Question of Attribution, The Door, Espionage, Love Is Old, Love Is New, Country, New World, Sun Child, She's Been Away (BBC; shown theatrically in U.S.), Never Come Back, Slowly Slowly in the Wind, As You Like It, Heart of Darkness, Fall from Grace, Hostage, Doomsday Gun, Headhunters, Fall From Grace, Gulliver's Travels, Armadillo, The Lost World, Hans Christian Andersen: My Life as a Fairy Tale, The Falklands Play, Trial & Retribution VI, Poirot: Death on the Nile, Marple: The Body in the Library, Colditz, Celebration, Margaret. *Mini-series:* Nancy Astor, Les Cadavres exquis de Patricia Highsmith, A Perfect Hero, The Old Curiosity Shop, The Choir, Kings in Grass Castles, Metropolis, Shaka Zulu: The Citadel, Cambridge Spies, Escape from Colditz. *Series:* Waking the Dead. *Guest:* More than 70 appearances.

FOX, JORJA
Actress. b. New York, NY, July 7, 1968.
PICTURES: Traveling Companion (comp. only), Kill-Off, Happy Hell Night, Dead Drunk, Dead Funny, The Jerky Boys, Velocity Trap, How to Make the Cruelest Month, The Hungry Bachelors Club, Memento, 3 Weeks to Daytona.
TELEVISION: *Movie:* Alchemy. *Mini-series:* Summer Stories: The Mall, House of Frankenstein 1997. *Series:* Missing Persons, ER, The West Wing, CSI: Crime Scene Investigation.

FOX, MEGAN
Actress. b. Rockwood, TN, May 16, 1986. m. actor Brian Austin Green.
PICTURES: Confessions of a Teenage Drama Queen, Transformers, How to Lose Friends & Alienate People, Transformers: Revenge of the Fallen, Jennifer's Body, Passion Play, Jonah Hex, Transformers 3.
TELEVISION: *Movie:* Crimes of Fashion. *Series:* Ocean Ave., The Help, Hope & Faith. *Guest:* More than 45 appearances.

FOX, MICHAEL J.
Actor. b. Edmonton, Alberta, Canada, June 9, 1961. r.n. Michael Andrew Fox. m. actress Tracy Pollan. Appeared in Vancouver TV series Leo and Me, and on stage there in The Shadow Box. Moved to Los Angeles at age 18.
PICTURES: Midnight Madness (debut, 1980), The Class of 1984, Back to the Future (Golden Globe nom. 1986), Teen Wolf, Light of Day, The Secret of My Success, Bright Lights Big City, Casualties of War, Back to the Future Part II, Back to the Future Part III, The Hard Way, Doc Hollywood, Homeward Bound: The Incredible Journey (voice), Life With Mikey, For Love or Money, Where the Rivers Flow North, Greedy, Coldblooded (also co-prod.), Blue in the Face, The American President, Homeward Bound II: Lost in San Francisco (voice), The Frighteners, Mars Attacks!, Stuart Little (voice), Atlantis: The Lost Empire (voice), Interstate 60, Stuart Little 2 (voice), A Christmas Carol.
TELEVISION: *Movies:* Letters From Frank, High School USA, Poison Ivy, Family Ties Vacation, Don't Drink the Water, I Am Your Child, Hench At Home (writer only), Magic 7 (voice). *Series:* Palmerstown U.S.A., Family Ties (3 Emmy Awards; 2 other nom. Golden Globe Award 1989; 3 other nom.), Spin City (3 Golden Globe Awards, 1998, 1999, 2000, 1 other nom.; Emmy Award, 2000; 4 other nom.), Otherwise Engaged (exec. prod. only), Boston Legal (Emmy nom. 2006), Rescue Me (Emmy Award 2009). *Specials/Documentaries:* Teachers Only, Time Travel: Fact Fiction and Fantasy, Dear America: Letters Home From Vietnam (reader), James Cagney: Top of the World (host), The Concert for New York City. *Director:* Brooklyn Bridge (episode), In Search of Ted Demme. *Guest:* More than 141 appearances.

FOX, RICHARD J.
Executive. b. New York, NY, Feb. 24, 1947. Joined Warner Bros. International as mgt. trainee in October 1975, working in Australia and Japan. 1977, named gen. mgr. of Columbia-Warner Dist., New Zealand. Served as gen. mgr. of WB in Tokyo, 1978\-1981. Joined WB in L.A. as exec. asst. to Myron D. Karlin, pres. of WB International, 1981; appt. v.p., sales, 1982; 1983, promoted to exec. v.p. of int'l. arm; 1985, named pres. of WB International, assuming post vacated by Karlin. 1992, promoted to exec. v.p., International Theatrical Enterprises, Warner Bros. Currently, executive v.p. of International at Warner Bros. Entertainment Inc.

FOX, VIVICA A.
Actress. b. Indianaplolis, IN, July 30, 1964. e. Golden West College.
PICTURES: Born on the Fourth of July, Don't Be a Menace to South Central While Drinking Your Juice in the Hood, Independence Day, Set It Off, Booty Call, Batman & Robin, Soul Food, Teaching Mrs. Tingle, Why Do Fools Fall in Love?, Idle Hands, Double Take, Kingdome Come, Two Can Play that Game, Juwanna Mann, Boat Trip, Ride or Die, Kill Bill, Ella Enchanted, Motives (also prod.), Blast!, Getting Played (also prod.),The Salon (also prod.), Kickin It Old Skool, Citizen Duane, Caught on Tape, Marble City, The Hard Corps, San Saba, Father of Lies, Cover, Three Can Play That Game (also prod.), Street, Major Movie Star, Caught on Tape, Miss Nobody, Hollywood & Wine, Shark City, Thorns from a Rose, Junkyard Dog, The Land of the Astronauts, Street.
TELEVISION: *Movies:* Out All Night, The Tuskegee Airmen, Solomon, A Saintly Switch, Hendrix, Kim Possible: A Sitch in Time (voice). *Series:* Days of Our Lives, The Young and the Restless, Arsenio, Generations, Out All Night, Getting Personal, Walking After Midnight, City of Angels, Ozzy & Drix, 1-800-Missing, Secrets of Life (host), Curb Your Enthusiasm, Glam God with Vivica A. Fox (judge). *Documentary:* Independence Day: The ID4 Invasion. *Guest:* More than 148 appearances.

FOXWORTH, ROBERT
Actor. b. Houston, TX, Nov. 1, 1941. e. Carnegie-Mellon U. Began acting at age 10 at Houston Alley Theatre and stayed with

stage part-time while completing formal education. Returned to theatre on full-time basis after graduation. Made TV debut in Sadbird, 1969.
THEATRE: *NY:* I Henry V, Terra Nova, The Crucible (Theatre World Award), Love Letters, Candida. *Regional:* Antony & Cleopatra, Uncle Vanya, Cyrano de Bergerac, Who's Afraid of Virginia Woolf?, Othello, Habeus Corpus, The Seagull, Macbeth, Honour, Proof.
PICTURES: Treasure of Matecumbe (debut, 1976), The Astral Factor, Airport '77, Damien: Omen II, Prophecy, The Black Marble, Beyond the Stars, Syriana, Transformers (voice), Kiss the Bride, Transformers: Revenge of the Fallen (voice).
TELEVISION: *Movies:* The Devil's Daughter, Frankenstein, Mrs. Sundance, The Questor Tapes (pilot), The FBI Story: The FBI Vs. Alvin Karpis, James Dean, It Happened at Lakewood Manor, Death Moon, The Memory of Eva Ryker, Act of Love, Peter and Paul, The Return of the Desperado, Double Standard, Face to Face, The Price of the Bride, With Murder in Mind, For Love and Glory. *Series:* The Storefront Lawyers, Falcon Crest, 2000 Malibu Road, Real Adventures of Johnny Quest (voice), Lateline, Six Feet Under, Star Trek: Enterprise, Justice League Unlimited (voice). *Documentaries/Specials:* Hogan's Goat, Another Part of the Forest, The Eruption of Mount St. Helens!, Ring of Fire, Epic Journeys: The Great Migrations. *Guest:* More than 95 appearances.

FOXX, JAMIE
Actor. b. Terrell, TX, December 13, 1967. Recipient of numerous industry awards.
PICTURES: Toys, The Truth About Cats & Dogs, The Great White Hype, The Player's Club, Booty Call, Any Given Sunday, Bait, Date From Hell, All Jokes Aside, Ali, Shade, Breakin' All the Rules, Ray (Academy Award/Best Actor, Golden Globe/Best Actor, BAFTA Award/Best Actor, 2005), Collateral (Academy Award nom. Best Supporting Actor, Golden Globe nom. 2005), Stealth, Jarhead, Inside Man (soundtrack performer), ATL (soundtrack performer), Miami Vice, Dreamgirls, The Kingdom, The Soloist, Law Abiding Citizen, Valentine's Day (also soundtrack performer), Due Date, Kane & Lynch.
TELEVISION: *Movies:* Redemption: The Stan Tookie Williams Story, Life Support (exec. prod. Golden Globe nom. 2005). *Series:* In Living Color, The Jamie Foxx Show (also prod.), C Bear and Jamal (voice), It's Black Entertainment, From G's to Gents (exec. prod., writer). *Special:* Inside TV Land: African Americans in Television, Jamie Foxx: I Might Need Security. *Guest:* More than 190 appearances.

FRAKER, WILLIAM A.
Cinematographer, Director. b. Los Angeles, CA, Sept. 29, 1923. e. U. of Southern California Film Sch. Worked as camera operator with Conrad Hall; moved to TV before feature films. Photographed and co-prod. doc. Forbid Them Not. ASC Lifetime Acheivemant Award 2000.
PICTURES: *Cinematographer:* Games, The Fox, The President's Analyst, Fade In, Rosemary's Baby, Bullitt, Paint Your Wagon, Dusty and Sweets McGee, The Day of the Dolphin, Rancho Deluxe, Aloha Bobby and Rose, Lipstick, The Killer Inside Me, Gator, Exorcist II--The Heretic, Looking for Mr. Goodbar (Academy Award nom. 1978), American Hot Wax, Heaven Can Wait (Academy Award 1979), Old Boyfriends, 1941 (2 Academy Award nom. 1980), The Hollywood Knights, Divine Madness, Sharky's Machine, The Best Little Whorehouse in Texas, WarGames (Academy Award nom. 1984), Irreconcilable Differences, Protocol, Fever Pitch, Murphy's Romance (Academy Award nom. 1986), SpaceCamp, Burglar, Baby Boom, Chances Are, An Innocent Man, The Freshman, Memoirs of an Invisible Man, Honeymoon in Vegas, Tombstone (also co-assoc. prod.), Street Fighter, Father of the Bride II, The Island of Dr. Moreau, Vegas Vacation, Rules of Engagement, Town & Country, Waking Up in Reno, Section B. *Director:* Monte Walsh, Reflection of Fear, Legend of the Lone Ranger.
TELEVISION: *Movies:* The Unknown, The Haunted, Fade-In, B.L. Stryker: The Dancer's Touch (dir.), Death in Small Doses. *Series:* Stony Burke, Outer Limits, Ozzie and Harriet, Daktari, Wiseguy, J.J. Starbuck, The Flash, Walker, Texas Ranger (dir.).
(d. May 31, 2010)

FRAKES, JONATHAN
Actor, Director. b. Bethlehem, PA, Aug. 19, 1952. m. Actress Genie Francis.
PICTURES: Gargoyles: The Heroes Awaken (voice), Star Trek: Generations, Star Trek: First Contact (also dir.), Trekkies, Star Trek: Insurrection (also dir.), Star Trek: Nemesis, *Director:* Clockstoppers, Thunderbirds.
TELEVISION: *Movies:* Beach Patrol, The Night the City Screamed, Star Trek: The Next Generation (pilot), The Cover Girl and the Cop, Dying to Live, Brothers of the Frontier, The Librarian 2: Return to King Solomon's Mines (also dir.), The Librarian: The Curse of the Judas Chalice (dir.). *Mini-series*: Beulah Land, North & South, North & South II, Dream West, Nutcracker: Money—Madness & Murder, North & South III, The Lot. *Series:* The Doctors, Bare Essence, Paper Dolls, Star Trek: The Next Generation (also dir.), Gargoyles (voice), University Hospital (dir. only), Gargoyles: The Goliath Chronicles (voice), Star Trek: Voyager, The Paranormal Borderline (host), Beyond Belief: Fact or Fiction, The Lot, Roswell, The Twilight Zone (dir., pilot). *Guest:* More than 100 appearances.

FRANCO, JAMES
Actor. b. Palo Alto, CA, April 19, 1978.
PICTURES: Never Been Kissed, Whatever It Takes, Spider-Man, Deuces Wild, Sonny, City by the Sea, The Company, Spider-Man 2, The Great Raid, Tristan + Isolde, Annapolis, Flyboys, The Wicker Man, The Dead Girl, Interview (voice), Finishing the Game: The Search for a New Bruce Lee, Spider-Man 3, In the Valley of Elah, Pineapple Express (Golden Globe nom. 2009), Milk, In Praise of Shadows, Howl, Date Night, Your Highness, Eat, Pray, Love, 127 Hours, Rise of the Apes.
TELEVISION: *Movies:* To Serve and Protect, At Any Cost, James Dean (Emmy nom.; Golden Globe Award 2002). *Series:* Freaks and Geeks, General Hospital.

FRANK, ALAN
Executive. b. Pittsburgh, PA. e. B.A. in journalism from Duquesne University; Master's degree in TV and radio from Syracuse Univ. He served in the U.S. Army as an officer in Vietnam. From 1971-1972 Frank was production manager for The David Frost Revue; exec. prod. at KPIX-TV, San Francisco from 1972-1974, and program mgr. at WJZ-TV, Baltimore from 1975-1978; Frank joined WDIV in 1979 as program manager. In 1986 he became v.p. of programming and production for Post-Newsweek Stations. Frank became president and CEO of Post-Newsweek Stations in Jan. 2000 and is the position he holds today. Frank is chairman of the Television Board of the National Association of Broadcasters (NAB) and the Network Affiliated Station Alliance (NASA) and serves on the board of directors of MSTV, the Broadcasters' Foundation and Internet Broadcasting. He also serves on the board of governors of the ABC Affiliate Association. In 2005 he was named Broadcasting and Cable's "Broadcaster of the Year." Frank was the founding chairman of the board of trustees of Sparky Anderson's charity for children and serves on the boards of various children's and other charities.

FRANK, SCOTT
Writer. b. 1960.
PICTURES: Plain Clothes (story), The Walter Ego, Little Man Tate, Dead Again, Malice, Get Shorty (Golden Globe nom.; WGA nom. 1996), Heaven's Prisoners, Out of Sight (Academy Award nom.; WGA Award 1999), The Caveman's Valentine, Minority Report (also second unit dir.), Dawn of the Dead (s.p.), The Flight of the Phoenix, A Walk Among the Tombstones, The Interpreter, Charlie and the Chocolate Factory (script consultant), The Lookout (also dir.), Marley & Me.
TELEVISION: *Series:* The Wonder Years, Fallen Angels, Karen Sisco.

FRANKLIN, CARL
Actor, Director. b. Richmond, CA April 11, 1949. e. Studied arts, UC Berkeley.
PICTURES: *Actor:* Five on the Black Hand Side, Eye of the Eagle 2: Inside the Enemy (also dir., s.p.), Last Stand at Lang Mei (also s.p.), Full Fathom Five (also dir.), In the Heat of Passion. *Director:* Punk, Nowhere to Run, One False Move, Devil in a Blue Dress (also s.p.), One True Thing, High Crimes, Out of Time.
TELEVISION: *Movies:* It Couldn't Happen to a Nicer Guy, The Legend of the Golden Gun, One Cooks, The Other Doesn't, Too Good to be True, Laurel Avenue (dir. only), Low Life (dir. only), The Riches (pilot dir.). *Mini-series:* The Pacific (dir.). *Series:* The A-Team, Partners, The Riches (dir.).

FRANKLIN, ROBERT A.
Executive. b. New York, NY, April 15. e. U. of Miami, B.B.A., 1958; Columbia Pacific U., M.B.A., 1979; Ph.D., 1980 majoring in marketing. Before entering film industry worked with House of Seagram, Canada Dry Corp., J. M. Mathes Adv. 1967, joined 20th Century-Fox as dir. of mkt. planning. Formed RP Marketing Intl. (entertainment consulting firm) in 1976 and World Research Systems (computer software marketer). 1981 joined MPAA; 1983, named v.p., admin. & info. services. 1986, named v.p. worldwide market research. Chmn., MPAA research comm.; member, AMA and ESOMAR.

FRANZ, DENNIS
Actor. b. Chicago, IL, Oct. 28, 1944. Started in Chicago Theatre.
PICTURES: Stony Island, Dressed to Kill, Blow Out, Psycho II, Body Double, A Fine Mess, The Package, Die Hard 2, The Player, American Buffalo, City of Angels.
TELEVISION: *Movies:* Chicago Story (pilot), Deadly Messages, Kiss Shot, Moment of Truth: Caught in the Crossfire (also co-prod.), Texas Justice, Bleacher Bums (s.p. only). *Series:* Chicago Story, Bay City Blues, Hill Street Blues, Beverly Hills Buntz, Nasty Boys, N.Y.P.D. Blue (Emmy Award, 1994, 1996, 1997, 1999, 4 other nom.; Golden Globe Award, 1995, 1 other nom.), Mighty Ducks (voice). *Documentaries/Specials:* Golden Anniversary of Snow White and the Seven Dwarfs, TV Guide Looks at Cops (host), America: A Tribute to Heroes, NYPD 24/7 (narrator), Above and Beyond: The Story of Cpl. William T. Perkins, Jr. *Guest:* More than 87 appearances.

FRASER, BRENDAN

Actor. b. Indianapolis, IN, Dec. 3, 1968. Raised in Holland, Switzerland, Canada. e. Actors' Conservatory, Cornish College of the Arts, Seattle. Member of Laughing Horse Summer Theatre in Ellensberg, WA.
THEATRE: Waiting for Godot, Arms and the Man, Romeo and Juliet, A Midsummer Night's Dream, Moonchildren, Four Dogs and a Bone.
PICTURES: Dogfight (debut, 1991), Encino Man, School Ties, Twenty Bucks, Younger and Younger, With Honors, Airheads, The Scout, Now and Then, The Passion of Darkly Noon, Mrs. Winterbourne, Glory Daze, George of the Jungle, Still Breathing, Gods and Monsters, Dudley Do-Right, Blast from the Past, The Mummy, Bedazzled, Monkeybone, The Mummy Returns, The Quiet American, Looney Tunes: Back in Action, Journey to the End of the Night, Crash, Accidental Husband, Singularity, Big Bug Man (voice), The Last Time, The Air I Breathe, Journey to the Center of the Earth 3D, Inkheart, The Mummy: Tomb of the Dragon Emperor, G.I. Joe: The Rise of Cobra, Extraordinary Measures, Furry Vengeance.
TELEVSION: *Movie:* Guilty Until Proven Innocent, The Twilight of the Golds. *Pilot:* My Old School. *Series:* The Fairly Odd Parents: Wishology Trilogy. *Guest:* More than 70 appearances.

FRAZIER, SHEILA E.

Actress, Producer. b. Bronx, NY, Nov. 13, 1948. e. Englewood, NJ. Was exec. sect'y. and high-fashion model. Steered to acting career by friend Richard Roundtree. Studied drama with N.Y. Negro Ensemble Co. and New Federal Theatre, N.Y., also with Bob Hickey at H.B. Studios, N.Y. Currently working as a TV producer.
PICTURES: Super Fly (debut), Superfly T.N.T., The Super Cops, California Suite, What Does It Take?, Three the Hard Way, The Hitter, I'm Gonna Git You Sucker, Two of a Kind, Jim Brown: All American, The Last Stand.
TELEVISION: *Movie:* Firehouse. *Mini-series:* King. *Series:* The Lazarus Syndrome, NCIS: Naval Criminal Investigative Service. *Documentary:* Jim Brown: All American (actor, prod.).

FREARS, STEPHEN

Director. b. Leicester, Eng., June 20, 1941. e. Cambridge, B.A in law. Joined Royal Court Theatre, working with Lindsay Anderson on plays. Later assisted Karel Reisz on Morgan: A Suitable Case for Treatment, Albert Finney on Charlie Bubbles, and Lindsay Anderson on If ... Worked afterwards mostly in TV, directing and producing. First directorial credit was 30-minute film The Burning, 1967.
PICTURES: Gumshoe (dir. debut 1971), Bloody Kids, The Hit, My Beautiful Laundrette, Prick Up Your Ears, Sammy and Rosie Get Laid, Dangerous Liaisons, The Grifters (Academy Award nom. 1991), Hero (GB: Accidental Hero), The Snapper, Mary Reilly, The Van, The Hi-Lo Country, High Fidelity, Liam, Dirty Pretty Things, Mrs. Henderson Presents, The Queen (Academy Award nom.; DGA nom.; Golden Globe nom. 2007), Chéri (also narr.), Jean Charles (exec. prod.), Tamara Drewe.
TELEVISION: *Movies:* A Day Out (1971), England Their England, Match of the Day, Sunset Across the Bay, Three Men in a Boat, Daft as a Brush, Playthings, Early Struggles, Last Summer, 18 Months to Balcomb Street, A Visit from Miss Protheroe, Abel's Will, Cold Harbour, Song of Experience; series of six Alan Bennett plays; Long Distance Information, Going Gently, Loving Walter, December Flower, Fail Safe (Emmy nom.; DGA nom. 2000), The Deal, Skip Tracer.

FREDERICKSON, H. GRAY, JR.

Producer. b. Oklahoma City, OK, July 21, 1937. e. U. of Lausanne, Switzerland, 1958\-59; U. of Oklahoma. B.A., 1960. Worked one yr. with Panero, Weidlinger & Salvatori Engineering Co., Rome Italy. In 1979 named v.p. of feature films, Lorimar Films. Currently President of Graymark Productions.
PICTURES: Candy, Inspector Sterling, Gospel 70, An Italian in America, The Man Who Wouldn't Die, The Good, the Bad and the Ugly, Intrigue in Suez, How to Learn to Love Women, God's Own Country, Wedding March, An American Wife, Natika, Echo in the Village, Little Fauss and Big Halsey, Making It, The Godfather (assoc. prod.), The Godfather Part II (co-prod; Academy Award for Best Picture, 1975), Hit (exec. prod.), Apocalypse Now (co.-prod.; Academy Award nom. 1980), One From the Heart, The Outsiders, UHF, The Godfather Part III (co-prod.), Ladybugs (exec. prod.), Bad Girls (story), Heaven's Prisoners, South of Heaven West of Hell, My 5 Wives (creative consultant), Cloud 9 (exec. prod.), Surveillance, Soul's Midnight (exec. prod. also first assist. dir. 2nd unit), Fingerprints (exec. prod. also unit prod. mngr.), The Hunt (exec. prod.), Agenda (prod. consult.), Ivory.
TELEVISION: The Return of Mickey Spillane's Mike Hammer, Houston Nights, Staying Afloat (exec. prod.). *Series:* Houston Knights. *Documentary:* Dream No Little Dream: The Life and Legacy of Robert S. Kerr.

FREEBORN, STUART

Make-Up. London, England, September 5, 1914.
PICTURES: I See A Dark Stranger, Captain Boycott, Oliver Twist, Silent Dust, Obsession, The Man Who Watched The Trains Go By, His MajestyO'Keefe, The Bridge on the River Kwai, The Naked Truth, I Was Monty's Double, Kidnapped, Mr.Topaze, The Hands of Orlac, The Devil's Daffodil, Foxhole in Cairo, Tarzan Goes to India, The Wrong Arm of the Law, Private Potter, Heaven's Above, Dr.Strangelove: Or How I Learned to Stop Worrying and Love the Bomb, Seance on a Wet Afternoon, 2001: A Space Odyssey, Oh! What A Lovely War, 10 Rillington Place, See No Evil, Young Winston, Alice's Adventures in Wonderland, Murder on the Orient Express, The Adventures of Sherlock Holmes' Smarter Brother, The Omen, Star Wars, Superman, The Empire Strikes Back, Superman II, The Great Muppet Caper, Return of the Jedi, Top Secret!, Santa Claus, Haunted Honeymoon.
TELEVISION: *Movies:* Spectre, The 'Star Wars' Holiday Special, Max and Helen. *Series/Documentary:* The Wonderful World of Disney (Kidnapped parts 1 and 2).

FREEMAN, MORGAN

Actor. b. Memphis, TN, June 1, 1937. e. LA City Coll. Served in Air Force 1955-59 before studying acting. Worked as dancer at NY's 1964 World's Fair. Broadway debut in Hello Dolly! with Pearl Bailey. Took over lead role in Purlie. Became known nationally when he played Easy Reader on TV's The Electric Company (1971-76).
THEATRE: NY: Ostrich Feathers, The Nigger Lovers, Hello Dolly!, Scuba Duba, Purlie, Cockfight, The Last Street Play, The Mighty Gents (Drama Desk & Clarence Derwent Awards), Coriolanus (Obie Award), Julius Caesar, Mother Courage, Buck, Driving Miss Daisy (Obie Award), The Gospel at Colonus (Obie Award), The Taming of the Shrew.
PICTURES: Who Says I Can't Ride a Rainbow? (debut, 1972), Brubaker, Eyewitness, Death of a Prophet, Harry and Son, Teachers, Marie, That Was Then...This Is Now, Street Smart (NY & LA Film Critics & Natl. Board of Review Awards; Academy Award nom.; Golden Globe nom. 1988), Clean and Sober, Lean on Me, Johnny Handsome, Glory, Driving Miss Daisy (Natl. Board of Review & Golden Globe Awards; Academy Award nom., 1990), The Bonfire of the Vanities, Robin Hood: Prince of Thieves, The Power of One, Unforgiven, Bopha (dir. only), The Shawshank Redemption (Academy Award nom.; Golden Globe nom. 1995), Outbreak, Seven, Moll Flanders, Chain Reaction, Hurricane (dir., prod., s.p., only), Kiss the Girls, Under Suspicion, Long Walk to Freedom, High Crimes, Along Came a Spider, Sum of All Fears, Tusker, Levity, Bruce Almighty, The Big Bounce, Danny the Dog, Million Dollar Baby (Academy Award, Golden Globe nom. 2005), An Unfinished Life, Tusker (voice), Unleashed, Colors Straight Up (also exec. prod.), Edison, Batman Begins, Lucky Number Slevin, Rope Burns, Long Walk to Freedom, Freedomland, Harry and the Butler, The Contract, Gone Baby Gone, Evan Almighty, Feast of Love, The Bucket List, Wanted, The Dark Knight, The Maiden Heist (also prod.), Invictus (also exec. prod., Academy Award nom.; Golden Globe nom. 2010), Red.
TELEVISION: *Movies:* Hollow Image, Attica, The Marva Collins Story, The Atlanta Child Murders, Resting Place, Flight For Life, Roll of Thunder Hear My Cry, Charlie Smith and the Fritter Tree, Clinton and Nadine, Mutiny. *Series:* The Electric Company, Ryan's Hope, Another World (1982-4). *Specials (narrator):* The Civil War, Follow the Drinking Gourd, The Promised Land, The Long Way Home, Declaration of Independence, Survivors of the Shoah: Visual History Foundation, Slavery and the Making of America, A Raisin in the Sun, Through the Wormhole (series, also exec. prod.). *Guest:* More than 201 appearances.

FRESTON, THOMAS E.

Executive. e. B.A. degree from St. Michael's College and M.B.A. from New York University. Freston began a career in advertising and in 1980 joined Warner Amex Satellite Entertainment Company (WASEC), the predecessor to MTV Networks. In 1981, he was one of the founding members of the team that launched MTV: Music Television. As the head of marketing, Freston oversaw the breakthrough "I want my MTV" campaign which helped propel the channel into a global entertainment network. Freston held a succession of positions with MTV Networks, culminating in the CEO position in 1987. In mid-2004, Freston was promoted to co-president and co-COO of MTV Networks' parent company, Viacom, Inc. At Viacom Freston acquired DreamWorks. Freston also initiated several campaigns and programs that addressed social issues. These included Nickleodeon's Big Help campaign. Other initiatives addressed issues ranging from discrimination to HIV/AIDS. While at MTV Networks, Freston shared a prestigious "diversity leadership" award from the Diversity Best Practices (DBP) Council. Freston resigned from Viacom during 2006 over disagreements on Internet strategy and Viacom Executive Chairman of the Board and Founder Sumner Redstone's disappointment over the price of Viacom stock. He is currently self-employed as a consultant and also started a private company, Firefly3 LLC, which invests and consults in the media and entertainment businesses. Recently, Firefly3 LLC became an investor in Veoh Networks, an Internet TV company. Freston received an honorary doctoral degree from Emerson College in 2007. In Sept. 2007, Freston was elected to the bd. of directors of DreamWorks Animation SKG Inc., and also serves on the Board of the American Museum of Natural History and the Board of Trustees for Emerson College in Boston. He is a member of the Broadcasting and Cable Hall of Fame, has received many industry awards and has worked closely with many charitable organizations like City of Hope, the Natural Resources Defense Council (NRDC), Riverkeeper and Phoenix House.

FREWER, MATT

Actor. b. Washington, D. C., Jan. 4, 1958. Raised in Victoria, British Columbia. Studied drama at the Bristol Old Vic Theatre, appearing in Romeo and Juliet, Macbeth, Waiting for Godot, Deathtrap.

PICTURES: The Lords of Discipline (debut, 1983), Supergirl, Spies Like Us, Ishtar, The Fourth Protocol, Far From Home, Speed Zone, Honey I Shrunk the Kids, Short Time, The Taking of Beverly Hills, Twenty Bucks, National Lampoon's Senior Trip, Lawnmower Man II, Hercules (voice), Dead Fire, 6ix, Cyberworld (voice), Whitecoats, Dawn of the Dead, A Home at the End of the World, Riding the Bullet, Piggy Bank Blues, Going the Distance, Weirdsville, Watchmen, Frankie and Alice.

TELEVISION: *Movies:* The Positively True Adventures of the Alleged Texas Cheerleader-Murdering Mom, The Day My Parents Ran Away, Kissinger and Nixon, Generation X, Apollo 11, Dead Man's Gun, Quicksilver Highway, Desert's Edge, Dead Man's Gun, In the Doghouse, Jailbait, The Hound of the Baskervilles, The Sign of Four, The Royal Scandal, The Case of the Whitechapel Vampire, Intelligence, Desperation. *Mini-series:* The Stand, Taken, Desperation. BBC: Tender is the Night, Robin of Sherwood; U.S. *Series:* Max Headroom, Doctor Doctor, Shaky Ground, The Pink Panther (voice), Outer Limits, Aladdin, Iron Man (voice), Dumb and Dumber (voice), The Incredible Hulk (voice), Hercules (voice), Toonsylvania (voice), The House of Mouse (voice), Eureka, Intelligence. *Guest:* More than 80 appearances.

FRICKER, BRENDA

Actress. b. Dublin, Ireland, Feb. 17, 1945. Appeared in short film The Woman Who Married Clark Gable. Theatre work with the RSC, Royal Court Theatre, and The National Theatre.

PICTURES: Quatermass Conclusion, Bloody Kids, Our Exploits at West Poley, My Left Foot (Academy Award, Golden Globe nom. best supporting actress, 1989), The Field, Utz, Home Alone 2: Lost in New York, So I Married an Axe Murderer, Angels in the Outfield, A Man of No Importance, Moll Flanders, A Time to Kill, Swann, Masterminds, Painted Angels, Resurrection Man, Pete's Meteor, The American, The War Bride, The Intended, Veronica Guerin, Conspiracy of Silence, Trauma, Rory O'Shea Was Here, Tara Road, How About You, The Day I Ran Into All My Ex-Boyfriends, Closing the Ring, Stone of Destiny, Locked In, Crossmaglen, Hotel Caledonia.

TELEVISION: *Movies:* Seekers, Alexander Graham Bell: The Sound and the Silence, Durango, Cupid & Cate, The American, Journey, Resurrection, Torso: The Evelyn Dick Story, Watermelon, Call Me: The Rise and Fall of Heidi Fleiss, Omagh. *Mini-series:* Brides of Christ, A Woman of Independent Means, Relative Strangers, I Was a Rat, No Tears. *Series:* Casualty, Cupid & Cate. *Specials:* Licking Hitler, The House of Bernarda Alba, The Ballroom Romance. *Documentary:* Out of Ireland. *Guest:* More than 50 appearances.

FRIEDKIN, WILLIAM

Director, Writer. b. Chicago, IL, Aug. 29, 1939. m. producer Sherry Lansing. Joined WGN-TV, 1957, worked for National Education TV, did TV documentaries before feature films. Dir. B'way play Duet for One.

PICTURES: Good Times (debut, 1967), The Night They Raided Minsky's, The Birthday Party, The Boys in the Band, The French Connection (Academy Award, Golden Globe Award, DGA Award 1971), The Exorcist (Academy Award nom.; Golden Globe Award, DGA nom. 1974), Sorcerer (also prod.), The Brink's Job, Cruising (also s.p.), Deal of the Century, To Live and Die in L.A. (also co-s.p.), Rampage (also s.p.), The Guardian (also co-s.p.), Blue Chips, Jade, Rules of Engagement, The Hunted, The Man Who Kept Secrets, Bug, Coco & Igor (dir.).

TELEVISION: *Movies:* C.A.T. Squad (also exec. prod.), C.A.T. Squad: Python Wolf, Jailbreakers, 12 Angry Men (Emmy nom.; DGA nom. 1998). *Series:* Tales From the Crypt (On a Dead Man's Chest). *Special:* Barbra Streisand: Putting It Together.

FRIEDMAN, PAUL

Executive. b. Brooklyn, NY. e. Princeton U. Woodrow Wilson School of Public & Int'l. Affairs, 1966, Master's of Science in Journalism from Columbia School of Journalism. 1967. Friedman began his journalism career as a reporter and writer in NY for WNBC Radio News (1967). From 1969-1970, reporter for WRC-TV Washington, D.C.; 1970-1972, field producer for NBC's The Huntley-Brinkley Report; 1972-1974, senior producer of NBC Weekend Nightly News; 1974-1975, executive producer of NewsCenter 4; 1975-1976, senior producer of NBC News' Nightly News; 1976-1979, executive producer of NBC News' Today; 1980-1981, executive prod. Primetime with Tom Snyder; 1981-1982, NBC Magazine with David Brinkley. Friedman then joined ABC News as a sr. producer in London, 1982-84; from 1984-1988, he was dir. of ABC news coverage for Europe, Africa, Middle East; In 1988, he created-American Agenda-an award-winning extended news feature covering current critical domestic issues for World News Tonight. Four years later, Friedman added Your Money - Your Choice, a weekly segment that analyzed how the federal government spends taxpayer money. 1988-1993, executive producer of ABC's World News Tonight with Peter Jennings. Returned to exec. prod. the newscast from 1997-2000. Under Friedman, the broadcast became the highest-rated evening news program. Friedman supervised live coverage of major breaking news events and served as the exec. prod. of ABC News' 9/11 and 9/11 anniversary coverage. From 2000-2003, he was the executive v.p. and managing editor of news coverage for ABC News. 2003-2005, moved to PBS and was exec. prod. of The Wall Street Journal's The Journal Report. In April 2006, Friedman moved to CBS as v.p. of news and now oversees all aspects of the network's hard news coverage and promoted to exec. v.p. 2009. Friedman has been an adjunct professor of journalism at Columbia University and New York University, as well as serving as a consultant through Friedman News Consultancy, Inc. from 2003-2006.

FRIEDMAN, ROBERT G.

Executive. Began in the mailroom of Warner Bros. and moved up to president of Worldwide Advertising & Publicity. Moved to Paramount and from 1996-July 2005 served as vice chmn. & COO of Paramount's Motion Picture Group. In April 2007 Friedman teamed with Patrick Wachsberger to create a new worldwide theatrical motion picture production and distribution studio—Summit Entertainment, LLC. Under the terms of a transaction with Merrill Lynch, Summit Ent. will have access to more than $1 Billion for development, production, acquisition, marketing and distribution of filmed entertainment across all media. The studio plans to release 10 to 12 films annually, with Friedman as co-chmn. & CEO. Friedman has been a faculty member of the Independent Producers' Program, UCLA Dept. of Theater, Film and Television; member, Next Generation Council for the Motion Picture & Television Fund Found., member of the board of directors, Motion Picture Pioneers, and Southern California Special Olympics.

FRIEDMAN, ROBERT L.

Executive. b. Bronx, NY, March 1, 1930. e. DeWitt Clinton H.S, Bronx. Started as radio announcer and commentator with Armed Forces Radio Service in Europe and U.S. sr. v.p., distrib. & mktg., United Artists Corp.; pres. domestic distribution, Columbia Pictures. 1984, named pres., AMC Entertainment Int'l. Inc. 1992, named pres. of AMC Entertainment—the Motion Picture Group. 2001-present, a senior advisor to Chanin Capital Partners' Entertainment and Media Goup. 2000, named pres. & CEO of Stereo Vision Entertainment. Member: Exec. div. of the Academy of Motion Picture Arts & Sciences (bd. of dir.—Center for Motion Picture Study), Variety Club of So. Ca., Motion Picture Pioneers of America, the Will Rogers Hospital, the Motion Picture Associates Found. Also, bd. of dir. of the Century City Chamber of Commerce—chmn. of ent. ind. committee.

FRIELS, COLIN

Actor. b. Scotland, Sept. 25, 1952. e. Australia Natl. Inst. of Dramatic Art. m. actress Judy Davis. First began acting with the State Theatre Co. of So. Australia and the Sydney Theatre Co. Theatre includes Sweet Bird of Youth and Hedda Gabler. TV includes special Stark.

PICTURES: Buddies, Monkey Grip, For the Term of His Natural Life, Kangaroo, Malcolm, High Tide, Ground Zero, Grievous Bodily Harm, Warm Nights on a Slow Moving Train, Darkman, Class Action, Dingo, A Good Man in Africa, Angel Baby, Back of Beyond, Cosi, Mr. Reliable, Dark City, The Man Who Sued God, Black and White, Max's Dreaming, The Illustrated Family Doctor, The Book of Revelation, Solo, A Heartbeat Away.

TELEVISION: *Movies:* For the Term of His Natural Life, Stark, Halifax f.p.: Hard Corps, Marriage Acts, Child Star: The Shirley Temple Story, My Husband My Killer, Black Jack, Temptation, The Mystery of Natalie Wood, BlackJack: Sweet Science, BlackJack: In the Money, BlackJack: Ace Point Game, BlackJack: Ghosts, BlackJack: Dead Memory, BlackJack: At the Gates, The Informant. *Mini-series:* The Farm, Seven Deadly Sins, Bastard Boys. *Series:* Water Rats.

FRIES, CHARLES W.

Executive, Producer. b. Cincinnati, OH, 1928. e. Ohio State U., B.S. Exec.-prod., Ziv Television; v.p., prod., Screen Gems; v.p., prod., Columbia Pictures; exec. v.p., prod. and exec. prod., Metromedia Prod. Corp., 1970-74; pres., exec. prod., Alpine Prods. and Charles Fries Prods. 1974-83; chmn. & pres., Fries Entertainment, 1984-1995; pres., Charles Fries Prods., 1996-present.

PICTURES: *Prod.:* Cat People, Flowers in the Attic, Troop Beverly Hills, Screamers, A Million Colours (exec. prod.).

TELEVISION: *Movies:* Maybe I'll Come Home in the Spring, A Tattered Web, Murder Once Removed, She Waits, Foosteps: Nice Guys Finish Last, Sandcastles, A Great American Tragedy, Go Ask Alice, The Norliss Tapes, Honor Thy Father, Message to My Daughter, Scream of the Wolf, It's Good to Be Alive, Hurricane, Terror on the 40th Floor, The Strange and Deadly Occurrence, Where Have All the People Gone?, Punch and Jody, Betrayal, The Hatfields and the McCoys, The Secret Night Caller, Someone I Touched, Last Hours Before Morning, Hey, I'm Alive!, The Right of the People, Foster and Laurie, Louis Armstrong — Chicago Style, Twin Detectives, The Call of the Wild, The Million Dollar Rip-Off, Francis Gary Powers: The True Story of the U-2

Spy Incident, How to Break Up a Happy Divorce, Stalk the Wild Child, Night Terror, The Spell, Terraces, The Amazing Spider-Man, The Trial of Lee Harvey Oswald, The Greatest Thing That Almost Happened, Halloween with the New Addams Family, Intimate Strangers, A Love Affair: The Eleanor and Lou Gehrig Story, Night Cries, The Initiation of Sarah, Are You in the House Alone?, Human Feelings, Crash, The Winds of Kitty Hawk, And Your Name Is Jonah, Bogie, A Rumor of War, Rage!, The Children of An Lac, A Cry for Love, High Noon, Part II: The Return of Will Kane, Leave 'em Laughing, Bitter Harvest, Twirl, The Ambush Murders, In Love with an Older Woman, Rosie: The Rosemary Clooney Story, Cocaine: One Man's Seduction, Carpool, Memorial Day, Through Naked Eyes, For Us the Living: The Medgar Evers Story, Dempsey, Jealousy, The Zany Adventures of Robin Hood, Sins of the Father, Toughlove, Bridge Across Time, The Right of the People, Samaritan: The Mitch Snyder Story, Timestalkers, Fight for Life, Blood Vows: The Story of a Mafia Wife, The Alamo: 13 Days to Glory, Intimate Betrayal, Drop Out Mother, Crash Course, Supercarrier, Bridge to Silence, The Case of the Hillside Strangler, The Neon Empire, Leona Helmsley: The Queen of Mean, Mission of the Shark: The Saga of the U.S.S. Indianapolis, Chance of a Lifetime, Deadly Web. Small Sacrifices, The Initiation of Sarah. *Mini-series:* The Word, The Martian Chronicles. *Series:* Here We Go Again, Baby, I'm Back, The Amazing Spider-Man. *Specials:* It's Howdy Doody Time: A 40 Year Celebration.

FRONS, BRIAN S.

Executive. e. B.A. in history from the State Univ. of New York at Fredonia and Master of Science in communications from Syracuse Univ. Began TV career in 1978 as a program mgt. trainee for CBS Entertainment. In the daytime programming field, Frons has held various executive positions, including vp, daytime programming, for NBC Entertainment, and director, daytime programming, for CBS Entertainment. He has also been vp, creative affairs, for NBC Productions. Earlier in his career he was pres., creative affairs, for New World Entertainment in Hollywood, where he directed program development and production for network, first-run syndication and international co-production. Before joining ABC Daytime, Frons was sr. vp of programming for London-based SBS Broadcasting, S.A. There, he oversaw all programming, promotion and research operations for 12 SBS-owned and operated channels reaching about 125 million European viewers. In Aug. 2002, Frons was named pres., ABC Daytime for ABC Television Network. In May 2006, Frons was promoted to pres., daytime, Disney-ABC Television Group. He oversees creation, production and delivery of all product on ABC Daytime, SOAPnet and Buena Vista Productions.

FRONTIERE, DOMINIC

Executive, Composer. b. New Haven, CT, June 17, 1931. e. Yale School of Music. Studied composing, arranging and conducting; concert accordionist, World's Champion Accordionist, 1943; An Hour with Dominic Frontiere, WNHC-TV, New Haven, 3 years, 1947; exec. vice-pres., musical dir., Daystar Prods. Composer or arranger over 75 films.
PICTURES: Giant, Gentlemen Prefer Blondes, Let's Make Love, High Noon, Meet Me in Las Vegas, 10,000 Bedrooms, Hit the Deck, Marriage-Go-Round, The Right Approach, One Foot in Hell, Hero's Island, Hang 'Em High, Popi, Barquero, Chisum, A for Alpha, Cancel My Reservation, Hammersmith is Out, Freebie and the Bean, Brannigan, The Gumball Rally, Cleopatra Jones and the Casino of Gold, The Stunt Man (Golden Globe Award 1981), Modern Problems, The Aviator, Road, Color of Night (Golden Globe nom.1995), Behind the Badge, Watchmen (soundtrack writer).
TELEVISION: *Composer-conductor/Movies:* Washington: Behind Closed Doors, The Haunted, The Immortal, Lost Flight, The Love War, The Sheriff, Revenge, Probe, Haunts of the Very Rich, Fer-de-Lance, The Mark of Zorro, Who Is the Black Dahlia?, Young Pioneers, Yesterday's Child, Perfect Gentlemen, Vega$, Shooting Stars, Dark Mirror, Velvet, Harry's Hong Kong, Palomino. *Mini-series:* Washington: Behind Closed Doors, Trade Winds. *Series:* The New Breed, Stoney Burke, Bankamericard commercials (Venice Film Fest. Award for best use of original classical music for filmed TV commercials), Outer Limits, Branded, Iron Horse, Rat Patrol, The Iron Horse, Flying Nun, The Invaders, Name of the Game, That Girl, Twelve O'Clock High, Zig Zag, Swing Out, Sweet Land (Emmy Award 1971), The Young Rebel, The Immortal, Chopper One, Fugitive, The Love War, Vega$, Matt Houston.

FROT-COUTAZ, CECILE

Executive. e. Insead, Paris. Frot-Coutaz joined the Pearson Group in London in 1994. 1995, when Pearson purchased the assets of Grundy Television, she was promoted to Corporate Strategy Executive. In 1998, she joined one of two teams that managed the integration of All-American Fremantle assets into the Pearson family as Deputy CEO, Southern Europe and Managing Director, France. she headed to San Francisco in 2000 to develop online and interactive strategies for Pearson before being appointed Exec. V. P., Commercial and Operations for FreemantleMedia North America. She was promoted to CEO in July of 2005 and manages all business and operations. As CEO, she is responsible for over 400 hours of television programming and makes decisions on multiple shows including the juggling of replacement judges on American Idol. She also oversaw a ratings surge at NBC's America's Got Talent while driving Let's Make a Deal into the daytime lineup at CBS, other programs include The Price Is Right and syndicated, The Family Feud.

FUCHS, FRED

Producer, Executive. e. graduate of Wesleyan University, 1977. Veteran Los Angeles producer and former pres. of American Zoetrope Studios. After more than a dozen years working with Coppola at American Zoetrope, Fuchs left Zoetrope in 1998 to start an independent film, TV and new media production company in San Francisco. A few years later, he relocated to Canada to work in the Canadian independent production community. In March 2006 Fuchs was tapped by the Canadian Broadcasting Corp. (CBC) to be its arts and entertainment chief, responsible for the network's drama.
PICTURES: *Exec. Prod.:* Vietnam War Story: The Last Days, The Spirit of '76, The Godfather: Part III, The Secret Garden, Mary Shelley's Frankenstein, Don Juan DeMarco, Haunted, Jack, Buddy, The Rainmaker. Producer: New York Stories (segment 2), Tucker: The Man and His Dream, Bram Stoker's Dracula, The Secret Garden, Frankenstein, Don Juan deMarco, Haunted, Jack, Buddy, The Rainmaker, The Virgin Suicides, The Third Miracle, Beautiful Joe, The End of Silence, Graduation.
TELEVISION: *Movies:* Dark Angel, Tecumseh: The Last Warrior, Titanic, Riot, The Odyssey (Emmy nom. 1997), Outrage, Moby Dick (Emmy nom. 1998). *Mini-series:* The Odyssey. *Series:* Faerie Tale Theater (Emmy nom. 1988; outstanding children's program), What It's Like Being Alone, Being Erica (exec. dir.).

FURIE, SIDNEY J.

Director, Writer, Producer. b. Toronto, Canada, Feb. 28, 1933. Ent. TV and films 1954. Canadian features include: Dangerous Age, A Cool Sound from Hell. Also dir. many Hudson Bay TV series. To England 1960. 1961 appt. exec. dir. Galaworldfilm Productions, Ltd.
PICTURES: The Snake Woman, Doctor Blood's Coffin, Wonderful to Be Young, Night of Passion (also prod., s.p.), The Young Ones, The Leather Boys, Wonderful Life, The Ipcress File (DGA nom. 1966), The Appaloosa, The Naked Runner, The Lawyer, Little Fauss and Big Halsy, Lady Sings the Blues, Hit!, Sheila Levine Is Dead and Living in New York, Gable and Lombard, The Boys in Company C, The Entity, Purple Hearts (also prod., s.p.), Iron Eagle, Superman IV: The Quest For Peace, Iron Eagle II (also co-s.p.), The Taking of Beverly Hills, Ladybugs, Hollow Point, Iron Eagle IV, The Rage (also story), Top of the World, The Rage, In Her Defense, The Collectors, Cord, My 5 Wives, Sonic Boom, A Firday Night Date, Going Back, Global Heresy, Donzi: The Legend, The Circle, Partners in Action, Direct Action, The Controller, American Soldiers.
TELEVISION: *Movies:* Married to a Stranger, The Collectors, Road Rage, Going Back (also writer) The Veteran. *Series:* Hudson's Bay, Petrocelli (writer/creator), Pensacola: Wings of Gold, V.I.P., 18 Wheels of Justice, Just Cause.

FURLONG, EDWARD

Actor. b. Glendale, CA, Aug. 2, 1977. Discovered by casting agent for Terminator 2, having no previous acting experience. Appeared in Aerosmith video Livin' on the Edge.
PICTURES: Terminator 2: Judgment Day (debut, 1991), Pet Sematary 2, American Heart, A Home of Our Own, Brainscan, Little Odessa, The Grass Harp, Before and After, Pecker, American History X, Detroit Rock City, The Animal Factory, The Knights of the Quest, Terminator 3, Three Blind Mice, Random Acts of Kindness, The Crow: Wicked Prayer, The Visitation, Cruel World, Warriors of Terra, Living & Dying, Dark Reel, Kingshighway, The Mortician, Crave, Conception, The Green Hornet, The Beautiful Outsiders.
TELEVISION: *Documentary:* 50 Films to See Before You Die.

GABLER, ELIZABETH

Executive. e. graduate of University of California-Santa Barbara, B.A. in English, 1977. m. agent/executive Lee Gabler. Began career as literary agent at ICM and creative exec., Columbia Pictures; v.p. of production, United Artists; exec. v.p. of production, Twentieth Century Fox, 1988. President, Fox 2000 Pictures, 1999-present. Gabler is a member of UC Santa Barbara's Center for Film, Television, and New Media Advisory Board and also is involved with numerous environmental and animal rights charities.

GABLER, LEE

Executive. b. New York, NY. m. executive Elizabeth Gabler. Began career in the mailroon of Ashely Steiner Famous Artists in New York (later ICM) where he became an agent in 1964. Promoted to v.p. in 1968. 1970, transferred to ICM in California as exec. v.p. and head of worlwide television. 1983, joined CAA where he was partner, co-chmn. and head of television through

Spring 2007, at which time he left the agency. Gabler joined David Letterman's Worldwide Pants, serving as a consultant for the New York production company. Gabler remains based in Los Angeles.

GAGHAN, STEPHEN

Writer.
PICTURES: Rules of Engagement, Traffic (Academy Award, Golden Globe Award, WGA Award 2001), Abandon (also dir.), Abandon (also dir.), The Alamo, Havoc, Syriana (Academy Award nom.; WGA nom. 2006).
TELEVISION: *Series:* New York Undercover, American Gothic, NYPD Blue (Emmy Award 1997), American Gothic, Sleepwalkers (co-prod.), The Practice.

GAIL, MAX

Actor. b. Grosse Ile, MI, Apr. 5, 1943. e. William Coll. B.A. Economics, Univ. of Mich M.B.A.
THEATRE: NY: The Babe, One Flew Over the Cuckoo's Nest (also S.F.). LA: Visions of Kerouac.
PICTURES: The Organization, Dirty Harry, D.C. Cab, Heartbreakers, Pontiac Moon, Mind Lies, Sodbusters, Ox and the Eye, Forest Warrior, Good Luck, Naturally Native, The Perfect Wife, Mind Lies, Facing the Enemy, Truth and Dare, Angst, The Tillamook Treasure, Act Your Age, Beautysleep Symphony.
TELEVISION: *Movies:* The Priest Killer, Like Mom Like Me, Desperate Women, The 11th Victim, The Aliens Are Coming, Fun and Games, Letting Go, The Other Lover, Killer in the Mirror, Intimate Strangers, Can You Feel Me Dancing?, Tonight's the Night, Man Against the Mob, The Outside Woman, Ride With the Wind, Robin Cook's Mortal Fear, Naomi & Winona: Love Can Build a Bridge, Secret Agent (prod.), Wrong Side of the Fence (prod.), Tell Me No Secrets, Not in This Town, The Perfect Wife. *Mini-series:* Pearl. *Series:* Barney Miller (2 Emmy nom.), Whiz Kids, Normal Life, Sons & Daughters, Gary Unmarried. *Guest:* More than 81 appearances.

GALE, BOB

Writer, Producer. b. St. Louis, MO, May 25, 1951. e. USC Sch. of Cinema. Joined with friend Robert Zemeckis to write screenplays, starting with episode for TV series, McCloud. Also co-wrote story for The Nightstalker series. Turned to feature films, co-writing with Zemeckis script for I Wanna Hold Your Hand, on which Gale also acted as assoc. producer. Exec. prod. of CBS animated series Back to the Future. Wrote and directed interactive feature Mr. Payback.
PICTURES: I Wanna Hold Your Hand (co-s.p., co-assoc. prod.), 1941 (co-s.p.), Used Cars (prod., co-s.p.), Back to the Future (co.-prod., s.p. Academy Award nom.; Golden Globe nom.; WGA nom. 1986), Back to the Future Part II (prod., co-s.p.), Back to the Future Part III (prod., s.p.), Trespass (co-exec. prod., co-s.p.), Tales From the Crypt: Bordello of Blood (co-s.p.).
TELEVISION: *Series:* Amazing Stories, Back to the Future (animated; exec. prod.), Tales From the Crypt (wrote, dir. House of Horror). *Documentary:* Time Travel: Fact, Fiction and Fantasy (exec. prod.).

GALLAGHER, PETER

Actor. b. New York, NY, Aug. 19, 1955. e. Tufts Univ.
THEATRE: NY: Hair (1977 revival), Grease, A Doll's Life (Theatre World Award), The Corn is Green, The Real Thing (Clarence Derwent Award), Long Day's Journey Into Night (Tony Award nom.; also London), Guys & Dolls.
PICTURES: The Idolmaker (debut, 1980), Summer Lovers, Dream Child, My Little Girl, High Spirits, Sex Lies and Videotape, Tune in Tomorrow, Late for Dinner, The Cabinet of Dr. Ramirez, The Player, Bob Roberts, Watch It, Malice, Short Cuts (Golden Globe Award 1994), Mother's Boys, The Hudsucker Proxy, Mrs. Parker and the Vicious Circle, While You Were Sleeping, The Underneath, Cafe Society, The Last Dance, To Gillian on Her 37th Birthday, The Man Who Knew Too Little, Johnny Skidmarks, American Beauty, House on Haunted Hill, Other Voices, Center Stage, Perfume, Lunar Girl, Protection, Mr. Deeds, The Adventures of Tom Thumb and Thumbelina (voice), How to Deal, The War Boys, Adam, Betty Anne Waters, Burlesque.
TELEVISION: *Movies:* Skag, Terrible Joe Moran, The Caine Mutiny Court-Martial, The Murder of Mary Phagan, I'll Be Home for Christmas, Love and Lies, An Inconvenient Woman, White Mile, Titanic, Path to Paradise, The Frightening Frammis, The Quiet Room, The Cabinet of Dr. Ramirez, Virtual Obsession, Brotherhood of Murder, Cupid & Cate, The Last Debate, A Tale of Two Wives, Covert Affairs. *Mini-series:* Brave New World, Feast of All Saints,
The Gathering. *Series:* Skag, The Secret Lives of Men, The O.C., Robot Chicken (voice), Californication. *Specials:* The Big Knife, Long Day's Journey Into Night, Private Contentment, Guys & Dolls: Off the Record. *Guest:* More than 86 appearances.

GALLIGAN, ZACH

Actor. b. New York, NY, Feb. 14, 1964. e. Columbia U.
PICTURES: Gremlins, Nothing Lasts Forever, Waxwork, Mortal Passions, Rising Storm, Gremlins II, Zandalee, Waxwork II: Lost in Time, Round Trip to Heaven, All Tied Up, Warlock: The Armageddon, Ice, Caroline at Midnight, The First to Go, Prince Valiant, Cupid, Storm Troopers, Arthur's Quest, The Storytellers, Raw Nerve, Point Doom, G-Men From Hell, What They Wanted What They Got, Little Insects (voice), Gabriela, Infested, The Pack, Let Them Chirp Awhile, Jewslim, Nightbeasts, Cut.
TELEVISION: *Movies:* Jacobo Timerman: Prisoner Without a Name Cell Without a Number, Surviving, Psychic, For Love and Glory, Momentum. *Pilot:* Interns in Heat. *Mini-series:* Crossings. *Specials:* The Prodigious Hickey, The Return of Hickey, The Beginning of the Firm, A Very Delicate Matter, The Hitchhiker: Toxic Shock.

GAMBON, SIR MICHAEL

Actor. b. Dublin, Ireland, Oct. 19, 1940. Ent. ind. 1966. Early experience in theatre. 1985-87 Acting at National Theatre and London's West End. 1988: in Harold Pinter's Mountain Language.
THEATRE: *London:* Endgame, Henry IV, The Norman Conquests (trilogy), Cressida, A Number.
PICTURES: Othello, The Beast Must Die, Turtle Diary, Paris By Night, The Rachel Papers, A Dry White Season, The Cook the Thief His Wife and Her Lover, Mobsters, Toys, Clean Slate, The Browning Version, Squanto: A Warrior's Tale, A Man of No Importance, Midnight in St. Petersberg, Bullet to Beijing, The Innocent Sleep, Nothing Personal, Mary Reilly, The Wings of the Dove, The Gambler, Plunkett & MacLeane, Dancing at Lughnasa, The Last September, The Monkey's Tale, The Insider, Sleepy Hollow, Dead On Time, High Heels and Low Lifes, Gosford Park, Boswell for the Defence, Charlotte Gray, Ali G Indahouse, Standing Room Only, Open Range, The Actors., Sylvia, Harry Potter and the Prisoner of Azkaban, Sky Captain and the World of Tomorrow, Layer Cake, The Life Aquatic, Being Julia, Harry Potter and the Goblet of Fire, Elizabeth Rex, My Boy, The Omen, The Good Night, The Good Shepherd, Amazing Grace, The Baker, Harry Potter and the Order of the Phoenix, The Alps (doc., narr.), Brideshead Revisited, Harry Potter and the Half-Blood Prince, Law Abiding Citizen, Fantastic Mr. Fox (voice), The Book of Eli, Harry Potter and the Deathly Hallows: Part I, The King's Speech, Albert Nobbs, Harry Potter and the Deathly Hallows: Part II.
TELEVISION: *Movies:* Uncle Vanya, Ghosts, The Holy Experiment, Absurd Person Singular, Heat of the Day, Maigret Sets a Trap, Samson & Delilah, The Wind in the Willows, The Willows in Winter, Longitude, Endgame, Perfect Strangers, Larry and Viven: The Oliviers in Love, Path to War (Emmy nom.; Golden Globe nom. 2002), The Lost Prince, Celebration, Joe's Palace. *Mini-series:* The Singing Detective, The Storyteller: Greek Myths, Wives and Daughters, Angels in America, Masterpiece Theatre: Cranford, Emma. *Series:* The Borderers, The Challengers, The Other One, Chalk and Cheese, Oscar, Inspector Maigret. *Guest:* More than 96 appearances.

GAMMON, JAMES

Actor. b. Newman, IL, Apr. 20, 1940. e. Boone H.S., Orlando, FL. Former television cameraman. First acting role was small part on Gunsmoke. Head of Los Angeles' Met Theatre for 10 years.
THEATRE: *B'way:* Burning Child. The Dark at the Top of the Stairs (L.A. Critics Circle Award, best actor), Bus Stop (L.A. Drama Critics award, best director), Curse of the Starving Class (NY, L.A.), A Lie of the Mind (NY, L.A.), Buried Child (Chicago).
PICTURES: Cool Hand Luke (debut, 1967), Journey to Shiloh, Macho Callahan, A Man Called Horse, Macon County Line, Black Oak Conspiracy, Urban Cowboy, Any Which Way You Can, Smithereens, Vision Quest, Sylvester, Silverado, Silver Bullet, Made in Heaven, Ironweed, The Milagro Beanfield War, Major League, Revenge, Coupe de Ville, I Love You to Death, Leaving Normal, Crisscross, The Painted Desert, Running Cool, Cabin Boy, Vegas Vice, Natural Born Killers, Wild Bill, Traveller, The Apostle, Point Blank, The Hi-Lo Country, The Man in the Iron Mask, Love From Ground Zero, The Iron Giant (voice), One Man's Hero, The Cell, Life or Something Like It, The Country Bears (voice), Cold Mountain, Silver City, Don't Come Knocking, Outlaw Trail: The Treasure of Butch Cassidy, The Far Side of Jericho, Altered, The Final Season, In the Electric Mist, Otis E, The New Daughter.
TELEVISION: *Movies:* Kansas City Massacre, Rage, Women of San Quentin, M.A.D.D.: Mothers Against Drunk Drivers, Hell Town, The Long Hot Summer, Roe vs. Wade, Dead Aim, Conagher, Stranger at My Door, Men Don't Tell, Truman, Two Mothers For Zachary, You Know My Name, Logan's War: Bound by Honor, Monte Walsh, Paradise, What I Did for Love, Jesse Stone: Sea Change. *Mini-series:* Lincoln. *Series:* Bagdad Cafe, Nash Bridges. *Guest:* More than 76 appearances.

GANDOLFINI, JAMES

Actor. b. NJ, 1961. e. Rutgers U.
THEATRE: *B'way:* God of Carnage (Tony nom. 2009).
PICTURES: A Stranger Among Us, True Romance, Mr Wonderful, Money for Nothing, Angie, Terminal Velocity, The New World, Crimson Tide, Get Shorty, The Juror, She's So Lovely, Night Falls on Manhattan, Perdita Durango, The Mighty, A Civil Action, Fallen, 8MM, The Mexican, The Man Who Wasn't There, The Last Castle, Catch Me if You Can, Before the Devil Knows You're Dead, Sharkslayer, Surviving Christmas, Be Cool, Romance & Cigarettes, The Set-Up, All the King's Men, Kiddie Ride, Miracle at St. Anna, Where the Wild Things Are (voice), Sexual Healing (also prod.), Welcome to the Rileys, In the Loop,

The Taking of Pelham 123, Where the Wild Things Are (voice), Mint Julep.
TELEVISION: *Movie:* 12 Angry Men. *Series:* Gun, The Sopranos (3 Emmy Awards, 3 other noms.; Golden Globe Award, 2000; 3 other noms.). *Documentary:* Alive Day Memories: Home from Iraq (Emmy nom. 2008). *Guest:* More than 48 appearances.

GANELESS, MICHELE
Executive. e. B.S. degree, Northwestern Univ. Worked as acct. mgr. at Young & Rubicam, 1989-1990. Ganeless then became a research mgr. for Comedy Central, 1990-1992; named v.p., research and planning at MTV, 1992-1995; returned to Comedy Central in 1996 as v.p., programming, and was promoted to senior v.p. in Jan. 2000. In that role, Ganeless was a key architect of the programming strategy that drove five straight years of ratings growth, and was a key member of the team that launched hits "The Daily Show" and "South Park." She was tapped to turn around the USA Network and was its executive v.p. and general mgr. from 2001-2004. While at USA Network, Ganeless had oversight of acquisitions, program scheduling, marketing, press, on-air promotion and research. She played a key role in that network's turnaround story, overseeing the launches of successful series including "Monk" and "The Dead Zone," and helped the network grow its ratings after the loss of wrestling. She returned to Comedy Central in 2004 as its executive v.p. and general mgr. In Sept. 2007, Ganeless was elevated to her current position, president, Comedy Central. She is based in New York and reports to Doug Herzog, pres., MTV Networks Entertainment Group.

GANIS, SIDNEY M.
Executive, Producer. b. New York, NY, Jan. 8, 1940. e. Brooklyn College. Staff writer, newspaper and wire service contact, 20th Century-Fox 1961-62; radio, TV contact and special projects, Columbia Pictures 1963-64. Joined Seven Arts Prod. 1965 as publicity mgr.; 1967, appt. prod. publicity mgr. Warner-7 Arts, Asst. prod., There Was a Crooked Man, 1969. Studio publicity dir., Cinema Center Films, 1970. Director of Ad-Pub for Mame, Warner Bros., 1973; Director of Advertising, Warner Bros., 1974; named WB v.p., worldwide adv. & pub., 1977; 1979, sr. v.p., Lucasfilm, Ltd.; 1982 Emmy winner, exec. prod., best documentary, The Making of Raiders of the Lost Ark. 1986, joined Paramount Pictures as pres., worldwide mktg; 1986, named pres., Paramount Motion Picture Group. 1988, elected trustee University Art Museum, Berkeley, CA. 1991, appointed exec. v.p., Sony Pictures Ent. Exec. v.p., pres. mktg. & distrib., Columbia Pictures, 1992. Also in 1992, elected for term on AMPAS bd. of governors. Became vice chmn., Columbia Pictures, 1994 and pres., worldwide mktg., Columbia TriStar. Pres./owner of Out of the Blue...Entertainment, since Sept. 1996. In 2008 Ganis elected to fourth consecutive one-year term as pres. of Motion Picture Arts & Sciences. 2009 became "immediate past president" meaning he serves on the exec committee and remains a resource for the org.
PICTURES: *Producer:* There was a Crooked Man (asst. to prod.), Deuce Bigalow: Male Gigolo, Big Daddy, Mr. Deeds (also actor), The Master of Disguise, Akeelah and the Bee (also actor), Iron Man (creative comm.). *Actor:* All the President's Men, Little Nicky, Anger Management, Montgomery West and the Wings of Death (short), Click, You Don't Mess with the Zohan.

GANZ, BRUNO
Actor. b. Zurich, Switzerland, March 22, 1941. Theatre debut in 1961. Founded the Berlin Theatre troupe, Schaubuehne, with Peter Stein in 1970.
THEATRE: Hamlet (1967), Dans La Jungle Des Villes, Torquato Tasso, La Chevauchee Sur Le Lac de Constance, Peer Gynt.
PICTURES: Der Sanfte Lauf (1967), Sommergaste, The Marquise of O, Lumiere, The Wild Duck, The American Friend, The Lefthanded Woman, The Boys from Brazil, Black and White Like Day and Night, Knife in the Head, Nosferatu the Vampyre, Return of a Good Friend, 5% Risk, An Italian Woman, Polenta, La Provinciale, La Dame Aux Camelias, Der Erfinder, Etwas Wird Sichtbar, Circle of Deceit, Hande Hoch, Logik Der Gerfuhls, War and Peace, In the White City, System Ohne Schatten, Der Pendler, Wings of Desire, Bankomatt, Strapless, The Last Days of Chez Nous, Especially on Sunday, Faraway So Close!, Heller Tag, Lumiere & Company, Saint-Ex, Eternity and a Day, WhoAfraidWolf, Bread and Tulips, Epstein's Night, The Power of the Past, Behind Me-Bruno Ganz (documentary), Luther, The Manchurian Candidate, The Downfall: Hitler and the End of the Third Reich, Vitus, Youth Without Youth, The Dust of Time, Der Baader Meinhof Komplex, The Reader, Der grosse Kater, Satte Farben vor Schwarz, La fine è il mio inizio, Unknown White Male.
TELEVISION: Father and Son, Todliches Schweigen, Ein Richter In Angst, Tatort — Schattenwelt (German TV), Gegen Ende der Nacht, Johann Wolfgang von Goethe: Faust, Have No Fear: The Life of Pope John Paul II, Copacabana, Ein Starker Abgang. *Mini-series:* Grande Fausto II. *Guest:* More than 54 appearances.

GANZ, LOWELL
Writer, Producer, Director. b. New York, NY, Aug. 31, 1948. e. Queens Col. Worked as staff writer on tv series The Odd Couple. Met writing partner Babaloo Mandel at The Comedy Store in the early 1970s. Was co-creator Laverne & Shirley. First teamed with Mandel on script for 1982 comedy Night Shift.
PICTURES: *Writer:* Night Shift, Splash (Academy Award nom., writing, s.p.; WGA nom. 1985; also actor), Spies Likes Us, Gung Ho, Vibes, Parenthood (also actor), City Slickers, A League of Their Own (also actor), Mr. Saturday Night (also actor), Greedy (also actor), City Slickers II: The Legend of Curly's Gold, Forget Paris, Multiplicity, Father's Day, EdTV, Where the Heart Is, Down and Under, Fifty First Kisses, National Treasure, The Last First Kiss, Robots, Fat Albert, Fever Pitch, Tooth Fairy.
TELEVISION: *Writer-Exec. Prod (series):* The Odd Couple, Happy Days, Busting Loose, The Ted Knight Show, Makin' It, Joanie Loves Chachi, Gung Ho, Knight and Dave, Parenthood, Hiller & Diller. *Producer:* Laverne & Shirley (also writer).

GANZ, TONY
Producer. b. New York, NY. e. studied film at Harvard U. Produced documentaries for PBS in N.Y. Moved to L.A. 1973 where in charge of dev., Charles Fries Productions. Then joined Ron Howard Productions, 1980. Left to form own prod. co. with Deborah Blum. Currently is in charge of features for Dick Wolf's Wolf Films, Inc. in Universal City, CA.
PICTURES: Gung Ho, No Man's Land (exec. prod.), Clean and Sober, Vibes.
TELEVISION: *Movies:* The Hatfields and the McCoys (assoc. prod.), Foster and Laurie (assoc. prod.), The Call of the Wild (assoc. prod.), The Greatest Thing That Almost Happened (assoc. prod.), Intimate Strangers (assoc. prod.), Crash (assoc. prod.). Bitter Harvest (prod.), Into Thin Air (exec. prod.), The Corpse Had a Familiar Face (exec. prod.). *Series:* American Dream Machine, Maximum Security (exec. prod.).

GARCIA, ANDY
Actor. r.n. Andres Arturo Garcia Menendez. b. Havana, Cuba, Apr. 12, 1956. Family moved to Miami Beach in 1961. e. Florida International U, Miami. Spent several years acting with regional theatres in Florida; also part of improv. group. Music producer of album: Cachao Master Sessions Vol. I (Grammy Award), Chachao Master Sessions Vol II (Grammy nom.).
PICTURES: The Mean Season, 8 Million Ways to Die, The Untouchables, Stand and Deliver, American Roulette, Black Rain, Internal Affairs, A Show of Force, The Godfather Part III (Academy Award nom.; Golden Globe nom. 1991), Dead Again, Hero, Jennifer Eight, Cachao... Como Su Ritmo No Hay Dos (Like His Rhythm There Is No Other; also dir., co-prod.), When a Man Loves a Woman, Steal Big Steal Little, Things to Do in Denver When You're Dead, Night Falls on Manhattan, Disappearance of Garcia Lorca, Hoodlum, Desperate Measures, Just the Ticket (also prod.), Sins of the Father, Avenging Angels, Lakeboat, The Unsaid, The Man From Elysian Fields (also prod.), Ocean's Eleven, Just Like Mona, Twisted, Confidence, Modigliani, Ocean's Twelve, The Lost City (also dir./exec. prod.), The Lazarus Child, The Air I Breathe, Smokin' Aces, Ocean's Thirteen, Beverly Hills Chihuahua (voice), The Line, The Last Full Measure, Pink Panther 2, City Island (also prod.), Magic City Memoirs (exec. prod.), Hemingway & Fuentes (also prod., dir., s.p.), Georgia.
TELEVISION: *Movies:* Clinton and Nadine, Swing Vote, The Arturo Sandoval Story (2 Emmy nom., Golden Globe nom. 2001), Classical Baby (I'm Grown Up Now): The Poetry Show. *Documentaries:* Cachao... Como Su Ritmo No Hay Dos, A Galaxy Far, Far Away, America: A Tribute to Heroes, Festival Pass with Chris Gore (series), Creating a Twisted Web of Intrigue (short), San Francisco: Scene of the Crime (short). *Guest:* More than 104 appearances.

GARNER, JAMES
Actor. r.n. James Baumgarner. b. Norman, OK, April 7, 1928. e. Norman H.S. Joined Merchant Marine, U.S. Army, served in Korean War. Prod. Paul Gregory suggested acting career. Studied drama at N.Y. Berghof School. Toured with road companies; Warner Bros. studio contract followed. Received Golden Globe Award for Most Promising Newcomer 1958.
PICTURES: Toward the Unknown (debut, 1956), The Girl He Left Behind, Shoot Out at Medicine Bend, Sayonara, Darby's Rangers, Up Periscope, Alias Jesse James (cameo), Cash McCall, The Children's Hour, Boys' Night Out, The Great Escape, The Thrill of It All, The Wheeler Dealers (Golden Globe nom. 1964), Move Over Darling, The Americanization of Emily, 36 Hours, The Art of Love, Mister Buddwing, A Man Could Get Killed, Duel at Diablo, Grand Prix, Hour of the Gun, The Pink Jungle, How Sweet It Is, Support Your Local Sheriff, Marlowe, A Man Called Sledge, Support Your Local Gunfighter, Skin Game, They Only Kill Their Masters, One Little Indian, The Castaway Cowboy, Health, The Fan, Victor/Victoria, Tank, Murphy's Romance (Academy Award nom.; Golden Globe nom. 1986), Sunset, The Distinguished Gentleman, Fire in the Sky, Maverick, My Fellow Americans, The Hidden Dimension, Twilight, Space Cowboys, Atlantis: The Lost Empire (voice), Divine Secrets of the Ya-Ya Sisterhood, The Notebook, The Ultimate Gift, The Magic Shoe, Terra (voice).
TELEVISION: *Movies:* The Rockford Files (pilot), The New Maverick (pilot), The Long Summer of George Adams, The Glitter Dome, Heartsounds (Emmy nom.; Golden Globe nom. 1985), Promise (also exec. prod. Emmy Award; 1 other nom.;

Golden Globe nom. 1987), Obsessive Love, My Name Is Bill W. (also exec. prod., 2 Emmy nom. 1989), Decoration Day (Emmy nom.; Golden Globe Award 1991), Barbarians at the Gate (Emmy nom.; Golden Globe Award 1993), The Rockford Files: I Still Love L.A. (also co-exec. prod.), The Rockford Files: A Blessing in Disguise (also co-exec. prod.), The Rockford Files: Godfather Knows Best, The Rockford Files: Friends and Foul Play, The Rockford Files: Crime and Punishment, Dead Silence, The Rockford Files: Murder and Misdemeanors, Legalese, The Rockford Files: If It Bleeds...It Leads, The Last Debate, Roughing It. *Mini-series:* Space, Shake Rattle and Roll: An American Love Story. *Series:* Maverick (Emmy nom. 1959), Nichols, The Rockford Files (Emmy Award 1977; 4 other nom.), Bret Maverick (Emmy nom.; Golden Globe nom. 1982), Man of the People, Chicago Hope, God the Devil and Bob, First Monday, 8 Simple Rules. *Specials:* Sixty Years of Seduction, Lily for President, Breathing Lessons (Emmy nom.; Golden Globe nom. 1994). *Guest:* More than 114 appearances.

GAROFALO, JANEANE

Actress. b. Newton, NJ, Sept. 28, 1964. Created I Hate Myself Productions. Began standup comedy career in 1985.
PICTURES: Late for Dinner, Reality Bites, Suspicious, I Shot a Man in Vegas, Bye Bye Love, Coldblooded, Now and Then, Kids in the Hall: Brian Candy, The Truth About Cats and Dogs, The Cable Guy, Larger than Life, Sweethearts, Touch, Romy and Michele's High School Reunion, Cop Land, The Matchmaker, Clay Pigeons, Dog Park, Thick as Thieves, Steal This Movie, 200 Cigarettes, Half Baked, Permanent Midnight, Mystery Men, The Minus Man, Dogma, Can't Stop Dancing, The Bumblebee Flies Anyway, The Adventures of Rocky and Bullwinkle, Titan A.E. (voice), Wet Hot Summer, The Cherry Picker, Nobody Knows Anything, The Search for John Gissing, Big Trouble, Martin and Orloff, Manhood, Wonderland, Jiminy Glick in Lalawood, Ash Tuesday, Stay, Duane Hopwood, The Wild (voice), Southland Tales, The Ten, Ratatouille, Labor Pains, For Better or for Worse.
TELEVISION: *Movies:* Fantastic Newness, Outlaw Comic: The Censoring of Bill Hicks (narrator), Slice o' Life (exec. prod.), Nadine in Date Land, Law Dogs, Girl's Best Friend. *Mini-series:* Tales of the City. *Series:* Saturday Night Live, The Larry Sanders Show (2 Emmy nom., 1996, 1997), The Ben Stiller Show, TV Nation, Jimmy Kimmel Live (guest host), The West Wing, Freak Show, 24. *Guest:* More than 146 appearances.

GARR, TERI

Actress. b. Lakewood, OH, Dec. 11, 1949. Began career as dancer, performing S.F. Ballet at 13. Later appeared with L.S. Ballet and in original road show co. of West Side Story. Several film appearances as a dancer incl. Fun in Acapulco, Viva Las Vegas, What a Way to Go, Roustabout, etc. Did commercials; appeared in film Head written by a fellow acting student, Jack Nicholson. Career boosted by appearance on TV as semi-regular on The Sonny and Cher Show.
PICTURES: Maryjane, Head, The Moonshine War, The Conversation, Young Frankenstein, Won Ton Ton the Dog Who Saved Hollywood, Oh God!, Close Encounters of the Third Kind, Mr. Mike's Mondo Video, The Black Stallion, Witches' Brew, Honky Tonk Freeway, One from the Heart, The Escape Artist, Tootsie (Academy Award nom. 1983), The Sting II, The Black Stallion Returns, Mr. Mom, Firstborn, Miracles, After Hours, Full Moon in Blue Water, Out Cold, Let It Ride, Short Time, Waiting for the Light, The Player, Mom and Dad Save the World, Dumb & Dumber, Ready to Wear (Pret-a-Porter), Michael, A Simple Wish, The Definite Maybe, Changing Habits, The Sky is Falling, Kill the Man, Dick, Ghost World, Life Without Dick, Searching for Debra Winger (documentary), Expired, Unaccompanied Minors, Kabluey.
TELEVISION: *Movies:* Law and Order, Doctor Franken, Prime Suspect, Winter of Our Discontent, To Catch a King, Intimate Strangers, Pack of Lies, A Quiet Little Neighborhood A Perfect Little Murder, Stranger in the Family, Deliver Them From Evil: The Taking of Alta View, Fugitive Nights: Danger in the Desert, Murder Live!, Nightscream, Half a Dozen Babies, A Colder Kind of Death. *Mini-series:* Fresno. *Series regular:* Shindig, The Ken Berry "Wow" Show, (1972), Burns and Schreiber Comedy Hour, Girl With Something Extra, The Sonny and Cher Comedy Hour, The Sonny Comedy Revue, Good and Evil, Good Advice, Women of the House. *Specials:* The Frog Prince (Faerie Tale Theatre), Drive She Said (Trying Times), Paul Reiser: Out on a Whim, Mother Goose Rock 'n' Rhyme, The Whole Shebang, Aliens for Breakfast. *Guest:* More than 153 appearances.

GARRETT, BETTY

Singer, Actress. b. St. Joseph, MO, May 23, 1919. e. scholarships: Annie Wright Seminary, Tacoma, WA; Neighborhood Playhouse, N.Y. Sang in night clubs, hotels, Broadway shows: Call Me Mister (Donaldson Award, 1946), Spoon River Anthology, A Girl Could Get Lucky, Meet Me in St. Louis (1989). Motion Picture Herald, Star of Tomorrow, 1949. Starred in one woman show, Betty Garrett and Other Songs, beginning in 1974 and touring through 1993 (Bay Area Critics & LA Drama Critics Awards); also in autobiographical show, No Dogs or Actors Allowed (Pasadena Playhouse, 1989), So There! (with Dale Gonyear; Pasadena Playhouse, 1993). Given Life Achievement Award by Los Angeles Drama Critics Circle, 1995. With Ron Rapaport author of Betty Garrett and Other Songs—A Life on Stage & Screen, 1998.
PICTURES: The Big City (debut, 1948), Words and Music, Take Me Out to the Ball Game, Neptune's Daughter, On the Town, My Sister Eileen, Shadow on the Window, Broadway: The Golden Age By the Legends Who Were There, Trail of the Screaming Forehead, Dark and Stormy Night.
TELEVISION: *Movies:* All the Way Home, Who's Happy Now, The Long Way Home. *Series:* All in the Family (Golden Globe Award 1975), Laverne and Shirley, Becker (Emmy nom. 2003 as guest). *Guest:* More than 50 appearances.

GASPIN, JEFF

Executive. e. State Univ. of New York at Binghamton, undergraduate degree. NYU Graduate School of Business Administration, M.B.A. During Gaspin's first five years at NBC, he was v.p., programming & development and helped develop and launch "Dateline NBC." Before that, he was responsible for the expansion of the "Today" franchise to seven days. Gaspin also served as dir. of financial planning for NBC News, overseeing production finance for "Late Night with David Letterman" and "Saturday Night Live," as well as for NBC's TV stations division. Gaspin joined VH1 in 1996 and served as executive v.p., programming & production. He created the acclaimed program "Behind the Music." Under Gaspin VH1's ratings more than doubled and its profits increased fivefold. He was responsible for overall programming strategies, as well as program development, production, acquisition, scheduling, on-air talent, news and studio operations. Also developed under his watch were "Divas Live" and the hit series "Pop-up Video," "Rock and Roll Jeopardy," "Storytellers" and "Before They Were Rock Stars." He returned to NBC in March 2001 as executive v.p., alternative series, long-form, specials and program strategy. There, he led the network's unscripted programming division, specials, movies and mini-series and developed the hit NBC programs "Deal or No Deal," "The Apprentice," "Fear Factor" and "Biggest Loser." In Dec. 2002, Gaspin was named president of the Bravo cable network where he guided the day-to-day operation, programming, and marketing when the network was acquired by NBC. Among his accomplishments are "Queer Eye for the Straight Guy," which was Bravo's highest-rated show in its 23-year history, and "Project Runway," which continues to break ratings records for Bravo. Under Gaspin's direction in 2003, Bravo increased its subscriber base from 68 million to 76 million and more than doubled revenue and profits. In 2004 Gaspin became president of NBC Universal cable entertainment and cross-network strategy. He added digital content to his responsibilities in November 2005. Under Gaspin, the NBC Universal entertainment cable division posted its strongest performance ever and traffic to all of the television group's entertainment websites more than doubled. Gaspin had served as President of NBC Universal Cable and Digital Content since February 2007. Gaspin was named president and COO of the Universal Television Group, in July 2007. In 2009 Gaspin was promoted to Chairman of NBC Universal Television Entertainment and his postion expanded to complete oversight of the conglom's network and cable entertainment operations. He is a member of the boards of the A&E Networks and the Sundance Channel. Gaspin reports to Jeff Zucker, President and CEO of NBC Universal.

GATES, WILLIAM H.

Executive. b. Seattle, WA, Oct. 28, 1955. e. Harvard University (three years). Started computer programming at age 13. While at Harvard, Gates developed a version of the programming language BASIC for the first microcomputer - the MITS Altair in 1974. In 1975, left Harvard and formed Microsoft to develop software for personal computers with his childhood friend, Paul Allen. Today, Gates is chmn. of Microsoft Corporation, the worldwide leader in personal computer software, services and solutions. Microsoft products are integrally intermingled with entertainment delivery in the digital arena. In 2006, Microsoft announced a broad agreement with DIRECTV Inc. that would open new ways for consumers to enjoy their digital media in the networked home and on portable devices. Microsoft and DIRECTV are working together to enable digital content to flow between Windows-based PCs, DIRECTV devices, PlaysForSure™-based portable media devices and Xbox 360. As of 2008, Gates still serves as Microsoft chmn. but will devote more time to developing the worldwide Gates Foundation. Gates also founded Corbis, which is a comprehensive digital archive of art and photography from public and private collections around the globe. He is also a member of the bd. of directors of Berkshire Hathaway Inc., which invests in companies engaged in diverse business activities.

GAZZARA, BEN

Actor. b. New York, NY, Aug. 28, 1930. e. Studied at CCNY 1947-49. Won scholarship to study with Erwin Piscator; joined Actor's Studio, where students improvised a play, End as a Man, which then was performed on Broadway with him in lead. Screen debut (1957) in film version of that play retitled The Strange One.
THEATRE: Jezebel's Husband, End as a Man, Cat on a Hot Tin Roof, A Hatful of Rain, The Night Circus, Epitaph for George Dillon, Two for the Seesaw, Strange Interlude, Traveler Without Luggage, Hughie, Who's Afraid of Virginia Woolf, Dance of

Death, Thornhill, Shimada.
PICTURES: The Strange One (debut, 1957), Anatomy of a Murder, The Passionate Thief, The Young Doctors, Convicts Four, Conquered City, A Rage to Live, The Bridge at Remagen, Husbands, The Neptune Factor, Capone, Killing of a Chinese Bookie, Voyage of the Damned, High Velocity, Opening Night, Saint Jack, Bloodline, They All Laughed, Inchon, Tales of Ordinary Madness, Road House, Quicker Than the Eye, Don Bosco, A Lovely Scandal, Girl from Trieste, Il Camorrista, Tattooed Memory, Beyond the Ocean (also dir., s.p.), Forever, Farmer & Chase, The Shadow Conspiracy, The Big Lebowski, The Spanish Prisoner, Buffalo 66, Illuminata, Happiness, The Thomas Crown Affair, Summer of Sam, Believe, Undertakers Paradise, Squirrels to the Nuts, Paradise Cove, Jack of Hearts, Blue Moon, Very Mean Men, The List, Nella terra di nessuno, Home Sweet Hoboken, Believe, Dogville, The Shore, ...and Quiet Flows the Don, je t'aime Paris, Looking for Palladin, Holy Money, 13, Christopher Roth.
TELEVISION: *Movies:* When Michael Calls, Maneater, QB VII, The Death of Ritchie, A Question of Honor, An Early Frost (Emmy nom. 1986), A Letter to Three Wives, Police Story: The Freeway Killings, Downpayment on Murder, People Like Us, Lies Before Kisses, Blindsided, Love Honor & Obey: The Last Mafia Marriage, Parallel Lives, Fatal Vows: The Alexandria O'Hara Story, Valentine's Day, Angelo Nero, Tre Stelle, Un Bacio nel buio, Brian's Song, Hysterical Blindness (Emmy Award, 2003), Pope John Paul II, Donne sbagliate, Empire State Building Murders, L'onore e il rispetto. *Series:* Arrest and Trial, Run for Your Life (2 Emmy noms. 1968; 3 Golden Globe noms.). *Guest:* More than 91 appearances.

GEARY, ANTHONY
Actor. b. Coalville, UT, May 29, 1947. e. U. of Utah.
THEATRE: The Inspector General, The Glass Menagerie, The Wild Duck, Barabbas.
PICTURES: Blood Sabbath (debut, 1969), Johnny Got His Gun, Private Investigations, Disorderlies, Penitentiary III, You Can't Hurry Love, Pass the Ammo, Dangerous Love, It Takes Two, UHF, Night Life, Crack House, Night of the Warrior, Scorchers, Teacher's Pet (voice), 3 Day Test, Carpool Guy.
TELEVISION: *Movies:* Intimate Agony, Sins of the Past, The Imposter, Kicks, Perry Mason: The Case of the Murdered Madam, Do You Know the Muffin Man? Special: Intimate Portrait: Genie Francis, Sunset Beat. *Series:* Bright Promise, General Hospital (1978-83; 1990- 6 Emmy Awards; 8 other noms.). *Guest:* More than 70 appearances.

GEDRICK, JASON
Actor. b. Chicago, IL, Feb. 7, 1965.
PICTURES: Massive Retaliation (debut, 1984), The Zoo Gang, The Heavenly Kid, Iron Eagle, Stacking, Promised Land, Rooftops, Born on the Fourth of July, Backdraft, Crossing the Bridge, The Force, Power 98, Silent Cradle, Summer Catch, One Eyed King, Jesus-Mary and Joey, Shannon's Rainbow, Sinatra Club.
TELEVISION: *Movies/Specials:* Dare to Love, EZ Streets (pilot), The Last Don, The Third Twin, The Last Don II, The Partners, A Date with Darkness: The Trial and Capture of Andrew Luster, Rapid Fire, Hidden Places, Kings of South Beach, Wisegal, Depth Charge, The Christmas Choir, Sand Serpents. *Series:* Class of 96, Murder One, Sweet Justice, EZ Streets, Falcone, The Beast, Boomtown, Windfall, Desperate Housewives. *Guest:* More than 46 appearances.

GEESON, JUDY
Actress. b. Arundel, Sussex, England, Sept. 10, 1948. e. Corona Stage Sch. Began professional career on British TV, 1960.
THEATRE: Othello, Titus Andronicus, Two Gentlemen of Verona, Section Nine, An Ideal Husband.
PICTURES: To Sir with Love, Berserk, Here We Go Round the Mulberry Bush, Prudence and the Pill, Hammerhead, Three into Two Won't Go, The Oblong Box, Two Gentlemen Sharing, The Executioner, Nightmare Hotel, 10 Rillington Place, Doomwatch, Fear in the Night, It's Not the Size That Counts, Brannigan, Diagnosis Murder, The Eagle Has Landed, Carry On England, Dominique, Horror Planet, The Plague Dogs (voice), Young Goodman Brown, The Duke, Everything Put Together, Alien Fury: Countdown to Invasion, Spanish Fly.
TELEVISION: Sam Hill: Who Killed Mr. Foster?, Dance of Death, Lady Windermere's Fan, Room with a View, The Skin Game, Star Maidens, Poldark, She, The Coronation, Murder She Wrote, Astronomy (Triple Play II), The Secret Life of Kathy McCormick, Joan Crawford: The Ultimate Movie Star (documentary), To Sir, with Love II, Houdini, Alien Fury. *Mini-series:* Poldark II. *Series:* The Newcomers, Poldark, Star Maidens, Danger UXB, Breakaway, Mad About You, Gilmore Girls. *Guest:* More than 60 appearances.

GEFFEN, DAVID
Executive, Producer. b. Brooklyn, NY, Feb. 21, 1943. Began in mailroom of William Morris Agency before becoming agent there and later at Ashley Famous. With Elliott Roberts founded own talent management co. for musicians. Founded Asylum Records, 1970. Pres. then chmn. Elektra-Asylum Records 1973-76. Sold co. to Warner Communications for whom he headed film prod. unit. Vice-chmn. Warner Bros. Pictures, 1975; exec. asst. to chmn., Warner Communications, 1977; Member music faculty Yale U., 1978. Formed Geffen Records 1980 and Geffen Pictures. Producer of Broadway shows Master Harold... and the Boys, Cats, Good, Dreamgirls, Social Security, Chess. 1990, sold record co. to MCA, Inc. With Steven Spielberg and Jeffrey Katzenberg formed DreamWorks entertainment company, 1995. DreamWorks was purchased by Paramount in 2005, David Geffen will stay on with Viacom until the end of 2008. He annually makes entertainment industry "power lists," and with a net worth of more than $4.6 billion is one of the richest Americans as reported by Forbes magazine.
PICTURES: *(Exec. prod./producer):* Personal Best, Risky Business, Lost in America, Beetle Juice, Defending Your Life, The Last Boy Scout, After Hours, Little Shop of Horrors, Men Don't Leave, 1991: The Year Punk Broke (documentary), M. Butterfly, Joe's Apartment, Michael Collins, Beavis and Butthead Do America, The Butcher Boy, Interview with the Vampire: The Vampire Chronicles.
TELEVISION: *Series:* Beetlejuice (exec. prod.).

GELFAN, GREGORY
Executive. b. Los Angeles, CA, Aug. 7, 1950. Was entertainment atty. with Kaplan, Livingston et. al., and Weissmann, Wolff et. al. before joining Paramount Pictures in 1983 as dir. of business affairs. 1985, named v.p., business affairs, for M.P. Group of Paramount; 1989 promoted to sr. v.p. in charge of business affairs. 1994, named exec. v.p. in charge of business & legal affairs, 20th Century Fox. He became exec. v.p. & general counsel for Fox Filmed Entertainment and exec. v.p. of Fox Entertainment Group and promoted to Sr. v.p.

GELLAR, SARAH MICHELLE
Actress. b. New York, NY, April 14, 1977.
PICTURES: Over the Brooklyn Bridge, Funny Farm, High Stakes, I Know What You Did Last Summer, Scream 2, Small Soldiers (voice), She's All That (cameo), Simply Irresistible, Cruel Intentions, The It Girl, Harvard Man, Scooby Doo, Happily N'Ever After (voice), Scooby Doo2: Monsters Unleashed, The Grudge, Southland Tales, Revolver, Happily N'Ever After (voice), The Grudge 2, The Return, The Air I Breathe, Teenage Mutant Ninja Turtles (TMNT, voice).
TELEVISION: *Movies:* An Invasion of Privacy, Beverly Hills Family Robinson, 2004: A Light Knight's Odyssey (voice), The Wonderful Maladys. *Mini-series:* A Woman Named Jackie. *Series:* Girl Talk, Swans Crossing, All My Children (Emmy Award 1995, 1 other nom.), Buffy the Vampire Slayer (Golden Globe nom. 2001), Buffy: The Animated Series (voice), Robot Chicken. *Guest:* More than 117 appearances.

GELLER, BRIAN L.
Executive. b. New York, NY, Feb. 3, 1948. e. Queens Coll. Entered industry with Columbia Pictures as sls. trainee in 1966, leaving in 1968 to go with American Intl. Pictures as asst. branch mgr. In 1969 joined Cinemation Industries as eastern div. sls. mgr.; 1978, left to become gen. sls. mr. of NMD Film Distributing Co. 1982, named dir. of dist., Mature Pictures Corp. 1983, gen. sls. mgr., Export Pix.; with Cinema Group as east. sls. mgr.; joined Scotti Brothers Pictures as national sales, mgr. Joined 20th Century Fox sls. dep't. Member of Motion Picture Bookers Club of N.Y.; Variety Tent 35, Motion Picture Pioneers.

GENDECE, BRIAN
Producer, Executive. b. St. Louis, MO, Dec. 3, 1956. e. Drury College, Springfield, MO. From 1981-85, Director of Business Affairs, Weinstein/Skyfield Productions and Skyfield Management. 1986-87, dir. of business affairs, Cannon Films; 1987-89, v.p., creative affairs, Cannon Film Group; 1989 co-pres., Sheer Entertainment; indie first look Epic Prods.; 1991 owner The Gendece Film Co.; 1991-93, prod./dir., 21st Century Film; 1993-96, dir. of mktg., Raleigh Film and Television Studios. 1997-98, pres., G & G Prods. Currently runs Gendece Entertainment Group, Los Angeles. The group manages choreographers, director/choreographers, artistic directors, stylists, composers, actors, singers and dancers in the entertainment industry. Served for several years on the bd. of dir. of the L.A. Dance Foundation and is currently a bd. member of the Academy of Dance on Film.
THEATRE: Jack Klugman as Lyndon, The Bob Fosse Awards.
PICTURES: Runaway Train, Salsa, Rope Dancin', The Hunters, The American Samurai, Ceremony.

GEORGE, LOUIS
Executive, Producer. b. Karavas, Kyrenia, Cyprus, June 7, 1935. e. Kyrenia Business Acad., Cyprus (honored 1951). Emigrated to U.S. in 1952. After brief stint in Foreign Exchange Dept. of City National Bank, New York, served in U.S. Army, 1953-55. Entered industry in 1956 as theatre manager with Loew's Theatres in N.Y. metro area, managing Metropolitan, Triboro, New Rochelle, between 1958-66. 1966 joined MGM as dir. of int'l. theatre dept. 1969 promoted to dir. of world-wide non-theatrical sales. 1972-74 served as regional dir. of MGM Far East operations. 1974 left MGM to establish Arista Films, Inc., an indep. prod./dist. co. Pres. & CEO, Arista Films, Inc. Sold Arista Films library in 1996 and closed co. Currently, George is v.p., Intl. sales & acquisitions for Four Point Entertainment. Also bd. mem-

ber, American Film Marketing Association, chmn. Copyright and Film Security Committee of the association.
PICTURES: Slaughterhouse Rock, Buying Time, Violent Zone (exec. prod.), Angels Brigade, Final Justice, Surf II, Crackdown, Perfect Profile (exec. prod.).

GEORGE, SUSAN
Actress, Producer. b. Surrey, England, July 26, 1950. m. actor-prod. Simon MacCorkindale. e. Corona Acad.
PICTURES: Billion Dollar Brain, The Sorcerers, Up the Junction, The Strange Affair, The Looking Glass War, All Neat in Black Stockings, Twinky (Lola), Spring and Port Wine, Eye Witness (Sudden Terror), Die Screaming Marianne, Fright, Straw Dogs, Sonny and Jed, Dirty Mary Crazy Larry, Mandingo, Out of Season, A Small Town in Texas, Tintorera, Tomorrow Never Comes, Enter the Ninja, Venom, The House Where Evil Dwells, Jigsaw Man, Lightning: The White Stallion, Stealing Heaven (exec. prod. only), That Summer of White Roses (also exec. prod.), Diana & Me, In Your Dreams, City of Life, 1066.
TELEVISION: *Movies:* Swallows and Amazons, Adam's Apple, Weaver's Green, Compensation Alice, The Right Attitude, Dracula, Lamb to the Slaughter, Royal Jelly, Masquerade, Czechmate, Hotel, Blacke's Magic, Jack the Ripper, The Castle of Adventure,The House That Mary Bought (also exec. prod.). *Series:* Swallows and Amazons, Weavers Green, Cluedo, Stay Lucky, EastEnders. *Guest:* More than 64 appearances.

GERARD, GIL
Actor. b. Little Rock, AK, Jan. 23, 1943. e. Arkansas State Teachers Coll. Appeared in over 400 TV commercials. On stage in I Do! I Do!, Music Man, Stalag 17, Applause, etc.
PICTURES: Some of My Best Friends Are (1971), Man on a Swing, Hooch (also co-prod.), Airport '77, Buck Rogers in the 25th Century, Soldier's Fortune, Looking for Bruce, Mom Can I Keep Her?, The Stepdaughter.
TELEVISION: *Movies:* Ransom for Alice, Killing Stone, Help Wanted: Male, Not Just Another Affair, Hear No Evil, Johnny Blue (pilot), For Love or Money, Stormin' Home, International Airport, Final Notice, The Elite, Last Electric Knight, Beyond, Action Hero Makeover (also prod.), Nuclear Hurricane, Bone Eater, Reptisaurus, Ghost Town. *Series:* The Doctors, Buck Rogers in the 25th Century, Nightingales, Sidekicks, E.A.R.T.H. Force, Fish Police (voices), Days of Our Lives, Code 3 (host), Star Trek New Voyages: Phase II. *Guest:* More than 52 appearances.

GERBER, DAVID
Executive, Producer. b. Brooklyn, NY. e. U. of the Pacific. m. actress Laraine Stephens. Joined Batten, Barton, Durstine and Osborn ad agency in N.Y. as TV supervisor. Left to become sr. v.p. of TV at General Artists Corp. 1956, named v.p. Sales at 20th-Fox TV where sold and packaged over 50 prime-time series and specials. Entered indep. prod. with The Ghost and Mrs. Muir, followed by Nanny and the Professor. 1970 was exec. prod. of The Double Deckers, children's series made in England. 1972 joined Columbia Pictures Television as indep. prod.; 1974 was named exec. v.p. worldwide prod. for CPT. 1976 returned to indep. prod. 1985, joined MGM/UA TV broadcasting group in charge of worldwide prod. 1986, named president, MGM/UA Television. 1988-92, chmn & CEO, MGM/UA Television Prods. group. Formed Gerber/ITC Development in 1992. 1995, became pres., All American TV Production. Currently, pres., David Gerber Co.
PICTURES: *Executive producer:* The Night the Animals Talked, Cry for Justice, Runaways, The Price of Love.
TELEVISION: *Exec. producer: Movies:* Prudence and the Chief (prod. only), Oh Nurse!, Incident on a Dark Street, Jarrett, Police Story (Emmy Award, best dramatic series; 1 other nom. 1976), The Girl on the Late Late Show, Nakia, To Sir With Love, Ernie-Madge & Artie, The Turning Point of Jim Malloy, Medical Story, The Quest: The Longest Drive, The Lindbergh Kidnapping Case (Emmy nom. 1976), The Quest, Cover Girls, The Magnificent Magical Magnet of Santa Mesa, A Killing Affair, Keefer, Doctors' Private Lives, To Kill a Cop, The Courage and the Passion, Pleasure Cove, The Billion Dollar Threat, Power, Once Upon a Spy, Beulah Land, The Night The City Screamed, Terror Among Us, Cry for the Strangers, The Neighborhood, Women of San Quentin, Lady Blue, George Washington II: The Forging of a Nation, Police Story: The Freeway Killings, The Man Who Fell to Earth, Royce, Nothing Lasts Forever, We the Jury, Countdown: The Sky's On Fire, On the Line, The Lost Battalion, Flight 93 (Emmy nom. 2006). *Mini-series:* Doctors' Private Lives, George Washington, The Last Days of Pompeii. *Series:* The Ghost & Mrs. Muir, Here Comes the Double Deckers!, Cade's County, Police Story, Born Free, Police Woman, Joe Forrester, Gibbsville, Quark, David Cassidy: Man Undercover, Eischied, Walking Tall, Riker, Today's FBI, Seven Brides for Seven Brothers, Jessie, CBS Summer Playhouse,The Adventures of Sinbad, Tarzan, Kids are in Charge: Family Vacaton.
(d. January 2, 2010)

GERBER, MICHAEL H.
Executive. b. New York, NY, Feb. 6, 1944. e. St. Johns U., B.A., 1969; St. Johns U. School of Law, J.D., 1969. Atty, for Screen Gems, 1969-71; asst. secy. & asst. to gen. counsel, Columbia Pictures Industries, 1971-74; corporate counsel and secretary, Allied Artists Pictures, 1974, v.p. corporate affairs, Allied Artists, 1978; v.p., business affairs, Viacom Int'l. 1980-86; 1986-89, sr. v.p.; 1989-93, pres., first run, int'l. distrib. & acquisitions, Viacom Enterprises. He formed Gerber Entertainment Group in 1992 to dev. and package TV programs and features. In 1999, he created and is currently pres., CEO and chmn of board, Victory Entertainment Corp. (live action and 3-D animation, etc. for Internet and worldwide distribution); he holds the position of company chairman.

GERE, RICHARD
Actor. b. Philadelphia, PA, Aug. 29, 1949. e. U. of Massachusetts. Started acting in college; later joined Provincetown Playhouse and Seattle Repertory Theatre. Composed music for productions of these groups.
THEATRE: *B'way:* Grease, Soon, Habeas Corpus, Bent (Theatre World Award), A Midsummer Night's Dream (Lincoln Center). Off-B'way in Killer's Head. *London:* Taming of the Shrew (with Young Vic).
PICTURES: Report to the Commissioner (debut, 1975), Baby Blue Marine, Looking for Mr. Goodbar, Days of Heaven, Bloodbrothers, Yanks, American Gigolo, An Officer and a Gentleman (Golden Globe nom. 1983), Breathless, Beyond the Limit, The Cotton Club, King David, Power, No Mercy, Miles From Home, Internal Affairs, Pretty Woman (Golden Globe nom. 1991), Rhapsody in August, Final Analysis (also co-exec. prod.), Sommersby (also co-exec. prod.), Mr. Jones (also co-exec. prod.), Intersection, First Knight, Primal Fear, Runaway Bride, Dr. T and the Women, Steinbeck's Point of View, The Mothman Prophecies, Unfaithful, Chicago (Golden Globe Award best actor in m.p. musical or comedy, 2003), Shabana! Actor-Activist-Woman (documentary short, as himself), Shall We Dance?, Bee Season, Emperor Zehnder, The Flock, The Hoax, I'm Not There, The Hunting Party, Nights in Rodanthe, Brooklyn's Finest, Hachiko: A Dog's Story (also prod.), Amelia, State of the Union, The Emperor's Children, Henry and Me (voice), Woodland Cross.
TELEVISION: *Movies:* Chelsea D.H.O., Strike Force, And the Band Played On (Emmy nom. 1994). Freedom: A History of Us (doc.). *Guest:* More than 136 appearances.

GERTZ, JAMI
Actress. b. Chicago, IL, Oct. 28, 1965. e. NYU. Won a nationwide talent search competition headed by Norman Lear to cast TV comedy series Square Pegs. Following series studied at NYU drama school. Los Angeles theater includes Out of Gas on Lovers' Leap and Come Back Little Sheba. On NY stage in Wrong Turn at Lungfish. Also appeared in the Julian Lennon music video Stick Around.
PICTURES: Endless Love (debut, 1981), On the Right Track, Alphabet City, Sixteen Candles, Mischief, Quicksilver, Crossroads, Solarbabies, The Lost Boys, Less Than Zero, Listen to Me, Renegades, Silence Like Glass, Don't Tell Her It's Me, Sibling Rivalry, Jersey Girl, Twister, Seven Girlfriends, Lip Service, Lucky 13, Keeping Up with the Steins.
TELEVISION: *Movies:* This Can't Be Love, Gilda Radner: It's Always Something, Undercover Christmas, Fighting the Odds: The Marilyn Gambrell Story, Lost Holiday: The Jim & Suzanne Shemwell Story. *Series:* Square Pegs, Dreams, Sibs, ER, Ally McBeal (Emmy nom. 2001 as guest), Still Standing, Entourage.

GETTY, BALTHAZAR
Actor. b. California, Jan. 22, 1975. Spotted by talent agent while at Bel Air Prep School, winning lead role in remake of Lord of the Flies. Parents are actors Gisela Getty and Paul Getty, Jr. Great Grandfather is the late Jean Paul Getty.
PICTURES: Lord of the Flies (debut, 1990), Young Guns II, My Heroes Have Always Been Cowboys, The Pope Must Die, December, Where the Day Takes You, Halfway House, Red Hot, Dead Beat, Natural Born Killers, Don't Do It, Terrified, Judge Dredd, City Scrapers, White Squall, Habitat, Lost Highway, Four Dogs Playing Poker, Big City Blues, Center of the World, Macarthur Park, Run for the Money, Sol Goode, In God We Trust, Deuces Wild, Ladder 49, Slingshot, West of Brooklyn, Feast, The Tripper, Struggle.
TELEVISION: *Movie:* The Turn of the Screw, Ghost Whisperer (pilot), Dirtbags, Brothers & Sisters: Family Album. *Mini-series:* Traffic, Into the West. *Series:* Pasadena, Rosebud, Corsairs, Charmed, Brothers & Sisters, Alias.

GETZ, JOHN
Actor. b. Davenport, IA, Oct. 15, 1946. e. Univ Iowa, Amer. Conservatory Theatre (SF). Appeared on B'way in They're Playing Our Song, M. Butterfly. LA stage: Money & Friends.
PICTURES: The Happy Hooker, Tattoo, Thief of Hearts, Blood Simple, The Fly, The Fly II, Born on the Fourth of July, Men at Work, Don't Tell Mom the Babysitter's Dead, Curly Sue, Fortunes of War, Playmaker, A Passion to Kill, Painted Hero, Some Girl, Held for Ransom, A Day Without a Mexican, Living 'til the End, Hard Four, Zodiac, Superhero Movie, A Line in the Sand, The Social Network.
TELEVISION: *Movies:* Killer Bees, A Woman Called Moses, Kent State, Rivkin: Bounty Hunter, Muggable Mary: Street Cop, Not in Front of the Children, Concrete Beat, The Execution, In My Daughter's Name, Betrayal of Trust, Untamed Love, Awake to Murder, The Late Shift, Zenon: The Sequel, Hunger Point, Mystery Woman: Sing Me a Murder. *Mini-series:* Loose Change.

Series: Rafferty, Suzanne Pleshette is Maggie Briggs, MacGruder & Loud, Mariah, Maggie, Joan of Arcadia. *Guest:* More than 74 appearances.

GIANNINI, GIANCARLO

Actor. b. Spezia, Italy, Aug. 1, 1942. Acquired degree in electronics but immediately after school enrolled at Acad. for Drama in Rome. Cast by Franco Zeffirelli as Romeo at age of 20. Subsequently appeared in a play also directed by Zeffirelli, Two Plus Two No Longer Make Four, written by Lina Wertmuller.
PICTURES: Rita la Zanzara, Arabella, Anzio, Fraulein Doktor, The Secret of Santa Vittoria, Love and Anarchy, The Seduction of Mimi, Swept Away by an Unusual Destiny in the Blue Sea of August, Seven Beauties (Academy Award nom. 1977), How Funny Can Sex Be?, A Night Full of Rain, The Innocent, Buone Notizie (also prod.), Revenge, Travels with Anita, Lili Marleen, Lovers and Liars, La Vita e Bella, Picone Sent Me, Immortal Bachelor, American Dreamer, Fever Pitch, Saving Grace, New York Stories (Life Without Zoe), I Picari, The Sleazy, Uncle, Snack Bar Budapest, Oh King, Blood Red, Brown Bread Sandwiches, Killing Time, Short Cut, Night Sun, Criminals, Once Upon a Crime, Giovanni Falcone, Colpo di Coda, Celluloide, A Walk in the Clouds, New York Crossing, Come Due Coccodrilli, La Frontiera, Broken Dreams, The Scirocco Room, The Last Target, Blood of a Poet, La Lupa, Heaven Before I Die, Lorca, Mimic, Vuoti o Perdere, Una Vacanza all'inferno, Beyond the Garden, Heaven Before I Die, La Cena, The Room of the Scirocco, No Deposit No Return, Sweet Idleness, Milonga, Terra bruciata, A Night with Sabrina Love, The Whole Shebang, Welcome Albania, Ciao America, Hannibal, A Long Long Long Night of Love, CQ, Francesca and Nunziata, Viper, Joshua, Darkness, Ti voglio bene Eugenio, God's Bankers, The Council of Egypt, A Heart Elsewhere, Man on Fire, The Shadow Dancer, Raul, Shadows in the Sun, Casino Royale, Estrenando sueños, Bastardi, Milano-Palermo: il ritorno, Liolà, Bastardi, Quantum of Solace, Boogie Woogie, Up (voice dubbing), I Looked in Obituaries.
TELEVISION: *Movies:* Jacob, Francesca and Nunziata, Pope John XXIII (voice), My House in Umbria. *Mini-series:* David Copperfield, Sins, Nessuno Escluso, Voglia Di Volare, World Cup '98, Frank Herbert's Dune, L' Dracula, L' Onore e il rispetto. Many more Italian language productions.

GIANNOLI, XAVIER

Director.
PICTURES: J'aime beaucoup ce que vous faites, Dialogue au sommet, L'Interview (Cannes Film Fest. Palme d'Or, 1998), Demonlover (prod. only), Les Corps impatients (also s.p. & cinematographer), Clean (prod.), À cause de la nuit, La Belle image (also writer), Une aventure (also writer), Quand j'étais chanteur (also writer), Je suis parti de rien, In the Beginning (also writer s.p.).

GIANOPULOS, JAMES N. (JIM)

Executive. President of International and Pay Television, Twentieth Century Fox, 1992-1994. Pres., Fox International Theatrical Distribution, 1994-2000. Co-chair and CEO Twentieth Century Fox and Fox Filmed Entertainment, July 2000-present. Shares position with Thomas E. Rothman. Board member, USC Entertainment Technology Committee and KCRW for National Public Radio.

GIBBS, MARLA

Actress. b. Chicago, IL, June 14, 1931. e. Cortez Peters Business School, Chicago. Worked as receptionist, switchboard operator, travel consultant (1963-74) before co-starring as Florence Johnston on the Jeffersons (1974-85). Formed Marla Gibbs Enterprises, Los Angeles, 1978. Member of CA State Assembly, 1980. Image Award NAACP, 1979-83.
PICTURES: Black Belt Jones, Sweet Jesus Preacher Man, The Meteor Man, Border to Border, Foolish, Lost & Found, The Visit, Stanley's Gig, The Brothers.
TELEVISION: *Movies:* The Missing Are Deadly, Tell Me Where It Hurts, Nobody's Child, Menu for Murder, Lily in Winter. *Mini-series:* The Moneychangers. *Series:* The Jeffersons (5 Emmy nom.; Golden Globe nom. 1985), Checking In, 227, Happily Ever After: Fairy Tales for Every Child, 101 Dalmatians: The Series (voice), The Hughleys. *Special:* You Can't Take It With You. *Guest:* More than 91 appearances.

GIBSON, MEL

Actor, Producer, Director. b. Peekskill, NY, Jan. 3, 1956. Emigrated in 1968 to Australia with family. Attended Nat'l Inst. of Dramatic Art in Sydney; in 2nd yr. was cast in his first film, Summer City. Graduated from NIDA, 1977. Joined South Australian Theatre Co. in 1978, appearing in Oedipus, Henry IV, Cedoona. Other plays include Romeo and Juliet, No Names No Pack Drill, On Our Selection, Waiting for Godot, Death of a Salesman.
PICTURES: Summer City (Coast of Terror; debut, 1977), Mad Max, Tim, Chain Reaction (unbilled), Attack Force Z, Gallipoli, The Road Warrior (Mad Max II), The Year of Living Dangerously, The Bounty, The River, Mrs. Soffel, Mad Max Beyond Thunderdome, Lethal Weapon, Tequila Sunrise, Lethal Weapon 2, Bird on a Wire, Air America, Hamlet, Lethal Weapon 3, Forever Young, The Man Without a Face (also dir.), Maverick, Braveheart (also dir., co-prod.; 2 Academy Awards, Golden Globe nom.; DGA nom. 1996), Casper (cameo), Pocahontas (voice), Ransom (Golden Globe nom. 1997), Father's Day (cameo), Conspiracy Theory, Lethal Weapon 4, Payback, The Million Dollar Hotel, The Patriot, What Women Want (Golden Globe nom. 2001), We Were Soldiers, Signs, The Singing Detective (also prod.), Mad Max: Fury Road, Payback: Straight Up - The Director's Cut, Edge of Darkness, The Beaver, How I Spent My Summer Vacation (also s.p.). *Producer:* The Passion of the Christ, (also dir., s.p.), Paparazzi, Apocalypto (also dir., writer), Leonard Cohen: I'm Your Man (doc., exec. prod.).
TELEVISION: *Movies:* Wallace and Grommmit Go Chicken, Breaking the News, The Three Stooges (exec. prod.), Invincible (exec. prod.), Family Curse (exec. prod.), Evel (exec. prod.). *Mini-series:* Peace Out (exec. prod.). *Series:* The Sullivans, Punishment, The Oracle, Drama School, Clubhouse (exec. prod.), Complete Savages (exec. prod. also actor), *Specials/Documentaries:* The Ultimate Stuntman: A Tribute to Dar Robinson, Australia's Outback: The Vanishing Frontier (host), Wallace and Grommit Go Chicken, Breaking the News (narr.), Leonard Cohen: I'm Your Man, Another Day in Paradise (prod.), Carrier (series, exec. prod.). *Guest:* More than 150 appearances.

GIBSON, THOMAS

Actor. b. Charleston, SC, July 3, 1962.
PICTURES: Far and Away, Love & Human Remains, The Age of Innocence, Sleep with Me, Men of War, Barcelona, To Love Honor and Deceive, The Next Step, The Flintstones in Viva Rock Vegas, Eyes Wide Shut, Psycho Beach Party, The Broken Hearts Club: A Romantic Comedy, Stardom, Jack the Dog, Virginia's Run, Manhood, First Time Caller, Come Away Home, Berkeley, I'll Believe You.
TELEVISION: *Movies:* Lincoln, The Kennedys of Massachusetts, Tales of the City, Secrets, Night Visitors, Inheritance, The Devil's Child, Nightmare Street, More Tales of the City, A Will of Their Own, The Lost Empire, Brush with Fate, Evil Never Dies, Raising Waylon, Category 6: Day of Destruction, In From the Night. *Series:* As the World Turns, Another World, Chicago Hope, Dharma & Greg (2 Golden Globe nom.), Criminal Minds.

GILBERT, ARTHUR N.

Producer. b. Detroit, MI, Oct. 17, 1920. Lt., Enlisted USMC Oct. 1941. In USMC for 37 years and also in reserves. e. U. of Chicago, 1946. Special investigator for Michigan LCC, 1946-53; world sales dir., Gen. Motors, Cadillac Div., 1953-59; investments in mot. pictures and hotel chains, 1957-70; produced motion pictures with associates beginning in 1965: exec. prod., Mondo Hollywood, 1965; exec. prod. Jeannie-Wife Child, 1966; assoc. prod., The Golden Breed, 1967 and many more. 1970-80, exec. prod. Jaguar Pictures Corp; Columbia, 1981-86; Indi Pic. Corp. Also exec. v.p. for Pacific Western Tours. Producer at Jonte Prods., U.S., France and U.K., 1990-present.
PICTURES: (prod./exec. prod.): The Glory Stompers, Fire Grass, Cycle Savages, Bigfoot, Incredible Two-Headed Transplant, Balance of Evil, The Life and Curious Death of Marilyn Monroe.

GILBERT, BRUCE

Producer. b. Los Angeles, CA, March 28, 1947. e. U. of California. Pursued film interests at Berkeley's Pacific Film Archive; in summer involved in production in film dept. of San Francisco State U. Founded progressive pre-school in Bay Area. Became story editor in feature film division of Cine-Artists; involved in several projects, including Aloha, Bobby and Rose. Formally partnered with Jane Fonda in IPC Films, Inc., then pres., American Filmworks.
PICTURES: Coming Home (assoc. prod.), The China Syndrome (exec. prod.). *Producer:* Nine to Five, On Golden Pond (Academy Award nom. 1982), Rollover, The Morning After, Man Trouble, Jack the Bear.
TELEVISION: *Movies:* The Dollmaker (exec. prod., (Emmy Award nom. 1984), By Dawn's Early Light (writer, exec. prod.), Red Alert (exec. prod). Glory & Honor (exec. prod). *Series:* Nine to Five (exec. prod.).

GILBERT, LEWIS, CBE

Producer, Writer, Director, Former Actor. b. London, England, Mar. 6, 1920. In RAF, W.W.II. Screen debut, 1932; asst. dir. (1930-39) with London Films, Assoc. British, Mayflower, RKO-Radio; from 1939-44 attached U.S. Air Corps Film Unit (asst. dir., Target for Today). In 1944 joined G.B.I. as writer and dir. In 1948, Gainsborough Pictures as writer, dir., 1949; Argyle Prod. 1950; under contract Nettlefold Films, Ltd. as dir.
PICTURES: *Actor.* Under One Roof, I Want to Get Married, Haunting Melody. *Director:* The Little Ballerina, Marry Me (s.p. only), Once a Sinner, Scarlet Thread, There Is Another Sun, Time Gentlemen Please, Emergency Call, Cosh Boy, Johnny on the Run, Albert R.N., The Good Die Young, The Sea Shall Not Have Them, Reach for the Sky, Cast a Dark Shadow, The Admirable Crichton, Carve Her Name with Pride, A Cry from the Street, Ferry to Hong Kong, Sink the Bismarck, Light Up the Sky, The Greengage Summer, H.M.S. Defiant, The Patriots, Spare the Rod, The Seventh Dawn, Alfie (Academy Award nom.; Golden Globe nom. 1967), You Only Live Twice, The Adventurers,

Friends (also prod., story), Paul & Michelle (also prod., story), Operation Daybreak, Seven Nights in Japan, The Spy Who Loved Me, Moonraker, Educating Rita (also prod.), Not Quite Paradise, Shirley Valentine (also prod.), Stepping Out (also co-prod.), Haunted (also s.p.), Before You Go.

GILBERT, MELISSA

Actress. b. Los Angeles, CA, May 8, 1964. m. actor Bruce Boxleitner. Made debut at age of 3 in TV commercial. Comes from show business family: father, late comedian Paul Gilbert; mother, former dancer-actress Barbara Crane. Grandfather, Harry Crane created The Honeymooners. NY Off-B'way debut A Shayna Madel (1987; Outer Critics Circle & Theatre World Awards). Two-time president of the Screen Actors Guild. Chose not to run for re-election in 2005.
PICTURES: Sylvester (debut, 1985), Ice House, Famous, Heart of the Storm, Betrayal of Trust.
TELEVISION: *Movies:* Christmas Miracle in Caulfield U.S.A., The Miracle Worker (Emmy nom. 1980), Splendor in the Grass, Choices of the Heart, Choices, Penalty Phase, Family Secrets, Killer Instincts, Without Her Consent, Forbidden Nights, Blood Vows: The Story of a Mafia Wife, Joshua's Heart, Donor, The Lookalike, With a Vengeance, Family of Strangers, With Hostile Intent, Shattered Trust: The Shari Karney Story, House of Secrets, Dying to Remember, Babymaker: The Dr. Cecil Jacobson Story, Against Her Will: The Carrie Buck Story, With Hostile Intent, Cries From the Heart, A Touch of Truth, Zoya, Seduction in a Small Town, Christmas in My Home Town, Childhood Sweetheart?, Me & My Hormones (dir.), A Holiday for Love, Her Own Rules, Murder at 75 Birch, The Soul Collector, Two Babies: Switched at Birth, A Vision of Murder: The Story of Donielle, Sanctuary, Then Came Jones, Hollywood Wives: The New Generation, Thicker Than Water, Sacrifices of the Heart. *Series:* Little House on the Prairie (Golden Globe nom. 1981), Stand By Your Man, Sweet Justice, The Adventures of Batman & Robin (voice). *Guest:* More than 110 appearances.

GILER, DAVID

Producer, Writer, Director. b. New York, NY. Son of Bernie Giler, screen and TV writer. Began writing in teens; first work an episode for ABC series, The Gallant Men. Feature film career began as writer on Myra Breckenridge (1970).
PICTURES: *Writer:* The Parallax View (WGA nom. 1975), Fun with Dick and Jane (s.p. 1977), The Blackbird (also dir.), Southern Comfort (also prod.). *Prod.:* Aliens (story), Rustlers' Rhapsody, Let It Ride, Alien3 (exec. prod., also writer), Demon Knight, Bordello of Blood, Ritual, Alien: Resurrection, Undisputed, AVP: Alien Vs. Predator, AVPR: Aliens vs Predator - Requiem.
TELEVISION: *Movies/Exec. Prod:* Two-Fisted Tales, Girls in Prison, Dragstrip Girl, W.E.I.R.D. World. *Series/Writer:* The Kraft Theatre, The Gallant Men, Burke's Law, The Man from U.N.C.L.E., The Girl from U.N.C.L.E., Tales From the Crypt (exec. prod.), Perversions of Science (prod.).

GILLIAM, TERRY

Writer, Director, Actor, Animator. b. Minneapolis, MN, Nov. 22, 1940. e. Occidental Coll. Freelance writer and illustrator for various magazines and ad agencies before moving to London. Animator for BBC series Do Not Adjust Your Set, We Have Ways of Making You Laugh. Member, Monty Python's Flying Circus (1969-76). Books incl. numerous Monty Python publications. Honorary degrees: DFA Occidental Col. 1987, DFA Royal Col. of Art 1989. Received Art Dir. Guild Award for Contribution to Cinematic Imagery Award 2007.
PICTURES: And Now for Something Completely Different (animator, co-s.p., actor), Monty Python and the Holy Grail (co-dir., co-s.p., actor, animator), Jabberwocky (dir., co-s.p.), Life of Brian (actor, co-s.p., animator), The Do It Yourself Animation Film, Time Bandits (prod., dir., co-s.p.), Monty Python Live at the Hollywood Bowl (actor, co-s.p., animator, designer), The Miracle of Flight (animator, s.p.), Monty Python's The Meaning of Life (co-s.p., actor, animator), Spies Like Us (actor), Brazil (Academy Award nom. 1986; co-s.p., dir.), The Adventures of Baron Munchausen (dir., co-s.p.), The Fisher King (Golden Globe nom. 1992; dir.), Twelve Monkeys (dir.), Fear and Loathing in Las Vegas (dir., s.p.), Lost in La Mancha (actor only), The Piano Tuner of Earthquakes (exec. prod.), Good Omens (dir., s.p.), The Brothers Grimm, Tideland, The Imaginarium of Doctor Parnassus (writer, dir.), The Man Who Killed Don Quixote (writer, dir.).
TELEVISION: *Movie:* Pleasure at Her Majesty's. *Series:* Monty Python's Flying Circus (also animator, dir.), Do Not Adjust Your Set, We Have Ways of Making You Laugh, The Mart Feldman Comedy Machine, The Last Machine (1995). *Guest:* More than 111 appearances.

GILMORE, WILLIAM S.

Producer. b. Los Angeles, CA, March 10, 1934. e. U. of California at Berkeley. Started career in film editing before becoming asst. dir. and prod. mgr. at Universal Studios, where worked on 20 feature films. Headed prod. for Mirisch Co. in Europe; then to Zanuck/Brown Co. as exec. in chg. prod. Sr. v.p./prod. of Filmways Pictures, supervising literary development, prod. and post-prod.
PICTURES: Jaws (prod. exec.), The Sugarland Express (prod. exec.), The Last Remake of Beau Geste, Defiance, Deadly Blessing, Tough Enough, Against All Odds, White Nights, Little Shop of Horrors, The Man in the Moon, The Player, A Few Good Men, Watch It, The Sandlot, Curse of the Starving Class, Fire Down Below, A Soldier's Sweetheart, Down, Roper & Goodie, Before the Devil Knows You're Dead, Main Street (line prod.).
TELEVISION: *Movies:* Just Me and You, One in a Million--The Ron Leflore Story, The Legend of Walks Far Woman, S.O.S. Titanic, Another Woman's Child, Women and Men: Stories of Seduction, Women & Men 2: In Love There Are No Rules, Silent Predators (co-exec. prod, s.p.), The Circuit (exec. prod.).

GILULA, STEPHEN

Executive. b. Herrin, IL, Aug. 20, 1950. e. Stanford U. Gilula began his career as a film booker/buyer at United Artists Theatre Circuit in San Francisco. He co-founded Landmark Theatres in 1974 and served as its president and CEO from 1974-1998. He grew the company from one screen, the NuArt Theatre in West Los Angeles, to a national chain of more than 140 screens, dominating specialty film exhibition. Gilula spent five years on the bd. of directors and executive committee of the National Association of Theatre Owners (NATO) and served as chairman of NATO of California/Nevada for six years. In that capacity, he supervised the expansion and management of ShoWest, the world's largest convention of theatre owners. In 2000, Gilula became Fox Searchlight Picture's president of distribution and was promoted to co-COO in 2006 with Nancy Utley who had been Searchlight's marketing president since 1999. The two, along with Searchlight President Peter Rice, have presided over the label's most successful releases to date, including the Academy Award®-winning "Sideways," which won the 2005 Oscar® for Best Adapted Screenplay and was nominated for four additional Oscars® including Best Picture. Other successful Searchlight films have included "Little Miss Sunshine," "Thank You For Smoking," "Garden State," "Napoleon Dynamite," "Bend It Like Beckham," "The Last King of Scotland," and "Juno," which grossed more than $100 million at the box office, a Searchlight record.

GINNANE, ANTONY I.

Executive, Producer. b. 1949. e. Melbourne U (law), 1976. In 1977, formed joint venture with financier William Fayman for Australian film production and distribution. 1981, established company Film and General Holdings Inc. for locating film projects/financing. Then, became pres. of Imparato Fay Management in Glendale, CA. Currently is president of IFM Film Associates, which handles worldwide distribution in all media of film, TV fiction and factual content. Will manage production and co-financing arrangements and provide co-production consulting services. IFM specializes in Australia, New Zealand, Canada and Eastern Europe, with budgets from $100,000 to $10 million.
PICTURES: *Producer or Exec. Prod:* Sympathy in Summer (debut, 1970; also dir.), Fantasm, Patrick, Snapshot, Thirst, Harlequin, Race for the Yankee Zephyr, Strange Behavior, Turkey Shoot, Prisoners, Second Tim Lucky, Mesmerized, Dark Age, Slate Wyn & Me, Initiation, High Tide, The Lighthorsemen, Time Guardian, Incident at Raven's Gate, The Everlasting Secret Family, The Dreaming, Grievous Bodily Harm, Boundaries of the Heart, Killer Instinct, Savage Justice, Outback, A Case of Honor, Siege of Firebase Gloria, Driving Force, Demonstone, Fatal Sky, No Contest, Screamers, Bonjour Timothy, The Whole of the Moon, Men with Guns, The Truth About Juliet, Sally Marshall Is Not an Alien, Reluctant Angel, Reaper, Captive, Torrent, Sweet Revenge, fIXers, Black Light, Blind Heat, The Big Red (doc.), Look @ Me, Ten Dead Men, Arctic Blast.
TELEVISION: *Movies:* Great Expectations—The Untold Story, Lawless: Dead Evidence, Lawless: Beyond Justice, The Risen. *Mini-series:* Emma: Queen of the South Seas.

GIRARDOT, ANNIE

Actress. b. Paris, France, Oct. 25, 1931. Studied nursing. Studied acting at the Paris Conservatory, made her acting debut with the Comedie Franccaise. Has acted on the French stage and in reviews in the Latin Quarter.
PICTURES: Trezie a Table (debut, 1955), Speaking of Murder, Inspector Maigret, Love and the Frenchwoman, Rocco and His Brothers, Le Rendezvous, Crime Does Not Pay, Vice and Virtue, The Organizer, La Bonne Soupe (Careless Love), Male Companion, The Dirty Game, The Witches, Live for Life, Les Galoises Bleues, Dillinger Is Dead, The Seed of Man, Trois Chambres a Manhattan (Venice Film Fest. Award), The Story of a Woman, Love Is a Funny Thing, Shock!, Where THere's Smoke, Juliette et Juliette, The Slap, It Is Raining in Santiago, No Time for Breakfast (Cesar Award), Dear Inspector, The Skirt Chaser, Traffic Jam, Jupiter's Thigh, Five Days in June, La Vie Continue, Prisonniers, Comedie D'Amour, Girls With Guns, Les Miserables, Les Bidochons, When I Will Be Gone, Preference, T'Aime, La Pianiste, This Is My Body, Epstein's Night, Des fleurs pour Irma, Hidden.
TELEVISION: 39 Various European productions. *Guest:* More than 65 appearances.

GISH, ANNABETH

Actress. b. Albuquerque, NM, Mar. 13, 1971. e. Duke U ('93). Started acting at age 8; several TV commercials in Iowa.
PICTURES: Desert Bloom, Hiding Out, Mystic Pizza, Shag,

Coupe de Ville, Wyatt Earp, The Red Coat, Nixon, The Last Supper, Beautiful Girls, Steel, S.L.C. Punk!, Double Jeopardy, Race to Space, Morning, Pursuit of Happiness, Buying the Cow, Knots, The Celestine Prophecy, Mojave Phone Booth.
TELEVISION: *Movies:* Hero in the Family, When He's Not a Stranger, The Last to Go, Lady Against the Odds, Silent Cries, Don't Look Back, to Live Again, God's New Plan, Different, The Way She Moves, Sealed With a Kiss, A Death in the Family, Life on Liberty Street, Detective, Desperation, Candles on Bay Street, At Risk, The Front. *Mini-series:* Scarlett, True Women, Who Named the Knife. *Series:* Courthouse, The X-Files, The West Wing, Brotherhood.

GIVENS, ROBIN
Actress. b. New York, NY, Nov. 27, 1964. e. Sarah Lawrence Col., Harvard Univ. Graduate Sch. of Arts & Sciences. While at college became model, made appearances on daytime dramas The Guiding Light and Loving.
PICTURES: A Rage in Harlem (debut, 1991), Boomerang, Foreign Student, Blankman, Dangerous Intentions, Secrets, Everything's Jake, Elite, The Expendables, Book of Love, A Cold Day in August, Antibody, Head of State, A Good Night to Die, 4-Bidden, Little Hercules in 3-D, The Family That Preys, Tulips, Under the Influence, Queen of Media, Enemies Among Us.
TELEVISION: *Movies:* Beverly Hills Madam, The Women of Brewster Place, The Penthouse, Dangerous Intentions, A Face to Die For, Spinning Out of Control, Hollywood Wives: The New Generation, Captive Hearts, The Verdict. *Series:* Head of the Class, Angel Street, Courthouse, Sparks, Hollywood Squares, Forgive or Forget (host), House of Payne, My Parents, My Sister & Me. *Guest:* More than 52 appearances.

GLASER, PAUL MICHAEL
Actor, Director. b. Cambridge, MA, March 25, 1943. e. Tulane U., Boston U., M.A. Did five seasons in summer stock before starting career in New York, making stage debut in Rockabye Hamlet in 1968. Appeared in numerous off-B'way plays and got early TV training as regular in daytime series, Love of Life and Love Is a Many Splendored Thing.
PICTURES: *Actor:* Fiddler on the Roof, Butterflies Are Free, Phobia, Something's Gotta Give, Starsky & Hutch Lego: The Adventures of Clutch Powers. *Director:* Band of the Hand, The Running Man, The Cutting Edge, The Air Up There, Kazaam (also prod., story), F-Stops, Game Theory (video doc. short).
TELEVISION: *Movies:* Trapped Beneath the Sea, The Great Houdinis, Wail Till Your Mother Gets Home!, Princess Daisy, Jealousy, Attack on Fear, Single Bars Single Women, Amazons (dir. only), And Never Let Her Go, Ladies Night, Faceless. *Series:* Starsky and Hutch, The Agencey (dir. episodes), Miami Vice (Emmy nom.; DGA nom. 1985), Robbery Homicide Division (dir. episodes), Third Watch (dir. episodes), The Lyon's Den (dir.), Las Vegas (dir.). *Guest:* More than 65 appearances.

GLASS, PHILIP
Composer, Actor, Writer. b. Baltimore, MD, Jan. 31, 1937.
PICTURES: Cenere, Chappaqua, Mark Di Suvero Sculptor, Four American Composers (also actor), Koyaanisqatsi, High Wire, Mishima: A Life in Four Chapters, Dead End Kids, Hamburger Hill, Einstein on the Beach: The Changing Image of Opera, The Thin Blue Line, Powaqqatsi, Le Chiesa, Mindwalk, Closet Land, Anima Mundi, Candyman, A Brief History of Time, Niki de Saint Phalle: Wer ist das Monster-du oder ich?, Jenipapo, Candyman: Farewell to the Flesh, The Secret Agent, Absence Stronger Than Presence, Bent, Kundun (Academy Award nom., Golden Globe nom., LA Film Critics Award, Best Musical Score, 1998), The Truman Show (actor, Golden Globe Award, Best Original Score, 1999), The Man in the Bath, The Source, The Eden Myth, Armonie dell'Estasi, Naqoyqatsi, The Baroness & the Pig, Special Delivery, The Hours (Academy Award nom.; Golden Globe nom. 2003), Secret Window, Taking Lives, Partition, Going Upriver: The Long War of John Kerry, Undertow, The Illusionist, The Reaping, No Reservations, Les Animaux amoureux (documentary), Pandemic: Facing AIDS (Emmy Award nom. 2004), Notes on a Scandal (Academy Award nom. 2007), Cassandra's Dream, Watchmen (soundtrack writer), Mr. Nice, The Goldberg Variations. *Documentaries:* Roving Mars,The Fog of War: Eleven Lessons from the Life of Robert S. McNamara, Glass: Enron: The Smartest Guys in the Room, A Portrait of Philip in Twelve Parts, Animals in Love, Objects and Memory, Certainty, Transcendent Man, When the Dragon Swallowed the Sun, Secret and Sacred: The Balinese Reincarnations. *Guest:* More than 52 appearances.

GLAZER, WILLIAM
Executive. b. Cambridge, MA. e. State U. of New York, Entered m.p. ind. with Ralph Snider Theatres 1967-69; General Cinema Corp. 1969-71; Loews Theatres 1971-73; Joined Sack Theatres/USA Cinemas 1973 as Dist. mgr.; 1974 Exec. Asst. to Pres.; 1976 Gen. Mgr.; 1980 V.P. Gen. Mgr.; 1982-86 Exec. V.P. Joined Interstated Theatres 1987 (Pres.); Fox Theatres 1993-95. m.p. industry consultant, 1988-present. In Sept. 2006, appointed to three-year term to the Broward (FL) Performing Arts Foundation. Past memberships: Bd. of Dir. Member of SMPTE; NATO (Exec. Bd.); Theatre Owners of New England (Pres. and Chairman)

GLEASON, LARRY
Executive. b. Boston, MA, Apr. 30, 1938. e. Boston College, M.A., 1960. Held various positions, western div., mgr., General Cinema Corp., 1963-73; gen. mgr., Gulf States Theatres, New Orleans, 1973-74; pres., Mann Theatres, 1974-85; joined DeLaurentiis Entertainment Group as pres., mktg./dist., 1985. Named sr. v.p., Paramount Pictures Corp, theatrical exhibition group, 1989. Named pres. Paramount Pictures Corp. theatrical exhib. group, 1991. Joined MGM/UA as pres. of Worldwide Distrib., 1994, a position he left in June 2001. In 2006, Gleason was retained by Big Sky Motion Pictures to negotiate and roll out the theatrical release of What Love Is. Past Memberships: Foundation of Motion Picture Pioneers v.p. Member, Variety Club, Will Rogers Foundation. Currently, Gleason is a member of the business advisory bd. of IndieVest Inc.

GLENN, CHARLES OWEN
Executive. b. Binghamton, NY, March 27, 1938. e. Syracuse U., B.A. in English & History, 1960; He is a also a graduate of the Joanne Barron/D.W. Brown School for the Dramatic Arts. U.S. Army, 1961-63. Asst. to dir. of adv., 20th Cent. Fox, 1966-67; asst. adv. mgr., Paramount, 1967-68; acct. supervisor & exec., MGM record & m.p. div., 1968-69; nat'l. adv. mgr., Paramount, 1969-70; nat'l. dir. of adv., Paramount, 1970-71; v.p. adv.-pub.-prom., 1971-73; v.p. marketing, 1974; v.p. prod. mktg., 1975; joined American Intl. Pictures as v.p. in chg. of adv./creative affairs, 1979. 1980, when Filmways took AIP over he was named v.p. in charge of worldwide adv./pub./promo.; joined MCA/Universal in 1982 as exec. v.p., adv.-promo.; 1984, appt. Orion Pictures adv.-pub.-promo. exec. v.p.; 1987, appt. Orion mktg. exec. v.p. In 1989 recipient, Outstanding Performance Award from Leukemia Society of Amer. for completing NYC Marathon. 1993, pres. mktg., Bregman/Baer Prods. In 2000, sr. v.p. of communications for Univision Online. In Sept. 2001 upped to v.p. of PR for Univision Communications Inc.; resigned post in June 2003. Founder of production company, GlennIris Entertainment with partner Barbara Cocks. Featured actor in 1993 film Philadelphia. Member: Acad. of Motion Picture Arts & Sciences, Motion Picture Pioneers & the Screen Actors Guild. Holder of NATO mktg. exec. of year (1983) award, Clio Award for U.S. adv. of Platoon.

GLENN, SCOTT
Actor. b. Pittsburgh, PA, Jan. 26, 1942. e. William & Mary Coll. Worked as U.S. Marine, newspaper reporter before going to New York to study drama at Actors Studio in 1968.
THEATRE: Off-B'way: Zoo Story, Fortune in Men's Eyes, Long Day's Jack Street, Journey into Night. B'way: The Impossible Years, Burn This, Dark Picture.
PICTURES: The Baby Maker (debut, 1970), Angels Hard as They Come, Hex, Nashville, Fighting Mad, More American Graffiti, Apocalypse Now, Urban Cowboy, Cattle Annie and Little Britches, Personal Best, The Challenge, The Right Stuff, The Keep, The River, Wild Geese II, Silverado, Verne Miller, Man on Fire, Off Limits, Miss Firecracker, The Hunt for Red October, The Silence of the Lambs, My Heroes Have Always Been Cowboys, Backdraft, The Player, Night of the Running Man, Tall Tale, Reckless, Edie and Pen, Courage Under Fire, Carla's Song, Lesser Prophets, Absolute Power, Larga Distancia, Firestorm, The Virgin Suicides, The Last Marshall, Vertical Limit, Training Day, Buffalo Soldiers, The Shipping News, Seabiscuit (documentary, voice), Puerto Vallarta Squeeze, Murder on the Hudson, Journey to the End of the Night, Camille, Freedom Writers, The Bourne Ultimatum, Surfer, Dude, Nights in Rodanthe, W., Magic Valley, Secretariat, Sucker Punch.
TELEVISION: *Movies:* Gargoyles, As Summers Die, Intrigue, The Outside Woman, Women & Men 2, Shadowhunter, Slaughter of the Innocents, Past Tense, Naked City: Justice with a Bullet, Naked City: A Killer Christmas, The Seventh Stream, A Painted House, Homeland Security, Faith of My Fathers, Code Breakers, Sons of Anarchy. *Mini-series:* Gone But Not Forgotten. *Series:* Mobile Suit Gundam, The American Experience (doc., narr.).*Guest:* More than 62 appearances.

GLESS, SHARON
Actress. b. Los Angeles, CA, May 31, 1943. m. producer Barney Rosenzweig. London stage: Misery.
PICTURES: Airport 1975, The Star Chamber, Ayn Rand: A Sense of Life (narr.), Bring Him Home, Once Fallen, Hannah Free.
TELEVISION: *Movies:* The Longest Night, All My Darling Daughters, My Darling Daughters' Anniversary, Richie Brockelman: Missing 24 Hours, The Flying Misfits, The Islander, Crash, Whisper in the Gloom (Disney), Hardhat and Legs, Moviola: The Scarlett O'Hara War, Revenge of the Stepford Wives, The Miracle of Kathy Miller, Hobson's Choice, The Sky's No Limit, Letting Go, The Outside Woman, Honor Thy Mother, Separated by Murder, Cagney & Lacey: The Return, Cagney & Lacey: Together Again, Cagney & Lacey: True Convictions, Cagney & Lacey: The View Through the Glass Ceiling, The Girl Next Door, Burn Notice. *Mini-series:* Centennial, The Immigrants, The Last Convertible, The State Within. *Series:* Marcus Welby M.D., Faraday and Co., Switch, Turnabout, House Calls, Cagney and Lacey (2 Emmy Awards, 1986, 1987; 4 other noms.; Golden Globe Award), The Trials of Rosie O'Neill (2 Emmy nom.; Golden Globe Award, 1 other nom.1991,), Queer As Folk, The State

Within, Burn Notice, Nip/Tuck (Emmy nom. 2008). *Guest:* More than 94 appearances.

GLICKMAN, DAN

Executive. e. B.A. in history from the Univ. of Michigan; J.D. from George Washington University. Member of the Kansas and District of Columbia Bars. Glickman began his career as a partner in the law firm of Sargent, Klenda and Glickman and worked as a trial attorney at the U.S. Securities and Exchange Commission. He also served as pres. of the Wichita, KS, School Board. He was elected to the U.S. Congress in 1976 and served for 18 years in the U.S. House of Representatives, representing Kansas' 4th Congressional District. During that time, he served on several committees: the House Agriculture Committee, including six years as chmn. of subcommittee over most federal farm policy issues; the House Judiciary Committee, where he was a leader on technology issues; and also served as chmn. of the House Permanent Select Committee on Intelligence. While in the House, he was a leading congressional expert on general aviation policy and wrote landmark legislation providing product liability protection for small airplane manufacturers. Glickman served as the Sec. of Agriculture from March 1995 until Jan. 2001. From Aug. 2002-Aug. 2004, Glickman was the director of the Institute of Politics located at Harvard University's John F. Kennedy School of Government. The Institute of Politics seeks to unite students, particularly undergraduates, with academics, politicians, activists, and policymakers on a nonpartisan basis, with the goal of stimulating and nurturing students' interest in public service and leadership. On Sept. 1, 2004, Glickman became pres. and CEO of the Motion Picture Association of America, Inc. Later became Chairman as well as CEO. As the organization's top executive, he serves as the voice and advocate of the American motion picture, home video and TV industries. In Sept. 2005 Glickman hired industry veteran Bob Pisano to be president and CEO of the MPAA, with Glickman retaining his Chairman/CEO title. 2010 Glickman resigned from his MPAA position and currently is pres. of Refugees International.

GLOBUS, YORAM

Producer. b. Israel, 1941. Came to U.S. 1979. Has co-produced many films with cousin and former partner Menahem Golan. Sr. exec. v.p., Cannon Group; Pres. and CEO Cannon Entertainment and Cannon Films; 1989 named chmn. and CEO Cannon Entertainment and officer of Cannon Group Inc.; then co-pres. Pathe Communications Corp. and chmn. and CEO Pathe Intl. Left MGM/Pathe in 1991.
PICTURES: *All as producer or exec. prod:* with Menahem Golan: Sallah; Trunk to Cairo; My Margo; What's Good for the Goose; Escape to the Sun; I Love You, Rosa; The House on Chelouch Street; The Four Deuces; Kazablan; Diamonds; God's Gun; Kid Vengeance, Operation Thunderbolt, The Uranium Conspiracy, Savage Weekend, The Magician of Lublin, The Apple, The Happy Hooker Goes to Hollywood, Dr. Heckyl and Mr. Hype, The Godsend, New Year's Evil, Schizoid, Seed of Innocence, Body and Soul, Death Wish II, Enter the Ninja, Hospital Massacre, The Last American Virgin, Championship Season, Treasure of Four Crowns, 10 to Midnight, Nana, I'm Almost Not Crazy..., John Cassavetes: The Man and His Work, The House of Long Shadows, Revenge of the Ninja, Hercules, The Wicked Lady, Sahara, The Ambassador, Bolero, Exterminator 2, The Naked Face, Missing in Action, Hot Resort, Love Streams, Breakin', Grace Quigley, Making the Grade, Ninja III-The Domination, Breakin' 2: Electric Boogaloo, Lifeforce, Over the Brooklyn Bridge, The Delta Force, The Assisi Underground, Hot Chili, The Berlin Affair, Missing in Action 2-The Beginning, Rappin', Thunder Alley, American Ninja, Mata Hari, Death Wish 3, King Solomon's Mines, Runaway Train, Fool for Love, Invasion U.S.A., Maria's Lovers, Murphy's Law, The Naked Cage, P.O.W.: The Escape, The Texas Chainsaw Massacre, Part 2, Invaders from Mars, 52 Pick-Up, Link, Firewalker, Dumb Dicks, The Nutcracker: The Motion Picture, Avenging Force, Hashigaon Hagadol, Journey to the Center of the Earth, Prom Queen, Salome, Otello, Cobra, America 3000, American Ninja 2: The Confrontation, Allan Quartermain and the Lost City of Gold, Assassination, Beauty and the Beast, Down Twisted, Duet for One, The Emperor's New Clothes, The Hanoi Hilton, The Barbarians, Dutch Treat, Masters of the Universe, Number One with a Bullet, Rumpelstiltskin, Street Smart, UnderCover, The Assault, Hansel and Gretel, Going Bananas, Snow White, Sleeping Beauty, Tough Guys Don't Dance, Shy People, Dancers, Red Riding Hood, King Lear, Braddock: Missing in Action III, Too Much, Die Papierene Brucke, Field of Honor, Barfly (exec. prod.), Surrender (exec. prod.), Death Wish 4: The Crackdown (exec. prod.), Gor (exec. prod.), Business as Usual (exec. prod.), Over the Top, Superman IV: The Quest for Peace, O Jerusalem (assoc. prod.). *Prod.:* Delta Force, Operation Crackdown, Manifesto, Stranglehold, Delta Force II, Cyborg, Step By Step, The Kitchen Toto, Doin' Time on Planet Earth, Kickboxer, Kinjite, A Man Called Sarge, The Rose Garden, The Secret of the Ice Cave, Mack the Knife, Journey to the Center of the Earth, Lambada, A Bit of Luck, Licking the Raspberry, Street Knight, Night Terrors, The Mummy Lives, Hellbound, American Cyborg: Steel Warrior, Chain of Command, Delta Force One: The Lost Patrol, Tipul Nimratz (TV series, prod.).
TELEVISION: *Movie:* Mortgage. *Series:* Tipul Nimratz. *Documentary:* Operation Thunderbolt: Entebbe.

GLOVER, CRISPIN

Actor. b. New York, NY, April 20, 1964. e. Mirman School. Trained for stage with Dan Mason and Peggy Feury. Stage debut, as Friedrich Von Trapp, The Sound of Music, Los Angeles, 1977. Wrote books, Rat Catching (1987), Oak Mot (1990), Concrete Inspection (1992), What It Is and How It Is Done (1995). Recorded album The Big Problem Does Not Equal the Solution-The Solution Equals Let it Be.
PICTURES: My Tutor, Racing with the Moon, Friday the 13th-The Final Chapter, Teachers, Back to the Future, At Close Range, River's Edge, Twister, Where the Heart Is, Wild at Heart, The Doors, Little Noises, Rubin and Ed, Thirty Door Key, What's Eating Gilbert Grape, Chasers, Even Cowgirls Get the Blues, Crime and Punishment, Dead Man, The People vs. Larry Flynt, Nurse Betty, Charlie's Angels, Crime and Punishment, Beaver Trilogy, Bartleby, Fast Sofa, Like Mike, Willard, Charlie's Angels: Full Throttle, What is It? (also dir., prod., s.p., editor), Drop Dead Sexy, Red Light Runners, The Wizard of Gore, It Is Fine. Everything Is Fine! (also dir., writer), Epic Movie, Beowulf, Freezer Burn: The Invasion of Laxdale, 9 (voice), Alice in Wonderland, Hot Tub Time Machine.
TELEVISION: *Movies:* Best of Times, The Kid with the 200 I.Q., High School U.S.A. *Special:* Hotel Room (Blackout).

GLOVER, DANNY

Actor. b. San Francisco, CA, July 22, 1947. e. San Francisco State U. Trained at Black Actors Workshop of American Conservatory Theatre. Appeared in many stage productions (Island, Macbeth, Sizwe Banzi Is Dead, etc.). On N.Y. stage in Suicide in B Flat, The Blood Knot, Master Harold... and the Boys (Theatre World Award).
PICTURES: Escape from Alcatraz (debut, 1979), Chu Chu and the Philly Flash, Out (Deadly Drifter), Iceman, Places in the Heart, Witness, Silverado, The Color Purple, Lethal Weapon, Bat-21, Lethal Weapon 2, To Sleep with Anger (also co-exec. prod.), Predator 2, Flight of the Intruder, A Rage in Harlem, Pure Luck, Grand Canyon, Lethal Weapon 3, Bopha!, The Saint of Fort Washington, Maverick (cameo), Angels in the Outfield, Operation Dumbo Drop, Gone Fishin', Wild America (cameo), Switchback, The Rainmaker (cameo), The Prince of Egypt (voice), Beloved, Antz (voice), Lethal Weapon 4, The Monster, Battu, Boesman and Lena, 3 AM, The Royal Tenenbaums, Just A Dream (dir. only), Saw, The Cookout, The Woodcutter, Woman Thou Art Loosed, Manderlay, Duplicity, The Shaggy Dog, Bamako (also exec. prod.), Barnyard (voice), Missing in America, Razor (also exec. prod.), Honeydripper, Be Kind Rewind, Shooter, Poor Boy's Game, Nujoma: Where Others Wavered, Dreamgirls, Toussaint (prod., dir.), Terra (voice), Gospel Hill, Por vida, Blindness (narr.), Night Train, Saw V, Soundtrack for a Revolution (doc., exec. prod.), Once Was Lost, The Harimaya Bridge (also exec. prod.), 2012, The Disappearance of McKinley Nolan (doc., exec. prod.), Son of Morning, Mooz-lum, Highland Park, Curse of the Dragon, Brother's Keeper, Bad Luck Snake Bite, Death at a Funeral, Dear Alice, Alpha and Omega, Playback (exec. prod.).
TELEVISION: *Movies:* Face of Rage, Mandela (Emmy nom. 1988), Dead Man Out, Buffalo Soldiers (also exec. prod.), Good Fences, Freedom Song (Emmy nom. 2000), The Exonerated. *Mini-series:* Chiefs, Lonesome Dove (Emmy nom. 1989), Queen, Life by the Numbers (host), Legend of Earthsea. *Series:* Storybook Classics (host), Civil War Journal (host),Courage (host, exec. prod.), The Real Eve, ER, Brothers & Sisters, Human Target (pilot). *Documentaries/Specials:* And the Children Shall Lead, How the Leopard Got Its Spots (narrator), A Place at the Table, A Raisin in the Sun, Override (dir. only), Shelley Duvall's Tall Tales and Legends: John Henry, Can't You hear the Wind Howl?: The Life & Music of Robert Johnson (voice), Scared Straight! 20 Years Later (voice), Just a Dream (Emmy nom. 2003), The John Garfield Story, The Hunger Heroes, The Real Eve, The Henry Lee Project (acting and prod.), XXI Century, Conakry Kas, Picture This: A Fight to Save Joe, In Pursuit of Happiness, Willie Francis Must Die Again, Africa Unite (narr. exec. prod.). *Guest:* More than 173 appearances.

GLOVER, JOHN

Actor. b. Kingston, NY, Aug. 7, 1944. e. Towson State Coll., Baltimore.
THEATRE: On regional theatre circuit; Off-B'way in A Scent of Flowers, Subject to Fits, The House of Blue Leaves, The Selling of the President, Love! Valour! Compassion! (also B'way; Tony Award, 1995). With APA Phoenix Co. in Great God Brown (Drama Desk Award), The Visit, Don Juan, Chermin de Fer, Holiday. Other NY stage: The Importance of Being Earnest, Hamlet, Frankenstein, Whodunnit, Digby. L.A.: The Traveler (L.A. Drama Critics Award), Lips Together Teeth Apart, Sorrows and Rejoicings.
PICTURES: Shamus, Annie Hall, Julia, Somebody Killed Her Husband, Last Embrace, Success, Melvin and Howard, The Mountain Men, The Incredible Shrinking Woman, A Little Sex, The Evil That Men Do, A Flash of Green, 52 Pick-Up, White Nights, Something Special, Masquerade, A Killing Affair, Rocket Gibraltar, The Chocolate War, Scrooged, Meet the Hollowheads, Gremlins 2: The New Batch, Robocop 2, Ed and His Dead

Mother, Night of the Running Man, In the Mouth of Madness, Schemes, Automatics, Batman and Robin, Love! Valour! Compassion!, Macbeth in Manhattan, Dead Broke, Payback, On Edge, Sex & Violence, Mid-Century, Sweet Union, Tricks, Walk Hard: The Dewey Cox Story (soundtrack performer).
TELEVISION: *Movies:* A Rage of Angels, The Face of Rage, Ernie Kovacs-Between the Laughter, An Early Frost (Emmy nom. 1986), Apology, Moving Target, Hot Paint, Nutcracker: Money Madness and Murder (Emmy nom. 1987), David, The Traveling Man (ACE nom.), Twist of Fate, Breaking Point, El Diablo, What Ever Happened to Baby Jane?, Dead on the Money, Drug Wars: The Cocaine Cartel, Grass Roots, Majority Rule, Assault at West Point, Dead by Midnight, The Tempest, Medusa's Child. *Mini-series:* Kennedy, George Washington, Nutcracker: Money, Madness & Murder. *Series:* Search for Tomorrow, The Adventures of Batman & Robin (voice), South Beach, Batman: Gotham Knights (voice), Brimstone, Smallville. *Specials:* An Enemy of the People, Paul Reiser: Out on a Whim, Crime and Punishment (Emmy nom. 1993). *Guest:* More than 74 appearances.

GLYNN, CARLIN

Actress. b. Cleveland, OH, Feb. 19, 1940. m. actor-writer-dir. Peter Masterson. Daughter is actress Mary Stuart Masterson. e. Sophie Newcomb College, 1957-58. Studied acting with Stella Adler, Wynn Handman and Lee Strasberg in NY. Debut, Gigi, Alley Theatre, Houston, TX 1959. Adjunct professor at Columbia U. film sch. Resource advisor at the Sundance Inst.
THEATRE: (NY debut, 1960) Waltz of The Toreadors, The Best Little Whorehouse in Texas (Tony, Eleanora Duse & Olivier Awards), Winterplay, Alterations, Pal Joey (Chicago; Jos. Jefferson Award), The Cover of Life, The Young Man From Atlanta (winner, Pulitzer Prize for Drama, 1995), Amazing Grace.
PICTURES: Three Days of the Condor, Continental Divide, Sixteen Candles, The Trip to Bgountiful, Gardens of Stone, Blood Red, Night Game, Convicts, Blessing, Judy Berlin, West of Here, Lost Junction.
TELEVISION: *Movies:* The Tenth Level, Day-O. *Mini-series:* A Woman Named Jackie. *Series:* Mr. President.

GODARD, JEAN-LUC

Writer, Director. b. Paris, France, Dec. 3, 1930. e. Lycee Buffon, Paris. Journalist, film critic Cahiers du Cinema. Acted in and financed experimental film Quadrille by Jacques Rivette, 1951. 1954: dir. first short, Operation Beton, followed by Une Femme Coquette. 1956, was film editor. 1957: worked in publicity dept. 20th Century Fox. Received the MPAA Governor's Award 2011.
PICTURES: *Director/Writer:* Breathless (A Bout de Souffle; feature debut, 1960), Le Petit Soldat, A Woman Is a Woman, My Life to Live, Les Carabiniers, Contempt, Band of Outsiders, The Married Woman, Alphaville, Pierrot le Fou, Masculine-Feminine, Made in USA, Two or Three Things I Know About Her, La Chinoise, Weekend, Sympathy for the Devil, Le Gai Savoir, Tout a Bien (co-dir.), Numero Deux, Every Man For Himself, First Name Carmen, Hail Mary, Aria (Armide segment), King Lear, Keep Up Your Right (also edit, actor), Nouvelle Vogue (New Wave), Helas Pour Moi (Oh Woe is Me). Germany Year, J.L.G. by J.L.G., The Kids Play Russian, Forever Mozart (also edit.), The Old Place, Eloge de l'Amour, Notre musique, je t'aime Paris, Socialisme.

GOLAN, MENAHEM

Producer, Director, Writer. b. Tiberias, Israel, May 31, 1929. e. NYU. Studied theatre dir. at Old Vic Theatre London, m.p. prod. at City Coll, NY. Co-founder and prod. with cousin Yoram Globus, Golan-Globus Prods., Israel, then L.A., 1962. Later Noah Films, Israel, 1963, Ameri-Euro Pictures Corp, before buying controlling share in Cannon Films, 1979. Sr. exec. v.p., Cannon Group; chmn. of bd., Cannon Ent. and Cannon Films. 1988, dir. and sr. exec. v.p. Cannon Group, chmn. and head of creative affairs, Cannon Entertainment when it became div. of Giancarlo Parretti's Pathe Communications Corp. Resigned March, 1989, to form 21st Century Film Corp as chmn. and CEO; ran company until company disbanded in 1996. Golan then headed New Cannon, Inc. (now called New Generation Films) through Aug. 2001. Golan remains active in the industry, working from Tel Aviv.
PICTURES: *Director/co-writer:* Kasablan, Diamonds, Entebbe (Operation Thunderbolt), Teyve and His Seven Daughters, What's Good for the Goose? Lepke, The Magician of Lublin, The Goodsend, Happy Hooker Goes to Hollywood, Enter the Ninja. *Producer-Writer-Director:* Mack the Knife, Hanna's War. *Producer-Director:* The Uranium Conspiracy, Delta Force, Over the Brooklyn Bridge, Over the Top, Crime & Punishment, Death Game, Open Heart. *Producer/Exec. prod.:* Sallah, Runaway Train, Sallah, Fool For Love, Maria's Lovers, Cobra, Evil Angels, I Love You Rosa, Body and Soul, Deathwish II, The Last American Virgin, That Championship Season, House of Long Shadows, Revenge of the Ninja, Hercules, The Movie Tales (12 children's fairy tales films), The Wicked Lady, Cobra, Barfly, Breakin', Missing in Action, Dancers, Surrender, Death Wish 4: The Crackdown, King Lear, Too Much, Powaqquatsi, Mercenary Fighters, Doin' Time on Planet Earth, Manifesto, Kinjite, Messenger of Death, Alien From L.A., Hero and the Terror, Haunted Summer, A Cry in the Dark, Delta Force-Operation Crackdown, A Man Called Sarge, Stranglehold: Delta Force II, Cyborg, The Rose Garden, Rope Dancing, The Phantom of the Opera, Escape to Grizzly Mountain, Rak Klavim Ratzim Hofshi.
TELEVISION: *Movies:* Hothouse (prod., dir.), Die Tunnelgangster von Berlin (dir.), Days of Love (prod.). *Series:* Love Hurts (actor).

GOLCHAN, FREDERIC

Producer. b. Neuilly sur Seine, France, Nov. 20, 1955. e. UCLA Film School, HEC in Paris, NYU Bus.Sch. Journalist/photographer for various European magazines. Worked for American Express, 1979-80. Started indept. investment banking firm, 1980-84. Started own production co., 1985. Directed Victory of the Deaf. V.P. French Hollywood Circle.
PICTURES: Flagrant Desire, Quick Change, Intersection, The Associate, Kimberly, All Men Are Mortal, Chaos Theory, Twelve (assoc. prod.).
TELEVISION: Freedom Fighter, Home by Midnight, In The Deep Woods.

GOLDBERG, LEONARD

Executive, Producer. b. Brooklyn, NY, Jan. 24, 1934. e. Wharton, U. of Pennsylvania. Began career in ABC-TV research dept.; moved to NBC-TV research div.; 1961 joined BBD&O ad agency in charge of overall broadcast coordinator. In 1963 rejoined ABC-TV as mgr. of program development. 1964-66, v.p., daytime programs. 1966, named v.p. in charge of network TV programming. Resigned in 1969 to join Screen Gems as v.p. in charge of prod. Left for partnership with Aaron Spelling in Spelling/Goldberg Prods.; later produced TV and theatrical films under own banner, Mandy Prods. 1986, named pres., COO, 20th Century Fox. Resigned, 1989. Currently, pres. of Mandy Films,Inc. and Panda Productions, Inc. which produce TV and feature films. Became of a director of the CBS Corporation in Jan. 2007.
PICTURES: *Producer:* All Night Long, WarGames, Space Camp, Sleeping With the Enemy, The Distinguished Gentleman, Aspen Extreme, Double Jeopardy, Charlie's Angels, Charlie's Angels: Full Throttle, Unknown White Male.
TELEVISION: *Movies:* Brian's Song (Peabody Award, Emmy Awards), The Daughters of Joshua Cabe (1972), No Place to Run, Say Goodbye Maggie Cole, Home for the Holidays, Every Man Needs One, The Chill Factor, Snatched, The Great American Beauty Contest, The Letters, The Bait, Satan's School for Girls Hijack, Letters from Three Lovers, The Affair, The Death Squad, The Girl Who Came Gift-Wrapped, Cry Panic, Savages, Death Sentence, Hit Lady, Death Cruise, Only With Married Men, The Daughters of Joshua Cabe Return, The Fireman's Ball, Murder on Flight 502, The Legend of Valentino, One of My Wives Is Missing, The New Daughters of Joshua Cabe, The Sad and Lonely Sundays, The Shrine of Lorna Love, The Boy in the Plastic Bubble, Fantasy Island, Little Ladies of the Night, Delta County USA, Fantasy Island II, Beach Patrol, Hart to Hart, This House Possessed, Paper Dolls, Deadly Lessons, Something About Amelia (Emmy Award, 1984), Sins of the Past, Beverly Hills Cowgirl Blues, Alex: The Life of a Child, Blood Sport, Love Letters, Runaway Virus, Critical Assembly, Limelight. *Series:* Firehouse, Chopper One, S.W.A.T., Starsky and Hutch, The Rookies, Family (Emmy nom. 1977, 1978, 1980), Fantasy Island, Hart to Hart, Charlie's Angels, T.J. Hooker, Paper Dolls, Class of '96.

GOLDBERG, WHOOPI

Actress. r.n. Caryn Elaine Johnson. b. New York, NY, Nov. 13, 1955. e. Sch. for the Performing Arts. Began performing at age 8 in N.Y. with children's program at Hudson Guild and Helena Rubenstein Children's Theatre. Moved to San Diego, CA, 1974, and helped found San Diego Rep. Theatre appearing in Mother Courage, Getting Out. Member: Spontaneous Combustion (improv. group). Joined Blake St. Hawkeyes Theatre in Berkeley, partnering with David Schein. Went solo to create The Spook Show, working in San Francisco and later touring U.S. & Europe. 1983 performance caught attention of Mike Nichols which led to B'way show (for which she received a Theatre World Award) based on it and directed by him. Founding member of Comic Relief benefits. Theatrical film debut in The Color Purple (1985; Image Award NAACP, Golden Globe). *Author:* Alice, Koi and the Kola Nuts, Book.
THEATRE: B'way prods. of Pippin, Hair, Jesus Christ Superstar. Living on the Edge of Chaos (tour, 1988), A Funny Thing Happened on the Way to the Forum, Whoopi (2004). Solo performance + playwright, Funny Girl, Thoroughly Modern Millie. *Off B'way:* Ma Rainey's Black Bottom. Host of her own radio show.
PICTURES: The Color Purple (debut, 1985; Academy Award nom.; Golden Globe Award 1986), Jumpin' Jack Flash, Burglar, Fatal Beauty, The Telephone, Clara's Heart, Beverly Hills Brats (cameo), Homer and Eddie, Ghost (Academy Award, Golden Globe Award, best supporting actress, 1991), The Long Walk Home, Soapdish, House Party 2 (cameo), The Player, Sister Act (Golden Globe nom. 1993), Wisecracks, Sarafina!, The Magic World of Chuck Jones, National Lampoon's Loaded Weapon 1 (cameo), Made in America, Sister Act 2: Back in the Habit, Naked in New York (cameo), The Lion King (voice), The Little Rascals, Corrina Corrina, Star Trek: Generations, Theodore Rex, The Pagemaster (voice), Liberation (narrator), Boys on the Side, Moonlight and Valentino, The Celluloid Closet, Bogus, Eddie, The Associate, Ghosts of Mississippi, An Alan Smithee Film: Burn

Hollywood Burn, How Stella Got Her Groove Back, The Rugrats Movie (voice), Monkey Bone, Get Bruce, The Deep End of the Ocean, Girl Interrupted, The Adventures of Rocky & Bullwinkle, More Dogs Than Bones, A Second Chance at Life (narr.), Mary Pickford: A Life on Film, Kingdom Come, Monkeybone, Rat Race, Golden Dreams, Searching for Debra Winger (documentary), You'll Never Wiez in This Town Again, Blizzard (voice), Baby Geniuses 2: Superbabies, Pinocchio 3000 (voice), Racing Stripes (voice), Sprung! The Magic Roundabout (voice), Doogal (voice), Farce of the Penguins (voice), Everyone's Hero, Earthbound, Toy Story 3 (voice).
TELEVISION: *Movies:* Kiss Shot, In the Gloaming, Cinderella, A Knight in Camelot, Leprechauns, Jackie's Back!, Alice in Wonderland, What Makes a Family, Willie Nelson: Live & Kicking, Ruby's Bucket of Blood (exec. prod.), Call Me Claus (also exec. prod.), It's a Very Merry Muppet Christmas Movie, Good Fences (also prod.), The Piano Man's Daughter (co-prod.), A Muppets Christmas: Letters to Santa. *Series:* Star Trek: The Next Generation, Bagdad Cafe, The Whoopi Goldberg Show (synd. talk show), Hollywood Squares (4 Emmy nom.), Foxbusters, Celebrity Dish, Strong Medicine (exec. prod., writer; developed by), Express Yourself, Whoopi (also exec. prod.), The Power Strikers (exec. prod.), Littleburg, Head to Toe (exec. prod.), Sketch Off (exec. prod.), Just for Kicks (exec. prod., writer), The View (co-host, Emmy Award 2009; 1 other nom.), Head Games (exec. prod.). *Specials:* Whoopi Goldberg Direct From Broadway, Comic Relief VII (Emmy nom. 1996), Whoopi: Back to Broadway - The 20th Anniversary (Emmy nom. 2005), Carol Carl Whoopi and Robin, Scared Straight: 10 Years Later, Funny You Don't Look 200, Comedy Tonight (host), My Past is My Own (Schoolbreak Special), Free to Be... a Family, The Debbie Allen Special, Cool Like That Christmas (voice), 34th Annual Grammy Awards (host), A Gala for the President's at Ford's Theatre (host), The 66th Annual Academy Awards (host, Emmy nom. 1994), The 68th Annual Academy Awards (host Emmy nom. 1996), America: A Tribute to Heroes, The 74th Annual Academy Awards (host), Beyond Tara: The Extraordinary Life of Hattie McDaniel (Emmy Award 2002), I Love Lucy's 50th Anniversary Special, The Word According to Whoopi (writer, exec. prod.). *Guest:* More than 338 appearances.

GOLDBLUM, JEFF

Actor. b. Pittsburgh, PA, Oct. 22, 1952. Studied at Sanford Meisner's Neighborhood Playhouse in New York. On B'way in Two Gentleman of Verona, The Moony Shapiro Songbook. Off-B'way: El Grande de Coca Cola, City Sugar, Twelfth Night.
PICTURES: Death Wish (debut, 1974), California Split, Nashville, Next Stop Greenwich Village, St. Ives, Special Delivery, The Sentinel, Annie Hall, Between the Lines, Remember My Name, Thank God It's Friday, Invasion of the Body Snatchers, Threshold, The Big Chill, The Right Stuff, The Adventures of Buckaroo Banzai, Into the Night, Silverado, Transylvania 6-5000, The Fly, Beyond Therapy, Vibes, Earth Girls Are Easy, Twisted Obsession, The Tall Guy, Mr. Frost, The Player, Deep Cover, The Favor the Watch and the Very Big Fish, Fathers and Sons, Jurassic Park, Hideaway, Nine Months, Powder, The Great White Hype, Independence Day, Mad Dog Time, The Lost World: Jurassic Park, Welcome to Hollywood, The Prince of Egypt (voice), Holy Man, The Prince of Egypt (voice), Playmate Pajama Party, Chain of Fools, One of the Hollywood Ten, Auggie Rose, Cats & Dogs, Igby Goes Down, Run Ronnie Run, Perfume (exec. prod. & actor), Dumpling Ground, Spinning Boris, Dallas 362, Incident at Loch Ness, The Life Aquatic with Steve Zissou, Mini's First Time, Fay Grim, Man of the Year, Adam Resurrected, The Switch, Morning Glory.
TELEVISION: *Movies:* Tenspeed and Brown Shoe, The Legend of Sleepy Hollow, Rehearsal for Murder, Ernie Kovacs: Between the Laughter, The Race for the Double Helix (BBC), Framed, Lush Life, The Story of Bean, Little Surprises (Academy Award nom. Best Short Film Live Action 1996). *Series:* Tenspeed and Brownshoe, Futurequest (host), War Stories, Crank Yankers (voice), Will & Grace (Emmy nom. 2005), Raines, Law & Order: Criminal Intent. *Guest:* More than 140 appearances.

GOLDEN, PAT

Casting Director, Director. b. Pittsburgh, PA, July 21, 1951. e. U. Pittsburgh, Carnegie-Mellon U. Has directed plays for theatre incl. Homeboy at Perry St. Th. in NY. Was in casting dept. of NY Shakespeare Festival Public Th. Served as assoc. prod. on PBS series The Negro Ensemble Company's 20th Anniversary. *Assoc. prod.:* Hallelujah (PBS); *Dir.:* House Party 2 documentary, My Secret Place (tv pilot).
PICTURES: Ragtime, Beat Street, Krush Groove, The Killing Fields, Blue Velvet (CSA nom. 1987), Platoon (CSA Award 1987), Dear America, The Handmaid's Tale, House Party 2 (assoc. prod.), New Jack City, True Identity, Fly by Night, Posse, Kalifornia, Heights, Shadowboxer (supvr. editor, Hong Kong).
TELEVISION: *Movies:* The Josephine Baker Story (casting consultant), Hallelujah. *Series:* Linc's.

GOLDEN, PETER

Executive. b. New York, NY. e. Bachelor's degree, English, Colby College. Began career as a casting director at Hughes/Moss in New York where his projects included "The Cosby Show." From 1986-1987, Golden was dir., casting for NBC and also a casting dir. at Universal Television. From 1987-1990, v.p., talent and casting of GTG Entertainment, Inc. From 1990-1992, Golden was v.p., talent and casting, for Stephen J. Cannell Productions, Inc., where credits included the hits series "Wiseguy" for CBS and "The Commish" for ABC. Golden was promoted to v.p., development for Cannell and served in that position from 1992-1995. He was briefly v.p., development for St. Clare Entertainment before joining CBS in Jan. 1996 as v.p., talent and casting. Since joining CBS, Golden has supervised casting on more than 100 series and on more than 200 movies and mini-series. In Aug. 1998, named senior v.p., talent and casting, CBS Entertainment. In Oct. 2004 Golden was promoted to executive v.p., talent and casting, with expanded responsibilities to include casting oversight of CBS Paramount Network Television. He oversees all talent and casting operations for CBS primetime and daytime series, television movies and mini-series, reality series and special programs.

GOLDMAN, BO

Writer. b. New York, NY, Sept. 10, 1932. e. Princeton U., B.A., 1953. Wrote lyrics for B'way musical version of Pride and Prejudice entitled First Impressions (1959). Assoc. prod. & script editor for Playhouse 90 1958-60; writer-prod., NET Playhouse 1970-71, Theater in America 1972-74. Received WGA Laurel Award for Screen Writing Achievement 1998.
PICTURES: One Flew Over the Cuckoo's Nest (co-s.p.; WGA & Academy Awards, Golden Globe Award 1976), The Rose (co-s.p.), Melvin and Howard (NY Film Critics, WGA & Academy Award, 1981), Shoot the Moon (WGA nom. 1983), Swing Shift (uncredited), Little Nikita (co-s.p.), Dick Tracy (uncredited), Scent of a Woman (Golden Globe Award, Academy Award nom.; WGA nom. 1993), First Knight (co-s.p.), City Hall (co-s.p.), Meet Joe Black, Children of Angels, Rififi (s.p.), The Colonel and Me.
TELEVISION: *Movie:* June Moon. *Series:* Repertory Theatre (assoc. prod.), The Seven Lively Arts (prod.), The Seven Lively Arts (prod.), The Tunnel (Assoc. prod.), Playhouse 90 (writer, assoc. prod).

GOLDMAN, MICHAEL F.

Executive. b. Manila, Philippines, Sept. 28, 1939. e. UCLA, B.S. in accounting, 1962 California C.P.A. certificate issued June, 1972. In 1962 incorporated Manson International, which was sold in 1986. Incorporated Quixote Prods., 1979. Also owner and sole proprietor Taurus Film co. of Hollywood, founded 1964. Co-founder and first CFO of American Film Marketing Association, sponsor of First American Film Market in Los Angeles in 1981; v.p. of AFMA 1982 and 1983, President AFMA 1984 and 1985. Chmn. AFMA, 1992-93. AFMA (since 2004 called Independent Film & Television Alliance) bd. mbr., 1981-87. Co-founder, Cinema Consultants Group, 1988. Produced feature, Jessi's Girls in 1975. Founded Manson Interactive, 1995. Member A.M.P.A.S. since 1979. Director, Foundation of Motion Picture Pioneers.

GOLDMAN, STEVE

Executive. e. Univ. of IL. 1980, joined Paramount as Midwest division mngr., Chicago. Then served in NY as v.p. Eastern regional mngr. 1983, to Hollywood office. 1985, exec. v.p., sls. & mktg. 1989, exec. v.p. 1992, pres. Paramount Domestic Television. 1995, named exec. v.p. of Paramount Television Group. Currently, exec. v.p. and Chief Administrative Officer for Paramount TV Group.

GOLDMAN, WILLIAM

Writer. b. Chicago, IL, Aug. 12, 1931. e. Oberlin College, B.A., Columbia U., M.A. Received WGA Laurel Award for Screen Writing Achievement 1985.
WRITER: The Temple of Gold, Your Turn to Curtsy—My Turn to Bow, Soldier in the Rain (filmed), Boys and Girls Together, No Way to Treat a Lady (filmed), Butch Cassidy and the Sundance Kid, The Thing of It Is, Father's Day, The Princess Bride (filmed, WGA nom. 1988), All the President's Men, Marathon Man (filmed), Magic (filmed), Tinsel, Control, Heat (filmed), The Silent Gondoliers, The Color of Light, Brothers, Absolute Power (filmed), Four Screenplays, Five Screenplays, The Ghost & The Darkness (filmed). Non-fiction: The Season: A Candid Look at Broadway, Adventures in the Screen Trade, Wait Until Next Year (w/Mike Lupica), Hype and Glory, Which Lie Did I Tell?: More Adventures in the Screen Trade, others.
PICTURES: Harper (WGA nom. 1967), Butch Cassidy and the Sundance Kid (Academy Award, Golden Globe nom.; WGA Award 1970), The Hot Rock, The Stepford Wives, The Great Waldo Pepper, All the President's Men (Academy Award, Golden Globe nom.; WGA Award 1977), Marathon Man (based on his novel; Golden Globe nom.; WGA nom. 1977), A Bridge Too Far, Magic (based on his novel, WGA nom. 1988), Mr. Horn, Heat (based on his novel), The Princess Bride (based on his novel), Misery, Memoirs of an Invisible Man (co-s.p.), Year of the Comet, Chaplin (co-s.p.), Last Action Hero (co-s.p.), Maverick, The Chamber, The Ghost and the Darkness (based on his novel), Fierce Creatures (co-s.p.), Absolute Power (based.on his novel), The General's Daughter, Jurassic Park III, Hearts in Atlantis, Dreamcatcher.
TELEVISION: *Movie:* Mr. Horn.

GOLDSTEIN, MILTON

Executive. b. New York, NY, Aug. 1, 1926. e. NYU, 1949. In exec.

capac., Paramount; foreign sales coord., The Ten Commandments, Psycho; v.p. foreign sales, Samuel Bronstonorg; asst. to Pres., Paramount Int'l, special prods., 1964; Foreign sales mgr., 1966; v.p., world wide sales, 1967, Cinerama; Sr. v.p. Cinema Center Films, 1969; pres., Cinema Center Films, 1971; v.p. Theatrical Mktg. & Sales, Metromedia Producers Corp., 1973; in March, 1974, formed Boasberg-Goldstein, Inc., consultants in prod. and dist. of m.p.; 1975, named exec. vice pres., Avco Embassy Pictures; 1978, named exec. v.p. & chief operating officer, Melvin Simon Prods. 1980, named pres.; 1985, pres. Milt Goldstein Enterprises, Inc.; 1990, chairman and CEO, HKM Films. 1991, pres., Introvision movies. In 2001, teamed with ent. attorneys Leroy Bobbitt and Virgil Roberts to form StreetSmart Pictures, as COO, a distribution company specializing in the release of African-American Films.

GOLDTHWAIT, BOBCAT (BOB)
Comedian, Actor. b. Syracuse, NY, May 1, 1962. Performed with The Generic Comics in early 1980's. Album: Meat Bob.
PICTURES: Police Academy 2: Their First Assignment (debut, 1985), One Crazy Summer, Police Academy 3: Back in Training, Burglar, Police Academy 4: Citizens on Patrol, Hot to Trot, Scrooged, Shakes the Clown (also dir., s.p.), Freaked, Radioland Murders, Destiny Turns on the Radio, Hercules (voice), Rusty: A Dog's Tale (voice), G-Men From Hell, Open Mic, Lion of Oz (voice), Blow, Hansel & Gretel, Grind, Sleeping Dogs Lie (dir., writer, exec. prod.), World's Greatest Dad (also dir., writer).
TELEVISION: *Movies:* Out There, Encino Woman, Back to Back, Windy City Heat, Leroy & Stitch (voices). *Series:* Capitol Critters (voice), Unhappily Ever After (voice), Bobcat's Big Ass Show, Hercules (voice), Hollywood Squares, Stories From My Childhood, Late Friday, Crank Yankers, The Man Show (dir.), Chappelle's Show (episodes dir.), House of Mouse (voice), Strip Mall (dir.), Buzz Lightyear of Star Command (voice), Jimmy Kimmel Live! (co-host, dir.), Important Things with Demetri Martin (dir.). *Specials:* Bob Goldthwait: Don't Watch This Show, Share the Warmth, Is He Like That All the Time? (also dir., writer), Bob Saget: In the Dream Suite, Comic Relief, Medusa: Dare to Be Truthful. *Guest:* More than 96 appearances.

GOLDWATER, CHARLES
Executive. b. New Orleans, LA. e. B.S. in Broadcasting & Film, Boston U. Began career with Walter Reade Organization as usher in 1971-74, promoted to manager. Sack Theatres/USA Cinemas 1974-88, began as manager, promoted to sr. v.p. & g.m. National Amusements, exec. dir. Project Development, 1988-90. Loews/Sony Theatres, sr. v.p. & g.m., 1990-1995. Pres. & CEO, Cinamerica/Mann Theatres, 1995-1998. Became pres., CEO and chairman of the bd., Iwerks Entertainment. March 1998-Feb. 2000. Pres., Clearview Cinemas, July 2000. From June 2002-Sept. 2004 pres./CEO of Digital Cinema Initiatives, an organization formed by a coalition of the seven major film studios to develop digital cinema technology. In August 2005 joined AccessIT as president & CEO of Christie/AIX and in July 2006 was named president of AccessIT's Media Services, Christie/AIX and Advertising and Creative Services divisions. 2008 AccessIT changed it's name to Cinedigm Digital Cinema Corp. Currently Sr. V.P.; Pres. of the Media Services Group; President of Phase 1 DC and Phase 2 DC. (Goldwater memberships have included: NATO bd. of dir.; Chmn. CARA / Product Committee, 1991-1996; Exec Comm.' Gen. chmn. ShowEast 1992-1995; a past chmn. of the bd. ShowEast, 1995; bd. of directors, Motion Picture Pioneers, Will Rogers. Past pres./chmn. of bd., Theatre Owners of New England. Past bd. of directors, Variety Clubs of New England & New York.

GOLDWYN, JOHN
Executive, Producer. Grandson of late Samuel Goldwyn, father is Samuel Goldwyn, Jr. Began career as exec. story editor, The Ladd Co., 1982; later promoted to v.p., creative affairs, served as exec. producer on Police Academy II. Became senior v.p., motion picture production, MGM/UA Entertainment Co., 1985, and was named exec. v.p., motion picture production for MGM in 1988. Joined Paramount Pictures in 1990 as exec. v.p., production and was promoted to president, Motion Picture Group/production, 1991. 1997, became president, Paramount Pictures. Then, elevated to vice chmn. & co-pres. of Paramount Pictures in 2002. During Goldwyn's tenure as a senior executive at the studio, Paramount Pictures took home three Best Picture Oscars for Forrest Gump, Braveheart and Titanic. He stepped down in 2004 and inked a long-term production deal with Paramount as an independent producer. In 2005 Goldwyn merged with producer Lorne Michaels to form the Michaels/Goldwyn Company at Paramount. Currently is President/Producer for John Goldwyn Productions.
PICTURES: Police Academy 2: Their First Assignment (exec. prod.), Hot Rod, I'm Not There., Baby Mama, MacGruber.
TELEVISION: *Series:* Dexter (exec. prod., 2 Emmy noms.).

GOLDWYN, SAMUEL, JR.
Producer. b. Los Angeles, CA, Sept. 7, 1926. e. U. of Virginia. Son of late Samuel Goldwyn. Father of actor Tony Goldwyn and producer John Goldwyn. U.S. Army, 1944; following war writer, assoc. prod., J. Arthur Rank Org.; prod. Gathering Storm on London stage; returned to U.S., 1948; assoc. prod., Universal; recalled to Army service, 1951; prod., dir., Army documentary films including Alliance for Peace (Edinburgh Film Festival prize); prod. TV shows, Adventure series for CBS, 1952-53; prod. TV series, The Unexpected, 1954; pres., The Samuel Goldwyn Company, 1955-. Also established Samuel Goldwyn Home Entertainment and Goldwyn Pavilion Cinemas.
PICTURES: Man With the Gun, The Sharkfighters, The Proud Rebel, The Adventures of Huckleberry Finn, The Young Lovers (also dir.), Cotton Comes to Harlem, Come Back Charleston Blue, The Golden Seal, Mystic Pizza (exec. prod.), Stella, The Preacher's Wife, Tortilla Soup, Master and Commander: The Far Side of the World (Academy Award nom. 2004).
TELEVISION: *Movie:* April Morning (exec. prod.). *Series:* Sneak Preview (prod.), The New Adventures of Flipper (exec. prod.). *Specials:* The 60th Academy Awards, (Emmy Award 1988).

GOLDWYN, TONY
Actor, Director. b. Los Angeles, CA, May 20, 1960. e. Brandeis U., London Acad. of Music & Dramatic Art.
THEATRE: Digby, The Foreigner, The Real Thing, Pride and Prejudice, The Sum of Us, Spike Heels, Inherit the Wind.
PICTURES: Friday the 13th Part VI: Jason Live, Gaby-A True Story, Ghost, Kuffs, Traces of Red, The Pelican Brief, Reckless, The Substance of Fire, Nixon, The Substance of Fire, Kiss the Girls, Trouble on the Corner, The Lesser Evil, Tarzan (voice), The 6th Day, Bounce, Someone Like You, An American Rhapsody, Joshua, Abandon, The Last Samurai, Ash Tuesday, Romance & Cigarettes, Ghosts Never Sleep, The Sisters, American Gun, The Last Kiss (dir. only), The Last House on the Left, Betty Anne Waters (dir., prod.).
TELEVISION: *Movies:* Favorite Son, Dark Holiday, Iran: Days of Crisis, Taking the Heat, Love Matters, Doomsday Gun, The Last Word, The Boys Next Door, Truman, The Song of the Lark. *Mini-series:* A Woman of Independent Means, From the Earth to the Moon. *Series:* Without a Trace (dir.), The L Word (dir.), Law & Order: Criminal Intent (actor). *Special:* The Last Mile. *Series: Dir., Episodes:* Grey's Anatomy, Dexter. *Guest:* More than 53 appearances.

GOLINO, VALERIA
Actress. b. Naples, Italy, Oct. 22, 1966. Raised in Athens, Greece. Was model at age 14 before being discovered by dir. Lina Wertmuller for film debut.
PICTURES: A Joke of Destiny (debut, 1983), Blind Date, My Son Infinitely Beloved, Little Fires, Dumb Dicks, Storia d'Amore (Love Story), Last Summer in Tangiers, The Gold-Rimmed Glasses, Three Sisters, Big Top Pee-wee, Rain Man, Torrents of Spring, The King's Whore, Traces of an Amorous Life, Hot Shots!, The Indian Runner, Hot Shots! Part Deux, Clean Slate, Immortal Beloved, Leaving Las Vegas, Four Rooms, Escape From L.A., The Acrobats, Side Streets, Le Acrobate, The Pear Tree, Harem Square, Spanish Judges, Things You Can Tell Just By Looking at her, Il Fratello minore, Ivansxtc, Against the Wind, Word of Honor, Hotel, L'Inverno, Boccanera, Respiro: Grazia's Island, Frida, Laria.
TELEVISION: *Movie:* Caesar. *Mini-series:* La Vita che verrà.

GOMEZ, NICK
Director, Writer. b. Sommerville, MA, 1963. Stunts in film, Powder. Acted in films Mob War and Blue Vengeance.
PICTURES: Laws of Gravity, New Jersey Drive (also story), Illtown, Drowning Mona.
TELEVISION: *Movies:* Final Jeopardy, Hunter: Return to Justice. *Series:* Homicide: Life on the Street, Oz, The Sopranos, Mondo Picasso, Final Jeopardy, Night Visions, Crossing Jordan, The Agency, The Shield, Push Nevada, Robbery Homicide Division, Talk to Me, Brotherhood, Sleeper Cell. Director of numerous series episodes.

GOODALL, CAROLINE
Actress. b. London, England, Nov. 13, 1959. e. Natl Youth Theatre of Great Britain; Bristol Univ. On stage with Royal Court Theatre, Royal Natl. Theatre, Royal Shakespeare Co. Toured Australia in Richard III for RSC, 1986.
PICTURES: Every Time We Say Goodbye (debut, 1986), Hook, The Silver Brumby, The Webbers' 15 Minutes, Cliffhanger, Schindler's List, Disclosure, Hotel Sorrento, White Squall, Casualties, Rhapsody in Bloom, The Secret Laughter of Women, Harrison's Flowers, The Princess Diaries, Shattered Glass, Chasing Liberty, The Princess Diaries 2: Royal Engagement, Haven, The Chumscrubber, Molding Clay, The Thief Lord, The Seven of Daran: Battle of Pareo Rock, My Life in Ruins, Dorian Gray.
TELEVISION: *Movies* (Australia): Cassidy, Ring of Scorpio, The Great Air Race, Diamond Swords (Fr.), The Sculptress, Opera Ball, Sex n' Death, Love and Murder, Me & Mrs. Jones. *Mini-series:* After the War, A Difficult Woman, The Mists of Avalon. *Series:* Murder in Mind.

GOODING, CUBA, JR.
Actor. b. Bronx, NY, Sept. 2, 1968. Son of rhythm and blues vocalist Cuba Gooding. Raised in California. Prof. debut as dancer backing up Lionel Richie at 1984 Olympic Games. Recipient of NAACP Image Awards for Boyz in the Hood and tv movie, Murder Without Motive. Voted by NATO/Showest as

Newcomer of the Year, 1992.
PICTURES: Coming to America (debut, 1988), Sing, Boyz in the Hood, Hitz, Gladiator, A Few Good Men, Judgment Night, Lightning Jack, Outbreak, Losing Isaiah, Jerry Maguire (Academy Award, Golden Globe nom.; Chicago Film Critics Award; Screen Actors Guild Award, 1997), Do Me a Favor (cameo), As Good As It Gets, What Dreams May Come, Welcome to Hollywood, Chill Factor, A Murder of Crows (also prod.), Instinct, Men of Honor, Pearl Harbor, Rat Race, In the Shadows, Zoolander, Snow Dogs, Boat Trip, Sweating Bullets (voice), The Fighting Temptations, Radio, Home on the Range (voice), Shadowboxer, End Game, Dirty, What Love Is, Norbit, Daddy Day Camp, American Gangster, Harold, The Way of War, Linewatch, Hero Wanted, The Devil's Tomb, Hardwired, Wrong Turn at Tahoe, Ticking Clock, Red Tails, Hit List.
TELEVISION: *Movies:* Murder Without Motive: The Edmund Perry Story, Daybreak, The Tuskegee Airmen, Gifted Hands: The Ben Carson Story. *Specials:* No Means No, America: A Tribute to Heroes. *Guest:* More than 97 appearances.

GOODMAN, ADAM,
Executive. e. Attended college at New York University and American University. Goodman began his career in the entertainment industry while still in his teens in Highland Park, IL. While in high school, he landed a job as a production assistant for the Chicago-based Hughes Entertainment, where he worked on such John Hughes comedies as "Home Alone" and "Only The Lonely." While in college, he continued to work on films, including "The Pelican Brief," "Backdraft" and "Waterworld." He joined DreamWorks in early 1996 and became a production executive only eight months later. Goodman was named head of production in 2004. Viacom Inc., parent of Paramount Pictures, acquired DreamWorks for $1.6 billion in 2006. By 2008, DreamWorks executives sought independence from the Paramount fold and in Oct. 2008, the two entities struck a pact to separate. Goodman remained with Paramount, as president of production of the DreamWorks-nurtured projects now in Paramount's pipeline. 2009, Goodman became president of Paramount's Film Group.

GOODMAN, DAVID Z.
Writer. e. Queens Coll., Yale School of Drama.
PICTURES: Lovers and Other Strangers (Academy Award nom.; WGA nom. 1971), Straw Dogs, Farewell My Lovely, Logan's Run, Eyes of Laura Mars, Fighting Back, Man Woman and Child (co.-s.p.), Straw Dogs (s.p. 1971).
TELEVISION: *Movies*: Freedom Road, Monte Walsh. *Series*: The Untouchables, Mr. Broadway.

GOODMAN, JOHN
Actor. b. Affton, MO, June 20, 1952. e. Southwest Missouri State U. Moved to NY in 1975 where he appeared on stage (incl. A Midsummer Night's Dream) and in commercials. On Broadway in Loose Ends, Big River. L.A. stage in Antony and Cleopatra. Co-owner, CG Parners Entertainment.
PICTURES: Eddie Macon's Run (1983, debut), The Survivors, Revenge of the Nerds, C.H.U.D., Maria's Lovers, Sweet Dreams, True Stories, Raising Arizona, Burglar, The Big Easy, The Wrong Guys, Punchline, Everybody's All-American, Sea of Love, Always, Stella, Arachnophobia, King Ralph, Barton Fink (Golden Globe nom. 1992), The Babe, Matinee, Born Yesterday, We're Back! A Dinosaur's Story (voice), The Flintstones, The Hudsucker Proxy (cameo), Pie in the Sky, Mother Night, The Borrowers, The Big Lebowski, Fallen, Blues Brothers 2000, Dirty Work (cameo), The Runner, Bringing Out the Dead, Coyote Ugly, What Planet Are You From, O Brother Where Art Thou? Happy Birthday, My First Mister, One Night at McCool's, The Emperor's New Groove (voice), Storytelling, Monsters Inc. (voice), Dirty Deeds, Masked & Anonymous, The Jungle Book 2 (voice), Home of Phobia, Clifford's Really Big Movie (voice), Beyond the Sea, Marilyn Hotchkiss' Ballroom Dancing and Charm School, Kronk's New Groove (voice), Cars (voice), Drunkboat, Evan Almighty, Bee Movie (voice), Death Sentence, In the Electric Mist, Speed Racer, Confessions of a Shopaholic, Gigantic, Spring Break '83, Thicker, The Princess and the Frog (voice), The Gatekeeper.
TELEVISION: *Movies*: The Face of Rage, Heart of Steel, The Mystery of Moro Castle, Murder Ordained, Kingfish: A Story of Huey P. Long (also co-prod., Emmy nom.1995), A Streetcar Named Desire (Emmy nom. 1996), The Jack Bull, On the Edge, The Year Without a Santa Claus, You Don't Know Jack. *Mini-series*: Chiefs. *Series*: Roseanne (7 Emmy nom.; Golden Globe Award 1993, 3 other nom.), Normal Ohio, Now and Again, Pigs Next Door (voice), Father of the Pride (voice), Center of the Universe, The Siegfried and Roy Fantasy Experience Movie, Studio 60 on the Sunset Strip (Emmy Award 2007), Baseball Bunch (exec. prod.), Treme. *Guest*: More than 103 appearances.

GOODRICH, ROBERT EMMETT
Exhibitor. b. Grand Rapids, MI, June 27, 1940. e. U. of Michigan, B.A., 1962; J.D., 1964; NYU. LL.M, 1966. Pres. & Secretary, Goodrich Quality Theaters, Inc., 1967-present; developed circuit from father's one theatre to 275 screens at 32 locations in 17 Michigan cities, five Indiana cities, four Illinois cities and three Missouri cities. Owns and operates a Radio Disney AM affiliate in Grand Rapids, MI. Goodrich is a NATO bd. member; bd. member of Michigan Millers Mutual Insurance Co.; bd. member of the Western Michigan ACLU branch; is on the Will Rogers Institute Advisory Committee and is a member of the State Bar of Michigan.

GOODWIN, RICHARD B.
Producer. b. Bombay, India, Sept. 13, 1934. e. Rugby. Entered film world by chance: while waiting to go to Cambridge U. took temporary job as tea boy at studio which led to 20-year-long association with producer Lord Brabourne.
PICTURES: *Prod. Mgr.:* The Sheriff of Fractured Jaw, Carve Her Name with Pride, The Grass Is Greener, Sink the Bismarck, HMS Defiant. *Prod.:* The Tales of Beatrix Potter. *Co-Prod.:* Murder on the Orient Express, Death on the Nile, The Mirror Crack'd, Evil Under the Sun, A Passage to India (Academy Award nom. 1985), Little Dorrit, Seven Years In Tibet (exec. prod.).

GOODWYN, BILL
Executive. e. Bachelor's degree in journalism, Univ. of North Carolina at Chapel Hill. Goodwyn joined Discovery Communications in 1987 and has spearheaded record-breaking distribution growth for each of the company's domestic cable channels. 2010 Goodwyn is pres., of global distribution and enterprises for Discovery Communications and is CEO of Discovery Education. He oversees the distribution sales and marketing efforts for Discovery's 13 U.S. cable networks including Discovery Channel, TLC, Animal Planet, Science Channel, Planet Green, Discovery Health and HD Theater, as well as five high definition network feeds. Goodwyn also directs distribution sales and marketing efforts for BBC America, BBC World and Cox Communications' Travel Channel, and manages Discovery's digital media content distribution efforts in broadband, mobile and video on demand. He also serves as pres. of Discovery Education, a leading provider of scientifically proven, standards-based digital media services that reach more than half of K-12 schools in the U.S. Honors include: the National Cable & Telecommunications Association's (NCTA) highest honor for Young Leadership (the Vanguard Award); hall of fame inductee at the Cable Center's Cable TV Pioneer Hall of Fame. Board positions: Cable & Telecommunications Association for Marketing (CTAM) Educational Foundation, the T. Howard Foundation (diversity in media), the Alexander Youth Network and the UNC-Chapel Hill Journalism and Communications School Board of Advisors.

GORDON, BRUCE
Executive. e. B.S. in bus. admin. from Syracuse Univ.; M.B.A. from Hofstra Univ. Career with Price Waterhouse and Company before joining ABC in 1981. 1981-1985 asst. dir./finance for KGO-TV, an ABC-owned TV station in San Francisco. 1985-1997, held sr. mgt. position at KABC-TV, the ABC-owned station in Los Angeles. There he led the station's finance, admin. & strategic planning operations. 1997-2001, pres. & gen. mgr. of WTVD-TV, the ABC-owned TV affiliate in Raleigh, NC. From 2001-present, Gordon is senior v.p. & CFO of the Walt Disney Internet Group, headquartered in North Hollywood, CA.

GORDON, CHARLES
Executive, Producer. b. Belzoni, MS, May 13, 1947. Began career as a talent agent with William Morris Agency. Left to write and develop television programming creating and producing 5 pilots and 3 series. Left TV to enter motion picture production in partnership with brother Lawrence Gordon. President and COO, The Gordon Company. Now an executive with Daybreak Productions.
PICTURES: *Prod./Exec. prod.:* Die Hard, Leviathan. Co-prod.: Night of the Creeps, The Wrong Guys, Field of Dreams (Academy Award nom. 1990), K-9, Lock Up, The Rocketeer, The Super, Unlawful Entry, Waterworld, Trojan War, October Sky, Small World, The Girl Next Door, Hitman.
TELEVISION: *Writer-creator*: When the Whistle Blows. *Exec. prod.*: The Renegades, Just Our Luck (also creator), Our Family Honor (also creator), Things That Go Bump.

GORDON, JEROME
Executive, Exhibitor. b. Newport News, VA, Mar. 1, 1915. Began movie career at age 10 as usher in father's theatre. At age 18, owned and operated two theatres. Spent one year in theater decorating business in Philadelphia. Worked for Fox West Coast circuit in Los Angeles, 1937-40. Returned to VA and developed small theater circuit with brothers. Served as pres. of Virginia NATO for 4 yrs. 1975, exec. dir., Virginia NATO; 1976, exec. dir., Maryland & D.C. NATO. Coordinated Mid-Atlantic NATO convention from 1975 until it merged with ShowEast in 1989. 1978-86, spec. asst. to pres., NATO; coordinated campaigns to pass Anti-Blind Bidding Laws in individual states. Edited Regional Presidents' NATO Handbook. Member, bd. of dirs., NATO; chmn., NATO Membership Development Committee; secretary NATO, 1996. Recipient of Distinguished Service Award, ShowEast, 1992; B.V. Sturdivant Award, NATO/ShowEast, 1992. (d. July 18, 2007)

GORDON, KEITH
Actor, Director, Writer. b. Bronx, NY, Feb. 3, 1961.
THEATRE: A Traveling Companion, Richard III, Album, Back to

Back The Buddy System, Third Street.
PICTURES: *Actor:* Jaws 2 (debut, 1978), All That Jazz, Home Movies, Dressed to Kill, Christine, The Legend of Billie Jean, Static (also co-s.p., co-prod.), Back to School, I Love Trouble, Delivering Milo. *Director and/or Writer:* The Chocolate War, A Midnight Clear. Mother Night (also prod.), Waking the Dead (also prod.), The Singing Detective, Billy Dead.
TELEVISION: *Movies:* Kent State, Single Bars Single Women, Combat High, Shadow Realm. *Mini-series*: Studs Lonigan. *Series:* Gideon's Crossing. *Director:* Wild Palms, Homicide (1 episode), Fallen Angels: The Black Bargain, House, M.D., Dexter. *Special:* My Palikari (Amer. Playhouse).

GORDON, LAWRENCE
Producer, Executive. b. Yazoo City, MS, March 25, 1936. e. Tulane U. (business admin.). Assist. to prod. Aaron Spelling at Four Star Television, 1964. Writer and assoc. prod. on several Spelling shows. 1965, joined ABC-TV as head of West Coast talent dev; 1966, TV and motion pictures exec. with Bob Banner Associates; 1968 joined AIP as v.p. in charge of project dev.; 1971 named v.p., Screen Gems (TV div. of Columbia Pictures) where he helped develop Brian's Song and QB VII. Returned to AIP as v.p. worldwide prod. Formed Lawrence Gordon Prods. at Columbia Pictures; 1984-86, pres. and COO 20th Century Fox. In 1987, he went independent again as head of Largo Productions. Currently pres. of Lawrence Gordon Productions. Also producer of B'way musical Smile.
PICTURES: Dillinger (1973), Hard Times, Rolling Thunder, The Driver, The End, Hooper, The Warriors, Xanadu, Paternity, Jekyll and Hyde, Together Again, 48 Hours, Streets of Fire, Brewster's Millions, Lucas, Jumpin' Jack Flash, Predator, The Couch Trip, The Wrong Guys, Die Hard, Leviathan (exec. prod.), K-9, Field of Dreams (Academy Award nom. 1990), Lock Up, Family Business, Another 48 HRS, Die Hard 2, Predator 2, The Rocketeer, Used People, The Devil's Own, Boogie Nights, Event Horizon, Tomb Raider, Thieves, Mystery Men, Thieves, Lara Croft Tomb Raider: The Cradle of Life, K-PAX, Hellboy, Hellboy II: The Golden Army, Watchmen.
TELEVISION: *Movies: Co-creator and co-exec. prod.:* The Missing Are Deadly, Dog and Cat, Stunts Unlimited, The Renegades, Our Family Honor, Hellboy Animated: Sword of Storms (Emmy nom. 2007), Hellboy Animated: Blood and Iron. *Series:* Dog and Cat, Matt Houston, Just Our Luck, Timecop.

GORDON, RICHARD
Producer. b. London, Eng., Dec. 31, 1925. e. U. of London, 1943. Served in Brit. Royal Navy, 1944-46; ed. & writer on fan magazines & repr. independent American cos. 1946, with publicity dept. Assoc. Brit. Pathe 1947; org. export-import business for independent, British and American product; formed Gordon Films, Inc., 1949; formed Amalgamated prod., 1956; formed Grenadier Films, Ltd. 1971. 1992, prod. of A Tribute to Orson Welles.
PICTURES: The Counterfeit Plan, The Haunted Strangler, Fiend Without a Face, The Secret Man, First Man into Space, Corridors of Blood, Devil Doll, Curse of Simba, The Projected Man, Naked Evil, Island of Terror, Tales of the Bizarre, Tower of Evil, Horror Planet, The Cat and the Canary.

GORDON, STUART
Director, Writer. b. Chicago, IL, Aug. 11, 1947. e. Univ. of WI. Worked at commercial art studio prior to founding Broom Street Theater in Madison, WI. Later founder and prod. dir. of Organic Theater Co. in Madison, then Chicago, 1969-85. Was fight choreographer on 1976 film The Last Affair.
PICTURES: *Director:* Re-Animator (also co-s.p.), From Beyond (also co-s.p.), Dolls, Robot Jox (also wrote story), Honey I Shrunk the Kids (co-story only), The Pit and the Pendulum, Honey I Blew Up the Kid (exec. prod., co-story only), Fortress, Body Snatchers (co-s.p. only), Castle Freak (also co-story), Space Truckers (dir., prod., co-story), The Wonderful Ice Cream Suit, Dagon, King of the Ants, Edmond, Stuck (also writer).
TELEVISION: *Movies: Director:* Bleacher Bums, Daughter of Darkness, Bleacher Bums (special).

GORDY, BERRY
Executive, Producer. b. Detroit, MI, Nov. 28, 1929. Was working on auto assembly line in Detroit when decided to launch record co., Motown. In 1961 wrote song, Shop Around; recording by Smokey Robinson made it his first million dollar record. Expanded into music publishing, personal mgt., recording studios, film and TV, also backing stage shows. Former bd. chmn., Motown Industries. Chmn. The Gordy Co. Received Business Achievement Award, Interracial Council for Business Opportunity, 1967; Whitney M. Young Jr. Award, L.A. Urban League, 1980; Inducted into Rock and Roll Hall of Fame, 1988. Recipient of NARAS Trustee Award, 1991. Other awards include: the Martin Luther King Jr. Leadership Award, Yale University's Gordon Grand Fellow Award, a star on the Hollywood Walk of Fame, and the Rainbow Coalition's Man of the Millennium Award. Author of To Be Loved (1994). Member BMI, NAACP, A.M.P.A.S., DGI, NARAS.
PICTURES: Lady Sings the Blues (prod.), Bingo Long Traveling All-Stars and Motor Kings (exec. prod.), Mahogany (dir.), Almost Summer, The Last Dragon (exec. prod.). *Composer:* Coming to America, Moonwalker, Ski Patrol, Sleepwalkers, Beethoven's 2nd, Blank Check, Milk Money, Dangerous Minds, Leaving Las Vegas, Empire Records, Now and Then, Happy Gilmore, Telling Lies in America, Trojan War, Drive Me Crazy, Dirty Dancing, Crooklyn, Duets, The Dish, Charlie's Angels, Drumline, Malibu's Most Wanted, Daddy Day Care, Honey, Lord of War, Jarhead, Clerks II, We Are Marshall, Daddy Day Camp, Mad Money, numerous credits as sountrack writer. *Documentaries:* Standing in the Shadows of Motown, In the Hands of the Gods.
TELEVISION: *Movie:* Babycakes (composer song). *Special:* Diana (prod.). *Documentaries:* TV Land Confidential, These Kids Mean Busines$.

GORE, MICHAEL
Composer, Producer. b. New York City, New York, March 5, 1951. e. Yale University and studied in Paris with composer Max Deustch. Began writing pop songs for his sister singer Lesley Gore; as a staff songwriter for Screen Gems-Columbia; and as a producer of classical recordings for CBS Records. Prod. for Philips Classics recording of The King and I (with Julie Andrews, Ben Kingsley). Wrote Whitney Houston's hit single All the Man That I Need.
PICTURES: Fame (2 Academy Awards for Best Score and Title Song, 1 other nom.; Golden Globe Award; 1 other nom. 1981), Terms of Endearment (Academy Award nom. 1984), Footloose, Pretty in Pink, Broadcast News, Defending Your Life, The Butcher's Wife, Mr. Wonderful, Superstar, Camp, Hot Rod many more credits as soudtrack writer.
TELEVISION: *Movies:* South Pacific. *Series:* Generations (theme); Fame (theme).

GOSSETT, LOUIS, JR.
Actor. b. Brooklyn, NY, May 27, 1936. e. NYU, B.S. Also nightclub singer during 1960s.
THEATRE: Take a Giant Step (debut, 1953), The Desk Set, Lost in the Stars, A Raisin in the Sun, Golden Boy, The Blacks, Blood Knot, The Zulu and the Zayda, My Sweet Charlie, Carry Me Back to Morningside Heights, Murderous Angels (L.A. Drama Critics Award).
PICTURES: A Raisin in the Sun (debut, 1961), The Bushbaby, The Landlord, Skin Game, Travels With My Aunt, The Laughing Policeman, The White Dawn, The River Niger, J.D.'s Revenge, The Deep, The Choirboys, An Officer and a Gentleman (Academy Award, best supporting actor; Golden Globe Award 1983), Jaws 3-D, Finders Keepers, Enemy Mine, Iron Eagle, Firewalker, The Principal, Iron Eagle II, Toy Soldiers, The Punisher, Aces: Iron Eagle III, Diggstown, Monolith, Flashfire, Blue Chips (unbilled), A Good Man in Africa, Iron Eagle IV, Inside, Managua, Bram Stoker's Legend of the Mummy, Y2K, The Highwayman, Delgo (voice), Cover, Daddy's Little Girls, The Perfect Game, The Least Among You, Dog Jack (voice), Shannon's Rainbow, Taking Woodstock (soundtrack writer), Dog Jack (voice), Why Did I Get Married Too?, 4Chosen (co-exec. prod.), The Grace Card, Sweetwater, Smitty, A Fonder Heart, Samuel Bleak, Redemption.
TELEVISION: *Movies:* Companions in Nightmare, It's Good to Be Alive, Sidekicks, Delancey Street, The Crisis Within, Don't Look Back, Little Ladies of the Night, To Kill a Cop, The Critical List, This Man Stands Alone, Sadat (Emmy nom.; Golden Globe nom. 1984), The Guardian, A Gathering of Old Men (Emmy nom. 1987), The Father Clements Story, Roots: The Gift, El Diablo, Sudie and Simpson, The Josephine Baker Story (Golden Globe Award 1992), Carolina Skeletons, Father & Son: Dangerous Relations (also co-exec. prod.), Ray Alexander: A Taste for Justice, A Father for Charlie (also co-exec. prod.), Curse of the Starving Class, Zooman, Ray Alexander: A Menu for Murder, Captive Heart: The James Mink Story, to Dance with Olivia, The Inspectors, Love Songs, Strange Justice, The Color of Love: Jacey's Story, Dr. Lucille, For Love of Olivia, What About Your Friends: Weekend Getaway, Momentum, Jasper Texas, Solar Strike, Lackawanna Blues. *Mini-series:* Roots (Emmy Award, 1977), Backstairs at the White House (Emmy nom. 1979), Return to Lonesome Dove. *Series:* The Young Rebels, The Lazarus Syndrome, Palmerstown, U.S.A. (Emmy nom. 1981), The Powers of Matthew Star, Gideon Oliver, The Great War (voice), Hercules (voice), Walking After Midnight, Resurrection Blvd., Stargate SG-1. *Specials:* I Love Liberty, Circus of the Stars #8 (ringmaster), Welcome Home, A Triple Play: Sam Found Out, Zora Is My Name, The Century Collection Presents Ben Vereen: His Roots (Emmy nom. 1978), In His Father's Shoes (Emmy Award; 1 other nom. 1998). *Documentaries:* Roots: One Year Later (narr.), A Celebration of Life: A Tribute to Martin Luther King, Jr. (host), Liberators: Fighting on Two Fronts in World War II (voice), Gridiron Gang (host), The Great War and the Shaping of the 20th Century (mini-series, voice), Small Steps, Big Strides: The Black Experience in Hollywood (narr.), Asthma: Fighting to Breathe (host), The Needs of Kim Stanley, The Distance (actor), ReNew Orleans (host, exec. prod.), For Love of Liberty: The Story of America's Black Patriots (voice, exec. prod.). *Guest:* More than 190 appearances.

GOTTERUP, MORTEN B.
Exhibitor. b. Walnut Creek, CA. e. St. Mary's College of Calif., undergraduate degree. Pepperdine Univ., master's degree in international business mgt. Began career in entertainment industry with MovieFone, Inc., as v.p. of sales working with national theatre chains and motion picture studios (five years). Gotterup also spent time as COO of Xpressreturns, Inc., a return

concierge service for Internet and catalog businesses. He then joined Clearview Cinemas, the second largest operator of movie theatres in the New York metro market, with 54 theatres located in mainly downtown, main street locations. He was v.p. of marketing and business development before assuming his current position of senior v.p. and general manager of Clearview Cinemas, which is a subsidiary of Cablevision and Rainbow Media Holdings. Gotterup sits on the bd. of directors for the National Association of Theatre Owners; is a bd. member for Variety, The Children's Charity, and supports various other charity efforts.

GOTTESMAN, STUART

Executive. b. New York, NY, June 11, 1949. Started career in mailroom of Warner Bros., 1972; later named promo. asst. to southwestern regional fieldman; promoted to that post which held for 10 years. 1987, named WB dir. field activities; 1990, appointed v.p. WB national field operations. 1997, named v.p. regional publicity and promo. for Paramount Pictures' m.p. group.

GOTTLIEB, CARL

Writer, Director, Actor. New York, NY, March 18, 1938. e. Syracuse U., B.S., 1960. Directed short film The Absent- Minded Waiter. Received WGA Morgan Cox Award 2010.
PICTURES: *Actor:* Maryjane, M*A*S*H, Up the Sandbox, Cannonball, The Sting II, Johnny Dangerously, The Committee, Into the Night, Clueless. *Director:* Caveman (also co-s.p.), Amazon Women on the Moon (co-dir.). *Co-Writer:* Jaws (also actor, Golden Globe nom.; WGA nom. 1976), Which Way Is Up?, Jaws II, The Jerk (also actor), Doctor Detroit, Jaws 3-D, The Sting II, Jonny Dangerously, Into the Night, Clueless.
TELEVISION: *Writer:* Smothers Bros. Comedy Hour (Emmy Award, 1969), The Odd Couple, Flip Wilson, Bob Newhart Show, The Super, Crisis at Sun Valley, The Deadly Triangle. *Director:* Paul Reiser: Out on a Whim, Partners In Life, Campus Cops, Honey I Shrunk the Kids, The Lot (consulting prod.). *Director-Co-creator:* Leo & Liz in Beverly Hills. *Co-creator:* George Burns' Comedy Week. *Actor:* Secrets of a Hollywood Nurse.

GOUGH, MICHAEL

Actor. b. Malaya, Nov. 23, 1917. e. Rose Hill Sch., Kent, England, and at Durham School. Studied at Old Vic School in London; first stage appearance in 1936 at Old Vic Theatre. N.Y. stage debut 1937 in Love of Women. London debut in 1938 in The Zeal of Thy House. Won 1979 Tony Award for Bedroom Farce.
PICTURES: Blanche Fury (debut, 1947), Anna Karenina, Saraband for Dead Lovers, The Small Back Room, The Man in the White Suit, Rob Roy, The Sword and the Rose, Richard III, Reach for the Sky, Horror of Dracula (Dracula), Horrors of the Black Museum, The Horse's Mouth, Konga, Candidate for Murder, I Like Money (Mr. Topaze), The Phantom of the Opera, Black Zoo, Dr. Terror's House of Horrors, The Skull, Berserk, They Came From Beyond Space, A Walk With Love and Death, Women in Love, Trog, Julius Caesar, The Go-Between, Savage Messiah, Legend of Hell House, Horror Hospital, Computer Killers, Galileo, The Boys from Brazil, Venom, The Dresser, Top Secret!, Oxford Blues, Out of Africa, Caravaggio, Memed My Hawk, The Fourth Protocol, The Serpent and the Rainbow, Batman, Strapless, Let Him Have It, Blackeyes, Batman Returns, Little Nemo (voice), The Age of Innocence, Wittgenstein, Uncovered, Batman Forever, Batman & Robin, What Rats Won't Do, The Whisper, St. Ives, Sleepy Hollow, The Cherry Orchard, Corpse Bride (voice), Alice in Wonderland (voice).
TELEVISION: *Movies:* Count of Monte Cristo, The Girl Who Loved Robots, Alice in Wonderland, Pride and Prejudice, Inside the Third Reich, Witness for the Prosecution, Another Flip for Dominick, Cymbeline, To the Lighthouse, The Biko Inquest, A Christmas Carol, Arthur the King, Vincent the Dutchman, Heart Attack Hotel, Dr. Who, Lace II, Shattered Spirits, Cariani and the Courtesans, The Shell Seekers, Children of the North, The Haunting of Helen Walker, Young Indiana Jones: Travels with Father, Dame Edna Live at the Palace. *Mini-series:* The Search for the Nile, Fall of Eagles, Shoulder to Shoulder, Six Wives of Henry VIII, QB VII, Notorious Woman, Brideshead Revisited, Smiley's People, The Citadel, Mistral's Daughter, Lace II, A Killing On the Exchange, After the War, Blackeyes, Sleepers, The Modern World: Ten Great Writers (reader). *Series:* The Little Vampire. *Documentaries:* Doctor Who: The Hartnell Years, Sleepy Hollow: Behind the Legend. *Guest:* More than 108 appearances.

GOULD, ELLIOTT

Actor. r.n. Elliott Goldstein. b. Brooklyn, NY, August 29, 1938. e. Professional Children's Sch., NY 1955. Vaudeville: appeared at Palace Theater, 1950. Broadway debut in Rumple (1957). Son is actor Jason Gould.
THEATRE: Rumple, Say Darling, Irma La Douce, I Can Get It for You Wholesale, On the Town (London), Fantasticks (tour), Drat the Cat!, Little Murders, Luv (tour), Hit the Deck (Jones Beach), Rumors, Breakfast With Les & Bess.
PICTURES: Quick Let's Get Married (debut, 1965), The Night They Raided Minsky's, Bob & Carol & Ted & Alice (Academy Award nom. 1970), M*A*S*H (Golden Globe nom. 1971), Getting Straight, Move, I Love My Wife, Little Murders (also prod.), The Touch, The Long Goodbye, Busting, S*P*Y*S!, California Split, Who?, Nashville (cameo), Whiffs, I Will I Will... For Now, Harry and Walter Go to New York, Mean Johnny Barrows, A Bridge Too Far, Capricorn One, Matilda, The Silent Partner, Escape to Athena, The Muppet Movie, The Last Flight of Noah's Ark, The Lady Vanishes, Falling in Love Again, The Devil and Max Devlin, Dirty Tricks, The Naked Face, Over the Brooklyn Bridge, The Muppets Take Manhattan, Inside Out, My First 40 Years, Lethal Obsession, The Telephone, The Big Picture, Dangerous Love, Night Visitor, The Wounded King, The Lemon Sisters, Judgment, Dead Men Don't Die, Bugsy, Strawanser, The Player, Exchange Lifeguards, Wet and Wild Summer, Naked Gun 33 1/3: The Final Insult (cameo), White Man's Burden, The Glass Shield, Kicking and Screaming, A Boy Called Hate, Johns, City of Industry (cameo), Camp Stories, Michael Kael in Katango, The Big Hit, American History X, Picking up the Pieces, Playing Mona Lisa, Boys Life 3, Ocean's Eleven, Puckoon, The Experience Box (also prod.), A Yiddish World Remembered (doc., narr.), Ocean's Twelve, Open Window, Ocean's Thirteen, The Ten Commandments (voice), The Deal, The Caller, Removal, Expecting Mary, Noah's Ark: The New Beginning (voice), Morning.
TELEVISION: *Movies:* The Rules of Marriage, Vanishing Act, Conspiracy: The Trial of the Chicago 8, Stolen: One Husband, Somebody's Daughter, Bloodlines: Murder in the Family, The Shining, Good As Gold, The Kentucky Derby, Kim Possible: A Sitch in Time, Bad Apple, Uncorked. *Mini-series:* St. Urbain's Horseman. *Series:* ER, Together We Stand, Sessions (HBO), Getting Personal, Baby Bob, Kim Possible. *Specials:* Once Upon A Mattress, Come Blow Your Horn, Jack and the Beanstalk (Faerie Tale Theater), Paul Reiser: Out on a Whim, Prime Time, Out to Lunch, Casey at the Bat (Tall Tales & Legends), Seasons in the Valley (narr.). *Guest:* More than 141 appearances.

GOULD, HAROLD

Actor. b. Schenectady, NY, Dec. 10, 1923. e. SUNY, Albany, B.A. Cornell U., MA., Ph.D. Instructor of theatre and speech, 1953-56, Randolph Macon's Woman's Col., Lynchburg, VA. Asst. prof. drama and speech, 1956-60, Univ. of Calif., Riverside.Acted with Ashland, OR Shakespeare Fest. in 1958 and Mark Taper Forum (The Miser, Once in a Lifetime). Won Obie Award for Off-B'way debut in The Increased Difficulty of Concentration, 1969. ACE Award for Ray Bradbury Theatre. L.A. Drama Critics Award, 1994.
THEATRE: The House of Blue Leaves, Fools, Grown Ups, Artist Descending a Staircase, I Never Sang for My Father, Freud (one man show), Love Letters, Incommunicado, King Lear (Utah Shakespearean Fest.), Mixed Emotions, Old Business, The Tempest (Utah Shakespearean Fest.), Substance of Five (San Diego Olde Globe).
PICTURES: Two for the Seesaw, The Couch, Harper, Inside Daisy Clover, Marnie, An American Dream, The Arrangement, The Lawyer, Mrs. Pollifax: Spy, Where Does It Hurt?, The Sting, The Front Page, Love and Death, The Big Bus, Silent Movie, The One and Only, Seems Like Old Times, Playing for Keeps, Romero, Flesh Suitcase, Killer, Lover's Knot, My Giant, Beloved, Patch Adams, Brown's Requiem, Stuart Little, Dying on the Edge, The Master of Disguise, Freaky Friday, Brother Bear (voice), English as a Second Language.
TELEVISION: *Movies:* To Catch a Star, Moviola: The Scarlett O'Hara War (Emmy nom. 1980), Washington Behind Closed Doors, Aunt Mary, Better Late Than Never, King Crab, Have I Got a Christmas for You, Man in the Santa Claus Suit, I Never Sang For My Father, Get Smart Again!, Mrs. Delafield Wants to Marry (Emmy nom. 1986), Love Bug, Fox Hope, McBride: Anybody Here Murder Marty?. *Series:* Rhoda (Emmy nom. 1978), Park Place, Police Story (Emmy nom. 1975), Foot in the Door, Under One Roof, Singer and Sons, Golden Girls, Feather and Father Gang, The Ray Bradbury Theater (Emmy nom. 1990). *Special:* The Sunset Gang. *Guest:* More than 155 appearances.

GOULD, JASON

Actor. b. New York, NY, Dec. 29, 1966. Son of actor Elliott Gould and actress, director, producer, Barbra Streisand.
PICTURES: Say Anything..., Listen to Me, The Big Picture, The Prince of Tides, Boys Life 3 (also dir., prod., and writer, segment Inside Out).

GOURLEY, SAMUEL D. (SONNY)

Executive. e. B.A. degree in English, Miami Univ. in Oxford, OH. Began career as asst. mgr. At AMC Woodhaven 4 near Philadelphia, PA, in 1975. After one year, promoted to gen. mgr., AMC East 5 theatre in Harrisburg, PA. In 1979, named a film buyer for AMC's Eastern div.; in 1990 became head film buyer for company's Southern div. By 1995, Gourley became executive v.p., film marketing and dir., national settlements. In this position he negotiated film rental payments and managed programming decisions for the chain's domestic screens. In 2005, Gourley was elevated to current position, pres., film programming for AMC Entertainment Inc. He oversees the programming of movies, negotiates film rental terms for each featured release and manages relationships with studios. Gourley currently serves on the advisory bd. of Tent 25 Variety-The Children's Charity located in Los Angeles, as well as serving on the bd. of the local Tent 8 Variety - The Children's Charity in Kansas City.

GRABOFF, MARC

Executive. e. Bachelor's degree in communications studies, UCLA, 1977; graduated magna cum laude from Loyola Law School in 1983. Began career in legal field as a founding partner of the firm Silverberg, Katz, Thompson and Braun. He then was a partner at the Los Angeles law firm Troop, Meisinger, Steuber and Pasich. Graboff then entered the TV industry with CBS, and had responsibility for business affairs for both the CBS Television Network and CBS Productions. Graboff joined NBC after serving as senior v.p., CBS Entertainment. In Nov. 2000, Graboff was appointed executive v.p., NBC West Coast, overseeing business affairs activities related to all NBC's Burbank-based divisions, including NBC Entertainment, NBC Studios and NBC Enterprises. In May 2004, he became executive v.p. NBC Universal Television Group. Jan. 2006 marked Graboff's promotion to president, NBC Universal Television, West Coast. In May 2007 Graboff was promoted to co-chairman, NBC Entertainment & Universal Media Studios. Graboff reported to Jeff Zucker, president & CEO of NBC Universal. 2009, Graboff became sole Chairman and reports to Jeff Gaspin.

GRADE, MICHAEL, C.B.E.

Executive. b. London, England, March 8, 1943. e. Stowe. Entered industry in 1966 as a theatrical agent with the Grade organization. Early career as newspaper columnist, became an executive at London Weekend Television then Embassy Television in Hollywood. Joined BBC Television, 1983 as controller of BBC One and director of programmes (TV), 1986. Joined Channel 4 as chief executive, 1988-1997. Became chief executive of First Leisure Corporation plc in 1997, where he oversaw that company's restructuring in 1999. He has been non-executive chmn. of Pinewood Shepperton plc since 2000. In May 2004 he was appointed chmn. of the BBC. He was also chairman of the UK's National Lottery operator Camelot. He resigned from BBC in Nov. 2006 and became executive chmn. of ITV in Jan. 2007. He is a trustee of the National Film and Television School. He is also the non-executive chmn. of Ocado (food delivery co.).

GRAFF, TODD

Actor, Writer. b. New York, NY, Oct. 22, 1959. e. SUNY / Purchase.
THEATRE: NY: Baby (Tony nom., Theatre World Award), Birds of Paradise.
PICTURES: *Actor:* Sweet Lorraine (also composed songs), Five Corners, Dominick & Eugene, The Abyss, An Innocent Man, Opportunity Knocks, City of Hope, Death to Smoochy. *Writer:* Used People, The Vanishing (also co-prod.), Fly by Night (also actor), Angie (also co-prod., cameo), The Beautician and the Beast, Camp (also dir.), Bandslam (dir., writer).
TELEVISION: *Movies:* Framed, The Marshall Chronicles (pilot). *Mini-series:* Summer Stories: The Mall. *Series:* The Electric Company, Vietnam War Story,

GRAHAM, HEATHER

Actress. b. Milwaukee, WI. Jan. 29, 1970.
PICTURES: License to Drive, Twins, Drugstore Cowboy, I Love You to Death, Shout, Guilty as Charged, Twin Peaks: Fire Walk With Me, Diggstown, Six Degrees of Separation, Even Cowgirls Get the Blues, The Ballad of Little Jo, Mrs. Parker and the Vicious Circle, Don't Do It, Terrified, Desert Winds, Swingers, Entertaining Angels: The Dorothy Day Story, Two Girls and a Guy, Boogie Nights, Nowhere, Scream 2, Committed, Bowfinger, Lost in Space, Austin Powers: The Spy Who Shagged Me, Kiss & Tell, Committed, Sidewalks of New York, When the Cat's Away, Alien Love Triangle, Killing Me Softly, From Hell, .45, Say It Isn't So, The Guru, Austin Powers in Goldmember, Hope Springs, Blessed, .45, Cake, Gray Matters, Mary, Broken, Bobby, Adrift in Manhattan, Seymour's Last Rule (also prod.), Miss Conception, Boogie Woogie, Baby on Board, Father of Invention, Son of Morning, The Hangover, Fallen Moon, Vengeance: A Love Story, Georgia, The Friday Principal.
TELEVISION: *Movies:* Student Exchange, O Pioneers!. *Series:* Twin Peaks, Scrubs, Emily's Reasons Why Not (also pilot).

GRAHAM, LAUREN

Actress. b. Honolulu, Hawaii. March. 16, 1967.
PICTURES: Nightwatch, One True Thing, Confessions of a Sexist Pig, Dill Scallion, Lucky 13, Chasing Destiny, Sweet November, Bad Santa, Seeing Other People, The Pacifier, The Moguls, Because I Said So, Evan Almighty, Flash of Genius, Birds of America, The Answer Man, Cloudy with a Chance of Meatballs (voice), It's Kind of a Funny Story.
TELEVISION: *Movies:* Chasing Destiny, Objects of Desire (exec. prod.), The Bridget Show. *Series:* Good Company, Caroline in the City, Townies, Conrad Bloom, M.Y.O.B, Gilmore Girls (Golden Globe nom. 2002), Parenthood. *Guest:* More than 56 appearances.

GRAMMER, KELSEY

Actor, Producer. b. St. Thomas, Virgin Islands, Feb. 20, 1955. e. Juilliard. Acting debut on tv in Another World. Supplied voice for Disney/Mickey Mouse short Runaway Brain. CEO of Grammnet Productions. Numerous commercial voice overs.
THEATRE: *B'way:* Sunday in the Park With George, Macbeth, Othello. *Boston:* Macbeth, Hamlet. *LA:* Sweeney Todd, Richard II.
PICTURES: Down Periscope, Star Trek: First Contact (cameo), Anastasia (voice), The Real Howard Spitz, Standing on Fishes, Toy Story 2 (voice), New Jersey Turnpikes, The Hand Behind the Mouse: The Ub Iwerks Story (narr.), 15 Minutes, Just Visiting, The Big Empty, Teacher's Pet (voice), The Good Humor Man (also exec. prod.), Even Money, X-Men: The Last Stand, The Simpsons Movie (voice), Swing Vote, An American Carol, Crazy on the Outside, Middle Men, Fame, Dorothy of OZ (voice).
TELEVISION: *Movies:* Macbeth, Mickey's 60th Birthday, Dance 'Til Dawn, Top of the Hill, Beyond Suspicion, The Innocent, London Suite, The Pentagon Wars, Influences: From Yesterday to Today (host), Animal Farm (voice), Mr. St. Nick, Benedict Arnold: A Question of Honor, A Christmas Carol: The Musical, Frasier: Analyzing the Laughter, My Ex Life, Dash 4 Cash, Action News, The Kelsey Grammer and Bill Zucker Comedy Hour (also prod.). *Mini-series:* Kennedy, George Washington, Crossings, Heroes of Comedy: Women on Top (doc.). *Series:* Cheers (2 Emmy nom.), Wings (Emmy nom. 1992), Frasier (4 Emmy Awards; 9 other nom.; 2 Golden Globe Awards, 6 other nom.; DGA nom. 1999), Fired Up (exec. prod. only), Gary the Rat (voice, exec. prod.), In-Laws (exec. prod.), World Cup Comedy (exec. prod.), Medium (exec. prod.), Kelsey Grammer Presents: The Sketch Show (also exec. prod.), Out of Practice (dir., pilot) The Simpsons (voice, Emmy Award 2006), The Game (prod. only), Back to You, Hank (exec. prod.). *Documentaries:* First Dogs (narr.), The American Revolution (voice), Keeli & Ivy: Chimps Like Us (narr.), The Real Allison DuBois (short), Generation Boom (narr.). *Guest:* More than 172 appearances.

GRANATH, HERBERT A.

Executive. e. Fordham U. Started with ABC TV in sales, marketing and production. 1979, became v.p. of Capital Cities/ABC Video Enterprises Inc.; 1982-93, served as pres. of same; Oct. 1993, named pres. ABC Cable and International Broadcast Group, sr. v.p. Capital Cities/ABC Inc. During this time he served as Chairman of the Board of ESPN, A&E, The History Channel, The Biography Channel and Lifetime Television. Internationally he was a founding partner and bd. member of Eurosport, the largest cable network in Europe. Until 2002, Director, Chairman Emeritus, ESPN. Senior Content Advisor, Callahan Associates International. Currently is non-executive vice chairman of the Bd. of Central European Media Enterprises and Director for Crown Media Holdings, Inc. Past-president of the International Council of the National Academy of Television Arts and Sciences. Trustee of the American Museum of the Moving Image. Past-president of the Veterans Bedside Network, past member of the New York City Council for Motion Pictures Radio and Television. Included in the numerous awards he has received are two Tony awards, along with six Tony nominations, an International EMMY (Lifetime Achievement in International TV), as well as a U.S. EMMY (Lifetime Achievement in Sports Television).

GRANT, DAVID MARSHALL

Actor. b. Westport, CT, June 21, 1955. e. Yale School of Drama.
THEATRE: NY: Sganarelle, Table Settings, The Tempest, Bent, The Survivor, Making Movies, Angels in America: Millenium Approaches/Perestroika, Three Sisters. Regional: Bent (also dir.), Once in a Lifetime, Lake Boat, Free and Clear, True West, The Wager, Rat in the Skull, Snakebit (author), The End of the Day.
PICTURES: French Postcards (debut, 1979), Happy Birthday Gemini, The End of August, American Flyers, The Big Town, Bat 21, Air America, Strictly Business, Forever Young, The Rock, The Chamber, Remembering Sex, People I Know, The Stepford Wives, The Devil Wears Prada.
TELEVISION: *Movies:* Kent State, Legs, Sessions, Dallas: The Early Years, What She Doesn't Know, Citizen Cohn, Through the Eyes of a Killer, Noriega: God's Favorite, Jenifer (s.p. only). *Series:* thirtysomething, Brothers & Sisters. *Special:* A Doonesbury Special (voice). *Pilot:* Graham. *Host:* The Legend of Billy the Kid (Emmy nom. 1994), Night Sins. *Guest:* More than 45 appearances.

GRANT, HUGH

Actor. b. London, England, Sept. 9, 1960. e. New Coll., Oxford U. Acted with OUDS before landing role in Oxford Film Foundation's Privileged. Acted at Nottingham Playhouse and formed revue group, The Jockeys of Norfolk.
PICTURES: Privileged (debut, 1982), Maurice, White Mischief, The Lair of the White Worm, The Dawning, Remando al Viento (Rowing With the Wind), Bengali Night, Impromptu, Crossing the Line, The Remains of the Day, Night Train to Venice, Sirens, Four Weddings and a Funeral (BAFTA & Golden Globe Awards 1995), Bitter Moon, The Englishman Who Went Up a Hill But Came Down a Mountain, Nine Months, An Awfully Big Adventure, Restoration, Sense and Sensibility, Extreme Measures (also prod.), Notting Hill (Golden Globe nom. 2000), Mickey Blue-Eyes, Small Time Crooks, Bridget Jones's Diary, About a Boy (Golden Globe nom. 2003), Two Weeks Notice, Love Actually, Bridget Jones: The Edge of Reason, American Dreamz, Music and Lyrics (also soundtrack performer), Did You Hear About the Morgans?.
TELEVISION: *Movies/Specials:* Handel: Honour, Profit and Pleasure, Jenny's War, The Demon Lover, The Lady and the Highwayman, Champagne Charlie, Lord Elgin and Some Stones

of No Value, 'Til We Meet Again, Our Sons (U.S.), The Changeling, The Trials of Oz. *Mini-series:* The Last Place on Earth, The Detective. *Series:* Ladies in Charge. *Guest:* More than 111 appearances.

GRANT, LEE

Actress, Director. r.n. Lyova Rosenthal. b. New York, NY, Oct. 31, 1931. m. producer Joseph Feury. Daughter is actress Dinah Manoff. At 4 was member of Metropolitan Opera Company; played princess in L'Orocolo. Member of the American Ballet at 11. e. Juilliard Sch. of Music, studied voice, violin and dance. At 18 with road co. Oklahoma as understudy. Acting debut: Joy to the World.
THEATRE: Acted in a series of one-acters at ANTA with Henry Fonda. Detective Story (Critics Circle Award, 1949), Lo and Behold, A Hole in the Head, Wedding Breakfast; road co. Two for the Seesaw, The Captains and the Kings; toured with Electra, Silk Stockings, St. Joan, Arms and the Man, The Maids (Obie Award), Prisoner of Second Avenue.
PICTURES: Detective Story (debut, 1951; Acad. Award nom. ; Golden Globe nom. 1952), Storm Fear, Middle of the Night, Affair of the Skin, The Balcony, Terror in the City, Divorce American Style, In the Heat of the Night (Golden Globe nom. 1968), Valley of the Dolls, Buona Sera Mrs. Campbell, The Big Bounce, Marooned, The Landlord (Academy Award nom.; Golden Globe nom. 1971), There Was a Crooked Man, Plaza Suite, Portnoy's Complaint, The Internecine Project, Shampoo (Academy Award, best supporting actress, Golden Globe nom. 1976), Voyage of the Damned (Academy Award nom.; Golden Globe nom. 1977), Airport '77, Damien: Omen II, The Swarm, The Mafu Cage, When You Comin' Back Red Ryder, Little Miss Marker, Charlie Chan and the Curse of the Dragon Queen, Visiting Hours, Teachers, The Big Town, Defending Your Life, Under Heat, It's My Party, The Substance of Fire, Poor Liza, Dr. T & the Women, The Amati Girls, Mulholland Dr. *Dir.:* Tell Me a Riddle, Willmar Eight, Staying Together.
TELEVISION: *Movies:* Night Slaves, The Love Song of Bernard Kempenski, BBC's The Respectful Prostitute, The Neon Ceiling (Emmy Award, 1971), Columbo: Ransom for a Dead Man (Emmy nom. 1971), The Shape of Things (Emmy nom. 1974), Lt. Schuster's Wife, Partners in Crime, What Are Best Friends For?, Perilous Voyage, The Spell, Million Dollar Face, For Ladies Only, Thou Shalt Not Kill, Bare Essence, Will There Really Be A Morning?, The Hijacking of the Achille Lauro, She Said No, Something to Live For: The Alison Gertz Story, In My Daughter's Name, Citizen Cohn (Emmy nom. 1993). *Mini-series:* Backstairs at the White House, Mussolini--The Untold Story. *Series:* Search for Tomorrow (1953-4), Peyton Place (Emmy Award, 1966), Fay (Emmy nom. 1976), Judd for the Defense (Emmy nom. 1969). *Specials:* Plaza Suite, Baghdad ER (exec. prod.). *Director:* Nobody's Child (DGA Award 1987), Shape of Things, When Women Kill, A Matter of Sex, Down and Out in America, No Place Like Home, Following Her Heart, "Intimate Portrait" series, A Father... A Son... Once Upon a Time in Hollywood, American Masters (narr., dir. one episode). *Guest:* More than 117 appearances.

GRANT, RICHARD E.

Actor. b. Mbabane, Swaziland, May 5, 1957. e. Cape Town U., South Africa (combined English and drama course). Co-founded multi-racial Troupe Theatre Company with fellow former students and members of Athol Fugard and Yvonne Bryceland's Space Theatre, acting in and directing contemporary and classic plays. Moved to London 1982 where performed in fringe and rep. theater. Nominated most promising newcomer in Plays and Players, 1985, for Tramway Road.
PICTURES: Withnail and I, Hidden City, How to Get Ahead in Advertising, Killing Dad, Mountains of the Moon, Henry and June, Warlock, L.A. Story, Hudson Hawk, The Player, Bram Stoker's Dracula, Franz Kafka's It's A Wonderful Life (short), The Age of Innocence, Ready to Wear (Pret-a-Porter), Jack and Sarah, Twelfth Night, The Portrait of a Lady, Spice World, Keep the Aspidstra Flying, The Serpent's Kiss, St. Ives, Cash in Hand, The Match, The Little Vampire, William Shakespeare, Cocozza's Way, Hildegarde, Gosford Park, Monsieur N. Bright Young Things, Tooth, The Story of an African Farm, Colour Me Kubrick, Wah-Wah (dir., writer only), Corpse Bride (voice), Garfield: A Tail of Two Kitties (voice), Penelope, Filth and Wisdom, Jackboots on Whitehall (voice), Nutcracker and the Rat King, Cosi, Zambezia Foster.
TELEVISION: *Movies/Specials:* Honest Decent and True, Codename Kyril, Thieves in the Night (also released theatrically), Here Is the News, Suddenly Last Summer, Hard Times, Bed, The Miracle Maker (voice) Moonshot-The Spirit of '69 (voice), Trial & Tribulation III, The Scarlet Pimpernel Meets Madame Guillotine, The Scarlet Pimpernel and the Kidnapped King, A Christmas Carol, Victoria's Secrets, The Miracle Maker, Victoria Wood with All the Trimmings, The Scarlet Pimpernel: A Good Name, We Know Where You Live, Case of Evil, The Hound of the Baskervilles, The 100 Greatest Movie Stars (documentary, narrator), The Secret Policeman's Ball, Marple: Nemesis, Freezing. *Mini-series:* Lizzie's Pictures, Cold Lazarus, Karaoke, The Scarlet Pimpernel, Doctor Who: Scream of the Shalka (voice), Above and Beyond. *Series:* Sweet Sixteen, Captain Star (voice), Posh Nosh, Home Farm Twins. *Guest:* More than 109 appearances.

GRANT, SUSANNAH

Writer b. New York, NY, January 4, 1963.
PICTURES: Pocahontas (s.p.), Ever After (s.p.), Erin Brockovich (Academy Award nom.; WGA nom. 2001), 28 Days, Unfaithful, In Her Shoes (s.p.), Catch and Release (also dir.), Charlotte's Web (s.p.), The Soloist (s.p.), Burlesque.
TELEVISION: *Series:* Party of Five (also prod. & dir.).

GRAVES, PETER

Actor. r.n. Peter Aurness. b. Minneapolis, MN, March 18, 1926. e. U. of Minnesota. Brother of actor James Arness. Played with bands, radio announcer, while at school; U.S. Air Force 2 yrs.; summer stock appearances.
PICTURES: Rogue River (debut, 1950), Fort Defiance, Red Planet Mars, Stalag 17, East of Sumatra, Beneath the 12-Mile Reef, Killers From Space, The Raid, Black Tuesday, Wichita, Long Gray Line, Night of the Hunter, Naked Street, Fort Yuma, Court Martial of Billy Mitchell, It Conquered the World, The Beginning of the End, Death in Small Doses, Poor White Trash (Bayou), Wolf Larsen, A Rage to Live, Texas Across the River, Valley of Mystery, The Ballad of Josie, Sergeant Ryker, The Five Man Army, Sidecar Racers, Parts: The Clonus Horror, Survival Run, Airplane!, Savannah Smiles, Airplane II: The Sequel, Number One With a Bullet, Addams Family Values.
TELEVISION: *Movies*: A Call to Danger, The President's Plane is Missing, Scream of the Wolf, The Underground Man, Where Have All the People Gone?, Dead Man on the Run, SST-Death Flight, The Rebels, Death on the Freeway, The Memory of Eva Ryker, 300 Miles for Stephanie, If It's Tuesday It Still Must Be Belgium, These Old Broads. *Mini-series*: Winds of War, War and Remembrance. *Series*: Fury, Whiplash, Court-Martial, Mission Impossible, New Mission: Impossible (Emmy nom.; 1969; Golden Globe Award 1971, 2 other nom.), With You in Spirit, 7th Heaven. *Host/narrator:* Discover! The World of Science, A&E Biography series narrator (Emmy Award 1997), Tarzan the Legacy of Edgar Rice Burroughs. *Guest:* More than 105 appearances.
(d. March 14, 2010)

GRAVES, RUPERT

Actor. b. Weston-Super-Mare, England, June 30, 1963. Before film debut worked as a clown with the Delta travelling circus in England.
THEATRE: The Killing of Mr. Toad, 'Tis Pity She's a Whore, St. Ursula's in Danger, Sufficient Carbohydrates, Amadeus, Torch Song Trilogy, Candida, Pitchfork Disney, History of Tom Jones, A Madhouse in Goa, A Midsummer Night's Dream, Design for Living.
PICTURES: A Room with a View, Maurice, A Handful of Dust, The Children, Where Angels Fear to Tread, Damage, The Madness of King George, The Innocent Sleep, Different for Girls, Mrs. Dalloway, Bent, The Revengers Comedies, Dreaming of Joseph Lees, All My Loved Ones, Room to Rent, Extreme Ops, Rag Tale, V for Vendetta, Intervention, Death at a Funeral, Made in Dagenham.
TELEVISION: *Movies:* Good and Bad at Games, The Plot to Kill Hitler, Royal Celebration, Open Fire, Vice Versa, All for Love, A Life of Puccini, Fortunes of War, The Sheltering Desert, Union Matters, Starting Out, Inspector Morse, Doomsday Gun, Cleopatra, Take a Girl Like You, Pride (voice), A Waste of Shame: The Mystery of Shakespeare and His Sonnets, To Be First, Clapham Junction, The Dinner Party, God on Trial, Marple: A Pocket Full of Rye, The Good Times Are Killing Me. *Mini-series:* Fortunes of War, The Tenant of Wildfell Hall, The Blonde Bombshell, The Forsyth Saga, Charles II: The Power & the Passion, The Forsyte Saga, Series II, The Last King, Son of the Dragon, Midnight Man. *Guest:* More than 47 appearances.

GRAY, LINDA

Actress. b. Santa Monica, CA, Sept. 12, 1940.
PICTURES: Under the Yum Yum Tree, Palm Springs Weekend, Dogs, Fun With Dick and Jane, Oscar, Star of Jaipur, Expecting Mary, The Flight of the Swan.
TELEVISION: *Movies:* The Big Ripoff, Murder in Peyton Place, The Grass is Always Greener Over the Septic Tank, Two Worlds of Jennie Logan, Haywire, The Wild and the Fire, Not in Front of the Children, The Entertainers, Highway Heartbreaker, Moment of Truth: Why My Daughter?, Bonanza: The Return, To My Daughter with Love, Accidental Meeting, Moment of Truth: Broken Pledges, When the Cradle Falls, Dallas: War of the Ewings, Doing Dallas, When Shoulderpads Ruled the World, After Dallas, Intimate Portrait: Linda Gray, McBride: It's Murder, Madam. *Series:* Dallas (Emmy nom. 1981; 2 Golden Globe nom.), Melrose Place, Models Inc., The Bold and the Beautiful. *Guest:* More than 97 appearances.

GRAY, THOMAS K.

Executive, Producer. b. New York City, N. Y., July 1, 1945. e. U. of Arizona, B.A., post grad work at American Graduate School of Int'l Management, Phoenix. Began career as management trainee with United Atists film exchange in Spain, 1970, and year later became managing director, UA, Chile. Also managing director for UA, New Zealand, 1972; Columbia, 1973; South and East Africa, 1974. Joined Cinema Int'l. Corp., London, as exec. assist.

to co-chairman, 1974, and moved up to managing director of CIC/Warner, South Africa, 1976. Returned to UA as vice pres. Far East, Latin America, Africa and Australia, 1977. Joined Golden Communications Overseas Ltd., London, as v.p., foreign sales in 1980. In 1984, joined Golden Harvest Films, Inc. as sr. vice. pres., production and became the executive in charge of prod. for Golden Harvest features. In 1992, Gray became pres. and CEO of Rim Film Distribution Inc. Served as Pres. and CEO of Imagi Entertainment. Currently Pres./CEO of Dalat Films.
PICTURES: Flying, The Protector, China O'Brien, China O'Brien II, A Show of Force, Teenage Mutant Ninja Turtles, Best of Martial Arts (prod.), Teenage Mutant Ninja Turtles II: Secret of the Ooze (prod.), Teenage Mutant Ninja Turtles III, Highlander: Vengeance, TMNT (prod.).

GRAYSON, KATHRYN

Actress, Singer. r.n. Zelma Hedrick. b. Winston-Salem, NC, Feb. 9, 1923. e. St. Louis schools.
THEATRE: Camelot, Rosalinda, Merry Widow, Kiss Me Kate, Showboat.
PICTURES: Andy Hardy's Private Secretary (debut, 1941), The Vanishing Virginian, Rio Rita, Seven Sweethearts, Thousands Cheer; Anchors Aweigh, Ziegfeld Follies, Two Sisters from Boston, Till the Clouds Roll By, It Happened in Brooklyn, The Kissing Bandit, That Midnight Kiss, The Toast of New Orleans, Grounds for Marriage, Show Boat, Lovely to Look At, The Desert Song, So This Is Love, Kiss Me Kate, The Vagabond King, A Century of Cinema, Too Damn Hot (video short).
TELEVISION: *Special:* Die Fliedermaus.
(d. February 17, 2010)

GRAZER, BRIAN

Producer. b. Los Angeles, CA, July 12, 1951. e. U. of Southern California. Started as legal intern at Warner Bros.; later script reader (for Brut/Faberge) & talent agent. Joined Edgar J. Scherick-Daniel Blatt Co.; then with Ron Howard as partner in Imagine Films Entertainment in 1986, where he currently remains co-chmn. alongside Howard. He has personally been nominated for three Academy Awards. Received NATO/ShoWest Producer of the Year Award, 1992. In 1998 he received a star on the Hollywood Walk of Fame. The Producers Guild of America bestowed on Grazer the David O Selznick Lifetime Achievement Award in 2001. In 2002 Grazer won the Best Picture Oscar for A Beautiful Mind. ShowWest awarded Grazer with a Lifetime Achievement Award in 2003.
PICTURES: Night Shift, Splash (also co-story, Academy Award nom. 1985), Real Genius, Spies Like Us, Armed and Dangerous (also co-story), Like Father Like Son, Vibes, The 'burbs, Parenthood, Cry-Baby (co-exec. prod.), Kindergarten Cop, The Doors (co-exec. prod.), Closet Land (co-exec. prod.), Backdraft (exec. prod.), My Girl, Far and Away, Housesitter, Boomerang, CB4 (co-exec. prod.), Cop and a Half, For Love or Money, My Girl 2, Greedy, The Paper, The Cowboy Way, Apollo 13 (Academy Award nom. 1996), Fear, Sgt. Bilko, The Nutty Professor, Ransom, Inventing the Abbotts, Liar Liar, Mercury Rising, Psycho, Life, Into thin Air, How to Eat Fried Worms, Edtv, Bowfinger, Sprockets, The Nutty Professor II, How the Grinch Stole Christmas, A Beautiful Mind (Academy Award 2002), D-Tox, Undercover Brother, Blue Crush, Stealing Harvard, 8 Mile, Intolerable Cruelty, The Cat in the Hat, The Missing, The Alamo, Friday Night Lights, Cinderella Man, Fun with Dick and Jane, Inside Man, The Incredible Shrinking Man, Flight Plan, Tru Blu, Ralph, Inside Deep Throat (doc.), The Da Vinci Code, Bra Boys (doc.), American Gangster, Frost/Nixon (Academy Award nom. 2009), Changeling, Robin Hood, Angels & Demons, Waterbug, Your Cheating Heart, The Emperor's Children, The Day Trader, Restless, Cowboys and Aliens, Hoover.
TELEVISION: *Executive Prod.: Movies:* Zuma Beach, Thou Shalt Not Commit Adultery, Splash Too, Student Affairs, Boarding School, Beyond, Nice Girls Don't Get the Corner Office, 24: Redemption. *Mini-series:* From Earth to the Moon (prod. Emmy Award 1998). *Series:* Shadow Chasers, Take Five, Ohara, Parenthood, Hiller & Diller, Felicity, Sports Night, The PJs (Emmy nom. 1999), Wonderland, The Beast, 24 (Emmy Award 2006; 5 Emmy noms.), Miss Match, Arrested Development (Emmy Award 2004; 2 Emmy Award nom. 2005, 2006), The Big House, The Inside, The F.B.I., Shark, Misconceptions, Friday Night Lights, Treasure Hunters (co-prod.), Curious George (2 Emmy noms. Emmy Award 2008), Lie to Me, Parenthood. *Special:* Poison (prod.).

GREATREX, RICHARDS

Cinematographer.
PICTURES: Forbidden Sun, For Queen and Country, War Requiem, A Foreign Field, Deadly Advice, Blue Juice, Mrs. Brown, Shakespeare in Love (Academy Award nom.; ASC nom. 1999), Where the Heart Is, A Knight's Tale, Happy Now, I Capture the Castle, Connie and Carla, The Upside of Anger, The Rocket Post, Chaos, The Detonator, Big Nothing, Flawless, Run, Fat Boy, Run, Resistance.
TELEVISION: *Movies:* Aderyn Papur...and Pigs Might Fly, Brond, The Plant, Truth or Dare, The Woman in White, Dalziel and Pascoe: Exit Lines, Tess of the D'Urbervilles, Getting Hurt, Warriors, The Last of the Blonde Bombshells, Sons and Lovers. *Mini-series:* Castle (doc.), Sea Wolf. *Series:* Moby Dick.

GREEN, JACK N.

Cinematographer. b. San Francisco, Nov. 18, 1946. Started as camera operator for Bruce Surtees. Received ASC Lifetime Achievement Award 2009.
PICTURES: *Camera operator:* Fighting Mad, Firefox, Honky Tonk Man, Risky Business, Sudden Impact, Tightrope, Beverly Hills Cop, City Heat, Pale Rider, Ratboy. *Cinematographer:* Heartbreak Ridge, Like Father Like Son, The Dead Pool, Bird, Pink Cadillac, Race for Glory, White Hunter Black Heart, The Rookie, Deceived, Unforgiven (Academy Award nom. 1993), Rookie of the Year, A Perfect World, Bad Company, The Bridges of Madison County (ASC nom. 1996), The Net, The Amazing Panda Adventure, Twister, Speed 2: Cruise Control, Midnight in the Garden of Good and Evil, True Crime, Girl Interrupted, Space Cowboys, Pretty When You Cry, Golden Dreams, Wounded, Against the Ropes, Secondhand Lions, 50 First Dates, Serenity, The 40 Year-Old Virgin, The Drummer, Click, The 1 Second Film (exec. prod.), Are We Done Yet?, My Best Friend's Girl (dir. of photog.), Sweetwater, Oy Vey! My Son Is Gay!! (visual consult.), Diary of a Wimpy Kid, Hot Tub Time Machine, The Letters, Sweetwater.

GREEN, SETH

Actor. b. Philadelphia, PA, Feb. 8, 1974.
PICTURES: The Hotel New Hampshire, Willy/Milly, Radio Days, Can't Buy Me Love, My Stepmother is an Alien, Big Business, Pump Up the Volume, Ticks, The Double 0 Kid, Airborne, White Man's Burden, To Gillian on Her 37th Birthday, Austin Powers: International Man of Mystery, Enemy of the State, The Attic Expeditions, Can't Hardly Wait, Austin Powers: The Spy Who Shagged Me, Stonebrook, Idle Hands, The Attic Expeditions, The Trumpet of the Swan, Knockaround Guys, Diary of a Mad Freshman, Rat Race, Josie and the Pussycats, America's Sweethearts, Knockaround Guys, Rock Star 101, Rat Race, Austin Powers in Goldmember, Party Monster, The Italian Job, Scooby-Doo 2: Monsters Unleashed, Without a Paddle, Family Guy: The Movie (voice), The Best Man, The 1 Second Film (prod.), Sex Drive, Old Dogs, Mars Needs Moms!.
TELEVISION: *Movies:* Stephen King's It, Our Shining Moment, Arcade, The Day My Parents Ran Away. *Series:* Good & Evil, The Byrds of Paradise, Buffy the Vampire Slayer, Temporarily Yours, Batman Beyond (voice), Family Guy (voice), Greg the Bunny, Robot Chicken (voice, also writer, dir., prod., creator, 4 Emmy noms.). *Guest:* More than 163 appearances.

GREENAWAY, PETER

Director, Writer. b. Newport, Wales, Apr. 5, 1942. Trained as a painter, first exhibition was at Lord's Gallery in 1964. Started making short films and documentaries in 1966, including: A Walk Through H, The Falls, Act of God, Vertical Features Remake. Directorial feature debut in 1982. Author of numerous books including, 100 Objects to Represent the World, The Physical Self, Les Bruits des Nuages.
PICTURES: The Draughtsman's Contract, A Zed and Two Noughts, The Belly of an Architect, Drowning By Numbers, The Cook The Thief His Wife and Her Lover, Prospero's Books, The Baby of Macon, The Pillow Book (also ed.), The Bridge, Death of a Composer (also act.), 8 1/2 Women, The Death of a Composer: Rosa, a Horse Drama, The Man in the Bath, The Tulse Luper Suitcases, Nighwatching.
TELEVISION: Death in the Seine, series of 9 Cantos from Dante's Inferno in collaboration with painter Tom Phillips, M Is for Man Music Mozart, Darwin.

GREENBURG, ROSS

Executive. e. B.A., political science, Brown University in Providence, RI. Greenburg carved out a niche and career at HBO Sports, starting with the unit in 1978. In 1985, he was named v.p. & executive producer. In Sept. 2000 Greenburg was named to his current post as president of HBO Sports. He has won more than 50 major TV sports awards, including five Peabody Awards, 20 Sports Emmy Awards,(r) 21 CableACE Awards, 12 Cine Golden Eagle Awards, five Monitor Awards from the Video Tape Production Association, and several accolades from the Chicago International Film Festival and the International Film and Television Festival of New York.

GREENE, ELLEN

Actress, Singer. b. Brooklyn, NY, Feb. 22, 1950. e. Ryder Coll. After coll. joined musical road show. Appeared in cabaret act at The Brothers & the Sisters Club and Reno Sweeney's, NY. Off-B'way debut, Rachel Lily Rosenbloom. B'way in the The Little Prince and The Aviator. With NY Shakespeare Fest. in In the Boom Boom Room, The Sorrows of Steven, The Threepenny Opera (Tony nom.). Film debut Next Stop, Greenwich Village (1976). Off B'way co-starred in musical Little Shop of Horrors 1982, repeated role in film. Also Off-B'way in Weird Romance. L.A. stage: David's Mother.
PICTURES: Next Stop Greenwich Village (debut, 1976), I'm Dancing as Fast as I Can, Little Shop of Horrors, Me and Him, Talk Radio, Pump Up the Volume, Stepping Out, Rock a Doodle (voice), Fathers and Sons, Naked Gun 33 1/3: The Final Insult, Wagons East!, The Professional, A Journal of Murder, Jaded, One Fine Day, States of Control, Alex in Wonder, The Cooler, Love Object, Privileged.

TELEVISION: *Movies:* Glory! Glory!, Dinner at Eight, Mystery Woman: Sing Me a Murder, Fielder's Choice, Re-Animated (voice). *Mini-series:* Seventh Avenue. *Series:* Rock Rainbow, Pushing Daisies, Out of Jimmy's Head. *Pilot:* Road Show. *Special:* Rock Follies.

GREENE, GRAHAM

Actor. b. Six Nations Reserve, Ontario, Canada, June 22, 1952. Member of the Oneida tribe. First show business job as audio technician for several rock bands. Began acting in theatre in England.
THEATRE: Diary of a Crazy Boy, Coming Through Slaughter, Crackwalker, Jessica, Dry Lips Oughta Move to Kapuskasing.
PICTURES: Running Brave, Revolution, Powwow Highway, Dances With Wolves (Academy Award nom. 1991), Thunderheart, Clearcut, Savage Land, Rain Without Thunder, Benefit of the Doubt, Maverick, North, Camilla, Die Hard With a Vengeance, Sabotage, The Pathfinder, Dead Innocent, Song of Hiawatha, Wounded, The Education of the Little Tree, Shattered Image, Bad Money, Grey Owl, The Green Mile, Desire, Christmas in the Clouds, Lost and Delirious, Skins, Snow Dogs, Duct Tape Forever, Phil the Alien, Transamerica, A Lobster Tale, The Legend of Secret Pass (voice), All Hat, New Moon, Breakfast with Scot, Valley of the Sun, Running Mates, Gunless.
TELEVISION: *U.S./Movies:* Unnatural Causes, The Last of His Tribe, Cooperstown, Huck and the King of Hearts, Rugged Gold, The Pathfinder, Stranger in Town, Wolf Lake, The New Beachcombers, Big Spender, Coyote Waits, A Thief of Time, Spirit Bear: The Simon Jackson Story, Buffalo Dreams, Luna: Spirit of the Whale. *Mini-series:* Shattered City: The Halifax Explosion, 500 Nations, Into the West. *Series:* Northern Exposure, Cover Me: Based on the True Life of an FBI Family, Wolf Lake, The Red Green Show. *Canada/Series:* 9B, Spirit Bay. *Movies:* Murder Sees the Light, The Great Detective, Street Legal. *Documentaries:* Earth and the American Dream (voice), The Way West (voice), Great Drives (mini-series, host), First Nation Blue (narr.), The Herd (voice), Exhibit A: Secrets of Forensic Science (host), Rocket Science (narr.), Freedom: A History of Us (series, voices), Declaration of Independence (video), The War That Made America (mini-series, narr.). *Guest:* More than 76 appearances.

GREENHUT, ROBERT

Producer. b. New York, NY. e. Univ. of Miami. Began career as prod. asst. on Arthur Hiller's The Tiger Makes Out, 1967. Worked as prod. manager and asst. director on such films as Pretty Poison, The Night They Raided Minsky's, Where's Poppa?, The Owl and the Pussycat, Husbands, Born to Win, Panic in Needle Park, The Last of the Red Hot Lovers. Received Crystal Apple from city of NY and Eastman Kodak Award for lifetime achievement.
PICTURES: *Prod./assoc. prod./exec. prod.:* Huckleberry Finn, Lenny, Dog Day Afternoon, The Front, Annie Hall (DGA Award 1978), Interiors, Hair, Manhattan, Stardust Memories, Arthur, A Midsummer Night's Sex Comedy, The King of Comedy, Zelig, Broadway Danny Rose, The Purple Rose of Cairo, Hannah and Her Sisters (Academy Award nom. 1987), Heartburn, Radio Days, September, Big, Another Woman, Working Girl, New York Stories, Crimes and Misdemeanors, Quick Change, Postcards From the Edge, Alice, Regarding Henry, Shadows and Fog, A League of Their Own, Husbands and Wives, Manhattan Murder Mystery, Renaissance Man, Wolf, Bullets Over Broadway, Mighty Aphrodite, Everyone Says I Love You, The Preacher's Wife, Mom's On the Roof, With Friends Like These, Siegfried and Roy: The Magic Box, White River Kid, Company Man, Seabiscuit (production exec.), Constellation, Stateside, Find Me Guilty, The Wedding Contract, A License to Steal (also dir.), Garfield: A Tail of Two Kitties (special teams coach), The Departed (unit prod. mngr), The Marconi Bros. (consult. prod.), August Rush (also unit prod. mngr.), Brooklyn's Finest, Trust.
TELEVISION: *Movies:* The Silence, Panic in Echo Park, Don't Drink the Water.

GREENSPAN, ALAN

Producer. Owner of International Arts Entertainment.
PICTURES: *Exec. Prod.:* Photographing Fairies, Donnie Brasco, Best Laid Plans, High Fidelity, My Little Eye, Bookies, Adrenaline (assoc. prod.), Fever Pitch (prod.), A Good Woman (prod.), I Really Hate My Job (prod.), Prizefighter (prod.).
TELEVISION: *Movie:* Stanley Park.

GREENWALD, ROBERT

Director, Producer, Teacher. b. New York, NY, Aug. 28, 1948. e. Antioch Coll., New School for Social Research. Teaches film and theatre at NYU, New Lincoln, New School. Formed Robert Greenwald Prods.
THEATRE: A Sense of Humor, I Have a Dream, Me and Bessie.
PICTURES: *Director:* Xanadu, Sweet Hearts Dance (also exec. prod.), Hear No Evil, Breaking Up (also prod.), Steal This Movie (also prod.), My Dark Places: An L.A. Crime Memoir, Bud & Bill (also dir.). *Documentaries:* Outfoxed: Rupert Murdoch's War on Journalism, Uncovered: The War on Iraq (co-prod./dir.), Iraq for Sale: The War Profiteers (prod., dir.), Querida Antonia (co-exec. prod.), Outfoxed: Rupert Murdoch's War on Journalism (also dir.), The Big Buy: Tom DeLay's Stolen Congress, Iraq for Sale: The War Profiteers, Rethink Afghanistan.
TELEVISION: *Movies: Prod.:* The Desperate Miles, 21 Hours at Munich Emmy nom. 1977), Delta Country USA, Escape From Bogen County, Getting Married, Portrait of a Stripper, Miracle on Ice, The Texas Rangers, The First Time, The Crooked E: The Unshredded Truth About Enron. *Exec. prod.:* My Brother's Wife, Hiroshima, Zelda, The Portrait, Daddy, Scattered Dreams, Murder in New Hampshire, Death in Small Doses, Blood on Her Hands, The Day Lincoln Was Shot, The Secret Path, Our Guys: Outrage at Glen Ridge, The Audrey Hepburn Story, Deadlocked, Livin' for Love: The Natalie Cole Story, Sharing the Secret, And Never Let Her Go, Disappearance, Redeemer, Unprecedented: the 2000 Presidential Election (documentary), The Book of Ruth, Plain Truth, Trump Unauthorized. *Director:* Sharon: Portrait of a Mistress, In the Custody of Strangers, The Burning Bed (Emmy nom.; DGA nom. 1985), Katie: Portrait of a Centerfold, Flatbed Annie and Sweetpie: Lady Truckers, Shattered Spirits (also exec. prod.), Forgotten Prisoners. *Mini-series:* A Woman of Independent Means (also co-exec. prod., Emmy nom. 1995), Beach Girls (exec. prod.). *Series:* Sierra Club Chronicles (exec. prod.), The ACLU Freedom Files (exec. prod.).

GREENWOOD, BRUCE

Actor. b. Noranda, Quebec, Canada, Aug. 14, 1956. e. Univ. of British Columbia, London Sch. of Speech and Learning, AADA. Worked in Canadian theater and as lead singer/guitarist with blues/rock band in Vancouver before arriving in LA in 1983.
PICTURES: Bear Island (debut, 1980), First Blood, Malibu Bikini Shop, Another Chance, Wild Orchid, Passenger 57, Exotica, Paint Cans, Dream Man, Father's Day, The Sweet Hereafter, Disturbing Behavior, Thick as Thieves, The Lost Son, Double Jeopardy, Here on Earth, Rules of Engagement, Cord, Thirteen Days, Below, Love Sex Drugs & Money, The Core, Hollywood Homicide, The Water Giant, Ararat, The Republic of Love, I-Robot, Being Julia, Racing Stripes, Capote, Antarctica, The World's Fastest Indian, Eight Below, Deja Vu, I'm Not There, Firehouse Dog, American Dog (voice), National Treasure: Book of Secrets, Cell 213, Star Trek, Mao's Last Dancer, Meek's Cutoff, Barney's Version, Dinner for Schmucks.
TELEVISION: *Movies:* Peyton Place: The Next Generation, Destination: America, In the Line of Duty: The FBI Murders, Perry Mason: The Case of the All-Star Assassin, Spy, Summer Dreams: The Story of the Beach Boys, The Great Pretender, Rio Diablo, Adrift, The Heart of a Child, Bitter Vengeance, Treacherous Beauties, The Companion, Servants of Twilight, Little Kindappers, Twist of Fate, Woman on the Run: The Lawrencia Bembenek Story, Dazzle, The Judds: Love Can Build a Bridge, Tell Me No Secrets, The Absolute Truth, The Color of Courage, The Soul Collector, Haven, The Magnificent Amberson, Meltdown, The Riverman, Saving Milly, John from Cincinnati, The Mermaid Chair. *Mini-series:* A Girl Thing, The Summit. *Series:* Legmen, St. Elsewhere, Knots Landing, Hardball, Nowhere Man, Sleepwalkers, Class of the Titans, John from Cincinnati. *Guest:* More than 80 appearances.

GREIST, KIM

Actress. b. Stamford, CT, May 12, 1958. e. New School.
THEATRE: Second Prize: Two Months in Leningrad, Twelfth Night (NY Shakespeare Fest.).
PICTURES: C.H.U.D. (debut, 1984), Brazil, Manhunter, Throw Momma from the Train, Punchline, Why Me?, Homeward Bound: The Incredible Journey, Houseguest, Homeward Bound II: Lost in San Francisco, The Rose Sisters, H-E Double Hockeysticks, Rockin' Good Times, A Smaller Place, Zoe.
TELEVISION: *Movies:* Payoff, Duplicates, Roswell, Last Exit to Earth.

GREY, BRAD

Executive, Producer. b. Dec. 29, 1957. e. SUNY Buffalo. Managed comedians and signed first client, Bob Saget, while still an undergraduate; mgr., for Garry Shandling, Dana Carvey, Dennis Miller. With manager Bernie Brillstein, formed the prod. co., Brillstein-Grey; later bought out Brillstein's share. During 2005, left Brillstein-Grey for his current position, chairman and CEO of Viacom's Paramount Pictures Corporation.
PICTURES: The Burning, Opportunity Knocks, The Celluloid Closet, Cat and Mouse, Happy Gilmore, The Cable Guy, Bulletproof, Dirty Work, What Planet Are You From? Screwed, Scary Movie, City by the Sea, A View from the Top, Charlie and the Chocolate Factory, Why Men Shouldn't Marry, Infernal Affairs, Running with Scissors, The Departed, The Assassination of Jesse James by the Coward Robert Ford (exec. prod.).
TELEVISION: *Movies:* Don't Try This at Home!, Dennis Miller: They Shoot HBO Specials, Don't They?, Dana Carvey: Critics' Choice, Fantastic Newness, Mr. Show and the Incredible, Fantastical News Report. *Series:* The Boys, The Larry Sanders Show (6 Emmy nom.), Mr. Show, The Naked Truth, The Steve Harvey Show, NewsRadio, Just Shoot Me, Alright Already, C-16: FBI, Politically Incorrect (5 Emmy noms.), The Sopranos (2 Emmy Awards; 5 other noms.), Sammy, Pasadena, According to Jim, Real Time with Bill Maher (exec. prod. 5 Emmy noms.), My Big Fat Greek Life, Married to the Kellys (prod.& exec. prod.), Cracking Up, Jake in Progress. *Documentaries:* Three Sisters: Searching for a Cure, In Memoriam: New York City (Emmy nom. 2002).

GREY, JENNIFER
Actress. b. New York, NY, Mar. 26, 1960. Father is actor Joel Grey. Appeared as dancer in Dr. Pepper commercial before making NY stage debut in Off-B'way play Album. B'way in The Twilight of the Golds.
PICTURES: Reckless (debut, 1984), Red Dawn, The Cotton Club, American Flyers, Ferris Bueller's Day Off, Dirty Dancing (Golden Globe nom. 1988), Bloodhounds of Broadway, Stroke of Midnight (If the Shoe Fits), Wind, Portraits of a Killer, Redbelt, Lover's Knot, Red Meat, The Secrets of My Heart, Bounce, Ritual, Keith.
TELEVISION: *Movies:* Murder in Mississippi, Criminal Justice, Eyes of a Witness, A Case for Murder, The West Side, Waltz, Outrage, Since You've Been Gone, Tales from the Crypt Presents: Revelation, Road to Christmas. *Series:* It's Like You Know..., John from Cincinnati.

GREY, JOEL
Actor, Singer, Dancer. r.n. Joel Katz. b. Cleveland, OH, April 11, 1932. Father was performer Mickey Katz; daughter is actress Jennifer Grey. e. Alexander Hamilton H.S., L.A. Acting debut at 9 years in On Borrowed Time at Cleveland Playhouse. Extensive nightclub appearances before returning to theatre and TV. Performed Silverlake in NY.
THEATRE: *NY:* Come Blow Your Horn, Stop the World—I Want to Get Off, Half a Sixpence, Harry: Noon and Night, Littlest Revue, Cabaret (Tony Award, 1967), George M!, Goodtime Charley, The Grand Tour, Cabaret (1987, B'way revival), Chicago, Wicked. *Regional:* Herringbone.
PICTURES: About Face (debut, 1952), Calypso Heat Wave, Come September, Cabaret (Academy Award, best supporting actor; Golden Globe Award 1973), Man on a Swing, Buffalo Bill and the Indians or Sitting Bull's History Lesson, The Seven Percent Solution, Remo Williams: The Adventure Begins...(Golden Globe nom. 1986), Kafka, The Player, The Music of Chance, The Fantasticks, My Friend Joe, The Empty Mirror, Reaching Normal, Dancer in the Dark, Choke.
TELEVISION: *Movies:* Man on a String, Queenie, A Christmas Carol, Just Deserts, On the Edge. *Mini-series:* Further Tales of the City, *Series:* Oz. *Specials:* Jack and the Beanstalk, George M!, The Wizard of Oz in Concert. *Guest:* More than 130 appearances.

GREYSON, JOHN
Director, Writer. b. Canada, 1960.
PICTURES: Kipling Meets the Cowboy (dir. only), The Jungle Boy (dir. only), Moscow Does Not Believe in Queers (dir. only), A Moffie Called Simon (dir. only), Pissoir, Zero Patience, Lilies (dir. only), Uncut (also prod.), The Law of Enclosures. *Documentaries:* After the Bath, Fig Trees (dir., writer, prod.).
TELEVISION: *Series:* The Industry, Queer as Folk, Paradise Falls.

GRIECO, RICHARD
Actor. b. Watertown, NY, 1966. Started with Elite Modeling Agency. Studied acting at Warren Robertson Theatre Workshop appearing in prods. of Orphans, Golden Boy. As musician released album Waiting for the Sky to Fall.
PICTURES: Born to Ride, If Looks Could Kill, Mobsters, Tomcat: Dangerous Desires, Bolt, The Demolitionist, Mutual Needs, Heaven or Vegas, Against the Law, A Night at the Roxbury, Blackheart, Vital Parts, Point Doom, Final Payback, Raging Silence, Last Cry, Sweet Revenge, Manhattan Midnight, Fish Don't Blink, Death-Deceit-And Destiny Aboard the Orient Express, Samhain, Wounded, Forget About It, Raiders of the Damned, The Ghost Riders (also exec. prod., writer, dir.).
TELEVISION: *Movies:* Sin and Redemption, A Vow to Kill, It Was Him or Us, When Time Expires, Sinbad: Battle of the Dark Knights Ultimate Deception, Webs, Phantom Force. *Series:* One Life to Live, 21 Jump Street, Booker, Marker.

GRIER, DAVID ALAN
Actor. b. Detroit, MI, June 30, 1955. e. U. of MI, Yale. Acted with Yale Rep.
THEATRE: *NY:* A Soldier's Play, The First (Theatre World Award), Richard III, Dreamgirls, The Merry Wives of Windsor.
PICTURES: Streamers (debut, 1983), A Soldier's Story, Beer, From the Hip, Amazon Women on the Moon, Off Limits, I'm Gonna Git You Sucka, Me and Him, Loose Cannons, Almost an Angel, The Player, Boomerang, In the Army Now, Blankman, Tales From the Hood, Jumanji, Top of the World, McHale's Navy, Return to Me, The Adventures of Rocky and Bullwinkle, 15 Minutes, I Shaved My Legs for This, The Woodsman, Gettin' the Man's Foot Outta Your Baadasssss!, Bewitched, Little Man, Kissing Cousins, The Poker House (also writer), An American Carol, Something Like a Business, The Hustle, Hoodwinked 2: Hood vs. Evil (voice), Dance Flick.
TELEVISION: *Movies:* A Saintly Switch, The '60s, King of Texas, The Muppets' Wizard of Oz, Thugaboo: Sneaker Madness (voice), Thugaboo: A Miracle on D-Roc's Street, Gym Teacher: The Movie. *Series:* All Is Forgiven, In Living Color, The Preston Episodes (also co-exec. prod.), Damon, Random Acts of Comedy, DAG, Premium Blend, Life with Bonnie. Crank Yankers, Jimmy Kimmel Live (guest host), Tough Crowd with Colin Quinn, My Wife and Kids, David Alan Grier's Chocolate News (also exec. prod., writer), Dancing with the Stars. *Specials:* Young Hollywood Awards (host, 2003). *Guest:* More than 123 appearances.

GRIER, PAM
Actress. b. Winston-Salem, NC, May 26, 1949.
PICTURES: The Big Doll House, Big Bird Cage, Black Mama White Mama, Cool Breeze, Hit Man, Women in Cages, Coffy, Scream Blacula Scream, Twilight People, The Arena, Foxy Brown, Bucktown, Friday Foster, Sheba Baby, Drum, Greased Lightning, Fort Apache The Bronx, Tough Enough, Something Wicked This Way Comes, The Vindicator, On the Edge, Stand Alone, The Allnighter, Above the Law, The Package, Class of 1999, Bill & Ted's Bogus Journey, Posse, Original Gangstas, Mars Attacks!, Jackie Brown (Golden Globe nom. 1998), Jawbreaker, Holy Smoke, Fortress 2, In Too Deep, Holy Smoke, Snow Day, Wilder, 3 a.m., It Conquered Hollywood! The Story of American International Pictures, Ghosts of Mars, Bones, The Adventures of Pluto Nash, Identity, The Invited, Just Wright.
TELEVISION: *Movies:* A Mother's Right: The Elizabeth Morgan Story, Family Blessings, Hayley Wagner: Star, 1st to Die, Ladies of the House. *Mini-series:* Roots: The Next Generations, Feast of All Saints, Happily Ever After: Fairy Tales for Every Child (Emmy nom. 2000). *Series:* Linc's, The L Word, Smallville. *Guest:* More than 70 appearances.

GRIFFITH, ANDY
Actor. b. Mount Airy, NC, June 1, 1926. e. U. of North Carolina. Began career as standup comedian, monologist, recording artist (What It Was Was Football, 1954). TV acting debut in U.S. Steel Hour production of No Time for Sergeants, which he later played on Broadway and film.
THEATRE: B'way: No Time for Sergeants (Theatre World Award), Destry Rides Again.
PICTURES: A Face in the Crowd (debut, 1957), No Time for Sergeants, Onionhead, The Second Time Around, Angel in My Pocket, Hearts of the West, Rustler's Rhapsody, Spy Hard, Daddy and Them, Waitress, Play the Game, Christmas Is Here Again (voice).
TELEVISION: *Movies:* Strangers in 7A, Go Ask Alice, Pray for the Wildcats, Winter Kill, Savages, Street Killing, Girl in the Empty Grave, Deadly Games, Salvage, Murder in Texas (Emmy nom. 1981), For Lovers Only, Murder in Coweta County, The Demon Murder Case, Fatal Vision, Crime of Innocence, Diary of a Perfect Murder, Return to Mayberry, Under the Influence, Matlock: The Vacation (also co-exec. prod.), The Gift of Love, Gramps, Scattering Dad, A Holiday Romance. *Mini-series:* Washington Behind Closed Doors, Centennial, From Here to Eternity, Roots: The Next Generations. *Series:* The Andy Griffith Show, The Headmaster, The New Andy Griffith Show, Salvage One, Matlock. *Guest:* More than 116 appearances.

GRIFFITH, MELANIE
Actress. b. New York, NY, Aug. 9, 1957. m. actor Antonio Banderas. Mother is actress Tippi Hedren. Moved to Los Angeles at 4. e. Catholic academies until Hollywood Prof. Sch., 1974. Did some modeling before being cast in Night Moves at 16. Studied acting with Stella Adler, Harry Mastrogeorge and Sandra Seacat.
PICTURES: The Harrad Experiment (debut, 1973), Smile, Night Moves, The Drowning Pool, One on One, Joyride, Underground Aces, Roar, Fear City, Body Double (Golden Globe nom. 1985), Something Wild (Golden Globe nom. 1987), Cherry 2000, The Milagro Beanfield War, Stormy Monday, Working Girl (Academy Award nom.; Golden Globe Award 1989), In the Spirit, Pacific Heights, The Bonfire of the Vanities, Paradise, Shining Through, A Stranger Among Us, Born Yesterday, Milk Money, Nobody's Fool, Now and Then, Two Much, Mulholland Falls, Lolita, Celebrity, Another Day in Paradise, Shadow of a Doubt, RKO 281, Crazy in Alabama, Forever Lulu, Life with Big Cats, Tart, Searching for Debra Winger, Stuart Little 2 (voice), Shade, Tempo, Around the World in 50 Years 3D (voice).
TELEVISION: *Movies:* Daddy, I Don't Like It Like This, Steel Cowboy, The Star Maker, She's in the Army Now, Golden Gate, Women & Men: Stories of Seduction (Hills Like White Elephants), Buffalo Girls (Golden Globe nom. 1996), RKO 281 (Emmy nom.; Golden Globe nom. 2000), Heartless. *Mini-series:* Once an Eagle. *Series:* Carter Country, Me & George, Twins. *Guest:* More than 104 appearances.

GRIFFITHS, RACHEL
Actress. b. Melbourne, Australia, Feb. 20, 1968.
PICTURES: Muriel's Wedding, Jude, Cosi, Children of the Revolution, Welcome to Woop Woop, To Have and to Hold, My Best Friend's Wedding, Hilary and Jackie (Academy Award nom. 1999), Among Giants, Amy, My Myself I, Blow Dry, Blow, The Rookie, The Hard Word, Ned Kelly, Step Up, Beautiful Kate.
TELEVISION: *Movies:* Since You've Been Gone, Plainsong, Angel, Brothers & Sisters: Family Album. *Mini-series:* After the Deluge, Comanche Moon. *Series:* Jimeoin, Six Feet Under (2 Emmy noms.; Golden Globe Award 2002, 1 other nom.), Brothers & Sisters (2 Emmy noms., 2 Golden Globe noms.). *Guest:* More than 47 appearances.

GRIMALDI, ALBERTO
Producer. b. Naples, Italy, Mar. 28, 1925. Studied law, serving as counsel to Italian film companies, before turning to production with Italian westerns starring Clint Eastwood and Lee Van Cleef.

Is owner of P.E.A. (Produzioni Europee Associate, s.r.l.).
PICTURES: For a Few Dollars More, The Good the Bad and the Ugly, The Big Gundown, Three Steps in Delirium, A Quiet Place in the Country, The Mercenary, Satyricon, Burn!, The Decameron, Man of the East, The Canterbury Tales, Last Tango in Paris, Bawdy Tales, Arabian Nights, Salo or the 100 Days of Sodom, Burnt Offerings, Fellini's Casanova, 1900, Illustrious Corpses, Lovers and Liars, Hurricane Rosy, Ginger and Fred, Gangs of New York (Academy Award nom. 2003).

GRODIN, CHARLES
Actor, Director, Writer. b. Pittsburgh, PA, April 21, 1935. e. U. of Miami. After time with Pittsburgh Playhouse studied acting with Uta Hagen and Lee Strasberg; began directing career in New York 1965 as asst. to Gene Saks. Has appeared in some 75 plays all over the country. Has also written scripts, produced plays. Books: It Would Be So Nice If You Weren't Here, How I Get Through Life, We're Ready for You Mr. Grodin.
THEATRE: Tchin-Tchin (B'way debut, 1962), Absence of a Cello, Same Time Next Year, It's a Glorious Day... And All That (dir., co-author), Lovers and Other Strangers (dir.), Thieves (prod., dir.), Unexpected Guests (prod., dir.), Price of Fame (also author), One of the All-Time Greats (author).
PICTURES: Sex and the College Girl (debut, 1964), Rosemary's Baby, Catch-22, The Heartbreak Kid (Golden Globe nom. 1973), 11 Harrowhouse (also adapt.), King Kong, Thieves, Heaven Can Wait, Real Life, Sunburn, It's My Turn, Seems Like Old Times, The Incredible Shrinking Woman, The Great Muppet Caper, The Lonely Guy, The Woman in Red, Movers and Shakers (also s.p., co-prod.), Last Resort, Ishtar, The Couch Trip, You Can't Hurry Love, Midnight Run, Taking Care of Business, Beethoven, Dave, So I Married an Axe Murderer, Heart and Souls, Beethoven's 2nd, Clifford, It Runs in the Family (My Summer Story), Fast Track, The Ex.
TELEVISION: *Movies:* Just Me and You, The Grass Is Always Greener Over the Septic Tank, Charley's Aunt, Grown-Ups, The Muppets at Walt Disney World. Specials (writer): Candid Camera (also dir.), The Simon & Garfunkel Special, Paul Simon Special (also dir.; Emmy Award for writing, 1978). *Mini-series:* Fresno. *Series:* Charles Grodin (talk), The Charles Grodin Show, 60 Minutes II. *Specials (dir.):* Acts of Love and Other Comedies, Paradise (also prod.), The World of Jim Henson (actor). *Guest:* More than 50 appearances.

GROENING, MATT
Writer, Animator, Cartoonist. b. Portland, OR, Feb. 14, 1954. Moved to LA in mid 1980s, started drawing comic strip named "Life in Hell". In 1988 created The Simpsons, originally filler in The Tracy Ullman show, later TV series, now entering its 19th season on the Fox network. Author of Kevin Newcombe (bio.).
PICTURES: Hair High (voice), Tales of the Rat Fink (voice), The Simpsons Movie (writer, creator, s.p., exec. prod.).
TELEVISION: *Movies:* Olive the Other Reindeer (Emmy nom. 2000), My Wasted Life (as himself). *Series:* The Tracey Ullman Show (3 Emmy noms. for writing), The Simpsons (exec. prod., creator, 10 Emmy Awards, 9 other noms.), Futurama (exec. prod., writer, creator, Emmy Award 2002; 4 other noms.). *Specials:* The Simpsons: America's First Family.

GROSS, KENNETH H.
Executive, Producer. b. Columbus, OH, Feb. 12, 1949. e. New School for Social Research, U. of London. Conducted film seminars at New School and active in several independent film projects. Published film criticism in various journals and magazines. Joined ABC Ent. 1971. Named supervisor of feature films for ABC-TV. Appt. mgr. of feature films, 1974. Promoted 1975 to program exec., ABC Ent. Prime Time/West Coast. Promoted to exec. prod., movies for TV, ABC Ent. 1976 in L.A.; 1978, with literary agency F.C.A. as partner in L.A.; 1979 prod. for Lorimar; then with Int'l. Creative Mgt; 1982, formed own literary talent agency, The Literary Group; 1985, merged agency with Robinson-Weintraub & Assoc. to become Robinson-Weintraub-Gross & Assoc. 1993, founding partner of Paradigm, a talent and literary agency. 1997, formed Ken Gross Management, a management and prod. co. based in Los Angeles, and currently is president and CEO.
PICTURES: One Tough Cop (Writer), Stealing Sinatra (prod.).
TELEVISION: Movies/Producer: Dead By Midnight, A Town Without Christmas, Finding John Christmas, When Angels Come to Town.

GROSS, MARY
Actress. b. Chicago, IL, March 25, 1953. Brother is actor Michael Gross. e. Loyola U. Is also student of the harp. In 1980 discovered by John Belushi who saw her perform as resident member of Chicago's Second City comedy troupe, where she won Chicago's Joseph Jefferson Award as best actress for the revue, Well, I'm Off to the Thirty Years War. First came to national attention as regular on Saturday Night Live, 1981-85.
PICTURES: Club Paradise, The Couch Trip, Casual Sex, Baby Boom, Big Business, Feds, Troop Beverly Hills, The Santa Clause, The Evening Star, Mixed Nuts (voice), Practical Magic, The Rugrats Movie (voice), 40 Days and 40 Nights, A Mighty Wind.
TELEVISION: *Movie:* Jailbait. *Series:* Saturday Night Live (Emmy nom. 1984), The People Next Door, Billy, Sabrina the Teenage Witch, Animaniacs (voice), Detention (voice), Boston Legal, General Hospital. *Specials:* Comic Relief I, The Second City 25th Anniversary Reunion, SNL 25 (Emmy nom. for writing 1984), Saturday Night Live: TV Tales. *Guest:* More than 55 appearances.

GROSS, MICHAEL
Actor. b. Chicago, IL, June 21, 1947. m. casting dir. Elza Bergeron. Sister is actress Mary Gross. e. U. Illinois, B.A., Yale School of Drama, M.F.A.
THEATRE: NY Shakespeare Fest. (Sganarelle, An Evening of Moliere Farces, Othello). *Off-B'way:* Endgame, No End of Blame (Obie Award), Put Them All Together, Geniuses, Territorial Rites. B'way: Bent, The Philadelphia Story. L.A. stage: Hedda Gabler, The Real Thing, Love Letters, Money & Friends.
PICTURES: Just Tell Me What You Want, Big Business, Tremors, Midnight Murders, Cool as Ice, Alan & Naomi, Tremors II: Aftershocks, Ground Control, Tremors III: Back to Perfection, Tremors 4, Combustion, An American in China, Broken Windows, Stay Cool.
TELEVISION: *Movies:* A Girl Named Sooner, FDR: The Last Year, Dream House, The Neighborhood, Little Gloria Happy at Last, Cook and Peary-The Race to the Pole, Summer Fantasy, Family Ties Vacation, A Letter to Three Wives, Right to Die, In the Line of Duty: The FBI Murders, A Connecticut Yankee in King Arthur's Court, Vestige of Honor, In the Line of Duty: Manhunt in the Dakotas, With a Vengeance, Snowbound: The Jim and Jennifer Stolpa Story, In the Line of Duty: The Price of Vengeance, Avalanche, Awake to Danger, Deceived by Trust, Hijacked: Flight 285, Ed McBain's 87th Precinct tv movies: Ice and Heatwave, Batman Beyond: The Movie (voice), Silent Killer, Mrs. Harris, 100 Million BC. *Series:* Family Ties, Tremors ER, The Drew Carey Show, The Young and the Restless. *Guest:* More than 63 appearances.

GROSSBART, JACK
Producer. b. Newark, NJ, Apr. 18, 1948. e. Rutgers Univ. Was agent, 1975-80, then personal manager, Litke-Grossbart Mgmt., 1980-87. Became tv prod., President of Jack Grossbart Prods., 1987.
TELEVISION: *Movies/Exec. prod./prod.:* Shattered Vows, The Seduction of Gina, Rockabye, Killer in the Mirror, Something in Common, Dangerous Affection, Echoes in the Darkness, She Was Marked for Murder, The Preppie Murder, Joshua's Heart, Lies Before Kisses, Honor Bright, Last Wish, Something to Live For: The Alison Gertz Story, A Jury of One, Comrades of Summer, The Woman Who Loved Elvis, One of Her Own, Leave of Absence, Between Love & Honor, Rage Against Time: A Search for Sara, Unforgivable, Breaking Through, A Father for Brittany, At the Mercy of a Stranger, Personally Yours, Phantom of the Megaplex, The One Day at a Time Reunion, Why I Wore Lipstick to My Mastectomy (Emmy nom. 2007), Heartless, Love Is a Four Letter Word (co-exec. prod.), A Stranger's Heart (co-exec. prod.), Mrs. Washington Goes to Smith. *Series/Exec. prod.:* Sydney, Cafe Americain.

GRUENBERG, ANDY
Executive. b. Minneapolis, MN, March 10, 1950. e. University of Wisconsin. Held various sales positions with 20th Century Fox and Warner Bros. from 1976 to 1984. Joined Columbia Pictures as asst. general sales mgr. Lorimar Pictures s.v.p. and general sales mgr. 1985-89. Hemdale Prods. pres. of distribution, 1989-91. Joined MGM/UA in 1991, as exec. v.p. of distribution. In 2002, Gruenberg teamed with Mike Marcus and Craig Baumgarten to form a new distribution outlet for indie films—MAC Releasing. Gruenberg was then hired by First Look Studios in Los Angeles in Dec. 2005 to be executive v.p. of theatrical distribution and is the position he holds today.

GRUENBERG, JERRY
Exhibitor. Gruenberg is a veteran of the film industry, which he began as owner /operator of G&C Theaters, a circuit located throughout Wisconsin. From 1967 to 1971, he was the Midwestern division manager for Twentieth Century Fox Film Corporation, based in Chicago, and was responsible for 30% of all domestic theatrical sales and marketing. From 1971-1979, Gruenberg served as senior v.p. for Allied Artist Pictures Corp., a public corp. involved in the distribution of motion pictures worldwide. Gruenberg then became president of his own company, Blossom Pictures, located in New York City, which represents producers and directors. In addition to running Blossom Pictures, he was the executive v.p. of film buying for Ft. Lauderdale-based Muvico Theaters and served as film buyer and booking agent for the circuit until 2006.

GRUSIN, DAVID
Composer, Conductor, Performer. b. Littleton, CO, June 26, 1934. Directed music for the Andy Williams Show on TV for 7 yrs in the 1960s, where he met Norman Lear and Bud Yorkin, producers of the series, who signed him to score their first feature film, Divorce, American Style (1967).
PICTURES: Waterhole No. 3, The Graduate, Candy, The Heart Is a Lonely Hunter, Winning, Where Were You When the Lights Went Out?, Generation, A Man Called Gannon, Tell Them Willie

Boy Is Here, Adam at 6 A.M., Halls of Anger, The Gang That Couldn't Shoot Straight, The Pursuit of Happiness, Shoot Out, Fuzz, The Great Northfield Minnesota Raid, The Friends of Eddie Coyle, The Midnight Ride, W.W. and the Dixie Dance Kings, The Yakuza, Three Days of the Condor, Murder By Death, The Front, Fire Sale, Mr. Billion, Bobby Deerfield, The Goodbye Girl, Heaven Can Wait (Academy Award nom. 1979), And Justice for All, The Champ (Academy Award nom. 1980), The Electric Horseman, My Bodyguard, Absence of Malice, On Golden Pond (Academy Award nom. 1982), Reds, Author! Author!, Tootsie (Academy Award nom. 1983), Scandalous, Racing with the Moon, The Pope of Greenwich Village, The Little Drummer Girl, Falling in Love, Lucas, The Goonies, The Milagro Beanfield War (Academy Award; Golden Globe nom. 1989), The Fabulous Baker Boys (Academy Award nom.; Golden Globe nom. 1990), Clara's Heart, Tequila Sunrise, A Dry White Season, Havana (Academy Award nom.; Golden Globe nom. 1991), The Bonfire of the Vanities, For the Boys (Golden Globe nom. 1992), The Cure, The Firm (Academy Award nom. 1994), Mulholland Falls, Selena, Hope Floats, Random Hearts, Ocean's Twelve, Rumor Has It... (writer: song), Even Money, It's Complicated (soundtrack writer).
TELEVISION: *Movies:* Deadly Dream, Prescription: Murder, Scorpio Letters, Eric, In the Gloaming, The Family Rico, The Death Squad, Dinner with Friends (Emmy nom. 2002), Hope, Recount. *Series:* The Virginian, The Andy Williams Show, The Wild Wild West, The Name of the Game, The Ghost & Mrs. Muir, Dan August (also theme), The NBC Mystery Movie, Maude, Assignment Vienna, The Girl with Something Extra, Good Times, Baretta, It Takes a Thief, The Girl From Uncle, St. Elsewhere.

GUBER, PETER

Producer. b. March 2, 1942. e. Syracuse U., B.A.; U. at Florence (Italy), S.S.P.; Sch. of Law, J.D., L.L.M. Recruited by Columbia Pictures as exec. asst. in 1968 while at NYU. Graduate Sch. of Business Adm. With Columbia Pictures seven yrs. in key prod. exec. capacities, serving last three as studio chief. Formed own company, Peter Guber's Filmworks, which in 1976 was merged with his Casablanca Records to become Casablanca Record and Filmworks where he was co-owner & chmn. bd. 1980 formed Polygram Pictures later bringing in Jon Peters as partner. 1983 sold Polygram and formed Guber-Peters. 1988 merged co. with Burt Sugarman's Barris Industries to form Guber-Peters-Barris Entertainment Co. Co-chmn. & man. dir. 1989 took full control of co. with Sugarman's exit and addition of Australia's Frank Lowy as new partner. 1989 became CEO of Columbia Pictures Ent.; 1992 became chairman and CEO of Sony Pictures Ent. Awards include: Producer of Year, NATO, 1979; NYU Albert Gallatin Fellowship; Syracuse U. Ardent Award. He has been a visiting prof., & chmn. producer's dept., UCLA Sch. of Theatre Arts. He is a member of NY, CA and Wash. DC Bars. Books: Inside the Deep, Above the Title.
PICTURES: The Deep (first under own banner), Midnight Express. Co-Prod. with Jon Peters: An American Werewolf in London, Missing, Flashdance (exec. prod.), D.C. Cab (exec. prod.), Endless Love, Vision Quest (exec. prod.), The Legend of Billie Jean, Head Office, Clan of the Cave Bear, Six Weeks (exec. prod.), The Pursuit of D.B. Cooper (exec. prod.), Clue (exec. prod.), The Color Purple (exec. prod.), The Witches of Eastwick (prod.), Innerspace (exec. prod.), Who's That Girl (exec. prod.), Gorillas in the Mist (exec. prod.), Caddyshack II, Rain Man (exec. prod), Batman (prod.), Johnny Handsome, Tango and Cash (prod.), Batman Returns, This Boy's Life (exec. prod.), With Honors (exec. prod.), Galapagos: The Enchanted Voyage, Alex & Emma (exec. prod), The Jacket, Into the Blue.
TELEVISION: *Exec. prod.: Movies*: Stand By Your Man, The Toughest Man in the World, Bay Coven, Oceanquest, Brotherhood of Justice, Nightmare at Bitter Creek, Finish Line.Television and the Presidency, Double Platinum, Angels Fall, Montana Sky, Blue Smoke, Carolina Moon, Northern Lights, Midnight Bayou, High Noon, Tribute. *Series:* Dreams, Rude Awakening, Square Off. *Documentary:* Mysteries of the Sea (Emmy Award), Oceanquest (series).

GUEST, CHRISTOPHER

Actor, Writer, Composer, Director. b. New York, NY, Feb. 5, 1948. m. actress Jamie Lee Curtis. Brother is actor Nicholas Guest. Wrote the musical score and acted in National Lampoon's Lemmings off-B'way. On B'way in Room Service, Moonchildren. Director for Go Film Co.
PICTURES: The Hospital (debut, 1971), The Hot Rock, Death Wish, The Fortune, Girlfriends, The Last Word, The Long Riders, Heartbeeps, This Is Spinal Tap (also co-s.p.), Little Shop of Horrors, Beyond Therapy, The Princess Bride, Sticky Fingers, The Big Picture (also dir. co-s.p., story), A Few Good Men, Waiting for Guffman (also dir.), Edwards and Hunt (also dir.), Small Soldiers (voice), Best in Show (WGA nom. 2001), A Mighty Wind (also s.p., dir. & composer/songs), Mrs. Henderson Presents, For Your Consideration (also dir., writer,, composer), Night at the Museum: Battle of the Smithsonian, The Invention of Lying.
TELEVISION: *Movies:* It Happened One Christmas, Haywire, Million Dollar Infield, A Piano for Mrs. Cimino, Attack of the 50 Ft. Woman (dir.), D.O.A. (actor, writer, prod.), The Thick of It (dir.), Glastonbury 2009. *Mini-series:* Blind Ambition. *Series:* Saturday Night Live (1984-5). *Specials:* The TV Show, The Chevy Chase Special (also writer), The Billion Dollar Bubble, Lily Tomlin (also writer, Emmy Award, 1976), A Nice Place to Visit (writer only), Spinal Tap Reunion (also co-writer). *Guest:* More than 123 appearances.

GUEST, LANCE

Actor. b. Saratoga, CA, July 21, 1960. e. UCLA.
PICTURES: Halloween II, I Ought to Be in Pictures, The Last Starfighter, Jaws-The Revenge, The Wizard of Loneliness, Plan B, Mach 2, The Least of These.
TELEVISION: *Movies:* Confessions of a Married Man, Stepsister From Planet Weird, The Jenny Project, Bitter Winter, Flu Bird Horror. *Mini-series:* Favorite Son. *Series*: Lou Grant, Knots Landing, Life Goes On. *Specials:* One Too Many, My Father My Rival, The Roommate.

GUILLAUME, ROBERT

Actor. b. St. Louis, MO, Nov. 30, 1937. e. St. Louis U., Washington U. Scholarship for musical fest. in Aspen, CO. Then apprenticed with Karamu Theatre where performed in operas and musicals. B'way plays and musicals include Fly Blackbird, Kwamina, Guys and Dolls, Purlie, Jacques Brel is Alive and Well and Living in Paris, Cyrano. In L.A. in Phantom of the Opera.
PICTURES: Super Fly T.N.T. (debut, 1973), Seems Like Old Times, Prince Jack, They Still Call Me Bruce, Wanted Dead or Alive, Lean On Me, Death Warrant, The Meteor Man, The Lion King I & II (voice), First Kid, Spy Hard, Silicon Towers, The 13th Child Legend of the Jersey Devil, The Land Before Time VIII: The Big Freeze (voice), The Adventures of Tom Thumb & Thumbelina (voice), Unchained Memories: Readings from the Slave Narratives, Big Fish, Satin, The Secrets of Jonathan Sperry, Columbus Circle.
TELEVISION: *Movies*: The Kid From Left Field, The Kid with the Broken Halo, You Must Remember This, The Kid with the 100 I.Q. (also exec. prod.), Perry Mason: The Case of the Scandalous Scoundrel, The Penthouse, Fire and Rain, Greyhounds, Children of the Dust, A Good Day to Die, Panic in the Skies!, Merry Christmas George Bailey, His Bodyguard, The Happy Prince. *Mini-series:* North and South, Pandora's Clock. *Series*: Soap (Emmy Award, 1979), Benson (2 Emmy Awards, 1979, 1985, 4 other noms.; 3 Golden Globe noms.), The Robert Guillaume Show, Saturdays, Pacific Station, Fish Police (voice), Sports Night. *Specials*: Purlie, 'S Wonderful 'S Marvellous 'S Gershwin, John Grin's Christmas, Martin Luther King: A Look Back A Look Forward, Living the Dream: A Tribute to Dr. Martin Luther King Jr. (host), The Debbie Allen Special, Carol & Company, Happily Ever After: Fairy Tales for Every Child (Emmy nom. 2000), Sister Kate, Story of a People (host), Mastergate, Cosmic Slop. *Pilot:* Driving Miss Daisy. *Guest*: More than 127 appearances.

GUMBEL, BRYANT

Announcer, News Show Host. b. New Orleans, LA, Sept. 29, 1948. e. Bates College. Started as writer for Black Sports Magazine, NY, 1971; sportscaster, then sports dir., KNBC, Los Angeles. Sports host NBC Sports NY 1975-82. New York Emmy Awards, 1976, 1977. A Host of the Today Show (1982-1997). When Gumbel left the Today Show, he signed a $5 million a year contract with CBS News.
PICTURES: Heaven Can Wait, The Hard Way, Contact.
TELEVISION: Super Bowl Games, '88 Olympics, Games People Play, The More You Know, The R.A.C.E, Real Sports with Bryant Gumbel (anchor), Public Eye With Bryant Gumbel, The Early Show (host, 1999-2002), ESPN SportsCentury (series documentary, 2000-2001.), Flashpoints USA with Bryant Gumbel and Gwen Ifill (series, 2003-2004), Real Sports with Bryant Gumbel (HBO series). *Documentaries/Specials: As Host:* Main Street (also writer), The Hard Way, Black to the Promised Land, Arthur Ashe: Citizen of the World, Macy's Thanksgiving Day Parade (host, 3 Emmy noms.), Muhammad Ali: The Whole Story, Survivor: The Reunion, Survivor: The Australian Outback - The Reunion, Survivor 3: The Reunion, The Roswell Crash: Startling New Evidence, The N-Word, National Health Test with Bryant Gumbel, Life on the Edge: A Global Crisis (Emmy nom. 2009). *Guest:* More than 82 appearances.

GUMPERT, JON

Executive. e. Cornell U. Law School. Sr. v.p., business affairs, MGM/UA Entertainment; 1983-1985, pres., World Film Services, Inc., independent prod. co. in N.Y. 1985, named v.p., business affairs, Warner Bros; 1986 sr. v.p. Vista Films. Named sr. v.p. legal bus. affairs, Universal Pictures 1990. Named exec. v.p., legal business affairs, Universal Pictures, 1994. Group executive v.p., Universal Pictures, 1996. Left Universal in Nov. 2001 to join production company IM Internationalmedia AG, where he currently is vice chmn., head of m.p. operations. He supervises worldwide motion picture operations, including the structuring and financing of film projects and the supervision of worldwide legal and business affairs.

GUNTON, BOB

Actor. b. Santa Monica, CA, Nov. 15, 1945. e. U. of Cal. Served in army during Vietnam War. Prof. acting debut at Cumberland County Playhouse in Tennessee U.S.A.
THEATRE: Off-B'way: Who Am I? (debut, 1971), How I Got That

Story (Obie Award), Tip Toes, The Death of Von Richtofen. B'way: Happy End (debut, 1977), Working, Evita (Drama Desk Award; Tony nom.), Passion, King of Hearts, Big River, Rozsa, Sweeney Todd (Drama Desk Award; Tony nom.).
PICTURES: Rollerover (debut, 1981), Static, Matewan, The Pick-Up Artist, Cookie, Born on the Fourth of July, Glory, JFK, Patriot Games, The Public Eye, Jennifer Eight, Demolition Man, The Shawshank Redemption, Dolores Claiborne, Ace Ventura: When Nature Calls, Broken Arrow, The Glimmer Man, Changing Habits, Midnight in the Garden of Good and Evil, Patch Adams, Bats, The Perfect Storm, Scenes of the Crime, Boat Trip, Dallas 362, I Heart Huckabees, Believe in Me, Numb, Fracture, Player 5150, Rendition, The Heaven Project, The Least of These, Tenure, The Irishman, The Trial, Highland Park.
TELEVISION: *Movies*: Lois Gibbs and the Love Canal, A Woman Named Jackie, Finnegan Begin Again, Adam: His Song Continues, Unconquered, Judgment, The Bride in Black, Perry Mason: The Case of the Glass Coffin, Ned Blessing: The True Story of My Life, Ladykiller, Sinatra, Dead Ahead: The Exxon Valdez Disaster, Murder in the Heartland, Outer Limits, Roswell, In Pursuit of Honor, Kingfish: A Story of Huey P. Long, The Siege at Ruby Ridge, Elvis Meets Nixon, Buffalo Soldiers, Running Mates, When Billie Beat Bobby, 61, Judas, The Pact, Iron Jawed Angels, Imperfect Union, Pandemic, 24: Redemption. *Mini-series*: A Woman Named Jackie, Wild Palms. *Series*: Comedy Zone, Hot House, Courthouse, Greg the Bunny, Peacemakers, Nip/Tuck, Desperate Housewives, Pepper Dennis, 24. *Documentaries:* Forever James Dean (narr.), World War Two - Behind Closed Doors (series). *Guest:* More than 73 appearances.

GUTTENBERG, STEVE

Actor. b. Brooklyn, NY, Aug. 24, 1958. e. Sch. of Performing Arts, N.Y. Off-B'way in The Lion in Winter; studied under John Houseman at Juilliard; classes with Lee Strasberg and Uta Hagen. Moved to West Coast in 1976; landed first TV role in movie, Something for Joey. B'way debut 1991 in Prelude to a Kiss.
PICTURES: Rollercoaster, The Chicken Chronicles, The Boys from Brazil, Players, Can't Stop the Music, Diner, The Man Who Wasn't There, Police Academy, Police Academy 2: Their First Assignment, Cocoon, Bad Medicine, Police Academy 3: Back in Training, Short Circuit, The Bedroom Window, Police Academy 4: Citizens on Patrol (also prod. assoc.), Amazon Women on the Moon, Surrender, Three Men and a Baby, High Spirits, Cocoon: The Return, Don't Tell Her It's Me, Three Men and a Little Lady, The Big Green, Home for the Holidays, It Takes Two, Zeus and Roxanne, Casper, Airborne, Home Team, Love and Fear, Sheer Bliss, P.S. Your Cat Is Dead, Snow Job, The Stranger (short), Mojave Phone Booth, Making Change, Jackson, Heidi 4 Paws (voice), Major Movie Star, Fatal Rescue, Cornered!, Shannon's Rainbow, The Gold Retrievers, Ay Lav Yu, The Science of Cool, Making Change (also exec. prod.), It's Not You (also exec. prod.), Eldorado.
TELEVISION: *Movies*: Something for Joey, To Race the Wind, Miracle on Ice, The Day After, Tower of Terror, Single Santa Seeks Mrs. Claus, The Poseidon Adventure, Meet the Santas. *Mini-series:* The Poseidon Adventure. *Series*: Billy, No Soap Radio, Veronica Mars. *Specials*: Gangs (co-prod.), Pecos Bill: King of the Cowboys. *Guest:* More than 55 appearances.

GUY, JASMINE

Actress. b. Boston, MA, March 10, 1964. Toured with Grease!, 1996-97.
PICTURES: School Daze, Harlem Nights, Kla$h, America's Dream, Cats Don't Dance (voice), Lillie, Guinevere, Madeline, Diamond Men, Dying on the Edge, Unchained Memories: Readings from the Slave Narratives (reader), Tru Loved.
TELEVISION: *Movies*: At Mother's Request, A Killer Among Us, Stomping at the Savoy, Perfect Crime, Carrie, Kasha and the Zulu King (voice). *Mini-series*: Alex Haley's Queen, A Century of Women, Feast of All Saints. *Series*: A Different World, Dead Like Me, The Vampire Diaries. *Guest*: More than 82 appearances.

GUZMÁN, LUIS

Actor. b. Puerto Rico, Jan. 1, 1957.
PICTURES: Short Eyes, Variety, Heartbeat, Crocodile Dundee 2, True Believer, Rooftops, Family Business, Black Rain, Q & A, The Hard Way, McBain, Jumpin' at the Boneyard, Empire City, Innocent Blood, Guilty As Sin, Mr. Wonderful, Carlito's Way, The Cowboy Way, Handgun, Stonewall, Lotto Land, The Substitute, The Brave, Boogie Nights, Out of Sight, Snake Eyes, One Tough Cop, The Limey, Mystery Men, The Bone Collector, Magnolia, Luckytown Blues, Traffic, Table One, Sam the Man, Home Invaders, Double Whammy, The Salton Sea, Welcome to Collinwood, The Count of Monte Cristo, Punch Drunk Love, Confidence, Anger Management, Dumb & Dumberer: When Harry Met Loyd, Runaway Jury, Lemony Snicket's A Series of Unfortunate Events, Carlito's Way: The Beginning, Waiting..., I Believe in America, School for Scoundrels, Maldeamores, Rogue, War, Cleaner, Beverly Hills Chihuahua (voice), Nothing Like the Holidays, Fighting, Still Waiting..., Parkside, The Taking of Pelham 1 2 3, Old Dogs, Thicker, The Caller, A Girl and a Gun.
TELEVISION: *Movies*: In The Shadow of a Killer, Double Deception, The Burning Season, Empire City, Quiet Killer, On Seventh Avenue, Pronto, Mind Prey, The Huntress, Thin Air, Lolo's Cafe (voice), How to Make It in America. *Mini-series:* To Catch a Killer. *Series*: House of Buggin', Oz, John from Cincinnati, Luis, Raines (pilot), How to Make It in America. *Guest:* More than 64 appearances.

GYLLENHAAL, JAKE

Actor. b. Los Angeles, CA, Dec. 19, 1980. Son of director Stephen Gyllenhaal and writer, producer Naomi Foner. Brother of actress Maggie Gyllenhaal.
PICTURES: City Slickers (debut), A Dangerous Woman, Josh and S.A.M., Homegrown, October Sky, Donnie Darko, Bubble Boy, Lovely & Amazing, The Good Girl, Moonlight Mile, The Day After Tomorrow, Proof, Brokeback Mountain (Academy Award nom. 2006), Jarhead, Me and My Monster, Nautica, Zodiac, Rendition, Brothers, Nailed, Prince of Persia: The Sands of Time, Love and Other Drugs, Source Code. *Guest:* More than 64 appearances.

GYLLENHAAL, MAGGIE

Actress. b. New York, NY, Nov. 16, 1977. e. Royal Academy of Dramatic Arts, London, B.A. Columbia University. Daughter of Director Stephen Gyllenhaal and Writer, Producer Naomi Foner. Sister of actor Jake Gyllenhaal.
PICTURES: Waterland (debut), A Dangerous Woman, Homegrown, Cecil B. DeMented, Donnie Darko, Riding in Cars with Boys, Secretary (Golden Globe nom. 2003), 40 Days and 40 Nights, Adaptation, Confessions of a Dangerous Mind, Casa de los babys, Mona Lisa Smile, Criminal, Happy Endings, The Great New Wonderful, Trust the Man, Sherrybaby (Golden Globe nom. 2007), je t'aime Paris, Monster House, World Trade Center, Stranger Than Fiction, The Dark Knight, South Solitary, Crazy Heart (Academy Award nom. 2010), Away We Go, Nanny McPhee and the Big Bang.
TELEVISION: *Movies:* Shattered Mind, The Patron Saint of Liars, Resurrection, Strip Search. *Mini-series:* Shake, Rattle and Roll: An American Love Story. *Series:* Independent Lens (host, doc.). *Guest:* More than 51 appearances.

GYLLENHAAL, STEPHEN

Director. b. Pennsylvania. e. Trinity Col, CT. Started career in NYC making industrial films. Directed short film Exit 10. m. writer-producer Naomi Foner. Father of Maggie Gyllenhaal and Jake Gyllenhaal.
PICTURES: Waterland, A Dangerous Woman, Losing Isaiah, Piece of My Heart, Homegrown, Crashing, Time Bomb, Crashing (writer).
TELEVISION: *Movies*: The Abduction of Kari Swenson, Promised a Miracle, Leap of Faith, Family of Spies, A Killing in a Small Town (Emmy nom. 1990), Paris Trout (DGA Award 1992), Shattered Mind, The Patron Saint of Liars, Resurrection, The Warden, Warden of Red Rock, Time Bomb, Manchild (pilot). *Mini-series*: Living with the Dead. *Series*: The Shield, Metro, Everwood, CBS Afternoon Playhouse (Emmy nom. 1983 for episode "Help Wanted"), Robbery Homicide Division, Lucky, Numb3rs.

H

HAAS, LUKAS

Actor. b. West Hollywood, CA, Apr. 16, 1976. Kindergarten school principal told casting dir. about him which resulted in film debut in Testament. NY theatre debut in Mike Nichols' Lincoln Center production of Waiting for Godot (1988). Appeared in AFI film The Doctor.
PICTURES: Testament (debut, 1983), Witness, Solarbabies, Lady in White, The Wizard of Loneliness, See You in the Morning, Music Box, Rambling Rose, Convicts, Alan and Naomi, Leap of Faith, Warrior Spirit, Boys, Johns, Palookaville, Mars Attacks!, Everyone Says I Love You, Boys, Mars Attacks!, Johns, In the Quiet Night, Breakfast of Champions, Running Free (voice), Kiss and Tell, Zoolander, The Pearl, Long Time Dead, Bookies, Brick, What We Do Is Secret, Last Days, Vinyl, Alpha Dog, Material Girls, Gardener of Eden, The Tripper, The Stillborn, The Cradle, Death in Love, While She Was Out, The Perfect Age of Rock 'n' Roll, Inception.
TELEVISION: *Movies*: Love Thy Neighbor, Shattered Spirits, The Ryan White Story, The Perfect Tribute, Kiss and Tell, David and Lisa, The Lathe of Heaven. *Series*: Heavy Gear: The Animated Series (voice), 24. *Pilot:* Brothers-in-Law. *Specials*: A Place at the Table, My Dissident Mom, Peacemaker (Triple Play II), Child Stars: Their Story. *Guest:* More than 43 appearances.

HACKFORD, TAYLOR

Director, Producer. b. Santa Barbara, CA, Dec. 31, 1944. e. USC, B.A., int'l. relations. m. actress Helen Mirren. Was Peace Corps volunteer in Bolivia 1968-69. Began career with KCET in Los Angeles 1970-77. As prod.-dir. won Oscar for short, Teenage Father, 1978. Theatrical film debut as dir. with The Idolmaker (1980). Received DGA Award, Robert B. Aldrich Achievement Award 2007. 2009 elected President of Directors Guild of America (DGA) for a two year term.
PICTURES: *Dir. &/or Prod.:* The Idolmaker, An Officer and a Gentleman (DGA nom. 1983), Against All Odds, White Nights,

Chuck Berry: Hail! Hail! Rock 'n' Roll, Everyone's All-American, Bound By Honor/Blood In Blood Out, Dolores Claiborne, The Devil's Advocate, Proof of Life, Ray (also writer 2 Academy Award noms. DGA nom. 2005), Love Ranch. *Prod.:* Rooftops, La Bamba, The Long Walk Home, Sweet Talker, Queens Logic, Defenseless, Mortal Thoughts, When We Were Kings, Greenwich Mean Time.
TELEVISION: *Movie:* Economic Love-in (dir.). *Series:* E-Ring (prod., dir., 1 episode also pilot). *Special:* Genius: A Night for Ray Charles.

HACKMAN, GENE

Actor. b. San Bernardino, CA, Jan. 30, 1930. First major broadway role in Any Wednesday. Other stage productions include: Poor Richard, Children from Their Games, A Rainy Day in Newark, The Natural Look, Death and the Maiden. Formed own production co., Chelly Ltd. *Author:* "Wake of the Perdido Sea" (co-author), "Justice for None". 2003 received Golden Globe, Cecil B. DeMille Award.
PICTURES: Mad Dog Coll (debut, 1961), Lilith, Hawaii, A Covenant With Death, Bonnie and Clyde (Academy Award nom. 1968), First to Fight, Banning, The Split, Riot, The Gypsy Moths, Downhill Racer, Marooned, I Never Sang for My Father (Academy Award nom. 1971), Doctors' Wives, The Hunting Party, The French Connection (Academy Award; Golden Globe Award 1972), Cisco Pike, Prime Cut, The Poseidon Adventure, Scarecrow, The Conversation (Golden Globe nom. 1975), Zandy's Bride, Young Frankenstein, Night Moves, Bite the Bullet, French Connection II (Golden Globe nom. 1976), Lucky Lady, The Domino Principle, A Bridge Too Far, March or Die, Superman, All Night Long, Superman II, Reds, Eureka, Under Fire (Golden Globe nom. 1984), Uncommon Valor, Misunderstood, Target, Twice in a Lifetime (Golden Globe nom. 1986), Power, Hoosiers, Superman IV, No Way Out, Another Woman, Bat-21, Split Decisions, Full Moon in Blue Water, Mississippi Burning (Academy Award nom. 1989), The Package, Loose Cannons, Postcards From the Edge, Narrow Margin, Class Action, Company Business, Unforgiven (Academy Award, 1993; Natl. Soc. of Film Critics, NY Film Critics, BAFTA, LA Film Critics & Golden Globe Awards, best supporting actor, 1992), The Firm, Geronimo: An American Legend, The Quick and the Dead, Crimson Tide, Get Shorty, Birdcage, Extreme Measures, The Chamber, Absolute Power, Antz (voice), Twilight, Enemy of the State, Under Suspicion, The Replacements, The Heist, Breakers, Behind Enemy Lines, The Royal Tenenbaums (Golden Globe Award 2002), Runaway Jury, Welcome to Mooseport.
TELEVISION: *Movie*: Shadow on the Land. *Guest*: More than 101 appearances.

HAGERTY, JULIE

Actress. b. Cincinnati, OH, June 15, 1955. Studied drama for six years before leaving for NY where studied with William Hickey. Made acting debut in her brother Michael's theatre group in Greenwich Village called the Production Company.
THEATRE: The Front Page (Lincoln Center), The House of Blue Leaves (Theatre World Award, 1986), Wild Life, Born Yesterday (Phil. Drama Guild), The Years, Three Men on a Horse, Wifey, A Cheever Evening, Raised in Captivity.
PICTURES: Airplane! (debut, 1980), A Midsummer Night's Sex Comedy, Airplane II: The Sequel, Lost in America, Goodbye New York, Bad Medicine, Beyond Therapy, Aria, Bloodhounds of Broadway, Rude Awakening, Reversal of Fortune, What About Bob?, Noises Off, The Wife, U Turn, Mel, Held Up, The Story of Us, Gut Feeling, Baby Bedlam, Freddy Got Fingered, Sotrytelling, Bridget, A Guy Thing, Adam & Steve, Pizza, Just Friends, She's the Man, If I Had Known I Was a Genius, Confessions of a Shopaholic.
TELEVISION: *Movies*: The Day the Women Got Even, Jackie's Back: Portrait of a Diva (host), London Suite, Tourist Trap, The Badge. *Series*: Lucky Luke, Princesses, Women of the House, Reunited, Malcolm in the Middle, Girlfriends, The Winner. *Specials:* The Visit (Trying Times), House of Blue Leaves, Necessary Parties.

HAGGARD, PIERS

Director. b. London, March 18, 1939. e. U. of Edinburgh. Son of actor Stephen Haggard; great grandnephew of author Rider Haggard. Began career in theatre in 1960 as asst. to artistic dir. at London's Royal Court. Named dir. of Glasgow Citizens' Theatre, 1962. 1963-65 worked with the National Theatre, where co-directed Hobson's Choice and The Dutch Courtesan. Has directed many prize winning TV commercials.
PICTURES: Wedding Night (debut, 1969; also co-s.p.), Blood on Satan's Claw (Satan's Skin), The Fiendish Plot of Dr. Fu Manchu, Venom, A Summer Story, Conquest.
TELEVISION: *Specials/Movies*: A Triple Play: Sam Found Out (Liza Minnelli special), The Fulfillment of Mary Gray, Back Home, Quatermass Conclusion, Chester Cycle of Mystery Plays, Mrs. Reinhardt, Knockback, Visitors, Heartstones, I'll Take Romance, Four Eyes and Six-Guns, Eskimo Day, The Double (s.p.), Lifeforce Experiment, Cold Enough for Snow, The Hunt, The Shell Seekers. *Mini-series:* Love for Lydia, Pennies from Heaven, Return to Treasure Island, Centrepoint. *Series*: Public Eye, Callan, The Jazz Age, Zodiac, Romance, Quatermass, Space Precinct, Big Bad World.

HAGMAN, LARRY

Actor. b. Fort Worth, TX, Sept. 21, 1931. e. Bard Coll. Son of late actress Mary Martin. First stage experience with Margo Jones Theatre in the Round in Dallas. Appeared in N.Y. in Taming of the Shrew; one year with London production of South Pacific. 1952-56 was in London with U.S. Air Force where produced and directed show for servicemen. Returned to N.Y. for plays on and off *B'way:* God and Kate Murphy (Theatre World Award), The Nervous Set, The Warm Peninsula, The Beauty Part.
PICTURES: Ensign Pulver, Fail Safe, In Harm's Way, The Group, The Cavern, Up in the Cellar, Son of Blob (aka: Beware! The Blob; also dir.), Harry and Tonto, Stardust, Mother Jugs and Speed, The Big Bus, The Eagle Has Landed, Checkered Flag or Crash, Superman, S.O.B., Nixon, Primary Colors.
TELEVISION: *Movies*: Three's a Crowd, Vanished, A Howling in the Woods, Getting Away from It All, No Place to Run, The Alpha Caper, Blood Sport, What Are Best Friends For?, Sidekicks, Hurricane, Sarah T.-Portrait of a Teenage Alcoholic, The Big Rip-Off, Return of the World's Greatest Detective, Intimate Strangers, The President's Mistress, Last of the Good Guys, A Double Life, Deadly Encounter, Dallas: The Early Years, Staying Afloat, In the Heat of the Night: Who Was Geli Bendl? (dir. only), Dallas: War of the Ewings, Dallas: Who Killed J.R.?, Dallas: J.R. Returns, The Third Twin, Dallas: War of the Ewings, Doing Dallas, When Shoulderpads Ruled the World. *Mini-series*: The Third Twin, The Rhinemann Exchange. *Series*: The Edge of Night, I Dream of Jeannie, The Good Life, Here We Go Again, Orleans, Dallas (2 Emmy noms.; 4 Golden Globe noms.), Nip/Tuck. *Specials:* Applause, Lone Star. *Guest:* More than 172 appearances.

HAHN, HELENE

Executive. b. New York, NY. e. Loyola U. Sch. of Law. Instructor of entertainment law at Loyola. Attorney for ABC before joining Paramount in 1977 in studio legal dept. 1979, moved to business affairs; promoted to dir. 1980, v.p., 1981; sr. v.p., 1983. Left in 1985 to join Walt Disney Pictures as sr. v.p., business & legal affairs for m.p. division. 1987, promoted to exec. v.p., Walt Disney Studios. She joined DreamWorks at its inception in Oct. 1994 and worked with the three principal partners, Steven Spielberg, Jeffrey Katzenberg and David Geffen, on preparing the company's 10-year business plan and structuring the equity investments. The business plan served as the blueprint for the organization of the company's production, distribution and marketing operations. She was DreamWork's COO until she retired in 2004.

HAID, CHARLES

Actor, Director, Producer. b. San Francisco, CA, June 2, 1943. e. Carnegie Tech. Appeared on NY stage in Elizabeth the First. Co-produced Godspell. Prod. & dir. short film The Last Supper.
PICTURES: *Actor:* The Choirboys, Who'll Stop the Rain, Oliver's Story, House of God, Altered States, Square Dance (co-exec. prod. only), Cop, The Rescue, Nightbreed, Storyville, The Third Miracle, Home on the Range. *Director:* Iron Will.
TELEVISION: *Movies*: The Execution of Private Slovik, Remember When, Things in Their Season, Kate McShane (pilot), Foster and Laurie, A Death in Canaan, The Bastard, Death Moon, Twirl, Divorce Wars, Children in the Crossfire (also co-prod.), Code of Vengeance, Six Against the Rock, Weekend War, The Great Escape II: The Untold Story, A Deadly Silence, Fire and Rain, Man Against the Mob: The Chinatown Murders, In the Line of Duty: A Cop for the Killing (also co-prod.), In the Line of Duty: Siege at Marion (dir. only), The Nightman (dir., prod. only), Cooperstown (also dir.), For Their Own Good, The Fire Next Time, Broken Trust, Sally Hemings: An American Scandal (dir. only), Life Is Ruff. *Series:* Kate McShane, Delvecchio, Hill Street Blues (2 Emmy nom.), Cop Rock (prod. only). *Dir./series:* NYPD Blue (Emmy nom.; DGA nom. 1994), Murder One (Emmy nom.; DGA nom. 1996), High Incident, Buddy Faro, Big Apple (also co-exec. prod.), The Guardian, Citizen Baines, Philly, The Court, Presidio Med, Threat Matrix (also pilot, co-exec.prod.), ER (DGA Award 1995), Third Watch, Criminal Minds, Nip/Tuck. *Specials:* Buffalo Soldiers (DGA nom. 1998).

HAIM, COREY

Actor. b. Toronto, Canada, Dec. 23, 1972. Performed in TV commercials at 10; regular on children's show, The Edison Twins.
PICTURES: Firstborn (debut, 1984), Secret Admirer, Silver Bullet, Murphy's Romance, Lucas, The Lost Boys, License to Drive, Watchers, Dream a Little Dream, Fast Getaway (also assoc. prod.), Prayer of the Roller Boys, The Dream Machine, Oh What a Night, Blown Away, The Double-O Kid, National Lampoon's Last Resort, Fast Getaway 2, Dream a Little Dream 2, Life 101 (also assoc. prod.), Snowboard Academy, Fever Lake, Demolition High, Busted, Never Too Late, Tales From the Crypt: Bordello of Blood, Demolition University (also exec. prod.), Universal Groove, The Back Lot Murders, Dickie Roberts: Former Child Star (soundtrack), Shark City, Crank: High Voltage, Decisions, A Detour in Life (exec. prod., dir.).
TELEVISION: *Movies*: A Time to Live, Just One of the Girls, Merlin, Without Malice. *Series*: The Edison Twins, Roomies, The Coreys: Return of the Lost Boys(also exec. prod.).
(d. March 10, 2010)

HAINES, RANDA

Director, Producer. b. Los Angeles, CA, Feb. 20, 1945. Raised in NYC. Studied acting with Lee Strasberg. e. School of Visual Arts. 1975 accepted into AFI's Directing Workshop for Women. Dir. & co-wrote short film August/September, which led to work as writer for series Family. Appeared in documentary Calling the Shots.
PICTURES: Children of a Lesser God (DGA nom. 1987), The Doctor, Wrestling Ernest Hemingway, A Family Thing (co-prod. only), Dance with Me, Antwone Fisher (prod. only)
TELEVISION: *Movies*: The Jilting of Granny Weatherall, Something About Amelia (Emmy nom.; DGA nom. 1984), The Outsider, The Ron Clark Story (Golden Globe nom.; WGA nom.; DGA nom. 2007). *Series*: Family (writer), Knots Landing, Tucker's Witch, Hill Street Blues (dir. of 4 episodes), Alfred Hitchcock Presents (Bang You're Dead). *Specials*: Under This Sky, Just Pals.

HALL, ANTHONY MICHAEL

Actor. r.n. Michael Anthony Hall. b. Boston, MA, Apr. 14, 1968.
PICTURES: Six Pack (debut, 1982), National Lampoon's Vacation, Sixteen Candles, The Breakfast Club, Weird Science, Out of Bounds, Johnny Be Good, Edward Scissorhands, A Gnome Named Gnorm, Into the Sun, Hail Caesar (also dir.), Six Degrees of Separation, Me and the Mob, The Grave, Exit in Red, Trojan War, The Killing Grounds, Cold Night Into Dawn, Blunt, Revenge, Dirt Merchant, Happy Accidents, 2 Little 2 Late, The Photographer, The Caveman's Valentine, Freddy Got Fingered, All About the Benjamins, Funny Valentine, Aftermath (also prod.), LA Blues, The Dark Knight, Aftermath (also prod.).
TELEVISION: *Movies*: Rascals and Robbers: The Secret Adventures of Tom Sawyer and Huck Finn, Running Out, A Bucket of Blood, Hijacked: Flight 285, A Touch of Hope, Pirates of Silicon Valley, Hysteria: The Def Leppard Story, Hitched. *Mini-series*: Texas, Final Approach. *Series*: Saturday Night Live (1985-86), Stephen King's Dead Zone. *Guest:* More than 62 appearances.

HALL, ARSENIO

Actor, Comedian. b. Cleveland, OH. Feb. 12, 1959. e. Kent State U. Became interested in magic at 7, which later led to own local TV special, The Magic of Christmas. Switched from advertising career to stand-up comedy, 1979. Discovered at Chicago nightclub by singer Nancy Wilson.
PICTURES: Amazon Women on the Moon (debut, 1987), Coming to America, Harlem Nights, Bopha! (exec. prod. only), Blankman (cameo), Black Dynamite, Igor (voice).
TELEVISION: *Movies*: Uptown Comedy Express, The Proud Family Movie (voice). *Series:* The 1/2 Hour Comedy Hour (1983, co-host), Thicke of the Night, Motown Revue, The Real Ghost Busters (voice), The Late Show (1987, host), The Arsenio Hall Show (3 Emmy noms.), The Party Machine With Nia Peeples (prod. only), Arsenio, Martial Law, Arsenio Jams, Star Search (host, 2002-). *Specials:* Happy Birthday Elizabeth: A Celebration of Life, Inside TV Land: African Americans in Television, 16th Annual Soul Train Music Awards, World's Greatest Commercials (co-host), 40 Years of Laughter: At the Improv. *Guest:* More than 100 appearances.

HALL, KURT C.

Executive. b. Burlington, VT. e. Univ. of VT. Served as dir. of financial reporting, dir. of finance, and v.p. & treas. of UA Entertainment before becoming v.p. & treas. of United Artists Theatre Circuit, 1990-91. Named exec. v.p. and CFO of United Artists Theatre Circuit, Inc. From 1998-Aug. 2002, pres. & CEO of United Artists Theatre Company. From May 2002 to May 2005, Hall served as co-chmn. and co-CEO of Regal Entertainment Group (REG) and pres. & CEO of its media subsidiary Regal CineMedia Corporation. In May 2005 Mr. Hall was appointed to his current position of pres., CEO and chmn. of National CineMedia LLC. The company, which provides cinema advertising and in-theatre events, was founded as a venture of AMC Entertainment, Inc., Cinemark USA, Inc. and Regal Entertainment Group, three of the world's leading exhibition companies. Hall also serves on the exec. committee of NATO's bd. of directors.

HALL, PHILIP BAKER

Actor. b. Toldeo, Ohio, September 10, 1931. e. Univ. of Toldeo.
PICTURES: Cowards, The Man With Bogart's Face, The Last Reunion, Dream On, Secret Honor, Three O'Clock High, Midnight Run, Ghostbusters II, Say Anything, An Innocent Man, How I Got Into College, Blue Desert, Live Wire, Cigarettes and Coffee, Kiss of Death, The Little Death, Eye for an Eye, Hit Me, Hard Eight, The Rock, Buddy, Air Force One, Boogie Nights, Sour Grapes, The Truman Show, Judas Kiss, Rush Hour, Enemy of the State, Psycho, Implicated, Cradle Will Rock, The Insider, Magnolia, The Talented Mr. Ripley, Let the Devil Wear Black, Rules of Engagement, The Contender, Lost Souls, A Gentleman's Game, The Sum of All Fears, Die Die Mommie, Bruce Almighty, Dogville, A House on a Hill, In Control of All Things, The Matador, Duck, Synergy, Mrs. Harris, The Amityville Horror, Zodiac, The Shaggy Dog, You Kill Me, The Lodger, Wonderful World, Fired Up!, All Good Things, The Chicago 8.
TELEVISION: *Movies*: The Last Survivors, Mayday at 40000 Feet, Man from Atlantis, Kill Me If You Can, The Bastard, Terror Out of the Sky, Samurai, The Night the Bridge Fell Down, This House Possessed, Games Mother Never Taught You, Who is Julia?, Goddess of Love, A Cry for Help: The Tracey Thurman Story, Incident at Dark River, Crash Landing; The Rescue of of Flight 232, Stormy Weathers, M.A.N.T.I.S, Roswell, Without Warning, Tempting Fate, Witness to the Mob, Path to War, Mrs. Harris, Wildlife. *Mini-series*: Jackie Bouvier Kennedy Onassis. *Series*: Mariah, Falcon Crest, Pasadena, Hollywood Squares, American Dragon: Jake Long (voice), The Loop. *Guest*: More than 88 appearances.

HALLSTRÖM, LASSE

Director. b. Stockholm, Sweden, June 2, 1946. m. actress Lena Olin. As teenager made 16mm film which was eventually screened on Swedish tv. Began professional career filming and editing inserts for Swedish TV. Directed program Shall We Dance? for Danish TV, followed by TV prod. on The Love Seeker, dir. of program Shall We Go to My or to Your Place or Each Go Home Alone?.
PICTURES: A Love and His Lass (debut, 1974), ABBA: The Movie, Father-to-Be, The Rooster, Happy We, The Children of Bullerby Village, More About the Children of Bullerby Village, My Life as a Dog (also co-s.p.; 2 Academy Award noms. for dir. & s.p.; DGA nom. 1988), Once Around (U.S. debut, 1991), What's Eating Gilbert Grape (also co-exec. prod.), Lumiere & Company, Something to Talk About, The Cider House Rules (Academy Award nom. 2000), Chocolat, The Shipping News, An Unfinished Life, Fever (exec. prod. only), Harry & Caresse (also prod.), Casanova, Open Window (exec. prod.), The Hoax, Hachiko: A Dog's Story, Dear John.
TELEVISION: *Movies:* Shall We Go to My Place or Your Place or Each Go Home Alone? (also writer, editor, cinematographer), New Amsterdam (also exec. prod., pilot).

HALMI, ROBERT, JR.

Producer. Father is Robert Halmi, Sr. Emmys for Outstanding Children's Special for: The Night They Saved Christmas (Emmy nom. 1985), A Gift of Love: The Daniel Huffman Story (Emmy nom. 2000), Run the Wild Fields (Emmy Award 2001, shared with Paul Rauch, Paul Kaufman & Rodney P. Vaccaro); and A Storm in Summer (Emmy Award 2001, shared with Renee Valente.), They Call Me Sirr (Emmy nom. 2002), Off Season (Emmy nom. 2002), Won Emmy-Outstanding Drama/Comedy Special in 1990 for The Incident. Currently President and CEO of RHI Entertainment.
PICTURES: Hugo the Hippo, Braxton, Ascent, Just a Dream, Back to the Secret Garden, Dinotopia: Curse of the Ruby Sunstone, Love's Abiding Joy, Swamp Devil.
TELEVISION: *Movies: Exec. Prod.*: Nairobi Affair, Pack of Lies (Emmy nom. 1987), April Morning, Mr. & Mrs. Bridge, The Wishing Tree, Bump In The Night, The Josephine Baker Story, Eyes of a Witness. The Fire Next Time, Blind Spot, The Yearling, Seasons of the Heart, The Ascent, Black Fox, Black Fox: The Price of Peace, Black Fox: Good Men & Bad, September, The Tale of Sweeney Todd, Still Holding On: The Legend of Cadillac Jack, Creature, The Ransom of Red Chief, The Baby Dance (Emmy nom. 1999), Hard Time, The Premonition, Alice in Wonderland, Cleopatra, Journey to the Center of the Earth, In A Class of His Own, Hostage Hotel, Aftershock: Earthquake in New York, Finding Buck McHenry, Jason & the Argonauts, Seventeen Again, Hamlet, David Copperfield, By Dawn's Early Light, The Lost Empire, Walter & Henry, The Infinite Worlds of H.G. Wells, Prince Charming, Snow White: The Fairest of Them All, They Call Me Sir, Off Season, Roughing It, Just A Dream, Gentle Ben (2002), Night of the Wolf, The Snow Queen, Gentle Ben 2, The Last Cowboy, Straight from the Heart, Love Comes Softly, Audrey's Rain, The King & Queen of Moonlight Bay, Hard Ground, Mystery Woman, Turning Homeward, Monster Makers, Til' the River Runs Dry, Frankenstein, Farscape: The Peacekeeper Wars, Just Desserts, Life on Liberty Street, A Christmas Romance, Murder Without Conviction, Love's Enduring Promise, Love, Clyde, The Hollywood Mom's Mystery, The Long Shot: Believe in Courage, The Trail to Hope Rose, Wedding Daze, A Boyfriend for Christmas, The Lion in Winter (Emmy nom. 2004), Home for Christmas, Angel in the Family, Back to You and Me, The Family Plan, Thicker Than Water, Out of the Woods, The Reading Room, Hogfather, Hybrid, Eye of the Beast, Pandemic, Mystery Woman: In the Shadows, Love Is a Four Letter Word, Jane Doe: Ties That Bind, Love's Unending Legacy, Something Beneath, A Stranger's Heart, Avenging Angel, Claire, Croc, Lone Rider, Black Widow, A Grandpa for Christmas, Love's Unfolding Dream, Dr. Jekyll & Mr. Hyde, Jane Doe: Eye of the Beholder, Journey to the Center of the Earth, The Hive, Murder 101: New Age, Black Widow, Shark Swarm, The Color of Magic, Lone Rider, A Gunfighter's Pledge, Mask of the Ninja, Infected, Ladies of the House, The Deadliest Lesson, Relative Stranger Do You Know Me, Hellhounds, Uncorked, High Plains Invaders, Always and Forever, The Phantom, Riverworld. *Mini-series*: Lonesome Dove (Emmy nom. 1989), Return to Lonesome Dove, The Old Curiosity Shop, Streets of Laredo, Dead Man's Walk, The 10th Kingdom, In the Beginning, A Girl Thing, Voyage of the Unicorn, Arabian Nights (Emmy nom. 2000), Dinotopia (Emmy nom. 2002), La Femme Musketeer, Gone But Not Forgotten, King Solomon's Mines, Legend of Earthsea, The Detective, Supernova, Merlin's Apprentice, Blackbeard, Pandemic, Tin Man (Emmy nom. 2008), The Last Templar (parts 1 & 2), Meteor: Path to Destruction, Alice. *Series*:

Chillers, Space Rangers, Lonesome Dove: The Outlaw Years, Farscape, Dinotopia: The Series, Flash Gordon, Knights of Bloodsteel, Meteor.

HALMI, ROBERT, SR.

Producer. b. Budapest, Hungary, Jan 22, 1924. Originally writer-photographer under contract to Life Magazine. CEO, Hallmark Entertainment. During 2006, the Halmis bought back the production company from Hallmark Cards and changed its name back to RHI Entertainment, LLC. Halmi Sr. is currently chairman of the new RHI.
PICTURES: Created documentaries for U.N. Features include: Hugo the Hippo, Visit to a Chief's Son, The One and Only, Brady's Escape, Cheetah, Mr. and Mrs. Bridge, Swamp Devil.
TELEVISION: *Movies*: Bold Journey (dir.-cin.), American Sportsman, The Oriental Sportsman, The Flying Doctor, The Outdoorsman, Julius Boros Series, Rexford, Who Needs Elephants, Calloway's Climb, Oberndorf Revisited, True Position, Wilson's Reward, Nurse, Buckley Sails, A Private Battle, My Old Man, Mr. Griffin and Me, When the Circus Came to Town, Best of Friends, Bush Doctor, Peking Encounter, Svengali, China Rose, Cook and Peary-The Race to the Pole, Terrible Joe Moran, Nairobi Affair, The Night They Saved Christmas (Emmy nom. 1985), Spies, Pack of Lies (Emmy nom. 1987), Lies and Naked Thighs. *Exec. prod.:* The Prize Pulitzer, Paradise, Bridesmaids, Face to Face, Margaret Bourke-White, The Incident, Josephine Baker Story, The Secret, An American Story, Call of the Wild, Blind Spot, Incident in a Small Town, Spoils of War, The Yearling, A Promise Kept: The Oksana Baiul Story, A Mother's Gift, Reunion, My Brother's Keeper, Gypsy (Emmy nom. 1994), White Dwarf, Secrets, Bye Bye Birdie, Kidnapped, Gulliver's Travels (Emmy Award, 1996), Captains Courageous, Dead Man's Walk, Mrs. Santa Claus, Forbidden Territory: Stanley's Search for Livingstone, A Christmas Memory, Mary and Tim, The Long Way Home, Crime and Punishment, Only Love, Rear Window, Alice in Wonderland, Noah's Ark, Cleopatra, Animal Farm, The Magical Legend of the Leprechauns, A Christmas Carol, The 10th Kingdom, Don Quixote, The Land of Oz, The Lost Empire, Mike Bassett: England Manager, Prince Charming, Snow White, King of Texas, The Snow Queen, DC 9/11: Time of Crisis, The Lion in Winter (Emmy nom. 2004), The Five People You Meet in Heaven, Earthsea, Hercules, Maneater (prod.), Hogfather, Hybrid, Eye of the Beast, Marco Polo (prod.), Something Beneath, Grizzly Rage, Maneater (prod.), Dr. Jekyll & Mr. Hyde, Journey to the Center of the Earth, The Hive, Mask of the Ninja, The Color of Magic, Infected, Rise of the Gargoyle, Hellhounds, High Plains Invaders, The Phantom, Riverworld. *Mini-series*: Spearfield's Daughter, Scarlett, Voyage of the Unicorn, The Infinite Worlds of H.G. Wells, Dinotopia (Emmy nom. 2002), Teenage Mutant Ninja Turtles, Legend of Middletown, America (documentary), The Oddysey (Emmy nom. 1997), In Cold Blood (Emmy nom. 1997), Moby Dick, (Emmy nom. 1998), Merlin (Emmy nom. 1998), Arabian Nights (Emmy nom. 2000), The Ten Commandments, Middletown, America (TV doc.), The Thief of Bagdad, Marco Polo (prod.), Tin Man (Emmy nom. 2008), The Last Templar (parts 1 & 2), Alice. *Series:* Flash Gordon, Knights of Bloodsteel.

HAMEL, VERONICA

Actress. b. Philadelphia, PA, Nov. 20, 1943. e. Temple U. Moved to NY and began a modelling career with Eileen Ford Agency. Off B'way debut: The Big Knife. Acted in dinner theater prods. Moved to L.A. 1975.
THEATRE: *B'way:* Rumors. *Off B'way:* The Big Knife, The Ballad of Boris K.
PICTURES: Cannonball, Beyond the Poseidon Adventure, When Time Ran Out, A New Life, Taking Care of Business, The Last Leprechaun, Determination of Death.
TELEVISION: *Movies:* The Gathering, Ski Lift to Death, The Gathering II, The Hustler of Muscle Beach, Valley of the Dolls, Sessions, Twist of Fate, She Said No, Stop at Nothing, Deadly Medicine (also co-exec. prod.), Baby Snatcher (also co-exec. prod.), The Disappearance of Nora, The Conviction of Kitty Dodds, Shadow of Obsession, A Child's Cry for Help, Intensive Care, Secrets, Here Come the Munsters, Blink of an Eye, Talk to Me, Stranger in My Home, Home Invasion, Bone Eater. *Mini-series*: 79 Park Avenue, Kane & Abel. *Series*: Hill Street Blues (4 Emmy noms.), Philly, Third Watch, Lost. *Guest:* More than 50 appearances.

HAMILL, MARK

Actor. b. Oakland, CA, Sept. 25, 1951. While studying acting at LA City Col. made prof. debut in episode of The Bill Cosby Show, 1970. Featured in CD-ROM interactive game Wing Commander III.
THEATRE: *NY:* The Elephant Man (B'way debut), Amadeus (also Natl. tour), Harrigan 'n' Hart, Room Service (off-B'way), The Nerd.
PICTURES: Star Wars (debut, 1977), Wizards (voice), Corvette Summer, The Empire Strikes Back, The Big Red One, The Night the Lights Went Out in Georgia, Britannia Hospital, Return of the Jedi, Slipstream, Midnight Ride, Black Magic Woman, Sleepwalkers (cameo), Time Runner, The Guyver, Batman: Mask of the Phantasm (voice), Village of the Damned, Laserhawk, Gen 13 (voice), Hamilton, Wing Commander (cameo, voice), Walking Across Egypt, Sinbad: Beyond the Veil of Mists (voice), Earth Day (voice), Jay and Silent Bob Strike Back, Thank You Good Night, Baxter and Bananas, Reeseville, Comic Book: The Movie (also dir.), Through the Moebius Strip, Ultimate Avengers II (video), Tom and Jerry: Shiver Me Whiskers (video, voice), Robotech: The Shadow Chronicles (voice), Quantum Quest: A Cassini Space Odyssey (voice), Minkow.
TELEVISION: *Movies*: Sarah T.-Portrait of a Teenage Alcoholic, Eric, Delancey Street: The Crisis Within, Mallory: Circumstantial Evidence, The City, Earth Angel, Body Bags, Hollyrock-a-Bye Baby (voice), When Time Expires, Sinbad: Beyond the Veil of Mists, Codename: Kids Next Door - Operation Z.E.R.O. (voice), Afro Samurai: Resurrection (voice, English version). *Mini-series:* The Red Planet, The Wrong Coast (voice also exec. prod/writer). *Series*: General Hospital, The Texas Wheelers, Batman (voice), The Incredible Hulk (voice), Bruno the Kid (voice), Wing Commander Academy (voice), Cow and Chicken, The Legend of Calamity Jane, Superstructures of the World, The Sci-Fi Files, The Powerpuff Girls, .COM, Justice League, Teamo Supremo (voice), Stripperella, Super Robot Monkey Team Hyperforce Go!, Codename: Kids Next Door, IGPX: Immortal Grand Prix (voice), Spawn: The Animation (voice), Justice League Unlimited, Metalocalypse (voice), Avatar: The Last Airbender (voice), The New Woody Woodpecker Show (voice). *Specials*: Get High on Yourself, Night of 100 Stars. *Guest*: More than 235 appearances.

HAMILTON, GEORGE

Actor. b. Memphis, TN, Aug. 12, 1939. e. Grammar, Hawthorne, CA; military sch., Gulfport, MS, N.Y. Hackley Prep Sch., FL, Palm Beach H.S. Won best actor award in Florida, high sch. contest.
PICTURES: Crime and Punishment USA (debut, 1959), Home From the Hill, All the Fine Young Cannibals, Where the Boys Are, Angel Baby, By Love Possessed, A Thunder of Drums, Light in the Piazza, Two Weeks in Another Town, Act One, The Victors, Looking for Love, Your Cheatin' Heart, Viva Maria, That Man George, Doctor You've Got to Be Kidding!, Jack of Diamonds, A Time for Killing, The Power, Togetherness, Evel Knievel (also co-p), Medusa (also exec. prod.), The Man Who Loved Cat Dancing, Once Is Not Enough, The Happy Hooker Goes to Washington, Love at First Bite (also co-exec. prod. Golden Globe nom. 1980), Sextette, From Hell to Victory, Zorro the Gay Blade (also co-prod. Golden Globe nom. 1982), The Godfather Part III, Doc Hollywood, Once Upon a Crime, Double Dragon, Amore!, Playback, Meet Wally Sparks, 8 Heads in a Duffel Bag, She's Too Tall, Bulworth (cameo), The Little Unicorn, Pets, Crocodile Dundee in Los Angeles, Off Key, The Trip (exec. prod. only), Hollywood Ending, The L.A. Riot Spectacular, Coma, My One and Only (exec. prod. only).
TELEVISION: *Movies*: Two Fathers' Justice, Monte Carlo, Poker Alice, Caution: Murder Can Be Hazardous to Your Health, The House on Sycamore Street, Two Fathers: Justice for the Innocent, Danielle Steel's Vanished, Rough Riders, The Hollywood Mom's Mystery, Too Cool for Christmas. *Mini-series*: Roots, P.T. Barnum. *Series:* The Survivors, Paris 7000, Dynasty, Spies, The Bold & the Beautiful, The George and Alana Show (also prod.), The Guilt, Jenny, Match Game, The Family (host, 2003), Dancing with the Stars. *Special:* The Veil. *Guest*: More than 148 appearances.

HAMILTON, GUY

Director. b. Paris, France, Sept. 24, 1922. Ent. m.p. industry 1939 as apprentice at Victorine Studio, Nice; Royal Navy, 1940-45, in England asst. dir., Fallen Idol, Third Man, Outcast of the Islands, African Queen.
PICTURES: The Ringer, The Intruder, An Inspector Calls, Dragnet (actor only), Colditz Story, Manuela, The Devil's Disciple, A Touch of Larceny, The Best of Enemies, The Party's Over, Man in the Middle, Goldfinger, Funeral in Berlin, Battle of Britain, Diamonds Are Forever, Live and Let Die, The Man with the Golden Gun, Force Ten from Navarone, The Mirror Crack'd, Evil Under the Sun, Remo Williams, Try This One For Size.

HAMILTON, LINDA

Actress. b. Salisbury, MD, Sept. 26, 1956. Appeared on NY stage in Looice and Richard III.
PICTURES: Tag: The Assassination Game, Children of the Corn, The Stone Boy, The Terminator, Black Moon Rising, King Kong Lives!, Mr. Destiny, Terminator 2: Judgment Day, Silent Fall, The Shadow Conspiracy, Dante's Peak, Unglued The Secret Life of Girls, Skeletons in the Closet, Wholey Moses, Smile, The Woodcutter, The Kid & I, Broken, In Your Dreams, Waters Rising, Terminator Salvation (voice), Holy Water, Refuge.
TELEVISION: *Movies*: Reunion, Rape and Marriage-The Rideout Case, Country Gold, Secrets of a Mother and Daughter, Secret Weapons, Club Med, Go Toward the Light, A Mother's Prayer (Golden Globe nom. 1996), Rescuers: Stories of Courage: Two Couples, On the Line, Point Last Seen, The Color of Courage, Batman Beyond: The Movie, Sex & Mrs X, Bailey's Mistake, Silent Night, Home by Christmas. *Mini-series:* A Girl Thing. *Series*: Secrets of Midland Heights, King's Crossing, Beauty and the Beast (Emmy nom.; 2 Golden Globe nom. 1988, 1989), Hercules, According to Jim, Thief (also pilot), The Weight, The Line. *Guest:* More than 67 appearances.

HAMLIN, HARRY

Actor. b. Pasadena, CA, Oct. 30, 1951. m. actress Lisa Rinna. e. U. of California, Yale U., 1974 in theatre, psychology. Awarded IT&T Fulbright Grant, 1977. 1974-1976 with the American Conservatory Theatre, San Francisco, then joined McCarter Theatre, Princeton (Hamlet, Faustus in Hell, Equus). B'way debut

Awake and Sing! (1984). Also performed in Henry V, Smoke.
PICTURES: Movie Movie (debut, 1978; Golden Globe nom. 1979), King of the Mountain, Clash of the Titans, Making Love, Blue Skies Again Maxie, Ebbtide, Save Me, The Celluloid Closet, Badge of Bertrayal, Allie & Me, Frogs for Snakes, Perfume, Roads to Riches, Shoot or Be Shot, Strange Wilderness.
TELEVISION: *Movies*: Laguna Heat, Deceptions, Deadly Intentions... Again?, Deliver Them From Evil: The Taking of Alta View, Poisoned By Love: The Kern County Murders, In the Best of Families: Marriage Pride & Madness, Tom Clancy's Op Center, Her Deadly Rival, The Hunted, Like Father Like Santa, Silent Predators, Quarantine, Sex Lies and Obsession, Disappearance, L.A. Law: The Movie, Family Gathering. *Mini-series*: Studs Lonigan, Master of the Game, Space, Favorite Son, Night Sins. *Series*: L.A. Law (3 Golden Globe noms.), Ink, Movie Stars, Veronica Mars, Harper's Island. *Documentary:* Retrosexual: The 80's (mini). *Guest:* More than 75 appearances.

HAMLISCH, MARVIN

Composer. b. New York, NY, June 2, 1944. e. Juilliard. Accompanist and straight man on tour with Groucho Marx 1974-75; debut as concert pianist 1975 with Minn. Orch. Scores of B'way shows: A Chorus Line (Tony Award & Pulitzer Prize); They're Playing Our Song, Smile, The Goodbye Girl. Composer of popular songs: Sunshine Lollipops and Rainbows, Nobody Does it Better. Winner 4 Grammy awards, 3 Oscars, 2 Emmys, 1 Tony, 3 Golden Globe awards. Autobiography, The Way I Was, 1992. Conductor for the Pittsburgh Symphony Orchestra, 1995; Baltimore Symphony Orchestra, 1996.
PICTURES: The Swimmer, Take the Money and Run, Bananas, Save the Tiger, Kotch (Academy Award nom.; golden Globe Award 1972), The Way We Were (2 Acad. Awards for orig. score and title song; Golden Globe award 1974), The Sting (Acad. Award for music adapt., 1974, The Spy Who Loved Me (2 Academy Award nom.; 2 Golden Globe nom. 1978), Same Time Next Year (Academy Award nom.; Golden Globe nom. 1979), Ice Castles (Academy Award nom.; Golden Globe nom. 1980), Chapter Two, Seems Like Old Times, Starting Over (Golden Globe nom. 1980), Ordinary People, The Fan, Sophie's Choice (Academy Award nom. 1983), A Chorus Line (Academy Award nom. 1986), Shirley Valentine (Academy Award nom.; Golden Globe nom. 1990), I Ought to Be in Pictures, Romantic Comedy, D.A.R.Y.L., Three Men and a Baby, Little Nikita, The January Man, The Experts, Frankie and Johnny, Open Season, The Mirror Has Two Faces (Academy award nom.; 2 Golden Globe nom. 1997), Austin Powers: The Spy Who Shagged Me, Standing Room Only, Lost in Translation, Connie and Carla, Bridget Jones: The Edge of Reason, The Sisterhood of the Traveling Pants, American Dreamz, ShowBusiness: The Road to Broadway, Shrek the Third, The Informant! (Golden Globe nom. 2010), Cloudy with a Chance of Meatballs.
TELEVISION: *Movies*: The Underground Man, The Prime of Miss Jean Brodie, The Entertainer (also prod.), A Streetcar Named Desire, The Two Mrs. Grenvilles, When the Time Comes, Women & Men: Stories of Seduction, Sam Found Out: A Triple Play (musical dir.), Switched at Birth, Seasons of the Heart. *Mini-series:* Triple Sensation. *Series*: Doc Elliot, Hot L Baltimore, Beacon Hill (also theme), The Nancy Walker Show, Good Morning America (theme), Brooklyn Bridge (Emmy nom. 1992), Omnibus, Bert. Specials: Barbra Streisand: The Concert (2 Academy Awards 1995), AFI's 100 Years... 100 Movies (Academy Award; 1 other nom.1999), Timeless: Live in Concert (Academy Award 2001). Many more soundtrack writing credits.

HAMM, JON

Actor. b. St. Louis, MO, March 10, 1971. e. University of Missouri.
PICTURES: Space Cowboys, Kissing Jessica Stein, We Were Soldiers, Ira & Abby, The Ten, The Day the Earth Stood Still, Stolen, A Single Man (voice), Howl, Shrek Forever After (voice), The A-Team, The Town, Sucker Punch, Bridesmaids.
TELEVISION: *Series:* The Trouble with Normal (pilot), Providence, The Division, Related (pilot), What About Brian, The Unit, 30 Rock (2 Emmy noms. as guest), Mad Men (3 Emmy noms.; Golden Globe Award 2008, 2 other noms.). *Guest:* More than 35 appearances.

HAMMER, BONNIE

Executive. e. Bachelor's degree, Communications, Boston Univ.; Master's degree, media and new technology, Boston Univ. Hammer entered the TV industry at entry level and has become one of the industry's top cable executives. Early in her career she developed reality-based programs and executive produced the talk show series Alive & Well in Los Angeles; she served as producer on Boston ABC affiliate WCVB's top morning talk show Good Day!, and the PBS series—This Old House, Infinity Factory, and the critically-acclaimed children's series Zoom. Hammer moved into cable TV as a programming executive at Lifetime Television Network from 1987 to 1989. The 1988 documentary, Gangs: Not My Kid, garnered Hammer the Women in Film Festival's Lillian Gish Award, the Cine Golden Eagle and the National Association for Youth's Mentor Award. She moved to Universal in 1989, taking on the dual role as senior v.p. of SCI FI programming and USA original productions. In this post, she had oversight of programming and scheduling at SCI FI and development of original programming for both SCI FI and the USA Network. She eventually became executive v.p. & gen. mgr. of the SCI FI Channel before being named its president in April 2001. In May 2004, she added pres., USA Network, to her titles and since then assumes overall responsibility for both USA Network & SCI FI. 2008 became pres. NBC Universal Cable Studio and will continue her duties for USA Network & SCI FI. Hammer has served on the NATPE bd. of directors; serves on the Celebration of Women's Achievements in Television and Radio steering committee for the Museum of Radio and Television; and is on the bd. of advisors for MPH Connective, which provides professional-grade media solutions for entertainment and education purposes — such as developing and producing educational film projects for museums, corporations, presidential libraries and medical centers, as well as a range of family-friendly films. Additionally, Hammer is a mentor for Women in Film & Television. Outside TV, Hammer's work as a photographer has been published in Time, The Boston Herald, The Los Angeles Times, and various Houghton-Mifflin and Little Brown books. In Jan. 2007, Hammer was a recipient of NATPE's Brandon Tartikoff Legacy Awards.

HAMNER, EARL

Producer, Writer. b. Schuyler, VA, July 10, 1923. e. U. of Richmond 1940-43, Northwestern U.; U. of Cincinnati, Coll. Conservatory of Music, B.F.A., 1958. With WLW, Cincinnati, as radio writer-prod.; joined NBC 1949 as writer; (The Georgia Gibbs Show, The Helen O'Connell Show); freelance 1961-71; writer, prod. Lorimar Prods. 1971-86; writer prod. Taft Entertainment 1986-; Pres. Amanda Prods.
PICTURES: Palm Springs Weekend, Spencer's Mountain, The Tamarind Seed, Charlotte's Web (writer, 1973), Where the Lilies Bloom, The Education of Little Tree, Charlotte's Web (2006).
TELEVISION: *Movies*: The Homecoming: A Christmas Story (writer only Emmy nom. 1972), You Can't Get There From Here (writer only), A Wedding on Walton's Mountain, Mother's Day on Walton's Mountain, A Day of Thanks on Walton's Mountain (also actor), The Gift of Love--A Christmas Story (also writer), A Walton Thanksgiving Reunion, A Walton Wedding, A Mother's Gift, A Walton Easter, The Education of Little Tree, The Night Before Christmas: A Mouse Tale. *Exec. prod./Series:* The Waltons (creator, co-prod., narr., Emmy nom. 1973), Apple's Way (creator), The Young Pioneers (creator), Joshua's World, Falcon Crest, Snowy River: The McGregor Saga (co-exec. prod.), Boone (also creator), Morning Star/Evening Star (also narrator) Night Visions (writer).

HAMPSHIRE, SUSAN

Actress. b. London, England,, May 12, 1941. O.B.E., 1995.
THEATRE: Expresso Bongo, Follow That Girl, Fairy Tales of New York, Ginger Man, Past Imperfect, She Stoops to Conquer, On Approval, The Sleeping Prince, A Doll's House, Taming of the Shrew, Peter Pan, Romeo & Jeanette, As You Like It, Miss Julie, The Circle, Arms and the Man, Man and Superman, Tribades, An Audience Called Edward, The Crucifer of Blood, Night and Day, The Revolt, House Guest, Blithe Spirit, Married Love, A Little Night Music, The King and I, Noel & Gertie, Relative Values, Susanna Andler, Black Chiffon.
PICTURES: The Three Lives of Thomasina, Night Must Fall, Wonderful Life, Paris Au Mois d'Aout, The Fighting Prince of Donegal, The Trygon Factor, Monte Carlo or Bust, Rogan, David Copperfield, A Room in Paris, Living Free, Time for Loving, Malpertius, Baffled, Neither the Sea nor the Sand, Roses and Green Peppers, David the King, Bang!.
TELEVISION: *Movies:* An Ideal Husband, David Copperfield, Baffled!, Dr. Jekyll and Mr. Hyde (musical), The Story of David, Cry Terror, Coming Home, Nancherrow, Sparkling Cyanide. *Mini-series:* The Forsyte Saga (Emmy Award 1970), Vanity Fair (Emmy Award 1973), The First Churchills (Emmy Award 1971), Barchester Chronicles. *Series:* The Andromeda Breakthrough, Katy, The Pallisers, The Lady Is a Liar, The Improbable Mr. Clayville, Leaving, Leaving II, Going to Pot (I, II, and III), Don't Tell Father, The Grand I & II, Monarch of the Glen, The Time Tunnel.

HAMPTON, JAMES

Actor, Director. b. Oklahoma City, OK, July 9, 1936. e. N. Texas St. Univ.
PICTURES: Fade In, Soldier Blue, The Man Who Loved Cat Dancing, The Longest Yard (Golden Globe nom. 1975), W.W. & The Dixie Dancekings, Hustle, Hawmps!, The Cat from Outer Space, Mackintosh & T.J., The China Syndrome, Hangar 18, Condorman, Teen Wolf, Teen Wolf Too, Police Academy 5, Pump Up the Volume, The Giant of Thunder Mountain, Sling Blade, Lost in the Pershing Point Hotel, Danny & Max, Fire from Below, The Coffin.
TELEVISION: *Movies*: Attack on Terror: The FBI Versus the Ku Klux Klan, Force Five, The Amazing Howard Hughes, Three on a Date, Thaddeus Rose and Eddie, Stand By Your Man, Through the Magic Pyramid, World War III, The Burning Bed. *Mini-series*: Centennial. *Series*: F Troop, The Doris Day Show, Love American Style, Mary, Maggie, B.A.D. Cats, The Dukes of Hazzard, Maggie, Teen Wolf (voice), Days of Our Lives. *Director*: Evening Shade (also writer), Hearts Afire (dir.), Grace Under Fire, Sister, Sister, Kirk, Hudson Street, Boston Common, American Pie, Smart Guy, Linc's, Sister, Sister, Zoe, Duncan, Jack & Jane. *Guest:* More than 85 appearances.

HANCOCK, JOHN
Director. b. Kansas City, MO, Feb. 12, 1939. e. Harvard. Was musician and theatre dir. before turning to films. Dir. play, A Man's a Man, NY 1962. Artistic dir. San Francisco Actors Workshop 1965-66, Pittsburgh Playhouse 1966-67. Obie for dir., Midsummer Night's Dream, NY 1968. Nominated for Academy Award, 1971 for short, Sticky My Fingers, Fleet My Feet.
PICTURES: Let's Scare Jessica to Death, Bang the Drum Slowly, Baby Blue Marine, California Dreaming, Weeds (also co-s.p.), Prancer, A Piece of Eden, Suspended Animation.
TELEVISION: *Movie*: Steal the Sky. *Series*: The Twilight Zone (1986), Lady Blue, Hill Street Blues.

HAND, BETHLYN J.
Executive. b. Alton, IL. e. U. of Texas. Entered motion picture industry in 1966 as administrative assistant to president of Motion Picture Association of America, Inc. In 1975 became associate dir. of advertising administration of MPAA. In 1976 became dir. of advertising administration; in 1979 became; v.p.-west coast activities, board of directors, Los Angeles. S.P.C.A. 1981, appointed by Governor to Calif. Motion Picture Council. 1983, elected vice chmn., California Motion Picture Council. 1990, named sr. v.p. MPAA. Hand retired full-time duties with MPAA March 28, 2003. She remains a member of the Academy of Motion Picture Arts and Sciences and serves on the exec. committee for public relations and the PR Coordinating Committee, which handles press during the Acad. Awards.

HANEKE, MICHAEL
Director, Writer. b. Munich, Germany, March 23, 1942.
PICTURES: The Seventh Continent, Benny's Video, 71 Fragments of a Chronology of Chance, The Age of the Wolves, Lumiere and Company (dir. only), The Moor's Head (s.p. only), The Castle, Funny Games, Code Unkown: Incomplete Tales of Several Journeys, The Piano Player, Le Temps du loup, Hidden, Funny Games, The White Ribbon (s.p.).
TELEVISION: *Movies*: After Liverpool, Sperrmull (dir. only), Drei Wege zum See, Variation, Wer war Edgar Allan?, Fraulein, Nachruf fur einen Morder, Die Rebellion.

HANKS, TOM
Actor, Producer. b. Concord, CA, July 9, 1956. m. actress Rita Wilson. Traveled around Northern CA. with family before settling in Oakland, CA. e. Chabot Jr. Col., California State U. Began career with Great Lakes Shakespeare Festival, Cleveland (3 seasons) and NY's Riverside Theater (Taming of the Shrew). Formed Production Company: Playtone Productions with Rita Wilson. 2009 elected to the Bd. of Governors of AMPAS for three year term.
PICTURES: He Knows You're Alone (debut, 1980), Splash, Bachelor Party, The Man With One Red Shoe, Volunteers, The Money Pit, Nothing in Common, Every Time We Say Goodbye, Dragnet, Big (Academy Award nom.; Golden Globe Award 1989), Punchline, The 'Burbs, Turner and Hooch, Joe Versus the Volcano, The Bonfire of the Vanities, Radio Flyer, A League of Their Own, Sleepless in Seattle (Golden Globe nom. 1994), Philadelphia (Academy Award, 1994; Golden Globe Award), Forrest Gump (Academy Award, 1995; Golden Globe Award), The Celluloid Closet, Apollo 13, Toy Story (voice), That Thing You Do! (also dir.), Saving Private Ryan (Academy Award nom.; Golden Globe nom. 1999), You've Got Mail, Toy Story 2 (voice), The Green Mile, Cast Away (Academy Award nom.; Golden Globe Award 2001), The Road to Perdition, Catch Me If You Can, The Terminal, The Ladykillers, The Polar Express (also exec. prod.), Cars (voice), The Da Vinci Code, The Great Buck Howard (also prod.), Charlie Wilson's War (also prod., Golden Globe nom. 2008), Angels & Demons, Boone's Lick, Toy Story 3 (voice), Larry Crowne (also dir., prod., s.p.). *As Producer:* Connie & Carla, The Spider and the Fly, The Great Hartford Elementary Heist, A Cold Case (also actor), A Wilderness of Monkeys (also exec. prod., dir.), Magnificent Desolation: Walking on the Moon 3D, The Ant Bully, The Risk Pool (also actor), They Marched Into Sunlight, Evan Almighty (exec. prod.), Starter for Ten, Where the Wild Things Are, City of Ember, Mamma Mia!, Surfer Dude, My Life in Ruins, Where the Wild Things Are.
TELEVISION: *Movies:* Rona Jaffe's Mazes and Monsters, Rutles 2: Can't Buy Me Lunch, We're with the Band (prod.). *Mini-series:* Band of Brothers (exec. prod. 2 Emmy Awards; 1 other nom. 2002), From the Earth to the Moon (Emmy Award 1 other nom. for dir. Part I, 1998), John Adams (co-exec. prod., Emmy Award 2008), The Pacific (exec. prod.). *Series:* Bosom Buddies, West Point (exec. prod.), My Big Fat Greek Life (exec. prod.), Big Love (exec. prod., Emmy nom. 2009). *Documentaries:* The Celluloid Closet, I Am Your Child, Return to Normandy, Shooting War, We Stand Alone Together (exec. prod. Emmy nom. 2002), America: A Tribute to Heroes, Horatio's Drive: America's First Road Trip (voice), World War II Memorial Dedication (guest speaker), Magnificent Desolation: Walking on the Moon 3D (short, narr., prod., writer), Neil Young: Heart of Gold (prod.). *Guest:* More than 245 appearances.

HANNAH, DARYL
Actress. b. Chicago, IL, Dec. 3, 1960. Niece of cinematographer Haskell Wexler. e. UCLA. Studied ballet with Maria Tallchief. Studied acting with Stella Adler.
PICTURES: The Fury (debut, 1978), The Final Terror, Hard Country, Blade Runner, Summer Lovers, Reckless, Splash, The Pope of Greenwich Village, Clan of the Cave Bear, Legal Eagles, Roxanne, Wall Street, High Spirits, Crimes and Misdemeanors, Steel Magnolias, Crazy People, At Play in the Fields of the Lord, Memoirs of an Invisible Man, Grumpy Old Men, The Little Rascals, The Tie That Binds, Two Much, Grumpier Old Men, The Real Blonde, The Gingerbread Man, Hi-Life, Wild Flowers, Speedway Junky, Enemy of My Enemy, Diplomatic Siege, My Favorite Martian, Zapatista, Cord, Dancing At the Blue Iguana, Ring of Fire, Jackpot, A Walk to Remember, Run for the Money, Searching for Debra Winger, Bank, Northfolk, Casa des los Babys, Kill Bill: Vol. 1, The Job, The Big Empty, Kill Bill: Vol. 2, Silver City, The King, Supercross, Lucky 13, Living Neon Dreams, Keeping Up with the Steins, White Lies, Vice, Dark Honeymoon, Vice (also exec. prod.), Dark Honeymoon, Shannon's Rainbow, A Closed Book, A Fonder Heart, Eldorado.
TELEVISION: *Movies*: Paper Dolls, Attack of the 50 Ft. Woman (also co-prod.), Rear Window, First Target, On the Edge of Blade Runner, All the Good Ones Are Married, Kung Fu Killer (also singer), Shark Swarm, Storm Seekers. *Mini-series*: The Last Don, The Last Don II, Jack and the Beanstalk: The Real Story, Final Days of Planet Earth. *Series*: Robert Altman's Gun. *Documentaries:* Zapatista (narr.), Strip Notes (also prod., cinematographer, dir. and editor), Searching for Debra Winger, So Right So Smart (narr.), Beyond Borders: John Sayles in Mexico, Sierra Club Chronicles (narr.), Natural Heroes, Dolphins and Whales 3D: Tribes of the Ocean (narr.), It's Easy Being Green, The Garden, Fierce Light: When Spirit Meets Action, Call + Response, So Right So Smart (narr.). *Guest:* More than 107 appearances.

HANNAH, JOHN
Actor. b. Kilbride, Scotland, UK, April 23, 1962. Was an apprentice electrician before entering mp industry.
PICTURES: Harbour Beat, Four Weddings and a Funeral, Madagascar Skin, The Innocent Sleep, The Final Cut, The James Gang, Sliding Doors, The Mummy, The Hurricane, The Intruder, Circus, Pandaemonium, The Mummy Returns, Camouflage, I'm With Lucy, Before You Go, I Accuse, Houseboat, Burns, The Last Legion, The Mummy: Tomb of the Dragon Emperor, Tea Shop Asylum, Jacob, Woodland Cross.
TELEVISION: *Movies*: Paul Calf's Video Diary, Pauline Calf's Wedding Video, Truth or Dare, Romance and Rejection, Circles of Deceit: Kalon, The Love Bug, Rebus: Black and Blue, Rebus: The Hanging Garden, Rebus: Dead Souls, Rebus: Mortal Causes, Dr. Jekyll & Mr. Hyde, Amnesia, Quite Ugly One Morning (exec. prod.), Marple: 4.50 from Paddington, Marple: What Mrs. McGillicuddy Saw, Cold Blood, Cold Blood 2, Cold Blood 3: Interference, Cold Blood 4: Dead and Buried, Cold Blood 5: The Last Hurrah. *Mini-series*: Predators, Amnesia, Cold Blood. *Series*: Out of the Blue, McCallum, MDs, New Street Law, Spartacus: Blood and Sand. *Guest:* More than 47 appearances.

HANNIGAN, ALYSON
Actress. r.n. Allison Lee Hannigan. b. Washington, DC, March 24, 1974.
PICTURES: My Stepmother Is an Alien, Dead Man on Campus, American Pie, Boys and Girls, American Pie 2, Beyond the City Limits, American Wedding, Date Movie, Farce of the Penguins (voice).
TELEVISION: *Movies*: Switched at Birth, A Case for Life, The Stranger Beside Me, For My Daughter's Honor, Indecent Seduction, Hayley Wagner, Star. *Series*: Free Spirit, Buffy the Vampire Slayer, Buffy: The Animated Series (voice), Veronica Mars, How I Met Your Mother. *Guest*: More than 77 appearances.

HANSON, CURTIS
Director, Writer. b. Reno, NV, March 24, 1945. Editor of Cinema magazine before becoming screenwriter.
PICTURES: *Writer:* The Silent Partner, White Dog, Never Cry Wolf. *Director:* Sweet Kill, Little Dragons, Losin' It, The Bedroom Window (also s.p.), Bad Influence, The Hand That Rocks the Cradle, The River Wild, L.A. Confidential (also co-s.p., prod., Academy Award, 2 other noms.; Best Adapted Screenplay, 2 Golden Globe noms.; DGA nom.; WGA Award, 1998), Wonder Boys (also prod.), 8 Mile (also prod.) Lucky You (also prod., writer, s.p.), In Her Shoes (also prod.), The Big Year (prod. only), Mavericks. *Actor:* The Goonies, Adaptation.
TELEVISION: *Movies:* Pigs Vs. Freaks, Killing at Hell's Gate, The Children of Times Square, Take My Advice: The Ann and Abby Story. *Series*: Greg the Bunny, Three Rivers (exec. prod.).

HARBERT, TED
Executive. e. Boston Univ. 1976-77, prod. of new dept. at WHDH radio in Boston. Joined ABC, 1977, as feature film coordinator; 1979, supervisor, feature film and late-night program planning, then assst. to v.p., program planning & scheduling; 1981, became dir. program planning & scheduling; 1984, v.p. program planning & scheduling; 1987, v.p. motion pictures and scheduling, ABC Entertainment; 1988, v.p., prime time, ABC Entertainment; 1989, became exec. v.p., Prime Time, ABC Entertainment; 1993, promoted to pres. of ABC Entertainment. Left ABC to become a producer with Dreamworks SKG, 1997. Named pres., NBC Studios, August, 1999. Left NBC June 2003. Harbert briefly served as a producer at 20th Century Fox

Television. From summer 2004 - October 2006, pres. and CEO, E! Networks. In Oct. 2006, promoted to newly created position of pres. & CEO of Comcast Entertainment Group, with oversight of the company's West Coast entertainment properties—E! Entertainment Television, Style Network and G4. Member, Dean's Advisory Board of the USC School of Theater, Film and Television; board member, USC School of Cinema-Television's Television Advisory Council; exec. committee, Boston University's School of Communications; bd. of governors, UCLA's Center for Communication Policy; bd. of directors, Friends of the L.A. Free Clinic. He is a past president of the Hollywood Radio & TV Society.

HARDEN, MARCIA GAY

Actress. b. La Jolla, CA, Aug. 14, 1959.
Father was naval captain. Schooled in Athens, Munich, then returned to states attending Univ. of TX, NYU. Stage work in Washington D.C. in Crimes of the Heart, The Miss Firecracker Contest.
THEATRE: *Off-B'way:* The Man Who Shot Lincoln (debut, 1989), Those the River Keeps, The Skin of Our Teeth, The Years, Simpatico. B'way: Angels in America: Millenium Approaches/ Perestroika (Theatre World Award; Tony nom.), God of Carnage (Tony Award 2009).
PICTURES: Miller's Crossing (debut, 1990), Late for Dinner, Used People, Crush, Safe Passage, The Spitfire Grill, The Daytrippers, The First Wives Club, Spy Hard, Desperate Measures, Flubber, Meet Joe Black, Labor of Love, Curtain Call, Space Cowyboys, Pollock (Academy Award 2001), Just Like Mona, Gaudi Afternoon, Mystic River (Academy Award nom. 2004), Casa de los Babys, Mona Lisa Smile, Welcome to Mooseport, P.S., Miller, American Gun, The Bad News Bears, American Dreamz, The Hoax, The Invisible, Home, The Dead Girl, Into the Wild, Rails & Ties, The Mist, Thomas Kinkade's Home for Christmas, Home, The Maiden Heist, Whip It, The No Game, The No Game (voice), If I Were You.
TELEVISION: *Movies*: Path to Paradise, Kojak: None So Blind, In Broad Daylight, Fever, Talking with, Convict Cowboy, Labor of Love, Spenser: Small Vices, Thin Air, See You In My Dreams, Hate, From Where I Sit, Walking Shadow, Guilty Hearts, King of Texas, She's Too Young, Felicity: An American Girl Adventure, In From the Night, The Tower, Sex and Lies in Sin City: The Ted Binion Scandal, The Courageous Heart of Irena Sendler (Emmy nom. 2009). *Mini-series*: Sinatra. *Series*: The Education of Max Bickford, Drift (pilot), Law & Order: Special Victims Unit (Emmy nom. 2007), Damages. *Guest:* More than 73 appearances.

HARDISON, KADEEM

Actor. b. Brooklyn, NY, July 24, 1966. Studied acting with Earl Hyman and at H.B.Studios.
PICTURES: Beat Street (debut, 1984), Rappin', School Daze, I'm Gonna Git You Sucka, Def by Temptation, White Men Can't Jump, Gunmen, Renaissance Man, Panther, Vampire in Brooklyn, Drive, The Sixth Man, Blind Faith, Dancing in September, Who's Your Daddy, Thank Heaven, Dunsmore, Thirty Years to Life, Showtime, Biker Boyz, Who's Your Daddy?, Face of Terror, Bratz, The Dark Party (dir., writer, co-exec. prod.), Made of Honor, Sister Switch, Zerosome, The Dark Party (also dir., co-exec. prod., s.p.).
TELEVISION: *Movies*: Go Tell It On the Mountain, House of Dies Drear, Dream Date, Ducktales: The Movie Special (host), Fire & Ice, Red Skies, Life Is Not a Fairytale: The Fantasia Barrino Story. *Series*: A Different World, Between Brothers, Static Shock, Livin' Large, Abby. *Specials*: The Color of Friendship, Amazing Grace, Don't Touch. *Guest:* More than 66 appearances.

HARE, DAVID

Writer, Director. b. St. Leonards, Sussex, England, June 5, 1947. e. Lancing Coll., Jesus Coll., Cambridge. After leaving univ. in 1968 formed Portable Theatre Company, experimental touring group. Hired by Royal Court Theater as literary manager, 1969. 1970, first full-length play, Slag, prod. at Hampstead Theatre Club. Resident dramatist, Royal Court (1970-71), and Nottingham Playhouse (1973). Assoc. dir., National Theatre. West End debut, Knuckle.
THEATRE: Slag, The Great Exhibition, Brassneck, Knuckle, Fanshen, Teeth 'n' Smiles, Plenty, A Map of the World, Pravda, The Bay at Nice, Secret Rapture, Racing Demon, Murmuring Judges, Rules of the Game (new version of Pirandello Play), The Absence of War, Skylight, adapted Bertolt Brecht's: The Life of Gailileo, Mother Courage, The Absence of War, My Zinc Bed.
PICTURES: *Writer:* Plenty, Wetherby (also dir.), Paris by Night (also dir.), Strapless (also dir.), Damage, The Secret Rapture (also prod.), Via Dolorosa, The Designated Mourner (dir., prod. only), Via Dolorosa, The Hours (Academy Award nom.; Golden Globe nom.; WGA Award 2003), The Reader (Academy Award nom.; Golden Globe nom. 2009), The Corrections, Murder in Samarkand.
TELEVISION: *Writer*: Licking Hitler (also dir.), Dreams of Leaving (also dir.), Saigon: Year of the Cat, Knuckle, Heading Home (also dir.), The Absence of War, My Zinc Bed.

HAREWOOD, DORIAN

Actor. b. Dayton, OH, Aug. 6, 1950. e. U. of Cincinnati.
THEATRE: Jesus Christ Superstar (road co.), Two Gentlemen of Verona, Miss Moffat, Streamers, Over Here, Don't Call Back (Theatre World Award), The Mighty Gents, Kiss of the Spider Woman.
PICTURES: Sparkle (debut, 1976), Gray Lady Down, Looker, Tank, Against All Odds, The Falcon and the Snowman, Full Metal Jacket, Pacific Heights, Solar Crisis, The Pagemaster (voice), Sudden Death, Space Jam (voice), Archibald the Rainbow Painter, Evasive Action, Glitter, Levity, Gothika, Assault on Precinct 13, Mayor Cupcake.
TELEVISION: *Movies:* Foster and Laurie, Panic in Echo Park, Siege, An American Christmas Carol, High Ice, Beulah Land, The Ambush Murders, I Desire, The Jesse Owens Story, Guilty of Innocence, God Bless the Child, Kiss Shot, Polly, Polly-Comin' Home!, Getting Up and Going Home, Bermuda Grace, Shattered Image, When the Cradle Falls, 12 Angry Men, A Change of Heart, The Last Debate, Walter and Henry, The Triangle, Framed, The Christmas Shoes, Hollywood Wives: The New Generation, Jane Doe: The Harder They Fall, Billy & Mandy's Big Boogey Adventure (voice), Grave Misconduct. *Mini-series:* Roots: The Next Generations, Amerika, Christianity: The First Two Thousand Years, Little House on the Prairie. *Pilot:* Half 'n' Half. *Series:* Strike Force, Trauma Center, Glitter, The Trials of Rosie O'Neill, Viper, The Tick (voice), Sonic the Hedgehog (voice), The Marvel Action Hour: Iron Man (voice), Mortal Kombat: The Animated Series (voice), The Hoop Life, Astro Boy (voice), The Buzz on Maggie (voice), Kyle XY (pilot), Biker Mice from Mars (voice), 7th Heaven, Boomtown, The Spectacular Spider-Man (voice). *Documentaries:* Hank Aaron: Chasing the Dream (Emmy nom. 1995), Christianity: The First Two Thousand Years (mini-series). *Guest:* More than 138 appearances.

HARGITAY, MARISKA

Actress. b. Santa Monica, CA, Jan. 23, 1964. e. UCLA. Daughter of late actors Jayne Mansfield and Mickey Hargitay. Founder and President of non-profit organization, The Joyful Heart Foundation which aids victims of rape.
PICTURES: Ghoulies, The Perfect Weapon, Bank Robber, Leaving Las Vegas, Lake Placid, Perfume, Tales from Earthsea (voice, English version), Santorini Blue (assoc. prod.).
TELEVISION: *Movies:* Finish Line, Blind Side, Gambler V: Playing for Keeps, Night Sins, The Advocate's Devil, Love American Style (segment), Plain Truth. *Series:* Downtown, Falcon Crest, Tequila and Bonetti, Can't Hurry Love, Prince Street, ER, Law & Order, Law & Order: Special Victims Unit (Emmy Award 2006; 5 other noms.; Golden Globe Award 2005; 1 other nom.). *Guest:* More than 70 appearances.

HARK, TSUI

Director, Producer. b. Vietnam, Jan. 2, 1951. e. University of Texas. Started filming 8mm movies at 13. Moved to Hong Kong in 1966, then in 1975 relocated to NY where he became editor for a local Chinese newspaper. Returned to Hong Kong in 1977 and made his directorial debut with The Butterfly Murders. In the 1990's played a major part in reviving "swordsfighting" and "kung-fu" movies.
PICTURES: *Director*: Dangerous Encounter, Hell Has No Door, All the Wrong Clues, Zu: Warriors From the Magic Mountain, Aces go Places III, Shanghai Blues, Working Class, Peking Opera Blues, A Better Tomorrow III, Once Upon A Time in China (also II, III, V), The Master, Green Snake, The Lovers, A Chinese Feast, Love In a Time of Twilight, Tri-Star, Blade, Double Team, Triangle (also exec. prod., prod.), The Eye 3, Missing (also prod.), She Ain't Mean (also prod.), D-Project (also prod.). *Co-director:* Swordsman, The Banquet, Chess King, Twin Dragons, D-Project (also prod.). *Producer*: A Chinese Ghost Story (also II, III) A Better Tomorrow, I Love Maria, Deception, Gunmen, Diary of a Big Man, The Big Heat, The Killer, Spy Games, The Raid, The Wicked City, Swordsman II, Dragon Inn, The East is Red, Once Upon a Time in China (also IV), The Magic Crane, Burning Paradise, Shanghai Grand, Black Mask, Once Upon a Time in China & America, Chinese Ghost Story: The Tsui Hark Animation, Time and Tide, Old Master Q2001, Zu Warrios, Black Mask 2: City of Masks, The Era of the Vampires.

HARKINS, DANIEL E.

Exhibitor. b. Mesa, AZ, Feb. 6, 1953. e. Arizona State U. Joined family business, Harkins Theatres, in 1968. The Scottsdale-based movie company was founded by Dwight "Red" Harkins in 1933. Harkins acquired company in 1975. Currently, Dan Harkins is CEO of Harkins Amusement Enterprises, Inc. He promoted Mike Bowers, who has been with the Harkins circuit since 1993, to president and COO in Sept. 2006. Harkins Theatres now has 344 screens in five states—Arizona, California, Colorado, Oklahoma and Texas. Harkins' memberships include: National NATO bd. member where he currently is treasurer; pres., Arizona Theatre Assoc.; v.p. of the Governor's Film Commission. He was a recipient of United Motion Picture Association's National Showman of the Year award in 1976, 1980, 1981. He received the Hollywood Reporter Marketing Concept award in 1983. Other awards include: Box Office Showmandizer award in 1976 and 1978; the Phoenix Artistic Achievement award, 1989; the American Institute of Architects award, 1996; the Arizona Best awards, 1991-1995; Entrepreneur of the Year finalist, 1998 and 2001; Entrepreneur of the Year Award, 1999; the Sedony Award, 1999; and the ATOA Lifetime Achievement Award, 2001.

HARLIN, RENNY
Director, Producer. b. Helsinki, Finland, March 15, 1959. e. Univ. of Helsinki film school. r.n. Lauri Mauritz Harjola. Formed prod. co. The Forge with actress Geena Davis. Currently Director, Producer and Executive with Midnight Sun Pictures.
PICTURES: Born American (debut, 1986), Arctic Heat (also s.p.), Prison, A Nightmare on Elm Street IV: The Dream Master, Die Hard 2, The Adventures of Ford Fairlane, Rambling Rose (prod. only), Cliffhanger, Speechless (co-prod. only), Cutthroat Island (also prod.), Exit Zero, The Long Kiss Goodnight (also prod.), Blast From the Past (prod. only), Deep Blue Sea, Driven, Mindhunters, A Sound of Thunder (prod. only), Exorcist: The Beginning, The Covenant, The Killer's Game, Land of Legend, A Sound of Thunder (prod. only), The Northmen, Cleaner, 12 Rounds, Mannerheim, Georgia (also prod.).
TELEVISION: *Movies*: Mistrial (exec. prod.), T.R.A.X. *Series:* Gladiaattorit (also prod./writer).

HARMON, MARK
Actor. b. Burbank, CA, Sept. 2, 1951. Son of actress Elyse Knox and football star Tom Harmon. m. actress Pam Dawber. Brother of actresses Kelly and Kristin Harmon. On stage in Wrestlers, The Wager (both L.A.), Key Exchange (Toronto).
PICTURES: Comes a Horseman, Beyond the Poseidon Adventure, Let's Get Harry, Summer School, The Presidio, Stealing Home, Worth Winning, Till There Was You, Cold Heaven, Wyatt Earp, Natural Born Killers (cameo), Magic in the Water, The Last Supper, Casualties, Fear and Loathing in Las Vegas (cameo), I'll Remember April, Local Boys, Freaky Friday, Chasing Liberty, Weather Girl.
TELEVISION: *Movies*: Eleanor and Franklin: The White House Years (Emmy nom. 1977), Getting Married, Little Mo, Flamingo Road (pilot), The Dream Merchants, Goliath Awaits, Intimate Agony, The Deliberate Stranger (Golden Globe nom. 1987), Prince of Bel Air, Sweet Bird of Youth, After the Promise (Golden Globe nom. 1988), Dillinger, Fourth Story, Long Road Home, Shadow of a Doubts (2 Golden Globe noms. 1992), For All Time, The Amati Girls, Crossfire Trail, And Never Let Her Go. *Mini-series*: Centennial, From the Earth to the Moon. *Series*: Sam, 240-Robert, Flamingo Road, St. Elsewhere, Reasonable Doubts (2 Golden Globe noms.), Charlie Grace, Chicago Hope, West Wing (Emmy nom. 2002), Boston Public (director), NCIS: Naval Criminal Investigative Service. *Guest:* More than 82 appearances.

HARNELL, STEWART D.
Executive. b. New York, NY. e. U. of Miami, UCLA, New School for Social Research. Entertainer with Youth Parade in Coral Gables, FL,1948-55, performing for handicapped children, Variety Club, etc. as singer, dancer, musician. Had own bands, Teen Aces & Rhythm Rascals, 1950-56; performed on Cactus Jim TV show and Wood & Ivory, 1953-54, WTVJ, Miami. Catskills,1954-55. Joined National Screen Service as exec. trainee in 1960 writing trailer scripts for major studio releases in L.A. Relocated to Chicago as booker & salesman. Transferred to NY home office in 1963 to manage special trailer production. Promoted to asst. general sales manager, 1964-66; New Orleans branch mgr., 1966-67; Atlanta division mgr., 1967-70. Formed own distribution co., 1970-76 Harnell Independent Productions. Resumed post as exec. v.p., worldwide general sales manager of NSS, New York, 1977-78. In 1978, founded Cinema Concepts Theatre Service Co., where he currently is chairman and CEO. The company serves motion picture, advertising and broadcast industries with high-end studio and editing services, preview and policy trailers, animation, digital production services, HD post/mastering/film-out and screening rooms. Chief barker of Variety Club of Atlanta, Tent 21, 1972, 1976,1979, 1988, 1989, 1993, 1994. Presidential Citation 1988. Motion Picture Pioneers Bd. of Directors (1990-present).

HARPER, JESSICA
Actress. b. Chicago, IL, Oct. 10, 1949. married m.p. exec. Thomas E. Rothman. e. Sarah Lawrence Coll. Understudied on Broadway for Hair for one year. Appeared in summer stock and off-B'way shows (Richard Farina: Long Time Coming Longtime Gone, Doctor Selavy's Magic Theatre.)
PICTURES: Taking Off, Phantom of the Paradise, Love and Death, Inserts, Suspiria, The Evictors, Stardust Memories, Shock Treatment, Pennies from Heaven, My Favorite Year, The Imagemaker, Dario Argento's World of Horror, The Blue Iguana, Big Man on Campus, Mr. Wonderful, Safe, Boys, Minority Report.
TELEVISION: *Movies:* When Dreams Come True, Once Again, On the Edge of Innocence, Dalziel and Pascoe: Great Escapes. *Mini-series*: Studs Lonigan, Aspen (The Innocent and the Damned). *Series*: Little Women, It's Garry Shandling's Show. *Special*: The Garden Party.

HARPER, TESS
Actress. b. Mammoth Springs, AR, August 15, 1952. e. Southwest Missouri State Coll., Springfield. Worked in Houston, then Dallas in children's theatre, dinner theatre, and commercials.
PICTURES: Tender Mercies (debut, Golden Globe nom. 1984), Amityville 3-D, Silkwood, Flashpoint, Crimes of the Heart (Academy Award nom. 1987), Ishtar, Far North, Her Alibi, Criminal Law, Daddy's Dyin'... Who's Got the Will?, My Heroes Have Always Been Cowboys, The Man in the Moon, My New Gun, Dirty Laundry, The Jackal, Lonely Place, The In Crowd, Morning, The Rising Place, No Prom for Cindy, Studio City (short), Jesus-Mary-And Joey, Loggerheads, Deadly, Jam, Broken Bridges, Broken, No Country for Old Men, Kiss the Bride, Saving Sarah Cain, A Root Beer Christmas.
TELEVISION: *Movies*: Kentucky Woman, Starflight: The Plane That Couldn't Land, Reckless Disregard, A Summer to Remember, Promises to Keep, Daddy, Little Girl Lost, Unconquered, Incident at Dark River, In the Line of Duty: Siege at Marion, Willing to Kill: The Texas Cheerleader Story, Christy, Death in Small Doses, The Road to Galveston, A Stranger to Love, The Secret, A Child's Wish, Beyond the Prairie: The True Story of Laura Ingalls Wilder, Beyond the Prairie, Part 2: The True Story of Laura Ingalls Wilder, Angel in the Family. *Mini-series*: Chiefs, Celebrity. *Series:* Christy, Early Edition (host), Jack & Bobby (also pilot), Breaking Bad, Crash. *Guest:* More than 52 appearances.

HARPER, VALERIE
Actress. b. Suffern, NY. Aug. 22, 1940. e. Hunter Coll, New Sch. for Social Research. Started as dancer in stage shows at Radio City Music Hall. First professional acting in summer stock in Conn.; actress with Second City Chicago 1964-69; Appeared on B'way. in Lil' Abner, Take Me Along, Wildcat, Subways Are for Sleeping, Something Different, Story Theatre, Metamorphoses. Won 3 Emmys, best comedy performance in supporting role for portrayal of Rhoda on The Mary Tyler Moore Show and 1 for best leading actress on Rhoda. Off B'way, Death Defying Acts (1995-96).
PICTURES: Rock Rock Rock, Lil Abner, Freebie and the Bean (Golden Globe nom. 1975), Chapter Two (Golden Globe nom. 1980), The Last Married Couple in America, Blame It on Rio, Eight Characters In Search of a Sitcom (documentary), Golda's Balcony.
TELEVISION: *Movies*: Thursday's Game, Night Terror, Fun and Games, The Shadow Box, The Day the Loving Stopped, Farrell for the People (pilot), Don't Go to Sleep, An Invasion of Privacy, Execution, Strange Voices, Drop Out Mother, The People Across the Lake, Stolen: One Husband, A Friend To Die For, The Great Mom Swap, Dog's Best Friend (voice), Mary & Rhoda, The Mary Tyler Moore Reunion, Dancing at the Harvest Moon. *Series*: The Mary Tyler Show (3 Emmy Awards; 1 nom.; 2 Golden Globe noms. 1971-1974), Rhoda (Emmy Award, 3 other noms.; 1 Golden Globe Award 1 nom. 1975-1978), Valerie, City, The Office, Melrose Place, Generator Gawl (voice). *Guest:* More than 95 appearances.

HARRINGTON, PAT
Actor. b. New York, NY, Aug. 13, 1929. e. Fordham U. Served USAF as 1st Lt., 1952-54. Time salesman for NBC, 1954-58. Voice in over 40 animation shorts.
PICTURES: The Wheeler Dealers, Move Over Darling, Easy Come Easy Go, The President's Analyst, 2000 Years Later, The Candidate, Every Little Crook and Nanny, The Nine Lives of Fritz the Cat (voice), Round Trip to Heaven, Ablaze.
TELEVISION: *Movies*: Savage, The Affair, The Healers, Columbo: An Exercise in Fatality, Let's Switch, Benny and Barney: Las Vegas Undercover, The New Love Boat, The Critical List, The Last Convertible, Between Two Brothers, A Garfield Christmas, I Yabba Dabba Do, Spring Fling, These Old Broads, The One Day at a Time Reunion. *Series*: The Steve Allen Show, The Danny Thomas Show, The Jack Paar Show, Stump the Stars (host), Mr. Deeds Goes to Town, One Day at a Time (Emmy Award, Golden Globe Award 1981; 3 other noms.) 1984). *Guest:* More than 132 appearances.

HARRIS, ED
Actor. b. Tenafly, NJ, Nov. 28, 1950. m. actress Amy Madigan. Played football 2 years at Columbia U. prior to enrolling in acting classes at OK State U. Summer stock. Grad. CA Institute of the Arts, B.F.A, 1975. Worked in West Coast Theatre.
THEATRE: NY: Fool For Love (Off-B'way debut; Obie Award), Precious Sons (B'way debut; Theatre World Award), Simpatico, Taking Sides. LA: Scar.
PICTURES: Coma (debut, 1978), Borderline, Knightriders, Dream On, Creepshow, The Right Stuff, Under Fire, Swing Shift, Places in the Heart, Alamo Bay, A Flash of Green, Sweet Dreams, Code Name: Emerald, Walker, To Kill a Priest, Jacknife (Golden Globe nom. 1990), The Abyss, State of Grace, Glengarry Glen Ross, The Firm, Needful Things, China Moon, Milk Money, Just Cause, Apollo 13 (Academy Award nom.; Golden Globe nom. 1996), Eye for an Eye, Nixon, The Rock, Absolute Power, The Truman Show (Academy Award nom.; Golden Globe Award 1999), Stepmom, The Third Miracle, Waking the Dead, The Prime Gig, Pollock (Academy Award nom. 2001), Enemy at the Gates, Absolute Zero, Buffalo Soldiers, A Beautiful Mind, The Hours (Academy Award nom.; Golden Globe nom. 2003), The Hours, Masked and Anonymous, Just a Dream, Radio, The Human Stain, Winter Passing, A History of Violence, Copying Beethoven, Gone, Baby, Gone, National Treasure: Book of Secrets, Cleaner, Appaloosa (also prod., dir., writer/s.p., writer/songs, performer), Once Fallen, The Way Back, What's Wrong with Virginia, Big Ginger, Salvation Boulevard.
TELEVISION: *Movies*: The Amazing Howard Hughes, The Seekers, The Aliens Are Coming (Alien Force), The Last Innocent Man, Paris Trout, Running Mates, Riders of the Purple Sage, Empire Falls (Emmy nom. 2005; Golden Globe nom.

2006). *Mini-series*: The Stand, The Seekers, Baseball (voice). *Guest:* More than 88 appearances.

HARRIS, JAMES B.

Producer, Director, Writer. b. New York, NY, Aug. 3, 1928. e. Juilliard Sch. U.S. film export, 1947; Realart Pictures, 1948; formed Flamingo Films, 1949; formed Harris-Kubrick Productions, 1954. formed James B. Harris Prods., Inc., 1963.
PICTURES: *Producer:* The Killing, Paths of Glory, Lolita, The Bedford Incident (also dir.), Some Call It Loving (also dir., s.p.), Telefon, Fast-Walking (also dir., s.p.), Cop (also dir., s.p.), Boiling Point (dir., s.p.), The Black Dahlia (exec. prod.).

HARRIS, JULIE

Actress. b. Grosse Pointe, MI, Dec. 2, 1925. e. Yale Drama Sch.
THEATRE: Sundown Beach, Playboy of the Western World, Macbeth, Young and the Fair, Magnolia Alley, Monserrat, Member of the Wedding, I Am a Camera (Tony Award, 1952), Colombe, The Lark (Tony Award, 1956), A Shot in the Dark, Marathon 33, Ready When You Are, C.B., Break a Leg, Skyscraper, Voices, And Miss Reardon Drinks a Little, 40 Carats (Tony Award, 1969), The Last of Mrs. Lincoln (Tony Award, 1973), In Praise of Love, The Belle of Amherst (Tony Award, 1973), Driving Miss Daisy (Natl. co.), Lucifer's Child, Lettice & Lovage (tour), The Fiery Furnace (Off-B'way debut, 1993), The Glass Menagerie.
PICTURES: The Member of the Wedding (debut, 1952; Acad. Award nom. 1953), East of Eden, I Am a Camera, The Truth About Women, The Poacher's Daughter, Requiem for a Heavyweight, The Haunting, Harper, You're a Big Boy Now, Reflections in a Golden Eye, The Split, The People Next Door, The Hiding Place, Voyage of the Damned, The Bell Jar, Nutcracker: The Motion Picture (voice), Gorillas in the Mist, Housesitter, The Dark Half, Carried Away, Passage to Paradise, Bad Manners, Frank Lloyd Wright, The First of May, Broadway: The Golden Age by the Legends Who Were There, The Way Back Home, The Golden Boys, The Lightkeepers.
TELEVISION: *Movies:* A Doll's House, The Heiress, The Power and The Glory, Victoria Regina (Emmy Award, 1962), Pygmalion, The House on Greenapple Road, The Holy Terror (Emmy nom. 1965), How Awful About Alan, Home for the Holidays, Columbo: Any Old Port in a Storm, The Greatest Gift, The Belle of Amherst, The Last of Mrs. Lincoln (Emmy nom. 1977), Stubby Pringle's Christmas, The Gift, Annihilator, The Woman He Loved (Emmy nom. 1988), Too Good To Be True, The Christmas Wife, Single Women Married Men, They've Taken Our Children: The Chowchilla Kidnapping, When Love Kills: The Seduction of John Hearn, One Christmas, Lucifer's Child, Secrets, The Christmas Tree, Ellen Foster (Emmy nom. 1998), Love Is Strange. *Mini-series*: Backstairs at the White House, Scarlett. *Series*: Thicker Than Water, The Family Holvak, Knots Landing (Emmy nom. 1982). *Documentaries/Specials*: Little Moon of Alban (Emmy Award, 1959), Johnny Belinda, Ethan Frome, The Good Fairy, The Lark, He Who Gets Slapped, Anastasia, Brooklyn Bridge, The Civil War, Baseball, Frank Lloyd Wright, Not for Ourselves Alone: The Story of Elizabeth Cady Stanton & Susan B. Anthony (Emmy Award 2000). *Guest:* More than 102 appearances.

HARRIS, MEL

Actress. r.n. Mary Ellen Harris. b. Bethlehem, PA, July 12, 1957. e. Columbia. Career as model before turning to acting in 1984. NY theatre debut in Empty Hearts, 1992 (Theatre World Award).
PICTURES: Wanted: Dead or Alive, Cameron's Closet, K-9, Raising Cain, Desperate Motive (Distant Cousins), Suture, The Pagemaster, Sonic Impact, Firetrap, Dynamite, The Veritas Project: Hangman's Curse, Purple Heart, Arc, Imagine That.
TELEVISION: *Movies*: Seduced, Harry's Hong Kong, Cross of Fire, My Brother's Wife, The Burden of Proof, Grass Roots, Child of Rage, With Hostile Intent, Desperate Journey: The Allison Wilcox Story, Ultimate Betrayal, The Spider and the Fly, The Women of Spring Break, Sharon's Secret, The Secretary, A Case for Life, Murder She Wrote: South by Southwest, The Retrievers, Another Pretty Face, Out of the Woods. *Series*: thirtysomething (Golden Globe nom. 1990), Something So Right, Saints & Sinners. *Guest:* More than 53 appearances.

HARRIS, NEIL PATRICK

Actor. b. Albuquerque, NM, June 15, 1973. While attending week-long theatre camp at New Mexico St. Univ. met writer Mark Medoff who suggested him for co-starring role in Clara's Heart.
THEATRE: Luck Pluck and Virtue (Off-B'way debut, 1995).
PICTURES: Clara's Heart (debut, Golden Globe nom. 1989), Purple People Eater, Hairspray, Starship Troopers, The Proposition, The Next Best Thing, The Mesmerist, Undercover Brother, Harold & Kumar Go to White Castle, Harold & Kumar Escape from Guantanamo Bay, Cloudy with a Chance of Meatballs (voice), The Best and the Brightest, Beastly, Rio (voice), The Smurfs.
TELEVISION: *Movies*: Too Good to Be True, Home Fires Burning, Cold Sassy Tree, Stranger in the Family, A Family Torn Apart, Snowbound: The Jim and Jennifer Stolpa Story, Not Our Son, My Antonia, The Man in the Attic, Legacy of Sin: The William Coit Story, The Christmas Wish, Joan of Arc, The Wedding Dress, Sweeney Todd: The Demon Barber of Fleet Street In Concert, The Christmas Blessing, Yes, Virginia (voice). *Series*: Doogie Howser M.D. (Golden Globe nom. 1992), Capitol Critters (voice), Stark Raving Mad, Spider Man: The Animated Series (voice), How I Met Your Mother (3 Emmy noms.; 2 Golden Globe noms.). *Host:* The 63rd Annual Tony Awards (2009), The 61st Primetime Emmy Awards (also prod., 2009). *Guest*: More than 140 appearances.

HARRIS III, PHILIP

Exhibitor. Harris, a third generation motion picture exhibitor, began his cinema exhibition career more than 35 years ago as an IATSE union projectionist in family-owned theatres in Davis, California. In 1982, Harris purchased a family business with partner Doug Stephens, but sold it in 1985 to form what would become Signature Theatres in 1988. By 2004, Harris had increased the company's initial 22 screens in three sites to a total of 281 screens, located at 31 sites in 25 cities in California, Hawaii, and Montana. In Sept. 2004, Regal Entertainment Group acquired and integrated San Ramon, CA, based Signature Theatres. In 2003, Harris was awarded the "ShoWester of the Year" award, which recognized Harris' dedication to improving the exhibition industry. He has been a member of the NATO Board of Directors since 1990 and has served as vice chair of the finance committee and was NATO chairman Jan. 1, 2005-Jan. 1, 2007. Harris has also been on the bd. of dir. of NATO California/Nevada for the past 20 years, and served as its chairman for five years. He previously served on the Board of Directors of the Northern California Variety Club Children's Charity Tent and the Motion Picture Pioneers. In May 2007, Harris received the Excellence of Service Award from NATO of Wisconsin and upper Michigan.

HARRIS, RICHARD A.

Editor.
PICTURES: The Bamboo Saucer, Downhill Racer, The Christian Licorice Store, Chandler, The Candidate, Catch My Soul, Smile, The Bad News Bears, Semi-Tough, The Bad News Bears Go to Japan, An Almost Perfect Affair, The Island, The Toy, The Survivors, Fletch, The Golden Child, Wildcats, The Couch Trip, Fletch Lives, L.A. Story, Terminator 2: Judgment Day (Academy Award nom.; ACE nom. 1992), The Bodyguard, Last Action Hero, True Lies (ACE nom. 1995), Titanic (Academy Award, ACE Award 1997), The X Files: I Want to Believe, Flying Lessons.
TELEVISION: *Movies*: Dracula, The Kansas City Massacre, Murder at the World Series, The Executioner's Song, Tiger Town, 14 Going on 30, My Boyfriend's Back, A Mother's Courage: The Mary Thomas Story, Indictment: The McMartin Trial (Emmy Award, ACE Award 1995), Running Mates.

HARRIS, ROBERT A.

Archivist, Producer. b. New York, NY, Dec. 27, 1945. e. NYU, School of Commerce and School of Arts, 1968. Worked as exec. trainee with 7 Arts assoc., NY while in school, 1960-68; worked in corp. communications, Pepsico, 1970-71; formed Center for Instructional Resources, SUNY Purchase, 1971-73; organized Images Film Archive, dist. of classic theatrical and non theat. films, 1974; pres., Images Video and Film Archive, 1985; formed Davnor Prods., pres., 1986; formed The Film Preserve, Ltd. in Bedford Hills, NY, in 1989, and continues its operations today; Harris is considered one of the top film restoration experts in the industry. From 1975-80: restored Abel Gance films Beethoven, J'Accuse, Lucretia Borgia; 1974-79: worked with Kevin Brownlow to complete restoration of Abel Gance's Napoleon. Partnered with Francis Coppola/Zoetrope Studios to present Napoleon at Radio City Music Hall, 1981 and worldwide tour; 1986-89 reconstruction and restoration of David Lean's Lawrence of Arabia for Columbia Pictures, released 1989; The Grifters (prod.); restoration and reconstruction of Stanley Kubrick's Spartacus for Univ. Pictures, 1991; restoration of George Cukor's My Fair Lady for CBS Video, 1994, restoration in SuperVistaVision 70 of Alfred Hitchcock's Vertigo, 1996.
PICTURES: *Producer:* Alien Space Avenger, The Grifters (1990).

HARRIS, ROSEMARY

Actress. b. Ashby, Suffolk, Sept. 19, 1930. e. India and England. Early career, nursing; studied Royal Acad. of Dramatic Art, 1951-52.
THEATRE: Climate of Eden (NY debut 1952), Seven Year Itch, Confidential Clerk (Paris Festival), and with Bristol Old Vic in The Crucible, Much Ado About Nothing, Merchant of Venice. With Old Vic, 1955-56; U.S. tour, 1956-57; U.S. stage, 1958-63. Chichester Festivals 1962 and 63; Nat'l Theatre 1963-64; You Can't Take It With You, 1965; The Lion in Winter (Tony Award, 1966), 1967, APA Repertory Co., Heartbreak House, The Royal Family, The New York Idea (Obie Award), Pack of Lies, Hay Fever, Lost in Yonkers, An Inspector Calls, A Delicate Balance.
PICTURES: Beau Brummell, The Shiralee, A Flea in Her Ear, The Boys from Brazil, The Ploughman's Lunch, Heartbreak House, Crossing Delancey, The Delinquents, The Bridge, Tom and Viv (Academy Award nom. 1995), Looking for Richard, Hamlet, World of Moses, My Life So Far, Sunshine, The Gift, Blow Dry, Spider-Man, Broadway: The Golden Age by the Legends Who Were There, Spider-Man 2, Being Julia, Before the Devil Knows You're Dead, Spider-Man 3, Is There Anybody There?, Radio Free Albemuth.
TELEVISION: *Movies*: The Royal Family, To the Lighthouse,

Heartbreak House, Strange Interlude, Death of a Salesman, The Little Riders, Belonging. *Mini-series*: Notorious Woman (Emmy Award, Golden Globe nom. 1976), Holocaust (Emmy nom.; Golden Globe Award 1979), The Chisholms, The Camomille Lawn. *Series*: The Chisholms. *Specials*: Cradle of Willow (debut, 1951), Othello, The Prince and the Pauper, Twelfth Night, Wuthering Heights, Blithe Spirit, Profiles in Courage, Tales From the Hollywood Hills: The Old Reliable.

HARRIS, TIMOTHY

Writer, Producer. b. Los Angeles, CA, July 21, 1946. e. Charterhouse, 1963-65; Peterhouse Coll., Cambridge, 1966-69, M.A. Honors Degree, Eng. lit. Author of novels, Knonski/McSmash, Kyd For Hire, Goodnight and Goodbye; author of novelizations, Steelyard Blues, Hit, Heatwave, American Gigolo.
PICTURES: *Co-writer with Herschel Weingrod:* Cheaper to Keep Her, Trading Places (BAFTA nom.; orig. s.p.; NAACP Image Awards, best m.p. 1983), Brewster's Millions, My Stepmother is an Alien, Paint It Black, Twins (People's Choice Award, best comedy, 1988), Kindergarten Cop, Pure Luck, Astro Boy. *Co-Prod.:* Falling Down, Space Jam (s.p. only).
TELEVISION: Street of Dreams (based on his novel Goodnight and Goodbye; also exec. prod.).

HARRISON, GREGORY

Actor, Producer, Director. b. Avalon, CA, May 31, 1950. Started acting in school plays; then joined Army (1969-71). Studied at Estelle Harman Actors Workshop; later with Lee Strasberg and Stella Adler. Formed Catalina Productions with Franklin R. Levy, 1981-1988.
THEATRE: Child's Play, Carnal Knowledge, Picnic, The Hasty Heart, Love Letters, Festival, Billy Budd, The Subject Was Roses, The Promise, The Music Man, Steel Peir, Paper Moon—The Musical, Chicago (also touring co.).
PICTURES: Jim: the World's Greatest (debut, 1976), Fraternity Row, Razorback, North Shore (also 2nd unit dir.), Voice of a Stranger (also 2nd unit dir.), Cadillac Girls, It's My Party, Hard Evidence, Air Bud: Golden Retriever, Love N' Dancing, Give 'em Hell, Malone.
TELEVISION: *Movies actor:* Tales of Terror, The Gathering, Enola Gay: The Men, the Mission, the Atomic Bomb, Trilogy in Terror, The Best Place To Be, The Women's Room, For Ladies Only (also co-prod.), The Hasty Heart, Thursday's Child, The Fighter, Seduced (also exec. prod.), Oceans of Fire, Picnic (also exec. prod.), Hot Paint, Red River, Dangerous Pursuit, Angel of Death, Bare Essentials, Breaking the Silence, Duplicates, Split Images, Caught in the Act, A Family Torn Apart, Lies of the Heart: The Story of Laurie Kellogg, Robin Cook's Mortal Fear, A Christmas Romance, A Dangerous Affair, When Secrets Kill, Father's Day, Running Wild, Murder at 75 Birch, First Daughter, Au Pair, First Target, Au Pair II, First Shot, Nurses (pilot), Au Pair III, Shark Biscuit (dir. only). *Exec. Prod.:* Thursday's Child, Legs, Pleasures, The Tower, Spot Marks the X, Samson & Delilah. *Mini-series*: Centennial, Fresno, 500 Nations (narr.), Nothing Lasts Forever. *Series*: Logan's Run, Trapper John M.D. (also dir. 6 episodes), Falcon Crest, The Family Man, True Detectives, Sisters, New York News, Safe Harbor, St. Sass, Ed, Judging Amy, Touched by an Angel, Strong Medicine, North Shore (unit dir. only), Reunion, Joey, One Tree Hill. *Guest*: More than 91 appearances.

HARROLD, KATHRYN

Actress. b. Tazewell, VA, Aug. 2, 1950. e. Mills Coll. Studied acting at Neighborhood Playhouse in N.Y., also with Uta Hagen. Appeared in Off-Off-B'way. plays for year; then joined experimental theatre group, Section Ten, touring East, performing and teaching at Connecticut Coll. and NYU. Cast in TV daytime serial, The Doctors.
PICTURES: Nightwing (debut, 1979), The Hunter, Modern Romance, The Pursuit of D.B. Cooper, Yes Gorgio, The Sender, Heartbreakers, Into the Night, Raw Deal, Someone to Love.
TELEVISION: *Movies*: Son-Rise: A Miracle of Love, Vampire, The Women's Room, Bogie, An Uncommon Love, Man Against the Mob, Dead Solid Perfect, Capital News, Rainbow Drive, Deadly Desire, The Companion, Rockford Files: The Crime & Punishment, Tell Me No Secrets, Outrage, The 70s, A Woman's A Helluva Thing, Mystery Woman: At First Sight. *Mini-series:* Women in White, The '70s. *Series*: The Doctors (1976-78), MacGruder and Loud, Bronx Zoo, I'll Fly Away, The Larry Sanders Show, Chicago Hope, Desperate Housewives. *Guest:* More than 45 appearances.

HARRON, MARY

Director, Writer. b. Canada, Jan. 12, 1956.
PICTURES: I Shot Andy Warhol, American Psycho, The Weather Underground, (doc.), The Notorious Bettie Page, This Film Is Not Yet Rated (doc.).
TELEVISION: *Movies*: A Darkness More Than Night (s.p. only). Hollywood High, (doc.). *Series*: The Late Show, Homicide: Life on the Street, Oz, Pasadena, The L Word. *Documentaries:* Edge (series, prod.), Winds of Change.

HARRYHAUSEN, RAY

Special Effects Expert, Producer, Writer. b. Los Angeles, CA, June 29, 1920. e. Los Angeles City Coll. While at coll. made 16mm animated film, Evolution, which got him job as model animator for George Pal's Puppetoons in early '40s. Served in U.S. Signal Corps; then made series of filmed fairy tales with animated puppets for schools and churches. In 1946 worked on Mighty Joe Young as ass't. to Willis O'Brien. Designed and created special visual effects for The Beast from 20,000 Fathoms; then began evolving own model animation system called Dynarama. In 1952 joined forces with prod. Charles H. Schneer, using new process for first time in It Came from Beneath the Sea. Subsequently made many films with Schneer in Dynamation. Received Gordon E. Sawyer Award for Academy of Motion Picture Arts & Sciences, 1992. Art Directors Guild Award, 2008, Contribution to Cinematic Imagery Award. Appeared in films Spies Like Us, Beverly Hills Cop III, Comic Book: The Movie.
PICTURES: Mighty Joe Young, The Beast From 20,000 Fathoms, It Came From Beneath the Sea, Earth Vs. the Flying Saucers, Animal World, Twenty Million Miles to Earth, 7th Voyage of Sinbad, The Three Worlds of Gulliver, Mysterious Island, Jason and the Argonauts, First Men in the Moon, One Million Years B.C., The Valley of Gwangi, The Golden Voyage of Sinbad, Sinbad and the Eye of the Tiger (also co-prod.), Clash of the Titans (also co. prod.), Spies Like Us, Beverly Hills Cop III, The Story of the Tortoise & the Hare, (short), Elf.

HART, MELISSA JOAN

Actress. b. Smithtown, NY, April 18, 1976.
PICTURES: Can't Hardly Wait (cameo), The Specials, Drive Me Crazy, The Bachelor and the Bobby-Soxer, Backflash, Rent Control, Jesus-Mary-And Joey, Satin, Nine Dead.
TELEVISION: *Movies*: Family Reunion: A Relative Nightmare, Sabrina the Teenage Witch (pilot), Twisted Desire, The Right Connections, Two Came Back, Silencing Mary, Sabrina Goes to Rome (also prod.), Sabrina Down Under, Child Star: The Shirley Temple Story (exec. prod.), Dirtbags, Holiday in Handcuffs, Ashes to Ashes, Whispers and Lies, My Fake Fiance. *Mini-series*: Kane & Abel. *Series*: Clarissa Explains It All, Sabrina the Teenage Witch, Witchright Hall, Express Yourself, Sabrina the Animated Series (prod., voice), Melissa & Joey (also exec. prod.). *Guest*: More than 104 appearances.

HARTLEY, HAL

Director, Writer, Composer. b. Long Island, NY, November 3, 1959. e. SUNY/Purchase (film). Following graduation made 3 short movies: Kid, The Cartographer's Girlfriend, Dogs. For PBS made the shorts Theory of Achievement, Ambition, Surviving Desire; also NYC 3/94, Opera No. 1. Music videos: The Only Living Boy in New York (Everything But the Girl), From a Motel 6 (Yo La Tengo), Iris.
PICTURES: *Director/Writer:* The Unbelievable Truth (debut, 1990), Trust, Simple Men, Amateur, Flirt (also actor, editor), Henry Fool (Cannes Film Festival Award, Best Screenplay, 1998), The Book of Life, Kimono, No Such Thing, The Cloud of Unknowing (prod), Milk and Honey (composer only), The Girl From Monday (also prod.), Fay Grim (also prod., editor).

HARTLEY, MARIETTE

Actress. b. New York, NY, June 21, 1940. Student Carnegie Tech. Inst. 1956-57; studied with Eva Le Gallienne. Appeared with Shakespeare Festival, Stratford 1957-60. Co-host Today Show, 1980. Co-host on CBS Morning Show, 1987. Returned to stage in King John (NYSF in Central Park), 1989. Nominated for 6 Emmys for Best Actress. Received 3 Clio Awards, 1979, 1980, and 1981, for acting in commercials. Autobiography: Breaking the Silence.
THEATRE: The Sisters Rosenweig, Deathtrap, Sylvia.
PICTURES: Ride the High Country (debut, 1962), Drums of Africa, Marnie, Marooned, Barquero, The Return of Count Yorga, Skyjacked, The Magnificent Seven Ride!, Improper Channels, O'Hara's Wife, 1969, Encino Man, Snitch, Baggage, Farewell to Raskolnikov's, Novel Romance, The Inner Circle.
TELEVISION: *Movies*: Earth II, Sandcastles, Genesis II, Killer Who Wouldn't Die, Last Hurrah (Emmy nom. 1978), M.A.D.D.: Mothers Against Drunk Drivers (Emmy nom. 1983), Drop-Out Father, One Terrific Guy, Silence of the Heart, Falling From the Sky!: Flight 174, Meet the Santas, Love Is a Four Letter Word. *Mini-series:* Passion and Paradise, Perry Mason: The Case of the Telltale Talk Show Host, My Two Loves, Murder C.O.D., Diagnosis of Murder, The House on Sycamore Street, Child of Rage, Heaven & Hell: North and South Book III, *Series*: Peyton Place, The Hero, Good Night Beantown (Emmy nom. 1983), The Incredible Hulk (Emmy Award 1979), WIOU, The Rockford Files (Emmy nom. 1980), To Have and to Hold, One Life to Live, Healthy Solution with Mariette Hartley, The Morning Program, Law & Order: Special Victims Unit, Dirt. *Documentaries/Specials*: Strong Kids, Safe Kids (short), A Baby's World, The Night Dracula Saved the World (Emmy nom. 1980), Wild About Animals (host), Niagara Falls (narr.). *Guest*: More than 122 appearances.

HARTNETT, JOSH

Actor. b. San Francisco, CA, July 21, 1978. e. SUNY Purchase. Voted 'Star of Tomorrow' in Quigley's Top Ten MoneyMakers Poll of 2001-2002.
PICTURES: Halloween H20: 20 Years Later, Debutante, The Faculty, The Virgin Suicides, Here on Earth, Member, Blow Dry, Town & Country, Pearl Harbor, O, Black Hawk Down, 40 Days

and 40 Nights, Halloween: Resurrection, Hollywood Homicide, Obsessed, Wicker Park, Mozart and the Whale, Sin City, The Black Dahlia, The Rum Diary, Lucky Number Slevin, Resurrecting the Champ, 30 Days of Night, The Prince of Cool, August (also prod.), I Come with the Rain, Bunraku, Nobody (exec. prod.), Bunraku.
TELEVISION: *Series*: Cracker: Mind Over Murder. *Special:* AFI's 100 Years, 100 Thrills: America's Most Heart-Pounding Movies, Young Hollywood Awards, 2003 MTV Movie Awards (himself).

HARVEY, ANTHONY
Director, Editor. b. London, England,, June 3, 1931. Royal Acad. of Dramatic Art. Two yrs. as actor. Ent. m.p. ind. 1949 with Crown Film Unit.
PICTURES: *Editor*: Private's Progress, Brothers-in-Law, Man in a Cocked Hat (Carlton Brown of the F.O.), I'm Alright Jack, The Angry Silence, The Millionairess, Lolita, The L-Shaped Room, Dr. Strangelove, The Spy Who Came In From the Cold, The Whisperers. *Director:* Dutchman (debut, 1966), The Lion in Winter (Academy Award nom.; DGA Award, Golden Globe nom. 1969), They Might Be Giants, Eagles' Wing, Players, The Abdication, Richard's Things, The Ultimate Solution of Grace Quigley.
TELEVISION: *Movies*: The Disappearance of Aimee, Svengali, The Patricia Neal Story, The Glass Menagerie (DGA nom. 1974), This Can't Be Love.

HARWOOD, RONALD
Writer. b. Cape Town, South Africa, November 9, 1934. e. Royal Acad. of Dramatic Art.
THEATRE: The Dresser, Interpreters, J.J. Farr, Another Time, Reflected Glory, Poison Pen, Taking Sides.
PICTURES: Barber of Stamford Hill, Private Potter, High Wind in Jamaica, Arrivederci Baby, Diamonds for Breakfast, Sudden Terror (Eye Witness), One Day in the Life of Ivan Denisovich, Operation Daybreak (Price of Freedom), The Dresser (also prod. Academy Award nom.; Golden Globe nom. 1984), The Doctor and the Devils, Tchin-Tchin, The Browning Version, Cry the Beloved Country, Taking Sides, The Pianist (Academy Award, ASA nom. 2003), The Statement, Being Julia, Oliver Twist (s.p), Love in the Time of Cholera, The Diving Bell and the Butterfly (Academy Award nom.; Golden Globe nom.; WGA nom. 2008), Australia.
TELEVISION: *Movies:* The Barber of Stamford Hill, Private Potter, Take a Fellow Like Me, The Lads, Convalescence, Guests of Honor, The Guests, The Deliberate Death of a Polish Priest, Mandela, Breakthrough at Rykjavik, Countdown to War, All the World's a Stage (series), Garderober, Majstor. *Series:* ITV Television Playhouse, Adapted several of the Tales of the Unexpected.

HASHEMI, HAMID
Exhibitor. e. graduate of Florida Atlantic University. A 20+ year veteran of the cinema exhibition industry, Hashemi founded and ran the Florida-based Muvico Theaters circuit he founded in 1984 until Jan. 2006 when Muvico's board replaced Hashimi with a new president and CEO, Michael Whalen. Before founding Muvico, Hashemi was pres. of Professional Services Realty, and was involved with real estate transactions for offices, shopping centers, motels and warehouses. The Carl DeSantis Business and Economics Center for the Study and Development of the Motion Picture and Entertainment Industry named Hashemi the "Motion Picture Business Leader of the Year" in 2000. He is an inner circle founder of the FAU football program and is also helping FAU outfit its new movie theatre at the DeSantis Center by supplying more than $200,000 in theatre equipment. Hashemi has a long association with the "Variety Club-The Children's Charity" and the Will Rogers Institute. Work with South Florida charities includes The Center for the Arts in Boca Raton, National Multiple Sclerosis and The Jewish National Fund. Hashemi's newest venture—IPic Entertainment—launched a new theatre complex concept in Glendale, WI, in summer 2007. In a single facility resides a tony restaurant, bar, luxury bowling, a live stage auditorium with cabaret-style seating and also six to 10 luxury movie theatres, all digitally projected deluxe movie screening rooms with every seat a love seat and every row 54 inches behind and 24 inches higher than the row in front. IPic is based in Ft. Lauderdale, FL, and Hashemi has Florida investors financing IPic's theatre and entertainment complex concept. He plans to roll out six more locations over the next two years in Wisconsin, Texas, California, Illinois and New York.

HASKINS, RICK
Executive. e. B.S. degree from Utah State University. For nearly 25 years, Haskins has enjoyed a career in marketing to both consumer and trade on number one brands across a diverse field of industries. From 1982 to 1988, Haskins was with Procter and Gamble, where he worked within brand management on a number of highly visible brands, including Crest toothpaste and Vidal Sassoon haircare products. His extensive marketing background extended to entertainment with his 1988-1996 association with The Walt Disney Company. From 1989-1993 Haskins served as both director and v.p. of marketing, Buena Vista Television and helped create and build their full-service marketing department, with responsibility for such series as Live with Regis & Kathie Lee and Home Improvement. He was dir. of development for Buena Vista Television from 1993-1996 with responsibility for the creation and development of reality-based programming. From 1996-1999, Haskins founded and managed the Haskins Group, an independent business and marketing consultancy, with clients that included Microsoft, Intel, and McDonald's. He is the author of the Random House-published book titled, *Brand Yourself: How to Create an Identity for a Brilliant Career*, published in January 2000. In 1999, Lifetime cable network brought Haskins on board as executive v.p. of the Lifetime brand, with responsibility for branding, marketing, online and brand extensions. In June 2003, he was promoted to executive v.p. and gen. mgr. of Lifetime Entertainment Services. Shortly after the announcement of a new TV network, The CW, in Jan. 2006, Haskins was named to his current position, executive v.p. of marketing and brand strategy, The CW.

HASSANEIN, SALAH M.
Executive. b. Suez, Egypt, May 31, 1921. e. British School, Alexandria, Egypt. Nat'l. Bank of Egypt, Cairo, 1939-42. Asst. division mgr. Middle East, 20th-Fox, Cairo, Egypt, 1942-44: U.S. armed forces, 1945-47; usher, asst. mgr., Rivoli Theatre, N.Y., 1947-48. Film buyer, booker, oper. v.p. U.A. Eastern Theas., 1948-59; pres. 1960; exec. v.p. U.A. Communications, Inc. 1960; v.p. United Artists Cable Corp., 1963. Exec. v.p., Todd-AO Corp., 1980. President, Warner Bros. International Theaters, 1988. President, Todd AO Corp., 1994-2000. Currently Hassanein is pres., SMH Entertainment; chmn. of the bd. of PointSource Technology and a member of the bd. of dir. of SeeBeyond. He is chmn. of the Board of Variety Boys & Girls Club of Queens, past bd. chmn. and pres. of Variety Clubs International, honorary chmn. of the Will Rogers Memorial Fund, past chmn. and pres. of the Foundation of Motion Picture Pioneers, a member of the New York State Motion Picture and Television Advisory Board, and advisory bd. member of the National Bank of New York City. He is a past member of the Board of Television & Film Committee of the United States Information Agency, a trustee of the North Shore Hospital, Manhasset, NY, and a member of the Board of Aging in America, Inc. He is also currently Chairman of the Variety International Lifeline Program.
PICTURES: *Exec. prod.:* Knightriders, Q, Creepshow, Day of the Dead, Compromising Positions, Flicks, Hello Again, Love or Money.

HASSELHOFF, DAVID
Actor. b. Baltimore, MD, July 17, 1952.
PICTURES: Starcrash, Starke Zeiten, Witchery, W.B. Blue and the Bean, The Final Alliance, Ring of the Musketeers, Dear God (cameo), The Big Tease, The Target Shoots First, Layover, The New Guy, Don't Call Me Tonto, EuroTrip, Dodgeball: A True Underdog Story, Click, The Legend of the Dancing Ninja.
TELEVISION: *Movies*: Pleasure Cove, Knight Rider: Knight of the Phoenix, Griffin and Phoenix, Semi Tough, The Cartier Affair, Bridge Across Time, Perry Mason: The Case of the Lady in the Lake, Baywatch: Panic at Malibu Pier, Fire & Rain, Knight Rider 2000, Avalanche, Baywatch: Forbidden Paradise, Gridlock, Nick Fury, Baywatch: White Thunder at Glacier Bay, One True Love, Baywatch: Hawaiian Wedding, Knight Rider, Anaconda 3: The Offspring. *Mini-series*: Shaka Zulu: The Citadel. *Series*: The Young and the Restless, Knight Rider, Baywatch, Baywatch Nights, America's Got Talent (judge), Gumball 3000. *Guest:* More than 167 appearances.

HASTINGS, DON
Actor. b. Brooklyn, NY, Apr. 1, 1934. e. Professional Children's Sch., Lodge H.S. On B'way in I Remember Mama, Summer and Smoke, etc.; Nat'l. co. of Life With Father; on various radio shows. Also wrote scripts for tv series The Guiding Light. Won Lifetime Achievement Emmy Award, 2004.
TELEVISION: *Movie:* Engaged to Kill. *Series*: The Secret Files of Captain Video, Captain Video, The Edge of Night, As the World Turns (1960-present, also writer).

HATFIELD, TED
Executive. e. Hot Springs, AR High School; U.S. Army-NCO Academy. Entered industry with ABC-Paramount Theatres, advancing from usher to district mgr. From 1970-1991 with MGM, asst. exploitation mgr.; national advertising coordinator; v.p. field operations, v.p. exhibitor relations. From 1991-1997, v.p. of exhibitor relations with SONY. Joined Regal Entertainment Group in 1998; currently is dir., film marketing for Regal Entertainment Group. Regal is the largest U.S. theatre circuit consisting of more than 6,000 screens in over 544 theatres in 39 states.

HATHAWAY, ANNE
Actress. b. Brooklyn, NY, Nov. 12, 1982. First and only teenager admitted to the acting program at the award-winning The Barrow Group in New York. 2008 voted 'Star of Tomorrow' in Quigley Publishing's annual Top Ten MoneyMakers Poll.
THEATRE: Carnival, Get Happy.
PICTURES: The Princess Diaries, The Other Side of Heaven, Nicholas Nickleby, Ella Enchanted (also soundtrack), The Princess Diaries 2: Royal Engagement, Hoodwinked! (voice, soundtrack), Brokeback Mountain, The Devil Wears Prada, Becoming Jane, Get Smart, Rachel Getting Married (Academy

Award nom. 2009, Golden Globe nom. 2008), Passengers, Bride Wars, The Fiance, Valentine's Day, Alice in Wonderland, Love and Other Drugs, Rio (voice).
TELEVISION: *Series:* Get Real. *Special:* Anne Hathaway/The Killers. *Guest:* More than 80 appearances.

HATOSY, SHAWN
Actor. b. Fredrick, MD, Dec. 29, 1975.
PICTURES: Home for the Holidays, In & Out, No Way Home, Inventing the Abbotts, All Over Me, The Postman, The Faculty, Simpatico, The Joyriders, Anywhere But Here, Outside Providence, Simpatico, Anywhere But Here, Down to You, Borstal Boy, Tangled, John Q., A Guy Thing, The Cooler, Deadrockstar, The Cooler, 11:14, Dallas 362, Swimmers, Alpha Dog, Nobel Son, Factory Girl, The Heaven Project, Familiar Strangers, The Lazarus Project, Bad Lieutenant: Port of Call New Orleans, Public Enemies.
TELEVISION: *Movies*: Inflammable, Double Jeopardy, Witness Protection, A Soldier's Girl, The Winning Season, Faith of My Fathers, Drive (series pilot), The Apostles. *Series:* Southland.

HAUER, RUTGER
Actor. b. Breukelen, Netherlands, Jan. 23, 1944. Stage actor in Amsterdam for six years.
PICTURES: Repelsteeltje (debut, 1973), Turkish Delight, Pusteblume, The Wilby Conspiracy, Keetje Tippel, Het Jaar van de Kreeft, Max Havelaar, Griechische Feigen, Soldier of Orange, Pastorale 1943, Femme Entre Chien et Loup, Mysteries (also co-prod.), Gripsta en de Gier, Spetters, Nighthawks, Chanel Solitaire, Blade Runner, Eureka, The Osterman Weekend, A Breed Apart, Ladyhawke, Flesh and Blood, The Hitcher, Wanted: Dead or Alive, The Legend of the Holy Drinker, Bloodhounds of Broadway, The Blood of Heroes, Blind Fury, Ocean Point, On a Moonlit Night, Past Midnight, Split Second, Buffy the Vampire Slayer, Arctic Blue, Beyond Forgiveness, Surviving the Game, Nostradamus, The Beans of Egypt Maine, Angel of Death, Hemoglobin, Deathline, Tactical Assault, Bone Daddy, New World Disorder, Partners in Crime, Wilder, Lying in Wait, The Room, Jungle Juice, God's Bankers, Flying Virus, Confessions of a Dangerous Mind, Warrior Angels, Scorcher, In the Shadow of the Cobra, Dracula II: The Ascension, Dracula III: Legacy, Batman Begins, Tempesta, Moving McAllister, Mirror Wars: Reflection One, Minotaur, Sin City, Tonight at Noon, Magic Flute Diaries, Spoon, Goal! 2: Living the Dream..., 7eventy 5ive, Happiness Runs, Bride Flight, Smoke and Ochre, Dazzle, The Mill and the Cross, Barbarossa, The 5th Execution, Tonight at Noon, Black Butterflies, Happiness Runs.
TELEVISION: *Movies*: Escape from Sobibor (Golden Globe Award 1988), Inside The Third Reich, Deadlock, Blind Side, Voyage, Amelia Earhart: The Final Flight, Fatherland (Golden Globe nom. 1995), Hostile Waters, Merlin, 'Salem's Lot, The Poseidon Adventure, Wild at Heart, Starting Over, The Prince of Motor City. *Mini-series*: Maketub: The Law of the Desert (Italy), The 10th Kingdom. *Series*: Floris (Netherlands TV). *Documentaries:* Terror in the Aisles, Floris. *Guest:* More than 67 appearances.

HAUSER, WINGS
Actor. b. Hollywood, CA, Dec. 12, 1947. Nickname derived from playing wing back on h.s. football team. Began studying acting in 1975.
PICTURES: First to Fight, Who'll Stop the Rain, Homework, Vice Squad, Deadly Force, Uncommon Valor (assoc. prod., story only), Night Shadows, A Soldier's Story, Jo Jo Dancer Your Life is Calling, 3:15, Tough Guys Don't Dance, Nightmare at Noon, The Wind, Hostage, Dead Man Walking, The Carpenter, The Siege of Firebase Gloria, No Safe Haven (also co-s.p.), Reason to Die, L.A. Bounty, Street Asylum, Pale Blood, Out of Sight Out of Mind, Nightmare at Noon, Living to Die, Exiled in America, Bedroom Eyes II, Wilding, The Killer's Edge, In Between, Frame Up, Cold Fire, Beastmaster 2: Through the Portal of Time, The Art of Dying, Mind Body & Soul, Frame-up III: The Cover Up, Watchers 3, Tales From the Hood, Victim of Desire, Life Among the Cannibals, Original Gangstas, Going Home, The Insider, Clean and Narrow, Savage Season, Irish Eyes, The Stone Angel, Rubber.
TELEVISION: *Movies*: Hear No Evil, Ghost Dancing, Sweet Revenge, The Long Hot Summer, Perry Mason: The Case of the Scandalous Scoundrel, Highway Man, Bump In the Night, Mystery Woman: Wild West Mystery, Avenging Angel. *Mini-series:* Kingpin. *Series*: The Young and the Restless, The Last Precinct, Lightning Force, Command 5, Roseanne, Beverly Hills 90210, High Tide. *Documentary:* Terror in the Aisles. *Guest*: More than 51 appearances.

HAUSMAN, MICHAEL
Producer. Former stockbroker and still photographer. Entered film industry as assoc. prod. and prod. mgr. on The Heartbreak Kid and Taking Off. Worked as head of prod. for Robert Stigwood on Saturday Night Fever.
PICTURES: I Never Promised You a Rose Garden, Alambrista!, Heartland, Rich Kids, One-Trick Pony, Ragtime (exec. prod., 1st asst. dir.), The Ballad of Gregorio Cortez, Silkwood, Amadeus (exec. prod. DGA Award 1985), Places in the Heart (exec. prod.), Desert Bloom, Flight of the Spruce Goose, No Mercy, House of Games, Things Change, Valmont, State of Grace, Homicide, Nobody's Fool, A Family Thing, Twilight, Man on the Moon, American Saint, Gangs of New York. Eternal Sunshine of the Spotless Mind (first asst. dir.), Brokeback Mountain (first asst. dir.; DGA Award 2006), All the King's Men (exec. prod.), Factory Girl, Be Kind Rewind (first asst. dir.), Taking Woodstock (first asst. dir.), The Green Hornet (first asst. dir.).
TELEVISION: *Movies*: The Ballad of Gregorio Cortez, Lip Service (exec. prod.), Thicker Than Blood, New Amsterdam (line prod., pilot), Recount (Emmy Award 2008; DGA Award 2009).

HAVERS, NIGEL
Actor. b. London, England,, Nov. 6, 1949. e. Leicester U., trained for stage at Arts Educational Trust. Father, Sir Michael Havers, was Attorney General of Britain. As child played Billy Owen on British radio series, Mrs. Dale's Diary. Records voiceovers and books for the blind.
THEATRE: Conduct Unbecoming, Richard II, Man and , Superman (RSC), Family Voices, Season's Greetings, The Importance of Being Earnest.
PICTURES: Pope Joan (debut, 1972), Full Circle, Who is Killing the Great Chefs of Europe?, Chariots of Fire, A Passage to India, Burke and Wills, The Whistle Blower, Empire of the Sun, Farewell to the King, Clichy Days, Prophecy, Element of Doubt, Paradise Lost, The Life and Death of Peter Sellers, Penelope.
TELEVISION: *Movies*: The Charmer, Private War of Lucina Smith, Lie Down With Lions, The Burning Season, The Gentleman Thief, Open Wide. *Mini-series*: The Glittering Prizes, Nicholas Nickleby, Pennies From Heaven, Winston Churchill: The Wilderness Years, Nancy Astor, The Little Princess, Death of the Heart, Naked Under Capricorn, Sleepers, The Afternoon Play. *Series*: A Horseman Riding By, Don't Wait Up, OK! TV, Murder in Mind, Manchild, The Afternoon Play, Brothers & Sisters, Lunch Monkeys, Coronation Street. *Guest*: More than 128 appearances.

HAVOC, JUNE
Actress. r.n. Hovick. b. Seattle, WA, Nov. 8, 1916. Sister was late Gypsy Rose Lee. Made film bow at 2 yrs. old in Hal Roach/Harold Lloyd productions billed as Baby June. Danced with Anna Pavlova troupe, then entered vaudeville in own act. Later, joined Municipal Opera Company, St. Louis, and appeared in Shubert shows. Musical comedy debut: Forbidden Melody (1936). To Hollywood, 1942. Author: Early Havoc (1959), More Havoc (1980).
THEATRE: Pal Joey, Sadie Thompson, Mexican Hayride, Dunnigan's Daughter, Dream Girl, Affairs of State, The Skin of Our Teeth, A Midsummer Night's Dream (Stratford, CT. American Shakespeare Fest., 1958), Tour for U.S. Dept. of St., 1961; wrote Marathon 33. The Ryan Girl, The Infernal Machine, The Beaux Strategem, A Warm Peninsula, Dinner at Eight, Habeas Corpus. An Unexpected Evening with June Havoc (one woman show, London 1985), The Gift (tour), Eleemosynary, The Old Lady's Guide to Survival, Do Not Go Gently.
PICTURES: Four Jacks and a Jill (debut, 1941), Powder Town, My Sister Eileen, Sing Your Worries Away, Hi Diddle Diddle, Hello Frisco Hello, No Time for Love, Casanova Burlesque, Timber Queen, Sweet and Low Down, Brewster's Millions, Intrigue, Gentleman's Agreement, When My Baby Smiles at Me, The Iron Curtain, The Story of Molly X, Red Hot and Blue, Chicago Deadline, Mother Didn't Tell Me, Once a Thief, Follow the Sun, Lady Possessed, Three for Jamie Dawn, The Private Files of J. Edgar Hoover, Can't Stop the Music, Return to Salem's Lot, Broadway: The Golden Age by the Legends Who Were There.
TELEVISION: *Movies:* Mr. Broadway, The Boy Who Stole the Elephant, Nightside. *Series*: Anna Christie, The Bear, Cakes and Ale, Daisy Mayme, The Untouchables, Willy, MacMillan & Wife, The Paper Chase, Murder She Wrote, Rodgers & Hart Story: Thou Swell, Thou Witty, Marlene: Inventing Dietrich. More Havoc (1964-65), Search for Tomorrow, General Hospital.
(d. March 28, 2010)

HAWKE, ETHAN
Actor. b. Austin, TX, Nov. 6, 1970. Attended NYU. Studied acting at McCarter Theatre in Princeton, NJ, the British Theatre Assn., Carnegie Mellon U. Stage debut in St. Joan. Co-founder of Malaparte Theatre Co. in NYC. Dir. & wrote short film Straight to One. Author of novel The Hottest State, 1996.
THEATRE: NY: Casanova (Off-B'way debut, 1991), A Joke, The Seagull (B'way debut, 1992), Sophistry, Hesh, The Great Unwashed.
PICTURES: Explorers (debut, 1985), Dead Poets Society, Dad, White Fang, Mystery Date, A Midnight Clear, Waterland, Alive, Rich in Love, Reality Bites, White Fang 2: Myth of the White Wolf (cameo), Quiz Show (cameo), Floundering, Before Sunrise, Search and Destroy, Gattaca, Snow Falling on Cedars, The Newton Boys, Great Expectations, Hamlet, Joe the King, Waking Life, Training Day (Academy Award nom. 2002), Tape, The Jimmy Show, Corso: The Last Beat, Before Sunset (Academy Award nom.; Best Writing/s.p., WGA nom. 2005) Taking Lives, Assault on Precinct 13, Lord of War, Fast Food Nation, Tonight at Noon, Before the Devil Knows You're Dead, New York, I Love You, What Doesn't Kill You, The Hottest State (also dir., writer/novel, s.p.), Staten Island, Brooklyn's Finest, Daybreakers, Tonight at Noon, The Woman in the Fifth. *Guest:* More than 52 appearances.
TELEVISION: *Series:* Moby Dick. *Guest:* More than 58 appearances.

HAWN, GOLDIE

Actress, Producer. b. Washington, DC, November 21, 1945. Started as professional dancer (performed in Can-Can at the N.Y. World's Fair, 1964), and made TV debut dancing on an Andy Griffith Special. Daughter is actress Kate Hudson.
PICTURES: The One and Only Genuine Original Family Band (debut, 1968), Cactus Flower (Academy Award, best supporting actress, Golden Globe Award, 1 other nom. 1970), There's a Girl in My Soup, $ (Dollars), Butterflies Are Free (Golden Globe nom. 1973), The Sugarland Express, The Girl From Petrovka, Shampoo (Golden Globe nom. 1976), The Duchess and the Dirtwater Fox (Golden Globe nom. 1977), Foul Play (Golden Globe nom. 1979), Private Benjamin (Academy Award nom.; also exec. prod.; Golden Globe nom. 1981), Seems Like Old Times, Lovers and Liars (Travels With Anita), Best Friends (Golden Globe nom. 1983), Swing Shift, Protocol (also exec. prod.), Wildcats (also exec. prod.), Overboard (also exec. prod.), Bird on a Wire, My Blue Heaven (co-exec. prod. only), Deceived, Crisscross (also co-exec. prod.), Housesitter, Death Becomes Her, Something to Talk About (exec. prod. only), The First Wives Club, Everyone Says I Love You, The Out-of-Towners, Town and Country, The Banger Sisters (Golden Globe nom. 2003).
TELEVISION: *Movies*: Hope (exec. prod., dir.), When Billie Beat Bobby (exec. prod.), The Matthew Shepard Story (exec. prod.). *Series*: Good Morning World, Rowan & Martin's Laugh-In (1968-70; 2 Emmy noms.). *Specials*: The Goldie Hawn Special, Goldie & Liza Together (Emmy nom. 1980), Goldie and the Kids: Listen to Us. *Guest:* More than 112 appearances.

HAYEK, SALMA

Actress. b. Coatzacoalcos, Veracruz, Mexico, Sept. 2, 1968. Began her acting career in the 1980's in Mexican TV soap operas. Was first noticed in 1995 for her role in Desperado.
PICTURES: My Crazy Life, Midaq Alley, Desperado, Fair Game, Four Rooms, From Dusk Till Dawn, Fled, Fools Rush In, Breaking Up, The Velocity of Gary, The Faculty, Dogma, 54, Wild Wild West, Forever Hollywood, Timecode, Chain of Fools, Traffic, La Gran Vida, Frida (Academy Award nom.; Golden Globe nom. 2003), Spy Kids 3-D: Game Over, Hotel, Once Upon a Time in Mexico, The Ground Beneath Her Feet, Searching for Debra Winger, After the Sunset, Sian Ka'an, Ask the Dust, Paint, Murphy's Law (also prod.), Bandidas, Lonely Hearts, Across the Universe, Keep Coming Back, La Banda (also prod.), Beverly Hills Chihuahua (voice), Cirque du Freak: The Vampire's Assistant, Grown Ups.
TELEVISION: *Movies*: Roadracers, The Hunchback, In the Time of the Butterflies, The Maldonado Miracle (sr. exec. prod., dir., Emmy Award; 1 other nom. 2004). *Series*: Teresa, The Sinbad Show, Ugly Betty (exec. prod., pilot exec. prod., 2 Emmy noms.), 30 Rock. *Guest*: More than 116 appearances.

HAYNES, TODD

Director, Writer, Producer, Editor, Actor. b. Jan. 2, 1961.
PICTURES: Superstar: The Karen Carpenter Story, He Was Once, Poison (Sundance Film Fest. Grand Jury Prize, 1991), Swoon, Safe (Seattle Int'l. Film Fest. Amer. Indep. Award, 1995), Velvet Goldmine (Cannes Film Fest., Best Art. Contribution, 1998), Far From Heaven (Academy Award nom.; Golden Globe nom.; WGA nom. 2003), Quinceañera (exec. prod.), Old Joy (exec. prod.), I'm Not There., Wendy and Lucy (exec. prod.).
TELEVISION: *Movie*: Dottie Gets Spanked, Sonic Youth Video Dose, Mildred Pierce (dir., s.p.).

HAYS, ROBERT

Actor. b. Bethesda, MD, July 24, 1947. e. Grossmont Coll., San Diego State U. Left school to join San Diego's Old Globe Theatre five years, appearing in such plays as The Glass Menagerie, The Man in the Glass Booth, Richard III.
PICTURES: Airplane! (debut, 1980), Take This Job and Shove It!, Utilities, Airplane II: The Sequel, Trenchcoat, Touched, Scandalous, Cat's Eye, Honeymoon Academy, Hot Chocolate, Homeward Bound: The Incredible Journey, Fifty Fifty, Raw Justice, Homeward Bound II: Lost in San Francisco, Dr. T & The Women, Alex in Wonder, Freezerburn, Universal Remote, Nicky's Birthday Camera (also prod.), Superhero Movie.
TELEVISION: *Movies*: Young Pioneers, Young Pioneers' Christmas, Delta County U.S.A., The Initiation of Sarah, The Girl The Gold Watch and Everything, California Gold Rush, The Fall of the House of Usher, The Day the Bubble Burst, Murder by the Book, Running Against Time, No Dessert Dad 'Til You Mow the Lawn, Deadly Invasion: The Killer Bee Nightmare, Danielle Steel's Vanished, Christmas Every Day, Unabomber: The True Story, The Abduction, I'll Be Home for Christmas, Nightworld: 30 Years to Life, Deadly Appearances, The Retrievers, The Santa Trap. *Mini-series*: Will Rogers: Champion of the People. *Specials:* Mr. Roberts, Partners. *Series*: Angie, Starman, FM, Cutters, Kelly Kelly, To Tell the Truth, Bette. *Guest*: More than 70 appearances.

HAYSBERT, DENNIS

Actor. b. San Mateo, CA, June 2, 1954.
THEATRE: Wedding Band, Yanks-3 Detroit-0 Top of the Seventh, Diplomacy, Othello, On the Death of, All Over Town, Blood Knot, No Place to Be Somebody, Jimmy Shine, The Time of Your Life, Ten Little Indians.
PICTURES: Major League, Navy SEALS, Mr. Baseball, Love Field, Suture, Major League 2, Amanda, Waiting to Exhale, Absolute Power, Heat, Prairie Fire, Insomnia, Standoff, How to Make the Cruelest Month, Major League 2: Back to the Minors, The Minus Man, The Thirteenth Floor, Random Hearts, What's Cooking, .Love and Basketball, Far From Heaven, The Hire: Ticker (short), Sinbad: Legend of the Seven Seas (voice), Jarhead, Goodbye Bafana, Breach, When the Dragon Swallowed the Sun (doc., narr., prod.), The Details.
TELEVISION: *Movies*: The Return of Marcus Welby, M.D., A Summer to Remember, Grambling's White Tiger, Just the Ten of Us, K-9000, Hallelujah, Widow's Kiss, The Writing on the Wall. *Mini-series*: Wilder Westen, Inclusive, Queen, Return to Lonesome Dove, Empire. *Series*: Buck Rogers in the 25th Century, Growing Pains, Code Red, Off the Rack, Now and Again, Static Shock (voice), 24, Justice League Unlimited, The Unit, 24 (Golden Globe nom. 2003). Return to Lonesome Dove, Empire, The Unit. *Specials*: The Upper Room, Hallelujah, Secrets of Pearl Harbor (host, narr.). *Guest*: More than 100 appearances.

HEAD, ANTHONY

Actor. b. Camden, London, England, February 20, 1954.
PICTURES: Lady Chatterly's Lover, A Prayer for the Dying, Woof Again! Why Me?, I'll Be There, Imagine Me & You, Scoop, Sparkle, Sweeney Todd: The Demon Barber of Fleet Street, Macbeth, Repo! The Genetic Opera.
TELEVISION: *Movies*: Royce, Roger Roger, Best Actress, And Starring Pancho Villa As Himself, Reversals, The Children's Party at the Palace, Him and Us, Comic Relief 2007: The Big One, Persuasion, Doctor Who: The Infinite Quest (voice), Free Agents. *Mini-series*: Lillie, Love in a Cold Climate. *Series*: The Mallens, Woof, VR.5, Buffy the Vampire Slayer, Jonathan Creek, Manchild, MI-5 Spooks, Ripper, Fillmore!, Monarch of the Glen, Little Britain, Totally Doctor Who (voice), Sold, Merlin, The Invisibles. *Guest*: More than 115 appearances.

HEADLY, GLENNE

Actress. b. New London, CT, March 13, 1957. e. High Sch. of Performing Arts. Studied at HB Studios. In Chicago joined St. Nicholas New Works Ensemble. Won 3 Joseph Jefferson awards for work with Steppenwolf Ensemble in Say Goodnight Gracie, Miss Firecracker Contest, Balm in Gilead, Coyote Ugly, Loose Ends. Directed Canadian Gothic.
THEATRE: NY: Balm in Gilead, Arms and the Man, Extremities, The Philanthropist (Theatre World Award).
PICTURES: Four Friends (debut, 1981), Dr. Detroit, Fandango, The Purple Rose of Cairo, Eleni, Making Mr. Right, Nadine, Stars and Bars, Dirty Rotten Scoundrels, Paperhouse, Dick Tracy, Mortal Thoughts, Grand Isle, Ordinary Magic, Gettingeven with Dad, Mr. Holland's Opus, Sgt. Bilko, 2 Days in the Valley, The X Files: Fight the Future, Babe: Pig in the City (voice), Breakfast of Champions, Timecode, Bartleby, What's the Worst That Could Happen, Don't You Cry For Me, Confessions of a Teenage Drama Queen, Eulogy, Around the Bend, The Namesake, Comeback Season, Raising Flagg, Kit Kittredge: An American Girl, The Joneses.
TELEVISION: *Movies*: Say Goodnight Gracie, Seize the Day, And the Band Played On, Pronto, Winchell, My Own Country, The Darkest Day, The Sandy Bottom Orchestra, On Golden Pond, Oomph!, Women vs. Men, The Burbs. *Mini-series*: Lonesome Dove (Emmy nom. 1989), A Girl Thing, Bastard Out of Carolina (Emmy nom. 1997). *Series*: David Lynch's Hotel Room, Encore! Encore!, Monk.

HEALD, ANTHONY

Actor. b. New Rochelle, NY, Aug. 25, 1944. e. Michigan St. Univ.
THEATRE: B'way: The Wake of Jamey Foster, The Marriage of Figaro, Anything Goes, A Small Family Business, Love! Valour! Compassion!, Inherit the Wind. Off-B'way: The Glass Menagerie, The Electra Myth, Inadmissible Evidence, Misalliance (Theatre World Award), The Caretaker, The Fox, The Philanthropist, Henry V, The Foreigner, Digby, Principia Scriptoriae, The Lisbon Traviata, Elliot Loves, Lips Together Teeth Apart, Pygmalion, Later Life, Love! Valour! Compassion! Regional: Quartermaine's Terms, J.B., Look Back in Anger, The Rose Tattoo, Bonjour la Bonjour, The Matchmaker.
PICTURES: Silkwood (debut, 1983), Teachers, Outrageous Fortune, Happy New Year, Orphans, Postcards From the Edge, The Silence of the Lambs, The Super, Whispers in the Dark, Searching for Bobby Fisher, The Ballad of Little Jo, The Pelican Brief, The Client, Kiss of Death, Bushwacked, A Time to Kill, Deep Rising, 8MM, Proof of Life, The Ruby Princess Runs Away, Red Dragon, X-Men: The Last Stand, Accepted.
TELEVISION: *Movies*: A Case of Deadly Force, Royce, Revenge of the Middle-Aged Woman. *Mini-series*: Fresno, LIBERTY! The American Revolution, Benjamin Franklin. *Series*: Boston Public, Boston Legal. *Pilot:* After Midnight. *Special:* Abby My Love.

HEARD, JOHN

Actor. b. Washington, D.C., Mar. 7, 1947. e. Catholic U. Career began at Organic Theatre, starring in Chicago & N.Y. productions of Warp. Other stage roles include Streamers, G.R. Point (Theatre World Award), Othello, Split, The Glass Menagerie, Total Abandon, The Last Yankee.

PICTURES: Between the Lines (debut, 1977), First Love, On the Yard, Head Over Heels (Chilly Scenes of Winter), Heart Beat, Cutter and Bone (Cutter's Way), Cat People, Best Revenge, Violated, Heaven Help Us, Lies, C.H.U.D., Too Scared to Scream, After Hours, The Trip to Bountiful, The Telephone, The Milagro Beanfield War, The Seventh Sign, Big, Betrayed, Beaches, The Package, Home Alone, End of Innocence, Awakenings, Rambling Rose, Deceived, Mindwalk, Radio Flyer, Gladiator, Waterland, Home Alone 2: Lost in New York, In the Line of Fire, Me and Veronica, The Pelican Brief, Before and After, My Fellow Americans, 187, Executive Power, Men, Snake Eyes, Desert Blue, Freak Weather, The Secret Pact, Jazz Night, Fish Out of Water, Animal Factory, The Photographer, Pollock, Above Ground, The Boys of Sunset Ridge, O, Dying on the Edge, Tracks, Researching Raymond Burke, White Chicks, Under the City, Edison, The Deal, The Chumscrubber, Steel City, Absolute Tangerine, The Guardian, The Great Debaters, Little Hercules in 3-D, The Lucky Ones, The Truth, Formosa Betrayed, Legends of Nethiah, Whisper Me a Lullaby, Two Mothers.
TELEVISION: *Movies*: Will There Really Be a Morning?, Legs, Out on a Limb, Necessity, Cross of Fire, Dead Ahead: The Exxon Valdez Disaster, There Was a Little Boy, Spoils of War, Because Mommy Works, The Wednesday Woman, The Big Heist, The Pilot's Wife, Monday Night Mayhem, Word of Honor, Locusts, The Line-Up, Skip Tracer, Generation Gap, The Quickening. *Mini-series*: The Scarlet Letter, Tender Is the Night, Perfect Murder Perfect Town. *Series*: John Grisham's The Client, CSI: Miami, Jack & Bobby, Prison Break, The Sopranos (Emmy nom. 1999), Cavemen. *Specials:* Edgar Allan Poe: Terror of the Soul, Dear America: Letters Home from Vietnam. *Guest:* More than 60 appearances.

HECHE, ANNE

Actress. b. Aurora, OH, May 25, 1969.
PICTURES: An Ambush of Ghosts, The Adventures of Huck Finn, A Simple Twist of Fate, Milk Money, I'll Do Anything, The Wild Side, Pie in the Sky, The Juror, Walking and Talking, Donnie Brasco, Volcano, I Know What You Did Last Summer, Six Days Seven Nights, Wag the Dog, Return to Paradise, Psycho, The Third Miracle, Karen Black: Actress At Work, Auggie Rose, Prozac Nation, Timepiece, John Q, Birth, What Love Is, Suffering Man's Charity, Spread, The Other Guys, Cedar Rapids.
TELEVISION: *Movies:* O Pioneers!, Against the Wall, Girls in Prison, Kingfish: A Story of Huey P. Long, If These Walls Could Talk, Subway Stories, One Kill, On the Edge, Gracie's Choice (Emmy nom. 2004), The Dead Will Tell (also prod.), Silver Bells, Fatal Desire. *Series:* Another World (Emmy Award 1991; 1 other nom.), Everwood, Nip/Tuck Men in Trees (also pilot), Hung. *Guest:* More than 72 appearances.

HECHT, ALBIE

Producer, Executive. b. Queens, NY. e. B.A., Columbia U. Exec. producer and founding principal of Chauncey Street Prods. Then became president of Viacom-owned Nickelodeon and Spike TV. He left the company in 2005 and in 2006 founded Worldwide Biggies, a new digital media content company with a goal to create content that cuts across both traditional and emerging distribution platforms. Hecht immediately struck a children's programming development deal with Nickelodeon and produced the Video Game Awards on Spike TV (which Hecht created and launched while network pres.). He also runs Shine Global, a non-profit subsidiary of Worldwide Biggies, with his wife, Dr. Susan MacLaury. The couple's first Shine Global documentary—War/Dance—was selected for the 2007 Sundance Film Festival Independent Film Documentary Competition. Shine Global's goal is to end the abuse and exploitation of children through the production of documentary films and media products that raise awareness and inspire social change. Hecht is the recipient of three CableACE Awards and an ACT Award for excellence in children's television; also the first recipient of the Children's Museum of Los Angeles Freedom Award.
PICTURES: *Exec. prod.:* Doom Runners, Rugrats in Paris: The Movie, How to Eat Fried Worms, Clockstoppers, The Wild Thornberrys, Rugrats Go Wild!, Lemony Snicket's A Series of Unfortunate Events, The Barnyard, Planet 51 (exec. prod.). *Prod:* Snow Day, Jimmy Neutron: Boy Genius, Hey Arnold! The Movie, The SpongeBob SquarePants Movie, War Dance (doc.), Swift, Harvest (doc.).
TELEVISION: *Movies/Exec. prod.:* Doom Runners, Cry Baby Lane, Back from Hell: A Tribute to Sam Kinison. *Series:* Clarissa Explains It All, Global Guts, You're On!, Pop Across America, The Adventures of Jimmy Neutron: Boy Genius, Danny Phantom, The Naked Brothers Band.

HECKERLING, AMY

Director. b. New York, NY, May 7, 1954. e. Art & Design H.S., NYU, (film and TV), American Film Institute. Made shorts (Modern Times, High Finance, Getting It Over With), before turning to features.
PICTURES: Fast Times at Ridgemont High, Johnny Dangerously, Into the Night (actor only), National Lampoon's European Vacation, Look Who's Talking, Look Who's Talking Too, Look Who's Talking 3 (co-exec. prod. only), Clueless (WGA nom.), A Night at the Roxbury (prod.,s.p.), Molly (exec. prod. only), The Loser (also prod., writer), Sweat (also prod.), No Place Like Home, I Could Never Be Your Woman (also writer), Vamps (also s.p.).
TELEVISION: George Burns Comedy Hour, They Came From Queens, Life on the Flipside. *Series*: Clueless (writer, creator, exec. prod., WGA nom. 1996), Fast Times (also prod.), Baby Talk (also writer).

HEDAYA, DAN

Actor. b. Brooklyn, NY, July 24, 1940. e. Tufts Univ. Taught junior high school for seven yrs. before turning to acting. Joined NY Shakespeare Fest. in 1973.
THEATRE: NY: Last Days of British Honduras, Golden Boy, Museum, The Basic Training of Pavlo Hummel, Conjuring an Event, Survivors, Henry V.
PICTURES: The Passover Plot (debut, 1976), The Seduction of Joe Tynan, Night of the Juggler, True Confessions, I'm Dancing As Fast As I Can, Endangered Species, The Hunger, The Adventures of Buckaroo Banzai, Blood Simple, Reckless, Tightrope, Commando, Wise Guys, Running Scared, Joe Vs. the Volcano, Pacific Heights, Tune in Tomorrow, The Addams Family, Boiling Point, Benny & Joon, Rookie of the Year, For Love or Money, Mr. Wonderful, Maverick, Search and Destroy, Clueless, Nixon, The Usual Suspects, To Die For, Marvin's Room, Freeway, Ransom, Daylight, In & Out, Alien: Resurrection, A Life Less Ordinary, A Night at the Roxbury, A Civil Action, Dick, The Hurricane, Shaft, The Crew, Down, Mulholland Dr., Quicksand, The Myersons, Swimf@n, New Suit.
TELEVISION: *Movies*: The Prince of Central Park, Death Penalty, The Courage, Slow Burn, A Smoky Mountain Christmas, Betrayal of Trust, Reluctant Agent, The Whereabouts of Jenny, The Garden of Redemption, Locked in Silence, Pizza My Heart. *Series*: The Tortellis, One of the Boys, ER, NYPD Blue (Emmy nom. 1994), The Book of Daniel. *Pilots:* The Earthlings, The Flamingo Kid, The Rock. *Special:* Just Like Family, Mama's Boy, Veronica Clare, The Second Civil War. *Guest*: More than 67 appearances.

HEDLUND, DENNIS

Executive, Producer. b. Hedley, TX, Sept. 3, 1946. e. U. of Texas, Austin, B.A., business admin., 1968. Captain U.S. Marine Corp, 1966-72. 1970-74, newscaster and disc jockey, KGNC Amarillo, TX; KOMA Oklahoma City, OK; WTIX New Orleans, LA; WFLA Tampa, FL. 1974-77, nat'l. sales mgr., Ampex Corp., NY. 1977-80, v.p., Allied Artists Video Corp., NY. 1980-present, founder and pres., Kultur International Films Ltd., distributor of over 800 performing arts programs on home video. 1990, created White Star Ent., prod. of original programs for TV, and marketer of over 400 non-theatrical home video titles. Acquired Duke Powersports, 1200 motorsports programs for TV and home video. 1993 was appointed a commissioner to NJN, the New Jersey Public Broadcasting Authority. 2001 Hedlund was appointed a commissioner to the New Jersey Motion Picture and Television Commission, where he still serves. He is also the founder and director of the New Jersey Comedy Festival.
TELEVISION: Roger Miller: King of the Road, Jackie Mason: An Equal Opportunity Offender, Merle Haggard: A Portrait of a Proud Man, History of Talk Radio, George Jones: Golden Hits, Raised Catholic: Still Catholic After All These Fears.
PICTURE: A Dangerous Place (actor only).

HEDREN, TIPPI

Actress. r.n. Nathalie Kay Hedren. b. Lafayette, MN, Jan. 18, 1935. Daughter is actress Melanie Griffith. Was hired by Alfred Hitchcock for leading role in The Birds after being spotted on a commercial on the Today Show. Author of The Cats of Shambala. Founder and pres. of The Roar Foundation. Founder of the Shambala preserve. Bd. member, The Wildlife Safari, The Elsa Wild Animal Appeal, The ASPCA, The American Heart Assoc.
THEATRE: Black Comedy, A Hatful of Rain, Love Letters.
PICTURES: The Birds (debut, 1963; Golden Globe Award 1964), Marnie, A Countess From Hong Kong, The Man and the Albatross, Satan's Harvest, Tiger By the Tail, Mr. Kingstreet's War, The Harrad Experiment, Where the Wind Dies, Roar (also prod.), Foxfire Light, Deadly Spygames, Pacific Heights, In the Cold of the Night, Inevitable Grace, Theresa's Tattoo, Mind Lies, The Devil Inside, Citizen Ruth, I Woke Up Early the Day I Died, The Breakup, Internet Love, Expose, The Storytellers, The Hand Behind the Mouse: The Ub Iwerks Story, Mind Rage, Life with Big Cats, Ice Cream Sundae, Mob Dot Com, I Heart Huckabee's, Diamond Zero, The Last Confederate: The Story of Robert Adams, Return to Babylon, The House of Good and Evil, Section B, Lizzie's World: The Secret of the Magic Trunk.
TELEVISION: *Movies*: Alfred Hitchcock Presents..., Through the Eyes of a Killer, Shadow of a Doubt, Perry Mason: The Case of the Skin-Deep Scandal, The Birds II: Land's End, Treacherous Beauties, Return to Green Acres, Kraft Suspense Theatre: The Trains of Silence, The Book of Virtues (voice), Freakazoid! (voice), Sixth Sense (short), Mulligans (short), The Darklings, Replacing Dad, 111 Gramercy Park, Tribute. *Series*: The Bold and the Beautiful, Dream On, Fashion House (also pilot). *Specials*: Inside The Birds, Terror in the Aisles. *Guest*: More than 92 appearances.

HEFFNER, RICHARD D.

Executive, Author, Educator. b. New York, NY, Aug. 5, 1925. e. A Phi Beta Kappa honors graduate of Columbia University, A.B., 1946; M.A., 1947. Instrumental in acquisition of Channel 13 (WNET) as New York's educational TV station; served as its first gen. mgr. Previously had produced and moderated Man of the Year, The Open Mind, etc. for commercial and public TV. Served as dir. of public affairs programs for WNBC-TV in NY. Was also dir. of special projects for CBS TV Network and editorial consultant to CBS, Inc. Editorial Board. Was radio newsman for ABC. Exec. editor of From The Editor's Desk on WPIX-TV in NY. Taught history at U. of California at Berkeley, Sarah Lawrence College, Columbia U. and New School for Social Research, NY. Served as American specialist in communications for U.S. Dept. of State in Japan, Soviet Union, Germany, Yugoslavia, Israel, etc. Former chmn. of classification and rating admin. rating board. 1994-95, sr. fellow, Freedom Forum Media Studies Center at Columbia Univ. Prof. of Communications and Public Policy at Rutgers U. from 1964-present. He commutes to Rutgers from New York City, where he produces and moderates The Open Mind, his prize-winning weekly public affairs TV program which has aired for more than 40 years on public stations around the U.S.

HEGEMAN, JOHN

Executive. Film industry marketing executive. From 1997-2000 Hegeman was president of worldwide marketing for Artisan Entertainment. He also launched and was president of Distant Corners Entertainment Group. In 2002, Hegeman became an exec. at Revolution Studios. In Sept. 2004, he moved to Lions Gate Entertainment as pres., worldwide marketing. At Lions Gate he oversaw the marketing campaigns of films such as Crash, Diary of a Mad Black Woman, as well as both Saw movies. He was also behind the online marketing for The Blair Witch Project. In Jan. 2006, Hegeman became the COO of Fox Filmed Entertainment's new young adult-focused division, Fox Atomic. The division's films are in the $10 million - $20-million range and are geared toward 17- to 24-year-olds. Hegeman was charged with releasing a modest slate in 2006-2007 which included: Turistas, The Hills Have Eyes 2, 28 Weeks Later, a remake of the 1984 classic Revenge of the Nerds and The Comebacks, a sports comedy. 2008 he became Exec. VP and Chief Marketing Officer of New Regency Prods. In his new role, the 20-year industry veteran will oversee the film and TV production company's marketing strategy and its plans from theatrical release through ancillary distribution windows.

HELGELAND, BRIAN

Writer, Director, Producer. b. Providence, RI, Jan. 17, 1961.
PICTURES: *Writer:* A Nightmare on Elm Street 4: The Dream Master, 976-EVIL, Highway to Hell, Assassins, L.A. Confidential (also co-prod., Academy. Award, Best Adapted Screenplay, WGA Award, Chicago Film Crits. Award, Golden Globe nom., LA Film Crits. Award, NY Film Crits. Awards Best Screenplay, 1998), Conspiracy Theory, The Postman, Payback (also dir.), A Knight's Tale, Blood Work, The Sin Eater, Mystic River (writer/s.p. Academy Award nom.; Golden Globe nom.; WGA nom. 2004), The Order, Man on Fire, Cirque du Freak, Green Zone, Robin Hood, The Taking of Pelham 1 2 3, Salt, Green Zone, Cirque du Freak: The Vampire's Assistant, Robin Hood (s.p.), Salt (s.p.).
TELEVISION: *Series*: Tales from the Crypt (dir.).

HELGENBERGER, MARG

Actress. b. North Bend, NE, Nov. 16, 1958. e. Northwestern U. Came to NY where she landed first professional job as regular on daytime serial Ryan's Hope.
PICTURES: After Midnight (debut, 1989), Always, Crooked Hearts, Distant Cousins, The Cowboy Way, Bad Boys, Species, My Fellow Americans, Fire Down Below, Species II, Erin Brockovich, Synergy, In Good Company, Mr. Brooks.
TELEVISION: *Movies*: Blind Vengeance, Death Dreams, The Hidden Room, Deadline (pilot), Through the Eyes of a Killer, The Tommyknockers, When Love Kills: The Seduction of John Hearn, Where Are My Children?, Red Eagle, Partners, Inflammable, Conundrum, Murder Live!, The Last Time I Commited Suicide, Gold Coast, Thanks of a Grateful Nation, Giving Up the Ghost, The Happyface Murders, Lethal Vows. *Mini-series*: When Love Kills: The Seduction of John Hearn, Perfect Murder, Perfect Town: Jon Benét and the City of Boulder. *Series*: Ryan's Hope, Shell Game, China Beach (Emmy Award, 1990, 2 other noms.; Golden Globe nom. 1991), Fallen Angels, Partners, CSI: Crime Scene Investigation (2 Emmy noms.; 2 Golden Globe noms.). *Special:* Fallen Angels. *Guest:* More than 80 appearances.

HELLER, PAUL M.

Producer. b. New York, NY, Sept. 25, 1927. e. Hunter Coll., Drexel Inst. of Technology. President, Intrepid Productions. Studied engineering until entry into U.S. Army as member of security agency, special branch of signal corps. Worked as set designer (Westport, East Hampton, Palm Beach) and in live TV and then on theatrical films. Produced the NY Experience and South Street Venture. Debut as film prod., David and Lisa, 1963. From 1964 to 1969 was president of MPO Pictures Inc. Joined Warner Bros. as prod. exec., 1970. Founded the Community Film Workshop Council for the American Film Institute. In 1972 founded Sequoia Pictures, Inc. with Fred Weintraub. Pres. of Paul Heller Prods. Inc. formed in 1978. Founded the Audrey Skirball-Kenis Theatre. Bd of dirs., the British Academy of Film and Television - Los Angeles, The Hearst Monument Foundation, The Geffen Theatre, Eternal.
PICTURES: David and Lisa, The Eavesdropper, Secret Ceremony, Enter the Dragon, Truck Turner, Golden Needles, Dirty Knight's Work, Outlaw Blues, The Pack, The Promise, First Monday in October, Withnail and I, My Left Foot (exec. prod.), The Lunatic, Fatal Inheritance, The Annihilation of Fish.
TELEVISION: *Movies*: Pygmalion, Falcon's Gold, The Disappearance of Christina, David & Lisa.

HELLMAN, JEROME

Producer. b. New York, NY, Sept. 4, 1928. e. NYU. Joined ad dept. of New York Times then went to William Morris Agency as apprentice. Made asst. in TV dept. Worked as agent for Jaffe Agency. After hiatus in Europe joined Ashley-Steiner Agency (later IFA) where clients included Franklin Schaffner, Sidney Lumet, George Roy Hill, John Frankenheimer. Functioned as TV prod., inc. Kaiser Aluminum Hour. Left to form own agency, Ziegler, Hellman and Ross. Switched to feature prod. with The World of Henry Orient in 1964.
PICTURES: The World of Henry Orient, A Fine Madness, Midnight Cowboy (Academy Award for Best Picture, 1970), The Day of the Locust, Coming Home (Academy Award nom. 1979), Promises in the Dark (also dir.), The Mosquito Coast.

HELLMAN, MONTE

Director, Editor. b. New York, NY, 1932. e. Stanford Univ., UCLA. Started by working for Roger Corman's company as dir., editor, 2nd Unit dir. Replaced deceased directors on the films The Greatest, Avalanche Express. *Dialogue Director:* St. Valentine's Day Massacre. Acted in The Christian Licorice Store, Someone to Love.
PICTURES: *Director*: Beast from Haunted Cave, Back Door to Hell, Flight to Fury (also story) , Ride in the Whirlwind (also edit., prod.), The Shooting (also edit., prod.), Two-Lane Blacktop (also edit.), Cockfighter, China 9 Liberty 37 (also prod.), Iguana (also s.p., edit.), Silent Night, Trapped Ashes, Road to Nowhere (also prod.). *Editor*: The Wild Angels, The Long Ride Home, How to Make It, The Killer Elite, Harry and Walter Go to New York, China 9 Liberty 37, The Awakening, Iguana, Deadly Night 3: Better Watch Out!, The Killing Box. *Second Unit Director:* Last Woman on Earth, Ski Troop Attack, Creature from the Haunted Sea, The Terror. *Exec. Prod.:* Reservoir Dogs.
TELEVISION: *Movie:* Baretta.

HELMOND, KATHERINE

Actress. b. Galveston, TX, July 5, 1934. Initial stage work with Houston Playhouse and Margo Jones Theatre, Dallas. Joined APA Theatre, NY, and Trinity Square Rep. Co., RI, Hartford Stage, CT and Phoenix Rep. NY. In 1950s opened summer stock theatre in the Catskills. Taught acting at American Musical and Dramatic Acad., Brown U. and Carnegie-Mellon U. 1983, accepted into AFI's Directing Workshop for Women. Directed Bankrupt.
THEATRE: The Great God Brown, House of Blue Leaves (Clarence Derwent, NY and LA Drama Critics Awards, 1972), Mixed Emotions.
PICTURES: The Hindenberg, Baby Blue Marine, Family Plot, Time Bandits, Brazil, Shadey, Overboard, Lady in White, Inside Monkey Zetterland, Amore!, The Flight of the Dove, Fear & Loathing in Las Vegas, The Perfect Nanny, Living in Fear, The Strand, Cars (voice), Longfellow.
TELEVISION: *Movies:* Dr. Max, Larry, Locusts, The Autobiography of Miss Jane Pittman, The Legend of Lizzie Borden, The Family Nobody Wanted, Cage Without a Key, The First 36 Hours of Dr. Durant, James Dean, Wanted: The Sundance Woman, Little Ladies of the Night, Getting Married, Diary of a Teenage Hitchhiker, Scout's Honor, World War III, For Lovers Only, Rosie: The Rosemary Clooney Story, Meeting of the Minds, Save the Dog, When Will I Be Loved?, The Perfect Tribute, Deception: A Mother's Secret, Grass Roots, Liz: The Elizabeth Taylor Story, Ms. Scrooge, How to Marry a Billionaire: A Christmas Tale, Mr. St. Nick, Bert & Becca, A Grandpa for Christmas. *Series*: Soap (4 Emmy noms.; Golden Globe Award 1981), Who's The Boss? (also episode dir, 2 Emmy noms.; 2 Golden Globe noms.), Benson (episode dir. only), Coach, Everybody Loves Raymond (Emmy nom. 2002 as guest). *Special:* Christmas Snow. *Guest:* More than 80 appearances.

HEMINGWAY, MARIEL

Actress. b. Ketchum, ID, Nov. 22, 1961. Granddaughter of writer Ernest Hemingway. Sister of late actress-model Margaux Hemingway.
PICTURES: Lipstick (debut, 1976, Golden Globe nom. 1977), Manhattan (Academy Award nom. 1980), Personal Best, Star 80, The Mean Season, Creator, Superman IV: The Quest for Peace, Sunset (Golden Globe nom. 1993), The Suicide Club (also co-prod.), Delirious, Falling From Grace, Naked Gun 33 1/3: The Final Insult, Deceptions II: Edge of Deception, Bad Moon, Road Ends, Little Men, Deconstructing Harry, Drop-Dead, American Reel, The Contender, Londinium, Perfume, Time of Change, In Her Line of Fire, The Golden Boys, My Suicide.
TELEVISION: *Movies:* I Want to Keep My Baby, Steal the Sky,

Into the Badlands, Desperate Rescue: The Cathy Mahone Story, September, The Crying Child, First Shot, Warning: Parental Advisory, See Arnold Run, The Prince, Between Truth and Lies. *Mini-series*: Amerika. *Series*: Civil Wars (Golden Globe nom. 1993), Central Park West. *Guest:* More than 63 appearances.

HENRIKSEN, LANCE
Actor. b. New York, NY, May 5, 1943. Appeared on B'way in The Basic Training of Pavo Hummel, Richard III.
PICTURES: It Ain't Easy (debut, 1972), Dog Day Afternoon, The Next Man, Mansion of the Doomed, Close Encounters of the Third Kind, Damien: Omen II, The Visitor, The Dark End of the Street, Prince of the City, Piranha II: The Spawning, Nightmares, The Right Stuff, Savage Dawn, The Terminator, Jagged Edge, Choke Canyon, Aliens, Near Dark, Deadly Intent, Pumpkinhead, Hit List, The Horror Show, Johnny Handsome, Survival Quest, The Last Samurai, Stone Cold, Comrades in Arms, Delta Heat, Alien3, Jennifer Eight, Excessive Force, The Outfit, Super Mario Bros., Hard Target, Man's Best Friend, No Escape, Color of Night, The Quick and the Dead, Powder, The Criminal Mind, Profile for Murder, No Contest II, Tarzan (voice), Scream 3, The Untold, The Lost Voyage, Unspeakable, The Mangler 2, The Invitation, Antibody, One Point O, Out for Blood, Modigliani, Starkweather, Madhouse, Alien Vs. Predator, The Chosen One (voice), Pirates of Treasure Island, Bone Dry, Deadwater, Dark Reel, Dying God, Appaloosa, The Lost Tribe, Necessary Evil, Blood Shot, Broken Lizard's the Slammin' Salmon, Punctured, Cyrus, Wild Michigan, Godkiller (voice), The Penitent Man, For the Love of Jade, Wilderness, The Genesis Code, Good Day for It, Blood Shot, Beautiful Wave, The Witches of Oz 3D, The Arcadian.
TELEVISION: *Movies*: Return to Earth, Question of Honor, Blood Feud, Reason for Living: The Jill Ireland Story, Wes Craven Presents Mind Ripper, The Day Lincoln Was Shot, Alien Evolution, The Omen Legacy, Harsh Realm, Lost Voyage, The Last Cowboy, Evel Knievel, Supernova, Pumpkinhead: Ashes to Ashes, Pumpkinhead: Blood Feud, In the Spider's Web, Ladies of the House. *Mini-series:* Into the West. *Series*: B.A.D. Cats, Ryan's Hope, Millenium (3 Golden Globe noms.), IGPX: Immortal Grand Prix (voice), Caminhos do Coração, Transformers: Animated (voice). *Guest:* More than 82 appearances.

HENRY, BUCK
Actor, Writer. r.n. Henry Zuckerman. b. New York, NY, Dec. 9, 1930. e. Dartmouth Coll. Acted in Life with Father, (tour, 1948), Fortress of Glass, Bernardine, *B'way:* 1952-54, U.S. Army; No Time for Sergeants (Nat'l. Co.), The Premise, improv. theatre, off-B'way.
PICTURES: *Actor*: The Secret War of Harry Frigg, Taking Off, The Man Who Fell to Earth, Old Boyfriends, Gloria, Eating Raoul, Aria, Dark Before Dawn, Rude Awakening, Tune in Tomorrow, Defending Your Life, The Player, The Linguini Incident, Short Cuts (Golden Globe Award 1994), Even Cowgirls Get the Blues, Grumpy Old Men Shotgun Freeway: Drives Through Lost L.A., The Real Blonde, Later Life, I'm Losing You, 1999, Curtain Call, Breakfast of Champions, Curtain Call, Famous, Serendipity, The Last Shot, The Loop. *Actor-Writer:* The Troublemaker, The Graduate (Academy Award nom.; Golden Globe nom.; WGA Award 1968), Is There Sex After Death?,Catch-22 (WGA nom. 1971), Heaven Can Wait (also dir.; Academy Award nom.; DGA nom. 1979), First Family (also dir.), To Die For, Town and Country. *Writer:* Candy, The Owl and the Pussycat (WGA nom. 1971), What's Up Doc? (WGA Award 1973), The Day of the Dolphin, Protocol, Get Smart (also creator).
TELEVISION: *Movies: Actor:* Keep the Change, Mastergate, Harrison Bergeron (prod. only). *Series (writer):* Garry Moore Show, Steve Allen Show (also performer), The Bean Show, That Was the Week That Was (also performer), Get Smart (co-creator, story ed.; Emmy Award 1967, 1 other nom.), Captain Nice (also exec. prod.), Alfred Hitchcock Presents (1985, also actor), Quark, The New Show (also performer), Falcon Crest (actor only), Trying Times: Hunger Chic (dir. only), Saturday Night Live. *Guest*: More than 58 appearances.

HENSON, BRIAN
Executive, Producer. Director, Writer, Performer. b. 1963. Henson is Co-CEO of The Jim Henson Company, alongside his sister and co-CEO, Lisa Henson. He also oversees the groundbreaking work at Jim Henson's Creature Shop, a character building, digital and physical visual effects facilities. Henson was part of the team that first created and utilized the Henson Performance Control Studio, a powerful custom-based interface for puppeteers, which won an Academy of Motion Picture Arts and Science Scientific and Engineering Award in 1992. Recently, he has been leading the Shop's work with its revolutionary puppeteered animation system.
PICTURES: The Great Muppet Caper (voice), Split Image (as Brian Hinson), The Muppets Take Manhattan (voice), Return to Oz (voice), Labyrinth (voice & puppeteer coord.), Little Shop of Horrors (principal puppeteer), The Witches (puppeteer), Teenage Mutant Ninja Turtles (chief puppeteer & second unit dir.), The Muppet Christmas Carol (prod., dir., soundtrack), Muppet Treasure Island (prod., dir., soundtrack), Buddy (exec. prod.), Muppets from Space (prod. & voice), The Adventures of Elmo in Grouchland (exec. prod.), Rat (exec. prod.), The Happytime Murders (prod., dir.).
TELEVISION: *Movies: As Exec. Prod./Voices:* Gulliver's Travels Emmy Award 1996), Poison (actor), Jack and the Beanstalk: The Real Story (also dir.,), It's a Very Merry Muppet Christmas Movie, Farscape: The Peacekeeper Wars (dir.), The Muppets' Wizard of Oz. *Mini-series:* The Storyteller: Greek Myths, Nightmares & Dreamscapes: From the Stories of Stephen King (dir. of episode). *Series:* Jim Henson Presents Mother Goose Stories (dir. & various characters, Emmy Award 1991), Living with Dinosaurs, The Jim Henson Hour (actor), Dinosaurs (also dir., Muppets Tonight (also dir., Emmy Award 1998, 1 other nom.), Aliens in the Family (exec. prod.), Animal Show (Emmy nom. 1999), The Wubbulous World of Dr. Seuss (prod., 2 Emmy noms. 1998), Bear in the Big Blue House (Emmy nom. 2000), B.R.A.T.S. of the Lost Nebula (exec. prod.), Farscape, Puppet Up! Uncensored, Tinseltown (also writer), Sid the Science Kid (Emmy nom. 2009), Simian Undercover Detective Squad, Pajanimals, Dinosaur Train.

HENSON, LISA
Executive, Producer. b. May 9, 1960. e. Harvard University, degree in folklore & mythology, 1983. She was the first femal pres. of The Harvard Lampoon. Father was performer-puppeteer-director Jim Henson. Joined Warner Bros., 1983, as exec. asst. to head of prod. 1985, named dir. of creative affairs. 1985, promoted to v.p., prod. 1992, became exec. v.p., production. 1993, named pres. of worldwide prod. of Columbia Pictures. 1994, named pres. of Columbia Pictures. Resigned in 1996 to form own production company. She then became a producer/partner in the Manifest Film Co. She currently is co-CEO of The Jim Henson Company, where she oversees all TV and feature film production. She is also producing the DVD animated series Frances based on the Frances Treasury best-selling books. Henson is currently a producer on the direct-to-DVD animated series Unstable Fables, feature-length irreverent retellings of popular fairy tales to be released by The Weinstein Company. Henson has previously served on the Bd. of Overseers for Harvard University, Tibet House and The Jim Henson Foundation for Puppetry.
PICTURES: The Muppet Movie, Zero Effect (prod.), The Weight of Water (exec. prod.), Ivansxtc (exec. prod. also actress), Ivansxtc (exec. prod.), High Crimes (exec. prod.), Good Boy! (prod), Five Children and It (prod.), MirrorMask (exec. prod.), The Kreutzer Sonata (exec. prod.), Unstable Fables: Tortise vs. Hare (prod.), Unstable Fables: 3 Pigs & a Baby (prod.), Unstable Fables: Goldilocks & 3 Bears Show (prod.), The Happytime Murders.
TELEVISION: *As Exec. Prod.: Movie:* The Muppets' Wizard of Oz. *Series:* Puppet Up! Uncensored, Pajanimals, Dinosaur Train, Sid the Science Kid (Emmy nom. 2009).

HEREK, STEPHEN
Director. b. San Antonio, TX, Nov. 10, 1958.
PICTURES: Critters (also s.p.), Bill & Ted's Excellent Adventure, Don't Tell Mom the Babysitter's Dead, The Mighty Ducks, The Three Musketeers, Mr. Holland's Opus, 101 Dalmatians, Holy Man (also prod.), Rock Star, Life or Something Like It, Cheer Up, Man of the House, The Census Taker.
TELEVISION: *Movie*: The Gifted One, The Cutting Edge: Fire & Ice. *Series*: Young MacGyver.

HERRMANN, EDWARD
Actor. b. Washington, DC, July 21, 1943. Raised in Grosse Pointe, MI. e. Bucknell U. Postgrad. Fulbright scholar, London Acad. Music and Dramatic Art 1968-69. Acted with Dallas Theater Center for 4 years.
THEATRE: *NY:* The Basic Training of Pavlo Hummel, Moonchildren, Mrs. Warren's Profession (Tony Award, 1976), Journey's End, The Beach House, The Philadelphia Story, Plenty, Tom and Viv, Julius Caesar, Not About Heroes, Life Sentences, The Deep Blue Sea. *London:* A Walk in the Woods.
PICTURES: Lady Liberty, The Paper Chase, The Day of the Dolphin, The Great Gatsby, The Great Waldo Pepper, The Betsy, Brass Target, Take Down, The North Avenue Irregulars, Harry's War, Reds, Death Valley, A Little Sex, Annie, Mrs. Soffel, The Purple Rose of Cairo, The Man With One Red Shoe, Compromising Positions, The Lost Boys, Overboard, Big Business, Hero (unbilled), Born Yesterday, My Boyfriend's Back, Foreign Student, Richie Rich, Critical Care, Frank Lloyd Wright, A Civil Action, Better Living, Walking Across Egypt, Miss Congeniality, Double Take, Down, The Cat's Meow, The Emperor's Club, Intolerable Cruelty, Welcome to Mooseport, The Aviator, Bereft, Relative Strangers, A Love of Time, Factory Girl, The Skeptic, I Think I Love My Wife, Son of Mourning, The Skeptic, Son of Morning, Born to Be a Star, A Root Beer Christmas.
TELEVISION: *Movies*: Eleanor and Franklin (Emmy nom. 1976), Eleanor and Franklin: The White House Years (Emmy nom. 1977), A Love Affair: The Eleanor and Lou Gehrig Story, Portrait of a Stripper, The Gift of Life, Memorial Day, So Proudly We Hail, Sweet Poison, Fire in the Dark, The Face on the Milk Carton, Hostile Waters, The Soul of the Game, Pandora's Clock, Liberty! The American Revolution, Saint Maybe, Atomic Train, Vendetta, James Dean, Bereft, Andrew Jackson (narr.), Hatching Pete. *Mini-series*: Freedom Road, The Korean War: Fire & Ice, A Season in Purgatory. *Series:* Beacon Hill, Our Century (host), The Practice, Oz, Gilmore Girls, The Revolution (narr.). *Specials*: Sorrows of Gin, The Private History of The Campaign That Failed, Murrow, Dear Liar, Concealed Enemies, The Return of

Hickey, The Beginning of the Firm, Last Act is a Solo, The End of a Sentence, A Foreign Field, Don't Drink the Water, The Face on the Milk Carton, Here Come the Munsters, Soul of the Game, What Loves Sees, Pandora's Clock, The Impressionists, Horror in the East, The World Trade Center: Rise and Fall of an American Icon, Bible Battles, Eighty Acres of Hell (narr.), Decoding the Past: Mysteries of the Bermuda Triangle, The Ten Commandments: Part 1 - The Laws of God (narr.) The Ten Commandments: Part 2 - The Laws of Man (narr.), Violent Earth: New England's Killer Hurricane (narr.), Mayan Doomsday Prophecy (narr.), The States (narr, series), Columbus: The Lost Voyage (narr), Christmas with the Mormon Tabernacle Choir Featuring Brian Stokes Mitchell and Edward Herrmann (narr.), many others. *Guest:* More than 112 appearances.

HERSHEY, BARBARA

Actress. r.n. Barbara Herzstein. b. Los Angeles, CA, Feb. 5, 1948. e. Hollywood H.S. Briefly, in the mid-1970's, acted under the name Barbara Seagull.
PICTURES: With Six You Get Eggroll (debut, 1968), Heaven With a Gun, Last Summer, The Liberation of L.B. Jones, The Baby Maker, The Pursuit of Happiness, Dealing, Boxcar Bertha, Angela (Love Comes Quietly), The Crazy World of Julius Vrooder, Diamonds, You and Me, The Last Hard Men, Dirty Knights' Work, The Stunt Man, Americana, Take This Job and Shove It, The Entity, The Right Stuff, The Natural, Hannah and Her Sisters, Hoosiers, Tin Men, Shy People (Cannes Film Fest. Award, 1987), A World Apart (Cannes Film Fest. Award, 1988), The Last Temptation of Christ (Golden Globe nom. 1989), Beaches, Tune in Tomorrow, Defenseless, The Public Eye, Falling Down, Swing Kids, Splitting Heirs, A Dangerous Woman, Last of the Dogmen, Portrait of a Lady (Academy Award nom.; LA Film Critics Award; Natl Society of Film Critics Award; Golden Globe nom. 1997), The Pallbearer, A Soldier's Daughter Never Cries, Frogs for Snakes, Breakfast of Champions, Passion, Drowning on Dry Land, Lantana, Uncross the Stars, Riding the Bullet, Albert Schweitzer, Black Swan, Answers to Nothing.
TELEVISION: *Movies:* Flood, In the Glitter Palace, Just a Little Inconvenience, Sunshine Christmas, Angel on My Shoulder, My Wicked Wicked Ways, The Legend of Errol Flynn, Passion Flower, A Killing in a Small Town (Emmy & Golden Globe Awards, 1991), Paris Trout (Emmy nom. 1991), Stay the Night, Abraham, The Staircase, Hunger Point, Ann Rule Presents: The Stranger Beside Me, Paradise Anne of Green Gables: A New Beginning. *Mini-series:* A Man Called Intrepid, Return to Lonesome Dove, Daniel Deronda. *Series*: The Monroes, From Here to Eternity, The Mountain, Agatha Christie: Poirot. *Special*: Working. *Guest:* More than 61 appearances.

HERSKOVITZ, MARSHALL

Producer, Director, Writer. b. Philadelphia, PA, Feb. 23, 1952. e. Brandeis U., BA, 1973; American Film Inst., MFA. 1975. Worked as freelance writer, dir., and prod. on several TV shows. Received Humanitas Award, 1983 and Writers Guild award, 1984.
PICTURE: Jack the Bear (dir.), Legends of the Fall (co-prod.), Dangerous Beauty, Executive Search, Traffic (Academy Award nom. 2001), I Am Sam, Lone Star State of Mind, The Last Samurai (s. p.), Blood Diamond (prod.), Defiance (exec. prod.), Love and Other Drugs (prod., s.p.). *Documentaries:* The Lions of Al-Rassan (prod.), America: A Tribute to Heroes (writer, Emmy nom. 2002).
TELEVISION: *Movies:* Special Bulletin (prod., writer, 2 Emmys for writing and dramatic special, WGA Award 1989), Extreme Close-Up exec. prod./writer), Women vs. Men (exec. prod. also actor), 1/4life (writer, exec. prod.) A Marriage (exec. prod., writer, dir.). *Series:* CHiPs (writer), Seven Brides for Seven Brothers (writer), Family (writer, dir.), White Shadow (writer), thirtysomething (exec. prod., co-writer, dir; creator, 2 Emmy awards for writing and dramatic series, 4 other noms.; 1988; Also Humanitas Award, DGA Award, 1988 & 1989, 1 other nom.; WGA Award, Peabody Award, 1989.), My So-Called Life (exec. prod.), Relativity (prod.), Once and Again (exec. prod., writer, creator, dir.), Quarterlife (prod./writer).

HERZFELD, JOHN

Writer, Director, Actor, Producer.
PICTURES: *Writer:* Voices, Hard Feelings, Two of a Kind (also dir.), The Last Winter, Ha-Kala, 2 Days in the Valley (also dir./music prod.), Turbulence, 15 Minutes (dir./prod./music prod.), Whitebread (prod.), The Death and Life of Bobby Z (dir.).
TELEVISION: *Movies*: Lieutenant Schuster's Wife (actor only), Cannonball (actor only), Shattered Spirits (actor only), Cobra (actor only), On Fire (also actor), Daddy (also dir.), The Ryan White Story (also actor, dir.), The Preppie Murder (also dir.), Casualties of Love: The Long Island Lolita Story (also dir., prod.), Barbara Taylor Bradford's 'Remember,' (also dir.), Don King: Only in America (dir. only, Emmy nom.; DGA Award, 1998), Point of Origin (prod.), S. I. S. (exec. prod., writer, dir.). *Series*: Tales from the Crypt (dir.), Bill Stanton Project (dir.), ABC Afterschool Specials (Emmy Award for episode "Stoned" 1981, 1 other nom.), Dr. Vegas (dir./writer, exec. prod., pilot).

HERZOG, DOUG

Executive. e. B.S. degree, mass comm., Emerson College, Boston, MA, 1981. Before beginning a 20-year assoc. with Viacom and MTV, Herzog he began his career in the early '80s as an assoc. producer with Turner Broadcasting System's newly launched Cable News Network (CNN) and SuperStation TBS. Herzog then became a segment producer on entertainment newsmagazine "Entertainment Tonight." Herzog's original stint at MTV began in 1984-hired as news director, music news; during next 11 years at MTV, Herzog rose to become: v.p., news and special programming; senior v.p., programs and development; and, ultimately, serving simultaneously as executive v.p., programming for the network and pres. of MTV Productions. Herzog was pres. of Comedy Central from 1995-1998. From 1998-2000, pres. of entertainment for FOX Broadcasting Company. where he was responsible for all FOX programming, scheduling and marketing. Herzog moved to USA Network as its pres. from 2001-May 2004 and returned to Comedy Central for a second round as its pres. in May 2004. In Feb. 2005 Herzog added the additional role of pres., Spike TV, and was charged with establishing the channel as the preeminent entertainment network for men. Herzog added oversight of TV Land to his responsibilities in Jan. 2006 and was named pres. of the newly formed Entertainment Group in Dec. 2006. Today, as pres. of MTV Networks Entertainment Group, Herzog guides the growth of the Comedy Central, Spike TV and TV Land cable channels and Internet sites Atom.com and GameTrailers.com He reports to Judy McGrath, chmn. & CEO of MTV Networks.

HERZOG, WERNER

Director, Producer, Writer. r.n. Werner Stipetic. b. Sachrang, Germany, September 5, 1942. e. U. of Munich, Duquesne U., Pittsburgh. Wrote first s.p. 1957; 1961 worked nights in steel factory to raise money for films; 1966, worked for U.S. National Aeronautics and Space Admin.
PICTURES: Signs of Life (debut, 1968), Precautions Against Fanatics, Even Dwarfs Started Small (also composer), Fata Morgana, The Land of Silence and Darkness, Aguirre—Wrath of God, The Great Ecstasy of Woodcarver Steiner, The Mysery of Kasper Hauser, Nobody Wants to Play With Me, How Much Wood Would a Woodchuck Chuck, Heart of Glass, Stroszek, La Soufriere, Nosferatu: The Vampyre (also cameo), Woyzeck, Garlic Is As Good As Ten Mothers (actor), Werner Herzog Eats His Shoe (actor), Fitzcarraldo, Burden of Dreams (actor), Man of Flowers (actor), Tokyo-Ga (actor), Where the Green Ants Dream, Les Gauloises, Cobra Verde, Scream of Stone, Lessons in Darkness, Bride of the Orient (actor), It Isn't Easy Being God (actor), Echoes of a Somber Empire, Burning Heart (actor), Mexico, My Best Friend, Invincible, Pilgrimage, Ten Minutes Older: The Trumpet, Wake for Galileo (dir.), Grizzly Man (doc., DGA Award 2006), Rescue Dawn (dir., writer), Mister Lonely (actor), The Grand (actor), Encounters at the End of the World (doc. dir., narr.), (Academy Award nom. 2009), Bad Lieutenant: Port of Call New Orleans, My Son, My Son, What Have Ye Done (also writer, s.p.).
TELEVISION: *Movies*: Huie's Sermon, Chambre 666, The Dark Glow of the Mountains, Ballad of the Little Soldier, Little Dieter Needs to Fly (Emmy nom. 1999), Herdsmen of the Sun, The Transformation of the World Into Music (actor), and many others. *Documentaries:* God's Angry Man, Gesualdo: Death for Five Voices, Wings of Hope, many more.

HESSEMAN, HOWARD

Actor. b. Salem, OR, Feb. 27, 1940. Started with the San Francisco group, The Committee and worked as a disc jockey in San Francisco in the late 1960's.
PICTURES: Petulia, Billy Jack, Steelyard Blues, Shampoo, The Sunshine Boys, Jackson County Jail, The Big Bus, The Other Side of Midnight, Silent Movie, Honky Tonk Freeway, Private Lessons, Loose Shoes, Doctor Detroit, This is Spinal Tap, Police Academy 2: Their First Assignment, Clue, My Chauffeur, Flight of the Navigator, Heat, Amazon Women on the Moon, Rubin and Ed, Little Miss Millions, Munchie Strikes Back (voice), Out of Sync, Boys Night Out, Gridlock'd, The Sky is Falling, The Mesmerist, Teddy Bears' Picnic, About Schmidt, Man About Town, Martian Child, Dirty Politics, All About Steve, Halloween II.
TELEVISION: *Movies*: Hustling, The Blue Knight (pilot), Tail Gunner Joe, The Amazing Howard Hughes, Tarantulas: The Deadly Cargo, The Ghost on Flight 401, The Comedy Company, More Than Friends, Outside Chance, The Great American Traffic Jam, Victims, One Shoe Makes It Murder, Best Kept Secrets, The Diamond Trap, Call Me Anna, Murder in New Hampshire: The Pamela Smart Story, Quiet Killer, Lethal Exposure, High Stakes, On the 2nd Day of Christmas, Crazy for Christmas. *Series*: WKRP in Cincinnati (2 Emmy noms.), One Day at a Time, Head of the Class, Boston Legal. *Guest*: More than 107 appearances.

HESSINGER, GREG

Executive. b. Allentown, PA. e. Lebanon Valley College, St. John's University School of Law, law degree, with honors, 1990. From 1990 to 1994, Hessinger practiced as a labor lawyer at the New York firm of Skadden, Arps, Slate, Meagher & Flom. In 1994, he joined Westinghouse Broadcasting Company, which later merged with CBS, Inc. While at Westinghouse/CBS, he negotiated and drafted numerous collective bargaining agreements with entertainment industry unions, including AFTRA, the WGA, DGA, IATSE and IBEW. Hessinger joined the American Federation of Television & Radio Artists (AFTRA) in June 1998 as nat'l. asst. exec. dir. for News/Broadcast. He acted as chief negotiator for AFTRA's collective bargaining agreements covering network newspersons and oversaw the negotiation and administration of several hundred TV and radio contracts nationwide. He also directed all legal, legislative, and organizing activities related to news and broadcast contracts. Hessinger was appointed AFTRA'S nat'l. exec. dir. in July 2000. He became the nat'l. exec. dir. & CEO for the Screen Actors Guild, the nation's largest labor union for working actors, was ousted by the SAG board Oct. 24, 2005. 2006 he became a partner with the law firm Curley & Mullen LLP resposible for a host of emplyment issues. Currently is a partner with Reed Smith a firm that specializes in labor and employment in the entertainment business. He also sits on the nat'l. bd. of advisors of The Actors Fund.

HEWITT, JENNIFER LOVE

Actress. b. Waco, TX, Feb. 21, 1979. President of prod. co. Love Spell Entertainment.
PICTURES: Munchie, Little Miss Millions, Sister Act 2: Back in the Habit, House Arrest, Trojan War, I Know What You Did Last Summer, Telling You, Can't Hardly Wait, I Still Know What You Did Last Summer, The Suburbans, The Adventures of Tom Thumb and Thumbelina (voice), The Hunchback of Notre Dame II, The Tuxedo, Why Can't I Be Audrey Hepburn?, The Devil and Daniel Webster, Garfield, The Truth About Love, Delgo (voice), Garfield: A Tail of Two Kitties, Cafe.
TELEVISION: *Movies*: Audrey Hepburn Story, The Magic 7, A Christmas Carol, Confessions of a Sociopathic Social Climber, The Magic 7, Yes, Virginia (voice). *Series:* Kids Incorporated, Shaky Ground, The Byrds of Paradise, McKenna, Party of Five, Time of Your Life, In the Game (also exec. prod.), Ghost Whisperer, Angry Little Girls (voice, exec. prod.). *Guest*: More than 120 appearances.

HEYER, STEVEN

Executive. b. New York, NY, June 13, 1952. e. Cornell U., BS industrial relations, 1974; Stern School of Business at NYU, MBA, 1976. Various positions with Booz, Allen & Hamilton, finally senior v.p./managing partner, 1976-92. Pres./COO Young & Rubicam Adv. Worldwide and exec. VP Young & Rubicam, Inc., 1992-94. Pres., Turner Broadcasting Sales Inc., 1994-98. Pres., worldwide sales/marketing/distribution/int'l. networks, Turner Broadcasting System, 1996-98. Pres/COO Turner Broadcasting System Inc., 1998-2000 where he was instrumental in launching 14 new TV networks, including Turner South, Boomerang, CNN En Espanol, the Cartoon Network in Japan and Brazil, and a partial-day, German language version of CNN, a European and Asian version of Turner Classic Movies. Led the effort to expand company's Internet presence, introducing 19 websites for its CNN, Cartoon Network, and its Turner Classic Movie brands in various languages. Acquired NASCAR rights, the renewal of the NBA contract, and the acquisition of over 200 world broadcast premier movies for TBS and TNT. Departed Time Warner to join Coca-Cola as exec. v.p., pres. and COO, Coca-Cola Ventures, and pres., Latin American Operations. Was CEO of Starwood Hotels & Resorts Worldwide, Inc. until March 31, 2007, when he was removed by the hotel company's board. He has served as a director of Lazard Ltd and Lazard Group since June 2005. Became co-chmn & CEO of Fathom Studios and vice chmn of Mistral Acquisition Co., he also currently serves on the bd. of dir. of the National Collegiate Athletic Association and the Special Olympics.

HEYMAN, JOHN

Producer. b. Germany, 1933. e. Oxford U. Started with Independent British Television creating,. writing and producing entertainment and documentary programs. Had 5 top-ten programs 1955-57. Expanded into personal management, forming International Artists, representing Elizabeth Taylor, Richard Burton, Richard Harris, Shirley Bassey, Laurence Harvey, Trevor Howard, among others. In 1963, formed World Film Services Ltd. to produce package and finance films and World Film Sales Ltd., the first major independent film sales co. Co-financed 250 major studio films 1969-91. In 1973, formed Genesis Project. In 1989 co-founded Island World and Islet. Island sold to Polygram, and in 1994, formed World Group of Companies Ltd., parent co. to World Production Ltd.
PICTURES: Hamlet, Privilege, Boom!, Secret Ceremony, Twinky, Bloomfield, The Go-Between (Grand Prix, Cannes 1971), Superstars, Hitler: The Last Ten Days, Black Gunn, Divorce His, Divorce Hers, The Hireling (Grand Prix, Cannes 1973), A Doll's House, Daniel, Beyond the Limit, The Dresser, A Passage to India (co-prod.), Martin's Day, Steaming, D.A.R.Y.L., Saturday Night Fever, Grease, Heaven Can Wait, Home Alone, Reds, Eddie the Eagle.
TELEVISION: *Movie*: Divorce His - Divorce Hers, Never Better.

HICKS, CATHERINE

Actress. b. New York NY, Aug. 6, 1951. e. St. Mary's Notre Dame; Cornell U. (2 year classical acting prog.). On B'way. in Tribute, Present Laughter.
PICTURES: Death Valley, Better Late Than Never, Garbo Talks, The Razor's Edge, Fever Pitch, Peggy Sue Got Married, Star Trek IV: The Voyage Home, Like Father Like Son, Child's Play, She's Out of Control, Cognac, Liebestraum, Dillinger and Capone, Eight Days a Week, Turbulence, Callers, The Genesis Code.
TELEVISION: *Movies*: Love for Rent, To Race the Wind, Marilyn-the Untold Story (Emmy nom. 1981), Valley of the Dolls 1981, Happy Endings, Laguna Heat, Spy, Hi Honey I'm Dead, Redwood Curtain, For All Time, Poison Ivy: The Secret Society, Stranger with My Face. *Series*: Ryan's Hope (1976-8), The Bad News Bears, Tucker's Witch, Winnetka Road, 7th Heaven, Celebrity Dish, Pushed. *Pilot*: The Circle Game.

HICKS, SCOTT

Director, Writer, Producer. b. Australia, March 4, 1953.
PICTURES: *Director:* Down the Wind (also prodr.), Freedom, Call Me Mr. Brown (also writer), Sebastian and the Sparrow (also writer & prodr.), Shine (also writer, DGA nom.; WGA nom.; Golden Globe nom., 2 Academy Award noms. 1997), Snow Falling on Cedars, Arkansas, Hearts in Atlantis (dir. only), No Reservations, Glass: A Portrait of Philip in Twelve Parts (doc. also cinematographer), The Boys Are Back (dir.).
TELEVISION: *As Dir.: Movie:* The Plumber. *Series:* Finders Keepers. *Documentaries:* The Space Shuttle (also writer), The Ultimate Athlete: Pushing the Limit.

HIGGINS, KEN

Exhibitor. Higgins has more than 30 years of experience in the film exhibition industry. From 1971 to 1987 Higgins was employed by Santikos Theatres, a San Antonio, TX, theatre circuit. Began career as a theatre manager; gained increasingly responsible positions through the years: operations manager, director of advertising, film buyer and v.p. of film/advertising/marketing. Joined Cinemark USA, Inc., in 1987. Currently Higgins is Cinemark's V.P. & international head film buyer for the circuit, which has more than 3,000 screens in North America and an int'l. presence in Argentina, Brazil, Canada, Chile, Colombia, Costa Rica, Ecuador, El Salvador, Honduras, Mexico, Nicaragua, Panama, Peru and Taiwan.

HILL, BERNARD

Actor: b. Manchester, England, Dec. 17, 1944. Joined amateur dramatic society in Manchester then studied drama at Manchester Art Coll. Joined Liverpool Everyman rep. co. West End debut as John Lennon in John, Paul, George, Ringo... and Burt. Also in Normal Service, Shortlist, Twelfth Night, Macbeth, Cherry Orchard, Gasping, A View From the Bridge.
PICTURES: Gandhi, The Bounty, The Chain, Restless Natives, No Surrender, Bellman and True, Drowning by Numbers, Shirley Valentine, Mountains of the Moon, Double X: The Name of the Game, Skallagrigg, Madagascar Skin, The Ghost and the Darkness, The Wind in the Willows, Titanic, The Mill on the Floss, A Midsummer Night's Dream, Blessed Art Thou, True Crime, The Loss of Sexual Innocence, The Red Door, The Titanic Chronicles, Blessed Art Thou, Einstein, Going Off Big Time, The Criminal, The Scorpion King, Lord of the Rings: The Two Towers, Gothika, Lord of the Rings: The Return of the King, Wimbledon, The League of Gentlemen's Apocalypse, Save Angel Hope, The Heart of the Earth, Exodus, Save Angel Hope, Franklyn, Valkyrie, The Kid.
TELEVISION: *Movies*: Hard Labour, Professional Foul, Henry VI, Parts One, Two and Three, The Tragedy of Richard the III, Squaring the Circle, Theban Plays: Antigone, The Great White Mountain, The Fremantle Conspiracy, New World, Dirtysomething, Great Expectations, Raphael: A Mortal God, Heatwave (narr.), A Very Social Secretary, Canoe Man. *Mini-series*: I Claudius, Squaring the Circle, Gambling Man, John Lennon: A Journey in the Life, St. Luke's Gospel, The Black Stuff, Boys from the Blackstuff, Burston Rebellion, Horizon, What Sank the Kursk, Lipstick on Your Collar, The Grid. *Series*: Rooms, Fox, Play for Today, Once Upon a Time in the North, Surviving Disaster, Sunshine, Five Days. *Documentaries: As Narr.:* The Last Tommy, Secrets of the Deep, Cruel Sea: The Penlee Disaster, No Go: The Free Derry Story, 30 Greatest Political Comedies, Wild China (series), Dispatches (series), Horizon (series). *Guest:* More than 80 appearances.

HILL, DAVID

Executive. Started career in 1964 as a newspaper copy boy and police reporter for the Sydney Daily Telegraph; In 1988, Hill helped News Corp. Chairman Rupert Murdoch launch Sky Television in Britain, and when it merged with British Sky Broadcasting in 1990, Hill became the head of BSkyB Sports Channel and created Sky Sports. He then joined Fox in the U.S. in 1993. From 1997 to 1999, Hill was chmn. of Fox Broadcasting Co., overseeing programming for the network. He became chmn. of Fox Sports in 1999. At Fox Sports, Hill earned a reputation for innovation. He instituted fixed scoreboards at the bottom of the screen, the yellow first-down line in professional football and "Catcher Cam" for Major League Baseball games. In April 2005, Murdoch tapped Hill to become pres. of the newly created DirecTV Entertainment group, with a goal of beefing up the satellite TV giant's offerings. Hill remained chmn. of Fox Sports TV Group but gave up day-to-day mgt. duties. (News Corp. owns Fox and is DirecTV's largest shareholder.) In March 2007 Hill resigned his DirecTV post and returned full-time to his position as chmn. and CEO, FOX Sports.

HILL, TERENCE

Actor, Director. r.n. Mario Girotti. b. Venice, March 29, 1939. Debuted as actor under his real name. First attracted attention as actor in Visconti's The Leopard, 1963. Gained fame in European-

made westerns. Formed Paloma Films.
PICTURES: as Mario Girotti: Vacanze col Gangster (debut, 1951), Villa Borghese, Il Viale della speranza, La Vena d'oro, The Wide Blue Road, Mary Magdalene, Anna of Brooklyn, Hannibal, Pecado de amor, Carthage in Flames, Joseph and His Brethren, The Wonders of Aladdin, Seven Seas to Calais, The Leopard, Games of Desire, Last of the Renegades, Arizona Wildcat, Duell vor Sonnenuntergang, Ruf de Walder, Rampage at Apache Wells, Flaming Frontier, Whom the Gods Destroy, Blood River; as Terence Hill: The Crazy Kids of the War, Io non protesto io amo, Preparati la bara!, Rita in the West, God Forgives I Don't, Viva Django, Boot Hill, Ace High, Barbagia, Blackie the Pirate, Anger of the Wind, They Call Me Trinity, The True and the False, A Reason to Live a Reason to Die, Trinity Is Still My Name, Man of the East, Baron Blood, All the Way Boys!, My Name Is Nobody, The Two Missionaries, The Genius, Crime Busters, Mr. Billion, March or Die, Odds & Evens, I'm for the Hippopotamus, Super Fuzz, Watch Out We're Mad, Double Trouble, Don Camillo (also dir.), Miami Supercops, Renegade Luke (also exec. prod.), Go for It!, Lucky Luke (also dir.), The F(N)ight Before Christmas (also dir.), Botte di Natale, Troublemakers, Cyberflic.
TELEVISION: *Series:* Don Matteo, Don Matteo II, Don Matteo III, Don Matteo IV, L' Uomo che cavalcava nel buio, Doc West. *Guest:* More than 78 appearances.

HILL, WALTER

Director, Writer, Producer. b. Long Beach, CA, Jan. 10, 1942. e. Michigan State U.; Mexico City College; U. of the Americas.
PICTURES: *Writer:* Hickey and Boggs, Thief Who Came to Dinner, The Getaway (1972), The Mackintosh Man, The Drowning Pool, Blue City (also prod.), Alien³ (prod./s.p.), The Getaway (1993; co-s.p.), The Warriors (s.p.). *Writer/Dir.:* Hard Times, The Driver, The Warriors, Southern Comfort , 48 HRS, Streets of Fire (also exec. prod.), Red Heat (also prod.). *Director:* The Long Riders, Brewster's Millions, Crossroads, Extreme Prejudice, Johnny Handsome, Another 48 HRS, Trespass, Geronimo: An American Legend (also co-prod.), Wild Bill, Last Man Standing, Undisputed, The Prophecy (video, dir.), Supernova, Walk On, Little Sister. *Other:* Alien (prod.), Aliens (exec. prod., story), Bordello of Blood (exec. prod.), Alien: Resurrection (prod.), Tales From the Crypt Presents Demon Knight (co-exec. prod.), AVP: Alien Vs. Predator (prod.), AVPR: Aliens vs Predator - Requiem (prod.), Warriors (writer of s.p. 1979), St. Vincent.
TELEVISION: *Movies*: Two-Fisted Tales, W.E.I.R.D. World, Madso's War (dir.). *Mini-series:* Broken Trail (prod., dir.; DGA Award, Emmy Award 2007). *Series:* Dog and Cat (creator, writer), Perversions of Science, Deadwood (dir.; Emmy Award, DGA Award, 2004), Tales From the Crypt. *exec. prod.; also dir. & writer of episodes:* The Man Who Was Death, Cutting Cards, Deadline (Cable ACE Award, Best Dir.).

HILLER, ARTHUR

Director. b. Edmonton, Alberta, Can., Nov. 22, 1923. e. U. of Alberta, U. of Toronto, U. of British Columbia. Worked for Canadian Broadcasting Corp. as dir. of live tv before moving to L.A. Pres. of DGA. 1993, became pres. of AMPAS where he served until 1997. Appeared in Beverly Hills Cop III. Chartable work includes: Motion Picture and Television Fund, KCET, Amnesty International, Inner City Filmmakers, the Los Angeles Central Library's reading program, the Deaf Arts Council, The Anti-Defamation League, Los Angeles County Museum programs on film and television, Humanitas, the Streisand Centre at UCLA and the Venice Family Clinic. Received Jean Hersholt Humanitarian Award 2002. Received DGA Awards Honorary Life Member Award 1993 and Robert B. Aldrich Achievement Award 1999.
PICTURES: The Careless Years (debut, 1957), Miracle of the White Stallions, The Wheeler Dealers, The Americanization of Emily, Promise Her Anything, Penelope, Tobruk, The Tiger Makes Out, Popi, The Out-of-Towners, Love Story (Academy Award nom.; Golden Globe Award, DGA nom. 1971), Plaza Suite, The Hospital, Man of La Mancha, The Crazy World of Julius Vrooder (also co-prod.), The Man in the Glass Booth, W. C. Fields and Me, Silver Streak, Nightwing, The In-Laws (also co-prod.), Making Love, Author Author, Romantic Comedy, The Lonely Guy (also prod.), Teachers, Outrageous Fortune, See No Evil Hear No Evil, Taking Care of Business, The Babe, Married to It, Beverly Hills Cop III (actor only), Wild Bill: A Hollywood Maverick (actor only), Carpool, An Alan Smithee Film: Burn Hollywood Burn, Speakeasy (acting only), A-List, The Trouble with Frank.
TELEVISION: *Movie*: Roswell. *Series*: Matinee Theatre, Playhouse 90, Climax, Alfred Hitchcock Presents, Perry Mason, Suspicion, Goodyear Theatre, Steve Canyon, The Rifleman, Gunsmoke, Ben Casey, Empire, Rte. 66, Naked City (Emmy nom. 1962), The Third Man, The Barbara Stanwyck Show, Route 66, Insight, The Dick Powell Show, Roswell (actor only), Frank Capra's American Dream (actor only), I'm Dickens, He's Fenster, The Addams Family.

HILLMAN, WILLIAM BRYON

Writer, Director, Producer. b. Chicago, IL, Feb. 3, 1951. e. Oklahoma Military Acad., UCLA. Head of production at Intro-Media Prod.; Fairchild Ent.; Spectro Prod.; Double Eagle Ent. Corp; Excellent Films Inc.; Creative consultant for The Hit 'Em Corp. Presently head of SpectroMedia Ent.
AUTHOR: Novels: Silent Changes, The Combination, The Liar, Additives The Perfect Crime, Why Me, The Loner.
PICTURES: *Dir.-Writer:* His Name is Joey (also exec. prod.), Tis the Season (also co-prod.), Strangers (also co-prod.), Back on the Street (also co-prod.), Loner (also co-prod.), Fast & Furious, The Master, Lovelines (s.p. only), Double Exposure (also co-prod.), The Passage, Campus, The Photographer (also prod.), The Man From Clover Grove (also co-prod.), Thetus, The Trail Ride (also co-prod.), Betta Betta (also prod.), Ragin' Cajun (also co-prod.), The Adventures of Ragtime, Quigley.
TELEVISION: Working Together (pilot writer), Disco-Theque Pilot (dir., writer), Everything Will Be Alright (writer), Money (dir., writer), RIPA (writer).

HINDERY, LEO JOSEPH, JR.

Media Co. Executive. b. Springfield, Ill, Oct. 31, 1947. e. Seattle U, BA, 1969; Stanford U, MBA, 1971. With U.S. Army, 1968-70. Asst. treas., Utah Internat, 1971-80. Treas. Natomas Co., 1980-82. Exec. v.p. fin. Jefferies & Co., 1982-83. CFO with A.G. Becker Paribas, 1983-85. Chief officer. planning & fin. Chronicle Pub. Co., 1985-88. Managing general partner Intermedia Partners, 1988. Became pres., Tele-Communications, Inc. and its affiliated companies, March 1997, then pres./CEO, AT&T Broadband, the successor company to TCI. Left TCI in Oct. 1999 and became chmn. & CEO, GlobalCenter Inc. In March 2000, became pres. & CEO, Global Crossing Ltd. In the summer of 2001 he formed YES Network, the TV home of the New York Yankees where he won five executive producer Emmys for outstanding programming. Hindery resigned the position in spring 2004. Board service has included: bd. of dir., Akamai Technologies and Knowledge Universe, Inc. and chmn., GT Group Telecom. Received International Cable Executive of the Year award, 1998; Foundation Award of the International Radio & Television Society, 1998; Executive Achievement Award of the National Association of Minorities in Cable, 1998; named Cable Television Operator of the Year, 1999; National Cable Television Association Distinguished Vanguard Award for Leadership, 1999; named by Business Week as one of its "Top 25 Executives of the Year", 1999. Vice chmn., Museum of Television & Radio; member, Stanford Business School Advisory Council. He currently is managing partner of InterMedia Partners VII, LLP, which makes mid-to-large-size media investments. InterMedia Partners VII follows on InterMedia Partners I through VI which were founded by Hindery in 1988, and by 1997-1999 when they were sold, were the ninth largest cable system operator in the country. Hindery is a dir. of the Daniels Fund, the Global Business Council on HIV/AIDS, the Library of Congress Trust Fund, the Milano School of New School University, Teach for America, and Victory Junction Gang Camp. He is a U.S. Senate appointed member of the HELP Commission, which seeks to improve U.S. development assistance and food aid around the globe. He is also a dir. of West Virginia Media Holdings LLC.

HIRSCH, JUDD

Actor. b. New York, NY, March 15, 1935. e. City Coll. of New York. Degree in physics but turned to acting; studied at Amer. Acad. of Dramatic Arts., HB Studios. First acting job in 1962 in Crisis in the Old Sawmill in Estes, Colorado; then to Woodstock Playhouse, before returning to N.Y.C.
THEATRE: NY: On the Necessity of Being Polygamous, Barefoot in the Park, Scuba Duba, Mystery Play, HotL Baltimore, King of the United States, Prodigal, Knock Knock, Chapter Two, Talley's Folly (Obie Award), I'm Not Rappaport (Tony Award), Conversations With My Father (Tony Award).
PICTURES: Serpico (debut, 1973), King of the Gypsies, Ordinary People (Acad. Award nom. 1981), Without a Trace, The Goodbye People, Teachers, Running on Empty, Independence Day, Out of the Cold, Man on the Moon, A Beautiful Mind.
TELEVISION: *Movies*: The Law, Fear on Trial, Legend of Valentino, The Keegans, Sooner or Later, Marriage is Alive and Well, Brotherly Love, First Steps, The Great Escape II: The Untold Story, She Said No, Betrayal of Trust, Color of Justice, Rocky Marciano, Who Killed the Federal Theatre (narr.). *Series*: Delvecchio, Taxi (2 Emmy Awards: 1981, 1983, 3 other nom.; 5 Golden Globe nom.), Detective in the House, Dear John (Golden Globe Award 1989; 1 other nom.), George & Leo, Regular Joe, Numb3rs, Studio 60 on the Sunset Strip (pilot). *Documentaries/Specials*: The Halloween That Almost Wasn't, I Love Liberty, Coney Island. *Guest:* More than 72 appearances.

HIRSCHFIELD, ALAN J.

Executive. b. Oklahoma City, OK, Oct.10, 1935. e. U. of Oklahoma, B.A., 1957; Harvard Business School, M.B.A.,1959. Hirschfield has extensive experience in the entertainment and finance fields, specializing in management and media, publishing, oil/gas and real estate. He began his career in investment banking after college. He entered the entertainment industry in 1967 as financial v.p. & director and CEO for Warner/Seven Arts; v.p. & dir., American Diversified Enterprises, 1969-73; pres. & CEO, Columbia Pictures Inc., 1973-78; consultant, Warner Communications, 1979. Hirschfield then joined Twentieth Century Fox Film Corporation as vice chairman in 1980 and was chairman and CEO from 1982-1986. From 1986-1990, he was a consultant/investor in the entertainment/media fields. From 1990-1992 he was the managing director of investment bankers

Wertheim Schroder & Co., Inc., From 1992-2000 he was involved with the Data Broadcasting Corporation, which merged with Financial Time/Pearsons Inc., to become Interactive Data Corp. He has served on various corporate boards, and has been a dir. of the Grand Teton Music Festival; has been v.p. and dir. of the Lymphoma Research Foundation and is a former trustee of the Dana-Farber Cancer Institute. Hirschfield has been a dir. of Carmike Cinemas, Inc. since April 2002 and currently serves as the chmn. of its audit committee, and a member of the exec. committee. He currently serves on the boards of directors of Cantel Medical Corp. (Vice-Chairman) and Leucadia National Corporation, a diversified holding company

HIRSHAN, LEONARD

Theatrical Agent. b. New York, NY, Dec. 27, 1927. e. NYU. Joined William Morris Agency as agent trainee, New York, 1951. Agent legit theatre & TV dept. 1952-54. Sr. exec. agent M.P. dept., California office, 1955; sr. v.p., 1983; head of m.p. dept., West Coast, 1986; named exec. v.p. and mem. bd. of dir., William Morris Agency, 1989; mem. bd. of dir., Center Theater Group, 1988; bd. governors Cedars-Sinai Hospital in L.A. 1987. Formed own management company, Leonard Hirshan Management, 2001, and still represents entertainment legends like Clint Eastwood and Sophia Loren.

HITZIG, RUPERT

Producer, Director. b. New York, NY, Aug. 15, 1942. e. Harvard. At CBS as doc. writer-prod.-dir.; later moved into dramas and comedy. Was Alan King's partner in King-Hitzig Prods. from mid 1970s - 1980. Currently Hitzig is pres., Rupert Productions, Los Angeles, CA.
PICTURES: *Producer:* Electra Glide in Blue, Happy Birthday Gemini, Cattle Annie and Little Britches, Wolfen (also 2nd unit dir.), Jaws 3-D, The Last Dragon, The Squeeze, Static. *Director:* Night Visitor, Backstreet Dreams, The Legend of O.B. Taggart, Nowhere Land.
TELEVISION: Much Ado About Nothing, The Wonderful World of Jonathan Winters, Playboy After Dark, How to Pick Up Girls, Return to Earth, Saturday Night Live, Birds of Prey, Date My Dad, Save Our Streets, Snakes and Ladders (prod., dir.), Real Stories of the Highway Patrol, NASCAR Victory Lane: All Access; annual comedy awards, TV series and numerous specials.

HOBBS, LANDEL C.

Executive. b. Fort Worth, TX. e. Angelo State University (San Angelo, TX), B.A. degree, 1984. From 1984-1990, senior mgr. with KPMG Peat Marwick. 1991-1993, senior v.p. & audit director for Banc One Illinois Corporation. From 1993-2000, senior v.p., controller & chief accounting officer for Turner Broadcasting System, Inc. Hobbs then became v.p., financial analysis & operations support for AOL Time Warner, where he oversaw budgeting,financial forecasts and profit improvement for the various AOL Time Warner divisions including AOL, Warner Bros., Time Warner Cable, Warner Music, Time, Inc., HBO, Turner, New Line Cinema and the WB Network. In 2001 Hobbs became executive v.p. & CFO for Time Warner Cable. He was responsible for finance, accounting, treasury, tax, facilities and information technology. In Aug. 2005 Hobbs was promoted to COO and is the position he holds today. Time Warner Cable Inc. is the second-largest cable operator in the U.S. and an industry leader in developing and launching innovative video, data and voice services. The system reaches approximately 26 million homes. He also serves as chairman of C-SPANS executive committee and serves on the Boards of Canoe Ventures, LLC, Women in Cable & Telecommunications (WICT) and the CTAM Education Foundation.

HOBERMAN, DAVID

Executive, Producer. b. 1953. Started career as prod. exec. with TAT Communications for five years. 1982-85, worked as m.p. agent with Writers and Artists Agency and later at Ziegler Associates and ICM. 1985, named v.p. of prod. for Walt Disney Pictures based at studio. 1987, promoted to sr. v.p., prod. 1988, named president, production. 1989, pres. Touchstone Pictures. 1994, appointed head of all motion pictures produced by Walt Disney. Resigned from Disney, 1995, to form Mandeville Films, where he was CEO. Went to MGM in 1999. In 2002, Hoberman re-formed Mandeville Films and Television at The Walt Disney Studios. Mandeville released the box office hit Bringing Down the House, Raising Helen, and The Last Shot at Disney, as well as Walking Tall and Beauty Shop at MGM. Hoberman is the creator and exec. prod. of the USA Network orig. series Monk. He is also a professor with UCLA's grad. school in the producers program. Member: bd. of the Starbright Foundation (for over 10 years); serves on the collections & acquisitions committee at L.A.'s Museum of Contemporary Art and has sat on the bd. of the Los Angeles Free Clinic. In Jan. 2006, Hoberman joined the bd. of the Anxiety Disorders Association of America.
PICTURES: *Producer:* American Raspberry (assoc. prod., 1977), Mr. Wrong (exec. prod.), The Sixth Man, George of the Jungle, Senseless, The Negotiator, I'll Be Home for Christmas, The Other Sister (exec. prod.), Antitrust (exec. prod.), What's the Worst That Could Happen (also exec. prod.), Original Sin (exec. prod.), Bandits, Moonlight Mile, Bringing Down the House, Walking Tall, Raising Helen, The Last Shot, Beauty Shop, Eight Below, The Shaggy Dog, Five Fingers (exec. prod.), The Heaven Project, Traitor, Beverly Hills Chihuahua, The Lazarus Project, The Proposal, Surrogates, Beverly Hills Chihuahua 2, The Fighter.
TELEVISION: *Exec. Prod.: Movies:* Toothless, Brink!, A.K.A., 187 Detroit. *Series:* Ryan Caulfield: Year One, Monk.

HOCK, MORT

Executive. Blaine-Thompson Agency; A. E. Warner Bros., 1948; David Merrick B'way Prod., 1958; asst. adv. mgr., Paramount Pictures Corp., 1960; adv. mgr., United Artists Corp., 1962; dir. adv., UA Corp., 1964; adv. dir., Paramount, 1965; v.p. adv. & PR, Paramount, 1968-71; v.p., marketing, Rastar Prods., 1971; exec. v.p., Charles Schlaifer & Co., 1974; sr. v.p. entertainment div., DDB Needham Worldwide Advertising, 1983; exec. v.p. DDB, 1994.

HODGE, PATRICIA

Actress. b. Cleethorpes, Lincolnshire, England, Sept. 29, 1946. Studied at London Acad. of Music and Dramatic Arts.
THEATRE: Popkiss, Two Gentlemen of Verona, Pippin, The Mitford Girls, Benefactors, Noel and Gertie, Separate Tables, The Prime of Miss Jean Brodie.
PICTURES: The Elephant Man, Betrayal, Sunset, Thieves in the Night, Diamond's Edge, The Leading Man, Lies and Whispers, Jilting Joe, Before You Go, N-Day.
TELEVISION: *Movies:* The Naked Civil Servant, Let's Face the Music of..., The One and Only Phyllis Dixey, Rumpole's Return, The Death of a Heart, Behind Enemy Lines, Hotel Du Lac, Thieves in the Night, The Heat of the Day, The Shell Seekers, The Secret Life of Ian Fleming, The Cloning of Joanna May, The Moonstone, The People's Passion, The Falklands Play, Marple: The Sittaford Mystery, Maxwell. *Mini-series:* Disraeli: Portrait of a Romantic, Edward and Mrs. Simpson, The Life and Loves of a She-Devil. *Series:* Rumpole of the Bailey, The Other 'Arf, Holding the Fort, Jemima Shore Investigates, Rich Tea and Sympathy, The Legacy of Reginald Perrin, Sweet Medicine, Miranda. *Documentary/Special:* RIP 2002, An Audience with Victoria Wood. *Guest:* More than 58 appearances.

HOFFMAN, DUSTIN

Actor. b. Los Angeles, CA, Aug. 8, 1937. m. actress Lisa Gottsegen. e. Los Angeles Conservatory of Music, Santa Monica Coll., Pasadena Playhouse, 1958. Worked as an attendant at a psychiatric institution, a demonstrator in Macy's toy dept., and a waiter. First stage role 1960 in Yes Is for a Very Young Man at Sarah Lawrence Coll. Acted in summer stock, television and dir. at community theatre. Asst. dir. Off-B'way of A View From the Bridge. Recipient of the Golden Globe Cecil B. DeMille Award, 1997.
THEATRE: *B'way and Off B'way:* A Cook for Mr. General (bit part, B'way debut), Harry Noon and Night, Journey of the Fifth Horse (Obie Award), Eh? (Vernon Rice & Theatre World Awards), Jimmy Shine, All Over Town (dir. only), Death of a Salesman (Drama Desk Award), The Merchant of Venice (also London).
PICTURES: The Tiger Makes Out (debut, 1967), Madigan's Millions, The Graduate (Academy Award nom.; Golden Globe Award, 1 other nom. 1968), Midnight Cowboy (Academy Award nom.; Golden Globe nom. 1970), John and Mary (Golden Globe nom. 1970), Little Big Man, Who Is Harry Kellerman and Why Is He Saying Those Terrible Things About Me?, Straw Dogs, Alfredo Alfredo, Papillon, Lenny (Academy Award nom.; Golden Globe nom. 1975), All the President's Men, Marathon Man (Golden Globe nom. 1977), Straight Time, Agatha, Kramer vs. Kramer (Academy Award; Golden Globe Award, 1980), Tootsie (Academy Award nom.; Golden Globe Award 1983), Ishtar, Rain Man (Academy Award; Golden Globe Award, 1989), Family Business, Dick Tracy, Billy Bathgate, Hook (Golden Globe nom. 1992), Hero, Outbreak, American Buffalo, Sleepers, Mad City, Wag the Dog (Academy Award nom.; Golden Globe nom. 1998), Sphere, Being John Malkovich, The Messenger: The Story of Joan of Arc, Shylock, Tuesday, Goldwyn, Moonlight Mile, Confidence, Runaway Jury, Finding Neverland, Meet the Fockers, The Lost City, Racing Stripes (voice), I Heart Huckabee's, Perfume: The Story of a Murderer, Stranger Than Fiction, Kung Fu Panda (voice), Mr. Magorium's Wonder Emporium, The Tale of Despereaux (voice), Last Chance Harvey (Golden Globe nom. 2009), Jews and Baseball: An American Love Story (narr.), Barney's Version, Meet the Fockers Sequel, Kung Fu Panda: The Kaboom of Doom (voice).
TELEVISION: *Movies*: The Point (narrator), Death of a Salesman (Emmy Award, 1 other nom.; Golden Globe Award, 1986), AFI's 100 Years, 100 Laughs: America's Funniest Movies. *Series*: Liberty's Kids: Est. 1776 (voice). *Specials*: Journey of the Fifth Horse, The Star Wagons, Free to Be You and Me, Bette Midler: Old Red Hair Is Back, Common Threads: Stories from the Quilt (narrator), The Earth Day Special, The Devil's Arithmetic (exec. prod., Emmy nom. 2000). *Guest*: More than 202 appearances.

HOFFMAN, MARK

Executive. e. B.A. degree in sociology, Univ. of California, Berkeley. M.A. degree in journalism, Univ. of Missouri. From 1983-1987 Hoffman served in a number of senior news mgt. positions at the ABC-owned stations in Chicago (WLS-TV) and New York (WABC-TV). From 1987-1991, news director at WAGA-TV in Atlanta, where the station won the Emmy Award for

Best News Operation and was considered one of the strongest CBS affiliates in the country. 1991-1993, Hoffman served as news director at WBBM-TV in Chicago. From 1993-1995 Hoffman served as v.p., news at KNBC-TV in Los Angeles, where the news team won the Emmy Award for Best Newscast during his tenure. Hoffman was v.p. and gen. mgr. of KDNL-TV in St. Louis, 1995-1996. In 1997, Hoffman became executive producer for CNBC post-market hours where he oversaw programming for "Market Wrap" and "The Edge," which he developed and launched, along with "Business Center." In 1999, Hoffman was v.p. and managing editor, business news for CNBC. At that time, he also served as acting pres. and managing director for CNBC Europe and developed and launched the digital cable network CNBC World. In 2001, became pres. and gen. mgr. of WVIT/NBC30, NBC's owned and operated station in Connecticut. Hoffman returned to CNBC and was named president in Feb. 2005 and is the position he holds today. He reports directly to Jeff Zucker, president and CEO of NBC Universal.

HOFFMAN, PHILIP SEYMOUR

Actor. b. Fairport, NY, July 23, 1967.
THEATRE: Defying Gavity, The Merchant Of Venice, Henry V, Mother Courage, Shopping And Fucking (off B'way), True West, Long Day's Journey into Night. *Dir. Off-B'way:* Jesus Hopped the A Train, The Glory of Living.
PICTURES: Triple Bogey On A Par Five Hole, My New Gun, Szuler, Scent of a Woman, Leap of Faith, My Boyfriend's Back, Money for Nothing, Joey Breaker The Getaway, The Yearling, Nobody's Fool, When A Man Loves A Woman, The Fifteen Minute Hamlet, Twister, Hard Eight, Boogie Nights (SAG nom.), Montana, Next Stop Wonderland, The Big Lebowski, Happiness, Patch Adams, Culture, Flawless, Magnolia (SAG nom.), The Talented Mr. Ripley, State And Main, Almost Famous (SAG nom.), Last Party 2000, Love Liza, Punch-Drunk Love, The Sweet Spot, Red Dragon, The 25th Hour, Voltage, Owning Mahowny, Captured, Cold Mountain, Along Came Polly, Strangers with Candy, Capote (also exec. prod., Academy Award, Golden Globe Award, 2006), Mission: Impossible III, The Savages, Before the Devil Knows You're Dead, Charlie Wilson's War (Academy Award nom.; Golden Globe nom. 2008), Synecdoche, New York, Doubt (Academy Award nom.; Golden Globe nom. 2009), Pirate Radio, Mary and Max (voice), The Invention of Lying, Jack Goes Boating (also exec. prod., dir.).
TELEVISION: *Movies*: The Yearling, Empire Falls (Emmy nom. 2005). *Mini-series*: LIBERTY! The American Revolution. *Guest:* More than 74 appearances.

HOGAN, P.J.

Director, Writer. b. Australia, 1962.
PICTURES: Getting Wet, The Humpty Dumpty Man, Sloth, Vicious!, Proof (unit dir.), Sloth (dir.), Muriel's Wedding (WGA nom. 1996), My Best Friend's Wedding (dir.), Unconditional Love, Peter Pan, Confessions of a Shopaholic (dir.).
TELEVISION: *Movies:* Philadelphia General (dir., exec. prod.), Nurses (dir., exec. prod.), The American Mall (writer). *Series/Writer*: The Flying Doctors, Skirts, The Miraculous Mellops, Lift Off.

HOLBROOK, HAL

Actor. r.n. Harold Rowe Holbrook Jr. b. Cleveland, OH, Feb. 17, 1925. m. the late actress Dixie Carter. e. Denison U., 1948. Summer stock 1947-53. Gained fame and several awards for performance as Mark Twain on stage in Mark Twain Tonight over a period of years throughout the U.S. and abroad.
THEATRE: Mark Twain Tonight (Tony Award, 1966), Do You Know the Milky Way?, Abe Lincoln in Illinois, American Shakespeare Fest., Lincoln Center Repertory (After the Fall, Marco Millions, Incident at Vichy, Tartuffe), The Glass Menagerie, The Apple Tree, I Never Sang For My Father, Man of La Mancha, Does a Tiger Wear a Necktie?, Lake of the Woods, Buried Inside Extra, The Country Girl, King Lear. Regional: Our Town, The Merchant of Venice, Uncle Vanya, Eye of God.
PICTURES: The Group (debut, 1966), Wild in the Streets, The People Next Door, The Great White Hope, They Only Kill Their Masters, Jonathan Livingston Seagull (voice), Magnum Force, The Girl From Petrovka, All the President's Men, Midway, Julia, Rituals (The Creeper), Capricorn One, Natural Enemies, The Fog, The Kidnapping of the President, Creepshow, The Star Chamber, Girls Night Out (The Scaremaker), Wall Street, The Unholy, Fletch Lives, The Firm, Carried Away, Hercules (voice), Cats Don't Dance, Eye of God, Judas Kiss, Hush, The Florentine, The Bachelor, Walking to the Waterline, Waking the Dead, Men of Honor, The Majestic, Purpose, Shade, Our Country (documentary short, narrator), Silent Wings: The American Glider Pilots of World War II (narr.), Into the Wild (Academy Award nom. 2008), Killshot, Flying Lessons, That Evening Sun, Good Day for It.
TELEVISION: *Movies*: Coronet Blue, The Whole World is Watching (Emmy nom. 1969), A Clear and Present Danger (Emmy nom. 1971), Travis Logan, Suddenly Single, Goodbye Raggedy Ann, That Certain Summer (Emmy nom. 1973), Murder by Natural Causes, Legend of the Golden Gun, When Hell Was in Session, Off the Minnesota Strip, The Killing of Randy Webster, Under Siege, Behind Enemy Lines, Dress Gray, The Fortunate Pilgrim, Three Wishes for Billy Grier, Emma, Queen of the South Seas, Day One, Sorry Wrong Number, A Killing in a Small Town, Bonds of Love, A Perry Mason Mystery: The Case of the Lethal Lifestyle, A Perry Mason Mystery: The Case of the Grimacing Governor, A Perry Mason Mystery: The Case of the Jealous Jokester, She Stood Alone: The Tailhook Scandal, Beauty, My Own Country, Haven, The Street Lawyer, Captain Cook's Extraordinary Atlas. *Mini-series:* North and South Books I & II, Celebrity, George Washington, Rockport Christmas, Lewis & Clark: The Journey of the Corps of Discovery, The Third Twin, Founding Fathers, Mark Twain. *Series*: The Bold Ones: The Senator (Emmy Award, 1971), Designing Women, Portrait of America (4 annual ACE Awards, 2 Emmy Awards, 1988, 1989), Evening Shade, Hercules (voice). *Specials*: Mark Twain Tonight (Emmy nom. 1967), Pueblo (2 Emmy Awards, 1974), Sandburg's Lincoln (Emmy Award, 1976), Our Town (Emmy nom. 1978), Plaza Suite, The Glass Menagerie, The Awakening Land (Emmy nom. 1978), The Oath: 33 Hours in the Life of God, Omnibus. *Guest:* More than 142 appearances.

HOLDRIDGE, LEE

Composer. b. Port-au-Prince, Haiti, March 3, 1944. e. Manhattan School of Music. Music arranger for Neil Diamond, 1969-73, with whom he collaborated on the score for Jonathan Livingston Seagull. Wrote score for B'way musical Into the Light (1986). With Alan Raph wrote score for the Joffrey Ballet's Trinity. One-act opera for L.A. Opera commission: Journey to Cordoba.
PICTURES: Jeremy, Jonathan Livingston Seagull, Forever Young Forever Free, Mustang Country, The Other Side of the Mountain—Part 2, The Pack, Moment By Moment, Oliver's Story, French Postcards, Tilt, American Pop, The Beastmaster, Mr. Mom, Micki and Maude, Splash, Sylvester, 16 Days of Glory, Transylvania 6-5000, The Men's Club, Big Business, Old Gringo, Pastime, Freefall, The Long Way Home, Family Plan, The Company, I Have Never Forgotten You: The Life & Legacy of Simon Wiesenthal (doc.), Brothers at War (doc.).
TELEVISION: *Movies/Mini-series*: East of Eden, Fly Away Home, The Day the Loving Stopped, For Ladies Only, The Sharks, The Story Lady, One Against the Wind, In Love With an Older Woman, Running Out, Thursday's Child, Wizards and Warriors, The Mississippi, Legs, I Want to Live, Letting Go, Fatal Judgment, The Tenth Man, I'll Take Manhattan, Do You Know the Muffin Man? (Emmy nom. 1990), Incident at Dark River, A Mother's Courage, World of Discovery (doc., Emmy Award 1991), In the Arms of a Killer, Face of a Stranger, Deadly Matrimony, Killer Rules, One Against the Wind, Call of the Wild (Emmy nom. 1993), Torch Song, Barcelona '92: 16 Days of Glory, Jack Reed: Badge of Honor, Incident in a Small Town, The Yearling, Heidi, Texas, Buffalo Girls (Emmy nom. 1995), The Tuskegee Airmen (Emmy nom. 1996), Nothing Lasts Forever, Twilight of the Golds, Into Thin Air, A Christmas Memory, Two for Texas, Her Own Rules, Replacing Dad, Mutiny (Emmy nom. 1999), Blue Moon, Love Letters, Atomic Train, Sealed with a Kiss, Anya's Bell, A Gift of Love: The Daniel Huffman Story, Take Me Home: The John Denver Story, Into the Arms of Strangers: Stories of the Kindertransport, The Mists of Avalon (Emmy nom. 2002), The Pilot's Wife, Almost a Woman, Sounder, 10.5, The Brooke Ellison Story, See Arnold Run, Saving Milly. *Series*: One Life to Live (2 Emmy Awards; 5 other noms.), Hec Ramsey, Moonlighting (Emmy nom. (pilot), 1985), Beauty and the Beast (Emmy Award, 1 other nom. 1988), Bob (Emmy nom. 1993), American Family, Korgoth of Barbaria (pilot). *Special:* Atlanta's Olympic Glory (Emmy Award 1998).

HOLLAND, AGNIESZKA

Director, Writer. b. Warsaw, Poland, Nov. 28, 1948. e. FAMU, Prague. Studied filmmaking in Czechoslovakia. Worked in Poland with dir. Andrzej Wajda. Moved to Paris in 1981.
PICTURES: *Dir./s.p.:* Screen Tests, Provincial Actors, Bez Znieczulenia (s.p. only), A Woman Alone (co-s.p.), Danton (co-s.p.), Interrogation (actor only), A Love in Germany (co-s.p.), Angry Harvest (co-s.p.), Anna (only s.p., story), Les Possedes (only co-s.p.), La Amiga (only co-s.p.), To Kill a Priest (co-s.p.), Korczak (s.p. only), Europa Europa (Academy Award nom. 1992), Olivier Olivier, Three Colors: Blue (s.p. only)The Secret Garden (dir. only), Total Eclipse (dir. only), Washington Square (dir. only), The Third Miracle (dir. only), Julie Walking Home, Golden Dreams (dir. only), The True Story of Janosik and Uhorcik, Magnificat, Copying Beethoven, Hidden (dir. only).
TELEVISION: *Movies*: Evening With Abdon, The Children of Sunday, Something for Something, Lorenzaccio, The Trial, Largo Desolato, Shot in the Heart (dir. only), A Girl Like Me: The Gwen Araujo Story(dir. only), Treme (dir.). *Series*: *Dir.:* Fallen Angels, Veronica Mars, The Wire, Cold Case. *Documentary:* Total Eclipse.

HOLLAND, TODD

Director. b. 1961.
PICTURES: The Wizard, Krippendorf's Tribe, Firehouse Dog.
TELEVISION: *Movies*: Kilroy, The Time Tunnel (also exec. prod.), Pizza Time (exec. prod.), Miss/Guided (also exec. prod.), Fugly. *Series*: Amazing Stories, Vietman War Story, Max Headroom, Tales from the Crypt, Twin Peaks, Eerie Indiana, Bill & Ted's Excellent Adventures, The Larry Sanders Show (Emmy Award, 1998, 6 other nom.; 4 DGA nom.), My So-Called Life, Friends, Maximum Bob, Felicity, Malcolm in the Middle (2 Emmy Awards;

1 other nom.; DGA Award 2002, 1 other nom.), D.C., Freaky Links (pilot), Ball & Chain, Wonderfalls (also exec. prod., creator, WGA nom. 2005 for episode), Girls Club, Miss Guided (exec. prod. episodes dir.), 30 Rock (Emmy nom. 2009 for episode) Sons of Tucson (exec. prod., dir.).

HOLLAND, TOM
Director, Writer. b. Highland, NY, July 11, 1945. e. Northwestern U. Started as actor, working at Bucks County Playhouse in PA and HB Studios in NY. Appeared on daytime serials Love of Life, Love is a Many-Splendored Thing. Turned to commercial prod. while attended UCLA law school, then took up screenwriting.
PICTURES: *Writer*: The Beast Within, The Class of 1984, Pyscho II (also actor), Scream for Help, Cloak and Dagger. *Director:* Fright Night (also s.p.), Fatal Beauty, Child's Play (also co-s.p.), The Temp, Stephen King's Thinner (also s.p.), Hatchet 2 (actor only).
TELEVISION: *Movies*: The Stranger Within, The Initiation of Sarah. *Mini-series*: Stephen King's The Langoliers (also writer, actor), The Stand. *Series*: Tales From the Crypt (dir. 3 episodes: Love Come Hack to Me-also co-writer, Four-Sided Triangle-also co-writer, King of the Road).

HOLLIMAN, EARL
Actor. b. Delhi, LA, Sept. 11, 1928. e. U. of Southern California, Pasadena Playhouse. Pres., Actors and Others for Animals.
THEATRE: Camino Real (Mark Taper Forum), A Streetcar Named Desire (Ahmanson).
PICTURES: Scared Stiff, The Girls of Pleasure Island, Destination Gobi, East of Sumatra, Devil's Canyon, Tennessee Champ, The Bridges at Toko-Ri, Broken Lance, The Big Combo, I Died a Thousand Times, Forbidden Planet, Giant, The Burning Hills, The Rainmaker (Golden Globe Award 1957), Giant, Gunfight at the OK Corral, Trooper Hook, Don't Go Near the Water, Hot Spell, The Trap, Last Train From Gun Hill, Visit to a Small Planet, Armored Command, Summer and Smoke, The Sons of Katie Elder, A Covenant With Death, The Power, Anzio, The Biscuit Eater, Good Luck Miss Wyckoff, Sharky's Machine, Bad City Blues, The Perfect Tenant.
TELEVISION: *Movies*: Tribes, Alias Smith and Jones, Cannon, The Desperate Mission, Trapped, Cry Panic, I Love You... Goodbye, Alexander: The Other Side of Down, The Solitary Man, Where the Ladies Go, Country Gold, Gunsmoke: Return to Dodge, American Harvest, P.S. I Luv You (pilot). *Mini-series*: The Thorn Birds. *Series*: Hotel de Paree, Wide Country, Police Woman, P.S. I Luv You, Delta (Golden Globe nom. 1993), Night Man. *Pilot:* Twilight Zone. *Specials*: The Dark Side of the Earth, The Return of Ansel Gibbs, Intimate Portrait: Lisa Hartman Black (himself). *Guest:* More than 85 appearances.

HOLLINGER, MARK
Executive. e. B.A. degree, summa cum laude, history and political science, Colgate Univ.; J.D., Yale Law School. Hollinger was a sr. associate in the ent. dept. of the law firm Paul, Weiss, Rifkind, Wharton & Garrison in New York City. He also lectured on entertainment law at Columbia Law School. 1991, Hollinger joined Discovery Communications as v.p. and deputy general counsel. In 1994, Hollinger became acting general mgr. for Discovery Channel Asia. Based in Hong Kong, he was responsible for overseeing and coordinating all activities related to the operation and launch of Discovery Channel Asia. Back in the U.S. in 1995, Hollinger was appointed v.p., international business development in addition to his role as v.p., deputy general counsel. Hollinger became Discovery's general counsel and was also given responsibility for Discovery's business affairs group in 1996. He assumed responsibility for the production mgt. dept. in 1999 and was named executive v.p., corporate operations in 2001. From 2003-2007, Hollinger was senior executive v.p., corporate operations and general counsel. He then became pres., global businesses and operations, and general counsel. In 2008, Hollinger was promoted to company COO. 2009 he became President and CEO of Discovery Networks International. He oversees Discovery Networks Intl. and Discovery Commerce, and manages all corporate operations. He also has responsibility for Discovery Studios, including the Discovery Films unit and Discovery's internal content production operations.

HOLLY, LAUREN
Actress. b. Bristol, PA, October 28, 1963.
PICTURES: Seven Minutes in Heaven, Band of the Hand, The Adventures of Ford Fairlane, Dragon: The Bruce Lee Story, Dumb & Dumber, Sabrina, Beautiful Girls,Down Periscope, Turbulence, A Smile Like Yours, No Looking Back, Entropy, Any Given Sunday, The Last Producer, What Women Want, Colored Eggs, Don't Cry For Me, Changing Hearts, Pavement, Counting Sheep, In Enemy Hands, Down and Derby, The Chumscrubber, The Godfather of Green Bay, The Pleasure Drivers, Fatwa, Chasing 3000, Raising Flagg, The Least Among You, The Perfect Age of Rock 'n' Roll, You're So Cupid!, Scream of the Banshee.
TELEVISION: *Movies*: Archie: To Riverdale and Back Again, Fugitive Among Us, Dangerous Heart, Vig, King of Texas, Santa Jr., Just Desserts Caught in the Act, Bounty Hunters, Untitled Camryn Manheim Pilot, Before You Say 'I Do', Too Late to Say Goodbye. *Mini-series*: Jackie, Ethel, Joan: The Women of Camelot. *Series*: All My Children (Emmy nom. 1988), The Antagonists, Picket Fences, Chicago Hope, Rocky Point, NCIS: Naval Criminal Investigative Service. *Guest:* More than 53 appearances.

HOLM, CELESTE
Actress. b. New York, NY, Apr. 29, 1919. e. Univ. Sch. for Girls, Chicago, Francis W. Parker, Chicago, Lyceae Victor Durui (Paris), U. of Chicago, UCLA. p. Theodor Holm and Jean Parke Holm. m. actor Wesley Addy.
THEATRE: *B'way:* Gloriana, The Time of Your Life, 8 O'Clock Tuesday, Another Sun, Return of the Vagabond, My Fair Ladies, Papa Is All, All the Comforts of Home, The Damask Cheek, Oklahoma!, Bloomer Girl, She Stoops to Conquer, Affairs of State, Anna Christie, The King and I, Interlock, Third Best Sport, Invitation to a March, Mame, Candida, Habeas Corpus, The Utter Glory of Morrissey Hall, I Hate Hamlet. *Off-B'way:* A Month in the Country. Theatre-in-Concert for the U.S. State Department in 8 countries May-July 1966. *Regional:* Janet Flanner's Paris Was Yesterday. Natl. Tour: Mame (Sarah Siddons Award), Hay Fever, Road to Mecca, Cocktail Hour.
PICTURES: Three Little Girls in Blue (debut, 1946), Carnival in Costa Rica, Gentleman's Agreement (Academy Award, best supporting actress; Golden Globe Award 1948), Road House, The Snake Pit, Chicken Every Sunday, Come to the Stable (Academy Award nom. 1950), A Letter to Three Wives (voice), Everybody Does It, Champagne for Caesar, All About Eve (Academy Award nom. 1951), The Tender Trap, High Society, Bachelor Flat, Doctor You've Got To Be Kidding, Tom Sawyer, Bittersweet Love, The Private Files of J. Edgar Hoover, Three Men and a Baby, Once You Meet a Stranger, Broadway: The Golden Age by the Legends Who Were There, Still Breathing, Alchemy, My Guaranteed Student Loan, Driving Me Crazy.
TELEVISION: *Movies*: Underground Man, Death Cruise, Love Boat II, Midnight Lace, The Shady Hill Kidnapping, This Girl for Hire, Murder by the Book, Polly, Polly-Comin' Home!, Home of the Brave, Once You Meet a Stranger. *Pilot:* Road Show. *Mini-series*: Backstairs at the White House (Emmy nom. 1979). *Series*: Honestly Celeste, Who Pays, Nancy, Jessie, Falcon Crest, Christine Cromwell, Loving, Promised Land, The Beat. *Specials*: A Clearing in the Wood, Play of the Week, Cinderella, Nora's Christmas Gift. *Guest*: More than 128 appearances.

HOLM, SIR IAN
C.B.E. Actor. r.n. Ian Holm Cuthbert. b. Ilford, Essex, England, Sept. 12, 1931. e. RADA. On British stage in Love Affair, Titus Andronicus, Henry IV, Ondine, Becket, The Homecoming (B'way: Tony Award, 1967), Henry V, Richard III, Romeo and Juliet, The Sea. Knighted, 1998.
PICTURES: The Bofors Gun (debut, 1968), A Midsummer Night's Dream, The Fixer, Oh! What a Lovely War, A Severed Head, Nicholas and Alexandra, Mary Queen of Scots, Young Winston, The Homecoming, Juggernaut, Robin and Marian, Shout at the Devil, March or Die, Alien, Chariots of Fire (Academy Award nom. 1982), Time Bandits, Return of the Soldier, Greystoke: The Legend of Tarzan Lord of the Apes, Dance With a Stranger, Wetherby, Dreamchild, Brazil, Laughterhouse, Another Woman, Henry V, Hamlet, Kafka, Naked Lunch, The Advocate, Mary Shelley's Frankenstein, The Madness of King George, Big Night, Night Falls On Manhattan, The Fifth Element, The Sweet Hereafter, A Life Less Ordinary, Joe Gould's Secret, eXistenZ, The Match, Wisconsin Death Trip, Shergar, Joe Gould's Secret, Esther Kahn, Beautiful Joe, Bless the Child, From Hell, The Emperor's New Clothes, The Lord of the Rings: The Fellowship of the Ring, The Lord of the Rings: The Return of the King, The Day After Tomorrow, The Aviator, Strangers with Candy, Chromophobia, Lord of War, Renaissance (voice), The Treatment, O Jerusalem, Ratatouille, This Side of the Looking Glass.
TELEVISION: *Movies*: Frankenstein, Les Miserables, S.O.S. Titanic, All Quiet on the Western Front, Man in the Iron Mask, Thief of Bagdad, Inside the Third Reich, Soft Targets, Mr. and Mrs. Edgehill, The Browning Version, Murder by the Book, The Endless Game, The Last Romantics, Uncle Vanya, The Deep Blue Sea, A Season of Giants, The Borrowers, The Return of the Borrowers, King Lear (Emmy nom. 1999), The Miracle Maker (voice), Alice Through the Looking Glass, Animal Farm (voice), The Last of the Blonde Bombshells (Emmy nom. 2001), D-Day 6.6.1944, Dragons: A Fantasy Made Real (narr. UK version). *Mini-series:* War of the Roses, Napoleon and Love, Jesus of Nazareth, Holocaust, The Lost Boys, We the Accused, Stalin, The Churchills (narr.). *Series:* The Wars of the Roses, The Man from Haven, The Bell, Television (narr.), Game Set and Match, Timewatch. *Documentaries:* Strike!, The Fever, The Seas of Zanzibar, Hiroshima: The Decision to Drop the Bomb, There Is a Light That Never Goes Out, Prisoner of Paradise. *Specials*: Tailor of Gloucester, The Unforgettable Joan Sims. *Guest:* More than 91 appearances.

HOLMES, KATIE
Actress. r.n. Kate Noelle Holmes. b. Toledo, OH, Dec. 18, 1978. m. actor Tom Cruise.
THEATRE: *NY:* All My Sons (debut).
PICTURES: The Ice Storm, Disturbing Behavior, Go, Muppets From Space, Teaching Mrs. Tingle, The Gift, The Wonder Boys, Abandon, Phone Booth, The Singing Detective, Pieces of April,

First Daughter, Batman Begins, Thank You for Smoking, Shame on You, Mad Money, The Extra Man, The Romantics (exec. prod.), Don't Be Afraid of the Dark, Son of No One.
TELEVISION: *Movies*: Christmas in Washington, Overrated in '06. *Series*: Dawson's Creek, Disney's Hercules (voice). *Guest:* More than 64 appearances.

HOLOFCENER, NICOLE

Director, Writer. b. New York, NY, March 22, 1960. e. NYU School of Film.
PICTURES: Hannah and Her Sisters (apprentice editor), Walking and Talking (dir., writer), Lovely & Amazing (dir., writer), Friends with Money (dir., writer), Please Give (dir., writer).
TELEVISION: *Series:* Ready or Not, Cold Feet, Sex and the City, Leap of Faith.

HOOKS, KEVIN

Actor, Director. b. Philadelphia, PA, Sept. 19, 1958. Son of actor-dir. Robert Hooks.
PICTURES: Sounder, Aaron Loves Angela, A Hero Ain't Nothin' But a Sandwich, Take Down, Innerspace, Strictly Business (also dir.), Passenger 57 (dir. only), Fled, Glory & Honor (also dir.), Black Dog (dir. only), Lie Detector.
TELEVISION: *Movies*: Just an Old Sweet Song, The Greatest Thing That Almost Happened, Friendly Fire, Can You Hear the Laughter?-The Story of Freddie Prinze, Roots: The Gift (dir.), Murder Without Motive: The Edmund Perry Story (dir.), Glory and Honor, Mutiny (dir.), The Color of Friendship (dir., DGA nom.; Emmy Award 2000), Sounder (dir., prod. DGA Award nom. 2004; Golden Globe nom. 1973)). *Mini-series*: Backstairs at the White House. *Series*: The White Shadow, He's the Mayor, The Hoop Life (dir.), City of Angels (dir.), Soul Food (dir.), Philly (dir.), Without A Trace (dir. only), Dragnet (dir., co-exec. prod.), 24 (episode dir.), Lincoln Heights (also pilot), Prison Break (exec. prod., dir., co-exec. prod.), Human Target (exec. prod., dir. episodes). *Special*: Home Sweet Homeless (dir.).

HOOKS, ROBERT

Actor, Director, Producer. b. Washington, D.C., April 18, 1937. Father of actor-dir. Kevin Hooks. Co-founder and exec. dir. Negro Ensemble Co. NY 1967-present. Founder DC Black Repertory Company, 1970-77. Co-star of TV series NYPD, 1967-69.
THEATRE: *B'way:* A Raisin In the Sun (B'way debut, 1960), A Taste of Honey, Tiger Tiger Burning Bright, Arturo Ui, The Milktrain Doesn't Stop Here Anymore, Where's Daddy? (Theatre World Award for last two), Hallelujah, Baby?. *Off B'way.:* The Blacks, Dutchman, Happy Ending, Day of Absence, Henry V, Ballad for Bimshire, Kongi's Harvest. A Soldier's Play (Mark Taper Forum, LA). Co-prod. (with Gerald S. Krone): Song of the Lusitanian Bogey, Daddy Goodness, Ceremonies in Dark Old Men, Day of Absence, The Sty of the Blind Pig, The River Niger, The First Breeze of Summer.
PICTURES: Sweet Love Bitter, Hurry Sundown, The Last of the Mobile Hot-Shots, Trouble Man, Aaron Loves Angela, Airport '77, Fast-Walking, Star Trek III: The Search For Spock, Passenger 57, Posse, Fled, Seventeen Again.
TELEVISION: *Movies*: Carter's Army, Vanished, The Cable Car Murder, Crosscurrent, Trapped, Ceremonies in Dark Old Men, Just an Old Sweet Song, The Killer Who Wouldn't Die, The Courage and the Passion, To Kill a Cop, A Woman Called Moses, Hollow Image, Madame X, The Oklahoma City Dolls, The Sophisticated Gents, Cassie and Co., Starflight-The Plane that Couldn't Land, Feel the Heat, Sister Sister, The Execution, Abandoned and Deceived, Glory and Honor, Free of Eden. *Series:* N.Y.P.D., Supercarrier, Seinfeld, Parenthood, Family Matters, Different World, Murder She Wrote, The Hoop Life. *Pilots:* The Cliff Dweller, Two for the Money, Down Home. *Guest:* More than 81 apearances.

HOOL, LANCE

Producer, Director. b. Mexico City, Mex., May 11, 1948. e. Univ. of the Americas.
PICTURES: *Producer:* Cabo Blanco, Ten to Midnight, The Evil That Men Do, Missing in Action (also s.p.), Missing in Action 2 (dir.), Steel Dawn (also dir.), Options, Damned River, Pure Luck, The Air Up There, Gunmen, Road Flower, Flipper, McHale's Navy, One Man's Hero, Crocodile Dundee in Los Angeles. *Exec. prod.:* Broken Lizard's Club Dread (also unit dir.), Man on Fire.
TELEVISION: *Movies*: The Tracker, Born To Run, Cover Girl Murders, Flashfire, Caught in the Act.

HOOPER, TOBE

Director. b. Austin, Texas, Jan. 25, 1943. e. Univ. of TX. Began film career making documentary and industrial films and commercials in Texas. Was asst. dir. of U. of Texas film program, continuing filmmaking while working with students. First feature film: documentary Peter Paul & Mary, followed by Eggshells. Directed Billy Idol video Dancing With Myself.
PICTURES: The Texas Chainsaw Massacre (also prod., co-s.p.), Eaten Alive (Death Trap), The Funhouse, Poltergeist, Lifeforce, Invaders from Mars, The Texas Chainsaw Massacre Part 2 (also co-prod., co- music), Spontaneous Combustion, Sleepwalkers (actor only), Night Terrors, The Mangler (also co-s.p.), Crocodile, The Toolbox Murders, Brew, Mortuary, The Texas Chainsaw Massacre: The Beginning.
TELEVISION: *Movies*: Salem's Lot, I'm Dangerous Tonight, Body Bags, The Apartment Complex, Shadow Realm. *Mini-series*: Taken. *Series:* The Equalizer, Freddy's Nightmares, Nowhere Man,Dark Skies, Perversions of Science, Masters of Horror. *Episodes:* Amazing Stories, No More Mr. Nice Guy, No Place Like Home, Tales from the Crypt, The Others, Night Visions, Masters of Horror. *Pilot*: Haunted Lives.

HOPE, TED

Producer. b. 1962.
PICTURES: Tiger Warsaw (assoc. prod.), The Unbelievable Truth, (1st asst. dir.), Theory of Achievement, Surviving Desire, Ambition, Pushing Hands (Tui Shou), I Was on Mars (also actor), Simple Men, The Wedding Banquet, Roy Cohn/Jack Smith, Eat Drink Man Woman, (assoc. prod.), Amateur, Safe (exec. prod.), The Brothers McMullen (exec. prod.), Flirt, Walking and Talking, She's the One, Little Cobras, Arresting Gena, The Myth of Fingerprints (exec. prod.), The Ice Storm, Office Killer, Love God, No Looking Back, The Lifestyle (exec. prod.), Ride with the Devil, The Tao of Steve, In the Bedroom, Storytelling, Human Nature, Lovely & Amazing, American Splendor (also exec. prod.), 21 Grams, The Door in the Floor, The Devil and Daniel Johnston (doc.), Thumbsucker (exec. prod.), Friends with Money, A Dirty Shame, The Hawk Is Dying (exec. prod.), Fast Track, The Savages, Towelhead, Fay Grim (exec. prod.) The Ex, Adventureland, Super, Longfellow (exec. prod.).
TELEVISION: *Movie:* Punch and Judy Get Divorced, The Laramie Project (Emmy nom. 2002). *Series:* Monsters (asst. dir.).

HOPKINS, SIR ANTHONY

C.B.E.: Actor. r.n. Philip Anthony Hopkins. b. Port Talbot, South Wales, Dec. 31, 1937. Trained at Royal Acad. of Dramatic Art; Welsh Coll. of Music & Drama. Joined National Theatre, gaining fame on stage in England, then TV and films. Appeared in short The White Bus. Recordings: Under Milk Wood (1988), Shostakovich Symphony No. 13 Babi Yar (reciting Yevtushenko's poem, 1994). *Dir.:* An Evening With Dylan Thomas, 1993. Evening Standard Film Awards Special Award for Body of Work, 1994; BAFTA Britannia Award for Outstanding Contribution to the International Film and TV Industry, 1995. Received Golden Globe: Cecil B. DeMille Award 2006. Several BAFTA Awards including special award at Montreal Film Festival for Career Excellence, 1992; Academy Fellowship Award 2008.
THEATRE: Julius Caesar (debut, 1964), Juno and the Paycock, A Flea in Her Ear, The Three Sisters, Dance of Death, As You Like It, The Architect and the Emperor of Assyria, A Woman Killed With Kindness, Coriolanus, The Taming of the Shrew, Macbeth, Equus (NY, 1974-75; Outer Critics Circle, NY Drama Desk, U.S. Authors & Celebrities Forum Awards), Equus (LA 1977, also dir.; LA Drama Critics Award), The Tempest, Old Times, The Lonely Road, Pravda (Variety Club Stage Actor Award, 1985; British Theatre Association Best Actor, Laurence Olivier & Observer Awards), King Lear, Antony and Cleopatra, M. Butterfly, August (also dir.), Timon Of Athens (London).
PICTURES: The Lion in Winter (debut, 1967), The Looking Glass War, Hamlet, When Eight Bells Toll, Young Winston, A Doll's House, The Girl from Petrovka, Juggernaut, Audrey Rose, A Bridge Too Far, International Velvet, Magic (Golden Globe nom. 1979), The Elephant Man, A Change of Seasons, The Tenth Man (Golden Globe nom. 1989) The Bounty (Variety Club UK Film Actor Award, 1983), 84 Charing Cross Road (Moscow Film Fest. Award, 1987), The Good Father, The Dawning, A Chorus of Disapproval, Desperate Hours, The Silence of the Lambs (Academy Award, Golden Globe nom.; Natl. Board of Review, NY Film Critics, Boston Film Critics & BAFTA Awards, 1991), Freejack, One Man's War, Howards End, The Efficiency Expert (Spotswood), Bram Stoker's Dracula, Chaplin, The Remains of the Day (Golden Globe nom.; BAFTA, Variety Club UK Film Actor, LA Film Critics, Japan Critics Awards, 1993), The Trial, Shadowlands (Natl. Board of Review & LA Film Critics Award, 1993, BAFTA, Best Actor-Leading, 1994), The Road to Wellville, Legends of The Fall, The Innocent, Nixon (Academy Award nom.; Golden Globe nom. 1996) August (also dir.), Surviving Picasso, The Edge, Amistad (Golden Globe nom. 1998), Meet Joe Black, The Mask of Zorro, Instinct, Titus, How the Grinch Stole Christmas (voice), Mission Impossible 2, Hannibal, Hearts in Atlantis, The Devil and Daniel Webster, Red Dragon, Bad Company, The Human Stain, Alexander, Proof, The World's Fastest Indian, Bobby, All the King's Men, Slipstream Dream (also dir., writer), Fracture, Beowulf, City of Your Final Destination, The Last Station, Bare Knuckles, The Wolfman, Hemingway & Fuentes, You Will Meet a Tall Dark Stranger, Thor.
TELEVISION: *Movies:* A Flea in Her Ear, The Great Inimitable Mr. Dickens, The Three Sisters, Danton, Uncle Vanya, Decision to Burn, Possessions, The Arcata Promise, A Heritage and Its History, Hearts and Flowers, Find Me, Cuculus Canorus, Lloyd George, A Childhood Friend, Dark Victory, All Creatures Great and Small, The Lindbergh Kidnapping Case (Emmy Award, 1976), Victory at Entebbe, Kean, Mayflower: The Pilgrim's Adventure, The Bunker (Emmy Award, 1981), Peter and Paul, Othello, The Hunchback of Notre Dame (Emmy nom. 1982), Little Eyolf, A Married Man, Corridors of Power, Strangers and Brothers, Guilty Conscience, Blunt, Arch of Triumph, Mussolini: The Rise and Fall of Il Duce (ACE Award), Across the Lake, The Dawning, Heartland, The Tenth Man, One Man's War, To Be the

Best, Selected Exits, Big Cats. *Mini-series:* The Edwardians, War and Peace, QB VII, Hollywood Wives, Great Expectations (Emmy nom. 1990). *Series:* Freedom: A History of Us (doc.). *Guest:* More than 176 appearances.

HOPKINS, BO

Actor. b. Greenwood, SC, Feb. 2, 1942. Studied with Uta Hagen in N.Y. then with Desilu Playhouse training school in Hollywood. Parts in several prods. for that group won him an agent, an audition with dir. Sam Peckinpah and his first role in latter's The Wild Bunch.
PICTURES: The Wild Bunch (debut, 1969), Monte Walsh, The Moonshine War, The Culpepper Cattle Co., The Getaway, White Lightning, The Man Who Loved Cat Dancing, American Graffiti, The Nickel Ride, The Day of the Locust, Posse, The Killer Elite, A Small Town in Texas, Tentacles, Midnight Express, More American Graffiti, The Fifth Floor, Sweet Sixteen, Night Shadows, Trapper Country, What Comes Around, War, The Bounty Hunter, The Stalker, Nightmare at Noon, The Tenth Man, Big Bad John, Center of the Web, Inside Monkey Zetterland, The Ballad of Little Jo, Cheyenne Warrior, Radioland Murders, Riders in the Storm, The Feminine Touch, Ben Johnson: Third Cowboy on the Right, Painted Hero, Fever Lake, U Turn, Uncle Sam, Lunker Lake, Phantoms, The Newton Boys, Getting to Know You, Time Served, South of Heaven West of Hell, Big Brother Trouble, Vice, The Thundering 8th, Ring of Fire, A Crack in the Door, Land of Canaan, Choosing Matthias, Don't Let Go, Mending Fences (also prod.), The Road Home, Shade (also exec. prod.).
TELEVISION: *Movies*: The Runaway Barge, Kansas City Massacre, Charlie's Angels (pilot), The Invasion of Johnson County, Dawn: Portrait of a Teenage Runaway, Thaddeus Rose and Eddie, Crisis in Sun Valley, Plutonium Incident, A Smoky Mountain Christmas, Beggerman Thief, Down the Long Hills, Last Ride of the Dalton Gang, Casino, Rodeo Girl, Ghost Dancing, Blood Ties, Movie Lover's Road Trip (himself, 2003), Cheyenne Warrior, OP Center, Shaughnessy, Time Served. *Series*: Doc Elliott, The Rockford Files, Dynasty. *Special*: Wyatt Earp: Return to Tombstone. *Guest:* More than 66 appearances.

HOPPER, DENNIS

Actor, Director. b. Dodge City, KS, May 17, 1936. e. San Diego, CA, public schools. Author: Out of the Sixties (1988; book of his photographs).
PICTURES: Rebel Without a Cause, I Died a Thousand Times, Giant, The Steel Jungle, The Story of Mankind, Gunfight at the OK Corral, From Hell to Texas, The Young Land, Key Witness, Night Tide, Tarzan and Jane Regained Sort Of, The Sons of Katie Elder, Queen of Blood, Cool Hand Luke, Glory Stompers, The Trip, Panic in the City, Hang 'Em High, True Grit, Easy Rider (also dir., co-s.p. Academy Award nom.; WGA nom.; DGA nom. 1970), The Last Movie (also dir., s.p.), Kid Blue, James Dean-The First American Teenager, Bloodbath (The Sky Is Falling), Mad Dog Morgan, Tracks, The American Friend, Douleur Chair, The Sorcerer's Appentices, L'Ordre et la Securite du Monde, Resurrection, Apocalypse Now, Out of the Blue (also dir.), King of the Mountain, Renacida, White Star, Human Highway, Rumble Fish, The Osterman Weekend, My Science Project, The Texas Chainsaw Massacre Part 2, Hoosiers (Academy. Award nom.; Golden Globe nom. 1987), Blue Velvet (Golden Globe nom. 1987), Black Widow, River's Edge, Straight to Hell, The Pick Up Artist, O.C. and Stiggs, Riders of the Storm, Blood Red, Colors (dir. only), Flashback, Chattachoochee, The Hot Spot (dir. only), Superstar: The Life and Times of Andy Warhol, The Indian Runner, Hearts of Darkness: A Filmmaker's Apocalypse, Midnight Heat, Eye of the Storm, Boiling Point, Super Mario Bros., True Romance, Red Rock West, Chasers (also dir.), Speed, Search and Destroy, Waterworld, Acts of Love, Basquiat, Carried Away, Star Truckers, The Blackout, Tycus, Meet the Deedles, The Source, The Prophet's Game, Lured Innocence, Jesus' Son, Bad City Blues, EDtv, Straight Shooter, Luck of the Draw, Listen With Your Eyes, Choke, Ticker, Knockaround Guys, Unspeakable, My Little Hollywood, LAPD: To Protect and to Serve, I Don't Know Jack, Firecracker, One Giant Leap, The Piano Player, Knockaround Guys, Leopold Bloom, Dumping Ground, Out of Season, The Keeper, The Crow: Wicked Prayer, Americano, House of 9, Legacy, Closing the Ring, Land of the Dead, 10th & Wolf, Hell Ride, Sleepwalking, Elegy, The Palermo Shooting, Forever, Swing Vote, An American Carol, The Last Film Festival (also prod.), Alpha and Omega.
TELEVISION: *Movies*: Wild Times, Stark, Stark: Mirror Image, Paris Trout (Emmy nom. 1991), Nails, Doublecrossed, Backtrack (also dir.), Nails, The Heart of Justice, Witch Hunt, Samson and Delilah, Jason and the Argonauts, Firestarter 2: Rekindled, The Piano Player, Suspense, The Last Ride, Gorillaz: Live in Manchester (narr.). *Series*: The Lieutenant, Flatland, E-Ring, Crash. *Guest*: More than 280 appearances.
(d. May 29, 2010)

HORN, ALAN

Executive. b. 1944. e. M.B.A. (awarded with distinction), Harvard Bus. School. Began career in brand management with Proctor & Gamble, then five years in the U.S. Air Force, rank of Captain. Entered entertainment as an executive for Tandem Prods., T.A.T. Communications, and as CEO for Embassy Communications (with Norman Lear and Jerry Perenchio), 1973-86. In 1986, he served as pres. & COO of 20th Century Fox Film Corp. Left 20th Century in 1987 to form Castle Rock Ent. as a co-founder, chair & CEO (1987-99). Named to current position of pres. & COO, Warner Bros. Entertainment, Inc. in Oct. 1999. He oversees all of Warner Bros.' theatrical and home ent. operations, including Warner Bros. Pictures (worldwide theatrical prod., distribution and marketing), Warner Independent Pictures, Warner Premiere (the studio's direct-to-DVD prod. arm) and Warner Home Video (with operations in 90 int'l. territories). Under Horn's leadership Warner Bros. Pictures' domestic and international divisions each had their sixth consecutive billion dollar-plus years at the box office (2006), and Warner Home Video was the industry's marketshare leader. In 2004, Horn received the Will Rogers Motion Picture Pioneers Foundation's Pioneer of the Year Award. Horn serves on the bd. of dir. of Univision Communications; as a Vice Chairman of the Natural Resources Defense Council (NRDC); on the bd. of trustees for the Autry National Center in Los Angeles; and the advisory bd. of the National Museum of the American Indian. He served for six years as a member of the Harvard Business School Board of Associates and in May 2007 received that group's Leadership Award. Horn is also a founding bd. member of the Environmental Media Association. Horn is also a member of the Acad. of Television Arts & Sciences , Acad. of Motion Picture Arts & Sciences, AFI, the Hollywood Radio and Television Society & the Museum of Broadcasting.

HORNER, JAMES

Composer. b. Los Angeles, CA, Aug. 14, 1953. e. Royal Col. of Music: London, USC, UCLA. Received Grammy Awards for the song Somewhere Out There (from the film An American Tail), and for instrumental composition from Glory. Has won 19 ASCAP awards for his film compositions and 3 Grammy Awards with 4 other noms.
PICTURES: The Lady in Red, Battle Beyond the Stars, Humanoids From the Deep, Deadly Blessing, The Hand, Wolfen, The Pursuit of D.B. Cooper, 48 HRS, Star Trek II: The Wrath of Khan, Something Wicked This Way Comes, Krull, Brainstorm, Testament, Gorky Park, The Dresser, Uncommon Valor, The Stone Boy, Star Trek III: The Search for Spock, Heaven Help Us, Cocoon, Volunteers, Journey of Natty Gann, Commando, Aliens (Academy Award nom. 1987), Where the River Runs Black, The Name of the Rose, An American Tail (Academy Award nom.; Golden Globe nom. 1987), P.K. and the Kid, Project X, Batteries Not Included, Willow, Red Heat, Vibes, Cocoon: The Return, The Land Before Time, Field of Dreams (Academy Award nom. 1990), Honey I Shrunk the Kids, Dad, Glory (Golden Globe nom. 1990), I Love You to Death, Another 48 HRS., Once Around, My Heroes Have Always Been Cowboys, Class Action, The Rocketeer, An American Tail: Fievel Goes West (Golden Globe nom.1992), Thunderheart, Patriot Games, Unlawful Entry, Sneakers, Swing Kids, A Far Off Place, Jack the Bear, Once Upon a Forest, Searching for Bobby Fischer, The Man Without a Face, Bopha!, The Pelican Brief, Clear and Present Danger, Legends of the Fall (Golden Globe nom. 1995), Braveheart (Academy Award nom.; Golden Globe nom. 1996), Casper, Apollo 13 (Academy Award nom. 1996), Jumanji, Courage Under Fire, Ransom, To Gillian on Her 37th Birthday, Titanic (2 Academy Awards, Best Dramatic Score, Best Orig. Song, 2 Golden Globe Awards, Best Orig. Score, Best Orig. Song, Chicago Film Crits. Award, Best Musical Score, 1998), The Devil's Own, Deep Impact, The Mask of Zorro, Mighty Joe Young, Bicentennial Man, The Perfect Storm, How the Grinch Stole Christmas, Enemy at the Gates, A Beautiful Mind (Academy Award nom.; Golden Globe nom. 2002), Iris, indtalkers, Four Feathers, The Land Before Time: Journey to Big Water (video), Soul Calibur, Beyond Borders, Radio, The Missing, House of Sand and Fog (Academy Award nom. 2004), Bobby Jones, Stroke of Genius, Troy, The Forgotten, The Chumscrubber, Flightplan, Legend of Zorro, The New World, All the King's Men, 10 Items or Less (soundtrack writer, song), Apocalypto, The Life Before Her Eyes (conduct.), The Good Shepherd, In Bloom, The Spiderwick Chronicles, Night at the Museum: Battle of the Smithsonian (soundtrack writer), Capitalism: A Love Story (doc., soundtrack writer), Avatar (Academy Award nom.; 2 Golden Globe noms. 2010), The Boy in the Striped Pyjamas (also conduct.), The Karate Kid.
TELEVISION: *Movies:*Angel Dusted, A Few Days in Weasel Creek, A Piano for Mrs. Cimino, Rascals and Robbers: The Secret Adventures of Tom Sawyer and Huck Finn, Between Friends, Surviving, Extreme Close-Up, Freedom Song. *Series:* Shelley Duvall's Faerie Tale Theatre, Amazing Stories, Tales from the Crypt, Fish Police, Crossroads (theme), CBS Evening News with Katie Couric. Many episode credits as soundtrack writer.

HOROWITZ, JIMMY

Executive. e. Tulane University, B.A. in political science, cum laude, 1983. George Washington University Law School, J.D. degree. Practiced labor law at Manatt, Phelps, et.al. and later at Greenberg Glusker, et.al. until 1990. Horowitz was counsel for the Alliance of Motion Picture and Television Producers before joining Universal Pictures in 1992 in the feature legal department. In Oct. 1999, he was named senior v.p., business & legal affairs. Horowitz was appointed executive v.p., business & legal affairs for Universal Pictures in Jan. 2002, where he was responsible for the day-to-day operations of the business & legal affairs departments, in addition to overseeing all matters relating to Universal's term deals. In July 2006, Horowitz was appointed co-president, production, and executive v.p. Universal Pictures. 2010 he was promoted to President of the movie studio. He will work in concert with Chairman Adam Fogelson, Co-Chairwoman Donna Langley and Chief Operating Officer Rick Finkelstein in helping strategize and execute domestic business initiatives and manage the day-to-day business operations.

HORTON, PETER

Actor, Director, Producer. b. Bellevue, DC, Aug. 20, 1953. e. Univ. of CA, Santa Barbara. Stage work includes appearances with Lobero Rep. Co. Theatre in Santa Barbara, Butterflies Are Free in L.A.
PICTURES: Serial, Fade to Black, Split Image, Children of the Corn, Where the River Runs Black, Amazon Women on the Moon (also co-dir.), Sideout, Singles, The Cure (dir. only), The Baby-sitters Club, 2 Days in the Valley, Death Benefit, T-Rex: Back to the Cretaceous, The Siege, The Dust Factory.
TELEVISION: *Movies*: She's Dressed to Kill, Miracle on Ice, Freedom, Choices of the Heart, Children of the Dark, Crazy Horse, One Too Many (dir. only), Murder Live!, Into Thin Air: Death on Everest, Sawyer and Finn (pilot), Capital City, While I Was Gone, Dirty Sexy Money (pilot), True Blue (dir.). *Mini-series*: From the Earth to the Moon. *Series*: Seven Brides for Seven Brothers, thirtysomething (also dir.), The Wonder Years (dir. only), Class of '96 (dir., actor), Brimstone (also prod.), The Geena Davis Show, Karen Sisco, MDs, Grey's Anatomy (co-exec. prod./also pilot; 2 DGA noms.; 3 Emmy noms.), Deterioration of the Fight or Flight Response (dir., exec. prod.), Masquerade (consult. prod.), Six Degrees (consult., exec. prod.), The Philanthropist (exec. prod. also pilot).

HOSKINS, BOB

Actor. b. Bury St. Edmunds, Suffolk, England, Oct. 26, 1942. Porter and steeplejack before becoming actor at 25. Veteran of Royal Shakespeare Co. Appeared with Britain's National Theatre (Man Is Man, King Lear, Guys and Dolls.)
PICTURES: The National Health (debut, 1973), Royal Flash, Inserts, Zulu Dawn, The Long Good Friday, Pink Floyd: The Wall, Beyond the Limit, Lassiter, The Cotton Club, Brazil, Sweet Liberty, Mona Lisa (Academy Award nom.; Golden Globe Award 1987), A Prayer for the Dying, The Lonely Passion of Judith Hearne, Who Framed Roger Rabbit (Golden Globe nom. 1989), The Raggedy Rawney (also dir., co-s.p.), Heart Condition, Mermaids, Shattered, The Inner Circle, The Favor the Watch and the Very Big Fish, Hook, Passed Away, Super Mario Bros., The Rainbow, The Secret Agent, Nixon, Balto (voice), Joseph Conrad's The Secret Agent, Michael, Spice World (cameo), Twenty Four Seven, Parting Shots, Captain Jack, Cousin Bette, The White River Kid, A Room for Romeo Bass, American Virgin, Felicia's Journey, Enemy at the Gates, Last Orders, The Sleeping Dictionary, Where Eskimos Live, Maid in Manhattan, Tortoise vs. Hare, Den of Lions, Danny the Dog, Beyond the Sea, Stay, Son of the Mask, Elizabeth Rex, Mrs. Henderson Presents (Golden Globe nom. 2006), Garfield: A Tail of Two Kitties (voice), Hollywoodland, Ruby Blue, Sparkle, Outlaw, Go Go Tales, Doomsday, A Christmas Carol, Made in Dagenham.
TELEVISION: *Movies:* The Bankrupt, Her Majesty's Pleasure, Schmoedipus, Cry Terror, Othello, New Scotland Yard, The Beggar's Opera, On the Move, Rock Follies, Mussolini: The Decline and Fall of Il Duce, The Dunera Boys, The Changeling, In the Looking Glass, Napoleon, Mussolini, Tube Tales, David Copperfield, Noriega: God's Favorite, Don Quixote, The Lost World, The Good Pope: Pope John XXIII, The Wind in the Willows, Pinocchio. *Mini-series:* Shoulder to Shoulder, Pennies from Heaven, Flickers, The Englishman's Boy. *Series:* Villains, Thick as Thieves, Big Jim and the Figaro Club (narr.), The Forgotten Toys. *Documentaries:* The Secret Policeman's Third Ball (narr.), World War II: When Lions Roared. *Guest:* More than 90 appearances.

HOU, HSIAO-HSIEN

Director. b. Meixian, China, April 8, 1947.
PICTURES: Cute Girl, Cheerful Wind, Six is Company (s.p. only), Growing Up (s.p., prod. only), The Green Green Grass of Home, All the Youthful Days, The Sandwich Man, A Summer at Grandpa's, The Time to Live and the Time to Die (also s.p.), Dust in the Wind, Daughter of the Nile, City of Sadness, Raise the Red Lantern (exec. prod. only), Dust of Angels (exec. prod. only), The Puppetmaster, A Borrowed Life (exec. prod. only), Good Men Good Women, Heartbreak Island (s.p., exec. prod. only), Goodbye South Goodbye, Flowers of Shanghai, Borderline (prod. only), Mirror Image (co-exec. prod.), Millenium Mambo, Three Times, Orsay, Flight of the Red Balloon (also writer), To Each His Cinema (segment dir.), One Day (exec. prod.).

HOUGH, JOHN

Director. b. London, England,, Nov. 21, 1941. Worked in British film prod. in various capacities; impressed execs. at EMI-MGM Studios, Elstree, London, so was given chance to direct The Avengers series for TV. Began theatrical films with Sudden Terror for prod. Irving Allen, 1971.
PICTURES: Sudden Terror, The Practice, Twins of Evil, Treasure Island, The Legend of Hell House, Dirty Mary Crazy Larry, Escape to Witch Mountain, Return From Witch Mountain, Brass Target, The Watcher in the Woods, The Incubus, Triumphs of a Man Called Horse, Biggles: Adventures in Time, American Gothic, Howling IV—The Original Nightmare, The Backyard (doc., exec. prod.), Something to Believe In (also prod., writer), Bad Karma, The Human Race (exec. prod.).
TELEVISION: *Movies*: A Distant Scream, Czech Mate, Black Carrion, Black Arrow, A Hazard of Hearts (also co-prod.), The Lady and the Highwayman (also prod.), A Ghost in Monte Carlo (also prod.), Duel of Hearts (also prod.). *Series*: The Avengers, The Champions, The Protectors, The Zoo Gang, The New Avengers, Dempsey & Makepeace. *Documentaries*: Making the Return Trip, What's a Carry On? (exec. prod.), Lovely War (prod.), Mr. Thunderbird: The Gerry Anderson Story (exec. prod.).

HOUNSOU, DJIMON

Actor. b. Benin, West Africa, April 24, 1964. Was model before he began acting.
PICTURES: Without You I'm Nothing, Unlawful Entry, Stargate, Amistad (Golden Globe nom. 1998), Ill Gotten Gains, Deep Rising, Gladiator, The Middle Passage, Dead Weight, Four Feathers, In America (Academy Award nom. 2004), Heroes (short), Biker Boyz, Lara Croft Tomb Raider: The Cradle of Life, Blueberry, Constantine, Beauty Shop, The Island, Eragon, Blood Diamond (Academy Award nom. 2007), Never Back Down, Push, The Tempest, Elephant White.
TELEVISION: *Series*: ER, Black Panther.

HOWARD, ARLISS

Actor. r.n.Leslie Richard Howard. b. Independence, MO, Oct. 18, 1955. e. Columbia Col., MO. m. actress Debra Winger.
THEATRE: American Buffalo, Lie of the Mind.
PICTURES: The Prodigal, Sylvester, Door to Door, The Ladies Club, The Lightship, Full Metal Jacket, Plain Clothes, Tequila Sunrise, Men Don't Leave, For the Boys, Ruby, Crisscross, The Sandlot, Wilder Napalm, Natural Born Killers, Wet, To Wong Foo—Thanks for Everything—Julie Newmar, Johns, Beyond the Call, The Lost World: Jurassic Park, Amistad, The Lesser Evil, A Map of the World, Big Bad Love, Dandelion, Birth, Weapons, Awake, The Time Traveler's Wife.
TELEVISION: *Movies*: Hands of a Stranger, I Know My First Name is Steven, Somebody Has to Shoot the Picture, Iran: Days of Crisis, Till Death Us Do Part, Those Secrets, The Infiltrator, The Man Who Captured Eichmann, Old Man, You Know My Name, The Song of the Lark, Word of Honor, Dawn Anna. *Series:* Medium.

HOWARD, CLINT

Actor. b. Burbank, CA, Apr. 20, 1959. Brother is dir. Ron Howard. Father is actor Rance Howard.
PICTURES: An Eye for an Eye, Gentle Giant, The Jungle Book (voice), Winnie the Pooh and the Blustery Day (voice), The Wild Country, The Grand Auto Theft, The Many Adventures of Winnie the Pooh (voice), Harper Valley P.T.A., Rock 'n' Roll High School, Evil Speak, Night Shift, Flip Out, Spalsh, Cocoon, Gung Ho, The Wraith, End of the Line, Freeway, B.O.R.N.,An Innocent Man, Parenthood, Tango and Cash, Silent Night Deadly Night 4: Initiation, Disturbed, Backdraft, The Rocketeer, Silent Night Deadly Night 5: The Toy Maker, Voice of a Stranger, Far and Away, Ticks, Forced to Kill, Carnosaur, Leprechaun 2, The Paper, Bigfoot: The Unforgettable Encounter, Not Like Us, The Ice Cream Man, Fist of the North Star, Dillinger and Capone, Digital Man, Baby Face Nelson, Forget Paris, Apollo 13, Twisted Love, That Thing You Do!, Rattled, Barb Wire, Unhook the Stars, Santa with Muscles, The Protector, Austin Powers: International Man of Mystery, Telling You, Twilight, The Dentist II, The Waterboy, Sparkle and Charm, Fortune Hunters, Austin Powers: The Spy Who Shagged Me, Arthur's Quest, Edtv, The Million Dollar Kid, My Dog Skip, Little Nicky, How the Grinch Stole Christmas, Sparkle and Charm, Ping!, Blackwoods, Austin Powers in Goldmember, Home Room, The House of the Dead, Searching for Haizmann, You'll Never Wiez in This Town Again (documentary), The Great Commission, Big Paw: Beethoven 5 (video), The Missing, The Sure Hand of God, Raising Genius, My Big Fat Independent Movie, Molding Clay, Taking Charge, Planet Ibsen (also co-prod.), Cinderella Man, Curious George (voice), Cinderella Man, Fun with Dick and Jane, Church Ball, How to Eat Fried Worms, Music Within, Halloween, A Plumm Summer, London Betty (narr.), Super Capers, Play the Game, Foreign Exchange, Holyman Undercover, The Haunted World of El Superbeasto (voice), Frost/Nixon, Ashley's Ashes, Alabama Moon, Super Capers, Night at the Museum: Battle of the Smithsonian, Speed-Dating, Pumping Up, Last Call, Bloodrayne: The Third Reich, House of Good and Evil (dir.), Night Club.
TELEVISION: *Movies*: The Red Pony, Huckleberry Finn, The Death of Richie, Cotton Candy (also writer), Skyward, Little White Lies, Cheyenne Warrior, Sawbones, Humanoids from the Deep, Rattled, Rapsittie Street Kids: Believe In Santa (voice), Skip Tracer, Arthur's Quest, Fur on the Asphalt: The Greg the Bunny Reunion Show. *Mini-series*: From the Earth to the Moon, The Clint Howard Variety Show (also exec. prod., dir.). *Series*: The Andy Griffith Show, The Baileys of Balboa, Gentle Ben, Salty, The Cowboys, Gung Ho, Space Rangers, Comedy Central

Roast of William Shatner. *Guest*: More than 102 appearances.

HOWARD, JAMES NEWTON

Composer. b. Los Angeles, CA, June 9, 1951. Started as keyboard player for Elton John, before composing and producing for such artists as Cher, Diana Ross, Barbra Streisand, Chaka Khan, Randy Newman. Has 31 ASCAP Awards: 1994-2006.
PICTURES: Tough Guys, Nobody's Fool, Head Office, Wildcats, 8 Million Ways to Die, Five Corners, Campus Man, Promised Land, Off Limits, Tap, Some Girls, Everybody's All-American, Major League, The Package, Marked for Death, Pretty Woman, Coupe de Ville, Flatliners, Three Men and a Little Lady, Dying Young, The Man in the Moon, My Girl, The Prince of Tides (Academy Award nom. 1992), Grand Canyon, Guilty by Suspicion, King Ralph, Dying Young, The Man in the Moon, Glengarry Glen Ross, Night and the City, American Heart, Diggstown, Alive, Falling Down, Dave, The Fugitive (Academy Award nom. 1994), The Saint of Fort Washington, Intersection, Wyatt Earp, Junior (Academy Award nom; Golden Globe nom. 1995), Restoration, Just Cause, Outbreak, Eye for an Eye, The Juror, Primal Fear, The Trigger Effect, The Rich Man's Wife, Space Jam, One Fine Day (Academy Award nom.; Golden Globe nom. 1997), Dante's Peak, Liar Liar, Fathers' Day, My Best Friend's Wedding (Academy Award nom. 1998), The Devil's Advocate, The Postman, Snow Falling on Cedars, A Perfect Murder, Runaway Bride, Stir of Echoes, The Sixth Sense, Mumford, Snow Falling on Cedars, Wayward Son, Dinosaur, Unbreakable, Vertical Limit, Atlantis: The Lost Empire, America's Sweethearts, Big Trouble, Signs, Treasure Planet, Unconditional Love, The Palace Thief, Dreamcatcher, Peter Pan, Hidalgo, Collateral, The Village (Academy Award nom. 2005), The Interpreter, Batman Begins, King Kong (Golden Globe nom. 2006), Freedomland, R.V., Lady in the Water, Michael Clayton (Academy Award nom. 2008), Miami Vice (soundtrack), Blood Diamond, The Lookout, The Water Horse: Legend of the Deep, I Am Legend, Charlie Wilson's War, The Great Debaters, Mad Money, The Dark Knight (also musician), The Happening, Defiance (Academy Award nom.; Golden Globe nom. 2009), Confessions of a Shopaholic, Duplicity, Nanny McPhee Returns, Gnomeo and Juliet, The Last Airbender, Salt, Inhale.
TELEVISION: *Movies*: The Image, Revealing Evidence: Stalking the Honolulu Stangler, Somebody Has to Shoot the Picture, Descending Angel, A Private Matter, It's All Gone King Kong (doc.), Angels Fall (score prod.), Blue Smoke (score prod.), Carolina Moon (score prod.), Northern Lights (score prod.), Midnight Bayou, Previously On: E.R., High Noon (score prod.). *Mini-series:* From the Earth to the Moon. *Series*: Men (Emmy nom. 1989) ER (Emmy nom. 1995), Gideon's Crossing (Emmy Award 2001), The Fugitive, The Sentinel.

HOWARD, KEN

Actor. b. El Centro, CA, March 28, 1944. e. Yale Drama Sch. Left studies to do walk-on in B'way. musical, Promises Promises. Elected President of the Screen Actors Guild in 2009 for a two year term.
THEATRE: Promises Promises, 1776 (Theatre World Award), Child's Play (Tony Award, 1970), The Norman Conquests, Seesaw, Equus, Little Black Sheep, 1600 Pennsylvania Avenue, Rumors, Camping With Henry and Tom.
PICTURES: Tell Me That You Love Me Junie Moon (debut, 1970), Such Good Friends, The Strange Vengeance of Rosalie, 1776, Second Thoughts, Oscar, Clear and Present Danger, The Net, Tactical Assault, At First Sight, Dreamer: Inspired by a True Story, In Her Shoes, Michael Clayton, Arc, Still Waters, Smother, Rambo, Two:Thirteen, The Beacon, 2:13, A Numbers Game.
TELEVISION: *Movies*: Manhunter, Superdome, Critical List, A Real American Hero, Damien: The Leper Priest, Victims, Rage of Angels, The Trial of George Armstrong Custer, He's Not Your Son, Rage of Angels: The Story Continues, Murder in New Hampshire: The Pamela Smart Story, Memories of Midnight, Hart to Hart Returns, Moment of Truth: To Walk Again, Tom Clancy's Op Center, Her Hidden Truth, Something Borrowed Something Blue, A Vow to Cherish, Chasing the Sun, Chasing the Sun (doc., narr.), Sacrifices of the Heart, Grey Gardens (Emmy Award 2009), Facing Kate. *Mini-series*: The Thorn Birds, Perfect Murder Perfect Town. *Series*: Adam's Rib, The Manhunter, The White Shadow, It's Not Easy, The Colbys, Dynasty, Dream Girl U.S.A., What Happened? (host), Crossing Jordan, Cane. *Specials*: Strange Interlude, The Man in the Brown Suit, Mastergate, The Body Human: Facts for Boys (Emmy Award 1981). *Guest*: More than 90 appearances.

HOWARD, RANCE

Actor. rn. Harold Rance Beckenholdt. b. Oklahoma, Nov. 17, 1928. Father of actor Clint Howard and actor, director, producer Ron Howard.
PICTURES: Frontier Woman, Village of the Giants, The Desert Raven, An Eye for an Eye, Gentle Giant, Deed of Daring-Do, Bloody Trail, Salty, Where the Lilies Bloom, Chinatown, Eat My Dust, The Legend of Frank Woods, Grand Theft Auto (also writer, assoc. prod.), Another Man, Another Chance, Mr. No Legs, Forever and Beyond, Love Letters, The Lonely Guy, Splash, Cocoon, The Big Picture, Gung Ho, Innerspace, B.O.R.N., Dark Before Dawn, The 'burbs, Listen to Me, Parenthood, Trust Me, Limit Up, 9 1/2 Ninjas!, Boris and Natasha, I Don't Buy Kisses Anymore, Far and Away, Universal Soldier, Snapdragon, Forced to Kill, Ed and His Dead Mother, Wishman, Fearless, Bigfoot: The Unforgettable Encounter, The Paper, The Cowboy Way, Ed Wood, Little Giants, Apollo 13, Sgt. Bilko, Independence Day, Mars Attacks!, Ghosts of Mississippi, Where Truth Lies, Traveller, Money Talks, Chairman of the Board, The Sender, Small Soldiers, Psycho, Happy, Texas, Love & Sex, How the Grinch Stole Christmas, Joe Dirt, Rat Race, A Beautiful Mind, D-Tox, Back by Midnight, The Missing, The Alamo, Eulogy, Cinderella Man, Georgia Rule, Walk Hard: The Dewey Cox Story, Within, Grizzly Park, Drillbit Taylor, Frost/Nixon, Play the Game, Play Dead, Boppin' at the Glue Factory, Audie & the Wolf, Scarlet Cross, Play Dead, Valentine's Day, Once Fallen, Timberwolf, The Trial, The Genesis Code, Algona, Wild Michigan, Night Club.
TELEVISION: *Movies:* The Red Pony, Locusts, Huckleberry Finn, The New Daughters of Joshua Cabe, Cotton Candy (also assoc. prod.), Scout's Honor, Skyward, The Miracle of Kathy Miller, Through the Magic Pyramid (writer, prod. only, Emmy nom. 1982), The Kid with the Broken Halo, Rita Hayworth: The Love Goddess, The Fantastic World of D.C. Collins, Finder of Lost Loves, Scandal Sheet, Playing with Fire, A Death in California, The Long Hot Summer, Return to Mayberry, A Smoky Mountain Christmas, Lucy & Desi: Before the Laughter, Switched at Birth, Runaway Daughters, Problem Child 3: Junior in Love, The Colony, The Second Civil War, Holiday in Your Heart, Skip Tracer. *Mini-series:* The Thorn Birds. Series: Numerous appearances 1956-2006. *Guest:* More than 112 appearances.

HOWARD, RON

Actor, Director, Producer. b. Duncan, OK, March 1, 1954. e. Univ. of So. Calif. Los Angeles Valley Col. Acting debut as Ronny Howard at age of 2 with parents, Rance and Jean Howard, in The Seven Year Itch at Baltimore's Hilltop Theatre. Two years later traveled to Vienna to appear in first film, The Journey. Brother is actor Clint Howard, also former child actor. Father is actor Rance Howard. Co-Chairman of Imagine Films Entertainment. 1990 received American Cinematheque Award. 2006 received American Cinema Editors USA Award, Golden Eddie Filmmaker of the Year Award. 2007 received American Society of Cinematographers, USA Award, Board of the Governors Award.
PICTURES: *Actor*: The Journey (debut, 1959), Door-to-Door Maniac, The Music Man, The Courtship of Eddie's Father, Village of the Giants, The Wild Country, American Graffiti, Happy Mother's Day... Love George, The Spikes Gang, Eat My Dust!, I'm a Fool, The Shootist (Golden Globe nom. 1977), The First Nudie Musical (cameo), More American Graffiti, The Magical World of Chuck Jones, Osmosis Jones (voice). *Director*: Grand Theft Auto (dir. debut, 1977; also actor, co-s.p.), Night Shift, Splash, Cocoon (DGA nom. 1986), Gung Ho (also exec. prod.), Willow, Parenthood (also co-story), Backdraft, Far and Away (also co-prod., co-story), The Paper, Apollo 13 (DGA Award, Golden Globe nom. 1996), Ransom, Edtv (also prod.), How the Grinch Stole Christmas, A Beautiful Mind (Academy Award, AFI nom.; BAFTA nom.; DGA Award, Golden Globe nom. 2002), The Missing, The Da Vinci Code, East of Eden, Frost/Nixon (also prod.), Angels & Demons (also prod.), Frost/Nixon (also prod., 2 Academy Award noms.; DGA nom.; Golden Globe nom. 2009), Cheaters. *Exec. prod/prod.:* Leo & Loree, No Man's Land, Vibes, Clean and Sober, Closet Land, Far and Away, The Chamber, Inventing the Abbotts, Edtv, Beyond the Mat, How the Grinch Stole Christmas, The Alamo, The Cinderella Man (also dir.), Curious George, The Da Vinci Code (also dir.), Changeling, The Emperor's Children, Restless, Cowboys and Aliens, Hoover.
TELEVISION: *Movies*: The Migrants, Locusts, Huckleberry Finn, Cotton Candy (dir., co-writer), Act of Love, Bitter Harvest, Fire on the Mountain, When Your Lover Leaves (also co.exec. prod.), Through the Magic Pyramid (exec. prod., dir., Emmy nom. 1982), Splash Too, Skyward (co-exec. prod., dir.), Into Thin Air (exec. prod.), Return to Mayberry, Frank Capra's American Dream, Boarding School (exec. prod). *Mini-series*: From the Earth to the Moon (Emmy Award 1998). *Series*: The Andy Griffith Show, The Smith Family, Happy Days (Golden Globe nom. 1978), Fonz and the Happy Days Gang (voice), Parenthood, Hiller & Diller (exec. prod), Felicity (prod.), The PJs (exec. prod., Emmy nom. 1999), Wonderland (exec. prod.), The Beast (exec. prod.), 24 (exec. prod.), Arrested Development (exec. prod., Emmy Award, 2004; 2 other noms.), The Inside (exec. prod.), Curious George (2 Emmy noms.; Emmy Award 2008), Parenthood (exec. prod.). *Documentaries/Specials:* Where Have All the Children Gone, Homeward Bound, Frank Capra's American Dream, One Vision, The Independent, Tell Them Who You Are, In the Shadow of the Moon. *Guest*: More than 217 appearances.

HOWELL, C. THOMAS

Actor. r.n. Christopher Thomas Howell. b. Los Angeles, CA, Dec. 7, 1966. Former junior rodeo circuit champion.
PICTURES: E.T.: The Extra Terrestrial (debut, 1982), The Outsiders, Tank, Grandview U.S.A., Red Dawn, Secret Admirer, The Hitcher, Soul Man, A Tiger's Tale, Young Toscanini, Side Out, Far Out Man, The Return of the Musketeers, Kid, Nickel and Dime, Breaking the Rules, First Force, That Night, Tattle Tale, Streetwise, To Protect and Serve, Gettysburg, Jailss Bate, Teresa's Tattoo, Power Play,

Treacherous, Payback, Dangerous Indiscretion, Hourglass (also dir.), Baby Face Nelson, Mad Dogs and Englishmen, Pure Danger (also dir.), The Big Fall (also dir.), Sleeping Dogs, Last Lives, Dilemma, The Prince and the Surfer, The Glass Jar, Felons, Fortune Hunters, Shepherd, Red Team, The Million Dollar Kid, Hot Boyz, Enemy Action, WillFull, XCU: Extreme Closeup, Separate Ways, Asylum Days, Nursie, Net Games, Gods and Generals, The Hitcher II: I've Been Waiting (video), The Keeper: The Legend of Omar Khayyam, Fighting Words, Mutant Vampire Zombies from the 'Hood!, House of Fallen, Big Game, A Killer Within, Toxic, Razor, The Stolen Moments of September (also co-prod.), Fuel, Secret at Arrow Lake, Cupid's Arrow, Commander and Chief, Camouflage, The Jailhouse, Street Poet, The Genesis Code (2nd dir.), Razor, Fight or Flight, Camel Spiders.
TELEVISION: *Movies*: It Happened One Christmas, Into the Homeland, Curiosity Kills, Acting on Impulse, Dark Reflection, Suspect Device, Dead. Fire, Night of the Wolf, Killer Bees!, Hope Ranch (s.p., prod.), Zolar, Ordinary Miracles, The Poseidon Adventure, Xenophobia, A Gunfighter's Pledge. *Mini-series:* The Poseidon Adventure. *Series*: Little People (only 4 yrs. old), Two Marriages, Kindred: The Embraced, Amazon, Ollie, 24, CMT's All Jacked Up (also exec. prod.), Criminal Minds, Southland. *Guest:* More than 56 appearances.

HUBBARD, STANLEY S.

Satellite Broadcast Executive. b. St. Paul, MN, May 28, 1933. B.A. Univ. MN 1955. Stanley S. Hubbard's father, the late Stanley E. Hubbard, began his broadcasting empire when he launched a Minneapolis radio station in 1923. The entity grew into Hubbard Broadcasting, which today owns seven TV stations and three radio stations in Minnesota, and has TV stations in New Mexico and New York. Its Hubbard Radio Network syndicates programming to stations throughout the Midwest. Hubbard sold its stake in United States Satellite Broadcasting to Hughes Electronics (now The DIRECTV Group) in 1999 for $1.25 billion. Stanley S. Hubbard has been with the family business—Hubbard Broadcasting—from 1950. He was named president in 1967, chmn. & CEO in 1983 and remains in these roles today. He also helped develop Conus Communications, the world's first satellite news gathering organization, and United States Satellite Broadcasting, a pioneer in Direct Broadcast Satellite television. Stanley S. Hubbard has served on the National Infrastructure Advisory Council, which advised Vice President Al Gore in developing the "information superhighway," on the FCC's Blue Ribbon Advisory Committee on Advanced Television Service, and as chmn. of the bd. of trustees of the National Academy of Television Arts and Sciences. He was named to the Broadcasting & Cable Hall of Fame in 1991; received a Distinguished Service Award from the National Association of Broadcasters with his late father in 1995. He was a charter inductee into the Museum of Broadcasting Hall of Fame in 2001.

HUDDLESTON, DAVID

Actor, Producer. b. Vinton, VA, Sept. 17, 1930. e. American Acad. of Dramatic Arts. Son is actor Michael Huddleston.
THEATER: A Man for All Seasons, Front Page, Everybody Loves Opal, Ten Little Indians, Silk Stockings, Fanny, Guys and Dolls, The Music Man, Desert Song, Mame. Broadway: The First, Death of a Salesman.
PICTURES: All the Way Home, A Lovely Way to Die, Slaves, Norwood, Rio Lobo, Fools, Parade, Bad Company, Blazing Saddles, McQ, The World's Greatest Lover, Capricorn One, Gorp, Smokey and the Bandit II, The Act, Santa Claus, Frantic, Life With Mikey, Cultivating Charlie. Something to Talk About (unbilled), Joe's Apartment, The Man Next Door, The Big Lebowski, G-Men From Hell, The Producers, Postal, Locker 13.
TELEVISION: *Movies*: Sarge: The Badge or the Cross, The Priest Killer, Suddenly Single, The Homecoming, Brian's Song, Tenafly (pilot), Brock's Last Case, Hawkins on Murder, Heatwave, The Gun and the Pulpit, The Oregon Trail, Shark Kill, Sherlock Holmes in New York, Kate Bliss and the Ticker Tape Kid, Oklahoma City Dolls, Family Reunion, Computerside, M.A.D.D.: Mothers Against Drunk Drivers, Finnegan Begin Again, Family Reunion, Spot Marks the X, The Tracker, Margaret Bourke-White, In a Child's Name. *Mini-series:* Once an Eagle. *Series*: Tenafly, Petrocelli, The Kallikaks, Hizzoner, The Wonder Years (Emmy nom. 1990 as guest). *Guest:* More than 104 appearances.

HUDSON, ERNIE

Actor. b. Benton Harbor, MI, Dec. 17, 1945. e. Wayne St. Univ., Yale Sch. of Drama. Former Actors Ensemble Theater while in Detroit. Stage debut in L.A. production of Daddy Goodness.
PICTURES: Leadbelly (debut, 1976), The Main Event, The Jazz Singer, Penitentiary II, Spacehunter: Adventures in the Forbidden Zone, Going Berserk, Ghostbusters, The Joy of Sex, Weeds, Leviathan, Ghostbusters II, The Hand That Rocks the Cradle, Sugar Hill, No Escape, The Crow, The Cowboy Way, Airheads, Speechless, The Basketball Diaries, Congo, The Substitute, Operation Delta Force, Levitation, Fakin' Da Funk, Mr Magoo, Stranger in the Kingdom, Butter, Lillie, Shark Attack, Paper Bullets, Interceptors, Hijack, Everything's Jake, Red Letters, The Watcher, Miss Congeniality, Anne B. Real, Halfway Decent, Clifford's Really Big Movie (voice), Marilyn Hotchkiss' Ballroom Dancing and Charm School, Miss Congeniality 2: Armed and Fabulous, Sledge: The Story of Frank Sledge, Nobel Son, Hood of Horror, Lonely Street, The Man in the Silo, All Hat, Lonely Street, Dragonball: Evolution, Balancing the Books, Pastor Brown, Machete Joe, A State of Hate.
TELEVISION: *Movies*: White Mama, Dirty Dozen: The Fatal Mission, Love on the Run, Clover, Tornado!, The Cherokee Kid, Miracle on the 17th Green, Nowhere to Land, Walking Shadow, A Town Without Christmas, Lackawanna Blues, The Ron Clark Story, Final Approach. *Mini-series*: Roots: The Next Generations, Wild Palms, Final Approach, Meteor: Path to Destruction. *Series*: Highcliffe Manor, The Last Precinct, Broken Badges, Oz, H.R.T., 10-8: Officers on Duty, Desperate Housewives, The Secret Life of the American Teenager, Law & Order. *Guest*: More than 111 appearances.

HUDSON, HUGH

Producer, Director. b. England. e. Eton. Began career as head of casting dept. with ad agency in London; left for Paris to work as editor for small film co. Returned to London to form Cammell-Hudson-Brownjohn Film Co., production house., turning out award-winning documentaries (Tortoise and Hare, A is for Apple). 1970, joined Ridley Scott to make TV commercials. 1975, formed Hudson Films to produce.
PICTURES: *Director*: Chariots of Fire (Academy Award nom.; DGA nom. 1982), Greystoke: The Legend of Tarzan Lord of the Apes (also prod.), Revolution, Lost Angels, Lumiere and Company, My Life So Far, I Dreamed of Africa.

HUGH-KELLY, DANIEL

Actor. b. Hoboken, NJ, Aug. 10, 1949. Began acting with the National Players touring U.S. in such plays as Henry IV Part 1, Charlie's Aunt, School for Wives.
THEATRE: Arena Stage (DC): An Enemy of the People, Once in a Lifetime, Long Day's Journey Into Night. Actors Theatre (Louisville): Much Ado About Nothing, The Best Man, The Taming of the Shrew, The Rainmaker. Off-B'way: Hunchback of Notre Dame, Miss Margarita's Way, Juno's Swans, Fishing, Short-Changed Revue. B'way: Born Yesterday, Cat on a Hot Tin Roof.
PICTURES: Cujo, Nowhere to Hide, Someone to Watch Over Me, The Good Son, Bad Company, Star Trek: Insurrection, Chill Factor, The In Crowd, Guardian, American Gun, Saw III (title designer).
TELEVISION: *Movies*: Nutcracker, Thin Ice, Murder Ink, Night of Courage, Citizen Cohn, Moment of Truth: A Mother's Deception, A Child's Cry for Help, The Tuskegee Airmen, Never Say Never: The Deidre Hall Story, No Greater Love, Stranger in My Home, Five Desperate Hours, Bad As I Wanna Be: The Dennis Rodman Story, Labor of Love, Atomic Dog, Passing Glory, Growing Up Brady, Joe and Max. *Mini-series*: From the Earth to the Moon, Jackie Ethel Joan: The Women of Camelot. *Series*: Chicago Story, Hardcastle and McCormick, Second Noah, Ponderosa, As the World Turns, Memphis Beat (also pilot). *Guest:* More than 46 appearances.

HUGHES, WENDY

Actress. b. Melbourne, Australia, July 29, 1952. Studied acting at National Institute of Dramatic Art, Sydney.
PICTURES: Petersen, Sidecar Racers, High Rolling, Newsfront, My Brilliant Career, Kostas, Lucinda Brayford, Touch and Go, Hoodwink, A Dangerous Summer, Partners, Duet for Four, Lonely Hearts, Careful He Might Hear You, My First Wife, Remember Me, An Indecent Obsession, Happy New Year, Echoes of Paradise, Warm Nights on a Slow Moving Train, Boundaries of the Heart, Luigi's Ladies (also co-s.p.), Wild Orchid II, Princess Caraboo, Lust & Revenge, Paradise Road.
TELEVISION: *Movies*: Coralie Landsdowne Says No, Puzzle, Promises to Keep, Can't Get Started, The Heist, Donor. *Mini-series:* Power Without Glory, Return to Eden, Amerika, A Woman Named Jackie. *Series*: Rush, Snowy River: The McGregor Saga, State Coroner, Darwin's Brave New World (doc., narr.).

HULCE, TOM

Actor. b. White Water, WI, Dec. 6, 1953. e. NC School of the Arts. Understudied and then co-starred in Equus on Broadway. Directorial stage debut Sleep Around Town. Appeared in IMAX film Wings of Courage. Recipient of Emmy Award, 1996.
THEATRE: A Memory of Two Mondays, Julius Caesar, Candida, The Sea Gull, The Rise and Rise of Daniel Rocket, Eastern Standard, A Few Good Men (Tony nom.), Hamlet.
PICTURES: September 30, 1955 (debut, 1978), National Lampoon's Animal House, Those Lips Those Eyes, Amadeus (Academy Award nom.; Golden Globe nom. 1985), Echo Park, Slamdance, Dominick and Eugene (Golden Globe nom. 1989), Parenthood, Shadowman, The Inner Circle, Fearless, Mary Shelley's Frankenstein, Wings of Courage, The Hunchback of Notre Dame (voice), Paul Monette: The Brink of Summer's End, Hunchback of Notre Dame II (voice), A Home at the End of the World (prod. only), Stranger Than Fiction, Jumper.
TELEVISION: *Movies:* Murder in Mississippi (Emmy nom.; Golden Globe nom. 1991), Black Rainbow, The Heidi Chronicles (Emmy Award, Golden Globe nom. 1996). *Mini-series:* The Adams Chronicles. *Specials:* Emily Emily, The Rise and Rise of Daniel Rocket, Song of Myself, Forget-Me-Not Lane, Tall Tales and Legends (John Henry).

HUNDT, REED

Executive. b. Ann Arbor, MI, March 3, 1948. B.A. Yale, 1969, magna cum laude with exceptional distinction in history; J.D. from the Yale Law School, 1974. Was member of the exec. bd. of the Yale Law Journal. Served on various U.S. circuit courts 1975-1980. Associate with Latham & Watkins, 1975; partner in 1982. Named to FCC in 1994 as chairman. Resigned 1997. Currently Hundt is a principal of Charles Ross Partners, a private investor and business advisory services. He is also an indep. adviser on information industries to McKinsey & Company, Inc., a mgt. consulting firm, and to the Blackstone Group, a private equity firm. He serves on the bd. of directors of Intel Corp. (since 2001), and is a member of the Mgt. Advisory Board at the Yale School of Management. In early 2007, he joined the bd. of directors of Data Domain, a Santa Clara storage appliance maker, and Vanu, Inc., a software radio innovator. He was a co-chmn. of The Forum on Communications and Society at The Aspen Institute. He is the author of "You Say You Want A Revolution: A Story of Information Age Politics."

HUNT, HELEN

Actress. b. Los Angeles, CA, June 15, 1963. Daughter of dir. Gordon Hunt.
THEATRE: Been Taken, Our Town, The Taming of the Shrew, Methusalem, Twelfth Night, *L.A.:* The Guys.
PICTURES: Rollercoaster, Girls Just Want to Have Fun, Peggy Sue Got Married, Project X, Miles From Home, Trancers, Stealing Home, Next of Kin, The Waterdance, Only You, Bob Roberts, Mr. Saturday Night, Kiss of Death, Twister, As Good as It Gets (Academy Award, Golden Globe Award, Best Actress, 1998), Twister: Ride it Out, Dr. T and the Women, Pay it Forward, Cast Away, What Women Want, The Curse of the Jade Scorpion, Pulse Pounders, Timepiece (co-prod. only), A Good Woman, Bobby, Then She Found Me (also dir., prod., s.p.), Every Day, Aline & Wolfe, Soul Surfer.
TELEVISION: *Movies*: Pioneer Woman, All Together Now, Death Scream, The Spell, Transplant, Angel Dusted, Child Bride of Short Creek, The Miracle of Kathy Miller, Sexual Healing, Quarterback Princess, Bill: On His Own, Sweet Revenge, Incident at Dark River, Into the Badlands, Murder in New Hampshire: The Pamela Smart Story, In the Company of Darkness, Twelfth Night, or What You Will, Empire Falls. *Series*: Swiss Family Robinson, Amy Prentiss, The Fitzpatricks, It Takes Two, Mad About You (4 Emmy Awards, 4 other nom.; 3 Golden Globe Awards, 3 other nom.). *Specials*: Weekend, Land of Little Rain. *Guest*: More than 158 appearances.

HUNT, LINDA

Actress. b. Morristown, NJ, Apr. 2, 1945. e. Interlochen Arts Acad., MI, and Chicago's Goodman Theatre & Sch. of Drama. Narrated documentary Ecological Design: Inventing the Future.
THEATRE: Long Wharf (New Haven): Hamlet, The Rose Tattoo, Ah Wilderness. NY: Mother Courage, End of the World (Tony nom.), A Metamorphosis in Miniature (Obie Award), Top Girls (Obie Award), Aunt Dan and Lemon, The Cherry Orchard. *Regional:* The Three Sisters.
PICTURES: Popeye (debut, 1980) The Year of Living Dangerously (Academy Award, Golden Globe nom. best supporting actress, 1984), The Bostonians, Dune, Silverado, Eleni, Waiting for the Moon, She-Devil, Kindergarten Cop, If Looks Could Kill, Rain Without Thunder, Twenty Bucks, Younger and Younger, Ready to Wear (Pret-a-Porter), Pocahontas (voice), The Relic, Eat Your Heart Out, Amazon, Paul Monette: The Brink of Summer's End, Amazon, Out of the Past, Pocahontas II: Journey to a New World (voice), Island of the Sharks, Dragonfly, Shadow Play: Indonesia's Year of Living Dangerously (documentary, narrator), A Lot Like Love, Yours, Mine and Ours, Stranger Than Fiction, The Crooked Eye (narr.), Sacred Earth (narr.).
TELEVISION: *Movies*: Ah, Wilderness!, The Room Upstairs, Basements, The Turn of the Screw. *Mini-series*: The Century. *Series*: Space Rangers, The Practice, Before We Ruled the Earth (host, voice), Carnivàle (voice), NCIS: Los Angeles. *Documentaries/Specials*: Chico Mendes: Voice of the Amazon, Ishi: The Last Yahi, Ecological Design: Inventing the Future, Paul Monette: The Brink of Summer's End, Out of the Past, Influenza 1918, Ah Wilderness, The Century (mini-series), Island of the Sharks, Before We Ruled the Earth (series), Woodrow Wilson and the Birth of the American Century, California and the American Dream (series, narr.), The American Experience (narr.). *Guest*: More than 50 appearances.

HUNT, MARSHA

Actress. b. Chicago, IL, Oct. 17, 1917.
THEATRE: B'way: Joy to the World, Devils Disciple, Legend of Sarah, Borned in Texas, Tunnel of Love, The Paisley Convertible.
PICTURES: The Virginia Judge (debut, 1935), College Holiday, Easy to Take, Blossoms in the Dust, Panama Hattie, Joe Smith American, These Glamour Girls, Winter Carnival, Irene, Pride and Prejudice, Flight Command, The Affairs of Martha, Kid Glove Killer, Seven Sweethearts, Cheers for Miss Bishop, Trial of Mary Dugan, Lost Angel, Cry Havoc, Bride by Mistake, Music for Millions, Valley of Decision, A Letter for Evie, Smash-Up, Carnegie Hall, The Inside Story, Raw Deal, Take One False Step, Actors and Sin, Happy Time, No Place to Hide, Back from the Dead, Bombers B-52, Blue Denim, The Plunderers, Johnny Got His Gun, Chloe's Prayer.
TELEVISION: *Movies*: Fear No Evil, Jigsaw, Terror Among Us. *Series*: Peck's Bad Girl. *Guest*: More than 58 appearances.

HUNT, WILLIE

Executive, Producer. b. Van Nuys, CA, Oct. 1, 1941. e. Utah State U., B.A., 1963. m. writer Tim Considine. Started in industry as secretary at Warner Bros., 1965; named exec. secty. to Ted Ashley, WB, 1969; story analyst, WB, 1974; story editor, WB, 1975; named West Coast story editor for WB, 1978; joined MGM in 1979 as v.p., motion picture development. Moved to U,A, as v.p.-prod., 1982. 1983 sr. v.p. of prod. at Rastar Prods.; 1984, indep. prod., Tri-Star; 1986, sr. v.p., Freddie Fields Prods. 1988: Loverboy (co-prod.) 1989, sr. v.p. Considine Prods. 1993, partner, Creative Entertainment Group.
PICTURE: Loverboy.

HUNTER, HOLLY

Actress. b. Conyers, GA. March 20, 1958. e. studied acting, Carnegie-Mellon Univ. Appeared Off-B'way in Battery (1981) and Weekend Near Madison. Appeared in 5 Beth Henley plays: The Miss Firecracker Contest (Off-B'way), as a replacement in Crimes of the Heart (B'way) The Wake of Jamey Foster (B'way), Lucky Spot (Williamstown Theater Festival), and Control Freaks (L.A.; also co-prod.). Also: A Lie of the Mind (L.A.).
PICTURES: The Burning (debut, 1981), Swing Shift, Raising Arizona, Broadcast News (NY Film Critics, LA Film Critics and Natl. Board of Review Awards, Academy Award nom.; Golden Globe nom. 1988), End of the Line, Miss Firecracker, Animal Behavior, Always, Once Around, The Firm (Academy Award nom. 1994), The Piano (Academy Award, Cannes Film Fest., LA Film Critics, NY Film Critics, Natl. Board of Review, Natl. Society of Film Critics & Golden Globe Award, 1994), Home for the Holidays, Copycat, Crash, A Life Less Ordinary, Living Out Loud, Woman Wanted, Jesus' Son, Things You Can Tell Just By Looking At Her, Timecode, O Brother Where Art Thou?, Down From the Mountain, Festival in Cannes, Searching for Debra Winger, Moonlight Mile, Levity, Thirteen (also exec. prod; Academy Award nom.; Golden Globe nom. 2004), The Incredibles (voice), The Big White, Little Black Book, Nine Lives, Frost Flowers, The Big White.
TELEVISION: *Movies*: Svengali, An Uncommon Love, With Intent to Kill, A Gathering of Old Men, Roe vs. Wade (Emmy Award, Golden Globe nom. 1989), Crazy in Love, The Positively True Adventures of the Alleged Texas Cheerleader-Murdering Mom (Emmy Award, Golden Globe nom. 1993), When Billy Beat Bobby (Emmy nom. 2001), Harlan County War (Emmy nom.; Golden Globe nom. 2000), Eco Challenge New Zealand (narr.). *Pilot:* Fame, Grace. *Series:* Saving Grace (Golden Globe nom.; 2 Emmy noms.). *Documentaries/Specials:* The Way West, Down From the Mountain, Abraham and Mary Lincoln: A House Divided (mini), Searching for Debra Winger, Rock That Uke. *Guest:* More than 72 appearances.

HUNTER, TIM

Director. b. Los Angeles, CA, June 15,1947. e. Harvard, AFI.
PICTURES: Over the Edge (co-s.p.). Dir.: Tex (also s.p.), Sylvester, River's Edge, Paint It Black, The Saint of Fort Washington, The Maker, Reflections of Eden, The Failures, Control, The Far Side of Jericho, New Orleans.
TELEVISION: *Movies*: Beverly Hills, 90210, The Colony, Lies of the Twins, People Next Door, Rescuers: Stories of Courage, Mean Streak, Anatomy of a Hate Crime, Video Voyeur: The Susan Wilson Story, Kings of South Beach. *Mini-series:* Out of Order. *Series*: Falcon Crest, Homicide: Life on the Street, Bakersfield, P.D., Chicago Hope, Nowhere Man, Central Park West, Sins of the City, Soul Food, Crossing Jordan, Dead Last, Carnivàle, The 4400, Mad Men.

HUNTSBERRY, FREDERICK

Executive. b. Born in the U.S. but educated in Germany and Switzerland. e. Boston University, College of General Studies, 1982. Graduate of Boston University School of Management, 1984. Straight from college Huntsberry entered General Electric's Financial Management program. During 12 years with GE, he held a broad range of finance and business development positions in medical systems, plastics and information services. Before leaving GE, Huntsberry was manager, mergers & acquisitions Europe. Huntsberry joined Universal in Jan. 1997 as v.p., TV business development where he led strategic planning and financial operations for the group. During 1997 promoted to senior v.p. & CFO for Universal Television & Networks group and is a position he held through 1999. From 1999-2002 he served as senior v.p., CFO, Universal Pictures and represented Universal on the operating committees of Universal International Pictures and United Cinemas International. From 2002-2004, he was executive v.p. and CFO, Vivendi Universal Entertainment. He was instrumental in the company's sale to GE in 2004, with the merged company forming NBC Universal. He spent the following two years working for Jeff Zucker, first as CFO and later as president, NBC Universal Television Distribution & Universal Pictures Group International Operations. One of Huntsberry's self-proclaimed career highlights was being responsible for NBC Universal's syndication business which generated success through shows like "Access Hollywood, "The Jerry Springer

Show" and "Maury Povich." In July 2006 Huntsberry left NBC Universal and became COO, Paramount Pictures. In this role today, Huntsberry is responsible for worldwide strategic planning and operations for the studio, including finance, human resources, industrial relations, lot operations and the office of the general counsel.

HUPPERT, ISABELLE

Actress. b. Paris, France, March 16, 1955. e. Conservatoire National d'Art Dramatique.
PICTURES: Faustine and the Beautiful Summer (Growing Up; debut, 1971), Cesar and Rosalie, Going Places, Rosebud, The Rape of Innocence, The Judge and the Assassin, The Lacemaker, Violette (Cannes Fest. Award, 1977), The Bronte Sisters, Loulou, Heaven's Gate, Coup de Torchon, Every Man for Himself, The True Story of Camille, Wings of the Dove, Deep Water, Entre Nous, The Trout, Cactus, Signed Charlotte, The Bedroom Window, The Possessed, Story of Women (Venice Fest Award, 1988), Milan Noir, Madame Bovary, Revenge of a Woman, Malina, Apres l'Amour (After Love), Amateur, The Separation, A Judgment in Stone, Love's Debris, The Elective Affinities, Les Palmes de M. Schultz, Rien ne va Plus, Keep it Quiet, Modern Life, False Servant, The King's Daughters, Les Destinees Sentimentales, Comedy of Innocence, Nightcap, Clara, La Pianiste, 8 femmes, La Vie Promise, Deux, Ghost River, Le Temps du loup, I Heart Huckabee's, Les Soeurs fâchées, Gabrielle, L' Ivresse du pouvoir, Medea Miracle, Private Property, Home, Sans queue ni tête, Copacabana.
TELEVISION: *Movies*: Médée, Gulliver's Travels (voice). *Mini-series*: Seobe. *Guest:* More than 50 appearances.

HURD, GALE ANNE

Producer. b. Los Angeles, CA, Oct. 25, 1955. e. Stanford U., Phi Beta Kappa, 1977. Joined New World Pictures in 1977 as exec. asst. to pres. Roger Corman, then named dir. of advertising and pub. and moved into prod. management capacities on several New World films. Left in 1982 to form own co., Pacific Western Productions. Honored by NATO with special merit award for Aliens. Served as juror, U.S. Film Fest., Utah, 1988 and for 1989 Focus Student Film Awards. Member, Hollywood Women's Political Committee. Board of Trustees, AFI. The Amer. Film Inst. created Gale Anne Hurd production grants for Institute's Directing Workshop for Women. Bd. of dir. The Independent Feature Project/West. Currently serves as Recording Secetary for the Producers Guild of America and is CEO/Producer for Valhalla Motion Pictures.
PICTURES: Smokey Bites the Dust (co-prod. with Roger Corman, 1981), The Terminator (Grand Prix, Avoriaz Film Fest.,France), Aliens (Hugo Award) Alien Nation (Saturn nom.), The Abyss, Downtown (exec. prod.), Tremors (exec. prod.), Terminator 2 (exec. prod.), The Waterdance, Raising Cain, No Escape, Safe Passage, The Relic, The Ghost and The Darkness, Dante's Peak, Switchback, Snake Eyes, Armageddon, Dead Man on Campus, Virus, Dick, Clockstoppers, The Hulk, Terminator 3: Rise of the Machines (exec. prod., writer), The Punisher, Æon Flux, Room Service, Welcome to the Jungle, The Incredible Hulk, Punisher: War Zone.
TELEVISION: *Movies*: Cast a Deadly Spell, Witch Hunt, Sugartime, The Coven, Breadwinners (exec. prod.), The Wronged Man (exec. prod.). *Series*: Alien Nation (consult.) Adventure Inc. (exec. prod.), Terminator: The Sarah Connor Chronicles (writer only), The Walking Dead (exec. prod., pilot).

HURLEY, ELIZABETH

Actress, Producer. b. Hampshire, England, June 10, 1965. Also model.
PICTURE: Rowing In the Wind, Aria, Kill Cruise, The Long Winter of '39, Passenger 57, Beyond Bedlam, Mad Dogs and Englishmen, Extreme Measures (prod. only), Dangerous Ground, Austin Powers: International Man of Mystery, Permanent Midnight, Austin Powers: The Spy Who Shagged Me, My Favorite Martian, Edtv, Mickey Blue Eyes (prod. only), The Weight of Water, Bedazzled, Double Whammy, Serving Sarah, Bad Boy, Psyclops (video, exec. prod.), Method (exec. prod.), The Last Guy on Earth.
TELEVISION: *Movies/Specials:* Christabel, Act of Will, Death Has a Bad Reputation, Orchid House, Sharpe's Enemy, The World of 007 (host), Samson and Delilah, The Human Face.

HURT, JOHN

Actor. b. Shirebrook, Derbyshire, Jan. 22, 1940. e. St. Martin's Sch. for Art, London, RADA.
THEATRE: The Dwarfs, Little Malcolm and His Struggle Against the Eunichs, Man and Superman, Belcher's Luck, Ride a Cock Horse, The Caretaker, Romeo and Juliet, Ruffian on the Streets, The Dumb Waiter, Travesties, The Arrest, The Seagull, The London Vertigo, A Month in the Country.
PICTURES: The Wild and the Willing (debut, 1962), This is My Street, A Man for All Seasons, The Sailor from Gibraltar, Before Winter Comes, Sinful Davey, In Search of Gregory, 10 Rillington Place, Mr. Forbush and the Penguins, The Pied Piper, Little Malcolm, The Naked Civil Servant, La Linea del Fiume, The Ghoul, East of Elephant Rock, The Disappearance, Midnight Express (Academy Award nom.; Golden Globe Award 1979), Watership Down (voice), The Lord of the Rings (voice), The Shout, Alien, The Elephant Man (Academy Award nom.; Golden Globe nom. 1981), Heaven's Gate, History of the World Part I, Night Crossing, Partners, The Plague Dogs (voice), The Osterman Weekend, Champions, The Hit, Success Is the Best Revenge, 1984, After Darkness, The Black Cauldron (voice), Jake Speed, From the Hip, Spaceballs, Aria, Vincent (voice), White Mischief, Little Sweetheart, Poison Candy, Bengali Night, Scandal, Frankenstein Unbound, The Field, King Ralph, Romeo-Juliet, Resident Alien, Windprints, I Dreamt I Woke Up, Lapse of Memory, Dark at Noon or Eyes and Lies, Monolith, Hans Christian Andersen's Thumbelina (voice), Even Cowgirls Get the Blues, Crime and Punishment, Great Moments in Aviation, Second Best, Betrayal (voice), Rob Roy, Wild Bill, Two Nudes Bathing, Saigon Baby, Dead Man, Love & Death on Long Island, Contact, The Climb, Bandyta, If... Dog... Rabbit, Desert Blue, The Commissioner, All the Little Animals, The Tigger Movie, Lost Souls, Crime and Punishment, Captain Corelli's Mandolin, Harry Potter and the Sorcerer's Stone, Tabloid, Miranda, Owning Mahowny, Dogville (narr.), Hellboy, Valiant (voice), The Skeleton Key, V for Vendetta, Shooting Dogs, Manderlay (narr.), The Proposition, Short Order, Perfume: The Story of a Murderer (narr.), The Oxford Murders, Outlander, Lesson 21, Indiana Jones and the Kingdom of the Crystal Skull, Hellboy II: The Golden Army, New York, I Love You, An Englishman in New York, The Limits of Control, Angel Makers, Lou, Brighton Rock, Harry Potter and the Deathly Hallows: Part I, Harry Potter and the Deathly Hallows: Part II, Immortals.
TELEVISION: *Movies*: Playboy of the Western World, A Tragedy of Two Ambitions, Green Julia, Nijinsky, Ten from the Twenties, The Peddler, The Naked Civil Servant, Spectre, Deadline, The Jim Henson Hour, King Lear, The Investigation: Inside a Terrorist Bombing, Journey to Knock, Six Characters in Search of an Author, Great Moments in Aviation, Shades of Fear, Prisoners in Time, Krapp's Last Tape, Bait, Hiroshima (narr.), Pride, Hellboy: Sword of Storms (voice), Hellboy Animated: Blood and Iron (voice), Recount, The Gruffalo. *Mini-series*: Crime and Punishment, I Claudius, The Storyteller, Red Fox, The Alan Clark Diaries. *Series*: Watership Down (voice), Merlin (voice). *Documentaries:* Förräderi, The Hidden Wars of Desert Storm (narr.), Shaolin Wheel of Life, The 'Alien' Saga, Dracula's Bram Stoker (narr.),The Plot Against Harold Wilson (narr.), Terror in the Aisles. *Guest:* More than 132 appearances.

HURT, MARY BETH

Actress. r.n. Mary Beth Supinger. b. Marshalltown, IA, Sept. 26, 1946. m. writer-dir. Paul Schrader. e. U. of Iowa, NYU Sch. of Arts. Stage debut in 1973 with N.Y. Shakespeare Fest. (More Than You Deserve, Pericles, The Cherry Orchard).
THEATRE: As You Like It (Central Park), 2 seasons with Phoenix Theater, Love For Love, Tralawny of the Wells, Secret Service, Boy Meets Girl, Father's Day, Crimes of the Heart, The Misanthrope, Benefactors, The Nest of the Wood Grouse, The Day Room, Othello, A Delicate Balance.
PICTURES: Interiors (debut, 1978), Head Over Heels (Chilly Scenes of Winter), A Change of Seasons, The World According to Garp, D.A.R.Y.L., Compromising Positions, Parents, Slaves of New York, Defenseless, Light Sleeper, My Boyfriend's Back, The Age of Innocence, Six Degrees of Separation, From the Journals of Jean Seberg, Alkali Iowa, Affliction, Boy's Life 2, Bringing Out the Dead, Autumn in New York, The Family Man, Red Dragon, The Exorcism of Emily Rose, Lady in the Water, The Dead Girl, The Walker, Untraceable, Lebanon, PA.
TELEVISION: *Movies*: Baby Girl Scott, Shimmer, After Amy. *Series*: Nick and Hillary, Working It Out, Tattingers. *Documentaries/Specials*: The Five-Forty-Eight, Secret Service (NET Theatre), From the Journals of Jean Seberg.

HURT, WILLIAM

Actor. b. Washington, DC, Mar. 20, 1950. Lived as child in South Pacific when father was dir. of Trust Territories for U.S. State Dept. e. Tufts as theology major, switched to drama in jr. year, Juilliard. Acted with Oregon Shakespearean Fest. Leading actor with New York's Circle Repertory Company (Theatre World Award), since 1976.
THEATRE: NY: The Fifth of July, My Life (Obie Award), Ulysses in Traction, The Runner Stumbles, Hamlet, Childe Byron, Beside Herself. NY Shakespeare Festival: Henry V, A Midsummer's Night's Dream, Hurlyburly (off-B'way and B'way). Regional: Good (S.F.), Ivanov (Yale).
PICTURES: Altered States (debut, 1980 Golden Globe nom. 1981), Eyewitness, Body Heat, The Big Chill, Gorky Park, Kiss of the Spider Woman (Academy Award, Golden Globe nom. 1986), Children of a Lesser God (Academy Award nom.; Golden Globe nom. 1987), Broadcast News (Academy Award nom.; Golden Globe nom. 1988), A Time of Destiny, The Accidental Tourist, I Love You to Death, Alice, The Doctor, Until the End of the World, Mr. Wonderful, The Plague, Trial by Jury, Second Best, Smoke, Jane Eyre, A Couch in New York, Michael, Loved, Dark City, The Proposition, Lost in Space, One True Thing, The Taste of Sunshine, The Big Brass Ring, The 4th Floor, The Simian Line, The Contaminated Man, Artificial Intelligence: AI, Rare Birds, Changing Lanes, Tuck Everlasting, Au plus pres du paradis, The Blue Butterfly, The Village, Downloading Nancy, Neverwas, The King, Syriana, A History of Violence (Academy Award nom. 2006), Goodnight, and Good Luck, A License to Steal, Noise, The Good Shepherd, Mr. Brooks, Vantage Point, Into the Wild,

Yellow Handkerchief, The Incredible Hulk, The Countess, Endgame, The River Why, Shadows, Late Bloomers, Robin Hood.
TELEVISION: *Movies*: Verna: USO Girl, All the Way Home, A Midsummer Night's Dream, The Miracle Maker, The Flamingo Rising, Varian's War, Master Spy: The Robert Hanssen Story, Hunt for Justice. *Mini-series*: Dune, Best of Families, Nightmares and Dreamscapes: From the Stories of Stephen King Frankenstein. *Series:* Damages (Emmy nom. 2009, Golden Globe nom 2010), Moby Dick. *Specials*: The Odyssey of John Dos Passos (voice). *Guest:* More than 64 appearances.

HUSSEY, OLIVIA
Actress. b. Buenos Aires, Apr. 17, 1951. Attended Italia Conti Stage School, London. Began acting at age 8.
PICTURES: The Battle of the Villa Fiorita (debut, 1965), Cup Fever, All the Right Noises, Romeo and Juliet (Golden Globe Award 1969), Summertime Killer, Lost Horizon, Black Christmas, Death on the Nile, The Cat and the Canary, Virus, The Man With Bogart's Face, Escape 2000, Distortions, The Jeweler's Shop, The Undeclared War, Save Me, Ice Cream Man, Bad English I: Tales of a Son of a Brit, Saving Grace, Shame Shame Shame, Tortilla Heaven, El Grito, Island Prey, Headspace, Three Priests.
TELEVISION: *Movies:* The Pirate, The Bastard, Ivanhoe, The Corsican Brothers, Psycho IV: The Beginning, Stephen King's IT, Save Me, Quest of the Delta Knights, H-Bomb, Dead Man's Island, Lonesome Dove, Shame, The Gardener, Mother Teresa of Calcutta. *Mini-series:* Jesus of Nazareth, Last Days of Pompeii.

HUSTON, ANJELICA
Actress. b. Santa Monica, CA, July 8, 1951. Father is late writer-dir.-actor, John Huston. Brother is dir. Danny Huston. Raised in St. Clerans, Ireland. Studied acting at the Loft Studio and with Peggy Furey, Martin Landau. Appeared in 3-D Disney short Captain Eo.
PICTURES: A Walk With Love and Death (debut, 1969), Sinful Davey, Swashbuckler, The Last Tycoon, The Postman Always Rings Twice, Frances, The Ice Pirates, This is Spinal Tap, Prizzi's Honor (Academy Award, best supporting actress; Golden Globe nom. 1986), Good to Go (Short Fuse), Gardens of Stone, The Dead, A Handful of Dust, Mr. North, Crimes and Misdemeanors, Enemies a Love Story (Academy Award nom. 1990), The Witches, The Grifters (Academy Award nom.; Golden Globe nom. 1991), The Addams Family (Golden Globe nom. 1994), The Player (cameo), Manhattan Murder Mystery, Addams Family Values, The Perez Family, The Crossing Guard (Golden Globe nom. 1996), Buffalo '66, Phoenix, Ever After: A Cinderella Story, Agnes Browne (also dir., prod.), The Golden Bowl, Time of Our Lives, The Man from Elysian Fields, The Royal Tenenbaums, Searching for Debra Winger, Blood Work, Barbie as Rapunzel (video, voice), Daddy Day Care, Kaena: The Prophecy (voice), The Life Aquatic with Steve Zissou, Art School Confidential, Living and Breathing, These Foolish Things, Material Girls, Seraphim Falls, The Darjeeling Limited, Martian Child, Choke, The Fantastic Mr. Fox, Spirit of the Forest, When in Rome, The Other Side.
TELEVISION: *Movies*: The Cowboy and the Ballerina, Family Pictures (Golden Globe nom. 1994), And the Band Played On, Buffalo Girls (Emmy nom. 1995), Iron Jawed Angels (Emmy nom.; Golden Globe Award 2005), Riding the Bus with My Sister, Covert One: The Hades Factor. *Mini-series*: Lonesome Dove (Emmy nom.; Golden Globe nom. 1989), The Mists of Avalon (Emmy nom. 2002), Bastard Out of Carolina (dir., DGA nom.; Emmy nom. 1997). *Series:* Huff, Medium (Emmy nom. 2008). *Specials*: Faerie Tale Theatre, A Rose for Miss Emily. *Guest:* More than 105 appearances.

HUSTON, DANNY
Actor, Director. b. Rome, Italy, May 14, 1962. Youngest son of dir.-actor John Huston and actress Zoe Sallis. Brother of actress Anjelica and screenwriter Tony Huston. e. Overseas School, Rome; Intl branch of Milfield School in Exeter, London Film School. A constant visitor to his father's sets throughout the world, he began working on his father's films, beginning in Cuernavaca, Mexico as second-unit dir. on Under the Volcano. Directed TV doc. on Peru and on making of Santa Claus: The Movie; and TV features Bigfoot and Mr. Corbett's Ghost.
PICTURES: Mr. North (debut, 1988), Becoming Colette, The Maddening, Amparo. *Actor:* Leaving Las Vegas, Ana Karenina, Susan's Plan, Spanish Fly, Rockin' Good Times, Timecode, Ivansxtc, Eden, Hotel, The Bacchae, 21 Grams, Birth, The Aviator, Silver City, The Constant Gardener, The Proposition, Alpha Male, Marie Antoinette, Children of Men, Fade to Black, I Really Hate My Job, The Number 23, The Kingdom, 30 Days of Night, The Kreutzer Sonata, Boogie Woogie, How to Lose Friends & Alienate People, X-Men Origins: Wolverine, The Warrior's Way, Edge of Darkness, Clash of the Titans, The Conspirator, Robin Hood, A Monster in Paris (voice).
TELEVISION: *Movies*: Bigfoot, Mister Corbett's Ghost, Eisprinzessin, Die, Covert One: The Hades Factor, You Don't Know Jack. *Mini-series:* John Adams.

HUTTON, LAUREN
Actress. r.n. Mary Laurence Hutton. b. Charleston, SC, Nov. 17, 1943. e. U. of South Florida, Sophie Newcombe Coll. As model featured on more covers than any other American. Stage debut at LA Public Theatre in Extremities.
PICTURES: Paper Lion (debut, 1968), Pieces of Dreams, Little Fauss and Big Halsy, Rocco Papaleo, The Gambler, Gator, Welcome to L.A., Viva Knievel!, A Wedding, American Gigolo, Paternity, Zorro the Gay Blade, Tout Feu tout Flamme (Hecate), Lassiter, Once Bitten, Flagrant Desire, Malone, Blue Blood, Bulldance (Forbidden Sun), Run For Your Life, Billions, Guilty as Charged, Missing Pieces, My Father the Hero, A Rat's Tale, 54, Loser Love, Just a Little Harmless Sex, The Venice Project, The Joneses.
TELEVISION: *Movies*: Someone Is Watching Me, Institute for Revenge, Starflight, The Cradle Will Fall, Scandal Sheet, The Return of Mike Hammer, Time Stalker, Monte Carlo, Perfect People, Fear, We the Jury, Caracara, The Last Witness, The Bunny Years. *Mini-series*: The Rhinemann Exchange, Sins. *Series*: Paper Dolls, Falcon Crest, Lauren Hutton and... (talk show), Central Park West, Manchild (pilot), Nip/Tuck. *Guest:* More than 60 appearances.

HUTTON, TIMOTHY
Actor, Director. b. Malibu, CA, Aug. 16, 1960. Father was late actor Jim Hutton. Debut in bit part in father's film Never Too Late. Acted in high school plays; toured with father in Harvey during vacation. Directed Cars video Drive (1984).
PICTURES: Never Too Late (debut, 1965), Ordinary People (Academy Award, best supporting actor, 1980; also 2 Golden Globe Awards & LA Film Critics Awards 1981), Taps (Golden Globe nom. 1982), Daniel, Iceman, The Falcon and The Snowman, Turk 182, Made in Heaven, A Time of Destiny, Betrayed (cameo), Everybody's All American, Torrents of Spring, Q&A, Strangers, The Temp, The Dark Half, French Kiss, Beautiful Girls, The Substance of Fire, City of Industry, City of Industry, Playing God, Deterrence, The General's Daughter, Deterrence, Just One Night, The Lucky Strike, Sunshine State, Secret Window, Kinsey, Lymelife, Heavens Fall, Last Holiday, Stephanie Daley, Off the Black, The Good Shepherd, The Last Mimzy, When a Man Falls, The Alphabet Killer, Reflections, Multiple Sarcasms, The Killing Room, Serious Moonlight, Brief Interviews with Hideous Men, Lymelife, Broken Hill, The Ghost Writer.
TELEVISION: *Movies*: Zuma Beach, Friendly Fire, The Best Place to Be, And Baby Makes Six, Young Love First Love, Father Figure, A Long Way Home (Golden Globe nom. 1982), Zelda, The Last Word, Mr. & Mrs. Loving, Dead by Midnight, Vig, Aldrich Ames: Traitor Within, Deliberate Intent, WWIII, 5ive Days to Midnight, Avenger. *Director:* Amazing Stories (Grandpa's Ghost). *Mini-series*: 5ive Days to Midnight. *Series*: A Nero Wolfe Mystery (also exec. prod.), Kidnapped, Leverage. *Guest:* More than 60 appearances.

HUVANE, KEVIN
Executive. b. New York, NY. e. Fordham U. Began career in mail-room of William Morris Agency in New York. Promoted to agent in motion picture talent department. 1988, joined Creative Artists Agency where he is currently a managing partner. He is the talent agent of film and TV stars, including: Angela Bassett, Geena Davis, Meryl Streep, Glenn Close, Oprah Winfrey, Brad Pitt, Jennifer Anniston, Nicole Kidman, Lindsay Lohan, Stanley Tucci and Orlando Bloom. He helped create the CAA Foundation which encourages philanthropy in the entertainment community and develops public/private partnerships to support educational programs and charities. Recipient of David Niven Award for his contribution to Project ALS (Lou Gehrig's Disease).

HUYCK, WILLARD
Writer, Director. b. Sept. 8, 1945. e. USC. Worked as reader for Larry Gordon, executive at American-International Pictures; named Gordon's asst., working on scene rewrites for AIP films. First screen credit on The Devil's Eight as co-writer with John Milius.
PICTURES: *Writer*: American Graffiti (Academy Award nom.; WGA nom. 1974), Dead People (also dir., prod.), Lucky Lady, More American Graffiti, French Postcards (also dir., prod.), Indiana Jones and the Temple of Doom, Best Defense (also dir.), Howard the Duck (also dir.), Radioland Murders.
TELEVISION: A Father's Homecoming (co-exec. prod., co-s.p.), American River (co-exec. prod., co-s.p.), Mothers-Daughters & Lovers (also exec. prod.), Secrets of a Hollywood Nurse (writer, actor/voice).

HYAMS, JOSEPH
Advertising & Publicity Executive. b. New York, NY, Sept. 21, 1926. e. NYU Ent. industry, 1947. Various publicity posts, 20th Century-Fox, Columbia Pictures, 1947-55; eastern pub. mgr., Figaro Prods., 1955-56; West Coast pub. mgr., Hecht-Hill-Lancaster, 1955-58; pub. adv. dir., Batjac Prods. 1959-60 national adv. & pub. dir., Warner Bros.-7 Arts, 1960. v.p., worldwide pub., Warner Bros., Inc., 1970-87; sr. v.p., special projects, 1987, became exec. v.p. special projects 1992. Sr. v.p. of publicity for Warner Bros.

HYAMS, PETER
Director, Writer, Cinematographer. b. New York, NY, July 26, 1943. e. Hunter College, Syracuse U. Joined CBS news staff N.Y. as anchor. Filmed documentary on Vietnam in 1966. Left CBS in 1970 and joined Paramount in Hollywood as writer. Hired by ABC

to direct TV features. Currently runs own production co., Peter Hyams Productions, Inc.
PICTURES: *Writer:* T.R. Baskin (also prod.), Telefon, The Hunter. *Exec. Prod.:* The Monster Squad. *Director:* Busting (dir. debut 1974; also s.p.), Our Time (also s.p.), Peeper, Capricorn One (also s.p..), Hanover Street (also s.p)., Outland (also s.p.), The Star Chamber (also s.p.), 2010 (also prod., s.p., photog.), Running Scared (also exec. prod., photog.), The Presidio (also photog.), Narrow Margin (also s.p., photog.), Stay Tuned (also photog.), Timecop (also photog.), Sudden Death (also photog.), The Relic (also photog.), End of Days, The Musketeer (also photog.), A Sound of Thunder (also dir. of photog.), Beyond a Reasonable Doubt (also prod.), Universal Soldier: Regeneration (prod., cinematographer).
TELEVISION: *Movies (dir., writer):* The Rolling Man, Goodnight My Love. *Series:* Threshold (dir.).

HYMAN, DICK

Composer. b. New York, NY, March 8, 1927.
PICTURES: Erased Off, French Quarter, Stardust Memories, Zelig, Broadway Danny Rose (also mus. supv.), The Purple Rose of Cairo, Moonstruck (ASCAP Award 1989), Thelonious Monk: Straight—No Chaser, Radio Days (mus. supv.), The Lemon Sisters, Alan & Naomi, Mighty Aphrodite, Everyone Says I Love You, Sweet & Lowdown, The Curse of the Jade Scorpion (band leader), Two Weeks Notice (performer), Melinda and Melinda (also performer).
TELEVISION: *Movies:* Bernice Bobs Her Hair, The Deadliest Season, The Last Tenant, The Henderson Monster, King Crab, Johnny Bull, Natica Jackson, Ask Me Again. *Series:* Search for Tomorrow, Arthur Godfrey and His Friends, Great Performances, Fame, Fortune and Romance, Tales from the Hollywood Hills, NBC Special Treat (Emmy Award 1981). *Special:* 25th Annual News and Documentary Emmy Awards.

I

IANNIELLO, JOSEPH

Executive. e. Bachelor degree, business admin., Pace University; MBA, Columbia University. Finance executive Ianniello spent seven years with KPMG in various capacities before joining CBS. From 1997-2000, Ianniello was dir., financial planning at CBS. He also spent time in the investor relations and internal audit departments. Moved to CBS parent, Viacom, and from 2000-2005, served in various financial roles, including senior v.p. and treasurer and v.p., corporate development. Ianniello was integrally involved in identifying and assessing potential mergers and acquisitions for Viacom. Major transactions included the divestiture of Blockbuster and the acquisitions of BET, Comedy Central and Sportsline. 2008 senior v.p., finance and treasurer for CBS Corporation. In this role, Ianniello is responsible for corporate development, corporate finance, worldwide treasury and risk management activities for CBS. 2009 he became Exec. V.P. and CFO of CBS Corp. He serves on the bd. of the charitable organization New Alternatives for Children. In addition, he is a member of the American Institute of Certified Public Accountants and the New York Society of Public Accountants.

ICE CUBE

Actor, Singer. r.n. O'Shea Jackson. b. Los Angeles, CA, June 15, 1969. e. Phoenix Inst. of Tech. Debuted as rap performer with group N.W.A. Solo debut 1990 with album Amerikkka's Most Wanted.
PICTURES: Boyz N the Hood (debut, 1991), Trespass, CB4 (cameo), Higher Learning, Friday (also co-s.p., co-exec. prod.), The Glass Shield, Anaconda, Dangerous Ground (also exec. prod.), The Players' Club (also co-s.p., co-exec. prod., dir.), I Got the Hook-up, Three Kings, Next Friday (also co-s.p., co-exec. prod.), Ghosts of Mars, All About the Benjamins, Friday After Next, Torque, Barbershop, Barbershop 2: Back in Business, The Extractors, Waist Deep (soundtrack performer), Beerfest (soundtrack writer), Are We There Yet? (also prod.), Beauty Shop (exec. prod.), Mr. Blandings Builds His Dream House, xXx 2: The Next Level (also prod.), Are We Done Yet? (also prod.), First Sunday (also prod.), The Longshots (also prod.), 10 (also prod.), Lottery Ticket.
TELEVISION: *Movie:* Sisters in the Name of Rap. *Mini-series:* Generation Kill (soundtrack). *Series:* Barbershop (exec. prod.), Black. White. (exec. prod.). Documentary: Journey of Dr. Dre (also composer), Friday: The Animated Series (exec. prod.), ESPN 30/30: Straight Outta LA. *Guest:* More than 115 appearances.

ICE-T

Actor, Singer. r.n. Tracy Marrow. b. Newark, NJ, February 16, 1958. Raised in Los Angeles. Served 4 yrs. as ranger in U.S. Army. Made debut as rap performer with 1982 single The Coldest Rap. Received Grammy Award 1990 for Back on the Block.
PICTURES: Breakin' (debut, 1984), Breakin' 2: Electric Boogaloo, New Jack City, Ricochet, Trespass, Who's the Man?, Surviving the Game, Tank Girl, Johnny Mnemonic, Below Utopia, Rhyme & Reason (cameo), The Deli, Crazy Six, Jacob Two Two Meets the Hooded Fang, Final Voyage, Corrupt, The Wrecking Crew, Sonic Impact, Point Doom, The Heist, The Alternate, Leprechaun in the Hood, The Luck of the Draw, Los Angeles, Ablaze, 3000 Miles to Graceland, Deadly Rhapsody, R-Xmas, Ticker, Crime Partners 2000, Out Kold, Ablaze, Space Station, Playback, Air Rage, Stranded, Tracks, Pimpin' 101 (video, host, composer, 2002), Pimpin' 101 (video, host, 2003), Hancock (soundtrack writer), The Taking of Pelham 1 2 3 (soundtrack writer), Sounds Like a Revolution, Crossed the Line (exec. prod.), Santorini Blue.
TELEVISION: *Movies:* Exiled, The Disciples, The Magic 7 (voice/composer). *Series:* Players, (writer/creator), Law & Order: Special Victims Unit, Ice T's Rap School (host). *Guest:* More than 143 appearances.

IDLE, ERIC

Actor, Writer. b. South Shields, England, March 29, 1943. e. Pembroke Coll., Cambridge, 1962-65. Pres. Cambridge's Footlights appearing at Edinburgh Fest. 1963-64. Member Monty Python's Flying Circus appearing on BBC, 1969-74.
THEATRE: Oh What a Lovely War, Monty Python Live at the Hollywood Bowl, Monty Python Live, The Mikado (English Natl. Opera, 1986).
BOOKS: Hello Sailor, The Rutland Dirty Weekend Book, Pass the Bulter; as well as co-author of Monty Python books: Monty Python's Big Red Book, The Brand New Monty Python Book, Monty Python and the Holy Grail, The Complete Works of Shakespeare and Monty Python.
PICTURES: And Now for Something Completely Different (also co-s.p.), Monty Python and the Holy Grail (also co-s.p.), Monty Python's Life of Brian (also co-s.p.), Monty Python Live at the Hollywood Bowl (also co-s.p.), Monty Python's The Meaning of Life (also co-s.p.), Yellowbeard, National Lampoon's European Vacation, Transformers (voice), The Adventures of Baron Munchausen, Nuns on the Run, Too Much Sun, Missing Pieces, Mom & Dad Save the World, Splitting Heirs (also s.p., exec. prod.), Casper, The Wind and the Willows, An Alan Smithee Film: Burn Hollywood Burn, Quest for Camelot, Dudley Do-Right, South Park: Bigger Longer and Uncut (voice), 102 Dalmations, Dudley Do-Right, Pirates: 3D Show (writer), Journey Into Your Imagination, It's Only Rock 'n' Roll (video documentary), Brightness (short), Pinocchio (voice, U.S. version), Hollywood Homicide, Ella Enchanted (narrator), Delgo (voice), The Wild, Shrek the Third (voice), Wolf Sheep, Not the Messiah: He's a Very Naughty Boy (also writer).
TELEVISION: *Movies:* Isadora (debut, 1965), Alice in Wonderland, All You Need is Cash, The Mikado, The Scream Team, Christmas Vacation 2: Cousin Eddie's Island Adventure, BCN aixeca el teló (soundtrack writer). *Mini-series:* Around the World in 80 Days. *Series:* The Frost Report (writer), At Last the 1948 Show, No, That's Me Over Here!, Do Not Adjust Your Set, According to Dora, We Have Ways of Making You Laugh, Broaden Your Mind, Hark at Barker, Monty Python's Flying Circus, Rutland Weekend Television, The Two Ronnies, Shelley Duvall's Faerie Tale Theatre (The Frog Prince; dir., writer ACE Award, 1982; The Pied Piper), Saturday Night Live, Nearly Departed, One Foot in the Grave (theme comp.), Mickey Mouse Works (voice), Suddenly Susan, House of Mouse, The Soul Patrol, Super Robot Monkey Team Hyperforce Go! (voice). *Documentaries/Specials:* Top Ten Comedy Records, Rutles 2: Can't Buy Me Lunch, Funny Business, The Sketch Show Story. *Guest:* More than 137 appearances.

IDZIAK, SLAVOMIR

Cinematographer. b. Poland, Jan. 25, 1945.
PICTURES: A Woman's Decision, The Scar, Partita for a Wooden Instrument, The Conductor, Constancy, The Contract, Imperative, The Year of the Quiet Sun, Power of Evil, Harmagedon, A Short Film About Killing, Yasemin, Wherever You Are, Inventory, The Double Life of Veronique, Blue, Weltmesiter, The Journey of August King, Lilian's Story, Mannerpension, Tears of Stone, Men With Guns, Gattaca, Commandments, I Want You, Love and Rage, The Last September, Paranoid, LiebesLuder, Proof of Life, Black Hawk Down (Academy Award nom. 2002), King Arthur, Harry Potter and the Order of the Phoenix (also dir. of photog.).
TELEVISION: *Movies*: Podrozni jak inni, Gory o zmierzchu, Pizama, The Underground Passage, From A Far Country: Pope John Paul, The Unapproachable, The Decalogue, Long Conversation with a Bird.

IGER, ROBERT A.

Executive. b. New York, Feb. 10, 1951. e. Ithaca College. Iger is a 30-year entertainment industry veteran who began his career at ABC in 1974 as a studio supervisor in New York; he then moved to ABC Sports, where he advanced over a 12-year period through a series of increasingly responsible management posts. He became programming v.p., responsible for all scheduling and program acquisitions for ABC Sports in 1987. He left ABC Sports in 1988 for a promotion to executive v.p. of the ABC Television Network and became pres. of ABC Entertainment in Los Angeles in 1989. Iger was promoted to president, ABC Television Network Group in New York, 1993; named president and CEO of ABC in 1994. Iger first became part of Disney's management team in 1996, when The Walt Disney Company acquired Capital

Cities/ABC, where Iger had been president and COO. Iger guided the complex merger of ABC with The Walt Disney Company and was chmn. of the ABC Group while simultaneously serving as pres. of Walt Disney International. Iger was named pres. and COO, The Walt Disney Company in January 2000. Elevated to pres. and CEO, The Walt Disney Company on Oct. 1, 2005 and is the position he holds today He is also a Disney bd. member and part of its executive mgt. committee. Iger is a member of the bd. of dir. of Lincoln Center for the Performing Arts, Inc. He is a trustee of the American Film Institute bd. and serves on the Executive Advisory Board of the Elizabeth Glaser Pediatric AIDS Foundation.

IMI, TONY

Cinematographer. b. London, March 27, 1937. Ent. ind. 1959.
PICTURES: The Raging Moon, Dulcima, The Slipper and the Rose, International Velvet, Brass Target, Ffolkes, The Sea Wolves, Night Crossing, Not Quite Jerusalem, Enemy Mine, Empire State, American Roulette, Options, Wired, Fire Birds, Pretty Hattie's Baby, Shopping, Downtime, Aimee and Jaguar, Dead of Night, Rancid Aluminium, The Testimony of Taliesin Jones, Goodbye Charlie Bright, Silent Cry, A Flight of Fancy, Lighthouse Hill, Chaos and Cadavers, School for Seduction, Survival Island, Three, Watchful Eyes, Victims, Perfect Life.
TELEVISION: *Movies:* Up the Junction, Cathy Come Home, A Tale of Two Cities, For Ladies Only, My Body, My Child, Inside the Third Reich, Dreams Don't Die, Little Gloria–Happy at Last, Princess Daisy, The Last Days of Frank and Jesse James, John Paul II, Sakharov, A Christmas Carol, Reunion at Fairborough, Oceans of Fire, Queenie, Babycakes, Old Man and the Sea, Coins in the Fountain, Fourth Story, The Last to Go, Our Sons, Carolina Skeletons, Against Her Will: An Incident in Baltimore, Child of Rage, Poisoned by Love: The Kern County Murders, Queen, Cobb's Law, For the Love of My Child: The Anissa Ayala Story, Blind Angel, The Sunshine Boys, The Haunting of Helen Walker, The Turn of the Screw, Dalva, The Abduction, Her Desperate Choice, Only Love, Victoria & Albert, Blackwater Lightship, The Shell Seekers, Candles on Bay Street, Starting Over. *Mini-series:* Edward the King, The Life and Adventures of Nicholas Nickleby, Scarlett (ASC nom. 1995). *Series:* Elephant Boy, The Return of Sherlock Holmes, Four Seasons.

IMMERMAN, WILLIAM J.

Producer, Attorney, Executive. b. New York, NY, Dec. 29, 1937. e. Univ. Wisconsin, BS, 1959; Stanford Law, J.D., 1963. 1963-65, served as deputy district attorney, LA County. 1965-72, assoc. counsel, v.p.-bus. affairs, American Int'l. Pictures. 1972-77, v.p., business affairs, sr. v.p. feature film division 20th Century-Fox. He represented Fox on the bd. of dir. of M.P.A.A. & the Assoc. of Motion Picture and Television Producers. 1977-1979, producer at Warner Bros. 1979-82, founder and chmn. of bd. of Cinema Group Inc., spec. vice chmn. Cannon Pictures, consultant to office of pres., Pathe Communications. 1989-90; 1986-90, dir. Heritage Ent., Inc. 1991, v.p. The Crime Channel, 1983-93. Has also practiced law as sr. entertainment atty. with the law firms of Barash & Hill, Kenoff & Machtinger and The Law Offices of William J. Immerman. Currently is COO of the Yari Film Group. Member of the Academy of Motion Picture Arts and Sciences and serves as an arbitrator for the American Film Marketing Association. Stage Productions: Berlin to Broadway (LA), The Knife Thrower's Assistant (LA, tour), The Wiz (B'way).
PICTURES: *Exec. prod.:* Highpoint, Southern Comfort, Hysterical, Mind Games, Take this Job and Shove It, Where the Red Ferns Grows Part II, The St. Tammany Miracle, The Lost Treasure of Sawtooth Island, Bring Him Home, Swimming Upstream, Danny Deckchair, The Game of Their Lives, Unchain My Heart, Ray, Sahara, The Game of Their Lives, A Sound of Thunder, Kickin It Old Skool (head of bus. & legal affairs), Nothing But the Truth (also actor), What Doesn't Kill You, The Payback Man (legal services only). *Prod.:* Primal Rage, Nightmare Beach (Welcome to Spring Break), Children on Their Birthdays.
TELEVISION: *Movie:* Partners (legal services).

IMPERIOLI, MICHAEL

Actor, Writer, Producer. b. Mount Vernon, NY, March 26, 1966. e. Studied acting at New York City's Stella Adler Conservatory.
THEATRE: *NY:* Aven' U Boys.
PICTURES: Lean on Me, Goodfellas, Jungle Fever, Fathers & Sons, Malcolm X, The Night We Never Met, Household Saints, Amateur, Post Cards from America, Bad Boys, The Basketball Diaries, Clockers, Flirt, Dead Presidents, The Addiction, I Shot Andy Warhol, Girls Town, Girl 6, Sweet Nothing, Trees Lounge, Last Man Standing, Office Killer, Em Fuga, Summer of Sam (also writer, exec. prod.), Love in the Time of Money, My Baby's Daddy, Shark Tale (voice), The Inner Life of Martin Frost, The Lovebirds, The Higher Force, The Hungry Ghosts (writer only), The Lovely Bones.
TELEVISION: *Movies:* Firehouse, Disappearing Acts, Hamlet, The Five People You Meet in Heaven, Oprah Winfrey Presents: Mitch Albom's For One More Day. *Series:* Law & Order, The Sopranos (also writer, consult. prod., Emmy Award 2004, 4 other noms.; 2 Golden Globe noms.), Life on Mars.

INGELS, MARTY

Actor, Former Comedian, Executive. b. Brooklyn, NY, Mar. 9, 1936. m actress-singer Shirley Jones. U.S. Infantry 1954-58. Ent. show business representing Army, Name That Tune. Stage: Sketchbook revue, Las Vegas. Pres., Celebrity Brokerage, packaging celebrity events and endorsements. Active in community affairs and charity funding.
PICTURES: The Ladies Man, Armored Command, The Horizontal Lieutenant, The Busy Body, Wild and Wonderful, A Guide for the Married Man, If It's Tuesday It Must be Belgium, For Singles Only, Instant Karma, Round Numbers, The Opposite Sex and How to Live with Them, Cops n Roberts, Kartenspieler, Wednesday Again, Parasomnia.
TELEVISION: *Series:* I'm Dickens... He's Fenster, The Pruitts of Southampton, The Phyllis Diller Show. Voice: The Cattanooga Cats, Motormouse, The New Tom & Jerry Show, The Great Grape Ape Show, Pac-Man, Z-Squad. *Guest:* More than 62 appearances.

INSDORF, ANNETTE

Film Professor, Critic, Translator, TV Host. b. Paris, France. e. 1963-68 studied voice, Juilliard Sch. of Music and performed as singer; Queens College (summa cum laude), B.A. 1972; Yale U., M.A., 1973; Yale U., Ph.D., 1975. 1973: soloist in Leonard Bernstein's Mass (European premiere in Vienna and BBC/WNET TV). 1975-87: professor of film, Yale U. Author of Francois Truffaut (1979; updated 1989), Indelible Shadows: Film and the Holocaust (1983, updated 1989). Since 1979: frequent contributor to NY Times (Arts and Leisure), Los Angeles Times, San Francisco Chronicle, Film Comment, and Premiere. Named Chevalier dans l'ordre des arts et lettres by French Ministry of Culture, 1986. Since 1987, dir. of Undergrad. Film Studies, Columbia U., and prof. Graduate Film Div. 1990 named chmn. of Film Div. 1987: exec.-prod. Shoeshine (short film nom. for Oscar). 1989: exec. prod., Tom Abrams' Performance Pieces (named best fiction short, Cannes Fest). 2002-2003, Host of Bravo Cable Network's Weekend at Cannes: Closing Ceremonies.

IRELAND, DAN

Producer, Director, Actor.
PICTURES: *Exec. Prod.:*The Unholy, Salome's Last Dance, Midnight Crossing, Paperhouse, The Lair of the White Worm, Paint It Black, The Rainbow, Em. *Prod.:* If You're Afraid to Say It... Just See It, The Whole Wide World (also dir.). *Dir.:* Passionada, Jolene, Mrs. Palfrey at the Claremont. *Actor:* Ivansxtc.
TELEVISION: *Movie:* Living Proof (dir.). *Series:* The Outer Limits (dir. episode "Skin Deep"), 2gether: The Series (dir. episode "Waxed").

IRELAND, JAY

Executive. e. B.A. from St. Lawrence University in 1977. After three years as an U.S. Army Officer, Ireland started his career with General Electric (GE) in 1980 in the financial mgt. program in Lynchburg, Virginia, and joined the corporate audit staff in 1982. In 1988, he transferred to GE Plastics in Pittsfield, Massachusetts, where he held several financial and product mgt. assignments. He then moved to Bergen op Zoom, Holland, in 1990, where he was managing director of Polymerland-Europe, a plastics distribution company. In March 1993, he returned to Fairfield, CT, as mgr., corporate investor communications. In May 1995, v.p., corporate audit staff. Before joining NBC (NBC Universal since the May 2004 merger), Ireland had been the CFO of GE Plastics since 1997. Ireland was named pres. of NBC Universal Television Stations and Network Operations in December 2006. In mid-July 2007, GE promoted Ireland, naming him the president and CEO of GE Asset Management. He also serves as a member of GE's corporate executive council and the GE Capital Board of Directors. The move puts Ireland in charge of one of GE's major businesses, a global investment firm with nearly $200 billion in assets under management.

IRONS, JEREMY

Actor. b. Isle of Wight, UK, Sept. 19, 1948. m. actress Sinead Cusack. e. Sherborne Sch., Dorset. Stage career began at Marlowe Theatre, Canterbury, where he was student asst. stage manager. Accepted at Bristol Old Vic Theatre Sch. for two-yr. course; then joined Bristol Old Vic Co. In London played in Godspell, Much Ado About Nothing, The Caretaker, Taming of the Shrew, Wild Oats, Rear Column, An Audience Called Edouard, etc. N.Y. stage debut, The Real Thing (Tony Award, 1984).
PICTURES: Nijinsky (debut, 1980), The French Lieutenant's Woman, Moonlighting, Betrayal, The Wild Duck, Swann in Love, The Mission (Golden Globe nom. 1987), Dead Ringers, A Chorus of Disapproval, Danny the Champion of the World (tv in U.S.), Australia, Reversal of Fortune (Academy Award, Golden Globe Award 1991), Kafka, Waterland, Damage, M. Butterfly, The House of the Spirits, The Lion King (voice), Die Hard With a Vengeance,Stealing Beauty, Lolita, The Man in the Iron Mask, Chinese Box, Longitude, Dungeons & Dragons, The Fourth Angel, The Night of the Iguana, Callas Forever, The Time Machine, And Now Ladies and Gentleman, Mathilde, Broadway: The Golden Age by the Legends Who Were There, Being Julia, Mathilde, Casanova, Kingdom of Heaven, The Merchant of Venice, Inland Empire, Eragon, Appaloosa, The Pink Panther 2,

The Master of Farnow.
TELEVISION: *Movies:* The Pallisers, Notorious Woman, Langrishe Go Down, The Captain's Doll, Autogeddon, Tales From Hollywood, The Dream of a Ridiculous Man, The Great War (voice), Ohio Impromptu, Last Call, Longitude, Fitzgerald, Elizabeth I (Emmy Award, Golden Globe Award 2006), The Magic 7 (voice), Georgia O'Keeffe (Golden Globe nom. 2010), The Borgias. *Mini-series:* Notorious Woman, Love for Lydia, Brideshead Revisited (Emmy nom.; Golden Globe nom. 1982). *Documentaries/Specials:* The Statue of Liberty, Sesame Street Special, The Civil War (mini), Russia's Last Tsar (narr.), The Great War and the Shaping of the 20th Century (mini, Emmy Award 1997), Ennio Morricone, Het, Korte leven van Anne Frank, Broadway: The Golden Age, by the Legends Who Were There, Freedom: A History of Us, Hittites (narr.), Predators at War, Gelibolu (narr.). *Guest:* More than 150 appearances.

IRONSIDE, MICHAEL
Actor. b. Toronto, Ontario, Canada, Feb. 12, 1950. e. Ontario Col. of Art.
PICTURES: Scanners, Visiting Hours, Spacehunter: Adventures in the Forbidden Zone, The Falcon and the Snowman, Jo Jo Dancer Your Life Is Calling, Top Gun, Extreme Prejudice, Nowhere to Hide, Hello Mary Lou: Prom Night II, Watchers, Total Recall, McBain, Highlander II: The Quickening, The Vagrant, Fortunes of War, The Killing Man, Free Willy, The Next Karate Kid, Major Payne, The Glass Shield, Starship Troopers, Desert Blue, Chicago Cab, Captive, Black Light, Going to Kansas City, One of Our Own, Ivory Tower, The Omega Code, Southern Cross, Ivory Tower, Crime and Punishment in Suburbia, Heavy Metal, The Perfect Storm, Cause of Death, Borderline Normal, Mindstorm, Down, Soulkeeper, Dead Awake, Extreme Honor, Fallen Angels, Fairtales & Pornography, Maximum Velocity, The Failures, The Machinist, Reeker, Prisoners of the Sun, The Veteran, The Alphabet Killer, Surveillance, Eve, Mutants, The Beacon, The Jazzman, Abduction of Jesse Bookman, Way of the Dolphin, Liberty, Eve, Terminator Salvation, Beneath the Blue.
TELEVISION: *Movies*: The Family Man, Clown White, The Sins of Dorian Gray, Murder in Space, Ford: The Man and the Machine, Murder by Night, Deadly Surveillance, Marked for Murder, Dead Man's Revenge, Probable Cause (also co-exec. prod.), Asian Connection: Road to Mandalay, Terminal, The Arrow, Voyage of Terror, Johnny 2.0, Jett Jackson: The Movie, The Red Phone: Manhunt, Hemingway vs. Callaghan, Alaska, The Red Phone: Checkmate, Bloodsuckers, Disaster Zone: Volcano in New York, The Veteran, Storm Cell, The Terrorist Next Door. *Mini-series:* V: The Final Battle, Race for the Bomb, Nuremberg, The Last Chapter, The Last Chapter II: The War Continues. *Series*: V, ER, SeaQuest 2032, The New Batman Superman Adventures, Young Blades, Ice Planet, Justice League Unlimited, Wolverine and the X-Men. *Documentaries/Specials:* The Moravian Massacre, A Supercarrier Is Burning: U.S.S. Enterprise, Inside the Kill Box: Fighting the Gulf War. *Guest:* More than 90 appearances.

IRVIN, JOHN
Director. b. Cheshire, England, May 7, 1940. In cutting rooms at Rank Organisation before making first film documentary, Gala Day, on grant from British Film Inst.; made other award-winning documentaries before turning to features.
PICTURES: The Dogs of War (debut, 1981), Ghost Story, Champions, Turtle Diary, Raw Deal, Hamburger Hill, Next of Kin, Eminent Domain, Widow's Peak, A Month by the Lake, City of Industry, Wisegirls, Shiner, The Fourth Angel, The Great Ceili War, The Boys & Girl From County Clare, Digital Reaper, Laughing Water (Mine-Ha Ha), The Moon and the Stars, The Garden of Eden, Red Gold.
TELEVISION: *Movies:* Possessions, Haunted: The Ferryman, Robin Hood (foreign theatrical), Crazy Horse, When Trumphets Fade, Noah's Ark. *Mini-series:* Tinker Tailor Soldier Spy. *Series:* The Nearly Man, Hard Times.

IRVING, AMY
Actress. b. Palo Alto, CA, Sept. 10, 1953. e. American Conservatory Theatre, London Acad. of Dramatic Art. Daughter of late theatre dir. Jules Irving and actress Priscilla Pointer.
THEATRE: NY: Amadeus, Heartbreak House, Road to Mecca, Broken Glass, Three Sisters, Ghosts. LA: The Heidi Chronicles.
PICTURES: Carrie (debut, 1976), The Fury, Voices, Honeysuckle Rose, The Competition, Yentl (Academy Award nom. 1984), Micki and Maude, Rumpelstiltskin, Who Framed Roger Rabbit (voice), Crossing Delancey (Golden Globe nom. 1989), A Show of Force, An American Tail: Fievel Goes West (voice), Benefit of the Doubt, Kleptomania, Acts of Love (also co- exec. prod.), I'm Not Rappaport, Carried Away, Deconstructing Harry, One Tough Cop, Blue Ridge Fall, The Confession, The Rage: Carrie 2, Blue Ridge Fall, Bossa Nova, Traffic, 13 Conversations About One Thing, Tuck Everlasting, Hide and Seek, Adam.
TELEVISION: *Movies*: James Dean, James A. Michener's Dynasty, Panache, Anastasia: The Mystery of Anna (Golden Globe nom. 1987). *Mini-series*: Once an Eagle, The Far Pavilions, The Impressionists, A Century of Women (voice). *Series:* Alias, Stories from My Childhood. *Specials*: I'm a Fool, Turn of the Screw, Heartbreak House, Twilight Zone: Rod Serling's Lost Classics: The Theater, The Impressionists, A Century of Women (voice), Terror in the Aisles, American Masters (voice).

IRWIN, BILL
Actor. b. Santa Monica, CA, April 11, 1950.
THEATRE: B'way: Accidental Death of an Anarchist, 5-6-7-8 Dance, Largely New York, Fool Moon. Off-B'way: The Regard of Flight, The Courtroom, Not Quite New York, Waiting for Godot. Regional: Scapin (also dir., adaptation).
PICTURES: Popeye (debut, 1980), A New Life, Eight Men Out, My Blue Heaven, Scenes From a Mall, Hot Shots!, Stepping Out, Silent Tongue, Manhattan by Numbers, Water Ride, Illuminata, Just the Ticket, A Midsummer Night's Dream, Stanley's Gig, How the Grinch Stole Christmas, The Laramie Project, Igby Goes Down, The Truth About Miranda, The Manchurian Candidate, Lady in the Water, Dark Matter, Across the Universe, Rachel Getting Married.
TELEVISION: *Movies*: Subway Stories: Tales from the Underground. *Series*: Sesame Street, The Moth. *Specials*: The Regard of Flight, Bette Midler—Mondo Beyondo, The Paul Daniels Magic Show (BBC), The Last Mile.

ISAACS, CHERYL BOONE
Executive. b. Springfield, MA. Entered m.p. industry 1977 as staff publicist for Columbia Pictures. Worked five years after that for Melvin Simon Prods., named v.p. Left to become dir. of adv./pub. for The Ladd Co. 1984, named dir., publicity & promotions, West Coast, for Paramount Pictures. Promoted to vice pres., Worldwide Publicity, Paramount, 1986; sr. v.p., Worldwide Publicity, Paramount, 1991; exec. v.p., Worldwide Publicity, Paramount, 1994. Pres., theatrical marketing, New Line until 1999. Boone Isaacs currently is a partner with Target Approach, Inc., a strategic marketing company. Member A.M.P.A.S. Board of Governors since 1988 and v.p. 2003-.

ISRAEL, NEAL
Writer, Director, Producer.
PICTURES: Cracking Up (s.p., actor), Americathon (dir., s.p.), Police Academy (s.p.), Bachelor Party (dir., s.p.), Johnny Dangerously (actor), Moving Violations (dir., s.p.), Real Genius (s.p.), It's Alive III (s.p.), Buy and Cell (co-s.p.), Look Who's Talking Too (co-prod., actor), Spurting Blood (exec. prod., s.p.), All I Want for Christmas (co-s.p.), Breaking the Rules (dir.), Surf Ninjas (dir., actor), Tunnelvision (co-dir.),Three O'clock High (co-prod.), Police Academy: Mission to Moscow (s.p.), The Adventures of Mary-Kate & Ashley: The Case of the Sea World Adventure & The Case of the Mystery Cruise (video, dir. s.p.), Chocolate for Breakfast (exec. prod.), The Runner (exec. prod.), Finding Neverland, Police Academy (writer), Bachelor Party 2: The Last Temptation (exec. prod.).
TELEVISION: *Movies*: The Cover Girl and the Cop (dir.), Woman With a Past (co-exec. prod.), Combat High (dir.), Taking the Heat (co-prod.), Dream Date (prod.), Bonnie and Clyde: The True Story (co-prod.), A Quiet Little Neighborhood (co-prod.), Foster's Field Trip (dir., writer), Family Reunion: A Relative Nightmare (dir., co-writer, co-prod.), National Lampoon's Dad's Week Off (dir., writer), The Patty Duke Show: Still Rockin' in Brooklyn Heights (s.p.), Hounded, The Poof Point, The Brady Bunch in the White House, Thanksgiving Family Reunion (dir.). *Series:* Twilight Theater, The Wonder Years (dir.), Harts of the West (dir.). Nash Bridges (dir.) Clueless (dir.), Love Boat: The Next Wave, Lizzie McGuire, Shasta McNasty, Even Stevens (dir.), The Mind of the Married Man (dir.), Family Affair (dir., 2002), Do Over, Miracles (co-prod.), Phil of the Future (dir.), Hidden Howie (exec. prod./dir.), About a Girl (pilot). *Specials:* Lola Falana Special (writer), Mac Davis Show, Ringo, Marie (prod.), Twilight Theatre (writer, prod.), Man of the People (co-prod.), Steve Martin: All Commercials (WGA Award 1981).

IVANEK, ZELJKO
Actor. b. Ljubljana, Yugoslavia, Aug. 15, 1957. Came to U.S. with family in 1960 and returned to homeland before settling in Palo Alto, CA, in 1967. Studied at Yale, majoring in theatre studies: graduated in 1978. Also graduate of London Acad. of Music and Dramatic Arts. Was member of Williamstown Theatre Festival, appearing in Hay Fever, Charley's Aunt, Front Page. B'way debut in The Survivor.
THEATRE: *B'way:* The Survivor, Brighton Beach Memoirs, Loot, Two Shakespearean Actors, The Glass Menagerie. *Regional:* Master Harold... and the Boys (Yale Rep. premiere prod.), Hamlet (Guthrie), Ivanov (Yale Rep.). *Off B'way:* Cloud 9, A Map of the World, The Cherry Orchard, Blue/Orange.
PICTURES: Tex, The Sender, The Soldier, Mass Appeal, Rachel River, School Ties, White Squall, Courage Under Fire, Infinity, The Associate, Donnie Brasco, Julian Po, Nowhere to Go, A Civil Action, Snow Falling on Cedars, Dancer in the Dark, Hannibal, Black Hawk Down, Unfaithful, Dogville, The Manchurian Candidate, Manderlay, The Hoax, Ascension Day, Live Free or Die Hard, In Bruges.
TELEVISION: *Movies*: The Sun Also Rises, Echoes in the Darkness, Aftermath: A Test of Love, Our Sons, My Brother's Keeper, Truman, After Jimmy, Ellen Foster, The Rat Pack, Dash and Lilly, Sally Hemmings: An American Scandal, Homicide: The Movie, The Reagans. *Mini-series*: From the Earth to the Moon, John Adams. *Series*: Homicide: Life on the Street, 24, Damages

(Emmy Award 2008), Heroes, Big Love. *Documentaries/Specials*: All My Sons, Anatomy of a 'Homicide: Life on the Street'. *Guest:* More than 68 appearances.

IVANY, PETER

Executive. b. Melbourne, Australia, Aug. 23, 1954. e. Monash U. Melbourne, B.A. Victoria Health Commission as strategic planning analyst, 1978-80. Kodak Australia, estimating and planning analyst, 1980-81. Joined Hoyts Corporation Pty Ltd. in 1982 as cinema mgr., then general mgr., Hoyts Video; general mgr., corporate development, 1988. CEO, Hoyts Corp. Resigned 1999 after selling out his share to Kerry Packer who bought Hoyts. Formed Ivany Investment Group in 1999 and is the CEO, taking over IMAX operations in Australia. He has taken three companies to IPO, raising in excess of $500 million. As well as Hoyts, these have included TV broadcasting and media outsourcing services and an entertainment and advertising business. The positions he currently holds include: appeal chmn. and chmn., major gifts, Jewish Communal Appeal; chmn., Sydney Swans Foundation; bd. member, Jewish Film Festival; Presidents' Council at the Art Gallery of NSW; bd. member, Museum of Contemporary Art (Sydney), bd. member, MacFarlane Burnet Medical Institute for Medical Research & Public Health Ltd.; bd. member, Australia Israel Cultural Exchange Patron and the Sydney University Australian Rules Club.

IVEY, JUDITH

Actress. b. El Paso, TX, Sept. 4, 1951. m. ind. prod., Tim Braine. e. Illinois State U. Stage debut in The Sea in Chicago, 1974.
THEATRE: Bedroom Farce, The Goodbye People, Oh Coward!, Design for Living, Piaf, Romeo and Juliet, Pastorale, Two Small Bodies, Steaming (Tony & Drama Desk Awards), Second Lady (off-B'way work she helped develop), Hurlyburly (Tony & Drama Desk Awards), Precious Sons (Drama Desk nom.), Blithe Spirit, Mrs. Dally Has a Lover, Park Your Car in Harvard Yard (Tony nom.), The Moonshot Tape (Obie Award), A Fair Country, A Madhouse in Goa.
PICTURES: Harry and Son (debut, 1984), The Lonely Guy, The Woman in Red, Compromising Positions, Brighton Beach Memoirs, Hello Again, Sister Sister, Miles from Home, In Country, Everybody Wins, Alice, Love Hurts, There Goes the Neighborhood, Washington Square, The Devil's Advocate, Without Limits, Mystery Alaska, The Stand-In, What Alice Found, Flags of Our Fathers, The Loop.
TELEVISION: *Movies*: The Shady Hill Kidnapping, Dixie: Changing Habits, We Are the Children, The Long Hot Summer, Jesse and the Bandit Queen, Decoration Day, Her Final Fury: Betty Broderick—The Last Chapter, On Promised Land, Almost Golden: The Jessica Savitch Story, What the Deaf Man Heard (Emmy nom. 1998), Texarkana, Life's Little Struggles, Pictures of Hollis Woods. *Mini-series*: Rose Red. *Series*: Down Home, Designing Women, The Critic (voice), The Five Mrs. Buchanans, Buddies, Past Life. *Special*: Other Mothers (Afterschool Special).

IVORY, JAMES

Director. b. Berkeley, CA, June 7, 1928. e. U. of Oregon, B.F.A., 1951; U. of Southern California, M.A. (cinema) 1956. First film Venice: Theme and Variations (doc. made as M.A. thesis, 1957). Early work: The Sword and the Flute, The Delhi Way. Formed Merchant Ivory Productions with prod. Ismail Merchant and script writer Ruth Prawer Jhabvala. Received D.W. Griffith Lifetime Achievement Award from DGA 1995, Commandeur Des Arts et Des Lettres, France 1996.
PICTURES: The Householder, Shakespeare Wallah (also co-s.p.), The Guru (also co-s.p.), Bombay Talkie (also co-s.p.), Savages, The Wild Party, Roseland, The Europeans (also cameo), Quartet, Heat and Dust, The Bostonians, A Room With a View (Academy Award nom.; DGA nom.; Golden Globe nom. 1987), Maurice (also co-s.p.), Slaves of New York, Mr. and Mrs. Bridge, Howards End (Academy Award nom.; DGA nom.; Golden Globe nom. 1993), The Remains of the Day (Academy Award nom.; DGA nom.; Golden Globe nom. 1994), Jefferson in Paris, Surviving Picasso, A Soldier's Daughter Never Cries (also s.p.), The Golden Bowl, Le Divorce (also s.p), Heights (prod.), The White Countess, Made in France (exec. prod.), City of Your Final Destination.
TELEVISION: *Movies:* Noon Wine (exec. prod.). *Dir:* Autobiography of a Princess (also released theatrically), Hullabaloo Over George and Bonnie's Pictures, Jane Austen in Manhattan (also released theatrically), The Five Forty Eight. *Documentaries:* Adventures of a Brown Man in Search of Civilization, The Courtesans of Bombay.

J

JACKMAN, HUGH

Actor, Producer. b. Sidney, New South Wales, Australia, October 12, 1968. e. U. of Technology, Sydney. Pursued drama at the Western Australian Academy of Performing Arts. Owner/Founder of production company, Seed Productions.
THEATRE: *London:* Beauty and the Beast, Oklahoma!. *Australia:* Sunset Boulevard, The Boy from Oz. *B'way:* Carousel, The Boy From Oz (Tony Award 2004), A Steady Rain.
PICTURES: X-Men, Someone Like You..., Swordfish, Kate & Leopold (Golden Globe nom. 2002), X2, Van Helsing, X-Men: The Last Stand, Scoop, The Fountain, The Prestige, Flushed Away (voice), Happy Feet (voice, soundtrack performer), Deception (also prod.), Australia, X-Men Origins: Wolverine (also prod.), Snow Flower and the Secret Fan, Unbound Captives, Selma, Real Steel, Butter, Avon Man (also prod.).
TELEVISION: *Movies:* Halifax f.p: Afraid of the Dark, Oklahoma!. *Series:* Correlli, Snowy River: The McGregor Saga, The Directors' Series (exec. prod.), Viva Laughlin (also pilot). *Specials:* The 2004 Tony Awards (host, Emmy Award 2005), The 59th Annual Tony Awards (host, Emmy Award nom. 2006), 81st Annual Academy Awards (Emmy nom. 2009). *Guest:* More than 133 appearances.

JACKSON, ANNE

Actress. b. Allegheny, PA, Sept. 3, 1926. e. Neighborhood Playhouse, Actors Studio. m. to actor Eli Wallach. Stage debut in The Cherry Orchard, 1944. Autobiography: Early Stages.
THEATRE: Major Barbara, Middle of the Night, The Typist and the Tiger, Luv, Waltz of the Toreadors, Twice Around the Park, Summer and Smoke, Nest of the Woodgrouse, Marco Polo Sings a Solo, The Mad Woman of Chaillot, Cafe Crown, Lost in Yonkers, In Persons, The Flowering Peach, Love Letters.
PICTURES: So Young So Bad (debut, 1950), The Journey, Tall Story, The Tiger Makes Out, How to Save a Marriage and Ruin Your Life, The Secret Life of an American Wife, The Angel Levine, Zig Zag, Lovers and Other Strangers, Dirty Dingus Magee, Nasty Habits, The Bell Jar, The Shining, Sam's Son, Funny About Love, Folks!, Man of the Century, Something Sweet, Broadway: The Golden Age by the Legends Who Were There, Lucky Days.
TELEVISION: *Movies*: The Family Man, A Woman Called Golda, Private Battle, Blinded By the Light, Leave 'em Laughing, Baby M, Rescuers: Stories of Courage: Two Women. *Series*: Everything's Relative, CBS Playhouse (Emmy nom. for episode "Dear Friends" 1968). *Special*: 84 Charing Cross Road. *Guest:* More than 60 appearances.

JACKSON, BRIAN

Actor, Film & Theatre Producer. b. Bolton, England, 1931. Early career in photography then numerous stage performances incl. Old Vic, Royal Shakespeare. Ent. film/TV industry 1958. Formed Quintus Plays, 1965; formed Brian Jackson Productions 1966; formed Hampden Gurney Studios Ltd. 1970. Co-produced The Others 1967; presented The Button, 1969; co-produced the documentary film Village in Mayfair, 1970; 1971: Formed Brian Jackson Films Ltd.; produced Yesterday, The Red Deer, The Story of Tutankhamen.
THEATRE: Mame, Drury Lane, Fallen Angels, In Praise of Love.
PICTURES: Incident in Karandi, Carry On Sergeant, Gorgo, Jack the Ripper, Taste of Fear, Heroes of Telemark, Only the Lonely, The Deadly Females, The Revenge of the Pink Panther, Deceptions, Shadowchaser, Cash and Curry, Coulda, Woulda, Shoulda.
TELEVISION: *Mini-series:* Walk a Crooked Mile. *Commercials:* featured as the man from Delmonte for 5 years.

JACKSON, GLENDA

Actress. b. Birkenhead, England, May 9, 1936. Stage debut: Separate Tales (Worthing, England, 1957). 1964 joined Peter Brooks' Theatre of Cruelty which led to film debut. Became Member of Parliament, 1992.
THEATRE: (Eng.): All Kinds of Men, Hammersmith, The Idiot, Alfie. Joined Royal Shakespeare Co in experimental Theatre of Cruelty season. Marat Sade (London, N.Y.), Three Sisters, The Maids, Hedda Gabler, The White Devil, Rose, Strange Interlude (N.Y.), Macbeth (N.Y.), Who's Afraid of Virginia Wolf? (L.A.).
PICTURES: The Persecution and Assassination of Jean-Paul Marat as Performed by the Inmates of the Asylum at Charenton Under the Direction of the Marquis de Sade (debut, 1967), Tell Me Lies, Negatives, Women in Love (Academy Award, Golden Globe nom. 1971), The Music Lovers, Sunday Bloody Sunday (Academy Award nom. 1972), Mary Queen of Scots (Golden Globe nom. 1972), The Boy Friend, Triple Echo, The Nelson Affair, A Touch of Class (Academy Award, Golden Globe Award 1974), The Maids, The Temptress, The Romantic Englishwoman, The Devil is a Woman, Hedda (Academy Award nom.; Golden Globe nom. 1976), The Incredible Sarah (Golden Globe nom. 1977), Nasty Habits, House Calls, Stevie (Golden Globe nom. 1979), The Class of Miss McMichael, Lost and Found, Health, Hopscotch, Giro City, The Return of the Soldier, Turtle Diary, Beyond Therapy, Business as Usual, Salome's Last Dance, The Rainbow, The Visit, King of the Wind, Doombeach,
TELEVISION: *Movies*: The Patricia Neal Story (Emmy nom.; Golden Globe nom. 1982), Sakharov (Golden Globe nom. 1985), Strange Interlude, Jerry Springer on Sunday,The House of Bernarda Alba, A Murder of Quality, The Secret Life of Arnold Bax. *Mini-series*: Elizabeth R (2 Emmy Awards, 1 other nom. 1972). *Specials*: Strange Interlude, A Murder of Quality, The House of Bernarda Alba, I Love a 1970s Christmas, William Shakespeare. *Guest:* More than 55 appearances.

JACKSON, JOSHUA
Actor. b. Vancouver, Canada, June 11, 1978.
PICTURES: Crooked Hearts, The Mighty Ducks, Digger, Andre, D2: The Mighty Ducks, Magic in the Water, Robin of Locksley, D3: The Mighty Ducks, Scream 2, Apt Pupil, Urban Legend, Cruel Intentions, Muppets From Space, The Skulls, Gossip, The Safety of Objects, Ocean's Eleven, The Laramie Project, Road To Hell (2002), I Love Your Work, Cursed, Aurora Borealis, Americano, Racing Stripes (voice), Shadows in the Sun, Bobby, Battle in Seattle, Shutter, One Week (also exec. prod.), U.F.O.
TELEVISION: *Movies*: Payoff, Robin of Locksley, Ronnie & Julie, The Laramie Project, On the Edge of Innocence, Capitol Law, Fringe (pilot). *Series*: Dawson's Creek, Fringe.

JACKSON, KATE
Actress. b. Birmingham, AL, Oct. 29, 1949. e. U. of Miss., Birmingham Southern U. Did stock before going to N.Y. to enter American Acad. of Dramatic Arts, appearing in Night Must Fall, The Constant Wife, Little Moon of Alban. Worked as model and became tour guide at NBC. First role on TV in Dark Shadows (series).
PICTURES: Night of Dark Shadows, Limbo, Thunder and Lightning, Dirty Tricks, Making Love, Loverboy, Error in Judgment, Larceny, No Regrets.
TELEVISION: *Movies*: Satan's School for Girls, Killer Bees, Death Cruise, Death Scream, Charlie's Angels (pilot), Death at Love House, James at 15 (pilot, Emmy nom. 1978), Topper, Inmates: A Love Story, Thin Ice, Listen to Your Heart, The Stranger Within, Quiet Killer, Homewrecker (voice), Adrift, Empty Cradle, Armed and Innocent, Justice in a Small Town, The Silence of Adultery, Murder on the Iditarod Trail, A Kidnapping in the Family, Panic in the Skies, What Happened to Bobby Earl, Satan's School for Girls, A Mother's Testimony, Charlie's Angels: TV Tales (doc.), Miracle Dogs, A Daughter's Conviction. *Series*: Dark Shadows, The Rookies, Charlie's Angels (2 Emmy noms.; 3 Golden Globe noms.), Scarecrow and Mrs. King (Golden Globe nom. 1985), Baby Boom. *Guest*: More than 108 appearances.

JACKSON, MICK
Director. b. Grays, England, October 4, 1943. e. Bristol Univ. Joined BBC as film editor, following post-grad work in film & tv. Produced and directed many documentaries for the BBC.
PICTURES: Chattahoochee, L.A. Story, The Bodyguard, Clean Slate, Volcano, Josiah's Canon, The First $20 Million is Always the Hardest, Temple Grandin.
TELEVISION: *Movies/Specials*: How to Pick Up Girls!, Threads, The Race for the Double Helix, Yuri Nosenko KGB (HBO), A Very British Coup, Indictment: The McMartin Trial (DGA Award, Emmy nom. 1996), Strange World, Tuesdays with Morrie (DGA Award 2000), Traffic, Live from Baghdad (DGA Award, Emmy nom.; 2003), Street Boss, Covert One: The Hades Factor, The Memory Keeper's Daughter, Temple Grandin. *Mini-series*: A Very British Coup. *Series*: The Practice, Strange World, Connections, That's Life, The Handler. *Pilot:* Numb3rs (pilot), In Justice (pilot).

JACKSON, PETER
Director, Writer, Producer. b. New Zealand, Oct. 31, 1961.
PICTURES: Bad Taste, Meet the Feebles, Dead Alive, Heavenly Creatures (Academy Award nom.; WGA nom. 1995), Forgotten Silver, The Frighteners, Contact (special effects only), The Lord of the Rings: The Fellowship of the Ring (3 Academy Award nom., AFI Award; DGA nom.; WGA nom.; Golden Globe nom. 2002), The Lord of the Rings: The Two Towers (Academy Award nom.; DGA Award nom.; Golden Globe nom. 2003), The Lord of the Rings: The Return of the King (3 Academy Awards; DGA Award, WGA nom.; Golden Globe Award 2004), King Kong (Golden Globe nom. 2006), The Lovely Bones (s.p.,), The Adventures of Tintin: Secret of the Unicorn, District 9 (prod., Academy Award nom. 2010).
TELEVISION: *Movies:* Hercules and the Lost Kingdom, Lord of the Brush (actor only). *Series:* Worzel Gummidge Down Under (sp. effects), Ship to Shore (co-exec. prod.).

JACKSON, SAMUEL L.
Actor. b. Washington, D.C., Dec. 21, 1948. e. Morehouse Col. m. actress LaTanya Richardson. Co-founder, member of the Just Us Theatre Co. in Atlanta.
THEATRE: Negro Ensemble Company: Home, A Soldier's Story, Sally/Prince, Colored People's Time. NY Shakespeare Fest: Mother Courage, Spell No. 7, The Mighty Gents. Yale Rep: The Piano Lesson, Two Trains Running. Seattle Rep: Fences.
PICTURES: Ragtime (debut, 1981), Eddie Murphy Raw, School Daze, Coming to America, Do the Right Thing, Sea of Love, A Shock to the System, Def by Temptation, Betsy's Wedding, Mo' Better Blues, The Exorcist III, GoodFellas, Jungle Fever (Cannes Film Fest. & NY Film Critics Awards, 1991), Strictly Business, Juice, White Sands, Patriot Games, Johnny Suede, Jumpin at the Boneyard, Fathers and Sons, National Lampoon's Loaded Weapon 1, Amos & Andrew, Menace II Society, Jurassic Park, True Romance, Hail Caesar, Fresh, The New Age, Pulp Fiction (Academy Award nom.; Golden Globe nom. 1995), Losing Isaiah, Kiss of Death, Die Hard With a Vengeance, Fluke (voice), The Great White Hype, A Time to Kill (Golden Globe nom. 1997), The Long Kiss Goodnight, 187, Eve's Bayou (also prod.), Jackie Brown (Golden Globe nom. 1998), The Red Violin, Sphere, Out of Sight (cameo), The Negotiator, Rules of Engagement, Deep Blue Sea, Star Wars: Episode I-The Phantom Menace, Forever Hollywood, Rules of Engagement, Shaft, Unbreakable, The Caveman's Valentine, Changing Lanes, 51st State, Mefisto in Onyx, Stars Wars: Episode 2: Attack of the Clones, XXX, No Good Deed, S.W.A.T., Basic, Kill Bill: Volume 1, Country of My Skull, The Blackout Murders, Twisted, Kill Bill: Vol. 2, The Incredibles (voice), All Day Long, xXx 2: The Next Level, The Man, Star Wars: Episode III - Revenge of the Sith, Flight 121, Freedomland, Snakes on a Plane, Home of the Brave, Black Snake Moan, Jumper, Resurrecting the Champ, 1408, Cleaner, Black Water Transit, Lakeview Terrace, Iron Man, Star Wars: The Clone Wars (voice), The Spirit, Soul Men, Rape: A Love Story, Blown, Inglourious Basterds (narr.), Quantum Quest: A Cassini Space Odyssey (voice), Unthinkable, Astro Boy (voide), Mother and Child, The Other Guys, Iron Man 2, Vengeance: A Love Story, xXx: The Return of Xander Cage.
TELEVISION: *Movies*: The Displaced Person, The Trial of the Moke, Uncle Tom's Cabin, Dead Man Out, Mob Justice, Simple Justice, Assault at West Point: The Court-Martial of Johnson Whittaker, Against the Wall (Golden Globe nom. 1995), 2004: A Light Knight's Odyssey (voice), Honor Deferred (narr.), Afro Samurai: Resurrection (voice, exec. prod.). *Mini-series:* Afro Samurai (voice, co-prod., exec. prod., Emmy nom. 2009). *Documentaries / Specials:* The Secret World of Spying, The American Experience, The Directors, The Journey of the African-American Athlete (narr.), Jazz (mini), America Beyond the Color Line with Henry Louis Gates Jr. (mini), Middle School Confessions (host), Unchained Memories: Readings from the Slave Narratives, Freedom: A History of Us, The N-Word, Unforgivable Blackness: The Rise and Fall of Jack Johnson, Extras (series). *Guest:* More than 242 appearances.

JACOBI, SIR DEREK
O.B.E. Actor. b. London, England, Oct. 22, 1938. e. Cambridge. On stage in Pericles, The Hollow Crown, Hobson's Choice, The Suicide, Breaking the Code (London, NY).
PICTURES: Othello (debut, 1965), Interlude, The Three Sisters, The Day of the Jackal, Blue Blood, The Odessa File, The Medusa Touch, The Human Factor, Enigma, The Secret of NIMH (voice), Little Dorrit, Henry V, Dead Again, Hamlet, Basil, Up at the Villa, Love Is the Devil, Molokai: The Story of Father Damian, Gladiator, Up at the Villa, The Body, Joan of Arc: Virgin Warrior, Revelation, Gosford Park, Fairy Feller, The Diaries of Vaslav Nijinsky, Two Men Went to War, A Revenger's Tragedy, Broadway: The Golden Age by the Legends Who Were There, Bye Bye Blackbird, Nanny McPhee, Venetian Heat, Underworld: Evolution, Guantanamero, The Riddle, Anastezsi, The Golden Compass, Adam Resurrected, A Bunch of Amateurs, Morris: A Life with Bells On, Endgame, There Be Dragons, Ironclad, Hippie Hippie Shake, The King's Speech, Anonymous.
TELEVISION: *Movies*: Much Ado About Nothing, King Richard the Second, Hamlet, Prince of Denmark, Othello, Three Sisters, Interlude, Charlotte, The Man Who Went Up in Smoke, The Hunchback of Notre Dame, Inside the Third Reich (Emmy nom. 1982), Cyrano de Bergerac, The Secret Garden, The Tenth Man (Emmy Award 1989, Golden Globe nom. 1988), Storyteller: The Greek Myths, Circle of Deceit, Witness Against Hitler, Breaking the Code, Animated Epics: Beowulf, The Wyvern Mystery, Jason and the Argonauts, The Great Escape: The Untold Story (narr.), Larry and Viven: The Oliviers in Love, The Gathering Storm, Inquisition, Manor House, Dinosaur Hunters (narr.), Mr. Ambassador, London, The Long Firm, Marple: The Murder at the Vicarage, Pinochet's Last Stand, Mist: The Tale of a Sheepdog Puppy, Mist: Sheepdog Tales, The Old Curiosity Shop, Margot, Joe Maddison's War. *Mini-series*: Man of Straw, The Strauss Family, Mr Pye, She Stoops to Conquer, I, Claudius, The Storyteller: Greek Myths, Philby, Burgess and MacLean, Hamlet, The Jury, Doctor Who: Scream of the Shalka, Diamonds. *Series*: The Pallisers, Minder, Tales of the Unexpected, Mr. Pye, The Leper of St. Giles, Cadfael, Flora Britannica, Mist: Sheepdog Tales. *Documentaries:* The Statue of Liberty (voice), The Civil War (mini, voice), Animating Shakespeare, Baseball (mini, voice), The West (mini, voice), Victoria Wood and All the Trimmings, Jazz (Mini, voices), Manor House (mini, narr.), Unforgivable Blackness: The Rise and Fall of Jack Johnson (voice). *Guest:* More than 100 appearances.

JACOBS, MICHAEL
Producer, Writer. b. New Brunswick, NJ. Studied at Neighborhood Playhouse in NY. Had first play, Cheaters, prod. on B'way when he was only 22 yrs. old.
PICTURE: 3:15 (writer only), Halloween 5 (writer only) Quiz Show Academy Award nom. 1995), Treehouse Hostage, Trapped: Beneath the Snow, Peace Virus, Fangs, Let Freedom Sing: How Music Inspired the Civil Rights Movement (doc., exec. prod.), Nanking (doc., prod.).
TELEVISION: *Movies*: *Exec. Prod.:* Wild Grizzly, Lightning: Fire From the Sky, Trapped: Buried Alive, Killer Flood: The Day the Dam Broke, Love Thy Neighbor, Absolute Zero, Christmas in Boston, Night of Terror, Past Sins, Lost in the Dark, Vivid Dreams A Decent Proposal, Seventeen & Missing, The Terrorist Next Door, Girl's Best Friend, The Watch, Flirting with Forty (co-prod.), Special Delivery. *Series*: *Creator/prod.:* Charles in Charge, No

Soap Radio, Together We Stand, Singer and Songs, My Two Dads (also dir.), Dinosaurs, The Torkelsons (Almost Home), Boy Meets World, Maybe This Time (writer), The Sinbad Show (exec. prod., writer), Where I Live, You Wish (writer), Misery Loves Company, The Brainiacs.com., Lost at Home, Boarding School, Beyond the Break. *Documentaries:* As Seen Through These Eyes (exec. prod.), Nanking (news doc., prod., Emmy Award 2009, 2 other noms).

JACOBSEN, JOHN M.

Producer, Executive. b. Oslo, Norway, Dec. 27, 1944. Produced number of feature films incl. Pathfinder (Acad. Award nom.), Shipwrecked, Head Above Water. Pres., Norwegian Film and HTV Producers Assn.; Pres. AB Svensk Filmindustri Norwegian Operation.
PICTURES: Prima Veras saga om Olav den hellige, Hard asfalt, Pathfinder, Showbiz - eller hvordan bli kjendis på en-to-tre!, Shipwrecked, Giftige logner, De Bla ulvene, Head Above Water (1993), Chasing the Kidneystone, Head Above Water (1996), Gurin with the Foxtail, Only Clouds Move the Stars, Sleepwalker, 37 1/2, Pathfinder (exec. prod.), Elias and the Royal Yacht, Max Manus.
TELEVISION: *Mini-series:* Sofies verdin. *Series*: Elias: The Little Rescue Boat.

JACOBSON, NINA

Executive. e. graduate of Brown Univ. Began career as documentary researcher for Arnold Shapiro Productions. In 1987, she joined the Disney Sunday Movie as a story analyst. In 1988, Jacobson moved to Silver Pictures as dir. of development. She went on to head development at MacDonald/Parkes Productions, before leaving to join the executive ranks at Universal as sr. v.p., production. While there she helped develop Twelve Monkeys, Dazed and Confused and Dragon-The Bruce Lee Story. She developed What Lies Beneath and originated the idea for DreamWorks' first animated feature ANTZ as a senior film executive at DreamWorks SKG. From 1998-2006, Jacobson was with Buena Vista Motion Pictures Group. She resigned as the group's president in 2006. She was responsible for developing scripts and overseeing film production for Walt Disney Pictures, Touchstone Pictures and Hollywood Pictures. She supervised production of The Sixth Sense, Remember the Titans, Pearl Harbor and The Princess Diaries, among others. In December 2006, she opened her own studio-based production shingle, and is a producer for Color Force, at DreamWorks. Over the past 10 years, Jacobson has consistently ranked among the most powerful women in entertainment.

JAFFE, STANLEY R.

Producer. b. New York, NY, July, 31, 1940. Graduate of U. of Pennsylvania Wharton Sch. of Finance. Joined Seven Arts Associates, 1962; named exec. ass't to pres., 1964; later, head of East Coast TV programming. Produced Goodbye, Columbus, in 1968 for Paramount; joined that company as exec. v.p., 1969. Named pres. of Paramount in 1970; resigned 1971 to form own prod. unit. Joined Columbia as exec. v.p. of global prod. in 1976, but resigned to be independent prod. Pres. & COO of Paramount Communications from 1991-1994. Owner of Jaffilms LLC, 1994-
PICTURES: Goodbye Columbus, A New Leaf, Bad Company, Man on a Swing, The Bad News Bears, Kramer vs. Kramer (Academy Award for Best Picture, 1980), Taps, Without a Trace (also dir.), Madeline (exec.). Co-prod.(with Sherry Lansing): Racing with the Moon, Firstborn, Fatal Attraction (Academy Award nom. 1988), The Accused, Black Rain, School Ties, I Dreamed of Africa, The Four Feathers.

JAFFE, STEVEN-CHARLES

Producer. b. Brooklyn, NY, 1954. e. U. of Southern California, cinema. First professional job as documentary prod. on John Huston's Fat City. Served as prod. asst. on The Wind and the Lion in Spain. Assoc. prod. on Demon Seed (written by brother Robert); served as location mgr. on Who'll Stop the Rain; assoc. prod. on Time After Time. On TV worked as 2nd unit dir. on The Day After. Managing Director for production company Mount Helix.
PICTURES: Those Lips Those Eyes, Motel Hell (also co-s.p.), Scarab (dir.), Flesh + Blood (2nd unit. dir.), Near Dark, Plain Clothes (exec. prod.), The Fly II, Ghost (exec. prod., 2nd unit dir.), Company Business, Star Trek VI: The Undiscovered Country, Strange Days, The Informant, The Weight of Water, K-19: The Widowmaker, Eddy Deco (dir., writer), I'll See You Again (dir.).
TELEVISION: *Movie:* The Day After.

JAGGER, MICK

Singer, Composer, Actor, Producer. b. Dartford, Kent, England, July 26, 1943. Lead singer with the Rolling Stones.
PICTURES: *Composer:* Songs appeared in the following: The Rolling Stones Rock and Roll Circus, Performance, Ned Kelly (actor), Popcorn, Gimme Shelter, Sympathy for the Devil, Ladies and Gentlemen: The Rolling Stones, The London Rock 'n' Roll Show, Let's Spend the Night Together, At the Max, Freejack (actor), Bent, My Best Friend, The Man From Elysian Fields, Enigma, The Mayor of Sunset Strip. Made in U.S.A, Zabriskie Point, Mean Streets, Coming Home, FM, Divine Madness!, Night Shift, The Big Chill, Jumpin' Jack Flash, Full Metal Jacket, Adventures in Babysitting, Flashback, Goodfellas, Interview with the Vampire, Nine Months, Assassins, Casino, Bottle Rocket, The Fan, The Devil's Advocate, Fallen, Hope Floats, Rushmore, The Other Sister, The Replacements, The Way of the Gun, The Family Man, Blow, The Royal Tenenbaums, Life or Something Like It, Moonlight Mile, Adaptation, A Mighty Wind, Bruce Almighty, S.W.A.T., Alfie (comp. Golden Globe Award, best orig. song, 2005), The Women (prod., short), Without a Paddle, Beyond the Sea, Layer Cake, V for Vendetta, Talladega Nights: The Ballad of Ricky Bobby, Children of Men, The Departed, Ruby Tuesday (prod., composer), Children of Men, The Hoax, Sicko, Salt of the Earth (doc.), Citizen Havel (doc.), Shine a Light (doc., exec. prod.), The Bank Job, Tropic Thunder, The Women (prod.), Adventureland (soundtrack writer), Pirate Radio (soundtrack writer), Fantastic Mr. Fox (soundtrack writer), The Bounty Hunter (soundtrack writer), Stones in Exile (doc., exec. prod.).
TELEVISION: *Series:* The Knights of Prosperity (actor, exec. prod.), Ready, Steady, Go! (actor), many more. *Specials*: The Nightingale (Faerie Tale Theatre), History of Rock 'N' Roll Pt. 3, 5 and 6, The Concert for New York City, America: A Tribute to Heroes, Being Mick. Numerous credits for soundtrack writing).

JAGGS, STEVE

Executive. b. London, England, June 29, 1946. Entered motion picture industry, 1964. Gained experience in the film production and laboratory areas with Colour Film Service and Universal Laboratories. Joined Agfa-Gevaert Ltd., Motion Picture Division, 1976. Appt. sales manager, 1979; divisional manager, 1989. Joined Rank Organisation, 1992. Became managing director of Pinewood Studios and acquired Shepperton Studios, Buckinghamshire, United Kingdom in 2003. In 2005, Jaggs received the Life Fellow honor from BKSTS: The Moving Image Society, based in England.

JAGLOM, HENRY

Director, Writer, Editor, Actor. b. London, Eng., Jan. 26, 1943. Studied acting, writing and directing with Lee Strasberg and at Actors Studio. Did off-B'way. shows; went to West Coast where guest-starred in TV series (Gidget, The Flying Nun, etc.). Shot documentary film in Israel during Six Day War. Hired as edit consultant for Easy Rider by producer Bert Schneider. Acted in Psych Out, Drive He Said, The Last Movie, Thousand Plane Raid, Lili Aime Moi, The Other Side of the Wind (Orson Welles' unreleased last film). Wrote and dir. first feature, A Safe Place, in 1971. Created The Women's Film Co. (to prod. and distrib. motion pictures by women filmmakers), and Jagfilms Inc., Rainbow Film Company, and Rainbow Releasing. Presented Academy Award winning documentary Hearts and Minds, 1974.
PICTURES: *Dir.-Writer-Prod.-Editor:* A Safe Place, Tracks, Sitting Ducks (also actor), National Lampoon Goes to the Movies (co-dir. only), Can She Bake A Cherry Pie?, Always (also actor), Someone To Love (also actor), New Year's Day (also actor), Eating, Venice Venice (also actor), Babyfever, Last Summer in the Hamptons (dir., co-s.p., edit., actor), Deja Vu (dir., s.p., edit.), Shopping, Festival in Cannes, Going Shopping, Hollywood Dreams, Irene in Time, Always, But Not Forever (writer).

JALBERT, JOE JAY

Executive. e. U. of Washington. Was ski captain in school and began film career as technical director on Downhill Racer, 1969, also cinematographer and double for Robert Redford. 1970, produced Impressions of Utah, documentary, with Redford. Won Emmy for cinematography on TV's Peggy Fleming Special. In 1970 formed Jalbert Productions Inc., where he serves as pres./owner to make feature films, TV sports, specials, commercials, etc. Co. has prod. Winter Sportscast and nine official films at Innsbruck Winter Olympics (1976), Lake Placid (1980), Sarajevo (1984). Albertville Winter Olympic Games official film, One Light One World, 1992. For more than 10 years the co. has been the official film prod. for the U.S. ski team. Jalbert Productions is based in Huntington, NY.

JAMES, CLIFTON

Actor. b. Portland, OR, May 29, 1925. e. U. of Oregon. Studied at Actors Studio. Made numerous appearances on stage and TV, as well as theatrical films.
THEATRE: NY: B'way: J.B., All the Way Home, The Shadow Box, American Buffalo. Off-B'way: All the King's Men.
PICTURES: On The Waterfront, The Strange One, The Last Mile, Something Wild, Experiment in Terror, David and Lisa, Black Like Me, The Chase, The Happening, Cool Hand Luke, Will Penny, The Reivers, ...tick...tick...tick..., WUSA, The Biscuit Eater, The New Centurions, Kid Blue, Live and Let Die, The Iceman Cometh, Werewolf of Washington, The Last Detail, Bank Shot, Juggernaut, The Man with the Golden Gun, Rancho DeLuxe, Silver Streak, The Bad News Bears in Breaking Training, Superman II, Where Are the Children?, Whoops Apocalypse, Eight Men Out, The Bonfire of the Vanities, Lone Star, Insterstate 84, Sunshine State, Counting Sheep, Raising Flagg.
TELEVISION: *Movies*: Runaway Barge, Friendly Persuasion, The Deadly Tower, Hart to Hart (pilot), Undercover With the KKK, Guyana Tragedy: The Story of Jim Jones, Carolina Skeletons, The John Vernon Story, The Summer of Ben Tyler. *Mini-series:* Captains and the Kings. *Series*: City of Angels, Lewis and Clark, All My Children.

JAMESON, JERRY

Director. b. Hollywood, CA. Started as editorial asst.; then editor and supv. editor for Danny Thomas Prods. Turned to directing.

PICTURES: Dirt Gang, The Bat People, Brute Core, Airport '77, Raise the Titanic, Land of the Free, Running Red (exec. prod.), Last Flight Out.
TELEVISION: *Movies*: Heatwave!, The Elevator, Hurricane, Terror on the 40th Floor, The Secret Night Caller, The Deadly Tower, The Lives of Jenny Dolan, The Call of the Wild, The Invasion of Johnson County, Superdome, A Fire in the Sky, High Noon--Part II, The Return of Will Kane, Stand By Your Man, Killing at Hell's Gate, Hotline, Starflight: The Plane That Couldn't Land, Cowboy, This Girl for Hire, Last of the Great Survivors, The Cowboy and the Ballerina, Stormin' Home, One Police Plaza, The Red Spider, Terror on Highway 91, Fire and Rain, Gunsmoke: The Long Ride, Bonanza: The Return, Gunsmoke: One Man's Justice, Gone in a Heartbeat, Too Close to Home, The Red Phone, The Red Phone 2, Safe Harbor. *Series*: The Six Million Dollar Man, Murder She Wrote, B.L. Stryker, Dr. Quinn: Medicine Woman, Walker Texas Ranger, Models Inc., Touched by an Angel, JAG, The Lazarus Man, The Magnificent Seven.

JANKOWSKI, GENE F.
Executive. b. Buffalo, NY, May 21, 1934. e. Canisius College, B.S., Michigan State U., M.A. in radio, TV and film. Joined CBS radio network sales, 1961 as acct. exec.; eastern sales mgr., 1966; moved to CBS-TV as acct. exec. 1969; gen. sales mgr. WCBS-TV, 1970; dir. sales, 1971; v.p. sales, CBS-TV Stations Divisions, 1973; v.p., finance & planning, 1974; v.p., controller, CBS Inc. 1976; v.p. admin., 1977; exec. v.p. CBS/Broadcast Group, 1977; pres., CBS/Broadcast Group, 1977; chmn. CBS/Broadcast Group, 1988-89; since 1989 chmn. Jankowski Communications Systems, Inc. Memberships: a past pres., Int'l. Council of National Acad. of Television Arts & Sciences; chairman emeritus of the American Film Institute; Member, Library of Congress Film Preservation Board; adjunct prof. telecommunications, Michigan State U. Since 2003, non-executive chairman of the bd. for Trans-Lux Corporation; an advisor-managing director of Veronis Suhler & Associates, Inc.; and former dir. of TV Azteca; formerly co-chmn. of St. Vincent's College and also a former trustee of St. Vincent's Medical Center.
AWARDS: Received Distinguished Communications Medal from South Baptist Radio & Television Commission; honorary Doctorate of Humanities, Michigan State U.; Humanitarian Award, National Conference of Christians and Jews.

JANNEY, ALLISON
Actress. b. Dayton, Ohio, November 19, 1960.
PICTURES: Who Shot Patakango?, Dead Funny, The Cowboy Way, Miracle on 34th Street, Wolf, Heading Home, Big Night, Faithful, Walking and Talking, The Associate, Flux, Private Parts, The Ice Storm, Julian Po, Anita Liberty, Primary Colors, The Object of My Affection, Six Days Seven Nights, Celebrity, The Impostors, 10 Things I Hate About You, Drop Dead Gorgeous, American Beauty, Nurse Betty, Leaving Drew, The Hours, Finding Nemo (voice), How to Deal, Winter Solstice, Piccadilly Jim, Our Very Own, The Chumscrubber, Over the Hedge (voice), Hairspray, Margaret, Pretty Ugly People, Juno, Forgiveness, Away We Go, A Thousand Words, The Oranges.
TELEVISION: *Movies*: Blind Spot, First Do No Harm, David and Lisa, Path to Paradise: The Untold Story of the World Trade Center Bombing. *Mini-series*: A Girl Thing. *Series*: The Guiding Light, The West Wing (4 Emmy Awards, 2 other noms.; 4 Golden Globe noms.), Shameless (pilot), Mr. Sunshine (pilot). *Guest:* More than 72 appearances.

JARMUSCH, JIM
Director, Writer, Composer, Actor. b. Akron, OH, 1953. e. attended Columbia U., went to Paris in senior year. NYU Film Sch., studied with Nicholas Ray and became his teaching asst. Appeared as an actor in Red Italy and Fraulein Berlin. Composed scores for The State of Things and Reverse Angle. Wrote and directed The New World using 30 minutes of leftover, unused film from another director. (Won International Critics Prize, Rotterdam Film Festival). Expanded it into Stranger Than Paradise.
PICTURES: *Director-Writer*: Permanent Vacation (dir. debut, 1980; also prod., music, edit.), Stranger Than Paradise (also edit., Golden Leopard, Locarno Film Festival; Camera d'Or best new director, Cannes), Down by Law, Mystery Train (also actor) Night on Earth (also prod.), When Pigs Fly (prod. only), Coffee and Cigarettes (also II & III), Dead Man, Year of the Horse, Ghost Dog: The Way of the Samurai (also prod.), Ten Minutes Older: The Trumpet. Actor: American Autobahn, Straight to Hell, Running Out of Luck, Helsinki Napoli All Night Long, Candy Mountain, Leningrad Cowboys Go America, The Golden Boat, Iron Horsemen, In the Soup, Tigrero: A Film That Was Never Made, Blue in the Face, The Typewriter the Rifle & the Movie Camera, Cannes Man, Sling Blade, Divine Trash, Year of the Horse, RIP: Rest in Pieces, Screamin' Jay Hawkins: I Put a Spell On Me. Ten Minutes Older: The Trumpet, Coffee and Cigarettes, Broken Flowers, Explicit Ills (exec. prod.), The Limits of Control Night at the Opera (exec. prod.).

JARROTT, CHARLES
Director. b. London, England, June 16, 1927. Joined British Navy; wartime service in Far East. After military service turned to theatre as asst. stage mgr. with Arts Council touring co. 1949 joined Nottingham Repertory Theatre as stage dir. and juvenile acting lead. 1953 joined new co. formed to tour Canada; was leading man and became resident leading actor for Ottawa Theatre. 1955 moved to Toronto and made TV acting debut opposite Katharine Blake whom he later wed. 1957 dir. debut in TV for Canadian Bdcstg. Co. Became CBC resident dir. Moved to London to direct for Armchair Theatre for ABC-TV. Then became freelance dir., doing stage work, films, TV. Received BAFTA Best Director Award, 1962. Golden Globe Awards, 1969, 1987.
THEATRE: The Duel, Galileo, The Basement, Tea Party, The Dutchman, etc.
PICTURES: Time to Remember (debut, 1962), Anne of the Thousand Days (Golden Globe Award 1970), Mary Queen of Scots, Lost Horizon, The Dove, The Littlest Horse Thieves, The Other Side of Midnight, The Last Flight of Noah's Ark, Condorman, The Amateur, The Boy in Blue, Morning Glory (co-s.p. only), Byron (s.p., dir.), The Secret Life of Algernon (also s.p.), Turn of Faith, Snow Prince.
TELEVISION: The Hot Potato Boys, Roll On, Bloomin' Death, Girl in a Birdcage, The Picture of Dorian Gray, Rain, The Rose Affair, Roman Gesture, Silent Song, The Male of the Species, The Young Elizabeth, A Case of Libel, Dr. Jekyll and Mr. Hyde. U.S. *Movies/Mini-series:* A Married Man, Poor Little Rich Girl: The Barbara Hutton Story, The Woman He Loved, Till We Meet Again (mini-series), Night of the Fox (mini-series), Lucy & Desi: Before the Laughter, Changes, Yes Virginia There is a Santa Claus, Stranger in the Mirror, Jackie Collins' Lady Boss, Treacherous Beauties, Trade Winds, A Promise Kept: The Oksana Baiul Story (Emmy Award for dir.), At The Midnight Hour, The Christmas List.

JAUTZ, KEN
Executive. e. B.S. degree, Cornell Univ., 1978; Master's degree, Columbia Univ., 1979. Jautz was an Associated Press correspondent, 1981-1989; CNN, German bureau chief, 1989-1995; Turner Broadcasting Europe, VP, business development, 1995-1999; N-TV Television, managing director, 1999-2001; CNN, executive VP, business news, 2001-2003; current position as executive v.p., CNN Worldwide since Nov. 2004. Jautz is also responsible for programming CNN's Headline News channel.

JAYSTON, MICHAEL
Actor. b. Nottingham, England, Oct. 28, 1935. Member of Old Vic theatre Co. & Bristol Old Vic.
PICTURES: A Midsummer Night's Dream, Cromwell, Nicholas and Alexandra, The Public Eye, Alice's Adventures in Wonderland, The Nelson Affair, Tales That Witness Madness, The Homecoming, Craze, The Internecine Project, Dominique, Zulu Dawn, From a Far Country, MacBeth, Element of Doubt.
TELEVISION: *Movies/Mini-series*: She Fell Among Thieves, Tinker Tailor Soldier Spy, Dust to Dust, Still Crazy Like a Fox, Shake Hands Forever, A Guilty Thing Surprised, Somewhere to Run, A Bit of a Do, 20,000 Leagues Under the Sea, A Dinner of Herbs. *Series*: Haggard, The Casebook of Sherlock Holmes, Outside Edge, Fun at the Funeral Parlour, Foyle's War, Emmerdale Farm, Holby City. *Documentary:* Timewatch (series, narr.). *Guest:* More than 75 appearances.

JEFFREYS, ANNE
Actress. b. Goldsboro, NC, Jan. 26, 1923. m. late actor Robert Sterling. Named by Theatre Arts Magazine as one of the 10 outstanding beauties of the stage. Trained for operatic career. Sang with NY's Municipal Opera Co. while supplementing income as a Powers model. Appeared as Tess Trueheart in Dick Tracy features.
THEATRE: B'way: in Street Scene, Kiss Me Kate, Romance, Three Wishes for Jamie, Kismet. Stock: Camelot, King & I, Kismet, Song of Norway, Bells Are Ringing, Marriage Go Round, No Sex Please, We're British, Take Me Along, Carousel, Anniversary Waltz, Do I Hear a Waltz, Ninotchka, Pal Joey, Name of the Game, Destry Rides Again, The Merry Widow, Bitter Sweet, Desert Song, High Button Shoes, Sound of Music.
PICTURES: I Married an Angel, Billy the Kid, Trapped, Joan of Ozark, The Old Homestead, Tarzan's New York Adventure, X Marks the Spot, Yokel Boy, Catterbox, Man from Thunder River, Nevada, Step Lively, Dillinger, Sing Your Way Home, Those Endearing Young Charms, Zombies on Broadway, Dick Tracy Vs. Cueball, Genius at Work, Step By Step, Vacation in Reno, Trail Street, Riffraff, Return of the Bad Men, Boys' Night Out, Panic in the City, Southern Double Cross, Clifford, Richard III.
TELEVISION: *Movies*: Beggarman Thief, A Message From Holly, American Movie Classics (host), Empire State Building Murders. *Series*: Topper, Love That Jill, Bright Promise, The Delphi Bureau (Golden Globe nom. 1973), General Hospital, Finder of Lost Loves, Baywatch Hawaii, Port Charles. *Guest*: More than 65 appearances.

JEFFRIES, LIONEL
Actor, Director. b. Forest Hill, London, England, June 10, 1926. e. Queens Elizabeth's Grammar Sch, Wimbone Dorset. Ent. m.p. ind. 1952.
THEATRE: Hello, Dolly!, See How They Run, Two Into One, Pygmalion (U.S.), The Wild Duck.
PICTURES: The Black Rider, The Colditz Story, No Smoking, Will Any Gentleman?, Windfall, All for Mary, Bhowani Junction, Eyewitness, Jumping for Joy, Lust for Life, Creeping Unknown (Quatermass Experiment), Baby and the Battleship, Decision Against Time, Doctor at Large, High Terrace, Hour of Decision,

Up in the World, Behind the Mask, Blue Murder at St. Trinian's, Dunkirk, Girls at Sea, Law and Disorder, Orders to Kill, Revenge of Frankenstein, Up the Creek, Bobbikins, The Vicious Circle, Idol on Parade, Nowhere to Go, The Nun's Story, Jazzboat, Let's Get Married, Trials of Oscar Wilde, Please Turn Over, Tarzan the Magnificent, Two-Way Stretch, Fanny, The Hellions, Life is a Circus, Kill or Cure, Mrs. Gibbons' Boys, Operation Snatch, The Notorious Landlady, The Wrong Arm of the Law, Call Me Bwana, The Crimson Blade, First Men in the Moon, The Long Ships, Murder Ahoy, The Secret of My Success, The Truth About Spring, You Must Be Joking!, Arrivederci Baby!, The Spy With a Cold Nose (Golden Globe nom. 1967), Oh Dad Poor Dad, Blast Off!, Camelot, Chitty Chitty Bang Bang, Sudden Terror, The Railway Children (dir., s.p. only), Lola, Who Slew Auntie Roo?, The Amazing Mr. Blunden (dir., s.p. only), Baxter (dir. only), Royal Flash, Wombling Free (voice, also dir., s.p.), The Water Babies (dir. only), The Prisoner of Zenda, Better Late Than Never, A Chorus of Disapproval.
TELEVISION: *Movies:* Cream in My Coffee, First and Last, Ending Up, Minder, Danny: the Champion of the World, Jekyll and Hyde, Boon Morse, Bed, Heaven on Earth. *Mini-series:* Look at It This Way. *Series:* Room at the Bottom, Father Charlie, Tom Dick and Harriet, Rich Tea and Sympathy, Woof!. *Documentaries:* Dors: The Other Diana, I Love 1970s, I Love a 1970s Christmas.
(d. February 19, 2010)

JENS, SALOME

Actress. b. Milwaukee, WI, May 8, 1935. e. Northwestern U. Member Actors Studio.
THEATRE: The Disenchanted, Far Country, Night Life, Winter's Tale, Mary Stuart, Antony and Cleopatra, After the Fall, Moon For the Misbegotten, The Balcony.
PICTURES: Angel Baby (debut, 1961), The Fool Killer, Seconds, Me Natalie, Cloud Dancer, Harry's War, Just Between Friends, Coming Out Under Fire (narr.), I'm Losing You, Cats and Dogs (voice).
TELEVISION: *Movies*: In the Glitter Palace, Sharon: Portrait of a Mistress, The Golden Moment: An Olympic Love Story, A Killer in the Family, Playing with Fire, Uncommon Valor, Grace Kelly, Cast the First Stone, The Lottery. *Mini-series:* From Here to Eternity, The Great War. *Series*: Falcon Crest, Mary Hartman, Mary Hartman, Melrose Place, Star Trek: Deep Space Nine, Superboy. *Guest*: More than 75 appearances.

JEWISON, NORMAN

Producer, Director. b. Toronto, Canada, July 21, 1926. e. Malvern Collegiate Inst., Toronto, 1940-44; Victoria Coll., U. of Toronto, 1946-50, B.A. Stage and TV actor 1950-52. Director, Canadian Broadcasting Corp 1953-58. Awarded 1988 Acad. of Canadian Cinema and Television Special Achievement Award. Made Companion Order of Canada, 1992. Received Academy Award, Irving G. Thalberg Award, 1999. ASC Bd. of Governors Award 2003. ACE Golden Eddie Filmmaker of the Year Award 2008. DGA Lifetime Achievemant Award 2010.
PICTURES: *Director:* 40 Pounds of Trouble (debut, 1962), The Thrill of It All, Send Me No Flowers, The Art of Love, The Cincinnati Kid. *Director-Producer:* The Russians Are Coming! The Russians Are Coming! (Academy Award nom. for picture, DGA nom. 1967), In the Heat of the Night (dir. only; Academy Award nom.; DGA nom.; Golden Globe nom. 1968), The Thomas Crown Affair, Gaily Gaily, Fiddler on the Roof (2 Academy Award noms. for dir. & picture, Golden Globe nom. 1972), Jesus Christ Superstar (also co-s.p.), Rollerball, F.I.S.T., ... And Justice for All, Best Friends, A Soldier's Story (Academy Award nom. for picture, DGA nom. 1985), Agnes of God, Moonstruck (2 Academy Award noms. for dir. & picture, 1988), In Country, Other People's Money, Only You, Bogus, The Hurricane (Golden Globe nom. 2000), The Statement, Bread and Tulips. *Producer:* The Landlord, Billy Two Hats, The Dogs of War (exec. prod.), Iceman, The January Man, Dance Me Outside (exec. prod.), A Brother's Kiss (exec. prod.).
TELEVISION: Exec. prod. of 8 episodes of The Judy Garland Show, Walter and Henry (Emmy nom. 2002). *Prod.-Dir.:* Judy Garland specials, The Andy Williams Show, Dinner with Friends (Emmy nom. 2002). *Dir. of Specials:* Tonight with Harry Belafonte, The Broadway of Lerner and Loewe.

JEUNET, JEAN-PIERRE

Director, Writer. b. Roanne, Loire, France, Sept. 3, 1953.
PICTURES: The Escape, Le Manege, The Bunker of the Last Gunshots, Pas du repos pour Billy Brakko, Things I Like, Things I Don't Like, Delicatessen (also s.p.), The City of Lost Children (also s.p.), Alien: Resurrection, Amélie (dir., s.p., Academy Award nom.; BAFTA Award, 2002), A Very Long Engagement, Life of Pi (also s.p.), Micmacs à tire-larigot.

JHABVALA, RUTH PRAWER

Writer. b. Cologne, Germany, May 7, 1927. Emigrated with her family to England, 1939. e. Hendon County Sch., Queen Mary Coll., London U. (degree in English). m. architect C.S.H. Jhabvala, 1951 and moved to Delhi. Has written most of the screenplays for the films of Ismail Merchant and James Ivory.
AUTHOR: To Whom She Will, Esmond in India, The Nature of Passion, The Householder, Get Ready for Battle, Heat and Dust, In Search of Love and Beauty, Three Continents, Poet and Dancer, Shards of Memory.
PICTURES: The Householder (debut, 1963; based on her novel), Shakespeare Wallah (with Ivory), The Guru (with Ivory), Bombay Talkie (with Ivory), Roseland, The Europeans, Quartet, Heat and Dust (based on her own novel; BAFTA Award), The Bostonians, A Room with a View (Academy Award, WGA Award 1987), Madame Sousatzka (co.-s.p. with John Schlesinger), Mr. and Mrs. Bridge (NY Film Critics Award), Howards End (Academy Award, Golden Globe nom.; WGA nom. 1993), The Remains of the Day (Academy Award nom.; Golden Globe nom.; WGA nom. 1994), Jefferson in Paris, Surviving Picasso, A Soldier's Daughter Never Cries, The Golden Bowl, Le Divorce, The City of Your Final Destination (s.p.).
TELEVISION: *Movie:* The Place of Peace. *Documentaries/Specials:* Hullabaloo Over Georgie and Bonnie's Pictures, The Courtesans of Bombay, Autobiography of a Princess, Jane Austen in Manhattan, In Ismail's Custody, The Wandering Company.

JOANOU, PHIL

Director. b. La Canada, CA, Nov. 20, 1961. e. UCLA, USC. Student film The Last Chance Dance won him first professional job directing 2 episodes of tv's Amazing Stories.
PICTURES: Three O'Clock High (debut, 1987), U2: Rattle and Hum (also edit., camera operator), State of Grace, Final Analysis, Heaven's Prisoners, Entropy, 14 Up in America, U2: The Best of 1980-1990 (music video documentary), Entropy (also s.p. and prod.), The Regulators, A Walk Among the Tombstones, Hammer Down, Sharky's Machine, Gridiron Gang.
TELEVISION: *Movies*: 14 Up in America, Naked Hotel, Starz Special: Gridiron Gang (actor). *Mini-series*: Wild Palms (co-dir.). *Series*: Fallen Angels (Dead-End for Delia). *Documentary:* 7-Up In America.

JOBS, STEVE

Executive. b. San Francisco, CA, Feb. 24, 1955. Jobs showed an interest in electronics from an early age and pursued his interest as an employee of Atari, the pioneering arcade game company. While at Atari, he met future partner, Steve Wozniak, a whiz at assembling electronic components. By April 1, 1976, Jobs and Wozniak launched Apple Computer, which revolutionized personal computing. Apple made its first public stock sale in 1980, making Jobs a millionaire before he was 30. Jobs left Apple after losing a bitter battle over control with CEO John Sculley, whom Jobs had recruited to Apple. He then founded NeXT, creating workstations for research and higher education. Jobs pulled the plug in 1993 after poor sales of the high-priced workstations, choosing to focus on software. While NeXT struggled, Jobs had success with Pixar Animation Studios, which he bought in 1986 for $10 million. After signing a deal with Disney to produce three movies, Pixar released the immensely successful Toy Story in Nov. 1995. The film was the first feature-length animated movie produced entirely with computers. Jobs became an instant billionaire when Pixar's stock went public. Pixar has won 20 Academy Awards and its films have grossed more than $3.2 billion at the worldwide box office to date. Jobs returned to Apple and is now CEO of both Apple and Pixar. In late Jan. 2006, Walt Disney announced the acquisition of Pixar Animation Studios for approx. $7.4 billion in stock. The deal put Apple Computer CEO Steve Jobs on Disney's board of directors and makes Jobs Disney's largest shareholder.

JOFFE, EDWARD

Producer, Director, Writer, Production Consultant. Worked in m.p., theatre, commercial radio and as journalist before ent. TV ind. in Britain as writer/prod with ATV. 1959-61 staff prod. Granada TV. 1962, dir., Traitor's Gate & Traveling Light for Robt Stigwood; prod. dir., numerous series for Grampian TV; 1967, dir. film The Price of a Record—Emmy finalist; 1967-68 films, Columba's Folk & So Many Partings ITV entries in Golden Harp Fest.; 1968, prod., dir. Tony Hancock Down Under in Australia, prod. dir. Up At The Cross; prod. dir. ind. film, Will Ye No' Come Back Again; dir., This Is... Tom Jones; prod. dir., The Golden Shot; 1971, senior production lecturer, Thomson TV College; dir., films for U.S. for London Television Service; Evening Standard Commercials for Thames TV. Co. prod. dir.,ind. film Sound Scene, 1972-8, Contract prod. dir. Thames TV various series: Magpie, Today, Opportunity Knocks, The David Nixon Show, Seven Ages of Man, Problems, Finding Out; 1980 production consultant, CBC-TV; 1978-82, prod. dir. series Writers' Workshop, About Books; 1978, film, Places & Things (British Academy Award nom.) film, Who Do You Think You Are? (British Academy Award nom., ITV's Japan Prize entry, Special Jury Award San Francisco Intl. Film Fest), 1981, Film Images, (British Academy Award nom.; Gold Plaque Chicago Intl. Film Fest.); The Protectors (medal winner Intl. Film & TV Festival, N.Y.). 1982-86: 1989-95, devised, prod., dir. Video View for ITV Network; Co-prod. & dir. 2 series Sprockets; dir. Challenge. Dir. Screen Scene Prods, String of Pearls, PLC, String of Pearls 2 PLC. Companies produced mopics Double X, Little Devils - The Birth, To Catch a Yeti, Big Game, Shepherd on the Rock.
TELEVISION: *Movies: Dir./Prod.:* Traitor's Gate, The Tony Hancock Special, Who Do You Think You Are?, Crime Story, The Protectors, Images, The Rainbow Coloured Disco Dancer, Preview, Challenge, Hancock & Joan (writer, book, Hancock's

Last Stand). *Series:* The David Nixon Show (dir.), Opportunity Knocks, Seven Ages of Man, Sprockets, Video View (also writer). *Documentaries:* War Games in Italy, So Many Partings, Flight 1977, Ghosts, Spinoffs (series), The Buzz (series).

JOFFÉ, ROLAND

Director, Producer. b. London, England, Nov. 17, 1945. e. Lycee Francaise, Carmel Col. Manchester U., England. Worked in British theatre with the Young Vic, the National Theatre and the Old Vic. 1973 became youngest director at National Theatre. 1978, moved into directing TV for Granada TV, then Thames and B.B.C. before feature debut in 1984 with The Killing Fields.
PICTURES: *Director:* The Killing Fields (debut, 1984, Academy Award nom.; DGA nom.; Golden Globe nom. 1985), The Mission (Academy Award nom.; DGA nom.; Golden Globe nom. 1987), Fat Man and Little Boy (also co-s.p.), City of Joy (also co-prod.), The Scarlett Letter (also prod.), Goodbye Lover, Vatel (also prod.), Captivity, You and I (Finding tATu), There Be Dragons (also prod.). *Producer:* Made in Bangkok, Super Mario Bros, Waterproof.
TELEVISION: *Movie:* Tis Pity She's a Whore. *Mini-series:* The Stars Look Down. *Series:* Coronation Street, Sam, Bill Brand, Headmaster, Undressed (exec. prod.). *Documentaries:* Rope, Ann, No Mama No. Plays: The Spongers, The Legion Hall Bombing, United Kingdom (also co-wrote).

JOHANSSON, SCARLETT

Actress. b. New York, NY, Nov. 22, 1984. e. Professional Children's School, NY. Named Star of Tomorrow in Quigley Publishing's Top Ten Money Makers Poll 2006.
THEATRE: *B'way:* South Pacific (2008), A View From The Bridge (Tony Award 2010). *Off B'way:* Sophistry.
PICTURES: North (debut, 1994), Just Cause, If Lucy Fell, Manny & Lo, Home Alone 3, The Horse Whisperer, Ghost World, The Man Who Wasn't There, An American Rhapsody, Eight Legged Freaks, Lost in Translation (Golden Globe nom. 2004), Girl with a Pearl Earring (Golden Globe nom. 2004), The Perfect Score, A Love Song for Bobby Long (Golden Globe nom. 2005), A Good Woman, The SpongeBob SquarePants Movie (voice), In Good Company, The Island, Match Point (Golden Globe nom. 2006), The Black Dahlia, Mission: Impossible III, A View From the Bridge, Scoop, The Prestige, The Nanny Diaries, The Other Boleyn Girl, He's Just Not That Into You, The Spirit, Vicky Cristina Barcelona, New York, I Love You (segment writer, dir.), Iron Man 2.
TELEVISION: *Series:* The Client (pilot). *Documentary:* Lost on Location (short). *Guest:* More than 70 appearances.

JOHNS, GLYNIS

Actress. b. Durban, South Africa, Oct. 5, 1923. e. in England. Daughter of Mervyn Johns, actor, and Alys Steele, pianist. On London stage from 1935 (Buckie's Bears, The Children's Hour, A Kiss for Cinderella, Quiet Week-End; Gertie, N.Y. stage, 1952; Major Barbara, N.Y., 1956-57.) Voted one of top ten British Money-making stars in Motion Picture Herald-Pathe poll, 1951-54.
THEATRE: Too Good to Be True (NY), The King's Mare, Come as You Are, The Marquise (tour), A Little Night Music (NY; Tony Award), Cause Celebre, Harold and Maude (Canada, Hay Fever (U.K. tour), The Boy Friend (Toronto), The Circle (NY).
PICTURES: South Riding (debut, 1938), Murder in the Family, Prison Without Bars, On the Night of the Fire, Mr. Brigg's Family, Under Your Hat, The Prime Minister, 49th Parallel, Adventures of Tartu, Half-Way House, Perfect Strangers, This Man Is Mine, Frieda, An Ideal Husband, Miranda, Third Time Lucky, Dear Mr. Prohack, State Secret, Flesh and Blood, No Highway in the Sky, Appointment With Venus (Island Rescue), Encore, The Magic Box, The Card (The Promoter), The Sword and the Rose, Rob Roy the Highland Rogue, Personal Affair, The Weak and the Wicked, The Seekers (Land of Fury), The Beachcomber, Mad About Men, Court Jester, Josephine and Men, Loser Takes All, All Mine to Give, Around the World in 80 Days, Another Time Another Place, Shake Hands with the Devil, The Sundowners (Academy Award nom. 1961), The Spider's Web, The Cabinet of Caligari, The Chapman Report (Golden Globe nom. 1963), Papa's Delicate Condition, Mary Poppins, Dear Brigette, Don't Just Stand There, Lock Up Your Daughters, Under Milk Wood, Vault of Horror, Zelly and Me, Nukie, The Ref, While You Were Sleeping, Superstar.
TELEVISION: *Movies:* Little Gloria... Happy at Last, Spraggue, Scooby-Doo and the Ghoul School, The Secret Garden (voice). *Mini-series:* Murder in the Family. *Series:* Glynis, Coming of Age. *Guest:* More than 48 appearances.

JOHNSON, DON

Actor. b. Flatt Creek, MO, Dec. 15, 1949. Worked at ACT (American Conservatory Theatre), San Francisco. On stage in Your Own Thing. In L.A. in Fortune and Men's Eyes. Recording: Heartbeat (1986).
PICTURES: The Magic Garden of Stanley Sweetheart (debut, 1970), Zachariah, The Harrad Experiment, A Boy and His Dog, Return to Macon County, Soggy Bottom USA, Cease Fire, Sweet Hearts Dance, Dead-Bang, The Hot Spot, Harley Davidson and the Marlboro Man, Paradise, Born Yesterday, Guilty as Sin, Tin Cup, Goodbye Lover, Moondance Alexander, When in Rome, Machete, Born to Be a Star, Vineyard Haven.
TELEVISION: *Movies*: First You Cry, Ski Lift to Death, Katie: Portrait of a Centerfold, Revenge of the Stepford Wives, Amateur Night at the Dixie Bar and Grill, Elvis and the Beauty Queen, The Two Lives of Carol Letner, In Pursuit of Honor, Word of Honor (also co-exec. prod.), Southern Discomfort. *Mini-series*: The Rebels, Beulah Land, The Long Hot Summer. *Series*: From Here to Eternity, Miami Vice (Emmy nom. 1985, Golden Globe Award 1986, 1 other nom.), Nash Bridges (also prod.), Just Legal. *Special:* Don Johnson's Heartbeat (music video, also exec. prod.). *Guest:* More than 96 appearances.

JOHNSON, LAMONT

Director, Producer. b. Stockton, CA, Sept. 30, 1922. e. UCLA. 4 time winner of Director's Guild Award for TV work. Directed plays The Egg, Yes Is For a Very Young Man. Dir. two operas, L.A. Philharmonic, 1964; founder, dir., UCLA Professional Theatre Group. Won DGA Award for most outstanding TV director, 1973.
PICTURES: A Covenant With Death (debut, 1967), Kona Coast, The McKenzie Break, A Gunfight, The Groundstar Conspiracy, You'll Like My Mother, The Last American Hero, Visit to a Chief's Son, Lipstick, One on One (also actor), Somebody Killed Her Husband, Cattle Annie and Little Britches, Spacehunter: Adventures in the Forbidden Zone.
TELEVISION: *Movies:* Deadlock, My Sweet Charlie (Emmy nom.; DGA Award 1971), That Certain Summer (Emmy nom.; DGA Award 1973), The Execution of Pvt. Slovik (Emmy nom.; DGA nom. 1975), Fear on Trial (Emmy nom.; DGA nom. 1976), Off the Minnesota Strip, Crisis at Central High, Escape from Iran, Dangerous Company, Life of the Party: The Story of Beatrice, Ernie Kovacs: Between the Laughter, Wallenberg: A Hero's Story (also co-prod.; Emmy Award,1 other nom. DGA nom. 1985), Unnatural Causes (Emmy nom. 1987), Gore Vidal's Lincoln (Emmy Award, DGA Award 1988), Voices Within: The Lives of Truddi Chase, Crash Landing: The Rescue of Flight 232 (Emmy nom. 1992), The Broken Chain (also prod.), The Man Next Door, All the Winters That Have Been. *Mini-series:* The Kennedys of Massachusetts (Emmy nom. 1990). *Series:* Have Gun - Will Travel, Peter Gunn, The Rifleman, Naked City, Johnny Ringo, Mr. Lucky, The Defenders, Dr. Kildare, The Nurses, Profiles in Courage (DGA Award 1965), Twilight Zone, Cimarron Strip, Judd for the Defense, The Name of the Game, Felicity. *Documentary:* The Animals (narr.).

JOHNSON, MARK

Producer. b. Washington, DC, Dec. 27, 1945. Moved to Spain at age 7, lived there for eleven years before returning to America. e. Univ. of VA, Univ. of IA. Joined Directors Guild training program receiving first credit on Next Stop Greenwich Village. Worked as prod. asst., then asst. dir. on High Anxiety, Movie Movie, The Brink's Job, and Escape From Alcatraz. Starting with Diner in 1982 served as executive prod. or prod. on all Barry Levinson films. With Levinson formed Baltimore Pictures in 1989.
PICTURES: Diner (exec. prod.), Kafka (co-exec. prod.), The Astronaut's Wife (exec. prod.), My Dog Skip (exec. prod.), Mouse Hunt (exec. prod.), What Lies Beneath (exec. prod.). *Producer:* The Natural, Young Sherlock Holmes, Tin Men, Good Morning Vietnam, Rain Man (Academy Award for Best Picture of 1989), Avalon, Bugsy (Academy Award nom. L.A. Film Critics & Golden Globe Awards for Best Picture of 1992), Toys, Sniper, Wilder Napalm, A Perfect World, A Little Princess, Donnie Brasco, Home Fries, An Everlasting Piece, Dragonfly, The Rookie, Moonlight Mile, The Banger Sisters, The Alamo, The Notebook, The Wendell Baker Story, The Chronicles of Narnia: The Lion, the Witch and the Wardrobe, How to Eat Fried Worms, Shooter, The Hunting Party, Lake City (exec. prod.), Ballast (exec. prod.), The Chronicles of Narnia: Prince Caspian, My Sister's Keeper, Flying Lessons (exec. prod.), The Chronicles of Narnia: The Voyage of the Dawn Treader, Don't Be Afraid of the Dark.
TELEVISION: *Series*: L.A. Doctors (exec. prod.), The Parkers (exec. in charge of prod.), Falcone (exec. prod.), The Guardian (exec. prod.), HRT (exec. prod.), Greetings from Tucson (exec. in charge of prod.), Hack (exec. in charge of prod.), Love Monkey (exec. prod.), Breaking Bad (Emmy nom. 2009). *Documentary:* War Wounds (segment prod.).

JOHNSON, RICHARD

Actor. b. Upminster, Essex, England, July 30, 1927. Studied at Royal Acad. of Dramatic Art. First stage appearance Opera House, Manchester, then with John Gielgud's repertory season, 1944. Served in Royal Navy 1945-48. Subsequent stage appearances incl. The Madwoman of Chaillot, The Lark. Visited Moscow with Peter Brook's production of Hamlet. Royal Shakespeare Thea.: Stratford, London, 1957-62. Royal Shakespeare Co. 1972-73. National Theatre, 1976-77. Founded United British Artists, 1983.
PICTURES: Captain Horatio Hornblower (debut, 1951), Calling Bulldog Drummond, Scotland Yard Inspector (Lady in the Fog), Saadia, Never So Few, Cairo, The Haunting, 80,000 Suspects, The Pumpkin Eater, The Amorous Adventures of Moll Flanders, Operation Crossbow, Khartoum, The Witch in Love, Deadlier Than the Male, The Rover, Danger Route, A Twist of Sand, Oedipus the King, Lady Hamilton, Some Girls Do, Julius Caesar, The Tyrant, The Beloved, Behind the Door, Hennessy, Night Child, The Cursed Medallion, Aces High, The Last Day of Spring,

The Comeback, Zombie, The Monster Club, Screamers, What Waits Below, Lady Jane, Turtle Diary, Foreign Student, Diving In, Milk, Lara Croft: Tombraider, The Dark (video short, voice), Scoop, Two Families, Jump!, The Boy in the Striped Pyjamas.
TELEVISION: *Movies:* Hamlet, Murder in Mind, Antony and Cleopatra, Moses the Lawgiver (narr.), The Flame is Love, Haywire, The Four Feathers, Portrait of a Rebel: Margaret Sanger, Cymbeline, The Biko Inquest, A Man For All Seasons, Treasure Island, The Secret Life of Ian Fleming, Voice of the Heart, The Crucifer of Blood, Duel of Hearts, Anglo Saxon Attitudes, Heavy Weather, Breaking the Code, Front Seat, The Echo, Happy Days, The Whistle-Blower, Whatever Love Means, Wallis & Edward, The Raven (narr.). *Mini-series:* Pride and Prejudice, The Camomile Lawn. *Series:* Epilogue to Capricorn, The Robinsons, MI-5. *Guest:* More than 80 appearances.

JOHNSON, TOM

Sound. e. Graduated from USC School of Cinema-Television (1981). Re-recording Mixer for Ardmore Sound, Ireland.
PICTURES: Star Wars: Return of the Jedi, Indiana Jones and the Temple of Doom, Seize the Day, Howard the Duck, Dirty Rotten Scoundrels, Colors, The Couch Trip, Tucker: The Man and His Dream, The Karate Kid III, To Cross the Rubicon, The Five Heartbeats, Terminator 2: Judgment Day (Academy Award, Best Sound, 1992), F/X2, Single White Female, Quiz Show, Forrest Gump (Academy Award nom.; CAS Award 1995), Nine Months, Strange Days, Stealing Beauty, Jack, One Fine Day, Titanic (Academy Award, Best Sound, CAS Award 1998), Beverly Hills Ninja, Contact (Academy Award nom.; CAS nom. 1998), Wag the Dog, Sphere, The Horse Whisperer (CAS nom. 1999), A Midsummer Night's Dream, Star Wars: Episode 1 - The Phantom Menace (Academy Award nom.; CAS nom. 2000), Liberty Heights, Galaxy Quest, The Yards, Requiem for a Dream, When the Sky Falls, Cirque du Soleil: Journey of Man, What Lies Beneath, Cast Away (Academy Award nom.; CAS nom. 2001), An Everlasting Piece, The Tailor of Panama, Atlantis: The Lost Empire, Bandits, Blood Work, The Magdalene Sisters, The Good Thief, The Ring, Maid in Manhattan, Peter Pan, In My Country, Ella Enchanted, Hotel Rwanda, Rory O'Shea Was Here, The Polar Express (Academy Award nom. 2005), Million Dollar Baby, Asylum, Charlie and the Chocolate Factory, Harry Potter and the Goblet of Fire, King Kong, Shrooms, Children of Men, Small Engine Repair, Becoming Jane, There Will Be Blood, Beowulf, The Water Horse: Legend of the Deep, Sweeney Todd: The Demon Barber of Fleet Street, Trapped, Two Lovers, Coraline, The Private Lives of Pippa Lee, Ondine, Where the Wild Things Are, A Christmas Carol, Alice in Wonderland.
TELEVISION: *Movies*: The Ewok Adventure, Ewoks: The Battle for Endor (Emmy nom. 1986), The Dreamer of Oz, Bobbie's Girl, George Gently: Gently Go Man.

JOHNSTON, JOANNA

Costume Designer.
PICTURES: Hellraiser, Who Framed Roger Rabbit, Indiana Jones and the Last Crusade, Back to the Future Part II, Back to the Future Part III, Far and Away, Death Becomes, Forrest Gump, French Kiss, Contact, Saving Private Ryan, The Sixth Sense, Unbreakable, Cast Away, About a Boy (CDG nom. 2003), Love Actually, The Polar Express, War of the Worlds, Munich, The Spiderwick Chronicles, Valkyrie, Pirate Radio.

JOLIE, ANGELINA

Actress. b. Los Angeles, CA, June 4, 1975. e. Lee Strasberg Theatre Institute, New York University. Father is actor Jon Voight. Has served as United Nations Good Will Ambassador for refugees.
PICTURES: Lookin' to Get Out, Cyborg 2: Glass Shadow, Angela & Viril (short), Hackers, Without Evidence, Mojave Moon, Foxfire, Love Is All There Is, Playing God, Pushing Tin, Hell's Kitchen, Dancing About Architecture, Girl Interrupted (Academy Award, Golden Globe Award 2000), The Bone Collector, Gone in Sixty Seconds, Original Sin, Tomb Raider, Beyond Borders, Life or Something Like It, Trading Women (documentary, narrator), Tomb Raider: The Cradle of Life, Beyond Borders, Lovesick (prod. only), Taking Lives, The World of Tomorrow, Shark Tale (voice), Sky Captain and the World of Tomorrow, Alexander, Trudell (doc., exec. prod.), Mr. and Mrs. Smith, The Good Shepherd, Beowulf (voice), A Mighty Heart (Golden Globe nom. 2007), Kung Fu Panda (voice), A Moment in the World (doc., dir.), Changeling (Academy Award nom.; Golden Globe nom. 2009), Wanted, Resilient (doc. exec. prod.), Salt, The Tourist, Kung Fu Panda: The Kaboom of Doom (voice).
TELEVISION: *Movies*: True Women, George Wallace (Emmy nom.; Golden Globe Award, 1998), Gia (Emmy nom.; Golden Globe Award 1998), True Women. *Guest:* More than 135 appearances.

JOLLEY, STAN

Producer, Director, Production Designer, Art Director. b. New York, NY, May 17, 1926. e. U. of Southern California, col. of architecture. Son of actor I. Stanford Jolley. In Navy in W.W.II. Has acted in capacities listed for many feature films and TV series. One of orig. designers of Disneyland.
PICTURES: *Prod./Prod. Designer:* Knife for the Ladies. *Assoc. Prod./ Prod. Designer:* The Good Guys and the Bad Guys. *2nd Unit Dir.:* Superman. *Prod. Designer:* Dutch, The Good Mother, Witness (Academy Award nom. 1986), Taps, Caddyshack, Cattle Annie and Little Britches, Americathon (also second unit director), The Swarm, Drum, Framed, Dion Brothers, Mixed Company, Walking Tall, Terror in the Wax Museum, Night of the Lepus (also second unit director), War Between Men and Women, Law Man, The Phynx. *Art Director:* Young Billy Young, Ride Beyond Vengeance, Broken Saber, The Restless Ones, Mail Order Bride, Toby Tyler, The Grass Harp, Mr. Ed. *Assoc. Prod./Prod. designer & 2nd unit dir.:* Happily Ever After.
TELEVISION: *Movies*: *2nd Unit Dir./Prod. Designer:* Walt Disney's Wonderful World of Color, Swiss Family Robinson, Adventures of the Queen, Woman Hunter, Abduction of Carrie Swenson, Eagle One, No Man's Land, Last of the Great Survivors, Like Normal People, Rescue From Gilligan's Island, Flood, Voyage of the Yes, The Stranger, Punch & Jody, City Beneath the Sea, Women of San Quentin. *Mini-series:* Howards, The Amazing Mr. Hughes. *Series*: *Dir./Prod. Designer:* MacGyver, Today's FBI. *Assoc. Prod./Prod. Designer:* Jessie. *Prod. Designer:* Walking Tall, For Love and Honor, Swiss Family Robinson (2nd unit dir.). *Art Dir.:* Pete and Gladys, Gunsmoke, Mr. Ed, Branded, Voyage to the Bottom of the Sea, Land of the Giants, O'Hara, U.S. Treasury, Adams of Eagle Lake, Shane, Acapulco, The Racers, *Docu-drama:* Under Fire, The Nine Lives of Elfego Baca, Ralph Edward's This Is Your Life Show. *Pilots*: Get Smart, Some Like It Hot. *Cartoon:* Donald in Mathmagic Land. *Documentary*: Crisis in the Wetlands (prod./dir.). *Writer*: Novel: "Dichotomy-Amish Justice," Chake (s.p.).

JONES, AMY HOLDEN

Director, Writer. b. Philadelphia, PA, Sept. 17, 1953. m. cinematographer, Michael Chapman. e. Wellesley Coll., B.A., 1974; film and photography courses, Massachusetts Inst. of Technology. Winner, first place, Washington National Student Film Festival, 1973.
PICTURES: *Editor:* Hollywood Boulevard (debut, 1976), American Boy, Corvette Summer, Second Hand Hearts. *Director:* Slumber Party Massacre, Love Letters (also s.p.), Mystic Pizza (s.p. only), Maid to Order (also co-s.p.), Rich Man's Wife (also s.p.). Writer: Beethoven (1, 2, 3, 4 & 5), Indecent Proposal, The Getaway, It Had to Be Steve (co-s.p.), The Relic (co-s.p.).
TELEVISION: *Movies*: Saturday's, Indecency, Complications (writer, exec. prod.). *Pilot:* Jack's Place (writer).

JONES, DEAN

Actor. b. Decatur, AL, Jan. 25, 1931. e. Asbury Coll., Wilmore, KY. Prof. debut as blues singer, New Orleans; U.S. Navy, 1950-54. Author: Under Running Laughter.
THEATRE: There Was a Little Girl, Under the Yum-Yum Tree, Company, Into the Light, Show Boat.
PICTURES: Tea and Sympathy (debut, 1956), The Rack, The Opposite Sex, These Wilder Years, The Great American Pastime, Designing Woman, Ten Thousand Bedrooms, Jailhouse Rock, Until They Sail, Imitation General, Torpedo Run, Handle with Care, Night of the Quarter Moon, Never So Few, Under the Yum-Yum Tree, The New Interns, That Darn Cat, Two on a Guillotine, Any Wednesday, The Ugly Dachshund, Monkeys Go Home, Blackbeard's Ghost, The Horse in the Grey Flannel Suit, The Love Bug, The Million Dollar Duck (Golden Globe nom. 1972), Snowball Express, Mr. Super Invisible, The Shaggy D.A., Herbie Goes to Monte Carlo, Born Again, Other People's Money, Beethoven, Clear and Present Danger.
TELEVISION: *Movies*: Guess Who's Sleeping in My Bed?, When Every Day Was the 4th of July, Long Days of Summer, Fire and Rain, The Great Man's Whiskers, Saved By the Bell: Hawaiian Style, The Computer Wore Tennis Shoes, The Love Bug Reunion, Who Is This Jesus? Scrooge and Marley. *Series*: Ensign O'Toole, The Chicago Teddy Bears, What's It All About World?, Herbie the Love Bug, Beethoven (animated; voice). *Specials*: Journey to Mars, Out of Jerusalem, The Age of Believing: The Disney Live Action Classics. *Guest:* More than 74 appearances.

JONES, GEMMA

Actress. b. London, Eng., Dec. 4, 1942. e. Royal Acad. of Dramatic Art.
THEATRE: Baal, Alfie, The Cavern, The Marriage of Figaro, And A Nightingale Sang, reaking the Silence, Howards End, A Midsummer Night's Dream, The Homecoming, Mount Morgan, The Winter's Tale.
PICTURES: The Devils, The Paper House, On the Black Hill, The Devils Feast of July, Sense and Sensibility, Wilde, The Winslow Boy, O.K. Garage, The Theory of Flight, Captain Jack, Cotton Mary, Bridget Jones's Diary, Don't Tempt Me, Harry Potter and the Chamber of Secrets, Shanghai Knights, Fragile, Bridget Jones: The Edge of Reason, Good, Harry Potter and the Half-Blood Prince, Forget Me Not, The Cellar, You Will Meet a Tall Dark Stranger.
TELEVISION: *Movies:* The Lie, The Way of the World, Dial a Deadly Number, The Merchant of Venice, The Importance of Being Earnest, Some Lie Some Die, The Return of the Borrowers, Faith, Wilderness, Jane Eyre, An Evil Streak, Longitude, Poirot: Five Little Pigs, Forget Me Not Lane, Call My Bluff, Dial M For Murder, The Way of the World, Churchill's People, The Cherry Orchard, The Lie, Man In A Sidecar, Shadows of Fear, Crimes of Passion, After The Dance, Ballet

Shoes. *Mini-series:* The Spoils of Poynton, Fall of Eagles, Chelworth, Devices and Desires, The Phoenix and the Carpet, Bootleg. *Series:* Rainbow City, The Jim Henson Hour, Inspector Morse, The Storyteller, All About George, MI-5, Trial & Retribution. *Guest:* More than 62 appearances.

JONES, GLENN R.

Executive. e. Bachelor's degree in economics, Allegheny College; juris doctor degree from University of Colorado School of Law. Completed executive program at Stanford Business School in 1973. Began career in law, representing cable TV cos. in acquisition efforts. Purchased his first cable TV system in 1967 which became part of Jones Intercable, Inc., founded 1970. Pres. and CEO of the corp. since its inception. Co. changed name to Jones International, Ltd. Currently, chmn. and CEO. 1987, founded cable network Mind Extension University. Renamed Knowledge TV in 1990s. Organization delivers college courses to viewers' TV sets, offering easy access to learning programs. Included in Jones' diverse business enterprises is Jones' entertainment companies. During the 1990s Jones formed Jones Media Networks, Ltd., a network content and e-commerce company that develops programming for radio TV, cable TV networks and the Internet. Jones' International Unviversity, a university which exists completely in cyberspace and was founded in 1993 by Jones, became the first online university to receive full accred-itaion from the nationally recognized Higher Learning Commission and was ranked in the top five for best online universities in 2010. Past memberships: Served as a member of the Board of Directors and the Executive Committee for the National Cable Television Association (NCTA) and as a member of the Board of Governors for the American Society for Training and Development (ASTD). Also former bd. member of the Board and Education Council of the National Alliance of Business (NAB). Founding member of the James Madison National Council. Recipient of numerous honors including: named Man of the Year by the Denver chapter of the Achievement Rewards for College Scientists (ARCS) and inducted into Broadcasting and Cable's Hall of Fame. He now serves on the Advisory Board for the Columbia Institute of Tele-Information at Columbia Business School. Locally, he serves on the Board of Trustees for the Denver Center for the Performing Arts and the Board of the Denver Area Council, Boy Scouts of America.

JONES, JAMES EARL

Actor. r.n. Todd Jones. b. Arkabutla, MS, Jan. 17, 1931. e. U. of Michigan. Son of late actor Robert Earl Jones. Awarded Hon. Doctor of Fine Arts (Yale, Princeton); Medal for Spoken Language (Amer. Acad. and Inst. of Arts and Letter; Hon. Doctor of Humane Letters (Columbia Coll. & U. of Mich.).
THEATRE: Moon on a Rainbow Shawl (Theatre World Award), The Cool World, Othello, Paul Robeson, Les Blancs, The Great White Hope (Tony Award, 1969), The Iceman Cometh, Of Mice and Men, A Lesson from Aloes, Master Harold ... and the Boys, Fences (Tony Award, 1986).
PICTURES: Dr. Strangelove, or: How I Learned to Stop Worrying and Love the Bomb (debut, 1964), The Comedians, King: A Filmed Record ... Montgomery to Memphis, End of the Road, The Great White Hope (Academy Award nom.; Golden Globe Award, 1 other nom. 1971), Malcolm X (narrator), The Man, Claudine (Golden Globe nom. 1975), Deadly Hero, Swashbuckler, The Bingo Long Travelling All-Stars and Motor Kings, The River Niger, The Greatest, Star Wars (voice), Exorcist II: The Heretic, The Last Remake of Beau Geste, A Piece of the Action, The Bushido Blade, The Empire Strikes Back (voice), Conan the Barbarian, Blood Tide (The Red Tide), Return of the Jedi (voice), City Limits, My Little Girl, Soul Man, Allan Quartermain and the Lost City of Gold, Gardens of Stone, Matewan, Pinocchio and the Emperor of the Night (voice), Coming to America, Three Fugitives, Field of Dreams, Best of the Best, The Hunt for Red October, Grim Prairie Tales, The Ambulance, True Identity, Convicts, Patriot Games, Sneakers, Sommersby, The Sandlot, The Meteor Man, Naked Gun 33 1/3: The Final Insult, Clean Slate, The Lion King (voice), Clear and Present Danger, Jefferson in Paris, Judge Dredd (voice), Cry the Beloved Country, Lone Star, A Family Thing, Good Luck (cameo), Gang Related, Summer's End, The Lion King II: Simba's Pride (voice), The Annihilation of Fish, Fantasia/2000, Undercover Angel, Quest for Atlantis, Antietam: A Documentary Drama, Finder's Fee, The Papp Project, Disney's American Legends (documentary, narrator), Robots (voice), Star Wars: Episode III - Revenge of the Sith, The Sandlot 2, The Benchwarmers (voice), Scary Movie 4 (narr.), Click (narr.), Welcome Home, Roscoe Jenkins, Jack and the Beanstalk (voice), Quantum Quest: A Cassini Space Odyssey (voice).
TELEVISION: *Movies*: King Lear, The UFO Incident, Jesus of Nazareth, The Greatest Thing That Almost Happened, Guyana Tragedy—The Story of Jim Jones, Golden Moment: An Olympic Love Story, Philby, Burgess and MacLean, The Atlanta Child Murders, The Vegas Strip War, Soldier Boys, Lone Star Kid, Teach 109 (short), By Dawn's Early Light (Emmy nom. 1990), Heat Wave (Emmy Award, 1991), Last Flight Out, The Last Elephant, Percy & Thunder, Hallelujah, Bailey's Bridge, Third and Oak: The Pool Hall, The Vernon Johns Story, Confessions: Two Faces of Evil, Alone, The Second Civil War, What the Deaf Man Heard, Merlin, Summer's End (Emmy Award 2000), Santa and Pete, In Search of Liberty Bell 7, 2004: A Light Knight's Odyssey, The Magic 7 (voice), The Reading Room. *Mini-series*: Roots: The Next Generations, Feast of All Saints. *Series*: As the World Turns, The Guiding Light, Vegetable Soup, Paris, Me and Mom, Mathnet, Gabriel's Fire (Emmy Award; Golden Globe nom. 1991), Pros & Cons (Golden Globe nom. 1992), Under One Roof (Emmy nom. 1995). *Documentaries/Specials*: King: A Filmed Record... Montgomery to Memphis, Malcolm X, Allen Boesak: Choosing for Justice, JFK: The Day the Nation Cried, When It Was a Game, Diamonds on the Silver Screen, Lincoln, Africa: The Serengeti, Countdown to Freedom: 10 Days That Changed South Africa, New York City... Come Visit the World, In Search of Liberty Bell 7, Ennis' Gift, Antietam: A Documentary Drama, The Papp Project, Black Indians: An American Story, The Great Year, Unforgivable Blackness: The Rise and Fall of Jack Johnson, The Clinton 12. *Host:* Black Omnibus, Summer Show, Long Ago and Far Away, Business World News. *Guest:* More than 227 appearances.

JONES, JEFFREY

Actor. b. Buffalo, NY, Sept. 28, 1947. e. Lawrence U., Wisconsin. While pre-med student, performed in 1967 prod. of Hobson's Choice and was invited by Sir Tyrone Guthrie to join Guthrie Theatre in Minneapolis. After short time in South America, studied at London Acad. of Music and Dramatic Arts before joining Stratford Theater in Ontario. 1973-74 worked with Vancouver touring children's theater co. Playhouse Holiday. Moved to N.Y. where performed on stage.
THEATRE: The Elephant Man (B'way debut), Trelawney of the Wells, Secret Service, Boy Meets Girl, Cloud Nine, Comedy of Errors, The Tempest, The Death of Von Richtoven, London Suite, Loot (MA).
PICTURES: The Revolutionary, The Soldier, Easy Money, Amadeus (Golden Globe nom. 1985), Transylvania 6-5000, Ferris Bueller's Day Off, Howard the Duck, The Hanoi Hilton, Beetlejuice, Without a Clue, Who Is Harry Crumb?, Valmont, The Hunt for Red October, Over Her Dead Body, Mom and Dad Save the World, Stay Tuned, Out on a Limb, Heaven and Earth (cameo), Ed Wood, Houseguest, The Pest, The Crucible, Sante Fe, Flypaper, The Pest, The Devil's Advocate, There Is No Fish Food in Heaven, Ravenous, Sleepy Hollow, Stuart Little, Robots of Mars, Company Man, Heartbreakers, Dr. Dolittle 2, How High, Par 6, Who's Your Caddy?.
TELEVISION: *Movies*: Kenny Rogers as The Gambler III—The Legend Continues, The Avenging Angel, Till Dad Do Us Part. *Mini-series*: George Washington: The Forging of a Nation, Fresno. *Series*: The People Next Door, Deadwood.

JONES, KATHY

Executive. b. Aug. 27, 1949. Began career as acct. exec. for m.p. clients, Stan Levinson assoc., Dallas. Joined Paramount Pictures in 1977 as sr. publicist in field marketing then exec. dir., field mktg. Left to join Time-Life Films as v.p., domestic mktg. for m.p. div. Returned to Paramount 1981 as v.p., domestic pub. & promo. 1984, appt. sr. v.p., domestic pub. & promo. for Motion Picture Group, Paramount. Formed m.p. consultancy with Buffy Shutt, 1987 and has worked with Shutt in various capacities and projects ever since. In 1989, appt. exec. v.p., marketing, Columbia Pictures. 1991, appt. exec. v.p. marketing, TriStar Pictures. 1994, joined Universal Pictures as co-president of marketing with Shutt. In 1998, Jones became an independent producer at Universal, and with Imagine Entertainment produced Blue Crush. Jones has taught and guest lectured on marketing and producing at UCLA, USC, Chapman University and The Art Center College of Design. Both Jones and colleague Buffy Shutt then joined Participant Productions as EVP, Marketing in Jan. 2007. The company's focus is to raise awareness about important social issues, educate audiences and inspire action through its films. Before joining Participant, she helped guide the company through the release of Good Night and Good Luck, Syriana and An Inconvenient Truth. Jones was recognized by Women in Film with its highest honor, the Crystal Award, in 1996. She is a member of the Academy of Motion Picture Arts and Sciences.
PICTURES: Blue Crush (exec. prod.).

JONES, QUINCY

Producer, Composer, Arranger, Recording Artist. b. Chicago, IL, March 14, 1933. e. Seattle U., Berklee Sch. Music, Boston Conservatory, Trumpeter and arranger for Lionel Hampton's orch. 1950-53, played with Dizzy Gillespie, Count Basie and arranged for orchs., singers-Frank Sinatra, Sarah Vaughn, Peggy Lee, Dinah Washington and led own orch. for European tours, and recordings. Prod. recordings for Michael Jackson, Tevin Campbell, Barbra Streisand, Donna Summer. Music dir. and v.p., Mercury Records 1961-64 before scoring films. Prod. & arranged We Are the World recording. Owns Qwest Records record company. During a career spanning more than six decades Jones has won more than 25 Grammy Awards. Among his numerous awards, Jones received the Academy Award: Jean Hersholt Humanitarian Award, 1995. Wrote autobiography in 2001, Q: The Autobiography of Quincy Jones. In 2007, Jones launched a series of video podcasts with behind-the-scenes segments of his projects with famous artists. Jones' digital efforts include www.quincyjones.com, a website launched in late 2007.
PICTURES: The Pawnbroker, Mirage, The Slender Thread,

Made in Paris, Walk Don't Run, Banning (Academy Award nom. 1968), The Deadly Affair, In the Heat of the Night, In Cold Blood (Academy Award nom. 1968), Enter Laughing, A Dandy in Aspic, For Love of Ivy (Academy Award nom. 1969), The Hell With Heroes, The Split, Up Your Teddy Bear, Jocelyn, McKenna's Gold, The Italian Job, Bob & Carol & Ted & Alice, The Lost Man, Cactus Flower (Golden Globe nom. 1970), Honky (Golden Globe nom. 1972), John and Mary, The Last of the Mobile Hotshots, The Out-of-Towners, They Call Me Mister Tibbs, Brother John, $ (Dollars), The Anderson Tapes, Yao of the Jungle, The Hot Rock, The New Centurions, Come Back Charleston Blue, The Getaway (Golden Globe nom. 1973), The Wiz (also cameo, Academy Award nom. 1979), The Color Purple (also co-prod.; 4 Academy Award nom.; Golden Globe nom.1986), Listen Up: The Lives of Quincy Jones, Steel, Austin Powers: International Man of Mystery, Austin Powers: The Spy Who Shagged Me, The Smokers (exec. prod. only), Vaccuums (exec. prod. only), Thug Angel (exec. prod. only), Austin Powers in Goldmember (also actor), Vacuums (exec. prod., prod), Keeping Time: The Life-Music & Photography of Milt Hinton (as himself), Kill Bill: Vol. 1, Kill Bill: Vol. 2, Get Rich or Die Tryin' (Composer, conductor), Date Movie (writer, theme), Hollywoodland (writer on soundtrack), Since I Don't Have You (soundtrack performer), Paul Mooney: Jesus Is Black - So Was Cleopatra - Know Your History (doc.), This Christmas, Paris (soundtrack performer), Semi-Pro, Hancock, Recording: The History of Recorded Music (doc., host, exec. prod.).
TELEVISION: *Movies*: Ironside, The Counterfeit Killer, Split Second to an Epitaph, The Palladium: Where Mambo Was King, Passing Glory (exec. prod.), Their Eyes Were Watching God (exec. prod.), Brando (doc., music consult.). *Mini-series*: Roots (Emmy Award, 1977), *Series*: *Exec. Prod.:* The Jesse Jackson Show (also prod.), Fresh Prince of Bel Air, In the House, Mad TV, Vibe, Star Camp. *As Comp:* Hey, Landlord, Ironside, The New Bill Cosby Show (musical dir., Emmy nom. 1970), In the Heat of the Night, Now You See It. *Specials:* An American Reunion (exec. prod.), The History of Rock 'N' Roll, Vol. 9 (Emmy nom. 1995), The 68th Annual Academy Awards (Emmy nom. 1996), Great Performances. Numerous documentaries. *Guest:* More than 216 appearances.

JONES, SAM J.
Actor. b. Chicago, IL, Aug. 12, 1954.
PICTURES: "10," Davinci's War, One Man Force, Night Rhythms, South Beach, Iron Fist, Where the Truth Lies, Evasive Action, Flash Gordon, Lady Dragon II, Last Breath, My Chauffeur, Under the Gun, Silent Assassins, Jane & the Lost City, White Fire, Trigon Factor, Driving Force, In Gold We Trust, Human Shields, Fists of Honor, Ballistic, American Strays, Texas Payback, Hard Vice, R.I.O.T., American Tigers, Baja Run, Earth Minus Zero, Baja Run, American Tigers, T.N.T., Evasive Action, The Killer Inside, Gangland, Down n' Dirty, Dead Sexy (video), Van Hook, Psychotic, Redemption, Revamped.
TELEVISION: *Movies*: This Wife for Hire, Ray Alexander. Pilot: Hat Squad, Cobra, Thunder in Paradise, Stunts Unlimited, No Man's Land, The Spirit. *Series*: Training Camp, Code Red, The Highwayman, Hollywood Safari.

JONES, SHIRLEY
Actress. b. Smithton, PA, March 31, 1934. m. agent-prod. Marty Ingels. Mother of actors Shaun and Patrick Cassidy. Former Miss Pittsburgh. Natl. chair, Leukemia Foundation. Book: Shirley & Marty: An Unlikely Love Story (Wm. Morrow, 1990). Received hon. Doctor of Humane Letters degree from Point Park College, 1991.
THEATRE: Appeared with Pittsburgh Civic Light Opera in Lady in the Dark, Call Me Madam. B'way: South Pacific, Me and Juliet, Maggie Flynn.
PICTURES: Oklahoma! (debut, 1955), Carousel, April Love, Never Steal Anything Small, Bobbikins, Elmer Gantry (Academy Award, best supporting actress, 1961), Pepe, Two Rode Together, The Music Man, The Courtship of Eddie's Father, A Ticklish Affair, Dark Purpose, Bedtime Story, Fluffy, The Secret of My Success, The Happy Ending, El Golfo, Oddly Coupled, The Cheyenne Social Club, Beyond the Poseidon Adventure, Tank, There Were Times Dear, Jack L. Warner: The Last Mogul, Cops n' Roberts, Gideon, Shriek If You Know What I Did Last Friday the Thirteenth (video), Ping!, The Adventures of Cinderella's Daughter, Manna From Heaven, Bloodhead, Raising Genius, The Creature of the Sunny Side Up Trailer Park, Grandma's Boy, Christmas Is Here Again (voice, singer), Johnny Blue.
TELEVISION: *Movies*: Silent Night Lonely Night (Emmy nom. 1970), But I Don't Want to Get Married, The Girls of Huntington House, The Family Nobody Wanted, Winner Take All, The Lives of Jenny Dolan, Yesterday's Child, Evening in Byzantium, Who'll Save Our Children? A Last Cry For Help, Children of An Lac, Intimates: A Love Story, Widow, Charlie, Dog's Best Friend, Intimate Portrait: Shirley Jones (as herself), We Are Family (documentary, as herself), Hidden Places (Emmy nom. 2006). *Series*: The Partridge Family (2 Golden Globe noms.), Shirley, The Slap Maxwell Story, Melrose Place, Monarch Cove, Days of Our Lives. *Guest*: More than 168 appearances.

JONES, TERRY
Writer, Actor, Director. b. Colwyn Bay, North Wales, Feb. 1, 1942. Worked with various rep. groups before joining BBC script dept. Was member of Monty Python's Flying Circus.
PICTURES: Actor: And Now for Something Completely Different (also co-s.p.), Monty Python and the Holy Grail (also co-dir., co-s.p.), Monty Python's Life of Brian (also dir., co-s.p.), Monty Python's The Meaning of Life (also co-s.p., dir., music), Labyrinth (s.p. only), Personal Services (dir. only), Erik the Viking (also dir., s.p.), LA Story, The Wind in the Willows, Magdalen, The Creator, Help I'm a Fish, Bitter Jester (doc.), Green Card Fever.
TELEVISION: *Movies:* Pleasure at Her Majesty's, The Mermaid Frolics (writer/stage dir.), Peter Cook & Co., Secrets, The Crusades (doc., writer). *Mini-series:* Ancient Inventions (host, writer), Dinotopia. *Series: As Writer:* The Frost Report, The Late Show (writer), A Series of Birds, Twice a Fortnight, Do Not Adjust Your Set, Marty, Horne A'Plenty, Broaden Your Mind, The Complete and Utter History of Britain, Monty Python's Flying Circus, The Two Ronnies, Black and Blue, Ripping Yarns, Bergerac, Blazing Dragons (also creator), So This Is Progress, It's the Monty Python Story, Crusades, Monty Python's Flying Circus: Live at Aspen, 30 Years of Monty Python: A Revelation, The Boy in Darkness, Top Ten Comedy Records, The Sketch Show Story, Medieval Lives (Emmy nom. 2004), The Legend of Dick & Dom (narr.). *Guest:* More than 116 appearances.

JONES, TOMMY LEE
Actor. b. San Saba, TX, Sept. 15, 1946. Worked in oil fields; graduated Harvard, where earned a degree, cum laude, in English. Broadway debut in A Patriot for Me; appeared on stage in Four in a Garden, Ulysses in Nighttown, Fortune and Men's Eyes.
PICTURES: Love Story (debut, 1970), Eliza's Horoscope, Jackson County Jail, Rolling Thunder, The Betsy, Eyes of Laura Mars, Coal Miner's Daughter (Golden Globe nom. 1981), Back Roads, Nate and Hayes, The River Rat, Black Moon Rising, The Big Town, Stormy Monday, The Package, Firebirds, JFK (Academy Award nom. 1992), Under Siege, House of Cards, The Fugitive (Academy Award, best supporting actor, 1994; LA Film Critics & Golden Globe Awards), Heaven and Earth, Blown Away, The Client, Natural Born Killers, Blue Sky, Cobb, Batman Forever, Men in Black, Volcano, U.S. Marshalls, Small Soldiers (voice), Rules of Engagement, Double Jeopardy, Space Cowboys, Men in Black II, The Hunted, The Missing, Cheer Up (also exec. prod.), Man of the House (also exec. prod.), The Three Burials of Melquiades Estrada (also dir., prod.), A Prairie Home Companion, No Country for Old Men, In the Valley of Elah (Academy Award nom. 2008), In the Electric Mist, The Company Men.
TELEVISION: *Movies*: Charlie's Angels (pilot), Smash-Up on Interstate 5, The Amazing Howard Hughes, The Executioner's Song (Emmy Award, 1983), Broken Vows, The Park is Mine, Yuri Nosenko: KGB, Gotham, Stranger on My Land, April Morning, The Good Old Boys (also dir., co-writer), The Sunset Limited (dir., exec. prod.). *Mini-series*: Lonesome Dove (Emmy nom.; Golden Globe nom. 1989). *Specials*: The Rainmaker, Cat on a Hot Tin Roof, Small Soldiers: Size Doesn't Matter (voice). *Guest:* More than 77 appearances.

JONES, TREVOR
Composer, Conductor. b. Cape Town, S. Africa, March 23, 1949.
PICTURES: The Dollar Bottom, Brothers and Sisters, The Beneficiary, The Appointment, Excalibur, The Sender, The Dark Crystal, Nate and Hayes, Runaway Train, From an Immigrant's Diary, Labyrinth, Angel Heart, Sweet Lies, A Private Life, Mississippi Burning, Just Ask For Diamond, Dominick and Eugene, Sea of Love, Bad Influence, Arachnophobia, Ture Colors, CrissCross, Blame It on the Bellboy, Freejack, The Last of the Mohicans (Golden Globe nom. 1993), In the Name of the Father, Cliffhanger, De Baby huilt, LochNess, Hideaway, Kiss of Death, Richard III, Brassed Off, Lawn Dogs, Roseanna's Grave, Talk of Angels, Desperate Measures, G.I. Jane, Titanic Town, Plunkett & MacLeane, Analyse This, Dark City, The Mighty (Golden Globe nom. 1999), Notting Hill, Molly, Frederic Wilde, From Hell, Crossroads, I'll Be There, The League of Extraordinary Gentlemen, Around the World in 80 Days, Chaos, Fields of Freedom, Three and Out, A Deal Is a Deal.
TELEVISION: *Movies*: Those Glory Glory Days, One of Ourselves, Aderyn Papur. and Pigs Might Fly, Those Glory Glory Days, Dr. Fischer of Geneva, A Private Life, Murder by Moonlight, By Dawn's Early Light, Chains of Gold, Death Train, Gulliver's Travels, Merlin (Emmy nom. 1998), Cleopatra, Blood and Oil. *Mini-series*: Joni Jones, The Last Place on Earth, The Last Days of Pompeii, Jim Henson Presents the World of International Puppeteering, Dinotopia. *Series:* Dinotopia, Jozi-H. *Documentaries:* Inside the Labyrinth, Guns: A Day in the Death of America,

JONZE, SPIKE
Actor, Director. b. Rockville, Maryland, 1969. r.n. Adam Speigel. Has directed many television commercials and music videos for artists. Is heir to the Spiegel mail order catalog. DGA nom. 2006 for Outstanding Commercial Direction.
PICTURES: Mi Vida Loca (actor), The Game (actor only), Being John Malkovich (Academy Award nom.; 2 DGA nom. 2000), Three Kings (actor only), Human Nature (prod. only), Hannibal (actor only), Adaptation (Golden Globe nom. 2003), Keep Your Eyes Open (actor only), Jackass (doc., writer, prod.), Adaptation (actor, dir.), Yeah Right! (video, dir. exec. prod.), The 1 Second Film (prod.), Jackass Number Two (doc., prod., writer), Heavy

Metal in Baghdad (doc., exec. prod.), Synecdoche, New York (prod.) Where the Wild Things Are (dir., writer, s.p.), I'm Here (writer, dir.), Jackass 3-D (doc., prod.).
TELEVISION: *Movies:* Sonic Youth Video Dose, Jackass Presents: Murderball (writer), Jackass: Gumball 3000 Rally Special (exec. prod.). *Series:* Jackass (exec. prod., prod., writer), Double Rush (dir., titles).

JORDAN, GLENN
Director, Producer, b. San Antonio, TX, April 5, 1936. e. Harvard, B.A.; Yale Drama Sch. Directed plays off-B'way and on tour.
PICTURES: *Dir.* Only When I Laugh, The Buddy System, Mass Appeal.
TELEVISION: *Movies*: *Director:* Frankenstein, The Picture of Dorian Gray, Shell Game, One of My Wives is Missing, The Displaced Person, Delta County U.S.A., In the Matter of Karen Ann Quinlan, Sunshine Christmas, Les Miserables (Emmy nom. 1979), The Women's Room (Emmy nom. 1981), Son Rise: A Miracle of Love, The Family Man, The Princess and the Cabbie, Lois Gibbs and the Love Canal, Heartsounds, Dress Gray (also prod., Emmy nom. 1986), Promise (also prod., 2 Emmy Awards 1987), Something in Common (also prod.), Echoes in the Darkness (also prod., Emmy nom. 1988), Jesse, Home Fires Burning (also prod.), Challenger, Sarah Plain & Tall (also prod., 2 Emmy nom. 1991), Aftermath: A Test of Love, The Boys (also prod.), O Pioneers (also prod.), Barbarians at the Gate (Emmy Award 1993, 1 other nom.; co-exec. prod.), To Dance with the White Dog (also prod., 2 Emmy nom. 1994), Jane's House (also prod.), My Brother's Keeper, A Streetcar Named Desire (1995), Jake's Women (also prod.), After Jimmy, Mary & Tim, A Christmas Memory, The Long Way Home, Legalese, Night Ride Home, Sarah Plain & Tall: Winter's End, Midwives, Lucy. *Mini-series:* Lives of Benjamin Franklin (prod., Emmy Award, 1 other nom. 1975). *Series*: Family (DGA Award 1977), Friends. *Specials*: Hogan's Goat, Paradise Lost, Eccentricities of a Nightingale, The Oath, The Court Martial of Gen. George Armstrong Custer.

JORDAN, NEIL
Director, Writer. b. Sligo, Ireland, Feb. 25, 1950. e. University Coll, B.A., 1972. *Novels:* The Past, Night in Tunisia, Dream of a Beast.
PICTURES: Traveller (s.p.), The Courier (co-exec. prod.). *Dir./Writer:* Angel, The Company of Wolves, Mona Lisa (LA Film Critics Award for s.p., Golden Globe nom.; WGA nom. 1987), High Spirits, We're No Angels (dir. only), The Miracle, The Crying Game (Academy Award, 1 other nom.; WGA & NY Film Critics Awards for s.p., DGA nom., 1993), Interview With the Vampire, Michael Collins, The Butcher Boy, In Dreams, The End of the Affair (Golden Globe nom. 2000), Not I (dir. only), The Good Thief, Borgia, The Actors (story only), Intermission (prod. only), Me and My Monster, Breakfast on Pluto (also prod.), The Brave One, A Film with Me in It, Ondine.
TELEVISION: *Movies:* Miracles and Miss Langan, Red Hot and Blue (segment dir.). *Series:* The Borgias (dir., exec. prod.).

JOSEPHSON, ERLAND
Actor, Director, Writer. b. Stockholm, Sweden, June 15, 1923. Acted in over 100 plays in Sweden. Joined Sweden's Royal Dramatic Theatre in 1956 replacing Ingmar Bergman as head of the theater, 1966-76. Closely associated with Bergman, with whom he staged plays in his late teens. Co-authored s.p. The Pleasure Garden and Now About These Women. Also has pub. poetry, six novels, and scripts for stage, screen and radio. American stage debut: The Cherry Orchard, 1988. In numerous movies on Swedish television.
PICTURES: It Rains on Our Love, To Joy (uncredited), Sceningang, Som man baddar, Brink of Life, The Magician, Hour of the Wolf, The Girls, Eva: Diary of Half Virgin, The Passion of Anna, Cries and Whispers, Scenes from a Marriage, Monismanien, Face to Face, A Look at Liv, Io ho paura, Beyond Good and Evil, Games of Love and Loneliness, I'm Afraid, Autumn Sonata, Die Erste Polka, To Forget Venice, One and One (also dir.), The Marmalade Revolution (also dir., s.p.), Karleken, Victor Sjostrom (voice), You Love Only Once, Montenegro, Sezona Mira u Parizu, Fanny and Alexander, Bella Donna, Nostalgia, House of the Yellow Carpet, Angela's War, Bakom jalusin, Behind the Shutters, A Case of Irresponsibility, Dirty Story, Amorosa, The Flying Devils, Garibaldi, The General, The Last Mazurka, The Sacrifice, The Malady of Love, Saving Grace, Le Testament d'un poete juif assassine, Unbearable Lightness of Being, Directed by Andrei Tarkovsky, Hanussen, Good Evening Mr. Wallenberg, The Wicked, Meeting Venus, Prospero's Books, The Ox, The Accidental Golfer, Sofie, Holozan, The Dancer, Dreamplay, Ulysses' Gaze, Vendetta, Waiting for Sunset, Kristin Lavransdatter, I Am Curious Film, Al la recherche de Erland Josephson, Magnetist's Fifth Winter, Light Keeps Me Company, Faithless, Hr. Boe & Co's Anxiety, Scener ur ett aktenskap II, Nu, Dobro ustimani mrtvaci, Wellkåmm to Verona.
TELEVISION: *Movies:* The Lie, After the Rehearsal, The Last Witness, The Good Pope: Pope John XXIII, Saraband. *Mini-series:* Rosenbaum, Vendetta.

JOSEPHSON, MARVIN
Executive. b. Atlantic City, NJ, March 6, 1927. e. Cornell U., B.A., 1949; L.L.B. NYU, 1952. Lawyer at CBS Television 1952-55; In 1955, founded and owned company which today is ICM Holdings Inc. ICM Holdings Inc. is the parent company of Intl. Creative Management Inc. and ICM Artists Ltd.

JOST, JON
Director, Writer, Cinematographer, Editor. b. May 16, 1943.
PICTURES: Speaking Directly, Angel City, Last Chants for a Slow Dance, Chameleon (also prod.), Stagefright, Psalm, Slow Moves, Bell Diamond, Rembrandt Laughing, Plain Talk & Common Sense, Blood Orgy of the Leather Girls (assoc. prod. only), All the Vermeers in New York, The Living End (exec. prod. only), Sure Fire, Frame Up, The Bed You Sleep In, One for You One for Me and One for Raphael, Albrecht's Wings, Frame Up, London Brief (doc.), Roman Walls, Homecoming (also prod.), Over Here (also prod.), Not Since You (ADR recordist).

JOY, ROBERT
Actor. b. Montreal, Canada, Aug. 17, 1951. e. Memorial Univ. of Newfoundland; Rhodes Scholar. Acted in regional and off-Broadway theatre. Off-B'way debut The Diary of Anne Frank (1978). Has composed music for stage, radio and film.
THEATRE: NY Shakespeare Fest. (Found a Peanut, Lenny and the Heartbreakers, The Death of von Richtofen), Life and Limb, Fables for Friends, Welcome to the Moon, What I Did Last Summer, Lydie Breeze, Romeo and Juliet (La Jolla Playhouse; Drama-Logue Award), Hay Fever (B'way debut), Big River (premiere), The Nerd, Hyde in Hollywood, The Taming of the Shrew, Shimada, Goodnight Desdemona (Good Morning Juliet), Abe Lincoln in Illinois, No One Will Be Immune, June Moon.
PICTURES: Atlantic City, Ragtime, Ticket to Heaven, Threshold, Terminal Choice, Amityville 3-D, Desperately Seeking Susan, Joshua Then and Now, Adventure of Faustus Bidgood (also co-prod. music), Radio Days, Big Shots, The Suicide Club, She's Back!, Millenium, Longtime Companion, Shadows and Fog, The Dark Half, Death Wish 5: The Face of Death, I'll Do Anything, Henry & Verlin, Waterworld, A Modern Affair, Pharoah's Army, Dangerous Offender, Harriet the Spy, The Divine Ryans, Fallen, Resurrection, The Divine Ryans, Advice From a Caterpillar, Bonhoeefer: Agent of Grace, Perfume, Sweet November, The Shipping News, Joe Somebody, The Lazarus Child, Land of the Dead, The Hills Have Eyes, It's a Boy Girl Thing, AVPR: Aliens vs Predator - Requiem, Superhero Movie.
TELEVISION: *Movies*: Escape from Iran: The Canadian Caper, Gregory K, Woman on the Run: The Lawrencia Bembenek Story, The High Life, Moonlight Becomes You, The Bookfair Murders, Cheaters, Haven, 61*, Just Ask My Children, Fargo, Killer Instinct: From the Files of Agent Candice DeLong, Helter Skelter, Sex Traffic. *Mini-series:* Seasons of Love, The '70s, Nuremberg, The National Dream: Building the Impossible Railway. *Series*: One Life to Live, The High Life, MDs, E-Ring (pilot), CSI: NY. *Specials*: The Prodigious Hickey, The Return of Hickey, The Beginning of the Firm, Hyde in Hollywood. *Guest*: More than 75 appearances.

JUDD, ASHLEY
Actress. r.n. Ashley Tyler Ciminella. b. Los Angeles, CA, April 19, 1968. Mother and sister are country singers, Naomi and Wynona Judd. Global ambassor for YouthAIDS.
PICTURES: Kuffs, Ruby in Paradise, The Passion of Darkly Noon, Smoke, Heat, A Time to Kill, Normal Life, The Locusts, Kiss the Girls, Simon Birch, Eye of the Beholder, Double Jeopardy, Where the Heart Is, Killing Priscilla (video documentary), Someone Like You, High Crimes, Frida, Divine Secrets of the Ya Ya Sisterhood, Star Trek: Nemesis, The Blackout Murders, Twisted, De-Lovely (Golden Globe nom. 2005), Come Early Morning, Bug, Crossing Over, Helen, Tooth Fairy.
TELEVISION: *Movies*: Till Death Us Do Part, Norma Jean and Marilyn (Emmy nom.; Golden Globe nom. 1996), The Ryan Interview. *Series*: Sisters. *Special*: Naomi & Wynona: Love Can Build a Bridge. *Guest:* More than 66 appearances.

JUDGE, MIKE
Animator, Actor, Director, Producer. b. Guayaquil, Ecuador, Oct. 17, 1962. e. UC San Diego. Shorts: Frog Baseball (also voices, dir., prod., s.p.), Inbred Jed (also voices, dir., prod., s.p.), Office Space (voice, composer, dir.).
PICTURES: Airheads (voice), Beavis & Butt-head Do America (also dir., prod., composer, voices), Mene Tekel (voices), Office Space (dir., s.p., act.), South Park: Bigger Longer and Uncut (voice), Spy Kids, Spy Kids 2: The Island of Lost Dreams, The Animation Show (co-prod. only), Spy Kids 3-D: Game Over (acting), 3001 (s.p., prod., dir.), The Animation Show 2 (prod.) Idiocracy (prod., dir., writer, s.p.), The Animation Show 2007 (prod.), Extract (dir., writer s.p.).
TELEVISION: *Movie:* Beavis and Butt-head Christmas Special, Monsignor Martinez (dir., s.p.,). *Series*: Beavis and Butt-head, (also dir., prod., composer, voices), King of the Hill (creator also prod., voices, Emmy Award 1999, 4 other noms.), The Goode Family (also exec. prod.). *Guest:* More than 45 appearances.

K

KAGAN, JEREMY
Director, Writer. b. Mt. Vernon, NY, Dec. 14, 1945. e. Harvard; NYU, MFA; student Amer. Film Inst. 1971. Film animator, 1968; multi-media show designer White House Conf. on Youth and Ed. Previously credited as Jeremy Paul Kagan. Received DGA, Robert B. Aldrich Achievement Award 2004.
PICTURES: Scott Joplin, Heroes, The Big Fix, The Chosen (Montreal World Film Fest. Prize, 1981), The Sting II, The Journey of Natty Gann (Gold Prize, Moscow Film Fest., 1987), Big Man on Campus, By the Sword.
TELEVISION: *Movies*: Unwed Father, Judge Dee and the Monastery Murders, Katherine (also writer), Courage, Roswell (also co-prod., co-story), My Dad Lives in a Downtown Hotel, Conspiracy: The Trial of the Chicago 8 (also writer; ACE Award, 1988), Descending Angel, The Hired Heart, The Ballad of Lucie Whipple, Crown Heights (DGA nom. 2005). Bobbie's Girl. *Mini-series:* Taken. *Series*: Columbo, The Bold Ones, Chicago Hope (Emmy Award, 1996), Ally McBeal, Family Law, The West Wing, Resurrection Blvd., Boomtown, The Handler. *Documentary:* The ACLU Freedom Files (series).

KAHN, MILTON
Publicist. b. Brooklyn, NY, May 3, 1934. e. Syracuse U., Ohio U., B.S.J. 1957. Formed Milton Kahn Associates, Inc. in 1958. Represented: Gregory Peck, Joan Crawford, Steve Allen, Glenn Ford, Lee Grant, Herb Alpert, Roger Corman, Robert Aldrich, Arthur Hiller, Chuck Norris, Bob Cousy, Gordie Howe, Michael Landon, Dean Hargrove, Bill Conti, etc. and New World Pictures (1970-83), Avco-Embassy, Vista Films, Roger Corman's Concorde (1983), Electric Shadow Prods. Named Publicist of the Year by Book Pub. of So. CA, 1996. Among his PR campaigns is the 2007 Stanley Alpert "The Birthday Party: A Memoir of Survival," which has been acquired by Tom Cruise and Paula Wagner to be produced as a United Artists film.

KALISH, EDDIE
Executive. b. New York, NY, April 27, 1939. Reporter/reviewer, Variety, 1959-64; sr. publicist, Paramount, 1964-65; adv./pub./promo dir., Ken Greengras Personal Management, 1965-66; pub. dir., Harold Rand & Co., 1966-67; indept. publicist overseas, 1967-75; rejoined Paramount in 1975 as dir. of intl. mktg.; later named v.p.; 1978, v.p., worldwide pub. & promo. 1979 appt. sr. v.p., worldwide mktg. 1980 joined UA as v.p. domestic mktg.; sr. v.p., adv., pub., promo, for MGM/UA 1981-82; became sr. v.p., worldwide mkt., PSO, 1982-1986. Now pres./owner, Kalish/Davidson Marketing, Inc. (KDM, Inc.), a full-service entertainment marketing agency based in Los Angeles, CA.

KAMINSKI, JANUSZ
Cinematographer. b. Ziembice, Poland, June 27, 1959. Second unit work on films: Watchers II, To Die Standing, One False Move.
PICTURES: The Terror Within II (debut, 1990), Grim Prairie Tales, The Rain Killer, Pyrates, Cool as Ice, Trouble Bound, Mad Dog Coll, The Adventures of Huck Finn, Schindler's List (Academy Award, ASC nom.; 1994), Little Giants, Tall Tale, How to Make an American Quilt, Jerry Maguire, Amistad (Academy Award nom.; ASC nom. 1998), The Lost World: Jurassic Park, Armageddon (addt'l), Saving Private Ryan (Academy Award, ASC nom. 1999),A.I., Minority Report, Collateral, Catch Me If You Can, Jumbo Girl (short), The Terminal, Indiana Jones 4, Vengeance, War of the Worlds, Munich, Hania (also dir.), The Diving Bell and the Butterfly (Academy Award nom.; ASC nom. 2008), The Trial of the Chicago 7, Indiana Jones and the Kingdom of the Crystal Skull, Funny People, How Do You Know (also dir. of photog.). *Dir:* Lost Souls, White Rose.
TELEVISION: *Movies*: Wildflower, Class of '61, Love, Cheat & Steal.

KANAKAREDES, MELINA
Actress. b. Akron, OH, April 23, 1967.
PICTURES: White Man's Burden, The Long Kiss Goodnight, Rounders, Dangerous Beauty, 15 Minutes, Percy Jackson & the Olympians: The Lightning Thief.
TELEVISION: *Movies*: Saint Maybe Into the Fire. *Series*: The Guiding Light (2 Emmy noms.), NYPD Blue, New York News, Leaving L.A., Providence, C.S.I.: NY.

KANE, CAROL
Actress. b. Cleveland, OH, June 18, 1952. e. Professional Children's Sch., NY. Began professional acting career at age 14, touring, then on B'way in The Prime of Miss Jean Brodie.
THEATRE: The Tempest, The Effect of Gamma Rays on Man-in-the-Moon Marigolds, Are You Now or Have You Ever Been? Arturo Ui, The Enchanted, The Tempest, Macbeth, Tales of the Vienna Woods, Frankie and Johnny in the Claire de Lune, Control Freaks.
PICTURES: Carnal Knowledge (debut, 1971), Desperate Characters, Wedding in White, The Last Detail, Dog Day Afternoon, Hester Street (Academy Award nom. 1976), Harry and Walter Go to New York, Annie Hall, Valentino, The World's Greatest Lover, The Mafu Cage, The Muppet Movie, When a Stranger Calls, Pandemonium, Norman Loves Rose, Over the Brooklyn Bridge, Racing With the Moon, The Secret Diary of Sigmund Freud, Transylvania 6-5000, Jumpin' Jack Flash, Ishtar, The Princess Bride, Sticky Fingers, License to Drive, Scrooged, Flashback, Joe Vs. the Volcano, My Blue Heaven, The Lemon Sisters, Ted and Venus, In the Soup, Addams Family Values, Even Cowgirls Get the Blues, Big Bully, The Pallbearer, Sunset Park, The Pallbearer, American Strays, Office Killer, Gone Fishin', The Tic Code, Jawbreaker, Man on the Moon, Tomorrow by Midnight, The Shrink Is In, The Office Party, My First Mister, D.C. Smalls, Love in the Time of Money, Confessions of a Teenage Drama Queen, The Pacifier, The Key Man, Four Christmases, The Bounty Hunter, My Girlfriend's Boyfriend, Pete Smalls Is Dead.
TELEVISION: *Movies*: An Invasion of Privacy, Burning Rage, Drop Out Mother, Dad the Angel and Me, Freaky Friday, Merry Christmas George Bailey, Audrey's Rain, Cosmopolitan, The Year Without a Santa Claus. *Series*: Taxi (2 Emmy Awards: 1982, 1983, Golden Globe nom. 1983), All Is Forgiven, American Dreamer, Pearl, Beggars and Choosers, The Grubbs, Chicago Hope (2 Emmy noms. episodes "Stand", "Marguerite Birch". *Specials:* Faerie Tale Theatre, Paul Reiser: Out on a Whim, Tales From the Crypt (Judy, You're Not Yourself Today), Noah's Ark. *Guest:* More than 80 appearances.

KANE, TOM
Executive. b. New York. Kane got his start in 1969 in the media dept. of Dancer, Fitzgerald & Sample. He then worked in a variety of sales positions for companies including H.R. Television; Peters, Griffin & Woodward; and Storer Television Sales, Inc. He then moved to the station side of the business and worked in a variety of positions at WABC, including gen. sales mgr. (1986-1993), sales mgr. (1982-1986) and account executive (1975-1977). In between, he served as an Account Executive for ABC Spot Sales in Detroit (1977-1978) and ABC's New York Spot Sales office (1978-1979), where he was promoted to Eastern Sales Manager (1979-1982). Kane worked for seven years as pres. and gen. mgr. of WABC-TV New York, the flagship station of the ABC Owned Station Group. He also previously served as pres. & gen. mgr. of WPVI-TV, the ABC O&O in Philadelphia. When he joined Viacom, Inc., Kane did stints as pres. of sales for the TV Stations Group; was pres. for TV Stations Spot Sales and in 2005 was named pres. and CEO of the Viacom TV Stations Group (now CBS TV Stations Group). 2009 Kane left CBS. In his role at CBS, he oversaw all operations of the group's 36 local TV stations properties. Kane serves as chairman of the IRTS, in addition to participating on a number of boards of organizations in the city and TV industry, including the New York State Broadcasters Association and Promesa, a Hispanic community service organization.

KANEW, JEFF
Director. b. New York, NY, Dec. 16, 1944.
PICTURES: The Wicked Die Slow (writer, actor), Black Rodeo (also prod., edit.), Natural Enemies (also s.p., editor), Ordinary People (editor), Eddie Macon's Run (also s.p., editor), Revenge of the Nerds, Gotcha!, Tough Guys, Troop Beverly Hills, V.I. Warshawski, Detective in High Heels, Babij Jar (doc. dir., editor), Adam and Eve (also Prod. and Editor.), Yippee (doc., editor, co-prod.), National Lampoon's The Legend Of Awesomest Maximus.
TELEVISION: *Series*: Alfred Hitchcock Presents (1985), Touched by an Angel.

KANFER, MICHAEL
Special Effects.
PICTURES: Color of Night, Interview with the Vampire: The Vampire Chronicles, Apollo 13 (Academy Award nom. 1996), Titanic (Academy Award, Best Visual Effects, 1998), Edtv, Lake Placid, Fight Club, Rules of Engagement, O Brother Where Art Thou, Harry Potter & the Sorcerer's Stone, We Were Soldiers (digital mastering supervisor), Looney Tunes: Back in Action, Sky Captain and the World of Tomorrow, Superman Returns.

KANTER, HAL
Writer, Director, Producer. b. Savannah, GA, Dec. 18, 1918. On B'way contributor to Hellzapoppin. Then began writing radio dramas before mil. service, WW II. Served as combat corresp. Armed Forces Radio; writer, Paramount, 1951-54; dir., RKO, 1956; writer, prod. for Lucille Ball Prods., 1979-80. Savannah Prods., 1982-86. Received Writers Guild Paddy Chayefsky Laurel Award, 1989. Writer (radio): Danny Kaye Show, Amos 'n Andy, Bing Crosby Show, Jack Paar, Beulah. Winner 3 Emmy Awards for writing, 1954, 1991, 1992; W.G.A.W. Valentine Davies award. Was member: bd. of dir., WGAW; bd. of govs. AMPAS; v.p. Writers Guild Foundation. Received WGA, Morgan Cox Award 2005.
PICTURES: *Writer*: My Favorite Spy, Off Limits, Road to Bali, Casanova's Big Night, About Mrs. Leslie, Money from Home, Artists and Models, The Rose Tattoo, I Married a Woman (dir. only), Loving You (also dir.), Mardi Gras, Once Upon a Horse (also dir., prod.), Let's Make Love (WGA nom. 1961), Blue Hawaii (WGA nom. 1962), Pocketful of Miracles, Bachelor in Paradise, Move Over Darling, Dear Brigitte, Ji ji (from 1961 s.p. "A Pocketful of Miracles), Oscar's Greatest Moments (doc., writer).
TELEVISION: *Writer*: Ed Wynn Show, George Gobel Show (also

creator, prod., Emmy Award 1955, 2 other nom.), Kraft Music Hall (also dir., prod.; 1958-59), Chrysler Theatre (also prod., dir.; 1966-67), Julia (also dir., prod., creator, Emmy nom. 1969), Jimmy Stewart Show (also prod., dir., creator), All In The Family (exec. prod.: 1975-76, Emmy nom. 1976), Chico & The Man (spv. prod., 1976-77), You Can't Take It With You. *Specials (writer):* AFI Life Achievement Awards for Henry Fonda & Alfred Hitchcock, 1991-2005 Academy Awards and many others, (2 Emmy awards 1991, 1992, WGA nom. 2004).

KANTOR, IGO

Producer, Music Editor. b. Vienna, Austria, Aug. 18, 1930. e. UCLA, A.A. 1950; B.S., 1952; M.S., 1954. Foreign corres., Portugal magazine, FLAMA, 1949-57, music supvr., Screen Gems, Columbia 1954-63; post-prod. supvr., film ed., features, TV; assoc. prod., 1963-64; prod., exec., International Entertainment Corp., 1965; pres., Synchrofilm, Inc., post-production co. and Duque Films Inc., production co. 1968-74. 1975-present, produced and edited films. 1982, pres., Laurelwood Prods; 1988, pres. Major Arts Corp.
PICTURES: *Assoc. Producer:* Bye Bye Birdie, Under the Yum Yum Tree, Gidget Goes to Rome, A House Is Not a Home, Pattern for Murder, Willy. Producer: Assault on Agathon (also edit.), FTA, Dixie Dynamite (assoc. prod., edit.), Kingdom of the Spiders (also edit., music spvr.), The Dark (assoc. prod.), Good Luck Miss Wyckoff (prod. spvr.), Hardly Working, Kill and Kill Again, Shaker Run, Act of Piracy, Legends of the West (doc. exec. prod.), In the Shadow of Wings.
TELEVISION: From Hawaii with Love (1984), The Grand Tour, It's a Wonderful World (prod.-dir.), Nosotros Golden Eagle Awards (prod.), United We Stand (pre-Olympic special), Legends of the West With Jack Palance, Mom U.S.A., A Desperate Affair, Holiday Classics Cartoons (special). *Series: As Music Editor:* I Told You So, Playhouse 90, Naked City, The Monkees, Battle of the Planets, Scope (also prod., dir., writer). *Specials:* The Bob Hope Christmas Special (ACE nom. 1969), The Bob Hope Christmas *Special:* Around the World with the USO (ACE nom. 1970).

KAPLAN, JONATHAN

Director, Writer. b. Paris, France, Nov. 25, 1947. Son of late-composer Sol Kaplan. e. U. of Chicago, B.A.; NYU, M.F.A. Made short film Stanley Stanley. Member of tech. staff Fillmore East, NY 1969-71. New World Pictures' Roger Corman post-grad. sch. of filmmaking, Hollywood, 1971-73. As actor on B'way in Dark at the Top of the Stairs. Appeared in films: Cannonball, Hollywood Boulevard.
PICTURES: *Director:* Night Call Nurses, Student Teachers, The Slams, Truck Turner, White Line Fever (also co-s.p.), Mr. Billion, Over the Edge, Heart Like a Wheel, Project X, The Accused, Immediate Family, Unlawful Entry, Love Field, The Firm (actor), Bad Girls, Brokedown Palace.
TELEVISION: *Movies*: The 11th Victim, The Hustler of Muscle Beach, The Gentleman Bandit, Girls of the White Orchid, Reform School Girl, In Cold Blood. *Series*: Fallen Angels, JAG, ER (5 Emmy noms.), The Court, Inconceivable (also pilot), Without a Trace (dir., co-exec. prod.).

KAPUR, SHEKHAR

Director. b. Lahore, Pakistan, 1945.
PICTURES: Masoom, Joshilar, Mr. India, Time Machine, Bandit Queen, From the Heart (exec. prod. only), Dushmani, Dil Se (exec. prod. only), Elizabeth (Golden Globe nom. 1999), We Stand United, Four Feathers, Phantom of the Opera, The Guru (exec. prod. only) Paani (also writer), Long Walk to Freedom, The Last Full Measure, Elizabeth: The Golden Age, Solace, Secrets of the Seven Sounds (exec. prod., writer: story/concept), New York, I Love You (segment dir.).
TELEVISION: *Series:* Tahqiqat. *Special:* 100 Greatest Movie Stars (doc., as himself).

KARANOVIC, SRDJAN

Director. b. Belgrade, Yugoslavia, November 17, 1945. 1994-1996, Guest Instructor, Boston University.
PICTURES: Stvar Srca, Pani Vratna, Neblbni, Drustvena Igra, If It Kills Me (s.p. only), Miris Poljskog Cveca, Bravo Maestro (s.p. only), Nesto Izmedju (also s.p.), Jagode U Grlu, A Film with No Name, Virdzina (also writer), Pavle Vuisic 1926-1988 (video documentary), Zoran Radmilovic 1933-1985 (video documentary), Loving Glances, Besa.
TELEVISION: *Movies*: Apotekarica, Dom, Pogledaj Me Nevernice. *Series*: Grlom U Jagode, Petria's Wreath (also s.p.), Lift (writer only).

KARDISH, LAURENCE

Curator, Dept. of Film, Museum of Modern Art. b. Ottawa, Ontario, Canada, Jan. 5, 1945. e. Carlton U. Ottawa, Canada, 1966, Honors B.A. in philosophy; Columbia U., Sch. of the Arts, 1968, M.F.A. in film, radio, and television. 1965-66: Canadian Film Inst., programmer for National Film Theatre, Ottawa; researched a history of Canadian filmmaking. 1965: founded first film society in Canada to exhibit Amer. avant-garde films (Carleton U. Cine Club); directed summer seminar on film, Carleton U., 1966. 1966-68: New American Cinema Group, Inc., NY, worked for the Film-Makers' Distribution Center. 1968: joined Dept. of Film, MOMA; made curator 1984 and is currently the department's senior curator. Since 1968 involved with Cineprobe prog. Since 1972 participated in selection of films for New Directors/New Films series; dir. exhibitions of surveys of national cinemas (Senegal, Scandinavia, French-speaking Canada) and retrospectives of ind. Amer. filmmakers (includ. Rudolph Burkhardt, Stan Brakhage, Shirley Clarke), The Lubitsch Touch, Columbia Pictures, Warner Bros., MGM, Universal, RKO, and directors. 1980: toured Europe with prog. of indep. Amer. films. Author: Reel Plastic Magic (1972); also essays and monographs. Dir.feature Slow Run (1968). On jury for Channel 13's Indep. Focus series and on Board of Advisors, Collective for Living Cinema, NY. 1982-82: bd. of dirs. of National Alliance of Media Arts Centers; 1987-89: on Jerome Foundation panel. 1986 on Camera d'Or jury, Cannes Film Fest. Received France's medal of the Order of Arts and Letters, June 2003. AUTHOR: Michael Balcon: The Pursuit of British Cinema, Rainer Werner Fassbinder, Reel Plastic Magic: A History of Films and Filmmaking in America.

KARMAZIN, MELVIN ALLEN

Executive. b. Aug. 24, 1944, New York. e. Pace University, B.A. in business administration, 1965. Station Mgr., CBS Radio, NY, 1960-70. VP and Gen'l Mgr. Metromedia Inc., 1970-81. Pres. Infinity Broadcast Corp., 1981-96. CEO Infinity Broadcast Corp., 1988-96. Chairman, CEO CBS Station Group, 1996-1998. 1999, Chairman & CEO, CBS, Inc. At CBS, Karmazin amassed over 160 major-market radio stations, along with the nation's premier outdoor advertising companies. He also orchestrated the spin-off of Infinity Broadcasting in the largest IPO in media history at the time. Additionally, he invested in Internet properties such as CBS MarketWatch, CBS SportsLine, and iWon.com. Upon merger of CBS and Viacom, Inc., became pres. & COO of Viacom in May 2000. In March 2003, Karmazin signed a three-year contract to remain in current position through May 2006, but resigned on June 1, 2004. Also in 2004, became a director and CEO of Sirius Satellite Radio. In Feb. 2007, XM Satellite Radio and Sirius Satellite Radio announced the companies had entered into an agreement to combine the companies in a tax- free, all stock, merger of equals. Under the agreement, Karmazin, will serve as CEO of the combined company, which in 2008 became Sirius XM Radio, Inc. after Liberty Media Corp. provided a $530 million dollar loan. Karmazin is also vice-chmn. of the board of trustees of The Paley Center for Media. He is an inductee into the Broadcasting Hall of Fame; a recipient of the NAB National Radio Award and the IRTS Gold Medal Award. He is also the creator of the Prism Fund to encourage minority ownership of media outlets.

KARP, ALLEN

Executive. b. Toronto, Ontario, Canada, Sept. 18, 1940. e. Univ. of Toronto, law degree, 1964; called to Ontario bar in 1966; masters of business law degree 1975, from Osgoode Hall Law School, York Univ. Upon graduation joined the firm of Goodman & Carr, became a partner in 1970. Served as business lawyer and sr. legal advisor, becoming dir. of Odeon Theatre Film circuit, 1977. 1986, named sr. exec. v.p. of Cineplex Odeon Corp; 1988, became pres. North American Theatres Division; 1989, pres. & COO; 1990, elected pres. & CEO Cineplex Odeon Canada (Loews Cineplex Ent. Corp.). Chmn. and CEO from 1998 - 2002. Karp has been chmn. of the trustees of IBI Income Fund since July 8, 2005 and trustee since August 24, 2004. He has been a director of Tucows Inc., since Oct. 2005; a director of Teknion Corp. since June 25, 1998 and serves as its lead director. He has been a director of Alliance Atlantis Communications Inc. since 1992 and is a member of its executive committee. He serves as a director of Alliance Communications Corporation; SMK Speedy Int'l. Inc. and Speedy Muffler King Inc. He has been an independent trustee of Royal Lepage Franchise Services Fund since February 18, 2003. He sits on the bd. of directors of the Canadian Film Centre; and until 2007 was chmn. of the Toronto International Film Festival Group and a member of all major committees. He has been chairman of the Festival's governance committee since 2007.

KARPEN, ANDREW

Executive. e. Washington University's School of Business, B.S. in business administration. New York University's Leonard N. Stern School of Business, M.B.A. Began industry career at Miramax Films, where Karpen's four-year stint saw him promoted to senior v.p., finance & operations. Next came a CFO role at Sunbow Entertainment, followed by another CFO post with Independent Pictures Inc. In March 2000, joined Oxygen Media, serving as senior v.p., finance & planning. At Oxygen, he managed the company's multi-year business plan, and oversaw the company's revenue objectives and forecasts. Karpen joined Focus Features directly from Oxygen Media. Focus was formed in May 2002, and Karpen joined the company as COO in August 2003. As COO, he was responsible for the company's worldwide finance, daily operations, and strategic planning. He was promoted to his current position, president, Focus Features, in May 2006 and also named co-president, Rogue Pictures with Andrew Rona. Karpen's duties now encompass broader oversight of all aspects of domestic and international activities for Focus, sibling company Rogue Pictures, and the Focus Features International division. All Rogue movies are handled domestically through Focus Features' existing marketing and distribution operations, and comparably overseas via Focus Features International.

KARPOWICZ, PAUL

Executive. e. Bachelor's degree in Bus. Admin., Univ. of Notre Dame, 1975. Karpowicz is a TV executive who rose through the ranks of TV station management, and was v.p. gen. mgr. of WLNE-TV in Providence, RI, before assuming a corp. role with LIN TV Corp. During his 20 years with LIN, Karpowicz grew its broadcasting group from 12 stations to 23. In Feb. 2005, Karpowicz became pres. of the Meredith Broadcasting Group, where he is responsible for the direction of Meredith's 14 TV stations — including six in Top 30 markets — that reach 9 percent of America's TV households. The Broadcasting Group accounts for over 25 percent of all Meredith Corporation revenues. Currently, Karpowicz serves on the Television Bureau of Advertising Board and was elected bd. chmn. in Feb. 2007. He is also serving on the Associated Press Television Advisory Board. He is a former chmn. of both the CBS Affiliates Board and the Television Board of the National Association of Broadcasters. He has also served on the executive committees of the Rhode Island and Indiana Broadcasters Associations.

KARTOZIAN, WILLIAM F.

Executive. b. San Francisco, CA, July 27, 1938. e. Stanford U., 1960; Harvard Law Sch., 1963. Deputy Attorney General State of CA, 1963-64; assoc. in law firm of Lillick, McHose Wheat Adams & Charles, San Francisco, 1964-65; corp. counsel and dir., Natl. Convenience Stores, Houston, 1965-67; v.p. and corp. counsel, UA Theatres, 1967-75; owner, Festival Enterprises, Inc., 1970-86; chmn. San Francisco Theatre Employers Assoc., 1973-76; Theatre Assoc. of CA, Inc., dir. 1972-86, v.p. 1974-75, pres. 1975-79, chmn. of bd. 1979-81; member, State of CA Industrial Welfare Comm. Amusement and Recreation Industries Wage Board, 1975-76; Nat'l. Assoc. of Theatre Owners: dir. 1976-86, v.p. 1980-86, president 1988-2000. Received "Career Achievement Award" at the 1999 ShowEast convention and received the Robert W. Selig ShoWest Award 2000. Former member: Calif. Film Commission.

KAR-WAI, WONG

Director, Writer, Producer. b. Shanghai, 1959. e. B.A. in graphic design, Hong Kong, 1980.
PICTURES: *Dir.:* As Tears Go By (also s.p.), The True Story of Ah Fei (also s.p.), Let's Go Slam Dunk, Fallen Angels (also prod., s.p.), Ashes of Time (also s.p.), Chunking Express (also s.p.), Fallen Angels, Happy Together (also prod., s.p., Cannes 2000, Best Dir.), In the Mood For Love (also prod., s.p.), The Hire: Follow, 2046, Six Days (video), My Blueberry Nights (also writer, prod.), The Lady from Shanghai (also dir., prod.), The Grand Master (also writer, prod.). *Writer:* Intellectual Trio, The Final Test, The Final Victory, The Haunted Copshop, Dragon and Tiger Fight, The Haunted Copshop II, Saviour of Souls, Beijing Summer, Eros, To Each His Cinema (also segment prod.). *Prod.:* The Eagle Shooting Heroes, First Love: A Litter on the Breeze, Chinese Odyssey 2002, Miao Miao (exec. prod.).

KARYO, TCHÉKY

Actor. b. Istanbul, Turkey, Oct. 4, 1953. Studied drama at the Cyrano Theatre and became a member of the Daniel Sorano Company, National Theatre of Strasbourg. Received the Jean Gabin Prize, 1986.
PICTURES: Vincent and Me, La Balance, The Return of Martin Guerre, All Night Long, La Java des ombres, The Outsider, Full Moon in Paris, Amour braque, L' Actor, États d'âme, Bleu comme l'enfer, L' Unique, Spirale, Sorceress, The Bear, Australia, La Fille des Collines, La Femme Nikita, Corps Perdus, Exposure, Isabelle Eberhardt, 1492: Conquest of Paradise, Sketch Artist, On Guard, Husbands and Lovers, And the Band Played On, The Black Angel, Nostradamus, Fear City: A Family-Style Comedy, Zadoc et le bonheur, GoldenEye, Operation Dumbo Drop, Bad Boys, Colpo di luna, Crying Freeman, Foreign Land, Albergo Roma, Gentle Into the Night, To Have and to Hold, Follow Your Heart, Les Mille merveilles de l'univers, Dobermann, Addicted to Love, Habitat, Que la lumière soit, World of Moss, Wing Commander, Babel, Comme un poisson hors de l'eau, My Life So Far, The Messenger: The Story of Joan of Arc, Saving Grace, The Patriot, The King is Dancing, Kiss of the Dragon, The Core, The Good Thief, Cinemagique, Utopía, Blueberry, Taking Lives, A Very Long Engagement, Clarion's Call, A Previous Engagement, The Gravedancers, Jacquou le croquant, The Lark Farm, Chrysalis, Boxes, Vampire Party, A Man and His Dog, The Way.
TELEVISION: *Movies*: Sketch Artist, And the Band Played On, Les Liens du coeur, Arabian Nights, Le Père Goriot, D'Artagnan et les trois mousquetaires, Les Rois maudits, S.A.C.: Des hommes dans l'ombre, Les Cerfs-volants, L' Affaire Bruay-en-Artois. *Mini-series*: From the Earth to the Moon, La Résistance. *Series:* Kaamelott. *Documentary:* Mode in France.

KASDAN, LAWRENCE

Writer, Director, Producer. b. West Virginia, Jan. 14, 1949. e. U. of Michigan. Clio award-winning adv. copywriter, Detroit and LA before becoming screen writer. Became dir. with Body Heat (1981). Received WGA Laurel Award 2006. Owmer of Kasdan Pictures.
PICTURES: *Dir./s.p./co-s.p.:* Star Wars: Episode V - The Empire Strikes Back (WGA nom. 1981), Raiders of the Lost Ark (WGA nom. 1982), Continental Divide, Body Heat (WGA nom. 1982), Return of the Jedi, The Big Chill (also co-exec. prod. Academy Award nom.; DGA nom.; Golden Globe nom.; WGA Award 1984), Into the Night (actor), Silverado (also prod), Cross My Heart (prod.), The Accidental Tourist (also co-prod., 2 Academy Award noms.; WGA nom. 1989), Immediate Family (exec. prod.), I Love You to Death (also actor), Grand Canyon (also co-prod., actor, Academy Award nom.; Golden Globe nom.; WGA nom. 1992), Jumpin at the Boneyard (exec. prod.), The Bodyguard (also co-prod.), Wyatt Earp (also co-prod.), French Kiss, Home Fires (prod.), Mumford, Dreamcatcher, The Risk Pool (s.p.), In the Land of Women (exec. prod.).

KASSAR, MARIO

Executive, Producer. b. Lebanon, Oct. 10, 1951. At age of 18 formed own foreign distribution co. Kassar Films International, specializing in sale, dist. and exhibition of films in Asia and Europe. In 1976 became partners with Andrew Vajna who had own dist. co., forming Carolco. First prod., First Blood, followed by Rambo: First Blood Part II. Became sole chmn. of Carolco in 1989 and ran company through 1995. Formed own production co., MK Productions in 1996. In 2007 Kassar and Erick Fietshan launched Magnetik Media, an international sales and distribution company. On its launch slate are 3:10 to Yuma, Forbidden Kingdom and Untouchables: Capone Rising.
PICTURES: *Exec. Prod.:* Angel Heart, Extreme Prejudice, Rambo III, Red Heat, Iron Eagle II, Deep Star Six, Johnny Handsome, Mountains of the Moon, Total Recall, Air America, Jacob's Ladder, L.A. Story, The Doors, Terminator 2: Judgment Day, Rambling Rose, Basic Instinct, Universal Soldier, Light Sleeper, Chaplin, Cliffhanger, Heaven & Earth, Stargate, Last of the Dogmen, Showgirls, Cutthroat Island, Lolita (prod.), Icarus (prod.), I Spy, Terminator 3: Rise of the Machines, Basic Instinct 2, Negative Space, Terminator Salvation.
TELEVISION: *Series:* Terminator: The Sarah Connor Chronicles (also pilot, exec. prod., co-prod.).

KASTNER, ELLIOTT

Producer. b. New York, NY, Jan. 7, 1933. e. U. of Miami, Columbia U. Was agent then v.p. with MCA, before becoming indep. prod., financing and personally producing 65 feature films in 25 yrs. Based in London, NY & LA.
PICTURES: Bus Riley's Back in Town, Harper, Kaleidoscope, The Bobo, Sweet November (1968), Sol Madrid, Michael Kohlaas, Laughter in the Dark, Night of the Following Day, Where Eagles Dare, A Severed Head, Tam Lin, The Walking Stick, X Y and Zee (Zee & Company), The Nightcomers, Big Truck and Poor Clare, Face to the Wind, Fear Is the Key, The Long Goodbye, Cops and Robbers, Jeremy, 11 Harrowhouse, Spot, Rancho Deluxe, 92 in the Shade, Farewell My Lovely, Russian Roulette, Breakheart Pass, The Missouri Breaks, Swashbuckler, Equus, A Little Night Music, The Medusa Touch, The Big Sleep, Absolution, Goldengirl, Yesterday's Hero, Ffolkes, The First Deadly Sin, Death Valley, Man Woman and Child, Garbo Talks, Oxford Blues, Nomads, Heat, Angel Heart, Black Joy, Spy Trap, Jack's Back, The Blob, White of the Eye, Zombie High, Never on Tuesday, Homeboy, A Chorus of Disapproval, The Last Party, Love is All There Is, Frank and Jesse, Sweet November (2001), Gold on Eagle Street, Opa!.
TELEVISION: *Movie:* Mr. Horn.
(d. June 30, 2010)

KATT, WILLIAM

Actor. b. Los Angeles, CA, Feb. 16, 1955. Son of actors Barbara Hale and Bill Williams. e. Orange Coast Coll. Majored in music, playing piano and guitar. Acted with South Coast Repertory Theatre, later working in productions at the Ahmanson and Mark Taper Theatres in L.A. Phoenix Rep (N.Y.): Bonjour La Bonjour. Regional: Sarah and Abraham, Days of Wine and Roses.
PICTURES: Carrie (debut, 1976), First Love, Big Wednesday, Butch and Sundance: The Early Days, Baby, Rising Storm, House, White Ghost, Wedding Band, Naked Obsession, Double X: The Name of the Game, House IV: Home Deadly Home, Desperate Motive (Distant Cousins), Tollbooth, The Paperboy, Stranger by Night, Cyborg 3: The Recycler, Rattled, Devil's Food, Daddy's Girl, Whacked, U'bejani, Mother Teresa: In the Name of God's Poor, Hyacinth, Jawbreaker, The Rage: Carrie 2, Twin Falls Idaho, Clean and Narrow, Learning to Surf, Circuit, Determination of Death, Treading Water, Descendent-Descendent, Nexus, Molding Clay (also Dir.), Instant Karma, The Man from Earth, Beautiful Loser, Big Game, Deadland, Mirrors 2, Earthling, The Secret Lives of Dorks, Super, A Pure Country Gift, Firedog (voice), The Encore of Tony Duran.
TELEVISION: *Movies*: Night Chase, The Daughters of Joshua Cabe, Can Ellen Be Saved?, Perry Mason Returns and several Perry Mason follow-ups (Case of the...Murdered Madam, Avenging Ace, Scandalous Scoundrel, Lady in the Lake, Notorious Nun, Shooting Star, Lost Love, Sinister Spirit, Swim Suit, Americanski Blues, Problem Child 3: Junior in Love, Piranha, Rough Riders, Hide and Seek, Gentle Ben, Mystery Woman: Game Time, Bone Eater. *Series*: The Greatest

American Hero, Top of the Hill, Good Sports, Models Inc. *Specials*: Pippin, The Rainmaker. *Guest:* More than 84 appearances.

KATZ, GLORIA

Producer, Writer. e. UCLA. Film Sch. Joined Universal Pictures as editor, cutting educational films. Later joined forces with Willard Huyck, whom she had met at U.C.L.A. Pair signed by Francis Ford Coppola to write and direct for his newly created company, American Zoetrope.
PICTURES: *Writer*: American Graffiti (Academy Award nom.; WGA nom. 1974), Lucky Lady, French Postcards (also prod.), Indiana Jones and the Temple of Doom, Best Defense (also prod.), Howard the Duck (also prod.), Radioland Murders.
TELEVISION: *Co-Producer, Co-Writer:* A Father's Homecoming, Mothers Daughters and Lovers.

KATZ, JAMES C.

Producer, Executive. b. New York, NY, March 17, 1939. e. Ohio St. U. Started in publicity dept. of United Artists, 1963, eventually serving as v.p. of publicity for UA, 1966-68. Publicity co-ord. on film Khartoum, 1964. To London, 1968 as unit publicist for The Charge of the Light Brigade, Joanna. Prod. & dir. for C.I.C. special shorts and documentaries. 1973-78, prod./dir. commercials for own company in London. 1980, pres. Universal Classics Dept.; 1984, v.p. prod, Universal Pictures. With Robert A. Harris worked on restoration of Spartacus, My Fair Lady and Alfred Hitchcock's Vertigo, Finding Rin Tin Tin (co-exec. prod.).
PICTURES: Three Sisters (co-prod.), Lust in the Dust (exec. prod.), Nobody's Fool (prod.), Scenes From the Class Struggle in Beverly Hills (prod.) Rear Window (1998 restoration), Finding Rin Tin Tin (co-exec. prod.).

KATZ, MARTY

Producer. b. Landsburg, West Germany, Sept. 2, 1947. e. UCLA, U. of Maryland. Served in Vietnam War as U.S. Army first lieut.; awarded Bronze Star as combat pictorial unit director. 1971, dir. of film prod., ABC Circle Films; 1976, exec. v.p., prod., Quinn Martin Prods; 1978-80, producer and consultant, Paramount Pictures' 1981-85, independent producer (Lost in America, Heart Like a Wheel). 1985, joined Walt Disney Prods. as sr. v.p., motion picture & TV prod. Named exec. v.p. motion picture and TV production, 1988-92. 1992-present, prod. Marty Katz Prods./Buena Vista.
PICTURES: The American Dreamer (doc., asst. camera), The Velvet Vampire (asst. dir.), Another Nice Mess (asst. dir.), Heart Like a Wheel, Lost in America, Man of the House, Mr. Wrong, Titanic (production consult.), Reindeer Games (also unit dir.), Imposter, Below, The Four Feathers, The Great Raid, Kissing Strangers, Love Ranch.
TELEVISION: *Exec./Production: Movies:* Tales of the Unexpected, Code Name: Diamond Head, Standing Tall, 11th Victim, The Day the Bubble Burst, Triplecross. *Series:* Barnaby Jones, The Streets of San Francisco, Most Wanted.

KATZ, NORMAN B.

Executive. b. Scranton, PA, Aug. 23, 1919. e. Columbia U. In U.S. Army 1941-46 as intelligence officer, airborne forces. Entered m.p. industry in 1947 with Discina Films, Paris, France, as prod. asst. Named exec. asst. to head of prod. in 1948. 1950 named v.p. Discina Int'l. Films and in 1952 exec. v.p. 1954 joined Associated Artists Prods. as foreign mgr.; named dir. of foreign operation in 1958. 1959 became dir. of foreign operations for United Artists Associated. 1961 joined 7 Arts Associated Corp. as v.p. in chg. of foreign optns.; 1964, named exec. v.p., 7 Arts Prods. Int'l.; 1967, exec. v.p. Warner Bros.-7 Arts Int'l. 1969 appt. exec. v.p. & CEO WB Int'l. & bd. member of WB Inc. 1974 named sr. v.p. int'l. div. of American Film Theatre. Pres. of Cinema Arts Assoc. Corp. 1979, exec. v.p. and bd. member, American Communications Industries and pres., & CEO of ACI subsidiary, American Cinema; 1983, pres., The Norkat Co., Also, bd. chmn., CEO, American Film Mktg. Assoc., 1985-87; chmn. Amer. Film Export Assn. 1988-92.

KATZENBERG, JEFFREY

Executive, Executive Producer. b. Dec. 21, 1950. Entered motion picture industry in 1975 as asst. to Paramount Pictures chmn. and CEO Barry Diller in NY. In 1977, became exec. dir. of mktg.; later same year moved to West Coast as v.p. of programming for Paramount TV. Promoted to v.p., feature production for Paramount Pictures in 1978; two years later assumed role of sr. v.p. prod. of m.p. div; 1982, pres. of prod., m.p. and TV, Paramount Pictures. Left to join The Walt Disney Company, 1984; chairman of The Walt Disney Studios, 1984-94. With Steven Spielberg and David Geffen formed DreamWorks SKG entertainment company, 1995. When DreamWorks SKG spun off its animation division with an initial public offering in late 2004, Katzenberg became CEO of DreamWorks Animation SKG, Inc. He serves on the boards of The Motion Picture and Television Fund, The Museum of Moving Image, Cedars-Sinai Medical Center, California Institute of the Arts and The Simon Wiesenthal Center. Katzenberg is co-chairman of each of the Creative Rights Committee of the Directors Guild of America, and the Committee on the Professional Status of Writers of the Writers Guild of America.
PICTURES: *Exec. Prod:* The Prince of Egypt, Road to El Dorado, Chicken Run, Shrek, Spirit: Stallion of the Cimarron (Academy Award nom. 2003), Sinbad: Legend of the Seven Seas (prod.), Shrek 2, Shark Tale, Wallace and Gromit: The Curse of the Were-Rabbit, Shrek the Third (exec. in charge of prod.).
TELEVISION: *Movie:* The Contender Rematch: Mora vs. Manfredo (exec. prod.). *Series*: Father of the Pride, The Contender.

KAUFFMAN, MARTA

Producer. b. Sept. 21,1956. Was partner in Kauffman-Crane Prods. and co-creator of the TV hit series Friends. She is now based at Warner Bros. TV.
PICTURE: Blessed Is the Match: The Life and Death of Hannah Senesh (doc.).
TELEVISION: *Movie:* Gifted. *Series*: Dream On (co-creator, Emmy nom. 1993), Friends (exec., co-creator, Emmy Award 2002, 6 other noms.), Veronica's Closet (exec., co-creator), Jesse (exec. prod.), Related (exec. prod.), Joey (writer). *Specials/Documentaries:* Independent Lens (series, episode exec. prod.).

KAUFMAN, AVY

Casting Director.
PICTURES: Little Man Tate, The Super, The Basketball Diaries, Home for the Holidays, Across thr Sea of Time, Lone Star (CSA nom. 1997), Boys Life 2, The Ice Storm (CSA nom. 1998), The Real Blonde, Critical Care, Snitch, Wide Awake, Rounders, Searching for Bobby Fischer (CSA nom. 1994), Claire Dolan, Walking and Talking (CSA nom. 1997), A Civil Action, The Sixth Sense (CSA nom. 2000), Music of the Heart, Ride With the Devil, A Map of the World, The Hurricane, O, Keeping the Faith (CSA nom. 2000), Dancer in the Dark, State and Main (CSA Award 2001), Blow, Save the Last Dance, Dinner with Friends (CSA nom. 2002), The Heist, Don't Say a Word, Divine Secrets of the Ya Ya Sisterhood, Moonlight Mile, Smack in the Kisser, Dogville, Hulk, The Human Stain, Garden State, Against the Ropes, Jersey Girl, Around the World in 80 Days, Birth, National Treasure, Dear Wendy, Lemony Snicket's A Series of Unfortunate Events, Whirlygirl, The Architect, Piccadilly Jim, Manderlay, Derailed, Syriana (CSA nom. 2006), Capote (CSA nom. 2006), Zathura, Brokeback Mountain (CSA Award 2006), Revolver, All the King's Men, The Sentinel, Love Life, Awake, 10 Items or Less, Off the Black, The Return, Marriage, Bill, American Gangster, 13, The Bourne Ultimatum, Love Life, True North, The Guitar, Married Life, My Blueberry Nights, Lions for Lambs, Awake, Sunshine Cleaning (CSA Award 2009), Phoebe in Wonderland (CSA nom. 2009), Stop-Loss, Summerhood (assoc. casting), What Happens in Vegas..., Mammoth (also UK), Body of Lies, Brothers, Jack Goes Boating, The Lovely Bones (NY casting), Baby Mama, State of Play (CSA nom. 2009), 13, Just Wright, Six Bullets from Now, Leaves of Grass, Chinese Wall, Amelia, Solitary Man, An Invisible Sign of My Own, Public Enemies, Taking Woodstock, Shanghai, Salt, The Conspirator, The Beaver, Let Me In, My Soul to Take, A Birder's Guide to Everything, Scream 4, Keeper of the Pinstripes.
TELEVISION: *Movies*: On Seventh Avenue, Gotti (CSA nom. 1997), In His Father's Shoes, Color of Justice, Dinner With Friends, Lathe of Heaven, Sometimes in April, Empire Falls (Emmy nom.; CSA Award 2005), Knights of the South Bronx, Rubicon. *Series*: The Job, Damages (pilot, CSA nom.; Emmy Award 2008).

KAUFMAN, CHARLIE

Producer, Writer.
PICTURES: Being John Malkovich (Academy Award nom.; Golden Globe nom.; WGA nom.; BAFTA Award, 2000), Human Nature, Adaptation (Academy Award nom.; Golden Globe nom.; WGA nom. 2003), Confessions of a Dangerous Mind, Eternal Sunshine of the Spotless Mind (exec. prod., Academy Award, Golden Globe nom.; WGA Award 2005), The 1 Second Film, Synecdoche, New York (also dir.), Kung Fu Panda: The Kaboom of Doom (writer).
TELEVISION: *Series*: Get A Life, The Edge, The Trouble with Larry, Ned and Stacey, Misery Loves Company, The Mug Root Beer Dana Carvey Show. *Special:* The 77th Annual Academy Awards (

KAUFMAN, HAL

Creative Director, TV Writer, Producer. b. New York, NY, Dec. 16, 1924. e. U. of TX, 1943-44; U. of MI, 1944-47. Started career as petroleum geologist, Western Geophysical Co., 1947-48; TV writer-prod-dir., KDYL-TV, Salt Lake City, 1948-49; prog. dir., LAV-TV, Grand Rapids, 1949-51; prod. mgr., WOOD-TV, Grand Rapids, 1951-54; TV writer-prod., Leo Burnett Co., Chicago, 1954-56; TV writer-prod., Gordon Best Company, Chicago, 1957-58; with Needham Louis & Brorby Inc.: 1959, sr. writer, TV/Radio creative dept.; 1962, v.p., asst. copy dir.; 1963, dir., tv, radio prod.; 1964, dir., b'cast design, production; assoc. creat. dir., asst. exec. v.p., Needham, Harper & Steers, Inc., 1965; creat. dir. L.A., 1966; sr. v.p. and mem. bd. of dir., 1966. 1969, creative & mktg consultant in Beverly Hills. 1970, exec. v.p., principle, Kaufman, Lansky Inc., Beverly Hills and San Diego; 1974 editor and publisher Z Magazine; prog. dir., Z Channel, Theta Cable TV. 1979, sr. v.p./adv. & p.r. & asst. to pres. & bd. chmn., World Airways, Inc.

1982, v.p., creative dir., Admarketing, Inc., Los Angeles. 1985, mktg. & adv. consultant copy dir., Teleflora, Inc.; pres. Hal Kaufman Inc., mktg. & adv. consultant; pres. Brochures on Video, library division, creators and prods. of promotional videos, distribs. religious videos to libraries; pres. Pious Publications, prods. and distribs. of religious videos. Member, DGA, SAG, AFTRA. 1974.

KAUFMAN, LLOYD

Executive, Producer. e. Yale Univ., 1969. From 1974-present, pres. of Troma, Inc., an entertainment company. Co-writer of book, All I Need To Know About Filmmaking I Learned from the Toxic Avenger.
PICTURES: *Dir./Prod.:* The Girl Who Returned (prod., dir., s.p.), Cry Uncle (prod. mgr.), Joe (prod. asst.), Sugar Cookie (exec. prod., s.p.), Silent Night Bloody Night (assoc. prod.), Battle of Love's Return (dir., prod., s.p., actor), Big Gus What's the Fuss (dir., prod.), Sweet Savior (prod. mgr.), Mother's Day (assoc. prod.), Rocky (pre-prod. spvr.), Slow Dancing in the Big City (prod. spvr.), The Final Countdown (assoc. prod.), Squeeze Play (dir., prod.), Waitress (Co-dir., prod.), Stuck on You (co-dir., co-prod., co-s.p.), The First Turn-On (co-dir., co-prod.), Screamplay (exec. prod.), When Nature Calls (assoc. prod.), The Toxic Avenger (co-dir., co-prod., co-s.p., story), Blood Hook (exec. prod.), Girl School Screams (exec. prod.), Class of Nuke 'Em High (co-dir., co-prod.), Lust for Freedom (exec. prod.), Monster in the Closet (exec. prod.), Troma's War (Co-dir., co-prod., co-s.p., story), Toxic Avenger Part II (co-dir., co-prod., co-s.p., story), Fortress of Amerikkka (prod.), Toxic Avenger III: The Last Temptation of Toxie (co-dir., co-s.p., co-prod.), Class of Nuke 'Em High Part II: Subhumanoid Meltdown (co-s.p., co-prod., story), Sgt. Kabukiman N.Y.P.D. (co-dir., co-prod., co-s.p.), The Good the Bad and the Subhumanoid (co-s.p., co-prod., co-story), Tromeo and Juliet (dir., co-s.p., co-prod.), Rowdy Girls (prod.), Terror Firmer (co-s.p., prod., dir.), Alien Blood, Sidney Pink on 'Pyro', Terror Firmer (prod., dir., writer, book), Kickball: The Movie! (assoc. prod.), Mother's Day (exec. prod.). *Actor:* Nowhere Man, Slither, Frankenstein Vs. the Creature From Blood Cove, Black Dahlia, Hoodoo for Voodoo, Die and Let Live, The Cops Did It, Monkfish, Misadventures in Space, Zeppo: Sinners from Beyond the Moon!, The Vampires of Zanzibar (interviewer), Klown Kamp Massacre, Bikini Bloodbath 3: Bikini Bloodbath Christmas, Craig (voice), Working Title, The Art of Pain, Jessicka Rabid, Dead in Love, For Unholy Reunion, Horrorween, Bryan Loves You, HellBilly 58, George's Intervention, Hanger, Nun of That, Crank: High Voltage, Gamer, Melvin, Not Another B Movie, Health Freaks, The Uh-oh Show, Night on Has Been Mountain, The Coffin, Terror Talk (also exec. prod.), Super, Outtake Reel, Noirland, Little Big Boy: The Rise and Fall of Jimmy Duncan, Killed on the Fourth of July, Incest Death Squad 2, For Christ's Sake, Don't Let's Start Bad Girls Burn in Hell, Atom the Amazing Zombie Killer, Killer Hoo-Ha!, Jon, Post Mortem, America 2021.

KAUFMAN, PHILIP

Writer, Director, Producer. b. Chicago, IL, Oct. 23, 1936. e. U. of Chicago, Harvard Law Sch. Was teacher in Italy and Greece before turning to film medium.
PICTURES: *Co-Writer:* The Great Northfield Minnesota Raid (also s.p., prod., WGA nom. 1973),The Outlaw Josey Wales, Raiders of the Lost Ark (WGA nom. 1982), Indiana Jones and the Kingdom of the Crystal Skull. *Director:* Goldstein (co-dir., co-s.p., co-prod.), Fearless Frank (also s.p., prod.), The White Dawn, Invasion of the Body Snatchers, The Wanderers (also co-s.p.), The Right Stuff (also s.p., DGA nom.; WGA nom. 1984), The Unbearable Lightness of Being (also co-s.p., Academy Award nom.; WGA nom. 1989), Henry & June (also co-s.p.), Rising Sun (also co-s.p.), Quills, Blackout, Twisted.

KAUFMAN, VICTOR

Executive. b. New York, NY, June 21, 1943. e. Queens College; NYU Sch. of Law, J.D., 1967. Taught criminal law at UCLA before joining Wall St. law firm, Simpson Thacher & Bartlett. Joined Columbia Pictures as asst. general counsel, 1974. Named chief counsel, 1975; then made vice chmn. Columbia Pictures. Later exec. v.p. Columbia Pictures Industries and vice chmn. Columbia Pictures motion picture div. when conceived a new studio as a joint venture between Coca-Cola, Time Inc.'s Home Box Office and CBS, Inc. forming Tri-Star Pictures. Named chmn. and CEO Tri-Star, 1983. When Columbia Pictures and Tri-Star merged in late 1987, became pres. and CEO of new entity, Columbia Pictures Entertainment. In June 1988, dropped title of chmn. of Tri-Star. 1993 became head of Savoy Pictures. CFO, USA Networks, Nov., 1997. Director of IAC (and its predecessors) since Dec. 1996 and vice-chmn. since Oct. 1999. He oversees all strategic planning, financial and legal matters for IAC. Also on boards of Ticketmaster as vice chairman, and Expedia as vice chairman, Director of Live Nation Entertainment, Inc.

KAUFMANN, CHRISTINE

Actress. b. Lansdorf, Graz, Austria, Jan. 11, 1945. e. school in Munich, Germany. Film debut as a dancer. Salto Mortale at age 7. Golden Globe Award for most promising newcomer, 1962.
PICTURES: The White Horse Inn, Salto Mortale, Der Klosterjager, Staatsanwaltin Corda, Rosenrosli (Little Rosie), Schweigende Engel (Silent Angel), Wenn die Alpenrosen Bluh'n, Ein Herz Schlagt fur Erika, Stimme der Sehnsucht, Witwer mit 5 Tochtern, Die Winzerin von Langenlois, Sag ja Mutti!, First Love, Madchen in Uniform, Embezzled Heaven, Winter Vacation, Madchen von denen man spricht, Everybody Loves Peter, Toto Fabrizio e i Giovani D'oggi, Der Letzte Fubganger, The Last Days of Pompeii, Red Lips, Un Trono Para Cristy, A Man Named Rocca, Town Without Pity, Via Mala, The Phony American, Swordsman of Siena, Taras Bulba (U.S debut), Escape from East Berlin, Constantine the Great, Neunzig Minuten nach Mitternacht, Wild & Wonderful, Love Birds, The Death of Maria Malibran, Murder in the Rue Morgue, Willow Springs, Goodbye with Mums, Auf Biegen oder Brechen, Goldflocken, Rich and Respectable, Orgie des Todes, It Can only Get Worse, Day of the Idiots, Egon Schiele - Exzesse, Lili Marleen, Lola, Ziemlich weit Weg, The Wild Fifties, The Excluded, Pankow '95, The Swing, Bagdad Cafe, Hard to Be a God, Der Geschichtenerzahler, The Talking Grave, War of Neighbours, The Sleeper, Blutiger Ernst, Haider lebt - 1. April 2021, Fahr zur Hölle Gott.
TELEVISION: *Movies*: World on a Wire, Immobilien, Inflation im Paradies, Birkenhof & Kirchenau, Weihnachten mit Willy Wuff II - Eine Mama fur Lieschen, Ein Flotter Dreier, Club der Träume - Marmaris, many more. *Mini-series*: Wie ein Blitz, Lockruf des Goldes, Monaco Franze - Der Ewige Stenz, many more.

KAURISMÄKI, AKI

Director, Writer. b. Finland, April 4, 1957. Brother is filmmaker Mika Kaurismaki. First film credit was acting and writing his brother's The Liar in 1980. Directed short subjects: Rocky VI, Thru the Wire, Those Were the Days, These Boots. Served as writer on brother's features: Jackpot 2, The Worthless (also actor), The Clan: Tshe Tale of the Frogs, Rosso.
PICTURES: *Director*: The Saimaa Gesture (co-dir., with Mika), Crime and Punishment, Calamari Union, Shadows in Paradise, Hamlet Goes Business, Ariel, Leningrad Cowboys Go America, The Match Factory Girl, I Hired a Contract Killer, La Vie de Boheme (The Bohemian Life), Leningrad Cowboys Meet Moses (also s.p., prod., edit.), Total Balalaika Show (also s.p.), Take Care of Your Scarf Tatiana (also s.p., prod., edit.), Drifting Clouds (also s.p.), Quiet Village, Juha, Kovat miehet, The Man Without a Past (Cannes Grand Jury Prize), Ten Minutes Older: The Trumpet, Aaltra, Lights in the Dusk (also prod., editor), To Each His Cinema (segment dir.), Bad Family (prod.), Le Havre (also writer, prod.).
TELEVISION: *Movies:* Likaiset kädet, I Hired a Contract Killer.

KAVNER, JULIE

Actress. b. Los Angeles, CA, Sept. 7, 1951. e. San Diego State U. Professional debut as Brenda Morgenstern on TV's Rhoda, 1974.
THEATRE: Particular Friendships (Off-B'way), Two for the Seesaw (Jupiter, FLA), It Had to Be You (Canada).
PICTURES: National Lampoon Goes to the Movies, Bad Medicine, Hannah and Her Sisters, Radio Days, Surrender, New York Stories (Oedipus Wrecks), Awakenings, Alice, This Is My Life, Shadows and Fog, I'll Do Anything, Forget Paris, Deconstructin Harry, Doctor Dolittle (voice), A Walk on the Moon, Judy Berlin, Cyberworld (voice), Someone Like You... (voice), Click, The Simpsons Movie, Chickadee.
TELEVISION: *Movies:* Katherine, No Other Love, The Revenge of the Stepford Wives, Don't Drink the Water, The Simpsons: America's First Family, Jake's Women, Stand Up to Cancer. *Pilot:* A Fine Romance. *Series*: Rhoda (Emmy Award,1978, 3 other noms.; 4 Golden Globe noms.), The Tracey Ullman Show (4 Emmy noms.) The Simpsons (voice, Emmy Award 1992), Tracey Takes On.... *Special:* The Girl Who Couldn't Lose (Afternoon Playbreak, Emmy nom. 1975).

KAZAN, LAINIE

Singer, Actress. b. New York, NY, May 15, 1942. e. Hofstra U.
PICTURES: Dayton's Devils, Lady in Cement, Romance of a Horse Thief, One from the Heart, My Favorite Year (Golden Globe nom. 1983), Lust in the Dust, The Delta Force, The Journey of Natty Gann, Harry and the Hendersons, Beaches, Eternity, 29th Street, I Don't Buy Kisses Anymore, The Cemetery Club, Love Is All There Is, The Associate, Movies Money Murder, The Unknown Cyclist, Allie & Me, The Big Hit, Permanent Midnight, Kimberly, What's Cooking?, If You Only Knew, Bruno, The Crew, My Big Fat Greek Wedding, Gigli, Red Riding Hood, Intervention, Bratz, Beau Jest, You Don't Mess with the Zohan, Oy Vey! My Son Is Gay!!, Expecting Mary.
TELEVISION: *Movies*: A Love Affair: The Eleanor and Lou Gehrig Story, A Cry for Love, Sunset Limousine, The Jerk Too, Obsessive Love, Prince for a Day, Safety Patrol, Tempted, The Engagement Ring. *Series*: The Dean Martin Summer Show, Tough Cookies, Karen's Song, My Big Fat Greek Life, In the Motherhood. *Pilot:* Family Business, The Lainie Kazan Show. *Guest*: More than 77 appearances.

KAZANJIAN, HOWARD G.

Producer. b. Pasadena, CA, July 26, 1943. e. U. of Southern California Film Sch.; DGA Training Program.
PICTURES: *Asst. dir.:* Cool Hand Luke, Camelot, Finian's Rainbow, The Wild Bunch, The Great Bank Robbery, I Love You Alice B. Toklas, Christine, The Arrangement, The Girl From Petrovka, The Front Page, The Hindenberg, Family Plot. *Exec. Producer:* Rollercoaster (prod. exec.) More American Graffiti (prod.), Raiders

of the Lost Ark, Return of the Jedi (prod.), The Rookie (prod.), Demolition Man, One Dozen, Rattled, Carlo's Wake, The Sky Is Falling, Extreme Days, The Homecoming of Jimmy Whitecloud, Shortcut to Happiness, The Bridge of San Luis Rey, Worlds Apart (suprv. prod.), South Dakota.
TELEVISION: *Movies:* Trapped, The Rockford Files, Rattled. *Series:* JAG (exec. prod.), Danger Rangers. *Specials:* The Making of More American Graffiti, The Making of Raiders of the Lost Ark (Emmy Award, 1982), The Making of Return of the Jedi, Amati Girls.

KAZURINSKY, TIM

Actor, Writer. b. Johnstown, PA, March 3, 1950. Raised in Australia. Worked as copywriter for Chicago ad agency. Took acting class at Second City and quit job to become actor and head writer for Second City Comedy Troupe. Co-starred with John Candy in CTV/NBC's series Big City Comedy, 1980. Joined cast of Saturday Night Live as writer-actor 1981-84.
PICTURES: *Actor*: My Bodyguard, Somewhere in Time, Continental Divide, Neighbors, Police Academy II: Their First Assignment, Police Academy III: Back in Training, About Last Night (also co-s.p.), Police Academy IV: Citizens on Patrol, For Keeps (s.p. only), Road to Ruin (also s.p.), Hot to Trot, Wedding Band, A Billion for Boris, Shakes the Clown, Plump Fiction, Poor White Trash, Betaville, I Want Someone to Eat Cheese With, Roll Bounce, Police Academy, Tapioca, Stash, The Root of All Evil, Chad Chucker, Ca$h!, The Mole Man of Belmont Avenue, Chad Chucka, The Return of Joe Rich.
TELEVISION: *Movies*: This Wife for Hire, Dinner at Eight, The Cherokee Kid (also s.p.), My Beautiful Son, Strange Relations (WGA nom. 2003). *Series:* Big City Comedy, Saturday Night Live (writer, Emmy Award nom. 2002), The Two Dinos.

KEACH, STACY

Actor, Director, Producer. b. Savannah, GA, June 2, 1942. Brother is actor James Keach. Began professional acting career in Joseph Papp's 1964 Central Park prod. of Hamlet.
THEATRE: Long Day's Journey into Night (Obie Award), Macbird (Drama Desk & Obie Awards), Indians (Drama Desk Award & Tony nom.), Hamlet, Deathtrap, Hughie, Barnum, Cyrano de Bergerac, Peer Gynt, Henry IV Parts I & II, Idiot's Delight, Solitary Confinement, Richard III, The Kentucky Cycle (Helen Hayes Award), Steiglitz Loves O'Keefe, Finishing The Picture, Frost/Nixon.
PICTURES: The Heart Is a Lonely Hunter (debut, 1968), End of the Road, The Traveling Executioner, Brewster McCloud, Doc, The New Centurions, Fat City, Watched!, The Life and Times of Judge Roy Bean, Luther, The Gravy Train, The Killer Inside Me, Conduct Unbecoming, Street People, The Squeeze, The Duellists (narrator), Slave of the Cannibal God, The Great Battle, Gray Lady Down, Up in Smoke, The Ninth Configuration (Twinkle Twinkle Killer Kane), The Long Riders (also exec. prod., co-s.p.), Nice Dreams, Road Games, Butterfly, That Championship Season, Class of 1999, False Identity, Milena, Raw Justice, Batman: Mask of the Phantasm (voice), New Crime City, Escape from L.A., Prey of the Jaguar, Sea Wolf, Future Fear, American History X, Birds of Passage, Olympic Glory, Icebreaker, Militia, Mercy Streets, Unshackled, Lightning: Fire From the Sky, Sunstorm, El Padrino, Jesus-Mary-And Joey, Galaxy Hunter, The Hollow, Keep Your Distance, Caught in the Headlights, Man with the Screaming Brain, Come Early Morning, Death Row, Honeydripper, W., The Portal, Chicago Overcoat, The Boxer, Around the World in 50 Years 3D (voice), White Knight, Connemara Days.
TELEVISION: *Movies*: All the Kind Strangers, Caribe, The Blue and the Gray, Princess Daisy, Murder Me Murder You, More Than Murder, Wait Until Dark, Mistral's Daughter, Hemingway (Emmy Award nom.; Golden Globe Award 1988), Mickey Spillane's Mike Hammer: Murder Takes All, The Forgotten, Mission of the Shark, Revenge on the Highway, Rio Diablo, Body Bags, Against Their Will: Women in Prison, Texas, Amanda & the Alien, Young Ivanhoe, Plague Fighters, The Pathfinder, Legend of the Lost Tomb, Savage Seas, Murder in My Mind, The Courage to Love, Warship, The Santa Trap, Frozen Impact, Miracle Dogs, Death Row, Lone Rider, Ring of Death, The Nanny Express, Hindenburg. *Mini-series:* Washington the Warrior, Blackbeard, Meteor: Path to Destruction. *Director:* Incident at Vichy, Six Characters in Search of an Author. *Series*: Nova (narr.), Caribe, Mickey Spillane's Mike Hammer, The New Mike Hammer (Golden Globe nom. 1985) Case Closed (host), Mike Hammer Private Eye, World's Most Amazing Videos, Stupid Behavior: Caught on Tape, Rods!, Titus, Totally Outrageous Behavior (narr.), Prison Break, Great Performances: Live from Lincoln Center (Camelot), Two and a Half Men. *Documentaries:* One by One, James Dean: The First American Teenager, The Search for Solutions, Missing Reward (series), Lindbergh, Lincoln, Warren Oates: Across the Border, The Lost Fleet of Guadalcanal, Reflections on Elephants, Plague Fighters, The Titanic's Lost Sister, Mysteries of Deep Space, Sea Monsters: Search for the Giant Squid, Savage Seas (mini), Tesla: Master of Lightning, Warship, Great Projects: The Building of America, Freedom: A History of Us (actor), The Mummy Who Would Be King (narr.). *Guest:* More than 150 appearances.

KEATON, DIANE

Actress, Director. r.n. Diane Hall. b. Santa Ana, CA, Jan. 5, 1946. e. Santa Ana Coll. Appeared in summer stock and studied at Neighborhood Playhouse in N.Y. Made prof. debut in B'way prod. of Hair (1968); then co-starred with Woody Allen in Play It Again Sam, repeating role for film version. Off-B'way: The Primary English Class. Author: photography books: Reservations (co-ed.), Still Life. Directed 1982 short What Does Dorrie Want?
PICTURES: Lovers and Other Strangers (debut, 1970), The Godfather, Play It Again Sam, Sleeper, The Godfather Part II, Love and Death, I Will I Will... for Now, Harry and Walter Go to New York, Annie Hall (Academy Award, Golden Globe Award 1977), Looking for Mr. Goodbar (Golden Globe nom. 1978), Interiors, Manhattan, Reds (Academy Award nom.; Golden Globe nom. 1982), Shoot the Moon, The Little Drummer Girl, Mrs. Soffel (Golden Globe nom. 1985), Crimes of the Heart, Radio Days, Heaven (dir. only), Baby Boom (Golden Globe nom. 1988), The Good Mother, The Lemon Sisters (also prod.), The Godfather Part III, Father of the Bride, Manhattan Murder Mystery (Golden Globe nom. 1994), Look Who's Talking Now (voice), Unstrung Heroes (dir. only), Father of the Bride 2, Marvin's Room (Academy Award nom. 1997), The First Wives Club, The Only Thrill, Northern Lights, Town and Country, The Other Sister, Hanging Up, Plan B, Elephant (exec. prod. only), Something's Gotta Give (Academy Award nom.; Golden Globe nom. 2004), Hating Her, Mad Money, Da Vinci's Mother, Mama's Boy, Smother, The Family Stone, Because I Said So, Morning Glory.
TELEVISION: *Movies*: Running Mates, Amelia Earhart: The Final Flight (Emmy Award nom.; Golden Globe nom. 1995), Northern Lights, Sister Mary Explains It All, Crossed Over, On Thin Ice, Surrender, Dorothy (also exec. prod.). *Mini-series:* Oh What a Time It Was (prod.). *Series:* Pasadena (dir., exec. prod.). *Director:* The Girl With the Crazy Brother, Twin Peaks, Wildflower (movie). *Guest:* More than 80 appearances.

KEATON, MICHAEL

Actor. r.n. Michael Douglas. b. Coraopolis, PA, Sept. 5, 1951. Speech major, Kent State U, 2 years. Drove cab and ice-cream truck, worked for PBS station in Pittsburgh and appeared in regional theatre prods. while performing in local coffeehouses. Became memb. of improvisational troupe Jerry Vale. Moved to L.A. where honed craft at Comedy Store and Second City Improv. Workshops as stand-up comic.
PICTURES: Night Shift (debut, 1982), Mr. Mom, Johnny Dangerously, Gung Ho, Touch and Go, The Squeeze, Beetlejuice, Clean and Sober, The Dream Team, Batman, Pacific Heights, One Good Cop, Batman Returns, Much Ado About Nothing, My Life, The Paper, Speechless, Multiplicity, Inventing the Abbotts (narrator), Jackie Brown, Desperate Measures, Out of Sight (cameo), Jack Frost, A Shot At Glory, Quicksand, First Daughter, White Noise, Herbie: Fully Loaded, Cars (voice), The Last Time, The Merry Gentleman (also dir.), Noah's Ark: The New Beginning (voice), The Post Grad, Toy Story 3 (voice), The Other Guys.
TELEVISION: *Movies*: Roosevelt and Truman, Live From Baghdad (Golden Globe nom. 2003). *Mini-series:* Studs Lonigan, The Company. *Series*: All's Fair, Mary, The Mary Tyler Moore Hour, Working Stiffs, Report to Murphy. *Special*: Frank Capra's American Dream, Fred Rogers: America's Favorite Neighbor (Emmy Award nom. 2004). *Guest:* More than 87 appearances.

KEENER, CATHERINE

Actress. b. Miami, FL, March 26, 1961. e. Wheaton College.
PICTURES: About Last Night, The Education of Allison Tate, Survival Quest, Catchfire, Switch, Johnny Suede, The Gun in Betty Lou's Handbag, Living in Oblivion, Boys, Walking and Talking, Box of Moonlight, The Destiny of Marty Fine, The Real Blonde, Out of Sight, Your Friends & Neighbors, 8MM, Being John Malkovich (Academy Award nom.; Golden Globe nom. 2000), Simpatico, Simone, How to Survive a Hotel Room Fire, Death to Smoochy, Full Frontal, S1m0ne, Adaptation, The Ballad of Jack and Rose, The Interpreter, Capote (Academy Award nom. 2006), The 40 Year-Old Virgin, Friends with Money, God Grew Tired of Us (doc., co-prod.) An American Crime, Into the Wild, What Just Happened?, Hamlet 2, Synecdoche, New York, Genova, Where the Wild Things Are, The Soloist, Nailed, Please Give, Cyrus, Percy Jackson & the Olympians: The Lightning Thief, Trust, The Oranges, Peace, Love, & Misunderstanding, The Croods (voice).
TELEVISION: *Movies:* Journeys North, Heroine of Hell, If These Walls Could Talk. *Mini-series:* An American Crime (Emmy nom. 2008, Golden Globe nom. 2009). *Series*: Ohara.

KEHELA-SHERWOOD, KAREN

Executive. e. B.A., communications, UCLA. Began at Imagine Entertainment in 1986 as Brian Grazer's asst. Kehela Sherwood rose through the ranks manning the following positions: assistant, story editor, dir. of development, vice president, senior v.p., president and, in 1997, to her current position as co-chair of Imagine Entertainment.

KEITEL, HARVEY

Actor. b. Brooklyn, NY, May 13, 1939. Served in U.S. Marine Corps. Studied with Frank Corsaro, Lee Strasberg, Stella Adler.

Member of the Actors' Studio. Debuted in Martin Scorsese's student film Who's That Knocking at My Door? President of Production Co., The Goatsingers. 2008 became co-president of The Actors Studio.
THEATRE: NY: Up to Thursday, Death of a Salesman, Hurlyburly, A Lie of the Mind.
PICTURES: Who's That Knocking at My Door? (debut, 1968), Mean Streets, Alice Doesn't Live Here Anymore, That's the Way of the World, Taxi Driver, Mother Jugs and Speed, Buffalo Bill and the Indians or: Sitting Bull's History Lesson, Welcome to L.A., The Duellists, Fingers, Blue Collar, Eagle's Wing, Deathwatch, Saturn 3, Bad Timing, The Border, Exposed, La Nuit de Varennes, Corrupt, Falling in Love, Knight of the Dragon (Star Knight), Camorra, Off Beat, Wise Guys, The Investigation (The Inquiry), The Pick-Up Artist, The Last Temptation of Christ, The January Man, The Two Jakes, Mortal Thoughts, Thelma & Louise, Two Evil Eyes, Bugsy (Academy Award nom.; Golden Globe nom. 1992), Sister Act, Reservoir Dogs (also co-prod.), Bad Lieutenant, Point of No Return, Rising Sun, The Piano, Dangerous Game, The Young Americans, Monkey Trouble, Pulp Fiction, Imaginary Crimes, Somebody to Love, Smoke, Clockers, Blue in the Face, Ulysses' Gaze, From Dusk Till Dawn, Head Above Water, Somebody to Love, City of Industry, Cop Land, Shadrach, Finding Graceland, Lulu on the Bridge, My West, Three Seasons, Prince of Central Park, Holy Smoke, U-571, Little Nicky, Taking Sides, La Soutane Tourquoise, Nailed, Je Viens Apres La Pluie, Jack Shepard and Jonathan Wild, Taking Sides, The Grey Zone, Viper, Je viens apres la pluie, Dreaming of Julia, Beeper, Nowhere, Red Dragon, Crime Spree, Who Killed the Idea?, The Galindez File, National Treasure, The Bridge of San Luis Rey, The Shadow Dancer, Be Cool, Red Light Runners, The Swedish Job, One Last Dance, The Gypsy's Curse, Go Go Tales, 13 French Street, Arthur and the Invisibles (voice), My Sexiest Year, Murder Trust (prod.), National Treasure: Book of Secrets, The Ministers, Wrong Turn at Tahoe, So I Say, Criminal Empire for Dummy's, A Beginner's Guide to Endings, The Job, The Last Godfather.
TELEVISION: *Movies*: The Virginia Hill Story, A Memory of Two Mondays, Fail Safe, The Path to 9/11. *Series:* Life on Mars. *Documentaries/Specials*: Dear America: Letters Home from Vietnam, Who Do You Think You're Fooling? (short), Jonas at the Ocean, Venice Report (short), Beyond the Skyline (short), Imagine New York (short), This Ain't Bebop (Amer. Playhouse), This Year in Czernowitz. *Guest:* More than 73 appearances.

KEITH, DAVID

Actor, Director. b. Knoxville, TN, May 8, 1954. e. U. of Tennessee, B.A., speech and theatre. Appearance at Good-speed Opera House in musical led to role in CBS sitcom pilot, Co-Ed Fever.
PICTURES: The Rose (debut, 1979), The Great Santini, Brubaker, Back Roads, Take This Job and Shove It, An Officer and a Gentleman (2 Golden Globe noms. 1983), Independence Day, The Lords of Discipline, Firestarter, The Curse (dir. only), White of the Eye, The Further Adventures of Tennessee Buck (also dir.), Heartbreak Hotel, The Two Jakes, Off and Running, Desperate Motive, Caged Fear, Raw Justice, Temptation, Major League II, Liar's Edge, Till the End of the Night, Born Wild, Gold Diggers: The Secret of Bear Mountain, Deadly Sins, The Indian in the Cupboard, A Family Thing, Invasion of Privacy, Secret of the Andes, Ambushed, Judge & Jury, Red Blooded American Girl II, If... Dog... Rabbit, U-571, Men of Honor, Cahoots, Epoch, World Traveler, Anthrax, License to Steal, Clover Bend, Sabretooth, Behind Enemy Lines, The Stick Up, Deep Shock, Daredevil, The Veritas Project: Hangman's Curse, Come Away Home, Raise Your Voice, Loggerheads, Expiration Date, Clean Breaks, In Her Line of Fire, Bottoms Up, Succubus: Hell Bent, Boys of Summerville, Clown Hunt, Beneath the Blue, Unrequited.
TELEVISION: *Movies*: Are You in the House Alone?, Friendly Fire, Gulag, Whose Child Is This?: The War for Baby Jessica, XXX's & OOO's (pilot), James Michener's Texas, If Looks Could Kill: From the Files of America's Most Wanted, Poodle Springs, Perfect Prey, A Memory in My Heart, Epoch, Love and Treason, Carrie, Epoch: Evolution, Stratosphere, Locusts: The 8th Plague, Midland. *Mini-series*: If Tomorrow Comes, Golden Moment: An Olympic Love Story, Guts and Glory: The Rise and Fall of Oliver North, The Great War (voice). *Series*: Co-ed Fever, Flesh 'N' Blood, Strangers, High Incident, Local Heroes, Still Life, The Class. *Documentary:* The Great War and the Shaping of the 20th Century (mini), City Confidential (series, narr.). *Guest:* More than 50 appearances.

KELLER, MARTHE

Actress. b. Basel, Switzerland, 1945. e. Stanislavsky Sch., Munich. Joined a Heidelberg repertory group and Schiller Rep. in Berlin. Started acting in France and attracted attention of U.S. directors after appearing in Claude Lelouch's And Now My Love. Has acted in over 50 plays in French, German, Eng. & Italian.
PICTURES: Funeral in Berlin (debut, 1967), The Devil by the Tail, ive Her the Moon, La Vieille Fille, The Loser, Elle Court (Love in the Suburbs), And Now My Love, Down the Ancient Staircase, Le Guepier, Marathon Man (Golden Globe nom. 1977), Black Sunday, Bobby Deerfield, Fedora, The Formula, Les Uns et les Autres, The Amateur, Wagner, Femmes de Personne, Joan Lui, I Come on Monday, Dark Eyes, Rouge Basier, The Artisan, Una Vittoria, Lapse of Memory, Mon Amie Max, According to Pereira, Nuits Blanches, K, Elles, The School of Flesh, From Behind, Time of the Wolf, Fragile, UV, Chrysalis, Cortex, Le Bouquet final, Hereafter.
TELEVISION: Liberez mon Fils, Mein oder Dein, The Charthouse of Parma, Wagner, Die Frau des Reporters, La Ruelle de Clair de Lune, The Nightmare Years, Family of Lies, Young Catherine, Turbulences, Im Kreis der Iris. *Mini-series:* La Prophétie d'Avignon, Le Sanglot des anges. *Documentary:* Die Frau des Reporters.

KELLERMAN, SALLY

Actress. b. Long Beach, CA, June 2, 1936. e. Hollywood H.S. Studied acting in N.Y. at the Actors Studio and in Hollywood with Jeff Corey. Recorded album Roll With the Feeling. Has done voice-overs for many commercials.
THEATRE: Women Behind Bars, Holiday.
PICTURES: Reform School Girl (debut, 1959), Hands of a Stranger, The Third Day, The Boston Strangler, The April Fools, M*A*S*H (Academy Award nom.; Golden Globe nom. 1971), Brewster McCloud, Last of the Red Hot Lovers, Lost Horizon, Slither, Reflection of Fear, Rafferty and the Gold Dust Twins, The Big Bus, Welcome to L.A., The Mouse and His Child (voice), Magee and the Lady, A Little Romance, Serial, Head On (Fatal Attraction), Foxes, Loving Couples, Moving Violations, Lethal (KGB: The Secret War), Back to School, That's Life!, Meatballs III, Three For the Road, Someone to Love, You Can't Hurry Love, Paramedics (voice), All's Fair, Limit Up, The Secret of the Ice Cave, The Player, Doppelganger, Happily Ever After (voice), Younger and Younger, Ready to Wear (Pret-a-Porter), Mirror Mirror 2: Raven Dance, It's My Party, The Maze, The Lay of the Land (also prod.), Live Virgin, Ugly, Open House, Delgo (voice), The Boynton Beach Club, A Modern Twain Story: The Prince and the Pauper, Night Club.
TELEVISION: *Movies*: For Lovers Only, Dempsey, Secret Weapons, September Gun, Drop Dead Gorgeous, Boris and Natasha (also assoc. prod.), Columbo: Ashes to Ashes, Bar Hopping, Verdict in Blood, Wishing Well. *Mini-series*: Centennial. *Specials*: Big Blonde, Verna: USO Girl, Elena, Faerie Tale Theatre, Dr. Paradise. *Guest*: More than 120 appearances.

KELLEY, DAVID E.

Producer, Writer. b. Waterville, ME, April 4, 1956. e. Princeton U., Boston U. Law. m. actress Michelle Pfeiffer. Formerly a lawyer and accociate at Fine & Ambrogne when in 1983 he wrote a film script based on some of his legal experiences. The script was optioned and later became the film "From the Hip." Was invited to L.A. by Steven Bochco and Terry Louise Fisher to become story editor for "L.A. Law". 1985 he was part of the television production division of Twentieth Century Fox. In 1987, became exec. story editor, then exec. prod. and writer after Bochco left. CEO, writer and exec. prod. at David E. Kelley Prods. in L.A. 2008 moved to Warner Bros. Television signing an exclusive multiyear development and production deal. All projects will be produced in association with either Warner Bros. Television or Warner Horizon Television, with Warner Bros. International Television acquiring global distribution rights. Honored with four George Foster Peabody Awards, the inaugural Television Academy Honors Award, a Television Showmanship Award from the Publicists Guild of America, the David Susskind Lifetime Achievement Award from the Producers Guild and the TV Guide Awards' inaugural Brandon Tartikoff Award, Kelley was also the subject of a tribute by the Museum of Television and Radio and was named a Broadcasting and Cable Hall of Fame honoree. He is the recipient of the Monte Carlo Television Festival's first Showman of the Year Award, the Casting Society of America's Lifetime Achievement Award, and has been honored by the Legal Aid Foundation of Los Angeles. In addition, he received the prestigious Humanitas Prize for two consecutive years for The Practice, and was presented with both The Paddy Chayefsky Lifetime Achievement Award and The Paul Selvin Award from the Writers Guild of America.
PICTURES: *Writer*: From the Hip, To Gillian on Her 37th Birthday (also prod.), Lake Placid, Mystery Alaska (also prod.), Chasing Montana (writer).
TELEVISION: *Movies*: Annie O (cam.), DeMarco Affairs, Life on Mars (also exec. prod.), Hollywood Station (writer, exec. prod.), Lake Placid 2 (writer; orig. concept), Life on Mars (also exec. prod.), Legally Mad (exec. prod.). *Series exec. prod.:* L.A Law (5 Emmy Awards, 8 other noms.; WGA nom. 1991), Doogie Howser M.D., Picket Fences (2 Emmy Awards, WGA nom. 1996) Chicago Hope (2 Emmy noms.), The Practice (2 Emmy Awards, 3 other noms.; WGA nom. 1999), Ally McBeal (Emmy Award, 1999, 3 other noms.), Snoops, Ally, Boston Public, Girls Club, Boston Legal (2 Emmy noms.), The Law Firm, Halley's Comet, The Wedding Bells (writer, exec. prod), Life on Mars.

KELLEY, SHEILA

Actress. b. Philadelphia, PA, Sept. 9, 1963.
PICTURES: Wish You Were Here, Hostile Witness, Staying Together, Some Girls, Breaking In, Mortal Passions, Where the Heart Is, Wild Blade, Soapdish, Pure Luck, Singles, Passion Fish, Passion to Kill, Mona Must Die, One Fine Day, Sante Fe, Nurse Betty, Dancing at the Blue Iguana, Matchstick Men, Mozart and the Whale, Provinces of Night.
TELEVISION: *Movies*: Tonight's the Night, The Betty Ford Story,

Terrorist on Trial: The United States vs. Salim Ajami, Fulfillment, The Chase, Deconstructing Sarah, The Secretary, Mind Prey, The Jennie Project. *Series*: L.A. Law, Sisters, Moving Story, MDs, Lost.

KELLY, FRANK
Executive. Was assoc. prod. of AM Los Angeles, then exec. prod./program dir. for KABC-TV prior to joining Paramount. 1983, named v.p. programming for Paramount domestic TV division; 1985, promoted to sr. v.p. 1989, became exec. v.p. programming. 1995, named pres. of creative affairs for domestic TV division of Paramount Television Group. Co-pres. with Joel Berman of Paramount Domestic Television Distribution from Sept. 1997-April 2001. From that post, took production deal and became exec. prod. of Entertainment Tonight Enterprises.

KELLY, MOIRA
Actress. b. Queens, NY, March 6, 1968. e. Marymount Col. In addition to acting also trained as violinist, operatic soprano.
PICTURES: The Boy Who Cried Bitch (debut, 1991), Billy Bathgate, The Cutting Edge, Twin Peaks: Fire Walk With Me, Chaplin, With Honors, The Lion King (voice), Little Odessa, The Tie That Binds, Entertaing Angels: The Dorothy Day Story, Unhook the Stars, Henry Hill, Drive She Said, Changing Habits, The Lion King II: Simba's Pride, Love Walked In, Dangerous Beauty, Hi-Life, Henry Hill, The Safety of Objects, Two Tickets to Paradise, Remember the Daze, City of Shoulders and Noses.
TELEVISION: *Movies*: Love Lies and Murder, Daybreak, Monday After the Miracle. *Series*: To Have & To Hold, The West Wing, One Tree Hill.

KEMENY, JOHN
Producer. b. Budapest, Hungary. Producer for National Film Board of Canada, 1957-69. Formed International Cinemedia Center, Ltd. in 1969 in Montreal, as partner.
PICTURES: Ladies and Gentlemen... Mr. Leonard Cohen, Don't Let the Angels Fall, Seven Times a Day, The Apprenticeship of Duddy Kravitz, White Line Fever, Shadow of the Hawk, Ice Castles, The Plouffe Family (exec. prod.), Quest for Fire (co-prod.), The Bad Boy, Murder in the Family (exec. prod.), The Wraith, The Boy in Blue, The Gate, Iron Eagle II, Gate 2: The Trespassers.
TELEVISION: *Movies*: Louisiane, The Blood of Others, Sword of Gideon (exec. prod.), The Park is Mine, Murderers Among Us: The Simon Wiesenthal Story (co-prod., Emmy nom. 1989), Abby Mann (Emmy nom. 1989), Red King White King, The Josephine Baker Story (Emmy nom. 1991), The Teamster Boss: The Jackie Presser Story, Dead Silence, When Trumpets Fade.

KEMPER, VICTOR J.
Cinematographer. b. Newark, NJ, April 14, 1927. e. Seton Hall, B.S./Engineer. Channel 13, Newark 1949-54; Tech. supervisor EUE Screen Gems NY 1954-56; v.p. engineering General TV Network. Pres. VJK Prods. Received ASC Lifetime Achievement Award 1998.
PICTURES: Husbands, The Magic Garden of Stanley Sweetheart, They Might Be Giants, Who is Harry Kellerman?, The Hospital, The Candidate, Last of the Red Hot Lovers, Shamus, The Friends of Eddie Coyle, Gordon's War, The Hideaways, The Gambler, The Reincarnation of Peter Proud, Dog Day Afternoon, Stay Hungry, The Last Tycoon, Mikey and Nicky, Slapshot, Audrey Rose, Oh God!, The One and Only, Coma, Eyes of Laura Mars, Magic, Night of the Juggler, And Justice for All, The Jerk, The Final Countdown, Xanadu, The Four Seasons, Chu Chu and the Philly Flash, Partner, Author! Author!, National Lampoon's Vacation, Mr. Mom, The Lonely Guy, Cloak and Dagger, Secret Admirer, Pee-wee's Big Adventure, Clue, Bobo, Hot to Trot, Cohen and Tate, See No Evil, Hear No Evil, Crazy People, FX2, Another You, Married to It, Beethoven, Tommy Boy, Eddie, Jingle All the Way, American Pie: Band Camp, Bring It On: All or Nothing.
TELEVISION: *Movies:* The Prince of Central Park, Kojak: The Price of Justice (ASC nom. 1988, Emmy nom. 1987), On Golden Pond. *Mini-series:* The Atlanta Child Murders, Too Rich: The Secret Life of Doris Duke.

KENDRICK, KATHERINE
Executive. e. B.A. in economics, Univ. of California, Berkeley. J.D. degree, Columbia University. Kendrick was an associate at the law firm of Latham & Watkins in Los Angeles specializing in corporate securities law before joining the legal department of Hollywood Pictures, a theatrical film division of Walt Disney Studios. Disney moved Kendrick to Paris in 1993, where she was v.p., European legal affairs for The Walt Disney Company. Joined DreamWorks Studios SKG in April 2006 as its general counsel and head of human resources. When DreamWorks spun off its animation unit in an IPO in Oct. 2004, Kendrick moved with the company's animation executives and became general counsel and corporate secretary for the new company-DreamWorks Animation SKG. 2009 she left the company to pursue ongoing work with philanthropic organizations. Kendrick has received several civic honors for her legal work and serves on the boards of numerous civic and charitable institutions, including The Next Generation Council of The Motion Picture and Television Fund, the advisory bd. of the Los Angeles Sports and Entertainment Commission, the Kernochan Center for Law, Media and the Arts for Columbia University School of Law, and Big Brothers/Big Sisters of Greater Los Angeles.

KENNEDY, GEORGE
Actor. b. New York, NY, Feb. 18, 1925. At 2 acted in touring co. of Bringing Up Father. At 7, disc jockey with his own radio show for children. Served in Army during WWII, earning two Bronze Stars and combat and service ribbons. In Army 16 years, became Capt. and Armed Forces Radio and TV officer. 1957, opened first Army Information Office, N.Y. Served as technical advisor to Phil Silvers's Sergeant Bilko TV series. Began acting in 1959 when discharged from Army.
PICTURES: The Little Shepard of Kingdom Come (debut, 1961), Lonely Are the Brave, The Man From the Diner's Club, Charade, Strait- Jacket, Island of the Blue Dolphins, McHale's Navy, Hush... Hush... Sweet Charlotte, Mirage, In Harm's Way, The Sons of Katie Elder, The Flight of the Phoenix, Shenandoah, Hurry Sundown, The Dirty Dozen, Cool Hand Luke (Academy Award, best supporting actor, Golden Globe nom. 1967), The Ballad of Josie, The Pink Jungle, Bandolero!, The Boston Strangler, The Legend of Lylah Claire, Guns of the Magnificent Seven, Gaily Gaily, The Good Guys and the Bad Guys, Airport (Golden Globe nom. 1971), ... tick ... tick ... tick ..., Zigzag, Dirty Dingus Magee, Fool's Parade, Lost Horizon, Cahill: U.S. Marshal, Thunderbolt and Lightfoot, Airport 1975, Earthquake, The Human Factor, The Eiger Sanction, Airport '77, Ningen no Shomei (Proof of the Man), Mean Dog Blues, Death on the Nile, Brass Target, The Concorde—Airport '79, Death Ship, The Double McGuffin, Steel, Virus, Just Before Dawn, Modern Romance, A Rare Breed, Search and Destroy, Wacko, The Jupiter Menace, Bolero, Chattanooga Choo Choo, Hit and Run, Savage Dawn, The Delta Force, Radioactive Dreams, Creepshow 2, Born to Race, Demonwarp, Counterforce, Nightmare at Noon, Private Roads, Uninvited, The Terror Within, The Naked Gun: From the Files of Police Squad, Esmeralda Bay, Ministry of Vengeance, Brain Dead, Hangfire, The Naked Gun 2 1/2: The Smell of Fear, Driving Me Crazy, Distant Justice, Naked Gun 33 1/3: The Final Insult, Cats Don't Dance (voice), Dennis the Menace 2, Bayou Ghost, Small Soldiers (voice), Truce, Don't Come Knocking (dir. only), The Man Who Came Back, Mad Mad Wagon Party, Mad Mad Wagon Party.
TELEVISION: *Movies*: See How They Run, Sarge: The Badge or the Cross, Priest Killer, A Great American Tragedy, Deliver Us From Evil, A Cry in the Wilderness, The Blue Knight, The Archer: Fugitive from the Empire, Jesse Owens Story, Liberty, International Airport, Kenny Rogers as the Gambler III, The Gunfighters, What Price Victory, Good Cops Bad Cops, Final Shot: The Hank Gathers Story, Dallas: J.R. Returns, Dallas: War of the Ewings, National Lampoon's Men in White, Holy War, Un-Holy Victory, Monster Makers, Sands of Oblivion. *Mini-series*: Backstairs at the White House. *Series*: The Blue Knight, Sarge, Counterattack: Crime in America, Dallas, Santo Bugito (voice), The Young and the Restless. *Guest*: More than 122 appearances.

KENNEDY, JAMES C.
Publishing & Media Executive. b. Honolulu, HI, 1947. e. U. Denver, BBA, 1970. Production asst. with Atlanta Newspapers, 1972-76, then exec. v.p. gen. mgr. 1976-79. Pres. Grand Junction newpapers, 1979-80. Pub. Grand Junction Daily Sentinel, 1980-85. V.P. Cox newspapers div. of privately held Cox Enterprises, Inc., 1985-86; exec. v.p. 1986-87; pres., COO, Exec. v.p., 1986-87; chmn., 1987-; CEO & chmn. of the bd., Cox Enterprises, Inc., 1988. Currently he is Chairman of Cox Enterprises. He is also chmn. of Cox Radio, Inc. Currently serves on the boards of Flagler System, Inc. Ducks Unlimited, Atlanta Committee for Progress, the PATH Foundation and is also president of Wetlands America Trust, Inc. He was inducted into Georgia State University's J. Mack Robinson College of Business Hall of Fame in 2004. Bestowed an honorary doctorate of humane letters from Kennesaw State University in 2003. Kennedy and his wife, Sarah, were recognized as the 2003 Philanthropists of the Year by the Greater Atlanta Chapter of the Association for Fund-raising Professionals.

KENNEDY, KATHLEEN
Producer. b. 1954. Raised in Weaverville and Redding in No. Calif. e. San Diego State U. Early TV experience on KCST, San Diego, working as camera operator, video editor, floor director and news production coordinator. Produced talk show, You're On. Left to enter m.p. industry as prod. asst. on Steven Spielberg's 1941. Was founding member and pres. of Amblin Entertainment. In 1992, with husband and partner Frank Marshall formed the Kennedy/Marshall Company. Elected to interim presidency of Producers Guild of America in 2001. Term ran through 2002.
PICTURES: Raiders of the Lost Ark (prod. assoc.), Poltergeist (assoc. prod.), E.T.: The Extra-Terrestrial (Academy Award nom. 1983), Twilight Zone: The Movie (co-assoc. prod.), Indiana Jones and the Temple of Doom (assoc. prod.). *Exec. prod. (with Frank Marshall):* Gremlins, The Goonies, Back to the Future, The Color Purple (Academy Award nom. 1986), Young Sherlock Holmes (co-prod.), An American Tail, Innerspace, Empire of the Sun, Batteries Not Included, Who Framed Roger Rabbit, The Land Before Time, Indiana Jones and the Last Crusade, (prod. exec.), Dad, Always, Joe Versus the Volcano, Gremlins II, Hook (co-prod.), Noises Off, Alive, A Far Off Place, Jurassic Park, Milk

Money, The Bridges of Madison County, Congo, The Indian in the Cupboard, Twister, The Thief of Always, The Sixth Sense (Academy Award nom. 2000), Snow Falling on Cedars, A Map of trhe World, Artificial Intelligence: AI, Jurassic Park III, Seabiscuit (Academy Award nom. 2004), The Young Black Stallion, The Talisman, Indiana Jones 4, Jurassic Park IV, Vengeance, This Is Serbia Calling, Emma's War, War of the Worlds, Munich (Academy Award nom. 2006), The Diving Bell and the Butterfly, Crossing Over, The Curious Case of Benjamin Button (Academy Award nom. 2009), The Adventures of Tintin: Secret of the Unicorn, Hereafter. *Exec. Prod:* Schindler's List, A Dangerous Woman, The Flintstones, The Lost World: Jurassic Park, Olympic Glory, Signs, Persepolis, The Spiderwick Chronicles, Indiana Jones and the Kingdom of the Crystal Skull, The Last Airbender.
TELEVISION: *Movies:* The Sports Pages (exec. prod.), Movies Rock (exec. prod.), The Special Relationship (exec. prod.). *Series:* Amazing Stories (spv. prod.), You're On (prod.), Roger Rabbit & the Secrets of Toontown (exec. prod.).

KENSIT, PATSY

Actress. b. London, England, March 4, 1968. Made film debut at the age of 4 in The Great Gatsby. Later appeared in commercials directed by Tony Scott and Adrian Lyne.
PICTURES: The Great Gatsby (debut, 1974), Alfie Darling, The Blue Bird, Hanover Street, Absolute Beginners, Lethal Weapon 2, A Chorus of Disapproval, Chicago Joe and the Showgirl, Timebomb, Twenty-One, Blue Tornado, Blame It on the Bellboy, Beltenebros, Kleptomania, The Turn of the Screw, Bitter Harvest, Angels and Insects, Grace of My Heart, Speedway Junky, Best, Janice Beard: 45 Words Per Minute, The Pavilion, Best, Things Behind the Sun, The One and Only, Bad Karma, Darkness Falling, Played.
TELEVISION: *Movies:* BBC: Great Expectations, Silas Marner: The Weaver of Raveloe, Tycoon: The Story of a Woman, Adam Bede, French & Saunders, Emmerdale Farm (series). U.S.: Quiet as a Nun, The Legend of King Arthur, The Adventures of Pollyanna, The Tragedy of Richard the Third, The Corsican Brothers, Full Eclipse, Fall from Grace, Love and Betrayal: The Mia Farrow Story, At the Midnight Hour, Human Bomb, The Last Don, Aladdin, Murder in Mind, Loves Music Loves to Dance, The All Star Comedy Show, A Bear's Christmas Tail. *Mini-series:* Dickens of London, Prince Regent, Great Expectations, Diana, The Last Don II. *Series:* Hannah, A Bear's Tail, Emmerdale Farm, Luna, Holby City. *Guest:* More than 106 appearances.

KENT, JOHN B.

Theatre Executive, Attorney. b. Jacksonville, FL, Sept. 5, 1939. e. Yale U., U. of FL, Law Sch., NYU grad. sch. of law (L.L.M. in taxation, 1964). Partner in Kent Ridge & Crawford, P.A.; pres. & dir, Kent Investments, Inc. 1977-; dir., v.p. & gen. counsel, Kent Theatres, Inc. 1970-; dir. & v.p., Kent Enterprises, Inc. 1961-; dir. & v.p. Kent Cinemas Inc. 1993-. Was pres. of Kent Theatres Inc. 1967-70; resigned to devote full time to law practice. NATO dir. 1972 and Presidents' Advisory Cabinet, 1979-; v.p./dir. NATO of FL, 1968-. Member of Rotary Club of Jacksonville, FL. Bar Association, American Bar Association.

KENT, PHILIP I.

Executive. e. Bachelor's degree, economics, Lehigh University. Kent began his career in 1975 at Blair Television. By 1981, he was on the two-person team that started Blair Entertainment, the TV syndication division of John Blair & Co. Over the next five years, Kent helped build Blair Entertainment into a major TV and radio production and syndication company. In 1984, he was promoted to v.p. of program development. From Blair, he went to Creative Artists Agency (CAA) as a packaging agent responsible for TV program packaging in first-run syndication and cable TV. After six years at CAA, Kent joined Turner Broadcasting. He's managed several areas of the company including serving as pres., Turner Home Entertainment, the former TBS, Inc. division comprised of the company's home video, new media, licensing & merchandising, feature distribution and book publishing operations; pres., Turner Broadcasting System International (TBSI), the division overseeing Turner's wide-ranging activities in Asia, Europe and Latin America, including all sales, distribution, business development, joint partnerships and business alliances outside the U.S. At the helm of TBSI, Kent led the strategy that introduced local-language versions of CNN and the Turner entertainment networks around the globe. From Aug. 2000 to Aug. 2001, Kent served as president and COO of CNN News Group, where he reorganized the news division, CNN Headline News and oversaw high-profile hires including Lou Dobbs and Paula Zahn. In Feb. 2003, Kent returned to TBS, Inc., becoming its chairman & CEO. In his current role, he has corporate oversight of the TBS, Inc. domestic and international entertainment, animation and news networks and businesses, including TBS, TNT and Turner Classic Movies; Cartoon Network, Adult Swim and Boomerang; GameTap; and the CNN News Group, which includes CNN/U.S., CNN Headline News, CNN International and CNN.com. Kent has overall responsibility for all news and entertainment advertising and distribution, both domestically and internationally, as well as for all corporate administrative functions and Turner Sports. Turner Broadcasting System, Inc., is a Time Warner company. Kent serves on the bd. of directors of the Ad Council, the National Cable and Telecommunications Association and Central Atlanta Progress. He sits on the bd. of trustees of the Woodruff Arts Center; and on the Dean's executive bd. of UCLA's School of Theatre, Film & Television.

KERASOTES, ANTHONY

Exhibitor. b. Springfield, IL, July 7, 1948. e. B.A. from Northwestern University, 1970. Anthony Kerasotes is the chairman & CEO of Kerasotes Showplace Theatres, a cinema circuit operating theatres in Illinois, Indiana, Iowa, Ohio, Missouri and Minnesota. The company currently has 853 screens in 95 locations. Anthony Kerasotes is the third generation of the family to manage the theatre circuit, which was founded by Gus Kerasotes in 1909 in Springfield, IL.

KERASOTES, DEAN

Exhibitor. b. Springfield, IL, April 12, 1950. e. B.S. from the Univ. of Illinois, 1972; Master's degree from Oklahoma State Univ., 1978; Ph.D. from Oklahoma State Univ., 1980. Dean Kerasotes is the president & COO of Kerasotes Showplace Theatres, a cinema circuit operating theatres in Illinois, Indiana, Iowa, Ohio, Missouri and Minnesota. The company currently has 853 screens in 95 locations. Dean Kerasotes is the third generation of the family to manage the theatre circuit, which was founded by Gus Kerasotes in 1909 in Springfield, IL. Kerasotes is a member of the National Assoc. of Theatre Owners.

KERGER, PAULA

Executive. e. University of Baltimore. Director of principal gifts for the Metropolitan Opera in New York in 1993. Served as director of development and alumni affairs for International House in New York, and as program development officer for the U.S. Committee for UNICEF. Kerger served for more than a decade at Educational Broadcasting Corporation (EBC), the parent company of Thirteen/WNET and WLIW New York, as Exec. V.P. and COO. Her tenure included WNET's completion in 1997 of the largest successful endowment campaign ever undertaken by a public television station. In 2002, Kerger was promoted to V. P. and station manager of Thirteen/WNET. Kerger oversaw local program acquisition, broadcast scheduling, communications, on-air promotion, and pledge production, she supervised individual giving, as well as Thirteen's volunteer program, viewer and member services, and government affairs. Kerger also directed the launch of four digital channels: ThirteenHD, Kids Thirteen, World and Create. The latter, launched in January 2006 through a partnership with WGBH/Boston and American Public Television, is public television's first 24-hour lifestyle channel. 2004, Kerger became Exec. V.P. and COO of EBC and a member of the office of the President. Joined PBS as its sixth president and chief executive in March 2006. Public Broadcasting Service, is the nation's largest non-commercial media organization with 356 member stations. Among her accomplishments are Ken Burns' and Lynn Novick's "The War," which earned the highest rating of any PBS series in the last 10 years; the debut of children's programs as "Curious George" (the number one show for children ages 2-5 since 2006), "Word World," "Super Why!," "Martha Speaks," and "Sid the Science Kid"; new primetime science and arts series; and comprehensive online sites for parents and caregivers -- PBS Parents -- and for educators -- PBS Teachers. PBS programs have been honored with 33 Emmys, including ten News and Documentary Emmys and nine Primetime Emmys; eight George Foster Peabody awards; and one Academy Award (for best animated short film). Innovative partnerships with companies as iTunes, YouTube, Microsoft's Xbox, Netflix, Amazon's Video on Demand, Hulu, and Vuze ensure that PBS programming is accessible across more than one platform and, increasingly, to a global audience. In addition to leading PBS, Kerger is President of the PBS Foundation, an independent organization that raises private sector funding for PBS, and a director of the International Academy of Television Arts and Sciences. For the since 2007, the Hollywood Reporter has included Ms. Kerger in the "Women in Entertainment Power 100,". In 2005, she was named to the Women's Forum, an organization of 300 leading women in New York's arts and business. In 2008, Kerger received the Woman of Achievement Award from Women in Development, New York.

KERKORIAN, KIRK

Executive. b. Fresno, CA, June 6, 1917. e. Los Angeles public schools. Served as capt., transport command, RAF, 1942-44. Commercial air line pilot from 1940; founder Los Angeles Air Service (later Trans Intl. Airlines Corp.), 1948; Intl. Leisure Corp., 1968; controlling stockholder, Western Airlines, 1970; chief exec. officer, MGM, Inc., 1973-74; chmn. exec. com., vice-chmn. bd., 1974-1978. Stepped down from exec. positions while retaining financial interest in MGM/UA. Repurchased MGM in the summer of 1996. He is an American billionaire and president/CEO of Tracinda Corp., his private holding company.

KERNER, JORDAN

Producer. e. Stanford U, A.B. Political Science & Comm.; U.C. Berkely, J.D.-M.B.A.. Bgean career in entertainment working for CBS affiliate KPIX-TV. Joined law firm of Ball, Hunt, Brown & Baerwitz. Talent & Program Negotiator for CBS. Worked for Universal Pictures & QM Prods., 1978-81. Joined ABC Entertainment as dir., Dramatic Series Develop-ment. Promoted to v.p., 1983. While at ABC, placed Moonlight-ing,

MacGyver, Dynasty, Spencer for Hire, Call To Glory. Founded the Avnet/Kerner Co. in 1986 with Avent. Currently dir., Allied Communications, Inc. Member, bd. of dirs., The Starbright Foundation, The Chrysalis Foundation. Member, President's Advisory Council for the City of Hope, Sen. Dianne Feinstein's California Cabinet, Planned Parenthood, Earth Communications Office, A.M.P.A.S., A.F.I. Former gov., Academy of Television Arts & Sciences. Founder and former co-chmn., Committee for the Arts of the Beverly Hills Bar Asoc. Founder, COMM/ENT, the Journal of Communications & Entertainment Law.
PICTURES: Less Than Zero, Funny About Love, The Mighty Ducks, Fried Green Tomatoes, The War, The Three Musketeers, When A Man Loves A Woman, D2: The Mighty Ducks, Miami Rhapsody (exec. prod.), Up Close and Personal, Swiss Family Robinson, Dinner For Two at the El Cortez, To Live For, Friday Night Lights, Blaze of Glory, D3: The Mighty Ducks, Red Corner, George of the Jungle, Thirty Wishes, Inspector Gadget, Snow Dogs, Charlotte's Web, Summer School, The Smurfs.
TELEVISION: *Movies: Exec. Prod.:* Side by Side, My First Love, Do You Know the Muffin Man?, Backfield in Motion, The Nightman, For Their Own Good, Poodle Springs, Mama Flora's Family, My Last Love, A House Divided, Red Skies, A Wrinkle in Time. *Prod.:* Breaking Point, Heat Wave, The Watchman, The Switch, The War, Love Can Build a Bridge, Uprising.

KERNS, JOANNA
Actress, Director. r.n. Joanna de Varona. b. San Francisco, CA, Feb. 12, 1953. Former gymnast, became dancer, appeared on tv commercials. Sister is Olympic swimmer and tv commentator Donna de Varona. NY stage: Ulysses in Nighttown.
PICTURES: Coma, Cross My Heart, Street Justice, An American Summer, No Dessert Dad Til You Mow the Lawn, No One Could Protect Her, Girl Interrupted, All Over the Guy, Knocked Up.
TELEVISION: *Movies*: The Million Dollar Rip-Off, Marriage Is Alive and Well, Mother's Day on Walton's Mountain, A Wedding on Walton's Mountain, A Day of Thanks on Walton's Mountain, The Return of Marcus Welby M.D., A Bunny's Tale, The Rape of Richard Beck, Stormin' Home, Mistress, Those She Left Behind, Like Mother Like Daughter, The Preppie Murder, Blind Faith, Captive, The Nightman, Not in My Family, The Man With 3 Wives, Shameful Secrets, No Dessert Dad 'Til You Mow the Lawn, Robin Cook's Mortal Fear, See Jane Run, Whose Daughter Is She?, Sisters and Other Strangers, Mother Knows Best, Morning Glory, Terror In the Family, Emma's Wish, At the Mercy of a Stranger, The Growing Pains Movie, Someone to Love, Growing Pains: Return of the Seavers. *Series*: The Four Seasons, Growing Pains (also wrote one episode). *As Dir.:* Hope & Gloria, Remember WENN, Suddenly Susan, Clueless, Ally McBeal, Dawson's Creek, Any Day Now, Felicity, Strong Medicine, Defending Our Kids: The Julie Posey Story, Related, That's Life, Titans, Boston Public, Leap of Faith, The O'Keefes, Men in Trees, Army Wives. *Guest*: More than 108 appearances.

KERSHNER, IRVIN
Director. b. Philadelphia, PA, April 29, 1923. e. Tyler Sch. of Fine Arts of Temple U., 1946; Art Center Sch., U. of Southern California. Designer, photography, adv., documentary, architectural; doc. filmmaker, U.S.I.S., Middle East, 1950-52; dir., cameraman, TV doc., Confidential File, 1953-55; dir.-prod.-writer, Ophite Prod. Appeared as actor in film The Last Temptation of Christ.
PICTURES: Stakeout on Dope Street (debut, 1958; also co-s.p.), The Young Captives, The Hoodlum Priest, A Face in the Rain, The Luck of Ginger Coffey, A Fine Madness, The Flim-Flam Man, Loving, Up the Sandbox, S*P*Y*S, The Return of a Man Called Horse, Eyes of Laura Mars, The Empire Strikes Back, Never Say Never Again, Robocop 2, On Deadly Ground, Angus, American Perfekt (prod.), Manhood (actor), Instant Dads (post prod. consult.), Berkeley (actor), Empires of the Deep (prod.).
TELEVISION: *Movies*: Raid on Entebbe (theatrical in Europe, Emmy nom. 1977), The Traveling Man. *Pilot:* SeaQuest DSV. *Series*: The Rebel, Naked City, numerous pilots and other nat'l. shows.

KERWIN, BRIAN
Actor. b. Chicago, IL, Oct. 25, 1949. e. USC.
THEATRE: *NY:* Emily (Theatre World Award), Lips Together Teeth Apart, Raised in Captivity. LA: Strange Snow (LA Drama Critics Award), Who's Afraid of Virginia Woolf?, A Loss of Roses, Torch Song Trilogy.
PICTURES: Hometown USA (debut, 1979), Nickel Mountain, Murphy's Romance, King Kong Lives, Torch Song Trilogy, S.P.O.O.K.S., Hard Promises, Love Field, Gold Diggers: The Secret of Bear Mountain, Getting Away With Murder, Jack, The Myth of Fingerprints, Mr. Jealousy, Debating Robert Lee, 27 Dresses.
TELEVISION: *Movies*: A Real American Hero, Power, Miss All-American Beauty, Intimate Agony, Wet Gold, The Greatest Thing That Almost Happened, Challenger, Switched at Birth, Against Her Will: An Incident in Baltimore, Abandoned and Deceived, It Came From Outer Space, Sins of Silence, Critical Choices, Volcano: Fire on the Mountain, Flash, The Hunt for the Unicorn Killer, Common Ground. *Mini-series*: The Chisholms, The Blue and the Gray, Bluegrass, A Girl Thing. *Series*: The Young and the Restless (1976-77), The Misadventures of Sheriff Lobo, Angel Falls, Beggars and Choosers, Nip/Tuck, The Virgin of Akron, Ohio (pilot), Big Love, One Life to Live (Emmy nom. 2008). *Special:* Natica Jackson. *Guest*: More than 68 appearances.

KHONDJI, DARIUS
Cinematographer. b. Tehran, Iran, Oct. 21, 1955. e. NYU, Film.
PICTURES: Rive droite, rive gauche (first assistant cameraman), Le Tresor des chiennes, Delicatessen, Prague, Shadow of a Doubt, Before the Rain, Marie-Lousie ou la permission, City of Lost Children, Se7en (ASC nom. 1997), Stealing Beauty, Evita (Academy Award nom.; ASC nom. 1997), Alien: Resurrection, In Dreams, The Ninth Gate, The Beach, The Panic Room, Anything Else, Wimbledon, The Interpreter, Funny Games, My Blueberry Nights, The Lady from Shanghai, The Ruins, Chéri.

KIAROSTAMI, ABBAS
Director, Producer, Writer, Editor. b. Teheran, Iran, June 22, 1940. Recipient of the 1997 UNESCO Fellini-Medal in Gold for achievement in film, freedem, peace & tolerance.
PICTURES: The Window, The Bread & Alley, The Breaktime, The Experience, The Traveller, So I Can, Two Solutions for One Problem, The Colours, Suit for Wedding, The Report (Gozaresh), Tribute to the Teachers, How to Make Use of Our Leisure Time?, Solution No. 1, First Case—Second Case, Dental Hygiene, Orderly or Unorderly, The Chorus, Fellow Citizen, Toothache, First Graders, Where is the Friend's Home, The Key, Homework, Close Up, And Life Goes on..., Journey to the Land of the Traveller, Under the Olive Trees, The Journey, Lumiere & Company, The White Balloon, The Taste of Cherry (Cannes Film Festival Palme d'Or, 1997), The Wind Will Carry Us, Volte sempre Abbas!, Willow and Wind, Ten, Crimson Gold, Tickets, Os Invisíveis, To Each His Cinema (segment dir.), Shirin, The Certified Copy.

KIDDER, MARGOT
Actress. r.n. Margaret Kidder. b. Yellowknife, Ca., Oct. 17, 1948.
PICTURES: The Best Damned Fiddler From Calabogie to Kaladar (debut, 1968), Gaily Gaily, Quackser Fortune Has a Cousin in the Bronx, Sisters, A Quiet Day in Belfast, The Gravy Train, Black Christmas, The Great Waldo Pepper, 92 in the Shade, The Reincarnation of Peter Proud, Superman, Mr. Mike's Mondo Video, The Amityville Horror, Willie and Phil, Superman II, Heartaches, Shoot the Sun Down, Some Kind of Hero, Trenchcoat, Superman III, Little Treasure, GoBots (voice), Superman IV: The Quest for Peace, Miss Right, Mob Story, White Room, Crime and Punishment, Maverick, Henry & Verlin, Beanstalk, The Pornographer, La Florida, Aaron Sent Me, Windrunner, Never Met Picasso, The Planet of Junior Brown, Silent Cradle, Shadow Zone: My Teacher Ate My Homework, The Clown at Midnight, The Annihilation of Fish, Tail Lights Fade, Nightmare Man, The Hi-Line, Tribulation, Crime and Punishment, Angel Blade, The Last Sign, Chicks with Sticks, The Ocean, Universal Signs, On the Other Hand, Death, A Single Woman, Halloween II, For Robbing the Dead.
TELEVISION: *Movies*: Suddenly Single, The Bounty Man, Honky Tonk, Louisiana, The Glitter Dome, Picking Up the Pieces, Vanishing Act, Body of Evidence, To Catch a Killer, One Woman's Courage, Bloodknot, Phantom 2040: The Story of Alex Kelly, Common Ground, Someone Is Watching, Society's Child, I'll Be Seeing You, Cool Money, Something Evil Comes. *Series*: Nichols, Shell Game, Robson Arms. *Specials:* Bus Stop, Pygmalion. *Guest*: More than 117 appearances.

KIDMAN, NICOLE
Actress. b. Hawaii, June 20, 1967. Raised in Australia. Made acting debut at 14 in Australian film Bush Christmas. On Australian stage in Steel Magnolias (Sydney Theatre Critics Award for Best Newcomer). Owner of Blossom Films.
PICTURES: Bush Christmas (debut, 1982), BMZ Bandits, Windrider, Dead Calm, Emerald City, Days of Thunder, Billy Bathgate (Golden Globe nom. 1992), Far and Away, Flirting, Malice, My Life, Batman Forever, To Die For (Golden Globe Award 1996), Portrait of a Lady, The Peacemaker, Practical Magic, Eyes Wide Shut, Birthday Girl, Moulin Rouge (Academy Award nom.; Golden Globe Award 2002), The Panic Room (voice), The Others (BAFTA nom.; Golden Globe nom. 2002), The Hours (Academy Award- best actress, BAFTA-best actress, Golden Globe Award 2003), Dogville, Cold Mountain (Golden Globe nom. 2004), The Human Stain, Birth (Golden Globe nom. 2005), In the Cut (prod. only), The Stepford Wives, The Interpreter, Bewitched, The Producers, Emma's War, American Darlings (also exec. prod.), Margot at the Wedding, Eucalyptus, Fur: An Imaginary Portrait of Diane Arbus, Happy Feet (voice), I Have Never Forgotten You: The Life & Legacy of Simon Wiesenthal (doc., narr.), The Invasion, His Dark Materials: The Golden Compass, Need, Australia, Nine (also soundtrack performer), The Danish Girl, Rabbit Hole (also prod.), Monte Carlo (prod.), Just Go with It.
TELEVISION: *Movies:* Skin Deep, Chase Through the Night, Matthew and Son, Room to Move, Un' Australiana a Roma. *Mini-series* (Australia): Five-Mile Creek, Vietnam, Bangkok Hilton. *Guest:* More than 183 appearances.

KIDRON, BEEBAN
Director. b. London, England, 1961. e. National Film School.

Made co-dir. debut (with Amanda Richardson) with documentary Carry Greenham Home (Chicago Film Fest. Hugo Award, 1983).
PICTURES: Antonia and Jane, Used People, Great Moments in Aviation, To Wong Foo—Thanks for Everything—Julie Newmar, Swept from the Sea (also prod.), Bridget Jones: The Edge of Reason, Hippie Hippie Shake.
TELEVISION: The Global Gamble, Vroom, Oranges Are Not the Only Fruit, Great Moments in Aviation, Texarkana, Cinderella, Murder. *Documentary:* Antony Gormley: Making Space (also prod.).

KIEL, RICHARD

Actor. b. Detroit, MI, Sept. 13, 1939. Former nightclub bouncer.
PICTURES: The Phantom Planet (debut, 1961), Eegah!, House of the Damned, The Magic Sword, Roustabout, The Human Duplicators, Las Vegas Hillbillies, A Man Called Dagger, Skidoo, The Longest Yard, Flash and the Firecat, Silver Streak, The Spy Who Loved Me, Force 10 from Navarone, Moonraker, The Humanoid, So Fine, Hysterical, Cannonball Run II, Pale Rider, Think Big, The Giant of Thunder Mountain (also co-s.p., co-exec. prod.), Happy Gilmore, Inspector Gadget (cameo), Confined.
TELEVISION: *Movies:* The Phantom, Now You See It Now You Don't, The Boy Who Stole the Elephant, *Series*: Land of the Lost, The Barbary Coast, Van Dyke & Company. *Pilot:* The Barbary Coast. *Guest:* More than 66 appearances.

KIER, UDO

Actor. b. Cologne, Germany, October 14, 1944.
PICTURES: Road to St. Tropez, Season of the Senses, Schamlos, La Horse, Satan, Provocation, Erotomaneis, The Salzburg Connection, Sexual Eroticism, Pan, Olifant, Andy Warhol's Frankenstein, Andy Warhol's Dracula, The Last Word, The Story of O, Trauma, Goldflocken, Spermula, Suspiria, Bolweiser, Belcanto oder Darf eine Nutte schluchzen?, Counterfeit Commandos, Das Funfte Gebot, Kretakor, The Third Generation, Hungarian Rhapsody, Lulu, Psyche, Deutschland privat, Lili Marleen, Lola, The Blood of Dr. Jekyll, Escape from Blood Plantation, The Wild Fifties, Pankow '95, Hur und Heilig, Seduction: The Cruel Woman, Der Unbesiegbare, Die Einsteiger, Egomania - Insel ohne Hoffmung, Die Schlacht der Idioten, Am nachsten Morgen kehrte der Minister nicht an seinen Arbeitsplatz zuruck, Mutters Mask, Epidemic, 100 Jahre Adolf Hitler- Die letzte Stunde im Fuhrerbunker, Blackest Heart, Europa, My Own Private Idaho, Der Unbekannte Deserteur, Terror 2000 - Intesivstation Deutschland, Even Cowgirls Get The Blues, Three Shake-A-Leg Steps to Heaven, Plotzlich und unerwarten, Josn and S.A.M, Ace Ventura: Pet Detective, For Love or Money, The Kingdom, Rotwang Must Go, Johnny Mnemonic, Over My Dead Body, Unter Druck, Paradise Framed, A Trick of the Light, Duke of Groove, Dog Daze, Ausgerstoben, United Trash, Barb Wire, Breaking the Waves, Pinocchio, Lea, The End of Violence, Prince Valiant, The Kingdom 2, Betty, Die 120 Tage von Bottrop, Armageddon, Blade, Modern Vampires, Ice, Simon Says, Guilty, Killer Deal, Besat, Spy Games, History is Made at Night, The Debtors, Under the Palms, The New Adventures of Pinocchio, End of Days, The Last Call, Doomsdayer, Shadow of the Vamprie, Dancer in the Dark, Just One Night, Red Letters, There's No Fish Food in Heaven, Invincible, Black Widow, Final Payback, Broken Cookies, Critical Mass, Citizens of Perpetual Indulgence, Cadillac Tramps, The Bloodcountess, All the Queen's Men, The 8th Day, The Last Minute, Revelation, Double Deception, Yuri's Revenge, Herz und Nieren, FearDotCom, Dogville, Broken Cookies, Evil Eyes, Modigliani, Wit's End, Sawtooth, Surviving Christmas, One More Round, Manderlay, Headspace, Holly, BloodRayne, Pray for Morning, Crusade in Jeans, Fall Down Dead, Tell, Mother of Tears, Halloween, Pars: Operation Cherry, Grindhouse, Tell, Lulu and Jimi, Far Cry, Night of the Templar, Sinners & Saints, House of Boys, Die Blutgräfin, Metropia (voice), My Son, My Son, What Have Ye Done, Night of the Templar, Melancholia, Der Himmel hat vier Ecken, Das Leben ist zu lang, Iron Sky.
TELEVISION: *Movies:* Medea, Jack Reed: Badge of Honor, Miss Diamond, Ice, Killer Deal, Final Run, He Sees You When You're Sleeping, 30 Days Until I'm Famous, Dracula 3000, 13 Graves. *Mini-series:* Joseph Balsamo, The Kingdom, The Kingdom II. *Series:* Polizeiruf 110, 4 gegen Z. *Documentary:* The Great War and the Shaping of the 20th Century. *Guest:* More than 83 appearances.

KIERZEK, TERRY

Executive. b. Chicago, IL, Feb. 15, 1951. e. U. of Il. Joined Paramount Pictures Domestic Distrib., as booker in Chicago, 1974. Promoted to Sales in 1976, Dallas, TX. Named branch mgr., Dallas/OK City, 1978. V.P., Eastern Division in Washington, D.C., 1982-84. V.P., Southern Division, Dallas, TX., 1984-86. V.P., Western Division, Los Angeles, 1986-89. Orion Pictures v.p., Western Division, 1990-92. Joined National Film Service in 1993 as v.p., sales & mktg. Named exec. v.p., 1995. Appointed pres., National Film Service in 1996. Bd. of Director for META.

KILAR, JASON

Executive. e. Graduated Phi Beta Kappa, bus. admin., journalism & mass. comm., Univ. of North Carolina, Chapel Hill; MBA, Harvard. Kilar began career with The Walt Disney Company, working in design and development. Began decade-long assoc. with Amazon.com Inc. in May 1997: product mgr. with Amazon.com Inc.; Feb. 2001-Oct. 2001 v.p., books, music, videos and DVD, Amazon.com Inc.; Oct. 2001-Feb. 2002 v.p. of marketplace, Amazon.com Inc.; From Feb. 2002-May 2003, served as v.p., worldwide application software, Amazon.com Inc.; May 2003-July 2007, Amazon's senior v.p., worldwide application software and also responsible for Amazon's marketplace business. Kilar wrote the original business plan for Amazon's entry into the video and DVD businesses and ultimately managed Amazon's North American media businesses, which included the company's books, music, video, and DVD categories. From July 2007-present, Kilar has been CEO of Hulu, LLC. Initially formed as a joint venture between NBC Universal (a unit of GE) and News Corp. (the parent of FOX), Hulu.com is a site that features video from more than 100 content providers. Hulu.com was launched in 2008; the following year Disney became a shareholder and content partner.

KILMER, VAL

Actor. b. Los Angeles, CA, Dec. 31, 1959. e. Hollywood Professional Sch., Juilliard, NY. Appeared in IMAX film Wings of Courage.
THEATRE: NY: Electra and Orestes, How It All Began (also co-writer), Henry IV Part One, Slab Boys (B'way debut), 'Tis Pity She's a Whore. Also: As You Like It (Gutherie MN), Hamlet (Colorado Shakespeare Fest.). *Author:* My Eden After Burns, 24 Days in Wonderland.
PICTURES: Top Secret! (debut, 1984), Real Genius, Top Gun, Willow, Kill Me Again, The Doors, Thunderheart, True Romance, The Real McCoy, Tombstone, Batman Forever, Heat, The Island of Dr. Moreau, The Ghost and the Darkness, The Saint, The Prince of Egypt (voice), Joe Henry, At First Sight, Pollock, Red Planet, The Salton Sea, Run For the Money, Mindhunters, The Missing, Prophet: The Story of Joseph Smith, Spartan, Stateside, Blind Horizon, Mindhunters, Alexander, Kiss Kiss Bang Bang, 10th & Wolf, What Love Is and What's It All About (also co-prod.), Déjà Vu, The Ten Commandments: The Musical, Have Dreams, Will Travel, Delgo (voice), Conspiracy, American Cowslip, Columbus Day, (also prod.), The Hard Ride, Felon, 2:22, The Thaw, Silver Cord, Bad Lieutenant: Port of Call New Orleans, Fake Identity, Provinces of Night, MacGruber, Abelar: Tales of an Ancient Empire, The Traveler, Georgia, Silver Cord, Riddle, Gun, Blood Out.
TELEVISION: *Movies*: Murders in the Rue Morgue, The Man Who Broke 1000 Chains, Gore Vidal's Billy the Kid. *Mini-series:* Comanche Moon, XIII: The Conspiracy. *Series:* Knight Rider (voice, 2009). *Guest:* More than 75 appearances.

KIMBROUGH, CHARLES

Actor. b. St. Paul, MN, May 23, 1936. e. Indiana U., Yale U.
THEATRE: NY: All in Love (debut, 1961), Cop-Out (B'way debut, 1969), Company (Tony nom.), Candide, Love for Love, The Rules of the Game, Secret Service, Mr. Happiness, Same Time Next Year, Drinks Before Dinner, The Dining Room, Sunday in the Park With George, Hay Fever. Several prods. with Milwaukee Rep. Theatre (1966-73).
PICTURES: The Front (debut, 1976), The Seduction of Joe Tynan, Starting Over, It's My Turn, Switching Channels, The Good Mother, The Hunchback of Notre Dame (voice), The Wedding Planner, Recess: School's Out (voice), Marci X.
TELEVISION: *Movies*: Secret Service, For Ladies Only, The Innocents Abroad, Concealed Enemies, A Doctor's Story, Sunday in the Park with George, Weekend War, Cast the First Stone. *Series*: Another World, Murphy Brown (Emmy nom. 1990). *Pilot*: The Recovery Room.

KIMMEL, JIMMY

Actor, Writer, Producer, Comedian, Host. b. Brooklyn, NY, Nov. 13, 1967. e. Attended University of Nevada, Las Vegas and Arizona State University. Started as co-host of morning radio show, The Me and Him Show at KZOK-FM in Seattle, Washington. With co-host Kent Voss, moved show to WRBQ-FM in Tampa, Florida. Hosted own show for KCMJ-FM in Palm Springs, CA. Kimmel landed a job with Mike Elliott at 93.7 KRQ in Tucson but then left after one year. Became comedy writer for KROQ-FM, Los Angeles, where he was known as "Jimmy, the Sports Guy". 1999 he became TV comedian working for cable station's Comedy Central game show, Win Ben Stein's Money. 2001 created and produced The Man Show and The Andy Milonakis Show for MTV2 under prod. company, Jackhole Industries, where he is currently a partner. Co-wrote feature film, Windy City Heat, which won Best Film at the Montreal Comedy Festival and aired on TV. Jan. 2003, became host of ABC late night talk show, Jimmy Kimmel Live! which was formerly known as The Jimmy Kimmel Project.
PICTURES: Delinquent's Derby (announcer, debut 1995), Down to You, Road Trip (voice), Like Mike, Garfield (voice), Patriot Act: A Jeffrey Ross Home Movie (doc.), Danny Roane: First Time Director, Certifiably Jonathan, Hellboy II: The Golden Army.
TELEVISION: *Movies:* Windy City Heat, Eminem's Making the Ass (voice), Mr. Warmth: The Don Rickles Project, Alligator Boots (exec. prod.), Ace in the Hole (exec. prod.). *Series:* Fox NFL Sunday, Hollywood Squares, Gerhard Reinke's Wanderlust (exec. pord.), Win Ben Stein's Money (2 Emmy noms.), The Adam Carolla Project (exec. prod.), Drawn Together (voice), The Andy Milonakis Show (exec. prod., writer), Robot Chicken

(voice), Crank Yankers (voices, writer, exec. prod.), The Man Show, ESPN 25: Who's #1?, Dancing with the Stars (2006-2008), Jimmy Kimmel Live! (host, exec. prod., writer), Big Night of Stars (special, WGA nom. 2009). *Specials As Host:* The 31st Annual American Music Awards, Playboy: 50 Years of Playmates, The 32nd Annual American Music Awards, Super Bowl XL Pre-Game Show, ESPY Awards, 2007 American Music Awards, 2008 American Music Awards. *Guest:* More than 114 appearances.

KIMMELMAN, KEN

Producer, Director, Animator. b. New York, NY. Aug. 6, 1940. e. School of Visual Arts. Has produced tv programs, political films, theatricals, TV commercials, and many films for Sesame Street. Consultant on the faculty of the Aesthetic Realism Roundation. Pres. of Imagery Film Ltd; prod. films for UN. Recipient of: National Emmy Award 1995 (The Heart Knows Better), Newark Black Film Festival's Paul Robeson Award; Atlanta Film Festival's Dir's. Choice Award; Cindy Award; ASIFA East's Best Children's Film Award. Taught and lectured at NYU, presently at School of Visual Arts, NY. Published numerous articles & letters.
TELEVISION: *Director/Producer:* People Are Trying to Put Opposites Together (documentary). *Series:* Drawing Power, Doug (Emmy nom., 1992, 93), The Head, Daria, Mr. Hiccup, Between the Lions.

KING, GRAHAM

Producer, Executive. b. England, Dec. 19, 1961. Raised in London, King came to the U.S. in 1981 on a student visa to study at the Univ. of California in Los Angeles. A summer job in the international TV distribution wing of Twentieth Century Fox led to promotion in foreign sales of B-pictures during a time when the American film and TV industry was opening up to the foreign market. From 1987 -1992, he worked for international sales company Cori Films. King then transferred to the Beverly Hills Producers Group, where he met future business partner Cindy Cowan. The two formed Initial Entertainment Group (IEG) in 1995, and began producing such films as Robert Altman's Dr. T & the Women. King soon purchased Cowan's share of the company and began taking chances on pricier films. King currently is pres. & CEO of IEG. The independent finance, production, and distribution company, with King at the helm, was the force that brought Steven Soderbergh's Academy Award-winning Traffic to the big screen; he bought the foreign film rights to Michael Mann's Ali and underwrote Martin Scorsese's Gangs of New York for $65 million. All were critical and box office successes. His willingness to gamble and ability to deliver at the box office put him among today's most successful producers. At the 2007 Academy Awards, King won a Best Picture Oscar for the ensemble crime thriller The Departed.
PICTURES: Ping! (2000), Dr. T and the Women, Traffic (exec. prod.), Ali (exec. prod.), The Dangerous Lives of Altar Boys (exec. prod.), Desert Saints, Gangs of New York (co-exec. prod.), The Aviator (BAFTA Best Film & Academy Award nom. 2005), The Ballad of Jack and Rose (exec. prod.), An Unfinished Life (exec. prod.), First Born (exec. prod.), The Departed (Academy Award 2007), Blood Diamond, First Born, Gardener of Eden (exec. prod.), Bangkok Dangerous, Next, The Young Victoria, Edge of Darkness, Silence, The Rum Diary, London Boulevard, Rango, The Town, The Tourist, The Invention of Hugo Cabret.
TELEVISION: *Mini-series:* Traffic (Emmy nom. 2004).

KING, LARRY

Talk Show Host, Writer. b. Brooklyn, NY, Nov. 19, 1933. Started as disc jockey on various Miami radio stations from 1958-64. Became host of radio talk show, broadcast from Miami before moving to Arlington, VA, in 1978. Host of CNN tv talk show since 1985, Larry King Live. Starred in tv special Larry King Extra. Columnist for Miami Beach Sun-Reporter, Sporting News, USA Today. King ended his 25 year run with Larry King LIve on CNN in 2010. He plans to stay on at CNN hosting reports on national and international issues. Holds the Guinness Book of World Records for having the longest running show with the same host in the same time slot. *Author:* Larry King by Larry King, Tell It to the King, Mr. King You're Having a Heart Attack, Tell Me More, How to Talk to Anyone Anytime Anywhere: The Secrets of Good Conversation, Anything Goes, Love Stories of WW II.
PICTURES: Ghostbusters, Lost in America, Eddie and the Cruisers II: Eddie Lives, The Exorcist III, Dave, Open Season, Courage Under Fire, The Long Kiss Goodnight, Contact, An Alan Smithee Film: Burn Hollywood Burn, Mad City, The Jackal, Primary Colors, Bulworth, Enemy of the State, The Kid, The Contender, America's Sweethearts, John Q., Shrek 2 (voice), Catching Kringle (voice), Shrek the Third (voice), Bee Movie (voice), Shrek Forever After (voice).
TELEVISION: Larry King Live, Sam Kinison: Why Did We Laugh?, I Love Lucy's 50th Anniversary Special, Roots: Celebrating 25 Years. *Guest:* More than 165 appearances.

KING, PETER

Executive, Barrister-At-Law. b. London, England, March 22, 1928. e. Marlborough, Oxford U. (MA, honors). Bd., Shipman & King Cinemas Ltd., 1956; borough councillor, 1959-61; chmn., London & Home counties branch, CEA, 1962-63; pres., CEA, 1964; mang. dir. Shipman & King Cinemas Ltd., 1959-68; chmn. & mang. dir. Paramount Pictures (U.K.) Ltd. Britain, 1968-70; mang. dir., EMI Cinemas and Leisure Ltd., 1970-74; chmn. & mang. dir. King Publications/pub. Screen Intl., 1974-89; pres., Screen Intl., 1989-90; chmn. & managing dir., Rex Publications Ltd., 1990-; pub., Majesty, 1990-; pub. Preview.

KING, PERRY

Actor. b. Alliance, OH, April 30, 1948. e. Yale. Studied with John Houseman at Juilliard. B'way debut 1990 in A Few Good Men.
PICTURES: Slaughterhouse-Five (debut, 1972), The Possession of Joel Delaney, The Lords of Flatbush, Mandingo, The Wild Party, Lipstick, Andy Warhol's Bad, The Choirboys, A Different Story, Search and Destroy (Striking Back), Class of 1984, Killing Hour (The Clairvoyant), Switch, A Cry in the Night, The Day After Tomorrow, The Discontents.
TELEVISION: *Movies*: Foster and Laurie, The Cracker Factory, Love's Savage Fury, City in Fear, Inmates: A Love Story, Golden Gate, Helen Keller: The Miracle Continues, The Hasty Heart (Golden Globe nom. 1984), Stranded, Perfect People, Shakedown on Sunset Strip, The Man Who Lived at the Ritz, Disaster at Silo 7, The Prize Pulitzer, Danielle Steel's Kaleidoscope, Only One Survived, Something to Live For, Sidney Sheldon's A Stranger in the Mirror, Jericho Fever, Good King Wenceslas, She Led Two Lives, Hijacked: Flight 285, Face of Evil, Their Second Chance, The Cowboy and the Movie Star, Titans, The Perfect Wife, Another Pretty Face, Stranger at the Door, The Perfect Neighbor, Home for the Holidays, Framed for Murder. *Pilot:* Half 'n' Half. *Mini-series*: Aspen, The Last Convertible, Captain and the Kings, I'll Take Manhattan, The Man Who Lived at the Ritz. *Series*: The Quest, Riptide, Almost Home, The Trouble With Larry, Melrose Place, Titans, Big Love. *Guest:* More than 80 appearances.

KING, STEPHEN

Writer. b. Portland, ME, Sept. 21, 1947. e. Univ. of Maine at Orono (B.S.). Best-selling novelist specializing in thrillers many of which have been adapted to film by others. Movie adaptations: Carrie, The Shining, The Dead Zone, Christine, Cujo, Children of the Corn, Firestarter, Cat's Eye, Stand By Me (The Body), The Running Man, Pet Sematary, Misery, Apt Pupil, The Lawnmower Man, The Dark Half, Needful Things, The Shawshank Redemption, The Mangler, Dolores Claiborne, Thinner, Night Flier, Apt Pupil, The Green Mile, Stud City (The Body), Desperation, Hearts in Atlantis, Secret Window. TV adaptations: Salem's Lot, It, The Stand, Trucks, The Tommyknockers, The Langoliers, The Shining, Rose Madder, The Diary of .Ellen Rimbauer, Dreamcatcher, Secret Window, Riding the Bullet (also exec. prod.), The Mangler Reborn, The Talisman, The Girl Who Loved Tom Gordon, Bag of Bones, From a Buick 8 (writer, novel), 1408 (writer, short story), Dolan's Cadillac (writer, novel).
PICTURES: Knightriders (actor), Creepshow (s.p., actor), Children of the Corn (s.p.), Silver Bullet (s.p.), Maximum Overdrive (dir., s.p., actor), Creepshow II (actor), Pet Sematary (s.p., actor), Sleepwalkers (s.p., actor), The Rage: Carrie 2 (char. writer), 1408 (writer short story), Diary of the Dead (voice), The Mist, From a Buick 8 (writer, novel), Dolan's Cadillac (writer, novel), Grey Matter (writer).
TELEVISION: *Movies/Mini-series*: Sometimes They Come Back (s.p.), The Stand (actor, Emmy nom. 1994), The Langoliers (actor), Sometimes They Come Back...Again (s.p.),Quicksilver Highway, Sometimes They Come Back..For More (s.p.), Storm of the Century (also prod.), Rose Red, Carrie, Kingdom Hospital, 'Salem's Lot, The Shining (Emmy nom. 1997), Desperation, Children of the Corn. Nightmares and Dreamscapes: From the Stories of Stephen King (also grip), Faithful: Two Diehard Boston Red Sox Fans Chronicle the Historic 2004 Season, Children of the Corn (writer, short story, teleplay). *Series*: Golden Years (creator, writer), Masters of Horror (writer/story), Stephen King's Dead Zone, Haven (writer).

KING, ZALMAN

Actor, Director, Writer. r.n. Zalman King Lefkowitz. b. Trenton, NJ, May 23, 1941. m. writer Patricia Knop.
PICTURES: *Actor:* The Ski Bum, You've Got to Walk It Like You Talk It or You'll Lose the Beat, Neither by Day Nor Night, Some Call It Loving, Trip with the Teacher, Sammy Somebody, The Passover Plot, Blue Sunshine, Tell Me a Riddle, Galaxy of Terror, Saint Francis. *Exec. Prod.:* Roadie (also co-story), Endangered Species, Siesta, Female Perversions, Boca, Business for Pleasure, In God's Hands, A Place Called Truth, Black Sea 213, Chromiumblue.com (also dir.), Body Count: Murder for Hire (doc.,), Crazy Again (doc., also prod., dir., cinematographer), Dance with the Devil (doc., also prod., dir., cinematographer), Scratching the Surface. *Prod./Writer:* 9 1/2 Weeks. *Director/Writer:* Wildfire, Two Moon Junction, Wild Orchid, Wild Orchid II: Two Shades of Blue, Delta of Venus, In God's Hands (also exec. prod.), Radio Silence, Red Shoe Diaries 12: Girl on a Bike (also exec. prod.), Red Shoe Diaries 17: Swimming Naked (also exec. prod.).
TELEVISION: *Movies*: The Iron Men, The Dangerous Days of Kiowa Jones, Stranger on the Run, The Young Lawyers (pilot), The Intruders, Don't Call the Police, Smile Jenny You're Dead, Like Normal People, Red Shoe Diaries (pilot, exec. prod.), Lake Consequence (co-prod., co-writer), ChromiumBlue.com, Austin

Angel. *Series*: Gunsmoke, The Young Lawyers (Golden Globe nom. 1971), Forty Deuce (also exec. prod.), Red Shoe Diaries: Las Vegas (exec. prod., creator, dir. episodes), Wind on Water, Body Language (dir., exec. prod.).

KINGSLEY, BEN

Actor. r.n. Krishna Banji. b. Snaiton, Yorkshire, England, Dec. 31, 1943. Started career with Salford Players, amateur co. in Manchester. Turned pro in 1966 and appeared on London stage at a Chichester Festival Theatre. 1967, joined Royal Shakespeare Co., appearing in A Midsummer Night's Dream, Tempest, Measure for Measure, Merry Wives of Windsor, Volpone, Cherry Orchard, Hamlet, Othello, Judgement. On NY stage in Kean. Played Squeers in Nicholas Nickleby in 1980 in London.
PICTURES: Fear Is the Key (debut, 1972), Gandhi (Academy Award, 2 Golden Globe Awards 1982), Betrayal, Turtle Diary, Harem, Maurice, Testimony, Pascali's Island, Without a Clue, Bugsy (Academy Award nom.; Golden Globe nom. 1992), Sneakers, Dave, Searching for Bobby Fisher (Innocent Moves), Schindler's List, Death and the Maiden, Species, Twelfth Night, The Assignment, Photographing Fairies, Parting Shots, Spooky House, Sexy Beast (Academy Award nom.; Golden Globe nom. 2002), Rules of Engagement, The Confession, A.I. Artificial Intelligence (voice), The Triumph of Love, Tuck Everlasting, All for Nothin', A Sound of Thunder, House of Sand and Fog (Academy Award nom.; Golden Globe nom. 2004), Thunderbirds, Suspect Zero, Valiant (voice), Oliver Twist, Mrs. Harris, Lucky Number Slevin, BloodRayne, Oskur Fishman, Gambit, You Kill Me (also co-exec. prod.), The Last Legion, The Ten Commandments (narr.), The Wackness, Transsiberian, Elegy, War, Inc., The Love Guru, Fifty Dead Men Walking, Shutter Island, Prince of Persia: The Sands of Time, Noah's Ark: The New Beginning (narr.), Crossmaglen, A Birder's Guide to Everything, The Invention of Hugo Cabret.
TELEVISION: *Movies*: Silas Marner: The Weaver of Raveloe, Kean, Oxbridge Blues, Camille, Murderers Among Us: The Simon Wiesenthal Story (Emmy nom.; Golden Globe nom. 1989), Lenin: The Train, The War That Never Ends, Joseph (Emmy nom. 1995), Moses, Weapons of Mass Distraction, The Tale of Sweeney Todd, Crime and Punishment, Alice in Wonderland, Anne Frank: The Whole Story (Emmy nom.; Golden Globe nom. 2001), Mrs. Harris (Emmy nom.; Golden Globe nom. 2006). *Mini-series:* Dickens of London. *Series:* Coronation Street. *Documentaries: As Narr.:* Liberation, The Lost Portrait (actor), Religions of the World (mini), Peace Is Every Step: Meditation in Action: The Life and Work of Thich Nhat Hanh, Islam: Empire of Faith, Unlikely Heroes, Imaginary Witness: Hollywood and the Holocaust (actor). *Guest:* More than 120 appearances.

KINSKI, NASTASSJA

Actress. r.n. Nastassja Nakszynski. b. Berlin, Germany, Jan. 24, 1960. Daughter of late actor Klaus Kinski.
PICTURES: Falsche Bewegung (The Wrong Move; debut, 1975), To the Devil a Daughter, Passion Flower Hotel, Stay as You Are, Tess (Golden Globe Award, 1 other nom. 1981), One From the Heart, Cat People, For Your Love Only, Exposed, The Moon in the Gutter, Unfaithfully Yours, The Hotel New Hampshire, Maria's Lovers, Paris Texas, Revolution, Symphony of Love, Harem, Malady of Love, Silent Night, Torrents of Spring, On a Moonlit Night, Magdalene, The Secret, Night Sun, Faraway So Close!, Crackerjack, Terminal Velocity, The Blonde, The Ring, One Night Stand, Little Boy Blue, Your Friends and Neighbors, Fathers' Day, The Magic of Marciano, Timeshare, Town and Country, The Claim, Off the Menu: The Last Days of Chasen's, Beyond City Limits, American Rhapsody, Say Nothing, .com for Murder, Diary of a Sex Addict, Paradise Found, Beyond the City Limits, All Around the Town, À ton image, Inland Empire.
TELEVISION: For Your Love Only, The Ring, Bella Mafia, Quarantine, A Storm in Summer, Blind Terror, The Day the World Ended, All Around the Town, The Lady Musketeer. *Mini-series:* Les Liasons Dangereuses.

KIRKLAND, SALLY

Actress. b. NY, NY, Oct. 31, 1944. e. Actors Studio, studied acting with Uta Hagen and Lee Strasberg. Achieved notoriety in the 1960s for on-stage nudity (Sweet Eros, Futz), for work in experimental off-off B'way theater and as part of Andy Warhol's inner circle. Appeared as featured actress in over 25 films and countless avant-garde shows, before winning acclaim (and Acad. Award nom.) as the star of Anna (1987). 1983 founded Sally Kirkland Acting Workshop, a traveling transcendental meditation, yoga and theatrical seminar. Formed Artists Alliance Prods. with Mark and David Buntzman, 1988.
THEATRE: The Love Nest, Futz, Tom Paine, Sweet Eros, Witness, One Night Stand of a Noisy Passenger, The Justice Box, Where Has Tommy Flowers Gone?, In the Boom Boom Room (L.A., Drama-Logue's best actress award, 1981), Largo Desolato.
PICTURES: The Thirteen Most Beautiful Woman (1964), Blue, Futz!, Coming Apart, Going Home, The Young Nurses, The Way We Were, Cinderella Liberty, The Sting, Candy Stripe Nurses, Big Bad Mama, Bite the Bullet, Crazy Mama, Breakheart Pass, A Star is Born, Pipe Dreams, Hometown U.S.A., Private Benjamin, The Incredible Shrinking Woman, Human Highway, Love Letters, Fatal Games, Talking Walls, Anna (Academy Award nom.; Golden Globe Award 1988), Melanie Rose (High Stakes), Crack in the Mirror (White Hot), Paint It Black, Cold Feet, Best of the Best, Revenge, Bullseye, Two Evil Eyes, JFK, In the Heat of Passion, The Player, Blast 'Em, Primary Motive, Double Threat, Forever, Paper Hearts (also co-exec. prod.), Eye of the Stranger, Gunmen, Little Ghost, Amnesia, Excess Baggage, Wilbur Falls, Paranoia, It's All About You (cameo), The Island, Edtv, Starry Night, Men Named Milo Women Named Greta, Wish You Were Dead, The Boys Behind the Desk, The Audit, Off the Black, Thank You Goodnight, The Rose Technique, A Month of Sunday, Mango Me, The Chocolate Fairy, Bruce Almighty, Neo Ned, A-List (also co-prod.), Spiritual Warriors, Factory Girl, Fingerprints, Big Stan, Under the Knife, Blind Spot (also assoc. prod.), Resurrection Mary, Richard III, Oak Hill (also prod.), Fast Track, The Last Gamble, One by One: Death's Door (also prod.), Lights Out, Make a Wish (also prod., co-exec. prod.), The Wayshower: Lord of the Realms.
TELEVISION: *Movies*: Kansas City Massacre, Death Scream, Stonestreet: Who Killed the Centerfold Model?, Georgia Peaches, Heat Wave, The Haunted (Golden Globe nom. 1992). Double Jeopardy, The Woman Who Loved Elvis, Double Deception, Another Woman's Husband, Night of the Wolf, Another Pretty Face. *Series*: General Hospital, Falcon Crest, Valley of the Dolls, Days of Our Lives, Head Case. *Specials*: Willow B—Women in Prison, Summer, Largo Desolato, The Westing Game, Brave New World. *Guest*: More than 100 appearances.

KIRKWOOD, GENE

Producer, Actor. b.New York, NY, April 21, 1945. The Kirkwood Company.
PICTURES: Rocky, New York New York (assoc. prod.), Comes a Horseman, Uncle Joe Shannon, The Idolmaker, Gorky Park, The Keep, The Pope of Greenwich Village, Ironweed, UHF, Guilty by Suspicion, Night and the City, What Makes Sammy Run, The Net, Gia a Thing of Beauty, The Crossing Guard, The Duke of Deception, At First Sight, Get Rich or Die Tryin' (exec. prod.), Nina (prod.).
TELEVISION: *Movie:* The Magnificent Ambersons (prod.). *Series:* Interscope Presents 'The Next Episode' (exec. prod.).

KITANO, TAKESHI

Director, Writer. b. Tokyo, Japan, Jan. 18, 1948. Also actor in numerous Japanese films.
PICTURES: Merry Christmas Mr. Lawrence (actor only), Yasha (actor only), Comic Magazine (actor only), Violent Cop (also actor), Boiling Point (also actor), A Scene at the Sea (also ed.), Sonatine (also ed., actor), Many Happy Returns (actor, novel only), Getting Any? (also actor, ed.), Johnny Mnemonic (actor only), The Five (actor only), Kids Return (also ed.), Fireworks (also actor, ed.), Tokyo Eyes (actor only), Kikujiro no natsu, Brother, Zatoichi (also editor), Izo (actor only), Blood and Bones, To Each His Cinema (segment dir.), Glory to the Filmmaker! (actor, editor), The Monster X Strikes Back: Attack the G8 Summit (voice), Achilles and the Tortoise (writer, dir., editor), Outrage (writer, dir., editor).

KLEIN, JONATHAN

Executive. e. Brown Univ., history degree, magna cum laude,1980. Klein began his TV career in 1980 as a news producer at WLNE in Providence, R.I., and the following year moved to a similar position at WPIX-TV/Independent Network News in New York. In 1982, joined CBS News as writer/news editor on the overnight broadcast, Nightwatch. He subsequently served as broadcast producer on CBS Morning News and then CBS Evening News Weekend Edition, where he won an Emmy Award for live coverage of the 1986 Reagan/Gorbachev summit in Reykjavik, Iceland. In 1988, Klein became field producers on prime-time magazine series 48 Hours, and won an Emmy Award for coverage of Hurricane Hugo and a Peabody Award for an hour he produced on the anti-abortion movement. Klein served as sr. producer for CBS' 1990 late-night series America Tonight with Charles Kuralt and Lesley Stahl as sr. producer for 1991 coverage of Gulf War; and later for the documentary Back to Baghdad. In 1993, Klein launched a prime-time documentary series, Before Your Eyes, with a two-hour movie-of-the-week format that explored social issues such as child abuse, AIDS and juvenile delinquency through the eyes of real people living through dramatic moments with the cameras rolling. The series, which Klein exec. produced and directed, was acclaimed for pioneering new forms of storytelling and received numerous national awards. In 1997, Klein conceived and executive produced the CBS documentary, Inside the Jury Room, in which network TV cameras were permitted for the first time to observe deliberations in a criminal trial. The documentary won a Columbia-DuPont Silver Baton. Klein also wrote the story for the TNT Original film, Buffalo Soldiers, a 1997 historical drama starring Danny Glover. In 1999, Klein became the pres. & CEO of The FeedRoom, a broadband video company he founded. Under his direction, The FeedRoom became one of the leading online broadcasters in the world, delivering more than 1 million video clips each day to customers including CBS, NBC, ESPN, Reuters, Tribune television stations and newspapers, USA Today, Business Week, General Motors, Cisco Systems, Sun Microsystems, General Mills and the U.S. Department of Defense. In Nov. 2004 Klein assumed his current position of pres. CNN/U.S. and is responsible for management oversight of all programming, editorial tone and strategic direction of the network. He reports to Jim Walton, president of CNN Worldwide.

KLEIN, ROBERT

Actor, Comedian. b. New York, NY, Feb. 8, 1942. e. Alfred U, Yale Drama School. Was member of Chicago's Second City comedy group. Comedy albums: Child of the '50s (Grammy nom.), Mind Over Matter, New Teeth, Let's Not Make Love.
THEATRE: NY: The Apple Tree, Morning Noon and Night, New Faces of 1968, They're Playing Our Song (Tony Award nom.), The Sisters Rosensweig.
PICTURES: The Landlord, The Owl and the Pussycat, Rivals, The Bell Jar, Hooper, Nobody's Perfekt, The Last Unicorn (voice), Tales from the Darkside—The Movie, Radioland Murders, Mixed Nuts, Jeffrey, One Fine Day, Next Stop Wonderland, Primary Colors, Suits, Labor Pains, The Safety of Objects, Pinero, People I know, Two Weeks Notice, How to Lose a Guy in 10 Days, Ira and Abby, Reign Over Me, Dirty Movie, Demoted, The Back-up Plan.
TELEVISION: *Movies*: Your Place or Mine, Poison Ivy, This Wife for Hire, Robert Klein: The Amorous Busboy of Decatur Avenue (actor, writer/book, composer, exec. prod.). *Series*: Comedy Tonight, Robert Klein Time, TV's Bloopers and Practical Jokes, Sisters, Bob Patterson, The Stones, Wyclef Jean in America. Also appeared in HBO comedy specials, including recent From Where I Sit and Child in His 50's (Emmy nom. 2001). *Guest*: More than 130 appearances.

KLEISER, RANDAL

Director, Producer. b. Lebanon, PA, July 20, 1946. e. U. of Southern California. For Disney Theme Parks dir. 70mm 3-D film Honey I Shrunk the Audience.
PICTURES: Street People (s.p.). Director: Grease, The Blue Lagoon, Summer Lovers (also s.p.), Grandview U.S.A., Flight of the Navigator, North Shore (exec. prod., co-story only), Big Top Pee-Wee, Getting it Right (also co-prod.), White Fang, Return to the Blue Lagoon (exec. prod. only), Honey I Blew Up the Kid, It's My Party, Shadow of Doubt, Vanilla Gorilla, Crazy in Alabama, Circuit, Red Riding Hood, Lovewrecked, Live Stream (also writer).
TELEVISION: *Movies*: All Together Now, Dawn: Portrait of a Teenage Runaway, The Boy in the Plastic Bubble, The Gathering (Emmy nom. 1978), Royal Standard, The O.Z. *Series*: Marcus Welby, M.D., The Rookies, Lucas Tanner, Starsky and Hutch, Family, New York News.

KLINE, JACK M.

Executive. b. West Point, NY, Dec. 11, 1950. e. B.A. degree in psychology, Univ. of Tampa. Kline received engineering training as a Combat Engineer Officer, United States Marine Corps, 1972 - 1976, and was honorably discharged as Captain. Kline joined Christie Digital Systems USA, Inc. in 1979 as a national sales representative. He was promoted to v.p., sales and marketing in 1988. In 1992, Kline helped engineer the merger of Christie with Xenon lamp manufacturer Ushio, Inc., a move that transformed the $4 million organization into a $70 million corporation operating on an international scale. In 1997, Jack was named executive v.p. & COO and he was appointed to his present position as president & COO in 1999. Among Kline's major accomplishments were Christie's new acquisition strategies that helped to rapidly establish Christie as a major force in the digital projection arena. The acquisition of Canadian digital projector manufacturer Electrohome Projection Systems in 1999 further strengthened Christie's increasingly dynamic leadership role in the industry's global conversion from 35mm film to cutting-edge digital cinema technology. In 2000, Christie became the world's first licensee of Texas Instruments' DLP® cinema technology, a move that catapulted the company from a 35mm analog manufacturer to a global provider of high powered, high performance digital projection products and the global leader in digital cinema development. In 2005, Kline played a critical role in designing the industry's first practical framework for the installation of digital cinema, successfully creating strategic partnerships with major Hollywood studios, exhibitors, projector manufacturers and technology providers that helped launch the digital cinema revolution. Kline is a member of the Society of Motion Picture & Television Engineers (SMPTE), Motion Picture Pioneers, and International Theatre Equipment Association (ITEA).

KLINE, KEVIN

Actor. b. St. Louis, MO, Oct. 24, 1947. e. Indiana U, School of Music. Studied at Juilliard Drama Center (1970-72), and became founding member of John Houseman's The Acting Company, touring in classics, incl. The School for Scandal, She Stoops to Conquer, The Lower Depths, The Way of the World. Associate prod., NY Shakespeare Festival, 1993-1997. m. actress Phoebe Cates.
THEATRE: Understudied Raul Julia in Lincoln Center's The Threepenny Opera; The Three Sisters (B'way debut, 1973), On the Twentieth Century (Tony Award, 1978), Loose Ends, The Pirates of Penzance (Tony Award, 1981), Richard III, Henry V (Central Park), Arms and the Man, Hamlet, Much Ado About Nothing, Hamlet (1990, also dir.), Measure for Measure, The Seagull, Henry IV, Mother Courage, The Play What I Wrote, Cyrano.
PICTURES: Sophie's Choice (debut, 1982, Golden Globe nom. 1983), The Pirates of Penzance, The Big Chill, Silverado, Violets Are Blue, Cry Freedom, A Fish Called Wanda (Academy Award for Best Supporting Actor, 1988), The January Man, I Love You to Death, Soapdish (Golden Globe nom. 1992), Grand Canyon, Consenting Adults, Chaplin, Dave (Golden Globe nom. 1994), George Balanchine's The Nutcracker (narrator), Princess Caraboo, French Kiss, Fierce Creatures, The Hunchback of Notre Dame (voice), The Ice Storm, In & Out (Golden Globe nom. 1998), Looking for Richard, Wild Wild West, A Midsummer Night's Dream, The Road to El Dorado, The Hunchback of Notre Dame II (voice), The Anniversary Party, Life As A House, The Palace Thief, Orange County, The Hunchback of Notre Dame II (voice), The Emperor's Club, Picasso at the Lapin Agile, De Lovely (Golden Globe nom. 2005), The Pink Panther, As You Like It, A Prairie Home Companion, Trade, The Tale of Despereaux (voice), Definitely, Maybe, Joueuse, The Extra Man, The Conspirator, Friends with Benefits.
TELEVISION: *Movies:* The Time of Your Life, Cyrano de Bergerac. *Series*: Search For Tomorrow (1976-77), Freedom: A History of Us (doc.). *Specials*: Hamlet (also co-dir.), The Pirates of Penzance, Merlin and the Dragons (narr.), Great Performances (Cyrano, Emmy nom. 2009). *Guest:* More than 82 appearances.

KLUGMAN, JACK

Actor. b. Philadelphia, PA, April 27, 1922. e. Carnegie Tech. Much tv work in 1950's incl. Captain Video, Tom Corbett— Space Cadet, U.S. Steel Hour, Kraft Television Theatre, Playhouse 90. *Author:* Tony and Me.
THEATRE: *B'way:* Saint Joan, Stevedore, Mister Roberts, Gypsy, I'm Not Rappaport, Three Men on a Horse. Tour/Stock: The Odd Couple.
PICTURES: Timetable (debut, 1956), Twelve Angry Men, Cry Terror, The Scarface Mob, Days of Wine and Roses, I Could Go on Singing, The Yellow Canary, Act One, Hail Mafia, The Detective, The Split, Goodbye Columbus, Who Says I Can't Ride a Rainbow?, Two Minute Warning, Dear God, Scene Smoking: Cigarettes, Cinema & the Myth of Cool, When Do We Eat?.
TELEVISION: *Movies*: Fame Is the Name of the Game, Poor Devil, The Underground Man, One of My Wives Is Missing, The Odd Couple: Together Again, Parallel Lives, The Twilight of the Golds. *Mini-series*: Around the World in 80 Days. *Series*: The Greatest Gift (daytime serial; 1954-55), Harris Against the World, The Defenders (Emmy Award 1964), The Odd Couple (2 Emmy Awards, 1971, 1973, 3 other noms.; Golden Globe Award 1974, 1 other nom.), Quincy M.E. (5 Emmy noms.), You Again? *Guest*: More than 131 appearances.

KNIGHT, SHIRLEY

Actress. b. Goessell, KS, July 5, 1936. e. Lake Forest Coll., D.F.A., 1978. Won 1976 Tony Award for Kennedy's Children; Joseph Jefferson Award for Landscape of the Body, 1977; New Jersey Drama Critics Awards for A Streetcar Named Desire, 1979.
THEATRE: *NY:* Cycling Past the Matterhorn, Necessary Targets. *Chicago:* The Landscape of the Body.
PICTURES: Five Gates to Hell (debut, 1959), Ice Palace, The Dark at the Top of the Stairs (Academy Award nom.; 2 Golden Globe noms. 1961) The Couch, Sweet Bird of Youth (Academy Award nom. 1963), House of Women, Flight from Ashiya, The Group, Dutchman (Venice Film Fest. Award), Petulia, The Counterfeit Killer, The Rain People, Juggernaut, Secrets, Beyond the Poseidon Adventure, Endless Love, The Sender, Prisoners, Color of Night, Stuart Saves His Family, Diabolique, Somebody Is Waiting, The Man Who Counted, As Good as It Gets, Little Boy Blue, 75 Degrees in July, The Center of the World, Angel Eyes, The Salton Sea, Divine Secrets of the Ya-Ya Sisterhood, A House on a Hill, Thanks to Gravity, Open Window, Grandma's Boy, Not Fade Away, The Other Side of the Tracks, Paul Blart: Mall Cop, The Private Lives of Pippa Lee, Listen to Your Heart, The Melancholy Fantastic.
TELEVISION: *Movies*: The Outsider, Shadow Over Elveron, Friendly Persuasion, Medical Story, Return to Earth, 21 Hours at Munich, The Defection of Simas Kudirka, Champions: A Love Story, Playing for Time (Emmy nom. 1981), Billionaire Boys Club, Bump in the Night, Shadow of a Doubt, To Save a Child, When Love Kills: The Seduction of John Hearn, A Mother's Revenge, Baby Brokers, The Yarn Princess, A Part of the Family, Children of the Dust, Indictment: The McMartin Trial (Emmy Award, 1995; Golden Globe Award, 1996), Stolen Memories: Secrets from the Rose Garden, Fudge-A-Mania, Dad the Angel and Me, A Promise to Carolyn, If These Walls Could Talk, The Uninvited, Mary & Tim, Convictions, Dying to Be Perfect: The Ellen Hart Pena Story, The Wedding (mini), A Father for Brittany, A Marriage of Convenience, My Louisiana Sky, Shadow Realm, Sudbury, Mrs. Ashboro's Cat, The Dan Show, Shark (pilot). *Series*: Maggie Winters, Desperate Housewives (Emmy nom. 2006). *Specials*: The Country Girl, The Lie. *Guest:* appearances including The Equalizer (Emmy nom. 1989), thirtysomething (Emmy Award, 1988, 1 other nom.), Law and Order (Emmy nom. 1992), NYPD Blue (Emmy Award, 1995). *Guest:* More than 128 appearances.

KOCH, HOWARD W., JR.

Producer. b. Los Angeles, CA, Dec. 14, 1945. Was asst. dir. and in other industry posts before turning to production. Pres. & chief exec. off., Rastar (Peggy Sue Got Married, The Secret of My

Success, Nothing in Common, Violets Are Blue, Amazing Chuck and Grace prod. under presidency); 1987, set up own prod. co. at De Laurentiis Entertainment Group. Oct. 1987: named president of the De Laurentiis Entertainment Group, Resigned April 1988 to produce independently. Treasurer Academy of Motion Picture Arts and Sciences (AMPAS).
PICTURES: Heaven Can Wait, The Other Side of Midnight, The Frisco Kid. *Exec./Co-prod./prod.:* The Idolmaker, Gorky Park, Honky Tonk Freeway, The Keep, A Night in Heaven, The Pope of Greenwich Village, Rooftops, The Long Walk Home, Necessary Roughness, Wayne's World, The Temp, Sliver, Wayne's World 2, Losing Isaiah, Virtuosity, Primal Fear, The Beautician and the Beast, Keeping the Faith (also actor), Frequency, Collateral Damage, Hostage (also unit prod. mngr.), Fear Itself, Blood and Chocolate, Fracture (also unit prod., mngr.), Untraceable (also unit prod., mngr.), Norman, Source Code (exec. prod.).
TELEVISION: *Movie:* The Riverman. *Special:* Frank Sinatra: Ol' Blue Eyes Is Back (stage mngr.).

KOCH, JOANNE
Executive Director. b. New York, NY, Oct. 7, 1929. e. Goddard College, B.A. political science, 1950. Dept. of Film, Museum of Modern Art, as circulation asst., film researcher, motion picture stills archivist, 1950. Early 1960s, technical dir., film dept. MOMA, supervised the implementation of MOMA's film preservation program. 1967, asst. to publisher of Grove Press, active in preparation of Grove's case in I Am Curious Yellow censorship trial. Joined film div., Grove, first in distribution then as tech. dir. and prod. coord. 1971 joined Film Society of Lincoln Center as prog. dir. of Movies-in-the-Parks. 1971 made admin. dir. Exec. dir. of N.Y. Film Festival, Film Comment magazine, Film-in-Education, New Directors/New Films, annual Film Society Tribute and Walter Reade Theater at Lincoln Center. Koch is currently director, new building project for the Film Society of Lincoln Center in New York.

KOEPP, DAVID
Writer. b. Pewaukee, WI, 1964.
PICTURES: Apartment Zero (also prod.), Bad Influence, Toy Soldiers, Death Becomes Her, Jurassic Park, Carlito's Way, The Paper (also prod.) The Shadow, Mission Impossible, Suspicious (dir. only), The Trigger Effect (also dir.), The Lost World: Jurassic Park (also actor), Snake Eyes, Stir of Echoes (also dir.), The Panic Room (also prod.), Spider-Man, Big Trouble (actor only), Secret Window, Spider-Man 2, Zathura, War of the Worlds, Indiana Jones and the Kingdom of the Crystal Skull (s.p.), Ghost Town (also dir.), Angels & Demons, Premium Rush (s.p., dir.).
TELEVISION: *Movies*: Hack. Suspense. *Series*: Hack.

KOENEKAMP, FRED J.
Cinematographer. b. Los Angeles, CA, Nov. 11, 1922. Father was special effects cinematographer Hans F. Koenekamp. Member of American Society of Cinematographers. Received ASC Lifetime Achievemant Award, 2005.
PICTURES: Doctor You've Got to Be Kidding, Sol Madrid, Stay Away Joe, Live a Little Love a Little, Heaven With a Gun, The Great Bank Robbery, Patton (Academy Award nom. 1971), Beyond the Valley of the Dolls, Flap, Skin Game, Billy Jack, Happy Birthday Wanda June, Stand Up and Be Counted, Kansas City Bomber, The Magnificent Seven Ride, Rage, Harry in Your Pocket, Papillon, Uptown Saturday Night, The Towering Inferno (Academy Award, 1975), The Wild McCullochs, Doc Savage, Posse, Embryo, Fun With Dick and Jane, The Other Side of Midnight, Islands in the Stream (Academy Award nom. 1978), The Bad News Bears in Breaking Training, The Dominic Principle, White Line Fever, The Swarm, The Champ, The Amityville Horror, Love and Bullets, When Time Ran Out, The Hunter, First Family, First Monday in October, Carbon Copy, Yes Giorgio, It Came From Hollywood, Two of a Kind, The Adventures of Buckaroo Banzai: Across the 8th Dimension, Stewardess School, Listen to Me, Welcome Home, Flight of the Intruder.
TELEVISION: *Movies*: Disaster on the Coastline, Tales of the Gold Monkey, Money on the Side, Return of the Man from U.N.C.L.E., Summer Fantasies, Whiz Kids, Flight 90—Disaster on the Potomac, Obsessive Love, City Killer, Las Vegas Strip War, A Touch of Scandal, Not My Kid, Hard Time on Planet Earth (pilot), Return of the Shaggy Dog, Foreign Exchange, Splash Too. *Series*: Kung Fu, Salvage 1, The Man From U.N.C.L.E. (Emmy nom.), Hard Time on Planet Earth.

KOENIG, WALTER
Actor, Writer. b. Chicago, Il, Sept. 14, 1936. e. Grinnell Coll. (IA), U. of California. Performed in summer stock; after college enrolled at Neighborhood Playhouse, N.Y.; first acting job in TV's Day in Court. *Author:* Chekov's Enterprise, Buck Alice and the Actor Robot. Creator and writer of comic book series Raver.
PICTURES: Strange Lovers, The Deadly Honeymoon, Star Trek—The Motion Picture, Star Trek II: The Wrath of Khan, Star Trek III: The Search for Spock, Star Trek IV: the Voyage Home, Star Trek V: the Final Frontier, Moontrap, Star Trek VI: The Undiscovered Country, Star Trek: Generations, Drawing Down the Moon, Trekkies, Mad Cowgirl, Star Trek: Of Gods and Men (video), InAlienable (writer, exec. prod.), Scream of the Bikini.
TELEVISION: *Movies*: The Questor Tapes, Goodbye Raggedy Ann, The Privateers, Antony and Cleopatra, Maximum Surge Movie, Bone Eater. *Writer:* Family, The Class of '65, The Powers of Matthew Starr. *Series*: Star Trek. *Guest*: More than 65 appearances.

KOHNER, SUSAN
Actress, b. Los Angeles, CA. Nov. 11, 1936. e. U. of California. m. late designer & author John Weitz. Sons Paul and Christopher Weitz are screenwriters. Mother, Lupita Tovar, was one of Mexico's leading film actresses. Father was talent rep. Paul Kohner. 1954-55. Received Golden Globe Awards, 1959 and 1960. Retired from acting in 1964. Co-chair, Juilliard Council, Juilliard Sch. NY.
THEATRE: Love Me Little, He Who Gets Slapped, A Quiet Place, Rose Tatoo, Bus Stop, St. Joan, Sunday in New York, Take Her She's Mine, Pullman Car, Hiawatha, as well as summer stock.
PICTURES: To Hell and Back (debut, 1955), The Last Wagon, Trooper Hook, Dino, Imitation of Life (Academy Award nom.; Golden Globe Award 1960), The Big Fisherman, The Gene Krupa Story, All the Fine Young Cannibals, By Love Possessed, Freud (Golden Globe nom. 1963).
TELEVISION: Alcoa Hour, Schlitz Playhouse, Four Star Theatre, Matinee Theatre, Climax, Suspicion, Playhouse 90, Route 66, Dick Powell Theatre.

KONCHALOVSKY, ANDREI
Director, Writer. a.k.a. Mikhalkov Konchalovski. b. Moscow, Soviet Union, Aug. 20, 1937. Great grandfather: painter Sourikov; grandfather: painter Konchalovski; father is a writer; mother poet Natalia Konchalovskaia; brother is director Nikita Mikhalkov. e. as pianist Moscow Conservatoire, 1947-57; State Film Sch. (VGIK) under Mikhail Romm (1964). Dir. debut with 1961 short film The Boy and the Pigeon. Worked as scriptwriter during 1960s especially with Andrei Tarkovsky. 1962: asst. to Tarkovsky on Ivan's Childhood. In 1980, moved to U.S. In 1991, moved back to Russia.
THEATRE/OPERA: The Seagull (Theatre de L'Odeon, Paris), Eugene Onegin (La Scala, Milan), La Pique Dame (La Scala, Milan & Bastille Opera, Pairs).
PICTURES: *Writer*: The Steamroller and the Violin, Andrey Rublev, Tashkent City of Bread, The Song of Manshuk, The End of Chieftain, Moscow Chill (also prod.). *Director:* The First Teacher (feature debut, 1965), Asya's Happiness, A Nest of Gentlefolk, Uncle Vanya, Romance for Lovers, Siberiade (Cannes Film Fest. Award, 1979), Maria's Lovers, Runaway Train, Duet for One, Shy People (also co-s.p.), Tango and Cash, Homer and Eddie, Ryaba, My Chicken (writer, dir.), The Inner Circle (also co-s.p.), Assia and the Hen with the Golden Eyes, The Royal Way, House of Fools (also prod./writer), The Forbidden City, Glyanets, To Each His Cinema (segment dir.), Moscow Chill (writer, prod.), The Last Station (exec. prod.), Nutcracker and the Rat King (s.p., dir., prod.).
TELEVISION: *Movies*: Split Cherry Terry (short), The Lion in Winter (Emmy nom. 2004). *Mini-series*: The Odyssey (Part I & II, Emmy Award, 1996).

KONIGSBERG, FRANK
Executive, Producer. b. Kew Gardens, NY, March 10, 1933. e. Yale, Yale Law Sch. Worked as lawyer at CBS for six years; moved to NBC 1960-65 in legal dept. as dir. prog. and talent administration. Left to package TV special for Artists Agency Rep. (later AFA) in Los Angeles; sr. v.p. of West Coast office seven years. Executive producer of many TV series, pilots, variety specials and made-for-TV movies. Currently executive with The Konigsberg-Smith Company based in Los Angeles, CA.
PICTURES: The Joy of Sex, Nine 1/2 Weeks (exec. prod.), Paris Trout, Living in Fear, Holy Water.
TELEVISION: *Movies (all exec. prod.):* Pearl, Ellis Island, Bing Crosby: His Life and Legend (Emmy nom. 1978), Dummy (Emmy nom. 1979), Before and After, Guyana Tragedy: The Story of Jim Jones (Emmy nom. 1980), A Christmas Without Snow, The Pride of Jesse Hallam, Hard Case, Divorce Wars, Coming Out of the Ice, The Glitter Done, Wet Gold, Surviving, Act of Vengeance, As Summers Die, Strong Medicine, Onassis: The Richest Man in the World, Dance til Dawn, Fourth Story, Paris Trout (Emmy nom. 1991), To Save a Child, In Sickness and in Health, Double Edge, Charles and Diana: Unhappily Ever After, Love Can Be Murder, The Tommyknockers, The Yarn Princess, Oldest Living Confederate Widow Tells All (Emmy nom. 1994), A Good Day to Die, A Face to Die for, Titanic, Sweet Temptation, A Loss of Innocence, Deadly Pursuits, The Price of Heaven, Bella Mafia, Like Mother Like Son: The Strange Story of Sante and Kenny Kimes, Caught in the Act, Sex and Lies in Sin City: The Ted Binion Scandal. *Mini-series*: Pearl, Ellis Island (Emmy nom. 1985), The Last Don (Emmy nom. 1997), Children of the Dust (Emmy nom 1995), Jesus (Emmy nom. 2000), The Last Don II, Ben Hur. *Series (exec. prod.):* It's Not Easy, Breaking Away, Dorothy, Rituals, Angel Falls.

KOONIN, STEVE
Executive. b. Atlanta, GA, June 6, 1957. e. B.A., marketing, University of Georgia, 1979. Began career as marketing mgr. for Hiram Walker Distillers. Joined Coca-Cola Co., promotions mgr. from 1986-1989; director of entertainment marketing, 1989-91; global advertising director, 1991-93; v.p., sports entertainment marketing, 1993-97; v.p., brand marketing, 1997-2000; senior

v.p., marketing and asset management, 2000; While at Coca-Cola Koonin worked on two Turner specials and caught the attention of Turner top executives who then recruited Koonin. He joined Turner in 2000 as executive v.p. & general manager of TNT and in mid-2003 added the executive v.p. & COO title with responsibilities for both the TNT and TBS networks. On Oct. 24, 2006, became president of Turner Entertainment Networks, adding TCM and truTV to his oversight. All are part of Turner Broadcasting System, Inc., a subsidiary of Time Warner Inc. The company is a major producer of news and entertainment product and a leading provider of programming for the basic cable industry. Koonin serves on the boards of the Georgia Aquarium and the Fox Theatre.

KOPELSON, ANNE

Producer. m. Producer, Arnold Kopelson.
PICTURES: *Exec. prod.:* Outbreak, Seven, Eraser, Murder at 1600, Mad City, Devil's Advocate, A Perfect Murder, U.S. Marshals, Don't Say a Word, Joe Somebody, Blackout, Twisted.
TELEVISION: *Movies*: Past Tense. *Series*: The Fugitive, Thieves.

KOPELSON, ARNOLD

Producer, Financier, Int'l. Distributor. b. New York, NY, Feb. 14, 1935. e. New York Law Sch., J.D., 1959; NYU, B.S. 1956. Has executive-produced, produced, packaged, developed or distributed with wife, Anne Kopelson over 100 films. Chmn. Arnold Kopelson Prods., Co-chmn. Inter-Ocean Film Sales, Ltd. Named NATO/ShoWest Producer of the Year, 1994. Became of director of the CBS Corp. board in March 2007. Currently runs own production company, Kopelson Entertainment in Hollywood.
PICTURES: *Exec. Prod.:* The Legacy, Lost and Found, Night of the Juggler, Dirty Tricks, Final Assignment, Gimme an "F", Fire Birds, Warlock. *Producer:* Foolin' Around, Platoon (Acad. Award for Best Picture, 1986), Triumph of the Spirit, Out for Justice, Falling Down, The Fugitive (Acad. Award nom.), Outbreak, Se7en, Eraser, Murder at 1600, Mad City, The Devil's Advocate, A Perfect Murder, U.S. Marshals, Don't Say a Word, Joe Somebody, Blackout, Twisted.
TELEVISION: *Movie*: Past Tense. *Series*: The Fugitive, Thieves.

KOPLOVITZ, KAY

Executive. b. Milwaukee, WI, April 11, 1945. e. U. Wis., 1967, BA, Mich. State U., M.A., Communications, 1968. Radio/TV prod., WTMJ-TV, Milwaukee 1967. Ed. Comm. Satellite Corp. 1968-72. Dir. Community Svcs. UA Columbia Cablevision 1973-75. VP, Exec. dir. UA Columbia Satellite Services, Inc. 1977-80. Founder, pres., CEO USA Network and Sci-Fi Channel 1980-1998. Jan-June 2001, CEO Working Women Network. Currently a principal of Koplovitz & Co., a media investment firm. Member Nat'l Cable TV Assn. 1984-. Nat'l. Acad. TV Arts and Sciences 1984-95. Women in Cable 1979-83. In 1998, President Bill Clinton appointed Koplovitz chair of the National Woman's Business Council, a bi-partisan commission to advance opportunities for women entrepreneurs. She then created and co-founded Springboard Enterprises, a national organization that raised nearly $2 billion in equity for women-led firms. Currently she is chmn & CEO of Koplovitz & Co. a media advisory and investment firm. She served as bd. chmn. of cable network, Reality Central in 2004. Koplovitz is a member on the corporate boards of Instinet and Liz Claiborne and previously served on the boards of Oracle, Nabisco and General Reinsurance Corporation. She is chair of the Board of Broadway Television Network, and serves on the Board if Miavita. Also on Board of Trustees for the Museum of Television and Radio in New York City, she heads the Corporate Partners Program for, and is a trustee of, the Central Park Conservancy, and serves on the board of the New York City Partnership and the International Tennis Hall of Fame.

KOPPEL, TED

TV News Correspondent, Anchor, Host. b. Lancashire, England, Feb. 8, 1940. To U.S. in 1953; became citizen, 1963. e. Syracuse U, Stanford U. Started as writer and news correspondent for WMCA radio in NYC. Joined ABC News in New York, 1963, serving as correspondent in Vietnam, 1967, 1969-71; Miami Bureau chief, 1968; Hong Kong Bureau chief, 1969-71; diplomatic correspondent, 1971-76, 1977-79. Anchor of NBC Saturday Night News, 1976-77. Host of Nightline, 1980-Nov. 2005. Joined Discovery Networks in Jan. 2006 with several of his former Nightline producers to produce six-10 programs a year in the documentary/special event news genre. The National Academy of Television Arts & Sciences (NATAS) honored Koppel with a lifetime achievement award at the 28th annual News & Documentary Emmy Awards in Sept. 2007. *Author:* The Wit and Wisdom of Adlai Stevenson, In the National Interest.
TELEVISION: *Series*: ABC News (1971-80), ABC Saturday Night News (1975-77); America Held Hostage (host), Nightline (1980-2005, 3 Emmy Awards, 2 other noms.), 20/20 (1986). Host/anchor/writer of many ABC news specials, Koppel on Discovery (exec. prod, host). *Special:* US Election Night (2008).

KOPPLE, BARBARA

Director, Producer.
PICTURES: *Dir.:* Harlan County USA (also prod., Academy Award, Best Doc., LA Film Crits. Special Award, 1976), American Dream (Academy Award, Best Doc., 1990, DGA Award, 1992, Cannes Film Festival Grand Jury Prize, 1991), Beyond JFK: The Question of Conspiracy, Woodstock '94 (also prod.), Wild Man Blues, A Conversation with Gregory Peck, My Generation (also s.p.). *Prod.:* American Standoff, WMD: Weapons of Mass Deception, Havoc, Shut Up & Sing, Kevorkian Chronicles (also dir.).
TELEVISION: *Movies/dir.:* Keeping On, The Hamptons Project. *Series/dir.:* Homicide: Life in the Street (DGA Award, 1998), Oz. *Mini-series/dir.:* A Century of Women (Emmy nom. 1995), The Hamptons. *Series:* I Married...(dir.). *Documentaries: As Dir./Prod:* Fallen Champ: The Mike Tyson Story (DGA Award, Emmy nom. 1994), Harlan County, U.S.A., American Dream, Beyond 'JFK': The Question of Conspiracy, Wild Man Blues, Woodstock '94, My Generation (also writer), American Standoff, Bearing Witness, High School Musical: The Music in You, Addiction (segment dir., prod.), Small Steps: Creating the High School for Contemporary Arts (prod.), The D.C. Sniper's Wife: A Barbara Kopple Film, Woodstock: Now & Then.

KORMAN, LEWIS J.

Executive. b. 1945. Partner, Kaye, Scholer, Fierman, Hays & Handler 1978; founding partner, Gelberg & Abrams where pioneered dev. of public limited partnerships, Delphi Partners, to help finance Columbia Pictures' and Tri-Star Pictures' films. 1986, became consultant to Tri-Star involved in negotiations that led to acquisition of Loews Theatre Corp. that year. Joined Tri-Star, 1987, as sr. exec. v.p. In 1988 appt. to additional post of COO and named dir. of Columbia Pictures Entertainment Inc.; 1989 also became chmn, Motion Picture Group. 1990, resigned his positions after Columbia sale to Sony. Co-founder, pres. & COO of Savoy Pictures Ent., Inc., 1992. Currently, vice-chmn., R.A.B. Holdings, Inc. and dir., The B. Manischewitz Company, LLC, pres., Delphi Film Enterprises, Ltd. Co-founder and current chairman of EpiCom Media, LLC.

KORTY, JOHN

Director, Producer, Writer, Animator. b. Lafayette, IN, June 22, 1936. e. Antioch Coll, B.A. 1959. President, Korty Films. Currently talent manager for The Coppage Co.
PICTURES: Crazy Quilt (1966), Funnyman, Riverrun, Alex and the Gypsy, Oliver's Story, Twice Upon a Time.
TELEVISION: *Movies*: The People, Go Ask Alice, Class of '63, The Autobiography of Miss Jane Pittman (Emmy & 2 DGA Awards, 1974), Farewell to Manzanar (Humanitas, Christopher Awards, Emmy nom. 1976), Forever, A Christmas Without Snow (also writer, prod.), The Haunting Passion, Second Sight: A Love Story, The Ewok Adventure, Resting Place (Emmy nom. 1986), Baby Girl Scott, Eye on the Sparrow, Winnie, Cast the First Stone, A Son's Promise, Line of Fire: The Morris Dees Story, Long Road Home, Deadly Matrimony, They, Getting Out, Redwood Curtain, Scrooge, Oklahoma City: A Survivor's Story, Gift of Love: The Daniel Huffman Story. *Documentaries:* Who Are the DeBolts? And Where Did They Get Nineteen Kids? (Academy Award, 1977; Emmy & DGA Awards, 1978-79). Short Films: The Language of Faces (AFSC, 1961), Imogen Cunningham: Photographer (AFI grant, 1970), The Music School. Animation: Breaking the Habit (Academy Award nom. 1965), Twice Upon a Time.

KOSSE, DAVID

Executive. e. B.A. in business admin. and journalism from Univ. of Oregon at Eugene, 1984. Kosse held positions with Ogily and Mather Worldwide and HBO Video before teaming with PolyGram Film International in 1993, as a sr. dir. of marketing-video, where he established the company's U.S. division. 1995, promoted to v.p.-marketing; 1997, upped to sr. v.p. for film, video & TV. From PolyGram, Kosse became chmn. of Universal Pictures UK. In that role he managed the day-to-day operations of Universal Pictures UK film and home entertainment distribution operations. Kosse then launched and headed independent film distrib. Momentum Pictures in April 2000 with financing from Canadian media company Alliance Atlantis. Kosse left Momentum in October 2003 when 49% of the company was sold as part of an income trust public offering. From 2004 to 2006, Kosse served as president, international marketing and distribution, for Universal Pictures' international theatrical interests. There, he oversaw the release of such international blockbusters as Bridget Jones: The Edge of Reason, The Bourne Supremacy, King Kong, and The Holiday. In July 2006, Kosse assumed his current position, president of Universal Pictures International, following the decision of Universal and Paramount to end their international joint venture, UIP, in major territories. On January 1, 2007, Universal Pictures International became the studio's overseas marketing and distribution company, with offices on four continents. Kosse is based in London and oversees Universal's theatrical operations and has strategic management responsibilities for international releases of all Universal films. Kosse sat on the British Academy of Film and Television Arts film committee and has headed two BAFTA juries.

KOTCHEFF, TED

Director. r.n. William Theodore Kotcheff. b. Toronto, Canada, April 7, 1931. Ent. TV ind. 1952. After five years with Canadian Broadcasting Corp. joined ABC-TV in London, 1957.
THEATRE: London: Progress the Park, Play with a Tiger, Luv,

Maggie May, The Au Pair Man, Have You Any Dirty Washing, Mother Dear?
PICTURES: Tiara Tahiti (debut, 1963), Life at the Top, Two Gentlemen Sharing, Wake in Fright, Outback, Billy Two Hats, The Apprenticeship of Duddy Kravitz, Fun with Dick and Jane, Who Is Killing the Great Chefs of Europe?, North Dallas Forty (also co-s.p.), First Blood, Split Image (also prod.), Uncommon Valor (also exec. prod.), Joshua Then and Now, The Check is in the Mail (prod. only), Switching Channels, Winter People, Weekend at Bernie's (also actor), Folks!, The Shooter, The Populist, Shattered Glass, Rambo (tech. consult), 1066 (prod.).
TELEVISION: *Movies*: A Family of Cops, A Husband a Wife and a Lover, Borrowed Hearts, Crime in Connecticut: The Story of Alex Kelly. *Series*: Buddy Faro, Law & Order: Special Victims Unit (dir., prod., exec. prod., co-exec. prod.). *Specials*: Of Mice and Men, Desperate Hours, The Human Voice.

KOTEAS, ELIAS

Actor. b. Montreal, Quebec, Canada, 1961. e. AADA.
PICTURES: One Magic Christmas, Some Kind of Wonderful, Gardens of Stone, Tucker: The Man and His Dream, Full Moon in Blue Water, Malarek, Blood Red, Friends Lovers and Lunatics, Teenage Mutant Ninja Turtles, Backstreet Dreams, Desperate Hours, Look Who's Talking Too, Almost an Angel, The Adjuster, Teenage Mutant Ninja Turtles III, Chain of Desire, Camilla, Exotica, The Prophecy, Hit Me, Crash, Gattaca, The Thin Red Line, Fallen, Apt Pupil, Divorce: A Contemporary Western, Dancing at the Blue Iguana, Harrison's Flowers, Lost Souls, Novocaine, Collateral Damage, Ararat, The Greatest Game Ever Played, Skinwalkers, Dark Streets, Zodiac, Shooter, The Girl in the Park, Two Lovers, The Haunting in Connecticut, The Curious Case of Benjamin Button, I Come with the Rain, Three Backyards, Defendor, The 4th Kind, Shutter Island, The Killer Inside Me, My Own Love Song, Let Me In, Dream House, Down and Dirty Pictures.
TELEVISION: *Movies:* Private Sessions, Onassis: The Richest Man in the World, The Habitation of Dragons, Sugartime, Shot in the Heart, Lights Out. *Mini-series:* Traffic. *Series:* Conviction (pilot), American Dad! (voice).

KOTTO, YAPHET

Actor. b. New York, NY, Nov. 15, 1937. Has many stage credits, including starring roles on Broadway in The Great White Hope, The Zulu and the Zayda. Off-B'way: Blood Knot, Black Monday, In White America, A Good Place To Raise a Boy.
AUTHOR: The Royalty (autobiography).
PICTURES: The Limit (also prod.), 4 for Texas, Nothing But a Man, 5 Card Stud, Thomas Crown Affair, The Liberation of L. B. Jones, Man and Boy, Across 110th Street, Bone, Live and Let Die, Truck Turner, Report to the Commissioner, Sharks' Treasure, Friday Foster, Drum, Monkey Hustle, Blue Collar, Alien, Brubaker, Fighting Back, Star Chamber, Eye of the Tiger, Warning Sign, Prettykill, The Running Man, Midnight Run, Nightmare of the Devil (also prod., dir.), Terminal Entry, Jigsaw, A Whisper to a Scream, Tripwire, Ministry of Vengeance, Hangfire, Freddy's Dead, Almost Blue, Intent to Kill, The Puppet Masters, Out-of-Sync, Two If By Sea, Witless Protection.
TELEVISION: *Movies*: Night Chase, Raid on Entebbe (Emmy nom. 1977), Rage, Playing With Fire, The Park Is Mine, Women of San Quentin, Badge of the Assassin, Harem, Desperado, Perry Mason: The Case of the Scandalous Scoundrel, Prime Target, After the Shock, Chrome Soldiers, It's Nothing Personal, Extreme Justice, The American Clock, The Corpse Had a Familiar Face, Deadline for Murder: From the Files of Edna Buchanan, Defenders: The Payback, Homicide: The Movie, The Ride, Stiletto Dance. *Mini-series:* Roots. *Series*: For Love and Honor, Homicide: Life on the Street (also writer). *Guest:* More than 65 appearances.

KOZAK, HARLEY JANE

Actress. b. Wilkes-Barre, PA, Jan. 28, 1957. e. NYU's School of the Arts. Member of Nebraska Repertory Theatre.
PICTURES: House on Sorority Row, Clean and Sober, When Harry Met Sally..., Parenthood, Sideout, Arachnophobia, Necessary Roughness, The Taking of Beverly Hills, All I Want for Christmas, The Favor, Magic in the Water, Dark Planet, The Lovemaster, The Red Queen.
TELEVISION: *Movies*: So Proudly We Hail, The Amy Fisher Story, The Android Affair, Unforgivable, A Friend's Betrayal, The Love Master, Emma's Wish. *Series*: The Guiding Light, Santa Barbara, Texas, Harts of the West, Bringing Up Jack, You Wish. *Mini-series*: Titanic.

KOZLOWSKI, LINDA

Actress. b. Fairfield, CT. Jan. 7, 1956. m. actor Paul Hogan. Began professional acting career soon after graduating from Juilliard Sch., N.Y., 1981. Stage debut in How It All Began at the Public Theatre. In regional theatre appeared in Requiem, Translations, Make and Break, as well as on Broadway and on tour with Dustin Hoffman in Death of a Salesman and the TV adaptation.
PICTURES: Crocodile Dundee (Golden Globe nom. 1987), Crocodile Dundee II, Pass the Ammo, Helena, Almost an Angel, The Neighbor, Backstreet Justice, Zorn, Village of the Damned, Crocodile Dundee in Los Angeles.
TELEVISION: *Movies*: Death of a Salesman, Zorn, Shaughnessy. *Mini-series:* Favorite Son.

KRABBÉ, JEROEN

Actor. b. Amsterdam, The Netherlands, Dec. 5, 1944. Trained for stage at De Toneelschool, Acad. of Dramatic Art, Amsterdam, 1965. Also studied at painting at Acad. of Fine Arts, grad. 1981. Founded touring theater co. in the Netherlands and translated plays into Dutch. Also costume designer. As a painter, work has been widely exhibited (one-man show at Francis Kyle Galleries, London). Author: The Economy Cookbook. Theatre dir. debut, new stage adaptation of The Diary of Anne Frank, 1985 in Amsterdam.
PICTURES: Soldier of Orange, A Flight of Rainbirds, Spetters, The Fourth Man, Turtle Diary, Jumpin' Jack Flash, No Mercy, The Living Daylights, Shadow of Victory, A World Apart, Crossing Delancey, Shadowman, Scandal, The Punisher, Melancholia, Till There Was You, Kafka, The Prince of Tides, For a Lost Soldier, The Fugitive, King of the Hill, Immortal Beloved, Farinelli, Blood of a Poet, Business for Pleasure, Lorca, Dangerous Beauty, Left Luggage (dir. debut), Dangerous Beauty, Ever After, An Ideal Husband, Ausverkauft, The Sky Will Fall, The Discovery of Heaven, Ocean's Twelve, Off Screen, Man with a Movie Camera, Deuce Bigalow: European Gigolo, Leef!, Transporter 3, Yankee Go Home, Schweitzer, Gangster Kittens.
TELEVISION: *Movies*: Danton's Death (debut, 1966), World War III. One for the Dancer, Family of Spies, Secret Weapon, Robin Hood (theatrical in Europe), Murder East Murder West, Dynasty: The Reunion, Stalin, Business for Pleasure, Only Love, Jesus. *Mini-series*: The Odyssey, After the War, The Great War, Willem van Oranje. Series: Verborgen gebreken.

KRAMER, LARRY

Writer, Producer. b. Bridgeport, CT, June 25, 1935. e. Yale U., B.A. 1957. Ent. m.p. ind. 1958. Story edit. Columbia Pictures, N.Y. London 1960-65. Asst. to David Picker and Herb Jaffe, UA, 1965. Assoc. prod. and additional dialogue Here We Go Round the Mulberry Bush, 1968. *Writer/prod.:* Women in Love (Academy Award nom. for s.p., 1971). Lost Horizon, 1973 (s.p.). *Novel:* Faggots (1978). *Theater:* The Normal Heart (NY Shakespeare Festival and throughout the world), Just Say No, The Destiny of Me. Cofounder: Gay Men's Health Crisis, Inc. (community AIDS org.). Founder: ACT UP: AIDS Coalition to Unleash Power (AIDS activist andprotest org.). *Book of Essays:* Reports from the Holocaust: The Story of an AIDS Activist (St. Martin's Press, 1995).

KRANE, JONATHAN

Executive, Producer. b. 1952. m. actress Sally Kellerman. e. St. Johns College, grad. with honors, 1972; Yale Law School, 1976. Joined Blake Edwards Entertainment in 1981, becoming pres. Formed talent management co. Management Company Entertainment Group representing clients such as John Travolta, Sally Kellerman, Kathryn Harrold, Sandra Bernhard, Howie Mandel, Drew Barrymore, others. Began producing vehicles for clients and transformed co. into production, distribution, management and finance co. Currently is producer/CEO/chairman of Jonathan Krane Group.
PICTURES: *Exec. prod./prod.:* Boardwalk, Honeymoon, Fly Away Home, The Man Who Loved Women, Micki & Maude, A Fine Mess, That's Life, The Chocolate War, The Experts, Fatal Charm, Boris and Natasha, Look Who's Talking, Chud II: Bud the Chud, Without You I'm Nothing (prod.), Look Who's Talking Too, Convicts, Cold Heaven, Breaking the Rules, Look Who's Talking Now, Face/Off, Lay of the Land, Primary Colors, Mad City, The General's Daughter, Battlefield Earth, Lucky Numbers, Swordfish, Domestic Disturbance, Standing Room Only, Basic, A Modern Twain Story: The Prince and the Pauper, Father of Invention (also writer).
TELEVISION: *Prod.: Movies:* Fatal Charm, Chains of Gold, Bar Hopping. *Series:* Good Grief, Howie Mandel Life at Carnegie Hall, Howie Mandel: The North American Watusi Tour, The Screening Room (prod., host).

KRAUSE, BRIAN

Actor. b. El Toro, California, February 1, 1969.
PICTURES: Return to the Blue Lagoon, December, An American Summer, Sleepwalkers, The Liars Club, Naked Souls, Breaking Free, Within the Rock, Mind Games, Get a Job, Trash, Dreamers, The HeadHunter, Protecting the King, Desertion, Jack Rio, The Thacker Case, Nowhere to Hide, Growth, The Gods of Circumstance, Cyrus (also 2nd unit dir.), You're So Cupid!, Next Stop Murder, Rain from Stars, Camel Spiders.
TELEVISION: *Movies:* Earth Angel, Teen Vid 2, American Eyes, Bandit: Bandit Goes Country, Bandit: Bandit Bandit, Bandit: Beauty and the Bandit, Bandit: Bandit's Silver Angel, Family Album, Extreme Blue, 919 Fifth Avenue, The Women of Charmed, Within the Rock, Ties That Bind, Return to Cabin by the Lake, Loch Ness, Beyond Loch Ness, Devil's Diary, Warbirds. *Series:* Another World, Charmed. *Guest:* More than 62 appearances.

KRIGE, ALICE

Actress. b. Upington, South Africa, June 28, 1954. Moved to London at 21 and studied at Central School of Speech and

Drama. Professional debut on British TV: The Happy Autumn Fields. In London prod. of Forever Yours, Maylou. West End debut, Arms and the Man, 1981. Two seasons with Royal Shakespeare Co. at Stratford and London (The Tempest, King Lear, The Taming of the Shrew, Cyrano de Bergerac, Bond's Lear.), Venice Preserved at the Almeida, 1995.
PICTURES: Chariots of Fire (debut, 1981), Ghost Story, King David, Barfly, Haunted Summer, See You in the Morning, S.P.O.O.K.S., Sleepwalkers, Habitat, Institute Benjamenta, Amanda, Star Trek: First Contact, Twilight of the Icenymphs, The Commissioner, The Little Vampire, Molokai: The Story of Father Damien, The Calling, Superstition, Falling, Reign of Fire, Shadow of Fear, Silent Hill, Lonely Hearts, Ten Inch Hero, The Contract, Skin, Solomon Kane, The Sorcerer's Apprentice.
TELEVISION: *Movies*: Wallenberg: A Hero's Story, Dream West, A Tale of Two Cities, Second Serve, Baja Oklahoma, Max and Helen, Iran: Days of Crisis, Ladykiller, Judgment Day: The John List Story, Double Deception, Jack Reed: Badge of Honor, Scarlet & Black, Sharpes Honour, Summer, Devil's Advocate, Donor Unknown, Joseph, Hidden in America, Like Father Like Son, Indefensible: The Truth About Edward Brannigan, Deep in My Heart, In the Company of Spies, Attila, The Death and Life of Nancy Eaton, The Mystery of Natalie Wood, Dynasty: The Making of a Guilty Pleasure, Persuasion, Persuasion, Heroes and Villains: Napoleon. *Mini-series*: Ellis Island, The Strauss Dynasty, The Scarlet and the Black, Dream West, Close Relations, Atilla, Dinotopia, Children of Dune, The Line of Beauty. *Series:* Deadwood, The 4400. *Guest:* More than 65 appearnces.

KRISTOFFERSON, KRIS

Actor, Singer. b. Brownsville, TX, June 22, 1936. e. Pomona Coll., Oxford U. (Rhodes Scholar). Joined U.S. Army briefly and taught English literature at West Point. Started writing songs (country music), hits have included Me and Bobby McGee, Why Me, Lord, Sunday Mornin' Comin' Down.
PICTURES: The Last Movie, Cisco Pike, Pat Garrett and Billy the Kid, Blume in Love, Bring Me the Head of Alfredo Garcia, Alice Doesn't Live Here Anymore, Vigilante Force, The Sailor Who Fell from Grace with the Sea, A Star Is Born (Golden Globe Award 1977), Semi-Tough, Convoy, Heaven's Gate, Rollover, Flashpoint, Songwriter (Academy Award nom. 1985), Trouble in Mind, Big Top Pee-wee, Millennium, Welcome Home, Original Intent, Night of the Cyclone, Sandino, No Place to Hide, Cheatin' Hearts, Lone Star, Fire Down Below, A Soldier's Daughter Never Cries, Girls' Night, Blade, Dance with Me, Limbo, The Joyriders, Payback, Molokai: The Story of Father Damien, Detox, Comanche, The Ballad of Ramblin' Jack, Planet of the Apes, Wooly Boys, Chelsea Walls, Eye See You, Disappearances, D-Tox, Blade II, Silver City, Blade: Trinity, The Wendell Baker Story, The Jacket, Breakfast on Pluto (singer), Dreamer: Inspired by a True Story, Fun with Dick and Jane (soundtrack writer), Disappearances, Fast Food Nation, Requiem for Billy the Kid, Southland Tales (soundtrack performer), The Last King of Scotland (singer), I'm Not There. (narr.), Powder Blue, For Sale by Owner, He's Just Not That Into You, Jump Out Boys, Watchmen (soundtrack writer), For Sale by Owner, The Last Rites of Ransom Pride, Yohan - Barnevandrer, The Greening of Whitney Brown, Shoedog.
TELEVISION: *Movies:* Freedom Road, The Lost Honor of Kathryn Beck, The Last Days of Frank and Jesse James, Blood and Orchids, Stagecoach, The Tracker, Dead or Alive, Pair of Aces, Another Pair of Aces: Three of a Kind, Miracle in the Wilderness, Christmas in Connecticut, Troubleshooters: Trapped Beneath the Earth, Sodbusters, Inflammable, Brothers' Destiny, Big Dreams & Broken Hearts: The Dottie West Story, Tad, Blue Rodeo, Outlaw Justice, Dead Man's Gun, Two for Texas, The Long Kill, NetForce, Perfect Murder, Perfect Town: JonBenét and the City of Boulder, Lives of the Saints, 14 Hours. *Mini-series*: Amerika, Netforce, American Roots Music (narr.), Lives of the Saints. *Series*: VH1 Legends, Dead Man's Gun (narr.). *Documentaries:* The Unbroken Circle: A Tribute to Mother Maybelle Carter, A Salute to American Imagination, America's Music: The Roots of Country (narr., mini-series), Adventures of the Old West, John Ford Goes to War (narr.), Trudell, Ricky Nelson Sings, The Life and Hard Times of Guy Terrifico (narr.), CMT: 20 Greatest Country Bands (narr.). *Guest:* More than 163 appearances.

KROLL, SUE

Executive. e. Glassboro State University in New Jersey, bachelor's degree, communications. Kroll worked seven years in New York for various Viacom divisions, including Showtime Networks Inc., The Movie Channel and Viewer's Choice. At Turner Network Television, she served as senior v.p. & managing dir. of TNT and Cartoon Network and headed up Turner's marketing dept., developing and directing marketing and promotional campaigns for the network and its programs. She joined Warner Bros. in 1994, heading programming & operations for its international channels. In this role, Kroll devised the strategy and launch of the studio's venture into the international branded cable channels business. Her success led to a promotion to the film group, where she became senior v.p., international marketing; she became president, international marketing in 2000. Since that appointment, Kroll has helped lead the division to seven consecutive years, 2001-2007, grossing over $1 billion, with 32 releases each grossing over $100 million internationally in that period. In 2004, Warner Bros. Pictures International crossed the $1 billion threshold in less than six months and went on to become the first studio ever to surpass the $2 billion dollar mark in a calendar year. In 2007, Warner Bros.' box office receipts shattered the record with a $2.4 billion total, both a Warner Bros. and industry record. Warner Bros. combined domestic and international marketing operations in 2008 and promoted Kroll to her current position, president, worldwide marketing, Warner Bros. Pictures. In this new post, she oversees the strategic creation and implementation of marketing campaigns in the U.S. and internationally, and directs all aspects of marketing, advertising, media planning, promotion, publicity and research.

KRUEGER, RONALD P.

Executive. b. St. Louis, MO, Oct. 19, 1940. e. Westminister College, 1961. Began working in theatres as teenager. Assumed presidency Wehrenberg Theatres, 1963. Currently is chairman and co-CEO. Son, Ronald P. Krueger II, serves as president. Member: NATO, bd. member; American Film Inst.; Motion Picture Pioneers; Demolay Legion of Honor; Mercantile Bank, bd. member; Big Game Hunters; World Presidents Org. Bd. trustees, Westminster College at Fulton, MO. Divan member. Moolah Temple Shrine. Past Master Tuscan Lodge 360 AF & AM. Scottish Rite 32 KCCH. Advisory bd. chmn., Salvation Army. Recipient of the NATO B.V. Sturdiviant award for Community Service. Member & past pres. of Safari Club Int'l.

KUDROW, LISA

Actress. b. Encino, CA, July, 30, 1963. e. Vassar College, NY, B.S., in biology. Member of The Groundlings improvisational theatre group, 1989-.
PICTURES: L.A. on $5 a Day, The Unborn, Dance with Death, In the Heat of Passion, Unfaithful, Behind Closed Doors, The Crazysitter, Mother, Hacks, Romy and Michele's High School Reunion, Clockwatchers, The Opposite of Sex, I Dream of Jeannie, Analyze This, All Over the Guy, I've Got 2 Babe, Analyze That, Bark, Marci X., Wonderland, Happy Endings, Kabluey, P.S. I Love You, The Deal, The Women, Powder Blue, Will, Hotel for Dogs, Paper Man, Love & Other Impossible Pursuits, Bandslam, Easy A.
TELEVISION: *Movies*: Murder in High Places, Picking Up and Dropping Off (exec. prod.), All In. *Series*: Bob, Mad About You, Friends (Emmy Award, 1998; Emmy noms. 1995, 1997-2001, Golden Globe nom. 1996), Hercules (voice), Hopeless Pictures (voice), The Comeback (also exec. prod., writer, Emmy nom. 2006), Who Do You Think You Are? (US) (doc., exec. prod.), Web Therapy (also writer, exec. prod.). *Guest*: More than 95 appearances.

KUHN, THOMAS G.

Executive, Executive Producer. e. Northwestern U., B.A.; USC, M.B.A. KNBC-TV sales; NBC business affairs; dir. live night time progs. Warner Bros. TV, v.p. prod. TV Pres., RCA Video Prods. Pres., Lightyear Ent., 1987. Received Academy Award of Commendation, 2007.
PICTURES: *Exec. prod.:* Aria, The Return of Swamp Thing, Heaven, The Lemon Sisters, Stories to Remember. With partner Fred Weintraub: The JFK Assassination: The Jim Garrison Tapes, Trouble Bound, Gypsy Eyes, Backstreet Justice, Guinevere, Young Connecticut Yankee, Under the Gun, Amazons and Gladiators, Undertow, Endangered Species, Warrior Angels, Iron Fist, Bruce Lee: Curse of the Dragon, Dream Warrior.
TELEVISION: *Movies: Exec. prod.:* Alice, Torn Between Two Lovers, The Jayne Mansfield Story, A Long Way Home. *Prod.:* Young Ivanhoe, Triplecross, The Devil's Arithmetic, Perilous. *Mini-series:* The Awakening Land (exec. prod.), The Lady Musketeer (prod.). *Series:* Really Naked Truth (exec. prod., writer), The New Adventures of Robin Hood (exec. prod., writer, creator).

KUREISHI, HANIF

Writer. b. South London, Eng., Dec. 5, 1956. e. King's Coll. (philosophy). At 18, first play presented at Royal Court Theatre where he ushered before becoming writer in residence. Early in career, wrote pornography as Antonia French. Stage and TV plays include: The Mother Country, Outskirts, Borderline and adaptations (Mother Courage). The Rainbow Sign, With Your Tongue Down My Throat (novella) and short stories have been pub. Anglo-Pakistani writer's first s.p. My Beautiful Laundrette earned Acad. Award nom., 1986 and began creative relationship with dir. Stephen Frears.
PICTURES: My Beautiful Laundrette (Academy Award nom. 1987), Sammy and Rosie Get Laid, London Kills Me (also dir.), My Son the Fanatic, Mauvaise passe, Intimacy, The Mother, Venus.
TELEVISION: *Mini-series*: The Buddha of Suburbia (s.p., also novel).

KURI, JOHN A.

Producer, Writer. b. Los Angeles, CA, Feb. 16, 1945. Son of set decorator and Disneyland co-designer, Emile Kuri. Began 13 yr. employment with Disney at age 16 in construction and maintenance at Disneyland. Progressed through mgmt. in Park Operations. 1969 transferred to Disney Studios in set decorating.

1973 became art director. 1975 at 20th Century Fox as exec. asst. to prod. Irwin Allen. 1976, formed own co., wrote and prod. both television and motion picture projects. 1979 thru 1982 developed and prod. television in partnership with Ron Howard. 1988 thru 1990 as pres. of Sheffield Ent. developed master broadcasting plan for KCMY TV, Sacramento, CA. Published works: Determined to Live: An American Epic, Remember Wes.
PICTURES: Captive Hearts (prod., co-s.p. 2nd unit dir., co-lyrics.) *Set decorator:* Apple Dumpling Gang, Leadbelly, Report to the Commissioner, Castaway Cowboy, Superdad, The Walking Dead.
TELEVISION: *Movies:* One More Mountain (prod., writer, 2nd unit dir.; Christopher Award, 1994), Conagher (prod.; Western Heritage Award from Cowboy Hall of Fame), Airwolf (2nd unit prod., dir.), Skyward (prod., 2nd unit dir.; Golden Halo Award), Skyward Christmas (prod., 2nd unit dir.), Through the Magic Pyramid (assoc. prod., art dir.). *Art dir.:* The Plutonium Incident, Scared Straight Another Story, Young Love First Love, Marriage is Alive and Well, Little Shots, The Red Pony (and set decorator, Emmy nom., 1973). *Set decorator:* Michael O'Hara IV, Bob & Carol & Ted & Alice (series), The Mouse Factory (22 episodes). *Series:* O'Hara (co-creator).

KURTZ, GARY

Producer, Director. b. Los Angeles, CA, July 27, 1940. e. USC Cinema Sch. Began prof. career during college. Has worked as cameraman, soundman, editor, prod. supervisor and asst. dir. on documentaries and features. Worked on many low budget features for Roger Corman including: The Terror, Beach Ball, Track of the Vampire, Planet of Blood, The Shooting, Ride in the Whirlwind. Drafted into Marines. Spent 2 yrs. in photo field as cameraman, editor and still photo.
PICTURES: The Hostage (prod. spvr., ed.), Two-Lane Blacktop (line prod.), Chandler (line prod.), American Graffiti (co.-prod., Academy Award nom. 1974), Star Wars (prod.), The Empire Strikes Back (prod.), Star Wars: Episode IV - A New Hope (Academy Award nom. 1978) The Dark Crystal (prod., 2nd unit dir.), Return to Oz (exec. prod.), Slipstream (prod.) The Steal (prod.), 5-25-77 (prod.), Gangster Kittens (exec. prod.), Panzer 88 (prod.).
TELEVISION: *Movie:* The Tale of Jack Frost (co-exec. prod.). *Mini-series:* The Animated Odyssey (animation supervisor). *Series:* Friends and Heroes.

KURTZ, SWOOSIE

Actress. b. Omaha, NE, September 6, 1944. e. Studied at U. Southern Calif., London Acad. of Music and Dramatic Art.
THEATRE: A History of the American Film (Drama Desk Award), Ah Wilderness (Tony nom.), Who's Afraid of Virginia Woolf? (with Mike Nichols and Elaine May), The Effect of Gamma Rays on Man-in-the Moon Marigolds, Fifth of July (Tony, Outer Critics Circle & Drama Desk Awards), House of Blue Leaves (Tony and Obie Awards), Uncommon Women and Others (Obie & Drama Desk Awards), Hunting Cockroaches (Drama League nom.), Six Degrees of Separation, Lips Together Teeth Apart.
PICTURES: Slap Shot, First Love, Oliver's Story, The World According to Garp, Against All Odds, Wildcats, True Stories, Vice Versa, Bright Lights Big City, Dangerous Liaisons, Stanley and Iris, A Shock to the System, Reality Bites, Storybook, Citizen Ruth, Liar Liar, Outside Ozona, The White River Kid, Cruel Intentions, Sleep Easy, Hutch Rimes, Get Over It, Bubble Boy, The Wild Girls, The Rules of Attraction, Duplex, An Englishman in New York.
TELEVISION: *Movies*: Walking Through the Fire, Marriage Is Alive and Well, Mating Season, A Caribbean Mystery, Guilty Conscience, A Time to Live, Baja Oklahoma (Golden Globe nom. 1989), The Image (Emmy & Cable ACE noms. 1990), Terror on Track 9, The Positively True Adventures of the Alleged Texas Cheerleader-Murdering Mom, And the Band Played On (Emmy & Cable Ace noms. 1994), One Christmas, Betrayed: A Story of Three Women, A Promise to Carolyn, Little Girls in Pretty Boxes, My Own Country, The Wilde Girls, Nadine in Date Land, Category 7: The End of the World, Living Proof, Mike and Molly. *Mini-series*: More Tales of the City. *Series*: As the World Turns (1971), Mary, Love Sidney (2 Emmy noms.), Carol & Company (Emmy Award as guest 1990). Sisters (2 Emmy noms. & SAG nom. 1993), Suddenly Susan, Love & Money, That's Life, Huff (2 Emmy noms.), Pushing Daisies, Rita Rocks. *Specials*: Uncommon Women, Fifth of July, House of Blue Leaves, The Visit (Trying Times). *Guest:* More than 77 appearances.

KURYS, DIANE

Director, Writer. b. Lyons, France, Dec. 3, 1948. In 1970 joined Jean-Louis Barrault's theatre group, acted for 8 years on stage, television and film. Adapted and translated staged plays. 1977, wrote screenplay for Dibolo Menthe (Peppermint Soda) which she also directed and co-prod. Film won Prix Louis Deluc, Best Picture. Co-prod. Alexandre Arcady's Coup de Sirocco and Le Grand Pardon.
PICTURES: *Dir./Writer:* Peppermint Soda (also co-prod.), Cocktail Molotov, Entre Nous, A Man in Love, C'est la vie, Apres L'amour, Six Days Six Nights, Children of the Century, I'm Staying!, L' Anniversaire (also prod.), Sagan (also prod.).

KUSHNER, DONALD

Producer, Executive. Exec. producer, all programming produced by The Kushner Locke Co. since 1983. Today. Kushner still owns the company, which distributes feature films and TV programming throughout the world. Kushner continues to produce as an executive with Junction Films, alongside Brad Wyman, Meriwether Tull & Daniel Jonathan Weisinger.
PICTURES: Animalympics, Tron, Nutcracker: The Motion Picture, Lady In Waiting, Andre, Dangerous Intentions, Last Gasp, The Adventures of Pinocchio, The Brave Little Toaster to the Rescue, The Whole Wide World, Shadow of the Night, The Grave, The Last Time I Committed Suicide, Little Ghost, The Incredible Genie, The Secret Kingdom, Girl, The Brave Little Toaster Goes to Mars, Basil, Possums, The Shrunken City, Small Time, Susan's Plan, Ringmaster, Denial, Bone Daddy, Murdercycle, Beowulf, Blooddolls, Freeway II: Confessions of a Trickbaby, But I'm a Cheerleader, The Boy with the X-Ray Eyes, Piking Up the Pieces, The Last Producer, Harvard Man, Monster, Blessed, Incubus, 7 Seconds, Snuff-Movie, Second in Command, The Hard Corps, True True Lie, Look (exec. prod.), Normal Adolescent Behavior (exec. prod.), The Six Wives of Henry Lefay (exec. prod.), The Uniter, The Marker (exec. prod.), Columbus Day (exec. prod.), Blitz, Gawd Bless America (exec. prod.), TRON: Legacy (exec. prod.).
TELEVISION: *Movies Exec. Prod.*: Automan, Your Mother Wears Combat Boots, Sweet Bird of Youth, Carolina Skeletons, The Brave Little Toaster (Emmy nom. 1988), Fire in the Dark, Father & Son: Dangerous Relations, Getting Gotti, A Husband, a Wife and a Lover, Every Woman's Dream (prod.), Jack Reed: Death and Vengeance, A Strange Affair, Unlikely Angel, Echo, Dragonworld: The Legend Continues, Search for the Jewel of Polaris: Mysterious Museum, They Nest, Dark Prince: The True Story of Dracula, Wolf Girl, Demonic Toys 3, Pumpkinhead: Ashes to Ashes (prod.), Pumpkinhead: Blood Feud. *Series*: 1st & Ten: The Championship, Gun.

KUSTURICA, EMIR

Director, Actor. b. Sarajevo, Yugoslavia, 1955. e. FAMU.
PICTURES: Do You Remember Dolly Bell? (debut, 1981), When Father Was Away on Business (Golden Palme at Cannes Film Fest., 1985), Time of the Gypsies (also co-s.p.), Arizona Dream, Underground (Golden Palme at Cannes Film Fest., 1995), White Cat Black Cat, Super 8 Stories, The Nose, The Good Thief, All the Invisible Children (dir., exec. prod. segment), Secret Journey (actor), Hermano, Maradona (doc., dir., writer), Promise Me This (dir., writer, prod.), Poslednji krug u Monci 2, Mamarosh, Maradona by Kusturica (doc., writer, dir.), Farewell, Cool Water.

KWAN, NANCY

Actress. b. Hong Kong, May 19, 1939. Trained as dancer at British Royal Ballet. 1961 received Golden Globe Award for most promising newcomer.
PICTURES: The World of Suzie Wong (debut, 1960,Golden Globe nom. 1961), Flower Drum Song, The Main Attraction, Tamahine, Fate Is the Hunter, The Wild Affair, Honeymoon Hotel, Arrivederci Baby, Lt. Robin Crusoe USN, The Corrupt Ones, Nobody's Perfect, The Wrecking Crew, The Girl Who Knew Too Much, The McMasters, Girl From Peking, Supercock, The Pacific Connection, Project: Kill, Night Creature, Streets of Hong Kong, Angkor, Walking the Edge, Night Children, Cold Dog Soup, Dragon: The Bruce Lee Story, Mr. P's Dancing Sushi Bar, Murder on the Yellow Brick Road, Ray of Sunshine (also prod.).
TELEVISION: *Movies*: The Last Ninja, Blade in Hong Kong, Miracle Landing, Babies. *Mini-series:* Noble House.

KWAN-RUBINEK, VERONIKA

Executive. e. Loyola Marymount University. She worked as a research consultant for the German American Chamber of Commerce and published several articles in the German American Business Review before joining the international marketing team for Lorimar Film Entertainment in the mid 1980s. Joined Warner Brothers Pictures as sales analyst in 1998 and became Senior Sales Analyst, Manager, International Sales; and Director of International Operations. Promoted to Sr. V. P. of International Distribution at Warner Bros. Pictures in 1997 and oversaw sales and distribution, including acting as a liaison with its various co-production partners and third-party producers and also responsible for regional and country management teams in analyzing and strategizing theatrical releases in the overseas marketplace. Named President of Distribution of Warner Brothers Pictures International in 2000. She reorganized the division to fully integrate Marketing and Sales/Distribution, maximizing the flow of communication and information to optimize a film's revenue-generating potential. She handled the international distribution of a number of the Studio's most successful films in terms of overseas box office, including, the entire Harry Potter franchise "Ocean's Thirteen," "300," "Flags of Our Fathers," "Letters From Iwo Jima," "Happy Feet" and "The Departed," and The Matrix series. Her accomplishments also include shepherding the first film ever to release simultaneously in every country at the same hour around the world ("The Matrix Revolutions"). Warner Brothers Pictures International has been the market leader in five of the previous nine years and has surpassed $1 billion in each year during Kwan-Rubinek's tenure. It was first to hit the $2 billion mark twice, in 2004 and 2007. She is a member of the Academy of Motion Picture Arts & Sciences and was ranked 12 in the Hollywood Reporter's 100 most powerful women in entertainment in 2010.

KWIETNIOWSKI, RICHARD
Director. b. London, England, March 17, 1957.
PICTURES: Alfalfa, Ballad of Reading Gaol, Flames of Passion, Proust's Favorite Fantasy, Cost of Love, Actions Speak Louder Than Words, I Was a Jewish Sex Worker (D.P. only), Love and Death on Long Island (also s.p.), Owning Mahowny.

L

LA BEOUF, SHIA
Actor. b. Los Angeles, CA, June 11, 1986. Attended Hamilton Academy of Music in Los Angeles. Voted Star of Tomorrow in Quigley Publishing's Top Ten Poll, 2007.
PICTURES: Holes (also soundtrack writer), Dumb and Dumberer: When Harry Met Lloyd, Charlie's Angels: Full Throttle, The Battle of Shaker Heights, I, Robot, Constantine, The Greatest Game Ever Played, A Guide to Recognizing Your Saints, Bobby, Disturbia, Surf's Up (voice), Transformers, Indiana Jones and the Kingdom of the Crystal Skull, New York, I Love You, Eagle Eye, Transformers 2: Revenge of the Fallen, Wall Street: Money Never Sleeps, Transformers 3, The Necessary Death of Charlie Countryman.
TELEVISION: *Movies:* Breakfast with Einstein, Hounded, Tru Confessions, The Even Stevens Movie. *Series:* Even Stevens (Emmy Award 2003). *Guest:* More than 75 appearances.

LA BUTE, NEIL
Director, Writer. b. Detroit, MI, March 19, 1963. Graduate of Brigham Young University Theatre and Film program.
PICTURES: In the Company of Men, Your Friends & Neighbors, Nurse Betty (dir. only), Possession, The Shape of Things, Vapor, The Wicker Man, Lakeview Terrace, The Vicious Kind (exec. prod.), Death at a Funeral (dir. only).
TELEVISION: *Movie:* Bash: Latter Day Plays. *Mini-series*: Lilac Lane.

LACHMAN, ED
Cinematographer. b. 1948. Son of a Morristown, NJ movie theater owner. e. Ohio U., BFA. Filmed documentaries Ornette: Made in America, Strippers, Huie's Sermon. Assisted Sven Nykvist on King of the Gypsies, Hurricane; Vittorio Storaro on Luna; Robby Muller on The American Friend and They All Laughed. Co-director of photography on Werner Herzog's La Soufriere and Stroszek and Wim Wendesrs' Lightning Over Water and A Tokyo Story.
PICTURES: Scalpel, Union City, Say Amen Somebody, Little Wars, Split Cherry Tree, Strippers, The Little Sister, Insignificance, Desperately Seeking Susan, True Stories, Making Mr. Right, Chuck Berry: Hail Hail Rock 'n' Roll, Less Than Zero, El Dia Que Me Quieras, Mississippi Masala, Light Sleeper, London Kills Me, My New Gun, My Family/Mi Familia, Selena, Why Do Fools Fall In Love, The Virgin Suicides, The Limey, Erin Brockovich, Sweet November, Simone, Far From Heaven (Academy Award nom.; ASC nom. 2003), Bad Santa, Moonlight Mile (photographer), Stryker, Posledniy poezd so stancii roppongi, A Prairie Home Companion, Hounddog, I'm Not There., Life for a Child (doc., short), Forgiveness, Howl, Paradies.
TELEVISION: *Movies:* The Little Sister, A Gathering of Old Men, Imaging America (Get Your Kicks on Route 66 dir., cinematography, American Playhouse.), Horse Opera Backtrack. *Series:* Tribeca.

LACK, ANDREW
Executive. b. New York, NY, May 16, 1947. e. Attended Sorbonne and received a bachelor of fine arts from the School of Fine Arts at Boston University in 1968. Starting in 1976, worked at CBS as prod. for Who's Who, 60 Minutes, CBS Reports. 1981, named sr. prod. of CBS Reports and CBS News correspondent. 1983 became exec. prod. Exec. prod. and creator of Face to Face with Connie Chung, West 57th, Crossroads, Our Times With Bill Moyers. Exec. prod. of Street Stories, specials The 20th Anniversary of Watergate, Malcolm X. Lack's broadcasts at CBS earned many honors, including 16 Emmy Awards, four Alfred I. DuPont-Columbia University Journalism Awards, five Ohio State Awards, an Oversees Press Club Award, two Gravel Awards from the American Bar Association, a George Polk Award and a Clarion Award. In 1993, appointed pres. of NBC News. Appointed pres. and CEO of NBC on June 4, 2001. CEO of Sony BMG Music Entertainment, Inc. from Aug. 2004-Feb. 2006. Currently, Chairman of Bd. Sony BMG Music Entertainment.

LADD, JR., ALAN
Executive, Producer. b. Los Angeles, CA, Oct. 22, 1937. Son of late actor Alan Ladd. M. P. agent, Creative Mgmt. Associates, 1963-69.; m.p. prod., 1969-73. Joined 20th Century-Fox in 1973 in chg. of creative affairs in feature div.; promoted to v.p., prod., 1974; 1975, named sr. v.p. for worldwide prod.; 1976, promoted to pres. of 20th Century-Fox Pictures. Resigned & formed The Ladd Co., 1979. 1985, appt. pres. & COO, MGM/UA Ent. Film Corp; appt. chmn. of bd., CEO, MGM Pictures Inc., 1986; resigned 1988. 1989, named co-chmn. Pathe Communications Corp. and chmn., CEO, Pathe Ent.; chmn., & CEO, MGM-Pathe Ent., 1989-92; chmn. & CEO MGM-Pathe Comm. Co., 1991-92; co-chmn. & co-CEO, MGM, 1992-93. Now president of The Ladd Company of Beverly Hills, CA.
PICTURES: *Prod.*: Walking Stick, A Severed Head, Tam Lin, Villian, Zee and Co., Fear Is the Key, Braveheart (Acad. Award), The Phantom, A Very Brady Sequel, An Unfinished Life, Gone Baby Gone. *Exec. prod.:* Nightcomers, Vice Versa, The Brady Bunch Movie, The Man in the Iron Mask.

LADD, CHERYL
Actress. r.n. Cheryl Stoppelmoor. b. Huron, S.D., July 12, 1951. Joined professional Music Shop Band while in high school; after graduation toured with group ending up in Los Angeles. Cast as voice of Melody character in animated Josie and the Pussycats. Studied acting with Milton Katselas. Did TV commercials, small parts in TV. Film debut 1972 in Jamaica Reef (unreleased).
PICTURES: Purple Hearts, Now and Forever, Millennium, Lisa, Poison Ivy, Permanent Midnight, Perfect Little Angels, A Dog of Flanders, Baggage.
TELEVISION: *Movies*: Satan's School for Girls, When She Was Bad, Grace Kelly Story, Romance on the Orient Express, A Death in California, Crossings, Deadly Care, Bluegrass, Kentucky Woman, Jekyll & Hyde, The Fulfillment of Mary Gray, The Girl Who Came Between Them, Crash: The Mystery of Flight 1501, Danielle Steel's Changes, Locked Up: A Mother's Rage, Dead Before Dawn, Broken Promises: Taking Emily Back, Dancing With Danger, The Haunting of Lisa, Kiss & Tell, Tangled Web, Kiss and Tell, Every Mother's Worst Fear, Michael Landon: The Father I Knew, Her Best Friend's Husband, Eve's Christmas, Though None Go with Me. *Series*: The Ken Berry "Wow" Show, Charlie's Angels, One West Waikiki, Las Vegas. *Specials*: Ben Vereen... His Roots, General Electric's All-Star Anniversary, John Denver and the Ladies; The Cheryl Ladd Special, Looking Back: Souvenirs, Scenes From a Special. *Guest:* More than 121 appearances.

LADD, DAVID ALAN
Actor, Producer, Motion Picture Executive. b. Los Angeles, CA, Feb. 5, 1947. e. USC. Son of late actor Alan Ladd. Received special Golden Globe Award 1959 for best juvenile actor along with Golden Globe nom. for most promising newcomer for The Proud Rebel. Had been exec. v.p. motion picture prod. at Pathe Entertainment and MGM. Now president of David Ladd Films.
PICTURES: *Actor:* The Big Land, The Proud Rebel (Golden Globe Award), The Sad Horse, A Dog of Flanders, Raymie, Misty, R.P.M., Catlow, Deathline (Raw Meat), The Klansman, The Day of the Locust, Wild Geese. *Producer:* The Serpent and the Rainbow, The Mod Squad, Hart's War, A Guy Thing, Leaving Barstow (exec. prod.).
TELEVISION: *Movies: Prod.:* When She Was Bad, Alan Ladd: The True Quiet Man. Various ABC Variety specials.

LADD, DIANE
Actress. r.n. Diane Rose Lanier. b. Meridian, MS. Daughter is actress Laura Dern. e. St. Aloysius Acad.; trained for stage with Curt Conway and Frank Corsaro. Member of Actors Studio. Worked as model, singer and as Copacabana nightclub dancer. At 17 in touring co. of Hatful of Rain. NY debut: Orpheus Descending.
THEATRE: Carry Me Back to Morningside Heights, One Night Stands of a Noisy Passenger. The Wall, The Goddess, The Fantastiks, Women Speak, Texas Trilogy; Lu Ann Hampton Laverty, Love Letters.
PICTURES: Wild Angels (debut, 1966), Rebel Rousers, The Reivers, Macho Calahan, WUSA, White Lightning, Chinatown, Alice Doesn't Live Here Anymore (Academy Award nom.; Golden Globe nom. 1975), Embryo, All Night Long, Sweetwater, The Reivers, Something Wicked This Way Comes, Black Widow, Plain Clothes, National Lampoon's Christmas Vacation, Wild at Heart (Academy Award nom.; Golden Globe nom. 1991), A Kiss Before Dying, Rambling Rose (Academy Award nom.; Golden Globe nom. 1992), The Cemetery Club, Forever, Carnosaur, Hold Me Thrill Me Kiss Me, Father Hood, Ghost of Mississippi, Primary Colors, Can't Be Heaven, 28 Days, The Law of Enclosures, Redemption of the Ghost, More Than Puppy Love, Daddy and Them, The Virgin, Rain, The World's Fastest Indian, Come Early Morning, When I Find the Ocean, Inland Empire, Jake's Corner, American Cowslip.
TELEVISION: *Movies*: The Devil's Daughter, Black Beauty, Thaddeus Rose and Eddie, Willa, Guyana Tragedy, Desperate Lives, Grace Kelly, Crime of Innocence, Bluegrass, Rock Hudson, The Lookalike, Shadow of a Doubt, Hush Little Baby, Mrs. Munck (also dir., writer), The Staircase, Late Last Night, Best Actress, Sharing the Secret, Christy: The Movie, Aftermath, Damaged Care, Gracie's Choice, Montana Sky, Menace. *Mini-series*: Christy, Choices of the Heart, Part II: A New Beginning, Living With the Dead, Kingdom Hospital. *Series*: The Secret Storm, Alice (Golden Globe Award, 1981), Enlightened. *Special*: The Gift. *Guest*: More than 95 appearances.

LAEMMLE, ROBERT

Exhibitor. b. Paris, France. Sept. 5, 1935. e. Cal State, Los Angeles, CA, bachelor's degree in business admin. Master's degree in finance from UCLA. While training to be a banker, temporarily ran family theatre business (started in late 1950s) when his parents took an extended trip. Today he is owner and chairman of Laemmle Theatres, a chain of art house theatres with 11 theatres, including West Hollywood's Sunset Five. His son, Greg is president of the company. Recently, the organization has branched out as a booking agent for other theatres.

LAGRAVENESE, RICHARD

Writer. b. Brooklyn, NY, Oct.30, 1959.
PICTURES: Rude Awakening, The Fisher King (also actor, Academy Award nom.; WGA nom. 1992), The Ref (also prod.), A Little Princess, The Bridges of Madison County, Unstrung Heroes, The Mirror has Two Faces, The Kiss (also dir.), The Horse Whisperer, Living Out Loud, Beloved, Blow (actor only), A Decade Under the Influence (also exec. prod.; Emmy nom. 2004), Monster-in-Law, The Secret Life of Walter Mitty, je t'aime Paris, (dir. segment), Pushing Dead (prod.), P.S., I Love You (dir., s.p.), Freedom Writers, Water for Elephants (s.p.). *Documentary:* In Search of Ted Demme (also exec. prod.).

LAHTI, CHRISTINE

Actress. b. Birmingham, MI, April 4, 1950. m. dir. Thomas Schlamme. e. U. of Michigan. Trained for stage at Herbert Berghof Studios with Uta Hagen. TV commercials. As a mime, performed with Edinburgh Scotland's Travis Theatre. N.Y. stage debut in The Woods, 1978.
THEATRE: The Zinger, Hooter (Playwrights Horizon), Loose Ends, Division St., The Woods (Theatre World Award), Scenes and Revelations, Present Laughter, The Lucky Spot, Summer and Smoke (LA), The Heidi Chronicles, Three Hotels.
PICTURES: ...And Justice For All (debut, 1979), Whose Life Is It Anyway?, Ladies and Gentlemen the Fabulous Stains, Swing Shift (Academy Award nom.; Golden globe nom. 1985), Just Between Friends, Housekeeping, Stacking, Running on Empty (Golden Globe nom. 1989), Miss Firecracker (cameo), Gross Anatomy, Funny About Love, The Doctor, Leaving Normal, Hideaway, Pie in the Sky, Judgment Day: The Ellie Nesler Story, Smart People, Yonkers Joe, Obsessed, Flying Lessons. *Director:* Lieberman In Love (also actress, short; Academy Award 1996), My First Mister.
TELEVISION: *Movies*: Dr. Scorpion, The Last Tenant, The Henderson Monster, The Executioner's Song, Love Lives On, Single Bars Single Women, No Place Like Home (Emmy nom. Golden Globe Award 1990), Crazy From the Heart, The Fear Inside, The Good Fight, The Four Diamonds, A Weekend in the Country, Subway Stories: Tales from the Underground, Hope, An American Daughter (Golden Globe nom. 2001), The Pilot's Wife, Oooph!, Gisella Perl, Women vs. Men, Open House, Out of the Ashes, The Book of Ruth, Revenge of the Middle-Aged Woman, Operating Instructions. *Mini-series*: Amerika (Emmy nom.; Golden Globe nom. 1987). *Series*: Chicago Hope (Golden Globe Award, 1 other nom.; Emmy Award, 3 other noms. 1998), Studio 60 on the Sunset Strip, Jack & Bobby (Golden Globe nom. 2005), Law & Order: Special Victims Unit. *Guest:* More than 70 appearances.

LAI, FRANCIS

Composer. b. France, April 26, 1932.
PICTURES: A Man and a Woman (2 Golden Globe noms. 1967), I'll Never Forget What's 'is Name, The Bobo, Three Into Two Won't Go, Hello Goodbye, Hannibal Brooks, The Games, Mayerling, House of Cards, Rider on the Rain, Love Story (Academy Award, Golden Globe Award 1970), Le Petit Matin, Another Man, Another Chance, Wanted: Babysitter, Bilitis, The Good and the Bad, Widow's Nest, Cat and Mouse, Live for Life (Golden Globe nom.1968) The Body of My Enemy, Emmanuelle 2; The Forbidden Room, International Velvet, Oliver's Story, Passion Flower Hotel, Robert and Robert, The Small Timers, By the Blood Brothers, Beyond the Reef, Bolero, A Second Chance, Edith and Marcel, My New Partner, Marie, A Man and a Woman: 20 Years Later, Bernadette, Itinerary of a Spoiled Child, Der Aten (The Spirit), La Belle Histoire, Le Provincial, Keys to Paradise, Il y a des jours... et des lunes, Stranger in the House, I'll Be Going Now, All That...For This?, The Thief and the Liar, Les Miserables, Men Women: A User's Manual, My Best Friend's Wedding, One 4 All, Une pour toutes, The Kid Stays In the Picture (documentary), Le Genre humain - 1: Les Parisiens, Bringing Down the House, Stranger Than Fiction (soundtrack performer/writer), Ocean's Thirteen (soundtrack writer), When Did You Leave Heaven!?!, The Nanny Diaries (soundtrack writer), A Nightmare on Elm Street (soundtrack writer).

LAKE, RICKI

Actress. b. New York, NY, Sept. 21, 1968. e. Manhattan's Professional Children's School. Won role in Hairspray while attending Ithaca Col. Theatre in LA: A Girl's Guide to Chaos.
PICTURES: Hairspray (debut, 1988), Working Girl, Starlight: A Musical Movie, Cookie, Cry-Baby, Last Exit to Brooklyn, Where the Day Takes You, Inside Monkey Zetterland, Cabin Boy, Serial Mom, Skinner, Mrs. Winterbourne, Cecil B. Demented, Hairspray, The Business of Being Born (doc., exec. prod.).
TELEVISION: *Movies*: Babycakes, The Chase, Based on an Untrue Story, Jackie's Back!, Murder She Purred: A Mrs. Murphy Mystery, Jackie's Back!, Matters of Life and Dating, Loving Leah (also exec. prod.). *Series*: China Beach, Gravedale High (voice), Ricki Lake (synd. talk show, Emmy nom. 1994), The King of Queens, The Middle (also pilot), Gameshow Marathon (host), Charm School with Ricki Lake (also exec. prod.). *Guest:* More than 68 appearances.

LAM, RINGO

Director. e. York University, Toronto. Started training as an actor in 1973 but switched to production as asst. until 1976, then as TV dir. until 1978. In 1981 he returned to Hong Kong and two years later made his dir. debut with Esprit D'Amour.
PICTURES: The Other Side of a Gentleman, Cupid One, Aces Go Places IV: Mad Mission, City on Fire, Prison on Fire, School on Fire, Wild Search, Undeclared War, Touch and Go, Prison on Fire II, Full Contact, Shuang long hui, Twin Dragons, Burning Paradise (Rape of the Red Temple), Maximum Risk, The Adventurers, The Exchange, Full Alert, The Suspect, Victim, Replicant, The Monk, Finding Mr. Perfect, Triangle (also prod., exec. prod.).

LAMAS, LORENZO

Actor. b. Los Angeles, CA, Jan. 20, 1958. e. Santa Monica City Coll. Son of the late actor Fernando Lamas and actress Arlene Dahl. Studied at Tony Barr's Film Actors Workshop (Burbank Studios). Appeared on commercials for Diet Coke, BVD, Coors.
PICTURES: Grease, Tilt, Take Down, Body Rock, Snakeater, Night of the Warrior, Snakeater II, Final Impact, Snakeater III: His Law, Killing Streets, The Swordsman, Bounty Tracker, Final Round, Bad Blood, Midnight Man, Gladiator Cop, CIA II Target: Alexa, Terminal Justice, Mask of Death, Black Dawn, The Rage, Undercurrent, Back to Even, The Muse, Raptor Island, Thralls, Lethal, 18 Fingers of Death!, Mexican Gold, The Stolen Moments of September, Chinaman's Chance, 30,000 Leagues Under the Sea, I Am Somebody, Mega Shark vs. Giant Octopus, Cathedral City.
TELEVISION: *Movies*: Detour to Terror, Snakeeater, La Carne e il diavolo, Hope Ranch, The Paradise Virus, Deep Evil. *Series*: California Fever, Secrets of Midland Heights, Falcon Crest (Golden Globe nom. 1983), Dancin' to the Hits (host), Renegade, Air American, The Immortal, Leave It to Lamas, The Bold and the Beautiful. *Guest:* More than 90 appearances.

LAMBERT, CHRISTOPHER (ALSO CHRISTOPHE)

Actor, Producer. b. Great Neck, NY, Mar. 29, 1957; reared in Geneva; parents French. Studied at Paris Conservatoire Drama Academy.
PICTURES: La Bar du Telephone (debut, 1981), Putain d'Historie d'Amour, Legitime Violence, Greystoke: The Legend of Tarzan Lord of the Apes, Love Songs, Subway (Cesar Award), Highlander, I Love You, The Sicilian, Love Dream, To Kill a Priest, Un Plan d'Enfer, Why Me?, Highlander 2: The Quickening, Priceless Beauty, Knight Moves, Fortress, Gunmen, Road Flower, Highlander III: The Sorcerer, The Hunted, Nine Months (exec. prod. only), Mortal Kombat, North Star (also exec. prod.), When Saturday Comes (exec. prod. only), Adrenalin, Hercule et Sherlock, Nirvana, Arlette, Mean Guns, Operation Splitsville (also prod.), Beowulf, Resurrection (also prod., story), Gideon (also prod.), Fortress 2, Highlander: Endgame, Druids, The Point Men, The Piano Player, Absolon, The Good Shepherd (exec. prod.), Day of Wrath, Southland Tales, Le Lièvre de Vatanen, Trivial, Limo Driver, White Material, Percussions, Abelar: Tales of an Ancient Empire, Mortal Kombat, The Job, Sweet Deceit.
TELEVISION: *Movie*: The Piano Player, Gesang der Wale. *Mini-series*: King of Bandit Jing (voice), Dalida. *Series:* The Ark.

LAMBERT, MARY

Director. b. Arkansas. e. attended U. of Denver, Rhode Island Sch. of Design where began making short films. Worked in variety of prod. jobs before moving to L.A. and directing TV commercials and music videos (includ. Madonna's Material Girl, Like a Virgin, Like a Prayer, others for Sting, Janet Jackson and Mick Jagger).
PICTURES: Siesta, Pet Sematary, Pet Sematary 2, Clubland, The In Crowd, In Between, 14 Women (doc.), The Attic, High Midnight.
TELEVISION: *Movies*: Dragstrip Girl, Face of Evil, My Stepson My Lover, Strange Frequency, Halloweentown II: Kalabar's Revenge. *Series:* On the Road in America, The Dark Path Chronicles (also writer).

LAMONT, PETER

Production Designer. b. England, Nov. 12, 1929.
PICTURES: Watch Your Stern, Night of the Eagle, This Sporting Life, On Her Majesty's Secret Service, Fiddler on the Roof (Academy Award nom. 1972), Daimonds Are Forever, Sleuth, Live and Let Die, The Dove, The Main with the Golden Gun, Inside Out, Seven-Per-Cent Solution, The Spy Who Loved Me (Academy Award nom. 1978), The Boys from Brazil, Moonraker, For Your Eyes Only, Octopussy, Top Secret!, A View to a Kill, Aliens (Academy Award nom. 1987), The Living Daylights, Consuming Passions, Licence to Kill, Eve of Destruction, The Taking of Beverly Hills, True Lies, GoldenEye, Titanic (Academy Award for Best Art Dir., Best Prod. Design, 1998), Wing

Commander, The World is Not Enough, Die Another Day, Casino Royale (ADG Award 2007), Sparkle (unit driver).

LANDAU, JON

Producer. b. New York, NY, July 23, 1960. e. USC.
PICTURES: *Prod.:* Campus Man (also unit prod. mgr.), Honey I Shrunk the Kids, Titanic (Academy Award, Best Pic.; DGA Award 1998), Mr. Hughes, Ding-a-ling-Less (assoc. prod.), Solaris, Godspeed, Avatar (Academy Award nom. 2010). *Unit prod. mgr.:* Manhunter, F/X, Making Mr. Right, Dick Tracy.
TELEVISION: Winter Break.

LANDAU, JULIET

Actress. b. Los Angeles, CA, March 30, 1965. Father is actor Martin Landau.
PICTURES: The Grifters, Pump Up the Volume, Neon City, Direct Hit, Ed Wood, Theodore Rex, Ravager, Citizens of Perpetual Indulgence, Carlo's Wake,Citizens of Perpetual Indulgence, Freedom Park, Repossessed, The Yellow Wallpaper, Hack!, Haunted Echoes, Land of Canaan, Monster Mutt, Material Lies.
TELEVISION: *Movie:* Fatal Reunion. *Series*: Buffy the Vampire Slayer, Angel: The Series, Justice League, Ben 10: Alien Force.

LANDAU, MARTIN

Actor. b. Brooklyn, NY, June 20, 1930. e. Pratt Inst., Art Students League, Was cartoon and staff artist on NY Daily News; studied at Actors Studio. Daughter is actress Juliet Landau. Recipient: Lifetime Achievement Awards from Houston Film Fest. and Charleston Film Fest. Spoken word recording, Harry Truman: The journey to Independence, 1997 (Grammy nom).
THEATRE: Middle of the Night, Uncle Vanya, Stalag 17, Wedding Breakfast, First Love, The Goat Song.
PICTURES: Pork Chop Hill (debut, 1959), North by Northwest, The Gazebo, Stagecoach to Dancer's Rock, Cleopatra, The Hallelujah Trail, The Greatest Story Ever Told, Decision at Midnight, Alien Attack, Nevada Smith, They Call Me Mister Tibbs, Situation Normal But All Fouled Up, A Town Called Hell, Black Gunn, Strange Shadows in an Empty Room, Meteor, Destination Moonbase Alpha, Without Warning, Trial By Terror, Cosmic Princess, Journey Through the Black Sun, The Last Word, The Return, Alone in the Dark, The Being, Access Code, Treasure Island, Run ... If You Can, Death Blow, W.A.R.: Women Against Rape, Sweet Revenge, Cyclone, Real Bullets, Empire State, Delta Fever, Tucker: The Man and His Dream (Academy Award nom.; Golden Globe Award 1989), Crimes and Misdemeanors (Golden Globe Award, Academy Award nom. 1990), Paint It Black, Firehead, Tipperary, The Color of Evening, Mistress, Eye of the Stranger, Sliver, Intersection, Time Is Money, Ed Wood (Academy Award, best supporting actor, 1995; also Golden Globe, SAG, American Comedy, NY Film Critics, LA Film Critics, Natl. Society of Film Critics, Boston Film Critics, Chicago Film Critics & Texas Film Critics Awards), City Hall, Pinocchio, B.A.P.S., The Elevator, The X Files: Fight the Future, Rounders, The Joy Riders, Edtv, The New Adventures of Pinocchio, Sleepy Hollow, Carlo's Wake, Ready to Rumble, Very Mean Men, Shiner, The Majestic, An Existential Affair, Hollywood Homicide, The Aryan Couple, Walk Two Moons, Harrison Montgomery, The Commission, Ivory, David & Fatima, City of Ember, Lovely, Still, Billy: The Early Years, The Company Men, 20% Fiction, 9 (voice), Life's a Beach (exec. prod.).
TELEVISION: *Movies*: Welcome Home Johnny Bristol, Savage, The Death of Ocean View Park, Harlem Globetrotters on Gilligan's Island, Fall of the House of Usher, Max and Helen (ACE Award nom.), The Neon Empire, By Dawn's Early Light (ACE Award nom.), Something to Live For: The Alison Gertz Story, Legacy of Lies (ACE Award), 12:01, Joseph, Merry Christmas, George Bailey, Bonanno: A Godfather's Story, Haven. *Mini-series*: In the Beginning. *Series*: Mission Impossible (1966-69; 3 Emmy noms.; Golden Globe Award 1968), Space 1999, In The Beginning, Haven, Rosebud, Without a Trace (2 Emmy noms.), The Evidence, Entourage (Emmy nom. 2007). *Guest*: More than 157 appearances.

LANDAU, YAIR

Executive. e. Univ. of Chicago, Phi Beta Kappa graduate; Stanford Univ. Graduate School of Business, M.B.A. Before entering entertainment industry, worked with Wasserstein, Perella & Co., a NY-based investment-banking firm. Joined Sony Pictures Entertainment in 1991. During his tenure, he served in many positions including exec. v.p. of corporate development and strategic planning. Served at Sony is vice chairman of Sony Pictures Entertainment and also pres. of Sony Pictures Digital Entertainment, which Landau formed in 1999—2008, bringing together all of Sony Pictures' digital artists and software engineers from Sony Pictures Imageworks, Sony Online Entertainment and Columbia Tristar Interactive into one division. Sony Pictures Imageworks has grown into a leading digital animation and visual effects company creating computer-generated imaging (CGI) for motion pictures. Landau supervised production of Imageworks' first animated short, The Chubbchubbs!, which won an Academy Award for Best Short Film (animated) in 2003. Building on this success, he established Sony Pictures Animation to develop and produce all-CGI animated features for SPE. Sony Online Entertainment has grown into the worldwide leader in massively multiplayer online (MMO) gaming, building upon EverQuest, with Star Wars Galaxies launched in partnership with Lucas Arts in 2003. Through Sony Pictures Digital, Landau developed the technology and formed the five-studio Movielink partnership, the first major studio Internet movie download service, launched in 2002. Most recently, he reorganized Sony Pictures Digital Networks to focus on emerging mobile entertainment, broadband video delivery and media software. Today this group includes Sony Pictures Mobile, SoapCity, and Sony Pictures Integrated Network (SPiN), the studio's online promotional presence. 2008, he will start a new games and animation venture to develop and produce multiplatform content as an exec. prod. for Sony Pictures Animation. He also served as vice Chairman of Sony Pictures Entertainment and President of Sony Pictures Digital. 2010 he joined venture capital firm, MK Capital, as a partner.

LANDES, MICHAEL S.

Executive, Producer. b. Bronx, NY, Feb. 4, 1939. e. Fairleigh Dickinson, B.A., 1961; Rutgers, J.D., 1964; NYU, L.L.M., 1965. Bars passed: NJ 1965, NY 1966, U.S. Supreme Ct. 1969. 17 years of corporate law and financing experience as sr. partner in law firm of Hahn and Hessen. Co-chmn of The ALMI Group formed, 1978. Co-chmn. & CEO of Almi Pictures Inc., formed 1982. 1986, Almi sold its 97-screen RKO Century Warner Theatre chain to Cineplex Odeon. 1986, purchased Video Shack Inc. assets and formed RKO Warner Video, Inc. and was chmn. and CFO. In 1988, became chmn, Damon Creations, Inc. which merged with Enro Holding Corp. and Enro Shirt Co. into Damon Creations. Sold Damon, 1988. Chmn./CEO, RKO Warner Int'l. Ltd. a video franchisor and chmn./CEO of The Lexington Group Ltd., org. 1990. By 2000, Landes returned to law practice and introduced a business method designed to cope with real estate problems associated with an increasing number of non-productive theatres. Landes' methodology involved property recycling services with the objective of eliminating or reducing ongoing tenant liability, as well as loss of profits by landlords.
PICTURES: Spaceship, The Big Score, I Am the Cheese, Rosebud Beach Hotel, B.C. Rock, The Bostonians, The Night Stalker.

LANDGRAF, JOHN

Executive. e. Pitzer College in Claremont, CA, B.A. degree. Landgraf began his TV career in 1988 as Sarabande Productions' dir. of development. He rose to sr. v.p. before departing to NBC in 1994. From 1994-1999, Landgraf was v.p., Primetime Series at NBC and was a key contributor to developing The West Wing, Profiler and Suddenly Susan. He also maintained daily oversight as current programming exec. on ER, Friends, Profiler, Jag and Suddenly Susan. Landgraf left NBC and became pres. of Jersey Television, a co. he co-founded along with former Jersey Films partners Danny DeVito, Michael Shamberg and Stacey Sher. Jersey Television produced acclaimed series Karen Sisco (ABC), Reno 911! (Comedy Central), UC: Undercover (NBC), The American Embassy (FOX) and Kate Brasher (CBS). Joined Fox as entertainment pres. in Jan. 2004. In May 2005, Landgraf was promoted to current position as pres. & gen. mgr. of FX Networks, replacing former FX Networks president and CEO Peter Liguori who joined FOX Broadcasting Company as its ent. pres.

LANDIS, JOHN

Director, Producer, Writer, Actor. b. Chicago, IL, Aug. 3, 1950. Raised in Los Angeles. Started in mailroom at 20th Century-Fox, then worked in Europe as prod. asst. and stuntman before making first low-budget film, Schlock.
PICTURES: *Director &/or Actor:* Schlock (also writer), The Kentucky Fried Movie, National Lampoon's Animal House, The Blues Brothers (also co-s.p.), An American Werewolf in London (also s.p.), Trading Places, Twilight Zone—The Movie (sequence dir., also s.p., co-prod.), Into the Night, Spies Like Us, Clue (co-exec. prod., co-story only), Three Amigos!, Amazon Women on the Moon (sequence dir.; also co-exec. prod.), Coming to America, Oscar, Innocent Blood, Beverly Hills Cop III, The Stupids, Battle for the Planet of the Apes, Death Race 2000, 1941, The Muppets Take Manhattan, Spontaneous Combustion, Darkman, Diva Las Vegas, Voice of a Stranger, Sleepwalkers, Venice/Venice, The Silence of the Hams, Vampirella, Mad City, Susan's Plan, Blues Brothers 2000, Diamonds, 2001 Maniacs, Spider-Man 2, Epic Proportions, Her Morbid Desires, Parasomnia, The Scenesters (actor only), Burke and Hare, Some Guy Who Kills People (exec. prod.).
TELEVISION: *Movies:* Psycho IV (actor), Quicksilver Highway, Slasher (doc., Masters of Horror, The Lost World. *Mini-series*: The Stand. *Series/Exec. prod.:* Dream On (also. dir., actor), Topper (also dir.), Weird Science, Sliders, Campus Cops. *Series*: Dream On, Sliders, Eek! the Cat (voice), Weird Science, Campus Cops, The Lost World, Honey, I Shrunk the Kids: The TV Show, Masters of Horror. *Specials*: B.B. King Into the Night, Disneyland's 35th Anniversary Celebration, Mr. Warmth: The Don Rickles Project (doc., prod., dir., actor, Emmy Award 2008), Starz Inside: Ladies or Gentlemen (doc.). *Videos*: Thriller, Black or White (both for Michael Jackson).

LANDSBURG, ALAN

Executive, Producer, Writer. b. New York, NY, May 10, 1933. e.

NYU. Producer for NBC News Dept., 1951-59; producer-writer, CBS, 1959-60; exec. prod., Wolper Productions/ Metromedia Producers Corp., 1961-70; founded Alan Landsburg Productions in 1971. Landsburg remains active in production through his current prod. co., Landsburg Company.
PICTURES: *Co-exec. prod.:* Jaws 3-D, Porky's II: The Next Day.
TELEVISION: *Exec. prod.:* Biography, National Geographic Specials (1965-70): The Undersea World of Jacques Cousteau; That's Incredible. Movies: Adam (Emmy nom. 1984), The Merchant of Scarsdale (Emmy Award 1970), Fear on Trial (Emmy nom. 1976), Parent Trap II, Adam: His Song Continues, The George McKenna Story, Long Gone, Strange Voices, Bluegrass, A Place at the Table, Bill (Emmy nom. 1982), Too Young the Hero, A Stoning in Fulham County, High Risk, Destined to Live, Quiet Victory: The Charlie Wedemeyer Story, The Ryan White Story, Unspeakable Acts (co-exec. prod., writer), A Mother's Right: The Elizabeth Morgan Story (writer), The Hunter (writer), The Lottery, Country Justice. Mini-series: The Chisholms, Kennedy. Series: Time-Life Specials: The March of Time, It Was a Very Good Year (exec. prod.), The Kids from C.A.P.E.R., That's Incredible!, The Future: What's Next?, True Confessions, In Search of (also creator). Documentaries: The Rise and Fall of the Third Reich (also narr.), Alaska Wilderness Lake (prod., Academy Award nom. 1972), The Outer Space Connection (prod. writer/book), In Search of Ancient Astronauts (exec. prod.), In Search of Ancient Mysteries (exec. prod.), In Search of...(series), Between the Wars (series, Emmy nom. 1978).

LANE, DIANE
Actress. b. New York, NY, Jan. 2, 1965. Acted in stage classics (Medea, Electra, As You Like It) at La Mama Experimental Theatre Club, NY. Addtl. stage: The Cherry Orchard, Agamemnon, Runaways, Twelfth Night.
PICTURES: A Little Romance (debut, 1979), Touched by Love, National Lampoon Goes to the Movies, Cattle Annie and Little Britches, Six Pack, Ladies and Gentlemen the Fabulous Stains, The Outsiders, Rumble Fish, Streets of Fire, The Cotton Club, The Big Town, Lady Beware, Priceless Beauty, Vital Signs, My New Gun, Chaplin, Knight Moves, Indian Summer, Judge Dredd, Wild Bill, Mad Dog Time, Jack, Murder at 1600, The Only Thrill, A Walk on the Moon, The Virginian, My Dog Skip, The Perfect Storm, Hardball, The Glass House, Just Like Mona, Unfaithful (Academy Award nom.; Golden Globe nom. 2003), Searching for Debra Winger, Under the Tuscan Sun (Golden Globe nom. 2004), Fierce People, Must Love Dogs, Hollywoodland, Killshot, Jumper, Untraceable, Nights in Rodanthe, Secretariat.
TELEVISION: *Movies*: Child Bride of Short Creek, Miss All-American Beauty, Descending Angel, Oldest Living Confederate Widow Tells All, Grace and Glorie, The Virginian. *Mini-series*: Lonesome Dove (Emmy nom. 1989). *Special*: Edith Wharton's Summer, Cool Women in History (host-season 2). *Guest:* More than 60 appearances.

LANE, NATHAN
Actor. r.n. Joseph Lane. b. Jersey City, NJ, Feb. 3, 1956. Received 1992 Obie Award for Sustained Excellence in Off-B'way Theatre.
THEATRE: *B'way:* Present Laughter (Drama Desk nom.), Merlin, The Wind in the Willows, Some Americans Abroad, On Borrowed Time, Guys & Dolls (Drama Desk & Outer Critics Circle Awards; Tony nom.), The Frogs, Laughter on the 23rd Floor, Love! Valour! Compassion! (Drama Desk, Outer Critics Circle and Obie Awards; also Off-B'way), A Funny Thing Happened On The Way To The Forum (2 Tony Awards), The Man Who Came to Dinner, The Producers (also London), Dedication or the Stuff of Dreams, The Odd Couple, Resurrection Blues, Butley, November. *Off-B'way*: A Midsummer Night's Dream, Measure for Measure, The Merry Wives of Windsor, She Stoops to Conquer, Claptrap, The Common Pursuit (Dramalogue Award), In a Pig's Valise, The Film Society, Uncounted Blessings, Hidden in This Picture, Love, The Lisbon Traviata (also L.A.; Drama Desk, Lucille Lortel, LA Drama Critics Circle & Dramalogue Awards), Bad Habits, Lips Together Teeth Apart (also L.A.).
PICTURES: Ironweed (debut, 1987), Joe Vs. the Volcano, The Lemon Sisters, He Said She Said, Frankie and Johnny, Life With Mikey, Addams Family Values, The Lion King (voice), Jeffrey (American Comedy Award nom.), The Birdcage (Golden Globe nom., American Comedy Award, SAG Award 1997), Mouse Hunt, Trixie, The Lion King II: Simba's Pride, Love's Labour's Lost, Isn't She Great, Get Bruce (cameo), At First Sight, Titan A.E. (voice), Trixie, Stuart Little 2 (voice), Nicholas Nickleby, Teacher's Pet (voice), Win a Date with Tad Hamilton!, The Producers (Golden Globe nom. 2006), Nutcracker: The Untold Story, Swing Vote, Astro Boy (voice), Nutcracker and the Rat King.
TELEVISION: *Movies*: Hallmark Hall of Fame's The Boys Next Door, Timon and Pumba (Emmy Award), Merry Christmas George Bailey, The Man Who Came to Dinner, Laughter on the 23rd Floor, A Muppets Christmas: Letters to Santa. *Series*: One of the Boys, Encore! Encore!, George and Martha (Emmy nom. 2000), Teacher's Pet (Emmy Award, voice 2001), One Saturday Morning (voice), Charlie Lawrence (also exec. prod.). *Specials*: Alice in Wonderland, The Last Mile, Co-host 1995 Tony Awards, 1995 Kennedy Center Honors, Host 1996 Tony Awards (American Comedy Award nom.), Recording 'The Producers': A Musical Romp with Mel Brooks. *Guest:* More than 95 appearances.

LANG, STEPHEN
Actor. b. Queens, NY, July 11, 1952. e. Swarthmore Col. Professional debut 1974 at Washington D.C.'s Folger Theatre.
THEATRE: NY: Rosencrantz and Guildenstern Are Dead, Henry V, Bloomsday on Broadway, The Shadow of a Gun, Saint Joan, Hamlet, Johnny on the Spot, Death of a Salesman, Barbarians, The Winter's Tale, A Few Good Men, The Speed of Darkness.
PICTURES: Twice in a Lifetime (debut, 1985), Band of the Hand, Manhunter, Project X, Last Exit to Brooklyn, The Hard Way, Another You, Guilty As Sin, Gettysburg, Tombstone, Tall Tale, The Amazing Panda Adventure, The Shadow Conspiracy, An Occasional Hell, Fire Down Below, Story of a Bad Boy, Trixie, The Proposal, After the Storm, D-Tox, The Treatment, Gods and Generals, Save Me, From Mexico with Love, Public Enemies, The Men Who Stare at Goats, Avatar, White Irish Drinkers Christina, Dancehall, Conan.
TELEVISION: *Movies*: King of America, Death of a Salesman, Stone Pillow, Babe Ruth, Taking Back My Life: The Nancy Ziegenmeyer Story, Darkness Before Dawn, Murder Between Friends, A Season of Hope, The Possession of Michael D., The Phantoms, Strangers, Escape: Human Cargo, A Town Has Turned to Dust, At the Mercy of a Stranger, After the Storm, Code 11-14, Matadors. *Series*: Crime Story, The Fugitive, The Bronx Is Burning. *Specials:* Anyone for Tennyson?, The Mother, Hubert Selby, Jr.: It/ll Be Better Tomorrow. *Guest:* More than 55 appearances.

LANGE, JESSICA
Actress. b. Cloquet, MN, Apr. 20, 1949. e. U. of Minnesota. Left to study mime 2 years under Etienne Decroux in Paris. Dancer, Opera Comique, Paris; model with Wilhelmina, NY. Worked in experimental theatre in New York. Broadway debut 1992 in A Streetcar Named Desire (Theatre World Award).
THEATRE: *B'way:* The Glass Menagerie. *London:* Long Days Journey Into Night.
PICTURES: King Kong (debut, 1976, Golden Globe Award 1977), All That Jazz, How to Beat the High Cost of Living, The Postman Always Rings Twice, Frances (Academy Award nom.; Golden Globe nom. 1983), Tootsie (Academy Award, best supporting actress, Golden Globe Award 1982), Country (also co-prod., Academy Award nom.; Golden Globe nom. 1985), Sweet Dreams (Academy Award nom. 1986), Crimes of the Heart, Far North, Everybody's All-American, Music Box (Academy Award nom.; Golden Globe nom. 1990), Men Don't Leave, Cape Fear, Night and the City, Blue Sky (Academy Award, Golden Globe Award 1995), Losing Isaiah, Rob Roy, A Thousand Acres (Golden Globe nom. 1998), Hush, Cousin Bette, Titus, Prozac Nation, Normal, Masked & Anonymous, Big Fish, Code 11-14, Neverwas, Aftershock, The Mermaids Singing, Don't Come Knockin', Bonneville, The Big Valley.
TELEVISION: *Movies*: The Best Little Girl in the World, Cat on a Hot Tin Roof, O Pioneers! (Golden Globe nom. 1993), A Streetcar Named Desire (Emmy nom.; Golden Globe Award 1996). Normal (Emmy nom.; Golden Globe nom. 2004), Sybil, Grey Gardens (Emmy Award 2009, Golden Globe nom. 2010). *Mini-series:* A Century of Women. *Series:* Stories from My Childhood (voice). *Specials / Documentaries:* SPFX: The Empire Strikes Back, A Century of Cinema, A Century of Women (voice), Nobel Peace Prize Concert (host), XXI Century, Vivien Leigh: Scarlett & Beyond, Myrna Loy Remembered, Peace by Peace: Women on the Frontlines (host), The Needs of Kim Stanley. *Guest:* More than 68 appearances.

LANGELLA, FRANK
Actor. b. Bayonne, NJ, Jan. 1, 1938. Studied acting at Syracuse U.; later in regional repertory, summer stock, and On- and Off-B'way. Joined Lincoln Ctr. Rep. Co., 1963.
THEATRE: *NY:* The Immoralist (Off-B'way debut, 1963), Benito Cereno, The Old Glory (Obie Award), Good Day (Obie Award), The White Devil (Obie Award), Long Day's Journey Into Night, Yerma, Seascape (B'way debut, 1975; Tony Award), Dracula, A Cry of Players, Cyrano de Bergerac, The Tooth of the Crime, Ring Around the Moon, Amadeus, Passion, Design for Living, Sherlock's Last Case, The Tempest, Booth, Present Laughter, Fortune's Fool (Tony Award). *L.A.*: The Devils, Les Liaisons Dangereuses, My Fair Lady, Scenes From an Execution, The Father.
PICTURES: Diary of a Mad Housewife (debut, 1970, Golden Globe nom. 1971), The Twelve Chairs, The Deadly Trap, The Wrath of God, Dracula, Those Lips Those Eyes, Sphinx, The Men's Club, Masters of the Universe, And God Created Woman, True Identity, 1492: Conquest of Paradise, Body of Evidence, Dave, Brainscan, Junior, Bad Company, Cutthroat Island, Eddie, Lolita, I'm Losing You, Small Soldiers, The Ninth Gate, Stardom, Sweet November, House of D, Back in the Day, How You Look to Me, Goodnight, and Good Luck, Rajapur, Superman Returns, Starting Out in the Evening, The Caller, Frost/Nixon (Academy Award nom.; Golden Globe nom. 2009), The Tale of Despereaux (voice), All Good Things, The Box, Wall Street: Money Never Sleeps, Unknown White Male.
TELEVISION: *Movies*: The Mark of Zorro, The Seagull, Eccentricities of a Nightingale, Sherlock Holmes: The Strange Case of Alice Faulkner, Liberty, Doomsday Gun, Moses, Kilroy,

Jason and the Argonauts, Cry Baby Lane, Now You See It..., 10.5: Apocalypse, Capitol Law, The Water Is Wide. *Series*: The Beast, Unscripted, Kitchen Confidential. *Specials/Documentaries:* Stella Adler: Awake and Dream! (narr.), Lincoln, Tennessee Williams: Orpheus of the American Stage, Mummies: Tales from the Egyptian Crypts, The Greatest Pharaohs, I, Leonardo: A Journey of the Mind (Emmy nom. 1983), Stephen Hawking's Universe, Inside 'High Noon' (narr.), Benito Cereno, The Good Day, The Ambassador, The American Woman: Portrait in Courage, Sherlock Holmes, Fortitude (Kurt Vonnegut's Monkey House), Small Soldiers: Size Doesn't Matter (voice). *Guest:* More than 74 appearances.

LANGLEY, DONNA

Executive. b. England. e. Kent College, England. Joined New Line Cinema in 1994 and rose to senior v.p., production before joining Universal Pictures as its senior v.p., production in 2001. Langley was named executive v.p., production in Oct. 2003 and in 2005 was made president, production for Universal Pictures. where she directed all aspects of production for Universal's feature film releases. Generating profits in excess of $1 billion, 2007 was the most successful year in the studio's long history, with "American Gangster," "The Bourne Ultimatum," "Knocked Up" and "I Now Pronounce You Chuck & Larry" all surpassing the $100 million mark in domestic ticket sales. October, 2009 Langley was promoted to co-chrm. of Universal with Adam Fogelson.

LANSBURY, ANGELA

Actress. b. London, England, Oct. 16, 1925. Brothers are producers Bruce and Edgar Lansbury. e. South Hampstead Sch. for Girls, England; Acad. of Music, London; Feagin Dramatic Sch., N.Y. Mother was actress Moyna Macgill. To NY 1940 to study drama. Signed to contract by MGM, 1944. Exercise and lifestyle video: Positive Moves, 1988. *Books:* Positive Moves, 1990, See Britain at Work, See Scotland at Work: A Guide to Factories & Craft Workshops Open to Visitors.
THEATRE: *B'way:* Hotel Paradiso (NY debut, 1957), A Taste of Honey, Anyone Can Whistle, Mame (Tony Award, 1966), Dear World (Tony Award, 1969), Prettybelle (closed out of town), All Over, Gypsy (Tony Award, 1975), Hamlet, The King and I, Sweeney Todd: The Demon Barber of Fleet Street (Tony Award, 1979), A Little Family Business, Mame (1983 revival), Deuce, Blithe Spirit (Tony Award 2009).
PICTURES: Gaslight (debut, 1944; Academy Award nom. 1945), National Velvet, The Picture of Dorian Gray (Academy Award nom. ; Golden Globe Award 1946), The Harvey Girls, The Hoodlum Saint, The Private Affairs of Bel Ami, Till the Clouds Roll By, If Winter Comes, Tenth Avenue Angel, State of the Union, The Three Musketeers, The Red Danube, Samson and Delilah, Kind Lady, Mutiny, Remains to Be Seen, The Purple Mask, A Lawless Street, The Court Jester, Please Murder Me, The Key Man (A Life at Stake), The Long Hot Summer, The Reluctant Debutante, The Summer of the 17th Doll (Season of Passion), The Dark at the Top of the Stairs, A Breath of Scandal, Blue Hawaii, All Fall Down, The Manchurian Candidate (Academy Award nom.; Golden Globe Award 1963), In the Cool of the Day, The World of Henry Orient, Dear Heart, The Greatest Story Ever Told, Harlow, The Amorous Adventures of Moll Flanders, Mister Buddwing, Something for Everyone (Golden Globe nom. 1971), Bedknobs and Broomsticks (Golden Globe nom. 1972), Death on the Nile, The Lady Vanishes, The Mirror Crack'd, The Last Unicorn (voice), The Pirates of Penzance, The Company of Wolves, Beauty and the Beast (voice), Beauty and the Beast: The Enchanted Christmas (voice), Anastasia (voice), Fantasia 2000, Forever Hollywood, Broadway: The Golden Age by the Legends Who Were There, The Last Unicorn, Nanny McPhee, Heidi 4 Paws (voice).
TELEVISION: *Movies*: Little Gloria... Happy at Last (Emmy nom. 1983), The Gift of Love: A Christmas Story (Golden Globe nom. 1984), The First Olympics: Athens 1896, A Talent for Murder, Lace, Rage of Angels: The Story Continues, Shootdown, The Shell Seekers, The Love She Sought, Mrs. Harris Goes to Paris, Mrs. Santa Claus, Murder She Wrote: South by Southwest, The Unexpected Mrs. Pollifax, Murder She Wrote: A Story to Die For, Murder She Wrote: The Last Free Man, AMC Backstory: The Long Hot Summer, Murder, She Wrote: The Celtic Riddle, The Blackwater Lightship (Emmy nom. 2004). *Series*: Pantomime Quiz, Murder She Wrote (also exec. prod., 10 Emmy noms.; 4 Golden Globe Awards, 6 other noms.), Poirot, Law & Order: Trial by Jury (Emmy nom. as guest 2005). *Specials*: Sweeney Todd: The Demon Barber of Fleet Street (Emmy nom. 1985), Elizabeth Taylor: England's Other Elizabeth, Circus of the Stars (ringmaster), Tournament of Roses Parade (grand marshal, 1993), The 43rd Annual Tony Awards (Emmy nom. 1987) *Guest*: More than 190 appearances.

LANSBURY, BRUCE

Executive. b. London, England, Jan. 12, 1930. Brother of Angela and twin Edgar. e. UCLA. Mother was actress Moyna Macgill. Writer, prod. KABC-TV, Los Angeles, 1957-59; joined CBS-TV, 1959, was ass't. dir., program dev., Hollywood, director for daytime and nighttime programs, and v.p., programs, New York; 1964-66, indep. prod., Broadway stage; 1966-69 producer, Wild Wild West, CBS series; 1969-72, prod. Mission: Impossible, Paramount Movies of Week; then v.p., creative affairs, Paramount TV.
TELEVISION: Murder, She Wrote: The Celtic Riddle (writer). Great Adventure (series; prod.), Wings of the Water (exec. prod.), Murder She Wrote.

LANSING, SHERRY

Executive, Producer. b. Chicago, IL, July 31, 1944. e. Northwestern Univ, B.S., 1966 (cum laude). m. director William Friedkin. Taught math and English in Los Angeles city schools, 1966-69. Acted in films (Loving, Rio Lobo) and numerous TV shows. Exec. story editor, movies, Wagner Int'l. Prod. Co, 1970-74; v.p., production, Heyday Prods., 1973-75; director, West Coast Develop., 1974-75; story editor, mgr., 1975-77, v.p., creative affairs, 1977, senior v.p., production, 1977-80, Columbia Pictures. Became president of production, 20th Century Fox, 1980-83, being the first woman to hold this position in the motion picture industry. Founded Jaffe-Lansing Prods. with Stanley Jaffe, 1983; independent producer, Jaffe-Lansing Prods., 1983-91. Chairman, Paramount Motion Pictures Group, 1992-2005. (Paramount Pictures Corporation is a unit of Viacom Entertainment Group). Recipient of a star on Hollywood Walk of Fame, 1996. In 2007, Lansing received the Jean Hersholt Award for her humanitarian work. Also in 2007 she became a dir. of Qualcomm. After her retirement from Paramount in 2005, she created The Sherry Lansing Foundation, a not-for-profit organization dedicated to cancer research, education, art and culture. Among Lansing's initiatives within the Foundation is PrimeTime LAUSD, a partnership with the Los Angeles Unified School District designed to engage retirees over 60 in improving the state of public education through targeted volunteerism. Her experience as a teacher has helped secure the place of education on the Foundation's slate of projects. Lansing sits on the boards of The Carter Center, Teach for America, and The American Association for Cancer Research. Additionally, she is a Regent of the University of California and serves as chair of the University Health Services Committee. Lansing also serves on California Governor Arnold Schwarzenegger's Committee on Education Excellence as well as the California State Superintendent of Education's P-16 Advisory Council. Other bd. involvement includes: the Executive Committee of the Board of Directors of Friends of Cancer Research, and on the board of the Lasker Foundation. Lansing also is on the American Red Cross Board of Governors and works with "Stop Cancer," a non-profit philanthropic group she founded in partnership with Dr. Armand Hammer.
PICTURES: *Co-prod:* Racing with the Moon, Firstborn (exec. prod.), Fatal Attraction (Academy Award nom. 1988), The Accused, Black Rain, School Ties, Indecent Proposal, The Kid Stays In the Picture (documentary), The Untouchables: Capone Rising.
TELEVISION: *Exec. producer:* When the Time Comes, Mistress.

LAPAGLIA, ANTHONY

Actor. b. Adelaidse, Australia, 1959. Former teacher, moved to U.S. in 1984. Made Off-B'way debut in Bouncers, followed by On the Open Road. B'way: The Rose Tattoo (Theatre World Award).
PICTURES: Slaves of New York (debut, 1989), Dangerous Obsession (Mortal Sins), Betsy's Wedding, He Said/She Said, One Good Cop, 29th Street, Whispers in the Dark, Innocent Blood, So I Married an Axe Murderer, The Client, The Custodian, Mixed Nuts, Bulletproof Heart, Lucky Break, Empire Records, The Funeral, Brilliant Lies, The Garden of Redemption, Phoenix, Summer of Sam, The House of Mirth, Sweet and Lowdown, Black and Blue, Company Man, Looking for Alibrandi, Autumn in New York, The Bank, The Salton Sea, I Fought the Law, Happy Hour, I'm With Lucy, The Guys, Winter Solstice (also exec. prod.), The Architect, The Constant Gardener, A View From the Bridge, Happy Feet (voice), $9.99, Overnight, Balibo.
TELEVISION: *Movies*: Police Story: Gladiator School, Criminal Justice, Keeper of the City, Black Magic, Past Tense, Never Give Up: The Jimmy V Story, The Garden of Redemption, Nitti: The Enforcer, Lansky, Black and Blue, On the Edge, The Other Side. *Mini-series*: Murder One: Diary of a Serial Killer. *Series*: Murder One, Normal Ohio, Frasier (3 Emmy noms. as guest), Without a Trace (Emmy nom.; Golden Globe Award 2004). *Documentaries:* The Needs of Kim Stanley, Nature (series, narr. 2 episodes), Johnny Warren's Football Mission, The Away Game (narr. exec. prod.). *Guest*: More than 72 appearances.

LARROQUETTE, JOHN

Actor. b. New Orleans, LA., Nov. 25, 1947. Disc jockey on FM radio during 1960s and early 70s. Acted on L.A. stage from 1973 (The Crucible, Enter Laughing, Endgame). Prof. debut, TV series Doctor's Hospital, 1976-78. Was narrator for film Texas Chainsaw Massacre.
PICTURES: Altered States, Heart Beat, Green Ice, Stripes, Cat People, Hysterical, Twilight Zone—The Movie, Choose Me, Meatballs Part II, Star Trek III: The Search for Spock, Summer Rental, Blind Date, Second Sight, Madhouse, Tune in Tomorrow, Richie Rich, Tales from the Crypt Presents: Demon Knight (cameo), Isn't She Great, The Texas Chainsaw Massacre (2003, narr.), Southland Tales, The Texas Chainsaw Massacre: The Beginning (narr.), Gun.
TELEVISION: *Movies:* Bare Essence, The Last Ninja, Hot Paint,

Convicted, One Special Victory (also co-exec. prod.), The Defenders: Payback, The Tenth Kingdom, Walter and Henry, Till Dad Do Us Part, The Heart Department, Wedding Daze, McBride: Murder Past Midnight, McBride: The Chameleon Murder, McBride: It's Murder, Madam, McBride: The Doctor Is Out, Really Out, McBride: Tune in for Murder, McBride: Anybody Here Murder Marty?, McBride: Requiem, McBride: Fallen Idol, McBride: Dogged, McBride: Semper Fi, Pleading Guilty. *Series*: Doctor's Hospital, Baa Baa Black Sheep, Night Court (4 Emmy Awards, 1985-88, Golden Globe nom.), The John Larroquette Show (Emmy nom. 1994), Payne, Rosebud, Corsairs, Happy Family, The Practice (Emmy Award, 1997, 1 other nom.), Boston Legal. *Guest*: More than 86 appearances.

LASSALLY, WALTER
Cinematographer. b. Berlin, Germany, Dec. 18, 1926. Entered indust. as clapper-boy at Riverside Studios. During 1950s allied himself with Britain's Free Cinema filmmakers working for Lindsay Anderson, Gavin Lambert, Tony Richardson and Karel Reisz. 2008 received ASC International Award.
PICTURES: A Girl in Black (feature debut, 1956), Beat Girl, A Taste of Honey, Electra, The Loneliness of the Long Distance Runner, Tom Jones, Zorba the Greek (Academy Award, 1964), The Day the Fish Came Out, Joanna, Oedipus the King, The Adding Machine, Three Into Two Won't Go, Something for Everyone, Twinky (Lola), Savages, Happy Mother's Day... Love George, To Kill a Clown, The Wild Party, Pleasantville, The Great Bank Hoax, The Woman Across the Way, Hullabaloo Over George and Bonnie's Pictures, Something Short of Paradise, The Blood of Hussain, Angel of Iron, Memoirs of a Survivor, Too Far to Go, Heat and Dust, Private School, The Bostonians, The Deceivers, Fragments of Isabella, The Perfect Murder, Ballad of the Sad Cafe, The Little Dolphins, Ta Delfinakia tou Amvrakikou, Silent Film (short), Aci gonul, Crescent Heart.
TELEVISION: *Movies*: Dan, Hullabaloo Over Georgie and Bonnie's Pictures, Too Far to Go, Gauguin the Savage, Life on the Mississippi, The Private History of a Campaign That Failed, The Mysterious Stranger, Pudd'nhead Wilson, Children in the Crossfire, Stone Pillow, Adventures of Huckleberry Finn, Mrs. Delafield Wants to Marry, The Man Upstairs. *Mini-series*: Nature Perfected: The Story of the Garden.

LASSER, LOUISE
Actress. b. New York, NY, April 11, 1939. e. Brandeis U., New School for Social Research. Appeared on stage before theatrical film debut in 1965 with What's New Pussycat? Won first Clio Award for best actress in a commercial.
THEATRE: I Can Get it For You Wholesale, The Third Ear, Henry Sweet Henry, Lime Green/Khaki Blue, The Chinese, Marie & Bruce, A Coupla White Chicks Sitting Around Talking.
PICTURES: What's Up Tiger Lily? (voice), Take the Money and Run, Bananas, Such Good Friends, Everything You Always Wanted to Know About Sex, Slither, Simon, In God We Trust, Stardust Memories, Crimewave, Nightmare at Shadow Woods (Blood Rage), Surrender, Sing, Rude Awakening, Modern Love, Frankenhooker, The Night We Never Met, Layin' Low, Sudden Manhattan, Happiness, Mystery Men, Requiem for a Dream, Fast Food, Fast Women, National Lampoon's Gold Diggers, Driving Me Crazy.
TELEVISION: *Movies*: Coffee, Tea or Me?, Isn't It Shocking?, Just Me and You (also writer), For Ladies Only, Club Land. *Series*: The Doctors, Mary Hartman Mary Hartman (Emmy nom. 1976), It's a Living.

LASSETER, JOHN
Executive, Director, Writer, Executive Producer.
b. Hollywood, CA, Jan. 12, 1957. e. California Institute of the Arts in Valencia, CA. In 1979 won Achievement Award for Animation of Lady and the Lamp from the Student Academy Awards, USA. Lasseter is a much-nominated animator who has received numerous awards, including an Oscar for Best Animated Short Film, Tin Toy, in 1988 (shared with William Reeves). In 1982 Disney hired Lasseter as an animator. He wanted to pursue computer animation, so in 1984 Lasseter left Disney in order to be on the cutting edge, with the computer animation division of Lucasfilm's Industrial Light and Magic. In 1986, Steve Jobs, co-founder and chairman of Apple Computer, Inc., purchased the computer division of Lucasfilm and incorporated it as an independent company, under the name Pixar Animation Studios. Jobs gave Lasseter the freedom to direct, produce, write, and create models for many projects, many of which were TV commercials. Lasseter directed the studio's first short film, 1986's Luxo, Jr, which starred a desk lamp and its precocious child. In 1988, Lasseter directed the short, Tin Toy, which would make history as the first computer animated film ever to win an Academy Award. Pixar's Toy Story received four Oscar nominations and Lasseter was presented with a Special Achievement Academy Award for his part in bringing the first feature-length computer animated film to the screen. Pixar merged with The Walt Disney in May 2006. Pixar is now a wholly owned subsidiary of The Walt Disney Company, and Lasseter serves as chief creative officer for Pixar Animation Studios and Walt Disney Animation. He also is principal creative adviser for Walt Disney Imagineering. 2004 received ADG Award for Contribution to Cinematic Imagery.
PICTURES: *Director:* Lady and the Lamp (debut, 1979), Mickey's Christmas Carol (creative collaboration only), Luxo Jr. (also prod., writer, models, animation), Red's Dream (also writer, animator), Tin Toy (also writer), Knick Knack (also writer), Toy Story (also writer, modeling & animation system development), A Bug's Life (also writer, additional voices), Toy Story 2 (also writer, additional voices), Cars (also writer, Academy Award nom. 2007). *Executive producer:* Geri's Game (short), For the Birds (short), Spirited Away, Monster's Inc., Finding Nemo, Boundin' (short), Howl's Moving Castle, The Incredibles, One Man Band (short), Ratatouille, Wall-E, Ponyo on the Cliff by the Sea (english version, prod.), Bolt, Up, The Princess and the Frog, Toy Story 3, Tangled. *Animator:* The Brave Little Toaster, Luxo Jr. in Surprise, and Light and Heavy (short). *Character Design & Animation:* The Adventures of André and Wally B. *Computer Animation:* Young Sherlock Holmes. *Executive creative consultant:* Porco rosso

LASZLO, ANDREW
Cinematographer. b. Papa, Hungary, Jan. 12, 1926. To U.S. in 1947, working as cameraman on tv before turning to feature films.
PICTURES: One Potato Two Potato, You're a Big Boy Now, The Night They Raided Minskys, Popi, The Out of Towners, Lovers and Other Strangers, The Owl and the Pussycat, Jennifer on My Mind, To Find a Man, The Effect of Gamma Rays on Man-in-the-Moon Marigolds, Class of '44, Countdown at Kusini, Thieves, Somebody Killed Her Husband, The Warriors, The Funhouse, Southern Comfort, I the Jury, First Blood, Streets of Fire, Thief of Hearts, Remo Williams: The Adventure Begins, Poltergeist II, Innerspace, Star Trek V: The Final Frontier, Ghost Dad, Newsies.
TELEVISION: *Specials/ Movies/Feature pilots:* The Happeners, The Cliffdwellers, Daphne, Teacher Teacher, Black Water Gold, Top of the Hill, Shogun, The Man Without a Country, Miracle on 34th Street, The Unwanted, Spanner's Key, Thin Ice, Love is Forever. *Mini-series*: Washington Behind Closed Doors, The Dain Curse, Top of the Hill, Shogun (Emmy nom. 1981). *Series*: The Phil Silvers Show, Joe and Mabel, Mama, Brenner, Naked City, The Nurses, Doctors and Nurses, Coronet Blue. Specials: New York New York, The Beatles at Shea Stadium, Ed Sullivan. *Documentaries*: High Adventure with Lowell Thomas, The Twentieth Century, and numerous commericals.

LATSIS, PETER C.
Publicist. b. Chicago, IL, Mar. 9, 1919. e. Wright Jr. College, Chicago. Newspaper reporter, Chicago Herald-American, 1942-45; Army, 1943; joined Fox West Coast Theatres, Los Angeles, in theatre operations 1945; adv.-pub. dept. 1946; asst. dir. adv.-pub. 1955; press rep. National Theatres, 1958; press relations dir., National General Corp., 1963; home office special field pub. repr., American International Pictures, 1973; Filmways Pictures, 1980-82; Recipient of Publicists Guild's Robert Yeager Award, 1983. Member, Motion Picture Pioneers. Unit rep., Executive Bd. of Publicists Guild of America, 1993-95.

LAUNER, DALE
Writer. b. Cleveland, OH. E. Cal State Northridge.
PICTURES: Ruthless People, Blind Date, Dirty Rotten Scoundrels, My Cousin Vinny, Love Potion No.9 (also dir.), Tom's Nu Heaven (also prod., dir.).

LAURENTS, ARTHUR
Writer, Director. b. New York, NY, July 14, 1917. e. Cornell U., B.A., 1937. First Professional writing as radio script writer in 1939. In Army 1941-45. Member of the Council of the Dramatists Guild; Theatre Hall of Fame.
THEATRE: *Author:* Home of the Brave (Sidney Howard Award), Heartsong, The Bird Cage, The Time of the Cuckoo, A Clearing in the Woods, Invitation to a March, West Side Story, Gypsy, Hallelujah, Baby! (Tony Award), Scream, The Enclave, Running Time, Jolson Sings Again, The Radical Mystique. *Dir:* Invitation to a March, I Can Get It for You Wholesale, La Cage aux Folles (Tony Award), Birds of Paradise. *Author-Director:* Anyone Can Whistle, Do I Hear a Waltz?, The Madwoman of Central Park West, Gypsy (revival), Nick and Nora.
PICTURES: *Writer*: Rope, The Snake Pit, Caught, Home of the Brave, Anna Lucasta, Anastasia (writer, play), Summertime, Bonjour Tristesse, West Side Story, Gypsy, The Way We Were (from his own novel, WGA nom. 1974), The Turning Point (also co-prod.; 2 Academy Award noms.; Golden Globe, WGA Award 1978), Anastasia (s.p.), Paragraph 175 (doc.), Tying the Knot (doc.). *Actor*: The Celluloid Closet, Leonard Bernstein Reaching for the Note, Broadway: The Golden Age by the Legends Who Were There.
TELEVISION: *Movie:* Gypsy.

LAURIA, DAN
Actor. b. Brooklyn, NY, April 12, 1947. e. So Conn. St. Col., Univ. of Conn. Served in U.S. Marine Corps., 1970-73.
PICTURES: Without a Trace, Stakeout, Another Stakeout, Excessive Force II: Force on Force, Dog Watch, Independence Day, Ricochet River, Justice, Rhapsody in Bloom, True Friends, Wide Awake, A Wake in Providence, Stranger in My House, Fear Runs Silent, Full Circle, High Times Potluck, The Empath, Contagion, The Signs of the Cross, The Book of Joe (dir., writer), Big Momma's House 2, The Waiter, Dear Me, In Search Of, Roney's Point, The Five, Donna on Demand, Alien Trespass, The

Waiter, Life of Lemon, Here's the Kicker.
TELEVISION: *Movies*: Johnny Brass, Johnny Bull, Doing Life, At Mother's Request, Angel in Green, David, Howard Beach: Making the Case for Murder, The Big One: The Great Los Angeles Earthquake, Overexposed, Dead and Alive, From the Files of Joseph Wambaugh: A Jury of One, In the Line of Duty: Ambush in Waco, In the Line of Duty: Hunt for Justice, Between Mother and Daughter, Terror in the Family The Bachelor's Baby, Prison of Secrets, Merry Christmas George Bailey, Backlash, Mr. Murder, From the Earth to the Moon, Justice, Common Ground, Hangman, Never Say Die, Behind the Camera: The Unauthorized Story of 'Charlie's Angels', The Path to 9/11, Finish Line. *Series*: Love of Life, One Life to Live, Hooperman, The Wonder Years, Amazing Grace, Party of Five, The Hoop Life, Costello, N.Y.U.K, JAG, The Bronx Is Burning. *Special*: Between Mother and Daughter. *Guest*: More than 106 appearances.

LAURIE, PIPER

Actress. r.n. Rosetta Jacobs. b. Detroit, MI, Jan. 22, 1932. e. Los Angeles H.S. Acted in school plays, signed by U.I. in 1949.
THEATRE: The Glass Menagerie (revival), Marco Polo Sings a Solo, The Innocents, Biography, Rosemary, The Alligators, The Last Flapper (tour), The Destiny of Me.
PICTURES: Louisa (debut, 1950), The Milkman, Francis Goes to the Races, The Prince Who Was a Thief, Son of Ali Baba, Has Anybody Seen My Gal, No Room for the Groom, Mississippi Gambler, Golden Blade, Dangerous Mission, Johnny Dark, Dawn at Socorro, Smoke Signal, Ain't Misbehavin', Kelly and Me, Until They Sail, The Hustler (Academy Award nom. 1962), Carrie (Academy Award nom.; Golden Globe nom. 1977), Ruby, The Boss's Son, Tim, Return to Oz, Children of a Lesser God (Academy Award nom. 1987), Distortions, Appointment with Death, Tiger Warsaw, Dream a Little Dream, Mother Mother, Other People's Money, Storyville, Rich in Love, Trauma, Wrestling Ernest Hemingway, The Crossing Guard, The Grass Harp, The Faculty, Palmer's Pick Up, The Rage: Carrie 2 (voice), The Mao Game, Eulogy, Bad Blood, The Dead Girl, Hounddog, Another Harvest Moon, Bad Blood... the Hunger, Saving Grace B. Jones, Hesher.
TELEVISION: *Movies*: In the Matter of Karen Ann Quinlan, Rainbow, Skag, The Bunker (Emmy nom. 1981), Mae West, Love Mary, Toughlove, Promise (Emmy Award, Golden Globe nom. 1987), Go To the Light, Rising Son, Poisoned By Love: The Kern County Murders, Lies and Lullabies, Shadows of Desire, Fighting for My Daughter, In the Blink of an Eye, Road to Galveston, Alone, Inherit the Wind, Possessed, Dario Argento: An Eye for Horror, Midwives, The Last Brickmaker in America. *Mini-series:* The Thorn Birds (Emmy nom.; Golden Globe nom. 1983), Tender is the Night, Intensity. *Series*: Skag, Twin Peaks (Golden Globe Award 1991, 2 Emmy noms.), Partners. *Specials:* Days of Wine and Roses (Emmy nom.), The Road That Led Afar (Emmy nom.), The Deaf Heart (Emmy nom.), The Secret Life of Margaret Sanger, St. Elsewhere (Emmy nom.), Studio One in Hollywood (Emmy nom. 1958), Playhouse 90 (Emmy nom. 1959), Frasier (Emmy nom. 1999). *Guest:* More than 91 appearances.

LAUTER, ED

Actor. b. Long Beach, NY, Oct. 30, 1940.
PICTURES: The New Centurions, Hickey & Boggs, The Last American Hero, Executive Action, Lolly Madonna XXX, The Longest Yard, French Connection II, Breakheart Pass, Family Plot, King Kong, The Chicken Chronicles, Magic, The Amateur, Death Hunt, Timerider, The Big Score, Eureka, Lassiter, Cujo, Finders Keepers, Death Wish 3, Girls Just Want to Have Fun, Youngblood, 3:15, Raw Deal, Chief Zabu, Revenge of the Nerds II, Gleaming the Cube, Fat Man and Little Boy, Tennessee Waltz, School Ties, Wagons East!, Trial by Jury, Girl in the Cadillac, Digital Man, Crash, Rattled, Coyote Summer, Mulholland Falls, Top of the World, Allie & Me, Out in Fifty, Farewell My Love, Civility, Python, Thirteen Days, Gentleman B., Blast, Not Another Teen Sex Movie, Go For Broke, Seabiscuit, Into the Fire, Purple Heart, Venice Underground, The Lost, Brothas in Arms, The Longest Yard, Camille, The American Standards, The Number 23, A Modern Twain Story: The Prince and the Pauper, Something's Wrong in Kansas, Taken by Force, Godspeed, The Prometheus Project, The American Standards, Sweetwater.
TELEVISION: *Movies*: Class of '63, The Migrants, The Godchild, Satan's Triangle, A Shadow in the Streets, Last Hours Before Morning, The Clone Master, The Jericho Mile, Love's Savage Fury, Undercover with the KKK, The Boy Who Drank Too Much, Guyana Tragedy—The Story of Jim Jones, AlcatrazThe Whole Shocking Story, In the Custody of Strangers, Rooster, The Seduction of Gina, Three Wishes of Billy Grier, The Last Days of Patton, The Thanksgiving Promise, Calendar Girl Cop Killer?: The Bambi Bembenek Story, Extreme Justice, The Return of Ironside, Secret Sins of the Father, Tuskegee Airmen, Ravenhawk, Under Wraps, Mercenary, A Bright Shining Lie, Dollar for the Dead, Python, Into the Fire, Expecting a Miracle. *Series*: B.J. and the Bear, ER. *Guest:* More than 103 appearances.

LAVIN, LINDA

Actress. b. Portland, ME, Oct. 15, 1937. e. Coll. of William & Mary. First professional job in chorus of Camden County (N.J.) Music Circus. Worked in plays both off and on Broadway before-returning to TV, where guest-starred on such series as Family, Rhoda, Phyllis and Harry O.
THEATRE: Oh Kay! (Off-B'way debut, 1960), A Family Affair (B'way debut), Revues: Wet Paint (Theatre World Award), The Game Is Up, The Mad Show, member acting co.: Eugene O'Neil Playwright's Unit, 1968; It's a Bird It's a Plane... It's Superman, Something Different, Little Murders (Outer Critics Circle & Sat. Review Awards), Cop Out, The Last of the Red Hot Lovers (Tony nom.), Story Theatre, Dynamite Tonight, Broadway Bound (Tony, Drama Desk, Outer Critics Circle & Helen Hayes Awards), Gypsy, The Sisters Rosensweig, Death Defying Acts.
PICTURES: The Muppets Take Manhattan, See You in the Morning, I Want to Go Home, The Back-up Plan.
TELEVISION: *Movies*: The Morning After, Like Mom and Me, The $5.20 an Hour Dream, A Matter of Life and Death (also exec. prod. & developed), Another Woman's Child, A Place to Call Home (also exec. prod. & developed), Lena: My Hundred Children, Room for Two, Stolen Moments, Secrets from the Rose Garden, A Dream Is a Wish Your Heart Makes, The Annette Funicello Story, The Ring, For the Children: The Irvine Fertility Scandal, Best Friends for Life, Collected Stories. *Series*: Barney Miller, Alice (2 Golden Globe Awards, 1 other nom.; Emmy nom. 1979), Room for Two (also co-exec. prod.), Conrad Bloom. *Documentaries:* CBS: On the Air (co-host, mini-series), Beneath the Airlie Oak (narr.), The Lady in Question Is Charles Busch. *Guest:* More than 80 appearances.

LAW, JUDE

Actor. b. London, England, Dec. 29, 1972.
PICTURES: Shopping, I Love You I Love You Not, Wilde, Gattaca, Bent, Midnight in the Garden of Good and Evil, Final Cut, Music From Another Room, The Wisdom of Crocodiles, The Talented Mr. Ripley (Academy Award nom.; Golden Globe nom. BAFTA Award 1999), eXistenZ, Love, Honour and Obey, A.I., Enemy at the Gates, Artificial Intelligence: AI (Golden Globe nom. 2002), The Road to Perdition, Marlowe, The Diary of a Young London Physician, Cold Mountain (Academy Award nom.; Golden Globe nom. 2004), Sky Captain and the World of Tomorrow, I Heart Huckabee's, Alfie, Closer, Lemony Snicket's A Series of Unfortunate Events (voice), The Aviator, Brideshead Revisited, All the King's Men, Breaking and Entering, The Holiday, My Blueberry Nights, Sleuth, Repossession Mambo, Rage, The Imaginarium of Doctor Parnassus, Sherlock Holmes, Repo Men, Contagion.
TELEVISION: *Movies*: The Marshal, Tube Tales. *Series*: The Casebook of Sherlock Holmes, Families. *Guest:* More than 90 appearances.

LAWRENCE, JOEY

Actor. b. Montgomery, PA, Apr. 20, 1976. e. USC.
PICTURES: Summer Rental, Oliver and Company (voice), Pulse, Radioland Murders, Tequila Body Shots, Urban Legends: Final Cut, Do You Wanna Know a Secret?, A Christmas Adventure from a Book Called Wisely's Tales (voice), Pandora's Box, R3, The 9th Passenger, Rest Stop, Together Again for the First Time, Killer Pad, Hit List, Sinatra Club.
TELEVISION: *Movies*: Chains of Gold, Prince for a Day, Brothers of the Frontier, Jumping Ship, Romantic Comedy 101, Love Rules, Confessions of a Sociopathic Social Climber, Android Apocalypse, My Fake Fiance. *Series*: Gimme a Break, Blossom, Brotherly Love, Express Yourself, American Dreams, Run of the House, Melissa & Joey. *Pilots:* Scamps, Little Shots. *Specials*: Andy Williams and the NBC Kids, Don't Touch, Alvin Goes Back to School, Umbrella Jack, Adventures in Babysitting, Disney's Countdown to Kids' Day, All That, Blossom in Paris, Kids' Choice Awards (host), Half & Half. *Guest:* More than 78 appearances.

LAWRENCE, MARTIN

Actor, Comedian. b. Frankfurt, Germany, 1965. Started as stand-up comic in Washington D.C.
PICTURES: Do the Right Thing (debut, 1989), House Party, Talkin' Dirty After Dark, House Party 2, Boomerang, You So Crazy (also exec. prod.), Bad Boys, Nothing to Lose, A Thin Line Between Love and Hate (also, exec. prod., dir., s.p.), Life, Blue Streak, Big Momma's House, What's the Worst that Could Happen?, Black Knight, National Security, Bad Boys II, Open Season (voice), Rebound (also exec. prod.), Big Momma's House 2 (also exec. prod.), Wild Hogs, The Better Man, Welcome Home, Roscoe Jenkins, College Road Trip, Death at a Funeral, Big Mommas: Like Father, Like Son.
TELEVISION: *Series*: What's Happening Now?, Kid 'n' Play (voice), Russell Simmons' Def Comedy Jam (host, prod. consultant), Martin (also creator, co-exec. prod.), 1st Amendment Stand Up (exec. prod.). *Pilots*: Hammer Slammer & Slade, A Little Bit Strange, Love That Girl! (exec. prod.). *Guest:* More than 63 appearances.

LAWRENCE, STEVE

Actor. r.n. Sydney Leibowitz. b. Brooklyn, NY, July 8, 1935. m. singer Eydie Gormé. Singer in nightclubs and on TV.
THEATRE: What Makes Sammy Run?, Golden Rainbow.
PICTURES: Stand Up and Be Counted, The Blues Brothers, The Lonely Guy, Blues Brothers 2000, Play It to the Bone, The Contract, The Yards, Ocean's Eleven, Mr. 3000 (soundtrack performer), Bewitched (soundtrack performer), Maxed Out: Hard Times, Easy Credit and the Era of Predatory Lenders (doc.,

soundtrack performer).
TELEVISION: *Movies*: Carol for Another Christmas, Express to Terror, Alice in Wonderland. *Specials*: Steve and Eydie Celebrate Irving Berlin (also co-exec. prod.; Emmy Award, 1979), Steve and Eydie: Our Love Is Here to Stay (Emmy nom. 1976), many specials. *Series*: Tonight, The Steve Lawrence-Eydie Gormé Show (1958), The Steve Lawrence Show (1965), Foul-Ups Bleeps and Blunders (host). *Guest:* More than 90 appearances.

LAYBOURNE, GERALDINE

Executive. e. Vassar College, B.A.; U. Penn, M.S. Laybourne joined Nickelodeon in 1980 and took over network management in 1984. Under her oversight, she built the Nickelodeon brand and in 1985 launched Nick at Nite, the successful lineup of retro sitcoms. While at Nickelodeon, the network won several Emmys, Peabodys, CableACE and Parent's Choice awards, among others. She expanded the brand internationally and developed theme park attractions and created the Nickelodeon movie, toy and publishing divisions. From 1996-1998 Laybourne was president of Disney/ABC Cable Networks and also took part in the creation and management of ABC's Saturday morning children's programming schedule. She resigned ABC/Cable post in 1998 and started own network/cable/Internet production company, Oxygen Media. NBC Universal purchased the cable network in Oct. 2007, with Laybourne announcing she would then step down as CEO by the end of 2007. She was ranked No. 1 among the 50 most influential women in the entertainment industry by The Hollywood Reporter in 1996 and named one of the 25 most influential people in America by Time magazine that same year. Her numerous awards include the Annenberg Public Policy Center's award for Distinguished Lifetime Contribution to Children and Television, the New York Women in Communications Matrix Award® for Broadcasting, and the Creative Coalition's Spotlight Award. Her other honors include the Grand Tam Award® from the Cable and Telecommunications Association for Marketing (CTAM), the Governor's Award® from the National Academy of Cable Programming, the American Women in Radio and Television Genii Award®, the Women in Cable Award®, and the Sara Lee Corporation's Frontrunner Award®. She also received both the Entrepreneur of the Year Award® from the University of Missouri at Kansas City and the New York Women in Film Muse Award®. In 1995, she was inducted into the Broadcasting & Cable Hall of Fame. In October of 2004 she was inducted into The Cable Center Hall of Fame. Laybourne sits on a number of boards and advisory committees, including The National Cable Television Association, The National Council for Families and Television, New York Women in Film & Television (Advisory Board), Cable Positive (Honorary Chair) and the Council of National Advisors of Springboard Enterprises. In 1997 she was elected to the Board of Trustees of Vassar College. Laybourne is also a member of the Board of Directors of Insight Communications, Move, Inc., Symantec Corp., Electronic Arts, Inc. and in 2009 joined the Bd. of Directors of J. C. Penney Company, Inc.

LAZARUS, PAUL N. III

Executive, Producer. b. New York, NY, May 25, 1938. e. Williams College, BA.; Yale Law School, L.L.B. Third generation film exec. Began career with Palomar Pictures Int'l. as exec. v.p.; joined ABC Pictures Corp. as v.p. in charge of creative affairs. Then became managing dir., CRM Productions, maker of educational films; v.p. for motion pictures, Marble Arch Productions; 1983, v.p. in charge of prod., Home Box Office. 1985, Film Commissioner, New Mexico; Since 1987, Dir. of Film Program, U. of Miami. In addition to motion pictures, Lazarus has produced 68 award-winning educational films for Psychology Today Films.
PICTURES: *Prod.*: Extreme Close-Up, Westworld, Futureworld, Capricorn One, Hanover Street, Barbarosa, Gringo Wedding (exec. prod.).

LAZENBY, GEORGE

Actor. b. Gouburn, Australia, Sept. 5, 1939. Appeared in Australian and British tv commericals before being chosen to star as James Bond.
PICTURES: On Her Majesty's Secret Service (debut, 1969, Golden Globe nom. 1970), Universal Soldier, Who Saw Her Die?, The Dragon Flies, Stoner, The Man From Hong Kong, The Kentucky Fried Movie, Death Dimension, The Falcon's Ultimatum, Saint Jack, L'ultimo Harem, Never Too Young to Die, Hell Hunters, Gettysburg, Eyes of the Beholder, Emmanuelle's Revenge, Emmanuelle's Love, Emmanuelle Forever, Death By Misadventure, Twin Sitters, Gut Feeling, Four Dogs Playing Poker, Bruce Lee: A Warrior's Journey, Bruce Lee in G.O.D, Sheer Bliss, Spider's Web, Snow Job.
TELEVISION: *Movies*: Is Anybody There?, Cover Girls, The Newman Shame, Evening in Byzantium, The Return of the Man From U.N.C.L.E., Batman Beyond: The Movie. *Series*: General Hospital, Rituals, The Adventures of Superboy, The Pretender, Batman Beyond (voice), Yu Yu Hakusho: Ghost Files (voice, English version). *Guest:* More than 92 appearances.

LEACHMAN, CLORIS

Actress. b. Des Moines, IA, April 30, 1926. e. Northwestern U. Broadway stage, television, motion pictures.
PICTURES: Kiss Me Deadly (debut, 1955), The Rack, The Chapman Report, Butch Cassidy and the Sundance Kid, Lovers and Other Strangers, The People Next Door, W.U.S.A., The Steagle, The Last Picture Show (Academy Award, best supporting actress, Golden Globe nom. 1972), Dillinger, Charlie and the Angel (Golden Globe nom. 1974), Happy Mother's Day... Love George, Daisy Miller, Young Frankenstein (Golden Globe nom. 1975), Crazy Mama, High Anxiety, The Mouse and His Child (voice), The North Avenue Irregulars, The Muppet Movie, Scavenger Hunt, Foolin' Around, Yesterday, Herbie Goes Bananas, History of the World—Part I, My Little Pony (voice), Shadow Play, Walk Like a Man, Hansel and Gretel, Prancer, Texasville, Love Hurts, My Boyfriend's Back, The Beverly Hillbillies, A Troll in Central park (voice), Now and Then, Beavis and Butt-Head Do America (voice), Never Too Late, Gen 13, The Iron Giant, Music of the Heart, Hanging Up, The Amati Girls, Animal, Manna From Heaven, Alex and Emma, The Californians, Mrs. Harris, Spanglish, The Longest Yard, Sky High, Scary Movie 4, Beerfest, Ponyo on the Cliff by the Sea (english version, voice), The Women, New York, I Love You, American Cowslip, The Oogieloves in the Big Balloon Adventure, Expecting Mary, You Again, Timberwolf, The Fields.
TELEVISION: *Movies*: Silent Night Lonely Night, Suddenly Single, Haunts of the Very Rich, A Brand New Life (Emmy Award, 1973), Crime Club, Dying Room Only, The Migrants (Emmy nom. 1974), Hitchhike!, Thursday's Game, Death Sentence, Someone I Touched, A Girl Named Sooner, Death Scream, Telly... Who Loves Ya Baby? (Emmy nom. 1976), The New Original Wonder Woman, The Love Boat (pilot), It Happened One Christmas (Emmy nom. 1978), Long Journey Back, Willa, Mrs. R's Daughter, S.O.S. Titanic, The Acorn People, Advice to the Lovelorn, Miss All-American Beauty, Dixie: Changing Habits, Demon Murder Case, Ernie Kovacs: Between the Laughter (Emmy nom. 1984), Deadly Intentions, Love Is Never Silent, Wedding Bell Blues, Danielle Steel's Fine Things, In Broad Daylight, A Little Piece of Heaven, Fade to Black, Without a Kiss Goodbye, Miracle Child, Double Double Toil and Trouble, Between Love and Honor, Annabella Wish, Mrs. Harris (Emmy nom. 2006), Crazy Love, Lake Placid 2, Love Takes Wing. *Mini-series:* Beach Girls. *Series*: Hold It Please, Charlie Wild: Private Detective, Bob and Ray, Lassie, Mary Tyler Moore Show (Emmy Awards 1974, 1975, 2 other noms.), Phyllis (Emmy nom,; Golden Globe Award 1976), The Facts of Life, The Nutt House, Walter & Emily, The Ellen Show, Thanks, Touched by an Angel, Malcolm in the Middle (2 Emmy Awards, 4 other noms.), Dancing with the Stars, Raising Hope. *Specials:* Oldest Living Graduate, Of Thee I Sing, Breakfast With Les and Bess, Screen Actors Guild 50th Anniversary Celebration (Emmy Award, 1984), The Woman Who Willed a Miracle (Emmy Award 1983). *As Guest*: Cher (Emmy Award, 1975), Love Boat, Promised Land (Emmy Award, 1997), Joan of Arcadia (Emmy nom. 2005). *Guest:* More than 240 appearances.

LEAR, NORMAN

Producer, Director, Writer. b. New Haven, CT, July 27, 1922. e. Emerson Coll. In public relations 1945-49. Began in TV as co-writer of weekly one-hour variety show, The Ford Star Revue in 1950. Followed as writer for Dean Martin and Jerry Lewis on the Colgate Comedy Hour and for the Martha Raye and George Gobel TV shows. With partner, Bud Yorkin, created and produced such specials as Another Evening with Fred Astaire, Henry Fonda and the Family, An Evening with Carol Channing, and The Many Sides of Don Rickles. In 1965 their company, Tandem Productions, also produced the original Andy Williams Show. Moved into motion pictures in 1963, writing and producing Come Blow Your Horn. Formed Act III Communications, 1987. Recipient of WGA Laurel Award 1993 and Valentine Davies Award 1978.
PICTURES: Come Blow Your Horn (co-prod., s.p.), Never Too Late (prod.), Divorce-American Style (prod., s.p., Academy Award nom.; WGA nom. 1968), The Night They Raided Minsky's (co.-prod., co-s.p.), Start the Revolution Without Me (exec. prod.), Cold Turkey (dir., s.p., prod.), The Princess Bride (exec. prod.), Fried Green Tomatoes (co-exec. prod.), Way Past Cool (exec. prod.), Juan Frances: Live (exec. prod.), Pete Seeger: The Power of Song (doc., exec. prod.).
TELEVISION: *Creator-dir.*: TV Guide Award Show (1962), Henry Fonda and the Family (1963), Andy Williams Specials, Robert Young and the Family. *Exec. prod. and creator or developer:* All in the Family (4 Emmy Awards, 5 other noms.), Maude (2 Emmy noms.), Good Times, Sanford and Son, The Jeffersons, Mary Hartman Mary Hartman (Emmy nom. 1976), One Day at a Time, All's Fair, A Year at the Top, All that Glitters, Fernwood 2 Night, The Baxters, Palmerstown, I Love Liberty (Emmy nom.; WGA Award 1982), Heartsounds (Emmy nom. 1985), Sunday Dinner, The Powers That Be, 704 Hauser, Channel Umptee-3, Maggie Bloom, All in the Family: 20th Anniversary Special (Emmy nom. 1991).

LEARNED, MICHAEL

Actress. b. Washington, DC, Apr. 9, 1939. Studied ballet and dramatics in school. Many stage credits include Under Milkwood, The Three Sisters, A God Slept Here, The Sisters Rosensweig, etc.; resident performances with Shakespeare festivals in Canada, Stratford, CT, and San Diego, CA. Gained fame on hit TV series, The Waltons, as the mother, Olivia.
PICTURES: Touched by Love, Shanghai Shadows (narrator), Power, Dragon: The Bruce Lee Story, Life During Wartime, For

the Love of May, Shallow End, Lethal Eviction, Loggerheads.
TELEVISION: *Movies:* Hurricane, It Couldn't Happen to a Nicer Guy, Widow, Little Mo, Nurse (pilot), Off the Minnesota Strip, A Christmas Without Snow, Mother's Day on Walton Mountain, The Parade, A Deadly Business, Mercy or Murder?, Roots: The Gift, Gunsmoke: The Last Apache, Aftermath: A Test of Love, Keeping Secrets, A Walton Thanksgiving Reunion, A Walton Wedding, A Father for Brittany. *Series*: The Waltons (3 Emmy Awards: 1973, 1974, 1976, 3 other noms.; 4 Golden Globe noms.), Nurse (Emmy Award, 1982, 1 other nom.), Hothouse, Living Dolls, Scrubs, General Hospital. *Specials*: All My Sons, Picnic. *Guest*: More than 71 appearances.

LEARY, DENIS

Actor. b. Boston, MA, Aug. 18, 1957. e. Emerson Coll. Performed with the New Voices Theater Company, Charlestown Working Theater. Debuted one-man stand-up show No Cure for Cancer at Edinburgh Intl. Arts Fest., then later in London, Off-B'way, and cable tv. Appeared in and dir. short film for Showtime, Thy Neighbor's Wife.
PICTURES: Strictly Business (debut), National Lampoon's Loaded Weapon 1, The Sandlot, Who's the Man?, Gunmen, Demolition Man, Judgment Night, The Ref, Operation Dumbo Drop, The Neon Bible, Two If by Sea (also co-s.p.), Suicide Kings, The Real Blonde, Underworld, The MatchMaker, Wag the Dog, Snitch, A Bug's Life (voice), Love Walked In, Wide Awake, Small Soldiers, The Thomas Crown Affair, Sand, Jesus' Son, True Crime, Company Man, Lakeboat, Double Whammy, Final, Dawg, Ice Age, The Secret Lives of Dentists, Ice Age: The Meltdown (voice), In Search of Ted Demme (doc., exec. prod.), Ice Age: Dawn of the Dinosaurs.
TELEVISION: *Movies*: Favorite Deadly Sins, The Second Civil War, Subway Stories: Tales from the Underground, Fashion Rocks (host), Ft. Pit (writer, exec. prod.), Recount (Emmy nom.; Golden Globe nom. 2008), Back from Hell: A Tribute to Sam Kinison. *Series*: Remote Control (also writer), Comics Come Home, The Job, Crank Yankers (voice), Shorties Watchin' Shorties (exec. prod.), Beached, Rescue Me (creator, writer, exec. prod., 3 Emmy noms.; Golden Globe nom. 2005), Canterbury's Law (exec. prod.), The Unusuals (exec. prod.). *Documetaries/Specials:* No Cure for Cancer (also writer, exec. prod., composer), Denis Leary: Lock 'N Load (also writer, exec. prod.,composer), True Crime: The Scene of the Crime, Lord Stanley's Cup: Hockey's Ultimate Prize (host), Contest Searchlight (exec. prod., co-exec. prod.). *Guest:* More than 105 appearances.

LÉAUD, JEAN-PIERRE

Actor. b. Paris, France, May 5, 1944. Parents were screenwriter Pierre Leaud and actress Jacqueline Pierreux. At 14 chosen to play Antoine Doinel in Truffaut's The 400 Blows and subsequent autobiographical films Love at 20, Stolen Kisses, Bed and Board, Love on the Run. Closely identified with major films by Jean-Luc Godard.
PICTURES: The 400 Blows, Boulevard, The Testament of Orpheus, Love at Twenty, Masculine-Feminine, Made in USA, Le Depart, La Chinoise, Weekend, Stolen Kisses, Le Gai Savoir, Pigsty, The Oldest Profession, Bed and Board, Two English Girls, Last Tango in Paris, Day for Night, Lola's Lolos, Love on the Run, Rebelote, Detective, Just a Movie, Seen by... 20 Years After, Treasure Island, The Grandeur and Decadence of a Small-Time Filmmaker, With All Hands, Time to Aim, Jane B, par Agnes V.; 36 Fillete, La Femme de Paille (The Straw Woman), The Color of the Wind, Bunker Palace Hotel, Treasure Island, I Hired a Contract Killer, Paris at Dawn, The Birth of Love, Nobody Loves Me, The Seducer's Diary, A Hundred & One Nights, Irma Vep, Mon Homme, Pour Rire!, Elizabeth, Innocent, A Question of Taste, The Marcorelle Affair, What Time Is It There?, Barra 68 - Sem Perder a Ternura, The Pornographer, The War in Paris, Folle embellie, I Saw Ben Barka Get Killed.

LEBLANC, MATT

Actor. b. Newton, MA, July 25, 1967.
PICTURES: The Killing Box, Lookin' Italian, Ed, Lost in Space, Charlie's Angels, All the Queen's Men, Broad Daylight, Charlie's Angels: Full Throttle, Jonah Hex (exec. prod. only).
TELEVISION: *Movies*: Anything to Survive, Reform School Girl, The Prince. *Series:* TV 101, Top of the Heap, Vinnie & Bobby, Friends (3 Emmy noms.; 2 Golden Globe noms.), Friends: The Stuff You've Never Seen, Joey (Golden Globe nom. 2005). *Guest*: More than 50 appearances.

LEDER, MIMI

Director, Script Supervisor. b. 1952. Daughter of late Producer, Director Paul Leder.
PICTURES: My Friends Need Killing (2nd unit camera op.), Ape (asst. dir., unit photog.), Red Light in the White House (script supv., asst. dir.), Sketches of a Strangler (asst. dir.), Computer Kid (script supv.), Spawn of the Slithis (script supv.), Borderline (script supv.), I'm Going to Be Famous (assoc. prod.), The Education of Allison Tate (assoc. prod.), The Peacemaker (dir.), Deep Impact (dir.), Sentimental Journey (dir.), Pay It Forward (dir.), Baltic Storm (exec. prod.), Thick as Thieves (dir.).
TELEVISION: *Script Supervisor:* Dummy, The Boy Who Drank too Much, A Long Way Home, A time to Live, L.A. Law. *Director*: L.A. Law, China Beach (4 Emmy noms.), Nightingales, Midnight Caller, A Little Piece of Heaven, A Woman with a Past, Marked for Murder, There Was a Little Boy, Rio Shannon, House of Secrets, Baby Brokers, ER (2 Emmy Awards, 1 other nom.; 3 DGA noms.), The Innocent, John Doe (also exec. prod.), U.S. Attorney (dir., exec. prod.), The Quinn-tuplets (dir.), The West Wing (Emmy nom. for episode, 2006). *Series Dir.:/Exec. Prod.:* The Beast, John Doe, Jonny Zero, Related (pilot), Vanished.

LEE, ANG

Director, Producer, Writer. b. Pingtung, Taiwan, Oct. 23, 1954.
PICTURES: Joe's Bed-Stuy Barbershop: We Cut Heads, Pushing Hands, The Wedding Banquet, Eat Drink Man Woman, Siao Yu, Sense and Sensibility (DGA nom.; BAFTA Award 1996), The Ice Storm, Ride with the Devil, Crouching Tiger Hidden Dragon (2 Academy Award noms.; BAFTA Award, DGA Award 2001), Tortilla Soup (s.p.), Hulk, Brokeback Mountain (Academy Award, DGA Award 2006), Lust, Caution, Taking Woodstock (dir., prod.).

LEE, CHRISTOPHER

Actor. b. London, England, May 27, 1922. e. Wellington Coll. Served RAF 1940-46. Ent. m.p. ind. 1947. *Autobiography:* Tall, Dark and Gruesome (1977).
PICTURES: Corridor of Mirrors (debut, 1947), One Night With You, A Song for Tomorrow, Scott of the Antarctic, Hamlet, The Gay Lady, Capt. Horatio Hornblower, Valley of the Eagles, The Crimson Pirate, Babes in Bagdad, Moulin Rouge, Innocents of Paris, That Lady, The Warriors, Cockleshell Heroes, Storm Over the Nile, Port Afrique, Private's Progress, Beyond Mombasa, Battle of the River Plate, Night Ambush, She Played With Fire, The Traitors, Curse of Frankenstein, Bitter Victory, Truth About Women, Tale of Two Cities, Dracula, Man Who Could Cheat Death, The Mummy, Too Hot to Handle, Beat Girl, City of the Dead (Horror Hotel), Two Faces of Dr. Jekyll, The Terror of the Tongs, The Hands of Orlac, Taste of Fear, The Devil's Daffodil, Pirates of Blood River, Devil's Agent, Red Orchid, Valley of Fear, Katharsis, Faust '63, The Virgin of Nuremberg, The Whip and the Body, Carmilla, The Devil Ship Pirates, The Gorgon, The Sign of Satan, The House of Blood, Dr. Terror's House of Horrors, She, The Skull, The Mask of Fu Manchu, Dracula, Prince of Darkness, Rasputin, Theatre of Death, Circus of Fear, The Brides of Fu Manchu, Five Golden Dragons, Vengeance of Fu Manchu, Night of the Big Heat, The Pendulum, The Face of Eve, The Devil Rides Out, The Blood of Fu Manchu, The Crimson Altar, Dracula Has Risen from the Grave, The Oblong Box, De Sade 70, Scream and Scream Again, The Magic Christian, Julius Caesar, One More Time, Count Dracula, Bloody Judge, Taste the Blood of Dracula, The Private Life of Sherlock Holmes, El Umbragolo, Scars of Dracula, The House That Dripped Blood, I Monster, Hannie Caulder, Dracula A.D. 1972, Horror Express, Death Line (Raw Meat), Nothing But the Night (also co-exec. prod.), The Creeping Flesh, The Wicker Man (Academy Award nom. 1979), Poor Devil, Dark Places, Satanic Rites of Dracula, Eulalie Quitte les Champs, The Three Musketeers, Earthbound, The Man with the Golden Gun, The Four Musketeers, Killer Force, Diagnosis—Murder, Whispering Death, The Keeper, To the Devil a Daughter, Dracula and Son, Airport '77, Starship Invasions, The End of the World, Return from Witch Mountain, Caravans, The Passage, Arabian Adventure (Academy Award nom. 1980), Jaguar Lives, Circle of Iron, 1941, Bear Island, Serial, The Salamander, An Eye for an Eye, Safari 3000, House of Long Shadows, The Return of Captain Invincible, The Rosebud Beach Hotel, Roadtrip, Dark Mission, The Howling II: Your Sister is a Werewolf, Olympus Force, Jocks, Murder Story, Mio In the Land of Faraway, The Girl, The Return of the Musketeers, Honeymoon Academy, The French Revolution, Gremlins 2: The New Batch, Curse III: Blood Sacrifice, The Rainbow Thief, L'Avaro, Jackpot, Double Vision, Shogun Mayeda, Special Class, Journey of Honor, Cybereden, Funny Man, Police Academy: Mission to Moscow, A Feast at Midnight, The Stupids, Sorellina, Jinnah, Russell Mulcahy's Tale of the Mummy, Sleepy Hollow, The Lord of the Rings: The Fellowship of the Ring, The Rocky Horror Interactive Show, Cries in the Night: Orloff, The Lord of the Rings: The Two Towers, Star Wars: Episode II: Attack of the Clones, The Last Unicorn, The Lord of the Rings: The Return on the King, Star Wars: Episode III - Revenge of the Sith, Charlie and the Chocolate Factory, The Corpse Bride (voice), The Golden Compass, Star Wars: The Clone Wars (voice), The Last Unicorn, May Day, Greyfriars Bobby, The Heavy, Boogie Woogie, Triage, Monstermania! (voice), Alice in Wonderland (voice), Season of the Witch, The Resident, Burke and Hare.
TELEVISION: *Movies:* The Disputation, Metier du Seigneur, Poor Devil, Harold Robbins' The Pirate, Captain America II, Once a Spy, Charles and Diana: A Royal Love Story, Goliath Awaits, Massarati and the Brain, Treasure Island, Young Indiana Jones, The Care of Time, Sherlock Holmes & the Leading Lady, Sherlock Holmes and the Incident at Victoria Falls, Death Train, Tales of Mystery & Imagination, Moses, Wyrd Sisters, The Odyssey, In the Beginning, Pope John Paul II, The Colour of Magic. *Mini-series:* How the West Was Won, The Far Pavilions, Shaka Zulu, Around the World in 80 Days, Ivanhoe, Gormenghast, Ghost Stories for Christmas. *Series:* Les Redoutables, Tales of Mystery and Imagination (host), The Tomorrow People, 100 Years of Horror (25 episodes), The New

Adventures of Robin Hood, Blue Heelers. *Guest:* More than 216 appearances.

LEE, DEBRA

Executive. b. Columbia, SC and raised in NC. e. Bachelor's degree, Political Science, with emphasis in Asian politics. J.D. degree from Harvard University Law School while simultaneously earning Master's degree in Public Policy from Harvard's John F. Kennedy School of Government in 1980. From Aug. 1980 through Sept. 1981, Lee served as a law clerk to the late Hon. Barrington Parker of the U. S. District Court for the District of Columbia. Then, an attorney for Washington, D.C.-based corporate law firm Steptoe & Johnson. Lee left the firm in 1986 to join one of the firm's clients, black-owned cable company BET — Black Entertainment Television — as v.p. & general counsel. Her responsibilities included managing BET's contract negotiations and legal affairs; She was instrumental in taking BET public in 1991 and again in 2000, when Viacom purchased the network for $3 billion. She has held several other positions during her 20-year tenure at BET, including corporate secretary; and president and publisher of BET's Publishing division. Before her appointment as COO in March 1996, Lee was the network's executive v.p. of strategic business development; then promoted to company president and CEO in June 2005. In January 2006, Lee succeeded BET founder Robert Johnson to become Chairman & CEO of BET Networks. She currently is the highest ranking African-American female executive at BET's parent company, Viacom, Inc. She serves on the corporate bd. of directors of Revlon, Marriott International and Eastman Kodak Company, and regionally for Washington Gas & Light Company. Lee is also a member of the national bd. of directors for the National Cable & Telecommunications Association (NCTA), Alvin Ailey Dance Theater, Girls Inc., National Symphony Orchestra, Center for Communication, and the Kennedy Center's Community & Friends Board. She is also a member of the Bd. of Trustees for Brown University and also serves on the boards of the Museum of Television and Radio and the Grammy Foundation. Lee received special recognition in 2005: the Madame C. J. Walker Award from Ebony magazine for best exemplifying the entrepreneurial spirit of the pioneering Black businesswoman.

LEE, JASON SCOTT

Actor. b. Los Angeles, CA, 1966. Raised in Hawaii. e. Fullerton Col., Orange County, CA.
PICTURES: Born in East L.A. (debut, 1987), Back to the Future II, Map of the Human Heart, Dragon: The Bruce Lee Story, Rapa Nui, Rudyard Kipling's The Jungle Book, Tale of the Mummy, Soldier, Arabian Nights (voice), Lilo & Stitch (voice), Dracula II: Ascencion, Dracula III: Legacy, Only the Brave, Nomad, Balls of Fury, Dance of the Dragon, Strange Frame: Love & Sax.
TELEVISION: *Movies*: The Lookalike, Vestige of Honor, Arabian Nights.

LEE, JOIE

Actress. b. 1968. e. Sarah Lawrence Col. Brother is director-writer Spike Lee. On NY stage in Mulebone. Appeared in short film Coffee and Cigarettes Part Two. Has also been billed as Joy Lee, Joie Susannah Lee.
PICTURES: She's Gotta Have It (debut, 1986), School Daze, Do the Right Thing, Bail Jumper, Mo' Better Blues, A Kiss Before Dying, Fathers and Sons, Crooklyn (also story, co-s.p., assoc. prod.), Losing Isaiah, Girl 6, Get on the Bus, Summer of Sam, Snapped (prod. only), Coffee and Cigarettes, She Hate Me, Full Grown Men, Starting Out in the Evening, Window on Your Present.

LEE, PAUL

Executive. e. Master's degree in modern languages, Oxford Univ. in England. TV executive with varied international experience, Lee's early career included work as a prod. mgr. for novellas at the Brazilian national network Rede Globo in Rio de Janeiro. He then joined the BBC in 1984, starting out as a reporter assigned to Belfast, Northern Ireland. Upon returning to London in 1987, he became a producer and director, going on to earn for BBC's flagship series Arena a British Academy Award and a BANFF award for his documentary portrait of Woody Guthrie. In 1990, Lee branched out into drama production, traveling to Moscow to direct Oblomov, starring George Wendt of Cheers fame. He also produced, directed and wrote TV movies. In 1998, Lee launched BBC America and was its gen. mgr. and COO before ultimately becoming the company's CEO. During his tenure, the hit comedy series "The Office" garnered two Golden Globes. Other shows under Lee's supervision included the BBC's "Changing Rooms" which formatted into TLC's signature show "Trading Spaces," the BBC version of "What Not to Wear," and the "Graham Norton show." From BBC America Lee was tapped to run ABC Family as pres. in April 2004. July, 2010 Lee became President of ABC Entertainment Group.

LEE, SHERYL

Actress. b. Augsburg, Germany, April 22, 1967.
PICTURES: Wild at Heart, I Love You to Death, Twin Peaks: Fire Walk With Me, Jersey Girl, Backbeat, Don't Do It, Fall Times, Notes From Underground, Homage, Mother Night, Bliss, This World, Then the Fireworks, The Blood Oranges, Vampire$, Kiss the Sky, Dante's View, Angel's Dance, Children on Their Birthdays, Paradise, Texas, Winter's Bone.
TELEVISION: *Movies*: Love, Lies, and Murder, Guinevere, Follow the River, David, Hitched, The Secrets of Comfort House. *Mini-series*: Kingpin. *Series*: Twin Peaks, L.A. Doctors, One Tree Hill, State of Mind, Dirty Sexy Money. *Guest:* More than 40 appearances.

LEE, SPIKE

Director, Producer, Writer, Actor. r.n. Shelton Jackson Lee. b. Atlanta, GA, Mar. 20, 1957. Son of jazz bass musician, composer Bill Lee. Sister is actress Joie Lee. e. Morehouse Coll B.A., Mass Comm., MFA NYU Film Sch. Completed 2 student features and hour-long thesis: Joe's Bed-Stuy Barbershop: We Cut Heads which won student Academy Award from Academy M.P. Arts & Sciences. Wrote, prod., dir., co-starred in indep. feature, She's Gotta Have It, budgeted at $175,000. Appeared in films Lonely in America, Hoop Dreams. Author of five books on his films. Director of numerous tv commercials for Nike, Levi's, Anheuser Busch Cos., ESPN and others. Director of over 35 music videos for Michael Jackson, Stevie Wonder, Miles Davis, and others.
PICTURES: Joe's Bed-Stuy Barbershop: We Cut Heads (co-prod., dir., s.p., editor). *Dir./Prod./Writer/Actor:* She's Gotta Have It (LA Film Critics Award for best new director, 1986), School Daze, Do the Right Thing (Academy Award nom.; 2 Golden Globe noms.; LA Film Critics Awards for best picture & dir., 1990), Mo' Better Blues, Jungle Fever, Malcolm X, Crooklyn, Clockers, Girl 6, Get On the Bus, 4 Little Girls (doc., Academy Award nom. 1998), He Got Game, Summer of Sam, Michael Jordan to the Max (actor only), Famous (actor), The Original Kings of Comedy, Bamboozled, Rent, (prod.), 25th Hour, She Hate Me, All the Invisible Children (dir.), The Night Watchman (dir.), Inside Man, Selling Time (dir./writer), Miracle at St. Anna. *Executive Producer:* Drop Squad (also actor), New Jersey Drive, Tales From the Hood, Subway Stories: Tales from the Underground, 3 AM, Dream Street, You're Nobody 'til Somebody Kills You, Evolution of a Criminal (doc.).
TELEVISION: *Dir.: Movies*: Freak, Good Fences (exec. prod.), Sucker Free City (also exec. prod.), 4 Little Girls (Emmy nom. 1998), M.O.N.Y, Passing Strange. *Mini-series*: The Blues, Miracle's Boys. *Series*: Sucker Free City, Shark (pilot). *Specials/Documentaries*: Seven Songs for Malcolm X, American Cinema, Pavarotti & Friends for the Children of Liberia, A Huey P. Newton Story, When the Levees Broke: A Requiem in Four Acts (2 Emmy Awards 2007), Kobe Doin' Work. *Guest:* More than 150 appearances.

LEGATO, ROBERT

Special Effects, Director.
PICTURES: Interview with the Vampire: The Vampire Chronicles, Apollo 13 (Academy Award nom. 1996), Titanic (Academy Award 1997), Armageddon, What Lies Beneath, Cast Away (consult), Harry Potter and the Sorcerer's Stone (AFI nom., BAFTA nom.), Bad Boys II (VES nom. 2004), The Aviator (VES Award 2005, 1 other nom.), Bewitched (2nd unit dir.), The Departed, The Good Shepherd, Shine a Light (doc.), Standard Operating Procedure (doc., visual effects supv.), Shutter Island, Avatar (virtual cinematography system creator, pipeline engineer), A Nightmare on Elm Street (2nd unit dir.), The Invention of Hugo Cabret (also 2nd unit dir.).
TELEVISION: *Movie*: Star Trek: Deep Space Nine-Emissary. *Series*: Star Trek: The Next Generation (also dir. Emmy Award 1992), Star Trek: Deep Space Nine (also dir., Emmy Award 1993), Vamped Out (cinematographer, editor).

LEGRAND, MICHEL JEAN

Composer, Conductor. b. France, Feb. 24, 1932. Son of well-known arranger, composer and pianist, Raymond Legrand. At 11 Michel, a child prodigy, entered Paris Cons. and graduated nine years later with top honors in composition and as solo pianist. In late fifties turned to composing for films and has composed, orchestrated and conducted scores of more than 140 films. Received ASCAP Henry Mancini Award 1998.
PICTURES: Lola, Eva, Vivre Sa Vie, La Baie des Anges, The Umbrellas of Cherbourg (3 Academy Award noms. 1966), Banda a Part, Un Femme Mariee, Une Femme est une Femme, The Young Girls of Rochefort (Academy Award nom. 1969), Ice Station Zebra, The Thomas Crown Affair (Academy Award for best song: The Windmills of Your Mind, 1 other nom.; Golden Globe Award, 1 other nom. 1968), Pieces of Dreams (Academy Award nom.; Golden Globe nom. 1971), The Happy Ending (Academy Award nom.; 2 Golden Globe noms. 1970), Picasso Summer, Wuthering Heights (Golden Globe nom. 1971), The Go-Between, Summer of '42 (Academy Award, Golden Globe nom. 1972), Le Mans (Golden Globe nom. 1972), Lady Sings the Blues (Golden Globe nom. 1973), The Nelson Affair, Breezy (2 Golden Globe noms. 1974), The Three Musketeers, Sheila Levine, Gable and Lombard, Ode to Billy Joe, The Savage, The Other Side of Midnight, The Fabulous Adventures of the Legendary Baron Munchausen, The Roads of the South, The Hunter, The Mountain Men, Atlantic City, Falling in Love Again, Best Friends (Academy Award nom. 1983), A Love in Germany, Never Say Never Again, Yentl (Academy Award, 2 other noms.; 2 Golden Globe noms. 1983), Hell Train, Micki and Maude, Secret Places, Spirale, Parking, Switching Channels, Three Seats for the 26th Cinq jours en juin (dir. debut, s.p., music), Dingo, The

Pickle, Ready to Wear (Pret-a-Porter), Les Miserables, The Children of Lumiere, Aaron's Magic Village, Madeline, Doggy Bag, Season's Beatings, And Now...Ladies and Gentlemen, The In-Laws, Connie and Carla, Breakfast on Pluto, The Legend of Simon Conjurer, Confetti, To Each His Own Cinema (soundtrack writer), Disco, Oscar and the Lady in Pink (theme).
TELEVISION: *Movies*: Brian's Song, The Jesse Owens Story, A Woman Called Golda (Emmy nom. 1982), As Summers Die, Crossings, Sins, Promises to Keep, Not a Penny More Not a Penny Less, The Burning Shore, The Ring. *Mini-series*: The Blue Bycicle.

LE GROS, JAMES
Actor. b. Minneapolis, MN, Apr. 27, 1962.
THEATRE: The Cherry Orchard, Galileo, Ceremony of Innocence, Table Settings, Curse of the Starving Class, American Buffalo, Bits and Bytes, Becoming Memories, Slab Boys.
PICTURES: Solarbabies, Near Dark, Fatal Beauty, Phantasm II, Drugstore Cowboy, Point Break, Blood & Concrete, Gun Crazy, The Rapture, Where the Day Takes You, Singles, My New Gun, Bad Girls, Floundering, Mrs. Parker and the Vicious Circle, Destiny Turns on the Radio, Panther, Safe, Living in Oblivion, Infinity, The Low Life, Boys, The Destiny of Marty Fine, Countdown, The Myth of Fingerprints, Wishful Thinking, The Pass, L.A. Without a Map, Thursday, Enemy of the State, Psycho, Jump, Drop Back Ten, If You Only Knew, There's No Fish Food in Heaven, Scotland, PA, Lovely and Amazing, World Traveler, Catch That Kid, Trust the Man, Zodiac, Sherman's Way, Visioneers, Vantage Point, Welcome to Academia, Thicker, Skateland, Bitter Feast.
TELEVISION: *Movies*: The Ratings Game, Marshal Law, Pronto, Border Line, Common Ground, Big Shot: Confessions of a Campus Bookie, Damaged Care, The Street Lawyer, Paradise, 1%. *Series*: Ally McBeal, Sleeper Cell, Mercy, Mildred Pierce.

LEGUIZAMO, JOHN
Actor. b. Bogota, Colombia, July 22, 1964. Moved to Queens, NY at age 5. e. NYU. Appeared in award-winning student film Five Out of Six, while in school. Studied acting with Lee Strasberg and Wynn Handman. Made professional debut on Miami Vice on tv.
THEATRE: A Midsummer Night's Dream, La Puta Vida, Parting Gestures, Mambo Mouth (also writer; Obie & Outer Critics Circle Awards), Spic-O-Rama (also writer).
PICTURES: Casualties of War, Revenge, Die Hard 2, Gentile Alouette, Street Hunter, Out for Justice, Hangin' With the Homeboys, Regarding Henry, Whispers in the Dark, Super Mario Bros., Night Owl, Carlito's Way, A Pyromaniac's Love Story, To Wong Foo—Thanks for Everything—Julie Newmar (Golden Globe nom. 1996), Executive Decision, Romeo and Juliet, The Pest, A Brother's Kiss, Spawn, Frogs for Snakes, Doctor Dolittle (voice), The Split, Summer of Sam, Joe the King (also exec. prod.), Moulin Rouge, Titan A.E. (voice), King of the Jungle, What's The Worst That Could Happen?, Collateral Damage, Empire, Spun, ZigZag, Ice Age (voice), Crónicas, Sueño, Assault on Precinct 13, The Alibi, The Honeymooners, Land of the Dead, The 1 Second Film (assoc. prod.), Ice Age: The Meltdown (voice), Tlatelolco: Mexico 68, Where God Left His Shoes, The Take, Love in the Time of Cholera, The Babysitters (prod.), Paraiso Travel, The Ministers, The Happening, Miracle at St. Anna, Righteous Kill, Nothing Like the Holidays, The Ministers, Rage, Ice Age: Dawn of the Dinosaurs (voice), Gamer, Vanishing on 7th Street, Tlatelolco: Mexico 68, The Lincoln Lawyer.
TELEVISION: *Movies*: N.Y.P.D. Mounted, Arabian Nights, Point of Origin, Undefeated (also exec. prod., dir., and writer), Edison. *Series*: House of Buggin', The Brothers Garcia (voice), The Gallant Hero & the Tragic Victor, ER, The Kill Point (also pilot). *Specials*: Talent Pool Comedy Special (ACE Award), Mambo Mouth (also writer), Spic-O-Rama (also writer; 3 Cable ACE Awards), Freak (Emmy Award, 1 other nom. 1999), Sexaholix: A Love Story. *Guest:* More than 80 appearances.

LEHMANN, MICHAEL
Director. b. San Francisco, CA, March 30, 1957. e. U. Cal, Berkeley, Columbia U. Started in industry supervising video systems used in the Francis Ford Coppola films One From the Heart, Rumble Fish, The Outsiders. Dir. short films for Saturday Night Live incl. Ed's Secret Life. Served as exec. prod. on Ed Wood.
PICTURES: Heathers (debut, 1989), Meet the Applegates, Hudson Hawk, Airheads, Ed Wood (exec. prod. only), The Truth About Cats and Dogs, My Giant, Killing Mrs. Duke, 40 Days and 40 Nights, Your Word Against Mine, Mary Warner, Because I Said So, Flakes.
TELEVISION: *Movie:* Trash. *Series*: The Larry Sanders Show (Emmy nom. 1996), Homicide: Life on the Street, Pasadena, Watching Ellie, Trash, Wonderfalls, The Comeback, Family of the Year (pilot), Big Love, True Blood. Many more series episodes.

LEHRER, JIM
News Anchor, Author. b. Wichita, KS, May 19, 1934. e. Victoria College, Univ. of MO. Served in U.S. Marine Corps. 1959-66, reporter for Dallas Morning News, Dallas Times-Herald; 1968 became Times-Herald's city editor before moving into TV as exec. dir. of public affairs, host and editor of news program on KERA-TV in Dallas. Then moved to Washington where he became public affairs coord. for PBS, then corresp. for the Natl. Public Affairs Center for Television. In 1973 he first teamed with Robert MacNeil to cover Senate Watergate hearings. By 1975, served as D.C. corresp. for the Robert MacNeil Report on PBS (show was renamed The MacNeil/Lehrer Report in 1976). 1983, started The MacNeil/Lehrer NewsHour. 1995, became exec. editor and anchor of new version of series, The NewsHour With Jim Lehrer. *Host of series:* Character Above All (1996).
AUTHOR: The Last Debate, Viva Max!.

LEIBMAN, RON
Actor. b. New York, NY, Oct. 11, 1937. m. actress Jessica Walter. e. Ohio Wesleyan U. Joined Actor's Studio in N.Y.; first professional appearance in summer theatre production of A View from the Bridge.
THEATRE: The Premise, Dear Me, The Sky Is Falling, We Bombed in New Haven (Theatre World Award), Cop Out, Room Service, I Oughta Be in Pictures, The Deputy, Bicycle Ride to Nevada, Doubles, Rumors, Angels in America: Millenium Approaches (Tony & Drama Desk Awards).
PICTURES: Where's Poppa (debut, 1970), The Hot Rock, Slaughterhouse Five, Your Three Minutes Are Up, Super Cops, Won Ton Ton the Dog Who Saved Hollywood, Norma Rae, Up the Academy, Zorro the Gay Blade, Romantic Comedy, Phar Lap, Rhinestone, Door to Door, Seven Hours to Judgment, Night Falls on Manhattan, Just the Ticket, Shylock, Dummy, Personal Velocity: Three Portraits, Auto Focus, Garden State, A Little Help.
TELEVISION: *Movies*: The Art of Crime, A Question of Guilt, Rivkin: Bounty Hunter, Many Happy Returns, Christmas Eve (Golden Globe nom. 1987), Terrorist on Trial: The United States vs. Salim Ajami, Don King: Only in America. *Series*: Kaz (Emmy Award 1979), Pacific Station, Central Park West, Law & Order: Special Victims Unit, Friends, Holding the Baby.

LEIDER, GERALD J.
Producer, Executive. b. Camden, NJ, May 28, 1931. e. Syracuse U., 1953; Bristol U., Eng., 1954, Fulbright Fellow-ship in drama. m. Susan Trustman. 1955 joined MCA, Inc., N.Y.; 1956-59 theatre producer in NY, London: Shinbone Alley, Garden District, and Sir John Gielgud's Ages of Man. 1960-61; director of special programs, CBS/TV; 1961-62, dir. of program sales, CBS-TV; 1962-69, v.p., tv optns., Ashley Famous Agency, Inc.; 1969-74, pres. Warner Bros. TV, Burbank; 1975-76, exec. v.p. foreign prod. Warner Bros. Pictures, Rome; 1977-82, ind. prod. under Jerry Leider Prods.; 1982-87, pres., ITC Prods., Inc; named pres. and CEO, ITC Entertain-ment Group, 1987-91. Leider once again ind. prod. under own banner, Jerry Leider Productions.
PICTURES: Wild Horse Hank, The Jazz Singer, Trenchcoat, Dr. Jekyll and Ms. Hyde, My Favorite Martian, Confessions of a Teenage Drama Queen, Just Peck, On the Road.
TELEVISION: *Movies*: And I Alone Survived, Willa, The Hostage Tower, The Scarlet and the Black, Secrets of a Married Man, The Haunting Passion, Letting Go, A Time to Live, The Girl Who Spelled Freedom, Unnatural Causes, Poor Little Rich Girl, Sydney Sheldon's The Sands of Time, Morning Glory, Home Song, Family Blessings, Trucks, Cadet Kelly, Fall From the Sky, Coast to Coast, Mayday. *Series*: Major Payne.

LEIGH, JENNIFER JASON
Actress. r.n. Jennifer Leigh Morrow. b. Los Angeles, CA, Feb. 5, 1962. Daughter of late actor Vic Morrow and TV writer Barbara Turner. At age 14 debuted in Disney tv movie The Young Runaway. Won L.A. Valley Coll. best actress award for stage prod. The Shadow Box (1979).
PICTURES: Eyes of a Stranger (debut, 1981), Wrong Is Right, Fast Times at Ridgemont High, Easy Money, Grandview U.S.A., The Hitcher, Flesh + Blood, The Men's Club, Undercover, Sister Sister, Heart of Midnight, The Big Picture, Miami Blues (NY Film Critics Award, 1990), Last Exit to Brooklyn (NY Film Critics Award, 1990), Backdraft, Crooked Hearts, Rush, Single White Female, Short Cuts (Golden Globe Award 1994), The Hudsucker Proxy, Mrs. Parker and the Vicious Circle (Golden Globe nom.; Natl. Society of Film Critics & Chicago Film Critics Awards, 1994), Dolores Claiborne, Georgia (also co-prod.), Kansas City, A Thousand Acres, Washington Square, eXistenZ, The King is Alive, Skipped Parts, Beautiful View, The Quickie, The Anniversary Party (also dir.), The Road to Perdition, Hey Arnold: The Movie (voice), In the Cut, The Machinist, Palindromes, The Jacket, Rag Tale, Margot at the Wedding, Synecdoche, New York, Greenberg (also prod., writer).
TELEVISION: *Movies*: The Young Runaway, Angel City, I Think I'm Having a Baby, The Killing of Randy Webster, The Best Little Girl in the World, The First Time, Girls of the White Orchid, Picnic, Buried Alive, The Love Letter, Thanks of a Grateful Nation, Crossed Over. *Series*: Spawn (voice). *Guest:* More than 65 appearances.

LEIGH, MIKE, OBE
Director, Writer. b. Salford, England, Feb. 20, 1943. e. RADA, Camberwell Art Sch., Central Sch. of Arts & Crafts, London Film Sch. Began career in experimental theatre. Plays include Waste Paper Guards, The Box Play, Neena, Individual Fruit Pies, Down Here and Up There, Big Basil, Epilogue, Bleak Moments, A Rancid Pong, Wholesome Glory, The Jaws of Death, Dick Whittington and His Cat, Babies Grow Old, The Silent Majority, Abigail's Party, Ecstacy, Goose-Pimples, Smelling the Rat, Greek Tragedy, It's a Great Big Shame, Two Thousand Years. Directed 1977 TV drama Abigail's Party. 1987 short: The Short

and Curlies. Recipient of 1995 BAFTA Award for Outstanding British Contribution to Cinema.
PICTURES: Bleak Moments, Hard Labour, Nuts in May, The Kiss of Death, Who's Who, Grown-Ups, Home Sweet Home, Meantime, Four Days in July, High Hopes, Life Is Sweet, Naked, Secrets & Lies (2 Academy Award noms. 1997, DGA nom.; WGA nom.; BAFTA, s.p.), Career Girls, Topsy-Turvy (Academy Award nom. 2000), All or Nothing, Vera Drake (2 Academy Award noms. 2005), Happy-Go-Lucky (Academy Award nom., s.p., 2009), Another Year.
TELEVISION: *Movies:* Hard Labour, Nuts in May (also writer), Kiss of Death, Abigail's Party (also writer), Who's Who, Grown-Ups (also writer), Home Sweet Home (also writer), Meantime (also writer), Four Days in July, A Mug's Game, Plays for Britain. *Series:* The Wednesday Play, Play for Today.

LEITCH, JR., DONOVAN

Actor. b. London, England, August, 16, 1968. Son of folksinger Donovan. Brother of actress Lone Skye. Acted in jr. high sch. musical then had bit part in PBS. show K.I.D.S.
PICTURES: And God Created Women (1988), The Blob, The In Crowd, Cutting Class, Glory, Gas Food Lodging, Dark Horse, I Shot Andy Warhol, One Night Stand, Love Kills, Cherry, Big City Blues, Men Make Women Crazy Theory, Sunset Strip (doc., co-prod.).
TELEVISION: *Movies*: But He Loves Me, For the Very First Time, The '60s. *Series*: Girls Club. *Documentary:* Schmatta: Rags to Riches to Rags (co-prod.).

LELAND, DAVID

Director, Writer, Actor. b. Cambridge, Eng., April 20, 1947. Began as actor at Nottingham Playhouse. Then joined newly formed company at Royal Court Theatre, London. Also appeared in films Time Bandits, The Missionary, and his own Personal Services (Peter Sellers Award for Comedy) and on TV in The Jewel in the Crown. As stage director specialized in complete seasons of new works at the Crucible in Sheffield and London venues. Wrote play Psy-Warriors.
PICTURES: Mona Lisa (co-s.p., Golden Globe nom.; WGA nom. 1987), Personal Services (s.p.), Wish You Were Here (dir., s.p.; BAFTA Award for s.p.), Checking Out (dir.), The Big Man (dir.; a.k.a. Crossing the Line), Land Girls (co-s.p., dir.), The White River Kid (also s.p.), Running Wild, The Decameron, Virgin Territory.
TELEVISION: *Movies*: Birth of a Nation (writer, 1982), Flying Into the Wind, Rhino, Made in Britain, Beloved Enemy, Ligmalion: A Musical for the 80s, Psy-Warriors. *Mini-series*: The Last of the Mohicans, The Hitch Hikers Guide to the Galaxy, The Jewel in the Crown, Band of Brothers (Emmy Award 2002). *Documentary:* Concert for George.

LE LOUCH, CLAUDE

Director, Writer, Producer, Cinematographer, Editor. b. Paris, France, Oct. 30, 1937. Began m.p. career with short subjects, 1956; French military service, motion picture department, 1957-60; formed Films 13, 1960; publicity Films and Scopitones, 1961-62.
PICTURES: Le Propre de l'Homme (The Right of Man; debut, 1960; also s.p., prod., actor), L'amour avec des Si (Love With Ifs; aalso prod., s.p.), La Femme Spectacle (Night Women; also prod., photog.), Une Fille et des Fusils (To Be a Crook; also co-s.p., prod., edit.), Les Grands Moments (also co-prod.), A Man and A Woman (also co-s.p., story, prod., photog., edit.; Academy Award for Best Foreign Language Film & Original Screenplay, DGA nom.; 1967; also Academy Award nom. for dir.; Golden Globe nom.), Live for Life (also co-s.p., co-photog. , edit.), Farm From Vietnam (segment), 13 Jours en France (Grenoble; co-dir., co-s.p.), Life Love Death (also co-s.p.), Love Is a Funny Thing (also photog., co-s.p.), The Crook (also co- photog., co-s.p.), Smic Smac Smoc (also prod., s.p., photog., actor), Money Money Money (also s.p., prod., photog.), La Bonne Annee (Happy New Year; also prod., s.p., co-photog.), Visions of Eight (segment: The Losers), And Now My Love (also s.p., prod.; Academy Award nom. 1976), Marriage (also co-s.p.), Cat and Mouse (also s.p.), The Good and Bad (also s.p., photog.), Second Chance (also s.p., prod.), Another Man Another Chance (also s.p.), Robert and Robert (also s.p.), Adventure for Two, Bolero (also s.p., prod.), Edith and Marcel (also prod., s.p.), Vive la Vie (also prod., s.p., photog.), Partier Revenir (also prod., co-s.p.), A Man and a Woman: 20 Years Later (also prod., co-s.p.), Bandits (also prod., s.p.), Itinerary of a Spoiled Child (also co-prod., s.p.), There Were Days and Moons (also prod., co-s.p.), Les Miserables., Lumiere and Company, Men Women: A User's Manual, Chance or Coincidence, All 4 One, And Now...Ladies and Gentlemen, Roman de gare (prod.), To Each His Cinema.
TELEVISION: Moliere (prod. only), là Ces amours.

LE MAT, PAUL

Actor. b. Rahway, NJ, Sept. 22, 1945. Studied with Milton Katselas, Herbert Berghof Studio, A.C.T., San Francisco, Mitchel Ryan-Actor's Studio.
PICTURES: American Graffiti (debut, 1973), Aloha—Bobby and Rose, Citizens Band (Handle With Care), More American Graffiti, Melvin and Howard, Death Valley, Jimmy the Kid, Strange Invaders, P.K. and the Kid, Rock & Rule (voice), The Hanoi Hilton, Private Investigations, Puppet Master, Easy Wheels, Deuce Coupe, Grave Secrets, Veiled Threat, Wishman, Caroline at Midnight, Sensation, Deep Down, The Outfitters, Big Bad Love, Stateside, Chrome Angels.
TELEVISION: *Movies*: Firehouse, The Gift of Life, The Night They Saved Christmas, The Burning Bed, Long Time Gone, Secret Witness, Into the Homeland, Blind Witness, In the Line of Duty: Siege at Marion, Woman With a Past, The Long Shot: Believe in Courage. *Mini-series*: On Wings of Eagles. *Series*: Lonesome Dove; The Outlaw Years.

LEMBERGER, KEN

Executive, Producer. e. B.A., Queen's College, CUNY and J.D., NYU School of Law. Began tenure with Sony Pictures Entertainment (SPE) in the legal dept., 1979-81; senior v.p., Studio Legal Affairs, 1981-83; senior v.p. & gen. counsel, SPE, 1983; vice chairman, TriStar Pictures, 1992-94; corporate exec. v.p., SPE, 1994-97. 1997,vice chairman of Sony Pictures Entertainment. 2001; named pres., Sony Pictures Entertainment. Retired from Sony, 2003. In 2004 became consultant to the Columbia TriStar Motion Picture Group. Currently founder and executive for JP Morgan Entertainment Advisors.
PICTURES: All the King's Men, When a Stranger Calls.

LENFEST, H. F. "GERRY"

Executive. b. Jacksonville, FL. e. Mercersburg Academy, graduate of Washington and Lee U., B.A., 1953; Columbia Law School, LL.B., 1958. Served in U.S. Navy, retired Captain. Practiced law at the New York firm of Davis Polk & Wardwell before becoming corporate counsel of Walter Annenberg's Triangle Publications in 1965. Became head of Triangle's Communications Div., 1970, which owned various media, including several radio, TV and cable stations, newspapers, TV Guide and SEVENTEEN magazine. There, he became the editorial director and publisher of SEVENTEEN, and president of CATV operations. Formed new co. in 1974 and bought two cable cos. from Triangle. His company, Lenfest Communications Inc., the parent company of the former Suburban Cable, eventually became one of the top 11 cable TV companies in the U.S. In 2000, he sold Lenfest Communications to Comcast Corporation. Serves as chmn of TelVue Corp. which provides services principally associated with Cable TV, Internet related businesses and the Telephone industry. Lenfest received Columbia University's Distinguished Achievement Award in 1997. He is permanent president of his class, and has served on his class fund committee since 1963. He served on the Columbia Law School Board of Visitors from 1988 to 2000, and the Law School Association Board from 1969 to 1973. Lenfest is also a member of the Dean's Council of the Law School. In addition, he serves or has served on the boards and councils of many non-profit organizations, including the Philadelphia Museum of Art, the Curtis Institute of Music, and the American Revolution Center, in each of which he serves as Chair of the Board of Trustees, the James Madison Council of the Library of Congress, and the Chesapeake Bay Foundation. He is a past trustee of Washington & Lee University and past president of the Board of Mercersburg Academy. Lenfest is a noted philanthropist, donating millions to the educational institutions he attended and to various other causes. In 2006, Lenfest received the Musser Award for Excellence in Leadership from Temple University's Fox School of Business and Management. He is also a Director for Environmental Tectonics Corporation.

LENO, JAY

Comedian, Actor. r.n. James Douglas Muir Leno. b. New Rochelle, NY, April 28, 1950. e. Emerson College, B.A. speech therapy, 1973. Raised in Andover, MA. Worked as Rolls Royce auto mechanic and deliveryman while seeking work as stand-up comedian. Performed in comedy clubs throughout the U.S. and as opening act for Perry Como, Johnny Mathis, John Denver and Tom Jones. Guest on numerous talk shows and specials. Since Johnny Carson's retirement in 1992, Leno has hosted The Tonight Show on NBC.
PICTURES: Fun With Dick and Jane, The Silver Bears, American Hot Wax, Americathon, Collision Course, What's Up Hideous Sun Demon? (voice), Dave, We're Back! (voice), Wayne's World 2, Major League 2, We're Back! A Dinosaur's Story (voice), The Flintstones, The Birdcage (cameo), Meet Wally Sparks, In & Out, Contact, Wag the Dog, EDtv, Space Cowboys, John Q., Stuck on You, Calendar Girls, Robots (voice), Ice Age: The Meltdown (voice), Cars (voice), Igor (voice), Christmas Is Here Again (voice).
TELEVISION: *Series*: The Marilyn McCoo & Billy Davis Jr. Show, The Tonight Show with Jay Leno (guest host: 1987-92; host: 1992; Emmy Award, 1995, 10 other noms.), Good Times (writer), The Fairly OddParents The Jimmy Timmy Power Hour 3: The Jerkinators! (voice). *Specials*: Jay Leno and the American Dream (also prod.), The Jay Leno Show, Our Planet Tonight, Jay Leno's Family Comedy Hour (WGA nom. 1989), Comedy Store: The E! True Hollywood Story, Jay Leno's Garage (Emmy nom. 2009).

LENZ, KAY

Actress. b. Los Angeles, CA, March 4, 1953.
PICTURES: Breezy (debut, 1973, Golden Globe nom. 1974), White Line Fever, The Great Scout and Cathouse Thursday, Moving Violation, Mean Dog Blues, The Passage, Fast-Walking, House, Stripped to Kill, Death Wish IV: The Crackdown, Headhunter, Physical Evidence, Fear, Streets, Falling From

Grace, Trapped in Space, Gunfighter's Moon, A Gun A Car A Blonde, The Adventures of Ragtime, Southside, The Secret Lives of Dorks.
TELEVISION: *Movies*: The Weekend Nun, Lisa, Bright and Dark, A Summer Without Boys, Unwed Father, The Underground Man, The FBI Story: The FBI Versus Alvin Karpis, Journey from Darkness, Rich Man, Poor Man (Emmy nom. 1976), The Initiation of Sarah, The Seeding of Sarah Burns, Sanctuary of Fear, The Hustler of Muscle Beach, Murder by Night, Heart in Hiding, How the West Was Won, Traveling Man, Escape, Hitler's Daughter, Against Their Will: Women in Prison, Trapped in Space, Shame II: The Secret, Journey of the Heart. *Mini-series:* Rich Man Poor Man—Book II. *Series:* Reasonable Doubts (2 Emmy noms.), The Tick (voice), Cover Me: Based on the True Life of an FBI Family, Midnight Caller (Emmy Award, 1 other nom.), The ABC Afternoon Playbreak (Emmy Award 1975). *Guest:* More than 80 appearances.

LEONARD, ROBERT SEAN
Actor. b. Westwood, NJ, Feb. 28, 1969. Raised in Ridgewood, NJ. Started acting at age 12 in local summer stock. Joined NY Shakespeare Festival at 15.
THEATRE: *Off-B'way:* Coming of Age in Soho, Sally's Gone—She Left Her Name, The Beach House, When She Danced, Romeo and Juliet, Good Evening, The Great Unwashed, Fifth of July. *B'way:* Brighton Beach Memoirs, Breaking the Code, The Speed of Darkness, Candida (Tony nom.), Philadelphia Here I Come!, The Iceman Cometh, Arcadia, The Invention of Love, (Tony Award), Long Day's Journey Into Night, The Violet Hour. *Regional:* Biloxi Blues (tour), Rocky and Diego,King Lear, The Double Inconstancy.
PICTURES: The Manhattan Project (debut, 1986), My Best Friend Is a Vampire, Dead Poets Society, Mr. & Mrs. Bridge, Swing Kids, Married to It, Much Ado About Nothing, The Age of Innocence, Safe Passage, Killer: A Journal of Murder, I Love You—I Love You Not, Ground Control, Stand Off, The Last Days of Disco, Tape, Driven, Chelsea Walls, The I Inside.
TELEVISION: *Movies*: My Two Loves, Bluffing It, The Boys Next Door, In the Gloaming, A Glimpse of Hell, A Painted House. *Pilot:* The Robert Klein Show. *Series*: Rosebud, Corsairs, House, M.D.

LEONI, TÉA
Actress. r.n. Elizabeth Téa Pantaleoni. b. New York, NY Feb. 25, 1966. e. The Putney School in Putney, VT. m. actor David Duchovny and together is co-owner of And Then Productions.
PICTURES: Switch, A League of Their Own, Wyatt Earp, Bad Boys, Flirting with Disaster, Deep Impact, There's No Fish Food In Heaven (also exec. prod.), The Family Man, Jurassic Park III, Hollywood Ending, People I Know, House of D, Spanglish, Fun with Dick and Jane, You Kill Me (also exec. prod.), Ghost Town, Manure.
TELEVISION: *Movies*: The Counterfeit Contessa. *Series*: Santa Barbara, Flying Blind, The Naked Truth.

LERNER, MICHAEL
Actor. b. Brooklyn, NY, June 22, 1941. e. Brooklyn Col., Univ. of CA, Berkeley. Prior to acting was professor of dramatic literature at San Francisco St. Col., 1968-69. Studied acting in London on Fullbright Scholarship. Was member of San Francisco's American Conservatory Theatre. On NY stage in Twelfth Night; L.A. stage in The Women of Trachis, Hurlyburly.
PICTURES: Alex in Wonderland (debut, 1970), The Candidate, Busting, Newman's Law, Hangup (Superdude), St. Ives, The Other Side of Midnight, Outlaw Blues, Goldengirl, Borderline, Coast to Coast, The Baltimore Bullet, The Postman Always Rings Twice, National Lampoon's Class Reunion, Threshold, Strange Invaders, Movers and Shakers, Anguish, Vibes, Eight Men Out, Harlem Nights, Any Man's Death, The Closer, Barton Fink (Academy Award nom. 1992), Newsies, Amos & Andrew, Blank Check, No Escape, Radioland Murders, The Road to Wellville, Girl in the Cadillac, A Pyromaniac's Love Story, The Beautician and the Beast, for Richer or Poorer, Russell Mulcahy's Tale of the Mummy, Godzilla, Celebrity, Safe Men, The Mod Squad, My Favorite Martian, Elf, The Calcium Kid, Poster Boy, When Do We Eat?, Art School Confidential, Love and Other Disasters, The Last Time, Slipstream Dream, Yonkers Joe, A Serious Man, The Bannen Way, Pete Smalls Is Dead.
TELEVISION: *Movies*: Thief, Marriage Year One, What's a Nice Girl Like You...?, Magic Carpet, Firehouse (pilot), Reflections of Murder, The Rockford Files (pilot), The Death of Sammy, A Cry for Help, Starsky and Hutch (pilot), Sarah T: Portrait of a Teenage Alcoholic, Dark Victory, F. Scott Fitzgerald in Hollywood, Scott Free, Killer on Board, A Love Affair: The Eleanor and Lou Gehrig Story, Vega$ (pilot), Ruby & Oswald, Hart to Hart (pilot), Moviola: This Year's Blonde, Gridlock, Blood Feud, Rita Hayworth: Love Goddess, The Execution, This Child is Mine, Betrayal of Trust, Hands of a Stranger, King of Love, Framed, Omen IV: The Awakening, The Comrades of Summer, Murder at the Cannes Film Festival, The Omen Legacy. *Mini-series:* Melba, Picture Windows: Language of the Heart, Kingdom Hospital. *Series*: Courthouse, Clueless. *Special:* The Missiles of October. *Guest*: More than 85 appearances.

LESHER, JOHN
Executive. b. Pittsburgh, PA. e. Graduate of Harvard University. Entered entertainment industry as a talent agent and spent 15 years with United Talent Agency, five of which he served as a partner there. In 2002, Lesher became a partner at Endeavor Talent Agency serving clients like Martin Scorsese. Lesher became president of Paramount Classics in Nov. 2005 which was renamed Paramount Vantage in 2006. His first release at the label was former U.S. Vice President Al Gore's documentary "An Inconvenient Truth," which won two 2006 Academy Awards, including Best Documentary and has since become one of the highest grossing documentaries of all time. Lesher was named president, Paramount Film Group in early 2008 and is the position he holds today He now has creative control over Paramount's picture labels Paramount Films, MTV Films, Nickelodeon Movies and Paramount Vantage. 2009 Lesher left Paramount and has started his own production company, Le Grisbi Prod., which has delivered several projects for HBO.

LESINSKI, THOMAS
Executive. e. Bachelor's and Master's degrees from Northwestern Univ. Lesinski began his career at the advertising agency BBDO in New York, where he worked on the Pepsi, Campbell Soup and Gillette accounts. He subsequently held the position of marketing director at Bristol Myers in New York. He then worked as managing dir. at the Los Angeles office of the adv. agency Foote Cone & Belding where he was responsible for the entertainment business. From the agency, he joined Warner Bros. in 1993 as dir. of marketing. He was promoted to v.p. of marketing in 1994 and to senior v.p. of marketing in 1996. Lesinski joined Warner Home Video and held key executive slots: executive v.p. of worldwide marketing with marketing responsibility in 78 countries and executive v.p. and gen. mgr., with responsibility for all U.S. activity. Lesinski joined Paramount in 2003 as president of Worldwide Home Entertainment for the Motion Picture Group of Paramount Pictures. On Feb. 1, 2006, Lesinski became president of the Paramount Pictures Digital Entertainment, a new division separate from the home entertainment group.

LESLIE, JOAN
Actress. r.n. Joan Brodell. b. Detroit, MI, January 26, 1925. e. St. Benedicts, Detroit; Our Lady of Lourdes, Toronto; St. Mary's Montreal; Immaculate Heart. H.S., L.A. Child performer on stage as part of The Three Brodels. Became model before going to Hollywood in 1936. Voted Quigley Publishing's Star of Tomorrow, 1946. Now on bd. of dir., St. Anne's Maternity Home, Damon Runyon Foundation.
PICTURES: (as Joan Brodel): Camille (debut, 1937), Men with Wings, Nancy Drew—Reporter, Love Affair, Winter Carnival, Two Thoroughbreds, High School, Young as You Feel, Star Dust, Susan and God, Military Academy, Foreign Correspondent, Laddie. (as Joan Leslie): Thieves Fall Out, The Wagons Roll at Night, High Sierra, The Great Mr. Nobody, Sergeant York, The Hard Way, The Male Animal, Yankee Doodle Dandy, The Sky's the Limit, This Is the Army, Thank Your Lucky Stars, Hollywood Canteen, Rhapsody in Blue, Where Do We Go From Here?, Too Young to Know, Janie Gets Married, Cinderella Jones, Two Guys From Milwaukee, Repeat Performance, Northwest Stampede, Born To Be Bad, The Skipper Surprised His Wife, Man in the Saddle, Hellgate, Toughest Man in Arizona, The Woman They Almost Lynched, Flight Nurse, Hell's Outpost, Jubilee Trail, The Revolt of Mamie Stover.
TELEVISION: *Movies*: Charley Hannah, The Keegans, Turn Back the Clock, Fire in the Dark.

LESTER, MARK
Actor. b. Oxford, England, July 11, 1958. Ent. m.p. ind. 1963.
THEATRE: The Murder Game, The Prince and the Pauper 1976.
PICTURES: Allez France (The Counterfeit Constable; debut, 1963), Spaceflight IC-1, Fahrenheit 451, Arrividerci Baby!, Our Mother's House, Oliver!, Run Wild Run Free, Sudden Terror (Eye Witness), Melody, Black Beauty, Who Slew Auntie Roo?, Redneck, Scalawag, Jungle Boy, Crossed Swords, 1066.
TELEVISION: The Boy Who Stole the Elephants, Graduation Trip, Danza Alla Porto Gli Olmi (Italian Entry Berlin '75), Seen Dimly Before Dawn.

LESTER, MARK LESLIE
Director. b. Cleveland, OH, Nov. 26, 1949. e. Cal. State Univ. Northridge, B.A.
PICTURES: Director and/or Producer: Steel Arena (debut, 1973; also co-prod., s.p.), Truck Stop Women (also co-s.p.), Bobbie Jo and the Outlaw, Stunts, Roller Boogie, The Funhouse (co-exec. prod. only), The Class of 1984 (also co-exec. prod., co-s.p.), Firestarter, Commando, Armed and Dangerous, Class of 1999 (also story), Showdown in Little Tokyo, Extreme Justice, Night of the Running Man, The Ex, Public Enemy #1, Double Take, Misbegotten, The Ex, Hitman's Run, Blowback, Betrayal, Pterodactyl (also prod.), Day of Wrath (exec. prod. only), Showgirls: Exposed (title creator), Groupie (also prod., exec. prod.), Sinbad and the Minotaur (prod.).
TELEVISION: *Movies:* Gold of the Amazon Women, Sacrifice (also prod.), Guilty As Charged (also prod.), Lost Colony (prod.), Wraiths of Roanoke (prod. only), Yeti: Curse of the Snow Demon (exec. prod.).

LESTER, RICHARD
Director. b. Philadelphia, PA, Jan. 19, 1932. e. Univ. of PA.

Started as stagehand at tv studio before becoming dir. and music. dir. CBS-TV in Philadelphia, then CBC-TV, Toronto. To England in 1956 where he resumed work as tv dir. TV dir. The Goon Shows. Composed (with Reg. Owen) Sea War Series. Short Film: composer and dir., The Running Jumping and Standing Still Film. Directed sequences for Mondo Teeno/Teenage Rebellion, Superman.
PICTURES: It's Trad Dad (debut, 1962; aka Ring-a-Ding Rhythm; also prod.), The Mouse on the Moon, A Hard Day's Night, The Knack... and How to Get It, Help!, A Funny Thing Happened on the Way to the Forum, How I Won the War (also prod.), Petulia, The Bed-Sitting Room (also co-prod.), The Three Musketeers, Juggernaut, The Four Musketeers, Royal Flash, Robin & Marian (also co-prod.), The Ritz, Butch and Sundance: The Early Days, Cuba, Superman II, Superman III, Finders Keepers (also exec. prod.), The Return of the Musketeers (tv in U.S.), Get Back (doc.).
TELEVISION: *Movie:* Curtains for Harry (also prod.). *Series:* The Vise, The Idiot Weekly, Price 2d (also prod.), A Show Called Fred (also prod.), Son of Fred (also prod.), After Hours (also writer).

LETTERMAN, DAVID
Performer, Writer. b. Indianapolis, IN, Apr. 12, 1947. e. Ball State U. Began career as weatherman and talk show host on Indianapolis TV before going to Hollywood. Cameo appearances in films Cabin Boy, Beavis and Butt-head Do America (voice), Private Parts, Man on the Moon, Meeting People Is Easy. Executive of production company World Wide Pants.
PICTURES: Cabin Boy, Beavis and Butt-Head Do America (voice), Strangers with Candy (exec. prod.).
TELEVISION: *Series Writer:* Good Times, Paul Lynde Comedy Hour. *Writer (specials):* John Denver Special, Bob Hope Special. *Series Performer:* The Starland Vocal Band (also writer), Mary (1978), Tonight Show (guest host 1978-82), The David Letterman Show (Daytime Emmy Award for writing, 1981), Late Night with David Letterman (1982-93, on NBC; 4 Emmy Awards for Writing), Late Show With David Letterman (1993-, on CBS, 4 Emmy Awards, 2 Daytimes Emmy Awards, 4 WGA noms.; Total Emmy noms. 41). *Series: Exec. Prod:* The Building, The Late Late Show with Tom Snyder, Bonnie, Everybody Loves Raymond, The High Life, The Late Late Show with Craig Kilborn, Ed (7 episodes), The Knights of Prosperity (exec. prod.), The Late Late Show with Craig Ferguson (exec. prod.).

LEVESQUE, MICHAEL
Exhibitor. b. Hartford, CT, 1958. e. Central Connecticut University. Currently is senior v.p. operations/East Division of Regal Entertainment Group. He also serves on the bd. of directors of the Regal Foundation. Regal is the largest U.S. theatre circuit consisting of more than 6,368 screens in over 529 locations in 39 states (as of June 2007).

LEVIN, GERALD M.
Executive. b. Philadelphia, PA, May 6, 1939. e. Haverford College, B.A., 1960' Univ. of PA Law School, LL.B., 1963. Associate of law firm Simpson, Thacher, and Bartlett, 1963-67; gen.mgr. and COO, Development and Resources Corp., 1967-71; representative, International Basic Economy Corp., in Tehran, Iran, 1971-72; v.p., programming, HBO, 1972; promoted to pres. & CEO, 1973-76; upped to chmn., 1976. chair and CEO, HBO, 1976-79; became group v.p. of video, Time, Inc., 1979-84; exec. v.p., 1984-88; vice-chairman and director, 1988-90; v.p. and director, Time-Warner, Inc., 1990; COO, 1991-92; chmn. & CEO of Time Warner Inc., 1993. Levin orchestrated the media company's $106 billion merger with AOL in 2000 and became CEO and dir., AOL Time Warner, Inc. after the merger and CEO, Time Warner Entertainment Group LP. He also served on the bd. of directors, AOL Time Warner. The company's post-merger lackluster performance resulted in Levin losing his CEO title, and he retired from the company in May 2002. Levin currently is a director Moonview Sanctuary, a California facility that treats ailments from drug abuse to depression and which was founded by Laurie Perlman, Levin's wife. Plans are under way to open a second facility in New York in 2008.

LEVIN, JULIAN
Executive. b. South Africa. Held various positions at Morgan Creek International, Vestron Motion Pictures and other independent production and distribution companies. Joined Fox in 1991, holding several exec. position in int'l. sales and distrib. 1995, promoted to exec. v.p., sales and distrib., Twentieth Century Fox Int'l. Played an integral role in the distribution of such films as Mrs. Doubtfire, Independence Day, Braveheart, Titanic, and Moulin Rouge. Feb. 2002, appointed to newly created position of exec. v.p., digital exhibition and non theatrical sales and distribution, Twentieth Century Fox. Responsible for development of corporate strategies for digital exhibition and analysis of key initiatives in new theatrical technologies. Levin is also the key exec. representing Twentieth Century Fox in NEWCO, (also known as "Digital Cinema Initiatives") the entity formed by the seven major studios to develop technical standards for digital cinema technology.

LEVIN, MARC
Director, Writer, Actor, Producer.
PICTURES: The Last Party, CIA: America's Secret Warriors, Slam (Cannes Film Fest. Awards, Camera d'Or, Grand Jury Prize, 1998) ,Whiteboys, Soldiers in the Army of God, Speak Truth to Power (dir. only), Brooklyn Babylon, Street Time (dir. only), Protocols of Zion (doc.), Mr. Untouchable (doc.), Cadillac Records (exec. prod.), Dirty Old Town (exec. prod.).
TELEVISION: *Series*: Cleghorne! (cinematographer), Street Time. *Mini-series/Series*: *Documentaries:* America Undercover, Moyers on Addiction: Close to Home, Gladiator Days: Anatomy of a Prison Murder, Thug Life in D.C. (DGA nom.; Emmy Award 1999), The Blues (dir. only), Back in the Hood: Gang War 2, Back in the Hood: Gang War II., Schmatta: Rags to Riches to Rags (dir., prod.), Brick City, Law & Order.

LEVIN, ROBERT B.
Executive. b. Chicago, IL, May 31, 1943. e. U. of Illinois, BS Journalism, 1965. Copywriter Sears Roebuck & Co. 1965-66, PR Natural Gas Pipeline Co. of Amer. 1966-69. Acct. Exec. Hurvis Binzer & Churchill 1969-70. McCann-Erickson 1975-82 Acct. Super. 1975-79, Mgmt. Super. Needham Harper Worldwide 1982-85. Pres. Mktg. WD Co. 1985-94, Chief Corp. Mktg. & Comm. 1994-95. Pres. Worldwide Mktg. Savoy Pictures 1995-96, Sony Pictures Entertainment, 1996. June 2001 became pres,. Worldwide Theatrical Mktg. & Distrib., MGM. In Sept. 2004, Levin formed an association with independent film co., MoviePartners, Inc., as both an advisor and as a film producer. He is also adjunct faculty at USC's School of Cinematic Arts.

LEVINE, PAMELA
Executive. Worked as v.p. of ent. mktg. at consulting firm MarketCast before joining Fox in 1995 as senior. v.p. market planning and research. In that post, she analyzed market research on domestic releases and crafted upfront marketing strategies. In May 2002, she was promoted to current position, co-president, domestic theatrical marketing for 20th Century Fox, alongside Tony Sella. In 2008, the pair received Advertising Age's Entertainment Marketers of the Year honor and also in 2008, Levine was ranked 31 in The Hollywood Reporter's Power 100 Women in Entertainment.

LEVINSON, BARRY
Director, Producer, Writer, Actor. b. Baltimore, MD, Apr. 6, 1942. e. American Univ. Wrote and acted in L.A. comedy show leading to work on network tv incl. writing and performing on The Carol Burnett Show. Co-wrote film scripts with Mel Brooks, and then-wife Valerie Curtin. Apppeared as actor in History of the World Part I, Quiz Show. Received WGA Laurel Award for Screen Writing Achievement 2010.
PICTURES: *Writer*: Silent Movie (also actor, WGA nom. 1977), High Anxiety (also actor), ... And Justice for All (Academy Award nom. 1980), Inside Moves, Best Friends, Unfaithfully Yours. *Director/Producer:* Diner (also s.p.; Academy Award nom. for s.p. WGA nom. 1983), The Natural, Young Sherlock Holmes, Tin Men (also s.p.), Good Morning Vietnam, Rain Man (also actor; Academy Award for Best Director, DGA Award Golden Globe nom. 1989), Avalon (also s.p.; WGA Award, DGA nom.; Academy Award nom. for s.p. Golden Globe nom. 1991), Bugsy (2 Academy Award noms.; DGA nom.; Golden Globe nom. 1992), Toys (also co-s.p.), Jimmy Hollywood (also s.p., co-prod.), Disclosure (also co-prod.), Sleepers (also s.p., co-prod.), Donnie Brasco (prod. only), Wag the Dog (also co-prod.), Sphere (also co-prod.), Liberty Heights (also prod.), The Perfect Storm (exec. prod.), An Everlasting Piece, Bandits (dir. only), Possession (prod. only), Analyze That, Deliver Us from Eva, Envy, My Italian Story, A View From the Bridge, Man of the Year, Bee Movie (voice), What Just Happened?, A Walk in the Woods, PoliWood (doc., prod.).
TELEVISION: *Movies*: The Second Civil War, Homicide: The Movie, American Tragedy, Shot in the Heart, Strip Search, M.O.N.Y., The Saint (exec. prod., pilot), You Don't Know Jack (dir., exec. prod.). *Series:* The Tim Conway Comedy Hour (writer), The Marty Feldman Comedy Machine (writer), The Carol Burnett Show (writer; 2 Emmy Awards: 1974, 1975, 1 other nom.), Harry (exec. prod.), Homicide: Life on the Streets (dir., co-exec. prod.; Emmy Award for directing, DGA nom. 1994), The Beat, Falcone, Baseball Wives, The Jury, The Bedford Diaries (exec. prod.), 3 lbs, The Philanthropist (prod., exec. prod.). *Pilot*: Diner (exec. prod., dir.), Oz (exec. prod.). *Specials*: Stopwatch 30 Minutes of Investigative Ticking (exec. prod.), Displaced Person (Emmy Award 1985).

LEVITAN, STEVEN
Producer.
TELEVISION: *Movies:* Quiet Killer, Say Uncle (co-exec. prod.). *Series*: Wings (co-exec. prod. and writer), Frasier (consult. and writer), The Larry Sanders Show (writer only, Emmy noms.; WGA nom. 1996), Just Shoot Me (also dir., creator), Yes, Dear (dir. only), Men Behaving Badly (writer only), Stark Raving Mad (exec. prod.), Greg the Bunny (exec. prod.), With You in Spirit (writer, exec. prod.), Oliver Beene, Stacked, The Saddle Club (exec. prod.), Train 48 (exec. prod.), Metropia (exec. prod.), Kaya (exec. prod.), Back to You (writer, exec. prod.), Modern Family (exec. prod., 2 WGA Awards; 1 other nom. 2010).

LEVITT, JOSEPH GORDON
Actor, Director, Editor. b. Los Angeles, CA, February 17, 1981.

e. Columbia U.
THEATRE: *B'way:* Slava's Snowshow. *Off B'way:* Uncle Bob (debut).
PICTURES: Beethoven, A River Runs Through It, Holy Matrimony, Angels in the Outfield, The Juror, Sweet Jane, Halloween H20: 20 Years Later, 10 Things I Hate About You, Manic, Treasure Planet (voice), Latter Days, Mysterious Skin, Brick, Shadowboxer, The Lookout, Stop-Loss, Miracle at St. Anna, Killshot, The Brothers Bloom, (500) Days of Summer (also soundtrack performer, Golden Globe nom. 2010), Uncertainty, G.I. Joe: The Rise of Cobra, Hesher, Elektra Luxx, Inception, Live with It, Premium Rush, Looper.
TELEVISION: *Movies:* Stranger on My Land, Settle the Score, Dark Shadows, Changes, Hi Honey - I'm Dead, Plymouth, Gregory K, The Great Elephant Escape. *Series:* Dark Shadows, The Powers That Be, Roseanne, 3rd Rock from the Sun.

LEVY, EUGENE

Actor, Writer, Director. b. Hamilton, Canada, Dec. 17, 1946. e. McMaster U. Acted with coll. ensemble theatre. Film debut in Ivan Reitman's Cannibal Girls, 1970.
PICTURES: Cannibal Girls, Running, Nothing Personal, double Negative, Heavy Metal (voice), National Lampoon's Vacation, Vacation, Strange Brew, Going Berserk, Splash, Tears Are Not Enough, Armed and Dangerous, Club Paradise, Speed Zone, Father of the Bride, Once Upon a Crime (also dir.), Stay Tuned, I Love Trouble, Father of the Bride 2, Multiplicity, Waiting for Guffman (also s.p.), Dogmatic, Almost Heroes, Holy Man, Akbar's Adventure Tours, The Secret Life of Girls, Unglued, America Pie, Best In Show (also s.p., WGA nom. 2001), The Ladies Man, Silver Man, Down to Earth, Josie and the Pussycats, American Pie 2, Serendipity, Repli-Kate, Like Mike, A Mighty Wind, In the Houze, Dumb and Dumberer: When Harry Met Lloyd, American Wedding, New York Minute, The Man, Curious George (voice), For Your Consideration, Over the Hedge (voice), Gooby, Punctured, Night at the Museum: Battle of the Smithsonian, Taking Woodstock, Astro Boy (voice).
TELEVISION: *Movies:* Partners 'n Love, Sodbusters (dir., co-writer, co-exec. prod.), Harrison Bergeron, D.O.A., Committed, Club Land, The Kid. *Series:* Stay Tuned, Second City TV (also writer), The Sunshine Hour, SCTV Network 90, SCTV Network (2 Emmy Awards 7 other noms.), Hiller & Diller, Hercules (voice), Greg the Bunny. *Specials:* The Canadian Conspiracy, Bully Crystal: Don't Get Me Started, *Biographies:* The Enigma of Bobbie Bittman. *Guest:* More than 96 appearances.

LEVY, MICHAEL

Executive, Producer. b. Brooklyn, NY. e. Brown U. Started in industry in editorial dept. of trade-paper Variety; held posts in New York with ABC Motion Pictures and with Diener/Hauser/Bates Advertising. Worked for Lawrence Gordon Productions as exec. asst. to Gordon and as story editor. Joined 20th Century Fox in Jan. 1985, as studio's dir. of creative affairs. 1986, named v.p., production, m.p. div., Fox; appointed sr. v.p. production, 20th Century Fox, 1988; named pres., Silver Pictures, 1989. In recent years has been independent producer working on projects with Lawrence Gordon Productions.
PICTURES: *Exec. Prod/Prod.:* Die Hard 2, The Adventures of Ford Fairlane, Predator 2, Ricochet, The Last Boy Scout, Demolition Man, Lara Croft: Tomb Raider, K-PAX.

LEWIS, GEOFFREY

Actor. b. San Diego, CA, July 31, 1935. Father of actress Juliette Lewis, actors Lightfield & Peter Lewis.
PICTURES: Welcome Home Soldier Boys, The Culpepper Cattle Company, Bad Company, High Plains Drifter, Dillinger, Thunderbolt and Lightfoot, Macon County Line, The Great Waldo Pepper, Smile, The Wind and the Lion, Lucky Lady, The Return of a Man Called Horse, Every Which Way But Loose, Tilt, Human Experiments, Tom Horn, Broncho Billy, Heaven's Gate, Any Which Way You Can, Shoot the Sun Down, I the Jury, Ten to Midnight, Night of the Comet, Lust in the Dust, Stitches, Fletch Lives, Out of the Dark, Pink Cadillac, Catch Me If You Can, Disturbed, Double Impact, The Lawnmower Man, Point of No Return, Wishman, The Man Without a Face, Only the Strong, Army of One, Maverick, White Fang II: Myth of the White Wolf, Last Resort, The Dragon Gate, An Occassional Hell, American Perfekt, Midnight in the Garden of Good and Evil, Five Aces, The Prophet's Game, The Way of the Gun, Highway 395, A Light in the Darkness, The New Guy, Something Borrowed, Formosa, Moving McAllister, The Fallen Ones, The Drummer (also writer, dir. and exec. prod.), The Devil's Rejects, Down in the Valley, Wicked Little Things, Moving McAllister, Retreat!, Cold Ones, Fingerprints, Thomas Kinkade's Home for Christmas, Chinaman's Chance, The Haunted World of El Superbeasto (voice), Miss Nobody, Pickin' & Grinnin', Retreat!.
TELEVISION: *Movies:* Moon of the Wolf, Honky Tonk, The Great Ice Rip-Off, Attack on Terror: The FBI Versus the Ku Klux Klan, The New Daughters of Joshua Cabe, The Great Houndinis, The Deadly Triangle, The Hunted Lady, When Every Day Was the Fourth of July, The Jericho Mile, Samurai, Salem's Lot, Belle Starr, The Shadow Riders, Life of the Party: The Story of Beatrice, The Return of the Man From U.N.C.L.E., Travis McGee, September Gun, Stormin' Home, Dallas: The Early Years, Day of Reckoning, Gambler V: Playing for Keeps, When the Dark Man Calls, Kansas, Trilogy of Terror II, Rough Riders, The Underworld, A Painted House, Plainsong, The Fallen Ones, Wild Hearts. *Mini-series:* Centennial. *Series:* Flo (Golden Globe nom. 1981), Gun Shy, Land's End, Maximum Security, My Life with Men. *Guest:* More than 140 appearances.

LEWIS, HAROLD G.

Executive. b. New York, NY, Sept. 18, 1938. e. Union Coll., 1960, electrical engineer. Joined ATA Trading Corp. in 1960 and has been pres. since 1977. Producer of feature animation. Importer and exporter for theatrical and TV features, documentaries, series, classics. Pres., ATA Trading Corp., and Favorite TV, Inc.

LEWIS, JERRY

Actor, Director, Writer, Producer. r.n. Joseph Levitch. b. Newark, NJ, Mar. 16, 1926. e. Irvington H.S. Parents Danny and Rae Lewis, prof. entertainers. Debut at 5 at a NY Borscht Circuit hotel singing Brother Can You Spare a Dime? 1946 formed comedy-team with Dean Martin at 500 Club, Atlantic City, NJ; then appeared on NBC TV, performed many theatres before being signed by Hal Wallis for m.p. debut. Voted Most Promising Male Star in Television in M.P. Daily's 2nd annual TV poll, 1950. Voted (as team) one of top ten money making stars in m.p. Herald-Fame poll: 1951-56 (including no. 1 position in 1952), voted as solo performer: 1957-59, 1961-64; named best comedy team in m.p. Daily's 16th annual radio poll, 1951-53. 1956 formed Jerry Lewis Prods. Inc., functioning as prod., dir., writer & star. National chmn. & bd. member, Muscular Dystrophy Association. Full professor USC; taught grad. film dir. Book: The Total Filmmaker (1971) based on classroom lectures. *Autobiography:* Jerry Lewis In Person (1982). Received Emmy Governor's Award 2005. Academy Award, Jean Hersholt Humanitarian Award, 2009.
THEATRE: Hellzapoppin (regional), Damn Yankees (B'way debut, 1995).
PICTURES: My Friend Irma (debut, 1949), My Friend Irma Goes West, At War With the Army, That's My Boy, Sailor Beware, Jumping Jacks, Scared Stiff, The Stooge, Road to Bali (cameo), The Caddy, Money From Home, Living It Up, Three Ring Circus, You're Never Too Young, Artists and Models, Pardners, Hollywood or Bust, The Delicate Delinquent (also prod.), The Sad Sack, Rock-a-Bye Baby, The Geisha Boy (also prod.), Don't Give Up the Ship, Li'l Abner (cameo), Visit to a Small Planet, Cinderfella (also prod.), The Bellboy (also dir., prod., s.p.), The Ladies Man (also dir., prod., co-s.p.), The Errand Boy (also dir., co-s.p.), It's Only Money, The Nutty Professor (also dir., co-s.p.), Who's Minding the Store?, It's a Mad Mad Mad Mad World (cameo), The Patsy (also dir., co-s.p.), The Disorderly Orderly, Boeing (707) Boeing (707) (Golden Globe nom. 1966), The Family Jewels (also dir., prod., co-s.p.), Three on a Couch (also dir., prod.), Way... Way Out, The Big Mouth (also dir., prod., co-s.p.), Don't Raise the Bridge Lower the River, Hook Line and Sinker (also prod.), Which Way to the Front? (also dir., prod.), One More Time (dir. only), The Day the Clown Cried (also dir., co-s.p.), Hardly Working (also dir., co-s.p.), The King of Comedy, Smorgasbord (Cracking Up; also dir., co-s.p.), Slapstick of Another Kind, Cookie, Mr. Saturday Night (cameo), Arizona Dream, Funny Bones, Off the Menu: The Last Days of Chasen's, Encounter in the Third Dimension, Nutty Professor II: The Klumps (exec. prod. and writer), The Nutty Professor (voice, prod., 2007, writer, exec. prod. 1963 original), Max Rose.
TELEVISION: *Movie:* Fight for Life. *Series:* Colgate Comedy Hour, The Jerry Lewis Show (1963), The Jerry Lewis Show (1967-69), Wiseguy, Super Force (dir.). Host for Muscular Dystrophy Telethon. *Guest:* More than 160 appearances.

LEWIS, JULIETTE

Actress. b. California, June 21, 1973. Father is actor Geoffrey Lewis.
PICTURES: My Stepmother Is an Alien (debut, 1988), Meet the Hollowheads, National Lampoon's Christmas Vacation, Crooked Hearts, Cape Fear (Acad. Award nom.), Husbands and Wives, That Night, Kalifornia, What's Eating Gilbert Grape, Romeo Is Bleeding, Natural Born Killers, Mixed Nuts, The Basketball Diaries, Strange Days, From Dusk Till Dawn, The Evening Star, The Audition, Full Tilt Boogie, The Other Sister, The 4th Floor, The Way of the Gun, Room to Rent, Picture Claire, Gaudi Afternoon, Armitage: Dual Matrix, Hysterical Blindness, Enough, Old School, Cold Creek Manor, Blueberry, Starsky & Hutch, Aurora Borealis, Grilled, The Drummer (exec. prod.), Lightfield's Home Videos, Darwin Awards, Daltry Calhoun, Catch and Release, Whip It!, Betty Anne Waters, Metropia (voice), Sympathy for Delicious, The Switch, Due Date, Different Kind of Love.
TELEVISION: *Movies:* Home Fires, Too Young to Die?, My Louisiana Sky, Hysterical Blindness, Chasing Freedom. *Series:* I Married Dora, A Family for Joe, Free for All (voice), Memphis Beat. *Guest:* More than 88 appearances.

LEWIS, MICHAEL J.

Composer. b. Aberystwyth, Wales, 1939. First film score 1969, The Mad Woman of Chaillot, won Ivor Novello Award for best film score. 1973: first Broadway musical, Cyrano, Grammy nomination '74, Caesar and Cleopatra (T.V. '76), The Lion the Witch and the Wardrobe (Emmy, 1979).
PICTURES: The Man Who Haunted Himself, Julius Caesar.

Upon This Rock, Unman Wittering and Zigo, Running Scared, Baxter, Theatre of Blood, 11 Harrowhouse, 92 in the Shade, Russian Roulette, The Stick-Up, The Medusa Touch, The Legacy, The Passage, The Unseen, Sphinx, Yes Giorgio, On the Third Day, The Naked Face.
TELEVISION: *Movies:* Kean, The Lion, the Witch and the Wardrobe, The Hound of the Baskervilles, The Rose and the Jackal, She Stood Alone.

LEWIS, RICHARD

Comedian, Actor. b. Brooklyn, NY, June 29, 1949. e. Ohio St. Univ. (marketing degree). Was copywriter for adv. agency before becoming stand-up comic performing in nightclubs in NYC, Las Vegas, 1971.
PICTURES: The Wrong Guys (debut, 1988), That's Adequate, Once Upon a Crime, Robin Hood: Men in Tights, Wagons East!, Leaving Las Vegas, Hugo Pool, Drunks, Game Day, Cinderella Man.
TELEVISION: *Movies:* Diary of a Young Comic (also writer), The Danger of Love: The Carolyn Warmus Story, A Weekend in the Country. *Series:* Harry, Anything But Love, Hiller & Diller, Rude Awakening, Curb Your Enthusiasm, 7th Heaven. *Specials*: Richard Lewis: I'm in Pain, Richard Lewis: I'm Exhausted, Richard Lewis: I'm Doomed, Living Against the Odds (also writer). *Pilot:* King of the Building. *Guest:* More than 102 appearances.

LI, GONG

Actress. b. Shenyang, Liaoning Province, China, Dec. 31, 1965.
PICTURES: Red Field, Red Sorghum, The Terracotta Warrior, Ju Dou, God of Gamblers III: Back to Shanghai, Raise the Red Lantern, The Story of Qiu Ju, Mary from Beijing, Farewell—My Concubine, Flirting Scholar, La Peintre, Semi-Gods and Semi-Devils, The Great Conqueror's Concubine, To Live, Shanghai Triad, Temptress Moon, Chinese Box, Breaking the Silence, The Assassin, Zhou Yu de huo che, Eros, Memoirs of a Geisha, Miami Vice, Curse of the Golden Flower, Hannibal Rising, Shanghai.

LIBERTINI, RICHARD

Actor. b. Cambridge, MA, May 21, 1933. Original member of Second City troupe in Chicago. With MacIntyre Dixon appeared as the Stewed Prunes in cabaret performances.
THEATRE: Three by Three (1961), Plays for Bleecker Street, The Cat's Pajamas, The Mad Show, . Bad Habits. Solo: The White House Murder Case, Don't Drink the Water, Paul Sill's Story Theatre, Ovid's Metamorphoses, The Primary English Class, Neopolitan Ghosts, Love's Labour's Lost, As You Like It.
PICTURES: The Night They Raided Minsky's, Don't Drink the Water, Catch-22, The Out-of-Towners, Lovers and Other Strangers, Lady Liberty, Fire Sale, Days of Heaven, The In-Laws, Popeye, Sharky's Machine, Soup for One, Best Friends, Deal of the Century, Going Berserk, Unfaithfully Yours, All of Me, Fletch, Big Trouble, Betrayed, Fletch Lives, Animal Behavior. Duck Tales: The Movie (voice), Lemon Sisters, Awakenings, The Bonfire of the Vanities, Cultivating Charlie, Nell, Lethal Weapon 4, Telling You, Grilled, Everybody Wants to Be Italian.
TELEVISION: *Movies*: Three on a Date, Fame, The Trial of Bernhard Goetz, Extreme Close-Up, House of Frankenstein, Cutty Whitman, Columbo: Ashes to Ashes, Vendetta, Drive/II, Bert & Becca, A Grandpa for Christmas. *Mini-series*: House of Frankenstein 1997. *Series*: Story Theatre, The Melba Moore-Clifton Davis Show, Soap, Family Man, The Fanelli Boys, Pacific Station, Pinky and the Brain. Pilots: Calling Dr. Storm, M.D., Fair Game. *Specials*: Let's Celebrate, The Fourth Wise Man, Fame (Hallmark Hall of Fame). *Guest*: More than 73 appearances.

LIEBERFARB, WARREN N.

Executive. e. Wharton Sch. of Commerce and Finance, U. of PA, B.S., economics; U. of Michigan. Started career in industry at Paramount Pictures as dir. of mktg. and exec. asst. to Stanley Jaffe, then pres. Later joined 20th-Fox as v.p., special market dist. (cable, pay-TV, non-theatrical). Joined Warner Bros. as v.p., exec. asst. to Ted Ashley, bd. chmn.; later named v.p., intl. adv.-pub. In 1979 joined Lorimar as v.p., of Lorimar Productions, Inc., the parent company, based in New York, Promoted to sr. v.p. 1982, named v.p. mktg., Warner Home Video; named pres., 1984. Chairman, and CEO Lieberfarb & Associates LLC. 2003-2008 dir.; Sirius Satellite Radio. In 1999, the Acad. of Television Arts & Sciences awarded him an Emmy for the development of DVD technology. Serves on the Bd. of Trustees of AFI; on bd. of directors for Digital Theater Systems, Inc., Director for Hughes Telematics, Inc. Bd. of Trustees of Univ. of PA and its Wharton Undergraduate exec. bd. Member of Academy of Motion Picture Arts & Sciences.

LIEBERMAN, ROBERT

Director, Producer. b. Buffalo, NY, July 16, 1947. e. Univ. of Buffalo. m. actress Marilu Henner. Moved to LA, became editor for Desort-Fisher commercial production house, which led to dir. tv ad spots. Formed own commercial company, Harmony Pictures.
PICTURES: *Dir.:* Table for Five, All I Want for Christmas, Fire in the Sky, D3: The Mighty Ducks, The Dead Zone, The Stranger.
TELEVISION: *Movies*: Fighting Back: The Story of Rocky Blier, The Craft, Will: The Autobiography of G. Gordon Liddy, To Save a Child (also exec. prod.), Abandoned and Deceived, Titanic, Rag and Bone, NetForce, Red Skies, Second String, Jake 2.0: The Tech, Final Days of Planet Earth. *Mini-series*: Legend of Earthsea. *Series*: thirtysomething, Dream Street (pilot), The Young Riders (pilot), Dream Street, Gabriel's Fire (also exec. prod.), Pros and Cons (exec. consultant), Under Suspicion (also exec. prod.), Medicine Ball (also exec. prod.), Harts of the West, Under Suspicion, Marilu, Moloney, Once and Again, Strong Medicine, Stephen King's Dead Zone, Jake 2.0, The Casino (creator, exec. prod., writer), Killer Instinct (pilot), Dexter, A.M.P.E.D. (exec. prod., dir. also pilot), Republic of Doyle.

LIEBERSON, SANFORD

Producer. b. Los Angeles, CA, 1936. Early career with William Morris Agency. 1961-62, agent in Rome for Grade Org. Returned to LA as Founding Member CMA agency then exec. in charge of European operations. 1979, named pres. of 20th-Fox Productions, which company he joined in 1977 as v.p. European production. Previously an independent producer forming Good Times. With David Putnam formed Visual Programming Systems to produce, acquire and consult in the Home Video area for CBS, Phillips, Time/Life, etc. As v.p. intl. prod. at Fox, spv. intl. release of such films as Star Wars, 1900, Alien, Chariots of Fire, Nine to Five, Quest for Fire. V.P. Intl. prod. for The Ladd Company. Outland, Body Heat, Blade Runner, The Right Stuff, Police Academy, etc. Chief of prod. at Goldcrest Harvest: Dance With a Stranger, Room With a View, Absolute Beginners, etc. Pres. intl. prod. MGM spv. Russia House, Thelma & Louise, Liebestraum, Not Without My Daughter, Criss Cross, etc. Currently head of prod. at the Natl. Film and Television School of Great Britain.
PICTURES: Melody, Pied Piper, Radio Wonderful, James Dean: First American Teenager, Bugsy Malone, Slade in Flame, Final Programme, Stardust, That'll Be the Day, Double Headed Eagle, Mahler (exec. prod.), Lisztomania, Jabberwocky, Rita Sue and Bob Too, Stars and Bars, The Mighty Quinn, Performance.
TELEVISION: *Movie*: Frank & Jessie (exec. prod.). *Documentaries:* Peacemaking 1919, Swastika, Radio Wonderful (short), Brother Can You Spare a Dime, All This and World War II.

LIEBMAN, JONATHAN

Executive. e. Graduated summa cum laude, Phi Beta Kappa, Yale College, 1981; Law degree from Yale Law School, 1985. Liebman clerked for U.S. District Judge Leonard B. Sand in Manhattan. He also served as an Assistant U.S. Attorney for the Southern District of New York under the Honorable Rudolph W. Giuliani, and was appointed Deputy Chief of the Criminal Division after four years in the U.S. Attorney's office. Liebman was a partner for 13 years at Parcher, Hayes & Liebman, a New York law firm whose clients included Paul Simon, Mariah Carey, Sony Pictures, Bruce Springsteen and the Rolling Stones. Liebman moved to Los Angeles in 1998, becoming vice chairman of Samax Inc., the holding company owned by Brad Grey that operated the Brillstein-Grey production and management companies. At that time he also became v.p. of the TV prod. company. In 2002, Liebman produced "In Memoriam: New York City 9/11/01," a highly acclaimed HBO documentary that raised over $1 million for the victims of the September 11 terrorist attacks. Liebman was nominated for a Prime Time Emmy Award in 2002 as exec. prod. of the documentary. In 2005, he and partner Cynthia Pett-Dante bought Brillstein-Grey from Brad Grey, who left company to run Paramount Pictures. In 2007, company renamed Brillstein Entertainment Partners LLC and now operates with Liebman at the helm as CEO.

LIGHT, JUDITH

Actress. r.n. Judith Ellen Licht. b. Trenton, NJ, Feb. 9, 1949. e. Carnegie-Mellon Univ. (BFA). Toured with USO in prod. of Guys and Dolls during college. Acted with Milwaukee and Seattle rep. companies. Made B'way debut in 1975 prod. of A Doll's House with Liv Ullmann. Other stage work: A Streetcar Named Desire, As You Like It, Richard III, Sorrows and Rejoicings, Wit. Landed role of Karen Wolek on daytime serial One Life to Live in 1977.
PICTURES: Paul Monette: The Brink of Summer's End, Save Me (also prod.).
TELEVISION: *Movies*: Intimate Agony, Dangerous Affection, The Ryan White Story, My Boyfriend's Back, In Defense of a Married Man, Wife Mother Murderer, Men Don't Tell, Betrayal of Trust, Against Their Will: Women in Prison, Lady Killer, A Husband, A Wife and A Lover, Murder at My Door, A Step Toward Tomorrow, Too Close to Home, Carriers. *Series*: One Life to Live (2 Emmy Awards), Who's the Boss?, Phenom, The Simple Life, Law & Order: Special Victims Unit, The Stones, Twenty Good Years (also pilot), Ugly Betty (Emmy nom. 2007). *Guest:* More than 63 appearances.

LIGHTCAP, CAROLINA

Executive. e. Columbia University. Lightcap began her career in media in 1986, working for Reuters Ltd. and Editorial Atlantida in New York and Buenos Aires. Executive Director, for Twentieth Century Fox Home Entertainment from 1996-99, serving Latin America, responsible for strategic development, supervision of trade and consumer marketing, sales for sell-through and rental video releases throughout Latin America. V. P., Programming, Sales and Marketing, Sky Latin America Partners, based in Miami, responsible for all sales and marketing for direct-to-home satellite television. V. P., Marketing, The Walt Disney Company, as Media Networks, Latin America, in 2000. In 2001 promoted to V. P., Marketing, On-air and Brand Strategy, and in 2004 she was elevated to Sr. V. P., Programming and Creative Affairs for Disney Channels in Latin America. Responsible for programming, production, on-air, marketing, research and publicity for Disney Channel, Disney XD and Playhouse Disney Channels, which includes 15 localized feeds in Spanish and Portuguese that are broadcast to 19 territories in Latin America. Ms. Lightcap also oversaw the successful rebrand of Jetix to Disney XD and the launch of Playhouse Disney Channel throughout the region. Ms. Lightcap spearheaded the Latin American launch of "High School Musical," which became the most watched movie among kids 4-17 in the channel's history. She became Chief Marketing Officer for The Walt Disney Company Latin America, where she led the integration of Disney's marketing departments into one organization. In 2006 she was named Chief Marketing Officer for The Walt Disney Company. She was promoted to her current role of President, Disney Channels Worldwide, part of the Disney ABC Television Group, in 2009. Lightcap manages the Company's successful global kids TV business, a total of 94 kid-driven, family inclusive entertainment channels and/or channel feeds available in 169 countries in 33 languages and includes Disney Channel, Disney XD, Playhouse Disney, Disney Cinemagic, Hungama and Jetix. She also has responsibility for Radio Disney which has set the radio industry standard for kid and family content. Disney Channel Worldwide's multiplatform strategy includes subscription video-on-demand and content-rich broadband websites DisneyXD.com and DisneyChannel.com -- which ranks as the #1 kids' (age 6-14) entertainment website. A global executive team representing Disney Channel's Programming and Production, Business Affairs, Business Planning and Development, Marketing, Brand Management, Advertising Sales and Radio Disney, reports to her.

LIGUORI, PETER

Executive. A former ad man with both Ogilvy & Mather and Saatchi & Saatchi, Liguori moved into television as vp, consumer marketing at HBO. From HBO Liguori segued to Fox/Liberty Networks, a new venture, in 1996 as senior vp, marketing. That unit included Fox Sports Net, FX, Fox Sports World, Speed, and the National Geographic Channel. Liguori also has had some experience in the feature film business, as a producer of the 1996 film Big Night. In 1998, Liguori became president and CEO of News Corp.'s FX Networks. In March 2005, Liguori was named president, entertainment for Fox Broadcasting Co. In July 2007, Liguori was given the nod as chairman, entertainment at Fox Broadcasting Co., with former NBC Universal exec. Kevin Reilly taking over Liguori's former role as ent. president. Liguori's expanded role will be developing new models for FOX broadcast content to best leverage the brands across all emerging platforms.

LILLARD, MATTHEW

Actor. b. Lansing, MI, Jan. 24, 1970.
PICTURES: Ghoulies 3: Ghoulies Go to College, Serial Mom, Ride for Your Life, Mad Love, Hackers, Tarantella, Scream, Telling You, Dish Dogs, The Curve, Senseless, Without Limits, S.L.C. Punk!, Love's Labour's Lost, She's All That, Wing Commander, Spanish Judges, Finder's Fee, Triangle Square, Summer Catch, Thir13en Ghosts, Scooby-Doo, The Perfect Score, Scooby Doo 2: Monsters Unleashed, Wicker Park, Without a Paddle, Bickford Shmeckler's Cool Ideas, The Groomsmen, What Love Is, One of Our Own (also co-prod.), In the Name of the King: A Dungeon Siege Tale, Parental Guidance Suggested, Endless Bummer, Spooner (also co-prod.), Messages Deleted, All's Faire in Love, The Pool Boys, Shrinking Charlotte, The Descendants, Adrenaline (prod. only).
TELEVISION: *Movies*: Vanishing Son IV, If These Walls Could Talk, The Devil's Child, It's a Very Merry Muppet Christmas Movie, 13 Graves, Area 57, Exit 19.

LIMAN, DOUG

Director, Producer. b. 1965. e. Brown University, USC Film.
PICTURES: Getting In, Swingers (also photog.), Go (also photog.), See Jane Run (prod. only), Kissing Jessica Stein (prod. only), The Bourne Identity, The Bourne Supremacy, Mail Order Bride, Cry Wolf (exec. prod.), Mr. and Mrs. Smith, The Bourne Ultimatum (exec. prod.), The Killing Floor (exec. prod.), Jumper (dir.), Fair Game (dir.), Three Musketeers.
TELEVISION: *Movie:* Business Class (exec. prod.). *Series*: The Moth (actor), The O.C. (exec. prod./dir. exec. consult.), Heist (exec. prod. also pilot), Mr. and Mrs. Smith (exec. prod., dir., also pilot), Knight Rider (exec. prod., also pilot), Covert Affairs (exec. prod.).

LINDBLOM, GUNNEL

Actress, Director. b. Gothenburg, Sweden, De. 18, 1931. Discovered by Ingmar Bergman while studying at drama school of Gothenburg Municipal Theatre, 1950-53; she moved to Malmo, where he was director of the local Municipal Theatre. Under Bergman's direction she played in Easter, Peer Gynt, Faust, etc. between 1954-59. Later appeared in many Bergman films. Since 1968 has been on staff of Stockholm's Royal Dramatic Theatre, assisting Bergman and then beginning to direct on her own. Made film debut as director with Summer Paradise in 1977.
PICTURES: *Actress*: Love, Girl in the Rain, Song of the Scarlet Flower, The Seventh Seal, Wild Strawberries, The Virgin Spring, Winter Light, The Silence, My Love Is a Rose, Rapture, Loving Couples, Hunger, Woman of Darkness, The Girls, The Father, Brother Carl, Scenes From a Marriage, Misfire, Bakom Jalusin, Capitan Escalaborns, Betraktelse (also dir., s.p.), Nadja, Lines From the Heart, Expectations, Passing Darkness, The Girl with the Dragon Tattoo. *Director*: Summer Paradise (also co-s.p.), Sally and Freedom, Summer Nights on Planet Earth (also s.p.).
TELEVISION: *Movies:* Rabies, The Lie, Hedda Gabler.

LINDE, DAVID

Executive. e. graduate, Swarthmore College, 1982. Linde joined Paramount Pictures Corp. in 1985, after graduating from Swarthmore College. At Paramount, he supervised the sales of select international theatrical rights. In 1988, he left Paramount for an international sales position at Fox/Lorber Associates, and in 1990 he was named v.p. At Fox/Lorber, where he directed the sales of over 300 independently produced film, documentary and TV titles. Linde joined Miramax Films in 1991 as v.p. of acquisitions. In 1992, he was named senior v.p. (and subsequently executive v.p. & head of sales) at the newly created Miramax International. In Jan. 1997, Linde joined Good Machine as a partner. Good Machine subsequently announced the formation of Good Machine International (GMI) at the Venice Film Festival with Linde as president. From GMI, Linde joined Universal Pictures in May 2002 as co-president (with James Schamus) of Universal's newly formed specialty unit, Focus Features. While at Focus, Linde oversaw a diverse and critically acclaimed slate including Roman Polanski's The Pianist, Sofia Coppola's Lost in Translation, Fernando Mereilles' The Constant Gardener and Ang Lee's Brokeback Mountain. During that time, the company garnered 53 Academy Award nominations, and 11 Academy Award wins. In addition to responsibilities at Focus Features, in 2004 Linde was named president of Universal's Rogue Pictures label. In March 2006, Linde was upped to co-chairman, Universal Pictures alongside chairman Marc Shmuger. Both Shmuger and Linde left Universal, October, 2009. 2010 Linde is exec. prod. with Dor Films.

LINDEN, HAL

Actor. b. Bronx, NY, March 20, 1931. e. City Coll. of New York. Began career as saxophone player and singer, playing with bands of Sammy Kaye, Bobby Sherwood, etc. Drafted and performed in revues for Special Services. After discharge enrolled at N.Y.'s American Theatre Wing; appeared on B'way in Bells Are Ringing, replacing Sydney Chaplin.
THEATRE: Wildcat, Something More, Subways Are for Sleeping, Ilya Darling, Anything Goes, Lessons (CA), The Apple Tree, The Education of H*Y*M*A*N K*A*P*L*A*N, On a Clear Day You Can See Forever, Three Men on a Horse, The Pajama Game, The Rothschilds (Tony Award, 1971), I'm Not Rappaport, Unfinished Stories, The Sisters Rosensweig.
PICTURES: Bells Are Ringing, When You Comin' Back Red Ryder?, A New Life, Out to Sea, The Others, Just Friends, Jump, Dumb Luck, Time Changer, Broadway: The Golden Age by the Legends Who Were There, Time Changer, Freezerburn, Light Years Away.
TELEVISION: *Movies*: Mr. Inside/Mr. Outside, The Love Boat (pilot), How to Break Up a Happy Divorce, Father Figure, Starflight: The Plane That Couldn't Land, The Other Woman, My Wicked Wicked Ways: The Legend of Errol Flynn, The O'Connors, Dream Breakers, The Colony, Killers in the House, Rockford Files: If It Bleeds It Leads, The Glow, A Kiss at Midnight. *Series*: Animals Animals Animals (host, Emmy nom. 1981 for episode "Llama"), Barney Miller (7 Emmy noms.; 4 Golden Globe noms.), Blacke's Magic, F.Y.I. (3 Emmy Awards, 1 other nom.), Jack's Place, The Boys Are Back, The Bold and the Beautiful. *Specials*: I Do! I Do!, The Best of Everything (host), CBS Schoolbreak Special (Emmy Award 1995 for episode "The Writing on The Wall"). *Guest:* More than 96 appearances.

LINDHEIM, RICHARD D.

Executive. b. New York, NY, May 28, 1939. e. Univ. of Redlands, USC. Admin. Asst. Story Dept., CBS, 1962-64. Project Dir. Entertainment Testing ASI Mkt. Research, 1964-69. VP Prog. Research NBC 1969-78, VP Dramatic Prog. 1978-79, Prod. Universal TV 1979-81, VP Current Prog. 1981-85, SVP Series Prog. 1986-87. Exec. VP Creative Affairs 1987-91, Exec. VP Prog. Strategy MCA TV Group 1991-92. Exec. VP Paramount TV 1992. Executive director Institute for Creative Technologies which he is the founder, U. So. Calif., Los Angeles, 1999-present, associated with ICT. Asst. Prof. CSU. Sr. Lecturer, USC, UCLA. Author: Primetime Network TV Programming (w/ Richard Blum) 1987, Inside TV Producing 1991.

LINDO, DELROY

Actor. b. London, England, Nov. 18, 1952. Received NAACP Image Awards for film Malcolm X and play A Raisin in the Sun.
THEATRE: B'way: Joe Turner's Come and Gone (Tony nom.), Master Harold and the Boys. Off-B'way: District Line, As You Like It, Romeo and Juliet, Spell #7, The Heliotrope Bouquet. Regional: Othello, Mrs. Ever's Boys, Cobb, A Raisin in the Sun, My Mark My Name, Union Boys, Macbeth, Black Branch, Home.
PICTURES: The Blood of Heroes (Salute to the Jugger; debut, 1990), Mountains of the Moon, Perfect Witness, The Hard Way, Bright Angel, Malcolm X, Bound by Honor, Mr. Jones, Behanzin,

Crooklyn, Congo, Clockers, Get Shorty, Feeling Minnesota, Broken Arrow, Ransom, The Devil's Advocate, A Life Less Ordinary, Glory & Honor, The Cider House Rules, The Book of Stars, Romeo Must Die, Gone In Sixty Seconds, Heist, The Last Castle, The One, The Core, Sahara, Hounddog, Domino, This Christmas, Up (voice), The Big Bang.
TELEVISION: *Movies*: Perfect Witness, Soul of the Game, First-Time Felon, Glory & Honor, Strange Justice, Profoundly Normal, Lackawanna Blues, The Exonerated, Ride Along (pilot). *Mini-series:* Jazz. *Series:* Kidnapped.

LINDSAY, ROBERT
Actor. b. Ilkeston, Derbyshire, Eng., Dec. 13, 1949. e. Gladstone Boys School, Ilkeston, Royal Acad. of Dramatic Art. With Manchester's Royal Exchange Theatre Co. (Hamlet, The Cherry Orchard, The Lower Depths). Also in Godspell, The Three Musketeers, Me and My Girl, (London—Olivier Award, NY—Tony, Theatre World & Drama Desk Awards, 1987), Becket (Olivier & Variety Club Awards), Cyrano de Bergerac.
PICTURES: That'll Be the Day, Bert Rigby You're a Fool, Strike It Rich, Fierce Creatures, Remember Me, Divorcing Jack, Wimbledon.
TELEVISION: *Movies*: Twelfth Night, All's Well That Ends Well, A Midsummer Night's Dream, Cymbeline, Much Ado About Nothing, King Lear, Confessional, Genghis Cohn, The Office, Brazen Hussies, Hornblower: The Even Chance, Hornblower: The Duchess and the Devil, Hornblower: The Frogs and the Lobsters, Jack the Ripper: On Going Mystery, Hornblower: Mutiny, Hornblower: Retribution, Horatio Hornblower 3, Hornblower: Duty, Friends & Crocodiles, A Very Social Secretary, Gideon's Daughter, The Trial of Tony Blair. *Mini-series*: The Wimbledon Poisoner, Jake's Progress, Oliver Twist, Hawk. *Series*: Citizen Smith, Give Us A Break, GBH, In Your Dreams, Jericho, My Family, The Heat Is On (narr.), Don't Eat the Neighbours. *Documentaries/Specials: As Narrator:* Secrets of the Ancients (mini), Jack the Ripper: An On-Going Mystery, Victoria Wood with All the Trimmings, Seven Wonders of the Industrial World (series), Celebrate the Sound of Music (performer). *Guest:* More than 82 appearances.

LINDSAY-HOGG, MICHAEL
Director. b. New York, NY, May 5, 1940. Mother is late actress Geraldine Fitzgerald.
PICTURES: Let It Be, Nasty Habits, The Object of Beauty (also s.p.), Frankie Starlight, Celebration: The Music of Pete Townshend and The Who, Rolling Stones Rock and Roll Circus, Guy, Waiting for Godot.
TELEVISION: *Movies:* A.D.A.M., Footprints in the Jungle, Skin Deep, Electra, Plaintiffs and Defendants, Two Sundays, Through the Night, Professional Foul, Ladies in Waiting, Master Harold and the Boys, As Is, The Importance of Being Earnest, Nazi Hunter: The Beate Klarsfeld Story, The Little Match Girl, Murder by Moonlight, The Strange Case of Dr. Jekyll and Mr. Hyde, Nightmare Classics, The Habitation of Dragons, Running Mates, For Love Alone: The Ivana Trump Story , Alone, Two of Us. *Mini-series:* Fall of Eagles, Brideshead Revisted (co-dir.). *Series:* Ready, Steady, Go!, The Informer, A Man of our Times, The Ronnie Barker Playhouse, Journey to the Unknown, The Protectors, Bill Brand, Loving (pilot), Marsalis on Music.

LINK, WILLIAM
Writer, Producer. b. Philadelphia, PA, Dec. 15, 1933. e. U. of Pennsylvania, B.S., 1956. With partner, late Richard Levinson, wrote and created numerous TV series and movies, specializing in detective-mystery genre. *Books:* Fineman, Stay Tuned: An Inside Look at the Making of Prime-Time Television, Off Camera. Stage incl.: Prescription Murder, Guilty Conscience, Merlin. Received WGA Laurel Award 1986.
PICTURES: The Hindenberg, Rollercoaster, Whispers in the Dark.
TELEVISION: *Movies/Writer/Prod.:* Prescription: Murder, Istanbul Express, Trial Run, The Whole World Is Watching, That Certain Summer (2 Emmy noms.), My Sweet Charlie (Emmy Award as writer, 1 other nom. 1970), McCloud: Who Killed Miss U.S.A.?, Children of the Lotus Eater, Sam Hill: Who Killed Mr. Foster?, The Judge and Jake Wyler, Savage (exec. prod., writer), The Execution of Private Slovik (2 Emmy noms.), Charlie Cobb: Nice Night for a Hanging, The Gun, A Cry for Help (prod. only), The Storyteller (Emmy nom. 1978), Murder by Natural Causes, Stone, Crisis at Central High, Rehearsal For Murder (also exec. prod.), Take Your Best Shot, Prototype (also exec. prod.), The Murder of Sherlock Holmes, The Guardian (also exec. prod.), Guilty Conscience (also exec. prod.), Vanishing Act (also exec. prod.), The United States Vs. Salim Ajami, Probe, The Boys, Over My Dead Body, The Cosby Mysteries, The NBC Mystery Movie (2 Emmy noms.). More than 65 Columbo movie credits as writer, creator. *Series/Writer/Creator:* Mannix, Honey West, Ellery Queen, McCloud, Tenafly, Banacek, Darkroom, Columbo (Emmy Award as writer, 1972), Murder She Wrote.

LINKLATER, RICHARD
Director, Writer, Producer. b. Houston, TX, July 30, 1961. Founded Austin Film Society, serving as artistic director. Filmed several super 8 films incl. feature It's Impossible to Learn to Plow by Reading Books.
PICTURES: *Director/Writer:* Slacker (also actor & prod.), Dazed and Confused (also co-prod.), Before Sunrise, The Underneath (actor only), SubUrbia, Beavis & Butt-Head Do America (voice), Before Sunset, (also prod. Academy Award nom.; WGA nom. 2005), The Newton Boys, Waking Life, Tape (dir. only), Spy Kids, The School of Rock, The Smoker(dir. only), The Bad News Bears (dir. only), A Scanner Darkly (dir., s.p.), Last Flag Flying (also prod), Inning by Inning: A Portrait of a Coach (doc.,dir.), RSO [Registered Sex Offender] (actor), Me and Orson Welles (dir., prod.).
TELEVISION: *Movie:* $5.15/Hr.

LINKLETTER, ART
Emcee, Producer, Author. b. Moose Jaw, Saskatchewan, Canada, July 17, 1912. Raised in San Diego. e. San Diego State Coll. Partner in production company, Linkletter/Atkins/Kritzer Productions Inc. Radio prg. mgr., San Diego Exposition, 1935; radio pgm. mgr. S.F. World's Fair, 1937-39; freelance radio announcer and m.c. 1939-42; m.c. series People Are Funny starting in 1942. Author: The Secret World of Kids, 1959; Kids Say the Darndest Things, 1957; Linkletter Down Under, 1969; Yes You Can, 1979; Old Age Is Not For Sissies, 1988; Cavalcade of the Golden West; Cavalcade of America. Recorded albums: Howls, Boners & Shockers and We Love You, Call Collect (Grammy Award winner, 1966). Bd. of dir., MGM, 1979-88. Received Emmy Lifetime Achievement Award 2003.
PICTURES: People Are Funny, Champagne for Caesar, The Snow Queen, Matinee, Off the Menu: The Last Days of Chasen's, Let Me In I Hear Laughter.
TELEVISION: *Movies:* Zane Grey Theatre, G.E. Theatre, Wagon Train: Kid at the Stick. *Series:* Art Linkletter's House Party, Life With Linkletter, People Are Funny (emcee), The Art Linkletter Show (emcee), Hollywood Talent Scouts, Kids Say the Darndest Things. *Specials*: Inside Salute to Baseball (exec. prod., host), Art Linkletter's Secret World of Kids (host), Ford Startime, Young Man With A Band, Linkletters Spend Christmas in the Holy Land, Kid's Eye View of Washington, Walt: The Man Behind the Myth, The Living Century (advisor). *Guest:* More than 74 appearances. (d. May 26, 2010)

LINN-BAKER, MARK
Actor, Director. b. St. Louis, MO, June 17, 1954. e. Yale Univ., Yale Sch. of Drama (M.F.A., 1979). Founding memb. American Repertory Th. in Cambridge, MA; founding prod./dir. NY Stage & Film Co. in NYC & Poughkeepsie. Co-founder of True Pictures, 1990.
THEATRE: *B'way:* Doonesbury, Laughter on the 23rd Floor, A Funny Thing Happened On The Way To The Forum.
PICTURES: Manhattan (bit), The End of August, My Favorite Year, Me and Him (voice only), Noises Off, Twelve and Holding, Adam, How Do You Know.
TELEVISION: *Movies*: Alice at the Palace, Wedding Bell Blues, Going to the Chapel, Bare Essentials, Laughter on the 23rd Floor. *Series:* Comedy Zone, Perfect Strangers, Hangin' With Mr. Cooper (dir. only), The Trouble with Larry dir. only), Twins. *Specials*: Doonesbury (voice of Kirby), The Ghost Writer (Amer. Playhouse). *Director/episodes:* Family Matters, Family Man, Going Places, Step by Step, The Trouble with Larry.

LINSON, ART
Producer, Director. b. Chicago, IL, 1942. e. UCLA; LLD. UCLA, 1967. Was rock music manager with record prod. Lou Adler and ran own record co., Spin Dizzy records before turning to film production. Debuted as director with Where the Buffalo Roam.
PICTURES: *Prod. &/or Dir.:* Rafferty and the Gold Dust Twins (co.-prod.), Car Wash, American Hot Wax (also co-s.p.), Where the Buffalo Roam, Melvin and Howard, Fast Times at Ridgemont High (co-prod.), The Wild Life, The Untouchables, Scrooged (co-prod.), Casualties of War, We're No Angels, Dick Tracy (exec. prod.), Singles, Point of No Return, This Boy's Life, Heat, The Edge, Pushing Tin, Great Expectations, Fight Club, Sunset Strip, Heist, Spartan, The Black Dahlia, Lords of Dogtown, Imaginary Heroes, What Just Happened? (prod., writer, s.p.,also novel), Into the Wild, The Runaways, The Untouchables: Capone Rising (prod.).
TELEVISION: *Series:* Sons of Anarchy (exec. prod.).

LIOTTA, RAY
Actor. b. Newark, NJ, Dec. 18, 1955. e. Univ. of Miami. First prof. job on tv commercial, followed by continuing role on daytime serial, Another World.
PICTURES: Something Wild (debut, 1983), The Lonely Lady, Dominick and Eugene, Field of Dreams, GoodFellas, Article 99, Unlawful Entry, No Escape, Corrina Corrina, Operation Dumbo Drop, Unforgettable, Turbulence, Cop Land, Phoenix, A Rumor of Angels, Forever Mine, Muppets from Space, Pilgrim, Blow, Hannibal, John Q, Heartbreakers, Point of Origin, Narc, Identity, Slow Burn (also co-exec. prod.), Control, The Last Shot, Jump Shot, Revolver, Take the Lead, Chlorine, The Poison Rose, The Night Job, In the Name of the King: A Dungeon Siege Tale, Smokin' Aces, Wild Hogs, Battle in Seattle, Bee Movie (voice), Powder Blue, Hero Wanted, Chasing 3000, Crossing Over, La Linea (also exec. prod.), Observe and Report, Crazy on the Outside, Youth in Revolt, Date Night, Ticket Out, Savage Innocent, Charlie St. Cloud, Things Fall Apart, The Son of No One, Entitled.
TELEVISION: *Movies*: Hardhat and Legs, Crazy Times, Our Family Honor, Women and Men 2: In Love There Are No Rules,

The Rat Pack, Point of Origin, Smith (pilot). *Series*: Another World, Casablanca, Our Family Honor, ER (Emmy Award as guest 2005) Criminal Behavior. *Guest:* More than 63 appearance.

LIPTON, PEGGY

Actress. b. New York, NY, Aug. 30, 1947. Former model. Co-wrote song L.A. is My Lady (recorded by Frank Sinatra). Recorded album Peggy Lipton.
PICTURES: The Purple People Eater, Kinjite (Forbidden Subjects), Twin Peaks: Fire Walk With Me, The Postman, The Intern, Skipped Parts, Jackpot, When in Rome.
TELEVISION: *Movies*: The Return of the Mod Squad, Addicted to His Love, Fatal Charm, The Spider and the Fly, Deadly Vows, Justice for Annie: A Moment of Truth Movie. *Mini-series:* Secrets, The '70s. *Series*: The John Forsythe Show, The Mod Squad (4 Emmy noms.; Golden Globe Award, 1971, 3 other noms.), Popular, Twin Peaks, Angel Falls, Crash.

LISI, VIRNA

Actress. r.n. Virna Pieralisi. b. Ancona, Italy, Nov. 8, 1936.
PICTURES: Desiderio e Sole, Violenza sul Lago, The Doll That Took the Town, Luna Nova, Vendicatta, La Rossa, Caterina Sforza, Il Mondo dei Miracoli, Duel of the Titans, Eva, Don't Tempt the Devil, The Black Tulip, The Shortest Day, How To Murder Your Wife, Casanova 70, The Possessed, A Virgin for a Prince, Kiss the Other Sheik, The Birds the Bees and the Italians, Made in Italy, La Bambole (The Dolls), Not With My Wife You Don't, Assault on a Queen, The 25th Hour, Anyone Can Play, The Girl and the General, Arabella, Better a Widow, The Girl Who Couldn't Say No, The Christmas Tree, The Secret of Santa Vittoria, If It's Tuesday This Must Be Belgium, Roma Bene, The Statue, Bluebeard, The Serpent, Ernesto, I Love N.Y., I Ragazzi di Via Panisperna, Beyond Good and Evil, Merry Christmas Happy New Year, Miss Right, Queen Margot (Cannes Film Fest. Award, 1994), A Hundred and One Nights, Follow Your Heart, The Best Day of My Life, Boogie Woogie.
TELEVISION: U.S.: Christopher Columbus. Several European movies and mini-series.

LISS, WALTER C.

Executive. Attended La Salle College in Philadelphia from 1961-1965, where he worked as announcer for WIBF-FM, an interest which started when Liss was 16 years old as host of his own radio program. Liss' early years in business were at John Blair and Company in New York, where he worked as associate creative director from 1969-71, and at Triangle Stations in Philadelphia, where he was asst. national promotion dir. from 1967 to 1969. He joined Capital Cities Communications (now ABC, Inc.) in 1971. He started as promotion manager at WPVI-TV in Philadelphia. In 1973, he moved to WKBW-TV, another Capital Cities station, in Buffalo, NY, where he served as program director. He was promoted to v.p. and gen. mgr. at KFSN-TV, the Capital Cities-owned station in Fresno, CA, where he worked from 1975 to 1981. He subsequently moved to Miami, FL, where he became v.p./gen. mgr. at WPLG-TV, a Post-Newsweek Television station. From 1983-1987, Liss was pres. of the broadcasting div. of Cox Enterprises, Inc. In that capacity, he directed the operations of eight TV stations, 12 radio stations and a national sales representative firm. In the late 1980s he became president and gen. mgr. of WABC-TV. He moved to Buena Vista Television as chairman in October 1996. He became pres., ABC Owned Television Stations, in May 1999. 2010 he announced his retirement from his position with ABC/Disney and took on the role of consultant during the transition for the Station Group.

LITHGOW, JOHN

Actor. b. Rochester, NY, Oct. 19, 1945. Father was prod. of Shakespeare Fests. in midwest. e. Harvard. Fulbright fellowship to study at London Acad. of Music and Dramatic Art. Interned in London with Royal Shakespeare Co. and Royal Court Theatre.
THEATRE: *NY:* The Changing Room (Tony & Drama Desk Awards, 1973), My Fat Friend, Trelawney of the Wells, Comedians, Anna Christie, A Memory of Two Mondays, Once in a Lifetime, Spokesong, Bedroom Farce, Salt Lake City Skyline, Division Street (also LA), Kaufman at Large (also dir., writer), Beyond Therapy, Requiem for a Heavyweight (Drama Desk Award), The Front Page, M Butterfly, Dirty Rotten Scoundrels (also LA). *Regional:* The Beggar's Opera, Pygmalion, Of Mice and Men, Troilus and Cressida, The Roar of the Greasepaint, What Price Glory?, The Lady's Not for Burning, Who's Afraid of Virginia Woolf? (LA Drama Critics Circle Award).
PICTURES: Dealing or The Berkeley-to-Boston Forty-Brick Lost-Bag Blues (debut, 1972), Obsession, The Big Fix, Rich Kids, All That Jazz, Blow Out, I'm Dancing as Fast as I Can, The World According to Garp (Academy Award nom. 1983), Twilight Zone—The Movie, Terms of Endearment (Academy Award nom. 1984), Footloose, The Adventures of Buckaroo Banzai: Across the Eighth Dimension, 2010, Santa Claus, The Manhattan Project, Mesmerized, Harry and the Hendersons, Distant Thunder, Out Cold, Memphis Belle, Ricochet, At Play in the Fields of the Lord, Raising Cain, Cliffhanger, The Pelican Brief, A Good Man in Africa, Princess Caraboo, Silent Fall, Hollow Point, Officer Buckle and Gloria, Johnny Skidmarks, A Civil Action, Homegrown, Rugrats in Paris: The Movie, C-Scam, Shrek, Orange County, Portofino, Shrek 2, Kinsey, Dreamgirls, The Smurfs, Confessions of a Shopaholic, Leap Year.
TELEVISION: *Movies*: Secret Service, The Oldest Living Graduate, Mom The Wolfman and Me, Not in Front of the Children, The Day After, The Glitter Dome, Resting Place, Baby Girl Scott, The Traveling Man, The Last Elephant (Ivory Hunters), The Boys, The Wrong Man, Love Cheat and Steal, My Brother's Keeper, World War II: When Lions Roared, Redwood Curtain, The Tuskegee Airmen, Don Quixote (also exec. prod.), The Life and Death of Peter Sellers, E=mc² (narr. English version), Classical Baby (I'm Grown Up Now): The Poetry Show. *Series*: Third Rock From the Sun (Emmy Award, 1996, 1997, 1999, 6 other noms.; Golden Globe Award, 1997, 2 other noms.), Freedom: A History of Us (doc.), Paloozaville, Twenty Good Years, Dexter (Golden Globe Award 2010). *Specials*: The Country Girl (TV debut, 1973), Secret Service, Big Blonde, The Oldest Living Graduate, Goldilocks and the Three Bears (Faerie Tale Theatre), Creating a Fairy Tale World: The Making of 'Shrek', Amazing Stories (Emmy Award, 1987). *Guest:* More than 106 appearances.

LITTLEFIELD, WARREN

Executive. b. Montclair, NJ. e. American Univ. in DC, School of Government and Public Admin.; Hobart Col. (psych. degree). 1975-79, Westfall Prods., developing prime-time specials and movies before being promoted to v.p., develop. & prod. 1979, served as WB TV dir., comedy develop. Joined NBC 1979, as mngr. comedy develop. 1981, v.p. current comedy programs at NBC. 1985, sr. v.p. series specials & variety progs., NBC Entertainment; 1987, exec. v.p., Prime-Time progs. NBC Entertainment. 1990, named pres. NBC Entertainment. Resigned, 1998. Head programming, Sony Pictures Entertainment, Inc., 1998. Formed the Littlefield Co. first producing programming with NBC and now with Paramount. Bd. mem. Launch Media Inc.

LITTMAN, LYNNE

Director, Producer. b. New York, NY, June 26. e. Sarah Lawrence. B.A., 1962; Student the Sorbonne 1960-61. Researcher for CBS News 1965; assoc. prod. Natl. Educational TV 1964-68; dir. NIMH film series on drug abuse UCLA Media Center 1970; prod., dir. documentary films, news and pub. affairs series KCET Community TV, So. Calif. 1971-77; dir. WNET non-fiction film, Once a Daughter 1979; exec. v.p., movies-for-TV, ABC, 1980-81; Received Ford Fdn. Grant 1978 and numerous awards. Acad. Award film tribute to women, 1993.
PICTURES: In the Matter of Kenneth (doc.), Wanted-Operadoras (doc.), Till Death Do Us Part (doc.), Number Our Days (doc. short; Academy Award 1977), Testament (co-prod., dir.), In Her Own Time (doc.), Freak City.
TELEVISION: *Movies*: Cagney & Lacey: True Convictions, Rescuers: Stories of Courage: Two Couples, Freak City, Having Our Say: The Delany Sisters' First 100 Years.

LITTO, GEORGE

Producer. b. Philadelphia, PA. e. Temple U. Joined William Morris Agency in New York and then became indep. literary agent. Opened own office in Hollywood, 1965. Packaged film and TV productions, including M*A*S*H, Hang 'Em High, Hawaii Five-O for TV prior to entering indep. prod.; 1981-82, chmn. bd. & CEO, Filmways; 1983-85 indep. prod. 20th Century Fox. CEO of George Litto Productions.
PICTURES: Thieves Like Us (exec. prod.), Drive-In (exec. prod.), Obsession (prod.), Over the Edge (prod.), Dressed To Kill (prod.). Blow Out (prod.), Kansas (prod.), Night Game (prod.), The Crew.

LITVINOFF, SI

Producer, Executive. b. New York, NY, April 5. e. Adelphi Coll., A.B.; NYU Sch. of Law, LL.B. Theatrical lawyer, personal and business manager in New York until 1967 when left firm of Barovick, Konecky & Litvinoff to produce plays and films. June, 1987: sr. v.p. for production and dev., Hawkeye Entertainment, Inc.
THEATRE: Leonard Bernstein's Theatre Songs, Cry of the Raindrop, Girl of the Golden West, Little Malcolm and His Struggle Against the Eunuchs, I and Albert (London).
PICTURES: The Queen, All the Right Noises, Walkabout, A Clockwork Orange (exec. prod.), Glastonbury Fayre (exec. in chg. prod.), The Man Who Fell to Earth (exec. prod.), Blue Gold: World Water Wars (doc., exec. prod.).
TELEVISION: *Exec. prod.:* 15th Annual Saturn Awards, Doobie Brothers Retrospective, Listen to the Music 1989. *Documentary:* The Queen.

LIU, LUCY

Actress. b. Jackson Heights, NY, Dec. 2, 1968.
PICTURES: The Big Bang Theory, Guy, Jerry Maguire, Flypaper, Gridlock'd, City of Industry, Payback, Love Kills, True Crime, The Mating Habits of the Earthbound Human, Play it To the Bone, Molly, Shanghai Noon, Charlie's Angels, Hotel, Ecks vs. Sever, Company Man, Chicago: The Musical, Charlie's Angels: Full Throttle, Kill Bill: Vol. 1, Kill Bill: Vol. 2, Lucky Number Slevin, Freedom's Fury (prod. only), 3 Needles, Domino, Code Name: The Cleaner (also exec. prod.), Rocket, Rise, Watching the Detectives, The Year of Getting to Know Us, Kung Fu Panda

(voice), Nomads, East Fifth Bliss, Kung Fu Panda: The Kaboom of Doom (voice).
TELEVISION: *Movies*: Riot, Cashmere Mafia (pilot), Little Spirit: Christmas in New York, Afro Samurai: Resurrection. *Series*: Pearl, Ally McBeal (Emmy nom. 1999), Game Over (voice), Maya & Miguel (voice), Cashmere Mafia, Dirty Sexy Money. *Guest*: More than 100 appearances.

LLOYD, CHRISTOPHER
Actor. b. Stamford, CT, Oct. 22, 1938. Studied at Neighborhood Playhouse, NY.
THEATRE: *NY:* Kaspar (Drama Desk & Obie Awards, 1973), Happy End, Red White and Maddox. Regional: The Father, Hot L Baltimore, The Possessed, A Midsummer Night's Dream.
PICTURES: One Flew Over the Cuckoo's Nest (debut, 1975), Goin' South, Butch and Sundance: The Early Days, The Onion Field, The Lady in Red, Schizoid, The Black Marble, The Postman Always Rings Twice, The Legend of the Lone Ranger, National Lampoon Goes to the Movies, Mr. Mom, To Be or Not to Be, Star Trek III: The Search for Spock, The Adventures of Buckaroo Banzai Across the Eighth Dimension, Joy of Sex, Back to the Future, Clue, Legend of the White Horse, Miracles, Walk Like a Man, Who Framed Roger Rabbit, Track 29, Eight Men Out, The Dream Team, Back to the Future Part II, Why Me?, Back to the Future Part III, Duck Tales: The Movie (voice), White Dragon, Suburban Commando, The Addams Family, Dennis the Menace, Twenty Bucks, Addams Family Values, Angels in the Outfield, Camp Nowhere, Radioland Murders, The Pagemaster, Things to Do in Denver When You're Dead, Cadillac Ranch, Changing Habits, Anastasia, Tom Sawyer, It Came from the Sky, Dinner at Fred's, Convegence, Baby Geniuses, My Favorite Martian, Man on the Moon, Dinner At Fred's, Wish You Were Dead, Happy Birthday, A Fate Totally Worse Than Death, Chasing Destiny, Kids World, Interstate 60, Hey Arnold! The Movie, Haunted Lighthouse, Admissions, 5-25-77, Chrome (voice), Peter Cottontail: The Movie (voice), Flakes, Fly Me to the Moon (voice), Jack and the Beanstalk, Call of the Wild, Foodfight! (voice), The Tale of Despereaux (voice), Thicker, Snowmen, Wolf Sheep, The Witches of Oz 3D, Serial Buddies, Last Call, Piranha 3-D, The Return of Captain Kidd.
TELEVISION: *Movies*: Lacy and the Mississippi Queen, The Word, Stunt Seven, Money on the Side, September Gun, The Cowboy and the Ballerina, T Bone N Weasel, Dead Ahead: The Exxon Valdez Disaster, It Came from the Sky, Wit, On the Edge, When Good Ghouls Go Bad, The Big Time, Admissions, Detective, A Perfect Day. *Mini-series:* Meteor: Path to Destruction. *Series*: Taxi (Emmy Awards: 1982, 1983), Back to the Future (voice for animated series), Deadly Games, Avonlea (Emmy Award, 1992). Cyberchase (Emmy nom. 2008), Clubhouse, Stacked. *Specials*: Earth Day Special, Pilgrim Farewell, The Penny Elf, Tales From Hollywood Hills: Pat Hobby—Teamed With Genius, In Search of Dr. Seuss, Knights of Bloodsteel. *Guest*: More than 100 appearances.

LLOYD, EMILY
Actress. r.n. Emily Lloyd Pack. b. North London, Eng., Sept. 29, 1970. Father is stage actor Roger Lloyd Pack, mother worked as Harold Pinter's secretary.
PICTURES: Wish You Were Here (Natl. Society of Film Critics & London Evening Standard Awards, 1987; BAFTA nom.), Cookie, In Country, Chicago Joe and the Showgirl, Scorchers, A River Runs Through It, Under the Hula Moon, When Saturday Comes, Dead Girl, Welcome to Sarajevo, Livers Ain't Cheap, Boogie Boy, Woundings, The Honeytrap, Hey Mr DJ.
TELEVISION: *Movies*: Override, Riverworld. *Series:* Denial.

LLOYD, EUAN
Producer. b. Rugby, Warwick, England, Dec. 6, 1923. e. Rugby. Entered m.p. ind. in 1939 as theatre manager, then pub. dir.; dir. of Publ. Rank, 1946; joined Associated British-Pathe, Ltd. in same capacity; 1952 asst. to prod., Warwick Film Prod. Ltd. v.p. Highroad Productions, 1962-64. Rep. Europe Goldwyn's Porgy & Bess 1959.
PICTURES: April in Portugal, Heart of Variety, Invitation to Monte Carlo, The Secret Ways, Genghis Khan, Poppy Is Also a Flower, Murderer's Row, Shalako, Catlow, The Man Called Noon, Paper Tiger, The Wild Geese, The Sea Wolves, Who Dares Wins, Wild Geese II, The Final Option.
TELEVISION: *Movie:* Riverworld.

LLOYD, NORMAN
Actor, Producer, Director. b. Jersey City, NJ, Nov. 8, 1914. e. NYU, 1932. Acted on B'way in: Noah, Liberty Jones, Everywhere I Roam, 1935-44; in various stock companies. Joined Orson Welles and John Houseman in the original company of Mercury Theatre, NY, 1937-38. Prod. asst. on films Arch of Triumph, The Red Pony. Produced film Up Above the World.
THEATRE: With the Civic Repertory Theatre, 1932-33 and The Living Newspapers of The Federal Theatre, 1936: Triple a Plowed Under, Injunction Granted. Regional: Power, Medicine Show, Ask My Friend, Sandy, Volpone. American Shakespeare Festival: Measure for Measure, Taming of the Shrew (also dir.). With La Jolla Playhouse, 1948-1955: Village Green, King Lear, The Cocktail Party, The Lady's Not for Burning, Madame Will You Walk, The Golden Apple, Major Barbara, The Will & Bart Show, Quiet City
PICTURES: *Actor:* Saboteur, Spellbound, The Southerner, A Walk in the Sun, A Letter for Evie, The Unseen, Green Years, The Beginning or The End, Limelight, Young Widow, No Minor Vices, The Black Book, Scene of the Crime, Calamity Jane and Sam Bass, Buccaneer's Girl, The Flame and the Arrow, He Ran All the Way, The Light Touch, Audrey Rose, FM, The Nude Bomb, Jaws of Satan, Dead Poets Society, Journey of Honor (Shogun Mayeda), The Age of Innocence, Jean Renoir, The Adventures of Rocky and Bullwinkle, In Her Shoes.
TELEVISION: *Assoc. prod./exec. prod.:* The Alfred Hitchcock Show. *Prod.-Dir.:* The Alfred Hitchcock Hour, The Name of the Game (Emmy nom. 1970), Hollywood Television Theater, Tales of the Unexpected, Steambath (Emmy nom. 1974), Omnibus (dir. of The Lincoln Films, 1952), Journey to the Unknown (series). *Actor*: St. Elsewhere (series), Harvest Home. *Movies (prod.-dir.):* The Smugglers, Companions in Nightmare, What's a Nice Girl Like You (prod.), The Bravos (prod.), Amityville: The Evil Escapes, The Battle Over Citizen Kane, Seven Days, Hitchcock: Shadow of a Genius, Fail Safe, The Song of the Lark. *Guest:* More than 95 appearances.

LOACH, KEN
Director, Writer. b. Nuneaton, England, June 17, 1936. e. Oxford (studied law). Served in Royal Air Force; then became actor. Began dir. career on British tv in early 1960's.
PICTURES: Poor Cow (debut, 1968; also co-s.p.), Kes (also co-s.p.), Family Life, Black Jack (also co-s.p.), Looks and Smiles (also co- s.p.), Fatherland (Singing the Blues in Red), Hidden Agenda, Riff-Raff, Rainisng Stones, Land and Freedom, Ladybird Ladybird, Carla's Song, The Flickering Flame, My Name is Joe, Bread and Roses, The Navigators, Sweet Sixteen, Tickets, These Times (dir., prod.), McLibel (doc.), The Wind That Shakes the Barley, To Each His Cinema (segment dir.), It's a Free World..., Looking for Eric, Route Irish.
TELEVISION: *Movies:* Diary of a Young Man, A Tap on the Shoulder, 3 Clear Sundays, The End of Arthur's Marriage, Up the Junction, Coming Out Party, Cathy Come Home, In Two Minds, The Golden Vision, The Big Flame, In Black and White, After a Lifetime, The Rank and the File, A Misfortune, The Price of Coal, Which Side Are You On. *Mini-series:* Days of Hope. *Series:* Z Cars, The Wednesday Play. *Documentaries: Dir., Prod.:* Auditions, A Question of Leadership (1981), The View From the Woodpile. *Dir.:* Questions of Leadership (1983), The Red and the Blue: Impressions of Two Political Conferences - Autumn 1982.

LOBELL, MICHAEL
Producer. b. Brooklyn, NY, May 7, 1941. e. Michigan State U. on athletic baseball scholarship. Worked briefly in garment indust. Entered film industry in 1974 by buying Danish distribution rights to The Apprenticeship of Duddy Kravitz. Formed Lobell/ Bergman Prods. with Andrew Bergman.
PICTURES: Dreamer, Windows, So Fine, The Journey of Natty Gann, Chances Are, The Freshman, White Fang, Honeymoon in Vegas, Undercover Blues, Little Big League, It Could Happen to You, Striptease, Isn't She Great, This Man This Woman, Hostile Rescue, Tears of the Sun.

LO BIANCO, TONY
Actor. b. New York, NY. Oct. 19, 1936. Performed on N.Y. stage as well as in films and TV. Former artistic dir. Triangle Theatre, NY.
THEATRE: Yanks 3—Detroit 0—Top of the Seventh (Obie Award), The Office, The Rose Tattoo, A View From the Bridge (Outer Critics Circle Award), The Royal Hunt of the Sun, Hizzoner, Other People's Money (tour).
PICTURES: The Honeymoon Killers (debut, 1970), The French Connection, The Seven Ups, Demon (God Told Me To), F.I.S.T., Bloodbrothers, Separate Ways, City Heat, Too Scared to Scream (dir. only), Mean Frankie and Crazy Tony, La Romana, City of Hope, The Spiders Web, Boiling Point, The Ascent, The Last Home Run (dir. only), The Juror, Sworn to Justics, Cold Night Into Dawn, Jane Austen's Mafia, The Pawn, The Day the Ponies Come Back, Friends and Family, Down n' Dirty, The Last Request, Endangered Species, Frame of Mind, The Irishman.
TELEVISION: *Movies/Mini-series*: Mr. Inside Mr. Outside, The Story of Joseph and Jacob, Magee and the Lady (She'll Be Sweet), Jesus of Nazareth, Hidden Faces, Legend of the Black Hand, Lady Blue, Marco Polo, Welcome Home Bobby, Blood Ties, A Last Cry for Help, Marciano, Another Woman's Child, The Last Tenant, Goldenrod, Shadow in the Streets, Eugene O'Neill's A Glory of Ghosts, Police Story: The Freeway Killings, The Ann Jillian Story, Body of Evidence, Off Duty, True Blue, Perry Mason: The Case of the Poisoned Pen, Malcolm Takes a Shot, In the Shadow of a Killer, Stormy Weathers, Teamster Boss: The Jackie Presser Story, The First Circle, The Maharajah's Daughter, Tyson, Rocky Marciano, Bella Mafia, Lucky Day, The Engagement Ring. *Specials*: Hizzoner (Emmy Award), A Glory of Ghosts. *Director:* Police Story, Kaz, Cliffhangers, When the Whistle Blows, The Duke. *Series*: Love of Life, Jessie, Palace Guard. *Guest:* More than 72 appearances.

LOCKE, PETER
Producer, Executive. Exec. producer, all programming produced by Kushner Locke. Producer, Stockard Channing Show, The Star Maker, The Hills Have Eyes, Parts I & II. Co-founder and

co-chairman & co-CEO, Kushner-Locke, 1983. Currently President of Peter Locke Productions.
PICTURES: *Producer*: The Hills Have Eyes, Nutcracker: The Motion Picture, Dorothy Meets Ozma of Oz, The Brave Little Toaster. *Exec. Producer:* Lady In Waiting, Adnre, Dangerous Intentions, Last Gasp, The Adventures of Pinocchio, The Whole Wide World, Shadow of the World, The Grave, The Last Time I Committed Suicide, Little Ghost, The Incredible Geneie, The Brave Little Toaster Goes to Mars, Possums, Basil, The Shrunken City, Small Time, Susan's Plan, Ringmaster, Teen Knight, Denial, Clockmaker, Bone Daddy, Phantom Town, Mudercycle, Beowulf, Girl, The Brave Little Toaster to the Rescue, Blooddolls, Freeway II: Confessions of a Trickbaby, But I'm a Cheerleader, The Boy with the X-Ray Eyes, Picking Up the Pieces, The Last Producer, Harvard Man, The Hills Have Eyes (prod.), The Hills Have Eyes II (prod.).
TELEVISION: *Exec. Producer:* Sweet Bird of Youth, Your Mother Wears Combat Boots, Carolina Skeletons, Fire in the Dar, Father & Son: Dangerous Relations, A Strange Affair, Jack Reed: Death and Vengeance, Unlikely Angel, Every Woman's Dream, Gun (series), Echo, Dragonworld: The Legend Continues, The Brave Little Toaster (Emmy nom. 1988), The Search for the Jewel of Polaris: Mysterious Museum, They Nest, Dark Prince: The True Story of Dracula, Wolf Girl. *Series:* 1st & Ten: The Championship, Divorce Court, Gun, Thrills.

LOCKHART, JUNE

Actress. b. New York, NY, June 25, 1925. p. actors, Gene and Kathleen Lockhart. B'way debut For Love or Money, 1947.
PICTURES: A Christmas Carol (debut, 1938), All This and Heaven Too, Adam Had Four Sons, Sergeant York, Miss Annie Rooney, Forever and a Day, White Cliffs of Dover, Meet Me in St. Louis, Son of Lassie, Keep Your Powder Dry, Easy to Wed, She-Wolf of London, Bury Me Dead, The Yearling, T-Men, It's a Joke Son, Time Limit, Butterfly, Deadly Games, Strange Invaders, Troll, Rented Lips, The Big Picture, Dead Women in Lingerie, Tis the Season, Sleep With Me, Lost in Space, Deterrence, Bongee Bear and the Kingdom of Rhythm (voice), Wesley, Super Capers.
TELEVISION: *Movies*: But I Don't Want to Get Married, The Bait, Who is the Black Dahlia?, Curse of the Black Widow, The Gift of Love, Walking Through the Fire, The Night They Saved Christmas, Perfect People, A Whisper Kills, Danger Island, The Au Pair II, Holiday in Handcuffs. *Mini-series*: Loose Change. *Series*: Who Said That? (panelist), Lassie (Emmy nom. 1959), Lost in Space, Petticoat Junction, General Hospital, Roseanne, Step By Step, Fired Up. *Guest*: More than 154 appearances.

LOCKLEAR, HEATHER

Actress. b. Los Angeles, CA, Sept. 25, 1961. e. UCLA. Appeared in commercials while in college.
PICTURES: Firestarter (debut, 1984), The Return of Swamp Thing, The Big Slice, Illusions, Wayne's World 2, The First Wives Club, Money Talks, Double Tap, Uptown Girls, Looney Tunes: Back in Action, The Perfect Man, Flying By, The Driver.
TELEVISION: *Movies*: Return of the Beverly Hillbillies, Twirl, City Killer, Blood Sport, Rich Men Single Women, Jury Duty: The Comedy, Her Wicked Ways, Dynasty: The Reunion, Body Language, Highway Heartbreaker, Fade to Black, Texas Justice, Too Many Lovers, Once Around the Park, Women of a Certain Age, Angels Fall, Flirting with 40. *Series*: Dynasty, T.J. Hooker, Fright Night Videos (host), Going Places, Melrose Place (4 Golden Globe noms.), Hercules (voice), Spin City (2 Golden Globe noms.), LAX (also pilot), See Jayne Run (also pilot), Melrose Place (2010). *Specials:* Battle of the Network Stars, Hollywood Starr, TV Guide 40th Anniversary Special (host). *Guest*: More than 108 appearances.

LOCKWOOD, GARY

Actor. r.n. John Gary Yusolfsky. b. Van Nuys, CA, Feb. 21, 1937. Began in Hollywood as stuntman.
PICTURES: Tall Story, Splendor in the Grass, Wild in the Country, The Magic Sword, It Happened at the World's Fair, Firecreek, 2001: A Space Odyssey, They Came to Rob Las Vegas, Model Shop, The Body, R.P.M., Stand Up and Be Counted, The Wild Pair, Night of the Scarecrow, Trekkies, A Bedfull of Foreigners.
TELEVISION: *Movies*: Earth II, Star Trek: Where No Man Has Gone Before, Manhunter, Alvin Karpis: Public Enemy No. 1, The Quest: The Longest Drive, The Ghost of Flight 401, The Incredible Journey of Doctor Meg Laurel, Top of the Hill, The Girl, the Gold Watch & Dynamite, Emergency Room, Half Nelson, The Return of the Six-Million-Dollar Man and the Bionic Woman. *Series*: Follow the Sun, The Lieutenant. *Guest*: More than 74 appearances.

LOCKWOOD, ROGER

Executive. b. Middletown, CT, June 7, 1936. e. Ohio Wesleyan U. Sports writer for Akron Beacon Journal, 1960-62. On executive staff of Lockwood & Gordon Theatres; exec. v.p. SBC Theatres, 1969-73. 1974 asst. to exec. v.p., General Cinema Corp. 1975 formed Lockwood/Friedman Theatres, buying-booking and exhibition organization. Pres., Theatre Owners of New England, 1971-72; pres., Young NATO 1965-67; bd. of dir. NATO, 1962-1968. Board of dir. Tone, 1968-present; pres., Jimmy Fund, present; 1979-80, Variety Club of New England, pres. Director, Dana-Farber Cancer Institute, 1983-present. 1988, formed Lockwood/McKinnon Company Inc. operating theatres and Taco Bell Restaurants.

LOEKS, JOHN D., JR.

Executive. b. Grand Rapids, MI, Feb. 24, 1945. e. Wheaton College, B.A., 1967; Wayne State Univ., J.D., 1970. Began own law practice in 1970 and practiced law there until 1990. President ShowSpan, Inc. Also owner and CEO Loeks Theatres, Inc. which is now known as Celebration! Cinema and is President of Jackson Entertainment, LLC. Board member of: AuSable Institute, Grand Rapids Symphony Orchestra, and the InterVarsity Christian Fellowship.

LOEWY, VICTOR

Executive. e. B.A., economics and German, McGill U., 1970. Co-founded Vivafilm, 1972; after Vivafilm became Alliance Communications Corp. in 1985, led that company to a dominant position in Canada's independent film distribution industry. Bd member, Canadian Film Centre, Toronto International Film Festival; chairman, National Assn. of Canadian Film Distributors; chairman, Alliance Atlantis Motion Picture Grp.; board member and member of Executive Committee, Alliance Atlantis Communications, Inc. In 2003 Loewy became chairman of Motion Picture Distribution, the leading Canadian indie distributor that was spun off from Alliance Atlantis. He was fired last summer for attempting to engineer a management buyout financed by British hedge fund Marwyn Investment Management. Loewy was quickly rehired by controlling shareholder Alliance Atlantis Communications as an independent consultant to appease output supplier New Line Cinema. In Sept. 2007 he was in negotiations to become chairman and CEO at MPD after it was sold earlier in 2007 to Goldman Sachs and its Canadian partner, EdgeStone Capital Partners. He became an independent consultant to MPD with the title of chairman emeritus. Recipient of the CFTPA for entrepreneurial excellence, honored by Cinémathèque Canada, Bd member of Canadian Film Centre and Chrmn of National Assoc. of Canadian Film Dist.
PICTURES: *Exec. Prod:* Shattered Image, New Waterford Girl.

LOGAN, JEFF

Executive. b. Mitchell, SD, Dec. 29, 1950. e. Dakota Wesleyan U. & U. of SD. Started working in family's Roxy Theatre at 9 yrs. old. Worked as announcer on KORN radio, 1969-70. Announcer, reporter & photgrapher KUSD-TV, 1970-71. Relief anchor KXON-TV, 1972-78. Took over management and is pres. of family theatre. Built co. into present circuit, Logan Luxury Theatres. Member Bd. of trustess Dakota Wesleyan U., 1990-present. Bd. of trustees Queen of Peace Hospital, 1991-1997. V.P. Variety Club of SD, 1994-96. Dir. NATO/North Central, 1980-90. V.P. VSDA of SD, 1989-1994. Dir., NATO, 1997-present. Chairman NATO Theatre Operations Committee, 1999.

LOGGIA, ROBERT

Actor. b. New York, NY, Jan. 3, 1930. e. U. of Missouri, B.A. journalism, 1951. Studied with Stella Adler and at The Actors Studio. Broadway debut, The Man with the Golden Arm, 1955.
THEATRE: Toys in the Attic, The Three Sisters, In the Boom Boom Room, Wedding Band.
PICTURES: Somebody Up There Likes Me (debut, 1956), The Garment Jungle, Cop Hater, The Lost Missile, Cattle King, The Greatest Story Ever Told, Che, First Love, Speed Trap, Revenge of the Pink Panther, The Ninth Configuration (Twinkle Twinkle Killer Kane), S.O.B., An Officer and a Gentleman, Trail of the Pink Panther, Psycho II, Curse of the Pink Panther, Scarface, Prizzi's Honor, Jagged Edge (Academy Award nom. 1986), Armed and Dangerous, That's Life, Over the Top, Hot Pursuit, The Believers, Gaby: A True Story, Big, Oliver & Company (voice), Relentless, S.P.O.O.K.S. (Code Name: Chaos), Triumph of the Spirit, Opportunity Knocks, The Marrying Man, Necessary Roughness, Gladiator, Innocent Blood, The Last Tattoo, Bad Girls, I Love Trouble, Man With a Gun, Independence Day, Lost Highway, Smilla's Sense of Snow, Wide Awake, The Proposition, Holy Man, American Virgin, The Suburbans, Return to Me, All Over Again, The Shipment, A Galaxy Far Far Away, Forget About It, The Deal, Funny Money, Wild Seven, Her Morbid Desires, The Least of These, Shrink, Room and Board, Harvest, Fake.
TELEVISION: *Movies*: Mallory: Circumstantial Evidence, Street Killing, Scott Free, Raid on Entebbe, No Other Love, Casino, A Woman Called Golda, A Touch of Scandal, Streets of Justice, Intrigue, Dream Breakers, Afterburn, Lifepod, Nurses on the Line: The Crash of Flight 7, White Mile, Jake Lassiter: Justice on the Bayou, Between Love and Honor, Mercy Mission: The Rescue of Flight 771, Right to Remain Silent, Joe Torre: Curveballs Along the Way, Hard Time: The Premonition, Dodson's Journey, Big Break All-Star Challenge. *Mini-Series*: Arthur Hailey's The Moneychangers, Echoes in the Darkness, Favorite Son, Wild Palms, Joan of Arc. *Series*: T.H.E. Cat, Emerald Point N.A.S., Mancuso FBI (Emmy nom. 1990), Sunday Dinner, Queens Supreme, Malcolm in the Middle (Emmy nom 2001 as guest). *Specials*: Miss Julie, The Nine Lives of Elfego Baca, Conspiracy: The Trial of the Chicago 8, Merry Christmas Baby, 3055 Jean Leon. *Guest:* More than 178 appearances.

LOHAN, LINDSAY
b. Cold Spring Harbor, NY, July 2, 1986.
Began her career at age three as a Ford model, and also made appearances in over sixty television commercials.
PICTURES: The Parent Trap (debut 1998), Freaky Friday, Confessions of a Teenage Drama Queen (also singer), Mean Girls, The Princess Diaries 2: Royal Engagement (singer), Herbie: Fully Loaded, Just My Luck, A Prairie Home Companion, Fashionistas, Bobby, I Know Who Killed Me, Georgia Rule, Chapter 27, Dare to Love Me, Labor Pains, Machete, Black Friday 3D, Lovelace.
TELEVISION: *Movies:* Life-Size, Get a Clue. *Series:* Another World, Bette (pilot only), Ugly Betty. *Guest:* More than 98 appearances.

LOLLOBRIGIDA, GINA
Actress. b. Subiaco, Italy, July 4, 1927. e. Acad. of Fine Arts, Rome. Film debut (Italy) L'aguila nera, 1946. Published several volumes of her photography incl. Italia Mia, The Wonder of Innocence. Received Golden Globe Henrietta Award 1961.
PICTURES: Pagliacci, The City Defends Itself, The White Line, Fanfan the Tulip, Times Gone By, Beat the Devil, Crossed Swords, The Great Game, Beauties of the Night, Wayward Wife, Bread Love and Dreams, Bread Love and Jealousy, Young Caruso, World's Most Beautiful Woman, Trapeze, Hunchback of Notre Dame, Solomon and Sheba, Never So Few, The Unfaithfuls, Fast and Sexy, Where the Hot Wind Blows, Go Naked in the World, Come September, Imperial Venus, Woman of Straw, That Splendid November, Hotel Paradiso, Buona Sera Mrs. Campbell (Golden Globe nom. 1969), Plucked, The Private Navy of Sgt. O'Farrell, Bad Man's River, King Queen Knave, The Lonely Woman, Bambole, Wandering Stars, A Hundred and One Nights, XXL.
TELEVISION: *Movies*: Deceptions, Cheer for Charlie. *Mini-series*: The Adventures of Pinocchio. *Series*: Falcon Crest (Golden Globe nom. 1985).

LOMIS, ERIK
Executive. b. Philadelphia, PA, November 21, 1958. e. B.S. Philadelphia Textile. Began career in 1979 at Sameric Theatres, where he held numerous positions including head film buyer. 1988-1993 United Artists Theatre Circuit, Sr. V.P. National Film Dept. 1993 joined MGM Distribution Co. as Sr. V.P. and G.S.M. From 2000 until 2005, Lomis held the post of MGM's president of domestic distribution. In May 2007 MGM appointed Lomis executive v.p., of international theatrical and home entertainment. He oversees the marketing and distribution of the international theatrical and home entertainment releases, which are handled by Fox. He is the primary executive working closely with the worldwide team at Twentieth Century Fox Home Entertainment as well as the theatrical team at Twentieth Century Fox International. Named President, Worldwide Theatrical Distribution, Home Entertainment & Acquisitions of MGM Studios, Inc.

LONDON, BARRY
Executive, Producer. Joined Paramount Pictures 1971 in L.A. branch office as booker; later salesman. 1973, sls. mgr., Kansas City-St. Louis; 1974, branch mgr. Transferred to San Francisco, first as branch mgr.; later as district mgr. 1977, eastern div. mgr. in Washington, DC, 1978-81, western div. mgr. 1981, named v.p., gen. sls. mgr. 1983, advanced to sr. v.p., domestic distrib.1984, named pres., domestic div., for Motion Picture Group of Paramount; 1985, named pres., marketing and domestic distrib.; 1988, named pres. worldwide distrib., Motion Picture Group. Producer, Barry London Co. Member: Variety Club NYC (VP, 1984-), Will Rogers Hospital Dist. Chmn., 1985-.
PICTURES: *Exec. Prod.:* Thomas and the Magic Railroad, Whipped, Beautiful.

LONDON, JASON
Actor. b. San Diego, CA, Nov. 7, 1972. Twin brother of actor Jeremy London. Raised in Oklahoma and Texas. Appeared in Aerosmith video Amazing.
PICTURES: The Man in the Moon (debut, 1991), December, Dazed and Confused, Safe Passage, To Wong Foo—Thanks for Everything—Julie Newmar, My Generation, Learning Curves, The Barefoot Executive, Fall Time, Countdown, Mixed Signals, Frontline, Broken Vessels, The Rage: Carrie 2, Goodbye Sunrise, Poor White Trash, $pent, Out Cold, Dracula II: Ascension, Grind, Wasabi Tuna, Dracula III: Legacy, Greed, Defining Moments (also prod.), Adventures of Johnny Tao: Rock Around the Dragon, The Good Mother, Throwing Stars, Shadows of Atticus, Alien vs. Alien, All Roads Lead Home, Sutures, Wrong Way, Killer Movie, The Devil's Tomb, Whole Lotta Love, Maskerade, Fight or Flight, 51, Snow Beast.
TELEVISION: *Movies*: Blood Ties, False Arrest, I'll Fly Away: Then and Now, A Matter of Justice, The Barefoot Executive, If These Walls Could Talk, Friends 'Til the End, Alien Cargo, Jason and the Argonauts, The Hound of the Baskervilles, Out of the Woods, Wishing Well, Monsterwolf. *Series:* Wildfire.

LONDON, JEREMY
Actor. b. San Diego, CA, Nov. 7, 1972. Twin brother of actor Jason London. Raised in OK and TX.
PICTURES: Breaking Free, The Babysitter, Mallrats, Levitation, Happenstance, Get a Job, Scene Smoking: Cigarettes, Cinema & the Myth of Cool, Gods and Generals, Julian & Chalice, Kiss Me Again, Nine Is Mine, Next of Kin, The Grift, Under the Knife, Trance, Lost Dream, Divided (also co-prod.), Chasing the Green, Drop Dead Gorgeous, Scratching the Surface, Lost Dream, The Divided (also co-prod.), House Under Siege, Drop Dead Gorgeous, Fight or Flight (also co-prod.), Trance, Scratching the Surface, Scavengers, Opponent, Hollywood & Wine, Rain from Stars.
TELEVISION: *Movies*: In Broad Daylight, A Seduction in Travis County, A Season of Hope, A Mother's Gift, Bad to the Bone, The Defenders: Taking the First, Journey to the Center of the Earth, Romantic Comedy 101, What I Did for Love, Basilisk: The Serpent King, Strokes, Ba'al, Do You Know Me, Wolvesbayne. *Series*: I'll Fly Away, Angel Falls, Party of Five, Hollywood Squares, 7th Heaven.

LONDON, JERRY
Director. b. Los Angeles, CA, Jan 21, 1937. Apprentice film editor, Desilu Prods., 1955; film ed., Daniel Boone, 1962; staged plays in local theater workshops; editor, assoc. prod., then dir. Hogan's Heroes. Formed Jerry London Prods., 1984.
PICTURE: Rent-a-Cop (feature debut, 1988).
TELEVISION: *Movies*: Bridget Loves Bernie (pilot). Killdozer, McNaughton's Daughter, Cover Girls, Evening in Byzantium, Swan Song, Women in White, Shogun, Father Figure, The Chicago Story, The Ordeal of Bill Carney (also prod.), The Gift of Life (also prod.), The Scarlet and the Black, Arthur Hailey's Hotel (also prod.), With Intent to Kill (exec. prod. only), Dark Mansions, Manhunt For Claude Dallas, Harry's Hong Kong, Family Sins (exec. prod. only), Macgruder and Loud (also prod.), Dadah Is Death (also prod.), Kiss Shot (also exec. prod.), The Haunting of Sarah Hardy (also exec. prod.), Vestige of Honor, A Season of Giants, Victim of Love, Grass Roots, Calendar Girl Cop Killer?: The Bambi Bembenek Story (also prod.), A Twist of the Knife, I Spy Returns, Labor of Love: The Arlette Schweitzer Story, A Mother's Gift, A Promise to Carolyn, A Holiday For Love, Get to the Heart: The Barbara Mandrell Story, I'll Be Home for Christmas, Stolen Women Captured Hearts, Beauty, As Time Runs Out, Take Me Home: The John Denver Story, Dr. Quinn Medicine Woman: The Heart Within, Attack on the Queen, Counterstrike. *Mini-series*: Wheels, Shogun (DGA, best dir., special award, Emmy nom. 1981), Women in White, Chiefs (also sprv. prod., Emmy nom. 1984), Ellis Island (also sprv. prod., Emmy nom. 1985), If Tomorrow Comes. *Series*: Hogan's Heroes, The Doris Day Show, Mary Tyler Moore Show, The Partridge Family, Temperatures Rising, The Paul Lynde Show, Love American Style, The Bob Newhart Show, Here We Go Again, Marcus Welby, M.D., The Brady Bunch, Kojak, Happy Days, The Six Million Dollar Man, Petrocelli, Harry O, Police Story, Rockford Files, Police Woman, Switch, Joe Forrester, The Bionic Woman, Delvecchio, The Feather and Father Gang, Dream On, Diagnosis Murder, Dream On, Dr. Quinn, Medicine Woman, Chicago Hope, The Cosby Mysteries, JAG, 100 Centre Street. Home, The Guardian, What About Brian.

LONE, JOHN
Actor. b. Hong Kong, Oct. 13, 1952. Studied at Chin Ciu Academy of the Peking Opera in Hong Kong, Moved to LA where he studied acting at Pasadena's American Acad. of Dramatic Art, becoming member of the East-West Players.
THEATRE: *NY*: F.O.B., The Dance and the Railroad (Obie Awards for both plays), Paper Angels (dir.), Sound and Beauty (also dir.).
PICTURES: Iceman (debut, 1984), Year of the Dragon (Golden Globe nom. 1986), The Last Emperor (Golden Globe nom. 1988), The Moderns, Echoes of Paradise, Shadow of China, Shanghai 1920, M. Butterfly, The Shadow, The Hunted, Task Force, Rush Hour 2, Paper Moon Affair, War.
TELEVISION: *Movies*: The Dance and the Railroad, Paper Angels (dir.), Kate Bliss and the Ticker Tape Kid.

LONG, SHELLEY
Actress. b. Ft. Wayne, IN, Aug. 23, 1949. e. Northwestern U. Was co-host, assoc. prod. of local tv show Sorting It Out.
PICTURES: A Small Circle of Friends (debut, 1980), Caveman, Night Shift, Losin' It, Irreconcilable Differences (Golden Globe nom. 1985), The Money Pit, Outrageous Fortune, Hello Again, Troop Beverly Hills, Don't Tell Her It's Me, Frozen Assets, The Brady Bunch Movie, A Very Brady Sequel, The Adventures of Ragtime, Dr. T. & the Women, A Fonder Heart, Pizza Man.
TELEVISION: *Movies*: The Cracker Factory, Princess and the Cabbie, Promise of Love, Voices Within: The Lives of Truddi Chase, Fatal Memories, A Message From Holly, The Women of Spring Break, Freaky Friday, Susie Q, A Different Kind of Christmas, Vanished Without a Trace, Jingle Bells (voice), Brady Bunch in the Whitehouse, The Santa Trap, Halloween Romance, Falling in Love with the Girl Next Door, Ice Dreams. *Series*: Cheers (Emmy Award, 1983, 4 other noms.; 2 Golden Globe Awards, 1 other nom.), Good Advice, Kelly Kelly. *Special*: Basic Values: Sex Shock & Censorship in the '90's. *Guest:* More than 109 appearances.

LOPEZ, GEORGE
Actor, Writer, Producer. b. Mission Hills, CA, April 23, 1961.

PICTURES: Ski Patrol, Fatal Instinct, Bread and Roses, Real Women Have Curves, Outta Time, The Adventures of Sharkboy and Lavagirl 3-D, Tortilla Heaven, Balls of Fury, Henry Poole Is Here, Swing Vote, El Superstar: The Unlikely Rise of Juan Frances (exec. prod.), Beverly Hills Chihuahua (voice), The Spy Next Door, Valentine's Day, Marmaduke (voice), Rio (voice), The Smurfs (voice).
TELEVISION: *Movies:* Fidel, Naughty or Nice, George Lopez: America's Mexican (writer, exec. prod.), Mr. Troop Mom (also exec. prod.), George Lopez: Tall, Dark & Chicano (also writer, exec. prod.). *Series:* Freddie, George Lopez, Dancing with the Stars, Reno 911!, Lopez Tonight. *Guest:* More than 90 appearances.

LOPEZ, GERARDO I. (GERRY)
Executive. b. Oriente, Cuba. e. B.S. degree in business admin. George Washington University; MBA, Harvard Business School. In his more than 25-year career, Lopez has served in a variety of executive mgt. positions with International Home Foods, Frito-Lay, Pepsi-Cola and the Procter & Gamble Company. Lopez was previously part of the entertainment industry from 2000-2004, serving as pres., Handleman Entertainment Resources, providing category mgt. and pre-recorded music dist. services to Wal-Mart, Best Buy and other major retailers in the U.S. and abroad. Most recently, Lopez served as executive v.p. of Starbucks Coffee Company and pres. of its Global Consumer Products, Seattle's Best Coffee and Foodservice divisions before joining exhibition giant AMC. Today, Lopez is CEO and pres. of AMC Entertainment Holdings, Inc.; Marquee Holdings Inc. and AMC Entertainment Inc. (AMC). He assumed this role in March 2009 when Peter C. Brown retired. Lopez is only the fourth CEO in the company's almost 90-year history. Lopez sits on the AMC's bd. of directors and is active on several public and private company boards, including TXU Corporation, Safeco Insurance and the supply chain startup SilkRoute Global. Recently Lopez was appointed to the bd. of National CineMedia, Inc., (NASDAQ: NCMI) a cinema advertising company; Digital Cinema Implementation Partners, LLC, a partnership implementing digital cinema deployment in theatres; and Midland Empire Partners, LLC. He was a member of the Cranbrook Institute of Science Board of Governors in Bloomfield Hills, MI, and has been recognized by Hispanic Business Magazine as one of the Top 100 Hispanic Business Leaders.

LOPEZ, JENNIFER
Actress. b. Bronx, NY, July 24, 1969. Actress/entertainer Lopez is also a principal in the production company Nuyorican Productios.
PICTURES: My Little Girl, My Family—Mi Familia, Money Train, Jack, Blood and Wine, Selena, Anaconda, U-Turn, Out of Sight, Antz (voice), Thieves, The Cell, The Wedding Planner, Angel Eyes, Enough, Uptown Girl, Gigli, Jersey Girl, Shall We Dance?, An Unfinished Life, Monster-in-Law, American Darlings, Bordertown, El Cantante (also prod.), Feel the Noise (also prod.), The Back-Up Plan.
TELEVISION: *Movies*: Nurses on the Line: The Crash of Flight 7. *Mini-series:* Como ama una mujer (exec. prod.). *Series*: Second Chances, South Central, Hotel Malibu, In Living Color, South Beach (exec. prod.). *Guest:* More than 240 appearances.

LORD, PETER
Director, Producer. b. England, 1953.
PICTURES: *Director*: On Probation, Late Edition, Early Bird, Babylon, My Baby Just Carres For Me, Going Equipped, War Story, Adam (Academy Award nom. 1993), Wat's Pig (Academy Award nom. 1997), Chicken Run. *Producer*: On Probation, Adam (exec.), Not Without My Handbag (exec.), Wallace & Gromit: The Wrong Trousers (exec.), Wat's Pig (exec.), Stage Fight (exec.), Chicken Run, Wee Wee (exec.), Superhero (exec.), Horror (exec.), Hardface (exec.), Chips (exec.), Buzz Off (exec.), Bone (exec.), Wallace and Gromit: The Great Vegetable Plot, Wallace & Gromit in The Curse of the Were-Rabbit, Flushed Away, (also writer), Pirates! (also exec. prod.), Arthur Christmas (exec. prod.).
TELEVISION: *Series: As Exec. Prod.:* The Amazing Adventures of Morph (dir.),Pee-wee's Playhouse (animation dir.), Purple and Brown (exec. prod.), Creature Comforts America (Emmy nom. 2008), Shaun the Sheep, Wallace and Gromit in 'A Matter of Loaf and Death'.

LOREN, SOPHIA
Actress. b. Rome, Italy, Sept. 20, 1934. e. Naples. m. late producer Carlo Ponti. Autobiography: Sophia: Living and Loving (with A.E. Hotchner, 1979). Received Honorary Academy Award, 1991. Won 4 Golden Globe Henrietta Awards. Received Golden Globe Cecil B. DeMille Award, 1995.
PICTURES: Africa Beneath the Seas, Village of the Bells, Good People's Sunday, Neapolitan Carousel, Day in the District Court, Pilgrim of Love, Aida, Two Nights with Cleopatra, Our Times, Attila, Scourge of God, Gold of Naples, Too Bad She's Bad, Scandal in Sorrento, Miller's Beautiful Wife, Lucky to Be a Woman, Boy on a Dolphin (U.S. debut, 1957), The Pride and the Passion, Legend of the Lost, Desire Under the Elms, The Key, Houseboat, The Black Orchid, That Kind of Woman, Heller in Pink Tights, It Started in Naples (Golden Globe nom. 1961), A Breath of Scandal, The Millionairess, Two Women (Academy Award, 1962), El Cid, Boccaccio 70, Madame Sans-Gene, Five Miles to Midnight, The Condemned of Altona, Yesterday Today and Tomorrow, The Fall of the Roman Empire, Marriage Italian Style (Academy Award nom. 1965), Operation Crossbow, Lady L, Judith, Arabesque, A Countess from Hong Kong, More than a Miracle, Ghosts—Italian Style, Sunflower, The Priest's Wife, Lady Liberty, White Sister, Man of La Mancha, The Voyage, The Verdict, The Cassandra Crossing, A Special Day, Angela, Brass Target, Firepower, Blood Feud, Ready to Wear ("Pret-a-Porter" Golden Globe nom. 1995), Grumpier Old Men, Messages, Soleil, Destinazione Verna, Francesca e Nunziata, Between Strangers, Nine (also soundtrack performer).
TELEVISION: *Movies/Specials*: Brief Encounter, Sophia Loren—Her Own Story, Softly Softly, Rivals of Sherlock Holmes, Fantasy Island, Aurora, Courage, Mario Puzo's Running Away, Sabato, domenica e lunedì, Francesca and Nunziata, La Casa dei gerani. *Mini-series*: The Fortunate Pilgrim, Lives of the Saints. *Guest:* More than 93 appearances.

LOUGHLIN, LORI
Actress. b. Queens, NY, July 28, 1964. Started modeling at age 7 for catalogues, then tv commercials. First professional acting job at 18 as regular on daytime serial The Edge of Night.
PICTURES: Amityville 3-D, The New Kids, Secret Admirer, Back to the Beach, The Night Before, Suckers, Critical Mass, Farce of the Penguins (video), Moondance Alexander, Old Dogs.
TELEVISION: *Movies*: North Beach and Rawhide, Brotherhood of Justice, A Place to Call Home, Doing Time on Maple Drive, A Stranger in the Mirror, Empty Cradle, One of Her Own, Abandoned and Deceived, In the Line of Duty: Blaze of Glory, Tell Me No Secrets, The Price of Heaven, Medusa's Child, Summerland (also prod.), Eastwick, Meet My Mom. *Series*: The Edge of Night, Full House, Hudson Street, Summerland (also prod/writer/creator), In Case of Emergency, 90210 (2009). *Guest:* More than 63 appearances.

LOUIS-DREYFUS, JULIA
Actress. b. New York, NY, Jan. 13, 1961. e. Northwestern Univ. Member of Second City comedy troupe which resulted in casting on Saturday Night Live.
PICTURES: Troll (debut, 1986), Hannah and Her Sisters, Soul Man, National Lampoon's Christmas Vacation, Jack the Bear, North, Deconstructing Harry, Father's Day, A Bug's Life (voice), Gilligan's Island, Sellevision.
TELEVISION: *Movies*: London Suite, Animal Farm (voice), Geppetto. *Series*: Saturday Night Live (1982-85), Day by Day, Seinfeld (Golden Globe, 1994, 1 other nom.; Emmy Award, 1996, 6 other noms.), Watching Ellie, Curb Your Enthusiasm, The New Adventures of Old Christine (Emmy Award 2006, 2 other noms.; Golden Globe nom. 2007). *Specials*: The Art of Being Nick, Spy Magazine's Hit List (host), Sesame Street's All-Star 25th Birthday. *Guest:* More than 95 appearances.

LOURD, BRYAN
Executive. b. New Iberia, LA. e. Cambridge U., George Washington U., U.S.C. Began as a page at CBS Studios. Joined William Morris Agency in the mailroom, 1983. Promoted to agent in motion picture dept. 1988, joined Creative Artists Agency. Lourd is currently one of six controlling partners, Managing Director and Co-Chairman at CAA. In 2005 joined Bd. of Directors. of InterActiveCorp. He received the David Niven Award for his contribution to Project ALS (Lou Gehrig's disease).

LOVETT, RICHARD
Executive. e. U. of Wisconsin, Madison. Began career in mailroom at Creative Artists Agency. Promoted from agent trainee to agent in motion picture department. Appointed pres., CAA, October 1995. He and his partners created the CAA Foundation which works to involve the entertainment community in philanthropy and encourages organizations to lend their support to educational programs. Named one of the most influential people in entertainment by numerous media outlets. Serves on the boards of Communities & Schools, the National Urban League, and the Artists Rights Foundation. Recipient of City of Angels Helen Bernstein Award and David Niven Award for his contribution to Project ALS.

LOVITZ, JON
Actor, Comedian. b. Tarzana, CA, July 21, 1957. e. U. of California at Irvine. Studied acting at Film Actors Workshop. Took classes at the Groundlings, 1982. Performed with Groundling's Sunday Company, before joining main company in Chick Hazzard: Olympic Trials. Developed comedy character of pathological liar which he later performed when he became regular member of Saturday Night Live in 1985, received 2 Emmy noms.
PICTURES: The Last Resort, Ratboy, Jumpin' Jack Flash, Three Amigos, Big, My Stepmother Is an Alien, The Brave Little Toaster (voice), Mr. Destiny, An American Tail: Fievel Goes West (voice), A League of Their Own, Mom and Dad Save the World, National Lampoon's Loaded Weapon 1, Coneheads, City Slickers II: The Legend of Curly's Gold, North, Trapped in Paradise, The Great White Hype, High School High, Happiness, The Wedding Singer, Happiness, Lost and Found, Small Time Crooks, Little Nicky, Sand In the Boom Boom Room, 2000 Miles to Graceland, Cats

and Dogs (voice), Rat Race, Good Advice, Eight Crazy Nights, Dickie Roberts: Former Child Star, The Stepford Wives, Bailey's Billion$ (voice), The Producers, The Bench Warmers, Farce of the Penguins (video, voice), Southland Tales, I Could Never Be Your Woman, Casino Jack.
TELEVISION: *Series*: Foley Square, Saturday Night Live (1985-90), The Critic (voice), NewsRadio, The Simpsons (voice). *Specials*: The Please Watch the Jon Lovitz Special, One Night With Robbie Williams. *Guest:* More than 118 appearances.

LOWE, CHAD
Actor. b. Dayton, OH, Jan. 15, 1968. Brother is actor Rob Lowe. Stage debut in L.A. production of Blue Denim. On NY stage in Grotesque Love Songs.
PICTURES: Oxford Blues (debut, 1984), Apprentice to Murder, True Blood, Nobody's Perfect, Highway to Hell, Driven, Floating, Do Me a Favor, The Way We Are, Suicide: The Comedy, The Audition, Take Me Home, Red Betsy, Unfaithful, Beautiful Ohio (dir., prod.).
TELEVISION: *Movies*: Silence of the Heart, There Must Be a Pony, April Morning, So Proudly We Hail, An Inconvenient Woman, Captive, Candles in the Dark, Fighting for My Daughter, In the Presence of Mine Enemies, Target Earth, Take Me Home: The John Denver Story, The Apartment Complex, Acceptable Risk, Fielder's Choice. *Series*: Spencer, Life Goes On (Emmy Award, 1993), Melrose Place, Now and Again, Popular, Hack, 24, Bones, Pretty Little Liars. *Special*: No Means No (Emmy nom.). *Guest:* More than 62 appearances.

LOWE, PHILIP M.
Executive. b. New Rochelle, NY, May 9, 1944. e. Deerfield Acad., Harvard Coll., cum laude in psychology, 1966; Columbia Business Sch., 1968. Work experience includes major marketing positions at General Foods, Gillette, Gray Advertising, and Estee Lauder Cosmetics before co-founding Cinema Centers Corp. and Theatre Management Services in Boston. Pres. of Lowe Group of Companies (cable television, broadcasting, hotels, real estate and management consulting). Past pres. and chmn. of the bd; National Association of Concessionaires (NAC); past director, National Association of Theatre Owners (NATO). Professor of Marketing, Bentley Coll., Waltham, MA.; Contributing Editor; The Movie Business Book, Prentice-Hall, Inc. 1983.

LOWE, ROB
Actor. r.n. Robert Helper Lowe. b. Charlottesville, VA, Mar. 17, 1964. Brother is Chad Lowe. Raised in Dayton, OH. Started acting as child appearing in commercials, local tv spots, summer stock. Family moved to California when he was 13 yrs. old.
PICTURES: The Outsiders (debut, 1983), Class, The Hotel New Hampshire, Oxford Blues, St. Elmo's Fire, Youngblood, About Last Night..., Square Dance (Golden Globe nom. 1988), Home Is Where the Heart Is, Masquerade, Illegally Yours, Mulholland Falls, Bad Influence, Stroke of Midnight (If the Shoe Fits), Desert Shield, The Dark Backward, The Finest Hour, Wayne's World, Tommy Boy, For Hire, Contact, Hostile Intent, Crazy Six, The Specials, Austin Powers: The Spy Who Shagged Me, Statistics, Dead Silent, The Specials, Under Pressure, Proximity, Austin Powers: Goldmember, A View From the Top, Thank You for Smoking, The Invention of Lying.
TELEVISION: *Movies*: Thursday's Child (Golden Globe nom. 1984), Frank and Jesse (also co-prod.), First Degree, Desert's Edge (s.p. dir.), Outrage, Atomic Train, Jane Doe, Framed, The Lyon's Den, 'Salem's Lot, Perfect Strangers, A Perfect Day, The Christmas Blessing, Stir of Echoes: The Homecoming, Brothers & Sisters: Family Album, Too Late to Say Goodbye. *Mini-series*: Stephen King's The Stand, Beach Girls. *Series*: A New Kind of Family, The West Wing (Emmy nom. 2001, 2 Golden Globe noms.), The Lyon's Den, Dr. Vegas, Brothers & Sisters. *Specials*: A Matter of Time, Schoolboy Father, Suddenly Last Summer, On Dangerous Ground, Midnight Man. *Guest:* More than 106 appearances.

LOWRY, DICK
Director. b. Oklahoma City, OK, Sept. 15, 1944. e. U. of Oklahoma. Commercial photographer before being accepted by AFI. Dir. short film The Drought.
PICTURE: The Drought (also prod.), Piranha (2nd unit dir.), Smokey and the Bandit Part 3.
TELEVISION: *Movies*: OHMS, Kenny Rogers as the Gambler, The Jayne Mansfield Story, Angel Dusted, Coward of the County, A Few Days in Weasel Creek, Rascals and Robbers: The Secret Adventures of Tom Sawyer and Huck Finn, Missing Children—A Mother's Story, Living Proof: The Hank Williams Jr.Story, Kenny Rogers as the Gambler—The Adventure Continues (also prod.), Off Sides (Pigs Vs. Freaks), Wet Gold, The Toughest Man in the World, Murder with Mirrors, American Harvest, Kenny Rogers as The Gambler III (also co-exec. prod.), Case Closed, In the Line of Duty: The FBI Murders, Unconquered (also prod.), Howard Beach: Making the Case For Murder, Miracle Landing (also prod.), Archie: To Riverdale and Back, In the Line of Duty: A Cop for the Killing (also prod.), In the Line of Duty: Manhunt in the Dakotas (also prod.), A Woman Scorned: The Betty Broderick Story (also co-prod.), In the Line of Duty: Ambush in Waco (also prod.), In the Line of Duty: The Price of Vengeance, One More Mountain, A Horse for Danny, In The Line of Duty: Hunt for Justice (also prod.), Forgotten Sins, Project Alf, In The Line of Duty: Smoke Jumpers (also prod.), Last Stand at Saber River, Blaze of Glory (also prod.), Mr. Murder, Atomic Train, A Murder on Shadow Mountain, Y2K, Atilla, Follow the Stars Home, The Diamon of Jeru, Little John, Heart of a Stranger, Category 6: Day of Destruction, Category 7: The End of the World, Silver Bells. *Mini-series*: Dream West, Texas Justice, Dean Koontz's Mr. Murder. *Series*: Barnaby Jones, Buck Rogers in the 25th Century, Island Son, NYPD Blue, Crossing Jordan.

LOWRY, HUNT
Producer. b. Oklahoma City, OK, Aug. 21, 1954. e. Rollins Coll., & Wake Forest. Abandoned plans to study medicine to enter film-making industry; first job for New World Pictures where he met Jon Davison, with whom was later to co-produce. Next made TV commercials as prod. asst. and then producer. Left to go free-lance as commercials producer. 1980, appt. assoc. prod. to Davison on Airplane! Producer for Roserock Films.
PICTURES: Humanoids from the Deep, Get Crazy, Top Secret!, Revenge, Career Opportunities, Only the Lonely, Last of the Mohicans, Striking Distance, My Life, First Knight, A Time to Kill, Instinct, The Kid, Donnie Darko, A Walk to Remember, Welcome to Collinwood, Divine Secrets of the Ya-Ya Sisterhood, White Oleander, What a Girl Wants, Grind, The Heart of Me, Company Man, Casa de los babys, A Home at the End of the World, A Cinderella Story, Duma, Shorts (exec. prod.), A Pure Country Gift (exec. prod.).
TELEVISION: *Movies/exec. prod.:* Rascals and Robbers: The Secret Adventures of Tom Sawyer and Huckleberry Finn, Baja Oklahoma, His Mistress, Surviving, Wild Horses, Hounded. *Mini-series*: Dream West (prod.). *Series*: L.A. Models.

LUCAS, GEORGE
Producer, Director, Writer. b. Modesto, CA, May 14, 1944. e. USC, cinema. Made short film called THX-1138 and won National Student Film Festival Grand Prize, 1967. Signed contract with WB. Ass't. to Francis Ford Coppola on The Rain People, during which Lucas made 2-hr. documentary on filming of that feature entitled Filmmaker. Appeared as actor in film Beverly Hills Cop III. Novel: Shadow Moon (1995). Chairman, Lucasfilms, Industrial Light & Magic. 2009 received Art Directors Guild Award for Contribution to Cinematic Imagery.
PICTURES: *Director/Writer*: THX-1138, American Graffiti, Star Wars: Episode IV-A New Hope, Star Wars: Episode I-The Phantom Menace (also exec. prod.), Star Wars: Episode II-Attack of the Clones (also prod.), Star Wars: Episode III-Revenge of the Sith (also prod.). *Executive Producer:* More American Graffiti, Star Wars: Episode V-The Empire Strikes Back (also story), Raiders of the Lost Ark (also co-story), Star Wars: Episode VI-Return of the Jedi (also co-s.p., story), Twice Upon a Time, Indiana Jones and the Temple of Doom (also story), Mishima, Labyrinth, Howard the Duck, Willow (also story), Tucker: The Man and His Dream, The Land Before Time, Indiana Jones and the Last Crusade (also co-story), Radioland Murders (also story), Indiana Jones and the Lost Continent, Star Wars: Episode III - Revenge of the Sith (writer, dir.), Indiana Jones and the Kingdom of the Crystal Skull (writer & exec. prod.), Star Wars: The Clone Wars (also writer), Red Tails (also writer), Star Wars: Star Tours II (exec. prod.).
TELEVISION: *Exec. Prod.: Movies:* The Ewok Adventure, Ewoks: The Battle for Endor. *Series:* The Young Indiana Jones Chronicles (series), The Adventures of Young Indiana Jones Documentaries, The Clone Wars (also writer).

LUCCHESI, GARY
Executive, Producer. b. San Francisco, CA, 1955. e. UCLA. Entered industry as a trainee with the William Morris Agency, 1977. Joined Tri-Star, 1983, as vice pres. of production, became sr. vice pres., 1985. Joined Paramount Pictures as exec. vice pres., April 1987; pres. of motion picture production division, 1987-92. Pres. of the Really Useful Film Company, Inc., 1994-1998. President LakeShore Entertainment, Oct. 1998.
PICTURES: *Producer/Executive Producer:* Jennifer Eight, Three Wishes, Virtuosity, Primal Fear, Gotti, Runaway Bride, Passion of Mind, The Next Best Thing, Autumn in New York, The Gift, The Mothman Prophecies, The Human Stain, Underworld, Wicker Park, Suspect Zero, Million Dollar Baby, The Cave, Underworld: Evolution, Undiscovered, The Exorcism of Emily Rose, Aeon Flux, Piece of My Heart, The Last Kiss, The Dead Girl, Blood and Chocolate, Silent Star, American Pastoral, The Feast of Love, Game, Untraceable, Elegy, Underworld: Rise of the Lycans, Pathology, The Midnight Meat Train, Crank: High Voltage, The Ugly Truth, Fame, Citizen Gamer, Thundercade, The Lincoln Lawyer, I, Frankenstein.
TELEVISION: *Movies:* Breast Men, Gotti (Emmy nom. 1997), Cats, Vendetta, Wild Iris.

LUCCI, SUSAN
Actress. b. Scarsdale, NY, Feb. 23, 1948. e. Marymount Col. Was semifinalist in NY State Miss Universe Pageant. First professional job as "color girl" for CBS, sitting for cameras as new lighting system for color tv was developed. Had bit parts in films Me Natalie and Goodbye Columbus. Performed on 1983 album Love in the Afternoon.
PICTURES: Daddy You Kill Me, Young Doctors in Love (cameo).

TELEVISION: *Movies*: Invitation to Hell, Mafia Princess, Anastasia: The Story of Anna, Haunted By Her Past, Lady Mobster, The Bride in Black, The Woman Who Sinned, Double Edge, Between Love and Hate, French Silk, Seduced and Betrayed, Ebbie, Blood on Her Hands. *Series*: All My Children (1970-; Daytime Emmy 1999, 20 other noms.). *Guest:* More than 77 appearances.

LUDDY, TOM

Producer. e. U. of California at Berkeley where he operated student film societies and rep. cinemas. Entered industry via Brandon Films. 1972, prog. dir. and curator of Pacific Film Archives. 1979, joined Zoetrope Studios as dir. of special projects where dev. and supervised revival of Gance's Napoleon and Our Hitler—A Film From Germany. Coordinated Koyaanis-qatsi, Every Man For Himself, Passion. A founder, Telluride Film Fest.
PICTURES: Mishima (co-prod.), Tough Guys Don't Dance (co-exec. prod.), Barfly, King Lear (assoc. prod.), Manifesto (exec. prod.), Powwaqatsi (assoc. prod.), Wait Until Spring Bandini, Wind, The Secret Garden (co-prod.), My Family (exec. prod.), Cachao: Uno Mas (doc.).

LUFT, LORNA

Actress, Singer. b. Hollywood, CA, Nov. 21, 1952. Daughter of actress-singer Judy Garland and producer Sid Luft. Has sung in nightclubs. Appeared on 1990 recording of Girl Crazy.
THEATRE: *NY*: Judy Garland at Home at the Palace, Promises Promises, Snoopy, Extremities.
PICTURES: I Could Go on Singing (cameo), Grease 2, Where the Boys Are, 54.
TELEVISION: *Movies*: Fear Stalk, Life with Judy Garland: Me and My Shadows (Emmy nom. 2001). *Series*: Trapper John, M.D., Rick & Steve the Happiest Gay Couple in All the World (voice). *Guest*: More than 74 appearances.

LUHRMANN, BAZ

Director, Writer. r.n. Bazmark Luhrmann. b. New South Wales, Australia, Sept. 17, 1962. President of Bazmark Films.
PICTURES: *Dir./Writer.:* Strictly Ballroom, Romeo + Juliet (also prod., BAFTA Award, Best Direction, Best Adapted Screenplay, 1997), Moulin Rouge (Academy Award nom., BAFTA nom., AFI nom.; Golden Globe nom.; DGA nom.; WGA nom. 2002), Rent, Australia (also prod.). *Actor*: Winter of Our Dreams, The Dark Room.
TELEVISION: *Movie:* La Bohème. *Series:* A Country Practice (actor).

LUMET, SIDNEY

Director. b. Philadelphia, PA, June 25, 1924. e. Professional Children's Sch.; Columbia U. Child actor in plays: Dead End, George Washington Slept Here, My Heart's in the Highlands, and films: The 400 Million, One Third of a Nation. U.S. Armed Forces, WWII, 1942-46; dir. summer stock, 1947-49; taught acting, H.S. of Prof. Arts. Assoc. dir. CBS, 1950, dir. 1951. Appeared in documentary Listen Up: The Lives of Quincy Jones. *Author:* Making Movies (Alfred A. Knopf, 1995). 1981 WGA, Evelyn F. Burkey Award 1997. Received DGA Honorary Life Member Award 1989, DGA Lifetime Achievement Award 1993. 2005 received Academy Honorary Award.
PICTURES: 12 Angry Men (debut, 1957, Academy Award nom.; DGA nom.; Golden Globe nom. 1958), Stage Struck, That Kind of Woman, The Fugitive Kind, A View From the Bridge, Long Day's Journey Into Night (DGA nom. 1963), Fail-Safe, The Pawnbroker (DGA nom. 1963), The Hill, The Group, The Deadly Affair (also prod.), Bye Bye Braverman (also prod.), The Sea Gull (also prod.), The Appointment, The Last of the Mobile Hotshots (also prod.), King: A Filmed Record... Montgomery to Memphis (co-dir., prod.), The Anderson Tapes, Child's Play, The Offence, Serpico (DGA nom. 1974), Lovin' Molly, Murder on the Orient Express (DGA nom. 1975), Dog Day Afternoon (Academy Award nom.; DGA nom.; Golden Globe nom. 1976), Network (Academy Award nom.; DGA nom.; Golden Globe Award 1977), Equus, The Wiz, Just Tell Me What You Want (also co-prod.), Prince of the City (also co-s.p., Academy Award nom.; Golden Globe nom.; WGA nom. 1982), Deathtrap, The Verdict (Academy Award nom.; Golden Globe nom. 1983), Daniel (also co-exec. prod.), Garbo Talks, Power, The Morning After, Running on Empty (Golden Globe nom. 1989), Family Business, Q & A (also s.p.), A Stranger Among Us, Guilty As Sin, Night Falls On Manhattan (also s.p.), Critical Care, The Beautiful Mrs. Seidelmann, Gloria, Whistle, The Manchurian Candidate (actor only), The Set-Up, Find Me Guilty (also writer), Before the Devil Knows You're Dead, How to Change in 9 Weeks (consult.).
TELEVISION: *Movies*: Mr. Broadway, All the King's Men, The Iceman Cometh (Emmy Award 1960), Strip Search. *Series episodes:* Mama, Danger, You Are There, Omnibus, Best of Broadway, Alcoa, Goodyear Playhouse, Kraft Television Theatre (Mooney's Kid Don't Cry, The Last of My Gold Watches, This Property is Condemned), Playhouse 90, Play of the Week (The Dybbuk, Rashomon, 100 Centre Street. *Specials*: The Sacco and Vanzetti Story (Emmy nom. 1961), John Brown's Raid, Cry Vengeance.

LUNDGREN, DOLPH

Actor. r.n. Hans Lundren. b. Stockholm, Sweden, Nov. 3, 1959. e. Washington State U., won Fulbright to Massachusetts Inst. of Technology, Royal Inst. of Technology, Stockholm, M.S.C. Was doorman at Limelight disco in NY while studying acting. Full Contact Karate champion. Made workout video, Maximum Potential. On stage in Another Octopus.
PICTURES: A View to a Kill, Rocky IV, Masters of the Universe, Red Scorpion, The Punisher, I Come in Peace, Cover-Up, Showdown in Little Tokyo, Universal Soldier, Army of One, Pentathlon, Men of War, Johnny Mnemonic, The Shooter, The Algonquin Goodbye, The Peacekeeper, The Minion, Sweepers, Storm Catcher, Bridge of Dragons, Storm Catcher, Jill Rips, The Last Patrol, Captured, Hidden Agenda, Straight Blast, Alien Agent, Retrograde, The Defender (also dir.), The Inquiry, Diamond Dogs (also prod., writer), Missionary Man (writer, dir., prod.), Double or Nothing (actor, exec. prod., prod.), Command Performance (also dir., writer, s.p., soundtrack), Direct Contact (also prod.), Universal Soldier: Regeneration, Icarus (also dir.), The Expendables.
TELEVISION: *Movies*: John Woo's Blackjack, The Final Inquiry. *Guest:* More than 65 appearances.

LUPONE, PATTI

Actress. b. Northport, NY, Apr. 21, 1949. e. Julliard.
THEATRE: School for Scandal, Three Sisters, The Beggars Opera, The Robber Bridegroom, Meaure for Measure, Edward II, The Water Engine, Working, Evita (Tony Award, 1980), Oliver!, Anything Goes, Les Miserables (London, Won Olivier Award), Sunset Boulevard (London), Master Class, The Old Neighborhood, Patti Lupone: Coulda Woulda Shoulda (also co-wrote), Noises Off, Gypsy (Tony Award 2008).
PICTURES: 1941, Fighting Back, Witness, Wise Guys, Driving Miss Daisy, Family Prayers, Summer of Sam, State and Main, 24 Hour Woman, Bad Faith, Heist, The Victim, City by the Sea.
TELEVISION: *Movies*: LBJ: The Early Years, The Water Engine, The Song Spinner, Her Last Chance, Bonanno: A Godfather's Story, Monday Night Mayhem, Strip Search. *Series*: Life Goes On, Falcone, Oz. *Special*: Sweeney Todd: The Demon Barber of Fleet Street In Concert, Great Performances: Live from Lincoln Center. *Guest:* More than 55 appearances.

LURIE, JOHN

Composer, Actor. b. Worcester, MA, Dec. 14, 1952.
PICTURES: *Composer:* The Offenders, The Loveless, Permanent Vacation, Stranger than Paradise, Variety, City Limits, Down By Law, Mystery Train, On the Beautiful Blue Danube, Blue in the Face, Get Shorty, Manny & Lo, Excess Baggage, Lulu on the Bridge, Clay Pigeons, The Animal Factory, Atlantic City Serenade. *Actor*: The Offenders, Subway Rider, Permanent Vacation, Paris, Texas, Stranger than Paradise, Desperately Seeking Susan, Down by Law, The Last Temptation of Christ, The Little Devil, Wild at Heart, John Lurie and the Lounge Lizard Live in Berlin, Smoke, Blue in the Face, Just Your Luck, New Rose Hotel, Sleepwalk.
TELEVISION: *Movies*: Police Story: Monster Manor, Are You Comfortable?, Late Night with Conan O'Brien: 10th Anniversary Special. *Series*: Oz, Animal Cops: Detroit (doc.), Animal Cops - Houston (narr.).

LYLES, A. C.

Producer. b. Jacksonville, FL. May 17, 1918. e. Andrew Jackson H.S. Paramount Publix's Florida Theatre, 1928; interviewed Hollywood celebrities, Jacksonville Journal, 1932; mail boy, Paramount Studios, Hollywood, 1937; publicity dept., 1938; hd. of adv., publ. dept., Pine-Thomas unit at Paramount, 1940; assoc. prod., The Mountain. President, A. C. Lyles Productions, Inc. (Paramount Pictures). Retired.
PICTURES: Short Cut to Hell, Raymie, The Young and the Brave, Law of the Lawless, Stage to Thunder Rock, Young Fury, Black Spurs, Hostile Guns, Arizona Bushwackers, Town Tamer, Apache Uprising, Johnny Reno, Waco, Red Tomahawk, Fort Utah, Buckskin, Rogue's Gallery, Night of the Lepus, The Last Day, The Hunt for Red October (advisor #1).
TELEVISION: *Movies*: The Last Day, Flight to Holocaust. *Series*: Rawhide (assoc. prod.), Here's Boomer, Dear Mr. President, Conversations With the Presidents, Deadwood (consult.).

LYNCH, DAVID

Director, Writer. b. Missoula, MT, Jan. 20, 1946. e. Pennsylvania Acad. of Fine Arts, where received an independent filmmaker grant from America Film Institute. Made 16mm film, The Grandmother. Accepted by Center for Advanced Film Studies in Los Angeles, 1970. Wrote and directed Eraserhead (with partial AFI financing). Acted in films Zelly & Me, Nadja (also exec. prod.). Daughter is director Jennifer Lynch.
PICTURES: *Director-Writer*: Eraserhead (also prod., edit., prod.-design, f/x), The Elephant Man (2 Academy Award noms.; Golden Globe nom. DGA nom.; WGA nom. 1981), Dune, Blue Velvet (Academy Award nom.; Golden Globe nom.; WGA nom. 1987), Wild at Heart, Twin Peaks: Fire Walk With Me (also co-exec. prod., actor), Lost Highway, The Straight Story (also s.p.), Mulholland Drive (Academy Award nom. 2 Golden Globe noms.; 2002), Darkened Room (also exec. prod.), Cabin Fever (exec. prod. only), The Company (lyricist only), To Each His Own Cinema (segment dir.), Surveillance (exec. prod.), King Shot (exec. prod.), My Son, My Son, What Have Ye Done (exec.

prod.), Change Begins Within (exec. prod.).
TELEVISION: *Series*: Twin Peaks (dir., exec. prod., writer, 3 Emmy noms.; 2 Emmy noms. for pilot, 1990), On the Air (exec. prod., dir., writer), Mulholland Drive (also exec prod.), Interview Project (prod.), The Cleveland Show (actor). *Special*: Hotel Room (co-dir., co-exec. prod.).

LYNCH, JANE
Actress. b. Dolton, ILL, July 14, 1960.
PICTURES: Vice Versa, Straight Talk, The Fugitive, Fatal Instinct, What Planet Are You From?, Best in Show, Collateral Damage, A Mighty Wind, Sleepover, Lemony Snicket's A Series of Unfortunate Events, The 40 Year Old Virgin, Talladega Nights: The Ballad of Ricky Bobby, For Your Consideration, Eye of the Dolphin, Smiley Face, The Hammer, Alvin and the Chipmunks, Walk Hard: The Dewey Cox Story, Adventures of Power, Tru Loved, The Rocker, Space Chimps (voice), Role Models, Weather Girl, Ice Age: Dawn of the Dinosaurs (voice), Julie & Julia, Post Grad, Shrek Forever After (voice), Paul.
TELEVISION: *Movies:* In the Best Interest of the Children, The Big Time, Area 57, The Adventures of Captain Cross Dresser (voice), Mr. Troop Mom. *Series:* Judging Amy (also pilot), Family Guy (voice), 7th Heaven, MDs, Illeanarama, Lovespring International, Help Me Help You, American Dad! (voice), Boston Legal, Criminal Minds, The L Word, Two and a Half Men (Emmy nom. 2010 as guest), Party Down, Glee (Emmy Award, Golden Globe nom. 2010), many more series episodes.

LYNCH, KELLY
Actress. b. Minneapolis, MN, Jan. 31, 1959. Former model.
PICTURES: Osa, Bright Lights Big City, Cocktail, Road House,Warm Summer Rain, Drugstore Cowboy, Desperate Hours, Curly Sue, For Better and For Worse, Three of Hearts, Imaginary Crimes, The Beans of Egypt Maine, Virtuosity, White Man's Burden, Heaven's Prisoners, Persons Unknown, Cold Around the Heart, Mr. Magoo, Homegrown, Charlie's Angels, Joe Somebody, The Slaughter Rule, Searching for Debra Winger, (documentary), Dallas and Rusty, The Jacket, At Last, The Visitation, Normal Adolescent Behavior, The Perfect Age of Rock 'n' Roll, Kaboom, A Good Funeral, Passion Play.
TELEVISION: *Movies*: For Better and for Worse, Brotherhood of Murder, Something in Common, Homeless to Harvard: The Liz Murray Story, Cyber Seduction: His Secret Life, The Hunters. *Pilot*: San Berdoo. *Series:* The L Word, 90210 (2010).

LYNCH, PAUL M.
Director.
PICTURES: Hard Part Begins, Blood and Guts, Prom Night, Cross Country, Flying, Blindside, Bullies, Mania, Flying, Blindside, No Contest, No Contest II, More to Love, Frozen With Fear, The Keeper, Nightmare Carnival.
TELEVISION: *Movies*: Cameo By Night, Going to the Chapel, She Knows Too Much, Murder by Night, Drop Dead Gorgeous, Savage Planet, Sharpshooter (2nd unit dir.). *Series:* Voyagers, Blacke's Magic, Murder She Wrote, In the Heat of the Night, Tour of Duty, Beauty and the Beast, Twilight Zone (1987), Moonlighting, Star Trek: The Next Generation, Dark Shadows, Tour of Duty, Top Cops, Mike Hammer, Hooperman, Bronx Zoo, Land's End, Viper, Xena: Warrior Princess, F/X: The Series, Poltergeist: The Legacy, Sliders, So Weird, various other series episodes.

LYNCH, RICHARD
Actor. b. Brooklyn, NY, Feb. 12, 1940. Trained with Lee Strasberg at Carnegie Hall. In 1970 became lifetime member of the Actors Studio, NY.
THEATRE: *NY:* The Devils (On and Off-B'way debut), The Basic Training of Pavlo Hummel, Lion in Winter, The Orphan, Arturo-U, The Lady From the Sea, One Night Stands of a Noisy Passenger, Action, Richard III, Live Like Pigs, The Man with the Flower in His Mouth, A View from the Bridge.
PICTURES: Scarecrow (debut, 1973), The Seven Ups, The Delta Fox, The Premonition, Steel, Open Season, The Formula, The Sword and the Sorcerer, Little Nikita, Savage Dawn, Invasion U.S.A., Cut and Run, Night Force, The Barbarians, Bad Dreams, The Ninth Configuration, Melanie Rose (High Stakes), Spirit, Aftershock, Return to Justice, One Man Force, The Forbidden Dance, October 32nd, Alligator II: The Mutation, Double Threat, H.P. Lovecraft's Necromonicon, Scanner Cop, Crime & Punishment, Loving Deadly, Deathmatch, Midnight Confessions, Terrified, Takedown, Dragon Fury, Destination Vegas, Werewolf, Warrior of Justice, Diamond Run, Under Oath, Total Force, Ground Rules, Divine Lovers, Armstrong, Love and War II, Lone Tiger, Breaking the Silence, Strike Zone, Enemy Action, Eastside, Battlestar Galactica: The Second Coming, First Watch, Ancient Warriors, Outta Time, Lewisburg, Luger of the Black Sun, Halloween, Laid to Rest, Lewisburg, Roney's Point, Gun of the Black Sun.
TELEVISION: *Movies*: Starsky and Hutch (pilot), Roger & Harry: The Mitera Target, Good Against Evil, Dog and Cat, Vampire, Alcatraz—The Whole Shocking Story, Sizzle, White Water Rebels, The Last Ninja. *Mini-series*: Noi siamo angeli, Thinking About Africa. *Series*: Battlestar Gallactica, The Phoenix, The Korean War. *Guest:* More than 81 appearances.

LYNE, ADRIAN
Director. b. Peterborough, England, March 4, 1941. Started as director of commercials. Owner of Victor Lyndon Productions.
PICTURES: Foxes, Flashdance, Nine 1/2 Weeks, Fatal Attraction (Academy Award nom.; DGA nom.; Golden Globe nom. 1988), Jacob's Ladder, Indecent Proposal, Lolita, Unfaithful, Two Minutes to Midnight.

LYNLEY, CAROL
Actress. b. New York, NY, Feb. 13, 1942. Was model as teenager. Golden Globe nom. 1959, Most Promising Newcomer.
PICTURES: The Light in the Forest (debut, 1958), Holiday for Lovers, Blue Denim, Hound-Dog Man, Return to Peyton Place, The Last Sunset, The Stripper, Under the Yum-Yum Tree, The Cardinal, The Pleasure Seekers, Shock Treatment, Harlow, Bunny Lake Is Missing, The Shuttered Room, Danger Route, Once You Kiss a Stranger, The Maltese Bippy, Norwood, Beware the Blob!, The Poseidon Adventure, Cotter, The Four Deuces, The Washington Affair, The Cat and the Canary, The Shape of Things to Come, Vigilante, Dark Tower, Blackout, Howling VI: The Freaks, Neon Signs, Off the Menu: The Last Days of Chasen's, Vic, Drowning on Dry Land, A Light in the Forest.
TELEVISION: *Movies*: Shadow on the Land, The Smugglers, The Immortal (pilot), Weekend of Terror, The Cable Car Murder, The Night Stalker, The Elevator, Death Stalk, Willow B, Women in Prison, Flood, Fantasy Island, Having Babies II, Cops and Robin, The Beasts Are on the Streets, In Possession, Best of Friends. *Series*: The Immortal, Another World. *Guest:* More than 84 appearances.

LYNN, JONATHAN
Director, Writer, Actor. b. Bath, England, Apr. 3, 1943. Was artistic dir. of Cambridge Theatre Company, 1976-81; Company Director of Natl. Theatre, 1987. Playwright: Pig of the Month. Books: A Proper Man, The Complete Yes Prime Minister, Mayday. Appeared as actor in Into the Night, Three Men and a Little Lady. Currently Producer for The Lynn Company.
PICTURES: The Internecine Project (s.p.). Director: Clue (also s.p.), Nuns on the Run (also s.p.), My Cousin Vinny, The Distinguished Gentleman, Greedy (also actor), Sgt. Bilko, Trial and Error (also prod.), The Whole Nine Yards, The Fighting Temptations, Vanity Fair (exec. prod.), He's Such a Girl (also exec. prod.), Wild Target (dir.).
TELEVISION: *Movies: Actor:* Bar Mitzvah Boy, Pleasure at Her Majesty's, Dinner at the Sporting Club, The Knowledge, Outside Edge, Suspicion, Life After Life. *Mini-series:* Diana (actor). *Series: Actor:* Twice a Fortnight, The Liver Birds, Doctor in the House, Turnbull's Finest Half-Hour, *As Writer:* On the Buses, Doctor at Large, Romany Jones, Doctor in Charge, Doctor at Sea, Doctor on the Go, My Name is Harry Worth, My Brother's Keeper (also actor), Yes, Minister (also creator), Yes, Prime Minister (also creator), Ferris Bueller (pilot), Life After Life.

LYNNE, MICHAEL
Executive. e. undergraduate degree, English literature, Brooklyn College, 1961. J.D. degree, Columbia Law School, 1964. Member of the New York Bar. Lynne was a partner for 20 years with Blumenthal & Lynne, specializing in entertainment law. He also worked with Barovick & Konecky, an entertainment law firm, and as resident counsel for Embassy Pictures. He then founded New Line Cinema Corporation in 1967 with Bob Shaye, a fellow classmate at Columbia Law School. Lynne, together with Shaye, was an executive producer of New Line's The Lord of the Rings trilogy, of which the final installment, The Return of the King, was the winner of 11 Academy Awards, including Best Picture, tying the record for most wins ever. On Feb. 28, 2008, Warner Bros. Pictures, A Time Warner Company, announced New Line Cinema would be absorbed into the Warner Bros. organization. With this reorganization, company co-chairmen and co-CEOs Shay and Lynne, departed the company. Lynne resigned in 2008. Serves as a trustee for Vornado Realty Trust (VNO) since 2005.

LYNTON, MICHAEL
Executive. Raised in the Netherlands. e. Harvard Business College and Harvard Business School. With a background in mergers and acquisitions from 1982-1985 with Credit Suisse First Boston in New York, London and Melbourne, Lynton entered the ent. industry when he joined Disney in 1987. Serving as pres., Lynton started and built Disney Publishing. From 1992-1996, Lynton served as pres. of Hollywood Pictures, a Disney division. He joined Time Warner from the international media company Pearson PLC, where he served as chmn. and CEO of Pearson's Penguin Group from 1996-2000. He led the turnaround of Penguin's global publishing operations, oversaw the successful acquisition and integration of Putnam, Inc., and extended the Penguin brand to music and the Internet. Lynton became chmn. and CEO of Sony Pictures Entertainment (SPE) in Jan. 2004. Lynton manages SPE's overall global operations, which include motion picture, television and digital content production and distribution, worldwide television channel investments and the development of new entertainment products, services and technologies. He reports directly to Howard Stringer, chmn. and CEO of Sony Corporation of America, and vice chmn., Sony Corporation.

LYONNE, NATASHA
Actress. r.n. Natasha Braunstein. b. NY, April 4, 1979.
PICTURES: Heartburn (debut, 1986), Dennis the Menace, Everyone Says I Love You, Slums of Beverly Hills, Krippendorf's Tribe, Modern Vampyres, Freeway II: Confessions of a Trickbaby, Detroit Rock City, But I'm a Cheerleader, American Pie, the Auteur Theory, When Autumn Leaves, Rat Girl, Plan B, Scary Movie 2, American Pie 2, The Grey Zone, Kate & Leopold, Zigzag, Night at the Golden Eagle, Fast Sofa, Comic Book Villains, Party Monster, Blade: Trinity, Robots (voice), Jelly, Outrage, Goyband, All About Evil, Night Club.
TELEVISION: *Movies/Specials*: If These Walls Could Talk 2, Old School, Loving Leah. *Series*: Pee-Wee's Playhouse.

LYONS, S. DANIEL
Executive. b. Toronto, Canada, Sept., 9, 1955. e. Brandeis Univ., B.A. magna cum laude 1977. Univ. of Toronto, LL.B. 1981. 1985, joined Astral Films as a lawyer. Promoted to dir. of bus. affairs, then v.p., Dist. for the Astral Entertainment Group. 1997, became v.p., Dist & Mktg., Coscient/Astral Dist. Author of: Public Strategy and Motion Pictures, and Showman (play, Cubiculo Theatre, NY).

M

MAATTA, JOHN
Executive. b. San Francisco, CA, Jan. 24, 1952. e. Undergraduate, Univ. of San Francisco, 1974. Law degree from Hastings College of Law, University of California, 1977. Began career as a trial lawyer with Lazzarini & Sheldon, Herron & Herron in San Francisco, 1978-86; moved to entertainment industry with Lorimar Telepictures, becoming the company's legal counsel, 1986-87; became v.p., business affairs, for Telepictures NIWS Division, 1988-91; With the Warner Bros. purchase of Lorimar, Maatta joined Warner Bros. as a legal counsel, 1991-93; became v.p., senior attorney, 1993-95; became one of the first employees for the The WB Television Network as its head of legal, 1995-97; then senior v.p., general counsel, 1997-2001; executive v.p., general counsel, 2001-05. In Jan. 2006, Maatta came on board as one of the first employees of new broadcast network, The CW, which combined programming and staff from the two networks shutting down in 2006: The WB and UPN. The CW is jointly owned and operated by CBS Corporation and Warner Bros., a Time Warner company. Maatta assumed his current role as COO & general counsel in Jan. 2006. The CW began broadcasting in mid-September 2006.

MACARTHUR, JAMES
Actor. b. Los Angeles, CA, Dec. 8, 1937. e. Harvard. Adopted son of actress Helen Hayes and writer Charles MacArthur. Stage debut, summer stock; The Corn Is Green, Life with Father.
PICTURES: The Young Stranger (debut, 1957), The Light in the Forest, Third Man on the Mountain, Kidnapped, Swiss Family Robinson, The Interns, Spencer's Mountain, Cry of Battle, The Truth About Spring, The Battle of the Bulge, The Bedford Incident, Ride Beyond Vengeance, The Love-Ins, Hang 'em High, The Angry Breed, JFK.
TELEVISION: *Movies*: Alcatraz—The Whole Shocking Story, The Night the Bridge Fell Down, Storm Chasers: Revenge of the Twister. *Series*: Hawaii Five-0.
Special: Willie and the Yank (Mosby's Marauders).

MACCHIO, RALPH
Actor. b. Long Island, NY, Nov. 4, 1962. Started in TV commercials at age 16 before winning role in series Eight Is Enough. Broadway debut in Cuba and His Teddy Bear, 1986; Off-B'way in Only Kidding.
PICTURES: Up the Academy (debut, 1980), The Outsiders, The Karate Kid, Teachers, Crossroads, The Karate Kid Part II, Distant Thunder, The Karate Kid Part III, Too Much Sun, My Cousin Vinny, Naked in New York, Dizzyland, Can't be Heaven, Popcorn Shrimp, The Office Party, A Good Night to Die, Beer League, Rosencrantz and Guildenstern Are Undead.
TELEVISION: *Movies*: Journey to Survival, Dangerous Company, The Three Wishes of Billy Grier, Garwood: Prisoner of War. *Series*: Eight Is Enough, Ugly Betty.

MACCORKINDALE, SIMON
Actor, Producer, Director, Writer. b. Isle-of-Ely, England, Feb. 2, 1952. m. actress Susan George. On stage in Dark Lady of the Sonnets, Pygmalion, French Without Tears, etc.
PICTURES: *Actor*: Death on the Nile, Quatermass Conclusion, Caboblanco, Robbers of the Sacred Mountain, The Sword and the Sorcerer, Jaws 3-D, The Riddle of the Sands, Sincerely Violet, The Dinosaur Hunter, Wing Commander: Space Will Never Be the Same, 13Hrs, A Closed Book. *Producer*: Stealing Heaven, That Summer of White Roses (also co-s.p.), The House That Mary Bought (also dir., co-s.p.), Such a Long Journey.
TELEVISION: *Movies*: Falcon's Gold, Twist of Fate, Obsessive Love, No Greater Love, At The Midnight Hour, A Family of Cops, While My Pretty One Sleeps, The Sands of Eden, Water War, Running Wild, The Girl Next Door, Casualty @ Holby City. *Mini-series:* Pursuit, The Way to Dusty Death, Jesus of Nazareth, The Manions of America, *Series:* The Doombolt Chase, Quatermass, Manimal, Falcon Crest, Counterstrike, Casualty, Casualty @ Holby City. *Specials:* I Claudius, Romeo and Juliet, Quatermass. *Series Prod.:* The Relic Hunter (also co-exec. prod.), Queen of Swords, Adventure Inc. *Guest:* More than 62 appearances.

MACCURDY, JEAN
Executive. Began career in the Children's Prog. dept., NBC TV network. Joined Warner Bros. Cartoons in 1979, as dir. of Animation and Prog.; named v.p. & gen. mngr, WB Cartoons & served as production exec., 1982. Named v.p., Children's Prog., 1983. Served as Production assist. for Marvel Production, and Hanna-Barbera. Returned to WB Animation as v.p. & gen. mgr., 1988; named sr. v.p. & gen. mgr., 1991; became first pres., WB TV Animation, 1992. In April 2001, stepped down as pres. and became creative consultant to the studio. Animated TV series created and produced under her guidance have earned 28 Emmy Awards, The George Foster Peabody Award, an Environmental Media Award and numerous Annie Awards, which honor excellence in animation.

MACDOWELL, ANDIE
Actress. r.n. Rose Anderson MacDowell. b. Gaffney, SC, April 21, 1958. Started as model for Elite Agency in NY appearing for L'Oreal Cosmetics, The Gap, Calvin Klein.
PICTURES: Greystoke: The Legend of Tarzan Lord of the Apes (debut, 1984), St. Elmo's Fire, Sex Lies and Videotape (L.A. Film Critics Award, 1989), Green Card, The Object of Beauty, Hudson Hawk, The Player, Groundhog Day, Short Cuts, Deception, Four Weddings and a Funeral, Bad Girls, Unstrung Heroes, Michael, Multiplicity, The End of Violence, Shadrach, Just the Ticket (also exec. prod.), Muppets from Space, The Muse, Reaching Normal, Harrison's Flowers, Ginostra, Town & Country, Crush, The Last Sign, Tara Road, Beauty Shop, Barnyard (voice), Intervention, Inconceivable, Happiness Runs, Daydream Nation, The 5th Quarter, Monte Carlo.
TELEVISION: *Movies*: Women and Men 2: In Love There Are No Rules, On the Edge, Dinner with Friends, Jo, Riding the Bus with My Sister, The Prince of Motor City, At Risk, The Front. *Mini-series (Italy)*: Sahara's Secret. *Series:* Insatiable. *Guest:* More than 58 appearances.

MACFARLANE, SETH
Actor, Writer, Producer. b. Kent, CT, October 26, 1973. e. Rhode Island School of Design.
PICTURES: Hellboy II: The Golden Army (voice), Tooth Fairy, The Drawn Together Movie: The Movie! (voice).
TELEVISION: *Series:* Jungle Cubs (writer), Ace Ventura: Pet Detective (writer), The Cleveland Show (voices, writer, creator, exec. prod.), Johnny Bravo (storyboard artist, writer), Dexter's Laboratory (storyboard artist, writer), Robot Chicken (voices), Crank Yankers (voices), Family Guy (voices, writer, creator, 2 Emmy Awards, 7 toher noms.), American Dad! (voices, writer, creator, exec. prod., Emmy nom. 2009). *Guest:* More than 40 appearances.

MACGILLIVRAY, GREG
Executive, Cinematographer, Director, Producer. President & co-founder, MacGillivray Freeman Films, which specializes in large format documentary films, 1965-present. He was nominated for an Academy Award for Best Documentary Short Subject for The Living Sea in 1995 and again in 2000 for Dolphins. The Library of Congress also selected the company's first IMAX theatre classic, To Fly!, for inclusion in America's film archives. To Fly! is the first large format film to be included in the archives. In 2002, MacGillivray was honored as one of the five most important contributors to the success of the large format industry over the last 25 years. Also in 2002, MacGillivray accepted the Bradford Washburn Award, the highest honor bestowed by Boston's Museum of Science, for his contribution for science education.
PICTURES: *Cinematographer:* Follow Me (doc.), Sky Riders (also aerial action director & s.p.), Speed (doc. short; also dir. and prod.), Island Child (documentary), Race the Wind (doc. short; also dir. & prod.), The Magic of Flight (doc. short; also dir. & prod.), Dolphins (doc. short; also dir. & prod., Academy Award nom. 2001, IDA nom. 2000), Adventures in the Wild (doc. short; also dir. & prod.), Journey Into Amazing Caves (doc. short; also dir. & prod.). *Director:* To Fly! (doc. short; also prod. & writer), To the Limit (doc. short; also prod.), At Sea (doc., also prod.), The Discoverers (short; also prod.), The Living Sea (doc. short; also prod., Academy Award nom. 1996), Stormchasers (doc. short; also prod.), Everest (doc. short; also prod. & additional camera operator), Coral Reef Adventure (doc. short; also prod.) Top Speed (doc. short; also prod.), Greece: Secrets of the Past (doc. short; also writer), Hurricane on the Bayou (doc.), Water Planet: Grand Canyon Adventure (also prod. doc.), Grand Canyon Adventure: River at Risk (also prod.), MacGillivray Freeman's Arabia (doc. short, also prod.), Hollywood Don't Surf! (doc. short). *Producer:* Mystery of the Nile (doc.), The Alps: Giants of Nature (doc.).

MACLACHLAN, KYLE
Actor. b. Yakima, WA, Feb. 22, 1959. e. Univ. of WA. Acted in high school and college, then in summer stock. Joined Oregon Shakespeare Festival (Romeo and Juliet, Julius Caesar, Henry V). Cast as lead in Dune by dir. David Lynch in a nationwide search.
THEATRE: NY: Palace of Amateurs (Off-B'way).
PICTURES: Dune (debut, 1984), Blue Velvet, The Hidden, Don't Tell Her It's Me, The Doors, Twin Peaks: Fire Walk With Me, Where the Day Takes You, Rich in Love, The Trial, The Flintstones, Showgirls, Trigger Effect, Mad Dog Time, One Night Stand, Hamlet, Timecode, XChange, Perfume, Me Without You, Miranda, Northfork, Touch of Pink, Free Jimmy (voice), The Sisterhood of the Traveling Pants 2, Manure, Mao's Last Dancer.
TELEVISION: *Movies*: Dream Breakers, Twin Peaks (pilot, Emmy nom. 1990), Against the Wall, Roswell, Windsor Protocol, Moonshine Highway, Thunder Point, Route 9, The Invisible Man, The Spring, The Librarian: Quest for the Spear, Mysterious Island, Lost Survivor Guide (narr.), Lost: The Answers (narr.). *Series*: Twin Peaks (Emmy nom.; Golden Globe nom. 1991), Sex and the City (recurring role 2000-2002), In Justice, Desperate Housewives. *Guest:* More than 74 appearances.

MACLAINE, SHIRLEY
Actress. r.n. Shirley MacLean Beaty. b. Richmond, VA, April 24, 1934. Brother is actor-prod. Warren Beatty. e. Washington and Lee H.S., Arlington, VA. Started as dancer; on B'way as understudy for Carol Haney in The Pajama Game, which resulted in contract with film prod. Hal Wallis. Prod., writer and co- dir. of Oscar-nominated film documentary: The Other Half of The Sky: A China Memoir. Returned to stage in Gypsy in My Soul, Shirley MacLaine on Broadway. Videos: Shirley MacLaine's Inner Workout, Relaxing Within. Received Golden Globe Newcomer Award 1955 also Won Special Award for most versatile actress 1959, another Golden Globe Award 1998; Cecil B. DeMille Award.
AUTHOR: Don't Fall off the Mountain, You Can Get There from Here, Out on a Limb, Dancing in the Light, It's All In the Playing, Going Within, Dance While You Can, My Lucky Stars. *Editor*: McGovern: The Man and His Beliefs (1972).
PICTURES: The Trouble With Harry (debut, 1955), Artists and Models, Around the World in 80 Days, Stranger with a Gun (aka The Sheepman), The Matchmaker, Hot Spell, Some Came Running (Academy Award nom.; Golden Globe nom. 1959), Ask Any Girl (Golden Globe nom. 1960), Career, Can-Can, The Apartment (Academy Award nom.; Golden Globe Award 1961), Ocean's Eleven (cameo), All in a Night's Work, Two Loves, My Geisha, The Children's Hour (Golden Globe nom. 1962), Two for the Seesaw, Irma La Douce (Academy Award nom.; Golden Globe Award 1964), What a Way to Go!, John Goldfarb Please Come Home, The Yellow Rolls Royce, Gambit (Golden Globe nom. 1967), Woman Times Seven (Golden Globe nom. 1968), The Bliss of Mrs. Blossom, Sweet Charity (Golden Globe nom. 1970), Two Mules for Sister Sara, Desperate Characters, The Possession of Joel Delaney, The Turning Point (Academy Award nom. 1978), Being There (Golden Globe nom. 1980), Loving Couples, A Change of Seasons, Terms of Endearment (Academy Award, Best Actress in Leading Role, Golden Globe Award 1984), Cannonball Run II, Madame Sousatzka (Golden Globe Award 1989), Steel Magnolias, Postcards From the Edge (Golden Globe nom. 1991), Waiting for the Light, Defending Your Life (cameo), Used People (Golden Globe nom. 1993), Wrestling Ernest Hemingway, Guarding Tess (Golden Globe nom. 1995), Mrs. Winterbourne, The Celluloid Closet (documentary), Evening Star, A Smile Like Yours (cameo), Kingdom Come (writer only), Looking for Lulu (documentary, narrator), Get Bruce (documentary), The Dress Code (aka Bruno; also dir.), Carolina, Broadway: The Golden Age by the Legends Who Were There (documentary), Bewitched, In Her Shoes (Golden Globe nom. 2006), Rumor Has It..., Closing the Ring, Valentine's Day, Anyone's Son, Egg Scape.
TELEVISION: *Movies*: Out on a Limb (also co-writer, Golden Globe nom. 1988), The West Side Waltz, Joan of Arc, These Old Broads, Hell on Heels: The Battle of Mary Kay (Golden Globe nom. 2003), Salem Witch Trials, Anne of Green Gables: A New Beginning. *Mini-series:* Coco Chanel (Emmy nom.; Golden Globe nom. 2009). *Series*: Shirley's World. *Documentaries/Specials:* The Other Half of the Sky: A China Memoir (also prod., co-writer, Academy Award nom. 1976), If They Could See Me Now (Emmy nom. 1975), Gypsy in My Soul (Emmy Award 1976) Where Do We Go From Here? (Emmy nom. 1977), Shirley MacLaine at the Lido (Emmy nom. 1979), Every Little Movement (Emmy Award for co-writing, 1980), Illusions, The Shirley MacLaine Show. *Guest:* More than 200 appearances.

MACLEOD, GAVIN
Actor. b. Mt. Kisco, NY, Feb. 28, 1930. e. Ithaca College.
PICTURES: I Want to Live, Compulsion, Pork Chop Hill, Operation Petticoat, Twelve Hours to Kill, High Time, The Crimebusters, War Hunt, McHale's Navy, The Sword of Ali Baba, McHale's Navy Joins the Air Force, The Sand Pebbles, Deathwatch, The Party, A Man Called Gannon, The Thousand Plane Raid, Billy Bright (1st dir. only), Kelly's Heroes, Time Changer, The Secrets of Jonathan Sperry.
TELEVISION: *Movies*: The Intruders, Only with Married Men, Ransom for Alice, Murder Can Hurt You, Student Exchange, The Love Boat: The Valentine Voyage, The Last Act Is A Solo, If I Die Before I Wake. *Mini-series*: Scruples. *Series*: McHale's Navy, The Mary Tyler Moore Show (2 Golden Globe noms.), The Love Boat (3 Golden Globe noms.), The King of Queens, Oz. *Guest:* More than 128 appearances.

MACMILLAN, MICHAEL
Executive. b. Scarborough, Ontario, Canada, 1956. e. B.A. in Honours Film Studies from Queen's Univ. in Kingston, Ontario. Co-founded and served as first cinematographer for Toronto-based Atlantis Films Ltd.,1978; Company later became Atlantis Communications Inc. In 1998, Atlantis Communications Inc. merged with Alliance Communications Corporation became Alliance Atlantis, where MacMillan served as exec. chairman and CEO. Currently is exec. chmn. Under MacMillan's leadership, the company operates 13 Canadian specialty television networks; co-owns and produces the TV hit CSI franchise and holds a 51% limited partnership in Motion Picture Distribution L.P., Canada's leading film distributor. 2007, he sold Alliance Atlantis. Co-founder and chmn. of Samara, which focuses on public services, political leadership and the media's contribution to public affairs. He is currently on the board of directors of the Canadian Stage Co., Toronto East General Hospital Foundation and The Canadian Film and Television Production Assn. He also is vice-chair Canadian Film Centre.

MACNICOL PETER
Actor. b. Dallas, TX, April 10, 1954. e. U. of Minnesota.
THEATRE: Manhattan Theatre Club: Crimes of the Heart. NY Shakespeare Fest: Found a Peanut, Rum and Coke, Twelfth Night, Richard II, Romeo & Juliet. Regional theatre includes Guthrie, Alaska Rep., Long Wharf, Dallas Theatre Center, Trinity Rep. B'way: Crimes of the Heart (Theatre World Award), The Nerd, Black Comedy/White Liars.
PICTURES: Dragonslayer (debut, 1981), Sophie's Choice, Heat, Ghostbusters II, American Blue Note, Hard Promises, Housesitter, Addams Family Values, Radioland Murders, Dracula: Dead and Loving It, Mojave Moon, Bean, Baby Geniuses, Recess: School's Out (voice), Balto II: Wolf Quest (voice), Breakin' All the Rules.
TELEVISION: *Movies*: Johnny Bull, By Dawn's Early Light, Roswell, Olive the Other Reindeer (voice), Abducted: A Father's Love, Silencing Mary, The Ponder Heart, Crazy Love. *Series*: Powers That Be, Chicago Hope, Ally McBeal (SAG award for outstanding ensemble peformance in Comedy Series, 1999; and Emmy, Supporting Actor in Comedy Series, 2001, 2 other Emmy noms.), Ally (also dir.), Boston Public (dir. only), This Just In (voice), Numb3rs, 24, The Spectacular Spider-Man. *Guest:* More than 46 appearances.

MACY, WILLIAM H.
Actor. b. Miami, FL, March 13, 1950. e. Goddard Col. m. actress Felicity Huffman.
THEATRE: *NY:* The Man in 605 (debut, 1980), Twelfth Night, Beaurecrat, A Call From the East, The Dining Room, Speakeasy, Wild Life, Flirtations, Baby With the Bathwater, The Nice and the Nasty, Bodies Rest and Motion, Oh Hell!, Life During Wartime, Mr. Gogol and Mr. Preen, Oleanna, Our Town (B'way).
PICTURES: Without a Trace, The Last Dragon, Radio Days, House of Games, Things Change, Homicide, Shadows and Fog, Benny and Joon, Searching for Bobby Fischer, The Client, Oleanna, Murder in the First, Mr. Holland's Opus, Down Periscope, Fargo (Academy Award nom. 1997), Ghosts of Mississippi, Boogie Nights, Air Force One, Wag the Dog, Pleasantville, Jerry & Tom, A Civil Action, Psycho, Mystery Men, Happy Texas, Magnolia, State and Maine, Panic, Jurassic Park III, Focus, Welcome to Collinwood, The Cooler, Stealing Sinatra, Seabiscuit (Golden Globe nom. 2004), Minnesota Nice (video short), Spartan, In Enemy Hands, Cellular, Transamerica (exec. prod. only), Sahara, Edmond, Yankee Irving (voice), Bobby, A Hole in the Earth (also prod.), Conquistadora, Everyone's Hero (voice), Wild Hogs, He Was a Quiet Man, Keep Coming Back (also dir.), The Deal (also writer/s.p.), Bart Got a Room, Hurricane Mary, Antique, The Maiden Heist (also prod.), The Tale of Despereaux (voice), Shorts, Marmaduke, Come Back to Sorrento, Keep Coming Back (also dir.), The Lincoln Lawyer, Dirty Girl, A Single Shot.
TELEVISION: *Movies:* In the Shadow of Evil, Andersonville, The Writing on the Wall, The Con (also writer), The Murder of Mary Phagan, Texan, A Murderous Affair, The Water Engine, Heart of Justice, A Private Matter, The Con, A Slight Case of Murder (Emmy nom. 2000), Night of the Headless Horseman (voice), Door to Door (also writer, 2 Emmy Awards, WGA nom. 2003), Just A Walk in the Park (writer only), Stealing Sinatra (Emmy nom. 2004) It's a Very Merry Muppet Christmas Movie, Reversible Errors, The Wool Cap (also writer, 2 Emmy noms.; Golden Globe nom.; WGA nom. 2005), Nightmares and Dreamscapes: From the Stories of Stephen King (Emmy nom. 2007), Family Man, Shameless (pilot). *Mini-series:* The Awakening Land, Out of Order. *Series:* ER (Emmy nom. 1997), The Lionhearts (voice), Sports Night (recurring role, Emmy nom. 2000), Curious George (narr.). *Guest:* More than 127 appearances.

MADDEN, BILL
Executive. b. New York, NY, March 1, 1915. e. Boston U. Joined Metro-Goldwyn-Mayer as office boy, 1930; student salesman,

1938; asst. Eastern div. sales mgr., 1939; U.S. Navy, 1942-46; Boston sales rep., MGM, 1947-53; Philadelphia branch mgr., 1954-59; Midwest div. sales mgr., 1960-68; roadshow sales mgr., 1969; v.p., gen. sales mgr., 1969-74, MGM; corp., v.p. & gen. sls. mgr., MGM, 1974; retired from MGM, 1975; 1976-? has been, exec. consultant to motion picture industry; lecturer and instructor at UCLA. Member: AMPAS, Motion Picture Associates, American Film Institute, Motion Picture Pioneers.

MADDEN, DAVID
Executive, Producer, Director. b. Chicago, IL, July 25, 1955. e. Harvard U., 1976; UCLA, M.A., 1978. Joined 20th Century-Fox in 1978 as story analyst. Named story editor, 1980; exec. story edi tor, 1982. Appointed v.p., creative affairs for 20th-Fox Prods., 1983; v.p., prod., 20th Century-Fox Prods; 1984, v.p., prod., Paramount Pictures. In 1987, joined Interscope Commun. as prod. Formed Cort Madden Co. at Paramount with Robert Cort in 1996. Joined Fox Television Studios in 2000 and in June 2007 renewed his contract as executive v.p. of Scripted Programming He is responsible for helping Fox Studios land three series on major cable networks in 2007 – The Riches on FX, Burn Notice on USA Network and Saving Grace on TNT.
PICTURES: *Director:* Separate Lives. *Producer:* Renegades, Blind Fury (exec. prod.), The First Power, Eve of Destruction, Jersey Girl, The Hand That Rocks the Cradle, Holy Matrimony, Operation Dumbo Drop, The Tie That Binds, The Associate (exec. prod.), Odd Couple II, The Out-of-Towners, Runaway Bride (exec. prod.), Save the Last Dance, Against the Ropes, Steppin' Up.
TELEVISION: *Movies*: *Director:* A Part of the Family (also writer). *Exec. Prod:* Body Language, In the Company of Spies (prod. only), Harlan County War, L.A. Law: The Movie, The Rats, Home Alone 4, Something the Lord Made (Emmy Award 2004), Knights of South Bronx, Iris Expanding.

MADDEN, JOHN
Director. b. Portsmouth, Hampshire, England. April 8, 1949.
PICTURES: Ethan Frome, Golden Gate, Her Majesty Mrs. Brown, Shakespeare in Love (Academy Award nom.; DGA nom.; Golden Globe nom. 1999), Captain Corelli's Mandolin, Proof, Killshot, The Debt.
TELEVISION: *Movies:* Grown-ups, A Wreath of Roses, The Widowmaker, The Storyteller: Greek Myths, Meat, Prime Suspect 4: The Lost Child, Truth or Dare. *Series:* The Return of Sherlock Holmes, Inspector Morse, The Casebook of Sherlock Holmes.

MADDIN, GUY
Director, Writer, Editor, Cinematographer. b. Winnipeg, Canada, Feb. 28, 1956.
PICTURES: *Director/Writer/Editor/Cinematographer:* Tales from the Gimli Hospital, Mauve Decade, BBB (documentary short), Tyro, Archangel (also art dir.), Indigo High-Hatters, Careful (also production designer, sound editor), Sissy Boy Slap Party, Imperial Orgies (short), Maldoror:Tygers (short), The Hoyden (short), Hospital Fragment (also prod.), The Heart of the World, Fleshpots of Antiquity (short), A Trip to the Orphanage (short), Sombra dolorosa (short), Death of the Reel. *Director:* The Dead Father (short; also writer, editor, prod.), The Pomps of Satan (also writer, editor), Sea Beggars (also writer & editor), Odilon Redon of The Eye Like a Strange Balloon Mounts Toward Infinity (short; also writer), The Hands of Ida, Twilight of the Ice Nymphs, The Cock Crew (also writer & editor), Dracula: Pages from a Virgin's Diary (also photographer), Cowards Bend the Knee (also cinematographer & writer), The Saddest Music in the World (also s.p.), The Brand Upon the Brain (also writer), Os Invisíveis.
TELEVISION: *Documentaries/Specials:* Fancy Fancy Being Rich (short; dir. & cinematographer).

MADIGAN, AMY
Actress. b. Chicago, IL, Sept. 11, 1950. m. actor Ed Harris. For 10 years traveled country performing in bars and clubs with band. Then studied at Lee Strasberg Inst., L.A. NY Stage: The Lucky Spot (Theatre World Award), A Streetcar Named Desire.
PICTURES: Love Child (debut, 1982, Golden Globe nom. 1983), Love Letters, Streets of Fire, Places in the Heart, Alamo Bay, Twice in a Lifetime (Academy Award nom.; Golden Globe nom. 1986), Nowhere To Hide, The Prince of Pennsylvania, Field of Dreams, Uncle Buck, The Dark Half, Female Perversions, Loved, With Friends Like These, Pollock, A Time for Dancing, The Sleepy Time Gal, Just a Dream, The Laramie Project, In the Land of Milk and Money, The Discontents, After the Past (prod. only), Admissions, Winter Passing, Gone, Baby, Gone, Gary's Walk, Once Fallen (also exec. prod.), What's Wrong with Virginia, Big Ginger.
TELEVISION: *Movies*: Crazy Times, The Ambush Murders, Victims, Travis McGee, The Day After, The Laundromat, Roe vs. Wade (Emmy nom.; Golden Globe Award 1989), Lucky Day, And Then There Was One, Riders of the Purple Sage, A Bright Shining Lie, Having Our Say: The Delany Sisters' First 100 Years, In the Name of the People, Shot in the Heart, The Ranch, Admissions, The Path to 9/11, Murder on Pleasant Drive. *Mini-series*: Eureka Stockade, Not for Ourselves Alone: The Story of Elizabeth Cady Stanton & Susan B. Anthony, Jazz. *Series:* Carnivàle, Grey's Anatomy. *Documentaries/Specials:* Baseball, The Way West, The West, Big Guns Talk: The Story of the Western, Mark Twain, Horatio's Drive: America's First Road Trip (voice), Unforgivable Blackness: The Rise and Fall of Jack Johnson (voices). *Guest:* More than 53 appearances.

MADONNA
Singer, Actress, Producer. r.n. Madonna Louise Veronica Ciccone. b. Pontiac, MI, Aug. 16, 1958. e. U. of Michigan. Gained fame as rock & recording star before professional acting debut in Desperately Seeking Susan, 1985. NY stage debut: Speed-the-Plow, 1988. Author: Sex (1992).
PICTURES: *Actress:* A Certain Sacrifice (debut, 1985), Vision Quest (also lyricist, singer & composer), Desperately Seeking Susan (also lyricist, singer, song producer & composer), Shanghai Surprise, Who's That Girl? (also lyricist, singer, song producer & composer, Golden Globe nom. for best song, 1988), Bloodhounds of Broadway (also singer), Dick Tracy, Truth or Dare (documentary, also exec. prod.), Shadows and Fog, A League of Their Own (also lyricist, singer, song producer & composer, Golden Globe nom. for best song 1993), Body of Evidence, Dangerous Game, Blue in the Face, With Honors (Golden Globe nom. for best song 1995), Four Rooms, Girl 6, Evita (Golden Globe Award for Actress, 1997), Torrance Rises (short; as herself), The Next Best Thing (also singer, song producer & composer), Swept Away, Agent Cody Banks (exec. prod. only), Agent Cody Banks 2: Destination London (exec. prod. only), Arthur and the Minimoys (voice), This Is America (prod. only), She Rocks (exec. prod. only), Arthur and the Invisibles (voice), Filth and Wisdom (exec. prod., dir.), I Am Because We Are (doc., exec. prod., writer). *Composer/Soundtrack Performer:* Flawless, Everybody's Famous!, Crossroads, Confidence, Pepsi More Music: The DVD Volume 1 (video). Singer: At Close Range (also lyricist, song prod.), Walk Like a Man, Nothing But Trouble, With Honors (also lyricist), Austin Powers: The Spy Who Shagged Me (also lyricist, song prod., Golden Globe nom. for best song 2000), Snatch: Pigs and Diamonds, 13 Going On 30, Bridget Jones: The Edge of Reason, Die Another Day (Golden Globe nom. for best song 2003), Cheaper by the Dozen 2, The Devil Wears Prada, Get Smart, The Wrestler, W.E. (s.p., dir.).
TELEVISION: *Guest:* More than 350 appearances on various documentaries, specials, talk shows, movies or series.

MADSEN, MICHAEL
Actor. b. Chicago, IL, Sept. 25, 1958. Sister is actress Virginia Madsen. Started acting with Chicago's Steppenwolf Theatre appearing in such plays as Of Mice and Men, A Streetcar Named Desire. On B'way in A Streetcar Named Desire (1992).
PICTURES: Against All Hope, WarGames, Racing With the Moon, The Natural, The Killing Time, Shadows in the Storm, Iguana, Kill Me Again, Blood Red, The End of Innocence, Fatal Instinct, The Doors, Thelma & Louise, Reservoir Dogs, Beyond the Law, Almost Blue, Straight Talk, Inside Edge, A House in the Hills, Trouble Bound, Free Willy, Money for Nothing, Season of Change, Dead Connection, The Getaway, Wyatt Earp, Species, Free Willy 2: The Adventure Home, Man With a Gun, Red Line, Mulholland Falls, The Winner, Surface to Air, The Sender (also assoc. prod.), Rough Draft, Papertrail, The Last Days of Frankie the Fly, Donnie Brasco, The Girl Gets Moe, The Maker, Catherine's Grove, Executive Target (also assoc. prod.), The Thief & The Stripper, Flat Out, Species II, Fait Accompli, The Stray, The Florentine, Detour, Love.com, Ides of March, The Ghost, Fall: The Price of Silence, Choke, Luck of the Draw, The Alternate, The Price of Air (also prod.), Pressure Point, Outlaw, L.A.P.D.: To Protect and Serve, Extreme Honor, Welcome to America, The Real Deal, Where's Angelo? (short, prod. only), Die Another Day, My Boss's Daughter, Kill Bill: Vol. 1, Vampires Anonymous, L.A. Dicks, Renegade, Kill Bill: Vol. 2, The Last Drop, Chasing Ghosts, Sin City, Bloodrayne, The Chronicles of Narnia: The Lion, the Witch and the Wardrobe (voice), Scary Movie 4, UKM: The Ultimate Killing Machine, Cosmic Radio, Hoboken Hollow, Living & Dying, King of Sorrow, All In, Canes, A License to Steal, Bob's Not Gay, Duplicity, Vice (also exec. prod.), House, Strength and Honour, Tooth & Nail (also exec. prod.), Deep Winter, Boarding Gate, Love and Virtue, Sin City 2, Hell Ride, Break, The Lion of Judah, Shannon's Rainbow, Last Hour, Serbian Scars, Put, Outrage, Hired Gun, Edgar Allan Poe's Ligeia, Chamaco, No Bad Days, 45 R.P.M., You Might as Well Live, The Bleeding, The Big I Am, Road Raiders, Road of No Return (also prod.), Lost in the Woods, Hired Gun (also prod.), Conflict of Interest, Black Box, The Way, Outrage, Nictophobia, Buttermilk Sky (also exec. prod.), Night Train, Code of Silence, Signed in Blood, The Portal, The Lion of Judah, The Killing Jar, Six Days in Paradise, Money to Burn, Let the Game Begin, The Big I Am, The 5th Execution, Threatened, The Witching Hour, The Visible Dark, The Throwaways, Road Raiders, Now Here (also prod.), Not Another Not Another Movie, Men Don't Lie, Krach, Federal, Code of Silence, Bed and Breakfast, A Detour in Life, 513, Madoff: Made Off with America, The Brazen Bull (also prod.), Magic Boys, Eldorado, Back2Hell, Corruption.Gov, Firedog (voice), White Widow, I'm in Love with a Church Girl, Egill: The Last Pagan (voice), Burn Off, Redemption.
TELEVISION: *Movies*: Our Family Honor, Montana, Baby Snatcher, Supreme Sanction, The Inspectors 2: A Shred of Evidence, Sacrifice, High Noon, 44 Minutes: The North

Hollywood Shoot-Out, Frankenstein, Croc, Crash N' Burn. *Pilot*: Diner. *Mini-series:* War and Remembrance. The North Hollywood Shoot-Out, Frankenstein. *Series:* Our Family Honor, The Outsiders, Vengeance Unlimited, Big Apple, Tilt, 24. *Documentaries/ Specials:* Steve McQueen: The King of Cool, Pet Star (series documentary; writer), Bullets Over Hollywood. *Guest:* More than 96 appearances.

MADSEN, VIRGINIA
Actress. b. Chicago, IL, Sept. 11, 1963. Mother is Emmy-winning Chicago filmmaker; brother is actor Michael Madsen. Studied with Chicago acting coach Ted Liss. Prof. debut, PBS, A Matter of Principle. Received Avoriaz & Saturn Awards for Best Actress for Candyman.
PICTURES: Class (debut, 1983), Electric Dreams, Dune, Creator, Fire With Fire, Modern Girls, Zombie High, Slam Dance, Mr. North, Hot to Trot, Heart of Dixie, The Hot Spot, Highlander 2: The Quickening, Candyman, Becoming Colette, Caroline at Midnight, Blue Tiger, The Prophecy, Ghosts of Mississippi, Suicide Kings, The Rainmaker, McClintocks Peach, The Florentine, Ballad of the Nightingale, Ambushed, The Haunting, All the Fine Lines, After Sex, Lying in Wait, American Gun, Almost Salinas, Artworks, Nobody Knows Anything!, Sideways (Numerous recognition for role, including: Academy Award nom.; Golden Globe nom.; Broadcast Film Critics Assoc. Award, Best Supporting Actress; Independent Spirit Awards, Best Supporting Actress; BFCA Best Acting Ensemble, 2005), Ripple Effect (also exec. prod.), Firewall, A Prairie Home Companion, The Astronaut Farmer, In the Shadow of Wings, The Number 23, Diminished Capacity, The Haunting in Connecticut, I Know a Woman Like That (doc., prod.), Father of Invention, Fighting Gravity (doc., exec. prod.).
TELEVISION: *Movies*: A Matter of Principle, The Hearst and Davies Affair, Long Gone, Gotham, Third Degree Burn, Ironclads, Victim of Love, Love Kills, Linda, A Murderous Affair: The Carolyn Warmus Story, Bitter Vengeance, Robert Ludlum's The Apocalypse Watch, Children of Fortune, Crossfire Trail, Just Ask My Children, Tempted, Brave New Girl. *Mini-series:* Mussolini: The Untold Story. *Series:* Unsolved Mysteries (co-host), American Dreams, Smith, Scoundrels. *Guest:* More than 80 appearances.

MAGNUSON, ANN
Actress, Writer, Performance Artist. b. Charleston, WV, Jan. 4, 1956. e. Denison U. Intern at Ensemble Studio Theatre when she came to NY in 1978. Ran Club 57, an East Village club, 1979. Has performed Off-B'way, in East Village clubs, downtown art spaces, on college campuses since 1980, and at Whitney Museum, Soguestu Hall (Tokyo), Walker Art Ctr. (Minn.), Lincoln Center, Serious Fun Festival, Joseph Papp's Public Theatre. Also performed with band Bongwater. Debut as solo recording artist on Geffen Records with The Luv Show, 1995.
PICTURES: Vortex, The Hunger, Perfect Strangers, Desperately Seeking Susan, Making Mr. Right, A Night in the Life of Jimmy Reardon, Sleepwalk, Mondo New York, Tequila Sunrise, Checking Out, Heavy Petting, Love at Large, Cabin Boy, Clear and Present Danger, Tank Girl, Before and After, Hugo Pool, Still Breathing, Levitation, Small Soldiers, I Woke Up Early The Day I Died, Still Breathing, Love & Sex, Friends & Lovers, Housebound, The Caveman's Valentine, Glitter, Panic Room, Night at the Golden Eagle, The United States of Leland, Ghost Light, Live Freaky Die Freaky (voice), Open House, Chasing Tchaikovsky, Woman's Picture, Small Pond.
TELEVISION: *Movies:* Tales from the Hollywood Hills: Natica Jackson, Tales from the Hollywood Hills: A Table at Ciro's, The Munster's Scary Little Christmas, The Groovenians (voice), Our House. *Mini-series:* From the Earth to the Moon. *Series*: Anything But Love, Postcards from America, Wanda at Large, All Grown Up.

MAGUIRE, TOBEY
Actor, Producer. b. Santa Monica, CA, June 27, 1975.
PICTURES: *Actor:* This Boy's Life, Revenge of the Red Baron, S.F.W., Joyride, The Ice Storm, Deconstructing Harry, Pleasantville, Fear and Loathing in Las Vegas, Wonder Boys, The Cider House Rules, Ride with the Devil, Cats & Dogs (voice), Don's Plum, Spider-Man, Seabiscuit (also exec. prod.), Spider-Man 2 The Good German, Spider-Man 3, Tropic Thunder, Brothers (Golden Globe nom. 2010), The Details, Pawn Sacrifice (also prod.). *Producer:* The 25th Hour, Whatever We Do (short), Tokyo Suckerpunch (short, also actor), The Hungry Rabbit Jumps, Love Don't Let Me Down.
TELEVISION: *Movies*: Hot Rod Brown Class Clown, In Spite of Love, A Child's Cry for Help, Seduced by Madness: The Diane Borchardt Story, Duke of Groove (short), Rock of Ages (exec. prod. only). *Series*: Great Scott!. *Guest:* More than 97 appearances.

MAHONEY, JOHN
Actor. b. Manchester, England, June 20, 1940. Mem. of Stratford Children's Theatre from age 10-13. Moved to U.S. at 19, taught Eng. at Western Illinois U. Then freelance ed. of medical manuscripts; assoc. ed., Quality Review Bulletin. At 35 quit medical book editing to become an actor. Studied acting, Chicago's St. Nicholas Theatre. Prof. debut, The Water Engine, 1977. Joined Steppenwolf Theatre Co., 1979.
THEATRE: Orphans (Theatre World Award), The House of Blue Leaves (Tony & Clarence Derwent Awards), The Subject Was Roses.
PICTURES: Mission Hill, Code of Silence, The Manhattan Project, Streets of Gold, Tin Men, Suspect, Moonstruck, Frantic, Betrayed, Eight Men Out, Say Anything..., Love Hurts, The Russia House, Barton Fink, Article 99, In the Line of Fire, Striking Distance, Reality Bites, The Hudsucker Proxy, The American President, Mariette in Ecstasy, Primal Fear, She's the One, Antz (voice), The Iron Giant (voice), The Broken Hearts Club, Almost Salinas, Atlantis: The Lost Empire (voice), Atlantis: Milo's Return (video; voice) Kronk's New Groove (video; voice), The Groomsmen, Dan in Real Life, Flipped.
TELEVISION: *Movies*: The Killing Floor, Chicago Story, First Steps, Listen to Your Heart, Dance of the Phoenix, First Steps, Trapped in Silence, Favorite Son, The Image, Dinner at Eight, The 10 Million Dollar Getaway, The Secret Passion of Robert Clayton, The Water Engine, Fathers and Sons. *Series*: Lady Blue, H.E.L.P., The Human Factor, Frasier (2 Emmy noms.; 2 Golden Globe noms.), In Treatment. *Documentaries/Specials:* The House of Blue Leaves Coney Island (voice). *Guest:* More than 62 appearances.

MAJORS, LEE
Actor. r.n. Lee Yeary. b. Wyandotte, MI, April 23, 1939. Star athlete in high school; turned down offer from St. Louis Cardinals in final year at Eastern Kentucky State Coll. to pursue acting career. In L.A. got job as playground supervisor for park dept. while studying acting at MGM Studio. Debuted in films under his real name in 1964.
PICTURES: Strait-Jacket (debut, 1964), Will Penny, The Liberation of L. B. Jones, The Norsemen, Killer Fish, Steel, Agency, The Last Chase, Scrooged, Keaton's Cop, Trojan War, Musketeers Forever, Chapter Zero, The Protector, New Jersey Turnpikes, Primary Suspect, Here, Out Cold, Big Fat Liar, Waitin' to Live, Fate, Arizona Summer, Strike the Tent When I Find the Ocean, TV: The Movie, The Brothers Solomon, Spring Break '83, The Adventures of Umbweki, Spring Break '83, Jerusalem Countdown, Johnny, Corruption.Gov.
TELEVISION: *Movies*: The Ballad of Andy Crocker, Weekend of Terror, The Gary Francis Powers Story, The Cowboy and the Ballerina, A Rocky Mountain Christmas, The Return of the Six Million Dollar Man and the Bionic Woman, Danger Down Under (exec. prod., actor), The Bionic Showdown: the Six Million Dollar Man and the Bionic Woman, Fire!, Trapped on the 37th Floor, Daytona Beach, The Cover Girl Murders, Bionic Ever After?, Lost Treasures of Dos Santos, Hotel, Hard Knox, The Trail to Hope Rose, Lightspeed, Me & Lee?. *Series*: The Big Valley, The Men From Shiloh, Owen Marshall-Counselor at Law, The Six Million Dollar Man (Golden Globe nom. 1977), The Fall Guy, Tour of Duty, Raven, Too Much Sun, The Game. *Guest:* More than 102 appearances.

MAKEPEACE, CHRIS
Actor. b. Montreal, Canada, April 22, 1964. e. Jarvis Collegiate Institute. Trained for stage at Second City Workshop.
PICTURES: Meatballs (debut, 1979), My Bodyguard, The Last Chase, The Oasis, The Falcon and the Snowman, Vamp, Captive Hearts, Aloha Summer, Memory Run, Short for Nothing, Silver Man (3rd asst. dir.), Tangled (3rd asst. dir.).
TELEVISION: *Movies:* The Terry Fox Story, The Mysterious Stranger, Mazes and Monsters, The Undergrads, A Holiday for Love. *Mini-series:* Handyman Superstar Challenge (constr. prod.). *Series:* Going Great (host, 1982-84), Drop the Beat (2nd asst. dir.).

MALICK, TERRENCE
Writer, Director, Producer. b. Bartlesville, OK, November 30, 1943. e. Harvard University. Former Rhodes Scholar. Malick's production company is Sunflower Productions LLC
PICTURES: *Writer*: Deadhead Miles, Pocket Money, The Gravy Train, Bear's Kiss, The Beautiful Country (also prod.). *Writer/Director*: Days of Heaven (Cannes Film Fest., best dir., Golden Globe nom. WGA nom. 1979), Badlands (also prod.), The Thin Red Line (2 Acad. Award noms for dir., s.p. adapt. DGA nom. 1999), The New World (also prod.), Tree of Life. *Producer*: Endurance (documentary), The Endurance: Shackleton's Legendary Antarctic Expedition, Happy Times (exec. prod.) Undertow, Amazing Grace.
TELEVISION: *Actor*: Golden Fiddles, The Beast.

MALIN, AMIR JACOB
Producer, Executive. b. Tel-Aviv, Israel, March 22, 1954. e. Brandeis U., 1972-76, Boston U. School of Law, 1976-79. Staff atty., WGBH-TV, Boston, 1979-81; president and co-CEO, Cinecom Entertainment Grp., Inc., 1982-88; co-president, October Films, Inc., 1989-97; president & CEO, Millennium Pictures, a joint venture with Nu-Image, Inc., Phoenician Films, and October Films; CEO, Artisan Entertainment, 1997-2003 (Artisan merged into Lions Gate Entertainment Corp. at end of 2003).
PICTURES: *Executive producer*: Swimming to Cambodia, Matewan, Miles From Home, Scenes from the Class Struggle in Beverly Hills, The Handmaid's Tale, Tune in Tomorrow, The Punisher, Stage Beauty.

MALKOVICH, JOHN
Actor, Producer, Director. b. Christopher, IL, Dec. 9, 1953. e. Illinois State U. Founding member Steppenwolf Ensemble in

Chicago with group of college friends, 1976. Starred in Say Goodnight Gracie and True West (Obie Award).Stage work includes Death of Salesman, Burn This, States of Shock. *Dir.:* Balm in Gilead, Arms and the Man, The Caretaker, Libra (also writer).
PICTURES: Places in the Heart (Academy Award nom. 1985), The Killing Fields, Eleni, Making Mr. Right, The Glass Menagerie, Empire of the Sun, Miles From Home, Dangerous Liaisons, The Accidental Tourist (co-exec. prod. only), The Sheltering Sky, Queens Logic, The Object of Beauty, Shadows and Fog, Of Mice and Men, Jennifer Eight, Alive, In the Line of Fire (Academy Award nom.; Golden Globe nom. 1994), The Convent, Beyond the Clouds, Mary Reilly, Mulholland Falls, Portrait of a Lady, Con Air, Rounders, The Man in the Iron Mask, Time Regained, Ladies Room, Being John Malkovich, The Messenger: The Story of Joan of Arc, Burned to Light, Shadow of the Vampire, Speak Truth to Power, Hotel, Knockaround Guys, Ripley's Game, I'm Going Home, Johnny English, A Talking Picture, The Libertine, (also prod.), The Hitchhiker's Guide to the Galaxy, Savage Grace, Klimt, Drunkboat (also prod.), Colour Me Kubrick, Art School Confidential (also prod.), Eragon, Beowulf, Mutant Chronicles, The Great Buck Howard, Burn After Reading, Gardens of the Night, Love and Virtue, Afterwards, Disgrace, Changeling, Jonah Hex, Secretariat, Red, Transformers 3. *Producer:* Kill the Poor, Found in the Street, Juno, Which Way Home (doc., exec. prod.), Perks of Being a Wallflower, Jeff Who Lives at Home.
TELEVISION: *Movies*: *Actor:* Word of Honor, American Dream, True West, Death of a Salesman (Emmy Award, Golden Globe nom. 1986), Rocket to the Moon, Santabear's First Christmas (voice), Santabear's High Flying Adventure (short; voice), Old Times, Heart of Darkness (Golden Globe nom. 1995), RKO 281 (Emmy nom. 2000), Dragans of New York (prod.), Good Canary (prod., stage dir.). *Mini-series*: Les Misérables, Napoléon (Emmy nom. 2003). *Documentaries/Specials*: The First Amendment Project: Some Assembly Required (prod. only), Which Way Home (exec. prod.). *Guest:* More than 96 appearances.

MALONE, DOROTHY
Actress. b. Chicago, IL, Jan. 30, 1925. e. Southern Methodist U., USC, AADA. Started as RKO starlet, 1943. Stage work incl. Little Me, Practice to Deceive.
PICTURES: The Big Sleep, Night and Day, One Sunday Afternoon, Two Guys From Texas, The Nevadan, The Bushwackers, Jack Slade, The Killer That Stalked New York, Scared Stiff, Torpedo Alley, The Lone Gun, Pushover, Security Risk, Private Hell 36, The Fast and the Furious, Young at Heart, Battle Cry, Sincerely Yours, Artists and Models, At Gunpoint, Five Guns West, Tall Man Riding, Pillars of the Sky, Tension at Table Rock, Written on the Wind (Academy Award, best supporting actress, Golden Globe nom. 1956), Man of a Thousand Faces, Quantez, The Tarnished Angels, Tip on a Dead Jockey, Too Much Too Soon, Warlock, The Last Voyage, The Last Sunset, Beach Party, Fate is the Hunter, Abduction, Golden Rendezvous, Good Luck Miss Wyckoff, Winter Kills, The Day Time Ended, The Being, Basic Instinct.
TELEVISION: *Movies*: The Pigeon, Little Ladies of the Night, Murder in Peyton Place, Katie: Portrait of a Centerfold, Condominium, Peyton Place: The Next Generation. *Mini-series*: Rich Man Poor Man. *Series*: Peyton Place (2 Golden Globe noms.). *Documentaries/Specials*: Gertrude Stein Story, The Family That Prays Together. *Guest:* More than 50 appearances.

MALONE, JOHN C.
Executive. b. Milford, CT, Mar. 7, 1941. e. Yale U, B.S. in electrical engineering and economics, 1963. While at Yale, was Phi Beta Kappa and a merit scholar. Earned Master of Science in Industrial Management from Johns Hopkins in 1964 and a Doctor of Philosophy (Ph.D.) in Operations Research from Johns Hopkins,1967. Began career in 1963 with Bell Telephone Labs/AT&T. Joined McKinsey & Co., 1968. 1970, became group v.p. at General Instrument Corp. Later named pres., Jerrold Electronics, a GI subsidiary. Joined Tele-Communications, Inc. in 1973. Pres. & CEO, TCI, 1973-1996. 1996-1999, chmn. & CEO, TCI until merger with AT&T. Chmn. & Bd. Dir., Chrm. Liberty Media. He is the chmn. & CEO of Discovery Communications Holding, LLC, 2005-Present. Malone served as director of the National Cable Television Assoc., 1974-1977 and 1980-1993. Was NCTA treasurer, 1977-1978. Merged DirecTV and Liberty Media, 2009. Industry recognition/awards include: TVC Magazine Man of the Year Award, 1981; recipient of the NCTA Vangaurd Award, 1983; Wall Street Transcript's Gold Award for the cable industry's best CEO, 1982, 1985, 1986 and 1987; Wall Street's Transcript Silver Award in 1984 and 1989; Women in Cable's Betsy Magness Fellowship Honoree; U. Penn Wharton School Sol C. Snider Entrepreneurial Center Award of Merit; American Jewish Committee Sherrill C. Corwin Human Relations Award; Denver U. Honorary Degree for Doctorate of Human Letters, 1992; Communications Technlogy Magazine Service And Technology Award; Bronze Award in 1993—Financial World CEO of the Year Competition; and 1994 Hopkins Distinguished Alumnus Award.

MAMET, DAVID
Writer, Director. b. Chicago, IL, Nov. 30, 1947. m. actress Rebecca Pidgeon. e. Goddard Coll. Artist-in-residence, Goddard Coll. 1971-73. Artistic dir. St. Nicholas Theatre Co., Chicago, 1973-75. Co-founder Dinglefest Theatre; assoc. artistic dir.,Goodman Theatre, Chicago. Appeared as actor in film Black Widow. *Novel:* The Village (1994). Received WGA Laurel Award for Screen Writing Achievement 2005.
THEATRE: Lakefront, The Woods, American Buffalo, Sexual Perversity in Chicago, Duck Variations, Edmond, A Life in the Theatre, The Water Engine, Prairie du Chien, Glengarry Glen Ross (Pulitzer Prize, Tony Award, 1984), Speed-the-Plow, Sketches of War (benefit for homeless Vietnam Veterans), Oleanna, An Interview (Death Defying Acts), The Cryptogram.
PICTURES: *Writer*: The Postman Always Rings Twice, The Verdict (Academy Award nom.; Golden Globe nom.; WGA nom. 1983), The Untouchables (WGA nom. 1988), House of Games (also dir., Golden Globe nom. 1988), Things Change (also dir.), We're No Angels, Homicide (also dir.), Hoffa, Vanya on 42nd Street (adaptation), Oleanna (also dir.), The Spanish Prisoner (also dir.), The Edge, Wag the Dog (Academy Award nom.; Golden Globe nom.; WGA nom. 1998), Ronin, The Winslow Boy (also dir.), State and Maine, Lakeboat, Hannibal, Heist, Spartan, Edmond, Whistle, Joan of Bark: The Dog that Saved France (also dir.), Redbelt (also dir.), Come Back to Sorrento (also dir.), Endangered (exec. prod. only).
TELEVISION: *Movies: Writer:* A Life in the Theater, Uncle Vanya, The Water Engine, Texan (short), Lansky (also exec. prod.). *Movies: Director:* Ricky Jay and His 52 Assistants. *Movies: Producer*: Lip Service. *Series: Writer:* Hill Stree Blues, The Unit (also creator, dir., exec. prod.). *Series: Director:* The Shield, The Unit (also writer).

MANASSE, GEORGE
Producer. b. Florence, Italy, Jan. 1, 1938. e. U. of North Carolina.
PICTURES: *Prod.*: Who Killed Mary What's 'er Name?, Squirm, Blue Sunshine, He Knows You're Alone. Prod. Mgr.: Greetings, Joe, Fury on Wheels, Slow Dancing in the Big City, Tribute, Porky's II: The Next Day, Neighbors, Death Wish III, Torch Song Trilogy, Indecent Proposal, Coneheads, Lassie, Die Hard With a Vengeance, Eraser, Chill Factor, The In Crowd, Juwanna Mann.
TELEVISION: *Movies*: *Prod. Mgr.:* Sanctuary of Fear, Muggable Mary Street Cop, Drop-Out Father, Running Out, John and Yoko: A Love Story, Intimate Strangers, Vengeance: The Story of Tony Cimo, The Diamond Trap, Roxanne: The Prize Pulitzer (also supervising prod.), Orpheus Descending (also prod.), Marilyn & Me, Legion of Fire: Killer Ants (also prod., dir.), The Hunley (also co-prod.). *Line prod.:* The Saint in Manhattan (pilot). *Series:* The District (unit prod. mangr.).

MANCIA, ADRIENNE
Film Curator-At-Large. b. New York, NY. e. U. of Wisconsin. B.A.; Columbia U., M.A. Worked in film distribution industry in New York prior to joining Dept. of Film & Video, Museum of Modern Art, 1964; responsible for film exhibition 1965-1998. In 1977, appointed curator. She restructured the Museums' Auditorium Exhibition Prog., creating a balance between classic cinema and contemporary work. Mancia initiated innovative programs such as Cineprobe and New Documentaries (formerly What's Happening?) and served on numerous int'l film juries. She is co-founder of New Directors/New Films. Chevalier de l'Ordre des Arts et des Lettres (France, 1985). Ufficiale dell Ordine al Merito della Repubblica Italiana, 1988. In 1998 she became the curator-at-large for the Brooklyn Academy of Music (BAM) Rose Cinemas and BAM Cinematek, a position she holds today. In this role she fills programming for the BAM Rose Cinemas.

MANCUSO, FRANK G.
Executive. b. Buffalo, NY, July 25, 1933. e. State U. of New York. Film buyer and operations supvr. for Basil Enterprises, theatre circuit, 1958-62. Joined Paramount as booker in Buffalo branch, 1962. Named sls. repr. for branch in 1964 and branch mgr. in 1967. 1970 appt. v.p./gen. sls. mgr., Paramount Pictures Canada, Ltd., becoming pres. in 1972. 1976 relocated with Paramount in U.S. as western div. mgr. in LA. 1977, appt. gen. sls. mgr. of NY, office; two months later promoted to v.p. domestic distribution; 1979, named exec. v.p., distrib. & mktg. 1983 made pres. of entire Paramount Motion Picture Group. 1984, appointed chmn. and CEO, Paramount Pictures; resigned 1991. Appointed chmn. and CEO, MGM in 1993. Retired from post, April 1999 but remained MGM director until company was sold in 2005. Named Motion Picture Pioneers Man of the Year, 1987. Member of Board: AMPAS, M.P. Assoc. of America, Variety Clubs Intl., Sundance Institute, Amer. Film Institute, Museum of Broadcasting, Motion Picture Pioneers. 1998 Women in film Mentor Award. 1998 Ellis Island Medal of Honor Award. Current chairman of the bd. of the Motion Picture & Television Fund Corp., Serves on Bd. of Dir. for Digital Entertainment Network, Inc. (DEN), Will Rogers Motion Picture Pioneers Foundation bd. of directors exec. committee (an honorary chairman). Named Chairman of The Geffen Playhouse 2007.

MANCUSO, JR., FRANK
Producer. b. Buffalo, NY, Oct. 9, 1958. Son of Frank G. Mancuso. e. Upsala Coll. Began with industry at age 14, booking short subjects in Canadian theatres. Worked in gross receipts dept. in Paramount corporate offices in New York and later with paralegal div. Initial prod. work as location asst. for Urban

Cowboy in Houston, TX. Served as assoc. prod. of Friday the 13th Part II and prod. of Friday the 13th Part III in 3-D.
PICTURES: Off the Wall, The Man Who Wasn't There, April Fool's Day, Friday the 13th, Part IV: The Final Chapter; Friday the 13th—A New Beginning (exec. prod.), Friday the 13th, Part VII (exec. prod.); Back to the Beach; Permanent Record, Internal Affairs, He Said/She Said, Species, Fled, Hoodlum, Toby's Story, Species II, Ronin, Stigmata, New Best Friend, Species III (video; exec. prod.), The Lost City (exec. prod.), Crossover (also exec. prod.), I Know Who Killed Me, Species: The Awakening (video, exec. prod.), April Fool's Day (video).
TELEVISION: *Movies: Exec. Prod.:* The Limbic Region, The Escape. *Series: Producer:* Friday the 13th (also writer), War of the Worlds (season 2).

MANDEL, BABALOO
Writer. r.n. Marc Mandel. b. 1949. Started as comedy writer for Joan Rivers, among others. First teamed with Lowell Ganz on script for 1982 film Night Shift.
PICTURES: Night Shift, Splash (Academy Award nom.; WGA nom. 1985, also actor), Spies Like Us, Gung Ho, Vibes, Parenthood, City Slickers, A League of Their Own, Mr. Saturday Night, Greedy, City Slickers II: The Legend of Curly's Gold, Forget Paris, Multiplicity, Father's Day, Edtv, Where the Heart Is, Robots, Fever Pitch, Sex Talk, Tooth Fairy.
TELEVISION: *Series co-writer:* Laverne and Shirley, Busting Loose, Take Five (also co-creator). Happy Days, Herndon, Knight & Daye (also creator), *Exec. prod.:* A League of Their Own, Hiller and Diller.

MANDEL, HOWIE
Actor. b. Toronto, Canada, Nov. 29, 1955.
PICTURES: Gremlins (voice), A Fine Mess, Walk Like a Man, Little Monsters, Gremlins 2: The New Batch (voice), Hansel & Gretel, Noah's Ark: The New Beginning (voice).
TELEVISION: *Movies:* The Princess Who Had Never Laughed, Mother Goose Rock 'n' Rhyme, David Copperfield (voice), Shake, Rattle and Rock!, In Search of Dr. Seuss (voice), Harrison Bergeron, Spinning Out of Control, Crown Heights, The Great Polar Bear Adventure (voice). *Series:* St. Elsewhere, Bobby's World, Good Grief, The Amazing Live Sea-Monkeys, Hidden Howie (also exec. prod.), Deal or No Deal (host, 2 Emmy noms.), Howie Do It (host, writer, exec. prod.). *Guest:* More than 140 appearances.

MANDEL, LORING
Writer. b. Chicago, IL, May 5, 1928. e. U. of Wisconsin, B.S. 1949. Long career writing scripts for TV, dating back to 1955 when penned Shakedown Cruise. Governor, Natl. Acad. of TV Arts & Sciences 1964-68; Pres. Writers Guild of America East 1975-77; Natl. Chmn. 1977-79. Received WGA Laurel Award 2004.
PICTURES: Countdown, Promises in the Dark, Little Drummer Girl.
TELEVISION: *Movies:* World's Greatest Robbery, Ambassador at Large, Do Not Go Gentle Into That Good Night (Emmy Award 1967), Shadow Game, To Confuse the Angel, Particular Men, The Whirlwind, The Trial of Chaplain Jensen, Breaking Up (Emmy nom. 1978), Project Immortality (Sylvania Award, 1959), Tom and Joann, The Lost Honor of Kathryn Beck, Conspiracy (Emmy Award, WGA Award 2001). *Mini-series:* Lincoln, The Best of Families. *Series:* Armstrong Circle Theatre, Lux Video Theatre, Lives of Ben Franklin (Emmy nom. 1975), The Kaiser Aluminum Hour, Playhouse 90 (Emmy nom. 1960), The Seven Lively Arts.

MANDEL, ROBERT
Director. e. Columbia Univ. Dean of American Film Institute Conservatory.
PICTURES: Night at O'Rears (also prod.), Independence Day, F/X, Touch and Go, Big Shots, School Ties, The Substitute, The King and I (exec. prod.).
TELEVISION: *Movies:* Hard Time on Planet Earth, The X Files (pilot), Kansas, Special Report: Journey to Mars, Thin Air, WWIII, A Season on the Brink, The Secret Life of Zoey. *Series:* Nash Bridges, The Practice, The District, Lost (1 episode), Prison Break (1 episode).

MANDOKI, LUIS
Director. b. Mexico City, Mexicom, 1954. e. San Francisco Art Institute, London Intl. Film School, London College's School of Film. Dir. short film Silent Music which won Intl. Amateur Film Fest. Award at 1976 Cannes Film Fest. Back in Mexico dir. shorts and documentaries for the Instituto Nacional Indignista Concaine, Centro de Produccionde Cortometraje. Won Ariel Award.
PICTURES: Mundo mágico, Campeche un estado de animo (documentary short; alos prod.), Papaloapan (doc.), Motel, Noche de Califas (prod. only), Gaby--A True Story, White Palace, Born Yesterday, When a Man Loves a Woman, Message in a Bottle, Amazing Grace, Angel Eyes, Trapped (also prod.), Innocent Voices (also s.p. and prod.; aka Casas de cartón), One More Day for Hiroshima, Amapola, The Winged Boy.
TELEVISION: *Movie:* The Edge. *Series: Exec. Prod.:* Utopia.

MANES, FRITZ
Producer. b. Oakland, CA, April 22, 1936. e. U.C., Berkeley, B.A. UCLA, 1956. Armed Service: 1951-54. U.S. Marines, Korea, Purple Heart. TV ad. exec. and stuntman before becoming exec. prod. on films for Clint Eastwood. Has formed own production co., Sundancer Prods. Holds membership in DGA and SAG.
PICTURES: *Executive Producer:* Firefox (also unit prod. mgr.), Honkytonk Man, Sudden Impact (also stunts), Pale Rider (also unit prod. mgr.), Heartbreak Ridge (also unit prod. mgr.). *Producer:* Any Which Way You Can (also second asst. dir.), Tightrope (also unit prod. mgr.), City Heat (also unit prod. mgr. & stunts), Ratboy (also unit prod. mgr.). *Associate Producer:* The Gauntlet (also acting), Every Which Way But Loose (also acting), Escape from Alcatraz (also acting), Bronco Billy (also acting). *Assistant to Producer:* The Outlaw Josey Wales, The Enforcer (also acting).

MANHEIM, CAMRYN
Actress. b. Caldwell, NJ, March 8, 1961. e. NYU.
PICTURES: The Bonfire of the Vanities, The Road to Wellville, David Searching, Jeffrey, Eraser, Romy and Michele's High School Reunion, Wide Awake, Mercury Rising, Fool's Gold, Happiness, Joe Henry, The Tic Code, You Are Here, What Planet Are You From?, East of A, Just Like Mona, The Laramie Project, Scary Movie 3, The Land Before Time XI: Invasion of the Tinysauruses (video; voice), Twisted, Marilyn Hotchkiss' Ballroom Dancing and Charm School, Dark Water, An Unfinished Life, Slipstream Dream, Fort McCoy.
TELEVISION: *Movies*: Deadley Whispers, The Loretta Claiborne Story, Kiss My Act, Jenifer, Snow Wonder, Jesse Stone: Thin Ice, Pregnancy Pact. *Mini-series*: The 10th Kingdom, A Girl Thing, Elvis (Emmy nom.; Golden Globe nom. 2005). *Series*: The Practice (Emmy Award 1998, 1 other nom.; Golden Globe Award 1999), The L Word, Ghost Whisperer. *Guest:* More than 76 appearances.

MANKIEWICZ, TOM
Writer, Director. b. Los Angeles, CA, June 1, 1942. e. Yale U.
PICTURES: *Writer:* The Sweet Ride (debut), Diamonds Are Forever, Live and Let Die, The Man with the Golden Gun, Mother Jugs and Speed (also prod.), The Cassandra Crossing, The Eagle Has Landed, Ladyhawke. *Exec. Prod.:* Hot Pursuit. *Creative consultant:* Superman, Superman II. *Director:* Dragnet (also s.p.), Delirious.
TELEVISION: *Movies*: *Writer:* The Beat of the Brass, Mother Juggs & Speed. *Director:* Hart to Hart, Taking the Heat, Hart to Hart: Till Death Do Us Hart. *Series: Writer:* Bob Hope Presents the Chrysler Theatre, Hart to Hart (pilot), Tales from the Crypt (episode). *Documentaries/Specials:* Movin' with Nancy, Cleopatra: The Film That Changed Hollywood.

MANN, MICHAEL
Director, Writer, Producer. b. Chicago, IL, Feb. 5, 1943. e. U. of Wisconsin, London Film Sch. Directed shorts, commercials and documentaries in England. Returned to U.S. in 1972. Wrote for prime-time TV.
PICTURES: *Director/Writer/Producer:* Thief (exec. prod.), The Last of the Mohicans, Heat, The Insider (3 Academy Award noms.; DGA nom.; 2 Golden Globe noms.; WGA nom. 2000), Ali, Public Enemies, Public Enemies. *Writer/Director:* The Keep, Manhunter (also camera operator). *Executive Producer:* Band of the Hand, Gettin' the Man's Foot Outta Your Baadasssss! *Producer:* 17 Days Down the Line (also dir. & cinematographer), Collateral (also dir.), The Aviator (Academy Award nom. 2005), Miami Vice (also writer, s.p.,dir.), The Kingdom, Tonight, He Comes, Arms and the Man (also writer, s.p. dir.), The Few (also dir.), Damage Control (also dir.), Hancock, The Fields.
TELEVISION: *Movies: Writer:* River of Promises, Vega$, The Jericho Mile (also dir., DGA Award, Emmy Award 1980), Swan Song, L.A. Takedown (also dir., exec. prod.), Miami Vice (also exec. prod., Emmy nom. 1985) *Prod./Exec. Prod:* Crime Story Miami Vice: Brother's Keeper. Drug Wars: The Cocaine Cartel (Emmy nom. 1992), Luck (also dir.). *Mini-series*: Drug Wars: The Camarena Story (also writer, Emmy Award 1990). *Series: Writer:* Police Story, Starsky and Hutch, Bronk, Vega$ (also dir.), Miami Vice (also exec. prod.). *Producer/Exec. Prod.:* Crime Story, Private Eye, Robbery Homicide Division.

MANNE, S. ANTHONY
Executive. b. New York, NY, July 19, 1940. e. Wharton School, Univ. of Pennsylvania, B.S. economics. Joined Columbia Pictures, 1963; intl. dept., 1964; asst. mgr., Brazil, 1968; mgr., Brazil, 1969-72. Joined JAD Films, 1976. V.p. United Artists, Latin American supervisor, 1980. V.p. Columbia Pictures Intl., continental mgr., 1981; sr. v.p., sales manager, 1984; exec. v.p., Tri-Star Intl, 1987; exec. v.p., Columbia Tri-Star Film Dist. Intl., 1988. Cine Asia Distributor of the Year, 1997. Intl. Consultant, Sony Pictures, 2002. Additionally, he created and managed Brazil's pioneer art-house distribution and exhibition company, Grupo Nacional de Diversões. He also served as a partner and manager of the independent international film sales organization, JAD Films, representing independent filmmakers, including Brian de Palma and John Carpenter Founded Bristol Media International, Inc. in 2002 and currently serves as president.

MANNING, MICHELLE
Executive, Producer, Director. Began production career at Zoetrope Studios as prod. supervisor, then VP Production, Orion Pictures. Sr. VP Production, Viacom, Inc., 1991; promoted to Exec. VP, 1993. Pres. production, Paramount Motion Pictures,

1997 - May 2004. Resigned from Paramount in 2004 to become an independent producer and president of M and M Productions.
PICTURES: The Outsiders (prod. supervisor), Sixteen Candles (assoc. prod.), The Breakfast Club (co-prod.), Blue City (dir.), Book of Skulls (prod.), The Eye (prod.).
TELEVISION: *Series: Director:* Miami Vice, Friday the 13th.

MANOFF, DINAH
Actress. b. New York, NY, Jan. 25, 1958. e. CalArts. Daughter of actress-dir. Lee Grant and late writer Arnold Manoff. Prof. debut in PBS prod., The Great Cherub Knitwear Strike. Guest starred on Welcome Back Kotter.
THEATRE: I Ought to Be in Pictures (Tony & Theatre World Awards, 1980), others.
PICTURES: Grease (debut, 1978), Ordinary People, I Ought to Be in Pictures, Child's Play, Staying Together, Bloodhounds of Broadway, Welcome Home Roxy Carmichael, The Amati Girls, Zigs, Bart Got a Room.
TELEVISION: *Movies*: Raid on Entebee, Night Terror, The Possessed, For Ladies Only, A Matter of Sex, The Seduction of Gina, Flight No. 90: Disaster on the Potomac, Classified Love, The Cover Girl and the Cop, Babies, Maid for Each Other (also co-exec. prod., co-story), The Lost Child, A Carol Christmas. *Mini-series*: Celebrity. *Series*: *Actress:* Soap, Empty Nest, State of Grace. *Director:* Sister Sister, Minor Adjustments, Brother's Keeper.

MANSON, ARTHUR
Executive. b. Brooklyn, NY, Feb. 21, 1928. e. City Coll. of New York, grad. Inst. Film Technique, 1945. Editor, American Traveler, U.S. Army, 1946. Advance agent, co. mgr., Henry V, U.S., 1948-50; producer's publ. rep., Stanley Kramer Distributing Corp., Samuel Goldwyn Productions, 1951-52, dir. of adv. and publ., MGM Pictures of Canada, Ltd., 1952-53; publ. and adv. rep., Cinerama widescreen process, 1953-58; dir. worldwide ad-pub Cinerama 1958-60; adv. mgr., Columbia Pictures, 1961-62; nat'l dir. of adv., publ., Dino De Laurentiis, 1962-64; exec. asst. to v.p. adv. & pub., 20th Century-Fox, 1964-67; v.p., adv. & pub. Cinerama. Inc., and Cinerama Releasing Corp.; 1967-74; exec. v.p., sales & marketing, BCP, service of Cox Broadcasting Corp., 1974-75; v.p. worldwide marketing Warner Bros., 1976. 1977 formed own company, CineManson Mkt. & Dist. Corp. In 2002, Manson was a ShowEast Hall of Fame inductee. He is also a former chairman of the AMPAS NY events committee.

MANTEGNA, JOE
Actor. b. Chicago, IL, Nov. 13, 1947. e. Morton Jr. Coll., Goodman Sch. of Drama, 1967-69. Member: The Organic Theatre Company, Chicago (The Wonderful Ice Cream Suit, Cops, and 2 European tours with ensemble). Later member of Goodman Theater where he began long creative assoc. with playwright-dir. David Mamet (A Life in the Theatre, The Disappearance of the Jews). In national co. of Hair, Godspell, Lenny. B'way debut: Working. Narrated documentaries Crack U.S.A. and Death on the Job.
THEATRE: Bleacher Bums (also conceived and co-author), Leonardo (L.A., co-author), Glengarry Glen Ross (Tony Award).
PICTURES: Who Stole My Wheels? (Towing), Second Thoughts, Compromising Positions, The Money Pit, Off Beat, Three Amigos, Critical Condition, House of Games, Weeds, Suspect, Things Change (Venice Film Fest. Award, 1988), Wait Until Spring Bandini, Alice, The Godfather Part III, Queens Logic, Homicide, Bugsy, Body of Evidence, Family Prayers, Searching for Bobby Fisher, Baby's Day Out, Airheads, Forget Paris, Eye for an Eye, For Better or Worse, Up Close and Personal, Underworld, Albino Alligator, Thinner, Persons Unknowns, The Wonderful Ice Cream Suit, Jerry & Tom (also exec. prod.), For Hire, Boy Meets Girl, Celebrity, Body And Soul, Error in Judgment, Airspeed, Liberty Heights, The Runner, More Dogs Than Bones, The Last Producer, Lakeboat, Fall: The Price of Silence, The Trumpet of the Swan (voice), Off Key, Mother Ghost, Uncle Nino, Pontormo: A Heretical Love, Stateside, Nine Lives, Elvis and Anabelle, Cougar Club, West of Brooklyn, My Suicide, Childless, Naked Fear, The Kid & I, The Book of Joe, The Simpsons Movie (voice), Hank and Mike, Witless Protection, The House That Jack Built, Redbelt, Lonely Street, Valentine's Day.
TELEVISION: *Movies*: Elvis, Comrades of Summer, The Water Engine, State of Emergency, Above Suspicion, A Call to Remember, Face Down, Merry Christmas George Bailey, The Rat Pack (Emmy nom.; Golden Globe nom. 1999), Spenser: Small Vices, My Little Assassin, Thin Air, Walking Shadow, And Thou Shalt Honor (narrator), Bleacher Bums (writer), Women vs. Men, A Very Married Christmas, The Last Hit Man. *Mini-series:* The Last Don (Emmy nom. 1997), The Last Don II, The Starter Wife (Emmy nom. 2007). *Series*: Comedy Zone, First Monday, Joan of Arcadia, The Simpsons (voice), Criminal Minds. *Documentaries/Specials*: Bleacher Bums (Emmy Award, writer/play, 1979). *Guest:* More than 116 appearances.

MARBUT, ROBERT GORDON
Broadcast Executive. b. Athens, GA, April 11, 1935. Bachelor Industrial Engineering, Georgia Tech, 1957. M.B.A., Harvard, 1963. Began career with Copley Newspapers, Esso Standard Oil and Harvard Business School. From 1970-991, pres. & CEO of San Antonio-based Harte-Hanks Communications. Started Argyle Television in 1992 and sold co. in 1994. Then co-founded Argyle II and took it public in 1995. Sold control to Hearst in 1997 and served as chairman and co-CEO of Hearst-Argyle Television through 2002. In Jan. 2003 co-founded and became chairman and CEO of San Antonio, TX, based SecTecGlobal, a company serving the electronic security industry.

MARCOVICCI, ANDREA
Actress, Singer. b. New York, NY, Nov. 18, 1948. e. Bennett Col. Studied acting with Herbert Berghof. Acted on NY stage in The Wedding of Iphigenia, The Ambassadors, Nefertiti, Hamlet, Any Given Day. Frequent performer in night clubs.
PICTURES: The Front (debut, Golden Globe nom. 1976), The Concorde: Airport 1979, The Hand, Spacehunter: Adventures in the Forbidden Zone, Kings and Desperate Men, The Stuff, Someone to Love, White Dragon, Jack the Bear, The Beatnicks, Who Is Henry Jaglom? (documentary), Irene in Time.
TELEVISION: *Movies:* Cry Rape!, Smile Jenny You're Dead, Some Kind of Miracle, A Vacation in Hell, Packin' It In, Spraggue, Velvet, The Canterville Ghost, The Water Engine. *Series*: Love Is a Many-Splendored Thing, Berrenger's, Trapper John M.D.

MARCUS, MICHAEL E.
Executive. b. Pittsburgh, PA, June 5, 1945. e. Penn State, 1963-67. Moved to LA where he started in industry in mailroom of General Artists Corp. Promoted to agent when co. merged with Creative Management Assocs. 1972 joined Bart/Levy Agency; 1980, became full partner and co-owner of Kohner/Levy/Marcus Agency. 1981, became sr. agent at Creative Artists Agency. 1993, named pres. & COO of MGM Pictures. Founder and a literary manager with Cornice Entertainment in Los Angeles and a Partner of MAC Releasing.

MARCUS, STEPHEN
Exhibitor. Marcus is chairman of the bd. and pres./CEO of Marcus Theatres Corporation, a publicly held Wisconsin corporation listed in the New York Stock Exchange (MCS). Founded in 1935 with a single theatre, the co. now operates theatres throughout Wisconsin, Illinois, Ohio and Minnesota. During 2007, Marcus Theatres Corp. expanded into Iowa and North Dakota, and bolstered its presence in Wisconsin and Minnesota, with the acquisition of 11 theatre complexes from Cinema Entertainment Corp. for $75.7 million. The company also operates a full-service hotel division, Marcus Hotels & Resorts. Marcus has been chmn. of the board since December 1991 and pres./CEO since December 1988. He has worked at the company for 42 years. Chairman of the board of the National Association of Theatre Owners through 2004.

MARGOLIN, STUART
Actor, Director, Writer. b. Davenport, IA, Jan. 31, 1940. Wrote play Sad Choices which was produced Off-B'way when he was only 20.
PICTURES: *Actor:* Women of the Prehistoric Planet, Don't Just Stand There, The Gamblers, Kelly's Heroes, Limbo, The Stone Killer, Death Wish, The Gambler, The Big Bus, Futureworld, Days of Heaven, S.O.B., Class, Running Hot, A Fine Mess, Iron Eagle II, Bye Bye Blues, Deep Sleep, Guilty By Suspicion, Guilty by Suspicion, Impolite, The Lay of the Land, The Hi-Line, The Hoax, Trooper, Will Gardner. *Director:* Paramedics, Salt Water Moose (DGA Award, 1997), Snatched. *Writer:* A Man A Woman And A Bank, Grizzly Falls.
TELEVISION: *Movies*: *Actor:* Ironside, The Intruders, A Summer Without Boys (voice), The Rockford Files, The California Kid, This Is The Way It Was, Lanigan's Rabbi, The Revolution of Antonio Deleon, Bret Maverick (also dir.), A Killer in the Family, The Glitter Dome (also dir., prod. & composer), Vendetta: Secrets of a Mafia Bride (also dir., writer & composer), To Grandmother's House We Go, The Rockford Files: I Still Love L.A., The Rockford Files: A Blessing in Disguise, The Rockford Files: If the Frame Fits, The Rockford Files: Godfather Knows Best, The Rockford Files: Friend and Foul Play (also dir.), The Rockford Files: Punishment and Crime, Mother Trucker: The Diana Kilmury Story, The Rockford Files: Murder and Misdemeanors, The Rockford Files: If It Bleeds It Leads (also dir.), The Bridge. *Director:* Suddenly Love, A Shining Season, The Long Summer of George Adams (also composer), Dirkham Detective Agency, The Room Upstairs, The Facts of Life Down Under, Medicine River, Double Double Toil And Trouble, How the West Was Fun, The Sweetest Gift (Emmy nom.; DGA nom. 1999), Stranger in Town. Composer: The Ballad of Andy Crocker (also writer and assoc. prod.), Evil Roy Slade, Rolling Man. *Series: Actor:* Occasional Wife, Nichols, The Rockford Files (Emmy Awards, 1979, 1980; also dir.), Bret Maverick (also dir.), Mr. Smith, Mom P.I., These Arms of Mine, Beggars and Choosers, Tom Stone (also episode dir.), Intelligence (also 3 episodes dir.). *Director:* The Texas Wheelers, The Hardy Boys/Nancy Drew Mysteries, The Hardy Boys Mysteries, The Fitzpatricks, The Love Boat, Hart to Hart, Crazy Like A Fox, The Ray Bradbury Theater, Salt Water Moose (DGA Award 1997), B.L. Stryker, Quantum Leap, Fly by Night, Touched By An Angel, Black Harbour, Promised Land, Da Vinci's Inquest, Wild Card. *Guest:* More than 116 appearances.

MARGULIES, JULIANNA
Actress. b. Spring Valley, NY, June 8, 1966. e. Sarah Lawrence College, BA.
PICTURES: Out of Justice, Paradise Road, Traveller, A Price Below Rubies, The Newton Boys, The Big Day, What's Cooking, Dinosaur (voice), The Man From Elysian Fields, Searching for Debra Winger (documentary), Ghost Ship, Evelyn, Slingshot, The Darwin Awards, Beautiful Ohio, Snakes on a Plane, Chlorine, City Island.
TELEVISION: *Movies:* ER, Jenifer, Hitler: The Rise of Evil, Where Is the Mango Princess?, Canterbury's Law. *Mini-series:* The Mists of Avalon (Golden Globe nom. 2002), Breast Health: New Hope (host and narrator), The Grid (Golden Globe nom. 2005), The Lost Room. *Series*: ER (Emmy Award, 1995, 5 other noms.; 4 Golden Globe noms.), Canterbury's Law, The Good Wife (Golden Globe nom. 2010). *Documentaries:* Searching for Debra Winger, Women on Top: Hollywood and Power, Autism Is a World (short, narr.). *Guest:* More than 64 appearances.

MARILL, ALVIN H.
Writer. b. Brockton, MA, Jan. 10, 1934. e. Boston U., 1955. Dir. music programming, writer/prod., WNAC, Boston 1961-65; dir. music prog., WRFM, NY 1966-67; publicity writer, RCA Records 1967-72; sr. writer/editor, RCA Direct Marketing 1972-80; partner, TLK Direct Marketing 1977-80; mgr., A & R Administration, RCA Direct Marketing 1980-83; exec. editor, CBS TV (1984-88); editor, Carol Publ. Group (1988-94); Television editor, Films in Review 1973-84. Writer/ researcher: The Great Singers (record/tape collections). Jury member: 1983 Locarno Film Fest. Television Movie Hall of Fame.
AUTHOR: Samuel Goldwyn Presents, Robert Mitchum on the Screen, The Films of Anthony Quinn, The Films of Sidney Poitier, Katharine Hepburn: A Pictorial Study, Boris Karloff—A Pictorial Biography, Errol Flynn—A Pictorial Biography, The Complete Films of Edward G. Robinson, More Theatre: Stage to Screen to Television, Movies Made for Television: The Telefeature and the Mini-Series, 1964 - 1979, Movies Made for Television: The Telefeature and the Mini-Series, 1964-1984, Movies Made for Television 1964-96, The Films of Tyrone Power, The Films of Tommy Lee Jones, Robert Mitchum on the Screen, Keeping Score, More Theatre, More Theatre: Stage to Screen to Television, 1993-2001, Mickey Rooney: His Films-Television Appearances-Radio Work-Stage Shows-And Recordings, Keeping Score (written with James L. Limbacher), The Films of Anthony Quinn.
BOOK EDITOR: Moe Howard & The 3 Stooges, The Ultimate John Wayne Trivia Book. *Assoc. editor:* Leonard Maltin's Movie & Video Guide.

MARIN, CHEECH (RICHARD)
Actor, Writer. b. Los Angeles, CA, July 13, 1946. e. California State U, B.S. Teamed with Tommy Chong in improvisational group, City Works (Vancouver). Comedy recordings include Sleeping Beauty, Cheech and Chong Big Bama, Los Cochinos, The Wedding Album (Grammy Award), Get Out of My Room.
PICTURES: *Actor:* Up in Smoke (also co-s.p.), Cheech and Chong's Next Movie (also co-s.p.), Cheech and Chong's Nice Dreams (also co-s.p.), Things Are Tough All Over (also co-s.p.), It Came from Hollywood, Still Smokin' (also co-s.p.), Yellowbeard, Cheech and Chong's The Corsican Brothers (also co-s.p.), After Hours, Echo Park, Born in East L.A. (also s.p., dir.), Fatal Beauty, Oliver & Company (voice), Troop Beverly Hills (cameo), Ghostbusters II (cameo), Rude Awakening, Far Out Man, The Shrimp on the Barbie, FernGully: The Last Rainforest (voice), A Million to Juan, The Lion King (voice), The Magic of the Golden Bear: Goldy III, Charlie's Ghost Story, Desperado, From Dusk Till Dawn, The Great White Hype, Tin Cup, Paulie, Picking Up the Pieces, Luminarias, It's Tough to Be a Bug, Spy Kids, Spy Kids 2: The Island of Lost Dreams, Pinocchio (voice: US version), Spy Kids 3-D: Game Over, Once Upon a Time in Mexico, Good Boy (voice), The Lion King 1½ (video, voice), Christmas With The Kranks, Underclassman, Cars (voice), Grindhouse, The Perfect Game, Beverly Hills Chihuahua (voice), Race to Witch Mountain, The Perfect Game, Hoodwinked Too! Hood VS. Evil, Machete.
TELEVISION: *Movies*: *Actor:* Mother Goose Rock 'n' Rhyme, La Pastorela, Ring of the Musketeers, The Cisco Kid, The Courtyard, Latino Laugh Festival (host), 2nd Annual Latino Laugh Festival (host), Funny Flubs & Screw-Ups V (host), Tracey Ullman in the Trailer Tales, Cheech Marin & Friends: Live from South Beach (also exec. prod.), Expecting a Miracle. *Series*: *Actor:* The Golden Palace, Santo Bugito (voice), Nash Bridges, Resurrection Blvd, Funny Flubs & Screw-Ups (host), The Ortegas, Judging Amy (recurring role), Lost (recurring role). *Documentaries/Specials*: Get Out of My Room (also dir., songs), Charlie Barnett—Terms of Enrollment, This So-Called Disaster: Sam Shepard Directs the Late Henry Moss, Chavez Ravine: A Los Angeles Story (narr.). *Guest:* More than 112 appearances.

MARK, LAURENCE M.
Producer, Executive. b. New York, NY. e. Wesleyan U., B.A., 1971; NYU, M.A. Started career as trainee and publicist for United Artists; also asst. to prod. on Lenny, Smile. Joined Paramount Pictures as mktg./prod. liaison dir. and then exec. dir., pub. for m.p. division in NY. Named v.p., prod./mktg. at Paramount Studio; named v.p., West Coast mktg, 1980; promoted in 1982 to v.p., prod. Joined 20th Century-Fox as exec. v.p., prod. (projects incl. The Fly, Broadcast News); Formed indep. prod. co. in 1986, Laurence Mark Productions, with offices at Fox; in 1989, moved headquarters to Walt Disney Studios. Headquarters relocated to Columbia Pictures at Sony Studios in 1998. Currently President of Laurence Mark Productions.
THEATRE: Brooklyn Laundry (L.A.), Big (N.Y.).
PICTURES: *Producer/Exec. prod.*: Black Widow, Working Girl , My Stepmother is an Alien, Cookie, Mr. Destiny, True Colors, One Good Cop, The Adventures of Huck Finn, Gunmen, Sister Act 2: Back in the Habit, Cutthroat Island, Tom & Huck, Jerry Maguire (Academy Award nom., 1997), Romy & Michele's High School Reunion, Deep Rising, As Good As It Gets, The Object of My Affection, Simon Birch, Anywhere But Here, Bicentennial Man, Hanging Up, Center Stage, Finding Forrester, Glitter, Riding In Cars With Boys, I Robot, Last Holiday, Dreamgirls, Six Shooters, The Anderson Tapes, The Lookout, Center Stage: Turn It Up , Julie & Julia, How Do You Know, Dream On.
TELEVISION: *Movies: Exec. prod.*: Sweet Bird of Youth, Oliver Twist, These Old Broads, Kiss My Act, Gypsy and Me, Mumbai Calling (pilot). *Special:* The 81st Annual Academy Awards (prod., Emmy nom. 2009).

MARKHAM, MONTE
Actor, Director, Producer. b. Manatee, FL, June 21, 1935. e. U. of Georgia. Military service in Coast Guard after which joined resident theatre co. at Stephens College, MO, where he also taught acting. Joined Actor's Workshop Theatre, San Francisco, for three years. Made TV debut in Mission: Impossible episode. In June 1992, formed Perpetual Motion Films with Adam Friedman.
THEATRE: *B'way*: Irene (Theatre World Award), Same Time Next Year.
PICTURES: *Actor:* Hour of the Gun, Project X, Guns of the Magnificent Seven, One Is a Lonely Number, Midway, Airport '77, Ginger in the Morning, Off the Wall, Jake Speed, Hot Pursuit, Defense Play (also dir.), Neon City (also dir., s.p.), Two Guys Talkin' About Girls (video), Frame by Frame, Silent Life.
TELEVISION: *Movies*: *Actor:* Death Takes a Holiday, The Astronaut, Visions, Hustling, Ellery Queen, Relentless, Drop-Out Father, Hotline, Finder of Lost Loves, Baywatch: Panic at Malibu Pier, Nikki and Alexander, Piranha, Millennium Man. *Mini-series: Actor:* Jack Holborn, Fly Past (narr, dir., prod.). *Series*: *Actor:* The Second Hundred Years, Mr. Deeds Goes to Town, The New Perry Mason, Dallas, Breakaway, (host), Rituals, Baywatch Hawaii (also dir. episodes), Melrose Place, Campus Cops. *Director/Producer:* Air Combat (also host), Masters of War, The Great Ships. *Documentaries/Specials: As narrator:* George Washington: Founding Father, Cleopatra: Destiny's Queen (voice), Attila the Hun: Scourge of God, Masters of Production: The Hidden Art of Hollywood, Biography. *Producer/Director:* Red Flag, Boneyard: Where Machines End Their Lives (exec. prod.), Boneyard: The Secret Life of Machines (exec. prod.). *Guest:* More than 100 appearances.

MARKLE, PETER
Director, Producer. b. Danville, PA, Sept. 24, 1952.
PICTURES: *Director/Producer:* The Personals (also s.p., cinematographer), Hot Dog ...The Movie (dir. only), Youngblood (also s.p.), Bat-21 (dir. only), Wagons East! (dir. only), The Last Days of Frankie the Fly, Virginia's Run (also s.p.).
TELEVISION: *Movies*: *Director:* Desperate, Nightbreaker, Breaking Point, El Diablo, Mob Justice, Through the Eyes of a Killer, Jake Lassiter: Justice on the Bayou, White Dwarf, Target Earth, Saving Jessica Lynch, Faith of My Fathers (also writer), Flight 93 (Emmy nom.; DGA nom. 2007), The Tenth Circle, High Noon. *Series*: *Director:* EZ Streets, L.A. Doctors, Strange World, Century City, Without a Trace. Also director of episodes for more than 16 additional TV series.

MARKOWITZ, ROBERT
Director. b. Irvington, NJ, Feb. 7, 1935. e. Boston Univ.
PICTURES: Voices (debut 1979).
TELEVISION: *Movies*: Children of the Night, Phantom of the Opera, The Deadliest Season, The Storyteller, Kojak: The Belarus File, My Mother's Secret Life, Pray TV, A Long Way Home, Alex: The Life of a Child, Adam: His Song Continues, The Wall, A Cry for Help: The Tracey Thurman Story, Too Young to Die, Decoration Day (Emmy nom. 1991), Love Lies and Murder, Afterburn, Overexposed, Murder in the Heartland, Because Mommy Works, The Tuskegee Airmen (DGA nom. 1996), Into Thin Air: Death on Everest, David, Nicholas' Gift, Spenser: Small Vices, The Great Gatsby, The Big Heist (also prod.), The Pilot's Wife (also prod.) Word of Honor, Heartless, Avenger. *Mini-series:* A Dangerous Life. *Series:* Delvecchio, Serpico. *Documentaries/Specials:* Twilight Zone: Rod Serling's Lost Classics.

MARKS, RICHARD E.
Executive. e. UCLA, B.A., magna cum laude; UCLA Sch. of Law, J.D. 1978-82, v.p., legal & business affairs for Ziegler/Diskant Literary Agency. Joined Paramount Pictures 1984 as sr. atty. for Network TV Div., as project atty. for Family Ties, Cheers, etc. 1985, named sr. atty. for M.P. Group for The Golden Child, Beverly Hills Cop II, etc.; 1987 joined Weintraub Ent. Group as v.p. business affairs; m.p. div. 1990; counsel for Disney projects

such as The Rocketeer, Beauty and the Beast. 1991, joined Media Home Entertainment as sr. v.p. in charge of all business and legal affairs. 1994, joined the Kushner-Locke Company as sr. v.p., business affairs for feature division and served as company's exec. v.p., gen. counselor. Previously, Marks also was v.p. of bus. & legal affairs at Universal Network Television. As a consultant, he worked for Nickelodeon Movies in the areas of development, production and distribution of its feature films for Paramount. In Jan. 2004, he joined the law firm of Greenberg Traurig, L.L.P. and practiced entertainment law in the firm's Los Angeles office. Professional and community involvement includes membership on the bd. of trustees of the Leo Baeck Temple and the bd. of directors for Jewish Big Brothers.

MARS, KENNETH
Actor. b. Chicago, IL, April 14, 1936.
PICTURES: The Producers, Butch Cassidy and the Sundance Kid, Desperate Characters, What's Up Doc?, The Parallax View, Young Frankenstein, Night Moves, The Apple Dumpling Gang Rides Again, Full Moon High, Yellowbeard, Protocol, Prince Jack, Beer, Fletch, Radio Days, For Keeps?, Illegally Yours, Rented Lips, Police Academy 6: City Under Siege, The Little Mermaid (voice), Shadows and Fog, We're Back (voice), The Land Before Time II: The Great Valley Adventure (voice), Thumbelina (voice), Land Before Time III, Rough Magic, Citizen Ruth, Teddy Bears' Picnic, Land Before Time--IV, V, VI, VII and VIII--(voice), The Little Mermaid II: Return to the Sea (voice), The Land Before Time: Journey to Big Water (voice), The Land Before Time X: The Great Longneck Migration (voice), The Land Before Time XI: Invasion of the Tinysauruses, The Land Before Time XII: The Great Day of the Flyers, The Little Mermaid 3 (video).
TELEVISION: *Movies:* Second Chance, Guess Who's Sleeping in My Bed?, It's A Bird-It's A Plane-It's Superman, Someone I Touched, The New Original Wonder Woman, Columbo: The Bye-Bye Sky-High I.Q. Murder Case, You Can't Take It With You, Before and After, Misfits of Science, Get Smart Again, I'll Take Romance, Basic Values: Sex Shock & Censorship in the '90s, Runaway Virus, How to Marry a Billionaire: A Christmas Tale. *Series:* He & She, The Don Knotts Show, Shepherd's Flock, Uncle Croc's Block, Sha Na Na, The Carol Burnett Show (1979), Shades of L.A., Malcolm in the Middle (recurring role). *Voice Roles:* The Jetsons, M-U-S-H, Laverne & Shirley in the Army, The Biskitts, The Mork & Mindy/Laverne & Shirley with the Fonz Show, Saturday Supercade, Challenge of the Gobots, A Pup Named Scooby-Doo, The Adventures of Raggedy Ann and Andy, Tale Spin, Fievel's American Tails, Dark Water, Darkwing Duck, The Little Mermaid, Bruno the Kid. *Guest:* More than 144 appearances.

MARSH, JEAN
Actress, Writer. b. London, England, July 1, 1934. NY stage debut in Much Ado About Nothing, 1959. As a child appeared in films: Tales of Hoffman; as principal dancer in Where's Charley. Co-creator, co-author and starred as Rose, in Upstairs, Downstairs.
THEATRE: *B'way:* Travesties, The Importance of Being Earnest, Too True to Be Good, My Fat Friend, Whose Life Is It Anyway?, Blithe Spirit.
PICTURES: Cleopatra, Unearthly Stranger, The Limbo Line, Jane Eyre, Frenzy, Dark Places, The Eagle Has Landed, The Changeling, Return to Oz, Willow, Monarch, The Heavy.
TELEVISION: *Movies:* The Moon and Sixpence, The Horsemasters, Heart to Heart, Danger Zone, Diary of a Young Man, Skin Deep, Goliath Awaits, The Corsican Brothers, Danny-The Champion of the World, A Connecticut Yankee in King Arthur's Court, Act of Will, Bejewelled, Adam Bede, Fatherland, The Pale Horse, The Mayor of Casterbridge, Julian Fellowes Investigates: A Most Mysterious Murder - The Case of the Croydon Poisonings. *Mini-series:* Master of the Game, Sense and Sensibility. *Series:* Upstairs Downstairs (Emmy Award, 1975,2 other noms.; 2 Golden Globe noms.), Nine to Five, No Strings, The House of Eliott (assoc. series creator only), The All New Alexei Sayle Show, Art of the Garden (documentary), Ghosthunter. *Guest:* More than 98 appearances.

MARSHALL, ALAN
Producer. b. London, England, Aug. 12, 1938. Co-founder Alan Parker Film Company, 1970. Formerly film editor. Received Michael Balcon Award, British Acad., Outstanding Contribution to Cinema, 1985.
PICTURES: Bugsy Malone, Midnight Express, Fame, Shoot the Moon, Pink Floyd: The Wall, Another Country (Cannes Film Fest. Award, 1984), Birdy (Special Jury Award, Cannes Film Fest., 1985), Angel Heart, Homeboy, Jacob's Ladder, Basic Instinct, Cliffhanger, Showgirls, Starship Troopers, Hollow Man, The Winter Queen.
TELEVISION: No Hard Feelings, Our Cissy, Footsteps.

MARSHALL, FRANK
Producer, Director. b. Sept. 13, 1946. Raised in Newport Beach, CA. Worked on first feature film in 1967 while still a student at UCLA. Protege of Peter Bogdanovich, working on his production crew and as asst. on Targets, location manager on The Last Picture Show, What's Up Doc?. Assoc. prod. on Paper Moon, Daisy Miller, Nickelodeon, etc. Line prod. on Orson Welles' The Other Side of the Wind (unreleased) and Martin Scorsese's The Last Waltz. Worked with Walter Hill on The Driver (assoc. prod.) and The Warriors (exec. prod.). Began collaboration with Steven Spielberg as prod. for Raiders of the Lost Ark. In 1992, with wife and partner Kathleen Kennedy, formed The Kennedy/Marshall Company. He received the Producer of the Year Award in 1982 from ShoWest.
PICTURES: *Producer:* Nickelodeon, Raider's of the Lost Ark (also pilot; Academy Award nom. for Best Picture, 1982), Poltergeist, The Color Purple (also second unit dir.; Academy Award nom. for Best Picture, 1986), The Money Pit, An American Tail, Empire of the Sun (also second unit dir.), Who Framed Roger Rabbit (also second unit dir.), Always (also second unit dir.), Hook, Noises Off...(also second unit dir.), Milk Money (also second unit dir.), The Indian in the Cupboard, Olympic Glory (documentary short; co-prod.), The Sixth Sense (Academy Award nom. for Best Picture, 2000), Snow Falling on Cedars (also second unit dir.), A Map of the World, Signs, Seabiscuit (also second unit dir. Academy Award nom. for Best Picture, 2004), The Young Black Stallion, The Bourne Supremacy, Hoot, Emma's War, Jurassic Park IV, The Diving Bell and the Butterfly, Crossing Over, The Bourne Ultimatum, Indiana Jones and the Kingdom of the Crystal Skull, The Curious Case of Benjamin Button (Academy Award nom. 2009), The Last Airbender. *Executive Producer:* The Warriors, Twilight Zone: The Movie, Indiana Jones and the Temple of Doom (also second unit dir.), Gremlins, Fandango, The Goonies, Back to the Future (also second unit dir.), Young Sherlock Holmes, Innerspace (co-exec. prod.), batteries not included, The Land Before Time (co-exec. prod.), Indiana Jones and the Last Crusade (also second unit dir.), Tummy Trouble (short; also dir.), Dad, Back to the Future II, Joe Versus the Volcano, Back to the Future III (also dir. of live action sequence), Roller Coaster Rabbit (short; also dir. of live action sequence), Gremlins 2: The New Batch, Arachnophobia (also dir.), Cape Fear, An American Tail: Fievel Goes West, Swing Kids, Trail Mix-Up, A Far Off Place, We're Back: A Dinosaur's Story, Congo (also dir.), The Best of Roger Rabbit (video), King Returns (short), The Bourne Identity, Mr. 3000, The Spiderwick Chronicles, Hereafter. *Production Executive on Videos:* Tiny Toon Adventures: How I spent My Vacation, Amazing Stories Book One, Amazing Stories Book Two, Amazing Stories Book Three, Amazing Stories Book Four, Amazing Stories Book Five. *Director:* Alive, Eight Below.
TELEVISION: *Movies: Executive Producer:* The Sports Pages, The Special Relationship. *Mini-series: Director:* From the Earth to the Moon (part six). *Series: Executive Producer:* Johnny Bago. *Production Executive:* Amazing Stories. *Documentaries/Specials: Executive Producer:* The Making of Goonies, The Secrets of the Back to the Future Trilogy, A Wish for Wings That Work, The Olympic Torch Relay *Producer:* The Making of Poltergeist (also dir.), The Making of Indiana Jones and the Temple of Doom (also writer & dir.). Documentary: Right to Play (dir.).

MARSHALL, GARRY
Producer, Director, Writer, Actor. r.n. Garry Marscharelli. b. New York, NY, Nov. 13, 1934. Sister is dir.-actress Penny Marshall. e. Northwestern U. Copy boy and reporter for NY Daily News while writing comedy material for Phil Foster, Joey Bishop. Was drummer in his own jazz band and successful stand-up comedian and playwright. Turned Neil Simon's play The Odd Couple into long running TV series (1970). Partner with Jerry Belson many years. Received Golden Eddie Filmaker of the Year Award 2004. 1990 received Creative Achievemant Award. Received WGA Valentine Davies Award 1995. *Playwright:* The Roast (with Belson, 1980), Wrong Turn at Lungfish (with Lowell Ganz, 1992; also dir., actor). *Autobiography:* Wake Me When It's Funny (1995).
PICTURES: *Writer-Producer:* How Sweet It Is, The Grasshopper. *Director:* Young Doctors in Love (also exec. prod.), The Flamingo Kid (also co-s.p.), Nothing in Common, Overboard, Beaches, Pretty Woman, Frankie and Johnny (also co-prod.), Exit to Eden, Dear God (also cameo), Runaway Bride (also cameo), The Other Sister (also story), The Princess Diaries, The Hollywood Sign, Raising Helen, The Princess Diaries 2: Royal Engagement, Georgia Rule, Valentine's Day, State of the Union. *Actor:* Psych-Out, Mary Jane, The Escape Artist, Lost in America, Jumpin' Jack Flash, Soapdish, A League of Their Own, Hocus Pocus, With Friends Like These, This Space Between Us, Can't Be Heaven, Never Been Kissed, Runaway Bride, Can't Be Heaven, This Space Between Us, It's A Shame About Ray, The Long Ride Home, Mother Ghost, Orange County, They Call Him Sasquatch, Devil's Knight, Lucky 13, Chicken Little (voice), Keeping Up with the Steins, Chronic Town, Race to Witch Mountain.
TELEVISION: *Movies*: *Executive Producer:* Beanes of Boston, The Twilight of the Golds (also acting). *Writer/Producer:* Evil Roy Slade. *Acting:* The Last Shot (TV short), But Seriously Folks (TV short; host), CHiPs '99. *Series: Writer:* Make Room For Daddy, Jack Paar Show, Joey Bishop Show, Bill Dana Show, Danny Thomas Show, The Dick Van Dyke Show, The Lucy Show, Gomer Pyle U.S.M.C., I Spy, Sheriff Who??, Hey Landlord (also prod.), Love American Style, The Odd Couple (also dir., exec. prod., 4 Emmy noms.), Barefoot in the Park, Me and the Chimp (also dir. and exec. prod.), Happy Days (also dir. & exec. prod.), Laverne & Shirley (also dir. & exec. prod.), Mork & Mindy (also dir. & exec.

prod., Emmy nom. 1979), Fonz and the Happy Days Gang. *Executive Producer:* Who's Watching the Kids, Joanie Loves Chachi, Herndon (also dir.). *Producer:* Blansky's Beauties (also dir.), Angie, Nothing In Common. *Series/Actor:* A League of Their Own (recurring guest role), Murphy Brown (also dir.), Father of the Pride (voice; recurring guest role). *Guest:* More than 117 appearances.

MARSHALL, PENNY
Actress, Director, Producer. b. New York, NY, Oct. 15, 1942. Father: industrial filmmaker and Laverne and Shirley prod., Tony Marscharelli. Brother is prod.-dir. Garry Marshall. Daughter is actress Tracy Reiner. Acted in summer stock and competed on The Original Amateur Hour before going to Hollywood to make TV debut in The Danny Thomas Hour (1967-68). 1992 received ACA Creative Achievement Award.
PICTURES: *Actress*: The Savage Seven, How Sweet It Is, The Grasshopper, How Come Nobody's on Our Side?, 1941, Movers and Shakers, The Hard Way, Hocus Pocus, Stateside, Looking for Comedy in the Muslim World, Alice, Everybody Wants to Be Italian, Blonde Ambition. *Director*: Jumpin' Jack Flash (debut, 1986), Big, Awakenings (also exec. prod.), A League of Their Own (also exec. prod.), Renaissance Man (also exec. prod.), The Preacher's Wife, Riding in Cars With Boys. *Producer:* Getting Away With Murder, With Friends Like These..., Risk, Cinderella Man, Bewitched, The Pottsville Maroons, The Fallen. *Executive Producer:* Calendar Girl. *Documentaries:* One Vision, Fathers of the Sport (consult).
TELEVISION: *Movies*: *Actress:* Wacky Zoo of Morgan City, The Feminist and the Fuzz, Evil Roy Slade, The Couple Takes a Wife, Let's Switch, The Crooked Hearts, More Than Friends, Love Thy Neighbor, Challenge of a Lifetime, The Odd Couple: Together Again, Laverne and Shirley Together Again, TV's Greatest Sidekicks (host), Women Without Men (also dir.). *Series*: *Actress:* The Odd Couple, The Bob Newhart Show, Friends and Lovers, Laverne and Shirley (also dir., 3 Golden Globe noms.), Laverne and Shirley in the Army (voice) *Series: Director*: Working Stiffs, Tracey Ullman Show, A League of Their Own (also prod.). *Documentaries/Specials*: *Executive Producer:* Crossover (aka Dynasties). The Laverne and Shirley Reunion. *Guest*: More than 140 appearances.

MARSHALL-DANIELS, MERYL
Executive, Producer. b. Los Angeles, CA, Oct. 16, 1949. e. UCLA, B.A. sociology, 1971. Loyola Marymount U., J.D., 1974. Deputy pub. defender, LA County, 1975-77. Partner, Markman & Markman, 1978-79. NBC: Sr. Atty., 1979-80. Dir. programs/contracts/bus. affairs, 1980; asst. general counsel, 1980-82; VP, compliance/practices, 1982-87. VP prog. affairs, Group W Prods., 1987-92. Founder and president, Two Oceans Ent. Grp., an independent production company, 1992-Present. Marshall-Daniels has been an active member of the Academy of Television Arts & Sciences (ATAS) since 1982; she was elected to three terms as Treasurer, two terms as Governor of the Production Executives Peer Group, was the chair of numerous committees and a member of the ATAS Foundation Board of Directors. She was chairman & CEO of ATAS in 1997 and re-elected in 1999. Marshall-Daniels spearheaded the development of the ATAS Foundation educational program S.T.A.R.T. Communications (Student and Teacher Achievement using the Resources of Television) for elementary students. Through S.T.A.R.T., students learn to examine, challenge and comprehend messages contained in television. Marshall-Daniels was a member of the 1998-99 class of Senior Fellows of the UCLA School of Public Policy and Social Research. She has lectured at UCLA, Peter F. Drucker Graduate School of Management and the University of Texas. Marshall has also moderated and participated on panels sponsored by Aspen Institute, the International Documentary Association, Prix Italia, Arts Inc. Leadership America and the National Association of Television Program Executives.
PICTURES: When Danger Follows You Home (prod.)
TELEVISION: *Movies*: Baby Monitor: Sound of Fear (exec. prod.). *Series*: Happily Ever After: Fairy Tales for Every Child (exec. prod.). *Documentaries/Specials*: Middle School Confessions (exec. prod.), Mother Goose: A Rappin' and Rhymin'.

MARTIN, ANDREA
Actress. b. Portland, ME, Jan. 15, 1947.
THEATRE: *NY*: My Favorite Year (Tony Award & Theatre World Award), The Merry Wives of Windsor.
PICTURES: Cannibal Girls, Soup for One, Club Paradise, Rude Awakening, Worth Winning, Too Much Sun, Stepping Out, All I Want for Christmas, Ted and Venus,. Bogus, Anastasia, Wag the Dog, The Rugrats Movie (voice), Believe, Hedwig and the Angry Inch, Recess: School's Out (voice), All Over the Guy, Jimmy Neutron: Boy Genius (voice), My Big Fat Greek Wedding, New York Minute, The Producers, Young Triffie's Been Made Away With, The TV Set, How to Eat Fried Worms, Black Christmas, The Toe Tactic (voice), Breaking Upwards.
TELEVISION: *Movies:* Torn Between Two Lovers, Martin Short: Concert for the North Americas, The Best of SCTV, The Trial of Red Riding Hood, Frosty Returns (TV short; voice), David Copperfield, Gypsy, Guitarman, In Search of Dr. Suess, Harrison Bergeron, Prince Charming, The Kid (voice), Kim Possible: A Sitch in Time (voice), Jimmy Neutron: Attack of the Twonkies. *Mini-series:* St. Urbain's Horseman. *Series*: The David Steinberg Show, The Sunshine Hour, SCTV (also writer), SCTV Network (2 Emmy Awards for writing, 1982 & 1983, 8 other noms.), SCTV Channel (also writer), Roxie, The Completely Mental Misadventures of Ed Grimley (voice), The Martin Short Show, Earthworm Jim (voice), Life...And Stuff, Recess (voice), Damon, Sesame Street, The New Woody Woodpecker Show, George and Martha, Committed (voice), The Adventures of Jimmy Neutron: Boy Genius (voice), My Big Fat Greek Life, Insatiable, Kim Possible, Dino Dan. *Documentaries/Specials:* Kid Safe: The Video, Andrea Martin... Together Again, Just for Laughs: Montreal Comedy Festival, Whether You Like It or Not: The Story of Hedwig. *Guest:* More than 118 appearances.

MARTIN, GARY
Executive. b. Santa Monica, CA, Aug, 14, 1944. e. CSU Northridge, 1962-65. Joined Columbia Pictures in 1981. V.P. of production, Columbia Pictures, 1984-86; exec. v.p., production, 1986-88. Pres. of production admin., Columbia Pictures and TriStar Pictures 1988-95; Columbia TriStar Motion Pictures Group president of production administration, 1995-present president of Sony Picture Studio Operations. Member, AMPAS., D.G.A.

MARTIN, JUDSON W.
Executive. Began career with Pricewaterhouse Coopers in Calgary, Alberta, Canada, 1979. Twenty years in various mgmt roles with affiliates of EdperBrascan Corp., including president & CEO, Trilon Securities Corp., v.p., corporate finance & treasurer, Trizec Hahn; senior exec. v.p., CEO, and director, MDC Corp. Currently director and non-exec. chairman, Board of Intl. Properties Group, Ltd.; director, TGS Properties, Ltd., served as senior exec. v.p. & CFO, Alliance Atlantis Communications, Inc.

MARTIN, KEVIN J.
Government Executive. b. Charlotte, NC, Dec. 14, 1966. e. Univ. of North Carolina at Chapel Hill, B.A. degree; a masters degree in Public Policy from Duke University; and a J.D. degree from Harvard Law School. Martin was a judicial clerk for U.S. District Court Judge William M. Hoeveler, Miami, FL. He previously worked as an associate at the Washington, DC law firm of Wiley, Rein & Fielding before serving in the Office of the Independent Counsel. Martin was an advisor to FCC Commissioner Harold Furchtgott-Roth before he became Deputy General Counsel for the Bush presidential campaign. He served on the Bush-Cheney Transition Team and was a Special Assistant to the President for Economic Policy. President George W. Bush nominated Martin to a Republican seat on the FCC , and Martin was sworn in on July 3, 2001. When FCC Chairman Michael Powell resigned his post, President Bush then designated Martin the new Commission chairman on March 18, 2005. President Bush renominated Martin to a new five year term on April 25, 2006. He was reconfirmed by the U.S. Senate on Nov. 17, 2006. January 15, 2009 Martin announced his resignation from the FCC effective January 20, 2009.

MARTIN, MILLICENT
Actress, Singer. b. Romford, England, June 8, 1934. Toured U.S. in The Boy Friend, 1954-57.
THEATRE: Expresso Bongo, The Crooked Mile, Our Man Crichton, Tonight at 8:30, The Beggar's Opera, Puss 'n Boots, Aladdin, Peter Pan, The Card, Absurd Person Singular, Aladdin, Side by Side by Sondheim, King of Hearts, Move Over Mrs. Markham, Noises Off, One Into Two, 42nd Street (N.Y. & L.A.), The Cemetery Club, Shirley Valentine, The Boyfriend, Noel, Follies, The Rivals, The Rise and Fall of Little Voice.
PICTURES: Libel, Invasion Quartet, The Girl on the Boat, Nothing But the Best, Those Magnificent Men in Their Flying Machines, Alfie, Stop the World I Want To Get Off, Mrs. Palfrey at the Claremont.
TELEVISION: *Movies:* The Horsemasters, ABC of Britain, Return to Halloweentown. *Series*: From a Bird's Eye View, The Picadilly Palace, Mainly Millicent, Millie, Downtown, Moon and Son, Days of Our Lives, Frasier (in recurring guest role).

MARTIN, PAMELA SUE
Actress. b. Westport, CT, Jan. 5, 1954. Did modeling and TV commercials before entering films.
PICTURES: To Find a Man, The Poseidon Adventure, Buster and Billie, Our Time, The Lady in Red, Torchlight (also assoc. prod. & s.p.), Flicks, A Cry in the Wild, Soupernatural, McTaggart's Fortune.
TELEVISION: *Movies*: The Girls of Huntington House, The Gun and the Pulpit, Human Feelings, Strong Medicine, Bay Coven, Sky Trackers. *Series*: The Hardy Boys/Nancy Drew Mysteries, Dynasty, The Star Games (host).

MARTIN, STEVE
Actor, Writer. b. Waco, TX, Aug. 14, 1945. e. Long Beach Col., UCLA. Raised in Southern California. Worked at Disneyland, teaching himself juggling, magic and the banjo. Partner/Exec. Prod. Martin/Stein Productions. Became writer for various TV comedy shows, incl. Smothers Brothers Comedy Hour (Emmy Award for writing, 1968-69), Glen Campbell Show, Sonny & Cher. Co-writer for special Van Dyke and Company. Wrote and starred

in Academy Award nominated short The Absent-Minded Waiter. *Author:* Cruel Shoes (1980), The Pleasure of My Company. *Albums:* Let's Get Small (Grammy Award, 1977), A Wild and Crazy Guy (Grammy Award, 1978), Comedy Is Not Pretty, The Steve Martin Brothers. Gold Record for single King Tut. Received ACA Lifetime Achievement Award 2000.
THEATRE: *Actor:* Waiting for Godot (Off-B'way debut, 1988), WASP. *Author:* Picasso at the Lapin Agile (regional, 1993), WASP (Off-B'way), Pure Drivel, Shopgirl: A Novella.
PICTURES: Sgt. Pepper's Lonely Hearts Club Band (debut, 1978), The Kids Are Alright, The Muppet Movie, The Jerk (also co-s.p.), Pennies From Heaven (Golden Globe nom. 1982), Dead Men Don't Wear Plaid (also co-s.p.), The Man With Two Brains (also co-s.p.), The Lonely Guy, All of Me (NY Film Critics & Natl. Board of Review Awards, Golden Globe nom. 1984), Movers and Shakers, Three Amigos! (also co-s.p., exec. prod.), Little Shop of Horrors, Roxanne (also s.p., exec. prod.; Natl. Society of Film Critics & L.A. Film Critics Awards for actor, WGA Award for adapt. s.p., Golden Globe nom. 1987), Planes Trains & Automobiles, Dirty Rotten Scoundrels, Parenthood (Golden Globe nom. 1990), My Blue Heaven, L.A. Story (also s.p., co-exec. prod.), Father of the Bride (Golden Globe nom. 1996), Grand Canyon, Housesitter, Leap of Faith, A Simple Twist of Fate (also s.p., exec. prod.), Mixed Nuts, Father of the Bride 2, Sgt. Bilko, The Spanish Prisoner, The Prince of Egypt (voice), The Out-of-Towners, Bowfinger (also s.p.), The Venice Project, Fantasia/2000, Joe Gould's Secret, Thin Ice, Novocaine, Bringing Down the House, Looney Tunes: Back in Action, Cheaper By the Dozen, The Pink Panther (also s.p.), Shopgirl (als s.p., exec. prod.), Cheaper by the Dozen 2, Baby Mama, Traitor (writer/idea, exec. prod.), Pink Panther 2 (also writer, s.p.), It's Complicated, Tangled (voice), The Big Year.
TELEVISION: *Movies*: The Jerk Too (exec. prod. only), And the Band Played On, The Rutles 2: Can't Buy Me Lunch, Mindy and Brenda (exec. prod.). *Series*: *Writer:* The Smothers Brothers Comedy Hour (Emmy Award for writing 1969), The Glen Campbell Goodtime Hour, The Sonny and Cher Show, The Downer Channel (also exec. prod.), Van Dyke and Company (Emmy nom. for writing 1976). *Executive Producer:* Domestic Life, George Burns Comedy Week, Leo & Liz in Beverly Hills, The Scholar (series). *Actor:* The Ray Stevens Show, Half the George Kirby Comedy Hour, The Sonny and Cher Comedy Hour (various characters, Emmy nom. for writing 1972), The Ken Berry "WOW" Show, The Smothers Brothers Show, Johnny Cash and Friends, Twilight Theater (various characters), 30 Rock (Emmy nom. 2009 as guest). *Documentaries/Specials: Writer:* Saturday Night Live: The Best of Steve Martin, Funny Business, Steve Martin: All Commercials (WGA Award 1981), The 73rd Annual Academy Awards (Emmy nom. 2001), The 75th Annual Academy Awards (host, writer WGA nom. 2004) and many others. *Guest:* More than 204 appearances.

MASLANSKY, PAUL
Producer. b. New York, NY, Nov. 23, 1933. e. Washington and Lee U., 1954. Moved to Europe performing as jazz musician in Paris, 1959-60. Entered film business with documentary, Letter from Paris. Asst. to prods. Charles Shneer and Irving Allen in England, Italy and Yugoslavia, 1961-62. In charge of physical-prod. in Europe for UA, 1965-67. Founder of production company, Paul Maslansky Productions.
PICTURES: Castle of the Living Dead, Revenge of the Blood Beast, Sudden Terror (Eye Witness), Raw Meat, Deathline, Sister of Satan, Big Truck, Poor Claire, Deathline, Sugar Hill (dir.), Race With the Devil (exec. prod.), Hard Times (exec. prod.), The Blue Bird, Circle of Iron, Damnation Alley (co-prod.), When You Comin' Back Red Ryder? (co-prod.), Hot Stuff (exec. prod.), The Villain (exec. prod.), Scavenger Hunt (co-prod.), The Salamander, Ruckus, Love Child, Police Academy, Police Academy 2: Their First Assignment, Return to Oz, Police Academy 3: Back in Training, Police Academy 4: Citizens on Patrol, Police Academy 5: Assignment Miami Beach, For Better or Worse (exec. prod.), Police Academy 6: City Under Siege, Ski Patrol (exec. prod.), Honeymoon Academy, The Russia House, Cop and ½, Police Academy: Mission to Moscow, Fluke.
TELEVISION: *Movie*: The Gun and the Pulpit. *Mini-series*: King (Emmy nom. 1978). *Series*: Police Academy: The Series (creator, writer, exec. prod.).

MASON, JACKIE
Comedian, Actor. b. Sheboygan, WI June 9, 1931. e. City College. Was a rabbi before becoming stand-up comedian. Records include The World According to Me! Has lectureship in his name at Oxford Univ. in England.
THEATRE: Enter Solly Gold (1965), A Teaspoon Every Four Hours (Amer. National Theatre & Academy Theatre), Sex-a-Poppin (revue, prod. only), The World According to Me! (one-man show, special Tony Award, 1987), Jackie Mason: Brand New, Politically Incorrect, Jackie Mason: Prune Danish, Jackie Mason: Freshly Squeezed.
PICTURES: Operation Delilah (debut, 1966), The Stoolie (also prod.), The Jerk, History of the World Part I, A Stroke of Genius (actor, prod. & s.p.), Stiffs (also exec. prod.), Caddyshack II.
TELEVISION: *Movie:* Jackie Mason at the London Paladium. *Series:* Chicken Soup, Jackie Mason (synd.), The Simpsons (Emmy Award 1992). *Specials:* Jack Paar is Alive and Well!, The World According to Me! (ACE Award), Jackie Mason on Broadway (Emmy Award for Writing), But...Seriously, The Royal Variety Performance 2001. *Guest:* More than 66 appearances.

MASON, JOHN DUDLEY
Executive. b. Ashland, KY, Oct 29, 1949. e. Amherst Coll., B.A., cum laude, 1971; Claremont Graduate Sch. and University Center, M.A., 1973; Amos Tuck Sch. of Business Administration, Dartmouth Coll., M.B.A., 1978. Program officer, National Endowment for the Humanities, 1972-76; analyst (1978-79), asst. mgr. (1979-80), mgr. (1980) strategic planning, Consolidated Rail Corp.; Consultant, Frito-Lay, Division, PepsiCo (1980-82); mgr, corporate planning, Dun & Bradstreet Corp. (1982-86); finance dir., anti-piracy (1986-90), v.p. finance, anti-piracy (1990-92), Motion Picture Association of America, Inc. Chmn., New Century Artists' Mgmt., 1990-98. Chmn., Finance Comm. and mem., bd. of dir. Association de Gestion Int'l. Collective des Oeuvres Audiovisuelles (AGICOA) 1987-88. Dir., Instituto Venezolano de Representacion Cinematografica (INVERECI), Caracas, Venezuela (1988-92). Dir.: Foundation for the Protection of Film & Video Works (FVWP), Taipei, Taiwan (1987-92). Dir. sec. Korean Federation Against Copyright Theft, 1990-92; Dir., Japan & Intl. M.P. Copyright Assn., Tokyo, 1990-92; Trustee and Treasurer, Design Industries Foundation for AIDS, 1990-94. Mng. dir., B.L. Nickerson & Associates, LLC, 1997-present.

MASON, MARSHA
Actress. b. St. Louis, MO, April 3, 1942. e. Webster Coll. Came to N.Y. to continue dramatic studies and embark on theatre career. Member of American Conservatory Theatre, San Francisco.
THEATRE: The Deer Park, Cactus Flower, The Indian Wants the Bronx, Happy Birthday Wanda June, King Richard III, Cactus Flower, Private Lives, You Can't Take It With You, Cyrano de Bergerac, A Doll's House, The Merchant of Venice, The Crucible, Twelfth Night, The Good Doctor, Old Times, The Big Love, Lake No Bottom. Escape from Happiness, Amazing Grace, Night of the Iguana. *Director:* Juno's Swans.
PICTURES: Hot Rod Hullabaloo (debut, 1966), Blume in Love, Cinderella Liberty (Academy Award nom.; golden globe Award 1974), Audrey Rose, The Goodbye Girl (Academy Award nom.; Golden Globe Award 1978), The Cheap Detective, Promises in the Dark (Golden Globe nom. 1980), Chapter Two (Academy Award nom.; Golden Globe nom. 1980), Only When I Laugh (Academy Award nom. 1982), Max Dugan Returns, Heartbreak Ridge, Stella, Drop Dead Fred, I Love Trouble, Nick of Time, 2 Days in the Valley, Balle Balle! Amritsar to L.A.
TELEVISION: *Movies*: *Actress:* Cyrano de Bergerac, The Good Doctor, Lois Gibbs and the Love Canal, Surviving, Trapped in Silence, The Image, Dinner at Eight, Broken Trust, Dead Aviators, Life With Judy Garland: Me and My Shadows, The Long Shot: Believe in Courage. *Director:* Little Miss Perfect. *Mini-series:* Nightmares and Dreamscapes: From the Stories of Stephen King. *Series*: *Actress:* Where the Heart Is, Love of Life, Young Dr. Kildare, Sibs, Frasier (recurring guest role, Emmy nom. 1997). *Guest:* More than 55 appearances.

MASSEY, ANNA
Actress. b. Sussex, England, Aug. 11, 1937. Daughter of late actor Raymond Massey. Brother is actor Daniel Massey. On London stage in The Reluctant Debutante (debut, 1958), The Prime of Jean Brodie, Slag, The Importance of Being Earnest, Spoiled, Doctor's Delimma, School for Scandal, With National Theatre, 1989.
PICTURES: Gideon of Scotland Yard, Peeping Tom, Bunny Lake Is Missing, DeSade, The Looking Glass War, David Copperfield (TV in U.S.), Frenzy, A Doll's House, Vault of Horror, A Little Romance, Sweet William, Another Country, The Chain, Five Days One Summer, Foreign Body, Mountains of the Moon, La Couleur du Vent, The Tall Guy, Killing Dad, Impromptu, Emily's Ghost, The Grotesque, Angels & Insects, Haunted, Sweet Angel Mine, Driftwood, The Slab Boys, Deja Vu, Captain Jack, Mad Cows, Room to Rent, Dark Blue World, The Importance of Being Earnest, An Angel for May, Possession, The Machinist, Mrs. Palfrey at the Claremont, The Gigolos, The Oxford Murders, Love and Virtue.
TELEVISION: *Movies:* A Midsummer Night's Dream, Hay Fever, Before the Party, David Copperfield, Rebecca, The Corn Is Green, Sakharov, Anna Karenina, Hotel du Lac (BAFTA Award),, Season's Greetings, The Christmas Tree, A Hazard of Hearts, Tears in the Rain, Sun Child, Shalom Joan Collins, The Man From the PRU, Sea Dragon, Murder in Mind, The Sleeper, Come and Go, Belonging, Agatha Christie: A Life in Pictures, A Good Murder, Pinochet's Last Stand, Oliver Twist, Affinity. *Mini-series:* The Mayor of Casterbridge, I Remember Nelson, Mansfield Park, Around the World in 80 Days, A Tale of Two Cities, A Respectable Trade, Manor House (voice), He Knew He Was Right, Tess of the D'Urbervilles. *Series:* The Return of Psammead, Nice Day at the Office, The Robinsons. *Guest:* More than 90 appearances.

MASTERS, BEN
Actor. b. Corvallis, OR, May 6, 1947. e. Univ. of Oregon.
THEATRE: The Cherry Orchard, Waltz of the Toreadors, Plenty, Captain Brassbound's Conversion, The Boys in the Band, Eden Court, What the Butler Saw, The White Whore and the Bit Player, Key Exchange, Long Day's Journey Into Night.
PICTURES: Mandingo, All That Jazz, Key Exchange, Dream

Lover, Making Mr. Right, Walker Texas Ranger 3: Deadly Reunion. TELEVISION: *Movies*: One of Our Own, The Shadow Box, The Neighborhood, Illusions, The Deliberate Stranger, Street of Dreams, Cruel Doubt, Running Mates, A Twist of the Knife, A Time to Heal, Lady Killer, The Second Civil War. *Mini-series*: Loose Change, Celebrity, Noble House. *Series*: Another World, Heartbeat, Pensacola: Wings of Gold, Harmony's Passions.

MASTERSON, MARY STUART
Actress. b. Los Angeles, CA, June 28, 1966. Daughter of writer-dir.-actor Peter Masterson and actress Carlin Glynn. e. Goddard Col. Made film debut at age 8 in The Stepford Wives (1975), which featured her father. Spent summer at Stage Door Manor in Catskills; two summers at Sundance Inst. Studied acting with Gary Swanson. Member of the Actor's Studio. Off-off B'way debut in Been Taken. Off-B'way debut in Lily Dale followed by The Lucky Spot (Manhattan Theatre Club). *Regional:* Moonlight and Valentines, Three Sisters.
PICTURES: The Stepford Wives (debut, 1975), Heaven Help Us, At Close Range, My Little Girl, Some Kind of Wonderful, Gardens of Stone, Mr. North, Chances Are, Immediate Family (Natl. Board of Review Award, 1989), Funny About Love, Fried Green Tomatoes, Mad at the Moon, Married to It, Benny & Joon, Bad Girls, Radioland Murders, Heaven's Prisoners, Bed of Roses, Dogtown, On the Second Day of Christmas, The Postman, The Florentine, Digging to China, The Book of Stars, West of Here, Leo, Last Man Running (prod. only), The Sisters, Intervention, The Cake Eaters (dir., prod.), Tickling Leo (prod.).
TELEVISION: *Movies: Actress:* Love Lives On, Lily Dale, On the 2nd Day of Christmas, Black and Blue, Three Blind Mice, Something the Lord Made. *Director/Writer:* On the Edge, The Other Side. *Series*: *Actress:* Kate Brasher (also prod.), R.U.S./H., Waterfront, Law & Order: Special Victims Unit, Mercy.

MASTERSON, PETER
Actor, Writer, Director. r.n. Carlos Bee Masterson, Jr. b. Houston, TX, June 1, 1934. m. actress Carlin Glynn. Daughter is actress Mary Stuart Masterson. e. Rice U., Houston, BA. 1957. NY stage debut, Call Me By My Rightful Name, 1961.
THEATRE: Marathon '33, Blues for Mr. Charlie, The Trial of Lee Harvey Oswald, The Great White Hope, That Championship Season, The Poison Tree, The Best Little Whorehouse in Texas (co-author, dir.), The Last of the Knucklemen (dir.).
PICTURES: *Actor*: Ambush Bay (debut, 1965), Counterpoint, In the Heat of the Night, Tomorrow, The Exorcist, Man on a Swing, The Stepford Wives, Gardens of Stone. *Writer*: The Best Little Whore House in Texas. *Director*: The Trip to Bountiful, Full Moon in Blue Water, Blood Red, Night Game, Convicts, Arctic Blue, The Only Thrill, Lost Junction, Whiskey School. *Producer:* Terra Nova
TELEVISION: *Movies: Actor:* Pueblo Affair, Delta County USA, The Quinns, The Storyteller, A Question of Guilt. *Writer:* City in Fear (also exec. prod.). *Director:* Lily Dale, Mermaid (Emmy nom. 2001).

MASTORAKIS, NICO
Writer, Director, Producer. b. Athens, Greece, April 28, 1941. Writer of novels and screenplays, including Fire Below Zero, and Keepers of the Secret (co-author). President and CEO, Omega Entertainment Ltd. since 1978.
PICTURES: *Writer/Director/Producer*: The Time Traveller, Blind Date, Sky High, The Zero Boys, The Wind, Terminal Exposure, Nightmare at Noon, Glitch, Ninja Academy, Hired to Kill, In the Cool of the Night, At Random, .com for Murder. *Prod.:* The Greek Tycoon, Red Tide, Grandmother's House, Darkroom, Bloodstone (prod., co-s.p.)., Nightmare at Noon, The Naked Truth.
TELEVISION: Director, executive producer and producer for several series produced and aired in Greece.

MASTRANTONIO, MARY ELIZABETH
Actress. b. Oak Park, IL, Nov. 17, 1958. e. U. of Illinois 1976-78 where she trained for opera. m. dir. Pat O'Connor. Worked as singer & dancer for summer at Opryland Theme Park in Nashville, TN. Came to New York as understudy and vacation replacement as Maria in West Side Story revival.
THEATRE: *NY*: Copperfield (1981), Oh Brother, Amadeus, Sunday in the Park With George (Playwright's Horizons), The Human Comedy, Henry V, The Marriage of Figaro, Measure for Measure, The Knife, Twelfth Night.
PICTURES: Scarface (debut, 1983), The Color of Money (Academy Award nom.; Golden Globe nom. 1987), Slamdance, The January Man, The Abyss, Fools of Fortune, Class Action, Robin Hood: Prince of Thieves, White Sands, Consenting Adults, A Day to Remember, Three Wishes, Two Bits, My Life So Far, Limbo, The Perfect Storm, Tabloid, Standing Room Only (short).
TELEVISION: *Movies:* The Brooke Ellison Story, Witness Protection, The Russell Girl. *Mini-series*: Mussolini: The Untold Story. *Series:* Without a Trace, Law & Order: Criminal Intent. *Documentaries/Specials*: Uncle Vanya (BBC).

MASUR, RICHARD
Actor. b. New York, NY, Nov. 20, 1948. Directed Oscar-nominated short, Love Struck, 1987. Pres., Screen Actors Guild, 1995.
THEATRE: *B'way*: The Changing Room.
PICTURES: Whiffs (debut, 1975), Bittersweet Love, Semi-Tough, Who'll Stop the Rain, Hanover Street, Scavenger Hunt, Heaven's Gate, I'm Dancing as Fast as I Can, The Thing, Timerider, Risky Business, Under Fire, Nightmares, The Mean Season, My Science Project, Head Office, Heartburn, The Believers, Walker, Rent-a-Cop, Shoot to Kill, License to Drive, Far from Home, Flashback, Going Under, My Girl, Encino Man, The Man Without a Face, Six Degrees of Separation, My Girl 2, Forget Paris, Multiplicity, Fire Down Below, Play It To the Bone, Palindromes, Lovely by Surprise.
TELEVISION: *Movies*: Having Babies, Betrayal, Mr. Horn, Walking Through the Fire, Fallen Angel, Money on the Side, An Invasion of Privacy, The Demon Murder Case, Adam, John Steinbeck's The Winter of Our Discontent, Flight #90: Disaster on the Potomac, The Burning Bed (Emmy nom. 1985), Obsessed With a Married Woman, Wild Horses, Embassy, Adam: His Song Continues, Roses Are for the Rich, Cast the First Stone, When the Bough Breaks, Settle the Score, Always Remember I Love You, Stephen King's IT, The Story Lady, And the Band Played On, Search for Grace, My Brother's Keeper, The Face on the Milk Carton, Hiroshima, It Was Him or Us, Undue Influence, Noriega: God's Favorite, 61, The One Day At A Time Reunion. *Mini-series*: *Actor:* East of Eden. *Director*: Torn Between Two Fathers (After School Special, DGA nom. 1990). *Series*: Hot L Baltimore, The Many Loves of Arthur, One Day at a Time, Empire. *Guest:* More than 89 appearances.

MATARAZZO, HEATHER
Actress. b. Long Island, NY, Nov. 10, 1982.
PICTURES: Welcome to the Dollhouse, Arresting Gena, The Devil's Advocate, The Deli, Hurricane Streets, 54, All I Wanna Do, Cuisine américaine , Getting To Know All About You, Cherry, Blue Moon, Scream 3, Company Man, The Princess Diaries, Sorority Boys, The Pink House, Home of Phobia, Saved!, The Princess Diaries 2: Royal Engagement, Believe in Me, Hostel: Part II, Mangus! (also prod.).
TELEVISION: *Movies:* Our Guys: Outrage at Glen Ridge, Stage on Screen: The Women. *Series*: The Adventures of Pete & Pete, Roseanne, Now & Again, St. Sass, Exes & Oh's.

MATHESON, TIM
Actor. b. Los Angeles, CA, Dec. 31, 1947. e. California State U. Debut on TV at age 12 in Window on Main Street. At 19, contract player for Universal. 1985, turned to direction: St. Elsewhere episode and music videos. Set up production co. at Burbank Studios in 1985; acted off-B'way in True West. With partner Daniel Grodnick bought National Lampoon from founder Matty Simons, becoming exec. officer and chmn. 1989; resigned in 1991.
PICTURES: Divorce American Style (debut, 1967), Yours Mine and Ours, How to Commit Marriage, Magnum Force, Almost Summer, National Lampoon's Animal House, Dreamer, The Apple Dumpling Gang Rides Again, 1941, House of God, A Little Sex, To Be or Not To Be, Up the Creek, Impulse, Fletch, Speed Zone, Drop Dead Fred, Solar Crisis, Black Sheep, A Very Brady Sequel, A Very Unlucky Leprechaun, She's All That, The Story of Us, Van Wilder, Chump Change, Don't Come Knocking, Redline.
TELEVISION: *Movies*: Owen Marshall: Counselor-at-Law, Lock Stock and Barrel, Hitched, Remember When, The Last Day, The Runaway Barge, The Quest, Mary White, Listen to Your Heart, Obsessed with a Married Woman, Blind Justice, Warm Hearts Cold Feet, Bay Coven, The Littlest Victims, Little White Lies, Buried Alive, Joshua's Heart, Stephen King's Sometimes They Come Back, The Woman Who Sinned, Quicksand: No Escape, Relentless: Mind of a Killer, Trial & Error, Dying to Love You, A Kiss to Die For, Robin Cook's Harmful Intent, Target of Suspicion, Breach of Conduct (dir., co-exec. prod. only), While Justice Sleeps, Fast Company, An Unfinished Affair, Buried Alive 2 (also dir.), Sleeping with the Devil, Forever Love, Catch Me If You Can, In the Company of Spies (also dir.), Fishing with John, At the Mercy of a Stranger, Navigating the Heart, Hell Swarm (also dir.), Sharing the Secret, Second Honeymoon, Wolf Lake, Moms on Strike, Martha Inc.: The Story of Martha Stewart, The King and Queen of Moonlight Bay, Judas, The World According to Barnes, To Love and Die in L.A., True Confessions of a Hollywood Starlet (dir.), Body Politic. *Pilot*: Nikki & Alexander. *Mini-series*: How the West Was Won, Jackie Bouvier Kennedy Onassis. *Series: Actor:* Window on Main Street, Jonny Quest (voice), The Virginian, Bonanza, The Quest, Tucker's Witch, Just in Time (also co-exec. prod.), Charlie Hoover, The Legend of Calamity Jane (voice), The West Wing (2 Emmy noms.), Breaking News. *Director:* The Twilight Zone, Without a Trace, Numb3rs, Threshold, Burn Notice. Has directed many series episodes. *Documentaries/Specials:* Bus Stop, Magnificent Desolation: Walking on the Moon 3D. *Guest:* More than 170 appearances.

MATHIS, SAMANTHA
Actress. b. New York, NY, May 12, 1970. Mother is actress Bibi Besch; grandmother was actress Gusti Huber. Began acting as teen landing role in tv pilot Aaron's Way at age 16.
PICTURES: The Bulldance (debut, 1988 in Yugoslav film), Pump Up the Volume, This Is My Life, FernGully ... The Last Rainforest (voice), Super Mario Bros., The Music of Chance, The Thing Called Love, Little Women, Jack and Sarah, How to Make an American Quilt, The American President, Broken Arrow, Waiting for Woody, Sweet Jane, Freak City, The Simian Line, American Psycho, Rules of Attraction, Searching for Debra Winger (doc.), The Punisher, Kids in America, Touched, Believe in Me, Local Color, Order of Chaos, The New Daughter, Lebanon, PA, Buried,

The Cellar, Good Day for It.
TELEVISION: *Movies*: Circle of Love, Cold Sassy Tree, Extreme Close Up, To My Daughter, 83 Hours 'Til Dawn, Freak City, Harsh Realm, Mermaid, Collected Stories, 'Salem's Lot, Fathers and Sons, Absolution, A Stranger's Heart, Oprah Winfrey Presents: Mitch Albom's For One More Day. *Mini-series*: The Mists of Avalon. *Series*: Knightwatch, Aaron's Way, Harsh Realm, First Years. Documentaries: Searching for Debra Winger, The Secret Life of Superfans. *Guest:* More than 44 appearances.

MATLIN, MARLEE
Actress. b. Morton Grove, IL, Aug. 24, 1965. e. John Hersey H.S., Chicago, public school with special education program for deaf; William Rainey Harper Coll.Performed at Children's Theatre of the Deaf in Des Plaines at age 8, playing many leading roles. Theatrical film debut in Children of a Lesser God. Production company, Solo One Productions.
PICTURES: Children of a Lesser God (debut, 1986; Academy Award, Golden Globe Award 1987), Walker, The Player, The Linguini Incident, Hear No Evil, It's My Party, Snitch, When Justice Fails, In Her Defense, Two Shades of Blue, What the Bleep Do We Know!? (doc.), What the Bleep!?: Down the Rabbit Hole (doc.), Silent Knights (also exec. prod.).
TELEVISION: *Movies:* Bridge to Silence, Against Her Will: The Carrie Buck Story, Dead Silence, Freak City, 90 Days At Hollyridge (also exec. prod.), Kiss My Act. Eddie's Million Dollar Cook-Off (exec. prod. only), Sweet Nothing in My Ear. *Series:* Reasonable Doubts (2 Golden Globe noms.), The Outer Limits, Picket Fences, The West Wing, Ollie, The L Word. *Documentaries/Specials:* Face the Hate, Meaning of Life, Free to Laugh, Creative Spirit, The Big Help, People In Motion (host). *Guest:* More than 78 appearances.

MATTHAU, CHARLES
Director, Producer, Actor. b. New York, NY, Dec. 10, 1962. Son of the late actor, Walter Matthau. e. U. of Southern California Film School. While at USC wrote and dir. The Duck Film, a silent comedy short (Golden Seal Award, London Amateur Film Fest. and C.I.N.E. Eagle Award.) Also dir. short, I Was a Teenage Fundraiser. President, The Matthau Company, organized 1990.
PICTURES: *Actor:* Charlie Varrick, The Bad News Bears, House Calls, Doin' Time on Planet Earth. (also dir., nom. Saturn Award, best dir., Acad. of Science Fiction.), The Grass Harp (also dir., prod.; Acad. of Family Films Award, Best Dir., 1996), Number One Fan, Hanging Up, An Ordinary Killer, Going Shopping, Dingo Dreaming, Queen of the Lot, Rachel's Return. *Associate Producer:* Buddy Buddy, I Ought to Be in Pictures. *Director:* Her Minor Thing, G'Day LA, Mikey & Dolores, Baby O, Freaky Deaky (also prod., writer-adaptation), Baby O.
TELEVISION: *Movies*: *Director:* Mrs. Lambert Remembers Love (also prod.; Golden Eagle, Golden Medal & Houston Fest. Grand & Angel Awards, 1993) , The Marriage Fool. *Associate Producer:* The Incident. *Actor:* The Stingiest Man in Town.

MAURA, CARMEN
Actress. b. Madrid, Spain, Sept. 15, 1945. e. Madrid's Catholic Inst. Daughter of ophthalmologist; faced family disapproval and custody battle when she became an actress. Met aspiring dir. Pedro Almodovar when they were cast in stage prod. of Sartre's Dirty Hands and starred in several of his films. Hosted weekly Spanish TV talk show, Esta Noche. More than 87 Spanish television appearances.
PICTURES: El Hombre Oculto (debut, 1970), El Love Feroz, The Petition, Paper Tigers, Que Hace una Chica Como tu en un Sitio Como Este?, Pepi Luci Bom... And Other Girls on the Heap (1980), El Cid Cabreador, Dark Habits, What Have I Done to Deserve This?, Extramuros, Se Infiel y No Mires Con Quien, Matador, Law of Desire, Women on the Verge of a Nervous Breakdown, Baton Rouge, How to Be a Woman and Not Die Trying, Ay Carmela!, Chatarra, Between Heaven and Earth, The Anonymous Queen, Shadows in a Conflict, Louis the Child King, How to Be Miserable and Enjoy It, The Flowers of My Secret, Una Pareja de Tres, El Palomo cojo, Happiness Is in the Field, Tortilla y cinema, Alliance cherche doigt, Elles, Vivir despeus, Alice and Martin, Enthusiasm, Superlove, The Comet, Lisbon, Harem of Madame Osmane, Common Wealth, To the End of the Road, Hold Up, Arregui la noticia del dia, Cara y Elena, Shutdown, Valentin, Le Ventre de Juliette, 800 balas (800 Bullets), Le Pacte du silence, 25 Degrees in Winter, Entre vivir y soñar, La Promesa, Reinas, Free Zone, Volver, El Menor de los males, Que parezca un accidente, The Garden of Eden, La Virgen negra, Tetro, Yours, Chicas, Le mac.
TELEVISION: Numerous Spanish credits.

MAXWELL, RONALD F.
Director, Writer, Producer. b. Jan. 5, 1947. e. NYU Coll. of Arts & Sciences; NYU Sch. of the Arts, Inst. of Film & Television Graduate Sch., M.F.A., 1970. Prod., dir,. for PBS Theater-in-America (1974-78).
PICTURES: *Director*: The Guest, Little Darlings, The Night the Lights Went Out in Georgia, Kidco, Gettysburg (also co-s.p.), Gods and Generals (also s.p. & prod.), Joan of Arc: The Virgin Warrior (also s.p. and prod.), Lincoln and Lee at Antietam: The Cost of Freedom (narr., doc.).
TELEVISION: *Movies: Director*: Sea Marks (also prod.), Verna: USO Girl (also prod., Emmy nom. 1978), Parent Trap II. *Series:* Hard Times (prod. only).

MAY, ELAINE
Actress, Director, Writer. b. Philadelphia, PA, April 21, 1932. Daughter is actress Jeannie Berlin. Father was prod.-dir. Jack Berlin whose traveling theatre she acted with from age 6 to 10. Repertory theatre in Chicago, 1954; comedy team with Mike Nichols starting in 1955. Appeared with improvisational theatre group, The Compass, Chicago. Co-starred in An Evening with Mike Nichols and Elaine May.
THEATRE: *Playwright*: A Matter of Position, Not Enough Rope, Hot Line, Better Point of Valour, Mr. Gogol & Mr. Preen, Hotline (Death Defying Acts), Adult Entertainment.
PICTURES: *Actress:* Luv, Enter Laughing, A New Leaf, (also dir. & s.p., Golden Globe nom.; WGA nom. 1972), California Suite, In the Spirit, Small Time Crooks. *Writer:* Such Good Friends, Mikey and Nicky, Heaven Can Wait (Academy Award nom.; WGA Award 1979), Ishtar (also dir. & composer), The Birdcage (WGA nom. 1997), Primary Colors (Academy Award nom.; WGA nom. 1999), Down to Earth (1978 s.p. for Heaven Can Wait).
TELEVISION: *Series regular*: Keep Talking (1958-59), Laugh Line (panelist).

MAY, JODHI
Actress. b. London, England, May 1975.
PICTURES: A World Apart, Isabelle Eberhardt, Eminent Domain, The Last of the Mohicans, Sister My Sister, Second Best, The Scarlet Letter (voice), The Woodlanders, The Gambler, The House of Mirth, The Escapist, The Dish, Spyhole (s.p. and dir.), Bye Bye Blackbird, Blinded, On a Clear Day, Land of the Blind, Nightwatching, Flashbacks of a Fool, Defiance.
TELEVISION: *Movies*: For the Greater Good, Max and Helen, Signs and Wonders, Warriors, The Turn of the Screw, Tipping the Velvet, The Other Boleyn Girl, Daniel Deronda, The Mayor of Casterbridge, Friends and Crocodiles, The Man-Eating Leopard of Rudraprayag, Einstein and Eddington, Sleep with Me, Blood and Oil. *Mini-series*: The Gift, Aristocrats, Emma. *Series:* The Amazing Mrs Pritchard, Strike Back.

MAYER, KEVIN
Executive. e. B.S.M.E. from Massachusetts Institute of Technology; MBA, Harvard, 1990; M.S.E.E. from San Diego State Univ. First joined The Walt Disney Company in 1993 as mgr., strategic planning. He spearheaded business dev. for all of Disney's interactive/Internet and TV businesses worldwide. Mayer left Disney and held variety of leading positions at interactive and Internet businesses, including chmn. and CEO of Clear Channel Interactive; pres. and CEO of Playboy.com Inc. Became partner in L.E.K. Consulting LLC, where he headed company's global media and entertainment practice. Responsibilities included global oversight of all media-related due diligence efforts for mergers and acquisitions, business strategies for new technology ventures such as portable music devices, online music services, video on demand and broadband ISP services, and creation of comprehensive anti-piracy strategies for motion picture studios and trade associations. He also devised plans for companies to offer electronic sell-through for movies, cable TV networks, TV programming and music. Mayer returned to Disney and in 2005 he was appointed executive v.p., corporate strategy, business dev. and technology group for The Walt Disney Company. In this role today, he and his group target emerging businesses new to Disney's existing portfolio, manage cross-divisional issues and opportunities, and evaluate new technology and business models.

MAYER, MICHAEL F.
Attorney, Executive. b. White Plains, NY, Sept. 8, 1917. e. Harvard Coll., B.S., 1939; Yale Law Sch., L.L.B., 1942. Armed Forces 1942-46, Air Medal (1945). V.P., Kingsley International Pictures Corp., 1954-62. Exec. dir. and gen. counsel, Independent Film Importers and Distributors of America Inc. (IFIDA), 1959-67. Special Counsel, French Society of Authors, Composers and Publishers, 1961-72; British Performing Rights Society, 1962-67. *Author:* Foreign Films on American Screens (1966), Divorce and Annulment (1967), The Libel Revolution: A New Look at Defamation and Privacy, What You Should Know About Libel and Slander (1968), Rights of Privacy (1972), The Film Industries (1973, revised ed. pub. in 1978). Teacher of courses on Business Problems in Film, New School (1971-82). Secty. of Film Society of Lincoln Center, Inc. (1972-88). Retired.

MAYER, ROGER LAURANCE
Executive. b. New York, NY, April 21, 1926. e. Yale U., B.A. 1948; Yale Law Sch., L.L.B. and J.D. 1951. In 1952 was practicing attorney; joined Columbia Pictures that year as atty. and named general studio exec., 1957. Left in 1961 to join MGM Studio as asst. gen. mgr. With MGM as follows: v.p., operations, 1964; v.p., administration, 1975-84. Also exec. v.p., MGM Laboratories, 1974-83. Named pres., MGM Laboratories and sr. v.p., studio admin.; MGM Entertainment Co. 1983-86; was Turner Entertainment Co. as pres. and COO Aug. 15, 1986 until his retirement on August 15, 2005. He is a member of the Los Angeles County Bar Assn., Calif. Bar Assn., Los Angeles Copyright Society, and is on the Board of Governors of the Academy of Motion Picture Arts & Sciences (AMPAS). He has

served on the Motion Picture & Television Fund (MPTF) for more than 25 years, with eight of them as chairman of its Bd. of Trustees. He is also the founding chair of the bd. of dir. of the National Film Preservation Foundation, created by the U.S. Congress in 1996 to preserve "orphan films," those films with no studio or other organization saving them. Mayer is a member of the National Film Preservation Board and provides advice on which films should be added to the National Film Registry and preserved at the Library of Congress. For these philanthropic activities and service to the Industry, Mayer received the Jean Hersholt Humanitarian Award from AMPAS at the 2005 Oscars.

MAYRON, MELANIE
Actress, Director. b. Philadelphia, PA, Oct. 20, 1952. e. American Academy of Dramatic Arts, 1972. Debut Godspell (tour), NY stage debut: The Goodbye People, 1979.
PICTURES: *Actress:* Harry and Tonto (debut, 1974), Gable and Lombard, Car Wash, The Great Smokey Roadblock, You Light Up My Life, Girlfriends (Locarno Film Fest. Award) Heartbeeps, Missing, The Boss' Wife, Sticky Fingers (also co-s.p., co-prod), Checking Out, My Blue Heaven, Drop Zone, East of A, Clockstoppers, Itty Bitty Titty Committee. *Director:* The Babysitters Club, Slap Her She's French, Zeyda and the Hitman.
TELEVISION: *Movies: Actress:* Hustling, The New Love Boat, Katie: Portrait of a Centerfold, Playing For Time, The Best Little Girl in the World, Lily: Sold Out, Will There Really Be a Morning?, Wallenberg: A Hero's Story, Wanted: A Man for Mom, Ordeal in the Arctic, Other Women's Children, Range of Motion, Toothless (also dir., DGA nom. 1998). *Dir:* Freaky Friday, Campus Confidential. *Series: Actress:* thirtysomething (Emmy Award, 1989, 2 other noms. also dir.). *Dir:* Sirens, Tribeca, New York Undercover, Nash Bridges, Dawson's Creek, Arli$$, Wasteland, Providence, State of Grace, Ed, In Treatment, The Naked Brothers Band, many more. *Documentaries/Specials:* Lily Tomlin: Sold Out, Cinder Ella: A Modern Fairy Tale, Wanted: The Perfect Guy.

MAYSLES, ALBERT
Director, Cinematographer. b. Boston, MA, Nov. 26, 1926. e. Syracuse (B.A.), Boston U (M.A.). Taught psychology there for 3 years. With late brother David (1932-87) pioneer in direct cinema documentary filmmaking. Entered filmmaking photographing Primary with D.A. Pennebaker, Richard Leacock and Robert Drew, 1960. Formed Maysles Films, Inc. 1962, making non-fiction feature films, commercials and corp. films. Received ASC President's Award 1998.
PICTURES: *Director:* Psychiatry in Russia, Youth in Poland, Showman (also cinematographer), With Love From Truman (also cinematographer), Meet Marlon Brando (doc. short; also cinematographer) Salesman (also cinematographer & prod.), Gimme Shelter (also cinematographer), Christo's Valley Curtain (also prod., Academy Award nom. 1974), Grey Gardens (also cinematographer & prod.), Running Fence (also cinematography) Muhammad and Larry (doc. short), Horowitz Plays Mozart (also cinematographer), Jessye Norman Sings Carmen (doc.), Christo in Paris (also cinematographer), Soldiers of Music (doc.; also cinematographer, DGA nom. 1992) Sports Illustrated: Swimsuit '92, Baroque Duet, Umbrellas (also cinematographer), Concert of Wills: Making the Getty Center (doc.; also cinematographer & writer), The Jew on Trial (also cinematographer, prod. & s.p.). *Cinematographer:* Yanki No!, Primary (also photographer), Sean O'Casey: The Spirit of Ireland (short), Paris vu par..., Monterey Pop, Jimi Plays Monterey (doc.), When We Were Kings, Deutschen Volke (doc.) The Paris Review: Early Chapters (video), A Dog's Life: A Dogamentary, In Good Conscience: Sister Jeannine Gramick's Journey of Faith, Stolen, This Is an Adventure (also dir., camera operator), Scapegoat on Trial (also prod.), American Prison: The Forgotten Jews (doc.), Sally Gross: The Pleasure of Stillness (doc., also dir.), Hollywood Renegade (doc. also cinematographer), Four Seasons Lodge, Soul Power, Hollywood Renegade (doc.), Radioman (doc., consult. prod.).
TELEVISION: *Documentaries: Cinematographer:* What's Happening-The Beatles in the USA (dir.), Islands (also dir.), Vladimir Horowitz: The Last Romantic (Emmy Award, 1987), Soldiers of Music: Rostopovich Returns to Russia (Emmy Award, 1991), Sports Illustrated: The Making of the Swimsuit Issue (co-dir.), Abortion: Desperate Choices (Emmy Award, 1992, Cable Ace Award), Letting Go: A Hospice Journey (Emmy Award, 1996), The Gates (also dir.), LaLee's Kin: The Legacy of Cotton (also dir.), With the Filmmaker: Portraits by Albert Maysles (dir. & cinematographer), The Jeff Koons Show, Pretty Things, Addiction (segment dir.), A Case of Mistaken Identity?, Close Up: Portraits (also dir.), Grey Gardens (exec. prod. only).

MAZURSKY, PAUL
Producer, Director, Writer, Actor. b. Brooklyn, NY, April 25, 1930. e. Brooklyn Coll. Started acting in 1951 Off-B'way (Hello Out There, The Seagull, Major Barbara, Death of a Salesman, He Who Gets Slapped), TV and films. Was nightclub comic 1954-1960 and directed plays. Began association with Larry Tucker by producing, directing, writing and performing in Second City, semi-improvisational revue. For four years they wrote the Danny Kaye TV show and created and wrote the Monkees series. First theatrical film I Love You Alice B. Toklas, 1968, which he wrote and exec. produced with Tucker. Exec. prod. of film Taking Care of Business.
PICTURES: *Director/Writer:* Bob and Carol and Ted and Alice (Academy Award nom.; WGA Award 1970). *Director/Producer/Writer/Actor:* I Love You, Alice B. Toklas! (2 WGA noms. 1969), Alex in Wonderland, Blume in Love (WGA nom. 1974), Harry and Tonto (Academy Award nom.; WGA nom. 1975), Next Stop Greenwich Village (dir., prod., s.p. only, WGA nom. 1977), An Unmarried Woman (2 Academy Award noms.; DGA nom.; 2 Golden Globe noms.; WGA nom. 1979), Willie and Phil, Tempest, Moscow on the Hudson, Down and Out in Beverly Hills (WGA nom. 1987), Moon Over Parador, Enemies: a Love Story (Academy Award nom. 1990), Scenes From a Mall, The Pickle, Faithful. *Actor:* Fear and Desire, Blackboard Jungle, Deathwatch, A Star Is Born, A Man a Woman and a Bank, History of the World Part 1, Into the Night, Punchline, Scenes From the Class Struggle in Beverly Hills, Man Trouble, Carlito's Way, Love Affair, Miami Rhapsody, Faithful, 2 Days in the Valley, Touch, Bulworth, Why Do Fools Fall in Love, Antz (voice), Crazy in Alabama, Stanley Kubrick: A Life in Pictures, Da wan (aka Big Shot's Funeral), The Majestic (voice), Do It For Uncle Manny, I Want Someone To Eat Cheese With, Cattle Call.
TELEVISION: *Movies: Actor:* Weapons of Mass Destruction, A Slight Case of Murder, Coast to Coast (also dir.) *Director:* Winchell. *Series: Actor:* Once and Again, Curb Your Enthusiasm. *Writer:* The Danny Kaye Show. *Documentaries:* A Decade Under the Influence, Bette Midler. *Guest:* More than 50 appearances.

MAZZELLO, JOSEPH
Actor. b. Rhinebeck, NY, Sept. 21, 1983. Made acting debut at age 5 in tv movie Unspeakable Acts. President/CEO of JJM Productions.
PICTURES: Presumed Innocent (debut, 1990), Radio Flyer, Jersey Girl, Jurassic Park, Shadowlands, The River Wild, The Cure, Three Wishes, The Lost World: Jurassic Park, Star Kid, Simon Birch, Wooly Boys, Raising Helen, The Hollow, Matters of Life and Death (also exec. prod, prod, dir. and writer), The Sensation of Sight, The Social Network.
TELEVISION: *Movies:* Unspeakable Acts, Desperate Choices: To Save My Child, A Father for Charlie. *Mini-series:* The Pacific. *Series:* Stories from My Childhood (voice).

McADAMS, RACHEL
Actress. b. Ontario, Canada, November 17, 1978. York U.
PICTURES: The Hot Chick, Mean Girls (also soundtrack per.), The Notebook, Wedding Crashers, Red Eye, The Family Stone, Married Life, The Lucky Ones, State of Play, The Time Traveler's Wife, Sherlock Holmes, Morning Glory, Midnight in Paris.
TELEVISION: *Movies:* Shotgun Love Dolls, Guilt by Association. *Series:* Slings and Arrows.

McBRIDE, JIM
Director, Writer. b. New York, NY, Sept. 16, 1941. e. NYU. m. costume designer Tracy Tynan. Began in underground film scene in New York. First film: David Holzman's Diary, 1967, which won grand prize at Mannheim and Pesaro Film Festivals, and was named to the Library of Congress' list of important American films designated for preservation in 1991. Appeared as actor in film Last Embrace.
PICTURES: *Director:* David Holzman's Diary (also prod.), My Girlfriend's Wedding (also s.p., editor), Glen and Randa (also s.p.), Hot Times (also s.p.), Breathless (also co-s.p.), The Big Easy, Great Balls of Fire (also co-s.p.), Uncovered (also co-s.p.), The Informant, Welcome to São Paulo (documentary; segment "Novo Mundo", also cinematographer)
TELEVISION: *Movies*: Blood Ties, The Wrong Man, The Informant, Pronto, Dead by Midnight. *Special*: Fallen Angels (Fearless), Dead Before Midnight, Meatloaf: To Hell and Back. *Series*: *Director:* The Wonder Years (3 episodes).

McCALLUM, DAVID
Actor. b. Glasgow, Scotland, Sept. 19, 1933. Early career in rep. theatres and dir. plays for Army. Entered industry in 1953.
PICTURES: The Secret Place (debut, 1957), Hell Drivers, Robbery Under Arms, Violent Playground, A Night to Remember, The Long and the Short and the Tall, Carolina, Jungle Street, Billy Budd, Freud, The Great Escape, The Greatest Story Ever Told, To Trap a Spy, The Spy With My Face, Around the World Under the Sea, One Spy Too Many, Three Bites of the Apple, Sol Madrid, Mosquito Squadron, The Kingfisher Caper, Dogs, King Solomon's Treasure, The Watcher in the Woods, Terminal Choice, The Wind, The Haunting of Morella, Hear My Song, Dirty Weekend, Healer, Fatal Inheritance, Cherry, xXx (singer), Batman: Gotham Knight (video, voice).
TELEVISION: *Movies*: The Unknown, The Helicopter Spies, Teacher Teacher (Emmy nom. 1969), Hauser's Memory, She Waits, The Six Million Dollar Man: Wine Women and War, Frankenstein: The True Story, The Invisible Man, The Return of the Man from U.N.C.L.E., The Corvini Inheritance, Behind Enemy Lines, Freedom Fighter, The Return of Sam McCloud, Shattered Image, Mortal Challenge, Coming Home, March in Windy City. *Mini-series:* Kidnapped, Mother Love (BBC), Lucky/Chances. *Series:* The Man from U.N.C.L.E. (2 Emmy noms.; Golden Globe nom. 1966), Colditz (BBC, 1972-74), The Invisible Man, Sapphire and Steel (BBC), As the World Turns, Trainer (BBC), Cluedo, VR.5, The Education of

Max Bickford (recurring role), The Replacements, Ben 10: Alien Force, Navy NCIS: Naval Criminal Investigative Service. *Documentaries:* The Big T.N.T. Show (narr.), Az, Aldozat, Ancient Prophecies (host), Titanic: Death of a Dream (narr.). *Guest:* More than 118 appearances.

McCARTHY, ANDREW
Actor. b. Westfield, NJ, Nov. 29, 1962. Raised in Bernardsville, NJ. e. NYU. While at college won role in film Class. Studied acting at Circle-in-the-Square.
THEATRE: *B'way:* The Boys of Winter. *Off B'way:* Bodies Rest and Motion, Life Under Water, Neptune's Hips, Mariens Kammer.
PICTURES: Class (debut, 1983), The Beniker Gang, Heaven Help Us, St. Elmo's Fire, Pretty in Pink, Mannequin, Waiting for the Moon, Less Than Zero, Kansas, Fresh Horses, Weekend at Bernie's, Quiet Days in Clichy, Dr. M, Year of the Gun, Only You, Weekend at Bernie's 2, The Joy Luck Club, Getting In, Night of the Running Man, Mrs. Parker & the Vicious Circle, Dream Man, Dead Funny, Mulholland Falls, Everything Relative, Things I Never Told You, Stag, I Woke Up Early the Day I Died, Bela Donna, A Breed Apart, New World Disorder, Jump, A Twist of Faith, New Waterford Girl, Nowhere in Sight, Standard Time, Diggity's Treasure, 2BPerfectlyHonest, News for the Church (short; dir., prod. & s.p.), The Orphan King, The Spiderwick Chronicles, The Good Guy, Camp Hope, Main Street, Snatched.
TELEVISION: *Movies:* Common Pursuit, The Courtyard, The Christmas Tree, Hostile Force, A Father For Brittany, Perfect Assassins, A Storm in Summer, The Sight, The Secret Life of Zoey, Straight From the Heart, The Hollywood Mom's Mystery, Crusader, The Way, Lipstick Jungle (pilot), The National Tree. *Mini-series:* Jackie Bouvier Kennedy Onassis. *Series:* Kingdom Hospital, E-Ring, Lipstick Jungle. *Guest:* More than 45 appearances.

McCARTHY, KEVIN
Actor. b. Seattle, WA, Feb. 15, 1914. Sister was late author Mary McCarthy. e. U. of Minnesota. Acted in sch. plays, stock; B'way debut in Abe Lincoln in Illinois. Served in U.S. Army.
THEATRE: *B'way:* Flight to West, Winged Victory, Truckline Cafe, Joan of Lorraine, The Survivors, Death of a Salesman (London), Anna Christie, The Deep Blue Sea, others.
PICTURES: Death of a Salesman (debut, 1951; Academy Award nom.; Golden Globe Award 1952), Drive a Crooked Road, The Gambler From Natchez, Stranger on Horseback, Annapolis Story, Nightmare, Invasion of the Body Snatchers, The Misfits, 40 Pounds of Trouble, A Gathering of Eagles, The Prize, The Best Man, An Affair of the Skin, Mirage, A Big Hand for the Little Lady, Three Sisters, Hotel, The Hell With Heroes, If He Hollers Let Him Go, Revenge in El Paso, Ace High, Kansas City Bomber, Alien Thunder, Order to Kill, Buffalo Bill and the Indians, Piranha, Invasion of the Body Snatchers (1978, cameo), Hero at Large, Those Lips Those Eyes, The Howling, My Tutor, Twilight Zone—The Movie, Hostage, Innerspace, UHF, Fast Food, Dark Tower, Love or Money, The Sleeping Car, Eve of Destruction, Final Approach, The Distinguished Gentleman, Matinee, Greedy, Just Cause, Steal Big Steal Little, Mommy, Addams Family Reunion (video), The Legend of Razorback, Looney Tunes: Back in Action, Trail of the Screaming Forehead, Her Morbid Desires, Wesley.
TELEVISION: Active on TV since 1949. *Movies*: U.M.C., A Great American Tragedy, Exo-Man, Mary Jane Harper Cried Last Night, Flamingo Road, Portrait of an Escort, Rosie: The Story of Rosemary Clooney, Making of a Male Model, Invitation to Hell, Deadly Intentions, The Midnight Hour, A Masterpiece of Murder, Poor Little Rich Girl: The Barbara Hutton Story, The Long Journey Home, Once Upon a Texas Train, In the Heat of the Night, Channel 99, The Rose and the Jackal, Dead on the Money, Duplicates, The Sister-in-Law, Liz: The Elizabeth Taylor Story, Marlon Brando: The Wild One, The Second World War, Elvis Meets Nixon. *Pilot*: Second Stage. *Mini-series:* Passion and Paradise. *Series*: The Colbys, The Survivors, Flamingo Road, Amanda's, Second Start. *Guest*: More than 160 appearances.

McCARTNEY, SIR PAUL
Singer, Musician. r.n. James Paul McCartney. b. Liverpool, England, June 18, 1942. Formerly with music groups The Beatles & Wings.
PICTURES: *Performer:* A Hard Day's Night, (debut, 1964; also songs) Help! (also songs), Yellow Submarine (cameo; also songs), Let It Be (also songs; Academy Award for best original song score, 1971), Rockshow (concert film), Give My Regards to Broad Street (also s.p., songs), Eat the Rich (cameo), Get Back (concert film), The Best of Ringo Starr & His All Starr Band So Far (narrator). *Composer/Songs for films:* Live and Let Die (title song; Academy Award nom. 1974), All This and World War II, Empty Hand (also prod.), Sgt. Pepper's Lonely Hearts Club Band, The Oriental Nightfish, I Wanna Hold Your Hand, Oh Heavenly Dog, Seaside Woman, Beatlemania, The World According to Garp, Beyond the Limit (title song), Once Upon A Time in America, Give My Regards to Broad Street (also s.p., Golden Globe nom. 1985), Mask, Twiice in a Lifetime, Spies Like Us (title song), Yesterday, Five Corners, Whispering Jack: Live, The Experts, Because (end credits song "Because"), Loaded Weapon 1, Bye Bye Love, Sól, sól skín á mig (short), Jerry Maguire, El Amor perjudica seriamente la salud (Spain), Grosse Pointe Blank, Father's Day, Armageddon, A Soldier's Daughter Never Cries, American Beauty, The Beatles Yellow Submarine Adventure, Heartbreakers, Moulin Rouge!, The Royal Tenenbaums, I Am Sam, Vanilla Sky (Academy Award nom.; Golden Globe nom. 2002), Bowling for Columbine (doc.), The In-Laws, Radio, The Cat in the Hat, Cheaper by the Dozen, 50 First Dates, Racing Stripes, Guess Who, Kicking & Screaming, Little Manhattan, The Lake House, Happy Feet, Shrek the Third, Evan Almighty, License to Wed, Across the Universe, American Gangster, Flunked (doc.), Ghost Town, Yes Man, Funny People, Everybody's Fine, Did You Hear About the Morgans?, Grown Ups. *Scores:* The Family Way, Beyond the Limit. *Dir.:* Grateful Dead (doc. short).
TELEVISION: Has appeared as an actor and/or composer on more than 50 TV movies and series; more than 465 appearances on various TV documentaries and specials.

McCLANAHAN, RUE
Actress. b. Healdton, OK, Feb. 21, 1934. e. U. of Tulsa (B.A. cum laude). Member: Actors Studio, NYC.
THEATRE: *On B'way* in Sticks and Bones, Jimmy Shine, California Suite. *Off-B'way*: Who's Happy Now? (Obie Award, 1970), After Play. Vienna: Lettice and Lovage. London: Harvey.
PICTURES: Five Minutes to Love, Hollywood After Dark, How to Succeed With Girls, They Might Be Giants, The People Next Door, The Pursuit of Happiness, Modern Love, This World Then The Fireworks, Dear God, Starship Troopers, Out to Sea, This Rusty: A Dog's Tale, Lugosi: Hollywood's Dracula, Border to Border, Blue's Big Treasure Hunt (video short), Nuncrackers (video), The Fighting Temptations, Wit's End.
TELEVISION: *Movies:* Having Babies III, Sgt. Matlovich Vs. the U.S. Air Force, Rainbow, Topper, The Great American Traffic Jam, Word of Honor, The Day the Bubble Burst, The Little Match Girl, Liberace, Take My Daughters Please, Let Me Hear You Whisper, To the Heroes, After the Shock, Children of the Bride, To My Daughter, The Dreamer of Oz, Baby of the Bride, Mother of the Bride (also co-exec. prod.), A Burning Passion: The Margaret Mitchell Story, Innocent Victims, A Christmas Love, Columbo: Ashes to Ashes, Blackbird Hall, A Saintly Switch, The Moving of Sophia Myles, Stage on Screen: The Women, Miracle Dogs, Back to You and Me, Generation Gap. *Mini-series*: Message From Nam. *Series*: Maude, Mama's Family, The Golden Girls (Emmy Award, 1987, 3 other noms.; 3 Golden Globe noms.), The Golden Palace, Apple Pie, Safe Harbor, The Lot, Sordid Lives: The Series. *Specials*: The Wickedest Witch, The Man in the Brown Suit, Nunsense 2: The Sequel. *Guest:* More than 146 appearances.
(d. June 3, 2010)

McCLUGGAGE, KERRY
Executive. b. 1955. e. USC, Harvard U. 1978, programming asst. at Universal; 1979, dir. of current srs. programming; 1980, became v.p., Universal TV. 1982, sr. v.p. creative affairs. Served as v.p. of production, Universal Pictures and supv. prod. on series Miami Vice. 1987-991, pres. of Universal Television. 1991, co-founder of UPN, joined Paramount as pres. of the Television Group. 1992, named chmn. of the Television Group of Paramount Pictures. Resigned Dec. 2001. Remains associated with Paramount as independent producer of programming. Chairman of Allumination Filmworks, a subsidiary of ContentFilm, a distributor of quality entertainment to broadcast, satellite and cable television as well as both the theatrical and home entertainment markets worldwide. Currently is the Owner/President of Craftsman Films. McCluggage also serves on the bd. of dir. for Peace Arch Productions, a new syndication and barter advertising firm.
TELEVISION: *Movies:* Exec. Prod.: Miami Vice: Brother's Keeper, Homeland Security. *Series:* Miami Vice (line prod., story, teleplay).

McCLURE, MARC
Actor. b. San Mateo, CA, March 31, 1957.
PICTURES: Freaky Friday, Coming Home, I Wanna Hold Your Hand, Superman, Superman II, Superman III, Supergirl, Back to the Future, Superman IV: The Quest for Peace, Amazon Women on the Moon, Perfect Match, Chances Are, After Midnight, Back to the Future Part III, Grim Prairie Tales, The Vagrant, Apollo 13, Sleepstalker, That Thing You Do, Menno's Mind, Storm, Python, Venomous, Landspeed, Freaky Friday, Coach Carter, Driftwood, Frost/Nixon.
TELEVISION: *Movies:* James at 15, The Sky Trap, Epoch, Python, Little John. *Series*: California Fever.

McCLURG, EDIE
Actress. b. Kansas City, MO, July 23, 1951. e. Syracuse Univ. Newswriter and documentary prod. for National Public Radio affiliate, KCUR-FM. Became member of the Groundlings Improv Comedy Revue.
PICTURES: Carrie (debut, 1976), Cheech and Chong's Next Movie, Oh God Book II, Secret of NIMH (voice), Pandemonium, Cracking Up, Eating Raoul, Mr. Mom, The Corsican Brothers, Ferris Bueller's Day Off, Back to School, The Longshot, Planes Trains and Automobiles, She's Having a Baby, Elvira: Mistress of the Dark, The Little Mermaid (voice), Curly Sue, A River Runs Through It, Stepmonster, Airborne, Natural Born Killers, Under

the Hula Moon, Carpool, Circuit Breaker, Casper: A Spirited Beginning, Flubber, Meeting Daddy, A Bug's Life (voice), Holy Man, The Rugrats Movie (voice), Can't Stop Dancing, The Manor, Hanging Up, Van Wilder, Colored Eggs, The Master of Disguise, Now You Know, Air Bud: Spikes Back (video), Dickie Roberts: Former Child Star, Fish Without a Bicycle, Home on the Range, Love Surreal, Breaking Dawn, Simple Things, Cars (voice), Holyman Undercover, Fired Up.
TELEVISION: *Movies*: Bill on His Own, Crash Course, Dance 'til Dawn, Menu for Murder, Columbo: Ashes to Ashes, Murder She Purred, Everything You Want, *Voice Characterizations/voice*: The Snorks, The 13 Ghosts of Scooby Doo, The New Jetsons, Casper, Problem Child, Bobby's World of Monsters, The Smurfs, Tale Spin, The Addams Family, Life with Louie, Crashbox, Clifford the Big Red Dog, Rocket Power: Race Across New Zealand, Everything You Want, The Life & Times of Tim. *Series*: Tony Orlando and Dawn, The Kallikaks, WKRP in Cincinnati, The Big Show, The David Letterman Show, Harper Valley PTA, No Soap Radio, Madame's Place, Small Wonder, Valerie, The Hogan Family, Drexell's Class, Caroline in the City, The Kids from Room 402, Higglytown Heroes, 7th Heaven, The Life & Times of Tim. *Documentaries/Specials*: Cinderella (Faerie Tale Theatre), The Pee-wee Herman Show, Martin Mull's History of White People in America, Once Upon a Brothers Grimm, The Chevy Chase Show, A Home Run for Love. *Guest*: More than 128 appearances.

McCONAUGHEY, MATTHEW
Actor. b. Uvalde, Texas, November 4, 1969. e. University of Texas at Austin.
PICTURES: Dazed and Confused, My Boyfriend's Back, Angels in the Outfield, The Return of the Texas Chainsaw Massacre, Boys on the Side, Scorpion Spring, Submission, Glory Daze, Larger Than Life, A Time to Kill, Lone Star, Amistad, Contact, Making Sandwiches, The Newton Boys, South Beach, Last Flight of the Raven (prod. only), Johnny Diamond, Edtv, U-571, Last Flight of the Raven, The Wedding Planner, Reign of Fire, Dexterity, 13 Conversations About One Thing, Frailty, Tiptoes, How to Lose a Guy in 10 Days, Sahara (also exec. prod.), Two for the Money, Failure to Launch, We Are Marshall, The Loop (also prod.), Dear Deliah (also prod.), Surfer Dude (also prod.), Fool's Gold, Tropic Thunder, Ghosts of Girlfriends Past, The Lincoln Lawyer.
TELEVISION: *Movie:* Absolute Evel: The Evel Knievel Story (host). *Series:* Freedom: A History of Us (doc.). *Guest:* More than 96 appearances.

McCORMICK, KEVIN
Executive. McCormick began his career at the Robert Stigwood Organization (RSO) in London, England, working on films including "Tommy," "Jesus Christ Superstar," "Grease" and "Saturday Night Fever," the last of which he executive produced. Following RSO, he formed a partnership with actress Sally Field to develop film projects and later had a production deal at Paramount Pictures. From 1995-1999 McCormick served as executive v.p., production at Fox 2000. McCormick moved to Warner Bros. in 1999, becoming executive v.p. production, Warner Bros. Pictures. In this role, he supervised films through each stage of development and production. Among his most recent projects for the studio were "Blood Diamond" and "No Reservations" as well as Tim Burton's "Sweeney Todd." In Jan. 2008, promoted to his current position of president, production, Warner Bros. Pictures. He maintains responsibility for the studio's creative team and the development of the movies produced by the company. In addition, he maintains oversight of the division's New York and London offices.

McCOWEN, ALEC
Actor. b. Tunbridge Wells, England, May 26, 1925. e. Royal Acad. of Dramatic Art. On stage in London in Hadrian the Seventh, among others. On B'way in Antony and Cleopatra, After the Rain, The Philanthropist, The Misanthrope, Equus, Someone Who'll Watch Over Me, etc.
PICTURES: The Cruel Sea, The Divided Heart, The Deep Blue Sea, The Good Companions, The Third Key (The Long Arm), Time Without Pity, Town on Trial, The Doctor's Dilemma, A Night to Remember, The One That Got Away, Silent Enemy, The Loneliness of the Long Distance Runner, In the Cool of the Day, The Devil's Own, The Hawaiians, Frenzy, Travels with My Aunt (Golden Globe nom. 1973), Stevie, Hanover Street, Never Say Never Again, The Assam Garden, Personal Services, Cry Freedom, Henry V, The Age of Innocence, Maria's Child, Gangs of New York.
TELEVISION: Numerous productions in the U.K. and U..S. *Movies: U.K.:* The Comedy of Errors, Luther, Ape and Essence, Twelfth Night, The Secret Adversary, A Dedicated Man, Squaring the Circle, The Importance of Being Earnest, The War that Never Ends, Cruel Train, The American, Victoria and Albert. *U.S.:* Longitude, David Copperfield. *Series: U.K.:* Private Lives, Mr. Palfrey of Westminster.

McCRANE, PAUL
Actor. b. Philadelphia, PA, Jan. 19, 1961. Stage debut at age 16 in NY Shakespeare Fest. prod. of Landscape of the Body.
THEATRE: *NY:* Dispatches, Runaway, Split, The House of Blue Leaves, The Palace of Amateurs, Hooters, The Hostage, Curse of an Aching Heart
PICTURES: Rocky II (debut, 1979), Fame (also score writer, Grammy nom. 1981), The Hotel New Hampshire, Purple Hearts, Robocop, The Blob, The Shawshank Redemption, The Last Producer, Last Mistake (short), New Suit, A Year And A Day.
TELEVISION: *Movies:* Baby Comes Home, We're Fighting Back, Money—Power—Murder, With Murder in Mind, The Portrait, Strapped, Zelda. *Mini-series*: North & South II, Heaven and Hell: North and South Book III, From the Earth to the Moon. *Series:* Cop Rock, Under Suspicion, ER, Champs, 24. *As Dir:* ER (several episodes), Third Watch, Without a Trace, Life, Miami Medical. Many more episode credits as Director.

McDERMOTT, DYLAN
Actor. b. Connecticut, Oct. 26, 1961. Raised in New York City. e. Fordham U., studied acting at Neighborhood Playhouse with Sanford Meisner.
THEATRE: The Seagull, Golden Boy, The Glass Menagerie, Biloxi Blues (B'way), Floating Rhoda and the Glue Man.
PICTURES: Hamburger Hill, The Blue Iguana, Twister, Steel Magnolias, Where Sleeping Dogs Lie, Hardware, In the Line of Fire, The Cowboy Way, Miracle on 34th Street, Destiny Turns on the Radio, Home for the Holidays, `Til There Was You, Three to Tango, Texas Rangers, Party Monster, Wonderland, Runaway Jury (uncredited), Unbeatable Harold, The Tenants, Edison, Mistress of Spices, The Messengers, Mercy, Burning Palms.
TELEVISION: *Movies*: The Neon Empire, Into the Badlands, The Fear Inside, A House Divided, Perfect Gentlemen. *Mini-series:* The Grid. *Series*: The Practice (Emmy nom. 1999, Golden Globe Award 1999, 2 other noms.), Big Shots, Dark Blue. *Documentaries:* In the Line of Fire: The Ultimate Sacrifice (video short), Music Behind Bars (host). *Guest:* More than 46 appearances.

McDONALD, JOHN D.
Exhibitor. b. Medford, OR, May 22, 1957. e. Attended California State Polytechnic University, Pomona. McDonald joined AMC Theatres in 1975 in California, earning promotions to manager, general manager and training director in the Company's West Division. In 1987 he became an area operations manager for the Company's South Division. In 1992 McDonald relocated to Kansas City, MO, to become manager of operations resources; in 1994 promoted to senior v.p. of corporate operations, and to his current position of EVP, North America Operations in 1998. Headquartered in Kansas City, Mo., AMC Entertainment Inc.has interests in 360 theatres with 5,140 screens in six countries. McDonald is a former board member for the National Association of Theatre Owners.

McDONALD, MARK A.
Executive. B.A. degree, economic history, USC, 1980. MBA, Univ. of California in Los Angeles, 1989. Began career with AMC Entertainment Inc. as a part-time mgr. at AMC Puente 6 in City of Industry, CA. Advanced to asst. dir., operations for AMC's Western region in 1987. Became v.p., finance in 1993. In 1995, McDonald moved to Tokyo, Japan, to oversee AMC's Asia venture as senior v.p., Asia and was promoted to executive v.p., intl. operations and film in 1998. McDonald has been involved with several innovative initiatives developed within the company, including the deployment of Self-Serve Box Office and Teleticketing systems in California during the late 1980s. Today, McDonald is executive v.p., intl. operations for AMC Entertainment International, Inc. He has worked for AMC for 30 years and oversees international business ventures which include wholly owned theatres in Europe and Mexico. AMC, based in Kansas City, MO, has interests in 307 theatres with 4,610 screens in 30 states and the District of Columbia and four countries outside the U.S., as of July 2009.

McDONNELL, MARY
Actress. b. Wilkes Bare, PA, April 28, 1952.
THEATRE: *NY:* Buried Child, Savage in Limbo, All Night Long, Black Angel, A Weekend Near Madison, Three Ways Home, Still Life, The Heidi Chronicles, Summer and Smoke. *Regional:* National Athems, A Doll's House, A Midsummer Night's Dream, The Three Sisters.
PICTURES: Matewan, Tiger Warsaw, Dances With Wolves (Academy Award nom.; Golden Globe Award 1991), Grand Canyon, Sneakers, Passion Fish (Academy Award nom.; Golden Globe nom. 1993), Blue Chips, Mariette in Ecstasy, Independence Day, You Can Thank Me Later, Spanish Fly (voice), Mumford, Fly Girls, Amargosa, Donnie Darko, Nola, Crazy Like a Fox.
TELEVISION: *Movies:* Courage, O Pioneers, The American Clock, Woman Undone, Two Small Voices, 12 Angry Men, Evidence of Blood, Behind the Mask, Replacing Dad, A Father's Choice, For All Time, Chestnut Hill, The Locket, Mrs. Harris, Battlestar Galactica: Razor, Killer Hair, Hostile Makeover. *Mini-series:* Battlestar Galactica. *Series:* As the World Turns, ER (Emmy nom. 2002 as guest), High Society, Ryan Caulfield: Year One, Battlestar Galactica. *Guest:* More than 50 appearances.

McDONOUGH, NEAL
Actor, Producer. b. Dorchester, MA, February 23, 1966. e.

Trained at the London Academy of Dramatic Arts and Sciences.
PICTURES: Darkman, Angels in the Outfield, Three Wishes, Star Trek: First Contact, Fire Down Below, Ravenous, Minority Report,Timeline, Walking Tall, Magnificent Desolation: Walking on the Moon 3D (doc. short), The Guardian, Flags of Our Fathers, The Hitcher, 88 Minutes, I Know Who Killed Me, Traitor, Forever Strong, Street Fighter: The Legend of Chun-Li, Ticking Clock, Little Birds, Captain America: The First Avenger.
TELEVISION: *Movies:* Babe Ruth, The Burden of Proof, Cruel Doubt, Ambush in Waco: In the Line of Duty, Jack Reed: Badge of Honor, White Dwarf, Blue River, Murder Live!, Invasion, Grace & Glorie, Balloon Farm. *Mini-series:* Band of Brothers, Tin Man. *Series:* The Incredible Hulk, Murder One, Diagnosis Murder, Martial Law, Boomtown, Medical Investigation, Traveler, Desperate Housewives.

McDORMAND, FRANCES
Actress. b. Illinois, June 23, 1957. e. Yale Drama School. m. dir. Joel Coen. Daughter of a Disciples of Christ preacher, traveled Bible Belt with family settling in PA at 8. Regional theatre includes Twelfth Night, Mrs. Warren's Profession, The Three Sisters, All My Sons. Two seasons with O'Neill Playwrights Conference.
THEATRE: Awake and Sing, Painting Churches, On the Verge, A Streetcar Named Desire (Tony nom.), The Sisters Rosensweig, The Swan.
PICTURES: Blood Simple, Raising Arizona, Mississippi Burning (Academy Award nom. 1989), Chattahoochee, Dark Man, Miller's Crossing (unbilled), Hidden Agenda, The Butcher's Wife, Passed Away, Short Cuts (Golden Globe Award 1994), Beyond Rangoon, Fargo (Academy Award, Best Actress, Golden Globe nom.; 1997; Chicago Film Critics Award; Screen Actors Guild Award; Independent Spirit Award), Lone Star, Primal Fear, Palookaville, Paradise Road, Johnny Skidmarks, Madeline, Talk of Angels, Wonder Boys, Almost Famous (Academy Award nom.; Golden Globe nom. 2001), Scottsboro: An American Tragedy, The Man Who Wasn't There, Searching for Debra Winger (documentary), City By the Sea, Laurel Canyon, Something's Gotta Give, Last Night (short), North Country (Academy Award nom.; Golden Globe nom. 2006), Æon Flux, Friends with Money, Miss Pettigrew Lives for a Day, Burn After Reading (Golden Globe nom. 2009), This Must Be the Place, Transformers 3.
TELEVISION: *Movies*: Vengeance: The Story of Tony Cimo, Crazy in Love, The Good Old Boys, Talking with, Hidden in America (Emmy nom. 1997), Precinct Hollywood (narr.). *Series*: Leg Work, State of Grace (voice, narr.).

McDOWELL, MALCOLM
Actor. b. Leeds, England, June 13, 1943. Was spearholder for the Royal Shakespeare Co. in season of 1965-66 when turned to TV and then to films. *NY stage:* Look Back in Anger (also on video), In Celebration, Another Time. *LA stage:* Hunting Cockroaches.
PICTURES: Poor Cow (debut, 1967), If..., Figures in a Landscape, The Raging Moon (Long Ago Tomorrow), A Clockwork Orange (Golden Globe nom. 1972), O Lucky Man!, Royal Flash, Voyage of the Damned, Aces High, The Passage, Time After Time, Caligula, Cat People, Britannia Hospital, Blue Thunder, Cross Creek, Get Crazy, Sunset, Buy and Cell, The Caller, Class of 1999, Disturbed, In the Eye of the Snake, Moon 44, The Maestro, Schweitzer, Assassin of the Tsar, The Player, Happily Ever After (voice), Chain of Desire, East Wind, Night Train to Venice, Bopha!, Milk Money, Star Trek: Generations, Tank Girl, Kids of the Round Table, Where Truth Lies, Hugo Pool, Mr. Magoo, The Gardener, The First 9 1/2 Weeks, Beings, Y2K, Southern Cross, My Life So Far, Stanley and Us, Gangster No. 1, Island of the Dead, Stanley Kubrick: A Life in Pictures, Just Visiting, The Void, Dorian, The Chemical Wedding, The Barber, Between Strangers, I Spy, Tempo, I'll Sleep When I'm Dead, Inhabited (video), The Company, Red Roses and Petrol (also assoc. prod.), Evilenko, Bobby Jones-Stroke of Genius, Tempesta, Pinocchio 3000 (voice), Dinotopia: Curse of the Ruby Sunstone (voice), Mirror Wars: Reflection One, Cut Off, Taking Charge, Funny Farm, Extreme Cities, The List, Halloween, Halloween II, Doomsday, Delgo (voice), Bolt (voice), Vivaldi, The Book of Eli, Barry Munday, Pound of Flesh, L.A., I Hate You, The Spider, Golf in the Kingdom, Easy A, The Beautiful Outsiders, Suing the Devil (also prod.), First Platoon.
TELEVISION: *Movies*: Arthur the King, Gulag, Monte Carlo, Seasons of the Heart, The Man Who Wouldn't Die, The Little Rider, Superman: The Last Son of Krypton, Can of Worms, The David Cassidy Story, St. Patrick: The Irish Legend, Faces of Evil, Princess of Thieves, Firestarter II: Rekindled, Shadow Realm, The Curse of King Tut's Tomb. *Mini-series*: Our Friends in the North, The Great War, Lexx: The Dark Zone, War and Peace, Coco Chanel. *Series:* Pearl, Fantasy Island, Captain Simian and the Space Monkeys, Pearl, Wing Commander Academy, Heroes, Metalocalypse. *Guest:* More than 137 appearances.

McEVEETY, STEPHEN
Producer, Writer. Son of late writer/director Joseph L. McEveety. Brother is Director Vincent McEveety. Worked on Herbie Goes Bananas as 2nd asst. dir. in 1980 marked entrance into industry. CEO/Partner of production company, Mpower Worldwide.
PICTURES: *Second Asst. Director:* Herbie Goes Bananas, Zorro the Gay Blade. *First Asst. Director:* Something Wicked This Way Comes (special effects), Baby: Secret of the Lost Legend, Real Genius. *Unit Production Manager:* The Trip to Bountiful (also first asst. dir.), Flatliners, Hot Shots (also assoc. prod.), Forever Young. *Production Manager*: Welcome Home Roxy Carmichael. *Producer:* Airborne (also s.p.), One Eight Seven, We Were Soldiers, The Passion of the Christ, Paparazzi, An American Carol, Snowmen, Left to Tell. *Executive Producer:* The Man Without a Face, Immortal Beloved, Braveheart, Anna Karenina, Payback, What Women Want, We Were Soldiers: Getting It Right (video doc. short), Bella, The Star of Bethlehem (video doc.).
TELEVISION: *Movies: First Assistant Director:* An Early Frost (DGA Award 1986), thirtysomething (DGA Award 1988), Street Dreams. *Production Manager:* Right To Die, The Revenge of Al Capone.

McGILLIS, KELLY
Actress. b. Newport Beach, CA, July 9, 1957. Studied acting at Pacific Conservatory of Performing Arts in Santa Maria, CA; Juilliard. While at latter, won role in film Reuben Reuben.
THEATRE: *D.C. Stage*: The Merchant of Venice, Twelfth Night, Measure for Measure, Much Ado About Nothing. *NY Stage*: Hedda Gabler.
PICTURES: Reuben Reuben (debut, 1983), Witness (Golden Globe nom. 1986), Top Gun, Once We Were Dreamers, Made in Heaven, The House on Carroll Street, The Accused, Winter People, Cat Chaser, Before and After Death, The Babe, North, Painted Angels, Morgan's Ferry, At First Sight, The Settlement, The Monkey's Mask, Stake Land, 1 a Minute (narr.), The Innkeepers.
TELEVISION: *Movies*: Sweet Revenge, Private Sessions, Grand Isle (also prod.), Bonds of Love, In the Best of Families: Marriage Pride & Madness, We the Jury, The Third Twin, Perfect Prey, Storm Chasers: Revenge of the Twister, Black Widower. *Series:* One Life to Live. *Documentaries/Specials:* Juilliard at 80 (host), Out of Ireland (narrator), Kate Chopin: A Re-Awakening (narr.), Journey to Planet Earth (narr.).

McGINLEY, JOHN C.
Actor. b. New York, NY, Aug. 3, 1959. e. NYU (M.F.A.), 1984.
THEATRE: *NY*: Danny and the Deep Blue Sea, The Ballad of Soapy Smith, Jesse and the Games, Requiem for a Heavyweight, Love as We Know It, Talk Radio, Florida Crackers, Breast Men.
PICTURES: Sweet Liberty, Platoon, Wall Street, Shakedown, Talk Radio, Lost Angels, Fat Man and Little Boy, Born on the Fourth of July, Point Break, Highlander 2: The Quickening, Article 99, Little Noises, A Midnight Clear, Fathers and Sons, Hear No Evil, Watch It (also co-prod.), Car 54 Where Are You?, On Deadly Ground, Surviving the Game, Suffrin' Bastards (also co-s.p.), Wagons East!, Born to Be Wild, Captive (co-prod. only), Seven, Nixon, Johns, The Rock, Nothing to Lose, A.W.O.L, Three to Tango, Any Given Sunday, Get Carter, The Animal, Summer Catch, Highway, Crazy As Hell, Stealing Harvard, Identity, American Crude, Dirt Nap, Easier, Softer Way, Wild Hogs, Are We Done Yet?.
TELEVISION: *Movies*: Clinton & Nadine, Cruel Doubt, The Last Outlaw, The Return of Hunter, Intensity, The Pentagon Wars, Target Earth, The Jack Bull, Back. *Mini-series:* Sole Survivor. *Series*: Another World, Scrubs, WordGirl. *Documentary:* Alien Planet (narr.). *Guest:* More than 55 appearances.

McGOVERN, ELIZABETH
Actress. b. Evanston, IL, July 18, 1961. Family moved to Southern California when she was 10. Acted in high school in North Hollywood; performance in prod. of The Skin of Our Teeth won her agency represenation. Studied at American Conservatory Theatre, San Francisco and Juilliard Sch. of Dramatic Art. Open audition for Ordinary People resulted in her film debut. Appeared in IMAX film Wings of Courage.
THEATRE: *NY*: To Be Young Gifted and Black (1981, debut), My Sister in This House (Theatre World, Obie Awards), Painting Churches, The Hitch-Hiker, A Map of the World, Aunt Dan and Lemon (L.A.), Two Gentlemen of Verona, A Midsummer Night's Dream (NY Shakespeare Fest.), Love Letters, Twelfth Night (Boston), Major Barbara (Alaska), Ring Aroung the Moon (D.C.), Maids of Honor, The Three Sisters, As You Like It.
PICTURES: Ordinary People (debut, 1980), Ragtime (Academy Award nom.; Golden Globe nom. 1982), Lovesick, Racing with the Moon, Once Upon a Time in America, Native Son, The Bedroom Window, She's Having a Baby, Johnny Handsome, The Handmaid's Tale, A Shock to the System, Tune in Tomorrow, King of the Hill, Me and Veronica, The Favor, Wings of Courage, Twice Upon a Yesterday The Wings of the Dove, The Misadventures of Margaret, Manila, The House of Mirth, Buffalo Soldiers, The Truth, Inconceivable, Kick-Ass, Clash of the Titans, Waska.
TELEVISION: *Movies*: Women and Men: Stories of Seduction (The Man in the Brooks Brothers Shirt), Broken Trust, The Summer of Ben Tyler, Broken Glass, Clover, The Scarlet Pimpernel Meets Madame Guillotine, The Scarlet Pimpernel and the Kidnapped King, Thursday the 12th, The Flamingo Rising, Daphne, Freezing, A Room with a View. *Mini-series*: The Scarlet Pimpernel, Hawk. *Series*: If Not for You, The Brotherhood of Poland New Hampshire,

Three Moons Over Milford, Downton Abbey. *Documentaries/Specials*: Ashenden, Tales From Hollywood, The Changeling (BBC), Dear America: Letters Home from Vietnam (voice).

McGRATH, JUDY
Executive. b. Scranton, PA, 1952. e. Cedar Crest Coll. With a career that began in the magazine world as copy chief of Glamour magazine and senior writer for Mademoiselle Magazine, McGrath jumped to cable television in 1981 when she joined Warner Amex Satellite Entertainment Company (WASEC). WASEC was MTV Networks' predecessor company, and McGrath worked as an on-air promotions writer. She moved up the ranks and became editorial director, MTV; executive v.p. & creative director, MTV; and most recently president, MTV Music Networks Group. In mid-2004, McGrath was promoted to chwn. & CEO MTV Networks with responsibilities for MTV, MTV2, VH1, CMT, Comedy Central, Nickelodeon, Nick at Nite, Spike TV, TV Land, LOGO, Noggin, The N, MTV Networks Digital Suite, MTV Networks International, and all of the company's related consumer products and digital businesses. Through the years, McGrath created Unplugged, MTV Books, MTV Online, Video Music Awards, MTV Movie Awards, Total Request Live, The Real World, The Osbournes, etc. 2006 ranked #12 on Fortune Magazine's most powerful women in business and ranked #18 in 2007. 2009 she won the American Women in Radio and Television Award (AWRT) which recognizes an individual who has made extraordinary strides and accomplished tremendous successes in the field of electronic media.

McGRATH, THOMAS J.
Producer, Attorney, Writer, Lecturer. b. New York, NY, Oct. 8, 1932. e. Washington Square Coll. of NYU, B.A., 1956; NYU Sch. of Law, Juris Doctor 1960. Served in Korea with U.S. Army, 1953-54. Partner with the law firm of Simpson Thacher & Bartlett from 1970 to retirement in 1995. Became independent movie producer with Deadly Hero in 1976.
AUTHOR: Carryover Basis Under The 1976 Tax Reform Act, published in 1977. Contributing author, Estate and Gift Tax After ERTA, 1982. He is also a writer for professional legal journals.
LECTURER: American Law Institute 1976-81; Practicing Law Institute, 1976-97. He is also a lecturer in continuing legal education at various bar associations throughout the U.S. including Law Center Tax Conference at USC. McGrath currently is the president of the American Austrian Foundation, Inc. (also a founding trustee) and is on the bd. of dir. of the New York Philharmonic; and is a founding trustee and Chairman Emeritus of the Tanzania Wildlife Fund. He remains active in business as chairman of Pret-a-Porter Custom Standards, Inc. and is a managing member of Twenty First Century Holdings, LLC (which owns and operates a chain of restaurants in Poland).

McGREGOR, EWAN
Actor. b. Crieff, Scotland, March 31, 1971. Formed Natural Nylon, a production company, with Johnny Lee Miller & Jude Law. Resigned from prod. co. in Oct. 2002; company folded in Jan. 2003.
THEATRE: Starring in London production of Guys and Dolls, June 2005.
PICTURES: Being Human, Shallow Grave, Blue Juice, The Pillow Book, Trainspotting, Emma, Brassed Off, The Serpent's Kiss, Nightwatch, A Life Less Ordinary, Velvet Goldmine, Little Voice, Desserts, Nightwatch, Rogue Trader, Nora, Star Wars: Episode I-The Phantom Menace, Eye of the Beholder, Moulin Rouge (Golden Globe nom. 2002), Nora, Killing Priscilla, Anno Domini, Black Hawk Down, Star Wars: Episode II-Attack of the Clones, Young Adam, Down With Love, Faster (narrator), Big Fish, Stay, Robots (voice), Valiant (voice), Star Wars: Episode III, The Island, Stay, Scenes of a Sexual Nature, Stormbreaker, The Great Pretender, Flora Plum, Miss Potter, Cassandra's Dream, The Tourist, Incendiary, Deception, Jackboots on Whitehall (voice), I Love You Phillip Morris, Angels & Demons, Amelia, The Men Who Stare at Goats, The Ghost Writer, Nanny McPhee Returns, The Last Word, Tangled (voice), The Raven, The Man Who Killed Don Quixote, Knockout, Beginners, Salmon Fishing in the Yemen.
TELEVISION: *Movies*: Lipstick on Your Collar, Family Style, Doggin' Around, Tube Tales (dir. only), Solid Geometry (short). *Mini-series*: Scarlet & Black, Karaoke. *Documentaries:* Faster (narr.), Long Way Round (mini-series also exec. prod., camera op.), Troy's Story (narr.), Long Way Down (mini series, also writer,, exec. prod.). *Guest:* More than 107 appearances.

McHATTIE, STEPHEN
Actor. b. Antigonish, Nova Scotia, Canada, Feb. 3, 1947. e. Acadia U. Trained for stage at American Acad. of Dramatic Arts.
PICTURES: Von Richthofen and Brown (debut, 1970), The People Next Door, The Ultimate Warrior, Moving Violation, Tomorrow Never Comes, Death Valley, Best Revenge, Belizaire the Cajun, Salvation!, Call Me, Sticky Fingers, Caribe, Bloodhounds on Broadway, Erik, The Dark, Geronimo: An American Legend, Beverly Hills Cop III, Art Deco Detective, Pterodactyl Woman From Beverly Hills, Nonnie & Alex, Theodore Rex, My Friend Joe, The Climb, BASEketball, The Highwayman, Secretary, Twist, The Lazarus Child, A History of Violence, The Fountain, The Covenant, 300, Kaw, All Hat, Shoot 'Em Up, Medium Raw, Watchmen, Pontypool, 2012, The Maiden Danced, This Movie Is Broken, Score: A Hockey Musical, Immortals.
TELEVISION: *Movies*: Search for the Gods, James Dean, Look What's Happened to Rosemary's Baby, Mary and Joseph: A Story of Faith, Roughnecks, Terror on Track 9, Jonathan Stone: Threat of Innocence, Deadlocked: Escape From Zone 14, Convict Cowboy, Visitors of the Night, Deadly Love, Midnight Flight, American Whiskey Bar, A Sordid Affair (Germany), Wall of Secrets, Stone Cold, One Dead Indian, Jesse Stone: Night Passage, Jesse Stone: Death in Paradise, Absolution, The Dark Room, Jesse Stone: Sea Change, Jesse Stone: Thin Ice, Who Is Clark Rockefeller?, Jesse Stone: No Remorse, Red. *Mini-series*: Centennial, Canada: A People's History, Killer Wave, Would Be Kings, The Trojan Horse, XIII, Guns, The Summit, Diamonds. *Series*: Highcliffe Manor, Mariah, Scene of the Crime, Emily of the New Moon, Cold Squad, Happy Town. *Guest:* More than 102 appearances.

McKEAN, MICHAEL
Actor, Writer. b. New York, NY, Oct. 17, 1947. e. NYU. Featured on L.A. radio show, The Credibility Gap.
THEATRE: Accomplice (Theatre World Award).
PICTURES: 1941, Used Cars, Young Doctors in Love, This is Spinal Tap (also co-s.p., co-wrote songs), D.A.R.Y.L., Clue, Jumpin' Jack Flash, Light of Day, Planes Trains and Automobiles, Short Circuit 2, Earth Girls Are Easy, The Big Picture (also co-s.p.), Hider in the House, Flashback, Book of Love, True Identity, Memoirs of an Invisible Man, Man Trouble, Coneheads, Airheads, Radioland Murders, Across the Moon, The Brady Bunch Movie, Edie and Pen, Jack, No Strings Attached, That Darn Cat, Nothing to Lose, With Friends Like These, Still Breathing, The Pass, Archibald the Rainbow Painter, Final Justice, Small Soldiers (voice), Teaching Mrs. Tingle, Kill the Man, True Crime, Mystery Alaska, Sugar: The Fall of the West, Best in Show, Beautiful, Little Nicky, My First Mister, Never Again, Dr. Dolittle 2 (voice), Teddy Bears' Picnic, The Guru, 100 Mile Rule, A Mighty Wind (Academy Award nom. 2004), Haunted Lighthouse, The Producers, Relative Strangers, For Your Consideration, Surf's Up (voice), Joshua, The Grand, Adventures of Power, Imps* (segment), Whatever Works.
TELEVISION: *Movies*: More Than Friends, Classified Love, Murder in High Places, MacShayne: The Final Roll of the Dice, The Sunshine Boys, Final Justice, The Master of Horror and Suspense, And Starring Pancho Villa as Himself, The Year Without a Santa Claus (also soundtrack perf.), The Thick of It. *Series*: Laverne & Shirley, Grand, Sessions, Saturday Night Live, Dream On, Road Rovers, Secret Service Guy, Totally Ridiculous (host), The Lone Gunmen, Clerks, Primetime Glick, Harvey Birdman: Attorney At Law, Hopeless Pictures. *Documentaries/Specials*: Spinal Tap Reunion, The Laverne and Shirley Reunion, The Aristocrats. *Guest:* More than 286 appearances.

McKEE, GINA
Actress. b. April 14, 1961.
PICTURES: The Lair of the White Worm, The Rachel Papers, The Misadventures of Mr. Wilt, Naked, Element of Doubt, Croupier, Wonderland, Notting Hill, The Loss of Sexual Innocence, Women Talking Dirty, Messenger: The Story of Joan of Arc, There's Only One Jimmy Gimble, The Zookeeper, The Reckoning, Divine Secrets of the Ya Ya Sisterhood, MirrorMask, Greyfriars Bobby, Mickybo and Me, Scenes of a Sexual Nature, And When Did You Last See Your Father?, Atonement, In the Loop.
TELEVISION: *Movies:* Treasure Seekers, Mothertime, Beyond Fear, Our Friends in the North, The Passion, The Real Yoko Ono, The Lost Prince, The Blackwater Lightship, The Baby War, The Lavender List, Tsunami: The Aftermath, The Old Curiosity Shop, Fiona's Story, Dive. *Mini-series*: Our Friends in the North, Dice, The Forsyte Saga I and II. *Series:* An Actor's Life for Me, The Lenny Henry Show, Brass Eye (recurring role), Premier Passions (doc., narr.). *Guest:* More than 53 appearances.

McKELLEN, SIR IAN
Actor. b. Burnley, England, May 25, 1939. e. Cambridge. C.B.E. 1979, Knighted 1991.
THEATRE: *London*: 'Ten Little Niggers' (debut 1953), A Scent of Flowers, Trelawny of the Wells, A Lily in Little India, The Man of Destiny, Black Comedy, Dr. Faustus, Henceforward, Bent, Uncle Vanya, Hamlet, Macbeth, Peter Pan, Enemy Of The People, Romeo & Juliet, Richard III, Richard the II, Aladdin, King Lear. *B'way:* The Promise, Amadeus (Tony Award, 1981), Hayfever, Uncle Vanya, Ian McKellen Acting Shakespeare, Wild Honey (also London), Richard III (Brooklyn), Othello, A Knight Out, The Dance Of Death. Assoc. Dir. Nat'l Theatre. Prof. of Contemporary Theatre, Oxford Univ., 1991.
PICTURES: Alfred the Great, Thank You All Very Much, A Touch of Love, Priest of Love, The Keep, Plenty, Zina, Scandal, Last Action Hero, The Ballad of Little Jo, Six Degrees of Separation, The Shadow, Jack & Sarah, Restoration, Thin Ice, Richard III (also co-s.p., Golden Globe nom. 1996), Apt Pupil, Gods and Monsters (Academy Award nom.; Golden Globe nom. 1999), X-Men, The Lord of the Rings: The Fellowship of the Ring (Academy Award nom. 2002), Cirque du Soleil: Journey of Man (voice), The Lord of the Rings: The Two Towers, X2, Emile, The Lord of the Rings: The Return of the King, Asylum, Sprung! The Magic Roundabout (voice), Neverwas, Displaced (voice), The Da Vinci Code, X-Men:

The Last Stand, Flushed Away (voice), Stardust (narr.), The Golden Compass, The Hobbit: Part 1, The Hobbit: Part 2.
TELEVISION: *Movies:* Sunday Out of Season, Hay Fever, Keats, Ross, The Tragedy of King Richard II, Edward II, Hedda Gabler, Hamlet, The Recruiting Officer, Macbeth, Dying Day, The Scarlet Pimpernel, Walter and June, Windmills of the Gods, Countdown to War, Othello, And the Band Played On (Emmy nom. 1994), Cold Comfort Farm, Rasputin (Emmy nom.; Golden Globe Award, 1997), David Copperfield, King Lear. *Mini-series:* Amud Ha'Esh, Sleepers, Tales of the City, Great Performances (Emmy nom. 2009). *Series:* Coronation Street, Extras (Emmy nom. 2007, segment guest), The Prisoner. *Documentaries: As Narrator:* Amud Ha'Esh (mini-series english ver.), A Bit of Scarlet, Surviving Friendly Fire, Churchill, Pavarotti: The Last Tenor, Muse of Fire: A Documentary. *Guest:* More than 165 appearances.

McKEON, DOUG
Actor, Director. b. Pompton Plains, NJ, June 10, 1966.
THEATRE: Dandelion Wine, Truckload, Brighton Beach Memoirs, Death of a Buick, The Big Day.
PICTURES: *Actor:* Uncle Joe Shannon (Golden Globe nom. 1979), On Golden Pond, Night Crossing, Mischief, Turnaround, Where the Red Fern Grows Part 2, The Empty Mirror, Courting Courtney, Sub Down, Critical Mass. *Director:* The Boys of Sunset Ridge (also s.p.), Whistlin' Dixie (short), Come Away Home, Silent Knights (also writer).
TELEVISION: *Movies*: *Actor:* Tell Me My Name, Daddy I Don't Like It Like This, The Comeback Kid, An Innocent Love, Desperate Lives, Silent Eye, Heart of a Champion: The Ray Mancini Story, Breaking Home Ties, Without Consent, Rocket's Red Glare. *Mini-series*: Centennial, At Mother's Request, From the Earth to the Moon. *Series*: Edge of Night, Big Shamus Little Shamus.

McKEON, NANCY
Actress. b. Westbury, NY, April 4, 1966.
PICTURES: Where the Day Takes You, Teresa's Tattoo, The Wrong Woman, Just Write.
TELEVISION: *Movies:* A Question of Love, The Facts of Life Goes to Paris, High School U.S.A., This Child Is Mine, Poison Ivy, Firefighter (also co-exec. prod.), The Facts of Life Down Under, Strange Voices (also co-exec. prod.), A Cry for Help: The Tracey Thurman Story, A Mother's Gift, Comfort and Joy, Category 6: Day of Destruction, Wild Hearts. *Series:* Stone, The Facts of Life, Can't Hurry Love, Style and Substance, The Division (aka Heart of the City; also directed several episodes), Sonny with a Chance. *Documentaries/Specials:* Schoolboy Father, Scruffy (voice), Please Don't Hit Me Mom, Candid Kids (co-host). *Guest:* More than 51 appearances.

McLAGLEN, ANDREW V.
Director. b. London, England, July 28, 1920. Son of late actor Victor McLaglen. e. U. of Virginia, 1939-40. Asst. m.p. dir., 1944-54.
PICTURES: Gun the Man Down (debut, 1956), Man in the Vault, The Abductors, Freckles, The Little Shepherd of Kingdom Come, McLintock!, Shenandoah, The Rare Breed, The Way West, Monkeys Go Home!, The Ballad of Josie. The Devil's Brigade, Bandolero, Hellfighters, The Undefeated, Chisum, Fool's Parade (also prod.), Something Big (also prod.), One More Train to Rob, Cahill: U.S. Marshal, Mitchell, The Last Hard Men, The Wild Geese, Breakthrough (Sergeant Steiner), ffolkes (North Sea Hijack), The Sea Wolves, Sahara, Return to the River Kwai, Eye of the Widow, Connemara Days (writer).
TELEVISION: *Movies*: Log of the Black Pearl, Stowaway to the Moon, Banjo Hackett: Roamin' Free, Murder at the World Series, Louis L'Amour's The Shadow Riders, Travis McGee, The Dirty Dozen: The Next Mission. *Mini-series*: The Blue and the Gray, On Wings of Eagles. *Series*: Gunsmoke, Have Gun—Will Travel, Perry Mason, Rawhide, The Virginian, Banacek, Hec Ramsey, The Lineup, The Lieutenant, Code R, The Fantastic Journey.

McLEAN, SEATON
Executive, Producer. b. Florida, raised in Montreal, Quebec, Canada. Founding partner, Atlantis Films, Ltd., 1978. Writer and editor of several award-winning films. Formerly in charge of Television Production for Alliance Atlantis. Left company in 2003 when Alliance Atlantis moved its focus away from the production business. He now owns and operates a winery and vineyard in Prince Edward County, Ontario, with his wife, actress Sonja Smits.
PICTURES: Formula 51, Morvern Callar (exec. prod.), The Good Thief, Owning Mahowny, Saint Ralph, The Stone Angel (exec. prod.).
TELEVISION: *Movies:* Brothers by Choice, Boys and Girls, A Child's Christmas in Wales, Glory! Glory!, Lost in the Barrens, Last Train Home, Lost in the Barrens II: The Curse of the Viking Grave, Deadly Betrayal: The Bruce Curtis Story, TekWar: TekLords (supr. prod.), Justice (exec. prod.). *Series:* The Twilight Zone, Air Waves, Mom P.I., White Fang (also writer), Traders (exec. prod.), Earth: Final Conflict (exec. prod.), Cold Squad, Amazon (exec. prod.), Ray Bradbury Theater, Marlowe (co-exec. prod.), Petticoat Wars (co- exec. prod.).

McMAHON, JOHN J.
Executive, Producer. b. Chicago, IL, 1932. e. Northwestern U. Served with U.S. Army in Korea, beginning career on WGN-TV, Chicago; associated with ZIV-United Artists TV Productions during 1950s; joined ABC in 1958; v.p. & gen. mgr., WXYTZ-TV, Detroit, then KABC-TV, Los Angeles, 1968; v.p., ABC, 1968-72; joined NBC in 1972 as v.p., programs, west coast, NBC-TV; president, Hollywood Radio & Television Society; board member, Permanent Charities Committee. 1980, named pres. of Carson Prods. (Johnny Carson's prod. co.).
TELEVISION: John & Yoko: A Love Story, If It's Tuesday It Still Must Be Belgium (exec. prod.), My Father My Son (exec. prod.), Passions, Brother of the Wind, Warning: Parental Advisory.

McMARTIN, JOHN
Actor. b. Warsaw, IN, Nov. 18, 1929. e. Columbia U. Off-B'way debut: Little Mary Sunshine (1959: Theatre World Award).
THEATRE: The Conquering Hero, Blood Sweat and Stanley Poole, Children from Their Games, A Rainy Day in Newark, Pleasures and Palaces (Detroit), Sweet Charity (Tony nom.), Follies, The Great God Brown (Drama Desk Award), Sondheim: A Musical Tribute, Forget-Me-Not-Lane (Mark Taper Forum), The Visit, Chemin de Fer, The Rules of the Game, A Little Family Business, Passion (Mark Taper), Solomon's Child, Julius Caesar, A Little Night Music (Ahmanson), Love for Love, Happy New Year, Don Juan (Drama Desk Award, Tony nom.), Artist Descending a Staircase, Henry IV (Kennedy Ctr.), Custer (Kennedy Ctr.), Money & Friends (L.A.), Show Boat (Tony nom.), High Society, Into the Woods (L.A.).
PICTURES: A Thousand Clowns, What's So Bad About Feeling Good?, Sweet Charity, All The President's Men, Thieves, Brubaker, Blow Out, Pennies From Heaven, Dream Lover, Legal Eagles, Native Son, Who's That Girl, A Shock to the System, Three Businessmen, The Dish, Kinsey, No Reservations.
TELEVISION: *Movies*: Ritual of Evil, Fear on Trial, The Defection of Simas Kudirka, The Last Ninja, Murrow, Day One, Roots: The Gift, Citizen Cohn, H.U.D. *Mini-series:* Further Tales of the City. *Series*: Falcon Crest, Beauty and the Beast, Law & Order. *Specials*: Edith Wharton Story, Rules of the Game, The Greatest Man in the World, Private Contentment, The Fatal Weakness, Concealed Enemies. *Documentary:* Broadway: The American Musical. *Guest*: More than 65 appearances.

McNAMARA, WILLIAM
Actor. b. Dallas, TX, March 31, 1965. e. Columbia U. Joined Act I theatre group at Williamstown Theatre Festival, 1986; studied acting at Lee Strasberg Institute.
PICTURES: Terror at the Opera, The Beat, Stealing Home, Dream a Little Dream, Stella, Texasville, Extreme Justice, Aspen Extreme, Radio Inside, Surviving the Game, Chasers, Storybook, Girl in the Cadillac, Copycat, Snitch, Dead Girl, The Brylcreem Boys, Sweet Jane, Something to Believe In, Stag, The Deli, Knockout, Implicated, Glam, Ringmaster, Paper Bullets, Just Sue Me, The Calling, The Kings of Brooklyn, Three 'S' a Crowd, The Still Life, The Fallen, A Dance for Bethany, April Moon, The Grift, The Bleeding, The Ascent, The Legend of Hell's Gate: An American Conspiracy, Beyond the Farthest Star, Risk for Honor.
TELEVISION: *Movies:* Wildflower (ACE Award nom.), Doing Time on Maple Drive, Honor Thy Mother, Sworn to Vengeance, Liz: The Elizabeth Taylor Story, Natural Enemy, Trapped, McBride: Murder Past Midnight, American Black Beauty. *Pilot*: The Wyatts. *Series*: Island Son, Beggars and Choosers, Nightmares and Dreamscapes: From the Stories of Stephen King. *Documentaries/Specials*: Soldier Boys (Afterschool Special), Secret of the Sahara, The Edge (Indian Poker), It's Only Rock 'n' Roll (Afterschool Special).

McNAUGHTON, JOHN
Director. b. Chicago, IL, Jan. 13, 1950.
PICTURES: Henry: Portrait of a Serial Killer, The Borrower, Sex Drugs Rock & Roll, Mad Dog and Glory, Girls in Prison, Normal Life, Veeck as a Wreck, Condo Painting, Wild Things, Speaking of Sex, Shoedog.
TELEVISION: *Movies:* Girls in Prison, Lansky. *Series*: Homicide: Life on the Street, Push Nevada.

McNEELY, JOEL
Composer.
PICTURES: The Pick-Up Artist (add'l. music score), Iron Will (orchestration), You Talkin' to Me?, Samantha, Police Story III: Supercop, Squanto: A Warrior's Tale, Iron Will, Terminal Velocity, Radioland Murders, Gold Diggers: The Secret of Bear Mountain, Flipper, Virus, Vegas Vacation, Wild America, Air Force One (add'l.), The Avengers, Zack and Reba, Soldier, Virus, Lover's Prayer (aka All Forgotten), Return to Never Land, The Jungle Book II, Ghosts of the Abyss (documentary), Holes, Uptown Girls, Stateside, America's Heart and Soul (documentary), The Stepford Wives, Pooh's Heffalump Movie, The Fox and the Hound 2 (video), I Know Who Killed Me, The Adventures of Young Indiana Jones: (video series), Tinker Bell, Tinker Bell and the Lost Treasure.
TELEVISION: *Movies*: Parent Trap III, Parent Trap Hawaiian Honeymoon, Frankenstein: The College Years, Buffalo Soldiers, Road Rage, Sally Hemmings: An American Scandal, Santa Who?. *Series*: Tiny Toon Adventures, The Young Indiana Jones Chronicles (Emmy Award 1993, 1 other nom.), Buddy Faro, Dark Angel, All Souls, The Court.

McRANEY, GERALD
Actor. b. Collins, MS, Aug. 19, 1948. m. actress Delta Burke. e. U. of Mississippi. Left school to become surveyor in oil fields after which joined acting company in New Orleans. Studied acting with Jeff Corey; landed guest role on TV series, Night Gallery.
PICTURES: Night of Bloody Horror, Keep Off My Grass, The

Neverending Story, American Justice, Blind Vengeance, Comanche, Hansel & Gretel, Saving Shiloh, Red Tails, The A-Team.
TELEVISION: *Movies*: Roots II, The Jordan Chance, Women in White, Trial of Chaplain Jenson, The Law, The Haunting Passion, A Hobo's Christmas, Where the Hell's That Gold?!!?, The People Across the Lake, Dark of the Moon, Murder By Moonlight, Blind Vengeance, Vestige of Honor, Love and Curses... And All That Jazz (also dir., co-exec. prod.), Fatal Friendship, Scattered Dreams: The Kathryn Messenger Story, Armed and Innocent, Motorcycle Gang, Deadly Vows, Someone She Knows, Not Our Son, Simon & Simon: In Trouble Again, The Stranger Beside Me, Nothing Lasts Forever, Home of the Brave, A Nightmare Come True, A Thousand Men and a Baby, A Holiday Romance, Take Me Home: The John Denver Story, Danger Beneath the Sea, Tornado Warning, Going for Broke, Ike: Countdown to D-Day. *Series*: Simon & Simon, Major Dad (also exec. prod.), Promised Land, The Protector, Mister Sterling, Deadwood, Jericho, Undercovers. *Special:* Fast Forward. *Guest:* More than 118 appearances.

McSHANE, IAN
Actor. b. Blackburn, England, Sept. 29, 1942. e. RADA.
THEATRE: *England*: The House of Fred Ginger, The Easter Man, The Glass Menagerie, Rashomon, Next Time I'll Sing to You, Loot, The Big Knife, The Admirable Crichton. *NY*: The Promise. *LA*: Inadmissible Evidence, Betrayal, As You Like It.
PICTURES: The Wild and the Willing (debut, 1962), The Pleasure Girls, Gypsy Girl (Sky West and Crooked), If It's Tuesday This Must Be Belgium, The Battle of Britain, Freelance, Pussycat Pussycat I Love You, The Devil's Widow (Tam-Lin), Villain, Sitting Target, The Left Hand of Gemini, The Last of Sheila, Ransom, Journey Into Fear, The Fifth Musketeer, Yesterday's Hero, Cheaper to Keep Her, Exposed, Torchlight, Ordeal By Innocence, Too Scared to Scream, Grand Larceny, Con Man, Sexy Beast, Bollywood Queen, Agent Cody Banks, Nemesis Game, Nine Lives, Kung Fu Panda (voice), Scoop, We Are Marshall, Hot Rod, His Dark Materials: The Golden Compass, The Seeker: The Dark Is Rising, Kung Fu Panda (voice), Coraline (voice), Shrek the Third (voice), Death Race, Pretty, Baby, Machine, Pirates of the Caribbean: On Stranger Tides.
TELEVISION: *Movies:* Funeral Games, Whose Life Is It Anyway?, The Lives of Jenny Dolan, Code Name: Diamond Head, The Pirate, High Tide, Chain Letter (pilot), Grace Kelly, Braker, Rocket to the Moon, The Murders in the Rue Morgue, The Great Escape II: The Untold Story, Young Charlie Chaplin, Dick Francis: Twice Shy, Dick Francis: In the Frame, Dick Francis: Blood Sport, Perry Mason: The Case of the Desperate Deception, Columbo: Rest in Peace Mrs. Columbo, White Goods, Soul Survivors, Babylon 5: The River of Souls, Man and Boy, Kings. *Mini-series:* Roots, Jesus of Nazareth, Life of Shakespeare, Disraeli: Portrait of a Romantic, A.D., Evergreen, War and Remembrance, The Pillars of the Earth. *Series:* You Can't Win, Wuthering Heights, Bare Essence, Lovejoy (also dir.), Dallas, Madson, Trust, Deadwood (Emmy nom.; Golden Globe Award 2005), Kings. *Guest:* More than 105 appearances.

McSLARROW, KYLE E.
Executive. e. Cornell University, undergraduate degree; University of Virginia School of Law, law degree. As a Captain in the U.S. Army, McSlarrow served in the Secretary of the Army's office as Asst. to the General Counsel of the Army from 1985-1989. McSlarrow was then an associate with the Washington, D.C. law firm of Hunton & Williams. He was the Republican nominee in Virginia's 8th Congressional District in 1992 and 1994. Served as deputy chief of staff and chief counsel for Senate Majority Leaders Bob Dole and Trent Lott between 1995 and 1997. In 1997, McSlarrow became chief of staff for the late U.S. Senator Paul Coverdell. In the political arena, held numerous positions, including serving as the national chairman for the Quayle 2000 Presidential Campaign from Nov. 1998 to Feb. 2000. McSlarrow served as vice president of Political and Government Affairs for Grassroots.com, a privately-held Internet company marketing web-based political tools and services. He then served as deputy secretary of the U.S. Dept. of Energy, an agency with more than 100,000 federal and contractor employees, 17 national labs, and a budget of $23 billion. In that role, he exercised policy and programmatic supervision over a diverse portfolio that included the nation's nuclear weapons complex, non-proliferation programs, and a research and development portfolio that includes high energy physics and the development of advanced technology to strengthen the nation's energy and homeland security. McSlarrow began his tenure as president & CEO of the National Cable & Telecommunications Association (NCTA) on March 1, 2005. In this role, McSlarrow is the cable industry's primary public policy advocate in Washington, D.C., and represents the industry's interests before Congress, the Federal Communications Commission and the Administration. NCTA is the primary trade association of the cable TV industry in the U.S., representing cable operators serving more than 90% of the nation's cable TV households and more than 200 cable program networks, as well as equipment suppliers and providers of other services to the cable industry. In 2007, McSlarrow was appointed to serve on the President's National Security Telecommunications Advisory Committee (NSTAC). The NSTAC informs and advises the President on telecommunications issues affecting national security and emergency preparedness.

McTEER, JANET
Actress. b. New Castle, England, May 8, 1961. Tony Award Winner in 1991 as Best Actress in a revival of Ibsen's "A Doll's House."
PICTURES: Half Moon Street, Hawks, I Dreamt I Woke Up, Prince, Wuthering Heights, Carrington, Saint-Ex, Velvet Goldmine (voice), Tumbleweeds (Academy Award nom.; Golden Globe Award 2000), Waking the Dead, Songcatcher, The King is Alive, The Intended (also s.p.), Tideland, As You Like It, Roadkill, Island, Albert Nobbs.
TELEVISION: *Movies:* Precious Bane, Portrait of a Marriage, Yellowbacks, A Masculine Ending, Don't Leave Me This Way, The Black Velvet Gown, Marple: The Murder at the Vicarage, Daphne, Into the Storm (Emmy nom. 2009; Golden Globe nom 2010). *Mini-series:* Five Days, Sense and Sensibility, Hunter. *Series:* Les Girls (UK), The Governor, The Amazing Mrs Pritchard, Psychoville.

McTIERNAN, JOHN
Director. b. Albany, NY, Jan. 8, 1951. e. Juilliard (acting), SUNY/Old Westbury (filmmaking). m. prod. Donna Dubrow. First effort was film The Demon's Daughter, unreleased to date. Appeared in film Death of a Soldier.
PICTURES: Nomads (also s.p.), Predator, Die Hard, The Hunt for Red October, Flight of the Intruder (exec. prod. only), Medicine Man, Last Action Hero (also co-prod.), Die Hard With a Vengeance (also prod.), Amanda (prod. only), The Thomas Crown Affair, The 13th Warrior (also prod.), Rollerball (also prod.), Basic.
TELEVISION: *Movies:* Robin Hood (exec. prod.), The Right to Remain Silent (prod.), Quicksilver Highway (exec. prod.).

MEADOWS, JAYNE
Actress. b. Wu Chang, China, Sept. 27, 1924. m. late performer Steve Allen. Sister of late actress Audrey Meadows. Parents were Episcopal missionaries. Came to U.S. in 1931. Studied acting with Stella Adler, Lee Strasberg, David Craig. Made B'way debut in 1941 in Spring Again.
THEATRE: *NY*: Once in a Lifetime (revival), The Gazebo, Spring Again, Another Love Story, Kiss Them for Me, Many Happy Returns, Odds on Mrs. Oakley. *Regional*: Lost in Yonkers, Love Letters, Cinderella, The Fourposter, Tonight at 8:30, Powerful Women in History (1 woman show).
PICTURES: Undercurrent (debut, 1946), Dark Delusion, Lady in the Lake, Luck of the Irish, Song of the Thin Man, David and Bathsheba, Enchantment, Norman Is That You?, The Fat Man, College Confidential, Da Capo (Finland), Murder by Numbers, City Slickers, City Slickers II: The Legend of Curly's Gold, The Player (as herself), Casino (as herself), The Story of Us.
TELEVISION: *Movies*: Alice in Wonderland, Alice Through the Looking Glass, Ten Speed and Brownshoe, Masterpiece of Murder, The Ratings Game, Miss All-American Beauty, The James Dean Story, Sex and the Married Woman, The Gossip Columnist, Parent Trap Hawaiian Honeymoon, Now You See It Now You Don't. *Series*: Meeting of Minds, Medical Center, I've Got a Secret, High Society (Emmy nom. 1996), It's Not Easy, The Steve Allen Show, Art Linkletter Show, Steve Allen Comedy Hour, Steve Allen's Laugh Back. *Guest*: More than 83 appearances.

MEANEY, COLM
Actor. b. Ireland, May 30, 1953. Started acting as a teen, appearing at Gate Theatre in Dublin in play, The Hostage. Studied at Abbey Theatre then joined London's 7-84 Theatre Co., Half Moon Theatre Co., Belt and Braces touring co. On NY stage in Breaking the Code.
PICTURES: The Dead, Dick Tracy, Die Hard 2, Come See the Paradise, The Commitments, The Last of the Mohicans, Under Siege, Far and Away, Into the West, The Snapper (Golden Globe nom. 1994), The Road to Wellville, The Englishman Who Went Up a Hill But Came Down a Mountain, The Van, The Last of the High Kings, Con Air, This is My Father, Snitch, October 22, Claire Dolan, Four Days, Chapter Zero, Mystery Alaska, Star Trek 3D, Most Important, How Harry Became a Tree, Backflash, Intermission, The Boys and Girl from County Clare, Renegade, Layer Cake, New France, Five Fingers, A Lobster Tale, The Metrosexual, A Deal Is a Deal, Clean Break, Kings, The Damned United, The Race, Ironclad, Law Abiding Citizen, Get Him to the Greek, Parked, Alleged, Bel Ami.
TELEVISION: *Movies:* Easter 2016, Playboy of the Western World, Kenny Rogers as The Gambler, Part III: The Legend Continues, Star Trek: The Next Generation: Encounter at Farpoint, Perfect Witness, Dr. Quinn Medicine Woman, Star Trek: Deep Space Nine, The Snapper, Star Trek: The Next Generation: All Good Things, The Magical Legend of the Leprechauns, King of Texas, Bad Apple, Caved In, Covert One: The Hades Factor, Life on Mars. *Mini-series:* Les Roses de Dublin, Scarlett, Random Passage, ZOS: Zone of Separation, Alice. *Series*: Star Trek: The Next Generation, Deep Space Nine, R.U.S./H., The Murdoch Mysteries. *Guest:* More than 75 appearances.

MEARA, ANNE
Actress, Writer. b. Brooklyn, NY Sept. 20, 1929. m. actor-writer Jerry Stiller. Son is actor-dir. Ben Stiller; daughter is actress Amy Stiller. e. Herbert Berghof Studio, 1953-54. Apprenticed in summer stock on Long Island and Woodstock NY, 1950-53. Acted with NY Shakespeare Fest. 1957 and 1988 (Romeo and Juliet).

With husband joined St. Louis improv. theatre The Compass, 1959 and Chicago's Medium Rare. They formed comedy act in 1962 appearing (34 times) on The Ed Sullivan Show and making the nightclub and comedy club circuit incl. The Village Gate, The Blue Angel, The Establishment. Formed own prod. company, writing, prod. and recording award-winning radio and TV commercials. With husband co-hosted video, So You Want to Be an Actor?
THEATRE: A Month in the Country, Maedchen in Uniform, Ulysses in Nightown, The House of Blue Leaves, Spookhouse, Bosoms and Neglect, Eastern Standard, Anna Christie (Tony nom.), After-Play (also author, Outer Critics Circle Award, 1996).
PICTURES: The Out-of-Towners, Lovers and Other Strangers, Nasty Habits, The Boys From Brazil, Fame, The Perils of P.K., The Longshot, My Little Girl, Awakenings, Highway to Hell, Reality Bites, Heavyweights, Kiss of Death, An Open Window, The Daytrippers, Brass Ring, Fish in the Bathtub, Brooklyn Thrill Killers, The Indepedent, Chump Change, Amy Stiller's Breast, Zoolander, Get Well Soon, Crooked Lines, Like Mike, The Yard Sale, Chump Change (casting dir. only), Night at the Museum, When the Evening Comes, Another Harvest Moon.
TELEVISION: *Movies*: Ninotchka, Kate McShane (pilot), The Other Woman (co-writer, WGA Award 1984), The Day They Came to Arrest the Book, What Makes a Family, The Sunset Gang, Love Off Limits, Jitters, After Play (writer only), What Makes a Family, Four Kings (pilot). *Series*: The Greatest Gift (1954 soap opera), The Paul Lynde Show, The Corner Bar, Take Five with Stiller and Meara (1977-78; synd.), Kate McShane (Emmy nom. 1976), Rhoda (Golden Globe nom. 1977), Archie Bunker's Place (Emmy nom. 1981), ALF, All My Children, Homicide: Life on the Street (Emmy nom. 1997 as guest), Four Kings (pilot), The King of Queens. *Documentaries:* In Our Hands, Keeping It Real: The Adventures of Greg Walloch, I Love the '70s (mini), Fired!. *Guest:* More than 106 appearances.

MECHANIC, WILLIAM M.
Executive, Producer. e. Michigan State University, 1973. V.P. & Head of Programming, Select TV Programming, Inc., 1978-82. V.p., pay TV & post-theatrical markets, Paramount; senior creative exec., Paramount Pictures; senior v.p. & v.p., pay TV sales, Walt Disney Co., 1984; president, Intl. Distribution & Worldwide Video, Walt Disney Studios, where he set up Buena Vista Intl; was chairman and CEO of Twentieth Century Fox Filmed Entertainment from 1994 to June 2000, where he oversaw production of such hits as Titanic, Braveheart and Boys Don't Cry. Currently, Mechanic is an independent producer with own production company, Pandemonium Films.
PICTURES: Dark Water (prod.), The New World (exec. prod.), Coraline (prod.).
TELEVISION: *Series:* Freedom. *Documentary:* Z Channel: A Magnificent Obsession. *Special:* The 82nd Annual Academy Awards (prod.).

MEDAK, PETER
Director. b. Budapest, Hungary, Dec. 23, 1940. Appeared in film Beverly Hills Cop III.
THEATRE: Miss Julie. *Operas*: Salome, La Voix Humaine, Rigoletto.
PICTURES: Negatives, A Day in the Death of Joe Egg, The Ruling Class, Ghost in the Noonday Sun, The Odd Job, The Changeling, Zorro the Gay Blade, The Men's Club, The Krays, Let Him Have It, Romeo Is Bleeding, Pontiac Moon, Species II, Fallen Moon.
TELEVISION: *Movies:* The Third Girl From the Left, Cosmic Princess, The Babysitter, Mistress of Paradise, Cry for the Strangers, Breakin' Through, David Copperfield, Marple: By the Pricking of My Thumbs. *Mini-series:* Feast of All Saints. *Series:* Court Martial, Space: 1999, The Professionals, Hart to Hart, Otherworld, The Twilight Zone (multiple episodes), Crime Story, Beauty and the Beast, Mount Royal, China Beach, Homicide: Life on the Street, Law & Order: Special Victims Unit. Also episode director for several series.

MEDAVOY, MIKE
Executive, Producer. b. Shanghai, China, Jan. 21, 1941. e. UCLA, grad. 1963 with honors in history. Lived in China until 1947 when family moved to Chile. Came to U.S. in 1957. Started working in mail room at Universal Studios and became a casting dir., then went to work for Bill Robinson as an agent trainee. Two years later joined GAC and CMA where he was a v.p. in the m. p. dept. 1971 joined IFA as v.p. in charge of m. p. dept. Represented American and foreign creative talents, incl. Jane Fonda, Donald Sutherland, Michelangelo Antonioni, Jean-Louis Trintignant, Karel Reisz, Steven Spielberg, Robert Aldrich, George Cukor, John Milius, Terry Malick, Raquel Welch, Gene Wilder and Jeanne Moreau. While at IFA was involved in packaging The Sting, Young Frankenstein, Jaws and others, before joining United Artists Corp. in 1974, as sr. v.p. in chg. of West Coast prod. While at UA, was responsible for One Flew Over the Cuckoo's Nest, Annie Hall and Rocky among others. 1978 named exec. v.p., Orion Pictures Co. where he was responsible for Platoon, Amadeus, Dances With Wolves and Silence of the Lambs. (In 1982 Orion team took over Filmways, Inc.). 1990, apptd. chmn. Tri-Star Pictures, & member Columbia Pictures Bd. of Dir. Resigned in 1994. Founded Phoenix Pictures in 1995 and became chmn. and CEO, a position he holds today. 1998 Orion Pictures became defunct due to bankruptcy and operates in name only under parent company MGM Studios. Co-chmn., St. Petersburg Film Festival, 1994. Chmn. of the Jury, Tokyo Film Festival, 1994. Member of Filmex; bd. of trustees, UCLA Foundation; chmn. advisory bd., College for Intl. Strategic Affairs at UCLA; steering comm. of Royce 270, UCLA; visiting comm., Boston Museum of Fine Arts; advisory bd., Tel Aviv U.; bd., Museum of Science & Industry; Co-Chmn.: Olympic Sports Federation, Music Center Unified Fund Campaign; founding bd. of governors, Sundance Inst. Recipient: Motion Picture Pioneer Award, 1993; Cannes Film Festival Award, 1998; UCLA Alumni Award for Excellence.
PICTURES: The 6th Day, Vertical Limit (exec. prod.), Basic, Holes, In My Country, Stealth, All The Kings Men, Pathfinder, Zodiac, Black Autumn, License to Wed, Shutter Island, Black Swan, Shanghai.
TELEVISION: *Movies:* Soul of the Game (exec. prod.), In the Time of the Butterflies, The Outsider (exec. prod.). *Series:* Shake, Rattle and Roll: An American Love Story (exec. prod.). *Documentaries:* Hollywood, D.C., A Decade Under the Influence, The Blockbuster Imperative, The American Ruling Class.

MEDOFF, MARK
Writer. b. Mt. Carmel, IL, March 18, 1940. e. U. of Miami, Stanford U. Honorary doctor of humane letters, Gallaudet Univ. Prof. & dramatist in residence, New Mexico St. Univ. Novel: Dreams of Long Lasting.
THEATRE: When You Comin' Back Red Ryder? (Obie Award), Children of a Lesser God (Tony Award), The Wager, Kringle's Window.
PICTURES: Good Guys Wear Black, Children of a Lesser God (Academy Award nom.; WGA nom. 1987), Clara's Heart, City of Joy, Homage (also prod.), Santa Fe, Children on Their Birthdays (dir. only), Refuge (also dir.).
TELEVISION: *Movies*: Apology, The Twilight of the Golds (actor only).

MEDWIN, MICHAEL
Actor, Writer, Producer. b. London, England, July 18, 1923. e. Institut Fischer, Switzerland. Stage debut 1940; m.p. acting debut in Root of All Evil, 1946. Acted with National Theatre 1977-78.
THEATRE: Spring and Port Wine, Joe Egg, Forget-me-not Lane, Chez Nous, Alpha Beta, Another Country, Crystal Clear, Interpreters, Orpheus, Noises Off.
PICTURES: *Actor*: My Sister and I, Mrs. Christopher, Gay One, Children of Chance, Operation Diamond, Black Memory, Just William's Luck, Ideal Husband, Picadilly Incident, Night Beat, Courtney's of Curzon Street, Call of the Blood, Anna Karenina, William Comes to Town, Woman Hater, Look Before You Love, Forbidden, For Them That Trespass, Queen of Spades, Trottie True, Boys in Brown, Trio, Long Dark Hall, Curtain Up, Street Corner, I Only Asked, Carry on Nurse, Wind Cannot Read, Heart of a Man, Crooks Anonymous, It's All Happening, Night Must Fall, I've Gotta Horse, 24 Hours To Kill, Scrooge, The Jigsaw Man, Just Ask for Diamond, Staggered, Fanny and Elvis, Invasion (short), Framed. *Producer*: Charlie Bubbles, If..., Spring and Port Wine, O Lucky Man! Gumshoe, Memoirs of a Survivor.
TELEVISION: *Movies: Actor:* Kid Flanagan, The Endless Game, Alice Through the Looking Glass, Cinderella, Twenty Thousand Streets Under the Sky. *Series:* The Army Game, The Love of Mike, Three Live Wires, Shoestring.

MELCHIOR, IB
Director, Writer. b. Copenhagen, Denmark, Sept. 17, 1917. Son of late singer Lauritz Melchior. e. Coll., Stenhus, Denmark, 1936; U. of Copenhagen, 1937. Actor. stage mgr., English Players, 1937-38; co-dir. 1938; actor in 21 stage prod. in Europe and U.S. on radio; set designer; stage man. dept., Radio City Music Hall, 1941-42; U.S. Military Intelligence, 1942-45; writer, dir., m.p. shorts for TV, 1947-48; TV actor, 1949-50; assoc. dir., CBS-TV, 1950; assoc. prod., G-L Enterprises, 1952-53; dir., Perry Como Show, 1951-54; dir. March of Medicine, 1955-56. Documentary writ. & dir., received Top Award by Nat'l. Comm. for Films for Safety, 1960. Golden Scroll Award, Acad. of Science Fiction, Best Writing, 1976; Hamlet Award, Shakespeare Society of America, excellence in playwriting, Hour of Vengeance, 1982.
AUTHOR: Order of Battle, Sleeper Agent, The Haigerloch Project, The Watchdogs of Abaddon, The Marcus Device, The Tombstone Cipher, Eva, V-3, Code Name: Grand Guignol, Steps & Stairways, Quest, Order of Battle: Hitler's Werewolves, Case by Case.
PICTURES: *Writer:* When Hell Broke Loose, Live Fast—Die Young, The Angry Red Planet (also dir.), The Case of Patty Smith (assoc. prod.), Reptilicus, Journey to the Seventh Planet, Robinson Crusoe on Mars, The Time Travellers (also dir.), Planet of the Vampires (Eng. version of Italy's Terrore nello spazio), Ambush Bay, Death Race 2000, Lost in Space (special advisor to Mark Koch, Death Race (1975 s.p.). *Director:* Where There's Smoke, Keep Off the Grass.
TELEVISION: *Series: Writer:* Men Into Space, The Outer Limits, Lost In Space (creator, uncredited). *Director:* Perry Como's Kraft Music Hall, Tom Corbett Space Cadet (technical director), The March of Medicine (series documentary).

MESTRES, RICARDO
Executive, Producer. b. New York, NY, Jan. 23, 1958. e.

Harvard U., A.B. 1980. Gained filmmaking experience during summers as prod. asst. on TV features. Joined Paramount Pictures as creative exec. 1981. Promoted to exec. dir. of production in 1982 and to v.p., prod. in 1984. Named v.p. of prod., Walt Disney Pictures, 1985. Promoted to sr. v.p., prod.,1986-88. Named pres. production, Touchstone Pictures, 1988-89. In 1989, became pres., Hollywood Pictures. Resigned, 1994. Co-founder Great Oaks Entertainment with John Hughes, 1995-1997. Principal of Ricardo Mestres Productions which is associated with Disney, 1997-present. Member, AMPAS.
PICTURES: *Prod.*: Jack, 101 Dalmatians, Flubber, Home Alone III, Reach the Rock, The Visitors, The Hunted.
TELEVISION: *Movie:* The Five Forty-Eight (prod. coordinator).

MELNIKER, BENJAMIN
Producer, Attorney. b. Bayonne, NJ. e. Brooklyn Coll., LL.B., Fordham Law Sch. Loew's Theatres usher; private law practice. Employed by Legal Department MGM; v.p. & gen. counsel, 1954-69; exec. v.p., 1968-70; resigned from MGM, 1971; President & CEO of Jerry Lewis Cinemas, 1972. Producer & exec. prod. for motion pictures and television movies and series, 1974 to present. Adjunct assoc. prof., NY Law Sch., 1976-77. Former m.p. chmn. Anti-Defamation League, B'nai Brith. Mem. Amer., NY State bar assns., Bar Assn. of City of NY, AMPAS.
PICTURES: *Executive producer:* Mitchell, Shoot, Batman, Batman Returns, Batman Forever, Batman & Robin, Catwoman, Batman Begins, The Dark Knight, The Spirit. *Producer:* Swamp Thing, The Return of Swamp Thing, Batman: Mask of the Phantasm, Constantine.
TELEVISION: *Movies: Executive producer:* :Three Sovereigns for Sarah, Harmful Intent. *Series: Executive producer:* Dinosaucers, Swamp Thing, Fish Police, Where on Earth is Carmen Sandiego? (Emmy Award 1995), Doomsday. *Producer:* The Adventures of Batman & Robin.

MELVIN, MURRAY
Actor. b. London, England, 1932. On stage with Theatre Workshop.
PICTURES: The Criminal (debut, 1960), A Taste of Honey, HMS Defiant (Damn the Defiant), Sparrows Can't Sing, The Ceremony, Alfie, Kaleidoscope, The Village (UK), Smashing Time, The Fixer, Start the Revolution Without Me, A Day in the Death of Joe Egg, The Devils, The Boy Friend, Ghost in the Noonday Sun, Barry Lyndon, The Bawdy Adventures of Tom Jones, Joseph Andrews, Comrades, Testimony, Little Dorrit, The Krays, Let Him Have It, Princess Caraboo, England My England, The Emperor's New Clothes, The Phantom of the Opera.
TELEVISION: *Movies:* Clouds of Glory: The Rime of the Ancient Mariner, The Soldier's Tale (UK), The Memorandum (UK), Surprises, A Christmas Carol, This Office Life (UK), Stuff of Madness (UK), Sunday Pursuit (UK, short), Prisoner of Honor, Doomsday Gun, Alice in Wonderland, David Copperfield, Tom's Christmas Tree, Hepzibah - Sie holt dich im Schlaf. *Mini-series:* Paradise Walk, Christopher Columbus, The Genius of Mozart. *Series:* Starhunter. *Guest:* More than 50 appearances.

MENDES, SAM
Director. England, UK, August 1, 1965. Runs the Donmar Warehouse in London.
PICTURES: Little Voice, American Beauty (Academy Award, Best Dir.; DGA Award, Golden Globe Award 2000), Road to Perdition (also prod.), Jarhead, Starter for Ten (exec. prod.), The Kite Runner (exec. prod.), Sweeney Todd (also prod.), Things We Lost in the Fire (prod. only), Revolutionary Road (also prod., Golden Globe nom. 2009), Away We Go.
TELEVISION: *Movies:* Cabaret (also stage dir.), Company (also actor, stage dir.), Stuart: A Life Backwards (exec. prod.).

MÉNÉGOZ, MARGARET
Producer, Director, Executive. Ménégoz is the president and chairman of Unifrance, the French Film Association, whose membership includes feature film and short film producers, sales agents, directors and actors. Active in French film since 1975, Ménégoz is an award-winning producer who has produced more than 40 films, including a BAFTA best foreign language film award for Danton in 1983. She has been a member of the bd. of directors of Auteurs Réalisateurs Producteurs and Cinémathèque française; managing director of Films du Losange, the French Distributor, as a Manager, Producer and Supervising Producer; and chmn. for Les Rendez-vous franco-allemands du cinema.
PICTURES: *Producer:* Goldflocken, Koko, a Talking Gorilla (documentary), Mountain Pass, Perceval le Gallois, Lady of the Camelias, The Aviator's Wife, Lettres d'amour en Somalie (documentary), Le Beau marriage, Danton (BAFTA award for best foreign language film, 1983), Pauline à la plage, Liberty Belle, Un jeu brutal, Tricheurs, Un amour de Swann, Full Moon in Paris, Le Tartuffe, Summer, Boyfriends and Girlfriends, Dandin, Les Possédés, De bruit et de fureur, Noce blanche, A Tale of Springtime, Europa Europe, Le Jour des rois, A Tale of Winter, La Règle du je, Louis, enfant roi, Conte d'été, Les Enfants de l'automne, À mort la mort, The Season of Men, Our Lady of the Assassins, Purely Coincidental (documentary), Le Temps du loup, Raja, Ne quittez pas!, The Feelings Factory (also exec. prod.), Das Weiße Band, The White Ribbon, Les mains en l'air. *Executive producer:* Le Pont du Nord, Autumn Tale, Hidden, La Fabrique des sentiments. *Associate producer:* Ne fais pas ca. *First assistant director:* Lautrec.

MENENDEZ, BELINDA
Executive. e. Menendez attended St. Andrews University in Scotland and holds a master's degree in theology. Began career running intl. sales for Televisa. Led intl. TV distribution operation's for Michael Solomon's S.I.E. then joined Studio Canal (formerly Canal Plus DA). As executive v.p. of sales, she oversaw intl. TV and video licensing for Latin America, Asia and the U.S., eventually managing these activities worldwide and taking on theatrical sales. Menendez first joined Universal Television Distribution in July 2001 with more than 15 years of international filmed entertainment sales experience, both as a buyer and seller. In the organization she became co-president, Universal Television Distribution, and president, Universal International Television. Menendez was named President, NBC Universal International Television Distribution in May 2004. In this role today, she oversees intl. free, pay, and new media television licensing for NBC Universal's current and library film and TV product outside of the U.S. and Canada. In 2007, Menendez made her debut on The Hollywood Reporter's prestigious Women in Entertainment Power 100 list at #35, ranked #6 on the publication's Latino Power 50 list, and also ranked #2 on The Hollywood Reporter's Hispanic Women in Entertainment Power 25 list. Additionally, she was named one of the 100 Most Influential Hispanics by Hispanic Business Magazine and was honored as one of the Most Powerful and Influential Latinos by the Imagen Foundation.

MENGES, CHRIS
Cinematographer, Director. b. Kington, England, Sept. 15, 1940. Received ASC International Award 2010.
PICTURES: *Cinematographer*: Kes, Gumshoe, The Empire Strikes Back (second unit), Local Hero, Comfort and Joy, The Killing Fields (Acad. Award, 1985), Marie, The Mission (Acad. Award, 1987), Singing the Blues in Red, Shy People, High Season, Michael Collins (LA Film Critics Award, 1997), The Boxer, The Pledge, The Honest Thief, Dirty Pretty Things, Criminal, Tickets, The Three Burials of Melquiades Estrada, North Country, Papa, Notes on a Scandal (also dir. of photog., camera op.), Yellow Handkerchief (also camera op.), Stop-Loss, The Reader (Academy Award nom.; ASC nom. 2009), Route Irish, London Boulevard. *Director*: A World Apart, Crisscross, Second Best, The Lost Son.
TELEVISION: *Movies: Cinematographer:* Made in Britain, Walter, Walter and June. *DocumentariesSpecials: Cinematographer:* Auditions, A Question of Leadership, World in Action (UK), The Red and the Blue: Impressions of Two Political Conferences, The Concert for George. *Director:* East 103rd Street.

MENKEN, ALAN
Composer. b. New York, NY, July 22, 1949. Raised in New Rochelle, NY. e. NYU. Began composing and performing at Lehman Engel Musical Theatre Workshop at BMI, where he met future partner, lyricist Howard Ashman. With Ashman made Off-B'way debut in 1979 with score of God Bless You Mr. Rosewater. Wrote music for workshop Battle of the Giants, and music and lyrics for Manhattan Theatre Club Prod. of Real Life Funnies. With Ashman wrote 1982 Off-B'way hit Little Shop of Horrors. Other theatre credits include: The Apprenticeship of Duddy Kravitz, Diamonds, Personals, Let Freedom Sing, Weird Romance, Beauty and the Beast, A Christmas Carol. His compositions have garnered 8 Oscars and numerous additional awards, including ASCAP Awards and Grammy Awards. Grammy Awards: The Little Mermaid (2), Beauty and the Beast (3), Aladdin (4), Pocahontas (1).
PICTURES: Little Shop of Horrors (Academy Award nom. for song Mean Green Mother From Outer Space 1987), The Little Mermaid (2 Academy Awards: best song, Under the Sea, and music score, 1 other nom.; 2 Golden Globe Awards, 1 other nom. 1989), Rocky V (song), Beauty and the Beast (2 Academy Awards: best song, title song, and music score, 2 other noms.; 2 Golden Globe Awards, 1 other nom. 1992), Newsies, Aladdin (2 Academy Awards: for song, A Whole New World, and music score, 1 other nom.; 2 Golden Globe Awards, 2 other noms. 1993), Home Alone 2: Lost in New York (song), Life With Mikey, Pocahontas (2 Academy Awards: best score & best orig. song, Golden Globe Award, 1 other nom. 1996), The Hunchback of Notre Dame (Academy Award nom.; Golden Globe nom. 1997), Hercules (Academy Award nom.; Golden Globe nom. 1998), Little Mermaid II: Return to the Sea, Mickey's PhilharMagic (uncredited for songs, "Be Our Guest," "Part of Your World," and "A Whole New World"), Home on the Range, Noel, The Shaggy Dog, Enchanted (3 Academy Award noms.; Golden Globe nom.; orig. song, 2008), She's Out of My League (soundtrack performer), Tangled.
TELEVISION: *Movies:* Cartoon All-Stars to the Rescue, Polly, Aladdin on Ice, Beauty and the Beast: A Concert on Ice, Michelle Kwan Skates to Disney's Greatest Hits, Michelle Kwan: Princess on Ice, A Christmas Carol: The Musical. *Mini-series:* Broadway: The American Musical (documentary) *Series:* Sesame Street (1995), Hercules. *Specials*: Lincoln, The 80th Annual Academy Awards (soundtrack).

MENZEL, JIRI
Actor, Director. b. Prague, Czechoslovakia (now Czech Republic), Feb. 23, 1938.
PICTURES: *Actor:* Defendant, Kdyby tisic klarinetu, Everday Courage, Closely Watched Trains (DGA nom. 1969), Return of the Prodigal Son, Soukroma vichrie, Hotel pro ciznice, Dita Saxova, Capricious Summer, The Cremator, Sechse kommen durch die ganze Welt, 30 panen a Pythagoras, The Apple Game, The Blue Planet, Magicians of the Silverscreen, Miniden szerdain, Koportos, Upir z Feratu, Szivzur, Buldoci a tresme, Srdecny pozdrav ze zemekoule, Fandy, O Fandy, Albert, Utekajme, uzide, Hard Bodies, Tender Barbarians, Larks on a String, The Elementary School, Long Conversation with a Bird, Everything I Like, The Little Apocalypse, Joint Venture, Vengeance is Mine, Jak si zaslouziat princeznu, Truck Stop, Every Sunday, Hannah's Ragtime, Velvet Hangover (documentary), Útek do Budína, Rokonok, Operace Dunaj. *Director:* Domy z panleu, Umrel nam pan Forester, Crime at the Girls School, Pearls of the Deep, Koncert 65, Closely Watched Trains, Capricious Summer, Zlocin v santanu, Promeny krajiny, Who Looks for Gold?, Seclusion Near A Forest, Magicians of the Silverscreen, Short Cut, Krasosmutneni, The Snowdrop Festival, My Sweet Little Village, Die Schokladenschnuffler, Prague, The End of Old Times, Larks on a String, The Beggar's Opera, Life and Extraordinary Adventures of Private Ivan Chonkin, Ten Minutes Older: The Cello, Útek do Budína, Világszám!, I Served the King of England (also writer).

MEREDITH, ANNE
Writer, Producer.
PICTURES: *Writer:* Bastard Out of Carolina (WGA Award 1998), Rated X, Cavedweller (WGA nom. 2005), Aftershock, (also dir.), Piece of My Heart.
TELEVISION: *Movies: Writer:* Losing Chase, (also assoc. prod.), Out of the Ashes (WGA Award 2006), The Human Betterment League.

MERHIGE, E. ELIAS
Director. b. Brooklyn, NY, 1964. r.n. Edmund Elias Merhige.
PICTURES: Implosion (also writer), Spring Rain (short), A Taste of Youth, Begotten (also s.p., prod., cinematography, film effects), Shadow of the Vampire (numerous film festival awards), Suspect Zero, Games they Play.

MERRILL, DINA
Actress. r.n. Nedenia Hutton. b. New York, NY, Dec. 29, 1925. Fashion model, 1944-46. Was a co-owner and vice-chmn., RKO Pictures, m.p. and TV prod. co.
THEATRE: *B'way*: Angel Street, Are You Now or Have You Ever Been?, On Your Toes.
PICTURES: The Desk Set (debut, 1957), A Nice Little Bank That Should Be Robbed, Don't Give Up the Ship, Operation Petticoat, The Sundowners, Butterfield 8, Twenty Plus Two, The Young Savages, The Courtship of Eddie's Father, I'll Take Sweden, Running Wild, The Meal, The Greatest, A Wedding, Just Tell Me What You Want, Twisted, Caddyshack II, True Colors, The Player, Open Season, The Point of Betrayal, Milk & Money (also exec. prod.), Mighty Joe Young, Shade.
TELEVISION: *Movies:* Westinghouse Presents: The Dispossessed, The Sunshine Patriot, Seven in Darkness, The Lonely Profession, Mr. & Mrs. Bo Jo Jones, Family Flight, The Letters, Kingston, The Tenth Month, The Brass Ring, Hot Pursuit, Turn Back the Clock, Fear, Not in My Family, Something Borrowed Something Blue, A Chance of Snow, The Magnificent Ambersons, The Glow. *Mini-series:* Roots: The Next Generations. *Series:* Hot Pursuit. *Guest*: More than 96 appearances.

METCALF, LAURIE
Actress. b. Edwardsville, IL, June 16, 1955. e. Illinois St. Univ. One of the original members of the Steppenwolf Theatre Company, 1982 Obie Award for Balm in Gilead. *B'way:* My Thing of Love.
PICTURES: Desperately Seeking Susan (debut, 1985), Making Mr. Right, Candy Mountain, Stars and Bars, Miles From Home, Uncle Buck, The Appointments of Dennis Jennings (short), Internal Affairs, Pacific Heights, JFK, Hollywood Mistress, A Dangerous Woman, Blink, Leaving Las Vegas, Toy Story (voice), Dear God, U Turn, Scream 2, Chicago Cab, Bulworth, Runaway Bride, Toy Story 2 (voice), Timecode, Treasure Planet (voice), Steel City, Beer League, Meet the Robinsons (voice), Georgia Rule, Stop-Loss, Toy Story 3 (voice).
TELEVISION: *Movies*: The Execution of Raymond Graham, Balloon Farm, Always Outnumbered, The Long Island Incident, The Virgin of Akron, Ohio (pilot), The Farm. *Series*: Saturday Night Live, Roseanne (3 Emmy Awards, 1 other nom.; 2 Golden Globe noms.), 3rd Rock from the Sun (Emmy nom. 1999 as guest), Norm, God the Devil and Bob, Charlie Lawrence, Monk (Emmy nom. 2006 as guest), Desperate Housewives (Emmy nom. 2007), Easy Money. *Documentary:* Two Mikes Don't Make a Wright. *Guest:* More than 45 appearances.

METZLER, JIM
Actor. b. Oneonta, NY, June 23, 1951. e. Dartmouth Coll.
PICTURES: Four Friends, Tex (Golden Globe nom. 1983), River's Edge, Hot to Trot, Sundown: The Vampire in Retreat, 976-EVIL, Old Gringo, Circuitry Man, Delusion, One False Move, Waxwork II: Lost in Time, A Weekend with Barbara und Ingrid, Gypsy Eyes, C.I.A. Trackdown, Plughead Rewired: Circuitry Man II, Children of the Corn III: Urban Harvest, Cadillac Ranch, A Gun A Car A Blonde, L.A. Confidential, St Patrick's Day, Under the Influence, Phantom Town, Warm Texas Rain, A Gun A Car A Blonde, Big Brass Ring, Bad City Blues, The Doe Boy, Megiddo: The Omega Code 2, What Matters Most, Under the Influence, The United States of Leland.
TELEVISION: *Movies*: Princess Daisy, Do You Remember Love, Christmas Star, The Alamo: 13 Days to Glory, The Little Match Girl, Perry Mason: The Case of the Musical Murder, Murder By Night, Crash: The Mystery of Flight 1501, Love Kills, French Silk, Don't Look Back, Apollo II, Little Girls in Pretty Boxes, A Wing and a Prayer, Hefner: Unauthorized, Witness Protection, A Family in Crisis: The Elian Gonzales Story, Amish Grace. *Mini-series*: North and South, North and South Book II, On Wings of Eagles. *Series*: Cutter to Houston, The Best Times. *Guest:* More than 48 appearances.

MEYER, BARRY M.
Executive. b. New York, NY, Nov. 28, 1943. e. B.A., U. of Rochester, J.D., Case Western Reserve U. School of Law. Began in legal & business affairs, ABC Television Network, 1968; director, Business Affairs, 1971; v.p., Business Affairs, 1972, Warner Bros. Television; exec. v.p., Television Division, Warner Bros., 1978; exec. v.p., Warner Bros., Inc., 1984, in charge of all television operations. Became CEO, Warner Bros., Inc., 1994. Named chairman & CEO, Warner Bros., Ent. Inc. 1999 and is the position he holds today. He is a member of the Board of Councilors of the USC School of Cinema-Television; a member of the bd. of dir. of the Motion Picture Association of America (MPAA); a bd. member of the Museum of Radio & Television; a member of the Academy of Motion Picture Arts & Sciences; a bd. member of the American Film Institute; a member and former Governor of the Academy of Television Arts & Sciences; a member and past bd. member of the Hollywood Radio and Television Society; a member of the Board of Trustees of the University of Rochester; Meyer is also involved in numerous charitable and civic activities, including serving on the Board of Directors of Human Rights Watch.

MEYER, BRECKIN
Actor. b. Minneapolis, MN, May 7, 1974.
PICTURES: Freddy's Dead: The Final Nightmare, Payback, Clueless, The Craft, Escape from L.A., Prefontaine, Touch, Dancer Texas Pop. 81, Can't Hardly Wait, 54, Go, The Insider, Tail Lights Fade, Road Trip, Josie and the Pussycats, Rat Race, Kate & Leopold, Pinocchio (voice, US version), Kim Possible: The Secret Files (video, voice), Garfield: The Movie, Blast!, Herbie: Fully Loaded, Rebound, Caffeine, Garfield: A Tail of Two Kitties, Blue State, Stag Night, The Ghosts of Girlfriends Past, The Maiden Heist.
TELEVISION: *Movies:* Camp Cucamonga, Betrayed: A Story of Three Women, Rocky Times, Robot Chicken: Star Wars (voice, Emmy nom. 2008). *Series:* Child's Play, Potato Head Kids, The Jackie Thomas Show, The Home Court, King of the Hill, The Near Future, Inside Schwartz, Kim Possible (voice), Married to the Kellys, A Portrait of the Artist as a Young Clown (voice), Dear Titan Maximum, Consumer, Robot Chicken (2 Emmy noms), Franklin & Bash.

MEYER, NICHOLAS
Director, Writer. b. New York, NY, Dec. 24, 1945. e. U. of Iowa. Was unit publicist for Love Story, 1969. Story ed. Warner Bros. 1970-71. Author: The Love Story Story, The Seven Percent Solution, Target Practice, The West End Horror, Black Orchid, Confession of a Homing Pigeon, The Canary Trainer.
PICTURES: *Writer:* Invasion of the Bee Girls, The Seven Percent Solution (Academy Award nom.; WGA nom. 1977), Time After Time (also dir.), Star Trek II: The Wrath of Khan (also dir.), Fatal Attraction, Company Business (also dir.) Star Trek VI: The Undiscovered Country (also dir), Sommersby (co-s.p.), Voices, The Informant (also exec. prod.), The Prince of Egypt (additional s.p.), The Human Stain, The Crimson Petal and White (s.p.), Elegy, The Politician's Wife, The Hessen Affair, Eddy Deco. *Director:* Volunteers, The Deceivers, Creation. *Executive producer:* Collateral Damage, Happy Endings.
TELEVISION: *Movies*: *Writer:* Judge Dee and the Monastery Murders, The Night That Panicked America (Emmy nom. 1976), Fall From the Sky, Orpheus (also exec. prod.). *Director:* The Day After (Emmy nom. 1984), Vendetta. *Executive producer:* The Odyssey (mini series, Emmy nom. 1997).

MEYER, RON
Executive. b. 1945. Served in U.S. Marine Corps. Agent with William Morris. 1975, co-founded, with Mike Ovitz, Creative Artists talent agency, eventually serving as pres. 1995, appointed his current position of pres. & COO of Universal Studios, which is now part of NBC Universal.

MEYERS, NANCY
Writer, Director, Producer. b. Philadelphia, PA, Dec. 8, 1949. e. American U., D.C. Began as story editor for Ray Stark. First teamed with Charles Shyer to write screenplay for Private

Benjamin.
PICTURES: *Writer:* Irreconcilable Differences, Protocol, Once Upon a Crime, Private Benjamin. *Writer/Producer:* Private Benjamin (Academy Award nom.; WGA Award 1981), Baby Boom, Father of the Bride, I Love Trouble, Father of the Bride II, Something's Gotta Give (also dir.). *Writer/Director:* The Parent Trap. *Producer/Director:* What Women Want, The Holiday (also writer), It's Complicated (also writer, Golden Globe nom. 2010).

MEYERS, ROBERT
Executive. b. Mount Vernon, NY, Oct. 3, 1934. e. NYU. Entered m.p. industry as exec. trainee in domestic div. of Columbia Pictures, 1956; sales and adv. 1956-60; transferred to sales dept. Columbia Pictures Int'l, NY: posts there included supervisor of int'l roadshows and exec. assistant. to continental mgr. Joined National General Pictures as v.p.-foreign sales, 1969. Created JAD Films International Inc. in Feb. 1974 for independent selling and packaging of films around the world. September, 1977, joined Lorimar Productions Inc. as sr. v.p. of Lorimar Distribution Intl. Became pres. in 1978. Joined Filmways Pictures in 1980, named pres. & COO. Pres. of American Film Mktg. Assn.; 1982, formed new co., R.M. Films International. Rejoined Lorimar 1985. as pres., Lorimar Motion Pictures, int'l distribution. 1988-92, pres., Orion Pictures Int'l. 1993-94, pres., Odyssey Entertainment. In 1995, joined Village Roadshow International as senior v.p. in charge of international aquisitions.

MICHAELS, JOEL B.
Producer. b. Buffalo, NY, Oct. 24, 1938. Studied acting with Stella Adler. Many co-prods. with Garth Drabinsky, Cineplex Corp. Pres. of Cineplex Odeon, 1986-90.
PICTURES: The Peace Killers, Your Three Minutes Are Up (prod. spvr.), Student Teachers (prod. spvr.), The Prisoners (assoc. prod.), Lepke (assoc. prod.), The Four Deuces (asso. prod.), Bittersweet Love, The Silent Partner, The Changeling, Tribute, The Amateur, Losin' It (exec. prod.), The Philadelphia Experiment, Black Moon Rising, Universal Soldier, Three of Hearts (exec. prod.), Stargate, Cutthroat Island (co-prod.), Last of the Dogmen, Lolita, Terminator 3: Rise of the Machines, The Gospel of John (exec. prod.), Half Light, Basic Instinct 2, Terminator Salvation.
TELEVISION: *Movies:* Harem (consulting prod.), Courage. *Series:* Terminator: The Sarah Connor Chronicles (exec. prod.).

MICHAELS, LORNE
Writer, Producer. b. Toronto, Canada, Nov. 17, 1944. e. U. of Toronto, 1966. Chairman, Broadway Video. Named B'caster of the Year by the International Radio and TV Society, 1992. A Co-creator, writer and exec. prod. of television's long-running Saturday Night Live (1975-).
THEATRE: Gilda Radner Live From New York (prod., dir.).
PICTURES: *Producer:* Gilda Live (also co-s.p.), Nothing Lasts Forever, Three Amigos (also co-s.p.), Wayne's World, Coneheads, Wayne's World 2, Lassie, Tommy Boy, Stuart Saves His Family, Black Sheep, Kids In the Hall: Brain Candy, A Night at the Roxbury, Superstar, The Ladies Man, Enigma, Mean Girls, Hot Rod, Baby Mama, MacGruber. Michaels has also produced several straight-to-video projects featuring former SNL performers. Has won 7 Emmy Awards with 21 others noms.; 3 WGA Awards, with 4 other noms. for Saturday Night Live.
TELEVISION: *Movies: Executive producer:* All You Need Is Cash, Simon and Garfunkel: The Concert in Central Park, The Coneheads (short), Saturday Night Live: Presidential Bash, Frosty Returns (short), Saturday Night Live: Best of the Clinton Scandal, Lookwell, SNL: 25 Years of Music, America's Most Terrible Things, Night of Too Many Stars, Late Night With Conan O'Brien: 10th Anniversary Special, SNL: The Best of Cheri Oteri, SNL: The Best of Christopher Walken, SNL: The Best of Tom Hanks, Saturday Night Live: The Best of Alec Baldwin, To Love and Die in L.A., The Gleib Show. *Writer:* Lily, Lily Tomlin (also prod., 2 Emmy Awards, 1 other nom.), Steve Martin's Best Show Ever (also prod.). *Producer:* Things We Did Last Summer, SNL: Game Show Parodies. *Series: Writer:* Barris & Company, Rowan & Martin's Laugh-In, The Beautiful Phyllis Diller Show, The Hart & Lorne Terrific Hour (also prod. & actor), Saturday Night Live (also creator, producer & exec. prod.). *Executive Producer:* Sunday Night, The Kids in the Hall, Late Night With Conan O'Brien (4 Emmy noms.), The Vacant Lot, The Colin Quinn Show, The Tracy Morgan Show, Thick and Thin, 30 Rock (3 Emmy Awards 2007, 2008, 2009), Late Night with Jimmy Fallon. *Documentaries/Specials: Writer:* The Paul Simon Special (also prod., Emmy Award 1978). *Executive producer:* Rolling Stone Presents Twenty Years of Rock & Roll (co-exec. prod.), Superman 50th Anniversary, Saturday Night Live: 15th Anniversary, Saturday Night Live Goes Commercial, Saturday Night Live: The Best of Phil Hartman, Saturday Night Live: The Best of Chris Farley, Saturday Night Live: The Best of Adam Sandler, Saturday Night Live: Presidential Bash 2000, 50 Years of NBC Late Night, Rutles 2: Can't Buy Me Lunch, NBC 75th Anniversary Celebration (also writer), Night of Too Many Stars, Late Night with Conan O'Brien: 10th Anniversary Special, Sons & Daughters (series), Late Night with Jimmy Fallon (series). *Producer:* Saturday Night Live: The Best of Steve Martin, Saturday Night Live: The Best of Dana Carvey, Saturday Night Live: The Best of Chris Rock, Saturday Night Live 25 (2 Emmy noms., 2 WGA Awards, 3 other noms.).

MICHEL, WERNER
Executive. e. U. of Berlin, U. of Paris, Ph.D., Sorbonne, 1931. Radio writer, dir., co-author two Broadway revues: From Vienna, 1939 and Reunion in New York, 1940. Broadcast dir., Voice of America, 1942-46. Prod. & dir., CBS, 1946-48; asst. prog. dir., CBS, 1948-50. Prod. Ford TV Theatre, 1950-52 Prod. DuMont TV network, 1952-55. Dir. Electronicam TV-Film Prod., 1955-56. Prod. of Edge of Night, Procter and Gamble, 1956-57. V.P. & dir., TV-radio dept., Reach, McClinton Advertising, Inc., 1957-62. Consultant, TV Programming & Comm'l-Prod., N.W. Ayer & Son Inc. V.P. & dir., TV dept., SSCB Advertising, 1963. Program exec. at ABC-TV Hollywood, 1975. Sr. v.p. of creative affairs, MGM-TV, 1977. Exec. v.p., Wrather Entertainment Intl., 1979. Returned to MGM-TV as sr. v.p., creative affairs, 1980-82. COO, Guber-Peters TV, 1982-84. Sr. v.p., corporate TV dept., Kenyon & Eckhart, & NY, 1984-86. Currently sr. v.p., sr. partner of TV dept., Bozell, Inc. NY.

MIDLER, BETTE
Actress, Singer. b. Honolulu, HI, Dec. 1, 1945. e. U. of Hawaii. Studied acting at Berghof Studios. Appeared on B'way in Fiddler on the Roof, Salvation; also in Tommy with Seattle Opera Co., 1971. Gained fame as singer-comic in nightclubs and cabarets. Has toured extensively with own stage shows: The Divine Miss M, Clams on the Half-Shell, Divine Madness, Art of Bust, Experience the Divine. Grammy Awards: The Divine Miss M, The Rose, Blueberry Pie (from In Harmony), Wind Beneath My Wings. *Author:* A View From a Broad, The Saga of Baby Divine. Special Tony Award, 1973. Many credits as soundtrack performer.
PICTURES: Hawaii (debut, 1966), The Rose (Academy Award nom.; 2 Golden Globe Awards 1980), Divine Madness (Golden Globe nom. 1981), Jinxed, Down and Out in Beverly Hills (Golden Globe nom. 1987), Ruthless People, Outrageous Fortune (Golden Globe nom. 1988), Big Business, Oliver & Company (voice), Beaches (also co-prod.), Stella, Scenes from a Mall, For the Boys (Academy Award nom., Golden Globe Award; also co-prod., 1992), Hocus Pocus, Get Shorty, First Wives Club, Divine Secrets of the Ya Ya Sisterhood (exec. prod. only), That Old Feeling, Isn't She Great, Get Bruce (documentary), Drowning Mona, What Women Want, The Stepford Wives, In the Pink, Then She Found Me, The Women, Cats & Dogs: The Revenge of Kitty Galore (voice), Sweet Baby Jesus.
TELEVISION: *Movies*: Gypsy (Emmy nom.; Golden Globe Award 1994), Jackie's Back!, Crossover, The Magic 7. *Series*: Bette. The Edge of Night, Vegetable Soup (voice), Bette (also singer of theme song, exec. prod. & composer, Golden Globe nom. 2001), Some of My Best Friends (exec. prod. only), Chocolate com Pimenta. *Documentaries/Specials:* The Fabulous Bette Midler Show, Ol' Red Hair is Back (Emmy Award, 1 other nom. 1978; also co-writer), Art or Bust (also prod., co-writer), Bette Midler's Mondo Beyondo (also creator, co-writer), Mud Will Be Flung Tonight, Bette Midler in Concert: Diva Las Vegas (Emmy Award, 1 other nom. 1997), Mississippi Rising. *Guest:* More than 156 appearances.

MILCH, DAVID
Writer, Producer, Consultant. Received WGA Laurel Award for TV writing achievement, 1999.
TELEVISION: *Movies:* Capital News (prod.), Last of the Ninth (s.p., exec. prod., pilot), Luck (s.p., exec. prod.). *Mini-series*: Murder One: Diary of a Serial Killer (creative consultant). *Series: Writer:* Hill Street Blues (Emmy, 1983, 7 other noms.), Capital News (creator & prod.), NYPD Blue (writer/creator & producer; 3 Emmy Awards, 5 other noms.), Murder One (also creative consultant, WGA nom. 1997), Total Security (also creator, exec. consultant), Big Apple (also exec. prod.), Deadwood (also creator & exec. prod., 2 Emmy noms.; 2 WGA noms.), John from Cincinnati (also exec. prod.). *Executive producer:* Brooklyn South.

MILCHAN, ARNON
Producer. b. Israel, Dec. 6, 1944. Began producing and financing films in Israel. CEO of New Regency Pictures.
PICTURES: *Producer:* Black Joy, Dizengoff 99, The King of Comedy, Once Upon A Time in America, Brazil, Legend, Man On Fire, Who's Harry Crumb?, The War of the Roses, Pretty Woman, Q & A, Gulty by Suspicion, The Mambo Kings, The Power of One, Under Siege, That Night, Heaven & Earth, Sommersby, Made in America, Striking Distance, Six Degrees of Separation, The Client, The New Age, Boys on the Side, Under Siege 2: Dark Territory, Empire Records, Copycat, The Sunchaser, Carpool, A Time to Kill, Bogus, The Mirror Has Two Faces, Murder at 1600, L.A. Confidential (Academy Award nom. 1998), Devil's Advocate, The Man Who Knew Too Little, Dangerous Beauty, The Negotiator, Tigerland, Don't Say A Word, Black Knight, High Crimes, Life or Something Like It, Daredevil, Runaway Jury, Man on Fire, First Daughter, Just My Luck, Mr. & Mrs. Smith, The Sentinel, Just My Luck, Beyond a Reasonable Doubt, My Super Ex-Girlfriend, The Fountain, Deck the Halls, Jumper. *Executive producer:* The Medusa Touch, Stripper (documentary), Switch, JFK, Memoirs of an Invisible Man, Falling Down, Free Willy, George Balanchine's The Nutcracker, Natural Born Killers, Second Best, Cobb, Free Willy 2: The Adventure

Home, Heat, Tin Cup, Free Willy 3: The Rescue, Breaking Up, City of Angels, Goodbye Lover, Simply Irresistible, A Midsummer Night's Dream, Entrapment, Fight Club, Up at the Villa, Big Momma's House, Freddy Got Fingered, Joy Ride, Joe Somebody, Unfaithful, Down With Love, The Girl Next Door, Stay, Bee Season, Date Movie, Epic Movie, Alvin and the Chipmunks, Meet the Spartans, Street Kings, What Happens in Vegas, Mirrors, Marley & Me, Fantastic Mr. Fox, Alvin and the Chipmunks: The Squeakquel, Knight and Day.
TELEVISION: *Movies*: *Executive producer:* Noriega: God's Favorite. *Producer:* The Hunt for the Unicorn Killer. *Mini-series:* Masada (supervising producer). *Series: Executive producer:* Free Willy, John Grisham's The Client, Michael Hayes.

MILES, AMY E.
Exhibitor. With a background in business/accounting, Miles was with PricewaterhouseCoopers, LLC from 1989 to 1998. She was a senior mgr. with Deloitte & Touche from 1998 to 1999. She joined Regal Cinemas, Inc. in April 1999 as senior v.p. of finance. Since Jan. 2000, Miles has served as executive v.p., principal accounting officer, CFO & Treasurer of Regal Cinemas, Inc.

MILES, SARAH
Actress. b. Ingatestone, England, Dec. 31, 1941. e. RADA. Was married to late writer Robert Bolt. Brother is director Christopher Miles. Appeared in short film Six-Sided Triangle.
PICTURES: Term of Trial (debut, 1962), The Servant, The Ceremony, Those Magnificent Men in Their Flying Machines, I Was Happy Here, Blow-Up, Ryan's Daughter (Academy Award nom.; Golden Globe nom. 1971), Lady Caroline Lamb, The Man Who Loved Cat Dancing, The Hireling, Bride to Be, The Sailor Who Fell From Grace With the Sea (Golden globe nom. 1977), The Big Sleep, Priest of Love, Venom, Ordeal by Innocence, Steaming, Hope and Glory, White Mischief, Dotkniecie reki (aka The Silent Touch), Jurij.
TELEVISION: *Movies:* Great Expectations, Ring Round the Moon, The Rehearsal, A Ghost in Monte Carlo, The Americans, Walter and June, Harem, Queenie, A Ghost in Monte Carlo. Poirot: The Hollow. *Mini-series:* Dandelion Dead.

MILES, SYLVIA
Actress. b. New York, NY, Sept. 9, 1932. Attended Pratt Inst., NYC. e. Washington Irving H.S., Actors Studio, Dramatic Workshop of the New School.
THEATRE: Rosebloom, The Iceman Cometh, The Balcony, The Riot Act, Vieux Carre, Before Breakfast, others.
PICTURES: Murder Inc. (debut, 1960), Parrish, Pie in the Sky, Violent Midnight, Terror in the City, Midnight Cowboy (Academy Award nom. 1970), The Last Movie, Who Killed Mary Whats'ername?, Heat, 92 in the Shade, Farewell My Lovely (Academy Award nom. 1976), The Great Scout and Cathouse Thursday, The Sentinel, Shalimar, Zero to Sixty, The Funhouse, Evil Under the Sun, No Big Deal, Critical Condition, Sleeping Beauty, Wall Street, Crossing Delancey, Spike of Bensonhurst, She-Devil, Denise Calls Up, Superstar: The Life and Times of Andy Warhol (documentary), High Times Potluck, Confessions of a Florist, Go Go Tales, Wall Street: Money Never Sleeps.
TELEVISION: *Movies:* No Big Deal, Cindy Eller: A Modern Fairy Tale. *Series*: All My Children, One Life To Live.

MILES, VERA
Actress. r.n. Vera Ralston. b. Boise City, OK, Aug. 23, 1929. e. public schools, Pratt and Wichita, KS.
PICTURES: Two Tickets to Broadway (debut, 1951), For Men Only, Rose Bowl Story, Charge at Feather River, So Big, Pride of the Blue Grass, Tarzan's Hidden Jungle, Wichita, The Searchers, 23 Paces to Baker Street, Autumn Leaves, Wrong Man, Beau James, Web of Evidence, FBI Story, Touch of Larceny, Five Branded Women, Psycho, Back Street, The Man Who Shot Liberty Valance, A Tiger Walks, Those Calloways, Follow Me Boys!, One of Our Spies Is Missing, The Spirit Is Willing, Gentle Giant, Sergeant Ryker, Kona Coast, It Takes All Kinds, Hellfighters, Mission Batangas, The Wild Country, Molly and Lawless John, One Little Indian, The Castaway Cowboy, Twilight's Last Gleaming, Thoroughbred, Run for the Roses, Brainwaves, Psycho II, The Initiation, Into the Night, Separate Lives.
TELEVISION: *Movies*: The Hanged Man, In Search of America, Cannon (pilot), Owen Marshall: Counselor at Law (pilot), A Howling in the Woods, Jigsaw, A Great American Tragedy, Baffled!, Runaway!, Live Again Die Again, Underground Man, The Strange and Deadly Occurence, NcNaughton's Daughter, Judge Horton and the Scottsboro Boys, Smash-up on Interstate 5, Fire!, And I Alone Survived, Roughnecks, Our Family Business, Rona Jaffe's Mazes and Monsters, Travis McGee, Helen Keller: The Miracle Continues, The Hijacking of the Achille Lauro. *Guest*: More than 153 appearances.

MILGRAM, HANK
Exhibitor. b. Philadelphia, PA, April 20, 1926. e. U. of PA, Wharton Sch. Exec. v.p., Milgram Theatres. Variety Club Board member, past president and chairman of the board of Variety Club of Philadelphia; past Variety Club Intl. v.p.; President's council. Served for 12 yrs. as bd. member, Hahneman Univ. until 1993.

MILIUS, JOHN
Writer, Director. b. St. Louis, MO. April 11, 1944. e. Los Angeles City Coll., U. of Southern California (cinema course). While at latter, won National Student Film Festival Award. Started career as ass't. to Lawrence Gordon at AIP. Began writing screenplays, then became dir. with Dillinger (1973). Appeared in documentary Hearts of Darkness.
PICTURES: *Writer:* The Devil's Eight (co-s.p.), Evel Knievel (co-s.p.), The Life and Times of Judge Roy Bean, Jeremiah Johnson (co-s.p.), Magnum Force (co-s.p.), The Wind and the Lion (also dir., WGA nom. 1976), Big Wednesday (also dir., co-s.p. & actor), Apocalypse Now (Academy Award nom.; WGA nom. 1980), 1941 (exec. prod. & co-s.p.), Conan the Barbarian (dir., co-s.p.), Red Dawn (dir. & co-s.p.), Extreme Prejudice (story), Farewell to the King (also dir.), Flight of the Intruder (dir. & co-s.p), Geronimo: An American Legend (co-s.p. & story), Clear and Present Danger (co-s.p.), Apocalypse Oz, Red Dawn (1984 s.p.). *Director:* Dillinger (also s.p.). *Executive producer:* Hardcore, Used Cars (co-exec. prod.), The Last Legion. *Producer:* Uncommon Valor (co-prod.).
TELEVISION: *Movies: Director:* Motorcycle Gang, Rough Riders, (also s.p.). *Series: Writer:* Miami Vice, Rome (also exec. prod., WGA nom. 2006).

MILLER, BARRY
Actor. b. Los Angeles, CA, Feb. 6, 1958. New York stage debut, My Mother My Father and Me, 1980.
THEATRE: Forty Deuce, The Tempest, Biloxi Blues (Tony, Theatre World, Outer Critics Circle and Drama Desk Awards, 1985), Crazy He Calls Me.
PICTURES: Lepke (debut, 1975), Saturday Night Fever, Voices, Fame, The Chosen, The Journey of Natty Gann, Peggy Sue Got Married, The Sicilian, The Last Temptation of Christ, Love at Large, The Pickle, Love Affair, Flawless, The Devil and Daniel Webster, Shortcut to Happiness.
TELEVISION: *Movies*: Brock's Last Case, Giving Birth, The Death of Richie, King of America, The Roommate, Conspiracy: The Trial of the Chicago 8, Equal Justice. *Series*: Joe and Sons, Szysznyk, Equal Justice (Golden Globe nom. 1991), The Practice (3 episodes).

MILLER, DENNIS
Comedian, Actor. b. Pittsburgh, PA, Nov. 3, 1953. e. Point Park Coll., (journalism degree). Began as stand-up comic in local clubs, then moved to NY appearing at Catch a Rising Star and the Comic Strip. Back in Pittsburgh wrote essays for PM Magazine and hosted Saturday-morning series for teens, Punchline. Recording: The Off-White Album.
PICTURES: Madhouse, Disclosure, The Net, Never Talk to Strangers, Tales From the Crypt: Bordello of Blood, Murder at 1600, Saturday Night Live Christmas Past (video), Joe Dirt, Thank You For Smoking, What Happens in Vegas...
TELEVISION: *Movies:* The Raw Feed (as himself, also writer, Emmy nom. 2003), Let Go, Dennis Miller: All In, The Monday Night Miracle (also writer). *Series*: Saturday Night Live (1985-91, also writer), The Dennis Miller Show (talk), Dennis Miller: State of the Union Undressed, Dennis Miller Live (also writer; 5 Emmy Awards for writing, 9 other noms.; 3 WGA Awards, 3 other noms.), Monday Night Football, Dennis Miller (series doc.), Amne$ia (host), The O'Reilly Factor (segment commentator). *Documentaries/Specials*: (also exec. prod./writer): Mr. Miller Goes to Washington, Dennis Miller: Black and White, They Shoot HBO Specials Don't They?, MTV Video Awards (host, 1996), Dennis Miller: Citizen Arcane (also exec. prod./writer; Emmy nom. 1996, WGA Award 1998), Real Time with Bill Maher., Sam Kinison: Why Did We Laugh?, The Millenium Special-1,000 years 100 laughs 10 Really Good Ones, Saturday Night Live: The Best of Phil Hartman, various SNL specials. *Guest:* More than 114 appearances.

MILLER, DICK (RICHARD)
Actor, Writer. b. New York, NY, Dec. 25, 1928. e. City Coll. of New York, Columbia U. Grad. NYU. Theater Sch. of Dramatic Arts. Commercial artist, psychologist (Bellevue Mental Hygiene Clinic, Queens General Hosp. Psychiatric dept.) Served in U.S. Navy, WWII. Boxing champ, U.S. Navy. Semi-pro football. Broadway stage, radio disc jockey, The Dick Miller Show, WMCA, WOR-TV. Over 500 live shows. Did first live night talk show with Bobby Sherwood, Midnight Snack, CBS, 1950. Wrote, produced and directed radio and TV shows in NY in early 1950s. Wrote screenplays: T.N.T. Jackson, Which Way to the Front, Four Rode Out and others. Has appeared on many major TV series and was a regular on Fame (3 years) and The Flash.
PICTURES: Has appeared in over 150 features, including: Apache Woman, Oklahoma Woman, It Conquered the World, The Undead, Not of This Earth, The Gunslinger, War of the Satellites, Naked Paradise, Rock All Night, Sorority Girl, Carnival Rock, A Bucket of Blood, Little Shop of Horrors, Atlas, Capture That Capsule, Premature Burial, X—The Man With the X Ray Eyes, The Terror, Beach Ball, Ski Party, Wild Wild Winter, Wild Angels, Hell's Angels on Wheels, The Trip, St. Valentine's Day Massacre, A Time for Killing, The Dirty Dozen, Targets, The Legend of Lilah Clare, Wild Racers, Target Harry, Which Way to the Front (also co-s.p.), Night Call Nurses, The Grissom Gang, Ulzana's Raid, Executive Action, The Slams, Student Nurses, Big Bad Mama, Truck Turner, Capone, T.N.T. Jackson, The Fortune,

White Line Fever, Crazy Mama, Moving Violation, Hustle, Cannonball, Vigilante Force, New York New York, Mr. Billion, Hollywood Boulevard, Grand Theft Auto, I Wanna Hold Your Hand, Piranha, Corvette Summer, Rock 'n' Roll High School, Lady in Red, Dr. Heckle and Mr. Hype, The Happy Hooker Goes Hollywood, Used Cars, The Howling, Heartbeeps, White Dog, Get Crazy, Lies, Heart Like a Wheel, All the Right Moves, Twilight Zone: The Movie, National Lampoon Goes to the Movies, Space Raiders, Swing Shift, Gremlins, The Terminator, Explorers, After Hours, Night of the Creeps, Project X, Armed Response, Chopping Mall, Amazon Women on the Moon, Innerspace, Angel III, The 'Burbs, Under the Boardwalk, Far From Home, Mob Boss, Gremlins 2: The New Batch, Unlawful Entry, Amityville 1992: It's About Time, Motorama, Matinee, Batman: Mask of the Phantasm (voice), Mona Must Die, Number One Fan, Tales From the Crypt Presents Demon Knight, Second Civil War, Small Soldiers, Route 666, It Conquered Hollywood! The Story of American International Pictures, Looney Tunes: Back in Action, Trail of the Screaming Forehead.
TELEVISION: *Movies:* The Andersonville Trial, The Lakeside Killer, W*A*L*T*E*R (short), Ghost Writer, The Woman Who Sinned, Shake, Rattle and Rock!, Midnight Runaround, Runaway Daughters, Attack of the 5 Ft. 2 Women, The Second Civil War, The Warlord: Battle for the Galaxy, Maximum Surge Movie. *Mini-series:* V: The Final Battle. *Series:* General Hospital, Miami Vice (dir. only), Fame. *Guest:* More than 81 appearances.

MILLER, (DR.) GEORGE
Director, Producer, Writer. b. Chinchilla, Queensland, Australia, March 3, 1945. Practiced medicine in Sydney; quit to work on films with Byron Kennedy, who became longtime partner until his death in 1983. They formed Kennedy Miller Productions where Miller still produces films. Early work: Violence in the Cinema Part One (short: dir., s.p.), Frieze—An Underground Film (doc.: editor only), Devil in Evening Dress (doc.: dir., s.p.). Achieved first worldwide success with Mad Max.
PICTURES: *Director:* In Search of Anna (1st asst. dir.), Mad Max (also s.p.), Mad Max 2: The Road Warrior (also s.p. & additional editor), Twilight Zone: The Movie (segment 4), Mad Max Beyond Thunderdome (also s.p. & prod.), The Witches of Eastwick, Lorenzo's Oil (also s.p. & prod., Academy Award nom.; WGA nom. 1993), 40,000 Years of Dreaming (documentary, also s.p., prod. & narrator, Babe: Pig in the City (also s.p. & prod.), Happy Feet (also prod., writer, Academy Award 2007), Mad Max 4, Happy Feet 2 in 3D (also prod., writer), Fury Road. *Producer:* The Chain Reaction (assoc. prod.), The Year My Voice Broke, Dead Calm (exec. prod., also 2nd unit dir.), Flirting, Video Fool For Love, Babe (also s.p., 2 Academy Award noms.; WGA nom. 1996).
TELEVISION: *Movies: Producer:* The Clean Machine, Fragments of War: The Story of Damien Parer. *Mini-series: Producer:* The Dismissal (exec. prod., co-writer & dir. of first episode). Bodyline: It's Not Just Cricket, Cowra Breakout, Vietnam, The Dirtwater Dynasty, Bangkok Hilton.

MILLER, GEORGE
Director. b. Scotland, 1945.
PICTURES: *Director:* In Search of Anna (asst. dir.), The Man from Snowy River, The Aviator, Cool Change, Les Patterson Saves the World, The Never Ending Story II, Over the Hill, Frozen Assets, Gross Misconduct, Andre, Zeus and Roxanne, Robinson Crusoe, Happy Feet (also prod., writer), Prey (writer). *Executive producer:* Heaven Before I Die.
TELEVISION: *Movies:* The Far Country, Miracle Down Under, Goodbye Miss 4th of July, Spooner, A Mom for Christmas, In the Nick of Time, The Great Elephant Escape, Silver Strand, Tidal Wave: No Escape, In the Doghouse (Emmy nom. 1999), Journey to the Center of the Earth, Cybermutt, Attack of the Sabertooth. *Mini-series:* Against the Wind, The Last Outlaw, All the Rivers Run, Anzacs, Tribe. *Series:* Homicide, Division 4, Matlock Police, Cash and Company, The Sullivans, Bluey, Young Ramsay, Five Mile Creek. *Documentary:* How Art Made the World (mini-series).

MILLER, JONATHAN
Executive. e. B.A. with honors from Harvard College. Began career in Boston with positions at WGBH (PBS) in educational programming and various advertising and video prod. roles. From 1987-1993, Miller was v.p., programming and co-general mgr. of NBA Entertainment. Developed and executed sports mktg. programs across electronic media, print and retail with NBA sponsors. From 1993-1997, managing dir. of Nickelodeon Intl., a unit of Viacom's MTV Networks. Simultaneously, also acted as CEO of several Nickelodeon and Paramount Pictures channels that were joint ventures with such partners as BSkyB in the UK and Foxtel in Australia. Under Miller's guidance, program distribution was extended to over 100 territories including sales to the BBC, ITV, Channel 4, ARD (Germany), ABC (Australia), and RAI (Italy). Then pres. & CEO of USA Broadcasting from July 1997-Oct. 1999. Pres. and CEO of USA Electronic Commerce Solutions, Oct. 1999-June 2000 when named pres. and CEO at USA Information and Services. Miller then served as a senior v.p., corporate development at Forbes Medi Tech Inc. until March 29, 2002. Miller assumed the highly visible role as CEO at AOL LLC (formerly America Online, Inc.) from 2002 until November 15, 2006 and was also an AOL director until November 15, 2006. While at AOL restructured core business lines, focused AOL on online advertising, including completing the highly successful 2004 acquisition of Advertising.com. Through his leadership, AOL delivered record annual profit growth of 21 percent and increased its online advertising growth, the centerpiece of its new business model, by 46 percent. When he left AOL, Miller was one of the founders and partners of Velocity Interactive Group (now called Fuse Capital), a leading investment and strategic equity mgt. firm that focuses on digital media. Known for his operational and strategic expertise in the digital arena, Miller was tapped in April 2009 by News Corp.'s Chairman and CEO Rupert Murdoch to become News Corp.'s chairman and CEO, Digital Media Group and its Chief Digital Officer. In this role, Miller drives the digital strategy across all News Corp. businesses and directs News Corp.'s stand-alone digital businesses, including MySpace, IGN Entertainment, Photobucket, as well as Jamba and the Hulu joint venture with NBC Universal. He serves on the bd. of the American Film Institute and serves as a trustee of both Emerson College and WNYC Public Radio in New York.

MILLER, MAX B.
Executive. b. Los Angeles, Feb. 23, 1937. e. UCLA. Father, Max Otto Miller, prod. silent features and shorts. Great grandfather was Brigham Young. e. Los Angeles Valley Coll., UCLA, Sherwood Oaks Coll. Writer of articles on cinema for American Cinematographer and other publications. Owns and manages Fotos Intl., entertainment photo agency with offices in 46 countries. Recipient of Golden Globe Award in 1976 for Youthquake, documentary feature. Owner of Hollywoodwires, distributor of Hollywood and entertainment news and photos. Also dir/Production mngr. of Films International (prod., Shoot Los Angeles) and pres. of MBM Prod., Inc. CEO of Fotos Internationsl, CEO Art & Entertainment Research. Contributor or consultant to many other industry publications. Active member of Hollywood Foreign Press Assn. (from 1974-82 bd member; twice chmn.), Independent Feature Project, Acad. of TV Arts & Sciences, L.A. Int'l, Film Exhibition, Soc. of M.P. & TV Engineers, Film Forum, Amer. Cinemateque. Member at BBC Film Network, Non-Fiction Exchange, Independent Film Project/WEST, FIND (Film Independent), Filmmakers Alliance, International Documentary Association, American Cinematheque, Organisation for Economic Co-operation and Development (United Nations), American Film Institute (Contributor Member), World Link (World Bank), Export-Import Bank (Electronic Information and Publications Office), The International Association for Media and History, China Trading Services, Society of American Archivists, AFCEA International, ZDNet UK, Development Gateway of the World Bank.

MILLER, PENELOPE ANN
Actress. b. Los Angeles, CA, Jan. 13, 1964. Daughter of actor-filmmaker Mark Miller and journalist-yoga instructor Bea Ammidown. e. studied acting with Herbert Berghof.
THEATRE: *NY*: The People From Work (1984), Biloxi Blues (B'way and LA), Moonchildren, Our Town (Tony nom.), On the Waterfront.
PICTURES: Adventures in Babysitting (1987, debut), Biloxi Blues, Big Top Pee-Wee, Miles From Home, Dead-Bang, Downtown, The Freshman, Awakenings, Kindergarten Cop, Other People's Money, Year of the Comet, The Gun in Betty Lou's Handbag, Chaplin, Carlito's Way (Golden Globe nom. 1994), The Shadow, The Relic, Rhapsody in Bloom, Little City, The Break Up, Outside Ozona, Chapter Zero, Lisa Picard Is Famous, Forever Lulu, Along Came a Spider, Funny Money, The Messengers, Blonde Ambition, Free Style, Robosapien: Rebooted, Flipped.
TELEVISION: *Movies*: Our Town, Witchhunt, The Hired Heart, Merry Christmas George Bailey, Ruby Bridges, Rocky Marciano, The Mary Kay Letourneau Story: All-American Girl, Killing Moon, Dodson's Journey, Dead in a Heartbeat, A Woman's A Helluva Thing, Scared Silent, Rudy: The Rudy Giuliani Story, Thanksgiving Family Reunion, Carry Me Home, Personal Effects, Detention, The Deadliest Lesson. *Mini-series:* The Last Don. *Series*: The Guiding Light, As the World Turns, The Popcorn Kid, The Closer, A Minute with Stan Hooper, Vanished, Men of a Certain Age. *Documentaries/Specials:* Tales From the Hollywood Hills: The Closed Set. *Guest:* More than 54 appearances.

MILLS, DONNA
Actress. b. Chicago, IL, Dec. 11, 1945. e. U. of Illinois. Left school to pursue career in theatre, beginning as dancer with stage companies around Chicago and touring. In NY became regular on soap opera, The Secret Storm. On B'way in Don't Drink the Water.
PICTURES: The Incident (debut, 1968), Play Misty for Me, Murph the Surf, Dangerous Intentions, Cursed Part III, Cage Free.
TELEVISION: *Movies*: Haunts of the Very Rich, Rolling Man, Night of Terror, The Bait, Someone at the Top of the Stair, One Deadly Owner, Live Again Die Again, Killer with Two Faces, Who Is the Black Dahlia?, Beyond This Place There Be Dragons, Look What's Happened to Rosemary's Baby, Smash-Up on Interstate 5, Bunco, Fire!, Curse of the Black Widow, The Hunted Lady, Superdome, Doctors' Private Lives, Hanging By A

Thread, Waikiki, Bare Essence, He's Not Your Son, Alice In Wonderland, Intimate Encounters, Outback Bound, The Lady Forgets, The World's Oldest Living Bridesmaid (also exec. prod.), Runaway Father (also exec. prod.), False Arrest, In My Daughter's Name (also exec. prod.), The President's Child, Remember, My Name Is Kate (also exec. prod.), An Element of Truth, The Stepford Husbands, Moonlight Becomes You, Too Cool for Christmas, Jane Doe: Yes, I Remember It Well, Love Is a Four Letter Word, Ladies of the House. *Mini-series:* Knots Landing: Back to the Cul-de-Sac. *Series:* The Secret Storm, Love Is A Many Splendored Thing, The Good Life, Knots Landing. *Guest*: More than 111 appearances.

MILLS, HAYLEY
Actress. b. London, England, April 18, 1946. Father is late actor Sir John Mills. Sister is actress Juliet Mills. e. Elmhurst Boarding Sch., Surrey, and Institute Alpine Vidamanette, Switz. Made m.p. debut in Tiger Bay, 1959, with father; then signed Disney contract, 1960. Received special Golden Globe Award for Most Promising Newcomer 1961.
THEATRE: The Wild Duck, Peter Pan, Trelawney of the Wells, The Three Sisters, A Touch of Spring, The Importance of Being Earnest, Rebecca, The Summer Party, Hush & Hide, My Fat Friend, Tally's Folly, Dial M for Murder, The Secretary Bird, Toys in the Attic, The Kidnap Game, The King and I (Australian tour), Fallen Angels (U.K., Australia, New Zealand), Dead and Guilty.
PICTURES: Tiger Bay, Pollyanna (Academy Award 1961), The Parent Trap (Golden Globe nom. 1962), Whistle Down the Wind, In Search of the Castaways, Summer Magic (Golden Globe nom. 1964), The Chalk Garden, The Moonspinners, That Darn Cat, The Truth About Spring, Sky West and Crooked (Gypsy Girl), The Trouble With Angels, The Family Way, A Matter of Innocence (Pretty Polly), Twisted Nerve, Take a Girl Like You, Mr. Forbush and the Penguins (Cry of the Penguins), Deadly Strangers, Endless Night, Silhouettes, What Changed Charley Farthing, The Kingfisher Caper, Appointment with Death, After Midnight, A Troll in Central Park (voice), 2BPerfectlIyHonest, Foster.
TELEVISION: *Movies:* Only A Scream Away, Parent Trap (II, III and Hawaiian Honeymoon), Back Home. *Mini-series:* The Flame Trees of Thika. *Series:* Good Morning Miss Bliss, Wild at Heart. *Documentaries/Specials:* The Love Goddesses, A&E Biography: Hayley Mills Seeing Double, Child Stars: Their Story. *Guest:* More than 50 appearances.

MILLS, JULIET
Actress. b. London, England, Nov. 21, 1941. m. actor Maxwell Caulfield. Father is late actor Sir John Mills. Mother is late writer Mary Hayley Bell. Sister is actress Hayley Mills. Made stage debut at 14 in Alice Through the Looking Glass. Also toured with Fallen Angels with sister; 1995, The Cherry Orchard, in Canada. Also in 1995, The Molière Comedies and Time of My Life; in 1996, It Could Be Any One of Us.
PICTURES: So Well Remembered, The History of Mr. Polly, No My Darling Daughter, Twice Round the Daffodils, Nurse on Wheels, Carry on Jack, The Rare Breed, Oh! What a Lovely War, Avanti! (Golden Globe nom. 1973), Beyond Obsession, The Second Power, Beyond the Door, Waxwork II: Lost in Time, The Other Sister.
TELEVISION: *Movies*: Mrs. Miniver, Wings of Fire, The Challengers, She Stoops to Conquer, Nanny and the Professor (Golden Globe nom. 1971), Letters from Three Lovers, Nanny and the Professor and the Phantom of the Circus, Demon Demon, Alexander: The Other Side of Dawn, Barnaby and Me, The Cracker Factory, Night of the Fox, Columbo: No Time to Die, A Stranger in the Mirror. *Mini-series*: QB VII (Emmy Award, 1975), Once an Eagle, Till We Meet Again, Four Seasons. *Series*: Nanny and the Professor, Harmony's Passions (Emmy nom. 2005), Wild at Heart. *Special*: She Stoops to Conquer. *Guest:* More than 82 appearances.

MILLS, SCOTT
Executive. b. New York. e. B.S. degree, economics, Wharton School of Business, Univ. of Pennsylvania. Early in career, served as deputy treasurer of Philadelphia; Later, v.p. with Lehman Brothers, a financial services firm, four years. Mills joined BET (Black Entertainment Television) in 1997 as senior v.p., strategy & business development, where he developed the business plan for BET.com and oversaw a number of BET's new business ventures. Next, Mills was executive v.p. and COO of BET Interactive, the operating entity for BET Network's flagship online portal BET.com. He became BET's CFO in 2003 and pres., digital media in Jan. 2007. In July 2007, Mills was named to his current position, pres. & COO.

MINER, STEVE
Director. b. Chicago, IL, June 18, 1951. e. Dean Junior College. Began career as prod. asst. on Last House on the Left (1970). Launched a NY-based editorial service, and dir., prod., edited sport, educational and indust. films.
PICTURES: Here Come the Tigers! (co-prod.), Manny's Orphans (co-prod., s.p.), Friday the 13th (assoc. prod.). *Director*: Friday the 13th Part 2 (also prod.), Friday the 13th Part 3, Soul Man, House, Warlock (also prod.), Wild Hearts Can't Be Broken, Forever Young, My Father the Hero, Big Bully, Halloween H20: Twenty Years Later, Lake Placid, Texas Rangers, Major Movie Star, Day of the Dead.
TELEVISION: *Movies:* Scarlett. *Series*: The Wonder Years (2 Emmy noms.), Laurie Hill, Diagnosis Murder, Chicago Hope, Raising Canes, Relativity, The Practice (multiple episodes), Dawson's Creek (also prod.), Felicity, Wasteland, Kate Brasher, The Third Degree, Home of the Brave, Jake 2.0, Miss Match. *Pilots*: The Wonder Years (sprv. prod., dir., DGA Award for pilot 1989), B-Men, Elvis, Against the Grain, Wildfire (series), Make It or Break It (also 3 series episodes).

MINNELLI, LIZA
Actress, Singer. b. Los Angeles, CA, March 12, 1946. p. late actress-singer Judy Garland & late dir. Vincente Minnelli. e. attended sch. in CA, Switzerland, and the Sorbonne. Left to tour as lead in The Diary of Anne Frank, The Fantastiks, Carnival and The Pajama Game. In concert with mother, London Palladium 1964. In concert Carnegie Hall, 1979, 1987, 1993. Film debut as child in mother's film In the Good Old Summertime (1949). Recordings incl. Liza with a Z, The Singer, Live at the Winter Garden, Tropical Nights, Live at Carnegie Hall, Liza Minnelli at Carnegie Hall, Results, Live at Radio City Music Hall, The Day After That.
THEATRE: Best Foot Forward (off-B'way debut, 1963, Theatre World Award), Flora The Red Menace (Tony Award, 1965), Liza at the Winter Garden (special Tony Award, 1974), Chicago, The Act (Tony Award, 1978), Are You Now or Have You Ever Been?, The Rink (Tony nom.), Minnelli on Minnelli, Victor/Victoria, Liza's at The Palace (Tony Award for special theatrical event 2009).
PICTURES: In the Good Old Summertime, Journey Back to Oz (voice; 1964, released in U.S. in 1974), Charlie Bubbles, The Sterile Cuckoo (Academy Award nom.; Golden Globe nom. 1970), Tell Me That You Love Me Junie Moon, Cabaret (Academy Award; also British Academy & Golden Globe Award 1973), That's Entertainment!, Lucky Lady (Golden Globe nom. 1976), Silent Movie, A Matter of Time, New York New York (Golden globe nom. 1978), Arthur (Golden globe nom. 1982), The Muppets Take Manhattan, That's Dancing!, Rent-a-Cop, Arthur 2: on the Rocks, Stepping Out. Many credits as soundtrack performer.
TELEVISION: *Movies*: The Dangerous Christmas of Red Riding Hood, A Time to Live (Golden Globe Award 1986), Parallel Lives, The West Side Waltz, The Sunshine Boys (singer-Old Friends). *Series:* Arrested Development. *Documentaries/Specials*: Many specials, including Judy and Liza at the London Palladium, Liza, Liza with a Z (Emmy Award, 1973). Goldie and Liza Together (Emmy nom. 1980), Baryshnikov on Broadway, Liza in London, Faerie Tale Theater (Princess and the Pea), Sam Found Out: A Triple Play, Frank Sammy and Liza: The Ultimate Event, Liza Minnelli Live From Radio City Music Hall (Emmy nom. 1993), Jackie's Back, My Favorite Broadway: The Leading Ladies, AFI's 100 Years...100 Stars, New York at the Movies, many more credits as soundtrack performer. *Guest:* More than 335 appearances.

MIOU-MIOU
Actress r.n. Sylvette Herry. b. Paris, France, Feb. 22, 1950. First job as apprentice in upholstery workshop. In 1968, helped to create Montparnasse cafe-theatre, Cafe de la Gare, with comedian Coluche. Returned to stage in Marguerite Duras' La Musica, 1985.
PICTURES: La Cavale (debut, 1971), Themroc, Quelques Messieurs Trop Tranquilles, Elle Court, Elle Court La Banlieue, Les Granges Brulees, The Mad Adventures of Rabbi Jacob, Going Places, Un Genie Deux Associes une Cloche, D'Amour et D'Eau Fraiche, Victory March, F... comme Fairbanks, On Aura Tout Vu, Jonah Who Will Be 25 in the Year 2000, Dites-lui Que Je l'aime, Les Routes du Sud, Le Grand Embouteillage, Memoirs of a French Whore, Au Revoir...a Lundi, La Femme Flic (Lady Cop), Est-ce Bien Raisonnable?, La Geule du Loup, Josepha, Guy De Maupassant, Coup de Foudre, Canicule, Le Vol du Sphinx, Blanche et Marie, Ménage, The Revolving Doors, La Lectrice, Milou in May, La Totale, Le Bal des Casse-Pieds, Tango, Montparnasse-Pondichery, Germinal., An Indian in Paris, My Woman Is Leaving Me, The Eighth Day, Dry Cleaning, Elles, Foul Play, Everything's Fine We're Leaving, Folle embelllie, Mariages!, L'Après-midi de monsieur Andesmas (Afternoon of Mr. Andesmas), Un reste, l'autre part L, Riviera, Les Murs porteurs, Les Poils du pinceau, Le Héros de la famille, The Science of Sleep, L' Hôte, Le Grand alibi, Affaire de famille, Pour un fils, Le concert, A Spot of Bother.
TELEVISION: Various French productions.

MIRISCH, DAVID
Executive. b. Gettysburg, PA, July 24, 1935. e. Ripon Coll. United Artists Corp., 1960-63. Former exec. with Braverman-Mirisch, adv. public rel. firm. Pres. of David Mirisch Ent., intl prom. firm. Also on Bd of Dirs. of Mirisch Film Co, which has produced Hawaii, West Side Story, Fiddler on the Roof, The Great Escape, The Pink Panther, Some Like it Hot, In the Heat of the Night and The Magnificent Seven.

MIRISCH, WALTER
Producer. b. New York, NY, Nov. 8, 1921. e. U. of Wisconsin, B.A., 1942; Harvard Grad. Sch. of Business Admin., 1943. In m.p. indust. with Skouras Theatres Corp., 1938-40; Oriental Theatre Corp., 1940-42. 1945 with Monogram/Allied Artists; apptd. exec. prod. Allied Artists, 1951 (spv. such films as The Big

Combo, The Phoenix City Story, Invasion of the Body Snatchers, Friendly Persuasion, Love in the Afternoon); established The Mirisch Company, supervising such films as Some Like It Hot, The Horse Soldiers, The Apartment, West Side Story, Irma La Douce, The Great Escape, The Pink Panther, A Shot in the Dark, The Fortune Cookie, The Russians Are Coming the Russians Are Coming, Fiddler on the Roof; 1960-61 Pres. of Screen Prod. Guild; 1962, mem. bd. dir., MPAA; bd. Gvnrs., AMPAS, 1964, 1972; 1967, pres., Center Thea. Group of L.A.; named pres. and exec. head of prod., The Mirisch Corporation, 1969; pres., Permanent Charities Committee 1962-63; pres., AMPAS, 1973-77. Recipient: Irving Thalberg Award 1978, Golden Globe Cecil B. DeMille Award 1977, Jean Hersholt Humanitarian Award 1984, Honorary Doctor of Humanities, Univ. of WI 1989, UCLA Medal 1989, the PGA Golden Laurel Awards-Lifetime Achievement in Motion Pictures, 1996.
PICTURES: *Producer or Executive producer*: Fall Guy, I Wouldn't Be in Your Shoes, Bomba on Panther Island, Bomba the Jungle Boy, Bomba and the Hidden City, County Fair, The Lost Volcano, Cavalry Scout, Elephant Stampede, Flight to Mars, The Lion Hunters, Rodeo, African Treasure, Wild Stallion, The Rose Bowl Story, Flat Top, Bomba and the Jungle Girl, Hiawatha, Safari Drums, The Maze, The Golden Idol, Killer Leopard, The Warriors, Annapolis Story, Lord of the Jungle, Wichita, The First Texan, The Oklahoman, The Tall Stranger, Fort Massacre, Man of the West, Cast a Long Shadow, Gunfight at Dodge City, The Man in the Net, The Magnificent Seven, By Love Possessed, Two for the Seesaw, Toys in the Attic, In the Heat of the Night (Academy Award for Best Picture, 1968), Sinful Davey, Some Kind of a Nut, Halls of Anger, The Hawaiians, They Call Me Mister Tibbs, The Organization, Scorpio, Mr. Majestyk, Midway, Gray Lady Down, Same Time Next Year, The Prisoner of Zenda, Dracula, Romantic Comedy.
TELEVISION: *Movies: Executive producer:* High Midnight, Desperado (prod.), Return of Desperado, Desperado: Avalanche at Devil's Ridge, Desperado: The Outlaw Wars, Desperado: Badlands Justice, Troubleshooters: Trapped Beneath the Earth, Lily In Winter, A Case for Life. *Series*: The Magnificent Seven.

MIRREN, DAME HELEN
Actress. b. London, England, July 26, 1945. r.n. Ilynea Lydia Mironoff. Made a DBE (Dame of the British Empire, June 2003.)
THEATRE: Troilus and Cressida, 2 Gentlemen of Verona, Hamlet, Miss Julie, Macbeth, Teeth 'n' Smiles, The Seagull, Bed Before Yesterday, Henry VI, Measure for Measure, The Duchess of Malfi, Faith Healer, Antony and Cleopatra, Roaring Girl, Extremities, Madame Bovary, Two Way Mirror, Sex Please We're Italian!, Woman in Mind (LA), A Month in the Country (also B'way).
PICTURES: A Midsummer's Night Dream (debut, 1968), Age of Consent, Savage Messiah, O Lucky Man!, Hamlet, Caligula, Hussy, The Fiendish Plot of Dr. Fu Manchu, Excalibur, The Long Good Friday, Cal, 2010, White Nights, Heavenly Pursuits, The Mosquito Coast, Pascali's Island, When the Whales Came, The Cook The Thief His Wife and Her Lover, The Comfort of Strangers, Where Angels Fear to Tread, Dr. Bethune, The Gift, The Hawk, Prince of Jutland, The Madness of King George (Academy Award nom.; Cannes Film Fest. Award 1995), Losing Chase, (Golden Globe Award, 1997), Some Mother's Son, Critical Care, The Prince of Egypt (voice), Teaching Mrs. Tingle, Green Fingers, Happy Birthday, The Pledge, Last Orders, Gosford Park (Academy Award nom.; Golden Globe nom. 2002), No Such Thing, Calendar Girls (Golden Globe nom. 2004), The Clearing, Raising Helen, The Hitchhiker's Guide to the Galaxy (voice), Shadowboxer, The Queen (Academy Award, Golden Globe Award 2007), National Treasure: Book of Secrets, Love Ranch, State of Play, Inkheart, The Last Station (Academy Award nom.; Golden Globe nom. 2010), The Tempest, Love Ranch, Brighton Rock, The Debt, Legend of the Guardians: The Owls of Ga'Hoole (voice), Red, Arthur.
TELEVISION: *Movies:* The Changeline, Kiss Kiss Kill Kill, The Applecart, Caesar and Claretta, The Little Minister, The Collection, The Country Wife, As You Like It, Blue Remembered Hills, SOS Titanic, A Midsummer Night's Dream, Mrs. Reinhardt, Soft Targets, Cymbeline, Cause célèbre, Red King White Knight, Losing Chase, The Passion of Ayn Rand (Emmy Award, Golden Globe nom. 1999), On the Edge (also dir.), Door to Door (Emmy nom.; Golden Globe nom. 2003), The Roman Spring of Mrs. Stone (Emmy nom.; Golden Globe nom. 2003), ExxonMobil Masterpiece Theatre: Prime Suspect 6 (Emmy nom. 2004), Pride (voice), Elizabeth I (Emmy Award, Golden Globe Award 2006), Prime Suspect 7: The Final Act (Emmy Award, Golden Globe nom. 2007). *Mini-series:* Cousin Bette, Prime Suspect (BAFTA Award), Prime Suspect 2 (Emmy nom. 1993), Prime Suspect 3 (Emmy Award, 1994), Prime Suspect 4 (Emmy Award 1996), Prime Suspect 5 (Emmy nom. 1997), Prime Suspect 6, Oresteia, Painted Lady (also assoc. prod.). *Series:* Georgetown. *Guest:* More than 174 appearances.

MISCHER, DON
Producer, Director. b. San Antonio, TX, March 5, 1941. e. U. of TX, B.A. 1963, M.A. 1965. Pres., Don Mischer Productions. Founded Don Mischer Productions, 1978. Recipient of 12 Emmy Awards, 9 Directors Guild Awards, 3 NAACP Image Awards, Peabody Award.
TELEVISION: *Producer*: Opening and closing ceremonies of the 1996 Centennial Olympics Games (Emmy Award, 1997), Michael Jackson's Super Bowl XXVII Halftime Show, The Kennedy Center Honors (Emmy Awards, 1981, 1987, 1994, 1996, DGA Award), Tony Awards (3 yrs; Emmy Awards, 1987, 1989), Shirley MacLaine... Illusions (DGA Award 1983), Carnegie Hall 100th Anniversary, Gregory Hines Tap Dance in America (DGA Award 1990), Opening of EuroDisney, The Muppets Celebrate Jim Henson, AFI Salutes to Billy Wilder and Gene Kelly, Irving Berlin's 100th Birthday (Emmy Award, 1988), Baryshnikov by Tharp, Motown 25: Yesterday Today Forever (Emmy Award, 1983), Motown Returns to the Apollo (Emmy Award, DGA Award 1986), Grand Reopening of Carnegie Hall, specials with Goldie Hawn, Liza Minnelli, Bob Hope, Robin Williams, Pointer Sisters. Also: The Great American Dream Machine, Donohue and Kids: Project Peacock (Emmy Award, 1981), The Presidential Inaugural, Timeless: Live in Concert (Emmy nom.; DGA nom. 2002), 6 Barbara Walters Specials, Great Performances (DGA Award 1997, Emmy nom. 2008), Ain't Misbehavin', It's Garry Shandling's Show, The Wayne Brady Show, 2002 ABC World Stunt Awards (exec. prod.), ABC's 50th Anniversary Celebration (exec. prod.), Lifetime's Achievement Awards: Women Changing the World (exec. prod.), 2003 ABC World Stunt Awards (exec. prod.), The 55th Annual Primetime Emmy Awards (exec. prod.), Democratic National Convention, The 56th Annual Primetime Emmy Awards (exec. prod.), Super Bowl XXXIX Pregame Show (exec. prod.), Super Bowl XXXIX Halftime Show, Super Bowl XLI Halftime Show (Emmy nom. 2007), Super Bowl XLIII (2 Emmy noms. for halftime show), From the Top: Live from Carnegie Hall (series, also exec. prod., Emmy nom. 2008, Emmy Award 2009), Movies Rock (also exec. prod.), Fashion Rocks, We Are One: The Obama Inaugural Celebration at the Lincoln Memorial (also dir., DGA Award 2010), The 61st Primetime Emmy Awards (exec. prod.).

MITCHELL, LEE ROY
Exhibitor. Mitchell has been engaged in the motion picture industry for nearly 46 years. He was president of Cinemark U.S.A., Inc. since the company's inception in 1987 and served in that capacity until March 1993. He also has been CEO and a company director since 1987. From 1985-1987, Mitchell was the president and CEO of a predecessor organization. From 1993 to 1996, he was vice chmn. of the bd. of directors. He became chmn. of the bd. in March 1996 and continues to carry out those duties today. Mitchell has served on the bd. of directors of the National Association of Theatre Owners since 1991. Cinemark has about 4,500 screens in nearly 400 theatres in the U.S. and Latin America. The company is based in Plano, TX. In early 2007 Cinemark filed to go public.

MITCHELL, TANDY
Exhibitor. b. Sept. 27, 1950. This theatre exhibition executive has been involved in the growth and operations of the Cinemark exhibition circuit since 1989. Mitchell has served as Cinemark executive v.p. since October 1989 and asst. secretary since December 2003. Mitchell is the wife of Cinemark Chairman Lee Roy Mitchell and as one of the company's top executives she supervises theatre operations and corporate projects. She also served as vice chairman of the board from March 1996 to April 2004. Mitchell served on the board of Variety Club of North Texas: The Children's Charity, and also supports numerous other charities, including Bill Glass Ministries, Peaceable Kingdom Retreat for Children, Young Life, SPCA of Texas and Operation Kindness. Cinemark has about 4,500 screens in nearly 400 theatres in the U.S. and Latin America. The company is based in Plano, TX. In early 2007 Cinemark filed to go public.

MOCIUK, YAR W.
Executive. b. Mylovania, Ukraine, Jan. 26, 1927. e. CCNY; World U.; Peoples U. of Americas, Puerto Rico. Expert in field of m.p. care and repair; holds U.S. patent for method and apparatus for treating m.p. film. Has also been film prod. and dir.. Founder and pres. of CM Films Service, Inc. until 1973. Now chmn. of bd. and pres. of Filmtreat International Corp. Member: M.P. & TV Engineers; Univ. Film Assn. Pres., Ukrainian Cinema Assn. of America. In 1998, received Emmy Award for Outstanding Achievement in Technical Advancement, Pioneering Development of Film Scratch Removal Systems for Telecines.

MODINE, MATTHEW
Actor. b. Loma Linda, CA, March 22, 1959. Raised in Utah. Studied acting with Stella Adler. Stage work incl. Our Town, Tea and Sympathy, The Brick and the Rose.
PICTURES: Baby It's You (debut, 1983), Private School, Streamers, The Hotel New Hampshire, Mrs. Soffel, Birdy, Vision Quest, Full Metal Jacket, Orphans, Married to the Mob, La Partita, Gross Anatomy, Pacific Heights, Memphis Belle, Wind, Equinox, Short Cuts (Golden Globe Award 1994), The Browning Version, Bye Bye Love, Fluke, Cutthroat Island., The Real Blonde, The Blackout, The Maker, If...Dog...Rabbit, Notting Hill (cameo), Any Given Sunday, Very Mean Men, Bamboozled, In the Shadows, Stanley Kubrick: A Life in Pictures, The Shipment, Nobody's Baby, Le Divorce, Hollywood North, Hairy Tale, Funky Monkey, Mary, Transporter 2, Opa!, Kettle of Fish, A West Texas Children's Story, Go Go Tales, The Garden of Eden, The

Neighbor, Sunchasers (doc., prod.), Little Fish, Strange Pond (also exec. prod.).
TELEVISION: *Movies*: And the Band Played On (Emmy nom. 1994), Jacob, What the Deaf Man Heard (Golden Globe nom. 1998), Flowers for Algernon, Redeemer, Hitler: The Rise of Evil, The Winning Season, Sex and Lies in Sin City. *Mini-series:* Jack and the Beanstalk, Into the West. *Series*: Texas (daytime serial), The Bedford Diaries, Weeds. *Documentaries/Specials*: The Way West (voice), Surviving the Dustbowl (voice), Amy and the Angel, Eugene O'Neill: Journey Into Greatness, Sovann komar (narr.), The American Experience (voice). *Guest:* More than 60 appearances.

MOFFAT, DONALD
Actor. b. Plymouth, England, Dec. 26, 1930. Studied acting Royal Academy of Dramatic Art, 1952-54. London stage debut Macbeth, 1954. With Old Vic before Broadway debut in Under Milkwood, 1957. Worked with APA-Phoenix Theatre Co. and as actor and dir. of numerous B'way and regional productions.
THEATRE: The Bald Soprano, Jack, Ivanov, Much Ado About Nothing, The Tumbler, Duel of Angels, A Passage to India, The Affair, The Taming of the Shrew, The Caretaker, Man and Superman, War and Peace, You Can't Take It With You, Right You Are... If You Think You Are, School for Scandal, The Wild Duck, The Cherry Orchard, Cock-a-Doodle Dandy, Hamlet, Chemin de Fer, Father's Day, Forget-Me-Not-Lane, Terra Nova, The Kitchen, Waiting for Godot, Painting Churches, Play Memory, Passion Play, The Iceman Cometh, Uncommon Ground, Love Letters, As You Like It, The Heiress.
PICTURES: Pursuit of the Graf Spee (The Battle of the River Plate; debut, 1957), Rachel Rachel, The Trial of the Catonsville Nine, R.P.M., The Great Northfield Minnesota Raid, Showdown, The Terminal Man, Earthquake, Land of No Return, Promises in the Dark, Health, On the Nickel, Popeye, The Thing, The Right Stuff, Alamo Bay, The Best of Times, Monster in the Closet, The Unbearable Lightness of Being, Far North, Music Box, The Bonfire of the Vanities, Class Action, Regarding Henry, Housesitter, Clear and Present Danger, Trapped in Paradise, The Evening Star, Just In Time, A Smile Like Yours, The Sleep Room, Cookie's Fortune.
TELEVISION: *Movies*: Devil and Miss Sarah, A Touch of the Poet, Call of the Wild, Waiting for Godot, Eleanor and Franklin: The White House Years, Exo-Man, Mary White, Tartuffe, Sergeant Matlovich vs. the U.S. Air Force, The Word, The Gift of Love, Strangers: The Story of a Mother and Daughter, Ebony Ivory and Jade, Mrs. R's Daughter, The Long Days of Summer, Jacqueline Bouvier Kennedy, Who Will Love My Children?, Through Naked Eyes, License to Kill, Houston: The Legend of Texas, Desperado, When the Time Comes, Necessary Parties, The Bourne Identity, Cross of Fire, Kojak: Flowers for Matty, A Son's Promise, Kaleidoscope, The Great Pretender, Babe Ruth, Columbo: No Time to Die, Teamster Boss: The Jackie Presser Story, Majority Rule, Love Cheat and Steal, Is There Life Out There?, 61. *Mini-series*: The Word, Wagner (narr.), Tales of the City. *Series*: One Life to Live, The New Land, Logan's Run, Bull. *Documentaries/Specials*: Forget-Me-Not Lane. *Guest*: More than 87 appearances.

MOGER, STANLEY H.
Executive, Producer. b. Boston, MA, Nov. 13, 1936. e. Colby College, Waterville, ME, B.A., 1958. Announcer/TV personality/WVDA and WORL (Boston) 1953-54; WGHM (Skowhegan) 1955-56; WTWO-TV (Bangor) 1955; WMHB (Waterville) 1956-57; WTVL (Waterville) 1957-58; unit pub. dir., Jaguar Prods., 1958-59; U.S. Army reserve, 1958-64, with calls to active duty in 1958-59, 1961-62. Account exec., NBC Films/California National Productions. Chicago 1959-60; asst. sales mgr., Midwest, RCA/NBC Medical Radio System, 1960; acct. exec. Hollingbery Co., Chicago, 1960-63; and NY 1963-66; acct. exec., Storer TV Sales, 1966-69; co-founded SFM Media Corp. 1969. Named pres. and CEO, SFM Entertainment, 1978, which distributes, packages and produces television programs for broadcast/cable and home video.
TELEVISION: *Executive producer:* Television-Annual, 1978-79: (ABC), Walt Disney's Mickey Mouse Club, The Adventures of Rin Tin Tin: Mobile Showcase Network, SFM Holiday Network, Your New Day with Vidal Sassoon, The Origins Game, Believe You Can and You Can, Walt Disney Presents Sport Goofy (series), The World of Tomorrow, March of Time ... on the March (England), Sports Pros and Cons, Unclaimed Fortunes (ABC), Sea World Summer Night Magic (ABC), America's Dance Honors (ABC), Allen & Rossi's 25th Anniversary Special, Paris '89 Celebration, U.S. Sports Academy Awards, K-Nite Color Radio (A&E), Into the Night With Brad Garrett (ABC), Family Film Awards (CBS), Sea World/Busch Gardens Annual Specials (CBS and Nickelodeon), Everybody Rides the Carousel (Lifetime), Gift of the Magi (Lifetime), Zoobilee Zoo (PBS), Pillar of Fire (History Channel), AFI Life Achievement Awards (CBS, ABC, NBC, Fox), AFI's 100 Years...100 Movies (CBS & TNT), The Journey Inside (Sci-Fi), Open Book (A&E), Indomitable Teddy Roosevelt (ABC), Ray Harryhausen Chronicles (AMC), Crusade in Europe (History/A&E), Visions of Light (PBS/Encore/Ovation), Alice Through the Looking Glass (Disney), Witness to the Execution (HBO/Cinemax), Grandma Got Run Over By A Reindeer (WB/The CW/Cartoon/Telefutura), The Flip Wilson Show (TV Land), Make Room for Daddy (Goodlife), The Real McCoy's ((TNN), Rowan & Martin's Laugh-In (Trio), The Ernie Kovacs Show (Trio), The Joey Bishop Show (TV Land), Moshe Dayan: A Warrior's Story (A&E/TBS/ABC), Instant Love, America's Last Frontier, 20,000 Leagues Under the Sea (ABC), Kings of the Ring (MSG), Pride & Predjudice: The Larry Doby Story (YES/OSN), Jesse Owens: Return to Berlin (YES), Wilma (YES), Jack L. Warner: The Last Mogul (WBV), Steve McQueen: An American Rebel, Blood Detectives (Discovery/Health), AFI's 100 Years/100 Movies (CBS/TNT), The following shown on CBS: AFI's 100 Movies/100 Stars, AFI's 100 Years/100 Laughs, AFI's 100 Years/100 Thrills, AFI's 100 Years/100 Passions, AFI's 100 Years/100 Heroes & Villains, AFI's 100 Years/100 Songs, AFI's 100 Years/100 Movie Quotes, AFI's 100 Years/100 Cheers. AFI's 100 Years/100 Movies (10th Anniversary), AFI's 100 Years/10 Top Ten.

MOL, GRETCHEN
Actress. b. Deep River, CT, November 8, 1972. e. William Esper Studio.
PICTURES: The Funeral, Girl 6, Donnie Brasco, The Last Time I Committed Suicide, The Deli, Rounders, The 13th Floor, Music From Another Room, Bleach, Too Tired to Die, Celebrity, Finding Graceland, New Rose Hotel, Music From Another Room, Cradle Will Rock, Sweet and Lowdown, Forever Mine, Just Looking, Rules of Attraction, Get Carter, The Shape of Things, Heavy Put-Away, The Notorious Bettie Page, Puccini for Beginners, Trainwreck: My Life as an Idiot, The Ten, Boy of Pigs, 3:10 to Yuma, Tenure, An American Affair.
TELEVISION: *Movies*: Calm at Sunset Calm at Dawn, Subway Stories: Tales from the Underground, Picnic, The Magnificent Ambersons, Freshening Up (short), The Valley of Light, The Memory Keeper's Daughter. *Mini-series*: Dead Man's Walk. *Series*: Girls' Club, Life on Mars, Boardwalk Empire.

MOLEN, GERALD R.
Producer. b. Jan. 6, 1935. Unit prod. mgr. on The Postman Always Rings Twice, Tootsie, Let's Spend the Night Together, A Soldier's Story. Assoc. prod. on Batteries Not Included. Joined Amblin Entertainment to oversee prod. of feature film projects. Currently CEO of WhiteLight Entertainment, a North Hollywood-based production company.
PICTURES: *Executive producer*: The Color Purple (DGA Award 1986), Bright Lights Big City, Rain Man (co- prod., DGA Award 1989), Days of Thunder, A Far Off Place, The Flintstones, The Little Rascals, Little Giants, Casper, Twister, The Trigger Effect. *Producer*: Hook, Jurassic Park, Schindler's List (Academy Award for Best Picture, 1994), The Lost World: Jurassic Park, View From the Swing, The Other Side of Heaven, Minority Report, The Legend of Johnny Lingo, Catch Me If You Can (actor), Playing with the Enemy.

MOLINA, ALFRED
Actor. b. London, England, May 24, 1953. e. Guildhall Sch. of Music and Drama. Began acting with the National Youth Theatre. Worked as stand-up comic for street theatre group. Joined Royal Shakespeare Co., 1977.
THEATRE: Frozen Assets, The Steve Biko Inquest, Dingo, Bandits, Taming of the Shrew, Happy End, Serious Money, Speed-the-Plow, Accidental Death of an Anarchist (Plays and Players' Most Promising New Actor Award), The Night of the Iguana, Molly Sweeney (off-B'way).
PICTURES: Raiders of the Lost Ark (debut, 1981), Meantime, Number One, Ladyhawke, Eleni, Water, Letter to Brezhnev, Prick Up Your Ears, Manifesto, Not Without My Daughter, Enchanted April, American Friends, The Trial, When Pigs Fly, Cabin Boy, White Fang 2: Myth of the White Wolf, Maverick, Hideaway, The Perez Family, The Steal, Nervous Energy, Species, Before and After, Dead Man, Scorpion Spring, Anna Karenina, Boogie Nights, The Man Who Knew Too Little, The Treat, The Imposters, The Odd Couple II, Dudley Do-Right, Texas Rangers, Magnolia, Chocolat, Texas Rangers, Frida, Undertaking Betty (aka Plots With a View), My Life Without Me, Identity, Coffee and Cigarettes, Luther, Spider-Man 2, Steamboy (voice), Sian Ka'an (voice), The Da Vinci Code, As You Like It, The Hoax, The Ten Commandments (voice), Nothing Like the Holidays, The Moon and the Stars, The Little Traitor, Silk, The Lodger, An Education, Humboldt Park, Pink Panther 2, The Tempest, The Good War, Lessons in Self-Defense (short), Carmel, Prince of Persia: The Sands of Time, The Sorcerer's Apprentice, Vivaldi, Abduction.
TELEVISION: *Movies:* Meantime, Number One, Virtuoso, Drowing in the Shallow End, The Trials of Oz, Hancock, Trust Me, Typhon's People, The Marshal, Requiem Apache, Rescuers: Stories of Courage: Two Couples, Virtuoso, Apocolyptic Butterflies, The Accountant, The Miracle Maker (voice), A Polish Practice, Murder on the Orient Express, Joan of Arc (narrator), Courtroom K, Yes, Virginia. *Mini-series*: Ashenden, Joni Jones, A Year in Provence, The Company. *Series:* The Losers, Nativity Blues, El C.I.D., Ladies Man, Bram and Alice. *Guest:* More than 67 appearances.

MOLL, RICHARD
Actor. b. Pasadena, CA, Jan. 13, 1943.
PICTURES: Caveman, The Sword and the Sorcerer, Metalstorm: The Destruction of Jared-Syn, The Dungeonmaster, House, Wicked Stepmother, Think Big, Driving Me Crazy,

National Lampoon's Loaded Weapon 1, Sidekicks, The Flintstones, Storybook, Galaxis, The Glass Cage, The Secret Agent Club, The Perils of Being Walter Wood, Jingle All the Way, The Elevator, Living in Peril, Me and the Gods, Little Cobras: Operation Dalmation, The Survivor, Snide and Prejudice, Route 66, Monkey Business, Dish Dogs, The Defectors, Big Monster on Campus, Foreign Correspondents, But I'm a Cheerleader, Shadow Hours, That Summer in L.A., Flamingo Dreams, Spiders II, Evolution, Scary Movie 2, No Place Like Home, Dumb Luck, Angel Blade, Pulse Pounders, The Biggest Fan, Uh Oh!, The Work and the Story, Icemaker, Cats and Mice, Boy-Next-Door, Diamond Zero, Thomas Kinkade's Home for Christmas, Razor, DaZe: Vol. Too (sic) - NonSeNse, Serpent Rising.
TELEVISION: *Movies*: The Jericho Mile, The Archer: Fugitive from the Empire, Bret Maverick, Through the Magic Pyramid, Combat High, Class Cruise, The Last Holloween, Words Up!, Summertime Switch, The Ransom of Red Chief, The Defectors, Call Me Claus. *Mini-series:* The Fantastic Two. *Series:* Night Court, Mighty Max, Batman, Batman: Gotham Knights (voice), Spider-Man (voice), 100 Deeds for Eddie McDowd, Detroit Docona (voice). *Guest:* More than 100 appearances.

MONICELLI, MARIO
Director, Writer. b. Rome, Italy, May 15, 1915. Ent. m.p. industry in production; later co-authored, collab., comedies.
PICTURES: *Director:* The Boys of Via Paal (also s.p.), Ballerine (asst. dir.), Marco Visconti (asst. dir.), Finalmente soli (asst. dir.), Pazzo d'amore (asst. dir., s.p.), Il Testimone (asst. dir.), Gioventù perduta (asst. dir.), Totò cerca casa (also s.p.), Fame and the Devil (also s.p.), Vita da cani (also s.p.), È arrivato il cavaliere! (also s.p.), Toto and the King of Rome (also s.p.), Guardie e ladri (also s.p.), Toto and the Women (also s.p.), The Unfaithfuls (also s.p.) Forbidden (also s.p.) Toto and Carolina (also s.p.), A Hero of Our Times (also s.p.), Donatella (also s.p.), Doctor and the Healer (also s.p.), A Tailor's Maid (also s.p.), Big Deal on Madonna Street (also s.p.), Lettere dei condannati a morte, The Great War (also s.p.), Risate di gioia, (also s.p.), The Organizer (also s.p., Academy Award nom. 1965), Casanova '70 (also s.p., Academy Award nom. 1966), The Queens, For Love and Gold (also s.p.), La Ragazza con la pistola, Oh Grandmother's Dead (also s.p.), Le Coppie, Brancaleone at the Crusades (also s.p.), Lady Liberty, Vogliamo i colonnelli (also s.p.), Romanzo popolare, Amici miei, Caro Michele, Signore e Signori Buonanotte, An Average Little Man (also s.p.), Viaggio con Anita, Temporale Rosy (also s.p.), Camera d'albergo (also s.p.), Il Marchese del Grillo (also s.p.), All My Friends Part 2 (also s.p.), Bertoldo Bertoldino and Cascacenno (also s.p.), Le Due vite di Mattia Pascal (also s.p.), Speriamo che sia femmina (also s.p.), Cari fottutissimi amici (also s.p.), Looking for Paradise (also s.p.), Dirty Linen (also s.p.), Un Amico magico: il maestro Nino Rota (documentary, also s.p.), Another World Is Possible (documentary), Letters from Palestine (documentary, also editor), Firenze il nostro domani (documentary), Under the Tuscan Sun (actor), The Roses of the Desert (also writer). Plus, various other italian films.

MONTENEGRO, FERNANDA
Actress. r.n. Arlette Pinheiro Monteiro Torres. b. Rio de Janeiro, Brazil, Oct. 16,1929.
PICTURES: Tudo Bem, A Hora da Estrela, O Que E Isso, Companheiro, Central Station (Academy Award nom.; Golden Globe nom. & winner of Silver Berlin Bear, best actress, Berlin Film Festival 1999), Treason, Gemeas, A Dog's Will, O Rendentor, The Other Side of the Street, Olga, House of Sand, Love in the Time of Cholera.
TELEVISION: *Movies:* O Auto da Compadecida. *Mini-series*: O Auto da Compadecida. *Mini-series:* Pastores da Noite, Hoje É Dia de Maria, Hoje É Dia de Maria 2, Queridos Amigos. *Series:* Pouco Amor Não É Amor, Redenção, Calúnia, A Muralha, Sangue do Meu Sangue, Cara a Cara, Baila Comigo, Brilhante, Guerra dos Sexos, Cambalacho, Rainha da Sucata, O Dono do Mundo, Renascer, O Mapa da Mina, Zazá, As Filhas da Mãe, Esperança, Belíssima. Many more credits in Spanish productions.

MOODY, RON
Actor. r.n. Ronald Moodnick. b. London, England, Jan. 8, 1924. e. London Sch. of Economics. *Novels:* The Devil You Don't, Very Very Slightly Imperfect, Off The Cuff, The Amazon Box.
THEATRE: *London:* Intimacy at Eight (debut, 1952), For Adults Only, Candide, Oliver! (also NY revival: Theatre World Award), Joey Joey (Bristol; also writer, composer, lyricist), Peter Pan, Hamlet, The Clandestine Marriage, The Showman (also writer), Sherlock Holmes—The Musical. *Author:* Saturnalia, Move Along Sideways.
PICTURES: Davy (debut, 1958), Follow a Star, Make Mine Mink, Five Golden Hours, The Mouse on the Moon, A Pair of Briefs, Summer Holiday, Ladies Who Do, Murder Most Foul, San Ferry Ann, The Sandwich Man, Oliver! (Academy Award nom.; Golden Globe Award 1969), The Twelve Chairs, Flight of the Doves, Dogpound Shuffle, Dominique, Unidentified Flying Oddball, Wrong Is Right, Where Is Parsifal?, A Kid in King Arthur's Court, Quality Time, The Three Kings, Revelation, Paradise Grove, Lost Dogs.
TELEVISION: *Movies:* David Copperfield (theatrical in U.K.), Dial M for Murder (U.S.), The Caucasian Chalk Circle, Hideaway, The Tales of the Gold Monkey, A Ghost in Monte Carlo, The People's Passion, Celebrate 'Oliver!'. *Mini-series:* The Word. *Specials:* Portrait of Petulia, Bing Crosby's Merrie Olde Christmas, Winter's Tale, Othello, Other Side of London, Baden Powell, Lights Camera Action, Last of the Summer Wine. *Series:* Nobody's Perfect, Into the Labyrinth, The Telebugs, The Animals of Farthing Wood (voice), EastEnders. *Guest:* More than 70 appearances.

MOONVES, LESLIE
Executive. b. New York, NY, Oct. 6, 1949. e. Bucknell Univ. Veteran TV executive. After college, Moonves pursued an acting career at New York's Neighborhood Playhouse, studying under the renowned Sanford Meisner. He performed in numerous stage and television productions before opting to produce plays on Broadway and in Los Angeles. From the stage, Moonves turned to the TV industry and was a v.p. of movies and mini-series for Twentieth Century-Fox Television, where he was also in charge of first-run syndication and pay/cable programming. He also had previously been v.p., development, for Saul Ilson Productions (in association with Columbia Pictures Television) and a development executive for Catalina Productions. From 1989 to 1993, Moonves was pres. of Lorimar Television. From 1993 to 1995, he was pres. of Warner Bros. Television (when Warner Bros. and Lorimar Television combined operations). Moonves joined CBS as pres., CBS Entertainment, in 1995, and was promoted in 1998 to pres. and CEO, CBS Television. Responsibility of UPN was added in Jan. 2002. In April 2003, Moonves was named chmn. of CBS. In June 2004, Moonves was named co-pres. and co-CEO of Viacom, Inc. in addition to his chmn. duties with CBS. He oversaw the operations of CBS, UPN, CBS Enterprises, King World, the Viacom Television Stations Group, Paramount Television, Infinity Broadcasting and Viacom Outdoor. In 2005, when Viacom's board unanimously approved a split of the company into Viacom, Inc. and CBS Corporation, Moonves was appointed CEO/Prresident/Dir. of the new CBS Corporation and is the position he holds today.

MOORE, DAN
Costumer Designer.
PICTURES: Southern Comfort, E.T. the Extra-Terrestrial (asst. costumer), Rocky III, Tex, Brewster's Millions, Blue City, Crossroads, Punchline, Red Heat, She's Out of Control, Johnny Handsome, Another 48 Hrs., Necessary Roughness, Trespass, Geronimo: An American Legend, Wild Bill, This World Then the Fireworks, Last Man Standing, Broken Arrow, Agua Dulce, Hart's War, Black Dawn, Annapolis (supervisor), X-Men: The Last Stand (supervisor), Deja Vu (supervisor), Bolden!, Louis, Jonah Hex (asst. costume designer), Shanghai (supervisor), Priest (supervisor).
TELEVISION: *Movies*: Twisted Desire, The Cherokee Kid, The Second Civil War, 12 Angry Men, Two for Texas, Houdini, 61* (CDG nom. 2002). *Series*: The Magnificent Seven (Emmy Award 1998, 1 other nom. 1999, 3 CDG noms.), The Bronx Is Burning.

MOORE, DEMI
Actress, Producer. r.n. Demetria Guynes. b. Roswell, NM, Nov. 11, 1962. m. actor Ashton Kutcher. Began modeling at age 16. *Off-B'way debut*: The Early Girl, 1987 (Theatre World Award).
PICTURES: *Actress:* Choices (debut, 1981), Parasite, Young Doctors in Love, Blame It on Rio, No Small Affair, St. Elmo's Fire, About Last Night, One Crazy Summer, Wisdom, The Seventh Sign, We're No Angels, Ghost (Golden Globe nom. 1991), Nothing But Trouble, Mortal Thoughts (also co-prod.), The Butcher's Wife, A Few Good Men, Indecent Proposal, A Century of Cinema, Disclosure, The Scarlett Letter, Now and Then (also co-prod.), The Juror, The Hunchback of Notre Dame (voice), Striptease, Destination Anywhere, G.I. Jane (also prod.), Deconstructing Harry, Passion of Mind, The Hunchback of Notre Dame 2 (voice), Charlie's Angels: Full Throttle, Half Light, Bobby (also singer), Flawless, Mr. Brooks, Happy Tears, Bunraku, The Joneses, LOL: Laughing Out Loud. *Producer:* Austin Powers: International Man of Mystery, Austin Powers: The Spy Who Shagged Me, Slugger, Austin Powers: Goldmember.
TELEVISION: *Movies*: If These Walls Could Talk (Emmy nom.; Golden Globe nom. 1997), The Magic 7 (voice). *Series*: General Hospital.*Guest:* More than 85 appearances.

MOORE, JULIANNE
Actress. b. Fayetteville, North Carolina, December 3, 1961. e. Boston Univ. Sch. for the Arts.
THEATRE: *Off-B'way*: Serious Money, Ice Cream/Hot Fudge, The Road to Nirvana, Hamlet, The Father.
PICTURES: Tales From the Darkside (debut, 1990), The Hand That Rocks the Cradle, Body of Evidence, Benny & Joon, The Fugitive, Short Cuts (Golden Globe Award 1994), Vanya on 42nd Street, Roommates, Safe, Nine Months, Assassins, Surviving Picasso, The Lost World: Jurassic Park, The Myth of Fingerprints, Boogie Nights (Academy Award nom.; Golden Globe nom.; LA Film Crits. Award, Best Supporting Actress, 1998), The Big Lebowski, Psycho, A Map of the World, Cookie's Fortune, An Ideal Husband (Golden Globe nom. 2000), The End of the Affair (Academy Award nom.; Golden Globe nom. 2000), Magnolia, The Ladies Man, Hannibal, Evolution, World Traveler, Not I, The Shipping News, The Hours (Academy Award nom. 2003), Far From Heaven (Academy Award nom.; Golden Globe

nom. 2003), Marie and Bruce (also exec. prod.), Laws of Attraction, The Forgotten, Savage Grace, The Prize Winner of Defiance Ohio, Freedomland,The Children of Men, Next, Savage Grace, I'm Not There., Blindness, Hateship, Friendship, Courtship (also exec. prod.), Shelter, The Private Lives of Pippa Lee, Chloe, A Single Man (Golden Globe nom. 2010), The Kids Are All Right, Elektra Luxx.
TELEVISION: *Movies*: I'll Take Manhattan, Money Power Murder, The Last to Go, Cast a Deadly Spell. *Series*: The Edge of Night, As the World Turns (Emmy Award 1988), 30 Rock. *Guest:* More than 93 appearances.

MOORE, MARY TYLER
Actress. b. Brooklyn. NY, Dec. 29, 1936. Began as professional dancer and got first break as teenager in commercials (notably the elf in Hotpoint appliance ads); then small roles in series Bachelor Father, Steve Canyon, and finally as the switchboard operator. in series Richard Diamond Private Detective (though only her legs were seen). Chairman of Bd., MTM Enterprises, Inc, which she founded with then-husband Grant Tinker.
THEATRE: *B'way*: Breakfast at Tiffany's (debut), Whose Life Is It Anyway? (special Tony Award, 1980), Sweet Sue.
PICTURES: X-15, Thoroughly Modern Millie, Don't Just Stand There, What's So Bad About Feeling Good?, Change of Habit, Ordinary People (Academy Award nom.; Golden Globe Award 1981), Six Weeks, Just Between Friends, Flirting With Disaster, Reno Finds Her Mom, Keys to Tulsa, Labor Pains, Cheats, Against the Current.
TELEVISION: *Movies*: Run a Crooked Mile, Mary's Incredible Dream, Cousins (exec. prod. only), First You Cry (Emmy nom. 1979), How to Survive the 70s and Maybe Even Bump Into Happiness, Heartsounds (Emmy nom. 1985), Finnegan Begin Again, Gore Vidal's Lincoln (Emmy nom. 1988), The Last Best Year, Thanksgiving Day, Stolen Babies (Emmy Award, 1993), Forbidden Memories, Stolen Memories: Secrets from the Rose Garden, Payback, Mary and Rhoda (also exec. prod.), Like Mother Like Son: The Strange Story of Sante and Kenny Kimes, Miss Lettie and Me, The Gin Game, (also co. exec. prod.), Blessings, The Dick Van Dyke Show Revisited, Snow Wonder. *Series*: Richard Diamond—Private Detective, The Dick Van Dyke Show (2 Emmy Awards: 1964, 1966), The Mary Tyler Moore Show (1970-77; 4 Emmy Awards: 1973, 1974 (2), 1976, 2 Golden Globe Awards and 6 other noms.), Mary (1978), The Mary Tyler Moore Hour (1979), Mary (1985-86), Annie McGuire, New York News. *Documentaries/Specials*: Dick Van Dyke and the Other Woman, How to Raise a Drugfree Child, Three Cats from Miami and Other Pet Practictioners (host). *Guest*: More than 159 appearances.

MOORE, MICHAEL
Director, Writer. b. Davison, MI, April 23, 1954. e. Univ. of MI. Was editor of The Michigan Voice and Mother Jones magazine, commentator on radio show All Things Considered, before gaining fame with first film Roger & Me. Established Center for Alternative Media to support independent filmmakers. Moore's work has won more than 30 awards internationally. Elected to the BD. of Governors of the Academy of Motion Picture Arts and Sciences for a three year term. This Bd. oversees the Oscars.
PICTURES: *Director/Producer./Writer/Actor:* Roger & Me (debut, 1989), Canadian Bacon, The Big One, Trade Off, Lucky Numbers, Fever Pitch (actor only), Bowling for Columbine (Academy Award for Best Doc., Features, 2003; & 55th Anniversary Prize, Cannes Film Fest., WGA Award), The Corporation (doc.), And Justice for All (doc., dir.), Fahrenheit 9/11 (Doc.; DGA nom. Palme d'Or Award from Cannes Film Festival, 2005), The Great '04 Slacker Uprising, Sicko (Academy Award nom.; WGA nom. 2008), Capitalism: A Love Story (WGA nom. 2010). *Writer:* A Brief History of the United States of America (short, writer), *Actor:* Edtv Lucky Numbers, The Fever.
TELEVISION: *Series*: *Director: Executive producer: Writer: Host:* TV Nation (Emmy Award, 1 other nom. 1995), The Awful Truth (tv series documentary, 2 Emmy noms. 1999, 2001, 2 WGA noms., 2000, 2001), Better Days (prod. only). *Documentaries/Specials*: Pets or Meat: The Return to Flint. *Guest:* More than 93 appearances.

MOORE, ROB
Executive. e. Pepperdine University, Bachelor's degree in business. Moore's early career was with Arthur Anderson and Co. in Los Angeles, CA, specializing in entertainment. Moore became a senior financial analyst for Walt Disney Pictures & Television in 1987. In 1990, he was named v.p., finance for The Walt Disney Studios. In 1992, he was promoted to senior v.p., planning and analysis. In 1994, Moore became senior v.p. and CFO of Walt Disney Television and Telecommunications and by 1996 assumed executive v.p. & CFO post at The Walt Disney Studios. By 1999, Moore was appointed executive v.p., finance & operations. In this role he oversaw business affairs for the studio's motion picture, television & video divisions in addition to finance and studio operations responsibilities. While at Disney, Moore played a key role in the acquisition of Miramax Films, the launch of Walt Disney Theatrical Productions and negotiated Disney's production and distribution agreement with Pixar Animation Studios. From 2000-2005, Moore was a founding member and a partner at Revolution Studios, where he developed the strategic plan and oversaw the formation of the company. He supervised all aspects of business affairs, finance, physical productions and operations. Moving to Paramount in 2005, Moore became Paramount Picture's president, worldwide marketing, distribution & operaions. In 2006 he was promoted to president, worldwide marketing, distribution & home entertainment. In Jan. 2008, Moore was promoted to his current position, vice chairman of Paramount Pictures, reporting to Paramount Pictures Corporation Chairman and CEO Brad Grey. Moore is a current member of the Academy of Motion Picture Arts & Sciences.

MOORE, ROGER
Actor. b. London, England, Oct. 14, 1927. e. art school, London; Royal Acad. of Dramatic Art. Had bit parts in British films Vacation From Marriage, Caesar and Cleopatra, Piccadilly Incident, Gay Lady. Appointed Special Ambassador for UNICEF, 1991. Recipient of Golden Globe Henrietta Award 1978.
THEATRE: Mr. Roberts, I Capture the Castle, Little Hut, others. *B'way*: A Pin to See the Peepshow.
PICTURES: The Last Time I Saw Paris, Interrupted Melody, The King's Thief, Diane, The Miracle, Gold of the Seven Saints, The Sins of Rachel Cade, Rape of the Sabines, Crossplot, The Man Who Haunted Himself, Live and Let Die, Gold, The Man With the Golden Gun, That Lucky Touch, Street People, Shout at the Devil, The Spy Who Loved Me, The Wild Geese, Escape To Athena, Moonraker, ffolkes, The Sea Wolves, Sunday Lovers, For Your Eyes Only, The Cannonball Run, Octopussy, The Curse of the Pink Panther, The Naked Face, A View to a Kill, The Magic Snowman (voice), Fire Ice and Dynamite, Bed and Breakfast, Bullseye!, The Quest, The Saint, Spice World, The Enemy, Na svoji vesni (as himself), Boat Trip, The Fly Who Loved Me (short; voice), Peter Cottontail: The Movie (voice), Agent Crush (voice), De vilde svaner (voice), Gnomes and Trolls: The Forest Trial (voice)Cats & Dogs: The Revenge of Kitty Galore, Connemara Days.
TELEVISION: *Movies*: This Happy Breed, Bacharach 74, Sherlock Holmes in New York, The Man Who Wouldn't Die (also co-exec. prod.), D.R.E.A.M. Team, Tatort-Schatten (as himself). *Series*: Ivanhoe, The Alaskans, Maverick, The Saint, The Persuaders, Return of the Saint, The Dream Team, Children with Childhood (narrator). *Guest:* More than 248 appearances.

MOORE, TERRY
Actress. r.n. Helen Koford. b. Los Angeles, CA, Jan. 7, 1929. Mother was Luella Bickmore, actress. Photographer's model as a child; acted on radio; with Pasadena Playhouse 1940. Voted Star of Tomorrow: 1958. *Author:* The Beauty and the Billionaire (1984). Formed Moore/Rivers Productions, 1988 with partner-manager Jerry Rivers. Has also acted as Helen Koford, Judy Ford, and Jan Ford.
PICTURES: Maryland (debut as Helen Koford, 1940), The Howards of Virginia, On the Sunny Side (billed as Judy Ford), A-Haunting We Hill Go, My Gal Sal, True to Life, Date With Destiny, Gaslight, Since You Went Away, Son of Lassie, Sweet and Low Down, Shadowed, Summer Holiday, Devil on Wheels, The Return of October (1st billing as Terry Moore), Mighty Joe Young, The Great Ruppert, He's a Cockeyed Wonder, Gambling House, The Barefoot Mailman, Two of a Kind, Sunny Side of the Street, Come Back Little Sheba (Academy Award nom. 1953), Man on a Tightrope, Beneath the 12-Mile Reef, King of the Khyber Rifles, Daddy Long Legs, Shack Out on 101, Postmark for Danger (Portrait of Alison), Between Heaven and Hell, Peyton Place, Bernardine, A Private's Affair, Cast a Long Shadow, Why Must I Die?, Platinum High School, City of Fear, Black Spurs, Town Tamer, Waco, A Man Called Dagger, Daredevil, Death Dimension, Double Exposure, Hellhole, W.A.R., Beverly Hills Brats (also co-prod., co-story), Mighty Joe Young, Second Chances, Final Voyage, Stageghost, The Still Life, Kill Your Darlings.
TELEVISION: *Movies*: Quarantined, Smash-Up on Interstate 5, Jake Spanner, Private Eye, Marilyn and Me. *Series*: Empire, America's Funniest (co-exec. prod.). *Guest:* More than 65 appearances.

MORALES, ESAI
Actor. b. Brooklyn, NY, October 1, 1963. e. NY's High School for the Performing Arts. NY stage debut at age 17 in NY Shakespeare Fest. prod. of The Tempest, 1981.
THEATRE: Short Eyes, Tamer of Horses, El Mermano, Salome.
PICTURES: Forty Deuce (debut, 1982), Bad Boys, L.A. Bad, Rainy Day Friends, La Bamba, The Principal, Bloodhounds of Broadway, Naked Tango, Amazon, Freejack, In the Army Now, Rapa Nui, My Family/Mi Familia, Scorpion Spring, The Disappearance of Garcia Lorca, Livers Ain't Cheap, The Wonderful Ice Cream Suit, Southern Cross, Doomsday Man, American Virgin, How to Go Out on a Date in Queens, Spin Cycle, Paid In Full, Isla Bella, Once Upon A Wedding, American Fusion, Fast Food Nation, Kill Kill Faster Faster, La Linea-The Line, King of the Avenue, Cherry, Beisbol (doc., exec. prod.), The Spanish Harlem Project.
TELEVISION: *Movies:* Bay City Story, The Burning Season, Deadlocked: Escape From Zone 14, Dying to Be Perfect: The Ellen Hart Pena Story, Circle of Deceit, Atomic Train, The Elian Gonzalez Story, Heartless, Company Town, The Cure, Caprica. *Mini-series:* On Wings of Eagles. *Series:* NYPD Blue, American

Family, Vanished, Jericho, Caprica (also pilot). *Documentaries/Specials:* The Great Love Experiment. *Guest:* More than 72 appearances.

MORANIS, RICK
Actor, Writer. b. Toronto, Canada, April 18, 1954. Began career as part-time radio engineer while still in high school. Hosted own comedy show on radio then performed in Toronto cabarets and nightclubs and on TV. Joined satirical TV series SCTV during its 3rd season on CBC, for which he won Emmy for writing when broadcast in U.S. Created characters of the McKenzie Brothers with Dave Thomas and won Grammy nom. for McKenzie Brothers album. With Thomas co-wrote, co-directed and starred in film debut Strange Brew, 1983. Supplied voice for cartoon series Rick Moranis in Gravedale High.
PICTURES: Strange Brew (debut, 1983; also co-dir., co-s.p.), Streets of Fire, Ghostbusters, The Wild Life, Brewster's Millions, Head Office, Club Paradise, Little Shop of Horrors, Spaceballs, Ghostbusters II, Honey I Shrunk the Kids, Parenthood, My Blue Heaven, L.A. Story, Honey I Blew Up the Kid, Splitting Heirs, The Flintstones, Little Giants, Big Bully, Brother Bear (voice).
TELEVISION: *Movies:* the Last Polka, Hockey Night, The Rocket Boy, Miss Spider's Sunny Patch Kids (voice). *Series:* 90 Minutes Live, SCTV (also writer, Emmy Award 1982, 3 other noms.), SCTV Network 90 (also writer), Twilight Theater, Gravedale High (voice), The Animated Adventures of Bob & Doug McKenzie, (voice), Bob & Doug (exec. prod., writer).

MOREAU, JEANNE
Actress. b. Paris, France, Jan. 23, 1928. e. Nat'l Conservatory of Dramatic Art. Stage debut with Comedie Francaise, acting there until 1952 when she joined the Theatre Nationale Populaire. Directorial debut: La Lumiere (film), 1976. Recipient of 1995 BAFTA Film Craft Fellowship Award. 2003 recipient of honorary Golden Palm from the Cannes Film Festival.
THEATRE: A Month in the Country, La Machine Infernale, Pygmalion, Cat on a Hot Tin Roof.
PICTURES: The She-Wolves, Elevator to the Scaffold, The Lovers, Le Dialogue Des Carmelites, Les Liaisons Dangereuses, Moderato Cantabile, La Notte, Jules and Jim, A Woman Is a Woman, Eva, The Trial, Bay of Angels, The Victors, Le Feu Follet, Diary of a Chambermaid, The Yellow Rolls-Royce, The Train, Mata Hari, Viva Maria, Mademoiselle, Chimes at Midnight, Sailor From Gibraltar, The Bride Wore Black, The Immortal Story, Great Catherine, Monte Walsh, Alex in Wonderland, The Little Theatre of Jean Renoir, Louise, The Last Tycoon, French Provincial, La Lumiere (also dir., s.p.), Mr. Klein, The Adolescent (dir., s.p. only), Plein Sud, Querelle, The Trout, Le Miracule, La Femme Nikita, The Suspended Step of the Stork, La Femme Farde, Until the End of the World, Alberto Express, The Lover (voice), Map of the Human Heart, Anna Karamazova, The Summer House, See You Tomorrow, My Name Is Victor, The Old Lady Who Walks in the Sea, Beyond the Clouds, I Love You I Love You Not, The Proprietor, Orson Welles: The One-Man Band, Amour et confusions, Un amour de sorciere, Ever After, The Prince's Manuscript, Fassbinder's Women (documentary), Lisa, Cet amour-là, The Will to Resist, The Birch Tree Meadow, (writer), Go West (also assoc. prod.), Une vieille maitresse, Time to Leave, Disengagement, Later, One Day You'll Understand, Face.
TELEVISION: *Movies:* Portrait: Orson Welles (short, narrator, L'Arbre, The Last Seance, The Summer House, Katharina die Große, Balzac: A Life of Passion, Zaïde un petit air de vengeance, Attila, Les Parents terribles, La Contessa di Castiglione, Wash This Blood Clean from My Hand, Château en Suède. *Mini-series:* Le Tiroir secret, Belle Époque, Les Misérables, Les Rois maudits.

MORENO, RITA
Actress. r.n. Rosa Dolores Alvario. b. Humacao, Puerto Rico, Dec. 11, 1931. Spanish dancer since childhood; night club entertainer. Has won all 4 major show business awards in U.S.: Oscar, Tony, 2 Emmys and Grammy (for Best Recording for Children: The Electric Company, 1972).
THEATRE: Skydrift (debut, 1945), The Sign in Sidney Brustein's Window, Gantry, Last of the Red Hot Lovers, The National Health (Long Wharf, CT), The Ritz (Tony Award, 1975), Wally's Cafe, The Odd Couple (female version), Sunset Boulevard (London), The Glass Menagerie (CA).
PICTURES: So Young So Bad (debut, 1950, as Rosita Moreno), Pagan Love Song, The Toast of New Orleans, Singin' in the Rain, The Ring, Cattle Town, Ma and Pa Kettle on Vacation, Latin Lovers, Fort Vengeance, Jivaro, El Alamein, Yellow Tomahawk, Garden of Evil, Untamed, Seven Cities of Gold, Lieutenant Wore Skirts, The King and I, The Vagabond King, The Deerslayer, This Rebel Breed, Summer and Smoke, West Side Story (Academy Award, best supporting actress, Golden Globe Award 1962), Cry of Battle, The Night of the Following Day, Marlowe, Popi, Carnal Knowledge, The Ritz (Golden Globe nom. 1977), The Boss' Son, Happy Birthday Gemini, The Four Seasons, Life in the Food Chain, The Italian Movie, Blackout, I Like It Like That, Angus, Slums of Beverly Hills, Carlo's Wake, Blue Moon, Speak Truth to Power, Piñero, Casa de los Babys, The Pursuit of Happiness, King of the Corner, April Showers, Play It by Ear, 4Chosen.
TELEVISION: *Movies*: Evita Peron, Anatomy of a Seduction, Working, Portrait of a Showgirl (Emmy nom. 1982), The Wharf Rat, The Spree, Resurrection, The Rockford Files: It It Bleeds...It Leads, Open House, Cop Shop. *Series*: Out to Lunch (Emmy nom. 1975), The Muppet Show (Emmy Award 1977), Rockford Files (Emmy Award 1978, 1 other nom.), The Electric Company, Nine to Five (Emmy nom.; Golden Globe nom. 1983), B.L. Styker, Top of the Heap, Raw Toonage (voice), The Magic Schoolbus (voice), The Cosby Mysteries, Where On Earth Is Carmen Sandiego? (voice), Oz (three ALMA awards for outstanding actress in series, 1998, 1999 & 2002...ALMA Awards honor the actors and directors who promote positive portrayals of Hispanics in the media.), The Remarkable Journey (as herself), American Family, Cane. *Guest*: More than 150 appearances.

MORGAN, ANDRE E.
Producer. b. Morocco, 1952. e. U. of Kansas. Golden Harvest Films prod., 1972-84. Exec. v.p., Golden Communications 1976-84. Formed Ruddy-Morgan Organization with Albert S. Ruddy, 1984. Exec. prod. with Golden Harvest.
PICTURES: Enter the Dragon, The Amsterdam Kill, The Boys in Company C, Cannonball Run II, High Road to China, Lassiter, Farewell to the King, Speed Zone, Impulse, Ladybugs, Bad Girls, The Scout, Heaven's Prisoners, Mr. Magoo, Solo, Lei ting zhan jing (aka China Strike Force), The White Countess (exec. prod.), Protégé, Warlords (also exec. prod.).
TELEVISION: *Movies*: Miracle in the Wilderness, Staying Afloat. *Series*: Walker Texas Ranger, Martial Law, Flatland.

MORGAN, DEBBI
Actress. b. Dunn, NC, Sept. 20, 1956.
PICTURES: Cry Uncle! (debut, 1971), Mandingo, Monkey Hustle, Dirty Mary, Eve's Bayou (Chicago Crits. Award, Best Supporting Actress, 1997), Asunder, She's All That, The Hurricane, Love & Basketball, Woman Thou Art Loosed, Coach Carter, Relative Strangers, Color of the Cross.
TELEVISION: *Movies:* Love's Savage Fury, Thornwell, The Jesse Owens Story, Guilty of Innocence: The Lenell Geter Story, The Less Than Perfect Daughter, Perry Mason: The Case of the Fatal Framing, The Runaway. *Mini-series:* Roots: The Next Generations. *Series*: Behind the Screen, All My Children (Emmy Award 1989, 2 other noms.), Generations, Loving, The City, Port Charles, Spawn, General Hospital, Soul Food, Charmed (recurring role), For the People, Touching Evil (pilot), The Bold and the Beautiful. *Guest:* More than 68 apperances.

MORIARTY, CATHY
Actress. b. Bronx, NY, Nov. 29, 1960. Raised in Yonkers, NY.
PICTURES: Raging Bull (debut, 1980; Academy Award nom.; 2 Golden Globes noms. 1981), Neighbors, White of the Eye, Burndown, Kindergarten Cop, Soapdish, The Mambo Kings, The Gun in Betty Lou's Handbag, Matinee, Another Stakeout, Me and the Kid, Pontiac Moon, Forget Paris, Casper, Foxfire, Opposite Corners, Cop Land, Hugo Pool, P.U.N.K.S., Digging to China, New Waterford Girl, But I'm A Cheerleader, Gloria, Crazy in Alabama, Red Team, Prince of Central Park, Little Pieces, Next Stop Eternity, Lady and the Tramp 2: Scamp's Adventure (voice), Analyze That, The Extra Man, The Bounty Hunter.
TELEVISION: *Movies*: Another Midnight Run, The Adventures of Captain Zoom in Outer Space (voice), Traces of Insanity, Casper Meets Wendy. *Series*: Bless This House, Stories from My Childhood (voice).

MORIARTY, MICHAEL
Actor. b. Detroit, MI, April 5, 1941. e. Dartmouth. Studied at London Acad. of Music and Dramatic Arts. Appeared with New York Shakespeare Festival, Charles Street Playhouse (Boston), Alley Theatre (Houston) and Tyrone Guthrie Theatre (Minneapolis). B'way debut in The Trial of the Catonsville Nine.
THEATRE: Find Your Way Home (Tony & Theatre World Awards, 1974), Richard III, Long Day's Journey Into Night, Henry V, GR Point, Whose Life Is It Anyway (Kennedy Center), The Ballad of Dexter Creed, Uncle Vanya, The Caine Mutiny Court-Martial, My Fair Lady.
PICTURES: Glory Boy (debut, 1971), Hickey and Boggs, Bang the Drum Slowly, The Last Detail, Shoot It Black Shoot It Blue, Report to the Commissioner, Who'll Stop the Rain, Reborn, The Sound of Murder, Q, Blood Link, Odd Birds, Pale Rider, The Stuff, Troll, The Hanoi Hilton, It's Alive III: Island of the Alive, Return to Salem's Lot, Dark Tower, The Hanoi Hilton, The Island of the Alive, Full Fathom Five, The Secret of the Ice Cave, Broken Silence, Shiloh, The Art of Murder, Courage Under Fire, Shiloh, Shiloh 2: Shiloh Season, Hitler Meets Christ, Cold Blooded, Woman Wanted, House of Luk, Out of Line, Mindstorm, Along Came a Spider, Swimming Upstream, Fugitives Run, Latter Days, Neverwas, The Yellow Wallpaper, Hitler Meets Christ (also writer), The Sons of Summer.
TELEVISION: *Movies*: A Summer Without Boys, The Glass Menagerie (2 Emmy Awards, 1974), The Deadliest Season, The Winds of Kitty Hawk, Too Far to Go (also distributed theatrically), Windmills of the Gods, Frank Nitti: The Enforcer, Tailspin: Behind the Korean Airline Tragedy, Born Too Soon, Children of the Dust, Cagney & Lacey: True Convictions, Calm at Sunset Calm at Dawn, Crime of the Century, The Arrow, Major Crime, Earthquake in New York, Galileo: On the Shoulders of Giants, Becoming Dick, Children of Fortune, Children of My Heart, James Dean (Emmy Award 2002), Mob Princess, Deadly Skies,

12 Hours to Live, Santa Baby. *Mini-series*: Holocaust (Emmy Award, 1978), Taken, Living With the Dead. *Series*: Law and Order (4 Emmy noms.; Golden Globe nom. 1994), Emily of New Moon, The 4400 (pilot). *Guest:* More than 55 appearances.

MORRICONE, ENNIO
Composer, Arranger. b. Rome, Italy, Nov. 10, 1928. Studied with Goffredo Petrassi at the Acad. of Santa Cecilia in Rome. Began career composing chamber music and symphonies as well as music for radio, TV and theatre. Wrote for popular performers including Gianni Morandi. Early film scores for light comedies. Gained recognition for assoc. with Italian westerns of Sergio Leone (under name of Dan Davio). Received Academy Honorary Award 2007.
PICTURES: Il Federal (1961, debut), A Fistful of Dollars, The Good the Bad and the Ugly, El Greco, Fists in the Pocket, Battle of Algiers, Matcheless, Theorem, Once Upon a Time in the West, Investigation of a Citizen, Fraulein Doktor, Burn, The Bird with the Crystal Plumage, Cat O'Nine Tails, The Red Tent, Four Flies in Grey Velvet, The Decameron, The Black Belly of the Tarantula, Bluebeard, The Serpent, Blood in the Streets, Eye of the Cat, The Human Factor, Murder on the Bridge, Sunday Woman, The Inheritance, Partner, Orca, Exorcist II: The Heretic, 1900, Days of Heaven (Academy Award nom. 1979), La Cage aux Folles, Bloodline, Stay as You Are, The Humanoid, The Meadow, A Time to Die, Travels With Anita (Lovers and Liars), When You Comin' Back Red Ryder?, Almost Human, La Cage aux Folles II, The Island, Tragedy of a Ridiculous Man, Windows, Butterfly (Golden Globe nom. 1982), So Fine, White Dog, Copkiller, Nana, The Thing, Treasure of the Four Crowns, Sahara, Once Upon a Time in America (Golden Globe nom. 1985), Thieves After Dark, The Cage, La Cage aux Folles III, The Forester's Sons, The Red Sonja, Repentier, The Mission (Academy Award nom.; Golden Globe Award 1987), The Venetian Woman, The Untouchables (Academy Award nom.; Golden Globe nom. 1988), Quartiere, Rampage, Frantic, A Time of Destiny, Casualties of War (Golden Globe nom. 1990), Cinema Paradiso, State of Grace, Hamlet, Bugsy (Academy Award nom.; Golden Globe nom. 1992), City of Joy, The Bachelor, In the Line of Fire, Wolf, Love Affair, Disclosure, Lolita, U Turn, Phantom of the Opera, Bulworth, The Legend of 1900 (Golden Globe Award 2000), Canone Inverso, Missions to Mars, Vatel, Before Night Falls, Malèna (Academy Award nom.; Golden Globe nom. 2001), Say It Isn't So, The Sleeping Wife, Another World Is Possible, Aida of the Trees, Senso '45, Ripley's Game, Kill Bill: Vol. 1, Marvelous Light, Al cuore si comanda, 72 Metres, Kill Bill: Vol. 2, Libertas, E ridendo l'uccise, Guardiani delle nuvole, Fateless, Sportsman of the Century, The Untouchables: Capone Rising, Leningrad, Hot Rod (soundtrack writer/performer), Madagascar: Escape 2 Africa (soundtrack writer), Seven Pounds (soundtrack writer), Baaria - La porta del vento, Couples Retreat (soundtrack writer), The Book of Eli (soundtrack writer), Spider Dance. Several more compositions for video releases.
TELEVISION: Composer for more than 90 internationally produced movies, mini-series and series. *U.S.: Movies & Mini-series:* Moses—The Lawgiver, Marco Polo, C.A.T. Squad, C.A.T. Squad: Python Wolf, The Endless Game, Voyage of Terror: The Achille Lauro Affair, Only One Survived, Abraham, Jacob, Joseph, Moses, Samson and Delilah, David, Solomon, The Fourth King, The Sands of Time, Esther, The Good Pope: Pope John XXIII, Pet Shop Boys: A Life in Pop (doc.), Karol - The Pope, the Man. *U.S. Special:* Josh Groban In Concert. *U.S. Series:* The Virginian (theme), Ally McBeal, many more credits for soundtrack writing. Many international/Italian compositions.

MORRIS, ERROL
Director, Producer, Writer. b. Hewlett, NY, Feb. 5, 1948. e. Univ. of WI, Univ. of CA/Berkeley Accomplished documentary director, producer and writer. DGA nom. for achievement in commercials, 2004.
PICTURES: *Director:* The Dark Wind. *Documentaries: Director:* Gates of Heaven (also prod. & editor), Vernon Florida (also prod.), The Thin Blue Line (also writer; International Documentary Association IDA Award, 1988), A Brief History of Time (Sundance Film Festival Filmmakers Trophy & Grand Jury Prize, 1991), Fast Cheap & Out Of Control (also prod.), Mr. Death: The Rise and Fall of Fred A Leuchter Jr. (also prod., DGA nom. 2000), The Fog of War: Eleven Lessons from the Life of Robert S. McNamara (also prod.; Academy Award for Best Documentary Feature, DGA nom. 2004. Also named Best Documentary by the National Board of Review, the Los Angeles Film Critics Association, the Chicago Film Critics and the Washington D.C. Area Film Critics. 2003 doc.), S.O.P.: Standard Operating Procedure (also prod.).
TELEVISION: *Series*: First Person (dir., prod., also host). *Specials:* The 74th Annual Academy Awards (Emmy nom. 2002), The 79th Annual Academy Awards.

MORRIS, GARRETT
Actor. b. New Orleans, LA, Feb. 1, 1937. e. Dillard Univ., Julliard Sch. of Music, Manhattan Sch. of Music. Was singer and arranger for Harry Belafonte Folk Singers and B'way actor before achieving fame as original cast member of Saturday Night Live.
THEATRE: Porgy and Bess, I'm Solomon, Show Boat, Hallelujah Baby!, The Basic Training of Pavlo Hummel, Finian's Rainbow, The Great White Hope, Ain't Supposed to Die a Natural Death, The Unvarnished Truth.
PICTURES: Where's Poppa? (debut, 1970), The Anderson Tapes, Cooley High, Car Wash, How to Beat the High Cost of Living, The Census Taker, The Stuff, Critical Condition, The Underachievers, Dance to Win, Motorama, Children of the Night, Almost Blue, Coneheads, Black Rose of Harlem, Black Scorpion II: Aftershock, Santa with Muscles, Black Rose of Harlem, Palmer's Pick Up, Twin Falls Idaho, Graham's Diner, Jackpot, How High, Connecting Dots, The Salon, Frank, Who's Your Caddy?, The Longshots, Diamond Dog Caper, Sonny Dream Weaver, Pickin' & Grinnin', Valley of the Sun, Pawn Shop.
TELEVISION: *Movies*: The Invisible Woman, Earth Angel, Maid for Each Other, Black Scorpion, Little Richard, Maniac Magee, Frangela. *Series*: Roll Out, Saturday Night Live (1975-80, also writer, Emmy nom. 1979), It's Your Move, Hunter, Roc, Martin, Cleghorne!, The Jamie Foxx Show. *Guest*: More than 87 appearances.

MORRIS, JOHN
Composer, Conductor, Arranger. b. Elizabeth, NJ, October 18, 1926. e. Juilliard Sch. Music 1946-48, U. of Washington. 1947, New Sch. Social Research 1946-49. Member: ASCAP, Acad. of M.P. Arts & Sciences, American Federation of Musicians.
THEATRE: *Composer*: *B'way:* My Mother My Father and Me, A Doll's House, Camino Real, A Time For Singing (musical), Take One Step, Young Andy Jackson, 15 Shakespeare plays for NY Shakespeare Fest. & Amer. Shakespeare Fest, Stratford CT. Musical supervisor, conductor, dance music arranger: Mack and Mabel, Much Ado About Nothing, Bells Are Ringing, Bye Bye Birdie and 23 other B'way musicals. *Off-B'way*: Hair.
PICTURES: The Producers, The Twelve Chairs, Blazing Saddles (Academy Award nom. 1975), Bank Shot, Young Frankenstein, The Adventure of Sherlock Holmes' Smarter Brother, Silent Movie, The Last Remake of Beau Geste, The World's Greatest Lover, High Anxiety, The In-Laws, In God We Trust, The Elephant Man (Academy Award nom. 1981), History of the World Part 1, Table for Five, Yellowbeard, To Be or Not to Be, The Woman in Red, Johnny Dangerously, The Doctor and the Devils, Clue, Haunted Honeymoon, Dirty Dancing, Spaceballs, Ironweed, The Wash, Second Sight, Stella, Life Stinks. *Soundtrack writer:* The Pelican Brief, Kiss of Death, Bring It On, The Mexican, Reign Over Me.
TELEVISION: *Movies: Composer*: Katherine Anne Porter, Ghost Dancing, The Firm, The Mating Season, Splendor in the Grass, The Electric Grandmother, Georgia O'Keeffe, The Adams Chronicles, The Franken Project, The Tap Dance Kid (Emmy Award, 1986), Make Believe Marriage, The Desperate Hours, The Skirts of Happy Chance, Infancy and Childhood, The Fig Tree, The Little Match Girl, The Last Best Year, The Last to Go, The Sunset Gang, Our Sons, When Lions Roared, Carolina Skeletons, The Fig Tree, Ellen Foster, Only Love, Murder in a Small Town, The Lady in Question, The Blackwater Lightship. *Mini-series: Composer:* The Scarlet Letter, Scarlett, Fresno, Favorite Son, *Themes*: ABC After School Special, Making Things Grow, The French Chef, Coach (5 ASCAP Awards 1992-1996). *Musical sprv., conductor, arranger Documentaries/Specials*: *Composer:* Anne Bancroft Special (Emmy Award), S'Wonderful S'Marvelous S'Gershwin (Emmy Award), With God On Our Side: The Rise of the Religious Right in America, Hallmark Christmas specials.
RECORDINGS: Wildcat, All-American, Bells Are Ringing, First Impressions, Bye Bye Birdie, Kwamina, Baker Street, Rodgers and Hart, George Gershwin Vols. 1 & 2, Jerome Kern, Lyrics of Ira Gershwin, Cole Porter, others.

MORRISSEY, PAUL
Writer, Director, Photographer. b. New York, NY, Feb. 23, 1938. e. Fordham U. 2nd lt. in Army. A writer, cameraman and dir. in independent film production prior to becoming Andy Warhol's mgr. in all areas except painting. Discovered and managed The Velvet Underground and Nico. Founded Interview magazine. Story, casting, dir. & photog. for Warhol Productions' Chelsea Girls, Four Stars, Bike Boy, I A Man, Lonesome Cowboys, Blue Movie, and San Diego Surf.
PICTURES: *Writer/Photographer/Editor/Director:* Flesh, Trash, Heat, L'Amour, Women in Revolt. *Writer/Director*: Flesh For Frankenstein, Blood for Dracula, The Hound of the Baskervilles, Madame Wang's, Mixed Blood, Beethoven's Nephew, Spike of Bensonhurst. *Director:* Forty Deuce, The Armchair Hacker, Beautiful Darling (doc., exec. prod.).

MORROW, ROB
Actor. b. New Rochelle, NY, Sept. 21, 1962.
THEATRE: *NY*: The Substance of Fire, Aven'U Boys, The Chosen, Scandal (workshop), Soulful Scream of a Chosen Son, The Boys of Winter, Slam, Third Secret.
PICTURES: Private Resort, Quiz Show, The Last Dance, Mother, Into My Hear, Other Voices, Touched, (also s.p., dir., prod.), Labor Pains, The Guru, The Emperor's Club, Night's Noontime, Going Shopping, The Bucket List, The Good Doctor.
TELEVISION: *Movies:* The Day Lincoln Was Shot, Only Love, The Thin Blue Lie, Jennifer Estes Story, Custody. *Series*: Tattinger's, Northern Exposure (2 Emmy noms.; 3 Golden Globe noms.), Nearly Yours, Street Time, Numb3rs. *Guest:* More than 52 appearances.

MORSE, DAVID
Actor. b. Beverly, MA, Oct. 11, 1953.
THEATRE: *B'way*: On the Waterfront.
PICTURES: Inside Moves, Desperate Hours, The Indian Runner, The Good Son, The Getaway, The Crossing Guard, Twelve Monkeys, The Rock, Contact, The Legend of Pig Eye, A.W.O.L., The Negotiator, The Green Mile, Dancer in the Dark, Bait, Von Trier's 100 Eyes, Proof of Life, Diary of a City Priest, Hearts in Atlantis, The Slaughter Rule, Double Vision, Down in the Valley, Nearing Grace, Dreamer: Inspired by a True Story, 16 Blocks, Hounddog, Disturbia, Passengers, The Hurt Locker, Shanghai, Mother and Child, Mint Julep, Longfellow, Drive Angry 3D.
TELEVISION: *Movies*: Pineapple Poll, Our Family Business, Prototype, Shattered Vows, When Dreams Come True, Six Against the Rock, Downpayment on Murder, Winnie, Brotherhood of the Rose, Cry in the Wild: The Taking of Peggy Ann, Two-Fisted Tales, Dead Ahead: The Exxon Valdez Disaster, Miracle on Interstate 880, Tecumseh: The Last Warrior, Murder Live!, Hack, Empire State. *Mini-series*: Stephen King's The Langoliers, Abraham and Mary Lincoln: A House Divided, John Adams (Emmy nom. 2008). *Series*: St. Elsewhere, Big Wave Dave's, Friday the 13th (dir. only), Action Man (voices), Madeline (voice), The American Experience, Hack, House M.D. (Emmy nom. 2007). *Special*: A Place at the Table. *Guest:* More than 60 appearances.

MORSE, ROBERT
Actor. b. Newton, MA, May 18, 1931. Served in U.S. Navy. Studied with American Theatre Wing, New York. Following radio work, appeared on B'way stage in The Matchmaker, 1956.
THEATRE: *B'way*: The Matchmaker, Say Darling (Theatre World Award), Take Me Along, How to Succeed in Business Without Really Trying (Tony Award, 1962), Sugar, So Long 174th Street, Tru (Tony Award, 1990).
PICTURES: The Proud and the Profane (debut, 1956), The Matchmaker, The Cardinal, Honeymoon Hotel, Quick Before It Melts, The Loved One, Oh Dad Poor Dad Mama's Hung You in the Closet and I'm Feeling So Sad, How to Succeed in Business Without Really Trying, A Guide for the Married Man, Where Were You When the Lights Went Out?, The Boatniks, Hunk, The Emperor's New Clothes, Broadway: The Golden Age by the Legends Who Were There (doc., as himself).
TELEVISION: *Movies*: Thieves Carnival, The Calendar Girl Murders, Tru (Emmy Award, 1993), Here Come the Munsters. *Mini-series*: Wild Palms. *Series*: The Secret Storm (1954), That's Life, All My Children, Monchichis (voice), Pound Puppies (voice), ProStars (voice), City of Angels, Mad Men (Emmy nom. 2008). *Documentaries/Specials*: The Stingiest Man in Town (voice), Kennedy Center Tonight—Broadway to Washington. *Guest:* More than 92 appearances.

MORTENSEN, VIGGO
Actor. b. New York, NY, Oct. 20, 1958.
PICTURES: Witness, Salvation!, Prison, Fresh Horses, Tripwire, Leatherface: Texas Chainsaw Massacre III, Young Guns II, The Reflecting Skin, The Indian Runner, The Young Americans, Ruby Cairo, Ewangelia wedlug Harry'ego, Carlito's Way, Boiling Point, Floundering, Desert Lunch, The Crew, American Yakuza, The Passion of Darkly Noon, Gimlet, Crimson Tide, The Prophecy, Albino Alligator, The Portrait of a Lady, Daylight, La Pistola de mi hermano, G. I. Jane, Blouse Man, A Perfect Murder, Psycho, A Walk on the Moon, 28 Days, Lord of the Rings: The Fellowship of the Ring, Lord of the Rings: The Two Towers, Lord of the Rings: The Return of the King (best acting ensemble awards from Broadcast Film Critics Assoc. (BFCA) National Board of Review (NBR) and Screen Actors Guild (SAG), 2003), Live Freaky Die Freaky (voice), Hidalgo, A History of Violence, Wild Horse Preservation (narrator), Alatriste, Eastern Promises (Academy Award nom.; Golden Globe nom. 2008), Good, Appaloosa, The Road, A Dangerous Method, The Girl with the Dragon Tattoo.
TELEVISION: *Movies*: Vanishing Point. *Mini-series*: George Washington. *Series:* Search for Tomorrow. *Guest:* More than 97 appearances.

MORTON, JOE
Actor. b. New York, NY, Oct. 18, 1947. e. Hofstra U.
THEATRE: *NY*: Hair (debut), Raisin (Theatre World Award), Oh Brother, Honky Tonk Nights, A Midsummer Night's Dream, King John, Cheapside, Electra, A Winter's Tale, Oedipus Rex, Julius Caesar, The Tempest. *Director:* Heliotrope Bouquet.
PICTURES: Between the Lines, And Justice for All, The Clairvoyant, Curse of the Pink Panther, The Brother From Another Planet, Trouble in Mind, Crossroads, Stranded, Zelly and Me, The Good Mother, Tap, Terminator 2: Judgment Day, City of Hope, Of Mice and Men, Forever Young, The Inkwell, Speed, The Walking Dead, Lone Star, Executive Decision, The Pest, Speed 2: Cruise Control, Trouble on the Corner, Blues Brothers 2000, Apt Pupil, When It Clicks, The Astronaut's Wife, What Lies Beneath, Bounce, Ali, Dragonfly, Crossing (short), Paycheck, Thoughtcrimes, Lenny the Wonder Dog, Breaking Dawn (also assoc. prod.), Stealth, The Night Listener, American Gangster, Badland, Wherever You Are, La Linea-The Line, The Mulberry Tree. *Director:* Sunday on the Rocks. *Executive producer:* Mitchellville.
TELEVISION: *Movies*: Lawman without a Gun, Death Penalty, We're Fighting Back, The Files on Jill Hatch, Terrorist on Trial: The United States vs. Salim Ajami, Alone in the Neon Jungle, Police Story: Burnout, Howard Beach: Making a Case for Murder, Challenger, Equal Justice, Legacy of Lies, In the Shadow of Evil, Jack Reed: Death and Vengeance, Miss Evers' Boys, Mutiny, Ali: An American Hero, Jasper Texas, Gone But Not Forgotten. *Series*: Search for Tomorrow, Grady, Another World, Equal Justice, A Different World, Tribeca, Under One Roof, New York News, Prince Street, Mercy Point, Smallville, The Fritz Pollard Story (host), All My Children, E-Ring, Eureka, The Good Wife. *Documentaries: As Narrator:* The Great Depression, Blood & Iron: The Story of the German War Machine (mini-series), American Cinema (series), The Black Press: Soldiers Without Swords, New York: A Documentary Film (mini-series), John Brown's Holy War (actor), Jazz (voices), Beyond Human, Africa (mini-series), War Birds: Diary of an Unknown Aviator, Unforgivable Blackness: The Rise and Fall of Jack Johnson (voices), The American Experience. *Guest*: More than 86 appearances.

MOSK, RICHARD M.
Executive. b. Los Angeles, CA, May 18, 1939. e. Stanford U, B.A., 1960; Harvard Law School, JD, 1963. Admitted to California Bar, 1964. Member of staff on Warren Commission, 1964. Clerk to California Supreme Court Justice Mathew Tobriner (1964-1965); Partner with Mitchell, Silverberg & Knupp (1965-1987). Principal in firm of Sanders Barnet Goldman Simons & Mosk from 1987-2000. Chair and co-chair, Classification and Rating Administration of Motion Picture Assoc. of America, 1994-2000. Member of the Christopher Commission, Judge, Iran-U.S. Claims Tribunal. Associate Justice for the California Court of Appeals, 2001.

MOSKO, STEVE
Executive. e. Univ. of Delaware. Began career in local radio and TV when he started in the sales division at Baltimore radio station WITH(AM) the day after graduating from the University of Delaware. After several sales positions in Baltimore, including local sales manager at WMAR-TV, Mosko was named general sales manager at WTAF-TV Philadelphia in 1983. In 1988, he moved over to WPHL-TV Philadelphia to become v.p. and station manager. In 1992, Mosko was asked to join Columbia TriStar TV Distribution, Sony's syndication unit in Los Angeles. He joined the sales team as v.p. of the Western region, where he handled distribution deals on everything from The Ricki Lake Show to off-network syndication runs of Seinfeld and Mad About You. In July 2000, Mosko was promoted to pres. atop CTTD. By Nov. 2001, Mosko had responsibility for all of Sony/Columbia's domestic TV assets. In 2005, with Sony's acquisition of MGM complete, Sony restructured its small-screen operations by placing all domestic TV units under the watch of Mosko as pres. of Sony Pictures Television. In addition he added all domestic pay cable and video-on-demand to his portfolio, which already included all other aspects of the studio's U.S. TV operations. He inked a four-year deal that keeps him at the studio until 2009. In 2004 Mosko was named chairman of the Academy of Television Arts & Sciences Foundation and served a two-year term. In addition to his work with the Academy, Mosko was chairman of NATPE in 2000.

MOSLEY, ROGER E.
Actor. b. Los Angeles, CA. Dec. 18, 1938. Planned career in broadcasting but turned to acting, first appearing in small roles on TV in: Night Gallery, Baretta, Kojak, Cannon, Switch.
PICTURES: The New Centurions (debut, 1972), Hit Man, The Mack, Sweet Jesus Preacher Man, Terminal Island, McQ, Darktown Strutters, Leadbelly, Stay Hungry, Big Time, The Greatest, Semi-Tough, Steel, The White Lions, Heart Condition, Unlawful Entry, Pentathlon, A Thin Line Between Love and Hate, Letters From a Killer, Hammerlock.
TELEVISION: *Movies*: The Next Howling Wind, Voyage Into Evil, I Know Why the Caged Bird Sings, The Jericho Mile, Attica, Magnum P.I. *Mini-series*: Roots: The Next Generations. *Series*: Magnum P.I., You Take the Kids, Hangin' With Mr. Cooper, Rude Awakening.

MOSS, CARRIE-ANNE
Actress. b. Vancouver, Canada, Aug. 21, 1967.
PICTURES: Flashfire, The Soft Kill, Terrified, Sabotage, Secret Life of Algernon, Lethal Tender, New Blood, The Crew, The Matrix, Memento, Red Planet, Chocolat, The Matrix Revisited, The Matrix Reloaded, The Matrix Revolutions, Suspect Zero, Sledge: The Untold Story, The Chumscrubber, Snow Cake, Mini's First Time, Mission: Impossible III, Fido, Disturbia, Normal, Fireflies in the Garden, Love Hurts, Unthinkable.
TELEVISION: *Movies:* Doorways, Suspect, Pretty/Handsome. *Series:* Dark Justice, Matrix, Spider-Man (voice), Models Inc., F/X: The Series. *Guest:* More than 50 appearances.

MOSS, IRWIN
Executive. e. Syracuse U., Harvard Law Sch. Member NY State Bar. Began industry career as dir. of package negotiations for CBS-TV; 1970-80, exec. v.p. & natl. head of business affairs for I.C.M.; 1978-80, sr. v.p., NBC Entertainment; 1980, pres., Marble Arch TV. 1982, joined Paramount Pictures as sr. v.p. for motion picture div. 1984, exec. v.p., D.L. Taffner Ltd.

MOSTEL, JOSH
Actor, Director. b. New York, NY, Dec. 21, 1946. Father was late actor Zero Mostel. e. Brandeis U., B.A. 1970. Part of The Proposition, a Boston improvisational comedy group. Stage debut, The Homecoming (Provincetown Playhouse, MA).
THEATRE: *Actor:* Unlikely Heroes, The Proposition, An American Millionaire, A Texas Trilogy, Gemini, Men in the Kitchen, The Dog Play, The Boys Next Door, A Perfect Diamond, Threepenny Opera, My Favorite Year, The Flowering Peach, Cranes. *Director:* Ferocious Kisses, Love As We Know It, Misconceptions, Red Diaper Baby.
PICTURES: Going Home (debut, 1971), The King of Marvin Gardens, Jesus Christ Superstar, Harry and Tonto, Deadly Hero, Fighting Back, Sophie's Choice, Star 80, Almost You, The Brother from Another Planet, Windy City, Compromising Positions, The Money Pit, Stoogemania, Radio Days, Matewan, Wall Street, Heavy Petting, Animal Behavior, City Slickers, Naked Tango, Little Man Tate, City of Hope, Searching for Bobby Fischer, The Chase, City Slickers II: The Legend of Curly's Gold, Billy Madison, The Basketball Diaries, The Maddening, Big Daddy, Rounders, The Out of Towners, Knockaround Guys, State of Play.
TELEVISION: *Movies:* The Boy Who Loved Trolls, Beverly Hills 90210, Thicker than Blood, Strip Search. *Mini-series:* Seventh Avenue. *Co-writer:* Media Probes: The Language Show. *Series:* Delta House, At Ease, Murphy's Law.

MOUND, FRED
Executive. b. St. Louis, MO, April 10, 1932. e. St. Louis U., Quincy Coll. 1946-52, assoc. with father, Charles Mound, at Park Theatre in Valley Park, Mo.; 1952-53, Universal Pictures (St. Louis); 1953, booker, UA, St. Louis; 1955 promoted to salesman in Kansas City; 1957, salesman, St. Louis; 1962, Indianapolis branch mgr. 1967 named UA regional mgr., Dallas and in 1970 became S.W. div. mgr; 1976-77, asst. gen. sls. mgr. for Southern, N.W. and S.W. div. operating out of Dallas. 1977 appt. v.p., asst. gen. sls. mgr. of UA; 1978, appt. v.p. gen sls. mgr. for AFD Pictures in Los Angeles; 1981, v.p. asst. gen. sls. mgr. for Universal; 1984, sr. v.p., gen. sls. mgr., Universal Pictures Distribution; named exec. v.p. 1988. Will Rogers Motion Picture Pioneers Foundation v.p., 1989, also past pres. Appointed pres. Universal distrib., 1990, v.p., creative svcs., Carsey-Werner. Retired.

MOUNT, THOM
Executive, Producer. b. Durham, NC, May 26, 1948. e. Bard Coll.; CA Institute of the Arts, MFA. Started career with Roger Corman and as asst. to prod., Danny Selznick at MGM. Moved to Universal under prod. exec. Ned Tanen. At 26, named pres. and head of prod. at Universal. During 8-year tenure, was responsible for dev. and prod. of more than 140 films (including Smokey and the Bandit, Animal House, others). Pres. of The Mount Co.
THEATRE: Open Admissions (co-prod.), Death and the Maiden.
PICTURES: *Executive producer:* My Man Adam, Pirates, The Indian Runner, Natural Born Killers, Real Men, A West Texas Children's Story, Have Dreams, Will Travel, How to Change in 9 Weeks (consult. prod.). *Producer:* Can't Buy Me Love, Frantic, Bull Durham (co-prod.), Stealing Home, Tequila Sunrise, Roger Corman's Frankenstein, Death and the Maiden, Night Falls on Manhattan, High Times, Mr. Blandings Builds His Dream House, Are We Done Yet?, Bathory, How to Change in 9 Weeks, Chéri.
TELEVISION: *Movie:* Open Admissions (exec. prod.).

MOYER, STEPHEN
Actor. b. Brentwood, England, October 11, 1969. e. London Academy of Music and Dramatic Art. m. actress Anna Paquin.
PICTURES: Quills, Undiscovered, 88 Minutes, Open House, The Caller, Master Class, Ice, The Double, A Dead Man in Deptford, Priest, The Big Valley.
TELEVISION: *Movies:* Lord of Misrule, The Secret, Princess of Thieves, Men Only, Uprising, Menace, Entrusted, The Final Quest, Empathy. *Mini-series:* The Starter Wife. *Series:* Conjugal Rites, Castles, The Grand, Life Support, NY-LON, Lilies, True Blood.

MOYERS, BILL
TV Correspondent. b. Hugo, OK, June 5, 1934. e. U. of Texas; Southwestern Baptist Theological Sem. Aide to Lyndon B. Johnson; assoc. dir., Peace Corps, 1961-62, and deputy dir., 1963. Spec. asst. to Pres. Johnson, 1963-65 and press secty., 1965-67. Editor and chief corr., CBS Reports. Bill Moyers Journal on PBS. Established Public Affairs TV, Inc., 1986. Currently, host of *Now with Bill Moyers* (weekly PBS series). Won Emmy Award 1978 for CBS Reports with the late Ed Bradley. Career Achievement Award from Intl. Documentary Assoc. 1991.
TELEVISION: *Documentaries/Specials:* The Power of the Past with Bill Moyers: Florence, Facing Hate, Songs Are Free (also exec. editor), Manufacturing Consent: Noam Chomsky and the Media, Free Speech for Sale, Hunting Bin Laden, Empire of Dreams: The Story of the Star Wars Trilogy, What Can We Do About Violence? (writer), Trade Secrets: A Moyers Report (also editor), Fooling with Words (editor), Earth on Edge (also editor). *Mini-series:* Vietnam: A Television History, Joseph Campbell and the Power of Myth, The Language of Life with Bill Moyers, The Wisdom of Faith with Huston Smith: A Bill Moyers Special. Moyers on Addiction: Close to Home, On Our Own Terms: Moyers On Dying, Bill Moyers on the Hudson (host/narr., writer), Bill Moyers on Faith & Reason. *Series:* Bill Moyers' Journal (Emmy nom. 1980, WGA Award 2009, 1 other nom.), Creativity with Bill Moyers (Emmy Award 1982), The American Parade, Healing and the Mind with Bill Moyers (Emmy Award 1993), Now with Bill Moyers (also writer), Now (host and writer, WGA Award, News/Documentary Emmy Award 2004), Becoming American: The Chinese Experience (WGA nom. 2004), Moyers on America (exec. editor).

MUDD, ROGER
Newscaster. b. Washington, DC, Feb. 9, 1928. e. Washington & Lee U., U. of North Carolina. Reporter for Richmond News-Leader, 1953; news. dir., WRNL, 1954; WTOP, Washington, 1956; joined CBS News 1961 as Congressional correspondent (2 Emmy Awards). 1977, Natl. Aff. corr.; 1978, corr., CBS Reports; 1980-87: NBC News as chief Washington corr., chief political corr., co-anchor; 1987 joined The MacNeil/Lehrer News Hour as special correspondent; essayist, and chief congressional correspondent. 1992 became contributing correspondent. Host of numerous specials and history series.

MUELLER-STAHL, ARMIN
Actor. b. Tilsit, East Prussia, Dec. 17, 1930. Moved to West Germany in 1980. e. Berlin Conservatory. Studied violin before turning to acting. *Author:* Verordneter Sonntag (Lost Sunday), Drehtage, Nuterwegs Nach Hause (On the Way Home).
PICTURES: Naked Among the Wolves, The Third, Jacob the Liar, The Flight, Lite Trap, Lola, Wings of Night, Veronika Voss, A Cop's Sunday, A Love in Germany, Thousand Eyes, Trauma, Colonel Redl, L'Homme blesse, God Doesn't Believe in Us Anymore, Angry Harvest, The Blind Director, Following the Fuhrer, Momo, The Jungle Mission, Lethal Obsession, Midnight Cop, Music Box, Das Spinnenetz, Just for Kicks, Avalon, Bronstein's Children, Kafka, The Power of One, Night on Earth, Utz, The House of the Spirits, Holy Matrimony, The Last Good Time, A Pyromaniac's Love Story, Taxandria, Shine (Academy Award nom. 1997), Theodore Rex, The Peacemaker, The Game, The Commissioner, The X Files: Fight the Future, Jakob the Liar, The Thirteenth Floor, The Third Miracle, Pilgrim, Mission to Mars, The Long Run, The Story of an African Farm, The Dust Factory, Where Love Reigns, Local Color, Leningrad, Ich bin die Andere, Eastern Promises, Die Buddenbrooks, The International, Angels & Demons, Virtuoso.
TELEVISION: *Movie:* 12 Angry Men. *Mini-series:* Collin, Amerika, Jesus, Crociati. Several German movies and specials. *Series:* The West Wing, The Power of Knowledge (host). *Guest:* More than 68 appearances.

MULGREW, KATE
Actress. b. Dubuque, IA, April 29, 1955. e. NYU. Stage work includes stints with American Shakespeare Festival, NY Shakespeare Festival, Seattle Rep. Theatre, Mark Taper Forum (LA). B'way: Black Comedy.
PICTURES: Lovespell, A Stranger Is Watching, Remo Williams: The Adventure Begins, Throw Momma from the Train, Camp Nowhere, Round Numbers, Camp Nowhere, Captain Nuke and the Bomber Boys, Trekkies, Star Trek: Nemesis, Star Trek: The Experience-Borg Invasion 4D (short), Perception, The Best and the Brightest.
TELEVISION: *Movies*: Alien Lover, The American Woman: Portraits, of Courage, Kate Loves a Mystery, Jennifer: A Woman's Story, A Time for Miracles, My Town, Roses Are For The Rich, Roots: The Gift, Heartbeat, Danielle Steel's Daddy, Fatal Friendship, For Love and Glory, Caretaker, Riddler's Moon. *Mini-series:* The Word, The Manions of America. *Series*: Ryan's Hope (1975-77), Kate Columbo (Kate Loves a Mystery, Golden Globe nom. 1980), Heartbeat, Man of the People, Gargoyles (voice), Star Trek: Voyager, The Black Donnellys, Mercy. *Documentaries:* Sisters in Resistance (narr.), Of Ashes and Atoms (actor). *Guest:* More than 56 appearances.

MULHERN, MATT
Actor, Director, Writer. b. Philadelphia, PA, July 21, 1960. e. Rutgers Univ.
THEATRE: *NY:* Biloxi Blues, Wasted, The Night Hank Williams Died.
PICTURES: *Actor:* One Crazy Summer, Extreme Prejudice, Biloxi Blues, Junior, Infinity, The Sunchaser, Walking the Waterline (also dir. & s.p.), Trainwreck: My Life as an Idiot. *Director:* Duane Hopwood (also s.p.).
TELEVISION: *Movies*: Gunsmoke: To the Last Man, Terror in the Night, A Burning Passion: The Margaret Mitchell Story. *Series*: The Ellen Burstyn Show, Major Dad.

MULL, MARTIN
Actor. b. Chicago, IL, Aug. 18, 1943. e. Rhode Island Sch. of Design. Started as humorist, making recordings for Warner Bros., Capricorn, ABC Records.
PICTURES: FM (debut, 1978), My Bodyguard, Serial, Take This Job and Shove It, Flicks, Mr. Mom, Bad Manners, Clue, O.C. and Stiggs, Home Is Where the Hart Is, Rented Lips (also s.p., exec. prod.), Cutting Class, Ski Patrol, Far Out Man, Think Big, Ted and Venus, The Player, Miracle Beach, Mrs. Doubtfire, Mr. Write, Edie and Pen, Jingle All the Way, Movies Money Murder, Zack and

Reba, Attention Shoppers, The Year That Trembled, Relative Strangers, Come Away Home, Killers, And They're Off.
TELEVISION: *Movies*: Sunset Limousine, The Jerk Too, Lots of Luck, California Girls, The History of White People in America (host, writer), The Vidiots, The History of White People in America: Vol. II (host), The Whole Shebang, Missing Parents, How the West Was Fun, Beverly Hills Family Robinson, Sister Mary Explains It All, The Nick At Nite Holiday Special, A Boyfriend for Christmas, Family Man. *Series:* Mary Hartman Mary Hartman, Fernwood 2Nite, America 2-Night, Domestic Life, His & Hers, Roseanne (also writer), The Jackie Thomas Show, Family Dog (voice), Sabrina the Teenage Witch, The Ellen Show, Teamo Supremo (voice) Thick and Thin, Hopeless Pictures, Danny Phantom, American Dad! (voice), 'Til Death. *Guest:* More than 141 appearances.

MULLAN, PETER
Actor. b. Glasgow, Scotland. 1954.
PICTURES: *Actor.* The Big Man, Shallow Grave, Ruffian Hearts, Good Day for the Bad Guys, Braveheart, Trainspotting, Fairy Tale: A True Story, My Name Is Joe (Cannes Film Fest. Award, Best Actor, 1998), Miss Julie, Mauvaise passe, Ordinary Decent Criminal, The Claim, Session 9, Young Adam, Kiss of Life, Out Of This World, Criminal, Blinded, Waves (short), On A Clear Day, The Last Legion, The Children of Men, Connolly, True North, The Last Legion, Stone of Destiny, Red Riding: In the Year of Our Lord 1974, Red Riding: In the Year of Our Lord 1983, Red Riding: In the Year of Our Lord 1980, Tyrannosaur, Cross My Mind, The Lion Inside. *Director.* Good Day for the Bad Guys, Fridge, Orphans, Magdalena Sisters, Neds (also writer, co-prod.).
TELEVISION: *Movies*: Opium Eaters, Jute City, Nightlife, Bogwoman, This Little Life, The Trial of Tony Blair. *Series:* Your Cheatin' Heart, Cardiac Arrest (dir.), Shoebox Zoo, The Fixer.

MULLEN, PATRICK J.
Executive. b. Pentwater, MI, July 6, 1955. e. Attended Univ. of Mich., speech communication & radio/television. Mullen began his career in 1979 as an account executive with WGTU-TV/WGTQ-TV, Traverse City, Mich., where he was promoted to sales manager in 1980. He served as general sales manager at WKFT-TV, Fayetteville, N.C., in 1982 and 1983, before joining WXMI-TV, Grand Rapids, Mich., as director/sales. He was named vice president/station manager of WXMI in 1988 and general manager in 1989. He was regional vice president of Tribune Television from 1998 to 2001 with management responsibility for 11 stations. Mullen has overseen the company's television group since March 2001, when he was appointed president of Tribune Television. He was named president of Tribune Broadcasting in Jan. 2003. He left Tribune and became the v.p. & gen. manager of Fox-owned stations WFLD-TV and WPWR-TV in Chicago in April 2006. He has served as chairman emeritus of the Fox Affiliates Board of Governors, and has been a bd. member of the Television Bureau of Advertising (TVB), The Association for Maximum Service Television (MSTV) and the National Association of Broadcasters (NAB). Mullen also is a past president and the founding chairman of the Michigan Association of Broadcasters Foundation. In addition, he is a member of the Quello Center Board of Advisors at Michigan State University and the Northwestern University Associates, and serves on the board of trustees of Aquinas College and the Davenport College Foundation. He also serves on the board of directors for Chicago's Shedd Aquarium.

MÜLLER, ROBBY
Cinematographer. b. Netherlands, April 4, 1940. e. Dutch Film Acad. Asst. cameraman in Holland before moving to Germany where he shot 9 films for Wim Wenders.
PICTURES: Alabama: 2000 Light Years, Summer in the City, Jonathan, Carlos, The Goalkeeper's Fear of the Penalty Kick, The Scarlet Letter, Die Reise Nach Wien, Kings of the Road, Alice in the Cities, Perahim Die Zweite Chance, Wrong Move, The American Friend, Mysteries, The Glass Cell, Opname, Saint Jack, Honeysuckle Rose, A Cop's Sunday, They All Laughed, Body Rock, Repo Man, Paris Texas, To Live and Die in L.A., The Longshot, Down By Law, Tricheurs, The Believers, Barfly, Il Piccolo Diavolo (The Little Devil), Mystery Train, Korczak, Until the End of the World, When Pigs Fly, The Ditvoorst Domains (actor only), Mad Dog and Glory, Breaking the Waves (NY Society of Film Critics Award and Natl Society of Film Critics Awards, 1997), Dead Man (NY Society of Film Critics Awards, 1997), Last Call, Beyond the Clouds, The Tango Lesson, Shattered Image, Ghost Dog: The Way of the Samurai, Buena Vista Social Club, Dancer in the Dark, My Brother Tom, 24 Hour Party People, Poem: I Set My Foot Upon the Air and It Carried Me, Coffee and Cigarettes, Visions of Europe, The Man from London.
TELEVISION: *Movies:* Der Fall Lena Christ, Eine Rose fur Jane, Marie, Die Eltern, Finnegan Begin Again, Red Hot and Blue.

MULRONEY, DERMOT
Actor. b. Alexandria, VA, Oct. 31, 1963. e. Northwestern Univ.
PICTURES: Sunset, Young Guns, Survival Quest, Staying Together, Longtime Companion, Career Opportunities, Bright Angel, Where the Day Takes You, Samantha, Point of No Return, The Thing Called Love, Silent Tongue, Bad Girls, Angels in the Outfield, There Goes My Baby, Living in Oblivion, Copycat, How to Make an American Quilt, Kansas City, Trigger Effect, My Best Friend's Wedding, Goodbye Lover, Where the Money Is, Trixie, Goodbye Lover, Where the Money Is, The Safety of Objects, Lovely & Amazing, Investigating Sex, About Schmidt, Undertow, The Wedding Date, The Family Stone, Must Love Dogs, Griffin and Phoenix, Dante's Inferno, Zodiac, Gracie, Georgia Rule, Jolene, Burn After Reading, Flash of Genius, Inhale, The Family Tree, Love, Wedding, Marriage (dir.).
TELEVISION: *Movies*: Sin of Innocence, The Drug Knot, Daddy, Unconquered, Long Gone, The Heart of Justice, Family Pictures, The Last Outlaw, Journeys North, Heroine of Hell, The Memory Keeper's Daughter. *Guest:* More than 50 appearances.

MUMY, BILL
Actor. r.n. Charles William Mumy Jr. b. El Centro, CA, Feb. 1, 1954. Began acting as Billy Mumy at age 6. Played with band America in 1970's, also with bands Bill Mumy & The Igloos, and The Jenerators. Has made 8 albums with Barnes & Barnes. With actor Miguel Ferrer, wrote comic books Comet Man and Trip to the Acid Dog. Has also written stories for Star Trek, The Hulk, and Spiderman comic books, and Lost in Space comic published by Innovation. Wrote music for Disney's Adventures in Wonderland series (Emmy nom.)
PICTURES: Tammy Tell Me True, Palm Springs Weekend, A Ticklish Affair, A Child is Waiting, Dear Brigitte, Rascal, Bless the Beasts and Children, Papillon, Twilight Zone—The Movie, Hard to Hold, Captain America, Double Trouble, Three Wishes, The Fantasy Worlds of Irwin Allen (host, writer).
TELEVISION: *Movies*: Sammy the Way Out Seal, For the Love of Willadean, Sunshine, The Rockford Files (pilot), Sunshine Christmas, Alfred Hitchcock Presents, Lost in Space Forever, A.I. Assault. *Series*: Lost in Space, Sunshine, Space Cases (writer only). A&E Biography (narrator of TV documentary specials since 1993) Backstory (series documentary; theme composer), Babylon 5. *Guest*: More than 80 appearances.

MURDOCH, ELISABETH
Executive. Murdoch founded Shine TV in 2001 and with a series of successful acquisitions, Shine TV is now The Shine Group and the United Kingdom's fourth largest indie producer. Shine Group Chairman and CEO Murdoch, who left billionaire father Rupert Murdoch's News Corp. organization and a senior exec. position at News Corp.'s BSkyB, is building a media empire of her own. Shine started out making shows in the UK for News Corp.'s Sky, a comprehensive multi-channel TV service in the UK and Ireland with nearly 10 million subscribers. Struggling in its early years, Shine's recent savvy acquisitions have made headlines. The Shine Group now includes: Shine Pictures, Princess Productions, Kudos Film & TV, Firefly (factual programs) and in 2008 Shine acquired one of the biggest U.S. indie producers, Reveille (of "Ugly Betty" and "The Office" fame), for $200 million. In Sept. 2009 Murdoch teamed with Joanna Shields, the former CEO of online social networking site Bebo.com, to launch a digital media content company, a move that will enable The Shine Group to join the growing cadre of companies racing to produce digital content that airs across multiple platforms. Murdoch sits on the bd. of dir. of the UK Film Council.

MURDOCH, JAMES
Executive. b. United Kingdom, Dec. 13,1972. Son of billionaire media tycoon K. Rupert Murdoch. Studied music at Harvard University. In 1995 with two partners, he set up Rawkus Records, an independent hip hop record label. In 1996, Rawkus was bought up by his father's company, and the younger Murdoch joined News Corporation (controlled by father, Rupert Murdoch). James Murdoch was appointed chairman and chief executive of subsidiary Star Television in Hong Kong in May 2000. At the time, the pan-Asian satellite broadcaster was losing money and the younger Murdoch was charged with turning the organization's fortunes around, which he did. He was appointed exec. v.p. of News Corp's 36.8 per cent-owned British satellite broadcasting arm, he became CEO of BSkyB, Nov. 2003. Became Chairman and CEO, Europe & Asia, News Corp.

MURDOCH, LACHLAN K.
Executive. e. B.A. in philosophy, Princeton University. Son of New Corp. Chairman Rupert Murdoch. After serving in an executive capacity for News Corporation since the mid-1990s, Lachlan Murdoch resigned all his executive positions within News Corporation in July 2005. He stepped down as deputy COO, a position he'd held since 2000, but remained a director of News Corporation with plans to advise the company in a number of areas. Previous positions with News Corp. included: pres. of Fox Television Stations, publisher of the New York Post, a director for Fox Entertainment Group, Inc.; involvement in other ventures included his role as deputy chmn. of STAR Group, a wholly owned unit of News Corporation since 1995, a non-executive dir. of NDS Group PLC since 2002, and a director for OmniSky Corporation. He also was a director of Gemstar-TV Guide International, Inc. from 2001-Dec. 2004. Murdoch set up his new company, Illyria Pty Ltd, on Aug. 3, 2005. In May 2007, Illyria Pty Ltd. (Australia) launched a 50:50 joint venture with Percept Holdings to launch Percept Talent Management. The company represents creative and technical talent in the fields of motion pictures, TV, fashion, music, sports & branded entertainment.

MURDOCH, K. RUPERT
Executive. b. Australia, March 11, 1931. e. Oxford U., England. Son of Sir Keith Murdoch, head of The Melbourne Herald and leading figure in Australian journalism. Spent two years on Fleet St. before returning home to take over family paper, The Adelaide News. Acquired more Australian papers and in 1969, expanded to Britain, buying The News of the World. Moved to U.S. in 1973, buying San Antonio Express and News. Conglomerate in 1985 included New York Post, New York Magazine, The Star, The Times of London, The Boston Herald, The Chicago Sun-Times along with TV stations, book publishing companies, airline, oil and gas companies, etc. In 1985, made deal to buy 20th Century-Fox Film Corp. from owner Martin Davis. Sold the NY Post, 1988, to conform with FCC regulations. Purchased Triangle Publications in 1988 (including TV Guide). Currently, Murdoch is chmn. & CEO at News Corporation Inc., where he has been the exec. director and chief executive since 1979. He has been a director of News Limited, News Corporation's principal subsidiary in Australia, since 1953, a director of News International, News Corporation's principal subsidiary in the U.K., since 1969 and a director of News America, News Corporation's principal subsidiary in the United States, since 1973. In the entertainment industry, Murdoch has been been a director of Fox Entertainment Group since 1985, chmn. since 1992 and CEO since 1995. He is the chmn. of the bd. of The DIRECTV Group, Inc. Murdoch has also served as a director of BSkyB since 1990 and chairman since 1999; since 2001, Murdoch has served as a director of Gemstar-TV Guide and China Netcom (Hong Kong) Limited (2001-2005).

MUREN, DENNIS E.
Visual Effects Creator. b. Glendale, CA, Nov. 1, 1946. AA Pasadena CC, 1966. Studied at UCLA. Freelance special effects 1968-75. Cameraman Cascade 1975-76. Dir. of photography, visual effects Industrial Light Magic 1976-80. AMPAS Scientific/Technical Award, 1981. Member ASC, AMPAS. 1981 received Academy Award for special achievement. Won Academy Award, 1982 for technical achievement. Received Visual Effects Society Award for Lifetime Achievement 2007.
PICTURES: Star Wars, Close Encounters of the Third Kind, The Empire Strikes Back (Academy Award), Dragonslayer (Academy Award nom. 1982), E.T.: the Extraterrestrial (Academy Award 1983), Star Wars: Episode VI - Return of the Jedi (Special Achievement Academy Award, BAFTA Award 1984), Indiana Jones and the Temple of Doom (Academy Award, BAFTA Award 1985), Young Sherlock Holmes (Academy Award nom. 1986), Captain Eo (short feature), Innerspace (Academy Award 1988), Empire of the Sun, Willow (Academy Award nom. 1989), Ghostbusters II, The Abyss (Academy Award 1990), Terminator 2: Judgment Day (Academy Award, BAFTA Award 1992), Jurassic Park (Academy Award, BAFTA Award 1994), Casper, Star Wars: Episode I - The Phantom Menace (Academy Award nom. 2000), The Lost World: Jurassic Park (Academy Award nom. 1998), Artifical Intelligence: AI (Academy Award nom. 2002), Star Wars: Episode II - Attack of the Clones, Hulk (VES Award nom. 2004), Star Wars: Episode III, War of the Worlds (Academy Award nom.; VES Award 2006), WALL·E (visual consult.).
TELEVISION: *Movies:* Battlestar Galactica, Caravan of Courage (Emmy), The Ewok Adventure (Emmy Award 1985).

MURPHY, BEN
Actor. b. Jonesboro, AR, March 6, 1942. e. U. of Illinois. Degree in drama from Pasadena Playhouse. Acted in campus productions and toured in summer stock. Film debut with small role in The Graduate, 1967.
PICTURES: Yours Mine and Ours, The Thousand Plane Raid, Sidecar Racers, Riding with Death, Hanging Up, Time Walker, To Protect and Serve, Freezerburn, The Uniform Motion of Folly, The Genesis Code.
TELEVISION: *Movies*: The Letters, Wild Bill Hickock, Bridger, Heat Wave, Runaway, This Is the West That Was, Gemini Man, Hospital Fire, The Cradle Will Fall, Stark: Mirror Image, McBride: Semper Fi. *Mini-series*: The Winds of War. *Series*: The Name of the Game, Alias Smith and Jones, Griff, Gemini Man, The Chisholms, Lottery!, Berrenger's, The Dirty Dozen. *Guest:* More than 63 appearances.

MURPHY, EDDIE
Actor. b. Brooklyn, NY, April 3, 1961. e. Roosevelt High Sch. Wrote and performed own comedy routines at youth centers and local bars at age 15. Worked on comedy club circuit; at 19 joined TV's Saturday Night Live as writer and performer. Recordings: Eddie Murphy, Eddie Murphy: Comedian, How Could It Be?, Love's Alright. Voted Top-Money Making Star of 1988 on Quigley Poll, NATO/ShoWest Star of the Decade for 1980s.
PICTURES: 48 HRS. (debut, 1982, Golden Globe nom. 1983), Trading Places (Golden Globe nom. 1984), Best Defense, Beverly Hills Cop (Golden Globe nom. 1985), The Golden Child, Beverly Hills Cop II, Eddie Murphy Raw (also s.p., exec. prod.), Coming to America (also story), Harlem Nights (also dir., s.p, exec. prod.), Another 48 HRS., Boomerang (also story), The Distinguished Gentleman, Beverly Hills Cop III, Vampire in Brooklyn (also co-prod.), The Nutty Professor (also co-exec. prod.; Nat'l Society of Film Critics Award, Golden Globe nom. 1997), Metro, Mulan (voice), Doctor Dolittle, Holy Man, Life, Bowfinger, The Nutty Professor II, Shrek, Dr. Dolittle 2, Showtime, The Adventures of Pluto Nash, I Spy, The Incredible Shrinking Man, Daddy Day Care, Shrek 2, Dreamgirls (Academy Award nom.; Golden Globe Award 2007), Shrek the Third (voice), Norbit (also prod.), Meet Dave, NowhereLand, Shrek Forever After (voice), Imagine That, A Thousand Words.
TELEVISION: *Movies:* Uptown Comedy Express (host), The Kid Who Loved Christmas (exec. prod.), What's Alan Watching? (exec. prod.), Shrek the Halls (voice). *Series:* Saturday Night Live (1981-84, also writer, 3 Emmy noms.), The PJs (also creator, writer & exec. prod., Emmy nom. 1999). *Guest:* More than 144 appearances.

MURPHY, MICHAEL
Actor. b. Los Angeles, CA, May 5, 1938. e. U. of Arizona. m. actress Wendy Crewson. Taught English and Drama in L.A. city school system, 1962-64. N.Y. stage debut as dir. of Rat's Nest, 1978.
PICTURES: Double Trouble (debut, 1967), Countdown, The Legend of Lylah Clare, The Arrangement, That Cold Day in the Park, M*A*S*H, Count Yorga: Vampire, Brewster McCloud, McCabe and Mrs. Miller, What's Up Doc?, The Thief Who Came To Dinner, Phase IV, Nashville, The Front, An Unmarried Woman, The Great Bank Hoax, The Class of Miss MacMichael, Manhattan, The Year of Living Dangerously, Strange Behavior, Cloak and Dagger, Salvador, Mesmerized, Shocker, Folks!, Batman Returns, Clean Slate, Bad Company, Kansas City, Private Parts, The Island, Magnolia, Tricks, Silver City, Heights, Childstar, X-Men: The Last Stand, Away from Her, Greta, The Trotsky.
TELEVISION: *Movies*: The Autobiography of Miss Jane Pittman, The Caine Mutiny Court-Martial, Tailspin: Behind the Korean Airlines Tragedy, Special Report: Journey to Mars, Breaking the Surface: The Greg Louganis Story, Indiscretion of An American Wife, The Day Reagan Was Shot, Live From Baghdad, Footsteps, In the Dark, H2O, Hunt for Justice, Mayday, Playing House, The Path to 9/11, The Wind in the Willows. *Mini-series:* Tanner on Tanner. *Series*: Two Marriages, Hard Copy, This Is Wonderland, Tilt, The American Experience (narr.), The Bridge. *Documentaries/Specials*: John Cheever's Oh Youth and Beauty, Tanner '88. *Guest:* More than 67 appearances.

MURPHY, RYAN
Writer, Director, Producer. b. Indianapolis, IN, 1966. e. Indiana University. Producer/Executive for Ryan Murphy Productions.
PICTURES: Running with Scissors, Eat Pray Love (s.p., dir.).
TELEVISION: Movies: St. Sass (exec. prod.), Pretty/Handsome (writer, exec. prod., dir.). Series: Popular (writer), Nip/Tuck (writer, exec. prod., dir.), Glee (writer, exec. prod., dir., exec. music prod., Emmy Award 2010, 1 other nom.; DGA nom.; 2 WGA noms. 2010).

MURPHY, THOMAS S.
Executive. e. Cornell Univ (B.S.M.E.), Harvard U. Grad. Sch. of Bus. Admin. (M.B.A.). Joined Capital Cities at its inception in 1954. Named a dir. in 1957, then pres. in 1964. Chmn. & CEO of Capital Cities, 1966-90. Company named Capital Cities/ABC Inc. in 1986 after acquistion of American Broadcasting Companies Inc. 1990-94, chmn. of bd. Resumed position of chmn. & CEO in Feb., 1994. Murphy retired in 1996 when The Walt Disney Co. purchased ABC. Murphy has been a board member of: Walt Disney, DoubleClick, Inc., New York University and Madison Square Boys and Girls Clubs. In Feb. 2005 he completed a seven-year term on the Bd. of Trustees of Save the Children. He continues as chair emeritus of Save the Children and also chairs the Save the Children campaign.

MURRAY, BILL
Actor. b. Wilmette, IL, Sept. 21, 1950. e. attended Regis Coll. Was pre-med student; left to join brother, Brian Doyle-Murray, in Second City the Chicago improvisational troupe. Appeared with brother on radio in National Lampoon Radio Hour, and in off-B'way revue, National Lampoon Show. Also on radio provided voice of Johnny Storm the Human Torch on Marvel Comics' Fantastic Four. Hired by ABC for Saturday Night Live with Howard Cosell; then by NBC for Saturday Night Live, 1977.
PICTURES: Jungle Burger (debut, 1975), Meatballs, Mr. Mike's Mondo Video, Where the Buffalo Roam, Loose Shoes, Caddyshack, Stripes, Tootsie, Ghostbusters (Golden Globe nom. 1985), The Razor's Edge (also co-s.p.), Nothing Lasts Forever, Little Shop of Horrors, Scrooged, Ghostbusters II, Quick Change (also co-dir., co-prod.), What About Bob?, Groundhog Day, Mad Dog and Glory, Ed Wood, Space Jam, Larger Than Life, Kingpin, The Man Who Knew Too Little, With Friends Like These, Veeck As in Wreck, Rushmore (Golden Globe nom. 1999), Wild Things, The Cradle Will Rock, Hamlet, Scout's Honor, Company Man, Charlie's Angels, Osmosis Jones, The Royal Tenenbaums, Speaking of Sex, Lost in Translation (Academy Award nom.; Golden Globe Award 2004), Coffee and Cigarettes, Garfield: The Movie (voice), The Life Aquatic with Steve Zissou, Broken Flowers, The Lost City, Garfield: A Tail of Two Kitties (voice), The Darjeeling Limited, City of Ember, The Limits of Control, The Fantastic Mr. Fox (voice), Get Smart, Get Low, Passion Play.
TELEVISION: *Movies*: All You Need Is Cash. *Series:* Saturday Night Live (1977-80; also writer; Emmy Award for writing 1977, 1 other nom.), The Sweet Spot, Stories from my Childhood (voice). *Documentaries/Specials*: It's Not Easy Being Me—The Rodney

Dangerfield Show, Steve Martin's Best Show Ever, Second City—25 Years in Revue, The Sweet Spot (series doc., writer, segment prod.). *Guest:* More than 112 appearances.

MURRAY, DON
Actor, Director, Writer. b. Hollywood, CA, July 31, 1929. e. AADA. Mother was a Ziegfeld Girl, father was dance dir. for Fox Studio.
THEATRE: *B'way*: Insect Comedy, The Rose Tattoo, The Skin of Our Teeth, The Hot Corner, Smith (musical), The Norman Conquests, Same Time Next Year. *National tours*: California Suite, Chicago.
PICTURES: Bus Stop (debut, 1956; Academy Award nom. 1957), The Bachelor Party, A Hatful of Rain, From Hell to Texas, These Thousand Hills, Shake Hands With the Devil, One Foot in Hell, The Hoodlum Priest (also co-prod., co-s.p. as Don Deer), Advise and Consent, Escape From East Berlin, One Man's Way, Baby the Rain Must Fall, Kid Rodelo, The Plainsman, Sweet Love Bitter, The Viking Queen, Childish Things (Confession of Tom Harris; also prod., co-s.p.), The Cross and the Switchblade (dir., co-s.p. only), Happy Birthday Wanda June, Conquest of the Planet of the Apes, Cotter, Call Me by My Rightful Name (also prod., co-s.p.), Deadly Hero, Damien (dir., s.p. only), Endless Love, I Am the Cheese, Radioactive Dreams, Peggy Sue Got Married, Scorpion, Made in Heaven, Ghosts Can't Do It, Island Prey, Elvis Is Alive (dir.), The Hard Ride.
TELEVISION: *Movies*: The Borgia Stick, Daughter of the Mind, The Intruders, The Girl on the Late Late Show, The Sex Symbol, A Girl Named Sooner, Rainbow, Crisis in Mid-Air, If Things Were Different, The Boy Who Drank to Much, Fugitive Family, Return of the Rebels, Thursday's Child, Quarterback Princess, License to Kill, A Touch of Scandal, Something in Common, Stillwatch, The Stepford Children, Mistress, My Dad Can't Be Crazy...Can He?, Hearts Adrift, Mr. Headmistress. *Series*: Made in America (panelist), The Outcasts, Knots Landing, Brand New Life, Sons and Daughters. *Documentaries/Specials*: For I Have Loved Strangers (also writer), Hasty Heart, Billy Budd, Winterset, Alas Babylon, Justin Morgan Had a Horse, Montana Crossroads (Emmy nom.). *Guest:* More than 75 appearances.

MURRAY, JONATHAN
Producer, Executive. b. New York, 1955. e. Univ. of Missouri, journalism degree. Murray got his start in local television, spending six years at WLUK-TV, WXIA-TV and WKYC-TV in news, station management (WOKR-TV) and programming. He then worked with the TV rep firm HRP, Inc., helping local stations buy and schedule their syndicated programming. In 1991, Murray and Mary Ellis Bunim pitched their idea for an unscripted drama series to MTV executives over breakfast. MTV bought the show before lunch time, and the landmark success of Bunim-Murray Productions was underway. Bunim's experience in scripted dramas with Murray's documentary and news expertise broke all the rules of TV production. The result - The Real World - quickly dominated the youth market. From the Real World's 1992 launch, Murray has created and exec. produced more than 50 seasons and close to 2000 hours of unscripted TV. Despite the loss of Bunim to cancer in early in 2004, Murray continues to lead the company they founded together as its chmn. and pres.
PICTURE: The Real Cancun (doc., prod.).
TELEVISION: *Movies as Exec. Prod.*: The Real World Reunion, Personally Yours, 2 Punk Rock 4 This: The Real World San Diego Reunion, An Eye for Alba. *Series as Exec. Prod.*: MTV Real World: Philadelphia, Road Rules (Emmy nom. 2001), Class Reunion, Road Rules All Stars, The Real World/Road Rules Challenge, The Real World/Road Rules Challenge 2000, The Real World/Road Rules Extreme Challenge, Lost in the USA, Love Cruise: The Maiden Voyage, The Real World/Road Rules Battle of the Seasons, Making the Band 2, The Real World/Road Rules Battle of the Sexes, Born to Diva, Real World/Road Rules Challenge: The Gauntlet, The Simple Life, Real World/Road Rules Challenge: The Inferno, The Simple Life 2: Road Trip, The Real World/Road Rules Challenge: Battle of the Sexes 2, The Rebel Billionaire: Branson's Quest for the Best, Real World/Road Rules Challenge: The Inferno II, The Bad Girls Club, Keeping Up With the Kardashians, Kourtney & Khloe Take Miami, America's Psychic Challenge, Reunited: The Real World Las Vegas, Starting Over (Emmy Award 2005, 2 other noms.), Living Lohan, Supreme Court of Comedy, The Real World Brooklyn (creator, writer), Styl'd, The Real World/Road Rules Challenge: The Ruins, Models of the Runway, Project Runway. *Documentaries/Specials:* The Real World Casting Special, The Real World: Tenth Anniversary Special, Playboy: Who Wants to be a Playboy Centerfold?, Autism: The Musical (Emmy Award 2008).

MUSANTE, TONY
Actor. b. Bridgeport, CT, June 30, 1936. e. Oberlin Coll. B.A. Directed local theatre, then appeared off-Broadway, in regional theater, and on Dupont Show of the Month (Ride With Terror).
THEATRE: *B'way*: The Lady From Dubuque, P.S. Your Cat Is Dead, 27 Wagons Full of Cotton, Memory of Two Mondays. *Off-B'way:* Grand Magic, Cassatt, A Gun Play, Benito Cereno, L'Histoire du Soldat, Match-Play, The Zoo Story, The Pinter Plays (The Collection), Kiss Mama, The Balcony, Snow Orchid, The Flip Side, Frankie and Johnny in the Claire de Lune. *Regional*: The Big Knife, A Streetcar Named Desire, The Taming of the Shrew, Widows, The Archbishop's Ceiling, Dancing in the Endzone, Two Brothers, Souvenir, APA Shakespeare Rep., Wait Until Dark, Anthony Rose, Mount Allegro, Double Play, Falling Man, Breaking Legs, Love Letters, The Sisters, Italian Funerals and Other Festive Occasions.
PICTURES: Once a Thief, The Incident, The Detective, The Mercenary, The Bird with the Crystal Plumage, The Grissom Gang, The Last Run, The Anonymous Venetian, Collector's Item, The Repenter, The Pisciotta Case, Goodbye and Amen, Break Up, Nocturne, The Pope of Greenwich Village, One Night at Dinner, Appointment in Trieste, Devil's Hill, The Deep End of the Ocean, The Yards, La Vita come viene, Promessa d'amore, We Own the Night.
TELEVISION: *Movies*: Ride with Terror, Toma, Judgment: The Court Martial of Lieutenant William Calley, The Desperate Miles, Nowhere to Hide, My Husband is Missing, The Thirteenth Day: The Story of Esther, Breaking Up is Hard to Do, High Ice, Rearview Mirror, Deep Family Secrets, Exiled. *Mini-series:* Roots of the Mafia, Il Barone, Nutcracker: Money Madness & Murder, The Seventh Scroll, Traffic, Pompei, ieri, oggi, domani. *Series:* Toma, Oz, As the World Turns.

MYERS, JULIAN F.
Public Relations Executive. b. Detroit, MI, Feb. 22, 1918. e. Wayne U., 1935-37, USC, 1937-39. Distribution, Loew's Detroit, 1941-42; asst. story editor, idea man, Columbia, 1942-46; publicist, 20th Century-Fox, 1948-62; public relations, Julian F. Myers, Inc., 1962; pres., Myers Studios, Inc., 1966; pres., New Horizons Broadcasting Corp., 1968-69; sr. publicist American Intl. Pictures, 1970-80. Pres., Hollywood Press Club; former member Variety Club; Academy of Motion Pictures Arts & Sciences; Board of Governors Film Industry Workshops, Inc. 1977, 1979, western v.p., Publicists Guild; Recipient of Publicists Guild's Robert Yeager Award. First male member Hollywood Women's Press Club. Co-founder HANDS (Hollywood Answering Needs of Disaster Survivors). Member, M.P. Pioneers. Winner, 1980 Publicists Guild Les Mason Award. Instructor in publicity, UCLA, 1979-present, and at Loyola Marymount U, 1991-present. Filmways Pictures, pub. dept., 1980-81. Exec. v.p., worldwide m.p. and TV pub./mktg., Hanson & Schwam Public Relations 1981-91. Author of Myersystem and Myerscope guides. Member: USC Cinema & TV Alumni Assn., West Coast P.R. Will Rogers Inst., Acad. TV Arts Sciences; p.r. coord. comm., Academy of Motion Picture Arts & Sciences. Bd. of dirs., Show Biz Expo. Publicist, Prods. Guild of America. Pres. Julian Myers Public Relations, nominated MoPic Showmanship of the Year, Publicists Guild of America, 1993. Columnist, Drama-Logue Magazine. Special Award of Merit, Publicists Guild of America, 1998. Member, Women in Film. Co-founder, with wife, of AmigoDay, which is a day to greet anyone, anywhere, on any month's first Sunday — around the world.

MYERS, MIKE
Actor. b. Scarborough, Ontario, Canada, May 25, 1963.
PICTURES: Elvis Stories (short), Wayne's World (also s.p.), So I Married an Axe Murderer(also s.p.), Wayne's World 2 (also s.p., singer), Austin Powers: International Man of Mystery (also s.p., prod.), 54, Pete's Meteor, Austin Powers: The Spy Who Shagged Me (also s.p., prod.), Mystery Alaska, Shrek (voice), Austin Powers:Goldmember (also s.p. & prod.), A View from the Top, The Cat in the Hat, Shrek 2, Shrek the Third (voice), The Love Guru (also writer, prod.), Inglourious Basterds, Shrek Forever After (voice).
TELEVISION: *Movie:* Shrek the Halls (voice). *Series:* Saturday Night Live (1989-1995, also writer, Emmy Award 1989, 2 other noms.), It's Only Rock and Roll, Mullarky & Myers, The Dave Thomas Comedy Show (writer). *Guest:* More than 160 appearances.

N

NAEGLE, SUE
Executive. Grew up in Rockaway, N.J.. Started in the mailroom at United Talent Agency and over 16 years with the agency worked way up to become a top TV agent. In April 2008, Naegle became entertainment president at HBO, Inc. As a TV agent, Naegle worked closely with HBO executives, helping bring the hit "Six Feet Under" on to the premium TV network. After the run of "The Sopranos" and "Sex and the City," HBO has struggled to find its next breakout hits, a trend it's hoping to reverse with Naegle at the programming helm.

NAIFY, ROBERT, ALLEN
Executive. b. Sacramento, CA. e. Attended Stanford U. Worked for United California Theatres starting in 1946 in various capacities including: theatre manager, purchasing agent, film buyer, general manager and president. 1963 became exec. v.p. United Artists Communications; 1971 became pres. & CEO until 1987. Naify later purchased half of the United Artists theatre chain. He also invested in cable TV in 1950s; sold to TCI in 1986 for cash, stock. Became senior v.p. marketing for Placer Sierra Bank. Also man-

aged public relations for Mattel Interactive, Dir. of communications for iSpheres Corporation also has held marketing positions with The Learning Company, Broderbund Software, and Mindscape. Now in his eighties, Naify is one of the world's wealthiest people with a net worth of approximately $1.4 billion.

NAIR, MIRA
Director, Producer. b. Bhubaneshwar, India, October 15, 1957. e. Irish Catholic Missionary School in India, Delhi U., Harvard U. A course in documentary filmmaking at Harvard led to directing 4 non-fiction films including India Cabaret (1985) and Children of Desired Sex.
PICTURES: *Director-Producer*: Salaam Bombay! (also s.p. Cannes Film Fest. Camera d'Or/Prix du Publique; Acad. Award nom.), Mississippi Masala (also s.p.), The Perez Family (dir. only), Kama Sutra: A Tale of Love (also s.p.), Monsoon Wedding, September 11 (dir. only. segment "India"), Vanity Fair, Still the Children Are Here (documentary), The Namesake, Shantaram, Little Zizou (co-prod., exec. prod.), New York, I Love You, 8 (segment dir.), Amelia.
TELEVISION: *Movies: Director:* My Own Country, Hysterical Blindness. *Specials/documentaries/Director:* India Cabaret, Children of a Desired Sex, The Laughing Club of India (short).

NATHANSON, MICHAEL
Executive, Producer. Began his career at NBC Sports, NY. In 1977 moved to LA and worked as prod. asst. on The Deep, Sinbad the Eye of the Tiger. 1980-85, v.p., prod., MGM, United Artists, Warner Bros. 1987, exec. v.p., prod., Columbia Pictures; 1989-94, pres. of Worldwide Prod. at Columbia Pictures; projects included: Awakenings, The Prince of Tides, Boyz N the Hood, A River Runs Through It, A League of Their Own, In the Line of Fire, Groundhog Day, Bram Stoker's Dracula, My Girl and others. 1994-97, chmn. & CEO, Regency Productions; In 1997, Nathanson became pres. & COO, MGM Pictures. With the completion of MGM's sale to Sony in 2005, Nathanson left MGM and entered into a multi-year producing deal at Columbia Pictures via his production company O.N.C. Entertainment.
PICTURES: *Producer:* Empire Records, Carpool, A Time to Kill, L.A. Confidential (Academy Award nom. 1998), The Man Who Knew Too Little, Tin Cup, Natural Born Killers, Heat, Species 2, Dirty Work, Yours Mine & Ours, Ball's Out: The Gary Houseman Story. *Exec. prod.:* Copy Cat, The Sunchaser, Bogus, Murder at 1600, Dangerous Beauty, Goodbye Lover, The Pink Panther, The Pool Guy.

NAUGHTON, DAVID
Actor, Singer. b. Hartford, CT, Feb. 13, 1951. Brother is actor James Naughton. e. U. of Pennsylvania, B.A. Studied at London Acad. of Music and Dramatic Arts. Numerous TV commercials, including music for Dr. Pepper. On B'way in Hamlet, Da, Poor Little Lambs.
PICTURES: Midnight Madness (debut, 1980), An American Werewolf in London, Separate Ways, Hot Dog... The Movie, Not for Publication, The Boy in Blue, Separate Vacations, Kidnapped, Quite By Chance, Beanstalk, The Sleeping Car, Overexposed, Wild Cactus, Desert Steel, Amityville: A New Generation, Beanstalk, Mirror Mirror III: The Voyeur, Ice Cream Man, Urban Safari, Little Insects (voice), A Crack in the Floor, Flying Virus, Sky Blue (voice), Rave On, Big Bad Wolf, Hallows Point, Nightmare Carnival, Brutal Massacre: A Comedy.
TELEVISION: *Movies*: The Other Side of Victory, Desire the Vampire, Getting Physical, Goddess of Love, Overexposed, Body Bags, Basic Values: Sex-Shock & Censorship in the 90s, Chance of a Lifetime, Out of the Wilderness, Mystery Woman: Sing Me a Murder. *Series*: Makin' It, At Ease, My Sister Sam. *Guest:* more than 51 appearances.

NAUGHTON, JAMES
Actor. b. Middletown, CT, Dec. 6, 1945. Brother is actor David Naughton. Father of actors Greg Naughton and Keira Naughton. e. Brown U., A.B., 1967; Yale U., M.F.A., drama, 1970.
THEATRE: *NY*: I Love My Wife (B'way debut, 1977), Long Day's Journey Into Night (Theatre World, Drama Desk and New York Critics Circle Awards, 1971), Whose Life Is It Anyway?, Losing Time, Drinks Before Dinner, City of Angels (Tony & Drama Desk Awards, 1990), Four Baboons Adoring the Sun. Regional: Who's Afraid of Virginia Woolf? (Long Wharf), The Glass Menagerie (Long Wharf), Hamlet (Long Wharf), Julius Caesar (Amer. Shakespeare Festival), 8 seasons at Williamstown Theatre Festival, Chicago (Tony Award, B'way, 1996-97).
PICTURES: The Paper Chase (debut, 1973), Second Wind, Diary of the Dead, A Stranger is Watching, Cat's Eye, The Glass Menagerie, The Good Mother, First Kid, The First Wives Club, Oxygen, Broadway: The Golden Age by the Legends Who Were There (documentary), Fascination, The Devil Wears Prada, Factory Girl, Childless, Clear Blue Tuesday.
TELEVISION: *Movies*: F. Scott Fitzgerald and the Last of the Belles, The Last 36 Hours of Dr. Durant, The Bunker, My Body My Child, Parole, The Last of the Great Survivors, Between Darkness and the Dawn, Sin of Innocence, Traveling Man, Antigone, The Cosby Mysteries (pilot), The Birds II: Land's End, Cagney & Lacey: The Return, Cagney & Lacey: Together Again, Raising Caines, Crime Stories: The Capture and Trial of Adolf Eichmann, The Truth About Jane, Our Town (dir. only). *Series*: Faraday and Company, Planet of the Apes, Making the Grade, Trauma Center, Raising Miranda, The Cosby Mysteries, Gossip Girl. *Documentaries/Specials:* Look Homeward Angel (1972). *Guest:* More than 79 appearances.

NEAL, PATRICIA
Actress. b. Packard, KY, Jan. 20, 1926. e. Northwestern U. Worked as doctor's asst., cashier, hostess, model, jewelry store clerk prior to prof. career as actress. In summer stock before B'way debut in The Voice of the Turtle, 1946. Autobiography: As I Am (with Richard DeNeut, 1988).
THEATRE: *NY*: The Voice of the Turtle, Another Part of the Forest (Tony, Donaldson & Drama Critic Awards), The Children's Hour, Roomful of Roses, The Miracle Worker. *England*: Suddenly Last Summer.
PICTURES: John Loves Mary (debut 1949), The Fountainhead, It's a Great Feeling, The Hasty Heart, Bright Leaf, Three Secrets, The Breaking Point, Raton Pass, Operation Pacific, The Day the Earth Stood Still, Weekend With Father, Diplomatic Courier, Washington Story, Something for the Birds, Stranger From Venus (Immediate Disaster), Your Woman, A Face in the Crowd, Breakfast at Tiffany's, Hud (Academy Award, BFA Award, Golden Globe Award 1964), Psyche '59, In Harm's Way (BFA Award, 1965), The Subject Was Roses (Academy Award nom. 1969), The Night Digger, Baxter, Happy Mother's Day Love George, "B" Must Die, The Passage, Ghost Story, An Unremarkable Life, Theremin: An Electronic Odyssey, From Russia to Hollywood: The 100-Year Odyssey of Chekhov and Shdanoff, Cookie's Fortune, For the Love of May, Broadway: The Golden Age by the Legends Who Were There (documentary), Flying By, Shattered Glory.
TELEVISION: *Movies*: Immediate Disaster, Special for Women: Mother and Daughter, The Homecoming: A Christmas Story (Emmy nom.; Golden Globe nom. 1972), Things in Their Season, Eric, The American Woman: Portraits of Courage (narr.), Tail Gunner Joe (Emmy nom. 1977), A Love Affair: The Eleanor and Lou Gehrig Story, All Quiet on the Western Front (Emmy nom. 1980), Shattered Vows, Love Leads the Way: A True Story, Glitter, Caroline?, A Mother's Right: The Elizabeth Morgan Story, Heidi. *Mini-series:* The Bastard. *Guest:* More than 76 appearances.
(d. August 8, 2010)

NEAME, RONALD
C.B.E. Cinematographer, Producer, Director. b. Hendon, Eng. April 23, 1911. e. U. Coll. Sch., London. p. Elwin Neame, London photog., & Ivy Close, m.p. actress. Entered m.p. ind. 1928; asst. cameraman on first full-length Brit. sound film, Blackmail, dir. by Alfred Hitchcock, 1929; became chief cameraman & lighting expert, 1934; in 1945 joint assoc. prod., Noel Coward Prods.
PICTURES: *Cinematographer*: Girls Will Be Boys (co-cine.), Happy (co-cine.), Elizabeth of England, Honours Easy (co-cine.), Joy Ride, Music Hath Charms, One of Our Aircraft Is Missing (Academy Award nom. 1943) The Crimes of Stephen Hawke, The Improper Dutchess, A Star Fell From Heaven, Against the Tide, Brief Ecstasy, Feather Your Nest, Keep Fit, Weekend Millionaire, Gaunt Stranger, The Phantom Strikes, The Crime of Peter Frame, Dangerous Secrets, Penny Paradise, Who Goes Next? Cheers Boys Cheer, Sweeney Todd: The Demon Barber of Fleet Street, Let's Be Famous, Trouble Brewing, The Ware Case, Let George Do It, Return to Yesterday, Saloon Bar, Four Just Men, Major Barbara, A Yank in the R.A.F. (Brit. flying sequence), In Which We Serve, This Happy Breed, Blithe Spirit, Brief Encounter (Academy Award nom. 1947), Great Expectations (also co-s.p., 2 Academy Award noms. 1948), Oliver Twist (also co-s.p.), A Young Man's Fancy, Passionate Friends. *Director*: Take My Life, Golden Salamander (also co-s.p.), The Card (The Promoter; also prod.), Man With a Million (The Million Pound Note), The Man Who Never Was, The Seventh Sin, Windom's Way, The Horse's Mouth, Tunes of Glory, I Could Go on Singing, The Chalk Garden, Mister Moses, Gambit, A Man Could Get Killed (co-dir.), Prudence and the Pill (co-dir.), The Prime of Miss Jean Brodie, Scrooge, The Poseidon Adventure, The Odessa File, Meteor, Hopscotch, First Monday in October, Foreign Body, The Magic Balloon (also s.p.).

NEEDHAM, HAL
Director, Writer, Actor. b. Memphis, TN, March 6, 1931. e. Student public schools. Served with Paratroopers, U.S. Army 1951-54. Founder Stunts Unlimited, Los Angeles, 1970; stuntman Stunts Unlimited, 1956-65; dir. and stunt coordinator second unit, 1965-75. Chmn. of bd., Camera Platforms International, Inc. 1985. Owner Budweiser Rocket Car (fastest car in the world). Member Screen Actors Guild, AFTRA, Writers Guild of America, Directors Guild of America. Received Academy Award for Science and Engineering, 1987. Received Lifetime Achievement, World Stunt Award 2001.
PICTURES: *Director:* Smokey and the Bandit (debut, 1977; also co-story), Hooper, The Villain, Smokey and the Bandit II, The Cannonball Run, Megaforce (also co-s.p.), Stroker Ace (also co-s.p.), Cannonball Run II (also co-s.p.), RAD, Body Slam, Street Luge (also stunt design).
TELEVISION: *Movies*: *Director:* Death Car on the Freeway (also actor), Stunts Unlimited (also actor), Bandit: Bandit Goes Country (also s.p. & exec. prod.), Bandit: Bandit Bandit (also s.p. & exec. prod.), Bandit: Beauty and the Bandit (also s.p.), Bandit:

Bandit and the Silver Angel (also s.p. & exec. prod.), Hostage Hotel. *Series*: Hal Needham's Wild World of Stunts (synd. series; also writer, star); stunt work on numerous series. *Guest:* More than 58 appearances.

NEESON, LIAM
Actor. b. Ballymena, Northern Ireland, June 7, 1952. m. late actress Natasha Richardson. Former amateur boxer. Was driving a fork lift truck for a brewery when he joined the Lyric Player's Theatre in Belfast. Made prof. debut in The Risen (1976) and stayed with rep. co. two years. Moved to Dublin as freelance actor before joining the Abbey Theatre.
THEATRE: The Risen People (debut), The Informer (Dublin Theatre Fest.), Translations (National Theatre, London). NY theatre debut 1992 in Anna Christie (Theatre World Award).
PICTURES: Excalibur (debut, 1981), Krull, The Bounty, Lamb, The Innocent, The Mission, Duet For One, A Prayer for the Dying, Suspect, Satisfaction, The Dead Pool, The Good Mother, High Spirits, Next of Kin, Dark Man, Crossing the Line (The Big Man), Shining Through, Under Suspicion, Husbands and Wives, Leap of Faith, Ethan Frome, Deception, Schindler's List (Academy Award nom.; Golden Globe nom. 1994), Nell, Rob Roy, Before and After, Michael Collins (Golden Globe nom. 1997), A Leap of Faith (voice), Alaska: Spirit of the Wild (voice), Ambrose Chapel, Everest (narrator), Les Miserables, The Haunting, Star Wars: Episode I-The Phantom Menace, Omagh the Legacy: Clarie and Stephen's Story (voice), Gun Shy, Endurance: Shackleton's Legendary Antarctic Expedition (voice), Journey into Amazing Caves (voice), Gangs of New York, Star Wars: Episode 2 - Attack of the Clones (voice), K-19: The Widowmaker, Love Actually, Kinsey (Golden Globe nom. 2005), Kingdom of Heaven, Batman Begins, Breakfast on Pluto, The Chronicles of Narnia: The Lion, the Witch and the Wardrobe (also voice), The White Rose, Seraphim Falls, Taken, The Chronicles of Narnia: Prince Caspian (voice), The Other Man, The Red Circle, Five Minutes of Heaven, The Red Circle, Chloe, After.Life, What's Wrong with Virginia, Clash of the Titans, The A-Team, Lincoln, The Next Three Days, The Chronicles of Narnia: The Voyage of the Dawn Treader (voice), Selma, Unknown White Male.
TELEVISION: *Movies:* Arthur the King, Hold the Dream, Sworn to Silence, Sweet As You Are, The Man Who Came to Dinner (host), Martin Luther (narr.), Across the Water (BBC), Xavier (narr.). *Mini-series:* A Woman of Substance, Ellis Island, If Tomorrow Comes, Evolution (narr.). *Series:* Liberty's Kids (voice). *Documentaries/Specials:* Out of Ireland, A Leap of Faith, Lumière and Company, Who Is Alan Smithee?, The Great War and the Shaping of the 20th Century, Nobel Peace Prize Concert (host), Patrick (narrator), Coral Reef Adventure (short), Everest (short), Omagh the Legacy: Claire and Stephen's Story, The Maze, The Greeks: Crucible of Civilization, Inside the Space Station (narr.), The Greeks (mini-series), Journey Into Amazing Caves, Revenge of the Whale (narr.), Imaginary Witness: Hollywood and the Holocaust, Patrick (narr.). *Guest:* More than 127 appearances.

NEILL, SAM
Actor. r.n. Nigel Neill. b. Northern Ireland, Sept. 14, 1947. Raised in New Zealand. e. U. of Canterbury. In repertory before joining N.Z. National Film Unit, acting and directing documentaries and shorts. 1992, awarded the O.B.E. for his services to acting. Co-directed, co-wrote and appeared in New Zealand documentary Cinema of Unease: A Personal Journey by Sam Neill.
PICTURES: Sleeping Dogs (debut, 1977), The Journalist, My Brilliant Career, Just Out of Reach, Attack Force Z, The Final Conflict, Possession, Enigma, Le Sang des Autres, Robbery Under Arms, Plenty, For Love Alone, The Good Wife, A Cry in the Dark (Australian Film Inst. Award), Dead Calm, The French Revolution, The Hunt for Red October, Until the End of the World, Hostage, Memoirs of an Invisible Man, Death in Brunswick, Jurassic Park, The Piano, Sirens, Rudyard Kipling's The Jungle Book, In the Mouth of Madness, Country Life, Restoration, Victory, Event Horizon, The Revengers' Comedies, The Horse Whisperer, My Mother Frank, Molokai: The Story of Father Damien, Bicentennial Man, The Magic Pudding (voice), Jurassic Park 3, The Zookeeper, Dirty Deeds, Wimbledon, Yes, Irresistible, Angel, Telepathy, How to Change in 9 Weeks, Dean Spanley, Daybreakers, Skin, Under the Mountain, Daybreakers, Ice, Legend of the Guardians: The Owls of Ga'Hoole (voice).
TELEVISION: *Movies:* Ivanhoe, The Country Girls, Robbery Under Arms, Strong Medicine, Leap of Faith, Fever, One Against the Wind (Golden Globe nom. 1992), Family Pictures, In Cold Blood, Merlin (Emmy nom.; Golden Globe nom. 1998), Sally Hemings: An American Scandal, Submerged, Framed, Stiff (also prod.), The Brush-Off (dir. & prod. only), Merlin's Apprentice. *Mini-series:* Kane & Abel, Amerika, Doctor Zhivago, Reilly: Ace of Spies (Golden Globe nom. 1985), Mary Bryant, The Triangle, Iron Road, To the Ends of the Earth, Iron Road. *Series:* The Sullivans, The Tudors, Happy Town, Crusoe. *Documentaries/Specials:* Telephone Etiquette (also dir., writer, editor), Cinema of Unease: A Personal Journey by Sam Neill (also dir., writer), Forgotten Silver (also dir.), Numero Bruno (as himself), Hyperspace, SuperCroc, Colin McCahon: I Am, Gelibolu, Gallipoli. *Guest:* More than 74 appearances.

NELLIGAN, KATE
Actress. r.n. Patricia Colleen Nelligan. b. London, Ontario, Canada, March 16, 1950.
THEATRE: Barefoot in the Park, A Streetcar Named Desire, Playboy of the Western World, Private Lives, Plenty, Serious Money, Spoils of War, Bad Habits.
PICTURES: The Romantic Englishwoman, Dracula, Mr. Patman, Eye of the Needle, Without a Trace, The Mystery of Henry Moore, Eleni, Frankie and Johnny (BAFTA Award), The Prince of Tides (Acad. Award nom.), Shadows and Fog, Fatal Instinct, Wolf, Margaret's Museum, How to Make an American Quilt, Up Close and Personal, U.S. Marshals, Rape: A Crime of War (documentary, narrator), Stolen Moments, Boy Meets Girl, The Cider House Rules, Premonition.
TELEVISION: *Movies*: The Arcata Promise, The Count of Monte Cristo, The Lady of the Camellias, Measure for Measure, Victims, Kojak: The Price of Justice, Love and Hate: The Story of Colin and Joanne Thatcher, Three Hotels, Old Times, Terror Stalks the Class Reunion, The Diamond Fleece, Liar-Liar: Between Father and Daughter, Shattered Trust: The Shari Karney Story, In Spite of Love, Million Dollar Babies, A Mother's Prayer, Captive Heart: The James Mink Story, Calm at Sunset Calm at Dawn, Love is Strange, Swing Vote, Blessed Stranger: After Flight 111, Walter and Henry, In From the Night. *Mini-series:* Thérèse Raquin, Golden Fiddles, A Wrinkle in Time, Human Cargo. *Series:* The Onedin Line, Eleventh Hour. *Documentaries: As Narrator:* Marcel Proust: A Writer's Life, Into the Deep (short), Rape: A Crime of War, Stolen Moments.

NELSON, BILL
Executive. e. Pace University, B.B.A. degree in accounting and finance; Pace University, M.B.A. Nelson also completed Harvard University's Program for Management Development. From 1975-1979, served as an audit supervisor for Ernst & Young, a public accounting firm in New York where he became a CPA. Worked for Time Inc. five years as a director, External Reporting and Risk Management. Nelson joined HBO in May 1984 as v.p. & asst. controller, responsible for overseeing the financial aspects of HBO's general management, international finance and sale and marketing groups. In July 1985, he was named v.p. & controller; promoted to senior v.p. & CFO Sept. 1991. In April 1994, he was made executive v.p., adding the areas of information technology, business affairs and technology operations to his responsibilities in February 2000. Nelson became COO in July 2002 and was elevated to current position, chairman & CEO, in June 2007. HBO, one of the largest premium television companies, operates multiple premium networks in the United States, branded joint ventures and On Demand services internationally as well as other ancillary businesses. Nelson also is a Vietnam combat veteran, having served with the US Army's 101st Airborne Division. Currently, he is a member of the American Institute of Certified Public Accountants and the New York State Society of Certified Public Accountants.

NELSON, CRAIG T.
Actor. b. Spokane, WA, April 4, 1946. Began career as writer/performer on Lohman and Barkley Show in Los Angeles. Teamed with Barry Levinson as a comedy writer. Wrote for Tim Conway Show, Alan King TV special; guest appearances on talk shows and Mary Tyler Moore Show. Produced series of 52 half-hour films on American artists, American Still. Returned to L.A. in 1978 and acting career.
PICTURES: And Justice for All (debut, 1979), Where the Buffalo Roam, Private Benjamin, Stir Crazy, The Formula, Poltergeist, Man Woman and Child, All the Right Moves, The Osterman Weekend, Silkwood, The Killing Fields, Poltergeist II, Red Riding Hood, Action Jackson, Rachel River, Me and Him, Troop Beverly Hills, Turner & Hooch, I'm Not Rappaport, Ghosts of Mississippi, The Devil's Advocate, Wag the Dog, Top of the World, The Skulls, All Over Again, The Incredibles (voice), The Family Stone, Blades of Glory, The Proposal, The Company Men, Soul Surfer.
TELEVISION: *Movies:* Diary of a Teenage Hitchhiker, Rage, Promise of Love, Inmates: A Love Story, Chicago Story, Paper Dolls, Alex: The Life of a Child, The Ted Kennedy Jr. Story, Murderers Among Us: The Simon Wiesenthal Story, Extreme Close-Up, The Josephine Baker Story, The Switch, The Fire Next Time, Ride With the Wind (also co-writer), Probable Cause, Take Me Home Again, If These Walls Could Talk, The Huntress, Dirty Pictures *Mini-series*: Drug Wars: The Camarena Story, To Serve and Protect, The Fifty, Creature, Family Shield, *Series*: Call to Glory, Coach (Emmy Award, 1992, 2 other noms.; 4 Golden Globe noms.), The District, Parenthood, My Name Is Earl, CSI: NY. *Documentaries:* The Ultimate Driving Challenge (host), The Fifty (narr.). *Guest:* More than 70 appearances.

NELSON, JUDD
Actor. b. Portland, ME, Nov. 28, 1959. e. Haverford/Bryn Mawr College Studied acting at Stella Adler Conservatory. NY theatre includes Carnal Knowledge.
PICTURES: Making the Grade (debut, 1984), Fandango, The Breakfast Club, St. Elmo's Fire, Blue City, Transformers (voice), From the Hip, Relentless, Far Out Man, New Jack City, The Dark Backward, Primary Motive, Entangled, Conflict of Interest, Caroline at Midnight, Hail Caesar, Every Breath (also s.p.), Flinch, Circumstances Unknown, Blackwater Trail, Steel,

Endsville, Light It Up, The Big Beat Heat, Falcon Down, The Cure for Boredom, Jay and Silent Bob Strike Back, Dark Asylum, Deceived, White Rush, The Freediver, Lethal Eviction, TV: The Movie, Nevermore, Netherbeast Incorporated, The I Scream Man, The Caretaker, Little Hercules in 3-D, Dirty Politics, Boondock Saints II: All Saints Day, A Single Woman, Buds, Fight or Flight, Endure, Mayor Cupcake, Here & Now.
TELEVISION: *Movies*: Billionaire Boys Club (Golden Globe nom. 1988), Hiroshima: Out of the Ashes, Conflict of Interest, Blindfold: Acts of Obsession, Circumstances Unknown, Cabin by the Lake, Mr. Rock 'n' Roll, The Spiral Staircase, The New Adventures of Spin and Marty: Suspect Behavior, Return to Cabin by the Lake, Strange Frequency, Lost Voyage, Santa Jr., Cybermutt, Three Wise Guys, The Black Hole, The Kidnapping, Infected, Brookwood Sleazebags (also exec. prod.). *Series*: Suddenly Susan. *Guest:* More than 58 appearances.

NELSON, LORI
Actress. r.n. Dixie Kay Nelson. b. Santa Fe, NM, Aug. 15, 1933. e. Canoga Park H.S. Started as child actress, photographer's model before film debut in 1952.
THEATRE: The Pleasure of His Company, Who Was That Lady I Saw You With, Affairs of Mildred Wilde, Sweet Bird of Youth, Picnic, 'Night Mother.
PICTURES: Ma and Pa Kettle at the Fair (debut, 1952), Bend of the River, Francis Goes to West Point, All I Desire, All-American, Walking My Baby Back Home, Tumbleweed, Underwater, Destry, Revenge of the Creature, I Died a Thousand Times, Sincerely Yours, Mohawk, Day the World Ended, Pardners, Hot Rod Girl, Ma and Pa Kettle at Waikiki, Gambling Man, Untamed Youth, Outlaw's Son, Mom Can I Keep Her?, Back to the Black Lagoon (documentary), The Naked Monster.
TELEVISION: *Movies:* Secret Sins of the Father. *Series*: How to Marry a Millionaire. *Special*: The Pied Piper of Hamelin.

NELSON, TRACY
Actress, Singer, Dancer. b. Santa Monica, CA, Oct. 25, 1963. e. Bard Coll. Daughter of late singer-actor Rick Nelson. Sister of singers Matthew & Gunnar Nelson. Studied acting in England.
THEATRE: Grease (Nat'l touring co. & B'way).
PICTURES: Yours Mine and Ours (debut, 1968), Maria's Lovers, Down and Out in Beverly Hills, Chapters, The Night Caller, The Bus Stop, The Perfect Tenant, The Perfect Nanny, Home the Horror Story, Fangs, Dumb Luck, Miracle At Sage Creek, Polar Opposites.
TELEVISION: *Movies*: Glitter, Pleasures, The Drug Knot, Katie's Secret, Tonight's the Night, If It's Tuesday It Still Must Be Belgium, Fatal Confessions: A Father Dowling Mystery, Highway Heartbreaker, Perry Mason: The Case of the Reckless Romeo, No Child of Mine, Ray Alexander: A Taste for Justice, For Hope, Touched by Evil, Ray Alexander: A Menu for Murder, The Promise, Her Perfect Spouse, A Killer Upstairs, The Rival, A Grandpa for Christmas. *Series*: Glitter, Square Pegs, Glitter, Father Dowling Mysteries, A League of Their Own, Snowy River: The McGregor Saga, Melrose Place.

NELSON, WILLIE
Composer, Singer, Actor. b. Abbott, TX, April 30, 1933. Worked as salesman, announcer, host of country music shows on local Texas stations; bass player with Ray Price's band. Started writing songs in the 60's; performing in the 70's; and is a six-time Grammy Award winner.
PICTURES: *Composer and/or Singer:* Puzzle (short), Renaldo and Clara, The Electric Horseman (also actor), Coal Miner's Daughter, Honeysuckle Rose (also actor, Academy Award nom. 1981), Ruckus, Songwriter (also actor), Sweet Dreams, Trespasses, Red-Headed Stranger (also actor, producer), Doc Hollywood, My Cousin Vinny, A Perfect World, Forrest Gump, The Big Green, The Long Kiss Goodnight, Michael, Gone Fishin' (also actor), Switchback, Bride of Chucky, Little Boy Blues, Space Cowboys, Shrek, World Traveler, The Rookie, Stevie, Brokeback Mountain, Broken Bridges, W.. *Actor:* Thief, Barbarosa, Dust to Dust, Starlight, Wag the Dog, Half Baked, Dill Scallion (cameo), Austin Powers: The Spy Who Shagged Me (cameo), Freedom Highway: Songs that Shaped a Century (documentary), Stardust, The Journeyman, The Country Bears (as himself), The Big Bounce, The Dukes of Hazzard, Angel from Montgomery, Fighting with Anger (also exec. prod.), Blonde Ambition, Shoot Out of Luck (also exec. prod.), The Boom Boom Room, Surfer Dude, Fields of Fuel, Beer for My Horses, The Watermelon, W., Zombieland, Legion, Valentine's Day, The Crazies, Get a Job.
TELEVISION: *Movies*: *Actor:* Coming Out of the Ice, The Last Days of Frank and Jesse James, Stagecoach (also composer & exec. prod.), Once Upon a Texas Train, Baja Oklahoma, Where the Hell's That Gold?!!?, Pair of Aces, Another Pair of Aces, Wild Texas Wind, Big Dreams & Broken Hearts: The Dottie West Story, Outlaw Justice, The Long Kill, CD Highway, The Dukes of Hazzard: The Beginning. *Series:* Trailer Court Justice (comp.). *Documentaries/Specials:* Willie Nelson—Texas Style (also prod.), America: A Tribute to Heroes, Korean War Stories, Farm Aid: The Tenth Anniv. Concert, Farm Aid '96 (documentary, himself & exec. prod.), many others. *Guest:* More than 240 appearances.

NEMEC, CORIN
Actor. r.n. Joseph Charles Nemec IV. b. Little Rock, AR, Nov. 5, 1971. Began acting in commercials at age 13.
PICTURES: Tucker: The Man and His Dream, Solar Crisis, Drop Zone, Operation Dumbo Drop, The War at Home, Mojave Moon, Quality Time, The First to Go, Goodbye America, Legacy, Hussy: Life is NIce 2000, Foreign Correspondents, Shadow Hours, Killer Bud, Free, Sit and Spin (short), Raging Sharks, Parzania, Gangsta Rap: The Glockumentary (co-prod.), RoboDoc (also assoc. prod.), The American Standards, Nuclear Family (also prod.).
TELEVISION: *Movies*: What's Alan Watching?, I Know My First Name is Steven (Emmy nom. 1989), For the Very First Time, My Son Johnny, The Lifeforce Experiment, Father's Day, Silencing Mary, Blackout, My Brother's Keeper, McBride: Murder Past Midnight, S.S. Doomtrooper, The Mars Shuttle Murders, The Sea Beast, House of Bones. *Mini-series*: The Stand. *Series*: Webster, Cadets, Parker Lewis Can't Lose, Stargate-SG1, Ghost Whisperer, Star-ving.

NERO, FRANCO
Actor. r.n. Franceso Spartanero. b. Parma, Italy, Nov. 23, 1942. e. Univ. La Bocconi, Milan.
PICTURES: Celestina (Made at Your Service; debut, 1964), The Deadly Diaphanoids, I Knew Her Well, Wild Wild Planet, The Third Eyes, The Bible, The Tramplers, Django, The Avenger, Hired Killer, The Brute and the Beast, Mafia, Camelot (Golden Globe nom. 1968), L'uomo l'Orgoglio la Vendetta, Island of Crime, The Mercenary, The Day of the Owl, A Quiet Place in the Country, The Battle of Neretva, Detective Belli, Sardinia: Ramsom, Companeros, Tristana, The Virgin and the Gypsy, Drop Out!, Confessions of a Police Commissioner, Killer From Yuma, Redneck, The Monk, The Vacation, Pope Joan, Deaf Smith and Johnny Ears, The Fifth Day of Peace, The Aquarian, High Crime, Blood Brothers, Cry Onion, The Anonymous Avenger, Challenge to White Fang, Death Drive, Violent Breed, Submission, The Last Days of Mussolini, Force Ten From Navarone, The Man With Bogart's Face, The Visitor, Shark Hunter, Blue-Eyed Bandit, Danzig Roses, Day of the Cobra, The Falcon, The Salamander, Sahara Cross, Enter the Ninja, Mexico in Flames, Querelle, Wagner, Sweet Country, The Girl, Garibaldi the General, Race to Danger, Marathon, Django Strikes Again, Top Line, Silent Night, Young Toscanini, The Betrothed, The Magistrate, Heart of Victory, The Repenter, The Forester's Sons, Die Hard 2, Brothers and Sisters, Crimson Down, Oro, Deep Blue, The Lucona Affair, Babylon Complot, A Breath of Life, Jonathan of the Bears, Conflict of Interest, The Dragon's Ring, Talk of Angels, The Secret Lies Within, La Voce del sanque (The Call of Blood), Uninvited, Winds of Passion, Chimera, Sacra Corona, Megiddo: The Omega Code 2, White Smoke, The Innocent Sleep, 8. Todsünde: Das Toskana-Karussell, Die, The King and Me, Two Families, Bastardi, Bathory, Albakiara, Liebling Mord ist mein Geschäft, Killing Is My Business, Rasputin, various others in Europe and USA.
TELEVISION: *Movies*: The Legend of Valentino, 21 Hours at Munich, The Pirate, Young Catherine, David, The Versace Murder, Das Babylon Komplott, Il Deserto di fuoco, St. Paul, The Uncrowned Heart, Summer Solstice, The Holy Family. *Mini-series*: The Last Days of Pompeii, Desideria, The Return of Sandokan, Bella Mafia, Painted Lady, Crociati, Love Lies Passion, Four Seasons. *Series:* Gil Angeli dell'isola verde, Augustine: The Decline of the Roman Empire. *Guest:* More than 74 appearances.

NETTER, DOUGLAS
Executive, Producer. b. Seattle, WA. 1955-57, gen. mgr. Todd A.O.; 1958-60, Sam Goldwyn Productions; 1961-67, formed own co. representing producers; 1968-69, Jalem Productions; 1969-75, exec. v.p. & COO MGM Studios. Founded Rattlesnake Productions in 1978.
PICTURES: The Ambushers (assoc. prod.), Mr. Ricco (prod.), The Wild Geese (co-prod.), Babylon 5: The Lost Tales - Voices in the Dark (video).
TELEVISION: *Movies: Prod.:* Louis L'Amour's The Sacketts, Wild Times, Roughnecks, Siringo, *Exec. Prod.:* The Buffalo Soldiers, Louis L'Amour's The Cherokee Train, Captain Power and the Soldiers of the Future, Babylon 5, Babylon 5: In the Beginning, Thirdspace, Babylon 5: The River of Souls, Babylon 5: A Call to Arms, Babylon 5: The Legend of the Rangers. Dan Dare: Pilot of the Future (series). *Series: Exec. Prod.:* Babylon 5, Hypernauts, Crusade, Five Mile Creek (Australian-based TV series for Disney Channel), *Documentaries/Specials:* The Wild West (prod., Emmy nom. 1993).

NEUFELD, MACE
Producer. b. New York, NY, July 13, 1928. e. Yale. Started as professional photographer, before becoming prod. asst. at Dumont Television Network. Wrote musical material for performers incl. Sammy Davis Jr., Dorothy Loudon, Ritz Brothers, etc., and theme for Heckle and Jeckle animated series. In 1951, formed independent TV prod. and personal mgmt. co. ProducedTV programs for Dick Van Dyke, Elaine May and Mike Nichols. Formed independent production co. with Nichols and Buck Henry. In 1980, created Neufeld-Davis Prods. with Marvin Davis. Formed Neufeld/Rehme Prods. with Robert G. Rehme in 1989; Mace Neufeld Prods., 1997. On B'way, prod. Flying

Karamazov Brothers show. Voted Producer of the Year by NATO/ShoWest, 1992.
PICTURES: *Producer*: The Frisco Kid, The Aviator, Transylvania 6-5000, The Hunt for Red October, Flight of the Intruder, Necessary Roughness, Patriot Games, Beverly Hills Cop III, Clear and Present Danger, The Saint, The General's Daughter, Bless the Child, The Sum of All Fears, Asylum, Sahara, Invictus. *Associate producer:* Damien: Omen II, The Final Conflict. *Executive producer:* The Omen, The Funhouse, No Way Out, Blind Faith, Lost In Space, Black Dog, Gods and Generals.
TELEVISION: *Movies: Executive producer:* Angel on My Shoulder, A Death in California, Omen IV: The Awakening, For the Future: The Irvine Fertility Scandal, Woman Undone, Escape: Human Cargo, Love and Treason. *Producer*: Gridlock. *Mini-series:* East of Eden (Emmy nom. 1981). *Series: Executive producer:* Quark (co-exec. prod.), Lightning Force. *Documentaries/Specials:* The Magic Planet, The Flying Karamazov Brothers, Blind Faith.

NEUWIRTH, BEBE
Actress. b. Newark, NJ, Dec. 31, 1958. e. Juilliard. Started as chorus dancer.
THEATRE: *NY*: Little Me, Dancin', Upstairs at O'Neal, The Road to Hollywood, Sweet Charity (Tony Award, 1986), Showing Off, Damn Yankees. *Tour*: A Chorus Line. Regional: Just So, Kicks (also choreog.), Chicago. *London*: Kiss of the Spider Woman.
PICTURES: Say Anything... (debut 1989), Green Card, Bugsy, Paint Job, Malice, Jumanji, All Dogs Go to Heaven (voice), The Adventures of Pinocchio, The Associate, The Faculty, Celebrity, An All Dogs Christmas Carol (voice), Summer of Sam, Getting to Know All About You, Liberty Heights, Tadpole, Le Divorce, How To Lose a Guy in 10 Days, The Big Bounce, Game 6, Adopt a Sailor, Fame.
TELEVISION: *Movies*: Without Her Consent, Unspeakable Acts, Dash and Lilly (Emmy nom. 1999), Cupid and Cate. *Mini-series*: Wild Palms. *Series*: The Edge of Night, Cheers (2 Emmy Awards), Aladdin (voice), All Dogs Go to Heaven: The Series (voice), Deadline, The X's, Frasier, Law & Order: Trial by Jury. *Documentaries/Specials:* Stand Up Comics Take a Stand (as herself), My Favorite Broadway: The Leading Ladies, My Favorite Broadway: The LoveSongs. *Guest*: More than 81 appearances.

NEVINS, SHEILA
Executive. b. New York, NY, April 6, 1939. e. Studied dance at the High School of the Performing Arts; B.A., English, Barnard College, 1960. Master's in Fine Arts (Three Arts Fellow), directing, Yale Univ., 1963. (She was one of only two women in the directing program.) She was an instructor for "Adventures in English," United States Information Agency: Television & Film Service, 1960s; producer, "The Great American Dream Machine," for National Educational Television (precursor to PBS), 1971-1973; field producer, "The Reasoner Report," ABC News, 1973; writer, Time-Life Films, 1973-1975; writer and producer, Children's Television Workshop, 1975-1976; producer, "Who's Who," CBS, 1977-1978. Nevins interviewed in 1979 for a new position at a fledgling cable channel—Home Box Office. She was hired as HBO's dir., documentary programming. She started with historical biographies and consumer reports, but soon realized everyone had a story to tell. Was dir., documentary programming, HBO, 1979-1982. She took a brief hiatus from HBO from 1982-1986, during which she created TV's first reality-sex show, "Eros America," and won a Peabody for producing the children's show "Braingames." Returned to HBO in 1986 as v.p., documentary and family programming, (1986-1995); senior v.p., original programming, HBO, 1995-1999; executive v.p., original programming, HBO, 1999-2003; pres., documentary and family programming, HBO-2004-present. In 1998 Nevins received the Lifetime Achievement Award from the International Documentary Association. She was inducted into the Broadcasting and Cable Hall of Fame in 2000. Nevins has personally amassed 54 Emmy® nominations and 22 wins, including 2008's "White Light/Black Rain: The Destruction of Hiroshima and Nagasaki" for Exceptional Merit in Nonfiction Filmmaking, "Classical Baby" for Outstanding Children's Program, "When the Levees Broke: A Requiem in Four Acts" for Exceptional Merit in Nonfiction Filmmaking; and "Ghosts of Abu Ghraib" for Outstanding Nonfiction Special in 2007, and many more. Most recently, Nevins received the Governors Award at the Creative Arts Emmy® Awards in 2009. The Academy of Television Arts & Sciences' Board of Governors bestows the honor to those who have made a substantial impact and demonstrated the extraordinary use of television.

NEWELL, MIKE
Director. b. St. Albans, Hertfordshire, England, March 28, 1942. e. Cambridge U. Took directorial training course at Granada Television.
PICTURES: *Director:* Big Soft Nelly Mrs. Mouse, The Awakening, Bad Blood, Dance With a Stranger, The Good Father, Amazing Grace and Chuck, Soursweet, Enchanted April, Into the West, Four Weddings and a Funeral (DGA nom. 1995), An Awfully Big Adventure, Donnie Brasco, Pushing Tin, Mona Lisa Smile, Harry Potter and the Goblet of Fire, Sealand, Love in the Time of Cholera, Prince of Persia: The Sands of Time. *Executive producer*: Photographing Fairies, 200 Cigarettes, Best Laid Plans, High Fidelity, Traffic, I Capture the Castle.
TELEVISION: *Movies: Director:* The Kindness of Strangers, The Visitors, Them Down There, The Gamekeeper, 69 Murder: The Blood Relation, Blood Relations, Death of a Dog, Arthur Wants You For A Sunbeam, Allergy, Mrs. Mouse Are You Within?, Just Your Luck, The New Word, A Face Of Your Own, Barbara's Wedding, Twelve Pound Look, The Melancholy Hussar, Silver Wedding, Ms. or Jill and Jack, The Gift of Friendship, Baa Baa Black Sheep, The Childhood Friend, Of the Fields Lately, Mrs. Ackland's Ghost, Lost Yer Tongue? Jack Flea's Birthday Celebration, Brassneck, The Boundary, The Midas Connection, Ready When You Are Mr. McGill, Buffet, Honey, The Fosdyke Saga, Charm, The Man in the Iron Mask, The Mayor's Charity, The Mayor's Charity, Little Girls Don't, Mr. and Mrs. Bureaucrat, Destiny, Birth of a Nation, Blood Feud, The Whole Hog, Common Ground, Jo. *Series: Director*: Thirty-Minute Theatre, Spindoe, Big Breadwinner Hog, Budgie, The Adventures of Don Quick, The Guardians, The Man from Haven, Wessex Tales, Smith and Jones in Small Doses, The Branch (also exec. prod.). *Series: Executive producer:* Huff (also pilot).

NEWHART, BOB
Actor, Comedian. b. Chicago, IL, Sept. 5, 1929. e. Loyola U. In Army 2 yrs., then law school; left to become copywriter and accountant. Acted with theatrical stock co. in Oak Park; hired for TV man-in-street show in Chicago. Recorded hit comedy album for Warner Bros., The Button-Down Mind of Bob Newhart (Grammy Award, 1960), followed by two more successful albums. Did series of nightclub engagements and then acquired own TV variety series in 1961. Grand Marshall: Tournament of Roses Parade, 1991. Inducted into TV Hall of Fame, 1993.
PICTURES: Hell Is for Heroes (debut, 1962), Hot Millions, Catch-22, On a Clear Day You Can See Forever, Cold Turkey, The Rescuers (voice), Little Miss Marker, First Family, The Rescuers Down Under (voice), In & Out, Legally Blonde 2: Red, White and Blonde, Elf.
TELEVISION: *Movies*: Thursday's Game, Marathon, The Entertainers, The Sports Pages, The Librarian: Quest for the Spear, The Librarian: Return to King Solomon's Mines, The Librarian: The Curse of the Judas Chalice (Emmy nom. 2009). *Series*: The Bob Newhart Show (1961-62, variety, Emmy nom. 1962), The Entertainers, The Bob Newhart Show (1972-78, sit-com, 2 Golden Globe noms.), Newhart (3 Emmy noms.; 4 Golden Globe noms.), Bob, George & Leo, Bob Newhart: In Search of Comedy (host, exec. prod.), ER (Emmy nom. 2004 as guest). *Guest:* More than 130 appearances.

NEWMAN, ALFRED S.
Executive. b. Brooklyn, NY, Nov. 16. e. NYU. Public relations for Equitable Life Insurance, Trans World Airlines prior to joining Columbia Pictures in 1968 as writer in publicity dept.; named New York publicity mgr., 1970; national publicity mgr., 1972; joined MGM as East adv.-pub. dir., 1972; named director of adv., pub. and promotion, 1974; named v.p., worldwide adv., pub.; promo., 1978; v.p., pub.-promo., MGM/UA, 1981. 20th Century-Fox as v.p. adv.-pub.-promo. for TV & corporate, 1984-85; joined Rogers & Cowan as sr. v.p. and head of film and corporate entertainment dept., 1985; named exec. v.p., 1987; Oct. 1988 named pres. and CEO Sterling Entertainment Co. and exec. v.p. worldwide marketing of parent co. MCEG; formed Newman & Associates, 1989; joined Hill and Knowl Entertainment as founding mng. dir., 1990. Re-opened Newman and Assocs., 1991. Joined Imax Corp. as Sr V.P. & Head of Worldwide Communications, 1996. Formed and is Pres. of Newman & Company, a public relations firm, 1998. Serves on Motion Picture & Television Fund (MPTF) Fund Board of Directors.

NEWMAN, BARRY
Actor. b. Boston, MA, Nov. 7, 1938. e. Brandeis U.
PICTURES: Pretty Boy Floyd (debut, 1960), The Moving Finger, The Lawyer, Vanishing Point, The Salzburg Connection, Fear is the Key, City on Fire, Amy, Daylight, Brown's Requiem, Goodbye Lover, The Limey, Bowfinger, G-Men From Hell, Jack the Dog, Good Advice, True Blue, 40 Days and 40 Nights, Manhood, What the Bleep Do We Know!? (doc.), What the Bleep!?: Down the Rabbit Hole (doc.).
TELEVISION: *Movies*: Night Games, Sex and the Married Woman, King Crab, Fantasies, Having It All, Second Sight: A Love Story, Fatal Vision, My Two Loves, The Mirror Crack'd (BBC), Der Blaue Diamont, MacShayne: Winner Takes All. *Series*: Petrocelli (Emmy nom. 1975, Golden Globe nom. 1976), Nightingales.

NEWMAN, DAVID
Composer, Conductor. b. Los Angeles, CA, Mar. 11, 1954. e. USC (masters degree). Son of late composer Alfred Newman. Cousin of composer Randy Newman. Music director at Robert Redford's Sundance Institute.
PICTURES: Critters, Vendetta, The Kindred, My Demon Lover, Malone, Dragnet, Throw Momma from the Train, Pass the Ammo, Bill & Ted's Excellent Adventure, Disorganized Crime, The Brave Little Toaster, Heathers, Little Monsters, Gross Anatomy, The War of the Roses, Madhouse, Fire Birds, The Freshman, DuckTales: The Movie, Mr. Destiny, Meet the Applegates, The Marrying Man, Talent for the Game, Don't Tell Mom the Babysitter's Dead, Bill & Ted's Bogus Journey, Rover Dangerfield, Paradise, Other People's

Money, The Runestone, The Mighty Ducks, Hoffa, The Sandlot, Coneheads, The Air Up There, My Father the Hero, The Flintstones, The Cowboy Way, Tommy Boy, Operation Dumbo Drop, The Phantom, Mathilda, The Nutty Professor, Out to Sea, Anatastasia (Academy Award nom. 1998), 1001 Nights, Never Been Kissed, Brokedown Palace, Bowfinger, Galaxy Quest, The Flintstones in Viva Rock Vegas, Nutty Professor II: The Klumps, Duets, Bedazzled, 102 Dalmatians, Dr. Dolittle 2, The Affair of the Necklace, Death to Smoochy, Ice Age, Life or Something Like It, Scooby Doo, How To Lose a Guy in 10 Days, Daddy Day Care, Duplex, The Cat in the Hat, Scooby Doo 2: Monsters Unleashed, Are We There Yet?, Man of the House, Kicking & Screaming, Monster-in-Law, Serenity, Marigold: An Adventure in India, I Married a Witch, Cheaper by the Dozen 2 (soundtrack music from Ice Age, Norbit, Welcome Home, Roscoe Jenkins, The Spirit, My Life in Ruins, Alvin and the Chipmunks: The Squeakquel, Crazy on the Outside, The Spy Next Door, Die Konferenz der Tiere.
TELEVISION: *Movies:* Spotlight on Location: Nutty Professor II: The Klumps, The Flamingo Rising, Scooby-Doo! The Mystery Begins.

NEWMAN, EDWIN
News Correspondent. b. New York, NY, Jan. 25, 1919. Joined NBC News in 1952, based in N.Y. since 1961. Reports news on NBC-TV and often assigned to anchor instant specials. Has been substitute host on Today, appeared on Meet the Press and has reported NBC News documentaries. *Series host:* Edwin Newman Reporting, The Nation's Future, What's Happening to America, Comment, Speaking Freely, Television (PBS series), Weekly World News, My Fellow Americans.

NEWMAN, GARY
Executive. b. Los Angeles, CA, May 24, 1954. e. Yale. American Studies, 1976. J.D., USC Law Center 1980. Joined Lillick, McHose & Charles as attorney, 1980-1983. Newman joined Columbia Pictures Television as counsel in 1983-1984 before moving to NBC in 1984 where he held a series of positions over six years as manager, director and then vice president of business affairs. Twentieth Century Fox Television (TCFTV) in 1990 as senior V.P., business and legal affairs. From 1992 to 1999 he served as executive V.P., business and legal affairs. Became Co-President, TCFTV in November of 1999, a position he shares with friend Dana Walden. Since that time, Newman and Walden have been responsible for overseeing operations for the studio and have been instrumental in building TCFTV into a leading supplier of programming across all media from broadcast and cable television to syndication, mobile and broadband. TCFTV is home to writers and producers working in the industry including Seth MacFarlane, Shawn Ryan, Greg Garcia, Ryan Murphy, David E. Kelly, Goward Gordon and Joel Surnow and they maintain an exclusive relationship with Imagine Television. In addition to its roster of live action scripted comedies and dramas which under their tenure included "24," "Bones," "How I Met Your Mother," "Prison Break," "My Name Is Earl," "Raising Hope" and "Glee." TCFTV has become the leader in animated comedies for prime time with such hits as "The Simpsons," and "Family Guy," among others. Newman and Walden also oversee the studio's Licensing and Merchandizing division for their entertainment properties in areas including publishing, videogames, promotions, e-commerce, retail and themed entertainment. They also drive the Licensing and Merchandising efforts of Fox Film, Fox Sports and the Microsoft Game Studios hit, "Halo." In 2002, Newman and Walden pioneered the now common industry practice of releasing television series on DVD immediately following each broadcast season, at the time, a revolutionary idea that helped drive the Fox drama "24" to blockbuster status in its second season. Newman and Walden have also been at the forefront of developing new production models, creating fox21 in 2004, a production house devoted to empowering writers to produce their "passion projects" by rethinking conventional television production economics. They have also produced a range of innovative content based on the studio's hit franchises for the worldwide wireless market. Gary Newman and Dana Walden were named Chairmen of TCFTV in 2007, a position they hold today.

NEWMAN, LARAINE
Actress. b. Los Angeles, CA, Mar. 2, 1952. Founding member of comedy troupe the Groundlings.
THEATRE: *B'way*: Fifth of July.
PICTURES: Tunnelvision (debut, 1976), American Hot Wax, Wholly Moses!, Stardust Memories (cameo), Perfect, Sesame Street Presents Follow That Bird (voice), Invaders from Mars, Problem Child 2, Witchboard II, Coneheads, The Flintstones, Jingle All the Way, Chow Bella, Alone in the Woods, Rusty: A Dog's Tale, Naked in the Cold Sun, Demolition University, Fear and Loathing in Las Vegas, I'm Losing You, The Modern Adventures of Tom Sawyer, Just Add Water, The Flunky, Endsville, Monsters, Inc. (voice), Jimmy Neutron Boy Genius (voice), The Wild Thornberrys Movie (voice), Finding Nemo, (voices), Ice Age: The Meltdown (voices), Cars (voices), The Wild (voice), Barnyard (voice), Happily N'Ever After (voices), The Twenty, Surf's Up (voice), Horton Hears a Who! (voice), The Haunted World of El Superbeasto (voice), Ponyo (voice, English version), The Twenty, Up (voice), Cloudy with a Chance of Meatballs (voice).
TELEVISION: *Movies*: Her Life as a Man, This Wife for Hire, My Town, Radiant City, Van Stone: Tour of Duty, Problem Child. *Series*: Manhattan Transfer, Saturday Night Live (Emmy nom. 1979), Canned Film Festival, As Told by Ginger, Danny Phantom, The Goode Family, Metalocalypse. *Voices:* Histeria!, The Rugrats: All Growed Up, Oswald, Grim & Evil, Pinky and the Brain, Sylvester & Tweetie, The Tick, Rapunzel, Superman, Wonder Woman, The Buzz on Maggie. *Documentaries/Specials*: Steve Martin's Best Show Ever, SNL Remembers John Belushi, Saturday Night Live: TV Tales, The Lily Tomlin Special, Bob Ray Jane Laraine & Gilda, Saturday Night Live: 25th Anniversary. *Guest*: More than 110 appearances.

NEWMAN, NANETTE
Actress, Writer. b. Northampton, Eng., May 29, 1934. m. prod.-dir.-writer Bryan Forbes. Ent. films in 1946 and TV in 1951.
AUTHOR: God Bless Love, That Dog, Reflections, The Root Children, Amy Rainbow, Pigalev, Archie, Christmas Cookbook, Summer Cookbook, Small Beginnings, Bad Baby, Entertaining with Nanette Newman and Her Daughters, Charlie the Noisy Caterpillar, Sharing, The Pig Who Never Was, ABC, 123, Cooking for Friends, Spider the Horrible Cat, There's a Bear in the Bath, Karmic Mothers, There's a Bear in the Classroom, The Importance of Being Ernest, The Earwig, Take 3 Cooks.
PICTURES: The Personal Affair, The League of Gentlemen, The Rebel, Twice Around the Daffodils, The L-Shaped Room, The Wrong Arm of the Law, Of Human Bondage, Seance on a Wet Afternoon, The Wrong Box, The Whisperers, Deadfall, The Madwoman of Chaillot, Captain Nemo and the Underwater City, The Raging Moon, The Stepford Wives, It's a 2'2" Above the Ground World, Man at the Top, International Velvet, Restless Natives, The Mystery of Edwin Drood.
TELEVISION: *Movies:* Jessie, The Endless Game, The Glorious Days, The Wedding Veil, Broken Honeymoon, At Home, Trial by Candlelight, Diary of Samuel Pepys, Faces in the Dark. *Mini-series:* Prometheus: The Life of Balzac. *Series:* Fun Food Factory (presenter & writer), Stay With Me Till Morning, Let There Be Love, Late Expectations.

NEWMAN, RANDY
Composer, Singer. b. Los Angeles, CA, Nov. 28, 1943. Nephew of musicians Lionel and Alfred Newman. Studied music at UCLA. Debut album: Randy Newman Creates Something New Under the Sun. Was music director on film Performance. Began writing songs and scores for films in 1971 with The Pursuit of Happiness. Composed opera, Faust. 4 Grammy Awards and 9 noms. for movie soundtracks.
PICTURES: *Composer:* Pursuit of Happiness, Cold Turkey, Herbstkatzen, Ragtime (2 Academy Award noms.; Golden Globe nom. 1982), The Natural (Academy Award nom. 1985), Gotcha!, Huey Long (documentary), Nine 1/2 Weeks, Three Amigos (also co-wrote s.p.), Overboard, Her Alibi, Major League, Parenthood (Academy Award nom.; Golden Globe nom. 1990), Avalon (Academy Award nom.; Golden Globe nom. 1991), Awakenings, The Paper (Academy Award nom. 1995), Maverick, James and the Giant Peach (Academy Award nom. 1997), Forest Gump, Toy Story (also orchestrator & singer, 2 Academy Award noms.; Golden Globe nom. 1996), Michael, Cat's Don't Dance, The Full Monty, Pleasantville (Academy Award nom. 1999), A Bug's Life (Academy Award nom.; Golden Globe nom. 1999), Babe: Pig in the City (Academy Award nom. 1999), Toy Story 2 (Academy Award nom.; Golden Globe nom. 2000), You've Got Mail, Meet the Parents (Academy Award nom. 2001), Monsters, Inc. (Academy Award 2002, 1 other nom.), Seabiscuit, Mr 3000, Meet the Fockers, Domino, Fun with Dick and Jane, Cars (Academy Award nom. 2007), Bonneville (soundtrack performer), Leatherheads, Toy Story 3 (soundtrack writer & performer), The Princess and the Frog (also conductor, Academy Award nom. 2010, 1 other nom.), Percy Jackson & the Olympians: The Lightning Thief (soundtrack writer).
TELEVISION: *Movies: Composer:* Every Man A King (song), The Hollywood Soundtrack Story (host). *Series: Composer:* The Marshall Chronicles, Cop Rock (Emmy Award 1991), Monk (theme song & singer, Emmy Award 2004). *Documentaries/Specials:* Funny You Don't Look 200: A Constitutional Vaudeville (singer), Party at the Palace: The Queen's Concerts Buckingham Palace (song composer); also singer/composer of songs used at various award specials.

NEWMAR, JULIE
Actress. r.n. Julie Newmeyer. b. Hollywood, CA, Aug. 16, 1933. e. UCLA. Studied acting with Lee Strasberg at the Actor's Studio. Holds patent for special panty hose design. Appeared in George Michael video Too Funky.
THEATRE: *NY*: Silk Stockings, Li'l Abner, The Marriage-Go-Round (Tony Award, 1959). Other: In the Boom Boom Room (L.A.), Damn Yankees, Irma La Douce, Guys and Dolls, Dames at Sea, Stop the World, The Women.
PICTURES: Just for You (debut, 1952), Seven Brides for Seven Brothers, The Rookie, Li'l Abner, The Marriage-Go-Round, For Love or Money, McKenna's Gold, The Maltese Bippy, Hysterical, Streetwalkin', Love Scenes, Body Beat, Nudity Required, Ghosts Can't Do It, Oblivion, Oblivion 2: Backlash, If...Dog...Rabbit.
TELEVISION: *Movies*: McCloud: Who Killed Miss U.S.A.?, The

Feminist and the Fuzz, A Very Missing Person, Columbo: Double Shock, Terraces, Return to the Batcave: The Misadventures of Adam and Burt. *Series*: My Living Doll (Golden Globe nom. 1965), Batman (frequent guest; as Catwoman). *Guest*: More than 60 appearances.

NEWTON-JOHN, OLIVIA
Actress, Singer. b. Cambridge, Eng. Sept. 26, 1948. Brought up in Melbourne, Australia, where won first talent contest at 15, winning trip to England. Stayed there 2 yrs. performing as part of duo with Australian girl singer Pat Carroll (Farrar) in cabarets and on TV. Started recording; several hit records. Became a regular guest on TV series, It's Cliff Richard. Gained worldwide prominence as singer, winning several Grammys and other music awards. 1983 opened Koala Blue, U.S. Clothing Stores featuring Australian style clothes and goods. 1999 Emmy Award for Original Song for As the World Turns.
PICTURES: *Actress:* Toomorrow (debut, 1970, also singer), Grease (also singer, Golden Globe nom. 1979), Xanadu (also singer), Two of a Kind (also singer, composer), It's My Party (also lyricist, singer, composer), Sordid Lives (also lyricist, singer, composer), 1 a Minute, Score: A Hockey Musical (also composer). *Singer:* Funny Things Happen Down Under, Hurry Up or I'll be 30, The Other Side of the Mountain, Whisper of the Heart, Face/Off, The Wedding Planner, The Guru, The Land Before Time X: The Great Longneck Migration (also lyricist), Meet the Fockers, Monster House, Good Luck Chuck (singer).
TELEVISION: *Movies*: *Actress:* A Mom for Christmas (also singer), A Christmas Romance (also lyricist, singer, composer), Snowden on Ice (voice), The Christmas Angel: A Story on Ice, The Wilde Girls (also exec. prod.), Kaleidoscope. *Series:* It's Cliff Richard, Sordid Lives: The Series. *Documentaries/Specials*: Various self-titled musical specials, The Golbal Forum, Madonna: Truth or Dare (as herself), Mariah Carey: Around the World, Not Under My Roof, The Main Event, The Magic 7, Big River Man (exec. prod.), others. *Guest:* More than 185 appearances.

NICHOLAS, DENISE
Actress, Writer. b. Detroit, MI, July 12, 1946. e. USC.
THEATRE: Performances with the Free Southern Theatre, The Negro Ensemble Company, Crossroads Theatre Co., New Federal Theatre, Los Angeles Theatre Company, Media Forum.
AUTHOR: Buses (play), Augustine, Myrtle, Marty and Me (short story, Essence Magazine), various published articles and poetry.
PICTURES: Ghost Dad, Capricorn One, A Piece of the Action, Let's Do It Again, Blacula, The Soul of Nigger Charley, Marvin and Tige, Ghost Dad, Ritual, Proudly We Served.
TELEVISION: *Movies*: Five Desperate Women, Ring of Passion, The Big Stuffed Dog, The Sophisticated Gents, Valley of the Dolls, And the Children Shall Lead, Heart and Soul, Vindicated: A Mother's War, On Thin Ice: The Tai Babilonia Story, In the Heat of the Night (appearances in six movies in role of Harriet Delong), The Rockford Files: Murder and Misdemeanors. *Series*: Room 222 (3 Golden Globe noms.), Baby I'm Back, In the Heat of the Night (also wrote 6 episodes). *Guest*: More than 56 appearances.

NICHOLS, MIKE
Director, Producer, Performer. r.n. Michael Igor Peschkowsky. b. Berlin, Germany, Nov. 6, 1931. m. news correspondent Diane Sawyer. e. U. of Chicago. Member of Compass Players; later teamed with Elaine May in night clubs.
THEATRE: *Director*: Barefoot in the Park (Tony Award), The Knack, Luv (Tony Award), The Odd Couple, The Apple Tree, The Little Foxes, Plaza Suite (Tony Award), Uncle Vanya, The Prisoner of 2nd Avenue (Tony Award), Streamers, Comedians, The Gin Game, Drinks Before Dinner, Annie (prod. only; Tony Award), The Real Thing (2 Tony Awards), Hurlyburly, Social Security, Waiting for Godot, Elliot Loves, Death and the Maiden, Mony Python's Spamalot (Won Tony Award for best Dir. 2005).
PICTURES: *Director*: Who's Afraid of Virginia Woolf? (debut, 1966, Academy Award nom.; DGA nom. Golden Globe nom. 1967), The Graduate (Academy Award, Best Dir., 1968, Golden Globe Award, Best Dir.; DGA Award), Catch-22, Carnal Knowledge, The Day of the Dolphin, The Fortune, Gilda Live, Silkwood (also co-prod.; Academy Award nom. Best Dir.; Golden Globe nom. 1984), The Longshot (exec. prod. only), Heartburn (also prod.), Biloxi Blues, Working Girl (Academy Award nom. Best Dir., DGA nom.; Golden Globe nom. 1989), Postcards From the Edge, Regarding Henry (also prod.), The Remains of the Day (co-prod. only, Academy Award nom. 1994), Wolf, The Birdcage, Primary Colors, What Planet Are You From? (also prod.), Closer (also prod., Golden Globe nom. 2005), 1001 Nights, Charlie Wilson's War.
TELEVISION: *Movies:* The Gin Game (dir.), Wit (also exec. prod. & writer; 2 Emmy Awards for Outstanding Directing, 2001, 1 other nom.), Whoopi: Back to Broadway - The 20th Anniversary (orig. stage production dir., orig. stage production prod.). *Mini-series:* Angels in America (also exec. prod.; DGA Award, Outstanding Directorial Achievement, 2004; 2 Emmy Awards for Outstanding Mini-series & Emmy for Outstanding Directing, 2003; PGA Golden Laurel Awards-TV Producer of the Year Award in Longform and Visionary Award, 2003), The Thorns. *Series:* Laugh LIne (panelist), Family (exec. prod. only, Emmy nom. 1977), Dismissed (exec. prod.). *Documentaries/Specials*: B'way, An Evening with Mike Nichols and Elaine May.

NICHOLS, NICHELLE
Actress. b. Robbins, IL, Dec. 28, 1936. Started singing and dancing with Duke Ellington and his band at age 16. Was appointee to the bd. of dirs. of the National Space Institute in the 1970's; recruited women and minority astronauts for Space Shuttle Program. Received NASA's distinguished Public Service Award. Member of the bd. of govs. of the National Space Society. One of the original founders of KWANZA Foundation. Awarded star on Hollywood Walk of Fame (1992). *Autobiography*: Beyond (1994). Novels: Saturn's Child (1995), Saturna's Quest (1996).
THEATRE: Horowitz and Mrs. Washington, Reflections (one woman show). Nominated for Sarah Siddons Award for performances in Kicks and Company, The Blacks.
PICTURES: Porgy and Bess, Mr. Buddwing, Made in Paris, Truck Turner, Star Trek: The Motion Picture, Star Trek II: The Wrath of Khan, Star Trek III: The Search for Spock, Star Trek IV: The Voyage Home, The Supernaturals, Star Trek V: The Final Frontier, Star Trek VI: The Undiscovered Country, Trekkies, Snow Dogs, Surge of Power, Are We There Yet?, Lady Magdalene's (exec. prod., soundtrack writer), Tru Loved, This Bitter Earth.
TELEVISION: *Movies*: Great Gettin' Up Mornin', Antony and Cleopatra, Commander Toad in Space (voice), The Adventures of Captain Zoom in Outer Space. *Series*: Star Trek, Star Trek: The Animated Adventures (voices), Gargoyles, Heroes, The Cabonauts (pilot). *Documentaries/Specials*: Moonshot: The Spirit of '69, Inside TV Land: African Americans in Television. *Guest:* More than 67 appearances.

NICHOLSON, JACK
Actor, Producer, Director, Writer. b. Neptune, NJ, April 22, 1937. Began career in cartoon department of MGM. Made acting debut in Hollywood stage production of Tea and Sympathy. Made directing debut with Drive, He Said (1971). Twelve Academy Award nominations and three wins. Recipient of American Film Institute's Life Achievement Award, 1994.
PICTURES: Cry Baby Killer (debut, 1958), Too Soon to Love, Little Shop of Horrors, Studs Lonigan, The Wild Ride, The Broken Land, The Raven, The Terror, Thunder Island (co-s.p. only), Back Door to Hell, Flight to Fury (also s.p.), Ensign Pulver, Ride in the Whirlwind (also co-prod., s.p.), The Shooting (also co-prod.), The St. Valentine's Day Massacre, Rebel Rousers, Hell's Angels on Wheels, The Trip (s.p. only), Head (also co-prod., co-s.p.), Psych-Out, Easy Rider (Academy Award nom.; Golden Globe nom. 1970), On a Clear Day You Can See Forever, Five Easy Pieces (Academy Award nom.; Golden Globe nom. 1971), Carnal Knowledge (Golden Globe nom. 1972), Drive He Said (dir., co-prod., co-s.p. only), A Safe Place, The King of Marvin Gardens, The Last Detail (Academy Award nom.; Golden Globe nom. 1974), Chinatown (Academy Award nom.; Golden Globe Award 1975), Tommy, The Passenger, The Fortune, One Flew Over the Cuckoo's Nest (Academy Award, Golden Globe Award, 1976), The Missouri Breaks, The Last Tycoon, Goin' South (also dir.), The Shining, The Postman Always Rings Twice, Reds (Academy Award nom.; Golden Globe nom. 1982), The Border, Terms of Endearment (Academy Award, Golden Globe Award 1984), Prizzi's Honor (Academy Award nom.; Golden Globe Award 1986), Heartburn, The Witches of Eastwick, Broadcast News, Ironweed (Academy Award nom.; Golden Globe nom. 1988), Batman (Golden Globe nom. 1990), The Two Jakes (also dir.), Man Trouble, A Few Good Men (Academy Award nom.; Golden Globe nom. 1993), Hoffa (Golden Globe nom. 1993), Wolf, The Crossing Guard, Mars Attacks!, The Evening Star, As Good As It Gets (Academy Award, Golden Globe Award, 1998), The Pledge, Stanley Kubrick: A Life in Pictures (doc., as himself), Velocity, About Schmidt (Academy Award nom.; Golden Globe Award 2004), Anger Management, Stuck on You, Something's Gotta Give (Golden Globe nom. 2004), The Departed (Golden Globe nom. 2007), The Bucket List, Everything You've Got.
TELEVISION: *Movie:* Elephant's Child (narr.). *Guest:* More than 148 appearances.

NICHOLSON, WILLIAM
Writer. b. England, 1948. e. Cambridge U. Was graduate trainee at BBC, becoming prod./dir./writer of over 40 documentaries.
THEATRE: Shadowlands, Map of the Heart.
PICTURES: The Vision, The March, Sarafina!, Shadowlands (Academy Award nom. 1994), Nell, First Knight, Firelight (also dir.), Grey Owl, Gladiator (Academy Award nom. 2001), The Last Castle (Re-writer), Long Walk To Freedom, Elizabeth: The Golden Age.
TELEVISION: *Movies:* Shadowlands, Sweet As You Are, Martin Luther, New World, Life Story, The Race for the Double Helix, Miss Sherri, Crime of the Century (Emmy nom. 1997). *Exec. Prod.*: Everyman, Global Report, Lovelaw.

NICITA, RICK
Executive. b. Dec. 15, 1945. e. Wesleyan U. m. agent/producer, Paula Wagner. Began career at William Morris Agency, 1968 where he worked in the Motion Picture Dept. until 1980. Joined Creative Artists Agency, 1980. Co-head, Motion Picture Dept., then Head of the Talent Dept. Resigned co-chmn., CAA 2008. Currently co-chmn. and COO Morgan Creek Productions with

founder James G. Robinson. He also serves on the American Cinematheque board as president and serves on the Motion Picture Arts Advisory Board of Interlochen Arts Academy. Nicita helped pioneer strategy of actor-based properties and prod. companies.

NICKSAY, DAVID
Executive, Producer. e. Mass., Hampshire Coll. Entered industry through Directors Guild of America's training program, apprenticing on Rich Man Poor Man and rising to second asst. dir. on Oh, God. Producer of many TV projects and theatrical films with Edgar Scherick prod. co. In 1986, joined Paramount Pictures as v.p., prod., for M.P. Group. Assoc. prod., prod. mgr.: I'm Dancing as Fast as I Can. Became sr. v.p., prod. Paramount, M.P. Group, 1987; resigned in 1989. From 1989 to 1992 was pres. and head of prod. at Morgan Creek Prods. During that time was executive producer for six of the company's films, including Robin Hood: Prince of Thieves, Pacific Heights and Young Guns II. He currently is a partner with Heliopolis Entertainment, a Los Angeles-based production company.
PICTURES: The One & Only, When I am King, Mrs. Soffel, Lucas, Young Guns II (co-exec. prod.), Pacific Heights (co-exec. prod.), Robin Hood:Prince of Thieves (exec. prod.), Freejack (exec. prod.), White Sands (exec. prod.), Stay Tuned (exec. prod.), Addams Family Values (exec. prod.), Up Close & Personal, Flubber (exec. prod.), The Negotiator (exec. prod.), The Adventures of Rocky & Bullwinkle (exec. prod.), AntiTrust, What's the Worst That Could Happen? (exec. prod.), Legally Blonde (co-prod.), A Guy Thing (prod. & unit prod. mgr.), Agent Cody Banks, Legally Blonde 2: Red White & Blonde (also unit prod. mgr), Agent Cody Banks 2: Destination London, Be Cool (also unit prod. mgr.), Married Life (exec. prod.), Step Up 2: The Streets (exec. prod., unit prod. mngr.), Surrogates (exec. prod.).
TELEVISION: Homeward Bound (assoc. prod.), Call to Glory (pilot), Little Gloria Happy at Last (Emmy nom. 1983).

NIELSEN, LESLIE
Actor. b. Regina, Sask., Canada, Feb. 11, 1926. e. Victoria H.S., Edmonton. Disc jockey, announcer for Canadian radio station; studied at Lorne Greene's Acad. of Radio Arts, Toronto and at Neighborhood Playhouse; N.Y. radio actor summer stock. Toured country in one-man show, Darrow, 1979. *Author:* The Naked Truth (1993), Leslie Nielsen's Stupid Little Golf Book (1995).
PICTURES: Ransom (debut, 1956), Forbidden Planet, The Vagabond King, The Opposite Sex, Hot Summer Night, Tammy and the Bachelor, The Sheepman, Night Train To Paris, Harlow, Dark Intruder, Beau Geste, The Plainsman, Gunfight in Abilene, The Reluctant Astronaut, Rosie!, Counterpoint, Dayton's Devils, How to Commit Marriage, Change of Mind, Four Rode Out, The Resurrection of Zachary Wheeler, The Poseidon Adventure, And Millions Will Die, Day of the Animals, Viva Knievel!, The Amsterdam Kill, City on Fire, Airplane!, Prom Night, The Creature Wasn't Nice, Wrong Is Right, Creepshow, The Patriot, Soul Man, Nightstick, Nuts, Home Is Where the Hart Is, The Naked Gun: From the Files of Police Squad!, Dangerous Curves, Repossessed, The Naked Gun 2 1/2: The Smell of Fear, All I Want for Christmas, Surf Ninjas, Naked Gun 33 1/3: The Final Insult, Dracula: Dead and Loving It, Spy Hard (also co-exec. prod.), Family Plan, Mr. Magoo, Wrongfully Accused, Camouflage, 2001: A Space Travesty, Men With Brooms, Kevin of the North, Scary Movie 3, Scary Movie 4, Music Within, Superhero Movie, An American Carol, The Naked Truth (also exec. prod., writer: book), Stan Helsing, Slam I Am (prod. only).
TELEVISION: *Movies*: See How They Run, Code Name: Heraclitus, Shadow Over Elveron, Hawaii Five-O: Cocoon, Companions in Nightmare, Trial Run, Deadlock, Night Slaves, The Aquarians, Hauser's Memory, Incident in San Francisco, Columbo: Lady in Waiting, They Call It Murder, Snatched, THe Letters, Can Ellen Be Saved, Columbo: Identity Crisis, Brinks: The Great Robbery, Little Mo, The Albertans, Institute for Revenge, Riel, The Return of Charlie Chan, OHMS, The Night the Bridge Fell Down, Cave-In!, Blade in Hong Kong, Striker's Mountain, Reckless Disregard, Fatal Confession: A Father Dowling Mystery, Nightstick, The Railway Dragon (narratory), Chance of a Lifetime, Rent-A-Kid, Harvey, Safety Patrol, Santa Who?, Noël Noël (English narrator), Lipshitz Saves the World. *Mini-series*: Backstairs at the White House, Al Oeming: Man of the North (host), Race for the Bomb. *Series*: Swamp Fox, The New Breed, Peyton Place, The Bold Ones: The Protectors, Bracken's World, Twilight Theater, Police Squad (Emmy nom. 1982), Shaping Up, Day by Day (Emmy nom. 1989), Katie and Orbie (narrator), Liography (host), Chilly Beach, Zeroman, Robson Arms. Past television includes more than 171 titles. *Documentaries/Specials:* Death of a Salesman, The Force (host, assoc. prod.). *Guest*: More than 268 appearances.

NIMOY, LEONARD
Actor, Director. b. Boston, MA, Mar. 26, 1931. e. Boston College. Joined Pasadena Playhouse. Along with active career in films, TV and stage, has been writer and photographer. Author of three books on photography and poetry, as well as autobiography, I Am Not Spock. Has also been speaker on college lecture circuit. Created comic book Primortals.
THEATRE: Full Circle, Equus, Sherlock Holmes, Vincent (also dir., writer; one-man show), Love Letters.
PICTURES: Queen for a Day, Rhubarb, Francis Goes to West Point, Them!, Satan's Satellite's (edited from serial Zombies of the Stratosphere), The Brain Eaters, The Balcony, Catlow, Invasion of the Body Snatchers, Star Trek—The Motion Picture, Star Trek II: The Wrath of Khan, Star Trek III: The Search for Spock (also dir.), Transformers: The Movie (voice), Star Trek IV: The Voyage Home (also. dir., co-story), Three Men and a Baby (dir. only), The Good Mother (dir. only), Star Trek V: The Final Frontier, Funny About Love (dir. only), Star Trek VI: The Undiscovered Country (also exec. prod., co-story), Holy Matrimony (dir. only), The Pagemaster (voice), Jellies & Other Ocean Drifters (voice), Carpati: 50 Miles, 50 Years (voice), A Life Apart: Hasidism in America (voice), Sinbad: Beyond the Veil of Mists, Trekkies, Armageddon: Target Earth (narr.), Rashi: A Light After the Dark Ages (doc., voice), Minyan in Kaifeng (documentary, voice), Atlantis: The Lost Empire (voice), Star Trek, Land of the Lost (voice).
TELEVISION: *Movies:* Star Trek, Star Trek: Where No Man Has Gone Before, Valley of Mystery, Assault on the Wayne, Baffled, Columbo: A Stitch in Crime, The Alpha Caper, The Missing Are Deadly, Seizure: The Story of Kathy Morris, A Woman Called Golda (Emmy nom. 1982), Never Forget, Bonanza: Under Attack, David, Brave New World. *Mini-series:* Marco Polo. *Series*: General Hospital, Star Trek (3 Emmy noms.), Mission: Impossible, Rod Serling's Night Gallery (dir. only), Star Trek: The Animated Adventures (voice), The Powers of Matthew Star (dir. only), Deadly Games (dir., exec. prod., creative consultant), Invasion America (voice), After They Were Famous, Fringe. *Documentaries/Specials:* Has narrated numerous tv documentaries, including In Search Of (also host, writer), Greenhouse Gamble (host), Seapower: A Global Journey (narr.) Ringers: Lord of the Fans, Star Trek: Beyond the Final Frontier (host). *Guest:* More than 226 appearances.

NIVEN, DAVID, JR.
Executive, Producer. b. London, England, Dec. 15, 1942. Son of late actor David Niven. e. Univ. of Grenoble; London Sch. of Economics. Joined William Morris Agency in Beverly Hills in 1963. Transferred same yr. to New York; over next five yrs. worked for agency's European offices in Rome, Madrid and London. 1968-72, Columbia Pictures' U.K. office as v.p. of production; 1972-76, mng. dir. and v.p. of Paramount Pictures in U.K. 1976 became indep. prod. West Coast corresp. & interviewer for Inside Edition. Appeared as actor in films Lisa, Cool Surface, and on tv series, America's Most Wanted. 1993, became chmn. of R.A.D.D. (Recording-Artists Against Drunk Driving)
PICTURES: *Producer*: The Eagle Has Landed, Escape to Athena, Monsignor, Better Late Than Never, Kidco, That's Dancing!, Pyscho Cop Returns (exec. prod.), Blue Flame (exec. prod.), Girl With the Hungry Eyes, Cool Surface (exec. prod., also actor), Rush Hour 3 (actor only).
TELEVISION: The Night They Saved Christmas (exec. prod., s.p., Emmy nom. 1985), Cary Grant: A Celebration, Minnelli on Minnelli: Liza Remembers Vincente (Emmy nom. 1987), The Wonderful Wizard of Oz. Panelist: To Tell the Truth (1991-92).

NIX, WILLIAM PATTERSON
Executive. b. Philadelphia, PA, April 10, 1948. e. Georgetown U., A.B., 1970; Antioch, M.A., 1971; Hofstra U. Sch. of Law, J.D., 1976; NYU Sch. of Law, LL.M., 1979. In 1999, joined Baker & Botts, LLP New York, NY. Formerly, V.P. Bus. Affairs, NBA Properties Inc., NY, ent. & media firm. Prior to that, was sr. v.p. of both the MPAA and Motion Picture Export Assoc. of America. Chmn. of MPAA committee on copyright and literary property matters, and COO of film industry's intellectual property protection division (1976-91). Lifetime voting member, AMPAS.

NIXON, AGNES
Writer, Producer. b. Nashville, TN, Dec. 10, 1927. e. Northwestern Sch. of Speech, Catholic U. Landed first job writing radio serial dialogue (Woman in White, 1948-51) three days after graduating from college. Became a freelance writer for TV dramatic series. Guest writer, New York Times 1968-72, and TV Guide. Trustee, Television Conference Inst., 1979-82. Received National Acad. of Television Arts & Sciences' Trustee Award, 1981; Junior Diabetic Assn. Super Achiever Award, 1982; Communicator Award for American Women in Radio and Television, 1984. Gold Plate Award, American Acad. Achievement, 1993; inducted into TV Hall of Fame, 1993. Popular Culture Lifetime Achievement Award, 1995; Public Service Award, Johns Hopkins Hospital, 1995. Humanitarian Award, National Osteoporosis Foundation, 1996. Member, Int'l Radio & TV Society; Nat'l Acad. of TV Arts & Sciences; bd. of Harvard Foundation; The Friars Club.
TELEVISION: *Series writer*: Studio One, Philco Playhouse, Robert Montgomery Presents, Somerset Maugham Theatre, Armstrong Circle Theatre, Hallmark Hall of Fame, My True Story, Cameo Theatre, Search For Tomorrow, As The World Turns, Guiding Light, Another World, The City (story consultant). *Mini-series*: The Manions of America. *Series creator-producer*: One Life to Live (Emmy nom. 1973), All My Children (7 Emmy Awards, 24 other noms.; 5 WGA Awards, 3 other noms.), Loving.

NIXON, CYNTHIA
Actress. b. New York, NY, April 9, 1966. e. Barnard Coll. Started stage career at age 14.

THEATRE: *B'way*: The Philadelphia Story (Theatre World Award), Hurlyburly, The Real Thing, The Heidi Chronicles, Angels in America: Millenium Aproaches/Perestroika, Indiscretions. *Off-B'way*: Moonchildren, Romeo and Juliet, The Balcony Scene, Servy N Bernice 4-Ever, On the Bum, The Illusion, The Scarlet Letter.
PICTURES: Little Darlings (debut, 1980), Tattoo, Prince of the City, I Am the Cheese, Amadeus, The Manhattan Project, Let It Ride, Addams Family Values, The Pelican Brief, Baby's Day Out, Marvin's Room, 'M' Word, The Out-of-Towners, Advice from a Caterpillar, Igby Goes Down, The Paper Mache Chase (short), Little Manhattan, The Babysitters, Sex and the City, Lymelife, An Englishman in New York, Sex and the City 2.
TELEVISION: *Movies*: The Private History of a Campaign that Failed, Rascals and Robbers: The Secret Adventrues of Tom Sawyer and Huck Finn, My Body My Child, Fifth of July, The Murder of Mary Phagan, The Love She Sought, Women & Wallace, Love Lies and Murder, Face of a Stranger, Papa's Angels, Stage on Screen: The Women, Warm Springs (Emmy nom.; Golden Globe nom. 2005). *Mini-series:* Tanner on Tanner. *Series:* Sex and the City (Emmy Award 2004, 2 other noms.; 4 Golden Globe noms.) Law & Order: Special Victims Unit (guest, Emmy Award 2008). *Guest:* More than 94 appearances.

NOLTE, NICK
Actor. b. Omaha, NE, Feb. 8, 1941. Attended 5 colleges in 4 yrs. on football scholarships, including Pasadena City College and Phoenix City College. Joined Actors Inner Circle at Phoenix and appeared in Orpheus Descending, After the Fall, Requiem For a Nun. Did stock in Colorado. In 1968, joined Old Log Theatre in MN and after 3 yrs. left for New York, appearing at Cafe La Mama. Went to L.A. and did plays The Last Pad and Picnic, as well as several guest spots on TV series before big break in mini-series, Rich Man Poor Man as Tom Jordache.
PICTURES: Return to Macon County (debut, 1975), The Deep, Who'll Stop the Rain, North Dallas Forty, Heart Beat, Cannery Row, 48 HRS., Under Fire, Teachers, Grace Quigley, Down and Out in Beverly Hills, Extreme Prejudice, Weeds (Golden Globe nom. 1988), Three Fugitives, New York Stories (Life Lessons), Farewell to the King, Everybody Wins, Q&A, Another 48 Hrs., Cape Fear, The Prince of Tides (Academy Award nom.; Golden Globe Award, 1992), The Player, Lorenzo's Oil, I'll Do Anything, Blue Chips, I Love Trouble, Jefferson in Paris, Mulholland Falls, Nightwatch, Mother Night, Afterglow, Affliction (Academy Award nom.; Golden Globe nom. 1999), U-Turn, Thin Red Line, Breakfast of Champions, Simpatico, The Best of Enemies, The Golden Bowl, Trixie, Investigating Sex, The Good Thief, Northfork, Hulk, Beautiful Country, Clean, Hotel Rwanda, Peaceful Warrior, The Rum Diary (also exec. prod.), Paris, je t'aime Over the Hedge (voice), Pride and Glory The Death of Harry Tobin, A Few Days in September, Off the Black, The Mysteries of Pittsburgh, The Spiderwick Chronicles, Nine Miles Down, Tropic Thunder, King Shot (also exec. prod.), Night Train, My Own Love Song, Arcadia Lost, Warrior, Cats & Dogs: The Revenge of Kitty Galore, Arthur.
TELEVISION: *Movies:* Winter Kill (pilot), The California Kid, Death Sentence, The Runaway Barge, Luck. *Mini-series:* Rich Man Poor Man (Emmy nom.; Golden Globe nom. 1977). *Series*: Adams of Eagle Lake,.Independent Lens (doc., episode Chicago 10). *Guest:* More than 58 appearances.

NOONAN, TOM
Actor, Writer. b. Greenwich, CT, Apr. 12, 1951. e. Yale.
THEATRE: Buried Child (Off-B'way debut, 1978), Invitational Farmyard, The Breakers, Five of Us, Spookhouse, What Happened Was (also writer), Wifey (also writer).
PICTURES: Heaven's Gate, Wolfen, Eddie Macon's Run, Easy Money, Best Defense, The Man with One Red Shoe, F/X, Manhunter, The Monster Squad, Collision Course, Mystery Train, Robocop 2, Last Action Hero, What Happened Was...(also composer, writer, dir., editor), The Wife, (also composer, writer, dir., editor), Heat, Phoenix, The Astronaut's Wife, Wang Dang (also writer, dir.), The Photographer, The Opportunists, The Pledge, Bullet in the Brain, Knockaround Guys, The Egoists, Madness and Genius, Hair High (voice), Seraphim Falls, Snow Angels, Follow the Prophet, The Alphabet Killer, Synecdoche, New York, The House of the Devil, Algona.
TELEVISION: *Movies*: *Actor*: Rage, The 10 Million Dollar Getaway, Heaven & Hell: North & South Book III. *Writer*: Red Wind. *Mini-series*: North & South III. *Series: Actor*: The Beat, Damages. *Writer:* Monsters (also dir.).

NORMAN, BARRY
Writer, Film Reviewer, Presenter. b. London, England, Aug. 21, 1933. Early career as show business editor London Daily Mail; then was humorous columnist for The Guardian; also worked for The Times and other publications as a freelancer before getting his big break into TV. Entered TV as writer, presenter of film review series FILM 1972-81 and 1983-98. In 1982, he left FILM to be a presenter for the arts program Omnibus. In 1998 Norman was lured to work for Sky where he made the show Film Night. *Writer/host:* Norman has written and presented four acclaimed series on The Hollywood Greats and a series on The British Greats in 1980. Best-selling books on The Hollywood Greats, Film Greats and Movie Greats followed each TV series. Radio work incl.: Going Places, The News Quiz, Breakaway, The Chip Shop, Countdown (host). He currently is a public speaker available through The Gordon Poole Entertainment Agency in the U.K.
AUTHOR: Norman's books include: To Nick A Good Body, End Product, Tales of the Redundance Kid, A Series of Defeats, Sticky Wicket, The Bird Dog Tapes, Death on Sunset, The Good Night In Guide, 100 Best Films of the Twentieth Century, Barry Norman's Video Guide, The Radio Times Family Video Guide and his memoir And Why Not?

NORRIS, CHUCK
Actor. r.n. Carlos Ray Norris. b. Ryan, OK, Mar. 10, 1940. World middle weight karate champion 1968-74. Owner of LA karate schools which led to film career.
PICTURES: The Wrecking Crew (debut, 1969), Slaughter in San Francisco, Return of the Dragon, The Student Teachers, Breaker! Breaker!, Good Guys Wear Black, Game of Death, A Force of One, The Octagon, An Eye for an Eye, Silent Rage, Forced Vengeance, Lone Wolf McQuade, Missing in Action, Missing in Action 2, Code of Silence, Invasion U.S.A. (also co-s.p.), Delta Force, Firewalker, Braddock: Missing in Action III (also co-s.p.), Hero and the Terror, Delta Force II, The Hitman, Sidekicks (also co-exec. prod.), Hellbound, Top Dog, Forest Warrior, The Bells of Innocence, Birdie and Bogey (exec. prod.), The Cutter.
TELEVISION: *Movies*: Logan's War: Bound by Honor, The President's Man, The President's Man: A Line in the Sand (also exec. prod.), Walker, Texas Ranger: Trial by Fire (also exec. prod.). *Series*: Chuck Norris's Karate Kommandos (animated series, voice), Walker: Texas Ranger (also co-exec. prod.), Sons of Thunder (writer, exec. prod.). *Documentaries/Specials*: The Ultimate Stuntman: A Tribute to Dar Robinson (host), Bruce Lee and Kung Fu Mania. *Guest:* More than 60 appearances.

NORTON, EDWARD
Actor, Producer, Director. b. Boston, MA, Aug. 18, 1969. e. Yale University. Board member of Edward Albee's Signature Company. Works as a board member of the Enterprise Foundation in New York.
PICTURES: *Actor:* Primal Fear (Academy Award nom.; Golden Globe Award 1997), The People vs. Larry Flynt, Everyone Says I Love You, Rounders, Out of the Past (voice), American History X (Academy Award nom. 1999), Fight Club (narrator), Keeping the Faith (also dir. and prod.), The Score, Death to Smoochy, Frida, Red Dragon, The 25th Hour (also co-prod.), The Italian Job, Dirty Work (doc., exec. prod.), Down in the Valley (also prod.), Kingdom of Heaven, The Illusionist, The Painted Veil (also prod.), Pride and Glory, The Incredible Hulk (also s.p.), The Invention of Lying, Leaves of Grass (also prod.), By the People: The Election of Barack Obama (doc., prod.), Stone. *Guest:* More than 85 appearances.

NOSSECK, NOEL
Director, Producer. b. Los Angeles, CA, Dec. 10, 1943. Began as editor with David Wolper Prods; made documentaries then turned to features.
PICTURES: *Director*: Best Friends (also prod.), Las Vegas Lady, Youngblood, Dreamer, King of the Mountain, What Kind of Mother Are You?.
TELEVISION: *Movies*: Return of the Rebels, The First Time, Night Partners, Summer Fantasies, A Different Affair, Stark, A Mirror Image, Roman Holiday, Full Exposure: The Sex Tapes Scandal, Follow Your Heart, Opposites Attract, A Mother's Justice, The Laurie Samuels Story, Born Too Soon, French Silk, The Sister-In-Law, Down Out and Dangerous, Justice For Annie: A Moment of Truth Movie, No One Would Tell, Tornado!, The Secret, Nightscream, The Fury Within, Silent Predators, Another Woman's Husband. *Series*: Adam-12, Downtown, Studio 5-B, Burke's Law, Charmed, Hunter. *Pilots*: Aaron's Way, Half 'n Half, Fair Game, Heaven Help Us.

NOURI, MICHAEL
Actor. b. Washington, DC, Dec. 9, 1945. e. Avon Old Farms, Rollins Coll., Emerson Coll. Studied for theatre with Larry Moss and Lee Strasberg. New York stage debut in Forty Carats, 1969.
THEATRE: Forty Carats, Victor/Victoria.
PICTURES: Goodbye Columbus (debut, 1969), Gangster Wars, Flashdance, Gobots (voice), The Imagemaker, The Hidden, Thieves of Fortune, Little Vegas, Fatal Sky, Total Exposure, Black Ice, Captain America, Psychic, No Escape No Return, Fortunes of War, Da Vinci's War, American Yakuza, Inner Sanctum II, Lady in Waiting, To the Limit, Hologram Man, Overkill, Picture This, Finding Forrester, Carman: The Champion, Lovely & Amazing, Terminal Error, Klepto, High Roller: The Stu Ungar Story, Searching for Bobby D, The Terminal, The Boynton Beach Club, Last Holiday, Invincible, Scarlet Cross, The Proposal, Easy Rider: The Ride Back, Sinatra Club.
TELEVISION: *Movies*: Contract on Cherry Street, Fun and Games, Secrets of a Mother and Daughter, Spraggue, Between Two Women, Rage of Angels: The Story Continues, Quiet Victory: the Charlie Wedemeyer Story, Shattered Dreams, Danielle Steel's Changes, In the Arms of a Killer, Exclusive, The Sands of Time, The Hidden 2, Eyes of Terror, Victor/Victoria, Between Love and Honor, This Matter of Marriage, Second

Honeymoon, 61*. *Mini-series*: The Last Convertible, Too Rich: The Secret Life of Doris Duke. *Series*: Beacon Hill, Search for Tomorrow (Emmy nom. 1976), The Curse of Dracula, The Gangster Chronicles, Bay City Blues, Downtown, Love and War, The Young and the Restless, Damages, The O.C., Army Wives. *Guest:* More than 66 appearances.

NOVELLO, DON
Writer, Comedian, Actor. b. Ashtabula, OH, Jan. 1, 1943. e. U. of Dayton, B.A., 1964. Best known as Father Guido Sarducci on Saturday Night Live. Was advertising copywriter before writing and performing on The Smothers Brothers Comedy Hour (1975). Writer for Van Dyke and Company, and writer-performer on Saturday Night Live 1978-80. *Producer:* SCTV Comedy Network (1982) and performer-writer on B'way in Gilda Radner—Live From New York (1979), as well as filmed version (Gilda Live!). *Recordings*: Live at St. Douglas Convent, Breakfast in Heaven. *Author*: The Lazlo Letters: The Amazing Real-Life Actual Correspondence of Lazlo Toth, American!, The Blade, Citizen Lazlo.
PICTURES: Gilda Live!, Head Office, Tucker: The Man and His Dream, New York Stories (Life Without Zoe), The Godfather Part III, Casper (cameo), One Night Stand, Jack, Touch, Nothing Sacred, Just the Ticket, The Adventures of Rocky & Bullwinkle, Just One Night, Atlantis: The Lost Empire (voice), Rent Control, Factory Girl.
TELEVISION: *Movies:* La Pastorela. *Mini-series:* Tales of the City. *Series:* Saturday Night Live (3 Emmy noms. for writing), SCTV Network (3 Emmy noms.) *Documentaries/Specials/:* Father Guido Sarducci Goes to College, Van Dyke and Company (Emmy nom. for writing 1977) The Vatican Inquirer—The Pope Tour. *Series:* Histeria!

NOYCE, PHILLIP
Director. b. Griffith, New South Wales, Australia, April 29, 1950. Began making films at school and university. Made first short film at age 15, Better to Reign in Hell. In 1980, became part-time mgr., Sydney Filmmaker's Co-operative and in 1973 was selected for Australian Nat'l Film School in Sydney, for year-long training program which resulted in shorts, Good Afternoon, Caravan Park, Castor and Pollux, God Knows Why But It Works, and 60-minute film Backroads.
PICTURES: Backroads (also prod., s.p.), Newsfront (also s.p.; Australian Acad. Awards for best dir. & s.p., 1978), Heatwave (also co-s.p.), Echoes of Paradise, Dead Calm, Blind Fury, Patriot Games, Sliver (also cameo), Clear and Present Danger, The Saint, The Bone Collector, Blast Off (also s.p.), The Repair Shop, Rabbit Proof Fence (also prod.), The Quiet American, Welcome to São Paulo (documentary; dir. segment "Marca Zero" & also cinematographer), Hotstuff, Catch a Fire, Foolproof (exec. prod.), Salt.
TELEVISION: *Movie:* Lights Out (exec. prod.). *Mini-series*: The Dismissal (also writer), Cowra Breakout (also writer), Vietnam (writer). *Series:* The Hitchhiker, Nightmare Cafe (dir. pilot), Tru Calling (episode dir. and exec. prod. of pilot), Brotherhood, Lights Out (exec. prod.).

NOZOE, YUKI
Executive. Began career with Sony Pictures Entertainment (SPE) in 1972. Director, senior v.p. & gen. mgr., Sony Electronics Consumer Video Co., 1986; exec. v.p. & senior v.p. of mktg., Consumer Products Group, Sony Electronics, Inc., 1993-96, where he was instrumental in developing and standardizing DVD format; co-president, SPE, 1999. Nozoe, a long-time strategist for Sony, corporate executive v.p. for Sony Corporation and co-pres. of Digital Entertainment. Currently president and chief executive for I & S BBDO, Japan.

NUNN, BILL
Actor. b. Pittsburgh, PA, Oct. 20, 1953. Teamed with friend Al Cooper as member of comedy team Nunn and Cooper in nightclubs, 1980-83. On stage with various theatrical companies including the Alliance, the Academy, Theatrical Oufit, Just Us Theatre.
THEATRE: T-Bone and Weasel, Split Second, Home, A Lesson From Aloes, A Soldier's Play, Macbeth, The River Niger, Fences.
PICTURES: School Daze, Do the Right Thing, Def by Temptation, Cadillac Man, Mo' Better Blues, New Jack City, Regarding Henry, Sister Act, National Lampoon's Loaded Weapon 1, The Last Seduction, Canadian Bacon, Things to Do in Denver When You're Dead, Candyman 2, Money Train, Mr. & Mrs. Loving, BulletProof, Extreme Measures, Kiss the Girls, Mad City, He Got Game, Ambushed, The Legend of 1900, The Tic Code, Foolish, The Hungry Bachelors Club, Lockdown, Spider-Man, People I Know, Runaway Jury, Spider-Man 2, Idlewild, Randy and the Mob, The Land, Firehouse Dog, Spider-Man 3.
TELEVISION: *Movies:* The Littlest Victims, The Affair, Carriers, Quicksilver Highway, Ellen Foster, Always Outnumbered, Stolen From the Heart, The Price of a Broken Heart, A Raisin in the Sun. *Series*: Traps, The Job, October Road (pilot). *Specials:* Native Strangers, Dangerous Heart, War Stories, A Yankee in King Arthur's Court.

O

O'BRIEN, CONAN
Performer, Writer. b. Brookline, MA, Apr. 18, 1963. e. Harvard, B.A., magna cum laude, 1985. Served two years as pres. of Harvard Lampoon before landing work as TV writer for The Simpsons, Saturday Night Live (Emmy Award, 1989), Winner WGA Award 1996-2003. Since 1993 had been host of NBC's Late Night With Conan O'Brien. June 2009 O'Brien became host of NBC's, The Tonight Show, taking over from Jay Leno who moved his show to an earlier time slot. Prod. of pilot Lookwell. 2010, O'Brien moved to Cable Network, TBS after Leno resumed hosting The Tonight Show at it's original time slot. Owner of Production Company, Conaco.
TELEVISION: *Movies:* Lookwell (writer, prod.), Beat Cops (exec. prod.), Robot Chicken: Star Wars (voice), Man of Your Dreams (exec. prod.), Telepathetic (exec. prod.). *Series:* Not Necessarily the News, Saturday Night Live (writer, 1987-1991, Emmy Award 1989,2 other noms.), The Simpsons (writer, prod.), NBC's Late Night With Conan O'Brien (host, writer, prod., Emmy Award, 2007, 13 Emmy noms.; 6 WGA Awards, 5 other noms.), Andy Barker, P.I. (writer, creator, exec. prod.), The Tonight Show with Conan O'Brien (host, consult. prod., writer 2009-2010, WGA nom. 2010), Outlaw (exec. prod.). *Documentaries/Specials:* Saturday Night Live: 25th Anniv. (writer). *Host*: Emmy Awards, 2002. *Guest*: More than 107 appearances.

O'BRIEN, MARGARET
Actress. r.n. Angela Maxine O'Brien. Los Angeles, CA, Jan. 15, 1938. Screen debut at 3 in Babes on Broadway (1941). Awarded special Academy Award as best child actress, 1944. Voted one of 10 best money-making stars in Motion Picture Herald-Fame Poll 1945-46.
PICTURES: Babes on Broadway (debut, 1941), Journey for Margaret, Dr. Gillespie's Criminal Case, Lost Angel, Thousands Cheer, Madame Curie, Jane Eyre, The Canterville Ghost, Meet Me in St. Louis, Music for Millions, Our Vines Have Tender Grapes, Bad Bascomb, Three Wise Fools, Unfinished Dance, Tenth Avenue Angel, The Big City, The Secret Garden, Little Women, Her First Romance, Two Persons Eyes (Jap.), Agente S3S Operazione Uranio (It.), Glory, Heller in Pink Tights, Anabelle Lee, Diabolic Wedding, Amy, Morella.
TELEVISION: *Movies*: Maggie, Death in Space, Split Second to an Epitaph, Elf Sparkle Meets Christmas the Horse, Elf Sparkle and the Special Red Dress. *Mini-series:* Testimony of Two Men. *Documentaries/Specials:* Hollywood's Children, The Story of Lassie, Homeward Bound, others. *Guest*: More than 86 appearances.

OBST, LYNDA
Producer. b. New York, NY, Apr. 14, 1950. e. Pomona College, 1972; attended grad school and studied Philosophy at Columbia Univ. After Columbia, she began her career as the editor/author of The Rolling Stone's History of the Sixties. Former editor for New York Times Magazine, 1976-79; then exec. at Polygram Pictures, 1979-81; Geffen Films, 1981-83, co-prod. at Paramount, 1983-85; prod. for Walt Disney, 1986, before moving over to Columbia. In 1989 Obst formed Lynda Obst Productions, a feature films prod. co. The company has a first-look deal with Paramount Pictures, and the co. is based at Paramount Pictures in Hollywood, CA. Obst is on the bd. of trustees for Pomona College, where she was awarded an Honorary Degree of Doctor of Fine Arts. She is a regular contributor to the New York Times Book Review, LA Times Book Review and does the annual Oscar coverage for Slate.com with film critic David Edelstein. Obst has taught a Master's screenwriting class at USC and a course in producing at the Univ. of Texas. She has also taught several courses at The Learning Annex, where she is one of their most requested lecturers and has given seminars on the film industry around the world; is a regular moderator and speaker at the annual LA Times Book Festival.
AUTHOR: Hello, He Lied and Other Truths From the Hollywood Trenches. The book debuted at #1 on the LA Times Best Seller list was recently adapted into a documentary which aired on AMC. *Co-Author*: Dirty Dreams (with Carol Wolper).
PICTURES: *Associate producer:* Flashdance. *Producer*: The Adventures in Babysitting, Heartbreak Hotel, The Fisher King, This Is My Life, Bad Girls, One Fine Day, Hope Floats, The Siege, The Wishbones, Someone Like You, Abandon, How to Lose a Guy in 10 Days, The Invention of Lying. *Executive producer*: Sleepless in Seattle, Bad Girls, Contact.
TELEVISION: *Mini-series:* The '60s (exec. prod.; Emmy nom. 1999). *Documentaries / Specials:* Hello, He Lied & Other Truths From the Hollywood Trenches (exec. prod., host, writer of book).

OCHS, MILLARD L.
Exhibitor. e. U. of Akron. Beginning in July 1946, worked as an usher, projectionist and concession manager and later as cinema manager for his father Lee A. Ochs, while in college. After graduation, became city mgr. for RKO Stanley Warner Theatre, Cincinnati, OH; followed by district mgr. for AMC, covering SW territories of AZ and S. CA. 1985, while with AMC, transferred to England and began developing the multiplex concept at Milton Keynes; over next three years, AMC opened eight locations in

England, then sold their interest to Univ./Paramount Studio Joint Venture of United Cinema Int'l.; stayed on with UCI until June 1993. Joined WB International Cinemas as exec. v.p.; July 1994, promoted to pres. and began working with Ira Stiegler, v.p., architecture & planning, to introduce the Looney Tune Themed lobby. Ochs, continues as president, WB International Cinemas today, expanding WB's cinema presence in overseas markets including managemant of the Mann Theatres chain in the U.S. He oversaw an agreement for Warner Brothers International Cinemas to be the first overseas cinema company to enter the Chinese market. Its 2004 agreement with Guangzhou Jinyi Film and Television Investment Co Ltd advances the development of 10 state-of-the-art multiplex theatres in Guangzhou and other cities in China, including Beijing, Xiamen, Hangzhous, Fuzhou and Xi'an. Awards have included: Exhibitor of the Year, Cinema Expo in Amsterdam, June 1996; co-recipient, Exhibitor of the Year, ShoWest, March 1998. The 2007 RAAM Awards honored Ochs for outstanding contribution to the UK and Irish cinema exhibition industry.

O'CONNELL, JACK
Producer, Director, Writer. b. Boston, MA. e. Princeton U., Harvard Business School. After being a creative group head in all media and doing 500 TV commercials entered feature films working with Fellini on La Dolce Vita, then asst. dir. to Antonioni on L'Avventura.
PICTURES: *Writer/Prod./Dir.:* Greenwich Village Story, Revolution, Christa (aka Swedish Flygirls), Up the Girls Means Three Cheers for Them All, That Hippie Revolution.

O'CONNOR, DAVID
Executive. e. Dartmouth College. Joined Creative Artists Agency 1983 as agent trainee and was soon promoted to motion picture literary agent. In 1996, created the CAA Foundation to involve the entertainment community in philanthropy, developing public/private partnerships at local and national levels. Currently, partner and managing dir., CAA. Serves on bd. of overseers, Dartmouth College and National Council for the Environmental Defense Fund. In April 2000, he received the David Niven Award for his contribution to Project ALS (Lou Gehrig's disease).

O'CONNOR, GLYNNIS
Actress. b. New York, NY, Nov. 19, 1955. Daughter of ABC News prod. Daniel O'Connor and actress Lenka Peterson. e. State U., NY at Purchase. Stage includes Domestic Issues (Circle Rep., NY, 1983), The Taming of the Shrew (Great Lakes Shakespeare Fest.), The Seagull (Mirror Rep.).
PICTURES: Jeremy (debut, 1973), Baby Blue Marine, Ode to Billy Joe, Kid Vengeance, California Dreaming, Those Lips Those Eyes, Night Crossing, Melanie, Johnny Dangerously, New Best Friend, Graduation, The Trouble with Cali, P.J.
TELEVISION: *Movies*: The Chisholms, Someone I Touched, All Together Now, The Boy in the Plastic Bubble, Little Mo, My Kidnapper, My Love, The Fighter, Love Leads the Way, Why Me?, Sins of the Father, The Deliberate Stranger, To Heal a Nation, Death in Small Doses, Past the Bleachers, Father's Day, Saint Maybe, Ellen Foster. *Mini-series*: Black Beauty. *Series*: As the World Turns, Sons and Daughters, Law & Order.

O'CONNOR, KEVIN J.
Actor. b. Nov. 15, 1964. e. DePaul Univ.'s Goodman Sch. of Drama. On stage in Colorado Catechism (NY), El Salvador (Chicago).
PICTURES: One More Saturday Night, Peggy Sue Got Married, Candy Mountain, The Moderns, Signs of Life, Steel Magnolias, Love at Large, F/X 2, Hero, Equinox, No Escape, Color of Night, Virtuosity, Lord of Illusions, Canadian Bacon, Hit Me, Amistad, Gods & Monsters, Chicago Cab, Deep Rising, If...Dog...Rabbit, Chill Factor, The Mummy, Van Helsing, Kettle of Fish, Seraphim Falls, Flight of the Living Dead, There Will Be Blood, G.I. Joe: The Rise of Cobra.
TELEVISION: *Movies*: The Caine Mutiny Court Martial, The Love Bug, Black Cat Run. *Series*: Birdland, The Others, Gideon's Crossing, The Beast. *Special*: Tanner 88.

O'CONNOR, PAT
Director. b. Ardmore, Ireland, 1943. After working in London at odd jobs (putting corks in wine bottles, paving roads), came to U.S. e. UCLA, B.A. Studied film and TV at Ryerson Institute in Toronto. 1970, trainee prod., dir. with Radio Telefis Eireann. 1970-78 prod. and dir. over 45 TV features and current affairs documentaries. (The Four Roads, The Shankhill, Kiltyclogher, One of Ourselves, Night in Ginitia). A Ballroom of Romance won BAFTA Award in 1981.)
PICTURES: Cal (debut, 1984), A Month in the Country, Stars and Bars, The January Man, Fools of Fortune, Circle of Friends, Sacred Hearts, Inventing the Abbotts, Dancing at Lughnasa, Sweet November, Private Peaceful.
TELEVISION: *Movies*: Force of Duty, Zelda.

O'DONNELL, CHRIS
Actor. b. Winetka, IL, June 26, 1970. e. Boston College.
THEATRE: The Man Who Had All the Luck (B'way).
PICTURES: Men Don't Leave (debut, 1990), Fried Green Tomatoes, School Ties, Scent of a Woman (Golden Globe nom. 1993), The Three Musketeers, Blue Sky, Circle of Friends, Mad Love, Batman Forever, The Chamber, In Love and War, Batman & Robin, Cookie's Fortune, Y2K (prod. only), The Bachelor (also exec. prod.), Vertical Limit, 29 Palms, Kinsey, The Sisters, Kit Kittredge: An American Girl, Max Payne, A Little Help, Cats & Dogs: The Revenge of Kitty Galore.
TELEVISION: *Movies:* Miracle on the 17th Green (exec. prod.), The Triangle (exec. prod.). *Mini-series:* The Company. *Series:* Head Cases, Grey's Anatomy (recurring role), NCIS: Los Angeles, NCIS: Naval Criminal Investigative Service, NCIS: Los Angeles. *Guest:* More than 55 appearances.

O'DONNELL, ROSIE
Actress. b. Commack, NY, March 21, 1962. e. Dickinson College, Boston Univ. Stand-up comic first gaining attention on series Star Search. Her production company is One Canvas Productions. 2010 hosts radio show on sattelite Sirius.
THEATRE: Grease! (B'way debut, 1994).
PICTURES: A League of Their Own, Sleepless in Seattle, Another Stakeout, Car 54 Where Are You?, I'll Do Anything, The Flintstones, Exit to Eden, Now and Then, Beautiful Girls, Harriet the Spy, A Very Brady Sequel (cameo), Wide Awake, Tarzan (voice), Get Bruce, The Flintstones in Viva Rock Vegas (voice), Secrets Through the Smoke (documentary), Artists and Orphans: A True Drama (documentary, narrator), Mina & the Family Treasure (documentary, exec. prod. only), After the Storm (doc., exec. prod.).
TELEVISION: *Movies:* The Twilight of the Golds, Pair of Jokers with Rosie O'Donnell & Bill Engvall, Rosie O'Donnell (Emmy nom. 1995) Riding the Bus with My Sister, Rosie's Variety Show (host, exec. prod.), America (prod., writer, WGA nom. 2010). *Series:* Gimme a Break, Stand-Up Spotlight (host), Stand By Your Man, The Rosie O'Donnell Show (host; 10 Emmy, Awards, 1 other nom.). The Caroline Rhea Show (exec. consultant.), Simply Sketch (exec. prod.), The View (co-host, 2006-2007, Emmy nom. 2007), Grey's Anatomy, The Big Gay Sketch Show (exec. prod.), Drop Dead Diva. *Documentaries/Specials:* Jackie's Back!, My Favorite Broadway: Leading Ladies, The 52nd Annual Tony Awards (Emmy Award 1999), The Gun Deadlock, The 42nd Annual Academy Awards, Elmopalooza!, Kids are Punny (voice, exec. prod., Emmy nom. 1999), All Aboard! Rosie's Family Cruise (Emmy nom. 2006). *Guest:* More than 154 appearances.

O'HARA, CATHERINE
Actress, Writer, Director. b. Toronto, Canada, Mar. 4, 1954. Professional debut in 1974 with Toronto's Second City. Co-founder of SCTV in 1976 (Emmy and Canadian Nellie Awards for writing).
PICTURES: Nothing Personal, Rock & Rule (voice), After Hours, Heartburn, Beetlejuice, Dick Tracy, Betsy's Wedding, Home Alone, Little Vegas, There Goes the Neighborhood, Home Alone 2: Lost in New York, The Nightmare Before Christmas (voice), The Paper, Wyatt Earp, A Simple Twist of Fate, Tall Tale, Last of the High Kings, Pippi Longstocking, Home Fries, The Life Before This, Best in Show, Edwurd Fudwupper Fibbed Big, Bartok the Magnificent (voice), Speaking of Sex, Orange County, Searching for Debra Winger (documentary), A Mighty Wind, (also composer, songs), Surviving Christmas, Lemony Snicket's A Series of Unfortunate Events, Game 6, Chicken Little (voice), Cat Tale (voice), Monster House, For Your Consideration, Over the Hedge (voice), Penelope, Temple Grandin, Where the Wild Things Are (voice), Away We Go, Killers, A Monster in Paris (voice).
TELEVISION: *Movies:* Really Weird Tales (also episode writer), I Martin Short Goes Hollywood, Andrea Martin Together Again, Hope, Late Last Night, The Wool Cap, Good Behavior, Temple Grandin. *Series*: SCTV (also writer, Emmy Award 1982, 4 other noms.), Steve Allen Comedy Hour, SCTV Network 90, The Completely Mental Misadventures of Ed Grimley (voice), Dream On (dir.), Committed (voice), Six Feet Under, Good Behavior (pilot), Glenn Martin DDS. *Guest*: More than 88 appearances.

O'HARA, MAUREEN
Actress. r.n. Maureen FitzSimons. b. Dublin, Ireland. Aug. 17, 1921. Abbey Sch. of Acting. Won numerous prizes for elocution. Under contract to Erich Pommer-Charles Laughton. Co-starred, Abbey & Repertory Theatre.
PICTURES: Kicking the Moon Around (debut, 1938), My Irish Molly, Jamaica Inn, The Hunchback of Notre Dame, A Bill of Divorcement, Dance Girl Dance, They Met in Argentina, How Green Was My Valley, To the Shores of Tripoli, Ten Gentlemen From West Point, The Black Swan, The Immortal Sergeant, This Land Is Mine, The Fallen Sparrow, Buffalo Bill, The Spanish Main, Sentimental Journey, Do You Love Me?, Miracle on 34th Street, Sinbad the Sailor, The Homestretch, The Foxes of Harrow, Sitting Pretty, Woman's Secret, Forbidden Street, Father Was a Fullback, Bagdad, Comanche Territory, Tripoli, Rio Grande, At Sword's Point, Flame of Araby, The Quiet Man, Kangaroo, Against All Flags, The Redhead From Wyoming, War Arrow, Fire Over Africa, The Magnificent Matador, Lady Godiva, Long Gray Line, Lisbon, Everything But the Truth, Wings of Eagles, Our Man in Havana, The Parent Trap, The Deadly Companions, Mr. Hobbs Takes a Vacation, McLintock!, Spencer's Mountain, The Battle of the Villa Fiorita, The Rare Breed, How Do I Love Thee?, Big Jake, Only the Lonely, A Century of Cinema.(doc.).
TELEVISION: *Movies*: Mrs. Miniver, The Red Pony, The Christmas Box, Cab to Canada, The Last Dance.

Documentaries/Specials: John Ford (as herself), Scarlet Pimpernel, Spellbound, High Button Shoes, Who's Afraid of Mother Goose.

OHLMEYER, DON
Executive, Producer, Director. b. New Orleans, LA, Feb. 3, 1945. e. U. of Notre Dame, B.A. (Communications), 1967. Producer and director at both ABC and NBC. Formed Ohlmeyer Communications Company, 1982 (diversified prod. and dist. of entertainment and sports prog.). Assoc. dir., ABC Sports, NY 1967-70; *Director*, ABC Sports, 1971-72 (dir. 1972 Olympic Games); *Prod.:* ABC Sports, NY 1972-77 (prod. and dir. 1976 Winter and Summer Olympics; prod. ABC's Monday Night Football, 1972-76); *Exec. prod.:* NBC Sports, NY 1977-82 (exec. prod., 1980 Olympics, The World Series, The Super Bowl). Special Bulletin (exec. prod.), John Denver's Christmas in Aspen (exec. prod.). Chmn. and CEO, Ohlmeyer Communications Co., LA, 1982. 1993, named pres. NBC West Coast. Resigned from post 1999. In 2003, Ohlmeyer initiated a "mentoring fellowship" at Pepperdine Univ.'s communications department, where he oversees student-produced sports broadcasts, teaches two courses and enlists media executives to mentor communications students. He is a recipient of more than 16 Emmy Awards, Humanitas Prize, Award for Excellence, National Film Board. Member: Directors Guild of America, Writer's Guild of America & Acad. of Television Arts & Sciences, Lifetime Achievement Award 2007.
TELEVISION: *Movies*: Cold Sassy Tree (exec. prod.), Crazy in Love (exec. prod.), The Golden Moment: An Olympic Love Story, Special Bulletin (exec prod., Emmy Award 1983), Under Siege, Right to Die. *Specials*: Heroes of Desert Storm (dir.), Us Against the World (also dir.) Disney's Christmas on Ice (dir.), Emmy Awards Show (prod.), The MTV Awards Show (creator & prod. w/ Bob Pittman), Walt Disney World's 4th of July Spectacular (also dir.), Season's Greetings--An Evening with John Williams and the Boston Pops Orchestra. *Series*: Lifestories (dir./exec. prod.), Fast Copy (creator & prod.), ABC's Wide World of Sports (Emmy Award 1976), Crimes of the Century (creator, prod.), Life Stories (prod.), The Skins Game.

O'KEEFE, MICHAEL
Actor. b. Larchmont, NY, April 24, 1955. e. NYU, AADA. Co-founder, Colonnades Theatre Lab, NY.
THEATRE: *B'way*: Mass Appeal (Theatre World Award), Fifth of July. *Off-B'way*: Killdere (NYSF), Moliere in Spite of Himself, Christmas on Mars, Short Eyes. *Regional*: Streamers, A Few Good Men (tour).
PICTURES: Gray Lady Down (debut, 1978), The Great Santini (Academy Award nom.; Golden Globe nom. 1981), Caddyshack, Split Image, Nate and Hayes, Finders Keepers, The Slugger's Wife, Ironweed, Out of the Rain, Me and Veronica, Nina Takes a Lover, Three Lovers, Edie and Pen, Ghosts of Mississippi, Herman U.S.A, Just One Night, The Pledge, The Glass House, Prancer Returns, Taking A Chance on Love, The Hot Chick, The Inner Circle, Delusion (short), Cherry Crush, Michael Clayton, Frozen River, Chasing 3000, American Violet, Crimes of Opportunity.
TELEVISION: *Movies*: The Lindbergh Kidnapping Case, Friendly Persuasion, Panache, The Dark Secret of Harvest Home, A Rumor of War, Unholy Matrimony, Bridge to Silence, Disaster at Silo 7, Too Young to Die?, In the Best Interest of the Child, Fear, Incident at Deception Ridge, The People Next Door, Defending Our Kids: The Julie Posey Story, Swing Vote. *Series*: Against the Law, Roseanne, Middle Ages, Life's Work, State of Mind (pilot), Eleventh Hour. *Guest:* More than 50 appearances.

OLDMAN, GARY
Actor. r.n. Leonard Gary Oldman. b. New Cross, London, England, March 21, 1958. Won scholarship to Rose Bruford Drama College (B.A. Theatre Arts) after studying with Greenwich Young People's Theatre. Acted with Theatre Royal, York and joined touring theatre co. Then in 1980 appeared with Glasgow Citizens Theatre in Massacre at Paris, Chinchilla, Desperado Corner, A Waste of Time (also touring Europe and South America). Received Evening Standard Film Award for Best Newcomer for Sid and Nancy, 1986.
THEATRE: *London*: Massacre at Paris, Desperado Cornor, Chinchilla, Entertaining Mr. Sloane, Summit Conference, A Waste of Time, Saved, Abel and Caine, Minnesota Moon, Summit Conference, Rat in the Skull, Women Beware Women, The War Plays, Real Dreams, The Country Wife, The Desert Air, Serious Money (Royal Shakespeare Co.), The Pope's Wedding (Time Out's Fringe Award, best newcomer 1985-86; British Theatre Assc. Drama Mag. Award, Best Actor 1985), Walk Right By Me (monologue).
PICTURES: Remembrance, Sid and Nancy, Prick Up Your Ears, Track 29, We Think the World of You, Criminal Law, Chattahoochee, State of Grace, Rosencrantz and Guildenstern Are Dead, Exile, Before and After Death, JFK, Bram Stoker's Dracula, True Romance, Romeo Is Bleeding, The Professional, Immortal Beloved, Murder in the First, Dead Presidents, The Scarlet Letter, Basquiat, Air Force One, Nil by Mouth (s.p., dir., prod. only; BAFTA Award, Outstanding Brit. Film, Best Orig. Screenplay, 1997), Lost in Space, Quest for Camelot (voice), The Contender, Anasazi Moon, Hannibal, Interstate 60, The Hire: Beat the Devil (short), Nobody's Baby, Sin, Tiptoes, Dead Fish, Harry Potter and the Prisoner of Azkaban, Batman Begins, Harry Potter and the Goblet of Fire, BackWoods, Zodiac, Harry Potter and the Order of the Phoenix, The Dark Knight, The Unborn, Rain Fall, Planet 51 (voice), A Christmas Carol, The Book of Eli, Easter Sixteen, Kung Fu Panda: The Kaboom of Doom (voice), Harry Potter and the Deathly Hallows: Part II, Tinker, Tailor, Soldier, Spy, Red Riding Hood. *Executive producer:* Plunkett & Macleane.
TELEVISION: *Movies:* Morgan's Boy, Meantime, Honest Decent and True, Rat in the Skull, The Firm, Heading Home. *Mini-series:* Jesus. *Series:* Friends (Emmy nom. 2001 as guest). *Guest:* More than 70 appearances.

OLIN, KEN
Actor, Director, Executive Producer. b. Chicago, IL, July 30, 1954. e. Univ. of PA. m. actress Patricia Wettig. Studied acting with Warren Robertson and Stella Adler. Made Off-B'way debut in Taxi Tales, 1978.
PICTURES: Ghost Story, Queen's Logic, White Fang 2: Myth of the White Wolf (dir.), 'Til There Was You.
TELEVISION: *Movies: Actor:* Women at West Point, Flight 90: Disaster on the Potomac, There Must Be a Pony, Tonight's the Night, Cop Killer, A Stoning in Fulham County, Goodnight Sweet Wife: A Murder in Boston, Telling Secrets, Nothing But the Truth, The Advocate's Devil, Evolution's Child, Countdown to Chaos, Say Uncle. *Director:* The Broken Cord, Doing Time on Maple Drive, In Pursuit of Honor, Phenomenon II. *Series*: *Actor*: The Bay City Blues, Hill Street Blues, Falcon Crest, thirtysomething (also dir, Golden Globe nom. 1990), EZ Streets (also dir.), L.A. Doctors (also dir.). *Director*: Felicity, Judging Amy, The West Wing, Freaks and Geeks, Alias, Breaking News (also exec. prod.), Eli Stone (pilot, exec. prod., dir.), Brothers & Sisters (actor, dir. & exec. prod.).

OLIN, LENA
Actress. b. Stockholm, Sweden, March 22, 1955. Royal Dramatic Theatre member in Stockholm. Daughter of actor-director Stig Olin. m. director Lasse Hallstrom.
THEATRE: *NY*: Miss Julie.
PICTURES: The Adventures of Picasso, Karleken, Fanny and Alexander, Grasanklingar, After the Rehearsal, A Matter of Life and Death, Friends, The Unbearable Lightness of Being (Golden Globe nom. 1989), S/Y Glädjen, Enemies: A Love Story (Academy Award nom. 1990), Havana, Mr. Jones, Romeo Is Bleeding, The Night and the Moment, Night Falls on Manhattan, Polish Wedding, Hamilton, Mystery Men, The Ninth Gate, Chocolat, Ignition, Darkness, Queen of the Damned, The Dark, The United States of Leland, Hollywood Homicide, Bang Bang Orangutang, Devil You Know, Awake, The Reader, Remember Me.
TELEVISION: *Movies:* Friaren som inte ville gifta sig, After the Rehearsal, Wallenberg: A Hero's Story, Glasmastarna, Komedianter, Hebriana, Hamilton. *Series:* Alias (Emmy nom. 2003.

OLMI, ERMANNO
Director, Writer, Producer, Editor. b. Bergamo, Italy, July 24, 1931. e. Accademia d'Arte Drammatica, Milan. Worked as a clerk for an electric company Edisonvolta 1949-52, until 1952 when he began directing theatrical and cinematic activities sponsored by co. 1952-61, directed or supervised over 40 short 16mm and 35mm documentary films. 1959 first feature film, semi-doc. Time Stood Still. With other friends and Tullio Kezich formed prod. co., 22 December S.P.A., 1961. 1982, Helped found Hypothesis Cinema, a sch. for aspiring dirs.
PICTURES: *Director: Writer*: Time Stood Still (debut, 1959), The Sound of Trumpets, The Fiances (also prod.), And There Came a Man (A Man Named John), One Fine Day (also edit.), The Tree of the Wood Clogs (Cannes Film Fest. Award, 1978; also photog., edit.), Camminacammina (also photog., edit., design), Milano '83 (also photog., edit.), Long Live the Lady (also co-photog., edit.), Legend of the Holy Drinker (also edit.), Il Segreto Del Bosco Vecchio, Singing Behind Screens, Tickets, Don't Touch the Axe (prod.), Centochiodi (also writer). *Documentaries:* Artigiani Veneti, Lungo Il Fiume, The Secret of the Old Woods, Genesis: The Creation and the Flood, 12 registi per 12 città, Il Denaro non esiste, Professions of Arms.
TELEVISION: *Movies:* The Crush, I Recuperanti, In The Summertime, La Circostanza, Genesis: The Creation & the Flood, Jérusalem (stage director).

OLMOS, EDWARD JAMES
Actor. b. East Los Angeles, CA, February 24, 1947. e. East Los Angeles City College, CA State U. m. actress Lorraine Bracco. Started as rock singer with group Eddie James and the Pacific Ocean. By the early 1970s acted in small roles on Kojak and Hawaii Five-O. 1978 starred in Luis Valdez's musical drama Zoot Suit at Mark Taper Forum (L.A. Drama Critics Circle Award, 1978), later on B'way (Theatre World Award, Tony nom.), and in film version. Formed YOY Productions with director Robert Young. Numerous awards for humanitarian work.
PICTURES: Aloha Bobby and Rose (debut, 1975), Alambrista!, Virus, Wolfen, Zoot Suit, Blade Runner, The Ballad of Gregorio Cortez (also assoc. prod., composer and musical adaptor), Saving Grace, Stand and Deliver (Academy Award nom.; Golden Globe nom. 1989, also co-prod.), Triumph of the Spirit, Talent for the Game, American Me (also dir., co-prod.), A Million to Juan, Mirage,

My Family/Mi Familia, Roosters, Caught, Selena, The Wonderful Ice Cream Suit, The Wall, Zaoatista (narr.), Zapatista (doc., narr., The Road to El Dorado (voice), Gossip, Jack & Marilyn (also prod., dir.), La Cerca (short; narr.), Walkout (dir.), Splinter, Divine Forces (prod.), Beverly Hills Chihuahua (voice), A Class Apart (narr.), The Green Hornet.
TELEVISION: *Movies*: Evening in Byzantium, 300 Miles for Stephanie, Menendez: A Killing in Beverly Hills, The Taking of Pelham One Two Three, Bonanno: A Godfather's Story, The Princess and the Barrio Boy, The Judge, In the Time of the Butterflies, Walkout (DGA nom. 2007), Battlestar Galactica: Razor, Battlestar Galactica: The Plan (also dir.). *Mini-series*: The Burning Season (Emmy nom.; Golden Globe Award 1995), Battlestar Galactica. *Series*: Miami Vice (Golden Globe Award 1986, 1 other nom.; Emmy Award 1985, 1 other nom. also dir. episodes), American Family, Battlestar Galactica, The Batman (voice). *Documentaries/Specials:* Sequin, Y.E.S. Inc, The Story of Fathers & Sons, Good Cop Bad Kid (host), Songs of the Homeland (host). *Guest:* More than 131 appearances.

O'LOUGHLIN, GERALD STUART
Actor. b. New York, NY, Dec. 23, 1921. e. Lafayette Col., U. of Rochester, Neighborhood Playhouse. U.S. Marine, WWII.
THEATRE: *B'way*: Streetcar (ANTA series), Shadow of a Gunman, Dark at the Top of the Stairs, A Touch of the Poet, Cook for Mr. General, One Flew Over the Cuckoo's Nest, Calculated Risk, Lovers and Other Strangers. *Off-B'way:* Who'll Save the Plowboy (Obie Award), Harry Noon and Night, Machinal.
PICTURES: Lovers and Lollipops, Cop Hater, A Hatful of Rain, Ensign Pulver, A Fine Madness, In Cold Blood, Ice Station Zebra, Desperate Characters, The Organization, The Valachi Papers, Twilight's Last Gleaming, Frances, Crimes of Passion, City Heat, Quicksilver, The Secret Kingdom, The Secret Kingdom, 3 Strikes.
TELEVISION: *Movies*: The D.A.: Murder One, Murder at the World Series, Something for Joey, A Love Affair: The Eleanor and Lou Gehrig Story, Crash of Flight 401, Detour to Terror, Pleasure Palace, A Matter of Life and Death, Under Siege, Perry Mason: The Case of the Notorious Nun, Child's Cry, In the Arms of a Killer, The Crime of the Century. *Mini-series*: Wheels, Roots: The Next Generations, Blind Ambition, Women in White, The Blue and the Gray. *Series*: The Storefront Lawyers (Men at Law), The Rookies, Automan, Our House. *Guest*: More than 91 appearances.

OLSON, DALE C.
Executive. b. Fargo, ND, Feb. 20, 1934. e. Portland State College, OR. Owner, Dale C. Olson & Associates; formerly sr. v.p. & pres., m.p. div., Rogers & Cowan public relations. Journalist on Oregonian newspaper, West Coast editor, Boxoffice Magazine, 1958-60; critic and reporter, Daily Variety, 1960-66; dir. of publ., Mirisch Corp., 1966-68; Rogers & Cowan, 1968-85. From 1985-1998 headed Dale C. Olson & Associates, industry p.r. firm. Retired from industry in 1998. Past pres., Hollywood Press Club; awarded Bob Yaeger and Les Mason award by Publicists Guild; v.p. Diamond Circle, City of Hope; delegate for U.S. to Manila International Film Festival. Chmn. PR coordin. committee & member nat'l bd. of trustees, AMPAS, 1989-91. Chmn. of Western Council, Actors Fund of America, 1991; on Nat'l Bd. of Trustees, 1992-present.

OLSON, NANCY
Actress. b. Milwaukee, WI, July 14, 1929. e. U. of Wisconsin, UCLA. No professional experience before films.
PICTURES: Canadian Pacific (debut, 1949), Sunset Boulevard (Academy Award nom. 1951), Union Station, Mr. Music, Submarine Command, Force of Arms, Big Jim McLain, So Big, The Boy From Oklahoma, Battle Cry, Pollyanna, The Absent-Minded Professor, Son of Flubber, Smith!, Snowball Express, Airport 1975, Making Love.
TELEVISION: *Series:* Kingston: Confidential, Paper Dolls.

OLYPHANT, TIMOTHY
Actor. b. Hawaii, May 20, 1968. e. USC.
PICTURES: The First Wives Club, A Life Less Ordinary, Scream 2, 1999, No Vacancy, Go, Advice From a Caterpillar, The Broken Hearts Club: A Romantic Comedy, Gone in Sixty Seconds, Auggie Rose, Head Over Heels, The Safety of Objects, Rock Star, Coastlines, Dreamcatcher, A Man Apart, The Girl Next Door, Catch and Release, Meet Bill, Live Free or Die Hard, Stop Loss, Hitman, High Life, A Perfect Getaway, Elektra Luxx, The Crazies, I Am Number Four, Rango (voice), Hitman 2.
TELEVISION: *Movies:* Ellen Foster, When Trumpets Fade, Shadow Realm. *Series:* Mr. & Mrs. Smith (pilot), Deadwood, Damages, Justified.

O'NEAL, RYAN
Actor. r.n. Patrick Ryan O'Neal. b. Los Angeles, CA, April 20, 1941. Parents, screenwriter-novelist, Charles O'Neal, and actress Patricia Callaghan. Daughter is actress Tatum O'Neal; son is actor Griffin O'Neal. Boxer, L.A. Golden Gloves, 1956-57. Began career as stand-in, stunt man, then actor in Tales of the Vikings series, in Germany, 1959; freelanced in Hollywood.
PICTURES: The Big Bounce (debut, 1969), The Games, Love Story (Academy Award nom.; Golden Globe nom. 1971), Wild Rovers, What's Up Doc?, Paper Moon (Golden Globe nom. 1974), The Thief Who Came to Dinner, Barry Lyndon, Nickelodeon, A Bridge Too Far, The Driver, Oliver's Story, The Main Event, So Fine, Green Ice, Partners, Irreconcilable Differences, Fever Pitch, Tough Guys Don't Dance, Chances Are, Faithful, Hacks, An Alan Smithee Film: Burn Hollywood Burn, Zero Effect, Coming Soon, The List, People I Know, Malibu's Most Wanted.
TELEVISION: *Movies*: Love Hate Love, Small Sacrifices, The Man Upstairs, Epoch, Farrah's Story. *Series*: Empire, Peyton Place, Good Sports, Miss Match, Bones. *Documentaries/Specials:* Liza Minnelli: A Triple Play. *Guest:* More than 66 appearances.

O'NEAL, TATUM
Actress. b. Los Angeles, CA, Nov. 5, 1963. p. actors Ryan O'Neal and Joanna Moore. NY stage debut 1992 in A Terrible Beauty, followed by Adroscoggin Fugue.
PICTURES: Paper Moon (debut, 1973; Academy Award 1974, best supporting actress, Golden Globe Award, 1 other nom.), The Bad News Bears, Nickelodeon, International Velvet, Little Darlings, Circle of Two, Certain Fury, Little Noises, Basquiat, The Scoundrel's Wife, The Technical Writer, My Brother, Saving Grace B. Jones, The Runaways, Sweet Lorraine, Night at the Carriage House, Mr. Sophistication.
TELEVISION: *Movies*: Woman on Trial: The Lawrencia Bembenek Story, Fab Five: The Texas Cheerleader Scandal. *Series:* Wicked Wicked Games, Rescue Me. *Documentaries/Specials:* 15 and Getting Straight.

O'NEILL, ED
Actor. b. Youngstown, OH, Apr. 12, 1946. e. Ohio Univ., Youngstown State. Taught social studies in Youngstown prior to becoming an actor. Made NY stage debut Off-Off-B'way in Requiem for a Heavyweight at SoHo Rep. Theatre. B'way debut in Knockout.
PICTURES: Deliverance, Cruising, The Dogs of War, Disorganized Crime, K-9, The Adventures of Ford Fairlane, Sibling Rivalry, Dutch, Wayne's World, Wayne's World 2, Blue Chips, Little Giants, Prefontaine, The Spanish Prisoner, The Bone Collector, Lucky Numbers, Nobody's Baby, Spartan, Redbelt.
TELEVISION: *Movies*: When Your Lover Leaves, Braker, Farrell for the People, The Day the Women Got Even, Popeye Doyle, A Winner Never Quits, Right to Die, Police Story: Gladiator School, The Whereabouts of Jenny, Nick's Game, W.E.I.R.D. World, The Tenth Kingdom, In the Game. *Series*: Married...With Children (2 Golden Globe noms.), Big Apple, L.A. Dragnet, The West Wing, John from Cincinnati, Modern Family. *Guest:* More than 57 appearances.

O'NEILL, EILEEN
Executive. e. Bowling Green State University. Started at Discovery Communications as an unpaid intern while earning a graduate degree in popular culture from Bowling Green in Ohio. Having successfully developed a programming library, she was hired by DCI's networks operation department immediately upon graduation. O'Neill served as director of business affairs, responsible for all contract negotiations concerning co-productions, commissioned programming and original work for Discovery Channel, TLC and Animal Planetand also director of scheduling for Travel Channel. O'Neill then served as Exec. V. P. and general manager of Discovery Health Channel. Became President and general manager of Planet Green, the first and only 24-hour eco-lifestyle television network. She is credited with launching the network from the ground up in less than 12 months, and with more than 250 hours of all-original programming. She drew an authoritative and diverse group of celebrities and personalities to share their passion for the planet through a host of entertaining series and specials. In 2007, she simultaneously ran Discovery Health and TLC on an interim basis during a period of management transition at TLC. Under O'Neill, Discovery Health earned record ratings in all day-parts, including the strongest delivery ever during August 2005. Standout shows developed under her leadership include "Mystery Diagnosis", "Dr. G Medical Examiner" and "Jon & Kate Plus 8", then the top-rated series on the channel. O'Neill was named President and GM at TLC in 2008. Key show launches since then have included "Cake Boss" and "Toddlers & Tiaras".

O'NEILL, JENNIFER
Actress. b. Rio de Janeiro, Brazil, Feb. 20, 1949. e. Dalton Sch. Model before entering films. Spokeswoman: CoverGirl cosmetics. Pres., Point of View Productions and Management.
PICTURES: Rio Lobo, Summer of '42, Such Good Friends, The Carey Treatment, Glass Houses, Lady Ice, The Reincarnation of Peter Proud, Whiffs, Caravans, The Psychic, The Innocent, A Force of One, Cloud Dancer, Steel, Scanners, Committed, I Love N.Y., Love is Like That, Invasion of Privacy, The Gentle People, Discretion Assured, The Corporate Ladder, The Ride, The Prince and the Surfer, Time Changer, Billy: The Early Years, Last Ounce of Courage, Doonby.
TELEVISION: *Movies*: Love's Savage Fury, The Other Victim, An Invasion of Privacy, Chase, Perry Mason: The Case of the Shooting Star, The Red Spider, Glory Days, Full Exposure: The Sex Tapes Scandal, Personals, Perfect Family, The Cover Girl Murders, Frame-up, Jonathan Stone: Threat of Innocence, Silver Strand, On

Music Row. *Mini-series*: A.D. *Series*: Bare Essence, Cover Up.

ONTKEAN, MICHAEL
Actor. b. Vancouver, British Columbia, Canada, Jan. 24, 1946. e. U. of New Hampshire. Son of Leonard and Muriel Cooper Ontkean, actors. Acting debut at four with father's rep. theatre. Child actor with Stratford Shakespeare Fest., CBC and Natl Film Bd. Attended college four years on hockey scholarship. Has performed with Public Theatre, NY, Willamstown Theatre Fest., Mark Taper Lab, The Kitchen, Soho.
PICTURES: The Peace Killers (debut, 1971), A Time to Every Purpose, Necromancy, Girls on the Road, Hot Summer Week, Slap Shot, Voices, Willie and Phil, Making Love, The Blood of Others, Just the Way You Are, The Allnighter, Maid to Order, Clara's Heart, Street Justice, Cold Front, Bye Bye Blues, Postcards From the Edge, Bayou Boy, The Toy Factory, Le Sang des Autres, Cutting Loose, Square Deal, Rapture, Swann, Nico the Unicorn, Summer of the Monkeys, Just A Little Harmless Sex, Bear with Me, The Descendants.
TELEVISION: *Movies*: The Rookies (pilot), The Blood of Others, Kids Don't Tell, The Right of the People, Twin Peaks (pilot), Defense of a Married Man, In a Child's Name, Legacy of Lies, Whose Child Is This? The War for Baby Jessica, Vendetta 2: The New Mafia, Danielle Steel's Family Album, The Man Next Door, Man From the South, The Stepford Husbands, A Chance of Snow, A Killing Spring, Mrs. Ashboro's Cat. *Series*: The Rookies, Twin Peaks, North Shore, Sophie. *Specials/Documentaries:* The Greenpeace Years (narr.). *Guest:* More than 40 appearances.

OPHÜLS, MARCEL
Director, Writer. r.n. Hans Marcel Oppenheimer. b. Frankfurt-am-Main, Germany, Nov. 1, 1927. Son of German director Max Ophuls. e. Occidental Coll., U. of California, Berkeley, Sorbonne (philosophy). Family moved to France, 1932, then to Hollywood, 1941. Military service with Occupation forces in Japan, 1946; performed with theatre unit, Tokyo. 1951 began working in French film industry as asst. dir., using name Marcel Wall. Asst. dir. on Moulin Rouge, Act of Love, Marianne de ma Jeunesse, Lola Montes. 1956-59, radio and TV story ed., West Germany. Later worked for French TV as reporter and dir. news mag. features. Dir. & wrote short film Henri Matisse. 1968 doc. dir. for German TV. 1975-78 staff prod. CBS News, then ABC News. MacArthur Fellowship 1991. Member of AMPAS.
PICTURES: *Director/Writer*: Love at 20 (dir. segment), Banana Peel, Fire at Will, Munich or Peace in Our Time, The Sorrow and the Pity (also prod.; Natl. Soc. of Film Critics, NY Film Critics & Prix de Dinard Awards, 1970), The Harvest at Mai Lai, A Sense of Loss, Le Chagrin et la pitié (Academy Award nom. 1972, doc.) The Memory of Justice, Hotel Terminus--The Life and Times of Klaus Barbie (doc., also prod.; Academy Award, Berlin Peace Prize, Cannes Jury Prize, 1988), November Days (doc.), The Troubles We've Seen (also prod., Intl. Film Critics Prize, 1994).
TELEVISION: *Movies:* The Harvest of My Lai, Clavigo, Zwei ganze Tage, Two Whole Days. *Mini-series:* America Revisited. *Documentaries/Specials:* Munich or Peace in Our Time.

OPOTOWSKY, STAN
Executive. b. New Orleans, LA, Apr. 13, 1923. e. Tulane U. Served in U.S. Marine Corps as combat corr. and later joined United Press, working in New Orleans, Denver, and New York. Published own weekly newspaper in Mississippi before returning to N.Y. to join New York Post as mgr. editor and traveling natl. corr. Is also cinematographer and film editor. Joined ABC News as TV assignment editor; named asst. assignment mgr. 1974 named dir. of operations for ABC News TV Documentaries. 1975 named dir. of TV News Coverage, ABC News.
TELEVISION: *Author*: The Big Picture, The Longs of Louisiana, The Kennedy Government, Men Behind Bars.

O'QUINN, TERRY
Actor. b. Michigan, July 15, 1952.
THEATRE: *B'way*: Foxfire, Curse of an Aching Heart. *Off-B'way:* Richard III, Groves of Academy, Total Abandon. *Regional*: Streamers, Measure for Measure, The Front Page.
PICTURES: Heaven's Gate, Without a Trace, All the Right Moves, Places in the Heart, Mrs. Soffel, Mischief, Silver Bullet, SpaceCamp, The Stepfather, Black Widow, Young Guns, Pin, Stepfather 2, Blind Fury, The Rocketeer, Prisoners of the Sun, Company Business, The Cutting Edge, Amityville: A New Generation, Tombstone, Lipstick Camera, American Outlaws, Primal Fear, Ghosts of Mississippi, Shadow Conspiracy, The X Files, Rated X, Hometown Legend, Old School.
TELEVISION: *Movies*: FDR: The Final Year, Prisoner Without a Name Cell Without a Number, Right to Kill, Unfinished Business, An Early Frost, Stranger on My Land, Women of Valor, When the Time Comes, Perry Mason: The Case of the Desperate Deception, Son of the Morning Star, The Last to Go, Deliver Them From Evil: The Taking of Alta View, Trial: The Price of Passion, Sexual Advances, Wild Card, The Good Fight, Born Too Soon, Visions of Murder, Heart of a Child, Don't Talk To Strangers, Justice in a Small Town, A Friend to Die For, Ray Alexander: A Menu for Murder, JAG, My Stepson My Lover, Murder in a Small Town, Harsh Realm, Rated X, Semper Fi (tv short), WWIII, The Locket, Phenomenon II. *Series:* The Doctors, JAG, Alias, Millennium, Harsh Realm, The West Wing, Lost (Emmy Award 2007, 1 other nom.). *Guest:* More than 97 appearances.

ORMOND, JULIA
Actress. b. England, Jan. 4, 1965. Studied acting at Webber Douglas Acad., London.
THEATRE: The Rehearsal, Wuthering Heights, Arms and the Man, The Crucible, Faith Hope and Charity (London Drama Critics Award, 1989).
PICTURES: The Baby of Mâcon, Nostradamus, Legends of the Fall, First Knight, Captives, Sabrina, Calling the Ghosts (documentary, prod. only), Smilla's Sense of Snow, The Barber of Siberia, The Prime Gig, Resistance, Inland Empire, I Know Who Killed Me, Surveillance, Guerrilla, Kit Kittredge: An American Girl, La Conjura de El Escorial, The Curious Case of Benjamin Button, Playground (doc., assoc. prod.), Albatross, Mr. Tambourine Man.
TELEVISION: *Movies:* The Best Man to Die, Young Catherine, Stalin, Animal Farm (voice), Varian's War, Iron Jawed Angels, The Way, The Wronged Man, Temple Grandin. *Mini-series:* Traffik, Beach Girls. Series: Nurse Jackie. *Documentaries:* Searching for Debra Winger, The Nazi Officer's Wife (voice).

ORTEGA, KENNY
Director, Choreographer. b. Palo Alto, CA. e. American Conserv. Theatre, Canada Coll. Started acting at age 13. Earned several scholarships to dance academies in San Francisco Bay area. Regional theatre roles in Oliver, Hair, The Last Sweet Days of Isaac, before staging shows for rock band The Tubes. First major TV job choreographing Cher special. Directed/choreographed concerts and/or music videos for such performers as Michael Jackson, Kiss, Elton John, Cher, Rod Stewart, Diana Ross, Madonna, Billy Joel, Oingo Boingo, Miami Sound Machine, Pointer Sisters, Toto. Artistic dir. and choreographer, 1996 Centennial Olympic Games opening and closing ceremonies. Received ACA Career Achievement Award 2004.
PICTURES: *Director/Choreographer*: Newsies, Hocus Pocus. *Choreographer*: Xanadu, One from the Heart, St. Elmo's Fire, Pretty in Pink, Ferris Bueller's Day Off, Dirty Dancing, And God Created Woman, Salsa (also assoc. prod., 2nd unit dir.), Shaq, Newsies, Wasteland, To Wong Foo Thanks for Everything, Julie Newmar, Quest for Camelot, Hannah Montana/Miley Cyrus: Best of Both Worlds Concert Tour (doc., stage dir., prod.), High School Musical 3: Senior Year (also exec. prod.), This Is It (doc., also prod.).
TELEVISION: *Movies:* The Way She Moves, High School Musical (dir, choreog., Emmy Award 2006, 1 other nom.; DGA Award 2007), The Cheetah Girls 2 (dir.), High School Musical 2 (dir., DGA nom., Emmy nom. 2008), Legally Mad (dir.). *Series: Director*: Dirty Dancing (also choreog.), Hull Street High (also choreog., Emmy nom. 1991), Chicago Hope (also choreog., ACA Award 1998), Fame L.A., Ally McBeal, Grounded for Life (Emmy nom. 2001), Gilmore Girls. *Documentaries/Specials: Choreographer:* American Music Awards, Academy Awards, NAACP Awards, 1996 Olympics (ACA Award 1997), Mickey's 60th Birthday, Totally Mine, America Picks the #1 Hit, Nosotros Awards, Good Time Rock 'n' Roll, Jump, Olivia Newton-John, Cher, The Pointer Sisters, Neil Diamond, Smokey Robinson, Cheryl Ladd, XIX Winter Olympics Opening Ceremony (also dir. & prod., ACA Award, 2 Emmy Awards, 1 other nom. 2002).

ORTENBERG, TOM
Executive. e. Undergraduate degree, Penn State Univ., 1982. Began film career with Columbia Pictures in 1985. After four years, left to join Hemdale Film Corporation, makers of such films as "Platoon" and "The Last Emperor," and ultimately became Hemdale's pres., distribution and marketing. Ortenberg was Lionsgate's first employee in Los Angeles in 1996, running the office with only the help of a part-time asst. Most recently Ortenberg was the pres. of theatrical films for Lionsgate Entertainment. Under Ortenberg, Lionsgate received dozens of Academy Award nominations and several notable wins, including Halle Berry's historic Oscar win for Best Actress for "Monster's Ball" and the Best Picture Academy Award win for "Crash," along with numerous Golden Globe, BAFTA, and many other Guild and Critics groups nominations and awards. In Jan. 2009, Ortenberg left Lionsgate to fill the newly created position, pres., theatrical films for The Weinstein Company.

O'SHEA, MILO
Actor. b. Dublin, Ireland, June 2, 1926. Member of Dublin Gate Theatre Co., 1944, before screen career.
THEATRE: *NY*: Staircase, Dear World, The Comedians, A Touch of the Poet, Waiting For Godot (Brooklyn Acad. of Music), Mass Appeal, My Fair Lady, Corpse!, Meet Me in St. Louis, Remembrance (Off-B'way), Philadelphia Here I Come!, Alive Alive Oh! (alo co-writer), Mrs. Warren's Profession. *London*: Treasure Hunt, Glory Be, Hans Andersen, Corpse, Can-Can.
PICTURES: Carry on Cabby, Never Put It in Writing, Ulysses, Romeo and Juliet, Barbarella, The Adding Machine, The Angel Levine, Paddy, Sacco and Vanzetti, Loot, Theatre of Blood, Digby: The Biggest Dog in the World, It's Not the Size That Counts, Arabian Adventure, The Pilot, The Verdict, The Purple Rose of Cairo, The Dream Team, Opportunity Knocks, Only the Lonely, The Playboys, The Butcher Boy, The Match Maker, Moonglow, Puckoon, Mystics.

TELEVISION: *Movies:* Waiting for Godot (presenter), Come Buttercup Come Daisy Come...?, Silent Song, Something in the Cellar, And No One Could Save Her, The Dobson Doughnut, Peter Lundy and the Medicine Hat Stallion, Portrait of a Rebel: The Remarkable Mrs. Sanger, Broken Vows, Angel in Green, Murder in the Heartland, Swing Vote. *Mini-series:* QB VII, The Best of Families, Ellis Island. *Series*: Me Mammy, Once A Hero.

OSMENT, HALEY JOEL
Actor. b. Los Angeles, CA, April 10, 1988.
PICTURES: Forrest Gump, Mixed Nuts, Bogus, For Better or Worse, The Sixth Sense (Academy Award nom.; Golden Globe nom. 2000), I'll Remember April, Discover Spot (voice), Pay It Forward, A.I., The Hunchback of Notre Dame II (voice), Beauty and the Beast: The Enchanted Christmas (voice), Edges of the Lord, Edwurd Fudwupper Fibbed Big (voice), The Jungle Book 2 (voice), The Country Bears (voice), Secondhand Lions, Home of the Giants, Truth & Treason, Montana Amazon (also exec. prod.).
TELEVISION: *Movies:* Lies of the Heart: The Story of Laurie Kellog, Last Stand at Saber River, The Lake, The Ransom of Red Chief, Cab to Canada. *Series:* Thunder Alley, The Jeff Foxworthy Show, Murphy Brown. *Guest:* More than 63 appearances.

OSMOND, DONNY
Singer, TV Host. b. Ogden, UT, Dec. 9, 1957. Seventh of nine children, he was fifth member of family to become professional singer. (Four brothers: Alan, Wayne, Merrill and Jay, were original members of Osmond Bros., who originally sang barbershop quartet.) Made debut at four on Andy Williams Show. Has had 12 gold albums. Was co-host with sister of Donny & Marie on TV.
THEATRE: Little Johnny Jones, Joseph and the Amazing Technicolor Dreamcoat.
PICTURES: Goin' Coconuts, The Great Brain (composer), Mulan (singing voice), The Land Before Time: Journey to Big Water (video, composer), Mulan II (singing voice), College Road Trip.
TELEVISION: *Movies*: The Wild Women of Chastity Gulch, Joseph and the Amazing Technicolor Dreamcoat. Inside The Osmonds. *Series*: The Andy Williams Show, Donny and Marie (4 Emmy noms.), Pyramid, (host and consulting prod., Emmy nom. 2003), Name That Tune (host), The Great American Dream Vote (host), Dancing With The Stars (celebrity contestant). *Documentaries / Specials:* Osmond Family Christmas Special, Reflections on Ice: Michelle Kwan Skates to the Music of Disney's Mulan (singing voice), We are Family. Various appearances on musical specials. *Guest*: More than 187 appearances.

OSTROFF, DAWN
Executive. e. B.S. degree in journalism, Florida International University, 1980. Ostroff began her career in news as a reporter for WINZ, a CBS affiliate in Miami. She also worked in local news at WPLG and WTVJ in Miami. She then moved to the entertainment side of TV and from 1984 to 1989, Ostroff served as v.p., development at the Kushner-Locke Company. While there she developed a number of series for cable, as well as several mini-series and TV movies for all the broadcast networks. She became pres. of Michael Jacobs Productions, where she produced and supervised the production of comedies such as Boy Meets World and Dinosaurs for ABC and The Torkelsons for NBC. At 20th Century Fox Television, Ostroff was senior v.p., creative affairs, involved with the slate for the 1996-97 season: King of the Hill for FOX, Buffy the Vampire Slayer for The WB and the Emmy Award-winning The Practice for ABC. Ostroff joined Lifetime cable TV network in October 1996 as senior v.p., programming and production. She became Lifetime's executive v.p., entertainment in Aug. 1999. While at Lifetime, the network rose from the sixth highest-rated network in cable to the number one cable network in prime time and built its reputation as a dynamic outlet for Hollywood's most talented women in front of and behind the camera. During Ostroff's tenure, Lifetime's line-up boasted the top three original dramas on basic cable, including Strong Medicine, Any Day Now and The Division. CBS recruited Ostroff and in Feb. 2002, she became the UPN Network's entertainment pres. She was promoted to pres., UPN in Feb. 2005. When UPN and The WB announced in Jan. 2006 the two networks would fold and merge into a combined network dubbed The CW, Ostroff was tapped to become entertainment pres. for The CW. Ostroff has received numerous awards and named to several "power lists" for the entertainment industry, including: an annual presence on Hollywood Reporter's "100 most powerful women in entertainment" since 2002 (no. 11 in 2006); for two consecutive years, Entertainment Weekly ranked Ostroff among Hollywood's top executives in their annual "Power List" issue.

O'TOOLE, ANNETTE
Actress. b. Houston, TX, April 1, 1953. e. UCLA.
PICTURES: Smile (debut, 1975), One on One, King of the Gypsies, Foolin' Around, Cat People, 48 HRS, Superman III, Bridge to Terabithia, Cross My Heart, Love at Large, Andre (voice), Imaginary Crimes, Here on Earth, Temptation (also prod.), A Mighty Wind, (composer, Academy Award nom. 2004), Falling Up.
TELEVISION: *Movies*: The Girl Most Likely To..., The Entertainer, The War Between the Tates, Love For Rent, Ladies in Waiting, Stand By Your Man, Vanities, The Best Legs in the 8th Grade, Copacabana, Arthur Hailey's Strong Medicine, Broken Vows, Guts & Glory: Rise and Fall of Oliver North, Stephen King's It, The Dreamer of Oz, A Girl of the Limberlost, Unpublished Letters, White Lie, Kiss of a Killer, Love Matters, A Mother's Revenge, On Hope (tv short), My Brother's Keeper, The Christmas Box, The Man Next Door, Keeping The Promise, Final Descent, Final Justice, The Huntress. *Mini-series*: The Kennedys of Massachusetts (Emmy nom.; Golden Globe nom. 1990), Jewels, Dead by Sunset. *Series:* Nash Bridges, The Huntress, Smallville. *Documentaries/Specials*: Vanities, Secret World of the Very Young, On Hope. *Guest:* More than 110 appearances.

O'TOOLE, PETER
Actor. b. Connemara, Ireland, Aug. 2, 1932. Studied at Royal Acad. of Dramatic Art. Early career with Bristol Old Vic. Partner with Jules Buck, Keep Films, Ltd. Autobiography: Loitering With Intent (1993). Received Honorary Academy Award 2003.
THEATRE: *London*: Major Barbara, Oh My Papa, The Long the Short and the Tall, Baal, Hamlet, Ride a Cock Horse, Macbeth, Man and Superman, Jeffrey Bernard is Unwell, Our Song. 1960, with the Stratford-on-Avon Company (The Taming of the Shrew, Merchant of Venice, etc). *Dublin*: Arms and the Man, Waiting for Godot. *Toronto*: Present Laughter, Uncle Vanya. B'way debut 1987: Pygmalion.
PICTURES: Kidnapped (debut, 1959), The Savage Innocents, The Day They Robbed the Bank of England, Lawrence of Arabia (Academy Award nom.; 2 Golden Globe noms. 1963), Becket (Academy Award nom.; Golden Globe Award 1965), Lord Jim, What's New Pussycat?, The Bible, How to Steal a Million, The Night of the Generals, Casino Royale (cameo), Great Catherine, The Lion in Winter (Academy Award nom.; Golden Globe Award 1969), Goodbye Mr. Chips (Academy Award nom.; Golden Globe Award 1970), Brotherly Love (Country Dance), Murphy's War, Under Milk Wood, The Ruling Class (Academy Award nom. 1973), Man of La Mancha (Golden Globe nom. 1973), Rosebud, Man Friday, Foxtrot, Caligula, Power Play, Zulu Dawn, The Stunt Man (Academy Award nom.; Golden Globe nom. 1981), Supergirl, Creator, Club Paradise, The Last Emperor, High Spirits, On a Moonlit Night, Helena, Wings of Fame, The Nutcracker Prince (voice), The Rainbow Thief, Isabelle Eberhardt, King Ralph, Rebecca's Daughters, The Seventh Coin, FairyTale: A True Story, Phantoms, The Manor, Molokai: The Story of Father Damien, The Sinister Saga of Making "The Stunt Man" The Final Curtain, My Favorite Year (Academy Award nom.; Golden Globe nom. 1983), Global Heresy, Bright Young Things, Troy, One Night With The King: The Call of Destiny, Lassie, One Night with the King, Venus (Academy Award nom.; Golden Globe nom. 2007), Ratatouille (voice), Stardust, Thomas Kinkade's Home for Christmas, Love and Virtue, Dean Spanley, Mary Mother of Christ, Eager to Die, Eldorado (narr.), Cristiada, Katherine of Alexandria.
TELEVISION: *Movies*: Rogue Male (BBC), Svengali, Kim, Crossing to Freedom, Civvies, Gulliver's Travels, Coming Home, Jeffrey Bernard is Unwell, Hitler: The Rise of Evil (Emmy nom. 2003), Imperium: Augustus, Casanova. *Mini-series*: Masada (Emmy nom.; Golden Globe nom. 1981), Heaven & Hell: North and South Book III, Joan of Arc (Emmy Award, Golden Globe nom. 1999), Iron Road. *Series*: Strumpet City (BBC), Heavy Weather, The Tudors. *Documentaries/Specials*: Present Laughter, Pygmalion, The Dark Angel. *Guest:* More than 81 appearances.

OVERALL, PARK
Actress. b. Nashville, TN, March 15, 1957. Attended British boarding school, earned teaching degree, before turning to acting.
THEATRE: *NY*: Biloxi Blues, Wild Blue, Only You, Loose Ends, Something About Baseball, Marathon '88.
PICTURES: Body Passion, Biloxi Blues, Mississippi Burning, Talk Radio (voice), Lost Angels, Kindergarten Cop, The Vanishing, House of Cards, Undercover Blues, Sparkler, Abilene, Slammed, Cut and Run (short), Beer for My Horses.
TELEVISION: *Movies*: Luck of the Draw: The Gambler Returns, Overkill: The Aileen Wuornos Story, Precious Victims, The Good Old Boys, Inflammable, Fifteen and Pregnant, The Price of a Broken Heart, When Andrew Came Home, Alligator Point. *Pilot*: The Line. *Series*: Empty Nest (3 Golden Globe noms.), Reba, The Critic (voice), Katie Joplin, Ladies Man.

OVITZ, MICHAEL
Talent Agent, Executive. b. Chicago, IL, Dec. 14, 1946. e. UCLA, B.A. in psychology, 1968. Began ent. career as a tour guide at Universal Studios. Started as a trainee at William Morris Agency before becoming agent, 1969-75. Co-founder of Creative Artists Agency, 1975; became chmn. and chief stock holder. 1995 named pres. The Walt Disney Company; left The Walt Disney Company, Jan. 1997. Co-founder of Artists Management Group (AMG), 1998. In 2002, sold off AMG assets to The Firm, an L.A.-based agency. Professional memberships have included: bd. dir. for Opsware Inc., D.A.R.E. America, the National Bd. of Advisors for the Children's Scholarship Fund, bd. of advisors at UCLA School of Theater Film & Television; exec. advisory bd. of the Pediatric Aids Foundation; bd. of trustees of the Museum of of Modern Art in NYC.
PICTURES: Gangs of New York (exec. prod.), Timeline (exec. prod.).

OXENBERG, CATHERINE
Actress. b. NY, NY, Sept. 21, 1961. Daughter of the exiled Princess Elizabeth of Yugoslavia, raised among int'l. jet set with Richard Burton acting as her tutor. Modeled before making TV

debut in The Royal Romance of Charles and Diana (1982).
PICTURES: The Lair of the White Worm, The Collectors, The Omega Code, Perilous.
TELEVISION: *Movies*: The Royal Romance of Charles and Diana, Still Crazy Like a Fox, Roman Holiday, Swimsuit, Trenchcoat in Paradise, Ring of Scorpio, Overexposed, K-9000, Sexual Response, Rubdown, Treacherous Beauties, Hide and Seek, Thrill Seekers, The Miracle of the Cards, Boys will be Boys, Arthur's Quest, Time Served, Sanctimony, Road Rage, The Flying Dutchman, The Vector File, Premonition. *Series:* Dynasty, Acapulco H.E.A.T., Watch Over Me. *Guest:* More than 52 appearances.

OZ, FRANK
Puppeteer, Director, Performer. r.n. Frank Oznowicz. b. Hereford, England, May 25, 1944. Gained fame as creator and performer of various characters on Sesame Street and the Muppet Show (Fozzie Bear, Miss Piggy, Animal, Cookie Monster, Grover and Bert). V.P., Jim Henson Prods. Received Cinematic Imagery Award from Art Dir. Guild 2002.
PICTURES: *Performer*: The Muppet Movie, The Blues Brothers, Star Wars: Episode V-The Empire Strikes Back, The Great Muppet Caper (also prod.), An American Werewolf in London, The Dark Crystal (also co-dir.), Star Wars: Episode VI-Return of the Jedi, Trading Places, The Muppets Take Manhattan (also dir., co-s.p.), Spies Like Us, Labyrinth, Innocent Blood, The Muppet Christmas Carol (also exec. prod.), Muppet Treasure Island (voice), Blues Brothers 2000, Star Wars: Episode I-The Phantom Menace (voice), Muppets from Space (voice), The Adventures of Elmo in Grouchland (voice), Muppet Race Mania, Star Wars 2: Attack of the Clones, Monsters Inc. (voice), Star Wars III: Revenge of the Sith (voice), Zathura: A Space Adventure (voice). *Director only*: Little Shop of Horrors, Dirty Rotten Scoundrels, What About Bob?, Housesitter, The Indian in the Cupboard, In & Out, Bowfinger, The Score, Ump, The Stepford Wives, Death at a Funeral.
TELEVISION: *Movies/Voice:* Hey Cinderella!, The Great Santa Claus Switch, Tales from Muppetland: The Frog Prince, Tales from Muppetland: The Muppet Musicians of Bremen, The Muppets Valentine Show, Out to Lunch (actor), The Muppet Show: Sex and Violence, Emmet Otter's Jug-Band Christmas (also creative consult.), Christmas Eve on Sesame Street,A Special Sesame Street Christmas, The Muppets Go Hollywood, John Denver and the Muppets: A Christmas Together, The Muppets Go to the Movies, The Fantastic Miss Piggy Show, Don't Eat the Pictures: Sesame Street at the Metropolitan Museum of Art, Big Bird in China, The Muppets: A Celebration of 30 Years, A Muppet Family Christmas, Sesame Street, Special, Sesame Street Jam: A Musical Celebration, Cinderelmo, The Funkhousers. *Series*: Sesame Street (3 Emmy Awards), The Muppet Show (Emmy Award, 1978, 4 other noms.), Saturday Night Live, Star Wars: The Clone Wars (voice). *Guest:* More than 145 appearances.

P

PACINO, AL
Actor. b. New York, NY, April 25, 1940. e. High Sch. for the Performing Arts, NY; Actors Studio, 1966; HB Studios, NY. Gained attention as stage actor initially at Charles Playhouse, Boston (Why Is a Crooked Letter, The Peace Creeps, Arturo Ui). Served as artistic dir. (with Ellen Burstyn), Actors Studio (1982-84). Received Golden Globe, Cecil B. DeMille Award 2001. Received AFI Lifetime Achievement Award for Acting 2007.
THEATRE: NY: The Indian Wants the Bronx (Obie Award), Does a Tiger Wear a Necktie? (Tony & Theatre World Awards, 1969), The Local Stigmatic, Camino Real, The Connection, Hello Out There, Tiger at the Gates, The Basic Training of Pavlo Hummel (Tony Award, 1977), Richard III, American Buffalo, Julius Caesar, Chinese Coffee, Salome, Hughie (also dir.).
PICTURES: Me Natalie (debut, 1969), The Panic in Needle Park, The Godfather (Academy Award nom.Golden Globe nom. 1973), Scarecrow, Serpico (Academy Award nom.; Golden Globe Award 1974), The Godfather Part II (Academy Award nom.; Golden Globe nom. 1975), Dog Day Afternoon (Academy Award nom. ; Golden Globe nom. 1976), Bobby Deerfield (Golden Globe nom. 1978), ... And Justice for All (Academy Award nom.; Golden Globe nom. 1980), Cruising, Author! Author! (Golden Globe nom. 1983), Scarface (Golden Globe nom. 1984), Revolution, Sea of Love (Golden Globe nom. 1990), Dick Tracy (Academy Award nom.; Golden Globe nom. 1991), The Godfather Part III (Golden Globe nom. 1991), Frankie and Johnny, Glengarry Glen Ross (Academy Award nom.; Golden Globe nom. 1993), Scent of a Woman (Academy Award, Golden Globe Award 1993), Carlito's Way, A Day to Remember, City Hall, Heat, Two Bits, Looking for Richard (also dir.), Donnie Brasco, The Devil's Advocate, The Insider, Any Given Sunday, Chinese Coffee (also dir.), S1m0ne, People I Know, Insomnia, The Recruit, Gigli, The Merchant of Venice, Two for the Money, 88 Minutes, Ocean's Thirteen, Righteous Kill, Rififi, Mary Mother of Christ, Wilde Salome (also writer, dir.), The Son of No One, King Lear.
TELEVISION: *Movie:* You Don't Know Jack. *Mini-series:* Angels in America (Emmy Award, Golden Globe Award 2004). *Documentaries/Specials:* America: A Tribute to Heroes. Looking for Richard (doc., dir., prod., writer, DGA Award 1997). Has appeared in numerous TV documentaries and awards specials. *Guest:* More than 108 appearances.

PACKER, JIM
Executive. b. Chicago, IL, April 3, 1963. e. B.S., business and marketing, University of Colorado, 1985. Packer began his career in 1986 with Buena Vista Domestic Television Distribution as an account exec. in New York. Advanced to dir. of sales/Eastern region. Promoted to exec. dir./Midwest Region in Chicago, before returning to New York to assume the position of vice president/Eastern Region. During his tenure at Buena Vista, Packer handled the distribution of off-network product, theatrical films, and first-run syndication of such high-profile properties as TV series Home Improvement, Live with Regis and Kathie Lee and Golden Girls, along with numerous movie packages. During Packer's 15 years with Buena Vista Domestic TV Distribution, he rose to VP/general sales manager, West, 1993; and senior VP/general sales manager, 1996; He moved to MGM in Jan. 2001 as executive VP, North America television distribution; was elevated to executive VP, worldwide TV distribution in April 2005 and was named to current position—president, MGM Worldwide Television Distribution Group—in Sept. 2006.

PACULA, JOANNA
Actress. b. Tomszowau, Poland, Jan. 2, 1957. Member of Polish National Theatre School. Model in Poland, France, then U.S. where she moved in early 1980s.
PICTURES: Gorky Park (Golden Globe nom. 1984), Not Quite Paradise, Death Before Dishonor, The Kiss, Sweet Lies, Options, Marked for Death, Husbands and Lovers, Tombstone, Warlock: The Armageddon, Private Lessons 2, Every Breath, The Silence of the Hams, Kim Novak is on the Phone, Deep Red, Timemaster, Not Like Us, Last Gasp, Captain Nuke and the Bomber Boys, In Praise of Older Women, Heaven Before I Die, Haunted Sea, My Giant, The White Raven, Error in Judgment, Virus, Crash and Byrnes, The Art of Murder, No Place Like Home, The Hit, Warrior Angels, Cupid's Prey, DinoCroc (video), Moscow Heat, El Padrino, Forget About It, The Cutter, Honor, Shannon's Rainbow, Black Widow, Madoff: Made Off with America.
TELEVISION: *Movies*: Escape From Sobibor, Breaking Point, Condition: Critical, Under Investigation, Business for Pleasure, Sweet Deception, Lightning: Bolts of Destruction *Mini-series:* Crossings. *Series*: Dom, Jan Serce, E.A.R.T.H. Force, Brutally Normal.

PADDEN, PRESTON
Executive. b.Washington, D.C., Nov. 26, 1948. e. Undergrad. degree, Univ. of Maryland; Law degree from George Washington Univ., Washington, D.C. In Jan. 1990, was senior v.p., Affiliates for Fox Broadcasting Co. Padden was promoted to pres., telecommunications and TV, for News Corp. and then tapped for chmn. and CEO job of American Sky Broadcasting (ASkyB), a satellite TV joint venture between News Corp. and MCI. Joined ABC in 1997, and became pres., ABC Television Network. In July 1998, Padden returned to Wash., D.C. area as Disney's executive v.p., govt. relations for The Walt Disney Company, and today still serves as Disney's top lobbyist in Washington.

PAGE, ANTHONY
Director. b. Bangalore, India, Sept. 21, 1935. e. Oxford. Stage work includes Inadmissible Evidence, Waiting for Godot, A Patriot for Me, Look Back in Anger, Uncle Vanya, Mrs. Warren's Profession, Alpha Beta, Heartbreak House, Absolute Hell.
PICTURES: Inadmissible Evidence (debut, 1968), Alpha Beta, I Never Promised You A Rose Garden, Absolution, The Lady Vanishes, Forbidden, Silent Cries, My Zinc Bed.
TELEVISION: *Movies*: The Parachute, Pueblo, The Missiles of October (Emmy nom. 1975), F. Scott Fitzgerald in Hollywood, Collision Course, F.D.R. The Last Year, The Patricia Neal Story (DGA nom. 1982), Bill, Johnny Belinda, Grace Kelly, Bill: On His Own, Murder: By Reason of Insanity, Second Serve, Monte Carlo, Heartbreak House, Pack of Lies, Scandal in a Small Town, Chernobyl: The Final Warning, Absolute Hell, Human Bomb, My Zinc Bed. *Mini-series*: The Nightmare Year, Middlemarch.

PAGE, ELLEN
Actress. b. Halifax, Nova Scotia, Feb. 21, 1987. e. Neptune Theater School. Named Star of Tomorrow by Quigley Publishing Poll for 2007.
PICTURES: Hard Candy, X-Men: The Last Stand, The Tracey Fragments, Juno (Academy Award nom.; Golden Globe nom. 2008), The Stone Angel, Smart People, Peacock, Whip It!, Inception, Super.
TELEVISION: *Movies:* Pit Pony, Mrs. Ashboro's Cat, Homeless to Harvard: The Liz Murray Story, Going for Broke, I Downloaded a Ghost, Tilda. *Series:* Pit Pony, Rideau Hall, Trailer Park Boys, ReGenesis.

PAGETT, NICOLA
Actress. r.n. Nicola Scott. b. Cairo, Egypt, June 15, 1945. e. Royal Acad. of Dramatic Art. Appeared with Citizen's Rep. Theatre, Glasgow.
THEATRE: Cornelia (debut, 1964, Worthing, U.K.), A Boston

Story (London debut, 1968), A Midsummer Night's Dream, Widowers' Houses, The Misanthrope, A Voyage 'Round My Father, The Ride Across Lake Constance, Ghosts, The Seagull, Hamlet, The Marriage of Figaro, A Family and a Fortune, Gaslight, Yahoo, Old Times (L.A.).
PICTURES: Anne of the Thousand Days, There's a Girl in My Soup, Operation Daybreak, Oliver's Story, Privates on Parade, An Awfully Big Adventure.
TELEVISION: *Movies*: Franken-stein: The True Story, The Sweeney, Aren't We All. *Mini-series*: A Woman of Substance, Anna Karenina, Up Rising. *Series*: Upstairs Downstairs. A Bit of a Do, Ain't Misbehavin'.

PALCY, EUZHAN
Director, Writer. b. Martinique, Jan. 13, 1957. e. Earned a degree in French lit., Sorbonne and a film degree from Vaugirard School in Paris. Began career working as TV writer and dir. in Martinique. Also made 2 children's records. In Paris worked as film editor, screenwriter and dir. of shorts. She received grant from French gov. to make 1st feature Sugar Cane Alley which cost $800,000 and won Silver Lion Prize at Venice Film Fest., 1983.
PICTURES: Sugar Cane Alley (also writer), The Devil's Workshop, Rue cases nègres, Wings Against the Wind (also story), Dionysos (writer), A Dry White Season (also co-s.p.), Simeon (also writer), Aime Cesaire: A Voice for History (documentary).
TELEVISION: *Movies:* The Messenger (dir., writer, prod.), Ruby Bridges (dir., co-prod.), The Killing Yard (dir.), Parcours de dissidents (dir., writer), Les mariées de l'isle Bourbon (dir., writer).

PALIN, MICHAEL, CBE
Actor, Writer. b. Sheffield, Yorkshire, England, May 5, 1943. e. Oxford. Performed there in Pinter's The Birthday Party and in revue Hang Your Head Down and Die (also in West End prod., 1964). At Oxford met Terry Jones, began writing comedy together, incl. TV series The Frost Report. Became member of Monty Python's Flying Circus. On stage with troupe both in London and on B'way.
PICTURES: And Now for Something Completely Different (also co-s.p.), Monty Python and the Holy Grail (also co-s.p.), Jabberwocky, Life of Brian (also co-s.p.), Time Bandits, The Secret Policeman's Other Ball, Monty Python Live at the Hollywood Bowl (also co-s.p.), The Missionary (also co-prod., s.p.), Monty Python's The Meaning of Life (also co-music, co-s.p.), A Private Function, Brazil, A Fish Called Wanda, American Friends (also co-s.p.), Fierce Creatures, The Wind In The Willows (voice), Not the Messiah: He's a Very Naughty Boy.
TELEVISION: *Movies: Actor:* How to Irritate People, Pleasure at Her Majesty's, Red Dress, All You Need Is Cash, The Wind in the Willows (voice), The Willows in Winter (voice). *Writer:* Marty Amok, Secrets, East of Ipswich. *Mini-series:* G.B.H. (actor), The Human Face. *Series: Writer:* The Frost Report, The Late Show, A Series of Bird's, Twice a Fortnight (also performer), Do Not Adjust Your Set, Horne A' Plenty, Broaden Your Mind (also characters), Complete and Utter History of Britain, Monty Python's Flying Circus, The Two Ronnies, Black and Blue, *Series: Actor:* Ripping Yarns, Tracey Ullman: A Class Act. *Documentaries/Specials:* More than 45 appearances in various documentaries, including Parrot Sketch Not Included: Twenty Years of Monty Python, Pole to Pole (also writer), It's... the Monty Python Story (also writer), Hemingway Adventure, Sahara with Michael Palin (mini-series), Himalaya with Michael Palin (mini-series), How to Use Your Coconuts (video documentary short), Monty Python's Flying Circus: Live at Aspen, Pythonland, The Unknown Peter Sellers, The Sketch Show Story, The Secret Life of Brian, New Europe (series), Around the World in 20 Years (narr., writer). *Guest*: More than 180 appearances.

PALMER, BETSY
Actress. b. East Chicago, IN, Nov. 1, 1926. e. DePaul U. Studied at Neighborhood Playhouse, HB Studio with Uta Hagen. On Broadway in The Grand Prize, South Pacific, Affair of Honor, Cactus Flower, Roar Like a Dove, Eccentricities of a Nightingale, Same Time Next Year and many regional prods.
PICTURES: Mister Roberts, The Long Gray Line, Queen Bee, The Tin Star, The True Story of Lynn Stuart, The Last Angry Man, Friday the 13th, Friday the 13th Part 2, Unveiled, The Fear: Resurrection, Bell Witch: The Movie.
TELEVISION: All major live shows such as Studio One, U.S. Steel Hour, Kraft Theatre. *Movies*: Isabel's Choice, Windmills of the Gods, Goddess of Love, Still Not Quite Human, Columbo: Death Hits the Jackpot, Not Quite Human III. *Series*: Masquerade Party (panelist), What's It For? (panelist), I've Got a Secret (panelist, 11 years), No. 96 (series), Candid Camera (host), The Today Show (host), Wifeline (host), Knots Landing. *Guest*: More than 77 appearances.

PALMER, PATRICK J.
Producer. b. Los Angeles, CA, Dec. 28, 1936. Began career with 10-year apprenticeship at Mirisch Company, involved in making of West Side Story, Seven Days in May, The Fortune Cookie, etc. 1966, began association with Norman Jewison, serving as assoc. prod. on The Landlord, Fiddler on the Roof, Jesus Christ Superstar, Rollerball. 1972, prod., with Jewison, Billy Two Hats; exec. prod. on The Dogs of War.
PICTURES: *Co-producer*: And Justice for All, Best Friends, Iceman, A Soldier's Story (Academy Award nom. 1985), Agnes of God, Children of a Lesser God (Academy Award nom. 1987), Moonstruck (Academy Award nom. 1988), Stanley & Iris, Mermaids, Paradise (also writer), Made in America, Don Juan Demarco. *Exec. producer:* Milk Money, Iron Will, Mrs. Winterbourne, The Rage: Carrie 2, Hellboy, After the Sunset, Little Children. *Producer:* Blade II, The Shrink Is In (also unit prod. mgr.), Rex-patriates.

PALMINTERI, CHAZZ
Actor, Writer, Director. r.n. Calogero Lorenzo Palminteri. b. Bronx, NY, May 15, 1951. e. Bronx Comm. Coll. NY stage in The Guys in the Truck (B'way), The King's Men, 22 Years, The Flatbush Faithful, A Bronx Tale (which he also wrote).
PICTURES: *Actor*: The Last Dragon, Oscar, Innocent Blood, There Goes the Neighborhood, A Bronx Tale (also s.p.), Bullets Over Broadway (Academy Award nom. 1995), The Perez Family, The Usual Suspects, The Last Word, Jade, Mulholland Falls, Hurlyburly, Analyze This, Scar City, Excellent Cadavers, Stuart Little (voice), Down to Earth, Lady and the Tramp II: Scamp's Adventure (voice), One-Eyed King, Poolhall Junkies, One Last Ride, Noel (also dir.), Running Scared, Dying for Dolly, Push, Little Man, A Guide to Recognizing Your Saints, Arthur and the Invisibles (voice), Body Armour, The Dukes (also co-prod.), Yonkers Joe, Jolene, Once More with Feeling, Cat Tale (voice), The Oogieloves in the Big Balloon Adventure, Hollywood & Wine, Henry and Me (voice), American Empire. *Producer*: Dante and the Debutante (also writer). *Director*: For Life (also writer).
TELEVISION: *Movies:* Peter Gunn, Boss of Bosses, Women vs. Men (dir. only), Drift. *Series:* Oz (dir.), Kojak (also pilot, 2005). *Guest:* More than 57 appearances.

PALTROW, GWYNETH
Actress. b. Los Angeles, CA, Sept. 28, 1972. p. actress Blythe Danner, and the late dir.-prod. Bruce Paltrow. Moved to NY when she was 11.
THEATRE: *Williamstown:* Picnic, The Adventures of Huck Finn, Sweet Bye and Bye, The Seagull.
PICTURES: Shout (debut, 1991), Hook, Malice, Flesh and Bone, Mrs. Parker and the Vicious Circle, Jefferson in Paris, Moonlight and Valentino, Seven, The Pallbearer, Sydney, Emma, Hush, Out of the Past, Sliding Doors, Great Expectations, A Perfect Murder, Duets, Shakespeare in Love (Academy Award, Golden Globe Award 1999), The Talented Mr. Ripley, The Intern, Duets (also sings), Bounce, Shallow Hal, The Anniversary Party, Pootie Tang, The Royal Tenenbaums, Searching For Debra Winger (documentary), Austin Powers in Goldmember, Possession, A View From the Top, Sylvia, Sky Captain and the World of Tomorrow, Proof (Golden Globe nom. 2006), Dealbreaker (short; dir. & writer only), Running With Scissors, Love and Other Disasters, Have You Heard?, The Good Night, Iron Man, Two Lovers, Iron Man 2, Love Don't Let Me Down, Contagion.
TELEVISION: *Movies*: Cruel Doubt, Deadly Relations, Classical Baby (I'm Grown Up Now): The Poetry Show. *Guest*: More than 103 appearances.

PANAMA, CHARLES A. (CHUCK)
Publicist, b. Chicago, IL, Feb. 2, 1925. e. Northwestern U., Beloit Coll., UCLA. Publicist, Los Angeles Jr. Chamber of Commerce; So. Calif. sports ed., Los Angeles bureau, INS; publicist, 20th Century-Fox Studios; adv.-pub. dir., Arcola Pics.; opened L.A. office, John Springer Associates; v.p. Jerry Pam & Assoc.; account exec., Rogers, Cowan & Brenner, Inc.; directed m.p. div., Jim Mahoney & Assoc.; v.p. Guttman & Pam, Ltd.; asst. pub. dir., Twentieth TV. Owner, pres. Chuck Panama P.R.; Panama was the winner of the 1990 Les Mason Award and 1993 Robert Yeager Award, Publicists Guild of America. He's been a Docent of the Museum of Flying in Santa Monica, CA.

PANKIN, STUART
Actor. b. Philadelphia, PA, April 8, 1946. e. Dickinson Coll., Columbia U. Stage debut 1968 in The War of the Roses.
THEATRE: *NY*: Timon of Athens, Tale of Cymbeline, Mary Stuart, The Crucible, Twelfth Night, Glorious Age, Wings, Gorky, Joseph and the Amazing Technicolor Dreamcoat, Three Sisters, The Inspector General.
PICTURES: Scavenger Hunt, Hangar 18, The Hollywood Knights, An Eye for an Eye, Earthbound, Irreconcilable Differences, The Dirt Bike Kid, Fatal Attraction, Love at Stake, Second Sight, That's Adequate, Arachnophobia, Mannequin 2 on the Move, The Vagrant, I Love Trouble, The Silence of the Hams, Squanto: A Warrior's Tale, Congo, Striptease, Honey We Shrunk Ourselves, Encounter in the Third Dimension, The Settlement, Chasing Destiny, Now You Know, Misadventures in 3D (short), Miss Castaway and the Island Girls, Public Interest.
TELEVISION: *Movies*: Valentine Magic on Love Island, Father & Scout, Down Out and Dangerous, Babylon 5: The River of Souls, Like Father Like Santa, Zenon: Girl of the 21st Century, Batman Beyond: The Movie, Uncle Gus in: For the Love of Monkeys, Zenon: The Zequel, Zenon: Z3, An Accidental Christmas. *Pilots*: Car Wash, Wonderful World of Philip Malley. *Series*: The San Pedro Beach Bums, No Soap Radio, Not Necessarily the News, Nearly Departed, Falcon Crest, Knots Landing, Bonkers (voice), Animaniacs (voices), Nick Freno: Licensed Teacher, For Your Love. *Documentaries/Specials:* Stuart Pankin (also co-exec. prod., co-writer). *Guest*: More than 80 appearances.

PANTOLIANO, JOE
Actor. b. Jersey City, NJ, Sept. 12, 1954.
THEATRE: *NY*: The Kitchen, The Off Season, The Death Star, Visions of Kerouac. *Regional*: One Flew Over the Cuckoo's Nest, Skaters, Brothers, Italian American Reconciliation (Dramalogue Award), Orphans (Dramalogue Award, Drama Critic Circle nomination), Pvt. Wars.
PICTURES: The Idolmaker, Monsignor, Risky Business, Eddie and the Cruisers, The Mean Season, The Goonies, Running Scared, La Bamba, The Squeeze, Amazon Women on the Moon, Empire of the Sun, The In Crowd, Midnight Run, Downtown, The Last of the Finest, Short Time, Zandalee, Used People, Three of Hearts, Goin' to Mexico, The Fugitive, Calendar Girl, Me and the Kid, Teresa's Tattoo, Baby's Day Out, Bad Boys, Congo (cameo), Steal Big Steal Little, Bound, The Immortals, Top of the World, Tinseltown, U.S. Marshals, The Taxman, New Blood, The Life Before This, Black and White, The Matrix, Ready to Rumble, Memento, Silver Man, Pray for the Cardinal, A Better Way to Die, Cats and Dogs (voice), The Adventures of Pluto Nash, Daredevil, Bad Boys II, Second Best (also prod.), Just Like Mona (s.p., dir. only), Perfect Opposites, Racing Stripes (voice), The Moguls, The Easter Egg Adventure, Larry the Cable Guy: Health Inspector, Unknown, Falling Up, Spring Break '83, The Job, No Kidding, Me Too! (doc., dir.), Percy Jackson & the Olympians: The Lightning Thief, Cats & Dogs: The Revenge of Kitty Galore (voice), The Legend of Secret Pass (voice).
TELEVISION: *Movies*: More Than Friends, Alcatraz: The Whole Shocking Story, Nightbreaker, Destination America, El Diablo, One Special Victory, Through the Eyes of a Killer, The Last (also co-assoc. prod.), EZ Streets (pilot), Ed McBain's 87th Precinct: Ice, Natural Enemy, Olive the Other Reindeer, Deceit. *Mini-series*: Robert F. Kennedy: His Life and Times, From Here to Eternity. *Series*: Free Country, The Fanelli Boys, Beethoven (voice), EZ Streets, Godzilla (voice), Sugar Hill, The Sopranos (Emmy Award 2003), The Handler, Dr. Vegas, Waterfront. *Guest*: More than 100 appearances.

PAPAS, IRENE
Actress. b. Chiliomodion, Greece, Sept. 3, 1926. Entered dramatic school at 12. At 16 sang and danced in variety shows before debuting in Greek films, 1950. 1958 appeared with Greek Popular Theatre in Athens. Received Salonika Film Fest. Awards for the films Antigone, Electra.
THEATRE: The Idiot, Journey's End, The Merchant of Venice, Inherit the Wind, That Summer, That Fall, Iphigenia in Aulis.
PICTURES: Lost Angels (debut, 1950), Dead City, The Unfaithful, Atilla the Hun, Theodora the Slave Empress, Whirlpool, Tribute to a Bad Man, Antigone, The Guns of Navarone, Electra, The Moon-Spinners, Zorba the Greek, We Still Kill the Old Way, The Desperate Ones, The Brotherhood, Anne of the Thousand Days, Z, A Dream of Kings, The Trojan Women, Roma Bene, Bambina, Mohammed: Messenger of God, Iphigenia, Bloodline, Eboli, Lion of the Desert, Erendira, Into the Night, The Assisi Underground, Sweet Country, High Season, Chronicle of a Death Foretold, Island, Drums of Fire, Banquet, Zoe, Up Down and Sideways, Party, Anxiety, Yerma, The Wog Boy, Captain Corelli's Mandolin, Returning in Autumn. A Talking Picture.
TELEVISION: *Movies:* Moses the Lawgiver, Les Tribulations de Manuel, Le Banquet, Jacob, The Odyssey. *Mini-series*: L'Odissea, A Mala de Cartão, Ocean.

PAQUIN, ANNA
Actress. b. Winnipeg, Manitoba, Canada, July 24, 1982.
PICTURES: The Piano (Academy Award, Best Actress in Supporting Role, 1994; Golden Globe nom.), Fly Away Home, Jane Eyre, Amistad, Hurlyburly, Begin the Beguine, A Walk on the Moon, Sleepless Beauty, Castle in the Sky (voice), All the Rage, She's All That, X-Men, Almost Famous, Finding Forrester, Buffalo Soldiers, Darkness, The 25th Hour, X2, Steamboy (voice), The Squid and the Whale, X-Men: The Last Stand, Margaret, Blue State (also exec. prod.), Trick 'r Treat, Flying Into Love, The Romantics, Open House.
TELEVISION: *Movies*: The Member of the Wedding, Joan of Arc (voice), Bury My Heart at Wounded Knee (Emmy nom.; 2007 Golden Globe 2008), The Courageous Heart of Irena Sendler (Golden Globe nom. 2010). *Series:* True Blood (also pilot, Emmy nom. 2007, Golden Globe Award 2009, 1 other nom.). *Guest:* More than 55 appearances.

PARÉ, MICHAEL
Actor. b. Brooklyn, NY, Oct. 9, 1959. e. Culinary Inst. of America, Hyde Park, NY. Worked as chef and model before being discovered by ABC talent agent.
PICTURES: Eddie and the Cruisers (debut, 1983), Streets of Fire, The Philadelphia Experiment, Under Cover (Aust.), Space Rage, Instant Justice, The Women's Club, World Gone Wild, Eddie and the Cruisers II: Eddie Lives, Moon 44, Dragon Fight, Concrete War, The Closer, Into the Sun, Midnight Heat, First Light, Point of Impact, Village of the Damned, Bad Moon, Coyote Run, Strip Search, Merchant of Death, Falling Fire, 2103: The Deadly Wake, Hope Floats, October 22, Back to Even, The Virgin Suicides, Men of Means, Space Fury, Sanctimony, Peril, A Month of Sundays, Blackwoods, Two Faced, Red Serpent, Heart of America, Fate, Bloodrayne, Inland Empire, Seed, Ninja Cheerleaders, Polycarp, Dark World, Postal, BloodRayne II: Deliverance, 100 Feet, The Perfect Sleep, Ninja Cheerleaders, 1968 Tunnel Rats, Direct Contact, Far Cry, Rampage, Cool Dog, Bloodrayne: The Third Reich, Amphibious 3D, The Lincoln Lawyer.
TELEVISION: *Movies*: Crazy Times, Houston Knights, Empire City, Triplecross, The Colony, Carver's Gate, The Malibu Branch, Falling Fire, Sanctimony, Komodo vs. Cobra (also exec. prod.), Saurian. *Series*: The Greatest American Hero, Houston Knights, Starhunter.

PARENT, MARY
Executive. b. 1968. e. Studied business at USC before taking an agent trainee job at ICM. In 1994, Parent moved to New Line Cinema in 1994 and became v.p., production while there. She originally joined Universal in 1997 as a senior v.p. and eventually became vice chairman in 2003, a position she held through 2005. Since 2005 she and Scott Stuber had an exclusive producing deal on the Universal lot. In March 2008, MGM recruited Parent to a newly created position of Chairperson, Worldwide Motion Picture Group. In this position Parent oversaw worldwide theatrical production, distribution, marketing and business affairs for MGM. She resigned her position with MGM October, 2010.

PARISH, JAMES ROBERT
Film Historian, Biographer. b. Cambridge, MA, April 21, 1944. e. U. of PA (BA, Phi Beta Kappa); U. of PA Law School (LLB). Member of NY Bar. Founder Entertainment Copyright Research Co., Inc. 1968-69, film reporter, Motion Picture Daily, Weekly Variety. 1969-70, entertainment publicist, Harold Rand & Co. (NY). Currently author, contributor to arts sections of major national newspapers and entertainment trade papers, on-air interviewee for cable/TV documentaries, and series editor of show business book series.
AUTHOR: Hollywood's Great Musicals, Prostitution in Hollywood Films, Ghosts & Angels in Hollywood Films, Hollywood Songsters, Prison Pictures From Hollywood, Hollywood Baby Boomers, The Great Detective Pictures, The Great Cop Pictures, The Great Science Fiction Pictures II, Complete Actors TV Credits (1948-88), The Great Combat Pictures, Black Action Pictures From Hollywood, The Great Detective Pictures, The Great Western Pictures II: The Great Gangster Pictures II: The Great Spy Pictures II, Actors TV Credits, The Best of MGM, The Forties Gals, The Great American Movies Book, Hollywood Happiness, The Funsters, Hollywood on Hollywood, The Hollywood Beauties, Elvis!, The Great Science Fiction Pictures, The Child Stars, The Jeannette MacDonald Story, Great Movie Heroes, Liza!, The RKO Gals, Vincent Price Unmasked, The George Raft File, The Emmy Awards, Hollywood Death Book, Gays & Lesbians in Mainstream Cinema, Hollywood Celebrity Death Book (updated), Let's Talk! America's Favorite TV Talk Show Hosts, Today's Black Hollywood, Pirates and Seafaring Swashbucklers, Rosie: Rosie O'Donnell's Story, The Unofficial 'Murder She Wrote' Casebook, Whoopi Goldberg: Her Journey From Poverty to Mega-Stardom, The Hollywood Book of Scandals: The Shocking, Often Disgraceful Deeds and Affairs of Over 100 American Movie and TV Idols.

PARK, NICK
Director, Writer, Animator. b. Preston, Lancashire, England, December 6, 1958. e. Sheffield Hallam University. Awarded honorary doctor of arts degree by Bath University, UK. Winner of three Academy Awards for Best Short Animated Film.
PICTURES: War Story (anim. only), Creature Comforts (Academy Award 1990), Wallace & Gromit: A Grand Day Out (Academy Award nom. 1991), Wallace & Gromit: The Wrong Trousers (Academy Award 1994), Wallace & Gromit: A Close Shave (Academy Award 1996), Wallace & Gromit: The Best of Aardman Animation, Wallace & Gromit: The Aardman Collection 2, Chicken Run (also prod.), The Wallace & Gromit Movie: Curse of the Were-Rabbit (also prod., Academy Award 2006), Flushed Away (voice), Wallace and Gromit in 'A Matter of Loaf and Death' (short, Academy Award nom. 2010).
TELEVISION: *Movie:* Wallace and Gromit in 'A Matter of Loaf and Death' (writer, dir.). *Series:* Shaun the Sheep (exec. prod., writer), Creature Comforts America (exec. prod., Emmy nom. 2008).

PARKER, ALAN
Director, Writer. b. Islington, London, England, Feb. 14, 1944. Worked way up in advertising industry from mail room to top writer and dir. of nearly 500 TV commercials between 1969-78. Appointed chmn. of British Film Institute, 1997.
PICTURES: Melody (s.p., 1968). *Director: Writer*: No Hard Feelings, Our Cissy, Footsteps, Bugsy Malone (Brit. Acad. Award for best s.p.), Midnight Express (Academy Award nom.; DGA nom.; Golden Globe nom. 1979, Brit. Acad. Award), Fame, Shoot the Moon, Pink Floyd—The Wall, Birdy, Angel Heart, Mississippi Burning (Academy Award nom.; DGA nom.; Golden Globe nom. 1989), Come and See the Paradise, The Commitments (also cameo; BAFTA Award for best dir., 1991), The Road to Wellville (also co-prod.), Evita (also prod., Golden Globe nom. 1997), Angela's Ashes (also prod.), The Life of David Gale (also prod.), The Ice at the Bottom of the World (also prod.), Coram Boy.
TELEVISION: The Evacuees (Brit. Acad. Award), Bomber (composer).

PARKER, COREY
Actor. b. New York, NY, July 8, 1965. e. NYU.

THEATRE: *NY:* Meeting the Winter Bike Rider (Off-B'way debut, 1984), Been Taken, The Bloodletters, The Semi-Formal.
PICTURES: Scream for Help (debut, 1984), Friday the 13th Part V: A New Beginning, Something Special, Nine 1/2 Weeks, Biloxi Blues, How I Got Into College, Big Man on Campus, White Palace, Flesh Suitcase, Fool's Paradise, Woman's Picture, One Came Home.
TELEVISION: *Movies*: Courage, At Mother's Request, Liz: The Elizabeth Taylor Story, A Mother's Prayer, Mr. & Mrs. Loving, Encino Woman. *Series:* Eddie Dodd, Flying Blind, Blue Skies, The Love Boat: The Next Wave, thirtysomething, The Love Boat: The Next Wave. *Specials*: Don't Touch, Teen Father, The Lost Language of Cranes. *Pilot:* Sons of Gunz.

PARKER, FESS
Actor. b. Fort Worth, TX, Aug. 16, 1924. e. USC. U.S. Navy, 1943-46; national co., Mr. Roberts, 1951.
PICTURES: Untamed Frontier (debut, 1952), No Room for the Groom, Springfield Rifle, Thunder Over the Plains, Island in the Sky, The Kid From Left Field, Take Me to Town, Them!, Battle Cry, Davy Crockett—King of the Wild Frontier (from Disney TV show), Davy Crockett and the River Pirates (from TV show), The Great Locomotive Chase, Westward Ho! the Wagons, Old Yeller, The Light in the Forest, The Hangman, Alias Jesse James (cameo), The Jayhawkers, Hell Is for Heroes, Smoky.
TELEVISION: *Movies*: Along the Oregon Trail, Climb an Angry Mountain. *Series*: Mr. Smith Goes to Washington, Daniel Boone. *Documentaries/Specials*: Walt: The Man Behind the Myth. *Guest*: More than 29 appearances.
(d. March 18, 2010)

PARKER, HUTCH
Executive. b. 1964. Birth name Joseph Hutchison Parker. e. graduate of Princeton University, 1986. From 1991 to 1995 Parker was senior v.p. of production at Orion Pictures and director of development at Simpson-Bruckheimer Productions. Parker joined News Corp.'s 20th Century Fox (TCF) in 1995 as senior v.p. of production and was named production president in 1999. In Jan. 2005, Parker was promoted to president, 20th Century Fox. In Jan. 2006, Parker, whose TCF division delivered over $2 billion dollars worldwide box office for movies released in 2006, was elevated to vice chairman, Twentieth Century Fox Film Group, adding oversight of Fox Animation to his duties at TCF. Currently chairman of New Regency, the largest Independent Studio.

PARKER, JAMESON
Actor. b. Baltimore, MD, Nov. 18, 1947. e. Beloit College. Professional stage debut in Washington Theatre Club production, Caligula. Acted with Arena Stage in DC; worked in dinner theatres and summer stock. Moved to N.Y., working in TV commercials and acted in play, Equus (Coconut Grove Playhouse).
PICTURES: The Bell Jar (debut, 1979), A Small Circle of Friends, White Dog, American Justice (also prod.), Jackals, Prince of Darkness, Curse of the Crystal Eye, The Secret of NIMH 2: Timmy to the Rescue (video, voice).
TELEVISION: *Movies*: Women at West Point, Anatomy of a Seduction, The Gathering Part II, The Promise of Love, Callie and Son, A Caribbean Mystery, Who Is Julia?, Spy, She Says She's Innocent, Dead Before Dawn, Simon & Simon: In Trouble Again, Have You Seen My Son?, Dead Man's Island; Something Borrowed Something Blue. *Series*: Somerset, One Life to Live, Simon and Simon, JAG.

PARKER, MARY-LOUISE
Actress. b. Ft. Jackson, SC, Aug. 2, 1964. e. Bard College. 1990, received Clarence Derwent Award for her work in the theatre.
THEATRE: *B'way*: Prelude to a Kiss (Theatre World Award). *Off-B'way*: Hayfever, The Girl in Pink, Babylon Gardens, Throwing Your Voice, Four Dogs and a Bone, Communicating Doors. *Regional*: The Importance of Being Earnest, Up in Saratoga, The Miser, Hay Fever, The Night of the Iguana, The Age of Pie.
PICTURES: Signs of Life (debut, 1989), Longtime Companion, Grand Canyon, Fried Green Tomatoes, Mr. Wonderful, Naked in New York, The Client, Bullets Over Broadway, Boys on the Side, Reckless, The Portrait of a Lady, Murder in Mind, The Maker, Let the Devil Wear Black, Goodbye Lover, The Five Senses, Pipe Dream, Red Dragon, Best Thief in the World, Saved!, Romance & Cigarettes, The Assassination of Jesse James by the Coward Robert Ford, The Spiderwick Chronicles, Les Passages, Solitary Man, Howl, Red.
TELEVISION: *Movies*: Too Young the Hero, A Place for Annie, The Simple Life of Noah Dearborn, Cupid & Cate, Master Spy: The Robert Hanssen Story, Miracle Run, Vinegar Hill, The Robber Bride (Emmy nom. 2007). *Mini-series:* Angels in America (Emmy Award, Golden Globe, Best Perf. By Actress, Supporting Role, 2004). *Series*: The West Wing (Emmy nom. 2002), Weeds (Golden Globe Award 2006, 3 other noms.; 3 Emmy noms.). *Guest:* More than 55 appearances.

PARKER, SARAH JESSICA
Actress. b. Nelsonville, OH, March 25, 1965. m. actor Matthew Broderick. President Pretty Matches Productions. Was dancer with Cincinnati Ballet and American Ballet Theatre. Professional debut at age 8 in TV special The Little Match Girl.
THEATRE: *NY*: The Innocents, By Strouse, Annie (title role for 2 yrs.), To Gillian on Her 37th Birthday, The Heidi Chronicles, The Substance of Fire, Sylvia, How To Succeed In Business Without Really Trying, Once Upon A Mattress, others.
PICTURES: Rich Kids (debut, 1979), Somewhere Tomorrow, Footloose, Firstborn, Girls Just Want to Have Fun, Flight of the Navigator, L.A. Story, Honeymoon in Vegas, Hocus Pocus, Striking Distance, Ed Wood, Miami Rhapsody, If Lucy Fell, The Substance of Fire, First Wives Club, Extreme Measures, Mars Attacks!, 'Til There Was You, Isn't She Great, Dudley Do-Right, State and Main, Life Without Dick, Strangers with Candy, The Family Stone (Golden Globe nom. 2006), Spinning Into Butter (also prod.), Slammer, Failure to Launch, Smart People, Sex and the City, Did You Hear About the Morgans?, Sex and the City 2 (also prod., soundtrack performer).
TELEVISION: *Movies*: My Body My Child, Going for the Gold: The Bill Johnson Story, A Year in the Life (pilot), The Room Upstairs, Dadah Is Death, Twist of Fate, The Ryan White Story, In the Best Interest of the Children, The Sunshine Boys, Sex and the Matrix, The Big Show. *Series*: Square Pegs, A Year in the Life, Equal Justice, Stories From My Childhood, Sex and the City (2 Emmy Awards, 8 other noms.; 4 Golden Globe Awards, 4 other noms.), Washingtonienne (also pilot, exec. prod.). *Documentaries/Specials*: The Almost Royal Family, Life Under Water, America: A Tribute to Heroes. *Guest:* More than 165 appearances.

PARKER, TREY
Actor, Writer, Producer. rn. Randolph Severn Parker, III, b. Conifer, CO, October 19, 1969. e. U. of Colorado.
PICTURES: Orgazmo (writer, prod., dir., editor), Terror Firmer (actor), BASEketball (actor, soundtrack writer), South Park: Bigger Longer & Uncut (actor, writer, prod., composer, Academy Award nom. 2000), Bowling for Columbine (doc., soundtrack writer), Team America: World Police (voices, writer, prod., dir., soundtrack writer).
TELEVISION: *Movie:* Time Warped (writer, prod., dir., voices). *Series:* 3 Friends & Jerry, That's My Bush! (writer, exec. prod., composer), Saul of the Mole Men (soundtrack), Kenny vs. Spenny (exec. prod.), How's Your News? (exec. prod.), South Park (4 Emmy Awards, 5 other noms). *Guest:* More than 40 appearances.

PARKES, WALTER F.
Producer, Writer. b. Bakersfield, CA. e. Yale, Stanford Univ. 1978 prod. & dir. documentary The California Reich which was nominated for Academy Award.
PICTURES: WarGames (s.p.; Academy Award nom.; WGA nom. 1984). *Producer: or Executive producer.*: Volunteers, Project X, True Believer, Awakenings (Academy Award nom. 1991), Sneakers (also co-s.p.), Little Giants; To Wong Foo,-Thanks for Everything-Julie Newmar; How to Make an American Quilt, Twister, The Trigger Effect, Amistad, Men In Black, The Peacemaker, Deep Impact, Small Soldiers, The Mask of Zorro, Gladiator, Artificial Intelligence: AI, The Time Machine, Minority Report, Men in Black II, Road to Perdition, The Tuxedo, Ring, Catch Me If You Can, The Terminal, The Ring 2, Lemony Snicket's A Series of Unfortunate Events, The Island, Just Like Heaven, Legend of Zorro, The Lookout, The Kite Runner (exec. prod.), Sweeney Todd: The Demon Barber of Fleet Street, The Burning Plain, The Uninvited, Dinner for Schmucks, Men in Black III.
TELEVISION: *Series*: Eddie Dodd (prod., writer). *Pilot*: Birdland (exec. prod., writer), Men In Black: The Series (exec. prod.).

PARKS, MICHAEL
Actor. b. Corona, CA, April 24, 1940. r.n. Harry Parks, Jr.
PICTURES: Wild Seed (debut, 1964), Bus Riley's Back in Town, The Bible, The Idol, The Happening, The Last Hard Men, Sidewinder One, ffolkes, Hard Country, Savannah Smiles, Spiker, Club Life, The Return of Josey Wales (also dir.), Spiker, Arizona Heat, Nightmare Beach, Prime Suspect, The Hitman, Storyville, Death Wish 5: The Face of Death, Stranger by Night, Sorceress, Niagra Niagra, Deceiver, Julian Po, Full Tilt Boogie, Wicked, Bullfighter, Big Bad Love, Kill Bill: Vol. 1, Fighting Words, Kill Bill: Vol. 2, The Listening, El Muerto, Miracle at Sage Creek, Three Priests, Fighting Words, Death Proof, The Assassination of Jesse James by the Coward Robert Ford, Noble Things, Street Poet, Palominas.
TELEVISION: *Movies*: Can Ellen Be Saved?, Savage Bees, Chase, Dangerous Affection, Gore Vidal's Billy the Kid, The China Lake Murders, SeaQuest DSV, Hart to Hart: Secrets of the Hart, The Player. *Series:* Then Came Bronson, The Colbys, Twin Peaks. *Guest:* More than 84 appearances.

PARKS, VAN DYKE
Composer, Actor. b. Jan. 3, 1941. Albums include: Song Cycle, Discover America, Clang of the Yankee Reaper, Jump!, Tokyo Rose, Orange Crate Art (with Brian Wilson).
PICTURES: *Actor:* The Swan, A Gift for Heidi, Loose Shoes, Popeye (also conductor & music arranger), Vibes, The Two Jakes (also composer), He Said She Said. *Composer*: Goin' South, Popeye (actor only), Sesame Street Presents Follow That Bird, Club Paradies, The Brave Little Toaster (songs), Casual Sex?, Out on a Limb, Wild Bill (also music arranger), Bastard Out of Carolina, Private Parts, Shadrach, My Dog Skip (additional

music), The Adventures of Ociee Nash, The Company, The Departed, Arctic Tale (doc. soundtrack writer), Walk Hard: The Dewey Cox Story (soundtrack writer), Fantastic Mr. Fox (soundtrack writer).
TELEVISION: *Movies*: *Composer*: Next Door, One Christmas, The Summer of Ben Tyler, Oliver Twist, A Chance of Snow, Borderline, Harlan County War, The Ponder Heart, Call Me Claus, Charms for the Easy Life, Monday Night Mayhem, Whitewash: The Clarence Bradley Story, Charms for the Easy Life, Broken Trail (Emmy nom. 2007). *Actor*: Mother Goose Rock 'n' Rhyme (actor only), *Series*: *Composer*: The Marshal, Harold and the Purple Crayon, Stuart Little (Emmy nom. 2004). *Actor:* Bonino. *Documentaries/Specials: Composer*: Chesapeake Borne, Norman Rockwell: An American Portrait.

PARSONS, ESTELLE
Actress. b. Marblehead, MA, Nov. 20, 1927. e. Connecticut College for Women, Bachelor's degree in political science. Attended Boston U. Law Sch. Helped harvest crops in England with the Women's Land Army. Was active in politics; worked for the Committee for the Nation's Health in Wash. and the Republican Finance Committee in Boston. Was elected to public office in Marblehead, Mass. Joined NBC-TV's Today Show as prod. asst.; then writer, feature prod. and commentator. Appeared in two Julius Monk revues, Jerry Herman's Nightcap.
THEATRE: Happy Hunting, Whoop Up, Beg Borrow or Steal, Mrs. Dally Has a Lover (Theater World Award), Next Time I'll Sing to You (Obie Award), In the Summer House (Obie Award), Ready When You Are C.B., Malcolm, The Seven Descents of Myrtle, ...And Miss Reardon Drinks a Little, The Norman Conquests, Ladies of the Alamo, Miss Margarida's Way, Pirates of Penzance, The Unguided Missile, Threepenny Opera, Lincoln Center Repertory Theatre, Mahagonny, Forgiving Typhoid Mary, Shimada, The Shadow Box, Twice Removed, Grace & Glorie.
PICTURES: Ladybug Ladybug (debut, 1963), Bonnie and Clyde (Academy Award, 1968), Rachel Rachel (Academy Award nom. 1969), Don't Drink the Water, Watermelon Man, I Walk the Line, I Never Sang for My Father, Two People, For Pete's Sake, Foreplay, Dick Tracy, The Lemon Sisters, Boys on the Side, That Darn Cat, Looking for Richard (doc.), Wilde Salome.
TELEVISION: *Movies*: Terror on the Beach, The Gun and the Pulpit, The UFO Incident, The Gentleman Bandit, Open Admissions, A Private Matter, The American Clock, Miss Sherri, The Love Letter, Freak City, Strip Search. *Mini-series*: Backstairs at the White House, Empire Falls. *Series*: Roseanne. *Documentaries/Specials:* The Front Page. *Guest*: More than 56 appearances.

PARSONS, RICHARD
Executive. b. Brooklyn, NY, April 4, 1948. e. undergraduate at Univ. of Hawaii. Earned his law degree from Union University's Albany Law School and outscored all other test takers of the 1971 New York State bar exam. Parsons began his career as assistant counsel to New York State Governor Nelson Rockefeller in 1971 and later served as a senior White House aide when Rockefeller became vice president under Gerald Ford. He left Washington in 1977, and moved into the private sector, first becoming a managing partner at the New York law firm Patterson, Belknap, Webb & Tyler. In his eleven years with Patterson, Parsons gained recognition as a skilled negotiator. He also took on such high-profile clients as Happy Rockefeller, the widow of Nelson Rockefeller, and cosmetics giant Estée Lauder. In 1988, he left the firm to help steer former client, Dimes, out of a financial crisis. He was key to helping the thrift lower its debt and ultimately merge with Anchor Savings Bank in 1995. As a result, Dime Bancorp became the largest thrift institution on the East Coast and the fourth largest in the United States. Parsons then joined Time Warner as its president in Feb. 1995, helping negotiate its merger with America Online, which created a $165-billion media empire in 2000. As president, he oversaw the company's filmed entertainment and music businesses, and all corporate staff functions, including financial activities, legal affairs, public affairs and administration. He then became the company's co-COO. In Dec. 2001 AOL Time Warner CEO Gerald Levin announced plans to retire in May 2002 and declared that Parsons would succeed him. Parsons became CEO in May 2002; chairman of the board in May 2003. January, 2008 Parsons retired from Time Warner but remained chmn. of the board. In its Jan. 2005 report on America's Best CEOs, Institutional Investor magazine named Parsons the top CEO in the entertainment industry. Parsons' civic and non-profit commitments include Co-Chairman of the Mayor's Commission on Economic Opportunity in New York; Chairman Emeritus of the Partnership for New York City; Chairman of the Apollo Theatre Foundation and service on the boards of Howard University, the Museum of Modern Art and the American Museum of Natural History. He also serves on the boards of Citigroup and Estée Lauder.

PARTON, DOLLY
Singer, Composer, Actress. b. Sevierville, TN, Jan. 19, 1946. Gained fame as country music singer, composer, radio and TV personality. Co-partner with Sandy Gallin, Sandollar Prods. *Author*: My Life and Other Unfinished Business (autobiography), Coat of Many Colors.
PICTURES: *Actress:* Nine to Five (debut, 1980; also wrote & sang title song, Academy Award nom.; 3 Golden Globe noms. 1981), The Best Little Whorehouse in Texas (singer, also wrote addtl. songs, Golden Globe nom. 1983), Rhinestone (also composer, singer), Steel Magnolias, Straight Talk (also composer, singer), The Beverly Hillbillies, Heartsong, Miss Congeniality 2 (as herself). *Composer:* Norma Rae (also singer), The Bodyguard, Office Space, Women Talking Dirty (also singer), Moulin Rouge!, Sweet Home Alabama (also singer), Garfield, Transamerica (also singer, Academy Award nom.; Golden Globe nom. 2006), First Dog. *Singer:* Beethoven's 2nd, The Love Guru, Whip It.
TELEVISION: *Movies*: *Actress*: A Smoky Mountain Christmas (also songs), Wild Texas Wind (also co-writer, co-prod., composer & singer), Dolly and Carol in Nashville, Unlikely Angel (also composer of two original songs & singer; exec. prod.), Blue Valley Songbird (composer of title song & singer; exec. prod.). *Series: Composer:* Butterflies, 9 to 5 (also singer). *Actress:* The Porter Wagoner Show (as herself, 1967-1974), Dolly (1976), Dolly (1987-88). *Documentaries/Specials:* The Nashville Sound, Cher...Special (Emmy nom. 1978), A Christmas Special..With Love...Mac Davis, Lily: Sold Out, Roy Acuff...50 Years the King of Country Music, Dolly in Concert, Kenny-Dolly-Willie: Something Inside So Strong, A Tennessee Mountain Thanksgiving,Kenny & Dolly: A Christmas to Remember, Kenny Rogers & Dolly Parton: Together, This Is Your Life, Naomi & Wynonna: Love Can Build a Bridge, Christmas At Home, Billy Ray Cyrus, Big Dreams & Broken Hearts: The Dottie West Story, Dolly Parton: Treasures, Graham Goes to Dollywood, CMT 40 Greatest Women of Country Music, Willie Nelson & Friends: Live and Kickin', Dolly Celebrates 25 Years of Dollywood, many more. *Guest*: More than 450 appearances.

PASCAL, AMY
Executive. b. March 25, 1958. e. UCLA, degree in international relations. Early in her career, Pascal worked for producer Tony Garnett at Kestral Films, an independent production company affiliated with Warner Bros. From 1986-1987, Pascal was v.p., production at 20th Century Fox. She was a studio executive for Columbia from 1987 to 1994, then was named pres., production for Turner Pictures for two years before rejoining Columbia in 1996. She was president of Columbia Pictures for three years before her promotion to chairman in 1999. Under her guidance, Columbia Pictures released such hits as Spider-Man (which grossed more than $820 million worldwide at the box office), Something's Gotta Give, 50 First Dates, Big Fish, Bad Boys 2, S.W.A.T., Once Upon A Time in Mexico, Charlie's Angels: Full Throttle, Panic Room, Mr. Deeds, Men in Black II, Big Daddy, Stuart Little and A Knight's Tale, among others. In December 2003, Pascal was promoted to chairman, motion picture group and vice chairman, Sony Pictures Entertainment. In Sept. 2006, she was promoted to her current position as co-chairman of Sony Pictures Entertainment alongside SPE Chairman & CEO Michael Lynton. She also continues as chairman of Sony's motion picture group. In 2006 ranked #41 by Fortune Magazine's most powerful women in business. She ranked #46 in 2007.

PASDAR, ADRIAN
Actor. b. Pittsfield, MA, April 30, 1965. e. Univ. of Central FL. Studied acting with People's Light and Theatre Co., Lee Strasberg Institute.
THEATRE: *Regional*: The Glass Menagerie, Shadow Box, Hotters, Sorry Wrong Number, Cold Foot, Monkey's Paw.
PICTURES: Top Gun (debut, 1986), Streets of Gold, Solarbabies, Near Dark, Made in USA, Cookie, Vital Signs, Torn Apart, Shang Hai yi jiu er ling, Grand Isle, Just Like a Woman, The Killing Box, Carlito's Way, The Last Good Time, The Pompatus of Love, Ties to Rachel, Wounded, A Brother's Kiss, Desert Son, Cement (dir. only), The Big Day, Secondhand Lions, Home Movie.
TELEVISION: *Movies*: Big Time, The Lost Capone, Shadows of Desire, Paddy Chayefsky's The Mother, A Mother's Gift, Slave of Dreams, Touched by Evil, Love in Another Town, The Perfect Getaway, Mutiny, Crossing the Line. *Mini-series:* House of Frankenstein (1997). *Series*: Profit, Feds, Mysterious Ways, Judging Amy, Heroes, Marvel Super Hero Squad (voice). *Guest:* More than 45 appearances.

PASETTA, MARTY
Producer, Director. b. June 16, 1932. e. U. Santa Clara. Director and/or producer of numerous awards shows, including 17 Acad. Awards presentations, beginning with the 44th in 1972..
TELEVISION: *Series:* The Smothers Brothers Comedy Hour, Temptation, The Everly Brothers Show, The Reel Game, Don Adams' Screen Test, Stumpers!, The Monte Carlo Show. *Documentaries/Specials:* AFI Salutes to Fred Astaire, John Huston, Lillian Gish, Alfred Hitchcock and Jimmy Stewart, Gene Kelly Special, Elvis Aloha From Hawaii, Academy Awards (17), Emmy (2) and Grammy (8) Award Shows, A Country Christmas (1978-81), The Monte Carlo Show, Texaco Star Theatre-Opening Night, Burnett Discovers Domingo (Emmy nom. 1984), Disneyland's 30th Anniversary Celebration, 15 Years of Cerebral Palsy Telethons, A Night at the Moulin Rouge, Soap Opera Awards, An All-Star Celebration Honoring Martin Luther King, Disneyland's Summer Vacation Party, Disney's Captain EO Grand Opening, 15th Anniversary of Disney World; Beach Boys... 25 Years Together, Super Night at the Superbowl, 20th

Anniversary of Caesars Palace, Paris by Night with George Burns, I Call You Friend Papal Spacebridge '87, Walt Disney World's Celebrity Circus, Las Vegas: An All-Star 75th Anniversary, Julio Iglesias—Sold Out, The Ice Capades with Kirk Cameron, American All-Star Tribute Honoring Elizabeth Taylor, The Ice Capades 50th Anniversary Special, The Movie Awards (doc. exec. prod.), My Night at the Grammys (segment dir.) many Academy Award Specials (6 Emmy noms.; 6 DGA noms.).

PASOLINI, UBERTO
Producer.
PICTURES: The Killing Fields, The Frog Prince, The Mission, Meeting Venus, Palookaville, The Full Monty (Academy Award nom.; BAFTA Award, Outstanding Brit. Film, 1998), The Closer You Get, The Emperor's New Clothes, Machan (also dir., writer), Bel Ami.
TELEVISION: *Movies*: A Dangerous Man: Lawrence After Arabia.

PASSER, IVAN
Director, Writer. b. Prague, Czechoslovakia, July 10, 1933. e. Film Faculty of Acad. of Musical Arts, Prague. 1961, asst. dir. to Milos Forman on Audition which led to scripting for Forman. 1969, moved to U.S.; worked in NY as longshoreman while studying Eng. U.S. dir. debut: Born to Win, 1971.
PICTURES: *Writer*: Loves of a Blonde, A Boring Afternoon, Fireman's Ball. *Director*: Intimate Lighting (also s.p.), Born to Win (also s.p.), Law and Disorder (also s.p.), Crime and Passion, The Silver Bears, Cutter's Way, The Big Picture, Haunted Summer, Pretty Hattie's Baby, The Wishing Tree (Emmy nom. 2001), Nomad.
TELEVISION: *Movies:* Fourth Story, Stalin, While Justice Sleeps, Kidnapped, Picnic. *Series:* Shelley Duvall's Faerie Tale Theatre (2-episode dir.). *Special:* The Wishing Tree (Emmy nom. 2001).

PASSMAN, S. DAVID, III
Executive. This exhibition industry executive has accounting background and is a former partner of Deloitte & Touche LLP, a public accounting firm. Passman served as Deloitte's managing partner of the Atlanta office from 1993-1996. Previously, Passman served as pres. of the Harland Printed Products and Harland Checks division of the John H. Harland Company, a provider of printed products and software and related services to the financial institution market, 1999-2003 (and CFO from 1996-1999). June 2005, Passman became pres. and CEO of IBS-STL, Inc., a book publishing and distribution company. Passman has been an independent dir. of Carmike Cinemas since June 2003. In Jan. 2009, Carmike removed its CEO, Michael Patrick, and elevated Passman to top role at the office of the chairman. In June 2009, the bd. named Passman its new pres. and CEO and is the role he holds today. As of March 2009, Carmike had 249 theatres with 2,288 screens in 35 states. Carmike's digital cinema footprint reaches 2,154 screens, including 193 theatres with 500 screens that are also equipped for 3D.

PASTER, GARY M.
Executive. b. St. Louis, MO, July 4, 1943. e. U. of MO, B.A.; UCLA, USC Graduate Sch. of Business. 1970, joined Burbank Studios as asst. to pres., treas.; 1976 v.p., admin. and chmn. of the exec. comm.; 1977 pres. Member: AMPAS, LA Film Dev. Council, Hollywood Radio & T.V. Society, Acad. of Television Arts and Sciences. Advisory Bd., Kaufman Astoria Studios, N.Y.

PATINKIN, MANDY
Actor. r.n. Mandel Patinkin. b. Chicago, IL, Nov. 30, 1952. e. U. of Kansas, Juilliard Sch. (Drama Div.; 1972-74). m. actress Kathryn Grody. In regional theatre before coming to New York where played with Shakespeare Festival Public Theater (Trelawny of the Wells, Hamlet, Rebel Women). Recordings: Mandy Patinkin, Dress Casual, Experiment.
THEATRE: Savages, The Shadow Box (B'way debut), Evita (Tony Award, 1980), Henry IV, Part I (Central Park), Sunday in the Park With George (Tony nom.), The Knife, Follies in Concert, A Winter's Tale, Mandy Patinkin: Dress Casual (solo concert), The Secret Garden, Falsettos, others.
PICTURES: The Big Fix (debut, 1978), Last Embrace, French Postcards, Night of the Juggler, Ragtime, Daniel, Yentl (Golden Globe nom. 1984), Maxie, The Princess Bride, The House on Carroll Street, Alien Nation, Dick Tracy, True Colors, Impromptu, The Doctor, The Music of Chance, Life With Mikey (cameo), The Last Great Warrior, Men with Guns, Lulu on the Bridge, The Adventures of Elmo in Grouchland, Piñero, Choking Man, Yankee Irving (voice), Everyone's Hero (voice), 4.3.2.1.
TELEVISION: *Movies*: Charleston, Follies in Concert, Sunday in the Park with George, Broken Glass, The Hunchback, Strange Justice, Everything That Rises, NTSB: The Crash of Flight 323. *Series*: Chicago Hope (Emmy Award, 1995, 1 other nom.; Golden Globe nom. 1995), Dead Like Me, Criminal Minds. *Guest:* More than 57 appearances.

PATMORE-GIBBS, SUZANNE
Executive. b. Chicago, IL. e. B.A. in English literature, Pomona College. Began career at Sean Daniel's Alphaville Productions, then segued to Chuck Gordon's Universal Studios-based Daybreak Productions ("Field of Dreams," "October Sky") as v.p. development. Patmore-Gibbs served as senior v.p., development at Bedford Falls, the production company founded by awar-winning director/writer/producers Edward Zwick and Marshall Herskovitz. She joined Touchstone Television in Dec. 2000 as v.p., drama series; promoted in Dec. 2002 to senior v.p., drama series; moved to network TV in 2004 as ABC's senior v.p., drama development. During her tenure, ABC developed the hit series "Desperate Housewives," "Grey's Anatomy" and "Lost," as well as "Brothers & Sisters," and the Golden Globe Award-winning "Ugly Betty." In June 2007, promoted to executive v.p., drama development, ABC Entertainment. Patmore-Gibbs was named to current position, executive v.p., network scripted creative for ABC Entertainment Group in June 2009. She provides creative direction, oversight and management of the network's entire prime-time scripted creative group, which includes drama development/current programming, comedy development/current programming, and made-for-TV movies and mini-series.

PATRIC, JASON
Actor. Jason Patric Miller Jr .b. Queens, NY, June 17, 1966. Son of playwright-actor Jason Miller. Grandson of performer Jackie Gleason. Began professional career with Vermont's Champlain Shakespeare Festival.
THEATRE: *NY*: Beirut. *LA*: Out of Gas on Lovers' Leap.
PICTURES: Solarbabies (debut, 1986), The Lost Boys, The Beast, Denial, After Dark My Sweet, Roger Corman's Frankenstein Unbound, Rush, Geronimo: An American Legend, The Journey of August King, Sleepers, Speed 2: Cruise Control, Incognito, Your Friends & Neighbors (also prod.), Narc, Cinema & the Myth of Cool (documentary, as himself), The Alamo, The Good Shepherd, Shortcut to Happiness, Expired, Downloading Nancy, In the Valley of Elah, My Sister's Keeper, The Losers, Keyhole.
TELEVISION: *Movies:* Tough Love, Tilda. *Special:* Teach 109.

PATRICK, MICHAEL W.
Executive. b. Columbus, GA, May 17, 1950. e. Columbus Coll., B.S., 1972. Joined Carmike Cinemas in 1970. President since Oct. 1981. Currently Chmn., Pres. & CEO. A director on bd. since 1982. Became bd. chmn. in Jan. 2002. Carmike owned, operated and had an interest in 270 theatres with 2,369 screens located in 37 states. Carmike sought Chapter 11 bankrupsy protection in 2000. The company now operates approx. 300 theatres. Carmike exited bankruptcy in 2002 after investing in new megaplex theatres. In 2005 the company purchased 30 theatres from the heirs of George Krasotes Corp. Carmike Cinemas, Inc., bd. of directors removed Patrick as it's chief executive in January 2009. Patrick sits on the bd. of directors of the Will Rogers Institute and is a member of bd. of trustees at Columbus State University Foundation, Inc. Memberships have included: Variety Int'l; Motion Picture Pioneers.

PATRICK, ROBERT
Actor. b. Marietta, GA. November 5, 1959.
PICTURES: Eye of the Eagle, Equalizer 2000, Killer Instinct, Hollywood Boulevard II, Future Hunters, Die Hard 2, Terminator 2: Judgment Day, Double Dragon, Body Shot, Fire in the Sky, Zero Tolerance, Hong Kong 97, The Cool Surface, Last Gasp, Decoy, Asylum, Striptease, Rosewood, Cop Land, Ravager (prod. only), The Big Twist, The Only Thrill, Ambushed, The Faculty, Rogue Force, The Vivero Letter, Tactical Assault, From Dusk Till Dawn 2: Texas Blood Money, Texas Funeral, All the Pretty Horses, Mexico City, Angels Don't Sleep Here, Spy Kids, Texas Rangers, Blackflash, D-Tox (aka Eye See You), Out of These Rooms, Pavement, Charlie's Angels: Full Throttle, Supercross, Ladder 49, Walk the Line, The Marine, Firewall, Flags of Our Fathers, We Are Marshall, Bridge to Terabithia, Balls of Fury, Fly Me to the Moon (voice), Strange Wilderness, Autopsy, Lonely Street, Alien Trespass, The Black Waters of Echo's Pond (also exec. prod.), The Men Who Stare at Goats, Kill Speed, The Wrath of Cain, Good Day for It, Freedom for Joe, Mr. Sophistication, Will Gardner, S.W.A.T.: Fire Fight.
TELEVISION: *Movies*: Resident Alien, Body Language, Within the Rock (prod. only), Rag and Bone, Perfect Assassins, The X-Files: The Truth, 1st to Die, Bad Apple, Stargate Atlantis: Rising, Edgar Floats. *Mini-series:* Elvis. *Series*: Real Adventures of Jonny Quest, Counter Force, The X-Files, The Sopranos, Disorderly Conduct (narr.), The Unit. *Guest:* More than 65 appearances.

PATTINSON, ROBERT
Actor. b. London, England, May 13, 1986.
PICTURES: Harry Potter and the Goblet of Fire, Harry Potter and the Order of the Phoenix, Little Ashes, Twilight (also soundtrack writer/prod.), The Twilight Saga: New Moon, Remember Me (also exec. prod.), The Twilight Saga: Eclipse, Water for Elephants, Bel Ami, The Twilight Saga: Breaking Dawn - Part 1.
TELEVISION: *Movies:* Curse of the Ring, The Haunted Airman, The Bad Mother's Handbook. *Guest:* More than 52 appearances.

PATTON, WILL
Actor. b. Charleston, SC, June 14, 1954. e. NC School of the Arts, 1975.
THEATRE: *NY*: Tourists and Refugees #2 (La Mama E.T.C., Obie Award), Fool For Love (Obie Award), Goose and Tomtom (Public Theatre), A Lie of the Mind.

PICTURES: King Blank, Silkwood, Variety, Desperately Seeking Susan, After Hours, Chinese Boxes, Belizaire the Cajun, No Way Out, Stars and Bars, Wildfire, Signs of Life, Everybody Wins, A Shock to the System, The Rapture, Cold Heaven, In the Soup, The Paint Job, Romeo Is Bleeding, Natural Causes, Midnight Edition, Tollbooth, The Client, The Puppet Masters, Copycat, The Spitfire Grill, Fled, Inventing the Abbotts, This World Then the Fireworks, The Postman, O.K. Garage, I Woke Up Early the Day I Died, Breakfast of Champions, Armageddon, I Woke Up Early the Day I Died, Breakfast of Champions, Entrapment, Jesus' Son, Gone In Sixty Seconds, Trixie, Remember the Titans, The Mothman Prophecies, The Rough South of Larry Brown (doc.), The Punisher, Road House 2: Last Call, Dog Days of Summer, These Woods, Code Name: The Cleaner, The List, A Mighty Heart, American Violet, The Loss of a Teardrop Diamond, The Canyon, Lucky Days, Wendy and Lucy, Waking Madison, Brooklyn's Finest, Princess Kaiulani, The Fourth Kind, Meek's Cutoff, Knucklehead.
TELEVISION: *Movies*: Kent State, A Gathering of Old Men, Dillinger, Deadly Desire, In the Deep Woods, Judicial Consent, A Child Lost Forever: The Jerry Sherwood Story, Taking the Heat, The Agency, Family Sins, The Last Ride, The Way. *Mini-series:* Into the West. *Series*: Ryan's Hope, Search for Tomorrow, VR.5, The Protector, The Agency, Numb3rs, The American Experience 24.

PAULEY, JANE
TV Host, Journalist. b. Indianapolis, IN, Oct. 31, 1950. m. Doonesbury creator Garry Trudeau. e. Indiana U. Involved in Indiana state politics before joining WISH-TV, Indianapolis, as reporter. Co-anchored midday news reports and anchored weekend news reports. Co-anchor of nightly news at WMAQ-TV, NBC station in Chicago. Joined Today Show in October, 1976, as featured regular, prior to which had made guest appearances on that program; co-host until 1990. Began own series Real Life With Jane Pauley in 1991. Dateline NBC (news documentary series, 1992-2003). 2004, host of The Jane Pauley Show, which aired for one season before ceasing prod. *Documentaries/Specials:* Common Threads: Stories from the Quilt, Sex, Teens & Public Schools (host); 100 Years of Hope and Humor (host), JFK: Breaking the News (narr.), Brando, Take One Step: Caring for Depression.

PAVLIK, JOHN M.
Executive. b. Melrose, IA, Dec. 3, 1939. e. U. of Minnesota, B.A., 1963. Reporter, Racine (WI) Journal-Times, San Bernardino (CA) Sun-Telegram, 1963-66; writer, News Bureau, Pacific Telephone, Los Angeles, 1966-68; asst. PR dir, Association of Motion Picture and Television Producers, 1968-72; dir. of PR, 1972-78; v.p., 1978-79; special consultant, California Motion Picture Council, 1974-79; member, exec. council, Los Angeles Film Dev. Committee, v.p., 1977-78; exec. admin., Academy of Motion Picture Arts and Sciences, 1979-82; member, bd. of dir., Permanent Charities Comm. of the Entertainment Industries, 1979-84; member, bd. of dir., Hollywood Chamber of Commerce, 1979-85; exec. dir., M.P. & TV Fund, 1982-88; consultant, 1988-89; member, advisory board, Assn. of Film Commissioners Int'l, 1988-91; dir. of endowment dev., Academy Foundation, 1989-92. Member, advisory board, USAF Entertainment Liaison Office, 1998-2003. Retired from his director of communications post at the Academy of Motion Picture Arts and Sciences (AMPAS) in 2007.

PAXSON, LOWELL W. "BUD"
Executive. b. Rochester, NY. e. Syracuse U. Media industry pioneer whose broadcast career spans more than 48 years. As teenager worked in Rochester radio and became announcer while attending Syracuse Univ. Purchased first broadcast entity, WACK radio in Newark NY, 1954. Began selling merchandise on a Florida AM station in 1977. Conceived and founded Home Shopping Network, 1982. Est. Silver King Communications, 1986. Sold interest in HSN and Silver King in 1990 but remains president emeritus at HSN. From 1991 to 1997, Paxson assembled a radio empire of 46 stations throughout Florida. Sold radio interests in 1997 and acquired The Travel Channel, which has since been sold to Discovery Communications, Inc. Paxson Communications Corp. was formed in 1991 and now owns and operates 61 TV stations. In 1998, Paxson launched PAX TV, the nation's seventh broadcast TV network, featuring family-oriented programming and airing over Paxson's broadcast, cable and satellite distribution system. The network reaches more than 96 million U.S. TV households. The network rebranded itself as the "i" network in 2006. Additionally, as a result of an agreement with 32 % stakeholder NBC Universal, Paxson stepped down as chairman and CEO in Nov. 2005 and served as the company's chairman emeritus. R. Brandon Burgess, a former NBC Universal executive took over as the company's CEO. The company also changed its corporate name to ION Media Networks in mid-2006.
AWARDS AND INDUSTRY RECOGNITIONS: American Free Enterprise Award, 1996; Broadcaster of the Year Award by the Florida Assoc. of Broadcasters, 1997; NIMA International Lifetime Achievement Award from the Worldwide Electronic Marketing Assoc., 1997; the Northwood University Outstanding Business Leader Award, 1998; the W. Clement Stone Business and Professional Leadership Award from The Religious Heritage of America Foundation, 1999; the Florida Entrepreneur of the Year Award (1994 & 1999); honorary doctor of laws degree from Barry Univ., 2000; first annual "Sonny" award by The Broadcasters' Foundation and the Touchdown Club of America, 2000; the Crystal Teddy Bear Award from the Christian Film and TV Commission presented at the 10th Annual Movieguide® Awards, 2002; inductee into the 12th Annual Broadcasting & Cable Hall of Fame, 2002. Dir. of Comm. for AMPAS.

PAXTON, BILL
Actor. b. Fort Worth, TX, May 17, 1955. e. NYU. First professional job as set dresser for film Big Bad Mamma. Studied acting with Stella Adler. Dir. short films Fish Heads, Scoop (also s.p.)
PICTURES: Stripes, The Lords of Discipline, Mortuary, Streets of Fire, Impulse, The Terminator, Weird Science, Commando, Aliens, Near Dark, Pass the Ammo, Slipstream, Next of Kin, Back to Back, Brain Dead, The Last of the Finest, Navy SEALS, Predator 2, The Dark Backward, One False Move, The Vagrant, Trespass, Indian Summer, Boxing Helena, Future Shock, Monolith, Tombstone, True Lies, Apollo 13, The Last Supper, Twister, The Evening Star, Titanic, Traveller, A Simple Plan, Mighty Joe Young, U-571, Vertical Limit, Frailty (also dir.), Spy Kids 2: The Island of Lost Dreams, Resistance, Spy Kids 3D: Game Over, Club Dread, Thunderbirds, Haven, The Greatest Game Ever Played (dir. only), Haywire.
TELEVISION: *Movies*: Deadly Lessons, An Early Frost, Frank and Jesse, A Bright Shining Lie (Golden Globe nom. 1999). *Mini-series*: The Atlanta Child Murders, Fresno, Reclaiming History: The Assassination of President John F. Kennedy. *Series:* The Six O'Clock Follies, Big Love (3 Golden Globe noms.). *Guest:* More than 74 appearances.

PAYMER, DAVID
Actor, Director. b. Oceanside, NY, Aug. 30, 1954. e. Univ. of Mich. First professional job with natl. company of Grease, which he later appeared in on B'way. Has taught acting at UCLA and the Film Actor's Workshop; performed stand-up comedy and served as staff writer on The New Leave It to Beaver Show.
PICTURES: The In-Laws (debut, 1979), Airplane II: The Sequel, Best Defense, Irreconcilable Differences, Perfect, Howard the Duck, No Way Out, Crazy People, City Slickers, Mr. Saturday Night (Academy Award nom.; Golden Globe nom. 1993), Searching for Bobby Fischer, Heart and Souls, City Slickers II: The Legend of Curly's Gold, Quiz Show, City Hall, The American President, Unforgettable, Nixon, Get Shorty, The Sixth Man, Amistad, The Long Way Home (voice), Gang Related, Mighty Joe Young, Chill Factor, The Hurricane, Mumford, Payback, Outside Ozona, State and Main, Bait, Enemies of Laughter, Bounce, Partners, Bartleby, Focus, The Burial Society, Alex and Emma, Checking Out, In Good Company, Marilyn Hotchkiss' Ballroom Dancing and Charm School, Checking Out, The Poison Rose, Resurrecting the Champ, Ocean's Thirteen, Redbelt, Drag Me to Hell.
TELEVISION: *Movies*: This House Possessed, Grace Kelly, Her Life as a Man, Love Mary, Pleasures, Rock 'n Roll Mom, The Absent-Minded Professor, In Search of Dr. Seuss, Cagney & Lacey: The Return, Cagney & Lacey: Together Again, Crime of the Century (Golden Globe nom. 1997), Dash and Lilly, Partners, From Where I Sit, The Arturo Sandoval Story, Joe and Max, RFK, School of Life, Capital City, Warm Springs. *Mini-series:* Into the West. *Series*: Downtown, The Commish, Santo Bugito (voice), Channel Umptee-3 (voice), Line of Fire, The Good Wife. Director of many series episodes. *Guest*: More than 110 appearances.

PAYNE, ALEXANDER
Director, Writer. b. Omaha, NE, Feb. 10, 1961.
PICTURES: The Passion of Martin (alos prod.), Citizen Ruth, Election (Academy Award nom. for s.p., WGA Award 2000), Jurassic Park III (s.p. only), About Schmidt (Golden Globe Award, Best s.p., 2002, 1 other nom.; WGA nom.), A Decade Under the Influence (doc.; Winner Golden Globe Award, best s.p. 2003), Sideways (dir. & s.p.; Academy Award for Best Writing/s.p.,; 1 other nom. 2004, Golden Globe Award Best s.p.; 1 other nom.; DGA nom.; WGA Award), Paris, je t'aime (segment dir.), I Now Pronounce You Chuck and Larry (s.p.), The Descendants (also prod.), Cedar Rapids (prod.). *Executive Producer:* The Assassination of Richard Nixon, Gray Matters, The Savages, The King of California.
TELEVISION: Series: Hung (exec. prod., pilot dir.).

PAYNTER, ROBERT
Cinematographer. b. London, England, March 12, 1928. e. Mercer Sch. First job in industry at 15 years as camera trainee with Government Film Dept.
PICTURES: Hannibal Brooks (debut, 1969), The Games, Lawman, The Nightcomers, Chato's Land, The Mechanic, Scorpio, The Big Sleep, Superman, Firepower, The Final Conflict, Superman II, An American Werewolf in London, Superman III, Trading Places, The Muppets Take Manhattan, Into the Night, National Lampoon's European Vacation, Spies Like Us, Little Shop of Horrors, When the Whales Came, Strike It Rich, Get Back.
TELEVISION: *Movie:* The Secret Garden. *Series:* The Zoo Gang.

PAYS, AMANDA
Actress. b. Berkshire, England, June 6, 1959. m. actor Corbin Bernsen. Began as a model. Studied French, art and pottery at

Hammersmith Polytechnic. Acting debut: Cold Room (HBO).
PICTURES: Oxford Blues, The Kindred, Off Limits, Leviathan, Age of Treason, Solitaire for Two, Subterfuge, Spacejacked, Ablaze.
TELEVISION: *Movies*: The Cold Room, 13 at Dinner, Minder on the Orient Express, Mr. and Mrs. Edgehill, Max Headroom, The Flash, Parker Kane, Dead on the Money, I Know My Son Is Alive, Hollywood Confidential, The Santa Trap. *Mini-series*: A.D. *Series*: Max Headroom, The Flash, Thief Takers, Breathing Room (host).

PAYSON, MARTIN D.
Executive. b. Brooklyn, NY, Jan. 4, 1936. e. Cornell U., NYU Sch. of Law, LLB, 1961. Practiced law privately before joining Warner Communications, Inc. as v.p. 1970. Later named exec. v.p., gen. counsel. 1987, appointed to three-member office of pres., WCI. Was vice chmn. Time Warner Inc., until Dec. 1992. Retired.

PEARCE, CRAIG
Actor, Writer.
PICTURES: *Actor:* I Can't Get Started, Nightmaster, Vicious!, Mad Bomber in Love, The Seventh Floor. *Writer*: Strictly Ballroom, Romeo + Juliet (BAFTA Award, Best Adapted Screenplay, 1997), Moulin Rouge! (also composer & lyricist. BAFTA nom.; WGA nom. 2002), The Third Witch (writer/s.p.), Charlie St. Cloud (s.p.).

PEARCE, RICHARD
Director, Cinematographer. b. San Diego, CA, Jan. 25, 1943. e. Yale U., B.A. degree in Eng. lit., 1965. New School for Social Research, M.A., degree in political economics. Worked with Don Pennebaker and Richard Leacock on documentaries. Photographed Emile de Antonio's America Is Hard to See. In 1970 went to Chile where he dir., photographed and edited Campamento, an award-winning documentary.
PICTURES: *As photographer (Acad. Award winning documentaries):* Woodstock, Marjoe, Interviews With My Lai Veterans, Hearts and Minds. *Cinematographer:* Rust Never Sleeps, Baby Snakes, Umbrellas, From Wharf Rats to Lords of the Docks (camera op.). *Director*: Heartland (debut, 1979), Threshold, Country, No Mercy, The Long Walk Home, Leap of Faith, A Family Thing. *Co-Prod.:* Food, Inc. (doc.)
TELEVISION: *Movies: Director*: Siege, No Other Love, Sessions, Dead Man Out, The Final Days (Emmy nom. 1990), Thicker Than Blood, Witness Protection, South Pacific, Plainsong, Fatal Contact: Bird Flu in America. *Mini-series:* The Blues (mini-documentary, dir. & cinematographer). *Series Director*: Alfred Hitchcock Presents, Homicide: Life on the Streets, Party of Five, Nothing Sacred. *Special:* The Judge and the General (Emmy nom. 2009).

PEDAS, JIM
Executive. b. Youngstown, OH. e. Thiel College. Opened Circle Theatre in Washington, D.C. in 1957 with brother Ted. 1984 formed Circle Releasing, serving as Secretary/ Treasurer; Circle Films, serving as v.p. See Ted Pedas entry for releases.

PEDAS, TED
Executive. b. Farrell, PA, May 6, 1931. e. B.S.B.A, Youngstown St. Univ. M.B.A., Wharton Sch. of Business at Univ. of PA. J.D., George Washington Univ. 1957, with brother Jim, opened Circle Theatre in Washington D.C. one of the first repertory houses. Circle/Showcase group of m.p. theatres expanded to over 80 quality screens before being sold in 1988. 1973-78, served on board of Cinema 5 in NY. 1984, pres. NATO D.C.; National Film Preservation Board, Joseph Wharton Award in 1988. Circle Releasing formed to distribute films with Ted serving as president. Releases include Blood Simple, The Navigator and the Killer. Circle Films has produced: Raising Arizona, Miller's Crossing, Barton Fink, Caught, Whatever, The Long Haul of A.I. Bezzerides (exec. prod.), BlackMale.

PEDOWITZ, MARK
Executive. b. Feb. 6, 1953, Brooklyn, N.Y. e. Rockford College, B.A. history, 1974; John Marshall Law School, J.D., 1978. MCA Inc.: attorney, 1979; Reeves Entertainment Group/Alan Landsburg Prods.: VP, business affairs, 1980-85; The Landsburg Co.: VP, business affairs and general counsel, 1985-87; MGM/UA Television Production Group: senior VP, business affairs and administration, 1987-91; ABC: senior VP, business affairs and contracts, 1991-99; ABC Entertainment Television Group, executive VP, 1999-present; ABC Studios president, 2004-present (unit formerly called Touchstone Television). Pedowitz currently sits on the BMI bd. of directors, the bd. of the Foundation for the Academy of Television Arts and Sciences (ATAS), and has served on the Executive Board of both the Academy of Television Arts and Sciences (ATAS) and the Hollywood Radio and Television Society (HRTS).

PEERCE, LARRY
Director. b. Bronx, NY. April 19, 1930. Father was late singer Jan Peerce.
PICTURES: One Potato Two Potato, The Big T.N.T. Show, The Incident, Goodbye Columbus (DGA nom. 1970), The Sporting Club, A Separate Peace, Ash Wednesday, The Other Side of the Mountain, Two Minute Warning, The Other Side of the Mountain—Part II, The Bell Jar (also exec. prod.), Why Would I Lie?, Love Child, Hard to Hold, Wired.
TELEVISION: *Movies*: A Stranger Who Looks Like Me, Love Lives On, I Take These Men, The Fifth Missile, Prison for Children, Queenie, Elvis and Me, The Neon Empire, The Court-Martial of Jackie Robinson, Child of Rage, Poisoned by Love: The Kern County Murders, Heaven & Hell: North and South Book III, A Burning Passion: The Margaret Mitchell Story, In Pursuit of Honor (co-exec. prod. only), An Element of Truth, The Abduction, Love-Struck, Christmas Every Day, Holy Joe, A Test of Love, A Secret Life, Second Honeymoon. *Series:* Touched by an Angel.

PEISINGER, JON
Executive. b. New York, NY, July 13, 1947. e. B.S. in accounting from Lehigh University. Began career in the music industry with executive positions with Polygram Distribution, Arista Records and Elektra/Asylum Records. Entered the home video business in 1980 as v.p. of marketing at Time Life Video. For over two decades Peisinger headed companies and Fortune 100 operating divisions in the entertainment industry. He was president and COO of Vestron Inc., a publicly traded (NYSE) company. Under his management, Vestron grew to be the world's largest independent motion picture production and distribution company. He also served as a member of the company's bd. of directors, chmn. for Vestron International Group and pres. of Vestron Video. From 1990-1992, Peisinger was pres. of Sony Video Enterprises, a division of Sony Music, where he launched a children's music and home video unit. From 1992-1997, he was pres. of Capital Cities/ABC Video Publishing, Inc., a unit of Capital Cities/ABC, Inc. (which became part of The Walt Disney Company) In 1998, Peisinger launched Creative Branding Systems, LLC, and as president, built a successful corporate consulting, merchandising, and licensing organization with clients in cable television, children's media, music, home video, television production and telecommunications. Peisinger has served as sr. v.p., TFN Enterprises, and manages many of the company's ancillary revenue-generating activities, including the footballnetwork.com website, merchandising and licensing, home shopping, video and DVD syndication and marketing, and event sales. He served on the bd. of dir. of The Football Network, Inc., Citicorp's Citifunds group and Event411, Inc. He is currently providing advisory services to the Media Development Authority, an initiative sponsored by the government of Singapore.

PEÑA, ELIZABETH
Actress. b. N.J., Sept. 23, 1961, of Cuban parents. Moved to New York in 1969 where she attended NY High School for Performing Arts. Off-B'way in Blood Wedding, Antigone, Romeo & Juliet, Act One & Only, Italian American Reconciliation, and many others.
PICTURES: El Super, Times Square, They All Laughed, Fat Chance, Crossover Dreams, Down and Out in Beverly Hills, La Bamba, Batteries Not Included, Vibes, Blue Steel, Jacob's Ladder, The Waterdance, Across the Moon, Free Willy 2: The Adventure Home, Dead Funny, Lone Star (Ind't Spirit Award, 1997), Strangeland, The Pass, Rush Hour, Strangeland, Seven Girlfriends, On the Bordeline, Things Behind the Sun, Tortilla Soup, Ten Tiny Love Stories, Imposter, Zigzag, Sueño, The Incredibles (voice), Transamerica, Keep Your Distance, The Lost City, Adrift in Manhattan, Dragon Wars: D-War, Goal II: Living the Dream, Nothing Like the Holidays, Love Comes Lately, Becoming Eduardo, A Single Woman, Down for Life, Mother and Child, Shrinking Charlotte.
TELEVISION: *Movies*: Fugitive Among Us, Roommates, It Came From Outer Space, Contagious, The Second Civil War, Border Line, The Hollywood Mom's Mystery, Suburban Madness, Racing for Time. *Mini-series*: Drug War, The Camarena Story, The Invaders, Aldrich Ames: America Betrayed. *Series*: Tough Cookies, I Married Dora, Shannon's Deal, Resurrection Blvd, Maya & Miguel (voice). *Guest:* More than 48 appearances.

PENDLETON, AUSTIN
Actor. b. Warren, OH, March 27, 1940. e. Yale Univ. Started acting with Williamstown Theatre Festival. Teaches acting at the Herbert Berghof Studio. Named artistic dir. of NY's Circle Rep. Theatre, 1995.
THEATRE: *Actor*: Oh Dad Poor Dad Mama's Hung You in the Closet and I'm Feeling So Sad, Fiddler on the Roof, The Little Foxes, The Last Sweet Days of Isaac (NY Drama Critics & Outer Critics Circle Awards), Educating Rita, Doubles, The Sorrows of Frederick, Grand Hotel, Hamlet, Sophistry. *Director*: The Runner Stumbles, Say Goodnight Gracie, John Gabriel Borkman, The Little Foxes.
Author: Booth, Uncle Bob.
PICTURES: Skidoo (debut, 1968), Catch-22, What's Up Doc?, Every Little Crook and Nanny, The Thief Who Came to Dinner, The Front Page, The Great Smokey Roadblock (The Last of the Cowboys), The Muppet Movie, Starting Over, Simon, First Family, My Man Adam, Off Beat, Short Circuit, Hello Again, Mr. & Mrs. Bridge, The Ballad of the Sad Cafe, True Identity, My Cousin Vinny, Charlie's Ear, Rain Without Thunder, My Boyfriend's Back, Searching for Bobby Fischer, Mr. Nanny, Greedy, Guarding Tess, Dangerous Minds, Two Much, Home for the Holidays, Sgt. Bilko, Trial and Error, 2 Days in the Valley, The Proprietor, The Associate, The Mirror Has Two Faces, Sue, Amistad, A River Made to Drown In, Charlie Hoboken, Joe the King, Men of Means, Brokendown

Love Story, The 4th Floor, Broke Even, Fast Food Fast Women, Erotic Tales IV, Clowns, Angela, The Acting Class, Queenie in Love, Manna From Heaven, A Beautiful Mind, Sex & Violence, Don't You Cry For Me, Finding Nemo (voice), Uptown Girls, Raising Flagg, The Civilization of Maxwell Bright, Christmas with the Kranks, Dirty Work (aka Southside), 77, Lovely by Surprise, Glass Houses.
TELEVISION: *Movies*: Alice in Wonderland, Lethal Innocence, Don't Drink the Water, Long Island Fever, Homicide: The Movie, Sick in the Head, Strip Search. *Mini-series:* LIBERTY! The American Revolution. *Series:* Cupid (also pilot). *Guest*: More than 55 appearances.

PENN, ARTHUR
Director. b. Philadelphia, PA, Sept. 27, 1922. e. Black Mountain Coll., Asheville, NC; U. of Perugia, U. of Florence in Italy. Began as TV dir. in 1953, twice winner of Sylvania Award. Appeared in 1994 film Naked in New York.
THEATRE: Two for the Seesaw, Miracle Worker (Tony Award, 1960), Toys in the Attic, All the Way Home, Golden Boy, Wait Until Dark, Sly Fox, Monday After the Miracle, Hunting Cockroaches.
PICTURES: The Left-Handed Gun (debut, 1958), The Miracle Worker (Academy Award nom.; DGA nom. 1963), Mickey One (also prod.), The Chase, Bonnie and Clyde (Academy Award nom.; DGA nom.; Golden Globe nom. 1968), Alice's Restaurant (Academy Award nom.; WGA nom. 1970, also co-s.p.), Little Big Man, Visions of Eight (dir. segment: The Highest), Night Moves, The Missouri Breaks, Four Friends (also co-prod.), Target, Dead of Winter, Penn and Teller Get Killed (also prod.), Lumiere and Company (documentary).
TELEVISION: *Movies*: Flesh and Blood, The Portrait, Inside. *Series*: American Playhouse 90 (Emmy nom. 1958), Law & Order (exec. prod., Emmy nom. 2001), 100 Centre Street.

PENN, ROBIN WRIGHT
Actress. b. Dallas, TX, April 8, 1966. m. actor Sean Penn. Was model at age 14 before making acting debut on TV series The Yellow Rose.
PICTURES: Hollywood Vice Squad (debut, 1986), The Princess Bride, Denial, State of Grace, The Playboys, Toys, Forrest Gump (Golden Globe nom. 1995), The Crossing Guard, Moll Flanders, Loved, She's So Lovely, Message In a Bottle, Hurlyburly, How to Kill Your Neighbor's Dog, Unbreakable, The Pledge, The Last Castle, White Oleander, Searching for Debra Winger (documentary), The Singing Detective, Virgin (also exec. prod.), A Home at the End of the World, Nine Lives, Sorry, Haters, Breaking and Entering, Hounddog (also exec. prod.), Beowulf, What Just Happened?, New York, I Love You, State of Play, The Private Lives of Pippa Lee, A Christmas Carol, The Conspirator, Moneyball.
TELEVISION: *Movies:* Empire Falls. *Mini-series:* A TV Dante. *Series*: Santa Barbara (3 Emmy noms.). *Pilot*: Home.

PENN, SEAN
Actor, Director, Writer. b. Burbank, CA, Aug. 17, 1960. Son of actor-dir. Leo Penn and actress Eileen Ryan. Brother of late actor Christopher Penn. Brother is musician Michael Penn. m. actress Robin Wright Penn. e. Santa Monica H.S. Served as apprentice for two years at Group Repertory Theatre, L.A. Acted in: Terrible Jim Fitch, Earthworms, The Girl on the Via Flaminia. First prof. appearance as guest star on TV's Barnaby Jones. On B'way in Heartland, Slab Boys. Also in Hurlyburly (Westwood Playhouse, LA), Goose & Tom Tom (Lincoln Center Theater). Directed, The Kindness of Women (Santa Monica Pink Theater); exec. prod., Remembrance (Santa Monica Playhouse).
PICTURES: *Actor*: Taps (debut, 1981), Fast Times at Ridgemont High, Bad Boys, Crackers, Racing with the Moon, Falcon and the Snowman, At Close Range, Shanghai Surprise, Colors, Judgment in Berlin, Casualties of War, We're No Angels, State of Grace, Carlito's Way (Golden Globe nom. 1994), Dead Man Walking (Academy Award nom.; Golden Globe nom. 1996), She's So Lovely (also exec. prod.; Cannes Film Festival Award, 1997), Loved (also prod.), U-Turn (also prod.), The Game, Hurlyburly, The Thin Red Line, Sweet and Lowdown (Academy Award nom.; Golden Globe nom. 2000), Being John Malkovich (cameo), Up at the Villa, Before Night Falls, The Weight of Water, Beaver Trilogy, I Am Sam (Academy Award nom. 2002), You'll Never Wiez in this Town Again, Scene Smoking: Cigarettes-Cinema-and the Myth of Cool, The Art of Dennis Hopper, It's All About Love, Mystic River (Academy Award, Golden Globe Award 2003), 21 Grams, The Assassination of Richard Nixon, The Interpreter, All the King's Men, In Search of Captain Zero (also prod.), Crossing Over, Milk (Academy Award, Golden Globe nom. 2009), Fair Game, Tree of Life, This Must Be the Place. *Director/Writer*: The Indian Runner, The Crossing Guard (also co-prod.), The Pledge (prod.), September 11, Into the Wild (also prod., DGA nom.; WGA nom. 2008).
TELEVISION: *Movies*: Hellinger's Law, The Killing of Randy Webster. *Documentaries/Specials*: Dear America (reader), Deflating the Elephant: Framed Messages Behind Conservative Dialogue (video, narr.). *Guest:* More than 120 appearances.

PENNEBAKER, D.A.
Director, Cinematographer. r.n. Donn Alan Pennebaker. b. Evanston, IL, July 15, 1925. e. Yale U. Studied engineering, set up own electronics firm. Worked in advertising, before writing and directing documentaries, as well as experimental films. 1958 joined Richard Leacock, Willard Van Dyke and Shirley Clarke in equipment-sharing film co-op, Filmakers. 1960 joined Robert Drew operating out of Time Life with Leacock, Albert Maysles and others. Set up Leacock Pennebaker with Leacock and made several films that were blown up from 16mm to 35mm and released in theatres. Currently works with co-dir. and wife, Chris Hegedus, and son Frazer Pennebaker, continuing to film unscripted dramas of real events in cinema verite style. Has directed many music videos.
PICTURES: Daybreak Express (1956,short), Opening in Moscow, Primary, David, Jane, Crisis, The Chair, On the Pole, Mr. Pearson, Don't Look Back, Monterey Pop, Beyond the Law, One P.M., Sweet Toronto, Maidstone, Ziggy Stardust and the Spiders From Mars, On the Pole, Town Bloody Hall, The Energy War, Dance Black America, Rockaby, Delorean, Happy Come Home, Depeche Mode: 101, The Music Tells You, The War Room (Academy Award nom. 1994), Keine Zeit, Moon Over Broadway, Down From the Mountain, Only the Strong Survive, The Cutman (short; exec. prod. only), Al Franken: God Spoke (doc.).
TELEVISION: *Documentaries:* Woodstock Diary (also ed.), Sessions at West 54th (series), Searching for Jimi Hendrix (also ed.), Elaine Stritch: At Liberty (Emmy nom. 2004), The First Amendment Project: Fox Vs. Franken, Assume the Position 201 with Mr. Wuhl (dir. only), Addiction (segmant dir.), The Return of the War Room.

PEPLOE, MARK
Writer. b. Kenya. Sister is writer Clare Peploe. Raised in England and Italy. e. Magdalen Coll., Oxford. Became researcher for documentary dept. of the BBC; then worked as researcher, writer and dir. for series Creative Persons.
PICTURES: The Pied Piper, The Passenger, The Babysitter, High Season, The Last Emperor (Academy Award and Golden Globe Award for Best s.p.; WGA nom. 1988), The Sheltering Sky, Afraid of the Dark (also dir.), Little Buddha, Victory (also dir.), The Triumph of Love (script consultant).
TELEVISION: *Movies: Director:* Samson and Delilah.

PEPPER, JOHN E., JR.
Executive. e. Yale University, B.A., 1960. From 1963-2002, Pepper served in various positions at Procter & Gamble (P&G), including director from 1984-2003; president, 1986-1995 and CEO and chairman from 1995-2002, his retirement from P&G. Pepper has extensive experience leading P&G international market expansion, including China. After leaving P&G, he served as v.p., finance & administration at Yale University from Jan. 2004 to Dec. 2005. Pepper's current role is chairman of the board for The Walt Disney Company, a position he assumed in Jan. 2007. Pepper serves on the board of Boston Scientific Corp. and is a member of the Executive Committee of the Cincinnati Youth Collaborative.

PERAKOS, SPERIE P.
Executive. b. New Britain, CT, Nov. 12, 1920. e. Cheshire Acad., Yale U., Harvard Law Sch. Student mgr., Stanley-Warner Theatres, 1939-40; Perakos Theatres 1940 to present; Capt., U.S.A. Intelligence with 35 inf. division. Fellow, Pierson Coll., Yale, 1946-present; Yale Alumni Bd., 1949 to present; Yale Alumni Film Bd. 1952 to 1980; member Alumni Council for Yale Drama Sch.; Past pres. Yale Club of New Britain, Conn.; dir. of Films & Filmings Seminars, Pierson Coll., Yale; prod. Antigone, 1964; pres. Norma Film Prod., Inc., 1962 to present. Past pres. and chmn. Yale's Peabody Museum Associates. Pres., Perakos Theatres, Conn. Theatre Associates, Inc. Past Pres., Connecticut Association of Theatre Owners, Secretary, ShowEast. *Member:* Exec. Board of Natl' Assn. of Theatre Owners, C.A.R.A.

PERENCHIO, A. JERROLD "JERRY"
Executive. b. Fresno, CA, Dec. 20, 1930. e. U. of California. Known as "Jerry Perenchio." Vice pres., Music Corp. of America, 1958-62; General Artists Corp., 1962-64; pres., owner, Chartwell Artists, Ltd., theatrical agency, Los Angeles, 1964; pres. & CEO, Tandem Productions, Inc., and TAT Communications Co., 1973-83, then became principal with Norman Lear in Embassy Communications. Held post of pres. & CEO of Embassy Pictures. Owned and been active in Chartwell Partners LLC, a media and communications investment co., since it was formed in 1983. Former chairman of the Board and CEO of Univision Communications, Inc. From Dec. 1992 through Jan. 1997, he was also the company's president. Univision was sold to a consortium of private investors in Sept. 2006. Investors included: Madison Dearborn Partners, Providence Equity Partners, Texas Pacific Group, Thomas H. Lee Partners and Saban Capital Group.

PEREIRA, VANESSA
Casting Director.
PICTURES: Jude, Hamlet, Welcome to Sarajevo, Under the Skin, Spice World, My Son the Fanatic, Resurrection Man, I Want You, Dark City, What Rats Won't Do, Appetite, Elizabeth, Hilary and Jackie, Alegria, The Lost Son, Heart, Jakob the Liar (casting for Hungary), Battle in Seattle (exec. prod.).
TELEVISION: *Movies:* Flowers of the Forest, The Ripper (U.K.), Moby Dick (U.K.). *Series*: The Hunger.

PEREZ, ROSIE
Actress. b. Brooklyn, NY Sept.6, 1964. Attended sch. in L.A. where she became a dancer on Soul Train; then choreographer for music videos and stage shows for such performers as Bobby Brown, The Boys, Diana Ross, LL Cool J, etc. Acting debut in Do the Right Thing.
PICTURES: Do the Right Thing (also choreog.; debut, 1989), White Men Can't Jump, Night on Earth, Untamed Heart, Fearless (Academy Award nom.; Golden Globe nom. 1994), It Could Happen to You, Somebody to Love, A Brother's Kiss, Perdita Durango, The 24 Hour Woman (also co-prod.), The Road to El Dorado (voice), King of the Jungle, Human Nature, Riding in Cars with Boys, From the 104th Floor (short, narrator), Just Like the Son, The Take, The Pineapple Express, In the Woods, The Hero of Color City, Pete Smalls Is Dead.
TELEVISION: *Movies:* Criminal Justice, In a New Light: Sex Unplugged (host), Subway Stories: Tales from the Underground (also exec. prod.). One World Jam (host), Copshop, Lackawanna Blues, Lolo's Cafe (voice), Lies in Plain Sight. *Mini-series:* Widows. *Series:* In Living Color (choreographer, 3 Emmy noms.), House of Buggin', Go, Diego! Go! (voice), Lipstick Jungle. *Documentaries/Specials:* Rosie Perez Presents Society's Ride (exec. prod.). *Guest:* More than 74 appearances.

PERKINS, ELIZABETH
Actress. b. Forest Hills, Queens, NY, Nov. 18, 1960. Grew up in Vermont. After high school moved to Chicago to study at Goodman School of Drama. Two months after moving to NY in 1984, landed a role in the national touring co. of Brighton Beach Memoirs, later performing part on Broadway. Acted with Playwright's Horizon, NY Ensemble Theater, Shakespeare in the Park and Steppenwolf Theatre Co.
PICTURES: About Last Night..., From the Hip, Big, Sweet Hearts Dance, Love at Large, Avalon, Enid Is Sleeping, He Said She Said, The Doctor, Indian Summer, The Flintstones, Miracle on 34th Street, Moonlight and Valentino, Lesser Prophets, I'm Losing You, Crazy in Alabama, 28 Days, Cats & Dogs,Try Seventeen, Finding Nemo (voice), Speak, Gilded Stones (short), Jiminy Glick in La La Wood, Kids in America, The Ring Two, The Thing About My Folks, Must Love Dogs.
TELEVISION: *Movies*: Teach 109 (tv short), For Their Own Good, Cloned, If These Walls Could Talk 2, What Girls Learn, My Sister's Keeper, Speak, Hercules. *Mini-series*: The Rescuers: Two Women, From the Earth to the Moon, Hercules. *Series:* Battery Park, Weeds (2 Emmy noms.; 2 Golden Globe noms. 2006, 2007).

PERKINS, MILLIE
Actress. b. Passaic, NJ, May 12, 1938. Was model when chosen by dir. George Stevens for starring role in The Diary of Anne Frank.
PICTURES: The Diary of Anne Frank (debut, 1959), Wild in the Country, Dulcinea, Ensign Pulver, Ride in the Whirlwind, The Shooting, Wild in the Streets, Cockfighter, Lady Cocoa, The Witch Who Came From the Sea, Table for Five, At Close Range, Jake Speed, Slam Dance, Wall Street, Necronomicon, Two Moon Junction, The Pistol, Bodily Harm, The Chamber, Yesterday's Dreams, The Lost City.
TELEVISION: *Movies*: A.D., The Thanksgiving Promise, Penalty Phase, Anatomy of an Illness, Shattered Vows, License to Kill, Strange Voices, Best Intentions, The Other Love, Haunting Passion, A Gun in the House, Model Mother, Macbeth, 72 Hours, The Writing on the Wall, God-The Universe-and Hot Fudge Sundaes, The Bounty Hunter: Miles To Go Before I Sleep, The Thanksgiving Promise, Penalty Phase, Strange Voices, Broken Angel, Call Me Anna, Murder of Innocence, Midnight Run for Your Life, Harvest of Fire, The Summer of Ben Tyler, A Woman's a Helluva Thing, Though None Go with Me. *Mini-series:* A.D., Elvis. *Series*: Knots Landing, Any Day Now, The Young and the Restless. *Guest:* More than 45 appearances.

PERKINS, ROWLAND
Executive. Active in ent. industry for more than 30 years. Vice-President, Creative Services, William Morris Agency, 1952–75. Founding President, Creative Artists Agency, 1975–95. Established The Rowland Perkins Company (a.k.a. Double Eagle Entertainment) in 1994 to develop and produce feature, network and cable films; television series and specials; Broadway shows. Currently chmn. of NPOWR Database, Inc., a company that creates practical technology and programming solutions for the dynamic iTV/VOD marketplace. Perkins is also chmn. of ieProducer.com, an integrated-Internet company, and is a founder and president of its profitable, wholly owned subsidiary Talentclick.com an Internet company servicing the casting needs of the media industry for motion picture, television, legitimate theatre, and commercial talent. Since Jan. 2005, Perkins has been a director at USA Video Interactive. Now a Bd member of MouseJockey which evaluates new media for advertisers.

PERLMAN, RHEA
Actress. b. Brooklyn, NY, March 31, 1948. e. Hunter Coll. m. actor-dir. Danny DeVito. Co-founder Colonnades Theatre Lab., NY and New Street prod. co with Danny DeVito.
PICTURES: Love Child, My Little Pony (voice), Enid is Sleeping (Over Her Dead Body), Ted & Venus, Class Act, There Goes the Neighborhood, Canadian Bacon, Sunset Park, Carpool, Matilda, 10 Items or Less, Love Comes Lately, East Fifth Bliss.
TELEVISION: *Movies*: I Want to Keep My Baby!, Stalk the Wild Child, Having Babies II, Intimate Strangers, Mary Jane Harper Cried Last Night, Like Normal People, Drop-out Father, The Ratings Game, Dangerous Affection, A Family Again, To Grandmother's House We Go, A Place to Be Loved, Spoils of War, In the Doghouse, Houdini, The Frasier Story, A Tail of Two Bunnies, Secret Cutting, How to Marry a Billionaire: A Christmas Tale, Other People's Business, Stroller Wars, The Christmas Choir. *Series*: Cheers (4 Emmy Awards, 6 other noms.; 6 Golden Globe noms.), Pearl (co-exec. prod.), Kate Brasher. *Documentaries/Specials*: Funny You Don't Look 200, Two Daddies (voice), The Last Halloween. *Guest:* More than 114 appearances.

PERLMAN, RON
Actor. b. New York, NY, April 13, 1950. While in high school, part of comedy team that played clubs. e. City U. of NY, U. of Minnesota, M.F.A. Joined Classic Stage Company, NY, for 2 years.
THEATRE: *NY*: The Architect and the Emperor of Assyria (also toured Europe), American Heroes, The Resistible Rise of Arturo Ui, Tiebele and Her Demon, La Tragedie de Carmen, A Few Good Men.
PICTURES: Quest for Fire, The Ice Pirates, The Name of the Rose, Sleepwalkers, The Adventures of Huck Finn, Double Exposure, Romeo Is Bleeding, Crime and Punishment, Cronos, Fluke, The City of Lost Children, The Last Summer, The Island of Dr. Moreau, Prince Valiant, Alien Resurrection, Tinsletown, The Protector, Betty, Frogs for Snakes, I Woke Up Early the Day I Died, Happy,Texas, Price of Glory, Bread and Roses, Titan A.E. (voice), The King's Guard, The Trial of Old Drum, Crime and Punishment, Enemy at the Gates, Down, Quiet Kill, Rtas, Night Class, How to Go Out on a Date in Queens, Boys on the Run, Blade 2, G-S.P.O.T., Star Trek: Nemesis, Two Soldiers, Shakedown, Hoodlum & Son, Absolon, Looney Tunes: Back in Action, The Second Front, Hellboy, Nightmare Blvd., Soloman's Turn, Missing in America, 5ive Girls, In the Name of the King: A Dungeon Siege Tale, Uncross the Stars, The Last Winter, The Poison Rose, Conan: Red Nails (video-voice), The Mutant Chronicles, Outlander, I Sell the Dead, Terra (voice), I Sell the Dead, Hellboy 2: The Golden Army, Spirit of the Forest (voice, English version), The Job, The Devil's Tomb, Killer by Nature, Acts of Violence, Season of the Witch, Crave, Bunraku, Tangled, The Legend of Secret Pass (voice), The Riot, Conan.
TELEVISION: *Movies*: Our Family Honor, A Stoning in Fulham County, Blind Man's Bluff, Arly Hanks, The Cisco Kid, Original Sins, The Adventures of Captain Zoom in Outer Space, Mr. Stitch, The Second Civil War, A Town Has Turned to Dust, Houdini, Primal Force, Operation Sandman, The Trial of Old Drum, Desperation, Hellboy Animated: Sword of Storms (voice), Hellboy Animated: Blood and Iron (voice), Hellboy Animated: The Phantom Claw (voice). *Mini-series:* Afro Samurai (voice, English version). *Series*: Ryan's Hope, Beauty and the Beast (2 Emmy noms.; Golden Globe Award 1989), The Magnificent Seven, Justice League, Sons of Anarchy. *Characterizations/voices on series:* Batman, Bonkers, Aladdin, Phantom 2040, Mortal Kombat: The Animated Series, Skwids, Batman: Gotham Knights, Teen Titans, Danny Phantom, The Batman. *Guest:* More than 137 appearances.

PERLMUTTER, DAVID M.
Producer. b. Toronto, Canada, 1934. e. U. of Toronto. Pres., Quadrant Films Ltd.
PICTURES: *Producer:* Vengeance Is Mine, It Seemed Like a Good Idea at the Time, Nothing Personal, Falling Through, Tempo. *Executive producer:* The Neptune Factor, Find the Lady, Fast Company, Best Revenge, Soft Deceit, Bloodknot, Undertow, Hostile Intent, Ms. Bear, Bone Daddy, Teen Knight, Teenage Space Vampires, The Excalibur Kid, Bear with Me, Time of the Wolf, Touching Wild Horses.
TELEVISION: *Movies: Executive producer:* Model by Day, 30 Years to Life, Nightworld: Lost Souls, Protector, Survivor (TV short), The Cyberstalking, Stiletto Dance, Murder Among Friends, Recipe for Murder, Drive Time Murders, Every Second Counts, The Last Jinn, You Lucky Dog. *Producer:* Zebra Lounge, Cybermutt, The Shrink, Still Small Voices, Between Truth and Lies, Cheaters' Club, Obituary, They Come Back, Lies and Crimes, Wide Awake. *Series: Executive producer:* The Hitchhiker, Strangers, Sins of the City.

PERMUT, DAVID A.
Producer. b. New York, NY, March 23, 1954. In 1974, became pres., Diversified Artists Intl.; 1975, pres., Theatre Television Corp.; 1979, formed Permut Presentations, Inc., and is pres. Production deals with Columbia Pictures (1979), Lorimar Productions (1981), Universal (1985), United Artists (1986), and New Line Cinema (1991).
PICTURES: Give 'Em Hell Harry, Fighting Back (exec. prod.), Blind Date, Richard Pryor—Live in Concert (exec. prod.), Dragnet, The Marrying Man, 29th Street, Captain Ron, Consenting Adults, The Temp, Three of Hearts, Surviving the Game, Trapped in Paradise, Eddie, Face/Off, Woodstuck, Double Take, Uncoupled, Route 52, Kings for a Day, DysFunktional Family (doc.), The Last Shot, Local Color, Farce of the Penguins (video), Charlie Bartlett, My Mom's New Boyfriend (exec. prod.),

Prayers for Bobby (exec. prod.), Respect (doc.), The Boys: The Sherman Brothers' Story (doc.), Youth in Revolt.
TELEVISION: *Movies:* Mistress (sprv. prod.), Love Leads the Way, Triumph of the Heart: The Ricky Bell Story, Breaking the Silence (exec. prod.), Prayers for Bobby (exec. prod., Emmy nom. 2009).

PERREAU, GIGI
Actress. r.n. Ghislaine Perreau. b. Los Angeles, CA, Feb. 6, 1941. e. Immaculate Heart H.S. & College. Many stage and TV guest appearances. Now teaching and directing. Among first 50 stars to be honored with star on Hollywood Walk of Fame.
PICTURES: Madame Currie (debut, 1943), Abigail, Dear Heart, Dark Waters, San Diego I Love You, Two Girls and a Sailor, The Master Race, The Seventh Cross, Mr. Skeffington, Yolanda and the Thief, Voice of the Whistler, God Is My Co-Pilot, To Each His Own, Alias Mr. Twilight, High Barbaree, Song of Love, Green Dolphin Street, Family Honeymoon, Enchantment, Sainted Sisters, Roseanna McCoy, Song of Surrender, My Foolish Heart, Shadow on the Wall, For Heaven's Sake, Never a Dull Moment, Reunion in Reno, The Lady Pays Off, Weekend with Father, Has Anybody Seen My Gal, Bonzo Goes to College, There's Always Tomorrow, The Man in the Gray Flannel Suit, Dance With Me Henry, Wild Heritage, The Cool and the Crazy, Girls' Town, Tammy Tell Me True, Look in Any Window, Journey to the Center of Time, Hell on Wheels, High Seas Hijack, Fly Me to the Moon 3D (voice), Time Again, Sammy's Adventures: The Secret Passage.
TELEVISION: *Series*: The Betty Hutton Show, Follow the Sun.

PERRINE, VALERIE
Actress. b. Galveston, TX, Sept. 3, 1943. e. U. of Arizona. Was showgirl in Las Vegas before discovered by agent Robert Walker who got her contract with Universal Pictures.
PICTURES: Slaughterhouse 5 (debut, 1972), The Last American Hero, Lenny (Academy Award nom.; Golden Globe nom. 1975), W. C. Fields & Me, Mr. Billion, Superman, The Magician of Lublin, The Electric Horseman, Can't Stop the Music, Superman II, Agency, The Border, Water, Maid to Order, Reflections in a Dark Sky, Bright Angel, Boiling Point, Girl in the Cadillac, The Break, My Girlfriend's Boyfirend, Curtain Call, 54, Shame Shame Shame, A Place Called Truth, Brown's Requiem, Picture This, My Girlfriend's Boyfriend, What Women Want, Project: Indie, The End of the Bar, The Amateurs, The Californians, Redirecting Eddie.
TELEVISION: *Movies*: The Couple Takes a Wife, Ziegfeld: The Man and His Women, Marian Rose White, Malibu, When Your Lover Leaves, Sweet Bird of Youth, Un Casa a Roma, Mountain of Diamonds. *Mini-series:* The Secrets of Lake Success. *Series:* Leo and Liz in Beverly Hills, As the World Turns. *Documentaries/Specials:* Steambath.

PERRY, DON
Executive. e. B.A., communications management, Ithaca College, NY, 1974. With General Electric Perry entered company's broadcast-management training program from 1975 to 1979; moved on to WNYT, Albany, NY, general manager, 1984 to 1995; as WOAI San Antonio, TX, general manager, 1996-2002; became Clear Channel Television regional v.p., Southwest Group, from 2002 to 2005; was upped to Clear Channel executive v.p. & COO in May 2005 and was named to the position of president and CEO of Clear Channel Television in Jan. 2006. Clear Channel Television owns and operates 51 television stations. He resigned this position in early 2008. Currently v.p. and general mngr. of CBS affiliate KPSP, CA. Perry is a past chairman of the Texas Association of Broadcasters, past chairman of the New York State Broadcasters, a former member of the board of directors of the NBC Affiliates Association, and has held leadership positions on the board of directors of the San Antonio Chamber of Commerce. He was recognized by the Texas Assn. of Broadcasters in 2005 as its Broadcaster of the Year.

PERRY, LUKE
Actor. r.n. Coy Luther Perry III. b. Mansfield, OH, Oct. 11, 1966. To LA then NY as teen to become actor, landing role on daytime serial Loving.
PICTURES: Scorchers, Terminal Bliss, Buffy the Vampire Slayer, At Home With the Webbers (cameo), 8 Seconds, Normal Life, American Strays, The Fifth Element, Lifebreath, The Florentine, Storm, The Heist, Attention Shoppers, The Enemy, Dirt, Fogbound, Dishdogz, The Real Catch, Alice Upside Down, Adopt a Sailor (co-exec. prod.), Swedish Midsummer Comedy, Upstairs, Sam Steele and the Junior Detective Agency, Good Intentions, Final Storm, Walls of Separation, Soho A Fine Step.
TELEVISION: *Movies*: Riot, Storm, Indiscreet, The Last Buckaroo, The Night of the Headless Horseman, The Triangle, Supernova, Descent, The Pledge, A Very Merry Daughter of the Bride, Angel and the Bad Man. *Mini-series*: Johnson County War. *Series*: Loving, Another World, Beverly Hills 90210, Mortal Kombat: The Animated Series (voice), The Incredible Hulk (voice), Pepper Ann (voice), Jeremiah (also exec. prod.), Oz, Windfall, John from Cincinnati. *Guest:* More than 86 appearances.

PERRY, MATTHEW
Actor. b. Williamstown, MA, Aug. 19, 1969. e. Ashbury College.
PICTURES: A Night in the Life of Jimmy Reardon, She's Out of Control, Getting In, Fools Rush In, Almost Heroes, Three to Tango, Imagining Emily (s.p. only), The Whole Nine Yards, The Kid, Serving Sarah, The Whole Ten Yards, The Beginning of Wisdom (also prod.), Numb (also exec. prod.), Birds of America, 17 Again, Down and Dirty Pictures.
TELEVISION: *Movies:* Dance 'til Dawn, Call Me Anna, Deadly Relations, Parallel Lives, The Ron Clark Story (Emmy nom.; Golden Globe nom. 2007). *Series:* Second Chance, Sydney, Home Free, Friends (Emmy nom. 2002), The West Wing (2 Emmy noms.), Studio 60 on the Sunset Strip, Mr. Sunshine (exec. prod., writer, also pilot). *Special*: Friends: The Stuff You've Never Seen. *Guest:* More than 91 appearances.

PERRY, SIMON
Producer, Writer. b. Farnham, England, Aug. 5, 1943. e. Cambridge Univ., 1965. Ent. ind. 1974. Early career in stage and television production. Prod. mini-budget feature Knots; prod. dir. Eclipse. Served on bureau staff of Variety. Ran the National Film Development Fund for two years. 1982 set up Umbrella Films. Was chief exec. of British Screen Finance from 1991 until Sept. 2000 when British Screen was absorbed by the newly established Film Council. In early 2003, was appointed director of co-productions at U.K. tax financier Ingenious Media. Since March 2004, pres., bd. of directors, of Ateliers du Cinéma Européen (ACE), which is a center for training and development helping independent European producers. President and exec. prod. for Shore View Entertainment.
PICTURES: Another Time Another Place, Loose Connections, Nineteen Eighty Four, Hotel Du Paradis, Nanou, White Mischief, The Favour, the Watch and the Very Big Fish, The Playboys, Innocent Lies, Becoming Jane.
TELEVISION: *Series:* The 4400 (exec. prod.).

PERRY, TYLER
Director, Producer, Actor. rn. Emmitt Perry, Jr. b. New Orleans, LA, September 14, 1969.
THEATRE: Why Did I Get Married? (writer), Madea Goes to Jail (writer).
PICTURES: Diary of a Mad Black Woman (writer, exec. prod., soundtrack writer), Madea's Family Reunion (dir., writer, exec. prod.), Daddy's Little Girls (dir., prod., s.p.), Why Did I Get Married? (dir., prod., writer (play), Meet the Browns (dir., writer,(play), prod.), The Family That Preys (dir., writer, prod., soundtrack arr.), Madea Goes to Jail (dir., writer, prod.), Star Trek (actor only), I Can Do Bad All by Myself (dir., writer, s.p., prod.), Georgia Sky (exec. prod.), Why Did I Get Married Too? (dir., writer, s.p., exec. prod., prod., actor), For Colored Girls Who Have Considered Suicide When the Rainbow Is Enuf (dir., prod., actor).
TELEVISION: *Series:* House of Payne (dir., writer, exec. prod.), Meet the Browns (writer, dir., exec. prod., prod.). *Guest:* More than 45 appearances.

PESCI, JOE
Actor. b. Newark, NJ, Feb. 9, 1943. Raised in Belleville, NJ. First show business job as child on TV's Star Time Kids. Worked as mason's laborer, restaurant owner, prior to becoming actor. Manager for Melissa Prophet Management.
PICTURES: Death Collector, Raging Bull (Academy Award nom.; Golden Globe nom. 1981), I'm Dancing as Fast as I Can, Dear Mr. Wonderful (Ruby's Dream), Easy Money, Eureka, Once Upon a Time in America, Man on Fire, Moonwalker, Lethal Weapon 2, Betsy's Wedding, Goodfellas (Academy Award, Golden Globe nom. 1991), Home Alone, The Super, JFK, My Cousin Vinny, Tuti Dentro, Lethal Weapon 3, The Public Eye, Home Alone 2: Lost in New York, A Bronx Tale, Jimmy Hollywood, With Honors, Casino, 8 Heads in a Duffel Bag, Gone Fishing, Lethal Weapon 4, The Good Shepherd, Love Ranch, Rising Star.
TELEVISION: *Movies*: Half Nelson (pilot), Backtrack. *Series*: Half Nelson, The Pink Panther (voice). *Documentary:* A Galaxy Far Far Away. *Guest:* More than 50 appearances.

PETERS, BERNADETTE
Actress. r.n. Bernadette Lazzara. b. New York, NY, Feb. 28, 1948. e. Quintano Sch. for Young Professionals, NY. Professional debut at age 5 on TV's Horn & Hardart Children's Hour, followed by Juvenile Jury and Name That Tune. Stage debut with N.Y. City Center production of The Most Happy Fella (1959).
THEATRE: Gypsy (1961), This is Goggle, Riverwind, The Penny Friend, Curley McDimple, Johnny No-Trump, George M! (Theatre World Award), Dames at Sea (Drama Desk Award), La Strada, W.C. & Me, On the Town (1971 revival), Tartuffe, Mack and Mabel, Sally and Marsha, Sunday in the Park With George, Song and Dance (Tony, Drama Desk & Drama League awards), Into the Woods, The Goodbye Girl, Come le formiche.
PICTURES: Ace Eli and Rodger of the Skies (debut, 1973), The Longest Yard, W.C. Fields & Me, Vigilante Force, Silent Movie (Golden Globe nom. 1977), The Jerk, Tulips, Pennies from Heaven (Golden Globe Award 1982), Heartbeeps, Annie, Slaves of New York, Pink Cadillac, Alice, Impromptu, Anastasia (voice), Hey Mr. Producer, Let it Snow, Wakko's Wish, A Few Good Years, It Runs in the Family, Coming Up Roses.
TELEVISION: *Movies*: The Islander, David, Fall from Grace, The Last Best Year, Into the Woods, The Odyssey, Cinderella, What the Deaf Man Heard, Holiday in Your Heart, Prince Charming,

Adopted, Bobbie's Girl (Emmy nom. 2003), Living Proof. *Mini-series*: The Martian Chronicles. *Series*: All's Fair (Golden Globe nom. 1977), The Closer, Ugly Betty. *Documentaries/Specials*: George M, They Said It with Music, Party at Annapolis, Rich Thin and Beautiful (host), Faerie Tale Theatre, The Last Mile. *Guest*: More than 140 appearances.

PETERS, JANICE C.
Executive. e. Wayne State U., BS, and Stanford U., masters in mgmt. Began in local/long distance telecom. field. Became pres., CEO, U S WEST NewVector Group, a cellular comm. co., and pres. of wireless ops., U S WEST MediaOne before becoming managing dir. of One 2 One, a cellular comm. co. in the UK in 1996. Retired president and CEO of MediaOne, whose broadband services company was merged into AT&T in 2000.
Currently serves on the Bd. of Dir. for 3Com Corp. Member: bd. of dir. of Primus, an E-service solutions company and 3Com Corporation.

PETERS, JON
Producer. b. Van Nuys, CA, June 2, 1945. Started hair-styling business; built it into multimillion-dollar firm before turning film producer. Formed Jon Peters Organization. 1980, joined with Peter Guber and Neil Bogart to form The Boardwalk Co. (dissolved 1981). Later Guber-Peters-Barris Company. 1989, became co-chairman of Columbia Pictures. Resigned, 1991.
PICTURES: *Producer:* A Star Is Born, Eyes of Laura Mars, The Main Event, Die Laughing, Caddyshack, My Fellow Americans, Rosewood, Wild Wild West, Ali, Superman Returns, The Guru (actor). *Co-producer/Co-Executiv producer: with Peter Guber.* An American Werewolf in London, Missing, Six Weeks, Flashdance, D.C. Cab, Vision Quest, Legend of Billie Jean, Clue, The Color Purple, Head Office, The Clan of the Cave Bear, Youngblood, The Witches of Eastwick, Innerspace, Who's That Girl, Gorillas in the Mist, Caddyshack II, Rain Man, Batman, Tango and Cash, The Bonfire of the Vanities, Batman Returns, This Boy's Life, With Honors, Money Train.
TELEVISION: *Movies*: *Executive prod.:* Brotherhood of Justice, Bay Coven, Nightmare at Bitter Creek, Finish Line. *Series:* Dreams (prod.), Oceanquest (TV series documentary; exec. prod.). *Documentaries/Specials:* Superman 50th Anniversary (exec. prod.).

PETERSEN, PAUL
Actor. b. Glendale, CA, Sept. 23, 1945. e. Valley Coll. Original Disney Mouseketeer (TV). Recorded hit songs She Can't Find Her Keys, and My Dad in 1962. In the late 1960's turned to writing beginning with a Marcus Welby script followed by paperback novels in 1970's. Author of book about Disney empire, Walt Mickey and Me (1977), and co-author of It's a Wonderful Life Trivia Book (1992). President and founder of A Minor Consideration, a support foundation for former kid actors with a current membership of 150 movie, tv and sports stars spanning the past 70 years. In 2004, recipient of Lifetime Achievement Award at Annual State Bros. Route 66 Rendezvous® Presented by Firestone.
PICTURES: Houseboat, This Could Be the Night, The Happiest Millionaire, A Time for Killing, Journey to Shiloh, Mommy II: Mommy's Day, Dickie Roberts: Former Child Star (soundtrack), The Portal, Soupernatural.
TELEVISION: *Movies*: In the Year 2889, Something for a Lonely Man, Gidget Grows Up, Scout's Honor, Mike Hammer: Murder Takes All. *Series*: The Mickey Mouse Club, The Donna Reed Show, Dream Girl of '67, General Hospital. *Documentaries/Specials*: Child Stars: Their Story.

PETERSEN, WILLIAM
Actor. b. Chicago, IL, Feb. 21, 1953. e. Idaho State U. Active in Chicago theatre; helped to found Ix, an ensemble acting group now called the Remains Theatre. Acted in Moby Dick, In the Belly of the Beast, A Streetcar Named Desire, etc. 1986, formed company with prod. Cynthia Chvatal called High Horse Prods.
THEATRE: *NY*: Night of the Iguana.
PICTURES: To Live and Die in L.A., Manhunter, Amazing Grace and Chuck, Cousins, Young Guns II, Hard Promises (also co-prod.), In the Kingdom of the Blind the Man with One Eye Is King, Passed Away, Fear, Mulholland Falls, Gunshy, Kiss the Sky, The Skulls, The Contender.
TELEVISION: *Movies*: Long Gone (HBO), Keep the Change (also co-prod.), Curacao, Present Tense Past Perfect, The Beast, 12 Angry Men, The Staircase, The Rat Pack, Haven. *Mini-Series*: The Kennedys of Massachusetts, Return to Lonesome Dove. *Series*: C.S.I.: Crime Scene Investigation (also co-exec. prod, 2003, exec. prod. 2004-2005, prod., spvr. prod. 2006, 3 Emmy noms.; Golden Globe nom. 2004).

PETERSEN, WOLFGANG
Director, Writer. b. Emden, Germany, March 14, 1941. Career as asst. stage dir. at Ernst Deutsch Theatre in Hamburg before entering four-year program at the German Film & TV Academy where he directed for television and later theatrical films.
PICTURES: *Director:* Der Eine - der Andere, Der (short), Die Rote Fahne (doc. short), Ich nicht (short), I Will Kill You Wolf, One or the Other, The Consequence (also s.p.), Das Boot (The Boat; also s.p.; 2 Academy Award noms. for dir.; DGA nom. 1983), The Neverending Story (also s.p.), Enemy Mine, Shattered (also s.p., co-prod.), In the Line of Fire (also co-exec. prod.), Outbreak (also co-prod.), Air Force One (also prod.), The Perfect Storm (also prod.), Troy (also prod.), Poseidon (also prod.). *Producer:* Bicentennial Man, A Spell for Chameleon. *Executive producer:* Red Corner, Instinct.
TELEVISION: *Movies*: Director of more than 15 German tv movie/minis, including Planübung, Schwarz und weiß wie Tage und Nächte, Das Boot. I Will Kill You Wolf (dir. debut 1970), Tatort (series), Smog (Prix Futura Award, 1975), For Your Love Only (also released theatrically), The Agency (exec. prod.), Avenger (exec. prod.). *Series*: Scene of the Crime, The Agency (exec. prod.).

PETERSON, RICHARD W.
Executive. b. Denver, CO, June 15, 1949. e. Col. Sch. of Broadcasting, Harper Coll. Joined Kennedy Theatres, Chicago, 1966. 1968 went with Great States Theatres (now Cineplex Odeon), Chicago. Was city mgr. of Crocker and Grove Theatres, Elgin, IL. 1973 joined American Automated Theatres, Oklahoma City, as dir. of adv., pub. Promoted to dir. of U.S. theatre operations. Worked for American International Pictures, Dallas, TX. Then moved to Dal Art Film Exchange and B & B Theatres as general mgr.; 1987 took over 7 screens from McLendon and formed own co., Peterson Theatres, Inc., CLT, Inc.

PETERSON, S. DEAN
Executive. b. Toronto, Canada, December 18, 1923. e. Victoria College, U. of Toronto. WWII service RCNVR; 1946 TV newsreel cameraman NBC; founded own prod. co. in 1947; incorporated Dordean Realty Limited to acquire new studios in 1959; formed Peterson Productions Limited in 1957 to make TV commercials and sponsored theatrical shorts; formed Studio City Limited in 1965 to produce TV series and features acquiring an additional studio complex and backlot in Kleinberg, Ontario; 1972 formed SDP Communications Ltd. to package M.P. and TV; 1970 incorporated Intermedia Financial Services Limited to provide specialized financing and consultation to companies in M.P. and TV industries. Past-President Canadian Film and Television Production Assn., mbr. Variety Club, Tent 28; Canadian Society of Cinematographers; Directors Guild of America, Directors Guild of Canada, SMPTE.

PETIT, HENRI-DOMINIQUE
Executive. b. Baden-Baden, Germany. e. Ecole Superieure de Physique et Chimie de Paris, Univ. of Paris. Earned post-graduate degree in nuclear physics, and a Ph.D. in corpuscular electronics from the University of Paris XI, France. He attended the Advanced Management Program, I.N.S.E.A.D., Fontainbleau, France. Joined Kodak 1975 as asst. mgr. of the Purchasing Division, Kodak Pathe, France. 1980, asst., then mgr. of Kodak Pathe Photofinishing Lab (1981). 1984, became bus. mgr. Business Information Systems and Corporate Accounts, Kodak Pathe. 1987, named bus. mgr. of Photofinishing Systems Division. 1989, appointed gen. mgr. and v.p. Motion Picture and Television Imaging, Europe/ Africa/Middle East Region. In December 1992, named v.p. and gen. mgr. Motion Picture and Television Imaging and relocated to the U.S. November 1995 named general manager of European, African and Middle Eastern Region. In September 1997, he was appointed Chief Operating Officer of Consumer Imaging. In February 2001, Petit was named chmn. & pres., Greater Asia Region/Vice President, Eastman Kodak Company, based in Shanghai, China. In April 2003, Petit was given additional responsibility to provide leadership for Kodak other non-US regions and was elected as a Senior Vice President of the company. Left Kodak and imaging industry in June 2004 to become CEO of Bacou-Dalloz, an org. which designs, manufactures and sells personal protective equipment.

PETRIE, DONALD
Director, Actor. b. New York, NY. Son of dir. Daniel Petrie. Moved to LA as teenager, becoming TV actor. Attended American Film Inst. dir. program, where he made short film The Expert. Was then hired to dir. Mister Magic esisode of Amazing Stories.
PICTURES: Mystic Pizza (debut, 1988), Opportunity Knocks, Grumpy Old Men, The Favor, Richie Rich, The Associate, My Favorite Martian, Miss Congeniality, How to Lose a Guy in 10 Days. Welcome to Mooseport, Just My Luck, Noah's Ark: The New Beginning (actor), My Life in Ruins, Where Rainbows End.
TELEVISION: *Movies: As Actor:* Thou Shalt Not Commit Adultery (actor), Haywire, Why Me?. *As Dir.:* Country Estates, Have You Tried Talking to Patty?. *Series: Dir:* The Equalizer, Men, Picket Fences, Chicago Hope, L.A. Law (Emmy nom.; DGA nom. 1987 for episode), Players, Opposite Sex, CBS Schoolbreak Special (DGA nom. 1987 for episode).

PETROU, DAVID MICHAEL
Writer, Producer, Corporate Executive. b. Washington, DC, Nov. 3, 1949. e. U. of Maryland, B.A.; Georgetown U., M.A. Publicity assoc., Psychiatric Institutes of America, Washington, DC, 1971; assoc. dir. of publicity & film liaison, Random House, 1974; guest lecturer, screen writing & film production, The American University Consortium, Washington, DC, spring, 1980; Woodrow Wilson Fellowship, 1971. Entered industry in 1975. Joined Salkind Organization as assistant producer for literary

projects. Worked in numerous senior production capacities on Crossed Swords, Superman, Superman II. 1977, exec. in chg. of literary development, Salkind. Wrote Crossed Swords (1978) and The Making of Superman. Co-authored screenplay, Shoot to Kill. 1978-79, executive consultant, Warner Bros.; 1980-83, dir., special projects, Joseph P. Kennedy, Jr. Foundation. 1983-84, sr. edit. for entertainment, Regardie's magazine; 1984-86, sr. exec., p.r. div., Abramson Associates; 1986-2005, pres. & COO, Eisner Petrou & Associates Inc. Baltimore-Wash., strategic communications consulting firm 2005. Corporate strategic planning and communications consultant. 1992, named chmn. of American Film Institute's Second Decade Council. Bd. Member: John F. Kennedy Center Community Advisory Board, Choral Arts Society of Washington, Clarice Smith Center for the Performing Arts, Foundation for Contemporary Mental Health, Washington Men's Camerata.

PETTY, LORI
Actress. b. Chattanooga, TN, March 23, 1964. Worked as graphic artist before turning to acting.
PICTURES: Cadillac Man, Point Break, A League of Their Own, Free Willy, Poetic Justice, In the Army Now, The Johnny Johnson Trial, Tank Girl, The Glass Shield, Relax...It's Just Sex, Clubland, MacArthur Park, Horrible Accident, Firetrap, Route 666, Prey for Rock & Roll, Richard III, Broken Arrows, The Last Guy on Earth, The Poker House (dir., writer), Chasing 3000.
TELEVISION: *Movies*: Bates Motel, Perry Mason: The Case of the Musical Murder. *Series*: The Thorns, Booker, Lush Life, Brimstone, House M.D.

PFEIFFER, MICHELLE
Actress. b. Santa Ana, CA, April 29, 1957. Sister of actress Deedee Pfeiffer. m. David E. Kelley. While attending jr. coll. and working as supermarket checkout clerk, won Miss Orange County beauty contest. Began taking acting classes in L.A. Stage debut in L.A. prod. of A Playground in the Fall. NY Theatre debut 1989 in Twelfth Night (Central Park).
PICTURES: The Hollywood Nights (debut, 1980), Falling in Love Again, Charlie Chan and the Curse of the Dragon Queen, Grease 2, Scarface, Into the Night, Ladyhawke, Sweet Liberty, The Witches of Eastwick, Amazon Women on the Moon, Married to the Mob (Golden Globe nom. 1989), Tequila Sunrise, Dangerous Liaisons (Academy Award nom. 1989), The Fabulous Baker Boys (Academy Award nom.; Golden globe Award 1990), The Russia House (Golden Globe nom. 1991), Frankie and Johnny (Golden Globe nom. 1992), Batman Returns, Love Field (Academy Award nom.; Golden Globe nom.1993), The Age of Innocence (Golden Globe nom. 1994), Wolf, Dangerous Minds, Up Close and Personal, To Gillian On Her 37th Birthday, One Fine Day (also exec. prod.), A Thousand Acres, A Midsummer Night's Dream, The Deep End of the Ocean (also prod.), Prince of Egypt (voice), The Story of Us, What Lies Beneath, I Am Sam, White Oleander, Sinbad: Legend of the Seven Seas (voice), I Could Never Be Your Woman, Hairspray, Stardust, Personal Effects, Chéri.
TELEVISION: *Movies:* The Solitary Man, Callie & Son, Splendor in the Grass, The Children Nobody Wanted, Tales from the Hollywood Hills: Natica Jackson. *Series:* Delta House, CHiPs, B.A.D. Cats. *Guest:* More than 75 appearances.

PHILLIPPE, RYAN
Actor. r.n. Matthew Ryan Phillippe. b. New Castle, DE, Sept. 10, 1974.
PICTURES: Crimson Tide, Invader, White Squall, Nowhere, I Know What You Did Last Summer, Playing by Heart, Homegrown, Little Boy Blue, 54, Cruel Intentions, The Way of the Gun, Anti-Trust, Company Man, Gosford Park, Igby Goes Down, The I Inside, Crash, Five Fingers, Flags of Our Fathers, Breach, Stop Loss, Franklyn, MacGruber, Tlatelolco: Mexico 68, Isolated (narr., exec. prod.), The Bang Bang Club, The Lincoln Lawyer.
TELEVISION: *Movies:* Deadly Invasion: The Killer Bee Nightmare. *Mini-series:* The Secrets of Lake Success. *Series:* One Life to Live.

PHILLIPS, LESLIE
Actor, Producer. b. London, England, April 20, 1924. Early career as child actor. Ent. m.p. ind. 1935.
PICTURES: A Lassie From Lancashire (debut, 1935), The Citadel, Rhythm Serenade, Train of Events, The Woman With No Name, Pool of London, The Galloping Major, Breaking the Sound Barrier, The Fake, The Limping Man, Time Bomb, The Price of Greed, Value for Money, The Gamma People, As Long as They're Happy, The Big Money, Brothers in Law, The Barretts of Wimpole Street, Just My Luck, Les Girls, The Smallest Show on Earth, High Flight, I Was Monte's Double, The Man Who Liked Funerals, The Angry Hills, Carry on Nurse, Ferdinand of Naples, This Other Eden, Carry on Teacher, Please Turn Over, The Navy Lark, Doctor in Love, Watch Your Stern, No Kidding, Carry on Constable, Inn for Trouble, Raising the Wind, In the Doghouse, Very Important Persons, Crooks Anonymous, The Longest Day, The Fast Lady, Father Came Too, Doctor in Clover, You Must Be Joking, Maroc 7, Some Will Some Won't, Doctor in Trouble, The Magnificent 7 Deadly Sins, Not Now Darling, Don't Just Lie There Say Something!, Spanish Fly, Not Now Comrade, Out of Africa, Empire of the Sun, Scandal, Mountains of the Moon, King Ralph, Carry on Columbus, August, Caught In The Act, The Jackal, Saving Grace, Lara Croft: Tomb Raider, Harry Potter and the Sorcerer's Stone (voice), Harry Potter and the Chamber of Secrets (voice), Thunderpants, Collusion, Churchill: The Hollywood Years, Colour Me Kubrick, Venus, Is There Anybody There?, Hotel Caledonia.
TELEVISION: *Movies:* Impasse (TV short), Monte Carlo, The Trials of Oz, Bermuda Grace, Two Golden Balls, The Changeling, Vanity Dies Hard, The Canterville Ghost, Die Katze von Kensington, Das Karussell des Todes, Time and Motion Man, Comedy Playhouse: Impasse, The Pale Horse, Dalziel and Pascoe: Recalled to Life, Cinderella, The Trials of Oz, Take a Girl Like You, Vanity Dies Hard, Outside the Rules, Ghosts of Albion, Marple: By the Pricking of My Thumbs, Things Talk (voices). *Mini-series:* Summer's Lease, Love On a Branch Line, Sword of Honour. *Series:* Our Man at St. Mark's, Foreign Affairs, The Culture Vultures, Casanova '73, Chancer, Honey for Tea, The House of Windsor, Revolver. *Guest:* More than 115 appearances.

PHILLIPS, LOU DIAMOND
Actor. r.n. Lou Upchurch. b. Philippines, Feb. 17, 1962. Raised in Corpus Christi, TX. e. U. of Texas, Arlington (BFA. drama). Studied film technique with Adam Roarke, becoming asst. dir./instructor with the Film Actor's Lab, 1983-86. Regional theatre includes: A Hatful of Rain, Whose Life Is It Anyway?, P.S. Your Cat Is Dead, The Lady's Not for Burning, Doctor Faustus, Hamlet.
THEATRE: *NY*: The King and I (Broadway debut, Tony nom.)
PICTURES: Angel Alley, Interface, Trespasses (also co-s.p.), Harley, La Bamba, Stand and Deliver (Golden Globe nom. 1989), Young Guns, Dakota (also assoc. prod.), Disorganized Crime, Renegades, The First Power, A Show of Force, Young Guns II, Ambition (also s.p.), The Dark Wind, Shadow of the Wolf, Extreme Justice, Dangerous Touch (also dir.), Teresa's Tattoo, Sioux City (also dir.), Undertow, Boulevard, Courage Under Fire, Another Day in Paradise (cameo), The Big Hit, Brokedown Palace, Bats, Supernova, Picking Up the Pieces, A Better Way to Die, Route 666, Knight Club, Lone Hero, Malevolent, Stark Raving Mad, Absolon, Hollywood Homicide, El Cortez, Death Toll, Never Forget, Guerrilla, Che: Part Two, The Invited, Transparency.
TELEVISION: *Movies*: Time Bomb, The Three Kings, Override (TV short), The Wharf Rat, In a Class of His Own, Hangman, Wolf Lake, Red Water, The Trail To Hope Rose, Murder at the Presidio, Alien Express, Sci Fi Inside: 'The Triangle', Termination Point, Lone Rider. *Mini-series:* Gone But Not Forgotten, The Triangle. *Series*: Wolf Lake, The Twilight Zone (dir. only), Laws of Chance, Numb3rs, SGU Stargate Universe. *Guest*: More than 90 appearances.

PHILLIPS, MICHAEL
Producer. b. Brooklyn, NY, June 29, 1943. e. Dartmouth College, B.A., 1965. NYU, Law Sch. J.D., 1968. Indep. m.p. prod. 1971.
PICTURES: Steelyard Blues, The Sting (Academy Award 1973), Taxi Driver (Academy Award nom. 1977), The Big Bus, Close Encounters of the Third Kind, Heartbeeps, Cannery Row, The Flamingo Kid, Don't Tell Mom the Babysitter's Dead (exec. prod.), Mom and Dad Save the World, Eyes of an Angel, Mimic (exec. prod.), Imposter (exec. prod.), The Last Mimzy.
TELEVISION: *Movies*: The Flamingo Kid (TV short; prod.), Jane's House (exec. prod.), The Companion, (prod.). *Series:* Trailer Park (prod., co-exec. prod.).

PHILLIPS, MICHELLE
Actress. r.n. Holly Michelle Gilliam. b. Long Beach, CA, June 4, 1944. Daughter is actress-singer Chynna Phillips. Former member of music group The Mamas and the Papas. Co-wrote hit single California Dreamin'. *Author:* California Dreamin': The Story of The Mamas and The Papas (1986).
PICTURES: Monterey Pop, The Last Movie, Dillinger (Golden Globe nom. 1974), Valentino, Sidney Sheldon's Bloodline, The Man With Bogart's Face, Savage Harvest, American Anthem, Let It Ride, Scissors, Army of One, Keep on Running, Lost in the Pershing Point Hotel, The Price of Air, March, Jane White is Sick and Twisted, Harry and Max, Unbeatable Harold, Kids in America (singer).
TELEVISION: *Movies*: The Death Squad, The California Kid, The Users, Moonlight, Mickey Spillane's Mike Hammer: Murder Me Murder You, Secrets of a Married Man, Covenant, Paint Me a Murder, Stark: Mirror Image, Assault and Matrimony, Mike Hammer: Murder Takes All, Trenchcoat in Paradise, No One Would Tell, Pretty Poison, Sweetwater, California Dreamin': The Songs of 'The Mamas & the Papas'. *Mini-series*: Aspen, The French Atlantic Affair. *Series*: Hotel, Knots Landing, Second Chances, Malibu Shores, Spicy City (voice), Beverly Hills 90210, Popular. *Guest*: More than 88 appearances.

PHILLIPS, SIÂN
Actress. b. Bettws, Wales, May 14, 1934. e. Univ. of Wales. Studied acting at RADA. London stage debut 1957 in title role in Hedda. Has made numerous recordings including Pal Joey, Gigi, A Little Night Music, Remember Mama.
THEATRE: Saint Joan, The Three Sisters, Taming of the Shrew, Duchess of Malfi, Lizard on the Rock, Gentle Jack, The Night of the Iguana, Ride a Cock Horse, Man and Superman, The Burglar, The Cardinal of Spain, Alpha Beta, Spinechiller, A Woman of No Importance, You Never Can Tell, Dear Liar, Pal

Joey (SWET nom.), Major Barbara, Gigi, Paris Match, Painting Churches, Vanilla, Ghosts (Artist of the Year nom.), Marlene, A Little Night Music (Olivier nom.), Snow Spider, many others. Broadway debut 1994 in An Inspector Calls.
PICTURES: Becket, Young Cassidy, Laughter in the Dark, Goodbye Mr. Chips (Golden Globe nom. 1970), Murphy's War, Under Milk Wood, Clash of the Titans, Dune, The Doctor and the Devils, Valmont, The Age of Innocence, House of America.
TELEVISION: *Movies*: Ewoks: The Battle for Endor–Dark River, The Two Mrs. Grenvilles, Out of Time, Dark River, The Black Candle, Heidi, The Borrowers, The Return of the Borrowers, The Vacillations of Poppy Carew, The Scold's Bridle, Alice Through the Looking Glass, The Magician's House, Cinderella, The Magician's House II, Come and Go, Attila, The Murder Room. *Mini-series:* Shoulder to Shoulder, Snow Spider, How Green Was My Valley (BAFTA Award), I Claudius (BAFTA & Royal TV Society Awards), Crime and Punishment, Chestnut Soldier (BAFTA nom.), Tinker Tailor Soldier Spy, Vanity Fair, Red Empire, Aristocrats (also narrator), Ivanhoe. *Documentaries/Specials*: Off to Philadelphia in the Morning, Sean O'Casey, How Many Miles to Babylon?, Lady Windermere's Fan, Language and Landscape, Heartbreak House, Don Juan in Hell, Summer Silence. *Guest:* More than 102 appearances.

PHOENIX, JOAQUIN
Actor. b.San Juan, Puerto Rico, Oct. 28, 1974. Brother of the late actor River Phoenix.
PICTURES: SpaceCamp, Russkies, Parenthood, To Die For, Inventing the Abbotts, U Turn, Return to Paradise, Clay Pigeons, 8 MM, The Yards, Gladiator (Academy Award nom.; Golden Globe nom. 2001), Quills, Buffalo Soldiers, Signs, It's All About Love, Brother Bear (voice), THe Village, Hotel Rwanda, Ladder 49, Walk the Line (Academy Award nom.; Golden Globe Award 2006), We Own the Night (also prod.), Reservation Road, Two Lovers.
TELEVISION: *Movies*: Backwards: The Riddle of Dyslexia, Kids Don't Tell, Secret Witness. *Series*: Morningstar/ Eveningstar, 4Real (exec. prod.).

PICARDO, ROBERT
Actor. b. Philadelphia, PA, Oct. 27, 1953. e. Yale. Studied acting at Circle in the Square Theater School.
THEATRE: *NY:* Sexual Perversity in Chicago, Gemini, Tribute.
PICTURES: The Howling, Star 80, Oh God You Devil, Explorers, Legend, Back to School, Munchies, Innerspace, Amazon Women on the Moon, Jack's Back, Dead Heat, The 'burbs, 976-EVIL, Loverboy, Total Recall, Gremlins II, Samantha, Motorama, Matinee, Wagons East!, The Pagemaster (voice), Menno's Mind, Star Trek: First Contact, Small Soldiers, Archibald the Rainbow Painter, The Amati Girls, Until Morning, Looney Tunes: Back in Action, Star Trek: The Experience-Borg Invasion 4D (short), 2004: A Light Knight's Odyssey (voice), Love Hollywood Style, Universal Signs, PJ, Sensored, Chasing the Green, Quantum Quest: A Cassini Space Odyssey (voice), Trail of Blood, Last Stop, Legends of Nethiah.
TELEVISION: *Movies:* The Dream Merchants, The Violation of Sarah McDavid, Lois Gibbs and the Love Canal, Dixie: Habits, The Other Woman, Runaway Daughters, Short Pfuse, White Mile, Out There, The Second Civil War, Pfish and Chip, The Lyon's Den, 2004: A Light Knight's Odyssey (voice), A.I. Assault, Ben 10: Race Against Time, The Odds, Monsterwolf, Morlocks. *Series:* China Beach, The Wonder Years (Emmy nom. 1989), Star Trek: Voyager, The Lyon's Den, Justice League, Stargate SG-1, Stargate: Atlantis. *Guest*: More than 108 appearances.

PICCOLI, MICHEL
Actor. r.n. Jacques Piccoli. b. Paris, France, Dec. 27, 1925. Since his film debut in The Sorcerer in 1945 has had impressive career on the French stage and in films working for major French dirs. Renoir, Bunuel, Melville, Resnais, Clouzot, Godard as well as Hitchcock. Until 1957 was mgr. of Theatre Babylone in Paris. Formed prod. co. Films 66. Produced: Themroc (1972); La Faille; Les Enfants Gates. Has appeared in more than 175 films/videos.
PICTURES: The Sorcerer, Le Point du Jour, French Can Can, The Witches of Salem, Le Bal des Espiona, Gina, Le Doulos, Contempt, Diary of a Chambermaid, Lady L, La Guerre Est Finie, The Young Girls of Rochefort, Un Homme de Trop, Belle de Jour, La Chamade, Dillinger Is Dead, L'Invasion, The Milky Way, Topaz, The Things of Life, Ten Days' Wonder, The Discreet Charm of the Bourgeoisie, Themroc, Wedding in Blood, La Grande Bouffe, The Last Woman, Leonor, 7 Deaths by Prescription, The Weak Spot, F For Fairbanks, Mado, Todo Modo, Rene the Cane, Spoiled Children, Strauberg Is Here, The Fire's Share, Little Girl in Blue Velvet, The Savage State, The Sugar, The Bit Between the Teeth, La Divorcement, Leap into the Void, The Price for Survival, Atlantic City, The Prodigal Daughter, Beyond the Door, The Eyes The Mouth, Passion, A Room in Town, Will the High Salaried Workers Please Raise Their Hands!!!, The General of the Dead Army, La Passante, The Prize of Peril, Adieu Bonaparte, Dangerous Moves, Danger in the House, Long Live Life!, Success Is the Best Revenge, The Sailor 512, Departure, Return, Mon Beau-Frere a Tue Ma Soeur, The Nonentity, The Prude, Bad Blood, Undiscovered Country, Blanc de Chine, Le Peuple Singe (narrator), The French Revolution, May Fools, La Belle Noiseuse, The Children Thief, Archipelago, Punctured Life, Martha and I, Everything's Fine We're Leaving, The Black Beach (writer, dir.), Je rentre à la maison, That Day, Little Lili, Mal de mer (short), Les Disparus, Seven Heroes, Sous les toits de Paris, On War, The Dust of Time, others.
TELEVISION: Numerous French movies.

PICERNI, PAUL
Actor. b. New York, NY, Dec. 1, 1922. e. Loyola U., Los Angeles. U.S. Air Force 1943-46; head of drama dept. Mt. St. Mary's College, 1949-50.
PICTURES: Breakthrough, Operation Pacific, I Was A Communist for the FBI, Inside the Wals of Folsom Prison, Fort Worth, Force of Arms, The Tanks Are Coming, Mara Maru, Cattle Town, Operation Secret, She's Back on Broadway, House of Wax, The System, The Desert Song, Drive a Crooked Road, The Shanghai Story, The Bounty Hunter, The Adventures of Hajji Baba, Dial Red O, Hell's Island Lord of the Jungle, Wiretapper, To Hell and Back, Bobby Ware Is Missing, Miracle in the Rain, The Come On, Flight to Hong Kong, The Shadow on the Window, The Big Caper, The Loves of Omar Khayyam, The Brothers Rico, Return to Warbow, The Deep Six, Marjorie Morningstar, The Man Who Died Twice, Torpedo Run, The Young Philadelphians, Strangers When We Meet, The Scalphunters, Che!, Land Raiders, Airport, Kotch, The Fearmaker, Capricorn One, Doublt Take, Beyond the Poseidon Adventure, Retirement, Three Days to Vegas.
TELEVISION: *Movies:* The Old Man Who Cried Wolf, Big Rose: Double Trouble, Something for Joey, The Last Hurrah, Marciano, Alcatraz: The Whole Shocking Story, The Dirty Dozen: The Deadly Mission. *Mini-series:* Women in White. *Series*: The Untouchables, The Young Marrieds, Capitol. *Guest*: More than 131 appearances.

PICKER, DAVID V.
Executive, Producer. b. New York, NY, May 14, 1931. e. Dartmouth College, B.A., 1953. Father Eugene Picker, exec. Loew's Theatres. Ent. industry in 1956 as adv. pub. & exploitation liaison with sales dept., United Artists Corp.; exec. v.p. U.A. Records; asst. to Max Youngstein, v.p.; v.p. U.A.; first v.p. UA; pres. 1969. Resigned 1973 to form own production co. 1976 joined Paramount Pictures as pres. of m.p. div.; v.p., Lorimar Productions; 1987, pres. & COO, Columbia Pictures. Resigned. In 1997, named president of Worldwide Production at Hallmark Entertainment Inc. V. P. of the Producers Guild of America (east region).
PICTURES: *Producer*: Royal Flash, Won Ton Ton the Dog Who Saved Hollywood, The One and Only, Oliver's Story, Bloodline, The Jerk, Dead Men Don't Wear Plaid, The Man with Two Brains, The Goodbye People, Beat Street, Traces of Red, Leap of Faith, The Saint of Fort Washington, The Crucible. *Executive producer:* Terror on the Britannic, Lenny, Smile, Stella, Back to the Secret Garden.
TELEVISION: *Movies*: *Executive producer:* Rear Window, Journey to the Center of the Earth, Aftershock: Earthquake in New York, In the Beginning, David Copperfield, Hans Christian Andersen: My Life As A Fairy Tale, Fidel. *Mini-series*: *Executive producer:* The Temptations (Emmy nom. 1999), P.T. Barnum (Emmy nom. 2000), Fidel.

PICKMAN, JEROME
Executive. b. New York, NY, Aug. 24, 1916. e. St. John's U.; Brooklyn Law School of St. Lawrence U., LL.B. Reporter N.Y. newspapers; U.S. Army World War II; Ad-pub exec. 20th-Fox, 1945-46; v.p., dir., adv. & pub., later v.p. domestic gen. sls. mgr., Paramount Pictures; sr. sls. exec. Columbia Pictures; pres. Motion Picture Div. of Walter Reade Org.; pres., Levitt-Pickman Film Corp.; sr. v.p., domestic distribution, Lorimar Productions; pres., Pickman Film Corp., Cineworld Enterprises Corp.; pres. Scotti Bros. Pictures Distribution, 1986. Consultant, various entertainment entities, legal and financial individuals and organizations.

PIDGEON, REBECCA
Actress. b. Cambridge, MA, October 10, 1963. m. writer-director David Mamet.
PICTURES: The Dawning, She's Been Away, Homicide, Oleanna (comp. only), The Spanish Prisoner, The Winslow Boy, State and Main, Catastrophe, Heist, Advice and Dissent (short), Shopgirl, Provoked: A True Story, Redbelt, The Lodger, Come Back to Sorrento (also writer, soundtrack performer).
TELEVISION: *Movies*: She's Been Away, Uncle Vanya, The Water Engine, Jesse Stone: Sea Change. *Mini-series*: Campaign. *Series:* The Unit,

PIERCE, DAVID HYDE
Actor. b. Saratoga Sprins, NY, April 3, 1959. e. Yale U.
THEATRE: *Off-B'way:* Summer, That's It Folks, Donuts, Hamlet, The Moderati, The Cherry Orchard, Zero Positive, Much About Nothing, Elliot Loves. *Broadway:* Beyond Therapy, The Heidi Chronicles, Monty Python's Spamalot. *Regional:* work with Long Wharf, Guthrie, Goodman, Doolittle Theatres.
PICTURES: Bright Lights Big City, Crossing Delancey, Rocket Gibraltar, The Fisher King, Little Man Tate, Sleepless in Seattle, Addams Family Values, Wolf, Nixon, The Mating Habits of the Earthbound Human, A Bug's Life (voice), Isn't She Great, Chain of Fools, The Tangerine Bear (voice), Happy Birthday, Wet Hot American Summer, Osmosis Jones (voice), Laud Weiner (short),

Treasure Planet (voice), Full Frontal, Down With Love, Stingray Sam (narr.), The Perfect Host.
TELEVISION: *Movies:* Jackie's Back!, On the Edge, The Amazing Screw-On Head (voice). *Series:* The Powers That Be, Frasier (4 Emmy Awards, 7 other noms.; 5 Golden Globe noms.), Hercules (voice), Mighty Ducks: The Animated Series (voice). *Documentaries/Specials:* The 100 Greatest TV Characters, Just for Laughs: Montreal Comedy Special, NBC's Funniest Outtakes, The 59th Annual Tony Awards, The 61st Annual Tony Awards, others. *Guest:* More than 83 appearances.

PIERCE, FREDERICK S.
Executive. b. New York, NY, April 8, 1933. e. Bernard Baruch School, B.A., City College of New York. Served with U.S. Combat Engineers in Korean War. Associated with Benj. Harrow & Son, CAP, before joining ABC in 1956. Served as analyst in TV research department; promoted to supervisor of audience measurements, 1957, named mgr. next year. 1961 made dir. of research; 1962 dir. of research, sales dev. Named dir. of sales planning, sales development 1962; became a v.p. in 1964 and made national dir. of sales for TV. In 1968 named v.p., planning; 1970 named asst. to pres.; 1972, named v.p, in chg. ABC TV planning and development and asst. to pres. ABC TV, 1973. Named sr. v.p., ABC TV, 1974. Elected pres., ABC Television Division, 1974. president and chief operations officer, ABC, Inc., 1983; resigned from ABC, Inc., 1986; formed the Frederick Pierce Company, Inc., 1988, and Pierce/Silverman Company with Fred Silverman, 1989.

PIERSON, FRANK
Director, Writer, Producer. b. Chappaqua, NY, May 12, 1925. e. Harvard U. Was correspondent for Time magazine before entering show business as story editor of TV series, Have Gun Will Travel. Later served as both prod. and dir. for show. Developed a number of properties for Screen Gems before writing theatrical screenplays. Elected annually from 2001-2004, president, Academy of Motion Picture Arts & Sciences (AMPAS). He served the maximum four, one-year terms allowed by the organization before stepping down in Aug. 2005. Received several WGA Awards including Valentine Davies Award 1991, Laurel Award for Screen Writing Achievement 1992, Edmund J. North Award 1999, Morgan Cox Award 2006.
PICTURES: *Writer:* Cat Ballou (Academy Award nom.; WGA nom. 1966), The Happening, Cool Hand Luke (Academy Award nom. 1968), The Anderson Tapes, Dog Day Afternoon (Academy Award, Golden Globe nom.; WGA Award 1976), In Country, Presumed Innocent. *Director-Writer:* The Looking Glass War, A Star Is Born, King of the Gypsies. *Ex. Prod.:* The Anderson Tapes.
TELEVISION: *Movies*: *Director:* The Neon Ceiling, Somebody Has to Shoot the Picture (dir.; ACE Award, 1990), Citizen Cohn (DGA nom.; Emmy nom. 1993), Lakota Woman: Siege at Wounded Knee, Truman (DGA nom. 1996), Dirty Pictures, Conspiracy (also exec. prod.; DGA Award, 2 Emmy noms. 2002), Soldier's Girl (Emmy nom. 2003), Paradise. *Writer:* Haywire (co-writer). *Series*: *Producer:* Have Gun Will Travel, Nichols (also dir. & writer), *Director:* The Bold Ones: The New Doctors, Alfred Hitchcock Presents. *Special:* 56th Annual Writers Guild Awards (segment contrib.).

PIGOTT-SMITH, TIM
Actor. b. Rugby, England, May 13, 1946. e. U. of Bristol, B.A., Bristol Old Vic Theatre Sch., 1969. Acted with Bristol Old Vic, Royal Shakespeare Co. Artistic Director of Compass Theatre, 1989-93.
THEATRE: *Actor:* As You Like It, Major Barbara, Hamlet, School for Scandal, Sherlock Holmes (B'way debut, 1974), Benefactors, Entertaining Strangers, The Winter's Tale, Antony and Cleopatra, Cymbeline, The Tempest, Jane Eyre, The Picture of Dorian Gray, Retreat. *Director:* Company, Royal Hunt of the Sun, Playing the Wife, Hamlet, The Letter, Retreat, Mary Stuart.
PICTURES: Aces High (debut, 1975), Man in a Fog, Sweet William, Richard's Things, Joseph Andrews, Clash of the Titans, Lucky Village, Victory, State of Emergency, The Remains of the Day, Safe Conduct, Bloody Sunday, Four Feathers, Gangs of New York, Johnny English, Alexander, V for Vendetta, Flyboys, Quantum of Solace, Alice in Wonderland.
TELEVISION: *Movies*: Eustace and Hilda, The Lost Boys, I Remember Nelson, Measure for Measure, Henry IV, Day Christ Died, The Hunchback of Notre Dame, Fame Is the Spur, Glittering Prizes, Dead Man's Folly, The Case of Sherlock Holmes (host), Life Story, Hannah, The True Adventures of Christopher Columbus, The Chief, Bullion Boys, The Shadowy Third, Calcutta Chronicles, The Inspector Lynley Mysteries: For the Sake of Elena, Eroica, Pompeii: The Last Day, The Private Life of Samuel Pepys, London, North & South, Poirot: Taken at the Flood, The Last Flight to Kuwait, On Expenses. *Mini-series*: Winston Churchill: The Wilderness Years, The Jewel in the Crown, The Challenge, The Great War. *Series*: Danger UXB, Hannah, Struggle, The Chief, The Major Years (narrator), The Vice, Dr. Who, Nightmares of Nature (voice), Holby Blue, Money. *Guest:* More than 77 appearances.

PIKE, CORNELIA M.
Executive. b. Holyoke, MA, 1933. e. Boston U. Sch. of Comm., BS Magna Cum Laude. Asst. promotion & publicity dir. WNAC/WNAC-TV 1954-56, Boston, MA. Women's dir./on-air personality: WKNE, Keene, NH, 1957-60; WSMN, Nashua, NH, 1963-67; WHOB, Nashua, NH, 1967-68. Mngr., Trade Winds Interior Design, Boston, MA, 1979-81; Sales Mngr./V.P. Pike Productions, Inc.,1981-present. Company produces and markets trailers to exhibitors in U.S., UK, Germany, Australia and New Zealand. Bd. Dirs., Variety Club of New England. Life Patron, Variety Clubs International.

PINCHOT, BRONSON
Actor. b. New York, NY, May 20, 1959. e. Yale U. Grew up in Pasadena. Studied acting at Yale. On NY stage in Poor Little Lambs, Zoya's Apartment.
PICTURES: Risky Business (debut, 1983), Beverly Hills Cop, The Flamingo Kid, Hot Resort, After Hours, Second Sight, Blame It on the Bellboy, True Romance, Beverly Hills Cop III, It's My Party, Courage Under Fire, The First Wives Club, Babes in Toyland, Slappy and the Stinkers, Quest for Camelot, Beach Movie, The All New Adventures of Laurel & Hardy: For Love or Mummy, Out of the Cold, Lady & the Tramp II: Scamp's Adventure, Winning Girls Through Psychic Mind Control, Straight No Chaser, Boardheads, IceMaker, Second Best, Diamond Zero, Cluster, Mr. Art Critic, From a Place of Darkness, The Tale of Despereaux, Hooking Up, You and I, Virgin Alexander.
TELEVISION: *Movies*: Jury Duty—The Comedy, Merry Christmas George Bailey, Putting It Together. *Mini-series*: Stephen King's The Langoliers. *Series*: Sara, Perfect Strangers (Emmy nom. 1987), Eek the Cat, The Trouble With Larry, Dumb and Dumber, Bruno the Kid, Meego, Step By Step, The Young and the Restless. *Guest:* More than 60 appearances.

PINE, CHRIS
Actor. b. Los Angeles, CA, August 26, 1980. Son of actress Gwynne Gilford and actor/dir. Robert Pine.
PICTURES: The Princess Diaries 2: Royal Engagement, Just My Luck, Blind Dating, Smokin' Aces, Bottle Shock, Small Town Saturday Night, Star Trek, Carriers, Quantum Quest: A Cassini Space Odyssey (voice), Unstoppable, This Means War.
TELEVISION: *Movie:* Surrender Dorothy. *Guest:* More than 45 appearances.

PINKETT-SMITH, JADA
Actress. b. Baltimore, MD, Sept. 18, 1971. m. actor Will Smith. Production company, 100% Womon.
PICTURES: Menace II Society, A Low Down Dirty Shame, Jason's Lyric, The Inkwell, Tales from the Crypt Presents: Demon Knight, The Nutty Professor, Set It Off, Scream 2, Love For Hire (writer only), Return to Paradise, Woo, Welcome to Hollywood, Bamboozled, Kingdom Come, Ali, The Matrix Reloaded, The Matrix Revolutions, Collateral, The Seat Filler (exec. prod. only), Madagascar (voice), Madagascar 2 (voice), Reign Over Me, The Human Contract (also writer, dir.), e Women, Madagascar: Escape 2 Africa (voice), The Karate Kid (prod. only).
TELEVISION: *Movies*: If These Walls Could Talk, Maniac Magee (narr.), MILF & Cookies (exec. prod.). *Series*: A Different World, All of Us (exec. prod., writer, co-creator), Hawthorne (also exec. prod.). *Guest:* More than 92 appearances.

PINSKER, ALLEN
Executive. b. New York, NY, Jan. 23, 1930. e. NYU. Mgr., Hempstead Theatre, 1950. 1954 joined Island Theatre Circuit as booker-buyer; named head buyer 1958. 1968 joined United Artists Eastern Theatres as film buyer; head buyer, 1969, v.p., 1970. Named v.p. United Artists Theatre Circuit, 1972. 1973. named UAET exec. v.p., member bd., 1974. Appt. pres. & COO, UA Communications, Inc., theatre division, 1987. 1987, named pres. and CEO, United Artists Theatre Circuit, Inc. and exec. v.p., United Artists Communications, Inc.; 1988, became member, bd. dir. Tele- Communications, Inc. Retired.

PINSKER, NEAL
Exhibitor. Started in industry with United Artists theatres as an usher, working his way to executive v.p., managing all divisions of theatre operations. Today, he is a senior v.p./west operations, of Regal Entertainment Group. A third generation theatre operator, Pinsker is committed to theatre charities and national organizations. Memberships: NATO of Cal/Nevada (bd. of directors); Will Rogers Foundations, Variety Club of Colorado (past chief barker); MPAA Classifications and Rating Board; Motion Picture Pioneers; NATO; named "Executive Concession Manager" by the National Assn. of Concessionaires; and bd. member of Regal Foundation. Regal consists of 6,355 screens in 526 locations in 39 states and the District of Columbia as of September 27, 2007.

PISANO, A. ROBERT
Executive. e. San Jose St. Univ., Boalt Hall School of Law at Univ. of CA, Berkeley. Was partner at law firm of O'Melveny & Myers prior to entering m.p. industry. 1985-91, exec. v.p. of Paramount Pictures serving as gen. counsel, member of office of chmn.; 1993, named exec. v.p. of MGM responsible for all business and legal affairs, home video and pay tv. In 1997, became Vice Chairman, with overall responsibility for business operations of MGM. Resigned, 1999. In September 2001, Pisano became CEO and executive director of the Screen Actors Guild. He resigned and left SAG in April 2005. In

September 2005, Pisano became the president & COO of the MPAA, reporting to MPAA CEO Dan Glickman, and is the position he holds today.

PISCOPO, JOE
Actor, Comedian. b. Passaic, NJ, June 17, 1951. Stage appearances in regional and dinner theatres in South and Northeast. Worked as stand-up comic at the Improvisation and the Comic Strip clubs, NY 1976-80. Author: The Piscopo Tapes. Television debut as regular on Saturday Night Live, 1980.
PICTURES: American Tickler or the Winner of 10 Academy Awards (1976), King Kong, Johnny Dangerously, Wise Guys, Dead Heat, Sidekicks, Huck and the King of Hearts, Two Bits & Pepper, Captain Nuke and the Bomber Boys, Open Season, Baby Bedlam, Bartleby, Spring Break '83.
TELEVISION: *Movies*: Huck and the King of Hearts. *Series*: Saturday Night Live (1980-84, 2 Emmy noms. for writing), 100 Deeds for Eddie McDowd (voice), Caribbean Fantasy (as himself). *Documentaries /Specials*: The Joe Piscopo New Jersey Special (host, writer, prod.), Joe Piscopo Live! (as himself, writer), Saturday Night Live 15th Anniv. Special (as himself), The Joe Piscopo Special (HBO), Dear Santa. Guest: More than 54 appearances.

PISIER, MARIE-FRANCE
Actress. b. Dalat, Indochina, May 10, 1944. Began appearing in French films at age 17. Returned to school at Univ. of Paris for degrees in law and political science; continued to work in films.
PICTURES: Qui ose nous Accuser? (debut, 1961), Love at Twenty (Truffaut episode), La Mort d'un Tueur, Les Yeux cernes, Trans-Europe Express, Stolen Kisses, Celine and Julie Go Boating, French Provincial, Cousin Cousine, Serail, Barocco, The Other Side of Midnight, Love on the Run, Les Apprentis Sourciers, The Bronte Sisters, French Postcards, La Banquiere, Chanel Solitaire, Der Zauberberg (The Magic Mountain), Miss Right, Hot Touch, The Prize of Peril, The Silent Ocean, L'Ami de Vincent, Les Nanas, Parking, Blue Note, Why is My Mother in My Bed?, Seven Sundays, Son of Gascogne, La Gazelle, Marion, Why Not Me?, The Ice Rink, Time Regained, Highway Melody, Love Torn in Dream, Inch'Allah Sunday, Like an Airplane, Ordo, Inside Paris, Paid, Forgive Me.
TELEVISION: *U.S.*: French Atlantic Affair, Scruples. Has appeared in numerous French tv movies,mini-series and series.

PITT, BRAD
Actor, Producer. r.n. William Bradley Pitt. b. Shawnee, OK, Dec. 18, 1963. Raised in Springfield, MO. Studied journalism at Univ. of MO at Columbia. Moved to L.A. to attend art school, instead studied acting with Roy London. Appeared in short film Contact. He is a principal in Plan B Entertainment, a production company-based in Beverly Hills, CA.
PICTURES: *Acting*: Cutting Class (debut, 1989), Happy Together, Across the Tracks, Thelma & Louise, Cool World, Johnny Suede, A River Runs Through It, Kalifornia, True Romance, The Favor, Interview With the Vampire. Legends of the Fall (Golden Globe nom. 1995), Se7en, Twelve Monkeys (Academy Award nom.; Golden Globe Award, 1996), Sleepers, The Devil's Own, Seven Years In Tibet, Meet Joe Black, Fight Club, Being John Malkovich (cameo), Snatch, The Mexican, Ocean's Eleven, Spy Game, Full Frontal (as himself), Confessions of a Dangerous Mind, Sinbad: Legend of the Seven Seas (voice), Troy, Ocean's Twelve, Mr. & Mrs. Smith, The Assassination of Jesse James by the Coward Robert Ford (also prod.), Babel (Golden Globe nom. 2007), Ocean's Thirteen, The Curious Case of Benjamin Button (Academy Award nom.; Golden Globe nom. 2009), State of Play, Dirty Tricks (also prod.), Burn After Reading, Inglourious Basterds, Tree of Life (also prod.), Moneyball, Megamind (voice), Happy Feet 2 in 3D. *Producer:* Running with Scissors, The Departed, Year of the Dog (exec. prod.), A Mighty Heart, The Time Traveler's Wife (exec. prod.), Shantaram, The Private Lives of Pippa Lee, Kick-Ass, World War Z, Eat- Pray-Love (exec. prod.), Selma.
TELEVISION: *Movies*: A Stoning in Fulham County, Too Young to Die, The Image, Two-Fisted Tales, Pretty/Handsome (exec. prod.). *Series*: Another World, Glory Days, Undaunted Courage (prod.). *Documentaries /Specials:* Town Meeting with Diane Sawyer: Celebrities vs. the Press, On Location: Growing up Grizzly (host, narrator), America: A Tribute to Heroes (as himself), Freedom: A History of Us. *Guest*: More than 173 appearances.

PIVEN, JEREMY
Actor. b. New York, NY. July 26, 1965. Raised in Chicago where parents ran Piven Theater Workshop. e. Drake Univ. Studied acting at Eugene O'Neill Theater Center, Natl. Theater of Great Britain, NYU. Eventually joined Chicago's Second City comedy troupe. Co-founded Chicago's New Criminals Theatre Company, 1988.
THEATRE: Fear & Loathing in Las Vegas, Peacekeeper, Methusalen, Knuckle, Macbeth.
PICTURES: Lucas, One Crazy Summer, Say Anything..., White Palace, The Grifters, Pay Dirt, The Player, Bob Roberts, Singles, Judgment Night, Twenty Bucks, Car 54 Where Are You?, Twogether, PCU, Miami Rhapsody, Dr. Jekyll and Ms. Hyde, Heat, Grosse Pointe Blank, Very Bad Things, Music From Another Room, Phoenix, The Crew, Red Letters, The Family Man, Serendipity, Highway, Black Hawk Down, Rush Hour 2, Highway, Old School, Scary Movie 3, Runaway Jury, Chasing Liberty, Lucky 13, Two For The Money, Smokin' Aces, Cars (voice), Keeping Up with the Steins, The Kingdom, RocknRolla, The Goods: Live Hard, Sell Hard, Waska.
TELEVISION: *Movies*: 12:01, Don King: Only in America, Partners. *Pilots:* Heads Will Roll, Ready or Not. *Series:* Carol and Company, Rugrats (voices), The Larry Sanders Show, Pride and Joy, Ellen, Cupid, Entourage (3 Emmy Awards, 1 other nom.; Golden Globe Award 2008, 5 other noms.). *Guest:* More than 70 appearances.

PLACE, MARY KAY
Actress, Writer. b. Tulsa, OK, Sept. 23, 1947. e. U. of Tulsa. Worked in production jobs and as Tim Conway's asst. for his TV show also as sect. for Norman Lear on Maude before starting to write for TV series (Mary Tyler Moore Show, Phyllis, Maude, M*A*S*H, etc.).
PICTURES: *Actress:* Bound For Glory (debut, 1976), New York New York, More American Graffiti, Starting Over, Private Benjamin, Modern Problems, Waltz Across Texas, The Big Chill, Terms of Endearment (voice), Smooth Talk, A New Life, Bright Angel, Captain Ron, Samantha, Teresa's Tattoo, Manny and Lo, Citizen Ruth, Eye of God, The Rainmaker, How to Make the Cruelest Month, Pecker, Nobody Knows Anything, Naturally Native, Judgment Day: The Ellie Nesler Story, Being John Malkovich, Girl Interrupted, Committed, My First Mister, Nailed, The Safety of Objects, Human Nature, Junk, Sweet Home Alabama, Evergreen, Death and Texas, Killer Diller, Silver City, Lonesome Jim, Nine Lives, War Eagle, Grace Is Gone, The Toe Tactic, Mama's Boy, City of Ember, Julie & Julia (voice), Youth in Revolt, It's Complicated, Leonie, Shrek Forever After (voice).
TELEVISION: *Movies*: *Actress:* Act of Love, Mom's On Strike, For Love or Money, The Girl Who Spelled Freedom, Out on the Edge, Traitor in My House, Crazy from the Heart, Bed of Lies, Just My Imagination, Telling Secrets, In the Line of Duty: The Price of Vengeance, Leslie's Folly, My Very Best Friend, For My Daughter's Honor, Love in Another Town, Point Last Seen, A Woman's a Helluva Thing. *Mini-series:* Tales of the City, Further Tales of the City. *Series*: *Writer:* Mary Tyler Moore, M*A*S*H (Emmy nom. 1974), Mary Hartman Mary Hartman (actress, Emmy Award, 1977), Forever Fernwood (actress), Big Love (actress), 12 Miles of Bad Road (actress). *Director:* Dream On, Baby Boom, Arli$$. *Documentaries/Specials*: John Denver Special, Martin Mull's History of White People in America I & II, Portrait of a White Marriage, The Gift. *Guest*: More than 71 appearances.

PLATT, OLIVER
Actor. b. Windsor, Ontario, Canada, January 12, 1960. Raised in Asia, Africa and Washington DC. e. Tufts Univ.
THEATRE: *Off-B'way*: The Tempest, Moon Over Miami, Sparks in the Park, Urban Blight, Ubu, Elliot Loves.
PICTURES: Married to the Mob (debut, 1988), Working Girl, Crusoe, Flatliners, Postcards From the Edge, Beethoven, Diggstown, The Temp, Indecent Proposal, Benny & Joon, The Three Musketeers, Tall Tale, Funny Bones, Executive Decision, A Time to Kill, Dangerous Beauty, Bulworth, Simon Birch, Lake Placid, Three to Tango, Bicentennial Man, Gun Shy, Ready to Rumble, Don't Say a Word, Zigzag, Liberty Stands Still, Ash Wednesday, Hope Springs, Pieces of April, Kinsey, The Ice Harvest, Casanova, The Ten, Martian Child, Frost/Nixon, Year One, 2012, Please Give, Love and Other Drugs, The Oranges, Dorothy of Oz (voice).
TELEVISION: *Movies*: The Infiltrator, Cinderelmo, !Huff, The Thick of It. *Series:* Deadline, The West Wing (Emmy nom. 2001), Queens Supreme, Huff (2 emmy noms.; Golden Globe nom. 2005), The Bronx Is Burning, Nip/Tuck (Emmy nom. 2008), The Big C (pilot).

PLESKOW, ERIC
Executive. b., Vienna, Austria, April 24, 1924. Served as film offcer, U.S. War dept., 1946-48; entered industry in 1948 as asst. gen. mgr., Motion Picture Export Association, Germany; 1950-51, continental rep. for Sol Lesser Prods.; joined United Artists in 1951 as Far East Sales Mgr.; named mgr., S. Africa, 1952; mgr., Germany, 1953-58; exec. asst. to continental mgr., 1958-59; asst. continental mgr., 1959-60; continental mgr., 1960-62; v.p. in charge of foreign distrib., 1962; exec. v.p. & CEO, Jan., 1973; pres. & CEO, Oct. , 1973. Resigned in 1978 to become pres. and CEO of Orion Pictures Co.; 1982, became pres. & CEO, Orion Pictures Corp; appointed chmn. of bd. 1991. Resigned 1992. Partner, Pleskow/Spikings Partnership, Beverly Hills, 1992. 1999 1999 Entered into producing partnership with Leon de Winter to form PlesWin, a production company that was a joint venture with Senator Films. *Prod.:* Beyond Rangoon.

PLIMPTON, MARTHA
Actress. b. New York, NY, Nov. 16, 1970. Daughter of actors Shelley Plimpton and Keith Carradine. Acting debut in film workshop of Elizabeth Swados' musical Runaways. At 11 gained recognition as model in Richard Avedon's commercials for Calvin Klein jeans. Troupe member of the Steppenwolfe Theater Company.
THEATRE: *NY:* Hedda Gabler (also Chicago), Pal Joey, The Hagadah, Pericles, The Heidi Chronicles, Robbers, subUrbia, The Great Unwashed, Sixteen Wounded, Boston Marriage,

Shining Cit, Coast of Utopia Part 1: Voyage, Top Girls, Cymbeline, Coast of Utopia Part 2: Shipwreck, Coast of Utopia Part 3: Salvage. *Chicago:* The Libertine, The Glass Menagerie, Absolution.
PICTURES: Rollover (debut 1981, in bit role), The River Rat, The Goonies, The Mosquito Coast, Shy People, Stars and Bars, Running on Empty, Another Woman, Parenthood, Stanley and Iris, Silence Like Glass, Samantha, Inside Monkey Zetterland, Josh and S.A.M., My Life's in Turnaround, Mrs. Parker and the Vicious Circle, The Beans of Egypt Maine, Last Summer in the Hamptons, Beautiful Girls, I Shot Andy Warhol, I'm Not Rappaport, Eye of God, Pecker, Music From Another Room, 200 Cigarettes, The Sleepy Time Gal, Searching for Debra Winger (documentary), Hair High (voice, also assoc. prod.), Dante's Inferno, Small Town Murder Scenes.
TELEVISION: *Movies*: A Woman at War, Daybreak, Chantilly Lace, The Defenders: Payback, The Defenders: Choice of Evils, The Defenders: Taking the First, The End of Steve. *Series:* Law & Order: Special Victims Unit (Emmy nom. 2002 as guest), How to Make It in America, Raising Hope (also pilot).

PLOWRIGHT, JOAN
C.B.E. Actress. b. Scunthrope, Brigg, Lincolnshire, England, Oct. 28, 1929. m. late actor, Lord Laurence Olivier. Trained for stage at Laban Art of Movement Studio, 1949-50; Old Vic Theatre Sch. 1950-52; with Michel St. Denis, Glen Byam Shaw and George Devine. London stage debut The Duenna, 1954. Broadway debut The Entertainer, 1958. Won Tony Award in 1961 for A Taste of Honey. With Bristol Old Vic Rep., Royal Court, National Theatre in numerous classics and contemporary plays.
RECENT THEATRE: Saturday Sunday Monday, The Seagull, The Bed Before Yesterday, Filumena, Enjoy, Who's Afraid of Virginia Woolf?, Cavell, The Cherry Orchard, The Way of the World, Mrs. Warren's Profession, Time and the Conways, If We Are Women, Absolutely! (Perhaps).
PICTURES: Moby Dick (debut, 1956), Time Without Pity, The Entertainer (Academy Award nom. 1993), Uncle Vanya, Three Sisters, Equus, Brimstone and Treacle, Britannia Hospital, Wagner (tv in U.S.), Revolution, The Dressmaker, Drowning By Numbers, I Love You to Death, Avalon, Enchanted April (Academy Award nom. Golden Globe Award 1993), Last Action Hero, Dennis the Menace, A Pin for the Butterfly, The Summer House, Widow's Peak, A Pyromaniac's Love Story, Hotel Sorrento, The Scarlett Letter, Jane Eyre, Mr. Wrong, Surviving Picasso, 101 Dalmatians, The Assistant, Dance with Me, Tom's Midnight Garden, Tea with Mussolini, Dinosaur (voice), Back to the Secret Garden, Global Heresy, Callas Forever, Bringing Down the House, I am David, Goose!, George and the Dragon, Mrs. Palfrey at the Claremont, Curious George (voice), The Spiderwick Chronicles, Knife Edge.
TELEVISION: *Movies:* The Comedy of Errors, Twelfth Night, The Merchant of Venice, Daphne Laureola, The Diary of Anne Frank, A Dedicated Man, The Importance of Being Ernest, The Birthday Party, And a Nightingale Sang, The House of Bernarda Alba, Stalin (Emmy nom.; Golden Globe Award 1993), The Summer House, On Promised Land, A Place for Annie, The Return of the Native, This Could be the Last Time, Aldrich Ames: Traitor Within, Frankie & Hazel, Christmas Glory 2000 (reader), Bailey's Mistake, Scrooge and Marley (narr.). *Mini-series:* Wagner. *Series:* Encore Encore!. *Pilot*: Driving Miss Daisy (U.S.).

PLUMMER, AMANDA
Actress. b. New York, NY, March 23, 1957. e. Middlebury Coll. Daughter of actors Christopher Plummer and Tammy Grimes.
THEATRE: Artichokes, A Month in the Country, A Taste of Honey (Theatre World Award), Agnes of God (Tony Award, 1982), The Glass Menagerie, A Lie of the Mind, Life Under Water, You Never Can Tell, Pygmalion, The Milk Train Doesn't Stop Here Anymore, The Lark (Canada).
PICTURES: Cattle Annie and Little Britches (debut, 1981), The World According to Garp, Daniel, The Hotel New Hampshire, Static, The Courtship, Made in Heaven, Prisoners of Inertia, Joe Versus the Volcano, California Casanova, The Fisher King, Freejack, So I Married an Axe Murderer, Needful Things, Nostradamus, Pulp Fiction, Pax, Butterfly Kiss, The Propechy, Drunks, Freeway, A Simple Wish, American Perfekt, You Can Thank Me Later, L.A. Without a Map, Elizabeth Jane, 8 1/2 Women, The Million Dollar Hotel, Seven Days to Live, Triggerman, Ken Park, Darkness, My Life Wihout Me, The Last Angel (short), Satan's Little Helper, Broadway: The Golden Age by the Legends Who Were There (doc.), Red, 45 R.P.M., Inconceivable (also writer), Samurai Avenger: The Blind Wolf, The Making of Plus One, Girlfriend, Thicker, Sophomore, 1,001 Ways to Enjoy the Missionary Position, Go Straight to Hell, Vampire.
TELEVISION: *Movies*: The Dollmaker, The Unforgivable Secret, Kojak: None So Blind, Miss Rose White (Emmy Award, Golden Globe nom. 1992), The Sands of Time, Last Light, Whose Child Is This?, Under the Piano, Don't Look Back, The Right to Remain Silent, The Apartment Complex, Get a Clue, Shadow Realm, Affinity. *Series:* Stories from my Childhood, L.A. Law (Emmy nom. 1989), Law & Order: Special Victims Unit (Emmy Award 2005). *Documentaries/Specials*: Gryphon, The Courtship. *Pilot*: True Blue.

PLUMMER, CHRISTOPHER
Actor. b. Toronto, Canada, Dec. 13, 1927. Daughter is actress Amanda Plummer. Stage & radio career began in Canada (French & English).
THEATRE: toured U.S. in The Constant Wife; B'way debut in The Starcross Story, 1953. *B'way*: The Dark is Light Enough, Home Is the Hero, J.B., The Lark, The Good Doctor, Cyrano (Tony Award, 1974), Othello (Tony nom.), Macbeth, No Man's Land. *London*: leading actor, Royal Shakespeare Theatre, 1961-62, Becket (Evening Standard Award), Natl. Theatre, 1969-70. *Canada*: leading actor, Stratford Festival (6 yrs.). *Ireland:* Lock Up Your Daughters.
PICTURES: Stage Struck (debut, 1958), Wind Across the Everglades, The Fall of the Roman Empire, The Sound of Music, Inside Daisy Clover, The Night of the Generals, Triple Cross, Oedipus the King, The High Commissioner (Nobody Runs Forever), The Battle of Britain, The Royal Hunt of the Sun, Lock Up Your Daughters, Waterloo, The Pyx, The Return of the Pink Panther, Conduct Unbecoming, The Man Who Would Be King, The Spiral Staircase, Aces High, Assassination at Sarajevo (The Day That Shook the World), The Assignment, The Disappearance, International Velvet, Murder by Decree, The Silent Partner, Hanover Street, Starcrash, RIEL, Highpoint, Somewhere in Time, Eyewitness, Being Different (narrator), The Amateur, Dreamscape, Ordeal by Innocence, Lily in Love, The Boy in Blue, The Boss' Wife, An American Tail (voice), Dragnet, Souvenir, Light Years (voice), Nosferatu in Venice, I Love N.Y., Shadow Dancing, Mindfield, Kingsgate, Red-Blooded American Girl, Where the Heart Is, Don't Tell Mom the Babysitter's Dead, Star Trek VI: The Undiscovered Country, Firehead, Rock-a-Doodle (voice), Money, Liar's Edge, Impolite, Malcolm X, Wolf, Dolores Claiborne, Twelve Monkeys, Skeletons, Babes in Toyland, Hidden Agenda, The Clown at Midnight, Blackheart, All the Fine Lines, The Insider, The Dinosaur Hunter, Dracula 2000, Star Trek: Klingon Academy, Lucky Break, Full Disclosure, A Beautiful Mind, Ararat, Ted Allan: Minstrel Boy of the Twentieth Century, Nicholas Nickleby, Blizzard, The Gospel of John (narrator), Cold Creek Manor, Alexander, National Treasure, Alexander, Our Fathers, Must Love Dogs, Syriana, The New World, Man in the Chair, Inside Man, The Lake House, Closing the Ring, Emotional Arithmetic, Already Dead, Caesar and Cleopatra (also exec. prod.), The Imaginarium of Doctor Parnassus, My Dog Tulip (voice), 9 (voice), The Last Station (Academy Award nom. ; Golden Globe nom. 2010), Up (voice), Beginners, Priest.
TELEVISION: *Movies/Specials*: Hamlet at Elsinore (Emmy nom. 1966), Don Juan in Hell (BBC), Little Moon of Alban, Prince and the Pauper, Steiglitz and O'Keefe, Oedipus Rex, Omnibus, After the Fall, Desperate Voyage, The Shadow Box, When the Circus Came to Town, Dial M for Murder, Little Gloria—Happy at Last, The Scarlet and the Black, The Velveteen Rabbit, Crossings, A Hazard of Hearts, A Ghost in Monte Carlo, Young Catherine, Danielle Steel's Secrets, Stranger in the Mirror, Liar's Edge, Madeline (narrator; Emmy Award 1994), Harrison Bergeron, We the Jury, The Conspiracy of Fear, The Arrow, Winchell, Celebrate the Century (narrator), Nuremberg, Possessed, American Tragedy (Golden Globe nom. 2001), Leo's Journey, On Golden Pond, Night Flight, Agent of Influence, Our Fathers (Emmy nom. 2005), Four Minutes. *Mini-series:* Arthur Hailey's the Moneychangers (Emmy Award, 1977), Jesus of Nazareth, The Thorn Birds (Emmy nom. 1983), Spearfield's Daughter, Crossings, Berlin Lady, The Summit. *Series*: Playdate (host), David the Gnome (narr.), Madeline (narr./voice), Counterstrike, The American Experience (narr.). *Guest:* More than 132 appearances.

PODELL, ALBERT N.
Attorney. b. New York, NY, Feb. 25, 1937. e. Cornell U., U. of Chicago, NYU Sch. of Law. Non-fiction ed., Playboy magazine, 1959-60; dir. of photog. and m.p. reviewer Argosy magazine, 1961-64; Author: Who Needs a Road? (Bobbs-Merrill, 1967; re-published, Wolfenden, 1999), mng. ed., The Players Magazine, 1965-66; acct. exec. on 20th Century-Fox at Diener, Hauser, Greenthal, 1966-68; natl. adv. mgr., Cinema Center Films, 1969; acct. supervisor and creative dir. on Columbia Pictures at Charles Schlaifer, 1969-72; creator & dir. of Annual Motion Picture Advertising Awards sponsored by Cinema Lodge, B'nai B'rith. Attorney specializing in litigation, matrimonial law, rep. of performers and producers (1976-present). Pres., 1990-95 Jean Cocteau Rep. Th. Chmn. of Trustees; 1980-90, Assn. for Development of Dramatic Arts. Pres., Far Above Films. 2006, NYU established the Albert Podell Global Scholar at Risk Fund. This new fund will be used in partnership with the existing Scholars at Risk (SAR) organization, an international network of more than 100 universities and colleges that defend the rights of scholars, researchers, faculty members, and intellectuals outside of the United States who face persecution in their home countries.
PICTURES: *Director & Writer:* A Class Above, The Class on the Cutting Edge, Lift the Chorus, This Is Christmas.

PODHORZER, NATHAN
Executive. b. Brody, Poland, Nov. 27, 1919. e. City Coll. of New York, Rutgers U., U. of Southern California. U.S. Army, 1942-46; documentary film prod., Israel, 1946-57; CEO, United Film Enterprises, Inc. U.S. purchasing agent for European Motion Picture and video tape distribution.

POEHLER, AMY
Actress, Writer, Producer. b. Burlington, MA, September 16, 1971. e. Boston College. m. actor Will Arnett.
PICTURES: Deuce Bigalow: Male Gigolo, Wet Hot American Summer, Martin & Orloff, Mean Girls, Envy, Southland Tales, Tenacious D in The Pick of Destiny, The Ex, Blades of Glory, Shrek the Third (voice), Mr. Woodcock, Hamlet 2, Horton Hears a Who! (voice), Baby Mama, Monsters vs Aliens (voice), Alvin and the Chipmunks: The Squeakquel (voice), Hoodwinked Too! Hood VS. Evil (voice), Freak Dance.
TELEVISION: *Movies:* Escape from It's a Wonderful Life (also voice, writer), North Hollywood, Sick in the Head, A.S.S.S.S.C.A.T.: Improv (performer, writer, exec. prod.), Saturday Night Live Weekend Update Halftime Special, Upright Citizens Brigade: Asssscat (also writer), Saturday Night Live: The Best of Amy Poehler, SNL Presents: A Very Gilly Christmas. *Series:* Apt. 2F (also pilot), Upright Citizens Brigade (also writer), Arrested Development, Saturday Night Live: Weekend Update Thursday, The Mighty B! (also writer, exec. prod., 2 Emmy noms.), Saturday Night Live (2 Emmy noms.), Parks and Recreation (also writer, prod., Emmy nom. 2010). *Guest:* More than 60 appearances.

POITIER, SIDNEY
Actor, Director. b. Miami, FL, Feb. 20, 1927. Raised in the Bahamas. m. actress Joanna Shimkus. e. Miami, FL. On stage with Amer. Negro Theatre in Days of Our Youth. Appeared in Army Signal Corps documentary From Whence Cometh My Help. Formed First Artists Prod. Co. Ltd., 1969, with Paul Newman and Barbra Streisand. *Autobiography*: This Life (1980). Recipient 1992 AFI Life Achievement Award. Won honorary Academy Award in 2002 for his unique screen presence and representing the industry with dignity, style and intelligence. Received Golden Globe honorary Awards: Henrietta Award, 1969 and Cecil B. DeMille Award 1982.
THEATRE: Strivers Road, You Can't Take It With You, Anna Lucasta (B'way debut, 1948), Lysistrata, Freight, A Raisin in the Sun.
PICTURES: *Actor:* No Way Out (debut 1950), Cry the Beloved Country, Red Ball Express, Go Man Go, Blackboard Jungle, Goodbye My Lady, Edge of the City, Something of Value, Band of Angels, Mark of the Hawk, The Defiant Ones (Academy Awards nom.; Golden Globe nom. 1959), Our Virgin Island, Porgy and Bess (Golden Globe nom. 1960), All the Young Men, A Raisin in the Sun (Golden Globe nom. 1962), Paris Blues, Pressure Point, Lilies of the Field (Academy Award, Golden Globe Award 1963), The Long Ships, The Greatest Story Ever Told, The Bedford Incident, The Slender Thread, A Patch of Blue (Golden Globe nom. 1966), Duel at Diablo, To Sir With Love, In the Heat of the Night (Golden Globe nom. 1968), Guess Who's Coming to Dinner, For Love of Ivy (also writer), The Lost Man, They Call Me Mister Tibbs, Brother John, The Organization, Buck and the Preacher (also dir.), A Warm December (also dir.), Uptown Saturday Night (also dir.), The Wilby Conspiracy, Let's Do It Again (also dir.), A Piece of the Action (also dir.), Shoot To Kill, Little Nikita, Sneakers, The Jackal, Scandalize My Name: Stories from the Blacklist, Ralph Bunche: An American Odyssey (documentary, narrator). *Director:* Stir Crazy, Hanky Panky, Fast Forward, Ghost Dad.
TELEVISION: *Movies*: Separate But Equal (Emmy nom.; Golden Globe nom. 1992), Children of the Dust, To Sir With Love II, Mandela and de Klerk (Emmy nom. 1997), David and Lisa, Free of Eden (also exec. prod.), The Simple Life of Noah Dearborn, The Last Bricklayer in America. *Guest:* More than 85 appearances.

POLANSKI, ROMAN
Director, Writer, Actor. b. Paris, France, Aug. 18, 1933. m. actress Emmanuelle Seigner. Lived in Poland from age of three. Early career, art school in Cracow; Polish Natl. Film Acad., Lodz 1954-59. Radio Actor 1945-47; on stage 1947-53; asst. dir., Kamera film prod. group 1959-61. Co-founder Cadre Films, 1964. Wrote, dir. and acted in short films: Two Men and a Wardrobe, When Angels Fall, The Fat and the Lean, Mammals. On stage as actor in Amadeus (and dir., Warsaw & Paris), Metamorphosis (Paris, 1988). *Autobiography*: Roman (1984). Won Received Lifetime Achievement Awards from: The Stockholm Film Festival in 1999; European Film Awards in 1999, The Polish Film Awards in 2003. Owner of R.P. Productions.
PICTURES: *Director/Writer*: Knife in the Water (feature debut, 1962), Repulsion, Cul-de-Sac, The Fearless Vampire Killers or: Pardon Me But Your Teeth Are in My Neck (also actor), Rosemary's Baby (Academy Award nom.; DGA nom.; WGA nom.; Golden Globe nom. 1969), A Day at the Beach (s.p. only), Weekend of a Champion (prod. only), Macbeth, What? (a.k.a. Che?; also actor), The Tenant (also actor), Tess (Academy Award nom.; Golden Globe nom. 1981), Pirates, Frantic, Bitter Moon (also prod.), The Ninth Gate (also prod.), The Ghost. *Director:* Chinatown (also acting: Academy Award nom.; Golden Globe Award, DGA nom. 1975), Death and the Maiden, The Pianist (also prod.; Academy Award, 1 other nom.; DGA nom.; BAFTA Director's Award 2003), Oliver Twist (also prod.), To Each His Cinema (segment), Pompeii (also prod.), The Ghost Writer (also prod.). *Writer:* A Taste for Women, The Girl Across the Way, A Day At the Beach (alsoprod.), The Boat on the Grass. *Actor:* The Generation, The Magic Christian, Andy Warhol's Dracula, Back in the U.S.S.R., A Pure Formality, Grosse Fatigue, the Story of X, Light Keeps Me Company, Tribute to Alfred Lepetit, The Revenge, Quiet Chaos. *Producer:* Castelnuovo.

POLL, MARTIN H.
Producer. b. New York, NY, Nov. 24, 1926. e. Wharton Sch., U. of Pennsylvania. Pres. Gold Medal Studios (1956-61). President of Hollane Corporation in Beverly Hills, CA. President of Martin Poll Films, Ltd.
PICTURES: A Face in the Crowd, Middle of the Night, The Goddess, Butterfield 8, Love Is a Ball, Sylvia, The Lion in Winter (Academy Award nom. 1969), The Appointment, The Magic Garden of Stanley Sweetheart, The Man Who Loved Cat Dancing, Night Watch, Love and Death (exec. prod.); The Man Who Would Be King, The Sailor Who Fell From Grace with the Sea, Somebody Killed Her Husband, Nighthawks, Gimme an F, Haunted Summer, My Heroes Have Always Been Cowboys, Spatula Boy (short; exec. prod.), Big Bucket Head's: The Warehouse (short; exec. prod.).
TELEVISION: *Movies*: Arthur the King, Stunt Seven, The Lion in Winter (Emmy nom. 2004). *Mini-series*: A Town Called Alice, The Dain Curse, Diana: Her True Story. *Series*: Car 54 Where Are You?

POLLAK, KEVIN
Actor. b. San Francisco, CA, Oct. 30, 1958. Started doing stand-up comedy in the San Francisco Bay area, then continued in L.A. clubs. Executive of Red Bird Cinema.
PICTURES: Million Dollar Mystery (debut, 1987), Willow, Avalon, L.A. Story, Another You, Ricochet, A Few Good Men, The Opposite Sex and How to Live With Them, Indian Summer, Wayne's World 2, Grumpy Old Men, Reality Bites, Clean Slate, Miami Rhapsody, The Usual Suspects, Canadian Bacon, Casino, Nowhere Man, Chameleon, House Arrest, Grumpier Old Men, That Thing You Do!, National Lampoon's The Don's Analyst, Truth or Consequences N.M., Buffalo 66, Outside Ozona, Steal This Movie, The Sex Monster, She's All That, Deterrence, The Whole Nine Yards, Deal of a Lifetime, The Wedding Planner, 3000 Miles to Graceland, Dr. Dolittle 2, Juwanna Mann, The Santa Clause 2, Stolen Summer, Rolling Kansas, Blizzard, Seven Times Lucky, The Whole Ten Yards, Our Time Is Up (short), Hostage, Niagara Motel, White Lies, The Santa Clause 3: The Escape Clause, Numb, Soulmates, 2:13, Middle Men, Choose, Cop Out, The Big Year, American Empire.
TELEVISION: *Movies*: The World According to Straw, The Don's Analyst, The Underworld (also writer), Ruby Bridges, Capitol Law, The Staircase Murders, Picture This!. *Mini-series*: From the Earth to the Moon, The Halifax Comedy Fest, The Lost Room. *Series*: Hot Flashes, Coming of Age, Morton and Hayes, The Drew Carey Show, Work with Me (also co-exec. prod.), Movie Lover's Road Trip (host), Celebrity Poker Showdown (host), Shark, Suitemates, Kevin Pollak's Chat Show (host, writer, exec. prod.), Vamped Out (dir., writer, exec. prod.). *Documentaries/Specials:* One Night Stand (also prod., writer), Stop With the Kicking (also prod., writer), The Seven Deadly Sins (also writer, dir.), Project Greenlight (as himself). *Guest:* More than 77 appearances.

POLLAN, TRACY
Actress. b. New York, NY, June 22, 1960. m. actor Michael J. Fox.
THEATRE: *B'way*: Jake's Women.
PICTURES: Baby It's You, Promised Land, Bright Lights Big City, A Stranger Among Us.
TELEVISION: *Movies*: Sessions, Trackdown: Finding the Goodbar Killer, The Little Sister, A Good Sport, The Baron and the Kid, The Abduction of Kari Swenson, A Special Friendship, Fine Things, Dying to Love You, Children of the Dark, 1st to Die, Natalee Holloway. *Mini-series:* The Kennedys of Massachusetts. *Series*: Family Ties, Anna Says (also exec. prod.), Law & Order: Special Victims Unit (Emmy nom. 2000 as guest).

POLLARD, MICHAEL J.
Actor. r.n. Michael J. Pollack. b. Passaic, NJ, May 30, 1939. e. Montclair Academy, Actors Studio.
THEATRE: Comes a Day, Loss of Roses, Enter Laughing, Bye Bye Birdie, Leda Had a Little Swan, Our Town.
PICTURES: Adventures of a Young Man (debut, 1962), The Stripper, Summer Magic, The Wild Angels, Caprice, Enter Laughing, Bonnie and Clyde (Academy Award nom.; 2 Golden Globe noms. 1968), Jigsaw, Hannibal Brooks, Little Fauss and Big Halsy, The Legend of Frenchie King, Dirty Little Billy, Between the Lines, Melvin and Howard, Heated Vengeance, America, The Patriot, Riders of the Storm, Roxanne, Scrooged, American Gothic, Fast Food, Season of Fear, Next of Kin, Tango and Cash, Night Visitor, Sleepaway Camp 3: Teenage Wasteland, Why Me?, Dick Tracy, I Come in Peace, Joey Takes a Cab, The Art of Dying, Another You, Enid Is Sleeping (Over Her Dead Body), Split Second, The Arrival, Arizona Dream, Motorama, Skeeter, Heartstopper, Mad Dog Time, The Unknown Cyclist, Stir, Merchants of Venus, Tumbleweeds, The Debtors, Forever Lulu, Danny and Max, Out of the Black, House of 1000 Corpses, Sunburnt Angels.
TELEVISION: *Movies*: The Smugglers, Stuck With Each Other, An American Murder, Working Tra$h, The Odyssey. *Series*: The

Many Loves of Dobie Gillis, Leo and Liz in Beverly Hills, The Toxic Crusaders (voice). *Guest:* More than 53 appearances.

POLLEY, SARAH
Actress. b. Canada, Jan. 8, 1979. Daughter of late actress and casting director Diane Polley.
PICTURES: One Magic Christmas, The Big Town, The Adventures of Baron Munchausen, Babar: The Movie (voice), Exotica, Joe's So Mean to Josephine, The Sweet Hereafter, The Planet of Junior Brown, The Hanging Garden, Last Night, Guinevere, Go, eXistenZ, The Life Before This, The Weight of Water, Love Come Down, The Law of Enclosures, The Claim, This Might Be Good, No Such Thing, I Shout Love (short, dir. & writer), All I Want For Christmas (dir. only), My Life Without Me, The Event, Dermott's Quest (short), The I Inside, Luck, Dawn of the Dead, Sugar, Siblings, Beowulf & Grendel, The Secret Life of Words, 3 Needles, Away from Her (dir., writer, Academy Award nom. 2008), Mr. Nobody, Splice, Trigger, Take This Waltz (dir., writer, prod.).
TELEVISION: *Movies:* Lantern Hill, Johann's Gift to Christmas, Take Another Look, White Lies. *Mini-series:* John Adams. *Series:* Ramona, Road to Avonlea, Straight Up, The Shields Stories (dir. & writer only), Slings and Arrows.

POLLOCK, DALE
Producer. b. Cleveland, OH, May 18, 1950. e. Brandeis U., B.A. anthropology, San Jose State, M.S., mass communication. Began journalistic career in Santa Cruz in early '70s, serving as reporter and film critic for Daily Variety, 1977-80. Joined Los Angeles Times as film writer, winning paper's Award for Sustained Excellence in 1984. He left the L.A. Times in 1985 to take post with The Geffen Film Co. as executive in charge of creative development. Joined A&M Films as v.p. in charge of prod. in 1986 and became pres. in 1990. Became president of Peak Productions in 1994, and continues in that role today. He also helms Green Street Productions, which was established in 2003. Since Jan. 1999, Pollock has been dean of the School of Filmmaking at the NC School of the Arts. *Author:* Skywalking (George Lucas biography). *Member:* Academy of Motion Picture Arts & Sciences, Producers Guild & Writers Guild of America.
PICTURES: *Executive producer:* The Beast, The Mighty Quinn, Bats. *Producer.* House of Cards, Worth Winning, Blaze, Crooked Hearts, A Midnight Clear, A Home of Our Own, S.F.W., Mrs. Winterbourne, Set It Off, Meet the Deedles (also s.p.).

POLLOCK, THOMAS
Executive. b. 1943. In 1971, after 3 years as business mgr. for American Film Institute's film marketing wing, formed law firm Pollock Bloom, and Dekom with young filmmakers such as George Lucas and Matthew Robbins as clients. Served as chmn. Filmex, 1973-81. 1986, named chmn. MCA's Universal motion picture group., then vice chmn., MCA, Inc. Currently, partner in the Montecito Picture Company and vice chair of AFI's bd. of dir.
PICTURES: *Executive producer:* Road Trip, Evolution, Old School, Eurotrip, Disturbia, The Uninvited, I Love You, Man, Up in the Air (prod.), Chloe (prod.), Post Grad, Girlfriend Experience (prod.).
TELEVISION: *Movie:* Killing Me Softly (exec. prod.). *Series:* Alienators: Evolution Continues (exec. prod.).

POP, IGGY
Composer, Singer, Actor. r.n. James Osterberg. b. MI, April 21, 1947. Has recorded 16 albums with band the Stooges and solo.
PICTURES: *Composer/songs:* Repo Man, Sid & Nancy (also acting), Dogs in Space, Slaves of New York (also singer), Va mourir, Trainspotting (also lyricist), The Crow: City of Angels, The Brave, Full Blast, Great Expectations, The Wedding Singer, Velvet Goldmine, Whatever, Two Smoking Barrels, Born to Lose, The Filth and the Fury, Almost Famous, Dogtown and Z-Boys (documentary), Killer Barbys vs. Dracula, Rugrats Go Wild!, Wonderland, The School of Rock, The Life Aquatic with Steve Zissou, Lords of Dogtown, Just Like Heaven, Ecstasy, The Jacket, House of Wax, Sleeping Dogs Lie, Smokin' Aces, Shoot 'Em Up, Halloween, Transporter 3. *Singer:* Arizona Dream, The Avengers, Intimacy, Freddy Got Fingered, The Jacket, The Weather Man. *Actor:* Rock & Rule, The Color of Money, Hardware, Cry-Baby, Tank Girl, Jim Jarmusch's Dead Man, Atolladero, The Crow: City of Angels, Private Parts (cameo), Snow Day, Coffee and Cigarettes, Suck, Art House.
TELEVISION: *Movie:* Bulles de Vian. *Mini-series*: Rock and Roll. *Series:* Tales from the Crypt (composer, several episodes), The Adventures of Pete and Pete (acting), Home to Rent (composer, theme song), Space Goofs (composer, theme song). *Documentaries/Specials*: 25 Years of Punk.

POPE, DICK
Cinematographer.
PICTURES: The Girl in the Picture, Coming Up Roses, The Fruit Machine, The Reflecting Skin, Life is Sweet, Dark City, Naked, The Air Up There, An Awfully Big Adventure, Nothing Personal, Secrets and Lies, Career Girls, Swept from the Sea, The Debt Collector, Topsy-Turvy, The Way of the Gun, 13 Conversations About One Thing, All or Nothing, Nicholas Nickleby, Vera Drake, The Chronicles of Narnia: The Lion, the Witch and the Wardrobe (dir. of photog.), The Illusionist (dir. of photog., Academy Award nom.; ASC nom. 2007), Man of the Year (dir. of photog.), Honeydripper, Happy-Go-Lucky, Angus, Thongs and Perfect Snogging, Me and Orson Welles, Another Year, It's a Wonderful Afterlife, Virtuoso, The Convincer.
TELEVISION: *Movies:* A Sense of History (TV short), The Blackheath Poisonings, Fool's Gold: The Story of the Brink's-Mat Robbery, Pleasure, Life's a Bitch, The Great Kandinsky, Cats, Deadly Voyage. *Mini-series:* Porterhouse Blue. *Series:* Forever Green.

POPE, KATHERINE
Executive. b. Glencoe, IL. e. Sarah Lawrence, Bachelor of Arts degree. m. Documentary filmmaker Richard E. Robbins. Early career spent as writer and producer of documentaries for CBS in New York. Also associate producer for cable TV A&E's "Biography." She moved to VH1 as writer/producer in May 1999. She joined NBC Studios as an associate in primetime series in January 2000. By Aug. 2000, promoted to manager, primetime series. In April 2001 became director, primetime series. She then managed drama development and current programs for the studio. As v.p., primetime series, NBC Studios, she supervised creative development for the hit drama series "Las Vegas," "Crossing Jordan," "American Dreams" and the Peabody Award-winning "Boomtown." From June 2003-June 2004, Pope was v.p., drama development, NBC Entertainment. She presided over the development of all of NBC's new drama pilots, including the hit drama "Medium." Continuing her rise at NBC, she served as senior v.p., drama series, NBC Universal Television Studios (now named Universal Media Studios). In this role, she developed and oversaw the first seasons of "House," "Battlestar Galactica" for SCI FI Channel, as well as "Psych" for the USA Network. Elevated to executive v.p., NBC Entertainment, Pope then managed all aspects of NBC's new series development, including the critically acclaimed series "Heroes," "Friday Night Lights" and "30 Rock." In mid-2007, Pope was named president, Universal Media Studios. She reported to NBC Entertainment and Universal Media Studios Co-Chairmen Marc Graboff and Ben Silverman. 2008 she left UMS. 2009 in talks with Peter Chernin to join his new production company.

PORTMAN, NATALIE
Actress. b. Jerusalem, Israel, June 9, 1981. r.n. Natalie Hershlag. e. Stagedoor Manor Performing Arts, Harvard.
THEATRE: *B'way:* The Diary of Anne Frank (debut), The Seagull. *Off B'way:* Ruthless.
PICTURES: The Professional, Heat, Everyone Says I Love You, Beautiful Girls, Mars Attacks!, South Beach, Prince of Egypt (voice), The Little Black Book, Anywhere But Here (Golden Globe nom. 2000), Star Wars: Episode I-The Phantom Menace, Where the Heart Is, Zoolander, Star Wars: Episode II: Attack of the Clones, Cold Mountain, Garden State, True, Closer (Academy Award nom.; Golden Globe Award 2005), Star Wars: Episode III, Free Zone, V for Vendetta, Paris, je t'aime, Goya's Ghosts, My Blueberry Nights, Mr. Magorium's Wonder Emporium, The Other Boleyn Girl, The Darjeeling Limited, New York, I Love You (also dir., writer), Brothers, Love & Other Impossible Pursuits (also exec. prod.), Your Highness, Black Swan, Pride and Prejudice and Zombies (also prod.), Thor.
TELEVISION: *Movie:* Armenian Genocide (doc., voice). *Series*: Hercules (voice). *Guest:* More than 83 appearances.

PORTMAN, RACHEL
Composer. b. Haslemere, England, Dec. 11, 1960.
PICTURES: Privileged, First Love, Last Day of Summer, Sharma and Beyond, 90 Degrees South, High Hopes, Oranges Are Not the Only Fruit, Life Is Sweet, Antonia and Jane, Where Angels Fear to Tread, Used People, Rebecca's Daughters, The Joy Luck Club, Great Moments in Aviation, Friends, Ethan Frome, Benny & Joon, War of the Buttons, Only You, Sirens, The Road to Wellville, To Wong Foo—Thanks for Everything! Julie Newmar, A Pyromaniac's Love Story, Smoke, The Adventures of Pinocchio, Emma (Academy Award 1997), Palookaville, Marvin's Room, Home Fries, Beauty and the Beast: The Enchanted Christmas, Addicted to Love, Mulan, Beloved, The Other Sister, Ratcatcher, Cider House Rules (Academy Award nom. 2000), The Legend of Bagger Vance, Chocolat (Academy Award nom.; Golden Globe nom. 2001), The Emperor's New Clothes, Hart's War, The Truth About Charlie, Nicholas Nickleby, The Human Stain, Mona Lisa Smile, The Manchurian Candidate, Because of Winn-Dixie, Flight Plan, Oliver Twist, The Lake House, Infamous, Miss Potter, The Sisterhood of the Traveling Pants 2, The Duchess (also score prod.), Never Let Me Go, Resistance.
TELEVISION: *Movies*: Reflections, Four Days in July, Good as Gold, The Short and Curlies, 1914 All Out, Sometime in August, Loving Hazel, Young Charlie Chaplin, The Woman in Black, Precious Bane, Monster Maker, Living with Dinosaurs, The Widowmaker, Shoot to Kill, Flea Bites, The Cloning of Joanna May, Mr. Wakefield's Crusade, Great Moments in Aviation, The Little Prince (Emmy nom. 2005, Great Performances series), Grey Gardens (Emmy nom. 2009). *Mini-series*: The Storyteller: Greek Myths. *Series:* Jim Henson's The Storyteller.

POSEY, PARKER
Actress. b. Laurel, MS, Nov. 8, 1968. e. NC School of the Arts; SUNY Purchase.

PICTURES: Joey Breaker, Dazed and Confused, Coneheads, Mixed Nuts, Dead Connection, Amateur, Sleep with Me, Frisk, Drunks, Party Girl, Kicking and Screaming, The Doom Generation, Flirt, Waiting for Guffman, The Daytrippers, Basquiat, Henry Fool, Dinner at Fred's, SubUrbia, Clockwatchers, The House of Yes, The Misadventures of Margaret, Cross Country, You've Got Mail, Dinner at Fred's, Scream 3, Best in Show, Josie and the Pussycats, The Anniversary Party, The Sweetest Thing, Personal Velocity: Three Portraits, The Event, A Mighty Wind, Adam & Steve, Laws of Attraction, Blade: Trinity, The OH in Ohio, Superman Returns, For Your Consideration, Fay Grim, Broken English, The Eye, Spring Breakdown, Happy Tears, Highland Park, Inside Out.
TELEVISION: *Movies:* Tracey Takes on New York, Hell on Heels: The Battle of Mary Kay (Golden Globe nom. 2003), Frankenstein. *Mini-series*: Tales of the City, More Tales of the City, Further Tales of the City. *Series*: As The World Turns, The Return of Jezebel James (also pilot). *Guest:* More than 52 appearances.

POSTER, STEVEN
Cinematographer. A.S.C. b. Chicago, IL, March 1, 1944. e. L.A. Art Center College. Started as commercial cinematographer before moving into feature films. 2nd unit work includes: Close Encounters of the Third Kind, Blade Runner. 2nd v.p., American Society of Cinematographers.
PICTURES: Blood Beach, Dead and Buried, Spring Break, Strange Brew, Testament, The New Kids, The Heavenly Kid, Blue City, The Boy Who Could Fly, Aloha Summer, Someone to Watch Over Me (ASC nom. 1988), Big Top Pee-wee, Next of Kin, Opportunity Knocks, Rocky V, Life Stinks, The Cemetery Club, A Midwife's Tale, Boy's Life 2, Rocket Man, Half a Chance, Donnie Darko, Stuart Little 2, Daddy Day Care, Looney Tunes: Back in Action, Southland Tales, The Box (also dir. of photog.), Spread, Cats & Dogs: The Revenge of Kitty Galore.
TELEVISION: *Movies*: The Grass is Always Greener, The Night Rider, The Beggarman Thief, Coward of the County, Mysterious Two, The Cradle Will Fall, Class of '65, Courage, Shanghai La Plaza, Roswell, Present Tense Past Perfect, Once You Meet a Stranger, The Color of Justice, Mrs. Harris (Emmy nom. 2006), The Danny Comden Project. *Mini-series:* I'll Take Manhattan. *Series:* What Really Happened to the Class of '65?, The Loop (also pilot), Raising the Bar (pilot). *Documentary:* The Miles Davis Documentary.

POSTLETHWAITE, PETE
Actor. b. Lancashire, England. Feb. 16, 1946.
THEATRE: *RSC:* Every Man and His Humour, A Midsummer Night's Dream, MacBeth, King Lear, The Taming of the Shrew, Treasure Island (U.K.)
PICTURES: The Duellists, A Private Function, Distant Voices Still Lives, The Dressmaker, To Kill a Priest, Hamlet, Alien^3, The Last of the Mohicans, Waterland, In the Name of the Father (Acad. Award nom.), Anchoress, The Usual Suspects, James and the Giant Peach (voice), Dragonheart, When Saturday Comes, William Shakespeare's Romeo + Juliet, Brassed Off, Bandyta, Amistad, The Serpent's Kiss, The Lost World: Jurrasic Park, Among Giants, The Divine Ryans, When the Sky Falls, Rat, The Shipping News, Triggermen, Between Strangers, The Limit, Strange Bedfellows, Red Mercury, The Constant Gardener, Æon Flux, Valley of the Heart's Delight, Ghost Son, The Omen, Closing the Ring, Solomon Kane, Ironclad, Clash of the Titans, Killing Bono.
TELEVISION: *Movies:* Horse in the House, Doris and Doreen, Afternoon Off, Cyrano de Bergerac, Coast to Coast, Tumbledown, Treasure Island, A Child From the South, Sharpe's Company, Sharpe's Enemy, Lost for Words, Alice in Wonderland, Butterfly Collectors, Animal Farm (voice), The Muscle Market, A Child From the South, The Night Rider, Beggarman Thief, Coward of the County, Mysterious Two, The Cradle Will Fall, Courage, Roswell, Present Tense Past Perfect (TV short), Once You Meet A Stranger, Color of Justice, Shattered City: The Halifax Explosion. *Mini-series:* I'll Take Manhattan, Shattered City: The Halifax Explosion, Criminal Justice. *Series*: Horse in the House, Tales of Sherwood Forest, Needle, Martin Chuzzlewit, What Really Happened to the Class of '65?, The Sins, Criminal Justice. *Guest:* More than 68 appearances.

POTTS, ANNIE
Actress. b. Nashville, TN, Oct. 28, 1952. e. Stephens College, Columbia, MO, BFA. Amateur stage debut at 12 in Heidi. Then in summer stock; on road in Charley's Aunt, 1976. Serves on auxilliary bd. of MADD (Mothers Against Drunk Driving). Ambassador for Women for the Amer. Arthritis Foundation.
PICTURES: Corvette Summer (debut, 1978, Golden Globe nom. 1979), King of the Gypsies, Heartaches, Ghostbusters, Crimes of Passion, Pretty in Pink, Jumpin' Jack Flash, Pass the Ammo, Who's Harry Crumb?, Ghostbusters II, Texasville, Breaking the Rules, Toy Story (voice), Toy Story 2 (voice).
TELEVISION: *Movies*: Black Market Baby, Flatbed Annie and Sweetie Pie, Cowboy, Why Me?, It Came Upon the Midnight Clear, The Man Who Fell To Earth, Her Deadly Rival, Defending Our Kids: The Julie Posey Story, Queen Sized, Single with Parents, Family Man, The Karenskys, Freshman Father. *Series*: Goodtime Girls, Stuck In the Middle with You, Designing Women, Love & War (Emmy nom. 1994), Dangerous Minds, Over the Top, Joan of Arcadia, Any Day Now, Hercules (voice), Law & Order: Special Victims Unit. *Guest*: More than 72 appearances.

POWELL, JANE
Actress, Singer. r.n. Suzanne Burce. b. Portland, OR, April 1, 1929. m. pub. relations exec. Dick Moore. Had own radio program over KOIN, Portland; singer on nat'l networks; Star of Tomorrow, 1948. Autobiography: The Girl Next Door ... and How She Grew (1988). Video: Jane Powell's Fight Back With Fitness.
THEATRE: Irene (B'way, 1974). After-Play (off-B'way, 1996). Toured nationally with South Pacific, Peter Pan, My Fair Lady, The Unsinkable Molly Brown, I Do I Do, Same Time Next Year.
PICTURES: Song of the Open Road (debut, 1944), Delightfully Dangerous, Holiday in Mexico, Three Daring Daughters, A Date With Judy, Luxury Liner, Nancy Goes to Rio, Two Weeks With Love, Royal Wedding, Rich Young and Pretty, Small Town Girl, Three Sailors and a Girl, Seven Brides for Seven Brothers, Athena, Deep in My Heart, Hit the Deck, The Girl Most Likely, The Female Animal, Enchanted Island, That's Entertainment, Tubby the Tuba (voice), That's Dancing, Marie, Picture This, Broadway: The Golden Age by the Legends Who Were There.
TELEVISION: *Movies*: The Letters, Mayday at 40,000 Feet, The Making of Seven Brides for Seven Brothers, The Sandy Bottom Orchestra. *Host*: The Movie Musicals. *Mini-series*: Perfect Murder Perfect Town. *Series*: Alcoa Theatre, Loving, As the World Turns, Growing Pains. *Documentaries/Specials*: Ruggles of Red Gap, Give My Regards to Broadway, Meet Me in St. Louis, Jane Powell Show. *Guest*: More than 66 appearances.

POWELL, ROBERT
Actor. b. Salford, England, June 1, 1944. e. Manchester U. Stage work includes Tovarich.
PICTURES: Robbery (debut, 1967), Far From the Madding Crowd, Joanna, The Italian Job, Walk a Crooked Path, Secrets, Running Scared, Asylum, The Asphyx, Mahler, Tommy, Oltre il Bene e il Male, Cocktails for Three, The Thirty-Nine Steps, The Dilessi Affair, Harlequin, Jane Austin in Manhattan, The Survivor, Imperative (Venice Film Fest. Award), The Jigsaw Man, What Waits Below, D'Annunio and I Down There in the Jungle, Romeo-Juliet (voice), The Sign of Command, Chunuk Bair, The Mystery of Edwin Drood, Hey Mr. DJ, Colour Me Kubrick
TELEVISION: *Movies*: Tower of London: The Innocent, Season of the Witch, Hunting of Lionel Crane, Mr. Rolls, and Mr. Royce, Lady Killer, Murder Is A One-Act Play, The Four Feathers, Pygmalion, The Hunchback of Notre Dame, Frankenstein, Pasternak, The First Circle, Merlin of the Crystal Cave, The Golden Years, Das Lange Gesprach mit dem Vogel, Pride of Africa, Marple: The Murder at the Vicarage. *Mini-series*: Sentimental Education, Jude the Obscure, The Edwardians, Jesus of Nazareth, Shaka Zulu, The Century of Welfare. *Series*: Doomwatch, Looking for Clancy, Hannay, The Detectives, Escape (narrator), Infamous Assassinations (narr.), Holby City, The Book Quiz (announcer). *Documentaries:* The Wandering Company, Max Ernst: Mein Vagabundieren - Meine Unruhe (english ver.), Titanic, The Century of Warfare (mini-series), Great Mysteries and Myths of the Twentieth Century (series), Secrets of World War II (series), Al-Ghazali: The Alchemist of Happiness (voice), H Side Story. *Guest:* More than 87 appearances.

POWERS, C. F. (MIKE), JR.
Executive. b. San Francisco, CA, March 6, 1923. e. Park Coll., MO, Columbia U., N.Y., graduated U. of Oregon. Entered film business with P.R.C. in Portland, OR, 1947. Became Eagle Lion branch mgr. in Portland, 1950, and then United Artists. Moved to Seattle, WA as branch mgr. of 20th Century Fox, 1960. Was then western division mgr. for 20th Century Fox until 1967, then western division mgr. for Cinerama until 1973. Became exec. v.p., head film buyer for Robert L. Lippert Theatres, Transcontinental Theatres and Affiliated Theatres until 1978. Western div. mgr. Orion Pictures, 1982-4. Mike Powers Ent. (a buying and booking combine and indept. film distrib.). 1984-86 Western district mgr. Embassy Pictures. Became western division mgr. for Filmways Pictures. Past president of Catholic Entertainment Guild of Northern Calif.; past pres. of Variety Club Tent 32, San Francisco. Consultant to U.S. Federal Govt. Retired.

POWERS, STEFANIE
Actress. r.n. Stefania Federkiewicz. b. Hollywood, CA, Nov. 2, 1942. After graduation from Hollywood High signed by Columbia Studios.
PICTURES: Tammy Tell Me True (debut, 1962), Experiment in Terror, The Young Sinner, The Interns, If a Man Answers, McClintock!, Palm Springs Weekend, The New Interns, Love Has Many Faces, Die Die My Darling, Stagecoach, Warning Shot, The Boatniks, Crescendo, The Magnificent 7 Ride, Herbie Rides Again, Gone With the West, It Seemed Like a Good Idea at the Time, Invisible Strangler, Escape to Athena, Rabbit Fever, Transfer at Aachen.
TELEVISION: *Movies*: Five Desperate Women, Paper Man, Sweet Sweet Rachel, Hardcase, No Place to Run, Shootout in a One-Dog Town, Skyway to Death, Sky Heist, Return to Earth, Family Secrets (also prod.), A Death in Canaan, Nowhere to Run, Mistral's Daughter, Deceptions, At Mother's Request, Beryl Markham: A Shadow on the Sun (also co-prod.), She Was Marked for Murder, Love and Betrayal, When Will I Be Loved?,

The Burden of Proof, Survive the Night, Hart to Hart Returns (also co-prod.), Hart to Hart: Home is Where the Hart Is, Hart to Hart: Crimes of the Hart (also co-prod.), Hart to Hart: Old Friends Never Die, The Good Ride, Good King Wenceslas, Hart to Hart: Secrets of the Hart, Hart to Hart: Til Death Do Us Hart, Someone Is Watching, Meet My Mom. *Mini-series*: Washington: Behind Closed Doors, Hollywood Wives. *Series*: The Girl From U.N.C.L.E., Feather and Father Gang, Hart to Hart (2 Emmy noms.; 5 Golden Globe noms.), Doctors, Dale's All Stars. *Guest:* More than 135 appearances.

PREISNER, ZBIGNIEW
Composer. b. Bielsko-Biala, Poland, May 20, 1955.
PICTURES: The Weather Forecast, No End, By Touch, Ucieczka, The Lullabye, Kocham Kino, To Kill a Priest, A Short Film About Killing, A Short Film About Love, The Last Schoolbell, Europa, Europa, The Double Life of Veronique, Eminent Domain, At Play in the Fields of the Lord (Golden Globe nom. 1992), Dismissed from Life, Olivier, Olivier, Damage, The Secret Garden, Three Colors: Blue (Golden Globe nom. 1994), Three Colors: White, Three Colors: Red, The Line of the Horizon, To Have and to Hold, Desire in Motion, Elisa, Feast of July, Kryszstof Kieslowski: I'm So-So, De Aegypto, Bridges, Fairy Tale: A True Story, The Island on Bird Street, Foolish Heart, Liv, The Last September, Dreaming of Joseph Lees, Aberdeen, Weiser, Between Strangers, It's All About Love, Strange Gardens SuperTex, The Beautiful Country, 2046 (soundtrack song), Sportsman of the Century, A Woman in Berlin, Certainty (doc.).
TELEVISION: *Mini-series*: Radetzkymarsch. *Series:* The Decalogue.

PRESLE, MICHELINE
Actress. r.n. Micheline Chassagne. b. Paris, France, Aug. 22, 1922. e. Raymond Rouleau Dram. Sch. m.p. debut in Je Chante; on stage in Colinette. Am. Stram Gram, Spectacle des Allies; to U.S., 1945; Flea in Her Ear, Magic Circus, Who's Afraid of Virginia Woolf? (tour), Gigi, Nuit de Valognes, Boomerang, Adriana Mont, etc. Has appeared in more than 123 films.
PICTURES: Jeunes Filles en Detresse, L'Histoire de Rire, La Nuit Fantastique, Felicie Nanteuil, Seul Amour, Faibalas, Boule de Suif, Jeux Sont Faix, Diable au Corps, Under My Skin, Some Kind of News, An American Guerilla in the Philippines, Adventures of Captain Fabian, Sins of Pompeii, House of Ricordi, Archipelago of Love, Thieves After Dark, Le Chien, At the Top of the Stairs, Fine Weather, But Storms Due Towards Evening, Confidences, Alouette je te plumerai, I Want to Go Home, La Fête des pères, Le Jour de Rois, Fanfan, The Blood of Others, Casque bleu, Les Miserables, Le Journal du seducteur, Bastard Brood, Citron amer, Les Mille et une recettes du cuisinier amoureux, Greve party, Venus beaute, Bad Company, Charming Fellow, Gender Bias, Tender Souls, Love Vertigo, Chouchou, Saltimbank, France Boutique, Un homme et son chien, Operation Weed, others.
TELEVISION: several European productions.

PRESSMAN, EDWARD R.
Producer. b. New York, N.Y, 1943. e. Fieldston School; grad., Stanford U.; studied at London School of Economics. Began career with film short, Girl, in collaboration with dir. Paul Williams in London. They formed Pressman-Williams Enterprises.
PICTURES: *Producer:* Out of It, The Revolutionary, Dealing: or the Berkeley to Boston Forty Brick, Lost Bag Blues, Sisters, Phantom of the Paradise, Despair, Old Boyfriends, Heart Beat, The Hand, The Pirates of Penzance, Plenty, Half Moon Street, Cherry 2000, Talk Radio, Blue Steel, Reversal of Fortune, Waiting for the Light, Homicide, Year of the Gun, Storyville, Bad Lieutenant, Hoffa, The Crow, Street Fighter, Judge Dredd, City Hall, The Island of Dr. Moreau, The Crow: City of Angels, (also exec. soundtrack prod.), The Winter Guest, Two Girls and a Guy, The Blackout, New Rose Hotel, American Psycho, The Crow: Salvation, Driving Lessons, Beautiful Country, Undertow, The Crow: Wicked Prayer, Amazing Grace, Sisters (2006), The Mutant Chronicles, Bad Lieutenant: Port of Call New Orleans, Wall Street: Money Never Sleeps, The Crow. *Exec. Prod:* Badlands, Paradise Alley, Das Boot, Conan the Barbarian, Crimewave, True Stories, Good Morning Babylon, Masters of the Universe, Walker, Wall Street, Paris By Night, To Sleep with Anger, Martians Go Home, Iron Maze (co-exec. prod.), Dream Lover, The Crow: World of Gods and Monsters, The Endurance: Shackleton's Legendary Antarctic Expedition (doc.), Black and White, Harvard Man, Happy Times (exec. prod./international), The Guys, 10th Victim, The Cooler, Party Monster, Owning Mahowny, The Hebrew Hammer, Straight from the Projects: Rappers That Live the Lyrics - Brownsville, Brooklyn (video doc.), Love Object, Rick, Never Die Alone, Straight from the Projects: Rappers That Live the Lyrics - 3rd Ward, New Orleans (video doc.), The King, Thank You For Smoking, Fur: An Imaginary Portrait of Diane Arbus, Border Crosses.
TELEVISION: *Series: Executive producer:* The Crow: Stairway to Heaven.

PRESSMAN, LAWRENCE
Actor. b. Cynthiana, KY, July 10, 1939. e. Kentucky Northwestern U. On B'way in Man in the Glass Booth, Play It Again, Sam.
PICTURES: Making It, Shaft, Vrooder's Hooch, The Man in the Glass Booth, Walk Proud, Nine to Five, The Hanoi Hilton, Honor Bound, Angus, The Sunchaser, Trial & Error, The Maker, My Giant, Very Bad Things, Mighty Joe Young, The Waterdance, American Pie, Alex in Wonder, American Wedding, Nine Lives, American Dreamz, Mentor, The Far Side of Jericho, Tickling Leo, Mother and Child. *Associate producer:* In Good Company.
TELEVISION: *Movies*: Cannon, The Snoop Sisters, The Marcus-Nelson Murder, Winter Kill, The First 36 Hours of Dr. Durant, Man from Atlantis, Mulligan's Stew, The Trial of Lee Harvey Oswald, The Gathering, Like Mom Like Me, The Gathering Part II, Cry for the Strangers, Rehearsal for Murder, The Red-Light Sting, The Three Wishes of Billy Grier, Victims for Victims: The Theresa Saldana Story, For Love or Money, Matlock: Diary of a Perfect Murder, A Fighting Choice, The Deliberate Stranger, The Drug Knot, Little Girl Lost, She Knows Too Much, Breaking Point, Fire and Rain, White Hot: The Mysterious Murder of Thelma Todd, To My Daughter with Love, The Enemy Within,The Rockford Files: I Still Love L.A. Whose Daughter is She?, The Late Shift, She Cried No, DC 9/11: Time of Crisis, Murder Without Conviction. *Mini-series:* Rich Man, Poor Man, Blind Ambition, The Winds of War, On Wings of Eagles. *Series:* The Edge of Night, Mulligan's Stew, Ladies' Man, Doogie Howser M.D., General Hospital. *Guest:* More than 133 appearances.

PRESSMAN, MICHAEL
Director, Producer. b. New York, NY, July 1, 1950. e. California Inst. of Arts. From show business family; was actor in college.
PICTURES: *Director*: The Great Texas Dynamite Chase, The Bad News Bears Breaking Training, Boulevard Nights, Those Lips Those Eyes (also prod.), Some Kind of Hero, Doctor Detroit, Teenage Mutant Ninja Turtles II: The Secret of the Ooze, To Gillian On Her 37th Birthday, Lake Placid, Frankie and Johnny Are Married (also writer).
TELEVISION: *Movies*: Like Mom Like Me, The Imposter, And the Children Shall Lead, The Christmas Gift, Secret Passions, Baby M (actor only), To Heal a Nation, Final Jeopardy, Private Sessions, Haunted by Her Past, Shootdown, The Revenge of Al Capone, Incident at Dark River, Man Against the Mob (also co-prod.), Joshua's Heart, Miracle Child, Quicksand: No Escape, Saint Maybe, A Season for Miracles, The Comic-Con Chronicles (TV doc., 4 episodes). *Series*: Picket Fences (2 Emmy Awardsfor), The Practice, Law & Order, Boston Public, The $treet, The Guardian, Chicago Hope (Emmy nom.; DGA nom. for episode 1995 The Brotherhood of Poland New Hampshire (pilot dir. exec. prod.).

PRESTON, CARRIE
Actress. b. Macon, GA, June 21, 1967. m. actor Michael Emerson.
THEATRE: *B'way:* Boys and Girls, Cycling Past the Matterhorn, Festen, The Rivals. *Regional:* No Foreigners Beyond This Point.
PICTURES: My Best Friend's Wedding, For Richer or Poorer, Mercury Rising, Guinevere, Cradle Will Rock, The Legend of Bagger Vance, Straight-Jacket, The Stepford Wives, Transamerica, Towelhead, Vicky Cristina Barcelona, Doubt, Duplicity, That Evening Sun, What's Wrong with Virginia, A Bag of Hammers, Sironia.
TELEVISION: *Movies:* Cutty Whitman, Five Houses, Grace & Glorie. *Series:* Emeril, Law & Order: Criminal Intent, True Blood.

PRESTON, KELLY
Actress. r.n. Kelly Kamalelehua Palzis. b. Honolulu, HI, Oct. 13, 1962. e. UCLA, USC. m. actor John Travolta.
PICTURES: Metalstorm: The Destruction of Jared-Syn (debut, 1983), Christine, Mischief, Secret Admirer, SpaceCamp, 52 Pick-Up, Amazon Women on the Moon, A Tiger's Tale, Love at Stake, Spellbinder, Twins, The Experts, Run, Only You, Love Is a Gun, Cheyenne Warrior, Waiting to Exhale, From Dusk Till Dawn, Citizen Ruth, Addicted to Love, Jerry Maguire, Nothing to Lose, Jack Frost, Holy Man, For Love of the Game, Bar Hopping, Battlefield Earth, Daddy and Them, Not Under My Roof, A View from the Top, What a Girl Wants, The Cat in the Hat, Eulogy, Return to Sender, Sky High, Angel from Montgomery, Broken Bridges, Death Sentence, Old Dogs, Casino Jack, The Last Song.
TELEVISION: *Movies*: For Love and Honor, The Perfect Bride, The American Clock, Cyeyenne Warrior, Little Surprises, Bar Hopping, The Tenth Circle. *Series*: Capitol, For Love and Honor, Fat Actress, Suburban Shootout. *Documentaries/Specials:* Off the Menu: The Last Days of Chasen's (as herself), Intimate Portrait: Kelly Preston, Welcome to Hollywood (herself), A&E Biography: John Travolta (herself). *Guest:* More than 63 appearances.

PREVIN, ANDRÉ
Composer, Conductor. b. Berlin, Germany, April 6, 1929. Composed and conducted over 50 m.p. scores. Music dir., Pittsburgh Symphony Orchestra, & conductor emeritus of London Symphony Orchestra. Music dir., Royal Philharmonic Orch., 1985-89. Guest conductor of most major symphony orchestras in U.S. and Europe. Music dir., Pittsburgh Symphony 1972-81. Conductor, London Symphony, 1968-78. Conductor Emeritus London Symphony, 1992-present. Received Knighthood of British Empire in 1996. Work has appeared in more than 70 films/videos since 1947 and includes films below.

PICTURES: Three Little Words (Academy Award nom. 1951), Cause for Alarm, Kiss Me Kate (Academy Award nom., 1954), It's Always Fair Weather (Academy Award nom. 1956), Bad Day at Black Rock, Invitation to the Dance, Catered Affair, Designing Woman, Silk Stockings, Gigi (Academy Award 1959), Porgy and Bess (Academy Award, 1960), The Subterraneans, Bells Are Ringing (Academy Award nom. 1961), Pepe (Academy Award nom., 1961), Elmer Gantry (Academy Award nom. 1961), The Four Horsemen of the Apocalypse, One Two Three, Two for the Seesaw (Academy Award nom., 1963), Long Day's Journey Into Night, Irma LaDouce (Academy Award 1964), My Fair Lady (Academy Award, 1965), Goodbye Charlie, Inside Daisy Clover, The Fortune Cookie, Thoroughly Modern Millie (Academy Award nom. 1968), Valley of the Dolls, Paint Your Wagon, The Music Lovers, Jesus Christ Superstar (Academy Award nom. 1974), One Trick Pony, The Music Lovers, Mrs. Pollifax, Bang Bang, Rollerball, The Elephant Man, Six Weeks (conductor), The Professional, Anastasia, Playing by Heart, Fight Club, Small Time Crooks.
TELEVISION: Jennie: Lady Randolph Churchill, A Streetcar Named Desire. Also musical director and/or conductor of numerous specials and awards shows,. including the Academy Awards (26th, 28th, 32nd and 33rd).

PRICE, FRANK
Executive, Producer. b. Decatur, IL, May 17, 1930. e. Michigan State U. and was assoc. editor of "The Spartan," a humor magazine. Before college served in U.S. Nave. Joined CBS in N.Y. in 1951 as story editor and writer. Moved to Hollywood in 1953, serving as story editor first at Columbia and then NBC (Matinee Theatre). In 1958 joined Universal as an assoc. prod. and writer. In 1961 named exec. prod. of The Virginian TV series. Appt. exec. prod. of Ironside; later did It Takes a Thief and several World Premiere movies. 1964 named v.p. of Universal TV; 1971, sr. v.p.; 1974, pres. Also v.p., MCA, Inc. 1978, left to join Columbia as pres. of new company unit, Columbia Pictures Productions. In 1979 named chmn. & CEO of Columbia Pictures. In 1983 joined MCA Universal as chmn., motion picture group; also pres. of Universal Pictures, and v.p. of MCA. In 1987 formed Price Entertainment Inc. as chmn. & CEO to produce movies and create TV shows for dist. through Columbia Pictures Entertainment, an exclusive relationship which lasted through Oct. 1991. Today Price serves as chmn. and CEO of Price Entertainment, Inc. Member: USC bd. of trustees and chmn, USC School of Cinema-Television Bd. of Councilors; has served on numerous other bds., including governor of the Acad. of Motion Picture Arts & Sciences, dir., MPAA; trustee of the Sundance Film Institute. Honors include: Motion Picture Pioneer of the Year Award, NATO Motion Picture Exec. of the Year award, honorary doctor of humanities degree from Mich. State U. in 2003.
PICTURES: The Bear, Gladiator, The Walking Dead, Circle of Friends, Marriette in Ecstasy, Getting Away with Murder, Zeus and Roxanne, Texas Rangers.
TELEVISION: *Movies*: Sullivan's Empire, Split Second to an Epitaph, Lost Flight, Alias Smith and Jones, The City, I Love a Mystery, The Tuskegee Airmen (exec. prod., Emmy nom. 1996). *Mini-series:* Rich Man, Poor Man. *Series*: Matinee Theater, The Virginian, Ironside, It Takes a Thief.

PRICE, PETER
Executive. e. Princeton University, graduated with honors, 1962; Yale Law School, law degree. Price then served as an officer in the U.S. Air Force Force before joining New York City government as counsel to the Taxi Commission. Began media career as a summer intern at the Wall Street Journal while attending Princeton. From 1966 to 1970 he held a series of management positions at TIME-LIFE magazine before becoming dir. of corporate development of TIME Incorporated. Became president of Media Networks, Inc. (MNI) and after selling the firm to 3M, managed MNI as a subsidiary until 1986. In 1987 he was named publisher of The New York Post and, subsequently, president and publisher of The National Sports Daily. Price first entered the television industry as the founder and president of Cable Networks, Inc., and was president of Liberty Cable Television from 1990 to 1997. His career has included stints as president of Television Tonight, a venture between the major TV networks and movie chains; and president of Television USA, a joint venture with the Wall Street Journal. Price was named president and CEO of The National Academy of Television Arts & Sciences in February 2002 and is the position he holds today. At the Academy he spearheaded the development of the business & financial reporting Emmy Awards and expanded the technology & engineering Emmy Awards, which honors patent holders of television technology, to also recognize the technical applications of patented technology via the New Media Technology Awards. Under his leadership, the Academy recently created a new Emmy Award for video content on new delivery platforms, including the Internet, mobile phones, iPods, PDAs and similar devices.

PRICE, RICHARD
Writer. b. Bronx, NY, Oct. 12, 1949. e. Cornell U., Columbia U.
AUTHOR: The Wanderers, Bloodbrothers, Ladies' Man, The Breaks, Clockers.
PICTURES: *Cameos:* The Wanderers, The Paper. *Writer:* The Color of Money (Academy Award nom. 1987), Streets of Gold, New York Stories (Life Lessons; also cameo), Sea of Love, Night and the City (also cameo), Mad Dog and Glory (also exec. prod., cameo), Ethan Frome (exec. prod. only), Kiss of Death (also co-prod., cameo), Clockers (also co-prod.), Ransom (also cameo), Shaft, Freedomland (writer, novel/ s.p.), The Cold Light of Day.
TELEVISION: *Series:* The Wire (WGA Award 2008, 1 other nom.).

PRIESTLEY, JASON
Actor. b. Vancouver, Canada, Aug. 28, 1969. First screen appearance was as baby in 1969 film That Cold Day in the Park, in which his mother had bit part. Child actor in many Canadian TV commercials. First major U.S. acting job in 1986 TV movie Nobody's Child. Moved to L.A. in 1987. Theatre includes The Addict, The Breakfast Club.
PICTURES: The Boy Who Could Fly, Nowhere to Run, Watchers, Calendar Girl, Tombstone, Coldblooded, Love and Death on Long Island, The Thin Pink Line, Conversations in Limbo (short, also exec. prod.), Standing on Fishes, Dill Scallion, Barenaked in America (documentary; also dir., prod.), Eye of the Beholder, The Highwayman (also exec. prod.), Choose Life, Zigs, Lion of Oz (voice), The Fourth Angel, Cherish, Cover Story, Time of the Wolf, Fancy Dancing, Dark Side, Die Mommie Die, Chicks with Sticks, Going the Distance, Hot Tamale, Made in Brooklyn, The Last Rites of Ransom Pride, Courage, Stingy Jack.
TELEVISION: *Movies*: Stacie (Canada), Teen Angel, Beverly Hills 90210 (movie), Teen Angel Returns, Choices of the Heart: The Margaret Sanger Story (narrator), Vanishing Point, Common Ground, Homicide: The Movie, Kiss Tomorrow Goodbye, (also exec. prod., dir.), Warning: Parental Advisory, The True Meaning of Christmas Specials, Sleep Murder, I Want to Marry Ryan Banks, Murder at the Presidio, Snow Wonder, Love Monkey (pilot), Shades of Black: The Conrad Black Story, Subs (also dir.), Luna: Spirit of the Whale, Termination Point, Don't Cry Now (also dir.), The Other Woman (dir.), A Very Merry Daughter of the Bride, Expecting a Miracle. *Mini-series:* Colditz, Above and Beyond, Everest. *Series*: Sister Kate, Beverly Hills 90210 (also co-prod., dir. & exec. prod., 2 Golden Globe noms.), Eek! The Cat (voice), Tru Calling, Love Monkey, Side Order of Life, Medium, The Secret Life of the American Teenager (dir.), The Day of the Triffids, Call Me Fitz. *Documentaries/Specials:* Biking USA (as himself), Ice & Asphalt: The World of Hockey (as himself), Predators from Beyond Neptune (as himself), Rides (host) and several Beverly Hills 90120 specials / documentaries/reunions. *Guest*: More than 120 appearances.

PRIMUS, BARRY
Actor. b. New York, NY, Feb. 16, 1938. e. Bennington College, City College of New York.THEATRE: The King and the Duke, The Nervous Set, Henry IV, Parts I and II, Creating the World, Teibele and the Demon, Lincoln Center Rep. (The Changling, After the Fall).
PICTURES: The Brotherhood, Puzzle of a Downfall Child, Been Down So Long It Looks Like Up to Me, Von Richtofen and Brown, Boxcar Bertha, The Gravy Train, New York New York, Avalanche, Autopsy, The Rose, Heartland, Night Games, Absence of Malice, The River, Down and Out in Beverly Hills, Jake Speed, Space Camp, Talking Walls, The Stranger, Big Business, Cannibal Women in the Avocado Jungle of Death, Torn Apart, Guilty by Suspicion, Mistress (dir., s.p. only), Night and the City, Flipping, Black & White, 15 Minutes, Life as a House, Break a Leg, Cross Bronx, When Will I Be Loved, Jackson, Mustang Sally, Righteous Kill, 20% Fiction (dir., writer).
TELEVISION: *Movies*: Incident at Vichy, Big Rose, Roger & Harry: The Mitera Target, Portrait of a Showgirl, Paper Dolls, The Shooting, I Want to Live, Heart of Steel, Brotherly Love, Stillwatch, The Women of Spring Break, Trade Off, Crime of the Century, Gold Coast, James Dean. *Mini-series*: Washington Behind Closed Doors. *Series*: Cagney and Lacey, V.I.P. (dir. only).

PRINCE
Singer, Composer, Actor. r.n. Prince Rogers Nelson. b. Minneapolis, MN, June 7, 1958. Rock musician, composer and recording artist.
PICTURES: *Actor:* Purple Rain (also wrote songs; Academy Award, Golden Globe nom. for best orig. song score, 1985), Under the Cherry Moon (also dir., s.p., songs), Sign O' the Times (also dir., songs), Graffiti Bridge (also dir., s.p., songs), Gett Off, Sexy MF, 3 Chains o' Gold (as himself; also composer, dir., prod.), The Sacrifice of Victor (also prod. as Paisley Park). *Composer/Songs only*: Summer Lovers, Still Smokin', Risky Business, Protocol, Bright Lights Big City, Batman (also singer), Pretty Woman, Show Girls, Girl 6, Striptease, Scream 2, Bamboozled, Head of State, Are We There Yet?, Get Rich or Die Tryin', The Lake House, Happy Feet (Golden Globe Award 2007), Her Best Move, License to Wed, Rush Hour 3, P.S. I Love You, Dan in Real Life, Forgetting Sarah Marshall.
TELEVISION: *Movies: Composer:* The Ryde Devine, Attention-Fragile. *Documentaries/Specials:* Ringo Starr and the All Starr Band 2003 (song composer), the History of Rock 'N' Roll-Vols. 5 & 10, Negermagasinet Prince & Spectrum (series).

PRINCE, HAROLD
Director. b. New York, NY, Jan. 30, 1928. e. U. of Pennsylvania. Worked as stage mgr. for George Abbott on three shows, later co-produced, produced and/or directed the following: The

Pajama Game (Tony Award), Damn Yankees (Tony Award), New Girl In Town, West Side Story, A Swim in the Sea, Fiorello! (Tony Award, Pulitzer Prize), Tenderloin, A Call on Kurpin, Take Her She's Mine, A Funny Thing Happened on the Way to the Forum (Tony Award), She Loves Me, The Matchmaker (revival), Fiddler on the Roof, Poor Bitos, Baker Street, Flora, The Red Menace, Superman, Cabaret (Tony Award), Zorba, Company, Follies, The Great God Brown, The Visit, Love for Love (the last three all revivals), A Little Night Music (Tony Award), Candide (Tony Award), Pacific Overtures, Side by Side by Sondheim, Some of My Best Friends, On the Twentieth Century, Evita (also London), Sweeney Todd (Tony Award 1979; also London), Merrily We Roll Along, A Doll's Life, Play Memory, End of the World, Diamonds, Grind, Roza, Cabaret (revival), Phantom of the Opera (Tony Award, 1988; also London), Grandchild of Kings (dir. & adapt.), Kiss of the Spider Woman (Tony Award, 1993), Show Boat (Tony Award, 1995); and also directed the operas Ashmadei, Silverlake, Sweeney Todd, Candide and Don Giovanni for N.Y. City Opera, Girl of Golden West for Chicago Lyric Opera Co. and San Francisco Opera; Willie Stark for Houston Grand Opera; Madama Butterfly for Chicago Lyric Opera and Turandot for Vienna State Opera and Faust for Metropolitan Opera.
AUTHOR: Contradictions: Notes on Twenty-Six Years in the Theatre (1974).
PICTURES: *Co-producer*: The Pajama Game, Damn Yankees. *Director*: Something for Everyone, A Little Night Music, The Phantom of the Opera (stage dir.), Sweeney Todd: The Demon Barber of Fleet Street (stage dir.).
TELEVISION: *Movies:* Sweeney Todd, Turandot, Follies in Concert, Candide.

PRINE, ANDREW
Actor. b. Jennings, FL, Feb. 14, 1936. e. U. of Miami. m. actress Heather Lowe. Mem. Actors Studio. On stage in Look Homeward, Angel, A Distant Bell, Mrs. Patterson, Borak. Ahmanson Theatre, LA: Long Day's Journey into Night, The Caine Mutiny. South Coast Rep.: Goodbye Freddy.
PICTURES: The Miracle Worker, Advance to the Rear, Texas Across the River, Bandolero!, The Devil's Brigade, This Savage Land, Generation, Chisum, Riding Tall, Simon: King of the Witches, Barn of the Naked Dead (Terror Circus), One Little Indian, The Centerfold Girls, Grizzly, The Town That Dreaded Sundown, Winds of Autumn, High Flying Lowe, The Evil, Amityville II: The Possession, Playing with Fire, Eliminators, Chill Factor, The Big One, Life on the Edge, Double Exposure, Gettysburg, Inferno, Dark Dancer, Gathering Evidence, Without Evidence, Serial Killer, The Shadow Men, Possums, X-Ray Boys, Critical Mass, Scooby-Doo, Sweet Home Alabama, Gods and Generals, Glass Trap, Daltry Calhoun, Sutures, Beyond the Farthest Star.
TELEVISION: *Movies*: And the Children Shall Lead, Roughing It, Callie & Son, The Deputies, Another Part of the Forest, Night Slaves, Split Second to an Epitaph, Along Came a Spider, Night Slaves, Wonder Woman, Law of the Land, Tail Gunner Joe, Last of the Mohicans, A Small Killing, Mind over Murder, M-Station Hawaii, Christmas Miracle in Caulfield, Young Abe Lincoln, U.S.A., Donner Pass: The Road to Survival, Mission of the Shark, Scattered Dreams: The Kathryn Messenger Story, The Avenging Angel, The Miracle Worker, James Dean, Hollis & Rae. *Mini-series*: V: The Final Battle. *Series*: The Wide Country, The Road West, W.E.B., Dallas, Room for Two, Weird Science. *Guest:* More than 138 appearances.

PRINZE, JR., FREDDIE
Actor. b. Los Angeles, CA, March 8, 1976. Son of late actor Freddie Prinze. Received Mr. Golden Globe Award 1996. m. actress Sarah Michelle Gellar.
PICTURES: To Gillian on Her 37th Birthday, The House of Yes, I Know What You Did Last Summer, Sparkler, I Still Know What You Did Last Summer, Down to You, She's All That, Wing Commander, Head Over Heels, Boys and Girls, Summer Catch, Scooby-Doo, Scooby-Doo 2: Monsters Unleashed, Happily N' Ever After (voice), Delgo (voice), Brooklyn Rules, Jack and Jill vs. the World, Manslaughter (exec. prod.).
TELEVISION: *Movies:* Too Soon for Jeff, Detention: The Siege at Johnson High, Kim Possible: A Sitch in Time (voice), Atlanta, No Heroics. *Series:* Freddie (also creator, writer & exec. prod.), 24. *Guest:* More than 70 appearances.

PROCHNOW, JÜRGEN
Actor. b. Berlin, Germany, June 10, 1941. Studied acting at the Folkwang-Schule. In provinical theatre before making TV debut on the series Harbour at the Rhine River, 1970.
PICTURES: Zoff (debut, 1971), Zartlichkeit der Wolfe, The Lost Honor of Katharina Blum, The Consequence, Einer von uns beiden, Das Boot (The Boat; Berlin Film Fest. Award), The Keep, Dune, Der Bulle und das Madchen, Killing Cars, Terminus, Beverly Hills Cop II, Devil's Paradise, The Seventh Sign, A Dry White Season, The Fourth War, The Man Inside, Twin Peaks: Fire Walk With Me, Interceptor, Body of Evidence The Last Border, Die Wildnis Der Fall Lucona, Trigger FAst, In the Mouth of Madness, Judge Dredd, The English Patient, DNA, Air Force One, The Replacement Killers, Chinadream, The Fall, Wing Commander: Space will never be the Same, Gunblast Vodka, The Last Stop, Elite, Jack the Dog, Last Run, Ripper, Dark Asylum, Heart of America, House of the Dead, The Poet, Baltic Storm, The Celestine Prophecy, The Da Vinci Code, Beerfest, Schroeder's Wonderful World, Primeval, The Eye, The Absinthe Drinkers, Sinners & Saints, Hour of the Gun.
TELEVISION: *Movies:* Unternehmer, Auf Befehl erschossen - Die Brüder Sass, einst Berlins große Ganoven, Tatort-Jaqdrevier, Shirins Hochzeit, Das Tatort - Mädchen von gegenüber, Kotte, Love Is Forever, Murder: By Reason of Insanity, Robin Hood, The Fire Next Time, Lie Down with Lions, Tödliche Wahl, Fesseln, Sorellina e il principe del sogno, On Dangerous Ground, Der Schrei der Liebe, Human Bomb, Esther, Der Blonde Affe, Heaven's Fire, Die Millenium-Katastrophe - Computer-Crash 2000, Poison, Padre Pio, Final Ascent, Davon stirbt man nicht, Julie-chevalier de Maupin, See Arnold Run, Ohne einander, Spear of Destiny. *Mini-series:* Das Boot/The Boat, Danielle Steel's Jewels. *Series:* 24. *Documentaries /Specials:* The Great War and the Shaping of the 20th Century (mini-series documentary, voice). *Guest:* More than 65 appearances.

PRYCE, JONATHAN
Actor. b. North Wales, June 1, 1947. e. Royal Acad. of Dramatic Art. Actor and artistic dir. of Liverpool Everyman Theatre Co.
THEATRE: *London*: Comedians, Taming of the Shrew, Antony and Cleopatra, Tally's Folly, Hamlet (Olivier Award), The Caretaker, Macbeth, The Seagull, Uncle Vanya, Miss Saigon (Olivier & Variety Club Awards), Oliver! *NY*: Comedians (Tony & Theatre World Awards, 1977), Accidental Death of an Anarchist, Miss Saigon (Tony & Drama Desk Awards, 1991).
PICTURES: Voyage of the Damned (debut, 1976), Breaking Glass, Loophole, The Ploughman's Lunch, Something Wicked This Way Comes, The Doctor and the Devils, Brazil, Haunted Honeymoon, Jumpin' Jack Flash, Man on Fire, Consuming Passions, The Adventures of Baron Munchausen, The Rachel Papers, Freddie as F.R.O. 7 (voice), Glengarry Glen Ross, The Age of Innocence, A Business Affair, Great Moments in Aviation, A Troll in Central Park (voice), Deadly Advice, Shopping, Carrington (Cannes Film Fest. Award, 1995), Evita, Tomorrow Never Dies, Ronin, Stigmata, The Testimony of Taliesin Jones, Very Annie Mary, The Suicide Club, Il Gioco, Bride of the Wind, The Affair of the Necklace, Who Shot Victor Fox, What a Girl Wants, Pirates of the Caribbean: The Curse of the Black Pearl, De-Lovely, The Brothers Grimm, The New World, Pirates of the Caribbean: Dead Man's Chest, The Moon and the Stars, Pirates of the Caribbean: At World's End, Leatherheads, Bedtime Stories, Echelon Conspiracy, G.I. Joe: The Rise of Cobra, Hysteria.
TELEVISION: *Movies:* After the Boom was Over, Spasms, Comedians, The Day Christ Died, Timon of Athens, Murder is Easy, Praying Mantis, The Man From the PRU, Barbarians at the Gate (Emmy nom.; Golden Globe nom. 1993), Daft as a Brush,Thicker than Water, Great Moments in Aviation, David, Victoria & Albert, Confessions of an Ugly Stepsister, HR, Baker Street Irregulars. *Mini-series:* Selling Hitler, Mr. Wroe's Virgins, Return to Cranford. *Series:* Roger Doesn't Live Here Anymore, The Union Game: A Rugby History (narrator), Clone (also pilot). *Guest:* More than 90 appearances.

PTAK, JOHN
Consultant, Agent, Producer. b. San Diego, CA. Graduated UCLA film department, 1968. Theatre mgr. and booker for Walter Reade Organization and Laemmle Theatres, 1966-1969. Admin. exec. at American Film Institute's Center for Advanced Studies, 1969-1971. International Famous Agency (ICM), 1971-1975, William Morris Agency, 1976-91, Creative Artists Agency, 1991-May2006. At CAA represented motion picture and television talent and was a film finance specialist, handling finance & dist. deals on more than 100 indie films. After leaving CAA, he immediately teamed with partner Philip Elway to form Arsenal, a firm that advises producers, distributors and private equity funds.
PICTURES: Corso: The Last Beat (doc., exec. prod.), Let Me In (exec. prod.), The Way Back (exec. prod.).

PULLMAN, BILL
Actor. b. Hornell, NY, Dec. 17, 1953. e. SUNY at Oneonta, Univ. of Mass. at Amherst. Worked with various theatre companies, most notably the Folger Theater Groupe and the Los Angeles Theater Center.
THEATRE: *NY*: Dramathon '84, Curse of the Starving Class. *LA*: All My Sons, Barabbas, Nanawatai, Demon Wine, Control Freaks.
PICTURES: Ruthless People (debut, 1986), Spaceballs, The Serpent and the Rainbow, Rocket Gibraltar, The Accidental Tourist, Cold Feet, Brain Dead, Sibling Rivalry, Bright Angel, Going Under, Newsies, A League of Their Own, Singles, Nervous Ticks, Sommersby, Sleepless in Seattle, Malice, Mr. Jones, The Favor, Wyatt Earp, While You Were Sleeping, Casper, Mr. Wrong, Independence Day, The End of Violence, Lost Highway, Zero Effect, The Virginian (also dir.), A Man is Mostly Water, The Guilty, Lake Placid, Brokedown Palace, Titan A.E. (voice), Lucky Numbers, Ignition, Igby Goes Down, 29 Palms, Rick, The Grudge, Dear Wendy, The Orphan King, The 1 Second Film (short; prod. only), Alien Autopsy, Scary Movie 4, You Kill Me, Bottle Shock, Nobel Son, Your Name Here, Surveillance, Phoebe in Wonderland, Peacock, Celestina, Kerosene Cowboys, The Killer Inside Me, Rio Sex Comedy, Bringing Up Bobby.
TELEVISION: *Movies*: Home Fires Burning, Crazy in Love,

Mistrial, The Last Seduction (also released theatrically), Merry Christmas George Bailey, The Virginian (also dir., prod.), Opening the Tombs of the Golden Mummies: Live (co-host), Tiger Cruise. *Mini-series:* Revelations. *Guest:* More than 52 appearances.

PURCELL, PATRICK B.
Executive. b. Dublin, Ireland, March 16, 1943. e. Fordham U., M.B.A., 1973. In pub. & acct., England, 1969-69; acct., Associated Hosp. Service, N.Y., 1968-70; joined Paramount Pictures, 1970; v.p., fin., 1980-83; exec. v.p. chief fin. & admin. officer 1983-1998. Purcell is a member of the Corporate Bd. of the Motion Picture & Television Fund.

PURI, OM
Actor. b. Ambala, India, October 18, 1950.
PICTURES: Ghashiram Kotwal, The Strange Fate of Arvind Desai, Sparsh, A Folk Tale, Cry of the Wounded, Gandhi, The Ascent, Market Place, Who Pays the Piper, Half Truth, The Wave, Party, The Crossing, The Festival of Fire, Spices, New Delhi Times, Genesis, Sam & Me, Narasimha, The Inner Voice, City of Dreams, City of Joy, In Custody, The Burning Season, Ankuram, The Kite, Wold, Target, Kartavya, Brothers in Trouble, The Ghost and the Darkness, Maachis, Ghatak, Droh Kaal, Mrityu Dand, Gupt, My Son the Fanatic, Such a Long Journey, China Gate, Chachi 420, East is East, Hey Ram, Zandagi Zindabad, Kunuwara, The Zookeeper, The Parole Officer, Happy Now, Mystic Masseur, Indian, Deewaanapan, Bollywood Calling, Pitaah, Ansh, Awara Paagal Deewana, Shararat, Ghaav: The Wound, Code 46, Magbool, Aan: Men at Work, Dev, Lakshya, Kyun...Ho Gaya Na, Kisna: The Warrior Poet, Mumbai Express (Hindi version), The Rising: Ballad of Mangal Pandey (narrator; voice), Amar Joshi Shahid Ho Gaya (writer only), Rang De Basanti, Is Pyaar Ko Kya Naam Doon, Chup Chup Ke, Don, Malamaal Weekly, Baabul, Delhii Heights, Fool and Final, Buddha Mar Gaya, Charlie Wilson's War, Shoot on Sight, Lovesongs: Yesterday, Today & Tomorrow, Yaariyan, Wanted Dead and Alive, Singh Is Kinng, Delhi-6, Billu, Kurbaan, London Dreams, West Is West, Society, Dabangg.
TELEVISION: *Movies:* Sadgati, Murder, Second Generation. *Mini-series:* The Jewel in the Crown, Darkness, White Teeth, The Canterbury Tales. *Series:* Mr. Yogi (also narrator).

PURL, LINDA
Actress. b. Greenwich, CT, Sept. 2, 1955. Moved to Japan at age 2. Appeared in Japanese theatre, TV. e. Toho Geino Academy. Back to U.S. in 1971.
THEATRE: The Baby Dance (New Haven, NYC), Hedda Gabler, The Real Thing (Mark Taper), The Merchant of Venice (Old Globe Theatre), Romeo & Juliet, Doll's House, Hallelujah Hallelujah (NYC), Three Penny Opera, Nora, All the Way Home, The Road to Mecca, Long Wharf, Beyond Therapy.
PICTURES: Jory, Crazy Mama, W.C. Fields & Me, Leo and Loree, The High Country, Visiting Hours, Viper, Natural Causes. Mighty Joe Young, Sunday, The Perfect Tennant, Fear of the Dark.
TELEVISION: *Movies*: Eleanor and Franklin, Little Ladies of the Night, Testimony of Two Men, A Last Cry for Help, Women at West Point, Like Normal People, The Flame is Love, The Night the City Screamed, The Adventures of Nellie Bly, The Last Days of Pompeii, The Manions of America, Addicted to His Love, Spies Lies and Naked Thighs, Before the Storm, Spy Games, Danielle Steel's Secrets, Body Language, Accidental Meeting, Incident at Deception Ridge, Born Free: A New Adventure, Absolute Truth, Holy Joe, The Griffin and the Minor Canon, Frozen Impact, Stranger at the Door, Criminal Intent, Maid of Honor. *Series*: The Secret Storm, Beacon Hill, Happy Days, Matlock, Under Cover, Young Pioneers, Robin's Hoods, Port Charles, First Monday, Cold Case. *Guest:* More than 82 appearances.

PUTNAM, KERI
Executive. e. B.A. degree, Harvard University. Began career as asst. at HBO, but left the company for two years to live in Washington, D.C., to work in lit. dept. of the Arena Stage and as dir. of development for Devillier Donegan Enterprises. 1992, Putnam returned to HBO as dir. of development, HBO Showcase, the New York drama division of HBO programming that later became HBO NYC. 1995, Putnam was promoted to v.p., HBO NYC Productions, at the inception of the newly named film division. Under the HBO NYC banner, Putnam was responsible for some of the division's most successful projects, including HBO's highest-rated original movie, "If These Walls Could Talk." In 1999, became senior v.p., HBO Films, and moved to Los Angeles in 2000 to oversee HBO Films productions, where the slate of films has garnered nominations for 197 Emmys® and 37 Golden Globes. In Oct. 2004, Putnam was promoted to executive v.p., HBO Films. In 2005, the slate she oversaw was nominated for a record 51 Emmy® Awards. In March 2006, Putnam left HBO for her current position at Miramax Films-president of production. Putnam is the recipient of the 2005 Excellence in Media Award from Women in Film for her work at HBO and annually makes the "Power 100" women in entertainment list published by The Hollywood Reporter (#72 in 2008).

PUTTNAM, LORD DAVID
Producer. CBE: Hon. LL.D Bristol 1983; Hon. D. Litt, Leicester 1986. Hon. Litt. D., Leeds 1992. Knighted by Queen Elizabeth II in 1995. b. London, England, Feb. 25, 1941. e. Michenden School. In advertising before joining VPS/Goodtimes Prod. Co. Dir. of Britain's National Film Finance Corp. (1980-85); Also served on Cinema Films Council and governing council of the British Acad. of Film & Television Arts. Officier dans L'Ordre des Arts et des Lettres, 1986. Chmn. National Film and Television Sch., 1988. Past Pres., Council for the Protection of Rural England; Fellow, Royal Soc. of Arts; Fellow, Royal Geographical Soc., Hon. Fellow, The Chartered Society of Designers. appt. Chmn. & CEO, Columbia Pictures. Resigned 1987. Received Eastman 2nd Century Award, 1988. 1988 formed a joint venture for his Enigma Productions Ltd. with Warner Bros., Fujisankei Comm. Gp. of Japan, British Satellite Broadcasting & Country Nat West to prod. 4 films. Appt. chmn. ITEL intl. TV dist. agency, 1989. Dir., Anglia Television Group and Survival Anglia. V.P., BAFTA. Founding pres., Atelier du Cinema European. Member, European Commission's 'Think Tank' for audio-visual policy.
PICTURES: *Producer*: Melody, The Pied Piper, That'll Be The Day, Stardust, Brother Can You Spare a Dime?, Lisztomania, The Duellists, Midnight Express (Academy Award nom. 1979), Foxes, Chariots of Fire (Academy Award 1982), Local Hero, Cal, The Killing Fields (Academy Award nom. 1985), The Mission (Academy Award nom. 1987), Memphis Belle, Meeting Venus, Being Human, War of the Buttons, Le Confessionnal, My Life So Far. *Exec. Prod.:* The Last Days of Man on Earth, Mahler, Bugsy Malone, Forever Young, The Frog Prince, Mr. Love, Defense of the Realm, Arthur's Hallowed Ground. *Co-produced documentaries:* Swastika, Double-Headed Eagle: Hitler's Rise to Power 1918-1933, We Are the People We've Been Waiting For.
TELEVISION: *Movies:* Those Glory Glory Days (exec, prod.), P'Tang Yang Kipperbang (exec, prod.), A Dangerous Man: Lawrence After Arabia, Secrets, The Josephine Baker Story (exec. prod., Emmy nom. 1991), Without Warning: The James Brady Story (exec. prod., Emmy nom. 1992) The Burning Season (exec. prod., Emmy nom. 1995). *Documentaries/Specials:* James Dean—The First American Teenager.

PYNE, BEN
Executive. e. B.A. degree, Princeton University; MBA, Harvard Business School. Began career with nonprofit associations. From 1985-1990, orchestra mgr. of the New Jersey Symphony. In 1992, joined Disney serving in increasingly senior sales, marketing and distribution roles in its TV business units. Under Pyne's guidance, Disney Channel transitioned from a pay cable service to an expanded basic service, growing from 6.5 million U.S. subscribers in 1992 to the more than 94 million it has today. From 2000-2004, Pyne was senior v.p., affiliate sales and marketing for Disney-ABC Cable Networks Group. He managed all cable and satellite distribution, local ad sales and affiliate marketing for the four basic cable networks within the Group: ABC Family, Disney Channel, SOAPnet and Toon Disney. From June 2004-Sept. 2005, Pyne was executive v.p., Disney and ESPN affiliate sales and marketing; Oct. 2005, promoted to pres., Disney & ESPN Networks affiliate sales and marketing; June 2007, promoted to current position-pres., global distribution, Disney Media Networks. He has chief responsibility for the intl. distribution and sales of entertainment and news content produced by The Walt Disney Company.

QUAID, DENNIS
Actor. b. Houston, TX Apr. 9, 1954. Brother is actor Randy Quaid. e. U. of Houston. Appeared in Houston stage productions before leaving for Hollywood. On N.Y. stage with his brother in True West, 1984. Performer with rock band The Electrics; wrote songs for films The Night the Lights Went Out in Georgia, Tough Enough, The Big Easy. Formed Summers/Quaid Productions with producer Cathleen Summers, 1989.
PICTURES: Crazy Mama (debut, 1975), I Never Promised You a Rose Garden, September 30, 1955, Our Winning Season, Seniors, G.O.R.P., Breaking Away, The Long Riders, All Night Long, Caveman, The Night the Lights Went Out in Georgia, Tough Enough, Jaws 3-D, The Right Stuff, Dreamscape, Enemy Mine, The Big Easy, Innerspace, Suspect, D.O.A., Everybody's All-American, Great Balls of Fire, Postcards From the Edge, Come See the Paradise, Wilder Napalm, Undercover Blues, Flesh & Bone, Wyatt Earp, Hideaway (co-prod. only), Something to Talk About, Dragonheart, Gang Related, Switchback, Playing by Heart, The Parent Trap, Savior, Any Given Sunday, Frequency, Traffic, Stranger than the Wheel, The Rookie, Far From Heaven (Golden Globe nom. 2003), Cold Creek Manor, The Alamo, The Day After Tomorrow, In Good Company, Flight of the Phoenix, Yours Mine & Ours, American Dreamz, Smart People, The Horsemen, Vantage Point, Terra (voice), The Horsemen, The Express, Legion, Pandorum, G.I. Joe: The Rise of Cobra, Soul Surfer.
TELEVISION: *Movies*: Are You in the House Alone?, Amateur Night at the Dixie Bar and Grill, Bill, Johnny Belinda, Bill: On His Own, Everything That Rises (also dir., exec. prod.), Dinner with Friends, Freedom: A History of Us (series doc.), The Special Relationship. *Guest:* More than 89 appearances.

QUAID, RANDY

Actor. b. Houston, TX, Oct. 1, 1950. Brother is actor Dennis Quaid. Discovered by Peter Bogdanovich while still junior at Drama Dept. at U. of Houston and cast in his Targets and The Last Picture Show, 1971. Off-B'way debut: True West (1983).
PICTURES: Targets (debut, 1968), The Last Picture Show, What's Up Doc?, Paper Moon, Lolly-Madonna XXX, The Last Detail (Academy Award nom.; Golden Globe nom. 1974), The Apprenticeship of Duddy Kravitz, Breakout, The Missouri Breaks, Bound for Glory, The Choirboys, Midnight Express, Three Warriors, Foxes, The Long Riders, Heartbeeps, National Lampoon's Vacation, The Wild Life, The Slugger's Wife, Fool for Love, The Wraith, Sweet Country, No Man's Land, Moving, Caddyshack II, Parents, Bloodhounds of Broadway, Out Cold, National Lampoon's Christmas Vacation, Martians Go Home!, Days of Thunder, Quick Change, Cold Dog Soup, Texasville, Freaked, The Paper, Major League 2, Bye Bye Love, The Last Dance, Independence Day, Kingpin, Vegas Vacation, P.U.N.K.S., Bug Buster, Hard Rain, The Adventures of Rocky and Bullwinkle, George Wallace: Settin' the Woods on Fire (narrator), Not Another Teen Movie, Under the Mimosa, The Adventures of Pluto Nash, Frank McKlusky C.I., Carolina, Kart Racer, Back By Midnight, Milwaukee / Minnesota, Carolina, Grind, Kart Racer, Black Cadillac, Home on the Range (voice), Brokeback Mountain, The Ice Harvest, Goya's Ghosts, Last Flag Flying, Real Time, Balls Out: The Gary Houseman Story, Last Flag Flying.
TELEVISION: *Movies*: Getting Away From It All, The Great Niagara, The Last Ride of the Dalton Gang, To Race the Wind, Guyana Tragedy: The Story of Jim Jones, Of Mice and Men, Inside the Third Reich, Cowboy, A Streetcar Named Desire (Emmy nom. 1984), LBJ: The Early Years (Emmy nom.; Golden Globe Award 1987), Dead Solid Perfect, Evil in Clear River, Murder in the Heartland, Frankenstein, Roommates, Next Door, Ed McBain's 87th Precinct, The Siege at Ruby Ridge, Woman Undone, Moonshine Highway, Sands of Eden, Water War, Protector, Purgatory, The Magical Legend of the Leprechauns, Mail to the Chief, The Thin Blue Lie, The Day the World Ended, Christmas Vacation 2: Cousin Eddie's Island Adventure, Category 6: Day of Destruction, 5 Days to Midnight. *Mini-series:* Streets of Laredo, Elvis (Emmy nom.; Golden Globe nom. 2005), Category 7: The End of the World, Texas Ranch House (narr.). *Series*: Saturday Night Live (1985-86), Davis Rules, Gun, The Grubbs, The Brotherhood of Poland-NH. *Documentaries/Specials:* Dear America: Letters Home from Vietnam (reader), George Wallace: Settin' the Woods on Fire (narrator). *Guest:* More than 64 appearances.

QUIGLEY, MARTIN, JR.
Writer, Educator. b. Chicago, IL, Nov. 24, 1917. e. A.B. Georgetown U.; M.A., Ed. D., Columbia U. M.P. Herald, Oct. 1939; special ed. rep., M.P. Herald & M.P. Daily, May, 1941. U.S. Office of Coordination of Info., 1942; U.S. Office of Strategic Services, Special Intelligence Div., Eire & Italy, 1943-45. Assoc. ed., Quigley Pub., Oct. 1945; ed. M.P. Herald, July 1949; also edit. dir. of all Quigley Pub., 1956; pres., Quigley Publishing Company, 1964-2001. Editor: New Screen Techniques, 1953; m.p. tech. section, Encyclopedia Brit., 1956. Pres., QWS, Inc., ed. cons., 1975-81. Adjunct prof. of higher ed., Baruch College Univ. City of N.Y. 1977-89; Teachers College, Columbia Univ., 1990. Village of Larchmont, N.Y., trustee, 1977-79; mayor, 1980-84. Bd. of trustees, American Bible Society, 1984-; Religious Ed. Association, treasurer, 1975-80 & chairperson, 1981-84; Laymen's Nat'l. Bible Association, chmn. ed. com., 1983-93; Will Rogers Institute, chmn. Health ed. com., 1980-97; dir., William J. Donovan Memorial Foundation, 1995-2002.
CO-AUTHOR: Catholic Action in Practice, 1963; Films in America, 1929-69, 1970.
AUTHOR: Great Gaels, 1944; Roman Notes, 1946; Magic Shadows—The Story of the Origin of Motion Pictures, 1948; Gov't. Relations of Five Universities, 1975; Peace Without Hiroshima, 1991; First Century of Film, 1995; A U.S. Spy In Ireland, 1999; American edition 2002; Community College Movement In Perspective, 2003. Martin Quigley and the Glory Days of the American Film - 1915-1965, 2006.

QUIGLEY, WILLIAM J.
Executive, Producer. b. New York, NY, July 6, 1951. e. Wesleyan U., B.A., 1973; Columbia U., M.S., 1983. From 1973 to 1974 was advertising circulation mgr. for Quigley Publishing Company. Taught school in Kenya in 1974; returned to U.S. to join Grey Advertising as media planner. 1975 joined Walter Reade Organization as asst. film buyer; promoted to head film buyer in 1977. Named v.p., 1982. In 1986 joined Vestron, Inc. as senior v.p. to establish Vestron Pictures. Named pres., Vestron Pictures, 1987-89. In 1990 joined Fair Lanes Entertainment, Inc. as v.p. mktg. 1993, joined United Artists Theatre Circuit as senior v.p.,marketing & new business. 1997, pres., Entertainment Express; partner, Spellbound Pictures. Executive V.P. Mann Theatres, 1998-99. Founder and pres., QP Media 1999-present. President, Quigley Publishing Company, Inc., 2001-present.
PICTURES: *Executive producer*: Steel Dawn, The Dead, Salome's Last Dance, The Unholy, Waxwork, Burning Secret, The Lair of the White Worm, Paint It Black, The Rainbow, Twister.

QUINLAN, KATHLEEN
Actress. b. Pasadena, CA, Nov. 19, 1954. Played small role in film, One Is a Lonely Number, while in high school.
THEATRE: Taken in Marriage (NY Public Theatre; Theatre World Award), Uncommon Women and Others, Accent on Youth (Long Wharf, CT), Les Liaisons Dangereuses.
PICTURES: One Is a Lonely Number (debut, 1972), American Graffiti, Lifeguard, Airport '77, I Never Promised You a Rose Garden (Golden Globe nom. 1978), The Promise, The Runner Stumbles, Sunday Lovers, Hanky Panky, Independence Day, Twilight Zone—The Movie, The Last Winter, Warning Sign, Wild Thing, Man Outside, Sunset, Clara's Heart, The Doors, Trial by Jury, Apollo 13 (Academy Award nom.; Golden Globe nom. 1996), Perfect Alibi, Zeus and Roxanne, Breakdown, Event Horizon, Lawn Dogs, A Civil Action, My Giant, The Battle of Shaker Heights, El Padrino, The Hills Have Eyes, Breach, Made of Honor, The River Why, After.
TELEVISION: *Movies*: Can Ellen Be Saved?, Lucas Tanner (pilot), Where Have All the People Gone?, The Missing Are Deadly, The Abduction of St. Anne, Turning Point of Jim Malloy, Little Ladies of the Night, She's in the Army Now, When She Says No, Blackout, Children of the Night, Dreams Lost Dreams Found, Trapped, The Operation, Strays, An American Story, Stolen Babies, Last Light, In the Lake of the Woods, Blessings, Perfect Romance, The Riverman, The Dead Will Tell, Empire State. *Mini-series:* Picture Window: Language of the Heart, Too Rich: The Secret Life of Doris Duke. *Series:* Hollywood Squares, Family Law, Prison Break. *Guest:* More than 60 appearances.

QUINN, AIDAN
Actor. b. Chicago, IL, March 8, 1959. Raised in Rockwell, IL, also spent time in Ireland as a boy and following high sch. graduation. Returned to Chicago at 19, worked as tar roofer before debuting on Chicago stage in The Man in 605, followed by Scheherazade, The Irish Hebrew Lesson, Hamlet.
THEATRE: Fool for Love (off-B'way debut), A Lie of the Mind, A Streetcar Named Desire (Theatre World Award).
PICTURES: Reckless (debut, 1984), Desperately Seeking Susan, The Mission, Stakeout, Crusoe, The Handmaid's Tale, The Lemon Sisters, Avalon, At Play in the Fields of the Lord, The Playboys, Benny & Joon, Blink, Mary Shelley's Frankenstein, Legends of the Fall, The Stars Fell on Henrietta, Haunted, Looking for Richard, Michael Collins, Commandments, The Assignment, This is My Father (also exec. prod.), Practical Magic, Songcatcher, Music of the Heart, In Dreams, Songcatcher, The Messiah XXI, Stolen Summer, Evelyn, Song for a Raggy Boy, Bobby Jones Stroke of Genius, Cavedweller, Shadow of Fear, Return to Sender, Proudly We Served, Nine Lives, Dark Matter, 32A, Wild Child, A Shine of Rainbows, The Eclipse, Handsome Harry, The 5th Quarter, Flipped.
TELEVISION: *Movies*: An Early Frost (Emmy nom. 1986), Perfect Witness, Lies of the Twins, Miss Sherri, Forbidden Territory: Stanley's Search for Livingstone, Two of Us, The Prince and the Pauper, Benedict Arnold: A Question of Honor, Plainsong, Miracle Run, The Exonerated, Mayday, Bury My Heart at Wounded Knee (Emmy nom. 2007). *Mini-series:* Empire Falls. *Series*: Project Greenlight (series documentary), The Book of Daniel, Canterbury's Law. *Documentaries/Specials*: Baseball (narrator; TV documentary), The Irish in America (voice), Out of Ireland (narrator; TV documentary), All My Sons, Lumière and Company, The Messiah XXI (narr.), Freedom: A History of Us (series). *Guest:* Morre than 66 appearances.

R

RABE, DAVID WILLIAM
Writer. b. Dubuque, IA, March 10, 1940. m. actress Jill Clayburgh. e. Loras Coll., B.A., 1962. Villanova Univ., M.A., 1968.
THEATRE: The Basic Training of Pavlo Hummel (Obie Award, 1971), Sticks and Bones (Tony Award, 1971), The Orphan, In the Boom Boom Room, Streamers, Hurlyburly, Those the River Keeps.
PICTURES: Sticks and Bones (play), I'm Dancing As Fast As I Can (also exec. prod.), Streamers (play and s.p.), Casualties of War, The Firm, Hurlyburly, The Untouchables: Capone Rising.
TELEVISION: *Documentaries/Specials:* Sticks and Bones.

RABINOVITZ, JASON
Executive. b. Boston, MA, e. Harvard Coll., B.A. where elected to Phi Beta Kappa. Following WWII service as military intelligence captain with paratroops, earned M.B.A. at Harvard Business School, 1948. Started in industry in 1949 as asst. to secty.-treas., United Paramount Theatres. Asst. controller, ABC, 1953; adm. v.p., ABC-TV, 1956; joined MGM as asst. treas., 1957; named MGM-TV gen. mgr., dir. of business & financial affairs, 1958; treas. & CFO, MGM, Inc., 1963; financial v.p. & CFO, 1967. 1971, named exec. v.p. & dir. Encyclopedia Britannica Education Corp.; sr. v.p., American Film Theatre, 1974-75. Rejoined MGM as v.p./exec. asst. to the pres., 1976. Elected v.p. finance, 1979; promoted to sr. v.p., finance & corporate admin., MGM Film Co. & UA Communications, Inc. Resigned, 1984. Now film & TV consultant and indep. prod. Dir., Pacific Rim Entertainment, 1993-95. Retired.

RADCLIFFE, DANIEL
Actor. b. Fulham, UK, July 23, 1989.

THEATRE: *London/B'way:* The Tailor of Panama, Equus.
PICTURES: The Tailor of Panama, Harry Potter and the Sorcerer's Stone, Harry Potter and the Chamber of Secrets, Harry Potter and the Prisoner of Azkaban, Harry Potter and the Goblet of Fire, Harry Potter and the Order of the Phoenix, December Boys, Harry Potter and the Half-Blood Prince, Harry Potter and the Deathly Hallows: Part I, Harry Potter and the Deathly Hallows: Part II.
TELEVISION: *Movies:* David Copperfield, The Children's Party at the Palace, My Boy Jack. *Guest:* More than 90 appearances.

RADFORD, MICHAEL
Director, Writer. b. New Dehli, India, Feb. 24, 1946. e. Oxford U. Worked briefly as a teacher before becoming documentary filmmaker.
PICTURES: *Director & Writer.* Another Time Another Place, Nineteen Eight-Four, White Mischief, The Postman (Academy Award nom., DGA nom. 1996), The Swedish Cavalier, B. Monkey, Dancing at the Blue Iguana, Ten Minutes Older: The Cello, The Merchant of Venice, The Mule (also co-prod.). *Director:* Delta of Venus, The Elixir, Tania, The Letters, Puss 'n Boots, Flawless, Michel Petrucciani (doc.), King Lear (also s.p.). *Producer:* Love Is Like a Violin (doc.).
TELEVISION: *Movies*: The White Bird Passes (dir.). *Series:* Ripping Yarns (photographer).

RADNITZ, ROBERT B.
Producer. b. Great Neck, NY, Aug. 9, 1924. e. U. of VA. Taught 2 years at U. of VA, then became reader for Harold Clurman; wrote several RKO This Is America scripts, then to Broadway where co-prod. The Frogs of Spring; prod. The Young and the Beautiful; to Hollywood working at United Artists, then as story consultant to Buddy Adler, head of prod., 20th Century-Fox, 1957-58. V.P., Producer Guild of America, 1982, 1984, 1985; has been a bd. member, Producers Branch, AMPAS. First producer with retrospective at Museum of Modern Art, and first producer honored by joint resolution of both houses of Congress for his work, 1973. Pres. Robert B. Radnitz Productions, Ltd.
PICTURES: *Producer.* A Dog of Flanders (debut, 1960; first U.S. film to win Golden Lion Award at Venice Film Fest.), Misty, Island of the Blue Dolphins, And Now Miguel, My Side of the Mountain, The Little Ark, Sounder (Academy Award nom. 1973), Where the Lilies Bloom, Birch Interval, Sounder 2, A Hero Ain't Nothin' But a Sandwich, Cross Creek.
TELEVISION: Mary White (Emmy & Christopher Awards), Never Forget (ACE Award nom.).
(d. June 10, 2010)

RAFELSON, BOB
Producer, Director, Writer. b. New York, NY, Feb. 21, 1933. e. Dartmouth, B.A. (philosophy). Left NY in teens to ride in rodeos in AZ. Worked on cruise ship, then played drums and bass with jazz combos in Acapulco. 1953 won Frost Natl. Playwriting competition. Dir. his award-winning play at Hanover Experimental Theatre, N.H. After Army Service did program promotion for a radio station, was advisor for Shochiku Films, Japan, then hired by David Susskind to read scripts for Talent Assocs. Writer-assoc. prod., DuPont Show of the Month and Play of the Week (also script supervisor). Joined Screen Gems in California, developing program ideas for Jackie Cooper, then head of TV prod. arm of Columbia. Later formed BBS Productions with Burt Schneider and Steve Blauner. Appeared as actor in 1985 film Always.
PICTURES: *Producer/Director/Writer:* Head, Five Easy Pieces (2 Academy Award noms.; 2 Golden Globe noms.; DGA nom. 1971), The King of Marvin Gardens, Stay Hungry (WGA nom. 1977). *Director/Writer:* Mountains of the Moon, Wet (short), Blood & Wine, Tales of Erotica, Erotic Tales - Porn.com (also editor). *Director:* Modesty, The Postman Always Rings Twice (also prod.), Black Widow, Man Trouble, The House on Turk Street, No Good Deed. *Co-Prod.*: Easy Rider, The Last Picture Show, Drive He Said. *Actor:* Mora, Always, Leaving Las Vegas, Who is Henry Jaglon (doc., as himself).
TELEVISION: *Movies:* Poodle Springs (dir.). *Mini-series:* Picture Windows: Language of the Heart (dir.). *Series*: The Monkees (1966-68, creator, writer, dir.; Emmy Award, 1967), Adapted 34 prods., Play of the Week. *Documentaries/Specials:* Afterthoughts (dir.).

RAFFIN, DEBORAH
Actress. b. Los Angeles, CA, March 13, 1953. Mother is actress Trudy Marshall. e. Valley Coll. Was active fashion model before turning to acting when discovered by Ted Witzer. Debut in 40 Carats (1973). Publisher Dove Books On Tape. Head of Dove Films, prod. co.
AUTHOR: Sharing Christmas (Vols. I & II).
PICTURES: 40 Carats, The Dove, Once Is Not Enough, God Told Me To, Assault on Paradise, The Sentinel, Touched by Love (Golden Globe nom. 1981), Dance of the Dwarfs, Death Wish 3, Claudia, Scanners II: The New Order, Wilde (exec. prod. only).
TELEVISION: *Movies*: A Nightmare in Badham County, Ski Lift to Death, How to Pick Up Girls, Willa, Mind Over Murder, Haywire, For the Love of It, Killing at Hell's Gate, For Lovers Only, Running Out, Sparkling Cyanide, Threesome, The Sands of Time, Morning Glory (also co-s.p.), A Perry Mason Mystery: The Case of the Grimacing Governor, Home Song, Family Blessings (prod., dir. only), Unwed Father (prod. only), Futuresport (exec. prod.), Book of Days. *Mini-series*: The Last Convertible, James Clavell's Noble House, Windmills of the Gods (also co-prod.). *Series*: Foul Play, 7th Heaven, The Secret Life of the American Teenager. *Guest:* More than 45 appearances.

RAGLAND, ROBERT O.
Composer. b. Chicago, IL, July 3, 1931. e. Northwestern U., American Conservatory of Music, Vienna Acad. of Music. Professional pianist at Chicago nightclubs. In U.S. Navy; on discharge joined Dorsey Bros. Orchestra as arranger. On sls. staff at NBC-TV, Chicago. 1970, moved to Hollywood to become composer for movies; has scored more than 58 feature films plus many TV movies and series segments. Has also written some 45 original songs.
PICTURES: The Touch of Melissa, The Yin and Yang of Mr. Go, The Thing with Two Heads, Project: Kill, Abby, Seven Alone, The Eyes of Dr. Chaney, Return to Macon County, The Daring Dobermans, Shark's Treasure, Grizzly, Pony Express Rider, Mansion of the Doomed, Mountain Family Robinson, Only Once in a Lifetime, Jaguar Lives, The Glove, Lovely But Deadly, "Q", The Day of the Assassin, A Time To Die, The Winged Serpent, Trial by Terror, The Guardian, Ten to Midnight, Dirty Rebel, Hysterical, Brainwaves, Where's Willie?, The Supernaturals, Nightstick, Pretty Kill, Deep Space, Messenger of Death, The Fifth Monkey, No Place to Hide, The Buffalo Soldiers, The Raffle, Morty, The Fear, Evil Obsession, Warhead, Top of the World, Plato's Run, Motel Blue, Pearl Harbor, Crime & Punishment, Downtown: A Street Tale.
TELEVISION: Photoplay's Stars of Tomorrow, Wonder Woman, Barnaby Jones, Streets of San Francisco, High Ice, The Girl on the Edge of Town, The Guardian, Conspiracy of Silence, Nightstick.

RAILSBACK, STEVE
Actor. b. Dallas, TX, Nov. 16,1948. Studied with Lee Strasberg. On stage in Orpheus Descending, This Property Is Condemned, Cherry Orchard, Skin of Our Teeth, etc.
PICTURES: The Visitors, Cockfighter, Angela, The Stunt Man (Golden Globe nom. 1981), Escape 2000, Deadly Games, Turkey Shoot, Veliki Transport, The Golden Seal, Torchlight, Lifeforce, Armed and Dangerous, The Wind (video), The Survivalist, Scenes from the Goldmine, Distortions, Blue Monkey, Deadly Intent (video), The Assassin, La Cruz de Iberia, Scissors, Alligator II: The Mutation, Forever, After-Shock (video), Calendar Girl, Save Me, Private Wars, Nukie, Final Mission (video), The Flight of the Dove (dir. only), The Stars Fell on Henrietta (assoc. prod.), Barb Wire, Street Corner Justice, Stranger in the House, Pressure Point, Disturbing Behavior, Made Men, Me and Will, In the Light of the Moon (also exec. prod.), Termination Man, Storytelling, Zigs, Slash, The Box, The Hitcher II: I've been Waiting, The In Between, Neo Ned, The Devil's Rejects, Plaguers, Plaguers, Follow the Prophet, Once Fallen.
TELEVISION: *Movies*: Helter Skelter, Charlie Siringo, Good Cops Bad Cops, The Forgotten, Sunstroke, Bonds of Love, Separated by Murder, Vanishing Point, Supernatural (pilot), Ready or Not (pilot). *Mini-series*: Spearfield's Daughter, From Here to Eternity. *Series:* The Visitor, Supernatural (pilot).

RAIMI, SAM
Director, Writer, Producer, Actor. b. Royal Oak, MI, Oct. 23, 1959. e. Michigan St. Univ. Formed Renaissance Pictures, Inc.
PICTURES: *Director.* It's Murder!, The Evil Dead (also s.p., exec. prod. & acting), Clockwork, Crimewave (also s.p.), Evil Dead II, Darkman (also s.p.), Army of Darkness (also s.p. & editor), The Quick and the Dead, A Simple Plan, For the Love of the Game, The Gift, Spider-Man, Spider-Man 2, Spider-Man 3 (also writer), Drag Me to Hell (also prod., writer), Warcraft (also prod.). *Writer:* The Nutt House (s.p. as Alan Smithee, Jr.), Easy Wheels (as Celia Abrams; also exec. prod.), The Hudsucker Proxy (also 2nd unit dir.). *Producer:* Timecop, Boogeyman, The Grudge, The Messengers, 30 Days of Night, Priest, Armored. *Executive producer:* The Dead Next Door (as The Master Cylinder), Lunatics: A Love Story, Hard Target, Rise, The Grudge 2, Rise: Blood Hunter. *Actor.* Stryker's War, Spies Like Us, Thou Shalt Not Kill...Except, Maniac Cop, Maniac Cop 2, Miller's Crossing, Innocent Blood, Indian Summer, Intruder, The Hudsucker Proxy (also co-writer), The Flintstones, Galaxis.
TELEVISION: *Movies*: *Actor:* Journey to the Center of the Earth, Body Bags, The Stand. *Writer:* M.A.N.T.I.S. (also exec. prod.). *Executive producer:* Hercules and the Amazon Women, Hercules and the Lost Kingdom, Hercules: The Legendary Journeys, Hercules in the Underworld, Hercules in the Maze of the Minotaur. *Mini-series:* The Shining (actor), Wizard's First Rule (dir., exec. prod.). *Series: Executive producer:* M.A.N.T.I.S., Hercules: The Lengendary Journeys, Xena: Warrior Princess, American Gothic, Spy Game, Young Hercules, Jack of All Trades, Cleopatra 2525, 13: Fear Is Real, Spartacus: Blood and Sand, Legend of the Seeker.

RAJSKI, PEGGY
Producer. b. Stevens Point, WI. e. Univ. of Wisconsin. Began film career as prod. manager on John Sayles film Lianna, before becoming producer. Prod. of Bruce Springsteen music videos, including Glory Days which won American Video Award.
PICTURES: The Brother From Another Planet, Matewan, Eight

Men Out, The Grifters, Little Man Tate (also 2nd unit dir.), Used People, Trevor (short, also dir., Academy Award 1995), Home for the Holidays, Boy's Life 2, The Scoundrel's Wife, Bee Season, Towelhead (exec. prod.), Grassroots.

RALPH, SHERYL LEE
Actress. b. Waterbury, CT, Dec. 30, 1956. e. Rutgers U. Studied with Negro Ensemble Company in NYC.
THEATRE: *NY*: Reggae, Dreamgirls. *LA*: Identical Twins From Baltimore.
PICTURES: A Piece of the Action (debut, 1977), Oliver & Company (voice), The Mighty Quinn, Skin Deep, To Sleep With Anger, Hollywood Mistress, The Distinguished Gentleman, Sister Act 2: Back in the Habit, The Flintstones, White Man's Burden, Bogus, Lover's Knot, Personals, Deterrence, Unconditional Love, Lost in the Pershing Point Hotel, Baby of the Family, Frankie D, The Cost of Heaven, Blessed and Cursed.
TELEVISION: *Movies*: The Neighborhood, Code Name: Foxfire, Pros & Cons, Sister Margaret and the Saturday Night Ladies, Luck of the Draw: The Gambler Returns, No Child of Mine, Acalpulco Black Film Festival, Witch Hunt, The Jennie Project, Odicie. *Series*: Search for Tomorrow, Code Name: Foxfire, It's a Living, New Attitude, Designing Women, George, Moesha, The Wild Thornberrys (voices), The Parkers (dir.), Exes & Oh's (pilot). *Specials*: Happy 100th Birthday Hollywood, Children of Africa, Voices That Care, Story of a People: The Black Road to Hollywood (host). *Guest*: More than 98 appearances.

RAMIS, HAROLD
Writer, Director, Actor, Producer. b. Chicago, IL, Nov. 21, 1944. e. Washington U., St. Louis, MO. Assoc. ed. Playboy Mag. 1968-70; writer, actor, Second City, Chicago 1970-73; National Lampoon Radio Show, 1974-75. Recipient of Chicago Film Critics "Commitment to Chicago" Award, 1997. 2001 inducted into the American Screenwriting Hall of Fame.
PICTURES: *Writer:* Animal House (WGA nom. 1079), Meatballs, Caddyshack (also dir.), Stripes (also acting), Ghost Busters, Back to School (also exec. prod.), Club Paradise (also dir.), Armed and Dangerous, Caddyshack II, Ghostbusters II (also acting), Rover Dangerfield, Groundhog Day (also dir., prod. & acting), Analyze This (also dir.), Bedazzled (also dir., prod.), Analyze That, È già ieri (Italian film; s.p. for Groundhog Day). *Director:* Vacation, Multiplicity (also prod.), Ice Harvest. *Actor:* Heavy Metal (voice), Baby Boom, Stealing Home, Airheads, Love Affair, As Good As It Gets, Orange County, I'm With Lucy, The Last Kiss, Knocked Up, Walk Hard: The Dewey Cox Story, Year One (also co-prod., writer, dir.). *Executive producer*: The First $20 Million Is Always the Hardest, I Want Someone to Eat Cheese With.
TELEVISION: *Movies:* The Inspector General (prod.), Atlanta (dir.). *Series*: *Writer:* SCTV (head writer, performer, 1976-78), The Real Ghost Busters, Rodney Dangerfield Show (head writer, prod.), Extreme Ghostbusters, The Office (dir., only). *Documentaries/Specials*: Will Rogers—Look Back and Laugh (exec. prod.), Comic Relief.

RAMPLING, CHARLOTTE
Actress. b. Sturmer, England, Feb. 5, 1945. e. Jeanne D'Arc Academie pour Jeune Filles, Versailles; St. Hilda's, Bushey, England.
PICTURES: The Knack...and How to Get It (debut, 1965), Rotten to the Core, Georgy Girl, The Long Duel, Sequestro di Persona, The Damned, Target: Harry, Three, The Ski Bum, Corky, Addio Fratello Crrudele, Asylum, The Night Porter, Giordano Bruno, Zardoz, Caravan to Vaccares, La Chair de L'orchidee, Farewell My Lovely, Foxtrot, Yuppi-Du, Orca, Purple Taxi, Stardust Memories, The Verdict, Viva La Vie, Tristesse et Beaute, On ne Meurt que deux Fois, Angel Heart, Mascara, D.O.A., Max My Love, Rebus, Paris By Night, Helmut Newton: Frames from the Edge (doc.), Hammers Over the Anvil, Time is Money, Invasion of Privacy, Asphalt Tango, Wings of the Dove, Varya, Signs and Wonders, Tribute to Alfred Lepetit, Aberdeen, Under the Sand, Clouds: Letters to My Son, The Fourth Angel, Supersitition, Voyez comme on danse, I'll Sleep When I'm Dead, Spy Game, Embrassez qui vous voudrez, Swimming Pool, The Statement, Immortal (ad vitam), Le Chiavi di casa (The Keys to the House), Lemming, Basic Instinct 2, Angel, Deception, Babylon A.D., Boogie Woogie, The Duchess, Purple America, Blame It on Mum, Life During Wartime, Never Let Me Go, Rio Sex Comedy, StreetDance 3D, The Mill and the Cross, The Eye of the Storm, Melancholia, Cleanskin.
TELEVISION: *Movies*: Sherlock Holmes in New York, Infidelities, La Femme Abandonnee, Murder In Mind, The Fantasists, Mystery of Cader Ifan, Samson Le Maqnifique, La Dernière Fête, Great Expectations, Imperium: Augustus, Le grand restaurant. *Mini-series:* Radetzkymarsch. *Series*: The Six Wives of Henry VIII, The Superlative Seven, The Avengers, My Uncle Silas, Fringe. *Guest:* More than 70 appearances.

RAMSEY, CRAIG R.
Executive. B.S. degree in accounting and business admin., Univ. of Kansas. Ramsey, a certified public accountant, began his career with AMC Entertainment Inc. in 1995 as dir., financial reporting. Promoted to v.p., finance in Jan. 1997; to senior v.p. in Aug. 1998; and to CFO in Feb. 2000. Today, Ramsey is executive v.p. & CFO. His professional affiliations include membership in the American Institute of Certified Public Accountants, the Financial Executives Institute and the Missouri Society of Certified Public Accountants. AMC, headquartered in Kansas City, MO, has interests in 307 theatres with 4,610 screens in 30 states and the District of Columbia and four countries outside the U.S., as of July 2009.

RAPAPORT, MICHAEL
Actor. b. New York, NY, March 20, 1970. Started as stand-up comic appearing at Improv in LA before becoming actor.
PICTURES: Zebrahead, Point of No Return, Poetic Justice, Money for Nothing, True Romance, The Scout, Hand Gun, The Foot Shooting Party, Higher Learning, Kiss of Death, The Basketball Diaries, Mighty Aphrodite, Beautiful Girls, The Pallbearer, Illtown, Metro, A Brother's Kiss, Kicked in the Head, Cop Land, Palmetto, Some Girl, The Naked Man, Deep Blue Sea, Kiss Toledo Goodbye, Next Friday, Small Time Crooks, Men of Honor, Bamboozled, Chain of Fools, Lucky Numbers, The 6th Day, Dr. Dolittle 2, King of the Jungle, Comic Book Villains, Paper Soldiers, Triggermen, 29 Palms (also exec. prod.), A Good Night to Die, This Girl's Life, Live Free or Die, Hitch, Assassination of a High School President, The Saints of Mt. Christopher, Tom Cool, Big Fan, A Day in the Life, Beats Rhymes and Life (doc., also dir.), Inside Out.
TELEVISION: *Movies:* Subway Stories: Tales from the Underground, Rescuers: Stories of Courage: Two Families, Thugaboo: Sneaker Madness (voice), Fugly. *Series:* Boston Public, The War at Home, My Name Is Earl, Prison Break, The Line (pilot). *Guest:* More than 58 appearances.

RAPHAEL, FREDERIC
Writer. b. Chicago, IL, Aug. 14, 1931. e. Charterhouse, St. John's Coll., Cambridge. Won the Royal TV Society Writer Award in 1976 for The Glittering Prizes.
AUTHOR: The Earlsdon Way, The Limits of Love, A Wild Surmise, The Graduate Wife, The Trouble With England, Lindmann, Orchestra and Beginners, Like Men Betrayed, Who Were You With Last Night?, April June and November, Richard's Things, California Time, The Glittering Prizes, Sleeps Six & Other Stories, Oxbridge Blues & Other Stories, Heaven & Earth, Think of England and other stories, After the War, A Double Life, The Latin over and other stories, Old Scores. Biographies: Somerset Maugham and His World, Byron. Translations: (with Kenneth McLeish), Poems of Catullus The Oresteia. Essays: Cracks in the Ice, Of Gods and Men.
THEATRE: From the Greek (1979), An Early Life.
PICTURES: Bachelor of Hearts, Why Bother to Knock, Nothing But the Best, Darling (Academy Award, 1966), Two for the Road (Academy Award nom. 1968), Far from the Madding Crowd, A Severed Head, Daisy Miller, Richard's Things, The King's Whore, Eyes Wide Shut, Rabbit Fever.
TELEVISION: *Movies:* Weiß gibt auf, Rogue Male, Of Mycenae and Men (short), School Play, The Man in the Brooks Brothers Shirt (also dir.; ACE Award best picture), Women and Men: Stories of Seduction (also dir.),Coast to Coast. *Mini-series:* Un monsieur bien rangé, The Glittering Prizes, Oresteia, Oxbridge Blues (ACE Award, best writer), After the War, Picture Windows: Language of the Heart. *Series:* The Best of Friends.

RAPPOPORT, GERALD J.
Executive. b. New York, NY, Aug. 25, 1925. e. NYU. U.S. Marine Corps. Pres., Major Artists Representatives Corp., 1954-58; dir. of Coast Sound Services, Hollywood, 1959-61; pres., International Film Exchange Ltd., 1960-91; CEO of IFEX Int'l, 1991-94; pres., CIFEX Corporation, 1995-present.

RASHAD, PHYLICIA
Actress-singer. b. Houston, TX, June 19, 1948. Sister is Debbie Allen. e. Howard U., B.F.A., magna cum laude, 1970. NY School of Ballet. Acted under maiden name of Phylicia Ayers-Allen. Recording, Josephine Superstar (1979). Conceived (with Michael Peters) and appeared in revue Phylicia Rashad & Co. in 1989 in Las Vegas.
THEATRE: Ain't Supposed to Die a Natural Death, The Duplex, The Cherry Orchard, The Wiz, Weep Not For Me, Zooman and the Sign, In an Upstate Motel, Zora, Dreamgirls, Sons and Fathers of Sons, Puppetplay, A Raisin in the Sun (Tony for Best Actress, 2004), Into the Woods, Jelly's Last Jam.
PICTURES: Once Upon A Time...When We Were Colored, Loving Jezebel, The Visit, Frankie and Alice, Just Wright, For Colored Girls Who Have Considered Suicide When the Rainbow Is Enuf.
TELEVISION: *Movies*: Uncle Tom's Cabin, False Witness, Polly, Polly—Comin' Home!, Jailbirds, Hallelujah, David's Mother, TV's Funniest Families (host), The Possession of Michael D, The Babysitter's Seduction, Free of Eden, The Old Settler (also exec.prod.). Murder She Wrote: The Last Free Man, A Raisin in the Sun (Emmy nom. 2008). *Series*: One Life to Live, The Cosby Show (2 Emmy noms.), Santa Barbara (as Phylicia Ayers-Allen), Cosby, Little Bill, Character Studies (host). *Documentaries/Specials*: Nell Carter—Never Too Old to Dream, Superstars and Their Moms, Our Kids and the Best of Everything, The Debbie Allen Special, Intimate Portrait: Madeline Kahn, Intimate Portrait: Phylicia Rashad, The Cosby Show: A Look Back. *Guest:* More than 92 appearances.

RATHER, DAN
News Correspondent, Anchor. b. Wharton, TX, Oct. 31, 1931. e. Sam Houston State Teachers Coll., BA journalism, 1953.

Instructor there for one year. Graduate of U. of Houston Law School, S. Texas School of Law. Began journalism career as Associated Press reporter in Huntsville, Texas, 1950. Later, reported for United Press International, 1950-1952. Radio: KSAM-Huntsville, 1950-1953; KTRH-Houston and the Houston Chronicle, 1954-55; became news dir. of KTRH in 1956 and a reporter for KTRK-TV Houston in 1959. Then, news dir. at CBS affiliate KHOU-TV Houston. Joined CBS News in 1962 as chief of southwest bureau in Dallas. Transferred overseas (including chief of London Bureau 1965-66), then Vietnam before returning as White House correspondent, 1966. White House correspondent, 1964-74. Covered top news events, from Democratic and Republican national conventions to President Nixon's trip to Europe (1970) and to Peking and Moscow (1972). Anchored CBS Reports, 1974-75. From March 1981 until his retirement from anchor duties in March 2005, Rather served as anchor and managing editor of the CBS Evening News; a contributor since 1981 to CBS News Radio with Dan Rather Reporting, a weekday broadcast of news and analysis. Rather positions have also included co-editor of 60 Minutes; correspondent, 60 Minutes, 1975-1981; correspondent for 48 Hours Investigates, 1988-2002; author of syndicated weekly newspaper column, launched in 1997 as "Part of our World" and now "Dan Rather Reporting" correspondent, 60 Minutes II, 1999-2005. Rather is the winner of numerous awards, including 5 Emmys, two Peabody Awards (which includes his 2005 Peabody for breaking the story of abuses at Abu Ghraib prison in a report that first revealed shocking photos of American soldiers mistreating Iraqi prisoners. The Report aired on "60 Minutes" Wednesday), and he's also received citations from critical, scholarly, professional and charitable organizations. In 1994, Sam Houston State Univ., Rather's alma mater, named its journalism and communications building after him. Resigned from CBS March 2005. Currently Rather produces segments for HDNET in the format "Dan Rather Reports" (Emmy Award 2008). The program covers topics including politics, the environment, the global economy, and international affairs and conflicts.
AUTHOR: The Palace Guard, 1974; The Camera Never Blinks, 1977; I Remember, 1991; The Camera Never Blinks Twice, 1994; Mark Sullivan's Our Times, editor only, 1995, Deadlines and Datelines, 1999, The American Dream, 2001.
TELEVISION: *Movies:* Legacy of Shame, Victory in the Pacific (co-host). *Series:* Dan Rather Reports. *Documentaries / Specials:* Who Killed JFK? Facts Not Fiction, The Real Malcolm X (narr./interviewer), The Last Party, We Were There: CBS News at 50, AFI's 100 Years...100 Movies, Breaking the News, Feeding the Beast: The 24-Hour News Revolution, Barbecue: A Texas Love Story, Why We Fight, TV Junkie: Faces of Addiction (video), Oswald's Ghost, What It Takes, A National Disgrace (narr., exec. prod.).

RAVEN, ABBE
Executive. e. B.A. in theater, Univ. of Buffalo, NY, 1974. M.A. in cinema and theatre from from Hunter College, where she was named a Brookdale Fellow, 1977. Raven began her career in cable TV in 1982 in production for daytime and arts, which later was spun into Lifetime Television and AETN (A&E Television Networks). AETN is a joint venture of The Hearst Corporation (37.5%), The Walt Disney Company's Disney-ABC Television Group (37.5%) and General Electric's NBC Universal (25%). Since AETN's launch in 1984, Raven has taken on a number of executive responsibilities. Most notably she grew the History Channel into a highly successful branded cable network as its executive v.p. & gen. mgr. She was promoted in 2002 to executive v.p. & gen. mgr. of A&E Network-USA and since Sept. 2004 was its president. Upon the retirement of Nickolas Davatzes in March 2005, Raven became the second pres. & CEO of AETN and is the position she holds today. In 1997, Raven was inducted into Hunter College's Hall of Fame. In 2001, Raven received the University of Buffalo's Distinguished Alumnus Award. A native New Yorker, Raven resides with her family in the New York area.

RAVETCH, IRVING
Writer, Producer. b. Newark, NJ, Nov. 14, 1920. e. UCLA. m. Harriet Frank, with whom he often collaborated. Received WGA Laurel Award for Screen Writing Achievement 1988.
PICTURES: *Writer:* Living in a Big Way, The Outriders, Vengeance Valley, Ten Wanted Men, The Long Hot Summer (WGA nom. 1959), The Sound and the Fury, Home from the Hill, The Dark at the Top of the Stairs, Hud (also co-prod., Academy Award nom.; WGA Award 1964), Hombre (also co-prod.), The Reivers (also prod., WGA nom. 1970), House of Cards (as James P. Bonner), The Cowboys, Conrack (WGA nom. 1975), Norma Rae (Academy Award nom.; Golden Globe nom.; WGA nom. 1980), Murphy's Romance, Stanley and Iris.
TELEVISION: *Movies:* Baby Makes Three.

RAYNOR, LYNN S.
Producer, Production Executive. b. Chicago, IL, Feb. 11, 1940. Produced West Coast premiere of The Balcony by Genet, The Crawling Arnold Review by Feiffer. Joined Television Enterprises, 1965; Commonwealth United, 1968 as business affairs exec. later prod. spvr. 1972 opened London branch of the Vidtronics Co. 1974, formed Paragon Entertainment & RAH Records. 1980-95, prod. of TV movies and mini-series. Prod. & editor of 12 minute tv vignettes, A Hall of Fame Story.
PICTURE: Freejack (production executive).
TELEVISION: *Movies*: A Winner Never Quits, The High Price of Passion, Stranger in My Bed, Common Ground, The Girl Who Came Between Them, Face of Love, The Rape of Doctor Willis, Quiet Killer, Love Honor & Obey: The Last Mafia Marriage, Tonya & Nancy: The Inside Story, Tecumseh: The Last Warrior, It Was Him Or Us, Never Give Up: The Jimmy V Story, True Women, The Lover Letter, Glory & Honor, The Wall, Double Platinum, The Virginian, American Tragedy, A Town Without Christmas (exec. prod.), Two Against Time, Obsessed (line prod.), Fallen Angel (co-prod.), The Reagans (Emmy nom. 2004), 3: The Dale Earnhardt Story, Four Minutes, Family Man, Flirting with Forty, Back, Matadors. *Mini-series:* On Wings of Eagles (Emmy nom. 1986), The Kennedys of Massachusetts (Emmy nom. 1990), True Women. *Series*: Camp Wilderness, Falcone, One Tree Hill, Runaway, The Beast, One Tree Hill. *Documentaries/Specials*: Waiting for Godot.

REA, STEPHEN
Actor. b. Belfast, Northern Ireland, Oct. 31, 1946. e. Queens Univ. (BA in English Lit.). Started acting at Abbey Theatre in Dublin. Formed the Field Day Theatre Co. in 1980 in Londonderry, acting in or directing most of their productions. Also acted with Royal Natl. Theatre.
THEATRE: Playboy of the Western World, Comedians, High Society, Endgame, Freedom of the City, Someone Who'll Watch Over Me (also B'way; Theatre World Award, Tony nom.).
PICTURES: Danny Boy (Angel), Loose Connections, The Company of Wolves, The Doctor and the Devils, The House, Life Is Sweet, The Crying Game (Acad. Award nom.), Bad Behavior, Angie, Princess Caraboo, Ready to Wear (Pret-a-Porter), Between the Devil and the Deep Blue Sea, Interview With A Vampire, All Men Are Mortal, ,Trojan Eddie, Michael Collins, A Further Gesture, Last of the High Kings, Hacks, Fever Pitch, Double Top, This Is My Father, Still Crazy, The Butcher Boy, Blue Vision, The Life Before This, Guinevere, In Dreams, The End of the Affair, On the Edge, Snow in August, The Musketeer, Bloom, FearDotCom, Evelyn, The I Inside, Proudly We Served, The Good Shepherd, Control, The Halo Effect, Fluent Dysphasia (short), Tara Road, V for Vendetta, Sixty Six, Until Death, The Reaping, Stuck, Heidi 4 Paws (voice), The Heavy, The Devil's Mercy, Ondine, Blackthorn.
TELEVISION: *Movies*: Color Him Dead, Early Struggles, Professional Foul, Comedians, Joyce in June, Shergar, The House, Four Days in July, Scout, Nobody Here But Us Chickens, Endgame by Samuel Beckett, Hedda Gabler, Citizen X, Shadow of a Gunman, Crime of the Century, Snow in August, Copenhagen, Celebration, Chaos. *Mini-series*: Lost Belongings. *Series*: I Didn't Know You Cared, Crossroads, Not With a Bang, Armadillo, Horrible Histories (narr. UK version), Father & Son. *Guest:* More than 58 appearances.

REARDON, BARRY
Executive. b. Hartford, CT, Mar. 8, 1931. e. Holy Cross College, economics degree. Trinity College. Began industry career with Paramount Pictures, 1967-1975; left to join General Cinema Theatres Corp. as EVP, Marketing & Film Buying, 1975-1978; joind Warner Bros. in 1978 and worked there until retirement in 1999. Most recently was Warner Bros. pres. of domestic distribution. Named ShoWester of the Year, 1998. Consultant for numerous companies. Now serves on the Board of various companies.

REDFORD, ROBERT
Actor, Director, Producer. r.n. Charles Robert Redford, Jr. b. Santa Monica, CA, Aug. 18, 1937. Attended U. of Colorado; left to travel in Europe, 1957. Attended Pratt Inst. and American Acad. of Dramatic Arts. Founded Sundance Film Institute, Park City, Utah, workshop for young filmmakers. 2002 received honorary Academy Award for actor, director, producer, creator of Sundance, inspiration to independent and innovative filmmakers everywhere. Won 3 Golden Globe Henrietta Awards and received Cecil B. DeMille Award.
THEATRE: *B'way*: Tall Story (walk on), The Highest Tree, Sunday in New York (Theatre World Award), Barefoot in the Park.
PICTURES: *Actor*: War Hunt (debut, 1962), Situation Hopeless But Not Serious, Inside Daisy Clover (Golden Globe Award 1966), The Chase, This Property Is Condemned, Barefoot in the Park, Butch Cassidy and the Sundance Kid, Downhill Racer (also exec. prod.), Tell Them Willie Boy is Here, Little Fauss and Big Halsy, The Hot Rock, The Candidate (also co-exec. prod.), Jeremiah Johnson, The Way We Were, The Sting (Academy Award nom. 1974), The Great Gatsby, The Great Waldo Pepper, Following the Tundra Wolf (documentary, as himself), Broken Treaty at Battle Mountain (documentary, narrator), Three Days of the Condor, All The President's Men (also exec. prod.), A Bridge Too Far, The Electric Horseman, Brubaker, The Natural, Out of Africa, Legal Eagles, Havana, Sneakers, Indecent Proposal, Up Close and Personal, Anthem, Forever Hollywood, New York in the 50's, Sundance 20, The Last Castle, Spy Game, The Clearing, An Unfinished Life, Charlotte's Web (voice), Aloft (also prod./dir.), Lions for Lambs (also prod., dir.), A Walk in the Woods (also prod.). *Executive producer*: The Solar Film (short), Promised Land, Some Girls, Yosemite: The Fate of Heaven (also narrator), The Dark Wind, Incident at Oglala (also narrator), Strawberry &

Chocolate (presenter), She's the One, No Looking Back, Slums of Beverly Hills, A Civil Action (prod.), How to Kill Your Neighbor's Dog, People I Know, The Motorcycle Diaries, The Unforeseen (doc., also actor). *Director*: Ordinary People (Academy Award, Golden Globe Award, DGA Award 1980), The Milagro Beanfield War (also co-prod.), A River Runs Through It (also prod., narrator, Golden Globe nom. 1993), Quiz Show (also prod. 2 Academy Award noms. for picture & dir.; Golden Globe nom.; DGA nom. 1995), The Horse Whisperer (also actor, prod., Golden Globe nom. 1999), The Legend of Bagger Vance (also prod.), Enredando Sombras, Forever Hollywood, The Conspirator (also prod.).
TELEVISION: *Movies:* The Iceman Cometh (acting), Grand Ave. (exec. prod.), Wallace Stegner: A Writer's Life (narrator), Skinwalkers (exec. prod.), Coyote Waits (exec. prod.), A Thief of Time (exec. prod.). *Documentaries/Specials:* Iconoclasts (series doc.; exec. prod.) *Guest:* More than 140 appearances.

REDGRAVE, CORIN
Actor. b. London, England, July 16, 1939. e. Cambridge. p. late Sir Michael Redgrave and Rachel Kempson. Brother of Vanessa and Lynn Redgrave.
THEATRE: On stage with England Stage Co.: A Midsummer Night's Dream, Chips with Everything. RSC: Lady Windermere's Fan, Julius Caesar, Comedy of Errors, Antony and Cleopatra. Young Vic: Rosmersholm.
PICTURES: A Man for All Seasons, The Deadly Affair, Charge of the Light Brigade, The Magus, Oh What a Lovely War, When Eight Bells Toll, Serail, Excalibur, Eureka, Between Wars, The Fool, In the Name of the Father, Four Weddings and a Funeral, Persuasion, England-My England, Honest, Die Erika und Klaus Mann Story, Enigma, Gypsy Woman, Close Your Eyes, To Kill a King, Enduring Love, Venus, La Rabbia, Eve, The Calling.
TELEVISION: *Movies:* The Fall of Kelvin Walker, Dracula, Tower of London: The Innocent, David Copperfield, Antony & Cleopatra, L'Ombre sur la plage, Measure for Measure, Circles of Deceit: Dark Secret, The Ice House, The Woman in White, Trial & Retribution IV, Shackleton, Sunday, Bertie and Elizabeth, Trial & Retribution VI, The Girl in the Cafe, The Relief of Belsen. *Mini-series:* The Gambler, Wagner, Ultraviolet, The Forsyte Saga. *Series*: The Big Spender, Shameless. *Guest:* More than 50 appearances.
(d. April 6, 2010)

REDGRAVE, LYNN
Actress. b. London, England, Mar. 8, 1943. Sister of Vanessa and late Corin Redgrave. p. late Sir Michael Redgrave and Rachel Kempson. Entered m.p. and TV industries, 1962. *Author:* Journal: A Mother and Daughter's Recovery from Breast Cancer.
THEATRE: *NY*: Black Comedy (B'way debut), My Fat Friend (1974), Mrs. Warren's Profession, Knock Knock, Misalliance, St. Joan, Twelfth Night (Amer. Shakespeare Fest), Sister Mary Ignatius Explains It All For You, Aren't We All?, Sweet Sue, A Little Hotel on the Side, The Master Builder, Shakespeare for My Father (also writer), The Constant Wife. *Regional:* The Importance of Being Earnest. *London:* A Midsummer's Night Dream, Slag, Noises Off. *LA*: Les Liaisons Dangereuses. *Washington D.C.:* Company.
PICTURES: Tom Jones (debut, 1963), Girl With Green Eyes, Georgy Girl (Academy Award nom.; Golden Globe Award, 1 other nom. 1967), The Deadly Affair, Smashing Time, The Virgin Soldiers, Last of the Mobile Hot-Shots, Los Guerilleros, Viva la Muerta—Tua!, Every Little Crook and Nanny, Everything You Always Wanted to Know About Sex* But Were Afraid to Ask, The National Health, The Happy Hooker, The Big Bus, Sunday Lovers, Morgan Stewart's Coming Home, Midnight, Getting It Right, Shine, Strike, Gods and Monsters (Academy Award nom.; Golden Globe Award 1998), Touched, The Annihilation of Fish, The Simian Line, The Next Best Thing, Deeply, How to Kill Your Neighbor's Dog, Venus and Mars, My Kingdom, Spider, Anita and Me, Hansel and Gretel, Charlie's War, Peter Pan, Kinsey, The White Countess, The Jane Austen Book Club, Confessions of a Shopaholic.
TELEVISION: *BBC*: Pretty Polly, Ain't Afraid to Dance, The End of the Tunnel, I Am Osango, What's Wrong with Humpty Dumpty, Egg On the Face of the Tiger, Blank Pages, A Midsummer Night's Dream, Pygmalion, William, Vienna 1900, Daft as a Brush, Not For Women Only, Calling the Shots. *United States: Co-host*: A.M. America.
Movies: Turn of the Screw, Sooner or Later, Beggarman Thief, Gauguin the Savage, Seduction of Miss Leona, Rehearsal for Murder, The Bad Seed, My Two Loves, Jury Duty: The Comedy, What Ever Happened to Baby Jane?, Toothless, Indefensible: The Truth About Edward Brannigan, White Lies, Different,Tales From the Hollywood Hills: The Old Reliable, A Season For Miracles, Varian's War, My Sister's Keeper, Nurses. *Mini-series*: Vienna 1900, Centennial. *Series*: House Calls (Golden Globe nom. 1981), CBS Afternoon Playhouse: The Shooting (Emmy nom. 1983) Teachers Only, Chicken Soup, Rude Awakening, Me, Eloise. *Guest*: More than 114 appearances.
(d. May 2, 2010)

REDGRAVE, VANESSA, C.B.E.
O.B.E. Actress. b. London, England, Jan. 30, 1937.m. actor Franco Nero. p. late Sir Michael Redgrave and Rachel Kempson. Sister of late Lynn and late Corin Redgrave. Mother of actress Joely and the late Natasha Richardson. Early career with Royal Shakespeare Company. Appeared in documentary Tonight Let's All Make Love in London. Autobiography, 1994. Received Bafta Academy Fellowship Award 2010.
THEATRE: Daniel Deronda, Cato Street, The Threepenny Opera, Twelfth Night, As You Like It, The Taming of the Shrew, Cymbeline, The Sea Gull, The Prime of Miss Jean Brodie, Antony & Cleopatra, Design for Living, Macbeth, Lady from the Sea, Ghosts, New Statesman, The Aspern Papers, Anthony and Cleopatra, Not About Nightingales (prod., co-dir.), Julis Ceasar, John Gabriel Borkman, Tomorrow Was War, A Touch of the Poet, Orpheus Descending, A Song at Twilight, Madhouse in Goa, The Three Sisters, When She Danced, Maybe, Heartbreak House, Vita & Virginia, A Song at Twilight, The Cherry Orchard, Lady Windermere's Fan, The Hollow Crown, A Year of Magical Thinking, Long Day's Journey Into Night, Euripides.
PICTURES: Behind the Mask (debut, 1958), Morgan!: A Suitable Case for Treatment (Academy Award nom.; Golden Globe nom. 1967), A Man for All Seasons, Blow-Up, The Sailor From Gibraltar, Red and Blue, Camelot (Golden Globe nom. 1968), The Charge of the Light Brigade, Isadora (Academy Award nom.; Golden Globe nom. 1969), Oh! What a Lovely War, The Sea Gull, A Quiet Place in the Country, Drop Out, The Trojan Women, La Vacanza, The Devils, Mary—Queen of Scots (Academy Award nom.; Golden Globe nom. 1972), Murder on the Orient Express, Out of Season, The Seven Percent Solution, Julia (Academy Award, Golden Globe Award 1977), Agatha, Yanks, Bear Island, The Bostonians (Academy Award nom.; Golden Globe nom. 1985), Steaming, Wetherby, Prick Up Your Ears (Golden Globe nom. 1988), Consuming Passions, Comrades, The Ballad of the Sad Cafe, Romeo-Juliet (voice), Howards End (Academy Award nom. 1993), Breath of Life, Sparrow, The House of the Spirits, Crime and Punishment, Mother's Boys, Great Moments in Aviation, Little Odessa, A Month by the Lake (Golden Globe nom. 1996), Mrs. Dalloway, Deep Impact, Lulu on the Bridge, A Rumor of Angels, Mirka, Girl Interrupted, The Cradle Will Rock, The 3 Kings, The Pledge, Searching for Debra Winger (documentary), Crime and Punishment, Good Boy! (voice), The Keeper: The Legend of Omar Khayyam, Short Order, The White Countess, Thief Lord, Venus, Cowboys for Christ, The Magic Snowman II (voice), The Riddle, How About You, Evening, Atonement, Eva, Coriolanus, Letters to Juliet, The Whistleblower, Miral, Anonymous.
TELEVISION: *Movies:* As You Like It, My Body My Child, A Man for all Seasons (Golden Globe nom. 1989), Young Catherine, Children of the Mist, Great Moments in Aviation, Down Came a Blackbird, The Wind in the Willows (also narrator), Two Mothers for Zachary, The Willows in Winter (narrator), Bella Mafia (Golden Globe nom. 1998), If these Walls Could Talk 2 (Emmy Award, Golden Globe Award 2000), Jack and the Beanstalk: The Real Story, The Gathering Storm (Emmy nom.; Golden Globe nom. 2002), The Locket, Byron, The Shell Seekers, Ein Job. *Mini-series:* A Farewell to Arms, Peter the Great (Emmy nom. 1986), The Day of the Triffids. *Series:* Nip/Tuck. *Documentaries/Specials*: Katherine Mansfield, Playing for Time (Emmy Award 1981), My Body My Child, Wagner (theatrical in Europe), Three Sovereigns for Sarah, Peter the Great, Second Serve (Emmy nom.; Golden Globe nom. 1986), Orpheus Descending, Young Catherine (Emmy nom. 1991), What Ever Happened to Baby Jane? *Guest:* More than 125 appearances.

REDSTONE, SUMNER M.
Executive, Attorney. b. Boston, MA, May 27, 1923. e. Harvard, B.A., 1944, LLB., 1947. Served to 1st Lt. AUS, 1943-45. Served in military intelligence, with the mission to break Japan's military and diplomatic codes. For his efforts, Redstone received, among other honors, two commendations from the Military Intelligence Division for his service, contribution and devotion to duty. He is also a recipient of the Army Commendation Award. He was admitted to MA Bar in 1947 and began his law career with the U.S. Ct. Appeals 1st Circuit in 1948; 8th Circuit 1950; 9th Circuit 1948; D.C. 1951; U.S. Supreme Court, 1952; law sec. of the U.S. Court of Appeals for 9th Circuit 1947-48; special asst. to U.S. Atty. General, 1948-51. Subsequently, he was a partner with the law firm of Ford, Bergson, Adams, Borkland & Redstone in Washington, D.C., from 1951-54. Became exec. v.p. Northeast Drive-In Theatre Corp., 1954-67; pres. Northeast Theatre Corp.; From July 1967-December 1999 pres. of National Amusements, Inc., a theatre circuit that has grown to approximately 1,500 screens in the U.S., U.K., Latin America and Russia, and which operates under the Showcase Cinemas, Multiplex Cinemas, Cinema de Lux and KinoStar brands. He has been CEO of National Amusements, Inc. since July 1967 and chmn. of the bd. since 1986. He was President of National Amusements from July 1967 to December 1999. National Amusements is the parent company of media giant Viacom, Inc., which split at the end of 2005 into two publicly traded entities: Viacom and CBS Corporation. Before the separation, Redstone had served as bd. chairman since June 1987 and Viacom CEO since January 1996. Sumner Redstone (chairman) and and his daughter, Shari Redstone (vice chairman-nonexecutive), have controlling interests in both companies and lead the boards of both companies.
MEMBERSHIPS*:* asst. pres. Theatre Owners of America, 1960-63; pres. 1964-65; bd. chmn, National Assoc. of Theatre Owners, 1965-66. Currently, he is a member of exec. committee of the National Assoc. of Theatre Owners; member of the bd. of

overseers of the Dana-Farber Cancer Institute, serving as v.p; member of the exec. comm. of the Will Rogers Memorial Fund; member of the Corporation of the Massachusetts General Hospital; on bd. of overseers of the Boston Museum of Fine Arts; member of exec. bd. of the Combined Jewish Philanthropies of Greater Boston. Redstone is a former chmn. of the Metropolitan Div. of the Combined Jewish Philanthropies and was a member of the Corporation of the New England Medical Center. He has served as a member of the Advisory Council for the Academy of Television Arts and Sciences Foundation and on the Board of Trustees for The Museum of Television and Radio. During President Jimmy Carter's Administration, he was appointed a member of the Presidential Advisory Comm. of the Arts for the John F. Kennedy Center for the Performing Arts; and in 1984, was appointed a dir. of the Kennedy Presidential Library Foundation. He also has served as a judge on the Foundation's select comm. to award the annual John F. Kennedy Profile in Courage Award each year since the award's inception in 1990. He is a founding trustee of the American Cancer Society.
INSTRUCTOR: While a law clerk in the Court of Appeals, Redstone taught at the Univ. of San Francisco Law School and Labor Management School in 1947. Was a professor, Boston U. Law Sch. 1982-83, 1985-86. While there, he created one of the nation's first courses in entertainment law. Was visiting professor, Brandeis University and a lecturer at the Harvard Law School. Recipient, Boston Latin School's Graduate of the Year, 1989. In 1994, Redstone received an honorary Doctor of Laws from Boston University.
AWARDS: (Entertainment-related): Communicator of the Year B'nai B'rith Communications, Cinema Lodge 1980; Man of the Year, Entertainment Industries div.; UJA-Federation, NY, 1988; Variety of New England Humanitarian Award, 1989; Motion Picture Pioneers Pioneer of the Year, 1991; Golden Plate Award American Acad. Achievement 32nd Annual Salute to Excellence Program; 1994, Man of the Year Award from MIPCOM, the Int'l Film and Programme Market for TV Video Cable and Satellite; 1995, Variety Club International Humanitarian Award; Hall of Fame Award, Broadcast & Cable Magazine, 1995; Honoree 7th Annual Fundraiser, Montefiore Medical Center; Expeditioner's Award, New York City Outward Bound Center, 1996; Patron of the Arts Award, Songwriter's Hall of Fame, 1996; Vision 21 Award and Doctor of Humane Letter, New York Institute of Technology, 1996; Trustees Award, The National Academy of Television Arts and Sciences, 1997; Gold Medal Award, International Radio and Television Society, 1998; the Robert F. Kennedy Memorial Ripple of Hope Award, 1998; and National Conference of Christians and Jews Humanitarian Award, 1998.

REDSTONE, SHARI E.
Executive. b. Washington, D.C., 1954. e. BS from Tufts University, 1975; earned a JD in 1978 and a master's degree in Tax Law in 1980 from Boston University. Daughter of Sumner Redstone, who is chairman and CEO of National Amusements, the parent company of media companies Viacom, Inc. and CBS Corporation. (Mr. Redstone is also chairman of CBS Corporation and Viacom, Inc.) Ms. Redstone practiced corporate law, estate planning and criminal law in greater Boston from 1978 through 1993. From 1994-2000, she was executive v.p. of National Amusements, Inc., a theatre circuit which owns and operates approximately 1,500 screens in the U.S., U.K., Latin America and Russia. Ms. Redstone has served as president of National Amusements since January 2000. As president of National Amusements, Inc., she is the third generation of her family to lead the Massachusetts-based movie theatre chain founded by her grandfather, Michael, in 1936. Ms. Redstone led the recent launch of the Cinema de Lux brand of theatres and the development of The Bridge: Cinema de Lux theatres in Los Angeles and Philadelphia. Ms. Redstone is non-executive vice chair of both Viacom, Inc. and CBS Corporation, positions to which she was elected Jan. 1, 2006. Ms. Redstone served on the Board of the former Viacom Inc., a predecessor of the Viacom and CBS Corp., since 1994. Ms. Redstone is a member of the bd. of directors and executive committee for the National Association of Theatre Owners, co-chairman and co-CEO of MovieTickets.com, Inc., chairman and CEO of CineBridge Ventures, Inc. and chairman and CEO of Rising Star Media. Ms. Redstone is a member of the board of several charitable organizations. Ms. Redstone is also a director of National Amusements and vice chairwoman of Midway Games Inc., she resigned from Midway in 2008. October, 2008 National Amusements Inc., sold $233 million of its Viacom and CBS stock to avoid breaching covenants on a $1.6 billion loan. Also many regional National Amusements Theatres were offered for sale. Ms. Redstone is a bd. member of the Combined Jewish Philanthropies, the National Center on Addiction and Substance Abuse at Columbia U. and the John F. Kennedy Library Foundation, and she also is on the board of trustees at the Dana Farber Cancer Institute. The USO named her Woman of the Year in 2007 for National Amusements support of military families. She teamed with the USO of Metropolitan New York and implemented several weeks of free summer movies, popcorn and soda for America's military families and instituted an ongoing military discount at National Amusement theatres. Ms. Redstone also received the 2007 Salah M. Hassanein Humanitarian Award at ShowEast in recognition of her philanthropic work.

REED, PAMELA
Actress. b. Tacoma, WA, Apr. 2, 1953. Ran day-care center and worked with Head Start children before studying drama at U. of Washington. Worked on Trans-Alaska pipeline. Off-Broadway showcases.
THEATRE: Curse of the Starving Class (Off-B'way debut, 1978), All's Well That Ends Well (Central Park), Getting Out (Drama Desk Award), Aunt Dan and Lemon, Fools, The November People (Broadway debut), Sorrows of Stephen, Mrs. Warren's Profession, Getting Through the Night, Best Little Whorehouse in Texas, Fen, Standing on My Knees, Elektra.
PICTURES: The Long Riders (debut, 1980), Melvin and Howard, Eyewitness, Young Doctors in Love, The Right Stuff, The Goodbye People, The Best of Times, Clan of the Cave Bear, Rachel River, Chattahoochee, Cadillac Man, Kindergarten Cop, Passed Away, Bob Roberts, Junior, Santa Fe, Bean, Santa Fe, Why Do Fools Fall in Love, Standing on Fishes, Proof of Life, Life of the Party, Asleep at the Wheel.
TELEVISION: *Movies*: Inmates—A Love Story, I Want To Live, Heart of Steel, Scandal Sheet, Caroline?, Woman With a Past, Born Too Soon, Deadly Whispers, The Man Next Door, Critical Choices, Carriers, Book of Days, Dynasty: The Making of a Guilty Pleasure, Jane Doe: Now You See It Now You Don't. *Mini-series*: Tanner '88, Hemingway, Tanner on Tanner. *Series:* The Andros Targets (TV debut, 1977), Grand, Family Album, The Home Court, Pepper Dennis, Jericho, Eli Stone (also pilot), Parks and Recreation.

REES, ROGER
Actor. b. Aberystwyth, Wales, May 5, 1944. e. Camberwell Sch. of Art, Slade Sch. of Fine Art. Stage debut Hindle Wakes (Wimbledon, U.K., 1964). With Royal Shakespeare Co. from 1967. Starred in the title role The Adventures of Nicholas Nickleby (London and NY, Tony Award), also on stage in Hapgood (London, L.A.), Indiscretions (NY). Off-B'way in The End of the Day. Assoc. dir. Bristol Old Vic Theatre Co., 1986-present. Playwright with Eric Elice of Double Double and Elephant Manse.
PICTURES: Star 80 (debut, 1983), Keine Storung Bitte, Mountains of the Moon, If Looks Could Kill, Stop! Or My Mom Will Shoot, Robin Hood: Men in Tights, Sudden Manhattan, Trouble on the Corner, Next Stop Wonderland, A Midsummer Night's Dream, Jump, The Bumblebee Flies Away, Blackmale, 3 A.M., Loop Dreams- The Making of a Low Budget Movie, Return to Neverland, The Scorpion King, The Palace Thief, Frida, Crazy Like a Fox, The Tulse Luper Suitcases Episode 3: From Sark to the Finish, The Emperor's Club, Going Under, The New World, The Pink Panther, Social Grace, The Treatment, The Story of a Mother (voice), Garfield's A Tale of Two Kitties, The Prestige, The Invasion, The Narrows, Happy Tears, Almost Perfect.
TELEVISION: *Movies*: A Christmas Carol (released theatrically in Europe), Place of Peace, Under Western Eyes, Bouquet of Barbed Wire, Saigon: The Year of the Cat, Imaginary Friends, The Adventures of Nicolas Nickleby (Emmy nom. 1983), The Comedy of Errors, Macbeth, The Voysey Inheritance, The Ebony Tower, The Finding, The Return of Sam McCloud, Charles & Diana: Unhappily Ever After, The Tower, The Possession of Michael D., Titanic, Double Platinum, The Crossing. *Series*: Cheers (recurring guest role), Singles, M.A.N.T.I.S., Liberty! The American Revolution, Damian Cromwell's Postcards from America, Boston Common, The West Wing, Grey's Anatomy, Warehouse 13. *Guest:* More than 58 appearances.

REESE, DELLA
Actress, Singer. r.n. Deloreese Patricia Early. b. Detroit, MI, July 6, 1932. e. Wayne St. Univ. As teen toured with Mahalia Jackson. Began recording in 1950's. Hit songs include Don't You Know.
PICTURES: *Actress:* Psychic Killer, Harlem Nights, A Thin Line Between Love and Hate, Dinosaur, (voice), Beauty Shop, If I Had Known I Was a Genius, Expecting Mary. *Singer:* Swept Away.
TELEVISION: *Movies*: *Actress:* The Voyage of the Yes, Twice in a Lifetime, Cop on the Beat, The Return of Joe Forrester, Nightmare in Badham County, The Kid Who Loved Christmas, You Must Remember This (voice), A Match Made In Heaven, Miracle in the Woods, Emma's Wish, The Secret Path, Mama Flora's Family, Having Our Say: the Delany sisters' First 100 Years, Anya's Bell, The Moving of Sophie Miles. *Mini-series*: Roots: The Next Generations. *Series*: The Della Reese Show, Chico and the Man, It Takes Two, Charlie & Company, A Pup Named Scooby Doo (voices), The Royal Family, Touched by an Angel (2 Emmy Award noms.; Golden Globe nom.), Happily Ever After: Fairy Tales for Every Child (voice). *Guest*: More than 117 appearances.

REEVES, KEANU
Actor. b. Beirut, Lebanon, Sept. 2, 1964. Lived in Australia and NY before family settled in Toronto. e. Toronto's High School for the Performing Arts, then continued training at Second City Workshop. Made Coca-Cola commercial at 16. At 18 studied at Hedgerow Theatre in PA for summer. Professional debut on Hanging In, CBC local Toronto TV show. Toronto stage debut in Wolf Boy; later on stage in Romeo and Juliet, Hamlet.
PICTURES: Youngblood (debut, 1986), River's Edge, The Night Before, Permanent Record, The Prince of Pennsylvania, Dangerous Liaisons, Bill and Ted's Excellent Adventure,

Parenthood, I Love You to Death, Tune in Tomorrow, Point Break, Bill and Ted's Bogus Journey, My Own Private Idaho, Bram Stoker's Dracula, Much Ado About Nothing, Freaked (cameo), Even Cowgirls Get the Blues, Little Buddha, Speed, Johnny Mnemonic, A Walk in the Clouds, Chain Reaction, Feeling Minnesota, The Last Time I Committed Suicide, The Devil's Advocate, Me and Will (cameo), The Matrix, The Replacements, The Watcher, The Gift, Sweet November, Hardball, The Matrix Reloaded, The Matrix Revisited, The Matrix Revolutions, Something's Gotta Give, Thumbsucker, Constantine, A Scanner Darkly, The Lake House, Street Kings, The Day the Earth Stood Still, The Private Lives of Pippa Lee, Henry's Crime (also prod.), Passengers.
TELEVISION: *Movies*: Letting Go, Brotherhood of Justice, Act of Vengeance, Young Again, Under the Influence, Babes in Toyland, Life Under Water. *Series*: Going Great, Bill & Ted's Excellent Adventures (voice). *Guest*: More than 121 appearances.

RÉGNIER, NATACHA
Actress. b. Belgium, April 11. 1974.
PICTURES: The Motorcycle Girl, Le nid tombe de l'oiseau, Dis-moi oiu..., Cecile mon enfant, Encore, La Mouette, The Dreamlife of Angels (Cannes Film Fest. Award, Best Actress, 1998), Harlem, Calino Maneige, Tempo dell ámore, Les amants criminels, Tout va bien- on s'en va, La fille de son pere, How I Killed My Father, Vert paradis, Demain on déménage, Ne fais pas ca, Trouble, Les Amitiés maléfiques, Intrusions, 1 Journée, Orly, Magma, Impasse du désir.
TELEVISION: *Movies*: Le Nid tombé de l'oiseau, Ange Espérandieu, Un monde meilleur, Carmen, Gaspard le bandit. *Mini-series:* Voici venir l'orage...

REHME, ROBERT G.
Executive, Producer. b. Cincinnati, OH, May 5, 1935. e. U. of Cincinnati. 1953, mgr., RKO Theatres, Inc., Cincinnati; 1961, adv. mgr., Cincinnati Theatre Co.; 1966, dir. of field adv., United Artists Pictures; 1969, named dir. of pub. and field adv./promotion, Paramount Pictures; 1972, pres., BR Theatres and v.p., April Fools Films, gen. mgr. Tri-State Theatre Service; 1976, v.p. & gen. sls. mgr., New World Pictures; 1978, joined Avco Embassy Pictures as sr. v.p. & COO, then named exec. v.p.; 1979, named pres., Avco Embassy Pictures, Inc.; 1981, joined Universal Pictures as pres. of distrib. & marketing; 1982, named pres. of Universal Pictures; 1983, joined New World Pictures as co-chmn. & CEO; elected pres., Academy Foundation, 1988; pres. Foundation of Motion Picture Pioneers, 1989; 1st v.p., AMPAS; 1989, partner, Neufeld/Rehme Prods. at Paramount; 1992, pres. of Academy of Motion Picture Arts & Sciences. 1997-2001, pres., AMPAS. 1999, appointed to 4-year term on bd. of directors of the National Film Preservation Board. Currently, Rehme is a principal of Rehme Productions in Los Angeles, CA. He also serves as secretary of the bd. of dir. of REPRISE! BROADWAY'S BEST, a non-profit corp. in Santa Monica, CA, which produces musical theatre.
PICTURES: *Producer:* Flight of the Intruder, Necessary Roughness, Patriot Games, Beverly Hills Cop III, Clear and Present Danger. *Executive producer:* Blind Faith, Lost in Space, Black Dog, Bless the Child, Gods and Generals, Asylum.
TELEVISION: *Movies:* Gridock, For the Future: The Irvine Fertility Scandal, Woman Undone, Escape: Human Cargo, Love and Treason, Conviction, Deacons for Defense. *Series:* Lightning Force.

REHR, DAVID K.
Executive. e. B.S. degree, business administration, Saint John's University. M.A. and doctorate in economics, George Mason University. With more than two decades of experience on Capitol Hill and in the lobbying community, Rehr is the President & CEO of the National Association of Broadcasters (NAB) in Dec. 2005. Before joining NAB, he was president of the National Beer Wholesalers Association (NBWA) from 2000-2005. Rehr has been named a "Top Association Lobbyist" by The Hill multiple times and has been featured in Beachum's Guide to Key Lobbyists.

REID, TIM
Actor, Writer, Director, Producer. b. Norfolk, VA, Dec. 19, 1944. m. actress Daphne Maxwell. Started as half of comedy team of Tim and Tom in 1969, before becoming solo stand-up comedian. Published photo/poetry collection As I Feel It, 1982. In 1987 writer of four videos: The Wonderful Wizard of Oz, Ozma of Oz, The Marvelous Land of Oz and The Emerald City of Oz.
PICTURES: *Actor:* Dead Bang, The Fourth War, Say A Little Prayer, Out of Sync (also prod.), For Real (also s.p. & dir.), On the One, Preaching to the Choir, Trade, The Cost of Heaven. *Director:* The Little Mermaid (dir., English version), Once Upon A Time...When We Were Colored (also prod.), Asunder (also prod.). *Producer:* Spirit Lost.
TELEVISION: *Movies*: *Actor:* Perry Mason: The Case of the Silenced Singer, Stephen King's It, Mastergate, Race to Freedom: The Underground Railroad (also co-exec. prod.), You Must Remember This, Simon & Simon: In Trouble Again, Las Vegas Warrior, About Sarah (exec. prod. only), Blue Moon, (exec. prod. only), Alley Cats Strike, You Wish!, The Reading Room. *Series*: Easy Does It... Starring Frankie Avalon, The Marilyn McCoo and Billy Davis Jr. Show, The Richard Pryor Show, WKRP in Cincinnati, Teachers Only, Simon and Simon, Frank's Place (also co-exec. prod., 2 Emmy noms.), Snoops (also co-exec. prod.), Sister Sister, Save Our Streets, Lincs (also exec. prod.), That '70s Show (recurring role), Treme. *Guest:* More than 95 appearances.

REID, TRAVIS
Executive. e. B.S. in business admin., California State, Hayward. V.p. with General Cinema Corporation's Midwest, Southwest and Western regions before joining Loews theatres in 1991 as v.p. of film. Promoted to sr. v.p. in 1993; by 1995, promoted to executive v.p., with expanded responsibilities for strategic planning, corporate development, and theatre circuit expansion. Named president of Loews Theatres, 1996. Company merged with Cineplex Odeon Corporation in 1998 and formed Loews Cineplex Entertainment (LCE). Reid then became president, Loews Cineplex United States, a division of LCE. In July 2004, the company was acquired by a corporation formed by Bain Capital, The Carlyle Group and Spectrum Equity Investors for US $1.5 billion and continued to operate under Loews' current management. Loews merged with AMC Entertainment, Inc., in Jan. 2006. Reid served as co-chair of an integration committee with AMC Chairman, CEO & President Peter C. Brown. In June 2006, Reid was named head of National CineMedia's plan to structure the financing of the conversion to digital cinema. His current role is president & CEO of Digital Cinema Implementation Partners, LLC (DCIP), a joint venture owned equally by AMC Entertainment, Inc., Cinemark USA, Inc. and Regal Entertainment Group. The DCIP was formed in Feb. 2007. Reid's charitable work has included service as pres. of the Foundation of Motion Picture Pioneers, chairman of the ShowEast programming committee, member of the bd. of directors-trustees of the Will Rogers Institute and chairman of the National Association of Theatre Owners' "Committee of the Whole." He received the Salah M. Hassanein Humanitarian Award at the 2002 ShowEast Convention. He also received the 2005 Will Rogers Motion Picture Pioneers Foundation "Pioneer of the Year" award.

REILLY, KEVIN
Executive. e. Cornell Univ., 1984. TV executive whose knack for making hits propelled him to the top of broadcast network entertainment executive ranks. During Reilly's varied tenures at NBC, FX and Brillstein-Grey Entertainment, he successfully supervised such critical and commercial hits as HBO's The Sopranos, FX's The Shield and Nip/Tuck and NBC's ER. Early in his career, Reilly held a variety of positions over a six-year period at NBC Entertainment: mgr., creative affairs for NBC Productions, 1988; dir., drama development/dir., current drama at NBC Entertainment, 1989-92; v.p., drama development from 1992-94; He joined Brillstein-Grey in 1994 and helped build the TV studio into a successful independent TV programming supplier. Reilly was pres. of Brad Grey Television when he left to become entertainment pres. for FX. At FX he promoted an ambitious lineup of distinctive original series and movies. Reilly then returned to NBC in fall 2003 as pres., primetime development. Next, he became president, NBC Universal Entertainment from May 2004-May 2007. By July, Reilly had a new post as FOX's entertainment president, reporting to FOX entertainment chairman Peter Liguori. Reilly is a past president of the Hollywood Radio & Television Society.

REINER, CARL
Actor, Director, Writer, Producer. b. New York, NY, March 20, 1922. Son is actor-director-writer Rob Reiner. Comedian on B'way: Call Me Mr., Inside U.S.A., Alive and Kicking. 1994 received WGA Laurel Award for TV Writing Achievement. Received DGA Honorary Life Member Award 2007. 2009 received WGA Valentine Davies Award.
AUTHOR: (novels) Enter Laughing, All Kinds of Love, Continue Laughing. *Playwright:* Something Different.
PICTURES: *Actor only*: Happy Anniversary, Gidget Goes Hawaiian, It's a Mad Mad Mad Mad World, The Russians Are Coming! The Russians Are Coming!, Don't Worry We'll Think of a Title, A Guide for the Married Man, Generation, The End, The Spirit of '76, Slums of Beverly Hills, The Adventures of Rocky & Bullwinkle, Ocean's Eleven, The Majestic (voice), Good Boy! (voice), Ocean's Twelve, Ocean's Thirteen. *Writer/Actor*: The Gazebo, The Thrill of It All (also co-prod., WGA nom. 1964), The Art of Love. *Director*: Enter Laughing (also co-s.p.), The Comic (also s.p., actor), Where's Poppa?, Oh God! (also actor), The One and Only, The Jerk (also actor), Dead Men Don't Wear Plaid (also co-s.p., actor), The Man With Two Brains (also co-s.p.), All of Me, Summer Rental, Summer School (also actor), Bert Rigby You're a Fool (also s.p.), Sibling Rivalry, Fatal Instinct (also actor), That Old Feeling.
TELEVISION: *Movies*: Salute to Stan Laurel (documentary, writer), Free to Be...You & Me (writer), Medical Story, Steve Martin: Comedy is not Pretty, Skokie, The 2000 Year Old Man (voice), The Right to Remain Silent, The Alan Brady Show (voice, writer, exec. prod.), The Dick Van Dyke Show Revisited (actor, writer, exec. prod.), The Siegfried and Roy Fantasy Experience Movie (voice). *Series*: The Fashion Story, Your Show of Shows (also writer, Emmy nom. 1954), The Fifty-Fourth Street Revue, Caesar's Hour (also writer; 2 Emmy Awards, 1 other nom.), Sid

Caesar Invites You, Eddie Condon's Floor Show, (also writer), Droodles (panelist), Keep Talking, Dinah Shore Chevy Show (writer), Take a Good Look (panelist), The Dick Van Dyke Show (also creator-prod.-dir.-writer; 2 Emmy Awards), Art Linkletter Show, The Celebrity Game (host), Good Morning World (prod.), The Dick Van Dyke Show Revisited (creator, prod., writer, Emmy nom. 2004), Good Heavens (also exec. prod.), Sunday Best (host), Hercules (voice), A Touch of Grace (dir.), Father of the Pride (voice). *Documentaries / Specials*: The Sid Caesar-Imogene Coca-Carl Reiner-Howard Morris Special (Emmy Award for writing, 1967).
RECORDINGS: Carl Reiner and Mel Brooks, The 2000 Year Old Man, The 2001 Year Old Man, The 2013 Year Old Man, Continue Laughing, A Connecticut Yankee in King Arthur's Court, Miracle on 34th Street, Jack and the Beanstalk, Aesop's Fables, The Prince and the Pauper. *Guest*: More than 200 appearances.

REINER, ROB
Actor, Director, Producer, Writer. b. New York, NY, March 6, 1947. Father is actor-writer-director-producer Carl Reiner. Worked as actor with regional theatres and improvisational comedy troupes. Wrote for the Smothers Brothers Comedy Hour. Breakthrough as actor came in 1971 when signed by Norman Lear for All in the Family. Directorial debut with This Is Spinal Tap, 1984. Co-founder of Castle Rock Entertainment. Received American Cinema Editors Award, Golden Eddie Filmmaker of the Year, 2010.
PICTURES: *Actor*: Enter Laughing, Halls of Anger, Where's Poppa?, Summertree, How Come Nobody's On Our Side?, Fire Sale, This is Spinal Tap (also s.p., dir.), Throw Momma From the Train, Postcards From the Edge, The Spirit of '76, Sleepless in Seattle, Bullets Over Broadway, Mixed Nuts, Bye Bye Love, For Better or Worse, The First Wives Club, Mad Dog Time, Primary Colors, Edtv, The Muse (cameo), The Story of Us (also prod., dir.), The Majestic (voice), Alex and Emma (also prod., dir.), Everyone's Hero (voice). *Director:* The Sure Thing, Stand by Me (DGA nom.; Golden Globe nom. 1987), The Princess Bride, Rumor Has It. *Director/Producer:* When Harry Met Sally (DGA nom.; Golden Globe nom. 1990), Misery, A Few Good Men (Academy Award nom.; DGA nom.; Golden Globe nom. 1993), North, The American President (Golden Globe nom. 1996), Ghosts of Mississippi, The Story of Us (also actor), Hail Syd Caesar! The Golden Age of Comedy (doc., narr.), Whiskey River, The Bucket List, Flipped (also prod.).
TELEVISION: *Movies*: *Actor:* Thursday's Game (aka The Berk), More Than Friends (also co-writer, co-exec. prod.), The T.V. Show (also writer, exec. prod.), Million Dollar Infield (also co-prod., co-writer), Billy Crystal: Don't Get Me Started, Live Earth. *Series*: The Glen Campbell Goodtime Hour (writer), All in the Family (also writer 2 Emmy Awards, 3 other noms.; 4 Golden Globe noms.), The Super (prod. only), Free Country (also co-writer), Likely Stories Vol. 1 (also writer, dir.), Morton & Hayes (also co-creator, co-exec. prod.), Hopeless Pictures (actor). *Documentaries/Specials:* Forever Hollywood (TV documentary, as himself), But...Seriously (exec. prod.), I Am Your Child (also dir., writer). *Guest*: More than 166 appearances.

REINHOLD, JUDGE
Actor. r.n. Edward Ernest Reinhold, Jr. b. Wilmington, DE, May 21, 1957. e. Mary Washington College, North Carolina Sch. of Arts. Acted in regional theatres including Burt Reynolds dinner theater in Florida before signed to TV contract at Paramount.
PICTURES: Running Scared (debut, 1979), Stripes, Pandemonium, Fast Times at Ridgemont High, Lords of Discipline, Roadhouse 66, Gremlins, Beverly Hills Cop, Head Office, Off Beat, Ruthless People, Beverly Hills Cop II, Vice Versa, Rosalie Goes Shopping, Daddy's Dyin', Enid is Sleeping, Zandalee, Near Misses, Baby on Board, Bank Robber, Beverly Hills Cop III, The Santa Clause, Crackerjack 2, Last Lives, Family Plan, Homegrown, Redemption High, My Brother the Pig, Beethoven's 3rd, Enemies of Laughter, Ping, Newsbreak, Mindstorm, Camp Ninja, Beethoven's 4th, No Place Like Home, The Meeksville Ghost, Hollywood Palms, Betaville, Dead in a Heartbeat, The Santa Clause 2, Whacked!, Clifford's Really Big Movie (voice), The Hollow, Crab Orchard, Checking Out, The Santa Clause 3: The Escape Clause, Swing Vote.
TELEVISION: *Movies*: Survival of Dana, Magnum P.I., A Matter of Sex, Promised a Miracle, Black Magic, Four Eyes and Six-Guns, The Parallax Garden, As Good as Dead, The Wharf Rat, Dad the Angel and Me, Special Report: Journey to Mars, The Right to Remain Silent, Runaway Car, Netforce, Coming Unglued, Dead in a Heartbeat, Thanksgiving Family Reunion. *Mini-series:* Into the West. *Series*: Secret Service Guy, Redemption High, Seinfeld (Emmy nom. 1994 as guest), The O'Keefes, Easy Money. *Guest:* More than 61 appearances.

REISENBACH, SANFORD E.
Executive. e. NYU. Associated with Grey Advertising for 20 years; exec. v.p. and pres./founder of Grey's Leisure & Entertainment division in N.Y. In August 1979, joined Warner Bros. as exec. v.p. of worldwide adv. & pub.; named pres. worldwide adv. & pub., 1985. Appt. corporate exec. of marketing and planning, Warner Bros., 1989. In 2002 received Hollywood Reporter's Key Art Tribute Award.for a lifetime contribution to m.p. marketing. 2001 became consultant to Warner Bros. During his 20-year-plus tenure at Warners, Reisenbach was involved in some 250 marketing campaigns for movies including franchise films Batman and Lethal Weapon, comedy hits Private Benjamin and Police Academy and Academy Award winner Chariots of Fire. Adjunct professor in the Business of Entertainment Program at USC's School of Cinema-Television.

REISER, PAUL
Actor. b. New York, NY, Mar. 30, 1957. e. SUNY/Binghamton. Started performing as a stand-up comic in such clubs as Catch a Rising Star, the Improv, and the Comic Strip.
AUTHOR: Couplehood (1994).
PICTURES: Diner (debut, 1982), Beverly Hills Cop, Aliens, Beverly Hills Cop II, Cross My Heart, Crazy People, The Marrying Man, Mr. Write, Bye Bye Love, Get Bruce (cameo), The Story of Us, One Night at McCool's, Purpose, The Thing About My Folks (also s.p. & prod.).
TELEVISION: *Movies*: Sunset Limousine, Diner (short), From Here to Maternity (short), You Ruined My Life, The Tower, Now That's Funny (host), Strange Relations, Women Vs. Men, I Did Not Know That (exec. prod.), Atlanta (prod., exec. prod., writer). *Pilot*: Just Married. *Series*: My Two Dads, Mad About You (writer/creator, prod. & theme composer, 10 Emmy noms.; 4 Golden Globe noms.), Loved by You (writer), Loco por ti (writer), Love Bites (prod., writer), The Paul Reiser Show (host, writer, creator, prod., exec. prod.). *Documentaries/Specials:* Paul Reiser—Out on a Whim. *Guest*: More than 64 appearances.

REISS, JEFFREY C.
Executive. b. Brooklyn, NY, April 14, 1942. e. Washington U., St. Louis, B.A., 1963. Consultant at NYU and Manhattanville College and instructor at Brooklyn College before entering industry. Agent in literary dept. for General Artists Corp., 1966. Supervised development in NY of Tandem Prods. for Norman Lear, 1968. Produced off-B'way plays 1968-70. Dir. of program acquisition devel. for Cartridge TV, Inc. (mfg. of first home video cassette players-recorders), 1970-73. Joined ABC Entertainment as director of network feature films, 1973-75. Founder and pres., Showtime Pay TV Network, 1976-80. Co-founder, pres. & CEO, Cable Health Network, 1981-83. 1983, named vice chmn. & CEO, Lifetime Cable Network following Cable Health Network merger with Daytime. Chmn. of the board, pres. & CEO, Reiss Media Enterprises, Inc. 1984. Founder & chmn. of board, Request Television (pay-per-view svc.), 1985. In 2001 Reiss formed a new company, TViFusion Inc. and is currently the chairman and CEO. TViFusion provides outsourced services in affiliate sales, advertising sales and technology services and distribution for digital cable channels.

REITMAN, IVAN
Director, Producer. b. Komarmo, Czechoslovakia, Oct. 26, 1946. Moved to Canada at age 4. e. McMaster U. Attended National Film Board's Summer Institute directing three short films including Orientation (1968) which received theatrical distribution. Produced Canadian TV show in 1970s.
THEATRE: *Producer:* The National Lampoon Show, The Magic Show, Merlin (also dir.).
PICTURES: *Director/Producer*: Orientation (short; also writer, debut 1968), Foxy Lady (also edit., music), Stripes, Ghostbusters, Legal Eagles (also co-story), Twins, Ghostbusters II, Kindergarten Cop, Dave, Junior, Father's Day, Six Days Seven Nights, Evolution, Over My Dead Body. *Producer:* My Secret Life (also cinematographer), They Came From Within (also music supervisor), Death Weekend (also musical dir.), Tigress, Animal House, Heavy Metal, Stop Or My Mom Will Shoot, Space Jam, Private Parts, Old School 2, Up in the Air (Academy Award nom. 2010), Chloe, Post Grad. *Director:* Meatballs, My Super Ex-Girlfriend. *Executive producer:* Cannibal Girls (also dir. & s.p.), Rage, Blackout, Spacehunter, Big Shots, Casual Sex?, Feds, Beethoven's 2nd, Commandments, Road Trip, Killing Me Softly, Old School, EuroTrip, Trailer Park Boys: The Movie, Disturbia, I Love You, Man, The Uninvited, Trailer Park Boys: Countdown to Liquor Day.
TELEVISION: *Movies:* The Magic Show (exec. prod. & prod.), The Late Shift (exec. prod.; Emmy nom. 1996), The First Gentleman (exec. prod.), That Guy (prod., exec. prod.). *Series*: *Executive producer:* Delta House, The Real Ghost Busters (exec. consultant), Beethoven, Alienators: Evolution Continues. *Director:* Cooking Lessons (pilot).

RELPH, SIMON
Producer, Director. b. London, Eng., April 13, 1940. Entered industry 1961.
PICTURES: *First assistant director:* Underworld Informers, McGuire Go Home!, Deadlier Than the Male, Sunday Bloody Sunday, Macbeth, The Triple Echo, The Nelson Affair, Yanks (also production supervisor). *Assistant director:* Agent 8 3/4, Carnaby M.D., The High Commissioner, Anne of the Thousand Days, Three Sisters, Mary Queen of Scots, A Touch of Class, It's Not the Size That Counts, Zardoz, Reds (also exec. prod.; DGA Award, 1982). *Director:* How To Enjoy Wine (documentary). *Producer:* The Return of the Soldier, Privates on Parade, The Ploughman's Lunch (also asst. dir.), Secret Places, Wetherby, Comrades, Damage (co-prod.), The Secret Rapture, Look Me In The Eye, Camilla, Blue Juice, The Slab Boys, The Land Girls.

Executive producer: Laughterhouse, Enchanted April, Hideous Kinky, Bugs! (doc. short), Get the Picture (short).

REMAR, JAMES
Actor. b. Boston, MA, Dec. 31, 1953. Studied acting at NY's Neighborhood Playhouse and with Stella Adler. Appeared on NY stage in Yo-Yo, Early Dark, Bent, California Dog Fight.
PICTURES: On the Yard (debut, 1979), The Warriors, Cruising, The Long Riders, Windwalker, Partners, 48 HRS, The Cotton Club, The Clan of the Cave Bear, Band of the Hand, Quiet Cool, Rent-a-Cop, The Dream Team, Drugstore Cowboy, Tales from the Darkside, Silence Like Glass, White Fang, Fatal Instinct, Blink, Renaissance Man, Miracle on 34th Street, Boys on the Side, Session Man (Academy Award, Best Action Short, 1991), Across the Moon, Judge Dredd (cameo), The Quest, The Phantom, Robo-Warriors, Tale From The Darkside: The Movie, WIld Bill, Exquisite Tenderness, The Phantom, Born Bad, Mortal Kombat: Annihilation, Psycho, Rites of Passage, Blowback, What Lies beneath, Inferno Hellraiser, Guardian, Dying on the Edge, Betrayal, Fear the X, Duplex, Down with the Joneses, 2 Fast 2 Furious.The Girl Next Door, Blade: Trinity, Ratatouille (voice), The Pineapple Express, The Unborn, 2B, St. Vincent, The City of Gardens, Red, The Killing Game, Gun.
TELEVISION: *Movies:* The Mystic Warrior, Desperado: The Outlaw Wars, Fatal Charm, Chameleon Blue, Kojak: None So Blind, Wedlock, Hollister, Session Man (tv short), Indecency, Cutty Whitman, Inferno, The Huntress, Guilty as Charged, The Survivors Club, Ike: Countdown to D-Day, Meltdown, Sharpshooter, The Christmas Hope. *Mini-series:* The Grid. *Series:* The Huntress, Sex & the City (recurring role), North Shore, Justice League Unlimited, Dexter, Jericho, The Batman, Ben 10: Alien Force. *Guest:* More than 62 appearances.

REMBUSCH, MICHAEL J.
Executive. b. Indianapolis, IN, April 8, 1950. e. Ball State U. Son of the late Trueman T. Rembusch. Began working for father's circuit, Syndicate Theatres, Inc., in 1967. From 1970-80, managed various theatres in circuit. 1980-85, v.p., operations. 1985-90, acquired Heaston circuit (Indianapolis). Became pres., Syndicate Theatres, Inc. 1987-90, chmn, Indiana Film Commission. 1992-2000, pres., Theatre Owners of Indiana; he still represents the organization's interests publicly to members of the Indiana legislature and to the public. Rembusch currently owns the Canary Creek Cinemas in Franklin, IN.

RENO, JEAN
Actor. r.n. Juan Moreno b. Casablanca, Morocco, July 30, 1948. To France in early 1970s to serve in French military. Began acting in Paris with theatre workshop, then established his own traveling acting company.
PICTURES: Claire de Femme, Le Dernier Combat, Subway, Signes Exterieurs de Richesse, Notre Histoire, I Love You, The Big Blue, La Femme Nikita, L'homme au Masque d'Or, L'Operation Corned Beef, Loulou Graffiti, The Professional , French Kiss, Les Truffes, Beyond the Clouds, Visitors (also s.p.), Mission Impossible, Le Jaguar, Roseanna's Grave, Witch Way Love, Le Couloirs du Temps, Godzilla, Ronin, Tripwire, The Crimson Rivers, Just Visiting, Wasabi, Jet Lag, Rollerball, Décalage horaire, Ruby & Quentin, Crimson Rivers 2: Angels of the Apocalypse, L' Enquête corse, L' Empire des loups, La Tigre e la neve, The Pink Panther (2005 version), Margaret, Flyboys, The Da Vinci Code, Flushed Away (voice), Margaret, Ca$h, The Pink Panther 2, Armored, The Round Up, Couples Retreat, 22 Bullets, La Rafle., Fantomas.
TELEVISION: *Movies*: Un homme comblé, Pour venger Pépère, Monsieur Benjamin, Flight from Justice. *Mini-series*: L'Aéropostale, courrier du ciel, Quelques hommes de bonne volonté, Tender is the Night. *Guest:* More than 50 appearances in French and Spanish productions.

RESNAIS, ALAIN
Director. b. Cannes, France, June 3, 1922. Began career as asst. dir. to Nicole Vedres on compilation of film for Paris 1900. During '50s worked as asst. editor and editor; experimented with making his own 16mm films. Directed or co-dir. several short films: Van Gogh, Gauguin, Guernica, The Statues Also Die, Night and Fog.
PICTURES: Pictura: Adventure in Art (Golden Globe Award 1952), Hiroshima Mon Amour (feature debut, 1959, DGA nom. 1961), Last Year at Marienbad, Muriel, La Guerre Est Finie (The War Is Over), Je t'Aime Je t'Aime (also co-s.p.), Stavisky, Providence, Life Is a Bed of Roses, L'Amour a Mort (Love Unto Death), Melo, I Want to Go Home, Smoking/No Smoking, On connaît la chanson (aka Same Old Song), Not on the Lips, Private Fears in Public Places, Les Herbes folles, Wild Grass.

RESNICK, JOEL H.
Executive. b. New York, NY, April 28, 1936. e. U. of PA, B.A., 1958; NY Law Sch. 1961, admitted to NY State Bar. 1962 received Masters of Law degree in taxation; 1961-66 served as associate with NY law firm, Phillips Nizer Benjamin Krim & Ballon; Was in-house counsel to United Artists Corp. 1967, joined UA as spec. asst. to the sr. v.p. & gen. mgr.; 1970, moved to American Multi-Cinema, Inc., Kansas City, as asst. to pres.; 1972, named v.p. in chg. dev.; 1976, promoted to v.p. in chg. film development; 1977, named exec. v.p.; 1983, elected exec. v.p. & dir., AMC Entertainment; 1984, appt. to office of pres. as chmn. & CEO, film mktg.; 1986, resigned to join Orion Pictures Distribution Corp. as pres.; has served as co-chmn. NATO trade practices comm. since 1979. 1982 elected pres., NATO; 1984, became chmn. NATO bd.; 1989, v.p. Foundation of Motion Picture Pioneers; 1990, resigned from Orion; pres., GKC Theatres, Springfield, IL, 1991-92. Became Counsel for International Development for Cinemark International Theatres. Lifetime member of the Academy of Motion Picture Arts & Sciences (AMPAS) and is a past director of the American Film Institute.

REUBENS, PAUL
Actor, Writer. r.n. Paul Rubenfeld. b. Peekskill, NY, Aug. 27, 1952. Raised in Sarasota, FL. e. Boston U., California Inst. of the Arts (1976). Also acted as Pee-Wee Herman. Pee-wee character made debut, 1978 at Groundlings, improvisational theatre, Los Angeles followed by The Pee-wee Herman Show, a live show which gave 5 months of sold-out performances at the L.A. rock club, Roxy, and was later taped for HBO special.
PICTURES: Midnight Madness, The Blues Brothers, Cheech & Chong's Next Movie, Cheech and Chong's Nice Dreams, Pandemonium, Meatballs Part II, Pee-wee's Big Adventure (also co-s.p.), Flight of the Navigator (voice), Back to the Beach, Big Top Pee-wee (also co-s.p., co-prod.), Batman Returns, Buffy the Vampire Slayer, Tim Burton's The Nightmare Before Christmas (voice), Dunston Checks In, Matilda, Buddy, Doctor Doolittle (voice), Mystery Men, South of Heaven-West of Hell, Blow, Teacher's Pet (voice), The Tripper, Reno 911!: Miami, Life During Wartime, Nailed, The Smurfs (voice).
TELEVISION: *Movie:* Re-Animated (voice). *Series*: Likely Stories Vol. 2, Pee-wee's Playhouse (also creator, co-dir., co-writer, exec. prod.; 3 Emmy Awards, 9 other noms.), Hercules (voice), You Don't Know Jack, Murphy Brown (Emmy nom. 1995), Hopeless Pictures. *Documentaries/Specials*: Pinocchio (Faerie Tale Theatre), Pee-wee Herman Show, Pee-wee's Playhouse Christmas Special (also exec. prod., co-dir. co-writer, Emmy nom. 1989). *Guest:* More than 74 appearances.

REVELL, GRAEME
Composer. b. New Zealand, Oct. 23, 1955. e. U. of Auckland.
PICTURES: Spontaneous Combustion, Dead Calm, Till There Was You, Child's Play 2, Love Crimes, Until the End of the Crime, Traces of Red, Deadly, The People Under the Stairs, The Hand That Rocks the Cradle, Hear No Evil, Ghost, in the Machine, The Crush, Body of Evidence, Boxing Helena, Hard Target, Street Fighter, S.F.W., No Escape, The Crow, Killer: A Journal of Murder, The Basketball Diaries, Tank Girl, Mighty Morphin Power Rangers: The Movie, The Tie That Binds, Strange Days, From Dusk Till Dawn, Race the Sun, The Craft, Fled, The Crow: City of Angels, Chinese Box, The Saint, Spawn, Suicide Kings, Lulu on the Bridge, The Big Hit, The Negotiator, Phoenix, Strike, Bride of Chucky, The Siege, Idle Hands, Three to Tango, Gossip, Bats, Red Planet, Doubletake, Blow, Human Nature, Anne Frank, Lara Croft: Tomb Raider, Don't Say a Word, Collateral Damage, High Crimes, Below, Daredevil, Freddy Vs. Jason, Out of Time, Open Water, Walking Tall, The Chronicles of Riddick, Assault on Precinct 13, Miss Congeniality 2: Armed and Fabulous, Sin City, The Adventures of Sharkboy and Lavagirl 3-D, The Fog, Æon Flux, Bordertown, Man of the Year, The Condemned, Marigold, Grindhouse (segment), Darfur Now (doc.), The Ruins, Street Kings, Days of Wrath, Pineapple Express, A Perfect Getaway (score prod.), Unthinkable.
TELEVISION: *Movies:* Psycho IV: The Beginning, Down Came a Blackbird. *Mini-series:* Bangkok Hilton, Dune, Anne Frank: The Whole Story. *Series:* CSI: Miami, Eleventh Hour, Dark Blue, The Forgotten.

REVILL, CLIVE
Actor. r.n. Clive Selsby. b. Wellington, New Zealand, Apr. 18, 1930. e. Rongotal Coll., Victoria U.
THEATRE: Irma La Douce, The Mikado, Oliver, Marat/Sade, Jew of Malta, Sherry, Chichester Season, The Incomparable Max, Sherlock Holmes, Lolita, Pirates of Penzance, Mystery of Edwin Drood, My Fair Lady, Bandido.
PICTURES: Reach for the Sky, The Headless Ghost, Bunny Lake Is Missing, Once Upon a Tractor, Modesty Blaise, A Fine Madness, Kaleidoscope, The Double Man, Fathom, Italian Secret Service, Nobody Runs Forever, Shoes of the Fisherman, Assassination Bureau, The Private Life of Sherlock Holmes, The Buttercup Chain, A Severed Head, Boulevard de Rhum, Avanti! (Golden Globe nom. 1973), Escape to the Sun, Ghost in the Noonday Sun, The Legend of Hell House, The Little Prince, The Black Windmill, One of Our Dinosaurs Is Missing, Galileo, Matilda, Zorro the Gay Blade, Transformers (voice), Rumpelstiltskin, The Emperor's New Clothes, Mack the Knife, CHUD II: Bud the Chud, Frog Prince, Let Him Have It, Robin Hood: Men in Tights, Crime and Punishment, Arabian Knight (voice), The Wacky Adventures of Dr. Boris and Nurse Shirley, Dracula—Dead and Loving It!, Possums, Intrepid, Crime & Punishment, Return to Neverland (voice), Polar Opposites, Gentlemen Broncos.
TELEVISION: *Movies:* She's Dressed to Kill, A Deadly Game, Moviola: The Scarlett O'Hara War, The Diary of Anne Frank,

Death Ray 2000, The Monkey Mission, The Sorcerer, The Mikado, Samson & Delilah, A Masterpiece of Murder, The Sea Wolf, Feast of All Saints. *Mini-series:* Centennial, George Washington. *Series:* Arthur of the Britons, Chico the Rainmaker, Wizards and Warriors, The Snorks (voice), Dragon's Lair (voice), The Transformers, Probe, MIdnight Patrol (voice), The Preston Episodes. *Guest*: More than 117 appearances.

REYNOLDS, BURT
Actor, Director. b. Waycross, GA, Feb. 11, 1936. Former Florida State U. football star; TV and film stunt performer. Won fame as actor on TV in series Riverboat. Founded the Burt Reynolds Dinner Theater in Jupiter, FL, 1979. *Autobiography*: My Life (1994).
THEATRE: Mister Roberts (NY City Center), Look We've Come Through (B'way debut, 1956), The Rainmaker.
PICTURES: Angel Baby (debut, 1961), Armored Command, Operation CIA, Navajo Joe, Fade In, Impasse, Shark, Sam Whiskey, 100 Rifles, Skullduggery, Fuzz, Deliverance, Everything You Always Wanted To Know About Sex, Shamus, White Lightning, The Man Who Loved Cat Dancing, The Longest Yard (Golden Globe nom. 1975), W.W. & The Dixie Dancekings, At Long Last Love, Hustle, Lucky Lady, Gator (also dir.), Silent Movie, Nickelodeon, Smokey and the Bandit, Semi-Tough, The End (also dir.), Hooper, Starting Over (Golden Globe nom. 1980), Rough Cut, Smokey and the Bandit II, Cannonball Run, Paternity, Sharky's Machine (also dir.), The Best Little Whorehouse in Texas, Best Friends, Stroker Ace, Smokey and the Bandit III (cameo), The Man Who Loved Women, Cannonball Run II, City Heat, Stick (also dir.), Uphill All the Way (cameo), Heat, Malone, Rent-a-Cop, Switching Channels, Physical Evidence, Breaking In, All Dogs Go to Heaven (voice), Modern Love, The Player (cameo), Cop and a Half, The Maddening, Devil Inside, Meet Wally Sparks, Striptease, Mad Dog Time, Citizen Ruth, Boogie Nights (Academy Award nom.; Golden Globe Award, 1998), Raven, Bean, Crazy Six, Pups, The Last Producer (also dir.), The Hunter's Moon, Mystery Alaska, The Crew, The Last Producer, The Hollywood Sign, Driven, Big City Blues, Tempted, Hotel, A Woman in Love, The Hermit of Amsterdam, Time of the Wolf, Without a Paddle, Forget About It, Cloud Nine, Grilled, The Longest Yard, The Dukes of Hazzard, End Game, Randy and the Mob, Broken Bridges, In the Name of the King: A Dungeon Siege Tale, Deal, Delgo (voice), Not Another Not Another Movie, A Bunch of Amateurs.
TELEVISION: *Movies*: Hunters Are for Killing, Run Simon Run, The Man Upstairs (co-exec. prod. only), The Man From Left Field (also dir.), Universal Soldier II: Brothers in Arms, Universal Soldier III: Unfinished Business, Hard Time (also dir.), Hard Time: Hostage Hotel, Hard Time: Hide and Seek, Hard Time: The Premonition, Miss Lettie and Me, Hard Ground. *Mini-series:* Founding Fathers (documentary), Johnson County War. *Series*: Riverboat, Gunsmoke, Hawk, Dan August (Golden Globe nom. 1971), Out of This World (voice), B.L. Stryker (also co-exec. prod.), Evening Shade (Emmy Award, 1991, Golden Globe Award 1992, 2 other noms.), Reel Classics with Burt Reynolds (host). *Documentaries/Specials:* Wind in the Wire. *Dir.*: Alfred Hitchcock Presents (1985), Johnson County War. *Guest:* More than 230 appearances.

REYNOLDS, DEBBIE
Actress. r.n. Mary Frances Reynolds. b. El Paso, TX, April 1, 1932. Daughter is actress Carrie Fisher. e. Burbank & John Burroughs H.S., Burbank, CA. With Burbank Youth Symphony during h.s.; beauty contest winner (Miss Burbank) 1948; signed by Warner Bros.; on stage in Personal Appearances, Blis-Hayden Theater. Voted Star of Tomorrow, 1952. Received 2 Lifetime Achievement Aawrds in Comedy (ACA). *Autobiography*: Debbie: My Life (1988).
THEATRE: *B'way*: Irene, Woman of the Year.
PICTURES: June Bride (debut, 1948), The Daughter of Rosie O'Grady, Three Little Words (Golden Globe nom. 1951), Two Weeks With Love, Mr. Imperium, Singin' in the Rain, Skirts Ahoy, I Love Melvin, Give a Girl a Break, The Affairs of Dobie Gillis, Susan Slept Here, Athena, Hit the Deck, The Tender Trap, The Catered Affair, Bundle of Joy (Golden Globe nom. 1957), Tammy and the Bachelor, This Happy Feeling, The Mating Game, Say One for Me, It Started with a Kiss, The Gazebo, The Rat Race, Pepe (cameo), The Pleasure of His Company, The Second Time Around, How the West Was Won, My Six Loves, Mary Mary, Goodbye Charlie, The Unsinkable Molly Brown (Academy Award nom.; Golden Globe nom. 1965), The Singing Nun, Divorce American Style, How Sweet It Is, What's the Matter with Helen?, Charlotte's Web (voice), That's Entertainment!, The Bodyguard (cameo), Heaven and Earth, That's Entertainment III, Mother (Golden Globe nom. 1997), In & Out, Zack & Reba, Rudolph the Red-Nosed Reindeer: The Movie (voice), Wedding Bell Blues (as herself), Keepers of the Frame (doc., as herself), Rugrats in Paris- The Movie (voice), Cinerama Adventure (doc., as herself), Rugrats in Paris: The Movie - Rugrats II (voice), Blaze of Glory.
TELEVISION: *Movies*: Sadie and Son, Perry Mason: The Case of the Musical Murders, Battling for Baby, Halloweentown, The Christmas Wish, Virtual Mom, These Old Broads, Halloween Town II, Halloweentown III, Halloweentown High, Return to Halloweentown. *Series*: The Debbie Reynolds Show (Golden Globe nom. 1970), Aloha Paradise, Will & Grace (recurring guest role, Emmy nom. 2000), Kim Possible (recurring role). *Documentaries /Specials:* Jack Paar Is Alive and Well, Gene Kelly-Anatomy of a Dancer, A Gift of Love: The Daniel Huffman Story (Emmy nom. 2000). *Guest*: More than 191 appearances.

REYNOLDS, FREDRIC G.
Executive. e. Univ. of Miami, B.B.A. in finance, 1972. As C.P.A. worked for PepsiCo Inc. from 1981-1994 in various financial positions, including senior v.p. & CFO PepsiCo Foods International, PepsiCo's Frito-Lay unit. He was also CFO at other PepsiCo units, including Kentucky Fried Chicken, PepsiCola International and Pizza Hut. From PepsiCo, Reynolds joined Westinghouse. He was elected executive v.p. & CFO for Westinghouse Electric Corporation in February 1994 and assumed the additional post of CFO, CBS Inc., in April 1996. More recently, Reynolds had been executive v.p. & CFO, Viacom, Inc., responsible for all Viacom's financial functions, including treasury, accounting, internal audit, insurance and risk management, tax, mergers and acquisitions, information systems and financial planning and business analysis. In 2001, he was tapped to run Viacom TV Stations Group. When Viacom split the company into two entities in 2006, Reynolds agreed to be the executive v.p. & CFO of the new CBS Corporation until 2009. Currently he is Director for Kraft Foods, Inc. and a Director for AOL, Inc.

REYNOLDS, GENE
Actor, Executive, Producer. b. Cleveland, OH, April 4, 1925. Acted from 1936-55. Past pres. Director's Guild of America, Inc.; currently on DGA's Western Directors Council. Received DGA Robert B. Aldrich Achievement Award 1993.
PICTURES: *Actor:* Thank You, Jeeves; Sins of Man, Thunder Trail, In Old Chicago, The Californian, Of Human Hearts, Love Finds Andy Hardy, The Crowd Roars, Boys Town, The Spirit of Culver, The Flying Irishman, Bad Little Angel, They Shall Have Music, Santa Fe Trail, The Mortal Storm, Gallant Sons, The Blue Bird; Edison, the Man; Andy Hardy's Private Secretary, Adventure in Washington, The Penalty, The Tuttles of Tahiti, Junior G-men of the Air, Eagle Squadron, Jungle Patrol, The Big Cat, Slattery's Hurricane, 99 River Street, Down Three Dark Streets, The Country Girl, The Bridges at Toko-Ri, How to Get There (dir. only).
TELEVISION: *Movies:* In Defense of Kids, Doing Life (also exec. prod.), The Whereabouts of Jenny (also prod.). *Series: Director:* Wanted: Dead or Alive, My Three Sons, Hogan's Heroes, F Troop, The Ghost and Mrs. Muir, Room 222 (Emmy Award 1970, 1 other nom.), M*A*S*H (also exec. prod., 2 DGA Awards, 3 Emmy Awards, 4 other noms.), Anna and the King, (also exec. prod.), The Fitzpatricks, Lou Grant (also exec. prod., writer, DGA Award 1979, 2 other noms.; 2 Emmy Awards, 9 other noms.), The Duck Factory, In the Heat of the Night, Studio 5-B, Blossom (exec. prod. only), Lois & Clark: The New Adventures of Superman, Second Chances, Christy, Touched by an Angel, Promised Land.

REYNOLDS, KEVIN
Director, Writer. b. Jan. 17, 1950. e. Texas Marine Acad., Trinity Univ., Baylor Univ. (law degree), USC film school. Student film Proof led to offer to do expanded feature version subsequently retitled Fandango. Former lawyer in the state of Texas.
PICTURES: Red Dawn (co-s.p.). *Director:* Fandango (dir. debut, 1985; also s.p.), White Water Summer (second unit dir.), The Beast of War, Robin Hood: Prince of Thieves, Rapa Nui (also s.p.), One Eight Seven, Waterworld, The Count of Monte Christo, Tristan & Isolde, Red Dawn (writer 1984 s.p.), Learning Italian (also prod.).

REYNOLDS, NORMAN
Production Designer, Art Director.
PICTURES: *Production Designer:* The Empire Strikes Back, Raiders of the Lost Ark (Academy Award, 1982), Return of the Jedi, Return to Oz, Young Sherlock Holmes, Empire of the Sun (Academy Award nom. 1988), Mountains of the Moon, Avalon, Alien 3, Alive, Clean Slate, Mission: Impossible, Sphere, Bicentennial Man. *Art Director:* The Old Curiosity Shop, Lucky Lady, The Incredible Sarah (Academy Award nom. 1977), Star Wars: Episode IV-A New Hope (Academy Award 1978), Superman, Star Wars: Episode V - The Empire Strikes Back (Academy Award nom. 1981), Star Wars: Episode VI - Return of the Jedi (Academy Award nom. 1984), Superman II, The Exorcist III (special effects unit director).

REYNOLDS, RYAN
Actor. b. Vancouver, Canada, October 23, 1976. m. actress Scarlett Johansson.
PICTURES: The Alarmist, Coming Soon, Dick, Van Wilder, The In-Laws, Harold & Kumar Go to White Castle, Blade: Trinity, The Amityville Horror, Waiting..., Just Friends, Smokin' Aces, The Nines, Chaos Theory, Definitely, Maybe, Adventureland, X-Men Origins: Wolverine, The Proposal (also soundtrack per.), Paper Man, Buried, Green Lantern, The Change-Up, The Croods (voice).
TELEVISION: *Movies:* My Name Is Kate, Serving in Silence: The Margarethe Cammermeyer Story, A Secret Between Friends: A Moment of Truth Movie, Sabrina the Teenage Witch, In Cold Blood, Tourist Trap, School of Life. *Series:* Fifteen, The Odyssey,

Two Guys, a Girl and a Pizza Place. *Guest:* More than 61 appearances.

REZNOR, TRENT

Composer. r.n. Michael Trent Reznor. b. Mercer, PA, May 17, 1965. Head of Nothing Records, a division of Interscope Records. Fronts industrial-rock band Nine Inch Nails. Composed music and sounds for id Software's computergame QUAKE.
PICTURES: Light of Day (actor), Se7en, Natural Born Killers, Lost Highway, Closure, Lara Croft: Tomb Raider, Nine Inch Nails Live: And All That Could Have Been, Resident Evil, World Traveler, (musician), Freeman (short), Man on Fire (consultant on musical score), Rory O'Shea Was Here (soundtrack writer), Doom, Southland Tales, Constantine (soundtrack writer), Doom (soundtrack writer), The Hitcher (soundtrack writer), Wetlands Preserved: The Story of an Activist Nightclub (doc.), Wanted (soundtrack writer).
TELEVISION: Many episode soundtracks for series.

RHAMES, VING

Actor. b. May 12, 1959. e. Juilliard Sch. of Drama.
THEATRE: *B'way:* The Boys of Winter. *Off-B'way:* Map of the World, Short Eyes, Richard III, Ascension Day. *Europe:* Ajax.
PICTURES: Native Son, Patty Hearst, Casualties of War, Jacob's Ladder, The Long Walk Home, Flight of the Intruder, Homicide, The People Under the Stairs, Stop! Or My Mom Will Shoot, Bound by Honor, Dave, The Saint of Fort Washington, Pulp Fiction, Drop Squad, Kiss of Death, Mission: Impossible, Striptease, Rosewood, Con Air, Dangerous Ground, The Split, Out of Sight, Mission: Impossible 2, Duets, Bringing Out the Dead, Entrapment, Baby Boy, Final Fantasy (voice), Undisputed, Lilo and Stitch (voice), Dark Blue, Stitch! The Movie (voice), Sin, Dawn of the Dead, Pool Hall Prophets, Night Train (also prod.), Mission: Impossible III, Idlewild, Day of the Dead, A Broken Life, Ascension Day, The Bridge to Nowhere, I Now Pronounce You Chuck and Larry, Phantom Punch (also prod.), Evil Angel, The Tournament, Echelon Conspiracy, Unshakable, Silver Cord, Rogue's Gallery, King of the Avenue (also prod.), Give 'em Hell, Malone, The Goods: Live Hard, Sell Hard, Surrogates, The Wrath of Cain, Operation Endgame, Master Harold... and the Boys, Piranha 3-D, Minkow, Love Chronicles: Secrets Revealed, King of the Avenue (also exec. prod.), Silver Cord, The Spanish Harlem Project, Death Race: Frankenstein Lives, Unshakable.
TELEVISION: *Movies:* Go Tell It on the Mountain, Rising Son, When You Remember Me, Iran: Days of Crisis, Terror on Track 9, Ed McBain's 87th Precinct: Lightning, Deadly Whispers, Don King: Only in America (Emmy nom.; Golden Globe Award, 1998), Holiday Heart, American Tragedy, Sins of the Father, Little John, RFK, Kojak, Leroy & Stitch (voice), Football Wives. *Series:* Another World, Men, ER, UC: Undercover, Kojak (also co-exec. prod.), American Gangster (narr.), Gravity. *Guest:* More than 63 appearances.

RHYS-DAVIES, JOHN

Actor. b. Salisbury, England, May 5, 1944. Grew up in Wales and East Africa. Began acting at Truro School in Cornwall at 15. e. U. of East Angelia where he founded school's dramatic society. Worked as teacher before studying at Royal Academy of Dramatic Art, 1969. Appeared in 23 Shakespearean plays.
PICTURES: The Black Windmill, Sphinx, Raiders of the Lost Ark, Victor/Victoria, Sahara, Sword of the Valiant, Best Revenge, King Solomon's Mines, In the Shadow of Kilimanjaro, Firewalker, The Living Daylights, Waxwork, Rising Storm, Indiana Jones and the Last Crusade, Young Toscanini, Journey of Honor, Unnameable II, The Seventh Coin, The Great White Hype, Glory Daze, Marquis de Sade, Echo of Blue, Cats Don't Dance (voice), Bloodsport 3, Aladdin and the King of Thieves (voice), The Protector, Secret of the Andes, Sinbad: Beyond the Veil of Mists (voice), The Gold Cross, The Lord of the Rings: The Fellowship of the Ring, Never Say Never Mind: The Swedish Bikini Team (video), Scorcher, Sabretooth, The Lord of the Rings: The Two Towers, Endangered Species, The Jungle Book 2 (voice), Vlad (narrator), The Medallion, Coronado, The Lord of the Rings: The Return of the King, The Lost Angel, The Princess Diaries 2: Royal Engagement, Catching Kringle (voice), Shadows in the Sun, One Night with the King: The Call of Destiny, The King Maker, In the Name of the King: A Dungeon Siege Tale, The Legend of Sasquatch (voice), Shark Bait (voice), One Night with the King, The Ferryman, 31 North 62 East, Medium Raw: Night of the Wolf, Prisoners of the Sun, Shadows from the Sky, Spider Dance, The Lion Inside.
TELEVISION: *Movies*: The Incredible Robert Baldick: Never Come Night, The Naked Civil Servant, The Nativity, Shogun, The Merchant of Venice, Peter and Paul, Ivanhoe, Sadat, Kim, No Man's Land, Nairobi Affair, Perry Mason: The Case of the Murdered Madam, The Little Match Girl, Higher Ground, Goddess of Love, The Trial of the Incredible Hulk, The Gifted One, Desperado: Badlands Justice, Secret Weapon, Under Cover, Perry Mason: The Case of the Fatal Framing, Ring of the Musketeers, A Flintstones Christmas Carol, Sliders, Katharina die Große, Boo to you Too! Winnie the Pooh (narrator, voice), Au Pair, Britannic, Helen of Troy, 12 Days of Terror, Dragon Storm, The Lady Musketeer, Chupacabra: Dark Seas, Kiss Me Deadly, Anaconda 3: The Offspring, Anaconda 4: Trail of Blood. *Mini-series:* I Claudius, Shogun (Emmy nom. 1981), Reilley: Ace of Spies, James Clavell's Noble House, War and Remembrance, Great Expectations, The Strauss Dynasty, Revelations. *Series:* Crossroads, Budgie, The Quest, Under Cover, Dark Water (voices), The Untouchables, Gargoyles (voice), Sliders, You Wish, The Secret Adventures of Jules Verne, Takezo Kensei: Sword Saint (narr.). *Guest*: More than 148 appearances.

RIBISI, GIOVANNI

Actor. b. Los Angeles, CA, March 31, 1976.
PICTURES: The Outpost, That Thing You Do!, The Grave, First Love Last Rites, Lost Highway, SubUrbia, The Postman, Scotch and Milk, Phoenix, Men, Saving Private Ryan, The Virgin Suicides (voice), The Mod Squad, The Other Sister, The Boiler Room, Gone in 60 Seconds, The Gift, According to Spencer, Heaven, Masked & Anonymous, Basic, Lost in Translation, I Love Your Work, Cold Mountain, Love's Brother, Sky Captain and the World of Tomorrow, Flight of the Phoenix, The Big White, 10th & Wolf, The Dog Problem, Perfect Stranger, The Dead Girl, Gardener of Eden, Spirit of the Forest (voice), Avatar, Public Enemies, Middle Men, Columbus Circle (also exec. prod.), The Other Side, St. Vincent, The Rum Diary.
TELEVISION: *Movies:* Promised a Mircle, Blossom, The Positively True Adventures of the Alleged Texas Cheerleader-Murdering Mom, Alptraum im Airport, Shot in the Heart. *Series:* My Two Dads, The Wonder Years, Davis Rules, Family Album, Friends, My Name Is Earl (Emmy nom. 2007). *Guest:* More than 60 appearances.

RICCI, CHRISTINA

Actress. b. Santa Monica, CA, February 12, 1980. Raised in Long Island, NY, and Montclair, NJ. Started acting career in commercials.
PICTURES: Mermaids (debut, 1990), The Hard Way, The Addams Family, The Cemetery Club, Addams Family Values, Casper, Gold Diggers: The Secret of Bear Mountain, Now and Then, Last of the High Kings, The Ice Storm, That Darn Cat, Souvenir, I Woke Up Early the Day I Died, Buffalo 66, 200 Cigarettes, The Opposite of Sex (Golden Globe nom. 1999), Fear and Loathing in Las Vegas, Pecker, Desert Blue, Small Soldiers (voice), No Vacancy, Sleepy Hollow, Bless the Child, The Man Who Cried, Prozac Nation (also prod.), All Over the Guy, The Laramie Project, Pumpkin (also prod.), Miranda, The Gathering Anything Else, I Love Your Work, Monster, Cursed, Black Snake Moan, Penelope, The White Rose, The 1 Second Film (doc. also assoc. prod.), Home of the Brave, Speed Racer, New York, I Love You, Long Time Gone, After.Life, The Hero of Color City (voice), Born to Be a Star, Alpha and Omega, Bel Ami.
TELEVISION: *Movies:* Still the Beaver, Promised a Miracle, Blossom, The Positively True Adventures of the Alleged Texas Cheerleader-Murdering Mom, Ellen (pilot), Alptraum im Airport, Shot in the Heart. *Series:* Davis Rules, The Wonder Years, Ally McBeal (recurring role), Friends (recurring role), Grey's Anatomy (recurring role, Emmy nom. 2006), My Name Is Earl (recurring role, Emmy nom. 2007), Saving Grace. *Guest:* More than 74 appearances.

RICE, PETER

Executive. b. United Kingdom. e. Univ. of Nottingham, degree granted in 1989. His father was a business associate of media mogul Rupert Murdoch, a family connection that helped Rice land an internship in the office of Tom Sherak, who was head of U.S. distribution and marketing for Fox Filmed Entertainment at the time. Rice rose through company ranks over the next decade becoming executive v.p. production at 20th Century-Fox and working on such blockbuster hits as "Independence Day," before being tapped to run Fox Searchlight Pictures in Jan. 2000. Fox Searchlight Pictures is a specialty film company that both finances and acquires motion pictures. It has its own marketing and distribution operations, and its films are distributed internationally by Twentieth Century Fox. Fox Searchlight Pictures is a unit of Fox Filmed Entertainment, a unit of Fox Entertainment Group. In 2005, Rice expanded his role at Fox and in 2007 also becaming president of the company's new teen label, Fox Atomic which was suttered in 2009. He became Fox Entertainment Cahirman in 2009.

RICH, JOHN

Producer, Director. b. Rockaway Beach, NY, 1925. e. U. of Michigan, B.A., Phi Beta Kappa, 1948; M.A. 1949; Sesquicentennial Award, 1967; bd. of dir., Screen Dir. Guild of America, 1954-1960; v.p. 1958-1960, Founder-Trustee, Producers-Directors Pension Plan, chmn. of bd. 1965, 1968, 1970; treasurer, Directors Guild of America, 1966-67; v.p. 1967-72. Awards: Directors Guild Award, Most Outstanding Directorial Achievement, 1972. Christopher Award: Henry Fonda as Clarence Darrow, 1975. NAACP Image Award, 1974; 2 Golden Globe Awards: All in the Family, 1972-73. DGA Robert B. Aldrich Award for 1992 also DGA Honorary Life Member Award 2003.
PICTURES: *Director*: Wives and Lovers, The New Interns, Roustabout, Boeing-Boeing, Easy Come Easy Go.
TELEVISION: More than 66 credits for directing and producing, including; *Movies / Series: Director:* Our Miss Brooks, I Married Joan, Colonel Humphrey Flack, Where's Raymond?, Screen Directors Playhouse, Conflict, Gunsmoke (1957-1969), The Rifleman, The Rough Riders, Riverboat, Hotel de Paree, Outlaws, The Andy Griffith Show The Americans, The Dick Van Dyke Show

(Emmy Award 1963, 1 other nom.), McKeever & the Colonel, Gomer Pyle USMC, Gilligan's Island, Run for your Life, I Spy, That Girl, My World and Welcome to It, The Brady Bunch, Make Room For Granddaddy, All in the Family (DGA Award 1972, 2 Emmy Awards, 3 other noms.), Sanford & Son, Maude, Good Times, The Jeffersons, Barney Miller, Sunshine, On the Rocks, Billy, Dorothy, Benson, Newhart, Condo, Amanda's by the Sea, Dear John, Baby Talk, The Man in the Family, Walter & Emily, The Second Half, If Not for You, Hudson Street, Mr. Rhodes, Something So Right, Payne. *Series: Executive producer:* MacGyver, Young MacGyver. *Documentaries/Specials: Director*: Academy Awards.

RICH, LEE
Producer, Executive. b. Cleveland, OH, Dec. 10, 1926. e. Ohio U. Adv. exec.; resigned as sr. v.p., Benton & Bowles, to become producer for Mirisch-Rich TV, 1965 (Rat Patrol, Hey Landlord). Resigned 1967 to join Leo Burnett Agency. Left to form Lorimar Productions in 1969 and served as pres. until 1986 when left to join MGM/UA Communications as chmn. & CEO. Resigned 1988; signed 3-year deal with Warner Bros. setting up Lee Rich Prods. there. Twice named Television Showman of the Year by Publishers' Guild of America.
PICTURES: *Producer*: The Sporting Club, Just Cause, The Amazing Panda Adventure, Big Bully. *Executive Producer*: The Man, The Choirboys, Who Is Killing the Great Chefs of Europe?, The Big Red One, Hard to Kill, Innocent Blood, Passenger 57, Just Cause, The Amazine Panda Adventure, Big Bully, Desperate Measures, Gloria, The Score.
TELEVISION: *Movies*: Do Not Fold Spindle or Mutilate, The Homecoming: A Christmas Story, The Crooked Hearts, Pursuit, The Girls of Huntington House, Dying Room Only, Don't Be Afraid of the Dark, A Dream for Christmas, The Stranger Within, Bad Ronald, The Runaway Barge, Runaways, Returning Home, Eric, Conspiracy of Terror, Widow, Green Eyes, Killer on Board, Desperate Women, Long Journey Back, Mary and Joseph: A Story of Faith, Mr. Horn, Some Kind of Miracle, Young Love, First Love, A Man Called Intrepid, Flamingo Road, Marriage Is Alive and Well, A Perfect Match, Reward, Skag, Killjoy, A Matter of Life and Death, Our Family Business, Mother's Day on Walton's Mountain, This is Kate Bennett, Two of a Kind, A Wedding on Walton's Mountain, A Day of Thanks on Walton's Mountain, One Cooks the Other Doesn't, The Face of Fear, Secret of Midland Heights, Face of Fear, Killer Rules, A Walton Thanksgiving Reunion, Dallas: J.R. Returns, A Walton Easter. *Mini-series*: The Blue Knight, Helter Skelter, Studs Lonigan. *Series: Executive producer:* The Good Life, The Waltons (Emmy Award, 1973, 2 other noms.), Dallas (Emmy nom. 1980), Knots Landing, Against the Grain, Apple's Way, The Blue Knight (Emmy nom. 1974), Hunter, Eight is Enough, Big Shamus Little Shamus, Flamingo Road, Against the Grain.

RICHARD, SIR CLIFF
O.B.E. Singer, Actor. r.n. Harry Webb. b. India, Oct. 14, 1940. Ent. show business 1958 in TV series Oh Boy. Other TV includes Sunday Night at the London Palladium, several Cliff Richard Shows; top British Singer, 1960-71. Voted top box-office star of Great Britain, 1962-63, 1963-64. Twice rep. U.K. in Eurovision Song Contest. Innumerable platinum, gold and silver discs. 1989 became first UK artist to release 100 singles; voted top male vocalist of the 80s by UK Indept. TV viewers. Has made numerous videos. Knighted, 1995.
THEATRE: Aladdin, Five Finger Exercise, The Potting Shed, Time.
PICTURES: Serious Charge (debut, 1959), Expresso Bongo, Wonderful to be Young, Summer Holiday, Swingers' Paradise (actor, composer), Finders Keepers, Thunderbirds are GO (voice), Two a Penny (also composer, songs), Take Me High, Xanadu (singer), many more credits as soundtrack performer.
TELEVISION: Movies: Big Beat '64, Heathcliff (narrator), The Girl with the Giggle in Her Voice, Losing Gemma (soundtrack performer). *Series:* Getaway with Cliff, The Case, It's Cliff and Friends. *Documentaries/Specials:* Comic Relief, The Grand Knockout Tournament, Stars 2001: Die-Aids-Gala, Party at the Palace, many more credits as soundtrack performer. *Guest:* More than 175 appearances.

RICHARDS, DENISE
Actress. b. Downers Grove, IL, Feb. 17, 1972.
PICTURES: Loaded Weapon I, Tammy and the T-Rex, Lookin' Italian, Nowhere, Starship Troopers, Wild Things, Drop Dead Gorgeous, The World is Not Enough, Tail Lights Fade, Valentine, The Third Wheel, Good Advice, You Stupid Man, Empire, Undercover Brother, Love Actually, Scary Movie 3, Whore, Elvis Has Left The Building, Edmond, Blonde and Blonder, Jolene, Deep in the Valley, Finding Bliss, Mother's Little Helpers.
TELEVISION: *Movies:* 919 Fifth Avenue, In the Blink of an Eye, Pier 66, I Do (But I Don't), Backstage: Hollywood Fashion. *Series:* Sex, Love & Secrets, Secrets of a Small Town (pilot), Denise Richards: It's Complicated (also exec. prod.). *Guest:* More than 77 appearances.

RICHARDS, MICHAEL
Actor. b. Culver City, July 14, 1950. e. California Inst. of Arts. Work as stand-up comedian led to appearances on TV including regular stint on series Fridays. Acted on stage with San Diego Rep. Co.
THEATRE: *LA:* The American Clock, Wild Oats.
PICTURES: Young Doctors in Love, Transylvania 6-5000, Whoops Apocalypse, UHF, Problem Child, Coneheads, So I Married an Axe Murderer, Airheads, Unstrung Heroes, Trial and Error, Bee Movie (voice), Cat Tale (voice).
TELEVISION: *Movies:* Jonathan Winters: On the Ledge (various characters), London Suite, David Copperfield. *Series*: Fridays, Marblehead Manor, Seinfeld (3 Emmy Awards, 2 other noms.), The Michael Richards Show. *Guest:* More than 76 appearances.

RICHARDSON, JOELY
Actress. b. London, Eng., January 9, 1965. Daughter of actress Vanessa Redgrave and director Tony Richardson, sister of the late actress Natasha Richardson. e. Lycee, St. Paul's Girl's School, London; Pinellas Park H.S. (Florida), The Thacher Sch. (Ojai, CA), Royal Acad. of Dramatic Art. London stage: Steel Magnolias, Beauty and the Beast (Old Vic); also at Liverpool Playhouse, RSC.
PICTURES: Wetherby (debut, 1985 with mother),Body Contact, Drowning By Numbers, About That Strange Girl, King Ralph, Shining Through, Rebecca's Daughters, I'll Do Anything, Sister My Sister, Hollow Reed, Lochness, 101 Dalmations, Event Horizon, Wrestling with Alligators, Under Heaven, Maybe Baby, Return to Me, The Patriot, The Affair of the Necklace, Shoreditch, The Last Mimzy, The Christmas Miracle of Jonathan Toomey, Anonymous.
TELEVISION: *Movies:* Behaving Badly, Heading Home, Lady Chatterley, The Tribe, The Echo, Fallen Angel, Lies My Mother Told Me, Wallis & Edward, Fatal Contact: Bird Flu in America, Freezing. *Series:* Nip/Tuck (2 Golden Globe noms.), The Day of the Triffids, The Tudors.

RICHARDSON, MIRANDA
Actress. b. Southport, England, March 3, 1958. Studied acting at the drama program at Bristol's Old Vic Theatre School. Began acting on stage, 1979. Appeared in Moving, at the Queen's Theatre and continued in All My Sons, Who's Afraid of Virginia Woolf?, The Life of Einstein in provincial theatres. Also A Lie of the Mind (London), The Changeling, Mountain Language.
PICTURES: Dance With a Stranger (debut, 1985), The Innocent, Empire of the Sun, Eat the Rich, Twisted Obsession, The Bachelor, Enchanted April (Golden Globe Award 1993), The Crying Game, Damage (Academy Award nom.; Golden Globe nom. 1993), Tom and Viv (Academy Award nom.; Golden Globe nom. 1995), Century, The Night and the Moment, Kansas City, The Evening Star, The Apostle, The Designated Mourner, St. Ives, Jacob Two Two Meets the Hooded Fang, The King and I (voice), Sleepy Hollow, Chicken Run (voice), Get Carter, Constance & Carlotta, The Hours, Spider, Nicholas Nickleby, The Rage in Placid Lake, The Actors, Falling Angels, The Prince & Me, Churchill: The Hollywood Years, The Phantom of the Opera, Harry Potter and the Goblet of Fire, Wah-Wah, Spinning Into Butter, Provoked: A True Story, Paris, je t'aime, Southland Tales, Fred Claus, Kis Vuk (voice), The Young Victoria, We Want Sex, Harry Potter and the Deathly Hallows: Part I, Made in Dagenham.
TELEVISION: *Movies:* The Death of a Heart, The Dream Lover, Sweet as You Are, After Pilkington, Blackadder's Christmas Carol, Ball-Trap on the Cote Sauvage, Redemption, Old Times, Mr. Wakefield's Crusade, Fatherland (Golden Globe Award 1995), Merlin (Golden Globe nom. 1999), The Scold's Bridle, Ted & Ralph, Alice in Wonderland, The Miracle Worker, Snow White: The Fairest of Them All, The Lost Prince (Golden Globe nom. 2005), Comic Relief 2003: The Big Hair Do, Gideon's Daughter, Merlin's Apprentice, Rubicon. *Mini-series:* A Woman of Substance, Sorrell and Son, A Dance to the Music of Time, The Big Brass Ring (Golden Globe nom. 2000). *Series:* Blackadder II, Die Kinder, True Adventures of Christopher Columbus, Absolutely Fabulous, The Life and Times of Vivienne Vyle, Rubicon (also pilot). *Guest:* More than 89 appearances.

RICHARDSON, PATRICIA
Actress. b. Bethesda, MD, Feb. 23, 1951. e. Southern Methodist Univ.
THEATRE: *NY:* Gypsy, Loose Ends, The Wake of Jamie Foster, The Collected Works of Billy the Kid, The Frequency, Vanities, The Miss Firecracker Contest, The Coroner's Plot, Fables for Friends. *Regional:* The Killing of Sister George, King Lear, The Philadelphia Story, Fifth of July, About Face.
PICTURES: Gas, C.H.U.D., You Better Watch Out, Lost Angels, In Country, Ulee's Gold, Viva Las Nowhere, Candy Paint (short), Out of Omaha, Lost Dream, Beautiful Wave.
TELEVISION: *Movies:* Yuri Nosenko KGB, Hands of a Stranger, Parent Trap III, Sophie and the Moonhanger, Steve Martini's Undue Influence, Blonde, The Jensen Project. *Series:* Double Trouble, Eisenhower and Lutz, FM, Home Improvement (4 Emmy noms.; 2 Golden Globe noms.), Storytime (PBS), Strong Medicine, The West Wing. *Guest:* More than 40 appearances.

RICHMAN, PETER MARK
Actor. b. Philadelphia, PA, April 16, 1927. e. Philadelphia College of Pharmacy & Science with Bachelor of Science Degree in Pharmacy. Previously acted as Mark Richman. Member of Actors Studio since 1954.
THEATRE: *B'way*: End as a Man, Masquerade, A Hatful of Rain. *Off B'way*: The Dybbuk, The Zoo Story, 4 Faces (also author). *Regional*: Blithe Spirit, The Night of the Iguana, 12 Angry Men,

Babes in Toyland, Funny Girl, The Best Man, Equus, The Rainmaker, 4 Faces.
PICTURES: Friendly Persuasion, The Strange One, The Black Orchid, Dark Intruder, Agent for H.A.R.M., For Singles Only, Friday 13th Part VIII—Jason Takes Manahattan, The Naked Gun 2 1/2: The Smell of Fear, Judgment Day, 4 Faces (actor, writer, prod.), The Shiver Shack (documentary; also prod. & dir as Mark Richman), Poolhall Junkies.
TELEVISION: *Movies*: House on Greenapple Road, Yuma, Mallory: Circumstantial Evidence, The Islander, The Psi Factor, Dempsey, Blind Ambition, City Killer, Bonanza: The Next Generation. *Series*: Longstreet, Dynasty, Cain's Hundred, My Secret Summer (Berlin), Santa Barbara. *Guest:* More than 150 appearances.

RICHTER, W. D.
Writer, Director. b. New Britain, CT, Dec. 7, 1945. e. Dartmouth Coll, B.A.; U. of Southern California Film Sch., grad. study.
PICTURES: *Writer*: Slither (WGA nom. 1974), Peeper, Nickelodeon, Invasion of the Body Snatchers (WGA nom. 1979), Dracula, Brubaker (Academy Award nom. 1981), All Night Long, Big Trouble in Little China, Home for the Holidays, Needful Things, Stealth. *Producer/Director*: Adventures of Buckaroo Banzai Across the Eighth Dimension, Late for Dinner.

RICKERT, JOHN F.
Executive. b. Kansas City, MO, Oct. 29, 1924. e. USC. Joined Universal Pictures in 1951; left in 1957 to start independent productions. 1960-68 handled indep. roadshow distribution (4-walling). 1969 formed Cineworld Corporation, natl. dist. co., and was pres. 1975-76 did tax shelter financing for 13 films. Currently involved in distribution, production packaging and intl. co-production as pres. of Coproducers Corp as a Sports Agent.

RICKLES, DON
Actor, Comedian. b. New York, NY, May 8, 1926. e. AADA.
PICTURES: Run Silent Run Deep, Rabbit Trap, The Rat Race, X: The Man With the X-Ray Eyes, Muscle Beach Party, Bikini Beach, Beach Blanket Bingo, Enter Laughing, The Money Jungle, Where It's At, Kelly's Heroes, Keaton's Cop, Innocent Blood, Casino, Toy Story (voice), Little Redux Riding Hood (voice), Quest for Camelot (voice), Quest for Camelot (voice), Dirty Work, Toy Story 2 (voice), Toy Story 3 (voice).
TELEVISION: *Movies*: Kibbe Hates Fitch, For the Love of It, The Wool Cap, The Catch. *Series*: The Don Rickles Show (1968), The Don Rickles Show (1972), C.P.O. Sharkey, Foul-Ups Bleeps and Blunders, Daddy Dearest, The Catch (mid-season pilot), Mr. Warmth: The Don Rickles Project (Emmy Award 2008). *Guest*: More than 176 appearances.

RICKMAN, ALAN
Actor. b. London, England, Feb. 21, 1946. Began as graphic designer before studying acting at RADA. Joined the Royal Shakespeare Co. where he starred in Les Liaisons Dangereuses; received Tony Award nomination for 1987 NY production.
THEATRE: *Royal Court London:* The Tempest, Love's Labour's Lost, Antony and Cleopatra, Captain Swing, Troilus and Cressida, As You Like It, Mephisto, Les Liaisons Dangereuses (also on B'way). *Royal National Theatre:* Antony and Cleopatra. *B'way:* Private Lives (Tony Award nom.), Sense and Sensibility. *Royal Court:* Commitments, The Last Elephant, The Grass Widow, Lucky Chance, The Seagull, Tango At the End of Winter, Hamlet.
PICTURES: Die Hard (debut, 1988), The January Man, Quigley Down Under, Closet Land, Truly Madly Deeply, Robin Hood: Prince of Thieves (BAFTA Award, 1991), Close My Eyes, Bob Roberts, Mesmer, An Awfully Big Adventure, Sense and Sensibility, Michael Collins, The Winter Guest (also dir.), Judas Kiss, Dogma, Dark Harbor, Galaxy Quest, Play, Blow Dry, Harry Potter and the Sorcerer's Stone, The Search for John Gissing, Willows (exec. prod. only), Harry Potter and the Chamber of Secrets, Love Actually, Harry Potter and the Prisoner of Azkaban, Harry Potter and the Goblet of Fire, The Hitchhiker's Guide to the Galaxy (voice), Snow Cake, Perfume: The Story of a Murderer, Nobel Son, Sweeney Todd: The Demon Barber of Fleet Street, Harry Potter and the Order of the Phoenix, Bottle Shock, Harry Potter and the Half-Blood Prince, Alice in Wonderland, The Wildest Dream (voice), Harry Potter and the Deathly Hallows: Part I, Harry Potter and the Deathly Hallows: Part II.
TELEVISION: *Movies*: Romeo & Juliet, Spirit of Man, Revolutionary Witness, Rasputin (Emmy Award 1996, Golden Globe Award 1997), Something the Lord Made (Emmy nom. 2004), We Know Where You Live (UK documentary). *Mini-series:* Thérèse Raquin, Smiley's People, The Barchester Chronicles. *Guest:* More than 54 appearances.

RIEGERT, PETER
Actor. b. New York, NY, Apr. 11, 1947. e. U. of Buffalo, B.A. Brief stints as 8th grade English teacher, social worker, and aide de camp to politician Bella Abzug 1970, before turned actor, off-off B'way. Appeared with improvisational comedy group War Babies. Film debut in short, A Director Talks About His Film.
THEATRE: Dance with Me (B'way debut), Minnie's Boys (as Chico Marx), Sexual Perversity in Chicago, Isn't it Romantic?, La Brea Tarpits, A Rosen By Any Other Name, The Nerd, Mountain Language/The Birthday Party, The Road to Nirvana.
PICTURES: National Lampoon's Animal House, Americathon, Head Over Heels, National Lampoon Goes to the Movies, Local Hero, City Girl, A Man in Love, Le Grand Carnaval, The Stranger, Crossing Delancey, That's Adequate, The Passport, A Shock to the System, The Object of Beauty, Beyond the Ocean, Oscar, The Runestone, Passed Away, Utz, The Mask, White Man's Burden, Coldblooded, Pie in the Sky, Infinity, Jerry and Tom, Hi - Life, Passion of Mind, In the Weeds, How to Kill your Neighbor's Dog, Traffic, C-Scam, By Courier (short, dir., writer, prod., Academy Award nom. 2001), King of the Corner (also dir., s.p.), Love Conquers Paul, White Irish Drinkers, The Chosen One, Oka Amerikee.
TELEVISION: *Movies*: News at Eleven, Barbarians at the Gate (Emmy nom. 1993), Gypsy, The Infiltrator, Element of Truth, North Shore Fish, Face Down, The Baby Dance, Bojangles, The Bleacher Bums, Back When We Were Grownups, Surrender Dorothy. *Mini-series*: Ellis Island. *Series*: The Middle Ages, The Beast, Law & Order: Special Victims Unit (recurring role), Damages, The Good Wife (recurring role). *Documentaries/Specials*: Concealed Enemies, The Hit List, W. Eugene Smith: Photography Made Difficult, The First Basket (narr.). *Guest:* More than 45 appearances.

RIFKIN, MONROE M.
Executive. e. New York U., BA Finance. Began career with Amer. TV and Communications Corp. as CEO, 1968-82, and Chairman, 1974-82. Bd. member, Nat'l. Cable TV Assoc., 1968-84, and as Chairman, 1983-84. He is the founder, and current chairman and CEO of Rifkin & Associates. The Cable Center inducted Rifkin into the Cable Television Hall of Fame in Oct. 2005.

RIFKIN, RON
Actor. b. New York, NY, Oct. 31, 1939. e. NYU.
THEATRE: *B'way:* Come Blow Your Horn, The Goodbye People, The Tenth Man. *Off-B'way:* Rosebloom, The Art of Dining, Temple, The Substance of Fire.
PICTURES: The Devil's 8 (debut, 1969), Flareup, Silent Running, The Sunshine Boys, The Big Fix, The Sting II, Husbands and Wives, Manhattan Murder Mystery, Wolf, Last Summer in the Hamptons, The Substance of Fire, I'm Not Rappaport, L.A. Confidential, The Negotiator, Drop Back Ten, Keeping the Faith, Sam the Man, The Majestic, Tadpole, Dragonfly, Sum of All Fears, Just a Kiss, Pulse, Peep World.
TELEVISION: *Movies*: Awake & Sing, Get Christie Love, The Dream Makers, In the Glitter Palace, A Question of Guilt, Columbo: Make Me a Perfect Murder, Mrs. R's Daughter, Another Woman's Child, Concealed Enemies, Do You Remember Love, Dress Gray, Courage, Conspiracy: The Trial of the Chicago 8, The Sunset Gang, Norma Jean & Marilyn, Flowers for Algernon, Deliberate Intent, The Warden. *Mini-series:* The Greatest Heroes of the Bible, The Winds of War, Evergreen, *Series:* Adam's Rib, When Things Were Rotten, Husbands Wives & Lovers, One Day at a Time, Falcon Crest, The Trials of Rosie O'Neill, Leaving L.A., Alias, Brothers & Sisters, American Masters (Emmy nom. 2009). *Guest:* More than 85 appearances.

RIGG, DAME DIANA
C.B.E. (1987). Actress. b. Doncaster, England, July 20, 1938. With the Royal Shakespeare Co. at Aldwych Theatre, 1962-64. Recent London stage: Follies, Medea (also B'way).
PICTURES: A Midsummer's Night Dream (debut, 1968), The Assassination Bureau, On Her Majesty's Secret Service, Julius Caesar, The Hospital (Golden Globe nom. 1972), Theatre of Blood, A Little Night Music, The Great Muppet Caper, Evil Under the Sun, Snow White, A Good Man in Africa, Parting Shots, Heidi, The Painted Veil.
TELEVISION: *Movies*: The Comedy of Errors, Married Alive, In This House of Brede (Emmy nom. 1975), The Marquise, Hedda Gabler, Little Eyolf, Witness for the Prosecution, King Lear, The Worst Witch, A Hazard of Hearts, Unexplained Laughter, Mrs. 'Arris Goes to Paris, Genghis Cohn, Running Delilah, Zoya, The Haunting of Helen Walker, The Fortunes and Misfortunes of Moll Flanders, Samson and Delilah, Rebecca (Emmy Award 1997), The Mrs. Bradley Mysteries: Speedy Death, In the Beginning, The American, Victoria & Albert (Emmy nom. 2002). *Mini-series:* Oresteia, Bleak House, Mother Love, The Last King. *Series*: The Avengers (2 Emmy noms.), Diana, Mystery! (host), The Mrs. Bradley Mysteries. *Guest:* More than 66 appearances.

RILEY, MICHAEL
Executive. b.Vancouver, BC. e. University of Western Ontario, London Business School, MBA. From 1996-97 Strategy consultant with the global advertising and media conglomerate WPP Group in London and New York, where he conducted strategic reviews of the group's specialist communication companies including Ogilvy and Mather and J Walter Thompson. Business consultant for Canadian Pacific conglomerate in Toronto from 1992-95, working across its Strategy and Information division including hotels, real estate, oil production, resorts and railroads. From 2004-06 he was vice president and general manager, Turner Broadcasting System France, with responsibility for all Turner channels in that market. From 2000-03 he was V. P. Turner Classic Movies, Europe, Middle East and Africa, and from 1997-2000 was V.P., Business Development, Television and Interactive

Media, Cartoon Network and Turner Classic Movies. Named Sr. V. P. and general manager, Turner Broadcasting System, Europe, Middle East and Africa where he was responsible for developing the CNN commercial strategy and the overall brand strategy for Cartoon Network, Boomerang, TCM, TNT and Adult Swim in Germany, Northern Europe, Middle East and Africa. Other key responsibilities included the management of advertising sales, marketing and interactive commerce functions, as well as supporting the company's programming development and acquisition strategy. He joined The Walt Disney Company in April 2008 as Sr. V.P. and general manager, Radio Disney, where he oversaw the strategic management of the Radio Disney network and its portfolio of 36 owned radio stations, leading them to record ratings through original multi-platform content achievements. He was named President, ABC Family in 2010, with oversight of original programming and acquisitions, management, marketing, sales and operations, and responsibility for the overall strategic and creative direction for the channel.

RINGWALD, MOLLY
Actress. b. Sacramento, CA, Feb. 16, 1968. Daughter of jazz musician Bob Ringwald; began performing at age 4 with his Great Pacific Jazz Band and at 6 recorded album, Molly Sings. Professional debut at 5 in stage play, The Glass Harp. Appeared in bit on TV's New Mickey Mouse Club, a West Coast stage production of Annie and in TV series, The Facts of Life, *Off-B'way debut*: Lily Dale (Theatre World Award, 1986).
PICTURES: Tempest (debut, 1982, Golden Globe nom. 1983), P.K. and the Kid, Spacehunter: Adventures in the Forbidden Zone, Sixteen Candles, The Breakfast Club, Pretty in Pink, The Pick-Up Artist, For Keeps?, King Lear, Fresh Horses, Strike It Rich, Betsy's Wedding, Face the Music, Seven Sundays, Malicious, Baja, Bastard Brood, Office Killer, Requiem for Murder, Teaching Mrs. Tingle, Kimberly, Cut, The Giving Tree, In the Weeds, The Translator, Cowboy Up, Not Another Teen Movie.
TELEVISION: *Movies*: Packin' It In, Surviving, Women and Men: Stories of Seduction (Dust Before Fireworks), Something to Live For: The Alison Gertz Story, Since You've Been Gone,Twice Upon a Time, The Big Time, The Wives He Forgot, Molly: An American Girl on the Home Front. *Mini-series*: The Stand. *Series*: The Facts of Life, Townies, The Secret Life of the American Teenager. *Guest:* More than 62 appearances.

RISHER, SARA
Executive, Producer. Former chair of production, New Line Productions, Inc. Currently president of Chick Flicks Productions.
PICTURES: *Co-producer/Associate producer*: Polyester, Alone in the Dark, The First Time, A Nightmare on Elm Street, Critters, Quiet Cool, A Nightmare on Elm Street 3: Dream Warriors, Stranded, My Demon Lover, Wrongfully Accused. *Executive producer*: A Nightmare on Elm Street 4: The Dream Master, A Nightmare on Elm Street 5: The Dream Child, Book of Love, Pump Up the Volume, Wide Sargasso Sea, Surf Ninjas, Blink, New Nightmare (co-exec. prod.), In Love & War, Last Man Standing, Deep Blue, The Last Mimzy. *Producer:* Raise Your Voice, Angel from Montgomery, Broken Bridges, The Politician's Wife.

RISSNER, DANTON
Executive, Producer. b. Brooklyn, NY, March 27, 1940. e. Florida So. Col. Began as agent with Ashley Famous (later Intl. Famous), 1967-69. 1969 joined Warner Bros. as v.p., chg. European prod.; 1970, moved to United Artists as v.p., chg. European prod.; 1973, named v.p. in chg. East Coast & European prod. for UA; 1975- 78, v.p. in chg. of world-wide prod.; 1981, exec. v.p., 20th Century-Fox.; 1984, joined UA as sr. v.p., motion pictures. Later joined Kensington Entertainment as sr. v.p. Joined Sports Finance & Management Group as sr. v.p. of entertainment.
PICTURES: *Producer:* Up the Academy, Backfire, A Summer Story, School Ties (exec. prod.), Gone, Baby, Gone, Edge of Darkness (exec. prod.).
TELEVISION: *Movies*: Fall From the Sky (exec. prod.)

RITCHIE, GUY
Writer, Director. b. Hatfield, Hertfordshire, England, Sept. 10, 1968.
PICTURES: The Hard Case, Lock Stock and Two Smoking Barrels (also cast. dir.), Snatch (also actor), What It Feels Like For a Girl (dir. only), Star, Mean Machine (exec. prod.), Swept Away, Revolver, RocknRolla (also prod.), Sherlock Holmes (dir.), Excalibur (dir.).
TELEVISION: *Movie:* Suspect (exec. prod., dir.). *Series:* Lock, Stock...(writer & exec. prod.).

RIVERA, CHITA
Actress, Dancer. r.n. Concita del Rivero. b. Washington, DC, Jan. 23, 1933. Trained for stage at American School of Ballet.
THEATRE: Call Me Madam (1952), Guys and Dolls, Can-Can, Shoestring Revue, Seventh Heaven, Mr. Wonderful, Shinbone Alley, West Side Story, Bye Bye Birdie, Bajour, Sondheim: A Musical Tribute, Chicago, Hey Look Me Over, Merlin, The Rink (Tony Award, 1984), Jerry's Girls, Kiss of the Spider Woman (Tony Award, 1993), Broadway- The Golden Age.
PICTURES: Sweet Charity (1969), Chicago- The Musical, Kalamazoo?.
TELEVISION: *Movies:* The Marcus-Nelson Murders, Once Upon A Brothers Grimm, Pippin: His Life & Times, Mayflower Madam. *Series:* One Life to Live, The New Dick Van Dyke Show. *Documentaries/Specials:* Kennedy Center Tonight—Broadway to Washington!, Toller Cranston's Strawberry Ice, TV Academy Hall of Fame, 1985. *Guest:* More than 85 appearances.

RIVERA, GERALDO
Journalist. b. New York, NY, July 4, 1943. e. U. of Arizona, Brooklyn Law School; 1969, Columbia School of Journalism. Started legal career first as lawyer with Harlem Assertion of Rights Community Action for Legal Services 1968-70. Switched to journalism and joined WABC-TV, New York, 1970. Made several TV documentaries on such subjects as institutions for retarded, drug addiction, migrant workers, etc. Chmn.: One-to-One Foundation, Maravilla Foundation. Joined cast of Good Morning America. Later joined ABC's 20/20 and had eight-year association with show as investigative reporter. In 1987 started producing and hosting The Geraldo Rivera Show, which aired 11 years. In 1998 he hosted a series of investigative specials for NBC. Rivera joined FOX News Channel in Nov. 2001 as a war correspondent. In July 2002, he joined Fox Broadcasting as investigative reporter on its summer news magazine The Pulse. He returned to volatile Iraq in early 2005 to cover elections from Baghdad. Currently appears regularly on the Fox News Channel, which airs segments "Geraldo at Large." Rivera has received more than 170 awards for journalism, including the prestigious George Foster Peabody Award, three national and seven local Emmys, two Columbia-Dupont and two additional Scripps Howard Journalism Awards.
PICTURES: Meet Wally Sparks, Contact, Copland, Primary Colors, The Bonfire of the Vanities, All About Steve, The Miracle of Spanish Harlem.
TELEVISION: *Movies:* Perry Mason: The Case of the Reckless Romeo, Back to Bedlam, Cheech & Chong: Roasted. *Series:* Good Morning America (contributor), ABC Late Night, 20/20, The Geraldo Rivera Show, Now It Can Be Told, Frontline, Rivera Live, Up Front Tonight (host), Geraldo at Large (host), Hannity (recurring panelist). *Documentaries/Specials:* The Mystery of Al Capone's Vault, American Vice: The Doping of a Nation, Innocence Lost: The Erosion of American Childhood, Sons of Scarface: The New Mafia, Murder: Live From Death Row, Devil Worship: Exposing Satan's Underground, Harvest of Empire, New World Order. *Guest:* More than 88 appearances.

RIVERS, JOAN
Actress, Writer, Director. r.n. Joan Molinsky. b. New York, NY, June 8, 1933. e. Barnard College (Phi Beta Kappa). Formerly fashion coordinator for Bond clothing stores. Performed comedy act in nightclubs, then with Second City 1961-62; TV debut: Johnny Carson Show, 1965; nat'l syndicated columnist, Chicago Tribune 1973-76; Hadassah Woman of the Year, 1983; Jimmy Award for Best Comedian 1981; Chair., National Cystic Fibrosis Foundation. 1978 created TV series Husbands Wives and Lovers.
AUTHOR: Having a Baby Can Be a Scream (1974), Can We Talk? (1983), The Life and Hard Times of Heidi Abramowitz (1984), Enter Talking (1986), Still Talking (1990).
THEATRE: *B'way*: Fun City (also co-writer), Broadway Bound, Sally Marr... and Her Escorts (also co-writer).
PICTURES: The Swimmer, Rabbit Test (also dir., s.p.), The Muppets Take Manhattan, Spaceballs (voice), Serial Mom, Goosed, Intern, Hip Edgy Quirky!, Napoleon (voice), Shrek 2 (voice), Joan Rivers: A Piece of Work (doc.).
TELEVISION: *Movies*: The Girl Most Likely To...(writer), How to Murder a Millionaire, Tears and Laughter: The Joan and Melissa Rivers Story, Lady Boss, Joan Rivers: Before Melissa Pulls the Plug (also writer), Arthur (Emmy nom. 2009). *Series*: The Electric Company (narr.), The Tonight Show (regular substitute guest host: 1983-86), The Late Show (host), The New Hollywood Squares, The Joan Rivers Show (morning talk show, Emmy Award 1990), Can We Shop?, Another World, Dave the Barbarian (voice), The Joan Rivers Position (presenter), The Apprentice, Spaceballs: The Animated Series. *Specials:* Joan & Melissa: Live at the Grammys, Joan & Melissa: Live at the Golden Globes, Joan & Melissa: Live at the Academy Awards (host), Z Rock. *Guest:* More than 237 appearances.

ROACHE, LINUS
Actor. b. Manchester, England, February 1, 1964.
THEATRE: *London:* A Question of Geography, Titus Andronicus, Julius Caesar, Richard II, Love's Labours Lost (Manchester), The Deep Blue Sea.
PICTURES: Link, Priest, The Wings of the Dove, Hart's War, Beyond Borders, The Chronicles of Riddick, The Forgotten, Batman Begins, Twelve and Holding, Find Me Guilty, The Namesake, Before the Rains, Yonkers Joe.
TELEVISION: *Movies:* Shot Through the Heart, The Gathering Storm, RFK (Golden Globe nom. 2003), The Ten Commandments, The Miraculous Year. *Mini-series:* How High the Moon. *Series:* Seaforth, Kidnapped, Law & Order, Coronation Street.

ROBARDS, SAM
Actor. b. New York, NY, December 16, 1961. Son of actress Lauren Bacall and late actor Jason Robards. e. National Theater Institute and studied with Uta Hagen at H.B. Studios.

THEATRE: *B'way:* The Man Who Had All the Luck, Absurd Person Singular, 39 Steps. *Off-B'way*: Album, Flux, Taking Steps, Moonchildren. Kennedy Center: Idiot's Delight and regional theatre.
PICTURES: Tempest, Not Quite Paradise, Fandango, Bright Lights Big City, Bird, Casualties of War, The Ballad of Little Jo, Mrs. Parker and the Vicious Circle, Donor Unknown, Beautiful Girls, Dinner and Driving, American Beauty, Bounce, Artificial Intelligence: AI, Life as a House, Catch That Kid, Marmalade, Surviving Eden, Awake, The Other Side of the Tracks, Che: Part One, The Rebound, Perestroika, Company Retreat, Homework.
TELEVISION: *Movies*: Jacobo Timerman: Prisoner Without a Name Cell Without a Number, Into Thin Air, Pancho Barnes, The Man Who Captured Eichmann, Black and Blue, Hamlet, The Warden, On Golden Pond, Obsessed, The Blackwater Lightship. *Series*: Movin' Right Along (PBS), TV 101, Get a Life!, Maximum Bob, My Life with Men, Clubhouse, The West Wing (recurring role), Gossip Girl.

ROBBINS, MATTHEW
Writer, Director. e. U.S.C. Sch. of Cinema. Wrote early scripts in collaboration with Hal Barwood, Robbins branched out into directing with Corvette Summer in 1978.
PICTURES: *Writer*: The Sugarland Express (1975, WGA nom. 1975), The Bingo Long Traveling All-Stars and Motor Kings (WGA nom. 1977), MacArthur, Corvette Summer (also dir.), Dragonslayer (also dir.), The Legend of Billie Jean, Warning Sign, *batteries not included (also dir.), Bingo (dir. only), Mimic (s.p.), The Concert, Don't Be Afraid of the Dark (s.p.).
TELEVISION: *Movie:* Mothers, Daughters and Lovers (dir.).

ROBBINS, RICHARD
Composer. b. Boston, MA, Dec. 4, 1940. Bachelor of Music and Graduate Studies at New England Conservatory of Music. Received Frank Huntington Beebe Fellowship to Austria where he studied musicology, chamber music. Later became dir. of Mannes College of Music Preparatory School, N.Y. Has worked closely with James Ivory and Ismail Merchant. Also dir. doc. films Sweet Sounds, Street Musicians of Bombay.
PICTURES: The Europeans (supr. score), Jane Austen in Manhattan, Quartet, Heat and Dust, The Bostonians, A Room with a View, Maurice, Sweet Lorraine, My Little Girl, Slaves of New York, Mr. & Mrs. Bridge, The Ballad of the Sad Cafe, Howards End (Academy Award nom. 1993), The Remains of the Day (Academy Award nom. 1994), Jefferson in Paris, Surviving Picasso, The Proprietor, The Hidden Dimension, A Soldier's Daughter Never Cries, Place Vendome, Cotton Mary, The Girl, The Golden Bowl, The Mystic Masseur, Le Divorce, The White Countess, City of Your Final Destination.
TELEVISION: *Movie:* Love and Other Sorrows. *Documentary:* Love and Loyalty: The Making of 'The Remains of the Day'.

ROBBINS, TIM
Actor, Director. b. West Covina, CA, Oct. 16, 1958. Son of Greenwich Village folksinger, worked as actor while in high school. e. NYU. Transferred to UCLA theatre program appearing in guest roles on TV. 1981, co-founder and artistic dir., The Actors Gang, in L.A.; dir. them in and co-authored Alagazam: After the Dog Wars, Violence: The Misadventures of Spike Spangle—Farmer, Carnage: A Comedy (also prod. in NY).
PICTURES: Toy Soldiers (debut, 1984), No Small Affair, Fraternity Vacation, The Sure Thing, Top Gun, Howard the Duck, Five Corners, Bull Durham, Tapeheads, Miss Firecracker, Twister (cameo), Erik the Viking, Cadillac Man, Jacob's Ladder, Jungle Fever, The Player (Cannes Film Fest. Award, Golden Globe Award 1993), Bob Roberts (also dir., s.p., co-wrote songs, Golden Globe nom. 1993), Short Cuts (Golden Globe Award 1994), The Hudsucker Proxy, The Shawshank Redemption, Ready to Wear (Pret-a-Porter), I.Q., Dead Man Walking (dir., Academy Award nom.; Golden Globe nom. 1996), Nothing to Lose, Arlington Road, The Cradle Will Rock (dir and prod.), The Spectre of Hope (prod. only), Mission to Mars, High Fidelity, Anti-Trust, Human Nature, The Truth About Charlie, The Day My God Died (narr.), Mystic River (Academy Award, Golden Globe Award 2003), Code 46, The Secret Life of Words, War of the Worlds, Zathura: A Space Adventure, Tenacious D in: The Pick of Destiny, Hotstuff, The White Rose, Noise, Grindhouse, The Lucky Ones, City of Ember, Green Lantern, Keeper of the Pinstripes, Cinema Verite.
TELEVISION: *Movies*: Quarterback Princess, Malice in Wonderland, Possible Side Effects (dir., exec. prod., writer). *Series:* Freedom: A History of Us (doc.), Queens Supreme, (dir. only). *Guest*: More than 141 appearances.

ROBERTS, BRIAN L.
Executive. b. Philadelphia, PA. e. Wharton School at U. of Penn., MBA. Son of Comcast Corporation founder Ralph J. Roberts. Joined Comcast Corporation, a major cable TV and cell. telephone network operating co., in 1982. Several mgt. positions, incl. exec. VP of ops., before becoming president in 1990. Currently, Roberts is chmn. and CEO of Comcast Corporation. He serves as chairman of CableLabs, the cable industry's research and development arm. He was chairman of NCTA from 1995 to 1996, when the landmark deregulatory 1996 Telecommunications Act became law. Roberts was the recipient of the 2004 Humanitarian Award from the Simon Wiesenthal Center and was the 2002 Walter Kaitz Foundation Honoree of the Year for his commitment to diversity in the cable industry. The Police Athletic League of Philadelphia honored Roberts with its 2002 award for his commitment to youth programs and community partnerships. He co-chaired the 2003 Resource Development Campaign for the United Way of Southeastern Pennsylvania and was a founding co-chair of Philadelphia 2000, the nonpartisan host committee for the 2000 Republican National Convention. Roberts has been listed in Forbes magazine's "World's Richest People" and "400 Richest Americans."

ROBERTS, ERIC A.
Actor. b. Biloxi, MS, April 18, 1956. Father founded Actors and Writers Workshop in Atlanta, 1963. Sister is actress Julia Roberts. Began appearing in stage prods. at age 5. Studied at American Acad. of Dramatic Arts. Stage debut in Rebel Women.
THEATRE: Mass Appeal, The Glass Menagerie (Hartford Stage Co.), A Streetcar Named Desire (Princeton's McCarter Theater), Alms for the Middle Class (Long Wharf), Burn This (B'way debut; Theatre World Award).
PICTURES: King of the Gypsies (debut, 1978, Golden Globe nom. 1979), Raggedy Man, Star 80 (Golden Globe nom. 1984), The Pope of Greenwich Village, The Coca Cola Kid, Runaway Train (Academy Award nom., Golden Globe nom. 1986), Nobody's Fool, Rude Awakening, Blood Red, Best of the Best, The Ambulance, Lonely Hearts, Final Analysis, Best of the Best 2, By the Sword, Freefall, Babyfever, Love Is a Gun, The Specialist, Nature of the Beast, The Grave, Heaven's Prisoners, It's My Party, From the Edge, The Immortals, Power 98, The Cable Guy, American Strays, TNT, The Shadow Men, Making Sandwiches, Most Wanted, Two Shades of Blue, The Prophecy II, La Cucaracha, Dead End, Bittersweet, Spawn 3: Ultimate Battle, Hitman's Run, Facade, The Alternate, No Alibi, Luck of the Draw, Cecil B. Demented. Tripfall, The King's Guard, Mercy Streets, Sanctimony, The Flying Dutchman, The Beat Nicks, Mindstorm, Raptor, Con Games, Wrong Number, Sol Goode, Fool Proof, Spun, Wolves of Wall Street, Endangered Species, Intoxicating, National Security, The Long Ride Home, The Civilization of Maxwell Bright, Break A Leg, Killer Weekend, Miss Cast Away and the Island Girls, Junior Pilot, Six: The Mark Unleashed, Sledge: The Story of Frank Sledge, Graves End, Comedy Hell, Worlds Apart, Princess, DOA: Dead or Alive, Phat Girlz, Geppetto's Secret (voice), Hollywood Dreams, A Guide to Recognizing Your Saints, Aurora, Blizhniy Boy: The Ultimate Fighter, Dark Honeymoon, Confessions of an Action Star, The Butcher, Witless Protection, The Dark Knight, Rock Slyde, Kingshighway, Hunt to Kill, Royal Kill, Shannon's Rainbow, The Whole Truth, Groupie, Baby O, Westbrick Murders, Enemies Among Us, Project Solitude, Intent, Terror Trap, First Dog, The Throwaways, The Expendables, Baby O, Dante's Inferno Animated (voice, English version), The Wayshower: Lord of the Realms, Silver Case.
TELEVISION: *Movies*: Pauls' Case, Slow Burn, To Heal a Nation, The Lost Capone, Descending Angel, Vendetta: Secrets of a Mafia Bride, Fugitive Among Us, Love Honor & Obey: The Last Mafia Marriage, Voyage, Love Cheat and Steal, Saved by the Light, The Odyssey, Dr. Who, Dark Angel, In Cold Blood, Purgatory, Lansky, Heaven's Fire, Race Against Time, Strange Frequency, Stiletto Dance, Walking Shadow, Rough Air: Danger on Flight 534, Roughing It, Christmas Rush, L.A. Confidential, Deceptively Yours, Pandemic, Fatal Desire, Southern Comfort, Depth Charge, Cyclops. *Series*: Another World, C-16: FBI, Less Than Perfect, Crash, Heroes. *Documentaries/Specials*: Miss Lonelyhearts, Walking After Midnight, Dear America: Letters Home from Vietnam (reader). *Guest:* More than 113 appearances.

ROBERTS, JULIA
Actress. b. Smyrna, GA, Oct. 28, 1967. r.n. Julie Fiona Roberts. Brother is actor Eric Roberts. Parents ran theatre workshop in Atlanta. m. cinematographer Daniel Moder. Moved to NY to study acting; modeled for the Click Agency before making prof. debut in brother's film Blood Red. Number one on Quigley's Top Ten MoneyMaking Stars of 1999; number two in 2000, number three in 2001, number five in 2003 and number five in 2005.
THEATRE: *B'way:* Three Days of Rain (debut 2006).
PICTURES: Blood Red (debut, 1986), Satisfaction, Mystic Pizza, Steel Magnolias (Academy Award nom., Golden Globe Award 1990), Pretty Woman (Academy Award nom., BAFTA nom., Golden Globe Award 1991), Flatliners, Sleeping With the Enemy, Dying Young, Hook, The Pelican Brief, I Love Trouble, Ready to Wear (Pret-a-Porter), Something to Talk About, Mary Reilly, Michael Collins, Everyone Says I Love You, My Best Friend's Wedding (Golden Globe nom. 1998), Conspiracy Theory, Step Mom (also exec. prod.), Notting Hill (Golden Globe nom. 2000), Runaway Bride, Erin Brockovich (Academy Award, Golden Globe Award 2001), The Mexican, America's Sweethearts, Ocean's Eleven, Full Frontal, Confessions of a Dangerous Mind, Mona Lisa Smile, Closer, Ocean's Twelve, Charlotte's Web (voice), The Ant Bully (voice), Charlie Wilson's War (Golden Globe nom. 2008), Fireflies in the Garden, Kit Kittredge: An American Girl Mystery (exec. prod.), Duplicity (Golden Globe nom. 2010), Valentine's Day, Eat, Pray, Love, Larry Crowne, Jesus Henry Christ (prod. only).

TELEVISION: *Movies*: Baja Oklahoma, Before Your Eyes: Angelie's Secret (narr., voice), Samantha: An American Girl Holiday (exec. prod.), Felicity: An American Girl Adventure (exec. prod.). *Series:* Queens Supreme (exec. prod.), Law & Order (Emmy nom. 1999 as guest). *Documentaries/Specials*: In the Wild, AFI's 100 Years...100 Stars, America: A Tribute to Heroes. *Guest*: More than 120 appearances.

ROBERTS, RALPH J.
Executive. b. Philadelphia, PA. Father of Comcast Corporation pres. & CEO Brian L. Roberts. e. Wharton School at U. of Penn. Served 4-year tour of duty in U.S. Navy. Began career in 1950s as acct. exec., Aitken Kynett Advertising Agency. VP, Muzak Corp. Exec. VP, dir. of advertising and later pres. and CEO of Pioneer Industries, a men's accessory co. Co-founder and former pres. and chairman, Comcast Corp., a cable TV and cell. tel. network operating co. Starting with the purchase of a single cable television system in Tupelo, Mississippi, in 1963, Roberts went on to create the largest cable television company in the United States employing more than 59,000 people nationwide. Roberts served as Chairman of the Company from 1989 to 2002. Prior to that, he served as President and Chairman. He currently is the chairman Emeritus, Director, Chairman of Executive & Finance Committee and Director of Comcast Cable Communications Inc. of Comcast Corporation and is president of Sural Corp. He is also Member of Advisory Board of Axiom Venture Partners, L.P., Director of QVC, Inc., Former Chairman of NTL Triangle LLC, Former Chairman of the Board of Jones Intercable, Inc.
Awards include: the Distinguished Vanguard Award for Leadership from the National Cable and Telecommunications Association; induction in the Broadcasting & Cable Hall of Fame; the Cable Television Hall of Fame Award; and the Walter Kaitz Foundation Award for contributing to the cable industry's diversity efforts. Recently Roberts received the William Penn Award given by the Greater Philadelphia Chamber of Commerce; the American Horizon Award for visionary leadership from the Media Institute in Washington, DC; the Trustees Award from the National Academy of Television Arts & Sciences; and (jointly with his son and the Company's President, Brian) the Steven J. Ross Humanitarian Award given by the United Jewish Appeal Federation.

ROBERTS, TONY
Actor. b. New York, NY, Oct. 22, 1939. e. Northwestern U.
THEATRE: *B'way*: How Now Dow Jones, Don't Drink the Water, Play It Again Sam, Promises Promises, Barefoot in the Park, Absurd Person Singular, Sugar, Murder at the Howard Johnson's, They're Playing Our Song, Doubles, Arsenic and Old Lace, Jerome Robbins' Broadway, The Seagull, The Sisters Rosensweig, Victor/Victoria, Xanadu. *Off-B'way*: The Cradle Will Rock, The Good Parts, Four Dogs and a Bone. *NY City Opera:* Brigadoon, South Pacific. *LA:* The Tale of the Allergist's Wife. *Dir*: One of the All-Time Greats (Off-B'way).
PICTURES: Million Dollar Duck, Star Spangled Girl, Play It Again Sam, Serpico, The Taking of Pelham One Two Three, Lovers Like Us, Annie Hall, Just Tell Me What You Want, Stardust Memories, A Midsummer Night's Sex Comedy, Amityville 3-D, Key Exchange, Hannah and Her Sisters, Radio Days, 18 Again, Popcorn, Switch, Apologies to Bunuel, Dead Broke, My Best Friend's Wife, Twelve and Holding.
TELEVISION: *Movies*: The Lindbergh Kidnapping Case, Girls in the Office, If Things Were Different, Seize the Day, Messiah on Mott Street, A Question of Honor, A Different Affair, Our Sons, Not in My Family, The American Clock, A Perry Mason Mystery: The Case of the Jealous Jokester, Victor/Victoria, My Favorite Broadway: The Leading Ladies, Sounds From a Town I Love. *Series*: Rosetti and Ryan, The Four Seasons, The Lucie Arnaz Show, The Thorns, The Carol Burnett Show, Bravo Profiles (narr.), Law & Order (recurring role). *Guest:* More than 62 appearances.

ROBERTSON, CLIFF
Actor, Writer, Director. b. La Jolla, CA, Sept. 9, 1925.
THEATRE: Mr. Roberts, Late Love, The Lady and the Tiger, Ghosts of 87 (one-man show). *B'way*: The Wisteria Tree, Orpheus Descending (Theatre World Award), Love Letters.
PICTURES: *Actor:* Picnic (debut, 1955), Autumn Leaves, The Girl Most Likely, The Naked and the Dead, Gidget, Battle of the Coral Sea, As the Sea Rages, All in a Night's Work, Underworld USA, The Big Show, The Interns, My Six Loves, PT 109, Sunday in New York, The Best Man, 633 Squadron, Love Has Many Faces, Masquerade, Up From the Beach, The Honey Pot, The Devil's Brigade (also s.p.), Charly (Academy Award, Golden Globe nom. 1968), Too Late the Hero, J.W. Coop (also dir., s.p.), The Great Northfield Minnesota Raid, Ace Eli and Rodger of the Skies, Man on a Swing, Out of Season, Three Days of the Condor, Shoot, Obsession, The Pilot (also dir.), Dominique, Fraternity Row (narrator), Class, Brainstorm, Star 80, Shaker Run, Malone, Wild Hearts Can't Be Broken, Wind, Renaissance Man, Dazzle, The Sunset Boys, Escape From L.A., Melting Pot, Assignment Berlin, Family Tree, Paranoid III, March 2, Falcon Down, The 13th Child (also writer), Spider-Man, Spider-Man 2, Riding the Bullet, Spider-Man 3, Accidental Icon: The Real Gidget Story.
TELEVISION: *Movies*: The Sunshine Patriot, Man Without A Country, A Tree Grows in Brooklyn, My Father's House, Return to Earth, Overboard, Two of a Kind, The Key to Rebecca, Dreams of Gold: The Mel Fisher Story, Ford: The Man and the Machine,Dead Reckoning, P.T. Barnum: America's Greatest Shoman (narrator), Dazzle. *Mini-series:* Washington: Behind Closed Doors. *Series*: The United States Steel Hour (Emmy nom. 1961), Rod Brown of the Rocket Rangers, Bob Hope Presents the Chrysler Theatre: The Game (Emmy Award 1966), Falcon Crest. *Documentaries/Specials*: Days of Wine and Roses (Playhouse 90). Also spokesman for AT&T. *Guest*: More than 106 appearances.

ROBERTSON, KATHLEEN
Actress. b. Hamilton, Canada, July 8, 1973.
PICTURES: Blown Away, Lapse of Memory, Nowhere, Dog Park, Splendor, Runaway Bride (cameo), Psycho Beach Party, Speaking of Sex, Scary Movie 2, Beautiful, I am Sam, XX/XY, I Love Your Work, Mall Cop, Control, Until the Night, Hollywoodland, Player 5150, Not Since You, A Night for Dying Tigers.
TELEVISION: *Movies:* Liar's Edge, Quiet Killer, Survive the Night, IN the Line of Duty: The Price of Vengeance, Torso: The Evelyn Dick Story, In the Dark, Last Exit, The Terrorist Next Door, Glitch. *Mini-series:* Tin Man. *Series:* Maniac Mansion, Beverly Hills 90210, Girls Club, The Business.

ROBERTSON, TIMOTHY B.
Executive. e. Univ of VA, BA in English. Masters of Divinity from Gordon-Conwell Thelogical Seminary, and exec. program in business admin. at grad. school of business, Columbia Univ. Manager of WXNE-TV in Boston, 1980-82; supervisor of Christian Broadcasting Network's TV facility; 1982-90, in charge of Middle East Television after purchase by CBN. Became pres. & CEO of International Family Entertainment Inc., whose holdings included The Family Channel, Fit TV, United Family Communications. IFE was acquired by Fox Kids Worldwide, Inc. (FKW), in Sept. 1997, and is now a wholly owned subsidiary of FKW. Robertson currently serves as chmn. of Bay Shore Enterprises, LLC, an investment holding company with activities in international media and Internet technology ventures. Its most significant investment is in FamilyClick.com, LLC, an online service provider marketing safe and filtered Internet access for families. Robertson has served on the boards of a variety of cable and industry groups such as the Nat'l. Cable Television Assoc., the Cable Television Advertising Bureau, the Walter Kaitz Foundation, the Nat'l. Acad. of Cable Programming and Cable in the Classroom. He is on the bd. of visitors for Univ. of Va. and is a recently appointed member of the Governor's Blue Ribbon Commission on Higher Education in Va. He also serves on the bd. of trustees for Regent University, the bd. of trustees for Norfolk Academy and the bd. of trustees for the DON'T QUIT Foundation. Member: Arts & Sciences Alumni Council for the Univ. of Va. and has served as past campaign co-chmn. on the United Way of Virginia Beach and on the bd. of directors of Operation Smile.

ROBINOV, JEFF
Executive. Robinov started his career as an agent at Writers & Artists. He then spent three years as an agent with International Creative Management, handling the careers of such writer-directors as the Wachowskis ("The Matrix") and Academy Award winner Chris McQuarrie ("The Usual Suspects"). 1997, moved to Warner Bros. Pictures as senior v.p., production; promoted to executive v.p., production and stayed in that role two years before being named president, production in 2002. Under his management, the division crossed the billion-dollar mark every year since then in both domestic and international box office grosses. Also during this time, Warner Bros. Pictures won Best Picture Academy Awards for "Million Dollar Baby" (2004) and "The Departed" (2006) and the Best Animated Feature Oscar for "Happy Feet" (2006). Robinov was named president, Warner Bros. Pictures Group upon its founding in November 2007 and is the position he holds today. In this position, Robinov has oversight of all aspects of production of the movies produced by Warner Bros. Pictures and its partner production entities. The heads of the studio's theatrical physical production, post production, worldwide marketing, and domestic and international distribution teams report directly to Robinov, and he shares oversight of the studio's direct-to-platform production arm, Warner Premiere, with the Warner Bros. Home Entertainment Group. Robinov reports directly to Alan Horn, president & COO, Warner Bros.

ROBINSON, BRUCE
Writer, Director, Actor. b. Kent, England, May 1, 1946. e. Central School of Speech and Drama. As actor appeared in 12 films but began writing novels and screenplays long before he gave up acting in 1975.
PICTURES: *Actor*: Romeo and Juliet (debut), The Story of Adele H., Still Crazy, Paid in Full. *Writer*: The Killing Fields (WGA Award for best s.p., Academy Award nom.; Golden Globe nom. 1985), Fat Man and Little Boy, Return to Paradise, In Dreams. *Director/Writer*: Withnail and I, How to Get Ahead in Advertising, Jennifer Eight, Harry's War, Jennifer Eight, The Rum Diary (s.p.).

ROBINSON, JAMES G.
Executive, Producer. e. Univ. of Maryland. Was prof. photographer and business entrepreneur prior to entering m.p. industry as co-prod. of The Stone Boy, and exec. prod. of Where the River Runs Black, Streets of Gold. Founded Morgan Creek Prods. in 1988, Morgan Creek Intl. in 1989, Morgan Creek Music Group in 1990, Morgan Creek Theatres and Morgan Creek International Theatres in 1992. Currently, co-chmn. & CEO of Morgan Creek Productions. 2008 shares co-chmn. with Rick Nicita.
PICTURES: *Executive prod. for Morgan Creek*: Young Guns, Skin Deep, Renegades, Enemies a Love Story, Nightbreed, Coupe de Ville, Young Guns II, The Exorcist III, Pacific Heights, Robin Hood: Prince of Thieves, Freejack, White Sands, The Last of the Mohicans, True Romance. *Producer for Morgan Creek:* Stay Tuned, The Crush, Ace Ventura: Pet Detective, Major League II, Chasers, Trial by Jury, Silent Fall, Imaginary Crimes, A Walk in the Clouds, Big Bully, Ace Ventura: When Nature Calls, Two If By Sea, Diabolique, Bad Moon, Wild America, Incognito, Major League: Back to the Minors, Wrongfully Accused, Soldier, The King and I, Chill Factor, The In Crowd, American Outlaws, Juwanna Mann, I'll Be There, Exorcist: The Beginning, Paul Schrader's Exorcist: The Original Prequel, Two For The Money, The Good Shepherd, Man of the Year, Georgia Rule, Sydney White, Passengers, Dream House.
TELEVISION: *Movie: Prod.:* Ace Ventura: Pet Detective Jr.

ROBINSON, PHIL ALDEN
Director, Writer. b. Long Beach, NY, Mar. 1, 1950. e. Union College, Schenectady. Wrote and directed training films for Air Force, before writing two episodes for series Trapper John M.D. In July 2004, elected to the bd. of governors of the Acad. of Motion Picture Arts & Sciences. Received WGA Valentine Davies Award 1994.
PICTURES: Rhinestone (co-s.p.), All of Me (s.p., assoc. prod.). *Dir./Writer*: In the Mood, Field of Dreams (Academy Award nom. DGA nom.; WGA nom. 1990), Sneakers. All the Queen's Men (exec. prod.), The Sum of All Fears (dir. only).
TELEVISION: *Movies:* Freedom Song (writer, dir. & exec. prod.; WGA Award 2001). *Mini-series:* Band of Brothers (Emmy Award 2002). *Series*: Trapper John M.D. (writer), The George Burns Comedy Week (dir.). *Special:* 81st Annual Academy Awards (Emmy nom. 2009).

ROCCO, ALEX
Actor. r.n. Alexander Federico Petricone Jr. b. Cambridge, MA, Feb. 29, 1936.
PICTURES: Motor Psycho, St. Valentine's Day Massacre, Blood Mania, The Godfather, Slither, Detroit 9000, Friends of Eddie Coyle, The Outside Man, Stanley, Freebie and the Bean, Three the Hard Way, Rafferty and the Gold Dust Twins, Hearts of the West, Fire Sale, House Calls, Rabbit Test, Voices, Herbie Goes Bananas, The Stunt Man, Nobody's Perfekt, The Entity, Cannonball Run II, Stick, Gotcha!, P.K. and the Kid, Return to Horror High, Dream a Little Dream, Wired, The Pope Must Die, That Thing You Do!, Just-Write, Dead of Night, A Bug's Life (voice), Dudley Do-Right, Goodbye Lover, The Last Producer, The Wedding Planner, Face to Face, The Country Bears, The Job, Restive Planet (short), Find Me Guilty, Crazylove, Jam, Smokin' Aces, Ready or Not, Now Here, And They're Off.
TELEVISION: Over 400 television shows incl: *Movies*: Hustling, The Blue Knight, A Question of Guilt, The Grass is Always Greener Over the Septic Tank, Badge of the Assassin, Rock 'n' Roll Mom, The First Time, A Quiet Little Neighborhood A Perfect Little Murder, An Inconvenient Woman, Boris & Natasha, Love Honor & Obey: The Last Mafia Marriage, Robin Cook's Harmful Intent, Big Shot: Confessions of a Campus Bookie. *Mini-series*: 79 Park Avenue. *Series*: The Best of Times, Three for the Road, The Famous Teddy Z (Emmy Award 1990), Sibs, The George Carlin Show, Heart of the City, ER, The Division. *Guest:* More than 98 appearances.

ROCCO, NIKKI
Executive. This history-making motion picture executive joined the Universal Pictures sales department in New York in 1967. Rocco was promoted to assistant to the general sales manager in 1981 and was named vice president of distribution in 1984. In 1990, she was named senior vice president of distribution and marketing. Then, in 1996, Rocco was appointed president, Universal Pictures distribution, becoming the first woman to head a major studio distribution operation in Hollywood's history. In addition to overseeing the studio's relations with theatre owners, she is responsible for all distribution functions and strategic planning, including sales, branch operations, print control and national accounting.

ROCK, CHRIS
Actor, Comedian. b. Brooklyn, NY, Feb. 7, 1966. Host and a writer for the 77th Annual Academy Awards in 2005.
PICTURES: Beverly Hills Cop II, I'm Gonna Git You Sucka, New Jack City, Boomerang, CB4 (also writer, co-prod.), The Immortals, Panther, Sgt. Bilko, Beverly Hills Ninja, Doctor Dolittle (voice), Lethal Weapon 4, Dogma, Nurse Betty, Spin Doctor, Bamboozled, Osmosis Jones, Down to Earth (also s.p. & exec. prod.), A.I. Artificial Intelligence (voice), Pootie Tang (also prod.), Jay and Silent Bob Strike Back, You'll Never Wiez in this Town Again, Bad Company, Head of State, The N-Word (doc., as himself), Oh What a Lovely Tea Party (documentary, as himself), Paparazzi, Madagascar (voice), The Longest Yard, The Gilmores of Beverly Hills (also writer), I Think I Love My Wife (also dir., writer, s.p.), Bee Movie (voice), You Don't Mess with the Zohan, Madagascar: Escape 2 Africa (voice), Death at a Funeral (also prod.), Grown Ups, Credit Is the Devil (also exec. prod., writer).
TELEVISION: *Movies:* Chris Rock: Never Scared (himself; writer & exec. prod.), Back from Hell: A Tribute to Sam Kinison, Guys Choice. *Series*: Saturday Night Live, In Living Color, The Moxy Show, The Chris Rock Show (himself; writer & exec. prod.; Emmy Award 1999, 6 other noms.), Happily Ever After: Fairy Tales for Every Child (voice), The Hughleys (exec. prod.), Everybody Hates Chris (narr., writer & exec. prod., WGA nom. 2006) *Documentaries/Specials:* Chris Rock: Bigger & Blacker (also exec. prod., 3 Emmy noms.), Jackie's Back!, Whatever Happened to Michael Ray?, Saturday Night Live: The Best of Chris Rock, Chris Rock: Bring the Pain (2 Emmy Awards for outstanding Comedy Special; outstanding writing, 1997), Chris Rock: Never Scared (2 Emmy noms.) Politically Incorrect (TV series doc., Emmy nom. 1997), The 77th Annual Academy Awards (host, writer), Chris Rock: Kill the Messenger - London, New York, Johannesburg (also exec. prod., writer, Emmy Award 2009, 1 other nom.), Good Hair (doc., exec. prod., writer, WGA nom. 2010). *Guest*: More than 195 appearances.

RODAT, ROBERT
Writer. b. 1953.
PICTURES: Tall Tale: The Unbelievable Adventures of Pecos Bill, Fly Away Home, Saving Private Ryan (s.p., Academy Award nom.; Golden Globe nom.; WGA nom. 1999), The Patriot.
TELEVISION: Comrades of Summer, The Ripper, 36 Hours to Die, Fallen Skies (exec. prod., writer).

RODDAM, FRANC
Director. b. Stockton, England, Apr. 29, 1946. Studied at London Film Sch. Spent two years as adv. copywriter/prod. with Ogilvy, Benson, Mather before joining BBC as documentary filmmaker. Founder of Union Pictures 1991.
PICTURES: Quadrophenia (also co-s.p.), The Lords of Discipline, Rain Forest (s.p. only), The Bride, Aria (sequence), War Party (also co-exec. prod.), K2.
TELEVISION: *Movies:* An Ungentlemanly Act (exec. prod.), Deadly Voyage (exec. prod.), Moby Dick (dir., prod. & s.p. Emmy nom. 1998), Cleopatra (dir.). *Mini-series:* The Canterbury Tales (exec. prod.). *Series:* Aufwiedersehen Pet (also exec. prod., creator), Making Out (exec. prod.), MasterChef: The Professionals (format writer), Celebrity Masterchef (format writer, exec. prod.), Masterchef Goes Large (format writer, exec. prod.).

RODRIGUEZ, ROBERT
Director, Writer, Producer, Editor. b. June 20,1968. e. Univ. of TX. While in college created comic strip Los Hooligans. Made many short films including Bedhead which won several festival awards.
PICTURES: *Director/Writer/Editor:* El Mariachi (feature debut, 1993; also co-prod., story, photog., editor, sound), Desperado (also prod. & Steadicam operator), Four Rooms (segment), Spy Kids (also prod., camera operator, composer, sound re-recording mixer & visual effects supervisor), Spy Kids 2: Island of Lost Dreams (also prod., composer, cinematographer, sound effects editor, visual effects supervisor and prod. designer), Spy Kids 3-D: Game Over (also prod., composer, cinematographer, visual effects supervisor, production designer), Sin City (also cinematographer, composer, sound re-recording mixer & visual effects supervisor), Once Upon A Time In Mexico (also prod., camera operator, composer, cinematographer, visual effects supervisor & prod. designer). *Director:* From Dusk Till Dawn (also exec. prod., editor, camera operator, & sound re-recording mixer), Mimic (second unit dir.), The Faculty (also editor, camera operator, sound re-recording mixer), Del Castillo: Live (cinematographer), The Adventures of Sharkboy and Lavagirl 3-D (also editor, writer, composer, cinematographer, re-recording mixer, visual effect superviso), Grindhouse (segment "Planet Terror"; dir., prod., writer, composer, cinematographer), Death Proof (prod.), Shorts (also writer, cinematographer, composer). *Actor:* Lisa Picard Is Famous, Bullfighter, Delayed, Machete (also prod.), Spy Kids 4: Armageddon (also prod.). *Producer:* Predators.
TELEVISION: *Movies:* Roadracers (dir./writer/editor), The Outsider (post-prod. supervisor), Addicto de Salsa (co-prod.).

ROEG, NICOLAS
Director, Cameraman, Cinematographer. b. London, England. Aug. 15, 1928. Entered film industry through cutting rooms of MGM's British Studios, dubbing French films into English. Moved into prod. as clapper boy and part of photographer Freddie Young's crew at Marylebone Studios London, 1947. Next became camera operator (Trials of Oscar Wilde, The Sundowners). First experience as cameraman on TV series was with Police Dog and Ghost Squad. Debut as director on Performance, co-directed with Donald Cammell. First solo dir. film, Walkabout. Received a Lifetime Achievement Award from the British Independent Film Awards in 1999.
PICTURES: *Cameraman*: The Miniver Story, The Trial of Oscar Wilde, The Sundowners, Lawrence of Arabia, Jazz Boat,

Information Received, The Great Van Robbery. *Dir. of Photography*: The Caretaker, Dr. Crippen, Nothing But the Best, Masque of the Red Death, A Funny Thing Happened on the Way to the Forum, Fahrenheit 451, Far from the Madding Crowd, The Girl-Getters, Petulia. *Director/Cameraman*: Performance (co.-dir.), Walkabout. *Director*: Don't Look Now, The Man Who Fell To Earth, Bad Timing, Eureka, Insignificance, Castaway, Aria (sequence, also co-s.p.), Track 29, The Witches, Without You I'm Nothing (exec. prod. only), Cold Heaven, Two Deaths, Hotel Paradise, The Sound of Claudia Schiffer (short), Puffball: The Devil's Eyeball, Night Train (also writer).
TELEVISION: *Movies*: *Director:* Sweet Bird of Youth, Heart of Darkness, Full Body Massage, Samson & Delilah.

ROËVES, MAURICE
Actor. b. Sunderland, England, Mar. 19, 1937. Ent. industry, 1964. Played Macduff to Alec Guinness's Macbeth, London stage. Early films: Ulysses, Oh! What a Lovely War, Young Winston, The Eagle Has Landed, Who Dares Wins. Directed many stage plays.
THEATRE: The Killing of Michael Malloy.
PICTURES: The Fighting Prince of Donegal, Ulysses, Oh What A Lovely War, When Eight Bells Toll, Young Winston, The Eagle Has Landed, Victory, The Final Option, Crossing the Line, Hidden Agenda, The Last of the Mohican, Judge Dredd, The Acid House, Beautiful Creatures, The Damned United.
TELEVISION: In *USA* and *UK* incl.: *Movies:* A Taste of Evil, Orkney, S.O.S. Titanic, Twelfth Night, Journal of Bridget Hitler, Inside the Third Reich, Heather Ann, The Negotiator, 919 Fifth Avenue, Moses, Hillsborough, David, Forgive and Forget, The Sight, Trial & Retribution XVII: Conviction. *Mini-series:* The Shadow of the Tower, North and South II, Grafters, Vanity Fair, Reach for the Moon. *Series:* A Family at War, Danger UXB, The Nightmare Man, Cruise of Deception: Days of our Lives, Tutti Frutti, Spender, EastEnders. *Guest*: More than 88 appearances.

ROGERS, IVAN
Actor, Producer, Writer. b. Indianapolis, IN, Sept. 20, 1954. e. Ball State Univ. on a music scholarship.
PICTURES: Tigershark (co-s.p. only), One Way Out (also prod., s.p.), Two Wrongs Make a Right (also s.p., prod.), Slow Burn, Ballbuster (also co-prod.), The Runner, Karate Commando: Jungle Wolf 3, Striking Point, Caged Women II (also co-prod., s.p., dir.), Laserhawk, Down N Dirty, Forgive Me Father (also prod., dir.), The Payback Man (also prod., writer, dir., soundtrack song).
TELEVISION: *Movies: Actor:* Slow Burn, Ballbuster (also prod.).

ROGERS, KENNY
Singer, Actor, Songwriter. b. Crockett, TX, Aug. 21, 1938. Country and western singer. Member Bobby Doyle Trio, Christy Minstrels, 1966-67; The First Edition 1967-76. On screen in Six Pack (1982).
PICTURES: *Singer:* Trackdown, Urban Cowboy, Tough Guys (Golden Globe nom. 1987), many more credits as soundtrack performer. *Actor:* Six Pack, Dead Girls Don't Tango, Jack of All Trades, The Pledge.
TELEVISION: *Movies*: The Dream Makers, Kenny Rogers as The Gambler, Coward of the County, Kenny Rogers as the Gambler: The Adventure Continues, Wild Horses; Kenny Rogers as The Gambler Part III: The Legend Continues, Christmas in America, The Gambler Returns: Luck of the Draw, Real West, Rio Diablo, MacShayne: Winner Takes All, MacShayne: The Final Roll of the Dice, Gambler V: Playing for Keeps, Big Dreams & Broken Hearts: The Dottie West Story (as himself). A Death in Malibu: The Murder of Charlie Minor (as himself), Christmas in Canaan (writer: book). *Series*: McShane (NBC Friday Night Mystery), Rollin' On The River (host), The Real West (narrator, host). *Documentaries/Specials:* Kenny, Dolly & Willie: Something Inside So Strong, Kenny Rogers and the American Cowboy, Kenny Rogers' America, Kenny Rogers and Dolly Parton: Together, CMT 100 Greatest Duets Concert (performer), Dolly Celebrates 25 Years of Dollywood (performer) and numerous others. *Guest:* More than 186 appearances.

ROGERS, MIMI
Actress r.n. Miriam Spickler. b. Coral Gables, FL, Jan. 27, 1959.
PICTURES: Blue Skies Again (debut, 1983), Gung Ho, Street Smart, Someone to Watch Over Me, The Mighty Quinn, Hider in the House, Desperate Hours, The Doors, The Rapture, The Palermo Connection, The Player, White Sands, Dark Horse, Monkey Trouble, Far From Home: The Adventures of Yellow Dog, Bulletproof Heart, Reflections in the Dark, The Mirror Has Two Faces, Austin Powers International Man of Mystery, Lost In Space, Seven Girlfriends, Ginger Snaps, The Upgrade, Dumb and Dumberer: When Harry Met Lloyd, Seeing Other People, The Door in the Floor, Dancing in Twilight, Penny Dreadful, Big Nothing, Falling Up, Frozen Kiss, Order of Chaos, Lucky, Unstoppable (prod. only), Abandoned, Balls to the Wall.
TELEVISION: *Movies*: Divorce Wars, Hear No Evil, You Ruined My Life, Fourth Story, Deadlock, Ladykiller, Bloodlines: Murder in the Family, A Kiss to Die For, Weapons of Mass Distraction, Full Body Massage, Tricks, The Devil's Arithmetic, Common Ground, Cruel Intentions 2, My Horrible Year!, Charms for the Easy Life, Cave In, Stone Cold, Selling Innocence, The Stranger Game, Storm Cell, Sins of the Mother. *Series*: The Rousters, Paper Dolls, The Geena Davis Show, The Loop. *Guest:* More than 70 appearances.

ROGERS, THOMAS S.
Executive. e. Wesleyan Univ., B.A. degree; Columbia Law School, J.D. From 1981-86, sr. counsel, U.S. House of Representatives Subcommittee on Telecommunications, Consumer Protection and Finance. From January 1987 until October 1999, Rogers held positions with NBC, Inc. including executive v.p. & pres. of NBC Cable. While at NBC, he led the creation of CNBC and the formation of the MSNBC partnership with Microsoft. Rogers first joined the TiVo board in 1999, spear-heading NBC's original investment in the company. TiVo pioneered a brand new category of products, developing the first commercially available digital video recorder (DVR). From Oct. 1999 until April 2003, Rogers was chairman and CEO of Primedia, Inc., a print, video, and online media company. He then rejoined TiVo's bd. in 2003, and became bd. vice chairman in October, 2004. At TiVo led the successful negotiation of a mass deployment deal with Comcast, the world's largest cable company. In addition to his work for TiVo, Rogers was sr. operating executive at Cerberus Capital Management, a large private equity firm. He became TiVo pres. & CEO July 1, 2005. When becoming pres. & CEO, Rogers resigned as TiVo bd. vice chairman and as a Class II Director and was immediately reappointed as a Class III Director.

ROGERS, WAYNE
Actor. b. Birmingham, AL, April 7, 1933. e. Princeton U. After graduation entered the army for three yrs.; studied at Sanford's Meisner's Neighborhood Playhouse and with Martha Graham.
PICTURES: Odds Against Tomorrow (debut, 1959), The Glory Guys, Chamber of Horrors, Cool Hand Luke, WUSA, Pocket Money, Once in Paris, The Gig, The Killing Time, Ghosts of Mississippi, Love Lies Bleeding, Frozen With Fear, 3 Days of Rain, Nobody Knows Anything.
TELEVISION: *Movies*: Lamp Unto My Feet, Attack on Terror: The FBI Versus the Ku Klux Klan, Making Babies II, It Happened One Christmas, The Top of the Hill, Chiefs, He's Fired She's Hired, The Lady from Yesterday, American Harvest, Drop-Out Mother, One Terrific Guy, Bluegrass, Passion and Paradise, Miracle Landing, The Goodbye Bird, Night of the Twisters, Money Plays (exec. prod. only), Miracle Dogs. *Mini-series*: Chiefs. *Executive producer*: Perfect Witness, Age-Old Friends, The Charlie Rose Special, AMC Hollywood Report (also host), Money Plays. *Series*: Edge of Night, Stagecoach West, M*A*S*H, City of the Angels, House Calls (Golden Globe nom. 1981), High Risk (host). *Guest:* More than 89 appearances.

ROHMER, ERIC
Director. Writer. r.n. Jean Maurice Scherer. b. Nancy, France, April 4, 1920. Professor of literature. Film critic for La Gazette du Cinema and its successor Cahiers du Cinema which he edited, 1957-63. With Claude Chabrol wrote book on Alfred Hitchcock as a Catholic moralist, 1957. 1959 directorial debut, Le Signe du Lion. 1962 began a series of 6 Moral Tales; from 1980 with The Aviator's Wife began another series of 7 films called Comedies and Proverbs. Staged Catherine de Heilbronn in Nanterre, 1979.
PICTURES: *Short films*: Presentation ou Charlotte et Son Steack (1961), La Boulangere de Monceau, Veronique et Son Cancre, Nadja a Paris, Place de L'etoile, Une Etudiante d'aujourd'hui, Fermiere a Montfaucon. *Feature films* (dir. & s.p.): Le Signe du Lion (The Sign of Leo; debut, 1959), La Carriere de Suzanne, Six in Paris (episode), La Collectionneuse, My Night at Maude's (Academy Award nom. 1971), Claire's Knee, Chloe in the Afternoon, The Marquise of O, Perceval, The Aviator's Wife, Le Beau Mariage, Pauline at the Beach, Full Moon in Paris, Summer, Boyfriends and Girlfriends, Four Adventures of Reinette and Mirabelle (also prod.), A Tale of Springtime, A Tale of Winter, The Tree, The Mayor and the Mediatheque, Citizen Langlois (actor), Rendezvous in Paris, A Summer's Tale; Autumn Tale, The Lady and the Duke, Triple Agent, I Think I Love My Wife (writer, "Chloe in the Afternoon".
TELEVISION: Carl Dreyer, Le Celluloid et le Marbre, Ville Nouvelle, Between 1964-69 directed series of documentaries for French TV: Les Cabinets et Physique du XVIII siecle, Les Metamorphoses du Paysage Industriel, Don Quichotte, Edgar Poe, Pascal, Louis Lumiere, Catherine de Heilbronn, Les Jeux de société, El Trio en mi Bernoll, many more.
(d. January 11, 2010)

ROIZMAN, OWEN
Cinematographer. b. Brooklyn, NY, Sept. 22, 1936. e. Gettysburg College. Received ASC Lifetime Achievement Award 1997.
PICTURES: The French Connection (Academy Award nom. 1972), The Gang That Couldn't Shoot Straight, Play It Again Sam, The Heartbreak Kid, The Exorcist (Academy Award nom. 1974), The Taking of Pelham 1-2-3, The Stepford Wives, Independence, Three Days of the Condor, The Return of the Man Called Horse, Network (Academy Award nom. 1977), Straight Time, Sgt. Pepper's Lonely Hearts Club Band, The Electric Horseman, The Black Marble, True Confessions, Absence of Malice, Taps, Tootsie (Academy Award nom. 1983),

Vision Quest, I Love You to Death, Havana, The Addams Family, Grand Canyon, Wyatt Earp (Academy Award nom.; ASC nom. 1995), French Kiss.
TELEVISION: *Special:* Liza with a Z: A Concert for Television (Emmy nom. 1973).

ROLLINS, JACK
Producer. b. 1914. Co-founder of talent management firm Rollins, Joffe, Mora and Brezner Inc. handling careers of Woody Allen, Nichols and May, Robin Williams, Robert Klein, David Letterman, Dick Cavett, Billy Crystal.
PICTURES: *Co-producer./Executive producer with Charles Joffe:* Take the Money and Run, Bananas, Everything You Always Wanted to Know About Sex, Sleeper, Love and Death, The Front, Annie Hall (Acad. Award for Best Picture, 1977), Interiors, Manhattan, Stardust Memories, Zelig, Broadway Danny Rose (also actor), The Purple Rose of Cairo, Hannah and Her Sisters, Radio Days, September, Another Woman, New York Stories (Oedipus Wrecks), Crimes and Misdemeanors, Alice, Shadows and Fog, Husbands and Wives, Manhattan Murder Mystery, Bullets Over Broadway, Mighty Aphrodite, Everyone Says I Love You, Deconstructing Harry, Celebrity, Sweet and Lowdown, Small Time Crooks, The Curse of the Jade Scorpion, Hollywood Ending, Anything Else, Melinda and Melinda, Match Point, Scoop, Cassandra's Dream, Vicky Cristina Barcelona, Whatever Works, You Will Meet a Tall Dark Stranger (co-exec. prod.). *Composer:* The Polar Express (song), Deck the Halls (song).
TELEVISION: *Movies*: Only the Truth is Funny (exec. prod.), The Marx Brothers in a Nutshell (doc., prod.). *Series*: The Late Night with David Letterman (exec. prod., 12 Emmy noms.).

ROMANO, ED
Executive. This 40+year Warner Bros. executive joined the company in 1968 after five years at the public accountancy firm of Peat, Marwick, Mitchell & Co. During his tenure with Warner Bros. Romano has served as assistant treasurer, controller, vice president & controller, and senior v.p. & controller before being promoted to his current post, executive v.p. & CFO, Warner Bros. Entertainment. Serving in this capacity since 1994, Romano is responsible for all financial activities of the company, including financial reporting, budgeting and planning for future business growth. In addition, he is also responsible for management information services. Beyond his company responsibilities, Romano is a member of both the Academy of Motion Pictures Arts & Sciences and the Academy of Television Arts & Sciences and currently serves as the chairman of the finance committee and the treasurer of the bd. of directors at the Providence Saint Joseph Medical Center Foundation in Burbank, CA. He is also on the bd. of directors for the Literacy Network of Greater Los Angeles and a member of their finance committee.

ROMERO, GEORGE A.
Director, Writer, Editor. b. New York, NY, Feb. 4, 1940. e. Carnegie-Mellon Univ.
PICTURES: *Dir./Writer/Cameraman*: Night of the Living Dead (debut, 1968), There's Always Vanilla, The Crazies, Jack's Wife (also edit.). *Director/Writer*: Martin (also edit., actor), Dawn of the Dead (dir. only), Knightriders, Creepshow (dir., co-edit. only), Day of the Dead, Monkey Shines, Night of the Living Dead (s.p., co-exec. prod. only), Two Evil Eyes, The Dark Half (also exec. prod.), Bruiser, The Ill (s.p.), The Girl Who Loved Tom Gordon, Dawn of the Dead (s.p. only from 1978), Land of the Dead, From a Buick 8, Diamond Dead, Night of the Living Dead 3D, Diary of the Dead, Day of the Dead, The I Scream Man (actor), Deadtime Stories (exec. prod.), Dead Country (actor), Into the Dark: Exploring the Horror Film (exec. prod.), Deadtime Stories (exec. prod., host), Deadtime Stories 2 (exec. prod., host), The Crazies (exec. prod., writer 1973 motion picture).
TELEVISION: Tales from the Dark Side (exec. prod., writer). *Series:* The Winners (also prod. doc.).

RONA, JEFF
Composer. b. March 3, 1957. 1998 Won ASCAP Award for Most Performed Underscore.
PICTURES: *Composer*: Lipstick Camera, White Squall, Do Me a Favor, Net Force, Mind Prey, The In Croud, Traffic, Exit Wounds, The Follow, Black Hawk Down, The Mothman Prophecies, Little Black Boot, Slow Burn, A Thousand Roads (short), The Quiet, Sharkwater (doc.), Whisper, Jonna's Body, Please Hold,, American Renegade: Confessions of a Radical Humanist (doc.), The Tortured, The Chosen One. *Additional Music*: Toys, The Net, Assassins, The Fan, Black Cat Run, Shelter Island, Bobby, Meet Bill, Henry Poole Is Here.
TELEVISION: *Movies*: Black Magic, Death in Small Doses, NetForce, Mind Prey, The Riverman, Category 6: Day of Destruction, Earthsea, Category 7: The End of the World, For the Love of a Child, Final Days of Planet Earth, Crash and Burn. *Mini-series:* Traffic, Legend of Earthsea. *Series*: The Critic, Chicago Hope, High Incident, Profiler, Gun, Teen Angel, Sleepwalkers, L.A. Doctors, Stephen King's Dead Zone, Hot Properties, Brotherhood (ASCAP Award 2008), Persons Unknown.

ROOKER, MICHAEL
Actor. b. Jasper, AL, April 6, 1955. e. Goodman School of Drama. Studied Japanese martial art of Aikido prior to establishing himself in Chicago theatre, where he appeared in Union Boys, The Crack Walker and Moon Children.
PICTURES: Streets of Fire (debut, 1984), Light of Day, Rent-a-Cop, Eight Men Out, Mississippi Burning, Sea of Love, Music Box, Henry: Portrait of a Serial Killer, Days of Thunder, JFK, The Dark Half, Cliffhanger, Tombstone, The Hard Truth, Mallrats, The Trigger Effect, Rosewood, Liar, The Replacement Killers, Renegade Force, Brown's Requiem, The Bone Collector, A Table for One, Here on Earth, The 6th Day, Newsbreak, Replicant, Undisputed, The Box, The Eliminator, Skeleton Man, Chasing Ghosts, Slither, Lenexa, 1 Mile, Jumper, The Hard Ride, The Lena Baker Story, Super Capers, The Great Observer, Penance, Blood Done Sign My Name, Freeway Killer, Louis, Bolden!, Super, Song of the Knife, Rogue River, Pure Shooter, Hypothermia, Cell 213, Atlantis Down, Louis, Palominas.
TELEVISION: *Movies*: Crime Story, L.A. Takedown, Afterburn, Johnny & Clyde, Back to Back, On Thin Ice, Skeleton Man, Saving Jessica Lynch, Matadors. *Mini-series:* Meteor: Path to Destruction. *Series:* HRT, Thief (also pilot). *Guest:* More than 45 appearances.

ROONEY, ANDREW A
Writer, Producer. b. Albany, NY, Jan. 14, 1919. e. Colgate U. Started career as writer at MGM 1946-7, then for Arthur Godfrey, Garry Moore; wrote and produced documentaries, including Black History: Lost Stolen or Strayed (Emmy Award, 1969), An Essay on War, An Essay on Bridges, In Praise of New York City, Mr. Rooney Goes to Washington, etc. Commentator, 60 Minutes (CBS), 1978-present. Syndicated newspaper columnist for Tribune Media Services, 1979-present.
AUTHOR: Air Gunner, The Story of the Stars and Stripes, Conqueror's Peace, A Few Minutes With Andy Rooney, And More Andy Rooney, Pieces of My Mind, Sweet and Sour, The Fortunes of War, Not That You Asked, Word for Word, My War, Better Together, Sincerely Andy Rooney.
PICTURE: Silent Wings: The American Glider Pilots of World War II (doc., actor).

ROONEY, MICKEY
Actor. r.n. Joe Yule, Jr. b. Brooklyn, NY, Sept. 23, 1920. Son of late actors Joe Yule & Nell Carter, vaudeville performers. U.S. Army, WWII. In vaudeville as child with parents and others before m.p. debut and after; from age of 5 to 12 (1926-33) created screen version of Fontaine Fox newspaper comic character Mickey McGuire in series of short subjects (also billed as Mickey McGuire). Adopted name of Mickey Rooney, returned to vaudeville, then resumed screen career in features. Special Academy Award 1940 for Andy Hardy characterization; voted among first 10 Money-Making Stars in M.P. Herald-Fame Poll: 1938-43. *Autobiographies:* i.e. (1965), Life is Too Short (1991). *Novel:* The Search for Sonny Skies (1994). Academy Award 1939, Juvenile Award. Received honorary Academy Award, 1983. Rooney has appeared in 232 films/videos.
THEATRE: *B'way*: Sugar Babies, The Will Rogers Follies. *Regional*: W.C., Lend Me a Tenor.
PICTURES: Orchids and Ermine (feature debut, 1927), Emma, The Beast of the City, Sin's Pay Day, High Speed, Officer Thirteen, Fast Companions, My Pal the King, The Big Cage, The Life of Jimmy Dolan, The Big Chance, Broadway to Hollywood, The World Changes, The Chief, Beloved, I Like It That Way, Love Birds, Half a Sinner, The Lost Jungle, Manhattan Melodrama, Upperworld, Hide-Out, Chained, Blind Date, Death on the Diamond, The County Chairman, Reckless, The Healer, A Midsummer Night's Dream, Ah Wilderness, Riff-Raff, Little Lord Fauntleroy, The Devil is a Sissy, Down the Stretch, Captains Courageous, Slave Ship, A Family Affair, Hoosier Schoolboy, Live Love and Learn, Thoroughbreds Don't Cry, You're Only Young Once, Love is a Headache, Judge Hardy's Children, Hold That Kiss, Lord Jeff, Love Finds Andy Hardy, Boys Town, Stablemates, Out West With the Hardys, The Adventures of Huckleberry Finn, The Hardys Ride High, Andy Hardy Gets Spring Fever, Babes in Arms (Academy Award nom. 1940), Judge Hardy and Son, Young Tom Edison, Andy Hardy Meets Debutante, Strike Up the Band, Andy Hardy's Private Secretary, Men of Boy's Town, Life Begins for Andy Hardy, Babes on Broadway, The Courtship of Andy Hardy, A Yank at Eton, Andy Hardy's Double Life, The Human Comedy (Academy Award nom. 1944), Girl Crazy, Thousands Cheer, Andy Hardy's Blonde Trouble, National Velvet, Love Laughs at Andy Hardy, Killer McCoy, Summer Holiday, Words and Music, The Big Wheel, Quicksand, He's a Cockeyed Wonder, The Fireball, My Outlaw Brother, The Strip, Sound Off, All Ashore, Off Limits, A Slight Case of Larceny, Drive a Crooked Road, The Atomic Kid (also prod.), The Bridges at Toko-Ri, The Twinkle in God's Eye, Francis in the Haunted House, The Bold and the Brave (Academy Award nom. 1957), Magnificent Roughnecks, Operation Mad Ball, Baby Face Nelson, Andy Hardy Comes Home, A Nice Little Bank That Should Be Robbed, The Last Mile, The Big Operator, Platinum High School, The Private Lives of Adam and Eve (also co-dir.), Breakfast at Tiffany's, King of the Roaring Twenties, Requiem for a Heavyweight, Everything's Ducky, It's a Mad Mad Mad Mad World, Secret Invasion, 24 Hours to Kill, The Devil in Love, Ambush Bay, How to Stuff a Wild Bikini, The Extraordinary Seaman, Skidoo, The Comic, 80 Steps to Jonah, The Cockeyed Cowboys of Calico County, Hollywood Blue, B.J. Lang Presents

(The Manipulator), Richard, Pulp, The Godmothers (also s.p., music), Ace of Hearts, Thunder County, That's Entertainment, Journey Back to Oz (voice), From Hong Kong With Love, Rachel's Man, Find the Lady, The Domino Principle, Pete's Dragon, The Magic of Lassie, The Black Stallion (Academy Award nom. 1980), Arabian Adventure, The Fox and the Hound (voice), The Emperor of Peru, The Black Stallion Returns, The Care Bears Movie (voice), Lightning the White Stallion, Erik the Viking, My Heroes Have Always Been Cowboys, Sweet Justice, The Legend of Wolf Mountain, Little Nemo (voice), Silent Night Deadly Night 5: The Toymaker, The Milky Life, Revenge of the Red Baron, That's Entertainment III, Animals, Internet Love, Topa Topa Bluffs, Paradise, Strike the Tent, To Kill a Mockumentary (video), Night at the Museum, Lost Stallions: The Journey Home, Wreck the Halls (also soundtrack performer), Bamboo Shark, Driving Me Crazy, Gerald, Now Here, Driving Me Crazy, Saddle Up with Dick Wrangler & Injun Joe, Bamboo Shark, The Voices from Beyond, Night Club, Holding God (exec. prod. only).
TELEVISION: *Movies:* Home for Christmas, The Gambler Returns: The Luck of the Draw, Brothers' Destiny, Phantom of the Megaplex, Bill (Emmy Award, Golden Globe Award 1982), Bill: On His Own (Emmy nom. 1984), The Greatest Show Ever, others. *Series*: Hey Mickey, One of the Boys, The Black Stallion. *Many specials including*: Playhouse 90 ("The Comedian", Emmy nom. 1958), Pinocchio, Alcoa Theatre ("Eddie" Emmy nom. 1959), Somebody's Waiting, The Dick Powell Theater. *Guest:* More than 255 appearances.

ROOS, FRED
Producer. b. Santa Monica, CA, May 22, 1934. e. UCLA, B.A. Directed documentary films for Armed Forces Radio and Television Network. Worked briefly as agent for MCA and story editor for Robert Lippert Productions. Worked as casting dir. in 1960s and served as casting dir. on The Godfather, beginning longtime association with filmmakers Francis Coppola and George Lucas. Received Lifetime Achievement Award from the Casting Society of America in 1988.
PICTURES: The Conversation, The Godfather Part II (Academy Award Best Picture 1975), Apocalypse Now (Academy Award nom. 1980), The Black Stallion, The Escape Artist (exec. prod.), The Black Stallion Returns, Hammett, One From the Heart, The Outsiders, Rumble Fish, The Cotton Club, One Magic Christmas, Seven Minutes in Heaven, Peggy Sue Got Married (special consultant), Barfly, Gardens of Stone (co-exec. prod.), Tucker: The Man and His Dream, New York Stories (Life Without Zoe), Wait Until Spring Bandini, The Godfather Part III, Hearts of Darkness: A Filmmaker's Apocalypse (exec. prod.), The Secret Garden, Radioland Murders, Jack (spec. consultant), The Rainmaker (exec. consultant), The Virgin Suicides, Town & Country, Lost in Translation (exec. prod.), The Young Black Stallion (prod.), 5-25-77, Marie Antoinette, Youth Without Youth (exec. prod.), Expired, Columbus Day, Tetro (exec. prod.), Somewhere (exec. prod.), Master Class (prod., casting dir.).
TELEVISION: *Movie*: Montana. *Series*: *As Casting Dir:* The Andy Griffith Show, Gomer Pyle, U.S.M.C., I Spy, That Girl, The Guns of Will Sonnett, Mayberry R.F.D. The Outsiders (exec. prod.).

ROSE, ALEX
Producer. r.n. Alexandra Rose. b. Jan. 20, 1946. e. U. of WI, BS. Started in m.p. distribution with Medford Films. Later became asst. sls. mgr. for New World Pictures.
PICTURES: *Co-prod.*: Drive-In, I Wanna Hold Your Hand, Big Wednesday, Norma Rae (Academy Award nom. 1980), Nothing in Common (solo prod.), Overboard (co-prod.), Quigley Down Under, Frankie and Johnny, Exit to Eden, The Other Sister (prod./writer), Changing Hearts (assoc. prod.).
TELEVISION: *Series:* Nothing in Common (co-exec. prod. with Garry Marshall), *Pilots*: Norma Rae, Just Us Kids.

ROSE, CHARLIE
Talk Show Host. b. Henderson, NC, Jan. 5, 1942. e. Duke Univ. (history, law). Was exec. prod. for Bill Moyers' Journal, 1975.
PICTURE: Elegy.
TELEVISION: *Series (host/anchor):* A.M. Chicago, The Charlie Rose Show (NBC, 1979, 1981), CBS News Nightwatch, E.D.J. Entertainment Daily Journal (Personalities), Charlie Rose (synd; also exec. prod., editor), 60 Minutes (correspondent). *Documentaries/Specials:* Public Debate With Charlie Rose, Jimmy Carter Man from Plains, In Concert at the United Nations (host).

ROSE, STEPHEN
Executive. Entered m.p. industry in 1964 with Columbia Pictures; named adv. dir. 1970 joined Cinema V Distributing, Inc. as dir. of adv.; left in 1971 to take post at Cinemation Industries, where was named v.p. and bd. member. 1975 joined Paramount Pictures as dir. of adv.; promoted to v.p./adv. 1979 formed Barrich Prods. with Gordon Weaver. 1982, rejoined Paramount as v.p., mktg; 1983, named v.p. of mktg. for Paramount; sr. v.p., mktg., 1983. Resigned in 1984. Joined Barrich Marketing with Gordon Weaver.

ROSEANNE
Actress. r.n. Roseanne Cherrie Barr. b. Salt Lake City, UT, Nov. 3, 1952. Started performing in bars; prod. showcase for women performers, Take Back the Mike at U. of Boulder. 1983 won Denver Laff-Off. Moved to Los Angeles where performed at The Comedy Store, and showcased on TV special Funny and The Tonight Show. Has previously performed under the names Roseanne Barr, Roseanne Arnold. *Autobiographies:* My Life as a Woman (1989), My Lives (1994).
PICTURES: She-Devil (debut, 1989), Look Who's Talking Too (voice), Freddy's Dead, Even Cowgirls Get the Blues, Blue in the Face, Meet Wally Sparks, Get Bruce, The Eyes of Tammy Faye, Cecil B. Demented, 15 Minutes, Blue in the Face, Home On the Range (voice).
TELEVISION: *Movies*: Backfield in Motion, The Woman Who Loved Elvis (also co-exec. prod.), I Am Your Child. *Series*: Roseanne (also co-exec. prod.; Golden Globe Awards for Best Series 1993, 4 other noms.; Emmy Award for Best Actress, 1993, 3 other noms.), Little Rosie (voice), The Jackie Thomas Show (co-exec. prod, guest), Tom (co-exec. prod.), The Roseanne Show (also exec. prod., Emmy nom. 1999). General Hospital, Saturday Night Special (prod.). *Documentaries/Specials*: Fast Copy, Rodney Dangerfield—It's Not Easy Bein' Me, Live From Minneapolis: Roseanne, Roseanne Arnold: Live From Trump Castle, I Am Your Child, The Real Roseanne Show (series documentary), Roseanne Barr: Blonde and Bitchin' (exec. prod., writer). *Guest:* More than 149 appearances.

ROSENBERG, ALAN
Actor. b. Passaic, NJ, Oct. 4, 1950. Emmy-nominated actor and Screen Actors Guild activist. Elected SAG president in fall 2005.
PICTURES: The Wanderers, Happy Birthday Gemini, Not For Publication, Stewardess School, White of the Eye, The Last Temptation of Christ, Miracle Mile, After Midnight, Impulse, Reaching Normal, The Bum (short), Robots (voice), Righteous Kill.
TELEVISION: *Movies*: Kojak: The Belarus File, Promise, The King of Love, The Revenge of Al Capone, Parker Kane, The Boys, ...And Then She Was Gone, On Hope (short), Witch Hunt, Freaky Friday, On Seventh Avenue, Steve Martini's Undue Influence, Breaking Through, Cloned, Giving Up the Ghost, The Temptations, A Touch of Hope, A Mother's Fight For Justice, On the Edge, L.A. Law: The Movie. *Mini-series:* Robert Kennedy & His Times, Lucky/Chances. *Series*: Civil Wars, NYPD Blue (dir. only), L.A. Law, Cybill, The Guardian, ER (Emmy nom. 1995 as guest). *Guest*: More than 54 appearances.

ROSENBERG, GRANT E.
Executive, Writer, Producer. b. San Francisco, CA, 1952. e. Univ. of California at Davis. Started career in research dept., NBC; 1977, joined Paramount in research and later in development; 1984, v.p., dramatic dev.; then sr. v.p., dev., for TV group, Paramount. 1985, named sr. v.p., network TV for Walt Disney Pictures; 1988, named pres., Lee Rich Productions, TV div., and exec. prod. of Molloy TV series. 1990, was a writer and producer for Paramount TV. Rosenberg has been an exec. producer and a writer for the TV series Tracker and Showtime's Jeremiah. He currently is a consulting producer for the TV series Masters of Horror for Showtime.
PICTURE: Valentine (exec. prod.).
TELEVISION: *Movies:* The Face of Fear (exec. prod.). *Series:* MacGyver (writer), Star Trek: The Next Generation (writer), Time Trax (writer/creator), Lois & Clark: The New Adventures of Superman (writer, co-prod.), Pointman (writer), The Outer Limits (writer, exec. prod., co-exec. prod.), Poltergeist: The Legacy (writer, exec. prod.), Tracker (writer, co-exec. prod.), Jeremiah (writer, co-exec. prod.), Masters of Horror (consulting prod.), Eureka (supv. prod.), Masters of Science Fiction (supv. prod.), Fear Itself (supv. prod.).

ROSENBERG, RICHARD K.
Executive, Producer, Attorney. b. Paterson, NJ, Apr. 4, 1942. e. Indiana Univ. Corporate & intl. entertainment attorney for major corps. and celebrities. Formed RKR Entertainment Group in 1977 with subsidiaries RKR Releasing, RKR Artists and RKR Productions. Subsequently, consolidated into RKR Pictures Inc. Films include Alice Sweet Alice (Holy Terror), Hell's Angels Forever, Mother Lode, Best Revenge, The Wild Duck, Primary Motive, Fatal Past, Dutchman's Creek. V.p., Cinetel Films, 1991-93. Exec. v.p. and bd. mem., Jones Entertainment Group Ltd., 1995.
AUTHOR: Negotiating Motion Picture Contracts.
PICTURES: Primary Motive (exec. prod.), Cottonwood (exec. prod.), Communion (prod.), Fatal Past.

ROSENBERG, RICK
Producer. b. Los Angeles, CA. e. Los Angeles City College, UCLA. Started career in mail room of Columbia Pictures, then asst. to prod. Jerry Bresler on Major Dundee and Love Has Many Faces. Asst. to Columbia v.p., Arthur Kramer. Was assoc. prod. on The Reivers and in 1970 produced first feature, Adam at Six A.M., with Bob Christiansen.
PICTURES: Major Dundee, The Reivers, Adam at Six A.M., Communion, Hide in Plain Sight, Fatal Past, Southern Man (also dir. & writer), Down in the Delta, Gambling.
TELEVISION: *Movies:* Suddenly Single, The Glass House, A Brand New Life, The Man Who Could Talk to Kids, The Autobiography of Miss Jane Pittman (Emmy Award 1974), I Love You... Goodbye, Queen of the Stardust Ballroom (Emmy nom.

1975), Born Innocent, A Death in Canaan (Emmy nom. 1978), Strangers, Kids Don't Tell, As Summers Die, Gore Vidal's Lincoln (Emmy nom. 1988), Red Earth White Earth, Heist, A House of Secrets and Lies, The Last Hit, Heart of Darkness, Tad, Kingfish: A Story of Huey P. Long, Redwood Curtain, Death Benefit, Beyond the Call, Sudden Terror: The Hijacking of School Bus #17, Home Invasion, Lost Treasure of Dos Santos, The Long Island Incident, Southern Man, The Crossing, Reckless Behavior: Caught on Tape, Accidental Friendship. *Mini-series:* Robert Kennedy and His Times (Emmy nom. 1985).

ROSENBLUM, BRUCE
Executive. e. University of Southern California, bachelor's degree, business administration; University of California, Los Angeles, juris doctor degree. After law school became entertainment attorney for Dern, Mason & Floum (now Del, Shaw, Moonves, Tanaka & Finkelstein). Rosenblum then joined Lorimar Telepictures in 1986. Rosenblum came to Warner Bros. as part of Warner Communications' 1989 acquisition of Lorimar Telepictures as v.p., business affairs. In 1994, became senior v.p., television business management, Warner Bros. Rosenblum also served as executive v.p. of television at Warner Bros.' studio for six years. He was named president, Warner Bros. Television Group (WBTG) in Sept. 2005. In this post, Rosenblum is charged with managing and growing the entire Warner Bros. portfolio of television businesses, including worldwide production, distribution and broadcasting. During his two decades with Warner Bros., Rosenblum has played a vital role in such milestone transactions as the creation of The WB Network and record-establishing license fee negotiations for the hits "ER," "Friends" and "The West Wing." Also one of the key architects of the deal creating a joint venture with CBS Corporation to form a new broadcast network, The CW, and with Barry Meyer, chairman & CEO, Warner Bros., oversees the company's interest in the network. (The WB ceased operating in Sept. 2006.) Under Rosenblum's guidance, the WBTG is rapidly developing new business models for the evolving television landscape, including video-on-demand, broadband, wireless and home video exploitation of its vast television content library. Most recently, WBTVG reached digital distribution agreements with ABC, CBS and NBC representing an industry first for a major studio with unaffiliated networks, and formed Studio 2.0, a digital production venture that will create original live-action and animated short-form programming for broadband and wireless devices. In July 2008, Rosenblum announced he would stay with Warner Bros. TV through at least 2013.

ROSENFELT, SCOTT
Producer, Director. b. Easton, PA, Dec. 20, 1955. e. NYU.
PICTURES: *Producer:* Teen Wolf, Extremities, Russkies, Mystic Pizza, Big Man on Campus (co-prod.), Home Alone, Family Prayers (dir.), Smoke Signals, Getting to Know You (exec. prod.), The Book of Stars, The Business of Fancydancing, Final Draft, Once Upon A Wedding, Lenny the Wonder Dog, Kids in America, The Californians, Valley of the Heart's Delight (exec. prod.), Gospel Hill, Minion, The Evil Tongue (doc.), The Deported (prod. consult.), Coming & Going, Standing Silent (doc., prod., dir.).
TELEVISION: *Movie*: T-Bone N Weasel (exec. prod.)

ROSENMAN, HOWARD
Producer. b. Brooklyn, NY, Feb. 1, 1945. e. Brooklyn Col. Asst. to Sir Michael Benthall on B'way show; prod., Benton & Bowles Agency; ABC-TV; RSO Prods. Co-pres., Sandollar Prods.; currently pres. Brillstein-Grey Motion Pictures.
PICTURES: Sparkle, The Main Event, Resurrection, Lost Angels, Gross Anatomy, True Identity, Father of the Bride, Shining Through, Straight Talk, A Stranger Among Us, Buffy the Vampire Slayer, Paragraph 175 (doc.), The Family Man, My First Mister, Noel, You Kill Me, Breakfast with Scot (exec. prod.), Milk (actor only), Jonah, The Monster of Longwood, Coming & Going (creator),Little Warriors: Big Fists (doc., exec. prod.).
TELEVISION: *Movies*: Isn't It Shocking? Altogether Now, Death Scream, Virginia Hill Story, Killer Bees, Tidy Endings, Bond Girls are Forever (doc., co-exec. prod.). *Series:* John from Cincinnati (exec. prod.). *Documentaries/Specials*: Common Threads: Stories from the Quilt (co-exec. prod.), The Celluloid Closet (Emmy nom. 1996) Tidy Endings.

ROSENTHAL, BUD
Executive, Producer. b. Brooklyn, NY, Mar. 21, 1934. e. Brooklyn Coll., B.A., 1954, NYU. U.S. Army, 1954-56; college correspondent, NY Times. Entered m.p. ind. as assoc. editor, Independent Film Journal, 1957-59. Publicist, Columbia Pictures, 1959-61.Natl. publ mgr., Columbia Pictures, 1962-67. Publ. dir. for Anderson Tapes, Such Good Friends, The Blue Bird; Story edit. and casting dir., Otto Preminger's Sigma Productions, 1972-75. Assoc. prod., Broadway play, Full Circle. Warner Bros. worldwide mtg. coordinator, Superman, Superman II, Superman III, Batman, Space Jam. Project coordinator, Time Warner Earth Day Special, Warner Bros. Studio Rededication, Celebration of Tradition. International mktg. consultant, 1976-present.
PICTURES: Something for Everyone (asst. prod.), Rosebud (assoc. prod.). *Int'l mktg. co-ord. on films*: Ghostbusters, Labyrinth, Tune in Tomorrow, Boyz 'N the Hood, Addams Family, Bugsy, Batman Returns, A Few Good Men, Last Action Hero, Jumanji, Star Trek: Insurrection, The Rugrats Movie, Spine Tingler: The William Castle Story (doc.).

ROSENTHAL, JANE
Executive, Producer. b. Denver, CO. e. NYU. 1976-84, dir. of film for TV at CBS; 1984-87, v.p. prod. Disney; 1987-88, v.p. of TV & Mini-Series, Warners TV; 1988-93, co-founder, Tribeca Prods., Tribeca Film Center; 1993-present, pres. of Tribeca Prods.; 1992-93, exec. prod. of series Tribeca. Co-chairman Tribeca Entertainment.
PICTURES: *Prod.*: Thunderheart, Night and the City, A Bronx Tale, Faithful, Marvin's Room, Wag the Dog, The Repair Shop, Analyze This, Entropy, Flawless, The Adventures of Rocky & Bullwinkle, Meet the Parents, Prison Song, Showtime, About a Boy, Analyze That, House of D, Stage Beauty, Meet the Fockers, Chaos, Rent, The Good Shepherd, Bridge and Tunnel, What Just Happened?, Public Enemies, Little Fockers.
TELEVISION: *Movies*: *Executive producer:* Witness to the Mob, Holiday Heart, Chicken Club. *Series: Producer:* Tribeca.

ROSENTHAL, RICK
Director. b. New York, NY, June 15, 1949. e. Harvard, B.A. cum laude, 1971. Launched career as filmmaker-in-residence with New Hampshire TV Network. Moved to Los Angeles to study at American Film Institute where filmed Moonface, 1973.
PICTURES: *Director:* Halloween II (debut, 1981), Bad Boys (also actor), American Dreamer, Russkies, Distant Thunder, Just a Little Harmless Sex (also prod.), Mean Creek (prod. only), Nearing Grace (also prod.), Kabluey (prod.). *Actor:* Johnny Dangerously, Better Off Dead, Halloween: Resurrection (also dir., 2002). *Writer:* Best Revenge.
TELEVISION: *Movies*: Fire on the Mountain, Code of Vengeance, Secrets of Midland Heights, Nasty Boys, Devlin, Birds II, The Land's End. *Series*: Life Goes On, Witches of Eastwick, The Practice, Feds, Early Edition, Dellaventura, Roar, LA Doctors, Providence, D.C., Falcone, The District, Strong Medicine, All Souls, She Spies, MDs, Hack, The Handler, Smallville, Flash Gordon (pilot), many credits as episode dir..

ROSS, DIANA
Singer, Actress. b. Detroit, MI, Mar. 26, 1944. Formed musical group at age 14 with two friends, Mary Wilson and Florence Ballard. In 1960 they auditioned for Berry Gordy, head of Motown Record Corp. and were hired to sing backgrounds on records for Motown acts. After completing high school, the trio was named the Supremes and went on tour with Motor Town Revue. Over period of 10 yrs. Supremes had 15 consecutive hit records and once had five consecutive records in the number one spot on charts. In 1969 Ross went on her own, appearing on TV and in nightclubs. Memoirs: Secrets of a Sparrow (1993). Many performances for soundtracks in movies and television.
PICTURES: *Actress:* Lady Sings the Blues (debut as actress, 1972; Academy Award nom. Golden Globe Award, 1 other nom. 1973), Mahogany (also singer), The Wiz, numerous credits as soundtrack performer.
TELEVISION: *Movies*: *Actress:* Out of Darkness (also co-exec. prod., Golden Globe nom. 1995), Diana (as herself; writer), Double Platinum (also exec. prod.). *Documentaries/Specials*: Diana! (also exec. prod. & writer), Motown 25: Yesterday Today Forever, Motown Returns to the Apollo, Diana's World Tour, Diana Ross: Red Hot Rhythm & Blues (also prod., writer), Diana Ross Live! The Lady Sings...Jazz & Blues: Stolen Moments (also exec. prod.), Motown 40: The Music Is Forever (host), Nobel Peace Prize Concert. Many sountrack performances. *Guest:* More than 139 appearances.

ROSS, KATHARINE
Actress. b. Los Angeles, CA, Jan. 29, 1943. m. actor Sam Elliott. e. Santa Rosa Coll. Joined the San Francisco Workshop, appeared in The Devil's Disciple, The Balcony. TV debut, 1962 in Sam Benedict segment.
PICTURES: Shenandoah (debut, 1965), Mister Buddwing, The Singing Nun, Games, The Graduate (Golden Globe Award, Acad. Award nom.), Hellfighters, Butch Cassidy and the Sundance Kid, Tell Them Willie Boy is Here, Fools, Get to Know Your Rabbit, They Only Kill Their Masters, The Stepford Wives, Voyage of the Damned, The Betsy, The Swarm, The Legacy, The Final Countdown, Wrong Is Right, Daddy's Deadly Darling, The Red-Headed Stranger, A Climate for Killing, Home Before Dark, Donnie Darko, Don't Let Go, Eye of the Dolphin.
TELEVISION: *Movies*: The Longest Hundred Miles, Wanted: The Sundance Woman, Murder by Natural Causes, Rodeo Girl, Murder in Texas, Marian Rose White, Shadow Riders, Travis McGee, Secrets of a Mother and Daughter, Conagher (also co-script), Houston: The Legend of Texas, Tattle: When to Tell on a Friend, Snow in August, Capital City. *Series:* The Colbys.

ROSS, RICH
Executive. b. New York. e. B.A. degree in international relations and English, Univ. of Pennsylvania, 1983; J.D. degree, Fordham Univ., 1986. From 1986-1993, Ross worked in cable TV at Nickelodeon and served as v.p., program enterprises, and was involved in all original-programming deals. In addition he launched "Nick News" with Linda Ellerbee into syndication, Nickelodeon's first syndication success, and was a part of the launch team for Nickelodeon's first international network,

Nickelodeon UK. Ross also built the Nickelodeon/Nick at Nite talent relations department, overseeing network casting and talent booking, and served as executive producer of Nickelodeon's "Kids' Choice Awards," the first televised kid-voted award show. From 1993-1996, Ross was senior v.p., development and production for FX Networks and part of the team that launched the network. He moved to Disney Channel and from 1996-1999 was senior v.p. programming and production; 1999-2002, gen. mgr. and executive v.p., programming and production; 2002-2004, Disney Channel president, entertainment; April 2004-became president, Disney Channels Worldwide, which is part of the Disney ABC Television Group, a division of The Walt Disney Company. Ross managed Disney's global kids' TV business, a total of 94 kid-driven, family inclusive entertainment channels and/or channel feeds available in 163 countries in 32 languages. They span Disney Channel, Disney XD, Playhouse Disney, Disney Cinemagic, Hungama, GXT, Jetix Radio Disney and Disney XD brands. The group's multiplatform strategy includes subscription video-on-demand and content-rich broadband websites DisneyXD.com and DisneyChannel.com. Ross also had responsibility for Radio Disney which, over the past decade, has set the radio industry standard for kid and family content. October 2009 Rich was named Chairman of the Studio and will oversee worldwide production, distribution and marketing for the company's live-action and animated film labels, including Walt Disney, Touchstone, Miramax and Disney/Pixar. He will also head Disney's theatrical and music groups.

ROSSELLINI, ISABELLA
Actress. b. Rome, Italy, June 18, 1952. Daughter of actress Ingrid Bergman and director Roberto Rossellini. Former model. Worked as translator for Italian News Bureau, 1972. Taught Italian at New Sch. for Social Research. Worked 3 years on second unit assignments for journalist Gianni Mina and as NY corresp. for Ital. TV series, The Other Sunday.
PICTURES: A Matter of Time (debut 1976; with her mother), The Meadow, Il Pap'Occhio, White Nights, Blue Velvet, Tough Guys Don't Dance, Siesta, Red Riding Hood, Zelly and Me, Cousins, Les Dames Galantes, The Siege of Venice, Wild at Heart, Death Becomes Her, The Pickle, Fearless, Wyatt Earp, Immortal Beloved, The Innocent, Big Night, Left Luggage, The Imposters, The Sky Will Fall, Empire, The Wedding Contract, The Tulse Luper Suitcases/Part 2: Vaux to the Sea, Roger Dodger, The Saddest Music in the World, King of the Corner, Heights, The Feast of the Goat, Wiseguys & Beyond: Italian Americans and the Movies (doc.), All Fall Down, The Architect, Infamous, The Accidental Husband, Two Lovers, My Dog Tulip, The Solitude of Prime Numbers, Paavo, Master of Ceremonies, Late Bloomers, Keyhole, Chiken with Plums.
TELEVISION: *Movies*: The Last Elephant, Lies of the Twins, The Crime of the Century (Golden Globe nom. 1997), The Odyssey, Merlin, Don Quixote, Monte Walsh, Legend of Earthsea, Filthy Gorgeous, Infected, The Phantom. *Mini-series:* Napoléon. *Series:* The Tracey Ullman Show, Chicago Hope (Emmy nom. 1997), Alias, 30 Rock, Green Porno (also dir., writer). *Documentaries/Specials*: The Gift, Fallen Angels (The Frightening Frammis), World Fashion Premiere from Paris (documentary, host). *Guest:* More than 97 appearances.

ROSSOVICH, RICK
Actor. b. Palo Alto, CA, August 28, 1957. e. Calif. St. Univ. Sacramento.
PICTURES: The Lords of Discipline (debut, 1983), Losin' It, Streets of Fire, The Terminator, Fast Forward, Warning Sign, Top Gun, Let's Get Harry, The Morning After, Roxanne, Paint It Black, The Witching Hour, Spellbinder, Navy SEALS, Cognac, Tropical Heat, New Crime City, Cover Me, Black Scorpion II, Truth or Consequences N.M., Telling You, Artworks, Sandbar.
TELEVISION: *Movies*: Deadly Lessons, The Gambler Returns: Luck of the Draw, Black Scorpion, Fatally Yours, 14 Going On 30, Legend of the Lost Tomb, Killer Deal, Miracle in Lane 2. *Series*: MacGruder and Loud, Sons and Daughters, Pacific Blue, ER.

ROTH, BOBBY
Director, Writer, Producer. b. 1950.
PICTURES: The Boss' Son, Circle of Power, Independence Day, Heartbreakers, The Man Inside, Amanda, Jack the Dog, Manhood, Berkeley.
TELEVISION: *Movies*: Tonight's the Night, The Man Who Fell to Earth, Dead Solid Perfect (dir., co-s.p.), Baja Oklahoma (dir., co-s.p.), The Man Inside, Rainbow Drive, Keeper of the City, The Switch, Judgment Day: The John List Story, Ride With the Wind, Nowhere to Hide, Separated by Murder (s.p.), In the Line of Duty: Kidnapped, Naomi & Wynonna: Love Can Build A Bridge, Tell Me No Secrets, Inheritance, The Devil's Child, Vengeance Unlimited, Her Own Rules, A Secret Affair, A Holiday Romance, Crossed Over, Dancing at the Harvest Moon, A Date with Darkness: The Trial and Capture of Andrew Luster, The Elizabeth Smart Story, Brave New Girl, Shattered. *Series*: Miami Vice, The Insiders, Crime Story, Boomtown, Numb3rs, Blind Justice, Prison Break, FlashForward.

ROTH, JOE
Executive, Producer, Director. b. New York, NY, June 13, 1948. e. Boston Univ., 1970. Began career working as prod. assistant on commercials and feature films in San Francisco. Also ran the lights for improv group Pitchel Players. Moved with them to Los Angeles, and prod. their shows incl. the $250,000 film, Tunnelvision. 1987, co-founder of independent film prod. co. Morgan Creek Productions. 1989, left to become chmn. of newly-formed Fox Film Corp., the theatrical film unit of 20th Century Fox Film Corp. Also named head of News Corp. unit. Resigned from Fox, 1993. Pres. & founder, Caravan Pictures, 1993. In Aug. 1994, became chmn. Walt Disney Motion Pictures Group. In Jan. 2000, left Disney to start own company, Revolution Studios, where he currently is pres. & CEO. Roth's awards have included: Variety Club's Man of the Year Award, 1991; the NCCJ Humanitarian Award, 1996; the American Museum of Moving Image Award, 1997; and in 1998 was honored by the APLA and the National Multiple Sclerosis Society. Roth is a graduate instructor on the faculty at UCLA's independent film and TV program and has been coaching AYSO soccer for the past 10 years.
PICTURES: *Producer*: Tunnelvision, Cracking Up, Americathon, Our Winning Season, The Final Terror, The Stone Boy, Where the River Runs Black, Bachelor Party, Off Beat, Streets of Gold (also dir. debut), Tall Tale, Angels in the Outfield, The Forgotten, The Fantastic Mr. Fox, The Great Debaters, Hellboy 2: The Golden Army, Alice in Wonderland, Knight and Day, xXx: The Return of Xander Cage. *Executive producer:* Revenge of the Nerds II: Nerds in Paradise (also dir.), Young Guns, Dead Ringers, Skin Deep, Major League, Renegades, Enemies a Love Story, Pacific Heights, The Three Musketeers, Angie, I Love Trouble, Angels in the Outfield, A Low Down Dirty Shame, Houseguest, Tall Tale, While You Were Sleeping, Before and After, Tears of the Sun, Daddy Day Care, Hollywood Homicide, Mona Lisa Smile, An Unfinished Life, Little Man. *Director:* Coupe de Ville, Tomcats, Butterfly, Hostile Rescue, America's Sweethearts, Christmas with the Kranks, Freedomland.
TELEVISION: *Movie:* Demons (exec. prod.). *Series:* Are We There Yet? (exec. prod.). *Documentaries/Specials:* The 76th Annual Academy Awards (prod., Emmy nom. 2004).

ROTH, PETER
Executive. b. Larchmont, NY. e. U. of Pennsylvania, graduated cum laude, Tufts U., 1972. Began career in television at ABC Television Network as manager, then director, Children's Programs, 1976; moving to director, Current Programs, 1979; became v.p., Current Primetime Series, 1981-86; president, Stephen J. Cannell Prods., 1986-92, president of production, Twentieth Network Television (currently 20th Century Fox Television), 1992; president, Twentieth Network Television, 1993; president, 20th Century Fox Television, 1994. Currently president, Warner Bros. Television.

ROTH, TIM
Actor. b. London, England, May 14,1961. Started acting with various fringe theatre groups such as Glasgow Citizen's Theatre, The Oval House, and the Royal Court. Also on London stage in Metamorphosis.
PICTURES: The Hit, A World Apart, The Cook the Thief His Wife and Her Lover, Vincent & Theo, Rosencrantz and Guildenstern Are Dead, Jumpin at the Boneyard, Reservoir Dogs, Backsliding, Bodies Rest and Motion, Pulp Fiction, Rob Roy (Academy Award nom.; Golden Globe nom. 1996), Little Odessa, Captives, Hoodlum, Four Rooms, Everyone Say I Love You, Liar, Animals, No Way Home, Gridlock'd, The Legend of 1900, The Million Dollar Hotel, Vatel, Lucky Numbers, Invincible, Planet of the Apes, The Musketeer, Inside Job, Emmett's Mark, Whatever We Do (short) To Kill a King (aka Cromwell & Fairfax), The Beautiful Country, With It (short), Silver City, New France, The Last Sign, Don't Come Knockin', Dark Water, Even Money, Decameron: Angels & Virgins, Youth Without Youth, My Blueberry Nights, Funny Games, Virgin Territory, The Other Side, Six Bullets from Now, The Incredible Hulk, King Conqueror, Pete Smalls Is Dead.
TELEVISION: *Specials/Movies* Meantime, Made in Britain, Metamorphosis, Knuckle, Yellow Backs, King of the Ghetto, Common Pursuit, Murder in the Heartland, Heart of Darkness, Tsunami: The Aftermath, Skellig. *Mini-series:* Sea-Wolf. *Series:* King of the Ghetto, Lie to Me. *Guest:* More than 72 appearances.

ROTHMAN, THOMAS E.
Executive. b. Baltimore, MD, Nov. 21, 1954. m. actress Jessica Harper. e. Brown U., B.A. 1976; Columbia Law School, J.D. 1980. Worked as law clerk with Second Circuit Court of Appeals 1981-82 before becoming partner at entertainment law firm, Frankfurt Garbus Klein & Selz 1982-87; exec. v.p. of production, Columbia Pictures; president of worldwide production, Samuel Goldwyn Co.; founder and president, Fox Searchlight Pictures; president of production, Twentieth Century Fox, 1995-2000. President, Twentieth Century Fox Film Group, Jan. - Aug. 2000; Co-Chairman, Fox Filmed Entertainment, since 2000, Also CEO, the position he holds today with James N. Gianopulos. Member, bd. of directors, Sundance Institute; recipient, Arthur B. Krim Award from Columbia U.
PICTURES: *Co-producer:* Down By Law (co-prod.), Candy Mountain. *Executive producer*: The Program.

ROTUNNO, GIUSEPPE
Cinematographer. b. Rome, Italy, March 19, 1923. Gained fame as leading cinematographer of Italian films working with Federico

Fellini. Later worked in Hollywood. Received ASC International Award 1999.
PICTURES: Tosca, Monte Carlo Story, White Nights, The Naked Maja, On the Beach, Fast and Sexy, The Angel Wore Red, Five Branded Women, Rocco and His Brothers, Boccaccio '70, The Leopard, The Organizer, Juliet of the Spirits, The Bible, Anizo, Candy, Spirits of the Dead, Fellini Satyricon, The Secret of Santa Vittoria, Carnal Knowledge, Fellini's Roma, Man of La Mancha, Amarcord, Love and Anarchy, Fellini's Casanova, All Screwed Up, End of the World in Our Usual Bed in a Night Full of Rain, Orchestra Rehearsal, All That Jazz (Academy Award nom. 1980), City of Women, Popeye, Rollover, Five Days One Summer, And the Ship Sails On, American Dreamer, Desire, Nothing Left to Do But Cry, The Red Sonja, Hotel Colonial, Julia and Julia, Rent-a-Cop, Rebus, Haunted Summer, The Adventures of Baron Munchausen, Regarding Henry, Once Upon a Crime, Wolf, The Night the Moment, Sabrina, La Sindrome di Stendhal, Marcello Mastroianni: I Remember.
TELEVISION: *Movies:* The Scarlet and the Black, Guglielmo Tell. *Mini-series:* Roots of the Mafia. *Documentaries/Specials:* E il Casnova di Fellini?

ROUNDTREE, RICHARD
Actor. b. New Rochelle, NY, July 9, 1942. e. Southern Illinos U. Former model, Ebony Magazine Fashion Fair; joined workshop of Negro Ensemble Company, appeared in Kongi's Harvest, Man Better Man, Mau Mau Room; played lead role in Philadelphia road company of The Great White Hope before film debut.
PICTURES: What Do You Say to a Naked Lady? (debut, 1970), Shaft (Golden Globe nom. 1972), Embassy, Charley One-Eye, Shaft's Big Score, Embassy, Shaft in Africa, Earthquake, Diamonds, Man Friday, Portrait of a Hitman, Escape to Athena, Game for Vultures, An Eye for an Eye, Inchon, Q, One Down Two to Go, The Big Score, Young Warriors, Killpoint, City Heat, Opposing Force, Jocks, Maniac Cop, Homer and Eddie, Angel III: The Final Chapter, The Party Line, Getting Even, American Cops, The Banker, Night Visitor, Crack House, Bad Jim, Lost Memories, Body of Influence, Deadly Rivals, Amityville: A New Generation, Gypsy Angels, Mind Twister, Seven, Once Upon A Time...When We Were Colored, Theodore Rex, Original Gangstas, George of the Jungle, Steel, Shaft, Antitrust, Hawaiian Gardens, Corkey Romano, Capone's Boys, Boat Trip, Max Havoc: Curse of the Dragon, Brick, Wild Seven, All the Days Before Tomorrow, Speed Racer, Set Apart, Retreat!, This Bitter Earth, The Confidant.
TELEVISION: *Movies*: Firehouse, The Fifth Missile, Daddy Can't Read, Just an Overnight Guest, Masquerade, Black as the Heart, The Baron and the Kid, Outlaws, Christmas in Connecticut, Bonanza: The Return, Moscacieca, Shadows of Desire, Bonanza: Under Attack, Buddies, 413 Hope St., Any Place but Home, Having our Say: The Delany Sisters' First 100 Years, Joe and Max, Painkiller Jane, Final Approach, Point of Entry, Ladies of the House. *Mini-series*: Roots, A.D., Y2K: A World in Crisis. *Series*: Shaft, Outlaws, Cadets, Masquerade (pilot), Amen, Generations, 21 Jump Street, Buddies, Cop Files (host), 413 Hope St., Rescue 77, Soul Food, As The World Turns, Desperate Housewives, Heroes, Diary of a Single Mom. *Guest:* More than 111 appearances.

ROURKE, MICKEY
Actor. r.n. Phillip Andre Rourke, Jr. b. Schenectady, NY, Sept. 16, 1956. Fought as an amateur boxer four years in Miami. Studied acting with Sandra Seacat while working as a nightclub bouncer, a sidewalk pretzel vendor and other odd jobs. Moved to LA, 1978. Debut: TV movie City in Fear (1978).
PICTURES: 1941 (debut, 1979), Fade to Black, Heaven's Gate, Body Heat, Diner (Natl. Society of Film Critics Award, 1982), Rumblefish, Eureka, The Pope of Greenwich Village, Year of the Dragon, 9-1/2 Weeks, Angel Heart, A Prayer for the Dying, Barfly, Homeboy (also wrote orig. story), Francesco, Johnny Handsome, Wild Orchid, Desperate Hours, Harley Davidson and the Marlboro Man, White Sands, F.T.W., Fall Time, Double Team, Another 9-1/2 Weeks, The Rainmaker, Buffalo 66, Thursday, Shades, Out in Fifty, Animal Factory, Get Carter, The Pledge, The Follow, Picture Claire, Spun, Once Upon a Time in Mexico, Masked & Anonymous, Man on Fire, Sin City, Domino, Alex Rider: Operation Stormbreaker, The Informers, The Wrestler (Academy Award nom.; Golden Globe Award 2009), Killshot, 13, Pretty, Baby, Machine, Iron Man 2, Passion Play, The Expendables, Immortals, Office Paranormal.
TELEVISION: *Movies*: City in Fear, Act of Love, Rape and Marriage: The Rideout Case, Act of Love, The Last Outlaw, Thicker than Blood. *Guest:* More than 100 appearances.

ROUSSELOT, PHILIPPE
Cinematographer. b. Meurthe-et-Moselle, France, 1945. e. Vaugirard Film School, Paris. Worked as camera assistant to Nestor Almendros on My Night at Maud's, Claire's Knee, Love in the Afternoon.
PICTURES: The Guinea Pig Couple, Adom ou le sang d'Abel, Paradiso, Pauline et l'ordinateur, Peppermint Soda, For Clemence, Cocktail Molotov, La Provinciale, A Girl From Lorraine, Diva, The Jaws of the Wolf, The Moon in the Gutter, Thieves After Dark, The Emerald Forest, Therese, Hope and Glory (Academy Award nom. 1988), Dangerous Liaisons (ASC nom. 1989), The Bear (ASC nom. 1990), We're No Angels, Too Beautiful for You, Henry and June (Academy Award nom. 1991), A River Runs Through It (Academy Award, ASC nom. 1993), Sommersby, Interview With the Vampire, Queen Margot, Mary Reilly, The People vs. Larry Flynt, Instinct, Random Hearts, Remember the Titans, The Tailor of Panama, Planet of the Apes, Antwone Fisher, Big Fish, Constantine, Charlie and the Chocolate Factory, X-Men: The Last Stand, The Brave One, Lions for Lambs, The Great Debaters, Peacock, Sherlock Holmes, The Loop, Larry Crowne.

ROWLANDS, GENA
Actress. r.n. Virginia Cathryn Rowlands. b. Cambria, WI, June 19, 1934. e. U. of Wisconsin. Son is actor Nicholas Cassavetes. Came to New York to attend American Acad. of Dramatic Arts, where she met and married John Cassavetes. Made B'way debut as understudy and then succeeded to role of The Girl in The Seven Year Itch. Launched as star with part in The Middle of the Night, which she played 18 mos.
PICTURES: The High Cost of Loving (debut, 1958), Lonely Are the Brave, The Spiral Road, A Child Is Waiting, Tony Rome, Faces, Machine Gun McCain, Minnie and Moskowitz, A Woman Under the Influence (Academy Award nom.; Golden Globe Award 1975), Two Minute Warning, The Brink's Job, Opening Night (Golden Globe nom. 1978), Gloria (Academy Award nom.; Golden Globe nom. 1981), Tempest, Love Streams, Light of Day, Another Woman, Once Around, Ted and Venus, Night on Earth, The Neon Bible, Something to Talk About, Unhook The Stars, She's So Lovely, Paulie, Hope Floats, Playing by Heart, The Mighty, The Weekend, Taking Lives, The Notebook, The Skeleton Key, Paris, je t'aime, The Book of Joe, Broken English, Persepolis (voice, English version).
TELEVISION: *Movies*: A Question of Love, Strangers: The Story of a Mother & Daughter, Thursday's Child (Golden Globe nom. 1984), An Early Frost (Emmy nom.; Golden Globe nom. 1986), The Betty Ford Story (Emmy Award, Golden Globe Award 1987), Montana, Face of a Stranger (Emmy Award, 1992), Crazy in Love (Golden Globe nom. 1993), Silent Cries, Parallel Lives, The Color of Love: Jacey's Story (Emmy nom. 2000), Best Friends for Life, Wild Iris (Emmy nom. 2002), Grace and Glorie, Charms for the Easy Life, Hysterical Blindness (Emmy Award, Golden Globe nom. 2003), The Incredible Mrs. Ritchie (Emmy Award 2004), What If God Were the Sun? (Emmy nom. 2007). *Series*: Top Secret USA, 87th Precinct, Peyton Place, Monk (Emmy nom. 2009 as guest). *Guest*: More than 94 appearances.

ROY, DEEP
Actor, Stunts.
PICTURES: *Actor:* The Pink Panther Strikes Again, The Man from S.E.X., Roots of Evil, Flash Gordon, Greystoke: The Legend of Tarzan-Lord of the Apes, The Neverending Story, Return to Oz, Starship, Alien from L.A., My African Adventure, Disturbed, The Most Dangerous Woman Alive, The Resurrected, How the Grinch Stole Christmas, Planet of the Apes, The Haunted Mansion, Big Fish, Surviving Eden, Charlie and the Chocolate Factory, Corpse Bride (voice), Star Trek, Transformers: Revenge of the Fallen. *Stunts:* Poltergeist II: The Other Side, Hook, Leprechaun, Freaked, The Little Rascals, New Nightmare, The War, The Jungle Book, Sudden Death, Matilda, Retroactive, The Adventures of Ragtime, BASEketball, The Kid, A Man Apart, Van Helsing, The Unborn.
TELEVISION: Desperado: The Outlaw Wars (actor), Evil Has a Face.

RUBEN, JOSEPH
Director. b. Briarcliff, NY, 1951. e. U. of Michigan, majoring in theatre and film; Brandeis U., B.A. Interest in film began in high school. Bought a Super-8 camera and filmed his first movie, a teenage love story. First feature, The Sister-in-Law, a low budget feature which he wrote and dir. in 1975.
PICTURES: *Director/Writer*: The Sister-in-Law (also prod.), The Pom-Pom Girls (also prod.), Joy Ride, Our Winning Season. *Director:* G.O.R.P., Dreamscape (also co-s.p.), The Stepfather, True Believer, Sleeping With the Enemy, The Good Son, Money Train, Return to Paradise, The Forgotten.
TELEVISION: *Series:* Breaking Away (pilot), Eddie Dodd.

RUBINEK, SAUL
Actor. b. Fohrenwold, Germany, July 2, 1948. Family moved to Canada when he was a baby. Acting debut at age 8 with local theatre groups. Founding member of the Toronto Free Stage Theatre.
PICTURES: Nothing Personal, Highpoint, Agency, Death Ship, Ticket to Heaven, Soup for One, Young Doctors in Love, By Design, Against All Odds, Martin's Day, Sweet Liberty, Taking Care, Wall Street, Obsessed, The Outside Chance of Maximillian Glick, The Bonfire of the Vanities, Man Trouble, Unforgiven, The Quarrel, True Romance, Undercover Blues, Death Wish V, Getting Even With Dad, I Love Trouble, Open Season, Nixon, Past Perfect, Bad Manners, Dick, The Contender, The Family Man, Lakeboat, Rush Hour 2, Night's Noontime (short), Triggermen, The Singing Detective, Hollywood North, Gettin' the Man's Foot Outta Your Baadasssss!, Whitecoats, Santa's Slay, Cruel But Necessary (dir. only), Partner(s), A Broken Life, Blackout, Julia, War, The Express, Oy Vey! My Son Is Gay!!, The Trotsky, Barney's Version, Knucklehead.
TELEVISION: *Movies:* Sanctuary of Fear, The Wordsmith, Clown White, The Terry Fox Story, Dusty, Concealed Enemies, The

Suicide Murders, Murder Sees the Light, Half a Lifetime, Prescription for Murder, Hitting Home, Woman on Trial: The Lawrencia Bembenek Story, And the Band Played On, The Android Affair, Hiroshima, Color of Justice, Blackjack, 36 Hours to Die, The Golden Spiders: A Nero Wolfe Mystery, The Bookfair Murders, Laughter on the 23rd Floor, Club Land (dir. only), Gleason, The Brady Bunch in the White House, And Starring Pancho Villa as Himself, Call Me: The Rise and Fall of Heidi Fleiss, Coast to Coast, Trump Unauthorized, Jesse Stone: Night Passage, Jesse Stone: Sea Change, Jesse Stone: No Remorse. *Mini-series:* The Trojan Horse. *Series:* Bizarre, Men, Ink, A Nero Wolfe Mystery, Frasier (recurring guest role), Blind Justice, Warehouse 13. *Guest:* More than 90 appearances.

RUBINSTEIN, JOHN
Actor, Composer, Director. b. Los Angeles, CA, December 8, 1946. e. UCLA. Son of concert pianist Arthur Rubinstein and dancer-writer Aniela Rubinstein.
THEATRE: Pippin (NY debut, 1972; Theatre World Award), Picture (Mark Taper, LA), Children of a Lesser God (Tony Award, Drama Desk, L.A. Drama Critics Awards, 1980), Fools, The Caine Mutiny Court-Martial, M. Butterfly, Kiss of the Spider Woman, Love Letters, Hurlyburly, Getting Away With Murder, Camelot, Ragtime, On A Clear Day You Can See Forever, Counsellor-at-Law (also dir; Drama-Logue, Ovation, L.A. Drama Critics Awards, 1995), Into the Woods (also dir.), Merrily We Roll Along, Streamers, The Tempest, Candida, Arms and the Man, Three Hotels, Broken Glass, Sight Unseen. *Director:* The Rover, Les Liaisons Dangereuses, Phantasie, Nightingale, The Old Boy, She Loves Me.
PICTURES: *Actor:* Journey to Shiloh (debut, 1968), The Trouble With Girls, Getting Straight, The Wild Pack, Zachariah (also composer), The Wild Pack, The Boys From Brazil, In Search of Historic Jesus, Daniel, Someone To Watch Over Me, Another Stakeout, Mercy, Red Dragon, 21 Grams, Jekyll, Sublime, Choose Connor, Rome & Jewel, Seducing Spirits, The Truth About Layla. *Composer:* The Candidate, Jeremiah Johnson, The Killer Inside Me, If China 9-Liberty 37.
TELEVISION: *Movies*: *Composer:* All Together Now (also actor), Stalk the Wild Child, Stickin' Together, The New Maverick, Champions: A Love Story, The Ordeal Of Patty Hearst, Amber Waves, To Race the Wind, Johnny Belinda, Secrets of a Mother & Daughter, The Dollmaker (also writer), Conspiracy of Love. *Actor:* Children of the Lotus Eater, A Howling in the Woods, Something Evil, The Streets of San Francisco, Mr. & Ms. and the Magic Stusssdio Mystery, The Quest: The Longest Drive, Corey: For the People, Happily Ever After, She's Dressed to Kill, Make Me an Offer, Moviola: The Silent Lovers, Killjoy, Skokie, M.A.D.D.: Mothers Against Drunk Drivers, Surprise-Surprise!, The Two Mrs. Grenvilles, Still Crazy Like a Fox, Beryl Markham: A Shadow in the Sun, Liberace, Voices Within: The Lives of Truddi Chase, In My Daughter's Name, The American Clock, Norma Jean & Marily, The Sleepwalker Killing, Perfect Murder-Perfect Town: JonBenet and the City of Boulder, Amber Frey: Witness for the Prosecution, Jane Doe: The Wrong Face, Sweet Nothing in My Ear. *Director:* A Matter of Conscience. *Mini-series: Actor:* Roots: The Next Generations, The French Atlantic Affair, Freedom to Speak. *Series: Actor:* Day Break, The Young and the Restless. *Series: Composer:* Family (Emmy nom. 1978 for episode acting), The Fitzpatricks, China Beach. *Actor:* Crazy Like a Fox, Kokaku kidotai: Stand Alone Complex (voice), The Closer (pilot), Barbershop, Cold Case, Day Break, The Young and the Restless, Desperate Housewives. *Guest:* More than 172 appearances.

RUBINSTEIN, RICHARD P.
Producer, Executive. b. New York, NY, June 15, 1947. e. American U. B.S. 1969, Columbia U. MBA 1971. Pres. & CEO, New Amsterdam Entertainment, Inc.
PICTURES: Martin, Dawn Of The Dead, Knightriders, Creepshow, Day Of The Dead, Creepshow 2, Pet Sematary, Tales From the Darkside: The Movie, Thinner, Stephen King's The Night Flier, Dawn of the Dead.
TELEVISION: *Movies: Executive producer:* Golden Years, Precious Victims, The Road to Freedom: The Vernon Johns Story, The Langoliers, Kiss and Tell, A Season in Purgatory. *Mini-series*: The Stand (Emmy nom. 1994), Dune, Children of Dune. *Series*: Tales from the Darkside, Monsters. *Producer/Director:* The Winners (TV series documentary).

RUDDY, ALBERT S.
Producer. b. Montreal, Canada, March 28, 1934. e. U. of Southern California, B.S. in design, Sch. of Architecture, 1956. Exec. prod. of 1991 TV movie Miracle in the Wilderness.
PICTURES: The Wild Seed, Little Fauss & Big Halsey, Making It, The Godfather (Academy Award 1973), The Longest Yard, Coonskin, Matilda, The Cannonball Run, Megaforce, Lassiter, Cannonball Run II, Farewell to the King, Paramedics, Speed Zone, Impulse, Ladybugs, Bad Girls, The Scout, Heaven's Prisoners, Mean Machine, Rope Burns, The Longest Yard (2005 exec. prod., writer), Cloud Nine (also writer), Million Dollar Baby (Academy Award 2005), Camille.
TELEVISION: *Movies*: The Macahans, Revenge for a Rape (writer), Miracle in the Wilderness (exec. prod.), Married to a Stranger (exec. prod.), Running Mates, Georgetown, Walker, Texas Ranger: Trial by Fire (writer/creator). *Mini-series:* How the West Was Won. *Series*: Hogan's Heroes (writer), How the West Was Won, Walker—Texas Ranger (exec. prod. & creator), Flatland (exec. prod.).

RUDIN, SCOTT
Executive, Producer. b. New York, NY, July 14, 1958. Began career as prod. asst. on B'way for producers Kermit Bloomgarden, Robert Whitehead; then casting director. 1984, became producer for 20th Century Fox; named exec. v.p. prod.; 1986, appt.pres. prod., 20th-Fox. Resigned 1987 becoming independent producer—Scott Rudin Productions in New York City.
PICTURES: I'm Dancing as Fast as I Can, Reckless, Mrs. Soffel, Flatliners (exec. prod.), Pacific Heights, Regarding Henry, Little Man Tate, The Addams Family, White Sands, Sister Act, Jennifer Eight, Life With Mikey, The Firm, Searching for Bobby Fisher, Addams Family Values, Sister Act 2: Back in the Habit, Nobody's Fool, I.Q., Clueless, Sabrina, Up Close and Personal, Marvin's Room, In & Out, The Truman Show, Civil Action, Southpark:Bigger, Longer and Uncut,Bringing Out the Dead, Angela's Ashes, Wonder Boys, Rules of Engagement, Shaft, Brokeback Mountain, Zoolander, The Royal Tennenbaums, Iris, Orange County, Changing Lanes, Marci X, The Hours (Academy Award nom. 2003), The School of Rock, The Stepford Wives, The Manchurian Candidate, The Village, I Heart Huckabees, Team America: World Police (exec. prod.), Closer, The Life Aquatic with Steve Zissou, Lemon Snicket's A Series of Unfortunate Events (exec. prod.), Freedomland, Failure to Launch, Margaret, Nothing Is Private (exec. prod.), Notes on a Scandal, I Could Never Be Your Woman, Venus, There Will Be Blood (exec. prod.), Goat, The Queen (exec. prod.), No Country for Old Men (Academy Award 2008), Margot at the Wedding, Stop Loss, Margaret, The Other Boleyn Girl, The Darjeeling Limited, The Reader, Jack and Diane (exec. prod.), Doubt, Revolutionary Road, Julie & Julia (exec. prod.), The Fantastic Mr. Fox, Greenberg, It's Complicated, Margaret, The Social Network, The Way Back (exec. prod.), True Grit, Moneyball, Cleopatra, The Girl with the Dragon Tattoo.
TELEVISION: *Movies*: Sanctuary of Fear, The Lathe of Heaven, Revenge of the Stepford Wives, Little Gloria... Happy at Last (exec. prod., Emmy nom. 1983), Passion, He Makes Me Feel Like Dancin' (Emmy Award 1984). *Series*: Clueless.

RUDNER, RITA
Actress, Writer. b. Miami, FL, Sept. 17, 1956. m. producer Martin Bergmann. Was stage dancer then stand-up comic. Author: Naked Beneath My Clothes, Rita Rudner's Guide to Men.
THEATRE: Annie (B'way), Promises Promises, Follies, Mack and Mabel.
PICTURES: The Wrong Guys (debut, 1988), Gleaming the Cube, That's Adequate, Peter's Friends (also co-s.p.), Hanging Out Hooking Up Falling in Love, Love Hurts.
TELEVISION: *Documentaries/Specials*: Women of the Night, One Night Stand: Rita Rudner, Rita Rudner: Born to Be Mild, The Rita Rudner Comedy Specials (also writer), Comic Relief, Rita Rudner: Married Without Children, Bitter Jester (documentary), When Stand Up Comics Ruled the World, The 75th Annual Academy Awards (WGA nom. 2004), Rita Rudner: Live from Las Vegas. *Series*: George Schlatter's Funny People (co-host), The Real Las Vegas (TV series documentary), Women of Las Vegas (series documentary), Ask Rita (host, writer). *Guest:* More than 55 appearances.

RUDOLPH, ALAN
Director, Writer. b. Los Angeles, CA, Dec. 18, 1943. Son of late director Oscar Rudolph, TV director of '50s and '60s. Made his screen debut in his father's The Rocket Man (1954). Began in industry doing odd jobs in Hollywood studios. 1969 accepted for Directors Guild assistant director's training program. Worked with Robert Altman as asst. dir. on California Split, The Long Goodbye and Nashville and co-writer on Buffalo Bill and the Indians.
PICTURES: *Director*: Welcome to L.A. (debut, 1977; also s.p.), Remember My Name (also s.p.), Roadie (also story), Endangered Species (also co-s.p.), Return Engagement, Songwriter, Choose Me (also s.p.), Trouble in Mind (also s.p.), Made in Heaven, The Moderns (also co-s.p.), Love at Large (also s.p.), Mortal Thoughts, The Player (actor only), Equinox (also s.p.), Mrs. Parker and the Vicious Circle (also co-s.p.), Afterglow, Trixie (also s.p.), Breakfast of Champions (also s.p.), Investigating Sex, The Secret Lives of Dentists.

RUEHL, MERCEDES
Actress. b. Queens, NY, Feb. 28, 1950. Raised in Silver Spring, MD. e. College of New Rochelle, B.A. English lit. Worked for years in regional theatre, mostly in classics.
THEATRE: *B'way*: I'm Not Rappaport, Lost in Yonkers (Tony Award, 1991), The Shadow Box, The Rose Tattoo. *Off-B'way*: American Notes, The Marriage of Bette and Boo (Obie Award), Coming of Age in Soho, Other People's Money.
PICTURES: The Warriors (debut, 1979), Four Friends, Heartburn, Radio Days, 84 Charing Cross Road, The Secret of My Success, Leader of the Band, Big, Married to the Mob, Slaves of New York, Crazy People, Another You, The Fisher King (Academy Award, Golden Globe Award 1991), Lost in Yonkers, Last Action Hero, Roseanna's Grave, Out of the Cold, The Minus Man, More Dogs Than Bones, The Amati Girls, What's Cooking?, Spooky House, Zeyda and the Hitman.
TELEVISION: *Movies*: Mom's on Strike, On Hope (short),

Indictment: The McMartin Trial, North Shore Fish, Subway Stories: Tales from the Underground, Gia, The Mary Kay Letourneau Story: All-American Girl, The Lost Child, Guilt by Association, Bad Apple, Mom at Sixteen, A Girl Like Me: The Gwen Araujo Story, Loving Leah. *Mini-series*: Widows. *Series*: Late Bloomer (pilot), Everyday Life (pilot).

RUIZ-ANCHIA, JUAN
Cinematographer. b. Bilbao, Spain, 1949. e. Escuela Official de Cinematografica, 1972. Worked on such Spanish prods. as 19/19, Cornica del Alba, Odd and Even, Soldier of Metal. Moved to L.A. Granted 2 yr. fellowship at American Film Inst. from which he graduated in 1981. First U.S. prod. was Reborn, 1982.
PICTURES: The Stone Boy, That Was Then This Is Now, In 'N Out, Maria's Lovers, At Close Range, Where the River Runs Black, House of Games, Surrender, The Seventh Sign, Things Change, Lost Angels, The Last of the Finest, Dying Young, Naked Tango, Liebestraum, Glengarry Glen Ross, A Far Off Place, Mr. Jones, The Jungle Book, Two Bits, The Adventures of Pinocchio, Lorca, Mararia, The Corrupter, The Crew, New Port South, Focus, No Good Deed, Confidence, Off the Map, Darkness Falls, Spartan, Innocent Voices, September Dawn, Sleepwalking, I Come with the Rain, Bunraku, A Pure Country Gift, Blackthorn.
TELEVISION: *Movies:* Miss Lonelyhearts, Single Bars-Single Women, Noon Wine.

RUSH, BARBARA
Actress. b. Denver, CO, Jan. 4, 1927. e. U. of CA. First stage appearance at age of ten, Loberto Theatre, Santa Barbara, CA, in fantasy, Golden Ball; won acting award in college for characterization of Birdie (The Little Foxes); scholarship, Pasadena Playhouse Theatre Arts Coll.
THEATRE: A Woman of Independent Means, 40 Carats, Same Time Next Year, Steel Magnolias, The Golden Age.
PICTURES: Molly (debut, 1950), The First Legion, Quebec, When Worlds Collide, Flaming Feather, Prince of Pirates, It Came From Outer Space (Golden Globe Award 1954), Taza—Son of Cochise, The Magnificent Obsession, The Black Shield of Falworth, Captain Lightfoot, Kiss of Fire, World in My Corner, Bigger Than Life, Flight to Hong Kong, Oh Men! Oh Women!, No Down Payment, The Young Lions, Harry Black and the Tiger, The Young Philadelphians, The Bramble Bush, Strangers When We Meet, Come Blow Your Horn, Robin and the 7 Hoods, Hombre, The Man, Superdad, Can't Stop the Music, Summer Lovers.
TELEVISION: *Movies*: Suddenly Single, Cutter, Eyes of Charles Sand, Moon of the Wolf, Crime Club, The Last Day, Death on the Freeway, The Seekers, Flamingo Road (pilot), The Night the Bridge Fell Down, Web of Deceit, Widow's Kiss. *Series*: Saints and Sinners, Peyton Place, The New Dick Van Dyke Show, Flamingo Road, Hearts Are Wild, All My Children, 7th Heaven (recurring guest role). *Guest:* More than 97 appearances.

RUSH, GEOFFREY
Actor. b. Toowomba, Queensland, Australia, July 6, 1951. Won 1996 Acad. Award for Best Actor in Leading Role for Shine.
THEATRE: Exit the King (Tony Award 2009).
PICTURES: Hoodwink, Starstruck, Twelfth Night, Dad and Dave: On Our Selection, Call Me Sal, Shine (Academy Award, Golden Globe Award 1996), Children of the Revolution, Les Miserables, A Little Bit of Soul, Oscar and Lucinda, Shakespeare in Love (Academy Award nom.; Golden Globe nom. 1999), Elizabeth, Mystery Men, The House on Haunted Hill, Quills (Academy Award nom.; Golden Globe nom. 2001), The Magic Pudding (voice), The Tailor of Panama, Lantana, Frida, The Banger Sisters, The Assumption of the Virgin, Swimming Upstream, Finding Nemo (voice), Ned Kelly, Intolerable Cruelty, The Assumption, Pirates of the Caribbean: The Curse of the Black Pearl, Harvie Krumpet (short, narrator-voice), Candy, Munich, Pirates of the Caribbean: Dead Man's Chest, Pirates of the Caribbean: At World's End, Elizabeth: The Golden Age, $9.99, Bran Nue Dae, The Warrior's Way, Legend of the Guardians: The Owls of Ga'Hoole (voice), The King's Speech, The Eye of the Storm, Pirates of the Caribbean: On Stranger Tides.
TELEVISION: *Mini-series:* Frontier, The Life and Death of Peter Sellers (Emmy Award, Golden Globe Award 2005). *Series:* Menotti, Mercury, Lowdown (voice). *Guest:* More than 67 appearances.

RUSH, HERMAN
Executive. b. Philadelphia, PA, June 20, 1929. e. Temple U., Sales mgr., Official Films Inc., 1952-57. Headed Flamingo Telefilms, Inc. 1957-60; 1960-71, pres., TV div. of Creative Mgt. Assoc.; pres., Herman Rush Assoc. Inc., 1971-77; 1977-78 chmn. bd., Rush-Flaherty Agency, Inc.; 1970 headed Marble Arch TV; 1980 named pres., Columbia TV; 1984, pres. of newly formed Columbia Pictures TV Group; 1986, chmn. of newly formed Coca-Cola Telecommunications, Inc.; 1988, chmn., Rush Entertainment Group; 1989, became creative consultant for CBN Producers Group; 1992, Katz/Rush Ent., partner; co-founder, dir. of Transactional Media, Informercial and Transactional Program Production Co.; 1993-94 exec. prod., Willard Scott's New Original Amateur Hour; 1994-95, exec. prod. Susan Powter Show; exec. prod. of The Montel Williams Show, 2003; formed Media Consulting Associates in 2004 with industry veterans Ave Butensky, Robert Friedman, Jerry Katzman and Joe Indelli. The firm enables new projects from content to marketing.

RUSH, RICHARD
Director, Producer, Writer. b. New York, NY, 1930.
PICTURES: *Director*: Too Soon To Love (also prod., s.p.), Of Love and Desire (also prod., s.p.), A Man Called Dagger, Fickle Finger of Fate, Thunder Alley, Hell's Angels on Wheels, Psych-Out (also s.p.), Savage Seven, Getting Straight (also prod.), Freebie and the Bean (also prod.), The Stunt Man (also prod., s.p.; 2 Academy Award noms.; DGA nom.; WGA nom.; Golden Globe nom. for best dir., s.p.), Air America (co-s.p.), Color of Night, Murder in the First (project consultant).

RUSSELL, CHUCK
Director. Asst. Dir., and Line Prod. b. Highland Park, IL, August 6, 1952. Many low-budget films for Roger Corman and Sunn Classics, including Death Race 2000.
PICTURES: Dreamscape (co-s.p., line prod.), Back to School (prod.), Nightmare on Elm Street III (dir., co-s.p.), The Blob (dir., co-s.p.), The Mask, Eraser, Bless the Child, The Scorpion King, Collateral (exec. prod.), Arabian Nights (dir., s.p.).
TELEVISION: Black Cat Run (exec. prod.).

RUSSELL, DAVID O.
Director, Writer. b. New York, NY, August 20, 1958.
PICTURES: Spanking the Monkey (also exec. prod.), Flirting with Disaster, Three Kings (WGA nom. 2000), The Slaughter Rule (prod. only), Adaptation (actor only), Anchorman: The Legend of Ron Burgundy (exec. prod.), Soldiers Pay (doc. short), I Heart Huckabees (also prod.), Nailed, The Fighter, Pride and Prejudice and Zombies (dir.).
TELEVISION: *Series:* Outer Space Astronauts (exec. prod.).

RUSSELL, KEN
Director, Producer, Writer. b. Southampton, England, July 3, 1927. e. Walthamstow Art Sch. Early career as dancer, actor, stills photographer, TV documentarian. Ent. TV ind. 1959. Made 33 documentaries for BBC-TV. Also made numerous pop videos.
PICTURES: French Dressing, Billion Dollar Brain, Women in Love (Academy Award nom.; Golden Globe nom. 1971), The Music Lovers (also prod.), The Devils (also prod., s.p.), The Boy Friend (also prod., s.p., WGA nom. 1972), Savage Messiah (also prod.), Mahler (also s.p.), Tommy (also prod., s.p.), Lisztomania (also s.p.), Valentino, Altered States, Crimes of Passion, Gothic, Aria (sequence), Salome's Last Dance (also s.p., actor), The Lair of the White Worm (also prod., s.p.), The Rainbow (also prod., co-s.p.), The Russia House (actor only), Whore (also s.p.), Mindbender, Lion's Mouth (short, dir. and s.p.), The Fall of the Louse of Usher (also actor), Color Me Kubrick (actor only), Trapped Ashes (segment dir., actor), Invasion of the Not Quite Dead (exec. prod.), Master Class (s.p.).
TELEVISION: *Movies: Director:* Old Battersea House, Preservation Man, Pop Goes the Easel, Mr. Chesher's Traction Engines, Lotte Lenya Sings Kurt Weill, Elgar (also writer), Lonely Shore, The Dotty World of James Lloyd, Bartok, The Debussy Film (also writer), Isadora Duncan, the Biggest Dancer in the World (also writer & prod.), Dante's Inferno (also writer & prod.), Song of Summer (also writer & prod.), Dance of the Seven Veils, Clouds of Glory: The Rime of the Ancient Mariner (also writer), Clouds of Glory: William and Dorothy (also writer), Méphistophélès, A British Picture (also writer), Women and Men: Stories of Seduction, The Strange Affliction of Anton Bruckner (also writer), Prisoner of Honor, The Secret Life of Arnold Bax (also writer & actor), The Mystery of Dr Martinu, Lady Chatterley (also writer & actor), Alice in Russialand, Dogboys (also prod.), Elgar: Fantasy of a Composer on a Bicycle (TV documentary), Marple: The Moving Finger (actor). *Series: Director:* Monitor.

RUSSELL, KERI
Actress. b. Fountain Valley, CA, March 23, 1976.
PICTURES: Honey I Blew Up the Kid, Eight Days a Week, Dead Man's Curve, Mad About Mambo, We Were Soldiers, The Upside of Anger, Butterfly: A Grimm Love Story, Waitress, August Rush, Mission: Impossible III, The Girl in the Park, Bedtime Stories, Leaves of Grass, Extraordinary Measures.
TELEVISION: *Movies:* Clerks, The Babysitter's Seduction, The Lottery, When Innocence Is Lost, Cinderelmo, The Magic of Ordinary Days. *Mini-series:* Into the West. *Series:* The Mickey Mouse Club, Emerald Cove, Daddy's Girls, Malibu Shores, Felicity, (Golden Globe Award 1999).

RUSSELL, KURT
Actor. b. Springfield, MA, March 17, 1951. Son of late former baseball player-turned-actor Bing Russell (deputy sheriff on Bonanza). At 12 got lead in TV series The Travels of Jamie McPheeters (1963-64). Starred as child in many Disney shows and films. Professional baseball player 1971-73. Host, Kurt Russell Celebrity Shoot Out, 4-day hunting tournament.
PICTURES: It Happened at the World's Fair (debut, 1963), Follow Me Boys, The One and Only Genuine Original Family Band, The Horse in the Grey Flannel Suit, The Computer Wore Tennis Shoes, The Barefoot Executive, Fools' Parade, Now You See Him Now You Don't, Charley and the Angel, Superdad, The Strongest Man in the World, Used Cars, Escape from New York, The Fox and The Hound (voice), The Thing, Silkwood (Golden

Globe nom. 1984), Swing Shift, The Mean Season, The Best of Times, Big Trouble in Little China, Overboard, Tequila Sunrise, Winter People, Tango and Cash, Backdraft, Unlawful Entry, Captain Ron, Tombstone, StarGate, Executive Decision, Escape From L.A., Breakdown, Soldier, 3000 Miles to Graceland, Vanilla Sky, Interstate 60, Dark Blue, Miracle, Sky High, Dreamer: Inspired by a True Story, Poseidon, Grindhouse, Death Proof, Waco, Undying.
TELEVISION: *Movies*: Search for the Gods, The Deadly Tower, The Quest (pilot), Christmas Miracle in Caulfield U.S.A., Elvis (Emmy nom. 1979), Amber Waves, 14 Hours (exec. prod. only). *Series*: The Travels of Jamie McPheeters, The New Land, The Quest. *Guest*: More than 120 appearances.

RUSSELL, THERESA
Actress. r.n. Theresa Paup. b. San Diego, CA, Mar. 20, 1957. e. Burbank H.S. Began modeling career at 12. Studied at Actors' Studio in Hollywood.
PICTURES: The Last Tycoon (debut, 1976), Straight Time, Bad Timing/A Sensual Obsession, Eureka, The Razor's Edge, Insignificance, Black Widow, Aria, Track 29, Physical Evidence, Impulse, Whore, Kafka, Cold Heaven, The Grotesque, Trade Off,The Spy Within, EroticTales II, Wild Things, Running Woman, Luckytown Blues, The Believer, Passionada, Now and Forever, The House Next Door, Project V.I.P.E.R., Searching for Debra Winger, Passionada, Now and Forever, Destiny, Water Under the Bridge, The Box, Live to Ride, Chinaman's Chance, Spider-Man 3, On the Doll, Dark World, Street, Baby O, 16 to Life, Rid of Me, Legends of Nethiah.
TELEVISION: *Movies*: A Woman's Guide to Adultery, Thicker Than Water, Trade Off, Once You Meet A Stranger, Earth vs. The Spider, Love Comes Softly, Blind Injustice, Empire Falls. *Mini-series:* Blind Ambition. *Series:* Glory Days, Good vs Evil, Nash Bridges.

RUSSO, JAMES
Actor. b. New York, NY, Apr. 23, 1953. e. NYU, where he wrote and starred in prize-winning short film Candy Store.
THEATRE: *NY:* Welcome to Andromeda, Deathwatch, Marat / Sade, Extremities (Theatre World Award).
PICTURES: A Strange Is Watching (debut, 1982), Fast Times at Ridgemont High, Vortex, Exposed, Once Upon a Time in America, Beverly Hills Cop, The Cotton Club, Extremities, China Girl, The Blue Iguana, Freeway, We're No Angels, State of Grace, A Kiss Before Dying, My Own Private Idaho, Cold Heaven, Dangerous Game, Bad Girls, Donnie Brasco, The Postman, Felons, Detour, Sonic Impact, Jimmy Zip, The Ninth Gate, Diamonds, The Unscarred, Sonic Impact, Paper Bullets, Deep Core, Pendulum, Shattered Lies, Microwave Park, The House Next Door, Double Deception, Stealing Sinatra, A Good Night to Die, Paris, The Box (also s.p.), Open Range, Target, Taking Charge, Straight Out of Compton 2, Dark World, Blue Lake Massacre, All In, Taken by Force, The Pink Conspiracy, Dark World, Machine, Little Red Devil, Kings of the Evening, Deadwater, Stiletto, Taken by Force, Love Sick Diaries, Never Surrender, Break, Public Enemies, One in the Gun, Dreams and Shadows, Dark Woods, Boy Wonder, An American Hero, Street Poet, The One Warrior, Resurrected, King of Vampires, The Gift Horse, Samuel Bleak.
TELEVISION: *Movies:* In the Shadow of a Killer, Intimate Stranger, Desperate Rescue: The Cathy Mahone Story, Double Deception, The Secretary, My Husband's Secret Life, Hidden War, Broken Trail. *Mini-series:* The Capture of the Green River Killer. *Series:* Dark Blue.

RUSSO, RENE
Actress. b. California, Feb. 17, 1955. Raised in Burbank. Worked as top fashion model for Eileen Ford Agency prior to acting.
PICTURES: Major League (debut, 1989), Mr. Destiny, One Good Cop, Freejack, Lethal Weapon 3, In the Line of Fire, Outbreak, Get Shorty, Tin Cup, Ransom, Buddy, Lethal Weapon 4, The Thomas Crown Affair, The Adventures of Rocky and Bullwinkle, Big Trouble, Showtime, Two for the Money, Yours-Mine-And-Ours, Frank and Cindy, Thor.
TELEVISION: *Series:* Sable.

RYAN, ARTHUR N.
Executive. Joined Paramount in N.Y. in 1967 as asst. treas; later made dir. of admin. and business affairs, exec. asst. to Robert Evans and asst. scty. 1970 appt. v.p.-prod. adm. 1975 named sr. v.p. handling all prod. operations for Paramount's m.p. and TV divisions; 1976, asst. to the chmn. & CEO; chmn. & pres. Magicam, Inc.; chmn. Fortune General Corp.; chmn. Paramount Communications; co-chmn. of scholarship comm. of AMPAS; trustee of Univ. Film Study Center in Boston; joined Technicolor in 1976 as pres., COO & dir.; vice chmn., 1983-85; chmn. & CEO, 1985; chmn. Technicolor Audio-Visual Systems International, Inc.; dir. Technicolor S.P.A.; dir. Technicolor, Film Intl.; and chmn. of exec. committee, Technicolor Graphics Services, Inc.; dir., Technicolor, Inc.; chmn., Technicolor Fotografica, S.A.; chmn. Technicolor Film Intl. Service Company, Inc.; dir. & deputy chmn. Technicolor Ltd.; chmn. & dir., The Vidtronics Company, Inc.; chmn. & CEO, Compact Video, Inc., 1984; dir, Four Star Int'l., 1983; dir., MacAndrews & Forbes, Inc. 1985; Permanent charities committee of the Ent. Industry; Hollywood Canteen Foundations. Vice-chmn. & dir., Calif. Inst. of Arts. Trustee: Motion Picture & Television Fund.

RYAN, MEG
Actress. r.n. Margaret Mary Emily Anne Hyra. b. Bethel, CT, Nov. 19, 1961. e. NYU. While studying journalism at NYU, supported herself by making commercials. Auditioned for and won first prof. role as Candice Bergen's daughter in film Rich and Famous.
PICTURES: Rich and Famous (debut, 1981), Amityville 3-D, Top Gun, Armed and Dangerous, Innerspace, Promised Land, D.O.A., The Presidio, When Harry Met Sally (Golden Globe nom. 1990), Joe Versus the Volcano, The Doors, Prelude to a Kiss, Sleepless in Seattle (Golden Globe nom. 1994), Flesh & Bone, When a Man Loves a Woman, I.Q., French Kiss, Restoration, Courage Under Fire, Addicted to Love, Anastasia (voice), Hurlyburly, City of Angels, You've Got Mail (Golden Globe nom. 1999), Hanging Up, Proof of Life, Kate and Leopold, Desert Saints (prod.), Searching for Debra Winger (documentary), In the Cut, Against the Ropes, In the Land of Women, Homeland Security, The Women, The Deal, My Mom's New Boyfriend, Serious Moonlight.
TELEVISION: *Movies*: Amy and the Angel, Northern Lights (exec. prod. only). *Series*: One of the Boys, As the World Turns (1982-84), Wild Side, Captain Planet and the Planeteers (voice). *Guest:* More than 70 appearances.

RYAN, MITCHELL
Actor. b. Louisville, KY, Jan. 11, 1928. Entered acting following service in Navy during Korean War. Was New York stage actor working off-B'way for Ted Mann and Joseph Papp; on B'way in Wait Until Dark. Member of Arena Stage group in Washington.
PICTURES: Monte Walsh, Glory Boy, The Hunting Party, Chandler, The Honkers, A Reflection of Fear, HIgh Plains Drifter, The Friends of Eddie Coyle, Magnum Force, Electra Glide in Blue, Two Minute Warning, Lethal Weapon, Winter People, Aces: Iron Eagle III, The Opposite Sex and How to Live With Them, Hot Shots Part Deux, Blue Sky, Speechless, Judge Dredd, Hall6ween, Ed, The Devil's Own, Liar Liar, Grosse Pointe Blank, Love For Rent.
TELEVISION: *More than 50 TV credits, including: Movies*: Angel City, The Five of Me, Death of a Centerfold—The Dorothy Stratten Story, Uncommon Valor, Medea, Kenny Rogers as the Gambler—The Adventure Continues, Robert Kennedy & His Times, Fatal Vision, Favorite Son, The Ryan White Story, Margaret Bourke-White, Judgment, In A Child's Name, Majority Rule, Hart to Hart: Home is Where the Hart Is, Gramps, Raven Hawk, Life of the Party: The Pamela Harriman Story, Aftershock: Earthquake in New York. *Mini-series:* Robert Kennedy & His Times, North and South, Favorite Son. *Series*: Dark Shadows, Chase, Executive Suite, Having Babies, The Chisolms, High Performance, All My Children (1985-1987), Santa Barbara (1989), 2000 Malibu Road, General Hospital (1993-1994), Dharma & Greg. *Guest:* More than 108 appearances.

RYDELL, MARK
Director, Producer, Actor. b. New York, NY March 23, 1934. e. Juilliard Sch. of Music. Studied acting with Sanford Meisner of NY Neighborhood Playhouse. Became member of Actors Studio. Was leading actor for six years on daytime CBS serial, As The World Turns. Made Broadway debut in Seagulls over Sorrento and film debut in Crime in the Streets. Went to Hollywood as TV director (Ben Casey, I Spy, Gunsmoke, etc.). Partner with Sydney Pollack in Sanford Prods., film, TV prod. co. Formed own production co., Concourse Productions.
PICTURES: *Director*: The Fox (debut, Golden Globe nom. 1968), The Reivers, The Cowboys (also prod.), Cinderella Liberty (also prod.), Harry and Walter Go To New York, The Rose, On Golden Pond (Academy Award nom.; DGA nom.; Golden Globe nom. 1982), The River, Man in the Moon (prod. only), For the Boys (also exec. prod.), Intersection (also co-prod.), Crime of the Century, Jump Shot (also prod.), Even Money (also prod.). *Actor:* Crime in the Streets, The Long Goodbye, Punchline, Havana, Hollywood Ending, An Unfinished Life (exec. prod. only)
TELEVISION: *Movies:* Crime of the Century (dir. only, Emmy nom. 1997), James Dean (dir., actor, exec. prod., 2 Emmy noms. 2002, DGA nom.). *Series:* The Edge of Night (actor), As the World Turns (actor), Ben Casey (dir. several episodes), Gunsmoke (dir. 1964-1966), I Spy (dir.), The Wild Wild West (dir.), Family (dir.).

RYDER, WINONA
Actress. r.n. Winona Horowitz. b. Winona, MN, Oct. 29, 1971. Grew up in San Francisco. At 7, moved with family to Northern CA commune. At 13 discovered by talent scout during a performance at San Francisco's American Conservatory theatre, where she was studying, and given screen test.
PICTURES: Lucas (debut, 1986), Square Dance, Beetlejuice, 1969, Heathers, Great Balls of Fire, Welcome Home Roxy Carmichael, Edward Scissorhands, Mermaids (Golden globe nom. 1991), Night on Earth, Bram Stoker's Dracula, The Age of Innocence (Academy Award nom.; Golden Globe Award 1994), Reality Bites, The House of the Spirits, Little Women (Academy Award nom. 1995), How to Make an American Quilt, Boys, Looking for Richard, The Crucible, Alien: Resurrection, Celebrity, Lost Souls, Girl Interrupted (also exec. prod.), Autumn in New York, Mr. Deeds, S1m0ne, The Day My God Died (narr./voice,

prod.), The Heart is Deceitful Above All Things, The Darwin Awards, A Scanner Darkly, Alpha Numeric, The Ten, Sex and Death 101, The Last Word, Water Pills, The Informers, The Private Lives of Pippa Lee, Stay Cool, Star Trek, Black Swan, Cheaters.
TELEVISION: *Movie:* When Love Is Not Enough: The Lois Wilson Story. *Guest:* More than 60 appearances.

RYDSTROM, GARY
Sound. b. 1959. Received two career achievement awards in 2004, one from the Motion Picture Sound Editors' at the org.'s Golden Reel Awards and the other from the Cinema Audio Society. Rydstrom is a seven-time Academy Award winner. 2004 received Cinema Audio Society Career Acheivement Award. Received Motion Pictures Sound Editors Lifetime Achievement Award 2005, he has 5 Golden Reel Awards and 7 noms.
PICTURES: Indiana Jones and the Temple of Doom, Cocoon, Luxo Jr., Red's Dream, Spaceballs, Tin Toy, Cocoon: The Return, Willow, Colors, Knickknack, Ghostbusters II, Always, Romero, The Hot Spot, Rush, Luxo Jr. in 'Surprise' and 'Light & Heavy,' Backdraft (2 Academy Award noms. 1992), Terminator 2: Judgment Day (2 Academy Awards, Best Effects/Sound Effects Editing, & Best Sound, 1992), F/X2, A River Runs Through It, Single White Female, Mrs. Doubtfire, Meteor Man, Jurassic Park, Quiz Show, Baby's Day Out, Casper, Strange Days, Toy Story, Jumanji, James and the Giant Peach, Mission: Impossible, Sleepers, Titanic (Academy Award, Best Sound, CAS Award 1998), Hercules, The Lost World: Jurassic Park (2 Academy Awards, Best Effects & Best Sound, CAS nom. 1994), A Bug's Life, The Horse Whisperer, Saving Private Ryan (2 Academy Awards, Best Effects & Best Sound, CAS Award 1999), Reach the Rock, Rules of Engagement, The Haunting, Star Wars: Episode I-The Phantom Menace (Academy Award nom.; CAS nom. 2000), Toy Story 2, It's Tough to be a Bug, The Yards, X-Men, The Legend of Bagger Vance, 102 Dalmatians, The Mexican, Atlantis: The Lost Empire, Artificial Intelligence, Monsters Inc. (Academy Award nom. 2002), Star Wars Episode II: Attack of the Clones, Punch Drunk Love, Minority Report (Academy Award nom. 2003), Amandla: A Revolution in Four Part Harmony, Finding Nemo (voice, Academy Award nom. 2004), Hulk, Mickey's PhilharMagic, Peter Pan, Lifted (sound designer, s.p., dir., Academy Award nom. 2007 for best animated short), Up.
TELEVISION: *Movie:* Ewoks: The Battle for Endor (sound tech).

SADLER, WILLIAM
Actor. b. Buffalo, NY, April 13, 1950. e. SUNY, Cornell U. Made stage debut in title role in Hamlet for Colorado Shakespeare Fest. Also acted with La Jolla Playhouse, Yale Rep.
THEATRE: *NY:* Ivanov (Off-B'way debut, 1975), Limbo Tales (Obie Award), Chinese Viewing Pavilion, Lennon, Necessary Ends, Hannah, Biloxi Blues (B'way debut, 1985; Clarence Derwent & Dramalogue Awards). *Regional:* Journey's End, A Mad World My Masters, Romeo and Juliet, Night Must Fall, etc.
PICTURES: Hanky Panky, Off Beat, Project X, K-9, Hard to Kill, Die Hard 2, The Hot Spot, Bill & Ted's Bogus Journey, Rush, Trespass, Freaked, The Shawshank Redemption, Tales From the Crypt Presents Demon Knight, Solo, Skippy, Rocket Man, Ambushed, Disturbing Behavior, Reach the Rock, The Green Mile, Stealth Fighter, Another Life, The Battle of Shaker Heights, Kinsey, Unspoken, Purple Heart, Confess, Jimmy and Judy, Nothing Sacred, The Mist, August Rush, Eagle Eye, The Hills Run Red, Red & Blue Marbles, Shadowheart, Silent But Deadly, Last Day of Summer, Switchback, Restitution, Melvin Smarty, Riddle.
TELEVISION: *Movies:* The Great Walendas, Charlie and the Great Balloon Race, Face of Fear, The Last to Go, Bermuda Grace, Witness Protection, Shawshank: The Redeeming Feature, The Path to 9/11, Jesse Stone: Sea Change, Jesse Stone: Thin Ice, Jesse Stone: No Remorse. *Mini-series:* The Pacific. *Series:* Private Eye, Roswell, Wonderfalls, Traveler. *Guest:* More than 72 appearances.

SADUSKY, VINCENT
Executive. e. B.S. degree in Accounting, graduating with honors from Pennsylvania State University, 1987; M.B.A., New York Institute of Technology, 1995. Sadusky has 20 years of business experience, including seven years with the assurance and consulting firm Ernst & Young. Entered television industry and became CFO and treasurer of Telemundo Holdings, Inc. where he was instrumental in selling Telemundo to General Electric Corp's NBC Broadcasting unit for $2.7 billion. Since 2004, Sadusky had been LIN TV's v.p., CFO and treasurer. In July 2006, Sadusky was named LIN TV pres. and CEO, replacing retiring CEO Gary Chapman. LIN TV is one of the top national TV station groups, owning and operating 30 TV stations in 18 mid-size markets. He has been a member of the following: Financial Executives Institute, the American Institute of Certified Public Accountants, the Florida Institute of Certified Public Accountants and the Broadcast Cable Financial Management Association.

SAFER, MORLEY
News Correspondent. b. Toronto, Ont., Nov. 8, 1931. e. U. of Western Ontario. Started as corresp. and prod. with Canadian Broadcasting Corp. Joined CBS News London Bureau 1964, chief of Saigon Bureau, 1965. Chief of CBS London bureau 1967-70. Joined 60 Minutes as co-editor in December 1970.
Series/Specials/Documentaries: W5, The Twentieth Century, The Cowboy, the Craftsman and the Ballerina, The Canadian Conspiracy, Sing! Sesame Street Remembers Joe Raposo and His Music, 60 Minutes: The Entertainers, We Were There: CBS News at 50, The American President, Breaking the News, 60 Minutes (3 WGA noms.), That's the Way It Is: Celebrating Cronkite at 90, An Unlikely Weapon, A Man Without a Country.

SAGAL, KATEY
Actress. b. Los Angeles, CA, Jan. 19, 1954.
PICTURES: Maid to Order, The Good Mother, Dropping Out, Recess: Schools Out (voice), Loose Cannons (soundtrack performer), Recess: School's Out (voice), I'm Reed Fish, Futurama: Bender's Big Score (voice), Futurama: The Beast with a Billion Backs (voice), Futurama: Bender's Game (voice), Futurama: Into the Wild Green Yonder (voice), Jack and the Beanstalk.
TELEVISION: *Movies:* The Failing of Raymond, Mother Goose Rock 'n' Rhyme, She Says She's Innocent, Trail of Tears, Mr. Headmistress, Chance of a Lifetime, God's New Plan, Smart House, When Angels Come to Town, Campus Confidential, Three Wise Guys. *Series:* Mary, Married...with Children (4 Golden Globe noms., 1991 through 1994), Recess (voice), Futurama (voice), Tucker, Imagine That, 8 Simple Rules, Boston Legal, Eli Stone, Lost, Chadam, Sons of Anarchy. *Guest:* More than 90 appearances.

SAGANSKY, JEFF
Executive. b. Wellesley, MA, Jan. 26, 1952. e. Harvard, B.A. degree; M.B.A. from Harvard Business School. Joined CBS 1976 in broadcast finance; 1977, NBC, assoc. in pgm. development.; 1977, mgr. film pgms.; 1978, dir. dramatic dev.; 1978, v.p., dev. David Gerber Co.; 1981, returned to NBC as series dev. v.p.; 1983, sr. v.p. series programming; 1985, joined Tri-Star Pictures as pres. of production; 1989 promoted to president of Tri-Star, later that year joined CBS as entertainment division president. Resigned, 1994. From Sept. 1994-Oct. 1996, with Sony Corp. of America, supervising Sony Theaters, the Sony Theater/Cineplex Odeon Theaters merger and the launch of the Sony Playstation. Then Joined Sony Pictures Entertainment as co-president with responsibilities for worldwide TV ops. and strategic planning. During this time spearheaded Sony's acquisition of Telemundo. From 1998-2002, Sagansky served as pres. & CEO of Paxson Communications. From Dec. 2002-Aug. 2003, vice chairman, Paxson Communications. In April 2005, Sagansky and Kerry McCluggage acquired the independent international distribution company Ardustry Home Entertainment, since renamed Allumination Filmworks. The award-winning company boasts a portfolio of nearly 200 quality theatrical films, in all major categories, as well as over 4,000 hours of TV programming, along with music specials and kids/family feature titles for television, cable and home video/DVD distribution markets worldwide. Sagansky has served on the boards of the International Council for the National Academy of Television Arts and Sciences and the American Jewish Committee. Currently Director of Scripps Networks Interactive, Inc.

SÄGEBRECHT, MARIANNE
Actress. b. Starnberg, Germany, Aug. 27, 1945. In 1977 conceived revue Opera Curiosa.
PICTURES: Die Schaukel (debut, 1983), Sugarbaby, Crazy Boys, Bagdad Cafe, Moon Over Parador, The War of the Roses, Rosalie Goes Shopping, Martha and I, The Milky Life, Dust Devil, Mr. Bluesman, Il Piccolo lord, Erotique, Mona Must Die, All Men Are Mortal, Lorenz Im Land Der Lugner, The Ogre, Soleil, Johnny, Left Luggage, Spanish Fly, Astérix et Obélix contre César, Großglocknerliebe.
TELEVISION: *Movies*: Herr Kischott, Eine Mutter Kampft un Ihren Sohn, My Lord, Und Plotzlich War Alles Anders, Frau Nach Mab Eine, Private Lies, Without Family, Marga Engel schlägt zurück, Marga Engel kocht vor Wut, many more. *Series:* Anderland, Liebesgeschichten, Lilalu im Schepperland, Sesamstraße. Many more German productions.

SAGET, BOB
Actor, Director, Writer. b. Philadelphia, PA, May 17, 1956. Started as stand-up comedian.
PICTURES: Through Adam's Eyes (dir. only), Spaced Out (voice), Full Moon High, Moving (also dir.), Devics, Critical Condition, For Goodness Sake, Dirty Work (dir. only), Meet Wally Sparks, Half Baked, Dumb and Dumberer: When Harry Met Lloyd, Madagascar (voice), Farce of the Penguins (narr., dir., writer, prod.).
TELEVISION: *Movies*: Father and Scout (also co-exec. prod.), Jitters (dir.), For Hope (dir. and exec.prod.), A Comedy Salute to Andy Kaufman, Becoming Dick (also dir.), Becoming Dick (dir.), Casper's Scare School (voice). *Series*: Full House, America's Funniest Home Videos (host), Raising Dad, How I Met Your Mother, Surviving Suburbia. *Guest:* More than 111 appearances.

SAINT, EVA MARIE
Actress. b. Newark, NJ, July 4, 1924. e. Bowling Green State U.,

Ohio, Actors Studio. Radio, TV actress; on Broadway in Trip to Bountiful before film debut.
THEATRE: Trip to Bountiful, The Rainmaker, Desire Under the Elms, The Lincoln Mask, Summer and Smoke, Candida, Winesburg Ohio, First Monday in October, Duet for One, The Country Girl, Death of a Salesman, Love Letters, The Fatal Weakness, On The Divide.
PICTURES: On the Waterfront (debut, 1954; Academy Award, best supporting actress 1955), That Certain Feeling, Raintree County, Hatful of Rain (Golden Globe nom. 1958), North by Northwest, Exodus, All Fall Down, 36 Hours, The Sandpiper, The Russians Are Coming! The Russians Are Coming!, Grand Prix, The Stalking Moon, Loving, Cancel My Reservation, Nothing in Common, Mariette in Ecstasy, I Dreamed of Africa, Because of Winn Dixie, Don't Come Knockin', Superman Returns.
TELEVISION: *Movies*: Carol for Another Christmas, The Macahans, A Christmas to Remember, When Hell Was in Session, Fatal Weakness, Curse of King Tut's Tomb, Best Little Girl in the World, Splendor in the Grass, Malibu, Jane Doe, Love Leads the Way, Fatal Vision, The Last Days of Patton, Norman Rockwell's Breaking Ties, I'll Be Home for Christmas, Voyage of Terror: The Achille Lauro Affair, People Like Us (Emmy Award, 1990), Danielle Steel's Palomino, Kiss of a Killer, My Antonia, After Jimmy, Titanic, Jackie's Back!, Papa's Angels, Open House. *Mini-series:* How the West Was Won (Emmy nom. 1977), A Year in the Life. *Series*: Campus Hoopla, One Man's Family, Moonlighting. *Documentaries/Specials*: Producers' Showcase (Emmy nom. 1954), Repertory Theatre (Emmy nom. 1955), Our Town, First Woman President, Taxi!!! (Emmy nom. 1978), Primary Colors: The Story of Corita. *Guest:* More than 100 appearances.

SAJAK, PAT
TV Host. b. Chicago, IL, Oct. 26, 1946. e. Columbia College, Chicago. Broadcasting career began as newscaster for Chicago radio station. 1968 drafted into Army, where served 4 years as disc jockey for Armed Forces Radio in Saigon, Vietnam. Moved to Nashville, where continued radio career while also working as weatherman and host of public affairs prog. for local TV station. 1977 moved to LA to become nightly weatherman on KNBC. Took over as host of daytime edition of Wheel of Fortune and later the syndicated nighttime edition. The Pat Sajak Show.
PICTURE: Airplane II: The Sequel, Merry Christmas Space Case (prod. only)
TELEVISION: *Series:* The Sunday Show (co-host), Wheel of Fortune (host; 1981 - 3 Emmy Awards, 10 other noms.), The Pat Sajak Show (host), Pat Sajak Weekend (series documentary; host), Days of Our Lives. *Documentaries/Specials:* Rated "R": Republicans in Hollywood, The Thanksgiving Day Parade (host), The Rose Parade (host).

SALDANA, THERESA
Actress. b. Brooklyn, NY, Aug. 20, 1954. Following attack by stalker founded advocacy group Victims for Victims. *Author:* Beyond Survival, 1986.
PICTURES: Nunzio, I Wanna Hold Your Hand, The Maestro, Defiance, Raging Bull, The Evil That Men Do, Of Men and Angels, Double Revenge, Angel Town, Carlo's Wake, Paradise, Gang Warz.
TELEVISION: *Movies*: Sophia Loren: Her Own Story, Miss Lonelyhearts, Victims for Victims: The Theresa Saldana Story, Confessions of a Crime, The Highwayman, Shameful Secrets, The Commish: In the Shadow of the Gallows, She Woke Up Pregnant, The Time Shifters, Thrill Seekers, Ready to Run. *Series*: The Commish (Golden Globe nom. 1994), All My Children.

SALEM, KARIO
Actor, Writer.
PICTURES: b. 1955. *Actor:* Some Kind of Hero, Nomads, Starlight: A Musical Movie, Underground Aces, Triumph of the Spirit, 1492: Conquest of Paradise, Killing Zoe, Savage. *Writer:* The Score, The Fast and the Furious: Tokyo Drift.
TELEVISION: *Movies*: *Actor:* Through the Magic Pyramid, Heart of the City, Under the Influence, The Red Spider, Shooter, Liberace, Kojak: Ariana, Without Warning, Mr. Stitch. *Writer:* Divas, Don King: Only in America (Emmy Award, 1998, WGA nom. 1999), The Rat Pack (writer Emmy Award nom. 1999). *Mini-series*: *Actor:* Once an Eagle, Testimony of Two Men, Centennial. *Series*: *Actor:* Heart of the City. *Writer:* The Beast (also prod., exec. prod.).

SALHANY, LUCIE
Executive. e. Kent State U., Kent, OH. Began career 1967 WKBF-TV, Cleveland, OH. Prog. mgr., WLVI-TV, Boston, 1975. VP, TV and cable prog., Taft Broadcasting Co., 1979-85. Pres. & CEO, Paramount Domestic TV, 1985. Chairman, 20th TV, 1991. Chairman, Fox Broadcasting Co., 1993. Pres., UPN, 1995 until she resigned in fall 1997. She then formed her own consultancy and acquisition venture, JH Media, which is still in operation. She briefly joined the digital firm LifeFX, leaving shortly before it closed. Since then, in 2003, she's formed Echo Bridge Entertainment, LLC, a privately funded distribution company, and currently is one of four managing partners. The independent sales and distribution company acquires filmed product for distribution in theatrical, television, cable, satellite and home video markets in the United States and throughout the world.

SALKIND, ILYA
Producer. b. Mexico City, July 27, 1947. e. U. of London. Grandfather, Michael Salkind, was one of the pioneers of silent films. Father is late producer, Alexander Salkind. First film job as production runner on The Life of Cervantes for father. Owner of production company The Ilya Salkind Company.
PICTURES: The Three Musketeers, The Four Musketeers, Superman, Superman II (exec. prod.), Supergirl (exec. prod.), Superman III (exec. prod.), Santa Claus, Christopher Columbus: The Discovery, Brasil (1500), Young Alexander the Great, The Forest, The Abominable Snowman, The Director.
TELEVISION: *Series:* The Adventures of Superboy.

SALOMON, MIKAEL
Cinematographer, Director. b. Copenhagen, Feb. 24, 1945.
PICTURES: *Europe*: The Dreamers, Z.P.G., Three From Haparanda, The Five, Me and My Kid Brothers, The Owlfarm Brothers, Five on the Run, Magic in Town, 24 Hours With Ilse, Why?, Bedside Freeway, My Sister's Children Goes Astray, Around the World, Tumult, Welcome to the Club, Violets Are Blue, Tintomare, Tell It Like It Is Boys, Cop, Elvis Elvis, Hearts Are Trump, The Marksman, The Flying Devils, Peter von Scholten, The Baron, Once a Cop..., Early Spring, The Wolf at the Door, *U.S.:* Zelly and Me, Torch Song Trilogy, Stealing Heaven, The Abyss (Academy Award nom.; ASC nom. 1990), Always, Arachnophobia, Backdraft (Academy Award nom. 1992), Far and Away, A Far Off Place (dir. only), Congo (2nd unit dir.), Hard Rain (dir.), Swing (dir.), Undefeated: The Rocky Marciano Story (dir.).
TELEVISION: *Movies*: *Cinematographer:* Stumpen, På flykt undan mina landsmän, The Man Who Broke 1,000 Chains (ACE Award). *Director:* Aftershock: Earthquake in New York, A Glimpse of Hell, The Agency (pilot), Young Arthur, Benedict Arnold: A Question of Honor, 'Salem's Lot, Fallen (also exec. prod.), Flirting with Forty, Natalee Holloway (also co-exec. prod.), Who Is Clark Rockefeller? (also co-exec. prod.), The Lost Future (also co-exec. prod.). *Mini-series*: *Cinematographer:* De Tre från Haparanda. *Director:* Sole Survivor, Band of Brothers (Emmy Award 2002), The Grid, The Company (also co-exec. prod., DGA nom.; Emmy nom. 2008) The Andromeda Strain (also co-exec. prod., Emmy nom., DGA nom. 2009). *Series: Cinematographer:* Een gang strømer. *Director:* Space Rangers, The Agency, Rome, Nightmares and Dreamscapes: From the Stories of Stephen King, Over There, Runaway (co-exec. prod., also pilot), Hawthorne (pilot dir., exec. prod.).

SAMMS, EMMA
Actress. b. London, England, Aug. 28, 1960. Former fashion model. Has worked as commercial photographer for such magazines as Ritz, Metro, and Architectural Digest. Co-founder of charitable org. the Starlight Foundation.
PICTURES: Arabian Adventure (debut, 1979), The Shrimp on the Barbie, Delirious, Fatal Inheritance, Terminal Voyage, The Little Unicorn, Pets, The Adventures of Tom Thumb and Thumbelina (voice).
TELEVISION: *Movies*: More Wild Wild West, Goliath Awaits, Agatha Christie's Murder in Three Acts, The Lady and the Highwayman, A Connecticut Yankee in King Arthur's Court, Bejeweled, Dynasty: The Reunion, Shadow of a Stranger, Robin Cook's Harmful Intent, Treacherous Beauties, Humanoids from the Deep, His Bodyguard (writer/story), Pretend You Don't See Her, Ghosts of Albion: Legacy (voice), Ghosts of Albion: Embers (voice). *Mini-series:* Ellis Island, Supernova. *Series*: General Hospital, Dynasty, The Colbys, Models Inc., Doctors, Holby City. *Guest:* More than 77 appearances.

SAMUELSON, PETER
Producer. b. London, England, October 16, 1951. e. Cambridge U., M.A., English literature. Early career as interpreter, production assistant, then prod. mgr. 1975, Return of the Pink Panther. 1979-85, exec. v.p., Interscope Comm., Inc. 1982-present, Intl. Pres., Starlight Foundation. 1986-present, pres., Film Associates, Inc. 1985-90 chmn., Samuelson Group, Inc. 1990-present, partner, Samuelson Prods. of L.A. and London.
PICTURES: Speed Merchants, High Velocity, One by One, Return of the Pink Panther, Santa Fe, A Man a Woman and a Bank, Revenge of the Nerds, Turk 182, Playmaker, Tom and Viv, Wilde, This is the Sea, The Commissioner (co-prod.), Arlington Road, Guest House Paradiso, Gabriel and Me, The Gathering, Things to do Before You're 30, The Libertine (exec. prod.), Tales not Told, Need, Chromophobia, The Last Time, Alex Rider: Operation Stormbreaker, The Mermaids Singing (exec. prod.), The Last Time, Borrowing Time (doc., co- exec. prod.), Man in the Chair (exec. prod.).
TELEVISION: *Movies:* Dog's Best Friend, The Pact.

SAN GIACOMO, LAURA
Actress. b. New Jersey, Nov. 14, 1962. e. Carnegie Melon Univ. m. Matt Adler (2000-present). Appeared Off-B'way in North Shore Fish, Beirut, The Love Talker, Italian American Reconciliation, Wrong Turn at Lungfish, Three Sisters.
PICTURES: Sex Lies and Videotape (debut, 1989, Golden Globe nom. 1990), Pretty Woman, Vital Signs, Quigley Down Under,

Once Around, Under Suspicion, Where the Day Takes You, Nina Takes a Lover, Stuart Saves His Family, Suicide Kings, Eat Your Heart Out, The Apocalypse, With Friends Like These, A House on a Hill, Checking Out, Havoc.
TELEVISION: *Movies*: For Their Own Good, The Right to Remain Silent, Sister Mary Explains It All, The Jenifer Estess Story, The Electric Piper (voice). *Mini-series*: Stephen King's The Stand. *Series*: Just Shoot Me (Golden Globe nom. 1999), Stories From My Childhood (voice), Snapped (narr.), Related (pilot), Saving Grace.

SANDERS, JAY O.
Actor. b. Austin, TX, April 16, 1953. e. SUNY/Purchase. First professional theatre experience with NY Shakespeare-in-the Park prods. of Henry V and Measure for Measure. Appeared in Abel's Sister for England's Royal Court Theatre.
THEATRE: *NY*: Loose Ends, The Caine Mutiny Court-Martial, Buried Child, In Trousers, Geniuses, The Incredibly Famous Willy Powers, Heaven on Earth, Girls Girls Girls, King John, Saint Joan, Three Birds Alighting on a Field.
PICTURES: Starting Over (debut, 1979), Hanky Panky, Eddie Macon's Run, Cross Creek, Tucker: The Man and His Dream, The Prince of Pennsylvania, Glory, Just Like in the Movies, Mr. Destiny, V.I. Warshawski, Defenseless, Meeting Venus, JFK, Angels in the Outfield, Kiss of Death, Down Came a Blackbird, The Big Green, Three Wishes, Kiss the Girls, Daylight, The Matchmaker, For Richer or Poorer, Wrestling With Alligators, The Odd Couple II, Tumbleweeds, Music of the Heart, Endsville, The Confession, Dead Dog, Along Came a Spider, Rumor Has It, Second Born, Abby Singer, Hair High, The Day After Tomorrow, Shooting Livien, Half Nelson, Wedding Daze, Greetings from the Shore, The Undying, The Dissection of Thanksgiving, Cadillac Records, Revolutionary Road, I Hate Valentine's Day, Horizon, Edge of Darkness,A Novel Romance, Green Lantern.
TELEVISION: *Movies*: The Day Christ Died, Living Proof: The Hank Williams Jr. Story, A Doctor's Story, Rage of Angels: The Story Continues, The Revolt of Mother, Private Eye, Cold Sassy Tree, Revealing Evidence: Stalking the Honolulu Strangler, Hostages, State of Emergency, Nobody's Children, Down Came a Blackbird, Rio Shannon, Silver Strand, The Prosecutors, Earthly Possessions, The Jack Bull, A.T.F., Boss of Bosses, Picnic, The Familiar Stranger, The Last Brickmaker in America, D.C. Sniper: 23 Days of Fear, The Valley of Light. *Mini-series:* The Scarlet Letter, Salem Witch Trials, Widows. *Series*: After MASH, Crime Story, Lonesome Dove. *Documentaries: As Narr:* Extreme Oil, Aging Out, Nature, Wide Angle, Hunting the Edge of Space: The Mystery of the Milky Way, Hunting the Edge of Space: The Ever-Expanding Universe, Nova. *Guest:* More than 57 appearances.

SANDERS, TERRY BARRETT
Producer, Director, Writer. b. New York, NY, Dec. 20, 1931. e. UCLA, 1951; Co-prod., photographed, A Time Out of War, 1954. Academy Award best two-reel subject, and won first prize Venice Film Festival, etc.; co-wrote The Day Lincoln Was Shot, CBS-TV; s.p. The Naked and the Dead; prod. Crime and Punishment—USA., prod., co-dir. War Hunt; prod. and dir. Portrait of Zubin Mehta for U.S.I.A. Assoc. dean, Film Sch., California Inst. of the Arts. *Prod.-Dir.:* Four Stones for Kanemitsu (Academy Award nom. 1974). *Prod.-Dir.-Writer:* Rose Kennedy: A Life to Remember (Academy Award nom. 1991), Never Give Up: The 20th Century Odyssey of Herbert Zipper (Academy Award nom. 1996). Professor, UCLA. Pres., American Film Foundation.
PICTURES: A Time Out of War (Academy Award 1955), Four Stones for Kanemitsu (Academy Award nom. 1074), Maya Lin: A Strong Clear Vision (prod., Academy Award 1995), Never Give Up: The 20th Century Odyssey of Herbert Zipper (prod., dir., writer, Academy Award nom.1996), Return with Honor (doc. prod. dir, writer), Bird by Bird with Annie (doc. cinematographer), Wrestling with Angels: Playwright Tony Kushner (doc. exec. prod.), Fighting for Life (doc. writer, prod, dir.), Slow Fires: On the Preservation of the Human Record (DGA nom. 1988).
TELEVISION: *Producer/Director*: Hollywood and the Stars, The Legend of Marilyn Monroe, National Geographic Society specials, The Kids from Fame, Film Bios Kennedy Center Honors, Slow Fires, Lillian Gish: The Actor's Life for Me (Emmy Award).

SANDLER, ADAM
Actor, Producer, Writer, Comedian. b. Brooklyn, NY, Sept. 9, 1966. e. NYU. Principal of Happy Madison Productions.
PICTURES: Going Overboard, Shakes the Clown, Coneheads, Mixed Nuts, Airheads, Billy Madison (also s.p.), Happy Gilmore (also s.p.), Bulletproof, The Wedding Singer (also comp. 2 songs), Dirty Work, The Waterboy (also s.p., exec. prod.), Big Daddy (also s.p., exec. prod.), Little Nicky (also s.p.), Joe Dirt (exec. prod.), The Animal (exec. prod.), Master of Disguise (exec. prod.), Punch-Drunk Love (Golden Globe nom. 2003), Mr. Deeds, 8 Crazy Nights (voice & exec.prod. and s.p.), The Hot Chick, Anger Management, Dickie Roberts: Former Child Star, (exec. prod.), 50 First Dates, Spanglish, Deuce Bigalow: European Gigolo (exec. prod.), Grandma's Boy (exec. prod.), The Longest Yard (also prod., 2005), The Benchwarmer (exec. prod., writer, prod.), Click (also prod., writer), Strange Wilderness (exec. prod.), Empty City, Reign Over Me, I Now Pronounce You Chuck and Larry (also prod.), You Don't Mess with the Zohan (also prod., writer), Bedtime Stories (also prod.), The House Bunny (prod.), Paul Blart: Mall Cop (prod.), The Shortcut (exec. prod.), Funny People (also exec. prod), Born to Be a Star (s.p., prod.), Grown Ups (also writer, prod.), The Zookeeper (voice, prod.), Jack and Jill (also prod.), Just Go with It (also writer, prod.).
TELEVISION: *Movie:* Gay Robot (exec. prod.). *Series:* Remote Control, Saturday Night Live (3 Emmy noms. for writing), The Mayor (exec. prod.), Rules of Engagement (exec. prod.). *Guest:* More than 170 appearances.

SANDRICH, JAY
Director. b. Los Angeles, CA, Feb. 24, 1932. e. UCLA.
PICTURES: X-15 (assist. dir.), Seems Like Old Times, Neil Simon's London Suite.
TELEVISION: *Movies:* The Crooked Hearts, What Are Best Friends For?, For Richer For Poorer, The Man Who Came to Dinner, London Suite. *Series:* Insight (Emmy Award for episode, 1984), The Dick Van Dyke Show, Get Smart (also prod.), That Girl, The Hero (prod.), Captain Nice (prod.), He & She, Julia, The Ghost & Mrs. Muir, The Governor & J.J., Nanny and the Professor, The Mary Tyler Moore Show (2 Emmy Awards: 1971, 1973, 2 other noms.), Arnie, The Odd Couple, Here We Go Again, Rhoda, Beacon Hill, Laverne & Shirley, Ball Four, Soap (2 Emmy noms.), WKRP in Cincinnati (also pilot), Phyllis (pilot), Tony Randall Show (pilot), Bob Newhart Show (pilot), Benson, The Stockard Channing Show, It's a Living, It Takes Two, Golden Girls (pilot; DGA Award, 1985), The Cosby Show (2 Emmy Awards: 1985, 1986; 1 other nom.; DGA Award 1985), A Different World (pilot), Empty Nest (pilot), Thea, The Office, Pearl, Ink, The Tony Danza Show, Built to Last, Style and Substance, LateLine, The Secret Lives of Men, Thanks, My Family, Three Sisters, Charlie Lawrence. *Special:* The Lily Tomlin Show (DGA Award, 1975).

SANDS, JULIAN
Actor. b. Yorkshire, England, Jan. 4,1958. e. Central School of Speech and Drama, London, 1979. Formed small theatre co. that played in schools and youth clubs. Professional debut in Derek Jarman's short, Broken English, and one-line part in Privates on Parade. Then opposite Anthony Hopkins in British TV series A Married Man (1981).
PICTURES: Privates on Parade (debut, 1982), Oxford Blues, The Killing Fields, After Darkness, The Doctor and the Devils, A Room with a View, Gothic, Siesta, Vibes, Wherever You Are, Manika: The Girl Who Lived Twice, Arachnophobia, Warlock, Night Sun, Impromptu, Naked Lunch, Wicked, Husbands and Lovers, Tale of a Vampire, Boxing Helena, Warlock: The Armageddon, Black Water, The Browning Version, Leaving Las Vegas, Never Ever, One Night Stand, Long Time Since, Phantom of the Opera, The Loss of Sexual Innocence, Autumn Heart, The Million Dollar Hotel, Mercy, Love Me, Timecode, Vatel, Pokemon: The Movie 2000, Hotel, The Scoundrel's Wife, The Visitors, Highbinders, The Medallion, Easy Six, Romasanta, Her Name is Carla, La Piste, The Trail, Bongee Bear and the Kingdom of Rhythm, Ocean's Thirteen, Heidi 4 Paws, Cat City, Quantum Heist, Blood and Bone, Assisting Venus, Golf in the Kingdom.
TELEVISION: *Movies*: A Married Man, Romance on the Orient Express, Harem, The Room, Murder By Moonlight, Grand Isle, Crazy in Love, Witch Hunt, The Great Elephant Escape, The Tomorrow Man, End of Summer, Kingdom in Twilight, Kenneth Tynan: In Praise of Hardcore, Marple: Towards Zero, The Haunted Airman, Beyond Sherwood Forest. *Mini-series:* The Sun Also Rises, Rose Red, Napoléon. *Series*: Jackie Chan Adventures (voice), Lipstick Jungle, 24, Bollywood Hero. *Guest:* More than 50 appearances.

SANDS, RICK
Executive. Began career as v.p. of distribution, Columbia Pictures, 1978; exec. v.p. & CFO, Miramax Films, 1990; exec. v.p. & CFO, Hallmark/RHI Entertainment, 1993; president, Miramax Intl., 1995. From 1997-Dec. 2004 with Miramax. Left COO position with Miramax to become pres. & COO of DreamWorks SKG in Jan. 2005. Left DreamWorks for MGM in Jan. 2006, where he served as COO. April 2008 left MGM and formed Rick Sands Entertainment, which represents clients in all segments of the entertainment business. Member, Board of Directors, AFMA, AMPAS, BAFTA, and IFP; awarded Distributor of the Year, Cinema Expo Int'l., 2000.

SAPERSTEIN, DAVID
Writer, Director. b. Brooklyn, NY. e. Bronx H.S. of Science, CCNY, Film Institute, Chemical Engineering. 1960-80 wrote, prod. and dir. documentary films, TV commercials. Also wrote lyrics and managed rhythm and blues and rock 'n roll groups. Assoc. Professor NYU Graduate Film & TV, Manhattan Marymount College. Has directed various music videos. Wrote libretto and lyrics for Blue Planet Blue, Clowns and Cocoon: The Musical.
AUTHOR: Cocoon, Metamorphosis, Red Devil, Funerama, Fatal Reunion, Dark Again.
PICTURES: Cocoon (story), Killing Affair (dir., s.p.), Personal Choice (dir., s.p.), Cocoon: The Return. Fatal Reunion (s.p.), Queen of America (s.p.), Torch, Sara Deri, Hearts & Diamonds, Vets, Do Not Disturb, Point of Honor, Snatched, Jack in the Box, Schoolhouse, Roberto: The Roberto Clemente Story, Roamers,

Joshua's Golden Band, Beyond the Stars (dir., s.p.), Bab's Labs (s.p.), Fighting Back (s.p.), Silyan (s.p.).
TELEVISION: *Movies:* A Christmas Visitor, The Vintage Years (pilot), Dance of the Athletes (dir., writer), Rodeo—A Matter of Style (dir., writer), Mama Sings, The Corky Project, OB/GYN (pilot), Reppies (prod.).

SARA, MIA
Actress. b. Brooklyn, NY, June 19, 1968. Started doing TV commercials; landed role in soap opera, All My Children.
PICTURES: Legend (debut, 1986), Ferris Bueller's Day Off, The Long Lost Friend, Apprentice to Murder, A Row of Crows, Imagination, Any Man's Death, Shadows in the Storm, A Stranger Among Us, By the Sword, Timecop, The Pompatus of Love, The Maddening, Undertow, Bullet to Beijing, Black Day Blue Night, Dazzle, Little Insects, The Impossible Elephant, Turn of Faith, Hoodlum & Son, The Witches of Oz 3D.
TELEVISION: *Movies*: Queenie, Big Time, Till We Meet Again, Daughter of Darkness, Blindsided, Call of the Wild, Bullet to Beijing, 20,000 Leagues Under the Sea, The Set Up, Hard Time, Jack and the Beanstalk- The Real Story, Lost in Oz. *Mini-series:* Till We Meet Again, Nightmares and Dreamscapes: From the Stories of Stephen King. *Series:* Birds of Prey, Tinseltown.

SARAFIAN, RICHARD C.
Director, Writer, Actor. b. New York, NY. April 28, 1935. Studied medicine and law before entering film industry with director Robert Altman making industrial documentaries.
PICTURES: *Writer:* Attila, The Notorious Mr. Monks, The Cool and the Crazy, The Man Who Died Twice, Terror at Black Falls (also dir., prod., editor), Andy (also writer, prod.), The Next Man (also dir.). *Director:* Run Wild-Run Free, Fragment of Fear, Vanishing Point, Man in the Wilderness, Lolly-Madonna XXX, The Man Who Loved Cat Dancing, Sunburn, Gangster Wars, The Bear, Eye of the Tiger, Street Justice, Solar Crisis (as Allen Smithee). *Actor:* Songwriter, Bugsy, Ruby, Gunmen, The Road Killers, Don Juan DeMarco, The Crossing Guard, Bound, Bulworth, Blink of an Eye, Blue Streak, Picking Up The Pieces, Dr. Dolittle 2 (voice), Masked and Anonymous.
TELEVISION: *Movies: Director:* Shadow on the Land, One of Our Own,A Killing Affair, Disaster on the Coastliner, The Golden Moment: An Olympic Love Story, Splendor in the Grass, Liberty (also actor). *Actor:* Long Time Gone, Miami Hustle, Gotti. *Mini-series:* The Gangster Chronicles. *Series: Director:* Maverick, Bronco, 77 Sunset Strip, Surfside 6, Dr. Kildare, The Gallant Men, I Spy, Gunsmoke (1965-1968), Batman, The Girl from U.N.C.L.E., Jericho, Cimarron Strip, The Guns of Will Sonnett, Premiere, Shannon, The Mississippi. *Guest:* More than 51 appearances.

SARANDON, CHRIS
Actor. b. Beckley, WV, July 24, 1942. e. U. of West Virginia. Mem. Catholic U.'s National Players touring U.S. in Shakespeare and Moliere. Acted with Washington, D.C. improvisational theater co. and Long Wharf. B'way debut, The Rothschilds.
THEATRE: Two Gentlemen of Verona, Censored Scenes from King Kong, Marco Polo Sings a Solo, The Devil's Disciple, The Soldier's Tale, The Woods, Nick & Nora.
PICTURES: Dog Day Afternoon (debut, 1975; Academy Award nom.; Golden Globe nom. 1976), Lipstick, The Sentinel, Cuba, The Osterman Weekend, Protocol, Fright Night, Collision Course, The Princess Bride, Child's Play, Slaves of New York, Forced March, Whispers, The Resurrected, Dark Tide, The Nightmare Before Christmas (voice), Just Cause, Tales From the Crypt: Bordello of Blood, Edie and Pen, Road Ends, Little Men, Let the Devil Wear Black, Reaper, Perfume, Loggerheads, The Chosen One (voice), Multiple Sarcasms.
TELEVISION: *Movies*: Thursday's Game, You Can't Go Home Again, The Day Christ Died, A Tale of Two Cities, This Child Is Mine, Broken Promises, Liberty, Frankenstein, Mayflower Madam, Goodbye, Miss 4th of July, Tailspin: Behind the Korean Airliner Tragedy, Shangri-La Plaza, The Stranger Within, Lincoln & Seward, Lincoln and the War Within, A Murderous Affair: The Carolyn Warmus Story, David's Mother, When the Dark Man Calls, The Underworld, Race Against Time, The Griffin and the Minor Canon, The Dead Will Tell, Crazy, God in America. *Series*: The Guiding Light, Chicago Hope, Felicity, The Court, Judging Amy. *Guest:* More than 73 appearances.

SARANDON, SUSAN
Actress. r.n. Susan Abigail Tomalin. b. New York, NY, Oct. 4, 1946. e. Catholic U. Raised in Metuchen, New Jersey. Returned to New York to pursue acting, first signing with Ford Model Agency.
THEATRE: *NY*: An Evening with Richard Nixon and..., A Coupla White Chicks Sitting Around Talking, Extremities.
PICTURES: Joe (debut, 1970), Lady Liberty, Lovin' Molly, The Front Page, The Great Waldo Pepper, The Rocky Horror Picture Show, Dragonfly (One Summer Love), Checkered Flag or Crash, The Last of the Cowboys (The Great Smokey Roadblock; also co-prod.), The Other Side of Midnight, Pretty Baby, King of the Gypsies, Something Short of Paradise, Loving Couples, Atlantic City (Academy Award nom. 1982), Tempest, The Hunger, The Buddy System, Compromising Positions, The Witches of Eastwick, Bull Durham (Golden Globe nom. 1989), Sweet Hearts Dance, The January Man, A Dry White Season, Through the Wire (narr.), White Palace (Golden Globe nom. 1991), Thelma & Louise (Academy Award nom.; Golden Globe nom. 1992), The Player, Light Sleeper, Bob Roberts, Lorenzo's Oil (Academy Award nom.; Golden Globe nom. 1993), The Client (Academy Award nom. 1995), Little Women, Safe Passage, The Celluloid Closet, Dead Man Walking (Academy Award, Golden Globe nom. 1996), James and the Giant Peach (voice), 187, Illuminata, Twilight, Stepmom (also exec. prod., Golden Globe nom. 1999), Joe Gould's Secret, The Cradle Will Rock, Anywhere But Here, Our Friend, Martin (voice), Rugrats in Paris: The Movie (voice), Cats & Dogs, Baby's in Black, The Banger Sisters, This Child of Mine, Igby Goes Down (Golden Globe nom. 2003), Uphill All the Way (voice), Rudyland (narr.), Moonlight Mile, Noel, Shall We Dance?, Alfie, Romance & Cigarettes, Irresistible, Elizabethtown, Mr. Woodcock, A Whale in Montana, Enchanted, Emotional Arithmetic, In the Valley of Elah, Speed Racer, Middle of Nowhere, The Lovely Bones, Peacock, The Greatest, Solitary Man, Leaves of Grass, Wall Street: Money Never Sleeps, Jeff Who Lives at Home.
TELEVISION: *Movies*: F. Scott Fitzgerald & the Last of the Belles, Mussolini: Decline and Fall of Il Duce, Women of Valor, Father Roy: Inside the School of Assassins, Earthly Possessions, Ice Bound, Cool Women in History (Emmy nom. 2002), The Exonerated, Bernard and Doris (Emmy nom. 2008, Golden Globe nom. 2009), You Don't Know Jack. *Mini-series*: A.D, Mythos (host), Children of Dune. *Series*: Search For Tomorrow, Friends (Emmy nom. 2001 as guest role), Malcolm in the Middle (Emmy nom. 2002 as guest role), Rescue Me. Numerous documentaries as narrator. *Guest*: More than 243 appearances.

SARDI, JAN
Writer.
PICTURES: Moving Out, Street Hero, Ground Zero, Breakaway, Secrets, Shine (Academy Award nom.; Golden Globe nom.; WGA nom. 1997), Love's Brother (also dir.), The Notebook (adaptation), Mao's Last Dancer (s.p.).
TELEVISION: *Movie:* Halifax f.p: Lies of the Mind. *Mini-series:* Winners. *Series:* The Flying Doctors, Mission Impossible, All Together Now, Phoenix, Snowy River: The McGregor Saga, Law of the Land, Sky Trackers.

SARGENT ALVIN
Writer. b. Philadelphia, PA, April 12, 1927. Began career as writer for TV, then turned to theatrical films. 1991 received WGA Laurel Award for Screen Writing Achievement.
PICTURES: Gambit (co-s.p.), The Stalking Moon, The Sterile Cuckoo, I Walk the Line, The Effect of Gamma Rays on Man-in-the-Moon Marigolds, Paper Moon (Academy Award nom.; Golden Globe Award 1974), Love and Pain (and the Whole Damn Thing), Julia (Academy Award, Golden Globe nom.; WGA Award 1978), Bobby Deerfield, Straight Time (co-s.p.), Ordinary People (Academy Award, Golden Globe Award 1981), Nuts (co-s.p.), Dominick and Eugene (co-s.p.), White Palace (co-s.p.), What About Bob? (co-story), Other People's Money, Hero (co-story), Bogus, Anywhere But Here, Unfaithful, Spider-Man 2, Spider-Man 3.
TELEVISION: *Movies*: Foosteps: Nice Guys Finish Last, The Impatient Heart. *Series*: The Naked City, Route 66, Ben Casey, Alfred Hitchcock Presents, The Doctors and the Nurses, Mr. Novak, Empire.

SARGENT, JOSEPH
Director. r.n. Giuseppe Danielle Sargente. b. Jersey City, NJ, July 25, 1925. e. studied theatre, New Sch. for Social Research 1946-49. Won DGA Award, 1974 for Most Outstanding Television Director.
PICTURES: One Spy Too Many, The Hell With Heroes, Colossus: The Forbin Project, White Lightning, The Taking of Pelham One Two Three, MacArthur, Goldengirl, Coast to Coast, Nightmares, Jaws—The Revenge (also prod.).
TELEVISION: *Movies*: The Sunshine Patriot, The Immortal (pilot), The Man, Tribes (Emmy nom. 1971), The Marcus-Nelson Murders (Emmy Award, DGA Award 1973), Maybe I'll Come Home in the Spring (also prod.), The Man Who Died Twice, The Night That Panicked America, Sunshine (also prod.), Friendly Persuasion, Amber Waves (Emmy nom. 1980), Hustling, Freedom, Tomorrow's Child, Memorial Day, Terrible Joe Moran, Choices of the Heart (also prod.), Space, Passion Flower, Of Pure Blood, There Must Be a Pony, The Karen Carpenter Story, Day One, The Incident, Caroline? (Emmy Award 1990), The Last Elephant, Never Forget, Miss Rose White (Emmy Award,1992), Somebody's Daughter (also prod.), Skylark (also prod.), Abraham, My Antonia, Mandela and de Klerk, Miss Evers' Boys (DGA nom. 1998), The Long Island Incident, The Wall, Crime and Punishment, A Lesson Before Dying (DGA nom.; Emmy nom. 2000), Bojangles, Gisella Perl, The Arturo Sandoval Story (DGA nom. 2001), Vola Sciusciù, Out of the Ashes, Something the Lord Made (DGA Award, 2005), Warm Springs (DGA Award, Emmy nom. 2006), Sybil, Sweet Nothing in My Ear (also prod.). *Mini-series*: The Manions of America, James Mitchener's Space, Love Is Never Silent (Emmy Award 1986), Streets of Laredo, Salem Witch Trials. *Series:* Gunsmoke, The Man from U.N.C.L.E., The Girl from U.N.C.L.E., Gallegher Goes West,

Garrison's Gorillas, It Takes a Thief. *Specials*: The Spy in the Green Hat, World War II: When Lions Roared.

SARNOFF, THOMAS W.
Executive. b. New York, NY, Feb. 23, 1927. e. Phillips Acad., Andover, MA, 1939-43, Princeton U., 1943-45, Stanford U. grad. 1948, B.S. in E.E.; Grad Sch. of Bus. Admin. 1948-49. Sgt., U.S. Army Signal Corps, 1945-46; prod. & sales, ABC-TV, Hollywood, 1949-50; prod. dept. MGM, 1951-52; asst. to dir. of finance and oper., NBC, 1952-54; dir. of prod. and bus. affairs, 1954-57; v.p., prod. and bus. affairs, 1957-60; v.p. adm. west coast, 1960-62; v.p. west coast, 1962; exec. v.p. 1965-77; bd. of dir., NBC prods 1961-77; bd of dir. Hope Enterprises 1960-75; dir. NABCAT, Inc. 1967-75; dir. Valley County Cable TV, Inc. 1969-75; Pres. NBC Entertainment Corp. 1969-77; pres. Sarnoff International Enterprises, Inc. 1977-81; pres., Sarnoff Entertainment Corp., 1981-; pres., Venturetainment Corp. 1986-93; past pres. Research Foundation at St. Joseph Hospital of Burbank; past pres. Permanent Charities of the Entertainment Ind.; past ch. bd. of trustees, National Acad. of TV Arts and Sciences. Pres. Acad. of TV Arts & Sciences Foundation 1990-99. chmn. & CEO Acad. of TV Arts & Sciences Foundation, 1999. Became chairman emeritus of NATAS. Also serves on the ATAS bd. of dir. Sarnoff has been a dir. of Multimedia Games Inc. since 1997.

SARRAZIN, MICHAEL
Actor. r.n. Jacques Michel Andre Sarrazin. b. Quebec, Canada, May 22, 1940. Began acting at 17 on CBC TV; signed by Universal, 1965.
PICTURES: Gunfight in Abilene (debut, 1967), The Flim-Flam Man, The Sweet Ride, Journey to Shiloh, A Man Called Gannon, Eye of the Cat, In Search of Gregory, They Shoot Horses Don't They?, The Pursuit of Happiness, Sometimes a Great Notion, Believe in Me, The Groundstar Conspiracy, Harry in Your Pocket, For Pete's Sake, The Reincarnation of Peter Proud, The Loves and Times of Scaramouche, The Gumball Rally, Caravans, Double Negative, The Seduction, Fighting Back, Joshua Then and Now, Captive Hearts, Mascara, Keeping Track, Malarek, Lena's Holiday, Bullet to Beijing, Crackerjack II, The Peacekeeper, The Second Arrival, FeardotCom.
TELEVISION: *Movies*: The Doomsday Flight, Frankenstein: The True Story, Passion and Paradise, Earthquake in New York, The Phone Call, Bullet to Beijing, Midnight Man, Thunder Point, Earthquake in New York, Tripping the Wire: A Stephen Tree Mystery, The Christmas Choir. *Mini-series:* Beulah Land. *Series:* Deep in the City.

SAUNDERS, DAVID
Executive, Producer. Pres., Triumph Films, Inc. from 1993 to 1997 when Sony closed this indie unit.
PICTURES: *Executive producer*: Hellraiser, High Spirits, Bat *21 (co-prod.), Wild Orchid, Wild Orchid II: Two Shades of Blue, The Assignment, Masterminds, In God's Hands, Baby Geniuses, Radio Silence, FearDotCom, Extreme Ops, Chromiumblue.com., Crazy Again (doc., exec. prod.), Dance with the Devil (doc., exec. prod.).
TELEVISION: *Movies*: Red Shoe Diaries, Red Shoes Diaries 3: Another Woman's Lipstick. *Series*: *Executive producer:* Red Shoe Diaries, ChromiumBlue.com, Forty Deuce (docudrama; co-producer), Red Shoes Diaries: Las Vegas, Body Language (prod.).

SAURA, CARLOS
Director. b. Huesca, Spain, January 4, 1932. e. educated as engineer. Worked as professional photographer from 1949. Studied at Instituto de Investigaciones y Experiencias Cinematograficos, Madrid, 1952-57 where he then taught from 1957-64 until being dismissed for political reasons. 1957-58 dir. shorts La tarde del domingo and Cuenca.
PICTURES: *Director and/or Writer*: Los Golfos (The Urchins), Lament for a Bandit, La Caza (The Hunt), Peppermint Frappe, Stress es Tres Tres, La Madriguera (The Honeycomb), The Garden of Delights, Anna and the Wolves, Cousin Angelica (Cannes Fest. jury prize, 1974), Cria! (Cannes Fest. jury prize, 1976), Elisa Vide Mia, Los ojos Vendados (Blindfold), Mama Turns 100, Hurry Hurry (Golden Bear, Berlin Fest., 1981), Blood Wedding, Dulces Horas (Sweet Hours), Antonieta, Carmen, Los Zancos (The Stilts), El Amor Brujo (Love the Magician), El Dorado, The Dark Night, Ay Carmela!, Sevillanas, Outrage, Flamenco, Taxi, Tango, Pajarico, Esa luz!, Goya, Bunuel and King Solomon's Table, The 7th Day, Iberia, Fados (doc., also prod. designer), Io, Don Giovanni, Flamenco, Flamenco.
TELEVISION: Numerous Spanish credits.

SAVAGE, FRED
Actor, Director. b. Highland Park, IL, July 9, 1976. e. Stanford Univ. While in kindergarten auditioned for commercial at local community center. Didn't get the job but called back by same dir. for two more tests. Chosen for Pac-Man vitamin ad which led to 27 on-camera TV commercials and 36 voice-over radio spots.
PICTURES: The Boy Who Could Fly, The Princess Bride, Vice Versa, Little Monsters, The Wizard, Guy Walks into a Bar, As You Wish: The Story of the Princess Bride, The Jungle Book: Mowgli's Story (voice), Austin Powers in Goldmember, The Rules of Attraction, Welcome to Mooseport, The Last Run, Daddy Day Camp (dir. only).
TELEVISION: *Movies*: Convicted: A Mother's Story, Run Till You Fall, When You Remember Me, Christmas on Division Street, No One Would Tell, Area 52, Mongoose & Luther (dir.), Single White Millionaire. *Series*: Morningstar/Eveningstar, The Wonder Years (2 Emmy noms.; 2 Golden Globe noms.), Working (also dir.), Even Stevens (dir.), All About Us (dir.), Oswald (voice), Boy Meets World (dir.), Absolutely Psychic (dir.), Unfabulous (dir.), Ned's Declassified School Survival Guide (dir.), Situation: Comedy (series doc., dir.), Zoey 101 (dir.), Kitchen Confidential (dir.), Crumbs, Phil of the Future (dir., prod., DGA nom. 2007), Wizards of Waverly Place (DGA nom. 2008), It's Always Sunny in Philadelphia (dir., prod.), Aliens in America (dir.), Party Down (dir., suprv. prod., prod.), Generator Rex (voice), Zeke and Luther (pilot, DGA nom. 2010). *Documentaries/Specials*: Runaway Ralph. *Guest:* More than 80 appearances.

SAVAGE, JOHN
Actor. r.n. John Youngs. b. Old Bethpage, Long Island, NY, Aug. 25, 1949. Studied at American Acad. of Dramatic Arts. In Manhattan organized Children's Theatre Group which performed in public housing. Won Drama Desk Award for performance in One Flew Over the Cuckoo's Nest (Chicago & LA).
THEATRE: Fiddler on the Roof, Ari, Siamese Connections, The Hostage, American Buffalo, Of Mice and Men.
PICTURES: Bad Company (debut, 1972), Steelyard Blues, The Killing Kind, The Sister in Law (also composed score), The Deer Hunter, Hair, The Onion Field, Inside Moves, Cattle Annie and Little Britches, The Amateur, Brady's Escape, Maria's Lovers, Salvador, Beauty and the Beast, Hotel Colonial, Soldier's Revenge, The Beat, Caribe, Do the Right Thing, Point of View, Any Man's Death, The Godfather Part III, Hunting, Primary Motive, My Forgotten Man, C.I.A. II: Target Alexa, Red Scorpion 2, Killing Obsession, Carnosaur 2, From the Edge, The Dangerous, Centurion Force, The Crossing Guard, White Squall, Where Truth Lies, American Strays, Little Boy Blue, The Mouse, Burning Down the House, Amnesia, Hostile Intent, Summer of Sam, Frontline, Message in a Bottle, Something Between Us, Christina's House, Redemption of the Ghost, Dead Man's Run, The Anarchists' Cookbook, Wounded, Fallacy, Iowa, Admissions, Downtown: A Street Tale, The New World, The Fallen, The Attic, From a Place of Darkness, Boiler Maker, My Soul to Take 2, The Violent Kind, The Grift, The Golden Boys, Shortcut to Happiness, Chatham, Buffalo Bushido, Mary-8, American Cowslip, The Thacker Case, Anytown, The Red Canvas, Handsome Harry, Buffalo Bushido, Sibling: Marcus Miller the Orphan Killer, Dreamkiller, The Right to Bear Arms, The Last Gamble, Hit List, Gasp, Colombian Interviews, Blossom, Bereavement, A Star for Rose, Serpent Rising, Bed & Breakfast, Nephilim, 7E.
TELEVISION: *Movies*: All the Kind Strangers, Eric (also wrote and performed songs), The Turning Point of Jim Malloy, Coming Out of the Ice, The Tender Age (The Little Sister), Silent Witness, The Nairobi Affair, Desperate, The Burning Shore, Daybreak, Shattered Image, Tom Clancy's Op Center, Before Women Had Wings, The Jack Bull, Dark Angel, The Virginian, Nightworld: Lost Souls, They Nest, Alien Lockdown, Sucker Free City, Admissions, Love's Long Journey. *Mini-series:* Great Expectations. *Series*: Gibbsville, James Cameron's Dark Angel, Carnivàle, Everwood. *Special*: Date Rape (After school Special). *Guest:* More than 60 appearances.

SAVOCA, NANCY
Director. b. July 23, 1959. e. NYU film sch. m. prod.-writer Richard Guay. While in school directed and wrote short films Renata and Bad Timing. Received Haig P. Manoogian Award for filmmaking at 1984 NYU Student Film Festival. Made feature debut with True Love which won Grand Jury Prize at 1989 United States Film Festival.
PICTURES: True Love (also co-s.p.), Dogfight, Household Saints (also co-s.p.), 24-Hour Woman, Reno: Rebel Without a Pause (also exec. prod.), Dirt (also writer, WGA nom. 2006), The Guest Room.
TELEVISION: *Movie:*If These Walls Could Talk. *Series:* Murder One, Dark Eyes, The Mind of the Married Man.

SAWYER, DIANE
News Correspondent, Anchor. b. Glasgow, KY, Dec. 22, 1945. m. director Mike Nichols. e. Wellesley College. Studied law before deciding on career in TV. Former Junior Miss winner and weather reporter on a Louisville TV station before arriving in Washington, 1970. Worked for Nixon Administration in press office from 1970-74; assisted Nixon in writing memoirs, 1975-78. Joined CBS News as reporter in Washington bureau in 1978; named correspondent in 1980. Served as CBS State Dept. correspondent 1980-81. Joined Charles Kuralt as co-anchor of the weekday editions of CBS Morning News in 1981; 1984-89 correspondent on 60 Minutes; 1989, signed by ABC News as co-anchor of Primetime Live news prog. with Sam Donaldson. 1994, co-anchor of Turning Point, 2000: The Millennium (Emmy Award 2000) Good Morning America (GMA, Emmy Award 2007) co-host, 1999-2009. Co-anchor ABC Evening News, 2006. January 2010 Sawyer became anchor for ABC's "World News Tonight" replacing retired Charles Gibson.

SAXON, JOHN
Actor. r.n. Carmine Orrico. b. Brooklyn, NY, Aug. 5, 1936.
PICTURES: Running Wild (debut, 1955), The Unguarded

Moment, Rock Pretty Baby, Summer Love, The Reluctant Debutante, This Happy Feeling, The Restless Years, The Big Fisherman, Cry Tough, Portrait in Black, The Unforgiven, The Plunderers, Posse from Hell, Mr. Hobbs Takes a Vacation, War Hunt, Evil Eye, The Cardinal, The Ravagers, The Cavern, The Appaloosa (Golden Globe nom. 1967), Queen of Blood, Night Caller From Outer Space, For Singles Only, Death of a Gunfighter, Company of Killers, Joe Kidd, Enter The Dragon, Black Christmas, Mitchell, The Swiss Conspiracy, Strange Shadows in an Empty Room, Moonshine County Express, Shalimar, The Bees, The Glove, The Electric Horseman, Battle Beyond the Stars, Beyond Evil, Blood Beach, Cannibal in the Streets, Wrong Is Right, The Big Score, Nightmare on Elm Street, Prisioners of the Lost Universe, Fever Pitch, Nightmare on Elm Street 3: Dream Warriors, Criminal Act, Death House (also dir.), My Mom's a Werewolf, Aftershock, Blood Salvage, Hellmaster, Crossing the Line, Maximum Force, No Escape No Return, Jonathan of the Bears, Killing Obsession, Beverly Hills Cop III, Wes Craven's New Nightmare, Nonstop Pyramid Action, The Killers Within, From Dusk till Dawn, Lancelot: Guardian of Time, The Path of the Dragon, Joseph's Gift, Criminal Mind, The Party Crashers, Final Payback, Living in Fear, Night Class, Outta Time, The Road Home, The Craving Heart, Trapped Ashes, The Mercy Man, Old Dogs, City of Shoulders and Noses.
TELEVISION: *Movies*: The Doomsday Flight, Winchester 73, Istanbul Express, The Intruders, Snatched, Linda, Can Ellen Be Saved?, Planet Earth, Crossfire, Strange New World, Raid on Entebbe, The Immigrants, Golden Gate, Rooster, Prisoners of the Lost Universe, Payoff, Blackmail, Liz: The Elizabeth Taylor Story, War Wolves. *Series*: The Bold Ones (The New Doctors), Falcon Crest, Dynasty, Another World, Unseen Hollywood. *Guest:* More than 123 appearances.

SAYLES, JOHN
Writer, Director, Editor, Actor. b. Schnectady, NY, Sept. 28, 1950. e. Williams College, B.S. psychology, 1972. Wrote two novels: Pride of the Bimbos, 1975 and Union Dues, 1978; also The Anarchist's Convention, collection of short stories and, Thinking in Pictures: The Making of the Movie Matewan (1987). Wrote and directed plays off-B'way (New Hope for the Dead, Turnbuckle). Directed Bruce Springsteen music videos (Born in the U.S.A., I'm on Fire, Glory Days). Recipient of MacArthur Foundation Grant for genius. Received WGA Ian McLellan Hunter Award 2005.
PICTURES: *Writer:* Piranha, The Lady in Red, Alligator, Battle Beyond the Stars, The Howling, The Challenge, The Clan of the Cave Bear, Wild Thing, Matewan (also actor, dir.), Eight Men Out (also actor, dir.), Breaking In, Men of War, Apollo 13 (re-writer), The Spiderwick Chronicles (s.p.), Accidents Happen (script adv.), A Cold Case (s.p.). *Writer/Director/Editor:* Return of the Secaucus 7 (also actor, WGA nom. 1981), Lianna (also actor), Baby It's You (also dir.), Enormous Changes at the Last Minute, The Brother from Another Planet, City of Hope (also actor), Passion Fish (Academy Award nom.; WGA nom. 1993 for s.p.), The Secret of Roan Inish, Lone Star (Academy Award nom.; Golden Globe nom.; WGA nom. 1997 for s.p.), Men with Guns, Limbo, Sunshine State (also lyricist), Casa de los Babys, Silver City, Fade to Black, Carlisle School, A Cold Case (s.p.), Jurassic Park IV, Honeydripper (also actor), Amigo. *Actor:* Hard Choices, Something Wild, Little Vegas, Straight Talk, Malcolm X, Matinee, My Life's In Turnaround, Gridlock'd, The Toe Tactic, In the Electric Mist. *Executive producer:* Santitos, Girlfight.
TELEVISION: *Movies*: A Perfect Match, Unnatural Causes (actor, writer, WGA Award 1987), Shannon's Deal (writer, creative consult.), Piranha. *Documentaries/Specials:* Mountain View (Alive From Off Center).

SCACCHI, GRETA
Actress. b. Milan, Italy, Feb. 18, 1960. e. England and Australia. Acted in Bristol Old Vic Theatre in England.
PICTURES: Das Zweiter Gesicht, Heat and Dust, The Coca Cola Kid, Burke & Wills, Defence of the Realm, A Man in Love, Good Morning Babylon, White Mischief, Paura e Amore (Fear and Love), Woman in the Moon, Presumed Innocent, Fires Within, Shattered, The Player, Turtle Beach, Desire, The Browning Version, Jefferson in Paris, Country Life, Cosi (cameo), Emma, The Serpent's Kiss, The Red Violin, Love and Rage, Tom's Midnight Garden, Ladies Room, Cotton Mary, The Manor, Looking for Alibrandi, One of the Hollywood Ten, Festival in Cannes, Baltic Storm, Under a False Name, Beyond the Sea, Flightplan, The Book of Revelation, L' Amour caché, Shoot on Sight, Brideshead Revisited, Ways to Live Forever.
TELEVISION: *Movies*: Ebony Tower, Dr. Fischer of Geneva, Camille, Rasputin (Emmy Award, Golden Globe nom. 1996), The Odyssey, Macbeth, Christmas Glory 2000, Jeffrey Archer: The Truth, Maigret: L'ombra cinese, Marple: By the Pricking of My Thumbs, Broken Trail (Emmy nom. 2007), Miss Austen Regrets. *Mini-series*: Waterfront (Australia), The Farm, Daniel Deronda, Nightmares and Dreamscapes: From the Stories of Stephen King, The Trojan Horse. *Guest:* More than 42 appearances.

SCARWID, DIANA
Actress. b. Savannah, GA. August 27, 1955. e. St. Vincent's Acad., American Acad. of Dramatic Arts, Pace U., 1975. Member of National Shakespeare Conservatory (Woodstock, NY) and worked in regional theatres before moving to Hollywood 1976.
PICTURES: Pretty Baby (debut, 1978), Honeysuckle Rose, Inside Moves (Academy Award nom. 1981), Mommie Dearest, Rumble Fish, Strange Invaders, Silkwood, The Ladies Club, Psycho III, Extremities, Heat, Brenda Starr, Gold Diggers: The Secret of Bear Mountain, The Cure, The Neon Bible, Bastard Out of Carolina, Angel of Pennsylvania Avenue, What Lies Beneath, The Angel Doll, A Guy Thing, Party Monster, The Clearing, Dream Boy.
TELEVISION: *Movies*: In the Glitter Palace, The Possessed, Forever, Battered, Guyana Tragedy: The Story of Jim Jones, Desperate Lives, Thou Shalt Not Kill, A Bunny's Tale, After the Promise, Night of the Hunter, Simple Justice, Labor of Love: The Arlette Schweitzer Story, Truman (Emmy nom. 1996), If These Walls Could Talk, Critical Choice, Ruby Bridges, Before He Wakes, Down Will Come Baby, Dirty Pictures, Path to War, Tribute. *Mini-series:* Studs Lonigan, A Will of Their Own, J.F.K.: Reckless Youth, From the Earth to the Moon. *Series*: Wonderfalls, Prison Break.

SCHAMUS, JAMES
Executive, Producer, Writer. b. Detroit, MI, Sept. 7, 1959. Univ. of California - Berkeley, Ph.D. in English. He also holds a faculty position at Columbia U. and was named a Presidential Fellow in the Humanities at the Univ. of Chicago. Schamus is an Academy Award®-nominated screenwriter, producer, and film executive. In 1992 Schamus began a long collaboration as writer and producer for director Ang Lee, which resulted in nine films, including "Brokeback Mountain," "Crouching Tiger Hidden Dragon," "The Ice Storm," "The Wedding Banquet," "The Hulk," "Lust," and "Caution." Schamus has also produced or executive produced many important American independent films of the past decade, among them "Safe" and "The Brothers McMullen." And his works have included four Grand Prize winners at the Sundance Film Festival. He also is a widely published film historian and theorist. In 1991, he co-founded Good Machine with Ted Hope, which became Focus Features, a fully independent specialty motion picture division of Universal Pictures in 2002. Schamus became co-president with David Linde under the new label. In May 2006, Schamus became Focus CEO and is the position he holds today. Schamus was honored with the Trailblazer Award at the 9th annual Woodstock Film Festival in Oct. 2008. The award recognized Schamus' excellence in both business and creativity, a unique skill set separating him from industry peers.

SCHAPIRO, KEN
Executive. e. B.A., UC Berkeley, graduate, Harvard Law School. Joined Morgan Creek films, 1990, where he was responsible for business & legal affairs on the production of all films; executive v.p., Morgan Creek Prods. & Morgan Creek Intl.; executive v.p., Artisan Entertainment, 1998; pres. & COO of Artisan from July 2000 until Dec. 2003 when Artisan acquired by Lions Gate Entertainment Corporation. Formed Qualia Capital, LLC. Bd. member Artisan Ent., Inc.

SCHATZBERG, JERRY
Director. b. New York, NY, June 26, 1927. e. U. of Miami, 1947-48. Early career in photography as asst. to Bill Helburn 1954-56. Freelance still photographer and TV commercials dir. 1956-69. Contrib. photographs to several magazines, incl. Life.
PICTURES: Puzzle of a Downfall Child (debut, 1970), The Panic in Needle Park, Scarecrow, Sweet Revenge (also prod.), The Seduction of Joe Tynan, Honeysuckle Rose, Misunderstood, No Small Affair, Street Smart, Reunion, The Day the Ponies Came Back, A Decade Under the Influence (documentary), No Direction Home: Bob Dylan (doc., still photog.).
TELEVISION: *Movie*: Clinton and Nadine.

SCHEINMAN, ANDREW
Producer. b. 1948. e. Univ. of VA, law degree. Professional tennis player before entering film business as producer of three Charlton Heston films. Became one of five founding partners of Castle Rock Entertainment.
PICTURES: *Producer/Executive producer:* The Mountain Man, The Awakening, Modern Romance, Mother Lode, The Sure Thing, Stand By Me, The Princess Bride, When Harry Met Sally..., Misery, A Few Good Men (Academy Award nom. 1993), North (also co-s.p.), Ghosts of Mississippi, Extreme Measures. *Director*: Little Big League. *Writer:* Bait, Flipped (s.p.).
TELEVISION: *Series*: Seinfeld (exec. prod., Emmy Award 1993, 1 other nom.)

SCHELL, MAXIMILIAN
Actor, Director. b. Vienna, Dec. 8, 1930. Sister is actress Maria Schell. e. Switzerland. Stage debut 1952. B'way debut in Interlock. Won Acad. Award for Best Actor in Leading Role for Judgment at Nuremberg, 1961.
PICTURES: Children Mother and the General (debut, 1955), The Young Lions (U.S. debut, 1958), Judgment at Nuremberg (Academy Award, Golden Globe Award 1962), Five Finger Exercise, The Reluctant Saint, The Condemned of Altona, Topkapi, Return from the Ashes, The Deadly Affair, Counterpoint, The Desperate Ones, The Castle (also prod.), Krakatoa—East of Java, Simon Bolivar, First Love (also dir., co-s.p., co-prod.), Trotta (co-s.p.), Pope Joan, Paulina 1880, The Pedestrian (also dir., prod., s.p.), The Odessa File, The Man in the Glass Booth

(Academy Award nom.; Golden Globe nom. 1976), End of the Game (also dir., co-prod., co-s.p.), St. Ives, The Day That Shook the World, A Bridge Too Far, Cross of Iron, Julia (Academy Award nom.; Golden Globe nom. 1978), Players, Avalanche Express, Together?, The Black Hole, Tales From the Vienna Woods (also prod., s.p.), The Chosen, Les Iles, Morgen in Alabama, Marlene (dir., s.p., interviewer), The Rose Garden, The Freshman, Labyrinth, A Far Off Place, Little Odessa, The Vampyre Wars, Telling Lies in America, Zwischen Rosen, The Fifteenth Angel, Left Luggage, Vampires, Deep Impact, On the Wings of Love, I Love You Baby, Fisimatenten, Hamlet in Hollywood, Festival in Cannes, Meine Schwester Maria (aka My Sister Maria, doc.), Light in the Sky, House of the Sleeping Beauties, The Brothers Bloom, Darkness.
TELEVISION: *Movies:* Judgment at Nuremberg (Playhouse 90), The Fifth Column, Hamlet, The Diary of Anne Frank, Turn The Key Deftly, Phantom of the Opera, Heidi, The Assisi Underground, Young Catherine, Miss Rose White (Emmy nom. 1992), Stalin (Emmy nom.; Golden Globe Award 1993), Candles in the Dark (also dir.), Abraham, Thorn Birds: The Missing Years, Joan of Arc, The Song of the Lark, Coast to Coast, The Return of the Dancing Master, Liebe eines Priesters, Die, The Shell Seekers, Alpenklinik, Die. *Mini-series:* Der Seidene Schuh, Peter the Great, Love-Lies-Passions. *Series:* Bernstein/Beethoven, Wiseguy, Der Fürst und das Mädchen, Giganten. *Guest:* More than 82 appearances.

SCHEPISI, FRED
Producer, Director, Writer. b. Melbourne, Australia, Dec. 26, 1939. e. Assumption Col., Marist Bros. Juniorate, Marcellin Col. Assessed student films at Melbourne's Swinburne Inst. of Tech.; worked on gov. sponsored experimental Film Fund; made TV commercials. Founded The Film House prod. co. Dir. short film The Party.
PICTURES: *Director:* Libido (co-dir.), Barbarosa, Iceman, Plenty, Roxanne, A Cry in the Dark (also co-s.p.; Australian Film Inst. Award for best dir. & s.p.; 2 Golden Globe noms. 1989), Fierce Creatures, Beast of Bataan, The Eye of the Storm. *Dir./Prod.:* The Devil's Playground (also s.p.), The Chant of Jimmie Blacksmith (also s.p.), The Russia House, Mr. Baseball, Six Degrees of Separation, I.Q., Fierce Creatures, It Runs in the Family, Last Man (dir., writer). *Producer:* That Eye, the Sky (exec. prod.), Levity, (exec. prod.).
TELEVISION: *Movie:* Empire Falls (dir., exec. prod., 2 Emmy noms. 2005, DGA nom. 2006). *Series:* Boys from the Bush (exec. prod.).

SCHIFRIN, LALO
Composer. b. Buenos Aires, Argentina, June 21, 1932. Father was conductor of Teatro Colon in B.A. for 30 years. Schifrin studied with Juan Carlos Paz in Arg. and later Paris Cons. Returned to homeland and wrote for stage, modern dance, TV. Became interested in jazz and joined Dizzie Gillespie's band in 1962 as pianist and composer. Settled in L.A. Pres. Young Musicians Fed. Music; dir. and conductor, Paris Philharmonic 1987.
PICTURES: El Jefe, Rhino!, Joy House/Les Felins, Once A Thief, Gone With the Wave, Dark Intruder, The Cincinnati Kid, Way...Way Out!, The Liquidator, I Deal in Danger, Blindfold, Who's Minding the Mint?, The Venetian Affair, Sullivan's Empire, The President's Analyst, Murderer's Row, Cool Hand Luke (Academy Award nom. 1968), Sol Madrid, Hell in the Pacific, The Fox (Academy Award nom. 1969), Coogan's Bluff, Bullitt, The Brotherhood/The Heroin Gang, The Eye of the Cat, Che!, W.U.S.A., Pussycat Pussycat I love You, Kelly's Heroes, Imago, I Love My Wife, THX-1138, Pretty Maids All in a Row, Mrs. Pollifax–Spy, The Hellstrom Chronicle, Dirty Harry, The Christian Licorice Store, The Beguiled, The Wrath of God, Rage, Prime Cut, Joe Kidd, The Neptune Factor, Magnum Force, Hit!, Harry in Your Pocket, Enter the Dragon, Charlie Varrick, Man On a Swing, Golden Needles, The Master Gunfighter, The Four Musketeers, Voyage of the Damned (Academy Award nom.; Golden Globe nom. 1977), St. Ives, Special Delivery, The Sky Riders, Return From Witch Mountain, Telefon, Rollercoaster, The Eagle Has Landed, The Day of the Animals, Nunzio, The Manitou, The Cat From Outer Space, Love and Bullets, Escape to Athena, Boulevard Nights, The Concorde: Airport '79, The Amityville Horror (Academy Award nom.; Golden Globe nom. 1980), When Time Ran Out, Serial, The Nude Bomb, The Competition (Academy Award nom.; Golden Globe nom. 1981), Brubaker, The Big Brawl, The Seduction, La Pelle, Loophole, Caveman, Buddy Buddy, Las Viernes de la Etertnidad, Fast-Walking, The Class of 1984, A Stranger Is Watching, Amytiville II–The Possession, Airplane II–The Sequel, Sudden Impact, The Sting II (Academy Award nom. 1984), The Osterman Weekend, Dr. Detroit, Tank, The New Kids, The Mean Season, The Ladies Club, Black Moon Rising, The Fourth Protocol, The Silence at Bethany, Little Sweetheart, The Dead Pool, Berlin Blues, Return to the River Kwai, Fridays to Eternity, Naked Tango, FX 2, The Beverly Hillbillies, Rice Beans & Ketchup, Scorpion Spring, Mission: Impossible, Tango, Something to Believe In, Money Talks, Rush Hour, Rush Hour 2, Kate & Leopold, Red Dragon (conductor), Bringing Down the House, Shrek 2, Longshot, Mission Impossible 2, The Bridge of San Luis Rey, Abominable, Mission: Impossible III, Rush Hour 3, Drag Me to Hell (soundtrack writer), Inglourious Basterds (soundtrack writer), Did You Hear About the Morgans? (soundtrack writer), Sweetwater.
TELEVISION: *Theme, Episode, Movie & Mini-series scores*: Mission Impossible, Mannix, Medical Center, T.H.E. Cat, Planet of the Apes, Starsky and Hutch, Bronk, Braddock, The Blue Light, Dr. Kildare, 90 Bristol Court, The Young Lawyers, The Black Cloak, The Cliff Dwellers, Ben Casey, I.F.M., Johnny Comes Home, Delancy Street, Foster and Laurie, Egan, How I Spent My Summer Vacation, The World of Jacques Cousteau, Three for Danger, Brenda Starr, Good Against Evil, The Chicago Story, The Victims, Starflight One, Princess Diasy, Sprague, House Detective, Command 5, Glitter, A.D., Hollywood Wives, Terror at London Bridge, Private Sessions, The Equalizer, Beverly Hills Madam, Out on a Limb, Hunter, The Doomsday Flight, Jericho, The Highest Fall of All, Maryk, The Nativity, Quest, Petrocelli, The President's Mistress, Pay the Piper, The Rise and Fall of the Third Reich, The Hidden World of Insects, The Way-Out Men, Sullivan Country, The Aquarians, Shipwreck, Sam Sheppard, Sixth Sense, Memo From Purgatory, Kraft Suspense Theatre, The Virginians, Wagon Train, Private Eye, Shakedown on the Sunset Strip, Earthstar Voyager, Neon Empire, Little White Lies, Face to Face, Original Sins, Berlin Blues, El Quixote, A Woman Named Jackie, Danger Theatre, Jackass.

SCHILLER, LAWRENCE J.
Producer, Director. b. New York, NY, Dec. 28, 1936. Photojournalist with Life Magazine & Saturday Evening Post, 1958-70; collaborated on numerous books including three by Norman Mailer: The Executioner's Song, Marilyn, and The Faith of Graffiti; also Muhammad Ali (with Wilfrid Sheed), Minamata (with Eugene Smith).
PICTURES: The Man Who Skied Down Everest (editorial concept & direction), Butch Cassidy & the Sundance Kid (conceived and executed special still montages & titles); The American Dreamer (prod., dir.).
TELEVISION: *Prod.:* Hey I'm Alive (also dir.), The Trial of Lee Harvey Oswald, The Winds of Kitty Hawk, Marilyn, The Untold Story, An Act of Love, The Executioner's Song (also dir.), Peter the Great (Emmy Award 1986), Margaret Bourke-White (also dir.), The Patricia Neal Story, The Executioner's Song, Murder: By Reason of Insanity, The Plot to Kill Hitler, Double Jeopardy, Master Spy: The Robert Hanssen Story, American Tragedy, Perfect Murder-Perfect Town: JonBenét and the City of Boulder, JonBenet: Anatomy of a Cold Case. *Series:* Trace Evidence: The Case Files of Dr. Henry Lee.

SCHLATTER, GEORGE
Producer, Director, Writer. b. Birmingham, AL, Dec. 31, 1932. m. former actress Jolene Brand. e. Pepperdine U. on football scholarship. First industry job was MCA agent in band and act dept. Then gen. mgr. and show producer Ciro's nightclub (where he met Dick Martin and Dan Rowan). Produced shows at Frontier Hotel and Silver Slipper, Las Vegas. Sang 2 seasons St. Louis Municipal Opera Co. On television, created Laugh-In and Real People (3 Emmys, 27 nominations).
TELEVISION: *Movie:* Tracey Ullman in the Trailer Tales. *Series:* The Dinah Shore Show (talent booker), Rowan & Martin's Laugh-In (exec. prod. & creator, 2 Emmy Awards, 3 Emmy noms.), Real People (3 Emmy noms.), Turn On (exec. prod.), Cher, (prod., 2 Emmy noms.), Speak Up America (series documentary, exec. prod.), She TV (prod.), Next Big Star (exec. prod.). *Documentaries/Specials with*: Goldie Hawn, Robin Williams, The Shirley MacLaine Special: Where Do We Go from Here? (Emmy nom. 1977), Doris Day, John Denver, Frank Sinatra, Jackie Gleason, Danny Thomas, Bob Hope, Milton Berle, Danny Kaye, George Burns, Dinah Shore, Lucille Ball, John Denver and Friend (Emmy nom. 1977), Goldie & Liza Together (Emmy nom. 1980), Salute to Lady Liberty, Las Vegas 75th Anniversary, Real Kids, Best of Times, Look At Us, Shape of Things, Magic or Miracle, Grammy Awards (first 5 years: also writer), also ABC American Comedy Awards (3 years), George Schlatter's Comedy Club, George Schlatter's Funny People, Beverly Hills 75th Anniversary, Humor and the Presidency, The 2nd Annual American Comedy Awards (Emmy nom. 1988), Frank Liza & Sammy..., Sammy Davis, Jr. 60th Anniversary Celebration (Emmy Award 1990), The Ultimate Event, Comedy Hall of Fame, Sinatra's 75th Birthday, The Best Is Yet to Come, Muhammad Ali's 50th Birthday, Welcome Home America, Sinatra: 80 Years My Way (Emmy nom. 1996, WGA nom. 1997), Laugh-In 25th Anniversary Reunion, Heroes of Comedy: Women on Top. Many more series episodes and documentary appearances.

SCHLÖNDORFF, VOLKER
Director. b. Wiesbaden, Germany, March 31, 1939. Studied in France, acquiring degree in political science in Paris. Studied at French Intl. Film Sch. (IDHEC) before becoming asst. to Jean-Pierre Melville, Alain Resnais, and Louis Malle.
PICTURES: Young Torless (debut, 1966; also s.p.), A Degree of Murder (also s.p.), Michael Kohlhass, Baal, The Sudden Fortune of the Poor People of Kombach, Die Moral der Ruth Halbfass, A Free Woman, The Lost Honor of Katharina Blum (also s.p.), Coup de Grace, The Tin Drum (also s.p.), Valeska Gert (also s.p.), Circle of Deceit, Swann in Love (also s.p.), The Handmaid's Tale, Voyager (also co-s.p.), The Ogre, Palmetto, Legend of Rita, The Ninth Day, Ulzhan (also co-prod.).
TELEVISION: *Movies:* Death of a Salesman (Emmy nom. 1986),

A Gathering of Old Men. *Mini-series:* Nouvelles de Henry James (Dir. & writer). *Series:* Billy How Did You Do It? *Documentary:* Billy Wilder Speaks (also writer, prod., editor).

SCHLOSSBERG, JULIAN
Producer, Distributor, Director, Radio & TV Host. b. New York, NY, Jan. 26, 1942. e. N.Y.U. Joined ABC-TV network 1964 as asst. acct. rep.; named act. rep. 1965; 1966, joined Walter Reade Organization as asst. v.p. chg. of TV; 1969, moved to WRO Theatre Div.; 1970, joined faculty of School of Visual Arts; 1971 named v.p. of WRO Theatres; 1976, joined Paramount Pictures as v.p. in charge of feature film acquisition. 1974, prod. & moderated An Evening with Joseph E. Levine at Town Hall, N.Y.; 1974-1980, host of radio show Movie Talk on WMCA (N.Y.), WMEX (Boston), WICE (Providence); 1982-83 host of syndicated TV show, Julian Schlossbergs' Movie Talk; producers' rep. for Dustin Hoffman, Elaine May and the late John Cassavetes and Elia Kazan,. Responsible for restored version of Orson Welles' Othello, re-released in 1992. Founded Castle Hill Productions in 1978 and currently is CEO.
THEATRE: Unexpected Man, Madame Melville, Vita & Virginia, Death Defying Acts, Moscow Stations, Below the Belt, Cakewalk, Beauty Queen of Leenane, Power Plays, Tennessee Willliams Remembered, If Love Were All, Street of Dreams, Taller Than A Dwarf, It Had To Be You, Adult Entertainment, Tommy Tune: White Tie & Tails and Fortune's Fool, Sly Fox.
PICTURES: Going Hollywood: The War Years, Hollywood Uncensored, Hollywood Ghost Stories, No Nukes, Going Hollywood: The '30s, In the Spirit, Whore 2, Widow's Peak (co-exec. prod.).
TELEVISION: Steve Allen's Golden Age of Comedy; All the Best, Steve Allen, Sex & Justice: The Anita Hill/Clarence Thomas Hearings, Slapstick Too, Elia Kazan: A Director's Journey (Emmy nom.), Nichols & May: Take Two, Claire Bloom's Shakespeare's Women, The Lives of Lillian Hellman.

SCHLOSSER, HERBERT S.
Executive. b. Atlantic City, NJ, April 21, 1926. e. Princeton U., Yale Law Sch. Joined law firm of Phillips, Nizer, Benjamin, Krim & Ballon, 1954; attorney, California National Productions
subsidiary of National Broadcasting Company) 1957; v.p. & gen. mgr., 1960; joined NBC-TV as director, talent & program admin., 1961; v.p., talent & program admin., 1962; v.p. programs, west coast, 1966-72; exec. v.p., NBC-TV, 1972; pres., 1973; pres. & COO, 1974-76; pres. & CEO, 1977-78; exec. v.p. RCA, 1978-85; during this time Schlosser was also pres., of RCA Audio Visuals, Inc. Left RCA and became a sr. advisor, broadcasting & entertainment with Schroder Wertheim & Co., 1986. Currently is chairman of the bd. of trustees of the American Museum of the Moving Image (AMMI).

SCHMOELLER, DAVID
Writer, Director. b. Louisville, KY, Dec. 8, 1947. e. Universidad de Las Americas, 1967-69, studied film and theatre under Luis Bunuel and Alejandro Jodorowsky; U. of TX, B.A., M.A., 1969-74. Wrote and directed seven short films while studying at college; won 27 intl. awards. In Hollywood spent 6 months working as intern to Peter Hyams on film, Capricorn One. Now heads own co., The Schmoeller Corp. Professional organization memberships have included: Writers Guild of America, Directors Guild of America, Screen Actors Guild, American Society of Composers, Authors & Publishers (ASCAP), Independent Filmmakers Project (west - IFP), American Film Institute.
AUTHOR: The Seduction.
PICTURES: *Writer:* The Day Time Ended, The Peeper, Last Chance Romance, Thrill Palace, Warriors of the Wind (Eng. adaptation), Ghost Town (story). *Director:* Tourist Trap (debut as dir.), Catacombs, The Seduction (also s.p.), Crawlspace (also s.p.), Curse of the Puppet Master, The Arrival, Netherworld, Catch the Wind (also s.p.), The Secret Kingdom, Please Kill Mr. Kinski, Malevolence, Thor at the Bus Stop (prod., add. stills, script).
TELEVISION: *Movies:* James at 15 (writer), Kid Flicks (writer, prod.), Search for the Jewel of Polaris: Mysterious Museum, Puppet Master vs. Demonic Toys (writer). *Series:* Silk Stalkings (dir.), Renegade (dir.).

SCHNEIDER, JOHN
Actor. b. Mount Kisco, NY, April 8, 1960. Active in drama club in high school in Atlanta. Worked as fashion model and played guitar singing own compositions in various Atlanta clubs. Active in local community theatre. Summer stock in New Hampshire. B'way debut 1991 in Grand Hotel.
PICTURES: Eddie Macon's Run, Cocaine Wars, The Curse, Speed Zone, Ministry of Vengeance, Exit to Eden, The Little CHP, Snow Day, Conjurer, Sydney White, Conjurer, Beautiful Loser, Set Apart, H2O Extreme, Holyman Undercover, The Rebound, The Gods of Circumstance, What Would Jesus Do?, Snow Beast, Doonby, Into the Darkness.
TELEVISION: *Movies*: Dream House, Happy Endings, Stagecoach, Christmas Comes to Willow Creek, Outback Bound, Gus Brown and Midnight Brewster, Highway Heartbreaker, Desperate Journey: The Allison Wilcox Story, Texas, Bandit: Bandit Bandit, Night of the Twisters, The Legend of the Ruby Silver, The Dukes of Hazzard: Reunion!, True Women, Michael Landon-The Father I Knew, Sam Churchill: Search for a Homeless Man, The Dukes of Hazzard: Hazzard In Hollywood, Lightning: Fire From the Sky, Christy: The Movie, Mary Christmas, The Nick at Nite Holiday Special, 10.5, Lake Placid 2, Ogre, Shark Swarm, Come Dance at My Wedding, Crash Test (exec. prod., writer-concept), Back Nine. *Mini-series:* Christy: Choices of the Heart-Part I: A Change of Seasons (exec. prod. only), Wild Jack, Christy: Choices of the Heart- Part II: A New Beginning (exec. prod. only), 10.5. *Series*: Dukes of Hazzard, Grand Slam, Dr. Quinn Medicine Woman, Ordinary/Extraordinary (host), Second Chances, Loving, Heaven Help Us, Smallville, Nip/Tuck, The Secret Life of the American Teenager, 90210, Hot in Cleveland (pilot), Stunted (also exec. prod.), Twentysixmiles. *Documentaries/Specials*: John Schneider—Back Home. *Guest:* More than 131 appearances.

SCHNEIDER, PETER
Executive. e. B.A., theatre, Purdue U., 1971. Theatrical director, The WPA, Playwrights Horizon, and Circle Repetory Theater, New York; producer & managing director, Chicago's St. Nicholas Theater; general mgr., Apollo Theater Productions; director, 1984 Olympic Arts Festival; president (1985) and supervisor of the development and production of all Disney animated motion pictures; president, Walt Disney Studios; supervised the release of Disney's most successful release to date, The Lion King. Chairman of The Walt Disney Studios through June 2001. Resigned to form independent theatrical co. in New York. Schneider recently directed a theatrical production of Grand Hotel-The Musical at Burbank's Colony Theatre (2004-2005 season).

SCHNEIER, FREDERICK
Executive. b. New York, NY, May 31, 1927; e. NYU, 1951, bus. admin.; NYU Grad. Sch., M.B.A., 1953. Dir. sls. planning, Mutual Broadcasting System, 1947-53; media research dir., RKO Teleradio, 1953-55; RKO Teleradio Advisory Comm., 1955-56; exec. staff RKO Teleradio & dir., marketing services, 1956-58; exec. vice-pres., Showcorporation, 1958-71; v.p. TV programming, RKO General, 1972-1973; v.p., Hemdale Leisure Corp., 1973-79; Viacom Enterprises v.p., feature films, 1979; sr. v.p., program acquisitions & motion pictures, 1980-83; sr. v.p., acquisitions, Showtime/The Movie Channel, 1983-85; sr. v.p. program acquisitions, program enterprises, 1985-87; exec. v.p., programming; 1987-89; pres. & CEO, Viacom Pictures Inc., 1989-92; Left for form independent production co., FSA Film Enterprises, and is pres. & CEO.

SCHOONMAKER, THELMA
Editor. b. January 3, 1940.
PICTURES: Finnegan's Wake, Who's That Knocking at My Door?, Woodstock (Academy Award nom. 1971), Street Scenes, Taxi Driver, Rock Show, Raging Bull (Academy Award, ACE Award 1981), The King of Comedy, After Hours, The Color of Money, Bad, The Last Temptation of Christ, New York Stories, Made in Milan, Goodfellas (Academy Award nom.; ACE nom. 1991), Cape Fear, The Age of Innocence, Casino (ACE nom. 1996), Grace of My Heart, Kundun, My Voyage to Italy (documentary), Bringing out the Dead, Gangs of New York (Academy Award nom.; ACE Award 2003), The Aviator (Academy Award, ACE Award 2005), The Departed (Academy Award, ACE Award 2007), Shutter Island, Hugo Cabret.
TELEVISION: *Movie:* AFI Life Achievement Award: A Tribute to Robert De Niro (Emmy nom. 2004).

SCHRADER, PAUL
Writer, Director. b. Grand Rapids, MI, July 22, 1946. m. actress Mary Beth Hurt. e. Calvin College (theology & philosophy); Columbia U., UCLA, M.A., cinema. Served as film critic for L.A. Free Press and Cinema 1970-72. Former professor at Columbia U. Received WGA Laurel Award for Screen Writing Achievement 1999. American Film Institute Franklin J. Schaffner Award, 2005.
PICTURES: *Writer and/or Director*: The Yakuza (co-s.p.), Taxi Driver (Golden Globe nom.; WGA nom. 1977), Rolling Thunder, Obsession, Blue Collar (co-s.p., dir). Hardcore, Old Boyfriends (co-s.p., exec. prod.), American Gigolo, Raging Bull (co-s.p., Golden Globe nom. 1981), Cat People, Mishima (co-s.p.), The Mosquito Coast, Light of Day, The Last Temptation of Christ, Patty Hearst, The Comfort of Strangers, Light Sleeper, City Hall (co-s.p.), Touch, Affliction, Forever Mine (dir., s.p.), Bringing out the Dead (s.p.), Auto Focus, Dino (s.p.), Dominion: Prequel to the Exorcist, The Walker, Adam Resurrected.
TELEVISION: *Movies*: Witch Hunt (dir.), The Hollywood Fashion Machine (act. only).

SCHREIBER, LIEV
Actor. b. San Francisco, CA, October 4, 1967. e. Yale School of Drama. Attended London's Royal Academy of Art and Hampshire College, Amherst, Mass.
PICTURES: Mixed Nuts, Denise Calls Up, Mad Love, Party Girl, Big Night, Walking and Talking, Ransom, Scream, The Daytrippers, Baggage, Scream 2, His and Hers, Phantoms, Sphere, Twilight, Desert Blue (voice), A Walk on the Moon, Jakob the Liar, The Hurricane, Spring Forward, Hamlet, Scream 3, Dial 9 For Love, The Sum of All Fears, Kate and Leopold, The Manchurian Candidate, Everything Is Illuminated (dir./writer), The Omen, The Painted Veil, The Ten, Sea Monsters: A Prehistoric Adventure (doc., narr.), Love in the Time of Cholera,

Defiance, Repossession Mambo, X-Men Origins: Wolverine, Taking Woodstock, Repo Men, Every Day, Salt.
TELEVISION: *Movies:* Janek: The Silent Betrayal, Buffalo Girls, The Sunshine Boys, Since You've Been Gone, Babe Ruth (voice), RKO 281 (Emmy nom.; Golden Globe nom. 2000), Bill Russell: My Life My Way (voice), When It Was a Game 3, Ali-Frazier 1: One Nation...Divisible (narrator), Playing the Field: Sports and Sex in America (narrator), Do You Believe in Miracles? The Story of the 1980 U.S. Hockey Team (narrator), Shot Heard 'Round the World (narrator), A Brilliant Madness, Hitler: The Rise of Evil, Lackawanna Blues, Oil Storm, Dare to Dream: The Story of the U.S. Women's Soccer Team (narr.). *Series:* The American Experience (narr.), CSI: Crime Scene Investigation. *Guest:* More than 95 appearances.

SCHRODER, RICK
Actor. b. Staten Island, NY, April 13, 1970. Started modelling while only four months; did many TV commercials before theatrical film debut in The Champ, at age eight.
PICTURES: The Champ (Golden Globe Award 1980), The Last Flight of Noah's Ark, The Earthling, Apt Pupil, Across the Tracks, There Goes My Baby, Crimson Tide, I Awoke Early the Day I Died, Poolhall Junkies, Face of Terror, Consequence, Black Cloud (also dir., writer), Raising Cole (dir., exec. prod.), Blood Done Sign My Name, Locker 13 (also dir., prod.).
TELEVISION: *Movies*: Little Lord Fauntleroy, Something So Right, Two Kinds of Love, A Reason to Live, Too Young the Hero, Terror on Highway 91, Out on the Edge, A Son's Promise, The Stranger Within (Golden Globe nom. 1991), Blood River, My Son Johnny, Miles From Nowhere, Call of the Wild, To My Daughter with Love, Texas, Heart Full of Rain, Ebenezer, Too Close To Home, Detention: The Siege at Johnson High, What we did that Night, Murder at Devil's Glenn, The Lost Batallion, 14 Hours, Journey to the Center of the Earth, Hellhounds. *Mini-series*: Lonesome Dove, Return to Lonesome Dove, The Andromeda Strain. *Series*: Silver Spoons, NYPD Blue, Country Music Television (dir.), Strong Medicine, 24. *Guest:* More than 73 appearances.

SCHROEDER, BARBET
Producer, Director. b. Teheran, Iran, Aug. 26, 1941. Critic for Cahiers du Cinema and L'Air de Paris, 1958-63. 1963: asst. to Jean-Luc Godard on Les Carabiniers. 1964: formed own prod. co. Les Films du Losange. As actor only: Paris vu par, La Boulangere de Monceau Roberte, Celline and Julie Go Boating, Beverly Hills Cop III, La Reine Margot, Mars Attacks!
PICTURES: *Producer*: La Boulangere de Monceau (26 mins.), La Carriere de Suzanne (52 mins.), Mediterrannee, Paris Vu Par, La Collectionneuse, Tu Imagines Robinson, My Night at Maud's, Claire's Knee, Chloe in the Afternoon, Out One (co-prod.), The Mother and the Whore (co-prod.), Celine and Julie Go Boating, Flocons D'Or, The Marquise of O, Roulette Chinoise (co-prod.), The American Friend (co-prod.), Le Passe-Montagne, The Rites of Death, Perceval Le Gallois, Le Navire Night, Le Pont du Nord, Mauvaise Conduite, Une Sale Historie. *Director & Producer*: More (1969), Sing-Sing (doc.), La Vallee, General Idi Amin Dada (doc.), Maitresse, Koko a Talking Gorilla (doc.), Charles Bukowski Tapes (doc.), Tricheurs, Barfly, Reversal of Fortune (Academy Award nom.; Golden Globe nom. 1991), Single White Female, Kiss of Death, Before and After, Desperate Measures, Shattered Image(prod.), Our Lady of the Assassins, Murder by Numbers, Paris, je t'aime (actor only), Don't Touch the Axe (actor only), The Duchess of Langeais (actor), Terror's Advocate (doc. dir., narr., DGA nom. 2008), The Darjeeling Limited (actor), The Counsel (actor).

SCHUCK, JOHN
Actor. b. Boston, MA, Feb. 4, 1940. e. Denison (BA). Cabaret act: An Evening With John Schuck.
THEATRE: *B'way*: Annie. *Off-B'way*: The Streets of NY, The Shrike. London: The Caine Mutiny. Regional incl. Long Day's Journey Into Night, As You Like It.
PICTURES: M*A*S*H, The Moonshine War, Brewster McCloud, McCabe and Mrs. Miller, Hammersmith Is Out, Blade, Thieves Like Us, Butch and Sundance: The Early Days, Just You and Me Kid, Earthbound, Finders Keepers, Star Trek VI: The Voyage Home, Outrageous Fortune, The New Adventures of Pippi Longstocking, My Mom's a Werewolf, Second Sight, Dick Tracy, Star Trek IV: The Undiscovered Country, Holy Matrimony, Pontiac Moon, Tales From the Crypt Presents Demon Knight, The Curse of the Jade Scorpion, String of the Kite (short).
TELEVISION: *Movies*: Once Upon a Dead Man, Hunter, Till Death Us Do Part, Project ALF, Run for the Dream: The Gail Devers Story, The Trial of Old Drum. *Mini-series*: Roots, Greatest Heroes of the Bible. *Series*: Shepherd's Flock, McMillan and Wife, Holmes and Yoyo, Turnabout, The New Odd Couple, The New Munsters, Law & Order: Special Victims Unit. *Guest*: More than 72 appearances.

SCHULMAN, JOHN A.
Executive. b. Washington, D.C., June 13, 1946. e. Yale U., 1968; law degree from Boalt Hall, U. of California, Berkeley, 1972. Founding partner in Beverly Hills law firm, Weissmann, Wolff, Bergman, Coleman & Schulman in 1981 after nine years with firm of Kaplan, Livingston, Goodwin, Berkowitz & Selvin. Joined Warner Bros. in 1984 as v.p. & gen. counsel; 1989 sr. v.p. and gen. counsel; In 1991, promoted to the position of exec. v.p. and general counsel of Warner Bros. Entertainment, Inc. Retired 2008.

SCHULMAN, TOM
Writer. b. Nashville, TN. e. Vanderbilt U, BA. V.P. of The Writers Guild of America.
PICTURES: Dead Poets Society (Academy Award, Golden Globe nom.; WGA nom. 1990), Honey I Shrunk the Kids, Second Sight, What About Bob?, Medicine Man, Indecent Proposal (exec. prod.), 8 Heads in a Duffel Bag (also dir.), Holy Man, Me Myself and Irene (exec. prod.), Welcome to Mooseport (also prod.), Morgan's Summit (also dir.).
TELEVISION: *Movies:* The Gladiator, (exec. prod.), Das Rattennest, Genius, Anatomy of Hope (also exec. prod.). *Series:* The Court (also co-creator).

SCHULTZ, DWIGHT
Actor. b. Baltimore, MD, Nov. 24, 1947. e. Townson St. Univ. Acted with Williamstown Theatre Fest. prior to NY stage work, incl. The Crucifer of Blood, The Water Engine, Night and Day.
PICTURES: The Fan (dir.), Alone in the Dark, Fat Man and Little Boy, The Long Walk Home, The Temp, Enola Gay and the Atomic Bombing of Japan (narrator), Star Trek: First Contact, Vampire Hunter D (voice), Matriculated (voice), Kaena: The Prophecy (voice, English version), Ultimate Avengers II (voice), Borg War (voice), The A-Team, Batman: Under the Red Hood (voice).
TELEVISION: *Movies*: Child of Rage, When Your Lover Leaves, Perry Mason: The Case of the Sinister Spirit, Perry Mason: The Case of the Musical Murder, A Woman With a Past, The Last Wish, A Killer Among Us, Victim of Love: The Shannon Mohr Story, Menendez: A Killing in Beverly Hills, The Barbara Mandrell Story, Star Trek Voyager (series), Spawn, CatDog: The Great Parent Mystery (voice), The Wild Thornberrys: The Origin of Donnie (voice). Mini-series: Afro Samurai (voice, English version), *Series*: The A-Team, Star Trek: The Next Generation, Spawn (voice), Reign: The Conqueror (voice), CatDog (voice), The Chimp Channel (voice), Ninja Scroll: The Series (voice), Ben 10, Chowder (various voices). *Guest:* More than 128 appearances.

SCHULTZ, MICHAEL
Director, Producer. b. Milwaukee, WI, Nov. 10, 1938. e. U. of Wisconsin, Marquette U.
THEATRE: The Song of the Lusitainian Bogey, Kongi's Harvest, Does a Tiger Wear a Necktie?, Operation Sidewinder, What the Winesellers Buy, The Cherry Orchard, Mulebone, Dream on Monkey Mountain.
PICTURES: *Director:* Together for Days, Honeybaby Honeybaby, Cooley High, Car Wash, Greased Lightning, Which Way Is Up?, Sgt. Pepper's Lonely Hearts Club Band, Scavenger Hunt, Carbon Copy, The Last Dragon, Krush Groove (also prod.), Disorderlies (also co-prod.), Livin' Large, Phat Beach (exec. prod. only), Woman thou Art Loosed.
TELEVISION: *Movies*: Benny's Place, For Us the Living: The Medgar Evers Story, The Jerk Too, Timestalkers, Rock 'n' Roll Mom, Tarzan in Manhattan, Jury Duty: The Comedy, Day-O, Shock Treatment, Young Indiana Jones and the Hollywood Follies, Young Indiana Jones: Travels with Father, Killers in the House, My Last Love, L.A. Law: The Movie. *Series*: The Rockford Files, Baretta, Starsky and Hutch, Picket Fences, Diagnosis Murder, Chicago Hope, The Young Indiana Jones Chronicles, City of Angels, Boston Public, Ally, Family Law, Charmed, Ally McBeal, Felicity, The Practice, Promised Land, Philly, Everwood (dir. 16 episodes and prod.), Brothers & Sisters. *Pilot*: Shock Treatment. *Documentaries/Specials*: To Be Young Gifted and Black, Ceremonies in Dark Old Men, For Us the Living, Fade Out: The Erosion of Black Images in the Media (documentary), Hollywood Follies, Travels With Father.

SCHUMACHER, JOEL
Director, Writer. b. New York, NY, Aug. 29, 1939. Worked as design and display artist for Henri Bendel dept. store in NY while attending Parson's School of Design. As fashion designer opened own boutique, Paraphernalia. Joined Revlon as designer of clothing and packaging before entering m.p. indus. as costume designer on Play It As It Lays, Sleeper, The Last of Sheila, Blume in Love, Prisoner of 2nd Avenue, Interiors. ShoWest Director of the Year Award in 1997. Owner of Joel Schumacher Productions.
PICTURES: *Writer*: Car Wash, Sparkle, The Wiz. *Director*: The Incredible Shrinking Woman (debut, 1981), D.C. Cab (also s.p.), St. Elmo's Fire (also s.p.), The Lost Boys, Cousins, Flatliners, Dying Young, Falling Down, The Client, Batman Forever, A Time to Kill, Batman & Robin, Tigerland, 8mm (also prod.), Flawless (also s.p., prod.), Gossip (exec. prod.), Tigerland, Phone Booth, Bad Company, Veronica Guerin (also writer), The Phantom of the Opera (also s.p.), The Number 23, Blood Creek, Twelve, Trespass.
TELEVISION: *Movies: Director:* The Virginia Hill Story (also writer), Amateur Night at the Dixie Bar & Grill (also writer). *Executive producer:* Slow Burn. *Series*: 2000 Malibu Drive.

SCHUMACHER, MARTHA
Producer. a.k.a Martha De Laurentiis. m. Dino De Laurentiis, producer. President of the Dino De Laurentiis Company.

PICTURES: Firestarter (assoc. prod.), Silver Bullet, Cat's Eye, King Kong Lives, Raw Deal, Maximum Overdrive, The Bedroom Window, Desperate Hours (exec. prod.). *As Martha De Laurentiis*: Once Upon a Crime (exec. prod.), Temptation (exec. prod.), Slave of Dreams, Unforgettable, Breakdown, U-571, Hannibal, Red Dragon, Hannibal Rising, The Last Legion, Virgin Territory.
TELEVISION: *Movies:* Solomon & Sheba, Slave of Dreams.

SCHUMACHER, THOMAS
Producer, Executive. e. UCLA. Began as production asst., Taper Mainstage, Taper Too, and the literary cabaret, Mark Taper Forum. Producer, three original productions for the Improvisational Theater Project. Olympic Arts Festival staff, 1984; asst. gen. mgr., Los Angeles Ballet; co-founder and assoc. dir., 1987 Los Angeles Festival of Arts. Responsible for the American premiere of Canada's Cirque du Soleil. Joined Walt Disney Feature Animation, 1988; named exec. v.p., Disney Feature Animation and Theatrical Productions, 1994-98. President of Walt Disney Feature Animation, Walt Disney Television Animation, and Buena Vista Theatrical Group through Jan. 2003 when Disney combined feature animation with its live action unit. Schumacher then moved over to Disney's stage productions and heads Disney Theatrical Productions as president. Schumacher has served on the Education Council, the Presentations Committee of the Performing Arts Center of Los Angeles County, and the board of directors of the Rachel Rosenthal Co.
PICTURES: The Rescuers Down Under (prod., 1990), The Lion King, (exec. prod.).

SCHWARTZ, SHERWOOD
Producer, Writer. b. Nov. 14, 1916. Also composed themes for television shows Gilligan's Island and The Brady Bunch.
PICTURES: *Writer:* The Wackiest Wagon Train in the West, The Brady Bunch Movie, A Very Brady Sequel, Tinseltown, The Blair Witch Project, The Ballad of Jack and Rose.
TELEVISION: *Movies:* Rescue from Gilligan's Island (exec., s.p.), The Invisible Woman (exec., s.p.), The Harlem Globetrotters on Gilligan's Island (s.p. only), The Brady Girls Get Married (s.p. only), The Brady Bunch in the White House, The Brady Bunch 35th Anniversary Reunion Special: Still Brady After All These Years (Emmy nom. 2005). *Series:* The Red Skelton Hour (Emmy Award 1961, 1 other nom.) Gilligan's Island (also creator), It's About Time, The Brady Bunch (exec.), The Brady Kids (exec. consult. only), Dusty's Trail, Big John Little John (exec., also creator), The Brady Bunch Hour, Harper Valley P.T.A., The Bradys (creator only), The Real Gilligan's Island (exec. prod.).

SCHWARY, RONALD L.
Producer. b. Oregon, May 23, 1944. e. U. of Southern California. Started as movie extra before becoming asst. dir.; served as assoc. prod. on The Electric Horseman.
PICTURES: Ordinary People (Academy Award, DGA Award 1980), Absence of Malice, Tootsie, A Soldier's Story (Academy Award nom. 1985), Batteries Not Included, Havana, Scent of a Woman, Cops and Robbersons, Sabrina, The Mirror Has Two Faces (co-exec. prod.), Meet Joe Black (exec. prod.), Random Hearts (exec. prod.).
TELEVISION: *Movies:* The Blue Knight, The Stranger Who Looks Like Me, In the Glitter Palace, Jo, Partners and Crime. *Series:* Tour of Duty, Sisters, Now and Again, Fling, M*A*S*H (DGA Award 1973), Medium (exec. prod., dir.).

SCHWARZENEGGER, ARNOLD
Actor. b. Graz, Austria, July 30, 1947. m. NBC reporter Maria Shriver. e. U. Wisconsin, B.A. Bodybuilding Titles: Junior Mr. Europe (at age 18), Mr. Universe (3 time winner), Mr. Olympia (7 times), Mr. Europe, Mr. World. Special Olympics weightlifting Coach (1989), Prison Weightlifting Rehabilitation Prog. Awards: Sportsman of the Year (1977, Assn. Physical Fitness Ctrs.), Golden Globe (best newcomer, 1977), ShoWest '85 Intl. Star., ShoWest Career Achievement Award, NATO Male Star of Yr. (1987). Elected Governor of California during 2003 gov. recall election. 2006 reelected as Governor of California.
AUTHOR: Arnold: The Education of a Bodybuilder, Arnold's Bodyshaping for Women, Arnold's Bodybuilding for Men, The Encyclopedia of Modern Bodybuilding, Arnold's Fitness for Kids (3 Vols.).
PICTURES: Hercules in New York (debut, 1970; billed as Arnold Strong), The Long Goodbye, Stay Hungry (Golden Globe Award 1977), Pumping Iron, The Villain, Scavenger Hunt, Conan the Barbarian, Conan the Destroyer, The Terminator, Red Sonja, Commando, Raw Deal, Predator, The Running Man, Red Heat, Twins, Total Recall, Kindergarten Cop, Terminator 2: Judgment Day, Beretta's Island (cameo), Dave (cameo), Last Action Hero (also exec. prod.), True Lies, Junior (Golden Globe nom. 1995), Eraser, Jingle All the.Way, Batman and Robin, End of Days, The 6th Day, Collateral Damage, Terminator 3: Rise of the Machines, Around the World in 80 Days, Cars (voice), The Expendables.
TELEVISION: *Movie*: The Jayne Mansfield Story. *Director*: Tales from the Crypt (The Switch), Christmas in Connecticut (movie). *Documentaries/Specials:* A Very Special Christmas Party (host). *Guest*: More than 240 appearances.

SCHWIMMER, DAVID
Actor. b. Queens, NY, Nov. 12, 1966.
THEATRE: B'way: The Caine Mutiny Court-Martial (debut 2006).
PICTURES: Flight of the Intruder, Crossing the Bridge, Twenty Bucks, Wolf, The Pallbearer, Apt Pupil, Kissing a Fool (also exec. prod.), Six Days Seven Nights, Love & Sex, Picking up the Pieces, Hotel, Humanoid (exec. prod.), Duane Hopwood, Madagascar (voice), Fly Like Mercury (exec. prod.), Run, Fat Boy, Run (dir.), Nothing But the Truth, Madagascar: Escape 2 Africa (voice), Trust (dir., prod.).
TELEVISION: *Movies:* A Deadly Silence, Breast Men, Since You've Been Gone (also dir.), Uprising, Americana (dir.). *Mini-series:* Band of Brothers. *Series:* The Wonder Years, Monty, Friends (also dir. of multiple episodes, Emmy nom. 1995), Little Britain USA (dir., only). *Guest:* More than 75 appearances.

SCHYGULLA, HANNA
Actress. b. Kattowitz, Germany, Dec. 25, 1943. Worked with Rainer Werner Fassbinder in Munich's Action Theatre; a founder of the ``anti-theatre" group. Made film debut in 1968 short Der Brautigam die Komodiantin und der Zuhalter (The Bridegroom, the Comedienne and the Pimp).
PICTURES: Love Is Colder Than Death, Gods of the Plague, Beware of a Holy Whore, The Merchant of Four Seasons, The Bitter Tears of Petra Von Kant, House by the Sea, Jail Bait, Effi Briest, The Marriage of Maria Braun, Berlin Alexanderplatz, Lili Marleen, The Night of Varennes, Passion, A Labor of Love, A Love in Germany, The Delta Force, The Future Is a Woman, Forever Lulu, Miss Arizona, The Summer of Ms. Forbes, Dead Again, Warszawa, Golem: The Ghost of Exile, Mavi Surgun, Life's Little Treasures, Hey Stranger, A Hundred and One Nights, Pakten, Night of the Filmmakers, Milim, Lea, Girl of Your Dreams, Life- Love & Celluloid, Blackout, Hanna Sings, Werckmeister Harmonies, Fassbinder in Hollywood, Promised Land, The Edge of Heaven, Faust.
TELEVISION: *U.S.*: Rio das Mortes, Peter the Great, Barnum, Casanova, Angelo Nero, Absolitude. Numerous French programs and productions.

SCIORRA, ANNABELLA
Actress. b. New York, NY, March 24, 1964. As teen studied acting at HB Studio; then AADA. Founded The Brass Ring Theatre Co. Won role of Sophia Loren's daughter in mini-series Fortunate Pilgrim.
THEATRE: Orpheus Descending, Bus Stop, Three Sisters, Snow Angel, Cries and Shouts, Trip Back Down, Love and Junk, Stay With Me, Those the River Keeps, Shyster (off B'way).
PICTURES: True Love (debut, 1989), Internal Affairs, Cadillac Man, Reversal of Fortune, The Hard Way, Jungle Fever, The Hand That Rocks the Cradle, Whispers in the Dark, The Night We Never Met, Mr. Wonderful, Romeo is Bleeding, The Cure, The Addiction, The Innocent Sleep, The Funeral, Cop Land, What Dreams May Come, New Rose Hotel, Little City, Above Suspicion, Once in the LIfe, Sam the Man, King of the Jungle, Domenica, Chasing Liberty, Twelve and Holding, Find Me Guilty.
TELEVISION: *Movies*: Prison Stories: Women on the Inside, Favorite Deadly Sins, Asteroid, Jenifer, The Madam's Family: The Truth About the Canal Street Brothel, Identity Theft: The Michelle Brown Story. *Mini-series*: The Fortunate Pilgrim. *Series*: The Sopranos (recurring guest role, Emmy nom. 2001), Queens Supreme, Law & Order: Criminal Intent, Mental.

SCOGGINS, TRACY
Actress. b. Galveston, TX, Nov. 13, 1953. Studied acting at H.B. Studies, Wynn Handman Studios. Appeared on stage in L.A. in The Sicilian Bachelor.
PICTURES: Some Kind of Hero, Toy Soldier, In Dangerous Company, The Gumshoe Kid, Watchers II, Time Bomb, Silhouette, Ultimate Desires, Alien Intruder, Dead On, A Crack in the Floor, Asylum of the Damned, Popstar, Mr. Hell (also assoc. prod.), The Cutter, The Strange Case of Dr. Jekyll and Mr. Hyde, Otis.
TELEVISION: *Movies*: Twirl, Jury Duty: The Comedy, The Raven Red Kiss-Off, Dan Turner: Hollywood Detective, Jake Lassiter: Justice on the Bayou, Dallas: J.R. Returns, Dallas: War of the Ewings, Babylon 5: The River of Souls, Babylon 5: A Call to Arms, Homeland Security, Saurian. *Mini-series:* Dante's Cove. *Series*: Renegades, Hawaiian Heat, The Colbys, Lois & Clark: The New Adventures of Superman, Dynasty, Lonesome Dove: The Outlaw Years, Babylon 5, Crusade, Dante's Cove. *Pilots*: The Naturals, High Life. *Guest*: More than 74 appearances.

SCOLA, ETTORE
Director, Writer. b. Trevico, Italy, May 10, 1931. e. U. of Rome. Began career in 1947 as journalist; 1950, wrote for radio shows. Then made first film as script write, 1954; debut as director-writer, 1964. Has written 50+ scripts for other directors.
PICTURES: *Director & Writer*: Let's Talk about Women (debut, 1964), La Congiuntura, Thrilling (segment: Il Vittimista), The Devil in Love, Will Your Heroes Find Their Friends Who Disappeared so Mysteriously in Africa?, Inspector Pepe, The Pizza Triangle, Rocco Papaleo, The Greatest Evening of My Life, We All Loved Each Other So Much, Down and Dirty, Signore e Signori Buonanotte (segment), A Special Day, Viva Italia! (segment), The Terrace, Passion d'Amore, La Nuit de Varennes, Le Bal, Macaroni, The Family, Splendor, What Time is It?, Le Capitain Fracassa, Mario Maria and Mario, Romanzo di un

Giovane Povero, Corti italiani, 1943-1997, La Cena, Concorrenza Sleale, Another World Is Possible, Letters from Palestine, Gente di Roma (doc.). *Creative consultant:* The Motorcycle Diaries.
TELEVISION: *Movies:* Passion (writer). *Series:* Piazza Navona (prod.).

SCOLARI, PETER
Actor. b. New Rochelle, NY, Sept. 12, 1954.
PICTURES: The Rosebud Beach Hotel, Corporate Affairs, Ticks, Camp Nowhere, That Thing You Do!, Buckle Up, Sorority Boys, The Polar Express, Mentor, A Plumm Summer, Imps* (segment), Letting Go, Larry Crowne.
TELEVISION: *Movies*: Missing Children: A Mother's Story, Carpool, Amazons, Fatal Confession: A Father Dowling Mystery, The Ryan White Story, Fire! Trapped on the 37th Floor, Perfect Harmony, Perry Mason: The Case of the Glass Coffin, The House on Sycamore Street, Stop the World I Want to Get Off, Talk to Me, For Hope, The Ultimate Christmas Present. *Mini-series:* From the Earth to the Moon. *Series*: Wally Brown, Goodtime Girls, Bosom Buddies, Baby Makes Five, Newhart (3 Emmy noms. also dir.), Family Album, The Mommies, Gargoyles (voice), Dweebs, Honey I Shrunk the Kids: The TV Show. *Guest*: More than 86 appearances.

SCORSESE, MARTIN
Writer, Director, Editor, Actor. b. New York, NY, Nov. 17, 1942. Began career while film arts student at NYU, doing shorts What's A Nice Girl Like You Doing in a Place Like This? (dir., s.p.), It's Not Just You Murray and The Big Shave. Other short films: Street Scenes, Italianamerican, American Boy, Mirror Mirror, Somewhere Down the Crazy River. *Dir.* 2 commercials for Armani. Currently campaigning for the preservation and restoration of historic films.1995 received American Society of Cinematographers Board of the Governors Award. Recipient of the American Film Institute Life Achievement Award, 1997. Writers Guild of America Evelyn F. Burkey Award 2003. Received Golden Globe Cecil B. DeMille Award 2010.
THEATRE: The Act.
PICTURES: *Actor*: Cannonball, Il Papocchio, Anna Pavlova, 'Round Midnight, Yume, Guilty by Suspicion, Quiz Show, Search and Destroy (also co-exec. prod.), Shark Tale (voice). *Editor*: Woodstock (also asst. dir.), Medicine Ball Caravan (also assoc. prod.),Elvis on Tour, Unholy Rollers (supervising editor). *Producer*: Item 72-D: The Adventures of Spa and Fon (short; consulting prod.), The Grifters, Mad Dog and Glory, Naked in New York (exec. prod.), Con gli occhi chiusi (aka With Closed Eyes; exec. prod.), Clockers, Search and Destroy (exec. prod. & actor), Grace of My Heart (exec. prod.), Kicked in the Head (exec. prod.), The Hi-Lo Country, You Can Count On Me (exec. prod.), Rain (exec. prod.), The Soul of a Man (documentary; exec. prod.), Something to Believe In (exec. prod.), Brides (exec. prod.), Hello Suckers! (co-prod.). *Director*: Versuvius VI (short), What's a Nice Girl Like You Doing In A Place Like This? (also s.p.), It's Not Just You Murray! (also s.p.), The Big Shave (also prod., s.p. & editor), Who's That Knocking at My Door? (also s.p., assoc. prod., actor), Boxcar Bertha (also actor), Mean Streets (also co-s.p., prod. & actor, WGA nom. 1991), Alice Doesn't Live Here Anymore, Taxi Driver (also actor, DGA nom. 1977), New York New York, The Last Waltz (doc.; also cameo), Raging Bull (Academy Award nom. 1981, Golden Globe nom.; DGA nom. 1981, also cameo), The King of Comedy (also actor), After Hours (also cameo), The Color of Money, The Last Temptation of Christ (Academy Award nom. 1989), New York Stories (Life Lessons; also cameo), Made in Milan (doc. short), GoodFellas (2 Academy Award noms. 2 Golden Globe noms. 1991, Golden Globe nom.; WGA nom. 1991, also co-s.p.; DGA nom.), Cape Fear, The Age of Innocence (Academy Award nom. 1994, Golden Globe nom.; DGA nom. 1994, also co-s.p., cameo), Casino (Golden Globe nom. 1996, also co-s.p.), Kundun, Bringing Out the Dead, Gangs of New York (Academy Award nom. 2003, Golden Globe Award, DGA nom. 2003, also actor), The Aviator (Academy Award nom.; DGA nom. 2005, Golden Globe nom. 2005 also exec. prod.), No Direction Home: Bob Dylan (doc.), The Departed (also prod., Academy Award, DGA Award, Golden Globe Award 2007), Lymelife (exec. prod.), Sabina (exec. prod.), Shine a Light (doc.), Frankie Machine, The Young Victoria (prod. only), Shutter Island (also prod.), Silence (also writer, s.p.), Hugo Cabret (alsp prod.).
TELEVISION: More than 229 appearances on various TV documentaries, specials and talk shows. 5 Emmy noms., 1995-2006.

SCOTT, CAMPBELL
Actor. b. New York, NY, July 19, 1962. e. Lawrence Univ. Son of George C. Scott and Colleen Dewhurst. Studied with Geraldine Page and Stella Adler.
THEATRE: *NY*: The Last Outpost, The Real Thing, Copper-head, The Queen and the Rebels, Hay Fever, A Man For All Seasons, Long Day's Journey Into Night, Measure for Measure, Pericles, On the Bum. *Regional*: Romeo and Juliet, Our Town, Gilette, School for Wives, Hamlet.
PICTURES: Five Corners (debut, 1988), From Hollywood to Deadwood, Longtime Companion, The Sheltering Sky, Dying Young, Dead Again, Singles, Mrs. Parker and the Vicious Circle, The Innocent, The Daytrippers, Big Night (also co-dir., prod.), The Spanish Prisoner, The Imposters, Hi-Life, Top of the Food Chain, Lush, Other Voices, Delivering Milo, Final, Rodger Dodger, The Secret Lives of Dentists, Off the Map (prod. & dir. only), Saint Ralph, The Dying Gaul (prod.),Stolen (documentary), Duma, The Exorcism of Emily Rose, Crashing, Music and Lyrics, Phoebe in Wonderland, One Week (narr.), Handsome Harry, Company Retreat (dir., writer), Beware the Gonzo, Eye of the Hurricane.
TELEVISION: *Movies*: The Perfect Tribute, The Love Letter, The Tale of Sweeney Todd, Follow the Stars Home, Hamlet (also prod./dir.), The Pilot's Wife. *Mini-series*: The Kennedys of Massachusetts, LIBERTY-The American Revolution, Final Days of Planet Earth. *Series:* Six Degrees, Royal Pains (also pilot), Damages. *Documentaries/Specials:* Would You Kindly Direct Me to Hell?: The Infamous Dorothy Parker (commentator), Kinsey (narrator), Civil War Stories (special), The American Experience (doc., narr.).

SCOTT, DEBORAH LYNN
Costume Designer. b. 1954.
PICTURES: The Private Eyes, Don't Answer the Phone!, E.T. the Extra-Terrestrial, Never Cty Wolf, Back to the Future, Armed and Dangerous, Blue City, About Last Night..., Who's That Girl?, Life Is Sweet, Coupe de Ville, Hear My Song, Defending Your Life, Eve of Destruction, Blame It on the Bellboy, Hoffa, Jack the Bear, Sliver, Legends of the Fall, Sister My Sister, Persuasion, Funny Bones, Jack and Sarah, The Indian in the Cupboard, Othello, Heat, Looking for Richard, To Gillian on Her 37th Birthday, Titanic (Academy Award, 1998), Wild Wild West, The Patriot, Minority Report, Bad Boys II, The Upside of Anger, The Lost City, The Island, Seraphim Falls, Reign Over Me, Transformers, Get Smart, Transformers: Revenge of the Fallen, The Invention of Lying, Avatar (CDG nom. 2010), Love and Other Drugs, Transformers 3.
TELEVISION: *Movies*: Dancing Queen, Naked Hotel.

SCOTT, RIDLEY
Director, Producer. b. South Shields, Northumberland, England, Nov. 30, 1937. Brother is director Tony Scott. e. Royal College of Art, London. Joined newly formed Film School. First film: Boy on Bicycle (short). Won design scholarship in NY. Returned to London and joined BBC as set designer (Z-Cars, The Informer series). Directed almost 3,000 commercials in 18 years. Formed Percy Main Prods. Also mng. dir. of Ridley Scott Associates. In 2001, Ridley and brother Tony Scott's production co., Scott Free Productions, signed a three-year production deal with Fox.
PICTURES: *Director*: The Duellists (debut, 1978), Alien, Blade Runner, Legend, Someone to Watch Over Me (also exec. prod.), Black Rain, Thelma & Louise (Academy Award nom.; DGA nom. 1992, also prod.), 1492: Conquest of Paradise (also prod.), White Squall (also exec. prod.), G.I. Jane (also prod.), Gladiator (Academy Award nom. 2001, Golden Globe nom.; DGA nom. 2001), Hannibal, Black Hawk Down (Academy Award nom.; DGA nom. 2002, also prod.), Matchstick Men (also prod.), Kingdom of Heaven (also prod.), A Good Year (also prod.), Body of Lies (also prod.), Robin Hood (also prod.). *Producer:* Monkey Trouble, The Browning Version, Clay Pigeons, Six Bullets from Now, In Her Shoes, Domino, Tristan + Isolde (exec. prod.), The Assassination of Jesse James by the Coward Robert Ford, Tripoli (development exec.), American Gangster (Golden Globe nom. 2008), Churchill at War (exec. prod.), Tell-Tale, Welcome to the Rileys, Cyrus (exec. prod.), Cracks (exec. prod.), Sidney Hall (exec. prod.), The A-Team, Life in a Day (doc., exec. prod.).
TELEVISION: *Movies: Production designer:* Reluctant Bandit, Some Lapse of Time. *Director:* Robert. *Executive producer:* RKO 281 (Emmy Award nom. 2000), The Last Debate, The Gathering Storm (Emmy Award 2002), Orpheus, Law Dogs, Into the Storm (Emmy nom. 2009), Nomads. *Mini-series: Executive producer:* The Andromeda Strain (Emmy nom. 2008), The Company, The Pillars of the Earth. *Series: Director:* Z Cars, Mogul, Adam Adamant Lives!, The Informer. *Production designer:* R3, Out of the Unknown, *Executive producer:* The Hunger, AFP: American Fighter Pilot (series doc.), The Good Wife, Numb3rs.

SCOTT, TONY
Director, Producer. b. Newcastle, England, July 21, 1944. Began career in TV commercials, being partnered with his brother Ridley in prod. co. Winner of numerous Clios, Gold & Silver Lions, and other awards. Entered m.p. industry 1972, directing half-hr. film, One of the Missing, for British Film Inst. and Loving Memory, one-hour feature for Albert Finney.
PICTURES: *Director:* Loving Memory (also cinematographer, editor & writer), One of the Missing, Top Gun, Beverly Hills Cop II, Revenge, Days of Thunder, The Last Boy Scout, True Romance, Cityscapes: Los Angeles Crimson Tide, The Fan, Enemy of the State, Spy Game, The Hire: Beat the Devil (short; also exec. prod.), Man on Fire (also prod.), Agent Orange, Domino (also prod.), Deja Vu, The Warriors (also prod.), Unstoppable (also prod.). *Cinematographer:* Forum. *Producer:* Welcome to the Rileys, Tell-Tale, The Taking of Pelham 123 (also dir.), The A-Team (also prod.). *Executive producer:* Clay Pigeons, Where the Money Is, Big Time (documentary), Six Bullets from Now, The Hire: Hostage (short), The Hire: Ticker (short), In Her Shoes, Tristan + Isolde, The Assassination of Jesse James by the Coward Robert Ford, Churchill at War, Sidney Hall, Cracks, Cyrus.
TELEVISION: *Movies:* Number One (actor only). *Executive pro*

ducer: RKO 281 (Emmy nom. 2000), The Last Debate, The Gathering Storm (Emmy Award 2002), Orpheus, Law Dogs, Into the Storm (Emmy nom. 2009), The Real Robin Hood (doc.), Nomads. *Mini-series:* Spearfield's Daughter (actor), The Company, The Andromeda Strain (Emmy nom. 2008), The Pillars of the Earth (exec. prod.). *Series: Executive producer:* AFP: American Fighter Pilot (exec. prod.), The Good Wife, Numb3rs.

SCOTT-THOMAS, KRISTIN
Actress. b. Redruth, Cornwall, England, May 24, 1960. Lived in France since age 18. e. Central School of Speech and Drama, London; Ecole Nationale des Arts et Technique de Theatre, Paris. Stage debut in La Lune Declinante Sur 4 Ou 5 Personnes Qui Danse. Other theatre work in Paris.
PICTURES: Djomel et Juliette, L'Agent Troube, La Meridienne, Under the Cherry Moon, A Handful of Dust, Force Majeure, Bille en tete, Autobus/In the Eyes of the World, The Governor's Party, The Bachelor, Bitter Moon, Somebody to Love, Four Weddings and a Funeral, An Unforgettable Summer, Mayday, The Confessional, Angels and Insects, Les Milles, Richard III, The Pompatus of Love, Portraits Chinois, Mission: Impossible, Microcosmos: Le Peuple de L'Herbe, The English Patient (Academy Award nom.; Golden Globe nom. 1997), Amour et Confusions, The Revengers' Comedies, The Horse Whisperer, Up at the Villa, Random Hearts, Play, Life as a House, Gosford Park, Small cuts, Arsène Lupin, Man to Man, Chromophobia, Tell No One, Mauvaise pente, The Walker, The Golden Compass (voice), The Other Boleyn Girl, Largo Winch, Easy Virtue, I've Loved You So Long (Golden Globe nom. 2009), Confessions of a Shopaholic, Leaving, Nowhere Boy, Contre toi, Crime d'amour, Elle s'appelait Sarah, The Woman in the Fifth, Bel Ami, The Galapagos Affair, Salmon Fishing in the Yemen.
TELEVISION: *Movies:* La Tricheuse, The Tenth Man, Framed, The Endless Game, The Secret Life of Ian Fleming, Weep No More My Lady, Gulliver's Travels. *Mini-series:* Mistral's Daughter, Titmuss Regained, Look At It This Way, Body and Soul, Belle Époque. *Guest:* More than 61 appearances.

SEAGAL, STEVEN
Actor, Director, Producer, Writer. b. Lansing, MI, April 10, 1951. Became skilled at martial arts at an early age, studying Aikido. Lived in Japan for 15 yrs. where he opened a martial arts academy. Opened similar academy upon his return to U.S. in Los Angeles. Was martial arts choreographer/coordinator on film The Challenge.
PICTURES: Above the Law (debut, 1988; also co-prod., co-story), Hard to Kill, Marked for Death (also co-prod.), Out for Justice (also co-prod.), Under Siege (also co-prod.), On Deadly Ground (also dir., co-prod.). Under Siege 2: Dark Territory (also co- prod.), Executive Decision, The Glimmer Man, Fire Down Below (also prod.), My Giant (cameo), The Patriot (also prod.), Get Bruce, Exit Wounds, Ticker, The Path Beyond Thought, Half Past Dead, The Foreigner, Out for a Kill (also prod.), Belly of the Beast (also prod.), Clementine, Out of Reach, (also exec. prod.), Into the Sun (also s.p. & prod.), Today You Die (also prod.), Submerged (also exec. prod.), Black Dawn, Harvester (also exec. prod.), Prince of Pistols (exec prod. only), The Onion Movie, The Keeper (also prod., writer), Driven to Kill (also exec. prod.), On the Run (also exec. prod.), Born to Raise Hell (also exec. prod., writer), Machete.
TELEVISION: *Series:* Steven Seagal: Lawman (also exec. prod.). *Guest:* More than 56 appearances.

SEAGROVE, JENNY
Actress. b. Kuala Lumpur, Malaysia, July 4, 1957. e. Bristol Old Vic. Theatre Sch. Stage debut 1979. Early TV: The Brack Report, The Woman in White, Diana. Recent stage: Jane Eyre, King Lear, Present Laughter, The Miracle Worker, Dead Guilty.
PICTURES: Moonlighting, Local Hero, Nate and Hayes, Appointment With Death, A Chorus of Disapproval, The Guardian, Bullseye!, Miss Beatty's Children, Don't Go Breaking My Heart, Zoe.
TELEVISION: *Movies:* Mark of the Devil, In Like Flynn, Hold The Dream, In Like Flynn, The Sign of Four, Killer, Lucy Walker, Magic Moments, Some Other Spring, The Betrothed, Deadly Game, The Incident at Victoria Falls, A Shocking Accident, Judge John Deed: Exacting Justice. *Mini-series:* The Woman in White, A Woman of Substance, Diana, I Promessi sposi. *Series:* The Brack Report, Judge John Deed, Identity.

SEALE, JOHN
Cinematographer. b. Warwick, Australia, Oct. 5, 1942. Camera operator on several films before becoming director of photography.
PICTURES: Deathcheaters, Fatty Finn, The Survivor, Doctors & Nurses, Fighting Back, Ginger Meggs, Goodbye Paradise, Careful He Might Hear You, BMX Bandits, Silver City, Witness (Academy Award nom. 1986), The Empty Beach, The Mosquito Coast, The Hitcher, Children of a Lesser God, Stakeout, Gorillas in the Mist, Rain Man (Academy Award nom.; ASC nom. 1989), Dead Poets Society, Till There Was You (dir. only), The Doctor, Lorenzo's Oil, The Firm, The Paper, Beyond Rangoon, The American President, Ghosts of Mississippi, The English Patient (Academy Award, ASC Award 1997), City of Angels, The Talented Mr. Ripley, At First Sight, The Perfect Storm (ASC nom. 2001), Harry Potter and the Sorcerer's Stone, Dreamcatcher, Cold Mountain (Academy Award nom.; ASC nom. 2004), Spanglish, Poseidon, Prince of Persia: The Sands of Time, The Tourist, The Rum Diary (dir. of photog.).
TELEVISION: *Movies:* Harness Fever, Dreamspeaker, Top Kid, New South Wales Images (documentary).

SEDGWICK, KYRA
Actress. b. New York, NY, Aug. 19, 1965. e. USC. m. actor Kevin Bacon.
THEATRE: *NY*: Time Was, Dakota's Belly Wyoming, Ah Wilderness (Theatre World Award), Maids of Honor, Twelfth Night. *LA*: Oleanna.
PICTURES: War and Love, Tai-Pan, Kansas, Born on the Fourth of July, Mr. & Mrs. Bridge, Pyrates, Singles, Heart & Souls, Murder in the First, Something to Talk About (Golden Globe nom. 1996), The Low Life, Losing Chase, Phenomenon, Montana (also assoc. prod.), Critical Care, Labor Pains, What's Cooking, Just A Kiss, Rumor Has It, Behind the Red Door, Secondhand Lions, The Woodsman, Cavedweller (also exec. prod.), Loverboy (also prod.), The Game Plan, Gamer, Chlorine.
TELEVISION: *Movies*: The Man Who Broke 1000 Chains, Women & Men II (In Love There Are No Rules), Miss Rose White (Golden Globe nom. 1993), Family Pictures, The Wide Net, Twelfth Night, or What You Will, Lemon Sky, Enter Fleeing, Door to Door, Something the Lord Made. *Series*: Another World, Talk to Me, Queens Supreme, The Closer (5 Emmy noms.; Golden Globe Award 2007, 4 other noms.). *Documentaries/Specials*: Cinder Ella: A Modern Fairy Tale, 100 Sexiest Artists (host). *Guest:* More than 74 appearances.

SEGAL, GEORGE
Actor. b. New York, NY, Feb. 13, 1934. e. Columbia U., B.A., 1955. Worked as janitor, ticket-taker, soft-drink salesman, usher and under-study at NY's Circle in the Square theatre. Acting debut: Downtown Theatre's revival of Don Juan. Formed a nightclub singing act with Patricia Scott. Record album of ragtime songs and banjo music: The Yama Yama Man. *Dir. debut*: Bucks County Playhouse prod. Scuba Duba.
THEATRE: The Iceman Cometh (1956 revival), Antony and Cleopatra N.Y. Shakespeare Festival, Leave It to Jane, The Premise (satiric improv revue), Gideon, Rattle of a Simple Man, The Knack, Requiem for a Heavyweight, The Fourth Wall.
PICTURES: The Young Doctors (debut, 1961), The Longest Day, Act One, The New Interns, Invitation to a Gunfighter, Ship of Fools, King Rat, Lost Command, Who's Afraid of Virginia Woolf? (Academy Award nom.; Golden Globe nom. 1967), The Quiller Memorandum, The St. Valentine's Day Massacre, Bye Bye Braverman, No Way to Treat a Lady, The Southern Star, The Bridge at Remagen, The Girl Who Couldn't Say No, Loving, The Owl and the Pussycat, Where's Poppa?, Born to Win, The Hot Rock, A Touch of Class (Golden Globe Award 1974), Blume in Love, The Terminal Man, California Split, Russian Roulette, The Black Bird, The Duchess and the Dirtwater Fox, Fun with Dick and Jane, Rollercoaster, Who Is Killing the Great Chefs of Europe?, Lost and Found, The Last Married Couple in America, Carbon Copy, Killing 'em Softly, Stick, All's Fair, Look Who's Talking, The Clearing, For the Boys, Look Who's Talking Now, Army of One, Direct Hit, Deep Down, Flirting With Disaster, The Cable Guy, The Feminine Touch, The Mirror Has Two Faces, Dinotopia: Curse of the Ruby Sunstone (voice), Heights, Retirement, Made for Each Other, 2012, Love and Other Drugs.
TELEVISION: *Movies*: Trackdown: Finding the Goodbar Killer, The Cold Room, The Zany Adventures of Robin Hood, Not My Kid, Many Happy Returns, Endless Game, Taking the Heat, Following Her Heart, Houdini, The Linda McCartney Story, The Making of a Hollywood Madam, The Electric Piper (voice), Fielder's Choice, Billy & Mandy's Big Boogey Adventure, Retired at 35. *Mini-series:* Picture Windows: Language of the Heart. *Series*: Take Five, Murphy's Law, High Tide, Just Shoot Me (2 Golden Globe noms.). *Documentaries/Specials:* Death of a Salesman, Of Mice and Men, The Desperate Hours, The Kiss. *Guest*: More than 92 appearances.

SEIDELMAN, ARTHUR ALLAN
Director, Producer, Writer. b. New York, NY, October 11. e. Whittier College, B.A.; UCLA, M.A. Former staff member, Repertory Theatre of Lincoln Center and Phoenix Theatre, NY.
THEATRE: *Director: LA*: The Sisters, Gypsy Princess, The Beautiful People, Five Finger Exercise, The Purification, etc. *Dir.: NY*: Awakening of Spring, Hamp, Ceremony of Innocence, The Justice Box, Billy, Vieux Carre, The World of My America, Awake and Sing, The Four Seasons, Inherit the Wind, The Most Happy Fella, as well as numerous regional prods. and national tours.
PICTURES: Hercules in New York, Children of Rage (dir., s.p.), Echoes, The Caller, Street Hunter, Trapped in Space, Walking Across Egypt, Peurto Vallarta Squeeze, The Sisters, Prep School (exec. prod.), In the Shadow of Wings, Chickadee.
TELEVISION: *Movies*: *Director*: The Ceremony of Innocence, My Other Mother, A Special Gift, Schoolboy Father, Which Mother Is Mine? (Emmy Award 1980), Matter of Time, I Think I'm Having a Baby (Emmy Award nom. 1981), She Drinks A Little (Emmy Award 1982), Sin of Innocence, Kate's Secret, Place At The Table, Glory Years, Poker Alice, An Enemy Among Us, Strange Voices, Look Away, Addicted to His Love, A Friendship in Vienna, The People Across the Lake, False Witness, The Kid Who Loved

Christmas, Body Language, Dying to Remember, Harvest of Fire, The Summer of Ben Tyler, Deep Family Secrets, Miracle in the Woods, Grace & Glorie, By Dawn's Early Light, Sex & Mrs. X, The Runaway, Like Mother-Like Son: The Strange Story of Sante and Kenny Kimes, A Christmas Carol: The Musical,The Kidnapping, The Venice Beach Hostel (exec. prod.). *Mini-series:* The Secrets of Lake Success (part 2). *Series: Director:* Family, The Paper Chase: The Third Year, Knots Landing, Hill Street Blues (Emmy Award nom. 1984), Paper Dolls, Fame, Murder She Wrote (five episodes), FBI: Untold Stories, Heaven Help Us. *Documentaries/Specials:* I Love Liberty (Emmy Award nom.; WGA Award 1982, writer).

SEIDELMAN, SUSAN
Director. b. Philadelphia, PA, Dec.11, 1952. e. Drexel Univ. B.A. Worked at a UHF television station in Phila., NYU film school M.F.A. Debut: 28-min. student film And You Act Like One Too. Then dir. Deficit (short, funded by AFI), and Yours Truly, Andrea G. Stern.
PICTURES: Smithereens (dir., prod., co-s.p.; 1st Amer. indep. feature accepted into competition at Cannes Film Fest., 1982), Desperately Seeking Susan, Making Mr. Right, Cookie (also exec. prod.), She-Devil, The Dutch Master (short, Academy Award nom. 1994), Tales of Erotica, Gaudi Afternoon, The Boynton Beach Club (also prod. & s.p.), Occupant (exec. prod.).
TELEVISION: *Movies:* Confessions of a Suburban Girl (BBC; also writer, actress), The Barefoot Executive, A Cooler Climate, Power and Beauty, The Ranch. *Series:* Early Edition, Sex and the City (pilot), Now and Again, Stella, The Electric Company.

SEINFELD, JERRY
Comedian, Actor, Writer. b. Brooklyn, NY, April 29, 1954. e. Queens College. Stand-up comic; guest host for The Tonight Show, Late Night With David Letterman. Received American Comedy Award for funniest male comedy stand-up, 1988.
AUTHOR: Seinlanguage (1993).
PICTURES: Pros and Cons (acting), A Uniform Used to Mean Something (writer), Hindsight is 20/20 (short; writer), Bee Movie (voice, writer).
TELEVISION: *Movies:* The Ratings Game (actor), Sincerely, Ted L. Nancy (writer, creator), The Marriage Ref (exec. prod.). *Series:* Benson, Seinfeld (also co-creator, writer, exec. prod. & prod. Emmy Award 1993, 12 other noms.; Golden Globe Award 1994, 3 other noms.), Stand Up America (as himself), The Marriage Ref (exec. prod., writer, panelist). *Pilot:* The Seinfeld Chronicles. *Documentaries/Specials:* Jerry Seinfeld—Stand-Up Confidential (also writer), Abott and Costello Meet Jerry Seinfeld (host), Jerry Seinfeld: "I'm Telling You for the Last Time" (as himself; also writer & exec. prod., Emmy nom. 1999), The Seinfeld Story (writer & exec. prod.). *Guest:* More than 142 appearances.

SELBY, DAVID
Actor. b. Morganstown, WV. Feb. 5, 1941. e. West Virginia U. Acted in outdoor dramas in home state and did regional theatre elsewhere. Was asst. instructor in lit. at Southern Illinois U.
PICTURES: Night of Dark Shadows, Up the Sandbox, Super Cops, Rich Kids, Raise the Titanic, Rich and Famous, Dying Young, Intersection, Headless Body in Topless Bar, White Squall, D3: The Mighty Ducks, The Affair., Shadow of Fear, Surviving Christmas, End Game, Unknown, Spin, Inhale, The Social Network.
TELEVISION: *Movies*: Telethon, The Night Rider, Love for Rent, Doctor Franken, King of the Olympics: The Lives and Loves of Avery Brundage, Grave Secrets: The Legacy of Hilltop Drive, Lady Boss, Alone, Soldier of Fortune, Larva, MorphMan, The Black Hole. *Mini-series*: Washington: Behind Closed Doors. *Series*: Dark Shadows, Flamingo Road, Falcon Crest, Soldier of Fortune, Inc., Tell Me You Love Me.

SELLECCA, CONNIE
Actress. b. Bronx, NY, May 25, 1955. m. John Tesh.
PICTURES: Eye of the Storm, I Saw Mommy Kissing Santa Claus, The Wild Stallion.
TELEVISION: *Movies*: The Bermuda Depths (debut, 1978), Flying High (pilot), Captain America II, She's Dressed to Kill, The Last Fling, International Airport, Downpayment on Murder, Brotherhood of the Rose, Turn Back the Clock, Miracle Landing, People Like Us, P.S.I. Luv U, A House of Secrets and Lies (also co-exec. prod.), Passport to Murder, She Led Two Lives, A Dangerous Affair, The Surrogate, A Holiday to Remember, Something Borrowed, Something Blue, Doomsday Rock, While My Pretty One Sleeps, Dangers Waters, Imminent Danger, Anna's Dream. *Series*: Flying High, Beyond Westworld, The Greatest American Hero, Hotel (Golden Globe nom. 1987), P.S. I Luv U, Second Chances. *Documentaries/Specials*: The Celebrity Football Classic, Celebrity Challenge of the Sexes, Circus of the Stars #5 (performer).

SELLECK, TOM
Actor. b. Detroit, MI, Jan. 29, 1945. e. U. of Southern California. Grew up in Southern California, appearing in several commercials before being signed to 20th Century Fox. First acting job was on TV series Lancer.
PICTURES: Myra Breckenridge (debut, 1970), Midway, The Washington Affair, Coma, High Road to China, Lassiter, Runaway, Three Men and a Baby, Her Alibi, An Innocent Man, Quigley Down Under, Three Men and a Little Lady, Folks!, Christopher Columbus: The Discovery, Mr. Baseball, In & Out, The Love Letter, Meet the Robinsons (voice), Killers.
TELEVISION: *Movies*: The Movie Murderer, A Case of Rape, Returning Home, Most Wanted, Bunco, Superdome, The Chinese Typewriter, The Sacketts, The Concrete Cowboys, Magnum P. I., Divorce Wars, Revealing Evidence: Stalking the Honolulu Strangler (exec. prod. only), Broken Trust, Ruby Jean and Joe (also exec. prod.), Last Stand at Saber River (also exec. prod.), Running Mates, Louis L'Amour's 'Crossfire Trail', Monte Walsh (also exec. prod.), 12 Mile Road, Reversible Errors, Ike: Countdown to D-Day, Stone Cold, Jesse Stone: Night Passage (also exec. prod.), Jesse Stone: Sea Change (also exec. prod., Emmy nom. 2007), Jesse Stone: Thin Ice (also exec. prod., writer), Jesse Stone: No Remorse (also exec. prod., writer). *Series*: The Young and the Restless, Magnum P.I. (Emmy Award, 1984; 5 other noms.; Golden Globe Award 1985, 6 other noms.), B.L. Stryker (exec. prod. only), The Closer (also exec. prod.), Friends (recurring role, Emmy nom. 2000), Boston Legal (recurring role), Las Vegas, Blue Bloods (pilot). *Specials/Documentaries:* The Magic of Flight, A&E Biography: Dwight D. Eisenhower - Supreme Commander-in-Chief, Dobe and a Company of Heroes, Kingdom of the Blue Whale (narr.). *Guest:* More than 140 appearances.

SELTZER, DAVID
Writer, Director. b. Highland Park, IL, 1940. m. flutist Eugenia Zukerman. e. Northwestern U. School for Film and Television. Moved to NY where worked on TV game show I've Got a Secret. Made short My Trip to New York. 1966 moved to LA to write for David Wolper's Incredible World of Animals. Then dir. and prod. Wolper documentaries. Worked as ghostwriter on film Willy Wonka and the Chocolate Factory.
PICTURES: *Writer*: The Hellstrom Chronicle (WGA nom. 1972), One Is a Lonely Number, The Omen (WGA nom. 1977), Damien: The Omen Part II, The Other Side of the Mountain, Six Weeks, Table for Five, Lucas (also dir.), Punchline (also dir.), Bird on a Wire, Shining Through (also dir., co-exec. prod.), The Eighteenth Angel, My Giant, Nobody's Baby (also dir.), Dragonfly, The Omen (2006), Cinema Verite.
TELEVISION: *Movies:* Larry, The Story of Eric, My Father's House, Green Eyes, Private Sessions, Omen IV: The Awakening. *Mini-series:* Revelations (also exec. prod.). *Documentaries / Specials:* Sophia: A Self-Portrait (writer), National Geographic Specials (prod., dir., writer), William Holden in Unconquered Worlds (prod., dir., writer), The Underworld World of Jacques Cousteau.

SEMEL, TERRY
Executive. b. New York, NY, Feb. 24, 1943. e. Long Island Univ., B.S. Accounting 1964. Warner Bros. sales trainee 1966. Branch mgr., Cleveland, Los Angeles. V.P. Domestic sls. mgr. for CBS, 1971-73. Buena Vista as v.p., gen. sls. mgr., 1973-5. 1975 went to Warner Bros. as pres. domestic sls. 1978 named exec. v.p. and COO WB Inc. Named pres., Warner Bros. & COO, 1980. Named Pioneer of the Year by Foundation of Motion Picture Pioneers, 1990. In 2001 Semel became chairman and CEO of Yahoo! Inc. Semel resigned Yahoo! post in June 2007 but remained as non-executive chairman. Resigned Jan. 2008.

SEMLER, DEAN
Cinematographer. b. Renmark, Australia, 1943. Served as 2nd unit dir. and cameraman on the mini-series Lonesome Dove, Son of the Morningstar.
PICTURES: The Earthling, The Coca Cola Kid, The Road Warrior, Hoodwink, Kitty and the Bagman, Razorback, Mad Max Beyond Thunderdome, The Coca-Cola Kid, Going Sane, The Lighthorsemen, Cocktail, Young Guns, Farewell to the King, K-9, Dead Calm, Impulse, Young Guns II, Dances With Wolves (Academy Award, ASC Award 1991), City Slickers, The Power of One, Super Mario Bros., Last Action Hero, The Three Musketeers, The Cowboy Way, Waterworld, Gone Fishin', Firestorm, The Bone Collector, The Nutty Professor II, The Patriot (dir.), D-Tox, Dragonfly, We Were Soldiers, XXX, The Adventures of Pluto Nash, Bruce Almighty, The Alamo, Stealth, The Longest Yard, Just My Luck, Click, Apocalypto (ASC nom. 2007), I Now Pronounce You Chuck and Larry, Get Smart (dir. of photog.), Appaloosa, 2012, Date Night, Secretariat.
TELEVISION: *Movies:* The Valley of Water (flr. mngr), Do I Have to Kill My Child?, A Good Thing Going, Cass (dir. of photog. 2nd unit), Passion Flower, The Clean Machine. *Mini-series:* The Dismissal, Return to Eden, Bodyline, Melba, Lonesome Dove.

SENA, DOMINIC
Director. b. Niles, Ohio, April 26, 1949.
PICTURES: Rhythm Nation 1814, Kalifornia, Gone in Sixty Seconds, Swordfish, A Normal Life, Whiteout, Season of the Witch.
TELEVISION: *Movie:* 13 Graves.

SERNA, ASSUMPTA
Actress. b. Barcelona, Spain, Sept. 16, 1957. Abandoned plans to be a lawyer, making stage debut 1978 with anti-Franco theatre company.
PICTURES: Sweet Hours (debut, 1980), The Hunting Ground, Crime of Cuenca, Revolt of the Birds, Circle of Passions, Tin

Soldier, Secret Garden, Extramuros, The Old Music, Lola, Matador, Ballad of Dogs, Lucky Ravi, La Brute, La Nuite de L'Ocean, What Belongs to Caesar, Neon Man, Wild Orchid, I the Worst of All, Rossini Rossini, Adelaide, Chain of Desire, Cracked Nut, Fencing Master, Green Henry, Nostradamus, Shortcut to Paradise, Belle al Bar, The Shooter, Como un Relampago, The Craft, Stolen Moments, Managua, Como un relampago, Why Not Me?, Nana, The Journeyman, Bullfighter, Le Intermittenze del cuore, Teresa Teresa, The Piano Tuner of Earthquakes, I Vicerè, Uncertainty, Trash, El asesino a sueldo.
TELEVISION: *Movies:* Valentina, Fur Elise, Drug Wars: The Cocaine Cartel, Revolver, Sharpe, Sharpe's Rifles, Sharpe's Eagle, Day of Reckoning, Sharpe's Company, Sharpe's Enemy, Les Derniers Jours de la Victime, Caligula, Nana, Henry VIII, Une autre vie, Los Recuerdos de Alicia, Don Quichotte ou Les mésaventures d'un homme en colère. *Mini-series:* Para Elisa. *Series:* Falcon Crest, Brigada central, Aquí no hay quien viva, 90-60-90. Diario secreto de una adolescente.

SEWELL, RUFUS
Actor. b. Twickenham, England, Oct. 29, 1967. e. London's Central School of Speech and Drama.
THEATRE: *London*: (stage debut) Making It Better, Arcadia. *B'way*: (debut) Translations.
PICTURES: Twenty-One, Dirty Weekend, A Man of No Importance, Victory, Cold Comfort Farm, Carrington, Hamlet, The Woodlanders, Illuminata, Dark City, The Very Thought of You, Dangerous Beauty, Martha Meet Frank Daniel and Laurence, Bless the Child, A Knight's Tale, Extreme Ops, Victoria Station (short), Legend of Zorro, Tristan + Isolde, Paris, je t'aime, Amazing Grace, The Holiday, Downloading Nancy, Vinyan, The Tourist.
TELEVISION: *Movies*: The Last Romantics, Dirtysomething, Cold Comfort Farm, Arabian Nights, She Creature, Helen of Troy, The Taming of the Shrew. *Mini-series*: Middlemarch, The Last King, John Adams, The Pillars of the Earth. *Series:* Gone to Seed, Eleventh Hour.

SEYMOUR, JANE
Actress. r.n. Joyce Frankenberg. b. Hillingdon, England, Feb. 15, 1951. Dancer with London Festival Ballet at 13. On B'way in Amadeus (1980). British Repetory including Canterbury, Harrogate, Sussex, Windsor.
PICTURES: Oh! What a Lovely, The Only Way, Young Winston, Live and Let Die, Sinbad and the Eye of the Tiger, Battlestar Galactica, Oh Heavenly Dog, Somewhere in Time, Lassiter, Head Office, The Tunnel, The French Revolution, Keys to Freedom, Quest for Camelot (voice), The New Swiss Family Robinson, Touching Wild Horses, Odd Girl Out, The Wedding Crashers, Blind Dating, After Sex, Wake, The Assistants, The Velveteen Rabbit, Freeloaders, Love, Wedding, Marriage, Scribble.
TELEVISION: *Movies:* Frankenstein, The Hanged Man, Here Come the Double Deckers, Frankenstein: The True Story, Benny and Barney: Las Vegas Undercover, Killer on Board, The Four Feathers, Battlestar Galactica, Love's Dark Ride, Dallas Cowboys Cheerleaders, The Badness Within Him, The Story of David, McCloud, The Scarlet Pimpernal, Phantom of the Opera, The Haunting Passion, Dark Mirror, Obsessed with a Married Woman, Jamaica Inn, The Woman He Loved (Golden Globe nom. 1989), Onassis: The Richest Man in the World (Emmy Award 1988), Jack the Ripper, Angel of Death, I Remember You, Are You Lonesome Tonight?, Matters of the Heart, Sunstroke (also exec. prod.), Dr. Quinn, Medicine Woman (pilot), Heidi, Praying Mantis (also co-exec. prod.), A Passion for Justice: The Hazel Brannon Smith Story (also co-exec. prod.), The Absolute Truth, A Marriage of Convenience, A Memory in My Heart, Murder in the Mirror, Enslavement: The True Story of Fanny Kemble (also exec. prod.), Yesterday's Children, Blackout, Dr. Quinn, Medicine Woman: The Heart Within, (also exec. prod.), Heart of a Stranger, Marple: Ordeal by Innocence, Dear Prudence. *Mini-series*: The Strauss Family, Our Mutual Friend, Captains and the Kings (Emmy nom. 1977), Seventh Avenue, The Awakening Land, East of Eden (Golden Globe Award 1982), The Sun Also Rises, Crossings, War and Remembrance (Emmy nom. ; Golden Globe nom. 1989), Memories of Midnight. *Series*: The Pathfinders, The Onedine Line, Dr. Quinn: Medicine Woman (2 Emmy noms.; Golden Globe, 1996, 3 other noms.), Smallville, Modern Men (also pilot). *Host*: The Heart of Healing. *Guest:* More than 200 appearances.

SHAFER, MARTIN
Producer, Executive. b. 1954. e. UCLA, 1975. J.D., Southwestern U. Law School, 1978. President of production, Embassy Pictures, 1985; exec. v.p., Twentieth Century Fox Film Corp. Motion Picture Division, 1986; co-founder, Castle Rock Entertainment, 1987. Currently he is chairman & CEO of Castle Rock Pictures, where he is responsible for the development, production, and distribution of all movies. In October 2000, Shafer received the Lifetime Achievement Award at Show East.
PICTURES: The Mountain Men, The Awakening (co-prod.), Modern Romance, Mother Lode (also writer), Music and Lyrics, Beowulf (exec. prod.), Chaos Theory (exec. prod.), Did You Hear About the Morgans?, Faster, Friends with Benefits.

SHAIMAN, MARC
Composer, Arranger. b. Newark, NJ, Oct. 22, 1959. Began career at 16 as vocal arranger for Bette Midler; became her Musical Director and Co-producer as well as writing special material for The Divine Miss M! Wrote music for Saturday Night Live; co-wrote musical material for Billy Crystal for the Academy Awards (Emmy Award for "Oscar Medleys"). Prod. and arranger for several Harry Connick, Jr. albums. Received Grammy noms. for "When Harry Met Sally" and "We Are In Love". Appeared on stage in Harlem Nocturne.
PICTURES: Divine Madness (music dir., arranger), The Cotton Club (music sprv., arranger), Broadcast News (cameo), Big Business (music sprv., arranger), Beaches (arranger), When Harry Met Sally... (music spvr.), Misery (music), Scenes From a Mall (music, adapt., cameo), City Slickers (music), Hot Shots (cameo), For the Boys (music sprv., arranger, co-composer), The Addams Family (music, cameo, co-wrote song "Mamuschka"), Sister Act (music, adapt.), Mr. Saturday Night (music, cameo), A Few Good Men (music), Life With Mikey (music spvr.), Sleepless in Seattle (musical spvr., co-wrote song "With a Wink and a Smile"; Academy Award nom. 1994), Hocus Pocus (music prod.), Heart and Souls (music, cameo), For Love or Money (co-composer), Addams Family Values (music), Sister Act 2: Back in the Habit (music, adaptations), That's Entertainment III (music spvr.), City Slickers II: The Legend of Curly's Gold (music), North (music, cameo), The American President (Academy Award nom. 1996), Speechless, Stuart Saves His Family, Forget Paris, The First Wives Club (Academy Award nom. 1997), Ghosts of Mississippi, Mother, George of the Jungle, In & Out, Patch Adams (Academy Award nom. 1999), My Giant, Simon Birch, The Out-of-Towners, South Park: Bigger Longer and Uncut (Academy Award nom. 2000), The Story of Us, The Kid, How Harry Met Sally, Get Over It, One Night at McCool's, What's the Worst that Could Happen, Down with Love, Alex and Emma, Marci X, The Cat in the Hat, Team America: World Police, Rumor Has It, Slammer, Bee Movie, The Bucket List, Hairspray (also music arr., exec. prod.), Bedtime Stories, Flipped.
TELEVISION: *Movies:* What's Alan Watching?, 61. *Mini-series:* From the Earth to the Moon (part eleven), Jackie's Back: Portrait of a Diva. *Series:* Bette, Greg the Bunny, Charlie Lawrence (theme), Saturday Night Live (Emmy nom. 1987). *Specials:* The 63rd Annual Academy Awards (Emmy nom. 1991), The 64th Annual Academy Awards (Emmy Award 1992), The 76th Annual Academy Awards Emmy nom. 2004), A Prayer for America: Yankee Stadium Memorial, The 79th Annual Academy Awards (Emmy nom. 2004), The A-List Awards, The 63rd Annual Tony Awards, The 82nd Annual Academy Awards (musical dir., Emmy nom. 2010).

SHALIT, GENE
Critic. b. New York, NY, March 25, 1932. e. U. of Illinois. Started as freelance writer; joined NBC Radio Network, working on Monitor, 1968. Has been book and film critic, sports and general columnist. Since 1973 has been featured regularly on NBC "Today" show. Edits newsletter Shalit's Sampler. *Host:* Mystery!

SHANDLING, GARRY
Actor, Comedian, Writer, Producer. b. Chicago, IL, Nov. 29, 1949. e. Univ. of AZ. Moved to LA where he became writer for such sitcoms as Sandford & Son, Welcome Back Kotter, Three's Company. Became stand-up comedian in nightclubs which led to appearances on The Tonight Show.
PICTURES: The Night We Never Met (debut, 1993), Love Affair, Mixed Nuts, Hurlyburly, Doctor Dolittle (voice), What Planet Are You From? (also s.p. & prod.), Town and Country, Tusker (voice), Over the Hedge (voice), Iron Man 2.
TELEVISION: *Movie:* Mother Goose Rock 'n' Rhyme. *Series*: Sanford and Son (writer), Welcome Back, Kotter (writer), It's Garry Shandling's Show (also exec. prod., writer; ACE Awards for Best Series & Actor), The Larry Sanders Show (also co-exec. prod., co-creator, co-writer, Emmy Award, 1998, 18 other noms.; 2 Golden Globe noms.; 2 WGA noms.). *Documentaries /Specials*: Garry Shandling—Alone in Las Vegas (also writer, prod.), It's Garry Shandling's Show—25th Anniversary Special (also exec. prod., writer), Grammy Awards (host), Garry Shandling: Stand-Up (also writer), Rutles 2: Can't Buy Me Lunch. *Guest:* More than 85 appearances.

SHANLEY, JOHN PATRICK
Writer, Director. b. New York, NY, 1950. e. NYU. Cameo role in 1988 film Crossing Delancey. Dir. and s.p. for short I am Angry.
THEATRE: *Writer*: Rockaway, Welcome to the Moon, Danny and the Deep Blue Sea, Savage in Limbo, Dreamer Examines His Pillow, Doubt (Won numerous awards including the Pulitzer Prize and Tony Award 2005). *Writer-Dir.:* Italian-American Reconciliation, Beggars in the House of Plenty, Four Dogs and Bone.
PICTURES: *Writer*: Moonstruck (Academy Award, WGA Award, Golden Globe nom. 1987), Five Corners (also assoc. prod.), The January Man, Joe Versus the Volcano (also dir.), Alive, We're Back!, Congo (s.p.), Papillionns de nuit, Bread and Tulips (s.p.), Doubt (s.p. also dir., Academy Award nom.; Golden Globe nom.; WGA nom. for s.p. 2009).
TELEVISION: *Movies:* Danny i Roberta, Live From Baghdad (Emmy nom. 2003).

SHAPIRO, LARRY
Executive. e. Bachelor's degree, Univ. of Pennsylvania. J.D., Univ. of Michigan. Shapiro was an associate at two Los Angeles-

area law firms-Weil, Gotshal & Manges, and O'Melveny & Myers-before joining The Walt Disney Company as v.p., counsel within Disney's corporate legal department, where he led numerous transactions, including Disney's acquisition of Starwave Corporation and its 1998 investment in Infoseek. Shapiro was a key player in the formation of Disney's Internet business division. Before the Nov. 1999 merger of Infoseek Corporation and Buena Vista Internet Group (BVIG), Shapiro was senior v.p., business and legal affairs. He currently is executive v.p., business development and operations for the Disney Interactive Media Group (DIMG). In this role, Shapiro leads global business development and strategy for the company across connected new media platforms including the Web, mobile devices and video game consoles. He also oversees DIMG's legal and public affairs functions.

SHAPIRO, NEAL B.
Executive. e. Tufts University. Graduated magna cum laude in 1980 with degrees in history and political science. Married to ABC News correspondent JuJu Chang. Served as the editor-in-chief of the Tufts Observer. He began broadcast career in 1980 as asst. to ABC News Vice President David Burke. He then held various positions including assignment editor for ABC News, producer for Nightline and producer in the ABC News Chicago bureau. While at ABC, Shapiro received a George Polk Award, two Emmy awards and an Investigative Reporter and Editors award. From 1986 until 1989, Shapiro was a special segment producer for World News Tonight, where he wrote and produced stories with Peter Jennings on Cuba, the Far East and the 1988 presidential campaign. He also was a producer for Chief Correspondent Richard Threlkeld. From 1989 to 1993, he served as broadcast producer of PrimeTime Live. Shapiro joined NBC in 1993 and served as exec. prod. of Dateline NBC until he was promoted to pres.- CEO NBC News in June 2001. Resigned NBC News President post Sept. 6, 2005. Became president and CEO of New York's WNET.ORG in Feb. 2007 which creates award-winning broadcast and web content in the areas of arts and culture, news and public affairs, science and natural history, documentaries, and children's programming for local, national and global audiences. WNET.ORG is the parent of New York public television stations Thirteen and WLIW21.

SHAPIRO, ROBERT W.
Producer. b. Brooklyn, NY, March 1, 1938. e. USC. Joined William Morris Agency, Inc., 1958; dir. and head of motion picture dept., William Morris Agency (UK) Ltd., 1969; mng. dir., 1970; 1974 v.p., head int'l. m.p. dept.; 1977 joined Warner Bros. as exec. v.p. in chg. of worldwide production; 1981, named WB pres., theatrical production div. Resigned 1983 to produce films.
PICTURES: Pee-Wee's Big Adventure, Empire of the Sun (exec. prod.), Arthur 2 On the Rocks, There Goes My Baby, Black Beauty, The Last Days of Paradise, Dr. Jekyll and Ms. Hyde, An Alan Smithee Film: Burn Hollywood Burn (actor only), My Favorite Martian, Baby Geniuses (production supervisor), 100 Mile Rule (production supervisor), Confessions of a Teenage Drama Queen.
TELEVISION: *Movies*: The Summer My Father Grew Up (exec. prod.), Cadet Kelly (exec. prod.).

SHARIF, OMAR
Actor. r.n. Michel Shahoub. b. Alexandria, Egypt, April 10, 1932. e. Victoria College, Cairo.; pres. of College Dramatic Society. Starred in 21 Egyptian (billed as Omar el Cherif or Omar Cherif) and two French films prior to English-language debut in Lawrence of Arabia. Left Egypt 1964. Champion contract bridge player. 1983 made rare stage appearance in The Sleeping Prince (Chichester, then West End).
PICTURES: The Blazing Sun (debut, 1954), Our Happy Days, La Chatelane du Liban, Goha, The Mameluks, Lawrence of Arabia (Academy Award nom.; 2 Golden Globe Awards 1963), The Fall of the Roman Empire, Behold a Pale Horse, Marco the Magnificent, Genghis Khan, The Yellow Rolls-Royce, Doctor Zhivago (Golden Globe Award 1966), The Poppy Is Also a Flower, The Night of the Generals, More Than a Miracle, Funny Girl, Mackenna's Gold, The Appointment, Mayerling, Che!, The Last Valley, The Horsemen, The Burglars, The Right to Love (Brainwashed), The Tamarind Seed, The Mysterious Island of Captain Nemo, Juggernaut, Funny Lady, Crime and Passion, The Pink Panther Strikes Again (cameo), Ashanti, Bloodline, The Baltimore Bullet, Oh Heavenly Dog, Green Ice, Chanel Solitaire, Top Secret!, The Possessed, Paradise Calling, The Blue Pyramids, Keys to Freedom, Novice, Mountains of the Moon, Michelangelo and Me, Drums of Fire, Le Guignol, The Puppet, The Rainbow Thief, Journey of Love, Mother, 588 Rue Paradis, Bridge Deluxe with Omar Sharif, Umm Kulthum, Lebanon: Imprisoned Splendour, Heaven Before I Die, Mysteries of Egypt, The 13th Warrior, The Parole Officer, Monsieur Ibrahim, Hidalgo, Fire at My Heart, One Night with the King: The Call of Destiny, Return of the Thief of Baghdad, 10,000 B.C. (narr.).
TELEVISION: *Movies:* Mysteries of the Great Pyramid (host), S*H*E, Pleasure Palace, Harem, Anastasia: The Mystery of Anna, Grand Larceny, Omar Sharif Returns to Egypt, The Mysteries of the Pyramids Live (host), Mrs. 'arris Goes to Paris, Lie Down with Lions, Gulliver's Travels, Katharina die Grosse, St. Peter, The Ten Commandments, Kronprinz Rudolf. *Mini-series:* The Far Pavilions, Peter the Great, Memories of Midnight, Mother, Shaka Zulu: The Citadel, The Ten Commandments, The Last Templar (parts 1 and 2). *Guest:* More than 97 appearances.

SHARP, ALAN
Writer. b. Glasgow, Scotland, 1934.
PICTURES: The Hired Hand, Ulzana's Raid, Billy Two Hats, Night Moves, The Osterman Weekend, Little Treasure (also dir.), Freeway, Cat Chaser (co-s.p.), Rob Roy, Dean Spanley.
TELEVISION: *Movies:* The Snoop Sisters, Coming Out of the Ice, Love and Lies, Descending Angel, Mission of the Shark: The Saga of the U.S.S. Indianapolis, The Last Hit, Betrayed by Love, The Poet, Lathe of Heaven, Reversible Errors, While I Was Gone, Avenger, Ben Hur. *Mini-series:* Nightmares and Dreamscapes: From the Stories of Stephen King (teleplay), Ben Hur.

SHATNER, WILLIAM
Actor. b. Montreal, Quebec, March 22, 1931. e. McGill U. Toured Canada in various stock, repertory companies before U.S. tv debut in 1956. *Author*: TekWar, TekLords, TekLab, Tek Vengeance, TekSecret, Believe, Star Trek Memories (co-author with Chris Kreski), Star Trek Movie Memories (co-author with Kreski), The Return, Man O'War.
THEATRE: *NY*: Tamburlaine the Great, The World of Susie Wong (Theatre World Award), A Shot in the Dark, L'Idiote.
PICTURES: The Brothers Karamazov (debut, 1958), Judgment at Nuremberg, The Explosive Generation, The Intruder, The Outrage, Incubus, White Comanche, Impulse, Big Bad Mama, The Devil's Rain, Kingdom of the Spiders, Land of No Return, Star Trek—The Motion Picture, The Kidnapping of the President, Visiting Hours, Star Trek II: The Wrath of Khan, Airplane II: The Sequel, Star Trek III: The Search for Spock, Star Trek IV: The Voyage Home, Star Trek V: The Final Frontier (also dir., orig. story), Bill & Ted's Bogus Journey (cameo), Star Trek VI: The Undiscovered Country, National Lampoon's Loaded Weapon 1, Star Trek: Generations, Trekkies, Land of the Free, Trinity and Beyond, Jefftowne, Free Enterprise, Nukes in Space, The First Men on the Moon, Miss Congeniality, Falcon Down, Osmosis Jones (voice), Festival in Cannes, Shoot or be Shot, Showtime, American Psycho II, Groom Lake, Dumb Fellas, Dodgeball: A True Underdog Story, Miss Congeniality 2: Armed and Fabulous, The Wild (voice), Over the Hedge (voice), Horrorween 3D (cameo), Quantum Quest: A Cassini Space Odyssey (voice), The Captains (doc., also dir., exec. prod., writer).
TELEVISION: *Movies*: Sole Survivor, Vanished, Owen Marshall: Counselor at Law (pilot), The People, The Hound of the Baskervilles, Incident on a Dark Street, Go Ask Alice, The Horror at 37000 Feet, Pioneer Woman, Indict and Convict, Pray for the Wildcats, Barbary Coast (pilot), Perilous Voyage, The Bastard, Little Women, Crash, Disaster on the Coastliner, The Baby Sitter, Secrets of a Married Man, North Beach and Rawhide, Broken Angel, Family of Strangers, Columbo: Butterfly in Shades of Grey, TekWar (also dir., co-exec. prod.), TekLab, TekWar: TekJustice, Janek: The Silent Betrayal, Prisoner of Zenda Inc., Dead Man's Island, The Kid (voice), A Carol Christmas, Last Laugh '05, Fire Serpent (writer, creator), Gotta Catch Santa Claus, Making a Scene (host). *Mini-series*: Testimony of Two Men, Voice of the Planet, A Twist in the Tale, Iron Chef, Everest. *Series*: For the People, Star Trek, Barbary Coast, Kung Fu: The Legend Continues (dir. only), T.J. Hooker, Rescue 911 (host), 3rd Rock from the Sun (Emmy nom. 1999), Perversions of Science (dir. only), A Twist in the Tale (narrator), TekWar: The Series (also dir., co-exec. prod.), Hercules (voice), The Practice (Emmy Award for guest actor 2004), Boston Legal (Emmy, Award 2005, 4 other noms.; Golden Globe Award 2005, 1 other nom.), $#*! My Dad Says, Aftermath with William Shatner (series doc., exec. prod.). *Documentaries/Specials*: The Andersonville Trial, TekPower, TekMoney, Ashes of Money, Trinity and Beyond. *Guest:* More than 397 appearances.

SHAVER, HELEN
Actress, Director. b. St. Thomas, Ontario, Canada, Feb. 24, 1951. e. Banff School of Fine Arts, Alberta. Worked on stage and screen in Canada before coming to Los Angeles 1978.
THEATRE: Tamara, Are You Lookin'? Ghost on Fire, A Doll's House, The Master Builder, The Hostage, Jake's Women (B'way debut; Theatre World Award).
PICTURES: Christina, Shoot, Starship Invasions, Outrageous!, High-Ballin', The Amityville Horror, In Praise of Older Women, Who Has Seen the Wind, Gas, Harry Tracy, The Osterman Weekend, Best Defense, Desert Hearts, The Color of Money, The Believers, The Land Before Time (voice), Walking After Midnight, Innocent Victim (Tree of Hands), Zebrahead, That Night, Dr. Bethune, Morning Glory, Change of Heart, Open Season, Born to Be Wild, The Craft, Rowing Through, Egg Salad, The Wishing Tree, We All Fall Down, Bear With Me, The Keeper, Numb.
TELEVISION: *Movies*: Lovey: Circle of Children II, Between Two Brothers, Many Happy Returns, The Park is Mine, Countdown To Looking Glass, No Blame, B.L. Stryker: The Dancer's Touch, Pair of Aces, Columbo: Rest in Peace Mrs. Columbo, Survive the Night, Poisoned By Love: The Kern County Murders, Trial & Error, The Forget-Me-Not Murders, Ride With the Wind, Without Consent, Janek: A Silent Betrayal, Falling for You, Trial & Error,

The Sweetest Gift, Summer's End (Emmy nom. 2000), Common Ground, Due East, The Risen, D.C. Sniper: 23 Days of Fear, The Man Who Lost Himself, The Stranger I Married, Ultra, A Very Merry Daughter of the Bride, Iris Expanding. *Series*: United States, Jessica Novak, Hill Street Blues (actor), WIOU, The Education of Max Bickford, Poltergeist: The Legacy (actor), Dead Like Me (dir.), Joan of Arcadia (dir.), Judging Amy (also series prod.), Law & Order: Special Victims Unit (episodes dir.). *Guest:* More than 80 appearances.

SHAW, MICHAEL M. (JOHN)
Executive. b. Ashland, KY, Jan. 10, 1945. e. Eastern KY Univ., Univ. of KY, Univ of MS. 1968-69, asst. booker, 20th Century Fox, Denver; 1969, head booker, Fox; 1970, salesman, Paramount Pictures, S.F.; 1970-71, head booker, sales Paramount L.A.; 1971-73, booker, Commonwealth Theatres; 1973, booker, McLendon theatres, Dallas; 1973-78, div. mngr. Mulberry Square Prods., Dallas; 1978-79, branch mngr. Filmways Pictures, Dallas; 1980-82, owner, Sequoyah Cinema Svc., Denver; 1983-87, head film buyer, Presidio Theatres, Austin; 1987-88, head film buyer, Santikos Theatres, San Antonio; 1988-present, pres./CEO, Film Booking Office Corp., Movieline Int'l, Dallas. Member: Motion Picture Pioneers, Variety Club.

SHAW, STAN
Actor. b. Chicago, IL, July 14, 1952. On stage received NAACP Image Award for West Coast premiere of Home, 1982.
PICTURES: The Bingo Long Travelling All-Stars and Motor Kings, Rocky, The Boys in Company C, The Great Santini, Tough Enough, Runaway, The Monster Squad, Harlem Nights, Fried Green Tomatoes, Body of Evidence, Rising Sun, Houseguest, Cutthroat Island, Daylight, Snake Eyes, Detonator.
TELEVISION: *Movies*: Call to Glory, Maximum Security, When Dreams Come True, The Gladiator, The Billionaire Boys Club, The Three Kings, Fear, Red River, The Court-Martial of Jackie Robinson, Lifepod, Rag and Bone, Freedom Song. *Mini-series*: Roots: The Next Generations, Heaven & Hell: North & South, Book III , When Love Kills: The Seduction of John Hearn. *Series*: The Mississippi.

SHAWN, WALLACE
Playwright, Actor. b. New York, NY, Nov. 12, 1943. Son of former New Yorker editor William Shawn. e. Harvard; Oxford U. Taught English in India on a Fulbright scholarship 1965-66. English, Latin and drama teacher, NY 1968-70.
THEATRE: *Writer*: Our Late Night (1975, Obie Award), The Mandrake (translation, also actor), A Thought in Three Parts, Marie and Bruce, The Hotel Play, Aunt Dan and Lemon (also actor), The Fever (Obie Award, 1991; also actor). *Opera*: The Music Teacher (with Allen Shawn). *Actor*: The Master and Margarita, Chinchilla, Wifey.
PICTURES: *Actor:* Manhattan (debut, 1979), Starting Over, All That Jazz, Cheaper to Keep Her, Simon, Atlantic City, My Dinner With Andre (also co-s.p.), The First Time, A Little Sex, Lovesick,Strange Invaders, Deal of the Century, Crackers, The Hotel New Hampshire, The Bostonians, Micki and Maude, Heaven Help Us, Nice Girls Don't Explode, Head Office, The Bedroom Window, Radio Days, Prick Up Your Ears, Princess Bride, The Moderns, She's Out of Control, Scenes From the Class Struggle in Beverly Hills, We're No Angels, Shadows and Fog, Mom and Dad Save the World, The Cemetery Club, The Meteor Man, Mrs. Parker and the Vicious Circle, Vanya on 42nd Street, The Wife, Kalamazoo (short), A Goofy Movie (voice), Clueless, Canadian Bacon, Toy Story (voice), All Dogs Go to Heaven II (voice), House Arrest, National Lampoon's Vegas Vacation, Just Write, Critical Care, My Favorite Martian, Toy Story 2 (voice), Buzz Lightyear of the Star Command: The Adventure Begins (voice), The Prime Gig, The Curse of the Jade Scorpion, Love Thy Neighbor, Personal Velocity, Duplex, The Haunted Mansion, Teacher's Pet (voice), Melinda and Melinda, The Incredibles (voice), Chicken Little (voice), Happily N' Ever After (voice), Southland Tales, Kit Kittredge: An American Girl, The Speed of Thought, Jack and the Beanstalk, Toy Story 3 (voice), Cats & Dogs: The Revenge of Kitty Galore (voice). *Writer:* The Designated Mourner, Marie and Bruce, The Fever.
TELEVISION: *Movies:* How to Be a Perfect Person In Just Three Days, Just Like Dad, Noah, Blind Men, Mr. St. Nick, Monte Walsh, Karroll's Christmas. *Mini-series:* Blonde. *Series:* One Life to Live, Clueless, The Lionhearts (voice), Teacher's Pet (voice), Star Trek: Deep Space Nine, The 12th Man (pilot), Crossing Jordan, The L Word, Gossip Girl, Kung Fu Panda: Legends of Awesomeness. *Guest:* More than 69 appearances.

SHAYE, ROBERT
Executive, Producer, Director, Actor. b. Detroit, MI, March 4, 1939. e. U. of Michigan, B.B.A.; Postgraduate, Sorbonne Univ., 1961. Columbia U. Law, J.D. degree, 1964. At 15 wrote, prod. dir. training film for father's supermarket staff. Later won first prize in Society of Cinematologists' Rosenthal Competition (best m.p. by American dir. under 25). Wrote, prod., dir., edited short films, trailers and TV commercials, including award-winning shorts, Image and On Fighting Witches (prod., dir.). Founded New Line Cinema, 1967 with Michael Lynne, a fellow classmate at Columbia Law School. Lynne, together with Shaye, was an executive producer of New Line's The Lord of the Rings trilogy, of which the final installment, The Return of the King, was the winner of 11 Academy Awards, including best picture, tying the record for most wins ever. On Feb. 28, 2008, Warner Bros. Pictures, A Time Warner Company, announced New Line Cinema would be absorbed into the Warner Bros. organization. With this reorganization, company co-chairmen and co-CEOs Shaye and Lynne, departed the company. Shay has been a member of the Motion Picture Pioneers bd. of dir.; member of NYC Friar's Club.
PICTURES: *Director:* Image (short), On Fighting Witches (also cinematographer), Book of Love, The Last Mimzy (also exec. prod.). *Producer/Executive Producer:* Stunts (also writer), Polyester The First Time, Alone in the Dark, Xtro, A Nightmare on Elm Street (also parts 2,3,4,5,6), Critters, Quiet Cool, My Demon Lover, The Hidden, Stranded, Critters 2, Hairspray, Heart Condition (assoc. prod.), Freddy's Dead: The Final Nightmare (also actor), Blink, Wes Craven's New Nightmare, Frequency, The Lord of the Rings: The Fellowship of the Ring (exec. prod./New Line Cinema), The Lord of the Rings: The Two Towers, Freddy Vs. Jason (also actor), The Lord of the Rings: The Return of the King, The Last Mimzy, Hairspray, The Golden Compass, A Nightmare on Elm Street. *Actor:* Man's Best Friend, Festival in Cannes, Cellular.
TELEVISION: *Series:* Freddy's Nightmares (exec. prod.).

SHEA, JOHN
Actor. b. Conway, NH, April 14, 1949. Raised in MA. e. Bates Coll., ME, B.A. 1970; Yale Drama School, M.F.A. 1973. Worked as asst. dir. Chelsea Theater; taught part-time at Pratt Inst.
THEATRE: Yentl (debut 1975, Off-B'way and B'way; Theatre World Award), Sorrows of Stephen, Long Day's Journey Into Night (Joseph Jefferson Award nom.), The Master and Margarita, Romeo and Juliet (Circle in the Sq.), American Days (Drama Desk Award), The Dining Room, End of the World (B'way), The Normal Heart (London, 1987), Animal Kingdom, Rosmersholm (La Mama), Impossible Spy (China's Golden Panda Award).
PICTURES: Hussy, Missing, Windy City (Best Actor Montreal Film Festival), A New Life, Unsettled Land, Honeymoon, Stealing Home, Freejack, Honey I Blew Up the Kid, A Weekend in the Country, Brass Ring (also dir., co-writer), Nowhere to Go, Southie, The Adventures of Sebastian Cole, Lost & Found, Getting Personal, Catalina Trust, Heartbreak Hospital, The Insurgents, Framed, Achchamundu! Achchamundu!, An Invisible Sign, Low Grounds: The Portal, The Italian Key, 51.
TELEVISION: *Movies*: The Nativity, Family Reunion, Coast to Coast (BBC), Hitler's S.S.: Portrait in Evil, A Case of Deadly Force, The Impossible Spy, Magic Moments, Baby M (Emmy Award 1988), Do You Know the Muffin Man, Small Sacrifices, Notorious, Ladykiller, Justice in a Small Town, See Jane Run, Forgotten Sins, A Weekend in the Country, The Apocalypse Watch. *Mini-series*: The Last Convertible, Kennedy, A Will of Their Own. *Series*: WIOU, Lois and Clark, Mutant X, Gossip Girl. *Documentaries/Specials*: Leslie's Folly, Lincoln (narr.). *Guest:* More than 47 appearances.

SHEARER, HARRY
Writer, Actor. b. Los Angeles, CA, Dec. 23, 1943. e. UCLA (pol. science); grad. work in urban gov., Harvard. At 7 appeared on The Jack Benny Show. Worked as freelance journalist for Newsweek, L.A. Times and publ. articles in New West, L.A. Magazine and Film Comment. Also taught h.s. Eng. and social studies and worked in CA State Legislature in Sacramento. Founding mem. The Credibility Gap, co-wrote, co-prod. and performed on comedy group's albums (A Great Gift Idea, The Bronze Age of Radio). Co-wrote, co-prod. Albert Brooks' album A Star is Bought. Performed with group Spinal Tap. Host of Le Show, L.A. radio prog. Writer-cast mem. Saturday Night Live (1979-80 & 1984-85).
THEATRE: Accomplice (Pasadena Playhouse).
PICTURES: Abbott and Costello Go to Mars (debut, as child, 1953), Cracking Up, Real Life (also co-s.p.), Animalympics (voice), The Fish That Saved Pittsburgh, Serial, One-Trick Pony, The Right Stuff, This is Spinal Tap (also co-s.p.), Plain Clothes, My Stepmother is an Alien (voice), Oscar, Pure Luck, Blood & Concrete, The Fisher King, A League of Their Own, Wayne's World 2, I'll Do Anything, Speechless, My Best Friend's Wedding, Godzilla, Encounters in the Third Dimension (voice), Almost Heroes, The Truman Show, Small Soldiers (voice), Dick, Edtv, Ghost Dog: The Way of the Samurai (voice), Cyber World (voice), Edwurd Fudwupper Fibbed Big (voice), Haiku Tunnel, Haunted Castle (voice), Teddy Bears' Picnic (also writer), A Mighty Wind (also composer), Chicke Little (voice), My Suicide, For Your Consideration, A Couple of White Chicks at the Hairdresser, Buster's Class Project, The Simpsons Movie (voices), Flood Streets.
TELEVISION: *Movies:* Serpico: The Deadly Game, National Lampoon Presents Disco Beaver from Outer Space (writer), The T.V. Show (various characters; also writer, composer & prod.), Million Dollar Infield, Viva Shaf Vegas (also writer, dir. & exec. dir.), The History of White People in America: Volume II (also dir.), State of the Union: Undressed, Live Earth. *Series*: Saturday Night Live '80 (various characters; also writer, 1979, 1980 & 1984 Emmy nom. 1980), Fernwood 2-Night (creative consultant), The Simpsons (voice, Emmy nom. 2009), America 2-Night (Emmy nom. 1978), Harry Shearer's News Quiz, Sunday Best (sketch

characters). *Documentaries/Specials*: Likely Stories, It's Just TV, Paul Shaffer: Comedy Hour, Portrait of a White Marriage (also dir.), The Magic of Live, Spinal Tap Reunion (also co-writer), The Simpsons Christmas Special (voices). *Guest:* More than 190 appearances.

SHEARMUR, ALLI

Executive. e. Undergrad of Univ. of Pennsylvania; J.D. from USC Law Center; Member of the California bar. Early in career, Shearmur served in a variety of positions at Columbia Pictures Entertainment/Sony Pictures, including dir., comedy development at Columbia Pictures Television. Became vice president for Stewart Pictures, where she acquired and helped develop children's classic, "Madeline." From 1994-1997, v.p., production for Walt Disney Pictures. Moved to Universal Pictures as executive v.p., production, overseeing such hits as "The Bourne Supremacy," "The Bourne Identity," "American Pie" trilogy, "Along Came Polly" and "Erin Brockovich." From 2005-2007, she was co-pres., production, Paramount Pictures, where she spearheaded such productions as ""Dreamgirls," "The Curious Case of Benjamin Button" among others. Left Paramount in 2007 amid exec. reshuffling and resurfaced in Aug. 2008 in current position-pres., motion picture production-for Lionsgate Motion Picture Group. She is responsible for producing six-to-eight films annually.

SHEEDY, ALLY

Actress. r.n. Alexandra Sheedy. b. New York, NY, June 13, 1962. e. USC. m. actor David Lansbury. Daughter of literary agent Charlotte Sheedy. As child performed with American Ballet Theatre. At age 12 wrote children's book, She Was Nice to Mice; later wrote pieces for NY Times, Village Voice, Ms. Published book of poetry: Yesterday I Saw the Sun. Began acting in TV commercials at 15. Chicago Theatre in Wrong Turn at Lungfish; NY stage debut in Advice from a Caterpillar.
PICTURES: Bad Boys (debut, 1983), WarGames, Oxford Blues, The Breakfast Club, St. Elmo's Fire, Twice in a Lifetime, Blue City, Short Circuit, Maid to Order, Heart of Dixie, Betsy's Wedding, Only the Lonely, Home Alone 2: Lost in New York (cameo), Tattletale, The Pickle, Man's Best Friend, One Night Stand, High Art, Sugar Town, Autmn Heart, I'll Take You There, Advice from a Caterpillar, Just A Dream, Happy Here and Now, A Good Night to Die, Searching for Debra Winger (documentary), Shelter Island, Noise, Shooting Livien, The Veteran, Day Zero, Perestroika, Life During Wartime, Ten Stories Tall.
TELEVISION: *Movies*: The Best Little Girl in the World, The Violation of Sarah McDavid, The Day the Loving Stopped, Splendor in the Grass, Deadly Lessons, We Are the Children, Fear, The Lost Capone, Lethal Exposure, Chantilly Lace, Ultimate Betrayal, Parallel Lives, The Haunting of Seacliff Inn, The Tin Soldier, The Fury Within, Our Guys: Outrage at Glen Ridge, Walking After Midnight, The Warden, The Interrogation of Michael Crowe, Life on the Line, The Veteran, Citizen Jane. *Series:* Kyle XY. *Guest:* More than 64 appearances.

SHEEN, CHARLIE

Actor. r.n. Carlos Irwin Estevez. b. Los Angeles, Sept. 3, 1965. Father is actor Martin Sheen. Brother of actors Emilio, Ramon and Renee Estevez. Made debut as extra in TV movie, The Execution of Private Slovik (starring father) and as extra in Apocalypse Now (also starring father).
PICTURES: Grizzly II—The Predator, Red Dawn, The Boys Next Door, Lucas, Ferris Bueller's Day Off, The Wraith, Platoon, Wisdom, Three for the Road, No Man's Land, Wall Street, Never on Tuesday, Young Guns, Eight Men Out, Major League, Beverly Hills Brats, Courage Mountain, Navy Seals, Men at Work, The Rookie, Cadence, Hot Shots!, National Lampoon's Loaded Weapon 1 (cameo), Hot Shots Part Deux!, DeadFall, The Three Musketeers, The Chase (also co-exec. prod.), Major League 2, Beyond the Law, Terminal Velocity, The Shadow Conspiracy, All Dogs Go to Heaven II (voice), The Arrival, Money Talks, Postmortem, No Code of Conduct, Free Money, Being John Malkovich (cameo), Five Aces, Rated X, Famous, Good Advice, Scary Movie 3, Deeper than Deep, The Big Bounce, Foodfight! (voice), Scary Movie 4, Wall Street: Money Never Sleeps, Guns of the Dead.
TELEVISION: *Movies*: The Execution of Private Slovik, Silence of the Heart, Backtrack, The Fourth Wise Man, Out of the Darkness. *Series:* Sugar Hill, Spin City (Golden Globe Award 2002), Two and a Half Men (4 Emmy noms.; 2 Golden Globe noms.). *Guest:* More than 103 appearances.

SHEEN, MARTIN

Actor. r.n. Ramon Antonio Gerard Estevez. b. Dayton, OH, Aug. 3, 1940. Father of actors Emilio Estevez, Charlie Sheen, Ramon Estevez and Renee Estevez. Wrote play (as Ramon G. Estevez) Down the Morning Line (prod. Public Theatre, 1969). Emmy Award as dir., exec. prod. Babies Having Babies (1986).
THEATRE: The Connection (debut, 1959 with the Living Theater), Women of Trachis, Many Loves, In the Jungle of Cities, Never Live Over a Pretzel Factory, The Subject Was Roses, The Wicked Crooks, Hamlet, Romeo and Juliet, Hello Goodbye, The Happiness Cage, Death of a Salesman (with George C. Scott), Julius Caesar, The Crucible.
PICTURES: The Incident (debut, 1967), The Subject Was Roses (Golden Globe nom. 1969), Catch-22, No Drums No Bugles, Rage, Pickup on 101, Badlands, The Legend of Earl Durrand, The Cassandra Crossing, The Little Girl Who Lives Down the Lane, Apocalypse Now, Eagle's Wing, The Final Countdown, Loophole, Gandhi, That Championship Season, Enigma, Man Woman and Child, The Dead Zone, Firestarter, The Believers, Siesta, Wall Street, Walking After Midnight, Da (also co-exec. prod.), Judgment in Berlin (also exec. prod.), Beverly Hills Brats, Cold Front, Beyond the Stars, The Maid, Cadence (also dir.), JFK (narrator), Hear No Evil, Hot Shots Part Deux (cameo), Gettysburg, Trigger Fast, Hits!, Fortunes of War, Sacred Cargo, The Break, Dillinger & Capone, Captain Nuke and the Bomber Boys, Ghost Brigade, The Cradle Will Rock, Dead Presidents, Dorothy Day, Gospa, The American President, The War At Home, Spawn, Taylor's Campaign, Stranger in the Kingdom, Snitch, Shadrach (voice), No Code of Conduct, Gunfighter, Free Money, Texas Funeral, Ninth Street, Lucky Town, O, The Papp Project, The Confidence Game, Catch Me If You Can, Mercy of the Sea, The Commission, Bordertown, The Departed, Bobby, Flatland: The Movie, Talk to Me, Chamaco, Echelon Conspiracy, Imagine That, Bhopal: A Prayer for Rain, Love Happens, The Way, Flatland: An IMAX 3D Experience, The Double.
TELEVISION: *Movies*: Then Came Bronson, Mongo's Back in Town, Welcome Home Johnny Bristol, That Certain Summer, Letters for Three Lovers, Pursuit, Catholics, Message to My Daughter, The Execution of Private Slovik (Emmy nom. 1974), The California Kid, The Missiles of October, The Story of Pretty Boy Floyd, Sweet Hostage, The Guardian, The Last Survivors, The Long Road Home (Emmy Award, 1981), In the Custody of Strangers, Choices of the Heart, Consenting Adult, Shattered Spirits, News at Eleven, Out of the Darkness, Samaritan, Conspiracy: The Trial of the Chicago 8, No Means No (exec. prod. only), Nightbreaker (also exec. prod.), Guilty Until Proven Innocent, The Water Engine (voice), The Last P.O.W.?: The Bobby Garwood Story, A Matter of Justice, One of Her Own, Roswell, Voyage of Terror, Babylon 5: The River of Souls, The Darklings, Storm, The Time Shifters, D.R.E.A.M. Team, Forget Me Never, Thrill Seekers, The Apostle Paul: The Man Who Turned the World Upside Down (narr.), Insight (Emmy Award 1981). *Mini-series*: Blind Ambition (Golden Globe nom. 1980), Kennedy (Golden Globe nom. 1984), Queen, Medusa's Child, The Atlanta Child Murders. *Series*: The Edge of Night, As the World Turns, Captain Planet and the Planeteers (voice), Stories from My Childhood (voice), Chicken Soup for the Soul, The West Wing (6 Emmy noms; Golden Globe Award, Best Actor in series, 2001, 4 Golden Globe noms.), Two and a Half Men (guest actor Emmy nom. 2006), CBS Schoolbreak Special (Emmy Award 1986 for best dir.). *Documentaries/Specials:* A Salute to American Imagination, In the Name of the People, Spaceflight, Broken Rainbow, Atocha: Quest for Treasure, Dear America: Letters Home from Vietnam, A China Odyssey: 'Empire of the Sun', a film by Steven Spielberg, Walking After Midnight, The More You Know, My Home, My Prison, Alive: 20 Years Later, 1968: The 25th Anniversary, Congo: Journey Into the Unknown, The Great War and the Shaping of the 20th Century, An Act of Conscience, Tudjman, Titanic: Anatomy of a Disaster, Croatia: Land of 1,100 Islands & 101 Dalmations, 187: Documented, Holes in Heaven, Cinema Combat, High Tension, Low Budget (The Making of a Letter From Death Row), War Dogs: America's Forgotten Heroes, The Vietnam War: A Descent Into Hell, Hollywood, D.C., Stockpile, The Papp Project, Fate Did Not Let Me Go, Rosy-Fingered Dawn: a Film on Terrence Malick, Straight Up: Helicopters in Action (narr.), Freedom: A History of Us (series doc., actor), All the Presidents' Movies, Tibet: Cry of the Snow Lion, Rebel Frontier (narr.), On the Line: Dissent in an Age of Terrorism, Bringing Down a Dictator (narr.), The Perilous Fight: America's World War II in Color (series doc. narr.), Rebel Frontier (narr.), Why Shakespeare? (short), James Dean: Forever Young (narr.), Aleut Story (narr.), Who Killed the Electric Car? (narr.), Between Iraq and a Hard Place (narr.), Ten Days That Unexpectedly Changed America: The Homestead Strike (narr.), Freedom: A History of Us, Return to El Salvador (narr.), Shay Cullen: A Life Story (voice), many more documentaries as himself or narrator. *Guest*: More than 302 appearances.

SHEEN, MICHAEL

Actor. b. February 5, 1969, Gwent, Wales. e. Bristol Old Vic Theatre School.
THEATRE: *London:* Moonlight, The U.N. Inspector, Charley's Aunt, The Ends of the Earth, The Dresser, Look Back In Anger, Caligula, Henry V, Don't Fool With Love, Moonlight, When She Danced, Romeo and Juliet, Peer Gynt, The Homecoming, The Seagull, Look Back in Anger. *London/B'way:* Amadeus.
PICTURES: Othello, Mary Reilly, Wilde, The Four Feathers, Bright Young Things, Underworld, Timeline, Laws of Attraction, Kingdom of Heaven, Underworld: Evolution, The Queen, Blood Diamond, Music Within (also soundtrack per.), Frost/Nixon, Underworld: Rise of the Lycans, The Damned United, My Last Five Girlfriends, New Moon, Unthinkable, Alice in Wonderland (voice), Tron Legacy, Beautiful Boy, Midnight in Paris, Jesus Henry Christ, The Twilight Saga: Breaking Dawn - Part 2.
TELEVISION: *Movies:* Doomwatch: Winter Angel (voice), The Deal, Dirty Filthy Love, Kenneth Williams: Fantabulosa!, HG Wells: War with the World, A Child's Christmases in Wales (voice), The Special Relationship (Emmy nom. 2010). *Mini-*

series: The Battle for Rome. *Series:* Gallowglass, 30 Rock. *Guest:* More than 63 appearances.

SHEFFER, CRAIG
Actor. b. York, PA, April 23, 1960. e. East Stroudsberg Univ., PA. Started career in TV commercials; in soap opera, One Life to Live. On NY stage in Fresh Horses, G.R. Point, Torch Song Trilogy (B'way & Off-B'way). Starred in IMAX film Wings of Courage.
PICTURES: That Was Then This Is Now (debut, 1985), Fire with Fire, Some Kind of Wonderful, Voyage of the Rock Aliens, Split Decisions, Kid Gloves, Nightbreed, Instant Karma (also prod.), Blue Desert, Eye of the Storm, A River Runs Through It, Fire in the Sky, The Program, Fire on the Amazon, The Road Killers, Sleep With Me, Bloodknot, Wings of Courage (short), The Grave, Head Above Water, Flypaper, Double Take, Bliss, The Fall, Rhapsody in Bloom, Shadow of Doubt, Merlin: The Return, Net Worth, Fear of Flying, Deep Core 2000, Hellraiser: Inferno, Touched, Deadly Little Secrets, Berserker, Flying Virus, Turnaround, Water Under the Bridge, Dracula II: Ascension, The Second Front, Prodigal Son (short; also dir.), Tom's Nu Heaven, While She Was Out, Ashley's Ashes. *Director:* American Crude (also s.p. & prod.). *Executive producer:* Demolition Man.
TELEVISION: *Movies*: Babycakes, In Pursuit of Honor, A Season in Purgatory, The Desperate Trail, Miss Evers' Boys, Merry Christmas George Bailey, Without Malice, Cabin Pressure, Long Lost Son, Lies Between Friends. *Mini-series:* Into the West. *Series*: One Life to Live, Hamptons, One Tree Hill.

SHEINBERG, SIDNEY JAY
Executive, Producer. b. Corpus Christi, TX, Jan. 14, 1935. e. Columbia College, A.B. 1955; LL.B., 1958. Admitted to California bar, 1958; assoc. in law U. of California School of Law, Los Angeles, 1958-59; joined MCA, Inc, 1959; pres., TV div., 1971-74; exec. v.p., parent co., 1969-73. Named MCA pres. & chief oper. off., 1973. Resigned from position 1995 to form company, The Bubble Factory, to produce films for MCA. 1990 received DGA Honorary Life Member Award.
PICTURES: *Producer:* The Pest, McHale's Navy, A Simple Wish, For Richer or Poorer, Slappy and the Stinkers, Playing Mona Lisa, A Fate Totally Worse than Death, The Devil's Tomb, Burden (exec. prod.), Blood Is Blood.

SHELDON, DAVID
Producer, Director, Writer. b. New York, NY. e. Yale U. School of Drama, M.F.A.; Principia College, B.A.; Actors Studio, directors unit. 1972-74 was exec. at American Int'l Pictures supervising development and production of 18 films. Was director and producer with The Gateway Playhouse in NY where dir. over 50 plays and musicals. Started the Sheldon/Post Company in 1991 with Ira Post. *Exec. prod./writer* of Secret of a Small Town. CEO Prod./Dir., Joda Productions.
PICTURES: *Producer:* Sheba Baby (also writer), Grizzly (also writer), Project: Kill, Lovely But Deadly (also writer & dir.), Just Before Dawn, Lady Samurai (consult. prod.). *Writer:* Grizzly II: The Predator. *Director:* Grizzly Adams and the Legend of Dark Mountain.

SHELLEY, CAROLE
Actress. b. London, England, Aug. 16, 1939. e. Arts Educational Sch., RADA.
THEATRE: *NY:* The Odd Couple (debut, 1965), The Astrakhan Coat, Loot, Sweet Potato, Little Murders, Hay Fever, Absurd Person Singular (Tony nom.), The Norman Conquests, The Elephant Man (Tony Award, 1979), Twelve Dreams (Obie Award), The Misanthrope, Noises Off, Stepping Out (Tony nom.), What the Butler Saw, The Miser, Maggie and Misha, The Destiny of Me, Later Life, London Suite, Show Boat, Billy Elliot: The Musical. *London:* Simon and Laura (debut, 1955), New Cranks, Boeing-Boeing, Mary Mary, Lettice and Lovage. Also appearances with Shaw Festival, Stratford Fest., Amer. Shakespeare Fest., etc.
PICTURES: Give Us this Day (debut, 1949), Cure for Love, It's Great to Be Young, Carry on Regardless, Carry on Cabby, The Odd Couple, The Boston Strangler, The Aristocats (voice), Robin Hood (voice), The Super, Little Noises, Quiz Show, The Road to Wellville, Hercules (voice), Jungle 2 Jungle, Bewitched.
TELEVISION: *Movie:* Devlin. *Series:* The Odd Couple, Another World, One Life to Live. *Documentaries/Specials:* Coconut Downs, Gabby, A Salute to Noel Coward.

SHELTON, RON
Writer, Director, Producer. b. Whittier, CA, Sept. 15, 1945. e. Westmont Coll., Santa Barbara, CA, 1967; U. of Arizona, Tucson, AZ, 1974. For 5 years played second base for Baltimore Orioles farm team. Cleaned bars and dressed mannequins to support his art: painting and sculpture. A script he wrote, A Player to Be Named Later (which he later filmed himself as Bull Durham), attracted attention of dir. Roger Spottiswoode who directed his first two scripts.
PICTURES: *Associate producer:* The Pursuit of D. B. Cooper Executive producer: Open Season, No Vacancy. *Writer:* Under Fire (also 2nd unit dir.), The Best of Times (also 2nd unit dir.), Bull Durham (also dir., Academy Award nom.; WGA Award 1989), Blaze (also dir.), White Men Can't Jump (also dir.), Blue Chips (also co-exec. prod.), Cobb (also dir.), The Great White Hype (co-s.p.), Tin Cup (also dir.), Play it to the Bone (also dir.), Hollywood Homicide (also dir.), Bad Boys II. *Director:* Dark Blue.
TELEVISION: *Movie:* Game of Shadows (writer, dir.). *Series:* 30 for 30 (dir.). Numerous video documentaries related to film production

SHEPARD, SAM
Writer, Actor. r.n. Samuel Shepard Rogers. b. Fort Sheridan, IL, Nov. 5, 1943. Raised in California, Montana and South Dakota. Worked as stable hand, sheep shearer, orange picker in CA, a car wrecker in MA and musician with rock group Holy Modal Rounders. Lived near San Francisco, where, in addition to writing, ran a drama workshop at the U. of California at Davis. Recipient of Brandeis U. Creative Arts Citation, 1976, and American Acad. of Arts and Letters Award, 1975.
THEATRE: *Playwright*: Icarus' Mother, Red Cross (triple bill—Obie Award, 1966), La Turista (Obie Award, 1967), Forensic and the Navigators, Melodrama Play, Tooth of Crime (Obie Award, 1973), Back Dog Beast Bait, Operation Sidewinder, 4-H Club, The Unseen Hand, Mad Dog Blues, Shaved Splits, Rock Garden, Curse of the Starving Class (Obie Award, 1978), Buried Child (Obie Award & Pulitzer Prize, 1979), True West, Fool For Love, A Lie of the Mind, Simpatico. *Novel:* Cruising Paradise.
PICTURES: *Actor*: Renaldo and Clara (debut, 1978), Days of Heaven, Resurrection, Raggedy Man, Frances, The Right Stuff (Academy Award nom. 1984), Country, Fool for Love (also s.p.), Crimes of the Heart, Baby Boom, Steel Magnolias, Bright Angel, Defenseless, Voyager, Thunderheart, The Pelican Brief, Safe Passage, The Only Thrill, Snow Falling on Cedars, Hamlet, Curtain Call, All the Pretty Horses, Kurosawa (documentary; narrator), The Pledge, Swordfish, Black Hawk Down, Leo, Blind Horizon, The Notebook, Don't Come Knockin' (also writer), Stealth, The Return, Charlotte's Web (narr.), The Accidental Husband, The Assassination of Jesse James by the Coward Robert Ford, Felon, Inhale, Border Crosses, Brothers, Fair Game, Shoedog, Blackthorn. *Writer*: Me and My Brother (co-s.p.), Zabriskie Point (co-s.p.), Oh Calcutta! (contributor), Renaldo and Clara (co-s.p.), Far North (also dir.), Silent Tongue (also dir.), Curse of the Starving Class, Simpatico.
TELEVISION: *Movies*: The Good Old Boys, Lily Dale, Purgatory, Dash and Lilly (Emmy nom.; Golden Globe nom. 2000), See You In My Dreams (writer), One Kill, After the Harvest, Shot in the Heart, True West (writer, play), Ruffian, Tough Trade. *Mini-series:* Streets of Laredo. *Guest:* More than 38 appearances.

SHEPHERD, CYBILL
Actress, Singer. b. Memphis, TN, Feb. 18, 1950. e. Hunter Coll., NYU, USC. Was fashion model (won Model of the Year title, 1968) before acting debut in 1971. Debut record album, Cybill Does It... To Cole Porter, 1974, followed by Stan Getz: Mad About the Boy, Vanilla, Somewhere Down the Road.
PICTURES: The Last Picture Show (debut, 1971, Golden Globe nom. 1972), The Heartbreak Kid, Daisy Miller, At Long Last Love, Taxi Driver, Special Delivery, Silver Bears, The Lady Vanishes, The Return, Chances Are, Texasville, Alice, Once Upon a Crime, Married to It, The Muse (cameo), The Last Picture Show: A Look Back, Marine Life, Open Window, 4Chosen, Barry Munday, Another Harvest Moon, Expecting Mary.
TELEVISION: *Movies*: A Guide for the Married Woman, Secrets of a Married Man, Seduced, The Long Hot Summer, Which Way Home, Memphis (also co-writer, co-exec. prod.), Stormy Weathers, Telling Secrets, There Was a Little Boy, Baby Brokers, For the Love of My Daughter, While Justice Sleeps, The Last Word, Journey of the Heart, Due East, Detective, Martha: Behind Bars, High Noon, Mrs. Washington Goes to Smith, Alligator Point, The Client List. *Mini-series:* Martha, Inc.: The Story of Martha Stewart, The Detective. *Series*: The Yellow Rose, Moonlighting (Emmy nom. 1986), Cybill (also co-exec. prod.; 3 Emmy noms.; Golden Globe Award 1996, 1 other nom.; 2 Golden Globe Awards, 1 other nom.), The L Word, Eastwick. *Documentaries/Specials:* Signs and Voices. *Guest:* More than 113 appearances.

SHERAK, THOMAS
Executive. e. B.A., marketing, New York City Community College. Began film career in distribution, Paramount Pictures, 1970; v.p. & head film buyer, General Cinema; president, domestic dist. & mktg, Twentieth Century Fox, 1983-84 & 1986-90; senior exec. v.p., Twentieth Century Fox. Former chairman, 20th Domestic Film Group; senior exec. v.p., Fox Filmed Entertainment, 1994-2000. Partner, Revolution Studios until 2008. Currently consultant for Marvel Studios. Board member, National Multiple Sclerosis Society, the Weizmann Institute, Fulfillment Fund of Southern Calif., and Southern Calif. Variety; member, Endowment Campaign Committee for the Academy Found.; chairman, Found. for Motion Picture Pioneers; bd. of dir. Motion Picture Television Fund. Has served as an AMPAS governor for seven years. Elected as Treasurer of the Board of Governors of AMPAS, 2008. Elected President of AMPAS 2009 for a one year term.

SHERIDAN, JAMEY
Actor. b. Pasadena, CA, July 12, 1951. e. UC Santa Barbara.
THEATRE: *Off-B'way:* Just a Little Bit Less Than Normal, The

Arbor, One Wedding Two Rooms Three Friends. *B'way:* The Man Who Came to Dinner, Hamlet, Biloxi Blues, All My Sons, Long Day's Journey Into Night, Ah Wilderness, The Shadow Box. *Regional*: Major Barbara, Loose Ends, Deathtrap, Homesteaders.
PICTURES: Jumpin' Jack Flash (debut, 1986), The House on Carroll Street, Distant Thunder, Stanley & Iris, Quick Change, Talent for the Game, All I Want for Christmas, A Stranger Among Us, Whispers in the Dark, White Squall, Sherwood's Travels, The Ice Storm, Wild America, Luminous Motion, Cradle Will Rock, The Amati Girls, Let the Devil Wear Black, The Simian Line, Life as a House, Rain, Desert Saints, The Warrior Class, Last Night (short), Syriana, Nothing But the Truth, Reunion, Handsome Harry (also prod.).
TELEVISION: *Movies*: One Police Plaza, Shannon's Deal (pilot), A Mother's Courage: The Mary Thomas Story, Murder in High Places, My Breast, Spring Awakening, Killer Rules, All Lies End in Murder, The Echo of Thunder, Beauty, The Lost Child, Hamlet, Video Voyeur: The Susan Wilson Story, Babylon Fields, Dear Prudence. *Mini-series*: The Stand. *Series*: Shannon's Deal, Chicago Hope, Law & Order:Criminal Intent, Trauma (also pilot).

SHERIDAN, JIM
Director, Writer. b. Dublin, Ireland, Feb. 6, 1949. e. Univ College in Dublin, NYU Inst. of Films & TV. Started as director-writer at Lyric Theatre in Belfast and Abbey Theatre in Dublin; also at Project Arts Theatre (1976-80), NY Irish Arts Center (1982-87) as artistic director. Founded Children's Theatre Company in Dublin. Director / Producer for Hell's Kitchen International.
THEATRE: *Writer*: Mobile Homes, Spike in the First World War (Edinburgh Festival Fringe Award for best play, 1983).
PICTURES: *Director:* My Left Foot (also writer, 2 Academy Award noms.; WGA nom. 1990), The Field (also writer), In The Name Of The Father (also prod. & s.p., 3 Academy Award noms.; WGA nom. 1994), The Boxer (also s.p. & prod., Golden Globe nom. 1998), In America (also s.p. & prod., Academy Award nom.; Golden Globe nom.; WGA nom. 2004), Get Rich or Die Tryin' (also prod.), Brothers, Shanghai, I Love You, Dream House. *Writer:* Into the West, Some Mother's Son (also prod.). *Producer:* Agnes Browne, Borstal Boy, On The Edge, Bloody Sunday (exec. prod.). *Actor:* The Bridge of San Luis Rey.

SHERIDAN, NICOLLETTE
Actress. b. Worthing, Sussex, England, Nov. 21, 1963. Moved to LA in 1973. Became model in NYC before turning to acting.
PICTURES: The Sure Thing (debut, 1985), Noises Off, Spy Hard, Beverly Hills Ninja, Raw Nerve, .com for Murder, Lost Treasure, Code Name: The Cleaner, Fly Me to the Moon 3D (voice), Noah's Ark: The New Beginning (voice).
TELEVISION: *Movies*: Dark Mansions, Agatha Christie's Dead Man's Folly, Jackie Collins' Lucky/Chances, Deceptions, A Time to Heal, Shadows of Desire, Robin Cook's Virus, Murder in My Mind, Knots Landing: Back to the Cul-de-Sac, Dead Husbands, The Spiral Staircase, Haven't We Met Before, Deadly Betrayal, Deadly Visions. *Series*: Paper Dolls, Knots Landing, Desperate Housewives (Golden Globe nom. 2005). *Guest:* More than 86 appearances.

SHERMAN, RICHARD M.
Composer, Lyricist, Screenwriter. b. New York, NY, June 12, 1928. e. Bard Coll., B.A., 1949. Brother is Robert B. Sherman. Info. & Educ. Br., U.S. Army, 1953-55. Songwriter, composer, Walt Disney Prods 1960-71, then freelance. With partner-brother Robert has won, 9 Acad. Award nom., 2 Grammys, 17 gold and platinum albums, 1st Prize, Moscow Film Fest. (for Tom Sawyer) and a star on Hollywood Walk of Fame. Have written over 500 pub. and recorded songs. Also wrote score for B'way musical Over Here (1974) and songs for Disney Theme Parks.
SONGS: Things I Might Have Been, Tall Paul, Christmas in New Orleans, Mad Passionate Love, Midnight Oil, The Ugly Bug Ball, You're Sixteen, That Darn Cat, The Wonderful Thing About Tiggers, It's a Small World, A Spoonful of Sugar, Supercalifragilistic, Feed the Birds, Let's Go Fly a Kite, Age of Not Believing, When You're Loved, Pineapple Princess, Let's Get Together, Maggie's Theme, Chim Chim Cheree (Acad. Award, 1964), Chitty Chitty Bang Bang, Hushabye Mountain, Winnie the Pooh, Fortuosity, Slipper and the Rose Waltz, many others. Comedy Album: Smash Flops.
PICTURES: Nightmare, The Cruel Tower, The Absent Minded Professor, The Parent Trap, Big Red, In Search of the Castaways, Moon Pilot, Bon Voyage, Legend of Lobo, Summer Magic, Miracle of the White Stallions, The Sword in the Stone, The Misadventures of Merlin Jones, Mary Poppins (2 Acad. Awards for song & score, 1964), Those Calloways, The Monkey's Uncle, That Darn Cat, Follow Me Boys!, Winnie the Pooh, Monkeys Go Home!, Chitty Chitty Bang Bang, The Gnome-Mobile, The Jungle Book, The Happiest Millionaire, The One and Only Genuine Original Family Band, The Aristocats, Bedknobs & Broomsticks, Snoopy Come Home, Charlotte's Web, Beverly Hills Cop III, The Mighty Kong. Songs & S.P.: Tom Sawyer, The Slipper and the Rose, The Magic of Lassie, Huckleberry Finn, Little Nemo: Adventures in Slumberland, The Tigger Movie, Piglet's Big Movie, Around the World in 80 Days (song), Pooh's Heffalump Movie (song), War of the Worlds, Bewitched, The Boys: The Sherman Brothers' Story (composer, doc.).
TELEVISION: *Soundtrack Writer:* Wonderful World of Color, Bell Telephone Hour, The Enchanted Musical Playhouse, Harry Anderson's Sideshow, The Horsemasters, Escapade in Florence, The Golden Horseshoe Revue, Bristle Face, A Boy Called Nuthin', The Young Loner, Goldilocks (also prod.), The Velveteen Rabbit, The Age of Believing: The Disney Live Action Classics. *Series:* Zorro, The Adventures of Gallegher, Texas John Slaughter, Welcome to Pooh Corner, The Timberwood Tales.

SHERMAN, ROBERT B.
Composer, Lyricist, Screenwriter. b. New York, NY, Dec. 19, 1925. e. Bard Coll., B.A., 1949. Brother is Richard M. Sherman. U.S. Army, WWII, 1943-45 (purple heart). Songwriter, 1952-60; pres., Music World Corp., 1958; songwriter, composer, Walt Disney, 1971, then freelance. Hon. Phd., Lincoln Col, 1990. With partner-brother Richard Sherman, has won, 9 Academy Award nom., 2 Grammys, 17 gold and platinum albums, 1st Prize, Moscow Film Fest. (for Tom Sawyer) and a star on Hollywood Walk of Fame. Have written over 500 pub. and recorded songs. Also wrote score for B'way musical Over Here (1974) and songs for Disney Theme Parks. (see Richard M. Sherman for co-writing credits.)

SHERMAN, SAMUEL M.
Producer, Director, Writer. b. New York, NY. April 23, 1940. e. CCNY, B.A. Entered m.p. ind. as writer, cameraman, film ed., neg. & sound cutter; nat'l mag. ed., Westerns Magazine 1959; pres., Signature Films; prod., dir., TV pilot, The Three Mesquiteers, 1960; prod., Pulse Pounding Perils, 1961; helped create, ed., dir., Screen Thrills Illustrated; exec. prod., Screen Thrills; v.p., Golden Age Films, 1962; prod., Joe Franklin's Silent Screen, 1963; NY rep., Victor Adamson Prods.; NY rep., Tal prods., Hlywd.; adv. & pub. Hemisphere Pictures; prod., writer, Chaplin's Art of Comedy, The Strongman; prod., Hollywood's Greatest Stuntman; story adapt., Fiend With the Electronic Brain; tech. consul., Hal Roach Studios, Music from the Land; 1968, NY rep. East West Pict. of Hollywood. 1968, N.Y. rep., Al Adamson Prods. of Hollywood; Ed.-in-chief, bk., The Strongman; pres., Independent-International Pictures Corp. (and tv div.); pres., Producers Commercial Productions, Inc. Chmn. of Creditors' Committee, Allied Artists Television Corp.; pres., Technovision Inc.; pres., Super Video, Inc.
PICTURES: *Producer:* Chaplin's Art of Comedy (also dir.), Satan's Sadists, Blood of Dracula's Castle, Hell's Bloody Devils, Dracula vs. Frankenstein (also s.p. & prod. supervisor), The Undying Brain (also s.p.), Blood of Ghastly Horror (assoc. prod.), angels' Wild Women, Dynamite Brothers (exec. prod.), I Spit on Your Corpse!, Naughty Stewardesses (also s.p.), The Jet Set (also s.p.), Cinderella 2000 (co-prod.), Team-Mates, Midnight (exec. prod.), Drive-In madness! (doc.), Night Club. *Writer:* Lash of Lust, Svengali, Raiders of the Living Dead (also s.p. & dir.).

SHESGREEN, DAVID A.
Exhibitor. Shesgreen began his career at Pacific Theatres and has nearly 40 years of theatrical exhibition experience. He is a 27-year veteran of Century Theatres and spent 17 years as executive v.p. of film programming and advertising. Then, as president & CEO, Shesgreen helped lead Century Theatres' expansion, growing the circuit from a strong regional exhibitor to a national presence. He was pres. & CEO until the company's acquisition by Cinemark USA, Inc. was completed in Oct. 2006. Shesgreen is on the bd. of directors for the Motion Picture Pioneers and the National Association of Theatre Owners.

SHIELDS, BROOKE
Actress. r.n. Christa Brooke Camille Shields. b. New York, NY, May 31, 1965. e. Princeton U. Honors in French Lit. Discovered at age 11 months by photographer Francesco Scavullo to pose in Ivory Soap ads.
THEATRE: *Off-B'way*: The Eden Cinema, The Exonerated. *B'way debut* 1994 in Grease! (Theatre World Award), Cabaret (revival), Wonderful Town (revival). *London:* Chicago.
PICTURES: Alice Sweet Alice (debut 1977), Pretty Baby, King of the Gypsies, Tilt, Wanda Nevada, Just You and Me Kid, The Blue Lagoon, Endless Love, Sahara, The Muppets Take Manhattan (cameo), Speed Zone (cameo), Back Street Dreams, Brenda Starr, An American Love (It.), The Seventh Floor, Freeway, The Misadventures of Margaret, Black and White, The Weekend, The Bachelor, After Sex, Massholes, Rent-a-Husband, The Easter Egg Adventure (voice), Bob the Butler, Midnight Meat Train, Furry Vengeance, Chalet Girl, Castro's Daughter, The Greening of Whitney Brown.
TELEVISION: *Movies*: After the Fall, The Prince of Central Park, Wet Gold, The Diamond Trap, I Can Make You Love Me: The Stalking of Laura Black; Nothing Lasts Forever; Almost Perfect Bank Robbery, What Makes a Family, Miss Spider's Sunny Patch Kids (voice), The Boy Who Cried Werewolf. *Mini-series:* Widows, Gone But Not Forgotten. *Series*: Suddenly Susan (2 Golden Globe noms.), That '70s Show (recurring role), Lipstick Jungle. *Guest*: More than 190 appearances.

SHIELDS, WILLIAM A.
Executive, Producer. b. New York, NY, 1946. e. El Camino College, California State Coll. at LA. Entered the motion picture industry in 1966 with Pacific Theatres, then MGM sales dept., L.A. and Denver, 1970; New World Pictures, 1972; 20th Century-

Fox, Washington, 1973; NY district manager, 20th Century-Fox, 1973-75; joined Mann Theatres Corp. of California as head booker in 1975; gen. sls. mgr., Far West Films, 1977-79; joined Avco Embassy as Western div. mgr., promoted to asst. gen. sls. mgr., 1980; promoted to v.p.-gen. sls. mgr., 1981; 1983 joined New World Pictures as exec. v.p., worldwide mktg. & acquisitions; promoted to pres., worldwide sls. & mktg., 1985; 1987, pres. CEO, New World Intl.; 1989, joined Trans Atlantic Pictures as pres., CEO when company purchased assets of New World's feature film division. Sold ownership in Trans Atlantic and formed G.E.L. Prod. & Distrib., 1992. Past chmn, American Film Mktg. Assn. (1987-91). Presently chmn. American Film Export Assn.
PICTURES: Au Pair (exec. prod.), Death Ring (exec. in charge of prod.) Uninvited (exec. prod.).

SHIRE, DAVID
Composer. b. Buffalo, NY, July 3, 1937. m. actress Didi Conn. e. Yale U., 1959, B.A. Composer of theater scores: The Sap of Life, Urban Blight, Starting Here Starting Now, Baby, Closer Than Ever, Big. Grammy Awards for Saturday Night Fever.
PICTURES: One More Train to Rob, Summertree, Drive, He Said; Skin Game, To Find a Man, Showdown, Two People, Steelyard Blues (adapt.), Class of '44, The Conversation, The Taking of Pelham 1-2-3, The Fortune, Farewell My Lovely, The Hindenberg, All the President's Men, The Big Bus, Harry and Walter Go to New York, Saturday Night Fever (adapt. & add. music, Golden Globe nom. 1978), Straight Time, The Promise (Academy Award nom. 1980), Old Boyfriends, Norma Rae (Academy Award for best song, 1980), Only When I Laugh, The Night the Lights Went Out in Georgia, Paternity, The World According to Garp, Max Dugan Returns, Oh God You Devil, 2010, Fast Break, Return to Oz, Short Circuit, 'night Mother, Vice Versa, Monkey Shines, Bed and Breakfast, One Night Stand, Ash Wednesday, The Tollbooth, Zodiac, Beyond a Reasonable Doubt. *Soundtrack Writer:* The Longest Yard, Take the Lead,
TELEVISION: *Movies*: Priest Killer, McCloud, Harpy, Three Faces of Love, Killer Bees, Tell Me Where It Hurts, The Defection of Simus Kudirka (Emmy nom. 1978), Three for the Road, Amelia Earhart, Something for Joey, Raid on Entebbe (Emmy nom. 1977), The Storyteller, Promise, Mayflower Madam, Echoes in the Darkness, Jesse, God Bless the Child, Common Ground, The Clinic, Convicted, The Women of Brewster Place, I Know My First Name is Steven, The Great Los Angeles Earthquake, The Boys, Sarah: Plain and Tall, Always Remember I Love You, Paris Trout, Four Eyes, Broadway Bound, Bed of Lies, Last Wish, Alison, Habitation of Dragons, Lily in Winter, Reunion, A Father for Charlie, Serving in Silence: The Margarethe Cammermeyer Story, My Brother's Keeper, My Antonia, The Heidi Chronicles, The Man Who Wouldn't Die, Lily in Winter, Tecumseh: The Last Warrior, Almost Golden: The Jessica Savitch Story, Murderous Intent, Jake's Women, Last Stand at Saber River, Ms. Scrooge, Alone, I Married a Monster, Rear Window, Double Platinum, Spenser: Small Vices, Sarah, Plain and Tall: Winter's End, Robert B. Parker's Thin Air, These Old Broads, Two Against Time. *Series themes*: Sarge, McCloud, The Practice, Sirota's Court, Joe & Sons, Lucas Tanner, Alice, Tales of the Unexpected, Brewster Place, Room for Two. *Mini-series:* The Kennedys of Massachusetts (Emmy nom. 1990), Streets of Laredo, Do You Remember Love (Emmy nom. 1985), Rear Window (Emmy nom. 1999). *Series:* The Virginian, McCloud, Getting Together, The Sixth Sense, Lucas Tanner (theme), Joe and Sons, The Practice, Alice, Tales of the Unexpected (theme), Flying High, Darkroom (theme).

SHIRE, TALIA
Actress. r.n. Talia Coppola. b. New York, NY, April 25, 1946. Raised on road by her father, arranger-conductor Carmine Coppola, who toured with Broadway musicals. After 2 yrs. at Yale Sch. of Drama she moved to L.A. where appeared in many theatrical productions. Brother is dir. Francis Ford Coppola. Started in films as Talia Coppola.
PICTURES: The Wild Racers, The Dunwich Horror, Gas-s-s-s, The Christian Licorice Store, The Outside Man, The Godfather, The Godfather Part II (Academy Award nom. 1975), Rocky (Academy Award nom.; Golen Globe nom. 1977), Old Boyfriends, Prophecy, Rocky II, Windows, Rocky III, Rocky IV, RAD, Lionheart (co-prod.), New York Stories (Life Without Zoe), Rocky V, The Godfather III, Bed and Breakfast, Cold Heaven, DeadFall, One Night Stand (dir. only), Lured Innocence, A River Made to Drown In, The Landlady, Divorce: A Contemporary Western, Can I Play?, Palmer's Pick Up, Caminho dos Sonhos, The Visit, Your Aura is Throbbing, The Whole Shebang, Pomegranate, Kiss the Bride, Dunsmore, I Heart Huckabees, Scratching the Surface, Andrassy Street 60., The Deported, Pizza with Bullets, Shadows from the Sky, The Return of Joe Rich, Minkow.
TELEVISION: *Movies*: Foster and Laurie, The Caryl Chessman Story, Kill Me If You Can, Daddy I Don't Like It Like This, Blood Vows: The Story of a Mafia Wife, Mark Twain and Me, For Richer For Poorer, Please, God, I'm Only Seventeen, Chantilly Lace, Born Into Exile, Blue Smoke, Christmas at Cadillac Jack's. *Mini-series*: Rich Man Poor Man, A Century of Women.

SHMUGER, MARC
Executive. e. Phi Beta Kappa graduate of Wesleyan University. In 1987, Shmuger wrote and produced the MGM film Dead of Winter. Since then, he's ascended through the executive ranks, first at Sony Pictures Entertainment and then within Universal Pictures. Shmuger joined Sony in 1991 as senior v.p., creative advertising for Columbia Pictures. In 1992, he was promoted to executive v.p. and creative director for Columbia and in 1994 was named executive v.p. of worldwide marketing for the combined Columbia TriStar motion picture companies. In 1996, Shmuger formed Art Of War, a Sony-based production company, which he ran until he joined Universal. From May 1998 to Dec. 2000 Shmuger was president of marketing for Universal Pictures. He became vice chairman of Universal Pictures in Dec. 2000 and while vice chairman also served as co-chairman of NBC Universal's Marketing Council, which oversees cross-promotion priorities for all film and TV properties owned by NBC Universal. In March 2006 he earned his most recent promotion to chairman, Universal Pictures. October, 2009 he left Universal Pictures. Among the many hits and franchises that Shmuger has launched at Universal are: King Kong, The Mummy franchise, the American Pie franchise, The Fast and the Furious franchise , The Bourne Identity franchise, the Bridget Jones franchise, the Meet The Parents franchise, Ray, Erin Brockovich, and 8 Mile, among many others. In 1999 and 2000 Shmuger was named one of "The 50 Most Powerful People in Marketing" by *Advertising Age* and was also honored in both 1999 and 2000 by *Advertising Age* as Entertainment Marketer of the Year, the first person ever to receive this distinction twice.

SHORE, HOWARD
Composer, Conductor, Musician. b. Oct., 18, 1946, Toronto, Ontario, Canada. Began as musical director for Saturday Night Live, 1975. Work has garnered three Academy Awards, 17 ASCAP Awards (American Society of Composers, Authors & Publishers), 3 Golden Globe Awards and numerous others.
PICTURES: I Miss You Hugs and Kisses, The Brood, Scanners, Gilda Live (actor), Videodrome, The Fly, Nothing Lasts Forever, After Hours, Fire with Fire, The Fly, Heaven, Belizaire the Cajun, Nadine, Moving, Big, Dead Ringers, Signs of Life, She-Devil, The Local Stigmatic, An Innocent Man, The Lemon Sisters, Made in Milan, Postcards From the Edge (musical numbers sprv.), The Silence of the Lambs, A Kiss Before Dying, Naked Lunch, Prelude to a Kiss, Single White Female, Sliver, Guilty as Sin, M. Butterfly, Mrs. Doubtfire, Philadelphia, Ed Wood, The Truth About Cats & Dogs, Striptease, Looking for Richard, Crash, That Thing You Do!, The Game, Cop Land, eXistenZ, Chinese Coffee, Dogma, Gloria, Analyze This, High Fidelity, The Yards, Esther Kahn, the Cell, Camera, The Score, The Lord of the Rings: The Fellowship of the Ring (Academy Award, Best Score, Golden Globe nom. 2002), The Lord of the Rings: The Two Towers, Gangs of New York, The Panic Room, Spider, The Lord of the Rings: The Return of the King (2 Academy Awards, Best Music, Original Score and Best Original Song- "Into the West," 2 Golden Globe Awards 2004), The Aviator (Golden Globe Award 2005), King Kong, A History of Violence, The Departed, The Last Mimzy (soundtrack writer), Eastern Promises (conductor, orchestrator, Golden Globe nom. 2008), Doubt (also conductor, orchestrator), Edge of Darkness (conductor, orchestrator), The Twilight Saga: Eclipse (also conductor, orchestrator, soundtrack writer).
TELEVISION: *Movie:* Lord of the Brush. *Series:* The Hart & Lorne Terrific Hour, Saturday Night Live, Scales of Justice, Late Night with Conan O'Brien, The Outer Limits (composer, one episode). *Documentaries/Specials:* Coca-Cola Presents Live: The Hard Rock, The Making of 'Panic Room', Late Night with Conan O'Brien: 10th Anniversary Special, P.O.V. (series doc.).

SHORE, PAULY
Actor. b. Los Angeles, CA, Feb. 1, 1968. r.n. Paul Montgomery Shore. Son of comedian Sammy Shore and nightclub owner Mitzi Shore. Worked as stand-up comedian at mother's club, The Comedy Store.
PICTURES: For Keeps? (debut, 1988), 18 Again!, Lost Angels, Phantom of the Mall, Wedding Band, Encino Man, Class Act, Son-in-Law, In the Army Now, Jury Duty, Bio-Dome, The Curse of Inferno, Junket Whore, Love and Fear, An Extremely Goofy Movie, Red Letters, The Wash, You'll Never Wiez in this Town Again (aka Pauly Shore Is Dead; writer, dir. & prod.), My Big Fat Independent Movie, The 1 Second Film (assoc. prod., doc.), Adopted (also writer, prod., dir.), Slam I Am.
TELEVISION: *Movies*: What's Alan Watching?, Dream Date, Home By Midnight, The Curse of Inferno, Casper Meets Wendy, The Bogus Witch Project (host), The Princess and the Barrio Boy. *Mini-series*: I Love the '70s. *Series*: Pauly, Minding the Store, America (also writer). *Special:* Pauly Does Dallas. *Guest:* More than 95 appearances.

SHORT, MARTIN
Actor, Comedian, Writer. b. Toronto, Canada. March 26, 1950. e. McMaster U. Trained as social worker but instead performed on stage in Godspell as well as in revues and cabarets in Toronto, 1973-78, including a stint as a member of the Toronto unit of the Second City comedy troupe, 1977-78. Created such characters as Ed Grimley, Jackie Rogers Jr. B'way debut 1993 in The Goodbye Girl (Theatre World Award; Tony nom.).
PICTURES: Lost and Found, The Outsider, Three Amigos!, Innerspace, Cross My Heart, Three Fugitives, The Big Picture, Pure Luck, Father of the Bride, Captain Ron, Clifford, The Pebble

and the Penguin (voice), Father of the Bride Part 2, An Indian in the City, Mars Attacks!, Jungle 2 Jungle, A Simple Wish, Mumford, Akbar's Adventure Tours, Prince of Egypt (voice), Get Over It, Jimmy Neutron: Boy Genius (voice), Treasure Planet (voice), Cinemamagique (short), Jiminy Glick in La La Wood (also s.p. & prod.), The Santa Clause 3: The Escape Clause, The Spiderwick Chronicles, Hoodwinked 2: Hood vs. Evil, Dorothy of OZ (voice).
TELEVISION: *Movies*: The Family Man, Sunset Limousine, Money for Nothing (BBC), Alice in Wonderland, Merlin (Emmy nom. 1998), Hot Millions, Sunset Limousine, Prince Charming. *Series*: The David Steinberg Show, Right On, Cucumber, The Associates, I'm a Big Girl Now, SCTV Network (Emmy Award for writing, 1983, 4 other noms.), Saturday Night Live (1985-86), The Completely Mental Misadventures of Ed Grimley (cartoon series), The Martin Short Show (also exec. prod., writer, 2 Emmy noms. 2000), Primetime Glick (Emmy nom. 2003, prod., exec. prod.), Damages (Emmy nom. 2010). *Documentaries/Specials*: All's Well That Ends Well, Really Weird Tales, Martin Short's Concert for the North Americas (SHO), Martin Short Goes Hollywood (HBO), The Show Formerly Known as the Martin Short Show (also exec. prod., co-writer), Martin Short Shorts (short; writer & prod.). *Guest:* More than 147 appearances.

SHUE, ELISABETH
Actress. b. South Orange, NJ, Oct. 6, 1963. e. Harvard.
PICTURES: The Karate Kid (debut, 1984), Adventures in Babysitting, Link, Cocktail, Back to the Future Part II, Back to the Future Part III, The Marrying Man, Soapdish, Twenty Bucks, The Underneath, Leaving Las Vegas (Academy Award nom. 1996, Golden Globe nom.), Trigger Effect, The Saint, Radio Inside, Palmetto, Deconstructing Harry, Cousin Bette (LA Film Critics Award), Molly, Hollow Man, Leo, Tuck Everlasting, (narrator, voice), Mysterious Skin, Hide and Seek, Dreamer: Inspired by a True Story, Gracie, First Born, Hamlet 2, Waking Madison, Don McKay, The Hard Ride, Piranha 3-D, Janie Jones.
TELEVISION: *Movies*: The Royal Romance of Charles and Diana, Call to Glory, Double Switch, Amy and Isabelle. *Series*: Call to Glory. *Documentaries/Specials:* The First Year (narr.), Penguin Safari (narr.).

SHUGRUE, J. EDWARD
Executive. Began career in theatre management with General Cinema Corp, 1970-71. Joined Columbia Pictures as sales manager, 1971; became branch manager, 1976. Eastern Div. Mgr., 20th Century Fox, 1981-1983. 1983-1987, exec. v.p., North American Distribution, TriStar Pictures. Pres., Columbia TriStar Film Distributors International, 1987-1996. Exec. v.p., Sony Pictures Entertainment and exec. v.p. Sony Retail Entertainment, 1996-1998. Named pres., Loews Cineplex International in 1998. In March 2005 formed Envoy Media Partners Ltd. The partnership will develop entertainment businesses in underserved markets overseas. It brings together the resources of Mekong Leisure Ltd. and Asian Capital Partners LLC. Shugrue is CEO.

SHULER-DONNER, LAUREN
Producer. b. Cleveland, OH. June 23, 1949. B.S. in film & broadcasting, Boston U. m. dir.-prod. Richard Donner. Began filmmaking career as ed. of educational films then camerawoman in TV prod., assoc. prod., story editor, creative affairs exec.; TV movie: Amateur Night at the Dixie Bar and Grill (prod.). Assoc. prod. on film Thank God It's Friday. Cameo in film Maverick. Currently producer for Donners' Company.
PICTURES: Mr. Mom, Ladyhawke, St. Elmo's Fire, Pretty in Pink, Three Fugitives, The Favor, Radio Flyer, Dave, Free Willy, Free Willy 2: The Adventure Home, Assassins, Volcano, Free Willy 3, Bulworth, You've Got Mail, Any Given Sunday, X-Men, Out Cold, X-Men 2, Just Married, X2, Timeline, Constantine, She's the Man, X-Men: The Last Stand, Unaccompanied Minors, Semi-Pro (exec. prod.), Hotel for Dogs, Cirque du Freak: The Vampire's Assistant, The Secret Life of Bees, X-Men Origins: Wolverine, X-Men: First Class.
TELEVISION: *Movie:* Amateur Night at the Dixie Bar and Grill. *Series:* Free Willy, Babes in the Wood. *Documentaries: As Camera Operator:* James Dean Remembered, Gable: The King Remembered.

SHUTT, BUFFY
Executive, Producer. e. Sarah Lawrence College. Joined Paramount 1973 as secretary with N.Y. pub. staff; 1975, natl. mag. contact. 1978, named dir. of pub.; later exec. dir. of pub. Promoted 1980 to v.p., pub. & promo. Resigned to join Time-Life Films as v.p. east coast prod; returned to Paramount in 1981 as sr. v.p. & asst. to pres. of Motion Picture Group. 1983, appointed pres. of mktg. 1986, resigned. Formed Shutt-Jones Communications, 1987, a marketing consultancy with Kathy Jones. 1989, pres. of marketing, Columbia Pictures & TriStar Pictures. 1991, pres. of marketing, TriStar Pictures. 1994, co-pres. of marketing, Universal Pictures. Was a partner with Kathy Jones in Shutt Jones Productions. Company produced first feature, Blue Crush, with Imagine Media. Both Shutt and colleague Jones then joined Participant Productions as EVP, Marketing in Jan. 2007. The company's focus is to raise awareness about important social issues, educate audiences and inspire action through its films. Before joining Participant, she helped guide the company through the release of Good Night and Good Luck, Syriana and An Inconvenient Truth.
TELEVISION: *Movies*: Heat Wave, Memphis. *Mini-series:* Tales of the City. *Series*: Twin Peaks, Beverly Hills, 90210 (pilot). *Specials*: Rock the Vote, Education First.

SHYER, CHARLES
Director, Writer. b. Los Angeles, CA. Oct. 11, 1941. e. UCLA. Was asst. dir. and prod. mgr. before becoming head writer for TV series The Odd Couple. First teamed with Nancy Meyers on Private Benjamin.
PICTURES: *Writer.* Smokey and the Bandit, House Calls (WGA nom. 1979), Goin' South, Private Benjamin (Academy Award nom.; WGA Award 1981 also prod.), The Parent Trap (also prod.). Irreconcilable Differences, Baby Boom, Father of the Bride, I Love Trouble, Father of the Bride Part II, The Affair of the Necklace, Alfie (also dir. & prod.).
TELEVISION: Movies: Cops (prod.), Lady Luck (writer), Him and Us (dir.). *Series:* The Mothers-In-Law. *Series/Writer:* The Odd Couple, Getting Together, Happy Days, Private Benjamin, Baby Boom.

SHYAMALAN, M. NIGHT
Writer, Director, Producer. b. Pondicherry, Tamil-Nadu province, India, August 6, 1970.
PICTURES: *Writer:* Praying With Anger (also actor, dir. & prod.), Wide Awake (also dir.), The Sixth Sense (also actor & dir., 2 Academy Award noms.; DGA nom.; Golden Globe nom.; WGA nom. 2000), Stuart Little (s.p. only), Unbreakable (also actor, dir. & prod.), Signs, (also actor, dir. & prod.), The Village (also dir., prod., exec. soundtrack prod.), Lady in the Water (actor, writer, dir., prod.), Life of Pi (s.p., prod.), The Happening (also voice, dir., prod.), The Last Airbender (also dir., prod.), Devil (also prod.).

SIEMASZKO, CASEY
Actor. r.n. Kazimierz Siemaszko. b. Chicago, IL, March 17, 1961. e. Goodman Theatre School of Drama, Chicago.
PICTURES: Class (debut, 1983), Secret Admirer, Back to the Future, Stand By Me, Gardens of Stone, Three O'Clock High, Biloxi Blues, Young Guns, Breaking In, Back to the Future Part II, Of Mice and Men, Teresa's Tattoo, My Life's in Turnaround, Milk Money, The Phantom, Bliss, The Taxman, Limbo, The Crew, Waltzing Anna, Public Enemies.
TELEVISION: *Movies*: Hard Knox, Miracle of the Heart: A Boys Town Story, American Harvest, The Chase, Children Remember the Holocaust, Black Scorpion, Rose Hill, Mistrial, Chameleon II: Death Match. *Mini-series*: Storm of the Century. *Series:* Oz, NYPD Blue, The Bronx Is Burning, Damages. *Documentaries:* Children Remember the Holocaust (narr.), The Polish Americans (narr.).

SIGHVATSSON, SIGURJON (JONI)
Producer. b. Reykjavik, Iceland, June 15, 1952. e. Iceland Community College, Univ. of Iceland. Came to U.S. in 1978. Also attended USC. Was film and music video prod. for Blue-Ice Prods. Founder and chairperson with Steve Golin of Propaganda Films.
PICTURE: *Assoc. Prod*: Hard Rock Zombies, American Drive-In. *Producer:* Private Investigations, The Blue Iguana, Kill Me Again, Fear Anxiety and Depression, Daddy's Dyin'... Who's Got the Will?, Wild at Heart, Truth or Dare, Ruby, A Stranger Among Us, Candyman, Kalifornia, Red Rock West, S.F.W., Lord of Illusions, Canadian Bacon, The Kids in the Hall: Brain Candy, Basquiat, A Thousand Acres, The Weight of Water, K-19 The Widowmaker, A Little Trip to Heaven, Brothers, The Killer Elite. *Executive producer:* 'Til There Was You , The Real Blonde, Polish Wedding, Phoenix, Homegrown, 200 Cigarettes, Arlington Road, Passion of Mind, Pretty Persuasion, The Last Winter, The Good Heart.
TELEVISION: *Movies*: Heat Wave, Memphis. *Mini-series:* Tales of the City (Emmy nom. 1994). *Series*: Twin Peaks, Beverly Hills, 90210 (pilot). *Specials*: Rock the Vote, Education First.

SIKKING, JAMES B.
Actor. b. Los Angeles, CA, March 5, 1934. e. UCLA, B.A. Theatre includes Waltz of the Toreadors, Plaza Suite, Damn Yankees, The Big Knife.
PICTURES: The Magnificent Seven, Von Ryan's Express, Chandler, The New Centurions, The Electric Horseman, Capricorn One, Ordinary People, Outland, The Star Chamber, Up the Creek, Star Trek III—The Search for Spock, Morons from Outer Space, Soul Man, Narrow Margin, Final Approach, The Pelican Brief, Dead Badge, Fever Pitch, American Primitive, Made of Honor, Imps* (segment).
TELEVISION: *Movies*: Gidget Gets Married, The Astronaut, Man on a String, Family Flight, Coffee, Tea or Me?, The Alpha Caper, The President's Plane Is Missing, Outrage, The Six Million Dollar Man: Solid Gold Kidnapping, Columbo: Publish or Perish, Alvin Karpis: Public Enemy No. 1, Young Joe, the Forgotten Kennedy, The Caryl Chessman Story, The Last Hurrah, A Woman Called Moses, The Jesse Owens Story, First Steps, Dress Gray, L.A. Law, Police Story: The Freeway Killings, Bay Coven, Ollie Hopnoodle's Haven of Bliss, Too Good to Be True, Brotherhood of the Rose, Too Good to be True, Desperado: Badlands Justice, Doing Time on Maple Drive, The Final Days, Jake Lassiter: Justice on the Bayou, In Pursuit of Honor, Seduced by Evil, Tyson, Dare to Love, Dead Badge, The Ring, Mutiny, Nowhere to Land, Submerged. *Mini-series*: Around the World in 80 Days.

Series: General Hospital, Turnabout, Hill Street Blues (Emmy nom. 1984) Doogie Howser, M.D., Brooklyn South, Invasion America (voice). *Documentaries/Specials*: Tales from the Hollywood Hills (Golden Land), Ollie Hopnoodle's Haven of Bliss. *Guest:* More than 119 appearances.

SILLECK, HAYDN
Exhibitor. CFO of Colorado Cinema Group, which is based in Aurora, CO. The company began operations in May 2000 and operates 11 theatres with 125 screens throughout Denver and its surrounding cities.

SILVER, CASEY
Executive, Producer. Chmn., Universal Pictures, Inc. Began career in motion picture industry as a screenwriter. Was asst. to dir. Adrian Lyne on Flashdance. Became dir. of devt. and prod. for Simpson-Bruckheimer Prods. V.P., prod., TriStar Pictures. Sr. v.p., prod., TriStar. Joined Universal Pictures as exec. v.p., prod., 1987. Became pres. of prod. in January, 1989; pres., Universal Pictures, June, 1994. Appointed chmn., Universal Pictures, November,. 1995. In October 1999, Silver formed Casey Silver Productions, a motion picture company.
PICTURES: *Producer:* Gigli, Hidalgo, Rebels, Ladder 49, Leatherheads, The Forbidden Kingdom, Cleo.

SILVER, JOAN MICKLIN
Writer, Director. b. Omaha, NB, May 24, 1935. m. producer Raphael Silver. Daughter is dir. Marisa Silver. e. Sarah Lawrence Coll. Began career as writer for educational films. Original s.p., Limbo, purchased by Universal Pictures. In 1972 Learning Corp. of Am. commissioned her to write and direct a 30-min. film, The Immigrant Experience. Also wrote and directed two children's films for same co; dir. & wrote short film Bernice Bobs Her Hair. First feature was Hester Street, which she wrote and directed.
THEATRE: *Director*: Album, Maybe I'm Doing It Wrong, My Name is Alice, My Name is Still Alice (co-conceived & co-dir. with Julianne Boyd).
PICTURES: *Director*: Hester Street (also s.p., WGA nom. 1976), Between the Lines, On the Yard (prod.), Head Over Heels (also s.p.; retitled Chilly Scenes of Winter), Crossing Delancey, Loverboy, Big Girls Don't Cry... They Get Even, A Fish In the Bathtub.
TELEVISION: *Movies:* Bernice Bobs Her Hair, How to Be a Perfect Person In Just Three Days, Finnegan Begin Again (dir.), The Nightingale: Faerie Tale Theatre (writer), Parole Board (Prison Stories: Women on the Inside), A Private Matter (dir.), Miss Sherri, In the Presence of Mine Enemies, Invisible Child, Charms for the Easy Life, Hunger Point.

SILVER, JOEL
Producer. b. South Orange, NJ, July 14, 1952. e. NYU. Made first film, a short called Ten Pin Alley; moved to Los Angeles with job as asst. to Lawrence Gordon. Named pres., Lawrence Gordon Prods.; developed with Gordon and produced and marketed Hooper, The End, The Driver, The Warriors (also assoc. prod.). At Universal Pictures as prod. v.p.; supervising Smokey and the Bandit II. Honored 1990 as NATO/Showest's Producer of the Year. Appeared in 1988 film Who Framed Roger Rabbit. Currently Silver is chairman of Silver Pictures, a motion picture and television production company based at Warner Bros.
PICTURES: Xanadu (co-prod.), Jekyll & Hyde ... Together Again (exec. prod.), 48 HRS., Streets of Fire, Brewster's Millions, Weird Science, Commando, Jumpin' Jack Flash, Lethal Weapon, Predator, Action Jackson, Die Hard, Road House, Lethal Weapon 2, The Adventures of Ford Fairlane, Die Hard 2, Predator 2, Hudson Hawk, Ricochet, The Last Boy Scout, Lethal Weapon 3, Demoliton Man, The Hudsucker Proxy, Richie Rich, Tales From the Crypt Presents Demon Knight (co-exec. prod.), Fair Game, Assassins, Executive Decision, Conspiracy Theory, Father's Day, Conspiracy Theory, The Matrix, Lethal Weapon 4, Romeo Must Die, The House on Haunted Hill, Made Men, Dungeon & Dragons, Exit Wounds, Chimera, Proximity, Swordfish, Thir13en Ghosts, Ritual, Adrenalynn, Macabre, The Matrix Reloaded, The Matrix 3, Cradle 2: The Grave, Adrenalynn, The Matrix Revolutions, Gothika, House of Wax, Kiss-Kiss/Bang-Bang, V for Vendetta, The Visiting, The Reaping, The Brave One, Fred Claus, The Invasion, RocknRolla, Speed Racer, Ninja Assassin, The Hills Run Red, Orphan, Whiteout, Sherlock Holmes, The Apparition, The Book of Eli, The Losers, The Factory, Unknown White Male, Project X (exec. prod.).
TELEVISION: *Movies: Executive producer:* Parker Kane, Two-Fisted Tales, W.E.I.R.D. World, Future Tense, Jane Doe, Bet Your Life, The Odds. *Series:* Tales from the Crypt, Perversions of Science, Secrets of the Cryptkeeper's Haunted House (Emmy nom. 1997), Action, The Strip, Freedom, Next Action Star, Veronica Mars, The Studio, Moonlight.

SILVERMAN, BENJAMIN
Executive, Producer. b. Pittsfield, MA, Aug. 15, 1970. Entered industry as agent at the William Morris Agency. While with William Morris, he was in the middle of many of the early deals that brought reality programs to American networks, including hits like "Who Wants to Be a Millionaire" and "Survivor." In 2001, formed production company, Reveille. One of first projects was bringing the British hit series, "The Office," to U.S. television. Much of Silverman's success as a producer can be attributed to his ability to spot which foreign shows would play well in the U.S. In May 2007, NBC Universal hired Silverman to be co-chairman, NBC Universal Entertainment & Universal Media Studios, alongside co-chairman Marc Graboff. Resigned 2009 and has partnered with IAC (Barry Diller) on future production ventures.
PICTURE: MacGruber (co-exec. prod.).
TELEVISION: *(All as exec. prod. unless noted). Movies:* The Celebrity Look-Alike Show, Bitch House, I'm With Stupid, Kath and Kim, Zip, Welcome to the Family. *Mini-series:* Celebrity Cooking Showdown. *Series:* Nashville Star, $25 Million Dollar Hoax, The Biggest Loser, Blow Out, Scream Play, The Restaurant, Bound For Glory, The Tudors, 30 Days (series doc.), The Club (series doc.), The Office (Emmy Award 2006, 3 other noms.), The Tudors, Ugly Betty (Emmy nom. 2007), The N's Student Body, Jet Set, Are You Smarter Than A 5th Grader?, Identity, House of Boateng, Life on an Indian Reservation, 30, Kath & Kim. *Special:* The 6th Annual TV Land Awards.

SILVERMAN, FRED
Producer. b. New York, NY, Sept.13, 1937. e. Syracuse U., Ohio State U., master's in TV and theatre arts. Joined WGN-TV, indep. sta. in Chicago. Came to NY for exec. post at WPIX-TV, where stayed only six weeks. CBS-TV hired him as dir. of daytime programs. Named v.p., programs 1970. 1975 left CBS to become pres., ABC Entertainment. 1978, named pres. and CEO of NBC. In 1981 left NBC to make programs via The Fred Silverman Company, where he is currently president.
TELEVISION: *Sampling of TV projects: Movies: Producer: Executive producer:* Farrell for the People, Gramps, My Very Best Friend, Special Report: Journey to Mars, Murder Among Friends, Recipe for Murder, Drive Time Murders, A Town Without Pity, Without Warning. *Series:* Zim Bomba, Supertrain, Meatballs and Spaghetti (also creator), Thicke of the Night, The Mighty Orbots, Perry Mason Movies, Morningstar/Eveningstar, Matlock, Jake and the Fatman, In the Heat of the Night, Jake and the Fatman, Father Dowling Mysteries, A Twist of the Knife, Diagnosis Murder, In the Heat of the Night: Give Me Your Life, Bone Chillers, Bedtime Stories, Twenty One.

SILVERMAN, JONATHAN
Actor. b. Los Angeles, CA, Aug. 5, 1966. e. USC, NYU.
THEATRE: *NY*: Brighton Beach Memoirs, Biloxi Blues, Broadway Bound. *LA*: The Illusion (Dramalogue Award), Pay or Play (Dramalogue Award), Sticks and Stones (Dramalogue Award).
PICTURES: Brighton Beach Memoirs (debut, 1986), Caddyshack II, Stealing Home, Weekend at Bernie's, Class Action, Breaking the Rules, Life in the Food Chain, Little Sister, Weekend at Bernie's II, Little Big League, Teresa's Tattoo, French Exit, At First Sight, Denial, 12 Bucks, The Odd Couple II, Just a Little Harmless Sex, Freak City, Men Named Milo-Women Named Greta, Dirk and Betty, Made, Lip Service, The Medicine Show, It is What it Is, The Cookout, Jekyll, Life Coach: The Movie, Laura Smiles, Coffee Date, Jam, Angel on My Shoulder, Jekyll, Swinging with the Finkels, Snatched, Inkubus, Conception, Dead Serious.
TELEVISION: *Movies*: Challenge of a Lifetime, Traveling Man, For Richer For Poorer, Broadway Bound, 12:01, Sketch Artist II: Hands That See, London Suite, The Inspectors, These Old Broads, Inspectors 2: A Shred of Evidence, Bobbie's Girl, Deacons for Defense, DeMarco Affairs, The Wilderness Family, Married Not Dead, Jack's Family Adventure. *Series*: Gimme a Break, The Single Guy, Free for All (voice), In Case of Emergency, Close to Home, Saved by Zeroes. *Guest:* More than 52 appearances.

SILVERSTEIN, ELLIOT
Director. b. Boston, MA, Aug. 3, 1927. e. Boston Coll., Yale U. Started career in television. 1985 received DGA Robert B. Aldrich Achievement Award, 1990 received DGA Honorary Life Member Award.
PICTURES: Cat Ballou (DGA nom. 1966), The Happening, A Man Called Horse, Deadly Honeymoon, The Car (also co-prod.), Flashfire.
TELEVISION: *Pilot*: Belle Sommers (debut, 1962). *Movies*: Betrayed by Innocence, Night of Courage, Fight for Life, Rich Men Single Women. *Series*: Tales From the Crypt.

SILVERSTONE, ALICIA
Actress. b. San Francisco, California, October 4, 1976. Made stage debut at Met Theater in Los Angeles in Carol's Eve. Starred in three Aerosmith videos including Cryin'. Formed own production co., First Kiss Prods.
PICTURES: The Crush (debut, 1993), The Babysitter, True Crime, Le Nouveau Monde, Hideaway, Clueless, Excess Baggage (also prod.), Batman & Robin, Love's Labour's Lost, Blast from the Past, Global Heresy, Scorched, Scooby-Doo 2: Monsters Unleashed, Beauty Shop, Alex Rider: Operation Stormbreaker, Elektra Luxx, Homework, Vamps, Butter.
TELEVISION: *Movies*: Torch Song, Shattered Dreams, The Cool and the Crazy, Pink Collar, Candles on Bay Street, Bad Mother's Handbook. *Series:* Braceface (voice also exec. prod., Emmy nom. 2002), Miss Match (Golden Globe nom. 2004), The Singles Table. *Guest:* More than 78 appearances.

SILVESTRI, ALAN
Composer, Conductor. b. March 26, 1950.
PICTURES: The Doberman Gang, The Amazing Dobermans, The Fifth Floor, Romancing the Stone, Summer Rental, Fandango,

Cat's Eye, Back to the Future, No Mercy, Flight of the Navigator, American Anthem, The Delta Force, The Clan of the Cave Bear, Overboard, Critical Condition, Predator, Outrageous Fortune, My Stepmother Is an Alien, Mac and Me, Who Framed Roger Rabbit, She's Out of Control, The Abyss, Back to the Future Part II, Downtown, Back to the Future Part III, Young Guns II, Predator 2, Father of the Bride, Dutch, Back to the Future... The Ride, Soapdish, Shattered (also orchestration), Ricochet, FernGully: The Last Rainforest, Stop! Or My Mom Will Shoot, The Bodyguard, Sidekicks, Death Becomes Her, Judgment Night, In Search of the Obelisk, Grumpy Old Men, Super Mario Bros., Cop & 1/2, Richie Rich, Clean Slate, Forrest Gump (Academy Award nom.; Golden Globe nom. 1995), Blown Away, The Quick and the Dead, The Perez Family, Judge Dredd, Father of the Bride Part II, Grumpier Old Men, Sgt. Bilko, Eraser, The Long Kiss Goodnight, Fools Rush In, Volcano, Contact, Mouse Hunt, The Odd Couple II, Holy Man, Practical Magic, Stuart Little, Reindeer Games, What Lies Beneath, Cast Away, What Women Want, The Mexican, The Mummy Returns, Serendipity, Lilo and Stitch, Stuart Little 2, Macabre, Uptown Girl, Showtime, Maid in Manhattan, Identity, Lara Croft Tomb Raider: The Cradle of Life, Something's Gotta Give, Van Helsing, The Polar Express (Academy Award nom.; Golden Globe nom. 2005), The Wild, Click, Night at the Museum, Beowulf, AVPR: Aliens vs Predator - Requiem, G.I. Joe: Rise of Cobra, A Christmas Carol, Night at the Museum: Battle of the Smithsonian, Hannah Montana: The Movie, The A-Team (also conductor), Predators (comp. themes).
TELEVISION: *Movie:* Two-Fisted Tales. *Series:* Starsky and Hutch, CHiPs, Manimal, Airwolf, Tales From the Crypt, Back to the Future, Stuart Little.

SIMMONS, JEAN
Actress. b. London, England, Jan. 31, 1929. e. Aida Foster Sch., London. Screen debut 1944 at age 14. Voted one of top ten British money-making stars in M.P. Herald-Fame Poll, 1950-51. London stage: A Little Night Music. Awards: Cannes Film Festival Homage 1988, Italian Outstanding Film Achievement Award 1989, French Govt. Commandeur de L'Ordre des Arts des Lettres. 1990.
PICTURES: Give Us the Moon (debut, 1944), Mr. Emmanuel, Meet Sexton Blake, Kiss the Bride Goodbye, Sports Day, Caesar and Cleopatra, Way to the Stars, Great Expectations, Hungry Hill, Black Narcissus, Uncle Silas, The Women In the Hall, Hamlet (Academy Award nom. 1949), Blue Lagoon, Adam and Evelyne, Trio, So Long at the Fair, Cage of Gold, The Clouded Yellow, Androcles and the Lion (U.S. film debut, 1953), Angel Face, Young Bess, Affair with a Stranger, The Actress, The Robe, She Couldn't Say No, A Bullet Is Waiting, The Egyptian, Desiree, Footsteps in the Fog, Guys and Dolls (Golden Globe Award 1956), Hilda Crane, This Could Be the Night (Golden Globe nom.; also won special award 1958), Until They Sail, The Big Country, Home Before Dark (Golden Globe nom. 1959), This Earth Is Mine, Elmer Gantry (Golden Globe nom. 1961), Spartacus, The Grass Is Greener, All the Way Home, Life at the Top, Mister Buddwing, Rough Night in Jericho, Divorce American Style, The Happy Ending (Academy Award nom.; Golden Globe nom. 1970), Say Hello to Yesterday, Mr. Sycamore, Dominique, Going Undercover, The Dawning, How to Make an American Quilt, Final Fantasy: The Spirits Within (voice), Howl's Moving Castle (voice), Through the Moebius Strip (voice), Shadows in the Sun.
TELEVISION: *Movies & Specials:* Heidi, Beggarman Thief, The Easter Promise, The Home Front, Golden Gate, Jacqueline Susann's Valley of the Dolls 1981, A Small Killing, Inherit the Wind, A Friendship in Vienna, Great Expectations, Sensibility and Sense, The Laker Girls, Perry Mason: The Case of Lost Love, People Like Us, Dark Shadows, They Do It with Mirrors, December Flower, One More Mountain, Daisies in December, Her Own Rules, On Cukor, The Oliviers in Love, Winter Solstice. *Mini-series*: The Dain Curse, The Thorn Birds (Emmy Award, Golden Globe nom. 1983), North and South, North and South Book II, Great Expectations. *Series*: Dark Shadows (1991), Angel Falls, Ancient Mysteries, Mysteries of the Bible III, Murder, She Wrote (Emmy nom. 1989). *Guest:* More than 60 appearances.
(d. January 22, 2010)

SIMMONS, MATTY
Producer. b. Oct. 3. As bd. chmn., National Lampoon, Inc. produced National Lampoon Radio Hour, National Lampoon Lemmings, National Lampoon Show. Resigned from National Lampoon Inc. 1989. Now heads Matty Simmons Productions.
PICTURES: National Lampoon's Animal House, National Lampoon's Vacation, National Lampoon Goes to the Movies, National Lampoon's Class Reunion, National Lampoon's European Vacation, National Lampoon's Christmas Vacation (exec. prod.), National Lampoon's Vegas Vacation (exec. prod.), The Trouble with Frank (also writer), Pucked (also s.p.).
TELEVISION: National Lampoon's Disco Beaver From Outer Space, National Lampoon's Class of '86 (exec. prod.), Delta House, Christmas Vacation 2: Cousin Eddie's Island Adventure (also exec. prod./writer).

SIMON, NEIL
Playwright, Screenwriter, Producer. r.n. Marvin Neil Simon. b. Bronx, NY, July 4, 1927. e. NYU. U.S. Army Air Force, 1945-46. Wrote comedy for radio with brother, Danny, (Robert Q. Lewis Show and for Goodman Ace), also TV scripts for Sid Caesar, Red Buttons, Jackie Gleason, Phil Silvers, Garry Moore, Tallulah Bankhead Show. With Danny contributed to B'way revues Catch a Star (1955), and New Faces of 1956.
THEATRE: *Playwright*: Come Blow Your Horn, Little Me, Barefoot in the Park, The Odd Couple (Tony Award, 1965), Sweet Charity, The Star Spangled Girl, Plaza Suite, Promises Promises, Last of the Red Hot Lovers, The Gingerbread Lady, The Prisoner of Second Avenue, The Sunshine Boys, The Good Doctor, God's Favorite, California Suite, Chapter Two, They're Playing Our Song, I Ought to Be in Pictures, Fools, Little Me (revised version), Brighton Beach Memoirs, Biloxi Blues (Tony Award, 1985), The Odd Couple (female version), Broadway Bound, Rumors, Lost in Yonkers (Pulitzer Prize, Tony Award, 1991), Jake's Women, The Goodbye Girl (musical), Laughter on the 23rd Floor, London Suite (Off-B'way), The Out-of-Towners, The Odd Couple II, The Heartbreak Kid (earlier s.p.).
PICTURES: After the Fox, Barefoot in the Park (also assoc. prod., WGA nom. 1968), The Odd Couple (Academy Award nom.; WGA Award 1969), The Out-of-Towners (WGA Award 1971), Plaza Suite, Last of the Red Hot Lovers, The Heartbreak Kid (Golden Globe nom. 1973), The Prisoner of Second Avenue (WGA nom. 1976), The Sunshine Boys (Academy Award nom.; Golden Globe nom.; WGA Award 1976), Murder by Death (WGA nom. 1977), The Goodbye Girl (Academy Award nom.; Golden Globe Award, WGA nom. 1978), The Cheap Detective, California Suite (Academy Award nom.; WGA nom. 1979), Chapter Two, Seems Like Old Times, Only When I Laugh (also co-prod.), I Ought to Be in Pictures (also co-prod.), Max Dugan Returns (also co-prod.), The Lonely Guy (adaptation), The Slugger's Wife, Brighton Beach Memoirs, Biloxi Blues (also co-prod.), The Marrying Man, Lost in Yonkers, The Odd Couple II, The Out-of-Towners (1999), The Heartbreak Kid (remake 2006), Circus Camp (stunt double).
TELEVISION: *Movies*: The Good Doctor, Barefoot in the Park, Plaza Suite, Broadway Bound (Emmy nom. 1992), The Odd Couple: Together Again, The Sunshine Boys, Jake's Women, London Suite, Sonny Boys, Laughter on the 23rd Floor (Emmy nom. 2001), The Goodbye Girl. *Series:* Caesar's Hour (2 Emmy noms. for writing), Cavalcade of Stars, Your Show of Shows, The Garry Moore Evening Show, The Phil Silvers Show, Stanley, The Garry Moore Show. *Documentaries/Specials*: The Trouble With People, Plaza Suite.

SIMON, PAUL
Singer, Composer, Actor. b. Newark, NJ, Oct. 13, 1941. e. Queens College, BA; postgrad. Brooklyn Law Sch. Teamed with Art Garfunkel in 1964, writing and performing own songs; they parted in 1970. Reunited for concert in New York, 1982, which was televised on HBO. Songs With Garfunkel incl.: Mrs. Robinson (Grammy Award), The Boxer, Bridge Over Troubled Water (Grammy Award).
ALBUMS: with Garfunkel: Wednesday Morning 3 a.m., Sounds of Silence, Parsley, Sage, Rosemary and Thyme, The Graduate (Grammy Award), Bookends, Bridge Over Troubled Water (Grammy Award), Simon & Garfunkel's Greatest Hits, Concert in the Park. *Solo*: Paul Simon, There Goes Rhymin' Simon, Live Rhymin', Still Crazy After All These Years (Grammy Award), Greatest Hits, One Trick Pony, Hearts and Bones, Graceland (Grammy Award), Negotiations and Love Songs, The Rhythm of the Saints, Paul Simon's Concert in the Park.
PICTURES: *Composer:* The Graduate (songs & singer), Shampoo, One Trick Pony (also writer & actor). *Soundtrack Writer:* Rockshow (documentary), Baby It's You, Less Than Zero, Forest Gump, The Other Sister, Girl Interrupted, Almost Famous, American Pie 2, 40 Days and 40 Nights, The Wild Thornberrys Movie (Academy Award nom.; Golden Globe nom. 2003), Maid in Manhattan, Old School, Intolerable Cruelty, Something's Gotta Give, Garden State, Dodgeball: A True Underdog Story, Zathura: A Space Adventure, Rumor Has It..., John Tucker Must Die, 10 Items or Less, The Holiday, The Pursuit of Happyness, Sicko, Watchmen, Taking Woodstock. *Actor:* Annie Hall, Henry and Me, Henry and Me (voice).
TELEVISION: *Documentaries/Specials*: The Fred Astaire Show, The Paul Simon Special (Emmy Award 1978), Home Box Office Presents Paul Simon, Graceland: The African Concert, Mother Goose Rock 'n' Rhyme, Paul Simon's Concert in the Park, Baileys in Tune: John Mayer and Paul Simon, Mississippi Rising (actor), Dancing on Ice. *Guest:* More than 128 appearances.

SINBAD
Actor. r.n. David Adkins. b. Benton Harbor, MI, Nov. 10, 1956. e. Univ. of Denver. Served in Air Force before becoming stand-up comic. Career was subsquently launched by appearances on TV series Star Search.
PICTURES: Necessary Roughness (debut, 1991), Coneheads, The Meteor Man, Houseguest, First Kid (also co-exec. prod.), Jingle All the Way, Homeward Bound II: Lost in San Francisco, First Kid, Jingle All the Way, Good Burger, Crazy as Hell, Hansel & Gretel (voice), Cuttin Da Mustard, Stompin' (also exec. prod.).
TELEVISION: *Movies:* Club Med, Sinbad: Brain Damaged, Circus of the Stars and Sideshow, Aliens for Breakfast, The Cherokee Kid, (also exec. prod.), Ready to Run, Inside TVLand: African Americans in Television, (documentary). *Series*: The Redd Foxx Show, Keep on Cruisin' (co-host), A Different World,

It's Showtime at the Apollo (host), The Sinbad Show (also exec. prod.), Vibe, The Remarkable Journey (himself), Just for Laughs, Slacker Cats. *Documentaries/Specials*: Afros and Bellbottoms, Take No Prisoners, Sinbad and Friends All the Way Live...Almost (also writer). *Guest:* More than 93 appearances.

SINDEN, DONALD
Actor. b. Plymouth, England, Oct. 9, 1923. Stage debut 1942 in fit-up shows; London stage includes There's a Girl in My Soup, The Relapse, Not Now Darling, King Lear, Othello, Present Laughter, Uncle Vanya, The School for Scandal, Two Into One, The Scarlet Pimpernel, Oscar Wilde, Major Barbara, Out of Order, Venus Observed, She Stoops to Conquer, Hamlet, That Good Night. B'way: London Assurance, Habeas Corpus. TV debut 1948.
PICTURES: Portrait From Life (The Girl in the Painting; debut, 1948), The Cruel Sea, Mogambo, A Day to Remember, You Know What Sailors Are, Doctor in the House, The Beachcomber, Mad About Men, An Alligator Named Daisy, Black Tent, Eyewitness, Tiger in the Smoke, Doctor at Large, Rockets Galore (Mad Little Island), The Captain's Table, Operation Bullshine, Your Money or Your Wife, The Siege of Sydney Street, Twice Around the Daffodils, Mix Me a Person, Decline and Fall, Villain, Rentadick, The Island at the Top of the World, That Lucky Touch, The Children, Hey Mr. Producer, Balto (voice), Labrats (voice).
TELEVISION: *Movies:* Bullet in the Ballet, Road to Rome, Dinner With the Family, Odd Man In, Love from Italy, The Frog, The Glove, The Mystery of Edwin Drood, Bullet in the Ballet, Road to Rome, Dinner With the Family, Odd Man In, Love from Italy, The Frog, The Glove, The Mystery of Edwin Drood, The Happy Ones, The Comedy of Errors, All's Well That Ends Well, The Confederacy of Wives, Tell It to the Chancellor, The Rivals, Treasure Seekers, The Canterville Ghost, Cuts, Richard II, Alice in Wonderland (voice), Nancherrow, Judge John Deed: Exacting Justice, How Proust Can Change Your Life, Marple: The Blue Geranium. *Mini-series:* War of the Roses. *Series:* The Happy Ones, Seven Days in the Life of Andrew Pelham, Our Man at St. Mark's, Father Dear Father, The Organisation, Two's Company, Never the Twain, Judge John Deed. *Guest:* More than 54 appearances.

SINGER, LORI
Actress. b. Corpus Christi, TX, Nov. 6, 1962. Brother is actor Marc Singer; father was symphony conductor Jacques Singer. Concert cellist while in teens. Won starring role in TV series Fame (1981).
PICTURES: Footloose (debut, 1984), The Falcon and The Snowman, The Man with One Red Shoe, Trouble in Mind, Summer Heat, Made in U.S.A., Warlock, Equinox, Sunset Grill, Luck-Trust-&-Ketchup: Robert Altman In Carver Country (doc.), Short Cuts (Golden Globe Award 1994), F.T.W., Bach Cello Suite #4: Sarabande, When Will I Be Loved.
TELEVISION: *Movies*: Born Beautiful, Storm and Sorrow, Inspired by Bach, Sensibility and Sense. *Series*: Fame, VR.5.

SINGER, MARC
Actor. b. Vancouver, B.C., Canada, Jan. 29, 1948. Brother of actress Lori Singer. Son of symphony conductor Jacques Singer. Trained in summer stock and regional theatre.
PICTURES: Go Tell the Spartans, If You Could See What I Hear, The Beastmaster, Born to Race, A Man Called Sarge, Watchers II, Body Chemistry, Dead Space, In the Cold of the Night, Beastmaster 2, Sweet Justice, The Berlin Conspiracy, Alien Intruder, Beastmaster 3, Streetcorner 3, Lancelot: Guardian of Time, Determination to Death, Angel Blade, What Lies Above, Eagle Eye, Dragonquest, House Hunting.
TELEVISION: *Movies*: Things in Their Season, Journey from Darkness, Something for Joey, Never Con a Killer, Sergeant Matlovich vs. the U.S. Air Force, The Two Worlds of Jennie Logan, For Ladies Only, Paper Dolls, V, Her Life as a Man, V—The Final Battle, Deadly Game, The Sea Wolf, Beastmaster III, Lesser Evil, The Republic. *Mini-series*: 79 Park Avenue, Roots: The Next Generation, V: The Second Generation. *Series*: The Contender, V, Dallas, The Young and The Restless, Beastmaster. *Guest:* More than 60 appearances.

SINGLETON, JOHN
Director, Writer. b. Los Angeles, CA, Jan. 6, 1968. Entered USC's Filmic Writing Program, where he received a Robert Riskin Writing Award and two Jack Nicholson Writing Awards. With debut feature Boyz N the Hood (1991) he became the first African-American and youngest person ever to be nominated for an Academy Award for Best Director. Appeared in film Beverly Hills Cop III.
PICTURES: *Director/Writer*: Boyz N the Hood (2 Academy Award noms.; WGA nom. for dir. & s.p., 1992), Poetic Justice (also co-prod.), Beverly Hills Cop III, Higher Learning (also co-prod.), Rosewood, Woo, (also exec. prod.), Shaft (also prod. & s.p.), Baby Boy (also prod.). *Actor:* Gettin' the Man's Foot Outta Your Baadasssss!. *Director:* 2 Fast 2 Furious, Four Brothers, Luke Cage, Tulia, The Wheelman, Abduction. *Executive producer:* Time Out. *Producer:* Hustle & Flow, Black Snake Moan, Illegal Tender (also music suprv.).

SINGLETON, PHILLIP M.
Exhibitor. b. Kansas City, MO, Aug. 2, 1946. e. California State University, B.S. in business admin.; University of South Florida, M.B.A. Singleton joined AMC Entertainment Inc. (AMC) in 1974 as a manager trainee after an eight-year career with the U.S. Marine Corps. Since then, he's served in such positions as general manager, district manager, and vice president of southeast operations in Clearwater, FL. In 1991, Singleton became senior v.p. and COO of American Multi-Cinema Inc., a subsidiary of AMC, and relocated to the company's Kansas City, MO, headquarters. He was named executive v.p. in 1994 and was elected president in 1997. He then became pres. & COO. Singleton retired from AMC in March 2007. The AMC circuit has interests in 382 theatres and 5,340 screens in 10 countries, including the United States.

SINISE, GARY
Actor, Director. b. Blue Island, Illinois, March 17, 1955. Co-founder and artistic dir. of Chicago's Steppenwolf Theatre Company, 1974.
THEATRE: *NY*: Balm in Gilead, True West, The Caretaker, The Grapes of Wrath. Chicago: Of Mice and Men, Getting Out. *Director*: True West (Obie Award), Orphans, Buried Child.
PICTURES: Miles From Home (dir. only), A Midnight Clear, Of Mice and Men (also dir., co-prod.), Jack the Bear, Forrest Gump (Academy Award nom.; Golden Globe nom. 1995), The Quick and the Dead, Apollo 13, Albino Alligator, Ransom., Snake Eyes, Bruno, All the Rage, The Green Mile, Reindeer Games, Mission to Mars, Imposter, A Gentleman's Game, Made Up, Mission: Space (short), The Human Stain, The Big Bounce, The Forgotten, Open Season (voice), Brothers at War (exec. prod. only).
TELEVISION: *Movies*: Family Secrets, My Name is Bill W, The Final Days, Truman (Golden Globe Award, Emmy nom. 1996), George Wallace (Emmy Award, Golden Globe nom. 1998), That Championship Season, Path to War, Fallen Angel. *Mini-series*: The Stand. *Series:* C.S.I.: NY. *Director*: Crime Story, thirtysomething, China Beach. *Guest:* More than 90 appearances.

SIZEMORE, TOM
Actor. b. Detroit, MI.September 29, 1964. e. Wayne St. Univ., Temple Univ.Stage incl. The Land of the Astronauts in NYC and Washington, D.C.
PICTURES: Lock Up, Rude Awakening, Penn and Teller Get Killed, Born on the Fourth of July, Blue Steel, Flight of the Intruder, Guilty by Suspicion, Harley Davidson and the Marlboro Man, A Matter of Degrees, Passenger 57, Watch It, Heart and Souls, True Romance, Striking Distance, Wyatt Earp, Natural Born Killers, Devil in a Blue Dress, Strange Days, Heat, The Relic, Enemy of the State (cameo), Saving Private Ryan, The Florentine, The Match, Bringing Out the Dead, Play It To The Bone, Red Planet, Pearl Harbor, Ticker, Big Trouble, Black Hawk Down, You'll Never Wiez in this Town Again, $windle, Dreamcatcher, Paparazzi, The Nickel Children, Piggy Banks, No Rules, Zyzzyx Rd., Fear Itself, Thieves (exec. prod.), The Furnace, Splinter, American Son, Red, Sky Kids, The Last Lullaby, Stiletto, The Grind, Super Capers, Shadows in Paradise, Double Duty, Big Money Rustlas, Corrado (also prod.), Contractor's Routine, Toxic, Commute, The Saints of Mt. Christopher, Hangar 14, Grace and Danger, Chlorine, Code of Silence, 513, Madoff: Made Off with America, C.L.A.S.S., Visible Scars, The Speak, The Sons of Summer, Morella, White Knight, Suing the Devil.
TELEVISION: *Movies:* An American Story, Witness to the Mob, Witness Protection (Golden Globe nom. 2000), Sins of the Father, Hustle, P Lo's House. *Mini-series:* Superstorm. *Series:* Acapulco Bay, Robbery Homicide Division, Dr. Vegas, Crash. *Guest:* More than 45 appearances.

SKARSGARD, STELLAN
Actor. b. Gothenburg, Vastergotland, Sweden, June 13, 1951.
PICTURES: Raid in the Summer, The Office Party, Brollopet, Anita, Taboo, Homeward in the Night, The Simple-Minded Murder, P & B, Ake and His World, False as Water, Peter-No-Tail in Americat, The Serpents Way, Jim and the Pirates, Hipp hipp hurra!, Time of the Wolf, Friends, The Unbearable Lightness of Being, S/Y Joy, Code Name Coq Rouge, The Women on the Roof, The Hunt for Red October, The Perfect Murder, The Ox, The Democratic Terrorist, Wind, The Slingshot, The Last Dance, Jonssonligans storsta kupp, Zero Kelvin, Hundarna i Riga, Harry och Sonja, Breaking the Waves, Insomnia, The Volcano Man, The Kingdom 2, Amistad, Good Will Hunting, Tranceformer - A Portait of Lars von Trier, My Son the Fanatic, The Glass-Blower's Children, Savior, Ronin, Deep Blue Sea, Passion of Mind, Light Keeps Me Company, Signs & Wonders, Timecode, Dancer in the Dark, Aberdeen, Kiss Kiss Bang Bang, Taking Sides, The Glass House, Powder Keg, Beneath the Banyan Trees, No Good Deed, Dogville, City of Ghosts, Exorcist IV: The Beginning, Downloading Nancy, Beowulf & Grendel, Pirates of the Caribbean: Dead Man's Chest, Goya's Ghosts, Pirates of the Caribbean: At World's End, Waz, Arn: The Knight Templar, Mamma Mia!, Angels & Demons, Boogie Woogie, Frankie and Alice, Metropia (voice), The Galapagos Affair, Regnskap, A Somewhat Gentle Man, Moomins and the Comet Chase, As If I'm Not There, Melancholia, Thor.
TELEVISION: *Movies:* Hustruskolan, Noon Wine, Den Tragiska historien om Hamlet, The Wild Duck, Förhöret, D-dag - Lise, D-dag, Harlan County War, Helen of Troy, God on Trial. *Mini-series:* Bombi Bitt och jag, Skärp dig, älskling, Babels hus, Farmor och vår herre, Strindberg, ett liv, S*M*A*S*H, Parker Kane, Rapport till himlen, The Kingdom II. *Guest:* More than 45 appearances.

SKERRITT, TOM
Actor. b. Detroit, MI, Aug. 25, 1933. e. Wayne State U., UCLA. Model for Guess? jeans ads.
PICTURES: War Hunt (debut, 1962), One Man's Way, Those Calloways, M*A*S*H, Wild Rovers, Fuzz, Harold and Maude, Run Joe Run, Big Bad Mama, Thieves Like Us, The Devil's Rain, La Madonna, The Turning Point, Up in Smoke, Ice Castles, Alien, Savage Harvest, The Silence of the North, A Dangerous Summer (The Burning Man), Fighting Back, The Dead Zone, Top Gun, Opposing Force (Hell Camp), SpaceCamp, Wisdom, Maid to Order, The Big Town, Poltergeist III, Steel Magnolias, Big Man on Campus, Honor Bound, The Rookie, Wild Orchid II: Two Shades of Blue, Poison Ivy, Singles, A River Runs Through It, Knight Moves, Contact, Not Like You, Smoke Signals, The Other Sister, Texas Rangers, Greenmail, Colored Eggs, Tears of the Sun, Swing, Expiration Date, Bonneville, Whiteout, For Sale by Owner, Beer for My Horses, The Velveteen Rabbit, Whiteout, For Sale by Owner, Black, White and Blues.
TELEVISION: *Movies*: A Bell for Adano, The Bird Men, The Last Day, Maneaters Are Loose!, Ryan's Four, The Calendar Girl Murders, A Touch of Scandal, Miles to Go, Parent Trap II, Poker Alice, Moving Target, Nightmare at Bitter Creek, The Heist, Red King White Knight, The China Lake Murders, Child of the Night, A Question About Sex, I'll Take Romance, Getting Up and Going Home, In Sickness and in Health, Divided by Hate (also dir.), What the Deaf Man Heard, Two for Texas, Into the Wild Blue, The Hunt for the Unicorn Killer, Aftershock: Earthquake in New York, An American Daughter, High Noon, Chestnut Hill, Voyage to Atlantis: The Lost Empire, Path to War, Homeland Security, Vinegar Hill, Category 7: The End of the World, Mammoth, Fallen, Dr. Jekyll and Mr. Hyde. *Mini-series:* Roots of the Mafia, Jackie Bouvier Kennedy Onassis, The Grid, Desperation, Fallen, The Trojan Horse, Killer Wave. *Series*: Ryan's Four, Cheers, Picket Fences (Emmy Award, 1993, 1 other nom.; 2 Golden Globe noms.), Brothers & Sisters. *Guest:* More than 134 appearances.

SKIPPER, JOHN
Executive. e. Univ. of North Carolina, bachelor's degree; Columbia Univ., master's degree. Skipper had a successful career in publishing before entering the TV industry. He spent 10 years with Straight Arrow Publishing, including eight years with Rolling Stone. At Straight Arrow, he rose to publisher of US magazine. He also held the title of pres. and publishing director at Spin magazine. He then joined the Disney Publishing Group, serving two years as senior v.p. in charge of all Disney's magazine, book and licensed publishing operations in the U.S. Since 1990, Skipper was v.p. of Disney Magazine publishing, overseeing Disney Adventures, Discover, FamilyFun and Family PC. He joined ESPN The Magazine and in 1997 was senior v.p. & gen. mgr. there. During the magazine's inaugural year, the magazine earned more than 20 awards, including "Best New Magazine" honors from both Advertising Age and AdWeek magazines. In 1999 it won the National Magazine Award for design. In Jan. 2000, he joined ESPN.com as senior v.p. & gen. mgr. From Dec. 2001 to Sept. 2002, Skipper served as senior v.p. & senior v.p. & gen. mgr. of ESPN.com and ESPN The Magazine from December 2001 to September 2002. ESPN The Magazine was named to Adweek's Top 10 Hot List of magazines five consecutive years (2001-2005), the only men's magazine to do so in the 25-year history of the list. In the Sporting News' 2004 Power 100, Skipper was named No. 1 in the Media Executives category, up from No. 3 in 2003. Skipper's been an executive v.p. at ESPN since September 2002 and during his tenure at ESPN also ran the organization's entire sales division. In October 2005, Skipper was named to his currect position, executive v.p., content creation and development. Skipper's wide-ranging responsibilities include content creation for six domestic ESPN networks, ABC Sports, ESPN Radio, ESPN.com, Mobile ESPN, ESPN360, ESPN The Magazine, ESPN New Media, ESPN Consumer Products, ESPN Books and SportsTicker.

SKLAR, MARTIN A.
Executive. e. UCLA, 1956. editor, the Daily Bruin, 1955. Began as asst. news editor, MAC (Media Agency Clients) Publications, 1956. Worked in publicity & mktg., Disneyland, 1956-61; writer, advertising and publicity, WED Enterprises (now Walt Disney Imagineering - WDI) where he served on a team assigned by Walt Disney to develop special projects for industry. Wrote personal materials for Showman of the World and other publications, television and special films aimed at communicating Walt Disney's visionary concepts. Primary strategist, Imagineering, 1960s-90s; v.p., concepts/planning, 1974; v.p., creative development, 1979; exec. v.p., 1982; president, 1987-96, Walt Disney Imagineering, responsible for the creation and expansion of Disney's theme parks and other creative initiatives. Currently vice chairman and principal creative executive, Walt Disney Imagineering (WDI), which is responsible for all aspects of every theme park project; featured speaker at numerous art design and recreation-related conferences. Elected member & president, Board of Education, Anaheim City School District, 1969 & 1973; former president, Orange Cty. School Board Assoc.; former City Commissioner, Anaheim; founding chairman, Michael L. Roston Creative Writing Awards; recipient, Community Service Award for Anaheim, 1977; Disney Legend Award, 1995; recipient, Lifetime Achievement Award, Themed Entertainment Assoc., 1995; member, Board of the Manned Space Flight Education Found.; president, Ryman-Carroll Found., which fosters the teaching of art and cultural diversity in public education.

SKOLIMOWSKI, JERZY
Director, Writer, Actor. b. Lodz, Poland, May 5, 1938. e. Warsaw U., State Superior Film Sch., Lodz, Poland. Scriptwriter for Wajda's Innocent Sorcerers (also actor), Polanski's Knife in the Water and Lomnicki's Poslizg.
AUTHOR: Somewhere Close to Oneself, Somebody Got Drowned.
PICTURES: *Director-Writer*: The Menacing Eye (short), Little Hamlet (short), Erotique (short), Your Money Or Your Life, Boxing, Rysopis (also art dir.), Walkover, Barrier, Le Départ, Dialogue, The Adventures of Gerard, Deep End, The Shout, Rece do góry, Moonlighting (also prod.), Success Is the Best Revenge (also prod.), Torrents of Spring, Ferdydurke. *Director:* King-Queen-Knave, The Lightship, America, Essential Killing (also prod.). *Writer:* Niewinni czarodzieje, Knife in the Water, Poslizq, Mesmerized, America. *Actor:* Sposob bycia, Die Fälschung, White Nights, Big Shots, Mars Attacks!, L.A. Without A Map, Before Night Falls, Eastern Promises.
TELEVISION: *Series:* Naznaczony.

SKYE, IONE
Actress. r.n. Ione Skye Leitch. b. London, England, Sept. 4, 1971. Daughter of folksinger Donovan (Leitch) and sister of actor Donovan Leitch. Raised in San Francisco, Connecticut, Los Angeles. Magazine photo led to audition for film River's Edge.
PICTURES: River's Edge (debut, 1987 as Ione Skye Leitch), Stranded, A Night in the Life of Jimmy Reardon, Say Anything..., The Rachel Papers, Mindwalk, Samantha, Guncrazy, Carmilla, Wayne's World, The Color of Evening, Gas Food Lodging, Four Rooms, Wayne's World, Guncrazy, The Size of Watermelons, One Night Stand, Dream for an Insomniac, Went to Coney Island on a Mission from God...Be Back by Five, Jump, The Good Doctor, Mascara, Men Make Women Crazy Theory, Southlander, Free, Chicken Night, Spin Shoot & Run, Return to Babylon, Fever Pitch, Zodiac, My Father's Will.
TELEVISION: *Movies*: Napoleon and Josephine, Girls in Prison, The Perfect Mother, The Sands of Time, The Clinic, Back When We Were Grownups, 12 Hours to Live. *Series*: Covington Cross. *Documentaries/Specials*: It's Called the Sugar Plum, Nightmare Classics (Carmilla).

SLATER, CHRISTIAN
Actor. r.n. Christian Michael Leonard Hawkins. b. New York, NY, Aug. 18, 1969. Mother is NY casting dir. Mary Jo Slater; father Los Angeles stage actor Michael Hawkins. Made prof. debut at 9 in The Music Man starring Dick Van Dyke, natl. tour, then on B'way Also on B'way in Macbeth, A Christmas Carol, David Copperfield and Merlin, The Glass Menagerie. Off-B'way in Landscape of the Body, Between Daylight and Boonville, Somewhere's Better. Also summer theatre. Directed 1992 L.A. prod. of The Laughter Epidemic. *London:* One Flew Over the Cuckoo's Nest (2005, revival 2006.
PICTURES: The Legend of Billie Jean (debut, 1985), Twisted, The Name of the Rose, Tucker: The Man and His Dream, Gleaming the Cube, Heathers, The Wizard, Tales from the Dark Side: The Movie, Beyond the Stars (Personal Choice), Young Guns II, Pump Up the Volume, Robin Hood: Prince of Thieves, Mobsters, Star Trek VI: The Undiscovered Country (cameo), Kuffs, FernGully...The Last Rainforest (voice), Where the Day Takes You, Untamed Heart, True Romance, Jimmy Hollywood, Interview With the Vampire, Murder in the First, Broken Arrow, Austin Powers: International Man of Mystery (cameo), Bed of Roses, Julian Po, Very Bad Things, Hard Rain, Basil, Love Stinks (cameo), The Contender, 3000 Miles to Graceland, Windtalkers, Who is Cletis Tout? Zoolander, In God We Trust, Naked Movie, Mindhunters, Masked & Anonymous, Churchill: The Hollywood Years, The Good Shepherd, Pursued, Alone in the Dark, The Deal (also exec. prod.), 2004: A Light Knight's Odyssey (voice), He Was a Quiet Man, Bobby, The Ten Commandments (voice), Slipstream, He Was a Quiet Man, Love Lies Bleeding, Igor (voice), Lies & Illusions, Dolan's Cadillac, Gideon's Gift, Without Men, Shadows of the White Nights, Guns, Girls and Gambling, Soldiers of Fortune, Sacrifice.
TELEVISION: *Movies*: Living Proof: The Hank Williams Jr. Story, Secrets, Desperate For Love, Merry Christmas George Bailey. *Series*: One Life to Live, Ryan's Hope, Prehistoric Planet (narr.), My Own Worst Enemy, The Forgotten. *Guest:* More than 101 appearances.

SLATER, HELEN
Actress. b. New York, NY, Dec. 15, 1963. *Off-B'way*: Responsible Parties, Almost Romance.
PICTURES: Supergirl (debut, 1984), The Legend of Billie Jean, Ruthless People, The Secret of My Succe$s, Sticky Fingers, Happy Together, City Slickers, A House in the Hills, Betrayal of the Dove, Lassie, The Steal, The Long Way Home (voice), Nowhere in SIght, Carlo's Wake, Seeing Other People, Power & Pride, Beautiful Wave.
TELEVISION: *Movies*: The Great Air Race, 12:01, Couples, Chantilly Lace, Parallel Lives, Toothless, Best Friends for Life,

American Adventure, Jane Doe: The Harder They Fall, Rock the House. *Series*: Capital News, The Adventures of Batman & Robin (voice), Gigantic.

SLOAN, HARRY E.
Executive. e. B.A. degree from UCLA,1971. J.D. degree from Loyola Law School, 1976. From 1976 to 1983, Sloan was a practicing entertainment lawyer with Sloan, Kuppin and Ament, a law firm which he founded in Los Angeles, CA. He purchased New World Entertainment in 1983 and served as chairman; led the company's initial public offering (IPO) in 1985; acquired Marvel Entertainment Group in 1986, and sold the business in 1989. Under Sloan's leadership, New World grew into a fully integrated, publicly traded media company releasing 30 films per year. It was also the third largest supplier of prime time TV programming to the U.S. networks and the largest U.S. independent film and video distributor. He then turned his attention to European broadcasting and started SBS in 1990. SBS became the second largest broadcaster in Europe with 16 TV stations, 21 premium pay channels and 11 radio networks, with a reach of 100 million people across Europe. He led SBS' IPO in 1993. In 1999, SBS became the largest shareholder of Lions Gate Entertainment, a premier independent producer and distributor of motion pictures, TV programming, home entertainment, and video-on-demand content. Sloan was Lions Gate bd. chairman until April 2005. In Oct. 2005, Sloan has named chairman and CEO of Metro-Goldwyn-Mayer Inc. (MGM). MGM is actively engaged in the worldwide production and distribution of motion pictures, TV programming, home video, interactive media and licensed merchandise. In 2008 Sloan signed a three-year agreement to continue in his position as chairman and CEO. In 2009 he stepped down as CEO but continued on MGM's bd. as nonexecutive chairman.

SLOCOMBE, DOUGLAS
Cinematographer. b. England, Feb. 10, 1913. Former journalist. Filmed the invasion of Poland and Holland. Under contract to Ealing Studios 17 years. Received the American Society of Cinematographer's International Award in 2002.
PICTURES: Dead of Night, The Captive Heart, Hue and Cry, The Loves of Joanna Godden, It Always Rains on Sunday, Saraband for Dead Lovers, Kind Hearts and Coronets, Cage of Gold, The Lavender Hill Mob, Mandy, The Man in the White Suit, The Titfield Thunderbolt, Man in the Sky, Ludwig II, Lease on Life, The Smallest Show on Earth, Tread Softly, Stranger, Circus of Horrors, The Young Ones, The Mark, The L-Shaped Room, Freud, The Servant (BAFTA Award), Guns at Batashi, A High Wind in Jamaica, The Blue Max, Promise Her Anything, The Vampire Killers, Fathom, Robbery, Boom, The Lion in Winter, The Italian Job, The Music Lovers, Murphy's War, The Buttercup Chain, Travels With My Aunt (Academy Award nom. 1973), Jesus Christ Superstar, The Great Gatsby, Rollerball, Hedda, The Sailor Who Fell From Grace With the Sea, Nasty Habits, Julia (Academy Award nom. 1978), Close Encounters of the Third Kind (co-photog.), Caravans, Lost and Found, The Lady Vanishes, Nijinsky, Raiders of the Lost Ark (Academy Award nom. 1982), The Pirates of Penzance, Never Say Never Again, Indiana Jones and the Temple of Doom, Water, Lady Jane, Indiana Jones and the Last Crusade.
TELEVISION: *Movie*: Love Among the Ruins.

SLUIZER, GEORGE
Director. b. Paris, France, June 25, 1932.
PICTURES: De Lage landen (short; also writer), Jolio en het mes, Twice a Woman, Joao (also writer), The Year of the Cancer (prod. only), Tiro (prod. only), Red Desert Penetentiary, Spoorloos (also writer, prod. & editor), Utz, The Vanishing, Dying to Go Home (also writer & prod.), Crimetime, The Commissioner (also writer), The Stone Raft (also writer & prod.), The Chosen One.

SMALL, JEFF
Executive. b Marietta, GA, Nov. 25, 1973. Graduate of Stanford University. Small broke into the film business as a financial analyst at the Walt Disney Motion Picture Group. Next, he moved to Universal Studios beginning in the corporate development group where he played key roles in mergers and acquisitions across film, television, and music areas, including the acquisitions of Polygram and the USA Network. He then transitioned to Universal Pictures as dir. of business development, where he was responsible for sourcing and analyzing new business opportunities and financing packages. Small moved on to Revolution Studios where he oversaw business and legal affairs, finance, physical production, and administration. His acumen led to promotions to the CFO post and ultimately to COO. In Nov. 2006, DreamWorks tapped Small to be its new COO and is the position he holds today.

SMART, JEAN
Actress. b. Seattle, WA, Sept. 13, 1959. e. Univ. of WA. Member of Oregon Shakespeare Fest, 1975-77; also with Hartford Stage Co., Pittsburgh Public Theatre Co., Intiman Theatre Co.
THEATRE: *Regional*: Equus, Much Ado About Nothing, A Moon for the Misbegotten, Terra Nova, Cat's Play, Saint Joan, A History of the American Film, Last Summer at Bluefish Cove (LA Drama Critics Circle, Dramalogue & LA Drama Desk Awards), Mrs. California, Strange Snow. *NY*: Last Summer at Bluefish Cove, Piaf (B'way debut, 1981).
PICTURES: Flashpoint (debut, 1984), Protocol, Fire With Fire, Project X, Mistress, Homeward Bound: The Incredible Journey, The Brady Bunch Movie, Edie & Pen, The Odd Couple II, Guinevere, Snow Day, The Kid, Forever Fabulous, Sweet Home Alabama, Bringing Down the House, Garden State, I Heart Huckabees, Lucky You, Hero Wanted, Barry Munday, Youth in Revolt, Life as We Know It.
TELEVISION: *Movies*: Single Bars Single Women, A Fight for Jenny, A Seduction in Travis County, A Stranger in Town (also co-prod.), The Yarn Princess, The Yearling, A Stranger in Town, Undue Influence, The Man Who Came to Dinner, Audrey's Rain, Killer Instinct: From the Files of Agent Candice DeLong, Kim Possible: A Sitch in Time (voice), A Very Married Christmas, Kim Possible: So the Drama (voice). *Series*: Reggie, Teachers Only, Designing Women, High Society, Hey Arnold, Style and Substance, The District, The Oblongs, Kim Possible, In Laws, Center of the Universe, 24 (2 Emmy noms.), Samantha Who? (Emmy Award 2008), Hawaii Five-0 (2010, pilot). *Documentaries / Specials*: Piaf, Maximum Security, Royal Match, A Place at the Table, Mississippi Rising. *Guest:* More than 73 appearances.

SMITH, CHARLES MARTIN
Actor, Director. b. Los Angeles, CA, Oct. 30, 1953. e. California State U. Father is animation artist Frank Smith.
PICTURES: *Actor:* The Culpepper Cattle Company (debut, 1972), Fuzz, Pat Garrett and Billy the Kid, American Graffiti, The Spikes Gang, Rafferty and the Gold Dust Twins, No Deposit No Return, The Curious Case of the Campus Corpse, The Buddy Holly Story, More American Graffiti, Herbie Goes Bananas, Never Cry Wolf (also co-wrote narr.), Starman, Trick or Treat (also dir.), The Untouchables, The Experts, The Hot Spot, Deep Cover, Boris and Natasha (also dir.), Fifty-Fifty (also dir.), I Love Trouble, Speechless, The Final Cut, Perfect Alibi, Wedding Bell Blues. Deep Impact, Here's To Life (also exec. prod.), Dead Heat (also exec. prod.), Lucky You. *Director:* Air Bud, The Snow Walker (also s.p.), Stone of Destiny (also s.p.), A Dolphin's Tale (also s.p.).
TELEVISION: *Movies*: *As Actor:* Go Ask Alice, The Deputies, Law of the Land, Cotton Candy, And the Band Played On, Roswell, Brother's Destiny, Dead Silence, Blackout Effect, The Apartment Complex, Roughing It, The Clinic, The Last Casino, Still Small Voices. *Mini-series*: Streets of Laredo, The Beast, P.T. Barnum, The Triangle. *Series:* Da Vinci's City Hall (actor and recurring dir.), Drive. *Guest:* More than 69 appearances.

SMITH, DAVID D.
Executive. Smith founded Comark Communications, Inc. in 1978, a company engaged in the manufacture of high power transmitters for UHF television stations, and was an officer and director of Comark until 1986. He also was a principal in other television stations prior to serving as a General Manager of WCWB from 1984 until 1986. In 1986, Smith was instrumental in the formation of Sinclair Broadcast Group, Inc. He has served as President and Chief Executive Officer since 1988 and has been Chairman of the Board of Sinclair Broadcast Group, Inc. since September 1990. He currently is a member of the bd. of dir. of Sinclair Ventures, Inc.; Acrodyne Communications, Inc.; G1440, Inc.; Summa Holdings, Ltd.; KDSM, Inc.; and Safe Waterways in Maryland.

SMITH, DAVID R.
Archivist. b. Pasadena, CA, Oct. 13, 1940. e. Pasadena City Coll., A.A., 1960; U. of California, Berkeley, B.A. 1962, MLS 1963. Writer of numerous historical articles. Worked as librarian at Library of Congress, 1963-65 and as reference librarian, UCLA 1965-70 before becoming archivist for The Walt Disney Co. 1970-present. Exec. dir., The Manuscript Society, 1980-; member, Society of CA Archivists, Fellow of the Manuscript Society, 1993. Received service award, ASIFA, and award of distinction, Manuscript Soc, 1983. *Co-Author:* The Ultimate Disney Trivia Book (1992, 1994, 1997), Disney: The First 100 Years (1999). *Author:* Disney A to Z: The Official Encyclopedia (1996, 1998).

SMITH, GORDON H.
Executive. b. Pendleton, OR, May 25, 1952. e. Undergrad degree, Brigham Young Univ., 1976; Law degree, Southwestern Univ. School of Law in Los Angeles, 1979; admitted to the New Mexico bar, 1979; Arizona bar, 1980; law clerk, New Mexico supreme court, 1979-1980; practiced law in Arizona; pres., family-owned Smith Frozen Foods; member, Oregon State senate 1992-1997 and its president, 1995-1997; unsuccessful candidate for election to the United States Senate in January 6, 1996, special election for the remainder of the term ending January 7, 1999, left vacant by the resignation of Robert W. Packwood; elected as a Republican to the U.S. Senate in 1996, becoming the first person to run for a state's two U.S. Senate seats in one calendar year; reelected in 2002, and served from January 3, 1997, to January 3, 2009; while in Senate, his committee assignments included the Senate Commerce Committee, the panel that oversees all broadcast-related legislation. Smith also served on the Senate Energy and Natural Resources Committee, the Senate Finance Committee, and the Senate Foreign Relations Committee. Smith's role on the Commerce Committee and as the chairman of a Senate High Tech Task Force helped foster his interest in new media and new technology issues. Smith was

unsuccessful in his bid for reelection in 2008. He returned to law with Covington & Burling LLP, and in Sept. 2009 was named to his current job as pres. and CEO of the National Association of Broadcasters (NAB).

SMITH, HY
Executive. b. New York, NY, June 3, 1934. e. Baruch Sch., CCNY, B.B.A. Joined Paramount Pictures 1967, foreign ad.-pub coordinator; 1969, joined United Artists as foreign ad.-pub mgr.; named intl. ad.-pub dir., 1970; named v.p., intl. adv.-pub. 1976; v.p. worldwide adv., publ. & promo., 1978; 1981, named first v.p., adv./pub./promo; 1982, joined Rastar Films as v.p., intl. project director for Annie; 1983, joined United Intl. Pictures as sr. v.p., adv/pub, based in London. 1984, named sr. v.p., mktg. 1995, promoted to exec. v.p., mktg. Left UIP and currently head of Hy Smith & Assoc. a London-based international marketing consultant.

SMITH, JACLYN
Actress. b. Houston, TX, Oct. 26, 1947. Started acting while in high school and studied drama and psychology at Trinity U. in San Antonio. Appeared in many commercials as model.
PICTURES: The Adventurers, Bootleggers, Nightkill, Deja Vu, Free Fall, 1 a Minute.
TELEVISION: *Movies*: Probe (Switch), Charlie's Angels (pilot), Escape From Bogen County, The Users, Jacqueline Bouvier Kennedy (Golden Globe nom. 1982), Rage of Angels, The Night They Saved Christmas, Sentimental Journey, Florence Nightingale, Rage of Angels: The Story Continues, Windmills of the Gods, The Bourne Identity, Settle the Score, Danielle Steel's Kaleidoscope, Lies Before Kisses, The Rape of Dr. Willis, In the Arms of a Killer, Nightmare in the Daylight, Love Can Be Murder, Cries Unheard: The Donna Yalich Story, Danielle Steel's Family Album, My Very Best Friend, Married to a Stranger, Before He Wakes, Three Secrets, Navigating the Heart, Ordinary Miracles, Farrah's Story. *Mini-series:* George Washington. *Series*: Oh Nurse, Charlie's Angels, Christine Cromwell, The District. *Guest:* More than 90 appearances.

SMITH, KEVIN P.
Director, Writer, Editor, Actor. b. Red Bank, NJ, Aug. 2, 1970. Also co-authored comic book series featuring Jay and Silent Bob characters.
PICTURES: Clerks (debut, 1994. also actor, editor, prod.), Mallrats (also actor), Drawing Flies (prod. only), Chasing Amy (also actor, editor), A Better Place (prod. only), Good Will Hunting (co-exec. prod. only), Vulgar (exec. prod., actor only), Dogma (also actor, editor), Coyote Ugly (s.p. only), The Blair Crown Project (actor only), Big Helium Dog (dir. & exec. prod.), Jay and Silent Bob Strike Back (also actor), Now You Know (actor only), Jersey Girl (also exec. prod.), Daredevil, Doogal (voice), Bottom's Up, Clerks II (also writer, prod., dir., editor, co-editor), Southland Tales, Catch and Release, TMNT (voice), Live Free or Die Hard, Zack and Miri Make a Porno, K-11 (actor), A Couple of Dicks (dir., editor), Red State (also editor).
TELEVISON: *Movies:* Reel Comedy: Jay and Silent Bob, Roadside Attractions, Clerks, Manchild. *Mini-series / Series:* Clerks, Manchild (pilot), Reaper. *Documentaries:* I Love the '90s, Independent's Day, Lucy You Love It, Judge Not: In Defense of Dogma, Wizard World Chicago 2002, Comic Book Superheroes Unmasked, Oh, What a Lovely Tea Party, Reel Paradise, Bear Nation (exec. prod.). *Guest:* More than 96 appearances.

SMITH, KURTWOOD
Actor. b. New Lisbon, WI, July 3, 1943. e. B.A. San Jose (1966), M.F.A. Stanford (1969). Starred in Oscar-nom short 12:01 P.M.
THEATRE: Plymouth Rock, The Price, Faces by Chekhov, Familiar Faces, Enemy of the People, The Debutante Ball (all in Calif.), The Lucky Spot (Williamston), Signature, Hamlet, Taming of the Shrew, and over 20 other Shakespeare productions in CA.
PICTURES: Roadie (debut, 1980), Zoot Suit, Going Berserk, Staying Alive, Flashpoint, Robocop, Rambo III, True Believer, Dead Poets Society, Heart of Dixie, Quick Change, Oscar, Company Business, Star Trek VI: The Undiscovered Country, Shadows and Fog, The Crush, Heart and Souls, Fortress, Boxing Helena, Under Siege 2: Dark Territory, Last of the Dogmen, To Die For, Broken Arrow, A Time to Kill, Citizen Ruth, Precious, Shelter, Prefontaine, Deep Impact, Girl Interrupted, Teddy Bears' Picnic, Hard Scrambled, Evil Remains, The Trouble with Dee Dee, Entry Level, Cedar Rapids.
TELEVISION: *Movies*: Murder in Texas, Missing Pieces, The Midnight Hour, International Airport, Deadly Messages, The Christmas Gift, Doorways, While Justice Sleeps, A Bright Shining Lie, Black Jaq, Grand Union, The Life and Times of Tim (voice), Billion Dollar Freshmen. *Mini-series*: North and South Book II, The Nightmare Years (Ace Award nom.), Robocop: Prime Detectives, Gary & Mike. *Series*: The Renegades, The New Adventures of Beans Baxter, Eek! the Cat (voice), Big Wave Dave's, Spawn (voice), That '70s Show, Gary & Mike (voice), The Zeta Project, (voice), Fillmore! (voice), Battle Force: Andromeda (voice), Squirrel Boy (voice), Insatiable (pilot), 24, Worst Week, Neighbors from Hell (voice). *Guest:* More than 87 appearances.

SMITH, DAME MAGGIE
D.B.E. C.B.E. Actress. b. Ilford, England, Dec. 28, 1934. Early career Oxford Playhouse. With the Old Vic 1959-60. Also with Stratford Ontario Shakespeare Fest. 1975-78, & 1980. Received C.B.E. 1970; D.B.E., 1990.
THEATRE: Twelfth Night (debut, 1952), Cakes and Ale, New Faces of 1956 (NY debut, as comedienne), Share My Lettuce, The Stepmother, What Every Woman Knows, Rhinoceros, The Rehearsal, The Private Ear, The Public Eye, Mary Mary, The Recruiting Officer, Othello, The Master Builder, Hay Fever, Much Ado About Nothing, Black Comedy, Miss Julie, Trelawney of the Wells, The Beaux Stratagem, The Three Sisters, Hedda Gabler, Design for Living (L.A.), Private Lives (London & NY), Slap, Peter Pan, As You Like It, Macbeth, Night and Day (London & NY), Virginia, Way of the World, Lettice and Lovage (London & NY, Tony Award), The Importance of Being Earnest, Three Tall Women.
PICTURES: Nowhere to Go (debut, 1958), Go to Blazes, The V.I.P.s (Golden Globe nom. 1964), The Pumpkin Eater, Young Cassidy, Othello (Academy Award nom.; Golden Globe nom. 1966), The Honey Pot, Hot Millions, The Prime of Miss Jean Brodie (Academy Award, BAFTA Award, Golden Globe nom. 1970), Oh! What a Lovely War, Travels With My Aunt (Academy Award nom.; Golden Globe nom. 1973), Love and Pain and the Whole Damn Thing, Murder by Death, Death on the Nile, California Suite (Academy Award, best supporting actress, Golden Globe Award 1979), Clash of the Titans, Quartet, Evil Under the Sun, The Missionary, Better Late Than Never, A Private Function (BAFTA Award, 1985), Lily in Love, A Room with a View (Academy Award nom.; Golden Globe Award 1987), The Lonely Passion of Judith Hearne, Romeo-Juliet (voice), Hook, Sister Act, The Secret Garden, Sister Act 2: Back in the Habit, Richard III, Washington Square, Tea With Mussolini, Curtain Call, Harry Potter and the Sorcerer's Stone, Gosford Park (Academy Award nom.; Golden Globe nom. 2002), The Divine Secrets of the Ya Ya Sisterhood, Harry Potter and the Chamber of Secrets, Harry Potter and the Prisoner of Azkaban, Ladies in Lavender, Harry Potter and the Goblet of Fire, Keeping Mum, Harry Potter and the Order of the Phoenix, Becoming Jane, From Time to Time, Harry Potter and the Half-Blood Prince, Nanny McPhee Returns, Harry Potter and the Deathly Hallows: Part I, Harry Potter and the Deathly Hallows: Part II, Quartet, Gnomeo and Juliet.
TELEVISION: *Movies:* Much Ado About Nothing, Man and Superman, On Approval, Home and Beauty, Mrs. Silly, Bed Among the Lentils, Memento Mori, Suddenly Last Summer (Emmy nom. 1993), All the King's Men, David Copperfield (Emmy nom. 2000), My House in Umbria (Emmy Award, Golden Globe nom. 2003), Capturing Mary (Emmy nom. 2010). *Series:* Downton Abbey. *Guest:* More than 60 appearances.

SMITH, QUINCY
Executive. Early career as investment banker. Smith spent five years at Netscape, where he ran investor relations and corporate development and played a role in over 20 joint ventures, investments and acquisitions including Netscape's ultimate sale to AOL. Smith was a founding partner of The Barksdale Group, a venture capital firm. Moving into Internet transactions, Smith became an exec. at Allen & Company, handling projects including multiple transactions for Google, Advertising.com's sale to AOL, the del.icio.us sale to Yahoo, Neopets' sale to Viacom, Loudeye's sale to Nokia and CNET's acquisition of Webshots, among other transactions. In this role he also worked with companies such as Comcast, the Weinstein Company and CBS, as well as investments for Allen & Company in SpotRunner, Fon, Ning and Sling Media, among others. He joined CBS in Nov. 2006 and served as pres., CBS Interactive, for CBS Corporation. He also works closely with CBS' financial team to identify new businesses that could complement core assets and build its digital presence. 2010 Launced own advisory firm, Code Advisors, which will seek to fill a gap in providing advisory services to digital media companies.

SMITH, WILL
Actor, Singer. b. Philadelphia, PA, Sept. 25, 1968. m. actress Jada Pinkett Smith. Teamed with musician Jeff Townes as rap duo D.J. Jazzy Jeff & the Fresh Prince. Albums: Rock the House, He's the DJ I'm the Rapper, And in This Corner, Homebase. Recipient of 2 Grammy Awards. Producer for production company Overbrook Entertainment.
PICTURES: Where the Day Takes You (debut, 1992), Made in America, Six Degress of Separation, Bad Boys, Independence Day, Men in Black, Enemy of the State, Wild Wild West, The Legend of Bagger Vance, Men in Black II, Ali (Academy Award nom.; Golden Globe nom. 2002), Bad Boys II, I, Robot (also exec. prod.), Shark Tale (voice), Saving Face (prod. only), Hitch (also prod.), ATL (prod.), Pursuit of Happyness (also prod., Academy Award nom.; Golden Globe nom. 2007), Tonight, He Comes (also prod.), I Am Legend, Hancock (also prod.), Lakeview Terrace (prod.), The Secret Life of Bees (prod.), Seven Pounds (also prod.), Old Boy (also prod.), The Karate Kid (prod.), This Means War (prod.), Men in Black III.
TELEVISION: *Movies*: The Perfect Date, Voices That Care, (lead vocals as Fresh Prince), MILF & Cookies (exec. prod.). *Series*: Fresh Prince of Bel Air (also co-exec. prod., 2 Golden Globe noms.), comp. and singer of theme), Happily Ever After: Fairy Tales for Every Child (voice), All of Us (exec. prod./writer/co-creator/story creator). *Guest:* More than 260 appearances.

SMITH, WILLIAM
Actor. b. Columbia, MO, March 24, 1934. e. Syracuse, U., BA;

UCLA, MA.
PICTURES: Darker Than Amber, C.C. and Company, The Losers, Run, Angel, Run, Blood and Guts, Seven, Fast Company, No Knife, Twilight's Last Gleaming, The Frisco Kid, Any Which Way You Can, Rumble Fish, Red Dawn, Eye of the Tiger, Commando Squad, Moon in Scorpio, Hell Comes to Frogtown, Maniac Cop, Red Nights, Nam, B.O.R.N., Action U.S.A., Deadly Breed, Evil Altar, Jungle Assault, L.A. Vice, Slow Burn, Terror in Beverly Hills, Hell on the Battleground, Forgotten Heroes, Instant Karma, Empire of Ash, Emperor of the Bronx, Rock n' Roll Cops, Broken Vessels, Merchants of Evil, The Last Riders, Last of the Warriors, Kiss and Be Killed, The Final Sanction, Cybernator, American Me, Third Rail, Shadow of the Dragon, Legend of Skull Canyon, The Feast, Dark Secrets, Road to Revenge, Hard Time Romance, Maverick, Manosaurus, Taken Alive, Raw Energy, Judee Strange, Big Sister 2000, Rasputin, Neon Signs, Deadly Currency, Uncle Sam, The Shooter, Interview with a Zombie, Hollywood Cops, Ground Zero, Broken Vessels, No Rest for the Wicked, Dogs of Damnation, Blood of His Own, Inspector Gadget, Wasteland Justice, Vice, Plastic Boy and His Jokers, Never Look Back, Elite, Dangerous Highway, Never Look Back, The Vampire Hunters Club, Scarlet Countess, Deadman's Bluff, The Killing Point, Zombiegeddon, Y.M.I., Jumper, Killer Story, Inner Rage, Her Morbid Desires.
TELEVISION: *Movies*: The Over-the-Hill Gang, Crowhaven Farm, The Rockford Files (pilot), The Sex Symbol, Death Among Friends, Manhunter, The Rebels, Wild Times, The Jerk Too, Slow Burn, Rasputin (voice), The Malibu Branch, The Colony. *Mini-series*: Rich Man Poor Man, The Rebels. *Series*: The Asphalt Jungle, Zero One, Laredo, Emerald Point N.A.S., Rich Man Poor Man: Book II, Hawaii 5-0, Wildside. *Documentaries:* Tales of the Apple Dumpling Gang, The Wonderful World of Disney (series). *Guest:* More than 125 appearances.

SMITROVICH, BILL
Actor. b. Bridgeport, CT, May 16, 1947. e. Univ. of Bridgeport, Smith Col. Studied acting at Actors and Directors Lab.
THEATER: *B'way*: The American Clock. *Off-B'way*: Never Say Die, Frankie and Johnny in the Claire de Lune, Seks. Regional: Requeim for a Heavyweight, Food from Trash, Of Mice and Men, The Love Suicide at Schofield Barracks.
PICTURES: A Little Sex, Without a Trace, Splash, Maria's Lovers, Key Exchange, Silver Bullet, Band of the Hand, Manhunter, A Killing Affair, Her Alibi, Renegades, Crazy People, Bodily Harm, The Phantom, The Trigger Effect, Independence Day, Air Force One, Around the Fire, Kiss Toledo Goodbye, Thirteen Days Which Shocked the World, Heavens Fall, The Contract, The Last Lullaby, Iron Man, Flash of Genius, Black Widow, Eagle Eye, Seven Pounds, The Second Time, The Rum Diary.
TELEVISION: *Movies*: Born Beautiful, Miami Vice: Brother's Keeper, Overdrawn at the Memory Bank, Crime Story, Muggable Mary, Gregory K: A Place to Be, Labor of Love: The Arlette Schweitzer Story, Children of the Dark, Texas Justice, Mr. Murder, Futuresport, The '60s, Batman Beyond: The Movie, The Golden Spiders: A Nero Wolfe Mystery, Fail Safe, Far East, The Reagans, While I Was Gone, Mrs. Harris, Me & Lee?. *Series*: Crime Story, Life Goes On, Millennium, The Practice, The Henry Lee Project, Without a Trace, The Event (pilot). *Documentaries: Video:* Independence Day: The ID4 Invasion, Roots of the Cuban Missile Crisis. *Guest*: More than 59 appearances.

SMITS, JIMMY
Actor. b. New York, NY, July 9, 1955. e. Brooklyn College, B.A.; Cornell U., M.F.A. Worked as community organizer before acting with NY Shakespeare Fest. Public Theater.
THEATRE: Hamlet (NY Shakespeare Fest., 1983), Little Victories, Buck, The Ballad of Soapy Smith, Death and the Maiden.
PICTURES: Running Scared (debut, 1986), The Believers, Old Gringo, Vital Signs, Fires Within, Switch, Gross Misconduct, My Family/Mi Familia, Marshal Law, Murder in Mind, Lesser Prophets, The Million Dollar Hotel, Bless the Child, Price of Glory, Star Wars: Episode II - Attack of the Clones, Angel, Star Wars: Episode III - Revenge of the Sith, The Jane Austen Book Club, Backyard, Mother and Child.
TELEVISION: *Movies*: Rockabye, The Highwayman, Dangerous Affection, Glitz, The Broken Cord, The Tommyknockers, The Cisco Kid, Solomon and Sheba, The Last Word, Marshal Law, Lackawanna Blues. *Series*: L.A. Law (Emmy Award, 1990, 5 other noms.; Golden Globe nom.), NYPD Blue (5 Emmy noms.; Golden Globe, 1996, 2 other noms.), The West Wing (recurring guest role), Cane (also exec. prod.), Dexter (Emmy nom. 2009). *Pilots*: Miami Vice, Outlaw. *Documentaries/Specials*: The Other Side of the Border (narrator), Happily Ever After Fairy Tales: Cinderella (voice), Hispanic Americans: The New Frontier (host), The Story of the Western, Mother Goose: A Rappin' and Rhymin' Special (voice). *Guest*: More than 105 appearances.

SMOTHERS, DICK
Comedian. b. New York, NY, Nov. 20, 1939. e. San Jose State. Brother is Tom Smothers. College. Films: The Silver Bears (debut, 1978).
PICTURES: Speed Zone, Casino, The Debtors, The Informant!.
TELEVISION: *Movies:* Alice Through the Looking Glass, Terror at Alcatraz. *Series:* The New Steve Allen Show, The Smothers Brothers Show, The Smothers Brothers Comedy Hour (Emmy nom. 1988), The Smothers Brothers Show (1975), Fitz and Bones. *Documentaries:* Off Your Duff, CBS: The First 50 Years, The '70s: The Decade That Changed Television, TV's Most Censored Moments, Uncensored Comedy: That's Not Funny!, The Aristocrats, Tales of the Rat Fink (voice). *Guest:* More than 109 appearances.

SMOTHERS, TOM
Comedian. b. New York, NY, Feb. 2, 1937. e. San Jose State College. Brother is Dick Smothers. Began career as coffeehouse folk singers with a bit of comic banter mixed in. After success at some of hipper West Coast clubs, appeared on Jack Paar's Tonight Show, The Jack Benny Show and as regulars on Steve Allen's show, 1961. 1962-65 had a series of popular albums. After starring in a situation comedy show, Tom and his brother, Dick, hosted their own variety program. On B'way in musical I Love My Wife.
PICTURES: *Actor:* Get to Know Your Rabbit, The Silver Bears, A Pleasure Doing Business, Serial, There Goes the Bride, Pandemonium, Speed Zone!, The Informant!. *Producer:* Another Nice Mess
TELEVISION: *Movies:* Terror at Alcatraz, Comedy In Bloom (narrator), Once Upon a Mattress. *Series*: The Steve Allen Show (1961), The Smothers Brothers Show (1965-66), The Smothers Brothers Comedy Hour (1967-69), The Smothers Brothers Show (1970), The Smothers Brothers Show (1975), Fitz and Bones, The Smothers Brothers Comedy Hour (Emmy nom. 1988), The Vegas Connection., The '70s: The Decade That Changed Television, TV's Most Censored Moments, Smothered: The Censorship Struggles of the Smothers Brothers Comedy Hour. *Specials*: The Smothers Brothers Reunion. *Guest:* More than 132 appearances.

SNELL, PETER R. E.
Producer. b. Nov. 17, 1941. Entered industry 1967. Appt. head of prod. and man. dir. British Lion 1973. Joined Robert Stigwood group 1975. Returned to indep. prod., 1978; Hennessy. Appt. chief exec., Britannic Film & Television Ltd. 1985, purchased British Lion Film Prods., Ltd. from Thorn/EMI 1986-87. 1988: chmn. and chief executive British Lion.
PICTURES: Winters Tale, Some May Live, A Month in the Country, Carnaby 68, Subterfuge, Julius Caesar, Goodbye Gemini, Antony and Cleopatra, The Wicker Man, Hennessy, Bear Island, Mother Lode, Lady Jane, Turtle Diary, A Prayer for the Dying, Letters from a Killer, Cowboys for Christ (exec. prod.), The Wicker Tree.
TELEVISION: *Movies:* The Hostage Tower, Tears in the Rain, Death Train, Nightwatch. *Exec. Prod.*: A Man For All Seasons, Treasure Island, The Crucifer of Blood.

SNIDER, STACEY
Executive. b. 1960. e. Univ. of Pennsylvania, graduate. UCLA, School of Law graduate, 1985. After graduation Snider began working in the mail room at the Triad Agency and soon became the assistant at Simpson-Bruckheimer Productions. Later she became dir. of development and, ultimately, executive v.p. at Guber-Peters Entertainment Company (GPEC). In 1992, she became TriStar Pictures pres. and was in charge of films such as "Sleepless in Seattle," "Philadelphia," "Jumanjii," and "Legends of the Fall." Snider joined Universal Pictures in December 1996 as co-president, production, was promoted to head of production in April 1998. In Nov. 1998 named president, production. She held the post of chairman since November 1999, when she was promoted from the role of Co-Chairman. She became CEO, 1999. During her tenure, Universal experienced a remarkable turnaround, with a consistent output of domestic and intl. box office hits which included the Academy Award®-winners "A Beautiful Mind," "Gladiator," "Erin Brockovich" and Focus Features' "The Pianist." Snider has consistently made lists of the most powerful women in entertainment and ranked 59 among Forbes' The Most Powerful Women In 2005. Became CEO and co-chair of DreamWorks Studios in 2006. Also in 2006 ranked #50 in Fortune Magazine's most powerful women list.

SNIPES, WESLEY
Actor. b. Bronx, NY, July 31, 1962. e. SUNY/Purchase. Performed with puppet theatre group called Struttin Street Stuff before landing NY stage work. Appeared in Michael Jackson video Bad.
THEATRE: *B'way*: The Boys of Winter, Death and the King's Horsemen, Execution of Justice.
PICTURES: Wildcats (debut, 1986), Streets of Gold, Critical Condition, Major League, Mo' Better Blues, King of New York, New Jack City, Jungle Fever, White Men Can't Jump, The Waterdance, Passenger 57, Boiling Point, Rising Sun, Demolition Man, Sugar Hill, Drop Zone, To Wong Foo—Thanks for Everything—Julie Newmar, Money Train, Waiting to Exhale, The Fan, Murder at 1600, Down in the Delta, Blade (also prod.), U.S. Marshals, One Night Stand, The Art of War, Blade 2, Undisputed, (also exec. prod.), Zigzag, Liberty Stands Still, Blade: Trinity, (also prod.), Unstoppable, Chaos, 7 Seconds, Chasing the Dragon, The Detonator (video), Hard Luck (video), Gallowwalker, Art of War: The Betrayal, Brooklyn's Finest, Game of Death.

TELEVISION: *Movies:* America's Dream, Futuresport, Disappearing Acts (also exec. prod.). *Series*: H.E.L.P. *Special*: Vietnam War Stories (ACE Award, 1989). *Guest*: More than 50 appearances.

SNOW, MARK
Composer. b. Brooklyn, NY, Aug. 26, 1946. e. Juilliard School of Music, 1968. As co-founder and member of New York Rock 'n' Roll Ensemble, appeared with the Boston Pops at Carnegie Hall concerts and on the college circuit in the 1960s and 1970s. Has won 28 ASCAP Film and Television Awards 1986-2006.
PICTURES: Skateboard, Something Short of Paradise, High Risk, Jake Speed, Born to Be Wild, The X-Files: Fight the Future, Disturbing Behavior, Crazy in Alabama, The Dancing Crow, Stranger in My House, Code Name Phoenix, Pearl Harbor II-PearlmageddonPearlmageddon, Bereft, Private Fears in Public Places, The X-Files: I Want to Believe (conductor), Wild Grass, The Kings of Appletown, White Irish Drinkers, The Hunters.
TELEVISION: *Movies*: The Boy in the Plastic Bubble, Overboard, The Return of the Mod Squad, Angel City, Games Mother Never Taught You, John Steinbeck's Winter of Our Discontent, Packin' It In, I Married a Centerfold, Something About Amelia (Emmy nom. 1984), Challenge of a Lifetime, California Girls, I Dream of Jeannie: Fifteen Years Later, Not My Kid, The Lady From Yesterday, Beverly Hills Cowgirl Blues, The Lost Capone (Emmy nom. 1991) Acceptable Risks, News at Eleven, The Girl Who Spelled Freedom (Emmy nom.), Murder By the Book, A Hobo's Christmas, The Father Clements Story, Still Crazy Like a Fox, Cracked Up, Roman Holiday, Pals, Murder Ordained, Louis L'Amour's Down the Long Hills, The Saint, The Return of Ben Casey, Bluegrass, Alone in the Neon Jungle, Those She Left Behind, Stuck With Each Other, Settle the Score, Archie: To Riverdale and Back Again, Child of the Night, Dead Reckoning, Follow Your Heart, The Girl Who Came Between Them, The Little Kidnappers, Miracle Landing, When He's Not a Stranger, Opposites Attract, Crash: The Mystery of Flight 1501, In the Line of Duty, The Marla Hanson Story, A Woman Scorned: The Betty Broderick Story, Highway Heartbreaker, Deliver Them From Evil: The Taking of Alta View, An American Story (Emmy nom. 1993), Telling Secrets, The Man With 3 Wives, Born Too Soon, In the Line of Duty: Ambush in Waco, Precious Victims, Scattered Dreams: The Kathryn Messenger Story, In the Line of Duty: The Price of Heaven, Murder Between Friends, Moment of Truth: Cradle of Conspiracy, Substitute Wife, Down Out and Dangerous, Cloned, The Day Lincoln Was Shot, Le Dernier Combat, Mr. Murder, A Memory in My Heart, A Touch of Hope, In the Name of the People, Another Woman's Husband, Dirty Pictures, For Love of Olivia, Wolf Lake, Ground Zero, D.C. Sniper: 23 Days of Fear, She's Too Young, Helter Skelter (Emmy nom. 2004), Kojak, Odd Girl Out. *Mini-series*: Blood and Orchids, Night Sins, Oldest Living Confederate Widow Tells All (Emmy nom. 1994), Children of the Dust (Emmy nom. 1995). *Series*: The Rookies, Starsky and Hutch, The Gemini Man, Family, The San Pedro Beach Bums, The Love Boat, The Next Step Beyond, Vega$, Hart to Hart, When the Whistle Blows, Dynasty, Falcon Crest, Strike Force, Cagney and Lacey, T.J. Hooker, The Family Tree, Lottery!, Double Trouble, Crazy Like a Fox, Hometown, The X-Files (pilot, Emmy nom. 1994, 5 Emmy noms for series), Millenium, Nowhere Man (Emmy nom. 1996), La Femme Nikita, Harsh Realm, Bull, Sole Survival, Dark Realm, Lone Gunmen, Special Unit 2, The Guardian, Pasadena, Smallville, The Twilight Zone, Ghost Whisperer (2 Emmy noms.), Haunted, One Tree Hill. *Specials*: Day-to-Day Affairs, Vietnam War Story.

SNYDER, BRUCE M.
Executive. b. New York, NY, July 1, 1946. e. Queens College. Began entertainment career with Paramount Pictures as a booker in San Francisco, 1968-69. Paramount sales, NY 1969-76. Became eastern div. mgr., 20th Century Fox, 1976-80. New York sales mgr., American Cinema Releasing, 1980-82. Eastern div. mgr., Embassy Pictures, 1982-83. Eastern div. mgr., TriStar Pictures, 1984-85. General sales mgr., 20th Century Fox, 1985-89. Pres., domestic distribution, 20th Century Fox, 1989-present.

SOADY, WILLIAM C.
Executive. b. Toronto, Canada, Oct. 7, 1943. Career with Universal Pictures started in 1970 when named Toronto branch mgr.; promoted to v.p. & gen. sls. mgr. of Universal Film (Canada) in 1971. Promoted to v.p. & gen. sls. mgr., Universal Pictures, 1981, in NY relocating to L.A. later that year. 1983 named pres. of Universal Pictures Distribution, new domestic dist. div. of Universal; resigned, 1988. Named exec. v.p. distrib., Tri-Star Pictures, 1988; pres. of distrib., 1992. Named pres. & CEO of Showscan Entertainment Inc. in 1994. Became pres. of distrib. for Polygram Films in 1997. Currently director of distribution and-marketing for Mathiis Chapell LLC, a motion picture development, production and distribution company.

SOAMES, RICHARD
Executive, Producer. b. London, England, June 6, 1936. Joined Film Finances Ltd. 1972; Appt. director Film Finances Ltd., 1977: Appt. man. dir. 1979. Appt. pres. Film Finances Canada Ltd. In 1982 appointed to his current position of president, Film Finances Inc. Also formed Doric Productions.
PICTURES: The Boss's Wife, The Principal, Honey I Shrunk the Kids, Tap.

SOBIESKI, LEELEE
Actress. r.n. Liliane Rudabet Gloria Elsveta Sobieski. b. New York, NY, June 10, 1982.
PICTURES: Jungle 2 Jungle, A Soldier's Daughter Never Cries, Deep Impact, Never Been Kissed, Eyes Wide Shut, Here on Earth, My First Mister, The Glass House, Joy Ride, Max, London, The Optimist, Heavens Fall, The Wicker Man, In the Name of the King: A Dungeon Siege Tale, 88 Minutes, Acts of Violence, Finding Bliss (also exec. prod.), Night Train, Public Enemies, Acts of Violence, The Mad Cow, The Last Film Festival.
TELEVISION: *Movies:* Reunion, A Horse for Danny, Joan of Arc, Uprising, Hercules. *Mini-series:* Les liasiones dangereuses, Hercules. *Series:* Charlie Grace.

SODERBERGH, STEVEN
Director, Writer, Editor, Producer. b. Atlanta, GA, Jan. 14, 1963. First major professional job was directing concert film for rock group Yes for Grammy-nominated video, 1986. Many credits under the pseudonym, Peter Andrews.
PICTURES: *Director-Editor*: Sex Lies and Videotape (debut, 1989; also s.p.; Cannes Fest. Palme d'Or Award; Academy Award nom.; Golden Globe nom.; WGA nom. for s.p. 1990), Kafka, King of the Hill (also s.p.), The Underneath (also s.p.), Schizopolis (also actor), Gray's Anatomy, Out of Sight, The Limey, Erin Brockovich (Academy Award nom.; DGA nom.; Golden Globe nom. 2001), Traffic (Academy Award, DGA nom.; Golden Globe nom. 2001), Ocean's Eleven, How to Survive a Hotel Room Fire, Bubble (also prod. & cinematographer), The Good German (also prod.), Guerrilla (also prod., writer), The Argentine (also prod.), The Informant!, The Girlfriend Experience (also cinematographer), Che: Part One (also cinematographer), Che: Part Two (also cinematographer), The Informant! (dir., cinematographer), And Everything Is Going Fine (doc., dir.), The Last Time I Saw Michael Gregg (dir., actor), Haywire (dir., cinematographer), Haywire (also cinematographer). *Producer*: The Day Trippers, Pleasantville, Welcome to Collinwood, Full Frontal, Solaris, The Informant!, Eros, The Jacket, Criminal (also s.p.), Keane, The Good German (also dir., cinematographer, editor), Guerrilla (also dir., writer), Niagara, Ocean's Thirteen (also dir., cinematographer, exec. prod.), Solitary Man, Night Train, Cleo (also dir.), Solitary Man, Contagion (also dir.). *Executive producer:* Suture, Insomnia, Far From Heaven, Nagoygatsi (doc.), Confessions of a Dangerous Mind, Able Edwards, Ocean's Twelve, (also dir., cinematographer), A Scanner Darkly, A Confederacy of Dunces (also writer), Good Night and Good Luck, Syriana, Rumor Has It, Wind Chill, Michael Clayton, I'm Not There., Leatherheads (also writer), Playground (doc.), Rebecca H. (Return to the Dogs), We Need to Talk About Kevin.
TELEVISION: *Series:* Games People Play (editor), Fallen Angels (The Quiet Room), K Street (exec. prod., dir., cinematoprapher), Unscripted (exec. prod. & pilot dir.). *Special:* Roman Polanski: Wanted and Desired (Emmy nom. 2009).

SOKOLOW, DIANE
Executive, Producer. b. New York, NY. e. Temple U. m. Mel Sokolow. 1975, v.p., East Coast operations, for Lorimar; with Warner Bros. 1977-81; served as v.p. of East Coast production. Left to form The Sokolow Co. with husband, Mel, to produce films. 1982, returned to WB as v.p., East Coast prod. 1984, joined Motown Prods. as exec. v.p.; producer, MGM-UA 1986-87. From 1996-2000, S.V.P., East Coast Production, Phoenix Pictures. Currently Sokolow is an independent producer.
PICTURES: *As Actress:* My Son's Brother (co-prod.), This Is My Life, Sleepless in Seattle, Mixed Nuts, You've Got Mail, Possum Trot Cloggers (prod. only).
TELEVISION: *Movies: Executive producer*: Miles from Nowhere, Trial: The Price of Passion, Casualties of Love: The Long Island Lolita Story, Fallen Champ: The Untold Story of Mike Tyson, Mother May I Sleep With Danger?, The Outsider, The Perfect Husband: The Laci Peterson Story. *Mini-series: Executive producer:* The Hamptons.

SOLONDZ, TODD
Director, Producer, Writer. b. Newark, NJ, October 15, 1959. e. NYU Film Sch. After first feature film release, left filmmaking to teach English as a Second Language. Returned with Welcome to the Dollhouse.
PICTURES: Feelings (NYU short), Babysitter (NYU short), Schatt's Last Shot (NYU short), Fear Anxiety and Depression, Married to the Mob (actor only), Welcome to the Dollhouse (Jury Prize, Sundance Film Fest.), Happiness (Golden Globe nom. 1999), Storytelling, Palindromes, Life During Wartime (dir., s.p.), Dark Horse (dir., s.p.). *Actor*: As Good as It Gets.
TELEVISION: How I Became a Leading Artistic Figure in New York City's East Village Cultural Landscape (short for Saturday Night Live).

SOLT, ANDREW W.
Producer, Writer, Director. b. London, England, December 13, 1947. e. UCLA. Founder of Andrew Solt Productions.
PICTURES: Imagine: John Lennon, This is Elvis, It Came From Hollywood. Many documentaries about Elvis Presley.
TELEVISION: Honeymooners' Reunion, The Muppets... A

Celebration of 30 Years, Cousteau's Mississippi, America Censored, Remembering Marilyn, Great Moments in Disney Animation, ET & Friends, Disney's DTV, Heroes of Rock 'n Roll, Bob Hope's Christmas Tours, Disney Goes To The Oscars, Cousteau: Oasis In Space (series, Emmy nom. 1978), Cousteau: Odyssey (Emmy nom. 1978), Best of the Ed Sullivan Show (4 specials Emmy nom. 1991), The History of Rock 'n' Roll, (vol. 1-10, Emmy nom. 1995 for vol. #9), Donald Duck's 50th Birthday (Emmy nom. 1985) All-Star 25th Birthday: Stars and Street Forever! (Emmy nom. 1994), Grammy's Greatest Moments, TV Guide's 40th Anniversary Special, 25x5: The Continuing Adventures of the Rolling Stones, Andy Griffith Show Reunion, Cousteau: Search for Atlantis I&II, All My Children 25th Anniversary Special, Hunt for Amazing Treasure, Great Moments in Disney Animation, Gimme Some Truth, 50 Years of NBC Late Night, NBC 75th Anniversary Celebration, Las Vegas Then & Now, Destination: The Strip, CBS at 75 (segment prod.), The 76th Annual Academy Awards (editor, Emmy nom. 2004), 'Smallville' Backstage Special (doc.), Ed Sullivan's Rock and Roll Classics: The 60s.

SOMMER, JOSEF
Actor. b. Greifswald, Germany, June 26, 1934. Raised in North Carolina. e. Carnegie-Mellon U. Studied at American Shakespeare Festival in Stratford, CT, 1962-64. U.S. Army, 1958-60. NY stage debut in Othello, 1970.
PICTURES: Dirty Harry (debut, 1971), Man on a Swing, The Front, Close Encounters of the Third Kind, Oliver's Story, Hide in Plain Sight, Absence of Malice, Reds, Rollover, Hanky Panky, Still of the Night, Sophie's Choice (narrator), Independence Day, Silkwood, Iceman, Witness, D.A.R.Y.L., Target, The Rosary Murders, Chances Are, Dracula's Widow, Forced March, Bloodhounds of Broadway, Shadows and Fog, The Mighty Ducks, Malice, Cultivating Charlie, Nobody's Fool, Strange Days, Moonlight & Valentino, The Chamber, The Proposition, Bulworth, Patch Adams, The Next Best Thing, Shaft, The Family Man, Searching for Paradise, The Sum of All Fears, Summer in Siam, The Elephant King, X-Men: The Last Stand, The Visiting, The Invasion, Stop-Loss, Little Witch on a Broomstick.
TELEVISION: *Movies*: Too Far to Go, Doctor Franken, The Henderson Monster, Sparkling Cyanide, The Betty Ford Story, A Special Friendship, Bridge to Silence, The Bionic Showdown: The Six Million Dollar Man and the Bionic Woman, Money Power Murder, Spy Games, An American Story, Citizen Cohn, Hostages, The Enemy Within, Don't Drink the Water, The Minutes, Kansas, Letter to My Killer, Hidden in America, Mistrial, The Widenet, The Impressionists. *Mini-series*: The Kennedys of Massachusetts, A Woman Named Jackie, Benjamin Franklin. *Series*: Hothouse, Under Cover. *Documentaries/Specials*: Morning Becomes Electra, The Scarlet Letter, Saigon. *Guest:* More than 57 appearances.

SONDHEIM, STEPHEN
Composer, Lyricist. b. New York, NY, March 22, 1930. e. Williams Coll. Writer for Topper TV series, 1953. Wrote incidental music for The Girls of Summer (1956), Invitation to a March (1961), Twigs (1971). Winner of 6 Grammy Awards: Cast Albums 1970, 1973, 1979, 1984, 1988 and song of the year 1975. Named Visiting Prof. of Contemporary Theater, Oxford U. 1990.
THEATRE: *Lyrics only:* West Side Story, Gypsy, Do I Hear a Waltz? *Music and lyrics*: A Funny Thing Happened on the Way to the Forum, Anyone Can Whistle, Company (Tony Award, 1971), Follies (Tony Award, 1972), A Little Night Music (Tony Award, 1973), The Frogs, Candide (new lyrics for revival), Pacific Overtures, Sweeney Todd, (Tony Award, 1979), Merrily We Roll Along, Sunday in the Park with George (Pulitzer Prize, 1985), Into the Woods (Tony Award, 1988), Assassins, Passion (Tony Award, 1994). Theater anthologies of his songs: Side By Side By Sondheim; Marry Me a Little, You're Gonna Love Tomorrow, Putting It Together. *Play:* Getting Away With Murder.
PICTURES: West Side Story (lyrics), Gypsy (lyrics), A Funny Thing Happened on the Way to the Forum (music, lyrics), The Last of Sheila (s.p.), Stavisky (score), A Little Night Music (music, lyrics), Reds (score), Dick Tracy (music, lyrics; Academy Award for best song, 2 Golden Globe noms. 1991), Postcards from the Edge, The Birdcage, Selena (lyricist), The Bridge (lyricist), Camp, Starsky & Hutch, Ella Enchanted, Connie and Carla, Where the Truth Lies, Last Holiday, Sweeney Todd: The Demon Barber of Fleet Street, Madagascar: Escape 2 Africa (soundtrack writer).
TELEVISION: *Movies:* Evening Primrose, June Moon, (actor), Sweeney Todd, Sunday in the Park with George, A Little Night Music, Into the Woods, Gypsy, The Sunshine Boys, Passion, Company, Putting It Together, Sweeney Todd: The Demon Barber of Fleet Street In Concert. *Series:* Topper (writer). *Specials*: Evening Primrose (music, lyrics; ABC Stage '67), Into the Woods. Many production credits as soundtrack writer.

SONNENFELD, BARRY
Director, Producer, Cinematographer. b. New York, NY April 1, 1953. Producer/Exec. for Right Coast Productions. Received Emmy Award for photography on series Out of Step.
PICTURES: *Cinematographer:* Blood Simple (debut, 1984), Compromising Positions, Raising Arizona, Three O'Clock High, Throw Momma From the Train, Big, When Harry Met Sally..., Miller's Crossing, Misery. *Director:* The Addams Family (debut, 1991), For Love or Money (also co-prod.), Addams Family Values (also cameo), Get Shorty (also exec. prod.), Men in Black, Wild Wild West, Big Trouble (also prod.), Men in Black II, White Noise (also prod.), R.V., Men in Black III. *Producer:* The Ladykillers, Enchanted, Space Chimps. *Executive producer:* Lemony Snicket's A Series of Unfortunate Events.
TELEVISION: *Movies*: *Cinematographer:* How to Be a Perfect Person In Just Three Days, Doubletake, Welcome Home Bobby, Classified Love, Hackett (dir. only), Let It Go (dir.). *Dir: Series:* Notes from the Underbelly (also exec. prod.). *Series: Producer or Executive producer:* Maximum Bob, Fantasy Island, Partners, Secret Agent Man, The Tick (also pilot), Karen Sisco, Pushing Daisies (DGA Award, Emmy Award 2008), Funny in Farsi, Notes from the Underbelly.

SOOK, PERRY
Executive. b. DuBois, PA, Feb. 26, 1958. e. B.S., communications, Ohio University,1980.
Sales/on-air talent, WPME(AM/FM) Punxsutawney, Pa., 1974-1976; sales/on-air talent, WATH/WXTQ (FM), Athens, Ohio, 1977-1980; news anchor, WDTV Clarksburg, W.Va., 1979; account executive, WFIV (AM) Kissimmee, Fla., 1980; account executive, WOWK Huntington, W.V., 1980-1981; account executive, WPXI Pittsburgh 1981-1983; national account executive, TeleRep Inc., 1983-1985; national sales manager, KTVT Dallas, 1985-1987; general sales manager/acting general manager, KXTX, 1987-1989; president/CEO, Seaway Communications Inc. 1990-1991; principal, Superior Communications Group Inc., 1991-1996; Founded Nexstar Broadcasting Group, Inc., 1996, and is currently Chairman, president & CEO. Headquartered in Irving, TX, Nexstar owns, operates and/or services 20 stations and focuses on the acquisition, development and operation of TV stations in medium-sized markets in the U.S. The Texas Association of Broadcasters named Sook its 2006 Broadcaster of the Year.

SORVINO, MIRA
Actress. b. Tenafly, NJ,September 28, 1967. Father is actor Paul Sorvino. e. Harvard U., A.B., 1990.
PICTURES: Amongst Friends (also assoc. prod.), Quiz Show, Parallel Lives, Barcelona, Tarantella, Sweet Nothing, Mighty Aphrodite (Academy Award, Golden Globe Award 1996), The Dutch Master (short), The Second Greatest Story Ever Told (short), Blue in the Face, Tales of Erotica, New York Cop, Beautiful Girls, Romy and Michele's High School Reunion, Mimic, The Replacement Killers, Too Tired to Die, Lulu on the Bridge, Free Money, At First Sight, Summer of Sam, Joan of Arc: The Virgin Warrior, The Triumph of Love, The Grey Zone, Angel of Death, Wise Girls, Gods and Generals, Between Strangers, The Final Cut, Leningrad, Reservation Road, Like Dandelion Dust, Multiple Sarcasms, The Trouble with Cali, The Presence (also exec. prod.), Drift.
TELEVISION: *Movies*: The Second Greatest Story Ever Told, Parallel Lives, Jake's Women, Norma Jean and Marilyn (Emmy nom.; Golden Globe nom. 1996), The Great Gatsby, Human Trafficking (Golden Globe nom. 2006), Covert One: The Hades Factor, The Last Templar. *Mini-series*: The Buccaneers, Human Trafficking (Golden Globe nom. 2006), The Hades Factor, The Last Templar. *Series*: The Guiding Light, Swans Crossing. *Guest:* More than 56 appearances.

SORVINO, PAUL
Actor. b. New York, NY, April 13, 1939. Daughter is actress Mira Sorvino.
THEATRE: Bajour, An American Millionaire, The Mating Dance, King Lear, That Championship Season, Marlon Brando Sat Right Here.
PICTURES: Where's Poppa? (debut, 1970), The Panic in Needle Park, Made for Each Other, A Touch of Class, The Day of the Dolphin, The Gambler, Shoot It Black Shoot It Blue, I Will I Will... For Now, Oh God, Bloodbrothers, Slow Dancing in the Big City, The Brink's Job, Lost and Found, Cruising, Reds, I The Jury, That Championship Season, Off the Wall, Very Close Quarters, Turk 182, The Stuff, A Fine Mess, Vasectomy, Dick Tracy, GoodFellas, The Rocketeer, Life in the Food Chain (Age Isn't Everything), The Firm, Nixon, Romeo + Juliet, Money Talks, American Perfekt, Most Wanted, Bulworth, Knock Off, Harlem Aria, Goodnight Joseph Parker, Dead Broke, Longshot, Ciao America, Perfume, See Spot Run, Plan B, Last Call, Rhode Island Blue, Irishman: The Legend of Danny Greene, The Cooler, Hey Arnold! The Movie, Mambo italiano, Goodnight Joseph Parker, Mr. 3000, Mr. Fix It, Greetings from the Shore, Last Hour, The Trouble with Cali (also dir.), Carnera: The Walking Mountain, Repo! The Genetic Opera, The Wild Stallion, The Irishman, Switchback.
TELEVISION: *Movies*: Tell Me Where It Hurts, It Couldn't Happen to a Nicer Guy, Dummy, A Question of Honor, My Mother's Secret Life, With Intent to Kill, Surviving, Don't Touch My Daughter, The Case of the Wicked Wives, Parallel Lives, Without Consent, Joe Torre: Curveballs Along the Way, Houdini, That Championship Season, Chearers, Thin Blue Lie, The Amati Girls, Mafia Doctor, Doc West, Santa Baby 2. *Mini-series*: Seventh Avenue, Chiefs. *Series*: We'll Get By, Bert D'Angelo: Superstar, Behind Bars,The Oldest Rookie, Law and Order, That's Life, Still Standing, Mogli a pezzi. *Documentaries/Specials*: The Big House (narr.), The Last Mile, Bullets Over Hollywood (narr., singer). *Guest:* More than 70

appearances.

SOUL, DAVID
Actor. r.n. David Solberg. b. Chicago, IL, Aug. 28, 1943.
PICTURES: Johnny Got His Gun, Magnum Force, Dog Pound Shuffle, The Hanoi Hilton, Appointment with Death, Pentathalon, Tabloid, Deadwood, Starsky & Hutch, Puritan, The Hitcher (soundtrack), Farewell, Eldorado.
TELEVISION: *Movies*: The Disappearance of Flight 412, Starsky and Hutch (pilot), Little Ladies of the Night, Salem's Lot, Swan Song (also co-prod.), Rage, Homeward Bound, World War III, Through Naked Eyes, The Fifth Missile, Harry's Hong Kong, In the Line of Duty: The FBI Murders, Prime Target, So Proudly We Hail, Bride in Black, A Cry in the Wild, The Taking of Peggy Ann, Perry Mason: The Case of the Fatal Framing, Grave Secrets: The Legacy of Hilltop Drive, Vents Contraires, Terror in the Mall, Poirot: Death on the Nile, Jerry Springer: The Opera. *Mini-series:* The Manions of America, Il Segreto del Sahara, Sandra princesse rebelle, Les Filles du Lido. *Series*: Here Come the Brides, Owen Marshall-Counselor at Law, Starsky and Hutch, Casablanca, Yellow Rose, Miami Vice (dir. only), Crime Story (dir. only), In the Heat of the Night (dir. only), China Beach (dir. only), Unsub. *Guest:* More than 116 appearances.

SOURIAN, MARK
Executive. Sourian, a one-time assistant to producer Scott Rudin, joined DreamWorks in 1997 as a development assistant and worked his way up the ranks. He has shepherded such films as "The Ring" and its sequel, "House of Sand and Fog," "Red Eye," "The Kite Runner," and "Sweeney Todd: The Demon Barber of Fleet Street." When DreamWorks and Paramount Pictures parted ways in Oct. 2008, production chief Adam Goodman remained with Paramount Pictures. To fill this vacancy, DreamWorks Co-Chairman & CEO Stacey Snider named Sourian and Holly Bario co-presidents, production at the newly independent DreamWorks.

SPACEK, SISSY
Actress. r.n. Mary Elizabeth Spacek. b. Quitman, TX, Dec. 25, 1949. m. director Jack Fisk. Cousin of actor Rip Torn. Attended acting classes in New York under Lee Strasberg. Had bit role in Andy Warhol's Trash. Worked as set decorator on films Death Game, Phantom of the Paradise.
PICTURES: Prime Cut (debut, 1972), Ginger in the Morning, Badlands, Carrie (Academy Award nom. 1977), Welcome to L.A., 3 Women, Heart Beat, Coal Miner's Daughter (Academy Award, Golden Globe Award 1981), Raggedy Man (Golden Globe nom. 1982), Missing (Academy Award nom. Golden Globe nom. 1983), The Man With Two Brains (voice), The River (Academy Award nom. Golden Globe nom. 1985), Marie, Violets Are Blue, 'night Mother, Crimes of the Heart (Academy Award nom.; Golden Globe Award 1987), The Long Walk Home, JFK, Hard Promises, Trading Mom, The Grass Harp, Affliction, Blast from the Past, Rage: Carrie 2, The Straight Story, In The Bedroom (Academy Award nom.; Golden Globe Award 2002), Tuck Everlasting, A Decade Under the Influence (doc.), A Home at the End of the World, The Ring 2, Nine Lives, An American Haunting, Gray Matters, Lake City, Hot Rod, Four Christmases, Get Low.
TELEVISION: *Movies*: The Girls of Huntington House, The Migrants, Katherine, A Private Matter, Verna: USO Girl, Miss Sherri, A Place for Annie, The Good Old Boys (Emmy nom. 1995), Beyond the Call, If These Walls Could Talk, Songs in Ordinary Time, Midwives, Last Call, Fitzgerald (Emmy nom. 2002), Pictures of Hollis Woods (Golden Globe nom. 2008). *Mini-series:* Streets of Laredo. *Series:* Big Love (Emmy nom. 2010). *Specials/Documentaries:* Voices that Care, Thomas Jefferson: A View from the Mountain. *Guest:* More than 64 appearances.

SPACEY, KEVIN
Actor, Producer, Director. r.n. Kevin Spacey Fowler. b. South Orange, NJ, July 26, 1959. Raised in southern CA. e. L.A. Valley Coll., appearing in stage productions as well as stand-up comedy clubs, before attending Juilliard Sch. of Drama. Has appeared in numerous regional and repertory productions including Kennedy Center (The Seagull), Williamstown Theatre Fest. and Seattle Rep. Theatre, and with New York Shakespeare Fest. Recipient of numerous industry awards, including two Acad. Awards.
THEATRE: Henry IV Part I, The Robbers, Barbarians, Ghosts, Hurlyburly, Long Day's Journey into Night, National Anthems, Lost in Yonkers (Tony Award, 1991), Playland, The Iceman Cometh. *London:* The Iceman Cometh, Cloaca (dir. only), National Anthems, The Philadelphia Story, Richard II, A Moon for the Misbegotten, Speed-The-Plow.
PICTURES: *Actor:* Heartburn (debut, 1986), Rocket Gibraltar, Working Girl, See No Evil Hear No Evil, Dad, A Show of Force, Henry and June, Glengarry Glen Ross, Consenting Adults, Iron Will, The Ref, Outbreak, Swimming With Sharks (also co-prod.), The Usual Suspects (Academy Award, Chicago Film Critics Award, Golden Globe nom. 1996), Se7en, A Time to Kill, L.A. Confidential, Midnight in the Garden of Good and Evil, The Negotiator, Hurlyburly, A Bug's Life (voice), American Beauty (Academy Award, best actor, Golden Globe nom. 2000), The Big Kahuna (also prod.), Ordinary Decent Criminal, Pay It Forward, K-Pax, The Shipping News (Golden Globe nom. 2002), The Tower of Babble (short; narrator), Austin Powers: Goldmember, President Clinton: Final Days (short; appears as himself), Looking for Richard (documentary), Shackleton's Antarctic Adventure (documentary short; narr.), The United States of Leland (also prod.), The Life of David Gale, Beyond the Sea (also s.p., dir. & prod.; Golden Globe nom. 2005), Edison, Superman Returns, Fred Claus, 21 (also prod.), Telstar, Shrink (also prod.), Moon (voice), The Men Who Stare at Goats, Casino Jack, Margin Call, Inseparable (also exec. prod.), Horrible Bosses. *Director:* Albino Alligator. *Executive producer:* Interstate 84, Uncle Frank (doc.), Mr. Gibb, The Social Network, Safe. *Producer:* Triggerstreet.com, Mini's First Time, The Sasquatch Dumpling Gang, Fanboys, Columbus Day, Father of Invention (also actor).
TELEVISION: *Movies*: The Murder of Mary Phagan, Fall from Grace, When You Remember Me, Darrow, Doomsday Gun, Recount (Golden Globe nom. 2009). *Series*: Wiseguy.. *Documentaries/Specials:* Long Day's Journey into Night, Steve McQueen: The King of Cool, Hitchcock: Shadow of a Genius, Come Together: A Night for John Lennon's Words and Music, America Rebuilds: A Year at Ground Zero, Freedom: A History of Us. *Guest:* More than 138 appearances.

SPADE, DAVID
Actor. b. Birmingham, MI, Juy 22, 1964. Raised in Scottsdale, AZ. e. Arizona State Univ., business degree, 1986. Performed stand-up comedy in clubs and colleges which led to debut on Saturday Night Live in 1990.
PICTURES: Light Sleeper (debut, 1982), Coneheads, Reality Bites, P.C.U., Tommy Boy, Black Sheep, 8 Heads in a Duffel Bag, Senseless, The Rugrats Movie (voice), Lost & Found (also s.p.), Loser, Little Nicky, The Emperor's New Groove (voice), Joe Dirt, Dickie Roberts: Former Child Star, Racing Stripes (voice), Grandma's Boy, The Benchwarmers, Hollywood & Wine, Grown Ups.
TELEVISION: *Series*: Saturday Night Live (3 Emmy noms. for writing), Beavis and Butt-head (voice), Just Shoot Me (Emmy nom.; 2 Golden Globe noms. 1999), Sammy (voice also exec. prod.), 8 Simple Rules, The Showbiz Show with David Spade (host, writer, exec. prod.), Saturday Night Live: The Best of David Spade (also writer), Carpet Bros, Rules of Engagement. *Guest:* More than 131 appearances.

SPADER, JAMES
Actor. b. Boston, MA, Feb. 7, 1960. e. Phillips Academy. Studied acting at Michael Chekhov Studio.
PICTURES: Endless Love (debut, 1981), The New Kids, Tuff Turf, Pretty in Pink, Mannequin, Baby Boom, Less Than Zero, Wall Street, Jack's Back, The Rachel Papers, Sex Lies and Videotape (Cannes Fest. Award, 1989), Bad Influence, White Palace, True Colors, Storyville, Bob Roberts, The Music of Chance, Dream Lover, Wolf, Stargate, 2 Days in the Valley, Crash, Critical Care, Curtain Call, Supernova, The Watcher, Slow Burn, Speaking of Sex, Secretary, Shorts.
TELEVISION: *Movies*: Cocaine: One Man's Seduction, A Killer in the Family, Starcrossed, Family Secrets, Keys to Tulsa, The Pentagon Papers. *Series*: The Family Tree, The Practice (Emmy Award 2004), Boston Legal (2 Emmy Awards, 1 other nom.; Golden Globe nom. 2005).

SPANO, VINCENT
Actor. b. New York, NY, Oct. 18, 1962. While attending Stuyvesant H.S. made stage debut at 14 in The Shadow Box (Long Wharf and B'way).
THEATRE: The Shadow Box, Balm in Gilead.
PICTURES: Over the Edge (debut, 1979), The Double McGuffin, The Black Stallion Returns, Baby It's You, Rumblefish, Alphabet City, Maria's Lovers, Creator, Good Morning Babylon, And God Created Woman, 1753: Venetian Red, High Frequency (Aquarium), Oscar, City of Hope, Alive, Indian Summer, The Ascent, The Tie That Binds, A Brooklyn State of Mind, The Unknown Cyclist, No Strings Attached, The Christmas Path, Goosed, Prophecy 3, The Deadly Look of Love, The Colony, Texas Rangers, Silence, Betrunner (short; dir. only), Nevermore, A Modern Twain Story: The Prince and the Pauper, Dante's Inferno Animated (voice, English version), Dante's Inferno Documented (voice), Dante's Purgatorio Documented.
TELEVISION: *Movies*: The Gentleman Bandit, Senior Trip, Blood Ties, Afterburn, Downdraft, Medusa's Child, The Deadly Look of Love, Jenifer, The Rats, Deathlands, Landslide, The Engagement Ring, Her Fatal Flaw, Pandemic, Grave Misconduct, Lone Rider. *Series*: Search for Tomorrow, Prince Street, Law & Order: Special Victims Unit.

SPEARS, JR., HAROLD T.
Executive. b. Atlanta, GA, June 21, 1929. e. U. of Georgia, 1951. With Floyd Theatres, Lakeland, FL, since 1953; Since 1996 has been president of Sun South Theatres, Inc.

SPECKTOR, FREDERICK
Executive. b. Los Angeles, CA, April 24, 1933. e. USC, UCLA. M.P. agent, Ashley Famous Agency, 1962-64; Artists Agency Corp., 1964-68; exec. M.P. dept., William Morris Agency, 1968-78; exec. Creative Artists Agency, 1978-present. Trustees Council, Education First, bd. of dirs., Amer. Jewish Committee. Bd. of dirs. for the ACLU and Center for Gun-Violence Prevention.

SPEEDMAN, SCOTT
Actor. b. London, England, Sept. 1, 1975.

PICTURES: Ursa Major, Kitchen Party, Duets, Dark Blue, My Life Without Me, The 24th Day, Underworld, xXx 2: The Next Level, Underworld: Evolutuion, Weirdsville, The Strangers, Anamorph, Adoration, The Strangers, The Last Rites of Ransom Pride, Good Neighbours, Barney's Version.
TELEVISION: *Movies:* Net Worth, A Brother's Promise: The Dan Jansen Story, Giant Mine, Rescuers Stories of Courage: Two Couples, Dead Silence, What Happened to Bobby Earl?, Every 9 Seconds. *Series:* Nancy Drew, Felicity.

SPELLING, TORI
Actress. r.n. Victoria Davey Spelling. b. Los Angeles, CA, May 16, 1973. Daughter of late producer Aaron Spelling.
PICTURES: Troop Beverly Hills, The House of Yes, Scream 2, Perpetrators of the Crime, Trick, Scary Movie 2, Naked Movie, Sol Goode, 50 Ways to Leave Your Lover, Cthulhu, Kiss the Bride.
TELEVISION: *Movies:* Shooting Stars, Beverly Hills 90210 (pilot), A Friend to Die For, Awake to Murder, Deadly Pursuits, Co-ed Call Girl, Mother May I Sleep with Danger?, The Alibi, A Carol Christmas, Hush, The Family Plan, Mind Over Murder, Housesitter. *Series:* Beverly Hills 90210, So Downtown, The Help, So NoTORIous, Tori & Dean: Inn Love (also exec. prod., 1 episode), 90210 (2008, pilot). *Guest:* More than 96 appearances.

SPENGLER, PIERRE
Producer. b. Paris, France, 1947. Appeared on stage at 15; returned to language studies at Alliance Franccaise. Entered film industry as production runner and office boy. Teamed for first time with friend Ilya Salkind on The Light at the Edge of the World, produced by Alexander Salkind. Exec. Prod./Founder of Production company Clubdeal.
PICTURES: Kill-Kill-Kill-Kill! (assoc. prod.), Bluebeard, The Three Musketeers (exec. in charge of prod.), The Four Musketeers (also exec. in charge of prod.), The Twist, Crossed Swords (also s.p.), Superman, Superman II, Superman III, Santa Claus: The Movie, The Return of the Musketeers, The Turn of the Screw (exec. prod.), Underground (exec. prod.), Snapshots, Summer in the Golden Valley (exec. prod.), Method, Stratosphere Girl (co-prod.), Blessed, Unleashed (co-prod.), 7 Seconds, Man With A Movie Camera, Revolver (co-prod.), Girls Club, The Detonator, Second in Command, The Hard Corps, Incubus (co-prod.), Shadow Man (prod.), Superman II (prod.), Attack Force (prod.), Flight of Fury (prod.), Tirza (exec. prod).
TELEVISION: *Movies:* Pumpkinhead: Ashes to Ashes, Pumpkinhead: Blood Feud.

SPHEERIS, PENELOPE
Director. b. New Orleans, LA, De. 2, 1945. e. UCLA. Film School, MFA.
PICTURES: Real Life (prod. only). *Director:* The Decline of Western Civilization (also prod., s.p.), Suburbia (also s.p.), The Boys Next Door, Summer Camp Nightmare (s.p. only), Hollywood Vice Squad, Dudes, The Decline of Western Civilization-Part II: The Metal Years, Wedding Band (actress only), Wayne's World, The Beverly Hillbillies, The Little Rascals, Black Sheep, The Decline of Western Civilization Part III: Gutterpunks, Senseless, The Thing in Bob's Garage, Hollywierd (documentary), Posers, Closers, We Sold Our Souls for Rock N' Roll (also cinematographer), The Kid & I (also prod.), Gospel According to Janis (also writer), Balls to the Wall.
TELEVISION: *Movies*: UFO Abductions, Prison Stories: Women on the Inside, Applewood 911, Dear Doughboy, The Crooked E: The Unshredded Truth About Enron. *Series:* Saturday Night Live (prod. only), Danger Theatre (co-creator, dir., co-writer). *Documentary:* Mississippi Rising (cinematographer).

SPIEGEL, LARRY
Producer, Writer, Director. b. Brooklyn, NY. e. Ohio U. With CBS-TV; Benton & Bowles; Wells, Rich, Green; BBDO. Now heads Appledown Films, Inc.
PICTURES: *Writer:* Hail, Book of Numbers, Spree (also dir.), Evil Town (also dir.). *Director:* God Bless Dr. Shagetz. *Producer:* Death Game, Remo Williams: The Adventure Begins, The Sunchaser, Soulmates.
TELEVISION: *Movies: Writer:* Alexander Alexander, Remo Williams (pilot ABC; prod.), Avenger (prod.). *Series:* Return to the Planet of the Apes (writer). *Documentaries/Specials: ABC Afterschool Specials:* Bear That Slept Through Christmas (writer), Never Fool With A Gypsy Ikon (writer).

SPIELBERG, STEVEN
Director, Producer. b. Cincinnati, OH, Dec. 18, 1946. e. California State College. m. actress Kate Capshaw. Made home movies as child; completed first film with story and actors at 12 yrs. old in Phoenix. At 13 won film contest for 40-min. war movie, Escape to Nowhere. At 16 made 140-min. film, Firelight. At California State Coll. made five films. First professional work, Amblin' led to a contract with Universal Pictures at age 20. In 1984, formed his own company, Amblin Entertainment, headquartered at Universal Studios. Received Irving G. Thalberg Memorial Award, 1987; American Film Institute Life Achievement Award, 1995. Parterned with David Geffen and Jeffrey Katzenberg to form independent film company DreamWorks SKG in 1995. After an 11-year run, co. execs sold DreamWorks SKG to Paramount Pictures in 2006. The transaction included more than $1 billion in cash and the assumption of DreamWorks' debt. Spielberg signed an employment contract to continue directing for the studio, which will continue producing films under the DreamWorks label. The Walt Disney Company, Disney will handle marketing and distribution of the studio's films around the world, except for India where Reliance subsidiary Reliance Big Entertainment will retain distribution rights. Other Honorary Awards: Golden Eddie Filmmaker of the Year Award, 1990, American Cinematheque Award 1989, American Film Institute,Life Acievement Award, 1995, American Society of Cinematographers, Board of Governors Award 1994, Art Directors Guild, Contribution to Cinematic Imagery Award 2006, DGA Lifetime Achievement Award 2000, International Emmy Awards, Founders Award 2006, National Board of Review, USA Billy Wilder Award 2001, Society of Camera Operators Governors Award 1995. Received Golden Globe, Cecil B. DeMille Award 2008. Lifetime Achievement Award from Visual Effects Society 2008.
PICTURES: *Director:* The Sugarland Express (debut, 1974; also story, WGA nom. 1975), Jaws (DGA nom.; Golden Globe nom. 1976), Close Encounters of The Third Kind (also s.p.; Academy Award nom. for dir., DGA nom.; 2 Golden Globe noms.; WGA nom. 1978.), 1941, Raiders of the Lost Ark (Academy Award nom.; DGA nom.; Golden Globe nom. 1982), E.T. The Extra-Terrestrial (also co-prod.; 2 Academy Award noms. for dir. & picture, DGA nom.; Golden Globe nom. 1982), Twilight Zone—The Movie (sequence dir.; also exec. prod.), Indiana Jones and the Temple of Doom, The Color Purple (also co-prod.; Academy Award nom. for picture, DGA Award, Golden Globe nom. 1986), Empire of the Sun (also co-prod. DGA nom. 1988), Indiana Jones and the Last Crusade, Always (also co-prod.), Hook, Jurassic Park, Schindler's List (also co-prod.; 2 Academy Awards for Best Director & Picture, 1993; DGA Award, Golden Globe & Natl. Society of Film Critics Awards for director; NY Film Critics, LA Film Critics, Natl. Board of Review. Natl. Society of Film Critics), The Lost World: Jurassic Park, Amistad (also prod., DGA nom.; Golden Globe nom. 1998), Saving Private Ryan (also prod.; Academy Award for Best Director, 1 other nom.; DGA Award, Golden Globe Award 1999), The Unfinished Journey, Artificial Intelligence: AI (also writer & prod., Golden Globe nom. 2002), Minority Report, Catch Me If You Can, The Terminal (also prod.), Taken, War of the Worlds, Munich (also prod., 2 Academy Award noms. Best Picture; Academy Award nom. Best Director, DGA nom.; Golden Globe nom. 2006), Indiana Jones and the Kingdom of the Crystal Skull, The Adventures of Tintin: The Secret of the Unicorn (also prod.), War Horse (also prod). *Executive producer:* I Wanna Hold Your Hand, Used Cars, Continental Divide, Gremlins, Goonies (also writer), Back to the Future, Young Sherlock Holmes, The Money Pit, An American Tail, Innerspace, batteries not included, Who Framed Roger Rabbit, The Land Before Time, Tummy Trouble (short), Dad, Back to the Future II, Joe Versus the Volcano, Yume (int'l. version), Back to the Future III, Roller Coaster Rabbit (short), Gremlins 2: The New Batch, Arachnophobia, Trail Mix-Up (short), We're Back: A Dinosaur's Story, I'm Mad (short), The Flintstones (as Steven Spielrock), Casper, Balto, Twister, The Lost Children of Berlin (documentary), Men In Black, Deep Impact, The Mask of Zorro, The Last Days (doc.), Eyes of the Holocaust (doc.), Jurassic Park III, Price for Peace, Men in Black II, The Talisman, Legend of Zorro, Monster House, Disturbia, Transformers: The Movie, Jurassic Park IV, Spell Your Name (doc.), Eagle Eye, Transformers: Revenge of the Fallen, The Lovely Bones, Hereafter, Super 8, I Am Number Four, Transformers 3, Real Steel, Men in Black III. *Producer:* An American Tail: Fievel Goes West, Memoirs of a Geisha, Flags of our Fathers, Red Sun, Black Sand, Letters from Iwo Jima (Academy Award nom. 2007), Transformers, The Trial of the Chicago 7, Old Boy (also dir.), Lincoln (also dir.), The Adventures of Tintin: The Secret of the Unicorn (also dir.), True Grit, Cowboys & Aliens. *Writer:* Ace Eli and Rodger of the Skies, Poltergeist (also prod.). *Actor:* The Blues Brothers, Listen Up: The Lives of Quincy Jones.
TELEVISION: *Movies: Director:* Columbo: Murder by the Book, Duel, Something Evil, The Savage File. *Executive producer:* A Wish for Wings That Work (short), SeaQuest DSV, Tiny Toons Spring Break, Tiny Toon Adventures: Night Ghoulery (Emmy nom. 1995), A Pinky & the Brain Christmas Special (Emmy Award 1996), Semper Fi, Dan Finnerty & the Dan Band: I Am Woman, Falling Skies (prod.). *Mini-series: Director:* Strokes of Genius. *Executive producer:* Band of Brothers (Emmy Award 2002), Taken (Emmy Award 2003), Nine Lives, Into the West (Emmy nom. 2006), The Talisman, The Pacific. *Series: Executive producer:* Steven Spielberg Presents...Tiny Toon Adventures (also writer/developer; Emmy Award, 1991,), The Plucky Duck Show, Family Dog, Animaniacs (also writer/several episodes, 3 Emmy noms.), SeaQuest 2032, ER, Pinky and the Brain (2 Emmy Awards, 1 other nom.), Freakazoid! (Emmy Awards1997), HIgh Incident, Toonsylvania, Pinky Elmyra & the Brain (2 Emmy Awards), On The Lot (exec. prod.), The United States of Tara (writer, consult. prod.). *Documentaries/Specials: Executive producer:* Shooting War (also editor), We Stand Alone Together (Emmy nom. 2002), Broken Silence, Burma Bridge Busters, Warner at War (narr. only), Rebuilding Ground Zero (series). *Guest:* More than 200 appearances.

SPIKINGS, BARRY
Executive, Producer. b. Boston, England, Nov. 23, 1939. Ent. m.p. ind. 1973. Joint man. dir. British Lion Films Ltd., 1975. Appt. jnt. man. dir. EMI Films Ltd., 1977. 1979, appt. chmn. & chief exec., EMI Film & Theatre Corp.; chmn. & chief exec, EMI Films, Ltd., chmn. EMI Cinemas, Ltd.; chmn., Elstree Studios, Ltd.; chmn. EMI-TV Programs, Inc., 1980; appt. chmn. chief exec., EMI Films Group, 1982; 1985 Barry Spikings Productions Inc. (U.S.A.); 1985 became director Galactic Films Inc. (with Lord Anthony Rufus Issacs); 1986, acquired Embassy Home Entertainment from Coca Cola Co., renamed Nelson Entertainment Inc., appointed pres. and COO. 1992, Pleskow/Spikings Partnership, film prod. and distrib. partnership with Eric Pleskow.
PICTURES: *Prod.*: Conduct Unbecoming, The Man Who Fell to Earth, The Deer Hunter (Academy Award, Best Picture, 1978), Texasville, Beyond Rangoon. *Executive producer.*: Convoy, The Favor, The Last Days of Paradise.

SPINELLA, STEPHEN
Actor. b. Italy, Oct. 11, 1956.
THEATRE: Angels in America: Millenium Approaches (Tony award), Angels in America: Perestroika (Tony award).
PICTURES: Tarantella, Virtuosity, Faithful, The Unknown Cyclist, Love! Valour! Compassion!, The Jackal, Ravenous, Out of the Past (voice), Great Expectations, David Searching, Ravenous, Cradle Will Rock, Bubble Boy, Connie and Carla, House of D, Stone & Ed, Milk, Rubber.
TELEVISION: *Movies:* And the Band Played On, What the Deaf Man Heard, Our Town. *Series:* The Education of Max Bickford, 24, Desperate Housewives.

SPINER, BRENT
Actor. b. Houston, TX, Feb. 2, 1949. Recorded album Ol' Yellow Eyes Is Back.
THEATRE: *NY:* The Seagull, The Three Musketeers, Sunday in the Park With George, Big River.
PICTURES: Stardust Memories, The Miss Firecracker Contest, Corrina Corrina, Star Trek: Generations, Independence Day, Phenomenon, Star Trek: First Contact, Out to Sea, Trekkies, Star Trek: Insurrection, South Park: Bigger Longer and Uncut (voice), Geppetto, Dude- Where's My Car?, I am Sam, Star Trek: Bridge Commander, Dating Service, Master of Disguise, Star Trek: Nemesis, The Aviator, Material Girls, Superhero Movie, Quantum Quest: A Cassini Space Odyssey (voice).
TELEVISION: *Movies:* Introducing Dorothy Dandridge, As Me No Questions, The Ponder Heart, An Unexpected Love, Jack. *Series:* Star Trek: The Next Generation, Threshold. *Guest:* More than 70 appearances.

SPINETTI, VICTOR
Actor. b. South Wales, Sept. 2, 1933. e. Monmouth School. Entered industry in 1955. Appeared on Broadway in Oh! What a Lovely War winning 1965 Tony and Theatre World Awards.
THEATRE: *London*: Expresso Bongo, Candide, Make Me an Offer, Oh What a Lovely War (also B'way), The Odd Couple, Cat Among the Pigeons.
PICTURES: A Hard Day's Night, The Wild Affair, Help!, The Taming of the Shrew, The Biggest Bundle of Them All, Can Hieronymous Merkin Ever Forget Mercy Humppe and Find True Happiness?, Under Milk Wood, The Little Prince, The Return of the Pink Panther, Under the Cherry Moon, The Krays, The Princess and the Goblin (voice), Julie and the Cadillacs.
TELEVISION: *Movies:* The Magical Mystery Tour, The 500 Pound Jerk, The Lion, the Witch and the Wardrobe (voice), Vincent Van Gogh, Paradise Club, The Attic: The Hiding of Anne Frank, The Secret Garden, Young Indiana Jones and the Attack of the Hawkmen. *Mini-series:* In the Beginning, Mistral's Daughter, Secrets. *Series:* Two in Clover, Take My Wife..., Sweet Sixteen, SuperTed (voice), An Actor's Life for Me, Bad Boyes, Harry and the Wrinklies, First Degree.

SPINOTTI, DANTE
Cinematographer. b. Tolmezzo, Italy, Aug. 22, 1943.
PICTURES: La Disubbidienza, Cinderella '80, Hearts and Armour, Sogno di una notte di meza estate, Softly Softly, Cosi parlo Bellavista, The Berlin Affair, The Dark Side of Love, Manhunter, Crimes of the Heart, Choke Canyon, From the Hip, The Legend of the Holy Drinker (actor), Illegally Yours, Fair Game, Beaches, Torrents of Spring, A Violent Life, The Comfort of Strangers, True Colors, Hudson Hawk, Frankie and Johnny, The Last of the Mohicans (ASC nom. 1993), The Secret of the Old Woods, The End Is Known, Blink, Nell, The Quick and the Dead, The Star Maker, Heat, The Mirror Has Two Faces, L.A. Confidential (Academy Award nom.; LA Film Crits. Award, Best Cinematography, 1998), Goodbye Lover, Other Sister, Man of the People, The Insider (Academy Award nom.; ASC nom. 2000), Wonder Boys, The Family Man, Bandits, Red Dragon, Pinocchio, After the Sunset, The Contract, Slipstream Dream, Deception, Public Enemies, Flash of Genius, State of Play, The Chronicles of Narnia: The Voyage of the Dawn Treader.
TELEVISION: *Movie*: Blue Blood. *Mini-series:* La Donna di picche, I Nicotera. *Series:* Women's Murder Club.

SPIRA, STEVEN S.
Executive. b. New York, NY, March 25, 1955. e. City College of New York, bachelor's degree cum laude. Benjamin Cardozo School of Law, graduated a Samuel Belkin Scholar and also was member of the Law Review. Spent 10 years with the New York-based law firm of Monasch, Chazen and Stream. Became senior counsel for Twentieth Century Fox before affiliating with Warner Bros. Pictures in 1985. In business affairs dept., served as v.p., business affairs and senior v.p.. theatrical business affairs before a promotion to executive v.p., theatrical business affairs in 1996. In Aug. 1999, became executive v.p., worldwide business affairs for Warner Bros. Pictures. In Jan. 2004, Spira was promoted to his current position, president, worldwide business affairs, Warner Bros. Pictures. He is responsible for the business aspects of the studio's worldwide operations as they pertain to development, production and distribution of theatrical films for Warner Bros. Pictures.

SPITZ, DAVID
Executive. Began ent. career as film buyer for Mann Theaters. Served two years as regional branch mgr. for MGM Distribution, followed by Western div. mgr. at LIVE Entertainment. Spitz joined Lionsgate predecessor Artisan Entertainment in 1997. Series of promotions led to current position, executive v.p. and general sales mgr., since 2007. Spitz's Lionsgate tenure has included the successful distribution of such hits as the "Saw" franchise, which has grossed more than $667 million worldwide at the box office. 2009 and currently serves as the head of film distribution operations and reports to Joe Drake, Lionsgate pres., motion picture group and Lionsgate co-COO.

SPODICK, ROBERT C.
Exhibitor. b. New York, NY, Dec. 3, 1919. e. CCNY, 1940; ent. NYC m.p. ind. as errand boy Skouras Park Plaza, Bronx 1932-33; reel boy, asst. mgr., Loew's Theatres; mgr., Little Carnegie and other art theatres; exploitation man, United Artists. Acquired Lincoln, New Haven art house in 1945 in partnership with cousin Leonard E. Sampson; developed Nutmeg Theatre circuit, which was sold in 1968 to Robert Smerling. Beginning in 1970, built Groton, CT., Cinemas I and II; Norwich Cinemas I and II, Mystic Village Cinemas I, II and III, and Westerley Triple Cinemas in RI as Gemini Cinema Circuit in partnership with Sampson and William Rosen. Gemini sold to Interstate Theatres, 1986. Presently operates York Square I & II with his son, Peter, managing operations, and The New Lincoln in New Haven. Pres., Allied of CT, 1962-64; Pres. NATO of Conn. 1968-73. Past Chmn. Exec. Comm., CT Association of Theatre Owners.

SPOTTISWOODE, ROGER
Director, Editor. b. England, Jan. 5, 1945. Film editor of TV commercials and documentaries before turning to direction.
PICTURES: *Editor*: Straw Dogs, The Getaway, Pat Garrett and Billy the Kid, Hard Times, The Gambler; Who'll Stop the Rain? (assoc. prod.), Baby: Secret of the Lost Legend (exec. prod.). *Director:* Terror Train (debut, 1980), The Pursuit of D.B. Cooper, Under Fire, The Best of Times, Shoot to Kill, Turner & Hooch, Air America, Stop Or My Mom Will Shoot, Mesmer, Tomorrow Never Dies, The 6th Day, Spinning Boris, Ripley Under Ground, The Spire, Jack and Jill vs. the World (exec. prod. only), Shake Hands with the Devil, The Children of Huang Shi, Forgiveness and Justice (doc., dir.).
TELEVISION: *Movies*: *Director:* The Renegades, The Last Innocent Man, Third Degree Burn, And the Band Played On (DGA nom.; Emmy nom. 1994), Hiroshima, Murder Live!, Noriega: God's Favorite, The Matthew Shepherd Story, Ice Bound. *Series:* Prince Street. *Documentaries / Specials*: Time Flies When You're Alive.

SPRINGER, PAUL D.
Executive. e. Brooklyn Law School. Served as assoc. for NY law firm, Johnson & Tannebaum. Later with legal dept. of Columbia Pictures. 1970, joined Paramount Pictures N.Y. legal dept.; promoted to v.p. Theatrical Distrib. Counsel, 1979; promoted to sr. v.p., chief resident counsel, 1987; promoted to his current position of sr. v.p., asst. general counsel in Los Angeles and is responsible for all legal functions for Paramount's domestic distribution division, motion picture group. Member of NY and California Bar Associations.

SQUIRES, BUDDY
Cinematographer. Works primarily on documentaries.
PICTURES: *Documentaries:* Brooklyn Bridge (1981, also assoc. prod.), In Our Hands, The Statues of Liberty (Academy Award nom.; Emmy nom. 1986), Hue Long, The Children's Storefront, The Other Side of the Moon, Chimps: So Like Us, Lindbergh, Compassion in Exile: The Life of the 14th Dalai Lama, High Lonesome: The Story of Bluegrass Music, Martha and Ethel (additional photog.), One Survivor Remembers (Emmy nom. 1995), Listening to Children: A Moral Journey with Robert Coles (also prod., dir.), Hasten Slowly: The Journey of Sir Laurens van der Post, The Last Days of Kennedy and King, Out of the Past, Frank Lloyd Wright, Scottsboro: An American Tragedy, George Wallace: Settin' the Woods on Fire, Free to Dance, Amato: A Love Affair with Opera, Ram Dass-Fierce Grace (also co-prod.), Ghosts of Attica (additional photog.), Tupac: Resurrection (additional camera operator), The Boys of 2nd Street Park, Unforgivable Blackness: The Rise and Fall of Jack Johnson, People's Poetry: A Populist Bacchanal (also dir. &

prod.), Ring of Fire: The Emile Griffith Story, After Innocence, Waiting for Hockney (also editor), Nanking, Fighting for Life, Soundtrack for a Revolution, Stonewall Uprising, Salinger (also prod.).
TELEVISION: *Movies:* Images of Life, Fatal Twisters: A Season of Fury Richard Rogers: The Sweetest Sounds. *Mini-series:* The Irish in America: Long Journey Home, The National Parks: America's Best Idea (Emmy nom. 2010). *Series:* American High, The American Experience (Emmy nom. 2002), The War, The National Parks: America's Best Idea, Masterclass. *Documentaries/Specials:* The Civil War, Coney Island (also prod.), Baseball (Emmy nom. 1995), The Way West, The West, Buckminster Fuller: Thinking Out Loud, Thomas Jefferson, Heart of a Child, Lewis & Clark, America's Endangered Species: Don't Say Good-bye (Emmy Award 1998), Influenza 1918, Not for Ourselves Alone: The Story of Elizabeth Cady Stanton and Susan B. Anthony, New York: A Documentary Film (Emmy nom. 2000), John Brown's Holy War, Hate.com: Extremists on the Internet, Indie Sex: Taboos, Jazz (Emmy nom. 2001), Beyond Tara: The Extraordinary Life of Hattie McDaniel, Mark Twain, Miss America, Law & Order: Crime & Punishment, Reporting America At War: Episode 2: Which Side Are You On?, Happy to Be Nappy and Other Stories of Me, Broadway: The American Musical, The Life and Times of Frida Kahlo, I Have Tourette's But Tourette's Doesn't Have Me (Emmy nom. 2006), American Masters, Hard Times for an American Girl: The Great Depression (short).

STAGGS, THOMAS O.
Executive. b. Illinois. e. B.S. in business, Univ. of Minnesota; MBA, Stanford Graduate School of Business. Staggs was active in Investment banking with Morgan Stanley & Co. before joining The Walt Disney Company. Joined Disney, 1990, as mgr., strategic planning. In 1995, Staggs named senior v.p., strategic planning and development; 1998, became executive v.p., and CFO. Staggs played an important role in Disney strategic and operating initiatives and various Disney strategic joint ventures and corporate transactions, including Capital Cities/ABC, Inc. acquisition. Staggs assumed the title, sr. executive v.p., and CFO, in Jan. 2000. He is also a member, Disney exec. mgt. committee. Staggs oversees the company's worldwide finance organization, corporate strategy and development, brand management, acquisitions, corporate alliances, investor relations, treasury and risk management activities, controller functions, information systems, corporate outreach, real estate and taxes. He also represents Disney on the Supervisory Board of Euro Disney S.C.A., which owns and operates Disneyland Resort Paris. 2010 became Chairman of Walt Disney Parks and Resorts and presides over the company's worldwide vacation and travel businesses, which include 11 theme parks at five destination resorts in the United States, Europe and Asiaand a cruise line.

STAHL, NICK
Actor. b. Dallas, TX, Dec. 5, 1979. Started acting at age 4.
PICTURES: The Man Without a Face, Safe Passage, Tall Tale, Eye of God, The Thin Red Line, Disturbing Behavior, Soundman, Sunset Strip, All Forgotten, In the Bedroom, The Sleepy Time Gal, Bully, Taboo, Bookies, Terminator 3: Rise of the Machines, Twist, Sin City, The Night of the White Pants, How to Rob a Bank, A Cool Breeze on the Underground, Quid Pro Quo, Sleepwalking, The Speed of Thought, Kalamity, My One and Only, Everything Will Happen Before You Die, Burning Palms, The Nth Degree, The Boarding House, Afghan Luke and the Burgundy of Hash.
TELEVISION: *Movies*: Stranger at My Door, Woman With a Past, Incident in a Small Town, Blue River, My Son Is Innocent, Wasted. *Mini-series:* Seasons of Love. *Series:* Carnivàle.

STAINTON, DAVID
Executive. e. Princeton Univ., bachelor's degree; Harvard, M.B.A. Stainton joined The Walt Disney Company in 1989 as manager of special projects for Walt Disney Pictures and Television. In 1991, he went to Disney Feature Animation, where he served in a series of positions, with each new role increasing the scope of his responsibilities. In January 1998, Stainton was named senior v.p., creative affairs, where he was charged with overseeing Disney's animation studio in Paris. The facility houses 150 artists from 13 countries. During his tenure, Stainton worked on numerous successful films including The Lion King, Toy Story, Mulan, Tarzan, Hercules, The Hunchback of Notre Dame, Pocahontas, and Dinosaur. Stainton returned to the Burbank studio as executive v.p. of Walt Disney Television Animation in Jan. 2000; became div. pres. in early 2002. In that role, Stainton oversaw the day-to-day operations for the division's animated television series, Disney Video Premieres and DisneyToons. In Jan. 2003, Stainton was promoted to pres. Walt Disney Feature Animation. When Disney bought Pixar Animation Studios in 2006, Stainton left Disney. Currently Founder, Chrmn. and CEO Henry's World Media, Inc. which creates family entertainment for all media.

STALLONE, SYLVESTER
Actor, Writer, Director. b. New York, NY, July 6, 1946. After high school taught at American Coll. of Switzerland instructing children of career diplomats, young royalty, etc. Returned to U.S. in 1967 and studied drama at U. of Miami, 1969. Came to New York to seek acting career, taking part-time jobs, including usher for Walter Reade Theatres. Then turned to writing, selling several TV scripts.
PICTURES: Party at Kitty and Studs (debut, 1970), Bananas, Rebel (A Man Called Rainbo), The Lords of Flatbush (also co-s.p.), The Prisoner of 2nd Avenue, Capone, Death Race 2000, Farewell My Lovely, Cannonball, Rocky (also s.p.; Academy Award noms. for actor & s.p., 2 Golden Globe noms.; WGA nom. 1977), F.I.S.T. (also co-s.p.), Paradise Alley (also s.p., dir.), Rocky II (also s.p., dir.), Nighthawks, Victory, Rocky III (also s.p., dir.), First Blood (also co-s.p.), Staying Alive (cameo; also dir., prod., co-s.p.), Rhinestone (also co-s.p.), Rambo: First Blood Part II (also co-s.p.), Rocky IV (also dir., s.p.), Cobra (also s.p.), Over the Top (also co-s.p.), Rambo III (also co-s.p.), Lock Up, Tango and Cash, Rocky V (also s.p.), Oscar, Stop Or My Mom Will Shoot, Cliffhanger (also co-s.p.), Demolition Man, The Specialist, Judge Dredd, Assassins, Daylight, Cop Land, Antz (voice), Get Carter, Driven (also s.p.), D-Tox, Avenging Angelo, Dolan's Cadillac, Shade, Spy Kids 3-D: Game Over, Notorious (also writer, dir., prod.) Rocky Balboa (also writer, dir., exec. prod.), Rambo (also dir., s.p.), The Expendables (also s.p., dir.), The Zookeeper (voice).
TELEVISION: *Movies:* Heart of a Champion: The Ray Mancini Story (exec. prod. & fight choreographer), Father Lefty (exec. prod., writer). *Series:* Liberty's Kids: Est. 1776 (voice), The Contender (host, exec. prod.). *Guest:* More than 112 appearances.

STAMOS, JOHN
Actor. b. Cypress, CA, Aug. 19, 1963. Landed role of Blackie Parrish on daytime serial General Hospital in 1982. Has toured with his own band John Stamos and the Bad Boyz.
THEATRE: *B'way*: How to Succeed in Business Without Really Trying, Cabaret (role of emcee), Nine.
PICTURES: Never Too Young to Die, Born to Ride, Dropping Out, Party Monster, Knots, I Am Stamos (short), Farce of the Penguins (voice), Father of Invention.
TELEVISION: *Movies*: Alice in Wonderland, Daughter of the Streets, Captive, The Disappearance of Christina, Fatal Vows: The Alexandra O'Hara Story, Private Parts, A Match Made in Heaven, The Marriage Fool, Sealed with a Kiss, The Beach Boys: An American Family, (exec. prod., Emmy nom. 2000), How to Marry a Billionaire: A Christmas Tale, United We Stand, (host), Martin and Lewis, (co-exec. prod.), The Reagans, Wedding Wars, A Raisin in the Sun, The Two Mr. Kissels (also prod.). *Series*: General Hospital (Emmy nom. 2000), Dreams, You Again?, Full House, Celebrity Profile, The List, Thieves (also prod.), Virgin Chronicles (series/documentary; prod. & exec. prod.), Jake In Progress, ER (2005-2009). *Guest:* More than 91 appearances.

STAMP, TERENCE
Actor. b. London, England, July 23, 1938. Stage experience including Alfie on Broadway. Recent stage: Dracula, The Lady from the Sea, Airborne Symphony. *Autobiography:* Coming Attractions (1988).
PICTURES: Billy Budd (debut 1962; Academy Award nom.; Golden Globe Award 1963), Term of Trial, The Collector (Cannes Film Fest. Award, 1965), Modesty Blaise, Far from the Madding Crowd, Poor Cow, Blue, Teorema, Spirits of the Dead, The Mind of Mr. Soames, A Season in Hell, Hu-Man, The Divine Nymph, Strip-Tease, Superman, Meetings with Remarkable Men, Together?, Superman II, Monster Island, Death in the Vatican, The Hit, The Company of Wolves, Link, Legal Eagles, The Sicilian, Wall Street, Young Guns, Alien Nation, Stranger in the House (also dir., co-s.p.), Genuine Risk, Beltenebros, The Real McCoy, The Adventures of Priscilla--Queen of the Desert (Golden Globe nom. 1995), Mindbender, Limited Edition, Bliss, Kiss the Sky, Love Walked In, The Limey, Bowfinger, Star Wars: Episode I-The Phantom Menace, Red Planet, Ma femme est une actrice, Revelation, Fellini: Je suis un gran menteur, Full Frontal, My Boss's Daughter, The Haunted Mansion, Dead Fish, Elektra, These Foolish Things, September Dawn, Zombie Island, Streetlight, 9/11: Inside the Twin Towers (narr.), Get Smart, Wanted, Yes Man, Valkyrie, Ultramarines (voice), The Adjustment Bureau.
TELEVISION: *Movies*: The Thief of Baghdad, Deadly Recruits, Cold War Killers, The Alamut Ambush. *Series:* Chessgame, The Hunger (host), Smallville.

STANFILL, DENNIS C.
Executive. b. Centerville, TN, April 1, 1927. e. Lawrenceburg H.S.; U.S. Naval Acad., B.S., 1949; Oxford U. (Rhodes Scholar), M.A., 1953; U. of S. Carolina, L.H.D. (hon.). Corp. finance specialist, Lehman Bros 1959-65; v.p. finance, Times Mirror Company, Los Angeles, 1965-69; exec. v.p. finance, 20th C.-Fox Film Corp., 1969-71, pres., 1971, chmn. bd./CEO, 1971-81; pres., Stanfill, Bowen & Co., venture capital firm, 1981-90; chmn. bd./CEO, AME, Inc., 1990-92; co-chmn. bd./co-CEO, MGM, 1992-93. Sr. advisor to Credit Lyonnais, 1993-95. President of the Dennis Stanfill Company in California, a non-profit private investment co., 1995-.

STANTON, HARRY DEAN
Actor. b. West Irvine, KY, July 14, 1926. Acting debut at Pasadena Playhouse. Billed in early film appearances as Dean Stanton.

PICTURES: Revolt at Fort Laramie (debut, 1957), Tomahawk Trail, The Proud Rebel, Pork Chop Hill, The Adventures of Huckleberry Finn, A Dog's Best Friend, Hero's Island, The Man From the Diner's Club, Ride in the Whirlwind, The Hostage, A Time for Killing, Rebel Rousers, Cool Hand Luke, Day of the Evil Gun, The Miniskirt Mob, Kelly's Heroes, Cisco Pike, Two-Lane Blacktop, Face to the Wind (Cry for Me Billy), Pat Garrett and Billy the Kid, Dillinger, Where the Lilies Bloom, Cockfighter, Zandy's Bride, The Godfather Part II, Rafferty and the Gold Dust Twins, Rancho Deluxe, Farewell My Lovely, 92 in the Shade, Win Place or Steal, The Missouri Breaks, Straight Time, Renaldo and Clara, Alien, The Rose, Wise Blood, Death Watch, The Black Marble, Private Benjamin, Escape From New York, One From the Heart, Young Doctors in Love, Christine, Repo Man, Red Dawn, The Bear, Paris Texas, The Care Bears Movie (voice), One Magic Christmas, Fool for Love, UFOria, Pretty in Pink, Slamdance, Stars and Bars, Mr. North, The Last Temptation of Christ, Dream a Little Dream, Twister, The Fourth War, Stranger in the House, Wild at Heart, Man Trouble, Twin Peaks: Fire Walk With Me, Blue Tiger, Never Talk to Strangers, Down Periscope, She's So Lovely, Fire Down Below, The Mighty, Fear and Loathing in Las Vegas, The Straight Story, The Green Mile, The Man Who Cried, Sand, Ginostra, The Pledge, Sonny, Anger Management, Chrystal, The Big Bounce, Alpha Dog, Alien Autopsy, Inland Empire, The Good Life, The Open Road, On Holiday, Rango (voice).
TELEVISION: *Movies*: The Dangerous Days of Kiowa Jones, Flatbed Annie & Sweetpie: Lady Truckers, The Intruders, The Oldest Living Graduate, I Want to Live, Monster Maker, Payoff, Hostages, Against the Wall. *Mini-series:* Dead Man's Walk, Alice. *Series:* Dead Man's Walk, Big Love. *Documentaries/Specials*: Hotel Room (Tricks), Alien Evolution. *Guest:* More than 103 appearances.

STAPLETON, JEAN
Actress. r.n. Jeanne Murray. b. New York, NY, Jan. 19, 1923. e. Wadleigh H.S. Summer stock in NH, ME, MA, and PA. Broadway debut in In the Summer House (1954). Chair, Advisory bd., Women's Research and Education Inst. (Wash., D.C.); bd.: Eleanor Roosevelt Val-kill, Hyde Park; trustee: Actors Fund of America.
THEATRE: Harvey, Damn Yankees, Bells Are Ringing, Juno, Rhinoceros, Funny Girl, Arsenic and Old Lace (B'way and tour), Mountain Language/The Birthday Party (Obie Award), The Learned Ladies, Bon Appetit, The Roads to Home, Night Seasons, Morning's at Seven, You Can't Take It With You, The Show-Off, The Mystery of Edwin Drood (natl. tour). and extensive regional work at the Totem Pole Playhouse, Fayetteville, PA, Pocono Playhouse, Mountain Home Pa; Peterborough Playhouse, N.H. and others. Operatic debut with Baltimore Opera Co. in Candide, then The Italian Lesson and Bon Appetit. Cinderella, NY City Opera. Starred in San Jose Civic Light Opera Co.'s Sweeney Todd. Off B'way in The Entertainer. The Matchmaker, A.C.T. San Francisco.
PICTURES: Damn Yankees (debut, 1958), Bells Are Ringing, Something Wild, Up the Down Staircase, Cold Turkey, Klute, The Buddy System, Michael, You've Got Mail, This Is My Father (documentary), Pursuit of Happiness.
TELEVISION: *Movies*: Tail Gunner Joe, Aunt Mary, Angel Dusted, Isabel's Choice, Eleanor: First Lady of the World (Emmy nom.; Golden Globe nom. 1983), A Matter of Sex, Dead Man's Folly, Fire in the Dark (Golden Globe nom. 1992), The Habitation of Dragons, Ghost Mom, Lily Dale, Chance of a Lifetime, Baby, Like Mother LIke Son: The Strange Story of Sante and Kenny Kimes. *Mini-series*: The Great War. *Series*: All in the Family (3 Emmy Awards, 5 other noms.; 2 Golden Globe Awards, 5 other noms.), Bagdad Cafe, Mrs. Piggle-Wiggle. *Documentaries/Specials*: You Can't Take It With You, Grown-Ups (ACE nom.), Jack and the Beanstalk and Cinderella (Faerie Tale Theatre), Something's Afoot, Let Me Hear You Whisper, Mother Goose Rock 'n' Rhyme, Parallax Garden. *Guest:* More than 89 appearances.

STARR, MIKE
Actor. b. Queens, N.Y, July 29, 1950. e. Hofstra Univ. Theatre debut with Manhattan Punchline.
THEATRE: NY: Requiem for a Heavyweight, The Guys in the Truck, Map of the World, Vesper's Ever.
PICTURES: Bushido Blade, Cruising, The Natural, The Last Dragon, Cat's Eye, The Money Pit, Violets Are Blue, Off-Beat, Collision Course, Five Corners, Funny Farm, Lean on Me, Blue Steel, Uncle Buck, Last Exit to Brooklyn, Miller's Crossing, Goodfellas, Billy Bathgate, Freejack, The Bodyguard, Mac, Mad Dog and Glory, Son of the Pink Panther, Cabin Boy, On Deadly Ground, The Hudsucker Proxy, Blown Away, Baby's Day Out, Trial by Jury, Ed Wood, Radioland Murders, Dumb & Dumber, A Pyromaniac's Love Story, Clockers, Two If By Sea, James & the Giant Peach, Blood & Wine, Hoodlum, The Deli, Frogs for Snakes, The Adventures of Ragtime, Summer of Sam, Gloria, The taxman, New Jersey Turnpikes, The Cactus, 3 A.M., Tempted, The Next Big Thing, Backflash, Anne B. Real, Mickey, Jersey Girl, Under the City, The Ice Harvest, The Black Dahlia, BuzzKill, bgFATLdy, Lonely Street, Chicago Overcoat, Black Dynamite, I Hate Valentine's Day, Wrong Turn at Tahoe, The Irishman, Ca$h, Walk a Mile in My Pradas.
TELEVISION: *Movies:* Nasty Hero, Frank Nitti: The Enforcer, Kojak: Fatal Flaw, Hot Paint, Kojak: Ariana, The 10 Million Dollar Getaway, The Shamrock Conspiracy, EZ Streets, Stone Pillow, Path to Paradise: The Untold Story of the World Trade Center Bombing, Murder in a Small Town, The lady in Question, Jesse Stone: Night Passage, Lone Rider. *Mini-series*: The Last Don. *Series:* Hardball, EZ Streets, Ed, Joan of Arcadia, The Middleman (pilot). *Guest:* More than 78 appearances.

STEADMAN, ALISON
Actress. b. Liverpool, England, Aug. 26, 1946. Studied acting with East 15 Acting School.
THEATRE: The Prime of Miss Jean Brodie, Hamlet, Wholesome Glory, The Pope's Wedding, The Anchor, The King, Abigail's Party, Joking Apart, Unlce Vanya, The Rise and Fall of Little Voice, Othello, Plotters of Cabbage Patch Corner.
PICTURES: Kipperbang (debut, 1982), Champions, Number One, A Private Function, Clockwise, Stormy Monday, The Misadventures of Mr. Wilt, Shirley Valentine, Life Is Sweet, Blame It on the Bellboy, Secrets & Lies, Topsy Turvy, Happy Now, Bob the Builder: A Christmas to Remember, The Life and Death of Peter Sellers, Confetti.
TELEVISION: *Movies:* Virtuoso, The Finding, Hard Labour, Nuts in May, Abigail's Party,P'tang Yang Kipperbang, Number One, Monster Maker, Throught the Night, Pasmore, Crapston Villas, Karaoke, No Bananas, The Missing Postman, Hans Christian Andersen: My Life as a Fairy Tale, Dalziel and Pascoe: Soft Touch, People Like Us, Marple: Ordeal by Innocence, Who Gets the Dog?. *Mini-series:* The Singing Detective, Selling Hitler, Gone to the Dogs, Pride and Prejudice, Adrian Mole: The Cappuccino Years. *Series:* Gone to Seed, Stressed Eric, Let Them Eat Cake, Fat Friends, The Worst Week of My Life, Gavin and Stacey. *Guest:* More than 85 appearances.

STEELE, BARBARA
Actress. b. Trenton Wirrall, England, Dec. 29, 1937. Studied to be painter prior to joining rep. cos. in 1957.
PICTURES: Bachelor of Hearts (debut, 1958), Sapphire, Your Money or Your Wife, Black Sunday, The Pit and the Pendulum, Revenge of the Mercenaries, The Horrible Dr. Hitchcock, 8 1/2, Danse Macabre (Castle of Blood), The Ghost, The Hours of Love, White Voices, Nightmare Castle, The Maniacs, Terror Creatures From the Grave, The She Beast, Young Torless, Crimson Cult, They Came From Within, Caged Heat, I Never Promised You a Rose Garden, Piranha, Pretty Baby, The Silent Scream, Key is in the Door, Deep Above, Hollywood Rated R, The Prophet, Her Morbid Desires, The Butterfly Room.
TELEVISION: *Movies:* Honeymoon with a Stranger, Dark Shadows. *Mini-series:* The Winds of War, War and Remembrance (Emmy Award 1989). *Series:* Dark Shadows, Queer Eye, (assoc. prod.), I Want to Work for Diddy (field prod., 1 episode).

STEENBURGEN, MARY
Actress. b. Newport, AR, Feb. 8, 1953. m. actor Ted Danson. Graduated from Neighborhood Playhouse. Received honorary doctorate degrees from Univ. of Ark. at Little Rock and Hendrix Col. in Conway, AR. On B'way stage 1993 in Candida.
PICTURES: Goin' South (debut, 1978, Golden Globe nom. 1979), Time After Time, Melvin and Howard (Academy Award, best supporting actress, Golden Globe Award 1981), Ragtime (Golden Globe nom. 1982), A Midsummer Night's Sex Comedy, Cross Creek, Romantic Comedy, One Magic Christmas, Dead of Winter, End of the Line (also exec. prod.), The Whales of August, Miss Firecracker, Parenthood, Back to the Future Part III, The Long Walk Home (narrator), The Butcher's Wife, What's Eating Gilbert Grape, Philadelphia, Clifford, It Runs in the Family (My Summer Story), Pontiac Moon, My Family/Mi Familia, Powder, The Grass Harp, Nixon, Wish You Were Dead, Nobody's Baby, The Trumpet of the Swan, Life as a House, I am Sam, Sunshine State, Hope Springs, Casa de los Babys, Elf, Marilyn Hotchkiss' Ballroom Dancing and Charm School, Nobel Son, The Dead Girl, Elvis and Anabelle, In the Electric Mist, Honeydripper, The Open Road, Step Brothers, Four Christmases, The Proposal, Did You Hear About the Morgans?, Dirty Girl.
TELEVISION: *Movies*: The Attic: The Hiding of Anne Frank (Emmy nom. 1988), Gulliver's Travels, About Sarah. Noah's Ark, Picnic, Surviving Love, It Must Be Love, Capital City, Reinventing the Wheelers, Happiness Isn't Everything, Southern Discomfort. *Mini-series*: Tender Is the Night, Living With the Dead. *Series*: Ink (also co-exec. prod.), Back to the Future (voice), Joan of Arcadia, Curb Your Enthusiasm. *Specials*: Faerie Tale Theatre (Little Red Riding Hood), The Gift. *Guest:* More than 67 appearances.

STEINBERG, DAVID
Actor, Writer, Director. b. Winnipeg, Canada, Aug. 9, 1942. e. U. of Chicago; Hebrew Theological Coll. Member Second City troupe; comedian at comedy clubs: Mr. Kelly's Hungry i, Bitter End. Starred in London and B'way stage prods. B'way includes Little Murders, Carry Me Back to Morningside Heights.
PICTURES: *Actor*. The Lost Man, The End, Something Short of Paradise, The Best of the Big Laff Off, The Tommy Chong Roast. *Director*. Paternity, Going Berserk (also co.-s.p.), Cats Don't Dance (exec. prod. only), The Wrong Guy, Kids in the Hall: Brain Candy (exec. prod. only), All Dogs Go to Heaven, (writer, story), My Giant, Judgment Day: The Ellie Nesler Story (exec. prod.).

TELEVISION: *Movies:* Women of the Night 3, (exec. prod.), Paula Poundstone: Cats, Cops, and Stuff (exec. prod.), Women of the Night 3 (exec. prod.), Only The Truth Is Funny (dir.), Switching Goals, (dir.), Robin Williams: Live on Broadway (exec. prod., Emmy nom. 2003), Cooked (dir.), Frangela (dir.). *Series*: Music Scene (writer, co-host), Tonight Show (guest host), Sit Down Comedy with David Steinberg, Good Grief (exec. prod.), Big Sound (actor, exec. prod.), Air Combat (cinematographer). *Director Series*: Newhart, The Popcorn Kid, It's Garry Shandling's Show, Seinfeld (DGA nom. 1992), The Ellen Burstyn Show, Designing Women, Eisenhower & Lutz, The Fanelli Boys, Evening Shade, Get A Life, The Rick Reynolds Show, The Parent 'Hood, Ink, Mad About You (DGA nom. 1997), Even Stevens, Curb Your Enthusiasm (DGA nom.; Emmy nom. 2003), Go Kinky (also exec. prod.), Sons & Daughters, Living in Your Car (exec. prod.). *Specials:* Robin Williams: Live on Broadway (Emmy nom. 2003), Midnight Train to Moscow (Emmy nom. 1990), The 63rd Annual Academy Awards (Emmy Award 1991 for writing), The 64th Annual Academy Awards (Emmy Award 1992 for writing), The 65th Annual Academy Awards, The 69th Annual Academy Awards. *Guest:* More than 93 appearances.

STEINMAN, MONTE
Executive. b. New York, NY, May 18, 1955. e. Wharton Sch. of Univ. of PA. Joined Paramount Pictures in 1980 as sr. financial analyst. Series of promotions followed, culminating in appt. as dir. of financial planning of Gulf & Western's Entertainment and Communications Group, 1984. 1985, named exec. dir., financial planning. 1990, joined Viacom Intl., as mgr. financial planning. 1993, dir. financial planning, MTV Networks. 1994, v.p. finance at MTV Networks. Currently is v.p., finance and administration for FUSE Networks LLC, a music video network which delivers content through television and the Internet.

STEMBLER, WILLIAM J.
Exhibitor. b. Atlanta, GA, Nov. 29, 1946. e. Westminster Sch., 1964; U. of FL, 1968; U. of GA Law Sch., 1971. 1st. lt. U.S. Army, 1971; capt., U.S. Army Reserve; resigned 1976. Enforcement atty., SEC, Atlanta office, 1972-73; joined Georgia Theatre Co., 1973; pres. 1983-86; joined United Artists Communications, Inc., 1986, as v.p.; Incorporated Value Cinemas 1988 and Georgia Theatre Co. II in 1991 as its chmn. & pres. Today, he is chairman & CEO of Georgia Theatre Co. II. Stembler is on NATO's executive committee and its bd. of dir; he is a member, NATO OF GA & is a past-pres., 1983-85; Rotary Club of Atlanta, pres. 1991-92.

STERN, DANIEL
Actor, Director. b. Bethesda, MD, Aug. 28, 1957. e. H.B. Studios. Appeared in 1984 short film Frankenweenie.
PICTURES: Breaking Away (debut, 1979), Starting Over, A Small Circle of Friends, Stardust Memories, It's My Turn, One- Trick Pony, Honky Tonk Freeway, I'm Dancing As Fast As I Can, Diner, Blue Thunder, Get Crazy, C.H.U.D., Key Exchange, The Boss' Wife, Hannah and Her Sisters, Born in East L.A., D.O.A., The Milagro Beanfield War, Leviathan, Little Monsters, Friends Lovers and Lunatics, Coupe de Ville, My Blue Heaven, Home Alone, City Slickers, Home Alone 2: Lost in New York, Rookie of the Year (also dir.), City Slickers II: The Legend of Curly's Gold, Bushwhacked (also exec. prod.), Celtic Pride, Very Bad Things, Otis, Whip It.
TELEVISION: *Movies*: Samson and Delilah, Weekend War, The Court-Martial of Jackie Robinson, Big Guns Talk: The Story of the Western, Tourist Trap, Partners. *Series*: Hometown, The Wonder Years (narrator; also episode dir.), Dilbert (voice), Danny (also exec. prod.), Regular Joe.

STERN, HOWARD
Radio Personality, Actor, Writer, Producer. b. Jackson Heights, NY, January 12, 1954. e. Boston University, BA, Communications. Was listed in Forbes Magazine as 100 most powerful celebrities, 1999. Morning radio show broadcast in over 50 markets (1986-2005). Moved show to Sirius Satellite radio Jan. 2006. *Author:* Private Parts (autobiography 1993), Miss America 1996. President of The Howard Stern Production Co. (motion picture, independent film and TV producer.)
PICTURE: Private Parts (also composer).
TELEVISION: *Series:* Son of the Beach (writer, exec. prod.), Howard Stern: The High School Years (writer, exec. prod.), Howard Stern (writer, co-prod.), Howard TV on Demand. *Guest:* More than 53 appearances.

STERN, SANDRA
Executive. e. UCLA Law School. Stern began her career in the Columbia Pictures Television legal department, followed by a stint as a television attorney with the law firm that is now Bloom, Hergott, Cook, Diemer & Klein. She previously served as COO of Artists Television Group, where she helped create and structure the company and directed its business affairs, legal, finance, administrative and production operations. Prior to that, was Sr. V. P., then Exec. V. P. of the Columbia TriStar Television Group at Sony Pictures Entertainment, working closely with Columbia TriStar Television Group head Jon Feltheimer (now Chairman and CEO of Lionsgate). From 1986 through 1991, Stern was Sr. V. P. in charge of business affairs and international development at New World Entertainment, where she put together the first ever international co-production for a U.S. broadcast network. Stern joined Lionsgate Television in 2003 when she was named Exec. V.P., business and legal affairs. She became COO of Lionsgate Television in 2005. Stern's contributions have been pivotal to Lionsgate's emergence as a leading supplier of content to cable and broadcast networks. One of the industry's most forward-thinking strategists and creative dealmakers, she has been instrumental in forging new relationships and business models that have paved the way for such Lionsgate productions as the multiple Emmy and Golden Globe-winning series "Mad Men", AMC's first original drama series; "Crash", "Weeds" Showtime's series "Nurse Jackie", "Scream Queens" for VH1and "Blue Mountain State". As part of Lionsgate's ongoing initiative to expand its television business, Stern created a television joint programming venture with Michael Hirschorn and Stella Stolper's Ish Entertainment, which entered into the partnership with a commitment for three TV series, including the reality competition series "Paris Hilton's My New BFF," "50 Cent: The Money and the Power" and "T.I's Road to Redemption" under a first-look deal with MTV Networks. She recently negotiated another new joint television venture with Lost Marble Productions' Marty Adelstein and Jon Kroll to produce original unscripted programming. She also helped guide Lionsgate into the emerging area of international format production. Stern has expanded Lionsgate's cost-efficient production opportunities by developing and managing relationships with the governments of New Mexico, New York, Pennsylvania, Louisiana and Canada. She also played a key role in forming the company's feature length documentary unit by creating the business model to finance these projects through co-productions with TV networks. The unit's first production was Werner Herzog's 2005 Sundance award-winning documentary "Grizzly Man", which debuted on Discovery Channel after its successful domestic theatrical run. Since then, Stern has served as an exec. prod. on all of the unit's subsequent productions. Other recent productions include "Guys 'n' Divas: Battle of the High School Musicals", produced with Spitfire Pictures and Showtime which aired on Showtime; and "Street Dogs of South Central", produced in partnership with Animal Planet. Stern has also been instrumental in launching Lionsgate's first foray into the area of live theater with the stage production of "Dirty Dancing". After sold-out performances in Australia, New Zealand, Germany, The Netherlands and on London's West End, the show began its U.S. tour in Chicago and made its West Coast premiere in Los Angeles in the spring of 2009.

STERNHAGEN, FRANCES
Actress. b. Washington, DC, Jan. 13, 1930. e. Vassar College, drama dept.; Perry-Mansfield School of Theatre. Studied with Sanford Meisner at Neighborhood Playhouse, NY. Was teacher at Milton Acad. in MA. Acted with Arena Stage, Washington, DC, 1953-54.
THEATRE: Thieves Carnival (off-B'way debut, 1955), The Skin of Our Teeth, The Carefree Tree, The Admirable Bashville, Ulysses in Night Town, Viva Madison Avenue!, Red Eye of Love, Misalliance, Great Day in the Morning, The Right Honorable Gentleman, The Displaced Person, The Cocktail Party, Cock-a-Doodle Dandy, Playboy of the Western World, The Sign in Sidney Brustein's Window, Enemies, The Good Doctor (Tony Award, 1974), Equus, Angel, On Golden Pond, The Father, Grownups, Summer, You Can't Take It With You, Home Front, Driving Miss Daisy, Remembrance, A Perfect Ganesh, The Heiress (Tony Award, 1995), Long Day's Journey Into Night.
PICTURES: Up the Down Staircase (debut, 1967), The Tiger Makes Out, The Hospital, Two People, Fedora, Starting Over, Outland, Independence Day, Romantic Comedy, Bright Lights Big City, See You in the Morning, Communion, Sibling Rivalry, Misery, Doc Hollywood, Raising Cain, Curtain Call, Ruth at Midnight (short), Landfall, The Rising Place, The Laramie Project, Highway, The Mist, Julie & Julia.
TELEVISION: *Movies*: Who'll Save Our Children?, Mother and Daughter: The Loving War, Prototype, Follow Your Heart, She Woke Up, Labor of Love: The Arlette Schweitzer Story, Reunion, Vault of Horror I, The Con, To Live Again. *Series*: Love of Life, Doctors, Golden Years, Under One Roof, Cheers (2 Emmy noms.), The Road Home, Sex and the City (recurring guest role, Emmy nom. 2002), ER (recurring guest role), The Closer. *Guest:* More than 51 appearances.

STEUER, ROBERT B.
Executive. b. New Orleans, LA, Nov. 18, 1937. e. U. of Illinois, & 1955-57; Tulane U., 1957-59, B.B.A. Booker-Southern D.I. circuit, New Orleans, 1959; assoc., prod., Poor White Trash; 1960; v.p. Cinema Dist. America, 1961; co-prod., Flesh Eaters, Common Law Wife, Flack Black Pussy Cat; partner, gen. mgr., radio station WTVF, Mobile, 1963; dir. special projects, American Intl. Pictures, 1967; so. div. sls. mgr., AIP, 1971; v.p. asst. gen. sls. mgr., AIP, 1974; partner, United Producers Organization, producing Screamers, 1977; v.p., sls., Ely Landau Org., 1979; v.p., gen. sls. mgr., Film Ventures Intl., 1981; exec. v.p. world-wide mktg., 1983; pres., FVI, 1986-89. 1987, exec. v.p. world-wide mktg. Film Ventures Intl; 1987-88 exec. prod. Operation: Take No Prisoners, Most Dangerous Women Alive, Tunnels, Criminal Act, Au Pair; 1989 sales consultant, 20th Century Fox. 1990-93 Prod. rep: When the Whales Came, China Cry, Twogether, Sweet and Short, Taxi to Soweto, Bound and Gagged: A Love Story, Skin Art, Yankee Zulu. 1994-97 formed Robert B. Steuer and Assoc.

distribution and sales consult. to ent. industry. U.S. Rep 1997-98 Marche International du Film (Cannes Film Market). 1998-present, partner in Encore Int'l. Group LTD, a marketing & public relations company.

STEVENS, ANDREW
Actor, Director, Writer, Producer. b. Memphis, TN, June 10, 1955. Mother is actress Stella Stevens. e. Antioch U., L.A., B.A. (psychology). L.A. stage includes Journey's End, Mass Appeal, Leader of the Pack, Billy Budd (also prod.), P.S. Your Cat is Dead, Bouncers (L.A. Drama Circle Critics Award). Pres., CEO Royal Oaks Entertainment Intl. Film Distributors.
PICTURES: *Actor:* Shampoo, Deportee (short), Vigilante Force, Massacre at Central High, Day of the Animals, The Boys in Company C (Golden Globe nom. 1979), The Fury, Death Hunt, The Seduction, 10 to Midnight, Scared Stiff, Counterforce, Blood Chase, The Terror Within, Fine Gold, Tusks, The Terror Within II (also s.p. & dir.), Red Blooded American Girl, Night Eyes (also s.p. & prod.), Down the Drain, Deadly Innocents, Eyewitness to Murder, Munchie, Maximum Force, Night Eyes II (also s.p. & supervising prod.), Double Threat, Deadly Rivals, Night Eyes III (also s.p. & dir.), Munchie Strikes Back, Scorned (also dir.), The Skateboard Kid II (also dir. & prod.), Illicit Dreams (also dir.), Night Eyes IV (also prod.), Desert Shooter (also prod.), Scorned 2 (also prod.), Active Stealth, The Kid With X-Ray Eyes, Venomous, Mach 2. *Director:* Virtual Combat, The White Raven, Tommy and the Cool Mule (also prod., s.p.), Breaking the Press (also prod., s.p.). *Producer:* Victim of Desire, Beneath the Bermuda Triangle, Steel Sharks, Moving Target, Dead of Night (also prod. mgr.), Over the Wire, Surface to Air, Strategic Command, Scorpio One, Night Shade, Maximum Revenge, Operation Cobra, Ghost Dog, Black Thunder, Memorial Day, Fallout, Evasive Action, Secret Santa, Crash Dive 2, The Boy Who Saved Christmas, Mom Can I Keep Her?, Freedom Strike, Hijack, The Confession, Angel in Training, Restraining Order, Five Acres, The Prophet, Storm Catcher, Final Voyage (also writer), If...Dog...Rabbit, Animal Factory, Mercy, Nautilus, Beyond Suspicion, Submerged, Space Station, Green Dragon, The Caveman's Valentine, 3000 Miles to Graceland, Ablaze, Heist, Poison, ZigZag, Half Past Dead, The Foreigner, Method, Blessed, Pursued, 7 Seconds, Harvester, The Detonator, Missionary Man, Fire from Below (also writer). *Executive producer:* Hard Bounty, Droid Gunner, Entropy, The Boondock Saints, The Third Miracle, The Big Kahuna, Things You Can Tell Just By Looking at Her, The Whole Nine Yards, Battlefield Earth: A Saga of the Year 3000, Get Carter, The Pledge, Driven, Angel Eyes, Plan B, Viva Las Nowhere, FearDotCom, Avenging Angelo, City by the Sea, Ballistic: Ecks vs. Sever, The In-Laws, Thralls, Glass Trap, Sea Ghost, The Whole Ten Yards, Popstar, A Sound of Thunder.
TELEVISION: *Movies*: *Actor:* The Werewolf of Woodstock, The Last Survivors, The Oregon Trail, The Bastard, Women At West Point, Topper (also exec. prod.), Beggarman Thief, Miracle On Ice, Code Red, Forbidden Love, Journey's End, Columbo: Murder in Malibu, Extralarge: Jo-Jo, Roger Corman Presents "Flash Frame" (also dir. & prod.), Night Eyes Four: Fatal Passion (actor, prod.), My Ghost Dog (prod.), Mongolian Death Worm (prod.), Unearthed (prod.). *Executive producer:* Bloodsuckers. *Mini-series: Actor:* Once An Eagle, The Rebels, Hollywood Wives. *Series: Actor:* The Oregon Trail, Code Red, Emerald Point N.A.S., Dallas. *Director:* Swamp Thing, Marker.

STEVENS, CONNIE
Actress. r.n. Concetta Ann Ingolia. b. Brooklyn, NY, August 8, 1938. e. Sacred Heart Acad., Hollywood Professional School. Began career as winner of several talent contests in Hollywood; prof. debut, Hollywood Repertory Theatre's prod. Finian's Rainbow; B'way in Star Spangled Girl (Theatre World Award); recordings include: Kookie Kookie Lend Me Your Comb, 16 Reasons, What Did You Wanna Make Me Cry For, From Me to You, They're Jealous of Me, A Girl Never Knows.
PICTURES: Eighteen and Anxious (debut, 1957), Young and Dangerous, Dragstrip Riot, Rock-a-Bye Baby, The Party Crashers, Parrish, Susan Slade, Palm Springs Weekend, Two on a Guillotine, Never Too Late, Way ... Way Out, The Grissom Gang, The Last Generation, Scorchy, Sgt. Pepper's Lonely Hearts Club Band (cameo), Grease 2, Back to the Beach, Tapeheads, Love Is All There Is, James Dean: Race With Destiny, Saving Grace (dir., writer, prod.), Double Duty, City of Shoulders and Noses.
TELEVISION: *Movies*: The Littlest Angel, Mister Jerico, Call Her Mom, Playmates, Every Man Needs One, The Sex Symbol, Love's Savage Fury, Murder Can Hurt You, Side Show, Bring Me the Head of Dobie Gillis, Race with Destiny: The James Dean Story, Becoming Dick, The Wedding Album. *Mini-series:* Scruples. *Series*: Hawaiian Eye, Wendy and Me, Kraft Music Halls Presents, The Muppet Show (singer), The Des O'Connor Show, Starting from Scratch, Titus. *Guest:* More than 110 appearances.

STEVENS, FISHER
Actor, Producer. b. Chicago, IL, Nov. 27, 1963. e. NYU. Artistic Director of Naked Angels Theatre Co. in NYC.
THEATRE: *NY:* Torch Song Trilogy (Off-B'way & B'way), Brighton Beach Memoirs, A Perfect Ganesh, Carousel.
PICTURES: *Actor:* The Burning, Baby It's You, The Brother From Another Planet, The Flamingo Kid, My Science Project, Short Circuit, The Boss' Wife, Short Circuit 2, Bloodhounds of Broadway, Reversal of Fortune, The Marrying Man, Mystery Date, Lift, Bob Roberts, Hero, When the Party's Over, Super Mario Bros., Nina Takes a Lover, Only You, Hackers, Cold Fever, Hackers, Four Days in September, The Taxman, The Tic Code, Sam the Man (also s.p. & prod.), 3 A.M., Prison Song, Piñero (also prod.), Undisputed, Uptown Girls (also prod.), Anything Else, Easy Six, Replay, On the Couch (short), Undiscovered, Bill (prod.), The Cove (prod., Academy Award 2010, Best doc. Feature), Rising Stars, Fake, The Experiment, Henry's Crime. *Director:* Phinehas (short), Just A Kiss, Once in a Lifetime (documentary, prod), Crazy Love (also prod., co-dir.), The Highest Tide (also s.p.). *Executive producer:* The Château, Swimf@n, Yes, Slow Burn (also prod.), The Pleasure of Your Company, Awake (prod.), Balls Out: The Gary Houseman Story, Tenderness, The Invisible Woman (prod.), Hollywood Renegade (doc.), .
TELEVISION: *Movies: Actor:* Columbo: Murder, Smoke & Shadows, The Right to Remain Silent, Jenifer, Is It College Yet?. *Series: Actor:* One Life to Live, Ryan's Hope, Key West, Early Edition (also dir.), Lost (voice). *Guest:* More than 45 appearances.

STEVENS, GAIL
Casting Director.
PICTURES: High Season, The Lair of the White Worm, The Rachel Papers, Antonia and Jane, Captives, Paprazzo, Trainspotting, Beautiful Thing, The Slab Boys, Swept From the Sea, The Woodlanders, Still Crazy, Bedrooms & Hallways, Mansfield Park, Hold Back the Night, Saving Grace, The Beach, 15 Minutes, (UK), Late Night Shopping, Blow Dry, The Affair of the Necklace, The One and Only, 28 Days Later..., Peter Pan, (UK), Calendar Girls, The Prince and Me, Millions, On A Clear Day, The Kinky boot Factory, Match Point, The Descent, Colour Me Kubrick, Revolver, The Chronicles of Narnia: The Lion, the Witch & the Wardrobe, Severance, Funny Farm, Sunshine, Scoop, Love Me Still, Death Defying Acts, Death at a Funeral, Becoming Jane, Sunshine, In Tranzit, Cassandra's Dream, Intervention, The Chronicles of Narnia: Prince Caspian, City of Ember, Slumdog Millionaire, Defiance, Espion(s), Lesbian Vampire Killers, Freakdog, High School Musical 3: Senior Year (UK casting), Within the Whirlwind, From Time to Time, The Descent: Part 2, Mediator, From Time to Time, Dread, Bunny and the Bull, Huge, Pelican Blood, Get Him to the Greek (UK casting), Your Highness, Gnomeo and Juliet, F, Wuthering Heights, Dark Tide, John Carter of Mars (UK casting).
TELEVISION: *Movies:* Living with Dinosaurs, A Woman at War, A Murder of Quality, The Affair, (UK), Deadly Voyage, Truth or Dare, Great Expectations, All the Kings Men, Ella and the Mothers, White Teeth, Best of Both Worlds, Spooks, Goodbye, Mr. Chips, Dinosaur Hunters, No Night Is Too Long, Poirot: Five Little Pigs, Poirot: Sad Cypress, Poirot: Death on the Nile, Poirot: The Hollow, Belonging, Fungus he Bogeyman, Bloodlines, Child of Mine, Blood and Oil. *Mini-series:* Oliver's Travels, Painted Lady, Touching Evil, Butterfly Collectors, Crime and Punishment, The Last Enemy. *Series:* Tough Love, Best of Both Worlds, MI-5.

STEVENS, JR., GEORGE
Director, Writer, Producer. b. Los Angeles, CA, April 3, 1932. Son of late director George Stevens. e. Occidental College, 1949-53, B.A. 1st Lieut. U.S. Air Force; TV dir., Alfred Hitchcock Presents, Peter Gunn, 1957-61; prod. asst. Giant Productions, 1953-54; prod. asst. Mark VII, Ltd., 1956-57; dir. M.P. Service, U.S. Information Agency 1962-67; chmn., U.S. deleg. to Film Festivals at Cannes (1962, 1964), Venice (1962, 1963), Moscow (1963); Founding director, American Film Institute, 1967-79; currently serves on AFI's bd. of directors. Writer and producer of various TV specials. Numerous Emmy Awards and nominations, 10 Emmy Awards and 21 Emmy noms., 7 WGA Awards and 4 noms. Received WGA Paul Selvin Honorary Award 1992.
PICTURES: The Diary of Anne Frank (assoc. prod.), The Five Cities of June (Academy Award nom. 1964), The Greatest Story Ever Told (assoc. prod.), John F. Kennedy: Years of Lightning Day of Drums (prod.), America at the Movies (prod.), George Stevens: A Filmmaker's Journey (dir., s.p., prod.; 1988 WGA Award for TV broadcast), The Thin Red Line, (exec. prod.).
TELEVISION: *Movies:* The Murder of Mary Phagan (co-writer, prod., 1988; Emmy Award for prod.; also Christopher & Peabody Awards), Separate But Equal (dir., writer, co-exec. prod.; Emmy Award for exec. prod.; also Christopher Award, Ohio State Award, Paul Selvin Award by the Writers Guild of America), George Stevens: D-Day to Berlin. *Documentaries/Specials*: American Film Institute's Salutes (exec. prod./writer, 1973-; received 1975 Emmy Award as exec. prod. of The American Film Institue Salute to James Cagney), The Stars Salute America's Greatest Movies (exec. prod.), The Kennedy Center Honors (prod./writer, 1978-; Emmy Awards: 1984, 1986, 1989, 1996), America Entertains Vice Premier Deng (prod./writer), Christmas in Washington, (exec. prod./writer, 1982-), Star Trek: 30 Years and Beyond , The Kennedy Center Honors (co. prod., co-writer; Emmy Award, 1996), AFI Salute to Martin Scorsese (writer & exec. prod.), The Kennedy Center Honors: A Celebration of the Performing Arts (prod., 1998, 1999, 2002; prod. & writer, 2001, 2003, 2004, 2005, 2006), Christmas in Washington (writer, exec. prod., 2001, 2002, 2003, 2004, 2005, 2006 many Emmy noms. and WGA noms. and Awards), We Are One: The Obama Inaugural Celebration at the Lincoln Memorial (exec. prod., writer).

STEVENS, STELLA
Actress, Director. r.n. Estelle Eggleston. b. Yazoo City, MS, Oct. 1, 1938. Mother of actor Andrew Stevens. e. Attended Memphis State U. Modeled in Memphis when she was discovered by talent scouts. Was briefly a term contract actress at 20th Century-Fox, later under exclusive contract to Paramount, then Columbia. Reveived Golden Globe Award 1960. *Director*: The American Heroine (feature length doc.), The Ranch (feature comedy). Creator/owner of Sexy Fragrances.
PICTURES: Say One For Me (debut, 1959), The Blue Angel, Li'l Abner, Man Trap, Girls! Girls! Girls!, Too Late Blues, The Nutty Professor, The Courtship of Eddie's Father, Advance to the Rear, Synanon, The Secret of My Success, The Silencers, Rage, Where Angels Go Trouble Follows, How to Save a Marriage and Ruin Your Life, Sol Madrid, The Mad Room, The Ballad of Cable Hogue, A Town Called Hell, Slaughter, Stand Up & Be Counted, The Poseidon Adventure, Arnold, Cleopatra Jones and the Casino of Gold, Las Vegas Lady, Nickelodeon, The Manitou, Wacko, Chained Heat, The Longshot, Monster in the Closet, Down the Drain, Last Call, The Terror Within II, Eye of the Stranger, The Guest, Exiled in America, The Nutty Nut, Hard Drive, Molly & Gina, Body Chemistry 3: Point of Seduction, Illicit Dreams, The Granny, Virtual Combat, Bikini Hotel, Size Em Up (short), The Long Ride Home, Glass Trap, Blessed, Popstar.
TELEVISION: *Movies*: In Broad Daylight, In Cold Blood, Climb an Angry Mountain, Linda, The Day The Earth Moved, Honky Tonk, New Original Wonder Woman (pilot), Kiss Me Kill Me, Wanted: The Sundance Woman, Charlie Cobb (pilot), The Night They Took Miss Beautiful, Murder in Peyton Place, The Jordan Chance, Cruise into Terror, New Love Boat (pilot), Friendship Secrets and Lies, Hart to Hart (pilot), The French Atlantic Affair, The Pendragon Affair (Eddie Capra Mystery pilot), Make Me an Offer, Children of Divorce, Twirl, Amazons, Women of San Quentin, No Man's Land, A Masterpiece of Murder, Fatal Confessions (Father Dowling pilot), Power, Passion and Murder, Adventures Beyond Belief, Man Against The Mob, In Cold Blood, Jake Spanner: Private Eye, Attack of the 5 Ft. 2 Women, Special: Attack of the 5'2" Woman, The Christmas List, Reunion in Hazzard, Subliminal Seduction, By Dawn's Early Light. *Series:* Ben Casey, Flamingo Road, Santa Barbara, General Hospital, Strip Mall. *Guest:* More than 113 appearances.

STEVENSON, CYNTHIA
Actress. b. Oakland, CA, Aug. 2, 1962. Raised in Washington, Vancouver.
THEATRE: Ladies Room.
PICTURES: The Player, The Gun in Betty Lou's Handbag, Watch It, Forget Paris, Home for the Holidays, Live Nude Girls, Happiness, Air Bud: Golden Receiver, Air Bud: Golden Receiver, Agent Cody Banks, Agent Cody Banks 2: Destination London, Full of It, Case 39, I Love You, Beth Cooper, Reunion, Jennifer's Body.
TELEVISION: *Movies*: Double Your Pleasure, From the Earth to the Moon, Will You Merry Me. *Series*: My Talk Show, Bob, Hope and Gloria, Oh Baby, Dead Like Me. The L Word, Men in Trees, According to Jim (recurring role), Surviving Suburbia, Life Unexpected.

STEVENSON, JULIET
Actress. b. England, Oct. 30, 1956. e. RADA.
THEATRE: Other Worlds, Measure for Measure, Breaking the Silence, Troilus and Cressida, As You Like It, Les Liaisons Dangereuses, Yerma, Hedda Gabler, On the Verge, Burn This, Death and the Maiden, Scenes From an Execution (LA), The Duchess of Malfi.
PICTURES: Drowning by Numbers (debut, 1988), Ladder of Swords, Truly Madly Deeply, The Trial, The Secret Rapture, Emma, Play, The Search for John Gissing, Food of Love, Bend it Like Beckham, The One and Only, Nicholas Nickleby, Mona Lisa Smile, Being Julia, Red Mercury, A Previous Engagement, Infamous, Breaking and Entering, And When Did You Last See Your Father?, Triage.
TELEVISION: *Movies:* Oedipus at Colonus, Pericles: Prince of Tyre, The Race for the Double Helix, Living With Dinosaurs, Aimée, A Doll's House, Who Dealt?, Stone Scissors Paper, Cider with Rosie, Trial by Fire, The Road from Coorain, The Pact, Hear the Silence, The Snow Queen, Miss Marple: Ordeal by Innocence, Dustbin Baby. *Mini-series:* Maybury, The Politician's Wife, From the Earth to the Moon. *Series:* The Mallens (TV debut, 1978), The World of Eric Carle (short; narr.), Place of Execution. *Documentaries:* Paris Was a Woman (narr.), A History of Britain (actress, voice), Horizon (narr.), In Search of Mozart (narr.). *Guest:* More than 59 appearances.

STEVENSON, PARKER
Actor. b. Philadelphia, PA, June 4, 1952. e. Princeton U. Began professional acting career by starring in film, A Separate Peace, while high school senior, having attracted attention through work on TV commercials.
PICTURES: A Separate Peace (debut, 1972), Our Time, Lifeguard, Stroker Ace, Stitches, Official Denial, Rough Ridin' Justice, Caddie Woodlawn, Not of this Earth, Loaded, McTaggart's Fortune.
TELEVISION: *Movies*: This House Possessed, Shooting Stars, That Secret Sunday, Shades of Love: The Rose Cafe, Probe, Baywatch: Panic at Malibu Pier, The Cover Girl and the Cop, All the Rivers Run 2, Are You Lonesome Tonight?, Shadow of a Stranger, Official Denial, Legion, Avalon: Beyond the Abyss, Trapped, Terror Peak. *Mini-series*: North & South Book II, *Series:* Hardy Boys Mysteries, Falcon Crest, Probe, Baywatch Hawaii, Melrose Place, Models Inc. (dir. only), Savannah (dir. only).

STEWART, JON
Writer, Producer, Actor, Host. rn. Jonathan Stuart Leibowitz. b. New York, NY, November 28, 1962. e. College of William and Mary.
Author: Naked Pictures of Famous People, America (The Book): A Citizen's Guide to Democracy Inaction.
PICTURES: Mixed Nuts, Half Baked, The Faculty, Playing by Heart, Big Daddy, Jay and Silent Bob Strike Back, Death to Smoochy, Doogal (voice), Evan Almighty, The Naturalized (doc., exec. prod.).
TELEVISION: *Movies:* Since You've Been Gone, Many movie credits associated with The Daily Show with Jon Stewart (host), *Series:* The Sweet Life (writer), The Jon Stewart Show (host, exec. prod., co-prod., writer), The Larry Sanders Show (actor, creative consult.), Important Things with Demetri Martin (exec. prod.), The Colbert Report (exec. prod., 4 Emmy noms.), The Daily Show with Jon Stewart (host, writer, exec. prod., co-prod., 13 Emmy Awards, 10 other noms., WGA Award 2010, 2 other noms.). *Documentary/Specials:* Sportsfan (exec. prod.), The 78th Annual Academy Awards (2006), The 80th Annual Academy Awards (host, Emmy nom. 2008). *Guest:* More than 100 appearances.

STEWART, PATRICK
Actor. b. Mirfield, England, July 13, 1940. Trained at Bristol Old Vic Theatre School. Made professional stage debut 1959 in Treasure Island with Lincoln Rep. Co. at the Theatre Royal in Lincoln.
THEATRE: *NY*: A Midsummer Night's Dream, A Christmas Carol, The Tempest. Numerous London theatre credits incl.: The Investigation, Henry V, The Caretaker, Body and Soul, Who's Afraid of Virginia Woolf?, Yonadab. Associate artist with Royal Shakespeare Co. since 1967; many appearances with them incl. Antony and Cleopatra for which he received the Olivier Award for Best Supporting Actor in 1979.
PICTURES: Hennessey, Hedda, Excalibur, The Plague Dogs (voice), Races, Dune, Lifeforce, Code Name: Emerald, Wild Geese II, The Doctor and the Devils, Lady Jane, L.A. Story, Robin Hood: Men in Tights, Gunmen, Star Trek: Generations, The Pagemaster (voice), Liberation (narrator), Jeffrey, Star Trek: First Contact, Conspiracy Theory, Masterminds, The Prince of Egypt (voice), Dad Savage, Star Trek: Insurrection, Safe House, X-Men, Jimmy Neutron: Boy Genius, X-Men 2, Boo Zino & the Snurks (voice), Steamboy (voice), The Game of Their Lives, Chicken Little (voice), Bambi II (voice), X-Men: The Last Stand, TMNT (voice), X-Men Origins: Wolverine, Sinbad: The Fifth Voyage, Gnomeo and Juliet, Dorothy of Oz (voice).
TELEVISION: *Movies*: Antony and Cleopatra, The Gathering Storm, North and South, The Madness, When the Actors Come, Hamlet Prince of Denmark, Pope John Paul II, The Devil's Disciple, Star Trek: The Next Generation: Encounter at Farpoint, Star Trek: Deep Space Nine-Emissary, Death Train, Star Trek: The Next Generation-All Good Things, In Search of Dr. Seuss, The Canterville Ghost, Moby Dick (Emmy nom.; Golden Globe nom. 1998), Safe House, Animal Farm, A Christmas Carol, King of Texas (also exec. prod.), The Lion in Winter (also exec. prod., Emmy nom.; Golden Globe nom. 2004), Dragons' World: A Fantasy Made Real (narr., voice), Mysterious Island, The Snow Queen, Hamlet (Emmy nom. 2010), Macbeth. *Mini-series*: Fall of Eagles, I Claudius, Tinker-Tailor-Soldier-Spy, Maybury, Smiley's People, Mysterious Island. *Series*: Star Trek: The Next Generation (U.S.), Hollywood Update (dir.), High Spirits with Shirley Ghostman (narr., voice), American Dad! (voice), Extras (recurring role, Emmy nom. 2006), Eleventh Hour. *Guest:* More than 181 appearances.

STIERS, DAVID OGDEN
Actor. b. Peoria, IL, Oct. 31, 1942. Guest conductor: 5O American orchestras incl. Chicago, San Diego, Dallas, Utah, and Chamber Orchestra of Baltimore. Resident conductor of Yaquina Chamber Orchestra in Oregon.
THEATRE: *NY*: The Magic Show, Ulysses in Nighttown, The Three Sisters, Beggar's Opera, Measure for Measure.
PICTURES: Drive He Said, THX 1138, Oh God!, The Cheap Detective, Magic, Harry's War, The Man With One Red Shoe, The Big Picture, Better Off Dead, Creator, Another Woman, The Accidental Tourist, Doc Hollywood, Beauty and the Beast (voice), Shadows and Fog, Porco rosso, Taking Liberty, Iron Will, Bad Company, Pocahontas (voice), Steal Big Steal Little, Mighty Aphrodite, Meet Wally Sparks, The Hunchback of Notre Dame (voice), Everyone Says I Love You, Napoleon, Meet Wally Sparks, Jungle 2 Jungle, Krippendorf's Tribe, The Assistant, Tomcats, Atlantis: The Lost Empire (voice), Spirited Away (voice), The Curse of the Jade Scorpion, The Majestic, Lilo and Stitch (voice), Teacher's Pet (voice), Geeks (documentary; narr., voice), Hoodwinked! The True Story of Red Riding Hood (voice), Together Again for the First Time, Not Dead Yet, Hoodwinked 2: Hood vs. Evil (voice).

TELEVISION: *Movies*: Charlie's Angels (pilot), A Circle of Children, A Love Affair: The Eleanor and Lou Gehrig Story, Sgt. Matlovich Vs. the U.S. Air Force, Breaking Up Is Hard to Do, Damien: The Leper Priest, The Day the Bubble Burst, Anatomy of an Illness, The First Olympics: Athens 1896, The Bad Seed, 5 Perry Mason Movies (Shooting Star, Lost Love, Sinister Spirit, Avenging Ace, Lady in the Lake), Mrs. Delafield Wants to Marry, The Alamo: 13 Days to Glory, The Kissing Place, Final Notice, The Final Days, How to Murder a Millionaire, Wife Mother Murderer, The Last of His Tribe, Without a Kiss Goodbye (aka The Laurie Samuels Story), To Face Her Past, Murder She Wrote: The Last Free Man, Cable Beach, Leroy & Stitch (voice). *Mini-series*: North and South (also Book II), Reagan, The Black River. *Series*: Doc, M*A*S*H (2 Emmy noms.), Two Guys and a Girl, Love and Money, Teacher's PetHouse of Mouse (voice), Stephen King's Dead Zone, Lilo & Stitch: The Series (voice), Justice League Unlimited (voice). *Documentaries/Specials:* The Oldest Living Graduate, The Innocents Abroad, Mastergate, Odyssey of Life (voice), MacArthur (narrator; voice), New York: A Documentary Film (narrator, voice), Jazz (voice), The First Olympics: Athens 1896 (Emmy nom. 1984), The Race For the Superbomb (voice), Commanding Heights: The Battle for the World Economy (narr., voice), The American Experience (narr.). *Guest:* More than 118 appearances.

STILES, JULIA
Actress. b. New York, NY, March 28, 1981. e. Columbia U.
PICTURES: I Love You I Love You Not, The Devil's Own, Wicked, Wide Awake, Hamlet, State and Main, Save the Last Dance, 10 Things I Hate About You, Down to You, O, The Bourne Identity, A Guy Thing, Carolina, Mona Lisa Smile, The Prince and Me, The Bourne Supremacy, A Little Trip to Heaven, Edmond, The Omen, The Bourne Ultimatum, Gospel Hill, The Bell Jar (also prod.), Cry of the Owl.
TELEVISION: *Movies:* Before Women Had Wings, The '60s. *Series:* Dexter. *Guest:* More than 45 appearances.

STILES, RYAN
Actor. b.Seattle, WA, April 22, 1959.
PICTURES: Hot Shots!, Hot Shots! Part Deux, Courting Courtney.
TELEVISION: *Movies:* Andrea Martin...Together Again, Memory Lanes (also exec. prod., writer, creator), Bless This Mess. *Series:* Whose Line Is It Anyway? (UK), The Drew Carey Show, Whose Line Is It Anyway? (USA, also exec. prod., Emmy nom. 2002), Two and a Half Men.

STILLER, BEN
Actor, Director, Producer. b. New York, NY, November 30, 1966. Son of performers Jerry Stiller and Anne Meara. e. UCLA. Made short film parody of The Color of Money, called The Hustler of Money which landed him work on Saturday Night Live. Acting debut in 1985 B'way revival of The House of Blue Leaves.
PICTURES: Hot Pursuit, Empire of the Sun, Fresh Horses, Next of Kin, That's Adequate, Stella, Highway to Hell, Reality Bites (also dir.), Heavyweights, Get Shorty, Flirting With Disaster, The Cable Guy (also dir.), If Lucy Fell, Permanent Midnight, Zero Effect, There's Something About Mary, Your Friends & Neighbors, Permanent Midnight, The Suburbans, Mystery Men, Black and White, The Independent, Keeping the Faith, Meet the Parents, Zoolander, The Royal Tenenbaums, Run Ronnie Run (as himself), Duplex (also prod.), What Makes Sammy Run (writer, prod. & dir.), Along Came Polly, Starsky and Hutch (also exec. prod.), Envy, Dodgeball: A True Underdog Story (also prod.), Anchorman: The Legend of Ron Burgundy, You'll Never Wiez in this Town Again (documentary), Meet the Fockers, Madagascar (voice), Danny Roane: First Time Director, School for Scoundrels, Tenacious D in: The Pick of Destiny (also exec. prod., prod.), The Mirror, Blades of Glory (prod. only), Night at the Museum, Used Guys (also prod.), Madagascar 2 (voice), The Heartbreak Kid, The Marc Pease Experience, The Ruins (prod. only), Tropic Thunder (also dir., prod., s.p.), Madagascar: Escape 2 Africa (voice), The Boys: The Sherman Brothers' Story (doc., prod.), Night at the Museum 2: Battle of the Smithsonian, The Marc Pease Experience, The Trial of the Chicago 7 (dir.), Submarine (exec. prod.), Greenberg, Hollywood Renegade (exec. prod.), Little Fockers, Megamind (exec. prod.), The Big Year (prod.), 30 Minutes or Less (prod.).
TELEVISION: *Movies*: The House of Blue Leaves, Working Trash, Derek Zoolander: Male Model (short), Derek Zoolander University (short), Heat Vision and Jack (exec. prod. & dir.), Mission Improbable (short), Night of Too Many Stars: An Overbooked Event for Autism Education, Elmo's Christmas Countdown (voice), The Station (dir., exec. prod.). *Series*: Saturday Night Live (also writer), The Ben Stiller Show (also creator, dir., writer; Emmy Award as writer 1993), Liberty's Kids: Est. 1776 (voice), Prehistoric Planet (narr., voice), Extras (Emmy nom. 2006), Arrested Development (reurring role). *Documentaries/Specials*: House of Blue Leaves, Colin Quinn Back in Brooklyn (dir., writer). *Guest:* More than 200 appearances.

STILLER, JERRY
Actor. b. New York, NY, June 8, 1929. m. actress Anne Meara. Son is actor Ben Stiller, daughter is actress Amy Stiller. With partner Meara gained recognition as comedy team in nightclubs, theatres and on TV, most notably The Ed Sullivan Show. Video with Meara, So You Want to Be An Actor?
THEATRE: *B'way*: The Ritz, Passione, Hurlyburly, Three Men on a Horse, What's Wrong With This Picture?, The Three Sisters.
PICTURES: The Taking of Pelham One Two Three, Airport 1975, The Ritz, Nasty Habits, Those Lips Those Eyes, Hot Pursuit, Nadine, Hairspray, That's Adequate, Little Vegas, Highway to Hell, The Pickle, Heavy Weights, A Rat's Tale, Camp Stories, Stag, The Deli, The Suburbans, A Fish In the Bathtub, The Independent, My 5 Wives, Zoolander, On the Line, Serving Sara, Teacher's Pet (voice), Chump Change, The Mirror, Hairspray (2007), The Heartbreak Kid, Swinging with the Finkels, Flicker Box.
TELEVISION: *Movies*: Madame X, The Other Woman, Seize the Day, Subway Stories: Tales from the Underground, Ice Dreams. *Series:* The Paul Lynde Show, Joe and Sons, Take Five With Stiller and Meara (synd), Tattingers, Seinfeld (Emmy nom. 1997), The King of Queens, Crashbox (host, voice), Teacher's Pet (voice), Bombshell. *Guest*: More than 128 appearances.

STING
Musician, Actor. r.n. Gordon Matthew Sumner. b. Newcastle-Upon-Tyne, England, Oct. 2, 1951. e. Warwick U. A school-teacher before helping form rock group, The Police. B'way debut, Threepenny Opera, 1989. Received American Screenwriters Association, David Angell Humanitarian Award 2004.
PICTURES: *Actor:* Quadrophenia, Radio On, The Great Rock 'n' Roll Swindle, The Secret Policeman's Other Ball, Brimstone and Treacle, Urgh! A Music War, Dune, The Bride, Plenty, Julia and Julia, Bring on the Night, Stormy Monday, The Adventures of Baron Munchausen, Gentlemen Don't Eat Poets, Resident Alien, The Music Tells You, The Grotesque, Two Smoking Barrels, The Filth and the Fury, Bee Movie (voice), Brüno, Vertical Farm (doc., writer). *Composer:* 48 Hrs, Stars and Bars,Four Weddings and a Funeral, The Professional, Leaving Las Vegas, Sabrina, White Squall, The Truth About Cats & Dogs, The Wedding Singer, The Mighty (Golden Globe nom. 1999), The X Files, Red Planet, The Emperor's New Groove (Academy Award nom.; Golden Globe nom. 2001), Moulin Rouge!, Rush Hour 2, Kate & Leopold (Academy Award nom.; Golden Globe Award 2002), Rugrats Go Wild!, Sting: Inside-The Songs of Sacred Love, Cold Mountain (Academy Award nom.; Golden Globe nom. 2004), 50 First Dates, Bridget Jones: The Edge of Reason, Racing Stripes, Ashura, Bewitched, A Guide to Recognizing Your Saints (exec. prod.), The Wedding Weekend, Tony Bennett: Duets - The Making of an American Classic, Young@Heart (doc.), An Englishman in New York.
TELEVISION: *Movies: Actor:* Artemis 81, Peter and the Wolf: A Prokofiev Fantasy (narr.), Sting... All This Time (Emmy Award 2002). *Series:* Captain Planet and the Planeteers (voice). *Guest:* More than 60 appearances.

STOCK, ALAN
Exhibitor.
Active in motion picture exhibition for more than 23 years. Employed by Consolidated Theaters from 1981-1985, rising to district mgr. position. Became dir. of operations for the theatre div. of the Texas Cinema Corporation from Jan. 1986 to Dec. 1987. Stock joined the founding management team of Cinemark in 1987 and was general mgr. until March 1992. During 1989, the company promoted him to senior vice pres. Stock has been both a director of the co. and COO since early 1992. Assumed role of pres. in March 1993. Today, Stock serves Cinemark as its CEO. The company is based in Plano, TX.

STOCKWELL, DEAN
Actor. r.n. Robert Dean Stockwell. b. Hollywood, CA, March 5, 1935. p. Harry and Betty Veronica Stockwell. Brother is actor Guy Stockwell. e. Long Island public schools and Martin Milmore, Boston. On stage in Theatre Guild prod. Innocent Voyage. Appeared on radio in Death Valley Days and Dr. Christian. Named in 1949 M.P. Herald-Fame Stars of Tomorrow poll; 1976 retired to Santa Monica as a licensed real estate broker but soon returned to acting.
PICTURES: Anchors Aweigh (debut, 1945), The Valley of Decision, Abbott and Costello in Hollywood, The Green Years, Home Sweet Homicide, The Mighty McGurk, The Arnelo Affair, The Romance of Rosy Ridge, Song of the Thin Man, Gentleman's Agreement (Golden Globe Award best juvenile actor, 1947), Deep Waters, The Boy With Green Hair, Down to the Sea in Ships, The Secret Garden, The Happy Years, Kim, Stars in My Crown, Kim, Cattle Drive, Gun for a Coward, The Careless Years, Compulsion, Sons and Lovers (Golden Globe nom. 1961), Long Day's Journey Into Night, Rapture, Psych-Out, The Dunwich Horror, The Last Movie, The Loners, The Werewolf of Washington, Win Place or Steal (The Big Payoff), Won Ton Ton The Dog Who Saved Hollywood, Stick Fighter (South Pacific Connection), Tracks, She Came to the Valley, Alsino and the Condor, Sandino, Human Highway (also co-dir., s.p.), Wrong Is Right, To Kill a Stranger, Paris Texas, Dune, The Legend of Billie Jean, To Live and Die in L.A., Blue Velvet, Gardens of Stone, Beverly Hills Cop II, Banzai Runner, The Blue Iguana, Tucker: The Man and His Dream, Married to the Mob (Academy Award nom. 1989), Palais Royale, Limit Up, Buying Time, Time Guardian, The Player, Chasers, Mr. Wrong, Air Force One, McHale's Navy, The Rainmaker, Water Damage, Rites of Passage, Inferno, Batman

Beyond: Return of the Joker, In Pursuit, The Flunky, C.Q., The Quickie, Buffalo Soliders, The Manchurian Candidate, The Deal, Al's Beef, The Darkest Evil.
TELEVISION: *Movies*: Paper Man, The Failing of Raymond, The Adventures of Nick Carter, The Return of Joe Forrester, Three for the Road, A Killing Affair, Born to Be Sold, Sweet Smell of Death (U.K.), The Gambler III: The Legend Continues, Son of the Morning Star, Backtrack, Shame, Fatal Memories, Bonanza: The Return, In the Line of Duty: The Price of Vengeance, Justice in a Small Town, The Innocent, Madonna: Innocence Lost, Deadline for Murder: From the Files of Edna Buchanan, Stephen King's The Langoliers, The Commish: In the Shadow of the Gallows, Twilight Man, Unabomber: The True Story, Close to Danger, What Katy Did, American Black Beauty, They Nest, The Nanny Express, Battlestar Galactica: The Plan, The Dunwich Horror. *Mini-series:* Greatest Heroes of the Bible. *Series*: Dr. Kildare, Quantum Leap (4 Emmy Award noms.; Golden Globe Award 1990, 3 other noms.), It's True, Popular Science (host), The Tony Danza Show, Phenomenon: The Lost Archives (host), It's True, JAG (recurring guest role), Battlestar Galactica. *Guest*: More than 116 appearances.

STODDARD, BRANDON
Executive. b. Brideport, CT, March 31, 1937. e. Yale U., BS Amer. Studies, 1958. Columbia Law Sch. Was program ass't. at Batton, Barton, Durstine and Osborn before joining Grey Advertising, 1962, where was successively prog. ops. supvr., dir. daytime prog., VP TV/radio prog. Joined ABC in 1970; named v.p. daytime programs for ABC Entertainment, 1972; v.p. children's programs, 1973. Named v.p., motion pictures for TV, 1974; 1976 named v.p., dramatic progs. and m.p. for TV; 1979, named pres., ABC Motion Pictures; 1985 appt. pres., ABC Entertainment. Resigned 1989 to head ABC Prods. unit to create and prod. series and movies for ABC and other networks. Resigned that position, 1995. He is currently a partner in Ancient Mariner Films and has been an adjunct professor at USC Graduate School of Cinema- Television.

STOLTZ, ERIC
Actor. b. Los Angeles, CA, Sept. 30, 1961. Moved to American Samoa at age 3; family returned to California when he was 8. Spent two years at U. of Southern California in theatre arts; left to study with Stella Adler and later William Traylor and Peggy Feury.
THEATRE: *Off-B'way*: The Widow Claire, The American Plan, Down the Road, The Importance of Being Earnest. *B'way*: Our Town (B'way debut; Theatre World Award, Tony nom. & Drama Desk nom., 1988), Two Shakespearean Actors, Three Sisters. *Regional*: Tobacco Road, You're a Good Man Charlie Brown, Working (all with an American Rep. Co. in Scotland), Arms and the Man, Glass Menagerie (Williamstown Theater Festival).
PICTURES: Fast Times at Ridgemont High (debut, 1982), Surf II, Running Hot, The Wild Life, The New Kids, Mask (Golden Globe nom. 1986), Code Name: Emerald, Some Kind of Wonderful, Lionheart, Sister Sister, Haunted Summer, Manifesto, The Fly II, Say Anything... (cameo), Memphis Belle, The Waterdance, Singles (cameo), Bodies Rest & Motion (also co-prod.), Naked in New York, Killing Zoe, Sleep With Me (also prod.), Pulp Fiction, Little Women, Rob Roy, Fluke, The Prophecy, Kicking and Screaming, Grace of My Heart, 2 Days in the Valley, Jerry Maguire, Highball, Keys to Tulsa, Anaconda, Mr. Jealousy (also exec. prod.), Hi-Life, The Passion of Ayn Rand, Jesus & Hutch, It's A Shame About Ray (short), The Simian Line, The House of Mirth, Things Behind the Sun, Harvard Man, The Rules of Attraction, Happy Hour, When Zachary Beaver Came to Town, The Butterfly Effect, Childstar, The Honeymooners, Milk, Fort McCoy (also prod.).
TELEVISION: *Movies*: The Grass Is Always Greener Over the Septic Tank, The Violation of Sarah McDavid, Paper Dolls, A Killer in the Family, Money, Our Town, A Woman At War, The Heart of Justice, Foreign Affairs, Roommates, Don't Look Back, Inside, Blackout Effect, Outrage in Glen Ridge, Common Ground, One Kill, The Last Dance, My Horrible Year (Emmy nom. 2002), Blank Slate, Caprica (pilot). *Mini-series:* The Seekers, Out of Order, The Triangle. *Series:* Chicago Hope, The Lot, Once and Again (dir. only), Character Studies (host), Close to Home, Caprica. *Documentaries/Specials*: Things Are Looking Up, Sensibility and Sense. Many series credits as Director. *Guest*: More than 85 appearances.

STONE, H. AUBREY, JR.
Executive. b. Charlotte, NC, Jan. 14, 1964. e. U. of NC-Chapel Hill. Joined Consolidated Theatres Inc. in 1987. Helped to found a new motion picture exhibition company, Consolidated Theatres/The Stone Group, 1990. V.P., Consolidated Theatres/The Stone Group, 1990-95. Assumed role of v.p./general mgr. in 1996. Left Consolidated in May 2003 to become executive v.p. of the Georgia Theatre Company, a circuit based in St. Simons Island, Ga. In March 2005, promoted to president and COO. Formerly on bd. of dir., NATO of NC & SC; pres., NATO of NC & SC, 1995-96. Bd of dir., National NATO, 1995-present; chmn., Programs & Services Committee, National NATO, present.

STONE, DEE WALLACE
Actress. r.n. Deanna Bowers. b. Kansas City, MO, Dec. 14, 1948. e. U. of Kansas, theatre and education. m. actor Christopher Stone until his death in 1995. m. film editor Skip Belyea. Taught high school English. Came to NY to audition for Hal Prince and spent two years working in commercials and industrial shows. First break in Police Story episode.
PICTURES: The Stepford Wives (debut, 1975), All the King's Horses, The Hills Have Eyes, 10, The Howling, E.T:. The Extra-Terrestrial, Jimmy the Kid, Cujo, Club Life, The Letter, Shadow Play, Bialy Smok, Critters, Alligator II: The Mutation, Popcorn, My Family Treasure, Lightning in a Bottle, Huck and the King of Hearts, Discretion Assured, Street Hunter, Temptress, The Skateboard Kid II, The Phoenix and the Magic Carpet, Best of the Best 3: No Turning Back, Skeletons, The Frighteners, Mutual Needs, Black Circle Boys, Nevada, The Christmas Path, Deadly Delusions, Pirates of the Plain, Killer Instinct, Flamingo Dreams, 18, Out of the Black, A Month of Sundays, Sex and the Teenage Mind, Fish Don't Blink, Paradise, Dead Canaries, Dead End Road, The Blue Rose, Yesterday's Dreams, Scar, Kalamazoo?, Boo!, Headspace, Spice of Life, The Lost, Expiration Date, Abominable, Bone Dry, J-ok'el, The Plague, Halloween, Little Red Devil, The Haunted World of El Superbeasto, The Stalker Within, The No Sit List, Exodus Fall, Beautysleep Symphony, The House of the Devil, Stem Cell, Stay Cool, The Mother of Invention, Pound of Flesh, Fuzz Track City, Death Keeps Coming, Curve of Earth, Blossom, Bedrooms, Raven, Cage Free, Sebastian, Walk a Mile in My Pradas, Fuzz Track City, Blossom, Bedrooms.
TELEVISION: *Movies*: The Sky's No Limit, Young Love First Love, The Secret War of Jackie's Girls, Child Bride of Short Creek, The Five of Me, A Whale for the Killing, Skeezer, Wait Til Your Mother Gets Home, Happy, I Take These Men, Hostage Flight, Sin of Innocence, Addicted to His Love, Stranger on My Land, Terror in the Sky, The Christmas Visitor, I'm Dangerous Tonight, Prophet of Evil: The Ervil LeBaron Story, Witness to the Execution, Search and Rescue, Moment of Truth: Cradle of Conspiracy, Huck and the King of Hearts, Subliminal Seduction, The Perfect Mother, To Love Honor and Betray, She's No Angel, The Perfect Husband: The Laci Peterson Story, The Magic 7. *Series*: Together We Stand, The New Lassie, High Sierra Search and Rescue, Sons & Daughters. *Guest*: More than 116 appearances.

STONE, OLIVER
Director, Writer, Producer. b. New York, NY, Sept. 15, 1946. e. Yale U., NYU, B.F.A., 1971. Teacher in Cholon, Vietnam 1965-66. U.S. Infantry specialist 4th Class. 1967-68 in Vietnam (Purple Heart, Bronze Star with Oak Leaf Cluster honors). Executive, Writer, Director for Ixtlan Corp.
PICTURES: Sugar Cookies (assoc. prod.), Seizure (dir., s.p., co-editor, 1974), Midnight Express (s.p.; Academy Award, Golden Globe Award, WGA Award 1978), The Hand (dir., s.p., cameo), Conan the Barbarian (co-s.p.), Scarface (s.p.), Year of the Dragon (co-s.p.), Salvador (dir., co-s.p., co-prod., WGA nom. 1987), 8 Million Ways to Die (co-s.p.), Platoon (dir., s.p., cameo; Academy Award, 1 other nom.; & DGA Award for Best Director, Golden Globe Award, 1 other nom.; WGA nom. 1986), Wall Street (dir., co-s.p., cameo), Talk Radio (dir., co-s.p.), Born on the Fourth of July (dir., co-s.p., cameo; Academy Award, 2 other noms; & DGA Award for Best Director, 2 Golden Globe Awards, WGA nom. 1989), Blue Steel (co-prod.), Reversal of Fortune (co-prod.), The Doors (dir., co-s.p., cameo), Iron Maze (co-exec. prod.), JFK (dir., co-prod., co-s.p., 3 Academy Award noms.; DGA nom.; Golden Globe Award, 1 other nom.; WGA nom. 1992), South Central (co-exec. prod.), Zebrahead (co-exec. prod.), Dave (actor), The Joy Luck Club (co-exec. prod.), Heaven and Earth (dir., co-prod., s.p.), Natural Born Killers (dir., co-prod., co-s.p., Golden Globe nom. 1995), The New Age (exec. prod.), Nixon (dir., co-s.p., co-prod.; Academy Award nom. 1996, Chicago Film Critics Award), Killer: A Journal of Murder (co-exec. prod.), The People vs. Larry Flynt (prod.), Evita, U-Turn, Savior (prod.), Scud: The Disposable Assassin (prod.), Any Given Sunday (dir., prod.), Comandante (doc.; writer, dir. & prod.), Persona Non Grata (documentary; dir.) Chains (exec. prod.), The Art of War (prod.), The Corruptor (prod.), Alexander (prod.), Torrente 3: El protector (cameo), World Trade Center (dir., prod.), W. (dir., prod.), South of the Border (doc., dir.), Money Never Sleeps (actor, dir., prod., writer), SecretStone (actor).
TELEVISION: *Movies:* Indictment: The McMartin Trial (co-exec. prod., Emmy Award 1995), Frank Capra's American Dream, The Day Reagan Was Shot. *Mini-series:* Wild Palms (co-exec. prod.). *Series:* Film School (documentary; appears as himself). *Documentaries/Specials:* Looking for Fidel (narr., writer & dir.), Make Your Own Damn Movie! (video). *Guest:* More than 60 appearances.

STONE, SHARON
Actress. b. Meadville, PA, March 10, 1958. e. Edinboro St. Univ. Started as model, appearing in several TV commercials.
PICTURES: Stardust Memories (debut, 1980), Deadly Blessing, Bolero, Irreconcilable Differences, King Soloman's Mines, Allan Quartermain and the Lost City of Gold, Cold Steel, Police Academy 4: Citizens on Patrol, Action Jackson, Above the Law, Blood and Sand, Beyond the Stars (Personal Choice), Total Recall, He Said/She Said, Scissors, Year of the Gun, Basic Instinct (Golden Globe nom. 1993), Diary of a Hit Man, Where Sleeping Dogs Lie, Sliver, Last Action Hero (cameo), Intersection, The Specialist, The Quick and the Dead (also co-

prod.), Casino (Academy Award nom.; Golden Globe Award 1996), The Last Dance, Diabolique, The Mighty (Golden Globe nom. 1999), Sphere, Gloria, Antz (voice), Simpatico, Picking up the Pieces, Gloria, The Muse (Golden Globe nom. 2000), Forever Hollywood, Beautiful Joe, CyberWorld, In the Shadow of Hollywood, Searching for Debra Winger (doc.), Cold Creek Manor, Catwoman, A Different Loyalty, Alpha Dog, Broken Flowers, Wassup Rockers (exec. prod. only), Basic Instinct 2, Bobby, The Year of Getting to Know Us (also exec. prod.), $5 a Day, Streets of Blood, The Invocation (doc., narr., exec. prod., writer), The Guest Room, Waco, Sweet Baby Jesus, The Burma Conspiracy.
TELEVISION: *Movies*: Not Just Another Affair, The Calendar Girl Murders, The Vegas Strip Wars, Tears in the Rain, The Sissy Duckling (narrator; voice), If These Walls Could Talk 2. *Mini-Series*: War and Remembrance. *Series*: Bay City Blues, Happily Ever After: Fairy Tales for Every Child (narr.).Harold and the Purple Crayon (narr.), Huff, Law & Order: Special Victims Unit. *Documentaries/Specials:* Beyond the Summit (narr.). *Guest*: More than 212 appearances.

STOPPARD, TOM

Writer, Director. r.n. Tomas Straussler. b. Zlin, Czechoslovakia, July 3, 1937. Playwright whose works include Rosencrantz and Guildenstern Are Dead, Jumpers, Travesties, The Real Thing, Hapgood, Arcadia.
PICTURES: *Writer:* The Romantic Englishwoman, Despair, The Human Factor, Squaring the Circle, Brazil (Academy Award nom. 1986), Empire of the Sun, The Russia House, Rosencrantz and Guildenstern Are Dead (also dir.), Billy Bathgate, Fifteen Minute Hamlet, Shakespeare in Love (Academy Award for orig. s.p.; Golden Globe Award, WGA Award 1999), Enigma, Vatel, Casanova.
TELEVISION: *Movies*: *Writer:* Der Spleen des George Riley, A Separate Peace, Teeth (short), Another Moon Called Earth (short), Neutral Ground, Ulazi slobodan covek, Three Men in a Boat, Travesties, Professional Foul, A Walk on the Water, On the Razzle, Squaring the Circle, Konsert för en sluten avdelning, The Dog It Was That Died, Vaclav Havel's 'Largo Desolato', Poodle Springs. *Series: Writer:* Thirty-Minute Theatre.

STORARO, VITTORIO

Cinematographer. b. Rome, Italy, June 24, 1940. Trained at Rome's Centro Sperimentale Cinematografia and began filming short films. His work as Bernardo Bertolucci's regular cinematographer won him an international reputation and award-winning work in Europe and America, including 3 Academy Awards.
PICTURES: Giovinezza Giovinezza (Youthful Youthful), The Gallery Murders, The Conformist, The Spider's Stratagem, The Fifth Cord, Malice, 'Tis Pity She's a Whore, Last Tango in Paris, Giordano Bruno, Footprints, The Driver's Seat, 1900, Submission, Agatha, Apocalypse Now (Academy Award 1979), La Luna, Reds (Academy Award 1981), One From the Heart, Wagner, Ladyhawke, Captain Eo, Ishtar, The Last Emperor (Academy Award, ASC nom. 1987), Tucker: The Man and His Dream, New York Stories (Life Without Zoe), Dick Tracy (Academy Award nom.; ASC nom. 1991), The Sheltering Sky, Tosca, Little Buddha, Roma! Imago Urbis, Flamenco, Taxi, Tango (Canne Film Fest. Award, Tech. Prize, 1998), Bulworth, Goya, Mirka, Picking Up the Pieces. Zapata, Exorcist IV: The Beginning, Dominion: Prequel to the Exorcist, I, Don Giovanni, El Día que me quieras, Dare to Love Me, L' Imbroglio nel lenzuolo, Kingdom Come.
TELEVISION: *Movies:* Eneide, Tosca, La Traviata à Paris, Caravaggio, Rigoletto. *Mini- series:* Orlando Furioso, Wagner, Peter the Great (Emmy nom. 1986), Dune (Emmy Award, ASC nom. 2001).

STOSSEL, JOHN

News Correspondent. b. 1947. e. Princeton U., B.A. in psychology, 1969. Started as producer-reporter with KGW-TV in Portland, OR. Joined WCBS-TV in New York as investigative reporter and consumer editor, winning 15 local Emmy Awards. 1981 joined ABC-TV, appearing on Good Morning America and 20/20 as Correspondent; co-anchor (2003-). Also provides twice-weekly consumer reports on ABC Radio Information Network. Sex, Drugs, and Freedom of Choice (doc.).
AUTHOR: Shopping Smart (1982). 2009 Stossel moved to the Fox Business Network to anchor his own show. He will also appear on Fox News Channel and host and produce a number of specials. Stossel has received more than 19 Emmy Awards. National Press Club honors five times for excellence in consumer reporting. Awards include the George Polk Award for Outstanding Local Reporting and the George Foster Peabody Award.
Movies: As Host: Junk Science: What You Know That May Not Be So (host), Freeloaders, The Power of Belief with John Stossel, Is America Number One? With John Stossel, You Can't Say That! What's Happening to Free Speech with John Stossel, John Stossel Goes to Washington. *Series:* 20/20, Stossel. *Documentaries: Host / Writer:* The Trouble with Lawyers with John Stossel, The Mystery of Happiness: Who Has It & How to Get It - With John Stossel, Love, Lust & Marriage: Why We Stray and Why We Stay, Sex, Drugs & Consenting Adults, Teens: What Makes Them Tick?, Hype with John Stossel, Tampering with Nature, A Lawyer Walks Into a Bar..., Boys & Girls Are Different: Men, Women & the Sex Difference, Common Sense with John Stossel, The In-Crowd and Social Cruelty with John Stossel, Help Me! I Can't Help Myself with John Stossel, I Want Your Money.

STOWE, MADELEINE

Actress. b. Los Angeles, CA, Aug. 18, 1958. e. USC. m. actor Brian Benben. Began acting at the Solari Theatre in Beverly Hills where she appeared in The Tenth Man.
PICTURES: Stakeout (debut, 1987), Tropical Snow, Worth Winning, Revenge, The Two Jakes, Closet Land, China Moon, Unlawful Entry, The Last of the Mohicans, Another Stakeout, Short Cuts (Golden Globe Award; best ensemble cast 1994), Blink, Bad Girls, Twelve Monkeys, The Proposition, Playing by Heart, The General's Daughter, Imposter, We Were Soldiers, Avenging Angelo, Octane.
TELEVISION: *Movies*: The Nativity, The Deerslayer, Amazons, Blood and Orchids, The Magnificent Ambersons, Saving Milly, Southern Comfort, The Christmas Hope. *Mini-series*: Beulah Land. *Series*: The Gangster Chronicles, Raines.

STRATHAIRN, DAVID

Actor. b. San Francisco, CA, Jan. 26, 1949. e. Williams Col.
THEATRE: Einstein and the Polar Bear, Blue Plate Special, Fen, I'm Not Rappaport, Salonika, A Lie of the Mind, The Birthday Party, Danton's Death, Mountain Language, L'Atelier, A Moon for the Misbegotten, Temptation.
PICTURES: Return of the Secaucus 7, Lovesick, Silkwood, Iceman, The Brother from Another Planet, When Nature Calls, Enormous Changes at the Last Minute, At Close Range, Matewan, Stars and Bars, Dominick and Eugene, Call Me, Eight Men Out, The Feud, Memphis Belle, City of Hope, Big Girls Don't Cry... They Get Even, A League of Their Own, Bob Roberts, Sneakers, Passion Fish, Lost in Yonkers, The Firm, A Dangerous Woman, The River Wild, Losing Isaiah, Dolores Claiborne, Mother Night, Home for the Holidays, Song of Hiawatha, L.A. Confidential, The Climb, With Friends Like These, Bad Manners, Simon Birch, Meschugge, A Midsummer Night's Dream, Limbo, A Map of the World, Harrison's Flowers, A Good Baby, The Victim, Ball in the House, Speak Easy, Blue Car, Twisted, Missing In America, Heavens Fall, Goodnight and Good Luck (Academy Award nom.; Golden Globe nom. 2006), Fracture, The Sensation of Sight (also prod.), We Are... Marshall, My Blueberry Nights, The Spiderwick Chronicles, The Bourne Ultimatum, Cold Souls, The Uninvited, The Tempest, Odysseus in America (narr.), Howl, The Whistleblower, No God, No Master.
TELEVISION: *Movies*: Day One, Son of the Morning Star, Heat Wave, Judgment, Without Warning: The James Brady Story, O Pioneers!, The American Clock, Beyond the Call, In the Gloaming, Evidence of Blood, Freedom Song, The Miracle Worker, Lathe of Heaven, Master Spy: The Robert Hanssen Story, Paradise, Take 3, Matadors, Temple Grandin (Emmy nom. 2010). *Series*: The Days and Nights of Molly Dodd, Big Apple, The Sopranos, The Supreme Court (narr.). *Guest:* More than 60 appearances.

STRAUSS, PETER

Actor. b. Croton-on-Hudson, NY., Feb. 20, 1947. e. Northwestern U. Spotted at N.U. by talent agent and sent to Hollywood. On stage at Mark Taper Theatre in Dance Next Door, The Dirty Man.
PICTURES: Hail Hero! (debut, 1969), Soldier Blue, The Trial of the Catonsville Nine, The Last Tycoon, Spacehunter: Adventures in the Forbidden Zone, Nick of Time, xXx 2: The Next Level, License to Wed.
TELEVISION: *Movies*: The Man Without a Country, Attack on Terror: The FBI Versus the Ku Klux Klan, Young Joe: The Forgotten Kennedy, The Jericho Mile (Emmy Award 1979), Angel on My Shoulder, Heart of Steel (Golden Globe nom. 1984), Under Siege, A Whale for the Killing, Penalty Phase, Proud Men, Brotherhood of the Rose, Peter Gunn, 83 Hours Till Dawn, Flight of Black Angel, Fugitive Among Us, Trial: The Price of Passion, Men Don't Tell (Golden Globe nom. 1994), Thicker Than Blood: The Larry McLinden Story, The Yearling, Reunion, Texas Justice, In the Lake of the Woods, Death in the Shadows, Joan of Arc, A Father's Choice, Murder on the Orient Express, 111 Gramercy Park, The Way, Jack's Family Adventure. *Mini-series*: Rich Man Poor Man (Emmy nom.; Golden Globe nom. 1976), Masada (Emmy nom. Golden Globe nom. 1981), Kane & Abel (Golden Globe nom. 1986), Tender Is The Night, Seasons of Love. *Series*: Moloney, Rich Man, Poor Man - Book II, Body & Soul, Biker Mice from Mars (voice), State of the Union (narr.). *Guest:* More than 74 appearances.

STRAUSS, PETER E.

Executive, Producer. b. Oct. 7, 1940. e. Oberlin College, London School of Economics, Columbia U. Sch. of Law, L.L.B., 1965. Vice pres., University Dormitory Dev. Co., 1965-68; v.p., Allart Cinema 16, 1968-69; v.p. prod., Allied Artists Pictures Corp., 1970; 1978-80, exec. v.p. Rastar Films, Inc.; left to form Panache Productions and served as pres. from 1980-86. In 1987, became pres., CEO and chairman of the International Movie Group, Inc. In 1998, Strauss became the Chairman of Lions Gate Pictures, Inc. Currently, Strauss is an executive vice president with the Mandalay Entertainment Group.

PICTURES: *Producer*: Best of the Best, Cadence, By the Sword, Best of the Best II (also exec. prod.), Best of the Best III, Best of the Best: Without Warning. *Executive producer:* Touched by Love, Dance of the Dwarfs, Thunder Run, W.B. Blue and the Bean, Killer Instinct, The Runestone, Night of the Cyclone, Cadence, Sunset Grill, Chrystal, The Jacket.
TELEVISION: *Movie:* Carolina Moon, Northern Lights, Midnight Bayou, High Noon, Tribute.

STREEP, MERYL
Actress. r.n. Mary Louise Streep. b. Summit, NJ, June 22, 1949. e. Vassar. Acted for a season with traveling theatre co. in VT. Awarded scholarship to Yale Drama School, 1972. NY stage debut: Trelawny of the Wells (1975) with New York Shakespeare Fest. Appeared in 1984 documentary In Our Hands.
THEATRE: *Off-B'way*: 27 Wagons Full of Cotton (Theatre World Award), A Memory of Two Mondays, Secret Service, Henry V, (NY Shakespeare Fest.), Measure for Measure (NYSF), The Cherry Orchard, Happy End (B'way debut, 1977), The Taming of the Shrew (NYSF), Taken in Marriage, Alice in Concert, Isn't It Romantic?
PICTURES: Julia (debut, 1977), The Deer Hunter (Academy Award nom.; Golden Globe nom. 1979), Manhattan, The Seduction of Joe Tynan, Kramer vs. Kramer (Academy Award, best supporting actress, Golden Globe Award, 1983), The French Lieutenant's Woman (Academy Award nom.; Golden Globe Award 1982), Still of the Night, Sophie's Choice (Academy Award, Golden Globe Award, 1982), Silkwood (Academy Award nom.; Golden Globe nom. 1984), Falling in Love, Plenty, Out of Africa (Academy Award nom.; Golden Globe nom. 1986), Heartburn, Ironweed (Academy Award nom. 1988), A Cry in the Dark (Academy Award nom.; Golden Globe nom. 1989), She-Devil (Golden Globe nom. 1990), Postcards From the Edge (Academy Award nom.; Golden Globe nom. 1991), Defending Your Life, Death Becomes Her (Golden Globe nom. 1993), The House of the Spirits, The River Wild (Golden Globe nom. 1995), The Bridges of Madison County (Academy Award nom.; Golden Globe nom. 1996), Before and After, Marvin's Room (Golden Globe nom. 1997), One True Thing (Academy Award nom.; Golden Globe nom. 1999), Antz (voice), Dancing at Lughnasa, Music of the Heart (Academy Award nom.; Golden Globe nom. 2000), Artificial Intelligence: AI (voice), Clint Eastwood: Out of the Shadows, The Papp Project, The Hours (Golden Globe nom. 2003), Adaptation (Academy Award nom.; Golden Globe Award 2003), The Manchurian Candidate (Golden Globe nom. 2005), Lemony Snicket's A Series of Unfortunate Events, Prime, The Devil Wears Prada (Academy Award nom.; Golden Globe Award 2007), A Prairie Home Companion, Ant Bully (voice), The Ant Bully (voice), Dark Matter, Evening, Rendition, Lions for Lambs, The Last Station, First Man, Dirty Tricks, Mamma Mia! (also soundtrack performer, Golden Globe nom. 2009), A Question of Mercy, Julie & Julia, Doubt (Academy Award nom.; Golden Globe nom. 2009), The Fantastic Mr. Fox (voice), It's Complicated (Golden Globe nom. 2010).
TELEVISION: *Movies*: Secret Service, The Deadliest Season, Uncommon Women...And Others, Alice at the Palace, First Do No Harm (Emmy nom.; Golden Globe nom. 1997). *Mini-series*: Holocaust (Emmy Award, 1978). Angels in America (Emmy Award, Golden Globe Award Best Actress in mini-series or TV Movie, 2004). *Documentaries/Specials* (PBS): Secret Service, Uncommon Women and Others, Age 7 in America (host), Freedom: A History of Us. *Guest:* More than 184 appearances.

STREISAND, BARBRA
Singer, Actress, Director, Producer. b. New York, NY, April 24, 1942. e. Erasmus H.S., Brooklyn. Son is actor Jason Gould. Appeared as singer in NY night clubs. NY stage debut: Another Evening with Harry Stoones (1961), followed by Pins and Needles. On Broadway in I Can Get It For You Wholesale, Funny Girl. Performed song Prisoner for 1978 film Eyes of Laura Mars. Appeared in 1990 documentary Listen Up. Received 4 Golden Globe Henrietta Awards. 2000 won Golden Globe Cecil B. DeMille Award.
PICTURES: Funny Girl (debut; Academy Award, Golden Globe Award 1968), Hello Dolly! (Golden Globe nom. 1970), On a Clear Day You Can See Forever, The Owl and the Pussycat (Golden Globe nom. 1971), What's Up Doc?, Up the Sandbox, The Way We Were (Academy Award nom.; Golden Globe nom. 1974), For Pete's Sake, Funny Lady (Golden Globe nom. 1976), A Star Is Born (also co-composer, exec. prod.; Academy Award for best song: Evergreen, 2 Golden Globe Awards 1976), The Main Event (also co-prod.), All Night Long, Yentl (also dir., prod., co- s.p. Golden Globe Award, 1 other nom. 1984), Nuts (also prod., co-composer, Golden Globe nom. 1988), The Prince of Tides (also dir., co-prod.; Academy Award nom.; DGA nom.; Golden Globe nom. 1992), The Mirror Has Two Faces (also dir., Academy Award nom.; 2 Golden Globe noms. 1997), City at Peace (documentary, exec. prod.), The King and I (Singer, "We Kiss in a Shadow" & "Something Wonderful"), Mona Lisa Smile (Singer, "Smile"), Meet the Fockers, Little Fockers.
TELEVISION: *Movies:* Serving in Silence: The Margarethe Cammermeyer Story (co-exec. prod. only, Emmy nom. 1995), Rescuers: Stories of Courage: Two Women (exec. prod.), The Long Island Incident (exec. prod.), Rescuers: Stories of Courage: Two Families (exec. prod.), Frankie & Hazel (exec. prod.), What Makes a Family (exec. prod.), Varian's War (exec. prod.), Mame (exec. prod.). *Series:* Kath & Kim (composer; song "Evergreen"). *Documentaries/Specials*: My Name Is Barbra (Emmy Award, 1965), Color Me Barbra, The Belle of 14th Street, A Happening in Central Park, Barbra Streisand...And Other Musical Instruments, Putting It Together, One Voice, Barbra Streisand: The Concert (also co-prod.; 2 Emmy Awards, 1 other nom. 1995), The Living Century (series documentary; exec. prod.), Timeless: Live in Concert (Emmy Award, DGA nom. 2002) Reel Models: The First Women of Film (Emmy Award 2001), Tony Bennett: An American Classic (performer), Streisand: Live in Concert (exec. prod., dir., writer, creator), One Night Only: Barbra Streisand and Quartet at the Village Vanguard - September 26,2009. *Guest:* More than 182 appearances.

STRICK, WESLEY
Writer. b. New York, NY, Feb. 11, 1954. e. Univ. of California at Berkeley, 1975. Was rock critic for magazines: Rolling Stone, Cream, Circus.
PICTURES: True Believer, Arachnophobia, Cape Fear, Final Analysis, Batman Returns, Wolf, The Tie That Binds (dir.), The Saint, Return to Paradise, The Glass House, Love is the Drug (also exec. prod.), Glass House: The Good Mother, A Nightmare on Elm Street.
TELEVISION: *Movies:* Trouble Shooters: Trapped Beneath the Earth, Hitched. *Series*: Eddie Dodd (pilot, also creator).

STRICKLAND, GAIL
Actress. b. Birmingham, AL, May 18, 1947. e. Florida St. Univ. NY Theatre includes Status Quo Vadis, I Won't Dance.
PICTURES: The Drowning Pool, Bittersweet Love, Bound for Glory, One on One, Who'll Stop the Rain, Norma Rae, Lies, Oxford Blues, Protocol, The Man in the Moon, Three of Hearts, When a Man Loves a Woman, How to Make an American Quilt, The American President, Quality Time.
TELEVISION: *Movies:* Ellery Queen, My Father's House, The Dark Side of Innocence, The Gathering, A Love Affair: The Eleanor and Lou Gehrig Story, The President's Mistress, Ski Lift to Death, Letters from Frank, King Crab, Rape and Marriage: The Rideout Case, A Matter of Life and Death, My Body My Child, Eleanor: First Lady of the World, A Mother's Prayer, Life of the Party: The Pamela Harriman Story, Starlight: The Plane That Couldn't Land, An Enemy Among Us, Heartbeat, The Burden of Proof, Silent Cries, Spies, Barbara Taylor Bradford's Remember, A Mother's Prayer. *Series:* The Insiders, What a Country, Heartbeat, Dr. Quinn Medicine Woman, Melrose Place, First Monday. *Guest:* More than 72 appearances.

STRINGER, HOWARD
Executive. b. Cardiff, Wales. Feb. 19, 1942. e. Oxford U., B.A., M.A., modern history/international relations. Moved to the U.S. in 1965 and became a U.S. citizen in 1985. Received Army Commendation Medal for meritorious achievement for service in Vietnam (1965-67). Knighted by Queen Elizabeth II in 1999. Maintains residences in New York and England. Joined CBS, 1965, at WCBS-TV, NY, rising from assoc. prod., prod. to exec. prod. of documentary broadcasts. Served as prod., dir. and writer of CBS Reports: The Palestinians (Overseas Press Club of America, Writers Guild Awards, 1974); The Rockefellers (Emmy Award, 1973). Won 9 Emmy Awards as exec. prod., prod., writer or dir: CBS Reports: The Boston Goes to China; CBS Reports: The Defense of the United States; CBS Evening News with Dan Rather: The Beirut Bombing; The Countdown Against Cancer; The Black Family. Exec. prod., CBS Reports; exec. prod., CBS Evening News with Dan Rather, 1981-84. Appointed exec. v.p., CBS News Division, 1984; pres., CBS News, 1986; pres., CBS/Broadcast Group, 1988-1995. Chmn. & CEO, Tele-TV, a broadband technology co., 1995-1997. Joined Sony Corporation of America as president in 1997. Chmn. & CEO, Sony Corp. of America, appointed vice Chmn., Sony Corporation 2003. In March 2005 promoted to chairman/CEO of Sony Corp., the first time a foreigner has been put in charge of a giant Japanese conglomerate. He retains all duties at Sony Corp. of America, with current execs at Sony Pictures Entertainment still reporting directly to Stringer.

STRITCH, ELAINE
Actress. b. Detroit, MI, Feb. 2, 1926. e. studied acting with Erwin Piscator at the New Sch. for Social Research. Major career on stage. B'way debut 1946 in Loco.
THEATRE: *NY*: Made in Heaven, Angel in the Wings, Call Me Madam, Pal Joey, On Your Toes, Sail Away, Who's Afraid of Virginia Woolf?, Show Boat, A Delicate Balance (Tony Award nom.). *London:* Gingerbread Lady, Small Craft Warnings, Company.
PICTURES: The Scarlet Hour (debut, 1955), Three Violent People, A Farewell to Arms, The Perfect Furlough, Who Killed Teddy Bear?, Sidelong Glances of a Pigeon Kicker, The Spiral Staircase, Providence, September, Cocoon: The Return, Cadillac Man, Out to Sea, Krippendorf's Tribe, Screwed, Small Time Crooks, Autumn in New York, Romance & Cigarettes.
TELEVISION: *Movies*: Stranded, Follies in Concert. Sparks: The Price of Passion, The Secret Life of Archie's Wife, An Inconvenient Woman (Emmy nom. 1991), Chance of a Lifetime, An Unexpected Life, Paradise. *Series*: Growing Paynes (1948),

Pantomine Quiz (regular, 1953-55, 1958), My Sister Eileen, The Trials of O'Brien, Two's Company (London), Nobody's Perfect (London; also adapt.) The Edge of Night, The Ellen Burstyn Show, One Life to Live, EGG: The Arts Show (narrator), Life's A Bitch, Law & Order (recurring role, Emmy Award 1993), 30 Rock (Emmy Award 2007, 3 other noms.). *Documentaries/Specials*: Company: the Making of the Album, Kennedy Center Tonight, Elaine Stritch at Liberty (as herself; Emmy Award, 2004). *Guest*: More than 93 appearances.

STROLLER, LOUIS A.
Producer. b. Brooklyn, NY, April 3, 1942. e. Nicholas College of Business Admin., BBA, 1963. Entered film business in 1963 doing a variety of jobs in local NY studios and TV commercials. Unit manager on The Producers. Moved to L.A. in 1970s. First asst. dir. Charley, Take the Money and Run, Lovers and Other Strangers, They Might Be Giants, Man on a Swing, 92 in the Shade. Prod. mgr.: Mortadella, Sisters, Sweet Revenge, The Eyes of Laura Mars, Telefon. *Assoc. prod.*: Badlands, Carrie, The Seduction of Joe Tynan.
PICTURES: *Exec. prod. or prod.*: Simon, The Four Seasons, Venom, Eddie Macon's Run, Scarface, Sweet Liberty, Real Men, A New Life, Sea of Love, Betsy's Wedding, Back in the U.S.S.R., The Real McCoy, Carlito's Way, The Shadow, The Rock, Nothing to Lose, Snake Eyes, The Bone Collector, The Adventures of Pluto Nash, Carolina.Lara Croft Tomb Raider: The Cradle of Life (co-prod.).
TELEVISION: Half a Lifetime (exec. prod.; nom. 4 ACE Awards), Blue Ice, Grease: You're the One That I Want! (exec. prod.).

STROUD, DON
Actor. b. Honolulu, Hawaii, Sept. 1, 1943. e. Kaimuki H.S. Was surfing champion, ranked 4th in the world.
PICTURES: Games, Madigan, Journey to Shiloh, What's So Bad About Feeling Good?, Coogan's Bluff, Bloody Mama, Explosion, Angel Unchained, Tick Tick Tick, Von Richtofen and Brown, Joe Kidd, Slaughter's Big Rip-Off, Scalawag, Murph the Surf, The Killer Inside Me, The House by the Lake, The Choirboys, The Buddy Holly Story, The Amityville Horror, The Night the Lights Went Out in Georgia, Search and Destroy, Sweet Sixteen, Armed and Dangerous, Licence to Kill, Down the Drain, The Divine Enforcer, King of the Kickboxers, Cartel, Mob Boss, Street Wars, Frogtown, Deady Avenger, Danger Sign, Carnosaur II, Of Unknown Origin, Sudden Death, Dillinger and Capone, Twisted Justice, Two to Tango, Ghost Ship, Precious Find, Wild America, Perdita Durango, Little Bigfoot, HauntedSea, Detonator, Sutures.
TELEVISION: *Movies*: Split Second to an Epitaph, Something for a Lonely Man, DA: Conspiracy to Kill, Deadly Dream, Daughters of Joshua Cabe, Rolling Man, The Elevator, Return of Joe Forrester, High Risk, Katie: Portrait of a Centerfold, Out on a Limb, I Want to Live, Manhunters, Murder Me Murder You, The Alien Within, Sawbones, Barefoot in Paradise, National Lampoon's Men in White. *Series*: Kate Loves a Mystery, Mike Hammer, The New Gidget, Dragnet, Good Morning Hawai'i (assoc. prod.). *Pilot*: Barefoot in Paradise. *Documentaries/Specials:* Hatful of Rain. *Guest*: More than 98 appearances.

STRUTHERS, SALLY
Actress. b. Portland, OR, July 28, 1948. First TV appearance was as dancer on a Herb Alpert special. Appeared on Broadway stage in Wally's Cafe.
PICTURES: The Phynx, Five Easy Pieces, The Getaway, The Others, Out of the Black, A Month of Sundays, Reeseville, Gettin' the Man's Foot Outta Your Baadasssss!, Hoodwinked!, Monster Heroes.
TELEVISION: *Movies*: The Great Houdinis, Aloha Means Goodbye, Hey I'm Alive, Intimate Strangers, My Husband is Missing, And Your Name is Jonah, A Gun in the House, A Deadly Silence, In the Best Interest of the Children, New Adventures of Mother Goose. *Series*: The Summer Smothers (1970), The Tim Conway Comedy Hour, All in the Family (2 Emmy Awards, 3 other noms.; 4 Golden Globe noms.), Pebbles and Bamm-Bamm (voice), Flintstones Comedy Hour (voice), Gloria, 9 to 5, Tale Spin (voice), Dinosaurs (voice), General Hospital, Gilmore Girls, Still Standing. *Guest:* More than 70 appearances.

STUBBS, IMOGEN
Actress. b. Newcastle-upon-Tyne, England, Feb. 2, 1961. Brought up in West London on sailing barge on the Thames. Grandmother was playwright Esther McCracken. e. Exeter College. First class degree at Oxford U. in English. Joined Oxford U. Dramatic Society appearing in revues and at Edinburgh Festival in play called Poison. Trained for stage at Royal Acad. of Dramatic Art. Prof. stage debut in Cabaret and The Boyfriend, in Ipswich. Acted with Royal Shakespeare Co. in The Two Noble Kinsmen, The Rover (promising newcomer critics award), Richard II, Othello, Heartbreak House, St. Joan, Uncle Vanya.
PICTURES: Privileged, A Summer Story, Nanou, Erik the Viking, True Colors, A Pin for the Butterfly, Sandra C'est la Vie, Jack & Sarah, Sense and Sensibility, Twelfth Night: Or What You Will.
TELEVISION: *Movies:* The Browning Version, The Rainbow, Fellow Traveller, Relatively Speaking, Pasternak (voice), Othello, Sandra c'est la vie, Mother Time, Blind Ambition, Township Opera, Marple: The Moving Finger, The Adventures of Daniel. *Series:* Anna Lee, Big Kids.

SUGAR, LARRY
Executive, Producer. b. Phoenix, AZ, May 26, 1945. m. Bonnie Sugar. e. Cheshire Acad., 1962; CSUN, B.A., 1967; U. of Southern Calif., J.D., 1971. Writer and co-author, Calif. Primary Reading Program, 1967-68. Joined Warner Bros. as dir., legal and corp. affairs, 1971-74; 20th Century Fox legal staff, 1974-77; co-owner with Bonnie Sugar, Serendipity Prods., 1977-81; named president, international., Lorimar Prods. 1981-84; executive v.p., distribution, CBS 1984-85; exec. v.p. worldwide distribution, Weintraub Entertainment Group 1987-89; formed Sugar Entertainment, chairman., 1989-1991; president, Republic Pictures International, Inc. 1991-93; since 1993 Sugar has been producing and writing. He has written and/or produced a series of films in association with Showtime. He's also produced various TV movies and series for the SciFi Network in the U.S., the Disney Channel and NBC. He's served as an adjunct professor at the College of Santa Fe for over 12 years, teaching "The Business of Entertainment," and is a guest lecturer at the university level, appearing at Brandeis, USC, UCLA and Tulane, among others. Sugar formed two companies since 2000, Vancouver-based dcinema Entertainment Inc. and the Creative Crib, which he calls an entertainment incubator. The company seeks the hottest new stories from writers trying to break into the industry and then works with them to get their work produced. Sugar's industry memberships include: the Acad. of Motion Picture Arts and Sciences, The Screen Actors Guild, the Writer's Guild of Canada, the Director's Guild of Canada and the British Columbia Motion Picture Association.
PICTURES: *Executive producer*: Slapstick, Steel Dawn, Write to Kill, Fatal Sky, Graveyard Shift, Shattered, Dark Horse, The Plague, Family Prayers, Boxing Helena, Nightwatching.
TELEVISION: *Movies*: *Producer:* The Prisoner of Zenda Inc., The Halfback of Notre Dame (also writer), Annie O, Robin of Locksley (also writer), Dead Man's Gun, Ronnie & Julie (also s.p.), Out of Time, Mermaid. *Series: Producer:* Dead Man's Gun (also dir.), So Weird (also dir.), Just Deal, Romeo, Barely Cooking (doc. also dir.). *Executive producer:* First Wave (also dir.), The Collector (also dir.), The Assistants, jPod, The Troop.

SUMMERS, GARY
Sound. Among his awards for outstanding achievement in sound, he is a winner of four Academy Awards for Best Sound: Saving Private Ryan, 1998; Titanic, 1997; Jurassic Park, 1993; and Terminator 2: Judgment Day, 1991. 3 Cinema Audio Society Awards and 2 other noms.
PICTURES: Star Wars: Episode IV-A New Hope, Star Wars: Episode V-The Empire Strikes Back, Raiders of the Lost Ark, Star Wars: Episode VI-Return of the Jedi (Academy Award nom. 1984), Indiana Jones and the Temple of Doom, Cocoon, Captain EO (short), Howard the Duck, Spaceballs, Willow, Big Time (documentary), Cocoon: The Return, Indiana Jones and the Last Crusade (Academy Award nom. 1990), Always, Avalon, To Cross the Rubicon, Rush, The Five Heartbeats, Terminator 2: Judgment Day (Academy Award, Best Sound, 1992), Backdraft (Academy Award nom. 1992), F/X2, Defenseless, The Addams Family, Rush, From Time to Time, House of Cards, Jurassic Park (Academy Award, Best Sound, CAS nom. 1994), The Saint of Fort Washington, Mrs. Doubtfire, Baby's Day Out, Miracle on 34th Street, Casper, Toy Story, Jumanji (CAS nom. 1996), James and the Giant Peach, Mission Impossible, The Arrival, Mars Attacks!, Volcano, Titanic (Academy Award, Best Sound, CAS Award 1998), The Lost World: Jurassic Park, In God's Hands, Saving Private Ryan (Academy Award, Best Sound, CAS Award 1999), Stepmom, A Bug's Life, Lake Placid, The Haunting, Komodo, Toy Story 2, Bicentennial Man, Titus, Frequency, Cirque du Soleil, Titan A.E., Legend of Bagger Vance, 102 Dalmatians, The Mexican, Artificial Intelligence, Jurassic Park 3, Monsters Inc., Hart's War, K-19: The Widowmaker, The Lord of the Rings: The Two Towers, Ghosts of the Abyss (doc.), Finding Nemo, Lara Croft Tomb Raider: The Cradle of Life, The Lord of the Rings: The Return of the King, Sky Captain and the World of Tomorrow, Team America: World Police, The Polar Express (IMAX version), Hoodwinked, xXx 2: The Next Level, Magnificent Desolation: Walking on the Moon 3D (doc., short), Cars, Zoom, Charlotte's Web, Fracture, The Bourne Ultimatum, Untraceable, Meet the Browns,The Mummy: Tomb of the Dragon Emperor, The Family That Preys, City of Ember, W., Shelter, Madea Goes to Jail, Transformers: Revenge of the Fallen (Academy Award nom.; CAS nom. 2010), Case 39, Avatar (Academy Award nom.; CAS nom. 2010), Shelter, Why Did I Get Married Too?, Iron Man 2, With Great Power: The Stan Lee Story.
TELEVISION: *Movie:* The Young Indiana Jones Chronicles (Emmy Award 1992, 1 other nom.), Young Indiana Jones and the Hollywood Follies (CAS Award 1995). *Series*: Fame L.A.

SUNSHINE, ROBERT HOWARD
Publisher. b. Brooklyn, NY, Jan. 17, 1946. e. U. of RI; Brooklyn Law Sch., 1971. Admitted to NY State Bar, 1971. President of Pubsun Corp., owner of Film Journal International (formerly Film Journal). Publisher of Film Journal International. Exec. dir., International Theatre Equipment Association, 1979-present; sec. and exec. dir. Foundation of the Motion Picture Pioneers, 1975-present; exec. dir., Natl. Assoc. of Theatre Owners of NY State,

1985-present; Producer of Variety Telethon, 1985-present; coordinator and producer, Show East Convention; coordinator and prod., Cinema Expo Intl., Amsterdam, Holland; coordinator and producer, CineAsia, Singapore. Executive director of Nielsen Business Media Film Group.

SURTEES, BRUCE
Cinematographer. b. Carmel, CA, July 27, 1937. Son of cinematographer Robert L. Surtees.
PICTURES: The Beguiled, Play Misty for Me, Dirty Harry, The Great Northfield Minnesota Raid, Conquest of the Planet of the Apes, Joe Kidd, The Outfit, High Plains Drifter, Blume in Love, Lenny (Academy Award nom. 1975), Night Moves, Leadbelly, The Outlaw Josey Wales, The Shootist, Three Warriors, Sparkle, Big Wednesday, Movie Movie (segment: Baxter's Beauties of 1933), Dreamer, Escape from Alcatraz, Ladies and Gentlemen the Fabulous Stains, White Dog, Firefox, Inchon, Honkytonk Man, Bad Boys, Risky Business, Sudden Impact, Tightrope, Beverly Hills Cop, Pale Rider, Psycho III, Out of Bounds, Ratboy, Back to the Beach, License to Drive, Men Don't Leave, Run, The Super, The Crush, That Night. Corrina Corrina, The Stars Fell on Henrietta, The Substitute, Just A Little Harmless Sex Joshua.
TELEVISION: *Movies:* Murder in a Small Town, That Championship Season, Dash and Lilly (Emmy nom. 1999), That Championship Season, Lethal Vows, The Lady in Question, Thin Air, American Tragedy, And Never Let Her Go.

SUSCHITZKY, PETER
Cinematographer. b. Poland, July 25, 1941. Spent long time in Latin America as documentatory cinematographer. Later made commercials in France, England and U.S. First feature was It Happened Here, 1962.
PICTURES: Over 30 features including: A Midsummer Night's Dream, Charlie Bubbles, Leo the Last, Privilege, That'll Be the Day, Lisztomania, The Rocky Horror Picture Show, All Creatures Great and Small (TV in U.S.), Valentino, The Empire Strikes Back, Krull, Falling in Love, In Extremis, Dead Ringers, Where the Heart Is, Naked Lunch, The Public Eye, The Vanishing, M. Butterfly, Immortal Beloved, Crash, Mars Attacks, The Man in the Iron Mask, eXistenZ, Red Planet, Spider, A History of Violence, Shopgirl, The Stone Council, Eastern Promises, A Dangerous Method.

SUTHERLAND, DONALD
Actor. b. St. John, New Brunswick, Canada, July 17, 1935. Son is actor Kiefer Sutherland. e. U. of Toronto, B.A., 1956. At 14 became a radio announcer and disc jockey. Worked in a mine in Finland. Theatre includes: The Male Animal (debut), The Tempest (Hart House Theatre, U. of Toronto), Two years at London Acad. of Music and Dramatic Art. Spent a year and a half with the Perth Repertory Theatre in Scotland, then repertory at Nottingham, Chesterfield, Bromley and Sheffield.
THEATRE: August for the People (London debut), On a Clear Day You Can See Canterbury, The Shewing Up of Blanco Posnet, The Spoon River Anthology, Lolita (B'way debut, 1981).
PICTURES: Castle of the Living Dead (debut, 1964), The World Ten Times Over, Dr. Terror's House of Horrors, Die Die My Darling (Fanatic), The Bedford Incident, Promise Her Anything, The Dirty Dozen, Billion Dollar Brain, Sebastian, Oedipus the King, Interlude, Joanna, The Split, M*A*S*H (Golden Globe nom. 1971), Start the Revolution Without Me, Act of the Heart, Kelly's Heroes, Alex in Wonderland, Little Murders, Klute, Johnny Got His Gun, F.T.A. (also co-prod., co-dir., co-s.p.), Steelyard Blues (also exec. prod.), Lady Ice, Alien Thunder (Dan Candy's Law), Don't Look Now, S*P*Y*S, The Day of the Locust, End of the Game (cameo), Fellini's Casanova, The Eagle Has Landed, 1900, The Disappearance, The Kentucky Fried Movie, National Lampoon's Animal House, Invasion of the Body Snatchers, The Great Train Robbery, Murder by Decree, Bear Island, A Man a Woman and a Bank, Nothing Personal, Ordinary People (Golden Globe nom. 1981), Blood Relatives, Gas, Eye of the Needle, Threshold, Max Dugan Returns, Crackers, Ordeal by Innocence, Heaven Help Us, Revolution, Wolf at the Door, The Rosary Murders, The Trouble With Spies, Apprentice to Murder, Lost Angels, Lock Up, A Dry White Season, Eminent Domain, Backdraft, Buster's Bedroom, JFK, Scream of Stone, Buffy the Vampire Slayer, Shadow of the Wolf, Benefit of the Doubt, Dr. Bethune (Bethune: The Making of a Hero), Younger and Younger, Six Degrees of Separation, Robert A. Heinlein's The Puppet Masters, Disclosure, Outbreak, Hollow Point, The Shadow Conspiracy, A Time to Kill, The Assignment, Free Money, Fallen, Without Limits (Golden Globe nom. 1999), Virus, Toscano, Instinct, The Setting Sun, The Art of War, Clint Eastwood: Out of the Shadows, Threads of Hope (narrator), Final Fantasy: The Spirits Within (voice), Big Shot's Funeral, Fellini: Je suis un gran menteur, Baltic Storm, Cold Mountain, The Italian Job, Aurora Borealis, American Gun, Lord of War (voice), Pride and Prejudice, Ask the Dust, Land of the Blind, An American Haunting, Reign Over Me, Fool's Gold, Astro Boy (voice), The Con Artist, The Mechanic, The Truth About the War in Heaven: Declaration of War, Man on the Train, The Eagle, Horrible Bosses.
TELEVISION: *Movies*: The Sunshine Patriot, The Winter of Our Discontent, Quicksand: No Escape, The Railway Station Man, The Lifeforce Experiment, Oldest Living Confederate Widow Tells All, Citizen X (Emmy Award 1995; Golden Globe Award 1996), Natural Enemy, The Hunley, The Big Heist, Uprising, 'Salem's Lot, Human Trafficking (Emmy nom. 2006), The Eastmans. *Mini-series:* Queen Victoria's Empire (voice), Path to War (Golden Globe Award 2003), Frankenstein, The Pillars of the Earth. *Series*: Great Books (narrator), Commander in Chief (Golden Globe nom. 2006), Dirty Sexy Money (Golden Globe nom. 2008), Moby Dick. *Documentaries / Specials*: (British) Marching to the Sea, The Death of Bessie Smith, Hamlet at Elsinore, Gideon's Way, The Champions, Bethune (Canada), Give Me Your Answer True, The Prize (narrator), People of the Forest: The Chimps of Gombe (narr.), For Love of Liberty: The Story of America's Black Patriots (voice). *Guest:* More than 128 appearances.

SUTHERLAND, KIEFER
Actor. r.n. William Frederick Dempsey George Sutherland. b. London, England, Dec. 18, 1966. Son of actor Donald Sutherland and actress Shirley Douglas. Moved to Los Angeles at age 4, then to Toronto at 8. Debut with L.A. Odyssey Theater at age 9 in Throne of Straw. Worked in local Toronto theatre workshops before landing starring role in The Bay Boy (1984) for which he won Canadian Genie Award.
PICTURES: Max Dugan Returns (debut, 1983), The Bay Boy, At Close Range, Stand By Me, Crazy Moon, The Lost Boys, The Killing Time, Promised Land, Bright Lights Big City, Young Guns, 1969, Renegades, Flashback, Chicago Joe and the Showgirl, Flatliners, Young Guns II, The Nutcracker Prince (voice), Article 99, Twin Peaks: Fire Walk With Me, A Few Good Men, The Vanishing, The Three Musketeers, The Cowboy Way, Teresa's Tattoo, Eye for an Eye, Freeway, A Time To Kill, The Last Days of Frankie the Fly, Truth or Consequences—N.M. (also dir.), Dark City, A Soldier's Sweetheart, Break Up, Ground Control, After Alice, Beat, Woman Wanted, Picking up the Pieces, The Right Temptation, Cowboy Up, To End All Wars, Desert Saints, Dead Heat, Behind the Red Door, Phone Booth (caller voice), Paradise Found, Taking Lives, Hope in Heaven (doc., narr.), The Wild (voice), The Sentinel, Dragonlance: Dragons of Autumn Twilight (voice), Monsters vs. Aliens (voice), Mirrors (also exec. prod.), Twelve (voice), Marmaduke (voice), Melancholia.
TELEVISION: *Movies*: Brotherhood of Justice, Trapped in Silence, Last Light (also dir.), Natural Selection (exec. prod. only), Duke of Groove (short; host), L.A. Confidential, The Flight That Fought Back (narr.), 24: Redemption (also exec. prod., Emmy nom. 2009), Monsters vs Aliens: Mutant Pumpkins from Outer Space (voice). *Series:* Watership Down (voice), 24 (also prod., 2 Emmy Awards, 8 other noms.; Golden Globe Award 2002, 5 other noms.). *Documentaries/Specials:* Ben Johnson: Drugs and the Quest for Gold (narrator). *Guest:* More than 110 appearances.

SUTTON, JAMES T.
Executive. b. California, Sept. 13. e. Columbia U. Film inspector, U.S. government; overseas m.p. service, WW II; co-owner, gen. mgr., Hal Davis Studios; hd. TV commercial div., Allan Sandler Films; Academy Art Pictures; pres., chmn. of bd., exec. prod., Royal Russian Studios, Inc., western hemisphere div.; pres. exec. prod. Gold Lion Prods., Inc.; pres. exec. prod. James T. Sutton-John L. Carpenter Prods.; pres., exec. dir., Airax Corp.; pres. of Skyax (div. of Airax).

SUVARI, MENA
Actress. b. Newport, RI, February 9, 1979. e. Providence High School, Burbank. m. cinematographer Robert Brinkmann.
PICTURES: Nowhere, Kiss the Girls, Slums of Beverly Hills, Snide and Prejudice, The Rage: Carrie 2, American Pie, American Beauty, American Virgin, Loser, Sugar & Spice, American Pie 2, The Musketeer, Spun, Sonny, Standing Still, Trauma, Beauty Shop, Domino, Edmond, Rumor Has It..., The Dog Problem, Factory Girl, Stuck, The Mysteries of Pittsburgh, Day of the Dead, The Garden of Eden, You May Not Kiss the Bride, Restitution, Last Stop.
TELEVISION: *Movies:* Atomic Train, Orpheus, Sex and Lies in Sin City: The Ted Binion Scandal. *Series:* Six Feet Under.

SUZMAN, JANET
Actress. b. Johannesburg, South Africa, Feb. 9, 1939. e. Kingsmead College, U. of Witwaterstrand. Trained at L.A.M.D.A. London stage debut in The Comedy of Errors. *Recent theatre*: Another Time, Hippolytos, The Sisters Rosensweig. *Director*: Othello for Market Theatre and Channel 4 (TV), Death of a Salesman, A Dream of People, The Deep Blue Sea.
PICTURES: Nicholas and Alexandra (Academy Award nom.; Golden Globe nom. 1972), A Day in the Death of Joe Egg, The Black Windmill, Nijinsky, Priest of Love, The Draughtsman's Contract, And the Ship Sails On, A Dry White Season, Nuns on the Run, Leon the Pig Farmer.
TELEVISION: *Movies*: The Comedy of Errors, Lord Raingo, St. Joan, The Three Sisters, Macbeth, Hedda Gabler, Antony and Cleopatra, The House on Garibaldi Street, The Midsummer Marriage, Revolutionary Witness, (short), The Zany Adventures of Robin Hood, Nobody Here But Us Chickens, Othello, The Secret Agent, Front Seat, Trial & Retribution: Sins of the Father, The Color of Magic. *Mini-series:* Lord Mountbatten: The Last Viceroy, The Singing Detective. *Series:* Play of the Month, Clayhanger, The War of the Roses.

SVENSON, BO
Actor, Director, Producer. b. Goteborg, Sweden, Feb. 13, 1941. e. UCLA, 1970-74. U.S. Marine Corps 1959-65. Founder of

Production Company, MagicQuest
PICTURES: *Actor:* Maurie (debut, 1973), The Great Waldo Pepper, Part 2: Walking Tall, Breaking Point, Special Delivery, Inglorious Bastards, Portrait of a Hitman, Final Chapter: Walking Tall, Our Man in Mecca, North Dallas Forty, Day of Resurrection, Thrilled to Death, Thunder, Deadly Impact, Thunder II, The Manhunt, Wizards of the Lost Kingom, Borthers in Blood, Choke Canyon, The Delta Force, Heartbreak Ridge, Maniac Killer, Delta Force Commando, Deep Space, Double Target, Wizards of the Lost Kingdom, White Phantom, The Bite, Andy Colby's Incredible Adventure, Primal Rage, Beyond the Door III, Tides of War, Steele's Law, Critical Action, Savage Land, Steel Frontier, Private Obsession, Cheyenne, Speed 2: Cruise Control, Crackerjack 3, Outlaw, (also s.p. & dir.), Legacy (also s.p., dir. & prod.), Kill Bill: Vol. 2., Hell to Pay, Raising Jeffrey Dahmer (also co- prod.), Jersey Justice, Inglourious Basterds, Icarus, The 7 Adventures of Sinbad. *Director:* He's Not Heavy, Raising Jeffrey Dahmer (also co-prod.), Kabuki (also prod., writer), Moomins and the Comet Chase (also voice).
TELEVISION: *Movies*: Hitched, The Bravos, Frankenstein, You'll Never See Me Again, Target Risk, Snowbeast, Gold of the Amazon Women, The Spirit of Adventure: Night Flight, Jealousy, Dirty Dozen: The Deadly Mission, 3 Days to Kill, Heartless, I'll Be Seeing You. *Mini-series:* Proof of the Man. *Series*: Here Come the Brides, Walking Tall, Kung Fu: The Legend Continues (dir. only), The Di Palma Forum at UNLV (co-host).

SWAIM, BOB
Director, Writer. b. Evanston, IL, Nov. 2, 1943. e. Calif. State U, B.A.; L'Ecole Nationale de la Cinematographie, Paris, BTS 1969. American director who has often worked in France. Began career making shorts: Le Journal de M Bonnafous, Self Portrait of a Pornographer, Vive les Jacques. Received Cesar award French Acad. M.P., 1982; Chevalier des Arts et des Lettres 1985.
PICTURES: *Director:* Masquerade, The Climb. *Director/Writer:* Autoportrait d'un pornographe, L' (short), Vive les Jacques (short), The Night of Saint Germain des Pres, La Balance, Half Moon Street, L' Atlantide, Nos amis les flics. *Actor:* Spies Like Us, A Soldier's Daughter Never Cries.
TELEVISION: *Movies: Actor:* Rainbow Drive, J'ai deux amours, Viens jouer dans la cour des grands. *Writer:* Le Violeur impuni, Un flic pourri, Un alibi en or. *Director:* Target of Suspicion, Femme de passions, La France Made in USA (doc.).

SWANK, HILARY
Actress, Producer. Bellingham, Washington, July 30, 1974.
PICTURES: Buffy the Vampire Slayer, The Next Karate Kid, Sometimes They Come Back...Again, Kounterfeit, Quiet Days in Hollywood, Heartwood, Boys Don't Cry (Academy Award, best actress, Golden Globe Award 2000), The Gift, The Affair of the Necklace, Insomnia, The Core, 11:14 (also exec. prod.), Red Dust, Million Dollar Baby (Academy Award, best actress, Golden Globe Award 2005), The Black Dahlia, The Reaping, Freedom Writers (also exec. prod.), P.S., I Love You, Birds of America, Amelia (also exec. prod.), The Resident (also exec. prod.), Conviction (also exec. prod.), Something Borrowed (prod.), Dreams of a Dying Heart.
TELEVISION: *Movies*: Cries Unheard: The Donna Yaklich Story, Terror in the Family, Dying to Belong, The Sleepwalker Killing, Iron Jawed Angels (Golden Globe nom. 2005). *Series*: Evening Shade, Camp Wilder, Beverly Hills 90210, Leaving L.A., Celebrity Charades (exec. prod.). *Guest:* More than 97 appearances.

SWANSON, DENNIS
Executive. b. Wilmar, CA, e. Univ. of IL. B.A. in journalism, 1961, M.S. in communications/political science, 1966. Served as an officer in the U.S. Marine Corp. from 1961-1963. 1966-67, news prod. & assignment mgr. for WGN radio & TV in Chicago; 1968-70, assign. edit. & field prod. for NBC news at WMAQ TV in Chicago; 1970-73, sportscaster and prod. WMAQ; worked for Television News, Inc. in Chicago from 1973-1976 in both sports and marketing positions; later dir. of news div. in NY. 1976, became exec. prod. of KABC-TV in Los Angeles, Ca., and in 1978 he won the George Foster Peabody Award for the station's coverage of the L.A. police dept; 1981, appointed station mngr. KABC-TV; 1983, v.p. & gen. mngr. WLS-TV, Chicago and gave Oprah Winfrey her first daytime talk show, which evolved into the Oprah Winfrey Show, the most successful daytime TV talk show in history; 1985, named pres. of ABC Owned TV Stations; 1986, became pres. of ABC Sports, a position he held until 1996. He then joined WNBC in New York in 1996 as pres. & general Imanager. In 1998, Swanson was named co-chair of NBC's Olympic Sports Committee. He was named Broadcasting & Cable's broadcaster of the year in 2002. He left WNBC in July 2002 to become the executive vice president and COO of the Viacom Television Stations Group. In October 2005 Swanson joined FOX Television Stations Group as president, station operations, and is the position he holds today. Swanson is a former pres. of the New York State Broadcasters Assoc. Personal awards include: George Foster Peabody Award (1978), Marine Corps Scholarship Foundation (1988), Jockey Club's Gold Medal (1988), Marine Corps Scholarship Foundation's Semper Fidelis Award (1992), National Academy of Television Arts and Science's Silver Circle Award, Chicago Chapter (1995), Illinois Broadcasters Hall of Fame (1997), Ellis Island Medal of Honor (1997), Mentoring USA (1998), Illinois News Broadcasters Association (INBA)'s, "Illinoisan of the Year" (1998), Presidential "Daily Point of Light" (1999), New York State Special Olympics Man of the Year.

SWANSON, KRISTY
Actress. b. Mission Viejo, CA, Dec. 12, 1969. Signed with modeling agency at age 9, appearing in over 30 commercials. Acting debut at 13 on Disney series Dreamfinders.
PICTURES: Pretty in Pink, Ferris Bueller's Day Off, Deadly Friend, Flowers in the Attic, Diving In, Mannequin Two on the Move, Hot Shots, Highway to Hell, Buffy the Vampire Slayer, The Program, The Chase, Getting In (Student Body), Higher Learning, The Phantom, Marshal Law, Lover Girl, 8 Heads in a Duffel Bag, Tinseltown, Supreme Sanction, Past Imperfect, Big Daddy, Meeting Daddy, Dude Where's My Car?, Soul Assassin, Silence, Living Death, What If..., A Christmas Wish.
TELEVISION: *Movies*: Miracle of the Heart: A Boys Town Story, Not Quite Human, Bad to the Bone, Supreme Sanction, Zebra Lounge, Red Water, Drowning, The Black Hole, Forbidden Secrets, Swamp Shark. *Series*: Dreamfinders, Knots Landing, Nightingales, Early Edition, Grapevine, 3Way. *Guest:* More than 45 appearances.

SWEENEY, ANNE
Executive. e. B.A., College of New Rochelle, and Ed. M. degree from Harvard University. Sweeney spent 12 years at Nickelodeon/Nick at Nite in various executive positions, rising to senior v.p. of Program Enterprises. Among her accomplishments there, she oversaw Nickelodeon's international expansion, including launching the channel in the United Kingdom, resulting in a joint venture with British Sky Broadcasting. 1993-1996, chmn. & CEO of FX Networks, Inc. While at Fox, she launched two basic cable networks, FX and FXM: Movies from Fox. FXM was Hollywood's first studio-based movie network. Sweeney joined The Walt Disney Company in February 1996 as president of the Disney Channel and executive v.p. of Disney/ABC Cable Networks. She enjoyed another successful cable launch in Jan. 2000 with SOAPnet, the 24-hour soap opera network, now seen in more than 39 million homes. From October 2000 to April 2004, Sweeney served as president of ABC Cable Networks Group and Disney Channel Worldwide. During 2004, Sweeney was promoted to co-chairman, media networks, The Walt Disney Company and president, Disney-ABC Television Group. In this role Sweeney is responsible for all of Disney's non-sports, cable, satellite and broadcast properties globally. These include the ABC Television Network, which encompasses ABC Entertainment, ABC Kids, ABC Daytime and ABC News; ABC Studios; and the Disney ABC Cable Networks Group, comprising Disney Channel Worldwide. She also oversees Walt Disney Television Animation and has responsibility for managing Disney's equity interest in the cable groups of Lifetime Entertainment Services, A&E Television Networks and E! Entertainment Networks. She was a founding member, Women in Cable, who awarded her Executive of the Year in 1994, Woman of the Year in 1997, and the 1998 Advocate Leader Award from the So. Calif. chapter. Sweeney received prestigious STAR Award from American Women in Radio and Television in 1995 and was inducted into the American Advertising Federation's Advertising Hall of Achievement in 1996. She was named one of the "The World's 100 Most Powerful Women" by Forbes. In 2002 she received Women in Film's esteemed Lucy Award and, in 2004, was awarded the Cable Television Public Affairs Association's President's Award. She is a recipient of the 2004 Muse Award from New York Women in Film and Television. In 2007 Sweeney was ranked #15 on Fortune Magazine's list of most powerful women in business.

SWEENEY, D. B.
Actor. r.n. Daniel Bernard Sweeney. b. Shoreham, NY, Nov. 14, 1961. e. NYU, 1984 B.F.A.
THEATRE: *NY*: The Caine Mutiny Court-Martial (B'way), The Seagull: The Hamptons: 1990, Distant Fires (L.A.), among others.
PICTURES: Power (debut, 1986), Fire With Fire, Gardens of Stone, No Man's Land, Eight Men Out, Memphis Belle, Blue Desert, Sons, Leather Jackets, Heaven Is a Playground, The Cutting Edge, A Day in October, Hear No Evil, Fire in the Sky, Roommates, Three Wishes (cameo), Spawn, Goosed, The Book of Stars, The Weekend, Dinosaur, X-Men, After Sex, Warriors of Might and Magic, Hardball, Greenmail, Brother Bear (voice), Speak, Entry Level, Stiletto, Miracle at St. Anna, Javelina, Fencewalker.
TELEVISION: *Movies*: Out of the Darkness, Miss Rose White, Introducing Dorothy Dandridge, Harsh Realm, Superfire, Going to the Mat, Swamp Shark. *Mini-series*: Lonesome Dove. *Series*: Strange Luck, C-16: FBI, Harsh Realm, Beyond the Glory (narr.; voice), Life As We Know It, Jericho, Crash.

SWERLING, JO, JR.
Executive, Producer. b. Los Angeles, CA, June 18, 1931. e. UCLA, 1948-51; California Maritime Acad., 1951-54. Son of writer Jo Swerling. Active duty U.S. Navy 1954-56. Joined Revue Prods./Universal Television, 1957-81, as prod. coordinator, assoc. prod., prod., assoc. exec. prod., exec. prod., writer, director, actor; currently sr. v.p. and supervising prod., The Cannell Studios.
TELEVISION: *Movies (prod.):* The Whole World Is Watching, The Lonely Profession, Do You Take This Stranger?, Sam Hill: Who

Killed Mr. Foster?, How to Steal an Airplane, Toma, Drive Hard Drive Fast, The Rockford Files (assoc. prod. & exec. prod.), The Story of Pretty Boy Floyd, This Is the West That Was, The 3,000 Mile Chase, The Jordan Chance, Hunter (supervising prod.), Stingray (supervising prod.), Wiseguy (supervising prod.). *Executive producer:* Target Risk, The Invasion of Johnson County, Hawaii-Five O (co-exec. prod.). *Mini-series*: Captains and the Kings (prod., Emmy nom. 1977), Aspen (prod.), The Last Convertible (exec. prod., dir.). *Series*: Kraft Suspense Theater (prod.), Run for Your Life (prod., writer, Emmy, nom. 1967), The Rockford Files (prod., writer), Alias Smith & Jones (assoc. exec. prod.), Cool Million (prod.), Baretta (prod., Emmy nom. 1976), City of Angels (exec. prod.), The Quest (prod.), The Greatest American Hero (prod.), The A-Team (writer & supervising prod.), Hardcastel and McCormick (prod.), Riptide (prod.), Hunter (supervising prod.), Singray (prod.), 21 Jump Street (prod.), Wiseguy (prod., Emmy nom. 1989), Sonny Spoon (prod.), Unsub (prod.), Booker (supervising prod.), The Commish (supervising prod.), Palace Guard (supervising prod.), Profit (pilot suprv. prod.)

SYKES, ERIC
O.B.E.: Writer, Comedian, Actor. b. Oldham, England, May 4, 1923. Early career as actor; 1948 wrote first three series, BBC's Educating Archie TV comedy series for Frankie Howerd, Max Bygraves, Harry Secombe. BBC panel show member. Sykes Versus TV, The Frankie Howerd Series. Long-term contract with ATV 1956. Own BBC series 1958-78, Sykes and A... *Specials*: Silent Movies for TV, The Plank (also dir. & s.p.), If You Go Down Into the Woods Today, Rhubarb, It's Your Move, Mr. H Is Late, 19th Hole, The Big Freeze.
THEATRE: Big Bad Mouse (tour: 1966-9 in America, Rhodesia, Australia, Canada), One Man Show (1982), Time and Time Again, Run for Your Wife, Two Into One, The 19th Hole.
PICTURES: Watch Your Stern, Very Important Person, Invasion Quartet, Village of Daughters, Kill or Cure, Heavens Above, The Bargee, One Way Pendulum, Those Magnificent Men in Their Flying Machines, Rotten to the Core, The Liquidator, The Spy With The Cold Nose, Shalako, Monte Carlo or Bust, Theatre of Blood, Boys in Blue, Gabrielle and the Doodleman, Absolute Beginners, Splitting Heirs, The Big Freeze, The Others, Harry Potter and the Goblet of Fire, Son of Rambow.
TELEVISION: *Movies:As Writer:* Korean Party, Nuts In May, The Frankie Howerd Show, Dress Rehearsal (also dir.), Opening Night (also actor, comedy dir.), Pantomania, or Dick Whittington (also actor, comedy dir.), The Howerd Crowd, Closing Night (alsoactor, dir.), Gala Opening (also actor, dir.), East of Howerd, Sykes Versus ITV (also actor), Howerd's Hour, Sykes: With the Lid Off (also actor), Eric Sykes Shows a Few of Our Favourite Things (also actor), The Likes of Sykes (also actor), The Eric Sykes 1990 Show (also prod.). *Mini-series:* Gormenghast. *Series:* The Howerd Crowd (writer), The Idiot Weekly, Price 2d (also actor), The Tony Hancock Show (writer), Sykes and A... (writer), That Was the Week That Was (writer), Curry & Chips (actor), Sykes and a Big Big Show (also actor), Sykes (also writer), The Nineteenth Hole (actor), Teletubbies (voice). *Guest:* More than 91 appearances.

SYLBERT, ANTHEA
Executive, Producer. b. New York, NY, Oct. 6, 1939. e. Barnard College, B.A.; Parsons School of Design, M.A. Early career in costume design with range of B'way (The Real Thing), off-B'way and m.p. credits (Rosemary's Baby, John & Mary, Carnal Knowledge, A New Leaf, The Heartbreak Kid, The Cowboys, Bad Company, Shampoo, The Fortune, The Last Tycoon, F.I.S.T.). Two Acad. award. nominations for costume designs for Julia and Chinatown. Joined Warner Bros. in 1977, as v.p., special projects, acting as liaison between creative execs., prod. dept., and creative talent producing films for company. 1978, named v.p., prod. (projects included One Trick Pony, Personal Best.). 1980 appointed v.p. prod., for United Artists, working on Jinxed, Still of the Night, Yentl, etc. 1982 became indept. prod. in partnership with Goldie Hawn (Hawn/Sylbert Movie Co.) producing Swing Shift, Protocol, Wildcats, Overboard, My Blue Heaven, Deceived, Crisscross, Something to Talk About.
TELEVISION: *Movies: Exec. Prod.:* Truman, Hope, Giving Up the Ghost (also writer), If You Believe (also writer).

SYMS, SYLVIA
Actress. b. London, England, January 6, 1934. e. Convent and Grammar School. British leading lady Sylvia Syms trained for her craft at RADA where she received The Gerald Lawrence Scholarship and an HM Tenants Award. Her first major film role came in 'My Teenage Daughter' in 1956 and she has graced our stage and screen ever since, receiving nominations for 'Best Actress' both home and abroad and a British Film Academy nomination for The Tamarind Seed.
PICTURES: My Teenage Daughter (debut, 1956), No Time For Tears, The Birthday Present, Woman in a Dressing Gown, Ice Cold in Alex (Desert Attack), The Moonraker, Bachelor of Hearts, No Trees in the Street, Ferry to Hong Kong, Expresso Bongo, Conspiracy of Hearts, The Virgins of Rome, The World of Suzie Wong, Flame in the Streets, Victim, The Quare Fellow, The Punch and Judy Man, The World Ten Times Over, East of Sudan, Operation Crossbow, The Big Job, Hostile Witness, Danger Route, Run Wild Run Free, The Desperados, Asylum, The Tamarind Seed, Give Us Tomorrow, There Goes the Bride, Absolute Beginners, A Chorus of Disapproval, Shirley Valentine, Shining Through, Dirty Weekend, Staggered, The House of Angelo, Food of Love, Deep Down (short) What a Girl Wants, I'll Sleep When I'm Dead, The Queen, Is There Anybody There?, Booked Out.
TELEVISION: *Movies:* Something to Declare, Bat Out of Hell, Department in Terror, Friends and Romans, Strange Report, Half-hour Story, The Root of All Evil, The Bridesmaid, Clutterbuck, Movie Quiz, My Good Woman, Looks Familiar, Love and Marriage, The Truth About Verity, I'm Bob, He's Dickie, Blankety Blank, The Story of Nancy Astor, Give Us a Clue, Sykes, Crown Court, A Murder Is Announced, Murder at Lynch Cross, Rockcliffes Follies, Dr. Who, Countdown, Ruth Rendell Mystery, May to December, Intimate Contact, Thatcher: The Final Days, Natural Lies, Mulberry, Peak Practice, Half the Picture, Master of the Moor, Original Sin, Ruth Rendell: The Orchard Walls, Neville's Island, The Poseidon Adventure, Child of Mine, Marple: Murder Is Easy. *Mini-series*: The Glass Virgin, The Jury, The Poseidon Adventure. *Series*: The Human Jungle, The Saint, The Baron, At Home with the Braithwaites, Above Suspicion 2: The Red Dahlia, EastEnders. *Guest:* More than 96 appearances.

SYUFY, JOSEPH
Exhibitor. b. San Francisco, CA, Aug. 22, 1965. e. B.A. degree from St. Mary's College of Moraga, CA, and M.B.A. from the Univ. of San Francisco. Syufy joined family business when he began at Century Theatres' home office in San Franciso. Syufy, who was mentored by his father, the late Raymond J. Syufy, spent time in every department, learning theatre management and operations first-hand. In 1995, the year his father died, Syufy became pres. of the theatre circuit, while with his brother, Raymond, Became CEO. Since then, the brothers ran the circuit as a team. In 2001, Joe and his brother, Raymond, were recognized as industry leaders and were honored with the 'ShoWesters of the Year' award. Joe sits on the Board of Directors the National Association of Theatre Owners (NATO), Will Rogers Institute and the San Jose Tech Museum. In 2004, Joe Syufy was named Vice-Chairman and CEO. Cinemark USA, Inc. acquired Century Theatres in Oct. 2006. Both Syufy brothers sit on Cinemark's bd. of directors.

SYUFY, RAYMOND W.
Exhibitor. b. San Francisco, CA, Oct. 21, 1962. e. B.A. degree from St. Mary's College of Moraga, CA, and M.B.A. from the Univ. of San Francisco. Syufy joined family business when he began at Century Theatres' home office in San Franciso. Century was started in 1941 by his father Raymond J. Syufy who opened the first theatre in Vallejo, California. Raymond spent time in every department, learning the entire operation. After his father passed away in 1995, Raymond Syufy became CEO of Century Theatres, and his brother, Joseph Syufy, became President. In 2001, the Syufy brothers were recognized as industry leaders, receiving the 'ShoWesters of the Year' award. In 2004, Raymond was named Century Theatres' Chairman and CEO. He is a trustee of St. Mary's College in Moraga, CA, is on NATO's bd. of directors and is also a founding bd. member of Fandango.com. Raymond Syufy has been a major proponent of bringing on-line ticketing access to the movie-going public. Cinemark USA, Inc. acquired Century Theatres in Oct. 2006. Both Syufy brothers sit on Cinemark's bd. of directors.

SZABÓ, ISTVÁN
Director. b. Budapest, Hungary, Feb. 18, 1938. e. Academy of Theatre and Film Art, Budapest, 1961. Debut Koncert (short, diploma film) 1961. Short films: Variations on a Theme, You, Piety, Why I Love It, City Map. Appeared in film Stand Off.
PICTURES: Age of Illusions (feature debut, 1964), Father, A Film About Love, 25 Fireman's Street, Premiere, Tales of Budapest, The Hungarians, Confidence (Silver Bear Award, Berlin Fest.), The Green Bird, Mephisto (Hungarian Film Critics Award; Acad. Award, Best Foreign Film, 1982), Bali, Colonel Redl, Hanussen (also co-s.p.), Opera Europa, Meeting Venus, Dear Emma—Sweet Bobe, Offenbach Titkai, Place Vendôme, Sunshine (also s.p., Golden Globe nom. 2001), Taking Sides, Ten minutes Older: The Cello (also writer, segment Ten Minutes After), Being Julia, Clara (co-prod.), Rokonok (also s.p.), I Served the King of England (actor), Albert Nobbs (s.p.).
TELEVISION: *Movies:* Ösbemutató, Levél apámhoz, Katzenspiel, Isten teremtményei (writer only), Offenbachs Geheimnis. *Mini-series:* Bors.

SZWARC, JEANNOT
Director. b. Paris, France, Nov. 21, 1939.
PICTURES: Extreme Close-Up, Bug, Jaws II, Somewhere in Time, Enigma, Supergirl, Santa Claus, Honor Bound, Hercule et Sherlock, Les Soeurs Soleil.
TELEVISION: *Movies:* Night of Terror, The Weekend Nun, The Devil's Daughter, You'll Never See Me Again, The Small Miracle, Lisa: Bright and Dark, A Summer Without Boys, Crime Club, Code Name: Diamond Head, Murders in the Rue Morgue, The Rockford Files: A Blessing in Disguise, Laura, Shrecklicher Verdacht, The Rockford Files: If the Frame Fits. *Series:* Ironside, To Catch a Thief, Kojak, Columbo, Night Gallery, Crime Club, True Life Stories, Twilight Zone, JAG, The Practice, Ally McBeal, Seven Days, Providence, Boston Public, JAG, Smallville, Without a Trace, Heroes, Cold Case.

T

MR. T
Actor. r.n. Lawrence Tero. b. Chicago, IL, May 21, 1953. Professional bodyguard when hired by Stallone in 1980 for Rocky.
PICTURES: Penitentiary II, Rocky III, D.C. Cab, Freaked, Spy Hard, The Magic of the Golden Bear: Goldy III, Inspector Gadget, Not Another Teen Movie, Judgment, Cloudy with a Chance of Meatballs (voice).
TELEVISION: *Movies*: The Toughest Man in the World, Alice Through the Looking Glass (voice), I Pity the Fool, Guys Choice. *Series*: Twilight Theater (co-host), The A Team, T & T, Eek the Cat (voices), Pecola. *Guest*: More than 92 appearances.

TAFFNER DONALD L., JR.
Executive, Producer. b. New York, NY. e. St. Johns U. William Morris Agency, 1950-59; Paramount Pictures. 1959-63. Currently pres. D. L. T., Ltd., 1963-present.
TELEVISION: *Exec. Producer:* Three's Company, Too Close For Comfort, My Family.

TAGAWA, CARY-HIROYUKI
Actor. b. Tokyo, Japan, Sept. 30, 1950. Studied at USC.
PICTURES: Armed Response, The Last Emperor, Spellbinder, Twins, The Last Warrior, License to Kill, Showdown in Little Tokyo, The Perfect Weapon, Kickboxer 2: The Road Back, Raven: Return of the Black Dragons, American Me, Nemesis, Rising Sun, Natural Causes, The Dangerous, Soldier Boyz, Picture Pride, Mortal Kombat, White Tiger, Provocateur, Danger Zone, The Phantom, Top of the World, American Dragons, Vampires, Bridge of Dragons, Snow Falling on Cedars, Fixations, The Art of War, The Ghost, Camp Ninja, Pearl Harbor, Planet of the Apes, Speedball: The Movie, Elektra, Memoirs of a Geisha, Duel of Legends (also prod.), Balls of Fury, Ligeia, Bodyguard: A New Beginning, By the Will of Chingis Khan, Tekken, Hachiko: A Dog's Story, Slaughter, Hype Nation, Tekken, Duel of Legends (also prod.).
TELEVISION: *Movies:* Star Trek: The Next Generation-Encounter at Farpoint, L.A. Takedown, Murder in Paradise, Vestige of Honor, Not of This World, Mission of the Shark: The Saga of the U.S.S Indianapolis, Raven: Return of the Black Dragons, Day of Reckoning, NetForce, Johnny Tsunami, Baywatch: Hawaiian Wedding, Faith of My Fathers, Teen Titans: Trouble in Tokyo, Johnny Kapahala: Back on Board, Ghost Voyage. *Series*: Nash Bridges, Hawaii. *Guest:* More than 48 appearances.

TAKEI, GEORGE
Actor. b. Los Angeles, CA, April 20, 1937. e. UCLA. Professional debut in Playhouse 90 production while training at Desilu Workshop in Hollywood. Gained fame as Sulu in Star Trek TV series. *Author*: Mirror Friend Mirror Foe (novel), To the Stars (autobiography; 1994).
PICTURES: Ice Palace, A Majority of One, Hell to Eternity, PT 109, Red Line 7000, An American Dream, Walk Don't Run, The Green Berets, Star Trek: The Motion Picture, Star Trek II: The Wrath of Khan, Star Trek III: The Search for Spock, Star Trek IV: The Voyage Home, Star Trek V: The Final Frontier, Return From the River Kwai, Prisoners of the Sun, Star Trek VI: The Undiscovered Country, Live by the Fist, Oblivion, Chongbal, Oblivion 2: Backlash, Star Trek: Starfleet Academy, Mulan (voice), Bug Buster, Trekkies, The Magic Pearl, Who Gets the House?, With Honors Denied (short; narrator), Patient 14, Ninja Cheerleaders, The Great Buck Howard, American Summer, The Red Canvas, The Pool Boys, Larry Crowne.
TELEVISION: *Movies*: Year of the Dragon, Kissinger and Nixon, The Best Bad Thing, Batman Beyond: The Movie (voice), DC 9/11: Time of Crisis. *Series:* Star Trek, Star Trek: Where No Man Has Gone Before (voice), General Hospital, Jonny Quest (voices), The Young and the Restless, Kim Possible (voice), Heroes, Star Trek: Beyond the Final Frontier (doc.). *Guest:* More than 188 appearances.

TAMBLYN, RUSS
Actor b. Los Angeles, CA, Dec. 30, 1934. e. No. Hollywood H.S. West Coast radio shows; on stage with little theater group; song-and-dance act in Los Angeles clubs, veterans hospitals. 1956 won Golden Globe Award for most promising newcomer.
PICTURES: The Boy with Green Hair, Reign of Terror, Samson and Delilah, Gun Crazy, Kid from Cleveland, The Vicious Years, Captain Carey U.S.A., Father of the Bride, As Young As You Feel, Father's Little Dividend, Cave of Outlaws, Winning Team, Retreat Hell, Take the High Ground, Seven Brides for Seven Brothers, Deep in My Heart, Many Rivers to Cross, Hit the Deck, Last Hunt, Fastest Gun Alive, The Young Guns, Don't Go Near the Water, Peyton Place (Academy Award nom. 1958), High School Confidential, Tom Thumb, Cimarron, West Side Story, Wonderful World of the Brothers Grimm, How the West Was Won, Follow the Boys, The Haunting, Long Ships, Son of a Gunfighter, War of the Gargantuas, Scream Free, Dracula Vs. Frankenstein, Satan's Sadists, The Female Bunch, The Last Movie, Win Place or Steal, Murder Gang, Human Highway, Aftershock, Commando Squad, Cyclone, Necromancer, B.O.R.N., Phantom Empire, Bloodscream, Wizards of the Demon Sword, Desert Steel, Cabin Boy, Attack of the 60 Ft. Centerfold, Johnny Mysto: The Boy Wizard, Little Miss Magic, Ghost Dog.
TELEVISION: *Movies:* Twin Peaks, Running Mates, Inherit the Wind. *Series*: Days of Our Lives, Twin Peaks, Joan of Arcadia (also voice), The Increasingly Poor Decisions of Todd Margaret.

TAMBOR, JEFFREY
Actor. b. San Francisco, CA, July 8, 1944. e. San Francisco St. (BA), Wayne St. (MA). Acted with Seattle Rep., Actors Theatre of Louisville, Loeb Drama Ctr. (Harvard), Milwaukee Rep. Theatre, Acad. Festival Theatre (Chicago), Old Globe Theatre in San Diego, South Coast Rep. Theatre. B'way in Measure for Measure, Sly Fox.
PICTURES: And Justice for All, Saturday the 14th, Mr. Mom, The Man Who Wasn't There, No Small Affair, Three O'Clock High, Lisa, City Slickers, Life Stinks, Pastime, Article 99, Brenda Starr, Crossing the Bridge, At Home with the Webbers, Face Dancer, Under Pressure, A House in the Hills, Radioland Murders, Heavyweights, Big Bully, Learning Curves, Bad with Numbers, Big Bully, Meet Joe Black, Teaching Mrs. Tingle, Doctor Dolittle, There's Something About Mary, Girl Interrupted, The Freshman, Muppets From Space, Pollock, How the Grinch Stole Christmas, Never Again, Get Well Soon, Scorched, Malibu's Most Wanted, My Boss's Daughter, Hellboy, The Spongebob SquarePants Movie (voice), Staar, Slipstream Dream, Superhero Movie, Hellboy 2: The Golden Army, Monsters vs Aliens (voice), The Hangover, The Mad Cow, Rogue's Gallery, The Invention of Lying, Operation Endgame, Meeting Spencer, Lucky, Paul, Tangled (voice), Win Win, Flypaper, The Hangover 2.
TELEVISION: *Movies*: Alcatraz: The Whole Shocking Story, A Gun in the House, The Star Maker, Take Your Best Shot, Cocaine: One Man's Seduction, Sadat, The Awakening of Candra, The Three Wishes of Billy Grier, The Burden of Proof, Honey Let's Kill the Neighbors, Another Midnight Run, The Man Who Captured Eichmann, Weapons of Mass Destruction, Eloise at the Plaza, Eloise at Christmastime, The Muppets' Wizard of Oz, Pooh's Super Sleuth Christmas Movie, Monsters vs Aliens: Mutant Pumpkins from Outer Space. *Mini-series:* Robert Kennedy & His Times. *Series*: The Ropers, Hill Street Blues, 9 to 5, Mr. Sunshine, Max Headroom, Studio 5-B, American Dreamer, The Larry Sanders Show (4 Emmy noms.), Me and George, The Lionhearts (Emmy nom. 1999), Everything's Relative, The Lot, Sammy (voice), That Was Then, 3-South (voice), Arrested Development (2 Emmy noms.), Twenty Good Years, Welcome to the Captain (also pilot), Good Behavior (also pilot), WordGirl, Archer. *Guest*: More than 135 appearances.

TARANTINO, QUENTIN
Writer, Director, Actor, Producer. b. Knoxville, TN, March 27, 1963. Graduate of Sundance Institute Director's Workshop and Lab. With producer Lawrence Bender, formed production co. A Band Apart. 2004 received Casting Society of America Career Achievement Award. Received American Cinema Editors Golden Eddie Filmmaker of the Year Award 2007.
PICTURES: Past Midnight (assoc. prod., co-s.p.), Reservoir Dogs (dir., s.p., actor), True Romance (s.p.), Killing Zoe (co-exec. prod.), Natural Born Killers (story), Sleep With Me (actor), Pulp Fiction (dir., s.p., co-story, actor; Cannes Film Fest. Award for Best Film; LA Film Critics, NY Film Critics, Natl. Soc. of Film Critics, Chicago Film Critics & Independent Spirit Awards for dir. & s.p.; Academy Award, 1 other nom.; Golden Globe for s.p., 1 other nom.; DGA nom.; Natl. Bd. of Review Award for dir., 1994), Destiny Turns on the Radio (actor), Somebody to Love (actor), Desperado (actor), Four Rooms (co-s.p., co-exec. prod., actor), From Dusk Till Dawn (s.p., actor, co-exec. prod.), Girl 6 (actor), Curdled (exec. prod.), God Said, Ha (actor); Full Tilt Boogie (actor), Jackie Brown, Forever Hollywood (actor), Little Nicky (actor), From Dusk Till Dawn 2: Texas Blood Money (exec. prod), From Dusk Till Dawn 3: The Hangman's Daughter (exec. prod.), Kill Bill (prod., s.p., dir.), Kill Bill: Vol. 2 (s.p., exec. sound track prod. & dir.), Sin City (special guest dir.), Freedom's Fury (prod.), Daltry Calhoun (exec. prod.), Killshot (exec. prod.), Grind House (writer, prod., dir. segment "death Proof), Hell Ride (prod.), Hostel: Part II (also exec. prod.), Hell Ride (exec. prod.), Inglourious Basterds (writer, dir., 2 Academy Award noms. for dir. and s.p., DGA nom.; 2 Golden Globe noms. for dir. and s.p 2010), Machete (prod.), The Man with the Iron Fist (prod.).
TELEVISION: *Series:* CSI: Crime Scene Investigation (WGA nom.; Emmy nom. for dir., 2006) *Guest*: More than 145 appearances.

TARNOFF, JOHN B.
Producer. b. New York, NY, Mar. 3, 1952. e. UCLA, motion pictures & TV, 1973-74; Amherst College, B.A., 1969-73. Named field exec. with Taylor-Laughlin Distribution (company arm of Billy Jack Enterprises) 1974; left in 1975 to be literary agent with Bart/Levy, Inc.; later with Michael Levy & Associates, Paul Kohner/Michael Levy Agency; Headed TV dept., Kohner/Levy, 1979. Joined MGM as production exec., 1979; v.p., development, 1979-80; sr. v.p. production & devel., 1981-82; exec. v.p., Kings Road Prods., 1983-84; v.p., prod., Orion Pictures Corp., 1985; exec. prod., Out of Bounds, Columbia Pictures, 1986; v.p., prod., De Laurentiis Entertainment Group, 1987. Head of production, DeLaurentiis Entertainment, Australia, 1987-88. Exec.

v.p. production, Village Roadshow Pictures, 1988. *Executive prod.:* The Delinquents, Blood Oath. 1990-93, personal mgr., Addis-Wechsler & Assoc. 1994, New Line Cinema/Overseas Film Group; prod., Nature of the Beast. 1995, founder, Newspeak Media Inc. 1996, founder, Personality Factory, Inc. 1998, exec. prod. Big Brother, cd-rom adventure based on Orwell's 1984; writer/designer, WarGames, CD-rom.

TARSES, JAMIE
Executive, Executive Producer. b. Pittsburgh, PA. e. Williams College. Prior to joining NBC, worked as a casting director for Lorimar Productions. Joined NBC in Sept. 1987 as Mgr., Creative Affairs for NBC Productions. In Dec. 1987, named Mgr., Current Comedy Programs, NBC Entertainment and was NBC's Program Exec. for such series as Cheers, Amen, 227 and A Different World. In 1988, named Mgr., Comedy Development. In Feb. 1989, promoted to Director, Comedy Development, NBC Entertainment. Was directly involved in the development of Friends, NewsRadio, Caroline in the City, Mad About You, Frasier and several other NBC programs. In Aug. 1994, was named to supervise one of NBC's two programming teams before being promoted in 1995 to senior v.p., Primetime Series. In June 1996, joined ABC Entertainment as President. Resigned, July 1999. President of Three Sisters Ent., 2000-June 2003. Currently is on the bd. of directors of The Young Storytellers Foundation. She continues to produce and/or executive produce TV series with partner Karey Burke via their production company, The Untitled Burke-Tarses Project.
PICTURES: Man on a Ledge, Primeval.
TELEVISION: *Movies:* Tikiville, Crazy Love, Americana, More Patience, The Angriest Man in Suburbia, Held Up, Eva Adams, Mad Love. *Series:* Studio 60 on the Sunset Strip (consult), Mr. Sunshine, Happy Endings, Franklin & Bash, My Boys (exec. prod.), Hawthorne (exec. prod.).

TARSES, JAY
Producer, Writer, Actor. b. Baltimore, MD, July 3, 1939. e. Williams Coll., Ithaca Coll., BFA theatre. Daughter is executive Jamie Tarses. Wrote and acted with little-theater co. in Pittsburgh, drove a truck in NY for Allen Funt's Candid Camera and worked in advertising and promotion for Armstrong Cork Co. in Lancaster, PA where he met Tom Patchett. Formed Patchett and Tarses, stand-up comedy team played coffeehouse circuit in the late 1960s. Later twosome became TV writing team and joined writing staff of Carol Burnett Show, winning Emmy in 1972, 1 other nom.
PICTURES: *Co-s.p. with Patchett*: Up the Academy, The Great Muppet Caper, The Muppets Take Manhattan. *Actor:* Teen Wolf.
TELEVISION: *Movie:* Touch 'Em All McCall (exec. prod.). *Series*: *Actor*: Make Your Own Kind of Music, Open All Night (also writer/creator & dir.), The Duck Factory, The Days and Nights of Molly Dodd (also writer/creator, dir. & prod., 4 Emmy noms.), My Boys. *Writer:* The New Dick Van Dyke Show (also exec. prod.), The Bob Newhart Show (also exec. prod., Emmy nom. 1977), The Tony Randall Show (also creator & exec. prod.), We've Got Each Other (also creator, & exec. prod.), Mary, Open All Night (also creator & prod.), Buffalo Bill (also exec. prod., 3 Emmy noms.), Smoldering Lust (also creator & prod.), Black Tie Affair (also prod. & dir.).*Director:* The Slap Maxwell Story (also prod.), Public Morals (also exec. prod.), Public Morals also exec. prod.). *Pilots*: The Chopped Liver Brothers (exec. prod., writer), The Faculty (exec. prod., dir., writer), Baltimore (creator, prod., writer), Harvey Berger: Salesman (co-creator, prod., writer), Jackass Junior High (creator, prod., writer).

TASHIE, JIMMY
Executive. e. Bachelor's degree in cultural anthropology and Master's degree in special education, Univ. of Memphis. Tashie has devoted more than 35 years to the film exhibition industry. He is the chmn. of the Memphis-Shelby Film Commission in Tennessee and served as the v.p. and gen. mgr. of Malco Theatres, Inc., a Memphis-based theatre circuit operating for nearly 100 years, now with over 300 screens in five states. Tashie hosts all the city's not-for-profit film festivals: The Indie Memphis Film Festival; On-Location: The Memphis International Film Festival; and The Outflix Film Festival. Among many career accomplishments, Tashie executed his dream to open a unique art/independent/foreign film theatre: Malco's Studio on the Square, which gives emerging filmmakers an accessible, professional venue for their film screenings and premieres. Currently he is Sr. V.P. of Operations.

TASSLER, NINA
Executive. Bachelor of Fine Arts in Theatre, Boston Univ. In early career, assisted all aspects of running the Roundabout Theatre Co. in New York, Manhattan's only regional theatre. Worked as a talent agent at Triad, managing overall operations of the TV talent dept. and ultimately became dir., TV and motion picture administration for Triad Artists, Inc. In 1990, joined Warner Bros. (then Lorimar Television) as dir., movies and mini-series. She headed drama development for Warner Bros. Television and was instrumental in the development and subsequent success of "ER," "Lois & Clark: The New Adventures of Superman" and "Sisters." Tassler joined CBS in Aug. 1997 as v.p., drama, CBS Productions before serving as senior v.p., drama development, CBS Entertainment from 1998-2003. Then was executive v.p., drama series development, where she developed such series as "Without a Trace," "Cold Case" and "NCIS." Tassler was named to her current position, pres., CBS Entertainment, in Sept. 2004.

TAVERNIER, BERTRAND
Director, Writer. b. Lyon, France, April 25, 1941. After two yrs. of law study, quit to become film critic for Cahiers du Cinema and Cinema 60. Asst. to dir. Jean-Pierre Melville on Leon Morin Priest (1961), also worked as film publicist. Wrote film scripts and a book on the Western and a history of American cinema. Partner for six years with Pierre Rissient in film promotion company, during which time he studied all aspects of filmmaking. 1963: directed episode of Les Baisers. Pres., Lumiere Inst., Lyon. Book: 50 Years of American Cinema, Qu'est ce Qu'on Attend?, Amis Americains.
PICTURES: *Director: Co-writer*: The Clockmaker (L'Horloger de Saint-Paul), Let Joy Reign Supreme (Que La Fête Commence), The Judge and the Assassin (Le Judge et l'Assassin), Spoiled Children (also co-prod.). *Director: Writer:* Death Watch (also co-prod.), Une semaine de vacances (also prod.), Clean Up, La 8ème génération (short), Mississippi Blues (documentary; also prod.), Un dimanche à la campagne (also prod.), 'Round Midnight, Life and Nothing But, Daddy Nostalgia, L.627, La Fille de d'Artagnan, Appât, L', Capitaine Conan, Ça commence aujourd'hui, Safe Conduct, Holy Lola, The Princess of Montpensier. *Director:* Ciné citron (short), Beatrice, La Guerre sans nom (documentary), Histoires de vies brisées: les 'double peine' de Lyon (documentary), In the Electric Mist. *Associate producer:* La Trace (also writer). *Writer:* Les Mois d'avril sont meurtriers, Der Grüne Berg, My Father Saved My Life, Lucifer et moi. *Technical Advisor:* Un été après l'autre, Ragazzi, Jalousie, Joan of Arc: The Virgin Warrior. *Producer:* Veillées d'armes (documentary), Don't Make Trouble (co-prod.). *Executive producer:* Fred.
TELEVISION: Phillippe Soupault, October Country (co-dir. with Robert Parrish), Lyon, le regard interieur, La Lettre, The Other Side of the Tracks, Les Enfants de Thies.

TAVIANI, PAOLO AND VITTORIO
Directors, Writers. b. San Miniato, Pisa, Italy, (Paolo: Nov. 8, 1931; Vittorio: Sept. 20, 1929); e. Univ. of Pisa (Paolo: liberal arts; Vittorio: law). The two brothers always work in collaboration from script preparation through shooting and editing. 1950: With Valentino Orsini ran cine-club at Pisa. 1954: In collab. with Caesare Zavattini directed short about Nazi massacre at San Miniato. 1954-59: with Orsini made series of short documentaries (Curatorne e Montanara; Carlo Pisacane; Ville della Brianza; Lavatori della pietra; Pitori in cita; I Pazzi della domenica; Moravia, Cabunara). Worked as assistant to Rosellini, Luciano Emmer and Raymond Pellegrini. 1960: collaborated on an episode of Italy Is Not a Poor Country.
PICTURES (all by both): A Man for Burning (debut, 1962; co-dir. with Valentino Orsini), Matrimonial Outlaws (co-dir. with Orsini), The Subversives, Under the Sign of Scorpio, Saint Michael Had a Rooster, Allonsanfan, Padre Padrone (Cannes Film Fest.: Grand Prix & Critics International Prize, 1977), The Meadow, The Night of the Shooting Stars (1981, Best Director Award, Natl. Society of Film Critics; Special Jury Prize, Cannes), Kaos, Good Morning Babylon, The Sun Also Shines at Night, Fiorile, The Elective Affinities (Le Affinata elettive), You're Laughing (Tu ridi), Un Altro mondo e possible, Another World Is Possible (doc.), The Lark Farm.
TELEVISION: *Movie:* Resurrection. *Mini-series:* Luisa Sanfelice.

TAVOULARIS, DEAN
Production Designer. b. Lowell, MA, 1932. Received Art Directors Guild Lifetime Achievement Award 2007.
PICTURES: Candy, Zabriskie Point, Little Big Man, The Godfather, The Godfather: Part II (Academy Award, Best Art Direction-Set Decoration, 1975), The Conversation, Farewell, My Lovely, The Brink's Job (Academy Award nom. 1979), Apocalypse Now (Academy Award nom. 1980), One From the Heart, The Escape Artist, Hammett, The Outsiders, Rumble Fish, Peggy Sue Got Married, Gardens of Stone, Tucker: The Man and His Dream (Academy Award nom. 1989), New York Stories, The Godfather: Part III (Academy Award nom. 1991), Final Analysis, Rising Sun, I Love Trouble, Jack, Bulworth, The Parent Trap, The Ninth Gate, Angel Eyes, CQ.
TELEVISION: *Movie:* The Young Loner (art dir.).

TAYLOR, DAN
Executive. Career began outside the movie industry as a senior tax manager with Arthur Anderson & Co. He started an association with MGM in 1983 and first joined the company in 1985. He left MGM in 1991 and before rejoining MGM in 1997, Taylor had been an executive with the Tracinda Corporation. He rejoined MGM as executive v.p., corporate finance. Most recently, Taylor was senior executive v.p. & CFO, where, in addition to financial activities, he oversaw all MGM's worldwide post-theatrical distribution and information services, while also a member of the management team responsible for MGM's corporate strategy. He was MGM president from spring 2005 through the completion of MGM's sale to a consortium of investors led by Sony Corporation of America. He resigned his post on Jan. 31, 2006. Chairman of the Board of Directors, since May 2009, and a member of the Audit Committee, Nominating and Governance Committee, since February 2008, of Delta Petroleum

Corporation.

TAYLOR, ELIZABETH
Actress. b. London, Eng., Feb. 27, 1932. e. Bryon House, London. When three years old danced before Princess Elizabeth, Margaret Rose. Came to U.S. at outbreak of WWII. *Author*: World Enough and Time (with Richard Burton; 1964), Elizabeth Taylor (1965), Elizabeth Takes Off (1988). Initiated Ben Gurion U.—Elizabeth Taylor Fund for Children of the Negev, 1982. Co-founded American Foundation for AIDS Research, 1985. Named Comdr. Arts & Letters (France) 1985, Legion of Honor, 1987. Established the Elizabeth Taylor AIDS Foundation in 1991. Developed various perfume products: Elizabeth Taylor's Passion, Passion Body Riches, Passion for Men, White Diamonds, Diamonds and Emeralds, Diamonds and Sapphires, Diamond and Rubies; 1993 launched Elizabeth Taylor Fashion Jewelry Collection. Won Special Golden Globe Award 1957. 1985 won Golden Globe Cecil B. DeMille Award. Recipient of AFI Life Achievement Award (1993), Jean Hersholt Humanitarian Award (1993).
THEATRE: *B'way*: The Little Foxes (also London), Private Lives.
PICTURES: There's One Born Every Minute (debut, 1942), Lassie Come Home, Jane Eyre, White Cliffs of Dover, National Velvet, Courage of Lassie, Life with Father, Cynthia, A Date With Judy, Julia Misbehaves, Little Women, Conspirator, The Big Hangover, Father of the Bride, Father's Little Dividend, A Place in the Sun, Callaway Went Thataway (cameo), Love Is Better Than Ever, Ivanhoe, The Girl Who Had Everything, Rhapsody, Elephant Walk, Beau Brummel, The Last Time I Saw Paris, Giant, Raintree County (Academy Award nom. 1958), Cat on a Hot Tin Roof (Academy Award nom. 1959), Suddenly Last Summer (Academy Award nom.; Golden Globe Award 1960), Scent of Mystery (cameo), Butterfield 8 (Academy Award, Golden Globe nom. 1961), Cleopatra, The V.I.Ps, The Sandpiper, Who's Afraid of Virginia Woolf? (Academy Award, Golden Globe nom. 1967), The Taming of the Shrew, Doctor Faustus, Reflections in a Golden Eye, The Comedians, Boom!, Secret Ceremony, The Only Game in Town, X Y and Zee (Zee and Company), Under Milk Wood, Hammersmith Is Out, Night Watch, Ash Wednesday (Golden Globe Award, 1 other nom. 1974), That's Entertainment!, The Driver's Seat, The Blue Bird, A Little Night Music, Winter Kills (cameo), The Mirror Crack'd, Genocide (narrator), Young Toscanini, The Flintstones.
TELEVISION: *Movies*: Divorce His/Divorce Hers, Victory at Entebbe, Return Engagement, Between Friends, Malice in Wonderland, There Must Be a Pony, Poker Alice, Sweet Bird of Youth, These Old Broads. *Mini-series*: North and South. *Guest*: More than 209 appearances.

TAYLOR, JULIET
Casting Director. e. Smith College, Massachussetts.
PICTURES: The Exorcist, The Stepford Wives, Love and Death, Taxi Driver, Next Stop, Greenwich Village, Network, The Front, Close Encounters of the Third Kind, Annie Hall, Julia, Between the Lines, Cindy, Pretty Baby, An Unmarried Woman, Manhattan, Stardust Memories, Willie and Phil, Arthur, Shoot the Moon, A Midsummer Night's Sex Comedy, Tempest, Still of the Night, Zelig, Terms of Endearment, Broadway Danny Rose, The Killing Fields, Falling in Love, Birdy, The Purple Rose of Cairo (CSA nom. 1986), Alamo Bay, The Mission, Heartburn, Hannah and Her Sisters (CSA Award 1987), September, Radio Days (CSA nom. 1988), Big (CSA nom. 1989), Another Woman, Working Girl (CSA nom. 1989), Mississippi Burning (CSA Award 1989), Dangerous Liasons, New York Stories, Crimes and Misdemeanors, The Grifters (CSA nom. 1991), The Sheltering Sky, Postcards from The Edge (CSA nom. 1991), Alice (CSA nom. 1991), Harley Davidson and the Marlboro Man, Regarding Henry, Shadows and Fog, This is My Life (CSA nom. 1992), Husbands and Wives (CSA nom. 1993), Hero, Sleepless in Seattle (CSA Award 1994), Schindler's List, Bullets Over Broadway (CSA Award 1995), Mixed Nuts, Wolf, The Road To Welville, Angie (CSA nom. 1994), Mighty Aphrodite (CSA nom. 1996), Mary Reilly, The Birdcage (CSA nom. 1996), Everyone Says I Love You (CSA nom. 1997), Deconstructing Harry, Primary Colors (CSA nom. 1998), Celebrity (CSA nom. 1999), Meet Joe Black, Sweet and Lowdown, Angela's Ashes, Small Time Crooks, The Curse of the Jade Scorpion, Hollywood Ending, People I Know, The Life of David Gale, The Blind Assassin, Anything Else, Marie and Bruce, The Stepford Wives, Melinda and Melinda, The Interpreter, Match Point, Scoop, Cassandra's Dream, Vicky Cristina Barcelona, Whatever Works, You Will Meet a Tall Dark Stranger, Midnight in Paris.
TELEVISION: *Movies:* Cindy, Don't Drink the Water, Wit (Emmy nom. 2001). *Mini-series:* Angels in America (Emmy Award 2004). *Series:* Beacon Hill.

TAYLOR, LILI
Actress. b. Chicago, Feb. 20, 1967.
THEATRE: *NY*: What Did He See, Aven U Boys. *Regional*: Mud, The Love Talker, Fun. *Director*: Collateral Damage.
PICTURES: Mystic Pizza (debut, 1988), Say Anything, Born on the Fourth of July, Bright Angel, Dogfight, Watch It, Household Saints, Short Cuts (Golden Globe Award for ensemble cast 1994), Rudy, Arizona Dream, Mrs. Parker and the Vicious Circle, Ready to Wear (Pret-a-Porter), The Addiction, Cold Fever, Four Rooms, Things I Never Told You, I Shot Andy Warhol, Girl's Town, Ransom, Pecker, Kicked in the Head, O.K. Garage, The Imposters, A Slipping Down Forward, Janis, The Haunting, High Fidelity, Julie Johnson, Gaudi Afternoon, Casa de los Babys, Factotum, The Notorious Bettie Page, The Secret, Starting Out in the Evening, The Secret, The Promotion, Public Enemies, Brooklyn's Finest.
TELEVISION: *Movies*: Family of Spies, Subway Stories: Tales from the Underground, Anne Frank: The Whole Story, Live From Baghdad, Penguins Behind Bars, Rubicon. *Series:* Deadline, Six Feet Under (Emmy nom. 2002), State of Mind.

TAYLOR, MESHACH
Actor. b. Boston, MA, April 11, 1947. e. Florida A & M Univ. Hosted Chicago TV show Black Life.
THEATRE: Streamers, Sizwe Banzi is Dead, The Island, Native Son, Wonderful Ice Cream Suit, Bloody Bess, Sirens of Titan, Night Feast, Huckleberry Finn, Cops.
PICTURES: Damien: Omen II, The Howling, The Beast Within, Explorers, Warning Sign, One More Saturday Night, From the Hip, Mannequin, The Allnighter, House of Games, Welcome to Oblivion, Mannequin 2: On the Move, Class Act, Jacks or Better, Friends and Family, Tranced, Hyenas, Wigger.
TELEVISION: *Movies*: An Innocent Man, How to Murder a Millionaire, Double Double Toil and Trouble, Virtual Seduction, The Right Connections. *Mini-series*: Nothing Lasts Forever. *Series*: Buffalo Bill, Designing Women (Emmy nom. 1989), Dave's World, To Tell the Truth, Field Trips, Permission Slips, Signs, and Weasels, Ned's Declassified School Survival Guide. *Guest*: More than 55 appearances.

TAYLOR, RENÉE
Actress, Writer. b. New York, NY, March 19, 1933. Wife of actor Joseph Bologna, with whom she collaborates in writing. Their B'way plays include Lovers and Other Strangers, It Had to Be You. *Stage actress*: One of the All-Time Greats.
PICTURES: *Actress*: The Errand Boy, The Detective, The Producers, A New Leaf, Lovers and Other Strangers (also s.p. Academy Award nom. for s.p.; WGA nom. 1971), Made for Each Other (also s.p.; WGA nom. 1972), Last of the Red Hot Lovers, Lovesick, It Had to Be You (also co-dir., co-s.p.), That's Adequate, White Palace, End of Innocence, Delirious, All I Want for Christmas, Forever, Love Is All There Is, Dr. Dolittle 2 (voice), Dying On the Edge, Returning Mickey Stern, National Lampoon's Gold Diggers, A-List, Alfie, Boynton Beach Club, Kalamazoo?, Ice Age: The Meltdown (voice), Opposite Day, Driving Me Crazy, Boston Girls, Life During Wartime, The Rainbow Tribe.
TELEVISION: *Movies: Writer*: Acts of Love...and Other Comedies (Emmy Award, 1973), Paradise, Calucci's Department, The American Dream Machine, Bedrooms (Writers Guild Award, 1984), The Lucille Ball/Jackie Gleason Special, Woman of the Year (also actress), A Cry for Love. *Actress:* 61, Pandemic, Early Bird. *Series: Actress:* The Jack Paar Show, Forever Fernwood, Mary Hartman Mary Hartman, Dream On, Daddy Dearest, The Nanny (Emmy nom. 1996). *Writer:* Lovers and Other Strangers (also prod., WGA nom. 1971), *Guest:* More than 70 apearances.

TAYLOR, ROD
Actor. b. Sydney, Australia, Jan. 11, 1930. e. East Sydney Fine Arts Coll. Started out as artist then turned to acting on stage. Formed own company, Rodler, Inc., for TV-film production.
PICTURES: The Sturt Expedition (debut, 1951), King of the Coral Sea, Long John Silver, Top Gun, The Virgin Queen, Hell on Frisco Bay, World Without End, The Rack, Giant, The Catered Affair, Raintree County, Step Down to Terror, Separate Tables, Ask Any Girl, The Time Machine, Seven Seas to Calais, 101 Dalmatians (voice), The Birds, A Gathering of Eagles, The V.I.Ps, Sunday in New York, Fate is the Hunter, 36 Hours, Young Cassidy, Do Not Disturb, The Glass Bottom Boat, The Liquidator, Hotel, Chuka (also prod.), Dark of the Sun, High Commissioner (Nobody Runs Forever), The Hell with Heroes, Zabriskie Point, Darker Than Amber, The Man Who Had Power Over Women, The Heroes, The Train Robbers, Trader Horn, The Deadly Trackers, Hell River, Blondy, Picture Show Man, A Time To Die, On the Run, Close Enemy, Open Season, Point of Betrayal, Welcome to Woop-Woop, Kaw, Inglourious Basterds.
TELEVISION: *Movies*: Powerkeg, Family Flight, The Oregon Trail, Cry of the Innocent, Jacqueline Bouvier Kennedy, Charles and Diana: A Royal Love Story, Outlaws, Danielle Steel's Palomino, Grass Roots, The Warlord: Battle for the Galaxy, K.A.W. *Series*: Hong Kong, Bearcats, Masquerade, The Oregon Trail, Outlaws, Falcon Crest, Walker, Texas Ranger. *Guest:* More than 57 appearances.

TAYLOR, RONNIE
Cinematographer. b. London, England, Oct. 27, 1924. Ent. m.p. ind. 1941 at Gainsborough Studios
PICTURES: Tommy, The Silent Flute, Circle of Iron, Savage Harvest, Gandhi (Academy Award 1983), High Road to China, Splitz, Champions, A Chorus Line, Foreign Body, Cry Freedom, Terror at the Opera (Italy), The Experts, Sea of Love, Popcorn, The Rainbow Thief, The Steal, The Phantom of the Opera, Sleepless.
TELEVISION: *Movies:* The Hound of the Baskervilles, Nairobi Affair, Age of Treason, Shadow of Obsession, Good King Wenceslas, Redwood Curtain. *Mini-series:* Master of the Game

(UK). *Series:* The Avengers.

TAYLOR-YOUNG, LEIGH
Actress. b. Washington, DC, Jan. 25, 1945. e. Northwestern U. B'way debut 1966 in Three Bags Full. Additional stage: The Beckett Plays (Off-B'way, LA), Knives, Sleeping Dogs.
PICTURES: I Love You Alice B. Toklas (debut, 1968, Golden Globe nom. 1969), The Games, The Big Bounce, The Adventurers, The Buttercup Chain, The Horsemen, The Gang That Couldn't Shoot Straight, Soylent Green, Can't Stop the Music, Looker, Secret Admirer, Jagged Edge, Honeymoon Academy, Accidents, Dreamrider, Bliss, Slackers, A-List, Dirty Laundry.
TELEVISION: *Movies*: Marathon, Napoleon and Josephine: A Love Story, Perry Mason: The Case of the Sinister Spirit, Who Gets the Friends, Bonnie and McCloud, Moment of Truth: Murder or Memory?, An Unfinished Affair, Stranger in My Home. *Series*: Peyton Place, The Devlin Connection, The Hamptons, Dallas, Picket Fences (Emmy Award, Golden Globe nom. 1994), Sunset Beach, Harmony's Passions. *Pilots*: Ghostwriter, Houston Knights. *Guest*: More than 47 appearances.

TEAGUE, LEWIS
Director. b. March 8, 1938. e. NYU. Editor and/or 2nd unit dir. on such films as Cockfighter, Crazy Mama, Death Race 2000, Avalanche, Fast Charlie: The Moonbeam Rider, The Big Red One.
PICTURES: Dirty O'Neil (co-dir.), Lady in Red (also editor), Alligator, Fighting Back, Cujo, Cat's Eye, The Jewel of the Nile, Collision Course, Navy SEALS, Wedlock.
TELEVISION: *Movies*: Shannon's Deal, T Bone N Weasel, Tom Clancy's Op Center, Saved by the Light, The Reunion: Dukes of Hazzard, Love and Treason, The Triangle. *Series:* Barnaby Jones, A Man Called Sloane, Fortune Hunter.

TÉCHINÉ, ANDRÉ
Director, Writer. b. Valence d'Agen, Tarn-et- Garonne, France, March 13, 1943.
PICTURES: Paulina s'en va (dir. only), French Provincial, Barocco, The Bronte Sisters, Hotel des Ameriques, La Matiouette, Rendez-vous, Scene of the Crime, The Innocents, Mauvaise Fille (s.p. only), I Don't Kiss, My Favorite Season, The Wild Reeds (won Cesar, NY Film Critics Circle Award), The Child of the Night, Transatlantique (s.p. only), Alice and Martin, Terminus des anges, Loin, Cafe de la plage (s.p. only), Strayed, Changing Times, Les Témoins, The Witnesses, The Girl on the Train, Terminus des anges.

TELLEM, NANCY
Executive. e. UC Berkeley, bachelor's degree; Hastings College of Law, J.D. A lawyer by training, Tellem spent her early career working in business affairs under long-time TV executive Leslie Moonves at Lorimar TV. Later, she was the executive v.p., business and financial affairs at Warner Bros. Television. In 1997, she followed Moonves to CBS, where she got her first taste of the development side of the business. In Aug. 1998, Tellem was entertainment pres., where she oversaw development of dramas, comedies and reality series, including the CSI franchise, Survivor, the hit comedy Two and a Half Men and many others. In Sept. 2004, Tellem was promoted to a newly created post of pres., CBS Paramount Network Television Entertainment Group and is the position she holds today. For several years Tellem has been ranked among the most powerful women in entertainment.

TELLER, IRA
Executive, b. New York, NY, July 3, 1940. e. City College of New York, 1957-61; NYU Graduate Sch. of Arts, 1961-62. Publicist, Pressbook Dept., 20th Century Fox., 1961-62; asst. to adv. mgr., Embassy Pictures Corp., 1962-63; asst. adv. mgr., Columbia Pictures Corp., 1963; adv. mgr., Columbia Pictures Corp., 1964, 1964-65; asst. to chmn. of bd., Diener, Hauser, Greenthal Agy., 1966; adv. mgr., 20th Century-Fox, 1966-67; 1967, adv. dir. 20th Cent.-Fox.; dir. of adv., Nat'l General Pictures Corp., 1969; eastern dir., adv.-pub., 1972; national dir., adv-pub., 1973; Bryanston Distributors, Inc. v.p. adv.-pub., 1974; Cine Artists Pictures Corp. v.p. adv-pub., 1975; Lorimar Productions, v.p., adv.-marketing, 1976-77; 1977, pres., Ira Teller and Company, Inc.; This Is It Productions. Currently instructor, UCLA Film School. Advisory Board Member for the Indian Film Festival.

TEMPLE, JULIEN
Director. b. London, England, Nov. 26, 1953. e. Cambridge, London's National Film School. Dir. many rock videos.
PICTURES: The Great Rock 'n' Roll Swindle (debut, 1979), The Secret Policeman's Other Ball, Undercover (also s.p.), Running Out of Luck (also s.p.), Absolute Beginners, Aria (segment: Rigoletto), Earth Girls Are Easy, Rolling Stones: At the Max (creative consultant), Bullet, Catching Fire, Vigo, The Filth and the Fury, Pandaemonium, Glastonbury (also cinematographer, documentary), Joe Strummer: The Future Is Unwritten, The Eternity Man (also writer), The Liberty of Norton Folgate (doc.), Oil City Confidential (doc.), Requiem for Detroit (doc.), Gun Girl.
TELEVISION: *Movie:* Paul Weller: Find the Torch (dir.).

TEMPLE (BLACK), SHIRLEY
Actress, Diplomat. b. Santa Monica, CA, April 23, 1928. In 1932 screen debut, Red Haired Alibi. In 1933 To the Last Man; then leading figure in series of Educational shorts called Baby Burlesque and Frolics of Youth, until breakthrough role in Stand Up and Cheer, 1934, which resulted in career as child and teen star. Received Juvenile Academy Award 1935. Voted one of ten best Money-Making Stars in Motion Picture Herald-Fame Poll, 1934-39. As an adult, turned her attention to government and international issues. Republican candidate for U.S. House of Representatives, 1967. Rep. to 24th General Assembly of U.N. (1969-70). Special asst. to chmn., President's Council on the Environment (1970-72). U.S. Ambassador to Ghana (1974-76). Chief of Protocol, White House (1976-77); member of U.S. delegation on African Refugee problems, Geneva, 1981; 1987 made 1st honorary U.S. Foreign Service Rep. for State Dept.; 1989, appt. Ambassador to Czechoslovakia under Pres. George H.W. Bush. She spent 27 years working for the State Department. *Autobiography*: Child Star (1988).
PICTURES: The Red-Haired Alibi (feature debut, 1932), To the Last Man, Out All Night, Mandalay, Carolina, Stand Up and Cheer, Baby Take a Bow, Now and Forever, Bright Eyes, Now I'll Tell, Change of Heart, Little Miss Marker, The Little Colonel, Our Little Girl, Curly Top, The Littlest Rebel, Captain January, Poor Little Rich Girl, Dimples, Stowaway, Wee Willie Winkle, Heidi, Rebecca of Sunnybrook Farm, Little Miss Broadway, Just Around the Corner, Little Princess, Susannah of the Mounties, The Blue Bird, Young People, Kathleen, Miss Annie Rooney. Since You Went Away, I'll Be Seeing You, Kiss and Tell, That Hagen Girl, Honeymoon, Bachelor and the Bobby-Soxer, Fort Apache, Mr. Belvedere Goes to College, Adventure in Baltimore, Story of Seabiscuit, Kiss for Corliss.
TELEVISION: *Movie:* Child Star: The Shirley Temple Story (based on book). *Series*: Shirley Temple's Storybook (host, performer). Various tributes and specials.

TENNANT, VICTORIA
Actress. b. London, England, Sept. 30, 1953. e. Central School of Speech & Drama. Daughter of ballerina Irina Baronova and talent agent Cecil Tennant.
THEATRE: Love Letters (Steppenwolf), Getting Married (NY), Taming of the Shrew (NY).
PICTURES: The Ragman's Daughter, Horror Planet, Sphinx, Strangers Kiss, All of Me, The Holocraft Covenant, Best Seller, Flowers in the Attic, Whispers, Zugzwang, The Handmaid's Tale, L.A. Story, The Plague, Edie & Pen, The Legend of the Mummy, Irene in Time.
TELEVISION: *Movies*: Maigret, Dempsey, Under Siege, Act of Will, Voice of the Heart, Sister Mary Explains It All (also exec. prod.). *Mini-series*: Voice of the Heart, Winds of War (Golden Globe nom. 1984), Chiefs, War and Remembrance. *Series:* Snowy River: The McGregor Saga.

TEWKESBURY, JOAN
Writer, Director. b. Redlands, CA, April 8, 1936. e. USC. Student American School of Dance, 1947-54. Was ostrich and understudy in Mary Martin's Peter Pan. Directed and choreographed Theatre prods. in L.A., London, Edinburgh Festival, Scotland. Taught dance and theory, American School of Dance 1959-64; taught in theatre arts depts. of two universities: USC, Immaculate Heart. Became script supvr. for Robert Altman on McCabe & Mrs. Miller. *Off-B'way*: Cowboy Jack Street (writer, dir.). Teacher in film dept. UCLA. Sundance advisor, 1992-93: directors lab-writers lab. American Musical Theatre Festival in Philadelphia. Chippy (dir.), Jammed (Edinburgh Festival; writer, dir.). Dance Card (Oregon Ballter Theatre; writer, dir., co-choreo.)
PICTURES: Thieves Like Us (co.-s.p.), Nashville, (s.p.; Golden Globe nom.; WGA nom. 1976), Old Boyfriends (dir.), Hampstead Center (doc. of Anna Freud, writer, dir.), A Night in Heaven (s.p.), The Player (actress), Strangers (dir.).
TELEVISION: *Movies*: *Director/Writer*: The Acorn People, The Tenth Month, Elysian Fields (also co-exec. prod.), Cold Sassy Tree, Scattering Dad. *Director:* Sudie & Simpson, Wild Texas Wind, On Promised Land. *Actress:* Peter Pan. *Series*: *Director*: Alfred Hitchcock Presents (also writer), Almost Grown, Shannon's Deal (also writer), Nothing Sacred, The Guardian (also consulting prod.).

THARP, JIM
Executive. Began his motion picture career in 1966 in the sales departments at Warner Bros. Joined General Cinema Corp. 1970 as assistant film buyer. During his 25-year career with General Cinema Corporation, Tharp held a number of senior management positions including Sr. V. P. of Film and Film Marketing. Tharp managed the company's 1,187-screen circuit, and played a key role in its operations and real estate departments. Promoted to regional film buyer for the southern U.S. region 1975. 1979 became regional V. P. 1983 was named Sr. V. P. of film. Tharp served as head of Distribution at DreamWorks for five years and managed the distribution for many Oscar winning films such as. Shrek, winner of the first-ever Academy Award for Best Animated Film, also Oscar winners Wallace & Gromit Curse of the Were-Rabbit, Gladiator, American Beauty and Saving Private Ryan which was the top grossing feature film of 1998. Tharp also managed the distribution of Shrek 2, the top-grossing animated feature of all time, and the computer animated hits Shark Tale, and Madagascar. Joined Paramount Pictures 2006 and managed a number of successful films such as Cloverfield, The Spiderwick

Chronicles, Sweeney Todd The Demon Barber of Fleet Street, Bee Movie, Beowulf, Shrek the Third, Transformers, Dreamgirls, Freedom Writers, Norbit, Zodiac, Shooter, Blades of Glory and Disturbia. Currently is Pres. of Domestic theatrical Dist. and is responsible for overseeing the U.S. distribution of theatrical releases from Paramount Pictures, DreamWorks Pictures, MTV Films, Nickelodeon Movies, and DreamWorks Animation SKG. In addition, he oversees theatrical distribution operations, in-theater marketing and non-theatrical, distribution.

THEODORAKIS, MIKIS
Composer. b. Chios, Greece, July 29, 1925.
PICTURES: Eva, Night Ambush, Shadow of the Cat, Phaedra, Five Miles to Midnight, Zorba the Greek (Golden Globe nom. 1965), The Day the Fish Came Out, The Trojan Women, State of Siege, Serpico, Iphigenia, Easy Road, Kostas, The Man With the Carnation, Les Clowns de Dieu, Misioni përtej detit, The Fog, Barluschke, Beware of Greeks Bearing Guns, The Sisterhood of the Traveling Pants (soundtrack writer).
TELEVISION: *Movies:* Élo Antigoné (Hungary), Nausicaa (France), The Story of Jacob and Joseph, Christophe Colomb (France). *Mini-series:* Le Dernier seigneur des Balkans. *Series:* Peri anemon kai ydaton (Greece), An thimitheis t' oneiro mou (Greece).

THERON, CHARLIZE
Actress, Producer. b. Benoni, South Africa, August 7, 1975. Trained as a dancer. Worked for Joffrey Ballet in New York prior to an injury that ended her ballet career.
PICTURES: *Actress:* Children of the Corn II, Two Days in the Valley, That Thing You Do!, Trial and Error, The Devil's Advocate, Celebrity, Mighty Joe Young, The Astronaut's Wife, The Cider House Rules, Reindeer Games, The Yards, Men of Honor, The Legend of Bagger Vance, Sweet November, 15 Minutes, The Curse of the Jade Scorpion, Waking Up in Reno, Trapped, The Italian Job, Monster (also prod.; Academy Award, Best Actress in Leading Role, Golden Globe Award 2004), Head in the Clouds, North Country (Academy Award nom.; Golden Globe nom. 2006), Æon Flux, The Ice at the Bottom of the World (also prod.), The Brazilian Job, East of Havana (doc.), Sleepwalking, Battle in Seattle, In the Valley of Elah, Hancock, The Burning Plain (also exec. prod.), The Road, Astro Boy (voice), Young Adult.
TELEVISION: *Movies:* Hollywood Confidential, The Life and Death of Peter Sellers (Emmy nom.; Golden Globe nom. 2005). *Series:* Arrested Development. *Guest:* More than 100 appearances.

THEWLIS, DAVID
Actor. b. Blackpool, England, March 20, 1963. e. Guildhall School of Music and Drama, The Barbicon, London. First professional job in breakfast food commercial.
PICTURES: Road, Vroom, Little Dorrit, Resurrected, Life Is Sweet, Afraid of the Dark, Swords at Teatime (short), Damage, The Trial, Naked (Cannes Film Fest., NY Film Critics & Natl. Soc. of Film Critics Awards, 1993), Black Beauty, Hello Hello Hello (short; dir. & writer), Total Eclipse, Restoration, James and the Giant Peach (voice), Dragonheart, The Island of Dr. Moreau, American Perfekt, Seven Years in Tibet, The Big Lebowski, Divorcing Jack, Besieged, Whatever Happened to Harold Smith?, Gangster No. 1, Goodbye Charlie Bright, Cheeky (also s.p. & dir.), Timeline, Harry Potter and the Prisoner of Azkaban, Kingdom of Heaven, The New World, Basic Instinct 2, The Omen, The Inner Life of Martin Frost, Harry Potter and the Order of the Phoenix, The Boy in the Striped Pyjamas, Harry Potter and the Half-Blood Prince, Veronika Decides to Die, Mr. Nice, London Boulevard, Harry Potter and the Deathly Hallows: Part I, Harry Potter and the Deathly Hallows: Part II, Anonymous, War Horse.
TELEVISION: *Movies:* Skulduggery, Oranges Are Not the Only Fruit, Screen One: Filipina Dreamgirls, Journey to Knock, Black and Blue, Prime Suspect 3, Love Story (short), The Miracle Maker (voice), Endgame, Hamilton Mattress (short; voice). *Mini-series*: The Singing Detective, Dandelion Dead, Dinotopia. *Series*: Max, A Bit of a Do.

THINNES, ROY
Actor. b. Chicago, IL, April 6, 1938. Made TV debut as teen on DuPont Theatre, 1957.
PICTURES: Journey to the Far Side of the Sun, Charlie One-Eye, Airport 1975, The Hindenburg, Mind Benders, Rush Week, A Beautiful Mind, Undone, The Eyes of Van Gogh, The Eyes of Van Gogh, Broken English, Leadcatcher.
TELEVISION: *Movies*: The Other Man, Children of the Lotus Eater, Black Noon, The Manhunter, The Horror at 37000 Feet, The Norliss Tapes, Satan's School for Girls, State of Division, Secrets, Code Name: Diamond Head, Stone, Return of the Mod Squad, Freedom, Sizzle, Dark Shadows, An Inconvenient Woman, Stormy Weathers, The Invaders, Bar Hopping. *Mini-series*: From Here to Eternity, Scruples. *Series*: General Hospital (1963-66), The Long Hot Summer, The Invaders, The Psychiatrist, From Here to Eternity, One Life to Live, Falcon Crest, Dark Shadows. *Guest:* More than 70 appearances.

THOMAS, BETTY
Director, Producer, Actress. b. St. Louis, MO, July 27, 1948. e. Ohio U, BFA, 1969. Chicago Art Inst., Roosevelt U. Former member of Chicago's Second City improv group.
PICTURES: *Actress*: Tunnelvision, Chesty Anderson—U.S. Navy, Loose Shoes, Used Cars, Homework, Troop Beverly Hills, Jackson County Jail. *Director*: Only You, The Brady Bunch Movie, Private Parts, Doctor Dolittle, 28 Days, I Spy (also prod.), R3 (documentary), The Dreyfus Affair: A Love Story, John Tucker Must Die, Alvin and the Chipmunks: The Squeakquel. *Producer:* Can't Hardly Wait, Charlie's Angels (exec. prod.), I Spy, Surviving Christmas, Guess Who (also exec. prod.).
TELEVISION: *Movies*: *Actress:* Outside Chance, Nashville Grab, When Your Lover Leaves, No Greater Gift, Prison for Children. *Director:* My Breast (DGA Award, Emmy nom. 1997), Couples, The Late Shift (DGA Award, Emmy nom. 1997), The Loop (pilot), That Guy (dir. only), Dash 4 Cash. *Series: Actress:* Hill Street Blues (Emmy Award, 1985, 6 other noms.). *Director:* Hooperman, Doogie Howser M.D., Mancuso FBI, Shannon's Deal, Dream On (Emmy nom, DGA nom. 1994), Parenthood, Sons and Daughters, On the Air, The Loop.

THOMAS, DAVE
Actor, Writer, Director. b. St. Catherines, Ontario, Canada, May 20, 1949. e. McMaster Univ.
PICTURES: *Actor:* Double Negative, Stripes Strange Brew (also co-dir., co-s.p.), My Man Adam, Sesame Street Presents Follow That Bird, Moving, Love at Stake, Boris and Natasha, Public Enemy #2, Cold Sweat, Coneheads, Pippi Longstocking (voice), MVP: Most Valuable Primate, Rat Race, Fancy Dancing, Trial And Error: The Making of Sequestered, Brother Bear (voice), Intern Academy (also s.p. & dir.), Deluxe Combo Platter, Santa's Slay, Take 22: Behind the Scenes of Sequestered. *Director:* The Experts. *Executive producer:* Catching Kringle. *Producer:* Ambushed. *Writer:* Spies Like Us, Girl, This Is America.
TELEVISION: *Movies: Actor:* Home to Stay, Riel, Martin Short: Concert for the North Americas, The Last Polka (narr.), The Rocket Boy (also writer & prod.), I, Martin Short, Goes Hollywood, Andrea Martin...Together Again, Picture Perfect, Kidz in the Wood, The New Beachcombers, A Beachcombers Christmas. *Director:* Ghost Mom (also s.p.). *Series: Actor:* The David Steinberg Show, SCTV (also writer), SCTV Network (Emmy Award 1982, 5 other noms.; also writer), Camp Candy (voice), The Red Green Show, Raw Toonage (voices), Grace Under Fire (also writer), Bob & Doug (also exec. prod.), Mission Hill (voice), King of the Hill (voice), Arrested Development, El Tigre: The Adventures of Manny Rivera (dir. only, Emmy nom. 2009). *Writer:* The Dennis Miller Show, Pet Star (also dir.), The Mullets (consulting prod.), Bob & Doug McKenzie's Two-Four Anniversary (doc., also actor), Good Morning World, Bob & Doug (also exec. prod.), Popzilla (also exec. prod.), Slacker Cats (animation exec., dir.), Buckley and Eddie Deceased (animation exec.). *Guest:* More than 96 appearances.

THOMAS, HENRY
Actor. b. San Antonio, TX, Sept. 9, 1971. Made film debut at the age of 9 in Raggedy Man, 1981. On stage in Artichoke, The Guardsman.
PICTURES: Raggedy Man (debut, 1981), E.T.: The Extra-Terrestrial (Golden Globe nom. 1983), Misunderstood, Cloak and Dagger, The Quest, Murder One, Valmont, Curse of the Starving Class, Fire in the Sky, Legends of the Fall, Bombshell, Suicide Kings, Niagara Niagara, Hijacking Hollywood, A Good Baby, Fever, All the Pretty Horses, I'm With Lucy, Dead in the Water, Gangs of New York, I Capture the Castle, Briar Patch, Honey Baby, 11:14, Dead Birds, The Hard Easy, The Deal, The Last Sin Eater, Red Velvet, Don't Look Up, Dear John, The Last Ride.
TELEVISION: *Movies*: The Steeler and the Pittsburgh Kid, Psycho IV: The Beginning, A Taste for Killing, Beyond Obsession, Indictment: The McMartin Trial (Golden Globe nom. 1996), Riders of the Purple Sage, Moby Dick, Happy Face Murders Desperation, Under. *Mini-series:* Nightmares and Dreamscapes: From the Stories of Stephen King.

THOMAS, JAY
Actor. b. New Orleans, LA, July 12, 1948. Started as stand-up comedian before pursuing acting career in NY. Appeared on NY stage with Playwrights Horizons and Off-B'way in Isn't It Romantic? Also morning DJ on L.A. radio station KPWR-FM.
PICTURES: C.H.U.D., The Gig, Straight Talk, Mr. Holland's Opus, A Smile Like Yours, Dirty Laundry, A Smile Like Yours, The Adventures of Ragtime, Last Chance, The Big Tease, Stranger in My House, Surfacing, Dragonfly, The Santa Clause 2: The Mrs. Clause, Teacher's Pet (voice), The Santa Clause 3: The Escape Clause, The Pool Boys, Material Lies, Labor Pains, Horrorween, Snatched, A Kiss for Jed Wood, The Pool Boys, Sex Tax: Based on a True Story, Material Lies.
TELEVISION: *Movies*: Justin Case, Miracle Landing, A Husband A Wife A Lover, Encino Woman, The Bachelor's Baby (co-exec. prod.), Killing Mr. Griffin, Deserts Edge, My Date with the President's Daughter, An American Daughter, Monday Night Mayhem. *Mini-series:* Master of the Game. *Series*: Mork & Mindy, Where's Rodney?, Married People, Cheers (recurring guest role), Love & War, Ink, Katie Joplin, Ghost Stories (narr.). *Guest*: Murphy Brown (2 Emmy Awards, 1 other nom.), More than 80 appearances.

THOMAS, JEREMY
Producer. b. London, Eng., July 26, 1949. e. Millfield School.

Son of dir. Ralph Thomas (Doctor comedies) and nephew of dir. Gerald Thomas (Carry On... comedies). Entered industry 1969. Worked as film edit. on Brother Can You Spare a Dime, 1974. Received Evening Standard Special Award for Outstanding Contribution to Cinema in 1990, BAFTA's Michael Balcon Award in 1991. Appointed chmn. of British Film Institute, 1992.
PICTURES: Mad Dog Morgan, The Shout, The Great Rock 'n' Roll Swindle, Bad Timing: A Sensual Obsession, Eureka, Merry Christmas Mr. Lawrence, The Hit, Insignificance, The Last Emperor (Academy Award, 1988), Everybody Wins, The Sheltering Sky, Let Him Have It (exec. prod.), Naked Lunch, Little Buddha, Stealing Beauty, Blood and Wine, The Brave, All the Little Animals (dir.), Phorpa, Gohatto, Brother, Sexy Beast, The Triumph of Love, Heaven and Hell, Rabbit-Proof Fence, Young Adam, The Dreamers, Travelers and Magicians (exec. prod.), Promised Land (exec. prod.), Don't Come Knocking (exec. prod.), Tideland, Glastonbury (doc. exec. prod.), Fast Food Nation, Stray, Vacation (exec. prod.), Mister Lonely (co-prod.), Two Fists, One Heart (exec. prod.), Palermo Shooting (exec. prod.), Franklyn, Creation, Pina (exec. prod.), Thirteen Assassins, The Man Who Killed Don Quixote, A Dangerous Method (prod.).
TELEVISION: *Movie:* Stephen Fry: The Secret Life of the Manic Depressive (doc., assoc. prod.). *Series:* Heimat 3 - Chronik einer Zeitenwende (exec. prod., UK), Meet the Browns (prod. assist.).

THOMAS, MARLO
Actress. b. Detroit, MI, Nov. 21, 1938. Daughter of late actor Danny Thomas. m. Phil Donahue. Brother is TV producer Tony Thomas. e. U. of Southern California. Started career with small TV roles, summer stock. Appeared in London stage prod. of Barefoot in the Park. Most Promising Newcomer Awards from both Fame and Photoplay for series That Girl. Conceived book, record and TV special Free to Be You and Me (Emmy Award, 1974).
THEATRE: *NY*: Thieves, Social Security, The Shadow Box.Regional: Six Degrees of Separation.
PICTURES: Jenny (Golden Globe nom. 1971), Thieves, In the Spirit, The Real Blonde, Starstruck, Deuce Bigalow: Male Gigalo, Playing Mona Lisa, In the Woods, LOL: Laughing Out Loud.
TELEVISION: *Movies*: It Happened One Christmas (also co-prod.), The Lost Honor of Kathryn Beck (also exec. prod.), Consenting Adult (Golden Globe nom. 1986), Nobody's Child (Emmy Award, Golden Globe nom. 1986), Leap of Faith (co-exec. prod. only), Held Hostage: The Sis and Jerry Levin Story, Ultimate Betrayal, Reunion (also co-exec. prod.), Two Against Time, Our Heroes Ourselves (host; exec. prod.), Deceit (also exec. prod.). *Series*: The Joey Bishop Show, That Girl (4 Emmy noms.; Golden Globe Award 1967), Law & Order: Special Victims Unit. *Specials*: Acts of Love and Other Comedies, Free To Be You and Me (also prod.; Emmy Award, 1974), The Body Human: Facts for Girls (Emmy Award, 1981), Love Sex... and Marriage (also exec. prod.), Free to Be a Family (host, exec. prod.; Emmy Award, 1989), Funny Women of Television, Kids Are Punny, Intimate Portrait: Gloria Steinem. *Guest*: More than 98 appearances.

THOMAS, PHILIP MICHAEL
Actor. b. Columbus, OH, May 26, 1949. e. Oakwood Coll.
PICTURES: Come Back Charleston Blue, Stigma, Book of Numbers, Mr. Ricco, Black Fist, Coonskin, Sparkle, The Dark, El Hombre de los hongos, Hey Good Lookin' The Wizard of Speed and Time, Miami Shakedown, Fate.
TELEVISION: *Movies*: Toma, The Beasts Are on the Streets, This Man Stands Alone, Valentine, Miami Vice: Brother's Keeper A Fight for Jenny, Motown Merry Christmas (host), False Witness, Extralarge: Moving Target, Extralarge: Miami Killer, Extralarge: Magic Power, Extralarge: Jo-Jo, Extralarge: Cannonball, Extralarge: Black Magic, Extralarge: Black and White, Perry Mason: The Case of the Ruthless Reporter. *Mini-series*: Roots: The Next Generations, Noi siamo angeli. *Series*: Miami Vice (Golden Globe nom. 1986). *Documentaries/Specials*: Disney's Totally Minnie, The Debbie Allen Special. *Guest:* More than 53 appearances.

THOMAS, RICHARD
Actor. b. New York, NY, June 13, 1951. e. Columbia U. Made TV debut at age 7 on Hallmark Hall of Fame, The Christmas Tree. That same year appeared on Broadway in Sunrise at Campobello.
THEATRE: Sunrise at Campobello, Everything in the Garden, Fifth of July, The Front Page, Love Letters, Square One, The Lisbon Traviata, Danton's Death, Richard II, Richard III.
PICTURES: Winning (debut, 1969), Last Summer, Red Sky at Morning, The Todd Killings, Cactus in the Snow, You'll Like My Mother, 9/30/55, Battle Beyond the Stars, Riding the Rails (documentary; narrator), Camping with Camus (short; prod. only), The Million Dollar Kid, Wonder Boys, Taking Woodstock.
TELEVISION: *Movies*: Homecoming, The Red Badge of Courage, The Silence, Getting Married, No Other Love, All Quiet on the Western Front, Barefoot in the Park, To Find My Son, Berlin Tunnel 21, Fifth of July, Johnny Belinda, Living Proof: The Hank Williams Jr. Story, Hobson's Choice, The Master of Ballantrae, Final Jeopardy, Andre's Mother, Glory Glory, Go To the Light, Common Ground, Stephen King's IT, Mission of the Shark, Yes Virginia There Is a Santa Claus, Crash Landing: The Rescue of Flight 232, I Can Make You Love Me: The Stalking of Laura Black, Precious Victims, Linda, A Walton Thanksgiving Reunion, Death in Small Doses, A Walton Wedding, Down Out and Dangerous, The Christmas Box, What Love Sees, Time Piece, A Walton Easter, A Thousand Men and a Baby, Flood: A River's Rampage, Big and Hairy, Beyond the Prairie: The True Story of Laura Ingalls Wilder, In the Name of the People, For All Time (co-exec. prod. only), Flight of the Reindeer, The Miracle of the Cards, Beyond the Prairie 2: The True Story of Laura Ingalls Wilder, Anna's Dream, Annie's Point, Wild Hearts. *Mini-series:* Nightmares and Dreamscapes: From the Stories of Stephen King. *Series*: One Two Three Go, As the World Turns, The Waltons (Emmy Award, 1973, 1 other nom.; 2 Golden Globe noms.), Just Cause, It's a Miracle (host). *Guest*: More than 115 appearances.

THOMAS, ROBERT G.
Producer, Director. b. Glen Ridge, NJ, July 21, 1943. e. U. of Bridgeport, Fairleigh Dickinson U. Prod. educational radio programs, 1962, WPKN-FM. Asst. stage mgr. Meadowbrook Dinner Theatre, 1963; 1964, began career as TV cameraman for NY stations. Worked both full-time and freelance for major TV and video tape studios. 1968, started Bob Thomas Productions, producing business/sales films and TV commercials. Has 8 awards from natl. film festivals; nominated for 5 Emmys for TV series called The Jersey Side he produced for WOR-TV. Inventor of Futurevision 2000 multi-imaging video system for conventions and exhibits and museums (American Museum of Natural History: Hall of Human Biology to be shown over 15 years). Inventor and pres. of Video Mail Marketing Inc., low cost, light weight paper board video cassettes for the direct mail video marketing industry. *Shorts:* Valley Forge with Bob Hope, New Jersey—200 Years, Road-Eo '77.
TELEVISION: The Jersey Side (talk/entertainment), Jersey People (weekly talk/entertainment prog.), Movies '89 (synd. film preview series).

THOMOPOULOS, ANTHONY D.
Executive. b. Mt. Vernon, NY, Feb. 7, 1938. e. Georgetown U. Began career in broadcasting at NBC, 1959, starting as mail-room clerk and moving to radio division in prod. & admin. Shortly named to post in int'l division sales, involved with programming for stations and in dev. TV systems for other nations. Joined Four Star Entertainment Corp. as dir. of foreign sales, 1964; named v.p., 1965; exec. v.p., 1969; 1970 joined RCA SelectaVision Div. as dir. of programming; 1971 joined Tomorrow Entertainment as v.p.; 1973 joined ABC as v.p., prime-time programs in N.Y.; 1974, named v.p., prime-time TV creative operations, ABC Entertainment; 1975 named v.p. of special programs, ABC Entertainment; 1976 made v.p., ABC-TV, assisting pres. Frederick S. Pierce in supervising all activities of the division; 1978 named pres. of ABC Entertainment; 1983 promoted to pres., ABC Broadcast Group in charge of all TV & radio operations; 1986-88, pres. & COO, United Artists Corp.; independent prod. with Columbia, 1989. Formed Thomopoulos Productions in 1989. Pres., Amblin Television, 1991-95. Responsible for the original placement of ER in addition to several other series on network television. From March 1995 to Dec. 1997, Thomopoulos was the CEO of MTM Entertainment and pres. of The Family Channel, both subsidiaries of International Family Entertainment, Inc. From July 1999 to April 2001, he was the vice chmn. of the bd. of OnVANTAGE, Inc., formerly Familyroom.com. Since July 2000, Thomopoulos has been a member of the bd. of dir. of the Media Arts Group, Inc. (aka The Thomas Kinkade Company) and has been chmn. of the bd. since June 2001. He served as interim CEO of the company from June 21 until Jan. 2002. Bd. member of Los Angeles Mission, Inc. Co-Founder of Promise Media Productions.

THOMPSON, CAROLINE
Writer. b. Washington, DC, Apr. 23, 1956. e. Amherst Col., Harvard. Started as free-lance journalist. Wrote novel First Born, which led to screenwriting.
PICTURES: Edward Scissorhands (also assoc. prod.), The Addams Family, Homeward Bound: The Incredible Journey, The Secret Garden (also assoc. prod.), The Nightmare Before Christmas, Black Beauty (also dir.), Buddy (also dir.), Perfume: The Story of a Murderer, Corpse Bride, City of Ember.
TELEVISION: Snow White: The Fairest of Them All (also dir.).

THOMPSON, EMMA
Actress, Writer. b. London, England, Apr. 15, 1959. e. Cambridge Univ. Daughter of actors Eric Thompson and Phyllida Law. Acted with the Footlights at the Edinburgh Fringe. At Cambridge co-wrote, co-produced, co-directed and co-starred in school's first all-female revue Woman's Hour, as well as solo show Short Vehicle.
THEATRE: *London*: Me and My Girl, Look Back in Anger. Renaissance Theatre Company (World Tour): A Midsummer Night's Dream, King Lear. *Author:* "The 'Sense and Sensibility' Screenplay Diaries."
PICTURES: Henry V, The Tall Guy, Impromptu, Dead Again, Howards End (Academy Award, BAFTA, NY Film Critics, LA Film Critics, Golden Globe, Nat'l Society of Film Critics & Nat'l Board of Review Awards for Best Actress of 1993), Peter's Friends, Much Ado About Nothing, The Remains of the Day (Academy Award

nom.; Golden Globe nom. 1994), In the Name of the Father (Academy Award nom.; Golden Globe nom. 1994), My Father the Hero, Junior (Golden Globe nom. 1995), Carrington, Sense and Sensibility (also s.p.; BAFTA Award, 1995; Academy Award for s.p.,1996, 1 other nom.; WGA Award, 1996; Golden Globe Award, 1 other nom. 1996), The Winter Guest, Judas Kiss, Primary Colors, Maybe Baby, Treasure Planet (voice), Imagining Argentina, Love Actually, Harry Potter and the Prisoner of Azkaban, Nanny McPhee (also s.p.), Stranger Than Fiction, Harry Potter and the Order of the Phoenix, Brideshead Revisited, Last Chance Harvey (Golden Globe nom. 2009), An Education, Pirate Radio, Nanny McPhee Returns (also writer, s.p., exec. prod.), Effie (writer), My Fair Lady (s.p.), Brave (voice).
TELEVISION: *Movies*: Cambridge Footlights Revue (also writer), The Crystal Cube, Look Back In Anger, The Winslow Boy, The Blue Boy, Hospital, Wit (also writer; 2 Emmy noms.; Golden Globe nom. 2001), The Song of Lunch. *Mini-series*: Fortunes of War (BAFTA Best Actress award), Angels in America (Emmy nom. 2004). *Series*: Alfresco (also writer), Assaulted Nuts, Tutti Frutti, Thompson (also writer). *Documentaries/Specials:* The Emma Thompson Special. *Guest:* More than 98 appearances.

THOMPSON, FRED (DALTON)
Actor. b. Sheffield, AL, Aug. 19, 1942. Raised in TN. e. Memphis St. U, Vanderbilt U, studying law. Was Federal prosecutor before going to DC to serve as minority counsel on the Senate Select Committee on Presidential Campaign Activities, which involved investigation of the Watergate scandal. Hired to serve as consultant on film Marie, then was asked to play himself in the movie, resulting in acting career. Elected 1994 to U.S. senate as Republican representative from Tennessee.
AUTHOR: At That Point in Time (1975).
PICTURES: Marie (debut, 1985), No Way Out, Feds, Fat Man and Little Boy, The Hunt for Red October, Days of Thunder, Die Hard 2, Flight of the Intruder, Class Action, Necessary Roughness, Curly Sue, Cape Fear, Thunderheart, White Sands, Aces: Iron Eagle III, Born Yesterday, In the Line of Fire, Baby's Day Out, Racing Stripes, Looking for Comedy in the Muslim World, Alleged, The Genesis Code, Secretariat.
TELEVISION: *Movies:* Unholy Matrimony, Bed of Lies, Keep the Change, Stay the Night, Day-O, Barbarians at the Gate, Evel Knievel, Conviction (pilot), Bury My Heart at Wounded Knee. *Series:* Law & Order: Special Victims Unit, Law & Order, Law & Order: Trial by Jury. *Guest:* More than 47 appearances.

THOMPSON, JACK
Actor. r.n. John Payne. b. Sydney, Australia, Aug. 31, 1940. e. Queensland U. Joined drama workshop at school; first part was in TV soap opera as continuing character. 1988, appt. to bd. of Australian Film Finance Corp. Formed Pan Film Enterprises.
PICTURES: The Savage Wild, Outback (Wake in Fright), Libido, Petersen, A Sunday Too Far Away, Caddie, Scobie Malone, Mad Dog Morgan, The Chant of Jimmie Blacksmith, The Journalist, Breaker Morant, The Earthling, The Club, The Man From Snowy River, Bad Blood, Merry Christmas Mr. Lawrence, Flesh + Blood, Burke & Willis, Ground Zero, Waterfront, Turtle Beach, Wind, A Far Off Place, Deception, The Sum of Us, The Last Dance, Excess Baggage, Midnight in the Garden of Good and Evil, Feeling Sexy, The Magic Pudding, The Yolngu Boy, Original Sin, Star Wars: Episode II-Attack of the Clones, The Assassination of Richard Nixon, Oyster Farmer, Man-Thing, Eucalyptus, December Boys, The Good German, December Boys, Ten Empty, Leatherheads, Australia, Mao's Last Dancer, Don't Be Afraid of the Dark.
TELEVISION: Human Target, Because He's My Friend, A Woman Called Golda, The Letter, Waterfront, The Last Frontier, The Letter, The Riddle of the Stinson, Kojak: The Price of Justice, Trouble in Paradise, After the Shock, Beryl Markham: A Shadow on the Sun, Thornbirds: The Missing Years, McLeod's Daughters, My Brother Jack, South Pacific, The Karenskys. *Mini-series:* Waterfront, A Woman of Independent Means, Bastard Boys. *Series:* Motel, Spyforce, Behind the Legend. *Guest:* More than 60 appearances.

THOMPSON, LEA
Actress. b. Rochester, MN, May 31, 1961. m. director Howard Deutch. Danced professionally since age of 14; won scholarship to Pennsylvania Ballet Co., American Ballet Theatre, San Francisco Ballet. Gave up that career for acting, appearing in several commercials for Burger King. *L.A. stage*: Bus Stop, The Illusion.
PICTURES: Jaws 3-D (debut, 1983), All the Right Moves, Red Dawn, The Wild Life, Back to the Future, SpaceCamp, Howard the Duck, Some Kind of Wonderful, Casual Sex?, Going Undercover, The Wizard of Loneliness, Back to the Future Part II, Back to the Future Part III, Article 99, Dennis the Menace, The Beverly Hillbillies, The Little Rascals, The Unknown Cyclist, Fish Don't Blink, Electric, Haunted Lighthouse, Come Away Home, Out of Omaha, Doubting Thomas, Senior Skip Day, Exit Speed, Balancing the Books, Rock Slyde, Splinterheads, Prettyface, Adventures of a Teenage Dragonslayer, Mayor Cupcake, The Convincer.
TELEVISION: *Movies*: Nightbreaker, Montana, Stolen Babies, The Substitute Wife, The Unspoken Truth, Right to Remain Silent, Stealing Christmas, Jane Doe: Vanishing Act, Jane Doe: Now You See It Now You Don't, Jane Doe: Til Death Do Us Part, Jane Doe: The Wrong Face, Jane Doe: The Brigadoon Effect, Jane Doe: Yes, I Remember It Well, Jane Doe: The Harder They Fall (also dir.), Jane Doe: Eye of the Beholder (also dir.), Jane Doe: Ties That Bind, A Life Interrupted, Final Approach, Jane Doe: Eye of the Beholder, The Christmas Clause, Uncle Nigel. *Mini-series*: A Will of Their Own. *Series*: Caroline in the City, For the People. *Guest:* More than 58 appearances.

THORNTON, BILLY BOB
Actor, Director, Writer. b. Hot Springs, AR, Aug. 4, 1955.
PICTURES: *Actor*: Hubter's Blood, South of Reno, Going Overboard, Cycle Sluts, For the Boys, Babes Ahoy, One False Move (also s.p.), The Killing Box, Trouble Bound, Indecent Proposal, Bound By Honor, Tombstone, Floundering, Some Call It a Sling Blade (short; also s.p., dir.), On Deadly Ground, Jim Jarmusch's Dead Man, Stars Fell on Henrietta, Sling Blade (also dir., s.p.; Academy Award, for best adapt. s.p.,; 1 other nom.; WGA Award 1997), The Winner, A Gun A Car A Blonde, Princess Mononoke (voice), U-Turn, The Apostle, Primary Colors, Homegrown, ,Armageddon, A Simple Plan (Academy Award nom.; Golden Globe nom. 1999), Pushing Tin, Franky Goes to Hollywood (short; documentary), The Last Real Cowboys (short), South of Heaven, West of Hell, All the Pretty Horses (dir., prod.), The Man Who Wasn't There (Golden Globe nom. 2002), Daddy and Them (also s.p. & dir.), Bandits (Golden Globe nom. 2002), Monster's Ball, The Badge, Waking Up in Reno, Levity, Intolerable Cruelty, Love Actually, Bad Santa (Golden Globe nom. 2004), Chrystal, The Alamo, Friday Night Lights, The Bad News Bears, The Ice Harvest, Mr. Woodcock, The Astronaut Farmer, School for Scoundrels, Eagle Eye, The Informers, Faster, St. Vincent. *Writer:* A Family Thing, The Gift, Camouflage
TELEVISION: *Movies*: *Actor:* Out There, Don't Look Back (also writer), CatDog: The Great Parent Myster (voice). *Series*: The Outsiders (actor), Hearts Afire (actor). *Special*: AMC: Film Preservation Classics: Film Preservation Classics with Billy Bob Thornton (Emmy nom. 2000). *Guest*: More than 109 appearances.

THURMAN, UMA
Actress. b. Boston, MA, Apr. 29, 1970. Named after a Hindu deity. Raised in Woodstock, NY and Amherst, MA where father taught Asian studies. Father's work took family to India where they lived three years. e. Professional Children's School, NY. Worked as model while still in high school.
PICTURES: Kiss Daddy Good Night (debut, 1988), Johnny Be Good, Dangerous Liaisons, The Adventures of Baron Munchausen, Where the Heart Is, Henry and June, Final Analysis, Jennifer Eight, Mad Dog and Glory, Even Cowgirls Get the Blues, Pulp Fiction (Academy Award nom.; Golden Globe nom. 1995), A Month by the Lake, The Truth About Cats and Dogs, Beautiful Girls, Batman and Robin, Gattaca, Les Miserables, The Avengers, Sweet and Lowdown, Vatel, The Golden Bowl, Tape, Chelsea Walls, Kill Bill: Volume 1 (Golden Globe nom. 2004), Paycheck, Kill Bill: Vol. 2 (Golden Globe nom. 2005), Be Cool, Prime, The Producers (also soundtrack performer), My Super Ex-Girlfriend, Bee Movie (voice), The Life Before Her Eyes, The Accidental Husband (also prod.), My Zinc Bed, Motherhood, Eloise in Paris, Girl Soldier (also prod.), Percy Jackson & the Olympians: The Lightning Thief, Ceremony, Bel Ami.
TELEVISION: *Movies:* Robin Hood, Hysterical Blindness (also exec. prod., Golden Globe Award 2003), My Zinc Bed, A Muppets Christmas: Letters to Santa. *Documentaries/Specials*: Without Lying Down: Frances Marion and the Power of Women in Hollywood. *Guest:* More than 95 appearances.

THURSTON, BARRY
Executive. b. Hackensack, NJ. e. B.S., economics, Lehigh U. Began career as broadcaster, director and producer for network telecasts, Sports Network; program mgr., Kaiser Broadcasting, and station mgr., WKBD, 1965-1970; dir. of programming, v.p., programming, Field Communications (formerly Kaiser Broadcasting); v.p., domestic synd., Embassy Communications, 1983-85; senior v.p., domestic synd., and president, Embassy Comm., 1985-86; president of syndication, Columbia/Embassy Television, 1986-87; president of syndication, Columbia Pictures Entertainment and Columbia Pictures Television, 1987-92; pres., Columbia Pictures Television Distribution (now Columbia TriStar Television Distribution - CTTD), 1992-July 1, 2000. He was responsible for ushering CTTD into new areas of first-run syndication and first-run production for cable, and formed Columbia TriStar Advertiser Sales, 1993. Thurston has served on the board for NATPE and Combined Broadcasting and was a member of INTV's planning committee. He also has been on the bd. of dir. of the Television Bureau of Advertising (TVB). Thurston was inducted into the Broadcasting and Cable Hall of Fame in 2001. He currently is president of The Thurston Group, a media company he founded in 2001 that specializes in strategic planning and marketing and is Chairman at Beaver Group a digital signage and audio visual solutions company.

TICOTIN, RACHEL
Actress. b. Bronx, NY, Nov. 1, 1958. Began career as dancer with the Ballet Hispanico of New York, before becoming a production assist. on such films as The Wanderers, Dressed to Kill

and Raging Bull.
PICTURES: Fort Apache: The Bronx, Critical Condition, Total Recall, One Good Cop, FX2, Where the Day Takes You, Falling Down, Criminal Passion, Natural Born Killers, Don Juan DeMarco, Steal Big Steal Little, Turbulence, Con-Air, Civility, Can't Be Heaven, Desert Saints, Something's Gotta Give, Man on Fire, The Sisterhood of the Traveling Pants, The Eye, The Sisterhood of the Traveling Pants 2, The Burning Plain, America.
TELEVISION: *Movies*: Love Mary, Rockabye, When the Bough Breaks, Spies Lies and Naked Thighs, Prison Stories: Women on the Inside, Keep the Change, From the Files of Joseph Wambaugh: A Jury of One, Thicker Than Blood: The Larry McLinden Story, Deconstructing Sarah, The Wharf Rat, First Time Felon, Aftershock: Earthquake in New York, Warden of Red Rock. *Series*: For Love and Honor, Ohara, Crime and Punishment, American Family, Skin.

TIERNEY, MAURA
Actress. b. Boston, MA, Feb. 3, 1965.
PICTURES: Dead Women in Lingerie, The Linguini Incident, White Sands, The Temp, Fly by Night, Primal Fear, Mercy, Liar Liar, Primary Colors, Oxygen (also exec. prod.), Forces of Nature, Instinct, Mexico City (voice), Scotland PA, Insomnia, Rooftop Kisses (short), The Nazi (short), Melvin Goes to Dinner, Welcome to Mooseport, The Go-Getter, Diggers, Baby Mama, Semi-Pro, Finding Amanda.
TELEVISION: *Movies:* Student Exchange, Crossing the Mob, Flying Blind, Out of Darkness. *Series:* The Van Dyke Show, 704 Hauser, NewsRadio, Sammy (voice), Rescue Me, Parenthood (also pilot), ER (Emmy nom. 2001), The Whole Truth (also pilot).

TIGHE, KEVIN
Actor. b. Los Angeles, CA, Aug. 13, 1944. e. Cal. State, B.A. in psychology; USC M.F.A. in performing arts. Served in U.S. Army, 1967-69. Received N.E.A. Director's Fellowship, Seattle Rep. Theatre, 1988-89.
PICTURES: The Graduate (debut, 1967), Matewan, Eight Men Out, K-9, Lost Angels, Road House, Another 48 HRS, Bright Angel, City of Hope, Newsies, School Ties, A Man in Uniform (Genie Award), Geronimo: An American Legend, What's Eating Gilbert Grape, Jade, Race the Sun, Scorpion Spring, Mumford, The Big Day, Fast Food High, The Tulse Luper Suitcases Part I: The Moab Story, My Bloody Valentine.
TELEVISION: *Movies*: Emergency, Greatest Rescues of Emergency!, Emergency: Survival on Charter #220, The Saint in Manhattan, Perry Mason: The Case or the Defiant Daughter, Face of a Stranger, Better Off Dead, Betrayal of Trust, The Avenging Angel, Escape to Witch Mountain, In Cold Blood, Winchell, The Darwin Conspiracy, The Sight, Nancy Drew. *Mini-series*: The Rebels, Rose Red. *Series*: Emergency, Murder One, Lost. *Guest:* More than 60 appearances.

TILL, STEWART
Executive. e. M.A. in American politics, Essex University, United Kingdom. Till's career includes work as deputy managing director of satcaster BSkyB; and positions in advertising at Saatchi & Saatchi and the music business. In the film business for the last 14 years, Till has held several key executive positions: president of Universal Pictures International; president & CEO of Signpost Films; executive with Polygram Filmed Entertainment, where he was responsible for all film acquisitions, and he oversaw international film, video and TV marketing and distribution. In 2003, Till was named chairman and CEO of United International Pictures (UIP), a leading distributor of feature length motion pictures to theatrical exhibitors. UIP, the international joint venture of Paramount Pictures and Universal Studios, is a leading distributor of feature length motion pictures to theatrical exhibitors. Till announced plans to leave UIP at the end of 2006 when the 24-year-old international distribution relationship between Paramount and Universal was scheduled to end. Till's involvement in the film industry includes: chairman of the UK's Film Council; vice chairman of Skillset, as well as chairman of the Film Skills Strategy Committee. From 1997 to 1999 he co-chaired, with the Minister of Film, the UK Government's policy review group to advise the Secretary of State for Culture, Media and Sport, on film policy. In 2005 Cinema Expo International recognized Till with its "International Distributor of the Year" award.

TILLY, JENNIFER
Actress. b. Harbour City, CA, Sept. 16, 1958. Sister is actress Meg Tilly.
THEATRE: One Shoe Off (Off-B'way debut, 1993; Theatre World Award).
PICTURES: No Small Affair, Moving Violations, Remote Control, Inside Out, He's My Girl, Johnny Be Good, Rented Lips, High Spirits, Far From Home, Let It Ride, The Fabulous Baker Boys, The Doors, Scorchers, Shadow of the Wolf, The Webbers, Made in America, Embrace of the Vampire, Double Cross, The Getaway, Bullets Over Broadway (Academy Award nom. 1995), Bird of Prey, Man With a Gun, Edie and Pen, The Pompatus of Love, House Arrest, Bound, American Strays, Liar Liar, The Wrong Guy, Relax...It's Just Sex, Hoods, Bride of Chucky, Music From Another Room, Goosed, The Muse (cameo), Do Not Disturb, Stuart Little, Cord, Bruno, The Crew, Dancing at the Blue Iguana, Dirt, Fast Sofa, The Cat's Meow, Ball in the House, Monsters Inc. (voice), The Civilization of Maxwell Bright, Jericho Mansions, Hollywood North, Haunted Mansion, Happy End, Return to Babylon, Second Best, Perfect Opposites, Home on the Range (voice), El Padrino, Saint Ralph, Deluxe Combo Platter, Bailey's Billion$, Tideland, Lady Godiva: Back in the Saddle, Funny Farm, Deal, The Caretaker, Inconceivable, The Making of Plus One, Imps*, Empire of Silver, The Secret Lives of Dorks, 30 Beats, Renaissance Girl.
TELEVISION: *Movies*: Heads, Bella Mafia, The Kid (voice), Sister Mary Explains It All, The Magnificent Ambersons, Stage on Screen: The Women, The Initiation of Sarah. *Series*: *Actress*: Shaping Up, Hill Street Blues, Key West, Family Guy (voice), Out of Practice, The Cleveland Show (pilot). *Writer:* Mary. *Guest*: More than 85 appearances.

TINKER, GRANT A.
Executive. b. Stamford, CT., Jan. 11, 1926. e. Dartmouth College, 1947. Joined NBC radio prog. dept. 1949. In 1954 with McCann-Erickson ad agency, TV dept. In 1958, Benton & Bowles Ad Agency, TV dept.; 1961-66 with NBC, v.p., programs, West Coast; v.p. in charge of programming, NY, 1966-67; joined Universal Television as v.p., 1968-69; 20th-Fox, v.p., 1969-70. Became pres. MTM Enterprises, Inc. 1970. Named NBC bd. chmn. & CEO, 1981-86. Received ATAS Governor's Award in 1987. Formed indep. prod. co. GTG. Entertainment, 1988. The GTG partnership was dissolved in 1990. May 16, 2005, Tinker received an Individual Peabody for a career in the entertainment industry that the Peabody board cited for fostering "creative opportunities that led to some of television`s most exciting work – and workers." The Peabody Awards are given annually by the by the University of Georgia's Grady College of Journalism and Mass Communication. Retired.

TINKER, MARK
Director, Producer. b. Stamford, CT, Jan. 16, 1951. Brother of John Tinker. Father is retired executive Grant A. Tinker.
PICTURE: Inside the Box (dir., exec. prod.).
TELEVISION: *Movies: Producer:* Thornwell. *Director:* Private Eye, Capital News, My Old School (short), Our Shining Moment, NYPD Mounted, Babe Ruth, Bonanza Under Attack, Inside the Box (also exec. prod.). *Series: Director:* Making the Grade, The White Shadow (2 Emmy noms.), St. Elsewhere (4 DGA noms.; Emmy Award 1988, 8 other noms.), L.A. Law, Capital News (also exec. prod.), NYPD Blue (also exec. prod.; 2 DGA noms.; 2 Emmy Awards, 5 other noms.), Civil Wars (also exec. prod.), Chicago Hope, Brooklyn South (also prod., Emmy nom., 1998), Philly, Deadwood (also exec. prod.), John from Cincinnati (dir., episodes, exec. prod.), Private Practice (exec. prod.).

TINKER, JOHN
Writer, Producer. Brother of Mark Tinker. Father is retired executive Grant A. Tinker.
TELEVISION: *Series: Writer:* St. Elsewhere (also prod., Emmy Award 1986, 5 other noms.), L.A. Law (also co-exec. prod.), Tattingers, Home Fires (also co-exec. prod. & dir.), Chicago Hope (also exec. prod., 3 Emmy noms.), The Practice (also exec. prod.), Judging Amy (creator, writer). *Executive producer:* Snoops, HRT, The Road Home (co-exec. prod.), The Book of Daniel (exec. prod.).

TISCH, STEVE
Producer. b. Lakewood, NJ, 1949. e. Tufts U. Son of Preston Tisch. Worked during school breaks for John Avildsen and Fred Weintraub. Signed upon graduation as exec. asst. to Peter Guber, then prod. head at Columbia Pics. Entered producer ranks with Outlaw Blues, 1977, collaborating with Jon Avnet with whom formed Tisch/Avnet Prods. Alliance with Phoenix Entertainment 1988.
PICTURES: Outlaw Blues, Almost Summer, Coast to Coast, Risky Business, Deal of the Century, Soul Man, Big Business, Hot to Trot, Heart of Dixie, Heart Condition, Bad Influence, Forrest Gump (Academy Award for Best Picture, 1995), Corrina Corrina. *Exec. Prod.:* The Long Kiss Goodnight, Dear God, Wild America, American History X, The Postman, Nico the Unicorn, Lock Stock and Two Smoking Barrels, Wayward Son, Looking for an Echo, Snatch: Pigs and Diamonds, Alex and Emma, The Weather Man, Need, Pursuit of Happyness, Seven Pounds, The Taking of Pelham 123, Knowing, The Back-Up Plan.
TELEVISION: *Movies:* The Missing Are Deadly, No Other Love, Homeward Bound, Prime Suspect, Something So Right, Calendar Girl Murders, The Burning Bed (Emmy nom. 1985), Triplecross, In Love & War, Evil in Clear River, Out on the Edge, Judgment, Lies of the Heart, Afterburn, Keep the Change, The People Next Door. *Series:* Dirty Dancing, Freshman Dorm, Mission Extreme (co-prod.).

TOBACK, JAMES
Writer, Producer, Director. b. New York, NY, Nov. 23, 1944. e. Harvard U. Taught literature at City Coll. of New York; contributed articles and criticism to Harper's, Esquire, Commentary, etc. Wrote book Jim, on actor-athlete Jim Brown (1971). First screenplay, The Gambler, filmed in 1974.
PICTURES: *Writer*: The Gambler, Fingers (also dir.), Love and Money (also dir., prod.), Exposed (also dir., prod.), The Pick-Up Artist (also dir.), The Big Bang (also dir., actor), Alice (actor),

Bugsy (also actor, Academy Award nom.; Golden Globe nom.; WGA nom. 1992), Two Girls and a Guy (also dir.), Black and White (also dir.), Love in Paris (also dir.), Harvard Man (also dir.), When Will I Be Loved (also actor & dir.), The Beat That My Heart Skipped (from previous s.p.), Tyson (doc.). *Actor*: Death of a Dynasty.

TOBEY, BRUCE

Executive. e. Law degree, UCLA School of Law, 1984. From 1986-2000 worked at law firm Troop Steuber Pasich Reddick & Tobey, LLB (originally known as Hill Wynne Troop & Meisinger) where he began as an associate and left as a partner and head of firm's entertainment dept. Tobey also was a member of firm's five-person Executive Committee. His clients primarily consisted of the major movie studios. He then became v.p. and general counsel for Broadband Sports, a sports-oriented, Internet-based business. From 2001-2005, executive v.p. at Paramount and responsible for Paramount's business, legal and administration operations, with oversight over the following departments: business and legal affairs, office of the general counsel, industrial relations, government relations, human resources, studio facilities, corporate development, information systems and Paramount digital entertainment. His role evolved to also include key components of both a COO and Chief Administrative Officer position. He also served as one of the two Paramount reps on the MPAA Board of Directors. Until June 2004, Tobey was also executive v.p., Viacom Entertainment Group, which was comprised of the various businesses that at the time were all controlled by Paramount. These businesses included TV production and distribution, print publication (Simon & Schuster), consumer products (Viacom Consumer Products), theatres (Famous Players, Mann Theatres) and music publishing (Famous Music). Tobey left Paramount and in 2006, consulted for a variety of companies and individuals in the feature film, TV and new media areas. In March 2007, named to current position, COO, CBS Films. In addition to establishing the films unit, Tobey is charged with oversight of CBS Films' finance, legal, and business affairs departments. He also oversees home video distribution of the film division's releases.

TOBOLOWSKY, STEPHEN

Actor. b. Dallas, TX, May 30, 1951. e. Southern Methodist Univ.
THEATRE: *Actor*: Whose Life Is It Anyway?, Crimes of the Heart, Godspell, Three Sisters, The Glass Menagerie, Barabass, The Wake of Jamey Foster, The Wild Duck, No Scratch, The Miss Firecracker Contest, The Importance of Being Earnest, Purlie, Whispers in the Wind. *Director*: The Miss Firecracker Contest, The Lucky Spot, The Bridgehead (Dramalogue Award), The Secret Rapture (Dramalogue Award), Our Town, The Debutante Ball.
PICTURES: Swing Shift, True Stories (co-s.p.), Nobody's Fool, Spaceballs, Mississippi Burning, Checking Out, Two Idiots in Hollywood (dir. & s.p.), Great Balls of Fire!, In Country, Breaking In, Bird on a Wire, Funny About Love, Welcome Home Roxy Carmichael, The Grifters, Thelma & Louise, Memoirs of an Invisible Man, Basic Instinct, Roadside Prophets, Single White Female, Where the Day Takes You, Sneakers, Hero, Groundhog Day, The Pickle, Calendar Girl, Josh and S.A.M., My Father the Hero, Radioland Murders, Murder in the First, Dr. Jekyll and Ms. Hyde, Power 98, The Glimmer Man, The Curse of the Inferno, The Curse of Inferno, The Brave Little Toaster Goes to Mars, Boys Life II, Mr. Magoo, An Alan Smithee Film: Burn Hollywood Burn, The Operator, Black Dog, One Man's Hero, The Insider, Bossa Nova, Alien Fury: Countdown to Invasion, The Prime Gig, Memento, Urban Chaos Theory, Sleep Easy Hutch Rimes, Freddy Got Fingered, Par 6, It Is What It Is, Country Bears, Love Liza, Adaptation, A View From the Top, National Security, Freaky Friday, Debating Robert Lee, Win A Date With Tad Hamilton, Frankie and Johnny Are Married, Garfield, Little Black Book, Robots (voice), Miss Congeniality 2: Armed and Fabulous, Pope Dreams, Living 'til the End, Love Hollywood Style, Failure to Launch, Blind Dating, Beethoven: The Reel Story, The Time Traveler's Wife, Buried, The Rainbow Tribe, Hard Breakers, You May Not Kiss the Bride, The Last Ride, Egg Scape, Peep World.
TELEVISION: *Movies*: Cocaine and Blue Eyes, Roe v. Wade, To the Moon Alice, Last Flight Out, Marla Hanson Story, Perry Mason: The Case of the Maligned Mobster, Tagget, Deadlock, Deadly Medicine, When Love Kills: The Seduction of John Hearn, Against the Grain, Night Visitors, Don't Look Under the Bed, Alien Fury, Gene Pool, On the Edge, Black River, The Day the World Ended, McBride: The Doctor is Out Really Out, American Men, The Valley of Light. *Mini-series:* Kingpin. *Series*: Blue Skies, A Whole New Ballgame, Dweebs, Mr. Rhodes, CSI: Miami, Deadwood, John from Cincinnati, Heroes, Glee (also pilot). *Guest*: More than 120 appearances.

TODD, BEVERLY

Actress, Director, Producer. b. Chicago, IL, July 11, 1946.
THEATRE: *NY*: Carry Me Back to Morningside Heights, Black Visions. *Producer*: A Tribute to Ella Fitzgerald. *Director*: I Need a Man, Sneaky.
PICTURES: The Lost Man, They Call Me Mister Tibbs!, Brother John, Vice Squad, Homework, The Ladies Club, Happy Hour, Baby Boom, Moving, Clara's Heart, Lean on Me, Exquisite Tenderness, Crash, The Bucket List, Hope & Redemption: The Lena Baker Story, I Will Follow.
TELEVISION: *Movies*: Deadlock, The Ghost of Flight 401, Having Babies II, The Jericho Mile, Don't Look Back, A Touch of Scandal, Class of '61, A Different Affair, Ali: An American Hero. *Mini-series*: Roots. *Series*: Love of Life, Having Babies, The Redd Foxx Show, Six Feet Under. *Documentaries/Specials:* A Laugh a Tear: The Story of Black Humor in America (prod.), Don't Hit Me Mom (Afterschool Special), The Class of '61. *Guest*: More than 47 appearances.

TOFFLER, VAN

Executive. b. New York. e. B.A. degree in economics, George Washington Univ. J.D. degree from Univ. of Pennsylvania. This attorney by training, left Park Avenue law firm Kaye, Scholer, Fierman, Hays and Handler to break into the TV business. The move led Toffler to MTV Networks in 1987, joining the network's law and business affairs dept. He worked mostly on Nickelodeon for a year before focusing solely on MTV. For almost 20 years Toffler has occupied a range of roles at the network, including executive v.p., programming enterprises, and president, MTV Productions. In 1996, he helped start MTV Films; he became MTV general manager in 1997; and by 2000, Toffler had risen to become the president of MTV and MTV2. In 2002, Toffler supervised the start of MTVU, the college-only channel, and in Oct. 2004 Toffler's ascent continued as he was named MTV Networks Group President, responsible for MTV, MTV2, VH1, CMT and LOGO. Currently Toffler is president of the MTV Networks Music/Logo/Films Group, which includes MTV, VH1, digital all-video networks and a film production studio.

TOLAN, PETER

Producer, Writer.
PICTURES: *Actor:* Alice. *Writer*: My Fellow Americans, Analyze This, What Planet Are You From?, Bedazzled, America's Sweethearts, Stealing Harvard, Analyze That, Guess Who, Just Like Heaven, Fun with Dick and Jane, Just Like Heaven (s.p.), Finding Amanda (also dir.).
TELEVISION: *Movies:* The Dave Chappelle Project, Fort Pit (also exec. prod.), H.M.O. (exec. prod.), Phil at the Gate (writer, exec. prod.), The Unusuals (exec. prod.), The End of Steve (dir., co-exec. prod., writer). *Series*: Murphy Brown (Emmy Award, 1992, 1 other nom.), Carol & Company, Wish You Were Here, Home Improvement, The Larry Sanders Show (also consulting prod.; Emmy Award, 1998, 8 other noms.; 2 WGA noms.), Good Advice (also co-prod.), Ellen, The George Wendt Show (also creator), Buddies, Style and Substance (also dir. & exec. prod.), The Job (also exec. prod.), My Adventures in Television (also dir. & exec. prod.), Rescue Me (dir., exec. prod., 3 Emmy noms.), The Unusuals (exec. prod., consult).

TOLKAN, JAMES

Actor. b. Calumet, MI, June 20, 1931. e. Univ. of Iowa.
THEATRE: *NY*: Abe Lincoln in Illinois, Once in a Lifetime, Three Sisters, The Cannibals, Mary Stuart, The Silent Partner, 42 Seconds from Broadway, Full Circle, Macbeth, Dream of a Blacklisted Actor, Jungle of Cities, Wings.
PICTURES: Stiletto, They Might Be Giants, The Friends of Eddie Coyle, Serpico, Love and Death, The Amityville Horror, Wolfen, Prince of the City, Author! Author!, Hanky Panky, Nightmares (voice), WarGames, Iceman, The River, Turk 182!, Flanagan, Back to the Future, Off Beat, Top Gun, Armed and Dangerous, Masters of the Universe, Made in Heaven, Viper, Split Decisions, True Blood, Second Sight, Back to the Future Part II, Family Business, Opportunity Knocks, Back to the Future Part III, Dick Tracy, Hangfire, Problem Child 2, Driving Me Crazy, Boiling Point, Love in Ambush, Robo Warriors, Underworld, Wings, Seven Times Lucky, Heavens Fall.
TELEVISION: *Movies*: Little Spies, Leap of Faith, Weekend War, The Case of the Hillside Stranglers, Sketch Artist, Beyond Betrayal, Sketch Artist II: Hands That See, Love in Ambush. *Series*: Mary, Sunset Beat, The Hat Squad, Cobra A Nero Wolfe Mystery (dir. only).

TOLKIN, MICHAEL

Writer, Director, Producer. b. New York, NY, Oct. 17, 1950. e. Middlebury College, VT. Started as writer for LA Times, Village Voice, before becoming story editor on TV series Delta House. Novels: The Player (1988), Among the Dead (1992).
PICTURES: *Writer*: Let's Go (short), Gleaming the Cube, The Rapture (also dir.), The Player (also co-prod., actor; WGA Award, Academy Award nom.; Golden Globe nom. 1993), Deep Cover (also story), The New Age (also dir.), Deep Impact, Changing Lanes, Nine (writer, s.p.).
TELEVISION: *Movies: Writer:* The Burning Season (co-writer, Emmy Award nom. 1995), The Player, 1% (also prod.). *Series: Writer:* Taxi. *Dir.:* Masters of Science Fiction.

TOLL, JOHN

Cinematographer.
PICTURES: *Cam. Op.:* Tom Horn, Norma Rae, Zorro: The Gay Blade, Scarface, The Falcon and the Snowman, Peggy Sue Got Married, Black Widow, Tequila Sunrise, The Milagro Beanfield War, Blaze, Always, Shine a Light (doc.). *Cinematographer:* Wind, Legends of the Fall (Academy Award, ASC nom. 1995), Braveheart (Academy Award, ASC Award 1996), Jack, The Rainmaker, The Thin Red Line (Academy Award nom.; ASC Award 1999), Simpatico, Almost Famous, Captain Corelli's Mandolin, Vanilla Sky, Orange County, The Last Samurai (ASC

nom. 2004), Elizabethtown, Seraphim Falls, Rise: Blood Hunter, Gone Baby Gone (also dir. of photog.), Wanted (dir. of photog., NY), The Burning Plain, Tropic Thunder, It's Complicated, The Adjustment Bureau.
TELEVISION: *Movies:* The Boy Who Drank Too Much (cam. op.), Hiroshima Maiden, The Kid (ASC nom. 1990), Good Night Sweet Wife: A Murder in Boston. *Series:* The Young Riders, Breaking Bad (pilot, Emmy nom. 2008).

TOLMACH, MATT

Executive. Tolmach is a film production executive who's been running production for Columbia Pictures with colleague Doug Belgrad since 2003. In March 2008, the pair were promoted to co-presidents of Columbia Pictures, A Sony Pictures Entertainment Company, and extended their contracts with the studio through 2011. They report to Amy Pascal and Michael Lynton, co-chairmen of the studio. Since Tolmach and Belgrad became Columbia's presidents of production in 2003, films under their guidance have grossed approximately $7.6 billion. Twenty-five titles developed and produced by them and their team opened #1. During their tenure, they have overseen one of the most lucrative and successful eras in Columbia Pictures history, guiding a string of hits that includes the blockbuster "Spider-Man" franchise, "Casino Royale," "Superbad," "Hitch," "The DaVinci Code," "Talladega Nights: The Ballad of Ricky Bobby," "Ghost Rider," "The Pursuit of Happyness," "Click," "50 First Dates," "The Grudge," and many others. Belgrad and Tolmach jointly oversee Columbia's slate of 12 to 14 films annually. They are members of the Academy of Motion Picture Arts & Sciences and serve on the bd. of directors of the Environmental Media Association.

TOMEI, MARISA

Actress. b. Brooklyn, NY, Dec. 4, 1964. e. Boston U.
THEATRE: Beiruit (L.A.). *NY*: Daughters (Theatre World Award), The Comedy of Errors, What the Butler Saw, Slavs!, Salome. *Boston:* Wait Until Dark.
PICTURES: The Flamingo Kid (debut, 1984), Playing for Keeps, Oscar, Zandalee, My Cousin Vinny (Academy Award, best supporting actress, 1993), Chaplin, Untamed Heart, Equinox, The Paper, Only You, The Perez Family, Four Rooms, A Brother's Kiss, Unhook the Stars, Welcome to Sarajevo, The Women, The Slums of Beverly Hills, Only Love, Happy Accidents, The Watcher, What Women Want, King of the Jungle, Dirk and Betty, In the Bedroom (Academy Award nom.; Golden Globe nom. 2002), Someone Like You, Just A Kiss, The Guru, The Wild Thornberrys (voice), Anger Management, Alfie, Marilyn Hotchkiss' Ballroom Dancing and Charm School, Factotum, Loverboy, Danika, Grace Is Gone, Wild Hogs, War, Inc., Before the Devil Knows You're Dead, The Wrestler (Academy Award nom.; Golden Globe nom. 2009), Cyrus, The Lincoln Lawyer, Salvation Boulevard, Crazy, Stupid, Love.
TELEVISION: *Movies*: Supermom's Daughter, Parker Kane, My Own Country, Since You've Been Gone, Only Love, Jenifer, I Was a Network Star, The Rich Inner Life of Penelope Cloud. *Series*: As the World Turns, Leg Work (pilot), A Different World, Rescue Me. *Guest:* More than 82 appearances.

TOMLIN, LILY

Actress, Comedienne. r.n. Mary Jean Tomlin. b. Detroit, MI, Sept. 1, 1939. e. Wayne State U. (studied pre-med). Studied mime with Paul Curtis. Started inventing characters for comedy sketches in college, used them in cafe and night club dates in Detroit. 1965 went to NY performing skits on coffee-house circuit, landed job on The Garry Moore Show. Moved to L.A. where she appeared on The Music Scene. 1969, first appeared on Laugh-In TV series, gaining national attention with such characters as telephone operator Ernestine and child Edith Ann.
RECORDS: This Is a Recording (Grammy Award, 1971), Modern Scream, And That's the Truth, Lily Tomlin On Stage.
THEATRE: Appearing Nitely (special Tony Award, 1977), The Search for Signs of Intelligent Life in the Universe (1985, on B'way and on tour; Tony Award).
PICTURES: Nashville (debut, 1975; NY Film Critics Award; Academy Award nom.; 2 Golden Globe noms. 1976), The Late Show (Golden Globe nom. 1978), Moment by Moment, Nine to Five, The Incredible Shrinking Woman, All of Me (Golden globe nom. 1985), Big Business, The Search for Signs of Intelligent Life in the Universe, Shadows and Fog, The Player, Short Cuts Golden Globe Award, best ensemble cast 1994), The Beverly Hillbillies, Blue in the Face, Getting Away With Murder, The Celluloid Closet (documentary; narrator), Flirting With Disaster, Krippendorf's Tribe, Get Bruce (cameo), The Kid, Tea with Mussolini, Picking Up the Pieces, Orange County, I Heart Huckabee's, The Ant Bully (voice), The Last Guy on Earth, A Prairie Home Companion (also soundtrack performer), The Walker, The Pink Panther 2.
TELEVISION: *Movies*: And the Band Played On. *Specials*: Lily (Emmy Award as writer, 1974), Lily Tomlin (Emmy Award as writer, 1976), The Paul Simon Special (Emmy Award as writer, 1978), Lily: Sold Out! (also exec. prod.; Emmy Award as exec. prod., 1981), The Muppets Go to the Movies, Lily for President?, Live—and in Person, Funny You Don't Look 200, Free to Be... a Family, Edith Ann: A Few Pieces of the Puzzle (voice, exec. prod.), Edith Ann: Homeless Go Home (voice, exec. prod.), Edith Ann's Christmas: Just Say Noel (voice, exec. prod; Peabody Award), The Search for Signs of Inteligent Life in the Universe (2 Emmy noms. 1993), And the Band Played On (Emmy nom. 1994), The Celluloid Closet (Emmy nom. 1996). *Series*: The Music Scene (host, 1969), Rowan and Martin's Laugh-In (1969-73, Emmy nom. Golden Globe nom. 1972), Magic School Bus (voice for animated series; Emmy Award 1995), Murphy Brown, The West Wing (recurring guest role), Homicide: Life on the Street (recurring role, Emmy nom. 1996). Citizen Reno (exec. prod. only), 12 Miles of Bad Road, Desperate Housewives, Damages (Emmy nom. 2010). *Documentaries/Specials:* The Paul Simon Special (writer), Lily for President, Funny You Don't Look 200: A Constitutional Vaudeville. *Guest:* More than 189 appearances.

TOPOL

Actor. r.n. Chaim Topol. b. Tel-Aviv, Israel, Sept. 9, 1935. Received Golden Globe Award for most promising newcomer 1965.
THEATRE: Fiddler on the Roof (London, 1967, 1994-95 also U.K. tour; NY 1989: Tony nom.; Canada & Japan tour) Chicester Fest. Theatre: Caucasian Chalk Circle, Romanov and Juliet, Othello, View From the Bridge.
PICTURES: Sallah, Cast a Giant Shadow, Ervinka, Before Winter Comes, Fiddler on the Roof (Academy Award nom.; Golden Globe Award 1972), The Public Eye, Galileo, Flash Gordon, For Your Eyes Only, Roman Behemshechim (aka Again Forever), Time Elevator, Left Luggage.
TELEVISION: Movies: The Going Up of Daid Lev, House on Garibaldi Street, Queenie. Mini-series: The Winds of War, War and Remembrance. Series (BBC): It's Topol, Topol's Israel.

TORN, RIP

Actor. r.n. Elmore Torn, Jr. b. Temple, TX, Feb. 6, 1931. e. Texas A & M U., U. of TX. Served in army. Signed as understudy for lead in Cat on a Hot Tin Roof on Broadway.
THEATRE: Orpheus Descending, Sweet Bird of Youth (Theatre World Award), Daughter of Silence, Macbeth, Desire Under the Elms, Strange Interlude, Blues For Mr. Charlie, The Kitchen, The Deer Park (Obie Award), The Beard, The Cuban Thing, Dream of a Blacklisted Actor, The Dance of Death, Anna Christie.
PICTURES: Baby Doll (debut, 1956), A Face in the Crowd, Time Limit, Pork Chop Hill, King of Kings, Hero's Island, Sweet Bird of Youth, Critic's Choice, The Cincinnati Kid, One Spy Too Many, You're a Big Boy Now, Beach Red, Sol Madrid, Beyond the Law, Coming Apart, Tropic of Cancer, Maidstone, Slaughter, Payday, Crazy Joe, Birch Interval, The Man Who Fell to Earth, Nasty Habits, The Private Files of J. Edgar Hoover, Coma, The Seduction of Joe Tynan, Heartland, One Trick Pony, First Family, A Stranger is Watching, The Beastmaster, Jinxed, Airplane II: The Sequel, Cross Creek (Academy Award nom. 1984), Misunderstood, Songwriter, Flashpoint, City Heat, Summer Rental, Beer, Extreme Prejudice, Nadine, The Telephone (also dir.), Cold Feet, Hit List, Blind Curve, The Hunt for Red October, Defending Your Life, Silence Like Glass, Beautiful Dreamers, Hard Promises, Robocop 3, Dolly Dearest, Where the Rivers Flow North, Canadian Bacon, How to Make an American Quilt, Down Periscope, Hercules (voice), Trial and Error, Men in Black, The Mouse, Senseless, Wonder Boys, Men in Black Alien Attack (short), Freddy Got Fingered, Men in Black II, Rolling Kansas, Love Object, Welcome to Mooseport, Dodgeball: A True Underdog Story, Eulogy, Forty Shades of Blue, Retirement, Yours, Mine and Ours, Marie-Antoinette, Zoom, Cat Tale (voice), Bee Movie (voice), Lucky Days, August, The Afterlight, American Cowslip, The Afterlight, Bridge of Names, The Legend of Awesomest Maximus, 3 Weeks to Daytona, Men in Black III.
TELEVISION: *Movies*: The President's Plane Is Missing, Attack on Terror: The FBI vs. the Ku Klux Klan, Betrayal, Steel Cowboy, A Shining Season, Sophia Loren—Her Own Story, Rape and Marriage—The Rideout Case, Laguna Heat, When She Says No, The Execution, The Atlanta Child Murders (Emmy nom. 1985), Manhunt for Claude Dallas, J. Edgar Hoover, The King of Love, April Morning, Sweet Bird of Youth, Pair of Aces, By Dawn's Early Light, Another Pair of Aces, My Son Johnny, Death Hits the Jackpot, T Bone N Weasel, A Mother's Right: The Elizabeth Morgan Story, Dead Ahead: The Exxon Valdez Disaster, She Stood Alone: The Tailhook Scandal, Letter to My Killer, Balloon Farm, Seasons of Love, Maniac Magee. *Mini-series*: Blind Ambition, The Blue and the Gray, Heaven & Hell: North and South Book III, Heart of a Child. *Series*: The Larry Sanders Show (Emmy Award, 1996, 5 other noms.), Hercules (voice), Chicago Hope (recurring role, Emmy nom. 1996), Ghost Stories (voice), The Lyon's Den, 30 Rock (Emmy nom. 2008). *Guest*: More than 115 appearances.

TORNATORE, GIUSEPPE

Director, Writer. b. Bagheria, Sicily, Italy, 1956. Made directorial debut at age 16 with short film Il Carretto. 1978- 85, served as pres. of the CLTC filmmaking cooperative.
PICTURES: *Writer:* Cento giorni a Palermo, The Professor (also dir.), Cinema Paradiso (also dir.; DGA nom. 1991), Everybody's Fine (also dir.), A Pure Formality (also dir., song composer & editor), The Star Maker (aka L'uomo delle stelle; also dir.), The Legend of 1900 (La Leggenda del pianista sull'oceano; also dir.), Malèna (also dir.), La Sconosciuta (also dir.), The Unknown Woman (also dir.), Baaria - La porta del vento (also dir.),

Everybody's Fine (orig, s.p. 1990). *Director:* Especially on Sunday (segment). *Executive producer:* The Son of Bakunin. *Producer:* The Prince's Manuscript.
TELEVISION: Portrait of a Thief, Metting With Francesco Rosi, Sicilian Writers and Films, Il Diario di Guttuso, Ethnic Minorities in Sicily (Salerno Film Fest. Prize), A Hundred Days in Palermo (also writer, 2nd unit dir.).

TOWERS, CONSTANCE
Actress. b. Whitefish, MT, May 20, 1933. m. John Gavin, actor and one-time pres. of the Screen Actors Guild. Gavin was also former U.S. Ambassador to Mexico. e. Juilliard School of Music. Stage work on Broadway, incl. singing opposite Yul Brynner in a 1970s prod. of The King and I. She's alo toured in Concert with John Raitt, 1998.
THEATRE: *B'way*: Ari, Anya, Engagement Baby, The King and I (1977-79 opp. Yul Brynner), Showboat. *Regional*: Steel Magnolias, Follies, Sound of Music, I Do I Do, Mame, 110 In the Shade, Carousel, Oklahoma, Dumas & Son, Guys & Dolls, Oh Coward.
PICTURES: Bring Your Smile Along, Horse Soldiers, Sergeant Rutledge, Fate Is the Hunter, Shock Corridor, Naked Kiss, Sylvester, Fast Forward, Nutty Nut, The Next Karate Kid, The Relic, A Perfect Murder.
TELEVISION: *Movies*: The Renegade, Matlock: The Suspect. *Mini-series:* On Wings of Eagles. *Series*: Love Is a Many Splendored Thing, CBS Daytime 90 (Emmy nom. 1974), VTV, Capitol, 2000 Malibu Road, The Young and the Restless, Sunset Beach, General Hospital (Emmy nom. 2002). *Guest*: More than 65 appearances.

TOWNE, ROBERT
Writer, Director, Producer. b. Los Angeles, CA, Nov. 23, 1934. Raised in San Pedro. Was member of Warren Beatty's production staff on Bonnie and Clyde and contributed to that screenplay. Also uncredited, wrote Pacino-Brando garden scene in The Godfather; script doctor on Marathon Man, The Missouri Breaks and others. Received Writers Guild of America Award, Laurel Award for Screen Writing Achievement 1997.
PICTURES: *Writer*: The Last Woman on Earth (as Edward Wain), The Tomb of Ligeia, Villa Rides, The Last Detail (Academy Award nom.; WGA nom. 1974), Chinatown (Academy Award, Golden Globe Award, WGA Award 1974), Shampoo (co-s.p.; Academy Award nom.; WGA Award 1976), The Yazuka (co-s.p.), Personal Best (also dir., prod.), Greystoke: The Legend of Tarzan (s.p., uncredited, Academy Award nom.; WGA nom. 1985), Tequila Sunrise (also dir.), Days of Thunder, The Two Jakes, The Firm (co-s.p.), Love Affair (co-s.p.), Mission: Impossible (co-s.p.), Without Limits (also dir.), Mission: Impossible II, A Decade Under the Influence (doc.), Ask the Dust (also dir.).
TELEVISION: *Movies:* In the Company of Spies. *Mini-series:* Cadillac Desert. *Series:* The Outer Limits, Breaking Point, The Man from U.N.C.L.E. *Documentaries:* A Decade Under the Influence, Budd Boetticher: A Man Can Do That (actor), The Outsider, (actor).

TOWNSEND, ROBERT
Actor, Producer, Director, Writer. b. Chicago, IL, Feb. 6, 1957. e.Illinois State U., Hunter Coll. Veteran of Experimental Black Actors Guild and Second City. TV commercials; stand-up comedy at NY Improvisation; taped Evening at the Improv.
PICTURES: *Actor*: Willie and Phil, Summer Jobs, Streets of Fire, A Soldier's Story, American Flyers, Ratboy, Hollywood Shuffle (also prod., dir., co-s.p.), The Mighty Quinn, That's Adequate, The Five Heartbeats (also dir., exec. prod., co-s.p.), The Meteor Man (also dir., s.p., co-prod.), Joseph's Gift, The Taxman, The Script, Undercover Brother, Black Listed (also s.p. & dir.), Tao of the Golden Mask, Of Boys and Men (also exec. prod.). *Director:* Eddie Murphy Raw, B.A.P.S., Phantom Punch, Why We Laugh: Black Comedians on Black Comedy (doc., also co-exec. prod, writer).
TELEVISION: *Movies*: Women at West Point, Senior Trip!, In Love With an Older Woman, Love Songs, Jackie's Back, Up Up and Away, Holiday Heart, I Was a Teenage Faust, 10,000 Black Men Named George, CeCe Winans Straight Up (exec. prod.). *Mini-series*: Bliss, Great Drives. *Series*: Another Page (PBS series), Townsend Television, The Parent 'Hood (also co-creator, exec. prod.), Thousand Dollar Bee (exec. prod.), Spoken (exec. prod.), Souled Out (exec. prod.), Lisa Knight and the Round Table (exec. prod.), Black College Talent Hour (exec. prod.), Partners in Crime (dir., exec prod.), The Envy Life exec. prod.), Playhouse 22 exec. prod.), Thou$and Dollar Bee on the Road (exec. prod.), Partners in Crime: The Next Generation Atlanta (exec. prod.), South of Nowhere (exec. prod.), Musical Theatre of Hope (writer, dir.), Diary of a Single Mom (dir., exec. prod.). *Documentaries/Specials*: Robert Townsend and His Partners in Crime, Take No Prisoners: Robert Townsend and His Partners in Crime II (HBO), Why We Laugh: Black Comedians on Black Comedy (doc., co-exec. prod., dir.).

TRAVANTI, DANIEL J.
Actor. b. Kenosha, WI, March 7, 1940. e. U. of Wisconsin (B.A.), Loyola Marymount Univ. (M.A.), Yale School of Drama. Woodrow Wilson fellow, 1961. Formerly acted as Dan Travanty. On stage in Twigs, Othello, I Never Sang for My Father, Only Kidding, The Taming of the Shrew, Les Liaisons Dangereuses, A Touch of the Poet, Antony & Cleopatra, A Touch of the Poet.
PICTURES: St. Ives, Midnight Crossing, Millenium, Megaville, Weep No More My Lady, Just Cause, Siao Yu, Who Killed Teddy Bear, Something Sweet, Design.
TELEVISION: *Movies*: The Love War, Adam, Aurora, Murrow, Adam: His Song Continues, I Never Sang for My Father, Fellow Traveler, Howard Beach: Making the Case for Murder, Tagget, Eyes of a Witness, The Christmas Stallion, In the Shadows Someone's Watching, My Name is Kate, Wasp Woman, A Case of Libel, To Sir With Love II, Murder in My House. *Series*: General Hospital, Hill Street Blues (Emmy Awards, 1981, 1982, 4 other noms.; Golden Globe Award, 1981, 4 other noms.), Missing Persons, Poltergeist: The Legacy. *Guest:* More than 76 appearances.

TRAVIS, NANCY
Actress. b. New York, NY, Sept. 21, 1961. Raised in Baltimore, MD, and Farmingham, MA. e. NYU. Attended Circle-in-the-Square Theatre school. Acted with NY Amer. Jewish Theatre before landing role in touring prod. of Brighton Beach Memoirs.3
THEATRE: *NY*: It's Hard to Be a Jew, The Signal Season of Dummy Hoy, I'm Not Rappaport (B'way). Tour: Brighton Beach Memoirs. *La Jolla Playhouse*: My Children My Africa, Three Sisters.
PICTURES: Three Men and a Baby (debut, 1987), Married to the Mob, Eight Men Out, Internal Affairs, Loose Cannons, Air America, Three Men and a Little Lady, Passed Away, Chaplin, The Vanishing, So I Married an Axe Murderer, Greedy, Destiny Turns on the Radio, Fluke, Bogus, The Sisterhood of the Traveling Pants, The Jane Austen Book Club.
TELEVISION: *Movies*: Malice in Wonderland, Harem, I'll Be Home for Christmas, Body Language, My Last Love (prod.), Talk Show Diaries, Running Mates, The Party Never Stops: Diary of a Binge Drinker, Safe Harbor, Pregnancy Pact, In My Shoes. *Mini-series*: Rose Red. *Series*: Almost Perfect, Work with Me, Becker, Boys Life, The Bill Engvall Show. *Special*: High School Narc (ABC Afterschool Special).

TRAVOLTA, JOHN
Actor. b. Englewood, NJ, Feb. 18, 1954. m. actress Kelly Preston. First stage role in Who Will Save the Plowboy? Did off-B'way prod. of Rain; then on Broadway in Grease (also on tour for 10 months), Over Here (with the Andrew Sisters). Author of Staying Fit, 1984. Received Golden Globe Henrietta Award 1979.
PICTURES: The Devil's Rain (debut, 1975), Carrie, Saturday Night Fever (Academy Award nom.; Golden Globe nom. 1978), Grease (Golden Globe nom. 1979), Moment by Moment, Urban Cowboy, Blow Out, Staying Alive, Two of a Kind, Perfect, The Experts, Look Who's Talking, Look Who's Talking Too, Shout, Eyes of an Angel, Look Who's Talking Now, Pulp Fiction (Academy Award nom.; Golden Globe nom. 1995), White Man's Burden, Get Shorty (Golden Globe Award 1996), Broken Arrow, Phenomenon, Michael, Face/Off, She's So Lovely (also exec. prod.), Mad City, The Thin Red Line, A Civil Action, Primary Colors (Golden Globe nom. 1999), The General's Daughter, Our Friend, Martin (voice), Forever Hollywood, Battlefield Earth (also prod.), Lucky Numbers, Swordfish, Domestic Disturbance, Basic, Austin Powers in Goldmember (cameo), The Punisher, A Love Song for Bobby Long, Ladder 49, Be Cool, 2004: A Light Knight's Odyssey (voice), The Shaggy Dog (soundtrack performer), Lonely Hearts, Lonely Hearts, Wild Hogs, Hairspray (Golden Globe nom. 2008), Old Dogs, Bolt (voice), The Taking of Pelham 123, From Paris with Love.
TELEVISION: *Movies*: The Boy in the Plastic Bubble, Chains of Gold, Boris & Natasha (cameo). *Series*: Welcome Back Kotter. *Documentaries/Specials*: The Dumb Waiter. *Guest*: More than 215 appearances.

TREUT, MONIKA
Director, Writer, Editor. b. West Germany, April 6, 1954.
PICTURES: Seduction: The Cruel Woman, Virgin Machine, My Father is Coming, Ai-mei (also co-prod.). *Documentaries:* Female Misbehavior, Erotique ("Taboo Parlor" segment), Danish Girls Show Everything (dir. only), Didn't Do It for Love, Gendernauts (also prod.), Warrior of Light (also prod.), Jump Cut: A Travel Diary (also prod., cinematographer), Axensprung (dir. only), Tigerwomen Grow Wings (also prod.), Ghosted (also co-prod.).
TELEVISION: *Documentary:* Made in Taiwan.

TRILLING, WENDI
Executive. e. B.A. degree in screen studies, Clark University, Worcester, MA. Began career as a copywriter at BBK Advertising in Boston. Joined CBS in 1990 in the current programs dept. Named mgr., comedy/drama series development in 1992 and upped to associate dir., comedy development in 1993. She was promoted to dir., comedy development in 1994; named a vice president in 1997 and elevated to senior v.p., comedy development in June 2000. Trilling was named to her current post as executive v.p., comedy development, CBS Entertainment in Sept. 2004. Trilling's programming triumphs include CBS' long running signature comedy: "Everybody Loves Raymond."

TRINTIGNANT, JEAN-LOUIS
Actor. b. Piolenc, France, Dec. 11, 1930. Theatre debut: 1951,

To Each According to His Hunger. Then Mary Stuart, Macbeth (at the Comedie de Saint-Etienne). 1955 screen debut.
PICTURES: Si Tous Les Gars du Monde, La Loi des Rues, And God Created Woman, Club de Femmes, Les Liaisons Dangereuses, L'Estate Violente, Austerlitz, La Millieme Fenetre, Pleins Feux sur L'Assasin, Coeur Battant, L'Atlantide, The Game of Truth, Horace 62, Les Sept Peches Capitaux (7 Capital Sins), Le Combat dans L'Ile, The Easy Life, Il Successo, Nutty Naughty Chateau, Les Pas Perdus, La Bonne Occase, Mata-Hari, Meurtre a L'Italienne, La Longue Marche, Un Jour a Paris, Is Paris Burning?, The Sleeping Car Murders, A Man and a Woman, Enigma, Safari Diamants, Trans-Europ-Express, Mon Amour, Mon Amour, Un Homme a Abattre, La Morte Ha Fatto L'Uovo, Les Biches, Grand Silence, Z, Ma Nuit Chez Maud (My Night at Maud's), The Conformist, The Crook, Without Apparent Motive, The Outside Man, The French Conspiracy, Simon the Swiss, Agression, Les Violons du Bal, The Sunday Woman, Under Fire, La Nuit de Varennes, Long Live Life!, Next Summer, Departure, Return, The Man With the Silver Eyes, Femme Je Personne, Confidentially Yours, A Man and a Woman: 20 Years Later, La Vallee Fantome; Rendezvous, Bunker Palace Hotel, Three Colors: Red, The City of Lost Children, Fiesta, Un homme est tombe dans la rue, L'Insoumise, Les Bidochon, C'est jamais loin, Self-Made Hero, Tykho Moon, Those Who Love Me Can Take the Train, Chez Gino.

TRIPPLEHORN, JEANNE
Actress. b. Tulsa, OK, 1963. e. Julliard School of Drama. On stage at NY's Public Theatre in The Big Funk, 'Tis Pity She's a Whore.
PICTURES: Basic Instinct (debut, 1992), The Night We Never Met, The Firm, Waterworld, Reality Bites (cameo), Office Killer, 'Til There Was You, Very Bad Things, Snitch, Sliding Doors, Steal This Movie, Mickey Blue Eyes, Timecode, Paranoid, Relative Values, Dial 9 For Love, Swept Away, The Amateurs, Winged Creatures, Grey Gardens, Crazy on the Outside, Morning.
TELEVISION: *Movies*: The Perfect Tribute, Old Man, My Brother's Keeper, Word of Honor, Grey Gardens (Emmy nom. 2009). *Series:* Big Love.

TRUMBULL, DOUGLAS
Director, Cinematographer. b. Los Angeles, CA, Apr. 8, 1942. Inventor Showscan Film process. Produced and directed Universal Studios attraction Back to the Future: The Ride; Luxor Las Vegas attractions. Won Academy Award for scientifc and engineering 1993. *Director:* Showscan short films New Magic, Let's Go, Big Ball, Leonardo's Dream, Night of the Dreams, Chevy Collector. Former Vice Chmn., The Imax Corp. Founded Entertainment Design Workshop in 1997 and currently is pres. & CEO. Received Academy Award for Scientific and Engineering Excellence 1993.
PICTURES: *Cinematographer.* 2001: A Space Odyssey, Silent Running (also dir.), The Andromeda Strain, Close Encounters of the Third Kind (Academy Award nom. 1978), Star Trek: The Motion Picture (Academy Award nom. 1980), Blade Runner (Academy Award nom. 1983), Brainstorm (also dir., prod.).
TELEVISION: *Movie:* The Starlost: Deception (exec. prod.). *Series:* The Starlost (prod.).

TSAI, MING-LIANG
Director, Writer. b. Kuching, Malaysia, Oct. 27, 1957.
PICTURES: Rebels of the Neon God, Vive L'Amour (Golden Horse Award, 1994), The River, Last Dance (dir. only), Dong, Fish Underground, Ni neibian jidian, What Time Is It Over There?, The Skywalk Is Gone, Good Bye Dragon Inn, The Missing (exec. prod. only), Tian bian yi duo yun, The Wayward Cloud, I Don't Want to Sleep Alone (also cinematographer), To Each His Cinema (segment dir.), Visages (also prod.), Face.

TSUJIHARA, KEVIN
Executive. e. Bachelor's degree, business admin., Univ. of Southern California. M.B.A., Stanford University. In between earning his degrees, Tsujihara spent four years in Ernst & Young's entertainment division working in the audit and merger and acquisitions areas. Upon graduation, he founded QuickTax, Inc., a company specializing in the electronic filing of tax and financial data. He joined Warner Bros.' film studio in 1994 to assist in the management of the company's interest in Six Flags. Promotions within Warner Bros. followed: to v.p., corporate projects; senior v.p., strategic planning and development; executive v.p., corporate business development & strategy; executive v.p., new media (He also had corporate oversight of Warner Bros. Online.) In October 2005 Warner Bros. Entertainment realigned its businesses involved in the digital delivery of entertainment content to consumers to create the Warner Bros. Home Entertainment Group and named Tsujihara its president and is the position he holds today. The group includes home video, online, wireless, games and anti-piracy and emerging technologies operations.

TUBB, BARRY
Actor. b. Snyder, TX, Feb. 13, 1963. Former rodeo star. Studied acting at Amer. Conservatory Theatre in SF.
THEATRE: Sweet Sue (B'way), The Authentic Life of Billy the Kid.
PICTURES: Mask, The Legend of Billie Jean, Top Gun, Valentino Returns, Warm Summer Rain, Guilty By Suspicion, The Big Day, American Outlaws, Grand Champion (dir. only), Truce, The Three Burials of Melquiades Estrada, The Legend of Hell's Gate: An American Conspiracy, Clown Hunt (also dir., writer), Baghdad Texas.
TELEVISION: *Movies*: Consenting Adult, The Billionaire Boys Club, Without Her Consent, Temple Grandin. *Mini-series*: Lonesome Dove, Return to Lonesome Dove. *Series*: Bay City Blues, Hill Street Blues, Friday Night Lights.

TUCCI, STANLEY
Actor. b. Peekskill, NY, Jan. 11, 1960. e. SUNY.
THEATRE: *B'way:* The Misanthrope, Brighton Beach Memoirs, The Iceman Cometh. Moon Over Miami, Scapin, Dalliance, Balm in Gilead.
PICTURES: Who's That Girl, Monkey Shines, Slaves of New York, Fear Anxiety and Depression, The Feud, Quick Change, Men of Respect, Billy Bathgate, Beethoven, Prelude to a Kiss, The Public Eye, In the Soup, Undercover Blues, The Pelican Brief, It Should Happen to You, Mrs. Parker and the Vicious Circle, Kiss of Death, A Modern Affair, The Daytrippers, Big Night (also co-dir; Ind't Spirit Awards, 1997.), Life During Wartime, The Eighteenth Angel, Deconstructing Harry, A Life Less Ordinary, Montana, The Imposters (also prod., dir., s.p.), A Midsummer Night's Dream, Joe Gould's Secret (also prod., dir.), In Too Deep, Sidewalks of New York, The Whole Shebang, America's Sweethearts, The Road to Perdition, Big Trouble, Maid in Manhattan, The Core, Spin, The Life and Death of Peter Sellers, The Terminal, Shall We Dance?, Robots (voice), Lucky Number Slevin, Cat Tale (voice) Four Last Songs, The Devil Wears Prada, The Hoax, Four Last Songs, Blind Date (also prod., dir.), What Just Happened?, Kit Kittredge: An American Girl, Swing Vote, Space Chimps (voice), The Lovely Bones, The Tale of Despereaux (voice), Saint John of Las Vegas (exec. prod.), Julie & Julia, The Lovely Bones (Academy Award nom.; Golden Globe nom. 2010), Easy A, Margin Call, Burlesque, Captain America: The First Avenger.
TELEVISION: *Movies:* Kojak: The Price of Justice, Revealing Evidence: Stalking the Honolulu Strangler, Winchell (Emmy Award, Golden Globe Award 1999), Conspiracy (Emmy nom.; Golden Globe Award 2001). *Series:* The Street, Wiseguy, Murder One (Emmy nom. 1996), Bull, 3 lbs., ER (Emmy nom. 2008). *Documentary:* Freedom: A History of Us (series). *Guest:* More than 67 appearances.

TUCKER, MICHAEL
Actor. b. Baltimore, MD, Feb. 6, 1944. m. actress Jill Eikenberry. e. Carnegie Tech. Drama Sch. Worked in regional theatre (Long Wharf, Washington's Arena Stage, Milwaukee Rep.) and with the NY Shakespeare Festival in Trelawney of the Wells, Comedy of Errors, Measure for Measure, The Merry Wives of Windsor. Also prod. revival of El Grande de Coca Cola (1986).
THEATRE: Moonchildren, Modigliani, The Goodbye People, The Rivals, Mother Courage, Waiting for Godot, Oh What a Lovely War, I'm Not Rappaport (American Place Theatre).
PICTURES: A Night Full of Rain (debut, 1977), An Unmarried Woman, Eyes of Laura Mars, Diner, The Goodbye People, The Purple Rose of Cairo, Radio Days, Tin Men, Checking Out, For Love or Money, D2: The Mighty Ducks, 'Til There Was You, Cold Souls, 25 Hill.
TELEVISION: *Movies:* Concealed Enemies, Vampire, Assault and Matrimony, Day One, Spy, Too Young to Die?, Casey's Gift: For Love of a Child, The Secret Life of Archie's Wife, In the Nick of Time, A Town Torn Apart, The Alibi, Growing Up Brady, L.A. Law: The Movie, Emile Norman: By His Own Design (prod.). *Series*: L.A. Law (3 Emmy noms.; 2 Golden Globe noms.). *Documentaries/Specials*: Love Sex... and Marriage, A Family Again, On Hope, Emile Norman: By His Own Design (prod.). *Guest:* More than 45 appearances.

TUCKERMAN, DAVID R.
Executive. b. Perth Amboy, NJ, Nov. 9, 1949. e. Monmouth College, F.L.U. 1967-70; B.S.B.A. Entered industry with A.I.T. Theatres, 1967; gen. mgr., Music Makers Theatres, 1973; v.p., Leigh Group, MMT, head film buyer, 1976; sr. v.p., MMT, 1980; Loews Film Buyer, 1986; Loews (now Sony) v.p. film, 1993. U.A., Head Film Buyer, Southeast region, 1998. New Line Cinema, Exec. V.P. and Gen. Sales Mgr., 1999. President of Theatrical Distribution, New Line Cinema, 2000-present. *Member:* SMPTE, Variety Int., MPBC, AFI, Motion Picture Pioneers.

TURMAN, LAWRENCE
Producer. b. Los Angeles, CA, Nov. 28, 1926. e. UCLA. In textile business 5 years, then joined Kurt Frings Agency; left in 1960 to form Millar-Turman Prods.
PICTURES: *Producer*: The Young Doctors, I Could Go on Singing, The Best Man. Formed own prod. co., Lawrence Turman, Inc., to make The Flim-Flam Man, The Graduate (Academy Award nom. 1968), Pretty Poison (exec. prod.), The Great White Hope, The Marriage of a Young Stockbroker (also dir.), The Nickel Ride (exec. prod.), The Drowning Pool, First Love, Heroes, Walk Proud, Tribute, Caveman, The Thing, Second Thoughts (also dir.), Mass Appeal, The Mean Season, Short Circuit, Running Scared, Short Circuit 2, Full Moon in Blue Water, Gleaming the Cube, The Getaway, The River Wild, The Getaway, Booty Call (exec. prod.), American History X (exec. prod.), Kingdom Come, What's the Worst That Could Happen?

(also exec. prod.).
TELEVISION: *Co-prod. with David Foster*: The Gift of Love, News at Eleven, Between Two Brothers. *Producer*: The Morning After, She Lives, Unwed Father. *Co-exec. prod.*: Jesse. *Executive producer*: Miracle on the Mountain: The Kincaid Family Story.

TURNER, JANINE
Actress. r.n. Janine Gauntt. b. Lincoln, NE, Dec. 6, 1962. Raised in Texas. Studied dance, joined Forth Worth Ballet. Started modeling at age 15 in NYC, enrolled in Professional Children's School. First major acting job was on series Dallas. On stage in Full Moon and High Tide in the Ladies Room.
PICTURES: Young Doctors in Love, Knights of the City, Tai-Pan, Monkey Shines, Steel Magnolias, The Ambulance, Cliffhanger, The Curse of the Inferno, Leave It to Beaver, Dr. T and the Women, Maggie's Passage, Black Widow.
TELEVISION: *Movies*: Stolen Women Captured Hearts, Circle of Deceit, Beauty, Fatal Error, A Secret Affair, Walker, Texas Ranger: Trial by Fire, Primal Doubt. *Series*: Behind the Screen, General Hospital (1982-83), Another World (1986-87), Santa Barbara (1984), Northern Exposure (Emmy nom. 1993, 3 Golden Globe noms.), Strong Medicine, Friday Night Lights.

TURNER, KATHLEEN
Actress. b. Springfield, MO, June 19, 1954. e. U. of Maryland, SMSU.
THEATRE: *B'way*: Gemini, Cat on a Hot Tin Roof (Theatre World Award), Love Letters, Mr. T, Toyer!, Gemini, Indiscretions. *Regional*: Camille (Long Wharf), A Midsummer Night's Dream (DC), Tallulah!, Toyer (DC), Who's Afraid of Virginia Woolf? (Tony Award nom., 2005), The Exonerated, Crimes of the Heart (dir.). *London:* Who's Afraid of Virginia Woolf?", The Graduate. Autobiography: Send Yourself Roses.
PICTURES: Body Heat (debut, 1981, Golden Globe nom. 1982), The Man With Two Brains, Romancing the Stone (Golden Globe Award 1985), Crimes of Passion, A Breed Apart, Prizzi's Honor (Golden globe Award 1986), The Jewel of the Nile, Peggy Sue Got Married (Academy Award nom.; Golden Globe nom. 1987), Julia and Julia, Switching Channels, Who Framed Roger Rabbit (voice), The Accidental Tourist, The War of the Roses (Golden Globe nom. 1990), V.I. Warshawski, Naked in New York, House of Cards, Undercover Blues, Serial Mom, Moonlight & Valentino, Bad Baby (voice), A Simple Wish, The Real Blonde, Baby Geniuses, The Virgin Suicides, Beautiful, Prince of Central Park, Monster House (voice), Marley & Me, Shrinking Charlotte, The Perfect Family.
TELEVISION: *Movies*: Friends at Last, Legalese, Cinderella. *Series*: Ancient Mysteries (hostess), The Doctors, Californication. *Documentaries/Specials*: American Cinema (narr.), Love in the Ancient World (hostess), American Masters: Dashiell Hammett: Detective-Writer (narrator), Dear America: Letters Home From Vietnam (reader), In Bad Taste (as herself). *Director*: Leslie's Folly. *Guest:* More than 111 appearances.

TURNER, TED
Executive. r.n. Robert Edward Turner. b. Cincinnati, OH., Nov. 19, 1938. e. Brown U. Began career in Savannah in family's outdoor adv. business, selling space on billboards. Inherited co. in 1963 and in 1970 entered broadcasting with purchase of a failing TV station in Atlanta which he turned into WTBS, a "super station" which in 1994 reached 95% of U.S. homes equipped with cable. 1980, established CNN a 24-hr. cable news service. Purchased MGM film library. Co-owner of two professional sports teams in Atlanta: Braves (baseball) and Hawks (basketball). Started Headline News, 1982; CNN International begins global news service, 1985; Turner Network Television, 1988; Sportsouth, 1990; Turner Foundation is formed, 1991. Also named Time Magazine's Man of the Year in 1991. CNN Airport Network launched in 1992. Cartoon Network launched in 1992. Acquired Castle Rock Entertainment in 1993 and also launches TNT and Cartoon Network in Europe; merger with New Line Cinema, 1994; started Turner Classic Movies, 1994; CNNfn Financial Network, 1995. Turner Broadcasting System, Inc. and Time Warner Inc. merge in 1996 with Turner becoming vice chmn. of the new entity. He oversaw the organization's cable networks division, which included the assets of Turner Broadcasting System, Inc. (TBS, Inc.), the CNN Newsgroup, as well as Home Box Office, Cinemax, and the company's interests in Comedy Central and Court TV. He also over saw New Line Cinema and the company's professional sports teams-the Atlanta Braves, Atlanta Hawks and Atlanta Thrashers. From Jan. 2001-May 2003 he was vice chmn. of AOL Time Warner. In June 2001, Turner announced the creation of two independent film production companies based in Atlanta, Ted Turner Pictures and Ted Turner Documentaries. In 2006 he resigned from the Time Warner boardroom. In Jan. 2001, Turner and former U.S. Senator Sam Nunn founded the Nuclear Threat Initiative (NTI). NTI's mission is to strengthen global security by reducing the risk of use and preventing the spread of nuclear, biological and chemical weapons. NTI seeks to raise public awareness, serve as a catalyst for new thinking and take direct action to reduce these threats. Initially supported by a pledge from Turner and other private contributions, NTI is now classified as a 501 (c) 3 public charity. Currently Turner is Pres./CEO WTBS. Turner is the recipient of numerous honorary degrees, industry awards and civic honors, including being Cable and Broadcasting's Man of the Century in 1999. Turner was inducted into the Cable TV Hall of Fame in 1999, and in June 2000 he received the World Ecology Award from the University of Missouri. In October 1995, Turner accepted the Atlanta Braves' first World Championship trophy on behalf of the team. In August 2000, he was inducted into the Atlanta Braves Hall of Fame.

TURTURRO, JOHN
Actor. b. Brooklyn, NY, Feb. 28, 1957. e. SUNY/New Paltz; Yale Drama School, 1983. m. actress Katherine Borowitz. Worked in regional theatre and off-B'way.
THEATRE: Danny and the Deep Blue Sea (Obie & Theatre World Awards, 1985), Men Without Dates, Tooth of the Crime, La Puta Viva, Chaos and Hard Times, The Bald Soprano, Of Mice and Men, The Resistible Rise of Arturo Ui, Death of a Salesman (B'way debut, 1984), Souls of Naples, A Spanish Play (dir.), Life (x) 3.
PICTURES: Raging Bull (debut, 1980), Exterminator II, The Flamingo Kid, Desperately Seeking Susan, To Live and Die in L.A., Hannah and Her Sisters, Gung Ho, Off Beat, The Color of Money, The Sicilian, Five Corners, Do the Right Thing, Mo' Better Blues, State of Grace, Miller's Crossing, Men of Respect, Jungle Fever, Barton Fink (Cannes Film Fest. Award), Brain Donors, Mac (also dir., co-s.p.), Fearless, Being Human, Quiz Show (Golden Globe nom. 1995), Search and Destroy, Clockers, Unstrung Heroes, Grace of My Hear, Box of Moonlight, Girl 6, The Search for One-eye Johnny, Lesser Prophets, Animals, O.K. Garage, Illuminata, The Big Lebowski, He Got Game, Rounders, The Cradle Will Rock, Summer of Sam, Company Man, O Brother, Where Art Thou?, Two Thousand and None, The Man Who Cried, The Luzhin Defence, Monkeybone, Thirteen Conversations About One Thing, Collateral Damage, Mr. Deeds, Rosy-Fingered Dawn: A Film on Terrence Malick, Fear the X, Secret Passage, Anger Management, Secret Window, 2 B Perfectly Honest, She Hate Me, The Moon and the Son (short; voice), Romance & Cigarettes (also s.p. & dir.), Quelques jours en septembre, The Good Shepherd, Slipstream, Transformers, Beyond Wiseguys: Italian Americans & the Movies (doc.,also exec. prod.), What Just Happened?, Margot at the Wedding, You Don't Mess with the Zohan, Miracle at St. Anna, The Taking of Pelham 123, Nutcracker in 3D, Passione (dir.), Transformers: Revenge of the Fallen, Somewhere Tonight, Transformers 3.
TELEVISION: *Movies:* Backtrack, Sugartime, Monday Night Mayhem. *Mini-series*: The Fortunate Pilgrim. *Series:* Monk (recurring role, Emmy Award 2004), The Bronx Is Burning. *Guest:* More than 55 appearances.

TUSHINGHAM, RITA
Actress. b. Liverpool, England, March 14, 1940. Student at Liverpool Playhouse.
THEATRE: The Giveaway, Lorna and Ted, Mistress of Novices, The Undiscovered Country, Mysteries.
PICTURES: A Taste of Honey (debut, 1961; BFA Award, Golden Globe Award 1963), The Leather Boys, A Place to Go, Girl With Green Eyes, The Knack... and How to Get It (Golden Globe nom. 1966), Doctor Zhivago, The Trap, Smashing Time, Diamonds for Breakfast, The Guru, The Bed Sitting Room, Straight on Till Morning, The Case of Laura C., Where Do You Go From Here?, Situation, Instant Coffee, The Human Factor, Rachel's Man, The Slum Boy, The Black Journal, Bread Butter and Jam, Mysteries, Felix Krull, Spaghetti Thing, Dream to Believe, Flying, Seeing Red, The Housekeeper, Resurrected, Dante and Beatrice in Liverpool, Hard Days Hard Nights, Paper Marriage, Desert Lunch, An Awfully Big Adventure, The Boy From Mercury, Under the Skin, Swing, Out of Depth, Being Julia, Telstar, The Calling, Seamonsters, Out of the Night.
TELEVISION: *Movies:* Little Red Riding Hood, Green Eyes, Pippi Longstocking, Dieter Gütt - ein Journalist, Spending Nights with Joan, The Stretford Wives, Life Beyond the Box: Margo, Marple: The Sittaford Mystery, Angel Cake. *Mini-series:* Bekenntnisse des Hochstaplers Felix Krull. *Series:* No Strings, Bread.

TYKWER, TOM
Director, Writer, Composer. b. Wuppertal, Germany, May 23, 1965.
PICTURES: Deadly Maria (also prod.), Winter Sleeper, Life Is All You Get (s.p. only), Winter Sleepers, Run Lola Run, Gigantics (prod.), Any Given Sunday, Der Krieger und die Kaiserin (The Princess and the Warrior), Head Over Heels, Heaven, True (short; composer, s.p. & dir.), Lautlos (prod.), Paris, je t'aime, Perfume: The Story of a Murderer (s.p.), Ein Freund von mir (prod.), The Condemned (soundtrack performer), Das Herz ist ein dunkler Wald (prod.), The International (dir.), Inglourious Basterds (translater for German), Soul Boy (supvr. dir., prod.), Drei (dir.).

TYLER, LIV
Actress. b. July, 1, 1977. Daughter of fashion model Bebe Buell and musician Steven Tyler. Began as a model at age 14.
PICTURES: Silent Fall (debut, 1994), Empire Records, Heavy, Stealing Beauty, That Thing You Do!, Inventing the Abbotts, U-Turn, Armageddon, Plunkett & MacLeane, Cookie's Fortune, Eugene Onegin, Franky Goes to Hollywood (documentary short), Dr. T and the Women, One Night at McCool's, The Lord of the Rings: The Fellowship of the Ring, The Lord of the Rings: The Two Towers, The Lord of the Rings: The Return of the King, Jersey Girl,

Lonesome Jim, Reign Over Me, Smother, The Strangers, The Incredible Hulk, The Strangers 2, Super, Max Rose, The Ledge.

TYRRELL, SUSAN
Actress. b. San Francisco, CA, March 18, 1946. Made first prof. appearance with Art Carney in summer theatre tour prod. of Time Out for Ginger. Worked in off-B'way prods. and as waitress in coffee house before attracting attention in Lincoln Center Repertory Co. prods. of A Cry of Players, The Time of Your Life, Camino Real.
THEATRE: The Knack, Futz, Father's Day, A Coupla White Chicks Sitting Around Talking, The Rotten Life.
PICTURES: Shoot Out (debut, 1971), The Steagle, Been Down So Long It Looks Like Up to Me, Shoot Out, Fat City (Academy Award nom. 1973), Catch My Soul, Zandy's Bride, The Killer Inside Me, Islands in the Stream, Andy Warhol's Bad, I Never Promised You a Rose Garden, Another Man Another Chance, September 30, 1955, Racquet, Loose Shoes, Forbidden Zone, Subway Riders, Night Warning, Fast-Walking, Liar's Moon, Tales of Ordinary Madness, Fire and Ice (voice), Angel, The Killers, Avenging Angel, Flesh and Blood, The Chipmunk Adventure (voice), The Offspring, Big Top Pee-Wee, Tapeheads, The Underachievers, Far From Home, Cry-Baby, Motorama, Powder, Digital Man, Poison Ivy: The Last Seduction, Pink As the Day She Was Born, Relax...It's Just Sex, Buddy Boy, Masked and Anonymous, Forbidden Zone 2: The Forbidden Galaxy.
TELEVISION: *Movies*: Lady of the House, Willow B: Women in Prison, Midnight Lace, Jealousy, Thompson's Last Run, Poker Alice, The Christmas Star, Poker Alice, Windmills of the Gods. *Mini-series*: If Tomorrow Comes. *Series*: Open All Night, Extreme Ghostbusters (voice).

TYSON, CICELY
Actress. b. New York, NY, Dec. 19, 1933. e. NYU. Studied at Actor's Studio. Former secretary and model. Co-founder, Dance Theatre of Harlem.
THEATRE: The Blacks, Moon on a Rainbow Shawl, Tiger Tiger Burning Bright, The Corn Is Green.
PICTURES: A Man Called Adam (debut, 1966), The Comedians, The Heart Is a Lonely Hunter, Sounder (Academy Award nom. ; Golden Globe nom. 1973), The Blue Bird, The River Niger, A Hero Ain't Nothin' But a Sandwich, The Concorde—Airport '79, Bustin' Loose, Fried Green Tomatoes, Hoodlum, Because of Winn Dixie, Diary of a Mad Black Woman, Madea's Family Reunion, Idlewild, Why Did I Get Married Too?, The Help.
TELEVISION: *Movies*: Marriage: Year One, The Autobiography of Miss Jane Pittman (2 Emmy Awards, 1974), Just An Old Sweet Song, Wilma, A Woman Called Moses, The Marva Collins Story (Emmy nom. 1982), Benny's Place, Playing with Fire, Acceptable Risks, Samaritan: The Mitch Snyder Story, The Women of Brewster Place, Heat Wave, The Kid Who Loved Christmas, Duplicates, When No One Would Listen, House of Secrets, Oldest Living Confederate Widow Tells All (Emmy Award 1994), Mama Flora's Family, Road to Galveston, Bridge of Time, Riot, The Price of Heaven, Ms. Scrooge, Always Outnumbered, A Lesson Before Dying (Emmy nom. 1999), Aftershock: Earthquake in New York, Jewel, The Rosa Parks Story, Relative Stranger (Emmy nom. 2009). *Mini-series*: Roots (Emmy nom. 1977), King (Emmy nom. 1978). *Series*: East Side West Side, The Guiding Light, Sweet Justice (Emmy nom. 1995). *Pilot*: Clippers. *Guest:* More than 122 appearances.

U

UGGAMS, LESLIE
Singer. b. New York, NY, May 25, 1943. e. Professional Children's School, grad., 1960. Juilliard School of Music. Began singing career at age 5. TV debut as Ethel Waters' niece on Beulah. Also on Johnny Olsen's TV kids at age 7, Your Show of Shows as singer, 1953; Recording artist for Columbia Records, Atlantic, Motown. Wrote The Leslie Uggams Beauty Book (1962).
THEATRE: Hallelujah Baby (Tony & Theatre World Awards, 1968), Her First Roman, Blues in the Night, Jerry's Girls, Anything Goes (natl. co. & Bdwy), Stringbean (Dallas), Into the Woods (Long Beach, CA).
PICTURES: Two Weeks in Another Town, Poor Pretty Eddie, Black Girl, Heartbreak Motel, Skyjacked, Sugar Hill, Broadway: The Golden Age by the Legends Who Were There (doc.), Toe to Toe.
TELEVISION: *Movie*: Sizzle. *Mini-series*: Roots (Emmy nom.; Golden Globe nom. 1977), Backstairs at the White House, Freedom to Speak. *Series*: Sing Along With Mitch, The Leslie Uggams Show (1969), Fantasy (Emmy Award, 1984), All My Children. *Documentaries/Specials*: The Book of Lists (co-host). I Love Men, 'S Wonderful - 'S Marvelous - 'S Gershwin, Sinatra and Friends, Placido Domingo Steppin' Out With the Ladies, Jerry Herman Tribute, Rooms for Improvement. *Guest*: More than 87 appearances.

ULANO, MARK
Sound.
PICTURES: Think Me Nothing, Hospital Massacre, Time Walker, Cujo, Lovelines, Once Bitten, Sweet Hearts Dance, Desperado, Rough Magic, The Winner, From Dusk Till Dawn, Titanic (Academy Award, Best Sound Mixing, CAS Award 1998), The Pest, Austin Powers: International Man of Mystery, Jackie Brown, The Patriot, Molly, Making Sandwiches, 68, Stuart Little, Molly, Spy Kids, The Majestic, Blue Crush, The Hot Chick, Two Paths, Kill Bill: Volume 1, Kill Bill: Volume 2, A Cinderella Story, The Wedding Crashers, Zathura: A Space Adventure, Grandma's Boy, Big Momma's House 2, Talladega Nights: The Ballad of Ricky Bobby, Rocky Balboa, Norbit, Disturbia, Grindhouse, Iron Man (CAS nom. 2009), State of Play, Terminator Salvation, Inglourious Basterds (Academy Award nom. 2010), Iron Man 2, The Tourist, The Next Three Days, Cowboys & Aliens.
TELEVISION: *Movies*: Uncommon Valor, High School U.S.A., The Parade, Shattered Vows, The Cartier Affair, The Long Hot Summer, Between the Darkness and the Dawn, Rags to Riches, Shattered Spirits, A Time to Triumph, Can You Feel Me Dancing?, On Fire, Daddy, Lena: My 100 Children, The Caine Mutiny Court-Marial, Dance Til Dawn, My Brother's Wife, How to Murder a Millionaire, Guess Who's Coming For Christmas?, Shadow of a Doubt, Without Warning: Terror in the Towers, Empty Cradle, A Walton Thanksgiving Reunion, Lies of the Heart: The Story of Laurie Kellog, Bitter Vengeance, A Walton Wedding, Thrill, A Walton Easter, 68, If These Walls Could Talk 2, Empire Falls. *Mini-series*: Drug Wars: The Camarena Story, Empire Falls. *Series*: The Trials of Rosie O'Neill, Morton & Hayes, Significant Others, Time of Your Life, The District, Medium (pilot).

ULLMAN, TRACEY
Actress, Comedian, Singer. b. Hackbridge, England, Dec. 30, 1959. m. British TV prod. Allan McKeown. e. won a performance sch. scholarship at 12. Attended the Italia Conti School for 4 years. Soon after appeared on British TV and onstage in Grease and The Rocky Horror Picture Show. Also performed in improvisational play Four in a Million (1981) at the Royal Court Theatre, London (London Theatre Critics Award). Recorded gold-selling album You Broke My Heart in Seventeen Places. Appeared in music video They Don't Know. U.S. TV debut, The Tracey Ullman Show (debuted April, 1987). Won Emmy Awards for guest appearances in Love & War (Emmy Award, 1993), Tracey Ullman: Takes on New York (Emmy Award, 1994), Tracey Takes On... (Emmy, Cable Ace Awards, 1997).
THEATRE: *NY*: The Taming of the Shrew, The Big Love.
PICTURES: Give My Regards to Broad Street, Plenty, Jumpin' Jack Flash, I Love You to Death, Happily Ever After (voice), Robin Hood: Men in Tights, Household Saints, I'll Do Anything, Bullets Over Broadway, Ready to Wear (Pret-a-Porter), Panic, Small Time Crooks (Golden Globe nom. 2001), Searching For Debra Winger (documentary), A Dirty Shame, Corpse Bride (voice), Flushed Away (consult.), I Could Never Be Your Woman, The Tale of Despereaux (voice).
TELEVISION: *Movies:* I Martin Short Goes Hollywood, The Best of the Tracey Ullman Show (Emmy Award, 1990), Tracey Ullman in the Trailer Tales (also dir, exec.prod., writer, Emmy nom. 2004), Once Upon A Mattress, Women of the Night IV (Emmy nom. 1995). *Series*: Mackenzie, Three of a Kind (BBC), A Kick Up the Eighties, Girls on Top, Tracey Ullman: A Class Act, The Little Lulu Show, Tracy Takes On New York (Emmy Award 1994), Visible Panty Lines, The Tracey Ullman Show (Emmy Awards, 1989, 1990, 5 other noms.; Golden Globe Award, 2 other noms.), The Best of Tracey Takes On... (2 Emmy noms.), Tracey Takes On... (Emmy Award 1997, 7 other noms.; Golden Globe nom.; WGA nom. 1997) Ally McBeal (recurring guest role), Love & War (recurring role, Emmy Award 1993), Tracey Ullman: Live and Exposed (Emmy nom. 2005), Mumbai Calling (voice), State of the Union (also creator, writer, exec. prod.). *Guest:* More than 85 appearances.

ULLMANN, LIV
Actress, Director, Writer. b. Tokyo, Japan, of Norwegian parents, Dec. 16, 1938. Accompanied parents to Canada when WWII began and later returned to Norway. Was catapulted to fame in a succession of Swedish films directed by Ingmar Bergman.
AUTHOR: Changing, Choices. Ambassador for UNICEF since 1980. Youngest person to date to receive the Order of St. Olav from the King of Norway. Recipient of 11 honorary doctorates.
THEATRE: *U.S.*: A Doll's House, Anna Christie, I Remember Mama (musical), Ghosts, Old Times.
PICTURES: Actress: Fjols til Fjells (debut, 1957), The Wayward Girl, Tonny, Kort ar Sommaren, De Kalte Ham Skarven, Persona, Hour of the Wolf, Shame, The Passion of Anna, The Night Visitor, Cold Sweat, The Emigrants (Academy Award nom.; Golden Globe Award 1973), Nybyggarna, Pope Joan, Cries and Whispers, Lost Horizon, Scenes From a Marriage (Golden Globe nom. 1975), 40 Carats (Golden Globe nom. 1974), The New Land, Zandy's Bride, The Abdication, Leonor, Face to Face (Academy Award nom.; Golden Globe nom. 1977), Couleur Chair, A Bridge Too Far, The Serpent's Egg, Autumn Sonata, Players (cameo), Richard's Things, The Wild Duck, Bay Boy, Dangerous Moves, Let's Hope It's a Girl, Gaby—A True Story. Moscow Adieu, The Girlfriend, The Rose Garden (Golden Globe nom. 1990), Mindwalk, Sadako and the Thousand Paper Cranes (short; narr.), Oxen, The Long Shadow, Drømspel, Through a Glass, Darkly. *Director:* Love, Sofie (also s.p.), Kristin Lavrandsdatter (also s.p.), Trolösa.
TELEVISION: *Movies: Actress:* Jacobo Timerman: Prisoner Without a Name Cell Without a Number, Zorn, Saraband. *Director:*

Private Confession. *Mini-series*: Jenny. *Guest:* More than 57 appearances.

ULRICH, SKEET
Actor. r.n. Bryan Ray Ulrich. b. NC, Jan. 20, 1970.
PICTURES: Albino Alligator, Last Dance, The Craft, Boys, Scream, Touch, As Good As It Gets, The Newton Boys, A Soldier's Sweetheart, Takedown, Ride with the Devil, Chill Factor, For Sale by Owner, Armored.
TELEVISION: *Movie:* The Magic of Ordinary Days, Back. *Mini-series:* Into the West. *Series:* Miracles, Jericho, Law & Order: Los Angeles (also pilot).

UNDERWOOD, BLAIR
Actor. b. Tacoma, WA, Aug. 25, 1964. e. Carnegie-Mellon Univ. NY stage: Measure for Measure.
PICTURES: Krush Groove, Posse, Just Cause, Set It Off, The Eighth Day, Gattaca, Deep Impact, Asunder, The Wishing Tree, Rules of Engagement, Free to Dance, Final Breakdown, The Art of Negotiating A Turn, G, Full Frontal, Malibu's Most Wanted, Straight Out of Compton 2 (also prod.), Something New, Madea's Family Reunion, The Bridge to Nowhere (dir.), Weather Girl, I Will Follow, Homework.
TELEVISION: *Movies*: The Cover Girl and the Cop, Heat Wave, Murder in Mississippi, Father & Son: Dangerous Relations (also assoc. prod.), Soul of the Game, Mistrial, Mama Flora's Family, Company Town, Covert One: The Hades Factor. *Mini-series:* Story of a People, The Hades Factor. *Series*: One Life to Live, Downtown, L.A. Law (Golden Globe nom. 1991), High Incident, City of Angels, Fatherhood, LAX, The New Adventures of Old Christine, In Treatment (Golden Globe nom. 2009), Dirty Sexy Money, The Event. *Guest*: More than 100 appearances.

UNDERWOOD, RON
Director. b. Glendale, CA, Nov. 6, 1953. e. USC, AFI.
PICTURES: Tremors (also co-story), City Slickers, Heart and Souls, Speechless, Mighty Joe Young, The Adventures of Pluto Nash, Stealing Sinatra, Dying for Dolly, In the Mix.
TELEVISION: *Movies:* The Mouse and the Motorcycle (Peabody Award), Runaway Ralph (Emmy nom. 1989), Back When We Were Grownups, Mary Christmas, Santa Baby, The Year Without a Santa Claus (DGA nom. 2007), Holidays in Handcuffs, Santa Baby 2.

UNGER, ANTHONY B.
Executive, Producer. b. New York, NY, Oct. 19, 1940. e. Duke U., USC. Prod. ass't Third Man, TV series, 1961. v.p. Unger Productions, Inc., 1964; v.p. Landau-Unger Co., Inc., 1965; v.p. Commonwealth United Entertainment in London, 1968; pres., Unger Prods. Inc., 1978-present.
PICTURES: The Desperate Ones. The Madwoman of Chaillot. The Battle of Neretva, The Magic Christian, Julius Caesar, The Devil's Widow, Don't Look Now, Force Ten From Navarone, The Unseen, Silent Rage, The Dark Side of Hollywood (doc., prod.).

UNGER, STEPHEN A.
Executive. b. New York, NY, May 31, 1946. e. NYU, Grad. Film and Television Instit. Started as independent prod. and dist. of theatrical and TV films. 1978, joined Universal Pictures Intl. Sales as foreign sls. mgr.; named v.p. Universal Theatrical Motion Pictures in 1979, responsible for licensing theatrical or TV features not handled by U.I.P. in territories outside U.S. & Canada and worldwide acquisitions; 1980 joined CBS Theatrical Films as intl. v.p., sls.; 1982-88, pres., Unger Intl. Distributors, Inc.; 1988 joined Korn/Ferry Intl. as exec. v.p., worldwide entertainment div. Promoted to mng. dir., 1989-91. Joined Spencer Stuart Exec. Search Consultants as mng. dir., Worldwide Ent. Div. 1991. Elected Partner, 1994-98. Joined Heidrick & Struggles in 1998 as Managing Partner Media, Entertainment, and Interactive Content. Currently is Partner-In-Charge, Entertainment/ Communications at Heidrick & Struggles (2005). COO of Academy of Television Arts & Sciences.

URBANSKI, DOUGLAS
Producer.
PICTURES: Nil By Mouth (BAFTA Award, Outstanding Brit. Film, 1997), Plunkett & MacLeane (exec. prod.), The Contender (also actor), Nobody's Baby, Tiptoes, BackWoods (exec. prod.), The Social Network (actor), Guns, Girls and Gambling (exec. prod.).

URMAN, MARK
Executive. b. New York, NY, Nov. 24, 1952. e. Union College, 1973; NYU, cinema, 1973-74. m. story analyst Deborah Davis. 1973, apprentice publicist, Universal Pictures; 1973-82, United Artists intl. dept. as assoc. publicist, sr. publicist and ultimately asst. to v.p. worldwide ad-pub.; 1982-84, dir., publicity and marketing, Triumph Films (Columbia/Gaumont); 1985-86, exec. dir. East Coast pub., Columbia Pictures; 1986-89, v.p. East Coast pub., Columbia Pictures. Joined Dennis Davidson Associates as v.p., 1989; promoted to sr. v.p., 1991. From DDA, he became co-president of Lions Gate Films Releasing. During his tenure at Lions Gate he oversaw a slate that included such films as Affliction, Gods and Monsters, Buffalo 66, The Red Violin, Dogma and American Psycho, garnering a total of nine Academy Award nominations and three Oscar wins. He also served as executive producer on the Oscar-winning Monster's Ball, directed by Marc Forster and starring Billy Bob Thornton and Halle Berry. In 2001, he became head of the U.S. Theatrical Division of distributor THINKFilm, and is based in New York. 2008 he resigned his position to become president of Senator Entertainment U.S., a newly formed distribution company. After nine months he left Senator Entertainment, 2009. Currently owner of Paladin an independent film company.

USLAN, MICHAEL E.
Producer, Writer. b. Bayonne, NJ, Junpresident ofe 2, 1951. e. Indiana U., A.B., M.S., J.D. Wrote 12 books, including Dick Clark's 1st 25 Years of Rock 'n' Roll; 1976-80 atty. with United Artists; writer of syndicated comic strip Terry and the Pirates; produced with Benjamin Melniker.
PICTURES: Swamp Thing (prod.), The Return of Swamp Thing (prod.), Batman (exec. prod.), Batman Returns (exec. prod.), Batman: The Animated Movie (prod.), Batman Forever (exec. prod), Batman & Robin (exec. prod.), Catwoman, Constantine, Batman Begins (exec. prod.), The Dark Knight (exec. prod.), The Spirit.
TELEVISION: *Movies: T*hree Sovereigns for Sarah (prod.), Harmful Intent (exec. prod.). *Series:* Dinosaucers (exec. prod., creator, writer), Swamp Thing (exec. prod. for both live-action and animated series), Where in the World Is Carmen Sandiego? (exec. prod., Emmy Award 1995), Fish Police (exec. prod.), The Adventures of Batman & Robin (prod.). *Documentaries/Specials:* South Korea cultural segments NBC Summer Olympics 1988 (exec. prod.), Television's Greatest Bits (prod., creator, writer), 1st National Trivia Quiz (prod., writer), Robin Cook's Harmful Intent (exec. prod.), Little Orphan Annie's Very Animated Christmas (exec. prod., writer); remakes of The Kiss, The Sneeze, The Great Train Robbery, The Barbershop, Streetcar Chivalry, Smashing a Jersey Mosquito (prod., dir.), Doomsday.

UTLEY, NANCY
Executive. e. Northwestern University, master's degree, journalism. Began career with Grey Advertising in New York as an asst. media dir. She left eight years later as v.p., associate media dir. Moved to BBDO and became senior v.p. of new business. From BBDO joined Twentieth Century Fox (TCF) in 1986 and has served Fox organization ever since in a variety of capacities, including posts at TCF as v.p., media; senior v.p., media & research; and executive v.p. of marketing, media and research. Before moving to Fox Searchlight Pictures, Utley was TCF's executive v.p. of marketing, with responsibility for all aspects of media, research and publicity and promotion for theatrical releases. During her tenure at TCF, she worked on such films as: "Independence Day," "There's Something About Mary," "Speed," "The X-Files," and the "Diehard" series, among others. She became marketing president for Fox Searchlight Pictures in 1999. In 2006, she was promoted to co-COO, alongside Stephen Gilula, who had been Searchlight's president of distribution before his promotion with Utley. 2009 she became co-president with Gilula. Utley has overseen the marketing of some of Fox Searchlight's most successful films to date including the Academy Award®-winning "Sideways," which won the 2005 Oscar® for Best Adapted Screenplay and was nominated for four additional Oscars including Best Picture. Other successful Searchlight films have included "Little Miss Sunshine," "Thank You For Smoking," "Garden State," "Napoleon Dynamite," "Bend It Like Beckham," "The Last King of Scotland," and "Juno," which grossed more than $100 million at the box office, a Searchlight record.

VACCARO, BRENDA
Actress. b. Brooklyn, NY, Nov. 18, 1939. e. Thomas Jefferson H.S., Dallas; studied two yrs. at Neighborhood Playhouse in N.Y. Was waitress and model before landing first B'way role in Everybody Loves Opal.
THEATRE: Everybody Loves Opal (Theatre World Award), Tunnel of Love (tour), The Affair, Children From Their Games, Cactus Flower (Tony Award, 1965), The Natural Look, How Now Dow Jones (Tony nom.), The Goodbye People (Tony nom.), Father's Day, The Odd Couple, Jake's Women.
PICTURES: Where It's At (debut, 1969, Golden Globe nom. 1970), Midnight Cowboy (Golden Globe nom. 1970), I Love My Wife, Summertree, Going Home, Jacqueline Susann's Once Is Not Enough (Academy Award nom.; Golden Globe Award 1976), Airport '77, House by the Lake (Death Weekend), Capricorn One, Fast Charlie the Moonbeam Rider, The First Deadly Sin, Zorro the Gay Blade, Supergirl, Water, Cookie, Heart of Midnight, Masque of the Red Death, Ten Little Indians, Lethal Games, Love Affair, The Mirror Has Two Faces, Sonny, Charlotte's Web 2: Wilbur's Great Adventure (voice), Boynton Beach Club.
TELEVISION: *Movies*: Travis Logan D.A., What's a Nice Girl Like You...?, The Shape of Things (Emmy Award 1974), Honor Thy Father, Sunshine, The Big Ripoff, Guyana Tragedy, The Pride of Jesse Hallam, The Star Maker, A Long Way Home, Deceptions, Julius and Ethel Rosenberg, Stolen: One Husband, Red Shoes Diaries, Following Her Heart, When Husbands Cheat, Just A

Walk in the Park, Just Desserts, You Don't Know Jack (Emmy nom. 2010). *Series*: Sara (Emmy nom. 1976), Dear Detective, Paper Dolls, The Golden Girls (recurring role, Emmy nom. 1991) Spawn, Johnny Bravo, The War at Home. *Guest*: More than 95 appearances.

VAJNA, ANDREW
Executive, Producer. b. Budapest, Hungary, Aug. 1, 1944. e. UCLA. Launched career with purchase of m.p. theaters in Far East. Founded Panasia Film Ltd. in Hong Kong. Exhibitor and dist. of feature films since 1970. In 1976, Vajna sold Panasia to Raymond Chow's Golden Harvest Company, and he and Mario Kassar founded Carolco Pictures. At first, Carolco specialized in the financing, distribution and sales of films, which did especially well internationally. Founder and Pres., American Film Mkt. Assn., 1982. Resigned from Carolco, 1989; formed independent production co., Cinergi Pictures Entertainment, 1989. He also set up the Summit Group, a joint venture among Cinergi, Bernd Eichinger's Constantin Films and Arnon Milchan's Regency International to handle foreign sales and distribution on their own and selected other projects. In his native Hungary, Vajna currently serves as pres. of InterCom, an international film, video and DVD distributor and cinema exhibitor in Hungary.
PICTURES: *Executive producer or Producer*: The Deadly China Doll, The Silent Partner, The Changeling, Victory, The Amateur, First Blood, Superstition, Rambo: First Blood Part II, Angel Heart, Extreme Prejudice, Rambo III, Red Heat, Iron Eagle II, Deepstar Six, Johnny Handsome, Music Box, Mountains of the Moon, Total Recall, Air America, Narrow Margin, Jacob's Ladder, Medicine Man, Tombstone, Renaissance Man, Color of Night, Die Hard With a Vengeance, Judge Dredd, The Scarlet Letter, The Shadow Conspiracy, Nixon, Evita, Alan Smithee Film: Burn Hollywood Burn, Out of Order, The 13th Warrior, Eyes of the Holocaust, Basic Instinct 2, An American Rhapsody, I Spy, Terminator 3.: The Rise of the Machines, Basic Instinct 2: Risk Addiction, Freedom's Fury (doc.), Children of Glory, Terminator Salvation.
TELEVISION: *Series:* Terminator: The Sarah Connor Chronicles (exec. prod.).

VALENTINE, DEAN
Executive. b. Romania, 1954. e. U. of Chicago, English major, honors grad. Began career in journalism at *Time, Life* and *The Saturday Review*. Dir., comedy programming, NBC. 1988, joined Walt Disney Television as dir. of TV dev't; 1990, sr. v.p.; appointed pres. of WD Television and WD Television Animation. 1997, appointed COO, United Paramount Networks, then chairman & CEO, UPN. Resigned, Jan. 2002. Valentine launched First Family Entertainment in 2004 with Richard Cohen, the former MGM Home Entertainment president, and the former EVP/chief strategic officer of Artisan Entertainment, Nicholas Van Dyk. The company creates niche-oriented, DVD-based family entertainment. Currently he is pres. of Symbolic Action, LLC, a media investment fund, focused on the convergence of content and technology.

VAN ARK, JOAN
Actress. b. New York, NY, June 16, 1943. e. Yale School of Drama. m. NBC news reporter John Marshall. Began career in touring co., then on Broadway and in London in Barefoot in the Park. Also appeared on B'way with the APA-Phoenix Rep. Co. in the 1970s. As a runner has competed in 12 marathons, incl. Boston Marathon. On TV also created voices for animated series Spiderwoman, Thundarr and Dingbat, Dumb and Dumber, Santo Bugito and the Creeps and special Cyrano de Bergerac. Estee Lauder spokesperson.
THEATRE: School for Wives (Tony Award nom.; Theatre World Award), The Rules of the Game (Theatre World Award). L.A.: Cyrano de Bergerac, Ring Around the Moon, Chemin de Fer, As You Like It (L.A. Drama Critics Award). Williamstown Theatre Fest.: Night of the Iguana, The Legend of Oedipus, Little Night Music. *Off-B'way & L.A.*: Love Letters, Three Tall Women.
PICTURES: *Actress:* Frogs, Held for Randsom, UP Michigan!, IceMaker, Net Games, Channels, Diamond Zero, Channels. *Director:* Dedication Day.
TELEVISION: *Movies*: The Judge and Jake Wyler, Big Rose, Shell Game, The Last Dinosaur, Red Flag—The Ultimate Game, Glitter, Shakedown on the Sunset Strip, My First Love, Always Remember I Love You, The Grand Central Murders, Tainted Blood, In the Shadows Someone's Watching (also co-exec. prod.), Moment of Truth: A Mother's Deception, When the Dark Man Calls, Loyal Opposition: Terror in the White House, Tornado Warning. *Mini-series*: Knots Landing: Back to the Cul-de-Sac. *Series*: Peyton Place, Cruise of Deception: Days of our Lives, Temperatures Rising, Testimony of Two Men, We've Got Each Tarzan and the Super 7, Spider Woman (voice), Dallas, Knots Landing, Thundarr the Barbarian, Second Chance (dir. only), Santo Bugito (voice), The Young and the Restless. *Documentaries/Specials*: Boys Will Be Boys (also dir.). *Guest*: More than 130 appearances.

VAN DAMME, JEAN-CLAUDE
Actor. r.n. Jean-Claude Van Varenberg. b. Brussels, Belgium, Oct. 18, 1960. Former European karate champion, began studying martial arts at 11 yrs. old. Won the European Professional Karate Association's middleweight championship. As teen established the California Gym in Brussels; also worked as a model before coming to U.S. in 1981. Resumed career teaching martial arts before landing first film role.
PICTURES: No Retreat No Surrender, Bloodsport, Black Eagle, Cyborg, Kickboxer (also co-story), Death Warrant, Lionheart (also co-s.p., story), Double Impact (also co-prod., co-s.p., co-story, fight choreog.), Universal Soldier, Nowhere to Run, Last Action Hero (cameo), Hard Target, Timecop, Street Fighter, Sudden Death, The Quest (also dir. & story), Maximum Risk, Double Team, Legionnaire (also s.p., prod.), Knock Off, Inferno, Universal Soldier: The Return (also prod.), Replicant, The Order, Derailed, In Hell, Narco, Wake of Death, Second in Command, Kumite (writer, dir.), Asterix at the Olympic Games, Sinav, Until Death, The Shepherd: Border Patrol, Codename: JCVD, The Eagle Path (also writer, prod., dir., editor), Universal Soldier: A New Beginning, Kung Fu Panda: The Kaboom of Doom (voice).

VAN DER BEEK, JAMES
Actor. b. Cheshire, CT, March 8, 1977.
PICTURES: Angus, I Love You I Love You Not, Castle in the Sky (voice), Varsity Blues, Harvest, Scary Movie, Storytelling, Jay and Silent Bob Strike Back, Texas Rangers, The Rules of Attraction, Standing Still, Formosa Betrayed, Stolen, The Big Bang.
TELEVISION: *Movies:* Sex, Power, Love & Politics, Football Wives, Eye of the Beast, Robot Chicken: Star Wars (voice),Eva Adams, Taken in Broad Daylight, Mrs. Miracle. *Series:* As the World Turns, Dawson's Creek, Total Access 24/7, Three, Mercy.

VAN DYK, NICOLAS
Executive. e. B.A., political science (Phi Beta Kappa), UCLA, M.B.A., Harvard Business School. Served as consultant, LEK Partnership, where he worked on strategies for clients in the media & entertainment industries; manager, The Walt Disney Co., where he was responsible for technology-related acquisitions and strategies for business units such as ABC, ESPN, Disney Regional Entertainment, and Disney Interactive, as well as the acquisition of Dream Quest Images. Became v.p. of strategic planning, Artisan Entertainment, 1997, helping to acquire LIVE Entertainment. EVP. & CSO, Artisan, and president, Artisan Digital Media. Left Artisan. In 2004, launched First Family Entertainment with entertainment execs Dean Valentine, the former chairman & CEO of UPN and and Richard Cohen, the former MGM Home Entertainment president. He is senior v.p. of corp. development and strategic planning. The company creates niche-oriented, DVD-based family entertainment.

VAN DYKE, DICK
Actor. b. West Plains, MO, Dec., 13, 1925. Brother is actor Jerry Van Dyke. Son is actor Barry Van Dyke. Served in USAF, WWII. After discharge from service, opened advertising agency in Danville, IL. Teamed with friend in nightclub act called Eric and Van, The Merry Mutes, and for 4 yrs. toured country doing a routine in which they pantomimed and lip-synched to records. 1953 hosted local TV show in Atlanta, then New Orleans. 1955 to NY as host of CBS Morning show. *Author:* Faith, Hope and Hilarity.
THEATRE: *NY*: The Girls Against the Boys (Theatre World Award), Bye Bye Birdie (Tony Award, 1961), The Music Man (revival).
PICTURES: Bye Bye Birdie (debut, 1963), What a Way to Go!, Mary Poppins (Golden Globe nom. 1965), The Art of Love, Lt. Robin Crusoe USN, Divorce American Style, Fitzwilly, Chitty Chitty Bang Bang, Some Kind of a Nut, The Comic, Cold Turkey, The Runner Stumbles, Dick Tracy, Curious George (voice), Night at the Museum.
TELEVISION: *Movies*: The Morning After (Emmy nom. 1974), Wrong Way Kid, Drop-Out Father, Found Money, The Country Girl, Ghost of a Chance, Keys to the Kingdom, Daughters of Privilege, The House on Sycamore Street, A Twist of the Knife, A Town Without Pity, Without Warning, The Gin Game, The Alan Brady Show, The Dick Van Dyke Show Revisited, Murder 101, Murder 101: College Can Be Murder, Murder 101: If Wishes Were Horses, Murder 101: New Age. *Pilot*: Harry's Battles. *Specials*: The Dick Van Dyke Special, Dick Van Dyke and the Other Woman, Julie and Dick in Covent Garden, The Confessions of Dick Van Dyke, CBS Library: The Wrong Way Kid (Emmy Award, 1984), Breakfast With Les and Bess, The Town Santa Forgot (narrator), The People's Choice Awards (host), I Love Christmas. *Series*: The Morning Show (host), CBS Cartoon Theatre (host), The Chevy Showroom, Pantomime Quiz, Laugh Line (emcee), The Dick Van Dyke Show (3 Emmy Awards: 1964, 1965, 1966, 1 other nom.), The New Dick Van Dyke Show (Golden Globe nom. 1972), Van Dyke and Company (Emmy Award 1977, 2 other noms.), The Carol Burnett Show, The Van Dyke Show, The Golden Girls (recurring role, Emmy nom. 1990) Diagnosis Murder. *Guest*: More than 172 appearances.

VAN DYKE, JERRY
Actor. b. Danville, IL, July 27, 1931. Brother is actor Dick Van Dyke. Served in U.S. Air Force before becoming standup comic, banjo player in nightclubs. Guested on The Dick Van Dyke Show, playing Van Dyke's brother.
PICTURES: The Courtship of Eddie's Father (debut, 1963), McLintock!, Palm Springs Weekend, Love and Kisses, Angel in My Pocket, W.A.R.: Women Against Rape, Run If You Can.
TELEVISION: *Movies*: To Grandmother's House We Go, The

Dick Van Dyke Show Revisted. *Pilots*: My Boy Googie, You're Only Young Twice, Merry Christmas, George Bailey. *Mini-series*: Fresno. *Series*: Picture This, The Judy Garland Show, My Mother the Car, Accidental Family, Headmaster, 13 Queens Boulevard, Coach (4 Emmy noms.), You Wish, Teen Angel, Yes, Dear. *Guest*: More than 64 appearances.

VAN PATTEN, DICK
Actor. b. New York, NY, Dec. 9, 1928. Sister is actress Joyce Van Patten. Father of actors James and Vincent Van Patten. Began career as child actor with B'way debut at 7 yrs., playing son of Melvyn Douglas in Tapestry in Gray.
THEATRE: The Lady Who Came to Stay, O Mistress Mine, On Borrowed Time, Ah, Wilderness, Watch on the Rhine, The Skin of Our Teeth, Kiss and Tell, Mister Roberts, Thieves.
PICTURES: Reg'lar Fellers (debut, 1941), Psychomania, Charly, Zachariah, Making It, Joe Kidd, Soylent Green, Dirty Little Billy, Westworld, Superdad, The Strongest Man in the World, Gus, Treasure of Matecumbe, The Shaggy D.A., Freaky Friday, High Anxiety, Spaceballs, The New Adventures of Pippi Longstocking, Robin Hood: Men in Tights, A Dangerous Place, Demolition High, Love Is All There Is, Big Brother Trouble, The Price of Air, Doesn't Texas Ever End, You'll Never Amount to Anything.
TELEVISION: *Movies:* Hec Ramsey (pilot), The Crooked Hearts, The Love Boat (pilot), The Bionic Boy, With This Ring, High Powder, The Hoboken Chicken Emergency, Diary of a Hitchhiker, Eight Is Enough: A Family Reunion, 14 Going on 30, Going to the Chapel, Picnic, Combat High, An Eight Is Enough Wedding, Jake Spanner - Private Eye, The Odd Couple: Together Again, The Gift of Love, Another Pretty Face, The Santa Trap. *Series*: Mama, The Partners, The New Dick Van Dyke Show, When Things Were Rotten, Eight Is Enough, WIOU. *Documentaries/Specials*: Jay Leno's Family Comedy Hour, A Mouse A Mystery and Me, 14 Going On 30. *Guest*: More than 170 appearances.

VAN PATTEN, JOYCE
Actress. b. New York, NY, March 9, 1934. Brother is actor Dick Van Patten. Mother of actress Talia Balsam.
THEATRE: *NY*: Spoon River Anthology, Same Time Next Year, The Supporting Cast, The Seagull, I Ought to Be in Pictures, Brighton Beach Memoirs, Murder at the Howard Johnson's, Rumors, Jake's Women.
PICTURES: Reg'lar Fellers (debut, 1941), Fourteen Hours, The Goddess, I Love You Alice B. Toklas, Making It, Something Big, Thumb Tripping, The Manchu Eagle Murder Caper Mystery, Mame, The Bad News Bears, Mikey and Nicky, The Falcon and the Snowman, St. Elmo's Fire, Billy Galvin, Blind Date, Trust Me, Monkey Shines, Infinity, Show and Tell, Marley & Me, Grown Ups.
TELEVISION: *Movies*: But I Don't Want to Get Married!, Winter Kill, The Stranger Within, Let's Switch, Winner Take All, To Kill a Cop, Murder at the Mardi Gras, The Comedy Company, Eleanor: First Lady of the World, Another Woman's Child, The Demon Murder Case, In Defense of Kids, Malice in Wonderland, Under the Influence, The Haunted, Maid for Each Other, Breathing Lessons, The Gift of Love, Grandpa's Funeral, Jake's Women. *Mini-series*: The Martian Chronicles. *Special*: Bus Stop. *Series*: The Danny Kaye Show, The Good Guys, The Don Rickles Show, Mary Tyler Moore Hour, Unhappily Ever After. *Guest*: More than 113 appearances.

VAN PEEBLES, MARIO
Actor, Director, Producer, Writer. b. Mexico D.F., Mexico, Jan. 15, 1957. Father is filmmaker Melvin Van Peebles. e. Columbia U., B.A. economics, 1980. Studied acting with Stella Adler 1983. Served as budget analyst for NY Mayor Ed Koch and later worked as a Ford model. Directed music videos for Kid Creole and the Coconuts, Nighttrain (also prod., cameo) and for film Identity Crisis. Appeared as child in father's film Sweet Sweetback's Baadasssss Song. Dir., prod., wrote and starred in short, Juliet. Exec. prod. of soundtracks for Posse and Gunmen.
THEATRE: Waltz of the Stork (B'way debut, 1984), Take Me Along, The Legend of Deadwood Dick, Champeen, Friday the 13th.
PICTURES: The Cotton Club, Delivery Boys, Exterminator II, 3:15, Rappin' (also wrote and performed 5 songs), South Bronx Heroes, Heartbreak Ridge (also songs), Last Resort, Jaws: the Revenge, Hot Shot, Identity Crisis (also s.p.), New Jack City (also dir.), Posse (also dir.), Gunmen, Highlander: The Sorcerer, Panther (also dir., prod.), Jaws IV: The Revenge, Solo, Los Locos (also s.p., prod., exec. prod.), Stag, Love Kills (also. dir., prod., s.p.), Crazy Six, Raw Nerve, Judgment Day, Blowback, Guardian, Ali, The Hebrew Hammer, Getting the Man's Foot Outta Your Baadasssss! (also s.p., dir. & prod.), Gang of Roses, Carlito's Way: Rise to Power, Hard Luck (also writer, dir., prod.), The Yellow Wood, Multiple Sarcasms, Bring Your 'A' Game (doc., dir., prod.), Kerosene Cowboys (also dir.), Fair Game? (doc., dir., prod.), Black, White and Blues (dir.), The Second Time (actor), We the Party (dir., exec. prod.), Things Fall Apart (dir., actor), The Exodus of Charlie Wright (actor).
TELEVISION: *Movies*: *Actor:* Crosscurrent, The Sophisticated Gents, Children of the Night (Bronze Halo Award), D.C. Cops, L.A. Law, The Facts of Life Down Under, The Child Saver, Blue Bayou, Triumph of the Heart: The Ricky Bell Story, Stompin' at the Savoy, In the Line of Duty: Street War, Full Eclipse, Protector, Director: Malcolm Takes a Shot, Mama Flora's Family, Killers in the House, Sally Hemmings: An American Scandal, 10,000 Black Men Named George, 44 Minutes: The North Hollywood Shoot-Out, Crown Heights, Sharpshooter, Way Black When. *Series: Actor:* One Life to Live, L.A. Law, Sonny Spoon (also dir.), Rude Awakening, Fiona, All My Children, Damages (dir., 3 episodes). *Director:* 21 Jump Street, Wiseguy, Top of the Hill. *Guest:* More than 90 appearances.

VAN PEEBLES, MELVIN
Producer, Director, Writer, Composer, Editor, Actor. b. Chicago, IL, Aug. 21, 1932. e. Ohio Wesleyan U., 1953. Father of actor, director, producer Mario Van Peebles. Was portrait painter in Mexico, cable car driver in San Francisco; journalist in Paris and (in 1970s) options trader on Wall Street. Dir. Funky Beat music video.
AUTHOR: *Books*: The Big Heart, A Bear for the FBI, Le Chinois de XIV, La Permission (Story of a Three Day Pass) La Fete a Harlem, The True American, Sweet Sweetback's Baadassss Song, Just an Old Sweet Song, Bold Money, No Identity Crisis (co-author with Mario Van Peebles), Panther.
ALBUMS: *Composer*: Brer Soul, Watermelon Man, Sweet Sweetback's Baadassss Song, As Serious as a Heart Attack, Don't Play Us Cheap, Ain't Suppose to Die a Natural Death, What the #*!% You Mean I Can't Sing, Ghetto Gothic.
THEATRE: *B'way* (writer, prod., dir.): Ain't Supposed to Die a Natural Death, Don't Play Us Cheap, Waltz of the Stork (also actor). *Off-B'way*: Champeen, Waltz of the Stork, Kickin the Science.
PICTURES: The Story of a Three-Day Pass (dir., s.p., music), Watermelon Man (dir., music), Sweet Sweetback's Baad Assss Song (prod., dir., s.p., edit., music, actor), Don't Play Us Cheap (prod., dir., s.p., edit., music), Greased Lightning (co-s.p.), America (actor), O.C. and Stiggs (actor), Jaws: The Revenge (actor), Identity Crisis (prod., dir., co-edit., actor), True Identity (actor), Boomerang (actor), Posse (actor), Last Action Hero (actor), Terminal Velocity (actor), Fist of the North Star (actor), Panther (s.p., actor, prod., co-edit.), Vrooom Vroom Vrooom (short; s.p., dir., composer, prod. & editor), Gang in Blue (actor, dir. & prod.), Love Kills (actor), Time of Her Time (actor), Bellyful (s.p., dir., composer & delegate prod.), The Hebrew Hammer (actor), Gettin' the Man's Foot Outta Your Baadassss! (writer), Blackout, Confessionsofa Ex-Doofus-ItchyFooted Mutha (dir., prod., s.p.), Black, White and Blues.
TELEVISION: *Movies: Actor:* The Sophisticated Gents (also writer, composer & assoc. prod.), Taking Care of Terrific, Calm at Sunset Calm at Dawn, Riot. *Writer:* The Day They Came to Arrest the Books (Emmy Award 1987). *Mini-series: Actor:* The Shining. *Series: Actor:* Sonny Spoon, Mario's Green House. *Guest:* More than 50 appearances.

VAN SANT, GUS
Director, Writer. b. Louisville, KY, July 24, 1952. Raised in Darien, CT, then moved to Oregon at age 17. e. Rhode Island School of Design, where he studied painting. Went to L.A. in 1976, becoming prod. asst. to dir. Ken Shapiro. Made first low-budget film, Alice in Hollywood, which was never released. Later made commercials for NY ad agency before returning to film-making.
PICTURES: *Director:* The Discipline of D.E. (short; also s.p., prod. & editor), Mala Noche (also s.p., prod. & editor), Ken Death Gets Out of Jail (short), Five Ways to Kill Yourself (short), My New Friend (short), Drugstore Cowboy (Natl. Soc. of Film Critics Awards for best dir. & s.p.; NY Film Critics & L.A. Film Critics Award for s.p.), Thanksgiving Prayer (short; also s.p. & prod.), My Own Private Idaho, Even Cowgirls Get the Blues (also exec. prod., s.p. & editor), To Die For, Four Boys in a Volvo (short), Ballad of the Skeleton (short; also s.p.), Good Will Hunting (also sound re-recording mixer; Academy Award nom.; DGA nom. 1998), Psycho (also prod.), Finding Forrester (also sound re-recording mixer), Gerry (also s.p. & editor), Elephant (also s.p. & editor; Best Dir. & Golden Palm, Cannes Film Festival, 2003), Last Days (also s.p. & prod.), Paris, je t'aime (segment dir., writer), To Each His Cinema (segment dir.), Paranoid Park (also s.p.), 8 (segment dir., editor), Milk (also sound, Academy Award nom.; DGA nom. 2009), Accidents Happen (script consult.), Restless. *Executive producer:* Kids, Speedway Junky, Tarnation (documentary), Wild Tigers I Have Known, What's Wrong with Virginia, Howl, On the Road.

VANCE, COURTNEY B.
Actor. b. Detroit, MI, Mar. 12, 1960. e. Harvard (B.A.), Yale Drama Sch. (M.A.).
THEATRE: *B'way:* Fences (Theatre World & Clarence Derwent Awards; Tony nom.), Six Degrees of Separation (Tony nom.). *Off-B'way:* My Children My Africa (Obie Award), Romeo and Juliet, Temptation. *Regional:* A Lesson From Aloes, Rosencrantz and Guildenstern Are Dead, Hamlet, Butterfly, Jazz Wives Jazz Lives, Geronimo Jones.
PICTURES: Hamburger Hill, The Hunt for Red October, Beyond the Law, The Emperor's New Clothes, The Adventures of Huck Finn, Holy Matrimony, Panther, Dangerous Minds, The Last Supper, The Preacher's Wife, Blind Faith, Ambushed, Love and Action in Chicago (also co-prod.), Cookie's Fortune, Space Cowboys, The Acting Class, D-Tox, Nothing But the Truth, Extraordinary Measures, The Divide.
TELEVISION: *Movies:* First Affair, In the Line of Duty: Street War, Percy and Thunder, Race to Freedom: The Underground

Railroad, The Piano Lesson, The Tuskegee Airmen, The Affair, The Boys Next Door, 12 Angry Men, Whitewash: The Clarence Brandley Story. *Mini-series:* Parting the Waters. *Series*: Boston Public, Law & Order: Criminal Intent, ER, Flash Forward. *Documentaries:* Culture Shock (mini-series, narr.), Unchained Memories: Readings from the Slave Narratives, Unforgivable Blackness: The Rise and Fall of Jack Johnson (voices), Nova (narr.), For Love of Liberty: The Story of America's Black Patriots (voice).

VAN GALDER, VALERIE

Executive. e. Undergraduate degree from UCLA. Began career in m.p. publicity dept. at Rogers and Cowan. Took v.p., mktg. and publicity role with Hard Rock America. Van Galder then joined the Fox Searchlight team as senior v.p., mktg. and publicity, where she launched such films as "The Full Monty," "The Ice Storm" and "The Brothers McMullen" among others. She then moved to Sony's film group as executive v.p., marketing for its Screen Gems unit in 2000. She garnered a promotion to pres., TriStar Pictures and received the nod to become pres., domestic marketing for the Columbia TriStar Marketing Group in early 2006. In June 2008, Sony Pictures Entertainment promoted Van Galder and Marc Weinstock co-presidents of Worldwide Theatrical Marketing, and charged them with developing and overseeing worldwide marketing campaigns for all films released by Columbia Pictures, Screen Gems and Sony Pictures Animation. The two have worked together for more than a decade, first joining forces at Fox Searchlight. Van Galder and Weinstock have been the mktg. architects for 28 #1 films. In June 2009, Van Galder announced she would not renew her contract at the end of 2009 but would continue in a consulting role for the company. 2010 was hired by Disney to market the film, Pirates of the Caribbean: On Stranger Tides.

VANGELIS

Composer, Conductor. r.n. Vangelis Papathanassiou. b. Greece, March 29, 1943. Began composing as child, performing own compositions at 6. Left Greece for Paris by late 1960s. Composed and recorded his symphonic poem Faire que Ton Reve Soit Plus Long que la Nuit, and album Terra. Collaborated with filmmaker Frederic Rossif for whom composed La Cantique des Creatures. Moved to London then to Greece in 1989. Formed band Formynx in Greece; then Aphrodite's Child in Paris. 2005 won World Soundtrack Award for Alexander.
PICTURES: Chariots of Fire (Academy Award, 1982), Antarctica, Missing, Blade Runner (Golden Globe nom. 1983), The Year of Living Dangerously, The Bounty, Wonders of Life, Wild and Beautiful, Nosferatu in Venice, Francesco, 1492: Conquest of Paradise (Golden Globe nom. 1993), Bitter Moon, Cavafy, How the Grinch Stole Christmas, Old School, Bruce Almighty, Collateral, Millions, Alexander, Kicking & Screaming (soundtrack performer), Madagascar (soundtrack performer), Stranger Than Fiction (soundtrack writer and performer), The Holiday, Are We Done Yet? (soundtrack performer), El Greco.

VAN NOY, FRED W.

Executive. Exhibition ind.executive with Carmike Cinemas, Inc. since 1975. Served as dist. mgr. From 1984-1985; Western div. mgr., 1985-1988, when he became v.p. and gen. mgr. In Dec. 1997, elected to senior v.p., operations. In Nov. 2000, became senior v.p. & COO. In Jan. 2009, appointed member of the Office of the Chairman, when company CEO Michael Patrick was removed. Van Noy continues to serve Carmike as its COO, reporting to new CEO, S. David Passman III. Headquartered in Columbus, GA, Carmike has 249 theatres with 2,288 screens in 35 states. Carmike's digital cinema footprint reaches 2,154 screens, including 193 theatres with 500 screens that are also equipped for 3D.

VANOCUR, SANDER

News Commentator. b. Cleveland, OH, Jan. 8, 1928. e. Northwestern U. Began career as journalist on London staff of Manchester Guardian 1954-5; City staff, NY Times 1956-57. Joined NBC in 1957, hosting First Tuesday series. Resigned in 1971 to be correspondent of the National Public Affairs Center for PBS. TV Critic for Washington Post, 1975-7. Vanocur held positions at ABC News from 1977 to 1992. These positions included Chief Diplomatic correspondent, Senior correspondent in Buenos Aires during the Falkland Islands War in 1982, and was anchor of Business World, the first regularly scheduled business program on television. He also covered the 1987, 1988 and 1989 Economic Summit meetings and was ABC News Chief overview correspondent during the 1980 and 1984 presidential elections. From 1995 to 2002, he was anchor of two programs at the History Channel: Movies in Time and History's Business. Before joining the History Channel, Vanocur was a visiting scholar at the Freedom Forum First Amendment Center at Vanderbilt University in Nashville. He was also co-host of Vanderbilt's Freedom Speaks, a weekly series produced by the Center and aired on PBS. Vanocur now lives in Santa Barbara, California, where he heads his company, Old Owl Communications, a full-service communications and consulting corporation.

VAUGHN, ROBERT

Actor. b. New York, NY, Nov. 22, 1932. e. L.A. State college, B.S. and M.A. Theatre Arts 1956; USC, Ph.D. Communications, 1970. Gained fame as Napoleon Solo in The Man From U.N.C.L.E. TV series. *Author*: Only Victims, 1972.
PICTURES: The Ten Commandments (debut, 1956), Hell's Crossroads, No Time to Be Young, Teenage Caveman, Unwed Mother, Good Day for a Hanging, The Young Philadelphians (Academy Award nom.; Golden Globe nom. 1960), The Magnificent Seven, The Big Show, The Caretakers, To Trap a Spy, The Spy With My Face, One Spy Too Many, The Glass Bottom Boat (cameo), The Venetian Affair, How to Steal the World, Bullitt, Bridge at Remagen, If It's Tuesday This Must Be Belgium (cameo), The Mind of Mr. Soames, Julius Caesar, The Statue, Clay Pigeon, The Towering Inferno, The Babysitter, Lucifer Complex, Demon Seed (voice), Starship Invasions, Brass Target, Good Luck Miss Wycoff, Hangar 18, Sweet Dirty Tony, Battle Beyond the Stars, Virus, S.O.B., Superman III, Black Moon Rising, The Delta Force, Rampage, Nightstick, Hour of the Assassin, Skeleton Coast, River of Death, Captive Rage, Nobody's Perfect, Fair Trade, Edgar Allan Poe's Buried Alive, That's Adequate, Blind Vision, C.H.U.D. II: Bud the Chud, Transylvania Twist, Going Under, Twilight Blue, Joe's Apartment, Vulcan, The Sender, Motel Blue, Milk and Money, Anakng Bulkan, An American Affair, McCinsey's Island, BASEketball, Cottonmouth, Pootie Tang, Happy Hour, Hoodlum & Son, The Warrior Class, Scene Stealers, 2BPerfectlyHonest, The Magnificent Eleven.
TELEVISION: *Movies*: Boston Terrier, The Helicopter Spies, The Woman Hunter, Columbo: Troubled Waters, Columbo: Last Salute to the Commodore, Kiss Me Kill Me, The Islander, The Gossip Columnist, The Rebels, Mirror Mirror, Doctor Franken, Fantasies, City in Fear, FDR: That Man in the White House, The Day the Bubble Burst, A Question of Honor, Inside the Third Reich, Intimate Agony, The Return of the Man From U.N.C.L.E. (2 Golden Globe noms.), Private Sessions, International Airport, Murrow, Prince of Bel Air, Nightstick, Desperado, Perry Mason: The Case of the Defiant Daughter, Dark Avenger, Tatort - Camerone, W.S.H., Escape to Witch Mountain, Dancing in the Dark, Host, BBC: One of Our Spies is Missing, The Spy in the Green Hat, The Karate Killers, Virtual Obsession, The Verdict. *Mini-series*: Captains and the Kings, Washington: Behind Closed Doors (Emmy Award 1978), Centennial, Greatest Heroes of the Bible, Backstairs at the White House (Emmy nom. 1979), The Rebels, The Blue and the Gray, The Last Bastion, Evergreen, Tracks of Glory. *Series*: The Lieutenant, The Man From U.N.C.L.E., The Protectors, Emerald Point N.A.S., The A-Team, Love at First Sight, Danger Theatre (host), As the World Turns, One Life to Live, The Magnificent Seven, Family of the Year, Hustle. *Guest:* More than 196 appearances.

VAUGHN, VINCE

Actor. b. Minneapolis, MN, March 28, 1970.
PICTURES: For the Boys, Rudy, At Risk, Swingers, Just Your Luck, The Locusts, The Lost World: Jurassic Park, A Cool Dry Place, Return to Paradise, Clay Pigeons, Psycho, South of Heaven, West of Hell, The Cell, The Prime Gig, Zoolander, Made (also prod.), Domestic Disturbance, Old School, Blackball, I Love Your Work, Starsky & Hutch, Dodgeball: True Underdog Story, Thumbsucker, Be Cool, Mr. and Mrs. Smith, The Wedding Crashers, The Break Up (also prod., writer), Wild West Comedy Show: 30 Days & 30 Nights - Hollywood to the Heartland (doc. also prod.), Into the Wild, Fred Claus, Four Christmases (also prod.), Couples Retreat (also prod., writer), The Dilemma (also prod.).
TELEVISION: *Movies:* Liles of the Heart, Sex and the Matrix (short). *Guest*: More than 67 appearances.

VEL JOHNSON, REGINALD

Actor. b. Queens, NY, Aug. 16, 1952. e. Long Island Inst. of Music and Arts, NYU.
THEATRE: *NY*: But Never Jam Today, Inacent Black, World of Ben Caldwell, Staggerlee.
PICTURES: Wolfen (debut, 1981), Ghostbusters, Remo Williams, Crocodile Dundee, Magic Sticks, Plain Clothes, Die Hard, Turner & Hooch, Die Hard 2, Posse, Ground Zero, Waitin' to Live, Like Mike, The King (short), Sunday Evening Haircut (also s.p., exec. prod.), Suits on the Loose, Death to the Supermodels, Retirement, Out at the Wedding, Jelly, Marriage Retreat, Sex Tax: Based on a True Story.
TELEVISION: *Movies*: Doing Life, Quiet Victory: The Charlie Wedemeyer Story, The Bride in Black, Jury Duty: The Comedy, Grass Roots, A Cool Like That Christmas (voice), One of Her Own, Deadly Pursuits, The Three Gifts. *Series*: Family Matters. *Guest:* More than 48 appearances.

VENORA, DIANE

Actress. b. Hartford, CT, Aug. 10, 1952. e. Juilliard Sch. (BFA degree). Member of Juilliard's Acting Company, Circle Repertory Co. and the Ensemble Studio Theatre.
THEATRE: A Midsummer Night's Dream, Hamlet (New York Shakespeare Festival), Uncle Vanya (at La Mama), Messiah (Manhattan Theatre Club), Penguin Toquet, Tomorrow's Monday (Circle Rep), Largo Desolato, School for Scandal, The Seagull, A Man for All Seasons (Roundabout Theatre Co.), Peer Gynt (Williamstown Fest.), The Winter's Tale, Hamlet (NYSF).
PICTURES: All That Jazz, Wolfen, Terminal Choice, The Cotton Club, F/X, Ironweed, Bird (NY Film Critics Award, 1988; Golden

Globe nom. 1989), Heat, Three Wishes, Surviving Picasso, The Subsitute, Romeo and Juliet, The Jackal, Young Girl and the Monsoon, Looking for an Echo, The 13th Warrior, The Joyriders, The Insider, Hamlet, True Crime, Meggido: The Omega Code 2, Heartbreak Hospital, Self Medicated, Stateside, Breaking Dawn, Touched, The Ministers, Stiletto, Follow the Prophet, All Good Things, Disappearing Bakersfield (consult. prod.).
TELEVISION: *Movies:* Getting There (short), A Midsummer Night's Dream, Cook & Peary: The Race to the Pole, Hamlet, Special Report: Journey to Mars, Race Against Time, C.S. Lewis: Beyond Narnia (doc.), The Wish List. *Mini-series:* A.D. *Series:* Thunder Alley, Chicago Hope.

VEREEN, BEN
Singer, Dancer, Actor. b. Miami, FL, Oct. 10, 1946. e. High School of Performing Arts.
THEATRE: *NY*: Hair, Sweet Charity, Jesus Christ Superstar (Theatre World Award), Pippin (Tony Award, 1973), Grind, Jelly's Last Jam, I'm Not Rappaport. *Chicago:* Wicked.
PICTURES: Sweet Charity, Gasss, Funny Lady (Golden Globe nom. 1976), All That Jazz, The Zoo Gang, Buy and Cell, Friend to Friend, Once Upon a Forest (voice), Why Do Fools Fall in Love, I'll Take You There, Idlewild, Mama, I Want to Sing!.
TELEVISION: *Movies*: Louis Armstrong—Chicago Style, The Jesse Owens Story, Lost in London, Intruders (Emmy nom. 1992), Fosse, An Accidental Friendship. *Mini-series*: Roots (Emmy nom. 1977), Ellis Island (Golden Globe nom. 1985), A.D., Feast of All Saints. *Series:* Oz, Ben Vereen...Comin' at Ya, Ten Speed and Brown Shoe, Webster, Zoobilee Zoo, You Write the Songs (host), J.J. Starbuck, Silk Stalkings. *Documentaries/Specials*: Ben Vereen - His Roots, Uptown - A Tribute to the Apollo Theatre, Jubilee! (Emmy nom. 1977). *Guest:* More than 128 appearances.

VERHOEVEN, PAUL
Director. b. Amsterdam, The Netherlands, July 18, 1938. e. U. of Leiden, Ph.D., (mathematics and physics) where he began making films.
PICTURES: Business Is Business, Turkish Delight, Keetje Tippel (Cathy Tippel), Soldier of Orange, Spetters, The Fourth Man, Flesh + Blood, Robocop, Total Recall, Basic Instinct, Showgirls, Starship Troopers, Hollow Man, Zwartboek (also writer), Black Book (also writer), The Winter Queen (prod.).
TELEVISION: *Movie:* Voorbij, voorbij. *Series:* Floris, Roughnecks: The Starship Troopers Chronicles (exec. prod. Emmy nom. 2001).

VETTER, RICHARD
Executive. b. San Diego, CA, Feb. 24, 1928. e. Pepperdine Coll., B.A., 1950; San Diego State Coll., M.A., 1953; UCLA, Ph.D., 1959. U.S. Navy: aerial phot., 1946-48, reserve instr., San Diego County Schools, 1951-54; asst. prof., audio-vis. commun., U.C.L.A., 1960-63. Inventor, co-dev., Dimension 150 Widescreen Process. 1957-63: formed D-150 Inc. Currently associated with Todd-AO Camera Dept. Associate member of ASC, 1963; exec. v.p. mem.: SMPTE, Technical & Scientific Awards Committee, AMPAS.

VIANE, CHUCK
Executive. e. B.S., marketing, De Paul U. Began as film buyer, v.p. & head buyer, General Cinema Theater Corp., 1973-85; v.p. & asst. gen. sales mgr., Buena Vista Pictures, 1986; senior v.p. & gen. sales mgr., Buena Vista Pictures, 1995. Currently president, Walt Disney Studios Motion Pictures Distribution, overseeing sales and distribution operations throughout U.S. and Canada for all motion pictures released by Walt Disney, Touchstone, and Hollywood Pictures. 2010 he also heads International film sales and distribution. He received the 2005 humanitarian award from the Variety Boys and Girls Club.

VICTOR, JAMES
Actor. r.n. Lincoln Rafael Peralta Diaz. b. Santiago, Dominican Republic, July 27, 1939. e. Haaren H.S., N.Y. Studied at Actors Studio West. Member of Academy of Mo. Pic. Arts & Sciences, Actors Branch. Recipient of Cleo Award, 1975, for Mug Shot; Golden Eagle Award, 1981, for consistent outstanding performances in motion pictures.
THEATRE: Bullfight, Ceremony for an Assassinated Blackman, Latina (Drama-Logue Critics Award, 1980), The Man in the Glass Booth, The M.C. (Drama-Logue Critics, and Cesar best actor awards, 1985), I Gave You a Calendar (Drama-Logue Critics Award, 1983), I Don't Have To Show You No Stinking Badges (Drama-Logue Critics Award, 1986), The Rooster and the Egg, One Hour Without Television, The Red Devil Battery Sign.
PICTURES: Girl in Gold Boots, Faces (assist. dir.), Fuzz, Rolling Thunder, Boulevard Nights, Defiance, Losin' It, Borderline, The Telephone (voice), Stand and Deliver, Gunfighter's Moon.
TELEVISION: *Movies*: Robert Kennedy and His Times, Twin Detectives, Remington Steel, The Streets of L.A., I Desire, Second Serve, Grand Slam, Falcon Crest, The Second Civil War. *Mini-series*: Streets of Laredo. *Series*: Viva Valdez, Condo, I Married Dora, Angelica Mi Vida, The New Zorro.

VIGODA, ABE
Actor. b. New York, NYU, Feb. 24, 1921.
PICTURES: The Godfather, The Don Is Dead, Newman's Law, The Godfather: Part II, The Cheap Detective, Cannonball Run II, Vasectomy - A Delicate Matter, Keaton's Cop, Plain Clothes, Look Who's Talking, Prancer, Joe vs. the Volcano, Fist of Honor, Me and the Kid, Batman: Mask of the Phantasm, Home of Angels, Sugar Hill, North, The Misery Brothers, Jury Duty, Love Is All There Is, Underworld, Farticus, A Brooklyn State of Mind, Good Burger, Just the Ticket, Crime Spree, Chump Change, The Driver, Mafioso II, Mobster Movie.
TELEVISION: *Movies*: The Devil's Daughter, Tomaa, Having Babies, How to Pick Up Girls, Death Car on the Freeway, Witness to the Mob. *Series*: Dark Shadow, Barney Miller (3 Emmy noms.), Fish, One Life to Live. *Guest*: More than 82 appearances.

VINCENT, FRANCIS T, JR.,
Executive. b. Waterbury, CT, May 29, 1938. e. Williams College, B.A., 1960; Yale Law Sch. LL.B., 1963. Bar, CT 1963; NY, 1964; D.C. 1969. 1969-78, partner in law firm of Caplin & Drysdale, specializing in corporate banking and securities matters; 1978, assoc. dir. of, Division of Corporation Finance of Securities & Exchange Commission; exec. v.p. of the Coca-Cola Company and pres. & CEO of its entertainment business sector. Also chmn. & CEO of Columbia Pictures Industries, Inc.; appt. pres. CEO, 1978; mem. bd. of dir. of The Coca-Cola Bottling Co. of NY. 1987-88; rejoined law firm of Caplin & Drysdale, Washington, D.C., 1988. Vincent was the eighth Commissioner of Baseball, elected in 1989 and serving until he resigned in Sept. 1992. Vincent served as a director of Time Warner Inc. from 1993 until its merger with America Online, Inc. in January 2001, and he has served as a independent director of Time Warner since that time. He currently is chmn. of Vincent Enterprises.

VINCIQUERRA, ANTHONY J.
Executive. b. Albany, NY. e. graduate, State Univ. of New York. Vinciquerra began his media career in advertising sales at the Albany, NY, "Times Union" and later moved into broadcasting with Hearst as a sales manager at Hearst Broadcasting's WTAE-TV Pittsburgh in the early 1980s. Was v.p. & general mgr. of KYW-TV in Philadelphia; executive v.p. of the CBS Television Station Group. He joined the Hearst Corporation's broadcasting group as group executive in 1997, becoming executive v.p. of Hearst-Argyle upon the company's formation in Aug. 1997. Vinciquerra advanced to executive v.p. and COO of Hearst-Argyle Television, Inc. before joining FOX. He was named pres. of the Fox Television Network in Jan. 2002 and became the CEO of the Fox Networks Group in June 2002, also named Chairman in 2010 the positions he holds today.

VITALE, RUTH
Executive. e. Tufts U., B.A.; Boston U., M.S. Prior to motion picture career, worked in advertising and media. Senior v.p., Vestron Pictures then s.v.p. of feature production at United Artists and management at Constantin Film Development before joining New Line. Joined New Line as exec. v.p. of worldwide acquisitions. Later promoted to pres., Fine Line Features, a wholly owned division of New Line Cinema. Left Fine Line to assume her current position of co-president, specialty film division, Paramount Classics, along with David Dinerstein. Resigned 2006. Became president of First Look Pictures during 2006, but resigned this post April 30, 2007. Currently executive/prod. for Film Collective.

VOIGHT, JON
Actor. b. Yonkers, NY. Dec. 29, 1938. e. Archbishop Stepinac H.S., White Plains, NY; Catholic U. of Amer., D.C. (B.F.A.) 1960; studied acting at the Neighborhood Playhouse and in private classes with Stanford Meisner, four yrs. Daughter is actress Angelina Jolie.
THEATRE: *B'way*: The Sound of Music (debut, 1959), That Summer That Fall (Theatre World Award), The Seagull. *Off-B'way*: A View From the Bridge (1964 revival). *Regional*: Romeo & Juliet, A Streetcar Named Desire, Hamlet.
PICTURES: Hour of the Gun (debut, 1967), Fearless Frank, Midnight Cowboy (Academy Award nom.; Golden Globe Award, 1 other nom. 1970), Out of It, Catch-22, The Revolutionary, Deliverance (Golden Globe nom. 1973), All-American Boy, Conrack, The Odessa File, End of the Game, Coming Home (Academy Award, Golden Globe Award 1978), The Champ (Golden Globe nom. 1980), Lookin' To Get Out (also co-s.p., prod.), Table for Five (also prod.), Runaway Train (Academy Award nom.; Golden Globe Award 1986), Desert Bloom, Eternity, Heat, Rosewood, Mission Impossible, Anaconda, U-Turn, Most Wanted, The Rainmaker (Golden Globe nom. 1998), The General, Enemy of the State, Varsity Blues, Baby Geniuses (co-exec. prod. only), A Dog of Flanders, Pearl Harbor, Lara Croft: Tomb Raider, Zoolander, Ali (Academy Award nom.; Golden Globe nom. 2002), A Decade Under the Influence (documentary), Holes, The Karate Dog (also exec. prod.), The Manchurian Candidate, SuperBabies: Baby Geniuses 2, National Treasure, The Uninvited, Glory Road, Pride and Glory, Transformers, Bratz, National Treasure: Book of Secrets, Clarkworld (doc.), Pride and Glory, An American Carol, Four Christmases, The Final Song (exec. prod.).
TELEVISION: *Movies*: Chernobyl: The Final Warning, The Last of His Tribe (Golden Globe nom. 1993), The Tin Soldier (also

dir.), Convict Cowboy, The Fixer, Noah's Ark, Second String, Uprising (Emmy nom. 2002), Jasper Texas, The Five People You Meet In Heaven, Pope John Paul II (Emmy nom. 2006), 24: Redemption. *Mini-series*: Return to Lonesome Dove, Jack and the Beanstalk: The Real Story. *Series:* 24, Lone Star (also pilot). *Special*: The Dwarf (Public Broadcast Lab). *Guest*: More than 152 appearances.

VON SYDOW, MAX
Actor. b. Lund, Sweden, April 10, 1929. Theatrical debut in a Cathedral School of Lund prod. of The Nobel Prize. Served in the Swedish Quartermaster Corps two yrs. Studied at Royal Dramatic Theatre School in Stockholm. Tour in municipal theatres. Has appeared on stage in Stockholm, London (The Tempest, 1988), Paris and Helsinki in Faust, The Legend and The Misanthrope. 1954 won Sweden's Royal Foundation Cultural Award. Appeared on B'way in Duet for One.
PICTURES: Bara en Mor (Only a Mother; debut, 1949), Miss Julie, Ingen Mans Kvinna, Ratten att Alska, The Seventh Seal, Prasten i Uddarbo, Wild Strawberries, Brink of Life, Spion 503, The Magician, The Virgin Spring, Brollopsdagen, Through a Glass Darkly, Nils Holgerssons Underbara Resa, Alskarinnen, Winter Light, 4x4, The Greatest Story Ever Told (English-language debut, 1965), The Reward, Hawaii (Golden Globe nom. 1967), The Quiller Memorandum, Hour of the Wolf, Here Is Your Life, Svarta Palmkronor, Shame, Made in Sweden, The Kremlin Letter, The Passion of Anna, The Night Visitor, The Touch, The Emigrants, Appelbriget, Embassy, The New Land, The Exorcist (Golden Globe nom. 1974), Steppenwolf, Egg! Egg!, Illustrious Corpses, Three Days of the Condor, The Ultimate Warrior, Foxtrot (The Other Side of Paradise), Cuore di Cane, Voyage of the Damned, Les Desert des Tartares, Exorcist II: The Heretic, March or Die, Brass Target, Gran Bolitto, Hurricane, Deathwatch, Venetian Lies, Flash Gordon, Victory, She Dances Alone (voice), Conan the Barbarian, Flight of the Eagle, Strange Brew, Never Say Never Again, Target Eagle, Dreamscape, Dune, Code Name: Emerald, Hannah and Her Sisters, Duet for One, The Second Victory, Wolf at the Door, Pelle the Conqueror (Academy Award nom. 1989), Katinka (dir.), Cellini: A Violent Life, Awakenings, A Kiss Before Dying, Until the End of the World, Zentropa (narrator), The Bachelor, The Best Intentions, The Ox, Father, Grandfather's Journey, Needful Things, The Silent Touch, Time Is Money, The Atlantic (narrator), Judge Dredd, Needful Things, Jerusalem, Hamsun, What Dreams May Come, Snow Falling on Cedars, Sleepless, Vercingétorix, Intact, Minority Report, Heidi, The Diving Bell and the Butterfly, Emotional Arithmetic, Truth & Treason, Rush Hour 3, Solomon Kane, Un homme et son chien, Shutter Island, Robin Hood, Moomins and the Comet Chase (narr.).
TELEVISION: *Movies:* Rabies, The Diary of Anne Frank, Samson and Delilah, Kojak: The Belarus File, Red King White Knight (Emmy nom. 1990), Hiroshima: Out of the Ashes, Citizen X, Private Confessions, Hostile Waters, La Principessa E Il Povero, Solomon, Nuremberg, Curse of the Ring, The Final Inquiry. *Mini-series*: I havsbandet (narr.), Quo Vadis?, The Last Place on Earth, Christopher Columbus, Brotherhood of the Rose, Radetzky March,A Que Punto E La Notte, Uncle Vanya, Fantasma Per Caso, La Fuga degli innocenti, Ring of the Nibelungs, Hidden Children. *Series:* The Tudors. *Guest:* More than 72 appearances.

VON TRIER, LARS
Director, Writer, Editor, Actor. r.n. Lars Trier. b. Copenhagen, Denmark, April 30, 1956. e. Danish Film Institute. Attracted international attention with Forbrydelsens Element (The Element of Crime). Is working on a film project taking a 3 minute shot every year from different locations all over Europe for a period of 33 years; begun in 1991, the premiere is expected in the year 2024.
PICTURES: *Director:* Orchidegartneren (1977), Menthe la bienheureuse, Nocturne (short; also writer), The Last Detail, Befrielsesbilleder (also s.p.), The Element of Crime (also actor, s.p.), Epidemic (also actor, s.p., edit.), Medea (also s.p.), Un Monde de Difference (actor only), Zentropa (a.k.a. Europa; also actor, s.p.), The Kingdom (orig. for Danish TV; also s.p.), Breaking the Waves (also s.p.; Grand Jury Prize, Cannes, 1996), The Kingdom 2 (orig. for Danish TV; also s.p.), The Idiots (also s.p.), Dancer in The Dark (also s.p., Academy Award nom.; Golden Globe nom. for best orig. song 2001), Dogville (also s.p. & camera operator), Manderlay (also s.p.), To Each His Cinema (segment dir.), Antichrist (also s.p.), Melancholia (also s.p.). *Producer:* Visions of Europe, South (co-prod. only), Mammoth, The Erotic Man. *Writer:* Dear Wendy, The Early Years: Erik Nietzsche Part 1 (also narr.).
TELEVISION: *Movies:* Medea, D-dag - Niels-Henning (assistant dir.), D-dag - Lise, D-dag - Carl (assistant dir.), D-dag - Boris (assistant dir.), D-dag, D-dag - Den færdige film. *Mini-series:* The Kingdom, The Kingdom II. *Series:* The Teacher's Room, Marathon, Kingdom Hospital (writer, exec. prod.). *Documentaries/Specials:* Kayaking on the Top of the World (exec. prod.), The 73rd Annual Academy Awards (soundtrack writer).

VON TROTTA, MARGARETHE
Director, Writer. b. Berlin, Germany, Feb. 21, 1942. e. Studied German and Latin literature in Munich and Paris. Studied acting in Munich and began career as actress. 1970 began collaborating on Volker Schlondorff's films as well as acting in them.
PICTURES: *Actress*: Hands Up!, Madchen zwischen Nacht und Morgen, Schrage Vogel, Brandstifter, Gotter der Pest, Baal, Drucker, Der Amerikanische Soldat, Gods of the Plague, Why Does Herr R. Run Amok?, The Sudden Wealth of the Poor People of Kombach (also co-s.p.), Beware the Holy Whore, Die Moral der Ruth Halbfass, Free Woman (also co-s.p.), Desaster, Ubernachtung in Tirol, Die Atlantikschwimmer, Bierkampf, Coup de Grace (also co-s.p.), Blaubart. *Dir./ Co-s.p.*: The Lost Honor of Katharina Blum (co-dir., co-s.p., with Schlondorff), The Second Awakening of Christa Klages, Sisters or the Balance of Happiness, Circle of Deceit, Marianne and Julianne, Friends & Husbands, Unerreichbare Nahe, Rosa Luxemburg, Felix, Paura e Amore (Three Sisters), The African Woman, The Long Silence, The Promise, Rosenstrasse.
TELEVISION: *Movies: Actress:* Brandstifter, Baal, Der Plötzliche Reichtum der armen Leute von Kombach, A Free Woman (also writer), Übernachtung in Tirol, Blaubart. *Director:* Winterkind, Mit fünfzig küssen Männer anders, Dunkle Tage, The Other Woman. Many more credits in German.

VON ZERNECK, FRANK
Producer. b. New York, NY, Nov. 3, 1940. e. Hofstra College, 1962. Has produced plays in New York, Los Angeles and on national tour. Partner, von Zerneck/Sertner Films. Devised Portrait film genre for TV movies: Portrait of a Stripper, Portrait of a Mistress, Portrait of a Centerfold, etc. Past chmn. of California Theatre Council; former officer of League of Resident theatres; member of League of New York Theatres & Producers; Producers Guild of America; chmn's council, the Caucus for Producers, Writers and Directors; Board of Directors, Allied Communications, Inc. Museum of Radio & Television in NYC, Hollywood Television & Radio Society, Acad. of TV Arts & Sciences, Natl. Acad. of Cable Programming. Received American Film Institute Charles Fries Producer of the Year Award.
PICTURE: Tunnel Vision, God's Lonely Man, Living In Oblivion.
TELEVISION: *Movies: Producer:* The Desperate Miles, 21 Hours at Munich (Emmy nom. 1977), Delta County USA, Escape from Bogen County, Getting Married, Disaster on the Coastliner, Professional Date, Miracle on Ice, Return of the Rebels, The Broken Chain, Take Me Home Again, Still Holding On: The Legend of Cadillac Jack, Gracie's Choice. *Executive producer:* Sharon: Portrait of a Mistress, Katie: Portrait of a Centerfold, Flatbed Annie & Sweetiepie: Lady Truckers, Anatomy of a Seduction, The Secret Life of Susie Hanson, The Babysitter, Lois Gibbs and the Love Canal, Forbidden Love, The First Time, Baby Sister, NIght Partners, Policewoman Centerfold, Invitation to Hell, Summer Fantasy, Obsessive Love, I Married a Centerfold, Challenge of a Lifetime, Romance on the Orient Express, Hostage Flight, Final Jeopardy, Dress Gray, Combat High, Queenie, Celebration Family, The Spirit, Proud Men, Man Against the Mob, To Heal a Nation, Maybe Baby, Lady Mobster, Full Exposure: The Sex Tapes Scandal, Billy the Kid, Man Against the Mob: The Chinatown Murders, Too Young to Die, The Court Martial of Jackie Robinson, Opposites Attract, The Big One: The Great Los Angeles Earthquake, Menu for Murder, White Hot: The Mysterious Murder of Thelma Todd, Survive the Savage Sea, Battling for Baby, Woman with a Past, Calendar Girl Cop Killer-The Bambi Bembenek Story, Danger Island, Fergie & Andrew: Behing the Palace Doors, Lady Boss, Beyond Suspicion Geronimo, French Silk, The Corpse Had a Familiar Face, Lakota Woman: Siege at Wounded Knee, Mortal Fear, Deadly Invasion: The Killer Bee Nightmare, The Other Woman, Seduced and Betrayed, Virus, Deadline for Murder: From the Files of Edna Buchanan, The West Side Waltz, Terminal, Terror in the Family, No One Would Tell, My Son Is Innocent, Tornado, Crazy Horse, Dying to Belong, Murder Live, Mother Knows Best, NIghtscream, Invasion, Two Came Back, Holiday in Your Heart, Host, Don't Look Down, Fatal Error, A Murder On Shadow Mountain, Silent Predators, Mr. Rock and Roll, Nowhere to Land, Inside the Osmonds, Within These Walls, After Amy, Three Days, We Were the Mulvaneys, Scared Silent, Just a Walk in the Park (also prod.), The Shoot Divas Don't They?, Heart of a Stranger, Tempted, More than Meets the Eye: The Joan Brock Story, Defending our Kids: The Julie Posey Story, See Jane Date, Killer Instinct: From the Files of Agent Candice DeLong, The Elizabeth Smart Story, The Mystery of Natalie Wood, Reversible Errors, I Do But I Don't, While I Was Gone, Category 6: Day of Destruction, Dynasty: The Making of a Guilty Pleasure, Vinegar Hill, Spring Break Shark Attack, Mom at Sixteen, Locusts (also prod.), Ambulance Girl, Haunting Sarah, The Hunt for the BTK Killer, Vampire Bats (also prod.), Category 7: The End of the World, For One Night, Fatal Desire, Relative Chaos, Girl Posi+ive, Queen Sized, Racing for Time, The Circuit, Flirting with Forty, Natalee Holloway, Acceptance, Sorority Wars, Pregnancy Pact, Beauty & the Briefcase, Revenge of the Bridesmaids. *Mini-series: Executive producer:* Too Rich: The Secret Life of Doris Duke.

WADSWORTH, STEVE
Executive. e. B.S. degree in engineering, Univ. of Virginia; MBA, UCLA Graduate School of Management. Wadsworth was a principal for the Windsor Park Group in Los Angeles with responsibilities for providing strategic, operational and financial management consulting services to companies primarily in the retail and consumer products industries. He hooked up with The Walt Disney Company in 1993, joining Disney's Consumer Products group as dir. of business planning. Wadsworth moved over to Disney Online, Disney's first Internet operation, at its inception in Sept. 1995. Before being named pres. of Disney's Internet operations in 1999, he served as the unit's senior v.p. & CFO, responsible for all strategic planning, business development, technology operations, finance, accounting and administrative functions. On July 10, 2008, Disney combined the Walt Disney Internet Group and Disney's video gaming unit, Disney Interactive Media Group, with Wadsworth at the helm as president. He resigned from this position September, 2010.

WAGNER, LINDSAY
Actress. b. Los Angeles, CA, June 22, 1949. Appeared in school plays in Portland, OR; studied singing and worked professionally with rock group. In 1968 went to L.A. Signed to Universal contract in 1971.
PICTURES: Two People, The Paper Chase, Second Wind, Nighthawks, High Risk, Martin's Day, Ricochet, Frog and Wombat, The Fourth Horseman, A Light in the Forest, The Surfer King, Billy: The Early Years.
TELEVISION: *Movies*: The Rockford Files (pilot), The Bionic Woman, The Incredible Journey of Dr. Meg Laurel, The Two Worlds of Jennie Logan, Scruples, Callie and Son, Memories Never Die, I Want to Live, Princess Daisy, Two Kinds of Love, Jessie, Passions, The Other Lover, This Child Is Mine, Stranger in My Bed, Child's Cry, Convicted, Young Again, The Return of the Six Million Dollar Man and the Bionic Woman, Student Exchange, Evil in Clear River, The Taking of Flight 847, Nightmare at Bitter Creek, Scandals, Police Story: Burnout, From the Dead of Night, The Bionic Showdown: The Six-Million Dollar Man and the Bionic Woman, Voices of the Heart, Shattered Dreams, Babies, Fire in the Dark, She Woke Up, Treacherous Crossing, To Be the Best, A Message From Holly, Nurses on the Line: The Crash of Flight 7, Danielle Steel's Once in a Lifetime, Bionic Ever After?, Fighting for My Daughter, Sins of Silence, A Mother's Instinct, Contagious, Their Second Chance, Voyage of Terror, Thicker Than Water, Four Extraordinary Women. *Series*: The Bionic Woman (Emmy Award, 1977, 2 Golden Globe noms.), Jessie, Against All Odds (host), Peaceable Kingdom. *Guest:* More than 96 appearances.

WAGNER, PAULA
Producer, Agent, Actress, Executive. b. Youngstown, OH, Dec. 12, 1946. e.Carnegie-Mellon University Pittsburgh, Pennsylvania, BFA Theatre. Agent for CAA, representing Tom Cruise and many others. Formed Cruise/Wagner Productions in 1993, producing with Paramount Pictures. Cruise/Wagner Prod. left Paramount Pictures in 2006. In November 2006, MGM enlisted the Cruise/Wagner team and named Wagner CEO of its United Artist label. Wagner has part ownership of UA with control of the company's production slate. She also served as head of one of the juries at the 2006 Venice Film Festival.
THEATRE: As Actress: Numerous Broadway, Off Broadway productions and Yale Repertory Theatre. Playwright: Co-authored Out of Our Father's House (1977).
PICTURES: Murder in the First (project consultant). *Prod:* Mission: Impossible (Nova Award 1997), Without Limits, Mission: Impossible II, Vanilla Sky, The Last Samurai (PGA, Golden Laurel Award 2004), Suspect Zero, Elizabethtown, Ask the Dust, Mission: Impossible III, The Eye, Death Race, Mission: Impossible IV. *Exec. Prod.:* The Others, Narc, Shattered Glass, War of the Worlds, Lions for Lambs, Valkyrie, Death Race 2.
TELEVISION: *Movie*: Out of Our Father's House (writer). *Mini-series:* Loose Change (actress), Nightmares and Dreamscapes: From the Stories of Stephen King (episode exec. prod.). *Series:* Jammin' (actress). *Documentary:* Women on Top: Hollywood and Power.

WAGNER, RAYMOND JAMES
Producer. b. College Point, NY, Nov. 3, 1925. e. Middlebury College, Williams College. Joined Young & Rubicam, Inc., as radio-TV commercial head in Hollywood, 1950-59. Head of pilot devt., Universal Studios, 1960-65. V.P. of prod. (features) for MGM, 1972-79. Presently independent producer.
PICTURES: *Prod.*: Petulia, Loving (exec. prod.), Code of Silence, Rent-a-Cop, Hero and the Terror, Turner and Hooch, Run, Fifty Fifty, Snow Day.
TELEVISION: *Movies:* The Hanged Man, Maniac Magee.

WAGNER, ROBERT
Actor. b. Detroit, MI, Feb. 10, 1930. e. Saint Monica's H.S. m. actress Jill St. John. Signed contract with 20th Century-Fox, 1950.
PICTURES: The Happy Years (debut, 1950), The Halls of Montezuma, The Frogmen, Let's Make It Legal, With a Song in My Heart, What Price Glory?, Stars and Stripes Forever (Golden Globe nom. 1953), The Silver Whip, Titanic, Beneath the 12-Mile Reef, Prince Valiant,
Broken Lance, White Feather, A Kiss Before Dying, The Mountain, Between Heaven and Hell, The True Story of Jesse James, Stopover Tokyo, The Hunters, In Love and War, Say One for Me, All the Fine Young Cannibals, Sail a Crooked Ship, The Longest Day, The War Lover, The Condemned of Altona, The Pink Panther, Harper, Banning, The Biggest Bundle of Them All, Don't Just Stand There, Winning, The Towering Inferno, Midway, The Concorde—Airport '79, Trail of the Pink Panther, Curse of the Pink Panther, I Am the Cheese, Delirious, The Player, Dragon: The Bruce Lee Story, Austin Powers: International Man of Mystery, Wild Things, Something to Believe In, No Vacancy, The Kidnapping of Chris Burden, Austin Powers: The Spy Who Shagged Me, Crazy in Alabama, Play It To The Bone, Love and Fear, Forever Fabulous, Jungle Juice, Sol Goode, Nancy & Frank: A Manhattan Love Story, Austin Powers in Goldmember, The Calling, El Padrino, Man in the Chair, Hoot, Everyone's Hero (voice), Netherbeast Incorporated, The Wild Stallion, Life's a Beach.
TELEVISION: *Movies*: How I Spent My Summer Vacation, City Beneath the Sea, The Cable Car Murder, Killer by Night, Madame Sin (also exec. prod.), Streets of San Francisco (pilot), The Affair, The Abduction of St. Anne, Switch (pilot), Death at Love House, Cat on a Hot Tin Roof, The Critical List, Hart to Hart (pilot), To Catch a King, There Must Be a Pony, Love Among Thieves, Windmills of the Gods, Indiscreet, This Gun for Hire, False Arrest, Daniel Steel's Jewels, Deep Trouble, Hart to Hart Returns (also co-exec. prod.), Hart to Hart: Home is Where the Hart Is, Hart to Hart: Crimes of the Hart, Hart to Hart: Old Friends Never Die, Parallel Lives, Hart to Hart: Secrets of the Heart, Fatal Error, Becoming Dick, Rocket's Red Glare, The Retrievers, The Fallen Ones, Mystery Woman, Category 7: The End of the World, Making It Legal, Pretty/Handsome. *Mini-series*: Pearl, Around the World in 80 Days, Heaven & Hell: North and South Book III, Camino de Santiago. *Series*: It Takes A Thief (Emmy nom.; Golden Globe nom. 1970), Colditz (UK), Switch, Hart to Hart (4 Golden Globe noms.), Lime Street, Hope & Faith, Two and a Half Men. *Guest:* More than 180 apppearances.

WAITE, RALPH
Actor. b. White Plains, NY, June 22, 1928. e. Bucknell U.; Yale U. Social worker, publicity dir., assistant editor and minister before turning to acting. Founder of the Los Angeles Actors Theatre.
THEATRE: *B'way*: Hogan's Goat, The Watering Place, Trial of Lee Harvey Oswald. *Off-B'way*: The Destiny of Me, The Young Man From Atlanta. *Regional*: Hometown Heroes.
PICTURES: Cool Hand Luke, A Lovely Way to Die, Last Summer, Five Easy Pieces, Lawman, The Grissom Gang, The Sporting Club, The Pursuit of Happiness, Chato's Land, The Magnificent Seven Ride, Trouble Man, Kid Blue, The Stone Killer, On theNickel (also dir., prod., s.p.), Crash and Burn, The Bodyguard, Cliffhanger, Sioux City, Homeward Bound II: Lost in San Francisco (voice), Timequest, Sunshine State, Silver City, Letters to God, 25 Hill.
TELEVISION: *Movies*: The Secret Life of John Chapman, Waiting for Godot, Red Alert, Ohms, Angel City, The Gentleman Bandit, A Wedding on Waltons Mountain, Mother's Day on Waltons Mountain, A Day for Thanks on Waltons Mountain, A Good Sport, Growing Pains, Crime of Innocence, Red Earth White Earth, Sparks: The Price of Passion, A Walton Thanksgiving Reunion, Keys to her Past, Sin and Redemption, A Season of Hope, A Walton Wedding, A Walton Easter, The Third Twin, The President's Man, Spirit, Blessings, Generation Gap, Ace Ventura: Pet Detective Jr. *Mini-series*: Roots (Emmy nom. 1977). *Series*: The Waltons (also dir., Emmy nom. 1978 for acting), The Mississippi, All My Children, Murder One, Orleans, Carnivàle, Days of Our Lives. *Guest:* More than 62 appearances.

WAITE, RIC
Cinematographer. b. Sheboygan, WI, July 10, 1933. e. Univ. of CO. Photographed more than 40 movies-of-the-week for TV, 1979-83.
PICTURES: The Other Side of the Mountain (debut, 1975), Defiance, On the Nickel, The Long Riders, The Border, Tex, 48 Hrs., Class, Uncommon Valor, Footloose, Red Dawn, Volunteers, Summer Rental, Brewster's Millions, Cobra, Adventures in Babysitting, The Great Outdoors, Marked for Death, Out for Justice, Rapid Fire, On Deadly Ground, Truth or Consequences—N.M, Woman Wanted, The Watcher, Fallacy, A Handful of Beans, Best Ribs in Town, Serpent Rising.
TELEVISION: *Movies:* Nakia, The November Plan, Tail Gunner Joe (Emmy nom. 1977), Every Man A King (Emmy nom. 1978), Red Alert, The Initiation of Sarah, A Question of Guilt, Leave Yesterday Behind, A Guide for the Married Woman, Amateur Night at the Dixie Bar and Grill, Charleston, Steeletown, And Baby Makes Six, Nero Wolfe, The Comeback Kid, A Perfect Match, Revenge of the Stepford Wives, Baby Comes Home, Dempsey, Midas Valley, You Ruined My Life, Police Story: Burnout, Scam, Last Light, Money Plays, Last Stand at Saber River, Heart Full of Rain, Hope, Absence of the Good, Ratz, A Mother's Fight for Justice, The Triangle. *Mini-series:* Captains and the Kings (Emmy Award, 1977), Andersonville (Emmy nom. 1996). *Series:* Emergency!, Police Story, City of Angels, The New Adventures of Wonder Woman.

WAITS, TOM
Singer, Composer, Actor. b. Pomona, CA, Dec. 7, 1949. Recorded numerous albums and received Acad. Award nom. for his song score of One from the Heart. Composed songs for On the Nickel, Streetwise, Paradise Alley, Wolfen, American Heart, Dead Man Walking, Night on Earth (score). Featured songs in Smoke and Things to Do in Denver When You're Dead. Has starred in Chicago's Steppenwolf Theatre Co.'s Frank's Wild Years (also co-wrote, wrote the music) and Los Angeles Theatre Co.'s Demon Wine. Wrote songs and music for opera The Black Rider (1990). Co-wrote songs and music for opera Alice by Robert Wilson. Received Grammy Award for album, Bone Machine, 1992.
PICTURES: *Actor*: Paradise Alley, Poetry in Motion, The Outsiders, Rumble Fish, The Cotton Club, Down by Law (also music), Ironweed, Candy Mountain, Big Time (also co-s.p.), Cold Feet, Bearskin, Night On Earth (music only), The Two Jakes, Queens Logic, The Fisher King, At Play in the Fields of the Lord, Bram Stoker's Dracula, Short Cuts (Golden Globe Award 1994, best ensemble), Luck, Trust & Ketchup: Robert Altman In Carver Country, Coffee and Cigarettes III, Guy Maddin: Waiting for Twilight, Mystery Men, Freedom Highway, Texas Lullaby, The Good Heart, The Imaginarium of Doctor Parnassus, The Book of Eli. *As Composer:* Léolo, American Heart, One from the Heart (Academy Award nom. 1983 for best music, score, original song and best adaptation), Smoke, Twelve Monkeys, Dead Man Walking, Fight Club, Liberty Heights, Gun Shy, Keeping the Faith, The Perfect Storm, Pollock, Big Bad Love, The United States of Leland, Coffee and Cigarettes, The Prince and Me, Hellboy, Shrek 2, Ramones Raw (doc.), Around the Bend, Robots, The Secret Life of Words, Domino, Daltry Calhoun, Jarhead, Wristcutters: A Love Story, The Diving Bell and the Butterfly.
TELEVISION: *Movies: As Composer:* The Black Rider, Bez pogovora, Badry's Alibi, Generation X. *Documentaries: Actor:* Guy Maddin: Waiting for Twilight (narr.), Mississippi Rising. *As Composer: Series:* True Life, Pensionatet, Forklædt som voksen, Sig det ikke til nogen..., Norah Jones & the Handsome Band: Live in 2004 (special), The Wire, Ole & Jarl.

WAJDA, ANDRZEJ
Director, Writer. b. Suwalki, Poland, March 6, 1926. e. Fine Arts Academy, Krakow, Poland, 1945-48; High School of Cinematography, Lodz, Poland, 1950-52. 1940-43, worked as asst. in restoration of church paintings. 1942, joined Polish gov. in exile's A.K. (Home Army Resistance) against German occupation. 1950-52, directed shorts (While You Sleep; The Bad Boy, The Pottery of Ilzecka) as part of film school degree; 1954, asst. dir. to Aleksander Ford on 5 Boys from Barska Street. 1981, concentrated on theatrical projects in Poland and film prods. with non-Polish studios. 1983, gov. dissolved his Studio X film prod. group. 1984, gov. demanded Wajda's resignation as head of filmmakers' assoc. in order to continue org.'s existence. 1989, appt. artistic dir. of Teatr Powszechny, official Warsaw theater. Also leader of the Cultural Comm. of the Citizen's Committee. 1989, elected senator. Short films: While You Sleep, The Bad Boy, The Pottery of Ilza, I Go to the Sun. Received Honorary Academy Award, 1998. Received Academy Award, Oscar Salute for extraordinary film direction, 2000.
PICTURES: *Director/Writer*: A Generation (debut, 1957), Kanal, Ashes and Diamonds, Lotna, Innocent Sorcerers, Samson, Siberian Lady Macbeth (Fury Is a Woman), Love at 20 (Warsaw Poland episode), Ashes, Gates to Paradise, Everything for Sale, Hunting Flies, Landscape After the Battle, The Wedding, Promised Land, Shadow Line, Man of Marble, Without Anesthetic, The Girls From Wilko, The Orchestra Conductor, Man of Iron (Golden Palm Award, Cannes, 1981), Danton, A Love in Germany, Chronicle of Love Affairs, The Possessed, Korczak, The Ring with a Crowned Eagle, Nastasja, Holy Week, Miss Nobody, Pan Nikt, Pan Tadeusz: The Last Foray in Lithuania, Kekcja polskiego kina (documentary), The Revenge, Katyn, Tatarak.
TELEVISION: *Movies:* Przekladaniec (short), Pilatus und andere, Umarla klasa, Wyrok na Franciszka Klosa. *Mini-series:* Les Français vus par, Broken Silence (consult. dir.). *Series:* Z biegiem lat, z biegiem dni.

WALDEN, DANA
Executive. e. University of Southern California. Walden began her career at the public relations firm Bender, Goldman & Helper. She served at the studio's creative department as V. P. of Current Programming since 1994 and served as Sr. V.P. at Media and in Corporate Relations at both Twentieth Television and Twentieth Century Fox Television (TCFTV). She was promoted to Co-Pres., TCFTV in November of 1999, a position shared with friend Gary Newman. Became Co-President, TCFTV in November of 1999, a position he shares with friend Dana Walden. Since that time, Newman and Walden have been responsible for overseeing operations for the studio and have been instrumental in building TCFTV into a leading supplier of programming across all media from broadcast and cable television to syndication, mobile and broadband. TCFTV is home to writers and producers working in the industry including Seth MacFarlane, Shawn Ryan, Greg Garcia, Ryan Murphy, David E. Kelly, Goward Gordon and Joel Surnow and they maintain an exclusive relationship with Imagine Television. In addition to its roster of live action scripted comedies and dramas which under their tenure included "24," "Bones," "How I Met Your Mother," "Prison Break," "My Name Is Earl," "Raising Hope" and "Glee." TCFTV has become the leader in animated comedies for prime time with such hits as "The Simpsons," and "Family Guy," among others. Newman and Walden also oversee the studio's Licensing and Merchandizing division for their entertainment properties in areas including publishing, videogames, promotions, e-commerce, retail and themed entertainment. They also drive the Licensing and Merchandising efforts of Fox Film, Fox Sports and the Microsoft Game Studios hit, "Halo." In 2002, Newman and Walden pioneered the now common industry practice of releasing television series on DVD immediately following each broadcast season, at the time, a revolutionary idea that helped drive the Fox drama "24" to blockbuster status in its second season. Newman and Walden have also been at the forefront of developing new production models, creating fox21 in 2004, a production house devoted to empowering writers to produce their "passion projects" by rethinking conventional television production economics. They have also produced a range of innovative content based on the studio's hit franchises for the worldwide wireless market. Gary Newman and Dana Walden were named Chairmen of TCFTV in 2007, a position they hold today

WALKEN, CHRISTOPHER
Actor. r.n. Ronald Walken b. Astoria, NY, Mar. 31, 1943. Began career in off-B'way play J.B. billed as Ronnie Walken. Won Acad. Award, Best Supporting Actor for role in Deer Hunter, 1978.
THEATRE: *NY:* Best Foot Forward (Clarence Derwent Award), Kid Champion (Obie Award), High Spirits (B'way debut, 1964), The Lion in Winter (Clarence Derwent Award), Him (also writer), The Rose Tattoo (Theatre World Award), Hurlyburly (B'way), The Seagull, The Dead. NY Shakespeare Festival: Coriolanus, Othello.
PICTURES: The Anderson Tapes (debut, 1971), The Happiness Cage, Next Stop Greenwich Village, The Sentinel, Annie Hall, Roseland, The Deer Hunter (Academy Award, Best Supporting Actor, Golden Globe nom. 1979), Last Embrace, Heaven's Gate, The Dogs of War, Shoot the Sun Down, Pennies from Heaven, Brainstorm, The Dead Zone, A View to a Kill, At Close Range, Deadline, The Milagro Beanfield War, Biloxi Blues, Puss in Boots, Homeboy, Communion, King of New York, The Comfort of Strangers, McBain, All-American Murder, Batman Returns, Mistress, Le Grand Pardon, Day of Atonement, True Romance, Wayne's World 2, A Business Affair, Pulp Fiction, Search and Destroy, The Prophecy, The Addiction, Wild Side, Things to Do in Denver When You're Dead, Nick of Time, The Funeral, Last Man Standing, Touch, Excess Baggage, Suicide Kings, Mouse Hunt, Trance, The Prophecy II, New Rose Hotel, Illuminata, Antz (voice), Vendetta, The Prophecy III: The Ascent, The Opportunists, Kiss Toledo Goodbye, Blast from the Past, Sleepy Hollow, Inside Job, Joe Dirt, The Papp Project, America's Sweethearts, Scotland PA, The Affair of the Necklace, Poolhall Junkies, Stuart Little 2 (voice), Down and Under, Plots With A View, The Country Bears, Catch Me If You Can (Academy Award nom. 2003), Gigli, Helldorado, Kangaroo Jack, Envy, The Rundown, Man on Fire, The Stepford Wives, Around the Bend, The Wedding Crashers, Romance & Cigarettes, Domino, Man of the Year, Fade to Black, Click, We Own the Night, Hairspray (also soundtrack performer), Balls of Fury, Five Dollars a Day, The Maiden Heist, The Irishman, Office Paranormal.
TELEVISION: *Movies*: Barefoot in Athens, The Three Musketeers, Valley Forge, Who Am I This Time?, Sarah: Plain and Tall (Emmy nom. 1991), Scam, Sarah Plain and Tall: Skylark, Sarah Plain and Tall: Winter's End, Vendetta. *Mini-series:* Caesar. *Series:* The Wonderful John Acton (as Ronnie Walken), Guiding Light (as Ronnie Walken). *Documentaries/Specials*: Saturday Night Live 25th Anniversary. *Guest:* More than 102 appearances.

WALLACE, JOHN P.
Executive. e. Providence College, bachelor's degree, English; Montclair State University, master's degree in political science. Began career at NBC in 1988 as a member of the NBC Page Program. Wallace then held various positions in the NBC network's affiliate relations, network operations, finance, and affiliate services departments. From 1998-2000 worked in sales mgt. at NBC 10 in Philadelphia. Wallace managed the local sales department after completing a two-year post as v.p. and chief quality officer for the stations division. During this time Wallace earned General Electric (GE) certification as a Master Blackbelt. In 2000, Wallace became senior v.p., broadcast operations, NBC Television Stations Division. While there, Wallace developed the broadcast hub model, which centralized the stations' master control operations into three regional broadcast centers. He then built a centralized graphics operation in Fort Worth, TX, which produces all graphics for the NBC and Telemundo owned-and-operated stations in a single location at lower cost with higher quality production capability. GE, NBC Universal's parent company, recognized Wallace for this innovative technological and operational achievement with the prestigious Edison Award in May 2005. Wallace helped the company achieve additional efficiency when he led the operational integration of NBC and Vivendi Universal in 2004, which resulted in $100 million of operations synergies for the new company. Also in 2004, Wallace

became executive v.p., television operations & productions services of the merged company. He was responsible for broadcast operations across NBC Universal's extensive TV properties, overseeing the field, production, studio, on-air, and distribution operations for the NBC and Telemundo broadcast television networks, cable networks, and owned-and-operated TV stations. One of his most significant achievements was to integrate NBC Universal's operational and technical TV assets into enterprise-wide platforms, eliminating legacy broadcast silos. As a result, distribution of network and cable content is processed through one operating center and system, resulting in millions of dollars in synergies. In Jan. 2007, Wallace received the GE Chairman's Award in the Technology category for his innovative work using cutting-edge technology to improve performance and reduce costs. He was named to his current position, president, NBC Owned-and-Operated Television Stations, in July 2007. He oversees NBC Universal's 10 English-language TV stations, which provide NBC network and local programming to nearly 30% of the nation's households. He reports directly to NBC Universal President & CEO Jeff Zucker.

WALLACE, MIKE

Broadcast Journalist. b. Brookline, MA, May 9, 1918. e. U. of Michigan, B.A., 1939. Served in U.S. Navy, 1943-46. Newscaster, announcer, and continuity writer, radio station WOOD WASH, Grand Rapids, Michigan, 1939-40; newscaster, narrator, announcer, WXYZ Radio, Detroit, Michigan, 1940-41 on such shows as The Lone Ranger and The Green Hornet; freelance radio worker, Chicago, Illinois, announcer for the soap opera Road of Life, 1941-42, Ma Perkins, and The Guiding Light; acted in The Crime Files of Flamon; news radio announcer, Chicago Sun's Air Edition, 1941-43, 1946-48; announced radio programs such as Curtain Time, Fact or Fiction, and Sky King; host, Mike and Buff with his wife, New York City, 1950-53; host, various television and radio shows and narrator, various documentaries 1951-59; star, Broadway comedy Reclining Figure, 1954.Night Beat, WABD, N.Y., 1956; The Mike Wallace Interview, ABC, 1956-58; newspaper col., Mike Wallace Asks, N.Y. Post, 1957-58; News Beat, WNTA-TV, 1959-61; The Big Surprise (Golden Globe Award 1958), The Mike Wallace Interview, WNTA-TV, 1959-61; Biography, 1962; correspondent, CBS News, 1963, CBS Radio; Personal Closeup, Mike Wallace at Large; Co-editor, 60 Minutes (Emmy Awards, 1971, 1972, 1973), CBS News, Host, 20th Century, 1994, Breaking the News, 2001). Recipient: 18 Emmy Awards; Peabody Awards, 1963 and 1971; DuPont Columbia Journalism Awards, 1971 and 1983. Retired from 60 Minutes after 38 years as reporter. Became correspondent emeritus for the show 2006. *Guest:* More than 88 appearances.

WALLACE, SCOTT

Exhibitor.. e. Stanford Graduate School of Business, M.B.A., 1980. Wallace currently is chmn. & CEO of the Wallace Theater Corporation, a domestic and international theatre circuit headquartered in Portland, OR. He is also chairman and CEO of its wholly owned subsidiary Hollywood Theaters. Prior to forming Wallace Theater Corporation in 1991, Wallace co-founded Act III Theaters Inc., which became the eighth largest motion picture exhibitor in the U.S., serving as president and CEO. Before co-founding Act III, Wallace served as a senior executive at AMC Entertainment Inc., the second largest theatre circuit in the world at the time. Memberships: Wallace has served on the Univ. of Nevada Foundation bd. of trustees.

WALLACH, BARRY

Executive. b. Stanford, CT. e. Syracuse Univ., bachelor's degree, business and communications. 1987, joined Genesis Entertainment as an account executive, Midwest division. 1988, promoted to vice president; 1990, became senior v.p., domestic sales. While at Genesis/New World Television, Wallach was executive v.p. of domestic sales and played a key role in the 1996 launch of "Access Hollywood" from NBC and New World Television. He then moved to CBS/Eyemark Entertainment and was executive v.p. of domestic syndication. He oversaw the launch and/or renewal of 27 programs during his four-year tenure with the company, including the off-net syndication sales of "Everybody Loves Raymond," "Touched By An Angel," "Caroline in the City," and the first-run daily series "Martha Stewart Living." Left for WorldNow, where he was executive v.p., distribution & marketing. He directed the expansion of the WorldNow Network, as well as all the company's marketing activities. Wallach then joined NBC Enterprises and as executive v.p., he was responsible for all domestic distribution sales of NBC-owned product, which included domestic first-run syndication sales, strategic marketing and ancillary exploitation of owned product in home video, merchandising, licensing, music and publishing, and also strategic production and co-production alliances and co-ventures. This programming includes all shows produced by NBC Studio, NBC News, CNBC and MSNBC. Wallach was named president, NBC Universal Domestic Television Distribution, in May 2004. In this role today, he oversees all domestic sales and distribution for NBC Universal Television Distribution. The division currently distributes more than a dozen first-run strip and weekly nationally syndicated programs, including "Access Hollywood," "The Martha Stewart Show," "The Jerry Springer Show," "Maury," "Reel Talk" and "The Chris Matthews Show." The division also distributes current and library NBC Universal film and television programs, including "The Office," "House" and the "Law & Order" series.

WALLACH, ELI

Actor. b. Brooklyn, NY, Dec. 7, 1915. e. U. of Texas at Austin, B.A., 1936. m. actress Anne Jackson. Capt. in Medical Admin. Corps during WWII. After college acting, appeared in summer stock. Charter member of the Actors Studio. Received the MPAA Governor's Award 2011.
THEATRE: Skydrift (B'way debut, 1945), Antony & Cleopatra, The Rose Tattoo (Tony Award, 1951), Mademoiselle Colombe, Camino Real, The Teahouse of August Moon (also London), Major Barbara, Rhinoceros, Luv, Twice Around the Park, Cafe Crown, The Price, In Persons (Off-B'way), The Flowering Peach, Visiting Mr. Green.
PICTURES: Baby Doll (debut, 1956; BFA Award, Golden Globe nom. 1957), The Line Up, The Magnificent Seven, Seven Thieves, The Misfits, Hemingway's Adventures of A Young Man, How the West Was Won, The Victors, Act One, The Moonspinners, Kisses for My President, Lord Jim, Genghis Khan, How to Steal a Million, The Good the Bad and the Ugly, The Tiger Makes Out, How to Save a Marriage and Ruin Your Life, MacKenna's Gold, A Lovely Way to Die, Ace High, The Brain, Zigzag, The People Next Door, The Angle Levine, The Adventures of Gerard, Romance of a Horse Thief, Cinderella Liberty, Crazy Joe, Stateline Motel, Don't Turn the Other Cheek, The Sentinel, Nasty Habits, The Deep, The Domino Principle, Girlfriends, Movie Movie, Circle of Iron, Firepower, Winter Kills, The Hunter, The Salamander, Sam's Son, Tough Guys, Nuts, Funny, The Two Jakes, The Godfather Part III, Article 99, Mistress, Night and the City, Two Much, The Associate, Keeping the Faith, Cinerama Adventure, Advice and Dissent, Broadway; The Golden Age by the Legends Who Were There (documentary), Mystic River, King of the Corner, The Moon and the Son (short; voice), The Easter Egg Adventure (narrator; voice), The Hoax, The Holiday, Vote and Die: Liszt for President, The Toe Tactic, Tickling Leo, New York, I Love You, The Ghost Writer, Wall Street: Money Never Sleeps.
TELEVISION: *Movies*: Cold Night's Death, Indict and Convict, Seventh Avenue, The Pirate, Fugitive Family, Pride of Jesse Halam, Skokie, The Wall, Anatomy of an Illness, Poppies Are Also Flowers (Emmy Award 1967), Murder: By Reason of Insanity, Something in Common (Emmy nom. 1987), Executioner's Song, Christopher Columbus, Embassy, The Impossible Spy, Vendetta: Secrets of a Mafia Bride, Legacy of Lies, Teamster Boss: The Jackie Presser Story, Vendetta 2: The New Mafia, Naked City: Justice with a Bullet, The Bookfair Murders, Monday Night Mayhem. *Series*: Our Family Honor, Character Studies, Studio 60 on the Sunset Strip (recurring role, Emmy nom. 2007), Nurse Jackie (Emmy nom. 2010 as guest). *Guest*: More than 160 appearances.

WALSH, DYLAN

Actor. b. Nov. 17, 1963. Raised in Africa, Indonesia, India, Washington D.C. e. Univ. of VA. On D.C. stage with Arena Stage and Studio Theatre, Heritage Rep. Co. Appearing in A Midsummer Night's Dream, Curse of the Starving Class, Romeo & Juliet, Death of a Salesman.
PICTURES: Loverboy, Where the Heart Is, Betsy's Wedding, Arctic Blue, Nobody's Fool, Congo, Eden, Changing Habits, Men, Final Voyage, Chapter Zero, Jet Boy, Deadly Little Secrets, We Were Soldiers, Par 6, Blood Work, Power Play, Antebody, Edmond, The Lake House, The Stepfather, Secretariat.
TELEVISION: *Movies:* When We Were Young, Chameleons, Telling Secrets, The Almost Perfect Bank Robbery, Radio Inside, The Lone Ranger, Divided by Hate, More Than Meets the Eye: The Joan Brock Story, Christmas Miracle, Lost Holiday: The Jim & Suzanne Shemwell Story. *Series:* Gabriel's Fire, Brooklyn South, Nip/Tuck, The Line (also pilot).

WALSH, M. EMMET

Actor. r.n. Michael Emmet Walsh. b. Ogdensburg, NY, Mar. 22, 1935. e. Clarkson Col. (B.B.A., 1958), American Academy of Dramatic Arts (1959-61).
THEATRE: *B'way*: Does the Tiger Wear a Necktie?, That Championship Season. *Off-B'way*: Shepherds of the Shelf, The Old Glory, The Outside Man, Death of the Well Loved Boy, Three From Column 'A', Are You Now or Have You Ever Been, Marathon '93. Extensive summer stock and regional theatre.
PICTURES: End of the Road, Midnight Cowboy, Alice's Restaurant, Stiletto, Loving, They Might Be Giants, The Traveling Executioner, Little Big Man, Escape from the Planet of the Apes, Get to Know Your Rabbit, The Gambler, The Prisoner of 2nd Avenue, What's Up Doc?, Kid Blue, The Fish That Saved Pittsburgh, Serpico, Mikey and Nicky, Cold Turkey, At Long Last Love, Nickelodeon, Bound for Glory, Airport '77, Slap Shot, Straight Time, The Jerk, Raise the Titanic, Brubaker, Ordinary People, Reds, Back Roads, Fast-Walking, The Escape Artist, Cannery Row, Blade Runner, Silkwood, Blood Simple, Scandalous, (Raw) Courage, Grandview USA, The Pope of Greenwich Village, Back to School, Critters, Missing in Action, Fletch, Wildcats, The Best of Times, Raising Arizona, Harry and the Hendersons, The Milagro Beanfield War, No Man's Land, Sunset, War Party, Clean and Sober, Catch Me If You Can,

Thunderground, Sundown: The Vampire in Retreat, Chattahoochee, Red Scorpion, The Mighty Quinn, Narrow Margin, Killer Image, The Naked Truth, White Sands, Equinox, Wilder Napalm, The Music of Chance, Bitter Harvest, Cops and Robbersons, Relative Fear, The Glass Shield, Probable Cause, Dead Badge, Camp Nowhere, Panther, Free Willy 2: The Adventure Home, Criminal Hearts, Portraits of a Killer, Albino Alligator, The Killing Jar, A Time to Kill, Romeo & Juliet, Retroactive, Carrot Top–Chairman of the Board, My Best Friend's Wedding, Legal Tender, Twilight, Wild Wild West, Iron Giant, Random Hearts (cameo), Me and Will, Eyeball Eddie, Poor White Trash, Jack of Hearts, Christmas In The Clouds, Snow Dogs, Baggage, Greener Mountains, Christmas with the Kranks, Racing Stripes, Man in the Chair, Chasing 3000, Big Stan, Your Name Here, Sherman's Way, The Assignment, Youth in Revolt, Sam Steele and the Junior Detective Agency, Roney's Point.
TELEVISION: *Movies*: Sarah T.—Portrait of a Teenage Alcoholic, Crime Club, Invasion of Johnson County, Red Alert, Superdome, A Question of Guilt, No Other Love, The Gift, Skag, City in Fear, High Noon Part II, Hellinger's Law, Night Partners, The Deliberate Stranger, Resting Place, Broken Vows, Hero in the Family, The Abduction of Kari Swenson, Murder Ordained, Brotherhood of the Rose, Love and Lies, Fourth Story, Wild Card, Four Eyes and Six-Guns, From the Mixed-Up Files of Mrs. Basil E. Frankweiler, The Lottery, Dogs, Monster, Tracey Ullman in the Trailer Tales. *Mini-series*: The French-Atlantic Affair, East of Eden. *Series*: The Sandy Duncan Show, Dear Detective, Unsub, The Mind of the Married Man. *Guest*: More than 100 appearances.

WALSH, RICHARD T.
Exhibitor. b. Rochester, NY, Sept. 26, 1953. e. Rockhurst College, BA in 1975, master's degree in business administration from Rockhurst in 1985. Walsh joined the AMC Theatres organization in 1975 in Kansas City. He held various positions managing local theatres before being promoted to National Training Director in 1981. Walsh became assistant operations manager for the Midwest Division in 1984, and was promoted to vice president and division operations manager in 1987. In 1992, Walsh was named VP and division operations manager of the Central Division. He served as senior v.p. of operations for the company's West Division from July 1, 1994 to September 29, 1999. From Sept. 29, 1999 to Nov. 9, 2001, he was EVP, Film Operations, AMC Film. In Nov. 2001, he became EVP/AMC Film Group Chairman, overseeing film, marketing and strategic development areas and the company's National Cinema Network cinema advertising subsidiary. Walsh left the company Aug. 17, 2007 after 32 years with the company.

WALTER, JESSICA
Actress. b. Brooklyn, NY, Jan. 31, 1944. m. actor Ron Leibman. e. H.S. of the Performing Arts. Studied at Bucks County Playhouse and Neighborhood Playhouse. Many TV performances plus lead in series, For the People. Broadway debut in Advise and Consent, 1961. Also, Photo Finish (Clarence Derwent Award), Night Life, A Severed Head, Rumors.
PICTURES: Lilith (debut, 1964), The Group, Grand Prix (Golden Globe nom. 1967), Bye Bye Braverman, Number One, Play Misty for Me (Golden Globe nom. 1972), Goldengirl, Going Ape, Spring Fever, The Flamingo Kid, Tapeheads, Ghost in the Machine, PCU, Dark Goddess, Slums of Beverly Hills, My Best Friend's Wife, Dummy, Unaccompanied Minors.
TELEVISION: *Movies*: The Immortal (pilot), Three's a Crowd, They Call It Murder, Women in Chains, Home for the Holidays, Hurricane, Having Babies, Victory at Entebbe, Black Market Baby, Wild and Wooly, Dr. Strange, Secrets of Three Hungry Wives, Vampire, She's Dressed to Kill, Miracle on Ice, Scruples, Thursday's Child, The Return of Marcus Welby M.D., The Execution, Killer in the Mirror, Leave of Absence, Mother Knows Best, Doomsday Rock, I Do (But I Don't), Retired at 35. *Mini-series*: Wheels. *Series*: For the People, Love of Life, Amy Prentiss (Emmy Award 1975), Bare Essence, The Streets of San Francisco (recurring role, Emmy nom. 1977), Aaron's Way, Trapper John, M.D. (Emmy nom. 1980), Dinosaurs (voice), The Round Table, One Life to Live, Oh Baby, Arrested Development (Emmy nom. 2005), 90210 (2008, also pilot), Archer, Saving Grace, Gravity. *Guest:* More than 145 appearances.

WALTER, TRACEY
Actor. b. Jersey City, NJ, Nov. 25, 1942.
PICTURES: Goin' South, Blue Collar, Hardcore, The Hunter, The Hand, Raggedy Man, Honkytonk Man, Timerider, Rumble Fish, Conan the Destroyer, Repo Man, At Close Range, Something Wild, Malone, Mortuary Academy, Married to the Mob, Under the Boardwalk, Out of the Dark, Batman, Homer and Eddie, Young Guns II, The Two Jakes, Pacific Heights, The Silence of the Lambs, City Slickers, Delusion, Amos and Andrew, Philadelphia, Mona Must Die, Destiny Turns on the Radio, Wild America, Road to Ruin, Dorothy Day, Junior, Amanda, Larger Than Life, Matilda, Desperate Measures, Playing God, Kiss the Girls, Beloved, Mighty Joe Young, Man on the Moon, Facade, Drowning Mona, Erin Brokovich, Blast, The Man From Elysian Fields, How High, Face Value, Imposter, Death to Smoochy, Ted Bundy, Masked and Anonymous, Duplex, The Manchurian Candidate, Berkeley, Relative Strangers, Nobel Son, One Part Sugar, Man in the Chair, The Death and Life of Bobby Z, Trailer Park of Terror, Dark Reel, Wasting Away, The Perfect Game, Midnight Son, Pickin' & Grinnin', I Spit on Your Grave, Politics of Love, Midnight Son, Alyce.
TELEVISION: *Movies*: Ride With the Wind, In the Line of Duty: Kidnapped, Buffalo Girls, Bill On His Own, Mad Bull, Out of this World, Tell Me No Secrets, The Devil's Child, Monster Makers, The Trail to Hope Rose, The Family Plan. *Series*: Best of the West, On the Air, Nash Bridges, Reno 911!. *Guest:* More than 70 appearances.

WALTERS, BARBARA
Broadcast Journalist. b. Boston, MA, Sept. 25, 1931. e. Sarah Lawrence Coll. Daughter of Latin Quarter nightclub impressario Lou Walters. Began working in TV after graduation. Joined The Today Show in 1961 as writer-researcher, making occasional on-camera appearances. In 1963, became full-time on camera. In April, 1974, named permanent co-host. Also hosted own synd. prog., Not for Women Only. In 1976, joined ABC-TV Evening News as the first woman to anchor a network evening newscast.
(1976-78), correspondent World News Tonight (1978); corresp. for 25 years with 20/20 (1979-2004). Host of The Barbara Walters Specials (1979-present, 1 Emmy Award, 11 Emmy noms.). *Author:* How to Talk with Practically Anybody About Practically Anything (1970), Audition: A Memoir (2008). Walters is co-owner, co-executive producer and co-host of The View. The View premiered in August 1997 and is broadcast live from New York City. Walters' numerous and timely interviews read like a "Who's Who" of newsmakers. She did the first interview for American television with Russia's President Vladimir Putin and through the years has interviewed such world figures as China's Premier Jiang Zemin, Great Britain's former Prime Minister Margaret Thatcher, Libya's Moammar Quadaffi and Iraq's President Sadaam Hussein. She has interviewed every American President and First Lady since Richard Nixon. She made journalism history by arranging the first joint interview with Egypt's President Anwar Sadat and Israel's Prime Minister Menachem Begin in November, 1977. Another of her "firsts" was an hour-long primetime conversation with Cuban President Fidel Castro — an interview shown all over the world. She has has received national recognition for her work, including: The Overseas Press Club's highest award, the President's Award, 1988; induction into the Academy of Television Arts and Sciences' Hall of Fame "for being acknowledged worldwide as one of television's most respected interviewers and journalists," 1990; the Lowell Thomas Award for a career in journalism excellence by Marist College, 1990; Lifetime Achievement Award, International Women's Media Foundation, 1991; Salute by the American Museum of the Moving Image, 1992; Lifetime Achievement Award, Women's Project and Productions, 1993; Honored by the Museum of Television & Radio for her contributions to broadcast journalism, 1996; The Muse Award from NY Women in Film and Television, 1997; Lifetime Achievement Award, National Academy of Television Arts and Sciences, 2000. Walters is the recipient of honorary doctoral degrees from Sarah Lawrence, her alma mater, as well as Ohio State University, Temple University, Marymount College, Wheaton College, Hofstra University and Ben-Gurion University in Jerusalem. The Barbara Walters Summer Special (series, host), Currently co-host, exec. prod. of The View (2 Emmy Awards, 21 Emmy noms.). *Guest:* More than 110 appearances.

WALTERS, JULIE
Actress. b. Birmingham, England, Feb. 22, 1950. Trained for 2 years to be a nurse before studying drama at Manchester Polytechnic, followed by year at Granada's Stables Theatre. Joined Everyman Theatre, Liverpool. Also toured Dockland pubs with songs, dance and imitations.
THEATRE: Breezeblock Park, Funny Perculiar, The Glad Hand, Good Fun, Educating Rita, Jumpers, Fool for Love, When I Was a Girl I Used to Scream and Shout, Frankie and Johnnie in the Claire de Lune, Macbeth, Having a Ball, The Rose Tattoo, Jumpers, Fool for Love, When I Was a Girl I Used to Scream and Shout, Frankie and Johnny.
PICTURES: Educating Rita (debut, 1983; Academy Award nom.; Golden Globe Award 2004), She'll Be Wearing Pink Pyjamas, Car Trouble, Personal Services, Prick Up Your Ears, Buster, Mack the Knife, Killing Dad, Stepping Out, Wide Eyed and Legless, The Summer House, The Wedding Gift, Just Like a Woman, Sister My Sister, Bath Time, Girls' Night, Titanic Town, Billy Elliot (Academy Award nom.; Golden Globe nom. 2001), All Forgotten, Harry Potter and the Sorcerer's Stone, Before You Go, Harry Potter and the Chamber of Secrets, Harry Potter and the Prisoner of Azkaban, Mickybo and Me, Wah-Wah, Driving Lessons, Becoming Jane, Harry Potter and the Order of the Phoenix, Mamma Mia!, Harry Potter and the Half-Blood Prince, Harry Potter and the Deathly Hallows: Part I, Harry Potter and the Deathly Hallows: Part II, Gnomeo and Juliet.
TELEVISION: *Movies:* Talent, Nearly a Happy Ending, Happy Since I Met You, Intensive Care, The Birthday Party, The Summer House, All Day Breakfast, Requiem Apache, Bambino mio, The Wedding Gift, Pat and Margaret, Brazen Hussies, Jack and the Beanstalk, Wetty Hainthropp Investigates (short), Strange Relations, Murder, The Return, Ahead of the Class, The Ruby in the Smoke, Filth: The Mary Whitehouse Story, A Short Stay in Switzerland, Mid Life Christmas, Mo. *Mini-series:* Boys from the Blackstuff, Talking Heads, G.B.H, Jake's Progress,

Melissa, Talking Heads 2, Oliver Twist, The Canterbury Tales. *Series:* Empire Road, Wood and Walters, Victoria Wood: As Seen on TV, The Secret Diary of Adrian Mole, Dinnerladies. *Guest:* More than 105 appearances.

WALTERS, MELORA
Actress. b. Saudi Arabia, Oct. 21, 1968.
PICTURES: Dead Poets Society, Underground, Beethoven, Twenty Bucks, Ed Wood, Cabin Boy, America's Deadliest Home Video, All Tied Up, Eraser, American Strays, Hard Eight, Boogie Nights, Los Locos, Magnolia, Desert Saints, Speaking of Sex, Wisegirls, Rain, The Big Empty, Matchstick Men, Cold Mountain, The Butterfly Effect, Harrison Montgomery, Brothers Three: An American Gothic, Hurt, bgFATLdy, Hurt, Case 219, Love Ranch, Missing Pieces.
TELEVISION: *Movies:* How to Murder a Millionaire, Telling Secrets, Dead Man's Revenge, Midnight Run for Your Life, Twice Upon a Time. *Series:* Roseanne, L.A. Doctors, Push Nevada, Threat Matrix, Big Love.

WALTON, JIM
Executive. e. Univ. of Maryland, bachelor's degree in Radio, TV & Film. Walton began his career in CNN's entry-level position as a video journalist in 1981. Since then he has held many positions in the television news business — from tape editor to executive producer. Two years after his arrival at CNN, Walton moved to CNN Sports editor and two years later, after helping to produce CNN's Olympic coverage, he was named an executive producer. From 1996-2000, Walton was the president of CNN's all-sports network, CNN/Sports Illustrated, while also in charge of the News Group's sports division. Walton then became pres., CNN News Group. His next stop at CNN was pres. & COO, overseeing editorial and financial operations for CNN Worldwide. His current assignment with CNN is pres., CNN Worldwide, with overall responsibility for the company's networks and services. Walton has won several awards, including multiple Cable Ace awards and an Emmy Award for coverage of the 1996 Olympic Park bombing.

WANG, GERI
Executive. e. Ithaca College. Wang began her career as a media research analyst at Grey Advertising in New York. She joined ABC in 1990 as an associate director of Daytime Sales Proposals. In 1991 she was promoted to associate director of Primetime Proposals, and in 1992 was promoted to account executive in Daytime Sales. In 1994 she became an account executive in Early Morning and Late-Night Sales, and in 1996 she was promoted to senior account executive in Primetime Sales. She was named V. P. of Primetime Sales in 1998 and Sr. V. P. of Primetime Sales in 2000. Was named Pres. of Sales & Marketing, ABC Television Network, in February 2010, reporting to Anne Sweeney, co-chair, Disney Media Networks and president, Disney/ABC Television Group. In this position Ms. Wang is responsible for sales and integrated marketing efforts for all dayparts of the ABC Television Network, including ABC Primetime, ABC Daytime, ABC News, ABC Late-Night, ABC Interactive and Sales Development. She also oversees Disney/ABC Unlimited, the cross-platform sales unit of The Walt Disney Company, as well as sales and integrated marketing efforts for SOAPnet.

WANG, WAYNE
Director. b. Hong Kong, Jan. 12, 1949. e. Came to U.S. to study photography at College of Arts and Crafts, Oakland, CA. m. actress Cora Miao. With a Master's Degree in film and television, returned to Hong Kong. Worked on TV comedy series. First dir. work, as asst. dir. for Chinese sequences of Golden Needle. First film was A Man, A Woman and a Killer. Won grant from AFI and National Endowment for the Arts, used to finance Chan is Missing (1982) which cost $22,000.
PICTURES: Chan is Missing (also s.p., editor, prod.), Dim Sum: A Little Bit of Heart (also prod., story), Slam Dance, Eat a Bowl of Tea, Life is Cheap... But Toilet Paper is Expensive (also exec. prod., story), The Joy Luck Club, Smoke, Blue in the Face (also co-s.p.), Chinese Box (also prod., s.p.), Anywhere But Here, Center of the World, Maid in Manhattan, Because of Winn-Dixie, Last Holiday, A Thousand Years of Good Prayers (also prod.), Snow Flower and the Secret Fan.

WARBECK, STEPHEN
Composer.
PICTURES: Skallagrigg, O Mary This London, Sister My Sister, Nervous Energy, Brothers in Trouble, Different for Girls, Element of Doubt, Her Majesty Mrs. Brown, My Son the Fanatic, Shakespeare in Love (Academy Award, Best Music for Original Musical or Comedy Score, 1999), Toy Boys, Heart, Mystery Men, Fanny and Elvis, Billy Elliot, Quills, Captain Corelli's Mandolin, Very Annie Mary, Gabriel & Me, Birthday Girl, Charlotte Gray, Mystics, Desire, Blackball, The Alzheimer Affair, Secret Passage, Love's Brother, Two Brothers, Everybody is a Killer, Oyster Farmer, On A Clear Day, Mickybo and Me, Travaux, Alpha Male, Killshot, Proof, Opa!, Cargo, Miguel and William, Goal II: Living the Dream, The Hessen Affair, Princess Kaiulani, Machan, The Winter Butterfly, Gallowwalker.
TELEVISION: *Movies:* Prime Suspect, Femme Fatale, The Mother, The Changeling, Bambino mio, Prime Suspect 4: The Lost Child, Prime Suspect 4: inner Circles, Devil's Advocate, Truth or Dare, Bright Hair, The Student Prince, A Christmas Carol, Very Annie Mary, The Prince of Hearts, DreamKeeper, Skellig. *Mini-series:* Prime Suspect 2, Prime Suspect 3, Prime Suspect 5: Errors of Judgment. *Series:* Bramwell IV.

WARD, DAVID S.
Writer, Director. b. Providence, RI, Oct. 24, 1947. Raised in Cleveland. e. Pomona College. (BA), UCLA (MFA).
PICTURES: *Writer:* Steelyard Blues, The Sting (Academy Award, Golden Globe nom.; WGA nom. 1974), Cannery Row (also dir.), The Milagro Beanfield War (co-s.p.), Major League (also dir.), King Ralph (also dir.), Sleepless in Seattle (co-s.p.; Academy Award nom.; WGA nom. 1994), The Mask of Zorro, The Program (also dir.), Major League II (also dir., prod.), The Best Man (also dir.), Flyboys (s.p.), Luna, Buddha (s.p.). *Director:* Down Periscope. *Producer:* Phase One.

WARD, FRED
Actor. b. San Diego, CA, Dec. 30, 1943. Raised in Louisiana and Texas. Studied at Herbert Berghof Studio. Moved to Rome to work in experimental theatre. Returned to U.S. to appear on San Fransico stage with Sam Shepard's Magic Theatre in Inacoma and Angel City. Additional stage work in The Glass Menagerie, One Flew Over the Cuckoo's Nest, Domino Courts, Simpatico.
PICTURES: Escape From Alcatraz (debut, 1979), Tilt, Carny, Southern Comfort, Timerider, The Right Stuff, Silkwood, Uncommon Valor, Swing Shift, Uforia, Secret Admirer, Remo Williams: The Adventure Begins, Off Limits, Big Business, The Prince of Pennsylvania, Tremors, Miami Blues (also co-exec. prod.), Henry and June, Thunderheart, The Player, Bob Roberts, The Dark Wind, Equinox, Short Cuts (Golden Globe Award for ensemble 1994), Naked Gun 33 1/3: The Final Insult, Two Small Bodies, The Blue Villa, Chain Reaction, Best Men, Dangerous Beauty, Circus, All the Fine Lines, The Crow: Salvation, Ropewalk, Road Trip, The Chaos Factor, Joe Dirt, Summer Catch, Corky Romano, Enough, A.K.A. Birdseye, Sweet Home Alabama, Abandon, Masked and Anonymous, Feast of Love, Exit Speed, Management, Farewell, Armored, The Wild Stallion, 30 Minutes or Less.
TELEVISION: *Movies*: Belle Starr, Noon Wine, Florida Straits, Cast a Deadly Spell, Backtrack, Four Eyes and Six-Guns, First Do No Harm, Wild Iris, Coast to Coast, The Last Ride, 10.5. *Mini-series:* Invasion: Earth, Jackie Bouvier Kennedy Onassis, Dice. *Series*: Georgetown. *Documentaries/Specials*: Noon Wine (Amer. Playhouse), Great Books: The Right Stuff (narr.), The West (voice), T-20 Years and Counting (short).

WARD, RACHEL
Actress. b. London, Sept. 12, 1957. m. actor Bryan Brown. Top fashion and TV commercial model before becoming actress. Studied acting with Stella Adler and Robert Modica.
PICTURES: Night School (debut, 1981), Sharky's Machine (Golden Globe nom. 1982), Dead Men Don't Wear Plaid, The Final Terror, Against All Odds, Hotel Colonial, Who's Zoomin' Who, How to Get Ahead in Advertising, After Dark My Sweet, Christopher Columbus: The Discovery, Wide Sargasso Sea, Double Obsession, The Ascent, The Big House (dir. & writer only), Blindman's Bluff (also writer, dir.), Martha's New Coat (dir. only), Beautiful Kate (dir., s.p.).
TELEVISION: *Movies:* Christmas Lillies of the Field, Fortress, And the Sea Will Tell, Black Magic, Double Jeopardy, My Stepson My Lover, On the Beach (Golden Globe nom. 2001), And Never Let Her Go, Bobbie's Girl, Johnson County War, Blackbeard. *Mini-series*: The Thorn Birds (Golden Globe nom. 1984), Shadow of the Cobra (U.K.), Seasons of Love, Blackbeard. *Series*: In the Name of Love, Monarch Cove, Rain Shadow, Rake (dir.).

WARD, SELA
Actress. b. Meridian, MS, July 11, 1956.
PICTURES: The Man Who Loved Women, Rustler's Rhapsody, Nothing in Common, Steel Justice, Hello Again, The Fugitive, My Fellow Americans, 54, Runaway Bride, Passion's Way, The Badge, Dirty Dancing: Havana Nights, The Day After Tomorrow, The Guardian, The Stepfather.
TELEVISION: *Movies:* Almost Golden: The Jessica Savitch Story (Cable Ace Award, Emmy nom. 1996), The Haunting of Sarah Hardy, Rainbow Drive, Child of Darkness, Child of Light, Bridesmaids, Killer Rules, Double Jeopardy, Rescuers: Stories of Courage: Two Women, Catch a Falling Star, (also exec. prod.), Suburban Madness. *Series:* Emerald Point N.A.S., Sisters (Emmy Award, Golden Globe nom. 1994), Once and Again (Emmy Award 2000, 1 other nom.; Golden Globe Award 2001, 2 other noms.), House, M.D. *Guest:* More than 57 appearances.

WARD, SIMON
Actor. b. London, England, Oct. 19, 1941. Ent. ind. 1964.
PICTURES: If... (debut, 1969), Frankenstein Must Be Destroyed, I Start Counting, Quest for Love, Young Winston (Golden Globe nom. 1973), Hitler—The Last Ten Days, The Three Musketeers, The Four Musketeers, Deadly Strangers. Aces High, Children of Rage, Battle Flag, The Chosen, Dominique, Zulu Dawn, La Sabina, The Monster Club, L'Etincelle, Supergirl, Leave All Fair,

Double X, Wuthering Heights.
TELEVISION: Movies: Calf Love, Spoiled, Bram Stoker's Dracula, Valley Forge, The Four Feathers, The Last Giraffe, The Corsican Brothers, Challenge (narrator), Atrapa-la. *Mini-series*: The Black Tulip, An Inspector Calls, A Taste For Death, Around the World in 80 Days, Kurtulus, Ruth Rendell: The Strawberry Tree. *Series:* The Misfit, Diamonds, Judge John Deed, The Tudors.

WARD, VINCENT
Director, Writer. b. New Zealand, 1956. e. Ilam Sch. of Art. At 21 dir. & co-wrote short film A State of Siege (Hugo Award, Chicago Film Fest.)
PICTURES: In Spring One Plants Alone (Silver Hugo, Chicago Film Fest.), Vigil (Grand Prix Awards, Madrid & Prades Film Fests), The Navigator (Australian Film Awards for Best Picture & Director), Alien^3 (story only), Map of the Human Heart, Leaving Las Vegas (actor only), The Shot (actor only), One Night Stand (actor only), What Dreams May Come, The Last Samurai (exec. prod.), Spooked (actor), Rain of the Children (doc., prod., researcher).

WARNER, DAVID
Actor. b. Manchester, England, July 29, 1941. e. Royal Acad. of Dramatic Art. Made London stage debut in Tony Richardson's version of A Midsummer Night's Dream (1962). Four seasons with Royal Shakespeare Co. Theater includes Afore Night Comes, The Tempest, The Wars of the Roses, The Government Inspector, Twelfth Night, I Claudius.
PICTURES: Tom Jones (debut, 1963), Morgan!, The Deadly Affair, A King's Story (voice), Work Is a Four Letter Word, A Midsummer's Night Dream, The Bofors Gun, The Fixer, The Seagull, Michael Kolhaus, The Ballad of Cable Hogue, Perfect Friday, Straw Dogs, A Doll's House, From Beyond the Grave, Little Malcolm (and His Struggle Against the Eunuch), Mr. Quilp, The Omen, Providence, The Disappearance, Cross of Iron, Silver Bears, Nightwing, The Concorde—Airport '79, Time After Time, The 39 Steps, The Island, The French Lieutenant's Woman, Time Bandits, Tron, The Man With Two Brains, The Company of Wolves, Hansel and Gretel, My Best Friend Is a Vampire, Waxworks, Mr. North, Silent Night, Office Party, Hanna's War, Pulse Pounders, Keys to Freedom, Star Trek V: The Final Frontier, S.P.O.O.K.S., Tripwire, Mortal Passions, Teenage Mutant Ninja Turtles II: The Secret of the Ooze, Star Trek VI: The Undiscovered Country, Blue Tornado, Drive, Unnameable II, Dark at Noon, In the Mouth of Madness, Ice Cream Man, Final Equinox, Felony, Beastmaster III: The Eye of Braxus, Seven Servants, The Leading Man, Money Talks, Titanic, Scream 2, The Little Unicorn, The Last Leprechaun, Wing Commander, Shergar, Back to the Secret Garden, The Code Conspiracy, Planet of the Apes, Superstition, Avatar, Straight Into Darkness, Ladies in Lavender, Black Death, Harmony.
TELEVISION: *Movies:* S.O.S. Titantic, Desperado, A Christmas Carol, Hitler's SS—Portrait in Evil, Perry Mason: The Case of the Poisoned Pen, The Secret Life of Ian Fleming, Cast a Deadly Spell, The House on Sycamore Street, Perry Mason: The Case of the Skin-Deep Scandal, John Carpenter Presents Body Bags, Danielle Steel's Zoya, Rasputin, Houdini, Cinderella, Hornblower: Mutiny, Hornblower: Retribution, The Investigation, Dr. Jekyll and Mr. Hyde, Hearts of Gold, Marple: What Mrs. McGillicuddy Saw, The Grim Adventures of Billy & Mandy (voice), Sweeney Todd, Hogfather, Perfect Parents, In Love with Barbara, Albert's Memorial. *Mini-series:* Holocaust (Emmy nom. 1978), Masada (Emmy Award, 1981), Marco Polo, Wild Palms, Signs and Wonders, The Choir, In the Beginning, The Battle for Rome. *Series:* Spider-Man (voice), Men in Black: The Series (voice), Three, Toonsylvania (voice), Battle Force: Andromeda (voice), Conviction, Doctor Who: Dreamland (voice), Wallander. *Documentaries/Specials:* Love's Labour's Lost, Uncle Vanya. *Guest:* More than 122 appearances.

WARNER, JULIE
Actress. b. New York, NY, Feb. 9, 1965. e. Brown Univ., B.A. in Theatre Arts.
PICTURES: Doc Hollywood (debut, 1991), Mr. Saturday Night, Indian Summer, The Puppet Masters, Tommy Boy, White Lies, Wedding Bell Blues, Pros and Cons, Stick It, Forever Strong, Radio Free Albemuth.
TELEVISION: Movies: Stolen: One Husband, Baseball Wives, Mr. Murder, Uncaged Heart, Crossroads: A Story of Forgiveness. *Series:* Pride and Joy, Family Law, Hidden Howie, Nip/Tuck.

WARNER, MALCOLM-JAMAL
Actor. b. Jersey City, NJ, Aug. 18, 1970. Raised in Los Angeles.
THEATRE: Three Ways Home (off-B'way debut, 1988).
PICTURE: Drop Zone (debut, 1994), A Fare To Remember, Restaurant, Reflections: A Story of Redemption (short), Contradictions of the Heart, Fool's Gold.
TELEVISION: *Movies:* A Desperate Exit, The Father Clements Story, Vindicated: A Mother's War, Kids Killing Kids (host), Tyson, The Tuskegee Airmen, Legend of the Candy Cane. *Series*: The Cosby Show (also dir. episode, Emmy nom. 1986), CBS Storybreak (host), Here and Now, Magic School Bus (voice), Malcolm & Eddie (also dir. of 15 episodes), Kenan & Kel (dir. only), Jeremiah, Lyric Cafe (host), Listen Up. *Guest:* More than 91 appearances.

WARNER, TIM
Exhibitor. b. Butte, MT, e. Western Montana College in Dillon. Warner has been active in theatre industry for more than 35 years. Industry involvement includes his work as president/owner of Theatre Operators Inc.; he was also owner/operator of Warner Marketing Film Buying. His experience includes a senior executive position with Excellence Theaters and long-time involvement with the National Association of Theatre Owners as president and CEO of NATO of California for seven years and general chairman of NATO/ShoWest. Since 1996, Warner has been pres. of Cinemark International, L.L.C. Texas-based Cinemark's international holdings include 107 theatres with 911 screens. Warner has been the recipient of various industry awards, including the International Exhibitor of the Year at ShoWest 2000.

WARREN, JENNIFER
Actress, Producer. b. New York, NY, Aug. 12, 1941. e. U. of Wisconsin, Madison, B.A. Graduate work at Wesleyan U. Studied acting with Uta Hagen at HB Studios. As part of AFI Women's Directing Workshop, directed Point of Departure, short film which received Cine Golden Eagle and Aspen Film Festival Awards. Formed Tiger Rose Productions, indep. film-TV prod. co., 1988. Exec. prod., You Don't Have to Die (Acad. Award, doc. short, 1989). Dir., The Beans of Egypt Maine, 1994. Recipient of two Spirit Awards.
THEATRE: Scuba Duba (off-B'way debut, 1967), 6 RMS RIV VU (Theatre World Award), Harvey, P.S., Your Cat Is Dead, B'way: Saint Joan, Volpone, Henry V (Guthrie Theatre).
PICTURES: Sam's Song, Night Moves, Slapshot, Another Man Another Chance, Ice Castles, Night Shadows, Fatal Beauty, The Beans of Egypt, Maine (also dir.), Partners in Crime (also dir.).
TELEVISION: *Movies*: After the Fall, Banjo Hackett: Roamin' Free, Shark Kill, First You Cry, Steel Cowboy, Champions: A Love Story, Butterflies, Angel City, The Choice, The Intruder Within, Freedom, Paper Dolls (pilot), Confessions of a Married Man, Amazons, Gambler, Full Exposure: The Sex Tapes Scandal, Dying to Belong. *Mini-series*: Celebrity. *Series*: The Smothers Brothers Comedy Hour, Paper Dolls.

WARREN, LESLEY ANN
Actress. b. New York, NY, Aug. 16, 1946. Studied acting under Lee Strasberg. Big break came in Rodgers and Hammerstein's 1964 TV prod. of Cinderella, where she was seen by Disney scout. Broadway debut in 110 in the Shade (1963, Theatre World Award), followed by Drat! The Cat! Appeared in Aerosmith video Janie's Got a Gun.
PICTURES: The Happiest Millionaire (debut, 1967), The One and Only Genuine Original Family Band, Pickup on 101, Harry and Walter Go to New York, Victor/Victoria (Academy Award nom.; Golden Globe nom. 1983), A Night in Heaven, Songwriter (Golden Globe nom. 1985), Choose Me, Race to the Yankee Zephyr, Clue, Burglar, Cop, Worth Winning, Life Stinks, Pure Country, Color of Night, Bird of Prey, The First Man, Going All the Way, Love Kills, Marriage Material, The Limey, Twin Falls Idaho, Ropewalk, Trixie, Teaching Mrs. Tingle, Losing Grace, Delivering Milo, The Quickie, Secretary, My Tiny Universe, Constellation, When Do We Eat?, Deepwater, 10th & Wolf, Stiffs, The Last Time I Made Straight A's, A Little Help.
TELEVISION: *Movies*: Seven in Darkness, Love Hate Love, Assignment Munich, The Daughters of Joshua Cabe, The Letters, The Legend of Valentino, Betrayal, The Dancing Princesses, The Secret Life of Susie Hanson, Portrait of a Stripper, Beulah Land, Portrait of a Showgirl, A Fight for Jenny, Apology, Baja Oklahoma, In Sickness and in Health, A Seduction in Travis County, In Sickness and in Health, Willing to Kill: The Texas Cheerleader Story, Family of Spies (Emmy nom.; Golden Globe nom. 1991), A Mother's Revenge, Joseph, Murderous Intent, Natural Enemy, Wolf Girl, Recipe for Disaster, St. Sass, 27 Wagons Full of Cotton, In Plain Sight. *Mini-series*: Harold Robbins' 79 Park Avenue (Golden Globe Award 1978), Pearl, Evergreen, Family of Spies (Emmy nom. 1990), Joseph, Beulah Land. *Series*: Mission: Impossible (Golden Globe nom. 1971), Snip, Desperate Housewives, In Plain Sight. *Specials*: The Saga of Sonora, It's a Bird It's a Plane It's Superman, A Special Eddie Rabbit. *Guest:* More than 92 appearances.

WASCO, DAVID
Production Designer.
PICTURES: Goldy: The Last of the Golden Bears, Smooth Talk, Student Confidential, Stacking, Rachel River, The Wash, Twister, In A Shallow Grave, Reservoir Dogs, Where the River Flows North, Killing Zoe, Pulp Fiction, Oleanna, Bottle Rocket, Touch, She's So Lovely, Jackie Brown, Rushmore, Bounce, Heist, The Royal Tenenbaums (Art Dir. Guild nom. 2002), Kill Bill: Volume 1 (Art Dir. Guild nom. 2004), Kill Bill: Volume 2, Collateral (Art Dir. Guild nom. 2005), Freedomland, Redbelt, Stop Loss, Inglourious Basterds, Cartel.
TELEVISION: *Movies:* Traveling Man, A Life in the Theater. *Documentaries/Specials:* Edgar Allan Poe: Terror of the Soul.

WASHINGTON, DENZEL
Actor. b. Mt. Vernon, NY, Dec. 28, 1954. e. Fordham U., B.A.,

journalism. Studied acting with American Conservatory Theatre, San Francisco.
THEATRE: *B'way:* When the Chickens Come Home to Roost (Audelco Award), Coriolanus, Spell #7, The Mighty Gents, Ceremonies in Dark Old Men, A Soldier's Play, Checkmates, Richard III, Julius Caesar, Fences (Tony Award 2010).
PICTURES: Carbon Copy (debut, 1981), A Soldier's Story, Power, Cry Freedom (Academy Award nom.; Golden Globe nom. 1988), The Mighty Quinn, For Queen and Country, Glory (Academy Award, best supporting actor, Golden Globe Award 1990), Heart Condition, Mo' Better Blues, Ricochet, Mississippi Masala, Malcolm X (NY Film Critics Award; Academy Award nom.; Golden Globe nom. 1993), Much Ado About Nothing, Philadelphia, The Pelican Brief, Crimson Tide, Virtuosity, Devil in a Blue Dress, Courage Under Fire, The Preacher's Wife, Fallen, He Got Game, The Siege, The Hurricane (Academy Award nom.; Golden Globe Award 2000), The Bone Collector, Remember the Titans, Training Day (Academy Award, Best Actor, Leading Role, Golden Globe nom. 2002), John Q, Antwone Fisher (also dir. & prod.), Out of Time, Man on Fire, The Manchurian Candidate, Inside Man, Deja Vu, American Gangster (Golden Globe nom. 2008), The Great Debaters (also dir.), The Taking of Pelham 123, Inside Man 2, The Book of Eli (also prod.), Unstoppable.
TELEVISION: *Movies*: Wilma, Flesh and Blood, License to Kill, The George McKenna Story, Jammin': Jelly Roll Morton on Broadway (narrator). *Series*: St. Elsewhere, Happily Ever After: Fairy Tales for Every Child (voice). *Documentaries/Specials:* Mother Goose: A Rappin' and Rhymin' Special, Hank Aaron: Chasing the Dream (Emmy nom. 1995), Half Past Autumn: The Life and Works of Gordon Parks (prod. only, Emmy nom. 2001). *Guest:* More than 131 appearances.

WASSON, CRAIG
Actor. b. Ontario, OR, March 15, 1954. Also musician/songwriter.
THEATRE: Godspell, All God's Chillun Got Wings, Death of a Salesman (also wrote incidental music), Jock, Children of Eden, M. Butterfly, Skin of Our Teeth, The Sisters (Pasadena Playhouse). Wrote incidental music for prod. of The Glass Menagerie and Death of a Salesman.
PICTURES: Rollercoaster, The Boys in Company C (also wrote and performed song Here I Am), Go Tell the Spartans, The Outsider, Carny, Schizoid, Ghost Story, Night at O'Rear's, Four Friends (Golden Globe nom. 1982), Second Thoughts (also wrote and performed music), Body Double, The Men's Club, A Nightmare on Elm Street 3, Bum Rap (also wrote and performed music), Midnight Fear (co-s.p.), Malcolm X, Velocity Trap, Tian shang ren jian, The Pornographer (also assoc. prod.), The Last Best Sunday, Danny and Max, Escape Under Pressure, New Alcatraz, Puerto Vallarta Squeeze, The Reckoning, Akeelah and the Bee, Sasquatch Mountain.
TELEVISION: *Movies*: The Silence, Mrs. R's Daughter, Skag, Thornwell, Why Me?, Strapped, Trapped in Space, The Calvin Mire Story, The Becky Bell Story, Sister in Law, The Tomorrow Man, Harvest of Fire, Deep Family Secrets, Epoch. *Series*: Phyllis (also wrote and performed orig. songs), Skag, For Jenny with Love, One Life to Live. *Documentaries/Specials*: A More Perfect Union, Innocents Abroad. *Guest:* More than 44 appearances.

WATANABE, GEDDE
Actor. b. Ogden, UT, June 26, 1955. Trained for stage at American Conservatory Theatre, San Francisco. Appeared with N.Y. Shakespeare Fest. Shakespeare in the Park series and with Pan Asian Repertory Theatre, N.Y.
THEATRE: Pacific Overtures (debut, as Tree Boy, B'way and on tour, 1976), Bullet Headed Birds, Poor Little Lambs, Dispatches, Music Lesson, Good Person.
PICTURES: Sixteen Candles (debut, 1984), Gremlins 2: The New Batch, Volunteers, Gung Ho, Vamp, UHF, Boys on the Side, That Thing You Do!, Nick and Jane, Booty Call, Mulan (voice), Guinevere, EDtv, Slackers, Alfie, Two for the Money, The Onion Movie, Forgetting Sarah Marshall, All Ages Night, Not Forgotten.
TELEVISION: *Movies*: Miss America: Behind the Crown, L.A. Law: The Movie. *Series*: Gung Ho, Sesame Street, ER.

WATERS, JOHN
Director, Writer, Actor. b. Baltimore, MD, April 22, 1946. First short film Hag in a Black Leather Jacket (1964) shot in Baltimore, as are most of his films. Other shorts include Roman Candles, Eat Your Makeup. Feature debut, Mondo Trasho. On TV in Homicide: Life on the Streets.
PICTURES: *Director/Writer*: Mondo Trasho (also photo., edit.), Multiple Maniacs (also ed., sound), Pink Flamingos (also photo., edit.), Female Trouble (also photo.), Desperate Living (also prod. & cinematographer), Polyester (also prod.), Hairspray (also co-prod., actor), Cry-Baby, Serial Mom, Pecker, Cecil B. Demented, A Dirty Shame, In the Land of Merry Misfits (narr.), Hairspray (2007), Fruitcake. *Actor:* Homer & Eddie, Sweet & Lowdown, Pie in the Sky: The Brigid Berlin Story (documentary; as himself), Welcome to Hollywood (documentary; as himself), Blood Feast 2: All U Can Eat, Seed of Chucky.
TELEVISION: *Documentaries/Specials:* In Bad Taste (documentary; as himself), Memories of Oz (documentary; as himself), This Filthy World (also writer). *Series:* 'Til Death Do Us Part (actor). *Guest:* More than 115 appearances.

WATERSTON, SAM
Actor. b. Cambridge, MA, Nov. 15, 1940. e. Yale U. Spent jr. year at Sorbonne in Paris as part of the Amer. Actors' Workshop run by American dir. John Berry. Broadway debut in Oh Dad Poor Dad ... (1963). Film debut, The Plastic Dome of Norma Jean (made 1965; unreleased). TV debut Pound (Camera Three). Has worked in New York Shakespeare Festival prods. since As You Like It (1963).
THEATRE: *N.Y.* Shakespeare Festival: As You Like It, Ergo, Henry IV (Part I & II), Cymbeline, Hamlet, Much Ado About Nothing, The Tempest. *Off-B'way*: The Knack, La Turista, Waiting for Godot, The Three Sisters. *B'way*: The Paisley Convertible, Halfway Up the Tree, Indian, Hay Fever, The Trial of Cantonsville Nine, A Meeting by the River, Much Ado About Nothing (Drama Desk and Obie Awards), A Doll's House, Lunch Hour, Benefactors, A Walk in the Woods, Abe Lincoln in Illinois.
PICTURES: Fitzwilly, Three, Generation, Cover Me Babe, Mahoney's Estate, Who Killed Mary What's 'er Name?, Savages, The Great Gatsby (2 Golden Globe noms. 1975), Journey Into Fear, Rancho Deluxe, Sweet Revenge, Capricorn One, Interiors, Eagle's Wing, Sweet William, Hopscotch, Heaven's Gate, The Killing Fields (Academy Award nom.; Golden Globe nom. 1985), Warning Sign, Hannah and Her Sisters, Just Between Friends, A Certain Desire, The Devil's Paradise, September, Welcome Home, Crimes and Misdemeanors, The Man in the Moon, Mindwalk, A Captive in the Land, Serial Mom, The Journey of August King (also co-prod.), The Proprietor, The Shadow Conspiracy, Le Divorce, The Commission.
TELEVISION: *Movies*: The Glass Menagerie (Emmy nom. 1974), Reflections of Murder, Friendly Fire, Games Mother Never Taught You, In Defense of Kids, Dempsey, Finnegan Begin Again, Love Lives On, The Fifth Missile, The Room Upstairs, Terrorist on Trial: The United States vs. Salim Ajami, Gore Vidal's Lincoln, Lantern Hill, The Shell Seekers, Assault at West Point: The Court-Martial of Johnson Whittaker, David's Mother, The Enemy Within, Miracle at Midnight, Exiled: A Law & Order Movie, A House Divided, The Matthew Shepard Story. *Mini-series*: The Nightmare Years, The Civil War (voice), Thomas Jefferson, Lewis & Clark, I'll Fly Away: Then and Now (Emmy nom. 1994). *Series*: Q.E.D., I'll Fly Away (2 Emmy noms.; Golden Globe Award 1993, 1 other nom.), Law & Order: Trial by Jury, Law & Order (3 Emmy noms.; Golden Globe nom. 1995). *Documentaries/Specials*: Pound, Robert Lowell, The Good Lieutenant, Much Ado About Nothing, Oppenheimer (Golden Globe nom. 1983), A Walk in the Woods, Lost Civilizations (Emmy Award 1996). *Guest:* More than 93 appearances.

WATROS, CYNTHIA
Actress. b. Sept. 2, 1968.
PICTURES: Cafe Society, His and Hers, Mercy Streets, Yellow Bird (short), P.S. Your Cat Is Dead, Duane Incarnate, Just Pray (short), American Crude, Frank, Mars, Calvin Marshall.
TELEVISION: *Movies:* The Rich Inner Life of Penelope Cloud, Avenging Angel. *Series*: Guiding Light (Emmy Award 1998), Another World, Titus, The Drew Carey Show, Lost.

WATSON, BARRY
Actor. r.n. Michael Barret Watson. b. Traverse City, MI, April 23, 1974.
PICTURES: Teaching Mrs. Tingle, When Strangers Appear, Sorority Boys, Deluxe Combo Platter, Boogeyman. Ocean's Eleven, Sorority Boys, Boogeyman.
TELEVISION: *Movies:* Fatal Deception: Mrs. Lee Harvey Oswald, Attack of the 50 Ft. Woman, Co-ed Call Girl. *Series:* Malibu Shores, 7th Heaven, What About Brian (also pilot), Samantha Who?.

WATSON, EMILY
Actress. b. London, England, Jan. 14, 1967.
PICTURES: Breaking the Waves (Academy Award nom.; 1997, Golden Globe nom.; NY Society of Film Critics Award, Nat'l Society of Film Critics Award), Mill on the Floss, Metroland, The Boxer, Hilary and Jackie (Academy Award nom.; Golden Globe nom. 1999), The Cradle Will Rock, Angela's Ashes, Trixie, The Luzhin Defence, Gosford Park, Punch-Drunk Love, Red Dragon, Equilibrium, Separate Lives, Boo Zino & the Snurks, The Corpse Bride (voice), Wah-Wah, The Proposition, Crusade in Jeans, Miss Potter, Fireflies in the Garden, The Water Horse: Legend of the Deep, Synecdoche, New York, Cold Souls, Within the Whirlwind, Oranges and Sunshine, Cemetery Junction.
TELEVISION: *Movies:* The Mill on the Floss, The Life and Death of Peter Sellers (Golden Globe nom. 2005), The Memory Keeper's Daughter.

WATTS, EMMA
Executive. e. UCLA, B.A. in English. Watts began her career as a creative executive at Def Pictures. Then, she joined Oliver Stone's Illusion Entertainment, where she was director of development, working on such projects as "Any Given Sunday" and "U-Turn." Watts joined Twentieth Century Fox in mid-1998 as a creative executive and was upped to v.p., production in 2001, promoted to senior v.p., production in June 2003 and elevated to executive v.p., production in Jan. 2006. She ascended to her current position, co-president, production, along with Alex Young, in Jan. 2007. Watts and Young report directly to Fox Filmed Entertainment Chairmen Tom Rothman and Jim Gianopulos. 2009 she became the sole President of Production. Watts has been on The Hollywood Reporter's Power 100 list of Women in

Entertainment for the past several years, most recently ranking 33 on the 2007 list.

WAX, MORTON DENNIS
Public Relations Executive. b. New York, NY, March 13, 1932. e. Brooklyn Coll., 1952. CEO, Chairman and Principal of Morton Dennis Wax & Assoc., Inc., p.r. and marketing firm servicing int'l creative marketplace, established 1956. Recent PR & Marketing for foreign films: Hungarian Fairy Tale, December Bride, Eden Valley. Contrib. writer to Box Office Magazine, Film Journal. Recent articles: Creativity (Advertising Age), Rolling Stone's Marketing Through Music, Words & Music, Campaign Magazine, Songwriters Guild of America National Edition. As sect. of VPA, conceptualized int'l Monitor Award, an annual event, currently under auspices of ITS. Public relations counsel to London Int'l Advertising Awards. Member of The Public Relations Society of America, Nat'l Academy of TV Arts & Sciences, Nat'l Academy of Recording Arts & Sciences, Publishers Publicity Association. Morton Dennis Wax & Assocs. in NY was awarded the first EPM Entertainment Marketing Cause Event Award for creating, developing and promoting a nat'l fund raising campaign to combat homelessness, called Brother Can You Spare a Dime Day.

WAYANS, DAMON
Actor, Writer, Producer. b. New York, NY, Sept. 4, 1960. Brothers are comedian-actors Keenen Ivory Wayans and Marlon Wayans. Started as stand up comedian.
PICTURES: Beverly Hills Cop (debut, 1984), Hollywood Shuffle, Roxanne, Colors, Punchline, I'm Gonna Git You Sucka, Earth Girls Are Easy, Look Who's Talking Too (voice), The Last Boy Scout, Mo' Money (also s.p., co-exec. prod.), Last Action Hero (cameo), Blankman (also co-s.p., exec. prod.), Major Payne (also co-s.p., co-exec. prod.), The Great White Hype, Bulletproof, Harlem Aria, Goosed, Bamboozled, All Jokes Aside, Marci X, Behind the Smile, Homey the Clown (also writer).
TELEVISION: *Movies:* Triplecross, The Wayans Underground (also writer, exec. prod.), Never Better (also exec. prod.), Eye Shat (writer, exec. prod.), Giuseppe (writer, dir., exec. prod.). *Series*: Saturday Night Live (1985-6), In Living Color (also writer, 4 Emmy noms.), Waynehead (exec. prod.), 413 Hope St., (also prod.), Damon, My Wife and Kids, The Underground (also dir., exec. prod., writer), Rodney (writer, creator). *Guest:* More than 66 appearances.

WAYANS, KEENEN IVORY
Actor, Director, Writer. b. NYC, June 8, 1958. e. Tuskegee Inst. Began as stand-up comic at The Improv in NYC and L.A. Brothers are comedian-actors Damon Wayans, Marlon Wayans.
PICTURES: Star 80 (debut, 1983), Hollywood Shuffle (also co-s.p.), Eddie Murphy Raw (co-prod., co-s.p. only), I'm Gonna Git You Sucka, The Five Heartbeats (co-s.p. only), A Low Down Dirty Shame (dir., writer), Don't Be A Menace to South Central While Drinking Your Juice in the Hood (also prod.), The Glimmer Man, Most Wanted (also s.p. & exec. prod.), Scary Movie (also dir. & prod.), Scary Movie 2 (dir. only), White Chicks (writer s. p., prod., dir.), Little Man (writer, prod., dir.), Dance Flick (also writer, prod.).
TELEVISION: *Movies:* For Love and Honor (actor), Hammer Slammer & Slade (writer & exec. prod.), Thugaboo: A Miracle on D-Roc's Street (exec. prod., writer). *Series*: For Love and Honor (actor), In Living Color (also exec. prod. & writer, Emmy Award 1990, 6 other noms.), Keenen Ivory Wayans Show (also exec. prod., writer), My Wife and Kids (writer, creator, exec. prod.), HGTV Showdown. *Documentaries/Specials:* The Best of Robert Townsend & His Partners in Crime (actor & exec. prod.). *Guest:* More than 41 appearances.

WAYANS, MARLON
Actor, Producer, Writer. b. NYC, July 23, 1972. E. School of Performing Arts, NY and Howard U. Brothers are comedian-actors Damon and Keenan-Ivory Wayans.
PICTURES: I'm Gonna Git You Sucka, Mo'Money, Above the Rim, Don't Be a Menace to South Central While Drinking Your Juice in the Hood (also exec. prod, s.p.), The Sixth Man, Senseless, Requiem for a Dream, Scary Movie (also prod., s.p.), The Tangerine Bear, Dungeons & Dragons, Scary Movie 2 (also co-exec prod., s.p.), Scary Movie 3: Episode 1—Lord of the Brooms, Behind the Smile, The Ladykillers, White Chicks (also writer s.p.-story/prod.), Scary Movie 4 (writer), Little Man (also writer, prod.), Norbit, Dance Flick (also writer, prod.), G.I. Joe: Rise of Cobra.
TELEVISION: *Movies:* The Best of Robert Townsend & His Partners in Crime (various characters), Thugaboo: Sneaker Madness (voice, writer, exec. prod.), Thugaboo: A Miracle on D-Roc's Street (also writer, creator, exec. prod.), The Life and Times of Marcus Felony Brown (writer, creator, exec. prod.). *Series*: In Living Color, The Wayans Brothers (also prod., writer), Waynehead (voice). *Documentaries/Specials:* The Best of Robert Townsend & His Partners in Crime. *Guest:* More than 62 appearances.

WAYNE, PATRICK
Actor. b. Los Angeles, July 15, 1939. e. Loyola U, 1961, BS in biology. Father was late actor John Wayne. Made film debut at age 11 in Rio Grande with father. Won Golden Globe Award for most promising newcomer 1958.
PICTURES: The Long Gray Line, Mister Roberts, The Searchers, The Alamo, The Comancheros, McClintock, Donovan's Reef, Cheyenne Autumn, Shenandoah, An Eye for an Eye, The Green Berets, The Deserter, Big Jake, The Gatling Gun, Beyond Atlantis, The Bears and I, Mustang Country, Sinbad and the Eye of the Tiger, The People Time Forgot, Rustler's Rhapsody, Young Guns, Her Alibi, Chill Factor, Deep Cover, Legend of Hell's Gate.
TELEVISION: *Movies*: Sole Survivor, Yesterday's Child, Flight to Holocaust, The Last Hurrah, Three on a Date. *Series*: Mr. Adams and Eve, The Rounders, Shirley, The Monte Carlo Show (host), Tic Tac Dough, All My Children. *Guest:* More than 58 appearances.

WEATHERS, CARL
Actor. b. New Orleans, LA, Jan. 14, 1948. e. San Diego State U.
PICTURES: Bucktown (debut, 1975), Friday Foster, Rocky, Close Encounters of the Third Kind, Semi-Tough, Force Ten From Navarone, Rocky II, Death Hunt, Rocky III, Rocky IV, Predator, Action Jackson, Hurricane Smith, Happy Gilmore, Little Nicky, Eight Crazy Nights (voice), The Sasquatch Dumpling Gang, The Comebacks.
TELEVISION: *Movies*: The Hostage Heart, The Bermuda Depths, Braker, The Defiant Ones, Dangerous Passion, In the Heat of the Night: Give Me Your Life, In the Heat of the Night: A Matter of Justice, In the Heat of the Night: Who Was Geli Bendl?, In the Heat of the Night: By Duty Bound, Tom Clancy's Op Center, In the Heat of the Night: Grow Old Along With Me, Assault on Devil's Island, Assault on Death Mountain, Alien Siege, Phoo Action. *Series*: Fortune Dane, Tour of Duty, Street Justice, In the Heat of the Night, Sheena, Spawn: The Animation (voice), Brothers (pilot). *Director*: Silk Stalkings (7 episodes). *Guest:* More than 68 appearances.

WEAVER, FRITZ
Actor. b. Pittsburgh, PA, Jan. 19, 1926. e. U. of Chicago.
THEATRE: The Chalk Garden (Theatre World Award), Miss Lonelyhearts, All American, A Shot in the Dark, Baker Street, Child's Play (Tony, 1970), The Price, The Crucible, The Professional, etc.
PICTURES: Fail Safe (debut, 1964), The Guns of August (narrator), The Maltese Bippy, A Walk in the Spring Rain, Company of Killers, The Day of the Dolphin, Marathon Man, Demon Seed, Black Sunday, The Big Fix, Jaws of Satan, Creepshow, Power, The Thomas Crown Affair.
TELEVISION: *Movies*: Jane Eyre, The Power and the Glory, The Borgia Stick, The Crucible, Double Jeopardy, Company of Killers, Berlin Affair, Heat of Anger, The Snoop Sisters, Hunter, Rx for the Defense, Antigone, A Touch of the Poet, The Legend of Lizzie Borden, Captains Courageous, Children of Divorce, Magnum P.I., Momma the Detective, Maid in America, Alice In Wonderland, The Hearst and Davies Affair, A Death in California, Under Siege, D.C. Cops, My Name is Bill W, Ironclads, Citizen Cohn, Blind Spot, Pointman, Spring Awakening, Floating Palaces (narrator), Rescuers: Stories of Courage: Two Women. *Mini-series*: Holocaust (Emmy nom. 1978), The Martian Chronicles, Dream West, I'll Take Manhattan. *Series:* All My Children, Against the Law. *Guest:* More than 127 appearances.

WEAVER, SIGOURNEY
Actress. r.n. Susan Weaver. b. New York, NY, Oct. 8, 1949. e. Stanford U., Yale U. Daughter of Sylvester (Pat) Weaver, former NBC pres. Mother, actress Elizabeth Inglis (one-time contract player for Warner Bros.). After college formed working partnership with fellow student Christopher Durang for off-B'way improv. productions. First professional appearance on stage in 1974 in The Constant Wife with Ingrid Bergman. Formed Goat Cay Prods.
THEATRE: *Off-Off-B'way*: The Nature and Purpose of the Universe. *Off-B'way*: Titanic/Das Lusitania Songspiel (also co-writer), Gemini, Marco Polo Sings a Solo, New Jerusalem, The Merchant of Venice, Beyond Therapy, The Guys. *B'way*: Hurlyburly, The Mercy Seat.
PICTURES: Madman (Israeli; debut, 1976), Annie Hall, Alien, Eyewitness, The Year of Living Dangerously, Deal of the Century, Ghostbusters, One Woman or Two, Aliens (Academy Award nom.; Golden Globe nom. 1987), Half Moon Street, Gorillas in the Mist: The Story of Dian Fossey (Academy Award nom.; Golden Globe Award 1989), Working Girl (Academy Award nom.; Golden Globe Award 1989), Ghostbusters II, Alien 3 (also co-prod.), 1492: Conquest of Paradise, Dave, Death and the Maiden, Jeffrey, Copycat, The Ice Storm (BAFTA Award, Best Supporting Actress, Golden Globe nom. 1997), Alien: Resurrection (also co-prod.), A Map of the World (Golden Globe nom. 2000), Get Bruce, Galaxy Quest, Company Man, Speak Truth to Power, Heartbreakers, Big Bad Love, Tadpole, The Guys, Holes, Imaginary Heroes, The Village, Snow Cake, The TV Set, Infamous, Happily N' Ever After (voice), Baby Mama, Baby Mama, Vantage Point, WALL·E (voice), The Tale of Despereaux (voice), Crazy on the Outside, You Again, Avatar, Paul, Night Train.
TELEVISION: *Movies:* The Sorrows of Gin, O Youth and Beauty, Gypsy and Me (also exec. prod.), Prayers for Bobby (Emmy nom. 2009). *Mini-series:* The Best of Families, Snow White: A Tale of Terror (Emmy nom. 1998). *Series*: Somerset. *Guest:* More than 114 appearances.

WEBB, CHLOE
Actress. b. New York, NY, 1960. e. Boston Conservatory of Music and Drama. On stage with Boston Shakespeare Co., Goodman Theatre in Chicago and Mark Taper Forum, L.A., improv. groups Imagination Theatre Co., Paul Sills Theatre.
THEATRE: Forbidden Broadway (Off-B'way and L.A.), Addiction, Family Album, The Model Apartment (LA Critics Circle & Dramalogue Awards), House of Blue Leaves (Dramlogue Award), School Talk, A Midsummer Night's Dream.
PICTURES: Sid and Nancy (debut, 1986; Natl. Society of Film Critics Award), Twins, Heart Condition, The Belly of an Architect, Queens Logic, Silent Cries, A Dangerous Woman, Love Affair, She's So Lovely, The Newton Boys, Practical Magic, Quit.
TELEVISION: *Movies*: China Beach, Lucky Day, The Ballad of Lucy Whipple. *Mini-series*: Tales of the City. *Series*: Thicke of the Night, China Beach (Emmy nom. 1989).

WEBER, STEVEN
Actor. b. March 4, 1961. e. Purchase Col. Acted with Mirror Rep. Co. Off-B'way.
THEATRE: *NY*: Paradise Lost, The Real Thing (B'way debut, 1985), Something About Baseball. *Regional:* Made in Bangkok, Come Back Little Sheba, Naked at the Coast, Death of a Salesman.
PICTURES: The Flamingo Kid, Flanagan, Hamburger Hill, Les Anges, Single White Female, The Temp, Jeffrey, Dracula: Dead and Loving It, I Woke Up Early the Day I Died, The Breakup, Sour Grapes, At First Sight, Timecode, Sleep Easy Hutch Rimes, The Moguls, Choose Connor, Farmhouse, Son of Mourning, My One and Only.
TELEVISION: *Movies:* Kojak: Fatal Flaw, When We Were Young, In the Line of Duty, Deception: A Mother's Secret, In the Company of Darkness, Betrayed by Love, Take Out the Beast, Stories From the Edge, Thanks of a Grateful Nation, Love Letters, Late Last Night, Common Ground, Club Land, The Twelve Days of Christmas Eve, Reefer Madness: The Movie Musical, More of Me. *Mini-series:* The Kennedys of Massachusetts, The Shining, Desperation, Nightmares and Dreamscapes: From the Stories of Stephen King. *Series:* As The World Turns, Wings, Hercules (voice), The Weber Show (also co-exec. prod.), All Dogs Go To Heaven (voice), The D.A., Studio 60 on the Sunset Strip (also pilot), Brothers & Sisters, Web Therapy. *Guest:* More than 77 appearances.

WEDGEWORTH, ANN
Actress. b. Abilene, TX, Jan. 21, 1935. e. U. of Texas. On stage in Thieves, Blues for Mr. Charlie, Chapter Two (Tony Award, 1978).
PICTURES: Andy, Bang the Drum Slowly, Scarecrow, The Catamount Killing, Law and Disorder, Dragonfly (One Summer Love), Birch Interval, Thieves, Handle With Care, No Small Affair, Sweet Dreams, The Men's Club, Made in Heaven, A Tiger's Tale, Far North, Miss Firecracker, Steel Magnolias, Green Card, Hard Promises, Love and a .45, The Whole Wide World, The Hunter's Moon, The Hawk Is Dying.
TELEVISION: *Movies*: The War Between the Tates, Bogie, Elvis and the Beauty Queen, Killjoy, Right to Kill?, A Stranger Waits, Cooperstown, A Burning Passion: The Margaret Mitchell Story, Fight for Justice: The Nancy Conn Story. *Series*: The Edge of Night, Another World, Somerset, Three's Company, Filthy Rich, Evening Shade. *Pilot*: Harlan & Merleen.

WEILL, CLAUDIA
Director. b. New York, NY 1947. e. Radcliffe, B.A., 1969. Teacher of acting, Cornish Institute, 1983; guest lecturer on film directing, NYU and Columbia U. Winner of Donatello Award, best director, 1979; Mademoiselle Woman of the Year, 1974; AFI Independent Filmmakers Grant, 1973. Worked as prod. asst. on doc., Revolution.
THEATRE: An Evening for Merlin Finch (debut, 1975, Williamstown), Stillife, Found a Peanut, The Longest Walk.
PICTURES: *Doc. shorts*: This Is the Home of Mrs. Levant Grahame, Roaches' Serenade, Joyce at 34. *Director*: The Other Half of the Sky—A China Memoir (also photog., edit.), Girlfriends (also prod., story), It's My Turn.
TELEVISION: *Movies*: Face of a Stranger, A Child Lost Forever: The Jerry Sherwood Story, Critical Choices, Giving Up the Ghost. *Series*: The 51st State, Sesame Street, Joyce at 34, The Great Love Experiment, thirtysomething, Birdland, My So-Called Life, Chicago Hope, Once and Again.

WEINGROD, HERSCHEL
Writer, Producer. b. Milwaukee, WI, Oct. 30, 1947. e. U. of Wisconsin, 1965-69; London Film Sch., 1969-71.
PICTURES: *Co-writer* with Timothy Harris: Cheaper to Keep Her, Trading Places (BAFTA nom.), Brewster's Millions, My Stepmother Is An Alien, Paint It Black, Twins, Kindergarten Cop, Pure Luck, Falling Down (prod. only), Tollbooth (exec. prod.), Space Jam (co-s.p.), The Final Season, Out of Iowa (dir.).
TELEVISION: *Movie:* Street of Dreams (exec. prod.).

WEINSTEIN, BOB
Executive. b. 1953. With brother Harvey, founded distribution company Miramax Films in 1979. Company branched into feature production in 1989 with film Scandal. In 1993 the Weinsteins sold the studio named for their parents, Miriam and Max, to The Walt Disney Co., with Disney financing their projects. They formed Dimension Films, a motion picture unit within Miramax Films, to produce and release genre films. This unit still exists within The Weinstein Co. The Weinsteins announced in April 2005 they would leave the Walt Disney Co.'s Miramax Films in September 2005 and immediately formed a new company, The Weinstein Co., where he serves as co-Chairman with his brother, Harvey. Miramax and the Weinstein Company garnered a total of 249 Academy Award nominations and 60 Academy Awards as of 2009.
PICTURES: Light Years (Bob: prod., Harvey: dir. of U.S. version). *Executive Producer*: Scandal, The Lemon Sisters, Hardware, A Rage in Harlem, The Miracle, Crossing the Line, The Night We Never Met, Benefit of the Doubt, True Romance, Into the West, Mother's Boys, Pulp Fiction, Ready to Wear (Pret-a-Porter), The Englishman Who Went Up a Hill But Came Down a Mountain, Smoke, The Crossing Guard, The Journey of August King, Last of the High Kings, Addicted to Love, Air Bud, Cop Land, The English Patient, Scream, Wishful Thinking, The Wings of the Dove, She's So Lovely, Mimic, Good Will Hunting, Scream 2, Jackie Brown, Velvet Goldmine, Shakespeare in Love (Acad. Award for Best Picture), Rounders, The Prophecy II, A Price Above Rubies, Playing by Heart, The Mighty, Little Voice, Heaven, Halloween H20: Twenty Years Later, The Faculty, B. Monkey, Phantoms, Senseless, Ride, Wide Awake, Nightwatch, 54, Talk of Angels, The Yards, Teaching Mrs. Tingle, Outside Providence, My Life So Far, Music of the Heart, Mansfield Park, Holy Smoke, Guinevere, The Cider House Rules, Allied Forces, She's All That, In Too Deep, Scream If You Know What I Did Last Halloween, Reindeer Games, The Yards, Boys and Girls, Scary Movie, Highlander: Endgame, Backstage, Chocolat, The Lord of the Rings: The Fellowship of the Ring, Scary Movie 2, Daddy and Them, The Others, Jay and Silent Bob Strike Back, Waking Up in Reno, Texas Rangers, Kate & Leopold, Impostor, Halloween: Resurrection, Full Frontal, The Shipping News, Ritual, The Art of Negotiating a Turn, Alone In The Dark, Alice, Below, Bad Santa, Spy Kids 2: The Island of Lost Dreams, Below, Equilibrium, The Lord of the Rings: The Two Towers, Gangs of New York, Chicago, Confessions of a Dangerous Mind, Spy Kids 3-D: Game Over, The Human Stain, Duplex, Kill Bill: Vol. 1, Scary Movie 3, The Lord of the Rings: The Return of the King, Cold Mountain, Mindhunters, Ella Enchanted, Kill Bill: Vol. 2, Paper Clips (doc.), Fahrenheit 9/11, Shall We Dance, The Aviator, Cursed, Sin City, Halloween 9, Backwater, The Great Raid, An Unfinished Life, The Brothers Grimm, Underclassman, Proof, Venom, Feast, Curandero, Derailed, Scary Movie 4, Clerks II, Pulse, Breaking And Entering, School for Scoundrels, Factory Girl, Grindhouse, Sicko (doc.), Death Proof, 1408, Planet Terror, Who's Your Caddy?, The Nanny Diaries, Halloween, Rogue, The Mist, Awake, The Great Debaters, Hell Ride, Rambo, The Promotion, Superhero Movie, Fanboys, The Longshots, Zack and Miri Make a Porno, Soul Men, Killshot, The Reader, Vicky Cristina Barcelona, Hurricane Season, Crossing Over, Inglourious Basterds, Hey Watch This (doc.), Halloween II, Capitalism: A Love Story (doc.), Youth in Revolt, Nine, Shanghai, Piranha, My Week with Marilyn, Scream 4, Spy Kids 4: All the Time in the World.
TELEVISION: *Movies:* Since You've Been Gone, Project Jay (doc.). *Series:* The Real Magees, David the Gnome, Wasteland, Clerks: The Animated Series, Project Greenlight (series doc.; Emmy nom. 2002), Glory Days, Tokyo Pig, Project Greelight 2 (series doc.; Emmy nom. 2004), Project Runway (series doc., 5 Emmy noms.), Models of the Runway, Project Greenlight 3 (Emmy nom. 2005), Project Jay (doc.), The No. 1 Ladies' Detective Agency.

WEINSTEIN, HARVEY
Executive. With brother Bob founded distribution company Miramax Films in 1979. Company branched into feature production in 1989 with film Scandal. In 1993 the Weinsteins sold the studio named for their parents, Miriam and Max, to The Walt Disney Co., with Disney financing their projects. Miramax garnered a total of 220 Oscar nominations and 53 wins in 12 years. The Weinsteins announced in April 2005 they would leave the Walt Disney Co.'s Miramax Films in September 2005 and immediately formed a new company, The Weinstein Co., where he serves as co-Chairman with his brother, Bob. (For list of films see Bob Weinstein).

WEINSTEIN, PAULA
Producer. b. Nov. 19, 1945. e. Columbia U. Daughter of late prod. Hannah Weinstein. Raised in Europe. Partnered with Gareth Wigan in WW Productions at Warner Brothers. Started as theatrical agent with William Morris and ICM. With Warner Brothers, 1976-78 as production v.p.; left to go to 20th Century-Fox in same capacity; named Fox sr. v.p., worldwide prod; 1980, appointed v.p., prod., the Ladd Company; 1981, joined United Artists as pres., m.p. div.; 1983, began own prod. company at Columbia Pictures, also serving as a consultant for Columbia; 1987, joined MGM as exec. consultant; With late husband Mark Rosenberg formed Spring Creek Prods. Currently, CEO of Spring Creek Productions in Beverly Hills, CA. Won Emmy for Outstanding Made-for-TV Movie, "Truman," 1995; shared with Anthea Sylbert and Doro Bachrach. Won PGA's Golden Laurel Ward for TV Producer of the Year for "Truman," 1995; shared with Anthea Sylbert & Doro Bachrach.

PICTURES: *Producer*: American Flyers, A Dry White Season, The Fabulous Baker Boys, Fearless,The House of the Spirits, Flesh and Bone, With Honors, Something to Talk About, The Incredible Mr. Limpet, Analyze This, Liberty Heights, The Perfect Storm, An Everlasting Piece, Possession, Bandits, Analyze That, Deliver Us from Eva, Looney Tunes: The Movie, ID, Envy, Looney Tunes: Back in Action, Envy, Monster-in-Law, Rumor Has It, The Astronaut Farmer, Blood Diamond, The Company Men.
TELEVISION: *Movies*: *As Exec. Prod.:* Bejewelled, The Rose and the Jackal, Citizen Cohn (Emmy nom. 1993), Truman (Emmy Award 1996), The Cherokee Kid, First-time Felon, Cloned, Giving Up the Ghost, If You Believe, Crossed Over, Iron Jawed Angels, Recount (Emmy Award 2008). *Mini-series:* Salem Witch Trials.

WEINSTOCK, MARC

Executive. Bachelor's degree in intl. relations with a minor in film studies, Emory Univ. Weinstock spent three years as dir. of mktg. for Fox Searchlight Pictures. In 2000 he joined Sony Pictures Entertainment and has held senior mktg. roles at Sony's Screen Gems and TriStar Pictures labels. In Jan. 2006, promoted to executive v.p., mktg., Screen Gems and to pres., mktg. in Oct. 2007. In June 2008, Weinstock and colleague Valerie Van Galder were promoted to co-president, worldwide theatrical marketing with development and oversight responsibilities for Columbia Pictures, Screen Gems and Sony Pictures Animation. The two have worked together for more than a decade, first joining forces at Fox Searchlight. Van Galder and Weinstock have been the mktg. architects for 28 #1 films. Van Galder didn't renew her contract which expired at the end of 2009. Sony marketing and distribution chief Jeff Blake directed Weinstock to absorb Van Galder's duties, and Weinstock is now the studio's sole marketing president.

WEINTRAUB, FRED

Executive, Producer. b. Bronx, NY, April 27, 1928. e. U. of PA, Wharton Sch. of Business. Owner of The Bitter End Coffeehouse to 1971. Personal management, Campus Coffee House Entertain-ment Circuit; TV Production Hootenanny, Popendipity; syndicated TV show host: From The Bitter End; motion picture prod.; v.p., creative services, Warner Bros. 1969; exec. in chg. Woodstock; prod. motion pictures, Weintraub-Heller Productions, 1974; then Fred Weintraub Productions, which became Weintraub/Kuhn Prods. in 1990.
PICTURES: Rage, Enter the Dragon, Black Belt Jones (also writer), Truck Turner, Golden Needles, The Barony, Dirty Knights Work, (also writer), Crazy Animals (documentary), Hot Potato, The Pack, The Promise, Jaguar Lives!, Tom Horn, The Big Brawl, Force: Five, High Road to China, Gymkata, Out of Control, The Women's Club, China O'Brien, China O'Brien II, Born to Ride, The JFK Assassination: The Jim Garrison Tapes (documentary), Curse of the Dragon (documentary), Trouble Bound, Backstreet Justice, Under the Gun (exec. prod.), Undertow, Perilous, Amazons and Gladiators, Endangered Species, Warrior Angels, Dream Warrior.
TELEVISION: *Movies:* Triplecross, The Devil's Arithmetic, Trouble Bound, Perilous. *Mini-series:* The Lady Musketeer. *Series:* Really Naked Truth (exec. prod.), The New Adventures of Robin Hood (exec. prod., writer & creator).

WEINTRAUB, JERRY

Producer. b. Bronx, NY, Sept. 26, 1937. Enlisted in Air Force following high school. After honorable discharge, returned to New York and became a page for the Steve Allen Show at NBC-TV. m. former singer Jayne Morgan. Went from mailroom at William Morris Agency to an agent at MCA talent agency, in just three weeks. After several years with MCA, formed his own management co. In 1964, Weintraub formed Management III and managed diverse acts from Jack Paar to the Muppets while producing more than 100 TV shows. He branched out as a Broadway theatre owner and producer. Later founded Concert West after successfully producing Elvis Presley's first national appearance tour. He went on to promote artists such as Bob Dylan, Led Zeppelin, Frank Sinatra and The Beach Boys. He also owned several independent record labels and music publishing companies. Weintraub began his filmmaking career in 1973 when director Robert Altman challenged him to come up with the financing for a script he had called Nashville. Weintraub set up financing in two days and the movie was released to critical acclaim. Since then, Weintraub has produced more than 22 films and is one of the first independent movie producers to receive a star on the Hollywood Walk of Fame. For television, he has produced myriad projects including the opening ceremonies of the 1984 Olympic Games. In 1985, named United Artists Corp. chmn. Resigned, 1986. In 1987, he formed his own film and TV production company, Weintraub Entertainment Group. In 1990, he formed Jerry Weintraub Productions based at Warner Bros. Studios and remains the CEO today. Industry recognitions include his being named Producer of the Year by the National Association of Theatre Owners in 1986. In March 1991, President George Bush appointed Weintraub to the Board of the John F. Kennedy Center for the Performing Arts, a position he held through the end of the decade. Weintraub has contributed to, received awards from and sits on the board of directors of more than 30 charitable organizations including the Hebrew Home for the Aged, The Urban League, the Elizabeth Glaser Pediatrics AIDS Foundation, the Columbia Presbyterian Hospital Department of Orthopedics, the American Heart Association, the George Bush Presidential Library Center, the Los Angeles Music Center, the Variety Club, the B'nai B'rith, the Mount Sinai Medical Center, the Children's Diabetes Foundation, the Crossroads School for Arts & Sciences, the Rose and Sam Weintraub Elementary School, Brown University, Cedars-Sinai Medical Center and the Jane and Jerry Weintraub Library of the Vista Del Mar School, among others. At the 2001 ShowEast Awards, he won the Kodak Award for Extraordinary Achievement in Filmmaking.
PICTURES: Nashville, Oh God!, Cruising, All Night Long, Diner, The Karate Kid, The Karate Kid Part II, The Karate Kid Part III, Pure Country, The Firm (actor), The Next Karate Kid, The Specialist, National Lampoon's Vegas Vacation, The Avengers, Soldier, The Independent, Ocean's Eleven, Full Frontal (actor), Confessions of a Dangerous Mind (actor), Ocean's Twelve, Oh, God!, Nancy Drew, Police Academy, Ocean's Thirteen, Kung Fu Kid.
TELEVISION: *Movies: Exec. Prod.:* Rocky Mountain Reunion, Diner (short), The Cowboy and the Ballerina, L'Chaim: To Life Telethon. *Documentaries/Specials:* Frank Sinatra: The Main Event, John Denver and Friend, Rocky Mountain Christmas (Emmy nom. 1976), The Dorothy Hamill Special, The Neil Diamond Special (Emmy nom. 1977), The Neil Diamond Special: I'm Glad You're Here with Me Tonight (Emmy nom. 1978), Dorothy Hamill Presents Winners, The Carpenters: Music, Music, Music, John Denver: Music and the Mountains, John Denver: The Higher We Fly.

WEIR, PETER

Director, Writer. b. Sydney, Australia, Aug. 21, 1944. e. Scots Coll. and Sydney U. Briefly worked selling real estate, traveled to England 1965. Entered Australian TV industry as stagehand 1967 while prod. amateur revues. *Dir. shorts*: Count Vim's Last Exercise, The Life and Times of Reverend Buck Shotte Homeside, Incredible Floridas, What Ever Happened to Green Valley? 1967-73.
PICTURES: *Director*: Three to Go (debut, 1970; segment: (Michael), The Cars That Ate Paris (also s.p., co-story; a.k.a. The Cars That Eat People), Picnic at Hanging Rock, The Last Wave (also s.p.), The Plumber (also s.p.; tv in Australia). Gallipoli (also story), The Year of Living Dangerously (also co-s.p.; WGA nom. 1984), Witness (Academy Award nom.; Golden Globe nom.; DGA nom. 1986), The Mosquito Coast, Dead Poets Society (Academy Award nom.; Golden Globe nom.; DGA nom. 1990), Green Card (also prod., s.p.; Academy Award nom.; WGA nom. 1991), Fearless, The Truman Show (Academy Award nom. for dir.; Golden Globe nom.; DGA nom. 1999), Master and Commander: The Far Side of the World (also prod. 2 Academy Award noms.; Golden Globe nom.; DGA nom. 2004), War Magician, The Way Back (also s.p.).
TELEVISION: *Movie:* The Plumber (dir. & writer). *Mini-series:* Luke's Kingdom (dir.).

WEISS, STEVEN ALAN

Executive. b. Glendale, CA, Oct. 19, 1944. e. Los Angeles City Coll., A.A., 1964; USC, M.S., 1966; Northwestern U., B.S., 1967; LaSalle Extension U., J.D., 1970. U.S. Navy-San Diego, Great Lakes, Vallejo & Treasure Island, 1966-67; shipyard liaison officer, Pearl Harbor Naval Shipyard, U.S. Navy, 1967-70; gen. mgr., Adrian Weiss Prods., 1970-74; organized Weiss Global Enterprises with Adrian Weiss 1974 for production, acquisition & distribution of films. Purchased with Tom J. Corradine and Adrian Weiss from the Benedict E. Bogeaus Estate nine features, 1974. Sec./Treas. of Film Investment Corp. & Weiss Global Enterprises which own, control or have dist. rights to over 300 features, many TV series, documentaries, etc. In 2004, the Weiss Global Enterprises library was sold to Kit Parker Films. CFO/COO Flo-Fowes, a full service telecommunications corp., 1992-present. Member of the Nat'l Assn. of TV Program Executive Int'l, National Cable TV Assn., AFI.

WEISWASSER, STEPHEN A.

Executive. e. Wayne St. Univ., B.A. with distinction; The Johns Hopkins Univ on a Woodrow Wilson National Fellowship for Graduate Education; Harvard Law School, J.D. degree magna cum laude. Partner at Wilmer Cutler & Pickering law firm until he joined Capital Cities/ABC in 1986. Weiswasser spent almost 10 years as senior vice president of Capital Cities/ABC, Inc. While serving as senior vice president, he also served as president of the Capital Cities/ABC Multimedia Group, executive vice president of ABC News and executive vice president of the ABC Television Network Group and general counsel of Capital Cities/ABC, Inc. until Oct. 1995. In Nov. 1995, became pres. & CEO of Americast, a joint venture of SBC Communications, Ameritech, BellSouth, GTE, Southern New England Telephone and The Walt Disney Company. He then became a partner at Covington & Burling's communications practice and remains an active partner today, providing legal and strategic counsel to companies in the media, telecommunications and new media industries. While at Covington & Burling, he also served as EVP and general counsel of Gemstar-TV Guide International, Inc. from July 1999 to January 2001. In April 2004, Weiswasser joined Ucentric Systems board of advisors. Ucentric is a provider of home media networking software.

WEITZNER, DAVID

Executive. b. New York, NY, Nov. 13, 1938. e. Michigan State U. Entered industry in 1960 as member Columbia Pictures adv. dep't; later with Donahue and Coe as ass't exec. and Loew's Theatres adv. dep't; later with Embassy Pictures, adv. mgr.; dir. of adv. and exploitation for Palomar Pictures Corp.; v.p. in charge of adv., pub., and exploitation for ABC Pictures Corp.; v.p., entertainment/leisure div., Grey Advertising; v.p., worldwide adv., 20th Century Fox; exec. v.p. adv./pub./promo., Universal Pictures; exec. v.p., mktg. & dist., Embassy Pictures; 1985, joined 20th Century-Fox Films as pres. of mktg. 1987, pres., mktg., Weintraub Entertainment Group; 1988 joined MCA/Universal as pres. worldwide marketing, MCA Recreation Services. Weitzner currently is an independent marketing consultant and has been an adjunct instructor with USC's School of Cinematic Arts.

WELCH, RAQUEL
Actress. r.n. Raquel Tejada. b. Chicago, IL, Sept. 5, 1940. e. La Jolla H.S. Theatre arts scholarship San Diego State Coll. Worked as model before landing bit parts in films. Broadway debut, Woman of the Year, 1981.
PICTURES: A House Is Not a Home (debut, 1964), Roustabout, Do Not Disturb, A Swingin' Summer, Fantastic Voyage, Shoot Loud Louder... I Don't Understand, One Million Years B.C., Fathom, The Oldest Profession, Bedazzled, The Biggest Bundle of Them All, Le Fate (The Queens), Bandolero, Lady in Cement, 100 Rifles, Flare Up, The Magic Christian, Myra Breckinridge, Restless, Hannie Caulder, Kansas City Bomber, Fuzz, Bluebeard, The Last of Sheila, The Three Musketeers: The Queen's Diamonds (Golden Globe Award 1975), The Four Musketeers, The Wild Party, Mother Jugs and Speed, Crossed Swords, L'Animal, Naked Gun 33 1/3: The Final Insult, Tortilla Soup, Legally Blonde, Forget About It.
TELEVISION: *Movies*: The Muppets Go Hollywood, The Legend of Walks Far Woman, Right to Die (Golden Globe nom. 1988), Scandal in a Small Town, Trouble in Paradise, Tainted Blood, Judith Krantz's Torch Song, Hollyrock-a-Bye Baby (voice), Central Park West, Hollywood at Your Feet (host). *Series:* American Family, Central Park West, Welcome to the Captain. *Documentaries/Specials:* Really Raquel, Raquel, FY2K: Graham Norton Live, 2000 Hispanic Heritage Awards (host). *Guest:* More than 125 appearances.

WELD, TUESDAY
Actress. r.n. Susan Weld. b. New York, NY, Aug. 27, 1943. e. Hollywood Professional Sch. Began modeling at 4 yrs.
PICTURES: Rock Rock Rock (debut, 1956), Rally 'Round the Flag Boys! The Five Pennies, Because They're Young, High Time, Sex Kittens Go to College, The Private Lives of Adam and Eve, Return to Peyton Place, Wild in the Country, Bachelor Flat, Soldier in the Rain, I'll Take Sweden, The Cincinnati Kid, Lord Love a Duck, Pretty Poison, I Walk the Line, A Safe Place, Play It As It Lays (Golden Globe Award nom. 1973), Looking for Mr. Goodbar (Acad. Award nom. 1978), Who'll Stop the Rain, Serial, Thief, Author! Author!, Once Upon a Time in America, Heartbreak Hotel, Falling Down, Feeling Minnesota, Investigating Sex, Chelsea Walls.
TELEVISION: *Movies*: Reflections of Murder, F. Scott Fitzgerald in Hollywood, A Question of Guilt, Mother and Daughter: The Loving War, Madame X, The Winter of Our Discontent (Emmy award nom 1983), Scorned and Swindled, Circle of Violence, Something in Common. *Series*: The Many Loves of Dobie Gillis (1959-60).

WELLER, PETER
Actor. b. Stevens Point, WI, June 24, 1947. Acting since 10 years old. e. North Texas State U. Studied at American Acad. of Dramatic Arts with Uta Hagen. Member, Actor's Studio.
THEATRE: Sticks and Bones (moved up from understudy, B'way debut), Full Circle, Summer Brave, Macbeth, The Wool-Gatherer, Rebel Women, Streamers, The Woods, Serenading Louie, Daddy Wolf.
PICTURES: Butch and Sundance: The Early Years (debut, 1979), Just Tell Me What You Want, Shoot the Moon, Of Unknown Origin, The Adventures of Buckaroo Banzai Across the 8th Dimension, Firstborn, Robocop, Shakedown, A Killing Affair, Leviathan, The Tunnel, Robocop 2, Cat Chaser, Naked Lunch, Fifty Fifty, Sunset Grill, The New Age, Screamers, Mighty Aphrodite, Beyond the Clouds, Partners (Academy Award nom. 1994 for best short film), Top of the World, Enemy of My Enemy, Diplomatic Siege, Shadow Hours, Ivansxtc, Falling Through, The Contaminated Man, Ivansxtc, Styx, The Order, Man of God, The Hard Easy, Undiscovered, Prey, Once Fallen.
TELEVISION: *Movies*: The Man Without a Country, The Silence, Kentucky Woman, Two Kinds of Love, Apology, Women & Men: Stories of Seduction (Dust Before Fireworks), Rainbow Drive, The Substitute Wife, The Road to Ruin, Decoy, Gold Coast (dir.), Lakota Woman: Siege at Wounded Knee, End of Summer, The Sands of Time, Dark Prince: The True Story of Dracula, Odyssey 5, The Poseidon Adventure. *Mini-series:* Mourning Becomes Electra. *Series*: Odyssey 5, Homicide: Life on the Street (dir.), Michael Hayes (dir.), 24. *Documentaries/Specials*: Partners (also dir., co-writer, Academy Award nom. 1994), Rome: Engineering an Empire, Egypt: Engineering an Empire (narr.), Engineering an Empire (host). *Guest:* More than 50 appearances.

WENDERS, WIM
Director, Writer. b. Dusseldorf, Germany, August 14, 1945. Studied film 1967-70 at Filmhochschule in Munich. Worked as film critic 1968-70 for Filmkritik and Die Suddeutsche Zeitung. 1967 made first short films (Schauplatze) and three others before first feature, Summer in the City.
PICTURES: *Director-Writer*: Summer in the City (debut, 1970; also prod., actor), The Scarlet Letter, The Goalie's Anxiety at the Penalty Kick, Alice in the Cities, Wrong Move (dir. only), Kings of the Road (also prod.), The American Friend, Lightning Over Water (also actor), Chambre 66 (dir., actor), Hammett (dir. only), The State of Things, Paris Texas (dir. only), I Played It for You (dir., actor only), Tokyo-Ga (also edit.), Wings of Desire (also prod.), Notebooks on Cities and Clothes (also photog.), Until the End of the World, Faraway So Close! (also prod.), Lisbon Story, Beyond the Clouds (co-dir. & co-s.p. with Michelangelo Antonioni), The End of Violence (also prod.), City of Angels (s.p. only), The Million Dollar Hotel (also prod.), Vill Passiert, Ten Minutes Older: The Trumpet, Land of Plenty, Don't Come Knockin' (exec. prod.), The Palermo Shooting (also prod.), 8 (segment dir., writer), The Open Road (exec. prod.), The Miso Soup (s.p.), Pina (s.p.). *Actor:* Long Shot, King Kong's Faust, Helsinki Napoli All Night Long, Motion and Emotion. *Producer:* Half the Rent, Junimond, Fools, Egoshooter, Musica cubana (exec. prod.), The Open Road (exec. prod.), Au revoir Taipei (exec. prod.). *Documentaries:* Buena Vista Social Club (Academy Award nom. 2000), Invisibles (segment dir., writer), To Each His Cinema (segment dir.).
TELEVISION: Movies: Polizeifilm (short), Der Fall Lena Christ (prod. mgr.), Red Hot and Blue (dir.), *Mini-series*: The Blues.

WENDT, GEORGE
Actor. b. Chicago, IL, Oct. 17, 1948. e. Rockhurst College. Joined Second City's acting troupe in 1973. Appeared in NBC pilot Nothing but Comedy.
PICTURES: My Bodyguard, Somewhere in Time, Airplane II: The Sequel, Jekyll & Hyde Together Again, The Woman in Red, Dreamscape, Thief of Hearts, No Small Affair, Fletch, House, Gung Ho, Plain Clothes, Guilty by Suspicion, Forever Young, The Little Rascals, Man of the House, Spice World, Anarchy TV, Space Truckers, The Lovemaster, Rupert's Land, Outside Providence, Kids in America, Life Coach: The Movie, Edmond, Saturday Morning, LA Blues, Bryan Loves You, Chad Chucka, Opposite Day, Santa Buddies.
TELEVISION: *Movies*: Oblomov (BBC), The Ratings Game, Hostage for a Day, Shame II: The Secret, Bye Bye Birdie, Alien Avengers, Alien Avengers II, The Price of Heaven, Alice in Wonderland, The Pooch and the Pauper, Strange Relations, Mary Christmas, Santa Baby, Imperfect Union, A Colbert Christmas: The Greatest Gift of All!. *Series*: Making the Grade, Cheers (6 Emmy noms.), The George Wendt Show, The Naked Truth, The Evolution of Man, House of Dreams (host), Sabrina, the Teenage Witch, Modern Men (also pilot). *Guest*: More than 118 appearances.

WERNER, PETER
Director. b. New York, NY, Jan. 17, 1947. e. Dartmouth College, AFI.
PICTURES: Hidden and Seeking (documentary), In the Region of Ice (short; Academy Award 1977), Don't Cry It's Only Thunder, No Man's Land, The Good Policeman.
TELEVISION: *Movies:* Battered, William Faulkner's Barn Burning, Sins of the Father, Aunt Mary, No Man's Land, Women in Song, No Man's Land, LBJ: The Early Years, (Emmy nom. 1987), Men (exec. prod., dir.; Emmy nom. 1987), The Image (Ace Award), Hiroshima: Out of the Ashes (D.G.A. nom. 1991), The Good Policeman, Doorways, Middle Ages (co-exec. prod.), Substitute Wife, The Four Diamonds, The Unspoken Truth, Inflammable, Almost Golden: The Jessica Savitch Story (D.G.A. nom.; Emmy nom. 1996), For the Love of Zachary, On the Edge of Innocence, Tempting Fate, Mama Flora's Family, Parallels, Hefner: Unauthorized, After Amy Ruby's Bucket of Blood, Call Me Claus, We Were the Mulvaneys, The Pact, Killer Instinct: From the Files of Agent Candice DeLong (also co-exec. prod.), Gracie's Choice (also co-exec. prod.), Vinegar Hill (also co-exec. prod.), Mom at Sixteen, Amber Frey: Witness for the Prosecution, Snow Wonder, Why I Wore Lipstick to My Mastectomy (Emmy nom. 2007), Girl Posi+ive, The Circuit (also co-exec. prod.). *Mini-series:* House of Frankenstein 1997, The '70s. *Series:* Family, Moonlighting (Emmy nom., DGA nom. 1986), Outlaws (also pilot), Hooperman, The Wonder Years, D.E.A. (pilot), Ned Blessing (pilot), Nash Bridges (also pilot), The Expert, Grounded for Life, Maybe It's Me, Philly, For the People, Boomtown, Ghost Whisperer, Medium.

WERNER, TOM
Producer. b. New York. e. Harvard University, cum laude graduate in English literature, 1971. Werner was an award-winning documentary producer before he moved into a successful TV career as part of the successful production team Carsey-Werner with partner Marcy Carsey. Werner started at ABC-TV in 1973 in the planning and development department, then became mgr., prime time program development, East Coast, in 1975. He took over Marcy Carsey's position as sr. v.p. of prime time series in Dec. 1980. A year later he joined Carsey in their independent production partnership, which has lasted 25 years. In 1996, Werner and Carsey were inducted into the Hall of Fame of the National Academy of Television Arts and Sciences, as well as in the Broadcasting and Cable Magazine Hall of Fame. Along with Carsey, he was honored by the Museum of Television

and Radio in 1999, and earned a place in the Museum of the American Dream by sharing the American Academy of Achievement's Golden Plate Award with Carsey, as two of the 20th century's most extraordinary achievers. He is currently co-owner of the Boston Red-Sox.
PICTURES: Let's Go to Prison (exec. prod.), The Brothers Solomon.
TELEVISION: *As Exec. Prod.: Movies:* These Guys, Are We There Yet?, Peep Show, Playing Chicken. *Series:* Oh Madeline (co-exec. prod.), Chicken Soup (co-exec. prod.), Grand (co-exec. prod.), A Different World, Davis Rules (co-exec. prod.), The Cosby Show (Emmy Award 1985, 2 other noms.), You Bet Your Life (co-exec. prod.), Frannie's Turn (co-exec. prod.), Grace Under Fire (co-exec. prod.), She TV, Cosby, Townies, Roseanne, Cybill, Damon, God, the Devil and Bob, Normal, Ohio, Grounded for Life, 3rd Rock from the Sun (2 Emmy noms.), You Don't Know Jack, The Downer Channel, That '80s Show, Whoopi, The Tracy Morgan Show, Game Over, The Scholar, That '70s Show, Twenty Good Years (also pilot, prod.), The Life and Times of Tim, Hank.

WERTHEIMER, THOMAS
Executive. b. 1938. e. Princeton U., B.A. 1960; Columbia U., LLB, 1963. V.p. business affairs subs. ABC 1964-72; joined MCA Inc, 1972; v.p. Universal TV dir.; corp. v.p. 1974 -83; exec. v.p. 1983; chmn., MCA Television and Home Entertainment Groups, 1992-Jan. 1996. Consultant, 1996-present: Wertheimer has been a member of the bd. of directors of Macrovision Corporation since 1997, Board Member of Kcrw Foundation. Currently consultant for Universal Studios.

WERTMULLER, LINA
Director, Writer. b. Rome, Italy, Aug. 14, 1926. m. late sculptor-set designer Enrico Job. e. Acad. of Theatre, Rome, 1951. Began working in theatre in 1951; Prod.-dir. avant-garde plays in Italy 1951-52; member puppet troupe 1952-62; actress, stage mgr., set designer, publicity writer, for theater, radio & TV, 1952-62. Began film career as asst. to Fellini on 8 1/2 in 1962. Following year wrote and directed first film, The Lizards. Had big TV success with series called Gian Burasca and then returned to theatre for a time. 1988, named Special Commissioner of Centro Sperimentale di Cinematografia. Was the first woman to be nominated for an Acad. Award for Best Director (Seven Beauties, 1976).
PICTURES: *Director-Writer:* The Lizards (dir. debut, 1963), Let's Talk About Men, The Seduction of Mimi, Love and Anarchy, All Screwed Up, Swept Away... By an Unusual Destiny in the Blue Sea of August, Seven Beauties (2 Academy Award noms. for dir. & s.p., DGA nom. 1976), The End of the World in Our Usual Bed in a Night Full of Rain, Blood Feud, A Joke of Destiny (Lying in Wait Around the Corner Like a Bandit), A Complex Plot About Women, Sotto Sotto (Softly Softly), Summer Night With Greek Profile Almond Eyes and a Scent of Basil, The Tenth One in Hiding, On a Moonlit Night, Saturday Sunday Monday, Ciao Professore!, The Nymph, Metalmeccanico e parrucchiera in un turbine di sesso e di politica, 12 registi per 12 citta, Ferdinando e Carolina, An Interesting State, Francesa e Nunziata, Swept Away (2002, s.p. only), Too Much Romance...It's Time for Stuffed Peppers (dir. only), Mannaggia alla miseria.
TELEVISION: *Movies:* Rita the Mosquito, Il Decimo Clandestino (Cannes Fest. Award), Sabato domenica e lunedi, Francesca and Nunziata.

WEST, ADAM
Actor. r.n. William West Anderson. b. Walla Walla, WA, Sept. 19, 1928. e. Whitman Col. (B.A.), Stanford Univ. Created classic Batman role. Appeared in interactive short film Ride for Your Life, and CD-ROM The Golden Nugget.
PICTURES: The Young Philadelphians, Geronimo, Soldier in the Rain, Tammy and the Doctor, Robinson Crusoe on Mars, The Outlaws Is Coming!, Mara of the Wilderness, Batman, The Girl Who Knew Too Much, Marriage of a Young Stockbroker, The Specialist, Hell River, Hooper, The Happy Hooker Goes to Hollywood, Blonde Ambition, One Dark Night, Young Lady Chatterly II, Zombie Nightmare, Doin' Time on Planet Earth, Omega Cop, Mad About You, Jungle Wolf II, Maxim Xul, The New Age, Ride for Your Life (short), Joyride, Redux Riding Hood (short; voice), An American Vampire Story, Behind the Sting (documentary), Gettin' the Man's Foot Outta Your Baadassss!, Tales From Beyond, Chicken Little (voice), Angels with Angles, Sexina: Popstar P.I., Meet the Robinsons (voice), Super Capers, Ratko: The Dictator's Son.
TELEVISION: *Movies*: The Eyes of Charles Sands, For the Love of It, I Take These Men, Nevada Smith, Poor Devil, The Last Precinct, Lookwell, Return to the Batcave: The Misadventures of Adam and Burt, 1775 (short), Hollywood's Hot Wheels (host), Monster Island. *Mini-series:* Partizani, Achieving the Glow (host). *Series*: The Detectives, Batman, Tarzan and the Super 7, The Last Precinct, Danger Theatre, The Clinic, The Adventures of Pete & Pete, The Secret Files of the SpyDogs (voice), Family Guy (voice), Black Scorpion. Pet Star (documentary, dir.), The Batman (voice). *Guest*: More than 188 appearances.

WEST, TIMOTHY
Actor. b. Yorkshire, England, Oct. 20, 1934. m. actress Prunella Scales. e. John Lyon Sch. Harow. Ent. ind. 1960. Began acting 1956 after two years as recording engineer. Worked in regional repertory, London's West End and for Royal Shakespeare Company. Dec., 1979 appointed artistic controller of Old Vic. Has directed extensively in the theatre.
PICTURES: Twisted Nerve, The Looking Glass War, Nicholas and Alexandra, The Day of the Jackal, Hedda, Joseph Andrews, The Devil's Advocate, Agatha, The Thirty Nine Steps, Rough Cut, Cry Freedom, Consuming Passions, Ever After, The Messenger: The Story of Joan of Arc, 102 Dalmatians, Iris, Sinbad: Legend of the Seven Seas (voice), Beyond Borders, Endgame.
TELEVISION: *Movies:* Edward VII, Hard Times, Crime and Punishment, Henry VIII, Churchill and the Generals, Brass, The Monocled Mutineer, The Good Doctor Bodkin Adams, What the Butler Saw, Harry's Kingdom, The Train, When We Are Married, Breakthrough at Reykjavik, Strife, A Shadow on the Sun, The Contractor, Blore, m.p., Survival of the Fittest, Oliver Twist, Why Lockerbie, Framed, Smokescreen, Eleven Men Against Eleven, Cuts, The Place of the Dead, Rebecca, Bramwell: Our Brave Boys, King Lear, Animated Epics: Beowulf (voice), Station Jim, Martin Luther, Dickens, The Alan Clark Diaries, Inspector Lynley Mysteries: In Pursuit of the Proper Sinner, London, Essential Poems for Christmas, Colditz, A Room with a View. *Mini-series:* The Alan Clark Diaries. *Series:* The Big Knights, Bedtime, Bleak House. *Guest:* More than 96 appearances.

WESTERLING, RICHARD S.
Exhibitor. b. Erie, PA, June 26, 1951. e. Florida State Univ. (1974). With AMC Entertainment from 1975-1999. Joined Regal Entertainment Group in 2000. Currently, senior v.p., marketing & advertising, Regal Entertainment Group. The company's theatre circuit, comprising Regal Cinemas, United Artists Theatres and Edwards Theatres, operates 6,355 screens in 526 locations in 39 states and the District of Columbia as of Oct. 2007. Memberships: NATO (bd. member); Will Rogers Motion Picture Pioneers Foundation (board); Variety Tent #81 (East Tenn.); Patricia Neal Golf Classic (chair).

WESTON, BRAD
Executive, Producer.
As a motion picture development executive, Weston headed up acquisitions and development for Millennium films from 1997 to 2000. From 2000 to 2005, he was co-pres. of Dimension Films, Miramax's genre film label. While there, he oversaw development of a number of high profile film and video releases for the studio, working closely with such renowned directors as Robert Rodriguez and Wes Craven. In April 2005, Weston became the co-pres. of production for Paramount Pictures, serving beside Alli Shearmur. When Shearmur left Paramount in Jan. 2007, Weston became president, production of Paramount Pictures, reporting directly to chairman and CEO Brad Grey. 2009, Weston left Paramount.
PICTURES: *Executive Producer, Producer or Assoc. Producer:* Super Mario Bros, Rolling Thunder, Guinevere, The 4th Floor, Takedown, How to Kill Your Neighbor's Dog, Scary Movie 2, Prozac Nation, The Grey Zone, Scary Movie 3, Bad Santa, Cursed, Venom, Footloose (prod. exec.).

WETTIG, PATRICIA
Actress. b. Cincinnati, OH, Dec. 4, 1951. m. actor Ken Olin. e. Temple Univ. Studied at Neighborhood Playhouse. Smith College, Master's Degree, playwriting, 2001. Began acting career with NY's Circle Repertory Company appearing in The Wool Gatherer, The Diviners and A Tale Told. Other theatre work includes The Dining Room, Talking With (LA), Threads, Innocent Thoughts, My Mother Said I Never Should. Finalist in 2005 for the Blackburn Prize, annual award for outstanding new English-language play by a woman for play "My Andy."
PICTURES: Guilty by Suspicion, City Slickers, Me & Veronica, City Slickers II: The Legend of Curly's Gold, Bongwater, Dancer Texas Pop. 81, Stranger in a Small Town.
TELEVISION: *Movies*: Silent Motive, Taking Back My Life: The Nancy Ziegenmeyer Story, Parallel Lives, Nothing But the Truth, Kansas, Lackawanna Blues, Brothers & Sisters: Family Album. *Mini-series*: Stephen King's The Langoliers. *Series*: Police Story: Cop Killer, St. Elsewhere, thirtysomething (3 Emmy Awards 1988, 1990, 1991, Golden Globe Award 1991), Courthouse, Alias, Prison Break, Brothers & Sisters.

WEXLER, HASKELL
Cinematographer, Director. b. Chicago, IL June 2, 1922. Photographed educational and industrial films before features. Documentaries as cinematographer include: The Living City, The Savage Eye, T. for Tumbleweed, Stakeout on Dope Street, Brazil—A Report on Torture, Interviews With Mai Lai Veterans, Interview—Chile's President Allende, Introduction to the Enemy. Elected by AMPAS to Bd. of Governors, Cinematographers Branch. 1991, elected by AMPAS to bd. of govs., Cinematographers Branch; 1993, received lifetime achievement award from American Society of Cinematographers. Received Society of Camera Operators Governors' Award 2007.
PICTURES: *Cinematographer:* Studs Lonigan, Five Bold Women, The Hoodlum Priest, Angel Baby, A Face in the Rain, America America, The Best Man, The Bus (also dir., prod.), The Loved One (also co-prod.), Who's Afraid of Virginia Woolf? (Academy Award 1966), In the Heat of the Night, The Thomas Crown Affair, Medium Cool (also dir., co-prod., s.p., DGA nom. 1970), Trial of Catonsville Nine, American Graffiti, One Flew Over the Cuckoo's Nest

(Academy Award nom. 1976), Bound for Glory (Academy Award 1977), Coming Home, Days of Heaven (addit. photog.), No Nukes (also co-dir.), Second Hand Hearts, Richard Pryor: Live on the Sunset Strip, Lookin' to Get Out, The Man Who Loved Women, Matewan (Academy Award nom.; ASC nom. 1988), Colors, Latino (dir., writer only), Three Fugitives, Blaze (Academy Award nom.; ASC Award 1990), Through the Wire, Other People's Money, Rolling Stones at the MAX, The Babe, The Secret of Roan Inish, Canadian Bacon, The Sixth Sun: Mayan Uprising in Chiapas, Mulholland Falls, The Rich Man's Wife, Mexico, Stakeout on Dope Street, Limbo, Bus Rider's Union, Good Kurds, Bad Kurds: No Friends But the Mountains (doc.), Bread and Roses, The Man on Lincoln's Nose, Silver City, From Wharf Rats to the Lords of the Docks, Tell Them Who You Are (doc.), The Big Empty (short; actor only), Who Needs Sleep? (doc.), From Wharf Rats to Lords of the Docks (also camera operator), Battle in Seattle, In the Name of Democracy: The Story of Lt. Ehren Watada (doc.).
TELEVISION: Steve McQueen: The King of Cool, 61* (Emmy nom. 2001).

WHALEY, FRANK
Actor. b. Syracuse, NY, July 20, 1963. e. SUNY, Albany. With his brother formed rock band the Niagaras. Member of Malaparte Theatre Co. in NY.
THEATRE: *NY*: Tigers Wild (debut, 1986), Face Divided, The Indian Wants the Bronx, The Years, Good Evening, Hesh, The Great Unwashed.
PICTURES: Ironweed (debut, 1987), Field of Dreams, Little Monsters, Born on the Fourth of July, The Freshman, Cold Dog Soup, The Doors, Career Opportunities, JFK, Back in the U.S.S.R., A Midnight Clear, Hoffa, Swing Kids, Pulp Fiction, I.Q., Swimming With Sharks, Homage, Cafe Society, Broken Arrow, Retroactive, Glam, When Trumpets Fade, Went to Coney Island on a Mission from God...Be Back By Five, The Wall, Curtain Call, Pursuit of Happiness, The Jimmy Show, Chelsea Walls (also singer), A Good Night to Die, Cherry Crush, World Trade Center, Crazy Eights, The Hottest State, Aftermath, Vacancy, Drillbit Taylor, Thicker, As Good as Dead, Aftermath.
TELEVISION: *Movies*: Soldier Boys, Unconquered, Flying Blind, Fatal Deception: Mrs. Lee Harvey Oswald, To Dance With the White Dog, The Desperate Trail, Dead Man's Gun, The Wall, Shake, Rattle, and Roll: An American Love Story, When Trumpets Fade, Love, Clyde, Detective, Mrs. Harris, Where There's a Will, Ruffian. *Series:* Buddy Faro, Stephen King's Dead Zone. *Pilot:* Flipside. *Documentaries/Specials*: Seasonal Differences.

WHALLEY, JOANNE
Actress. b. Manchester, England, Aug. 25, 1964. Began stage career while in teens including season of Edward Bond plays at Royal Court Theatre (Olivier Award nom.) and The Three Sisters, The Lulu Plays. *NY*: What the Butler Saw (Theatre World Award).
PICTURES: Dance with a Stranger, No Surrender, The Good Father, Willow, To Kill a Priest, Scandal, Kill Me Again, Navy SEALS, Crossing the Line, Shattered, Storyville, Mother's Boys, The Secret Rapture, Trial by Jury, A Good Man in Africa, The Man Who Knew Too Little, A Texas Funeral, Run the Wild Fields, The Guilty, Breathtaking, Virginia's Run, Before You Go, The Californians, Flood, 44 Inch Chest, Gardel, Golf in the Kingdom.
TELEVISION: *Movies:* A Christmas Carol, Run the Wild Fields, 40, Child of Mine, Life Line, Diverted. *Mini-series:* Reilly: Ace of Spies, The Singing Detective, A TV Dante, A Quiet Life, Edge of Darkness, Save Your Kisses, Will You Love Me Tomorrow, Scarlett, Jackie Bouvier Kennedy Onassis, The Virgin Queen. *Series:* Coronation Street, Emmerdale Farm, A Kind of Loving.

WHEATON, WIL
Actor. r.n. Richard William Wheaton III. b. Burbank, CA, July 29, 1972. Began acting in commercials at age 7. Graduated L.A. Professional H.S., June, 1990.
PICTURES: The Secret of NIMH (voice), The Buddy System, Hambone and Hillie, The Last Starfighter, Stand by Me, The Curse, Toy Soldiers, December, The Liars' Club, Boys Night Out (short), Pie in the Sky, Tales of Glamour and Excess, Flubber, Fag Hag, The Girls' Room, Foreign Correspondents, Deep Core 2000, Python, Speechless (short), The Good Things (short), Jane White is Sick & Twisted, Fish Don't Blink, Star Trek: Nemesis, Neverland, Brother Bear (voice), Americanizing Shelley, The Science of Cool.
TELEVISION: *Movies*: A Long Way Home (debut, 1981), The Shooting, The Defiant Ones, Young Harry Houdini, The Man Who Fell to Earth, Star Trek: The Next Generation - Encounter at Farpoint, The Last Prostitute, Mr. Stitch, The Day Lincoln Was Shot, The Flintstones: On the Rocks, It Was Him or Us, Book of Days. *Series*: Star Trek: The Next Generation, Arena, Teen Titans (voice), Ben 10: Alien Force. *Pilots*: Long Time Gone, 13 Thirteenth Avenue, The Man Who Fell to Earth. *Documentaries/Specials*: Lifestories (A Deadly Secret). *Guest:* More than 87 appearances.

WHEDON, JOSS
Writer. b. June 23, 1964. e. Wesleyan University.
PICTURES: Buffy the Vampire Slayer, Toy Story (Academy Award nom. 1996), Alien: Resurrection, Titan A.E, Atlantis: The Lost Empire, Serenity, The Cabin in the Woods.
TELEVISION: *Series*: Roseanne, Parenthood, Angel (dir. and prod. only), Buffy the Vampire Slayer (also prod. and dir.; Emmy nom. 2000), Angel: The Series, Boy Meets World (prod. and dir. only), Ripper (creator), Buffy The Animated Series exec. prod. and creator), Firefly: The Series, Dr. Horrible's Sing-Along Blog (Acts I, II, III also exec. prod, lyricist) Dollhouse (also exec. prod.).

WHITAKER, FOREST
Actor, Director. b. Longview, TX, July 15, 1961. Raised in Los Angeles. e. Pomona College, studying music; USC, studying opera and drama. Prof. debut in prod. of The Beggar's Opera. Directed Whitney Houston's "Exhale (Shoop Shoop)" video.
THEATRE: Swan, Romeo and Juliet, Hamlet, Ring Around the Moon, Craig's Wife, Whose Life Is It Anyway?, The Greeks (all at Drama Studio London); School Talk (LA), Patchwork Shakespeare (CA Youth Theatre), The Beggar's Opera, Jesus Christ Superstar. *Dir.*: Look Back in Anger, Drums Across the Realm.
PICTURES: *Actor:* Everybody Gets It In The End (aka Tag: The Assassination Game; debut, 1982), Fast Times at Ridgemont High, Vision Quest, The Color of Money, Platoon, Stakeout, Good Morning Vietnam, Bloodsport, Bird (Cannes Film Fest. Award, Golden Globe nom. 1989), Johnny Handsome, Downtown, Rage in Harlem (also co-prod.), Diary of a Hit Man, Article 99, The Crying Game, Consenting Adults, Body Snatchers, Bank Robber, Body Snatchers, Blown Away, Jason's Lyric, Ready to Wear (Prêt-à-Porter), Smoke, Species, Phenomenon, Body Count, Light It Up, Battlefield Earth: A Saga of the Year 3000, Four Dogs Playing Poker, Green Dragon (also exec. prod.), The Fourth Angel, The Panic Room, Phone Booth, A Little Trip to Heaven, Jump Shot, American Gun (also exec. prod.), Mary, Ripple Effect (also exec. prod.), The Marsh, The Air I Breathe, Federal, The Last King of Scotland (Academy Award, Golden Globe Award 2007), Street Kings, Kassim the Dream (doc., exec. prod.), Winged Creatures, The Great Debaters, Where the Wild Things Are (voice), Vantage Point, Powder Blue (also prod.), Hurricane Season, My Very Own Love Song, The Experiment, Lullaby for Pi, Repo Men, Jekyll and Hyde, Family Wedding. *Director:* Waiting to Exhale, Hope Floats (also exec. soundtrack prod.), First Daughter (also voice, exec. prod.). *Producer:* Chasing Papi.
TELEVISION: *Movies*: *Actor:* Hands of a Stranger, Criminal Justice, Last Light, Lush Life, The Enemy Within, Rebound: The Legend of Earl 'The Goat' Manigault, Witness Protection, Deacons for Defense. *Director:* Strapped (dir. only), Black Jag (also exec. prod.). *Executive producer:* Door to Door (co-exec.prod.; Emmy Award 2003). *Mini-series*: North and South Parts I & II, Feast of All Saints. *Series*: The Twilight Zone (host), ER (Emmy nom. 2007), The Shield, Brick City (doc., exec. prod.). *Guest:* More than 106 appearances.

WHITE, BETTY
Actress. b. Oak Park, IL, Jan. 17, 1922. Graduated from Beverly Hills H.S. Performed on radio beginning in early 1940s on such shows as Blondie, The Great Gildersleeve, This Is Your FBI. Became local L.A. TV personality in early 1950s prior to starring in her first series to be seen nationwide, Life With Elizabeth, in 1953. Was married to late TV host Allen Ludden. Inducted into Academy of Television Arts & Sciences Hall of Fame, 1994. Recipient of Comedy Lifetime Achievement Award, from the American Comedy Awards, 1990. Emmy Award for Outstanding Guest Actress in a Comedy, The John Larroquette Show, 1993, 4 other Emmy guest noms.
AUTHOR: Betty White's Pet Love (1983), Betty White In Person (1987), The Leading Lady: Dinah's Story (1991), Here We Go Again: My Life in Television (1995).
PICTURES: Advise and Consent, Hard Rain, Lake Placid, The Story of Us, Holy Man, Whispers: An Elephant's Tale (voice), Bringing Down the House, The Third Wish, Love N' Dancing, The Proposal, You Again.
TELEVISION: *Movies*: Vanished, With This Ring, The Best Place to Be, Before and After, The Gossip Columnist, Chance of a Lifetime, Eunice, A Weekend in the Country, The Story of Santa Claus, The Retrievers, The Wild Thornberrys: The Origin of Donnie, Return to the Batcave: The Misadventures of Adam and Burt, Stealing Christmas, Annie's Point. *Host*: Macy's Thanksgiving Parade for 10 yrs, Tournament of Roses Parade (20 yrs.). *Series*: Life With Elizabeth, Make the Connection (panelist), Date With the Angels, The Betty White Show (1958), The Jack Paar Show, The Pet Set, The Mary Tyler Moore Show (2 Emmy Awards: 1975, 1976, 1 other nom.), Match Game P.M. (panelist), Liar's Club (panelist), The Betty White Show (1977-78), Just Men (host; Emmy Award 1983, 1 other nom.), Mama's Family, The Golden Girls (Emmy Award, 1985, 6 other noms.; 4 Golden Globe noms.), The Golden Palace, The John Larroquette Show (recurring role, Emmy Award 1996), Suddenly Susan (recurring role, Emmy nom. 1997), Yes, Dear (recurring role, Emmy nom. 2003), The Practice (recurring role, Emmy nom. 2004), Bob, Maybe This Time, The Lionhearts (voice), Ladies Man, Joey, Boston Legal, The Bold and the Beautiful. *Guest*: More than 231 appearances.

WHITE, ROY B.
Executive, Exhibitor. b. Cincinnati, OH, July 30, 1926. e. U. of

Cincinnati. U.S. Air Force during WWII; sales department of 20th Century-Fox, 1949-52; began in exhibition, 1952; past pres., Mid-States Theatres; chmn. R. M. White Management, Inc.; past president, National Association of Theatre Owners, past Chairman of the Board, NATO, Board of Trustees—American Film Inst.; bd.of dirs. NATO of Ohio, Motion Picture Pioneers Foundation; Will Rogers Hospital, Nat'l. Endowment for Arts.

WHITELAW, BILLIE
C.B.E., D.Litt.: Actress. b. Coventry, England, June 6, 1932. Acted on radio and television since childhood. Winner of the TV Actress of the Year and 1972, Guild Award, Best Actress, 1960. British Acad. Award 1969; U.S. National Society of Film Critics Award best supp. actress, 1968. Evening News, Best Film Actress, 1977; best actress Sony Radio Radio Award 1987, 1989. 1988 Evening Standard Award for Best Actress.
THEATRE: England Our England (revue), Progress to the Park, A Touch of the Poet, Othello; 3 yrs. with Natl. Theatre of Great Britain; Trelawney of the Wells, After Haggerty, Not I, Alphabetical Order, Footfalls, Molly, The Greeks, Happy Days, Passion Play, Rockaby (also in N.Y. and Adelaide Festival), Tales from Hollywood, Who's Afraid of Virginia Woolf?
PICTURES: The Fake (debut, 1953), Companions in Crime, The Sleeping Tiger, Room in the House, Small Hotel, Miracle in Soho, Gideon of Scotland Yard, Carve Her Name With Pride, Bobbikins, Mania, Hell Is a City, Make Mine Mink, No Love for Johnnie, Mr. Topaze (I Like Money), Payroll, The Devil's Agent, The Comedy Man, Charlies Bubbles, The Adding Machine, Twisted Nerve, Start the Revolution Without Me, Leo the Last, Eagle in a Cage, Gumshoe, Frenzy, Night Watch, The Omen, Leopard in the Snow, The Water Babies, An Unsuitable Job for a Woman, The Dark Crystal (voice), Tangier, Slayground, Shadey, The Chain, Murder Elite, Maurice, The Dressmaker, Joyriders, The Krays, Freddie as F.R.O.7 (voice), Deadly Advice, Skallagrigg, Jane Eyre, The Canterbury Tales (voice), The Lost Son, Quills, Hot Fuzz, The Power of the Dark Crystal (voice).
TELEVISION: Over 100 leading roles including: *Movies:* No Trams to Lime Street, Lena, O My Lena, Lady of the Camelias, Resurrection, Beyond the Horizon, Anna Christie, You and Me, A World of Time, Dr. Jekyll and Mr. Hyde, Poet Game, Sextet (8 plays for BBC), Wessex Tales, The Fifty Pound Note, Supernatural (2 plays), Four plays by Samuel Beckett, Eustace and Hilda, The Oresteia of Aeschylus, The Haunted Man, Jamaica Inn, Happy Days, Camille, The Secret Garden, The Picnic, A Tale of Two Cities, The Fifteen Streets, Three Beckett plays, Lorna Doone, Duel of Love, A Murder of Quality, The Cloning of Joanna May, Merlin, Shooting the Past, The Entertainer, The Last of the Blonde Bombshells. *Mini-series:* Napoleon and Love, Private Schulz, Imaginary Friends, Firm Friends, Changing Stages, A Dinner of Herbs. *Series:* Dixon of Dock Green, Time Out for Peggy, The Sextet, Born to Run. *Guest:* More than 64 appearances.

WHITEMORE, HUGH
Writer. b. England, 1936. Studied acting at Royal Acad. of Dramatic Art. Has since written for television, film, theatre.
THEATRE: Stevie, Pack of Lies, Breaking the Code, The Best of Friends, It's Ralph.
PICTURES: All Neat in Black Stockings, Man at the Top, All Creatures Great and Small, The Blue Bird, Three Dangerous Ladies, Mrs. Amworth, Stevie, The Return of the Soldier, 84 Charing Cross Road, Utz, Jane Eyre, Into the Storm (also tele-play).
TELEVISION: *Movies:* Angus Slowly Sinking?, Macready's Gala, Final Demand, Frankenstein Mark II, Amerika, Too Many Cooks, The Three Fat Women of Antibes, The Closed Shop, Act of Betrayal, Thinking Man As Hero, The Adventures of Don Quixote, Goodbye, Cider With Rosie (Writers' Guild Award 1971), Country Matters (Writers' Guild Award, 1972), Dummy (RAT—Prix Italia, 1979), Moll Flanders, State of Emergency, Brensham People, Daphne Laureola, Rebecca, A Dedicated Man, Concealed Enemies (Emmy & Neil Simon Awards, 1984), Pack of Lies (Emmy nom. 1987), The Final Days (Emmy nom. 1990), The Best of Friends, The Rector's Wife, The Haunting of Helen Walker, Breaking the Code, The Gathering Storm (Emmy Award, WGA Award 2002), My House in Umbria (Emmy nom. 2003), Into the Storm (also co-prod.). *Mini-series:* Elizabeth R (Emmy Award, 1971), The Shadow of the Tower, A Fall of Eagles, Shoulder to Shoulder, David Copperfield, I Remember Nelson, My Cousin Rachel, Boy in the Bush, A Dance to the Music of Time, Churchill at War. *Series:* Compact, The Wednesday Thriller, Thirty-Minute Theatre, Hadleigh, Late Night Horror, Menace, The Guardians, No Exit, Dead of Night, Romance.

WHITMAN, STUART
Actor. b. San Francisco, CA., Feb. 1, 1926. Army Corp. of Engineers (1945-1948), at Fort Lewis, WA; while in army, competed as light heavyweight boxer. Studied drama under G.I. Bill at Ben Bard Drama School and L.A. City College. Performed in Heaven Can Wait and became member of Michael Chekhov Stage Society and Arthur Kennedy Group. Entered films in early 1950's. TV debut on 26 episodes of Highway Patrol.
PICTURES: When Worlds Collide, The Day The Earth Stood Still, Rhapsody, Seven Men From Now, War Drums, Johnny Trouble, Darby's Rangers, Ten North Frederick, The Decks Ran Red, China Doll, The Sound and the Fury, These Thousand Hills, Hound Dog Man, The Story of Ruth, Murder Inc., Francis of Assisi, The Fiercest Heart, The Mark (Academy Award nom. 1962), The Comancheros, Convicts 4, The Longest Day, The Day and the Hour (Fr./It.), Shock Treatment, Rio Conchos, Those Magnificent Men In Their Flying Machines, Sands of the Kalahari, Signpost to Murder, An American Dream, The Invincible Six, The Last Escape, Captain Apache (U.S./Sp.), Night Of The Lepus, Welcome To Arrow Beach (Tender Flesh), Crazy Mama, Call Him Mr. Shatter, Assault on Paradise (Maniac/Ransom), Mean Johnny Barrows, Las Vegas Lady, Eaten Alive!, Tony Saitta/Tough Tony (It.), Strange Shadows In An Empty Room, Ruby, The White Buffalo; Delta Fox, Thoroughbred (Run for the Roses), Oil (It. as Red Adair), La Murjer de la Tierra Caliente (Sp./It.); Guyana: Cult of the Damned, Cuba Crossing, Jamaican Gold, The Monster Club, Demonoid, Butterfly, Treasure of The Amazon, John Travis: Solar Survivor, Deadly Reactor, Moving Target, Mob Boss, Private Wars, Trail by Jury, Improper Conduct, Land of Milk and Honey, Second Chances.
TELEVISION: *Movies*: The Man Who Wanted to Live Forever, City Beneath the Sea, Revenge, The Woman Hunter, The Man Who Died Twice, Cat Creature, Go West Young Girl, The Pirate, Condominium, Beverly Hills Cowgirl Blues, Stillwatch, Once Upon a Texas Train, Wounded Heart, Shaughnessy, The President's Man. *Mini-series*: The Last Convertible, Hemingway, Women in White, The Seekers. *Series*: Cimarron Strip, Roughcuts, Superboy, Knots Landing, Shaunessy (pilot). *Guest*: More than 92 appearances.

WHITMORE, JAMES
Actor. r.n. James Allen Whitmore, Jr. b. White Plains, NY, Oct. 1, 1921. e. Yale U. In Yale Drama Sch. players; co-founder Yale radio station, 1942; U.S. Marine Corps, W.W.II; in USO, in American Wing Theatre school, in stock. Broadway debut in Command Decision, 1947.
THEATRE: Give 'em Hell Harry, Will Rogers USA, Almost an Eagle.
PICTURES: The Undercover Man (debut, 1949), Battleground (Academy Award nom.; Golden Globe Award 1950), The Asphalt Jungle, The Next Voice You Hear, Mrs. O'Malley and Mr. Malone, The Outriders, Please Believe Me, Across the Wide Missouri, It's a Big Country, Because You're Mine, Above and Beyond, The Girl Who Had Everything, All the Brothers Were Valiant, Kiss Me Kate, The Command, Them!, Battle Cry, The McConnell Story, The Last Frontier (Savage Wilderness), Oklahoma!, Crime in the Streets, The Eddie Duchin Story, The Deep Six, Face of Fire, Who Was That Lady?, Black Like Me, Chuka, Waterhole No. 3, Nobody's Perfect, Planet of the Apes, Madigan, The Split, Guns of the Magnificent Seven, Tora! Tora! Tora!, Chato's Land, The Harrad Experiment, Where the Red Fern Grows, Give 'em Hell Harry (Academy Award nom.; Golden Globe nom. 1976), The Serpent's Egg, Bully, The First Deadly Sin, The Adventures of Mark Twain (voice), Nuts, Old Explorers, The Shawshank Redemption, The Relic, Old Hats, Here's to Life!, The Majestic.
TELEVISION: *Movies*: The Tenderfoot, The Challenge, If Tomorrow Comes, I Will Fight No More Forever, All My Sons, Rage, Mark I Love You, Glory! Glory!, Sky High, Swing Vote, A Ring of Endless Light. *Mini-series*: The Word, Celebrity, Favorite Son. *Series*: The Law and Mr. Jones, Survival, My Friend Tony, Temperature's Rising, Comeback, The Practice (recurring role, Emmy Award 2000), Mister Sterling (Emmy nom. 2003). *Guest:* More than 117 appearances.
(d. February 6, 2009)

WHITTON, MARGARET
Actress. b. Baltimore, MD, Nov. 30, 1950. Raised in Haddonfield, NJ. Has written articles for Village Voice, The National.
THEATRE: *NY*: Nourish the Beast (Off-B'way debut, 1973), Another Language, The Art of Dining, Chinchilla, Othello, One Tiger to a Hill, Henry IV Part 1, Don Juan, Steaming, Aunt Dan and Lemon, Ice Cream/Hot Fudge. *Regional*: Hamlet, Camille, Time and the Conways, The House of Blue Leaves.
PICTURES: National Lampoon Goes to the Movies (debut, 1981), Love Child, The Best of Times, 9-1/2 Weeks, The Secret of My Succe$s, Ironweed, Major League, Little Monsters, Big Girls Don't Cry...They Get Even, The Man Without a Face, Major League 2, Trial by Jury, Been Rich All My Life (doc., assoc. prod), The Loop (prod.).
TELEVISION: *Movies*: Kojak: None So Blind, Summer My Father Grew Up, Menendez: A Killing in Beverly Hills. *Series*: The Doctors, Search for Tomorrow, Hometown, A Fine Romance, Good and Evil, Cutters.

WIEST, DIANNE
Actress. b. Kansas City, MO, March 28, 1948. e. U. of Maryland. Studied ballet but abandoned it for theatre. Did regional theatre work (Yale Repertory, Arena Stage), performed with NY Shakespeare Festival, toured with American Shakespeare Co. Emmy Award for guest appearance on The Road to Avonlea, 1996.
THEATRE: *Regional*: Arena Stage (DC): Heartbreak House, Our Town, The Dybbuk, Inherit the Wind. *Yale Rep.*: Hedda Gabler, A Doll's House. *NY*: Ashes (NY debut, 1977, at Public Theatre), Agamemnon, Leave It to Beaver Is Dead, The Art of Dining (Obie & Theatre World Awards), Bonjour La Bonjour, Frankenstein (B'way), Three Sisters, Othello, Beyond Therapy, Other Places,

Serenading Louie (Obie Award), After the Fall, Not About Heroes (dir.; also at Williamstown Fest.), Hunting Cockroaches, Square One, In the Summer House, Blue Light, The Shawl (Off B'way), One Flea Spare (NY Public Theatre), All My Sons (B'way).
PICTURES: It's My Turn (debut, 1980), I'm Dancing as Fast as I Can, Independence Day, Footloose, Falling in Love, The Purple Rose of Cairo, Hannah and Her Sisters (Academy Award, supporting actress, Golden Globe nom. 1987), Radio Days, The Lost Boys, September, Bright Lights Big City, Parenthood (Academy Award nom.; Golden Globe nom. 1990), Cookie, Edward Scissorhands, Little Man Tate, Cops and Robbersons, The Scout, Bullets Over Broadway (Academy Award, best supporting actress, Golden Globe Award 1995, NY Film Critics, LA Film Critics, Natl. Bd. of Review Awards), Drunks, The Birdcage, The Associate, Practical Magic, The Horse Whisperer, Not Afraid, Not Afraid, I Am Sam, Merci Docteur Rey, Robots (voice), Dedication, Barry Munday, A Guide to Recognizing Your Saints, Passengers, Dan in Real Life, Synecdoche, New York, Rage, Rabbit Hole.
TELEVISION: *Movies*: Zalmen: or, The Madness of God, Out of Our Father's House, The Wall, The Face of Rage, The Simple Life of Noah Dearborn (Emmy nom. 1999), The Blackwater Lightship, Category 6: Day of Destruction. *Mini-series:* The 10th Kingdom. *Series*: Road to Avonlea (recurring role, Emmy Award 1997), Law and Order, In Treatment (Emmy Award 2008, 1 other nom.; Golden Globe nom. 2009).

WIGAN, GARETH
Executive. b. London, England. e. Oxford U.. Began career in the industry as theatrical agent and film producer. v.p. of production, Twentieth Century Fox, 1975-79; partner & producer, The Ladd Co. (Warner Communications), 1979-83; producer, American Flyers, produced by his own company with Paula Weinstein under Warner Bros., 1983-87; consultant, exec. of production, exec. v.p., Columbia Pictures, 1987-97. Became co-vice chairman 1997 and became Chairman of Columbia TriStar Motion Picture Group. 2008 became strategic advisor to Sony Pictures Entertainment's international film business
PICTURES: *Producer:* Unman Wittering and Zigo, Running Scared, Ghost in the Noonday Sun, American Flyers.
TELEVISION: *Movie: Producer:* Divorce His-Divorce Hers.
(d. February 13, 2010)

WILBY, JAMES
Actor. b. Rangoon, Burma, Feb. 20, 1958. Lived a nomadic childhood moving from Burma to Ceylon, then Jamaica and finally England. e. Durham U. Trained at Royal Acad. of Dramatic Art where he played Shakespearean roles and landed a part in Oxford Film Foundation's Privileged (1982). West End stage debut Another Country. Also acted in regional theatre. 1988: The Common Pursuit.
PICTURES: Privileged (debut, 1982), Dutch Girls, Dreamchild, Maurice, A Handful of Dust, A Summer Story, Conspiracy, Immaculate Conception, Howards End, Une Partie d'Echec, Behind the Lines, An Ideal Husband, Regeneration: Tom's Midnight Garden, Jump Tomorrow, Cotton Mary, Gosford Park, De-Lovely, C'est Gradiva qui vous appelle, Lady Godiva, Shadows in the Sun, We Need to Talk About Kieran.
TELEVISION: *Movies:* Dutch Girls, Tell Me That You Love Me, Adam Bede, Lady Chatterly, You Me + It , Treasure Seekers, Witness Against Hitler, The Woman in White, The Dark Room, Trial & Retribution IV, Adrian Mole: The Cappuccino Years, Bertie and Elizabeth, Sparkling Cyanide, Marple: The Sittaford Mystery, Little Devil, The Last Days of the Raj, Clapham Junction, Futureshock: Comet, A Risk Worth Taking. *Mini- series:* A Tale of Two Cities, Mother Love, Crocodile Shoes, Adrian Mole: The Cappuccino Years, Island at War, Ancient Rome: The Rise and Fall of an Empire. *Series:* Original Sin.

WILDE, ARTHUR L.
Publicist. b. San Francisco, CA, May 27, 1918. S.F. Daily News; Matson Lines; pub. dept., Warner Bros., 1936; photo editor at Columbia Pictures, RKO Pictures, Universal Pictures; dir. exploitation, CBS; pub. dir., Hal Wallis Prod.; pub. dept., Paramount; pub., Hecht-Hill-Lancaster; v.p., Arthur Jacobs, public rel.; Blowitz-Maskell Publicity Agency; pub. dir., C. V. Whitney Pictures; gen. v.p., 1958; owner, pub.-ad. agency, The Arthur L. Wilde Co., 1961-65; freelance publicist, 1965-66; pub. rel. consultant, Marineland of Florida 1965; unit publicity dir., United Artists, National General, Paramount, 1966-69; freelance publicity, 1971; unit publicist, MGM, Paramount, United Artists, 1972-74; staff position; Features Publicity at Paramount Pictures, 1973. Freelance unit publicist again in 1976 at Universal, Paramount and Lorimar Productions. 1978-79, Columbia Pictures & Universal Studios; 1980, Marble Arch. Prods. & Northstar Intl. Pictures; 1981, studio pub. mgr. 20th Century-Fox; recently staff unit publicist for 20th-Fox; 1984-89; currently freelance unit publicist for feature films.
PICTURES: ...And Justice for All, Coal Miner's Daughter. *Unit:* Raise the Titanic, The Postman Always Rings Twice, The Star Chamber, Lust in the Dust, Tennessee Waltz.
(d. April 15, 2009)

WILDER, GENE
Actor, Director, Writer. r.n. Jerry Silberman. b. Milwaukee, WI, June 11, 1933. e. U. of Iowa. Joined Bristol Old Vic company in England, became champion fencer; in NY, worked as chauffeur, fencing instructor, etc. before NY off-B'way debut in Roots. Co-founder of Gilda's Club, a cancer support center in Manhattan, named for wife, Gilda Radner, who died of cancer in 1989. Currently married to Karen Boyer.
THEATRE: *B'way*: The Complacent Lover, Mother Courage, Luv, One Flew Over the Cuckoo's Nest.
PICTURES: Bonnie and Clyde (debut, 1967), The Producers (Acad. Award nom.), Start the Revolution Without Me, Quackser Fortune Has a Cousin in the Bronx, Willy Wonka and the Chocolate Factory, Everything You Always Wanted to Know About Sex* But Were Afraid to Ask, Rhinoceros, Blazing Saddles, The Little Prince, Young Frankenstein (also co-s.p.), The Adventure of Sherlock Holmes' Smarter Brother (also dir., s.p.), Silver Streak, The World's Greatest Lover (also dir., s.p., prod.), The Frisco Kid, Stir Crazy, Sunday Lovers (also dir. & s.p.; episode: Skippy), Hanky Panky, The Woman in Red (also dir., s.p.), Haunted Honeymoon (also dir., s.p., prod.), See No Evil Hear No Evil (also co-s.p.), Funny About Love, Another You.
TELEVISION: *Movies*: The Scarecrow, The Berk, Murder in a Small Town, Alice in Wonderland, The Lady in Question. *Series*: The Electric Company, Something Wilder. *Documentaries/Specials*: The Man Who Refused to Die, Death of a Salesman (1966), The Scarecrow, Acts of Love—And Other Comedies, The Trouble With People, Marlo Thomas Special. *Guest:* More than 53 appearances.

WILKINSON, TOM
Actor. b. Leeds, West Yorkshire, UK, Dec. 12, 1948.
PICTURES: A Pocketful of Rye, Wetherby, Sylvia, Sharma and Beyond, Paper Mask, In the Name of the Father, Priest, All Things Bright and Beautiful, Business Affair, Sense and Sensibility, The Ghost and the Darkness, Wilde, Smilla's Sense of Snow, The Full Monty (BAFTA Award, Best Supporting Actor, 1997), Oscar and Lucinda, The Governess, Rush Hour, Shakespeare in Love, Molokai: The Story of Father Damien, Ride with the Devil, The Patriot, Essex Boys, Chain of Fools, In the Bedroom (Academy Award nom. 2002), Another Life, Black Knight, The Importance of Being Ernest, Before You Go, An Angel for May, Girl with a Pearl Earing, Separate Lives, If Only, Eternal Sunshine of the Spotless Mind, Stage Beauty, A Good Woman, Ripley Under Ground, Batman Begins, Living and Breathing, The Exorcism of Emily Rose, Separate Lies, The Last Kiss, The Night of the White Pants, Dedication, Cassandra's Dream, Michael Clayton (Academy Award nom.; Golden globe nom. 2008), Jackboots on Whitehall, RocknRolla, Valkyrie, 44 Inch Chest, Duplicity, The Ghost, The Debt, Jackboots on Whitehall (voice), After the Wedding.
TELEVISION: *Movies*: Sakharov, Shake Hands Forever, The Woman He Loved, The Attic: The Hiding of Anne Frank, First and Last, Prime Suspect, Resnick: Lonely Hearts, Eskimo Day, Interview Day, Crossing the Floor, Cold Enough for Snow, David Copperfield, The Gathering Storm, An Angel for May, Normal (Emmy nom.; Golden Globe nom. 2003), A Number, Recount, The Gruffalo. *Mini-series*: Spyship, Martin Chuzzlewit, John Adams (Emmy nom. 2008, Golden Globe Award 2009). *Guest:* More than 60 appearances.

WILLENBORG, GREGORY H.
Producer. b. Miami, FL, Feb. 18, 1959. e. George Washington U., B.B.A. 1981; UCLA M.B.A. Marketing & Strategic Planning 1983. During grad. school, worked at the political fundraising firm of Lynn, Bryan & Associates. In 1983, he formed Willenborg & Associates, a consulting group specializing in marketing and fundraising. Raised 25 million for the Bob Hope Cultural Center in Palm Desert, CA.
TELEVISION: America's Hope Awards (creator), America's Dance Awards (creator), America's Hope Award Honoring Bob Hope, America's All-Star Tribute to Elizabeth Taylor, Ray Charles: 50 Years in Music, An All-Star Tribute to Oprah Winfrey, Jerry Herman's Broadway at the Hollywood Bowl.

WILLIAMS, ANDY
Singer, Performer. b. Wall Lake, IA, Dec. 3, 1927. Sang as teen with brothers, performing on radio in Des Moines, Chicago, and Los Angeles. William Brothers were back up singers on Bing Crosby's hit recording of Swinging on a Star. Andy dubbed singing voice of Lauren Bacall in To Have and Have Not. Went solo after group disbanded in early 1950s.
PICTURES: 55 Days at Peking (singer), Something to Sing About, I'd Rather Be Rich, The Life and Times of Judge Roy Bean (singer), Where the Red Fern Grows. More than 31 soundtrack credits.
TELEVISION: Movie: My House in Umbria (singer). *Series:* The College Bowl, Tonight (with Steve Allen; 1954-57), The Andy Williams and June Valli Show, The Chevy Showroom, The Andy Williams Show (1958), The Andy Williams Show (1962-67, 1969-71, 2 Emmy noms.; Golden Globe nom.1968), The Andy Williams Show (synd.: 1976-77). *Documentaries/Specials:* Love Andy, Kaleidoscope Company, Magic Lantern Show Company, The NBC Kids Search for Santa, The NBC Kids Easter in Rome, NBC 75th Anniversary Celebration, many Christmas specials. Many soundtrack credits. *Guest:* More than 117 appearances.

WILLIAMS, BILLY DEE
Actor. b. New York, NY, April 6, 1937. e. National Acad. of Fine

Arts and Design. Studied acting with Paul Mann and Sidney Poitier at actor's workshop in Harlem. Was child actor in the Firebrand of Florence with Lotte Lenya; Broadway adult debut in The Cool World in 1961.
THEATRE: A Taste of Honey, Hallelujah Baby, I Have a Dream, Fences.
PICTURES: The Last Angry Man (debut, 1959), The Out-of-Towners, The Final Comedown, Lady Sings the Blues, Hit!, The Take, Mahogany, The Bingo Long Travelling All-Stars and Motor Kings, Scott Joplin, Star Wars: Episode V-The Empire Strikes Back, Nighthawks, Star Wars: Episode VI-Return of the Jedi, Marvin and Tige, Fear City, Number One with a Bullet, Deadly Illusion, Batman, Driving Me Crazy, Giant Steps, Alien Intruder, Steel Sharks, The Prince, Mask of Death, Moving Target, The Contract, Fear Runs Silent, The Visit, The Ladies Man, Very Heavy Love, Good Neighbor, The Last Place on Earth, Undercover Brother, Oedipus (short; voice), Constellation, Fanboys, iMurders, The Perfect Age of Rock 'n' Roll, This Bitter Earth, Barry Munday.
TELEVISION: *Movies*: Lost Flight, Carter's Army, Brian's Song (Emmy nom. 1972), The Glass House, Christmas Lilies of the Field, Children of Divorce, Shooting Stars, Time Bomb, The Hostage Tower, The Imposter, Courage, The Return of Desperado, Oceans of Fire, The Right of the People, Dangerous Passion, The Jacksons: An American Dream, Marked for Murder, Percy & Thunder, Message from Nam, Heaven & Hell: North and South Book III, Falling for You, Triplecross, The Fourth King, Hard Time, Epoch: Evolution. *Mini-series*: Chiefs. *Series*: Another World, The Guiding Light, Double Dare, Dynasty, Code Name: Eternity, 18 Wheels of Justice, The Andy Williams Show (Emmy Award 1963, 1966, 1967; Emmy nom. 1963 through 1967, Golden Globe nom. 1964, 1968), General Hospital: Night Shift. *Guest:* More than 131 appearances.

WILLIAMS, CARL W.
Executive. b. Decatur, IL, March 9, 1927. e. Illinois State Normal U., B.S., 1949; UCLA, M.A., 1950. dir. adv. photo., Clark Equipment Co., 1951-54; film dir., WKAR-TV, E. Lansing, MI, 1954-56; Prod., dir., Capital Films, E. Lansing, MI, 1957; dir., A-V Laboratory, U.C.L.A., 1957-63; co-dev. Dimension 150 Widescreen process, 1957; formed D-150 Inc., 1963; Filbert Co., 1970, v.p., 1977; founder and president/CEO of Cinema Equipment Sales of Calif., Inc. Member: AMPAS, SMPTE and the International Theatre Equipment Association.

WILLIAMS, CINDY
Actress. b. Van Nuys, CA., Aug. 22, 1947. e. Los Angeles City College. Appeared in high school and college plays; first professional role in Roger Corman's film Gas-s-s-s.
PICTURES: Gas-s-s-s (debut, 1970), Beware! the Blob, Drive He Said, The Christian Licorice Store, Travels With My Aunt, American Graffiti, The Conversation, Mr. Ricco, The First Nudie Musical, More American Graffiti, UFOria, The Creature Wasn't Nice, Rude Awakening, Big Man on Campus, Bingo, Father of the Bride I & II (co-prod. only), Meet Wally Sparks, The Biggest Fan, Timberwolf.
TELEVISION: *Movies*: The Migrants, Helped Wanted: Kids, Save the Dog, Tricks of the Trade, The Leftovers, Perry Mason: The Case of the Poisoned Pen, Menu for Murder (Murder at the PTA Luncheon), Earth Angel, The Patty Duke Show: Still Rockin' in Brooklyn Heights, Escape From Terror: The Teresa Stamper Story, The Stepford Husbands, Entertainment Tonight Presents: Laverne and Shirley Together Again, Intimate Portrait: Kathy Ireland. *Pilots*: Steel Magnolias, The Neighbors, TV's Greatest Sidekicks (host). *Series*: The Funny Side, Laverne and Shirley (Golden Globe nom. 1978), Normal Life, Getting By, Strip Mall, Drive. *Guest:* More than 107 appearances.

WILLIAMS, CLARENCE, III
Actor. b. New York, NY, Aug. 21, 1939. B'way stage: Slow Dance on the Killing Ground (Tony nom.; Theatre World Award), The Great Indoors, Night and Day.
PICTURES: The Cool World, Purple Rain, 52 Pick-Up, Tough Guys Don't Dance, I'm Gonna Git You Sucka, Maniac Cop 2, My Heroes Have Always Been Cowboys, Deep Cover, Dead Fall, Sugar Hill, Judgment, Tales From the Hood, The Immortals, The Silencers, The Brave, Sprung, Hoodlum, Last Rites, Half Baked, Frogs for Snakes, Starstruck, The Legend of 1900, Life, The General's Daughter, Reindeer Games, Civility, Ritual, Mindstorm, Blue Hill Avenue, Impostor, Happy Here and Now, The Extreme Team, Constellation, The Way of War, A Day in the Life.
TELEVISION: *Movies*: The Return of the Mod Squad, House of Dies Drear, The Last Innocent Man, Father & Son: Dangerous Relations, Against the Wall, Road to Galveston, Encino Woman, Rebound: The Legend of Earl 'The Goat' Manigault, George Wallace, The Love Bug, Ali: An American Hero, Mystery Woman: The Mystery Weekend, Mystery Woman: Snapshot, Mystery Woman: Sing Me a Murder, Mystery Woman: Vision of Murder, Mystery Woman: Redemption, Mystery Woman: At First Sight, Mystery Woman: Wild West Mystery, Mystery Woman: In the Shadows. *Series*: The Mod Squad, Crazy Love, American Dragon: Jake Long. *Guest*: More than 63 appearances.

WILLIAMS, ELMO
Film Editor, Director, Producer. b. Oklahoma City, OK, Apr. 30, 1913. Film editor 1933-39, with British & Dominion Studio, England. Since then with RKO-Radio as film editor for numerous major productions; mgr., dir., 20th Century Fox Prod. Ltd. v.p., worldwide production, 20th Century-Fox Film 1971. President Ibex Films. Exec. v.p., Gaylord Prods., 1979; promoted to pres., worldwide prods. 1971 received Golden Eddie Filmaker of the Year Award. Received American Cinema Editor's Career Achievement Award 1990.
PICTURES: High Noon (edit; Academy Award, 1952), Tall Texan (dir., edit.), The Cowboy (prod., dir., edit.), 20,000 Leagues Under the Sea (edit., Academy Award nom. 1955), Apache Kid (dir.), The Vikings (2nd unit dir., film ed.), The Big Gamble (2nd Unit dir.), The Longest Day (assoc. prod.), Zorba the Greek (exec. prod.), Those Magnificent Men in Their Flying Machines (exec. prod.), The Blue Max (exec. prod.), Tora! Tora! Tora! (prod.), Sidewinder One (edit.), Caravans (edit.), Man Woman and Child (prod.), Ernest Goes to Camp.

WILLIAMS, JOBETH
Actress. b. Houston, TX, Dec. 6, 1948. m. director John Pasquin. e. Brown U. One of Glamour Magazine's top 10 college girls, 1969-70. Acted with rep. companies in Rhode Island, Philadelphia, Boston, Washington, DC, etc. Spent over two years in New York-based daytime serials, Somerset and The Guiding Light.
THEATRE: Ladyhouse Blues (1979), A Coupla White Chicks Sitting Around Talking, Gardenia.
PICTURES: Kramer vs. Kramer (debut, 1979), Stir Crazy, The Dogs of War, Poltergeist, Endangered Species, The Big Chill, American Dreamer, Teachers, Desert Bloom, Poltergeist II, Memories of Me, Welcome Home, On Hope (Academy Award nom. 1995 for live action short film), Switch, Dutch, Stop Or My Mom Will Shoot, Me Myself & I, Wyatt Earp, Jungle 2 Jungle, Just Write, Little City, When Danger Follows You Home, Winona's Web (dir. only), Repossessed (short), The Rose Technique, Fever Pitch, Crazylove, Call It Fiction, In the Land of Women, TiMER, The Last Film Festival.
TELEVISION: *Movies*: Fun and Games, The Big Black Pill, Feasting with Panthers, Jabberwocky, The Day After, Adam (Emmy nom. 1984), Kids Don't Tell, Adam: His Song Continues, Murder Ordained, Baby M (Emmy nom.; Golden Globe nom. 1988), My Name is Bill W, Child of the Night, Bump in the Night (co-exec. prod. only), Victim of Love, Jonathan: The Boy Nobody Wanted, Sex Love and Cold Hard Cash, Chantilly Lace, Final Appeal, Parallel Lives, Voices From Within, A Season of Hope, Ruby Jean and Joe, Breaking Through, A Chance of Snow, It Came From the Sky, Jackie's Back: Portrait of a Diva, Backlash, Trapped in a Purple Haze, Frankie & Hazel (dir.), The Ponder Heart, Homeward Bound, 14 Hours, Stroller Wars, Sybil. *Mini-series:* From the Earth to the Moon. *Series*: Somerset, The Guiding Light, Fish Police (voice), John Grisham's The Client, Stories from My Childhood (voice), Payne, Frasier (recurring role, Emmy nom. 1995) Night Visions, 14th Annual Screen Actors Guild Awards (SAG prod.). *Guest:* More than 90 appearances.

WILLIAMS, JOHN
Composer. b. New York, NY, Feb. 8, 1932. e. UCLA, Juilliard Sch. Worked as session musician in '50s; began career as film composer in late '50s. Considerable experience as musical director and conductor as well as composer. Since 1977 conductor of Boston Pops; current role with Boston Pops' is laureate conductor.
PICTURES: I Passed for White, Because They're Young, The Secret Ways, Bachelor Flat, Diamond Head, Gidget Goes to Rome, The Killers, None But the Brave, John Goldfarb Please Come Home, The Rare Breed, How to Steal a Million, The Plainsman, Not with My Wife You Don't, Penelope, A Guide for the Married Man, Fitzwilly, Valley of the Dolls (Academy Award nom. 1968), Daddy's Gone A-Hunting, Goodbye Mr. Chips (music supvr. & dir.; Academy Award nom. 1970), The Reivers (Academy Award nom. 1970), Fiddler on the Roof (musc. dir.; Academy Award 1972). The Cowboys, Images (Academy Award nom. 1973), Pete 'n' Tillie, The Poseidon Adventure (Academy Award nom.; Golden Globe nom. 1973), Tom Sawyer (musc. supvr.; Academy Award nom.; Golden Globe nom. 1974), The Long Goodbye, The Man Who Loved Cat Dancing, The Paper Chase, Cinderella Liberty (2 Academy Award noms.; Golden Globe nom. 1974), Conrack, The Sugarland Express, Earthquake (Golden Globe nom. 1975), The Towering Inferno (Academy Award nom. 1975), The Eiger Sanction, Jaws (Academy Award, Golden Globe Award 1975), Family Plot, The Missouri Breaks, Midway, Black Sunday, Star Wars: Episode IV-A New Hope (Academy Award, Golden Globe Award 1978), Raggedy Ann & Andy, Close Encounters of the Third Kind (Academy Award nom.; Golden Globe nom. 1978), The Fury, Jaws II, Superman (Academy Award nom.; Golden Globe nom. 1979), Meteor, Quintet, Dracula, 1941, Star Wars: Episode V-The Empire Strikes Back (Academy Award nom.; Golden Globe nom. 1981), Raiders of the Lost Ark (Academy Award nom. 1982), Heartbeeps, E.T.: The Extra-Terrestrial (Academy Award, Golden Globe Award 1983), Yes Giorgio (Academy Award nom.; Golden Globe nom. 1983), Monsignor, Star Wars: Episode VI-Return of the Jedi (Academy Award nom. 1984), Indiana Jones and the Temple of Doom (Academy Award nom. 1985), The River (Academy Award nom.; Golden Globe nom.1985), SpaceCamp, The Witches of Eastwick (Academy Award nom. 1988), Empire of the Sun (Academy Award nom.; Golden Globe nom. 1988), The Accidental Tourist (Academy Award nom.; Golden Globe nom. 1989), Indiana

Jones and the Last Crusade (Academy Award nom. 1990), Born on the Fourth of July (Academy Award nom. Golden Globe nom. 1990), Always, Stanley & Iris, Presumed Innocent, Home Alone (2 Academy Award noms. 1991), Hook (Academy Award nom. 1992), JFK (Academy Award nom. 1992), Far and Away, Home Alone 2: Lost in New York, Jurassic Park, Schindler's List (Academy Award, Golden Globe nom. 1994), Sabrina (2 Academy Award noms.; Golden Globe nom. 1996), Nixon (Academy Award nom. 1996), The Lost World: Jurassic Park, Sleepers (Academy Award nom. 1997), Seven Years In Tibet (Golden Globe nom. 1998), Amistad (Academy Award nom. 1998), Rosewood, Stepmom, Saving Private Ryan (Academy Award nom.; Golden Globe nom. 1999), Angela's Ashes (Academy Award nom. Golden Globe nom. 2000), The Patriot (Academy Award nom. 2001), Star Wars: Episode I-The Phantom Menace, Artificial Intelligence: AI (Academy Award nom.; Golden Globe nom. 2002), Star Wars: Episode II–Attack of the Clones, Minority Report, Harry Potter and the Sorcerer's Stone (Academy Award nom. 2002), Catch Me If You Can (Academy Award nom. 2003), Harry Potter and the Prisoner of Azkaban (Academy Award nom. 2005), The Terminal, Star Wars: Episode III - Revenge of the Sith, War of the Worlds, Memoirs of a Geisha (Academy Award nom.; Golden Globe Award 2006), Munich (Academy Award nom. 2006), An Inconvenient Truth (doc.), Failure to Launch (soundtrack writer), The Astronaut Farmer (soundtrack writer), The Holiday (soundtrack writer), Sicko (doc., soundtrack writer), Harry Potter and the Order of the Phoenix (composer theme, also soundtrack writer), Superman Returns (main theme), Indiana Jones and the Kingdom of the Crystal Skull (conductor, comp.), Yes Man (soundtrack), Transformers: Revenge of the Fallen (theme), Harry Potter and the Half-Blood Prince (theme comp.), Lincoln.
TELEVISION: Once Upon a Savage Night, Jane Eyre (Emmy Award 1972), Sergeant Ryker, Heidi (Emmy Award 1969), The Ewok Adventure, Warner at War (doc.). *Series themes*: Checkmate, Alcoa Premiere (Emmy nom. 1962), Wide Country, Lost in Space, The Time Tunnel, NBC News Theme, Amazing Stories, Jack & Bobby. *Soundtrack Writer:* The 46th Annual Academy Awards, The 48th Annual Academy Awards, The 55th Annual Academy Awards, The 63rd Annual Academy Awards, The 64th Annual Academy Awards, The 68th Annual Academy Awards, The 74th Annual Academy Awards (Emmy nom. 2002). More than 80 soundtrack credits for movies, mini-series and series.

WILLIAMS, KENNETH S.

Executive. b. Tulsa, OK, Dec. 31, 1955. e. Harvard College, B.A. 1978; Columbia U., M.S. 1985. Began as team leader of Chase Manhattan's motion picture lending group 1978-81. Joined Sony Pictures Entertainment in Jan. 1982 as director of corporate finance, was promoted to asst. treasurer, Oct. 1982. Became treasurer in Feb. 1984 and named assistant v.p. in Nov. 1984. Served as v.p. & treas. of both Columbia Pictures Industries, Inc. and the Entertainment Business Sector of the Coca-Cola Co. (Sony Pictures previous parent co.), 1986-87. 1987-90, corporate v.p. & treas. of Sony Pictures Entertainment and was then promoted to senior v.p., Corporate Operations. Was named executive v.p. of Sony Pictures Entertainment in Aug. 1995. Named pres. of Digital Division of Sony Pictures in Jan. 1997. During this time at Sony Picturers, he co-founded Sony Pictures Imageworks, a three-time Academy Award nominated visual effects, animation and multimedia company. He then joined Stan Lee Media to oversee the development and global distribution of branded content. He left to become pres. of Technicolor Digital Cinema LLC, a joint venture between Technicolor and Qualcomm, While there he oversaw the commercial rollout of digital cinema systems worldwide. Williams joined Ascent Media Group in 2002 as COO and was promoted to his current position of president and CEO in 2003. He was a keynote speaker at the National Association of Broadcasters 2005 convention, and addressed "New Technologies for Digital Media."

WILLIAMS, MICHELLE

Actress. b. Kalispell, MT, Sept. 9, 1980.
PICTURES: Lassie, Species, Timemaster, A Thousand Acres, Halloween H20: Twenty Years Later, Dick, But I'm a Cheerleader, Me Without You, Prozac Nation, The United States of Leland, The Station Agent, Imaginary Heroes, A Hole In One, Land of Plenty, The Baxter, The Hawk Is Dying, Brokeback Mountain (Academy Award nom.; Golden Globe nom. 2006), The Hottest State, I'm Not There. Deception, Wendy and Lucy, Synecdoche, New York, Mammoth, Shutter Island, Blue Valentine.
TELEVISION: *Movies:* My Son Is Innocent, Killing Mr. Griffin, If These Walls Could Talk 2. *Series:* Raising Caines, Dawson's Creek.

WILLIAMS, PAUL

Actor, Composer. b. Omaha, NE, Sept. 19, 1940. Began career at studios as set painter and stunt parachutist. Bit and character parts in commercials followed. Became song writer, collaborating briefly with Biff Rose and later with Roger Nichols, with whom wrote several best-sellers, including We've Only Just Begun, Rainy Days and Mondays, Just an Old-Fashioned Love Song.
PICTURES: *Actor*: The Loved One (debut, 1965), The Chase, Watermelon Man, Battle for the Planet of the Apes, Phantom of the Paradise (also songs), Smokey and the Bandit, The Cheap Detective, The Muppet Movie (also songs), Stone Cold Dead, Smokey and the Bandit II, Smokey and the Bandit 3, Twelfth Night, The Chill Factor, Solar Crisis (voice), The Doors, Police Rescue, A Million to Juan, Markus 4, Headless Body in Topless Bar, The Rules of Attraction, The Princess Diaries 2: Royal Engagement, Nowhere Man, Georgia Rule, The Ghastly Love of Johnny X. *Songs for Films*: Cinderella Liberty, Bugsy Malone (also vocals), Lifeguard, A Star Is Born (co-composer; Academy Award for best song: Evergreen, 1976), One on One, The End, Agatha, Ishtar, The Muppet Christmas Carol, The Sum of All Fears (lyricist), Mr. Deeds, Starsky & Hutch, Raising Helen, Picasso at the Lapin Agile (lyricist), The Break-Up, Park, 1408, Lucky Ducks (doc., composer).
TELEVISION: *Movies (actor):* Flight to Holocaust, The Wild Wild West Revisted, Rooster, The Night They Saved Christmas, People Like Us, Hart to Hart Returns. *Series*: Sugar Time! (songs, music spvr.), The Love Boat (theme song), Another Day (theme song), The Paul Williams Show, Dark Water (voice), Batman: The Animated Series, Phantom 2040 (voice), Batman: Gotham Knights (voices), The Love Boat: The Next Wave (theme song), Kath & Kim (lyricist "Evergreen"). *Guest:* More than 112 appearances.

WILLIAMS, PAUL

Director. b. New York, NY, Nov. 12, 1943. e. Harvard (Phi Beta Kappa, 1965). First gained attention as director of film short, Girl, which won Golden Eagle award, made in collaboration with producer Edward R. Pressman, with whom he formed Pressman-Williams Enterprises. Now with Fulcrum Productions.
PICTURES: Out of It (also s.p.), The Revolutionary, Dealing: or the Berkeley-to-Boston Forty-Brick Lost-Bag-Blues (also s.p.), Nunzio, Miss Right (also story), The November Men (also actor), Mirage (also actor), Men (prod.), Breaking Up With Paul (actor only), Men (prod.), Charades (prod.), The Best Ever (dir., prod. & s.p.).

WILLIAMS, RICHARD

Producer, Painter, Film Animator. b. March 19, 1933, Toronto, Canada. Entered industry in 1955. Founded Richard Williams Animation Ltd. in 1962, having entered films by producing The Little Island (1st Prize, Venice Film Festival) in 1955. His co. produces TV commercials for England, America, France and Germany, entertainment shorts and animated films. Designed animated feature titles/sequences for What's New Pussycat?, A Funny Thing Happened On The Way To The Forum, Casino Royale, The Charge of the Light Brigade, A Christmas Carol (Academy Award for best animated short, 1972), Who Framed Roger Rabbit (dir. of animation), Arabian Knight (dir., prod., co-s.p.). Awards: at Festivals at Venice, Edinburgh, Mannheim, Montreal, Trieste, Melbourne, West Germany, New York, Locarno, Vancouver, Philadelphia, Zagreb, Hollywood, Cork, Los Angeles. 1989, Academy Award, BAFTA Award, AMPAS Award, special effects, also Special Achievement Awards for work over 30 years, esp. Roger Rabbit by both BAFTA and AMPAS, Arabian Knight (dir./writer).

WILLIAMS, ROBIN

Actor, Comedian. b. Chicago, IL, July 21, 1951. e. Claremont Men's College. (CA), Coll. of Marin (CA), studying acting at latter. Continued studies at Juilliard with John Houseman in New York augmenting income as a street mime. As San Francisco club performer appeared at Holy City Zoo, Intersection, The Great American Music Hall and The Boardinghouse. In Los Angeles performed as stand-up comedian at The Comedy Store, Improvisation, and The Ice House. First TV appearance on 1977 Richard Pryor series followed by The Great American Laugh Off. Guest on Happy Days as extraterrestrial Mork from Ork, led to own series. Received Golden Globe Cecil B. DeMille Award 2005.
PICTURES: Can I Do It...Til I Need Glasses? (debut, 1977), Popeye, The World According to Garp, The Survivors, Moscow on the Hudson, The Best of Times, Club Paradise, Good Morning Vietnam (Acad. Award nom.), The Adventures of Baron Munchausen, Dead Poets Society (Acad. Award nom.), Cadillac Man, Awakenings, Dead Again, The Fisher King (Acad. Award nom.), Hook, Shakes the Clown, FernGully... The Last Rainforest (voice), Aladdin (voice), Toys, Mrs. Doubtfire (also co-prod.), Being Human, Nine Months, To Wong Foo—Thanks for Everything—Julie Newmar, Jumanji, Birdcage, Jack, Hamlet, Good Will Hunting (Acad. Award, Best Supporting Actor, 1997), Flubber, What Dreams May Come, Patch Adams, Jakob the Liar, Bicentennial Man, A.I. (voice), One Hour Photo, Insomnia, Death to Smoochy, Insomnia, The Final Cut, House of D, Robots (voice), The Big White, The Night Listener, R.V., Man of the Year, Happy Feet, (voice), August Rush, Night at the Museum, License to Wed, Old Dogs, World's Greatest Dad, Shrink, Night at the Museum: Battle of the Smithsonian.
TELEVISION: *Movies*: Jonathan Winters: On the Ledge, A Wish for Wings That Work (voice), In Search of Dr. Seuss, Robin Williams: Live on Broadway (2 Emmy noms. 2003), Carol, Carl, Whoopi and Robin (Emmy Award 1987), Weapons of Self-Destruction. *Series*: The Richard Pryor Show (1977), Laugh-In (1977-78 revival; later aired as series in 1979), Mork and Mindy (Emmy nom. 1979), Shakespeare: The Animated Tales (host), Homicide: Life on the Street (recurring role, Emmy nom. 1994), Comic Relief VII (Emmy nom. 1996), Freedom: A History of Us, Law & Order: Special Victims Unit (guest role, Emmy nom.

2008). *Guest*: More than 288 appearances.

WILLIAMS, TREAT
Actor. r.n. Richard Williams. b. Rowayton, CT, Dec. 1, 1951. e. Franklin and Marshall College. Landed role on B'way in musical, Over Here! also played leading role in Grease on B'way.
THEATRE: Over Here, Bus Stop (Equity Library Theatre), Once in a Lifetime, The Pirates of Penzance, Some Men Need Help, Oh Hell, Oleanna.
PICTURES: Deadly Hero (debut, 1976), The Ritz, The Eagle Has Landed, Hair (Golden Globe nom. 1980), 1941, Why Would I Lie?, Prince of the City (Golden Globe nom. 1982), The Pursuit of D. B. Cooper, Once Upon a Time in America, Flashpoint, Smooth Talk, The Men's Club, Dead Heat, Sweet Lies, Heart of Dixie, The Third Solution, Where the Rivers Flow North, Hand Gun, Things to Do in Denver When You're Dead, Mulholland Falls, The Phantom, The Devil's Own, Deep Rising, The Deep End of the Ocean, Skeletons in the Closet, Critical Mass, Crash Point Zero, The Circle, Venomous, Hollywood Ending, Miss Congeniality 2: Armed and Fabulous, What Happens in Vegas, Howl.
TELEVISION: *Movies:* Dempsey, A Streetcar Named Desire (Golden Globe nom. 1985), Some Men Need Help, J. Edgar Hoover, Echoes in the Darkness, Third Degree Burn, Max and Helen, Final Verdict, The Water Engine, Deadly Matrimony, Bonds of Love, Parallel Lives, Vault of Horror I, In the Shadow of Evil, Johnny's Girl, The Late Shift (Emmy nom. 1996), Escape: Human Cargo, The Substitute 2: School's Out, 36 Hours to Die, The Substitute 3: Winner Takes All, Journey to the Center of the Earth, Guilty Hearts, The Staircase Murders, Miles from Nowhere. *Mini-series:* Drug Wars: The Camarena Story. *Series:* Eddie Dodd, Good Advice, Everwood, Brothers & Sisters, As We Are So Wonderfully Done with Each Other, Heartland, Good Behavior (pilot), The Storm (Parts 1 & 2). *Guest:* More than 62 appearances

WILLIAMS-JONES, MICHAEL
Executive. b. England, June 3, 1947. Joined United Artists as trainee, 1967; territorial mgr., South Africa, 1969; territorial mgr., Brazil, 1971; territorial mgr., England, 1976; appt. v.p., continental European mgr., 1978; sr. v.p. foreign mgr., 1979; 1982 joined United Intl. Pictures as sr. v.p. intl. sls., based in London. 1984, named pres. UIP motion picture group; 1986, named pres. & CEO. In Dec. 1996, retired from UIP to create own production co., Merlin Anglesey U.K. Ltd. Went on to become president of Miramax International in 2004, a post he held until his March 1, 2005 resignation. Fellow of the Royal Geographical Society.

WILLIAMSON, FRED
Actor, Director, Producer, Writer. b. Gary, IN, March 5, 1938. e. Northwestern U. Spent 10 yrs. playing pro football before turning to acting.
PICTURES: M*A*S*H (debut, 1970), Tell Me That You Love Me Junie Moon, Fist of Fear Touch of Death, Taxi Killer (prod.), The Legend of Nigger Charlie, Hammer, That Man Bolt, The Soul of Nigger Charlie, Hell Up in Harlem, Black Caesar, Three Tough Guys, Three Days to a Kill (also dir., s.p.), Justice Done (also dir.), Soda Cracker (also dir., prod.), Three the Hard Way, Crazy Joe, Black Eye, `Boss Nigger, Death Journey (also dir., prod.), Bucktown, The Black Bounty Killer (also prod.), Adios Amigo (also dir., prod., s.p.), Take a Hard Ride, Mean Johnny Barrows (also dir., prod.), Joshua, No Way Back (also dir., prod., s.p.), Quel Maledetto Treno Blindato, Mr. Mean (also dir., prod.), Hell's Heroes, Blind Rage, Express to Terror, Fist of Fear Touch of Death, Vigilante, Warriors of the Wasteland, One Down Two to Go (also dir., prod.), The Last Fight (also dir., s.p.), Warriors of the Year 2072, The Big Score (also dir.), 1990: The Bronx Warriors, Warrior of the Lost World, White Fire, Deadly Impact, Foxtrap (also dir., prod.), Delta Force Commando, The Black Cobra, Deadly Intent, Taxi Killer (prod. only), The Kill Reflex (also dir.), Detective Malone, Steele's Law (also dir.), Critical Action (also dir.), Delta Force Commando II: Priority Red One, South Beach (also dir., prod.), Silent Hunter (also dir.), From Dusk Till Dawn, Original Gangstas (also prod.), Full Tilt Boogie, Ride, Whatever It Takes, Down 'n Dirty, (also dir. & prod.), Submerged, Deadly Rhapsody, Shadow Fury, On the Edge (also dir.), Fighting Words, Starsky & Hutch, Last Ounce of Courage, Resist Evil Part Two: God Is Missing! Let Us Quest for God!, Resist Evil Part Three: Don't Stop or We'll Die, 4-Bidden (also prod.), I Wanna Dance, Shoot the Hero, Last Ounce of Courage.
TELEVISION: *Movies*: Deadlock, 3 Days to a Kill, Half Nelson, Blackjack, Carmen: A Hip Hopera. *Mini-series*: Wheels. *Series*: Julia, Monday Night Football, Half Nelson, Fast Track, Sexual Predator Alert (host), Hello Paradise. *Guest*: More than 54 appearances.

WILLIAMSON, KEVIN
Writer, Producer. b. New Bern, NC, March 14, 1965.
PICTURES: *Writer:* Scream, I Know What You Did Last Summer, Scream 2 (also exec. prod., actor), Halloween H20: Twenty Years Later (also co-exec. prod.), The Faculty, Teaching Mrs. Tingle (also dir.), Scream 3 (also prod.), Her Leading Man (prod.), Cursed (also prod.), Backwater (prod.), Venom (prod.), Scream 4.
TELEVISION: *Series:* Another World (actor), Kidsongs, Dawson's Creek (writer, exec. prod., creator), Wasteland (writer & exec. prod.), Glory Days (writer, creator, exec. prod.), Hidden Palms (also exec. prod.), The Vampire Diaries (also pilot, exec. prod.).

WILLIAMSON, NICOL
Actor. b. Hamilton, Scotland, Sept. 14, 1938. Has played many classical roles with Royal Shakespeare Co., including Macbeth, Malvolio, and Coriolanus. Starred on Broadway in Uncle Vanya, Inadmissible Evidence, Rex (musical debut), Macbeth, I Hate Hamlet, Hamlet, Shakespeare in Jazz, Cyrano de Bergerac. *London*: Jack.
PICTURES: Inadmissible Evidence (debut, 1968), The Bofors Gun, Laughter in the Dark, The Reckoning, Hamlet, The Jerusalem File, The Monk, The Wilby Conspiracy, Robin and Marian, The Seven Percent Solution, The Goodbye Girl (cameo), The Cheap Detective, The Human Factor, Excalibur, Venom, I'm Dancing as Fast as I Can, Return to Oz, Black Widow, The Exorcist III, The Hour of the Pig, Apt Pupil, The Advocate, The Wind in the Willows, Spawn.
TELEVISION: *Movies*: Of Mice and Men, Columbo: How to Dial a Murder, Macbeth, Sakharov, Passion Flower. *Mini-series*: Lord Mountbatten: The Last Viceroy, The Word, Christopher Columbus. *Documentaries/Specials*: I Know What I Meant, Hamlet Revisited: Approaches to Hamlet.

WILLIS, BRUCE
Actor. r.n. Walter Bruce Willis. b. Germany, March 19, 1955. Moved to New Jersey when he was 2. After graduating high school, worked at DuPont plant in neighboring town. First entertainment work was as harmonica player in band called Loose Goose. Formed Night Owl Promotions and attended Montclair State Coll. NJ, where he acted in Cat on a Hot Tin Roof. *NY stage debut*: Heaven and Earth. Member of Barbara Contardi's First Amendment Comedy Theatre; supplemented acting work by doing Levi's 501 jeans commercials and as bartender in NY nightclub, Kamikaze. Appeared as extra in film The First Deadly Sin. Star on the Hollywood Walk of Fame, 1998.
THEATRE: Fool for Love, True West.
PICTURES: Blind Date, Sunset, Die Hard, In Country (Golden Globe nom. 1990), Look Who's Talking (voice), That's Adequate, Die Hard 2, Look Who's Talking Too (voice), The Bonfire of the Vanities, Mortal Thoughts, Hudson Hawk (also co-story), Billy Bathgate, The Last Boy Scout, The Player, Death Becomes Her, National Lampoon's Loaded Weapon 1 (cameo), Striking Distance, North, Color of Night, Pulp Fiction, Nobody's Fool, Die Hard With a Vengeance, Twelve Monkeys, The Fifth Element, Last Man Standing, Mercury Rising, Armageddon, The Jackal, Mercury Rising, The Siege, The Sixth Sense, Breakfast of Champions, Franky Goes to Hollywood, The Story of Us, The Kid, The Whole Nine Yards, Unbreakable, Hart's War, Bandits, Hart's War, The Crocodile Hunter: Collision Course (exec. prod.), Man of War, Tears of the Sun, Rugrats Go Wild!, Charlie's Angels: Full Throttle, The Whole Ten Yards, Alpha Dog. Hostage, Sin City, Lucky Number Slevin, 16 Blocks, Just My Luck (prod. only), Over the Hedge (voice), The Hip Hop Project (doc., also exec. prod.) The Astronaut Farmer, Grindhouse, Perfect Stranger, Live Free or Die Hard, Assassination of a High School President, What Just Happened, Surrogates, Red, A Couple of Dicks, The Expendables, Pinkville.
TELEVISION: *Movie:* True West (also exec. prod.). *Series*: Moonlighting (Emmy nom. 1986, Emmy Award, Golden Globe Award, 1987, 2 other noms.), Bruno the Kid (exec. prod. lyricist, singer, theme song), Friends (guest, Emmy Award 2000), Touching Evil (exec. prod.). *Guest:* More than 140 appearances.

WILLIS, GORDON
Cinematographer. b. May 28, 1931. Acted two summers in stock at Gloucester, MA, where also did stage settings and scenery. Photographer in Air Force; then cameraman, making documentaries. In TV did commercials and documentaries. 1995 received Lifetime Achievement Award from American Society of Cinematographers.
PICTURES: End of the Road, Loving, The Landlord, The People Next Door, Little Murders, Klute, The Godfather, Bad Company, Up the Sandbox, The Paper Chase, The Parallax View, The Godfather Part II (ASC nom. 1991), The Drowning Pool, All the President's Men, Annie Hall, Interiors, September 30, 1955, Comes a Horseman, Manhattan, Stardust Memories, Pennies from Heaven, A Midsummer Night's Sex Comedy, Zelig, Broadway Danny Rose, The Purple Rose of Cairo, Perfect, The Money Pit, The Pick-Up Artist, Bright Lights Big City, Presumed Innocent, The Godfather Part III, Malice, The Devil's Own (also prod.). *Director*: Windows (1980; debut).
TELEVISION: *Movie*: The Lost Honor of Kathryn Beck.

WILSON, ELIZABETH
Actress. b. Grand Rapids, MI, April 4, 1921.
THEATRE: *B'way*: Picnic (debut, 1953), The Desk Set, The Tunnel of Love, Little Murders, Big Fish Little Fish, Sheep on the Runway, Sticks and Bones (Tony Award, 1972), Uncle Vanya, Morning's at Seven, Ah! Wilderness, The Importance of Being Earnest, You Can't Take It With You, A Delicate Balance.
Off-B'way: Sheep on the Runway, Token in Marriage (Drama Desk Award), Three Penny Opera, Salonika, Ante Room, Eh?, All's Well That Ends Well. Tour: The Cocktail Hour.
PICTURES: Picnic (debut, 1955), Patterns, The Goddess, The

Tunnel of Love, Happy Anniversary, A Child is Waiting, The Birds, The Tiger Makes Out, The Graduate, Jenny, Catch-22, Little Murders, Day of the Dolphin, Man on a Swing, The Happy Hooker, The Prisoner of Second Avenue, Nine to Five, The Incredible Shrinking Woman, Grace Quigley, Where Are the Children?, The Believers, Regarding Henry, The Addams Family, Quiz Show, Nobody's Fool, Rocky Road.
TELEVISION: *Movies*: Miles to Go Before I Sleep, Once Upon a Family, Million Dollar Infield, Sanctuary of Fear, Morning's at Seven, Nutcracker: Money Madness and Murder (Emmy nom. 1987), Conspiracy of Love, Skylark, In the Best of Families: Marriage Pride & Madness, Bitter Blood, In the Best Families, Spring Awakening, Journey to Mars. *Mini-series*: Queen, Scarlett, Promised Land, Delaventure. *Series*: East Side West Side, Doc, Morningstar/ Eveningstar, Delta. *Documentaries/Specials*: Patterns, Happy Endings, You Can't Take It With You. *Guest:* More than 44 appearances.

WILSON, HUGH
Producer, Director, Writer. b. Miami, FL, Aug. 21, 1943. e. Univ. of FL., 1965. Gained fame for creating, writing, producing and directing TV series. Feature film dir. debut with Police Academy (1984).
PICTURES: *Director &/or Writer*: Stroker Ace, Rough Riders, Police Academy, Rustler's Rhapsody, Burglar, Guarding Tess (also voice), Down Periscope (co-s.p.), Blast From the Past, The First Wives Club, Southie, Blast From the Past (also prod. & actor), Dudley Do-Right, Mickey (also actor), Police Academy.
TELEVISION: *Movies:* Rough Riders. *Series:* The Tony Randall Show, WKRP in Cincinnati (3 Emmy noms.), Frank's Place - The Movie, Frank's Place (Emmy Award 1988, 1 other nom.), The Famous Teddy Z (2 Emmy noms 1990).

WILSON, LUKE
Actor. b. Dallas, TX, Sept. 21, 1971. Brother is actor-writer Owen Wilson. Debuted in short film Bottle Rocket, which was later expanded to a feature.
PICTURES: Bottle Rocket, Telling Lies in America, Best Men, Scream 2, Rushmore, Home Fries, Dog Park, Bongwater, My Dog Skip, Kill the Man, Committed, Blue Streak, Preston tylk, Charlie's Angels, Soul Survivors, The Third Wheel, Legally Blonde, The Royal Tenenbaums, The Third Wheel, Charlie's Angels: Full Throttle, Old School, Legally Blonde 2: Bigger, Bolder, Blonder, Around the World in 80 Days, Anchorman: The Legend of Ron Burgundy, The Wendell Baker Story, Mini's First Time, Hoot, The Family Stone, My Super Ex-Girlfriend, Idiocracy, You Kill Me, Blades of Glory, Vacancy, 3:10 to Yuma, Blonde Ambition, Henry Poole Is Here, Tenure, Middle Men, Death at a Funeral.
TELEVISION: *Guest:* The X Files. *Guest:* More than 45 appearances.

WILSON, OWEN
Actor. b. Nov. 18, 1968. Brother is actor Luke Wilson. Debuted in short film Bottle rocket, which he co-wrote and later expanded to feature.
PICTURES: Bottle Rocket (also co-s.p.), The Cable Guy, Anaconda, As Good As It Gets (assoc. prod. only), Rushmore (also co-s.p., exec. prod.), Permanent Midnight, Armageddon, The Minus Man, The Haunting, Breakfast of Champions, Shangai Noon, Kingdom of the Sun (voice), Meet the Parents, Zoolander, Behind Enemy Lines, I Spy, The Royal Tenenbaums (also exec. prod., s.p., Academy Award nom.; WGA nom. 2002), Shanghai Knights, The Big Bounce, Starsky & Hutch, Around the World in 80 Days, The Life Aquatic with Steve Zissou, The Wendell Baker Story, The Wedding Crashers, Cars (voice), You, Me and Dupree (also prod.), Night at the Museum, The Darjeeling Limited, Drillbit Taylor, Marley & Me, Year One (exec. prod.), Night at the Museum 2: Battle of the Smithsonian, Fantastic Mr. Fox (voice), Little Fockers.
TELEVISION: *Movie:* Heat Vision and Jack (voice). *Guest:* More than 52 appearances.

WILSON, SCOTT
Actor. b. Atlanta, GA, March 29, 1942. Was college athlete on basketball scholarship when injured and had to leave school. Moved to L.A. and enrolled in local acting class.
PICTURES: In the Heat of the Night (debut, 1967), In Cold Blood, The Gypsy Moths, Castle Keep, The Grissom Gang, The New Centurions, Lolly Madonna XXX, The Great Gatsby, The Ninth Configuration (Golden Globe nom. 1981), The Right Stuff, The Aviator, On the Line, A Year of the Quiet Sun, Blue City, Malone, Johnny Handsome, The Exorcist III, Young Guns II, Femme Fatale, Pure Luck, Flesh and Bone, Geronimo: An American Legend, Tall Tale, Judge Dredd, The Grass Harp, Dead Man Walking, Saving Shiloh, Come Early Morning, Shiloh 2: Shiloh Season, South of Heaven, West of Hell, G.I. Jane, Our God's Brother, Clay Pigeons, Pride, The Way of the Gun, The Animal, Pearl Harbor, The Last Samurai, Monster, Junebug, Open Window, The Host, Behind the Mask: The Rise of Leslie Vernon, The Sensation of Sight, The Heartbreak Kid, Big Stan, Saving Grace B. Jones, Radio Free Albemuth, For Sale by Owner, Bottleworld.
TELEVISION: *Movies*: The Tracker, Jesse, Elvis and the Colonel, Soul Survivors, The Jack Bull, California Quartet, Guide Season. *Series:* CSI: Crime Scene Investigation.

WINCER, SIMON
Director. b. 1943. Australia. Directed over 200 hours of dramatic programs for Australian TV, including Cash and Company, Tandarra, Ryan, Against the Wind, The Sullivans, etc. Exec. prod. of The Man from Snowy River, then the top-grossing theatrical film in Australia.
PICTURES: Snapshot (The Day After Halloween), Harlequin, Phar Lap, D.A.R.Y.L., The Lighthorsemen (also co.-prod.), Quigley Down Under, Harley Davidson and the Marlboro Man, Free Willy, Lightning Jack (also co-prod.), Operation Dumbo Drop, The Phantom, Flash, Crocodile Dundee in Los Angeles, The Young Black Stallion, NASCAR: The IMAX Experience (doc., short).
TELEVISION: *Movies*: The Haunting of Hewie Dowker, The Last Frontier, Bluegrass, Flash, Lonesome Dove (Emmy Award, 1989), The Girl Who Spelled Freedom, Escape: Human Cargo, The Echo of Thunder, Murder She Purred: A Mrs. Murphy Mystery, Louis L'Amour's 'Crossfire Trail', Monte Walsh. *Mini-series*: Against the Wind, Lonesome Dove (Emmy Award 1989, DGA nom. 1990), P.T. Barnum, Into the West, Comanche Moon. *Series*: Homicide (prod.) Matlock Police, The Box, Cash & Company, Tandarra, The Sullivans, Young Ramsey, Chopper Squad, Prisoner, The Young Indiana Jones Chronicles, Ponderosa.

WINCOTT, MICHAEL
Actor. b. Canada, Jan. 21, 1958. Studied acting at Juilliard. NY stage incl. Talk Radio, States of Shock. President of Edith Grove Productions.
PICTURES: Wild Horse Hank (debut, 1979), Circle of Two, Ticket to Heaven, Curtains, The Sicilian, Talk Radio, Suffering Bastards, Bloodhounds of Broaway, Born on the Fourth of July, The Doors, Robin Hood: Prince of Thieves, 1492: Conquest of Paradise, The Three Musketeers, Romeo Is Bleeding, The Crow, Panther, Strange Days, Dead Man, Basquiat, Alien: Resurrection, Metro, Gunshy, Before Night Falls, Along Came a Spider, The Count of Monte Cristo, Treasure Planet (voice), The Assassination of Richard Nixon, Animal, Seraphim Falls, The Diving Bell and the Butterfly, What Just Happened?, A Lonely Place for Dying.
TELEVISION: *Movies*: An American Christmas Carol, Tragedy of Flight 103: The Inside Story, The Darkest Day, The Red Phone, Remembering Charlie.

WINDOM, WILLIAM
Actor. b. New York, NY, Sept. 28, 1923.
PICTURES: To Kill a Mockingbird (debut, 1962), Cattle King, For Love or Money, One Man's Way, The Americanization of Emily, Hour of the Gun, The Detective, The Gypsy Moths, The Angry Breed, Brewster McCloud, Fool's Parade, Escape From the Planet of the Apes, The Mephisto Waltz, The Man, Now You See Him Now You Don't, Echoes of a Summer, Mean Dog Blues, Separate Ways, Last Plane Out, Grandview U.S.A., Prince Jack, Space Rage, Funland, Pinocchio and the Emperor of the Night (voice), Planes Trains and Automobiles, Committed, She's Having a Baby, Funland, Street Justice, Uncle Buck (voice), Sommersby, Miracle on 34th Street, True Crime, The Thundering 8th (short), Early Bird Special, Raising Dead, Dismembered, Star Trek: New Voyages, Dopamine, Yesterday's Dreams, Madness.
TELEVISION: *Movies*: Seven Times Monday, Prescription: Murder, U.M.C., The House on Greenapple Road, Assault on the Wayne, Escape, A Taste of Evil, Columbo: Short Fuse, Marriage: Year One, The Homecoming, Second Chance, A Great American Tragedy, Pursuit, The Girls of Huntington House, The Day the Earth Moved, The Abduction of St. Anne, Journey from Darkness, Guilty or Innocent: The Sam Sheppard Murder Case, Bridger, Richie Brockelman: Missing 24 Hours, Hunters of the Reef, Portrait of a Rebel: Margaret Sanger, Leave 'Em Laughing, Side Show, Desperate Lives, The Rules of Marriage, Why Me?, Off Sides, Velvet, Surviving, There Must Be a Pony, Dennis the Menace, Chance of a Lifetime, Attack of the 50 Ft. Woman, Fugitive X: Innocent Target. *Mini-series*: Once an Eagle, Seventh Avenue, Blind Ambition. *Series*: The Farmer's Daughter, My World and Welcome to It (Emmy Award, 1970), The Girl With Something Extra, Brothers and Sisters, Murder She Wrote, Parenthood., Sky Commanders, Sonic the Hedgehog (voice). *Guest*: More than 212 appearances.

WINFREY, OPRAH
Executive, TV Talk Show Hostess, Actress, Producer, Philanthropist. b. Kosciusko, MS, Jan. 29, 1954. e. Tennessee State U. Started as radio reporter then TV news reporter-anchor in Nashville. Moved to Baltimore in same capacity, later co-hosting successful morning talk show. Left for Chicago to host own show AM Chicago which became top-rated in only a month; expanded to national syndication in 1986. In 1988, she established Harpo Studios, a production facility in Chicago, making her the third woman in the American entertainment industry, after Mary Pickford and Lucille Ball, to own a studio. Subsequently, Winfrey assumed ownership and production of The Oprah Winfrey Show, and is seen by an estimated 30 million viewers a week in the U.S. and is broadcast internationally in 109 countries. In 1990, Winfrey established Harpo Films, and struck a long-term

deal with ABC Television to produce "Oprah Winfrey Presents" TV movies. Harpo Films' 2005 production was "Their Eyes Were Watching God," based on the Zora Neale Hurston novel and starred Oscar winner Halle Berry. In addition to on-camera interview skills, Winfrey debuted her acting acumen in 1985 in Steven Spielberg's "The Color Purple," for which she received both Golden Globe and Academy Award nominations. In 1998, Winfrey co-founded Oxygen Media, a 24-hour cable television network for women (NBC Universal paid $925 million for the Oxygen cable network in Oct. 2007.). In 2000, Winfrey and Hearst Magazines introduced "O, the Oprah Magazine," a monthly women's lifestyle magazine and has more than 2 million readers each month, making "O" one of the most successful new magazines in recent history. A follow-up to "O" launched in 2004 was "O at Home." In Sept. 2002 she debuted "Oprah After the Show," an original unscripted half-hour show taped immediately following "The Oprah Winfrey Show." The series airs on the Oxygen Network. Extending her reach beyond television, Winfrey also operates Oprah.com, a women's lifestyle website that offers comprehensive advice to women; in 2003 she launched an interactive multimedia workshop online, which was based on her "Live Your Best Life" sold-out national speaking tour. In the second half of 2009 the Oprah Winfrey Network, LLC will debut on cable TV. It will be 50/50 owned by Discovery Communications and Harpo. OWN staff and operations will be based in Los Angeles. OWN will be a multi-platform media venture available in more than 70 million homes, and on the award-winning digital platform, Oprah.com.
PHILANTHROPY: Formed The Oprah Winfrey Foundation in 1987, to support the education & empowerment of women, children and families in the U.S. and around the world. Winfrey has awarded hundreds of grants to organizations that carry out this vision. In 1997, Winfrey established "Oprah's Angel Network," a public charity to encourage people to use their lives to make a difference in the lives of others. One hundred percent of audience donations go to non-profit organizations around the world. Winfrey initiated the National Child Protection Act in 1991, which culminated in the establishment of a national database of convicted child abusers. On Dec. 20, 1993, Pres. Bill Clinton signed the national "Oprah Bill" into law. For all her efforts to enrich, enlighten, educate and entertain others, Winfrey has been the recipient of numerous awards and recognitions.
AWARDS/RECOGNITION: George Foster Peabody Awards, Individual Achievement, 1995; International Radio & Television Society Foundation, Gold Medal Award, 1996; TV Guide, Television Performer of the Year, 1997; Newsweek, Most Important Person in Books and Media, 1997; Time Magazine, 100 Most Influential People of the 20th Century, 1998; National Academy of Television Arts & Sciences, Lifetime Achievement Award, 1998. (The following year, after accepting the lifetime achievement honor, Winfrey removed herself from future Emmy consideration and the show followed suit in 2000. Oprah and "The Oprah Winfrey Show" received nearly 40 Daytime Emmy Awards: seven for outstanding host; nine for Outstanding Talk Show; 21 in the Creative Arts categories; and one for Oprah's work as supervising producer of the ABC After School Special, "Shades of Single Protein."); the National Book Foundation, 50th Anniversary Gold Medal, 1999; the "Broadcasting & Cable" Hall of Fame, 2002; the 54th Annual Primetime Emmy Awards, Bob Hope Humanitarian Award, 2002; Association of American Publishers, AAP Honors Award, 2003; National Assoc. of Broadcasters, Distinguished Service Award, 2004; Hall of Fame Honoree at the 36th NAACP Image Awards, 2005, Time Magazine, 100 Most Influential People in the World, 2004-2007.
PICTURES: The Color Purple (debut, 1985; Academy Award nom.; Golden Globe nom. 1986), Native Son, Throw Momma From the Train (cameo), Listen Up: The Lives of Quincy Jones, Malcolm X, Beloved, Charlotte's Web (voice), Bee Movie (voice), The Great Debaters (prod. only), Precious: Based on the Novel Push by Sapphire (exec. prod.), The Princess and the Frog (voice).
TELEVISION: *Movies*: The Women of Brewster Place (actress, co-exec. prod.), There Are No Children Here, Lincoln (voice), Before Women Had Wings, About Us: The Dignity of Children, (as exec.prod./prod), Overexposed (exec. prod.), The Wedding (exec. prod.), David and Lisa (exec. prod.), Tuesdays with Morrie (exec. prod.), Amy & Isabelle (prod. & exec. prod.), Their Eyes Were Watching God (exec. prod.). *Series*: The Oprah Winfrey Show (also sup. prod.,many Emmy Awards), Brewster Place (also exec. prod.), Use Your Life. *Documentaries/Specials*: Peewee's Playhouse Christmas Special, Scared Silent: Ending and Exposing Child Abuse, Lincoln, Quincy Jones. The First 50 Years, A Celebration: 100 Years of Great Women, Our Friend, Martin, A Prayer for America: Yankee Stadium Memorial (Emmy nom. 2002), The Kennedy Center Honors: A Celebration of the Performing Arts, Unchained Memories: Readings from the Slave Narratives, Emmanuel's Gift (narr.), Legends Ball (exec. prod.). *Guest:* More than 138 appearances.

WINGER, DEBRA
Actress. b. Cleveland, OH, May 16, 1955. e. California State U. Began career on TV series Wonder Woman.
PICTURES: Slumber Party '57 (debut, 1977), Thank God It's Friday, French Postcards, Urban Cowboy (2 Golden Globe noms. 1981), Cannery Row, An Officer and a Gentleman (Academy Award nom.; Golden Globe nom. 1983), Terms of Endearment (Academy Award nom.; Golden Globe nom. 1984), Mike's Murder, Legal Eagles, Black Widow, Made in Heaven, Betrayed, Everybody Wins, The Sheltering Sky, Leap of Faith, Wilder Napalm, A Dangerous Woman (Golden Globe nom. 1994), Shadowlands (Academy Award nom. 1994), Forget Paris, Rumi: Poet of the Heart (documentary; narr.), Big Bad Love, Searching for Debra Winger (documentary), Radio, Eulogy, Rachel Getting Married.
TELEVISION: *Movies*: Special Olympics, ...Sometimes in April, Dawn Anna (Emmy nom. 2005). *Documentaries/Specials*: The Wizard of Oz in Concert: Dreams Come True, In the Wild: Pandas.

WINKLER, HENRY
Actor, Producer, Director. b. New York, NY, Oct. 30, 1945. e. Emerson Coll., Yale Sch. of Drama, MA. Appeared with Yale Repertory Co.; returned to N.Y. to work in radio. Did 30 TV commercials before starring in The Great American Dream Machine and Masquerade on TV. Formed Fairdinkum Productions with Ann Daniel.
PICTURES: *Actor*: Crazy Joe (debut, 1974), The Lords of Flatbush, Heroes (Golden Globe nom. 1978), The One and Only, Night Shift (Golden Globe nom. 1983), Scream, Ground Control, The Waterboy, Ugly Naked People (short), Elevator Seeking, P.U.N.K.S, Dill Scallion, Down To You, I Shaved My Legs for This, Holes, Berkeley, Unbeatable Harold, The Kid & I, Click, A Plumm Summer, You Don't Mess with the Zohan. *Executive producer*: The Sure Thing, Sightings 6 Years, Dead Man's Gun. *Director*: Memories of Me, Cop and a Half.
TELEVISION: *Movies*: *Actor:* Katherine, An American Christmas Carol, Happily Ever After (voice), Absolute Strangers, The Only Way Out, Truman Capote's One Christmas, A Child Is Missing (also prod.), Dad's Week Off, Detention: The Siege at Johnson High. *Director*: A Smoky Mountain Christmas, All the Kids Do It (also exec. prod.; Emmy Award as exec. prod., 1985). *Executive producer*: Who Are the DeBolts and Where Did They Get 19 Kids?, Scandal Sheet, Ryans Four, When Your Lover Leaves, Starflight, Second Start, Morning Glory (pilot), MacGyver: Lost Treasure of Atlantis, MacGyver: Trail to Doomsday, A Family Again, Starting Now (short), Dead Man's Gun, Sightings: Heartland Ghost, Young MacGyver, Unexplained Mysteries, Knots Landing Reunion: Together Again, Dynasty Reunion: Catfights & Caviar. *Series*: *Actor:* Happy Days (3 Emmy noms.; 2 Golden Globe Awards), Fonz and the Happy Days Gang (voice), The Mork & Mindy/Laverne & Shirley with the Fonz Show (voice), Monty (also exec. prod.), The Practice (guest, Emmy nom. 2000), Clifford's Puppy Days (voice, Emmy nom. 2004, Emmy Award 2005), Arrested Development, Out of Practice, Sit Down, Shut Up. *Director:* Joanie Loves Chachi, Dave's World, Too Something, Clueless, Sabrina, the Teenage Witch. *Executive producer*: Mr. Sunshine (co-exec. prod.), Young MacGyver, A Life Apart, WinTuition, Young MacGyver (exec. prod.), Dead Man's Gun, So Weird, Hollywood Squares (Emmy nom. 2003). *Documentaries/Specials*: Henry Winkler Meets William Shakespeare, America Salutes Richard Rodgers (host), Dallas Reunion: Return to Southfork (exec. prod.), Who Are the DeBolts? [And Where Did They Get 19 Kids?] (Emmy nom. 1979), CBS Schoolbreak Special: All the Kids Do It (Emmy Award, 1 other nom. 1985). *Guest*: More than 197 appearances.

WINKLER, IRWIN
Producer, Director. b. New York, NY, May 28, 1934. e. NYU. Received the Board of Governors Award from American Society of Cinematographers 2004.
PICTURES: *Producer*: Double Trouble, Blue, The Split, They Shoot Horses Don't They?, The Strawberry Statement, Leo the Last, Believe in Me, The Gang That Couldn't Shoot Straight, The Mechanic, The New Centurions, Up the Sandbox, Busting, S*P*Y*S, The Gambler, Breakout, Peeper, Rocky (Academy Award 1976), Nickelodeon, New York New York, Valentino, Comes a Horseman, Uncle Joe Shannon, Rocky II, Raging Bull (Academy Award nom. 1981), True Confessions, Rocky III, Author! Author!, The Right Stuff (Academy Award nom. 1984), Rocky IV, Revolution, 'Round Midnight, Betrayed, Music Box, Goodfellas (Academy Award nom. 1991), Rocky V, The Juror, Rocky Balboa (exec. prod.), Streets of Blood, The Mechanic. *Director*: Guilty by Suspicion (also s.p.), Night and the City, The Net (also co-s.p., co-prod.), At First Sight (also s.p., prod.), Life As A House, The Shipping News, Enough, De-Lovely, Man on Third, Home of the Brave (also writer).
TELEVISION: *Movies:* Scandal Sheet, Nobody's Children. *Series:* The Net (exec. prod./writer).

WINNER, MICHAEL
Producer, Director, Writer. b. London, England, Oct. 30, 1935. e. Cambridge U. Ent. m.p. ind. as columnist, dir., Drummer Films. *Presenter*: Michael Winner's True Crimes. *Actor*: For the Greater Good, Decadence, Calliope, Kenny Everett Show, The Full Wax, Birds of a Feather. PICTURES: *Writer*: Man With A Gun. *Director:* Old Mac, Play It Cool, West 11, The Games. *Director/Writer*: Haunted England (also prod.), Shoot to Kill, Swiss Holiday, Climb Up the Wall, Out of the Shadow, Some Like It Cool, Girls Girls Girls, It's Magic, Behave Yourself, The Cool Mikado, You Must Be Joking. *Director/Producer*: The System

(The Girl-Getters), I'll Never Forget What's 'is Name, The Jokers, Hannibal Brooks (also s.p.), Lawman, The Nightcomers, Chato's Land, The Mechanic (dir. only), Scorpio (also s.p.), The Stone Killer, Death Wish, Won Ton Ton the Dog Who Saved Hollywood, The Sentinel (also s.p.), The Big Sleep (also s.p.), Firepower (also s.p.), Death Wish II, The Wicked Lady (also s.p.), Scream for Help, Death Wish III (dir. only), Appointment With Death (also s.p.), A Chorus of Disapproval (also s.p.), Bullseye (also s.p.), Dirty Weekend (also s.p.), Parting Shots (also s.p., ed.).
TELEVISION: *Movie:* For the Greater Good (actor). *Series*: White Hunter, Dick and the Duchess, Camcorder. *Guest:* More than 70 appearances.

WINNINGHAM, MARE
Actress. r.n. Mary Megan Winningham. b. Phoenix, AZ, May 16, 1959. TV debut at age 16 as a singer on The Gong Show. Debut solo album What Might Be released in 1992.
PICTURES: One-Trick Pony, Threshold, St. Elmo's Fire, Nobody's Fool, Made in Heaven, Shy People, Miracle Mile, Turner and Hooch, Hard Promises, Sexual Healing, Teresa's Tattoo, Wyatt Earp, The War, Georgia (Academy Awrd nom. 1996), Swing Vote, Brothers.
TELEVISION: *Movies*: Special Olympics, The Death of Ocean View Park, Amber Waves (Emmy Award, 1980), Off the Minnesota Strip, The Women's Room, Freedom, A Few Days in Weasel Creek, Missing Children: A Mother's Story, Helen Keller: The Miracle Continues, Single Bars Single Women, Love Is Never Silent (Emmy nom. 1986), Who is Julia, A Winner Never Quits, Eye on the Sparrow, God Bless the Child, Love and Lies, Crossing to Freedom, Fatal Exposure, She Stood Alone, Those Secrets, Intruders, Better Off Dead, Betrayed by Love, Letter to My Killer, The Boys Next Door (Emmy nom. 1996), The Deliverance of Elaine, George Wallace (Emmy Award, Golden Globe nom. 1998), Little Girl Fly Away, Everything That Rises, The Poet, Sharing the Secret, Snap Decision, Tru Confessions, The Maldonado Miracle (Emmy nom. 2004), The Magic of Ordinary Days. *Mini-series*: The Thorn Birds, Studs Lonigan, Too Rich: The Secret Life of Doris Duke. *Series:* The Brotherhood of Poland/New Hampshire, Law & Order: Special Victims Unit (guest, Emmy nom. 2004), Clubhouse, Grey's Anatomy. *Guest:* More than 66 appearances.

WINSLET, KATE
Actress. b. Reading, England, Oct. 5, 1975. m. Oscar-winning director Sam Mendes. Began studying drama at age 11.
THEATRE: *U.K. Regional*: Adrian Mole, Peter Pan, What the Butler Saw, A Game of Soldiers.
PICTURES: Heavenly Creatures, Sense and Sensibility (Golden Globe nom.; Academy Award nom. 1996), A Kid In King Arthur's Court, Jude, Hamlet, Titanic (Academy Award nom.; Golden Globe nom. 1998), Hideous Kinky, Plunge, Holy Smoke, Faeries (voice), Quills, Therese Raquin, Enigma, Christmas Carol: The Movie (voice), Iris (Academy Award nom.; Golden Globe nom. 2005), Plunge: The Movie, The Life of David Gale, Eternal Sunshine of the Spotless Mind (Academy Award nom.; Golden Globe nom. 2005), J.M. Barrie's Finding Neverland, Romance & Cigarettes, All the King's Men, Llittle Children (Academy Award nom.; Golden Globe nom. 2007), Flushed Away (voice), The Holiday, The Fox & the Child (voice), The Reader (Academy Award, Golden Globe Award 2009), Revolutionary Road (Golden Globe Award 2009).
TELEVISION: *Movies:* Anglo Saxon Attitudes, Pride (voice). *Series*: Casualty, Dark Season, Get Back. *Documentary:* Deep Sea 3D (narr.), Extras (guest, Emmy nom. 2006). *Guest:* More than 120 appearances.

WINTER, ALEX
Actor, Director, Writer, Producer. b. London, England, July 17, 1965. e. NYU. At age 4 began studying dance. Played opposite Vincent Price in St. Louis Opera production of Oliver! Co-founder of Stern-Winter Prods. Produced videos for Red Hot Chili Peppers, Human Radio, Ice Cube, etc. Co-directed TV special Hard Rock Cafe Presents: Save the Planet.
THEATRE: *B'way*: The King and I (1977 revival), Peter Pan (1979 revival). *Off-B'way*: Close of Play.
PICTURES: Death Wish III, The Lost Boys, Haunted Summer, Bill & Ted's Excellent Adventure, Rosalie Goes Shopping, Bill & Ted's Bogus Journey, Freaked (also co-dir., co-s.p., co-prod.), Fever (dir., s.p.), The Gate (dir.).
TELEVISION: *Movies*: Gaugin the Savage, Ben 10: Race Against Time (dir., exec. prod.), Ben 10: Alien Swarm (dir., exec. prod.). *Series*: Bill & Ted's Excellent Adventures, Idiot Box (also co-creator, co-dir., co-writer), Jimmy Kimmel Live (dir.), Saul of the Mole Men (voice).

WINTERS, DAVID
Producer, Choreographer, Actor, Director. b. London, April 5, 1939. Acted in both Broadway and m.p. version of West Side Story (as A-rab). Directed and acted in number of TV shows. Pres., A.I.P. Distribution, A.I.P. Productions and A.I.P. Home Video. 1989, formed Pyramid Distributors.
PICTURES: *Choreographer*: Viva Las Vegas, Billie, Send Me No Flowers, Bus Riley's Back In Town, Tickle Me, Pajama Party, Girl Happy, The Swinger, Made in Paris, Easy Come, Easy Go, The Island of Doctor Moreau, Roller Boogie, A Star is Born, Blame It on the Night. *Director:* Welcome to My Nightmare, Racquet, The Last Horror Show, The Last Horror Film (also prod., s.p., act.), Thrashin', Rage to Kill (also exec. prod. & s.p.), The Mission... Kill (also prod.), Space Mutiny (also prod.), Code Name Vengeance (also prod.), Fever (also writer). *Producer*: Young Lady Chatterley, Future Force, Raw Nerve, Operation Warzone, Raw Justice, Good Cop Bad Cop, The Dangerous, Codename: Silencer, Rapid Fire, Chase, Battleground, Born Killer, Firehead, Night Wars, Center of the Web, Blood on the Badge, Armed for Action, Body Count, Rhythm & Blues, Devil's Harvest, The King Maker. *Executive producer:* Killer Workout, Phoenix the Warrior, Mankillers, Dead End City, Deadly Prey, Shooters, Order of the Eagle, Deadly Reactor, The Bounty Hunter, Jungle Assault, White Fury, Future Force, Deadly Dancer, Rapid Fire, Chase, Operation Warzone, Future Zone, Invasion Force (also writer), Battleground, The Final Sanction, Lock 'n' Load, Presumed Guilty, Maximum Breakout, The Last Ride, Cop-Out, Firehead, Night Wars, The Lost Platoon, Raw Nerve, Blood on the Badge, Armed for Action Center of the Web, Double Threat, Night Trap, Raw Justice, Devil's Harvest. *Actor*: Roogie's Bump, Rock Rock Rock, West Side Story, The New Interns, Mama, Chasing the Dragon (co-prod.).
TELEVISION: *Movies*: *Choreographer:* The George Kirby Show, Firehead, Raw Nerve, Center of the Web, Double Vision, The Star Wars Holiday Special, Diana, Pirates: The True Story of Blackbeard (actor). *Producer:* The Darin Invasion, The 5th Dimension Traveling Sunshine Show, Dr. Jekyll and Mr. Hyde (also dir.), Saga of Sonora. *Mini-series: Actor:* Blackbeard. *Series*: *Actor:* The Buick-Berle Show, Studio One, Suspense, Lux Video Theatre, Love Of Life, Hallmark Hall of Fame, The Red Buttons Show, Campbell Summer Soundstage, The Plymouth Playhouse, Jimmy Hughes Rookie Cop, Atom Squad. *Choreographer:* Breaking Point, Shindig!, Hullabaloo, The Steve Allen Comedy Hour, Donny and Marie (Osmond), The Big Show. *Producer:* The Barbara McNair Show, The Leslie Uggams Show, Story Theatre, Rollin' on the River. *Executive producer:* Half the George Kirby Comedy Hour. *Documentaries/Specials starring:* Joey Heatherton, Nancy Sinatra (Movin' with Nancy, Emmy nom. 1968), Diana Ross, Raquel Welch, Ann Margret (Ann-Margret: From Hollywood with Love, Emmy nom. 1970), Lucille Ball.

WINTERS, JONATHAN
Actor. b. Dayton, OH, Nov. 11, 1925. e. Kenyon Coll.; Dayton Art Inst., B.F.A. Disc jockey, Dayton and Columbus stations; night club comedian performing at Blue Angel and Ruban Bleu (NY), Black Orchid (Chicago), Flamingo, Sands, Riviera (Las Vegas), then on B'way in John Murray Anderson's Almanac.
AUTHOR: Mouse Breath, Conformity and Other Social Ills, Winters Tales, Hang Ups (book on his paintings). Recorded 7 comedy albums. Won Grammy Award for "Crank Calls" comedy album, 1996.
PICTURES: Alakazam the Great! (voice), It's a Mad Mad Mad Mad World (Golden Globe nom. 1964), The Loved One, The Russians Are Coming the Russians Are Coming, Penelope, Oh Dad Poor Dad Mama's Hung You in the Closet and I'm Feeling So Sad, Eight on the Lam, Viva Max, The Fish That Saved Pittsburgh, The Longshot, Say Yes, Moon Over Parador, The Flintstones, The Shadow, Arabian Knight (voice), Santa vs. the Snowman, The Adventures of Rocky & Bullwinkle, Swing.
TELEVISION: *Movies*: Now You See It—Now You Don't, More Wild Wild West, Jonathan Winters: On the Loose. *Series*: And Here's the Show, NBC Comedy Hour, The Jonathan Winters Show (1956-57), Masquerade Party (panelist), The Andy Williams Show, The Jonathan Winters Show (1967-69), Hot Dog, The Wacky World of Jonathan Winters, Mork and Mindy, Hee Haw, The Smurfs (voice of Papa Smurf), The Completely Mental Misadventures of Ed Grimley (voices), Davis Rules (Emmy Award, 1991), Fish Police (voice), Life with Bonnie (guest, Emmy nom. 2003). *Documentaries/Specials*: The Jonathan Winters Special, The Jonathan Winters Show (1964, 1965), Jonathan Winters Presents 200 Years of American Humor, 'Tis the Season to Be Smurfy (voice). *Guest*: More than 115 appearances.

WISDOM, NORMAN
O.B.E. Actor, Singer, Comedian. b. London, England, Feb. 4, 1915. Awarded Order of the British Empire (O.B.E.), 1995. Many London West End stage shows including royal command performances. N.Y. B'way shows include Walking Happy and Not Now Darling.
PICTURES: A Date With a Dream (debut, 1948), Meet Mr. Lucifer, Trouble in Store, One Good Turn, As Long as They're Happy, Man of the Moment, Up in the World, Just My Luck, The Square Peg, Follow a Star, There Was a Crooked Man, The Bulldog Breed, The Girl on the Boat, On the Beat, A Stitch in Time, The Early Bird, Press for Time, The Sandwich Man,
The Night They Raided Minsky's, What's Good for the Goose, Double X: The Name of the Game, Five Children and It.
TELEVISION: *Movies:* Androcles and the Lion, Dalziel and Pascoe: Mens Sana. *Mini-series:* Between the Sheets. *Series:* Norman, Music Hall, Nobody Is Norman Wisdom, A Little Bit of Wisdom. *Guest:* More than 30 appearances.

WISEMAN, FREDERICK
Documentary Filmmaker, Producer, Director & Editor. b. Boston, MA, Jan. 1, 1930. e. Williams College, B.A., 1951; Yale

Law Sch., L.L.B., 1954. Member: MA Bar. Private law practice, Paris, 1956-57. Lecturer-in-Law, Boston U. Law Sch., 1959-61; Russell Sage Fndn. Fellowship, Harvard U., 1961-62; research assoc., Brandeis U., dept. of sociology, 1962-66; visiting lecturer at numerous universities. Author: Psychiatry and Law: Use and Abuse of Psychiatry in a Murder Case (American Journal of Psychiatry, Oct. 1961). Co-author: Implementation (section of report of President's Comm. on Law Enforcement and Administration of Justice). Fellow, Amer. Acad. of Arts & Sciences, 1991; John D. and Catherine T. MacArthur Foundation Fellowship, 1982-87; John Simon Guggenheim Memorial Foundation Fellowship, 1980-81. Films are distributed through his Zipporah Films, located in Cambridge, MA. Awards include 3 Emmys, Peabody Award, Intl. Documentary Assn. Career Achievement Award, 3 Columbia Dupont Awards for Excellence in Broadcast Journalism, among others. American Society of Cinematographers Special Achievement Award 2006.
PICTURES: Titicut Follies, High School, Law and Order, Hospital, Basic Training, Essene, Juvenile Court, Primate, Welfare, Meat, Canal Zone, Sinai Field Mission, Manoeuvre, Model, Seraphita's Diary, The Store, Racetrack, Deaf, Blind, Multi-Handicapped, Adjustment and Work, Missile, Near Death, Central Park, Aspen, Zoo, High School II, Ballet, La Comedie Francaise, Public Housing, Belfast, Maine, Cinéma Vérité: Defining the Moment, Domestic Violence, The Last Letter, Domestic Violence 2, The Garden, State Legislature.
TELEVISION: *Documentaries:* Hospital (2 Emmy Awards 1970), Law and Order (news doc., Emmy Award 1969).

WITHERS, GOOGIE
Actress. b. Karachi, India, Mar. 12, 1917. Trained as a dancer under Italia Conti, Helena Lehmiski & Buddy Bradley; stage debut Victoria Palace in Windmill Man, 1929. Best Actress Award, Deep Blue Sea, 1954. Began screen career at 18. TV also. Theatrical tours Australia, Sun Award, Best Actress, 1974. Awarded officer of the Order of Australia (A.O.) 1980. U.S. ACE Cable award, best actress for Time After Time, 1988.
THEATRE: *Britain*: Winter Journey, Deep Blue Sea, Hamlet, Much Ado About Nothing. *Australia*: Plaza Suite, Relatively Speaking, Beckman Place, Woman in a Dressing Gown, The Constant Wife, First Four Hundred Years, Roar Like a Dove, The Cherry Orchard, An Ideal Husband. *London*: Getting Married, Exit the King. *New York*: The Complaisant Lover. Chichester Festival Theatre and Haymarket, London, in The Circle, The Kingfisher, Importance of Being Earnest, The Cherry Orchard, Dandy Dick, The Kingfisher (Australia and Middle East), Time and the Conways (Chichester), School for Scandal (London), Stardust (UK tour). 1986: The Chalk Garden, Hay Fever, Ring Round the Moon, The Cocktail Hour (UK, Australian tour), High Spirits (Aus. tour), On Golden Pond (UK tour).
PICTURES: Windfall, Dark World, The Girl in the Crowd, The Love Test, All At Sea, She Knew What She Wanted, King of Hearts, Crime Over London, Accused, Her Last Affaire, Crown vs. Stevens, Pearls Bring Tears, Action for Slander, Gaiety Girls, You're the Doctor, Paid in Error, Queen of Crime, If I Were Boss, Strange Boarders, The Lady Vanishes, Murder in the Night, The Amazing Mr. Forrest, Convict 99, Trouble Brewing, She Couldn't Say No, Haunted Honeymoon, Bulldog Sees It Through, Jeannie, Back-Room Boy, One of Our Aircraft Is Missing, The Silver Fleet, On Approval, They Came To A City, Dead of Night, Pink String and Sealing Wax, Once Upon A Dream, It Always Rains on Sunday, Miranda, Traveler's Joy, Night and the City, The Magic Box, White Corridors, Lady Godiva Rides Again, Derby Day, Devil on Horseback, Port of Escape, Nickel Queen, Time After Time, Country Life, Shine.
TELEVISION: *Movies*: Hotel Du Lac, Northanger Abbey, Ending Up. *Mini-series:* Melba. *Series*: Within These Walls.

WITHERS, JANE
Actress. b. Atlanta, GA, April 12, 1927. By 1934 attracted attention as child player on screen, after radio appearance in Los Angeles and experimental pictures parts, in 1934 in Fox production Bright Eyes, Ginger; thereafter to 1942 featured or starred in numerous 20th-Fox prod. Voted Money-Making Star M.P. Herald-Fame Poll, 1937, 1938. Starred as Josephine the Plumber in Comet TV commercials. TV Movie: All Together Now.
PICTURES: Handle With Care (debut, 1932), Bright Eyes, Ginger, This Is the Life, The Farmer Takes a Wife, Paddy O'Day, Pepper, Gentle Julia, Little Miss Nobody, Can This Be Dixie?, Wild and Woolly, The Holy Terror, Checkers, Angel's Holiday, Forty-Five Fathers, Always in Trouble, Rascals, Keep Smiling, Arizona Wildcat, Pack Up Your Troubles, Chicken Family Wagon, Boy Friend, Shooting High, High School, Youth Will Be Served, The Girl From Avenue A, Golden Hoofs, A Very Young Lady, Her First Beau, Small Town Deb, Young America, The Mad Martindales, Johnny Doughboy, The North Star, My Best Gal, Faces in the Fog, The Affairs of Geraldine, Danger Street, Giant, The Right Approach, Captain Newman M.D., The Hunchback of Notre Dame (voice).
TELEVISION: *Movies:* All Together Now, Zack & the Magic Factory. *Series:* Mickey Mouse Works (voice), House of Mouse (voice). *Guest:* More than 37 appearances.

WITHERSPOON, REESE
Actress. r.n. Laura Jean Reese Witherspoon. b. Nashville, TN, March 22, 1976.
PICTURES: The Man in the Moon, Jack the Bear, A Far Off Place, S.F.W., Fear, Freeway, Pleasantville, Overnight Delivery, Twilight, Cruel Intentions, Election (Golden Globe nom. 2000), Best Laid Plans, American Psycho, Little Nicky, The Trumpet of the Swan, Slow Motion, Legally Blonde (Golden Globe nom. 2002), Sweet Home Alabama, The Importance of Being Ernest, Legally Blonde 2: Red, White & Blonde, Vanity Fair, Walk the Line (Academy Award, Golden Globe Award 2006), Just Like Heaven, Penelope (also prod.), Rendition, Four Christmases (also prod.), Monsters vs. Aliens (voice), Under the Bridge (prod.).
TELEVISION: *Movies:* Wildflower, Desperate Choices: To Save My Child. *Mini-series:* Return to Lonesome Dove. *Series:* Freedom: A History of Us (doc). *Guest:* More than 92 appearances.

WITT, PAUL JUNGER
Producer. b. New York, NY, Mar. 20, 1943. e. Univ. of VA. Was assoc. prod., prod. and dir. for Screen Gems, starting in 1965; prod. for Spelling-Goldberg Prods., 1972; Prod.-exec. prod. for Danny Thomas Prods., 1973. With Tony Thomas became co-founder, exec. prod. of Witt/Thomas Prods., 1975.
PICTURES: Firstborn, Dead Poets Society (Academy Award nom. 1990), Final Analysis, Mixed Nuts, Three Kings, Insomnia.
TELEVISION: *Movies*: Brian's Song (Emmy Award, 1972), No Place to Run, Home for the Holidays, A Cold Night's Death, The Letters, Blood Sport, Remember When, The Gun and the Pulpit, Satan's Triangle, Griffin and Phoenix, High Risk, Trouble in High Timber Country, Radiant City. *Series*: Here Come the Brides, The Partridge Family, The Rookies, Soap (3 Emmy noms.), Benson, It's a Living, I'm a Big Girl Now, It Takes Two, Condo, Hail to the Chief, The Golden Girls (Emmy Awards: 1986, 1987), Beauty and the Beast (Emmy nom. 1988), Empty Nest, Blossom, Good and Evil, Herman's Head, Nurses, Woops, Golden Palace, The John Larroquette Show, Brotherly Love, Minor Adjustments, Common Law, Pearl, Local Heroes, The Secret Lives of Men, Everything's Relative.

WOLF, DICK
Producer, Writer. b. New York, NY, Dec. 20, 1946. e. Univ. of PA. Started in advertising winning three Clio Awards for excellence.
PICTURES: *Prod./Writer:* Skateboard, Gas, No Man's Land, Masquerade (exec. prod., writer, actor), School Ties (s.p., story only), Twin Towers (short; prod.)
TELEVISION: *Movies:* Power (prod.), Bury My Heart at Wounded Knee (exec. prod., Emmy Award 2007), Lost & Found. *Series: Writer:* Hill Street Blues. *Executive producer/Writer:* Miami Vice, Gideon Oliver, Christine Cromwell (also creator), Nasty Boys (also creator), H.E.L.P. (also creator), Law and Order (also creator, 2 Emmy Awards, 10 noms.), Mann and Machine, The Human Factor, Crime and Punishment (also creator), South Beach (also creator), New York Undercover (also creator), The Wright Verdicts (also creator), FEDS (creator), Players (prod.), D.C., Law & Order: UK, Law & Order: Special Victims Unit, Deadline, Arrest & Trial (exec.prod., creator), Law & Order: Criminal Intent, Law & Order: Crime & Punishment (exec.prod.), L.A. Dragnet (also creator), Conviction, Paris Criminal Inquiries (artistic adv.). *Producer:* Law & Order: Trial by Jury (also writer).

WONG, ANDREA
Executive. b. California, 1966. e. MIT, B.S. in electrical engineering; Stanford Univ. Graduate School of Business, M.B.A. Wong joined ABC in Aug. 1993 as a researcher for ABC News' "PrimeTime Live." In June 1994, named executive asst. to the president, ABC Television Network. 1995, appointed executive asst. to the president, ABC, Inc. In Sept. 1997, expanded duties with a promotion to vice president & executive asst. to the president, ABC, Inc. By 1998, she was appointed v.p., alternative series & specials, ABC Entertainment, and in 2000 was promoted to senior v.p. By May 2004, Wong was exec. v.p., alternative programming, specials and late night, ABC Entertainment. In that role, Wong's non-scripted programming for ABC received both critical acclaim and huge viewership. The first franchise Wong brought to the network which became a true pop culture phenomenon was the relationship reality series, "The Bachelor," and its sister show, "The Bachelorette." Since it launched in 2002, more than 14 editions of the franchise have successfully aired. In June 2005, she brought the UK phenomenon, "Dancing with the Stars," to American audiences — and the hit show has consistently topped the competition with record ratings. Another of her series, "Extreme Makeover: Home Edition," has won two Emmys for Outstanding Reality Program. In the specials area, Wong led the team that brought country music's crown jewel to ABC in 2006 — "The CMA Awards." Wong was named president and CEO, Lifetime Entertainment Services in April 2007 and oversaw all the day-to-day operations for Lifetime Television, Lifetime Movie Network, Lifetime Real Women and Lifetime Digital (including myLifetime.com), including advertising sales, affiliate sales, research, programming, public affairs, marketing, business and legal affairs, and strategic planning and operations. 2010 Wong left this position after the aquisition of Lifetime by A & E Networks. Currently she is on the Bd. of Directors for Liberty Media Corp.

WOO, JOHN
Director, Producer. r.n. Yusen Wu. b. Guangzhou, China, May

1, 1946. e. Matteo Ricci College, Hong Kong. Started making experimental 16 mm films in 1967. Joined film industry in 1969 as prod. asst. for Cathay Film Co., then asst. dir. 1971 joined Shaw Brothers working as asst. dir. to Zhang Che. Formed Tiger Hill Entertainment in 2003 in conjunction with Sega. The companies have a multi-year partnership to co-create and publish video games of John Woo and Sega properties. Woo's producing partner is Terence Chang and entertainment executive Brad Foxhoven. The company is a hybrid between a Hollywood and video game studio.
PICTURES: *Director:* Sijie (short; also writer as Ng Yu Chen), Accidentaly, Ma yong zhen (asst. dir.), Sui woo juen (asst. dir.), Chi ma (asst. dir.), Fists of the Double K, Tie han rou qing (also actor, writer), Nu zi tai quan qun ying hui (also writer), Dinü hua (also writer as Yusen Wu), Shao Lin men (also actor & writer), Qian zuo quai (also writer), Fa qian han (also writer), Hao xia (also writer), Ha luo ye qui ren (also co-prod. & writer), Da sha xing yu xiao mei tou (also actor & writer) Mo deng tian shi (also writer & editor), Hua ji shi dai (also writer), Ba cai Lin Ya Zhen (also actor & writer), Xiao jiang (also prod. & writer), Ying xiong wei lei (also prod. & writer), The Essence of Heroes (also actor, prod. & writer), A Better Tomorrow II (also writer), The Killer (also writer), Just Heroes, Bloodshed in the Streets (also actor, prod., editor & writer), Once a Thief (also writer), Hard-Boiled (also actor, editor & writer), Hard Target, Broken Arrow, Face/Off, Mission Impossible II, Windtalkers (also prod.), The Hire: Hostage (short), Paycheck (also prod.), Red Cliff (also writer), Red Cliff II (also prod., s.p.), Jianyu Jianghu (also prod.). *Producer:* A Better Tomorrow III: Love and Death in Saigon, The Peace Hotel, Somebody Up There Likes Me (also exec. prod.), The Replacement Killers (exec. prod. only), The Big Hit (exec. prod. only), Bulletproof Monk, The Red Circle (exec. prod.). *Actor:* Heng cai san gian wan, Gam ye sing qwong chaan laan, Yong chuang tian xia, Party of a Wealthy Family, Shuang long hui (actor as John Wu), Yit huet jui keung, Jian guo da ye.
TELEVISION: *Movies*: John Woo's Once a Thief (dir. & exec. prod.), Black Jack (dir. & exec. prod.), Red Skies (exec. prod.). *Series:* Once a Thief (exec. prod.).

WOOD, ELIJAH
Actor. b. Cedar Rapids, IA, Jan. 28, 1981. Started in commercial modeling. Landed first acting job in Paula Abdul video Forever Your Girl.
PICTURES: Back to the Future Part II (debut, 1989), Internal Affairs, Avalon, Paradise, Radio Flyer, Forever Young, The Adventures of Huck Finn, The Good Son, North, The War, Flipper, The Ice Storm, The Faculty, Deep Impact, The Bumblebee Flies Away, Black and White, Chain of Fools, The Lord of the Rings: The Fellowship of the Ring, Ash Wednesday, Try Seventeen, The Lord of the Rings: The Two Towers, Spy Kids 3-D: Game Over, The Lord of the Rings: The Return of the King, Eternal Sunshine of the Spotless Mind, Hooligans, Sin City, Everything Is Illuminated, Happy Feet (voice), Bobby, Day Zero, The Oxford Murders, The Legend of Spyro (voice), Made in Japan (doc., narr., exec. prod.), The Home (exec. prod.).
TELEVISION: *Movies*: Child of the Night, The Witness (short), Day-O, Cranberries: Ridiculous Thoughts, Oliver Twist. *Special:* Saving a Species: The Great Penguin Rescue (Emmy nom. 2007) *Guest:* More than 113 appearances.

WOOD, TERRY
Executive. Began a broadcasting career as a news producer at WSMV-TV in Nashville, TN; then to KFMB-TV in San Diego as exec. prod.; moved to New York and WCBS-TV, where Wood created first noon newscast in the market and went on to exec. produce all the station's newscasts. Spent eight years with CBS News, where Wood garnered multiple Emmy® Awards for her work as a producer on "60 Minutes," "Eye to Eye With Connie Chung" and the "Evening News With Dan Rather." Wood then served as executive dir., development for Oprah Winfrey's Harpo Entertainment, where she produced the award-winning special "Dinner With Oprah" as part of the launch of the Oprah Book Club. In 1998, Wood joined Paramount Domestic Television as v.p. programming, responsible for overseeing "Entertainment Tonight" and "Hard Copy." In Oct. 2006, Wood was recognized as part of the team inducted with "Entertainment Tonight" into the Broadcasting & Cable Hall of Fame. She was promoted to executive v.p. programming and in 2004 she headed up the development, production and launch of "The Insider," which premiered as the highest-rated debut of any newsmagazine in syndication since 1996. She also spearheaded the development, production and launch of "Dr. Phil," which debuted higher than any other syndicated talk show since 1986. Since Jan. 2005 Wood was the pres. of creative affairs and development for both CBS Paramount Domestic Television and King World and with the merger of King World in Sept. 2006 became pres., creative affairs and development of the combined group, CBS Television Distribution, and is the position she holds today.

WOODARD, ALFRE
Actress. b. Tulsa, OK, Nov. 8, 1952. e. Boston U., B.A. Soon after graduation landed role in Washington, D.C. Arena Stage Theater in Horatio, and Saved. Won Emmy Awards for guest appearances on TV series: Hill Street Blues (Emmy Award, 1984) & L.A. Law (Emmy Award, 1987).
THEATRE: A Christmas Carol, Bugs Guns, Leander Stillwell, For Colored Girls Who Have Considered Suicide/When the Rainbow Is Enuf, A Map of the World, A Winter's Tale, Two By South.
PICTURES: Remember My Name, Health, Cross Creek (Academy Award nom. 1984), Extremities, Scrooged, Miss Firecracker, Grand Canyon, The Gun in Betty Lou's Handbag, Passion Fish (Golden Globe nom. 1993), Rich in Love, Heart and Souls, Blue Chips, Crooklyn, How to Make an American Quilt, Primal Fear, Star Trek: First Contact, Follow Me Home, Mumford, Down in the Delta, Dinosaur, Brown Sugar, What's Cooking?, Love & Basketball, K-PAX, Searching for Debra Winger, The Wild Thornberrys Movie (voice), The Core, Radio, The Forgotten, Beauty Shop, Something New, Take the Lead, Reach for Me, American Violet, The Family That Preys.
TELEVISION: *Movies*: Freedom Road, Sophisticated Gents, The Ambush Murders, Go Tell It on the Mountain, Sweet Revenge, L.A. Law (pilot, Emmy Award 1987), Unnatural Causes (Emmy nom. 1987), The Killing Floor, Mandela, A Mother's Courage: The Mary Thomas Story (Emmy nom. 1990), The Child Saver, Blue Bayou, Race to Freedom: The Underground Railroad, Aliens for Breakfast, The Piano Lesson (Emmy nom. 1995), Gulliver's Travels (Emmy nom. 1996), The Wizard of Oz in Concert: Dreams Come True, Member of the Wedding, Miss Evers' Boys (Emmy Award, Golden Globe Award, 1998), Funny Valentines, Holiday Heart (Golden Globe nom. 2001), The Water is Wide (Emmy nom. 2006), Pictures of Hollis Woods (Emmy nom. 2008), Maggie Hill. *Mini-series*: Cadillac Desert, A Wrinkle in Time. *Series*: Tucker's Witch, Sara, St. Elsewhere (2 Emmy noms.), Homicide: Life on the Street (guest, Emmy nom. 1998), The Practice (guest, Emmy Award 2003), Inconceivable, Desperate Housewives (Emmy nom. 2006), My Own Worst Enemy, Black Panther (voice). *Documentaries/Specials*: Malcolm X: Make It Plain (narr.), A Century of Women (mini-series, voice), Countdown to Freedom: 10 Days That Changed South Africa (narr.), Frederick Douglass: When the Lion Wrote History (narr.), People's Century: 1900-1999 (narr. U.S.), The Underground Railroad (narr.), Eleanor Roosevelt (narr.), The Tulsa Lynching of 1921: A Hidden Story, The Kennedy Center Presents: Speak Truth to Power, Nat Turner: A Troublesome Property, (narr.), All Our Sons: Fallen Heroes of 9/11 (short, narr.), King Leopold's Ghost (voice), For Colored Girls Who Haved Considered Suicide/When the Rainbow Is Enuf, Trial of the Moke, Words by Heart (Emmy nom. 1985), The Wishing Tree (Emmy nom. 2001), Medal of Honor (narr.), For Love of Liberty: The Story of America's Black Patriots (narr.). *Guest:* More than 101 appearances.

WOODS, CLARK
Executive. e. B.A. School of Communication, American University, 1978. A theatrical distribution vet, Woods began his 25-year career with Paramount Pictures in 1978, when he was hired as a clerk in the Washington, D.C. branch. He moved up to sales and branch mgr. positions before being upped to v.p. of Paramount's Midwest div. in Chicago, IL, from 1986 to 1989. Subsequently he was v.p., Western div.; and then senior v.p., asst. gen. sales manager for North America and finally executive v.p and general sales manager for domestic distribution before moving over to Metro-Goldwyn-Mayer Inc. in March 2006, becoming MGM's president of domestic theatrical distribution. Left MGM 2008.

WOODS, JAMES
Actor. b. Vernal UT, Apr. 18, 1947. e. Massachusetts Inst. of Technology (appeared in 36 plays at MIT, Harvard and Theatre Co. of Boston). Left college to pursue acting career in New York.
THEATRE: Borstal Boy (B'way debut, 1970), followed by Conduct Unbecoming (off-B'way, Obie Award), Saved, Trial of the Catonsville Nine, Moonchildren (Theatre World Award), Green Julia (off-B'way), Finishing Touches.
PICTURES: The Visitors (debut, 1971), Hickey and Boggs, The Way We Were, The Gambler, Distance, Night Moves, Alex and the Gypsy, The Choirboys, The Onion Field (Golden Globe nom. 1980), The Black Marble, Eyewitness, Fast-Walking, Split Image, Videodrome, Against All Odds, Once Upon a Time in America, Cat's Eye, Joshua Then and Now, Salvador (Academy Award nom. 1986), Best Seller, Cop (also co-prod.), The Boost, True Believer, Immediate Family, The Hard Way, Straight Talk, Diggstown, Chaplin, The Getaway, The Specialist, For Better or Worse, Casino, Nixon, Killer: A Journal of Murder, Ghosts of Mississippi (Academy Award nom.; Golden Globe nom. 1997), Hercules (voice), Contact, Another Day in Paradise, John Carpenter's Vampires, The Virgin Suicides, True Crime, Any Given Sunday, The General's Daughter, Race to Space, Play it to the Bone, Final Fantasy (voice), Riding In Cars With Boys, Scary Movie 2, John Q, Stuart Little 2 (voice), Falling in Love in Ponga Ponga (short; dir. & writer only), Northfork (also exec. prod.), This Girl's Life, Pretty Persuasion, The Easter Egg Adventure (voice), Be Cool, Night Train, End Game, Surf's Up, An American Carol, Exit 102.
TELEVISION: *Movies*: Footsteps, A Great American Tragedy, Foster and Laurie, F. Scott Fitzgerald in Hollywood, The Disappearance of Aimee, Raid on Entebbe, Billion Dollar Bubble, The Gift of Love, The Incredible Journey of Dr. Meg Laurel, And Your Name Is Jonah, Badge of the Assassin, Promise (Emmy Award, Golden Globe Award 1987), In Love and War (Golden

Globe nom. 1988), My Name is Bill W. (Emmy Award, 1989), Women & Men: Stories of Seduction (Hills Like White Elephants), The Boys, Citizen Cohn (Emmy nom.; Golden Globe nom. 1993), Jane's House, Next Door, Curse of the Starving Class, Indictment: The McMartin Trial (Emmy nom.; Golden Globe nom. 1995), The Summer of Ben Tyler (Golden Globe nom. 1997), Dirty Pictures (Golden Globe nom. 2001), Robbie the Reindeer in Legend of the Lost Tribe (short; narrator), Rudy: The Rudy Giuliani Story (Emmy nom. 2003). *Mini-series*: Holocaust. *Series:* House of Mouse (voice), Hercules (Emmy Award 2000), ER (guest, Emmy nom. 2006), Shark. *Documentaries/Specials*: All the Way Home, Crimes of Passion (host), Wildfire (host), Mobs and Mobsters (host), Fallen Angels, A Salute to Martin Scorcese, America's Endangered Species: Don't Say Goodbye (narrator), World's Deadliest Earthquakes, Founding Fathers (mini-series documentary; voice) *Guest:* More than 135 appearances.

WOODWARD, EDWARD
O.B.E.: Actor, Singer. b. Croydon, England, June 1, 1930. e. Royal Acad. of Dramatic Art. As singer has recorded 11 LPs. 2 Gold Discs. Television Actor of the Year, 1969-70; also Sun Award, Best Actor, 1970-72.
THEATRE: With Royal Shakespeare Company, 1958-59; Cyrano, 20 West End plays and musicals, including The Art of Living, The Little Doctor, A Rattle of a Simple Man (West End/B'way), The High Bid, The Male of the Species, High Spirits (B'way musical), The Best Laid Plans, On Approval, The Wolf, Richard III, The Assassin.
PICTURES: Where There's a Will (debut, 1955), Becket, File on the Golden Goose, Incense for the Damned, Young Winston, Sitting Target, Hunted, Wicker Man, Callan, Stand Up Virgin Soldiers, Breaker Morant, The Appointment, The Final Option (Who Dares Wins), Champions, King David, Mister Johnson, Deadly Advice, The House of Angelo, Marcie's Dowry (short), The Abduction Club, Hot Fuzz, A Congregation of Ghosts.
TELEVISION: *Movies*: A Magnum for Schneider, Wanted (short), Julius Caesar, Evelyn, Blunt Instrument, Wet Job, Love is Forever, Killer Contract, A Christmas Carl, Arthur the King, Uncle Tom's Cabin, Memories of Manon, Codename: Kyril, The Man in the Brown Suit, Over My Dead Body, Hands of a Murderer, Christmas Reunion, The Shamrock Conspiracy, Gulliver's Travels, Harrison: Cry of the City, Messiah, Night Flight. *Mini-series:* Winston Churchill: The Wilderness Years, Five Days. *Series*: Emergency-Ward 10, Magnolia Street, Sword of Honour, Callan, The Edward Woodward Hour, 1990, Nice Work, The Equalizer (5 Emmy noms.; Golden Globe Award 1987, 1 other nom.), Over My Dead Body, In Suspicious Cirumstances, Common As Muck, CI5: The New Professionals, The Bill, EastEnders. *Guest:* More than 96 appearances.

WOODWARD, JOANNE
Actress. b. Thomasville, GA, Feb. 27, 1930. m. late actor Paul Newman. e. Louisiana State U. Studied at Neighborhood Playhouse Dramatic Sch. and the Actors Studio. Appeared in many TV dramatic shows. Won Best Actress Academy Award for The Three Faces of Eve, 1957.
THEATRE: Picnic, The Lovers, Baby Want a Kiss, Candida, The Glass Menagerie (Williamstown, The Long Wharf), Golden Boy (dir., the Blue Light Theatre Company).
PICTURES: Count Three and Pray (debut, 1955), A Kiss Before Dying, Three Faces of Eve (Academy Award, Golden Globe Award 1957), No Down Payment, The Long Hot Summer, Rally 'Round the Flag Boys, The Sound and the Fury, The Fugitive Kind, From the Terrace, Paris Blues, The Stripper, A New Kind of Love (Golden Globe nom. 1964), Signpost to Murder, A Big Hand for the Little Lady, A Fine Madness, Rachel Rachel (Academy Award nom. Golden Globe Award 1969), Winning, WUSA, They Might Be Giants, The Effect of Gamma Rays on Man-in-the-Moon Marigolds (Golden Globe nom. 1973), Summer Wishes Winter Dreams (Academy Award nom. 1974), The Drowning Pool, The End, Harry and Son, The Glass Menagerie, Mr. and Mrs. Bridge (Academy Award nom.; Golden Globe nom. 1991), The Age of Innocence (narrator), Philadelphia, Even If A Hundred Ogres (voice).
TELEVISION: *Movies*: Sybil (Emmy nom. 1977), Come Back Little Sheba, See How She Runs (Emmy Award, 1978), A Christmas to Remember, The Streets of L.A., The Shadow Box, Crisis at Central High (Emmy nom.; Golden Globe nom. 1981), Passions, Do You Remember Love? (Emmy Award, Golden Globe nom. 1985), Foreign Affairs, Blind Spot (also co-prod., Emmy nom. 1993), Breathing Lessons (Emmy nom.; Golden Globe Award 1994), Our Town (exec. prod.), Empire Falls (Emmy nom.; Golden Globe nom. 2005). *Series:* Family (dir. only). *Documentaries/Specials*: Broadway's Dreamers: The Legacy of The Group Theater (host, co-prod.; Emmy Award, 1990, 1 other nom.), James Dean: A Portrait (documentary), Family Thanksgiving Special (dir. only). *Guest:* More than 88 appearances.

WOOLDRIDGE, SUSAN
Actress. b. London, England, 1952. e. Central Sch. of Speech & Drama/Ecole/Jacques LeCoq. Paris. Ent. ind. 1971.
THEATRE: Macbeth, School for Scandal, Merchant of Venice, The Cherry Orchard, Look Back in Anger, 'night Mother, Map of the Heart.
PICTURES: The Shout, Butley, Loyalties, Hope and Glory, How to Get Ahead in Advertising, Bye Bye Blues, Twenty-One, Afraid of the Dark, Just Like a Woman, The Hummingbird Tree.
TELEVISION: *Movies:* The Naked Civil Servant, Dead Man's Folly, The Commander: Virus, The Commander: Blackdog, Twenty Thousand Streets Under the Sky, Pinochet's Last Stand. *Mini-series:* Napoleon and Love, The Racing Game, The Jewel in the Crown, The Last Place on Earth, A TV Dante, Crossing to Freedom, An Unwanted Woman, Underworld. *Series:* Emmerdale Farm, Rep, All Quiet on the Preston Front. *Guest:* More than 55 appearances.

WOPAT, TOM
Actor. b. Lodi, WI, Sept. 9, 1951. e. U. of Wisconsin. Left school to travel for two years with rock group as lead singer and guitarist. Spent two summers at Barn Theater in MI. Came to New York; *Off-B'way* in A Bistro Car on the CNR. *On B'way* in I Love My Wife, City of Angels, Guys and Dolls.
PICTURES: Bonneville, The Understudy, Taking Chance.
TELEVISION: *Movies*: Christmas Comes to Willow Creek, Burning Rage, Just My Imagination, Contagious, The Dukes of Hazzard: Reunion!, Meteorites, The Dukes of Hazzard: Hazzard in Hollywood, Taking Chance, The Hive. *Series*: The Dukes of Hazzard, Blue Skies, A Peaceable Kingdom, Cybill, Prime Time Country (host), All My Children, Standoff (pilot). *Guest:* More than 55 appearances.

WORKMAN, CHUCK
Director, Writer, Producer. b. Philadelphia, PA, June 5. e. Rutgers U., B.A.; Cornell U. Pres., International Documentary Assoc. 1987-88; Member: Directors Guild of America, National Board. Lecturer, U. of Southern California. Pres. Calliope Films, Inc. Winner Clio Award, 1969, 1970. Acad. Award, 1987; ShowEast Achievement Award, 1996; Cable Ace Award, 1996.
THEATRE: Bruno's Ghost (1981, writer, dir.), Diplomacy (writer, dir.), The Man Who Wore White Shoes (writer), Bloomers (writer).
PICTURES: Monday's Child (1967, editor), Traitors of San Angel (editor), San Sebastian The Money (dir.), Protocol (dir., media sequences), Cuba Crossing (dir. & s.p.), Stoogemania (dir., prod. & writer), Precious Images (Academy Award, Best Live Action Short, 1986, dir., editor & prod.), 50 Years of Bugs Bunny in 3 1/2 Minutes (short; dir. & prod.), Superstar: The Life and Times of Andy Warhol (dir., editor, prod. & writer), Words (Best Short, Houston Fest., N.Y. Film Fest., 1988), Pieces of Silver, 100 Years at the Movies (documentary short; dir. & prod.), That Good Night (short; dir., prod. & writer), The Spirit of America (short; dir.), A House on the Hill (dir., prod. & writer), Visions of Cody (dir., prod. & writer), Callers (actor only).
DOCUMENTARIES: 1746 in 1968 (documentary short; editor), The Director and the Image (CINE Golden Eagle Award, 1980), The Game, The Best Show in Town (CINE Golden Eagle), And the Winner Is..., The Keeper of the Light.
TELEVISION: *Movie:* And the Band Played On (consult.). *Specials: As Editor:* The 62nd Annual Academy Awards (Emmy nom. 1990), The 72nd Annual Academy Awards (Emmy nom. 2000), The 73rd Annual Academy Awards(Emmy nom. 2001), The 74th Annual Academy Awards Emmy nom. 2002), The 75th Annual Academy Awards (Emmy nom. 2003), The 76th Annual Academy Awards (Emmy nom. 2004), The 77th Annual Academy Awards (Emmy nom. 2005), The 78th Annual Academy Awards (Emmy nom. 2006), The 79th Annual Academy Awards (Emmy nom. 2007), The 80th Annual Academy Awards (Emmy nom. 2008). *Documentaries:* 100 Years at the Movies (short, dir., prod.), The First 100 Years: A Celebration of American Movies (also dir., prod.), The Source (also dir., prod., writer), CBS at 75 (segment dir.), Martin Luther King, Jr. Day: The Making of a Dream (short, dir.).

WORONOV, MARY
Actress. b. Brooklyn, NY, Dec. 8, 1943. e. Cornell. On NY stage with In the Boom Boom Room (Theatre World Award).
PICTURES: The Chelsea Girls, Kemek: It's Controlling Your Mind, Sugar Cookies, Seizure, Cover Girl Models, Death Race 2000, Cannonball, Jackson County Jail, Hollywood Boulevard, Bad Georgia Road, Mr. Billion, The One and Only, The Lady in Red, Rock 'n' Roll High School, National Lampoon Goes to the Movies, Angel of H.E.A.T., Heartbeeps, Eating Raoul, Get Crazy, Night of the Comet, Hellhole, My Man Adam, Nomads, Movie House Massacre, Chopping Mall, Terrorvision, Black Widow, Scenes From the Class Struggle in Beverly Hills, Let It Ride, Watcher's II, Mortuary Academy Warlock, Dick Tracy, Buster's Bedroom, Motorama, Where Sleeping Dogs Lie, The Living End, Good Girls Don't, Grief, Number One Fan, Glory Daze, Secrets of a Chambermaid, Sweet Jane, Mom Can I Keep Her?, Zoo, Perfect Fit, Citizens of Perpetual Indulgence, Straight Right, The New Women, Prison-A-Go-Go, Looney Tunes: Back in Action, The Halfway House, Frog-g-g!, I Pass For Human, The Devil's Rejects, The House of the Devil.
TELEVISION: *Movies*: In the Glitter Palace, Challenge of a Lifetime, A Bunny's Tale, Eyes of a Stranger, Shake, Rattle and Rock!, Here Come the Munsters, The Munsters' Scary Little Christmas. *Series:* Somerset, Flying Blind, Women: Stories of Passion (dir. writer many episodes).

WOWCHUK, HARRY N.
Stunts, Executive. b. Philadelphia, PA. Oct. 16, 1948. e. Santa

Monica City College, UCLA, theatre arts, 1970. Started film career as actor, stunt-driver-photographer. T.V. and commercial credits include: TV Guide, Seal Test, Camel Cigarettes, Miller High Life, American Motors, Camera V, AW Rootbeer. Former exec. v.p. International Cinema, in chg. of prod. and distribution; V.P. J. Newport Film Productions; pres., United West Productions. Member of AFTRA & SAG.
PICTURES: *Stunts:* The Lost Dutchman, Las Vegas Lady, This Is a Hijack, Tidal Wave, Tunnel Vision, Incredible 2-Headed Transplant, Jud, Bad Charleston Charlie, Some Call It Loving, Summer School Teachers, Five Minutes of Freedom, Pushing Up Daisies, Money-Marbles-Chalk, The Models, Love Swedish Style, Up-Down-Up, Sunday's Child, Soul Brothers, Freedom Riders, Perilous Journey, Claws of Death, Georgia Peaches, The Pom Pom Girls, The Last American Virgin, Up the Creek, Murphy's Law, Sister-Sister, License to Drive, Phantasm II, Alien Nation, Messenger of Death, See No Evil, Hear No Evil, Robocop 2, Marked for Death,The Hard Way, Deep Cover, The Cowboy Way, Die Hard: With a Vengeance, The Usual Suspects, Batman Forever, Assassins, Carpool, Chain Reaction, Set It Off, City of Industry, Volcano,The End of Violence, Air Force One, Conspiracy Theory, An Alan Smithee Film: Burn Hollywood Burn, The Replacement Killers, The Gingerbread Man, Bulworth, Lethal Weapon 4, Without Limits, Magnolia, The Adventures of Rocky & Bullwinkle, Rush Hour 2,Jay and Silent Bob Strike Back, Bandits, Frailty, Ocean's Eleven, Red Dragon, Star Trek: Nemesis, S.W.A.T., The Last Shot, After the Sunset, National Treasure, Shackles, Bewitched, H.G. Wells' War of the Worlds, Elizabethtown, All In, Borat: Cultural Learnings of America for Make Benefit Glorious Nation of Kazakhstan, The Bucket List, Hancock, N-Secure (stunt coordinator), The Last Airbender (utility stunts).
TELEVISION:*Movies: Stunts:* The Georgia Peaches, Call to Glory, Beverly Hills Cowgirl Blues, Streets of Justice, Fear, Black Scorpion, Host, Missing Pieces, Dirt. *Mini-series: Stunts:* House of Frankenstein 1997, Meteor. *Series: Stunts:* Hill Street Blues, St. Elsewhere, The A-Team, Spenser: For Hire, Melrose Place, The Burning Zone, Players, Harmony's Passions, Heart of the City, Everwood, Fear Factor, Lost, Huset, A Nightmare on Elm Street: Real Nightmares, Ghost Whisperer, Numb3rs, Invasion, In Justice, Dirt, Ghost Whisperer, Harmony's Passions. *Special:* Behind the Action: Stuntmen in the Movies.

WOWCHUK, NICHOLAS
Executive, Producer, Writer, Editor, Financier. b. Philadelphia, PA. e. St. Basil's College, UCLA. Founder-publisher: All-American Athlete Magazine, Sports and Health Digest, The Spectator. Former sports writer: Phila. Evening Public Ledger; Phila. Daily Record; Phila. Inquirer. Founder & bd. chmn.: Mutual Realty Investment Co.; Mutual Mortgage Co., Beverly Hills, CA. President: Mutual General Films, Bev. Hills, CA; Abbey Theatrical Films, NY; Mutual Film Distribution Co.; Mutual Recording & Broadcasting Enterprises.
PICTURES: *Executive producer*: Perilous Journey, The Incredible 2-Headed Transplant, Pushing Up Daisies, Money-Marbles-Chalk, Five Minutes of Freedom, The Campaign, Claws of Death. *Producer*: The Erotic Adventures of Pinocchio (assoc. prod.), Scorpion's Web, Pursuit, Brave Men, Sea of Despair, Cossacks in Battle, The Straight White Line, Tilt, Rooster, To Live... You Gotta Win.

WRIGHT, AMY
Actress. b. Chicago, IL, Apr. 15, 1950. e. Beloit College. Studied acting with Uta Hagen; 1976, joined Rip Torn's Sanctuary Theatre. B'way in Fifth of July, Noises Off, Mrs. Klein.
PICTURES: Not a Pretty Picture, Girlfriends, The Deer Hunter, Breaking Away, The Amityville Horror, Heartland, Wise Blood, Stardust Memories, Inside Moves, Off Beat, The Telephone, Crossing Delancey, The Accidental Tourist, Miss Firecracker, Daddy's Dyin', Deceived, Love Hurts, Hard Promises, Josh and S.A.M., Tom and Huck, Where the Rivers Flow North, The Scarlet Letter, Joe Henry, Besotted, Winning Girls Through Psychic Mind Control, Messengers, The Namesake, The Good Shepherd, Synecdoche, New York.
TELEVISION: *Movies*: Trapped in Silence, Settle the Score,Vaclav Havel's 'Largo Desolato', In the Line of Duty: Manhunt in the Dakotas, Final Verdict, Lethal Innocence, To Dance With the White Dog, Amy & Isabelle. *Special*: Largo Desolato. *Pilot*: A Fine Romance.

WRIGHT, ROBERT C.
Executive. b. Hempstead, NY, April 23, 1943. e. College, Holy Cross, B.A. history, 1965; U. of Virginia, LLB 1968. Mem. NY, VA, MA, NJ Bar. 1969, joined General Electric; lawyer in plastics div. Later moved into product & sls. management in plastics div. 1980, moved to Cox Cable as pres. Returned to GE in 1983, heading small appliances div.; moved to GE Financial Services & GE Credit Corp. as pres., posts he held when named head of NBC following purchase of NBC's parent RCA by GE in 1986. He became chairman & CEO on June 4, 2001. In May 2004, Wright became chairman and CEO of NBC Universal in conjunction with the combining of NBC and Vivendi Universal Entertainment. Wright stepped down from his role at NBC Universal in Feb. 2007, but remained an executive officer at parent company GE; vice chairman of the board and executive officer of GE until 2008. He now serves as senior advisor to Lee Equity Partners, LLC. Wright's past honors include: 2007 Cable Hall of Fame honoree; the 2005 Humanitarian Award from the Simon Wiesenthal Center; the Columbia Business School honored Wright with its Distinguished Leadership in Business Award, 2005; the Golden Mike Award from the Broadcasters' Foundation, the Steven J. Ross Humanitarian of the Year award from the UJA-Federation of New York, and the Gold Medal Award from the International Radio & Television Society Foundation. He has been honored by the Center for Communication for his industry leadership and has received the Ad Council's Public Service Award in recognition of his commitment to public service in both the public and private sectors. He has also been inducted into the Broadcasting & Cable Hall of Fame. Along with his wife, Suzanne, Wright serves as co-founder of Autism Speaks, a new initiative dedicated to raising public awareness and research funds to find the answers to autism.

WUHL, ROBERT
Actor, Writer. b. Union, NJ, Oct. 9, 1951. e. Univ. of Houston. Worked as stand-up comedian and joke writer. Was story editor on series Police Squad! Appeared in 1988 Academy Award winning short Ray's Male Heterosexual Dance Hall.
PICTURES: The Hollywood Knights (debut, 1980), Flashdance, Good Morning Vietnam, Bull Durham, Batman, Blaze, Wedding Band, Hollywood Mistress, The Bodyguard, A Kiss Goodnight, Blue Chips, Cobb, Dr. Jekyll and Ms. Hyde, Open Season (also dir., s.p.), Good Burger.
TELEVISION: *Movies:* Percy & Thunder, A Kiss Goodnight, *Writer*: Police Squad, Sledge Hammer, Grammy Awards (1987-89), Academy Awards (Emmy Award, 1991, 1992). *Mini-series:* The Last Don, The Last Don II. *Series*: Police Squad!, Sledge Hammer!, Arli$$ *Pilots*: Rockhopper, Sniff. *Documentaries/Specials*: The Big Bang (also dir.), Comic Relief IV, The Earth Day Special, The Real Deal, Assume the Position with Mr. Wuhl (writer, exec. prod., WGA nom. 2007), The 63rd Annual Academy Awards (Emmy Award 1991), The 64th Annual Academy Awards (Emmy Award 1992).

WYNN, TRACY KEENAN
Writer. b. Hollywood, CA, Feb. 28, 1945. e. UCLA Theatre Arts Dept., BA in film/TV division, 1967. Fourth generation in show business: son of actor Keenan Wynn, grandson of Ed Wynn, great-grandson of Frank Keenan, Irish Shakespearean actor who made B'way debut in 1880.
PICTURES: The Longest Yard (1974), The Drowning Pool (co-s.p.), The Deep (co. s.p.), Robinson Crusoe, Mean Machine, The Longest Yard (2005, s.p.).
TELEVISION: *Movies*: The Glass House Emmy & WGA nom. 1972), Tribes (also assoc. prod.: Emmy & WGA Awards, 1971), The Autobiography of Miss Jane Pittman (Emmy Award & WGA Awards, 1974), Hit Lady (dir. only), The Quest, The Quest: The Longest Drive, In the Line of Duty: The F.B.I. Murders, Bloody Friday (also co-prod.), Capone in Jail, Carolina Skeletons. *Series:* The Net.

Y

YABLANS, FRANK
Executive, Producer, Screenwriter. b. Brooklyn, NY, Aug. 27, 1935. Entered m.p. ind. as Warner Bros. booker, 1957. Warner Bros. salesman in N.Y., Boston, Milwaukee, Chicago, 1957-59. Milwaukee br. mgr. Buena Vista, 1959-66. Midwest sales mgr., Sigma III, 1966. Eastern sales mgr., 1967, sales v.p. 1968. V.P. general sales mgr., Paramount Pic. Corp., 1969; v.p.-dist., 1970; sr. v.p.-mkt., 1970; exec. v.p., 1971; named pres. 1971. 1975, became an indep. prod. for his company, Frank Yablans Presentations Inc. 1983, MGM/UA Entertainment Co. as bd. chmn. & CEO. Held titles of bd. chmn. & CEO with both MGM and UA Corp when resigned, 1985. Same year teamed with PSO Delphi to form Northstar Entertainment Co.; 1986, non-exclusive deal with Empire Entertainment; 1988, non-exclusive 3-year deal with Columbia Pictures; 1989, pres. Epic Prods., pres., CEO Nova Intl. Films Inc. Currently, Yablans is CEO of Promenade Pictures, a full-service production, distribution, and marketing company whose mission is: to create and distribute life-affirming, family-safe entertainment that celebrates the positive endeavors of the human spirit.
PICTURES: *Producer*: Silver Streak (exec. prod.), The Other Side of Midnight, The Fury, North Dallas Forty (also co-s.p.), Mommie Dearest (also co-s.p.), Monsignor (co.-prod), Star Chamber, Kidco, Buy and Cell, Lisa, Congo (exec. prod.), Baby Geniuses (exec. prod.), A Dog of Flanders, The Ten Commandments (exec. prod.), Noah's Ark: The New Beginning (exec. prod.).
TELEVISION: *Series:* Rome (prod.).

YABLANS, IRWIN
Executive, Producer. b. Brooklyn, NY, July 25, 1934. Brother of Frank Yablans. Began career in industry at WB in 1956 after two-yr. stint with U.S. Army in Germany. Held m.p. sales posts in Washington, DC, Albany, Detroit, Milwaukee and Portland. In 1962 joined Paramount as L.A. mgr.; in 1964 made western sales mgr. In 1972 entered production as assoc. prod. on Howard W. Koch's Badge 373. Pres. of Compass Int'l. Pictures. Exec. v.p., low budget films, Lorimar Productions. Resigned June, 1984. In

1985 named chmn., Orion Pictures Distributing Corp. 1988: named chmn. and CEO of Epic Pictures.
PICTURES: The Education of Sonny Carson. *Exec. prod.*: Halloween, Roller Boogie (also story), Fade To Black (also story), Seduction (prod.), Halloween II, Halloween III: Season of the Witch, Parasite, Tank, Hell Night, Prison Arena, Why Me?, Men at Work, Arena.

YAFFE, PHYLLIS
Executive. Involved in the entertainment industry for the past two decades, Yaffe was CEO of Toronto-based Alliance Atlantis Communications Inc. She oversaw Alliance Atlantis' worldwide operations, including its Canadian specialty television channels, its international television distribution business and the TV hit CSI franchise, which the company co-owns and co-produces with CBS Productions. She was the Pres./CEO of Alliance Atlantis' Broadcast Group and managed the company's 13 Canadian specialty television networks and also oversaw Alliance Atlantis' involvement and ownership interest of four other specialty channels: Historia, Series+, One: the Body, Mind and Spirit Channel and SCREAM. She was pres. of Alliance Atlantis Broadcasting and returned to Atlantis as CEO and Director. She is on the Bd. of Dir. for Cineplex Entertainment. Her industry work has included being the Chair of the Foundation to Underwrite New Drama for Pay Television (FUND), now known as The Harold Greenberg Fund, from its inception in 1986 through until 1993; she also serves on the Radio Arts Advisory Committee at Ryerson Polytechnic University, the World Wildlife Fund Board and is chair of the Canadian Abilities Foundation Board and is currently a Director for Astral Media, Inc., and lead Director for Torstar Corp. and also serves on the Bd. of Lionsgate. Yaffe was selected as the Canadian Women in Communications 1999 Woman of the Year, and received the Lifetime Achievement Award from Women in Film and Television in April 2000.

YATES, PETER
Producer, Director. b. Ewshoot, England, July 24, 1929. e. Royal Acad. of Dramatic Art. Entered m.p. ind. as studio mgr. and dubbing asst. with De Lane Lea. Asst. dir.: The Entertainer, The Guns of Navarone, A Taste of Honey, The Roman Spring of Mrs. Stone. *Stage dir.*: The American Dream, The Death of Bessie Smith, Passing Game, Interpreters.
PICTURES: *Assistant director:* A Touch of Larceny, Cover Girl Killer, Sons and Lovers, The Entertainer, The Guns of Navarone, A Taste of Honey, The Roman Spring of Mrs. Stone. *Director:* Summer Holiday, One Way Pendulum, Robbery (also co-s.p.), Bullitt, John and Mary, Murphy's War, The Hot Rock, The Friends of Eddie Coyle, For Pete's Sake, Mother Jugs and Speed (also prod.), The Deep, Breaking Away (Academy Award nom., Golden Globe nom. 1980, also prod.), Eyewitness (also prod.), Krull, The Dresser (Academy Award nom. Golden Globe nom. 1984, also prod.), Eleni, Suspect, The House on Carroll Street (also prod.), An Innocent Man, Year of the Comet (also co-prod.), Needful Things (exec. prod. only), Roommates, The Run of the Country (also co-prod.), Curtain Call.
TELEVISION: *Movies:* Koroshi, Nunsense (still photographer), Don Quixote, A Separate Peace (Emmy Award nom. 2005). *Series*: The Saint (7 episodes), Danger Man (Secret Agent).

YELLEN, LINDA
Producer, Director, Writer. b. New York, NY, July 13, 1949. e. Barnard College, B.A.; Columbia U., M.F.A., Ph.D. Lecturer Barnard College, Yale U.; asst. professor, City U. of N.Y. Member: exec. council, DGA.
THEATRE: Chantilly Lace (dir., prod., writer), Parallel Lives (dir., prod. writer).
PICTURES: The End of Summer, Looking Up (prod., dir.), Prospera, Come Out Come Out, Everybody Wins (exec. prod.), The Simian Line, The Last Film Festival.
TELEVISION: *Movies*: Mayflower: The Pilgrims' Adventure (prod.), Playing for Time (exec. prod.; Emmy Award 1981), Hardhat and Legs (prod.), The Royal Romance of Charles and Diana (exec. prod., co-writer), Prisoner Without a Name Cell Without a Number (prod., dir., co-writer; Peabody & WGA Awards), Second Serve (exec. prod.), Liberace: Behind the Music (exec. prod.), Sweet Bird of Youth (exec. prod.), Rebound (dir., co-writer), Chantilly Lace (prod., dir., writer, story), Parallel Lives (prod., dir,. writer, story), End of Summer (exec. prod., dir., written by), Northern Lights (dir.).

YEOH, MICHELLE
Actress. r.n. Yeoh Chu-Kheng. b. Ipoh, Malaysia, August 6, 1962. Has acted under the name Michelle Khan.
PICTURES: In the Line of Duty, Magnificent Warriors, The Heroic Trio, Police Story 3: Supercop, Butterfly Sword, Heroic Trio 2: Executioners, Seven Maidens, Tai-Chi, Wing Chun, The Stunt Woman, The Soong Sisters, Tomorrow Never Dies, Moonlight Express, Crouching Tiger-Hidden Dragon, The Touch, Silver Hawk also exec. prod. & prod.), Memoirs of a Geisha, Sunshine, Purple Mountain, The Children of Huang Shi, The Mummy: Tomb of the Dragon Emperor, Babylon A.D., Remembering History (doc., prod.), True Legend, Jianyu Jianghu (also prod.).

YORK, MICHAEL
Actor. r.n. Michael York-Johnson. b. Fulmer, England, March 27, 1942. Early career with Oxford U. Dramatic Society and National Youth Theatre; later Dundee Repertory, National Theatre. Chmn., California Youth Theatre. 1992 *Autobiography*: Accidentally on Purpose (Simon & Schuster).
THEATRE: Any Just Cause, Hamlet, Ring Round the Moon (Los Angeles), Cyrano de Bergerac, Ira Gershwin At 100. *B'way*: Outcry, Bent, The Little Prince and the Aviator, Whisper in the Mind, The Crucible, Someone Who'll Watch Over Me, Nora.
PICTURES: The Taming of the Shrew, Accident, Red and Blue, Smashing Time, Romeo and Juliet, The Strange Affair, The Guru, Alfred the Great, Justine, Something for Everyone, Zeppelin, La Poudre D'Escampette, Cabaret, England Made Me, Lost Horizon, The Three Musketeers, Murder on the Orient Express, The Four Musketeers, Conduct Unbecoming, Logan's Run, Seven Nights in Japan, The Last Remake of Beau Geste, The Island of Dr. Moreau, Fedora, The Riddle of the Sands (also assoc. prod.), Final Assignment, The White Lions, The Weather in the Streets, Success Is the Best Revenge, Dawn, Lethal Obsession (Der Joker), The Return of the Musketeers, Phantom of Death, Megiddo, The Secret of the Sahara, Midnight Cop, The Wanderer, The Long Shadow, Wide Sargasso Sea, Rochade, Discretion Assured, The Shadow of a Kiss, Gospa, Goodbye America, Austin Powers: International Man of Mystery, Dark Planet, The Treat, Perfect Little Angels, Wrongfully Accused, 54, Austin Powers: The Spy Who Shagged Me, The Omega Code, The Haunting of Hell House, Puss in Boots, Borstal Boy, Megiddo: The Omega Code 2, In Search of Peace (doc. voice), Austin Powers: Goldmember, Quantum Heist, Mika i Alfred, Transformers: Revenge of the Fallen (voice), The Mill and the Cross.
TELEVISION: *Movies*: Great Expectations, The Phantom of the Opera, The Master of Ballantrae, Space, For Those I Loved, The Far Country, Dark Mansions, Sword of Gideon, Four Minute Mile, The Lady and the Highwayman, The Heat of the Day, Till We Meet Again, Night of the Fox, A Duel of Love, The Road to Avonlea, Charles Dickens' David Copperfield (voice), Fall from Grace, Tek War: Tek Lab, September, A Young Connecticut Yankee in King Arthur's Court, Not of This Earth, The Out of Towner, Danielle Steel's The Ring, True Women, The Ripper, Glory Glory, Perfect Little Angels, A Knight in Camelot, Crusader, Icon, Four Seasons. *Mini-series:* Jesus of Nazareth, A Man Called Intrepid, Au nom de tous les miens, Il Segreto del Sahara, Till We Meet Again, La Nouvelle tribu, The Great War and the Shaping of the 20th Century, La Femme Musketeer, Four Seasons. *Series:* The Forsyte Saga, Knots Landing, The Human Adventure, Orson Welles Tales from the Black Museum, Liberty's Kids (voice). *Host*: The Hunt for Stolen War Treasure, The Magic Paint Brush, Gardens of the World. *Documentaries/Specials*: Rebel in the Grave, True Patriot, Much Ado About Nothing, Founding Fathers. *Guest:* More than 145 appearances.

YORK, SUSANNAH
Actress. b. London, England, Jan. 9, 1941. Ent. TV in 1959; m.p. 1960. Author: In Search of Unicorns, Lark's Castle.
THEATRE: A Cheap Bunch of Flowers, Wings of the Dove, Singular Life of Albert Nobbs, Man and Superman, Mrs. Warren's Profession, Peter Pan, The Maids, Private Lives, The Importance of Being Earnest, Hedda Gabler (N.Y.), Agnes of God, The Human Voice, Penthesilea, Fatal Attraction, The Apple Cart, Private Treason, Lyric for a Tango, The Glass Menagerie, A Streetcar Named Desire, September Tide. Produced The Big One, a variety show for peace, 1984.
PICTURES: Tunes of Glory (debut, 1960), There Was a Crooked Man, Greengage Summer (Loss of Innocence), Freud (Golden Globe nom. 1963), Tom Jones, The Seventh Dawn, Sands of the Kalahari, Kaleidoscope, A Man for All Seasons, Sebastian, Duffy, The Killing of Sister George, Oh What a Lovely War, The Battle of Britain, Lock Up Your Daughters, They Shoot Horses Don't They? (Academy Award nom.; Golden Globe nom. 1970), Brotherly Love (Country Dance), Zee & Co. (X Y & Zee), Happy Birthday Wanda June, Images, The Maids, Gold, Conduct Unbecoming, That Lucky Touch, Sky Riders, The Silent Partner, Superman, The Shout, Falling in Love Again, The Awakening, Superman II, Loophole, Yellowbeard, Land of Faraway, Superman IV (voice), Prettykill, Bluebeard Bluebeard, A Summer Story, American Roulette, Diamond's Edge, Melancholia, En Håndfull tid, Piccolo grande amore, The HIgher Mortals, Loop, Romance and Rejection, Jean (short), Visitors, Franklyn, The Calling.
TELEVISION: *Movies*: The Crucible, The Fall of the House of Usher, The Golden Gate Murders, Nelly's Version, A Christmas Carol, Star Quality, The Rebel and the Soldier, The First Gentleman, The Richest Man in the World, Slaughter of St. Teresa's Day, Kiss On A Grass Green Pillow, Fallen Angels, Second Chance, Betjeman's Briton, Jane Eyre (Emmy nom. 1972), A Christmas Carol, Macho, Return Journey, After the War, The Man From the Pru, Illusions, Dark Blue Perfume, St. Patrick: The Irish Legend. *Mini-series:* Prince Regent, After the War, Devices and Desires *Series*: Second Chance, We'll Meet Again,Trainer, Holby City. *Guest:* More than 67 appearances.

YORKIN, BUD
Producer, Director. r.n. Alan Yorkin. b. Washington, PA, Feb. 22, 1926. e. Carnegie Tech., Columbia U. U.S. Navy, 1942-45. Began career in tv in NBC's engineering dept. Moved into prod., first as stage mgr., then assoc. dir. of Colgate Comedy Hour (Martin and

Lewis) and dir. of Dinah Shore Show. Formed Tandem Productions with Norman Lear; 1974 formed own production co.
PICTURES: Come Blow Your Horn (dir., co-prod., adapt.), Never Too Late (dir), Divorce American Style (dir.), The Night They Raided Minsky's (exec. prod.), Inspector Clouseau (dir.), Start the Revolution Without Me (prod., dir.), Cold Turkey (exec. prod.), Thief Who Came to Dinner (prod., dir.), Deal of the Century (prod.), Twice in a Lifetime (prod., dir.), Arthur 2: On The Rocks (dir.), Love Hurts (prod., dir.), For the Boys (actor), Intersection (co-prod.).
TELEVISION: *Movies:* I Love Liberty. *Series dir.* Songs at Twilight, Martin & Lewis Show, Abbott and Costello Show, Spike Jones Show, The Soldiers, Tony Martin Show (also prod., writer), The Colgate Comedy Hour , George Gobel Show, The Ford Show Starring Tennesse Ernie Ford (also prod.), The Andy Williams Show. *Series co-prod.:* All In The Family, Sanford and Son, Maude, Good Times, What's Happening!, Carter Country, Sanford Arms, Diff'rent Strokes, Archie Bunker's Place, One in a Million. *Documentaries/Specials (dir.)*: An Evening with Fred Astaire (Emmy Award, 1959), Another Evening with Fred Astaire, The Jack Benny Hour Specials (Emmy Award, 1960), Henry Fonda and the Family, We Love You Madly with Duke Ellington, TV Guide Awards Show, Bobby Darin and Friends, Danny Kaye Special, Where It's At with Dick Cavett, Many Sides of Don Rickles, Robert Young and the Family, I Love Liberty.

YOUNG, ALAN
Actor. r.n. Angus Young. b. North Shield, Northumberland, England, Nov. 19, 1919. First acted as monologist for 13 years in Canada; radio comedian 10 yrs. in Canada and U.S. Served in Canadian Navy as sub-lt. 1942-44. Wrote, dir. and acted in comedy broadcasts.
AUTHOR: Mister Ed and Me.
PICTURES: Margie (debut, 1946), Chicken Every Sunday, Mr. Belvedere Goes to College, Aaron Slick from Punkin Crick, Androcles and the Lion, Gentlemen Marry Brunettes, Tom Thumb, Baker's Hawk, The Cat from Outer Space, The Great Mouse Detective (voice), Duck Tales: The Movie (voice), Beverly Hills Cop III, The Time Machine, Breakfast on Pluto (soundtrack writer).
TELEVISION: *Movies:* Earth Angel, Hart to Hart: Home is Where the Hart Is. *Series*: The Alan Young Show (Emmy Award, 1950), Saturday Night Revue, Mr. Ed, Coming of Age, Tale Spin (voice), The Ren & Stimpy Show (voice), Mickey Mouse Works (voice), House of Mouse (voice). *Guest:* More than 96 appearances.

YOUNG, BURT
Actor, Writer. b. New York, NY, April 30, 1940. Worked at variety of jobs (boxer, trucker, etc.) before turning to acting and joining Actor's Studio. Appeared in off-B'way plays which led to Hollywood career. On B'way in Cuba and His Teddy Bear.
PICTURES: The Gang that Couldn't Shoot Straight, Carnival of Blood, Across 110th Street, Cinderella Liberty, Chinatown, The Gambler, Murph the Surf, You Can't Steal Love, The Killer Elite, Rocky (Academy Award nom. 1977), Harry & Walter Go to New York, Twilight's Last Gleaming, The Choirboys, Uncle Joe Shannon (s.p. only), Convoy, Uncle Joe Shannon (also s.p.), Rocky II, Blood Beach, ...All the Marbles, Rocky III, Lookin' To Get Out, Amityville II: The Possession, Over the Brooklyn Bridge, Once Upon a Time in America, The Pope of Greenwich Village, Rocky IV, Back to School, Bandini, Going Overboard, Blood Red, Beverly Hills Brats, Last Exit to Brooklyn, Medium Rare, Betsy's Wedding, Wait Until Spring Bandini, Diving In, Backstreet Dreams, Rocky V, Bright Angel, Red American, Club Fed, Excessive Force, North Star, Red Blooded American Girl II, The Undertaker's Wedding, She's So Lovely, Kicked in the Head, Heaven Before I Die, Firehouse, The Deli, The Mouse, Mickey Blue-Eyes, Loser Love, The Florentine, Blue Moon, The Adventures of Pluto Nash, Kiss the Bride, Crooked Lines, Shut Up and Kiss Me, Land of Plenty, Downtown: A Street Tale, Firedog (voice), Transamerica, Oliviero Rising, Blue Lake Massacre, Hack!, Rocky Balboa, Kingshighway, Carnera: The Walking Mountain, New York, I Love You, Sweetwater, Firedog (voice).
TELEVISION: *Movies*: The Great Niagara, Hustling, Serpico: The Deadly Game, Woman of the Year, Daddy I Don't Like It Like This (also s.p.), Murder Can Hurt You, A Summer to Remember, Vendetta: Secrets of a Mafia Bride, Double Deception, Vendetta 2: The New Mafia, Before Women Had Wings, Firehouse. *Mini-series*: The Maharaja's Daughter, Crocodile Shoes, The Last Don. *Series*: Roomies, Thinking About Africa, Alternate Realities. *Guest:* More than 53 appearances.

YOUNG, CHRIS
Actor. b. Chambersburg, PA, April 28, 1971. Stage debut in college production of Pippin, followed by On Golden Pond.
PICTURES: The Great Outdoors (debut, 1988), The Runestone, Book of Love, December, Warlock: The Armageddon, Conversations in Public Places, PCU, Deep Down, Falling Sky, 1001 NIghts (shorts; co-prod. only)
TELEVISION: *Movies*: Jake's Journey, Dance 'Til Dawn, Breaking the Silence, MacShayne: The Final Roll of the Dice, Runaway Daughters, Killing Mr. Griffin, The Proud Family Movie (prod. only). *Series*: Max Headroom, Live-In, Married People, The Adventures of A.R.K. (dir.), The New Adventures of A.R.K. (exec. prod, dir.). *Pilot*: Jake's Journey. *Documentaries/Specials:* Square One.

YOUNG, CHRISTOPHER
Composer. b. Redbank, NJ, April 28, 1957.
PICTURES: *Composer:* Godzilla 1985: The Legend Is Reborn (US version), The Bride (2nd asst. editor), A Nightmare on Elm Street Part 2: Freddy's Revenge, Flowers in the Attic, Bat*21, The Fly II, Bright Angel, Rapid Fire, Jennifer Eight, The Dark Half, Unforgettable, Set It Off, Hush, Judas Kiss, Playing by Heart (soundtrack writer), Entrapment, Bless the Child, The Gift, Madison (orig. themes), Swordfish (also soundtrack per.), The Glass House (also soundtrack writer), The Shipping News (Golden Globe nom. 2002), The Country Bears, Shade, Runaway Jury, Something's Gotta Give, Spider-Man 2 (also soundtrack writer), The Grudge, Miss Congeniality 2: Armed & Fabulous (soundtrack writer) An Unfinished Life, The Grudge 2, Ghost Rider, Spider-Man 3 (also soundtrack writer), Sleepwalking, The Informers, The Uninvited, Drag Me to Hell, Creation, Love Happens, Unthinkable, When in Rome. *Also Orchestrator:* Hellraiser, Trick or Treat, Invaders from Mars, Hellbound: Hellraiser II, Murder in the First, Tales from the Hood, Species, Virtuosity, Copycat, Murder at 1600, The Man Who Knew Too Little (also score prod.), Hard Rain, Rounders, Urban Legend, In Too Deep, The Big Kahuna, The Hurricane, Wonder Boys, Sweet November, Bandits, The Core, Beauty Shop, The Exorcism of Emily Rose (also score prod.), Lucky You, Untraceable (also score prod.).
TELEVISION: *Movies:* American Harvest, Max and Helen, Last Flight Out (Emmy nom. 1990), Norma Jean & Marilyn (Emmy nom. 1996), The Warden, Something the Lord Made.

YOUNG, KAREN
Actress. b. Pequonnock, NJ, Sept. 29, 1958. Trained at Image Theatre/Studio in NYC.
THEATRE: A Lie of the Mind, 3 Acts of Recognition, Five of Us, Mud People.
PICTURES: Deep in the Heart (debut, 1983), Almost You, Birdy, 9-1/2 Weeks, Heat, Jaws the Revenge, Torch Song Trilogy, Criminal Law, Night Game, The Boy Who Cried Bitch, Hoffa, Love & Human Remains, The Wife, Daylight, Pants on Fire, Joe Henry, Falling Like This, Mercy, Factotum, Heading South, Sibling: Marcus Miller the Orphan Killer, Betty Anne Waters.
TELEVISION: *Movies*: The High Price of Passion, Wild Things, To the Moon Alice (short), The Summer My Father Grew Up, The 10 Million Dollar Getaway, Drug Wars: The Cocaine Cartel, On the Edge of Innocence. *Series:* The Sopranos.

YOUNG, ROBERT M.
Director. b. New York, NY, Nov. 22, 1924. e. Harvard.
PICTURES: Nothing But a Man (prod., co-s.p.), The Plot Against Harry (co-prod., photog.), Short Eyes, Rich Kids, One-Trick Pony, The Ballad of Gregorio Cortez (also s.p. adapt.), Alambrista! (also s.p., photog.), Extremities, Saving Grace, Dominick and Eugene, Triumph of the Spirit, Talent for the Game, American Me (co-prod. only), Children of Fate (exec. dir. & exec. prod. only), Roosters, Caught, China: The Panda Adventure, Human Error, Berkeley (additional cinematographer)
TELEVISION: *Movies*: J.T., Solomon and Sheba, We Are the Children, Slave of Dreams, Walkout (co-exec. prod., 2nd unit dir.). *Series*: Visions, Tales of the Unexpected (writer), Battlestar Galactica. *Documentaries/Specials*: Sit-In, Angola—Journey to a War (Peabody Award), The Inferno (Cortile Cascino; also prod., writer, edit.), Anatomy of a Hospital, The Eskimo: Fight for Life (Emmy Award, 1971).

YOUNG, SEAN
Actress. r.n. Mary Sean Young. b. Louisville, KY, Nov. 20, 1959. e. Interlochen Arts Acad., MI, studied dance, voice, flute and writing. After graduating, moved to N.Y., and signed with ICM. Shortly after signing with ICM debuted in Jane Austen in Manhattan. On L.A. Stage in Stardust.
PICTURES: Jane Austen in Manhattan (debut, 1980), Stripes, Blade Runner, Young Doctors in Love, Dune, Baby: The Secret of the Lost Legend, No Way Out, Wall Street, Arena Brains, The Boost, Cousins, Fire Birds, A Kiss Before Dying, Forever, Love Crimes, Once Upon a Crime, Blue Ice, Hold Me Thrill Me Kiss Me, Fatal Instinct, Ace Ventura: Pet Detective, Even Cowgirls Get the Blues, Mirage, Dr. Jekyll and Ms. Hyde, The Proprietor, Motel Blue, Exception to the Rule, The Invader, Men, Out of Control, Special Delivery, Poor White Trash, The Amati Girls, Night Class, Sugar & Spice, Mockingbird Don't Sing, Aftermath, The House Next Door, Threat of Exposure, The Drop, In the Shadow of the Cobra, A Killer Within, Until the Night, Ghosts Never Sleep, River to Havilah, LIving the Dream, Headspace, Dark Honeymoon, The Man Who Came Back, Haunted Echoes, Parasomnia, Serpent Rising.
TELEVISION: *Movies*: Blood and Orchids, The Sketch Artist, Blue Ice, Witness to the Execution, Model by Day, Evil Has a Face, Barbara Taylor Bradford Trilogy: Everything to Gain, The Cowboy and the Movie Star, Secret Cutting, 1st to Die, The King and Queen of Moonlight Bay, Before I Say Goodbye, Third Man Out, Home for the Holidays, A Job to Kill For, Jesse Stone: Sea Change. *Mini-series*: Tender Is the Night, Kingpin, Esenin. *Series:* A Force of One. *Documentaries/Specials*: Under the Biltmore Clock. *Guest:* More than 60 appearances.

YU, JESSICA
Director. b. 1966. e. Yale University.
PICTURES: Sour Death Balls, The Conductor, Picture Bride (script advisor), Maya Lin: A Strong Clear Vision (documentary; assoc. prod.), Breathing Lessons: The Life and Work of Mark O'Brien (doc. short; also edit., prod., s.p.; Academy Award, 1997), Better Late (short), The Living Museum (doc.; also editor & writer.; nom. Grand Jury prize, Sundance Film Fest.), The Kinda Sutra (doc., short).
TELEVISION: *Movie:* The Lyon's Den (pilot). *Series:* The Guardian, American Dreams, Mister Sterling, The Lyon's Den, In the Realms of the Unreal (doc.; also dir., editor, prod. & writer, Emmy nom. WGA nom. 2006), Grey's Anatomy.

YULIN, HARRIS
Actor. b. Los Angeles, Nov. 5, 1937. On B'way in Watch on the Rhine, A Lesson from Aloes, etc. Founder of the Los Angeles Classic Theatre.
THEATRE: Numerous productions including: The Little Foxes, Who's Afraid of Virginia Woolf?, Becket, The Entertainer, Uncle Vanya, Tempest, Timon of Athens, The Seagull, A Midsummer Night's Dream, Hamlet, Julius Caesar, Tartuffe, Henry V, The Visit (B'way), Arms and the Man, It's a Mad Mad World, Arts and Leisure, Diary of Anne Frank, The Visit. *Director:* Baba Goya, The Front Page, The Guardsman, Sheba, The Man Who Came to Dinner, Guns of Carrar, Cuba Si, Candida, Don Juan in Hell, Jitta's Atonement, As You Like It, The Rehearsal, After the Fall, Winterplay, Last Meeting of the Knights of the White Magnolia.
PICTURES: End of the Road, Doc, The Midnight Man, Night Moves, Steel, Scarface, The Believers, Fatal Beauty, Candy Mountain, Bad Dreams, Judgement in Berlin, Another Woman, Ghostbusters II, Narrow Margin, Final Analysis, There Goes the Neighborhood, Clear and Present Danger, Stuart Saves His Family, The Baby-sitters Club, Looking for Richard, Multiplicity, Loch Ness, Bean,Cradle Will Rock, The Hurricane, The Million Dollar Hotel, Rush Hour 2, American Outlaws, Training Day, Chelsea Walls, The Emperor's Club, King of the Corner, The Treatment, Fur: An Imaginary Portrait of Diane Arbus.
TELEVISION: *Movies*: Melvin Purvis: G-Man, The Greatest Gift, Alvin Karpis: Public Enemy No. 1, The Kansas City Massacre, The Americans, Victory at Entebbe, The Thirteenth Day—The Story of Esther, The Night Rider, When Every Day Was the Fourth of July, Missiles of October, Conspiracy: Trial of the Chicago Seven, Last Ride of the Dalton Gang, Robert Kennedy and His Times, Tailspin: Behind the Korean Airlines Tragedy, Daughter of the Streets, Face of a Stranger, The Heart of Justice, The Last Hit, Incident at Vichy, How the West Was Won, Truman, If These Walls Could Talk, Hostile Waters, The Virginian, Loving Leah. *Series*: As the World Turns, WIOU, Mister Sterling, Frasier (guest, Emmy nom. 1996), 24. *Documentaries/Specials:* American Photography: A Century of Images (narrator), Judy Garland: By Myself (narr.). *Guest:* More than 75 appearances.

YUN-FAT, CHOW
Actor. b. May 18, 1955, Nam Nga Island, Hong Kong. Has won several awards in Asia, including Hong Kong Film Award for Best Actor three times, Taiwan Golden Horse Best Actor Award twice, and Asian Pacific Festival Best Actor Award. CineAsia, the Asian Theatre Owners Convention, named him the Star of the Decade.
PICTURES: Massage Girls, Heroic Cops, Miss O, See-Bar, Patrol Horse, Woo Yuet's Story, Blood Money, Shanghai Beach, Shanghai Beach 2, The Head Hunter, Flower City, Love in a Fallen City, The Occupant, Waiting for Daybreak, Woman, Witch from Nepal, The Story of Rose, The Phantom Bride, The Seventh Curse, A Better Tomorrow, A Hearty Response, 100 Ways to Murder Your Wife, You Will I Will, Dream Lovers, Lunatic's True Story, Love Unto Waste, The Missed Date, Blacklist, A Better Tomorrow II, Heroic Hero, Scared Stiff, City on Fire, An Autumn's Tale, Dragon and Tiger Fight, Drifter Love, Prison Turbulence, The Romancing Star, Goodbye My Friend, Legend of Yu Ta Fu,City War, Tiger Goes on the Beat, The Greatest Lover, Diary of a Big Man, Fractured Follies, The Eighth Happiness, All About Ah-Long, A Better Tomorrow III, Brotherhood, The Inside Story, The Fun The Luck and the Tycoon, God of Gamblers, The Killer, Wild Search, Once a Thief, Black Vengeance, Prison on Fire II, Full Contact, Now You See Love Now You Don't, Hard-Boiled, All for the Winner, Treasure Hunt, God of Gamblers Returns, The Peach Hotel, The Replacement Killers, The Corruptor, Anna and the King, Crouching Tiger, Hidden Dragon, King's Ransom, Bulletproof Monk, Curse of the Golden Flower, Pirates of the Caribbean: At World's End, The Children of Huang Shi, The Red Circle, Dragonball: Evolution, Shanghai, Confucius, Jian guo da ye.
TELEVISION: *Movies:* The Reincarnation. *Series:* Saat sau qi shi er siu si, Keung yan, Sou hat yi, Fo fung wong, San jaat si hing-juk jaap, Dai heung kong.

Z

ZAENTZ, SAUL
Producer. b. Passaic, NJ. Feb. 28, 1921. Irving R. Thalberg Award, 1997. American Cinema Editors Golden Eddie Filmaker of the Year Award 1998.
PICTURES: One Flew Over the Cuckoo's Nest (Academy Award 1976), Three Warriors, The Lord of the Rings, Amadeus (Academy Award 1985), The Mosquito Coast (exec. prod.), The Unbearable Lightness of Being, At Play in the Fields of the Lord, The English Patient (Academy Award 1997), Goya's Ghosts (exec. prod.).

ZAGIN, DAVID
Executive. e. B.S. degree, Syracuse Univ. Began career in cable, 1987, with MTV Networks-hired in affiliate sales & mktg. as acct. mgr.; promoted to acct. dir.; and then sales dir., responsible for several territoritories including the New York DMA. In March 1996, Zagin joined NBC Cable and was part of the successful launch of MSNBC. While at NBC Cable, Zagin rose to v.p., affiliate sales, local ad sales and alternate technology. In 1999, Zagin joined A&E Networks and rose to senior v.p. of affiliate sales and marketing. In March 2005, Zagin was promoted to his current job as executive v.p., distribution for AETN. He oversees all affiliate sales revenue and distribution for AETN's 10 U.S. cable networks: A&E Network (A&E), A&E HD, The History Channel (THC), The History Channel HD, The Biography Channel (BIO), The Biography Channel HD, History International, Military History Channel, Crime & Investigation, and The History Channel en Español. Zagin also oversees all revenue, distribution and mktg. efforts for A&E and A&E HD in Canada. In addition, Zagin is responsible for AETN's new media & business development for cable, satellite, and Telco distributors including: Video On Demand, broadband, interactivity, gaming, and mobile distribution. Zagin serves on the AETN executive operating committee and has served on industry boards, including: the Cable & Telecommunications Association for Marketing (CTAM) and the Women in Cable & Telecommunications (WICT) Foundation board.

ZAHN, STEVE
Actor. b. Marshall, MN, Nov. 13, 1968.
PICTURES: Rain Without Thunder, Reality Bites, Crimson Tide, That Thing You Do!, Race the Sun, SubUrbia, The Object of My Affection, Out of Sight, Safe Men, You've Got Mail, Hamlet, Freaks Talk About Sex, Forces of Nature, Happy Texas, Stuart Little (voice), Hamlet, Chain of Fools, Squelch, Saving Silverman, Dr. Dolittle 2 (voice), Joy Ride, Chelsea Walls Riding in Cars with Boys, Stuart Little 2 (voice), National Security, Daddy Day Care, Shattered Glass, Employee of the Month, Speak, Sahara, Chicken Little (voice), Bandidas (voice), Strange Wilderness, Unstable Fables: 3 Pigs & a Baby (voice), Night Train, A Perfect Getaway, Salesmen, Calvin Marshall, Diary of a Wimpy Kid.
TELEVISION: *Movies:* SUBWAYStories: Tales from the Underground, Speak. *Mini-series:* Picture Windows: Language of the Heart, From the Earth to the Moon, Comanche Moon. *Series:* Treme.

ZAILLIAN, STEVEN
Writer. Director. b. Fresno, CA, Jan. 30, 1953. e. San Francicso State University with a degree in Cinema.
PICTURES: Kingdom of the Spiders (editor), The Falcon and the Snowman, Awakenings (Academy Award nom.; WGA nom. 1991), Jack the Bear, Searching for Bobby Fischer (also dir.), Schindler's List (Academy Award, WGA Award, Golden Globe Award 1994), Clear and Present Danger (co-s.p.), Mission: Impossible (co-s.p.), Amistad, A Civil Action (WGA nom. 1999), Hannibal, Gangs of New York (Academy Award nom.; WGA nom. 2003), The Interpreter, All the King's Men (also prod.), American Gangster, Welcome to the Rileys (exec. prod.).

ZALAZNICK, LAUREN
Executive. e. Brown University. Zalaznick's early career was focused on film, producing a number of independent feature films including the award-winning Larry Clark film, "Kids" (Cannes 1995); Todd Haynes' "Safe" (Cannes 1995) and the award-winning Jim McKay film "Girls Town" (1996 Sundance Film Festival Filmmakers Trophy and Special Jury Prize). She began her career in television at VH1 where she served as Sr. V. P., original programming and development. Named Pres. of Bravo in May 2004. Expanded her oversight in May 2007 with the announcement the formation of Bravo Media. Under her watch, Bravo has become the No.1 ranked entertainment cable network for upscale, educated and engaged television viewers. Since NBC Universal acquired Oxygen in 2007, under Zalaznick's oversight the network has shattered every previous ratings record and recorded its best year ever in 2008 across all demographic, on-air, on-line, and financial metrics. Previously, Zalaznick held the role of Pres. of the critically acclaimed Universal-owned TRIO arts and pop culture network from May 2002 to December 2005. She was named Pres., NBC Universal Women and Lifestyle Entertainment Networks in May 2008, when she added iVillage and announced the launch of Women@NBCU, a sales and marketing initiative designed to create custom solutions for advertisers seeking to connect with a highly targeted female demographic. Zalaznick is co-chair of Peacock Equity, a joint investment fund of GE Capital's Media, Communications & Entertainment business and NBC Universal. In addition, she chairs the Women@NBCU advisory board, comprised of senior executive women across numerous industries. Zalaznick also sits

on Brown University Women's Leadership Council, as well as the Brown University Creative Arts Council. In 2009, Time magazine named Zalaznick "The Time's 100 World's Most Influential People." Vanity Fair named her on their "New Establishment" list and Fortune included her in their "50 Most Powerful Women" issue and she was ranked 18 in the Hollywood Reporters Most Powerful Women in Entertainment.

ZANE, BILLY
Actor. b. Chicago, IL, Feb. 24, 1966. Sister is actress Lisa Zane. Studied acting at American School in Switzerland. To Hollywood in 1984 landing small role in Back to the Future. On stage in American Music (NY), The Boys in the Backroom (Actors' Gang, Chicago).
PICTURES: Back to the Future (debut, 1985), Critters, Dead Calm, Back to the Future Part II, Megaville, Memphis Belle, Blood & Concrete: A Love Story, Millions, Femme Fatale, Sniper, Posse, Orlando, Flashfire, Tombstone, The Silence of the Hams, Cyborg Agent, Only You, Tales From the Crypt Presents Demon Knight, Reflections in the Dark, Danger Zone, The Phantom, Titanic, This World—Then the Fireworks, Head Above Water, Susan's Plan, I Woke Up Early the Day I Died, Taxman, Morgan's Ferry, Claim, The Believer, C.Q, Silver City, Dead Fish, Big Kiss, Silver City, The Pleasure Drivers, Mem-o-re, The Last Drop, Bloodrayne, Perfect Hideout, The Man Who Came Back, The Gold Retrievers, Mama, I Want to Sing!, Magic Man, Love N' Dancing, The Hessen Affair, Surviving Evil, Enemies Among Us, Darfur, Evil - In the Time of Heroes, The Confidant, 4Chosen.
TELEVISION: *Movies*: Brotherhood of Justice, Police Story: Monster Manor, The Case of the Hillside Stranglers, Lake Consequence, Running Delilah, The Set Up, Cleopatra, Howard Hughes: His Women and His Movies, Hendrix, The Diamond of Jeru, Invincible, Bet Your Life, Finnegan, Blue Seduction, Journey to Promethea. *Mini-series:* Sole Survivor. *Series*: Twin Peaks (recurring guest role), Boston Public, Charmed, The Deep End (pilot), Samantha Who?. *Guest:* More than 57 appearances.

ZANE, DEBRA
Casting Director.
PICTURES: Days of Thunder, Cadillac Man, Delirious, The Addams Family ,My Cousin Vinny, Whitesands, Hoffa, Joshua Tree, Addams Family Values, Mr. Wonderful, Ghost in the Machine, The War, The Firm, Disclosure, The Last Supper, Get Shorty (CSA nom. 1996), The Truth About Cats & Dogs, Men In Black, Washington Square, Wag the Dog (CSA nom. 1998), Red Meat, A Cool, Dry Place, Home Fries, Pleasantville (CSA nom. 1999), Maximum Bob (2 CSA noms. 1999) The Limey, American Beauty, Liberty Heights, Stuart Little, Galaxy Quest (CSA nom. 2000), American Beauty (CSA Award 2000), The Legend of Bagger Vance, Traffic (CSA Award 2001), K-PAX, Ocean's Eleven (CSA nom. 2002), Dragonfly, Road to Perdition (CSA nom. 2003), Full Frontal, Seabiscuit (CSA nom. 2004), Solaris, Catch Me If You Can, Terminal, Ocean's Twelve, Kingdom of Heaven, Fun with Dick and Jane, War of the Worlds, Jarhead, Little Children, The Good German, Dreamgirls (CSA Award 2007), Ocean's Thirteen, Things We Lost in the Fire, Indiana Jones and the Kingdom of the Crystal Skull, The Burning Plain, Revolutionary Road, The Uninvited, X-Men Origins: Wolverine, The Tale of Despereaux, Away We Go, Morning, Battle: Los Angeles.
TELEVISION: *Movies*: The Nightman, The Last Seduction, David and Lisa, Hard Times. *Series:* Tracey Takes On..., Maximum Bob.

ZANUCK, LILI FINI
Producer, Director. b. Leominster, MA, April 2, 1954. e. Northern VA Community Coll. m. Richard D. Zanuck. Worked for Carnation Co. in LA prior to entering film business. Joined Zanuck/Brown Company in 1978 working in development and various phases of production; 1984-present, prod. Made directorial debut in 1991 with Rush. Named Producer of the Year (1985) by NATO, along with Richard D. Zanuck and David Brown; Producer of the Year (1989) by Producers Guild of America, with R. Zanuck.
PICTURES: Cocoon, Cocoon: The Return, Driving Miss Daisy (Academy Award 1989), Rush (dir.), Rich in Love, Clean Slate, Wild Bill, Mulholland Falls, The Double, True Crime, Reign of Fire.
TELEVISION: *Movies*: Rush, Into Thin Air, Dead Lawyers. *Mini-series*: From the Earth to the Moon, The Decalogue. *Series:* Revelations. *Special:* The 72nd Annual Academy Awards (Emmy nom. 2000).

ZANUCK, RICHARD DARRYL
Executive, Producer. b. Los Angeles, CA, Dec 13, 1934. e. Stanford U. 1952-56. Father was exec. Darryl Zanuck. Story dept., 20th Century Fox, 1954; NY pub. dept., 1955; asst. to prod.: Island in the Sun, The Sun Also Rises, The Longest Day; v.p. Darryl F. Zanuck Prods. 1958; first credit as prod. Compulsion (1959); president's prod. rep., 20th Century Fox Studio, 1963; v.p. charge prod., 20th Fox; pres., 20th Fox TV exec. v.p. in charge of prod.; 1968 Chmn. of Bd., Television div., 20th Century Fox, 1969 Pres., 20th Century Fox Film Corp. Joined Warner Bros., 1971, as sr. exec. v.p.; resigned 1972 to form Zanuck-Brown Production Company, Universal Pictures. Joined 20th Century-Fox, 1980-83. To Warner Bros., 1983. To MGM Entertainment, 1986. 1988, dissolved 16-year partnership with David Brown. The Zanuck Company, formed in 1988, scored a phenomenal success with its debut production, Driving Miss Daisy. Nominated for nine Academy Awards and winner of four, the film grossed in excess of $100 million at the domestic box office and with its cost of $5 million now ranks as one of the most profitable releases in Warner Bros. history. Mr. Zanuck's 1998 release, Deep Impact, for DreamWorks SKG and Paramount, grossed close to $349 million worldwide. He continues to be associated with box office winners. Charlie and the Chocolate Factory's 2005 release has grossed more than $405 million worldwide. Recipient: Irving Thalberg Award (1991). This particular Thalberg Award makes Zanuck the only second-generation recipient ever, in company with his father, Darryl F. Zanuck.
PICTURES: Compulsion, The Chapman Report, Sssssss, The Sting (Academy Award 1973), The Sugarland Express, Willie Dynamite, The Black Windmill, The Girl from Petrovka, The Eiger Sanction, Jaws (Academy Award nom. 1976), MacArthur, Jaws 2, The Island, Neighbors, The Verdict (Academy Award nom. 1983), Cocoon, Target, Cocoon: The Return, Driving Miss Daisy (Academy Award 1989), Rush, Rich in Love, Clean Slate, Wild Bill, Mulholland Falls, Chain Reaction, Deep Impact, True Crime, Rules of Engagement, Planet of the Apes, Reign of Fire, Road to Perdition, Big Fish, Charlie and the Chocolate Factory, Sweeney Todd: The Demon Barber of Fleet Street, Yes Man, The Book of Eli, Alice in Wonderland.
TELEVISION: Movies: Driving Miss Daisy, Dead Lawyers. *Special:* The 72nd Annual Academy Awards (Emmy nom. 2000).

ZARGHAMI, CYMA
Executive. For this veteran TV executive, work is all about kids and family. Ms. Zarghami began her career with the cable children's network Nickelodeon in 1985. Was instrumental in the company's marketing partnerships, initiatives and growth, including the launch of Nickelodeon UK in 1993 and Nick at Nite's TV Land launch in 1996. Named gen. mgr. of Nickelodeon in 1996, she helped launch all of Nickelodeon's major dayparts, including Nick Jr., SNICK (Saturday Night Nickelodeon) and TEENick. Zarghami, as Nickelodeon pres., has through the years introduced many of Nickelodeon's signature programming and breakthrough packaging concepts such as Slime Time Live and U Pick Live. In 2005, Zarghami was named pres. of the newly formed MTVN Kids and Family Group and is the position she currently holds with this Viacom, Inc., subsidiary. The group includes Nickelodeon Television, Nick at Nite, Nick Online, Nick Movies, Noggin/The N, Nicktoons Television, Nickelodeon Games and Sports (Nick GAS), as well as Nickelodeon's magazine and recreation divisions and Nickelodeon's new digital businesses, including Neopets. She was named "2006 Woman of the Year" by WICT, Women In Cable Telecommunications. Zarghami is on the board of the Children's Museum of Manhattan in NY.

ZASLAV, DAVID
Executive. E. Boston University School of Law, graduated with honors. Early in career, Zaslav was an attorney with the New York firm of LeBouef, Lamb, Leiby & MacRae. Zaslav joined NBC in 1989 and was instrumental in developing and launching CNBC that same year. He played a key role in creating MSNBC in 1996. His responsibilities extended to Bravo, CNBC World, SCI FI, ShopNBC, Sleuth, Telemundo, Telemundo Puerto Rico, mun2, Trio, Universal HD, USA Network, NBC Weather Plus and the Olympics on cable. Zaslav also oversaw NBC Universal's interests in A&E, The History Channel, The Biography Channel, National Geographic International, the Sundance Channel and TiVo. He became president of NBC Universal's Cable and Domestic TV and New Media Distribution, where he oversaw content distribution to all forms of TV, led negotiations for cable and satellite carriage of NBC Universal networks, and forged new-media partnerships, including a pioneering video-on-demand deal with the leading cable operator, Comcast. Zaslav also brought films and TV shows to consumers through new paths including the Web, cell phones and other wireless devices. Zaslav joined Discovery Communications in Jan. 2007 as president & CEO. At Discovery, he sets the strategy and oversees the operations of the world's leading nonfiction media company, with over 100 TV networks reaching more than 1.5 billion cumulative subscribers and new-media businesses that spread knowledge to schools and homes.

ZEFFIRELLI, FRANCO
Director, Writer. b. Florence, Italy, Feb. 12, 1923. e. Florence Univ. Was stage director before entering film industry. Set designer 1949 -52 for Visconti plays (A Streetcar Named Desire, The Three Sisters). Worked as asst. dir. on La Terra Trema, Bellissima, Senso. Director of operas.
PICTURES: *Director/Writer*: The Taming of the Shrew (also co-prod.), Romeo and Juliet (also exec. prod., Academy Award nom.; DGA nom.; Golden Globe nom. 1969), Brother Sun Sister Moon, The Champ (dir. only), Endless Love (dir. only), La Traviata (also prod. design, Academy Award nom. 1983), Othello, Young Toscanini (also story), Hamlet, Jane Eyre, Tea with Mussolini (also story), Callas Forever, Omaggio a Roma (short).
TELEVISION: *Movies:* Much Ado About Nothing, Otello (stage dir., prod. designer & costume designer), Pagliacci (Emmy Award

1985), Cavalleria Rusticana, Carmen, La Bohème, Tosca, Turandot, Don Giovanni, Don Carlo, Falstaff, La Fille du régiment, La Traviata. *Mini-series*: Jesus of Nazareth. *Series:* Great Performances (Emmy Award 1986). Opera Director, Stage Director, Production Designer, Art Supervisor, Costume Designer for numerous operas filmed for television broadcast.

ZELLWEGER, RENÉE
Actress. b. Katy, TX, April 25, 1969. e. Univ. of Texas, Radio-Television-Film major, 1991. Much-nominated actress whose recent performances have garnered an Acad. Award, and nods from the Golden Globes, SAG and BAFTA.
PICTURES: A Taste for Killing, My Boyfriend's Back, Murder in the Heartland, Shake-Rattle and Rock!, The Return of the Texas Chainsaw Massacre, The Low Life, 8 Seconds, Reality Bites, Love and a .45, Empire Records, Jerry Maguire, The Whole Wide World, A Price Above Rubies, One True Thing, Nurse Betty (Golden Globe Award 2001), Me, Myself, and Irene, Bridget Jones' Diary (Academy Award nom. Golden Globe nom. 2002), White Oleander, Chicago (Golden Globe, Academy Award nom. 2003) Down With Love, Cold Mountain (Academy Award, Golden Globe Award 2003), Sharkslayer (voice), Bridget Jones: The Edge of Reason (Golden Globe nom. 2005), Cinderella Man, Bee Movie (voice), Leatherheads, Miss Potter (also exec. prod., Golden Globe nom. 2007), Case 39, Appaloosa, New in Town, My One and Only, Monsters vs Aliens (voice), My Own Love Song.
TELEVISION: *Movies*: A Taste for Killing, Murder in the Heartland, Shake Rattle and Rock, Shark Tale: Gettin' Fishy with It, Living Proof (exec. prod.). *Guest:* More than 103 appearances.

ZELNICK, STRAUSS
Executive. b. Boston, MA, June 26, 1957. e. Wesleyan U. B.A., 1979 (Summa Cum Laude); Harvard Grad. School of Business Administration, M.B.A., 1983; Harvard Law School, J.D., 1983 (Cum Laude). 1983-86, VP Int'l. TV for Columbia Pictures. 1988-89, pres. & COO, Vestron, Inc.; 1989-93, pres. & COO, 20th Century Fox. CEO, Crystal Dynamics, pres. & CEO of BMG Entertainment North America, 1994-1998, pres.& CEO of BMG Entertainment. Left BMG and founded ZelnickMedia in 2001 and is also a partner. Chrmn of Take-Two Interactive Software, Inc., 2008, after aquisition from ZelnickMedia. He is an associate member of the National Academy of Recording Arts and Sciences and served on the bd. of directors of the Recording Industry Association of America and the Motion Picture Association of America. Named to the bd. of dir. of Anglo-Dutch conglomerate Reed Elsevier in April 2005. Zelnick also serves on numerous boards of corporations.

ZEMECKIS, ROBERT
Director, Writer. b. Chicago, IL, May 14, 1952. e. U. of Film Awards sponsored by M.P. Academy of Arts & Sciences, plus 15 intl. honors. m. actress Mary Ellen Trainor. Has film editing background, having worked as cutter on TV commercials in Illinois. Also cut films at NBC News, Chicago, as summer job. After schooling went to Universal to observe on set of TV series, McCloud. Wrote script for that series in collab. with Bob Gale. Turned to feature films, directing I Wanna Hold Your Hand and co-writing s.p. with Gale.
PICTURES: *Director*: I Wanna Hold Your Hand (also co-s.p.), Used Cars (also co-s.p.), Romancing the Stone, Back to the Future (Academy Award nom.; Golden Globe nom.; WGA nom. 1986), Who Framed Roger Rabbit (DGA nom. 1989), Back to the Future II (also story), Back to the Future III (also story), Death Becomes Her (also co-prod.), Forrest Gump (Academy Award, Golden Globe Award, DGA Award 1995), Contact (also prod.), House on Haunted Hill (prod.), What Lies Beneath (also prod.), Cast Away (also prod.), Macabre (also prod.), The Polar Express (also prod.), Beowulf (also prod.), A Christmas Carol (also prod., writer). *Producer:* Thir13en Ghosts, Revelation, Clink, Inc., Ritual, Ghost Ship, Gothika, House of Wax, The Prize Winner of Defiance Ohio, Magick, The Reaping, Mars Needs Moms!. *Executive producer:* The Public Eye, Tales From the Crypt Presents Demon Knight, The Frighteners, Tales From the Crypt Presents Bordello of Blood, Trespass (also writer), Matchstick Men, Last Holiday, Monster House. *Writer:* 1941.
TELEVISION: *Movies: Director:* Two-Fisted Tales (also exec. prod.). *Executive producer:* W.E.I.R.D. World. *Series:* Tales From the Crypt (exec. prod.; also dir.), Perversions of Science (exec. prod., prod.), *Writer:* Back to the Future. *Documentaries/Specials:* The 20th Century: The Pursuit of Happiness (dir.).

ZERBE, ANTHONY
Actor. b. Long Beach, CA, May 20, 1936. Studied at Stella Adler Theatre Studio.
THEATRE: *NY*: Solomon's Child, The Little Foxes.
PICTURES: Cool Hand Luke, Will Penny, The Liberation of L.B. Jones, The Molly Maguires, The Call Me Mister Tibbs, Cotton Comes to Harlem, The Omega Man, The Life and Times of Judge Roy Bean, The Strange Vengeance of Rosalie, The Laughing Policeman, Papillon, The Parallax View, Farewell My Lovely, Rooster Cogburn, The Turning Point, Who'll Stop the Rain, The First Deadly Sin, The Dead Zone, Off Beat, Opposing Force, Private Investigation, Steel Dawn, Listen to Me, See No Evil Hear No Evil, Licence to Kill, Touch, Star Trek: Insurrection, True Crime, The Matrix Reloaded, The Matrix Revolutions, Veritas-Prince of Truth.
TELEVISION: *Movies*: The Priest Killer, The Hound of the Baskervilles, Snatched, She Lives, The Healers, In the Glitter Palace, KISS Meets the Phantom of the Park, Child of Glass, Attica, The Seduction of Miss Leona, Rascals and Robbers: The Secret Adventures of Tom Sawyer and Huck Finn, A Question of Honor, The Return of the Man from U.N.C.L.E., One Police Plaza, Independence, Baja Oklahoma, Onassis: The Richest Man in the World, Columbo: Columbo Goes to the Guillotine, To Save a Child, Treasure Island: The Adventure Begins, Memories of Manon, The Craft, On Seventh Avenue, Jack Reed: Death and Vengeance, Asteroid. *Mini-series*: Once an Eagle, How the West Was Won, Centennial, The Chisholms, George Washington, A.D., North and South II, Dream West. *Series*: Harry-O (Emmy Award, 1976), The Young Riders. *Guest:* More than 77 appearances.

ZETA-JONES, CATHERINE
Actress. b. Swansea, Wales, Sept. 25, 1969. m. actor Michael Douglas. Starred in the Yorkshire Television comedy/drama series "Darling Buds of May" (1991). The show was a smash hit and made Jones one of the United Kingdom's most popular television actresses.
THEATRE: *B'way:* A Little Night Music (Tony Award 2010).
PICTURES: Les 1001 Nuits, Out of the Blue, Christopher Columbus: The Discovery, Splitting Heirs, Blue Juice, The Phantom, The Mask of Zorro, The Haunting, Entrapment, High Fidelity, Traffic (Golden Globe nom. 2001), America's Sweethearts, Chicago (Academy Award, Golden Globe nom. 2003), Intolerable Cruelty, Sinbad: Legend of the Seven Seas (voice), The Terminal, Ocean's Twelve, The Legend of Zorro, No Reservations, Death Defying Acts, Cleo, The Rebound.
TELEVISION: *Movies:* Out of the Blue, The Cinder Path, The Return of the Native, Catherine the Great, Titanic. *Series:* Darling Buds of May. *Guest:* More than 101 appearances.

ZIDE, LARRY M.
Executive. b. Flushing, NY, Oct. 16, 1954. 3rd generation in mp. industry. Started 1972 with American Intl. Pictures in sls. & adv.; 1973, named branch sls. mgr., Memphis. 1975, joined Dimension Pictures as print controller; 1978, formed Zica Films Co. serving m.p. industry; 1985, Zica merged with Filmtreat Intl. Corp; named pres., of Filmtreat West Corp.

ZIDE, MICHAEL (MICKEY)
Executive. b. Detroit, MI, May 31, 1932. Joined m.p. ind. with American Intl. Pictures as print controller; 1962, promoted to asst. gen. sls. mgr. Named v.p., special projects, 1970; 1972, joined Academy Pictures as v.p. of prod. Later went with Zica Film Co.; 1985, named exec. v.p., Filmtreat West Corp. Zide founded Transfilm, Inc. in 1997 and is president. The company is a film processing/recycling company located in Sun Valley, California. The company obtains the decommissioned movie film (feedstock) from the major and minor film studios located in Southern California.and recycles the feedstock, using components of the film for new moldable plastic products from the film's recycled materials.

ZIEFF, HOWARD
Director. b. Chicago, IL, Oct. 21, 1927. e. Art Center School in Los Angeles. Started as artist and photographer, working as newsreel photographer for L.A. TV station. Went to N.Y. to do still photography; became top photo artist in advertising. Turned to film direction with Slither.
PICTURES: Slither (debut, 1973), Hearts of the West, House Calls, The Main Event, Private Benjamin, Unfaithfully Yours, The Dream Team, My Girl, My Girl 2.
(d. February 21, 2009)

ZIMBALIST, EFREM, JR.
Actor. b. New York, NY, Nov. 30, 1918. e. Fay Sch., Southboro, MA; St. Paul's, Concord, NH; Yale. Son of violinist Efrem Zimbalist and soprano Alma Gluck. Daughter is actress Stephanie Zimbalist. Studied drama, Neighborhood Playhouse. N.Y. Stage debut, The Rugged Path. Shows with American Repertory Theatre; Henry VIII, Androcles and the Lion, What Every Woman Knows, Yellow Jack, Hedda Gabler, Fallen Angels. Co-prod., The Medium, The Telephone, The Consul. Gave up acting after death of his wife and served as asst. to father, Curtis Inst. of Music for 4 years. Returned to acting, stock co., Hammonton, NJ, 1954.
PICTURES: House of Strangers (debut, 1949), Bombers B-52, Band of Angels, The Deep Six, Violent Road, Girl on the Run, Too Much Too Soon, Home Before Dark (Golden Globe nom.1959), The Crowded Sky, A Fever in the Blood, By Love Possessed, The Chapman Report, The Reward, Harlow, Wait Until Dark (Golden Globe nom. 1968), Airport 1975, Elmira, Hot Shots!, Batman: Mask of the Phantasm (voice), The Street Corner Kids, The Street Corner Kids: The Sequel.
TELEVISION: *Movies*: Cosa Nostra-Arch Enemy of the FBI, Who Is the Black Dahlia?, A Family Upside Down (Emmy nom. 1978), The Revenge of the Savage Bees, The Best Place to Be, The Gathering Part II, Family in Blue, Beyond Witch Mountain, Baby Sister, Shooting Stars, Batman/Superman Adventures: World's

Finest, Cab to Canada, The First Day. *Host*: You Are the Jury, The Tempest. *Mini-series*: Trade Winds, Scruples. *Series*: Concerning Miss Marlowe (daytime serial), Maverick, 77 Sunset Strip (Emmy nom. 1959), The FBI (Golden Globe nom. 1969), Remington Steele, Hotel, Zorro, Prince Valiant (voice), Batman: The Animated Series (voice), Spiderman the Series, The Marvel Action Hour: Iron Man, Batman: Gotham Knights, A Year to Remember (host). *Guest*: More than 82 appearances.

ZIMBALIST, STEPHANIE
Actress. b. New York, NY, Oct. 8, 1956. Father is actor Efrem Zimbalist Jr.; grandparents: violinist Efrem Zimbalist and soprano Alma Gluck; aunt: novelist Marcia Davenport.
THEATRE: *LA*: Festival, The Tempest, American Mosaic, Love Letters, The Baby Dance, The Crimson Thread, AdWars, Sylvia. Williamstown Theatre Festival: Barbarians, Summer and Smoke, Threepenny Opera. *Tours*: My One and Only, Carousel. *Regional*: The Philadelphia Story, The Cherry Orchard, The Baby Dance.
PICTURES: The Magic of Lassie, The Awakening, The Prophet's Game, Borderline Normal, Malpractice.
TELEVISION: *Movies*: Yesterday's Child, In the Matter of Karen Ann Quinlan, The Gathering, The Long Journey Back, Forever, The Triangle Factory Fire Scandal, The Best Place to Be, The Baby Sitter, The Golden Moment—An Olympic Love Story, Elvis and the Beauty Queen, Tomorrow's Child, Love on the Run, A Letter to Three Wives, Celebration Family, The Man in the Brown Suit, Caroline? (Golden Globe nom. 1991), Personals, The Killing Mind, The Story Lady, Some Kind of Love, Breaking the Silence, Sexual Advances, Jericho Fever, Incident in a Small Town, Voices From Within, The Great Elephant Escape, Whose Daughter Is She? Stop the World—I Want to Get Off, Dead Ahead, Prison of Secrets. *Mini-series*: Centennial. *Series*: Remington Steele. Guest: More than 48 appearances.

ZIMMER, HANS
Composer. b. Germany, Sept. 12, 1957. Member of the Buggles, producing hit song Video Killed the Radio Star. Pioneered use of digital synthesizers with computer technology and traditional orchestras.
PICTURES: Burning Secret, A World Apart, Rain Man (Academy Award nom. 1989), Paperhouse, Wonderland, Black Rain, Driving Miss Daisy, Bird on a Wire, Days of Thunder, Pacific Heights, Green Card, Thelma & Louise, Backdraft, Radio Flyer, The Power of One, K-2, A League of Their Own, Toys, Younger and Younger, True Romance, Cool Runnings, I'll Do Anything, The House of the Spirits, Renaissance Man, The Lion King (Academy Award, Golden Globe, 1995), Drop Zone, Crimson Tide, Nine Months, Something to Talk About, Beyond Rangoon, Muppet Treasure Island, Broken Arrow, The Preacher's Wife (Academy Award nom. 1997), Smilla's Sense of Snow, The Peacemaker, As Good As It Gets (Academy Award nom. 1998), The Thin Red Line (Academy Award nom. 1999), The Prince of Egypt (Academy Award nom. Golden Globe nom. 1999), The Last Days, Gladiator (Academy Award nom. Golden Globe Award, 2000), Chill Factor, The Road to El Dorado, Mission Impossible II, The Pledge, Hannibal, Pearl Harbor (Golden Globe nom. 2002), Invincible, Riding in Cars With Boys, Black Hawk Down, Spirit: Stallion of the Cimarron (Golden Globe nom. 2003), The Ring, Tears of the Sun, Pirates of the Caribbean: The Curse of the Black Pearl, Matchstick Men, The Last Samurai (Golden Globe nom. 2004), Something's Gotta Give, King Arthur, Thunderbirds, Shark Tale, Lauras Stern, Spanglish (Golden Globe nom. 2005), The Ring Two, Madagascar, Batman Begins, Der Kleine Eisbär 2, The Weather Man, Over the Hedge, Pirates of the Caribbean: Dead Man's Chest, The Simpsons Movie, The Da Vinci Code (Golden Globe nom. 2007), August Rush (theme), Kung Fu Panda, The Dark Knight (also musician), The Burning Plain, Frost/Nixon (Golden Globe nom. 2009), Madagascar: Escape 2 Africa, Angels & Demons, Transformers: Revenge of the Fallen, Sherlock Holmes, Inception, Rango. *Executive score producer:* Ella Enchanted, Ask the Dust, Bee Movie, Iron Man, Babylon A.D.
TELEVISION: *Movies:* Wild Horses, Comeback, Die Motorrad-Cops: Hart am Limit, Live From Baghdad. *Mini-series:* First Born. *Series:* Space Rangers, Iron Chef, The Critic, High Incident, Fame L.A., Die Motorrad-Cops: Hart am Limit, El Candidato, What About Joan, Carnivàle, Threat Matrix, The Contender (reality series documentary), Blood+ (music prod.).

ZINNEMANN, TIM
Producer. b. Los Angeles, CA. e. Columbia U. Son of late dir. Fred Zinnemann. Entered m.p. ind. as film editor; then asst. dir. on 20 films. Production mgr. for 5 projects; assoc. prod. on The Cowboys and Smile. Prod., Straight Time for Warners with Stanley Beck.
PICTURES: *Assistant director:* Cast A Giant Shadow, The Happening, Bullitt, The Great White Hope, Carnal Knowledge, The Cowboys (also assoc. prod.), The King of Marvin Gardens, Cinderella Liberty (first asst. dir. & prod. mgr.), The Day of the Locust, Farewell My Lovely (first asst. dir. & unit prod. mgr.), Smile. *Production manager:* The Day of the Dolphin. *Producer:* Straight Time, A Small Circle of Friends, The Long Riders, Tex, Impulse, Fandango, Crossroads, The Running Man. *Executive producer:* Pet Sematary, Street Fighter, The Island of Dr. Moreau.
TELEVISION: *Movies:* The Jericho Mile (Emmy nom. 1979), Lies of the Twins. *Series:* Miami Vice.

ZISKIN, LAURA
Producer. b. San Fernando Valley, CA, March 3, 1950. e. USC Cinema School. Worked as game show writer, development exec. before joining Jon Peters' prod. co. where she worked on A Star is Born, Eyes of Laura Mars (assoc. prod.). Formed Fogwood Films with Sally Field. She was tapped to head 20th Century-Fox's new division, Fox 2000, in 1994 and helmed the division until Nov. 1999. She currently is an independent producer and president of Laura Ziskin Productions in Culver City, CA.
PICTURES: Murphy's Romance, No Way Out, D.O.A., The Rescue, Everybody's All American, Pretty Woman (exec. prod.), What About Bob? (also writer), The Doctor, Hero (also co-story), To Die For, As Good As It Gets (exec. prod.), Spider-Man, Spider-Man 2, Stealth, Spider-Man 3.
TELEVISION: *Movies:* One Cooks the Other Doesn't, Fail Safe (exec. prod.), How I Learned to Drive, Dinner with Friends (exec. prod. Emmy nom. 2002), Stand Up to Cancer (exec. prod.). *Series:* Tarzan, The Spaces, Three Moons Over Milford (exec. prod.). *Documentaries/Specials:* The 74th Annual Academy Awards (also exec. prod. Emmy Award nom. 2002), The 79th Annual Academy Awards (also exec. prod., Emmy nom. 2007).

ZSIGMOND, VILMOS
Cinematographer. b. Szeged, Hungary, June 16, 1930. e. National Film Sch. Began career photographing Hungarian Revolution of 1956. Later escaped from Hungary with friend Laszlo Kovacs, also a cinematographer. Winner of Academy Award and British Academy Award for cinematography, also several int'l and domestic awards as dir. of TV commercials.
PICTURES: The Time Travelers (1964), The Sadist, The Name of the Game Is Kill, Futz, Picasso Summer, The Monitors, Red Sky at Morning, McCabe and Mrs. Miller, The Hired Hand, The Ski Bum, Images, Deliverance, Scarecrow, The Long Goodbye, Cinderella Liberty, The Sugarland Express, The Girl From Petrovka, Sweet Revenge, Death Riders, Obsession, Close Encounters of the Third Kind (Academy Award 1978), The Last Waltz, The Deer Hunter (Academy Award nom. 1979), Winter Kills, The Rose, Heaven's Gate, Blow Out, The Border, Jinxed, Table for Five, No Small Affair, The River (Academy Award nom. 1985), Real Genius, The Witches of Eastwick, Fat Man and Little Boy, The Two Jakes, Journey to Spirit Island, The Bonfire of the Vanities, The Long Shadow (dir.), Sliver, Intersection, Maverick (also actor), The Crossing Guard, Assassins, The Ghost and the Darkness (A.S.C. nom. 1997), Playing by Heart, Bánk Bán, The Body, Life as a House, Timeline (dir. of photog.), Jersey Girl, Melinda and Melinda, The Black Dahlia (Academy Award nom.; ASC nom. 2007), Cassandra's Dream, The Great Observer, Bolden!, King Shot, Louis, The Maiden Danced to Death.
TELEVISION: *Movies:* Flesh and Blood, Stalin (Emmy Award, ACE Award, ASC Award 1993), Surrender Dorothy. *Mini-series:* The Mists of Avalon (Emmy Award nom. 2002). *Documentaries:* The Market, Who Needs Sleep? (actor), Torn from the Flag.

ZORADI, MARK
Executive. e. B.A. economics and sociology, Westmont College, 1976. M.B.A., Marketing & Finance, UCLA Graduate School of Management, 1980. Mktg. mgr., Walt Disney Home Video. Participated in Home Video and Disney Channel start-ups in the early 1980s, and growth of Buena Vista Pictures Distribution in the mid 1980s; mktg. dir., The Disney Channel, 1983-85; dir. of sales, establishing national adverstising sales division generating $100 million in first-yr. sales, Buena Vista Pictures Distribution, 1985-87; senior v.p. & gen. mgr., Buena Vista Television, 1987-92; president, Buena Vista Intl., 1992-99. Until July 2006, Zoradi was president, Buena Vista Intl. (BVI) and Buena Vista Home Entertainment (BVHE) Intl. He was named pres. of Disney Motion Picture Group in July 2006-2009. Currently he is a strategic advisor for Imax Corp. and is on the Bd. of Directors for Rave Cinemas which is the 5th largest theatre chain in the US. Member, Los Angeles chapter of Young Presidents Org. and board of trustees, Westmont College.

ZUCKER, DAVID
Producer, Director, Writer. b. Milwaukee, WI, Oct. 16, 1947. e. U. of Wisconsin, majoring in film. With brother, Jerry, and friend Jim Abrahams founded the Kentucky Fried Theatre in Madison in 1971 (moved theater to L.A., 1972); later wrote script for film of that name released in 1977.
PICTURES: *Director:* Airplane (also exec. prod. & writer, WGA Award 1981), Top Secret (also exec. prod. & writer), Ruthless People, The Naked Gun: From the Files of the Police Squad (also exec. prod. & writer), The Naked Gun 2 1/2 (also actor & writer), For Goodness Sake (also prod. & writer), Naked Gun 33 1/3 (also prod.), BASEketball (also prod., exec. music prod. & writer), My Boss' Daughter, Scary Movie 3, Scary Movie 4 (also exec. prod., voice), Superhero!, An American Carol (also prod., writer). *Producer:* A Walk in the Clouds, For Goodness Sake II, High School High (also writer), Phone Booth, The Onion Movie, Superhero Movie.
Writer: The Kentucky Fried Movie (also actor).
TELEVISION: *Movies*: Our Planet Tonight (exec. prod.), H.U.D. (dir. & writer). *Series:* Police Squad (creator, dir., exec. prod. & writer, Emmy nom. 1982), Absolutely True (exec. prod.)

ZUCKER, JEFF
Executive. b. Miami, FL, April 9, 1965. e. Harvard, degree in American History, 1986. Pres. of the Harvard Crimson from 1985-1986. From 1986-1988 researcher for NBC Sports' coverage of Olympic Games in Seoul, Korea. Traveled world compiling and writing background information used by NBC commentators before and during the Olympics. In 1989, Zucker joined NBC News as a field producer for Today Show correspondents. By 1990, he became Katie Couric's producer when she became the Today Show national correspondent. He also worked with Couric as exec. prod. for the TV newsmagazine, Now, which was hosted by Couric and Tom Brokaw. In 1992, at 26, he became the youngest exec. prod. in the Today Show's history, a position he held from Jan. 1992- May 1993. During 1993, he also served as exec. prod. for the NBC Nightly news with Tom Brokaw. Zucker has been tapped by the network to exec. prod. several major news events during the past decade, including the network's "Decision 2000" election night broadcast, the 1996 and 2000 political conventions, and the 1993 and 1997 presidential inaugurations. From Sept. 1994 - Dec. 2000, he again served as exec. prod. for The Today Show, during which time the show earned "most-watched" morning news program status and achieved the highest viewership in the show's 49-year history. In Dec. 2000, Zucker was named pres., NBC Entertainment, and in late 2003 was promoted to pres., NBC Entertainment, News and Cable Group. In May 2004, he was named president of the NBC Universal Television Group and was promoted to CEO of the NBC Universal Television Group in Dec. 2005. When Bob Wright stepped down in Feb. 2007, Zucker was named president and CEO of NBC Universal. 2010 Zucker resigned from NBC Universal as Comcast Corp. bought a 51% share of the company from the General Electric Co.

ZUCKER, JERRY
Producer, Director, Writer. b. Milwaukee, WI, March 11, 1950. e. U. of Wisconsin. With brother, David, and friend Jim Abrahams founded the Kentucky Fried Theatre in Madison in 1970 and wrote script for film of that name released in 1977.
PICTURES: The Kentucky Fried Movie (co-s.p., actor), Airplane! (co-dir., co-s.p.), Top Secret (co-dir., co-s.p.), Ruthless People (co-dir.), The Naked Gun (exec. prod., co-s.p.), Ghost (dir.), The Naked Gun 2-1/2 (exec. co-prod.), Brain Donors (co-exec. prod.), My Life (co-prod.), Naked Gun 33-1/3 (co-exec. prod.), First Knight (dir., co-prod.), A Walk in the Clouds (co-prod.), First Knight, My Best Friend's Wedding (prod.), Rat Race (prod.), Unconditional Love (prod.), Fair Game.
TELEVISION: *Movie:* Our Planet Tonight (exec. prod.). *Series*: Police Squad! (co-exec. prod., dir.; co-wrote first episode).

ZUNIGA, DAPHNE
Actress. b. Berkeley, CA, October 28, 1962. e. UCLA.
PICTURES: Pranks (debut, 1982), The Dorm That Dripped Blood, The Initiation, Vision Quest, The Sure Thing, Modern Girls, Spaceballs, Last Rites, The Fly II, Gross Anatomy, Staying Together, Eight Hundred Leagues Down the Amazon, Cityscrapes: Los Angeles, Charlie's Ghost Story, Stand-ins, Naked in the Cold Sun, Enermies of Laughter, Artificial Lies, A-List, The Scene.
TELEVISION: *Movies*: Quarterback Princess, Stone Pillow, The Eyes of the Panther, Pandora's Clock, Loss of Faith, Ghost Dog: A Detective Tail, Secret Lives, The Obsession, Christmas Do-Over, Mail Order Bride. *Mini-series:* Degree of Guilt. *Series*: Melrose Place, Stories from My Childhood, Beautiful People, One Tree Hill, Spaceballs: The Animated Series, Novel Adventures. *Guest:* More than 52 appearances.

ZWICK, EDWARD
Writer, Producer, Director. b. Chicago, IL, Oct. 8, 1952. e. Harvard U., B.A., 1974; AFI Advanced Film Studies, M.F.A., 1976. Editor and feature writer, The New Republic and Rolling Stone, 1972-74. Author: Literature and Liberalism (1975). Formed Bedford Falls Production Co. with Marshall Herskovitz.
PICTURES: *Director*: About Last Night... (debut, 1986), Glory (Golden Globe nom. 1990), Leaving Normal, Legends of the Fall (also co-prod., Golden Globe nom. 1995), Courage Under Fire, Against All Enemies, The Siege (also prod.), The Last Samurai (also prod. & s.p.), The Blood Diamond (also prod., s.p.). *Prod.:* Shakespeare in Love (Academy Award 1999), Dangerous Beauty, Executive Search, Traffic (Academy Award nom. 2001), I Am Sam, Lone Star State of Mind, Abandon, Defiance (also s.p.).
TELEVISION: *Movies (dir.)*: Paper Dolls, Having It All, Special Bulletin, Extreme Close-Up (also co-exec. prod., co-story), Relativity (pilot), Women vs. Men, 1/4life, A Marriage. *Series*: Family (writer, then story editor, dir., prod., Emmy nom. 1980), thirtysomething (co-exec. prod.; Emmy Award, 1988, 3 Emmy Award noms.; DGA nom. WGA Award 1989), Dream Street (exec. prod.), My So-Called Life (also ep. dir.), Relativity, Once and Again (exec. prod), Quarterlife (also creator). *Documentaries/Specials:* Special Bulletin (Emmy Award nom. Won 2- Emmy Awards, DGA Award, WGA Award 1983) America: A Tribute to Heroes (writer, Emmy Award nom. 2002).

ZWICK, JOEL
Director. b. Brooklyn, NY, Jan. 11, 1942. e. Brooklyn Coll., M.A.
THEATRE: Dance with Me, Cold Storage, Esther, Cafe La Mama.
PICTURES: *Exec. prod.:* Myopia, Parker, Sold (co-exec. prod.). *Producer*: Can't Be Heaven (also exec. prod.). *Director*: Second Sight, My Big Fat Greek Wedding, Elvis Has Left The Building, Fat Albert, Coming Out, Did U Get My Text.
TELEVISION: *Movies*: Adventures in Babysitting, Hey Hey Hey: Behind the Scenes of "Fat Albert". *Series*: Happy Days, Laverne and Shirley, Mork and Mindy, Makin' It, It's a Living, Bosom Buddies, America 2100, Goodtime Girls, Hot W.A.C.S. (also exec. prod.), Little Darlings, Joanie Loves Chachi, The New Odd Couple (also supv. prod.), Webster, Street Hawk, Brothers (supv. prod.), Perfect Strangers (also pilot), Full House (also pilot), Family Matters, Step by Step, Getting By (also prod.), The Trouble with Larry, On Our Own, Kirk, Meego, The Wayans Brothers, The Parent 'Hood, The Love Boat: The Next Wave, Two of a Kind, Guys Like Us. *Pilots*: Angie, Bosom Buddies, Struck by Lightning, Family Matters, Adventures in Babysitting, Morning Glory, Star of the Family, Up to No Good, Going Places, Hangin' With Mr. Cooper, Life Happens, On Our Own, Making Out, Nowhere Fast.

Obituaries

(October 2009 - October 2010)

Andy Albeck....September 29, 2010
Corey Allen....June 27, 2010
Dede Allen....April 17, 2010
Paul Anderson....March 8, 2010
Norbert Auerbach....December 12, 2009
Val Avery....December 12, 2009
John Aylesworth....July 28, 2010
Roy Ward Baker....October 5, 2010
Carl Ballantine....November 3, 2009
Gene Barry....December 9, 2009
Dan Barton....December 13, 2009
Margery Beddow....January 3, 2010
Barbara Billingsley....October 16, 2010
David Blewitt....July 8, 2010
Barry Blitzer....January 27, 2010
Tom Bosley....October 19, 2010
Joe Boston....July 14, 2010
Robert F. Boyle....August 2, 2010
Gary Brockette....January 1, 2010
David Brown....February 1, 2010
Sergio "Gino" Campagnola....November 3, 2009
Stephen J. Cannell....September 30, 2010
John Carlen....December 10, 2009
Dixie Carter....April 10, 2010
Christopher Cazenove....April 7, 2010
Claude Chabrol....September 12, 2010
Norman Chandler Fox....July 15, 2010
Maury Chaykin....July 27, 2010
Art Clokey....January 8, 2010
Gary Coleman....May 28, 2010
Alain Corneau....August 29, 2010
Nick Counter....November 6, 2009
Robert Culp....March 24, 2010
Tony Curtis....September 29, 2010
Suso Cecchi d'Amico....July 31, 2010
Charles Davis....December 12, 2009
Edward O. Denault....August 21, 2010
Michael Dennison....September 2, 2010
George DiCenzo....August 9, 2010
Roy E. Disney....December 16, 2009
Donal Donnelly....January 4, 2010
Clive Donner....September 6, 2010
David Dortort....September 5, 2010
Harold Dow....August 21, 2010
William DuBay....April 15, 2010
Allyn Ferguson....June 23, 2010
Elliot Fischoff....July 1, 2010
Eddie Fisher....September 22, 2010
Michael R. Fisher....December 31, 2009
Marshall Flaum....October 1, 2010
Irene Cagen Forrest....July 25, 2010
John Forsythe....April 1, 2010
William Fraker....May 31, 2010
Alvin M. Frank....November 7, 2009
Eric Freiwald....January 29, 2010
James Gammon....July 16, 2010
David Gerber....January 2, 2010
Jackson Gillis....August 19, 2010
Carl Gordon....July 20, 2010
Harold Gould....September 11, 2010
Peter Graves....March 14, 2010
Kathryn Grayson....February 17, 2010
Regina Gruss....August 1, 2010
Corey Haim....March 10, 2010
Dave Hettler....February 27, 2010
Steven Hodgson....June 16, 2010
Arthur E. Holch....September 23, 2010
Ron Holloway....December 16, 2009
Dennis Hopper....May 29, 2010
Lena Horne....May 9, 2010
Umetsugu Inoue....February 11, 2010
Gaby Monet Jacoby....October 31, 2009
John Jefferies, Sr.....March 25, 2010
Lionel Jeffries....February 19, 2010
Jennifer Jones....December 17, 2009
Michael Jordan....May 25, 2010
Elliott Kastner....June 30, 2010
Norman Katz....April 1, 2010
Larry Keith....July 17, 2010
Noel Kendall....December 26, 2009
John Kenley....October 23, 2009
Jack Kerness....January 9, 2010
James J. Kilpatrick....August 15, 2010
Kip King....July 15, 2010
John W. Kluge....September 7, 2010
Satoshi Kon....August 24, 2010
Kim Kurumada....November 19, 2009
Mick Lally....August 31, 2010
Rudy Larriva....February 19, 2010
Jan Leighton....November 16, 2009
Aleen Leslie....February 2, 2010
Ed Limato....July 3,, 2010
Art Linkletter....May 26, 2010
William "Bill" Littlejohn....September 17, 2010
David Lloyd....November 10, 2009
William Lubtchansky....May 4, 2010
Simon MacCorkindale....October 14, 2010
Allan Manings....May 12, 2010
Tom Mankiewicz....July 31, 2010
Joe Maross....November 7,, 2009
Nan Martin....March 4, 2010
Quinnie Martin....July 8, 2010
Kevin Mc Carthy....September 11, 2010
Rue McClanahan....June 3, 2010
Sally Menke....September 27, 2010
Justin Mentell....February 1, 2010
Werner Michel....August 27, 2010
Mitch Miller....July 31, 2010
David Mills....March 30, 2010
Marvin Minoff....November 11, 2009
James Mitchell....January 22, 2010
Judith Paige Mitchell....February 10, 2010
Brittany Murphy....December 20, 2009
Paul Naschy....November 30, 2009
Patricia Neal....August 8, 2010
Ronald Neame....June 16, 2010
Edwin Newman....August 13, 2010
Beverly Nix-Meier....May 13, 2010
Dan O'Bannon....December 17, 2009
Ken Ober....November 15, 2009
Merlin Olsen....March 11, 2010
Ken Orsatti....August 31, 2010
Fess Parker....March 18, 2010
Michael Pataki....April 16, 2010
Arthur Penn....September 28, 2010
Sultan Pepper....October 20,, 2009
Carla Princi....January 18, 2010
Dorothy Provine....April 25, 2010
Robert B. Radnitz....June 10, 2010
Robert Rappaport....January 28, 2010
Irving Raveth....September 19, 2010
Corin Redgrave....April 6,, 2010
Lynn Redgrave....May 2, 2010
Frances Reid....February 3, 2010
Marc E. Reshovsky....November 20, 2009
Steven Reuther....June 5, 2010
Michael Rhodes....October 7, 2010
Shari Rhodes....December20, 2009
Shirley Rich....December 28, 2009
Pernell Roberts....January 24, 2010
Eric Rohmer....January 11, 2010
Irwin Rosten....May 23, 2010
Aaron Ruben....January 30, 2010
Zelda Rubinstein....January 27, 2010
Paul Ryan Rudd....August 12, 2010
J.D. Salinger....January 27, 2010
Elena Santaballa....October 12, 2010
Furio Scarpelli....April 28, 2010
Karen Schmeer....January 29, 2010
Daniel Schorr....July 23, 2010
Sande Scoredos....August 14, 2010
Nathan Scott....February 27, 2010
Erich Segal....January 17, 2010
Johnny Seven....January 22, 2010
Glenn Shadix....September 7, 2010
Steffi Sidney-Splaver....February 22, 2010

Chet Simmons..March 25, 2010
Jean Simmons..January 22, 2010
George Simpson ....November 1, 2009
Arnold Stang...December 20, 2009
Richard Stapley...March 5, 2010
Gloria Stuart ....September 26, 2010
Jack Sydow ....May 28, 2010
Eleanor Bolta Taffner ....September 15, 2010
John Tiffin ....March 4, 2010
Richard Todd...December 3, 2009
Jack Wakefield...July 2, 2010
Clyde Ware ....August 30, 2010
Bernie Weintraub ....January 16, 2010
Paul Wendkos ....November 12, 2009
Bernie West ....July 29, 2010
Gareth Wigan ....February 13, 2010
Myles Wilder ....April 20, 2010
Dean Wilson ....July 20, 2010
Sir Norman Wisdom ....October 4, 2010
Ken Wlaschin ....November 10, 2009
David Wolper...August 10, 2010
Robin Wood ....December 18, 2009
Edward Woodward ....November 16, 2009
Lois Zetter ....November 17, 2009

Motion Pictures

U.S. Motion Picture Releases

(October 1, 2009—September 30, 2010)

This list includes motion pictures from major studios and independents. Many release dates are review or festival release dates.

2012

A Sony Pictures Entertainment release of a Columbia Pictures presentation of a Centropolis production. Producers: Harald Kloser, Mark Gordon, Larry Franco. Executive producers: Roland Emmerich, Ute Emmerich, Michael Wimer. Co-producers: Volker Engel, Marc Weigert, Aaron Boyd. Director: Roland Emmerich. Screenplay: Harald Kloser. Roland Emmerich. Camera: Dean Semler. Editors: David Brenner, Peter S. Elliot. Music: Harald Kloser, Thomas Wander. In Deluxe color, Panavision. Release date: Nov. 3, 2009. MPAA Rating: PG-13. Running time: 158 Min.
Cast: John Cusack, Adrian Helmsley - Chiwetel Ejiofor, Amanda Peet, Oliver Platt, Thandie Newton, Danny Glover, Woody Harrelson, Tom McCarthy, George Segal.

A CHRISTMAS CAROL

A Walt Disney Studios Motion Pictures release of a Walt Disney Pictures and ImageMovers Digital presentation. Producers: Steve Starkey, Robert Zemeckis, Jack Rapke. Co-producer: Steven Boyd. Director/Writer: Robert Zemeckis, based on the novella by Charles Dickens. Camera: Robert Presley. Editor: Jeremiah O'Driscoll. Music: Alan Silvestri. In Deluxe prints (Domestic), Technicolor prints (International), widescreen, 3D. Release date: Oct. 28, 2009. MPAA Rating: PG. Running time: 95 Min.
Cast: Jim Carrey, Marley, Gary Oldman, Colin Firth, Bob Hoskins, Robin Wright Penn, Dick Wilkins, Cary Elwes, Fionnula Flanagan.

A NIGHTMARE ON ELM STREET

A Warner Bros. release of a New Line Cinema presentation of a Platinum Dune production. Producers: Michael Bay, Andrew Form, Brad Fuller. Executive producers: Richard Brenner, Walter Hamada, Dave Neustadter, Robert Shayne, Michael Lynne, Mike Drake. Co-producer: John Rickard. Director: Samuel Bayer. Screenplay: Wesley Strick, Eric Hessler, from a story by Strick, based on characters created by Wes Craven. Camera: Jeff Cutter. Editor: Glen Scantlebury. Music: Steve Jablonsky. In color, Panavision widescreen. Release date: April 28, 2010. MPAA Rating: R. Running time: 95 Min.
Cast: Jackie Earle Haley, Kyle Gallner, Rooney Mara, Katie Cassidy, Thomas Dekker, Kellan Lutz, Clancy Brown, Connie Britton.

AFTER.LIFE

An Anchor Bay Films release of an Anchor Bay Films and Lleju Prods. presentation of a Plum Pictures production in association with Constellation Entertainment. Producers: Brad Michael Gilbert, William O. Perkins III, Celine Rattray. Executive producers: Cooper Richey, Catherine Kellner, Edwin L. Marshall, James Swisher. Co-producers: Joy Goodwin, Riva Marker. Director: Agnieszka Wojtowicz-Vosloo. Screenplay: Wojtowicz-Vosloo, Paul Vosloo, Jakub Korolczuk. Camera: Anastas N. Michos. Editor: Niven Howe. Music: Paul Haslinger. In color, widescreen. Release date: April 1, 2010. MPAA Rating: R. Running time: 103 Min.
Cast: Christina Ricci, Liam Neeson, Justin Long, Chandler Canterbury, Celia Weston, Josh Charles.

ALICE IN WONDERLAND

A Walt Disney Studios Motion Pictures release of a Walt Disney Pictures presentation of a Roth Films/Zanuck Co. production. Producers: Richard D. Zanuck, Suzanne Todd, Jennifer Todd, Joe Roth. Executive producers: Peter Tobyansen, Chris Lebenzon. Co-producers: Katterli Frauenfelder, Tom Peitzman. Director: Tim Burton. Screenplay: Linda Woolverton, based on the books "Alice's Adventures in Wonderland" and "Through the Looking Glass" by Lewis Carroll. Camera: Dariusz Wolski. Editor: Chris Lebenzon. Music: Danny Elfman. In Technicolor; Deluxe prints (Domestic), Technicolor prints (International), 3D. Release date: Feb. 23, 2010. MPAA Rating: PG. Running time: 108 Min.
Cast: Johnny Depp, Mia Wasikowska, Helena Bonham Carter, Anne Hathaway, Crispin Glover, Matt Lucas, Lindsay Duncan, Geraldine James, Tim Pigott-Smith, Martin Csokas, Leo Bill, Frances de la Tour, Jemma Powell, John Hopkins.

ALPHA AND OMEGA

A Lionsgate release presented with Crest Animation. Producers: Richard Rich, Ken Katsumoto, Steve Moore. Executive producers: Noah Fogelson, Max Madhavan, Michael Paseornek. Director: Anthony Bell, Ben Gluck. Screenplay: Christopher Denk, Steve Moore, from a story by Moore. Editor: Joseph L. Campana. Music: Chris Bacon. In Color, 3D. Release date: Sept. 8, 2010. MPAA Rating: PG. Running time: 88 Min.
Voices: Justin Long, Hayden Panettiere, Dennis Hopper, Danny Glover, Larry Miller, Eric Price, Vicki Lewis, Christina Ricci, Chris Carmack.

ALVIN AND THE CHIPMUNKS: THE SQUEAKQUEL

A 20th Century Fox release of a Fox 2000 Pictures and Regency Enterprises presentation of a Bagdasarian Co. production. Producer: Janice Karman, Ross Bagdasarian. Executive producers: Karen Rosenfelt, Arnon Milchan, Michele Imperato Stabile, Steve Waterman. Director: Betty Thomas. Screenplay: Jon Vitti, Jonathan Aibel, Glenn Berger, based on the characters Alvin and the Chipmunks created by Ross Bagdasarian and the Chipettes created by Janice Karman. Camera: Anthony B. Richmond. Editor: Matthew Friedman. Music: David Newman. In Deluxe color. Release date: Dec. 19, 2009. MPAA Rating: PG. Running time: 89 Min.
Cast: Zachary Levi, David Cross, Jason Lee, Justin Long, Matthew Gray Gubler, Jesse McCartney, Amy Poehler, Anna Faris, Christina Applegate, Wendie Malick, Anjelah Johnson, Kathryn Joosten, Kevin G. Schmidt, Chris Warren, Jr., Bridgit Mendler.

AMELIA

A Fox Searchlight release of a Fox Searchlight and Avalon Pictures presentation. Producer: Ted Waitt, Kevin Hyman, Lydia Dean Pilcher. Executive producers: Ron Bass, Hilary Swank. Co-producer: Don Carmody. Director: Mira Nair. Screenplay: Ron Bass, Anna Hamilton Phelan, based on the books "East to the Dawn" by Susan Butler and "The Sound of Wings" by Mary S. Lovell. Camera: Stuart Dryburgh. Editors: Allyson C. Johnson, Lee Percy. Music: Gabriel Yarel. In Deluxe color/B&W archival, Panavision widescreen. Release date: Oct. 16, 2009. MPAA Rating: PG. Running time: 111 Min.
Cast: Hilary Swank, Richard Gere, Ewan McGregor, Christopher Eccleston, Joe Anderson, Cherry Jones, Mia Wasikowska, William Cuddy.

AMERICAN, THE

A Focus Features release of a This Is That/Greenlit/Smokehouse production in association with Twins Financing. Producer: Anne Carey, Jill Green, Ann Wingate, Grant Heslov, George Clooney. Executive producer: Enzo Sisti. Director: Anton Corbijn. Screenplay: Rowan Joffe, based on the novel "A Very Private Gentleman" by Martin Booth. Camer: Martin Ruhe. Editor: Andrew Hulme. Music: Herbert Gronemeyer. In color, widescreen. Release date: Aug. 30, 2010. MPAA Rating: R. Running time: 105 Min.
Cast: George Clooney, Violante Placido, Thekla Reuten, Paolo Bonacelli, Johan Leysen.

ARMORED

A Sony Pictures Entertainment release of a Screen Gems presentation of a Stars Road Entertainment production, in association with Farah Films. Producers: Joshua Donen, Dan Farah. Executive producers: Debra James, Russell Hollander. Co-executive producers: Luis Guerrero, Chris Lemos. Director: Nimrod Antal. Screenplay: James V. Simpson. Camera: Andrzej Sekula. Editor: Armen Minasian. Music: John Murphy. In Deluxe color, Panavision widescreen. Release date: Dec. 4, 2009. Running time: 88 Min.
Cast: Matt Dillon, Jean Reno, Laurence Fishburne, Amaury Nolasco, Fred Ward, Milo Ventimiglia, Ty Hackett, Jimmy Hackett, Jamal Kinney.

ASTRO BOY

A Summit Entertainment (in U.S.) release of a Summit Entertainment (U.S.)/Imagi Studios (Hong Kong) presentation of an Imagi Studios (Hong Kong) production. Producer: Maryann Garger. Executive producers: Francis Kao, Cecil Kramer, Ken Tsumura, Paul Wang. Director: David Bowers. Screenplay: Timothy Hyde Harris, Bowers. Story: Bowers, based on the manga by Tezuka Osamu. Camera: Pepe Valencia. Editor: Robert Anich. Music: John Ottman. In color. Release date: MPAA Rating: PG. Running time: 94 Min.
Voices: Freddie Highmore, Kristen Bell, Nathan Lane, Eugene Levy, Matt Lucas, Bill Nighy, Donald Sutherland, Charlize Theron, Samuel L. Jackson, Nicolas Cage.

AVATAR

A 20th Century Fox release presented in association with Dune Entertainment and Ingenious Film Partners. Producers: James Cameron, Jon Landau. Executive producers: Colin Wilson, Laeta Kalogrios. Co-producers: Brooke Breton, Josh McLaglen. Directed/Writer: James Cameron. Camera: Mauro Fiore. Editors: Stephen Rivkin, John Refoua, Cameron. Music: James Horner. In Deluxe color, widescreen, HD, 3D. Release date: Dec. 10, 2009. MPAA Rating: PG-13. Running time: 163 MIN. Sam Worthington, Zoe Saldana, Sigourney Weaver, Stephen Lang, Michelle Rodriguez, Giovanni Ribisi, Joel David Moore, CCH Pounder, Wes Studi, Laz Alonso, Dileep Rao, Matt Gerald.

BACK-UP PLAN, THE

A CBS Films release of an Escape Artists production. Producer: Todd Black, Jason Blumenthal, Steve Tisch. Executive producers: Rodney

Liber, David Bloomfield. Co-producers: Lance Johnson, Christine Coggins. Director: Alan Poul. Screenplay: Kate Angelo. Camer: Xavier Perez Grobet. Editor: Priscilla Nedd-Friendly. Music: Stephen Trask. In Deluxe color: Release date: April 6, 2010. MPAA Rating: PG-13. Running time: 104 Min.
Cast: Jennifer Lopez, Alex O'Loughlin, Michaela Watkins, Eric Christian Olsen, Anthony Anderson, Noureen DeWulf, Melissa McCarthy.

BLIND SIDE, THE
A Warner Bros. release of an Alcon Entertainment presentation of a Gil Netter production. Producer: Netter, Andrew A. Kosove, Broderick Johnson. Executive producers: Molly Smith, Timothy M. Bourne, Erwin Stoff. Co-producers: Yolanda T. Cochran, Steven P. Wegner, K.C. Hodenfield. Director/Writer: John Lee Hancock, based on the book "The Blind Side: Evolution of a Game" by Michael Lewis. Camera: Alar Kivilo. Editor: Mark Livolsi. Music: Carter Burwell. In Technicolor. Release date: Nov. 9, 2009. MPAA Rating: PG-13. Running time:128 Min.
Cast: Sandra Bullock, Tim McGraw, Quinton Aaron, Jae Head, Lily Collins, Ray McKinnon, Kim Dickens, Adriane Lenox, Kathy Bates.

BOOK OF ELI
A Warner Bros. release of an Alcon Entertainment presentation of a Silver Pictures production. Producer: Joel Silver, Denzel Washington, Broderick Johnson, Andrew A. Kosove, David Valdes. Executive producers: Steve Richards, Susan Downey, Erik Olsen. Co-producers: Steven P. Wegner, Yolanda T. Cochran, John David Washington. Director: Hughes Brothers. Screenplay: Gary Whitta. Camera: Don Burgess. Editor: Cindy Mollo. Music: Atticus Ross, Claudia Sarne, Leopold Ross. In Technicolor, Panavision widescreen, DV. Release date: Jan. 5, 2010. MPAA Rating: R. Running time: 118 Min.
Cast: Denzel Washington, Gary Oldman, Mila Kunis, Ray Stevenson, Jennifer Beals, Frances de la Tour, Evan Jones, Joe Pingue, Tom Waits, Michael Gambon.

BOONDOCK SAINTS II
An Apparition release of a Stage 6 Films presentation of a Don Carmody/Chris Brinker production. Producer: Brinker, Carmody. Executive producers: Lloyd Segan, Rob Fried. Director/Writer: Troy Duffy, based on a story by Troy Duffy, Taylor Duffy. Camera: Miroslaw Baszak. Editor: Bill Deronde, Paul Kumpata. Music: Jeff Danna. Release date: Oct. 27, 2009. MPAA Rating: R. Running time: 115 Min.
Cast: Sean Patrick Flanery, Norman Reedus, Billy Connolly, Clifton Collins Jr., Julie Benz, Peter Fonda, Judd Nelson, David Della Rocco, Bob Marley, Brian Mahoney, David Ferry.

BOUNTY HUNTER
A Sony Pictures Entertainment release of a Columbia Pictures presentation in association with Relativity Media of an Original Film production. Producer: Neal H. Moritz. Executive producers: Wink Mordaunt, Robyn Meisinger, Ryan Kavanaugh, Donald J. Lee Jr., Ori Marmur. Director: Andy Tennant. Screenplay, Sarah Thorp. Camera: Oliver Bokelberg. Editor: Troy Takaki. Music: George Fenton. In Deluxe color prints, Arri widescreen. Release date: March 16, 2010. MPAA Rating: PG-13. Running time: 110 Min.
Cast: Gerard Butler, Jennifer Aniston, Jason Sudeikis, Jeff Garlin, Cathy Moriarty.

BOX, THE
A Warner Bros. release of a Media Rights Capital presentation of a Darko Entertainment production. Producer: Sean McKittrick, Richard Kelly, Dan Lin. Executive producers: Sue Baden-Powell, Edward H. Hamm Jr., Ted Field, Paris Kasidokostas Latsis, Terry Douglas. Director/Writer: Richard Kelly, based on the short story "Button, Button" by Richard Matheson. Camera: Steven Poster. Editor: Sam Bauer. Music: music, Win Butler, Regine Chassagne, Owen Pallett. In Technicolor, Panavision widescreen. Release date: Oct 12, 2009. MPAA Rating: PG-13. Running time: 113 Min.
Cast: Cameron Diaz, James Marsden, Frank Langella, James Rebhorn, Holmes Osborne, Gillian Jacobs, Sam Oz Stone.

CATS & DOGS: THE REVENGE OF KITTY GALORE
A Warner Bros. release presented in associated with Village Roadshow Pictures of a Mad Chance/Polymorphic Pictures production. Producer: Andrew Lazar, Polly Johnsen. Executive producers: Brent O'Connor, Bruce Berman. Co-producer: Miri Yoon. Director: Brad Peyton. Screenplay: Ron J. Friedman, Steve Bencich, based on characters created by John Requa, Glen Ficarra. Steven Poster. Editor: Julie Rogers. Music: Christopher Lennertz. In Technicolor. Release date: July 24, 2010. MPAA Rating: PG. Running time: 82 Min.
Cast: Chris O'Donnell, Jack McBrayer, Fred Armisen, Paul Rodriguez Voices: James Marsden, Nick Nolte, Christina Applegate, Katt Williams, Bette Midler, Neil Patrick Harris, Sean Hayes, Wallace Shawn, Roger Moore, Joe Pantoliano, Michael Clarke Duncan.

CEMETERY JUNCTION
A Sony Pictures Entertainment release of a Columbia Pictures presentation of a Gervais/Merchant production. Producer: Sarah Baden-Powell, Charlie Hanson. Executive producers: Ricky Gervais, Stephen Merchant. Director/Writer: Ricky Gervais, Stephen Merchant. Camera: Remi Adefarasin. Editor: Valerio Bonelli. Music: Tim Atack. In color. Release date: Aug. 6, 2010. MPAA Rating: R. Running time: 95 Min.

With: Tom Hughes, Ricky Gervais, Christian Cooke, Ralph Fiennes, Matthew Goode, Jack Doolan, Emily Watson, Steve Speirs, Felicity Jones, Stephen Merchant.

CLASH OF THE TITANS
A Warner Bros. release presented in association with Legendary Pictures of a Thunder Road Film/Zanuck Co. production. Producer: Basil Iwanyk, Kevin De La Noy. Executive producers: Richard D. Zanuck, Thomas Tull, Jon Jashni, William Fay. Director: Louis Letterier. Screenplay: Travis Beacham, Phil Hay, Matt Manfredi, based on the motion picture directed by Desmond Davis and written by Beverley Cross. Review date: MPAA Rating: PG-13. Running time: 106 Min.
Cast: Sam Worthington, Liam Neeson, Ralph Fiennes, Jason Flemyng, Gemma Arterton, Tine Stapelfeldt, Mads Mikkelsen.

COP OUT
A Warner Bros. release of a Marc Platt production. Producer: Platt, Polly Johnsen, Michael Tadross. Executive producers: Adam Siegel, Robb Cullen, Mark Cullen. Director/Editor: Kevin Smith. Screenplay: Robb Cullen, Mark Cullen. Camera: David Klein. Music: Harold Faltermeyer. In color. Release date: Feb. 22, 2010. MPAA Rating: R. Running time: 113 Min.
Cast: Bruce Willis, Tracy Morgan, Adam Brody, Kevin Pollack, Ana de la Reguera, Guillermo Diaz, Michelle Trachtenberg, Seann William Scott, Jason Lee, Sean Cullen.

CRAZIES
An Overture Films release presented with Participation Media in association with Imagenation of an Aguilar/Georgaris production. Producer: Michael Aguilar, Dean Georgaris, Rob Cowan. Executive producers: George A. Romero, Jeff Skoll, Jonathan King. Director: Breck Eisner. Screenplay: Scott Kosar, Ray Wright. Camera: Maxime Alexandre. Editor: Billy Fox. Music: Mark Isham. In color. Release date: Feb. 24, 2010. MPAA Rating: R. Running time: 101 Min.
Cast: Timothy Olyphant, Radha Mitchell, Joe Anderson, Danielle Panabaker, Christie Lynn Smith, Brett Rickaby, Preston Bailey, John Aylward, Joe Reegan, Glenn Morshower, Larry Cedar, Gregory Sporleder, Mike Hickman, Lisa K. Wyatt, Justin Welborn, Lynn Lowry.

CRAZY HEART
A Fox Searchlight release of an Informant Media/Butcher's Run Films production. Producer: Robert Duvall, Rob Carliner, Judy Cairo, T Bone Burnett. Executive producers: Jeff Bridges, Michael A. Simpson, Eric Brenner, Leslie Belzberg. Director/writer: Scott Cooper, based on the novel by Thomas Cobb. Camera: Barry Markowitz. Editor: John Axelrad. Music: Stephen Bruton, T Bone Burnett. In FotoKem color, Panavision widescreen. Release date: Nov. 27, 2009. MPAA Rating: R. Running time: 112 Min.
Cast: Jeff Bridges, Maggie Gyllenhaal, Robert Duvall, Tom Bower, Colin Farrell, James Keane, William Marquez, Ryan Bingham, Paul Herman, Rick Dial, Jack Nation.

CRAZY ON THE OUTSIDE
A Freestyle Releasing release of a Boxing Cat Films production. Producer: Brian Reilly, Brett Gregory, Anastasia Stanecki. Executive producers: Justin Moritt, Richard Baker. Director: Tim Allen. Screenplay: Judd Pillot, John Peaslee. Camera: Robbie Greenberg. Editor: Scott Conrad. Music: David Newman. In Deluxe color. Release date: Jan. 8, 2010. MPAA Rating: PG-13. Running time: 96 Min.
Cast: Tim Allen, Sigourney Weaver, Ray Liotta, Jeanne Tripplehorn, J.K. Simmons, Julie Bowen, Kelsey, Grammer, Jon Gries, Helen Slayton-Hughes, Malcolm Goodwin, Kenton Duty.

CYRUS
A Fox Searchlight release of a Scott Free production in association with Dune Entertainment. Producer: Michael Costigan. Executive producers: Tony Scott, Ridley Scott. Co-producer: Chrisann Verges. Director/Writer: Mark Duplass, Jay Duplass. Camera: Jas Shelton. Editor: Jay Deuby. Music: Michael Andrews. In color, HD. Release date: Jan. 23, 2010. Running time: 91 Min.
Cast: John C. Reilly, Jonah Hill, Marisa Tomei, Catherine Keener, Matt Walsh.

DATE NIGHT
A 20th Century Fox release of a 21 Laps production in association with Dune Entertainment. Producer: Shawn Levy. Executive producers: Joe Caracciolo, Jr., Josh McLaglen, Tom McNulty. Director: Shawn Levy. Screenplay: Josh Klausner. Camera: Dean Semler. Editor: Dean Zimmerman. Music: Christophe Beck. In Deluxe color. Release date: March 25, 2010. MPAA Rating: PG-13. Running time: 88 Min.
Cast: Steve Carell, Tiney Fey Taraji P. Henson, Jimmi Simpson, Common, William Fichtner, Mark Wahlberg.

DEAR JOHN
A Sony Pictures Entertainment release of a Screen Gems presentation in association with Relativity Media of a Temple Hill and Relativity Media production. Producer: Marty Bowen, Wyck Godfrey, Ryan Kavanaugh. Executive producers: Jeremiah Samuels, Toby Emmerich, Michele Weiss, Tucker Tooley. Co-producers: Kenneth Halsband, Jamie Linden. Director: Lasse Hallstrom. Screenplay, Linden, based on the novel by Nicholas Sparks. Camera: Terry Stacey. Editor: Kristina Boden. Music: Deborah Lurie. In Technicolor, Panavision widescreen. Release date: Feb. 1, 2010. MPAA Rating: PG-13. Running time: 107 Min.
Cast: Channing Tatum, Amanda Seyfried, Richard Jenkins, Henry Thomas, Scott Porter, D.J. Cotrona.

DESPICABLE ME

A Universal release of a Chris Meledandri, Illumination Entertainment production. Producer: Meledandri, Janet Healy, John Cohen. Executive producers: Nina Rowan, Sergio Pablos. Director: Chris Renaud, Pierre Coffin. Screenplay: Cinco Paul, Ken Daurio. Story, Sergio Pablos. Editors: Pamela Ziegenhagen-Shefland, Gregory Perler. Music: Pharrell Williams, Heitor Pereira. In color, HD, 3D. Release date: June 9, 2010. MPAA Rating: PG. Running time: 95 Min.
Cast: Steve Carell, Jason Segel, Russell Brand, Julie Andrews, Will Arnett, Kristen Wiig, Miranda Cosgrove, Dana Gaier, Elsie Fisher.

DEVIL

A Universal release presented with Media Rights Capital presentation of a Night Chronicles production. Producer: M. Night Shyamalan, Sam Mercer. Executive producers: Drew Dowdle, Trish Hofmann. Co-producers, Ashwin Rajan, John Rusk. Director: John Erick Dowdle. Screenplay: Brian Nelson. Story: M. Night Shyamalan. Camera: Tak Fujimoto. Editor: Elliot Greenberg. Music: Fernando Velazquez. In color. Release date: Sept. 17, 2010. MPAA Rating: PG-13. Running time: 80 Min.
Cast: Chris Messina, Logan Marshall-Green, Geoffrey Arend, Bojana Novakovic, Jenny O'Hara, Bokeem Woodbine, Matt Craven, Jacob Vargas.

DIARY OF A WIMPY KID

A 20th Century Fox release of a Fox 2000 Pictures presentation of a Color Force production in association with Dune Entertainment and DayDay Films. Producer: Nina Jacobson, Brad Simpson. Executive producer: Jeff Kinney. Co-producer: Ethan Smith. Director: Thor Freudenthal. Screenplay, Jackie Filgo, Jeff Filgo, Gabe Sachs, Jeff Judah, based on the novel by Jeff Kinney. Camera: Jack Green. Editor: Wendy Greene Bricmont. Music: Theodore Shapiro. In Deluxe color. Release date: March 16, 2010. MPAA Rating: PG. Running time: 92 Min.
Cast: Zachary Gordon, Robert Capron, Rachael Harris, Devon Bostick, Cloe Grace Moretz, Steve Zahn, Grayson Russell, Laine MacNeil, Karan Brar, Connor Fielding, Owen Fielding.

DINNER FOR SCHMUCKS

A Paramount release presented with DreamWorks and Spyglass Entertainment of a Parkes/MacDonald, Everyman Pictures production in association with Reliance Big Entertainment. Producer: Walter F. Parkes, Laurie MacDonald, Jay Roach. Executive producers: Francis Veber, Sacha Baron Cohen, Amy Sayres, Jon Poll, Roger Birnbaum, Gary Barber. Director: Jay Roach. Screenplay: David Guion, Michael Handelman, inspired by the film "Le Diner de cons" (The Dinner Game). Director/Writer: Francis Veber. Camera: Jim Denault. Editors: Alan Baumgarten, Jon Poll. Music: Theodore Shapiro. In Deluxe color. July 15, 2010. MPAA Rating: PG-13. Running time: 114 Min.
Cast: Steve Carell, Paul Rudd, Zach Galifianakis, Jemaine Clement, Stephanie Szostak, Lucy Punch, Bruce Greenwood, David Walliams.

EAT PRAY LOVE

A Sony Pictures Entertainment release of a Columbia Pictures presentation of a Plan B Entertainment production. Producer: Dede Gardner. Executive producers: Brad Pitt, Jeremy Kleiner, Stan Wlodkowski. Director: Ryan Murphy. Screenplay: Murphy, Jennifer Salt, based on the book by Elizabeth Gilbert. Camera: Robert Richardson. Editor: Bradley Buecker. Music: Dario Marianelli. In Deluxe color prints. Release date: Aug. 10, 2010. MPAA Rating: PG-13. Running time: 140 Min.
Cast: Julia Roberts, James Franco, Richard Jenkins, Viola Davis, Billy Crudup, Javier Bardem.

EDGE OF DARKNESS

A Warner Bros. (in U.S.) release presented in association with GK Films of a GK Films (U.S.)/BBC Films (U.K.)/Icon Prods. (U.S.) production. Producers: Graham King, Tim Headington, Michael Wearing. Executive producers: Dan Rissner, David M. Thompson, Suzanne Warren, Gail Lyon, E. Bennett Walsh. Co-executive producer: Jamie Laurenson. Co-producers: Lucienne Papon, Kwame L. Parker. Director: Martin Campbell. Screenplay: William Monahan, Andrew Bovell, based on the television series written by Troy Kennedy Martin. Camera: Phil Meheux. Editor: Stuart Baird. Music: Howard Shore. In Technicolor, Panavision widescreen. Release date: Jan. 20, 2010. MPAA Rating: R. Running time: 117 Min.
Cast: Mel Gibson, Ray Winstone, Danny Huston, Bojana Novakovic, Shawn Roberts, David Aaron Baker, Jay O. Sanders, Denis O'Hare.

EVERYBODY'S FINE

A Miramax Films release presented in association with Radar Pictures of a Hollywood Gang production. Producer: Gianni Nunnari, Ted Field, Vittorio Cecchi Gori, Glynis Murray. Executive producers: Craig J. Flores, Meir Teper, Mike Weber, Joe Rosenberg, Callum Greene. Co-producer: Nathalie Peter-Contesse. Director/Writer: Kirk Jones, based on the 1990 film "Stanno tutti bene" Director: Giuseppe Tornatore; Screenplay: Tornatore, Tonino Guerra, Massimo de Rita. Camera: Henry Braham. Editor: Andrew Mondschein. Music: Dario Marianelli. In color. Review date: Nov. 3, 2009, Nov. 3, 2009. MPAA Rating: PG-13. Running time: 95 Min.
Cast: Robert De Niro, Drew Barrymore, Kate Beckinsale, Sam Rockwell, Melissa Leo, Lucian Maisel, Damian Young, James Frain.

EXPENDABLES, THE

A Lionsgate release presented with Millennium Films of a NuImage production. Producer: Avi Lerner, John Thompson, Kevin King Templeton. Executive producers: Danny Dimbort, Boaz Davidson, Trevor Short, Les Weldon, Jon Feltheimer, Jason Constantine, Eda Kowan, Basil Iwanyk, Guymon Casady. Co-producers: Robert Earl, Matt O'Toole. Director: Sylvester Stallone. Screenplay: David Callaham, Stallone. Story: Callaham. Camera: Jeffrey Kimball. Editors: Ken Blackwell, Paul Harb. Music: Brian Tyler. In color, widescreen. Release date: Aug. 3, 2010. MPAA Rating: R. Running time: 103 Min.
Cast: Sylvester Stallone, Jason Statham, Jet Li, Dolph Lundgren, Eric Roberts, Randy Couture, Steve Austin, David Zayas, Giselle Itie, Charisma Carpenter, Gary Daniels, Terry Crews, Mickey Rourke.

EXTRAORDINARY MEASURES

A CBS Films release of a Double Feature Films production. Producer: by Michael Shamberg, Stacey Sher, Carla Santos Shamberg. Executive producers: Harrison Ford, Nan Morales. Director: Tom Vaughan. Screenplay: Robert Nelson Jacobs, from the book "The Cure" by Geeta Anand. Camera: Andrew Dunn. Editor: Anne V. Coates. Music: Andrea Guerra. In Deluxe color, Panavision widescreen. Release date: Jan. 19, 2010. Rating: PG. Running time: 106 Min.
Cast: Brendan Fraser, Harrison Ford, Keri Russell, Meredith Droeger, Diego Velazquez, Jared Harris, Patrick Bauchau, Alan Ruch, David Clennon, Dee Wallace, Courtney B. Vance, Ananna Berkshire.

FANTASTIC MR. FOX

A 20th Century Fox release presented in association with Indian Paintbrush and Regency Enterprises of an American Empirical picture. Producer: Allison Abbate, Scott Rudin, Wes Anderson, Jeremy Dawson. Executive producers: Steven Rales, Arnon Milchan. Co-producer, Molly Cooper. Director: Wes Anderson. Screenplay: Anderson, Noah Baumbach, based on the book by Roald Dahl. Camera: Tristan Oliver: Editor: Andrew Weisblum. Music: Alexandre Desplat. In Deluxe color. Release date: Oct. 12, 2009. MPAA Rating: PG. Running time: 88 Min.
Cast: George Clooney, Meryl Streep, Jason Schwartzman, Bill Murray, Wally Wolodarsky, Eric Anderson, Michael Gambon, Willem Dafoe, Owen Wilson, Jarvis Cocker.

FLIPPED

A Warner Bros. release of a Castle Rock Entertainment presentation of a Rob Reiner/Alan Greisman production. Producer: Reiner, Greisman. Executive producers: Martin Shafer, Liz Glotzer, David Siegel. Co-producer: Frank Capra III. Director: Rob Reiner. Screenplay: Reiner, Andrew Scheinman, from the novel by Wendelin Van Draanen. Camera: Thomas del Ruth. Editor: Robert Leighton. Music: Marc Shaiman. In color. Release date: July 26, 2010. MPAA Rating: PG. Running time: 90 Min.
Cast: Madeline Carroll, Callan McAuliffe, Rebecca De Mornay, Anthonay Edwards, John Mahoney, Aidan Quinn, Penelope Ann Miller, Kevin Weisman.

FOURTH KIND, THE

A Universal release presented with Gold Circle Films of a Chambara Pictures, Dead Crow Pictures production, in association with SagaFilms, Focus Films. Producer: Paul Brooks, Joe Carnahan, Terry Lee Robbins. Executive producers: Scott Niemeyer, Norm Waitt, Ioana A. Miller. Co-producers: Guy A. Danella, Jeff Levine, Michele Greco. Co-executive producers: David Pupkewitz, Jon Bjarnii Gudmundsson, Vinca Liane Jarrett. Director/Writer: Olatunde Osunsanmi. Story: Osunsanmi, Terry Lee Robbins. Camera: Lorenzo Senatore. Editor: Paul J. Covington. Music: Atli Orvarsson. In color, widescreen. Review date: Nov. 3, 2009. MPAA Rating: PG-13. Running time: 98 Min.
Cast: Milla Jovovich, Will Patton, Elias Koteas, Corey Johnson, Enzo Cilenti, Hakeem Kae-Kazim, Alisha Seaton, Daphne Alexander, Mia McKenna-Bruce, Olatunde Osunsanmi.

FURRY VENGEANCE

A Summit Entertainment release presented in association with Participant Media and Imagenation Abu Dhabi of a Robert Simonds production. Producer: Simonds, Keith Goldberg. Executive producers: Ira Shuman, Brendan Fraser, Jeff Skoll, Jonathan King. Co-producer: Terri Goddard. Director: Roger Kumble. Screenplay: Michael Carnes, Josh Gilbert. Camera: Peter Lyons Collister. Editor: Lawrence Jordan. Music: Edward Shearmur. In Deluxe color. Release date: April 25, 2010. MPAA Rating: PG. Running time: 91 Min.
Cast: Brendan Fraser, Brooke Shields, Matt Prokop, Ken Jeong, Angela Kinsey, Toby Huss, Skyler Samuels, Samantha Bee.

GET HIM TO THE GREEK

A Universal release presented in association with Relativity Media and Spyglass Entertainment of an Apatow production. Producer: Judd Apatow, Nicholas Stoller, David Bushell, Rodney Rothman. Executive producer: Richard Vane. Co-producer: Jason Segel. Director/Writer: Nicholas Stoller, Based on characters created by Jason Segel. Camera: Robert Yeoman. Editors: William Kerr, Mike Sale. Music. Lyle Workman. In color, Panavision widescreen. Release date: May 26, 2010. MPAA Rating: R. Running time: 108 Min.
Cast: Jonah Hill, Russell Brand, Elisabeth Moss, Rose Byrne, Colm Meaney, Sean Combs.

GOING THE DISTANCE

A Warner Bros. release of a New Line Cinema presentation of an Offspring Entertainment production. Producer: Adam Shankman, Jennifer Gibgot, Garrett Grant. Executive producers: Dave Neustadter, Richard Brener, Michael Disco. Director: Nanette Burstein.

Screenplay: Geoff LaTulippe. Camera: Eric Steelberg. Editor: Peter Teschner. Music: Mychael Danna. In Deluxe color prints, 35mm/HD-to-35mm, widescreen. Release date: Aug. 18, 2010. MPAA Rating: R. Running time: 102 Min.
Cast: Drew Barrymore, Justin Long, Charlie Day, Jason Sudeikis, Christina Applegate.

GREEN ZONE

A Universal release presented in association with StudioCanal and Relativity Media of a Working Title production. Producer: Tim Bevan, Eric Fellner, Lloyd Levin, Paul Greengrass. Executive producer: Debra Hayward, Liza Chasin. Co-producers: Mairi Bett, Michael Bronner, Christopher Rouse, Kate Solomon. Director: Paul Greengrass. Screenplay: Brian Helgeland, inspired by the book "Imperial Life in the Emerald City" by Rajiv Chandrasekaran. Camera: Barry Ackroyd. Editor: Christopher Rouse. Music: John Powell. In color, widescreen. Release date: March 1, 2010. MPAA Rating: R. Running time: 114 Min.
Cast: Matt Damon, Greg Kinnear, Brendan Gleeson, Amy Ryan, Khalid Abdalla, Jason Isaacs.

GREENBERG

A Focus Features release of a Scott Rudin production. Produced by Rudin, Jennifer Jason Leigh. Executive producer: Lila Yacoub. Director/Writer Noah Baumbach. Story, Jennifer Jason Leigh, Baumbach. Camera: Harris Savides. Editor: Tim Streeto. Music: James Murphy. In Deluxe color, Panavision widescreen. Release date: Feb. 9, 2010. (In Berlin Film Festival -- competing.) MPAA Rating: R. Running time: 107 Min.
Cast: Ben Stiller, Greta Gerwig, Rhys Ifans, Jennifer Jason Leigh, Brie Larson, Juno Temple, Chris Messina, Susan Traylor, Mark Duplass.

GROWN UPS

A Sony Pictures Entertainment release of a Columbia Pictures presentation in association with Relativity Media of a Happy Madison production. Producer: Adam Sandler, Jack Giarraputo. Executive producers: Barry Bernardi, Tim Herlihy, Allen Covert, Steve Koren. Co-producer: Kevin Grady. Director: Dennis Dugan. Screenplay, Adam Sandler, Fred Wolf. Camera: Theo Van de Sande. Editor: Tom Costain. Music: Rupert Gregson-Williams. In Deluxe color. Release date: June 23, 2010. MPAA Rating: PG-13. Running time: 102 Min.
Cast: Adam Sandler, Kevin James, Chris Rock, David Spade, Rob Schneider, Salma Hayek, Maria Bello, Maya Rudolph, Joyce Van Patten, Ebony Jo-Ann, Di Quon.

HOT TUB TIME MACHINE

An MGM release of a Metro-Goldwyn-Mayer Pictures and United Artists presentation of a New Crime production. Producer: John Cusack, Grace Loh, Matt Moore. Executive producer: Michael Nelson. Director: Steve Pink. Screenplay: Josh Heald, Sean Anders, John Morris. Story: Heald. Camera: Jack Green. Editors: George Folsey Jr., James Thomas. Music: Christophe Beck. In color. Release date: March 24, 2010. MPAA Rating: R. Running time: 99 Min.
Visit Variety.com to become a Variety subscriber.
Cast: John Cusack, Rob Corddry, Craig Robinson, Clark Duke, Crispin Glover, Lizzy Caplan, Sebastian Stan, Chevy Chase.

HOW TO TRAIN YOUR DRAGON

A Paramount release of a DreamWorks Animation presentation. Producer: Bonnie Arnold. Executive producers: Kristine Belson, Tim Johnson. Co-producers: Karen Foster, Doug Davison, Roy Lee, Michael Connolly. Director: Chris Sanders, Dean DeBlois. Screenplay: Will Davies, Sanders, DeBlois, based on the book by Cressida Cowell. Editors: Darren Holmes, Maryann Brandon. Music: John Powell. In Deluxe color and Technicolor, widescreen, 3D. Release date: March 11, 2010. MPAA Rating: PG. Running time: 98 Min.
Cast: Jay Baruchel, Gerard Butler, Craig Ferguson, America Ferrera, Johah Hill, Christopher Mintz-Plasse, T.J. Miller, Kristen Wiig. Editors: Darren Holmes, Maryann Brandon.

INCEPTION

A Warner Bros. release presented in association with Legendary Pictures of a Syncopy production. Producer: Emma Thomas, Christopher Nolan. Executive producers: Chris Brigham, Thomas Tull. Co-producer: Jordan Goldberg. Director/Writer: Christopher Nolan. Camera: Wally Pfister. Editor: Lee Smith. Music: Hans Zimmer. In Technicolor, Panavision widescreen. Release date: July 2, 2010. MPAA Rating: PG-13. Running time: 148 Min.
Cast: Leonardo DiCaprio, Ken Watanabe, Joseph Gordon-Levitt, Marion Cotillard, Ellen Page, Tom Hardy, Cillian Murphy, Tom Berenger, Michael Caine, Dileep Rao, Pete Postlethwaite.

INVICTUS

A Warner Bros. release presented in association with Spyglass Entertainment of a Revelations Entertainment/Mace Neufeld and Malpaso production. Producer: Clint Eastwood, Lori McCreary, Robert Lorenz, Neufeld. Executive producers: Morgan Freeman, Tim Moore, Gary Barber, Roger Birnbaum. Director: Clint Eastwood. Screenplay: Anthony Peckham, based on the book "Playing the Enemy" by John Carlin.
Cast: Morgan Freeman, Matt Damon, Tony Kgoroge, Julian Lewis Jones, Adjoa Andoh, Patrick Mofokeng, Matt Stern, Leleti Khumalo.

IRON MAN 2

A Paramount release presented with Marvel Entertainment of a Marvel Studios production in association with Fairview Entertainment. Producer: Kevin Feige. Executive producers: Alan Fine, Stan Lee, David Maisel, Denis L. Stewart, Louis D'Esposito, Jon Favreau, Susan Downey. Co-producers: Jeremy Latcham, Victoria Alonso. Director: Jon Favreau. Screenplay: Justin Theroux, based on the Marvel comicbook by Stan Lee, Don Heck, Larry Lieber, Jack Kirby. Camera: Matthew Libatique. Editors: Richard Pearson, Dan Lebental. Music: John Debney.
Cast: Robert Downey, Jr., Gwyneth Paltrow, Don Cheadle, Scarlett Johansson, Sam Rockwell, Mickey Rourke, Samuel L. Jackson, Clark Gregg, John Slattery, Garry Shandling.

IT'S COMPLICATED

A Universal release presented in association with Relativity Media of a Waverly Films/Scott Rudin production. Producer: Nancy Meyers, Rudin. Executive producers: Ilona Herzberg, Suzanne Farwell. Director/Writer: Nancy Meyers. Camera: John Toll. Editors: Joe Hutshing, David Moritz. Music: Hans Zimmer, Heitor Pereira. In color. Release date: Dec. 8, 2009. MPAA Rating: R. Running time: 118 Min.
Cast: Meryl Streep, Steve Martin, Alec Baldwin, John Krasinski, Lake Bell, Mary Kay Place, Rita Wilson, Alexandra Wentworth, Hunter Parrish, Zoe Kazan, Caitlin Fitzgerald, Nora Dunn, Bruce Altman, Robert Curtis Brown.

JANKY PROMOTERS, THE

A Third Rail Releasing release of a Dimension Pictures presentation of a Cube Vision production. Producers: Ice Cube, Matt Alvarez. Executive producers: Bob Weinstein, Harvey Weinstein, Neil Machlis. Co-producer: David K. Hebenstreit. Director: Marcus Raboy. Screenplay: Ice Cube. Camera: Tom Priestly. Editor: Robert Ivison. Music: John Murphy. In Technicolor. Release date: Oct. 21, 2009. MPAA Rating: R. Running time: 85 MIN.
With: Ice Cube, Mike Epps, Young Jeezy, Lahmard Tate, Julio Oscar Mechoso, Tamala Jones, "Lil' JJ" James Lewis, Glenn Plummer, Juanita Jennings.

JONAH HEX

A Warner Bros. release presented in association with Legendary Pictures of a Mad Chance/Weed Road production. Producer: Akiva Goldsman, Andrew Lazar. Executive producers: Ravi Mehta, Thomas Tull, Jon Jashni, William Fay, Matt LeBlanc, John Goldstone. Co-producers: Richard Middleton, Miri Yoon, Margot Lulick. Director: Jimmy Hayward. Screenplay: Neveldine & Taylor. Story, William Farmer, Neveldine & Taylor, based on comicbooks written by John Albano, illustrated by Tony DeZuniga, published by DC Comics. Camera: Mitchell Amundsen. Editors: Fernando Villena, Tom Lewis. Music: Marco Beltrami. In Technicolor, Panavision widescreen. Release date: June 16, 2010. MPAA Rating: PG-13. Running time: 81 Min.
Cast: Josh Brolin, John Malkovich, Megan Fox, Michael Fassbender, Will Arnett, Aidan Quinn.

KARATE KID

A Sony Pictures Entertainment (in U.S.) release of a Columbia Pictures presentation of an Overbrook Entertainment/Jerry Weintraub production in association with China Film Group Corp. Producer: Weintraub, Will Smith, Jada Pinkett Smith, James Lassiter, Ken Stovitz. Executive producers: Dany Wolf, Susan Ekins, Han San-ping. Co-producer: Solon So. Director: Harald Zwart. Screenplay, Christopher Murphey. Story, Robert Mark Kamen. Camera: Roger Pratt. Editor: Joel Negron. Music: James Horner. In Deluxe color, Arri widescreen. Release date: June 2, 2010. MPAA Rating: PG. Running time: 140 Min.
Cast: Jaden Smith, Jackie Chan, Taraji P. Henson, Han Wenwen, Yu Rongguang, Wu Zhensu, Wang Zhiheng, Wang Zhenwei.

KICK-ASS

A Lionsgate release presented with MARV of a MARV Films/Plan B production. Producer: Matthew Vaughn, Brad Pitt, Kris Thykier, Adam Bohling, Tarquin Pack, David Reid. Executive producers: Pierre Lagrange, Stephen Marks, Mark Millar, John S. Romita Jr., Jeremy Kleiner. Co-producer: Jane Goldman. Director: Matthew Vaughn. Screenplay: Jane Goldman, Vaughn, based on the comicbook by Mark Millar, John S. Romita Jr. Camera: Ben Davis. Editors: Jon Harris, Pietro Scalia, Eddie Hamilton. Music: John Murphy, Henry Jackman, Marius De Vries, Ilan Eshkeri.
Cast: Aaron Johnson, Christopher Mintz-Plasse, Mark Strong, Chloe Grace Moretz, Clark Duke, Lyndsy Fonseca, Evan Peters, Nicolas Cage, Michael Rispoli, Omari Hardwick, Xander Berkeley, Jason Flemyng.

KILLER INSIDE ME

A Hero Entertainment presentation of a Stone Canyon, Muse, Revolution production in association with Wild Bunch, Curiously Bright Entertainment and Indion Entertainment Group. (International sales: Wild Bunch Paris.) Producer: Chris Hanely, Bradford L. Schlei, Andrew Eaton. Executive producers: Lilly Bright, Chad Burris, Alan Liebert, Randy Mendelsohn, Fernando Sulichin. Co-producers: Susan Kirr, Bob Film & Film I Vast with Anna Croneman, Tomas Eskilsson. Director: Michael Winterbottom. Screenplay: John Curran, based on the novel by Jim Thompson. Marcel Zyskind. Editor: Mags Arnold. Music: Melissa Parmenter, Joel Cadbury. In Technicolor, Panavision widescreen. Release date: Jan 25, 2010. Running time: 108 Min.
Cast: Casey Affleck, Kate Hudson, Jessica Alba, Simon Baker, Bill Pullman, Ned Beatty, Elias Koteas, Tom Bower, Brent Briscoe, Jay R. Ferguson, Liam Aiken, Matthew Maher, Ali Nazary.

KILLERS

A Lionsgate release of an Aversano Films, Katalyst Films, Lionsgate

production. Producer: Scott Aversano, Ashton Kutcher, Jason Goldberg, Mike Karz. Executive producers: Christopher Pratt, Chad Marting, William S. Beasley, Josie Rosen, Peter Morgan, Michael Paseornek, John Sacchi. Co-producers: Hernany Perla, Karyn Spencer Murphy. Director: Robert Luketic. Screenplay: Bob DeRosa, T.M. Griffin, from a story by DeRosa. Camera: Russell Carpenter. Editors: Richard Francis-Bruce, Mary Jo Markey. Music: Rolfe Kent. In Deluxe color, Arri widescreen. Release date: June 4, 2010. MPAA Rating: PG-13. Running time: 100 Min.
Cast: Katherine Heigl, Ashton Kutcher, Tom Selleck, Catherine O'Hara, Katheryn Winnick, Kevin Sussman, Lisa Ann Walter, Casey Wilson, Rob Riggle, Martin Mull, Alex Borstein.

KNIGHT AND DAY

A 20th Century Fox release presented with Regency Enterprises of a Pink Machine/Todd Garner/Tree Line Film production in association with Dune Entertainment. Producer: Cathy Konrad, Steve Pink, Garner. Executive producers: Joe Roth, Arnon Milchan, E. Bennett Walsh. Director: James Mangold. Screenplay, Patrick O'Neill. Camera: Phedon Papamichael. Editors: Michael McCusker, Quincy Z. Gunderson. Music: John Powell. In Deluxe color prints, Panavision widescreen. Release Date: June 15, 2010. MPAA Rating: PG-13. Running time: 109 Min.
Cast: Tom Cruise, Cameron Diaz, Peter Sarsgaard, Viola Davis, Jordi Molla, Paul Dano, Maggie Grace, Marc Blucas, Celia Weston. Dale Dye.

LAST AIRBENDER

A Paramount release presented with Nickelodeon Movies of a Blinding Edge Pictures, Kennedy/Marshall Co. production. Producer: M. Night Shyamalan, Sam Mercer, Frank Marshall. Executive producers: Kathleen Kennedy, Scott Aversano, Michael Dante DiMartino, Bryan Konietzko. Co-producer: Jose L. Rodriguez. Director: Writer: M. Night Shyamalan, based on the series "Avatar: The Last Airbender" created by Michael Dante DiMartino, Bryan Konietzko. Camera: Andrew Lesnie. Editor: Conrad Buff. Music: James Newton Howard. In color, widescreen, 3D. Release date: June 29, 2010. MPAA Rating: PG. Running time: 103 Min.
Cast: Noah Ringer, Dev Patel, Nicola Peltz, Jackson Rathbone, Shaun Toub, Aasif Mandvi, Cliff Curtis, Seychelle Gabriel.

LAST EXORCISM, THE

A Lionsgate release of a Strike Entertainment, StudioCanal presentation of an Arcade Pictures production. Producer: Eric Newman, Eli Roth, Marc Abraham, Thomas A. Bliss. Executive producers: Huck Botko, Andrew Gurland, Phil Altmann, Ron Halpern. Co-producers: Patty Long, Gabrielle Neimand. Co-executive producers: Doug Plasse, Patrick Curd. Director: Daniel Stamm. Screenplay: Huck Botko, Andrew Gurland. Camera Zoltan Honti. Editor: Shilpa Khanna. Music: Nathan Barr. In color, HD. Release date: June 24, 2010. MPAA rating: PG-13. Running time: 90 Min.
With: Patrick Fabian, Ashley Bell, Iris Bahr, Louis Herthum, Caleb Landry Jones, Tony Bentley.

LAST SONG

A Walt Disney Studios Motion Pictures release of a Touchstone Pictures presentation of an Offspring Entertainment production. Producers: Adam Shankman, Jennifer Gibgot. Executive producer: Tish Cyrus. Co-producer: Dara Weintraub. Director: Julie Anne Robinson. Screenplay: Nicholas Sparks, Jeff Van Wie, from the novel by Sparks. Camera: John Lindley. Editor: Nancy Richardson. Music: Aaron Zigman. In Deluxe color, Deluxe prints (Domestic), Technicolor prints (International). Release date: March 25, 2010. MPAA Rating: PG. Running time: 108 Min.
Cast: Miley Cyrus, Greg Kinnear, Bobby Coleman, Liam Hemsworth, Hallock Beals, Kelly Preston, Nick Lashaway, Carly Chaikin, Kate Vernon, Nick Searcy.

LAW ABIDING CITIZEN

An Overture Films release presented with the Film Department of a Warp Film production in association with the Evil Twins. Producer: Lucas Foster, Gerard Butler, Alan Siegel, Mark Gill, Kurt Wimmer, Robert Katz. Executive producers: Neil Sacker, Michael Goguen. Co-producers: Jeff Waxman, Ian Watermeier. Director: F. Gary Gray. Screenplay, Kurt Wimmer. Camera: Jonathan Sela. Editor: Tariq Anwar. Music: Brian Tyler. Music: Brian Tyler. In Technicolor, widescreen. Release date: Oct. 14, 2009. MPAA Rating: R. Running time: 108 Min.
Visit Variety.com to become a Variety subscriber.
Cast: Jamie Foxx, Gerard Butler, Bruce McGill, Colm Meaney, Leslie Bibb, Regina Hall, Michael Irby.

LEGEND OF THE GUARDIANS: THE OWLS OF GA'HOOLE

A Warner Bros. Pictures presentation in association with Village Roadshow Pictures of a Village Roadshow and Animal Logic production. Producer: Zareh Nalbandian. Executive producer: Donald De Line, Deborah Snyder, Lionel Wigram, Chris de Faria, Kathryn Lasky, Bruce Berman. Director: Zack Snyder. Screenplay, John Orloff, Emil Stern, based on the novels "Guardians of Ga'Hoole" by Kathryn Lasky. Editor: David Burrows. Music: David Hirschfelder. In color 3D. Release date: September 16, 2010. MPAA Rating: PG. Running time: 91 Min.
Voices: Jim Sturgess, Emily Barclay, Ryan Kwanten, Anthony LaPaglia, Hugo Weaving, Helev Mirren, Sam Neill, Geoffrey Rush, Abbie Cornish, Miriam Margolyes, David Wenham, Adrienne de Faria, Joel Edgerton.

LEGION

A Sony Pictures Entertainment release of a Screen Gems presentation of a Bold Films production. Producer: David Lancaster, Michel Litvak. Executive producers: Gary Michael Walters, Scott Stewart, Jonathan Rothbart. Co-producers: Steve Beswick, Marc Sadeghi. Director: Scott Stewart. Screenplay: Peter Schink, Stewart. Camera: John Lindley. Editor: Steven Kemper. Music: John Frizzell. In Deluxe color. Release date: Jan. 22, 2010. MPAA Rating: R. Running time: 104 Min.
Cast: Paul Bettany, Lucas Black, Tyrese Gibson, Adrianne Palicki, Charles S. Dutton, Jon Tenney, Kevin Durand, Willa Holland, Kate Walsh, Dennis Quaid, Jeanette Miller, Doug Jones.

LETTERS TO GOD

A Vivendi Entertainment release of a Possibility Pictures production in association with DNP Studios and Vertical Innovations. Producer: Cameron Kim Dawson, David Nixon. Executive producer, Tom Swanson. Co-producer: Sandra Thrift. Director: David Nixon. Co-director: Patrick Doughtie. Screenplay: Doughtie, Art D'Alessandro, Sandra Thrift, Cullen Douglas. Camera: Bob M. Scott. Editor: Patrick Tyler. Music: Colin O'Malley. In Technicolor. Release date: April 7, 2010. MPAA Rating: PG. Running time: 113 Min.
With: Robyn Lively, Jeffrey S.S. Johnson, Maree Cheatham, Tanner Maguire, Michael Christopher Bolten, Bailee Madison, Ralph Waite.

LETTERS TO JULIET

A Summit Entertainment release of an Applehead Pictures, Mark Canton production. Producer: Canton, Caroline Kaplan, Ellen Barkin. Executive producer: Ron Schmidt. Co-producer: George Barkin. Director: Gary Winick. Screenplay: Jose Rivera, Tim Sullivan. Camera: Marco Pontecorvo. Editor: Bill Pankow. Music: Andrea Guerra. In color, widescreen. Release date: April 25, 2010. MPAA Rating: PG. Running time: 101 Min.
Cast: Amanda Seyfried, Vanessa Redgrave, Christopher Egan, Gael Garcia Bernal, Franco Nero, Oliver Platt, Luisa Ranieri.

LOSERS, THE

A Warner Bros. release, presented in association with Dark Castle Entertainment/StudioCanal/Studio Babelsberg Motion Pictures, of a Weed Road Pictures production. Producer: Joel Silver, Akiva Goldsman, Kerry Foster. Executive producer: ndrew Rona, Steve Richards, Sarah Aubrey, Stuart Besser. Co-producers: Carl Woebcken, Christoph Fisser, Henning Molfenter, Adam Kuhn. Director: Sylvain White. Screenplay: Peter Berg, James Vanderbilt based on the comicbook series by Andy Diggle, Jock, published by DC Comics/Vertigo. Camera: Scott Kevan. Editor: David Checel. Music: John Ottman. In Technicolor, Panavision widescreen. Release date: April 15, 2010. MPAA Rating: PG-13. Running time: 97 Min.
Cast: Jeffrey Dean Morgan, Zoe Saldana, Chris Evans, Idris Elba, Columbus Short, Oscar Jaenada, Jason Patric, Holt McCallany.

LOTTERY TICKET

A Warner Bros. release of an Alcon Entertainment presentation of a Burg-Koules and Cube Vision production. Producer: Andrew A. Kosove, Broderick Johnson, Matt Alvarez, Mark Burg, Oren Koules. Executive producers: Ice Cube, Timothy M. Bourne, Steven P. Wegner. Co-producers: Yolanda T. Cochran, Carl Rogers, Jesse Israel, H.H. Cooper, Brad Kaplan, Andrew Wilson. Director: Erik White. Screenplay, Abdul Williams. Story, Williams, White. Camera: Patrick Cady. Editor: Harvey Rosenstock. Music: Teddy Castellucci. In Technicolor prints. Release date: Aug. 11, 2010. MPAA Rating: PG-13. Running time: 95 Min.
Cast: Bow Wow, Brandon T. Jackson, Naturi Naughton, Keith, Charlie Murphy, Gbenga Akinnagbe, Terry Crews, Loretta Devine, Ice Cube.

MACHETE

A 20th Century Fox release and presentation of an Overnight production in association with Troublemaker Studios. Producer: Robert Rodriguez, Elizabeth Avellan, Rick Schwartz. Executive producers: Ashok Amritraj, Edward Borgerding, Alan Bernon, Myles Nestel. Co-executive producers: Peter Fruchtman, Jerry Fruchtman, Jacky Gilardi Jr., Darby Parker, Alastair Burlingham, Steve Robbins, Anthony Gudas. Director: Robert Rodriguez, Ethan Maniquis. Screenplay: Robert Rodriguez, Alvaro Rodriguez. Camera: Jimmy Lindsay. Editors: Robert Rodriguez, Rebecca Rodriguez. Music: Chingon. In Deluxe color. Release date: Aug. 26, 2010. (Venice Film Festival) MPAA Rating: R. Running time: 104 Min.
Cast: Danny Trejo, Robert De Niro, Jessica Alba, Steven Seagal, Michelle Rodriguez, Jeff Fahey, Cheech Marin, Don Johnson, Shea Whigham, Lindsay Lohan, Tom Savini, Daryl Sabara, Gilbert Trejo, Billy Blair.

MARMADUKE

A 20th Century Fox release presented in association with Regency Enterprises of a Davis Entertainment Co. production. Producer: John David. Executive producers: Jeffrey Scott, Derek Dauchy, Arnon Milchan, Tariq Jalil. Director: Tom Dey. Screenplay: im Rasmussen, Vince Di Meglio, based on the comic created by Brad Anderson, Phil Leeming.
Cast: Lee Pace, Judy Greer, Caroline Sunshine, Finley Jacobsen, Many Haines, Milana Haines, David Walliams, William H. Macy.
Voices: Owen Wilson, Emma Stone, George Lopez, Christopher Mintz-Plasse, Steve Coogan, Fergie, Kiefer Sutherland, Marlon Wayans, Damon Wayans, Jr., Sam Elliott.

MICHAEL JACKSON'S THIS IS IT

A Sony Pictures Entertainment release of a Columbia Pictures presentation in association with the Michael Jackson Co. and AEG Live. ProduceRS: Randy Phillips, Kenny Ortega, Paul Gongaware. Executive producers: John Branca, John McClain. Co-producers: Chantal Feghali, Frank Dileo. Director: Kenny Ortega. Camera: Tim Patterson, Sandrine Orabona. Editors: Don Brochu, Brandon Key, Patterson, Kevin Stitt. Music: Michael Bearden. In Deluxe color. Release date: Oct. 27, 2009. MPAA Rating: PG. Running time: 111 Min.

With: Michael Jackson, Kenny Ortega, Michael Bearden, Travis Payne, Judith Hill, Orianthi Panagaris, Tommy Organ, Mo Pleasure, Stacy Walker, Tony Testa. Documentary.

NINJA ASSASSIN

A Warner Bros. release, presented in association with Legendary Pictures, Dark Castle Entertainment, of a Silver Pictures production, in association with Anarchos Prods. Producers: Joel Silver, Andy Wachowski, Larry Wachowski, Grant Hill. Executive producers: Thomas Tull, Jon Jashni, Steve Richards. Director: James McTeigue. Screenplay: Matthew Sand, J. Michael Straczynski, bsed on a story by Sand. Camera: Karl Walter Lindenlaub. Editors: Gian Ganziano, Joseph Jett Sally. Music: Ilan Eshkeri. In color/B&W, widescreen. Release date: Oct. 13, 2009. (Also in Fantastic Fest, Austin.) MPAA Rating: R. Running time: 99 Min.

Cast: Rain, Naomie Harris, Ben Miles, Rick Yune, Sho Kosugi, Guido Foehrweisser, Stephen Marcus, Wladimir Tarasjanz, Randall Duk Kim, Sung Kang.

OLD DOGS

A Walt Disney Pictures release of a Tapestry Films production. Producer: Andrew Panay, Robert L. Levy, Peter Abrams. Executive producer: Garrett Grant. Director: Walt Becker. Screenplay, David Diamond, David Weissman. Camera: Jeffrey L. Kimball. Editors: Tom Lewis, Ryan Folsey. Music: John Debney. In color. Release date: November 21, 2009. MPAA Rating: PG. Running time: 88 Min.

Cast: John Travolta, Robin Williams, Kelly Preston, Conner Rayburn, Ella Bieu Travolta, Lori Loughlin, Seth Green, Bernie Mac, Matt Dillion, Ann-Margret, Rita Wilson.

OPERATION: ENDGAME

An Anchor Bay Films release presented with Infinity Media of an Infinity and Darko Entertainment production. Producer: Sean McKittrick, Michael Ohoven, Kevin Turen. Executive producers: Chadwick Clough, Jeff Culotta, Albert T. Dickerson III, Ted Hamm, Bill Johnson, Richard Kelly, Jim Seibel. Co-producer: Rani Aliahmad. Director: Fouad Mikati. Screenplay: Sam Levinson, Brian Watanabe.

With: Joe Anderson, Odette Yustman, Zach Galifianakis, Ellen Barkin, Rob Corddry, Adam Scott, Ving Rhames, Bob Odenkirk, Jeffrey Tambor, Maggie Q, Emilie de Ravin.

OTHER GUYS, THE

A Sony Pictures Entertainment release of a Columbia Pictures presentation of a Gary Sanchez/Mosaic production. Producer: Will Ferrell, Adam McKay, Jimmy Miller, Patrick Crowley. Executive producers: David Householter, Chris Henchy, Kevin Messick. Co-producers: Josh Church, Jessica Elbaum. Director: Adam McKay. Screenplay: McKay, Chris Henchy. Camera Oliver Wood. Editor: Brent White. Music: Jon Brion. In Deluxe color, Panavision widescreen. Release date: July 29, 2010. MPAA Rating: PG-13. Running time: 107 Min.

Cast: Will Ferrell, Mark Wahlberg, Eva Mendes, Michael Keaton, Steve Coogan, Ray Stevenson, Samuel L. Jackson, Dwayne Johnson.

OUR FAMILY WEDDING

A Fox Searchlight release of a Sneak Preview Entertainment and Edward Saxon productiON. Producer: Saxon, Steven J. Wolfe. Co-producer: Scott G. Hyman. Director: Rick Famuyiwa. Screenplay: Wayne Conley, Malcolm Spellman, Famuyiwa. Story: Conley. Camera: Julio Macat. Editor: Dirk Westervelt. Music: Transcenders. In Deluxe color, widescreen. Release date: Feb. 19, 2010. MPAA Rating: PG-13. Running time: 101 Min.

Cast: Forest Whitaker, America Ferrera, Carlos Mencia, Regina King, Lance Gross, Diana Maria Riva.

PIRANHA

A Dimension Films release and presentation of a Mark Canton/IPW production in association with Aja/Levasseur Prods. Producer: Mark Canton, Marc Toberoff, Alexandre Aja, Gregory Levasseur. Executive producers: Bob Weinstein, Harvey Weinstein, Alix Taylor, Louis G. Friedman, J. Todd Harris, Chako van Leeuwen. Director: Alexandre Aja. Screenplay: Peter Goldfinger, Josh Stolberg. Camera: John R. Leonetti. Editor: Baxter. Music: Michael Wandmacher.

Cast: Elisabeth Shue, Adam Scott, Jerry O'Connell, Ving Rhames, Jessica Szohr, Steven R. McQueen, Christopher Lloyd, Richard Dreyfuss.

PLANET 51:

A Sony Pictures Entertainment (in U.S.) release of a TriStar Pictures (U.S.) presentation of an Ilion Animation Studios (Spain) production in association with Handmade Films Intl. (U.K.). Producers: Ignacio Perez Dolset, Guy Collins. Executive producers: Juan Antonio Perez Ramirez, Peter Graves, Michael Ryan, Jose A. Rodriguez Diaz, Javier Perez Dolset, Albie Hecht, Patrick Meehan, Mercedes Gamero, Mercedes Rey, Stephen Margolis, Ricardo Garcia Arrojo, Albert Martinez-Martin. Director: Jorge Blanco. Co-director: Javier Abad, Marcos Martinez. Screenplay: Joe Stillman; original idea, Abad, Blanco, Martinez, Ignacio Perez Dolset. Editor: Alex Rodriguez. Music: James Brett. In color. Release date: Nov. 14, 2009. MPAA Rating: PG. Running time: 91 Min.

Dwayne Johnson, Jessica Biel, Justin Long, Gary Oldman, William Scott, John Cleese.

PRECIOUS:

A Lee Daniels Entertainment and Smokewood Entertainment presentation. (International sales: Elephant Eye Films, New York.) Producers: Daniels, Sarah Siegel-Magness, Gary Magness. Executive producers: Lisa Cortes, Tom Heller. Co-producer: Mark Mathis. Director: Lee Daniels. Screenplay: Damien Paul, based on the novel by Sapphire. Camera: Andrew Dunn. Editor: Joe Klotz. Music: Mario Grigorov. In Technicolor. Release date: Jan. 17, 2009 Running time: 109 Min.

Cast: Gabourey "Gabby" Sidibe, Mo'Nique, Paula Patton, Lenny Kravitz, Mariah Carey, Sherri Shepherd.

PREDATORS

A 20th Century Fox release of a Troublemaker Studios/Davis Entertainment Co. production in association with Dune Entertainment. Producer: Robert Rodriguez, John Davis, Elizabeth Avellan. Executive producer: Alex Young. Co-producer: Bill Scott. Director: Nimrod Antal. Screenplay: Alex Litvak, Michael Finch, based on characters created by Jim Thomas, John Thomas. Camera: Gyula Pados. Editor: Dan Zimmerman. Music: John Debney. In color, Panavision widescreen. Release date: July 7, 2010. MPAA Rating: R. Running time: 107 Min.

Cast: Adrien Brody, Topher Grace, Alice Braga, Walton Goggins, Oleg Taktarov, Laurence Fishburne.

PRINCE OF PERSIA: THE SANDS OF TIME

A Walt Disney Studios Motion Pictures release of a Walt Disney Pictures and Jerry Bruckheimer Films presentation. Producer: Bruckheimer. Executive producers: Mike Stenson, Chad Oman, John August, Jordan Mechner, Patrick McCormick, Eric McLeod. Director: Mike Newell. Screenplay: Boaz Yakin, Doug Miro, Carlo Bernard; screen story, Jordan Mechner, based on the videogame series "Prince of Persia" created by Mechner. Camera: John Seale. Editors: Michael Kahn, Mick Audsley, Martin Walsh. Music: Harry Gregson-Williams. In Technicolor, widescreen. Release date: May 7, 2010. MPAA Rating: PG-13. Running time: 115 Min.

Cast: Jake Gyllenhaal, Gemma Arterton, Ben Kingsley, Alfred Molina, Steve Toussaint, Toby Kebbell, Richard Coyle, Ronald Pickup, Will Foster, Gisli Orn Gardarsson.

PRINCESS AND THE FROG, THE

A Walt Disney Studios Motion Pictures release of a Walt Disney Pictures presentation. Producer: Peter Del Vecho. Executive producers: John Lasseter, Aghi Koh. Director: John Musker, Ron Clements. Screenplay: Clements, Musker, Rob Edwards. Story, Clements, Musker, Greg Erb, inspired in part by "The Frog Princess" by E.D. Baker. Editor: Jeff Draheim. Music: Randy Newman. In Deluxe color (domestic), Technicolor (international). Release date: Nov. 14, 2009. MPAA Rating: G. Running time: 95 Min.

Voices: Anika Noni Rose, Bruno Campos, Keith David, Leon Wooley, Jennifer Cody, Jim Cummings, Peter Bartlett, Jenifer Lewis, Oprah Winfrey, Terrence Howard, John Goodman.

RAMONA AND BEEZUS

A 20th Century Fox release of a Fox 2000 Pictures and Walden Media presentation of a Di Novi Pictures production. Producer: Denise Di Novi, Alison Greenspan. Co-producer: Brad Van Arragon. Director: Elizabeth Allen. Screenplay: Laurie Craig, Nick Pustay, based on the novels by Beverly Cleary.

REMEMBER ME

A Summit Entertainment release of an Underground Films production. Producer: Nicholas Osborne, Trevor Engelson. Executive producers: Carol Cuddy, Robert Pattinson. Director: Allen Coulter. Screenplay: Will Fetters. Camera: Jonathan Freeman. Editor: Andrew Mondshein. Music: Marcelo Zarvos. In Deluxe color. Release date: March 4, 2010. MPAA Rating: PG-13. Running time: 113 Min.

Cast: Robert Pattinson, Emilie de Ravin, Chris Cooper, Lena Olin, Tate Ellington, Ruby Jerins, Pierce Brosnan, Kate Burton, Gregory Jbara.

REPO MEN

A Universal release presented in association with Relativity Media of a Stuber Pictures production. Producer: Scott Stuber. Executive producers: Miguel Sapochnik, Jonathan Mone, Mike Drake, Valerie Dean, Andrew Z. Davis. Director: Miguel Sapochnik. Screenplay: Eric Garcia, Garrett Lerner, based on the novel "The Repossession Mambo" by Garcia. Camera: Enrique Chediak. Editor: Richard Francis-Bruce. Music: Marco Beltrami. In Technicolor, Panavision widescreen. Release date: March 15, 2010. MPAA Rating: R. Running time: 111 Min.

Cast: Jude Law, Forest Whitaker, Liev Schreiber, Alice Braga, Carice van Houten.

ROAD, THE

A Dimension Films release presented with 2929 Prods. of a Nick Wechsler and Chockstone Pictures production. Producers: Wechsler, Paula Mae Schwartz, Steve Schwartz. Executive producers: Todd Wagner, Mark Cuban, Marc Butan, Rudd Simmons. Director: John Hillcoat. Screenplay: Joe Penhall, based on the novel by Cormac McCarthy. Camera: Javier Aguirresarobe. Editor: Jon Gregory. Music:

Nick Cave, Warren Ellis. In Technicolor, widescreen. Release date: Aug 27, 2009 (premier), Nov. 2009 (U.S. release). MPAA Rating: R. Running time: 110 Min. MPAA Rating: R. Running time: 110 Min.
Cast: Viggo Mortensen, Kodi Smit-McPhee, Charlize Theron, Robert Duvall, Guy Pearce, Molly Parker, Michael Williams, Garret Dillahunt.

THE RUNAWAYS

An Apparition release of a River Road Entertainment and Linson Entertainment production. Producer: John Linson, Art Linson and Bill Pohlad. Executive producers: Joan Jett, Kenny Laguna, Brian Young. Co-producers: Frank Hildebrand, David Grace. Director: Floria Sigismondi. Screenplay: Sigismondi, based on the book "Neon Angel: The Cherrie Currie Story" by Currie. Camera: Benoit Debie. Editor: Richard Chew. In color, Super 16-to-35mm. Release date: Jan. 24, 2010. MPAA Rating: R. Running time: 102 Min.
Cast: Kristen Stewart, Dakota Fanning, Alia Shawkat, Scout Taylor-Compton, Michael Shannon.

SALT

A Sony Pictures Entertainment release of a Columbia Pictures presentation in association with Relativity Media. Producer: Lorenzo di Bonaventura, Sunil Perkash. Executive producers: Ric Kidney, Mark Vahradian, Ryan Kavanaugh. Director: Phillip Noyce. Screenplay, Kurt Wimmer. Camera: Robert Elswit. Editors: Stuard Baird, John Gilroy. Music: James Newton Howard. In Deluxe color, Panavision widescreen. Release date: July 15, 2010. MPAA Rating: PG-13. Running time: 100 Min.
Cast: Angelina Jolie, Liev Schreiber Peabody, Daniel Olbrychski, Andre Braugher.

SAW VI

A Lionsgate release of a Twisted Pictures presentation of a Burg/Koules/Hoffman production. Producer: Greg Hoffman, Oren Koules, Mark Burg. Executive producers: Daniel Jason Heffner, James Wan, Leigh Wannell, Stacey Testro, Peter Block, Jason Constantine. Co-producer: Troy Begnaud. Director: Kevin Greutert. Screenplay: Patrick Melton, Marcus Dunstan. Camera: David A. Armstrong. Editor: Andrew Coutis. Music: Charlie Clouser. In Deluxe color. Release date: Oct. 23, 2009. MPAA Rating: R. Running time: 90 Min.
Cast: Tobin Bell, Costas Mandylor, Betsy Russell, Mark Rolston, Peter Outerdridge, Shawnee Smith, Athena Karkanis, Samantha Lemole, Caroline Cave, George Newbern, Tanedra Howard.

SCOTT PILGRIM VS. THE WORLD

A Universal release of a Marc Platt, Big Talk Films, Closed on Mondays production. Producer: Platt, Eric Gitter, Nira Park, Edgar Wright. Executive producers: Ronaldo Vasconcellos, J. Miles Dale, Jared LeBoff, Adam Siegel. Co-producers: Joe Nozemack, Lisa Gitter, Steven V. Scavelli. Director: Edgar Wright. Screenplay: Michael Bacall, Wright, based on the Oni Press graphic novels by Bryan Lee O'Malley. Camera: Bill Pope. Editors: Jonathan Amos, Paul Machliss. Music: Nigel Godrich. In color. Release date: July 22, 2010. MPAA Rating: PG-13. Running time: 112 Min.
Cast: Michael Cera, Mary Elizabeth Winstead, Kieran Culkin, Chris Evans, Anna Kendrick, Alison Pill, Brandon Routh, Jason Schwartzman, Brie Larson, Aubrey Plaza, Johnny simmons, Stephen Stills, Mae Whitman, Ellen Wong.

SERIOUS MAN, A

A Focus Features release presented in association with StudioCanal and Relativity Media of a Working Title production. Producer: Joel Coen, Ethan Coen. Executive producers: Tim Bevan, Eric Fellner, Robert Graf. Directors/Writers: Joel Coen, Ethan Coen. Camera: Roger Deakins. Editor: Roderick Jaynes. Music: Carter Burwell. In Deluxe color. Release date: Sept. 11, 2009. MPAA Rating: R. Running time: 104 Min.
Cast: Michael Stuhlbarg, Richard Kind, Fred Melamed, Sari Lennick, Adam Arkin, Amy Landecker, Alan Mandell, Fyvush Finkel, Allen Lewis Rickman, Yelena Schmulenson, Peter Breitmayer, Brent Braunschweig, Simon Helberg, David Kang, Aaron Wolff, Jessica McManus, Ari Hoptman, Michael Tezla, George Wyner, Michael Lerner.

SEX AND THE CITY 2

A Warner Bros. and Village Roadshow Pictures release of a New Line Cinema presentation in association with Home Box Office and Village Roadshow of a Darren Star production. Producers: Michael Patrick King, Sarah Jessica Parker, Darren Star, John Melfi. Executive producers: Toby Emmerich, Richard Brener, Marcus Viscidi. Director/Writer: Michael Patrick King, based on the TV series created by Star, based on characters from the book by Candace Bushnell. Camera: John Thomas. Editor: Michael Berenbaum. Music: Aaron Zigman. In Panavision widescreen, Deluxe color. Release date: May 20, 2010. MPAA Rating: R. Running time: 146 Min.
Cast: Sarah Jessica Parker, Kim Cattrall, Kristin Davis, Cynthia Nixon, Chris Noth, John Corbett, David Eigenberg, Evan Handler, Jason Lewis, Willie Garson, Mario Cantone.

SHE'S OUT OF MY LEAGUE

A Paramount release of a DreamWorks presentation of a Mosaic Media Group production. Producers: Jimmy Miller, David Householter. Executive producer: George Gatins. Director: Jim Field Smith. Screenplay: Sean Anders, John Morris. Camera: Jim Denault. Editor: Dan Schalk. Music: Michael Andrews. In Deluxe color. Release date: Feb. 25, 2010. MPAA Rating: R. Running time: 106 Min.
Jay Baruchel, Alice Eve, T.J. Miller, Mike Vogel, Nate Torrence, Lindsay Sloane, Kyle Borheimer, Jessica St. Clair, Krysten Ritter, Debra Jo Rupp, Adam LeFevre.

SHERLOCK HOLMES

A Warner Bros. release presented in association with Village Roadshow Pictures of a Silver Pictures and Wigram production. Producer: Joel Silver, Lionel Wigram, Susan Downey, Dan Lin. Executive producers: Michael Tadross, Bruce Berman. Co-producer: Steve Clark-Hall. Director: Guy Ritchie. Screenplay: Michael Robert Johnson, Anthony Peckham, Simon Kinberg. Screen story: Lionel Wigram, Johnson; Sherlock Holmes and Dr. Watson created by Arthur Conan Doyle. Camera: Philippe Rousselot. Editor: James Herbert. Music: Hans Zimmer. In Technicolor. Release date: Dec. 3, 2009. MPAA Rating: MPAA Rating: PG-13. Running time: 128 Min.
Cast: Robert Downey, Jr., Jude Law, Rachel McAdams, Mark Strong, Eddie Marsan, Kelly reilly, James Fox, Hans Matheson, Geraldine James.

SHREK FOREVER AFTER

A Paramount release of a DreamWorks Animation presentation. Producer: Gina Shay, Teresa Cheng. Executive producers: Aron Warner, Andrew Adamson, John H. Williams. Director: Mike Mitchell. Screenplay: Josh Klausner, Darren Lemke, based on the book by William Steig. Editor: Nick Fletcher. Music: Harry Gregson-Williams. In Technicolor prints. Release date: April 21, 2010. MPAA Rating: PG. Running time: 95 Min.
Voices: Mike Myers, Eddie Murphy, Cameron Diaz, Antonio Banderas, Julie Andrews, John Cleese, Walt Dohrm.

SHUTTER ISLAND

A Paramount release of a Phoenix Pictures production in association with Sikelia Prods. and Appian Way. Producer: Mike Medavoy, Arnold W. Messer, Bradley J. Fischer, Martin Scorsese. Executive producers: Chris Brigham, Laeta Kalogridis, Dennis Lehane, Gianni Nunnari, Louis Phillips. Co-producers: Joseph Reidy, Emma Tillinger, Amy Herman. Director: Martin Scorsese. Screenplay: Laeta Kalogridis, based on the novel by Dennis Lehane. Camera: Robert Richardson. Editor: Thelma Schoonmaker. In Deluxe color, Panavision widescreen. Release date: Feb. 10, 2010. (Berlin Film Festival) MPAA Rating: R. Running time: 138 Min.
Cast: Leonardo DiCaprio, Mark Ruffalo, Ben Kingsley, Max von Sydow, Michelle Williams, Emily Mortimer, Patricia Clarkson, Jackie Earle Haley, Ted Levine, John Carroll, Elias Koteas.

SORCERER'S APPRENTICE

A Walt Disney Studios Motion Pictures release of a Walt Disney Pictures and Jerry Bruckheimer Films presentation of a Saturn Films/Broken Road production. Producer: Bruckheimer. Executive producers: Todd Garner, Nicolas Cage, Norman Golightly, Mike Stenson, Chad Oman, Barry Waldman. Director: Jon Turteltaub. Screenplay: Matt Lopez, Doug Miro, Carlo Bernard. Screen story: Lawrence Konner, Mark Rosenthal, Matt Lopez. Camera: Bojan Bazelli. Editor: William Goldenberg. Music: Trevor Rabin. In Technicolor (domestic), Technicolor, widescreen (international). Release date: July 8, 2010. MPAA Rating: PG. Running time: 108 Min.
Cast: Nicolas Cage, Jay Baruchel, Alfred Molina, Teresa Palmer, Monica Bellucci, Toby Kebbell, Alice Krige, Jake Cherry, Omar Benson Miller, Gregory Woo, James A. Stephens.

SPY NEXT DOOR

A Lionsgate release of a Relativity Media production. Producer: Robert Simonds. Executive producers: Ryan Kavanaugh, Tucker Tooley, Ira Shuman, Solon So. Co-producer, Kenneth Halsband. Director: Brian Levant. Screenplay: Jonathan Bernstein, James Greer, Gregory Poirier. Story: Bernstein, Greer. Camera: Dean Cundey. Editor: Lawrence Jordan. Music: David Newman. In Technicolor. Release date: Jan. 5, 2010. MPAA Rating: PG. Running time: 92 Min.
Cast: Jackie Chan, Amber Valletta, Madeline Carroll, Will Shadley, Alina Foley, Magnus Scheving, Katherine Boecher, Lucas Till, Billy Ray Cyrus, George Lopez.

STEP UP 3D

A Walt Disney Studios Motion Pictures release of a Touchstone Pictures and Summit Entertainment presentation of a Summit Entertainment production in association with Offspring Entertainment. Producer: Patrick Wachsberger, Erik Feig, Adam Shankman, Jennifer Gibgot. Executive producers: Bob Hayward, David Nicksay, Meredith Milton. Co-producer: Amy Herman. Director: Jon M. Chu. Screenplay: Amy Andelson, Emily Meyer, based on characters created by Duane Adler. Camera: Ken Seng. Editor: Andrew Marcus. Music: Bear McCreary. In color, 3D. Release date: July 31, 2010. MPAA Rating: PG-13. Running time: 106 Min.
Cast: Rick Malambri, Adam G. Sevani, Sharni Vinson, Alyson Stoner.

STEPFATHER, THE

A Sony Pictures Entertainment release of a Screen Gems presentation of a Maverick Films/Imprint Entertainment/Granada production. Producers: Mark Morgan, Greg Mooradian. Executive producers: Meredith Zamsky, J.S. Cardone, Guy Oseary, Robert Green, Julie Meldal-Johnsen. Co-producer: Jay Dykes. Director: Nelson McCormick. Screenplay: J.S. Cardone based on a screenplay by Donald E. Westlake; story, Carolyn Starin, Brian Garfield, Westlake. Camera: Patrick Cady. Editor: Eric L. Beason. Music: Charlie Clouser. In Deluxe color. Release date: Oct. 16, 2009. MPAA Rating: PG-13. Running time: 101 Min.
Cast: Dylan Walsh, Sela Ward, Penn Badgley, Amber Heard,

Stringfield, Paige Turco, Jon Tenney.

SWITCH

A Miramax release of a Miramax and Mandate Pictures presentation of a Bona Fide/Echo Films production. Producer: Albert Berger, Ron Yerxa. Executive producers: Jennifer Aniston, Kristin Hahn, Nathan Kahane. Co-producers: Brian Bell, Kelli Konop, Mary Lee, Allan Loeb, Steven Pearl. Directors: Josh Gordon, Will Speck. Screenplay: Allan Loeb, based on the short story "Baster" by Jeffrey Eugenides. Camera: Jess Hall. Editor: John Axelrad. Music: Alex Wurman. In color, Deluxe prints. Release date: Aug. 12, 2010. MPAA Rating: PG-13. Running time: 101 Min.
Cast: Jennifer Aniston, Jason Bateman, Thomas Robinson, Patrick Wilson, Jeff Goldblum, Juliette Lewis.

TAKERS

A Sony Pictures Entertainment release of a Screen Gems presentation of a Rainforest Films production in association with Grand Hustle Films. Producer: Will Packer, Tip "T.I." Harris, Jason Geter. Executive producers: Glenn S. Gainor, Gabriel Casseus, Chris Brown, Morris Chestnut. Co-producer: Nicolas Stern. Director: John Luessenhop. Screenplay: Peter Allen, Gabriel Casseus, Luessenhop, Avery Duff. Camera: Michael Barrett. Editor: Armen Minasian. Music: Paul Haslinger. In Deluxe color, Panavision widescreen. Release date: Aug. 13, 2010. MPAA Rating: PG-13. Running time: 107 Min.
Cast: Chris Brown, Hayden Christensen, Matt Dillon, Michael Ealy, Idris Elba, Steve Harris, Tip "T.I." Harris, Jay Hernandez, Johnathon Schaech, Paul Walker.

TOOTH FAIRY

A 20th Century Fox release presented with Walden Media of a Mayhem Pictures/Blumhouse production. Producers: Jason Blum, Mark Ciardi, Gordon Gray. Executive producer: Jim Piddock. Co-producer: Kevin Halloran. Director: Michael Lembeck. Screenplay: Lowell Ganz, Babaloo Mandel, Joshua Sternin, Jeffrey Ventimilia, Randi Mayem Singer. Story: Jim Piddock. David Tattersall. Editor: David Finfer. Music: George S. Clinton. In Deluxe color. Release date: Jan. 7, 2010. MPAA Rating: PG. Running time: 101 Min.
Cast: Dwayne Johnson, Ashley Judd, Stephen Merchant, Ryan Sheckler, Seth McFarlane, Julie Andrews, Chase Ellison, Destiny Grace Whitlock, Brandon T. Jackson, Billy Crystal.

TOY STORY 3

A Walt Disney Studios Motion Pictures release of a Walt Disney Pictures presentation of a Pixar Animation Studios production. Producer: Darla K. Anderson. Executive producer: John Lasseter. Director: Lee Unkrich. Screenplay: Michael Arndt. Story: John Lasseter, Andrew Stanton, Unkrich. Camera: Jeremy Lasky. Editor: Ken Schretzmann. Music: Randy Newman. In color, 3D. Release date: May 27, 2010. (In Taormina Film Festival) MPAA Rating: G. Running time: 102 Min.
Voices: Tom Hanks, Tim Allen, Joan Cusack, Ned Beatty, Don Rickles, Michael Keaton, Wallace Shawn, John Ratzenberger, Estelle Harris, John Morris, Jodi Benson, Emily Hahn.
With: Laurie Metcalf, Blake Clark, Teddy Newton, Bud Luckey, Beatrice Miller, Javier Fernandez-Pena, Timothy Dalton, Lori Alan, Charlie Bright, Kristen Schaal, Jeff Garlin, Bonnie Hunt, John Cygan, Jeff Pidgeon, Whoopi Goldberg, Jack Angel, R. Lee Ermey, Jan Rabson, Richard Kind.

THE TWILIGHT SAGA: ECLIPSE

A Summit Entertainment release and presentation of a Temple Hill production, in association with Maverick/Imprint, Sunswept Entertainment. Producers: Wyck Godfrey, Karen Rosenfelt. Executive producers: Marty Bowen, Greg Mooradian, Mark Morgan, Guy Oseary. Co-producer: Bill Bannerman. Director: David Slade. Screenplay: Melissa Rosenberg, based on the novel "Eclipse" by Stephenie Meyer. Camera: Javier Aguirresarobe. Editors: Art Jones, Nancy Richardson. Music: Howard Shore. In Deluxe color, Panavision widescreen. Release date: June 25, 2010. MPAA Rating: PG-13. Running time: 124 Min.
Cast: Kristen Stewart, Robert Pattinson, Taylor Lautner, Bryce Dallas Howard, Billy Burke, Dakota Fanning, Peter Facinelli, Elizabeth, Jackson Rathbone, Kellan Lutz, Ashley Greene, Nikki Reed.

THE TWILIGHT SAGA: NEW MOON

A Summit Entertainment (in U.S.)/SND Groupe M6 (in France) release of a Temple Hill production in association with Imprint Entertainment and Sunswept Entertainment. Producers: Wyck Godfrey, Karen Rosenfelt. Executive producers: Marty Bowen, Greg Mooradian, Mark Morgan, Guy Oseary. Co-producer: Bill Bannerman. Director: Chris Weitz. Screenplay: Melissa Rosenberg, based on the novel "New Moon" by Stephenie Meyer. Camera: Javier Aguirresarobe. Editor: Peter Lambert. Music: Alexandre Desplat. In Deluxe color, Panavision widescreen. Release date: Nov. 18, 2009. MPAA Rating: PG-13. Running time: 130 Min.
Cast: Kristen Stewart, Robert Pattinson, Taylor Lautner, Ashley Greene, Rachelle Lefevre, Bill Burke, Peter Facinelli, Nikki Reed, Kellan Lutz, Jackson Rathbone, Anna Kendrick, Michael Sheen, Dakota Fanning.

VALENTINES DAY

A Warner Bros. release of a New Line Cinema presentation of a Wayne Rice/Karz Entertainment production. Producer: Mike Karz, Rice. Executive producers: Toby Emmerich, Samuel J. Brown, Michael Disco, Diana Pokorny, Josie Rosen. Director: Garry Marshall. Screenplay: Katherine Fugate; Story: Fugate, Abby Kohn, Marc Silverstein. Camera: Charles Minsky. Editor: Bruce Green. Music: John Debney. In color. Release date: Feb. 4, 2010. MPAA Rating: PG-13. Running time: 124 Min.
Cast: Jessica Alba, Kathy Bates, Jessica Biel, Bradley Cooper, Eric Dane, Patrick Dempsey, Hector Elizondo, Jamie Foxx, Jennifer Garner, Topher Grace, Anne Hathaway, Carter Jenkins, Ashton Kutcher, Queen Latifah, Taylor Lautner, George Lopez, Shirley MacLaine, Emma Roberts, Bryce Robinson, Taylor Swift.

WHEN IN ROME

A Walt Disney Studios Motion Pictures release of a Touchstone Pictures presentation of a Gary Foster production. Producers: Gary Foster, Mark Steven Johnson, Andrew Panay. Executive producers: Mindy Farrell, Steven Roffer, Ezra Swerdlow. Co-producers: Rikki Lea Bestall, Kim Winther. Director: Mark Steven Johnson. Screenplay: David Diamond, David Weissman. Camera: John Bailey. Editors: Andrew Marcus, Ryan Folsey. Music: Christopher Young. In Technicolor. Release date: Jan. 27, 2010. MPAA Rating: PG-13. Running time: 91 Min.
Cast: Kristen Bell, Josh Duhamel, Anjelica Huston, Danny DeVito, Will Arnett, Jon Heder, Dax Shepard, Alexis Dziena, Kate Micucci, Peggy Lipton, Luca Calvani, Keir O'Donnell.

WINNING SEASON

A Lionsgate (in North America/U.K.) release of a Gigi Films and Plum Pictures presentation. Producers: Gia Walsh, Kara Baker, Daniela Taplin Lundberg, Celine Rattray, Galt Niederhoffer. Executive producers: Pamela Hirsch, Sam Rockwell, Joseph C. Grano, Andrea Grano, Daniel Crown, Nick Quested, Reagan Silber, Jeanne O'Brien, David Sweeney, Jamie Carmichael, Erick Kwak. Co-producers: George Paaswell, Riva Marker, Joy Goodwin. Director/writer: James C. Strouse. Camera: Frankie DeMarco. Editor: Joe Klotz. In 35mm-to-HD. Release date: Sept. 3, 2010. Running time: 100 Min.
Cast: Sam Rockwell, Emma Roberts, Shareeka Epps, Emily Rios, Rooney Mara, Meaghan Witri, Melanie Hinkle, Margo Martindale, Rob Corddry, Shana Dowdeswell.

WOLFMAN

A Universal release presented in association with Relativity Media of a Stuber Pictures production. Producers: Scott Stuber, Beneicio Del Toro, Rick Yorn, Sean Daniel. Executive producers: Bill Carraro, Jonathan Mone, Ryan Kavanaugh. Director: Joe Johnston. Screenplay: Andrew Kevin Walker, David Self, based on the motion picture screenplay by Curt Siodmak. Camera: Shelly Johnson. Editors: Dennis Virkler, Walter Murch. Music: Danny Elfman. In color. Release date: Feb. 8, 2010. MPAA Rating: R. Running time: 102 Min.
Cast: Benicio Del Toro, Anthony Hopkins, Emily Blunt, Hugo Weaving, Geraldine Chaplin, Art Malik, Antony Sher, David Schofield.

YOU AGAIN

A Walt Disney Studios Motion Pictures release of a Touchstone Pictures presentation of a Frontier Pictures production. Producers: John J. Strauss, Eric Tannenbaum, Andy Fickman. Executive producer: Mario Iscovich. Co-producer: Betsy Sullenger. Director: Andy Fickman. Screenplay: Moe Jelline. Camera: David Hennings. Editors: David Rennie, Keith Brachmann. Music: Nathan Wang. In Deluxe (domestic), Technicolor (international), widescreen. Release date: Sept. 22, 2010. MPAA Rating: PG. Running time: 105 Min.
With: Sean Wing, Kyle Bornheimer, Billy Unger, Christine Lakin, Meagan Holder, Patrick Duffy, Reginald VelJohnson, Daryl Hall, John Oates

YOUTH IN REVOLT

A Dimension Films release of a David Permut/Shangri-La Entertainment production. Producer: David Permut. Executive producers: Bob Weinstein, Harvey Weinstein, Nan Morales. Co-producers: Steve Longi, Miranda Freiberg. Director: Miguel Arteta. Screenplay: Gustin Nash, based on the novel "Youth in Revolt: The Journals of Nick Twisp" by C.D. Payne. Camera: Chuy Chavez. Editor: Pamela Martin, Andy Keir. Music: John Swihart. In color. Release date: Jan. 7, 2010. MPAA Rating: R. Running time: 90 Min.
With: Christa B. Allen, Ari Graynor, Adhir Kalyan, Erik Knudsen, Justin Long, Rooney Mara, M. Emmet Walsh, Fred Willard, Jonathan B. Wright.

ZOMBIELAND

A Sony Pictures Entertainment release of a Columbia Pictures presentation in association with Relativity Media of a Pariah production. Producer: Gavin Polone. Esecutive Producers: Ezra Swerdlow, Paul Wernick, Rhett Reese, Ryan Kavanaugh. Director: Ruben Fleischer. Screenplay: Rhett Reese, Paul Wernick. Camera: Michael Bonvillain. Editors: Peter Amundson, Alan Baumgarten. Music: David Sardy. In Deluxe color, Panavision widescreen. Release date: Sept. 23, 2009. MPAA Rating: R. Running time: 87 Min.
Cast: Woody Harrelson, Jesse Eisenberg, Emma Stone, Abigail Breslin, Amber Heard, Bill Murray, Derek Graf.

FOREIGN FEATURE FILMS

(OCTOBER 1, 2009—SEPTEMBER 30, 2010)

The distributor is followed by the release date, country of origin, the director (in parentheses), running time, and cast.

13 ASSASSINS
Sept. 8, 2010. Japanese, U.K. (Takashi Miike) Running time: 125 Min. Koji Yakusho, Takayuki Yamada, Yusuke Iseya, Goro Inagaki, Masachika Ichimura, Mikijiro Hira, Hiroki Matsukata, Ikki Sawamura, Arata Furuta, Tsuyoshi Ihara, Masataka Kubota, Sousuke Takaoka, Seiji Rokkaku, Koen Kondo, Yuma Ishigaki, Kazuki Namioka, Kazue Fukiishi, Koshiro Matsumoto, Mitsuki Tanimura, Takumi Saito, Shinnosuke Abe, Masaaki Uchino, Ken Mitsuishi, Ittoku Kishibe.

14 BLADES
INTERCONTINENTAL FILM DISTRIBUTORS. March 22, 2010. Chinese. (Daniel Lee) Running time: 113 Min.

22 BULLETS
EUROPACORP. March 29, 2010. French. (Richard Berry) Running time: 115 Min. Jean Reno, Kad Merad, Jean-Pierre Darroussin, Marina Fois, Luc Palun, Richard Berry, Joey Starr, Dominique Thomas, Martial Bezot, Daniel Lundh, Max Baissette De Malglaive.

4.3.2.1
UNIVERSAL. June 2, 2010. U.K. (Noel Clarke, Mark Davis) Running time: 117 Min. Emma Roberts, Tamsin Egerton, Ophelia Lovibond, Shanika Warren-Markland, Noel Clarke, Gregg Chillin, Adam Deacon, Eve, Susannah Fielding, Kevin Smith, Jacob Anderson, Mandy Patinkin, Michelle Ryan, Ben Miller, Camille Coduri, Helen McCrory, Kate Magowan, Sean Pertwee.

72 TENANTS OF PROSPERITY
MEGA-VISION PICTURES (IN HONG KONG). Feb 11, 2010. Chinese. (D) Running time: 97 Min.

7TH DIMENSION, THE
KALEIDOSCOPE HOME ENTERTAINMENT. July 6, 2010. U.K. (Brad Watson) Running time: 95 Min. Kelly Adams, Jonathan Rhodes, Lucy Evans, Calita Rainford, David Horton.

A SURPRISE IN TEXAS
PETER ROSEN PRODS. May, 2010. Japanese. (Peter Rosen) Running time: 92 Min. Nobuyuki Tsujii, Zhang Haochen, Yeol Eum-son, Di Wu, Evgeni Bozhanov, Mariangela Vacatello, Menahem Pressler, John Giorrano, James Condon, John Davidson, Carol Davidson. Documentary.

ABACUS AND SWORD
ASMIK ACE/SHOCHIKU. Sept. 1, 2010. Japanese. (Yoshimitsu Morita) Running time: 129 Min. Masato Sakai, Yukie Nakama, Keiko Matsuzaka, Masahiko Nishimura, Mitsuko Kusabue, Masatoshi Nakamura.

ABOUT HER BROTHER
SHOCHIKU. Feb. 20, 2010. Japanese. (Yoji Yamada) Running time: 126 Min. Sayuri Yoshinaga, Tsurube Shofukutei, Yu Aoi, Ryo Kase, Yuriko Ishida, Takashi Sasano, Fumiyo Kohinata, Nenji Kobayashi, Haruko Kato, Gajiro Satoh, Koen Kondo, Leo Morimoto, Midoriko Kimura, Rasaru Ishii, Akio Yokoyama, Medaka Ikeno, Sotaro Tanaka.

AFRICA UNITED
PATHE (IN U.K.). Sept. 16, 2010. U.K., South African, Rwandan. (Debs Gardner-Paterson) Running time: 85 Min. Eriya Ndayambaje, Roger Nsengiyumva, Sanyu Joanita Kintu, Yves Dusenge, Sherrie Silver. Narrator: Eriya Ndayambaje.

ALL ABOUT LOVE
A. Sept. 13, 2010. Chinese. (Ann Hui) Running time: 105 Min. Sandra Ng, Vivian Chow, Eddie Cheug, William Chan, Joey Meng, Jo Koo.

AMPHETAMINE
Jan. 19, 2010. Chinese. (Scud) Running time: 97 Min. Byron Pang, Thomas Price, Linda So, Winnie Leung, Simon Tam, Peng Lihua, Sun Cheng-kok, Tung Wai-keung, Liu Wing-yiu, Lam Tin-yan, Paul Fonoroff.

ANIMAL KINGDOM
A. Jan. 22, 2010. Austrailian. (David Michod) Running time: 112 Min. Ben Mendelsohn, Joel Edgerton, Guy Pearce, Luke Ford, Jacki Weaver, Sullivan Stapleton, James Frencheville, Dan Wyllie, Anthony Hayes, Laura Wheelwright, Mirrah Foulkes, Justin Rosniak, Susan Prior, Clayton Jacobson, Anna Lisa Phillips.

ANOTHER YEAR
SONY PICTURES CLASSICS. May 15, 2010. U.K. (Mike Leigh) Running time: 129 Min. Jim Broadbent, Ruth Sheen, Lesley Manville, Oliver Maltman, Peter Wight, David Bradley, Martin Savage, Karina Fernandez, Michele Austin, Phil Davis, Imelda Staunton.

ANPO: ART X WAR
Sept. 11, 2010. Japanese, U.S. (Linda Hoaglund) Running time: 89 Min. Ishiuchi Miyako, Nakamura Hiroshi, Yokoo Tadanori, Aida Makoto, Asakura Setsu.

ARBOR, THE
April 12, 2010. U.K. (Clio Barnard) Running time: 94 Min. Manjinder Virk, Christine Bottomley, Neil Dudgeon, Monica Dolan, Danny Webb, Kathryn Pogson, Natalie Gavin, Jonathan Haynes, Jimi Mistry, George Costigan.

ARTHUR AND THE REVENGE OF MALTAZARD
EUROPACORP DISTRIBUTION. Dec., 2009. French. (Luc Besson) Running time: 93 Min. Freddie Highmore, Mia Farrow, Ronald Crawford, Robert Stanton, Penny Balfour, Jean Bejote Njamba, Lou Reed, Selena Gomez, Snoop Dogg, Stacy Ferguson. (Luc Besson)

BEAUTIFUL ISLANDS
ELEVEN ARTS (IN U.S.). July 3, 2010. Japanese. (Tomoko Kana) Running time: 106 Min. Enele Sopoaga, Davide Signoretto, Claudio Staderini, Raymond Weyiouanna, Melanie Weyiouanna. Documentary.

FIRST BEAUTIFUL THING, THE
MEDUSA. Jan., 2010. Italian. Valerio Mastandrea, Micaela Ramazzotti, Stefania Sandrelli, Claudia Pandolfi, Marco Messeri, Fabrizia Sacchi, Aurora Frasca, Giacomo Bibbiani, Giulia Burgalassi, Francesco Rapalino, Sergio Albelli, Isabella Cecchi, Emanuele Barresi, Dario Ballantini, Paolo Ruffini, Fabrizio Brandi, Bobo Rondelli, Michele Crestacci, Isabelle Adriani, Paolo Giommarelli, Marco Risi. (Paolo Virzi) Running time: 122 Min.

BENEATH HILL 60
TRANSMISSION, PARAMOUNT. April 7, 2010. Austrailian. (Jeremy Hartley Sims) Running time: 121 Min. Brendan Cowell, Steve Le Marquand, Gyton Grantley, Chris Haywood, Jacqueline McKenzie, Harrison Gilbertson, Aden Young, John Stanton.

BEYOND THE POLE
Jan. 8, 2010. U.K. (David L. Williams) Running time: 87 Min.

BLACK DEATH
Feb. 11, 2010. U.K., German. (Christopher Smith) Running time: 101 Min.

BLACK SHEEP, THE
BIM DISTRIBUZIONE. Sept. 2010. Italian. (Ascanio Celestini) Running time: 96 Min. Ascanio Celestini, Giorgio Tirabassi, Maya Sansa, Luisa De Santis, Nicola Rignanese, Barbara Valmorin, Luigi Fedele, Teresa Saponangelo.

BLACK VENUS
MK2. Sept. 7, 2010. French. (Abdellatif Kechiche) Running time: 165 Min. With: Yahima Torres, Andre Jacobs, Olivier Gourmet, Elina Lowensohn, Francois Marthouret, Michel Gionti, Jean-Christophe Bouvet. (Afrikaans, French, English, Dutch dialogue)

BLAME
ROADSHOW FILMS. Sept. 13, 2010. Austrailian. (Michael Henry) Running time: 89 Min. Damian de Montemas, Sophie Lowe, Kestie Morassi, Simon Stone, Mark Leonard Winter, Ashley Zuckerman, Greg McNeill.

BONDED BY BLOOD
REVOLVER FILMS. Aug 20, 2010. U.K. (Sacha Bennett) Running time: 96 Min. Tamer Hassan, Vincent Regan, Terry Stone, Adam Deacon, Neil Maskell, Kierston Wareing, Dave Legeno, Alex MacQueen, Michael Socha.

BOX: THE HAKAMADA CASE
SLOW LEARNER. Sept. 3, 2010. Japanese. (Banmei Takahashi) Running time: 117 Min. Masato Hagiwara, Hirofumi Arai, Ryo Ishibashi, Naoki Hosaka, Riona Hazuki.

BRIGHTON ROCK
Sept. 12, 2010. U.K. (Rowan Joffe) Running time: 111 Min. Sam Riley, Andrea Riseborough, Phil Davis, Sean Harris, John Hurt, Helen Mirren.

CAMERAMAN: THE LIFE & WORK OF JACK CARDIFF
OPTIMUM RELEASING. May 4, 2010. U.K. (Craig McCall) Running time: 86 Min. Jack Cardiff, Martin Scorsese, Kirk Douglas, Lauren Bacall, Charlton Heston, Kim Hunter, John Mills, Alan Parker, Thelma Schoonmaker, Freddie Francis, Raffaella De Laurentiis, Richard Fleischer, Peter Yates, Kathleen Byron, Christopher Challis, Kevin McClory, Ian Christie, Moira Shearer, Michel Ciment, Peter Handford, George E. Turner, Michael Powell.

CASE 39
PARAMOUNT VANTAGE. Sept. 29, 2010. Canadian. (Christian Alvart) Running time: 104 Min. Renee Zellweger, Jodelle Ferland, Ian McShane, Bradley Cooper.

CATERPILLAR
Feb. 14, 2010. Japanese. (Koji Wakamatsu) Running time: 84 Min. Shinobu Terajima, Shima Ohnishi, Ken Yoshizawa, Keigo Kasuya, Emi Masuda, Sabu Kawahara, Maki Ishikaw, Katsuyuki Shinohara.

CENTURION
WARNER BROS. Feb. 12, 2010. U.K. (Neil Marshall) Running time: 97 Min. Michael Fassbender, Dominic West, J.J. Feild, Lee Ross, David Morrissey, Ulrich Thomsen, Ryan Atkinson, Paul Freeman, Olga Kurylenko, Liam Cunningham, Noel Clarke, Dimitri, Riz Ahmed, Imogen Poots.

CHATROOM
May 14, 2010. U.K. (Hideo Nakata) Running time: 97 Min. Aaron Johnson, Imogen Poots, Hannah Murray, Daniel Kaluuya, Matthew Beard, Megan Dodds, Jacob Anderson, Rebecca McLintock, Richard Madden.

CHICO AND RITA
Sept. 4, 2010. Spanish. (Fernando Trueba, Javier Mariscal, Tono Errando) Running time: 93 Min.

CHILD'S EYE 3D, THE
UNIVERSE ENTERTAINMENT. Sept. 4, 2010. Chinese. (Danny Pang) Running time: 96 Min. Rainie Yang, Elanne Kwong, Lam Ka Tung, Jo Koo, Ciwi Lam, Izz Xu, Rex Ho, Shawn Yue.

CIRKUS COLUMBIA
July 23, 2010. Bosnia, Herzegovina, France, U.K., Slovenia, Germany, Belgium, Serbia. (Danis Tanovic) Miki Manojlovic, Mira Furlan, Jelena Stupljanin, Boris Ler, Mario Knezovic.

COLD FISH
Sept. 7, 2010. Japanese. (Sion Sono) Running time: 145 Min. Mitsuru Kukikoshi, Denden, Asuka Kurosawa, Megumi Kagurazaka, Hikari Kajiwara, Tetsu Watanabe.

CONFESSIONS
TOHO CO. July 1, 2010. Japanese. (Tetsuya Nakashima) Running time: 106 Min. Takako Matsu, Yukito Nishii, Kaoru Fujiwara, Ai Hashimoto, Masaki Okada, Yoshino Kimura.

COPACABANA
MARS DISTRIBUTION. May 5, 2010. French, Belgian. (Marc Fitoussi. Running time: 105 Min. Isabelle Huppert, Lolita Chammah, Aure Atika, Jurgen Delnaet, Chantal Banlier, Magali Woch, Nelly Antignac, Guillaume Gouix, Joachim Lombard, Noemie Lvovsky, Luis Rego.

CROSSING HENNESSY
A. June 11, 2010. Chinese. (Ivy Ho) Running time: 108 Min. Jacky Cheung, Tang Wei, Paw Hee-ching, Danny Lee, Andy On, Maggie Cheung Ho-yee, Mimi Chu, Lam Wai, Kwok Fung, Gill Mohindepaul Singh, Lowell Lo.

CRYING WITH LAUGHTER
FILMBUFF (IN U.S.). March 17, 2010. U.K. (Justin Molotnikov) Running time: 93 Min. Stephen McCole, Malcolm Shields, Andrew Neil, Jo Hartley, Olivia McEwan, Paul McCole, Laura Keenan.

DARK LOVE
FANDANGO. Sept. 1 2010. Italian. (D) Running time: 109 Min. Irene De Angelis, Gabriele Agrio, Luisa Ranieri, Corso Salani, Valeria Golino, Anna Ammirati.

DEBT, THE
MIRAMAX FILMS . Aug. 25, 2010. U.K. (John Madden) Running time: 112 Min. Sam Worthington, Helen Mirren, Tom Wilkinson, Ciaran Hinds, Jessica Chastain, Marton Csokas, Jesper Christensen.

DETECTIVE DEE AND THE MYSTERY OF PHANTOM FLAME
HUAYI BROTHERS MEDIA CORP. Sept. 5, 2010. Chinese. (Tsui Hark) Running time: 123 Min. Andy Lau, Li Bingbing, Carina Lau, Deng Chao, Tony Leung Ka-fai.

DEVIL'S PLAYGROUND
May 15, 2010. U.K. (Mark McQueen) Running time: 92 Min. Danny Dyer, Craig Fairbrass, MyAnna Buring, Colin Salmon, Shane Taylor, Jaime Murray, Lisa McAllister, Jack Healy, Craig Conway, Del Henney.

DIRTY GIRL
WEINSTEIN CO. Sept. 12, 2010. U.K. (Abe Sylvia) Running time: 106 Min. Jeremy Dozier, Juno Temple, Milla Jovovich, William H. Macy, Mary Steenburgen, Dwight Yoakam.

DRAQUILA - ITALY TREMBLES
BIM. May, 2010. Italian. (Sabina Guzzanti) Running time: 94 Min. Massimo Cialento, Stefania Pezzopane, Giovanni Lolli, Angelo Venti, Giustino Masciocco, Giuliano Santelli, Paola Agnello Modica, Giovanni Ciancio, Marta La Ponzina, Riccardo Corbucci, Manuele Bonaccorsi, Georg Frisch, Fausto Corti, Carlo Costantini, Antonio Ingroia, Vincenzo Macri, Fabrizio Curcio, Roberto De Marco, Enzo Boschi. Documentary.

DREAM HOME
EDKO FILM. May 14, 2010. Chinese. (Pang Ho-cheung) Running time: 94 Min. Josie Ho, Eason Chan, Derek Tsang, Lawrence Chou, Juno Mak, Michelle Ye, Norman Chui, Wong Ching, Eason Chan.

EXIT THROUGH THE GIFT SHOP
PARANOID PICTURES FILM/CINETIC (INTERNATIONAL). Jan. 24, 2010. U.K. (Banksy) Running time: 86 Min. Narrator: Rhys Ifans.

EXTRAORDINARY ORDINARY LIFE OF JOSE GONZALEZ, THE
FOLKETS BIO. Feb. 2, 2010. Swedish. (Fredrik Egerstrand, Mikel Cee Karlsson) Running time: 75 Min. Jose Gonzalez, Yukimi Nagano, Erik Bodin. Documentary.

F
OPTIMUM RELEASING. Sept. 14, 2010. U.K. (Johannes Roberts) Running time: 79 Min. David Schofield, Eliza Bennett, Ruth Gemmell, Finlay Robertson, Roxanne McKee, Juliet Aubrey, Emma Cleasby, Tom Mannion, Max Fowler, Jamie Kenna.

FIRE OF CONSCIENCE
A. March 23, 2010. Chinese. (Dante Lam) Running time: 108 Min.

FIRST GRADER, THE
Sept. 6 , 2010. U.K. (Justin Chadwick) Running time: 99 Min.

FIVE CARDINAL POINTS, THE
April 12, 2010. Austrian. (Fridolin Schoenwiese) Running time: 94 Min. Maria Esther Solis, Miguel de la o Ochoa.

FOUR LIONS
FILM4. Jan. 22, 2010. U.K. (Chris Morris.) Running time: 102 Min. Riz Ahmed, Arsher Ali, Nigel Lindsay, Kayvan Novak, Adeel Akhtar, Benedict Cumberbatch, Julia Davis, Craig Parkinson, Preeya Kalidas, Wasim Zakir, Mohammad Aqil.

FROM PARIS WITH LOVE
LIONSGATE. Jan. 27, 2010. French. (Pierre Morel) Running time: 92 Min. John Travolta, Jonathan Rhys Meyers, Kasia Smutniak, Richard Durden, Bing Yin, Amber Rose Revah, Eric Godon, Chems Eddine Dahmani.

FROZEN
ANCHOR BAY FILMS. Jan. 26, 2010. Chinese. (Adam Green) Running time: 93 Min. Emma Bell, Shawn Ashmore, Kevin Zegers.

GAINSBOURG (VIE HEROIQUE)
UNIVERSAL PICTURES FRANCEA. French. (Joann Sfar) Running time: 134 Min. Eric Elmosnino, Lucy Gordon, Laetitia Casta Doug Jones, Anna Mouglalis, Mylene Jampanoi, Sara Forestier, Kacey Mottet-Klein.

GALLANTS
July 8, 2010. Chinese. (Derek Kwok) Running time: 97 Min. Bruce Leung, Chen Kuan-tai, Teddy Robin, J.J. Jia, Chan Wai-man, Susan Shaw, Wong You-nam, MC Jin.

GENPIN
Sept. 17, 2010. Japanese. (Naomi Kawase) Running time: 92 Min. Tadashi Yoshimura. Documentary.

GHOST WRITER, THE
PATHE (IN FRANCE)/KINOWELT (IN GERMANY)/CONTENDER (IN U.K.)/SUMMIT ENTERTAINMENT (IN U.S.). Feb. 12, 2010. French, German, U.K. (Roman Polanski) Running time: 126 Min. Ewan McGregor, Pierce Brosnan, Kim Cattrall, Olivia Williams, Tom Wilkinson, Timothy Hutton, James Belushi, Robert Pugh, Eli Wallach, Jon Bernthal.

GIRL WHO KICKED THE HORNET'S NEST, THE
NORDISK FILM. March 15, 2010. U.K. (Daniel Alfredson) Running time: 146 Min. Noomi Rapace, Michael Nyqvist, Annika Hallin, Per Oscarsson, Lena Endre, Peter Andersson, Jacob Ericksson, Sofia Ledarp, Johan Kylen, Tanja Lorentzon, Mirja Turestedt, Anders Ahlbom Rosendahl, Magnus Krepper, Michalis Koutsogiannakis, Niklas Hjulstrom, Hans Alfredson, Aksel Morisse.

GOLDEN SLUMBER
TOHO CO. Jan. 23, 2010. Japanese. (Yoshihiro Nakamura) Running time: 140 Min. Masato Sakai, Yuko Takeuchi, Hidetaka Yoshioka, Gekidan Hitori, Nao Omori, Sango Kitamura, Ken-ichi Takito, Shihori Kanjiya, Kiyohiko Shibukawa, Saki Aibu, Fumio Ito, Kenjiro Ishimaru, Zheng Longjin, Raita Ryu, Teruyuki Kagawa.

HAPPY FAMILY
01 DISTRIBUTION. Mar. 2010. Italian. (Gabriele Salvatores) Running time: 92 Min. Fabio De Luigi, Diego Abatantuono, Fabrizio Bentivoglio, Margherita Buy, Carla Signoris, Valeria Bilello, Gianmaria Biancuzzi, Alice Croci, Corinna Agustoni, Sandra Milo, Man Lo Zhang.

HAPPY FEW
LE PACTE. Sept. 2, 2010. French. (Antony Cordier) Running time: 104 Min. Marina Fois, Elodie Bouchez, Roschdy Zem, Nicolas Duvauchelle, Jean-Francois Stevenin, Alexia Stresi, Blanche Gardin.

HARIMAYA BRIDGE, THE
ELEVEN ARTS (IN U.S.). March 27, 2010. Japanese. (Aaron Woolfolk) Running time: 120 Min. Ben Guillory, Saki Takaoka, Misa Shimizu, Danny Glover, Victor Grant, Misono, Miho Shiraishi.

HEARTBREAKER
UNIVERSAL PICTURES INTL. FRANCE (IN FRANCE). March 18, 2010. French, U.K. (Pascal Chaumeil) Running time: 104 Min. Romain Duris, Vanessa Paradis, Julie Ferrier, Francois Damiens, Helena Noguerra, Andrew Lincoln, Jacques Frantz, Amandine Dewasmes, Jean-Yves Lafesse, Jean-Marie Paris.

HOW TO LIVE FOREVER
Feb. 14, 2010. Japanese. (Mark Wexler) Running time: 94 Min. Phyllis Diller, Jack LaLanne, Jonathan Gold, Aubrey de Grey, Suzanne

Somers.

HUMAN RESOURCES MANAGER, THE
Aug. 9, 2010. Israeli, German, French, Romanian. (D) Running time: 103 Min. Mark Ivanir, Guri Alfi, Noah Silver, Rozina Cambos, Julian Negulesco, Bogdan Stanoevitch, Gila Almagor, Irina Petrescu, Papil Panduru, Ofir Weil, Roni Koren, Galina Ozerner.

I HATE LUV STORYS
July 9, 2010. Indian. (Punit Malhotra) Running time: 133 Min. Sonam Kapoor, Imran Khan, Sammir Dattani, Samir Soni, Bruna Abdalah, Aseem Tiwari.

ILLUSIONIST, THE
Feb. 16, 2010. U.K., French (Sylvain Chomet) Running time: 78 Min.

INFIDEL, THE
TRIBECA FILM. Apr. 10, 2010. U.K. (Josh Appignanesi) Running time: 104 Min. Omid Djalili, Richard Schiff, Archie Panjabi, Amit Shah, Igal Naor, Mina Anwar, Soraya Radford.

INVISIBLE EYE, THE
PYRAMIDE DISTRIBUTION (IN FRANCE). May 14, 2010. U.K. (D) Running time: 97 Min. Julieta Zylberberg, Osmar Nunez, Marta Lubos, Gaby Ferrero, Diego Vegezzi, Pablo Sigal.

ITO - A DIARY OF AN URBAN PRIEST
May 5, 2010. Finish. (Pirjo Honkasalo) Running time: 111 Min. Documentary.

IT'S A WONDERFUL AFTERLIFE
Jan. 26, 2010. U.K. (Gurinder Chadha) Running time: 99 Min. Shabana Azmi, Goldy Notay, Sendhil Ramamurthy, Sally Hawkins, Sanjeev Bhaskar, Shaheen Khan, Jimi Mistry, Zoe Wanamaker, Mark Addy, Adlyn Ross, Ash Varrez, Ray Panthaki, Jack Gordon, Jamie Sives, Don Warrington.

JACKBOOTS ON WHITEHALL
June 18, 2010. U.S., U.K. (Edward McHenry, Rory McHenry) Running time: 93 Min. Ewan McGregor, Alan Cumming, Richard E. Grant, Richard Griffiths, Rosamund Pike, Sanjeev Bhaskar, Timothy Spall, Dominic West, Tom Wilkinson, Stephen Merchant, Richard O'Brien.

JULIA'S EYES
UNIVERSAL PICTURES INTL. SPAIN. Aug 25, 2010. Spanish. (Guillem Morales) Running time: 112 Min. Belen Rueda, Lluis Homar, Pablo Derqui, Francesc Orella, Joan Dalmau, Boris Ruiz, Andrea Hermosa, Julia Gutierrez Caba.

KARTHIK CALLING KARTHIK
EROS ENTERTAINMENT. March 1, 2010. Indian. (Vijay Lalwani) Running time: 135 Min.

KHATTA MEETHA
HARI OM ENTERTAINMENT CO., SHREE ASHTAVINAYAK CINEVISION (IN INDIA)/EROS INTL. (INTERNATIONAL). July 25, 2010. Indian. (Priyadarshan) Running time: 155 Min. Akshay Kumar, Trisha Krishnan, Makrand Deshpande, Kainaat Arora.

KINGS OF MYKONOS, THE
TRANSMISSION, PARAMOUNT. May 4, 2010. Austrailian. (Peter Andrikidis) Running time: 101 Min. Nick Giannopoulos, Vince Colosimo, Alex Dimitriades, Zeta Makrypoulia, Cosima Coppola, Kevin Sorbo, Costas Kilias.

KISS ME AGAIN
MEDUSA. Jan. 2010. Italian, French. (Gabriele Muccino) Running time: 139 Min. Stefano Accorsi, Vittoria Puccini, Pierfrancesco Favino, Claudio Santamaria, Giorgio Pasotti, Marco Cocci, Sabrina Impacciatore, Daniela Piazza, Primo Reggiani, Francesca Valtorta, Adriano Giannini, Valeria Bruni Tedeschi, Sara Girolami, Andrea Calligari.

KITES
RELIANCE BIG PICTURES (WORLDWIDE). May 17, 2010. Indian. (Anurag Basu) Running time: 133 Min. Hrithik Roshan, Barbara Mori, Kangana Ranaut, Kabir Bedi, Nick Brown, Anand Tiwari, Yuri Suri.

LABOR COURT
LOOK NOW!. Aug. 8, 2010. Swiss. (Stephane Goel) Running time: 88 Min. Philippe Colelough, Valerie Foray.

LAST CIRCUS, THE
Sept. 6, 2010. Spanish, French. (Alex de la Iglesia) Running time: 105 Min.

LEGEND OF THE FIST: THE RETURN OF CHEN ZHEN
MEDIA ASIA DISTRIBUTION. Aug. 31, 2010. Chinese. (Andrew Lau) Running time: 104 Min. Donnie Yen, Shu Qi, Anthony Wong, Huang Bo, Kohata Ryuichi, Huo Si-yan, Zhou Yang, Shawn Yu, Kurata Yasuaki, Akira.

LIGHTS OUT
A. May 3, 2010. French. (Fabrice Gobert) Running time: 84 Min. Jules Pelissier, Ana Girardot, Serge Riaboukine, Laurent Capelluto, Arthur Mazet, Laurent Delbecque, Yan Tassin, Selma El Mouissi, Esteban Carvajal-Alegria, Audrey Bastien.

LITTLE BIG SOLDIER
A. Feb. 16, 2010. Chinese. (Ding Sheng) Running time: 95 Min. Jackie Chan, Wang Leehom, Steve Yoo, Lin Peng, Du Yuming, Jin Song, Xu Dongmei, Low Houi-kang, Yu Rongguang, Wu Yue, Wang Baoqiang, Niu Ben.

LITTLE WHITE LIES
EUROPACORP DISTRIBUTION. Aug. 30, 2010. French. (Guillaume Canet) Running time: 154 Min. Francois Cluzet, Marion Cotillard, Magimel, Gilles Lellouche, Jean Dujardin, Laurent Lafitte, Velerie Bonneton, Pascale Arbillot.

LOOSE CANNONS
DOMENICO PROCACCI. Feb., 2010. Italian. (Ferzan Ozpetek) Running time: 112 Min. Riccardo Scamarcio, Nicole Grimaudo, Alessandro Preziosi, Ennio Fantastichini, Lunetta Savino, Ilaria Occhini, Elena Sofia Ricci, Bianca Nappi, Massimiliano Gallo, Paola Minaccioni, Emanuela Gabrieli, Carolina Crescentini, Giorgio Marchese, Matteo Taranto, Carmine Recano, Daniela Pecci, Gianluca De Marchi, Mauro Bonaffini.

LOVE IN A PUFF
MEDIA ASIA DISTRIBUTION. June 11, 2010. Chinese. (Pang Ho-cheung) Running time: 92 Min. Miriam Yeung, Shawn Yue, Cheung Tat-ming, Maio Felin, Chui Tien-you.

MADE IN DAGENHAM
SONY PICTURES CLASSICS (IN U.S.). Sept. 10, 2010. U.K. (Nigel Cole) Running time: 112 Min. Sally Hawkins, Bob Hoskins, Miranda Richardson, Geraldine James, Rosamund Pike, Andrea Riseborough, Daniel Mays, Jaime Winstone.

MAI MAI MIRACLE
A. March 6, 2010. Japanese. (Sunao Katabuchi) Running time: 95 Min.

MAKE BELIEVE
June 24, 2010. Japanese. (Clay Tweel) Running time: 89 Min. Hiroki Hara, Bill Koch, Krystyn Lambert, Derek McKee, Siphiwe Fangase, Nkumbuzo Nkonyana, Jeff McBride, Lance Burton, Chris Angel. Documentary.

MANOLETE
A. April 4, 2010. Spanish, U.K., U.S., French. (Menno Meyjes) Running time: 90 Min. Adrien Brody, Penelope Cruz, Santiago Segura, Juan Echanove, Ann Mitchell, Josep Lineusa, Nacho Aldeguer, Pedro Casablanc.

MATCHMAKER, THE
6 SALES. Sept. 11, 2010. Israeli. (Avi Nesher) Running time: 110 Min. Adir Miller, Maya Dagan, Dror Keren, Dov Navon, Tuval Shafir, Neta Porat, Yarden Bar-Kochva, Bat-el Papura, Kobi Farag, Yael Leventhal, Tom Gal, Eyal Shechter.

MIYOKO
WIDES SHUPPAN. Jan. 29, 2010. Japanese. (Yoshifumi Tsubota) Running time: 85 Min. Kenji Mizuhashi, Marie Machida, Shoichi Honda, Yuya Matsuura, Anji, Kan Mikami, Seichi Hayashi, Shiro Sano Documentary.

MONSTERS
MAGNET RELEASING (IN U.S.). March 19, 2010. U.K. (Gareth Edwards) Running time: 97 Min. Scoot McNairy, Whitney Able.

MOUTH OF THE WOLF, THE
BIM DISTRIBUZIONE. Dec. 2010. Italian. (Pietro Marcello) Running time: 67 Min. Narrator: Franco Leo. Documentary.

MR. NICE
INDEPENDENT. March 14, 2010. U.K. (Bernard Rose) Running time: 120 Min. Rhys Ifans, Chloe Sevigny, David Thewlis, Luis Tosar, Elsa Pataky, Omid Djalili, Crispin Glover, Jamie Harris, Christian McKay, Jack Huston.

MY DARLING IS A FOREIGNER
March 23, 2010. Japanese. (Kazuaki Ue) Running time: 96 Min. March 23, 2010. Mao Inoue, Jonathan Sherr, Jun Kunimura.

MY KIDNAPPER
Aug. 6, 2010. U.K., Colombian, German. (Mark Henderson, Kate Horne) Running time: 83 Min. Mark Henderson, Reinihilt Weigel, Ido Guy, Erez Eltawil.

MY NAME IS KHAN
FOX SEARCHLIGHT (IN U.S.). Feb. 18, 2010. Indian. (Karan Johar.) Running time: 160 Min. Shah Rukh Khan, Kajol, Katie Keane, Kenton Duty, Benny Nieves, Christopher B. Duncan, Jimmy Shergill, Sonya Jehan, Parvin Dabbas, Arjun Mathur, Sugandha Garg, Zarina Wahab, Tanay Chedda, S.M. Zaheer, Arif Zakaria, Vinay Pathak, Sumeet Raghavan, Tarun Mansukhani, Navneet Nishan, Sheetal Menon, Arjan Aujla, Yuvaan Makar, Jennifer Echols, Adrian Kali Turner, Michael Arnold, Dominic Renda.

MY PERESTROIKA
Jan. 25, 2010. U.S., U.K. (Robin Hessman) Running time: 87 Min. Olga Durikova, Borya Meyerson, Lyuba Meyerson, Mark Meyerson, Ruslan Stupin, Andrei Yevgrafov.

NAINSUKH
Sept. 8, 2010. Indian, Swiss. (Amit Dutta) Running time: 96 Min. Manish Soni, Nitin Goel, K. Rajesh, Sriniwas Joshi, Yamini Joshi, Sat Salarwi, Mohan Singh, Anil Raina, Gautam Vyathit, Ankit Raina, Pushpendra Singh, Brahmaswaroop Mishra, Shubham Vardhan, Dhananjai Singh, Samarth Dixit, Amit Singh, Ajit Singh Rathore, Vishnu Tailor.

NANNY MCPHEE AND THE BIG BANG
March 18 2010. U.K., U.S., French. (Susanna White) Running time: 109 Min. Emma Thompson, Maggie Gyllenhaal, Rhys Ifans, Maggie Smith, Sam Kelly, Sinead Matthews, Katy Brand, Oscar Steer, Asa Butterfield, Lil Woods, Eros Vlahos, Rosie Taylor-Ritson, Daniel Mays, Ralph Fiennes, Ewan McGregor.

NEDS
Sept. 16, 2010. U.K., French, Italian. (Peter Mullan) Running time: 124 Min. Conor McCarron, Gregg Forrest, Joe Szula, Mhairi Anderson, Gary Milligan, John Joe Hay, Christopher Wallace, Martin Bell, Peter Mullan, Louise Goodall, Marianna Palka, Laurie Ventry.

NEVER LET ME GO
FOX SEARCHLIGHT (IN U.S.). Sept. 3, 2010. U.K. (Mark Romanek) Running time: 104 Min. Carey Mulligan, Andrew Garfield, Keira Knightley, Isobel Meikle-Small, Ella Purnell, Charlie Rowe, Charlotte Rampling, Sally Hawkins, Nathalie Richard, Andrea Riseborough, Domhnall Gleeson.

NOBODY TO WATCH OVER ME
TOHO. Jan. 9, 2010. Japanese. (Ryoichi Kimizuka) Running time: 118 Min. Koichi Sato, Mirai Shida, Ryuhei Matsuda, Yuriko Ishida, Kuranosuke Sasaki, Shiro Sano, Yoshino Kimura Toshiro Yanagiba.

NORWEGIAN WOOD
Sept. 1, 2010. Japanese. (Tran Anh Hung) Running time: 133 Min. Kenichi Matsuyama, Rinko Kikuchi, Kiko Mizuhara, Reika Kirishima, Kengo Kora, Eriko Hatsune, Tetsuji Tamayama.

ONCE A GANGSTER
MEDIA ASIA. May 29, 2010. Chinese. (Felix Chong) Running time: 94 Min. Ekin Cheng, Jordan Chan, Alex Fong, Chan Chi-chung, Wilfred Lau, Michelle Ye, Yu On-on, Derrek Tsang.

OUR LIFE
01 DISTRIBUTION. May, 2010. Italian. (Daniele Luchetti) Running time: 100 Min. Elio Germano, Raoul Bova, Isabella Ragonese, Luca Zingaretti, Stefania Montorsi, Giorgio Colangeli, Alina Madalina Berzunteanu, Marius Ignat, Awa Ly, Emiliano Campagnola.

OUTRAGE
WARNER BROS. (INTERNATIONAL). May 16, 2010. Japanese. (Takeshi Kitano) Running time: 110 Min. Beat Takeshi, Kippei Shiina, Ryo Kase, Tomokazu Miura, Jun Kunimura, Tetta Sugimoto, Takashi Tsukamoto, Hideo Nakano, Renji Ishibashi, Fumiyo Kohinata, Soichiro Kitamura.

PARADE
Oct. 12, 2009. Japanese. (Isao Yukisada) Running time: 118 Min. Tatsuya Fujiwara, Karina, Shihori Kanjiya, Kento Hayashi, Keisuke Koide.

PEEPLI LIVE
UTV. Jan. 28, 2010. Indian. (Anusha Rizvi) Running time: 105 Min. Omkar Das Manikpuri, Raghubir Yadav, Malaika Shenoy, Nawazuddin Siddiqui, Shalini Vatsa, Farrukh Jaffer, Vishal Sharma.

PELICAN BLOOD
June 22, 2010. U.K. (Karl Golden) Running time: 99 Min. Harry Treadaway, Emma Booth, Ali Craig, Arthur Darvill, Christopher Fulford, Emma Clifford, Daniel Hawksford, John Hollingworth.

PERRIER'S BOUNTY
May 14, 2010. Irish. (Ian Fitzgibbon) Running time: 88 Min. Cillian Murphy, Jodie Whittaker, Jim Broadben, Brendan Gleeson, Liam Cunningham, Michael McElhatton, Gabriel Byrne.

RAAJNEETI
GRAVITAS VENTURES. June 18, 2010. Indian. (Prakash Jha) Running time: 169 Min. Arjun Rampal, Manoj Bajpai, Ajay Devgan, Nana Patekar, Ranbir Kapoor, Katrina Kaif, Sarah Thompson Kane, Shruti Seth, Nikhila Trikha, Chetan Pandit, Vinay Apte.

RAAVAN
RELIANCE BIG PICTURES. June 16, 2010. Indian. (Mani Ratnam) Running time: 136 Min. Abhishek Bachchan, Aishwarya Rai Bachchan, Vikram, Govinda.

RELEASE
A. Sept. 26, 2009. U.K. (Darren Flaxstone, Christian Martin) Running time: 87 Min. Daniel Brocklebank, Garry Summers, Bernie Hodges, Wayne Virgo, Dymphna Skehill.

RIDE THE WAVE JOHNNY
Oct. 15, 2009. Indian. (Sudhir Mishra) Running time: 113 Min. Sikander Agarwal, Neil Nitin Mukesh, Shahana Goswami, Soha Ali Khan, Kay Kay Menon, Karan Nath, Saurabh Shukla, Vijay Maurya.

ROBIN HOOD
UNIVERSAL. May 4, 2010. U.S., U.K. (Ridley Scott) Running time: 139 Min. Russell Crowe, Cate Blanchett, William Hurt, Mark Strong, Mark Addy, Oscar Isaac, Danny Huston, Kevin Durand, Scott Grimes, Matthew Macfayden, Eileen Atkins, Simon McBurney, Max von Sydow.

ROBINSON IN RUINS
BFI. Sept. 2, 2010. U.K. (Patrick Keiller) Running time: 100 Min. Vanessa Redgrave.

ROUTE IRISH
May 18, 2010. U.K., French, Belgian, Italian, Spanish. (Ken Loach) Running time: 109 Min. Mark Womack, Andrea Lowe, John Bishop, Jack Fortune, Geoff Bell, Talib Rasool, Craig Lundberg, Trevor Williams, Russell Anderson, Jamie Michie, Bradley Thompson, Daniel Foy, Najwa Nimri.

SAYONARA ITSUKA
March 31, 2010. South Korean. (John H. Lee) Running time: 150 Min. Miho Nakayama, Hidetoshi Nishijima, Yuriko Ishida.

SEX & DRUGS & ROCK & ROLL
ENTERTAINMENT FILM DISTRIBUTORS. Jan. 8, 2010. U.K. (Mat Whitecross) Running time: 114 Min. Andy Serkis, Olivia Williams, Naomie Harris, Bill Milner, Toby Jones, Tom Hughes, Noel Clarke, Mackenzie Crook, Ray Winstone, Wesley Nelson, Ralph Ineson.

SHOCK LABYRINTH, THE
May 14, 2010. Japanese. (Takashi Shimizu) Running time: 88 Min. Yuya Yagira, Ai Maeda, Ryo Katsuji, Susuki Matsuo, Shoichiro Masumoto, Misako Renbutsu, Erina Mizuno.

SKELETONS
Feb. 2, 2010. U.K. (Nick Whitfield) Running time: 94 Min. Ed Gaughan, Andrew Buckley, Paprika Steen, Tuppence Middleton, Jason Isaacs, Josef Whitfield.

SOLITUDE OF PRIME NUMBERS
MEDUSA FILM. Sept., 2009. Italian, German.France. (Saverio Costanzo) Running time: 118 Min. Alba Rohrwacher, Luca Marinelli, Isabella Rossellini, Martina Albano, Arianna Nastro, Tommaso Neri, Vittorio Lomartire, Aurora Ruffino, Giorgia Pizzo, Maraurizio Donadoni, Roberto Sbaratto, Filippo Timi.

SON OF BABYLON
Jan. 20, 2010. U.K., Iraqi, French. (Mohamed al-Daradji) Running time: 91 Min.

SONA, THE OTHER MYSELF
Jan. 28, 2010. Japanese. (Yang Yonghi) Running time: 81 Min. Yang Sona, Yang Geon-hwa, Yang Geon-seon, Gang Jeong-heui, Hye Gyeong.

SOUL BOY
Feb. 6, 2010. German, U.K., Kenyan. (Hawa Essuman) Running time: 60 Min.

STREETDANCE
VERTIGO FILMS. May 26, 2010. U.K. (Max Giwa) Running time: 98 Min. Nichola Burley, Richard Winsor, Ukweli Roach, Frank Harper, Ashley Banjo, George Sampson, Charlotte Rampling, Eleanor Bron, Patrick Baladi, Teneisha Bonner, Lex Milczarek, Kofi Agyemang-Prempeh, Hugo Cortes, Sianad Gregory, Jennifer Leung, Rachel McDowall, Rhimes Lecointe, Sacha Chang, Bradley Charles, Lil Steph (Nguyen), Brooke Milliner, Jeremy Sheffield.

SUBMARINE
WEINSTEIN CO. (IN U.S./CANADA). Sept. 12, 2010. U.K. (Richard Ayoade) Running time: 96 Min. Craig Roberts, Yasmin Paige, Noah Taylor, Paddy Considine, Steffan Rhodri, Sally Hawkins.

SUMMER WARS
WARNER BROS. JAPAN. June 10, 2010. Japanese. (Mamoru Hosoda) Running time: 114 Min. Nanami Sakuraba, Ryonosuke Kamiki, Ayumu Saito, Mitsuki Tanimura, Sumiko Fuji, Takahiro Yokokawa.

SUPER
IFC FILMS (IN U.S.). Sept. 11, 2010. U.K. (James Gunn) Running time: 96 Min. Rainn Wilson, Ellen Page, Liv Tyler, Kevin Bacon, Nathan Fillion, Gregg Henry, Michael Rooker, Andre Royo, William Katt, Rob Zombie.

SWEET LITTLE LIES
July 8, 2010. Japanese. (Hitoshi Yazaki) Running time: 117 Min. Miki Nakatani, Nao Omori, Chizuru Ikewaki, Juichi Kobayashi, Mei Kurokawa, Ando Sakura, Akiko Kazami, Yuko Oshima.

TAMARA DREWE
SONY PICTURES CLASSICS (IN NORTH AMERICA). May 17, 2010. U.K. (Stephen Frears) Running time: 110 Min. Gemma Arterton, Roger Allam, Dominic Cooper, Luke Evans, Tamsin Greig, Jessica Barden, Charlotte Christie.

TERE BIN LADEN
BSK NETWORK & ENTERTAINMENT. July 22, 2010. Indian. (Abhishek Sharma) Running time: 108 Min. Ali Zafar, Pradhuman Singh, Sugandha Garg, Nikhil Ratnaparkhi, Piyush Mishra, Rahul Singh, Barry John.

THE BUTCHER, THE CHEF AND THE SWORDSMAN
A. Sept. 15, 2010. Chinese. (Wuershan) Running time: 95 Min. Masanobu Ando, Kitty Zhang, You Benchang, Liu Xiaoye, Ashton Xu.

THE KING'S SPEECH
WEINSTEIN CO. Sept. 1, 2010. U.K. (Tom Hooper) Running time: 118 Min. Colin Firth, Geoffrey Rush, Helena Bonham Carter, Guy Pearce, Timothy Spall, Derek Jacobi, Jennifer Ehle, Anthony Andrews, Claire Bloom, Eve Best, Michael Gambon.

THE REBOUND
WARNER ENTERTAINMENT JAPAN (IN JAPAN). Oct. 17, 2009. (Bart Freundlich) Running time: 104 Min. Catherine Zeta-Jones, Justin Bartha, Kelly Gould, Andrew Cherry, Jake Cherry, Sam Robards, Art Garfunkel, Joanna Gleason, Stephanie Szostak, John Schneider.

TIGER FACTORY, THE
May 21, 2010. Malaysian, Japanese. (Woo Ming Jin) Running time: 88 Min. Lai Fooi Mun, Pearlly Chua, Susan Lee Fong Zhi, Cheong Woai Loon, Rum Nun Cung, Lesly Leon Lee.

TOMORROW WHEN THE WAR BEGAN
PARAMOUNT. Aug. 16, 2010. Austrailian. (Stuart Beattie) Running time: 103 Min. Caitlin Stasey, Rachel Hurd-Wood, Lincoln Lewis, Deniz Akdeniz, Phoebe Tonkin, Chris Pang, Ashleigh Cummings, Andrew Ryan, Colin Friels.

TONY
REVOLVER ENTERTAINMENT. Jan. 28, 2010. U.K. (Gerard Johnson) Running time: 72 Min. Peter Ferdinando, Greg Kam, George Russo, Francis Pope, Cyrus Desir, Vicky Murdock, Neil Maskell, Jill Keen, Lucy Flack, Ish, Mark Mooney, Lorenzo Camporese, Darren Jones, Ian Kilgannon, Ian Groombridge.

TREE, THE
A LE PACTE. May 21, 2010. French. Australian. (Julie Bertuccelli) Running time: 101 Min.

UDAAN
May 19, 2010. Indian. (Vikramaditya Motwane) Running time: 137 Min. Rajat Barmecha, Ronit Roy, Aayan Boradia, Ram Kapoor, Manjot Singh, Anand Tiwari, Suman Mastkar.

TRIP, THE
Sept. 12, 2010. U.K. (Michael Winterbottom) Running time: 109 Min. Steve Coogan, Rob Brydon.

UNCLE BOONMEE WHO CAN RECALL HIS PAST LIVES
May 20, 2010. U.K., Thai, French, German, Spanish. (Apichatpong Weerasethakul) Running time: 113 Min. Thanapat Saisaymar, Jenjira Pongpas, Sakda Kaewbuadee, Natthakarn Aphaiwonk, Geerasak Kulhong, Kanokporn Thongaram, Samud Kugasang, Wallapa Mongkolprasert, Sumit Suebsee, Vien Pimdee.

VILLAIN
TOHO. Sept. 6, 2010. Japanese. (Lee Sang-il) Running time: 139 Min. Satoshi Tsumabuki, Eri Fukatsu, Masaki Okada, Hikari Mitsushima, Akira Emoto, Kirin Kiki, Sansei Shiomi.

WANDERER, THE
SOPHIE DULAC DISTRIBUTION. May 17, 2010. Israeli. (Avishai Sivan) Running time: 86 Min. Omri Fuhrer, Ali Nassar, Ronit Peled, Shani Ben-Haim, Tzahi Grad.

WE ARE WHAT WE ARE
A. May 15, 2010. Mexican. (Michel Grau) Running time: 89 Min. Francisco Barreiro, Alan Chavez, Paulina Gaitan, Carmen Beato, Jorge Zarate, Esteban Soberanes, Humberto Yanez.

WE BELIEVED
01 DISTRIBUTION. Sept., 2010. Italian. French. (Mario Martone) Running time: 202 Min. Luigi Lo Cascio, Valerio Binasco, Francesca Inaudi, Andrea Bosca, Edoardo Natoli, Luigi Pisani, Guido Caprino, Michele Riondino, Andrea Renzi, Renato Carpentieri, Ivan Franek, Stefano Cassetti, Franco Ravera, Roberto de Francesco, Toni Servillo, Luca Barbareschi, Fiona Shaw, Luca Zingaretti, Anna Bonaiuto, Alfonso Santagata, Peppino Mazzotta.

WAY BACK, THE
NEWMARKET FILMS (IN U.S.). Sept. 4, 2010. U.K. (Peter Weir) Running time: 133 Min. Jim Sturgess, Ed Harris, Colin Farrell, Alexandru Potocean, Sebastian Urzendowsky, Gustaf Skarsgard, Dragos Bucur, Saoirse Ronan, Mark Strong.

WEST IS WEST
Sept. 15, 2010. U.K., Indian. (Andy De Emmony) Running time: 102 Min. Om Puri, Aqib Khan, Linda Bassett, Ila Arun, Emil Marwa, Vijay Raaz, Nadim Sawalha, Leslee Nicol, Raj Bhansali, Zita Sattar.

WHO KILLED NANCY?
PEACE ARCH. July 26, 2010. U.K. (Alan G. Parker) Running time: 96 Min. Glen Matlock, Steve Dior, Peter Kodick, John Tiberi, Hellin Killer, Elaine Albertine, Don Letts, John Holstrum, Howie Pyro. Documentary.

WOMB
Aug. 25, 2010. German, Hungarian. (Benedek Fliegauf) Running time: 111 Min. Eva Green, Matt Smith, Hannah Murray, Tristan Christopher, Ruby O. Fee, Peter Wight, Istvan Lenart, Natalia Tena, Ella Smith, Wunmi Mosaku, Lesley Manville, Jesse Hoffman.

ZEBRAMAN 2: ATTACK ON ZEBRA CITY
TOEI CO. Sept. 8, 2010. Japanese. (Takaski Miike) Running time: 106 Min. Show Aikawa, Riisa Naka, Tsuyoshi Abe, Masahiro Inoue, Naoki Tanaka, Gadarukanaru Taka

FEATURE FILMS

JANUARY 1, 2005 – SEPTEMBER 30, 2009

In the following listings, the distributor is followed by the release date, country of origin, the director (in parentheses), and cast.

4
June, 2007. Australian-U.S. (Tim Slade) Sayaka Shoji, Niki Vasiliakis, Cho-liang Lin, Pekka Kuusisto.

9
FOCUS FEATURES. July 30, 2009. (Shane Acker) Elijah Wood, John C. Reilly, Jennifer Connelly, Christopher Plummer, Crispin Glover, Marin Landau, Fred Tatasciore, Alan Oppenheimer, Tom Kane, Helen Wilson.

300
WARNER BROS. Feb., 2007. (Zack Snyder) Gerard Butler, Lena Headey, Dominic West, David Wenham, Vincent Regan, Michael Fassbender, Tom Wisdom, Andrew Pleavin, Andrew Tiernan, Rodrigo Santoro, Peter Mensah, Stephen McHattie.

1408
MGM. June, 2007. (Mikael Hafstrom) John Cusack, Samuel L. Jackson, Mary McCormack, Jasmine Jessica Anthony.

2012
SONY PICTURES ENTERTAINMENT. Nov. 3, 2009. (Roland Emmerich) John Cusack, Adrian Helmsley - Chiwetel Ejiofor, Amanda Peet, Oliver Platt, Thandie Newton, Danny Glover, Woody Harrelson, Tom McCarthy, George Segal.

10,000 BC
WARNER BROS. March, 2008. (Roland Emmerich) Steven Strait, Camilla Belle, Cliff Curtis, Joel Virgel, Ben Badra, Mo Zainal, Nathanael Baring, Mona Hammond, Marco Khan, Reece Ritchie, Joel Fry. Narrator: Omar Sharif.

3 NEEDLES
WOLFE RELEASING. Nov., 2006. Canadian. (Thom Fitzgerald) Shawn Ashmore, Stockard Channing, Tanabadee Chokpikultong, Olympia Dukakis, Lucy Liu, Sandra Oh, Ian Roberts, Chloe Sevigny.

3:10 TO YUMA
LIONSGATE. Aug., 2007. (James Mangold) Russell Crowe, Christian Bale, Peter Fonda, Gretchen Mol, Ben Foster, Dallas Roberts, Alan Tudyk, Vinessa Shaw, Logan Lerman, Kevin Durand, Luce Rains, Johnny Whitworth, Benjamin Petry.

7 DAYS
PRIME ENTERTAINMENT. Jan., 2008. South Korea. (Won Shin-yeon) Kim Yun-jin, Kim Mi-suk, Park Heui-sun, Lee Jeon-heon, Jang Hang-seon, Yang Jin-woo, Lee Ra-hye, Oh Gwang-rok, Ok Ji-yeong, Choi Myeong-su.

7 DAYS
XENON PICTURES. Aug., 2007. (Fernando Kalife) Eduardo Arroyuelo, Martha Higareda, Jaime Camil, Julio Bracho, Roberto D'Amico, Dino Garcia, Alex Hank, Harry Porter, Beto Cuevas, Sofia Vergara, Lumi Cavazos.

8 DATES
ALTA CLASSICS. April, 2008. Spanish. (Peris Romano, Rodrigo Sorogoyen) Fernando Tejero, Belen Lopez, Javier Rey, Veronica Echegui, Jordi Vilches, Raul Arevalo, Marta Hazas, Ana Wagener, Alfonso Basave, Arturo Valls, Javier Pereira, Adriana Ozores, Miguel Angel Sola, Maria Ballesteros, Jesus Caba, Jose Luis Garcia Perez, Belen Rueda.

12 ROUNDS
20TH CENTURY FOX. March 27, 2009. (Renny Harlin) John Cena, Aidan Gillen, Ashley Scott, Steve Harris, Brian White, Gonzalo Menendez, Taylor Cole, Kyle Clements, Peter Navy Tuiasosopo, Travis Davis, Nick Gomez.

13 ROSES
ALTA CLASSICS. Oct., 2007. Spanish-Italian. (Emilio Martinez-Lazaro) Pilar Lopez de Ayala, Veronica Sanchez, Marta Etura, Nadia de Santiago, Gabriella Pession, Felix Gomez, Fran Perea, Enrico Lo Verso, Asier Etxeandia, Adriano Giannini, Goya Toledo.

14 KILOMETERS
WANDA VISION. Dec., 2007. Spanish. (Gerardo Olivares) Adoum Moussa, Illiassou Mahamadou Alzouma, Aminata Kanta.

15 DAYS WITH YOU
SOLIDO. May, 2005. Spanish. (Jesus Ponce) Isabel Ampudia, Sebastian Haro, Mercedes Hoyos, Jose Maria Pena, Pepa Diaz Meco, Joan Dalmau, Manolo Caro.

16 BLOCKS
WARNER BROS. Feb., 2006. (Richard Donner) Bruce Willis, Mos Def, David Morse, Jenna Stern, Casey Sander, Cylk Cozart CQ, David Zayas, Robert Racki.

17 AGAIN
WARNER BROS. April 8, 2009. (Burr Steers) Zac Efron, Leslie Mann, Thomas Lennon, Michelle Trachtenberg, Sterling Knight, Melora Harding, Matthew Perry, Allison Miller, Hunter Parrish.

20 CENTIMETERS
WARNER SOGEFILMS. June, 2005. Spanish-French. (Ramon Salazar) Monica Cervera, Pablo Puyol, Miguel O'Dogherty, Concha Galan, Lola Duenas, Pilar Bardem, Rossy de Palma, Najwa Nimri, Richard Shaw, Inma Olmos.

20TH CENTURY BOYS
Nov., 2008. Japanese. (Yukihiko Tsutsumi) Toshiaki Karasawa, Etsushi Toyokawa, Takako Tokiwa.

27 DRESSES
20TH CENTURY FOX. Dec., 2007. (Anne Fletcher) Katherine Heigl, James Marsden, Malin Akerman, Judy Greer, Edward Burns, Melora Hardin, Brian Kerwin, Maulik Pancholy.

28 WEEKS LATER
20TH CENTURY FOX (IN U.K.)/FOX ATOMIC (IN U.S.). April, 2007. (Juan Carlos Fresnadillo) Robert Carlyle, Rose Byrne, Jeremy Renner, Harold Perrineau, Catherine McCormack, Mackintosh Muggleton, Imogen Potts, Idris Elba, Emily Beecham, Shahid Ahmed.

30 DAYS OF NIGHT
SONY PICTURES ENTERTAINMENT. Oct., 2007. (David Slade) Josh Hartnett, Melissa George, Danny Huston, Ben Foster, Mark Boone Junior, Mark Rendall, Amber Sainsbury, Manu Bennett, Megan Franich, Joel Tobeck, Elizabeth Hawthorne, Nathaniel Lees, Craig Hall, Peter Feeney, Min Windle, Camille Keenan, Jack Walley, Elisabeth McRae.

56 DROPS OF BLOOD
Oct., 2007. Hungarian. (Attila Bokor) Attila Kaszas, Monika Veres, Tamas Palcso, Robert Alfoldi, Zoltan Miller, Monika Hoffman, Tibor Szakacs.

88 MINUTES
SONY PICTURES ENTERTAINMENT (U.S.), U.S.-German. (Jon Avnet) Al Pacino, Alicia Witt, Leelee Sobieski, Amy Brenneman, William Forsythe, Deborah Kara Unger, Benjamin McKenzie, Neal McDonough, Leah Cairns, Stephen Moyer, Christopher Redman, Brendan Fletcher, Michael Eklund, Tammy Hui, Vicky Huang, Victoria Tennant.

90 MILES
DIORAMA. June, 2005. Spanish. (Francisco Rodriguez) Alexis Valdes, Claudia Rojas, Jorge Herrera, Sergio Lucas, Enrique Molina, Daisy Granados, Joel Guillen, Emilio Aragon.

99 FRANCS
PATHE. SEPT., 2007. French. (Jan Kounen) Jean Dujardin, Jocelyn Quivrin, Patrick Mille, Vahina Giocante, Elisa Tovati, Nicolas Marie, Frederic Beigbeder, Dominique Bettenfeld.

100 WAYS TO KILL LOVE
INDIGOMEDIA. Feb., 2006. Spanish. (Vicente Perez Herrero) Sergi Calleja, Rosana Pastor, Carme Elias, Cristina Plazas, Carlos Bardem, Gines Garcia Millan, Maria Almudever; Carmela Quijano, Paulina Galvez, Alicia Martinez, Juli Mira.

500 DAYS OF SUMMER
FOX SEARCHLIGHT. Jan 17, 2009. (Marc Webb) Joseph Gordon-Levitt, Zooey Deschanel, Geoffrey Arend, Chloe Grace Moretz, Matthew Gray Gubler, Clark Gregg, Rachel Boston, Minka Kelly.

THE 3 LITTLE PIGS
TFM DISTRIBUTION (IN FRANCE)/CHRISTAL FILMS (IN CANADA). Aug, 2008. Canadian. (Patrick Huard) Claude Legault, Guillaume Lemay-Thivierge, Paul Doucet, France Castel, Sophie Pregent, Julie Perreault, Isabel Richer, Mahee Paiement, Maxim Gaudette, Marie-Helene Gendreau.

THE 40-YEAR-OLD-VIRGIN
UNIVERSAL. Aug., 2005. (Judd Apatow) Steve Carell, Catherine Keener, Paul Rudd, Romany Malco, Seth Rogen, Elizabeth Banks, Leslie Mann, Jane Lynch.

...SO GOES THE NATION
IFC. Oct., 2006. (James D. Stern, Adam Del Deo) Paul Begala, Mary Beth Cahill, Tad Devine, Terry McAuliffe, Matthew Dowd, Ed Gillespie, Mark McKinnon, Ken Mehlman. Documentary.

A

A BATTLE OF WITS
EDKO. Dec., 2006. Hong Kong-Chinese-South Korean-Japanese. (Jacob Cheung) Andy Lau, Ahn Sung-ki, Wang Zhiwen, Fan Bingbing, Choi Si-won, Nicky Wu, Wu Ma, Chin Siu-hou, Sany Hung.

A BEAUTIFUL LIFE
NEW FILMS INTL. Sept. 24, 2009. (Alejandro Chomski) Angela Sarafyan, Jesse Garcia, Bai Ling, Debi Mazar, Dana Delany, Jonathan LaPaglia, Meltem Cumbul, Rena Owen.

A BOYFRIEND FOR YASMINA
ALTA FILMS. July, 2008. Spanish-Moroccan. (Irene Cardona) Sanaa Alaoui, Jose Luis Garcia Perez, Maria Luisa Borruel, Francisco Olmo, Paca Velardiez, Jose Antonio Lucia, Malayo Ben, Fermin Nunez, Olga Lozano, Candido Gomez.

A BROKEN SOLE
PRISM PLAYHOUSE. Nov. 3, 2007. (Antony Marsellis) Danny Aiello, Margaret Colin, Judith Light, Bob Dishy, Laila Robins, John Shea.

A DECENT FACTORY
FIRST RUN, ICARUS FILMS. June, 2005. Finnish-British-French. (Thomas Balmes) Hanna Kaskinen, Louise Jamison. Documentary.

A DIRTY CARNIVAL
CJ ENTERTAINMENT. July, 2006. South Korean. (Yoo Ha) Jo In-seong, Cheon Ho-jin, Nam-gung Min, Lee Bo-yeong, Yun Je-mun, Jin Gu, Park Hyo-jun, Heo Yi-jae, Jo Jin-woong, Gweon Tae-weon.

A FRENCH GIGOLO
GAUMONT. Oct., 2008. French. (Josiane Balasko) Nathalie Baye, Eric Caravaca, Isabelle Carre, Josiane Balasko, Catherine Hiegel, Marilou Berry, Felicite Wouassi, George Aguilar.

A LOT LIKE LOVE
BUENA VISTA. April, 2005. (Nigel Cole) Ashton Kutcher, Amanda Peet, Kathryn Hahn, Kal PennKal Penn, Ty Giordano.

A PAIN IN THE ASS
TFM DISTRIBUTION. Jan., 2009. French. (Francis Veber) Richard Berry, Patrick Timsit, Pascal Elbe, Virginie Ledoyen, Laurent Paolini, Michel Aumont.

A PERFECT GETAWAY
ROGUE PICTURES. Aug. 4, 2009. (David Twohy) Timothy Olyphant, Milla Jovovich, Kiele Sanchez, Steve Zahn, Marley Shelton, Chris Hemsworth.

A PROMISE
Nov., 2007. Chinese. (Cui Yi) Tse Kwan-ho, Yin Shuo, Hu Lifang, Lu Yingxing, Zhang Ming, Jin Lin, Ma Jun, Lu Ying, Yan Feng, Liu Jia, Xu Yating, Hong Fuxiang.

A QUESTION OF THE HEART
01 DISTRIBUTION. April, 2009. Italian. (Francesca Archibugi) Antonio Albanese, Kim Rossi Stuart, Micaela Ramazzotti, Francesca Inaudi, Andrea Calligari, Nelsi Xhemalaj, Chiara Noschese, Paolo Villaggio, Stefania Sandrelli, Carlo Verdone, Paolo Virzi, Paolo Sorrentino, Daniele Lucchetti, Adriano Apra.

A SERIOUS MAN
FOCUS FEATURES. Sept 11, 2009. (Joel Coen, Ethan Coen) Michael Stuhlbarg, Richard Kind, Fred Melamed, Sari Lennick, Adam Arkin, Amy Landecker, Alan Mandell, Fyvush Finkel, Allen Lewis Rickman, Yelena Schmulenson, Peter Breitmayer, Brent Braunschweig, Simon Helberg, David Kang, Aaron Wolff, Jessica McManus, Ari Hoptman, Michael Tezla, George Wyner, Michael Lerner.

A SINGLE MAN
WEINSTEIN CO. (IN U.S./GERMANY). Sept 11, 2009. (Tom Ford) Colin Firth, Julianne Moore, Nicholas Hoult, Matthew Goode, Jon Kortajarena, Paulette Lamori, Ryan Simpkins, Ginnifer Goodwin, Teddy Sears, Aaron Sanders, Lee Pace, Jon Hamm

A SONG OF INNOCENCE
OCEAN DISTRIBUTION. Aug., 2005. French. (Antoine Santana) Isild Le Besco, Emilie Dequenne, Gregoire Colin, Anemone, Frederic Pierrot, Bernard Blancan, Christian Gasc.

A SOUND OF THUNDER
WARNER BROS. Aug., 2005. (Peter Hyams) Edward Burns, Catherine McCormack, Ben Kingsley, Jemina Rooper, David Oyelowo, Wilfried Hochholdinger, August Zirner, Corey Johnson.

A TALE OF TWO PIZZAS
Sept., 2005. (Vincent Sassone) Vincent Pastore, Frank Vincent, Patti D'Arbanville, Louis Guss, Conor Dubin, Robin Paul, Angela Pietropinto.

A WALK TO BEAUTIFUL
ENGEL ENTERTAINMENT. Dec. 26, 2007. (Mary Olive Smith) Documentary.

A WORLD WITHOUT THIEVES
HUAYI BROTHERS (IN CHINA)/MEDIA ASIA (IN HONG KONG). March, 2005. Chinese-Hong Kong. (Feng Xiaogang) Andy Lau, Rene Liu, Ge You, Li Bingbing, Wang Baoqiang, Zhang Hanyu, Lin Jiadong, You Yong, Fu Biao, Fan Wei, Feng Yuanzheng, Xu Fan.

A YEAR IN MY LIFE
TFM DISTRIBUTION. March, 2006. French. (Daniel Duval) Jean-Paul Rouve, Anne Brochet, Lorant Deutsch, Raphael Katz, Annie Giradot, Denis Podalydes, Philippe Khorsand.

AAJA NACHLE
YASH RAJ. Dec., 2007. Indian. (Anil Mehta) Madhuri Dixit, Konkona Sen, Kunal Kapoor, Divya Dutta, Vinay Pathak, Ranvir Shorey, Yashpal Sharma, Akhilendra Mishra, Jugal Hansraj, Sushmita Mukherjee, Akshaye Khanna, Irrfan Khan, Uttara Baokar, Vinod Nagpal, Asha Sachdev, Darshan Jariwala, Raghuveer Yadav, Felix D'Alviella, Nowaz, Dalai.

THE ABANDONED
LIONSGATE. Feb., 2007. Spanish-British-Bulgarian. (Nacho Cerda) Anastasia Hille, Karel Roden, Valentin Ganev, Carlos Reig-Plaza.

ABOMINABLE
FREESTYLE. April, 2006. (Ryan Schifrin) Matt McCoy, Haley Joel, Christien Tinsley, Ashley Hartman, Mike Deak, Sheriff Halderman, Lance Henriksen.

ABOUT SARA
SONET FILM. Sept., 2005. Swedish. (Othman Karim) Linda Zilliacus, Alexander Skarsgard, Hugo Emretsson, Alexander Karim, Siw Erixon, Saman, Eva Rydberg, Alf Jonsson, Claes-Goran Turesson, Cecilia Zwick Nash, Birgitta Johansson, Per Ullberg, Mats Olausson.

ABOUT THE LOOKING FOR AND THE FINDING OF LOVE
March, 2006. German. (Helmut Dietl) Moritz Bleibtreu, Alexandra Maria Lara, Uwe Ochesenknecht, Anke Engelke, Heino Ferch, Justus Von Dohnanyi, Marily Milia, Richard Beek, Christoph Maria Herbst, Harald Schmidt.

ACCEPTED
UNIVERSAL. Aug., 2006. (Steve Pink) Justin Long, Jonah Hill, Blake Lively, Maria Thayer, Adam Herschman, Lewis Black, Anthony Heald, Columbus Short, Travis Van Winkle, Diora Baird, Ann Cusack, Mark Derwin, Robin Lord Taylor, Kellan Lutz, Brendan Miller.

ADAM
FOX SEARCHLIGHT (IN NORTH AMERICA/U.K.). Jan 20, 2009. (Max Mayer) Hugh Dancy, Rose Byrne, Frankie Faison, Mark Linn-Baker, Amy Irving, Peter Gallagher.

ADULTHOOD
Pathe. June, 2008. British. (Noel Clarke) Noel Clarke, Adam Deacon, Scarlett Alice Johnson, Jacob Anderson, Ben Drew, Danny Dyer, Femi Oyeniran, Shanika Warren-Markland, Red Madrell, Cornell John, Madeleine Fairley, Arnold Oceng.

ADVENTURELAND
MIRAMAX. Jan 20, 2009. (Greg Motolla) Jesse Eisenberg, Kristen Stewart, Martin Starr, Kristen Wiig, Bill Hader, Ryan Reynolds.

THE ADVENTURES OF SHARKBOY AND LAVAGIRL IN 3-D
DIMENSION FILMS. May, 2005. (Robert Rodriguez) Taylor Lautner, Taylor Dooley, Cayden Boyd, George Lopez, David Arquette, Kristen Davis, Jacob Davich, Sasha Pieterse, Rico Torres, Rebel Rodriguez, Racer Rodriguez, Rocket Rodriguez.

AEON FLUX
PARAMOUNT. Dec., 2005. (Karyn Kusama) Charlize Theron, Marton Csokas, Jonny Lee Miller, Sophie Okonedo, Frances McDormand, Pete Postlethwaite, Amelia Warner, Caroline Chikezie, Nikolai Kinski.

AFGHAN STAR
Jan., 2009. Afghan, U.K. (Havana Marking) Setara Hussainzada, Rafi Nabaazda, Hameed Sahkizada, Lema Sehar, Daoud Sediqi. Documentary.

AFTER THE WEDDING
NORDISK FILM. March, 2006. Danish. (Susanne Bier) Mads Mikkelsen, Rolf Lassgard, Sidse Babett Knudsen, Stine Fischer Christensen, Christian Tafdrup, Mona Malm, Neeral Mulchandani, Meenal Petal.

AGATHE CLERY
PATHE. Dec., 2008. French. (Etienne Chatiliez) Valerie Lemercier, Anthony Kavanagh, Dominique Lavanant, Isabelle Nanty, Jacques Boudet, Artus de Penguern, Jean Rochefort.

THE AGE OF STUPID
SPANNER FILMS. May., 2009. U.K. (Franny Armstrong) Pete Postlethwaite, Jamila Bayyoud, Adnan Bayyoud, Alvin DuVernay, Piers Guy, Layefa Malemi, Fernand Pareau, Jeh Wadia. Documentary.

THE AGENT
PINTER & MARTIN. July, 2009. U.K. (Lesley Manning) William Beck, Stephen Kennedy, Maureen Lipman.

THE AGGRESSIVES
SEVENTH ART RELEASING. Oct., 2005. (Daniel Peddle). Documentary.

AIN'T SCARED
GAUMONT. July, 2007. French. (Audrey Estrougo) Emilie de Preissac, Terry Nimajimbe, Salome Stevenin, Eye Haidara, Paco Boublard, Oumar Diaw, Lili Canobbio, Salome Stevenin, Jimmy Woha, Djena Tsimba.

THE AIRPLANE
PATHE DISTRIBUTION. July, 2005. French-German. (Cedric Kahn) Romeo Botzaris, Isabelle Carre, Vincent Lindon, Nicolas Briancon.

AKEELAH AND THE BEE
LIONSGATE, 2929 PRODS. AND STARBUCKS ENTERTAINMENT. March, 2006. (Doug Atchison) Laurence Fishburne, Angela Bassett, Keke Palmer, Curtis Armstrong, Tzi Ma, Lee Thompson Young, J.R. Villarreal, Sahara Garey, Sean Michael Afable, Erica Hubbard, Julito McCullum, Dalia Phillips.

AKOIBON
GEMINI FILMS. April, 2005. French. (Edouard Baer) Jean Rochefort, Nader Boussandel, Marie Denarnaud, Edouard Baer, Chiara Mastroianni, Benoit Poelvoorde, Francois Rolli, Atmen Kelif, Francis Van Litsenborgh, Gilles Gaston-Dreyfus, Lea Drucker, Pierre-Louis Lanier, Samir Guesmi, Josee Dayan, Christophe Meynet.

ALATRISTE
20TH CENTURY FOX. Aug., 2006. Spanish. (Agustin Diaz Yanes) Viggo Mortensen, Eduardo Noriega, Alex O'Dogherty, Nacho Perez, Juan Echanove, Enrico Lo Verso, Blanca Portello, Javier Camara, Ariadna Gil, Unax Ugalde, Elena Anaya.

ALHAMBRA DAYDREAMS
Nov., 2005. Spanish. (Jose Sanchez Montes) Enrique Morente, Pat Metheny, Ute Lemper, Tomatito, Cheb Khaled, Blanca Li, Estrella Morente, Israel Galvan, Juan Habichuela. Documentary.

ALIAN
Oct., 2005. Chineese. (Wei Xueqi) Meng Qiaohui, Luo Honglou, Tan Zhenghua, Chen Yujiao, Liang Jiwei, Zhang Qiang.

ALIEN AUTOPSY
WARNER BROS. (IN U.K.) April, 2006. British-U.S.-German. (Jonny Campbell) Ant McPartlin, Declan Donnelly, Bill Pullman, Goetz Otto, Morwenna Banks, Omid Djalili, Harry Dean Stanton, Orson Bean, David Threlfall, Jimmy Carr, Nichole Hiltz, John Cater, Madeleine Moffat, John Shrapnel, Lee Oakes, Martin McDougall, Gary Shoefield, Ray Santilli.

ALIENS IN THE ATTIC
20TH CENTURY FOX July 31, 2009. (John Schultz) Carter Jenkins, Austin Butler, Ashley Tisdale, Ashley Boettcher, Henri Young, Regan Young, Doris Roberts, Robert Hoffman, Kevin Nealon, Gillian Vigman, Andy Richter, Tim Meadows, Thomas Haden Church, Josh Peck, J.K. Simmons, Kari Wahlgren.

ALIENS VS. PREDATOR - REQUIEM
20TH CENTURY FOX. Dec. 25, 2007. (Colin Strause, Greg Strause) Steven Pasquale, Reiko Aylesworth, John Ortiz, Johnny Lewis, Ariel Gade, Kristen Hager, Sam Trammell, Robert Joy, David Paetkau, Tom Woodruff, Jr., Ian Whyte.

ALIENS OF THE DEEP
BUENA VISTA PICTURES. Jan., 2005. (James Cameron, Steven Quale) Dijanna Figueroa, Pan Conrad, Kelly Snook, Kevin Hand, James Cameron. Documentary. 3D Imax.

ALL ABOUT STEVE
20TH CENTURY FOX. Sept. 2, 2009. (Phil Traill) Sandra Bullock, Thomas Haden Church, Bradley Cooper, Ken Jeong, DJ Qualls, Howard Hesseman, Keith David, Beth Grant.

ALL DOLLED UP: A NEW YORK DOLLS STORY
Dec., 2005. (Bob Gruen, Nadya Beck) David Johansen, Arthur Kane, Jerry Nolan, Sylvain Sylvain, Johnny Thunders. Documentary.

ALL FOR LOVE
CJ ENTERTAINMENT. Oct., 2005. South Korean. (Min Gyu-dong) Eom Jeong-hwa, Im Chang-jeong, Kim Su-ro, Hwang Jeong-min, Ju Hyeon, Cheon Ho-jin, Yun Jin-seo, Jeong Gyeong-ho, Seo Yeong-heui, Oh Mi-heui, Jeon Hye-jin, Kim Tae-hyeon, Lee Byeong-jun, Kim Yu-jeong, Ha Ji-weon, Kim Su-rol.

THE ALL TOGETHER
LIONSGATE U.K. May, 2007. British. (Gavin Claxton) Martin Freeman, Corey Johnson, Velibor Topic, Danny Dyer, Richard Harrington, Amanda Abbington.

ALONE IN THE DARK
LIONS GATE FILMS. Jan., 2005. (Uwe Boll) Christian Slater, Tara Reid, Stephen Dorff, Frank C. Turner, Matthew Walker, Will Sanderson, Mark Acheson, Darren Shahlavi, Karin Konoval, Craig Bruhnanski, Kwesi Ameyaw, Catherine Lough Haggquist, Ed Anders.

ALPHA MALE
VERVE PICTURES. July, 2006. British. (Dan Wilde) Danny Huston, Jennifer Ehle, Mark Wells, Patrick Baladi, Christopher Egan, Amelia Warner, Trudie Styler, Jemma Powell, Arthur Duncan, Katie Knight.

THE ALPS
MACGILLIVRAY FREEMAN FILMS. March, 2007. (Stephen Judson). John Harlin III, Adele and Siena Harlin, Robert Jasper, Daniela Jasper, Bruno Messerli. Narrator: Michael Gambon. Documentary.

ALTERNATE WEEKS (AND HALF THE VACATION)
TFM DISTRIBUTION.Aug., 2009. French. (Ivan Calberac) Mathilde Seigner, Bernard Campan, Bertille Chabert, Gregori Derangere, Judith Davis, Daniele Lebrun, Jean-Baptiste Fonck, Keyne Cuypers, Manon Valentin.

ALVIN AND THE CHIPMUNKS
20TH CENTURY FOX. Dec. 8, 2007. (Tim Hill). Jason Lee, David Cross, Cameron Richardson, Jane Lynch, Justin Long, Matthew Gray Gubler, Jesse McCartney.

ALWAYS: SUNSET ON THIRD STREET 2
TOHO CO. Nov., 2007. Japanese. (Takashi Yamazaki) Hidetaka Yoshioka, Shinichi Tsutsumi, Koyuki, Maki Horikita, Hiroko Yakushimaru, Kazuki Koshimizu, Kenta Suga, Ayame Koike, Yosuke Asari, Fumiyo Kohinata.

AMBITIOUS
PYRAMIDE DISTRIBUTION. Jan. 2007. French. (Catherine Corsini) Karin Viard, Eric Caravaca, Jacques Weber, Gilles Cohen, Helene Babu, Jacqueline Danno, Claire Maurier, Chantal Neuwirth, Renan Carteaux.

AMELIA
FOX SEARCHLIGHT. Oct. 16, 2009. (Mira Nair) Hilary Swank, Richard Gere, Ewan McGregor, Christopher Eccleston, Joe Anderson, Cherry Jones, Mia Wasikowska, William Cuddy.

AMERICA THE BEAUTIFUL
FIRST INDEPENDENT PICTURES. July 25, 2008. (Darryl Roberts) Gerren Taylor, Michelle Taylor, Elizabeth Arden, Chris Elder, Jill Ishkarian, Paris Hilton, Eve Ensler, Anthony Griffin, Martin Short, Anne Becker. Documentary.

AMERICAN GANGSTER
UNIVERSAL. Sept. 18, 2007. (Ridley Scott) Denzel Washington, Russell Crowe, Chiwetel Ejiofor, Cuba Gooding, Jr., Josh Brolin, Ted Levine, Armand Assante, Clarence Williams, III, John Ortiz, John Hawkes, RZA, Lymari Nadal, Yul Vazquez, Ruby Dee, Idris Elba, Carla Gugino, Joe Morton, Jon Polito, Kevin Corrigan, Rodger Guenveur Smith, Malcolm Goodwin, Ric Young, Roger Bart, Tip Harris, Kadee Strickland, Ruben Santiago-Hudson, Norman Reedus.

THE AMITYVILLE HORROR
MGM (IN U.S.)/DIMENSION FILMS (INTERNATIONAL). March, 2005. (Andrew Douglas) Ryan Reynolds, Melissa George, Jesse James, Jimmy Bennett, Chloe Grace Moretz, Rachel Nichols, Philip Baker Hall, Isabel Conner, Brendan Donaldson, Annabel Armour, Rich Komenich, David Gee, Danny McCarthy, Nancy Lollar, Jose Taitano.

AMONG ADULTS
TFM DISTRIBUTION. Jan., 2007. French. (Stephane Brize) Edith Merieau, Vincent Dubois, Jeanne Ferron, Philippe Fauconnier, Celine Gorget, Vincent Rocher, France Ducateau, Cyril Couton, Charlotte Smither, Karim Hammiche, Veronique Dossetto, Dominique Coquelin.

AMREEKA
E1 FILMS. Jan., 2009. Canadian. (Cherien Dabis) Nisreen Faour, Melkar Muallem, Hiam Abbass, Yussef Abu-Warda, Joseph Ziegler, Alia Shawkat.

AN AMERICAN AFFAIR
SCREEN MEDIA FILMS. Feb. 24, 2009. (William Sten Olsson) Gretchen Mol, James Rebhorn, Cameron Bright, Mark Pellegrino, Perrey Reeves, Noah Wyle.

AN AMERICAN CAROL
VIVENDI ENTERTAINMENT. Oct. 3, 2008. (David Zucker) Kevin Farley, Kelsey Grammer, Trace Adkins, Robert Davi, Geoffrey Arend, Serdar Kalsin, Leslie Nielsen, Jon Voight, Gail O'Grady, Travis Schuldt, Kevin Sorbo, Nikki Deloach, David Alan Grier, Paris Hilton, Dennis Hopper, Chriss Anglin, Jesse Heiman, Simon Rex, Gary Coleman, Fred Travalena, Zachary Levi, James Woods, Bill O'Reilly.

AN EDUCATION
SONY PICTURES CLASSICS. Dec., 2008. U.K. (Lone Scherfig) Peter Sarsgaard, Carey Mulligan, Alfred Molina, Dominic Cooper, Rosamund Pike, Olivia Williams, Emma Thompson, Cara Seymour, Matthew Beard, Sally Hawkins.

AN UNFINISHED LIFE
MIRAMAX (IN U.S.), BUENA VISTA (IN U.K.). Aug., 2005. (Lasse Hallstrom) Robert Redford, Morgan Freeman, Jennifer Lopez, Becca Gardner, Josh Lucas, Damian Lewis, Camryn Manheim, Bart the bear.

ANAMORPH
IFC FILMS April 7, 2008. (H.S. Miller) Willem Dafoe, Scott Speedman, Clea Duvall, James Rebhorn, Peter Stormare.

AND LAUGHINGLY KILLED HIM
ISTITUTO LUCE. April, 2005. Italian. (Florestano Vancini) Manlio Dovi, Sabrina Colle, Ruben Rigillo, Marianna De Micheli, Giorgio Lupano.

AND THEN CAME LOVE
FOX MEADOW. June, 2007. (Richard Schenkman) Vanessa Williams, Kevin Daniels, Michael Boatman, Jeremy Gumbs, Eartha Kitt,

Stephen Spinella, Eileen Alana, Ben Vereen.

ANGEL

Sept., 2005. (Jim McKay) Rachel Griffiths, Jonan Everett, Denis O'Hare, Wallace Little, Jon Norman Schneider, Catherine Kellner, David Zayas.

ANGEL-A

EUROPACORP DISTRIBUTION. Dec., 2005. French. (Luc Besson) Jamel Debbouze, Rie Rasmussen, Gilbert Melki, Serge Riaboukine, Akim Chir, Olivier Claverie, Solange Milhaud, Franck Olivier Bonnet, Michel Chesneau.

ANGELS & DEMONS

SONY PICTURES ENTERTAINMENT. May 4, 2009. (Ron Howard) Tom Hanks, Ewan McGregor, Ayelet Zurer, Stellan Skarsgard, Pierfrancesco Favino, Nikolaj Lie Kaas, Armin Mueller-Stahl, Thure Lindhardt, David Pasquesi, Cosimo Fusco, Victor Alfieri.

ANGELS WITH ANGLES

Dec., 2005. (Scott Edmund Lane) Julie Carmen, Frank Gorshin, Rodney Dangerfield, Scott Edmund Lane, David Proval, Branscombe Richmond, Henry Darrow, Adam West, Soupy Sales.

ANGUS, THONGS AND PERFECT SNOGGING

PARAMOUNT (IN U.S./U.K.). July, 2008. British-U.S. (Gurinder Chadha) Georgia Groome, Alan Davies, Karen Taylor, Aaron Johnson, Steve Jones, Eleanor Tomlinson, Manjeevan Grewal, Georgia Henshaw, Sean Bourke, Kimberley Nixon, Liam Hess, Tommy Bastow, Eva Drew.

ANNAPOLIS

BUENA VISTA. Jan., 2006. (Justin Lin) James Franco, Tyrese Gibson, Jordana Brewster, Donnie Wahlberg, Vicellous Shannon, Roger Fan, McCaleb Burnett, Wilmer Calderon, Chi McBride.

ANTHONY ZIMMER

MARS DISTRIBUTION. April, 2005. French. (Jerome Salle) Sophie Marceau, Yvan Attal, Sami Frey, Gilles Lellouche, Daniel Olbrychski, Samir Guesmi, Dimitri Rataud.

ANTHONY, WARRIOR OF GOD

01 DISTRIBUTION. June, 2006. Italian. (Antonello Belluco) Jordi Molla, Arnoldo Foa, Paolo De Vita, Matt Patresi, Andrea Ascolese, Marta Jacopini, Franco di Francescantonio, Damir Todorovic, Michele Melega, Nuccio Siano, Luca Lionello, Mattia Sbragia, Eleonora Daniele.

THE ANTIDOTE

WARNER BROS. PICTURES FRANCE. Jan., 2005. French. (Vincent De Brus) Christian Clavier, Jacques Villeret, Agnes Soral, Annie Gregorio, Francois Morel, Francois Levantal, Alexandra Lamy, Daniel Russo, Thierry Lhermitte.

THE ANT BULLY

WARNER BROS. July, 2006. (John A. Davis) Julia Roberts, Nicolas Cage, Meryl Streep, Paul Giamatti, Zach Tyler Eisen, Regina King, Bruce Campbell, Lily Tomlin, Cheri Oteri, Larry Miller, Allison Mack, Ricardo Montalban, Myles Jeffrey, Jake T. Austin, Rob Paulsen, S. Scott Bullock, Mark DeCarlo, Frank Welker. Animated.

ANTS IN THE MOUTH

FILMAX. March, 2005. Spanish-Cuban. (Mariano Barroso) Eduard Fernandez, Ariadna Gil, Jorge Perugorria, Jose Luis Gomez, Samuel Claxton.

ANOTHER GAY SEQUEL: GAYS GONE WILD!

TLA RELEASING. August 5, 2008. (Todd Stephens) Jonah Blechman, Jake Mosser, Aaron Michael Davies, Jimmy Clabots, RuPaul, Lady Bunny, Will Wikle, Euriamis Losada, Brandon Lim, Issac Webster, Brent Corrigan, Lypsinka, Jim Verraros, Colton Ford, Amanda LePore, Michael Lucas, Ashlie Atkinson, Stephanie McVay, Andersen Gabrych, Perez Hilton, Scott Thompson.

APOCALYPTO

BUENA VISTA. Nov., 2006. (Mel Gibson) Rudy Youngblood, Dalia Hernandez, Jonathan Brewer, Morris Birdyellowhead, Carlos Emilio Baez, Amilcar Ramirez, Israel Contreras, Israel Rios, Isabel Diaz, Espiridion Acosta Cache, Raoul Trujillo, Gerardo Taracena, Rodolfo Palacios, Fernando Hernandez, Maria Isidra Hoil, Aquetzali Garcia.

APRIL SHOWERS

FILMES DO TEJO II. Feb., 2009. Portugeuse. (Ivo M. Ferreira) Goncalo Waddington, Joana Seixas, Hugo Tourita, Adelaide Joao, Lidia Franco, Candido Ferreira, Juan Jesus Valverde.

AQUA TEEN HUNGER FORCE COLON MOVIE FILM FOR THEATERS

FIRST LOOK PICTURES. March, 2007. (Matt Maiellaro, Dave Willis) Dana Snyder, Dave Willis, Carey Means, Andy Merrill, Mike Schatz, Matt Maiellaro, Fred Armisen, Bruce Campbell, C. Martin Croker, George Lowe, Chris Kattan, Neal Peart, Tina Fey. Animated.

AQUAMARINE

20TH CENTURY FOX. Feb., 2006. (Elizabeth Allen) Emma Roberts, Joanna "JoJo" Levesque, Sara Paxton, Jake McDorman, Arielle Kebbel, Claudia Karvan, Bruce Spence, Tammin Sursok, Roy Billing, Julia Blake, Shaun Micallef.

THE ARCHITECT

MAGNOLIA PICTURES. Nov., 2006. (Matt Tauber) Anthony LaPaglia, Viola Davis, Isabella Rossellini, Hayden Panettiere, Sebastian Stan, Paul James, Serena Reeder.

ARE WE DONE YET?

SONY PICTURES ENTERTAINMENT. March 2007. (Steve Carr) Ice Cube, Nia Long, John C. McGinley, Aleisha Allen, Philip Daniel Bolden, Dan Joffre, Pedro Miguel Arce, Linda Kash, Hayes MacArthur.

ARE WE THERE YET?

SONY PICTURES ENTERTAINMENT. Jan., 2005. (Brian Levant) Ice Cube, Nia Long, Jay Mohr, M.C. Gainey, Aleisha Allen, Philip Daniel Bolden, Tracy Morgan, Nichelle Nichols.

ARRANGED

FILM MOVEMENT. Dec. 10, 2007. (Diane Cresco) Zoe Lister-Jones, Francis Benhamou, John Rothman, Mimi Lieber, Laith Nakli, Marcia Jean Kurtz.

ARTHUR AND THE INVISIBLES

MGM. Dec., 2006. French. (Luc Besson) Freddie Highmore, Mia Farrow. Voices: David Bowie, Madonna, Snoop Dogg, Jimmy Fallon, Robert De Niro, Anthony Anderson, Chazz Palminteri, Jason Bateman, Harvey Keitel, Emilio Estevez, Adam LeFevre, Ron Crawford, Penny Balfour, Doug Rand, Jean Bejote Njamba. Narrator: CK. Live-action. Animated.

ASHES FROM THE SKY

UNIVERSAL PICTURES INTL. Spanish. Nov., 2008. Spanish. (Jose Antonio Quiros) Celso Bugallo, Clara Segura, Gary Piquer, Fran Sariego, Beatriz Rico, Txema Blasco.

ASSAULT ON PRECINCT 13

ROGUE PICTURES. Jan., 2005. (Jean-Francois Richet) Ethan Hawke, Laurence Fishburne, John Leguizamo, Maria Bello, Jeffrey "Ja Rule" Atkins, Drea de Matteo, Matt Craven, Brian Dennehy, Gabriel Byrne, Aisha Hinds, Dorian Harewood.

ASTERIX AND THE VIKINGS

SND. March, 2006. French. (Stefan Fjeldmark, Jesper Moller) Voices: Roger Carel, Lorant Deutsch, Sara Forestier, Jacques Frantz, Pierre Palmade, Pierre Tchernia. Animated.

ASTERIX AT THE OLYMPIC GAMES

PATHE DISTRIBUTION (IN FRANCE)/CONSTANTIN FILM (IN GERMANY)/WARNER BROS. ITALIA (IN ITALY)/PATHE (IN U.K.) Feb., 2008. French-German-Spanish-Italian. (Frederic Forestier, Thomas Langmann) Clovis Cornillac, Gerard Depardieu, Benoit Poelvoorde, Alain Delon, Stephane Rousseau, Vanessa Hessler, Michael Bully Herbig, Santiago Segura, Jean-Pierre Cassel, Jamel Debbouze, Zinedine Zidane, Michael Schumacher, Tony Parker, Amelie Mauresmo.

AT A GLANCE

01 DISTRIBUTION. March, 2008. Italian. (Sergio Rubini) Sergio Rubini, Riccardo Scamarcio, Vittoria Puccini, Richard Sammell, Paola Barale, Emanuele Salce, Giancarlo Ratti, Giorgio Colangeli, Alexandra Prusa, Flavio Parenti.

ATL

WARNER BROS. March, 2006. (Chris Robinson) Tip Harris, Lauren London, Evan Ross, Lonette McKee, Antwan Andre Patton, Mykelti Williamson, Keith David, Jackie Long, Albert Daniels, Jason Weaver, Khadijah, Malika, Tyree Simmons..

THE AURA

ALTA FILMS. Sept. 2005. Argentinian-Spaish-French. (Fabian Bielinsky) Ricardo Darin, Dolores Fonzi, Alejandro Awada, Pablo Cedron, Jorge D'Elia, Manuel Rodal, Rafael Castejon, Walter Reyno.

AURORE

LES FILMS DU LOSANGE. March, 2006. French. (Nils Tavernier) Margaux Chatelier, Carole Bouquet, Francois Berleand, Nicolas Le Riche, Monique Chaumette, Thibault de Montalembert, Kader Belarbi, Yann Bridard, Yutaka Takei.

AVRIL

HAUT & COURT. June, 2006. French. (Gerald Hustache-Mathieu) Sophie Quinton, Miou-Miou, Clement Sibony, Nicolas Duvauchelle, Richaud Valls.

AUSTRALIA

20TH CENTURY FOX. Nov. 19, 2008. Austrailian-U.S.-British. (Baz Luhrmann) Nicole Kidman, Hugh Jackman, David Wenham, Bryan Brown, Jack Thompson, David Gulpilil, Brandon Walters, David Ngoombujarra, Ben Mendelsohn, Essie Davis, Barry Otto, Kerry Walker, Sandy Gore, Ursula Yovich, Lillian Crombie, Yuen Wah, Angus Pilakui, Jacek Koman, Tony Barry, Ray Barrett, Max Cullen, Arthur Dignam, Bruce Spence.

AUTOPSY

AFTER DARK FILMS. Jan. 10, 2009. (Adam Gierasch) Robert Patrick, Jessica Lowndes, Jenette Goldstein, Michael Bowen, Robert LaSardo, Ross Kohn, Ashley Schneider, Arcadiy Golubovich, Ross McCall, Janine Venable, Eric F. Adams.

AWAKE

MGM. Nov. 30, 2007. (Joby Harold) Hayden Christensen, Jessica Alba, Terrence Howard, Lena Olin, Christopher McDonald,

Sam Robards, Arliss Howard, Fisher Stevens, Georgina Chapman.

AWAY WE GO

FOCUS FEATURES. April 28, 2009. (Sam Mendes) John Krasinski, Maya Rudolph, Catherine O'Hara, Jeff Daniels, Carmen Ejogo, Allison Janney, Jim Gaffigan, Maggie Gyllenhaal, Josh Hamilton, Chris Messina, Melanie Lynskey, Paul Schneider.

BAABUL

ADLABS. Dec., 2006. Indian. (Ravi Chopra) Amitabh Bachchan, Hema Malini, Salman Khan, Rani Mukherji, John Abraham, Om Puri, Rajpal Yadav, Sarika.

THE BAADER MEINHOF COMPLEX

CONSTANTIN FILM. Sept., 2008. German. (Uli Edel) Martina Gedeck, Moritz Bleibtreu, Johanna Wokalek, Bruno Ganz, Nadja Uhl, Jan Josef Liefers, Stipe Erceg, Niels Bruno Schmidt, Vinzenz Kiefer, Simon Licht, Alexandra Maria Lara, Hannah Herzsprung, Daniel Lommatzsch, Sebastian Blomberg, Heino Ferch, Tom Schilling, Bernd Stegemann.

BAB EL WEB

PYRAMIDE DISTRIBUTION. March, 2005. French-Algerian. (Merzak Allouache) Julie Gayet, Faudel, Samy Naceri, Hacene Benzerari, Boualem Benani, Bakhta Benouis.

BABY MAMA

Universal. April 16, 2008. (Michael McCullers) Tina Fey, Amy Poehler, Greg Kinnear, Dax Shepard, Romany Malco, Sigourney Weaver, Steve Martin, Maura Tierney, Holland Taylor, John Hodgman, Siobhan Fallon Hogan, Denis O'Hare, Stephen Mailer, James Rebhorn.

BABYLON A.D.

20TH CENTURY FOX (In U.S.)/STUDIOCANAL (In France). Aug 20, 2008. French-U.S. (Mathieu Kassovitz) Vin Diesel, Melanie Thierry, Michelle Yeoh, Lambert Wilson, Mark Strong, Jerome Le Banner, Charlotte Rampling, Gerard Depardieu, Joel Kirby, Souleymane Dicko, David Belle, Radek Bruna, Jan Unger, Abraham Belaga, Gary Cowan, David Gasman, Lemmy Constantine.

BACKSEAT

TRULY INDIE. March 22, 2008. (Bruce Van Dusen) Josh Alexander, Rob Bogue, Aubrey Dollar, Will Janowitz, Mark Rosenthal, Helen Coxe, Sarah Lord, Danny Mastrogiorgio.

BAD FAITH

Nov., 2006. French-Belgium. (Roschdy Zem) Roschdy Zem, Cecile de France, Pascal Elbe, Leila Bekhti, Jean-Pierre Cassel, Martine Chevallier, Berangere Bonvoisin, Naima Elmcherqui, Antoine Chappey, Mickael Masclet, Abdelhafid Metalsi, Xavier Beauvois.

BAD NEWS BEARS

PARAMOUNT PICTURES. July, 2005. (Richard Linklater) Billy Bob Thornton, Greg Kinnear, Marcia Gay Harden, Sammi Kane Kraft, Ridge Canipe, Brandon Craggs, Jeffrey Davis, Timmy Deters, Carlos Estrada, Emmanuel Estrada, Troy Gentile, Kenneth "K.C." Harris, Aman Johal, Tyler Patrick Jones, Jeffrey Tedmori.

BADLAND

COPEX DISTRIBUTION. Nov. 25, 2007. (Francesco Lucente) Jamie Draven, Grace Fulton, Vinessa Shaw, Chandra West, Joe Morton, Tom Carey, Patrick Richards, Jake Church, Louie Campbell.

THE BALL

Nov., 2007. Italian. (Claudio Antonini) Laura Morante, Antonio Catania, Umberto Morelli, Edoardo Baietti, Giorgia Brunaccini, Giordano DiPietro.

BALLS OF FURY

ROGUE PICTURES. Aug., 2007. (Robert Ben Garant) Dan Fogler, Christopher Walken, George Lopez, Maggie Q, James Hong, Terry Crews, Robert Patrick, Diedrich Bader, Aisha Tyler, Thomas Lennon.

BANDSLAM

SUMMIT ENTERTAINMENT. Aug. 4, 2009. Aly Michalka, Vanessa Hudgens, Gaelan Connell, Scott Porter, Ryan Donowho, Charlie Saxton, Lisa Kudrow, David Bowie.

BANDHOBI

INDIESTORY RELEASE OF A KT&G. Nov., 2009. South Korean. (Shin Dong-il) Mahbub Alam Pollob, Baek Jin-heui, Lee Il-hwa, Park Hyeok-gweon, Jeong Dong-gyu, Kim Jae-rok, Hyeon Weon-heui, Choi In-suk, Jean Sebastian, Park Yeong.

THE BANK JOB

LIONSGATE. (in U.S./U.K.). Feb 26, 2008. (Roger Donaldson) Jason Statham, Saffron Burrows, Stephen Campbell Moore, Daniel Mays, James Faulkner, Alki David, Michael Jibson, Richard Lintern, David Suchet, Peter De Jersey, Hattie Morahan.

BANKING ON HEAVEN

June, 2006. (Dot Reidelbach) Ruth Cooke, Elaine Jeffs, Carolyn Jessup, Penny Peterson, Jon Krakauer, Terry Goddard, Flora Jessup, Russ and Lori Chatwin, Gary Engels, Laureen Jessup, Seth Cooke, Ed Smart, Marilyn Jarrett. Documentary.

BANGKOK DANGEROUS

LIONSGATE (in U.S.)/TFM DISTRIBUTION (in France). Aug. 27, 2008. (the Pang Brothers) Nicolas Cage, Shahkrit Yamnarm, Charlie Young, Panward Hemmanee, Nirattisai Kaljareuk, Dom Hetrakul, Namngen Jaruvijit, Napasaranh Mittiraroch.

BANGKOK LOVE STORY

SAHAMONGKOLFILM INTL. Nov., 2007. Thai. (Poj Arnon) Rattanabunlung Tosawart, Chayawart Sang Thong, Weeradit Srimalai, Chatcha Rujinanoun, Utumporn Silapran.

BARELY LEGAL

SONY PICTURES ENTERTAINMENT. Oct., 2005. U.S.-German. (David Mickey Evans) Erik von Detten, Vince Vieluf, Sarah-Jane Potts, Tony Denman, Riley Smith, Daniel Farber, Samm Levine, Tom Arnold, Horatio Sanz, Amy Smart, Rachel Dratch, Chris Parnell.

BARNYARD

PARAMOUNT. Aug., 2006. (Steve Oedekerk) Kevin James, Courteney Cox, Sam Elliott, Danny Glover, Wanda Sykes, Andie MacDowell, David Koechner, Jeff Garcia, Cam Clarke, Rob Paulson, Tino Insana, Dom Irrera, Maria Bamford, Steve Oedekerk, Scott Bullock, John DiMaggio, Maurice LaMarche, Madeline Lovejoy, Nathaniel Stroman. Animated.

BARRIO CUBA

Nov., 2005. Spanish-Cuban. (Humberto Solas) Luisa Maria Jimenez, Jorge Perugorria, Isabel Santos, Mario Limonta, Adela Legra, Rafael Lahera, Ana Dominguez, Yeandro Tamayo.

BASIC INSTINCT 2

SONY PICTURES ENTERTAINMENT. March, 2006. (Michael Caton-Jones) Sharon Stone, David Morrissey, David Thewlis, Charlotte Rampling, Hugh Dancy, Flora Montgomery, Anne Caillon, Iain Robertson, Stan Collymore, Indira Varma, Heathcote Williams.

BASTARDY

FILM CAMP/PALACE FILMS. June, 2009. Australian. (Amiel Courtin-Wilson) Jack Charles, Amiel Courtin-Wilson, Artie Charles, Alkinos Tsilimidos.

BATMAN BEGINS

WARNER BROS. June, 2005. (Christopher Nolan) Christian Bale, Michael Caine, Liam Neeson, Katie Holmes, Gary Oldman, Cillian Murphy, Tom Wilkinson, Rutger Hauer, Ken Watanabe, Mark Boone Junior, Linus Roache, Morgan Freeman, Gus Lewis.

BE COOL

MGM. Feb., 2005. (F. Gary Gray) John Travolta, Uma Thurman, Vince Vaughn, Cedric the Entertainer, Andre Benjamin, Steven Tyler, Robert Pastorelli, Christina Milian, Paul Adelstein, Debi Mazar, Greg Alan Williams, Harvey Keitel, The Rock, Danny DeVito, James Woods.

THE BEAUTIFUL PERSON

LE PACTE. Sept., 2008. French. (Christophe Honore) Louis Garrel, Lea Seydoux, Gregoire Leprince-Ringuet, Esteban Carjaval-Alegria, Agathe Bonitzer, Simon Truxillo, Anais Demoustier, Valerie Lang, Martin Simeon.

BEAUTIFUL TRUTH

CINEMA LIBRE. Nov. 6, 2008. (Steve Kroschel) Garrett Kroschel, Charlotte Gerson, David Kennedy, John Olney, Hal Huggins, Jay Kordich, Russell Blaylock, Wallace Sampson.

BECAUSE I SAID SO

UNIVERSAL. Jan., 2007. (Michael Lehmann) Diane Keaton, Mandy Moore, Gabriel Macht, Tom Everett Scott, Lauren Graham, Piper Perabo, Stephen Collins, Ty Panitz, Matt Champagne, Colin Ferguson, Tony Hale.

BECAUSE OF WINN-DIXIE

20TH CENTURY FOX. Jan., 2005. (Wayne Wang) Anna Sophia Robb, Jeff Daniels, Cicely Tyson, Eva Marie Saint, Dave Matthews, Courtney Jines, Elle Fanning, Nick Price, Luke Benward.

BECOMING JANE

BUENA VISTA INTL. (IN U.K.)/MIRAMAX (IN U.S.). March, 2007. British-U.S. (Julian Jarrold) Anne Hathaway, James McAvoy, Julie Walters, James Cromwell, Maggie Smith, Joe Anderson, Lucy Cohu, Laurence Fox, Ian Richardson, Anna Maxwell Martin, Leo Bill, Jessica Ashworth, Michael James Ford, Tom Vaughan-Lawlor, Helen McCrory.

BEE MOVIE

PARAMOUNT. Oct. 19, 2007. (Simon J. Smith) Jerry Seinfeld, Renee Zellweger, Matthew Broderick, John Goodman, Patrick Warburton, Chris Rock, Kathy Bates, Barry Levinson, Larry King, Ray Liotta, Sting, Oprah Winfrey, Larry Miller, Megan Mullally, Rip Torn, Michael Richards, Mario Joyner.

BEER FOR MY HORSES

ROADSIDE ATTRACTIONS. Aug. 3, 2008. (Michael Salomon) Toby Keith, Rodney Carrington, Claire Forlani, Ted Nugent, Willie Nelson, Barry Corbin, Greg Serano, Tom Skerritt, Carlos Sanz, Lonnie M. Tillis.

BEERFEST

WARNER BROS. Aug. 2006. (Jay Chandrasekhar) Jay Chandrasekhar, Kevin Heffernan, Steve Lemme, Paul Soter, Erik Stolhanske, Will Forte, Ralf Moeller, Mo'Nique, Eric Christian Olsen,

Juergen Prochnow, Cloris Leachman.

BEESWAX
Feb. 6, 2009. (Andrew Bujalski) Tilly Hatcher, Maggie Hatcher, Alex Karpovsky, Katy O'Connor, David Zellner, Kyle Henry, Anne Dodge, Nathan Zellner, Janet Pierson.

BEFORE TOMORROW
ALLIANCE FILM. Oct., 2008. Canadian. (Marie-Helene Cousineau, Madeline Ivalu) Madeline Piujuq Ivalu, Paul-Dylan Ivalu, Peter-Henry Arnatsiaq, Mary Qulitalik, Tumasie Sivuarapik.

BEING CYRUS
EROS ENTERTAINMENT IN (U.K) March, 2006. Indian. (Homi Adajania) March, 2006. Naseeruddin Shah, Dimple Kapadia, Saif Ali Khan, Boman Irani, Honey Chhaya, Simone Singh, Manoj Pahwa.

BEOWULF
PARAMOUNT (in U.S.)/WARNER BROS. (International). Nov. 4, 2007. (Robert Zemeckis) Ray Winstone, Anthony Hopkins, John Malkovich, Robin Wright Penn, Brendan Gleeson, Crispin Glover, Alison Lohman, Angelina Jolie.

THE BEST DAY OF MY LIFE
SND. Jan., 2005. French-Belgium. (Julie Lipinski) Helene de Fougerolles, Jonathan Zaccai, Francois Berleand, Marisa Berenson, Michel Duchaussoy, Eva Darlan, Alexandre Brasseur, Elise Larnicol, Valerie Donzelli, Stephane Metzger, Annelise Hesme, Laurent Bateau, Vanessa Valence.

BETWEEN LIVING AND DREAMING
AURUM. Feb., 2005. Spanish. (Alfonso Albacete, David Menkes) Carmen Maura, Alex Brendemuhl, Thierry Lhermitte, Marta Etura, Manuel Manquina, Soledad Silveyra.

BEVERLY HILLS CHIHUAHUA
WALT DISNEY PICTURES. Sept. 27, 2008. (Raja Gosnell) Piper Perabo, Manolo Cardona, Jamie Lee Curtis, Vasquez - Jose Maria Yazpik. Voices: Drew Barrymore, Andy Garcia, George Lopez.

BEWITCHED
SONY PICTURES ENTERTAINMENT. June, 2005. (Nora Ephron) Nicole Kidman, Will Ferrell, Shirley MacLaine, Michael Caine, Jason Schwartzman, Kristin Chenoweth, Heather Burns, Jim Turner, Stephen Colbert, David Alan Grier, Steve Carell.

BEYOND THE YEARS
BEAR ENTERTAINMENT, PRIME ENTERTAINMENT. April, 2007. South Korean. (Im Kwon-taek) Jo Jae-hyeon, Oh Jeong-hae, Oh Seung-eun, Yu Seung-ryong, Im Jin-taek, Yun Je-weon, Hwang Shi-on, Bang Eun-mi, Jang Min-ho, Ahn Byeong-gyeong, Gweon Tae-weon.

BIENVENUE CHEZ LES CH'TIS
PATHE. March, 2008. French. (Dany Boon) Kad Merad, Dany Boon, Zoe Felix, Philippe Duquesne, Line Renaud, Michel Galabru, Stephane Freiss, Guy Lecluyse, Anne Marivin, Patrick Bosso, Zinedine Soualem, Jerome Commandeur, Christophe Rossignon, Yael Boon, Alexandre Carriere.

THE BIG BUY: TOM DELAY'S STOLEN CONGRESS
BRAVE NEW FILMS. May, 2006. (Mark Birnbaum, Jim Schermbeck). Documentary.

BIG FAN
FIRST INDEPENDENT. Jan. 20, 2009. Jan. 20, 2009. (Robert Siegel) Patton Oswalt, Kevin Corrigan, Marcia Jean Kurtz, Michael Rapaport, Matt Servitto, Gino Cafarelli, Serafina Fiore, Jonathan Hamm, Joe Garden, Polly Humphries.

BIG MOMMA'S HOUSE 2
20TH CENTURY FOX. Jan., 2006. (John Whitesell) Martin Lawrence, Nia Long, Emily Procter, Zachary Levi, Mark Moses, Kat Dennings, Chloe Grace Moretz, Marisol Nichols.

BIG NOTHING
PATHE. Dec., 2006. British. (Jean-Baptiste Andrea) David Schwimmer, Simon Pegg, Alice Eve, Jon Polito, Natascha McElhone, Mimi Rogers, Billy Asher, Mitchell Mullen.

THE BIG SHOT-CALLER
STELLA FILMS. May 8, 2009. (Marlene Rhein) David Rhein, Marlene Rhein, Laneya Wiles, Robert Costanzo, Leslie Eva Glaser.

BIGGER THAN THE SKY
MGM. Feb., 2005. (Al Corley) Marcus Thomas, John Corbett, Amy Smart, Sean Astin, Clare Higgins, Patty Duke, Allan Corduner, Greg Germann.

THE BIRTHDAY
MARS DISTRIBUTION. Sept., 2005. French. (Diane Kurys) Lambert Wilson, Michele Laroque, Jean-Hugues Anglade, Pierre Palmade, Isabella Ferrari, Antoine Dulery, Florence Thomassin, Fabio Sartor, Zoe Felix, Philippe Bas.

THE BITCH'S DIARY
BIOSCOP. April, 2007. Czech Republic. (Irena Pavlaskova) Danica Jurcova, Karel Roden, Marek Vasut, Tomas Matonoha, Miroslav Etzler.

BLACK
YASH RAJ FILMS. Feb., 2005. Indian. (Sanjay Leela Bhansali) Amitabh Bachchan, Rani Mukerji, Ayesha Kapur, Shernaz Patel, Dhritiman Chaterji, Nandana Sen.

BLACK
ZOOTROPE FILMS. July, 2009. French. (Pierre Laffargue) MC Jean Gab'1, Carole Karemera, Francois Levantal, Anton Yakovlev, Mata Gabin, Thierno Ndaye Doss, Ibrahima MBaye, Michel Duperial, Tapha Gueye, Nicky Naude, Louis-Karim Nebati, Youssef Hajdi, Francois Bredon.

BLACK AND WHITE
01 DISTRIBUTION. Jan., 2008. Italian. (Cristina Comencini) Fabio Volo, Ambra Angiolini, Aissa Maiga, Eriq Ebouaney, Anna Bonaiuto, Franco Branciaroli, Teresa Saponangelo, Katia Ricciarelli, Bob Messini, Awa Ly, Billo Thiernothian.

THE BLACK BOX
EUROPACORP. Sept., 2005. French. (Richard Berry) Jose Garcia, Marion Cotillard, Michel Duchaussoy, Bernard Le Coq, Gerald Laroche, Helena Noguerra, Marisa Borini.

BLACK CLOUD
March, 2005. (Rick Schroder) Eddie Spears, Julia Jones, Tim McGraw, Saginaw Grant, Branscombe Richmond, Rick Schroder, Russell Means, Pooch Hall, Wayne Knight, Peter Greene, Nathaniel Arcand.

BLACK CHRISTMAS
MGM. Dec., 2006. (Glen Morgan) Katie Cassidy, Mary Elizabeth Winstead, Lacey Chabert, Michelle Trachtenberg, Oliver Hudson, Andrea Martin, Crystal Lowe, Kristen Cloke, Jessica Harmon, Leela Savasta, Kathleen Kole, Karin Konoval, Howard Siegel, Peter Wilds, Cainan Wiebe, Robert Mann, Christina Crivici, Dean Friss.

BLACK DYNAMITE
SONY WORLDWIDE. Jan. 18, 2009. (Scott Sanders) Michael Jai White, Kym Whitley, Tommy Davidson, Kevin Chapman, Byron Minns, Salli Richardson-Whitfield, Cedric Yarbrough, Mykelti Williamson, Brian McKnight, Bokeem Woodbine, Arsenio Hall, John Salley, James McManus, Nicole Sullivan.

BLACK HOUSE
CJ ENTERTAINMENT. July, 2007. South Korean. (Shin Tae-ra) Hwang Jeong-min, Yu Seon, Gang Shin-il, Kim Seo-hyeong.

BLACK MAGIC
CINETEVE DISTRIBUTION. Jan., 2006. French. (Djibril Glissant) Gregoire Colin, Romane Bohringer, Jacky Berroyer.

BLACK WATER
ALL INTERACTIVE DISTRIBUTION (IN AUSTRALIA)/THE WORKS (IN U.K.). Jan., 2008. Australian-British. (Andrew Traucki, David Nerlich) Diana Glenn, Maeve Dermody, Andy Rodoreda, Ben Oxenbould, Fiona Press.

BLACKBALLED: THE BOBBY DUKES STORY
April, 2006. (Brant Sersen) Rob Corddry, Paul Scheer, Dannah Feinglass, Rob Riggle, Curtis Gwinn, Seth Morris, Rob Huebel, Jamie Denbo, DJ Hazard, Ed Helms.

BLADES OF GLORY
PARAMOUNT. March, 2007. (Will Speck, Josh Gordon) Will Ferrell, Jon Heder, Amy Poehler, Will Arnett, Craig T. Nelson, Jenna Fischer, William Fichtner.

BLESSED
ICON FILMS. Aug., 2009. Australian. (Ana Kokkinos) Frances O'Connor, Miranda Otto, Deborra-lee Furness, Victoria Haralabidou, Monica Maughan, Wayne Blair, William McInnes, Sophie Lowe, Anastasia Baboussouras, Harrison Gilbertson, Eamon Farren, Eva Lazzaro, Reef Ireland, Kellie Jones, Tasma Walton, Neil Pigot, Brett Climo.

BLONDE AMBITION
SONY HOME ENTERTAINMENT. Jan. 28, 2008. (Scott Marshall) Jessica Simpson, Luke Wilson, Rachael Leigh Cook, Penelope Ann Miller, Andy Dick, Larry Miller, Drew Fuller, Willie Nelson, Penny Marshall.

BLOOD: THE LAST VAMPIRE
DESTINATION FILMS/SAMUEL GOLDWYN FILMS (IN U.S.) RELEASE OF AN EAST WING HOLDINGS CORP. (HONG KONG)/SAJ (FRANCE) . Jun., 2009. Chinese, French. (Chris Nahon) Gianna, Allison Miller, Liam Cunningham, J.J. Field, Koyuki, Yasuaki Kurata, Larry Lamb.

BLOOD AND CHOCOLATE
MGM. Jan., 2007. (Katja von Garnier) Agnes Bruckner, Olivier Martinez, Hugh Dancy, Bryan Dick, Katja Riemann.

BLOOD AND TEARS: THE ARAB-ISRAELI CONFLICT
THINKFILM. Aug., 2007. (Isidore Rosmarin) Akbar Ahmed, Eve Harow, Saeb Erekat, Izzeldine Abuelaish, Benjamin Netanyahu, Ehud Barak, Shimon Peres, Yossi Klein Haveil, Renee Yakira, Ameed Al Masri, Sari Nusseibeh, Abdel Aziz al-Rantisi, Joseph Farah, Rashid Khalidi, Bernard Lewis, Michael Oren, Khalil Shikaki, Fouad Ajami, Alan Dershowitz. Documentary.

BLOOD DIAMOND
WARNER BROS. Nov., 2006. (Edward Zwick) Leonardo DiCaprio, Djimon Hounsou, Jennifer Connelly, Kagiso Kuypers, Arnold Vosloo, Anthony Coleman, Michael Sheen, Benu Mabhena.

BLOOD IN MAY
ALTA CLASSICS. Oct., 2008. Spanish. (Jose Luis Garci) Quim Gutierrez, Paula Echevarria, Manuel Galiana, Lucia Jimenez, Enrique Villen, Miguel Rellan, Tina Sainz, Natalia Millan, Manuel Tejada, Paco Algora, Fernando Guillen Cuervo.

BLOODLINE
CINEMA LIBRE DISTRIBUTION. April 30, 2008. (Bruce Burgess) Bruce Burgess, Ben Hammott, Nicolas John Shelby Spong, Margaret Starbird, Lionel Fanthorpe, Robert Eisenman, Aidan Dobson, Gabriel Barkay, Robert Howells, Gino Sandri.

BLOODRAYNE
ROMAR ENTERTAINMENT. Jan., 2006. (Uwe Boll) Kristanna Loken, Michael Madsen, Matt Davis, Michelle Rodriguez, Ben Kingsley, Will Sanderson, Udo Kier, Meat Loaf Aday, Michael Pare, Billy Zane, Geraldine Chaplin.

THE BLUE TOOTH VIRGIN
REGENT ENTERTAINMENT/HERE FILMS. Sept 21, 2009. (Russell Brown) Austin Peck, Bryce Johnson, Karen Black, Tom Gilroy, Roma Maffia, Lauren Stamile, Amber Benson.

BLUFFMASTER!
UTV MOTION PICTURE. Dec., 2005. Indian. (Rohan Sippy) Abhishek Bachchan, Priyanka Chopra, Riteish Deshmukh, Boman Irani, Nana Patekar.

BOLT
WALT DISNEY STUDIOS MOTION PICTURES. Nov 12, 2008. (Chris Williams, Byron Howard) Voices: John Travolta, Miley Cyrus, Susie Essman, Mark Walton, Malcolm McDowell, James Lipton, Greg Germann. Animated.

THE BOOK OF REVELATION
July, 2006. Australian-British. (Ana Kokkinos) Tom Long, Greta Scacchi, Colin Friels, Anna Torv, Deborah Mailman, Zoe Coyle, Zoe Naylor, Odette Joannidis, Nadine Garner, Olivia Pigeot, Ana Maria Belo, Belinda McClory, Sibylla Budd.

BOOGEYMAN
SONY PICTURES ENTERTAINMENT. Feb., 2005. (Stephen Kay) Barry Watson, Emily Deschanel, Skye McCole Bartusiak, Tory Mussett, Andrew Glover, Lucy Lawless, Charles Mesure, Phillip Gordon, Aaron Murphy, Jennifer Rucker, Robyn Malcolm.

THE BOONDOCK SAINTS II: ALL SAINTS DAY
APPARITION. Oct. 27, 2009. (Troy Duffy) Sean Patrick Flanery, Norman Reedus, Billy Connolly, Clifton Collins, Jr., Julie Benz, Peter Fonda, Judd Nelson, David Della Rocco, Bob Marley, Brian Mahoney, David Ferry.

THE BORGIAS
DEAPLANETA. Oct., 2006. Spanish-Italian. (Antonio Hernandez) Lluis Homar, Sergio Peris-Mencheta, Sergio Muniz, Maria Valverde, Eloy Azorin, Roberto Alvarez, Antonio Dechent, Antonio Hernandez, Eusebio Poncela, Paz Vega, Angela Molina, Linda Batista.

BORN IN '68
PYRAMIDE DISTRIBUTION. May, 2008. French. (Olivier Ducastel, Jacques Martineau) Laetitia Casta, Yannick Renier, Yann Tregouet, Christine Citti, Marc Citti, Sabrina Seyvecou, Theo Frilet, Edouard Collin, Kate Moran, Slimane Yefsah.

THE BOTTLE
PREMIUM CINE (IN SPAIN) RELEASE OF A QUIMERA FILMS (SPAIN)/ZARLEK PRODUCCIONES (ARGENTINA). April, 2009. Spanish, Argentinian. (Alberto Lecchi) Dario Grandinetti, Leticia Bredice, Martin Piroyansky, Nicolas Scarpino.

BOTTOMS UP
REZO FILMS. Jan., 2005. French. (Marion Vernoux) Emmanuelle Beart, Edouard Baer, Atmen Kelif, Yves Verhoeven, Jean-Michel Tinivelli, Claude Peron, Jackie Berroyer, Marina Fois.

BOUDU
PATHE DISTRIBUTION. March, 2005. French. (Gerard Jugnot) Gerard Depardieu, Catherine Frot, Gerard Jugnot, Constance Dolle, Bonnafet Tarbouriech, Hubert Saint-Macary.

THE BOURNE ULTIMATUM
UNIVERSAL. July, 2007. (Paul Greengrass) Matt Damon, Julia Stiles, David Strathairn, Scott Glenn, Paddy Considine, Edgar Ramirez, Albert Finney, Joan Allen, Tom Gallop, Corey Johnson, Daniel Bruhl, Joey Ansah, Colin Stinton.

THE BOX
WARNER BROS. Oct 12, 2009. (Richard Kelly) Cameron Diaz, James Marsden, Frank Langella.

THE BOY IN THE STRIPED PAJAMAS
WALT DISNEY STUDIOS MOTION PICTURES U.K. (IN U.K.)/MIRAMAX FILMS (IN U.S.). July, 2008. British-U.S. (Mark Herman) Vera Farmiga, David Thewlis, Rupert Friend, David Hayman, Asa Butterfield, Jack Scanlon, Amber Beattie, Sheila Hancock, Richard Johnson, Jim Norton, Cara Horgan.

THE BOYS ARE BACK
MIRAMAX FILMS. SEPT. 2009. Australian. (Scott Hicks) Clive Owen, Emma Booth, Laura Fraser, George MacKay, Nicholas Mcaunulty.

THE BOYS FROM BAGHDAD HIGH
Dec., 2007. British-French-U.S. (Ivan O'Mahoney, Laura Winter) Ali Shadman, Anmar Refat, Hayder Khalid, Mohammad Ra'ed. Documentary.

BOYTOWN
ROADSHOW FILMS. Sept., 2006. Australian. (Kevin Carlin) Glenn Robbins, Mick Molloy, Bob Franklin, Wayne Hope, Gary Eck, Sally Phillips, Lachy Hulme, Sarah Walker, Lois Ramsey.

BRA BOYS
HOPSCOTCH FILMS. Feb., 2007. Australian. (Sunny Abberton) Narrator: Russell Crowe. Documentary.

BRATZ
LIONSGATE. July, 2007. (Sean McNamara) Nathalia Ramos, Janel Parrish, Logan Browning, Skyler Shaye, Chelsea Staub, Anneliese van der Pol, Malese Jow, Stephen Lunsford, Lainie Kazan, Jon Voight.

THE BRAVE ONE
WARNER BROS. Aug., 2007. (Neil Jordan) Jodie Foster, Terrence Howard, Naveen Andrews, Carmen Ejogo, Nicky Katt, Mary Steenburgen, Lenny Venito, Zoe Kravitz.

BREACH
UNIVERSAL. Feb., 2007. (Billy Ray) Chris Cooper, Ryan Phillippe, Laura Linney, Dennis Haysbert, Caroline Dhavernas, Gary Cole, Bruce Davison, Kathleen Quinlan.

THE BREAK-UP
UNIVERSAL PICTURES. May, 2006. (Peyton Reed) Vince Vaughn, Jennifer Aniston, Joey Lauren Adams, Cole Hauser, Jon Favreau, Jason Bateman, Judy Davis, Justin Long, Ivan Sergei, John Michael Higgins, Ann-Margret.

BREATH
SPONGE. April, 2007. South Korean. (Kim Ki-duk) Chang Chen, Zia, Ha Jeong-woo, Gang In-hyeong.

BRICE DE NICE
TFM DISTRIBUTION. April, 2005. French. (James Huth) Jean Dujardin, Bruno Salomone, Clovis Cornillac, Elodie Bouchez, Alexandra Lamy, Francois Chattot, Mathias Mlekuz.

BRIDE FLIGHT
A-FILM. June, 2008. Dutch. (Ben Sombogaart) Karina Smulders, Elise Schaap, Anna Drijver, Waldemar Torenstra, Rutger Hauer, Pleuni Touw, Petra Laseur, Willeke van Ammelrooy, Micha Hulshof, Marc Klein Essink.

BRIDE WARS
20TH CENTURY FOX. Jan. 6, 2009. (Gary Winick) Kate Hudson, Anne Hathaway, Kristen Johnston, Bryan Greenberg, Chris Pratt.

BRIDESHEAD REVISITED
Miramax (in North America)/Buena Vista Intl. (in U.K.). June, 2007. British-U.S. (Julian Jarrold) Matthew Goode, Ben Whishaw, Hayley Atwell, Emma Thompson, Michael Gambon, Greta Scacchi, Jonathan Cake, Patrick Malahide.

THE BRIDGE OF SAN LUIS REY
Jan., 2005. British-Spanish-French. (Mary McGuckian) Robert De Niro, F. Murray Abraham, Kathy Bates, Gabriel Byrne, Geraldine Chaplin, Emilie Dequenne, Adriana Dominguez, Harvey Keitel, Pilar Lopez de Ayala, John Lynch, Mark Polish.

BRIDGE TO TERABITHIA
BUENA VISTA. Feb., 2007. (Gabor Csupo) Josh Hutcherson, AnnaSophia Robb, Robert Patrick, Zooey Deschanel, Bailey Madison, Kate Butler, Devon Wood, Emma Fenton, Grace Brannigan, Latham Gaines, Judy McIntosh, Patricia Aldersley, Lauren Clinton, Isabelle Rose Kircher, Cameron Wakefield, Elliot Lawless, Carly Owen, Jen Wolfe, James Gaylyn.

BRIGHT STAR
PATHE, SCREEN AUSTRALIA, BBC, UK FILM COUNCIL. May 2009. (Jane Campion) Abbie Cornish, Ben Whishaw, Paul Schneider, Kerry Fox, Edie Martin, Thomas Brodie-Sangster, Claudie Blakley, Gerard Monaco. Antonia Campbell-Hughes.

BROKEBACK MOUNTAIN
FOCUS FEATURES. Dec., 2005. (Ang Lee) Heath Ledger, Jake Gyllenhaal, Linda Cardellini, Anna Faris, Anne Hathaway, Michelle Williams, Randy Quaid, Graham Beckel, Scott Michael Campbell, David Harbour, Kate Mara, Roberta Maxwell, Peter McRobbi.

BROKEN BRIDGES
PARAMOUNT CLASSICS. Sept., 2006. (Steven Goldman) Toby Keith, Kelly Preston, Lindsey Haun, Burt Reynolds, Tess Harper, Willie Nelson.

BROKEN EMBRACES
WARNER SOGEFILMS (IN SPAIN) SONY (IN U.S.). March 2009. (Pedro Almodovar) Penelope Cruz, Lluis Homar, Jose Luis Gomez, Blanca Portillo, Lola Duenas, Ruben Ochandiano, Tamar Novas,

Kira Miro, Chus Lampreave, Carmen Machi.

BROKEN FLOWERS

FOCUS FEATURES. May, 2005. (Jim Jarmusch) Bill Murray, Jeffrey Wright, Sharon Stone, Frances Conroy, Jessica Lange, Tilda Swinton, Julie Delpy, Mark Webber, Chloe Sevigny, Christopher McDonald, Alexis Dziena, Larry Fessenden, Chris Bauer, Pell James, Heather Alicia Simms, Brea Frazier.

BRONSON

VERTIGO FILMS. Jan., 2009. U.K. (Nicolas Winding) Tom Hardy, Hugh Ross, Juliet Oldfield, Jonny Phillips, James Lance.

BROTHERS AT WAR

SAMUEL GOLDWYN. March 20, 2009. (Jake Rademacher) Jake Rademacher, Capt. Isaac Rademacher, Jenny Rademacher, Sgt. Joseph Rademacher, Danelle Fields, Dr. Dennis Rademacher, Nikki Rademacher, Sgt. Edward Allier.

THE BROTHERS SOLOMON

SONY PICTURES ENTERTAINMENT. Sept., 2007. (Bob Odenkirk) Will Arnett, Will Forte, Chi McBride, Kristen Wiig, Malin Akerman, Lee Majors.

BRUNO

UNIVERSAL. June 22, 2009. (Larry Charles) Sacha Baron Cohen, Gustaf Hammarsten.

BUDDY

LAUREL HILL FILMS. May, 2007. (Cherry Arnold) Narrator: James Woods. Documentary.

BUNKER PARADISE

EUROPACORP DISTRIBUTION (IN FRANCE). March, 2006. Belgium-French. (Stefan Liberski) Jean-Paul Rouve, Francois Vincentelli, Audrey Marnay, Bouli Lanners, Sacha Bourdo, Yolande Moreau, Jean-Pierre Cassel.

BUNTY AUR BABLI

YASH RAJ FILMS. June, 2005. Indian. (Shaad Ali Sahgal) Abhishek Bachchan, Rani Mukerji, Amitabh Bachchan, Kiran Joneja Sippy, Puneet Issar, Raj Babbar, Prem Chopra, Rameshwari, Pratima Kazmi, Aishwarya Rai.

BUSTIN' DOWN THE DOOR

SCREEN MEDIA FILMS. July 21, 2008. (Jeremy Gosch) Wayne "Rabbit" Bartholomew, Ian Cairns, Mark Richards, Shaun Tomson, Michael Tomson, Peter Townend, Drew Kampion, Eddie Rothman, Fred Hemmings, Barry Kanaiaupuni, Jeff Rakman, Clyde Aikau, Dave Gilovich, Rob Machado, Kelly Slater. Narrator: Edward Norton. Documentary.

BURMA VJ

MAGIC HOUR FILMS. Dec., 2009. Danish. (Anders Ostergaard).

BUT WHEN DO THE GIRLS GET HERE?

ANTONIO AVATI AND RAI CINEMA PRESENTATION AN 01 DISTRIBUTION. Feb., 2005. Italian. (Pupi Avati) Claudio Santamaria, Vittoria Puccini, Paolo Briguglia, Johnny Dorelli, Augusto Fornari, Alessio Modica, Enrico Salimbeni.

BY FORCE

SONY PICTURES. Nov., 2005. Spanish. (Juan Vicente Cordoba) Natalia Verbeke, Daniel Guzman, Juana Acosta, Maria Vazquez, Marian Alvarez, Zay Nuba, Andres Gertrudis, Alfredo Villa, Maria Reyes.

BY THE LIGHT OF DAY

MIKADO. Jan., 2005. Italian. (Roberto Faenza) Luca Zingaretti, Alessia Goria, Corrado Fortuna, Giovanna Bozzolo, Francesco Foti, Piero Nicosia, Lollo Franco, Mario Giunta, Pierlorenzo Randazzo, Gabriele Castagna, Salvo Scelta.

BY THE PRICKING OF MY THUMBS

UGC. April, 2005. French. (Pascal Thomas) Catherine Frot, Andre Dussollier, Genevieve Bujold, Laurent Terzieff, Valerie Kaprisky.

C

THE CABINET OF DR. CALIGARI

Oct., 2006. (David Lee Fisher) Judson Pearce Morgan, Daamen Krall, Doug Jones, Lauren Birkell, Neil Hopkins, William Gregory Lee, Randy Mulkey, Time Winters, Richard Herd, Scott Lincoln.

CACHIMBA

CIVITE. April, 2005. Chilean-Spanish-Argentinian. (Silvio Caiozzi) Pablo Schwarz, Mariana Loyola, Julio Jung, Patricio Contreras, Jesus Guzman.

CACTUS

HOYTS DISTRIBUTION. March, 2008. Australian. (Jasmine Yuen-Carrucan) Travis McMahon, David Lyons, Bryan Brown, Shane Jacobson.

THE CACTUS

UGC DISTRIBUTION. Dec., 2005. French. (Gerard Bitton, Michel Munz) Clovis Cornillac, Pascal Elbe, Alice Taglioni, Pierre Richard, Jean-Pierre Darroussin, Anne Suarez, Christian Charmetant, Eric Seigne.

CADILLAC RECORDS

SONY PICTURES ENTERTAINMENT. Nov. 18, 2008. (Darnell Martin) Adrien Brody, Jeffrey Wright, Gabrielle Union, Columbus Short, Cedric the Entertainer, Emmanuelle Chriqui, Eamonn Walker, Mos Def, Beyonce Knowles, Kevin Mambo.

CAFFEINE

STEAMING HOT COFFEE. March, 2007. (John Cosgrove) Mena Suvari, Marsha Thomason, Katherine Heigl, Andrew Lee Potts, Mike Vogel, Breckin Meyer, Callum Blue, Mark Pellegrino, Roz Witt, Sonya Walger, Orlando Seale, Andrew Abelson, Mark Dymond, Jules Leyser, Daz Crawford, Neil Dickson.

CALL OF THE WILD

BRAEBURN ENTERTAINMENT. June 12, 2009. (Richard Gabai) Christopher Lloyd, Ariel Gade, Wes Studi, Aimee Teegarden, Devon Graye, Kameron Knox, Jaleel White, Joyce DeWitt, Veronica Cartwright, Timothy Bottoms, Devon Iott.

CALL + RESPONSE

FAIR TRADE. Oct. 13, 2008. (Justin Dillon) Julia Ormond, Ashley Judd, Madeleine Albright, Nicholas Kristof, Moby, Natasha Bedingfield, Talib Kweli, Matisyahu, Cold War Kids, Emmanuel Jal, Imogen Heap.

CALLBACK: THE UNMAKING OF 'BLOODSTAIN'

JAFFLE PRODS. Sept. 21, 2008. (Eric M. Wolfson) Jeff Parise, Johnny Moreno, Michael DeGood, Kate Orsini, Jennifer Hall, Burnadean Jones, Darrin Reed.

THE CAMDEN 28

FIRST RUN FEATURES. July, 2007. (Anthony Giacchino) Michael Doyle, John Swinglish, Bob Hardy, Michael Giocondo, Joan Reilly, Howard Zinn, many others. Documentary.

CAMPING

PATHE. April, 2006. French. (Fabien Onteniente) Gerard Lanvin, Mathilde Seigner, Franck Dubosc, Claude Brasseur, Mylene Demongeot, Antoine Dulery, Christine Citti, Frederique Bel, Laurent Olmedo, Francois Levantal, Armonie Sanders.

CAMPING A LA FERME

PAN EUROPEENNE. July, 2005. French. (Jean-Pierre Sinapi) Roschdy Zem, Julie Gayet, Nadine Marcovici, Julie Delarme, Jean-François Stevenin, Dominique Pinon, Bruno Lochet, Mickael Masclet, Rafik Ben Mebarek, Jean-Noel Cridlig-Veneziano, Hassan Ouled-Bouarif, Yves Michel, Aghmane Ibersiene.

CANARY

BANDAI VISUAL, IMAGINASIAN PICTURES (IN U.S.). July, 2008. Japanese. (Akihito Shiota) Hoshi Ishida, Mitsuki Tanimura, Hidetoshi Nishijima, Miyako Koda, Ryo, Tsugumi.

CANDY LAND: THE GREAT LOLLIPOP ADVENTURE

PARAMOUNT HOME VIDEO. Feb., 2005. (Davis Doi) Voices: Jane Mortifee, Alberto Ghisi, Britt McKillip, Scott McNeil, Ian James Corlett, Doug Parker, Mark Oliver, Kathleen Barr, Ellen Kennedy. Animated.

CAPOTE

SONY PICTURES CLASSICS. Sept., 2005. (Bennett Miller) Philip Seymour Hoffman, Catherine Keener, Clifton Collins, Jr., Chris Cooper, Bruce Greenwood, Bob Balaban, Amy Ryan, Mark Pellegrino.

CAPITALISM: A LOVE STORY

OVERTURE FILMS. Sept. 5, 2009. (Michael Moore) Michael Moore, Frank Moore.

CAPTIVITY

LIONSGATE. July, 2007. (Roland Joffe) Elisha Cuthbert, Daniel Gillies, Pruitt Taylor Vince, Michael Harney, Laz Alonso.

CARRIERS

PARAMOUNT. Sept. 4, 2009. (Alex Pastor, David Pastor) Lou Taylor Pucci, Chris Pine, Piper Perabo, Emily VanCamp, Chris Meloni, Kiernan Shipka.

CARS

BUENA VISTA PICTURES. June, 2006. (John Lasseter) Owen Wilson, Paul Newman, Bonnie Hunt, Larry the Cable Guy, Cheech Marin, Tony Shalhoub, Guido Quaroni, Jenifer Lewis, Paul Dooley, Michael Wallis, George Carlin, Katherine Helmond, John Ratzenberger, Joe Ranft, Michael Keaton, Richard Petty. Animated.

CARLITOS AND THE FIELD OF DREAMS

HISPANO FOXFILM. Sept., 2008. Spanish. (Jesus del Cerro) Gustavo Salmeron, Irene Visedo, Jose Maria Pou, Guillermo Campra, David Becerra, Vicente Diez, Inigo Navares, Alejandra Lorenzo, Jennifer Manzano, Miliki.

CARNERA: THE WALKING MOUNTAIN

MEDUSA. May, 2008. Italian. (Renzo Martinelli) Andrea Iaia, Anna Valle, Paolo Seganti, Burt Young, Paul Sorvino, F. Murray Abraham, Kasia Smutniak, Eleonora Martinelli, Antonio Cupo, Stefano Meglio, Bruno Bilotta, Nino Benvenuti, Joe Capalbo, Carlo di Blasi, Lucrezia Maier, Florin Busuioc, Alexandru Pavel, Paolo Ginocchio, Nicolae Urs, Adriana Schiopu, Razvan Oprea, Vlad Radescu, Aura Clarasu, Mihai Dinvale, Ilie Petrica, Fiorenti Emanoil.

CASH

TFM DISTRIBUTION. April, 2008. French. (Eric Besnard) Jean Dujardin, Jean Reno, Valeria Golino, Alice Taglioni, Francois Berleand, Caroline Proust, Jocelyn Quivrin, Ciaran Hinds, Clovis Cornillac.

CASI DIVAS

MAYA ENTERTAINMENT (IN U.S.) Aug., 2009. Mexico. (Issa Lopez) Patricia Llaca, Julio Bracho, Maya Zapata, Ana Layevska, Daniela Schmidt, Diana Garcia.

CASINO ROYALE

SONY PICTURES ENTERTAINMENT. Nov., 2006. (Martin Campbell) Daniel Craig, Eva Green, Mads Mikkelsen, Judi Dench, Jeffrey Wright, Giancarlo Giannini, Caterina Murino, Simon Abkarian, Issach De Bankole, Jesper Christensen, Ivana Milicevic, Tobias Menzies.

CASTING ABOUT

KINO INTL. June, 2005. (Barry J. Hershey). Documentary.

CATCH AND RELEASE

SONY PICTURES ENTERTAINMENT. Jan., 2007. (Susannah Grant) Jennifer Garner, Timothy Olyphant, Sam Jaeger, Kevin Smith, Juliette Lewis, Joshua Friesen, Fiona Shaw.

THE CATERPILLAR WISH

PALACE FILMS. March, 2006. Australian. (Sandra Sciberras) Susie Porter, Victoria Thaine, Wendy Hughes, Phillip Quast, Robert Mammone, Khan Chittenden.

CAVALCADE

MARS DISTRIBUTION. May, 2005. French. (Steve Suissa) Titoff, Marion Cotillard, Richard Bohringer, Berenice Bejo, Laurent Bateau, Vincent Martinez, Bruno Todeschini, Stephan Guerin-Tillie, Axelle Laffont, Estelle Lefebure, Eric Berger, Jean-Claude Bouillon, Steve Suissa, Elodie Navarre, Maria Jurado.

THE CAVE

SONY PICTURES ENTERTAINMENT. Aug., 2005. (Bruce Hunt) Cole Hauser, Morris Chestnut, Eddie Cibrian, Rick Ravanello, Marcel Iures, Kieran Darcy-Smith, Daniel Dae Kim, Lena Headey, Piper Perabo.

THE CAYMAN

SACHER DISTRIBUZIONE. March, 2006. Italian-French. (Nanni Moretti) Silvio Orlando, Margherita Buy, Jasmine Trinca, Michele Placido, Jerzy Stuhr, Nanni Moretti, Antonio Catania, Valerio Mastrandrea, Toni Bertorelli, Anna Bonaiuto, Giuliano Montaldo, Tatti Sanguineti, Paolo Virzi, Paolo Sorrentino, Dario Cantarelli, Carlo Mazzacurati, Cecilia Dazzi, Daniele Rampello.

THE CELESTINE PROPHECY

April, 2006. (Armand Mastroianni) Matthew Settle, Thomas Kretschmann, Sarah Wayne Callies, Annabeth Gish, Hector Elizondo, Joaquim Almeida, Jurgen Pronchnow, Obba Babatunde, Robyn Cohen, John Aylward, Castulo Guerra.

CELIBATAIRES

BAC FILMS. March, 2006. French. (Jean-Michel Verner) Guillaume Depardieu, Olivia Bonamy, Patrick Mille, Serge Hazanavicius, Cartouche.

CHAK DE! INDIA

YASH RAJ FILMS. Aug., 2007. Indian. (Shimit Amin) Shah Rukh Khan, Sagarika Ghatge, Chitrashi Rawat, Shilpa Shukla, Vidya Malvade, Tanya Abrol, Anaitha Nair, Shubhi Mehta, Seema Azmi, Nisha Nair, Sandia Furtado, Arya Menon, Masochon V. Zimik, Kimi Laldawla, Kimberly Miranda, Nichola Sequeira, Raynia Mascarenhas, Aanjjan Srivastav, Javed Khan, Vibha Chibber, Mohit Chauhan, Nakul Vaid, Joyoshree Arora, Vivaan Bhathena.

CHANDNI CHOWK TO CHINA

WARNER BROS. (IN U.S.). Jan., 2009. Indian. (Nikhil Advani) Akshay Kumar, Deepika Padukone, Gordon Liu, Mithun Chakraborty, Ranvir Shorey, Roger Yuan.

THE CHANGELING

May, 2007. (Jay Stern) Wendy Herlich, Clyde Baldo, Chris Brady, James Prendergast, Bruce Meakem, Mary Micari, Mickey Ryan, Craig Wichman, Holiday Segal.

CHAOS

DINSDALE. Aug., 2005. (David DeFalco) Kevin Gage, Sage Stallone, K.C. Kelly, Maya Barovich, Chantal Degroat, Stephen Wozniak, Deborah Lacey, Scott Richards.

CHAOS THEORY

WARNER BROS. March 3, 2008. (Marcos Siega) Ryan Reynolds, Emily Mortimer, Stuart Townsend, Sarah Chalke, Mike Erwin, Constance Zimmer, Matreya Fedor, Elisabeth Harnois, Chris William Martin, Jocelyne Loewen.

CHARLIE AND THE CHOCOLATE FACTORY

WARNER BROS. June, 2005. (Tim Burton) Johnny Depp, Freddie Highmore, David Kelly, Helena Bonham Carter, Noah Taylor, Missi Pyle, James Fox, Deep Roy, Christopher Lee, Adam Godley, Franziska Troegner, Annasophia Robb, Julia Winter, Jordon Fry, Philip Wiegratz, Blair Dunlop, Liz Smith, Eileen Essell, David Morris. Narrator: Geoffrey Holder.

CHARLIE WILSON'S WAR

UNIVERSAL. Nov. 26, 2007. (Mike Nichols) Tom Hanks, Julia Roberts, Philip Seymour Hoffman, Amy Adams, Ned Beatty, Emily Blunt, Om Puri, Ken Stott, John Slattery, Denis O'Hare, Jud Tylor, Peter Gerety, Brian Markinson, Christopher Denham, Tracy Phillips, Wynn Everett, Mary Bonner Baker, Rachel Nichols, Shiri Appleby.

CHARLOTTE'S WEB

PARAMOUNT. Dec., 2006. (Gary Winick) Julia Roberts, Dakota Fanning, Steve Buscemi, John Cleese, Oprah Winfrey, Cedric the Entertainer, Kathy Bates, Reba McEntire, Robert Redford, Thomas Haden Church, Andre Benjamin, Dominic Scott Kay, Sam Shepard, Kevin Anderson, Gary Basaraba, Beau Bridges, Essie Davis, Siobhan Fallon Hogan, Nate Mooney.

CHAW

LOTTE ENTERTAINMENT. July, 2009. South Korean. (Shin Jeong-weon) Eom Tae-woong, Jeong Yu-mi, Jang Hang-seon, Yun Je-mun, Park Hyeok-gweon, Jeong Yun-min, Heo Yeon-hwa, Go Seo-heui, Park Hye-sin.

CHEAPER BY THE DOZEN 2

20TH CENTURY FOX. Dec., 2005. (Adam Shankman) Steve Martin, Eugene Levy, Bonnie Hunt, Tom Welling, Piper Perabo, Carmen Electra, Jaime King, Hilary Duff, Taylor Lautner, Alyson Stoner, Jonathan Bennett, Jacob Smith, Liliana Mumy, Morgan York, Kevin G. Schmidt, Forrest Landis, Brent Kinsman, Shane Kinsman, Blake Woodruff, Alexander Conti, Melanie Tonello, Robbie Amell, Courtney Fitzpatrick, Madison Fitzpatrick, Shawn Roberts.

CHEATING LOVE

TFM DISTRIBUTION. June, 2006. French. (Ivan Calberac) Julien Boisselier, Alexandra Lamy, Gilles Lellouche, Melanie Doutey, Patrick Chesnais, Claire Nebout, Melanie Page, Matthieu Roze, Anne Consigny.

CHEF'S SPECIAL

WARNER BROTHERS PICTURES INTL. SPAIN. April, 2008. Spanish. (Nacho Garcia Velilla) Javier Camara, Lola Duenas, Fernando Tejero, Chus Lampreave, Benjamiín Vicuna, Junio Valverde, Luis Varela.

CHÉRI

PATHE (IN U.K/FRANCE)/MIRIMAX (IN U.S.),Feb., 2009. (Stephen Frears) Min.U.K., French, German. Michelle Pfeiffer, Rupert Friend, Kathy Bates, Felicity Jones, Bette Bourne, Iben Hjejle, Nichola McAuliffe, Anita Pallenberg, Frances Tomelty, Harriet Walter, Stephen Frears.

CHICKEN LITTLE

BUENA VISTA. Oct., 2005. (Mark Dindal) Zach Braff, Garry Marshall, Joan Cusack, Steve Zahn, Amy Sedaris, Don Knotts, Harry Shearer, Patrick Stewart, Wallace Shawn, Fred Willard, Catherine O'Hara, Adam West, Patrick Warburton. Animated.

CHICKEN TIKKA MASALA

FILM INC./SEVEN SPICE PRODS. March, 2005. British. (Harmage Singh Kalirai) Chris Bisson, Saeed Jaffrey, Sally Bankes, Peter Ash, Zohra Segal, Katy Clayton, Jinder Mahal, Sushil Chudasama, Louisa Eyd, Shobu Kapoor, Jamila Massey, Harish Patel.

THE CHILD

DIAPHANA (IN FRANCE)/CINEART (IN BELGIUM). May, 2005. Belgium-French. (Jean-Pierre Dardenne and Luc Dardenne) Jeremie Renier, Deborah Francois, Jeremie Segard, Fabrizio Rongione.

THE CHILDREN

PATHE DISTRIBUTION. Jan., 2005. French. (Christian Vincent) Gerard Lanvin, Karin Viard, Brieuc Quiniou, Nicolas Jouxtel, Phareelle Onoyan, Martin Combes, Nathalie Richard, Anne Rousselet, Leopold Szabatura, Aurelie Namur, Geraldine Barbe, Lucy Samsoen.

THE CHILDREN OF HUANG SHI

SONY PICTURES CLASSICS (IN U.S.). April, 2008. Australian-U.S.-Chinese-German. (Roger Spottiswoode) Jonathan Rhys Meyers, Radha Mitchell, Chow Yun-fat, Michelle YeohBarnes, Guang Li, Jin Shuyuan.

THE CHINESE BOTANIST'S DAUGHTERS

EUROPACORP (IN FRANCE)/CHRISTOL FILMS (IN CANADA). April, 2006. French-Canadian. (Dai Sijie) Mylene Jampanoi, Li Xiaoran, Dongfu Lin, Wang Weidong, Nguyen Van Quang, Nguyen Nhur Quynh, Nguyen Thi Xuan Thuc, Yang Jun, le Tung Linh, Chu Hung, Tuo Jilin.

CHRISTMAS IN MIAMI

FILMAURO. Dec., 2005. Italian. (Neri Parenti) Massimo Boldi, Christian De Sica, Massimo Ghini, Vanessa Hessler, Francesco Mandelli, Giuseppe Sanfelice, Paolo Ruffini, Raffaella Berge, Caterina Vertova, Sofola Fatu.

CHRISTMAS ON MARS

CINEMA PURGATORIO/WARNER BROS. RECORDS. Sept. 14, 2008. (Wayne Coyne) Steven Drozd, Wayne Coyne, Michael Ivins, Kliph Scurlock, H. Michelle Martin-Coyne, Steve Burns, Fred Armisen, Adam Goldberg.

THE CHRONICLES OF NARNIA: PRINCE CASPIAN

WALT DISNEY STUDIOS. May 8, 2008. (Andrew Adamson) Georgie Henley, Skandar Keynes, William Moseley, Anna Popplewell, Ben Barnes, Peter Dinklage, Pierfrancesco Favino, Warwick Davis, Vincent Grass, Damian Alcazar, Alicia Borrachero, Sergio Castellitto, Liam Neeson, Tilda Swinton.

THE CHRONICLES OF NARNIA: THE LION, THE WITCH AND THE WARDROBE
BUENA VISTA. Nov., 2005. (Andrew Adamson) Tilda Swinton, Georgie Henley, Skandar Keynes, William Moseley, Anna Popplewell, James McAvoy, Jim Broadbent, Kiran Shah, James Cosmo, Judy McIntosh, Elizabeth Hawthorne. Voices: Liam Neeson, Ray Winstone, Dawn French, Rupert Everett, Cameron Rhodes, Philip Steuer, Jim May, Sim Evan-Jones.

CHUCK CLOSE
ART KALEIDOSCOPE. Dec 20, 2007. (Marion Cajori) Janet Fish, Robert Rauschenberg, Leslie Close, Alex Katz, Elizabeth Murray, Kirk Varnedoe, Philip Glass, Joe Zucker, Dorothea Rockburne, Mark Greenwold, Lucas Samaras, Arne Glimcher, Bruce Marden, Robert Storr, Kiki Smith. Documentary.

CINDERELLA MAN
UNIVERSAL PICTURES. May, 2005. (Ron Howard) Russell Crowe, Renee Zellweger, Paul Giamatti, Craig Bierko, Paddy Considine, Bruce McGill, Ron Canada, David Huband, Connor Price, Ariel Waller, Patrick Louis, Rosemarie DeWitt, Linda Kash.

CIRQUE DU FREAK: THE VAMPIRE'S ASSISTANT
UNIVERSAL. Sept. 26, 2009. (Paul Weitz) John C. Reilly, Ken Watanabe, Josh Hutcherson, Chris Massoglia, Ray Stevenson, Patrick Fugit, Willem Dafoe, Salma Hayek.

CITY OF EMBER
20TH CENTURY FOX. Oct. 8, 2008. (Gil Kenan) Saoirse Ronan, Harry Treadaway, Bill Murray, Martin Landau, Mary Kay Place, Toby Jones, Marianne Jean-Baptiste, Mackenzie Crook, Tim Robbins, Amy Quinn, Catherine Quinn.

CJ7
SONY PICTURES HONG KONG (IN HONG KONG)/CHINA FILM GROUP, POLYBONA FILM DISTRIBUTION (IN CHINA)/SONY PICTURES CLASSICS (IN U.S.). Feb., 2008. Hong Kong-Chinese. (Stephen Chow) Stephen Chow, Xu Jiao, Kitty Zhang, Lee Sheung-ching, Fun Min-hun, Huang Lee, Yao Wenxue, Han Yong-wua, Lam Tze-chung, Hu Qianlin.

CLARA
KINOWELT/ARTHAUS (IN GERMANY). Nov., 2008. German-French-Hungarian. (Helma Sanders-Brahms) Martina Gedeck, Pascal Greggory, Malik Zidi, Peter Takatsy, Bela Fesztbaum, Brigitte Annessy, Christine Oesterlein, Walter Theil.

CLASH OF EGOS
NORDISK FILM. Jan., 2007. Danish. (Tomas Villum Jensen) Ulrich Thomsen, Nikolaj Lie Kaas, Mille Dinesen, Line Kruse, Kristian Halken, Nicolaj Kopernikus, Jakob Cedergren, Lars Brygmann, Niels Olsen, Peter Mygind, Ellen Hillingso, Mikael Caroe, Christian Heldbo Wienberg, Frederikke Thomassen.

CLICK
SONY PICTURES ENTERTAINMENT. June, 2006. (Frank Coraci) Adam Sandler, Kate Beckinsale, Christopher Walken, Henry Winkler, David Hasselhoff, Julie Kavner, Jennifer Coolidge, Sean Astin.

CLOSING ESCROW
MAGNOLIA PICTURES. Aug., 2007. (Armen Kaprelian, Kent Llewellyn) April Barnett, Rob Brownstein, Colleen Crabtree, Andrew Friedman, Wendi McLendon-Covey, Bruce Thomas, Patty Wortham, Cedric Yarbrough.

CLOUDY WITH A CHANCE OF MEATBALLS
SONY PICTURES ENTERTAINMENT. Sept. 12, 2009. (Phil Lord, Christopher Miller) Bill Hader, Anna Faris, James Caan, Andy Samberg, Bruce Campbell, Mr. T, Bobb'e J. Thompson, Benjamin Bratt.

CLOVERFIELD
PARAMOUNT. Jan 14, 2008. (Matt Reeves) Lizzy Caplan, Jessica Lucas, T.J. Miller, Michael Stahl-David, Mike Vogel, Odette Yustman.

COACH CARTER
PARAMOUNT. Jan., 2005. (Thomas Carter) Samuel L. Jackson, Robert Richard, Rob Brown, Ashanti, Debbi Morgan, Rick Gonzalez, Antwon Tanner, Nana Gbewonyo, Channing Tatum, Texas Battle.

COACHELLA
Jan., 2006. (Drew Thomas) Spearhead, Squarepusher, The Mars Volta, Belle & Sebastian, Nu Mark & Cut Chemist, The White Stripes, Iggy Pop & the Stooges, Fischerspooner, Prodigy, Oasis, Bjork, Roni Size, Radiohead, The Polyphonic Spree, Kool Keith, Saul Williams, The Arcade Fire, Bright Eyes, Chemical Brothers, The Crystal Method, Morrissey, Pixies, Red Hot Chili Peppers, The Flaming Lips, Zero 7. Documentary.

COWEB
Joy Charm Enterprise (Hong Kong)/Beijing Channel Pictures Co. (China). July, 2009. Chinese. (Xiong Xinxin) Jiang Luxia, Sam Lee, Eddie Cheung, Kane Kosugi, Chan Kwok-pong, Peggy Zeng, He Zhonglin, Zhang Zuofeng, Mike Moeller, Eskindir Tesfay, Andy Taylor.

COCAINE COWBOYS
MAGNOLIA PICTURES. Oct., 2006. (Billy Corben) Jon Roberts, Mickey Munday, Jorge "Rivi" Ayala, Dr. Joseph Davis, Sgt. Al Singleton. Documentary.

COCO BEFORE CHANEL
WARNER BROS. (IN FRANCE)/SONY PICTURES CLASSICS (IN U.S.) April 2009. French. (Anne Fontaine) Audrey Tautou, Benoit Poelvoorde, Alessandro Nivola, Marie Gillain, Emmanuelle Devos.

CODE 68
BAC FILMS. Aug., 2005. French. (Jean-Henri Roger) Judith Cahen, Stanislas Merhar, Ariane Ascaride, Gerard Meylan, Jacno, Jean-Pierre Kalfon, Marie Balmelle, Yves Afonso.

CODE NAME: THE CLEANER
NEW LINE CINEMA. Jan., 2007. (Les Mayfield) Cedric the Entertainer, Lucy Liu, Nicollette Sheridan, Mark Dacascos, Callum Keith Rennie, Niecy Nash, DeRay Davis, Will Patton.

COLD FEET
COLUMBIA TRISTAR NORDISK FILM DISTRIBUTORS. May, 2007. Norwegian. (Alexander Eik) Lasse Valdal, Sarah Elise Steensby, Andreas Blix Henriksen, Hanna Kavli Lund.

COLD PREY II
NORDISK. Nov., 2008. Norwegian. (Mats Stenberg) Ingrid Bolso Berdal, Marthe Snorresdotter Rovik, Kim Wifladt, Johanna Mork, Fridtjov Saheim, Mats Eldoen, Robert Follin, Per Shaaning, Vetle Qvenild Werring, Mads Sjogaard Pettersen, Inger Joanne Ravn.

COLD SOULS
TWO LANE PICTURES and WINNER ARTS. Jan. 17, 2009. (Sophie Barthes) Paul Giamatti, David Strathairn, Dina Korzun, Katheryn Winnick, Lauren Ambrose, Emily Watson.

THE COLLECTOR
FREESTYLE RELEASING. July 31, 2009. (Marcus Dunstan) Josh Stewart, Michael Reilly Burke, Andrea Roth, Karley Scott Collins, Madeline Zima, Juan Fernandez, Tom Gulager, Patrick Melton.

COLLEGE
MGM. Aug. 28, 2008. (Deb Hagan) Drake Bell, Kevin Covais, Andrew Caldwell, Haley Bennett, Nick Zano, Ryan Pinkston, Camille Mana, Nathalie Walker, Verne Troyer, Alona Tal, Gary Owen.

COLLEGE ROAD TRIP
WALT DISNEY PICTURES. March 3, 2008. (Roger Kumble) Martin Lawrence, Raven-Symone, Donny Osmond, Brenda Song, Will Sasso, Eshaya Draper, Kym E. Whitley, Arnetia Walker, Margo Harshman, Josh Meyers, Michael Landes, Lucas Grabeel, Adam Lefevre.

THE COLOR OF OLIVES
ARAB FILM DISTRIBUTION. July, 2006. Mexican. (Carolina Rivas) Documentary.

COLOR OF THE CROSS
ROCKY MOUNTAIN PICTURES. Oct., 2006. (Jean Claude LaMarre) Jean Claude LaMarre, Debbi Morgan, David Gianopoulos, Elya Baskin, Pacinto Taras Riddick, Akiva David, Johann Jean, JR Dziengel, Marjan Faritous, John-Pierre Parent, Adam Green, Michael Govia, Shervin Daratzan, Melvin Weiss, Marc Winn.

COLORS OF PASSION
Nov., 2008. Indian. (Ketan Mehta) Randeep Hooda, Nandana Sen, Jim Boeven, Paresh Rawal, Rachna Shah, Ferena Wazeir, Tripta Parashar, Ashish Vidyarthi, Prroshant Narayannan, Darshan Jariwala, Sachin Khedekar, Vipin Sharma, Chirag Vohra, Tom Alter, Rajat Kapoor, Vikram Gokhle, Suhasini Mulay, Shreevallabh Vyas, Gaurav Dwivedi, Reema Vohra.

COLUCHE
MARS DISTRIBUTION. Oct., 2008. French. (Antoine de Caunes) Francois-Xavier Demaison, Lea Drucker, Olivier Gourmet, Laurent Bateau, Jean-Pierre Martins, Alexandre Astier, Denis Podalydes, Valerie Crouzet, Serge Riaboukine.

COME AWAY WITH ME
MEDUSA FILM. April, 2005. Italian. (Carlo Ventura) Mariangela Melato, Enrico Lucci, Daniele Passaro, Dino Nole, Alex Feldman, Dylan Fergus, Marta Mondelli, Adam Kaufman, Adrienne Williams, Irma St. Paule, Hal Hughes, Vincenzo Scalise, Michael Mandell.

COMING ATTRACTIONS: THE HISTORY OF THE MOVIE TRAILER
April, 2006. (Michael J. Shapiro) Joe Dante, Rob Friedman, Stewart Harnell, Vinzenz Hediger, Stephen Herek, Paul Hirsch, Lisa Kernan, Andrew Kuehn, Leonard Maltin, Greg Morrison, Joel Schumacher. Narrator/Host: Robert Osborne. Documentary.

THE COMEBACKS
20TH CENTURY FOX. Oct. 19, 2007. (Tom Brady) David Koechner, Carl Weathers, Melora Hardin, Matthew Lawrence, Brooke Nevin, Nick Searcy, George Back, Noureen DeWulf, Jesse Garcia, Jackie Long, Robert Ri'chard, Martin Spanjers, Jermaine Williams, Dennis Rodman, Andy Dick.

COMPLETELY MAD
FOLKETS BIO. May, 2005. Swedish. (Rafael Edholm) Gorel Crona, Rafael Edholm, Rogelio de Badajoz, Anett Duran, Yaba Holst, Hannu Kiviaho, Emilio Castillo, Rocio Sanchez Millan, Luis Rubio, Benito Abella, Miguel Abellan.

THE CONDEMNED
LIONSGATE. April, 2007. (Scott Wiper) Steve Austin, Vinnie Jones,

Robert Mammone, Victoria Mussett, Manu Bennett, Madeleine West, Samantha Healy, Christopher Baker, Luke Pegler, Rick Hoffman, Masa Yamaguchi, Emelia Burns, Dasi Ruz, Marcus Johnson, Nathan Jones, Andy McPhee, Rai Fazio, Angie Milliken, Sullivan Stapleton, Grant Piro, Neil Pigot.

CONFESSIONS OF A SHOPAHOLIC
WALT DISNEY STUDIOS MOTION PICTURES. Feb. 10, 2009. (P.J. Hogan) Isla Fisher, Hugh Dancy, Joan Cusack, John Goodman, John Lithgow, Kristin Scott Thomas, Leslie Bibb, Fred Armisen, Julie Hagerty, Krysten Ritter, Robert Stanton, Christine Ebersole, Clea Lewis, Wendie Malick, Lynn Redgrave.

CONFETTI
20TH CENTURY FOX INTL. (IN U.K.)/FOX SEARCHLIGHT (IN U.S.). March, 2006. British-U.S. (Debbie Isitt) Martin Freeman, Jessica Stevenson, Stephen Mangan, Meredith MacNeill, Robert Webb, Olivia Colman, Vincent Franklin, Jason Watkins, Jimmy Carr, Felicity Montagu, Alison Steadman, Mark Wootton, Sarah Hadland, Ron Cook.

CONNECTED
EMPEROR MOTION PICTURES (IN HONG KONG)/POLYBONA FILMS (IN CHINA). Sept., 2008. Hong Kong-Chinese. (Benny Chan) Louis Koo, Barbie Hsu, Nick Cheung, Liu Ye, Gong Beibi, Eddie Cheung, Fan Siu-wong, Flora Chan, David Rock, Robbin Harris, Daniel Whyte, Ankie Beilke.

THE CONSTANT GARDENER
FOCUS FEATURES. Aug., 2005. British-German. (Fernando Meirelles) Ralph Fiennes, Rachel Weisz, Danny Huston, Bill Nighy, Pete Postlethwaite, Richard McCabe, Donald Sumpter, Juliet Aubrey, Hubert Kounde, Archie Panjabi, Gerard McSorley, Samuel Otage, Anneke Kim Sarnau.

CONSTANTINE
WARNER BROS. Jan., 2005. (Francis Lawrence) Keanu Reeves, Rachel Weisz, Shia LeBeouf, Djimon Hounsou, Max Baker, Pruitt Taylor Vince, Gavin Rossdale, Tilda Swinton, Peter Stormare.

CONSTANTINE'S SWORD
FIRST RUN FEATURES/RED ENVELOPE ENTERTAINMENT. April 3, 2008. (Oren Jacoby) James Carroll, Liev Schreiber, Phillip Bosco, Natasha Richardson, Eli Wallach. Documentary.

CONTRACT LOVER
Nov., 2007. Chinese. (Alfred Cheung) Richie Jen, Fan Bingbing, Yuen Wah, Kate Tsui, Liu Yi, Ian Powers, Liu Yiwei, Yang Zhiying, You Hang, Yu Molin, Liang Tiejian, Zhang Jinrong, A Min.

CONVERSATIONS WITH GOD
SAMUEL GOLDWYN FILMS. Oct., 2006. (Stephen Simon) Henry Czerny, Vilma Silva, Bruce Page, Ingrid Boulting, Abdul Salaam el Razzac, Zillah Glory.

THE COTTAGE
PATHE INTL. March, 2008. British. (Paul Andrew Williams) Andy Serkis, Reece Shearsmith, Jennifer Ellison, Steven O'Donnell, Logan Wong, Jonathan Chan-Pensley, Simon Schatzberger, David Legeno.

COULD THIS BE LOVE?
STUDIOCANAL. Jan., 2007. French. (Pierre Jolivet) Vincent Lindon, Sandrine Bonnaire, Francois Berleand, Kad Merad, Liane Foly, Helene de Saint-Pierre, Guilaine Londez, Albert Dray, Pierre Diot, Mar Sodupe, Venantino Venantini, Brian Bigg.

COUPLES RETREAT
UNIVERSAL. Oct. 6, 2009. (Peter Billingsley) Vince Vaughn, Jason Bateman, Jon Favreau, Faizon Love, Kristin Davis, Malin Akerman, Kristen Bell, Temuera Morrison, Jean Reno, Kali Hawk.

COUNTER INVESTIGATION
PATHE DISTRIBUTION. Jan., 2007. French. (Franck Mancuso) Jean Dujardin, Laurent Lucas, Agnes Blanchot, Aurelien Recoing, Jean-Pierre Cassel, Jacques Frantz, Alexandra Goncalvez, Jean-Francois Garreaud.

THE COURAGE TO LOVE
July, 2005. French. (Claude Lelouch) Mathilde Seigner, Maiwenn, Arielle Dombasle, Agnes Soral, Massimo Ranieri, Michel Leeb, Ticky Holgado, Alessandra Martines, Francis Perrin, Pierre Santini, Gregori Derangere, Constantin Alexandrov, Michele Bernier, Cyrielle Clair, Mathilde Vitry, Regis Bouquet, Xavier Deluc, Patrick Fierry, Robert Namias, Richard Gotainer, Yannick Soulier, Antoine Dulery.

THE COVE
OCEANIC PRESERVATION SOCIETY. Jan. 18, 2009. (Louie Psihoyos) Richard O'Barry, Louie Psihoyos, Simon Hutchins, Mandy-Rae Cruickshank, Kirk Krack, David Rastovich, Scott Baker.

THE COVENANT
SONY PICTURES ENTERTAINMENT. Sept., 2006. (Renny Harlin) Steven Strait, Sebastian Stan, Laura Ramsey, Taylor Kitsch, Toby Hemingway, Jessica Lucas, Chace Crawford, Wendy Crewson.

COVER
AMERICAN CINEMA INTL. Feb 25, 2008. (Bill Duke) Aunjanue Ellis, Raz Adoti, Leon, Lou Gosset, Jr., Paula Jai Parker, Richard Gant, Mya Harrison, Victoria Platt Tilford, Vivica A. Fox.

COWARDS
FILMAX. April, 2008. Spanish. (Jose Corbacho, Juan Cruz) Lluis Homar, Elvira Minguez, Paz Padilla, Antonio de la Torre, Eduardo Espinilla, Eduardo Gare, Ariadna Gaya, Frank Crudele.

CRANK
LIONSGATE. Sept., 2006. (Mark Neveldine, Brian Taylor) Jason Statham, Amy Smart, Jose Pablo Cantillo, Efren Ramirez, Dwight Yoakam, Carlos Sanz, Reno Wilson, Edi Gathegi, Glenn Howerton, Jay Xcala, Keone Young, Valarie Rae Miller.

CRAZY EIGHTS
AFTER DARK FILMS. Nov. 12, 2007. (James Koya Jones) Traci Lords, Dina Meyer, George Newbern, Gabrielle Anwar, Dan DeLuca, Frank Whaley.

CRAZY LOTTERY
Nov., 2007. Chinese. (Gong Yingtian) Li Yixiang, Zhao Chunyang, Ding Liuyuan, Huang Juan, Xu Jun, Zi Qi, Zhang Cheng Xiaoyong, Liu Yuhuan, Liao Weiwei, Ji Ning, Dong Hui, Hong Liu, Ge Yaming.

CRAZY RACER
CHINA FILM GROUP. July, 2009. Chinese. (Ning Hao) Huang Bo, Jiu Kong, Rong Xiang, Jack Kao, Wang Shuangboa, Ba Duo, Wang Xun, Xu Zheng, Ma Shaohua, Worapoj Thuantanon, Liu Gang, Da Gang, Zhao Ben, Dong Lifan, Da Cheng, Zhang Ting.

CRAZY STONE
WARNER CHINA FILM HG CORP. (IN CHINA)/FOCUS FILMS (IN H.K.). June, 2006. Chineese-Hong Kong. (Ning Hao) Guo Tao, Liu Hua, Huang Bo, Yue Xiaojun, Teddy Lin, Hou Shu, Chen Zhenghua, Peng Bo, Wang Xun, Xu Zheng, Wang Jianing.

CRIME INSIDERS
MARS DISTRIBUTION. Jan., 2007. French. (Frederic Schoendoerffer) Benoit Magimel, Philippe Caubere, Beatrice Dalle, Olivier Marchal, Mehdi Nebbou, Tomer Sisley, Ludovic Schoendoerffer, Anne Marivin, Alain Figlarz, Andre Peron, Cyril Lecomte, Ichem Saibi, Christophe Maratier.

CRIME IS OUR BUSINESS
STUDIOCANAL. Oct., 2008. French. (Pascal Thomas) Catherine Frot, Andre Dussollier, Claude Rich, Annie Cordy, Chiara Mastroianni, Hippolyte Girardot, Melvil Poupaud, Christian Vadim, Alexandre Lafaurie, Yves Afonso, Laura Benson, Marie Lorna, Valerianne de Villeneuve, Florence Maury, Agathe Hazard, Ornella Bes, Barbara Jaquaniello.

CRIME NOVEL
WARNER BROS. PICTURES ITALIA. Sept., 2005. Italian-British-French. (Michele Placido) Kim Rossi Stuart, Anna Mouglalis, Pierfrancesco Favino, Claudio Santamaria, Stefano Accorsi, Riccardo Scamarcio, Jasmine Trinca.

THE CROSS: THE ARTHUR BLESSITT STORY
GENER8XION ENTERTAINMENT. March 28, 2009. (Matthew Crouch) Arthur Blessitt.

CROSSFIRE
SND. June, 2008. French. (Claude Michel Rome) Richard Berry, Pascal Elbe, Zabou Breitman, Aissa Maiga, Bernard Blancan, Aure Atika, Guilaine Londez, Moussa Maaskri, Fred Saurel, Gerald Laroche.

CROSSING OVER
WEINSTEIN CO. Feb 11, 2009. (Wayne Kramer) Harrison Ford, Ray Liotta, Ashley Judd, Jim Sturgess, Cliff Curtis, Alice Braga, Alice Eve, Summer Bishil, Jacqueline Obradors, Justin Chon, Melody Khazae.

CROSSOVER
SONY PICTURES ENTERTAINMENT. Aug., 2006. (Preston A. Whitmore II.) Anthony Mackie, Wesley Jonathan, Wayne Brady, Kristen Wilson, Lil' J.J., Phillip "Hot Sauce" Champion, Eva Pigford, Alecia Fears.

CRUDE IMPACT
PORCHLIGHT ENTERTAINMENT. March, 2007. (James Jandak Wood) Tundi Agardy, Guy Caruso, Cindy Cohn, Kenneth Deffeyes, Steve Donziger, Emeka Duruigbo, Michael Economides, Christopher Flavin, Amy Goodman, Thom Hartmann, Richard Heinberg, Santiago Kawarim, Terry Lynne Karl, Michael Klare, Kavita Ramdas, William Rees, Matthew Simmons, Lynne Twist. Narrator: Natalia Bortolotti. Documentary.

CRY WOLF
ROGUE PICTURES. Sept., 2005. (Jeff Wadlow) Lindy Booth, Julian Morris, Jared Padalecki, Kristy Wu, Sandra McCoy, Paul James, Jon Bon Jovi, Jesse Janzen, Gary Cole, Anna Deveare Smith.

CTHULHU
REGENT RELEASING. Aug. 17, 2008. (Daniel Gildark) Jason Cottle, Scott Patrick Green, Cara Buono, Tori Spelling, Dennis Kleinsmith, Nancy Stark, Ian Geoghegan, Greg Michaels.

THE CULT OF THE SUICIDE BOMBER
May, 2006. (David Batty, Kevin Toolis) Robert Baer. Documentary.

CURIOUS GEORGE
UNIVERSAL. Jan., 2006. (Matthew O'Callaghan) Will Ferrell, Drew Barrymore, David Cross, Eugene Levy, Dick Van Dyke, Frank Welker.

Animated.

CURIOSITY KILLS THE CAT
Nov., 2006. Chinese. (Zhang Yibai) Carina Lau, Hu Jun, Liao Fan, Song Jia, Lin Yuan, Chen Chen, Peng Jiayi, Xiaojian, Yan Yan.

THE CURIOUS CASE OF BENJAMIN BUTTON
PARAMOUNT (IN U.S.)/WARNER BROS. (FOREIGN). Nov. 22, 2008. (David Fincher) Brad Pitt, Cate Blanchett, Taraji P. Henson, Julia Ormond, Jason Flemyng, Mahershalalhashbaz Ali, Jared Harris, Elias Koteas, Phyllis Somerville, Tilda Swinton, Lance Nichols, Rampai Mohadi, Elle Fanning, Madisen Beaty.

CURSED
DIMENSION FILMS. Feb., 2005. (Wes Craven) Christina Ricci, Joshua Jackson, Jesse Eisenberg, Judy Greer, Scott Baio, Milo Ventimiglia, Kristina Anapau, Portia de Rossi, Shannon Elizabeth, Mya.

CUT LOOSE
KINEPOLIS FILM DISTRIBUTION. Nov., 2008. Belgium. (Jan Verheyen) Pepijn Caudron, Koen De Graeve, Sana Mouziane, Jaak Van Assche, Sofie Van Moll, Karin Tanghe, Stany Crets, Youssel el-Mousaoui, Achmed Akkabi.

CYCLES
ZELIG FILMS DISTRIBUTION. July, 2008. French. (Cyril Gelblat) Miou-Miou, Charles Berling, Giovanna Mezzogiorno, Shulamit Adar, Dominique Reymond, Anais Demoustier, Julie Judd, Romain Goupil, Andre Oumansky.

D

THE DA VINCI CODE
SONY PICTURES ENTERTAINMENT. May, 2006. (Ron Howard) Tom Hanks, Audrey Tautou, Ian McKellen, Jean Reno, Paul Bettany, Alfred Molina, Jurgen Prochnow, Jean-Yves Berteloot, Etienne Chicot, Jean-Pierre Marielle, Marie-Francoise Audollent.

DACHIMAWA LEE
SHOWBOX/MEDIAPLEX. June, 2009. South Korean. (Ryoo Seungwan) Im Weon-heui, Gong Hyo-jin, Park Shi-yeon, Hwang Bo-ra, Kim Byeong-ok, Kim Su-hyeon, Ahn Gil-kang, Ryu Seung-beom, Jeong Seok-yong, Oh Ji-hye.

DADDY DAY CAMP
SONY PICTURES ENTERTAINMENT. Aug., 2007. (Fred Savage) Cuba Gooding, Jr., Lochlyn Munro, Richard Gant, Tamala Jones, Paul Rae, Joshua McLerran, Spencir Bridges, Brian Doyle-Murray.

DADDY'S LITTLE GIRLS
LIONSGATE. Feb., 2007. (Tyler Perry) Gabrielle Union, Idris Elba, Louis Gossett, Jr., Tasha Smith, Malinda Williams, Gary Sturgis, Tracee Ellis Ross, Terri J. Vaughn, Sierra McClain, China McClain, Lauryn McClain, Juanita Jennings, Craig Robinson.

DALTRY CALHOUN
MIRAMAX FILMS. Oct., 2005. (Katrina Holden Bronson) Johnny Knoxville, Juliette Lewis, Elizabeth Banks, Kick Gurry, David Koechner, Sophie Traub, Andrew Prince, Beth Grant, James Parks, Matthew Sharp.

THE DAMNED
BENECE. Sept., 2009. Spanish. (Isaki Lacuesta) Daniel Fanego, Arturo Goetz, Leonor Manso, Maria Fiorentino, Juana Hidalgo, Barbara Lennie, Nazareno Casero.

THE DAMNED UNITED
SONY PICTURES ENTERTAINMENT. March, 2009. U.K. (Tom Hooper) Michael Sheen, Timothy Spall, Colm Meaney, Henry Goodman, Maurice Roeves, Jim Broadbent, Stephen Graham, Brian McCardie, Peter McDonald, Giles Alderson, Martin Compston, Joe Dempsie, Elizabeth Carling, Gillian Waugh.

DAN IN REAL LIFE
BUENA VISTA. Oct 20, 2007. (Peter Hedges) Steve Carell, Juliette Binoche, Dane Cook, Dianne Wiest, John Mahoney, Emily Blunt, Alison Pill, Brittany Robertson, Marlene Lawston, Norbert Leo Butz, Amy Ryan, Jessica Hecht, Frank Wood.

DANCE FLICK
PARAMOUNT. May 19, 2009. (Damien Dante Wayans) Shoshana Bush, Damon Wayans, Jr., Essence Atkins, David Alan Grier, Amy Sedaris, Brennan Hillard.

DANGEROUS MEN
SIMA SIM INTL. Oct., 2005. (John S. Rad) Melody Wiggins, Kelay Miller, Michael Gradilone, Annali Aeristos, Bryan Jenkins.

DANNY THE DOG
EUROPACORP DISTRIBUTION (IN FRANCE)/UIP (IN U.K.)/ROGUE PICTURES (IN U.S.). Feb., 2005. French-British. (Louis Leterrier) Jet Li, Bob Hoskins, Morgan Freeman, Kerry Condon, Michael Jenn, Vincent Regan, Dylan Brown, Phyllida Law.

DANTE 01
WILD BUNCH DISTRIBUTION. Dec., 2007. French. (Marc Caro) Lambert Wilson, Linh Dan Pham, Simona Maicanescu, Dominique Pinon, Bruno Lochet, Francois Levantal, Gerald Laroche, Francois Hadji-Lazaro, Lotfi Yahya-Jedidi, Yann Collette, Dominique Bettenfeld, Antonin Maurel.

DARE
NEXT WEDNESDAY/GIGANTIC PICTURES (IN U.S.)/CINETIC MEDIA, NEW YORK (INTERNATIONAL). Jan 19, 2009. (Adam Salky) Emmy Rossum, Zach Gilford, Ashley Springer, Ana Gasteyer, Rooney Mara, Sandra Bernhard, Alan Cumming.

DARE NOT WALK ALONE
INDICAN PICTURES. April 29, 2008. (Jeremy Dean) Andrew Young, Errol Jones, James Brock, Christoff, Corrine Brown, David Nolan. Documentary.

DARK STREETS
SAMUEL GOLDWYN FILMS. Dec. 8, 2008. (Rachel Samuels) Gabriel Mann, Bijou Phillips, Izabella Miko, Elias Koteas, Michael Fairman, Toledo.

DARK WATER
BUENA VISTA. June, 2005. (Walter Salles) Jennifer Connelly, John C. Reilly, Tim Roth, Dougray Scott, Pete Postlethwaite, Camryn Manheim, Ariel Gade, Perla Haney-Jardine.

DATE MOVIE
20TH CENTURY FOX. Feb., 2006. (Aaron Seltzer) Alyson Hannigan, Adam Campbell, Sophie Monk, Eddie Griffin, Meera Simhan, Fred Willard, Jennifer Coolidge, Marie Matiko, Judah Friedlander, Carmen Electra, Tony Cox.

DAVE CHAPPELLE'S BLOCK PARTY
ROGUE PICTURES. Feb., 2006. (Michel Gondry) Kanye West, Mos Def, Talib Kweli, Common, The Fugees, Dead Prez, Erykah Badu, Jill Scott, The Roots, Dave Chappelle. Documentary.

THE DAY THE EARTH STOOD STILL
20TH CENTURY FOX. Dec. 8, 2008. (Scott Derrickson) Keanu Reeves, Jennifer Connelly, Kathy Bates, Jaden Smith, John Cleese, Jon Hamm, Kyle Chandler, Robert Knepper, James Hong, John Rothman, Brandon T. Jackson.

DAY NIGHT DAY NIGHT
IFC FIRST TAKE. May, 2006. (Julia Loktev) Luisa Williams, Josh P. Weinstein, Gareth Saxe, Nyambi Nyambi, Frank Dattolo, Annemarie Lawless, Tschi-Hun Kim, Richard Morant, Jennifer Camilo, Rosemary Apolinaris, Jennifer Restrepo, Julissa Pere.

DAY WATCH
(Russia)
GEMINI FILM INTL. (IN RUSSIA)/FOX SEARCHLIGHT (IN U.S.). April, 2006. Russian. (Timur Bekmambetov) Konstantin Khabensky, Maria Poroshina, Vladimir Menshov, Viktor Verzhbitsky, Galina Tyunina, Gosha Kutsenko, Aleksei Chadov, Valery Zolotukhin, Zhanna Friske, Rimma Markova, Dima Martinov.

DE PROFUNDIS
ALTA FILMS. Jan., 2007. Spanish-Portugese. (Miguelanxo Prado) Animated.

DEAD COOL
July, 2005. British. (David Cohen) Imogen Stubbs, Steven Geller, James Callis, Anthony Calf, Liz Smith, Rosanna Arquette, Gemma Lawrence, Olivia Wedderburn, Aaron Johnson, Martin Cole, Patricia England, David Cohen.

DEAD MAN RUNNING
REVOLVER ENTERTAINMENT. Nov., 2009. U.K. (Alex De Rakoff) Tamer Hassan, Danny Dyer, Brenda Blethyn, Curtis "50 Cent" Jackson, Monet Mazur, Ashley Walters, Phil Davis, Omid Djalili, Blake Ritson, Bronson Webb, Alan Ford.

DEAD SILENCE
UNIVERSAL. March, 2007. (James Wan) Ryan Kwanten, Amber Valletta, Donnie Wahlberg, Michael Fairman, Joan Heney, Judith Roberts.

DEAD SNOW
IFC FILMS (IN U.S.). Jan., 2009. Norwegian. (Tommy Wirkola) Vegard Hoel, Stig Frode Henriksen, Charlotte Frogner, Jenny Skavlan, Jeppe Beck Laursen, Lasse Valdal, Evy Kasseth Rosten, Orjan Gamst, Bjorn Sundquist, Ane Dahl Torp.

DEAL
METRO-GOLDWYN-MAYER & SEVEN ARTS PICTURES. April 22, 2008. (Gil Cates) Burt Reynolds, Bret Harrison, Shannon Elizabeth, Charles Durning, Jennifer Tilly, Maria Mason.

DEATH AT A FUNERAL
MGM. March, 2007. (Frank Oz) Matthew Macfadyen, Keeley Hawes, Andy Nyman, Ewen Bremner, Daisy Donovan, Alan Tudyk, Jane Asher, Kris Marshall, Rupert Graves, Peter Egan, Peter Dinklage.

DEATH IN LOVE
BOAZ YAKIN. Jan. 22, 2008. (Boaz Yakin) Josh Lucas, Jacqueline Bisset, Lukas Haas, Morena Baccarin, Betty Gilpin, Vanessa Kai, Emma Bell, Carrington Vilmont, Adam Brody.

DEATH NOTE; DEATH NOTE: THE LAST NAME
DEATH NOTE
WARNER BROS. JAPAN. March, 2007. Japanese. (Shusuke Kaneko)

Tatsuya Fujiwara, Kenichi Matsuyama, Asaka Seto, Shigeki Hosokawa, Erika Toda, Shunji Fujimura, Takeshi Kaga, Yu Kashii, Hikari Mitsushima, Michiko Godai, Shido Nakamura.

DEATH NOTE: THE LAST NAME
WARNER BROS. JAPAN. March, 2007. Japanese. (Shusuke Kaneko) Tatsuya Fujiwara, Kenichi Matsuyama, Erika Toda, Shunji Fujimura, Takeshi Kaga, Hikari Mitushima, Nana Katase, Sakura Uehara, Miyuki Komatsu, Michiko Godai, Shido Nakamura.

DEATH RACE
UNIVERSAL. Aug. 20, 2008. (Paul W.S. Anderson) Jason Statham, Tyrese Gibson, Ian McShane, Joan Allen, Natalie Martinez, Max Ryan, Jason Clarke, Fred Koehler, Jacob Vargas, Justin Mader, Robert Lasardo, Robin Shou, Janaya Stephens.

DEATH SENTENCE
20TH CENTURY FOX. Aug., 2007. (James Wan) Kevin Bacon, Garrett Hedlund, Kelly Preston, Aisha Tyler, John Goodman, Jordan Garrett, Stuart Lafferty, Edi Gathegi, Matthew O'Leary, Leigh Whannell, Hector Atreyu Ruiz.

THE DEATHS OF IAN STONE
AFTER DARK FILMS. Nov. 12, 2007. (Dario Piana) Mike Vogel, Jaime Murray, Christina Cole, Michael Feast, Mamix Van Den Broeke, Jeff Peterson, Bill Nash, James Bartle, Andrew Buchan, Michael Dixon, Jason Durran.

DECEMBER BOYS
WARNER INDEPENDENT PICTURES (IN U.S.)/VILLAGE ROADSHOW ENTERTAINMENT (IN AUSTRALIA). July, 2007. Australian. (Rod Hardy) Daniel Radcliffe, Lee Cormie, Christian Byers, James Fraser, Teresa Palmer, Victoria Hill, Sullivan Stapleton, Jack Thompson, Kris McQuade, Frank Gallacher.

DECK THE HALLS
20TH CENTURY FOX. Nov., 2006. (John Whitesell) Danny DeVito, Matthew Broderick, Kristin Davis, Kristin Chenoweth, Alia Shawkat, Dylan Blue, Kelly Aldridge, Sabrina Aldridge, Jorge Garcia, Fred Armisen.

DEEP SEA
IMAX. Feb., 2006. (Howard Hall) Johnny Depp, Kate Winslet. Documentary. IMAX.

DEFENDOR
DARIUS FILMS. Sept., 2009. Canadian. (Peter Stebbings) Woody Harrelson, Elias Koteas, Michael Kelly, Kat Dennings, Lisa Ray, Sandra Oh.

DEFIANCE
PARAMOUNT. Nov. 9, 2008. (Edward Zwick) Daniel Craig, Liev Schreiber, Jamie Bell, Alexa Davalos, Allan Corduner, Mark Feuerstein, Tomas Arana, Jodhi May, Kate Fahy, Iddo Goldberg, Iben Hjejle, Martin Hancock, Ravil Isyanov, Jacek Koman, George Mackay, Jonjo O'Neill, Sam Spruell, Mia Wasikowska, Mark Margolis, Markus von Lingen, Rolandas Boravskis.

DEJA VU
BUENA VISTA PICTURES. Nov., 2006. (Tony Scott) Denzel Washington, Val Kilmer, Paula Patton, Bruce Greenwood, Adam Goldberg, Elden Henson, Jim Caviezel, Erika Alexander.

DEJATE CAER
ALTA FILMS. Feb., 2008. Spanish. (Jesus Ponce) Ivan Massague, Dario Paso, Juanfra Juarez, Pilar Crespo, Mercedes Hoyos, Isabel Ampudia, Ana Cuesta, Fanny De Castro, Benito Pocino, Jesus Carroza.

DELGO
FREESTYLE ENTERTAINMENT. Dec. 5, 2008. (Marc F. Adler) Voices: Freddie Prinze Jr., Chris Kattan, Jennifer Love Hewitt, Anne Bancroft, Val Kilmer, Malcolm McDowell, Michael Clarke Duncan, Louis Gossett Jr., Eric Idle, Burt Reynolds, Kelly Ripa. Animated.
Narrator: Sally Kellerman.

DELHI-6
UTV MOTION PICTURES. Feb., 2009. India. (Rakeysh Omprakash Mehra) Abhishek Bachchan, Sonam Kapoor, Om Puri, Waheeda Rahman, Rishi Kapoor, Atul Kulkarni, Divya Dutta, Cyrus Sahukar, Vijay Raaz.

DELTA FARCE
LIONSGATE. May, 2007. (C.B. Harding) Larry the Cable Guy, Bill Engvall, D.J. Qualls, Keith David, Danny Trejo, Marisol Nichols.

THE DEPARTED
WARNER BROS. Sept., 2006. (Martin Scorsese) Leonardo DiCaprio, Matt Damon, Jack Nicholson, Mark Wahlberg, Martin Sheen, Ray Winstone, Vera Farmiga, Anthony Anderson, Alec Baldwin, James Badge Dale, David Patrick O'Hara, Mark Rolston, Kevin Corrigan.

DERAILED
WEINSTEIN CO. Nov., 2005. (Mikael Hafstrom) Clive Owen, Jennifer Aniston, Vincent Cassel, Melissa George, Giancarlo Esposito, David Morrissey, Georgina Chapman, Denis O'Hare, Tom Conti, Addison Timlin, Xzibit, RZA.

DESCENT
CITY LIGHTS PICTURES. July, 2007. (Talia Lugacy) Rosario Dawson, Chad Faust, Marcus Patrick.

THE DESCENT
PATHE PICTURES. July, 2005. British. (Neil Marshall) Shauna Macdonald, Natalie Mendoza, Alex Reid, Saskia Mulder, Nora-Jane Noone, MyAnna Buring, Oliver Milburn, Molly Kayll.

DESERT BAYOU
CINEMA LIBRE. Nov. 1, 2007. (Alex LeMay) Art Hoyle. With: Master P, Tamu Smith, Curtis Pleasant, Shmuley Boteach, Beverly Wright, Karyn Dudley, Rocky Anderson. Documentary.

DESERT WIND
Feb., 2006. Canadian- Swiss. (Francois Kohler) Documentary.

DEUCE BIGALOW: EUROPEAN GIGOLO
SONY PICTURES ENTERTAINMENT. Aug., 2005. (Mike Bigelow) Rob Schneider, Eddie Griffin, Jeroen Krabbe, Til Schweiger, Douglas Sills, Carlos Ponce, Charles Keating, Hanna Verboom.

THE DEVIL WEARS PRADA
20TH CENTURY FOX. June, 2006. (David Frankel) Meryl Streep, Anne Hathaway, Stanley Tucci, Simon Baker, Emily Blunt, Adrian Grenier, David Marshall Grant, James Naughton, Tracie Thoms, Daniel Sunjata, Rebecca Mader, Rich Sommer.

THE DEVIL'S REJECTS
LIONS GATE FILMS. June, 2005. (Rob Zombie) Sid Haig, Bill Moseley, Sheri Moon Zombie, Ken Foree, Matthew McGrory, Leslie Easterbrook, Geoffrey Lewis, Priscilla Barnes, William Forsythe, Kate Norby, Lew Temple, Dave Sheridan, EG Daily, Danny Trejo.

THE DHAMMA BROTHERS
BALCONY RELEASING. March 26, 2008. (Jenny Phillips, Andrew Kukura, Anne Marie Stein) Grady Bankhead, Edward Johnson, Ben Oryang, Rick Smith, Jonathan Crowley, Bruce Stewart, Ron Cavanaugh. Documentary.

DHOOM:2
YASH RAJ. Nov., 2006. Indian. (Sanjay Gadhvi) Hrithik Roshan, Abhishek Bachchan, Aishwarya Rai, Uday Chopra, Bipasha Basu, Rimi Sen.

DIARY OF A MAD BLACK WOMAN
LIONS GATE FILMS. Feb., 2005. (Darren Grant) Kimberly Elise, Steve Harris, Shemar Moore, Tamara Taylor, Lisa Marcos, Tiffany Evans, Cicely Tyson, Tyler Perry.

DIGGERS
MAGNOLIA PICTURES. Sept., 2006. (Katherine Dieckmann) Paul Rudd, Lauren Ambrose, Ron Eldard, Josh Hamilton, Sarah Paulson, Ken Marino, Maura Tierney.

DIKKENEK
EUROPACORP DISTRIBUTION. June, 2006. French-Belgium. (Olivier Van Hoofstadt) Marion Cotillard, Dominique Pinon, Jean-Luc Couchard, Jeremie Renier, Melanie Laurent, Francois Damiens, Florence Foresti, Catherine Jacob.

DIRTY DEEDS
GREEN DIAMOND ENTERTAINMENT. Aug., 2005. (David Kendall) Milo Ventimiglia, Lacey Chabert, Tom Amandes, Matthew Carey, Mark Derwin, Charles Durning, Michael Milhoan, Billy L. Sullivan, Zoe Saldana.

DIRTY MIND
KFD. April, 2009. Belgian. (Pieter Van Hees) Wim Helsen, Robbie Cleiren, Kristine Van Pellicom, Peter Van Den Begin, Maaike Neuville, Sien Eggers, Frank Focketyn.

DIRTY SANCHEZ: THE MOVIE
PATHE DISTRIBUTION. Oct., 2006. British. (Jim Hickey) Lee Dainton, Mike "Pancho" Locke, Mathew Pritchard, Dan Joyce, Myke Hawke Pierce, Howard Marks.

DISASTER MOVIE
LIONSGATE. Aug. 29, 2008. (Jason Friedberg) Matt Lanter, Vanessa Minnillo, Gary "G-Thang" Johnson, Nicole Parker, Crista Flanagan, Kim Kardashian, Ike Barinholtz, Tad Hilgenbrinck, Jason Boegh, Carmen Electra.

DISCO
STUDIO CANAL. April, 2008. French. (Fabien Onteniente) Franck Dubosc, Emmanuelle Beart, Gerard Depardieu, Samuel Le Bihan, Abbes Zahmani, Annie Cordy, Isabelle Nanty, Chloe Lambert, Jacques Sereys, Daniele Lebrun, Annie Cordy, Christine Citti, Francois-Xavier Demaison. Documentary.

DISNEY'S A CHRISTMAS CAROL
WALT DISNEY STUDIOS MOTION PICTURES. Oct. 28, 2009. (Robert Zemeckis) Jim Carrey, Gary Oldman, Colin Firth, Bob Hoskins, Robin Wright Penn, Dick Wilkins, Cary Elwes, Fionnula Flanagan.

THE DISTANCE
FILMAX. Sept., 2006. Spanish. (Inaki Dorronsoro) Miguel Angel Silvestre, Jose Coronado, Federico Luppi, Belen Lopez, Lluis Homar, Carlos Kaniowsky.

DISTRICT 9
SONY PICTURES ENTERTAINMENT. (IN NORTH AMERICA) July 28, 2009. New Zealand. (Neill Blomkamp) Sharlto Copley, Jason Cope, David James, Vanessa Haywood, Mandla Gaduka, Kenneth Nkosi, Eugene Khumbanyiwa, Louis Minnaar, William Allen Young.

DIVE!!
KADOKAWA PICTURES. May, 2008. Japanese. (Naoto Kumazawa) Kento Hayashi, Sosuke Ikematsu, Junpei Mizobata, Asaka Seto, Misako Renbutsu, Ken Mitsuishi, Toru Emori.

DOA: DEAD OR ALIVE
DIMENSION FILMS. June, 2007. U.S.-German-British. (Cory Yuen) Jaime Pressly, Holly Valance, Sarah Carter, Devon Aoki, Kane Kosugi, Natassia Malthe, Matthew Marsden, Eric Roberts, Steve Howey, Brian White, Kevin Nash, Collin Chou.

DOC
DOC TANK. Jan. 17, 2008. (Immy Humes) Harold L. Humes, Norman Mailer, William Styron, George Plimpton, Timothy Leary, Paul Auster, Russell Hemenway. Documentary.

DOGHEAD
ALTA CLASSICS. Oct., 2006. Spanish. (Santo Amodeo) Juan Jose Ballesta, Adriana Ugarte, Julian Villagran, Ana Wagener, Eugenio Roca, Jorge Roelas, Ana Gracia, Mariano Pena, Manuel Alexandre.

DOGHOUSE
VERTIGO. June, 2009. U.K.. (Dan Schaffer) Danny Dyer, Noel Clarke, Stephen Graham, Emil Marwa, Lee Ingleby, Keith-Lee Castle, Christina Cole, Terry Stone, Neil Maskell, Emily Booth.

DOMINICK DUNNE: AFTER THE PARTY
Nov., 2008. Australian. (Kirsty de Garis, Timothy Jolley) Dominick Dunne, Robert Evans, Graydon Carter, Joan Didion, Ben Pesta, Griffin Dunne, Mart Crowley, Liz Smith, Tina Brown, Anne Fulenwider. Documentary.

DOMINO
NEW LINE CINEMA. Sept., 2005. (Tony Scott) Keira Knightley, Mickey Rourke, Edgar Ramirez, Delroy Lindo, Mo'Nique, Lucy Liu, Christopher Walken, Mena Suvari, Macy Gray, Jacqueline Bisset, Dabney Coleman, Brian Austin Green, Ian Ziering, Stanley Kamel, Peter Jacobson, T.K.Carter, Kel O'Neill, Shondrella Avery, Lew Temple, Tom Waits, Rizwan Abbasi.

DONKEY XOTE
FILMAX. Dec., 2007. Spanish. (Jose Pozo) Voices: Jose Luis Gil, Luis Posada, Andreu Buenafuente, David Fernandez, Sancho Gracia, Sonia Ferrer. Animated.

DON'T MAKE MOVIES!
March, 2005. Belgium. (Oren Nataf) Marc Levie, Yann Chely, Lou Broclain, Sacha Kollich, Michel Van Laer. Documentary.

DOOM
UNIVERSAL. Oct., 2005. (Andrzej Bartkowiak) Karl Urban, Rosamund Pike, DeObia Oparei, Ben Daniels, Raz Adoti, Richard Brake, Dexter Fletcher, Al Weaver, Brian Steele, The Rock, Yao Chin.

DOOMSDAY
ROGUE PICTURES. March 14, 2008. (Neil Marshall) Rhona Mitra, Bob Hoskins, Adrian Lester, Alexander Siddig, David O'Hara, Malcolm McDowell, Craig Conway, MyAnna Buring, Lee-Anne Liebenberg, Sean Pertwee, Darren Morfitt, Leslie Simpson, Nora-Jane Noone, Rick Warden, John Carson, Cokey Falkow, Nathalie Boltt.

DOSTANA
YASH RAJ FILMS. Nov., 2008. Indian. (Tarun Mansukhani) Abhishek Bachchan, John Abraham, Priyanka Chopra, Bobby Deol, Kirron Kher, Sushmita Mukherjee, Shrey Bawa, Boman Irani, Shilpa Shetty.

DRAG ME TO HELL
UNIVERSAL. May 12, 2009. (Sam Raimi) Alison Lohman, Justin Long, Lorna Raver, Dileep Rao, David Paymer, Adriana Barraza, Chelcie Ross, Reggie Lee.

DRAGONBALL EVOLUTION
20TH CENTURY FOX. March, 2009. Japanese. (James Wong) Justin Chatwin, Emmy Rossum, Jamie Chung, James Marsters, Joon Park, Eriko Tamura, Randall Duk Kim, Ernie Hudson, Chow Yun-fat, Texas Battle, Megumi Seki, Ian Whyte.

DRAGON HUNTERS
Dec., 2008. French. (Guillaume Ivernel, Arthur Qwak) Forest Whitaker, Rob Paulson, Mary Mouser, Dave Wittenberg, Nick Jameson, Jess Harnell. Animated.

DR. BRONNER'S MAGIC SOAPBOX
BALCONY RELEASING. June, 2007. (Sara Lamm) Emanuel Bronner, Ralph Bronner, Jim Bronner, Trudy Bronner, Gladys Bronner, Eldridge Cleaver. Documentary.

DREAM HOUSE
PATHE DISTRIBUTION. June, 2006. French. (Dany Boon) Dany Boon, Michele Laroque, Daniel Prevost, Zinedine Soualem, Laurent Gamelon, Line Renaud, Michel Vuillermoz, Gaelle Bona, Didier Flamand.

DREAMGIRLS
PARAMOUNT. Nov., 2006. (Bill Condon) Jamie Foxx, Beyonce Knowles, Eddie Murphy, Danny Glover, Anika Noni Rose, Keith Robinson, Jennifer Hudson, Sharon Leal, Hinton Battle, Loretta Devine.

DR. SEUSS' HORTON HEARS A WHO!
20TH CENTURY FOX. March 6, 2008. (Jimmy Hayward) Jim Carrey, Steve Carell, Carol Burnett, Will Arnett, Seth Rogen, Dan Fogler, Isla Fisher, Jonah Hill, Amy Poehler, Jaime Pressly. Narrator: Charles Osgood.

DRILLBIT TAYLOR
PARAMOUNT. March 18, 2008. (Steven Brill) Owen Wilson, Leslie Mann, Nate Hartley, Troy Gentile, David Dorfman, Alex Frost, Josh Peck, Danny R. McBride, Jonathan Lane, Valerie Tian, Shane Ryan, Lisa Ann Walter, Ian Roberts, Beth Littleford.

DRINK DRANK DRUNK
FILM UNLIMITED (IN H.K.)/MILKYWAY STUDIO-MIRACLE (IN U.K.). Jan., 2006. Hong Kong-Chineese. (Derek Yee) Daniel Wu, Miriam Yeung, Alex Fong, Vincent Kok, Hu Jing, Ella Koon, Renee Dai, Toby Leung, Chin Ka-lok, Terence Yin, Andrew Lin, Tony Ho, Ken Wong, Henry Fong, Paul Fonoroff.

DROP
KADOKAWA PICTURES. April, 2009. Japanese. (Hiroshi Shinagawa) Hiroki Narimiya, Hiro Mizushima, Yuika Motokariya, Yusuke Kamiji, Noriko Nakagoshi, Daisuke Miyagawa, Show Aikawa, Yuji Abe, Toru Wakatsuki.

DUCK
RIGHT BRAINED RELEASING. June, 2005. (Nic Bettauer) Philip Baker Hall, Amy Hill.

THE DUKES OF HAZZARD
WARNER BROS. July, 2005. (Jay Chandrasekhar) Johnny Knoxville, Seann William Scott, Jessica Simpson, Burt Reynolds, Joe Don Baker, Willie Nelson, Lynda Carter, M.C. Gainey.

DUPLICITY
UNIVERSAL. March 12, 2009. (Tony Gilroy) Julia Roberts, Clive Owen, Tom Wilkinson, Paul Giamatti, Tom McCarthy, Denis O'Hare, Kathleen Chalfant, Wayne Duvall, Carrie Preston, Oleg Stefan, Rick Worthy, Khan Baykal, Ulrich Thomsen, Christopher Denham

DYING IN SAN HILARIO
FILMAX. June, 2005. Spanish. (Laura Mana) Lluis Homar, Ana Fernandez, Ferran Rane, Ulises Oscar Dumont, Juan Echanove.

DYING OR FEELING BETTER
BAC FILMS. July, 2008. (Laurence Ferreira Barbosa) Florence Thomassin, Francois Civil, Marine Barbosa, Karine Barbosa, Thomas Cerisola, Valerie Lang, Emile Berling.

DYING TO LIVE
HOMESTAN. March 9, 2008. (Ben Mittleman) Ben Mittleman, Valerie Crawford Mittleman, Anne Mittleman.

EAGLE EYE
DREAM WORKS/PARAMOUNT. Sept. 24, 2008. (D.J. Caruso) Shia LaBeouf, Michelle Monaghan, Rosario Dawson, Michael Chiklis, Anthony Mackie, Billy Bob Thornton, Anthony Azizi, Cameron Boyce.

EASY VIRTUE
EALING STUDIOS. Sept. 9, 2008. (Stephan Elliott) Jessica Biel, Colin Firth, Kristin Scott Thomas, Ben Barnes, Kris Marshall, Kimberley Nixon, Katharine Parkinson, Pip Torrens, Christian Brassington, Charlotte Riley.

EATING OUT: ALL YOU CAN EAT
ARIZTICAL ENTERTAINMENT. Aug. 19, 2009. (Glenn Gaylord) Rebekah Kochan, Daniel Skelton, Chris Salvatore, Michael E.R. Walker, Julia Cho, John Stallings, Maximiliano Torandell, Cristina Balmores, Mink Stole, Leslie Jordan.

ECHELON CONSPIRACY
AFTER DARK FILMS. March 1, 2009. (Greg Marcks) Shane West, Ed Burns, Ving Rhames, Jonathan Pryce, Tamara Feldman, Sergey Gubanov, Martin Sheen.

EDEN LAKE
WEINSTEIN CO. (IN U.S.). Oct., 2008. British. (James Watkins) Kelly Reilly, Michael Fassbender, Jack O'Connell, Thomas Turgoose, Finn Atkins, James Burrows, Thomas Gill, Jumayn Hunter, James Gandhi.

EDEN LOG
BAC FILMS DISTRIBUTION (IN FRANCE)/MAGNET (IN U.S.) Dec., 2007. French. (Franck Vestiel) Clovis Cornillac, Vimala Pons.

THE EDGE OF LOVE
Lionsgate. June, 2007. British. (John Maybury) Keira Knightley, Sienna Miller, Matthew Rhys, Cillian Murphy, Anne Lambton, Camilla Rutherford, Alastair Mackenzie, Suggs.

EDISON

Sept., 2005. (David Burke) Morgan Freeman, Kevin Spacey, Justin Timberlake, LL Cool J, Dylan McDermott, John Heard, Cary Elwes, Roselyn Sanchez, Damien Dante Wayans, Garfield Wilson, Marco Sanchez, Darryl Quon, Andrew Jackson, Tim Paul Perez.

THE EDUCATION OF FAIRIES

ALTA CLASSICS. July, 2006. Spanish-French-Argentine-Portugese. (Jose Luis Cuerda) Ricardo Darin, Irene Jacob, Bebe, Victor Valdivia, Jordi Bosch, Gloria Roig.

EDY

MARS DISTRIBUTION. June, 2005. French. (Stephan Guerin-Tillie) Francois Berleand, Philippe Noiret, Yves Verhoeven, Marion Cotillard, Laurent Bateau, Julien Lepers, Pascal Parmentier, Philippe Sejourne, Dominique Bettenfeld, Steve Suissa, Joel Demarty, Cyrille Thouvenin.

EIGHT BELOW

BUENA VISTA. Feb., 2006. (Frank Marshall) Paul Walker, Bruce Greenwood, Moon Bloodgood, Jason Biggs, Gerard Plunkett, August Schellenberg, Wendy Crewson, Belinda Metz.

EIGHT MILES HIGH

DOKUMENT FILMS (IN U.S.)/WARNER BROS. (IN GERMANY). July, 2008. German. (Achim Bornhak) Natalia Avelon, David Scheller, Rainer Langhans, Alexander Scheer, Friederike Kempter, Victor Noren.

EKLAVYA: THE ROYAL GUARD

EROS INTL. Feb., 2007. Indian. (Vidhu Vinod Chopra) Amitabh Bachchan, Sanjay Dutt, Saif Ali Khan, Vidya Balan, Jackie Shroff, Jimmy Shergill, Boman Irani, Raima Sen, Swanand Kirkire, Parikshit Sahani, Sharmila Tagore, Rama Vij.

EL CALENTITO

BUENA VISTA INTL. June, 2005. Spanish. (Chus Gutierrez) Veronica Sanchez, Juan Sanz, Macarena Gomez, Ruth Diaz, Nuria Gonzalez, Jordi Vilches, Lluvia Rojo, Nilo Mur, Aitor Merino, Antonio Dechent, Isabel Ordaz, Mariano Pena.

EL CANTOR

SHELLAC. March, 2006. French. (Joseph Morder) Lou Castel, Luis Rego, Francoise Michaud, Talila Rosette, Pierre-Francois Desgeorge, Lucette Filiu, Abraham Leber, Solange Najman, Robi Morder, Henri de Camaret, Alexandra Stewart.

EL CORTEZ

BRAZOS PICTURES. Oct., 2006. (Stephen Purvis) Lou Diamond Phillips, Tracy Middendorf, Bruce Weitz, James McDaniel, Glenn Plummer, Peter Onorati.

THE EL ESCORIAL CONSPIRACY

SONY PICTURES (IN SPAIN). July, 2008. Spanish-Italian. (Antonio del Real) Jason Isaacs, Julia Ormond, Jurgen Prochnow, Jordi Molla, Joaquim de Almeida, Juanjo Puigcorbe, Blanca Jara, Fabio Testi, Rosana Pastor, Tony Peck.

ELEKTRA

20TH CENTURY FOX. Jan., 2005. (Rob Bowman) Jennifer Garner, Terence Stamp, Kirsten Prout, Goran Visnjic, Cary-Hiroyuki Tagawa, Will Yun Lee.

ELSA & FRED

ALTA FILMS. Nov., 2005. Spanish-Argentinian. (Marcos Carnevale) Manuel Alexandre, China Zorrilla, Blanca Portillo, Roberto Carnaghi, Jose Angel Egido, Carlos Alvarez-Novoa, Federico Luppi.

EM 4 JAY

Sept., 2006. Australian. (Alkinos Tsilimidos) Laura Gordon, Nick Barkla, Chloe Armstrong, Kat Stewart, Jeremy Taylor, David Campbell.

EMMENEZ-MOI!

MARS DISTRIBUTION. July, 2005. French. (Edmond Bensimon) Gerard Darmon, Zinedine Soualem, Lucien Jean-Baptiste, Damien Jouillerot, Witold Heretynski, Patrick Brasseur, Sophie Hermelin, Oranne Dutoit, Nathalie Levy-Lang, Charles Aznavour.

EMPIRE OF THE WOLVES

GAUMONT COLUMBIA TRISTAR FILMS. April, 2005. French. (Chris Nahon) Jean Reno, Jocelyn Quivrin, Arly Jover, Laura Morante.

EMPLOYEE OF THE MONTH

LIONSGATE. Sept., 2006. (Greg Coolidge) Dane Cook, Jessica Simpson, Dax Shepard, Andy Dick, Tim Bagley, Brian George, Efren Ramirez, Marcello Thedford, Danny Woodburn, Harland Williams, Sean Whalen, Barbara Dodd Ramsen.

THE EMPTY ACRE

CINEMA EPOCH ENTERTAINMENT. April, 2007. (Patrick Rea) Jennifer Plas, John Wilson, Robert Paisley, Ari Bavel, Sally Bremenkamp.

EMPTY TOWN

Sept., 2007. Chinese. (Hu Yaozhi) Zhang Lingxin, Li Haozhen, Tie Weiguang, Jiao Junyan, Li Yiling, Zhou Dehua, Luo Shiping, Zhao Zhigang, Zhai Huaxiu.

ENCHANTED

WALT DISNEY STUDIOS. Nov. 15, 2007. (Kevin Lima) Amy Adams, Patrick Dempsey, James Marsden, Timothy Spall, Idina Menzel, Rachel Covey, Susan Sarandon, Narrator: Julie Andrews.

THE END OF POVERTY?

CINEMA LIBRE. Feb. 14, 2009. (Philippe Diaz) John Christensen, Clifford Cobb, William Easterly, Susan George, Edgardo Lander, Chalmers Johnson, Alvaro Garcia Linera, John Perkins, Amartya Sen, Joseph Stiglitz, Eric Toussaint, Michael Watts. Narrator: Martin Sheen.

END OF THE SPEAR

M. POWER RELEASING. Jan., 2006. (Jim Hanon) Louie Leonardo, Chad Allen, Chase Ellison, Sara Kathryn Bakker, Cara Stoner, Jack Guzman, Christina Souza.

ENLIGHTEN UP!: A SKEPTIC'S JOURNEY INTO THE WORLD OF YOGA

BALCONY RELEASING. March 25, 2009. (Kate Churchill) Nick Rosen, B.K.S. Iyengar, Pattabhi Jois, Norman Allen, Sharon Gannon, David Life, Dharma Mittra, Diamond Dallas Page, Sharath Rangaswamy, Madan Kataria, Rodney Yee, Cindi Lee, Gurmukh Kaur Khalsa, Alan Finger, Baron Baptiste, Beryl Bender Birch, Natasha Rizopoulos.

ENLIGHTENED BY FIRE

ALTA FILMS. Sept., 2005. Argentine-Spanish. (Tristan Bauer) Gaston Pauls, Jose Luis Alfonzo, Cesar Albarracin, Pablo Ribba, Cesar Albarracin, Hugo Carrizo, Virginia Innocenti, Juan Leyrado.

EPIC MOVIE

20TH CENTURY FOX. Jan., 2007. (Jason Friedberg, Aaron Selzer) Kal Penn, Adam Campbell, Jennifer Coolidge, Jayma Mays, Faune Chambers, Crispin Glover, Fred Willard, Hector Jiminez, Darrell Hammond, Carmen Electra, David Carradine.

EPISODE 3: 'ENJOY POVERTY'

Dec., 2008. Dutch. (Renzo Martens) Renzo Martens. Documentary.

ERAGON

20TH CENTURY FOX. Dec., 2006. (Stefen Fangmeier) Ed Speleers, Jeremy Irons, Sienna Guillory, Robert Carlyle, Djimon Hounsou, Garrett Hedlund, Joss Stone, Rachel Weisz, John Malkovich, Alun Armstrong, Chris Egan, Gary Lewis, Steve Speirs, Caroline Chikezie.

ERREUR DE LA BANQUE EN VOTRE FAVEUR

WILD BUNCH. April, 2009. French. (Gerard Bitton) Gerard Lanvin, Jean-Pierre Darroussin, Philippe Magnan, Barbara Schluz, Jennifer Decker, Scali Delpeyrat, Roger Van Hool, Eric Berger, Eric Naggar, Martin Lamotte, Laourent Gamelon.

ESPACE DÉTENTE

ARP SELECTION. Feb., 2005. French. (Bruno Solo, Yvan Le Bolloc'h) Bruno Solo, Yvan Le Bolloc'h, Thierry Fremont, Sylvie Loeillet, Gerard Chaillou, Shirley Bousquet, Alexandre Pesle, Armelle, Alain Bouzigues, Jeanne Savary, Valerie Decobert, Marc Andreoni, Philippe Cura, Noemie Elbaz-Kapler, Karim Adda, Chantal Neuwirth, Jean-Francois Gallotte.

EVAN ALMIGHTY

UNIVERSAL. June, 2007. (Tom Shadyac) Steve Carell, Morgan Freeman, Lauren Graham, Johnny Simmons, Graham Phillips, Jimmy Bennett, John Goodman, Wanda Sykes, John Michael Higgins, Jonah Hill, Molly Shannon.

EVEN MONEY

YARI FILM GROUP. May, 2007. (Mark Rydell) Kim Basinger, Nick Cannon, Danny DeVito, Kelsey Grammer, Ray Liotta, Jay Mohr, Tim Roth, Forest Whitaker, Carla Gugino, Charlie Robinson, Grant Sullivan, Larry Burnett, Mark Rydell.

EVENING

FOCUS FEATURES. June, 2007. (Lajos Koltai) Claire Danes, Toni Collette, Vanessa Redgrave, Patrick Wilson, Hugh Dancy, Natasha Richardson, Mamie Gummer, Eileen Atkins, Meryl Streep, Glenn Close, Ebon Moss-Bachrach, Barry Bostwick.

EVERY OTHER WEEK

BUENA VISTA INTL. (SWEDEN). Dec., 2005. Swedish. (Felix Herngren, Mans Herngren, Hannes Holm, Hans Ingemansson) Felix Herngren, Mans Herngren, Cecilia Frode, Anja Lundqvist, Anna Bjork, Sofia Ledarp, Vera Herngren, Vilhelm Backer, Pal Strobaek, Dennis Fredriksson, Adam Nordlund.

EVERYBODY WANTS TO BE ITALIAN

ROADSIDE. Sept. 3, 2008. (Jason Todd Ipson) Jay Jablonski, Cerina Vincent, John Kapelos, John Enos, III, Richard Libertini, Marisa Petroro, Perry Anzilotti, Anthony Russell, Tammy Pescatelli, Dan Cortese, Judith Scarpone, P.J. Marino, Penny Marshall.

EVERYBODY'S FINE

MIRAMAX FILMS. Nov. 3, 2009. (Kirk Jones) Robert De Niro, Drew Barrymore, Kate Beckinsale, Sam Rockwell, Melissa Leo, Lucian Maisel, Damian Young, James Frain.

EVERYONE'S HERO

20TH CENTURY FOX. Sept., 2006. (Christopher Reeve, Daniel St. Pierre, Colin Brady) Rob Reiner, Whoopi Goldberg, Jake T. Austin, William H. Macy, Mandy Patinkin, Raven-Symone, Robert Wagner, Forest Whitaker, Brian Dennehy, Dana Reeve, Joe Torre, Robin Williams. Animated.

THE EX-LOVE OF MY LIFE
WARNER BROS. PICTURES FRANCE. Jan., 2005. French. (Josiane Balasko) Thierry Lhermitte, Karin Viard, Josiane Balasko, Nadia Fares, Nicolas Silberg, Didier Flamand, Micheline Dax.

EXECUTED IN FLORESTA
March, 2006. Argentinian. (Diego Hernan Ceballos) Documentary.

EXIT: THE RIGHT TO DIE
FIRST RUN/ICARUS FILMS. Oct., 2006. Swiss. (Fernand Melgar) Dr. Jerome Sobel, Marianne Tendon. Documentary.

EXPELLED: NO INTELLIGENCE ALLOWED
ROCKY MOUNTAIN PICTURES. March 28, 2008. (Nathan Frankowski) Ben Stein, Richard Sternberg, Mark Souder, Guillermo Gonzalez, Caroline Crocker, Richard Dawkins, P.Z. Myers, Eugenie Scott, Christopher Hitchens, Michael Shermer, John Lennox, David Berlinski, Alister McGrath, Stephen C. Meyer.

THE EXPRESS
UNIVERSAL. Sept. 23, 2008. (Gary Fleder) Rob Brown, Dennis Quaid, Omar Benson Miller, Darrin DeWitt Henson, Charles S. Dutton, Justin Martin, Geoff Stults.

EXPIRATION DATE
ROADKILL PRODS. Sept., 2006. (Rick Stevenson) Robert Guthrie, Sascha Knopf, Dee Wallace Stone, David Keith, Brandon Whitehead, Ben Ratner, Ned Romero, Nakotah LaRance.

THE EXTRA
HOYTS. April, 2005. Australian. (Kevin Carlin) Jimeoin, Rhys Muldoon, Katherine Slattery, Bob Franklin, Helen Dallimore, Kristy Hinze, Shaun Micallef, Tayler Kane.

EXTRACT
MIRAMAX FILMS. Aug. 11, 2009. (Mike Judge) Jason Bateman, Mila Kunis, Kristen Wiig, J.K. Simmons, David Koechner, Clifton Collins, Jr., Gene Simmons, Ben Affleck.

EYE OF THE DOLPHIN
MONTEREY MEDIA. Aug., 2007. (Michael D. Sellers) Carly Schroeder, Adrian Dunbar, George Harris, Jane Lynch, Christine Adams, Katharine Ross, Rudy Levarity, Joey Jam, Vivica Watkins.

F

FACING THE GIANTS
SONY PICTURES ENTERTAINMENT RELEASING. Sept., 2006. (Alex Kendrick) Alex Kendrick, Shannen Fields, Steve Williams, Bailey Cave, Jason McLeod, Tracy Goode, Chris Willis, Mark Richt.

FACTORY GIRL
MGM. Dec., 2006. (George Hickenlooper) Sienna Miller, Guy Pearce, Hayden Christensen, Jimmy Fallon, Mena Suvari, Shawn Hatosy, Ileana Douglas, Jack Houston, Beth Grant, James Naughton, Edward Herrmann, Sally Kirkland, Mary Kate Olsen, Don Novello, Armin Amiri, Tara Summer.

FACTS ABOUT THE MAGLIANA GANG
ISTITUTO LUCE. June, 2005. Italian. (Daniele Costantini) Francesco Pannofino, Roberto Brunetti, Francesco Dominedo, Fabio Grossi, Tommaso Capogreco, Mario Contu, Lucio Sinisi, Gianfranco Zuncheddu, Fanny Cadeo, Leo Gullotta.

FADED MEMORIES
ROCKY MOUNTAIN PICTURES. Nov. 12, 2008. (Anne-Sophie Dutoit) Dutoit, Brock Kelly, Ely Pouget, Kim Morgan Greene, Conni Marie Brazelton, Robert Sampson, Nick James, Patrick Ryan Anderson, Cory Williams.

FAILURE TO LAUNCH
PARAMOUNT. Feb., 2006. (Tom Dey) Matthew McConaughey, Sarah Jessica Parker, Zooey Deschanel, Justin Bartha, Bradley Cooper, Terry Bradshaw, Kathy Bates.

FAIR PLAY
TFM DISTRIBUTION. July, 2006. French-Belgium-Czech Republic. (Lionel Bailliu) Benoit Magimel, Marion Cotillard, Jeremie Renier, Eric Savin, Melanie Doutey, Jean-Pierre Cassel, Malcolm Conrath.

FALLING
MAIN STREET MOVIE CO. April 4, 2008. 9 (Richard Dutcher) Virginia Reece, Tennison Hightower, Frank Uzzolino, Maria Eberline, Anthony Tavera, Cesar Garcia, Lynn Elliot, Carmen Rojas, Miro.

FAME
MGM. Sept. 23, 2009. (Kevin Tancharoen) Debbie Allen, Charles S. Dutton, Kelsey Grammer, Megan Mullally, Bebe Neuwirth, Asher Book, Kristy Flores, Paul Iacono, Paul McGill, Naturi Naughton, Kay Panabaker, Kherington Payne, Collins Pennie, Walter Perez, Anna Maria Perez de Tagle.

FAMILY HERO
UGC DISTRIBUTION. Dec., 2006. French-Italian. (Thierry Klifa) Gerard Lanvin, Catherine Deneuve, Geraldine Pailhas, Emmanuelle Beart, Miou-Miou, Claude Brasseur, Michael Cohen, Valerie Lemercier, Pierrick Lilliu, Gilles Lellouche, Claire Maurier, Pierre Perrier, Lorenzo Balducci, Evelyne Buyle.

THE FAMILY STONE
20TH CENTURY FOX. Nov., 2005. (Thomas Bezucha) Claire Danes, Diane Keaton, Rachel McAdams, Dermot Mulroney, Craig T. Nelson, Sarah Jessica Parker, Luke Wilson, Ty Giordano, Brian White, Elizabeth Reaser, Paul Schneider.

FANBOYS
MGM. July 24, 2008. (Kyle Newman) Sam Huntington, Dan Fogler, Jay Baruchel, Kristen Bell, Christopher Marquette, Carrie Fisher, Allie Grant, Jaime King, Danny McBride, Jason Mewes, Ray Park, Seth Rogen, William Shatner, Kevin Smith, Ethan Suplee, Danny Trejo, Billy Dee Williams.

FANTASTIC FOUR
20TH CENTURY FOX. July, 2005. (Tim Story) Ioan Gruffudd, Jessica Iba, Chris Evans, Michael Chiklis, Julian McMahon, Hamish Linklater, Kerry Washington, Laurie Holde.

FANTASTIC FOUR: RISE OF THE SILVER SURFER
20TH CENTURY FOX. June, 2007. (Tim Story) Ioan Gruffudd, Jessica Alba, Chris Evans, Michael Chiklis, Julian McMahon, Kerry Washington, Andre Braugher, Doug Jones, Beau Garrett, Brian Posehn, Zach Grenier, Kenneth Welsh. Voice: Laurence Fishburne.

FANTASTIC MR. FOX
20TH CENTURY FOX. Oct. 12, 2009. (Wes Anderson) Voices: George Clooney, Meryl Streep, Jason Schwartzman, Bill Murray, Wally Wolodarsky, Eric Anderson, Michael Gambon, Willem Dafoe, Owen Wilson, Jarvis Cocker. Animated.

THE FAR SIDE OF JERICHO
FIRST LOOK PICTURES. May, 2007. (Tim Hunter) Suzanne Andrews, Judith Burnett, Lissa Negrin, Patrick Bergin, Lawrence Pressman, James Gammon, John Diehl, C. Thomas Howell, Jason Connery.

THE FAST AND THE FURIOUS: TOKYO DRIFT
UNIVERSAL. June, 2006. (Justin Lin) Lucas Black, Bow Wow, Nathalie Kelley, Brian Tee, Sung Kang, Leonardo Nam, Brian Goodman, JJ Sonny Chiba, Zachery Bryan, Nikki Griffin, Jason Tobin, Keiko Kitagawa, Lynda Boyd, Vincent Laresca.

FAST TRACK
MGM. Dec., 2006. (Jesse Peretz) Zach Braff, Amanda Peet, Jason Bateman, Charles Grodin, Mia Farrow, Lucien Maisel, Paul Rudd, Amy Adams, Donal Logue, Fred Armisen, Amy Poehler.

FAST & FURIOUS
UNIVERSAL. April 2, 2009. (Justin Lin) Vin Diesel, Paul Walker, Michelle Rodriguez, Jordana Brewster, John Ortiz, Laz Alonso, Sung Kang, Tego Calderon, Gal Gadot, Don Omar, Jack Conley, Liza Lapira, Shea Whigham.

FC VENUS
COLUMBIA TRISTAR NORDISK FILM DISTRIBUTORS OY. April, 2006. Finnish. (Joona Tena) Minna Haapkyla, Petteri Summanen, Laura Malmivaara, Taneli Makela, Noora Peltokukka, Jukka Rasila, Lotta Lehtikari.

FEARLESS
ROGUE PICTURES (IN U.S.). March, 2006. Chineese-Hong Kong. (Ronny Yu) Jet Li, Betty Sun, Dong Yong, Shidou Nakamura, Collin Chou, Paw Hee-ching, Nathan Jones, Masato Harada, Anthony De Longis, Jean-Claude Leuyer, Brandon Rhea, Mike Leeder.

FEAST
DIMENSION PICTURES. Sept., 2006. (John Gulager) Balthazar Getty, Henry Rollins, Navi Rawat, Judah Friedlander, Josh Zuckerman, Jason Mewes, Jenny Wade, Krista Allen, Clu Gulager, Duane Whitaker, Eileen Ryan, Diane Goldner, Tyler Patrick Jones, Anthony "Treach" Criss, Eric Dane.

FEAST OF LOVE
MGM. Aug., 2007. (Robert Benton) Morgan Freeman, Greg Kinnear, Radha Mitchell, Billy Burke, Selma Blair, Alexa Davalos, Toby Hemingway, Stana Katic, Jane Alexander, Fred Ward.

FEED
SHOWBOX ENTERTAINMENT/MIRACLE. Jan., 2006. Australian. (Brett Leonard) Alex O'Loughlin, Patrick Thompson, Gabby Millgate, Jack Thompson, Matthew Le Nevez, David Field, Rose Ashton, Sherly Sulaiman, Marika Aubrey.

FEEL THE NOISE
SONY PICTURES ENTERTAINMENT. Oct. 5, 2007. (Alejandro Chomski) Omarion Grandberry, Zulay Henao, James McCaffrey, Kellita Smith, Melonie Diaz, Victor Rasuk, Giancarlo Esposito.

FELON
STAGE 6 FILMS. July 9 2008. (Ric Roman Waugh) Stephen Dorff, Harold Perrineau, Val Kilmer, Marisol Nichols, Anne Archer, Sam Shepard, Nick Chinlund, Johnny Lewis.

FERMAT'S ROOM
MANGA FILMS. Nov., 2007. Spanish. (Luis Piedrahita, Rodrigo Sopena) Alejo Sauras, Elena Ballesteros, Santi Millan, Lluis Homar, Federico Luppi.

FESTIVAL

PATHE U.K. June, 2005. British. (Annie Griffin) Lyndsey Marshal, Amelia Bullmore, Daniela Nardini, Chris O'Dowd, Billy Carter, Raquel Cassidy, Stephen Mangan, Jonah Lotan, Clive Russell, Lucy Punch, Gabriel Quigley.

THE FEVER

01 DISTRIBUTION. March, 2005. Italian. (Alessandro D'Alatri) Fabio Volo, Gisella Burinato, Valeria Solarino, Vittorio Franceschi, Massimo Bagliani, Arnoldo Foa, Thomas Trabacchi, Gianluca Gobbi, Paolo Jannacci, Alessandro Garbin, Lucilla Agosti, Julie Depardieu.

FEVER PITCH

TWENTIETH CENTURY FOX. April, 2005. (Peter Farrelly, Bobby Farrelly) Drew Barrymore, Jimmy Fallon, James B. Sikking, JoBeth Williams, Willie Garson, Evan Helmuth, Ione Skye, Kadee Strickland.

FICTION

ALTA CLASSICS. Nov., 2006. Spanish. (Cesc Gay) Eduard Fernandez, Javier Camara, Montse German, Carme Pla, Agata Roca.

THE FIELD OF STARS

MANGA FILMS. Jan., 2008. Spanish. (Mario Camus) Alvaro de Luna, Marian Aguilera, Rodolfo Sancho, Oscar Abad, Mari Gonzalez, Jose Manuel Cervino, Antonio de la Torre.

FIGHTING

UNIVERSAL. April 16, 2009. (Dito Montiel) Channing Tatum, Terrence Howard, Zulay Henao, Luis Guzman, Roger Guenveur Smith, Brian White.

FIGHTING FOR LIFE

TRULY INDIE. March 4, 2008. (Terry Sanders) Crystal Davis, David Welling, Daniel Inouye.

FILM IS A GIRL & A GUN

LOOP MEDIA. Aug., 2009. Austrian. (Gustav Deutsch) Documentary.

FILMMAKERS VS. TYCOONS

M.C. DISTRIBUCION. July, 2005. Spanish. (Carlos Benpar) Marta Belmonte, Santiago Laperira, Enric Sunol. Documentary.

FINAL ARRANGEMENTS

GAUMONT. Nov., 2008. French. (Michel Delgado) Didier Bourdon, Marc-Andre Grondin, Berenice Bejo, Gerard Depardieu, Marthe Keller.

THE FINAL DESTINATION

WARNER BROS. (IN U.S.)/METROPOLITAN FILM EXPORT (IN FRANCE). Aug. 26, 2009. (David R. Ellis) Bobby Campo, Shantel VanSanten, Nick Zano, Haley Webb, Mykelti Williamson, Krista Allen, Andrew Fiscella, Justin Welborn.

FINAL DESTINATION 3

NEW LINE CINEMA. Feb., 2006. (James Wong) Mary Elizabeth Winstead, Ryan Merriman, Kris Lemche, Texas Battle, Alexz Johnson, Jesse Moss, Gina Holden, Sam Easton, Crystal Lowe, Chelan Simmons, Amanda Crew.

THE FINAL SEASON

YARI FILM GROUP. Oct. 3, 2007. (David Mickey Evans) Sean Astin, Powers Boothe, Rachael Leigh Cook, James Gammon, Larry Miller, Marshall Bell, Tom Arnold, Michael Angarano, Angela Paton.

FIRED UP!

SONY PICTURES ENTERTAINMENT. Feb. 9, 2009. (Will Gluck) Nicholas D'Agosto, Eric Christian Olsen, Sarah Roemer, Molly Sims, Danneel Harris, David Walton, Adhir Kalyan, Annalynne McCord, Juliette Goglia, Philip Baker Hall, John Michael Higgins.

FIREHOUSE DOG

20TH CENTURY FOX. April, 2007. (Todd Holland) Josh Hutcherson, Bruce Greenwood, Dash Mihok, Steven Culp, Bill Nunn, Bree Turner, Scotch Ellis Loring, Mayte Garcia, Teddy Sears. Dogs: Arwen, Frodo, Rohan, Stryder.

FIREWALL

WARNER BROS. Feb., 2006. (Richard Loncraine) Harrison Ford, Paul Bettany, Virginia Madsen, Mary Lynn Rajskub, Robert Patrick, Robert Forster, Alan Arkin, Carly Schroeder, Jimmy Bennett.

THE FIRST DAY OF THE REST OF YOUR LIFE

STUDIOCANAL. July, 2008. French. (Remi Bezancon) Jacques Gamblin, Zabou Breitman, Deborah Francois, Marc-Andre Grondin, Pio Marmai, Roger Dumas, Cecile Cassel.

FIRST DESCENT: THE STORY OF THE SNOWBOARDING REVOLUTION

UNIVERSAL. Nov., 2005. (Kevin Harrison, Kemp Curley) Shaun White, Hannah Teter, Shawn Farmer, Nick Perata, Terje Haakonsen, Travis Rice, Chuck Barfoot, Jake Barton, Tom Sims. Narrator: Henry Rollins. Documentary.

FIRST SNOW

YARI FILM GROUP. March, 2007. (Mark Fergus) Guy Pearce, Piper Perabo, William Fichter, J.K. Simmons, Shea Whigham, Rick Gonzales.

FIRST SUNDAY

SONY PICTURES ENTERTAINMENT. Jan. 3, 2008. (David E. Talbert) Ice Cube, Katt Williams, Tracy Morgan, Loretta Devine, Michael Beach, Keith David, Regina Hall, Malinda Williams, Chi McBride, Olivia Cole.

FISH STORY

FISH STORY FILM PARTNERS. April, 2009. Japanese. (Yoshihiro Nakamura) Atsushi Ito, Kora Kengo, Mikako Tabe, Dakaku Hama, Mirai Moriyama, Kenjiro Ishimaru, Nao Omori.

FIVE MINUTES OF HEAVEN

PATHE PICTURES. Jan, 2009. U.K., Irish. (Oliver Hirschbiegel) Liam Neeson, James Nesbit, Anamaria Marinca, Richard Dormer, Mark Davison, Kevin O'Neill.

FIXED

March, 2005. (Neil Matsumoto) Jason Van Over, Tina Holmes, Stephen DeCordova, Royana Black, Terry Anderson, Jill Jacobson, Steven Shaw.

FLAGS OF OUR FATHERS

PARAMOUNT (IN U.S.)/WARNER BROS. (INTERNATIONAL). Sept., 2006. (Clint Eastwood) Ryan Phillippe, Jesse Bradford, Adam Beach, John Benjamin Hickey, John Slattery, Barry Pepper, Jamie Bell, Paul Walker, Robert Patrick, Neal McDonough, Melanie Lynskey, Tom McCarthy, Chris Bauer, Judith Ivey, Myra Turley, Joseph Cross, Benjamin Walker, Alessandro Mastrobuono, Scott Reeves, Stark Sands, George Grizzard, Harve Presnell, George Hearn, Len Cariou, Christopher Curry.

FLAMENCO INHERITANCE

DOCFILM. June, 2005. German-Spanish. (Michael Meert) Juan Carmona, Antonio Carmona, Jose Miguel Carmona, Juan Habichuela, Pepe Habichuela. Documentary.

FLICKA

20TH CENTURY FOX. Oct., 2006. (Michael Mayer) Alison Lohman, Tim McGraw, Maria Bello, Ryan Kwanten, Dallas Roberts, Nick Searcy, Danny Pino, Kaylee DeFer, Jeffrey Nordling, Dey Young.

FLIGHTPLAN

BUENA VISTA PICTURES. Sept., 2005. (Robert Schwentke) Jodie Foster, Peter Sarsgaard, Erika Christensen, Sean Bean, Kate Beahan, Marlene Lawston, Greta Scacchi, Judith Scott, Michael Irby, Brent Sexton.

FLOOR 17

MOVIEMAX. March, 2006. Italian. (Marco Manetti, Antonio Manetti). Giampaolo Morelli, Elisabetta Rocchetti, Enrico Silvestrin, Giuseppe Soleri, Antonino Iuorio, Massimo Ghini.

FLUSHED AWAY

PARAMOUNT. Oct., 2006. (David Bowers, Sam Fell) Voices: Hugh Jackman, Kate Winslet, Jean Reno, Bill Nighy, Andy Serkis, Shane Richie, Ian McKellen, Kathy Burke, David Suchet, Miriam Margolyes. Animated.

FLY ME TO THE MOON

SUMMIT ENTERTAINMENT. July 10, 2008. (Ben Stassen) Trevor Gagnon, Kelly Ripa, Philip Daniel Bolden, David Gore, Christopher Lloyd, Nicollette Sheridan, Tim Curry, Buzz Aldrin.

FLYBOYS

MGM. Sept., 2006. (Tony Bill) James Franco, Martin Henderson, David Ellison, Jennifer Decker, Jean Reno, Tyler Labine, Abdul Salis, Philip Winchester, Daniel Rigby, Barry McGee, Augustin Legrand, Lex Shrapnel, Keith McErlean, Michael Jibson, Christien Anholt, Pip Pickering, Kyle Hesner Smith, Adrien Boublil, Lauren Downing, Hayley Downing.

FLYING LESSONS

01 DISTRIBUTION. April, 2007. Italian-British-Indian-French. (Francesca Archibugi) Giovanna Mezzogiorno, Andrea Miglio Risi, Tom Karumathy, Anna Galiena, Flavio Bucci, Roberto Citran, Angela Finocchiaro, Douglas Henshall, Mariano Rigillo, Emanuela Sparta, Riccardo Zinna, Maria Paiato, Sabina Vannucchi.

THE FOG

SONY PICTURES ENTERTAINMENT. Oct., 2005. (Rupert Wainwright) Tom Welling, Maggie Grace, Selma Blair, DeRay Davis, Kenneth Welsh, Adrian Hough, Sara Botsford, Rade Sherbedgia.

FOOD BEWARE: THE FRENCH ORGANIC REVOLUTION

FIRST RUN FEATURES (IN U.S.). Oct., 2009. French. (Jean-Paul Jaud) John Peterson Myers, Perico Legasse, Dominique Belpomme.

FOOL'S GOLD

WARNER BROS. Jan. 30, 2008. (Andy Tennant) Matthew McConaughey, Kate Hudson, Donald Sutherland, Alexis Dziena, Ewen Bremner, Ray Winstone, Kevin Hart, Malcolm-Jamal Warner, Brian Hooks, David Roberts.

FOON

PYRAMIDE DISTRIBUTION. Jan., 2006. French. (Benoit Petre, Deborah Saiag, Mika Tard, Isabelle Vitari) Alexandre Brik, Mayane Delem, Morgan Perez, Benoit Petre, Vanessa Pivain, Deborah Saiag, Mika Tard, Isabelle Vitari, Martine Chevallier, Michel Fau, Dominique Frot, Roland Menou, Stephane Metzgzer, Cecile Cassel, Ludivine Sagnier, Thierry Lhermitte.

FOOTY LEGENDS
ICON. July, 2006. Australian. (Khoa Do) Anh Do, Angus Sampson, Lisa Saggers, Jason McGoldrick, Claudia Karvan, Dao Minh Sinh.

THE FORBIDDEN KINGDOM
LIONSGATE/THE WEINSTEIN CO. April 9, 2008. (Rob Minkoff) Jackie Chan, Jet Li, Collin Chou, Liu Yifei, Li Bing Bing, Michael Angarano, Morgan Benoit.

FOREVER STRONG
CRANE MOVIE CO. Sept. 28, 2008. (Ryan Little) Gary Cole, Sean Faris, Arielle Kebbel, Julie Warner, Penn Badgley, Sean Astin, Neal McDonough, Michael Pagan.

FORFEIT
CORNDOG PRODS. Nov. 25, 2007. (Andrew Brendan Shea) Billy Burke, Sherry Stringfield, John Aylward, Gregory Itzin, Phil Reeves, Kirk Baltz, Robert Rusler, Lee Garlington, Chris McKenna, Steven Williams, Wayne Knight.

FORTAPASC
01 DISTRIBUTION. May, 2009. Italian. (Marco Risi) Libero De Rienzo, Valentina Lodovini, Michele Riondino, Massimiliano Gallo, Ernesto Mahieux, Salvatore Cantalupo, Gigio Morra, Gianfranco Gallo, Antonio Buonomo, Ennio Fantastichini, Duccio Camerini, Renato Carpentieri, Gianfelice Imparato, Marcello Mazzarella, Daniele Pecci.

THE FOUNDING OF A REPUBLIC
CHINA FILM GROUP. Oct., 2009. Chinese. (Han Sanping) Tang Guoqiang, Zhang Guoli, Xu Qing, Vivian Wu, Wang Wufu, Shi Xin, Wang Xueqi, Liu Jin, Hu Jun, You Yong, Zong Liqun, Wang Jian, Jin Xin, Xiu Zongdi, Liu Sha, Jiang Shan, Lu Liping, Wang Bing, Chen Kun, Feng Xiaogang, Chen Hao, Leon Lai, Huang Shengyi, Andy Lau, Sun Honglei, Tong Dawei, Wu Gang, Jet Li, Liu Hua, Chen Daoming, Jiang Wen, Ge You, Chen Kaige, Vicki Zhao, Donnie Yen, Yang Ruoxi, Che Yongli, Gong Beibi, He Lin, Chen Hong, Tao Zeru, Liu Yiwei, Lian Jin, Huang Xiaoming, Shen Aojun, Deng Chao, Zhang Ziyi, Wang Yajie, Ning Jing, Xu Fan, Fan Wei, Feng Fan, Tony Leung Kar-fai, Dong Xuan, Miao Pu, Guo Degang, Chen Shu, Zhang Hanyu, Wang Baoqiang, Chen Baoguo, Jackie Chan, John Leighton Stuart, Donald Freeman, Alexander Pavlov, Donald Eugene McCoy, Leslie H. Collings.

FOUR BROTHERS
PARAMOUNT. Aug., 2005. (John Singleton) Mark Wahlberg, Tyrese Gibson, Andre Benjamin, Garrett Hedlund, Terrence Howard, Josh Charles, Sofia Vergara, Fionnula Flanagan, Chiwetel Ejiofor, Taraji P. Henson, Barry Shabaka Henley, Jernard Burks, Kenneth Welsh.

FOUR CHRISTMASES
WARNER BROS. Nov. 19, 2008. (Seth Gordon) Vince Vaughn, Reese Witherspoon, Robert Duvall, Sissy Spacek, Jon Voight, Jon Favreau, Mary Steenburgen, Dwight Yoakam, Tim McGraw, Kristin Chenoweth, Katy Mixon, Colleen Camp.

THE FOURTH KIND
UNIVERSAL. Nov. 3, 2009. (Olatunde Osunsanmi) Milla Jovovich, Will Patton, Elias Koteas, Corey Johnson, Enzo Cilenti, Hakeem Kae-Kazim, Alisha Seaton, Daphne Alexander Mia McKenna-Bruce, Olatunde Osunsanmi.

FOUR WOMEN
Sept., 2007. Indian. (Adoor Gopalakrishnan) Padmapriya, Geetu Mohandas, Manju Pillai, Nandita Das, Sreejith, M. R. Gopakumar, Nandulal, Rosilin, Mukesh, Kavya Madhavan, Lalita.

THE FOURTH PIECE OF THE WOMAN SLICED IN THREE
LES FILMS DU PARADOXE. March, 2007. French. (Laure Marsac) Laure Marsac, Denis Podalydes, Claire Borotra, Alexia Stresi, Justine Gallou, Gisele Casadesus, Ivan Taieb, Emmanuelle Lepoutre.

FRACTURE
NEW LINE CINEMA. March, 2007. (Gregory Hoblit) Anthony Hopkins, Ryan Gosling, David Strathairn, Rosamund Pike, Embeth Davidtz, Billy Burke, Cliff Curtis, Fiona Shaw, Bob Gunton, Josh Stamberg, Xander Berkeley.

FRAGILE
ON PICTURES. March, 2005. Spanish. (Juanma Bajo Ulloa) Muriel, Julio Perillan, Imma Colomer, Paula Pizzi, Maria Bazan, Bibiana Schonhofer, Violaine Esterez, Kandido Uranga.

FRANKENSTEINS BLOODY NIGHTMARE
JRH FILMS. Oct., 2006. (John R. Hand) John R. Hand, Amy Olivastro, Christopher Delacruz, Chip Chisum, Mike Ensley, Wade Best, Karl Borst.

FRANKLYN
CONTENDER FILMS. Oct., 2009..U.K. (Gerald McMorrow) Eva Green, Ryan Phillippe, Sam Riley, Bernard Hill, James Faulkner, Stephen Walters, Art Malik, Susannah York, Richard Coyle, Kika Markham.

FRAUD: MEXICO 2006
MAYA RELEASING (IN U.S). Oct., 2008. Mexican. (Luis Mandoki) Andres Manuel Lopez Obrador. Narrator: Guillermina Campuzano. Documentary.

FRED CLAUS
WARNER BROS. Nov. 5, 2007. (David Dobkin) Vince Vaughn, Paul Giamatti, John Michael Higgins, Miranda Richardson, Rachel Weisz, Kathy Bates, Trevor Peacock, Chris "Ludacris" Bridges, Elizabeth Banks, Jeremy Swift, Elizabeth Berrington, Kevin Spacey.

FREE FIGHT
BAC FILMS. Jan., 2007. French. (Julien Seri) Clovis Cornillac, Francis Renaud, Olivier Marchal, Caroline Proust, Karole Rocher, Jerome Le Banner, Tony Mpoudja.

FREE STYLE
SAMUEL GOLDWYN FILMS (IN U.S.). July 28, 2009. (William Dear) Corbin Bleu , Madison Pettis, Sandra Echeverria, Jesse Moss, Matt Bellefleur, David Reivers, Penelope Ann Miller, Scott Patey, Tegan Moss, Gustavo Febres.

FREEDOMLAND
SONY PICTURES ENTERTAINMENT. Feb., 2006. (Joe Roth) Samuel L. Jackson, Julianne Moore, Edie Falco, Ron Eldard, William Forsythe, Aunjanue Ellis, Anthony Mackie, LaTanya Richardson Jackson, Clarke Peters.

FRENCH MEN 2
PATHE. Nov., 2007. French. (Marc Esposito) Gerard Darmon, Bernard Campan, Jean-Pierre Darroussin, Marc Lavoine, Zoe Felix, Valerie Stroh, Fabienne Babe, Valerie Kaprisky, Florence Thomassin, Catherine Wilkening, Ludmila Mikael.

FRIDAY'S SOLDIERS
IRANIAN FILM SOCIETY. June, 2005. Iranian. (Massoud Kimiayi) Mohammed Reza Foroutan, Bahram Radan, Poulad Kimiayi, Pezman Bazghi, Merila Zarei, Anidesheh Fouladvand, Saeed Pirdoust, Bahzad Javanbakhsh.

FRIENDS WITH MONEY
SONY PICTURES CLASSICS. Jan., 2006. (Nicole Holofcener) Jennifer Aniston, Joan Cusack, Catherine Keener, Frances McDormand, Jason Isaacs, Scott Caan, Simon McBurney, Greg Germann, Ty Burrell, Bob Stephenson.

FROM MEXICO WITH LOVE
ROADSIDE ATTRACTIONS. Oct. 12, 2009. (Jimmy Nickerson) Kuno Becker, Steven Bauer, Stephen Lang, Alex Nesic, Danay Garcia, Bruce McGill.

FROM WITHIN
AFTER DARK FILMS. Jan. 10, 2009. (Phedon Papamichael) Elizabeth Rice, Thomas Dekker, Kelly Blatz, Laura Allen, Adam Goldberg, Rumer Willis, Margo Harshman, Brittany Robertson, Jared Harris, Steven Culp, Amanda Babin, Shiloh Fernandez.

FROST/NIXON
UNIVERSAL. Oct. 13, 2008. (Ron Howard) Frank Langella, Michael Sheen, Rebecca Hall, Toby Jones, Matthew Macfadyen, Sam Rockwell, Patty McCormack, Andy Miller, Kate Jennings Grant, Eve Curtis.

FULL OF IT
NEW LINE CINEMA. Feb., 2007. (Christian Charles) Ryan Pinkston, Kate Mara, Craig Kilborn, John Carroll Lynch, Cynthia Stevenson, Amanda Walsh, Derek McGrath, Josh Close, Teri Polo, Carmen Electra.

FUN WITH DICK AND JANE
SONY PICTURES ENTERTAINMENT. Dec., 2005. (Dean Parisot) Jim Carrey, Tea Leoni, Alec Baldwin, Richard Jenkins, Angie Harmon, John Michael Higgins, Richard Burgi, Carloss Jacott, Aaron Michael Drozin, Gloria Garayua.

FUNNY GAMES
TARTAN(in U.K.)WARNER INDEPENDENT PICTURES (in U.S.) U.S.-British-French-German-Italian. (Michael Haneke) Naomi Watts, Tim Roth, Michael Pitt, Brady Corbet, Devon Gearhart, Boyd Gaines, Siobhan Fallon, Robert LuPone, Linda Moran.

FUNNY PEOPLE
UNIVERSAL. July 22, 2009. (Judd Apatow) Adam Sandler, Ira Wright, Seth Rogen, Leslie Mann, Eric Bana, Leo Koenig - Jonah Hill, Mark Taylor Jackson - Jason Schwartzman, Aubrey Plaza, RZA, Iris Apatow, Maude Apatow, Torsten Voges, Allan Wasserman.

G-FORCE
WALT DISNEY PICTURES. July 22, 2009. (Hoyt H. Yeatman) Bill Nighy, Will Arnett, Zach Galifianakis, Kelli Garner, Tyler Patrick Jones, Piper Mackenzie Harris, Nicolas Cage, Sam Rockwell, Jon Favreau, Penelope Cruz, Steve Buscemi, Tracy Morgan.

G.I. JOE: THE RISE OF COBRA
PARAMOUNT. Aug. 6, 2009. (Stephen Sommers) Adewale Akinnuoye-Agbaje, Christopher Eccleston, Joseph Gordon-Levitt, Byung-hun Lee, Sienna Miller, Rachel Nichols, Ray Park, Jonathan Pryce, Said Taghmaoui, Channing Tatum, Marlon Wayans, Dennis Quaid.

GABAI GRANNY
March, 2006. Japanese. (Hitoshi Kurauchi) Kazuko Yoshiyuki, Youma

Suzuki, Koshin Ikeda, Soma Ikeda, Youki Kudoh, Miyoko Asada, Ken Ogata.

GABRIEL
SONY PICTURES RELEASING INTL. Nov., 2007. Australian. (Shane Abbess) Andy Whitfield, Dwaine Stevenson, Samantha Noble, Michael Piccirilli, Jack Campbell, Erika Heynatz, Harry Pavlidis, Kevin Copeland, Matt Hylton Todd, Brendan Clearkin.

GAL
AURUM. Nov., 2006. Spanish-French. (Miguel Courtois) Jose Garcia, Natalia Verbeke, Jordi Molla, Ana Alvarez, Merce Llorens, Abel Folk, Jose Angel Egido, Tomas del Estal, Jose Coronado, Bernard le Coq.

GALLIPOLI
TOO COOL. Nov., 2005. Turkish. (Tolga Ornek) Narrators: Jeremy Irons, Sam Neill.

THE GAME OF THEIR LIVES
IFC FILMS. April, 2005. (David Anspaugh) Gerard Butler, Wes Bentley, Jay Rodan, Gavin Rossdale, Costas Mandylor, Louis Mandylor, Zachery Bryan, Jimmy Jean-Louis, Patrick Stewart, Terry Kinney, John Rhys Davies.

THE GAME PLAN
BUENA VISTA. Sept., 2007. (Andy Fickman) Dwayne "The Rock" Johnson, Madison Pettis, Kyra Sedgwick, Roselyn Sanchez, Morris Chestnut, Hayes Macarthur, Brian White, Jamal Duff, Paige Turco, Gordon Clapp, Jackie Flynn, Marv Albert, Boomer Esiason, Jim Gray, Stuart O. Scott, Steven Levy.

GAMER
LIONSGATE. Sept. 4, 2009. (Mark Neveldine) Gerard Butler, Michael C. Hall, Amber Valletta, Logan Lerman, Alison Lohman, Terry Crews, John Leguizamo, Zoe Bell, Chris "Ludacris" Bridges, Keith David, Kyra Sedgwick.

GANDHI MY FATHER
EROS INTL. July, 2007. Indian. (Feroz Abbas Khan) Darshan Jariwala, Akshaye Khanna, Bhumika Chawla, Shefali Shah, Daniel Janks, Vinay Jain, Natalie Hughes, Ilanit Shapiro, Gregg Viljoen.

GARDEN PARTY
ROADSIDE ATTRACTIONS. July 7, 2008. (Jason Freeland) Vinessa Shaw, Willa Holland, Richard Gunn, Patrick Fischler, Fiona Dourif, Erik Scott Smith, Alex Cendese, Ross Patterson, Christopher Allport, Jeff Newman.

GARFIELD: A TAIL OF TWO KITTIES
20TH CENTURY FOX. June, 2006. (Tim Hill) Breckin Meyer, Jennifer Love Hewitt, Billy Connolly, Ian Abercrombie, Roger Rees, Lucy Davis. Voices: Bill Murray, Tim Curry, Bob Hoskins, Sharon Osbourne, Jane Leeves, Jane Horrocks, Richard E. Grant, Vinnie Jones, Rhys Ifans, Roscoe Lee Browne.

GASHOLE
FILM RACKET. June 10, 2008. (Jeremy Wagener) Joshua Jackson, Curtis Wright, Sherwood Boehlert, Anna Eshoo, Jamie Court, Mark Brinkerhoff, Les Manns, Brian Pauwels. Narrator: Peter Gallagher.

THE GENIUS CLUB
ELEVEN ARTS. Oct. 28, 2007. (Tim Chey) Carol Abney, Stephen Baldwin, Jacob Bonneva, Tricia Helfer, Matt Medrano, Philip Moon, Paula Jai Parker, Huntley Ritter, Jack Scalia, Tom Sizemore.

GENTLEMEN BRONCOS
FOX SEARCHLIGHT. Sept. 24, 2009. (Jared Hess) Michael Angarano, Jennifer Coolidge, Halley Feiffer, Hector Jimenez, Sam Rockwell, Jemaine Clement, Mike White.

GEORG
Dec., 2007. Estonian-Finnish-Russian. (Peeter Simm). Marko Matvere, Anastasiya Makeyeva, Renars Kaupers, Elle Kull, Tonu Kark, Mirtel Pohla, Karin Toart, Rein Oja, Aleksandr Okunev.

GEORGIA RULE
UNIVERSAL. May, 2007. (Garry Marshall) Jane Fonda, Lindsay Lohan, Felicity Huffman, Dermot Mulroney, Cary Elwes, Garrett Hedlund, Hector Elizondo.

GET RICH OR DIE TRYIN'
PARAMOUNT. Oct., 2005. (Jim Sheridan) Curtis "50 Cent" Jackson, Terrence Howard, Joy Bryant, Bill Duke, Adewale Akinnuoye-Agbaje, Omar Benson Miller, Viola Davis, Tory Kittles, Marc John Jefferies, Sullivan Walker, Russell Hornsby, Ashley Walters, Serena Reeder, Mpho Koaho.

GET SMART
WARNER BROS. May 29, 2008. (Peter Segal) Steve Carell, Anne Hathaway, Dwayne Johnson, Alan Arkin, Terence Stamp, Ken Davitian.

THE GET-TOGETHER DINNER
MEDUSA FILM. March, 2007. Italian. (Pupi Avati) Diego Abatantuono, Vanessa Incontrada, Violante Placido, Ines Sastre, Francesca Neri, Blas Roca Rey, Fabio Ferrari, Osvaldo Ruggieri, Marica Pellegrinelli, Gaia Zoppi, Gaston Troiano, Gianfranco Barra, Manuela Morabito, Renato Cortesi.

GHAJINI
BIG PICTURES (IN U.S.)/INDIAN FILM CO. (IN INDIA). Jan., 2009. Indian. (A.R. Murugadoss) Aamir Khan, Asin Thottumkal, Jiah Khan, Pradeep Rawat, Riyaz Khan, Tinnu Anand.

GHOST RIDER
SONY PICTURES ENTERTAINMENT. Feb., 2007. (Mark Steven Johnson) Nicolas Cage, Eva Mendes, Wes Bentley, Sam Elliott, Donal Logue, Matt Long, Peter Fonda, Brett Cullen, Raquel Alessi.

GHOST TOWN
PARAMOUNT. Sept. 7, 2008. (David Koepp) Ricky Gervais, Greg Kinnear, Tea Leoni, Dana Ivey, Aasif Mandvi, Kristen Wiig.

THE GIGOLOS
PUNK CINEMA. March, 2007. British. (Richard Bracewell) Sacha Tarter, Trevor Sather, Susannah York, Sian Phillips, Angela Pleasence, Anna Massey, Ben Willbound, Basil Moss, Anna Hourmouzios.

THE GIRL FROM AUSCHWITZ
FOLKETS BIO. Aug., 2005. Swedish. (Stefan Jarl) Cordelia Edvardsson, Angelo Di Ponziano, Anita Molander. Documentary.

THE GIRL WITH THE DRAGON TATTOO
NORDISK. April, 2009. Swedish. (Niels Arden Oplev) Michael Nyqvist, Noomi Rapace, Lena Endre, Sven-Bertil Taube, Peter Haber, Peter Andersson, Marika Lagercrantz, Ingvar Hirdwall, Bjorn Granath.

THE GIRLFRIEND EXPERIENCE
MAGNOLIA PICTURES. April 13, 2009. (Steven Soderbergh) Sasha Grey, Chris Santos, Philip Eytan, Glenn Kenny, Timothy Davis, David Levien, Marc Jacobsen.

GLASS LIPS
INTL. FILM CIRCUIT (IN U.S.) Nov., 2007. Polish. (Lech Majewski) Patryk Czajka, Joanna Litwin, Grzegorz Przybyl.

GLORY ROAD
BUENA VISTA PICTURES. Jan., 2006. (James Gartner) Josh Lucas, Derek Luke, Austin Nichols, Jon Voight, Evan Jones, Schin A.S. Kerr, Alphonso McAuley, Mehcad Brooks, Sam Jones, III, Damaine Radcliff, Emily Deschanel, Al Shearer.

GO FAST
EUROPACORP DISTRIBUTION. Oct., 2008. French. (Olivier Van Hoofstadt) Roschdy Zem, Olivier Gourmet, Jil Milan, Xavier Maly, Catalina Denis, Jean-Michel Fete.

GO GO 70S
SHOWBOX/MEDIAPLEX. Oct., 2008. South Korean. (Choi Ho) Jo Seung-woo, Shin Min-ah, Cha Seung-woo, Son Gyeong-ho, Choi Min-cheol, Kim Min-gyu, Hong Gwang-ho, Lee Cheong-min.

GOAL II: LIVING THE DREAM
PEACE ARCH ENTERTAINMENT. Aug. 29, 2008. (Jaume Collet-Serra) Kuno Becker, Stephen Dillane, Anna Friel, Leonor Varela, Rutger Hauer, Alessandro Nivola, Elizabeth Pena, Jorge Garcia Jurado, Frances Barber, David Beckham, Ronaldo, Zinedine Zidane, Robinho, Thierry Henry, Freddy Ljungberg, Cesc Fabregas.

GOING SHOPPING
RAINBOW. Sept., 2005. (Henry Jaglom) Victoria Foyt, Rob Morrow, Lee Grant, Mae Whitman, Bruce Davison, Jennifer Grant, Cynthia Sikes, Martha Gehman, Pamela Bellwood, Juliet Landau.

GOING UNDER
ARGOT PICTURES. May, 2007. (Eric Werthman) Roger Rees, Geno Lechner, Kit Flanagan, Jenny Sterlin, Phyllis Somerville, Angela Forrest, Richard Eagan, Brian J. Keane, Beau van Donkelaar, Wendy Scharfman, Miho Nikaido.

GOLDA'S BALCONY
SEVENTH ART. Oct. 6, 2007. (Jeremy Kagan) Valerie Harper.

THE GOLDEN COMPASS
NEW LINE CINEMA. Nov. 27, 2007. (Chris Weitz) Nicole Kidman, Dakota Blue Richards, Daniel Craig, Sam Elliott, Eva Green, Christopher Lee, Tom Courtenay, Derek Jacobi, Ben Walker, Simon McBurney, Jim Carter, Clare Higgins, Jack Shepherd, Magda Szubanski, Edward De Souza, Ian McKellen, Ian McShane, Freddie Highmore, Kathy Bates, Kristin Scott Thomas.

GONE
UNIVERSAL. Dec., 2006. British-Australian-U.S. (Ringan Ledwidge) Scott Mechlowicz, Amelia Warner, Shaun Evans, Zoe Tuckwell-Smith.

GONE SHOPPING
GOLDEN VILLAGE ENTERTAINMENT. Oct., 2007. Singapore. (Wee Li-lin) Kym Ng, Aaron Kao, Sonya Nair, Adrian Pang, Charmaine Ang, Magdalene Tan, Brandon Lee, Raman Putra, Selena Tan.

THE GOOD GERMAN
WARNER BROS. Nov., 2006. (Steven Soderbergh) George Clooney, Cate Blanchett, Tobey Maguire, Beau Bridges, Tony Curran, Leland Orser, Jack Thompson, Robin Weigert, Ravil Isyanov, Christian Oliver, Don Pugsley.

GOOD HAIR
HBO FILMS. Jan. 18, 2009. (Jeff Stilson) Chris Rock, Maya Angelou, Warren Berry, Eric Bias, Sheila Bridges, Marvet Britto,

A'Lelia Bundles, Vanessa Bell Calloway, Elgin Charles, Rhonda Cowan, Joe Dudley, Eunice Dudley, Eve, Veronica Forbes, Melyssa Ford, Meagan Good, Vijay Madupali Gupta, Andre Harrell, Ice-T, Sarah Jones, Scott Julion, KRS-One, Lauren London, Nia Long, Melanye MacLin-Carroll, Jailyn Minor, Paul Mooney, Willie Morrow, Valerie Price, Salli Richardson, Salt-n-Pepa, Al Sharpton, Raven Symone, Tracie Thoms, T-Pain.

GOOD LUCK CHUCK

LIONSGATE. Sept., 2007. (Mark Helfrich) Dane Cook, Jessica Alba, Dan Fogler, Ellia English, Sasha Pieterse, Lonny Ross, Chelan Simmons.

THE GOOD SHEPHERD

UNIVERSAL. Dec., 2006. (Robert De Niro) Matt Damon, Angelina Jolie, Alec Baldwin, Tammy Blanchard, Billy Crudup, Robert De Niro, Keir Dullea, Michael Gambon, Martina Gedeck, William Hurt, Timothy Hutton, Mark Ivanir, Gabriel Macht, Lee Pace, Joe Pesci, Eddie Redmayne, John Sessions, Oleg Stefan, John Turturro.

THE GOODS: LIVE HARD * SELL HARD

PARAMOUNT. Aug. 11, 2009. (Neal Brennan) Jeremy Piven, Ving Rhames, James Brolin, David Koechner, Kathryn Hahn, Ed Helms, Jordana Spiro, Tony Hale, Ken Jeong, Rob Riggle, Alan Thicke, Charles Napier.

THE GOSPEL

SONY PICTURES ENTERTAINMENT/SCREEN GEMS. Oct., 2005. (Rob Hardy) Sean Nelson, Dwayne Boyd, Boris Kodjoe, Idris Elba, Clifton Powell, Aloma Wright, Donnie McClurkni, Omar Gooding, Tamyra Gray, Keshia Knight Pulliam, Nona Gaye, Michael J. Pagan.

GOYA'S GHOSTS

WARNER BROTHERS PICTURES INTL. Nov., 2006. Spanish-U.S. (Milos Forman) Javier Bardem, Natalie Portman, Stellan Skarsgard, Randy Quaid, Jose Luis Gomez, Michael Lonsdale, Blanca Portillo, Mabel Rivera, Unax Ugalde.

GRACIE

PICTUREHOUSE. May, 2007. (Davis Guggenheim) Carly Schroeder, Elisabeth Shue, Dermot Mulroney, Andrew Shue, Jesse Lee Soffer, Joshua Caras, Julia Garro, John Doman, Christopher Shand.

GRAN TORINO

WARNER BROS. Nov. 13, 2008. (Clint Eastwood) Clint Eastwood, Bee Vang, Ahney Her, Christopher Carley, Brian Haley, Geraldine Hughes, Brian Howe, Dreama Walker, William Hill, John Carroll Lynch, Brooke Chia Thao, Chee Thao.

GRANDMA'S BOY

20TH CENTURY FOX. Jan., 2006. (Nicholaus Goossen) Linda Cardellini, Allen Covert, Peter Dante, Shirley Jones, Shirley Knight, Joel David Moore, Kevin Nealon, Doris Roberts, Nick Swardson, Jonah Hill, Kelvin Yu, Abdoulaye N'Gom.

THE GREAT ALIBI

UGC DISTRIBUTION. May, 2008. French. (Pascal Bonitzer) Miou-Miou, Lambert Wilson, Valeria Bruni-Tedeschi, Pierre Arditi, Anne Consigny, Mathieu Demy, Caterina Murino, Maurice Benichou, Celine Sallette, Agathe Bonitzer, Emmanuelle Riva, Dany Brillant.

THE GREAT BUCK HOWARD

BRISTOL BAY PRODS. Jan. 19, 2008. (Sean McGinly) John Malkovich, Colin Hanks, Emily Blunt, Ricky Jay, Debra Monk, Griffin Dunne, Adam Scott, Patrick Fischler, Wallace Langham, Steve Zahn, Tom Hanks, Regis Philbin, Kelly Ripa, Jon Stewart, Martha Stewart, David Blaine, Tom Arnold, George Takai.

THE GREAT DEBATERS

MGM. Dec. 3, 2007. (Denzel Washington) Denzel Washington, Forest Whitaker, Nate Parker, Jurnee Smollett, Denzel Whitaker, Jermaine Williams, Gina Ravera, John Heard, Kimberly Elise.

THE GREAT WARMING

REGAL CINEMAS. Oct., 2006. (Michael Taylor) Narrators: Alanis Morissette, Keanu Reeves. Documentary.

THE GREAT RAID

MIRAMAX FILMS. July, 2005. (John Dahl) Benjamin Bratt, James Franco, Connie Nielsen, Joseph Fiennes, Marton Csokas, Motoki Kobayashi, Robert Mammone, Natalie Mendoza, Cesar Montano.

THE GREATEST GAME EVER PLAYED

BUENA VISTA. Sept., 2005. (Bill Paxton) Shia LaBeouf, Stephen Dillane, Josh Flitter, Peyton List, Elias Koteas, Marnie McPhail, Stephen Marcus, Peter Firth, Michael Weaver, James Paxton, Matthew Knight.

GREECE: SECRETS OF THE PAST

March, 2006. (Greg MacGillivray) Christos Doumas, Georges Vougioukalakis. Narrator: Nia Vardalos. Documentary. Imax.

GREG & GENTILLON

ODEON FILMS. Aug., 2007. Canadian. (Matthiew Klinck) Louis Durand, Thomas Michael, Paolo Mancini, Nadia Mansouri.

GREY SOULS

WARNER BROS. PICTURES FRANCE. Sept., 2005. French. (Yves Angelo) Jean-Pierre Marielle, Jacques Villeret, Denis Podalydes, Marina Hands, Michel Vuillermoz, Serge Riaboukine, Thomas Blanchard, Agnes Sourdillon, Nicole Dubois, Franck Manzoni, Josephine Japy.

GREEN RIVER

VANGUARD. May 4, 2008. (Sam Taybi) Kristina Hughes, Danielle Franke, Peter Bruce, Robert Lee.

GRIDIRON GANG

SONY PICTURES ENTERTAINMENT. Sept., 2006. (Phil Joanou) The Rock, Jade Yorker, Xzibit, Leon Rippy, Kevin Dunn, David Thomas, Setu Taase.

GRINDHOUSE

DIMENSION FILMS. March, 2007. Rodriguez/Tarantino double feature.
PLANET TERROR
June, 2007. (Robert Rodriguez) Rose McGowan, Freddy Rodríguez, Josh Brolin, Marley Shelton, Jeff Fahey, Michael Biehn, Rebel Rodriguez, Bruce Willis, Naveen Andrews, Julio Oscar Mechoso, Stacy Ferguson, Nicky Katt, Hung Nguyen, Cecilia Conti, Tommy Nix.

DEATH PROOF

May, 2007. (Quentin Tarantino) Kurt Russell, Zoe Bell, Rosario Dawson, Vanessa Ferlito, Sydney Tamiia Poitier, Tracie Thoms, Rose McGowan, Jordan Ladd, Mary Elizabeth Winstead, Quentin Tarantino, Marcy Harriell, Eli Roth, Omar Doom, Michael Bacall, Monica Staggs.

THE GROCER'S SON

FILM MOVEMENT (IN NORTH AMERICA)/LES FILMS DU LOSANGE (IN FRANCE). March, 2008. French. (Eric Guirado) Nicolas Cazale, Clotilde Hesme, Daniel Duval, Jeanne Goupil, Stephan Guerin Tillie, Liliane Rovere, Chad Chenouga, Paul Crauchet.

THE GRUDGE 2

SONY PICTURES ENTERTAINMENT. Oct., 2006. (Takashi Shimizu) Sarah Michelle Gellar, Amber Tamblyn, Arielle Kebbel, Jennifer Beals, Edison Chen, Christopher Cousins, Takako Fuji, Oga Tanaka, Kim Miyori, Teresa Palmer, Joanna Cassidy, Sarah Roemer, Matthew Knight, Shaun Sipos, Jenna Dewan, Eve Gordon, Misako Uno.

THE GUARDIAN

BUENA VISTA. Sept., 2006. (Andrew Davis) Kevin Costner, Ashton Kutcher, Melissa Sagemiller, Bonnie Bramlett, Clancy Brown, Sela Ward, Neal McDonough, John Heard, Brian Geraghty.

GUN OF MERCY

CHINA FILM GROUP/SHANGHAI FILM GROUP. Sept., 2007. Chinese. (Xiao Feng) Liu Peiqi, Jiang Wu, David Wu, Li Bin, Cao Ying.

GURU

Jan., 2007. Indian. (Mani Ratnam) Mithun Chakraborty, Abhishek Bachchan, Aishwarya Rai, Madhavan, Vidya Balan, Mallika Sherawat, Roshan Seth, Arya Babbar, Manoj Joshi, Rajendra Gupta.

HABANA BLUES

WARNER SOGEFILMS. March, 2005. Spanish-Cuban-French. (Benito Zambrano) Alberto Joel Garcia Osorio, Roberto Sanmartin, Yailene Sierra, Zenia Marabal, Marta Calvo, Roger Pera, Julie Ladagnous.

HACHI: A DOG'S STORY

SONY PICTURES WORLDWIDE ACQUISITIONS GROUP. June 11, 2009. (Lasse Hallstrom) Richard Gere, Joan Allen, Cary-Hiroyuki Tagawa, Jason Alexander, Erick Avari, Kevin Decoste.

HAEUNDAE

CJ ENTERTAINMENT.July. 2009. South Korean. (Yun Je-gyun) Seol Gyeong-gu, Ha Ji-weon, Park Jung-hun, Eom Jeong-hwa, Lee Min-gi, Gang Ye-weon, Kim In-gweon, Cheon Bo-geun, Song Jae-ho.

HAIRSPRAY

NEW LINE CINEMA. June, 2007. (Adam Shankman) John Travolta, Michelle Pfeiffer, Christopher Walken, Amanda Bynes, James Marsden, Queen Latifah, Brittany Snow, Zac Efron, Elijah Kelley, Allison Janney, Jerry Stiller, Paul Dooley, Nikki Blonsky, Taylor Parks.

HALF LIFE

Feb., 2008. Slovakian. (Vlado Fischer) Jan Kroner, Tana Pauhofova, Klara Trojanova Pollertova, Iva Janzurova, Matej Landl, Diana Morova, Marek Geisberg, Slavka Halcakova, Ady Hajdu, Kristina Turjanova, Henrieta Rabova.

HALLOWEEN 2

DIMENSION FILMS. Aug. 28, 2009. (Rob Zombie) Malcolm McDowell, Tyler Mane, Sheri Moon Zombie, Brad Dourif, Scout Taylor-Compton, Danielle Harris, Brea Grant, Howard Hesseman, Mary Birdsong, Chase Vanek, Margot Kidder, Al Yankovic, Angela Trimbur.

HANCOCK

SONY PICTURES ENTERTAINMENT. June 23, 2008. (Peter Berg) Will Smith, Charlize Theron, Jason Bateman, Eddie Marsan, Johnny Galecki, Thomas Lennon, Jae Head.

HANDY MAN

PYRAMIDE DISTRIBUTION. Aug., 2006. French. (Michel Leclerc) Elsa Zylberstein, Kad Merad, Claude Brasseur, Patrick Chesnais, Guillaume Toucas, Liliane Rovere, Sarah Martins.

THE HANGOVER

WARNER BROS. May 20, 2009. (Todd Phillips) Bradley Cooper, Ed Helms, Zach Galifianakis, Justin Bartha, Heather Graham, Sasha Barrese, Jeffrey Tambor, Ken Jeong, Rachel Harris, Himself, Mike Epps.

HANNAH MONTANA & MILEY CYRUS: BEST OF BOTH WORLDS CONCERT

WALT DISNEY PICTURES. Jan. 29, 2008. (Bruce Hendricks) Miley Cyrus, Joe Jonas, Kevin Jonas, Nick Jonas, Kenny Ortega, Billy Ray Cyrus. Documentary.

HANNIBAL RISING

MGM. Feb., 2007. (Peter Webber) Gaspard Ulliel, Gong Li, Rhys Ifans, Kevin McKidd, Dominic West, Richard Brake, Stephen Walters, Ivan Marevich, Goran Kostic, Charles Maquignon, Richard Leaf, Ingeborda Dapkunaite, Aaron Thomas, Helena-Lia Tachovska.

THE HAPPENING

20TH CENTURY FOX. June 10, 2008. (M. Night Shyamalan) Mark Wahlberg, Zooey Deschanel, John Leguizamo, Betty Buckley, Frank Collison, Ashlyn Sanchez, Spencer Breslin, Robert Bailey, Jr., Jeremy Strong, Alan Ruck, Victoria Clark, M. Night Shyamalan.

HAPPILY EVER AFTER

SHOCHIKU CO. Oct., 2007. Japanese. (Yukihiko Tsutsumi) Miki Nakatani, Hiroshi Abe, Toshiyuki Nishida, Kenichi Endo, Carousel Maki.

HAPPILY N'EVER AFTER

LIONSGATE. Dec., 2006. (Paul J. Bolger) Voices: Sarah Michelle Gellar, Freddie Prinze, Jr., Andy Dick, Wallace Shawn, Patrick Warburton, George Carlin, Sigourney Weaver, Terrence Evans, Kathy Lamkin, Marietta Marich, Cyia Batten, Lew Temple. Animated.

HAPPY FEET

WARNER BROS. Oct., 2006. (George Miller) Voices: Elijah Wood, Robin Williams, Brittany Murphy, Hugh Jackman, Nicole Kidman, Hugo Weaving, Anthony LaPaglia, E.G. Daily, Magda Szubanski, Miriam Margolyes, Steve Irwin. Animated.

HARDSET. A MURDER IN PARIS

OCEAN FILMS DISTRIBUTION. Jan., 2006. French. (Philippe Collin) Elie Semoun, Ludmila Mikael, Philippe Uchan, Laurent Stocker, Henri Garcin, Jean-Quentin Chatelain, Fabienne Babe.

HAROLD

CITY LIGHTS PICTURES. July 8, 2008. (T. Sean Shannon) Spencer Breslin, Cuba Gooding, Jr., Ally Sheedy, Nikki Blonsky, Chris Parnell, Stella Maeve, Suzanne Shepherd, Fred Willard, Colin Quinn.

HARRY POTTER AND THE GOBLET OF FIRE

WARNER BROS. Nov., 2005. (Mike Newell) Daniel Radcliffe, Rupert Grint, Emma Watson, Robbie Coltran, Ralph Fiennes, Michael Gambon, Brendan Gleeson, Jason Isaacs, Gary Oldman, Miranda Richardson, Alan Rickman, Maggie Smith, Timothy Spall, Frances de la Tour, Pedja Bjelac, David Bradley, Warwick Davis, Tom Felton, Robert Hardy, Shirley Henderson, Roger Lloyd Pack, Mark Williams, Stanislav Ianevski, Robert Pattinson, Clemence Poesy, David Tennant, James Phelps, Oliver Phelps.

HARRY POTTER AND THE HALF-BLOOD PRINCE

WARNER BROS. July 1, 2009. (David Yates) Daniel Radcliffe, Rupert Grint, Emma Watson, Helena Bonham Carter, Jim Broadbent, Robbie Coltrane, Michael Gambon, Alan Rickman, Maggie Smith, Timothy Spall, David Thewlis, David Bradley, Warwick Davis, Tom Felton.

HARRY POTTER AND THE ORDER OF THE PHOENIX

WARNER BROS. June, 2007. (David Yates) Daniel Radcliffe, Rupert Grint, Emma Watson, Helena Bonham Carter, Robbie Coltrane, Ralph Fiennes, Michael Gambon, Brendan Gleeson, Richard Griffiths, Jason Isaacs, Gary Oldman, Alan Rickman, Fiona Shaw, Maggie Smith, Imelda Staunton, David Thewlis, Emma Thompson, David Bradley, Warwick Davis, Tom Felton, Robert Hardy, Julie Walters, Mark Williams, Katie Leung, Matthew Lewis, Evanna Lynch, Bonnie Wright.

HARSH TIMES

Sept., 2005. (David Ayer) Christian Bale, Freddy Rodriguez, Eva Longoria, Terry Crews, Noel Guglielmi, Chaka Forman, Blue Mesquita, Michael Monks, J.K. Simmons, Armando Riesco, Emilio Rivera, Tammy Trull.

HATCHET

ANCHOR BAY ENTERTAINMENT. Sept., 2007. (Adam Green) Joel David Moore, Tamara Feldman, Deon Richmond, Kane Hodder, Mercedes McNab, Parry Shen, Joel Murray, Joleigh Fioreavanti, Richard Riehle, Patrika Darbo.

THE HAUNTING IN CONNECTICUT

LIONSGATE. March 17, 2009. (Peter Cornwell) Virginia Madsen, Kyle Gallner, Elias Koteas, Amanda Crew, Martin Donovan, Sophi Knight, Ty Wood, Erik Berg.

THE HAUNTING OF MOLLY HARTLEY

FREESTYLE RELEASING. Oct. 31, 2008. (Mickey Liddell) Haley Bennett, Chace Crawford, Jake Weber, Shannon Woodward, Marin Hinkle, Annalynne McCord, Shanna Collins, Nina Siemaszko, Ron Canada, Kevin Cooney, Jessica Lowndes.

HEADRUSH

Dec., 2006. French. (Jean Marboeuf) Pierre Arditi, Marie-Christine Barrault, Sandrine Le Berre, Bernard Haller, Jean-Paul Bazziconi, Fadila Belkebla.

HEADSPACE

March, 2007. (Jethro Senger) Tommy Sunshine, DJ Heather, Sean 7, DJ Hell, Louis Osborne, Red Nose Distrikt. Documentary.

THE HEART IS A DARK FOREST

X VERLEIH. Jan., 2008. German. (Nicolette Krebitz) Nina Hoss, Devid (cq) Striesow, Franziska Petri, Marc Hosemann, Monica Bleibtreu, Otto Sander, Angelika Taschen, Max Herbrechter, Guenther Maria Halmer, Jonathan Meese, Bruno Brunnet.

THE HEART OF THE EARTH

ON PICTURES. April, 2007. Spanish-British-Portugese. (Antonio Cuadri) Catalina Sandino Moreno, Sienna Guillory, Philip Winchester, Bernard Hill, Joaquim de Almeida, Ana Fernandez, Jorge Perugorria, Fernando Ramallo, Natalia Quesnel.

HEARTBREAK HOTEL

SVENSK FILMINDUSTRI. March, 2006. Swedish. (Colin Nutley) Helena Bergstrom, Maria Lundkvist, Claes Mansson, Johan Rabaeus, Erica Braun, Marie Robertson, Christoffer Svensson, Niki Gunke Stangertz, Jan Waldecrantz, Jill Johnson, Vas Blackwood.

HEAVEN, HELL... EARTH

CONTINENTAL FILM. June, 2009. Slovakian. (Laura Sivakova) Zuzana Kanocz, Bronislaw Wroclawski, Jiri Korn, Dagmar Blahova, Helena Polakova, Dagmar Edwards, Lukas Latinak, Ivan Martinka.

HELL

SND. Jan., 2006. French. (Bruno Chiche) Sara Forestier, Nicolas Duvauchelle, Christiane Millet, Didier Sandre, Anne-Marie Philipe, Michel Vuillermoz, May Alexandrov, Sarah-Laure Estragnat, Louise Monot.

HELL RIDE

THIRD RAIL. Aug. 4, 2008. (Larry Bishop) Larry Bishop, Michael Madsen, Eric Balfour, Vinnie Jones, Leonor Varela, David Carradine, Dennis Hopper, Michael Beach, Laura Cayouette, Julia Jones, Francesco Quinn, Cassandra Hepburn, David Grieco, Dean Delray.

HELLBOY II: THE GOLDEN ARMY

UNIVERSAL PICTURES. June 28, 2008. (Guillermo del Toro) Ron Perlman, Selma Blair, Doug Jones, John Alexander, James Dodd, Seth MacFarlane, Luke Goss, Anna Walton, Jeffrey Tambor, John Hurt.

HELLO SCHOOLGIRL

CJ ENTERTAINMENT. July, 2009. South Korean. (Ryu Jan-ha) Yu Ji-tae, Lee Yeon-heui, Chae Jeong-an, Gang In, Choi Su-yeong, Shin Chun-shik, Lee Ju-shil, Hwang Seok-jeong, Kim Gang-woo, Kang Full.

HELLPHONE

STUDIOCANAL. March, 2007. French. (James Huth) Jean-Baptiste Maunier, Jennifer Decker, Benjamin Jungers, Vladimir Consigny, Edouard Colin, Baptiste Caillaud, Anais Demoustier, Judith Chemla, Christian Hecq, Clotilde Mollet.

HELLSINKI

NORDISK FILM. April, 2009. Finish. (Aleksi Makela) Samuli Edelmann, Peter Franzen, Pihla Viitala, Kari Hietalahti, Juha Veijonen, Jasper Paakkonen, Pekka Valkeejarvi, Hiski Gronstrand.

HER WHOLE LIFE AHEAD OF HER

MEDUSA FILM. March, 2008. Italian. (Paolo Virzi) Isabella Ragonese, Sabrina Ferilli, Massimo Ghini, Valerio Mastandrea, Elio Germano, Micaela Ramazzotti, Mary Cipolla, Tatiana Farnese, Caterina Guzzanti, Valentina Carneluti, Paola Tiziana Cruciani, Niccolo Senni. Narrator: Laura Morante.

HERBIE: FULLY LOADED

BUENA VISTA PICTURES. June, 2005. (Angela Robinson) Lindsay Lohan, Michael Keaton, Matt Dillon, Breckin Meyer, Justin Long, Cheryl Hines, Jimmi Simpson, Jill Ritchie, Thomas Lennon, Jeremy Roberts, Jim Cody Williams, Allen Bestwick, Benny Parsons, Jeff Gordon, Jimmie Johnson, Dale Jarrett, Tony Stewart, Stuart Scott.

HERBIE HANCOCK: POSSIBILITIES

HDNET FILMS. March, 2006. (Doug Biro, Jon Fine) Herbie Hancock, Christina Aguilera, Sting, John Mayer, Raul Midon, Trey Anastasio, Damien Rice, Lisa Hannigan, Carlos Santana, Angelique Kidjo, Paul Simon, Brian Eno, Greg Phillinganes, Annie Lennox, Jonny Lang, Joss Stone, Wayner Shorter, Lionel Louke. Documentary.

HEROINE

ALTA FILMS. May, 2005. Spanish. (Gerardo Herrero) Adriana Ozores, Javier Pereira, Maria Bouzas, Carlos Blanco, Mercedes Castro, Cesar Cambeiro, Luis Iglesia.

HEY HEY IT'S ESTHER BLUEBURGER

WALT DISNEY STUDIOS MOTION PICTURES AUSTRALIA. March, 2008. Australian. (Cathy Randall) Keisha Castle-Hughes, Danielle Catanzariti, Essie Davis, Russell Dykstra, Christian Byers, Toni Collette.

HIDDEN

WARNER SOGEFILMS. Nov., 2005. Spanish-British-Italian. (Antonio

Hernandez) Laia Marull, Leonardo Sbaraglia, Angie Cepeda, Gerardo Malla, Joaquin Climent.

HIDE AND SEEK

20TH CENTURY FOX. Jan., 2005. (John Polson) Robert De Niro, Dakota Fanning, Famke Janssen, Elisabeth Shue, Amy Irving, Dylan Baker, Melissa Leo, Robert John Burke, Molly Grant Kallins, David Chandler, Amber McDonald, Josh Flitter, Alicia Harding.

THE HIDEOUT

01 DISTRIBUTION. Dec., 2007. Italian. (Pupi Avati) Laura Morante, Rita Tushingham, Burt Young, Treat Williams, Yvonne Brulatour Scio, Peter Soderberg, Giovanni Lombardo Radice, Angela Pagano, Sydne Rome, Angela Goodwin, Marin Jo Finerty, Chiara Tortorella, Tom Rottger-Morgan, Marina Ninchi.

HIGH SCHOOL MUSICAL 3: SENIOR YEAR

WALT DISNEY PICTURES. Oct. 16, 2008. (Kenny Ortega) Zac Efron, Vanessa Hudgens, Ashley Tisdale, Lucas Grabeel, Corbin Bleu, Monique Coleman, Olesya Rulin, Chris Warren Jr., Ryne Sanborn, Kaycee Stroh, Bart Johnson, Alyson Reed, Matt Prokop, Justin Martin, Jemma McKenzie-Brown.

THE HILLS HAVE EYES

20TH CENTURY FOX. Feb., 2006. (Alexandre Aja) Aaron Stanford, Kathleen Quinlan, Vinessa Shaw, Emilie de Ravin, Dan Byrd, Tom Bower, Billy Drago, Robert Joy, Ted Levine, Desmond Askew, Ezra Buzzington, Michael Bailey Smith, Laura Oritz.

THE HILLS HAVE EYES 2

20TH CENTURY FOX. March, 2007. (Martin Weisz) Michael McMillian, Jessica Stroup, Daniella Alonso, Jacob Vargas, Flex Alexander, Lee Thompson Young, Eric Edelstein, Michael Bailey Smith.

HIS MAJESTY MINOR

STUDIOCANAL DISTRIBUTION. Sept., 2007. French-Spanish. (Jean-Jacques Annaud) Jose Garcia, Vincent Cassel, Sergio Peris-Mencheta, Melanie Bernier, Claude Brasseur, Rufus, Jean-Luc Bideau, Taira, Marc Andreoni, Bernard Haller, Alice Fremont, Rosine Favey.

THE HISTORY BOYS

20TH CENTURY FOX. Oct., 2006. British-U.S. (Nicholas Hytner) Richard Griffiths, Frances de la Tour, Stephen Campbell Moore, Samuel Barnett, Dominic Cooper, James Corden, Jamie Parker, Russell Tovey, Samuel Anderson, Sacha Dhawan, Andrew Knott, Clive Merrison, Penelope Wilton, Adrian Scarborough.

HITCH

SONY PICTURES ENTERTAINMENT. Feb., 2005. (Andy Tennant) Will Smith, Eva Mendes, Kevin James, Amber Valletta, Julie Ann Emery, Michael Rapaport, Adam Arkin.

THE HITCHHIKER'S GUIDE TO THE GALAXY

BUENA VISTA. April, 2005. U.S.-British. (Garth Jennings) Martin Freeman, Mos Def, Sam Rockwell, Zooey Deschanel, Warwick Davis, Alan Rickman, John Malkovich, Bill Nighy, Thomas Lennon.

THE HITCHER

ROGUE PICTURES. Jan., 2007. (Dave Meyers) Sean Bean, Sophia Bush, Zachary Knighton, Neal McDonough.

HITMAN

20TH CENTURY FOX. Nov. 19, 2007. (Xavier Gens) Timothy Olyphant, Dougray Scott, Olga Kurylenko, Robert Knepper, Ulrich Thomsen, Henry Ian Cusick, Michael Offei.

HOLDING TREVOR

REGENT. June 25, 2008. (Rosser Goodman) Brent Gorski, Jay Brannan, Melissa Searing, Eli Kranski, Chris Wyllie.

HOLE

NOTRO FILMS. Aug., 2006. Spanish. (Carlos Martin Ferrera) Jaume Garcia Arija, Isak Ferriz, Enric Lopez.

THE HOLIDAY

SONY PICTURES ENTERTAINMENT. Nov., 2006. (Nancy Meyers) Cameron Diaz, Kate Winslet, Jude Law, Jack Black, Eli Wallach, Edward Burns, Rufus Sewell, Miffy Englefield, Emma Pritchard, Sarah Parish, Shannyn Sossamon, Bill Macy, Shelley Berman, Kathryn Hahn, John Krasinski.

HOLLYWOODLAND

FOCUS FEATURES. Aug., 2006. (Allen Coulter) Adrien Brody, Diane Lane, Ben Affleck, Bob Hoskins, Lois Smith, Robin Tunney, Larry Cedar, Jeffrey DeMunn, Caroline Dhavernas, Brad William Henke, Dash Mihok, Molly Parker, Kathleen Robertson, Joe Spano, Gareth Williams, Zach Mills.

HOME

PPR. June, 2009. French. (Yann-Arthus Bertrand) Jacques Gamblin. Documentary.

HOME SWEET HOME

REZO FILMS. Nov., 2008. French. (Didier Le Pecheur) Judith Godreche, Patrick Chesnais, Daniel Prevost, Alexandre Astier, Raphael Lenglet, Gerard Loussine, Gabriel Valensi, Lorant Deutsch, Nicolas Gob.

HOMECOMING

PAPER STREET FILMS/ANIMUS FILMS. June 29, 2009. (Morgan J. Freeman) Mischa Barton, Jessica Stroup, Matt Long, Michael Landes, Robert Haley.

THE HONEYMOONERS

PARAMOUNT PICTURES. June, 2005. (John Schultz) Cedric the Entertainer, Mike Epps, Gabrielle Union, Regina Hall, Eric Stoltz, Jon Polito, John Leguizamo, Carol Woods, Ajay Naidu, Kim Chan.

HONOR DE CAVALLERIA

May, 2006. Spanish. (Albert Serra) Lluis Carbo, Lluis Serrat, Glynn Bruce, Lluis Cardenal, Bartomeu Casellas, Jimmy Gimferrer, Xavier Gratacos, Eliseu Huertas, Enric Junca, Josep Pages, Jordi Pau, Rufino Pijoan, Eduard Sancho, Jordi Sancho, Albert Pla.

HOODWINKED!

WEINSTEIN CO. Dec., 2005. (Cory Edwards) Anne Hathaway, Glenn Close, Jim Belushi, Patrick Warburton, Anthony Anderson, David Ogden Stiers, Xzibit, Chazz Palminteri, Andy Dick, Cory Edwards, Benjy Gaither. Animated.

HOOT

NEW LINE CINEMA. April, 2006. (Wil Shriner) Luke Wilson, Logan Lerman, Brie Larson, Tim Blake Nelson, Cody Linley, Neil Flynn, Clark Gregg, Kiersten Warren, Jessica Cauffiel, Dean Collins, Eric Phillips, Robert Wagner.

HORSEMEN

LIONSGATE. (in U.S.)/METROPOLITAN FILMEXPORT (IN FRANCE) April 14, 2009. (Jonas Akerlund) Dennis Quaid, Ziyi Zhang, Lou Taylor Pucci, Clifton Collins, Jr., Patrick Fugit, Peter Stormare, Liam James.

HOSTEL

LIONS GATE FILMS. Jan., 2006. (Eli Roth) Jay Hernandez, Derek Richardson, Eythor Gudjonsson, Barbara Nedeljakova, Jan Vlasak, Jana Kaderabkova, Jennifer Lim.

HOSTEL: PART II

LIONSGATE. June, 2007. (Eli Roth) Lauren German, Roger Bart, Heather Matarazzo, Bijou Phillips, Richard Burgi, Vera Jordanova, Milan Knazko, Stanislav Ianevski.

HOT FUZZ

UNIVERSAL (IN U.K.)/ROGUE PICTURES (IN U.S.) Feb., 2007. British-U.S. (Edgar Wright) Simon Pegg, Nick Frost, Jim Broadbent, Paddy Considine, Timothy Dalton, Billie Whitelaw, Edward Woodward, Rafe Spall, Olivia Colman, Paul Freeman, Martin Freeman, Bill Nighy, Steve Coogan, Bill Bailey, Julia Deakin, Kenneth Cranham, Patricia Franklin, Anne Reid, Stuart Wilson, Peter Wright, Kevin Eldon, Karl Johnson.

HOT ROD

PARAMOUNT. June, 2007. (Akiva Schaffer) Andy Samberg, Isla Fisher, Jorma Taccone, Bill Hader, Danny McBride, Ian McShane, Sissy Spacek, Will Arnett, Chris Parnell.

HOTEL FOR DOGS

DREAMWORKS. Jan. 8, 2009. (Thor Freudenthal) Emma Roberts, Jake T. Austin, Don Cheadle, Lisa Kudrow, Kevin Dillon, Johnny Simmons, Kyla Pratt, Troy Gentile, Robinne Lee.

THE HOTTIE AND THE NOTTIE

REGENT. Jan. 31, 2008. (Tom Putnam) Paris Hilton, Joel David Moore, Christine Lakin, Johann Urb, Adam Kulbersh, Marianne Muellerleile, Kathryn Fiore.

THE HOUSE OF ADAM

HOLLYWOOD INDEPENDENTS. Aug. 21, 2008. (Jorge Ameer) John Shaw, Jared Cadwell, Alexis Karriker, Thomas Michael Kappler, Tiffany McFarland, Reeve Howard.

THE HOUSE BUNNY

SONY PICTURES ENTERTAINMENT. Aug. 19, 2008. (Fred Wolf) Anna Faris, Colin Hanks, Emma Stone, Kat Dennings, Katharine McPhee, Rumer Willis, Tyson Ritter, Christopher McDonald, Beverly D'Angelo, Hugh Hefner.

HOUSE

ROADSIDE ATTRACTIONS. Nov. 9, 2008. (Robby Henson) Michael Madsen, Allana Bale, J.P. Davis, Reynaldo Rosales, Bill Moseley, Leslie Easterbrook, Julie Ann Emery.

THE HOUSE OF THE DEVIL

MAGNET. Oct. 6, 2009. (Ti West) Jocelin Donahue, Greta Gerwig, Mary Woronov, Tom Noonan, AJ Bowen, Danielle Noe.

HOUSE OF THE SLEEPING BEAUTIES

FIRST RUN FEATURES (IN U.S.). Oct., 2008. German. (Vadim Glowna) Vadim Glowna, Angela Winkler, Maximilian Schell, Birol Unel, Mona Glass.

HOUSE OF WAX

WARNER BROS. April, 2005. Australian-U.S. (Jaume Collet-Serra) Elisha Cuthbert, Chad Michael Murray, Brian Van Holt, Paris Hilton, Jared Padalecki, Jon Abrahams, Robert Richard.

HOW MUCH DO YOU LOVE ME?

PAN-EUROPEENNE EDITION. Sept., 2005. French-Italian. (Bertrand Blier) Monica Bellucci, Bernard Campan, Gerard Depardieu,

Jean-Pierre Darroussin, Edouard Baer, Farida Rahouadj, Sara Forestier, Michel Vuillermoz, Francois Rollin.

HOW TO EAT FRIED WORMS

NEW LINE CINEMA. Aug., 2006. (Bob Dolman) Luke Benward, Hallie Kate Eisenberg, Adam Hicks, Austin Rogers, Alexander Gould, Andrew Gillingham, Ryan Malgarini, Philip Daniel Bolden, Ty Panitz, James Rebhorn, Tom Cavanagh, Kimberly Williams-Paisley.

HOW TO LOSE FRIENDS & ALIENATE PEOPLE

MGM. (in U.S.)/PARAMOUNT AND CHANNEL FOUR FILMS (U.K.). Sept. 29, 2008. (Robert Weide) Simon Pegg, Kirsten Dunst, Danny Huston, Gillian Anderson, Megan Fox, Miriam Margolyes, Bill Paterson, Max Minghella, Diana Kent, Jeff Bridges.

HOW TO ROB A BANK

IFC FILMS. Feb. 4, 2008. (Andrew Jenkins) Nick Stahl, Erika Christensen, Gavin Rossdale, Terry Crews, David Carradine.

HUMPDAY

SEASHEL PICTURES. Jan. 16, 2009. (Lynn Shelton) Mark Duplass, Joshua Leonard, Alycia Delmore, Lynn Shelton, Trina Willard.

HUNT ANGELS

Sept., 2006. Australian. (Alec Morgan) Ben Mendelsohn, Victoria Hill, Eloise Oxer, Robert Bruning, Charles "Bud" Tingwell, Andrew Pike, Paul F. Kathner, Allan Peters, Barry Noonan. Documentary.

HUNTING AND GATHERING

PATHE DISTRIBUTION. March, 2007. French. (Claude Berri) Audrey Tautou, Guillaume Canet, Laurent Stocker, Francoise Bertin, Firmine Richard, Helene Surgere, Daniele Lebrun, Sandrine Mazeas, Philippe Van Eeckhout.

THE HUNTING PARTY

WEINSTEIN CO. Aug., 2007. (Richard Shepard) Richard Gere, Terrence Howard, Jesse Eisenberg, Diane Kruger, Joy Bryant, James Brolin, Ljubomir Kerekes, Kristina Krepela, Dylan Baker, Mark Ivanir.

HUSTLE & FLOW

PARAMOUNT. Jan., 2005. (Craig Brewer) Terrence Howard, Anthony Anderson, Taryn Manning, Taraji P. Henson, Paula Jai Parker, Elise Neal, Isaac Hayes, DJ Qualls, Ludacris.

I

I AM LEGEND

WARNER BROS. Dec. 4, 2007. (Francis Lawrence) Will Smith, Alice Braga, Dash Mihok, Charlie Tahan, Salli Richardson, Willow Smith.

I CAN'T THINK STRAIGHT

REGENT RELEASING/HERE FILMS (IN U.S.). Nov., 2008. British. (Shamim Sarif) Lisa Ray, Sheetal Sheth, Antonia Frering, Amber Rose Revah, Rez Kempton, Anya Lahiri, Siddiqua Akhtar, Daud Shah.

I DO

MARS DISTRIBUTION. Nov., 2006. (Eric Lartigau) Alain Chabat, Charlotte Gainsbourg, Bernadette Lafont, Wladimir Yordanoff, Gregoire Oestermann, Veronique Barrault, Marie-Armelle Deguy, Katia Lewkowicz, Louise Monot, Luce Mouchel, Christiane Millet, Aissa Maiga, Tatiana Gousseff, Alix de Konopka.

I HATE VALENTINE'S DAY

IFC FILMS. June 27, 2009. (Nia Vardalos) Nia Vardalos, John Corbett, Stephen Guarino, Amir Arison, Zoe Kazan, Gary Wilmes, Mike Starr, Jason Mantzoukas, Judah Friedlander, Rachel Dratch, Jay O. Sanders.

I HOPE THEY SERVE BEER IN HELL

FREESTYLE RELEASING. Sept. 22, 2009. (Bob Gosse)

I KNOW WHO KILLED ME

SONY PICTURES ENTERTAINMENT. July, 2007. (Chris Sivertson) Lindsay Lohan, Julia Ormond, Neal McDonough, Brian Geraghty, Garcelle Beauvais-Nilon, Spencer Garrett, Gregory Itzin, Art Bell, Eddie Steeples.

I LOVE YOU

DOORS ART FOUNDATION. Jan., 2007. Croatian. (Dalibor Matanic) Kresimir Mikic, Ivana Roscic, Ivana Krizmanic, Bohan Navojec, Angelo Jurkas.

I LOVE YOU, BETH COOPER

20TH CENTURY FOX. July 2, 2009. (Chris Columbus) Hayden Panettiere, Paul Rust, Jack T. Carpenter, Lauren London, Lauren Storm, Shawn Roberts, Alan Ruck.

I LOVE YOU IN EVERY LANGUAGE IN THE WORLD

MEDUSA. Dec., 2005. Italian. (Leonardo Pieraccioni) Leonardo Pieraccioni, Giorgio Panariello, Marjo Berasategui, Rocco Papaleo, Massimo Ceccherini, Giulia Elettra Gorietti, Francesco Guccini, Barbara Enrichi, Elisabetta Rocchetti, Pietro Ghislandi, Fabrizio Pizzuto, Yoon C. Joyce, Barbara Tabita, Luis Molteni.

I LOVE YOU, MAN

PARAMOUNT. March 3, 2009. (John Hamburg) Paul Rudd, Jason Segel, Rashida Jones, Andy Samberg, J.K. Simmons, Jane Curtin, Jon Favreau, Jaime Pressly, Rob Huebel, Thomas Lennon, Sarah Burns, Lou Ferrigno.

I NOW PRONOUNCE YOU CHUCK AND LARRY

UNIVERSAL. July, 2007. (Dennis Dugan) Adam Sandler, Kevin James, Jessica Biel, Dan Aykroyd, Ving Rhames, Steve Buscemi, Nicholas Turturro, Allen Covert.

I THINK I LOVE MY WIFE

20TH CENTURY FOX. March, 2007. (Chris Rock) Chris Rock, Kerry Washington, Gina Torres, Steve Buscemi, Edward Herrmann, Welker White.

I WANT CANDY

BUENA VISTA INTL. March, 2007. British-Luxembourgors. (Stephen Surjik) Tom Riley, Tom Burke, Carmen Electra, Eddie Marsan, Michelle Ryan, Mackenzie Crook, John Standing, Felicity Montagu, Philip Jackson, Jimmy Carr.

I'LL BELIEVE YOU

STAND UP FILMS. Nov. 10, 2007. (Paul Francis) David Alan Basche, Patrick Warburton, Cece Pleasants, Patrick Gallo, Fred Willard, Chris Elliott, Doc Dougherty, Siobhan Fallon, Thomas Gibson, Ed Helms, Chris MacKenzie, Mo Rocca.

I'M GROWING SCARCE

Gemini Films. June, 2006. (Dante Desarthe) Dante Desarthe, Colas Gutman, Valerie Niddam, Michel Lascault, Raoul Saada, David Lescot, Sophie Gueydon, Fabrice Guez, Serge Saada, Sarah Leroy, Micha Lescot, Olga Grumberg.

ICE AGE: DAWN OF THE DINOSAURS

20TH CENTURY FOX. June 21, 2009. (Carlos Saldanha)
Voices: Ray Romano, John Leguizamo, Denis Leary, Simon Pegg, Queen Latifah, Seann William Scott, Josh Peck, Bill Hader, Kristen Wiig, Chris Wedge. Animated.

ICE AGE: THE MELTDOWN

20TH CENTURY FOX. March, 2006. (Carlos Saldanha) Ray Romano, John Leguizamo, Denis Leary, Seann William Scott, Josh Peck, Queen Latifah, Will Arnett, Jay Leno. Animated.

ICE PRINCESS

BUENA VISTA PICTURES. Feb., 2005. (Tim Fywell) Joan Cusack, Kim Cattrall, Michelle Trachtenberg, Hayden Panettiere, Trevor Blumas, Connie Ray, Kirsten Olson, Juliana Cannarozzo, Jocelyn Lai, Michelle Kwan, Brian Boitano.

IDIOCRACY

TWENTIETH CENTURY FOX. Sept., 2006. (Mike Judge) Luke Wilson, Maya Rudolph, Dax Shepard, Terry Alan Crews, David Herman, Andrew Wilson, Brad "Scarface" Jordan, Thomas Haden Church. Narrator: Earl Mann.

IDIOT LOVE

MANGA FILMS. Feb., 2005. Spanish. (Ventura Pons) Santi Millan, Cayetana Guillen-Cuervo, Merce Pons, Marc Cartes.

IDLEWILD

UNIVERSAL. Aug., 2006. (Bryan Barber) Andre Benjamin, Antwan A. Patton, Paula Patton, Terrence Howard, Malinda Williams, Macy Gray, Ben Vereen, Ving Rhames, Faizon Love, Patti LaBelle, Bill Nunn, Cicely Tyson, Bruce Bruce.

IF YOU ARE THE ONE

ROTHERS MEDIA CORP. (CHINA)/MEDIA ASIA FILMS (HONG KONG) . March, 2009. Chinese. (Feng Xiaogang) Ge You, Shu Qi, Fan Wei, Alex Fong, Vivian Hsu, Feng Yuanzheng, Hu Ke, Uzaki Issoh, Che Xiao, Gong Xinliang, He Jiayi, Luo Haiqiong.

IF YOU LOVE ME FOLLOW ME

PYRAMIDE DISTRIBUTION. July, 2006. French. (Benoit Cohen) Mathieu Demy, Romane Bohringer, Julie Depardieu, Eleonore Pourriat, Mathias Mlekuz, Fabio Zenoni, Warren Zavatta, Rufus, Thomas Chabrol.

IGOR

MGM. Sept. 9, 2008. (Tony Leondis) Steve Buscemi, John Cleese, Jennifer Coolidge, John Cusack, Arsenio Hall, Sean Hayes, Eddie Izzard, Jay Leno, James Lipton, Molly Shannon, Christian Slater.

ILLEGAL TENDER

UNIVERSAL. Aug., 2007. (Franc. Reyes) Rick Gonzalez, Wanda De Jesus, Dania Ramirez, Antonio Ortiz, Tego Calderon, Jessica Pimentel, Manny Perez.

IMAGINATION

ALBINO FAWN PRODS. Oct. 23, 2007. (Eric Leiser) Edmund K. Gildersleeve, Nikki Haddad, Jessi Haddad, Courtney Sanford, Travis Poelle.

IMAGINE THAT

PARAMOUNT. June 6, 2009. (Karey Kirkpatrick) Eddie Murphy, Thomas Haden Church, Yara Shahidi, Nicole Ari Parker, Ronny Cox, Martin Sheen.

IN DEBT WE TRUST: AMERICA BEFORE THE BUBBLE BURSTS

Nov., 2006. (Danny Schechter) Danny Schechter, Sheila Jackson Lee, Robert Manning, Roy Barnes, Joel Sucher, Travis Plunkett,

Kevin Phillips, Roy Barnes. Documentary.

IN A DREAM

INDIEPIX. March 30, 2009. (Jeremiah Zagar) Isaiah Zagar, Julia Zagar, Ezekiel Zagar, Jeremiah Zagar.

IN HER SHOES

20TH CENTURY FOX. Sept., 2005. (Curtis Hanson) Cameron Diaz, Toni Collette, Shirley MacLaine, Mark Feuerstein, Ken Howard, Candice Azzara, Francine Beers, Norman Lloyd, Jerry Adler, Brooke Smith, Richard Burgi.

IN THE LAND OF WOMEN

WARNER INDEPENDENT PICTURES. May, 2006. (Jonathan Kasdan) Adam Brody, Kristen Stewart, Meg Ryan, Olympia Dukakis, Makenzie Vega, Elena Anaya, Clark Gregg.

IN THE LOOP

OPTIMUM. Jan., 2009. U.K. Peter Capaldi, Tom Hollander, Gina McKee, James Gandolfini, Chris Addison, Anna Chlumsky, Paul Higgins, Mimi Kennedy, Alex MacQueen, Olivia Poulet, David Rasche, Steve Coogan, Zach Woods, Enzo Cilenti, Johnny Pemberton, Joanna Scanlan.

IN LOVE WITH THE DEAD

GALA FILM. Feb., 2008. Hong Kong. (Danny Pang) Shawn Yu, Stephy Tang, Yoka Yue, Zeng Qiqi, Kiki Sheung, Raymond Cho, Ken Wong, Patrick Tam.

IN THE MIX

LIONS GATE FILMS. Nov., 2005. (Ron Underwood) Usher, Chazz Palminteri, Emmanuelle Chriqui, Robert Davi, Matt Gerald, Robert Costanzo, Anthony Fazio, Geoff Stults, K.D. Aubert, Kevin Hart.

IN THE NAME OF THE KING: A DUNGEON SIEGE TALE

FREESTYLE RELEASING. Jan. 11, 2008. Jason Statham, John Rhys-Davies, Ray Liotta, Matthew Lillard, Leelee Sobieski, Burt Reynolds, Ron Perlman, Claire Forlani, Kristanna Loken, Will Sanderson, Brian White, Mike Dopud.

IN SEARCH OF MOZART

DIRECT CINEMA. June, 2007. (Phil Grabsky) Julian Rachlin, Jonathan Miller, Imogen Cooper. Narrator: Juliet Stevenson. Documentary.

IN YOUR DREAMS

MARS DISTRIBUTION. April, 2005. French. (Denis Thybaud) Disiz La Peste, Blandine Bury, Vincent Elbaz, Edouard Montoute, Beatrice Dalle, Lea Drucker, Simon Abkarian, Jean-Pierre Cassel, Firmine Richard, Alex Descas, Khalid Maadour, Tony Mpoudja, Simon Buret, Youssef Diawara, Ali Karamoko.

INCREDIBLE HULK

UNIVERSAL. June 10, 2008. (Louis Leterrier) Edward Norton, Liv Tyler, Tim Roth, William Hurt, Tim Blake Nelson, Ty Burrell, Christina Cabot.

INDIAN CINEMAS: FROM NORTH TO SOUTH

Dec., 2008. French. (Hubert Niogret) Aruna Vasudev, Krishnan Hariharan, Nasreen Munni Kabir, Premendra Mazumdar, Raj Narayan, Shyam Benegal, Buddhadeb Dasgupta, Goutam Ghose, Mrinal Sen, Ritaban Ghatak, Girish Kasaravalli, Adoor Gopalakrishnan, Shabana Azmi, Sharmila Tagore. Documentary.

THE INFORMANT!

WARNER BROS. Sept. 1, 2009. (Steven Soderbergh) Matt Damon, Scott Bakula, Joel McHale, Melanie Lynskey, Rick Overton, Tom Papa, Tom Wilson, Clancy Brown, Tony Hale, Ann Cusack, Allan Havey, Rusty Schwimmer, Tom Smothers, Dick Smothers.

THE INFORMERS

SENATOR ENTERTAINMENT. Jan. 20, 2009. (Gregor Jordan) Billy Bob Thornton, Kim Basinger, Mickey Rourke, Winona Ryder, Jon Foster, Amber Heard, Austin Nichols, Lou Taylor Pucci, Brad Renfro, Chris Isaak, Fernando Consagra, Aaron Himelstein, Mel Raido, Rhys Ifans.

INGLOURIOUS BASTERDS

WEINSTEIN CO. (in U.S.)/UNIVERSAL PICTURES INTL. (FOREIGN) May 20, 2009. (Quentin Tarantino) Brad Pitt, Melanie Laurent, Christoph Waltz, Eli Roth, Michael Fassbender, Diane Kruger, Daniel Bruhl, Til Schweiger, Gedeon Burkhard, Jacky Ido, B.J. Novak, Omar Doom, August Diehl, Denis Menochet, Sylvester Groth, Martin Wuttke, Mike Myers, Julie Dreyfus, Richard Samuel, Rod Taylor.

INKHEART

WARNER BROS. Dec. 8, 2008. (Iain Softley) Brendan Fraser, Paul Bettany, Helen Mirren, Jim Broadbent, Andy Serkis, Sienna Guillory, Eliza Hope Bennett, Rafi Gavron, Lesley Sharp, Jamie Foreman, Matt King, Steve Speirs, Stephen Graham, John Thomson.

INSIDE MAN

UNIVERSAL. March, 2006. (Spike Lee) Denzel Washington, Clive Owen, Jodie Foster, Christopher Plummer, Willem Dafoe, Chiwetel Ejiofor.

THE INTERNATIONAL

SONY PICTURES ENTERTAINMENT. Jan. 29, 2009. (Tom Tykwer) Clive Owen, Naomi Watts, Armin Mueller-Stahl, Ulrich Thomsen, Brian F. O'Byrne, Jack McGee, Felix Solis, Nilaja Sun, Haluk Bilginer, James Rebhorn, Alessandro Fabrizi, Luca Giorgio Barbareschi, Patrick Baladi, Jay Villiers.

THE INTERPRETER

UNIVERSAL. March, 2005. (Sydney Pollack) Nicole Kidman, Sean Penn, Catherine Keener, Jesper Christensen, Yvan Attal, Michael Wright, Earl Cameron, George Harris, Tsai Chin, Clyde Kusatsu, Eric Keenleyside.

INTO THE BLUE

SONY PICTURES ENTERTAINMENT. Sept., 2005. (John Stockwell) Paul Walker, Jessica Alba, Scott Caan, Ashley Scott, Josh Brolin, James Frain, Tyson Beckford.

THE INVASION

WARNER BROS. Aug., 2007. (Oliver Hirschbiegel) Nicole Kidman, Daniel Craig, Jeremy Northam, Jackson Bond, Jeffrey Wright, Veronica Cartwright, Josef Sommer, Celia Weston, Roger Rees.

THE INVENTION OF LYING

WARNER BROS. Sept. 13, 2009. (Ricky Gervais) Ricky Gervais, Jennifer Garner, Jonah Hill, Louis C.K., Jeffrey Tambor, Fionnula Flanagan, Rob Lowe, Tina Fey, Stephanie March, Ruben Santiago-Hudson, John Hodgman, Nate Corddry, Jimmi Simpson, Martin Starr, Christopher Guest, Alton Fitzgerald White, Bobby Moynihan, Jason Bateman, Philip Seymour Hoffman, Edward Norton.

THE INVESTIGATOR

Feb., 2008. Hungarian. (Attila Gigor) Zsolt Anger, Judit Rezes, Sandor Terhes, Ildiko Toth, Eva Kerekes, Zsolt Zagoni.

INVINCIBLE

BUENA VISTA PICTURES DISTRIBUTION. Aug., 2006. (Ericson Core) Mark Wahlberg, Greg Kinnear, Elizabeth Banks, Kevin Conway, Michael Rispoli, Kirk Acevedo, Dov Davidoff, Michael Kelly, Sal Darigo, Nicoye Banks, Turron Kofi Alleyne, Cosmo Dematteo, Stink Fisher, Michael Mulheren, Michael Nouri, Jack Kehler, Lola Glaudini, Paige Turco. Voices: Merrill Reese, Mike Quick.

INVISIBLE

SHARPSHOOTER PICTURES. Nov., 2006. (Adam Watstein) James Tupper, Kit Pongetti, David Mogentale, Joe Mellis.

THE INVISIBLE

BUENA VISTA PICTURES. April, 2007. (David S. Goyer) Justin Chatwin, Margarita Levieva, Marcia Gay Harden, Chris Marquette, Alex O'Loughlin, Callum Keith Rennie.

IRENE IN TIME

RAINBOW RELEASING. June 15, 2009. (Henry Jaglom) Tanna Frederick, Andrea Marcovicci, Victoria Tennant, Karen Black, Lanre Idewu, Jack Maxwell, David Proval, Kelly De Sarla, Sabrina Jaglom, Simon O. Jaglom.

IRON MAN

PARAMOUNT. April 18, 2008. (Jon Favreau) Robert Downey, Jr., Terrence Howard, Jeff Bridges, Gwyneth Paltrow, Leslie Bibb, Shaun Toub, Faran Tahir, Clark Gregg, Bill Smitrovich, Sayed Badreya.

IRRESISTIBLE

PALACE FILMS DISTRIBUTION. Oct., 2006. Australian. (Ann Turner) Susan Sarandon, Sam Neill, Emily Blunt, Bud Tingwell, William McInnes, Georgie Parker.

INTRUSIONS

REZO FILMS. Sept., 2008. French. (Emmanuel Bourdieu) Natacha Regnier, Denis Podalydes, Amira Casar, Jacques Weber, Eric Elmosnino, Francoise Gillard, Francis Leplay.

THE ISLAND

DREAMWORKS. July, 2005. (Michael Bay) Ewan McGregor, Scarlett Johansson, Djimon Hounsou, Sean Bean, Michael Clarke Duncan, Ethan Phillip, Max Baker, Steve Buscemi.

ISLAND ETUDE

Nov., 2007. Taiwanese. (Chen Huai-en) Tung Ming-hsiang, Teng An-ning, Saya, Huang Teng-te, Yuen-lun, Chen Hsiu-hui, Ruta Palionyte, Lin Chao-hsin, Hsu Hsiao-shun, Hung Jui-li, Yang Li-yin, Wu Nien-chen, Chang Chou-chieh, Hong Liu, Chen Yueh-nu, Wang Pao-hsin.

IT'S A BOY GIRL THING

ICON ENTERTAINMENT INTL. Nov., 2006. British. (Nick Hurran) Samaire Armstrong, Kevin Zegers, Mpho Koaho, Brooke D'Orsay, Emily Hampshire, Sherry Miller, Robert Joy, Maury Chaykin, Sharon Osborne.

IT'S ALL JUDAS' FAULT

WARNER BROS. April, 2009. Italian. (Davide Ferrario) Kasia Smutniak, Fabio Troiano, Gianluca Gobbi, Luciana Littizzetto, Cristiano Godano, Francesco Signa, Paolo Ciarchi, Linda Messerklinger, Angela Vuolo, Christian Konabite, Valentina Taricco, Kaas, Ladislao Zanini, Dante Cecchin, Michele Telesca, Sergio Settimo, Enzo Cardinale, Marco Trovato, Francesco Trovato, Marco De Marchi, Giuseppe Ruggiero, Salvatore Canni.

IT'S COLD OVER THERE

ARC EN CIEL FILMS. Oct., 2008. French. (Mansur Tural) Farzin Karim Sharos, Ahmet Zirek, Rohani Tural.

IT'S OUR LIFE!
BAC DISTRIBUTION. Dec., 2005. French. (Gerard Krawczyk) Sylvie Testud, Josiane Balasko, Eric Cantona, Michel Muller, Catherine Hiegel, Danny Martinez, Carole Weiss, Maroussia Dubreuil, Celia Rosich.

IZNOGOUD
TFM DISTRIBUTION. Feb., 2005. French. (Patrick Braoude) Michael Youn, Jacques Villeret, Arno Chevrier, Elsa Pataky, Franck Dubosc, Magloire, Rufus, Kad, Olivier, Bernard Farcy, Juliette Poissonnier, Maurice Lamy, Mathias Jung.

JAB WE MET
STUDIO 18 (IN U.K.). Nov., 2007. Indian. (Imtiaz Ali) Shahid Kapur, Kareena Kapoor, Tarun Arora, Dara Singh, Pawan Malhotra, Kiran Juneja, Saumya Tandon.

JACK AND JILL VS. THE WORLD
LANTERN LANE. April 14, 2008. (Vanessa Parise) Freddie Prinze, Jr., Taryn Manning, Robin Dunne, Robert Forster, Hannah Lochner, Vanessa Parise, Kelly Rowan, Peter Stebbings.

JACKASS NUMBER TWO
PARAMOUNT. Sept., 2006. (Jeff Tremaine) Johnny Knoxville, Bam Margera, Chris Pontius, Steve-O, Dave England, Ryan Dunn, Wee Man, Preston Lacy, Ehren McGhehey, John Waters, Spike Jonze.

JACQUOU LE CROQUANT
PATHE DISTRIBUTION. Jan., 2007. French-German. (Laurent Boutonnat) Gaspard Ulliel, Léo Legrand, Marie-Josee Croze, Albert Dupontel, Tcheky Karyo, Olivier Gourmet, Jocelyn Quivrin, Malik Zidi, Gerald Thomassin, Judith Davis, Bojana Panic, Dora Doll, Jérôme Kircher, Clemence Gautier, Julia Lumanare.

THE JANKY PROMOTERS
THIRD RAIL RELEASING. Oct. 21, 2009. (Marcus Raboy) Ice Cube, Mike Epps, Young Jeezy, Lahmard Tate, Julio Oscar Mechoso, Tamala Jones, "Lil' JJ" James Lewis, Glenn Plummer, Juanita Jennings.

JARHEAD
UNIVERSAL. Oct., 2005. (Sam Mendes) Jake Gyllenhaal, Peter Sarsgaard, Lucas Black, Brian Geraghty, Jacob Vargas, Laz Alonso, Evan Jones, Ivan Fenyo, Chris Cooper, Dennis Haysbert, Scott MacDonald, Jamie Foxx, Kareem Grimes, Peter Gail, Jamie Martz, Jocko Sims.

JEAN-PHILIPPE
MARS DISTRIBUTION. April, 2006. French. (Laurent Tuel) Fabrice Luchini, Johnny Hallyday, Guilaine Londez, Antoine Dulery, Elodie Bollee, Olivier Gueritee, Jackie Berroyer, Caroline Cellier, Barbara Schulz.

JENNIFER'S BODY
20TH CENTURY FOX. Sept. 9, 2009. (Karyn Kusama) Megan Fox, Amanda Seyfried, Johnny Simmons, J.K. Simmons, Amy Sedaris, Adam Brody, Kyle Gallner, Chris Pratt, Cynthia Stevenson, Valerie Tian.

JODHAA AKBAR
UTV MOTION PICTURES. Feb., 2008. Indian. (Ashutosh Gowariker) Hrithik Roshan, Aishwarya Rai Bachchan, Sonu Sood, Punam Sinha, Kulbhushan Kharbanda, Suhasini Mulay, Raza Murad, Rajesh Vivek, Pramod Moutho, Ila Arun, Surendra Pal, Visshwa Badola, Prathmesh Mehta, Shaji Chaudhary, Manava Naik, Disha Vakani, Abeer Abrar, Indrajit Sarkar, Aman Dhaliwal.

JOHN TUCKER MUST DIE
20TH CENTURY FOX. July, 2006. (Betty Thomas) Jesse Metcalfe, Brittany Snow, Ashanti, Sophia Bush, Arielle Kebbel, Penn Badgley, Jenny McCarthy.

JONAS BROTHERS: THE 3D CONCERT EXPERIENCE
WALT DISNEY PICTURES. Feb. 24, 2009. (Bruce Hendricks) Kevin Jonas, Joe Jonas, Nick Jonas, "Big Rob" Feggans, Demi Lovato, Taylor Swift.

THE JOURNEY TO ARMENIA
DIAPHANA. July, 2006. (Robert Guediguian) Ariane Ascaride, Gerard Meylan, Simon Abkarian, Serge Avedikian, Chorik Grigorian, Roman Avinian, Kristina Hovakimian, Madeleine Guediguian, Marcel Bluwal, Jalil Lespert, Jean-Pierre Darroussin.

JOURNEY TO THE CENTER OF THE EARTH
WARNER BROS. June 25, 2008. (Eric Brevig) Brendan Fraser, Anita Briem, Josh Hutcherson, Seth Meyers, Jean-Michel Pare, Jane Wheeler, Frank Fontaine, Giancarlo Caltabiano, Kaniehtiio Horn, Garth Gilker.

JULIE & JULIA
SONY PICTURES ENTERTAINMENT. July 14, 2009. (Nora Ephron) Meryl Streep, Amy Adams, Stanley Tucci, Chris Messina, Linda Emond, Mary Lynn Rajskub, Jane Lynch, Frances Sternhagen.

JUMPER
20TH CENTURY FOX. Feb. 11, 2008. (Doug Liman) Hayden Christensen, Jamie Bell, Samuel L. Jackson, Rachel Bilson, Diane Lane, Michael Rooker, AnnaSophia Robb, Max Thierot.

JUST ADD WATER
KINDRED MEDIA GROUP/VIRGIL FILMS. March 25, 2008. (Hart Bochner) Dylan Walsh, Tracy Middendorf, Danny DeVito, Justin Long, Jonah Hill, Anika Noni Rose, Brad Hunt, Will Rothhaar, Michael Hitchcock.

JUST BURIED
Oct., 2008. Canadian. (Chaz Thorne) Jay Baruchel, Rose Byrne, Graham Greene, Nigel Bennett, Thomas Gibson, Sergio DiZio, Reagan Pasternak, Slavko Negulic, Jeremy Akerman, Brian Downey, Christopher Shore.

JUST FRIENDS
NEW LINE CINEMA. Nov., 2005. (Roger Kumble) Ryan Reynolds, Amy Smart, Anna Faris, Julie Hagerty, Christopher Marquette, Stephen Root, Fred Ewanuick, Chris Klein.

JUST LIKE HEAVEN
DREAMWORKS. Aug., 2005. (Mark Waters) Reese Witherspoon, Mark Ruffalo, Donal Logue, Dina Waters, Ben Shenkman, Jon Heder, Ivana Milicevic.

JUST MY LUCK
20TH CENTURY FOX. May, 2006. (Donald Petrie) Lindsay Lohan, Chris Pine, Faizon Love, Missi Pyle, Bree Turner, Samaire Armstrong, Tovah Feldshuh, Carlos Ponce, Makenzie Vega.

KABHI ALVIDA NAA KEHNA
YASH RAJ FILMS. Aug., 2006. Indian. (Karan Johar) Amitabh Bachchan, Shah Rukh Khan, Abhishek Bachchan, Rani Mukerji, Preity Zinta, Kirron Kher, Arjun Rampal, Ahsaas Channa, Kajol, John Abraham, Saira Mohan.

KAMINEY
UTV MOTION PICTURES. Aug., 2009. Indian. (Vishal Bhardwaj) Shahid Kapoor, Priyanka Chopra, Amole Gupte, Tenzing Nima, Chandan Roy Sanyal.

THE KEEPER: THE LEGEND OF OMAR KHAYYAM
ARRIVAL PICTURES. Jan., 2006. (Kayvan Mashayekh) Adam Echahly, Bruno Lastra, Moritz Bleibtreu, Rade Sherbedgia, Vanessa Redgrave, Christopher Simpson, Marie Espinosa, Diane Baker, C. Thomas Howell.

KEEPING MUM
ENTERTAINMENT FILM DISTRIBUTORS. Dec., 2005. British. (Niall Johnson) Rowan Atkinson, Kristin Scott Thomas, Maggie Smith, Patrick Swayze, Tamsin Egerton, Toby Parkes, Liz Smith, Emilia Fox, James Booth.

KEINOHRHASEN
WARNER BROS. PICTURES GERMANY. Jan., 2008. German. (Til Schweiger) Til Schweiger, Nora Tschirner, Matthias Schweighoefer, Alwara Hoefels, Juergen Vogel, Rick Kavanian, Armin Rohde, Wolfgang Stumph, Barbara Rudnik, Christian Tramitz, Brigitte Zeh, Paul Maximilian Schueller, Florentine Lahme, Nina Proll, Wladimir Klitschko, Yvonne Catterfeld.

KENNY
MADMAN ENTERTAINMENT. Aug., 2006. Australian. (Clayton Jacobson) Shane Jacobson, Eve von Bibra, Ronald Jacobson, Jesse Jacobson, Chris Davis, Ian Dryden, Morihiko Hasebe.

KICKIN' IT OLD SKOOL
YARI FILM GROUP. April, 2007. (Harv Glazer) Jamie Kennedy, Miguel A. Nunez, Jr., Maria Menounos, Michael Rosenbaum, Bobby Lee, Aris Alvarado, Debra Jo Rupp, Christopher McDonald, Vivica A. Fox, Alexander Calvert, Jesse "Casper" Brown, Erik Estrada, David Hasselhoff, John Ratzenberger, Emmanuel Lewis, Roddy Piper.

KICKING & SCREAMING
UNIVERSAL. May, 2005. (Jesse Dylan) Will Ferrell, Robert Duvall, Mike Ditka, Kate Walsh, Musetta Vander, Dylan McLaughlin, Josh Hutcherson, Steven Anthony Lawrence, Jeremy Bergman, Elliot Cho, Erik Walker, Dallas McKinney, Francesco Liotti, Alessandro Ruggiero.

THE KID AND I
SLOWHAND CINEMA. Nov., 2005. (Penelope Spheeris) Tom Arnold, Eric Gores, Linda Hamilton, Henry Winkler, Richard Edson, Joe Mantegna, Shannon Elizabeth, Arielle Kebbel, Brenda Strong, Penelope Spheeris.

KIDS IN AMERICA
LAUNCHPAD RELEASING AND SLOWHAND RELEASING. Oct., 2005. (Josh Stolberg) Gregory Smith, Stephanie Sherrin, Malik Yoba, Julie Bowen, Nicole Camille Richie, Caitlin Wachs, Emy Coligado, Crystal Celeste Gant, Chris Morris, Alex Anfanger, Adam Arkin, George Wendt, Andrew Shaifer, Rosanna Arquette, Elizabeth Perkins, Charles Shaughnessy, W. Earl Brown, Kim Coles, Samantha Mathis.

KIDULTHOOD

REVOLVER ENTERTAINMENT. Jan., 2006. British. (Menhaj Huda) Aml Ameen, Red Madrell, Adam Deacon, Jaime Winstone, Femi Oyeniran, Madeleine Fairley, Cornell John, Kate Magowan, Pierre Mascolo, Rafe Spall, Noel Clarke, Katelin Okoro.

KILLSHOT

WEINSTEIN CO. HOME ENTERTAINMENT. June 9, 2009. (John Madden) Diane Lane, Mickey Rourke, Thomas Jane, Joseph Gordon-Levitt, Rosario Dawson, Hal Holbrook, Lois Smith.

THE KILLER

UGC DISTRIBUTION. Jan., 2008. French. (Cedric Anger) Gilbert Melki, Gregoire Colin, Melanie Laurent, Sophie Cattani, Xavier Beauvois.

KING CORN

BALCONY RELEASING. Oct. 19, 2007. (Aaron Woolf) Ian Cheney, Curt Ellis, Stephen Macko, Chuck Pyatt, Ricardo Salvador, Dawn Cheney, Rich Johnson, Al Marth, Michael Pollan, Scott McGregor, Bob Bledsoe, Sue & Dean Jarrett, Allen Trenkele, Loren Cordain, Audrae Erickson, Fray Mendez, Farida Khan, Sabita Moktan, Earl Butz. Documentary.

KING KONG

UNIVERSAL. Dec., 2005. (Peter Jackson) Naomi Watts, Jack Black, Adrien Brody, Thomas Kretschmann, Colin Hanks, Jamie Bell, Evan Parke, Lobo Chan, Kyle Chandler, Andy Serkis.

THE KING OF KONG: A FISTFUL OF QUARTERS

PICTUREHOUSE. May, 2007. (Seth Gordon) Steve Wiebe, Billy Mitchell, Walter Day, Nicole Wiebe, Steve Sanders, Robert Mruczek, Brian Kuh. Documentary.

THE KINGDOM

UNIVERSAL. Aug., 2007. (Peter Berg) Jamie Foxx, Chris Cooper, Jennifer Garner, Jason Bateman, Ashraf Barhom, Ali Suliman, Jeremy Piven.

KINGDOM OF HEAVEN

20TH CENTURY FOX. April, 2005. British-Spanish-U.S.-German. (Ridley Scott) Orlando Bloom, Eva Green, Jeremy Irons, David Thewlis, Brendan Gleeson, Marton Csokas, Michael Sheen, Liam Neeson, Edward Norton, Ghassan Massoud, Alexander Siddig, Khaled Nabawy, Kevin McKidd, Velibor Topi, Jon Finch, Ulrich Thomsen, Nikolaj Coster-Waldau, Iain Glen.

KING'S RANSOM

NEW LINE CINEMA. April, 2005. (Jeff Byrd) Anthony Anderson, Jay Mohr, Kellita Smith, Nicole Parker, Regina Hall, Loretta Devine, Donald Faison, Charlie Murphy, Brooke D'Orsay, Leila Arcieri, Jackie Burroughs.

KIRIKOU AND THE WILD BEASTS

GEBEKA FILMS. Sept., 2005. French. (Michel Ocelot, Benedicte Galup) Voices: Pierre-Ndoffe Sarr, Awa Sene Sarr, Robert Liensol, Marie-Philomene Nga, Emile Abossolo M'Bo, Pascal N'Zonzi, Marthe N'Dome, Emilie Gaydu. Animated.

KISMAT KONNECTION

UTV MOTION PICTURES. July, 2008. Indian. (Aziz Mirza) Shahid Kapoor, Vidya Balan, Juhi Chawla, Om Puri, Vishal Malhotra, Himani Shivpuri.

KIT KITTREDGE: AN AMERICAN GIRL

PICTUREHOUSE. June 9, 2008. (Patricia Rozema) Abigail Breslin, Chris O'Donnell, Julia Ormond, Joan Cusack, Madison Davenport, Glenne Headley, Jane Krakowski, Zach Mills, Colin Mochrie, Wallace Shawn, Willow Smith, Max Thieriot, Stanley Tucci.

KNOWING

SUMMIT ENTERTAINMENT. March 18, 2009. (Alex Proyas) Nicolas Cage, Rose Byrne, Chandler Canterbury, Ben Mendelsohn, Lara Robinson, Nadia Townsend, Danielle Carter, Alethea McGrath, Alan Hopgood, D.G. Maloney.

KOKODA

PALACE FILMS. April, 2006. Australian. (Alister Grierson) Jack Finsterer, Travis McMahon, Simon Stone, Luke Ford, Tom Budge, Christopher Baker, Angus Sampson, Steve Le Marquand, Shane Bourne, William McInnes.

THE KOVAK BOX

FILMAX ENTERTAINMENT (IN SPAIN)/FIRST LOOK PICTURES (IN U.S.) Spanish-British. Jan., 2007. (Daniel Monzon) Timothy Hutton, Lucia Jimenez, David Kelly, Gary Piquer, Georgia McKenzie, Annette Badland.

L

L FOR LOVE, L FOR LIES

NEWPORT. April, 2008. Jong Kong. (Patrick Kong) Stephy Tang, Alex Fong, Alice Tzeng, Leila Tong, Stephen Wong, Terry Wu, Miki Yeung.

LA FILLE COUPEE EN DEUX

WILD BUNCH DISTRIBUTION. Aug., 2007. French-German. (Claude Chabrol) Ludivine Sagnier, Francois Berleand, Benoit Magimel, Mathilda May, Caroline Sihol, Etienne Chicot, Marie Bunel, Valeria Cavalli, Thomas Chabrol, Jeremie Chaplain, Jean-Marie Winling, Didier Benureau, Edouard Baer.

LA MAISON DE NINA

TFM. Nov., 2005. French. (Richard Dembo) Agnes Jaoui, Sarah Adler, Katia Lewkowicz, Arie Elmaleh, Charles Berling, Adele Csech, Jeremy Sitbon, Vincent Rottiers, Tomas Le Marquis, Alexis Pivot, Max Levy, Lola Naymark, Claire Bouanich, Arnaud Marciszewer, Gaspard Ulliel, David Mambouch.

LA PETITE CHARTREUSE

Jan., 2005. French. (Jean-Pierre Denis) Olivier Gourmet, Marie-Josee Croze, Bertille Noel-Bruneau, Marisa Borini, Yves Jacques.

LA SENAL

WANDA VISION. Sept., 2007. Spanish-Argentinian. (Ricardo Darin, Martin Hodara) Ricardo Darin, Diego Peretti, Julieta Diaz, Andrea Pietra, Luis Solanas.

LA TERRA

MEDUSA. Feb., 2006. Italian. (Sergio Rubini) Fabrizio Bentivoglio, Paolo Briguglia, Massimo Venturiello, Emilio Solfrizzi, Claudia Gerini, Giovanna Di Rauso, Sergio Rubini, Marisa Eugeni, Alisa Bistrova, Daniela Mazzacane, Maurizio Rega.

LA VIE D'ARTISTE

HAUT & COURT DISTRIBUTION. July, 2007. French. (Marc Fitoussi) Sandrine Kiberlain, Emilie Dequenne, Denis Podalydes, Valerie Benguigui, Marilyne Canto, Camille Japy, Gregoire Leprince-Ringuet, Magali Woch, Claire Maurier, Aure Atika, Jean-Pierre Kalfon, Maria Schneider, Stephane Guillon, Jean-Marie Winling, Eric Savin, Solenn Jarniou, Jean-Noel Broute, Francis Leplay, Thibault Vincon.

LAAGA CHUNARI MEIN DAAG: JOURNEY OF A WOMAN

YASH RAJ FILMS. Oct., 2007. Indian. (Pradeep Sarkar) Jaya Bachchan, Rani Mukerji, Konkona Sen Sharma, Abhishek Bachchan, Kunal Kapoor, Anupam Kher, Amey Pandya, Baby Shriya Sharma, Hema Malini, Murli Sharma, Kamini Kaushal, Tinu Anand, Harsh Chhaya, Sushant Singh, Taraana Raja, Suchitra Pillai, Ninad Kamat.

LADRON QUE ROBA A LADRON

LIONSGATE. Aug., 2007. (Joe Menendez) Fernando Colunga, Miguel Varoni, Julie Gonzalo, Oscar Torre, Gabriel Soto, Ivonne Montero, Saul Lisazo, Sonya Smith.

LADY CHATTERLEY

AD VITAM. Nov., 2006. French-Belgium. (Pascale Ferran) Marina Hands, Jean-Louis Coulloc'h, Hippolyte Girardot, Helene Alexandridis, Helene Fillieres.

LADY GODIVA

LADY GODIVA. Jan., 2008. British. (Vicky Jewson) Phoebe Thomas, Matthew Chambers, James Wilby, Isabelle Amyes, Eric Carte, Simon Williams, Petra Markham, Nicholas Parsons.

LADY IN THE WATER

WARNER BROS. July, 2006. (M. Night Shyamalan) Paul Giamatti, Bryce Dallas Howard, Jeffrey Wright, Bob Balaban, Sarita Choudhury, Cindy Cheung, M. Night Shyamalan, Freddy Rodriguez, Bill Irwin, Mary Beth Hurt.

LAKE DEAD

AFTER DARK FILMS. Nov. 12, 2007. (George Bessudo) Alex A. Quinn, Kelsey Crane, Jim Devoti, Kelsey Wedeen, Tara Gerard, Vanessa Viola, James C. Burns, Pat McNeely, Edwin Craig, Christian Stokes, Trevor Torseth, Dan Woods, Maela Richardson.

THE LAKE HOUSE

WARNER BROS.June, 2006. (Alejandro Agresti) Keanu Reeves, Sandra Bullock, Dylan Walsh, Shohreh Aghdashloo, Christopher Plummer, Ebon Moss-Bachrach, Willeke Van Ammelrooy, Lynn Collins.

LAKEVIEW TERRACE

SONY PICTURES. Aug. 7, 2008. (Neil LaBute) Samuel L. Jackson, Patrick Wilson, Kerry Washington, Ron Glass, Justin Chambers, Jay Hernandez, Regine Nehy, Jaishon Fisher, Robert Pine, Keith Loneker, Caleeb Pinkett.

LAND OF THE DEAD (GEORGE A. ROMERO'S)

UNIVERSAL. June, 2005. (George A. Romero) Simon Baker, John Leguizamo, Asia Argento, Robert Joy, Dennis Hopper, Eugene Clark, Jennifer Baxter, Boyd Banks, Joanne Boland, Krista Bridges, Pedro Miguel Arce.

LAND OF THE LOST

UNIVERSAL. June 1, 2009. (Brad Silberling) Will Ferrell, Anna Friel, Danny McBride, Jorma Taccone, John Boylan.

LAND MINES: A LOVE STORY

April, 2005. Australian-British. (Dennis O'Rourke). Documentary.

LARRY FLYNT: THE RIGHT TO BE LEFT ALONE

Aug., 2007. (Joan Brooker-Marks) Larry Flynt, Liz Flynt. Documentary.

LARRY THE CABLE GUY: HEALTH INSPECTOR

LIONSGATE. March, 2006. (Trent Cooper) Larry the Cable Guy, Iris Bahr, Bruce Bruce, Joanna Cassidy, Brooke Dillman, Tony Hale, David Koechner, Lisa Lampanelli, Megyn Price, Tom Wilson, Joe Pantoliano, Kid Rock, Jerry Mathers.

LASSIE

ENTERTAINMENT FILM DISTRIBUTORS (IN THE U.K.). Dec., 2005. British-Irish-french-U.S. (Charles Sturridge) Peter O'Toole, Samantha Morton, John Lynch, Peter Dinklage, Steve Pemberton, Jemma Redgrave, Jonathan Mason, Hester Odgers, Edward Fox, John Standing, Gregor Fisher, Kelly Macdonald, Jamie Lee, Robert Hardy, Nicholas Lyndhurst.

LAST CHANCE HARVEY

OVERTURE FILMS. Nov. 3, 2008. (Joel Hopkins) Dustin Hoffman, Emma Thompson, Liane Balaban, James Brolin, Eileen Atkins, Kathy Baker, Richard Schiff.

THE LAST CONFEDERATE: THE STORY OF ROBERT ADAMS

THINKFILM. June, 2007. (A. Blaine Miller, Julian Adams) Julian Adams, Gwendolyn Edwards, Eric Holloway, Amy Redford, Nelson McCord, Tippi Hedren, Mickey Rooney.

LAST HOLIDAY

PARAMOUNT PICTURES. Jan., 2006. (Wayne Wang) Queen Latifah, LL Cool J, Timothy Hutton, Giancarlo Esposito, Alicia Witt, Gerard Depardieu, Jane Adams, Mike Estime, Susan Kellermann, Jascha Washington, Matt Ross, Ranjit Chowdhry, Michael Nouri, Julia Lashae, Emeril Lagasse, Shirl Cieutat.

THE LAST HOUSE ON THE LEFT

ROGUE PICTURES. March 10, 2009. (Dennis Iliadis) Tony Goldwyn, Monica Potter, Garret Dillahunt, Spencer Treat Clark, Riki Lindhome, Martha MacIsaac, Michael Bowen, Sara Paxton, Aaron Paul.

THE LAST LEGION

MGM/WEINSTEIN CO. Aug., 2007. (Doug Lefler) Colin Firth, Ben Kingsley, Aishwarya Rai, Peter Mullan, Kevin McKidd, John Hannah, Thomas Sangster, Iain Glen.

LAST RIDE

MADMAN CINEMA. May , 2009. Australian. (Glendyn Ivin) Hugo Weaving, Tom Russell, John Brumpton, Anita Hegh, Sonya Suares, Kelton Pell.

THE LAST SIGN

CARRERE GROUP DISTRIBUTION. April, 2005. French-British-Canadian. (Douglas Law) Andie MacDowell, Samuel Le Bihan, Tim Roth, Margot Kidder, Mimi Kuzyk, Tyler Hynes, Amanda Jane Tilson, Lila Bata-Walsh, Barry Flatman, Cory Bertrand.

THE LAST SIN EATER

BIGGER PICTURE. Feb., 2007. (Michael Landon, Jr.) Louise Fletcher, Henry Thomas, Liana Liberato, Soren Fulton, A.J. Buckley, Stewart Finlay-McLennan, Peter Wingfield, Elizabeth Lackey, Thea Rose, Kim Myers, Gabrielle Fitzpatrick, Valerie Wildman.

THE LAST STATION

EGOLI TOSSELL FILM/ZEPHYR FILMS. Sept. 5, 2009. (Michael Hoffman) Helen Mirren, Christopher Plummer, Paul Giamatti, James McAvoy, Anne-Marie Duff, Kerry Condon, John Sessions, Patrick Kennedy.

LAST STOP FOR PAUL

MANDT BROTHERS PRODS. March 2, 2008. (Neil Mandt) Neil Mandt, Marc Carter, Greg Poppen, Eric Wing, Heather Petrone, Ron Carlson.

THE LAST TIME

DESTINATION FILMS. May, 2006. (Michael Caleo) Michael Keaton, Brendan Fraser, Amber Valletta, Daniel Stern, Neal McDonough, Michael C. Hagerty, Michael Lerner, Richard Kuhlman, Alexis Cruz, William Ragsdale.

THE LAST TRAPPER

TFM DISTRIBUTION. Jan., 2005. French-Canadian-German-Italian-Swiss. (Nicolas Vanier) Norman Winther, May Loo, Alex Van Bibber.

LATE GRADUATES

BAC FILMS. June, 2006. French. (Renaud Bertrand) Jacques Gamblin, Kad Merad, Rufus, Anne Brochet, Helene Vincent, Edouard Collin, Valerie Kaprisky, Stephanie Sokolinski.

LAW ABIDING CITIZEN

OVERTURE FILMS. Oct. 14, 2009. (F. Gary Gray) Jamie Foxx, Gerard Butler, Bruce McGill, Colm Meaney, Leslie Bibb, Regina Hall, Michael Irby.

LE PETIT NICOLAS

WILD BUNCH DISTRIBUTION (IN FRANCE). Oct., 2009. French. (Laurent Tirard) Valerie Lemercier, Kad Merad, Sandrine Kiberlain, Francois-Xavier Demaison, Maxime Godart, Vincent Claude, Charles Vaillant, Victor Carles, Benjamin Averty, Germain Petit Damico.

THE LEAGUE OF GENTLEMEN'S APOCALYPSE

UIP. May, 2005. British-U.S. (Steve Bendelack) Mark Gatiss, Steve Pemberton, Reece Shearsmith, David Warner, Michael Sheen, Bernard Hill, Victoria Wood, Emily Woof, Liam Cunningham, Kate O'Toole, Peter Kay, Simon Pegg, Alan Morrissey.

LEATHERHEADS

UNIVERSAL. March 27, 2008. (George Clooney) George Clooney, Renee Zellweger, John Krasinski, Jonathan Pryce, Peter Gerety, Jack Thompson, Stephen Root, Wayne Duvall, Keith Loneker, Robert Baker, Matt Bushell, Malcolm Goodwin, Tim Griffin, Tommy Hinkley, Nick Paonessa, Max Casella, Mike O'Malley, Heather Goldenhersh, Marian Seldes.

THE LEGEND OF ZORRO

SONY PICTURES ENTERTAINMENT. Oct., 2005. (Martin Campbell) Antonio Banderas, Catherine Zeta-Jones, Rufus Sewell, Nick Chinlund, Julio Oscar Mechoso, Shuler Hensley, Michael Emerson, Adrian Alonso.

LEMMING

DIAPHANA FILMS. May, 2005. French. (Dominik Moll) Laurent Lucas, Charlotte Gainsbourg, Charlotte Rampling, Andre Dussollier.

LES BRONZES 3: FRIENDS FOREVER

WARNER BROS. DISTRIBUTION FRANCE. Feb., 2006. French. (Patrice Leconte) Josiane Balasko, Michel Blanc, Marie-Anne Chazel, Christian Clavier, Gerard Jugnot, Thierry Lhermitte, Ornella Muti, Dominique Lavanant, Martin Lamotte, Bruno Moynot, Caterina Murino, Doris Kunstmann, Arthur Jugnot, Eric Naggar.

LET IT RAIN

STUDIOCANAL. Sept., 2008. French. (Agnes Jaoui) Agnes Jaoui, Jean-Pierre Bacri, Jamel Debbouze, Pascale Arbillot, Guillaume de Tonquedec, Frederic Pierrot, Mimouna Hadji, Florence Loiret-Caille.

LET'S BE FRIENDS

MARS DISTRIBUTION. Jan., 2005. French. (Eric Toledano, Olivier Nakache) Gerard Depardieu, Jean-Paul Rouve, Tilly Mandelbort, Lionel Abelanski, Annie Girardot, Isabelle Renauld, Yves Jacques, Elisabeth Vitali, Xavier de Guillebon, Valerie Benguigui, Cassandra Harrouche.

LET'S DANCE!

UGC DISTRIBUTION. Nov., 2007. French-Swiss. (Noemie Lvovsky) Jean-Pierre Marielle, Valeria Bruni-Tedeschi, Sabine Azema, Bulle Ogier, Bakary Sangare, Arie Elmaleh, Nicolas Maury, Judith Chemla, Daniel Emilfork.

LET'S GO TO PRISON

UNIVERSAL. Nov., 2006. (Bob Odenkirk) Dax Shepard, Will Arnett, Chi McBride, David Koechner, Dylan Baker, Michael Shannon.

LETTERS FROM IWO JIMA

WARNER BROS. Nov., 2006. (Clint Eastwood) Ken Watanabe, Kazunari Ninomiya, Tsuyoshi Ihara, Ryo Kase, Shidou Nakamura.

LEUR MORALE ... ET LA NOTRE

GAUMONT. Aug., 2008. French. (Florence Quentin) Andre Dussollier, Victoria Abril, Samir Guesmi, Micha Lescot, Francoise Bertin.

THE LIBERTINE

ENTERTAINMENT FILM DISTRIBUTORS (IN U.K.)/THE WEINSTEIN CO. (IN U.S.). Oct., 2005. British. (Laurence Dunmore) Johnny Depp, Samantha Morton, John Malkovich, Rosamund Pike, Tom Hollander, Johnny Vegas, Kelly Reilly, Jack Davenport, Richard Coyle, Francesca Annis, Rupert Friend, Claire Higgins.

LICENSE TO WED

WARNER BROS. June, 2007. (Ken Kwapis) Robin Williams, Mandy Moore, John Krasinski, Eric Christian Olsen, Christine Taylor, Josh Flitter, DeRay Davis, Peter Strauss, Mindy Kaling, Angela Kinsey, Brian Baumgartner.

LICU'S HOLIDAY

A 50 NOTTURNO. June, 2007. Italian. (Vittorio Moroni) Muhammad Moazzem Hossain Licu, Fancy Khanam, Giulia Di Quilio, Khokan Miah, Anwar Khan, Andrea Wu, Syed Mohammed Ali. Documentary.

LIES AND FAT GIRLS

SONY PICTURES RELEASING. April, 2009. Spanish. (Alfonso Albacete) Yon Gonzalez, Mario Casas, Hugo Silva, Ana Polovorosa, Miriam Giovanelli, Marieta Orozco.

LIFE IN COLOR

ALTA CLASSICS. Jan., 2006. Spanish. (Santiago Tabernero) Junio Valverde, Silvia Abascal, Miguel Angel Silvestre, Joan Dalmau, Ana Wagener, Carmen Machi, Andres Lima, Natalia Abascal, Nadia De Santiago, Maru Valdivielso, Adolfo Fernandez, Pep Guinyol, Jose Manuel Munoz "Cheto," Fernando Ransanz, Silvia Casanova, Fernando Cayo.

LIFE IN THE ABYSS

FILMAX. Jan., 2007. Spanish. (Ventura Pons) Oscar Jaenada, Jose Sospedra, Antonio Valero, Juli Mira, Nausica Bonnin, Karme Malaga.

LIFE IS HOT IN CRACKTOWN

LIGHTNING MEDIA. June 17, 2009. (Buddy Giovinazzo) Kerry Washington, Victor Rasuk, Evan Ross, Desmond Harrington, Shannyn Sossamon, Edoardo Ballerini, Melissa Wilfley, Vondie Curtis-Hall, Brandon Routh, RZA, Thomas Ian Nichols, Tony Plana, Carmine Giovinazzo, Richard Portnow, Jeremy West, Ridge Canipe, Ariel Winter, Illeana Douglas, Lara Flynn Boyle.

LIFELINES

KANBAR ENTERTAINMENT. Oct. 11, 2008. (Rob Margolies) Jane Adams, Josh Pais, Jacob Kogan, Robbie Sublett, Dreama Walker, Joe Morton.

LIKE A STAR SHINING IN THE NIGHT
JML DISTRIBUTION. Dec., 2008. French. (Rene Feret) Salome Stevenin, Nicolas Giraud, Jean-Francois Stevenin, Maryline Canto, Guillaume Verdier, Sabrina Seyvecou, Aurelia Petit.

LIKE MINDS
DENDY FILMS (IN AUSTRALIA)/REDBUS FILM DISTRIBUTION (IN U.K.)/THE WEINSTEIN CO. (IN U.S.). Nov., 2006. Australian-British. (Gregory J. Read) Eddie Redmayne, Tom Sturridge, Toni Collette, Richard Roxburgh, Patrick Malahide, Kate Maberly, Jonathan Overton, Amit Shah, David Threlfall, Cathryn Bradshaw, Hugh Sachs.

THE LIMITS OF CONTROL
FOCUS FEATURES. Apil 15, 2009. (Jim Jarmusch) Isaach De Bankole, Alex Descas, Jean-Francois Stevenin, Luis Tosar, Paz de la Huerta, Tilda Swinton, Youki Kudoh, John Hurt, Gael Garcia Bernal, Hiam Abbass, Bill Murray.

LISSI AND THE WILD EMPEROR
CONSTANTIN FILM. Dec., 2007. German. (Michael Bully Herbig) Voices: Michael Bully Herbig, Christian Tramitz, Rick Kavanian, Lotte Ledl, Gerd Knebel, Waldemar Kobus, Henni Nachtsheim, Monika John. Animated.

THE LISTENING
DIGIWORLD STUDIOS. Dec., 2006. Italian. British. (Giacomo Martelli) Michael Parks, Maya Sansa, Andrea Tidona, James Parks, Matt Patresi, Bruce McGuire.

LITTLE ASHES
REGENT RELEASING (IN U.S.). May, 2009. Spanish, U.K. (Paul Morrison) Javier Beltran, Robert Pattinson, Matthew McNulty, Marina Gatell, Arly Jover.

LITTLE BOX OF SWEETS
OCEANSONIC PICTURES. Jan., 2008. British. (Meneka Das) Joe Anderson, Meneka Das, Sheenu Das, Helena Michell, Rahul Vohra, Mohini Mathur, Raja Zutshi, Tillotama Shome.

LITTLE CHENIER
DORE PRODS. Dec. 11, 2006. (Bethany Ashton) Johnathon Schaech, Fred Koehler, Clifton Collins, Jr., Chris Mulkey, Jeremy Davidson, Marshall Bell, Tamara Braun.

LITTLE MANHATTAN
20TH CENTURY FOX. Sept. 2005. (Mark Levin) Josh Hutcherson, Bradley Whitford, Cynthia Nixon, Charlie Ray, Willie Garson.

LITTLE MAN
SONY PICTURES ENTERTAINMENT. July, 2006. (Keenen Ivory Wayans) Marlon Wayans, Shawn Wayans, Kerry Washington, John Witherspoon, Tracy Morgan, Lochlyn Munro, Chazz Palminteri, Linden Porco, Gabe Pimental, Molly Shannon, David Alan Grier, Dave Sheridan, Fred Stoller, Brittany Daniel, Alex Borstein, Kelly Coffield Park, Damien Dante Wayans.

LITTLE MOSCOW
SYRENA ENTERTAINMENT GROUP. Dec., 2008. Polish. (Waldemar Krzystek) Svetlana Khodchenkova, Leslaw Zurek, Dmitrij Ulianov, Elena Leszczynska, Artem Tkachenko, Jurij Itskov, Aleksiej Gorbunov.

LITTLE TRAITOR
WESTCHESTER FILMS (IN U.S.). Oct., 2009. Israel. (Lynn Roth) Alfred Molina, Ido Port, Rami Heuberger, Gilya Stern, Theodore Bickel.

LOCKED OUT
UGC DISTRIBUTION. March, 2006. French. (Albert Dupontel) Albert Dupontel, Claude Perron, Nicolas Marie, Roland Bertin, Philippe Duquesne, Gilles Gaston-Dreyfus, Bouli Lanners, Patrick Ligardes, Bruno Lochet, Yolande Moreau, Philippe Uchan, Helene Vincent, Serge Riaboukine, Yves Pignot, Jackie Berroyer, Terry Gilliam, Terry Jones.

THE LODGER
SAMUEL GOLDWYN FILMS. Dec. 10, 2008. (David Ondaatje) Alfred Molina, Hope Davis, Shane West, Simon Baker, Rachael Leigh Cook, Donal Logue , Philip Baker Hall.

LOFT
INDEPENDENT FILMS. Nov., 2008. Belgium. (Erik Van Looy) Koen De Bauw, Filip Peeters, Bruno Vanden Broecke, Matthias Schoenaerts, Koen de Graeve, Veerle Baetens, Ann Miller, Jan Decleir.

LONDON DREAMS
INDIAN FILMS (IN U.K.). NOV., 2009. U.K., Indian. (Vipul Amrutlal Shah) Salman Khan, Ajay Devgan, Asin, Rannvijay Singh, Aditya Roy Kapoor, Om Puri, Manoj Pahwa, Brinda Parekh, Paul Gregory, Louise Cole.

THE LONGSHOTS
MGM. Aug. 11, 2008. (Fred Durst) Ice Cube, Keke Palmer, Dash Mihok, Tasha Smith, Jill Marie Jones, Matt Craven, Miles Chandler, Glenn Plummer.

THE LONGEST PENALTY IN THE WORLD
ALTA CLASSICS. March, 2005. Spanish. (Roberto Santiago) Fernando Tejero, Maria Botto, Marta Larralde, Carlos Kaniowsky, Javier Gutierrez, Enrique Villen, Fernando Cayo, Hector Colome, Luis Callejo, Cristina Alcazar, Benito Sagredo.

THE LONGEST YARD
PARAMOUNT PICTURES. May, 2005. (Peter Segal) Adam Sandler, Chris Rock, Burt Reynolds, Nelly, James Cromwell, William Fichtner, Michael Irvin, David Patrick Kelly, Bill Romanowski, Bill Goldberg, Brian Bosworth, Kevin Nash, Steve Austin, Bob Sapp, Dalip Singh, Cloris Leachman, Nicholas Turturro, Tracy Morgan, Terry Crews.

LOOKING FOR CHEYENNE
LES FILMS DU PARADOXE. March, 2006. French. (Valerie Minetto) Mila Dekker, Aurelia Petit, Laurence Cote, Malik Zidi, Guilaine Londez, Eleonore Michelin, Miglen Mirtchev, Pierre Hiessler.

LOOKING FOR COMEDY IN THE MUSLIM WORLD
WARNER INDEPENDENT PICTURES. Dec., 2005. (Albert Brooks) Albert Brooks, Sheetal Sheth, John Carroll Lynch, Jon Tenney, Homie Doroodian, Amy Ryan, Fred Dalton Thompson, Penny Marshall, Victoria Burrows, Avinash Kaur, Juliet Touzene, Sunny Raina, Rima Laham, Duncan Bravo, Barbara Ali, Kavi Raz.

LOOKING FOR PALLADIN
WILDCAT RELEASING. Oct. 28, 2009. (Andrzej Krakowski) Ben Gazzara, David Moscow, Talia Shire, Pedro Armendariz Jr. Vincent Pastore, Angelica Aragon, Bahman Soltani, Jerry Carlson, Robert Youngs.

LORD OF WAR
LIONS GATE FILMS. Aug., 2005. (Andrew Niccol) Nicolas Cage, Jared Leto, Bridget Moynahan, Ian Holm, Ethan Hawke, Eamonn Walker, Sammi Rotibi.

LORDS OF DOGTOWN
SONY PICTURES ENTERTAINMENT. May, 2005. (Catherine Hardwicke) Emile Hirsch, Victor Rasuk, John Robinson, Michael Angarano, Nikki Reed, Heath Ledger, Rebecca De Mornay, Johnny Knoxville.

LOST
SILVERCREST ENTERTAINMENT. May, 2005. (Darren Lemke) Dean Cain, Ashley Scott, Danny Trejo, Irina Bjorklund, Justin Henry, Griffin Armstorff.

THE LOST BEAUTY
Dec., 2007. Moroccan. (Lahcen Zinoun) Sanaa Alaoui, Mohamed Miftah, Hanane Zouhdi, Touria Jabrane, Mohamed Afifi, Chemseddine Zinoun, Hassan Sqali, Raouia, Khouloud, Fatima Atif, Abdessadeq Majdouline, Omar Sayed, Salamat Mustafa, Hamoudy Mahmoudy, Abdellatif Ben Mama, Izda Ahmed, Oujoud Boujemaa, Founou, Hijiu el-Hassan, Salah Gzouly, Boutaina el-Baaj.

LOVE EXPRESSO
BUENA VISTA INTL. (SPAIN). July, 2007. Spanish. (Alvaro Diaz Lorenzo) Alejo Sauras, Lucia Jimenez, Asier Etxeandia, Elena Ballesteros, Inma Cuesta, Diego Paris, Javier Godino, Terele Pavez.

THE LOVE GURU
PARAMOUNT. June 16, 2008. (Marco Schnabel) Mike Myers, Jessica Alba, Justin Timberlake, Romany Malco, Verne Troyer, Meagan Good, Manu Narayan, John Oliver, Stephen Colbert, Jim Gaffigan, Ben Kingsley, Deepak Chopra.

LOVE HAPPENS
UNIVERSAL. Sept. 16, 2009. (Brandon Camp) Aaron Eckhart, Jennifer Aniston, Dan Fogler, John Carrol Lynch, Martin Sheen, Judy Greer, Frances Conroy.

LOVE IS IN THE AIR
TFM DISTRIBUTION. June, 2005. French. (Remi Bezancon) Vincent Elbaz, Gilles Lelouche, Marion Cotillard, Elsa Kikoine, Didier Bezace, Tom Novembre, Philippe Nahon, Cecile Cassel.

LOVE ME NO MORE
Feb., 2008. French. (Jean Becker) Albert Dupontel, Marie-Josee Croze, Pierre Vaneck, Alessandra Martines, Cristiana Reali, Mathias Mlekus, Claire Nebout, Francois Marthouret, Anne Loiret, Jose Paul.

LOVE N' DANCING
SCREEN MEDIA FILMS. April 30, 2009. (Robert Iscove) Tom Malloy, Amy Smart, Billy Zane, Nicola Royston, Leila Arcieri, Caroline Rhea, Rachel Dratch, Gregory Harrison, Jordan Frisbee, Tatiana Mollman, Benji Schwimmer, Heidi Groskreutz, Marcus Smith, Deonna Ball, Parker Dearborn, Jessica Cox.

THE LOVE OF SIAM
Feb., 2008. Thai. (Matthew Chookiat Sakveerakul) Sinja Plengpanich, Songsit Roongnophakunsri, Chemarn Boonyasak, Pimpan Buranapim, Mario Maurer, Witwisit Hiranyawongkul.

LOVE SONGS IN LOLITA'S CLUB
AZETA CINEMA. Dec., 2007. Spanish. (Vicente Aranda) Eduardo Noriega, Flora Martinez, Belen Fabra, Hector Colome, Carla Sanchez, Sonia Madrid, Vicente Gil.

LOVE'S ABIDING JOY
20TH CENTURY FOX. Oct., 2006. (Michael Landon, Jr.) Erin Cottrell, Logan Bartholomew, John Laughlin, Dale Midkiff, Drew Tyler Bell, Mae Whitman.

LOWER LEARNING
ANCHOR BAY ENTERTAINMENT. Oct. 8, 2008. (Mark Lafferty) Jason Biggs, Eva Longoria Parker, Monica Potter, Will Sasso, Kyle Gass, Jill Latiano, Rob Corddry.

LUCKY COUNTRY
FOOTPRINT FILMS. June, 2009. Australian. (Kriv Stenders) Aden Young, Toby Wallace, Pip Miller, Hanna Mangan-Lawrence, Neil Pigot, Eamon Farren, Robert Menzies, Helmut Bakaitis.

LUCKY LUKE
UGC DISTRIBUTION. Oct., 2009. French. (James Huth) Jean Dujardin, Michael Youn, Sylvie Testud, Daniel Prevost, Alexandra Lamy, Melvil Poupaud, Andre Oumansky, Jean-Francois Balmer, Mathias Sandor, Bruno Salomone.

LUCKY YOU
WARNER BROS. May, 2007. (Curtis Hanson) Eric Bana, Drew Barrymore, Robert Duvall, Debra Messing, Horatio Sanz, Charles Martin Smith, Saverio Guerra, Jean Smart.

LYNCH
ABSURDA. Oct., 2007. Danish. David Lynch, Laura Dern. Documentary.

M

MADAGASCAR
DREAMWORKS. May, 2005. (Eric Darnell, Tom McGrath) Voices: Ben Stiller, Chris Rock, David Schwimmer, Jada Pinkett Smith, Sacha Baron Cohen, Cedric the Entertainer, Andy Richter. Animated.

MADAGASCAR: ESCAPE 2 AFRICA
PARAMOUNT. Oct. 26, 2008. (Eric Darnell, Tom McGrath) Voices: Ben Stiller, Chris Rock, David Schwimmer, Jada Pinkett Smith, Sacha Baron Cohen, Cedric the Entertainer, Andy Richter, Bernie Mac, Alec Baldwin, Sherri Shepherd, will.i.am, Elisa Gabrielli, Tom McGrath, Chris Miller, Christopher Knights, Conrad Vernon. Animated.

MADE IN YUGOSLAVIA
TRIANGELFILM. Dec., 2005. Swedish. (Miko Lazic) Sasha Drakulic, Pavle Martinoski, Sloboadan Boda Ninkovic, Natasa Ninkovic, Dragan Gagi Jovanavic, Milorad Mandic Manda, Velimir "Bata" Zivojinovic.

MADE OF HONOR
SONY PICTURES ENTERTAINMENT. April 24, 2008. (Paul Weiland) Patrick Dempsey, Michelle Monaghan, Kevin McKidd, Kathleen Quinlan, Sydney Pollack, Chris Messina, Busy Philipps, Kevin Sussman, Richmond Arquette, Kadeem Hardison, Selma Stern, Whitney Cummings, Emily Nelson.

MADEA'S FAMILY REUNION
LIONSGATE. Feb., 2006. (Tyler Perry) Tyler Perry, Blair Underwood, Lynn Whitfield, Boris Kodjoe, Henry Simmons, Lisa Arrindell Anderson, Maya Angelou, Rochelle Aytes, Jennifer Lewis, Keke Palmer, Cicely Tyson.

MADISON
MGM. April, 2005. (William Bindley) James Caviezel, Jake Lloyd, Mary McCormack, Bruce Dern, Brent Briscoe, Paul Dooley, Reed Diamond, Frank Knapp, Chelcie Ross, Byrne Piven, William Shockley, Matt Letscher.

MADONNAS
Feb., 2007. German-Swiss-Belgium. (Maria Speth) Sandra Hueller, Olivier Gourmet, Susanne Lothar, Luisa Sappelt, Gerti Drassel, Coleman Orlando Swinton, Martin Goossens.

MAGIC
PARAMOUNT PICTURES FRANCE (IN FRANCE). Oct., 2008. French-Canadian. (Philippe Muyl) Marie Gillain, Cali, Antoine Dulery, Louis Dussol, Benoit Briere, Holly O'Brien, Rachel Gauthier, Stephane Breton, Evelyne de la Cheneliere.

THE MAGIC ROUNDABOUT
PATHE (IN U.K., FRANCE)/MIRAMAX (IN U.S.). Feb., 2005. British-French. (Jean Duval, Frank Passingham, Dave Borthwick) Voices: Tom Baker, Jim Broadbent, Joanna Lumley, Ian McKellen, Kylie Minogue, Bill Nighy, Robbie Williams, Ray Winstone, Lee Evans.

MAGICIANS
UNIVERSAL PICTURES. May, 2007. British. (Andrew O'Connor) Robert Webb, David Mitchell, Jessica Stevenson, Andrea Riseborough, Darren Boyd, Peter Capaldi, Sarah Hadland, Steve Edge.

MAGNIFICENT DESOLATION: WALKING ON THE MOON
IMAX CORP. Oct., 2005. (Mark Cowen) John Corbett, Matt Damon, Morgan Freeman, Scott Glenn, Tim Matheson, Matthew McConaughey, Paul Newman, Bill Paxton, Barry Pepper, Kevin Pollak, Peter Scolari, Gary Sinise, John Travolta, Donnie Wahlberg. Narrator: Tom Hanks. Documentary. IMAX.

THE MAID
FORASTERO, DIRORIRO. Jan., 2009. Chilean. (Sebastian Silva) Catalina Saavedra, Claudia Celedon, Mariana Loyola, Alejandro Goic, Anita Reeves, Delfina Guzman, Andrea Garcia-Huidobro, Mercedes Villanueva, Agustin Silva.

MAIKO HAAAAN!!!
June, 2007. Japanese. (Nibou Mizuta) Sadawo Abe, Shinichi Tsutsumi, Kou Shibasaki, Saori Koide.

MAJOR DUNDEE: THE EXTENDED VERSION
SONY PICTURES. March, 2005. (Sam Peckinpah) Charlton Heston, Richard Harris, Jim Hutton, James Coburn, Michael Anderson, Jr., Senta Berger, Mario Adorf, Brock Peters, Warren Oates, Ben Johnson, R.G. Armstrong, L.Q. Jones, Slim Pickens.

MAMA'S BOY
WARNER BROS. Dec. 1, 2007. (Tim Hamilton) Jon Heder, Diane Keaton, Jeff Daniels, Anna Faris, Eli Wallach, Dorian Missick, Sarah Chalke, Mary Kay Place.

MAMMA MIA! THE MOVIE
UNIVERSAL (in U.S.)/UNITED INTL. PICTURES (in U.K.). July 4, 2008. (Phyllida Lloyd) Meryl Streep, Pierce Brosnan, Colin Firth, Stellan Skarsgard, Julie Walters, Dominic Cooper, Amanda Seyfried, Christine Baranski.

MAMMOTH
MEMFIS FILM (SWEDEN)/ZENTROPA ENTERTAINMENTS BERLIN (GERMANY)/ZENTROPA ENTERTAINMENTS 5 APS (DENMARK). Feb., 2009. Swedish, German, Danish. (D) Min.Gael Garcia Bernal, Michelle Williams, Marife Necesito, Sophie Nyweide, Run Srinikornchot, Tom McCarthy, Jan Nicdao, Martin Delos Santos, Maria del Carmen.

THE MAN
NEW LINE CINEMA. Aug., 2005. (Les Mayfield) Samuel L. Jackson, Eugene Levy, Luke Goss, Miguel Ferrer, Susie Essman, Anthony Mackie, Horatio Sanz, Rachael Crawford.

MAN OF THE HOUSE
SONY PICTURES ENTERTAINMENT. Feb., 2005. (Stephen Herek) Tommy Lee Jones, Cedric the Entertainer, Christina Milian, Paula Garces, Monica Keena, Vanessa Ferlito, Kelli Garner, Anne Archer, Brian Van Holt, Shea Whigham, Terry Parks, R. Lee Ermey, Paget Brewster, Shannon Marie Woodward, Liz Vassey, Curtis Armstrong, James Richard Perry.

MAN OF THE YEAR
UNIVERSAL. Sept., 2006. (Barry Levinson) Robin Williams, Laura Linney, Christopher Walken, Lewis Black, Jeff Goldblum, Rick Roberts.

MANUAL OF LOVE
LUIGI AND AURELIO DE LAURENTIIS PRESENT A FILMAURO. March, 2005. Italian. (Giovanni Veronesi)

MARCH OF THE PENGUINS
WARNER INDEPENDENT PICTURES, NATIONAL GEOGRAPHIC FEATURE FILMS (U.S.). June, 2005. French. (Luc Jacquet) Narrator: Morgan Freeman. Documentary.

MARGARET CHO: ASSASSIN
REGENT. Aug., 2005. (Kerry Asmussen) Margaret Cho. Documentary.

MARIA, HE DOESN'T LIKE IT!
CONSTANTIN FILM VERLEIH. Aug., 2009. German. (Neele Leana Vollmar) Lino Banfi, Christian Ulmen, Mina Tander, Maren Kroymann, Gundi Ellert, Peter Prager, Paolo De Vita, Ludovica Modugno, Lucia Guzzardi, Nino Bellomo, Leonardo Nigro, Pierluigi Ferrandini, Sergio Rubini, Marleen Lohse, Enzo Salomone, Massimo Sarchielli, Nicola Nocella.

MARIGOLD
ADLABS FILMS. July, 2007. U.S.-British-Australian-Indian-Canadian. (Willard Carroll) Ali Larter, Salman Khan, Suchitra Pillai, Vikas Bhalla, Simone Singh, Vijayendra Sinhrao Ghatge, Nandana Sen, Ian Bohen.

THE MARINE
20TH CENTURY FOX. Oct., 2006. (John Bonito) John Cena, Robert Patrick, Kelly Carlson, Anthony Ray Parker, Abigail Bianca, Jerome Ehlers, Manu Bennett, Damon Gibson, Drew Powell, Frank Carlopio.

MAROA
ALTA CLASSICS. July, 2005. Spanish-Venezuelan. (Solveig Hoogesteijn) Tristan Ulloa, Yorlis Dominguez, Elba Escobar, Luke Grande, Enghel Alejo.

MARRIAGE IRANIAN STYLE
BITA FILMS. Aug., 2006. Iranian. (Hassan Fathi) Dariush Arjmand, Fatemeh Goudarzi, Shila Khodadad, Daniel Holmes, Ladan Tabatabaee, Saeed Kangarani, Mohammad Reza Sharifinia, Hesam Navab-Savafi, Mehri Mehrnia, Bagher Sahraroodi, Amir-Hossein Bidgoli.

MARTA
BONTON. April, 2007. Czech Repbulic. (Marta Novakova) Petra Spalkova, Vojtech Stepanek, Jan Novotny.

MARRIED LIFE
SONY PICTURES CLASSICS. Sept. 12, 2007. (Ira Sachs) Pierce Brosnan, Chris Cooper, Patricia Clarkson, Rachel McAdams, David Wenham.

MARTIAN CHILD

NEW LINE CINEMA. Oct. 19, 2007. (Menno Meyjes) John Cusack, Amanda Peet, Sophie Okonedo, Oliver Platt, Bobby Coleman, Joan Cusack, Anjelica Huston.

MARTYRS

WILD BUNCH (IN FRANCE)/WEINSTEIN CO. (IN U.S.). Sept., 2008. French-Canadian. (Pascal Laugier) Morjana Alaoui, Mylene Jampanoi, Catherine Begin, Robert Toupin, Patricia Tulasne, Juliette Gosselin, Xavier Dolan-Tadros, Jessie Pham.

MARY AND MAX

SCREEN AUSTRALIA. Jan., 2009. Australian. (Adam Elliot) Toni Collette, Philip Seymour Hoffman, Barry Humphries, Eric Bana, Bethany Whitmore.

MATERIAL GIRLS

MGM. Aug., 2006. (Martha Coolidge) Hilary Duff, Haylie Duff, Anjelica Huston, Lukas Haas, Maria Conchita Alonso, Brent Spiner, Marcus Coloma, Obba Babatunde, Reagan Dale Neis, Colleen Camp, Judy Tenuta, Henry Cho, Ty Hodges, Carl Lewis.

MAX PAYNE

20TH CENTURY FOX. Oct 15, 2008. (John Moore) Mark Wahlberg, Mila Kunis, Beau Bridges, Chris "Ludacris" Bridges, Chris O'Donnell, Donal Logue, Amaury Nolasco, Kate Burton, Olga Kurylenko, Marianthi Evans.

MAY 18

CJ ENTERTAINMENT. Oct., 2007. South Korea. (Kim Ji-hoon) Ahn Seong-gi, Kim Sang-gyeong, Lee Yo-weon, Lee Yun-gi, Park Cheol-min, Park Weon-sang, Song Jae-ho, Na Mun-heui, Son Byeong-ho.

MCDULL KUNG FU KINDERGARTEN

SHANGHAI MEDIA GROUP. Oct., 2009. Chinese. (Brian Tse) Min.

MCLIBEL

CINEMA LIBRE. June, 2005. British. (Franny Armstrong) Helen Steel, Dave Morris, Eric Schlosser, Morgan Spurlock, Colin Campbell, Sue Dibb, Dan Gallin, Stephen Gardner, Geoff Giuliano, Charlie Kervons, Howard Lyman, Charles O'Leary, Paul Preston. Documentary.

ME AND YOU AND EVERYONE WE KNOW

IFC FILMS. Jan., 2005. (Miranda July) John Hawkes, Miranda July, Miles Thompson, Brandon Ratcliff, Carlie Westerman, Natasha Slayton, Najarra Townsend.

ME TWO

STUDIO CANAL. June, 2008. French. (Nicolas & Bruno) Daniel Auteuil, Alain Chabat, Marina Fois, Francois Damiens, Denis Marechal, Fred Tousch.

MEET THE ROBINSONS

BUENA VISTA. March, 2007. (Stephen Anderson) Voices: Daniel Hansen, Jordan Fry, Wesley Singerman, Angela Bassett, Tom Selleck, Harland Williams, Laurie Metcalf, Nicole Sullivan, Adam West, Ethan Sandler, Tom Kenney, Stephen John Anderson. Animated.

MEET THE SPARTANS

20TH CENTURY FOX. Jan. 25, 2008. (Jason Friedberg, Aaron Seltzer) Sean Maguire, Carmen Electra, Ken Davitian, Kevin Sorbo, Diedrich Bader, Method Man, Jareb Dauplaise, Travis Van Winkle, Phil Morris.

MEETING RESISTANCE

NINE LIVES. Oct. 17, 2007. (Steve Conners) Documentary.

MEIN FUHRER: THE TRULY TRUEST TRUTH ABOUT ADOLF HITLER

WARNER BROS. Jan., 2007. German. (Dani Levy) Helge Schneider, Ulrich Muehe, Sylvester Groth, Adriana Altaras, Stefan Kurt, Ulrich Noethen, Lambert Hamel, Udo Kroschwald, Torsten Michaelis, Axel Werner, Wolfgang Becker, Katja Riemann, Meret Becker.

MELISSA P.

COLUMBIA TRISTAR FILMS ITALIA. Nov., 2005. Italian-Spanish. (Luca Guadagnino) Maria Valverde, Geraldine Chaplin, Primo Reggiani, Fabrizia Sacchi, Elio Germano, Nilo Mur, Letizia Ciampa, Claudio Santamaria, Pier Giorgio Bellocchio, Marcello Mazzarella.

MEMOIRS OF A GEISHA

SONY PICTURES ENTERTAINMENT. Nov., 2005. (Rob Marshall) Ziyi Zhang, Ken Watanabe, Michelle Yeoh, Koji Yakusho, Youki Kudoh, Kaori Momoi, Tsai Chin, Cary-Hiroyuki Tagawa, Suzuka Ohgo, Gong Li, Randall Duk Kim, Mako, Kenneth Tsang, Thomas Ikeda, Zoe Weizenbaum, Shizuko Hoshi.

MEMORY

ECHO BRIDGE ENTERTAINMENT. March, 2007. (Bennett Davlin) Billy Zane, Ann-Margret, Dennis Hopper, Tricia Helfer, Terry Chen.

MEMORY TRAIN

ALTA FILMS. June, 2005. Spanish. (Marta Arribas, Ana Perez) Josefina Cembrero, Leonor Mediavilla, Victoria Toro, Heinz Seidel, Hans Peter Steber.

THE MEN WHO STARE AT GOATS

OVERTURE FILMS. Sept. 8, 2009. (Grant Heslov) George Clooney, Jeff Bridges, Ewan McGregor, Kevin Spacey, Robert Patrick, Stephen Lang, Stephen Root, Glenn Morshower, Waleed Zuaiter, Rebecca Mader.

MENDY: A QUESTION OF FAITH

May, 2006. (Adam Vardy) Ivan Sandomire, Gabriela Dias, Spencer Chandler, Deana Barone, Jonathan Hova.

MEREDITH MONK: INNER VOICE

FIRST RUN FEATURES (IN U.S.). Oct., 2009. Dutch. (Babeth M. VanLoo) Meredith Monk, Katie Geissinger, Allison Sniffin, Theo Bleckmann, Ellen Fisher, Ching Gonzalez, Brue Rameker.

THE MERRY WIDOW

GAUMONT. Jan., 2008. French. (Isabelle Mergault) Michele Laroque, Jacques Gamblin, Wladimir Yordanoff, Tom Morton, Valerie Mairesse, Claire Nadeau, Eva Darlan, Caroline Raynaud, Paul Crachet, Michel Lagueyrie, Choukri Gabteni, Franck Pitiot, Julien Cafaro, Agnes Boury, Tadrina Hocking.

MES AMIS, MES AMOURS

PATHE DISTRIBUTION (IN FRANCE/U.K.). Aug., 2008. French-British. (Lorraine Levy) Vincent Lindon, Pascal Elbe, Virginie Ledoyen, Florence Foresti, Bernadette Lafont, Mar Sodupe, Garance Le Guillermic, Mathias Mlekuz.

THE MESSENGER

OMNILAB MEDIA GROUP. Jan. 19, 2009. (Oren Moverman) Ben Foster, Woody Harrelson, Samantha Morton, Jena Malone, Steve Buscemi, Eamonn Walker.

THE MESSENGERS

SONY PICTURES ENTERTAINMENT. Feb., 2007. (Danny Pang, Oxide Pang) Kristen Stewart, Dylan McDermott, Penelope Ann Miller, John Corbett, Evan Turner, Theodore Turner, Dustin Milligan.

MESSY CHRISTMAS

X VERLEIH. Nov., 2007. German. (Vanessa Jopp) Martina Gedeck, Heino Ferch, Meret Becker, Jasmin Tabatabai, Roeland Wiesnekker, Rainer Sellien, Andreas Windhuis, Rosa Enskat, Matthias Matschke, Ursula Doll, Alexandra Neldel, Petra Kelling, Bjarne Ingmar Maedel, Feo Aladag, Eva Loebau.

MIAMI VICE

UNIVERSAL. July, 2006. (Michael Mann) Colin Farrell, Jamie Foxx, Gong Li, Naomie Harris, Ciaran Hinds, Justin Theroux, Barry Shabaka Henley, Luis Tosar, John Ortiz, Elizabeth Rodriguez.

MICHAEL JACKSON'S THIS IS IT

SONY PICTURES ENTERTAINMENT. Oct. 27, 2009. (Kenny Ortega) Michael Jackson, Kenny Ortega, Michael Bearden, Travis Payne, Judith Hill, Orianthi Panagaris, Tommy Organ, Mo Pleasure, Stacy Walker, Tony Testa.

MIDSUMMER DREAM

BUENA VISTA INTL. July, 2005. Spanish-Portuguese. (Angel de la Cruz, Manolo Gomez) Voices: Gabino Diego, Carmen Machi, Yolanda Mateos, Luis Bajo, Juan Perucho, Jose Luis Gil, Sara Vivas, Antonio Galvez, Viky Angulo, Emma Penella, Gemma Cuervo , Isabel Ordaz. Animated.

MIGUEL AND WILLIAM

WARNER BROS. ENTERTAINMENT SPAIN. Feb., 2007. Spanish-British. (Ines Paris) Elena Anaya, Juan Luis Galiardo, Will Kemp, Jose Maria Pou, Malena Alterio, Geraldine Chaplin.

MILK

FOCUS FEATURES. Oct. 31, 2008. (Gus Van Sant) Sean Penn, Emile Hirsch, Josh Brolin, Diego Luna, James Franco, Alison Pill, Victor Garber, Denis O'Hare, Joseph Cross, Stephen Spinella, Lucas Grabeel, Brandon Boyce, Zvi Howard Rosenman, Kelvin Yu, Jeff Koons.

MINDHUNTERS

MIRAMAX. May, 2005. British-Dutch-Finnish-U.S. (Renny Harlin) LL Cool J, Jonny Lee Miller, Kathryn Morris, Patricia Velasquez, Clifton Collins, Jr., Eion Bailey, Will Kemp, Val Kilmer, Christian Slater.

THE MIDNIGHT MEAT TRAIN

LIONSGATE. Aug. 1, 2008. (Ryuhei Kitamura) Bradley Cooper, Leslie Bibb, Brooke Shields, Vinnie Jones, Roger Bart, Tony Curran, Barbara Eve Harris, Ted Raimi.

MILITARY INTELLIGENCE AND YOU!

ANYWHERE ROAD. Feb. 22, 2008. (Dale Kutzera) Patrick Muldoon, Elizabeth Bennett, Mackenzie Astin, John Rixley Moore, Eric Jungman.

MIRRORS

20TH CENTURY FOX. Aug. 15, 2008. (Alexandre Aja) Kiefer Sutherland, Paula Patton, Amy Smart, Mary Beth Peil, Cameron Boyce, Erica Gluck, Julian Glover, John Shrapnel.

MISCONCEPTIONS

REGENT RELEASING/HERE. June 24, 2009. (Ron Satlof) Sam Ball, Sarah Carter, A.J. Cook, Orlando Jones, David Moscow, David Sutcliffe.

MISS CONCEPTION

FIRST LOOK STUDIOS (IN U.S.) May, 2008. British. (Eric Styles) MPAA Rating: R. Heather Graham, Tom Ellis, Mia Kirshner, Ruta Gedmintas, Orlando Seale, Will Mellor, Edward MacLiam.

MISS CONGENIALITY 2: ARMED AND FABULOUS
WARNER BROS. March, 2005. (John Pasquin) Sandra Bullock, Regina King, Enrique Murciano, William Shatner, Ernie Hudson, Heather Burns, Diedrich Bader, Treat Williams, Abraham Benrubi, Nick Offerman.

MISS MARCH
FOX SEARCHLIGHT. March 11, 2009. (Zach Cregger) Zach Cregger, Trevor Moore, Craig Robinson, Raquel Alessi, Molly Stanton, Cedric Yarbrough, Carla Jimenez, Geoff Meed.

MISS PETTIGREW LIVES FOR A DAY
FOCUS FEATURES. Feb. 27, 2008. (Bharat Nalluri) Paul Englishby. In Deluxe color, Panavision widescreen. Release date: Feb. 27, 2008. MPAA Rating: PG-13. Running time: 92 Min. Frances McDormand, Amy Adams, Lee Pace, Ciaran Hinds, Shirley Henderson, Mark Strong, Tom Payne, Christina Cole.

MISS POTTER
WEINSTEIN CO. Dec., 2006. (Chris Noonan) Renee Zellweger, Ewan McGregor, Emily Watson, Barbara Flynn, Bill Paterson, Matyelok Gibbs, Lloyd Owen, Anton Lesser, David Bamber, Phyllida Law, Lucy Boynton, Oliver Jenkins.

MISSING
BUENA VISTA INTL. Oct., 2005. Spanish. (Daniel Calparsoro) Ariadna Gil, Jordi Molla, Nacho Perez, Omar Munoz, Mar Sodupe, Alex Brendemuhl.

THE MISSING LYNX: PAWS ON THE RUN
AURUM. Oct., 2009. Spanish. (Manuel Sicilia) Jose Luis Martinez, Stephen Hughes, Thisbe Burns, Craig Stevenson, Kate Petrie.

MISSISSIPPI CHICKEN
REVERSAL FILMS. Dec. 7, 2007. (John Fiege).

THE MIST
MGM. Nov. 1, 2007. (Frank Darabont) Thomas Jane, Marcia Gay Harden, Laurie Holden, Andre Braugher, Toby Jones, William Sadler, Jeffrey DeMunn, Frances Sternhagen, Alexa Davalos, Nathan Gamble, Chris Owen, Sam Witwer, Robert C. Treveiler, David Jensen.

THE MISTRESS OF SPICES
ENTERTAINMENT FILM DISTRIBUTORS. April, 2006. British-U.S. (Paul Mayeda Berges) Aishwarya Rai, Dylan McDermott, Nitin Chandra Ganatra, Adewale Akinnuoye-Agbaje, Caroline Chikezie, Anupam Kher, Padma Lakshmi, Ayesha Dharker, Nina Young, Zohra Segal, Bansree Madhani.

MODERN LOVE
PATHE DISTRIBUTION (IN FRANCE)/ALLIANCE ATLANTIS VIVAFILM (IN CANADA). March, 2008. French-Canadian. (Stephane Kazandjian) Alexandra Lamy, Stephane Rousseau, Berenice Bejo, Pierre Francois Martin-Laval, Clotilde Courau, Stephane Debac, Melanie Bernier, Valerie Karsenti, Kad Merad, David La Haye, Thomas Jouannet, Francis Leplay, Raphaelle Agogue, Eric Naggar, Mai Ahn Le, Annie Gregorio.

MOLIERE
WILD BUNCH DISTRIBUTION. Jan., 2007. French (Laurent Tirard) Romain Duris, Fabrice Luchini, Laura Morante, Edouard Baer, Ludivine Sagnier, Fanny Valette, Melanie Dos Santos, Gonzague Montuel, Gilian Petrovsky, Sophie-Charlotte Husson, Arie Elmaleh, Eric Berger.

MONSTER HOUSE
SONY PICTURES ENTERTAINMENT. June, 2006. (Gil Kenan) Steve Buscemi, Nick Cannon, Maggie Gyllenhaal, Jon Heder, Kevin James, Jason Lee, Catherine O'Hara, Kathleen Turner, Fred Willard, Mitchel Musso, Sam Lerner, Spencer Locke. Animated.

MONSTERS VS. ALIENS
PARAMOUNT. March 14, 2009. (Rob Letterman, Conrad Vernon) Reese Witherspoon, Seth Rogen, Hugh Laurie, Will Arnett, Kiefer Sutherland, Rainn Wilson, Paul Rudd, Stephen Colbert.

MONOTONY
Dec., 2007. Latvian. (Juris Poskus) Iveta Pole, Varis Pinis, Artuss Kaimins, Andis Strods, Madara Melberga.

MONSTER-IN-LAW
NEW LINE CINEMA. April, 2005. (Robert Luketic) Jennifer Lopez, Jane Fonda, Michael Vartan, Wanda Sykes, Adam Scott, Monet Mazur, Annie Parisse, Will Arnett, Elaine Stritch.

MOON
STAGE 6 FILMS (IN U.S.). Jan. 16, 2009. (Duncan Jones) Sam Rockwell, Dominique McElligott, Kaya Scodelario, Benedict Wong, Matt Berry, Malcolm Stewart, Kevin Spacey.

THE MOON IN A BOTTLE
HISPANO FOXFILM. Nov., 2007. Spanish-British. (Grojo) Edu Soto, Barbara Goenaga, Dominique Pinon, Pep Jove, Leigh Zimmerman, Michael Jenn, Jagvier Mejia.

MORNING LIGHT
WALT DISNEY PICTURES. Oct. 7, 2008. (Mark Monroe) Roy E. Disney, Robbie Haines, Chris Branning, Graham Brant-Zawadzki, Chris Clark, Charlie Enright, Jesse Fielding, Robbie "Turtle" Kane, Steve Manson, Chris Schubert, Kate Theisen, Mark Towill, Genny Tulloch, Piet van Os, Chris Welch, Kit Will, Jeremy Wilmot. Narrator: Patrick Warburton.

MOUTH TO MOUTH
SONET FILM. Dec., 2005. Swedish. (Bjorn Runge) Marie Richardson, Peter Andersson, Sofia Westberg, Magnus Krepper, Magdalena Jansson, Anton Jarlos Gry, Pernilla August, Ann Petren, Marie Goranzon, Anna Pettersson, Camilla Larsson, Liv Omsen, Ingvar Hirdvall, Leif Andree, Fyr Thorwald.

MOVING MCALLISTER
FIRST INDEPENDENT PICTURES. Sept., 2007. (Andrew Black) Ben Gourley, Mila Kunis, Jon Heder, Rutger Hauer, Hubbel Palmer, Billy Drago, Peter Jason, Cathrine Grace, Patrika Darbo, William Mapother, Zach Ward.

MR 73
GAUMONT. March, 2008. French. (Olivier Marchal) Daniel Auteuil, Olivia Bonamy, Catherine Marchal, Francis Renaud, Gerald Laroche, Guy Lecluyse, Philippe Nahon, Virginia Anderson, Yasmine Lafitte, Swan Demarsan, Didier Nobletz, Jean-Paul Zehnacker, Moussa Maaskri, Louise Monot.

MR. BEAN'S HOLIDAY
UNIVERSAL. March, 2007. (Steve Bendelack) Rowan Atkinson, Emma de Caunes, Max Baldry, Willem Dafoe, Jean Rochefort, Karel Roden, Steve Pemberton.

MR. BROOKS
MGM. May, 2007. (Bruce A. Evans) Kevin Costner, Demi Moore, Dane Cook, William Hurt, Marg Helgenberger, Ruben Santiago-Hudson, Danielle Panabaker.

MR. & MRS. SMITH
20TH CENTURY FOX. May, 2005. (Doug Liman) Brad Pitt, Angelina Jolie, Vince Vaughn, Adam Brody, Kerry Washington, Keith David, Chris Weitz, Rachael Huntley.

MR. MAGORIUM'S WONDER EMPORIUM
20TH CENTURY FOX. Nov. 7, 2007. (Zach Helm) Natalie Portman, Dustin Hoffman, Jason Bateman, Zach Mills.

MR. NOBODY
PATHE DISTRIBUTION. Sept., 2009. French. Jared Leto, Sarah Polley, Diane Kruger, Linh-Dan Pham, Rhys Ifans, Natasha Little, Toby Regbo, Juno Temple, Clare Stone, Thomas Byrne, Audrey Giacomini, Laura Brumagne, Allan Corduner, Daniel Mays, Noa de Constanzo.

MR. WOODCOCK
NEW LINE CINEMA. Sept., 2007. (Craig Gillespie) Billy Bob Thornton, Seann William Scott, Susan Sarandon, Ethan Suplee, Melissa Sagemiller, Kurt Fuller, Bill Macy, Brent Briscoe, M.C. Gainey, Amy Poehler, Kyley Baldridge.

MRS. HARRIS
Sept., 2005. (Phyllis Nagy) Annette Bening, Ben Kingsley, Ellen Burstyn, Frances Fisher, Philip Baker Hall, Cloris Leachman, Mary McDonnell, Chloe Sevigny, Bill Smitrovich, Frank Whaley.

MT. TSURUGIDAKE
TOEI CO. Sept., 2009. Japanese. (Daisaku Kimura) Tadanobu Asano, Teruyuki Kagawa, Ryuhei Matsuda, Toru Nakamura, Aoi Miyazaki, Koji Yakusho.

THE MUD BOY
FILMAX. May, 2007. Spanish-Argentinian. (Jorge Algora) Maribel Verdu, Daniel Freire, Chete Lera, Juan Ciancio, Cesar Bordon, Abel Ayala.

MUETTER
EUROZOOM. Feb., 2006. French. (Dominique Lienhard) Stanislas Merhar, Sophie Quinton, Aurelian Recoing, Agathe de La Boulaye, Andree Meyer-Benjamin.

THE MUMMY: TOMB OF THE DRAGON EMPEROR
UNIVERSAL. July 28, 2008. (Rob Cohen) Brendan Fraser, Jet Li, Maria Bello, John Hannah, Michelle Yeoh, Luke Ford, Chau Sang Anthony Wong, Isabella Leong, Liam Cunningham, David Calder, Russell Wong.

MUNICH
UNIVERSAL (IN U.S.), DREAMWORKS (INTERNATIONAL). Dec., 2005. (Steven Spielberg) Eric Bana, Daniel Craig, Ciaran Hinds, Mathieu Kassovitz, Hanns Zischler, Ayelet Zurer, Geoffrey Rush, Michael Lonsdale, Mathieu Amalric, Lynn Cohen, Marie-Josee Croze, Makram Khoury, Igal Naor, Omar Metwally, Moritz Bleibtreu, Mostefa Djadjam, Gila Almagor, Moshe Ivgy, Yvan Attal, Hiam Abbass.

MUSIC AND LYRICS
WARNER BROS. Jan., 2007. (Marc Lawrence) Hugh Grant, Drew Barrymore, Brad Garrett, Kristen Johnston, Haley Bennett, Aasif Mandvi, Campbell Scott, Jason Antoon, Matthew Morrison.

MUSIC WITHIN
MGM. Oct. 21, 2007. (Steven Sawalich) Ron Livingston, Melissa George, Michael Sheen, Yul Vazquez, Rebecca De Mornay, Hector Elizondo.

MUST LOVE DOGS
WARNER BROS. July, 2005. (Gary David Goldberg) Diane Lane,

John Cusack, Elizabeth Perkins, Dermot Mulroney, Stockard Channing, Christopher Plummer.

MUTANT CHRONICLES

MAGNET. April 24, 2009. (Simon Hunter) Thomas Jane, Ron Perlman, Devon Aoki, Benno Furmann, Sean Pertwee, John Malkovich, Anna Walton, Luis Echegaray, Tom Wu, Steve Toussaint.

MY ANGEL

MK2 DIFFUSION. Jan., 2005. French-Belgium. (Serge Frydman) Vanessa Paradis, Vincent Rottiers, Eduardo Noriega, Claude Perron, Eric Ruf, Thomas Fersen.

MY BEST ENEMY

FILMAURO. March, 2006. Italian. (Carlo Verdone) Carlo Verdone, Silvio Muccino, Ana Caterina Morariu, Agnese Nano, Paolo Triestino.

MY BEST FRIEND'S GIRL

LIONSGATE. Sept. 19, 2008. (Howard Deutch) Dane Cook, Kate Hudson, Jason Biggs, Alec Baldwin, Diora Baird, Lizzy Caplan.

MY BLOODY VALENTINE

LIONSGATE. Jan 15, 2009. (Patrick Lussier) Jensen Ackles, Jaime King, Kerr Smith, Betsy Rue, Edi Gathegi, Tom Atkins, Kevin Tighe, Megan Boone, Karen Baum, Rich Walters.

MY BROTHER

CODEBLACK ENTERTAINMENT. March, 2007. (Anthony Lover) Vanessa Williams, Nashawn Kearse, Rodney Henry, Fredro Starr, Tatum O'Neal, Christopher Scott, ,Donovan Jennings.

MY BROTHER IS AN ONLY CHILD

WARNER BROS. (ITALIA). April, 2007. Italian-French. (Daniele Luchetti) Elio Germano, Riccardo Scamarcio, Diane Fleri, Alba Rohrwacher, Angela Finocchiaro, Vittorio Emanuele Propizio, Massimo Popolizio, Luca Zingaretti, Anna Bonaiuto, Ascanio Celestini, Claudio Botosso, Ninni Bruschetta.

MY BROTHER'S WIFE

LIONSGATE. March, 2006. (Ricardo de Montreuil) Barbara Mori, Christian Meier, Manolo Cardona, Bruno Bichir, Angelica Aragon, Beto Cuevas.

MY CAREER AS A TEACHER

Sept., 2007. Chinese. (Zheng Kehong) Tony Leung Ka-fai, Qin Hailu, Guo Xiaodong, Luo Deyuan, He Wenchao, Zhang Xiaodao.

MY DAD IS INTO TERRORISM

REZO FILMS DISTRIBUTION. Jan., 2006. French. (William Karel) Narrator: Elsa Zylberstein. Clemence Boulouque. Documentary.

MY DNA SAYS I LOVE YOU!

SERENITY (IN TAIWAN)/CHENGTIAN (IN CHINA). Oct., 2007. Taiwanese-Chinese. (Robin Lee) Terri Kwan, Yu Nan, Peter Ho, Eddie Peng, Lin Yu-lun.

MY DATE WITH DREW

SLOW HAND RELEASING. Aug., 2005. (Jon Gunn, Brian Herzlinger, Brett Winn). Documentary.

MY LIFE IN RUINS

FOX SEARCHLIGHT. April 29, 2009. (Donald Petrie) Nia Vardalos, Richard Dreyfuss, Maria Adanez, Sheila Bernette, Maria Botto, Rachel Dratch, Alexis Georgoulis, Ralph Nossek, Bernice Stegers, Harland Williams.

MY NAME IS BRUCE

IMAGE ENTERTAINMENT. Dec. 17, 2008. (Bruce Campbell) Bruce Campbell, Grace Thorsen, Taylor Sharpe, Ted Raimi, Ben McCain, Ellen Sandweiss, Tim Quill, Danny Hicks.

MY NAME IS JUANI

MANGA FILMS. Nov., 2006. Spanish. (Bigas Luna) Veronica Echegui, Laya Marti, Dani Martin, Gorka Lasaosa, Jose Chaves, Mercedes Hoyos, Marcos Campos, Ferran Madico, Joana Lopez.

MY QUICK WAY OUT

WARNER SOGEFILMS. Jan., 2006. Spanish. (Miguel Albaladejo) Borja Navas, Fernando Tejero, Mariola Fuentes, Alex Casanovas, Mar Regueras, Jose Luis Garcia-Perez.

MY SISTER'S KEEPER

WARNER BROS. June 18, 2009. (Nick Cassavetes) Cameron Diaz, Abigail Breslin, Alec Baldwin, Jason Patric, Sofia Vassilieva, Heather Wahlquist, Joan Cusack, Thomas Dekker, Evan Ellingson, David Thornton.

MY SUPER EX-GIRLFRIEND

20TH CENTURY FOX. July, 2006. (Ivan Reitman) Uma Thurman, Luke Wilson, Anna Faris, Eddie Izzard, Rainn Wilson, Wanda Sykes.

THE MYSTERIES OF PITTSBURGH

GROUNDSWELL. Jan. 20, 2008. (Rawson Marshall) Jon Foster, Peter Sarsgaard, Sienna Miller, Nick Nolte, Mena Suvari, Omid Abtahi, Keith Michael Gregory.

MYSTERY TEAM

DERRICK COMEDY. Jan. 17, 2009. (Dan Eckman) Donald Glover, D.C. Pierson, Aubrey Plaza, Dominic Dierkes, Bobby Moynihan, Matt Walsh.

MYWAY

BADITRI. Feb., 2008. Spanish. (J. A. Salgot) Jordi Sanchez, Joan Dalmau, Asuncion Balaguer, Jaume Garcia Arija, Silvia Marso, Ariel Casas, Miquel Folch, Ramon Pujol, Susana Fawaz, Ana Fibla.

MY WIFE'S FIRST LOVER

SONET FILM. Dec., 2005. Swedish. (Hans Ake Gabrielsson) Marika Lagercrantz, Mikael Samuelsson, Philip Zanden, Sissela Kyle, Carl Kjellgren, Pontus Gustafsson, Cecilia Frode, Mats Bergman, Wera Westholm, Sverrir Gudnason, Melinda Wrede, Nassim Al Fakir.

MY WORDS, MY LIES, MY LOVE

A. Lila Lila, 2009. German. (Alain Gsponer) Daniel Bruhl, Hannah Herzsprung, Henry Hubchen, Kirsten Block.

MYSTERY OF THE NILE

MACGILLIVRAY FREEMAN FILMS. Feb., 2005. U.S.-Spanish. (Jordi Llompart) Pasquale Scaturro, Gordon Brown, Saskia Lange, Mohamed Megahed, Myriam Seco, Michel l'Huillier. Documentary.

N

N (NAPOLEON AND ME)

Oct., 2006. Italian-French-Spanish. (Paolo Virzi) Daniel Auteuil, Elio Germano, Monica Bellucci, Francesca Inaudi, Sabrina Impacciatore, Valerio Mastandrea, Massimo Ceccherini, Omero Antonutti, Margarita Lozano, Jose Angel Egidio, Achille Brugnini, Vincent Lo Monaco, Vittorio Amandola, Emanuele Barresi, Carlo Monni, Fausto Caroli.

NACHO LIBRE

PARAMOUNT. June, 2006. (Jared Hess) Jack Black, Ana del la Reguera, Hector Jimenez, Darius A. Rose, Moises Arias, Diego Eduardo Gomez, Carlos Maycotte, Richard Montoya, Cesar Gonzalez, Peter Stormare.

THE NAKED YEARS – CLASSIFIED 'S'

UNIVERSAL PICTURES INTL. SPAIN. Oct., 2008. Spanish. (Felix Sabroso, Dunia Ayaso) Candela Pena, Goya Toledo, Mar Flores, Antonio de la Torre, Luis Zahera.

NAMASTEY LONDON

EROS INTL. March, 2007. Indian. (Vipul Amrutlal Shah) Rishi Kapoor, Akshay Kumar, Katrina Kaif, Upen Patel, Javed Sheikh, Ritesh Deshmukh, Tiffany Mulheron, Clive Standen, Shaana Diya, Liam Evans Ford, Richard Field, Paul Williamson.

NANCY DREW

WARNER BROS. June, 2007. (Andrew Fleming) Emma Roberts, Josh Flitter, Max Thieriot, Rachael Leigh Cook, Tate Donovan, Barry Bostwick, Laura Elena Harring, Daniella Monet, Kelly Vitz, Marshall Bell.

NANNY MCPHEE

UIP (IN U.K.)/UNIVERSAL (IN U.S.). Oct., 2005. British-U.S. (Kirk Jones) Emma Thompson, Colin Firth, Kelly MacDonald, Derek Jacobi, Patrick Barlow, Celia Imrie, Imelda Staunton, Thomas Sangster, Angela Lansbury, Eliza Bennett, Jenny Daykin, Raphael Coleman, Samuel Honywood, Holly Gibbs, Hebe Barnes, Zinnia Barnes.

NATIONAL LAMPOON'S HOMO ERECTUS

NATIONAL LAMPOON. June 9, 2008. (Adam Rifkin) Adam Rifkin, Ali Larter, Hayes MacArthur, David Carradine, Talia Shire, Carol Alt, Gary Busey, William A. Tyree, Ron Jeremy, Tom Arnold.

NATIONAL LAMPOON'S VAN WILDER 2: THE RISE OF TAJ

MGM. Nov., 2006. (Mort Nathan) Kal Penn, Lauren Cohan, Daniel Percival, Glen Barry, Anthony Cozens, Steven Rathman, Holly Davidson.

NATIONAL LAMPOON PRESENTS ELECTRIC APRICOT: QUEST FOR FESTEROO

NATIONAL LAMPOON. Nov. 10, 2007. (Les Claypool) Les Claypool, Adam Gates, Bryan Kehoe, Jonathan Korty, Jason McHugh, Kyle McCulloch, Brian Kite, Dian Bachar, Seth Green, Matt Stone, Bob Weir, Mike Gordon, Warren Hynes.

NATIONAL TREASURE: BOOK OF SECRETS

WALT DISNEY PICTURES. Dec. 19, 2007. (Jon Turteltaub) Nicolas Cage, Jon Voight, Harvey Keitel, Ed Harris, Diane Kruger, Justin Bartha, Bruce Greenwood, Michael Maize, Timothy Murphy, Alicia Coppola, Armando Riesco, Albert Hall, Helen Mirren, Joel Gretsch.

THE NATIVITY STORY

NEW LINE CINEMA. Nov., 2006. (Catherine Hardwicke) Keisha Castle-Hughes, Oscar Isaac, Hiam Abbass, Shaun Toub, Ciaran Hinds, Shohreh Aghdashloo, Stanley Townsend, Alexander Siddig, Nadim Sawalha, Eriq Ebouaney, Stefan Kalipha, Alessandro Giuggioli, Farida Ouchani, Said Amadis.

NEAL 'N' NIKKI

YASH RAJ. Dec., 2005. Indian. (Arjun Sablok) Uday Chopra, Tanisha Mukerji, Richa Pallod, Gaurav Gera, Priya Sachdev, Alexander Montez, Kristy McQuade, Serinda Swan, Samantha McLeod, Sana Abou Khazal, Kamini Khanna, Chander Khanna, Abhishek Bachchan.

THE NEAR EAST
SOGEPAQ (IN SPAIN). Sept., 2006. Spanish. (Fernando Colomo) Javier Cifrian, Nur Al Levi, Asier Etxeandia, Ash Varrez, Lalita Ahmed, Laura Cepeda, Victor Benjumea.

NEG MARON
MARS DISTRIBUTION. Feb., 2005. French. (Jean-Claude Flamand Barny) Admiral T, D. Daly, Stomy Bugsy, Alex Descas, Francois Levantal, Jocelyne Beroard.

NEVER AGAIN LIKE BEFORE
MEDUSA. Dec., 2005. Italian. (Giacomo Campiotti)Marco Casu, Marco Velluti, Natalia Piatti, Nicola Cipolla, Laura Chiatti, Federico Battilocchio, Pino Quartullo, Lidia Broccolino, Francesco Salvi, Mariella Valentini, Fabio Sartor.

NEVER BACK DOWN
SUMMIT ENTERTAINMENT. March 11, 2008. (Jeff Wadlow) Sean Faris, Amber Heard, Cam Gigandet, Evan Peters, Leslie Hope, Djimon Hounsou, Wyatt Smith.

NEVER BEEN THAWED
Sept., 2005. (Sean Anders) Allen Zwolle, Sean Anders, Shelly Frasier, John Morris, John Angelo, Mike Gordon, Scott Isham, Charles Arnold.

NEVER SAY NEVER!
SND. Aug., 2005. French. (Eric Civanyan) Gerard Jugnot, Jean Dujardin, Melanie Doutey, Marie-France Santon, Michele Garcia, Patrick Haudecoeur, Arno Chevrier, Henri Garcin, Jean-Luc Porraz, Jacques Herlin.

NEVERWAS
Sept., 2005. (Joshua Michael Stern) Aaron Eckhart, Ian McKellan, Brittany Murphy, William Hurt, Nick Nolte, Alan Cumming, Jessica Lange, Bill Bellamy, Vera Farmiga, Michael Moriarty, Cynthia Stevenson, Ryan Drescher.

THE NEW MAN
SONET FILM. Jan., 2007. Swedish. (Klaus Haro) Julia Hogberg, Maria Lundqvist, Lo Kauppi, Ellen Mattson, Anna Littorin, Ann-Sofie Nurmi, Nadja Mirmiran, Christoffer Svensson, Tobias Aspelin, Linda Kulle, Monica Edvardsson, Happy Jankell.

THE NEW PROTOCOL
STUDIO CANAL. March, 2008. French. (Thomas Vincent) Clovis Cornillac, Marie-Josee Croze, Dominique Reymond, Stephane Hillel, Gilles Cohen, Carole Richert.

NEW TOWN ORIGINAL
NEW TOWN FILMS. April, 2005. British. (Jason Ford) Elliott Jordan, Katharine Peachey, Nathan Thomas, Richard Gooch, Kal Aise, Jamie Palmer, Steve Gibbs, Terry Bird, Paul McNeilly, Laura Pennycard, Lynn Verral.

THE NEW WORLD
NEW LINE CINEMA. Dec., 2005. (Terrence Malick) Colin Farrell, Q'Orianka Kilcher, Christopher Plummer, Christian Bale, August Schellenberg, Wes Studi, David Thewlis, Yorick Van Wageningen, Ben Mendelsohn, Raoul Trujillo, Brian F. O'Byrne, Irene Bedard, John Savage, Jamie Harris, Alex Rice, Michael Greyeyes, Kalani Queypo, Noah Taylor, Jonathan Pryce, Alexandra Malick.

NEW YORK
YASH RAJ FILMS. July, 2009. Indian. (Kabir Khan) John Abraham, Katrina Kaif, Neil Nitin Mukesh, Irrfan.

NEXT
PARAMOUNT. April, 2007. (Lee Tamahori) Nicolas Cage, Julianne Moore, Jessica Biel, Thomas Kretschmann, Tory Kittles, Peter Falk, Jim Beaver, Enzo Cilenti, Jason Butler Harner, Jose Zuniga.

NEXT!
EUROPACORP DISTRIBUTION. June, 2006. French. (Jeanne Biras) Alexandra Lamy, Clovia Cornillac, Jerry Rudes, Rastko Jankovic, Juliette Roudet.

NEXT DAY AIR
SUMMIT ENTERTAINMENT. May 6, 2009. (Benny Boom) Donald Faison, Mike Epps, Wood Harris, Omari Hardwick, Darius McCrary, Cisco Reyes, Debbie Allen, Mos Def, Emilio Rivera, Lobo Sebastian, Malik Barnhardt, Lauren London, Yasmin Deliz.

NICE BOMBS
SEVENTH ART RELEASING. July, 2007. (Usama Alshaibi) Usama Alshaibi, Kristie Alshaibi, Hameed Alshaibi, Tareef Alshaibi. Documentary.

NIGHT AT THE MUSEUM
20TH CENTURY FOX. Dec., 2006. (Shawn Levy) Ben Stiller, Carla Gugino, Dick Van Dyke, Mickey Rooney, Bill Cobbs, Jake Cherry, Ricky Gervais, Robin Williams, Kim Raver, Patrick Gallagher, Rami Malek, Pierfrancesco Favino, Charlie Murphy, Steve Coogan, Mizuo Peck, Owen Wilson.

NIGHT AT THE MUSEUM: BATTLE OF THE SMITHSONIAN
20TH CENTURY FOX. May 18, 2009. (Shawn Levy) Ben Stiller, Amy Adams, Owen Wilson, Hank Azaria, Robin Williams, Christopher Guest, Alain Chabat, Steve Coogan, Ricky Gervais, Bill Hader, Jon Bernthal.

NIGHT BEFORE FINALS
01. March, 2006. Italian. (Fausto Brizzi) Nicolas Vaporidis, Cristiana Capotondi, Giorgio Faletti, Andrea De Rosa, Sarah Maestri, Riccardo Minggio, Valeria Fabrizi.

NIGHT BUS
01 DISTRIBUTION. June, 2007. Italian-Polish. (Davide Marengo) Giovanna Mezzogiorno, Valerio Mastandrea, Ennio Fantastichini, Anna Romantowska, Roberto Citran, Francesco Pannofino, Ivan Franek, Antonio Catania, Iaia Forte, Marcello Mazzarella, Marek Barbasiewicz, Renato Nicolini, Paolo Calabresi, Massimo De Santis, Manuela Morabito, Alice Palazzi, Mario Rivera.

THE NIGHT OF THE BROTHER
ALTA FILMS. Aug., 2005. Spanish. (Santiago Garcia de Leaniz) Jan Cornet, Maria Vazquez, Pablo Rivero, Joan Dalmau, Iciar Bollain, Luis Tosar, Jose Angel Egido.

NIGHT RAID
Nov., 2007. Chinese. (An Lan) Wang Yongming, Liu Tianzuo, He Dandan, Xu Honghao, Zhang Yongxiang, Jin Liang, Zhang Zhijian, Yu Junhao, Dai Huikang, Wang Wenjie, Liu Lin, Zhang Qingpeng.

NIGHTMARE MAN
VALKHN FILMS. July, 2006. (Rolfe Kanesky) Tiffany Shepis, Blythe Metz, Hanna Putnam, James Ferris, Jack Sway, Luciano Szafir, Aaron Sherry, Richard Moll.

NIGHTS IN RODANTHE
WARNER BROS. Sept. 18, 2008. (George C. Wolfe) Richard Gere, Diane Lane, Christopher Meloni, Viola Davis, Becky Ann Baker, Scott Glenn, James Franco.

NIM'S ISLAND
20TH CENTURY FOX .April 1, 2008. (Mark Levin) Abigail Breslin, Jodie Foster, Gerard Butler, Michael Carman, Mark Brady, Anthony Simcoe, Christopher Baker, Maddison Joyce, Peter Callan, Rhonda Doyle.

NINA FRISK
SONET FILM. Feb., 2007. Swedish. (Maria Blom) Sofia Helin, Daniel Gotschenhjelm, Vilde Helmersson, Gunilla Nyroos, Urban Eldh, Sven Ahlstrom, Mia Poppe.

NINA'S JOURNEY
SVENSK FILMINDUSTRI. Jan., 2006. Spanish. (Lena Einhorn) Nina Einhorn, Agnieszka Grochowska, Maria Chwalibog, Andrzej Brzeski, Pawel Iwanicki, Iwona Sitkowska, Malgorzata Zajaczkowska, Artur Chamski, Dominika Bednarczyk, Adam Malecki, Marek Wojciechowski, Maria Kaniewska, Halina Rasiakowna, Dorota Liliental, Adam Bauman.

NINETTE
DEAPLANETA. Aug., 2005. Spanish (Jose Luis Garci) Elsa Pataky, Carlos Hipolito, Enrique Villen, Beatriz Carvajal, Fernando Delgado, Mar Regueras, Miguel Rellan.

NO RESERVATIONS
WARNER BROS. July, 2007. (Scott Hicks) Catherine Zeta-Jones, Aaron Eckhart, Abigail Breslin, Bob Balaban, Brian F. O'Byrne, Patricia Clarkson, Celia Weston, Stephanie Berry, John McMartin, Lily Rabe, Jenny Wade.

NOAH'S ARC: JUMPING THE BROOM
LOGO FEATURES (IN U.S.). Oct., 2008. Canadian. (Patrik-Ian Polk) Darryl Stephens, Rodney Chester, Doug Spearman, Christian Vincent, Jensen Atwood, Gregory Kieth, Jonathan Julian, Jason Steed, Gary LeRoi Gray, Tonya Pinkins, Phoebe Snow.

NOBODY'S PERFECT
LORDER FILMS (IN U.S.). Oct., 2009. German. (Niko von Glasow) Stefan Fricke, Sofia Plich, Bianca Vogel, Sigrid Kwella, Doris Pakendorf, Theo Zavelberg, Petra Uttenweiler, Andreas Meyer, Kim Morton, Fred Dove, Mat Fraser, Niko von Glasow, Mandel von Glasow. Documentary.

NOBODY'S SHADOW
MANGA FILMS. Dec., 2006. Spanish. (Pablo Malo) Jose Luis Garcia Perez, Philippine Leroy-Beaulieu, Maria Jesus Valdes, Manuel Moron, Andres Gertrudix, Vicente Romero, Andrea Villanueva.

NOELLE
GENER8XION ENTERTAINMENT. Dec. 8, 2007. (David Wall) David Wall, Kerry Wall, Sean Patrick Brennan, Jean Bates, Curt Dewitz, Daffyd Rees, Brennan Wall.

NORBIT
PARAMOUNT. Feb., 2007. (Brian Robbins) Eddie Murphy, Thandie Newton, Terry Crews, Clifton Powell, Lester "Rasta" Speight, Cuba Gooding, Jr., Eddie Griffin, Katt Williams, Marlon Wayans, Khamani Griffin, Austin Reid, Lindsey Sims-Lewis, China Anderson.
Voice: Charles Murphy.

NORTH COUNTRY
WARNER BROS. Oct., 2005. (Niki Caro) Charlize Theron, Frances McDormand, Sean Bean, Richard Jenkins, Jeremy Renner, Michelle Monaghan, Woody Harrelson, Sissy Spacek, Rusty Schwimmer, Jillian Armenante, Thomas Curtis, Elizabeth Peterson, Linda Emond, Amber Heard, Cole Williams.

NOT EASILY BROKEN

SONY PICTURES ENTERTAINMENT. Jan. 7, 2009. (Bill Duke) Morris Chestnut, Taraji P. Henson, Maeve Quinlan, Kevin Hart, Wood Harris, Eddie Cibrian, Jenifer Lewis, Niecy Nash, Cannon Jay, Albert Hall.

NOT HERE TO BE LOVED

REZO FILMS. Aug., 2005. French. (Stephane Brize) Patrick Chesnais, Anne Consigny, Georges Wilson, Lionel Abelanski, Cyril Couton, Genevieve Mnich, Helene Alexandridis, Anne Benoit, Olivier Claverie.

NOTES ON A SCANDAL

20TH CENTURY FOX. Nov., 2006. (Richard Eyre) Judi Dench, Cate Blanchett, Bill Nighy, Andrew Simpson, Phil Davis, Michael Maloney, Juno Temple, Max Lewis, Joanna Scanlan, Julia McKenzie, Shaun Parkes.

NOTHING LIKE THE HOLIDAYS

OVERTURE FILMS. Dec. 3, 2008. (Alfredo de Villa) Alfred Molina, Elizabeth Pena, Freddy Rodriguez, Luis Guzman, Jay Hernandez, John Leguizamo, Debra Messing, Vanessa Ferlito, Melonie Diaz.

NOTORIOUS

FOX SEARCHLIGHT. Jan. 7, 2009. (George Tillman, Jr.) Angela Bassett, Derek Luke, Jamal Woolard, Anthony Mackie, Antonique Smith, Naturi Naughton, Kevin Phillips, Dennis L.A. White, Marc John Jefferies, Julia Pace Mitchell, Aunjanue Ellis, John Ventimiglia, C. Malik Whitfield, Christopher Jordan, Wallace.

NOUVELLE-FRANCE

METROPOLITAN FILMEXPORT. July, 2005. Canadian-British-French. (Jean Beaudin) Noemie Godin-Vigneau, David La Haye, Sebastien Huberdeau, Juliette Gosselin, Irene Jacob, Tim Roth, Gerard Depardieu, Vincent Perez, Jason Isaacs.

THE NUMBER 23

NEW LINE CINEMA. Feb., 2007. (Joel Schumacher) Jim Carrey, Virginia Madsen, Logan Lerman, Danny Huston, Rhona Mitra, Lynn Collins, Mark Pellegrino, Paul Butcher, Ed Lauter.

O JERUSALEM

SAMUEL GOLDWYN FILMS. Oct. 17, 2007. French-Greek-British-Italian-Israeli-German-U.S. (Elie Chouraqui) J.J. Feild, Said Taghmaoui, Daniel Lundh, Mel Raido, Patrick Bruel, Maria Papas, Peter Polycarpou, Ian Holm, Tovah Feldshuh, Elie Chouraqui.

OBSERVE AND REPORT

WARNER BROS. March 16, 2009. (Jody Hill) Seth Rogen, Ray Liotta, Michael Pena, Anna Faris, Dan Bakkedahl, Jesse Plemons, John Yuan, Matthew Yuan, Celia Weston, Collette Wolfe, Aziz Ansari.

OBSESSED

SONY PICTURES ENTERTAINMENT. April 24, 2009. (Stephen Shill) Idris Elba, Beyonce Knowles, Ali Larter, Bruce McGill, Matthew Humphreys, Scout Taylor-Compton, Jerry O'Connell, Bonnie Perlman, Christine Lahti.

ODETTE TOULEMONDE

PATHE. March, 2007. French-Belgium. (Eric-Emmanuel Schmitt) Catherine Frot, Albert Dupontel, Jacques Weber, Alain Doutey, Camille Japy, Fabrice Murgia, Nina Drecq, Laurence D'Amelio, Jacqueline Bir.

OFF AND RUNNING

WARNER BROS. FRANCE. April, 2008. French. (Tonie Marshall) Nathalie Baye, Edouard Baer, Guy Marchand, Maurice Benichou, Melanie Bernier, Joey Starr, Sandrine Le Berre, Park Jung-hak, Park Sang-kiu, Hippolyte Girardot, Michel Vuillermoz, Bulle Ogier.

THE OFFSIDERS

Dec., 2008. Polish. (Kasia Adamik) Marcin Dorocinski, Rafal Fudalej, Piotra Jagielski, Marek Kalita, Krzysztof Kiersznowski, Eryk Lubos, Maciej Nowak, Dimitri Piersin, Jacek Poniedzialek, Dariusz Toczek, Bartolmiej Topa.

OLE!

ARP SELECTION. Nov., 2005. French. (Florence Quentin) Gerard Depardieu, Gad Elmaleh, Sabine Azema, Valeria Golino, Bob Swaim.

OLE

MEDUSA. Dec., 2006. Italian. (Carlo Vanzina) Massimo Boldi, Vincenzo Salemme, Daryl Hannah, Enzo Salvi, Natalia Estrada, Francesca Lodo, Armando De Razza, Federico Zanandrea, Niccolo Contrino, Brigitta Boccoli, Fabrizia Martano, Ashley Burryt.

OM SHANTI OM

EROS INTL. Nov., 2007. Indian. (Farah Khan) Shah Rukh Khan, Arjun Rampal, Kirron Kher, Shreyas Talpade, Deepika Padukone, Jawed Sheikh, Asawari Joshi, Bindu, Satish Shah, Nitish Pandey, Uvika Chaudhary, Shawar Ali.

OMKARA

EROS ENTERTAINMENT. July, 2006. Indian. (Vishal Bhardwaj) Ajay Devgan, Saif Ali Khan, Viveik Oberoi, Kareena Kapoor, Konkona Sen Sharma, Bipasha Basu, Naseeruddin Shah, Deepak Dobroyal.

THE OMEN

20TH CENTURY FOX. May, 2006. (John Moore) Julia Stiles, Liev Schreiber, Mia Farrow, David Thewlis, Pete Postlethwaite, Michael Gambon, Seamus Davey-Fitzpatrick.

ON PROBATION

NOTRO FILMS. May, 2006. Argentinian. (Damian Szifron) Diego Peretti, Luis Luque, Oscar Ferreiro, Gabriela Izcovich, Martin Adjemian, Tony Lestingi.

ONCE UPON A TIME IN THE OUED

GAUMONT COLUMBIA TRISTAR. Nov., 2005. French-Arabic. (Djamel Bensalah) Julien Courbey, David Saracino, Karina Testa, Marilou Berry, Sid Ahmed Agoumi, Amina Annabi, Medy Kerouani, Mouss Benia, Adrien Saint-Jore, Stephane Soo Mongo, Elie Semoun, Atmen Kelif, Olivier Barroux, Eric Judor, Ramzy Bedia, David Elmaleh.

ONE

MARS DISTRIBUTION. Oct., 2009. French. (Jean-Albert Lievre) Documentary.

ONE FINE DAY

MARS DISTRIBUTION. March, 2006. French. (Philippe Le Guay) Benoit Poelvoorde, Anne Consigny, Rufus, Bernard Bloch, Constance Dolle, Anne Le Ny.

ONE FOR THE ROAD

WILD BUNCH DISTRIBUTION. Oct., 2009. French. (Philippe Godeau) Francois Cluzet, Melanie Thierry, Michel Vuillermoz, Eric Naggar, Lionnel Astier, Raphaeline Goupilleau, Eva Mazauric, Ninon Bretecher, Francoise Pinkwasser, Marilyne Canto, Arthur Moncla, Bernard Campan, Anne Consigny.

ONE HUNDRED NAILS

MIKADO. March, 2007. Italian. (Ermanno Olmi) Raz Degan, Luna Bendandi, Amina Syed, Michele Zattara, Damiano Scaini, Franco Andreani.

ONE MISSED CALL

WARNER BROS PICTURES. Jan. 3, 2008. U.S.-German-Japanese-British. (Eric Valette) .Shannyn Sossamon, Edward Burns, Ana Claudia Talancon, Ray Wise, Azura Skye, Johnny Lewis, Jason Beghe, Margaret Cho, Meagan Good, Rhoda Griffis.

ONE NIGHT

Feb., 2005. Iranian. (Niki Karimi) Hanieh Tavasoli, Saeed Ebrahimifar, Abdolreza Fakhar, Nader Torkaman.

ONE NIGHT WITH THE KING

GENER8XION ENTERTAINMENT. Oct., 2006. (Michael O. Sajbel) Tiffany Dupont, Luke Goss, John Rhys-Davis , John Noble, Tommy "Tiny" Lister, James Callis, Jonah Lotan, Peter O'Toole, Omar Sharif.

ONE OUT OF TWO

01 DISTRIBUTION. March, 2007. Italian. (Eugenio Cappuccio) Fabio Volo, Anita Caprioli, Ninetto Davoli, Giuseppe Battiston, Tresy Taddei, Agostina Belli, Paola Rota, Francesco Crescimone, Emanuela Sparta, Luca Martella, Pino Calabrese.

ONE TO ANOTHER

A STRAND RELEASING, RED ENVELOPE ENTERTAINMENT June, 2007. French. (Pascal Arnold, Jean-Marc Barr) Lizzie Brochere, Arthur Dupont, Guillaume Bache, Pierre Perrier, Nicolas Nollet, Karl E. Landler.

ONE WAY

UNIVERSAL (GERMANY) Jan., 2007. German-Canadian-U.S. (Reto Salimbeni) Til Schweiger, Lauren Lee Smith, Stefanie von Pfetten, Sebastien Roberts, Art Hindle, Sonja Smits, Eric Roberts, Michael Clarke Duncan, Kenneth Welsh, Daniel Kash, Allan Royal, Ned Bellamy, Elisa Moolecherry, Sandra Hess, Jennifer Steele.

ONE WORD FROM YOU

ALTA FILMS. Aug., 2008. Spanish. (Angeles Gonzalez-Sinde) Malena Alterio, Esperanza Pedreno, Antonio de la Torre, Maria Alfonsa Rosso, Chiqui Fernandez, Juan Sanz.

THE OPEN ROAD

ANCHOR BAY. Aug. 28, 2009. (Michael Meredith) Jeff Bridges, Justin Timberlake, Kate Mara, Harry Dean Stanton, Lyle Lovett, Mary Steenburgen, Ted Danson.

OPEN SEASON

SONY PICTURES ENTERTAINMENT. Sept., 2006. (Jill Culton, Roger Allers) Martin Lawrence, Ashton Kutcher, Gary Sinise, Debra Messing, Billy Connolly, Jon Favreau, Georgia Engel, Jane Krakowski, Gordon Tootoosis, Patrick Warburton. Animated.

OPERATION HOMECOMING: WRITING THE WARTIME EXPERIENCE

Feb., 2007. (Richard E. Robbins) Brian Turner, Jack Lewis, Sangjoon Han, Ed Hrivnak, John McCary, Mike Strobl, Colby Buzzell, Tim O'Brien, Joe Haldeman, James Salter, Yusef Komunyakaa, Paul Fussell, Anthony Swofford, Tobias Wolff, Richard Currey. Readers: Beau Bridges, Robert Duvall, Aaron Eckhart, Blair Underwood. Documentary.

ORANGE WINTER
May, 2007. (Andrei Zagdansky) Narrator: Matthew Gurewitsch. Documentary.

ORCHESTRA SEATS
MARS DISTRIBUTION. Feb., 2006. French. (Daniele Thompson) Cecile De France, Valerie Lemercier, Albert Dupontel, Claude Brasseur, Dani, Christopher Thompson, Laura Morante, Sydney Pollack, Suzanne Flon, Annelise Hesme, Michel Vuillermoz.

ORPHAN
WARNER BROS. July 21, 2009. (Jaume Collet-Serra) Vera Farmiga, Peter Sarsgaard, Isabelle Fuhrman, CCH Pounder, Jimmy Bennett, Margo Martindale, Karel Roden, Aryana Engineer, Rosemary Dunsmore.

OSS 117: CAIRO - NEST OF SPIES
GAUMONT COLUMBIA TRISTAR FILMS. April, 2006. French. (Michel Hazanavicius) Jean Dujardin, Berenice Bejo, Aure Atika, Philippe Lefebvre, Constantin Alexandrov, Said Amadis, Laurent Bateau, Claude Brosset, Francois Damiens, Youssef Hamid, Khalid Maadour, Arsene Mosca, Abdallah Moundy, Eric Prat, Richard Sammel.

OTHER DAYS WILL COME
ALTA FILMS. Oct., 2005. Spanish. (Eduard Cortes) Cecilia Roth, Antonio Resines, Fernando Guillen, Nacho Aldeguer, Nadia de Santiago, Reyes Calzado, Alex Angulo.

THE OTHER END OF THE LINE
MGM. Oct. 31, 2008. (James Dodson) Jesse Metcalfe, Shriya Saran, Anupam Kher, Sara Foster, Austin Basis, Larry Miller.

OUR CITY DREAMS
DI SAN LUCA FILMS. Oct. 16, 2008. (Chiara Clemente) Swoon, Ghada Amer, Kiki Smith, Marina Abramovic, Nancy Spero.

THE OUTCOME
CINEMA INDIEGROUP. Oct., 2005. Spanish. (Juan Pinzas) Jose Sancho, Beatriz Rico, Carlos Bardem, Javier Gurruchaga, Miquel Insua, Isabel de Toro, Víctor Rueda, Fernando Epelde.

OUTSIDERS
BADITRI. Nov., 2008. Spanish. (Ventura Pons) Anna Lizaran, Joan Pera, Joan Borras, Dafnis Balduz.

OUTLAW
PATHE. Jan., 2007. British. (Nick Love) Sean Bean, Bob Hoskins, Danny Dyer, Rupert Friend, Lennie James, Sean Harris, Rob Fry, Dave Legeno, Andrew Parfitt, John Standing.

OVER HER DEAD BODY
NEW LINE CINEMA. Jan 14, 2008. (Jeff Lowell) Eva Longoria Parker, Paul Rudd, Lake Bell, Jason Biggs, Lindsay Sloane, Stephen Root.

OVER THE GW
SEVENTH ART RELEASING. June, 2007. (Nick Gaglia) George Gallagher, Kether Donohue, Albert Insinnia, Nicholas Serra, Julia Moriarty.

OVER THE HEDGE
PARAMOUNT. April, 2006. (Tim Johnson, Karey Kirkpatrick) Bruce Willis, Garry Shandling, Steve Carell, Wanda Sykes, William Shatner, Nick Nolte, Thomas Haden Church, Allison Janney, Eugene Levy, Catherine O'Hara, Avril Lavigne, Omid Djalili. Animated.

THE OXFORD MURDERS
WARNER BROS. PICTURES INTL. (IN SPAIN). Jan., 2008. Spanish-British-French. (Alex de la Iglesia) Elijah Wood, John Hurt, Leonor Watling, Julie Cox, Jim Carter, Anna Massey, Alex Cox, Dominique Pinon, Burn Gorman.

P.S. I LOVE YOU
WARNER BROS. Dec. 5, 2007. (Richard LaGravenese) Hilary Swank, Gerard Butler, Lisa Kudrow, Gina Gershon, James Marsters, Kathy Bates, Harry Connick, Jr.

P2
SUMMIT ENTERTAINMENT. Nov. 7, 2007. (Frank Khalfoun) Wes Bentley, Rachel Nichols.

THE PACIFIER
BUENA VISTA. March, 2005. (Adam Shankman) Vin Diesel, Lauren Graham, Faith Ford, Brittany Snow, Max Thieriot, Chris Potter, Morgan York, Scott Thompson, Carol Kane, Brad Garrett, Denis Akiyama, Mung-Ling Tsui.

PAHELI
EROS ENTERTAINMENT. June, 2005. Indian. (Amol Palekar) Shah Rukh Khan, Rani Mukerji, Anupam Kher, Dilip Prabhavalkar, Neena Kulkarni, Padma Rani, Mohan Bhandari, Aditi Govitrikar, Rajpal Yadav, Amitabh Bachchan, Juhi Chawla, Suniel Shetty, Aasif Sheikh, A.K. Hangal, Naseeruddin Shah, Ratna Pathak.

PAINTBALL
FILMAX .July , 2009. Spanish. (Daniel Benmayor) Brendan Mackey, Robert Maskell, Patrick Regis, Jennifer Matter, Peter Vives, Anna Casas.

PAINTED SKIN
GOLDEN SUN FILMS (IN HONG KONG)/EASTERN MORDOR (In China). Sept., 2008. Hong Kong Chinese-Singapore. (Gordon Chan) Donnie Yen, Zhou Xun, Chen Kun, Vicki Zhao, Sun Li, Qi Yuwu, Jiu Song.

THE PAINTED VEIL
WARNER INDEPENDENT PICTURES. Dec., 2006. U.S.-Chinese. (John Curran) Naomi Watts, Edward Norton, Liev Schreiber, Toby Jones, Diana Rigg, Anthony Wong.

PALAIS ROYAL!
GAUMONT COLUMBIA TRISTAR FILMS. Nov., 2005. French. (Valerie Lemercier) Valerie Lemercier, Lambert Wilson, Catherine Deneuve, Michel Aumont, Mathilde Seigner, Denis Podalydes, Michel Vuillermoz, Gisele Casadesus, Gilbert Melki, Etienne Chicot, Maurane, Noel Godin, Franck De La Personne, Pierre Vernier, Veronique Barrault, Michel Fortin.

PANDORUM
OVERTURE FILMS. Sept. 24, 2009. (Christian Alvart) Dennis Quaid, Ben Foster, Cam Gigandet, Antje Traue, Cung Le, Eddie Rouse, Norman Reedus, Andre M. Hennicke.

PAPA
GAUMONT COLUMBIA TRISTAR FILMS. June, 2005. French. (Maurice Barthelemy) Alain Chabat, Martin Combes, Yael Abecassi, Judith Godreche, Anne Benoit, Michel Scourneau.

PAPER HEART
ANCHOR BAY ENTERTAINMENT. Jan. 17, 2009. (Nicholas Jasenovec) Charlyne Yi, Michael Cera, Jake M. Johnson.

PARADISE
(Michael Almereyda) Colin Farrell, Terrence Malick, Sonic Youth, Elina Lowensohn.

PARADISE NOW
Oct., 2005. Dutch-Israeli-German-French. (Hany Abu-Assad) Kais Nashef, Ali Suliman, Lubna Azabal, Amer Hlehel, Hiam Abbass, Ashraf Barhoum, Mohammad Bustami, Mohammad Kosa, Ahmad Fares, Olivier Meidinger.

THE PARALLEL
PIANDARYAN FILMS. May, 2007. (Jack Piandaryan) Margaret Scarborough, Taylor Hart, Darla Gordon, Jeff Swarthout, Elliot V. Kotek, L.G. Ross.

PARANOID PARK
IFC FILMS. May 21, 2007. (Gus Van Sant) Gabe Nevins, Taylor Momsen, Jake Miller, Dan Liu, Lauren McKinney, Scott Green.

PARK BENCHES
UGC. Aug., 2009. French. (Bruno Podalydes) Denis Podalydes, Isabelle Candelier, Pierre Arditi, Michael Lonsdale, Thierry Lhermitte, Josiane Balasko, Benoit Poelvoorde, Bruno Podalydes, Catherine Deneuve, Emmanuelle Devos, Mathieu Almaric, Chaira Mastroianni, Nicole Garcia, Olivier Gourmet, Amira Casar, Julie Depardieu.

PARIS
MARS DISTRIBUTION. Feb., 2008. French. (Cedric Klapisch) Juliette Binoche, Romain Duris, Fabrice Luchini, Albert Dupontel, Francois Cluzet, Karin Viard, Gilles Lellouche, Melanie Laurent, Zinedine Soualem, Julie Ferrier, Olivia Bonamy, Maurice Benichou, Sabrina Ouazani, Kingsley Kum Abang.

PARTLY PRIVATE
6291635 CANADA. April, 2009. Canadian. (Danae Elon) Danae Elon, Philip Touitou, Howard Shaw, Buster Morango, Martin Bergmann, Amos Elon, Kamal Ozkan, James Williams, Dodi Ben Ami. Documentary.

PASSENGERS
SONY PICTURES ENTERTAINMENT. Oct. 24, 2008. (Rodrigo Garcia) Anne Hathaway, Patrick Wilson, David Morse, Andre Braugher, Clea DuVall, Dianne Wiest.

PASSING POSTON
FLY ON THE WALL. Feb. 23, 2008. (Joe Fox, James Nubile) Ruth Okimoto, Kiyo Sato, Mary Higashi, Leon Uyeda. Documentary.

PASSION & POWER: THE TECHNOLOGY OF ORGASM
WABI SABI. Jan. 30, 2008. (Wendy Slick, Emiko Omori) Rachel P. Maines, Dell Williams, Reno, Joanne Webb, BeAnn Sisemore, Pat Davis, Kathryn Young, Nina Townsend, Betty Dodson.
Narrator: Gerri Lawlor.

PASSPORT TO LOVE
EVEREST PRODS. Oct., 2009. Vietnamese. (Victor Vu) Binh Minh, Huy Khanh, Kathy Uyen, Ngoc Diep, Tang Bao Quyen.

PATHFINDER
20th Century Fox. April, 2007. (Marcus Nispel) Karl Urban, Moon Bloodgood, Russell Means, Clancy Brown, Jay Tavare, Ralf Moeller.

PATHOLOGY
MGM. April 18, 2008. (Marc Scholermann) Cast: Milo Ventimiglia, Michael Weston, Alyssa Milano, Lauren Lee Smith, Johnny Whitworth,

John de Lancie, Mei Melancon, Keir O'Donnell, Buddy Lewis, Dan Callahan, Larry Drake.

PAUL BLART: MALL COP

SONY PICTURES ENTERTAINMENT. Jan 8, 2009. (Steve Carr) Kevin James, Keir O'Donnell, Jayma Mays, Raini Rodriguez, Shirley Knight, Stephen Rannazzisi, Peter Gerety, Bobby Cannavale, Adam Ferrara.

PEACE, PROPAGANDA & THE PROMISED LAND

ARAB FILM DISTRIBUTION. March, 2005. (Bathsheba Ratzkoff, Sut Jhally) Seth Ackerman, Rabbi Arik Ascherman, Gila Svirsky, Robert Fisk, Hanan Ashrawi, Noam Chomsky, Neve Gordon, Toufic Haddad, Sam Husseini, Hussein Ibish, Robert Jensen, Rabbi Michael Lerner, Karen Pfeifer, Alisa Solomon, Major Stav Adivi. Narrator: Loretta Alper. Documentary.

PEACEFUL WARRIOR

LIONSGATE. April, 2006. (Victor Salva) Nick Nolte, Scott Mechlowicz, Amy Smart, Tim Dekay, Paul Wesley, Ashton Holmes, Agnes Bruckner, B.J. Britt, Ray Wise.

THE PEARL

FREESTYLE RELEASING. Aug., 2005. U.S.-Mexican. (Alfred Zacharias) Lukas Haas, Tere Tarin, G. Paul "Litefoot" Davis, Jorge Rivero, Richard Harris.

THE PERFECT HOLIDAY

YARI FILM GROUP. Dec. 5, 2007. (Lance Rivera) Morris Chestnut, Gabrielle Union, Terrence Howard, Malik Hammond, Charlie Murphy, Khail Bryant, Faizon Love, Katt Williams, Jeremy Gumbs, Jill Marie Jones, Rachel True. Narrator: Queen Latifah.

PERFECT MAN

WARNER BROS. PICTURES ITALIA. April, 2005. Italian. (Luca Lucini) Francesca Inaudi, Gabriella Pession, Riccardo Scamarcio, Giampaolo Morelli.

THE PERFECT MAN

UNIVERSAL PICTURES. June, 2005. (Mark Rosman) Hilary Duff, Heather Locklear, Chris Noth, Mike O'Malley, Ben Feldman, Vanessa Lengies, Caroline Rhea, Kym Whitley, Aria Wallace.

PERFECT MATCH...

ARP SELECTION. Jan., 2008. French. (Anne-Marie Etienne) Carole Bouquet, Marc Lavoine, Florence Foresti, Jean Senejoux, Francois-Eric Gendron, Jean-Claude Adelin, Marc Fayet, Jean-Paul Bonnaire, Gregory Montel, Yves Lambrecht, Yvan Varco, Ariane Moret.

THE PERFECT SLEEP

CINEMA EPOCH. March 10, 2009. (Jeremy Alter) Anton Pardoe, Roselyn Sanchez, Patrick Bauchau, Peter J. Lucas, Tony Amendola, Sam Thakur, Dominique Vandenberg, Cameron Daddo, Michael Pare.

PERFECT STRANGER

SONY PICTURES ENTERTAINMENT. April, 2007. (James Foley) Halle Berry, Bruce Willis, Giovanni Ribisi, Richard Portnow, Gary Dourdan, Florencia Lozano, Nicki Aycox, Kathleen Chalfant.

PERFUME: THE STORY OF A MURDERER

CONSTANTIN FILM (IN GERMANY)/PARAMOUNT (IN U.S.) Oct. 4, 2006. German-French-Spanish. (Tom Tykwer) Ben Whishaw, Dustin Hoffman, Alan Rickman, Rachel Hurd-Wood, John Hurt, Karoline Herfurth, David Calder, Simon Chandler, Sian Thomas, Jessica Schwarz, Corinna Harfouch, Paul Berrondo, Timothy Davies, Sam Douglas, Harris Gordon, Sara Forestier, Joanna Griffiths, Birgit Minichmayr, Alvaro Roque, Franck Lefeuvre, Jaume Montane, Anna Diogene.

PHAT GIRLZ

20TH CENTURY FOX. April, 2006. (Nnegest Likke) Mo'Nique, Jimmy Jean-Louis, Godfrey, Kendra C. Johnson, Joyful Drake, Jack Noseworthy, Eric Roberts.

PHOBIA 2

GMM TAI HUB CO..Oct., 2009. Thai.

THE PHOTOGRAPHER, HIS WIFE, HER LOVER

FIRST RUN/ICARUS FILMS. July, 2006. U.S.-British. (Paul Yule) Documentary.

PIECE BY PIECE

Nov., 2005. (Nic Hill) Narrator: Senor One. Documentary.

PIERREPOINT

LIONSGATE U.K. (IN U.K.), IFC (IN U.S.). March, 2006. British. (Adrian Shergold) Timothy Spall, Juliet Stevenson, Cavan Clerkin, Eddie Marsan, Christopher Fulford, Ian Shaw, Maggie Ollerenshaw.

PINEAPPLE EXPRESS

SONY PICTURES ENTERTAINMENT. July 15, 2008. (David Gordon Green) Seth Rogen, James Franco, Gary Cole, Rosie Perez, Danny McBride, Kevin Corrigan, Craig Robinson, Amber Heard, Ed Begley, Jr., Nora Dunn, Bobby Lee, James Remar.

THE PINK PANTHER

SONY PICTURES ENTERTAINMENT. Jan., 2006. (Shawn Levy) Steve Martin, Kevin Kline, Jean Reno, Emily Mortimer, Henry Czerny, Kristin Chenoweth, Roger Rees, Beyonce Knowles.

THE PINK PANTHER 2

SONY PICTURES ENTERTAINMENT. Feb. 2, 2009. (Harald Zwart) Steve Martin, Jean Reno, Alfred Molina, Emily Mortimer, Aishwarya Rai Bachchan, Andy Garcia, Lily Tomlin, John Cleese, Yuki Matsuzaki, Geoffrey Palmer, Jeremy Irons, Johnny Hallyday.

PIRATES OF THE CARIBBEAN: AT WORLD'S END

BUENA VISTA. May, 2007. (Gore Verbinski) Johnny Depp, Geoffrey Rush, Orlando Bloom, Keira Knightley, Jack Davenport, Bill Nighy, Jonathan Pryce, Lee Arenberg, Mackenzie Crook, Kevin R. McNally, David Bailie, Stellan Skarsgard, Tom Hollander, Naomie Harris, Chow Yun-fat, Keith Richards.

PIRATES OF THE CARIBBEAN: DEAD MAN'S CHEST

BUENA VISTA. June, 2006. (Gore Verbinski) Johnny Depp, Orlando Bloom, Keira Knightley, Stellan Skarsgard, Bill Nighy, Jack Davenport, Kevin R. McNally, Jonathan Pryce, Lee Arenberg, Mackenzie Crook, Tom Hollander, Naomie Harris, Alex Norton, David Bailie, Martin Klebba, David Schofield.

THE PIRATES WHO DON'T DO ANYTHING: A VEGGIETALES MOVIE

UNIVERSAL. Jan. 5, 2008. (Mike Nawrocki) Phil Vischer, Mike Nawrocki, Cam Clarke, Laura Gerow, Yuri Lowenthal, Alan Lee.

THE PIXAR STORY

July, 2007. (Leslie Iwerks) Brad Bird, Loren Carpenter, Ed Catmull, Diane Disney Miller, Roy Disney, Michael Eisner, Bob Iger, Steve Jobs, Ollie Johnston, Glen Keane, John Lasseter, George Lucas, Alvy Ray Smith, Andrew Stanton, Frank Thomas. Narrator: Stacy Keach. Documentary.

PLATO'S ACADEMY

Aug, 2009. Greek, German. (Filippos Tsitos) Antonis Kafetzopoulos, Anastas Kozdine, Titika Saringouli, Giorgos Souxes, Konstantinos Koronaios, Panayiotis Stamatakis, Maria Zorba.

PLAY THE GAME

SLOWHAND CINEMA RELEASING. Aug. 19, 2009. (Marc Fienberg) Paul Campbell, Andy Griffith, Doris Roberts, Marla Sokoloff, Liz Sheridan, Clint Howard, Rance Howard, Geoffrey Owens, Juliette Jeffers.

THE POET

AMERICAN WORLD PICTURES (IN U.S.) May, 2008. Canadian. (Damian Lee) Jonathan Scarfe, Nina Dobrev, Zachary Bennett, Daryl Hannah, Kim Coates, Roy Scheider, Colm Feore, Lara Daans.

POISON FRIENDS

STRAND RELEASING (IN U.S.)/LES FILMS DU LOSANGE (In France). May, 2006. (Emmanuel Bourdieu) Malik Zidi, Natacha Regnier, Alexandre Steiger, Thibault Vincon, Thomas Blanchard, Jacques Bonnaffe, Dominique Blanc, Francoise Girard, Botum Dupuis.

THE POKER CLUB

RAM FILMS. Oct. 28, 2008. (Tim McCann) Johnathon Schaech, Johnny Messner, Judy Reyes, Loren Dean, Michael Risley, Lori Heuring, Jana Kramer.

POOH'S HEFFALUMP MOVIE

BUENA VISTA PICTURES. Feb., 2005. (Frank Nissen) Voices: Jim Cummings, John Fiedler, Nikita Hopkins, Kath Soucie, Ken Sansom, Peter Cullen, Brenda Blethyn, Kyle Stanger. Animated.

POSEIDON

WARNER BROS. April, 2006. (Wolfgang Petersen) Josh Lucas, Kurt Russell, Jacinda Barrett, Richard Dreyfuss, Emmy Rossum, Mia Maestro, Mike Vogel, Kevin Dillon, Freddy Rodriguez, Jimmy Bennett.

POSSESSED

SHOWBOX/MEDIAPLEX. Oct., 2009. South Korea. (Lee Yong-ju) Nam Sang-mi, Ryu Seung-ryong, Kim Bo-yeon, Shim Eun-gyeong, Mun Heui-gyeong, Jang Yeong-nam, Lee Chang-jin, Oh Ji-eun, Shin Eun-jeong, Kim Yu-jeong.

POST GRAD

20TH CENTURY FOX. July 30, 2009. (Vicky Jenson) Alexis Bledel, Zach Gilford, Michael Keaton, Jane Lynch, Bobby Coleman, Carol Burnett, Rodrigo Santiago, Catherine Reitman, Fred Armisen, Andrew Daly, Kirk Fox, Craig Robinson, J.K. Simmons, Barbara Snaff.

POSTAL

FREESTYLE. Aug., 2007. (Uwe Boll) Zack Ward, Dave Foley, Chris Coppola, Michael Benyaer, Jackie Tohn, J.K. Simmons, Ralf Moeller, Verne Troyer, Chris Spencer, Larry Thomas, Michael Pare, Jodie Stewart, David Huddleston, Seymour Cassel, Erick Avari, Lonelle New, Holly Eglington, Lucie Guest, Uwe Boll, Vince Desiderio, Brent Mendenhall.

PREACHING TO THE CHOIR

FREESTYLE. April, 2006. (Charles Randolph Wright) Billoah Greene, Darien Sills-Evans, Adewale Akinnuoye-Agbaje, Janine Green, Novella Nelson, Tuffy Questell, Eartha Kitt, Patti LaBelle.

PRECIOUS: BASED ON THE NOVEL 'PUSH' BY SAPPHIRE

LEE DANIELS/SMOKEWOOD ENTERTAINMENT (IN U.S.)/ ELEPHANT EYE FILMS, NEW YORK (INTERNATIONAL).

Jan. 17, 2009. (Lee Daniels) Gabourey "Gabby" Sidibe, Mo'Nique, Paula Patton, Lenny Kravitz, Mariah Carey, Sherri Shepherd.

PREMONITION
SONY PICTURES ENTERTAINMENT. Feb., 2007. (Mennan Yapo) Sandra Bullock, Julian McMahon, Nia Long, Kate Nelligan, Amber Valletta, Peter Stormare, Courtney Taylor Burness, Shyann McClure.

THE PRESTIGE
BUENA VISTA. Oct., 2006. (Christopher Nolan) Hugh Jackman, Christian Bale, Michael Caine, Piper Perabo, Rebecca Hall, Scarlett Johansson, Samantha Mahurin, David Bowie, Andy Serkis, Daniel Davis, Jim Piddock, Mark Ryan, Roger Rees.

THE PRICE TO PAY
WILD BUNCH DISTRIBUTION. April, 2007. French. (Alexandra Leclere) Christian Clavier, Nathalie Baye, Gerard Lanvin, Geraldine Pailhas, Patrick Chesnais, Anais Demoustier.

PRICELESS
TFM. Dec., 2006. French. (Pierre Salvadori) Audrey Tautou, Gad Elmaleh, Marie-Christine Adam, Vernon Dobtcheff, Jacques Spiesser, Annelise Hesme.

PRIDE
LIONSGATE. March, 2007. (Sunu Gonera) Terrence Howard, Bernie Mac, Kimberly Elise, Tom Arnold, Brandon Fobbs, Alphonso McAuley, Regine Nehy, Nate Parker, Kevin Phillips, Scott Reeves, Evan Ross, Gary Sturgis.

PRIDE & PREJUDICE
UIP (IN U.K.)/FOCUS FEATURES. Nov., 2005. British-U.S. (Joe Wright) Keira Knightley, Matthew Macfadyen, Brenda Blethyn, Donald Sutherland, Tom Hollander, Judi Dench, Rosamund Pike, Jena Malone, Kelly Reilly, Claudie Blakley, Peter Wight, Penelope Wilton, Simon Woods, Rupert Friend, Carey Mulligan, Talulah Riley, Tamzin Merchant.

PRIME
UNIVERSAL. Oct., 2005. (Ben Younger) Meryl Streep, Uma Thurman, Bryan Greenberg, Jon Abrahams, Zak Orth, Annie Parisse.

PRIMEVAL
BUENA VISTA. Jan., 2007. (Michael Katleman) Dominic Purcell, Orlando Jones, Brooke Langton, Jurgen Prochnow, Gideon Emery, Dumisani Mbebe, Gabriel Malema.

PRINCESS OF THE SUN
REZO FILMS. March, 2007. French-Belgium-Hungarian. (Philippe Leclerc) Voices: Coralie Vanderlinden, David Scarpuzza, Arnaud Leonard, Catherine Conet, Philippe Allard, Mathieu Moreau. Animated.

PRINCESSES
WARNER SOGEFILMS. Aug., 2005. Spanish. (Fernando Leon de Aranoa) Candela Pena, Micaela Nevarez, Mariana Cordero, Llum Barrera, Violeta Perez, Monica van Campen, Flora Alvarez, Maria Ballesteros, Alejandra Lorente, Luis Callejo, Antonio "Morris" Duran, Alberto Ferreiro.

THE PRIZE WINNER OF DEFIANCE, OHIO
GO FISH PICTURES. Sept., 2005. (Jane Anderson) Julianne Moore, Woody Harrelson, Laura Dern, Trevor Morgan, Ellary Porterfield, Simon Reynolds.

THE PRODUCERS
UNIVERSAL (IN U.S.), COLUMBIA (INTERNATIONAL). Nov., 2005. (Susan Stroman) Nathan Lane, Matthew Broderick, Uma Thurman, Will Ferrell, Gary Beach, Roger Bart, Eileen Essell, David Huddleston, Michael McKean, Debra Monk, Andrea Martin, Jon Lovitz.

PROM NIGHT
SONY PICTURES. April 11, 2008. (Nelson McCormick) Brittany Snow, Scott Porter, Jessica Stroup, Dana Davis, Collins Pennie, Kelly Blatz, James Ransone, Brianne Davis, Kellan Lutz, Mary Mara, Ming Wen, Johnathon Schaech, Idris Elba.

THE PROMISE
Jan., 2006. Chinese-U.S. (Chen Kaige).

THE PROMPTER
EUROPACORP DISTRIBUTION. Jan., 2005. French. (Guillaume Pixie) Guillaume Pixie, Frederic Diefenthal, Linda Hardy, Elodie Navarre, Stephane Olivie-Bisson, Vanessa Guedj.

PROOF
MIRAMAX FILMS. July, 2005. (John Madden) Gwyneth Paltrow, Anthony Hopkins, Jake Gyllenhaal, Hope Davis, Gary Houston, Roshan Seth.

THE PROPOSAL
WALT DISNEY STUDIOS MOTION PICTURES. June 13, 2009. (Anne Fletcher) Sandra Bullock, Ryan Reynolds, Mary Steenburgen, Craig T. Nelson, Betty White, Denis O'Hare, Malin Akerman, Oscar Nunez, Aasif Mandvi, Michael Nouri.

THE PROPOSITION
SONY PICTURES. July, 2005. Australian-British. (John Hillcoat) Guy Pearce, Ray Winstone, Emily Watson, Danny Huston, John Hurt, David Wenham, Noah Taylor, David Gulpilil, Leah Purcell, Richard Wilson, Tom E. Lewis.

PROVOKED: A TRUE STORY
EROS INTL. March, 2007. Indian-British. (Jag Mundhra) Aishwarya Rai, Miranda Richardson, Naveen Andrews, Rebecca Pidgeon, Nandita Das, Robbie Coltrane, Steve McFadden, Raji James, Nicholas Irons, Deborah Moore, Lorraine Bruce, Ray Panthaki, Leena Dhingra, Julie T. Wallace, Maxine Finch, Claire Louise Amias, Wendy Albiston, Karen David, Guy Siner.

PSYCHOPATHIA SEXUALIS
KINO INTL. June, 2006. (Bret Wood) Jane Bass, Bryan Davis, Veronika Duerr, Sandra L. Hughes, Ted Manson, Daniel May, Rob Nixon, Lisa Paulsen, Daniel Pettrow, Rachel Sorsa.

PULSE
WEINSTEIN CO. Aug., 2006. (Jim Sonzero) Kristen Bell Dexter, Ian Somerhalder Stone, Zach Grenier, Kel O'Neill, Sam Levine, Octavia L. Spencer, Ron Rifkin, Christina Milian, Jonathan Tucker, Brad Dourif.

PUNISHER: WAR ZONE
LIONSGATE.(IN U.S.). Dec. 1, 2008. (Lexi Alexander) Ray Stevenson, Dominic West, Doug Hutchison, Colin Salmon, Wayne Knight, Dash Mihok, Julie Benz, Stephanie Janusauskas.

THE PURSUIT OF HAPPYNESS
SONY PICTURES ENTERTAINMENT. Nov., 2006. (Gabriele Muccino) Will Smith, Thandie Newton, Jaden Christopher Syre Smith, Brian Howe, James Karen, Dan Castellaneta, Kurt Fuller.

QUANTUM HOOPS
GREEN FOREST FILMS. Oct. 26, 2007. (Rick Greenwald) Roy Dow, Jordan Carlson, Chris Yu, Ben Sexon, Robert Grubbs. Narrator: David Duchovny. Documentary.

QUANTUM OF SOLACE
SONY PICTURES ENTERTAINMENT. Oct. 24, 2008. (Marc Forster) Daniel Craig, Olga Kurylenko, Mathieu Amalric, Judi Dench, Giancarlo Giannini, Gemma Arterton, Jeffrey Wright, David Harbour, Jesper Christensen.

QUARANTINE
SONY PICTURES ENTERTAINMENT. Oct. 10, 2008. (John Erick Dowdle) Jennifer Carpenter, Steve Harris, Jay Hernandez, Johnathon Schaech, Columbus Short, Andrew Fiscella, Rade Sherbedgia, Greg Germann, Bernard White, Dania Ramirez.

QUEENS
WARNER SOGEFILMS. April, 2005. Spanish. (Manuel Gomez Pereira) Betiana Blum, Veronica Forque, Carmen Maura, Marisa Paredes, Mercedes Sampietro, Betiana Blum, Gustavo Salmeron, Unax Ugalde, Hugo Silva, Daniel Hendler, Paco Leon, Raul Jimenez, Tito Valverde, Lluis Homar, Jorge Perugorria.

QUO VADIS, BABY?
MEDUSA. May, 2005. Italian. (Gabriele Salvatores) Angela Baraldi, Gigio Alberti, Claudia Zanella, Andrea Renzi, Elio Germano, Luigi Maria Burruano, Alessandra D'Elia.

RABBIT WITHOUT EARS
WARNER BROS. PICTURES GERMANY. Jan., 2008. German. (Til Schweiger) Til Schweiger, Nora Tschirner, Matthias Schweighoefer, Alwara Hoefels, Juergen Vogel, Rick Kavanian, Armin Rohde, Wolfgang Stumph, Barbara Rudnik, Christian Tramitz, Brigitte Zeh, Paul Maximilian Schueller, Florentine Lahme, Nina Proll, Wladimir Klitschko, Yvonne Catterfeld.

RAB NE BANA DI JODI
YASH RAJ FILMS. Dec., 2008. Indian. (Aditya Chopra) Shah Rukh Khan, Anushka Sharma, Vinay Pathak, Bobby Bedi, Kajol, Bipasha Basu, Preity Zinta, Lara Dutta, Rani Mukerji.

RACE
UTV MOTION PICTURES. April, 2008. Indian. (Abbas Burmawalla, Mustan Burmawalla). Anil Kapoor, Saif Ali Khan, Akshaye Khanna, Bipasha Basu, Katrina Kaif, Sameera Reddy, Dilip Tahil, Johny Lever.

RACE TO WITCH MOUNTAIN
WALT DISNEY PICTURES. March 11, 2009. (Andy Fickman) Dwayne Johnson, AnnaSophia Robb, Carla Gugino, Ciaran Hinds, Alexander Ludwig, Tom Everett Scott, Billy Brown, Richard "Cheech" Marin, Garry Marshall, Kim Richards, Iake Eissinmann.

RACING DREAMS
GOOD/WHITE BUFFALSO ENTERTAINMENT/FIRE TOWER FILMS. April 29, 2009. (Marshall Curry) Annabeth Barnes, Josh Hobson, Brandon Warren.

RAMBO
LIONSGATE. Jan. 23, 2008. (Sylvester Stallone) Sylvester Stallone, Julie Benz, Paul Schulze, Matthew Marsden, Graham McTavish, Tim Kang, Rey Gallegos, Jake La Botz, Maung Maung Khin, Ken Howard.

RANDY AND THE MOB
CAPRICORN PICTURES. Oct. 20, 2007. (Ray McKinnon) Ray McKinnon, Walton Goggins, Lisa Blount, Tim DeKay, Bill Nunn, Brent Briscoe, Paul Ben-Victor, Sam Frihart, Burt Reynolds.

RANG DE BASANTI
UTV MOTION PICTURES. Jan., 2006. Indian. (Rakeysh Omprakash Mehra) Aamir Khan, Siddharth, Atul Kulkarni, Kunal Kapoor, Sharman Joshi, Alice Patten, Soha Ali Khan, Madhavan, Kirron Kher, Om Puri, Waheeda Rehman, Anupam Kher, Steven McKintosh, Mohan Agashe, K.K. Raina, Lekh Tandon.

RAP DREAMS
March, 2006. (Kevin Epps) Kev Kelley, Hectic, Mistah FAB, Shock G, Sway, King Tech, JT Bigga Figga, Herm Lewis, Ray Luv, MacMall, T-Kash, Messy Marv. Documentary.

RATATOUILLE
BUENA VISTA. June, 2007. (Brad Bird) Voices: Patton Oswalt, Ian Holm, Lou Romano, Brian Dennehy, Peter Sohn, Peter O'Toole, Brad Garrett, Janeane Garofalo, Will Arnett, Julius Callahan, James Remar, John Ratzenberger, Teddy Newton, Tony Fucile, Jake Steinfeld, Brad Bird. Narrator: Stephane Roux. Animated.

RAUL - THE RIGHT TO KILL
WARNER BROS. PICTURES ITALIA. April, 2005. Italian. (Andrea Bolognini) Stefano Dionisi, Violante Placido, Nicola Farron, Ernesto Mahieux, Maurizio Mattioli, Laura Betti, Alessandro Haber, Giancarlo Giannini, Guia Jelo, Claudio Spadaro, Pino Ferrara, Laura Troschel.

RAZZLE DAZZLE: A JOURNEY INTO DANCE
PALACE FILMS. Dec., 2006. Australian. (Darren Ashton) Kerry Armstrong, Ben Miller, Shayni Notelovitz, Denise Roberts, Tara Morice, Nadine Garner, Clancy Ryan, Jane Hall, Toni Lamond, Barry Crocker.

THE READER
WEINSTEIN CO. (in U.S.). Nov. 24, 2008. (Stephen Daldry) Kate Winslet, Ralph Fiennes, David Kross, Lena Olin, Bruno Ganz, Matthias Habich, Susanne Lothar, Karoline Herfurth, Alexandra Maria Lara, Volker Bruch, Burghart Klaussner, Hannah Herzsprung, Vijnessa Ferkic.

REAL, THE MOVIE
WARNER SOGEFILMS. Aug., 2005. Spanish. (Borja Manso) Javier Albala, Carlos Coppo, Jessica Bohl, Lair Torrent, Moussa Faye, Maguette Coly, Guillermo Herrera, Manuel Escolano, Keiichirou Sasaki, Ari Ohta.

REALLY SSSUPERCOOL: CHAPTER TWO
01 DISTRIBUTION. Jan., 2006. Italian. (Carlo Vanzina) Diego Abatantuono, Carlo Bucirosso, Ugo Conti, Mauro Di Francesco, Luigi Maria Burruano, Tony Sperandeo, Nino Frassica, Anna Maria Barbera, Sabrina Ferilli.

THE REAPING
Warner Bros. March, 2007. (Stephen Hopkins) Hilary Swank, David Morrissey, Idris Elba, AnnaSophia Robb, Stephen Rea, William Ragsdale, John McConnell, David Jensen, Yvonne Landry, Samuel Garland, Myles Cleveland, Andrea Frankle, Mark Lynch.

REBOUND
20TH CENTURY FOX. June, 2005. (Steve Carr) Martin Lawrence, Wendy Raquel Robinson, Breckin Meyer, Horatio Sanz, Oren Williams, Patrick Warburton, Megan Mullally, Eddy Martin, Steven Christopher Parker, Steven Anthony Lawrence, Logan McElroy, Gus Hoffman, Tara Correa, Amy Bruckner, Alia Shawkat.

[REC]2
FILMAX ENTERTAINMENT. Sept., 2009. Spanish. (Jaume Balaguero, Paco Plaza) Jonathan Mellor, Oscar Sanchez Zafra, Ariel Cassas, Alejandro Casaseca, Pablo Rosso, Manuela Velasco, Andrea Ros, Alex Batllori, Pau Poch.

RED 71
RED 71. July 22, 2008. (Patrick Roddy) Nathan Ginn, Michelle Belegrin, Ted Parks, Josh Marcantel, Angus Scrimm.

THE RED BARON
WARNER BROS. GERMANY. April, 2008. German. (Nikolai Muellerschoen) Matthias Schweighoefer, Lena Headey, Til Schweiger, Joseph Fiennes, Volker Bruch, Maxim Mehmet, Hanno Koffler, Tino Mewes, Steffen Schroeder, Axel Prahl, Ralph Misske, Gitta Schweighoefer, Jan Vlasak, Karsten Kaie.

RED CLIFF
CHINA FILM GROUP CORP. (IN CHINA)/AVEX ENTERTAINMENT (IN JAPAN)/CMC ENTERTAINMENT, TWENTIETH CENTURY FOX (IN TAIWAN)/SHOWBOX (IN SOUTH KOREA). July, 2008. Chinese-Japanese-Taiwanese-South Korean-U.S. (John Woo) Tony Leung Chiu-wai, Takeshi Kaneshiro, Zhang Fengyi, Chang Chen, Vicki Zhao, Hu Jun, Shido Nakamura, Lin Chi-ling, You Yong, Hou Yong, Tong Dawei, Song Jia, Basenzabu, Zang Jinsheng, Zhang Shan, Wang Hui, Shi Xiaohong, Wang Qingxiang, Wang Ning, He Yin, Sun Chun, Jiang Tong, Kou Shixun, Koyuki, Li Hong, Menghe Wuliji, Wang Yuzhang, Zhang Yi, Wu Qi, Chen Changhai, Zhao Chengshun, Wang Zaolai, Xie Gang, Yi Zhen, Jia Hongwei, Guo Chao, Cui Yugui, Xu Fengnian, Ma Jing, Hu Xiaoguang, Ye Hua.

RED CLIFF II
CHINA FILM GROUP CORP. Jan., 2009. Chinese, Japanese, Taiwanese, South Korean, U.S. (John Woo) Tony Leung Chiu-wai, Takeshi Kaneshiro, Fengyi Zhang, Chen Chang, Vicki Zhao, Jun Hu, Shido Nakamura, Chiling Lin, Yong You, Yong Hou, Tong Dawei, Jia Song, Basenzabu, Jinsheng Zang, Shan Zhang, Hui Wang, Xiaohong Shi.

THE RED SHOES
SHOWBOX/MEDIAPLEX. July, 2005. South Korean. (Kim Yong-gyun) Kim Hye-su, Kim Seong-su, Park Yeon-ah, Go Su-heui, Seo Ha-rim, Kim Ji-eun, Son Se-gwang, Lee Eol, Sa Hyeon-jin.

RED-EYE
DREAMWORKS PICTURES. Aug., 2005. (Wes Craven) Rachel McAdams, Cillian Murphy, Brian Cox, Jayma Mays, Jack Scalia.

REDLINE
CHICAGO PICTURES. April, 2007. (Andy Cheng) Nathan Phillips, Nadia Bjorlin, Angus Macfadyen, Tim Matheson, Eddie Griffin, Jesse Johnson.

REFUSENIK
ABRAMORAMA. April 1, 2008. (Laura Bialis) Zev Yaroslavsky, Vladimir Slepak, Anatoly Shcharansky, Yuli Edelstein, Valery Panov, Elie Wiesel, Alan Dershowitz, George Shultz, Mikhail Gorbachev.

RENAISSANCE
PATHE DISTRIBUTION (IN FRANCE). March, 2006. French-Luxembourgors-British. (Christian Volckman) Actors/Voices: Robert Dauney, Patrick Floersheim, Crystal Shepherd-Cross, Laura Blanc, Isabelle Van Waes, Virginie Mery, Max Hayter, Gabriel Le Doze, Marco Lorenzini, Marc Cassot, Jerome Causse, Bruno Choel, Jean-François Wolff, Marc Alfos. Animated.

RENO 911!: MIAMI
20TH CENTURY FOX (IN U.S.) AND PARAMOUNT PICTURES (INTERNATIONAL). Feb., 2007. (Robert Ben Garant) Carlos Alazraqui, Mary Birdsong, Robert Ben Garant, Kerri Kenney-Silver, Thomas Lennon, Wendi McLendon-Covey, Niecy Nash, Cedric Yarbrough.

RENT
SONY PICTURES ENTERTAINMENT. Nov., 2005. (Chris Columbus) Anthony Rapp, Adam Pascal, Rosario Dawson, Jesse L. Martin, Wilson Jermaine Heredia, Idina Menzel, Tracie Thoms, Taye Diggs, Aaron Lohr, Sarah Silverman, Wayne Wilcox, Anna Deveare Smith, Daryl Edwards, Daniel London, Aisha de Haas.

RESIDENT EVIL: EXTINCTION
SONY PICTURES ENTERTAINMENT. Sept., 2007. Canadian-British. (Russell Mulcahy) Milla Jovovich, Oded Fehr, Ali Larter, Iain Glen, Ashanti, Christopher Egan, Spencer Locke, Matthew Marsden, Linden Ashby, Jason O'Mara, Mike Epps.

THE RETURN
ROGUE PICTURES. Nov., 2006. (Asif Kapadia) Sarah Michelle Gellar, Peter O'Brien, Adam Scott, Kate Beahan, J.C. Mackenzie, Erinn Allison, Sam Shepard, Darrian McClanahan.

REVOLUTIONARY ROAD
PARAMOUNT. Nov. 15, 2008. (Sam Mendes) Leonardo DiCaprio, Kate Winslet, Kathy Bates, Michael Shannon, Kathryn Hahn, David Harbour, Dylan Baker, Richard Easton, Zoe Kazan, Jay O. Sanders, Max Casella.

RIGHTEOUS KILL
OVERTURE FILMS. Sept. 10, 2008. (Jon Avnet) Robert De Niro, Al Pacino, Curtis Jackson, Carla Gugino, Donnie Wahlberg, Trilby Glover, Shirly Brener, Melissa Leo, Oleg Taktarov, Alan Rosenberg, Alan Blumenfeld, Rob Dyrdek, Brian Dennehy, John Leguizamo.

THE RING FINGER
MEMENTO FILMS. June, 2005. French-German-British. (Diane Bertrand) Olga Kurylenko, Marc Barbe, Stipe Erceg, Edith Scob, Hanns Zischler, Sotigui Kouyate, Doria Achour, Anne Benoit, Louis de Winter.

THE RING TWO
DREAMWORKS. March, 2005. (Hideo Nakata) Naomi Watts, Simon Baker, David Dorfman, Elizabeth Perkins, Gary Cole, Sissy Spacek, Ryan Merriman, Emily VanCamp, Daveigh Chase, Kelly Overton, James Lersure.

THE RINGER
20TH CENTURY FOX. Dec., 2005. (Barry W. Blaustein) Johnny Knoxville, Brian Cox, Katherine Heigl, Geoffrey Arend, Edward Barbanell, Bill Chott, Leonard Flowers, Leonard Earl Howze, Jed Rees, John Taylor, Luis Avalos, Zen Gesner, Steve Levy.

RIP! A REMIX MANIFESTO
June, 2009. Canadian. (Brett Gaylor) Girl Talk, Marybeth Peters, Cory Doctorow, Lawrence Lessig, Dan O'Neill, Mark Hosler, Jammie Thomas, Bruce Lehman. Gilberto Gil.

RISE: BLOOD HUNTER
SONY PICTURES ENTERTAINMENT. April, 2007. (Sebastian

Gutierrez) Lucy Liu, Michael Chiklis, Carla Gugino, James D'Arcy, Samaire Armstrong, Robert Forster, Cameron Goodman, Margo Harshman, Nick Lachey, Marilyn Manson, Julio Oscar Mechoso, Allan Rich, Cameron Richardson, Kevin Wheatley.

RIVALS

STUDIO CANAL. March, 2008. French. (Jacques Maillot) Guillaume Canet, Francois Cluzet, Clotilde Hesme, Marie Denarnaud, Helene Foubert, Eric Bonicatto, Olivier Perrier, Carole Franck, Mehdi Nebbou, Lui Thuillier, Marie Gili-Pierre, Fred Ulysse, Nadia Fossier, Pierre Pellet, Cyril Couton, Marc Bodnard, Thierry Levaret.

RIVALS

ON PICTURES. June, 2008. Spanish. (Fernando Colomo) Ernesto Alterio, Gonzalo de Castro, Santi Millan, Kira Miro, Juanjo Puigcorbe, Maria Pujalte, Jorge Sanz, Rosa Maria Sarda, Goya Toledo, Adrian Portugal.

ROAD TO ITALY

SONET FILM. Nov., 2005. Swedish. (Daniel Lind Lagerlof) Livia Millhagen, Karl Linnertorp, Adam Palsson, Anna Lyons, Johan Holmberg, Maria Fahl Vikander, Mats Andersson.

ROADSIDE ROMEO

YASH RAJ FILMS (IN INDIA/U.S.). Oct., 2008. Indian-U.S. (Jugal Hansraj) Saif Ali Khan, Kareena Kapoor, Javed Jaffrey, Vrajesh Hirjee, Tannaz Irani, Suresh N. Menon, Kiku Sharda, Sanjay Mishra. Animated.

ROBOTS

20TH CENTURY FOX. March, 2005. (Chris Wedge) Voices: Ewan McGregor, Halle Berry, Robin Williams, Greg Kinnear, Mel Brooks, Drew Carey, Jim Broadbent, Amanda Bynes, Jennifer Coolidge, Stanley Tucci, Dianne Wiest, Paul Giamatti, Natasha Lyonne, Terry Bradshaw, Dan Hedaya, James Earl Jones, Jay Leno, Al Roker, Stephen Tobolowsky, Harland Williams. Animated.

ROCK BOTTOM: GAY MEN AND METH

OUTCAST FILMS. March, 2007. (Jay Corcoran) Documentary.

THE ROCKER

20TH CENTURY FOX. July 22, 2008. (Peter Cattaneo) Rainn Wilson, Christina Applegate, Josh Gad, Teddy Geiger, Emma Stone, Will Arnett, Fred Armisen, Bradley Cooper, Jeff Garlin, Lonny Ross, Jason Sudeikis.

THE ROCKET: THE LEGEND OF ROCKET RICHARD

PALM PICTURES (IN U.S.). Dec., 2007. Canadian. (Charles Biname) Roy Dupuis, Stephen McHattie, Julie LeBreton, Michel Barrette, Pierre-Francois Legendre, Philip Craig, Patrice Robitaille, Remy Girard.

ROCKY BALBOA

MGM. Nov., 2006. (Sylvester Stallone) Sylvester Stallone, Burt Young, Antonio Tarver, Geraldine Hughes, Milo Ventimiglia, Tony Burton, A.J. Benza, James Francis Kelly, III, Lou DiBella, Mike Tyson, Woodrow W. Paige, Skip Bayles, Jay Crawford, Brian Kenny, Dana Jacobson, Chuck Johnson, Jim Lampley, Larry Merchant, Max Kellerman, LeRoy Neiman, Bert Randolph Sugar, Bernard Fernandez, Michael Buffer, Talia Shire.

ROGUE

ROADSHOW FILMS (in Australia)/THE WEINSTEIN CO. Weinstein Co. (in U.S.). Nov. 8, 2007. (Greg McLean) Radha Mitchell, Michael Vartan, Sam Worthington, John Jarratt, Stephen Curry, Heather Mitchell, Geoff Morrell, Mia Wasikowska, Robert Taylor, Caroline Brazier, Celia Ireland.

ROLE MODELS

UNIVERSAL. Oct. 8, 2008. (David Wain) Seann William Scott, Paul Rudd, Christopher Mintz-Plasse, Jane Lynch, Bobb'e J. Thompson, Elizabeth Banks.

ROLL BOUNCE

20TH CENTURY FOX. Sept., 2005. (Malcolm D. Lee) Bow Wow, Chi McBride, Mike Epps, Wesley Jonathan, Kellita Smith, Meagan Good, Khleo Thomas, Nick Cannon, Rick Gonzalez, Marcus T. Paulk, Brandon T. Jackson, Jurnee Smollett, Charlie Murphy, Paul Wesley, Wayne Brady.

ROLLIN WITH THE NINES

FRAMEWORK/MAIDEN VOYAGE. April, 2006. British. (Julian Gilbey) Vas Blackwood, Robbie Gee, Naomi Taylor, Terry Stone, Roffem Morgan, Billy Murray, Jason Flemyng, Simon Webbe, George Calil, Dominic Alan-Smith, William Gilbey, Kingsley Pilgrim, Ian Virgo, Patrick Regis.

ROMANTIC ISLAND

SBSI CO. April, 2009. South Korean. (Kang Chul-woo) Lee Sun-kyun, Lee Soo-kyung, Lee Min-ki, Eugene, Lee Mun-shik.

ROMULUS, MY FATHER

March, 2007. Australian. (Richard Roxburgh) Eric Bana, Franka Potente, Kodi Smit-McPhee, Marton Csokas, Russell Dykstra, Jacek Koman.

THE ROSES OF THE DESERT

MIKADO. Dec., 2006. Italian. (Mario Monicelli) Michele Placido, Giorgio Pasotti, Alessandro Haber, Claudio Bigagli, Moran Atias, Tatti Sanguineti.

ROUND TWO

WARNER SOGEFILMS. Nov., 2005. Spanish. (Daniel Cebrian) Dario Grandinetti, Alex Gonzalez, Eva Marciel, Alberto Ferreiro, Maru Valdivielso, Laura Aparicio, Pepo Oliva, Francesc Orella.

ROVING MARS

BUENA VISTA PICTURES. Jan., 2006. (George Butler) Steve Squyres, Rob Manning, Dr. Charles Elachi, Wayne Lee. Narrator: Paul Newman. Documentary.

RUDO Y CURSI

Sony Pictures Classics (in North America). Jan., 2009. Mexican. (Carlos Cuaron) Gael Garcia Bernal, Diego Luna, Guillermo Francella, Dolores Heredia, Adriana Paz, Jessica Mas.

THE RUINS

DREAMWORKS-PARAMOUNT. March 3, 2008. (Carter Smith) Jonathan Tucker, Jena Malone, Shawn Ashmore, Laura Ramsey, Joe Anderson, Dimitri Baveas, Sergio Calderon.

RULES OF DATING

CJ ENTERTAINMENT. July, 2005. South Korean. (Han Jae-rim) Park Hae-il, Gang Hye-jeong, Park Jun-myeong, Galina Park.

RULES OF SILENCE

March, 2005. French. (Orso Miret) Mathieu Demy, Natacha Regnier, Thierry de Peretti, Muriel Solvay, Angele Massei, Pierre-Marie Mosconi.

RUMOR HAS IT...

WARNER BROS. Dec., 2005. (Rob Reiner) Jennifer Aniston, Kevin Costner, Shirley MacLaine, Mark Ruffalo, Richard Jenkins, Christopher McDonald, Steve Sandvoss, Mena Suvari.

RUNAWAY HORSE

CONCORDE FILMVERLEIH. Nov., 2007. German. (Rainer Kaufmann) Ulrich Noethen, Ulrich Tukur, Katja Riemann, Petra Schmidt-Schaller.

RUNNING SCARED

NEW LINE CINEMA. Feb., 2006. (Wayne Kramer) Paul Walker, Cameron Bright, Vera Farmiga, Karel Roden, Johnny Messner, Ivana Milicevic, Chazz Palminteri, Alex Neuberger, Michael Cudlitz, Bruce Altman, Elizabeth Mitchell, Arthur Nascarella, John Noble, Idalis DeLeon, David Warshofsky.

RUNNING WITH SCISSORS

SONY PICTURES ENTERTAINMENT. Oct., 2006. (Ryan Murphy) Annette Bening, Brian Cox, Joseph Fiennes, Evan Rachel Wood, Alec Baldwin, Joseph Cross, Jill Clayburgh, Gwyneth Paltrow, Gabrielle Union, Kristin Chenoweth, Patrick Wilson, Colleen Camp, Dagmara Dominczyk, Jack Kaeding.

RUSH HOUR 3

NEW LINE CINEMA. July, 2007. (Brett Ratner) Jackie Chan, Chris Tucker, Hiroyuki Sanada, Youki Kudoh, Max Von Sydow, Yvan Attal, Noemie Lenoir, Zhang Jingchu, Tzi Ma, Dana Ivey, Henry O., Sun Ming Ming, Julie Deparadieu.

RUSSIAN DOLLS

MARS DISTRIBUTION. June, 2005. French-British. (Cedric Klapisch) Romain Duris, Audrey Tautou, Cecile De France, Kelly Reilly, Kevin Bishop, Evguenya Obraztsova, Irene Montala, Lucy Gordon, Gary Love, Aissa Maiga, Olivier Saladin, Martine Demaret, Pierre Cassignard, Cristina Brondo, Federico D'Anna, Barnaby Metschurat, Christian Pagh, Pierre Cohen Victor, Zinedine Soualem.

RV

SONY PICTURES ENTERTAINMENT. April, 2006. (Barry Sonnenfeld) Robin Williams, Jeff Daniels, Cheryl Hines, Kristin Chenoweth, Joanna "JoJo" Levesque, Josh Hutcherson, Will Arnett, Hunter Parrish, Brendan Fletcher, Rob LaBelle, Brian Markinson.

SAAWARIYA

SONY PICTURES ENTERTAINMENT. Nov., 2007. Indian. (Sanjay Leela Bhansali) Ranbir Kapoor, Sonam Kapoor, Rani Mukerji, Salman Khan, Zohra Segal, Begum Para.

SACCO AND VANZETTI

FIRST RUN FEATURES. March, 2007. (Peter Miller) Howard Zinn, Nunzio Pernicone, Michael Topp, Lincoln Robbins, Mary Anne Trasciatti, Anton Coppola, Arlo Guthrie, Studs Terkel, Guiliano Montaldo. Readers: Tony Shalhoub, John Turturro. Documentary.

SACRED HEART

MEDUSA FILM. Feb., 2005. Italian. (Ferzan Ozpetek) Barbora Bobulova, Camille Dugay Comencini, Lisa Gastoni, Massimo Poggio.

SAHARA

PARAMOUNT PICTURES. April, 2005. (Breck Eisner) Matthew McConaughey, Steve Zahn, Penelope Cruz, Lambert Wilson, Glynn Turman, Delroy Lindo, William H. Macy, Lennie James, Rainn Wilson.

SAINT JACQUES... LA MECQUE

UGC DISTRIBUTION. Nov., 2005. French. (Coline Serreau) Muriel Robin, Artus de Penguern, Jean-Pierre Darroussin, Pascal Legitimus,

Marie Bunel, Marie Kremer, Flore Vannier-Moreau, Aymen Saidi, Nicolas Cazale.

SALAAM NAMASTE

YASH RAJ FILMS. Sept., 2005. Indian. (Siddharth Raj Anand) Saif Ali Khan, Preity Zinta, Arshad Warsi, Tania Zaetta, Jugal Hansraj, Ravi Khote, Kunal Vijaykar, Kavita Kapoor, Javed Jaffrey, Maria Goretti, Abhishek Bachchan.

SALAAM-E-ISHQ

Jan., 2007. Indian. (Nikhil Advani) Vidya Balan, John Abraham, Govinda, Anil Kapoor, Anjana Sukhani, Juhi Chawla, Shannon Esrechowitz, Priyanka Chopra, Salman Khan, Akshaye Khanna, Ayesha Takia, Sohail Khan, Isha Koppikar, Aroon Bakshi, Prem Chopra, Mangal Kenkre, Kamini Khanna, Manoj Pahwa, Atul Parchure, Kushal Punjabi, Deepak Qazir, Saurabh Shukla. Voice: Karan Johar.

SAMSON & DELILAH

FOOTPRINT FILMS. March, 2009. Australian. (Warwick Thornton) Marissa Gibson, Rowan McNamara, Scott Thornton, Mitjili Gibson.

SANS ARME, HI HAINE, NI VIOLENCE

MARS DISTRIBUTION. April, 2008. French. (Jean-Paul Rouve) Jean-Paul Rouve, Alice Taglioni, Gilles Lellouche, Maxime Leroux, Patrick Bosso, Anne Marivin, Renan Carteaux, Jean-Philippe Puymartin, Pom Klementieff, Arsene Mosca.

THE SANTA CLAUSE 3: THE ESCAPE CLAUSE

BUENA VISTA. Nov., 2006. (Michael Lembeck) Tim Allen, Elizabeth Mitchell, Judge Reinhold, Wendy Crewson, Ann-Margret, Eric Lloyd, Spencer Breslin, Liliana Mumy, Alan Arkin, Martin Short, Abigail Breslin, Art LaFleur, Aisha Tyler, Kevin Pollak, Jay Thomas, Michael Dorn.

SANTOS

BUENA VISTA INTERNACIONAL (IN SPAIN). Sept., 2008. Spanish-Chilean. (Nicolas Lopez) Javier Gutierrez, Elsa Pataky, Pablo Pinedo, Leonardo Sbaraglia, Guillermo Toledo.

SARAH LANDON AND THE PARANORMAL HOUR

FREESTYLE RELEASING. Oct. 19, 2007. (Lisa Comrie) Rissa Walters, Dan Comrie, Brian Comrie.

SATURN IN OPPOSITION

MEDUSA. Feb., 2007. Italian-French-Turkish. (Ferzan Ozpetek) Stefano Accorsi, Margherita Buy, Pierfrancesco Favino, Serra Yilmaz, Ennio Fantastichini, Ambra Angiolini, Luca Argentero, Isabella Ferrari, Michelangelo Tommaso, Filippo Timi, Luigi Diberti, Lunetta Savino, Milena Vukotic, Benedetta Gargari, Gabriele Paolino.

SAVING SHILOH

NEW DOG DISTRIBUTION. May, 2006. (Sandy Tung) Jason Dolley, Scott Wilson, Gerald McRaney, Ann Dowd, Jordan Garrett.

SAW III

LIONSGATE. Oct., 2006. (Darren Lynn Bousman) Tobin Bell, Shawnee Smith, Angus MacFadyen, Bahar Soomekh, Dina Meyer, Mpho Koaho, Barry Flatman.

SAW IV

LIONSGATE. Oct. 26, 2007. (Darren Lynn Bousman) Tobin Bell, Costas Mandylor, Scott Patterson, Betsy Russell, Lyriq Bent, Athena Karkanis, Billy Otis, Donnie Wahlberg, Angus Macfadyen, Shawnee Smith, Bahar Soomekh, Dina Meyer, Justin Louis.

SAW V

LIONSGATE. Oct. 24, 2008. (David Hackl) Tobin Bell, Costas Mandylor, Scott Patterson, Betsy Russell, Mark Rolston, Julie Benz, Carlo Rota, Mike Butters, Meagan Good, Joris Jarsky.

SAW VI

LIONSGATE. Oct. 23, 2009. (Kevin Greutert) Tobin Bell, Costas Mandylor, Betsy Russell, Mark Rolston, Peter Outerbridge, Shawnee Smith, Athena Karkanis, Samantha Lemole, Caroline Cave, George Newbern, Tanedra Howard.

SAY GOOD DAY TO DAD

Nov., 2005. Spanish-Cuban. (Fernando Vargas) Isabel Santos, Paola Rios, Jose Veliz, Bismark Virhuez, Soledad Ardaya, Fabrizio Prada.

THE SCAR

CAMERA OSCURA. Aug., 2005. Spanish. (Pablo Llorca) Angela Pugh, Ludovic Tattevin, Joan Keary, Santi Olmo.

SCARY MOVIE 4

DIMENSION FILMS. April, 2006. (David Zucker) Anna Faris, Regina Hall, Craig Bierko, Simon Rex, Anthony Anderson, Carmen Electra, Dr. Phil, Leslie Nielsen, Shaquille O'Neal, Cloris Leachman, Bill Pullman, Chris Elliott, Molly Shannon, Michael Madsen, Kevin Hart, Conchita Campbell, Chris Williams, Charlie Sheen, Alonzo Bodden, Dave Attel, D-Ray, Chingy, Lil' Jon, Young Bloodz, Fabolous.

SCENES OF A SEXUAL NATURE

MIRACLE COMMUNICATIONS. Oct. 2006. British. (Ed Blum) Holly Aird, Eileen Atkins, Hugh Bonneville, Tom Hardy, Douglas Hodge, Adrian Lester, Andrew Lincoln, Ewan McGregor, Gina McKee, Sophie Okonedo, Eglantine Rembauville, Mark Strong, Catherine Tate, Polly Walker, Benjamin Whitrow.

SCHOOL FOR SCOUNDRELS

MGM. Sept., 2006. (Todd Phillips) Billy Bob Thornton, Jon Heder, Jacinda Barrett, Michael Clarke Duncan, Luis Guzman, David Cross, Horatio Sanz, Sarah Silverman, Matt Walsh, Todd Louiso, Jon Glaser, Paul Scheer, Ben Stiller.

SCOOP

FOCUS FEATURES. June, 2006. (Woody Allen) Woody Allen, Hugh Jackman, Scarlett Johansson, Ian McShane, Charles Dance, Romola Garai, Fenella Woolgar, Julian Glover, Victoria Hamilton.

SEA OF DREAMS

SUCCESS FILMS. Sept., 2007. (Jose Bojorquez) Johnathon Schaech, Sendi Bar, Angelica Maria, Nicholas Gonzalez, Seymour Cassel, Sonia Braga, Julio Bekhor, Gaston Melo, Tina Romero, Pablo Santos, Daniela Schmidt, Jessica Valdes.

SEA MONSTERS: A PREHISTORIC ADVENTURE

NATIONAL GEOGRAPHIC GIANT SCREEN FILMS. Oct. 8, 2007. (Sean Phillips) Narrator: Liev Schreiber. Documentary.

THE SEASON OF MISTS

Aug., 2008. Russian-British. (Anna Tchernakova) Marina Blake, Ifan Huw Dafydd, Sergey Chonishvilli, Dudley Sutton, Alexandra-Maria Bryars, Heather Chasen, Eve Pearce, Janet Henfrey, Larissa Panchenko, Yuri Nifontov, Alexander Miakushko, Alexander Rezalin.

THE SECOND CHANCE

SONY PICTURES ENTERTAINMENT. Feb., 2006. (Steve Taylor) Michael W. Smith, Jeff Obafemi Carr, J. Don Ferguson, Lisa Arrindell Anderson, David Alford, Henry Haggard, Kenda Benward, Jonathan Thomas, Calvin Hobson, Bobby Daniels, Shirley Cody, Peggy Walton Walker, Vilia Steele.

SECRET

SONY PICTURES TAIWAN (IN TAIWAN)/EDKO (IN HONG KONG). Sept., 2007. Taiwan-Hong Kong. (Jay Chou) Jay Chou, Guey Lun-mei, Anthony Wong, Alice Tzeng, Su Ming-ming, Huang Chun-lang.

SECRETS OF STATE

UGC DISTRIBUTION. Oct., 2008. French. (Philippe Haim) Gerard Lanvin, Vahina Giocante, Nicolas Duvauchelle, Simon Abkarian, Rachida Brakni, Medhi Nebbou, Aurelien Wiik, Nicolas Marie, Katia Lewkowicz, Catherine Hiegel.

SEE NO EVIL

LIONSGATE. May, 2006. (Gregory Dark) Kane (Glen Jacobs), Christine Vidal, Michael J. Pagan, Samantha Noble, Steven Vidler, Cecily Polson, Luke Pegler, Rachael Taylor, Penny McNamee, Craig Horner, Mikhail Wilder, Tiffany Lamb.

THE SEEKER

20TH CENTURY FOX. Oct. 2, 2007. (David L. Cunningham) Alexander Ludwig, Christopher Eccleston, Frances Conroy, Ian McShane, Wendy Crewson, John Benjamin Hickey, Gregory Smith, James Cosmo, Jim Piddock, Drew Tyler Bell, Amelia Warner, Edmund Entin, Gary Entin, Emma Lockhart, Jonathan Jackson.

SEMEN, A LOVE STORY

DEAPLANETA. July, 2005. Spanish-British. (Ines Paris, Daniela Fejerman) Ernesto Alterio, Leticia Dolera, Hector Alterio, Maria Pujalte, Maria Isbert.

THE SENTINEL

20TH CENTURY FOX. April, 2006. (Clark Johnson) Michael Douglas, Kiefer Sutherland, Eva Longoria, Martin Donovan, Ritchie Coster, Kim Basinger, Blair Brown, David Rasche, Kristin Lehman, Raynor Scheine, Chuck Shamata, Paul Calderon, Clarque Johnson.

SEOUL RAIDERS

MEDIA ASIA. April, 2005. Hong Kong. (Jingle Ma) Tony Leung Chiu-wai, Richie Ren, Shu Qi, James Kim, Jeong Jin, Momo Tian, Saki Seto, Hanna Jo, Choi Yeo-jin, Jo Su-hyeon.

SEPARATE LIES

20TH CENTURY FOX. Aug., 2005. British. (Julian Fellowes) Tom Wilkinson, Emily Watson, Rupert Everett, Linda Bassett, David Harewood, John Neville, Hermione Norris.

SEPTEMBER DAWN

SLOW HAND RELEASING/BLACK DIAMOND PICTURES. April, 2007. (Christopher Cain) Jon Voight, Trent Ford, Tamara Hope, Jon Gries, Taylor Handley, Huntley Ritter, Krisinda Cain, Shaun Johnston, Lolita Davidovich, Dean Cain, Terence Stamp.

THE SEPTEMBER ISSUE

A&E INDIEFILMS. Jan. 17, 2009. Thakoon Panichgul, Andre Leon Talley, Grace Coddington, Anna Wintour, Mario Testino, Patrick Demarchelier, Oscar de la Renta, Vera Wang, Jean Paul Gaultier.

SEPTEMBERS

SAGRERA TV. July, 2007. Spanish. (Carles Bosch) Documentary.

SERIOUS MOONLIGHT

NIGHT & DAY PICTURES and ALL FOR A FILMS. April 25, 2009. (Cheryl Hines) Meg Ryan, Timothy Hutton, Kristen Bell, Justin Long

SERKO

GEBEKA FILMS. April, 2006. French. (Joel Farges) Aleksei Chadov, Jacques Gamblin, Marina Kim, Larissa Batourova, Nicolas Gouraid,

Anya Petoushinova, Roman Jilkin, Nicolai Smirnov.

SEVEN MINUTES IN HEAVEN

Nov., 2008. Israeli-French-Hungarian. (Omri Givon) Reymond Amsalem, Eldad Fribas, Nadav Nates, Benjamin Jagendorf.

SEVEN POUNDS

SONY PICTURES ENTERTAINMENT. Dec. 3, 2008. (Gabriele Muccino) Will Smith, Rosario Dawson, Woody Harrelson, Michael Ealy, Barry Pepper, Elpidia Carrillo, Bill Smitrovich, Robinne Lee, Tim Kelleher, Joseph A. Nunez, Gina Hecht.

SEVIGNE

SHERLOCK FILMS. April, 2005. Spanish. (Marta Balletbo-Coll) Anna Azcona, Marta Balletbo-Coll, Josep Maria Pou, Eduard Farelo.

SEX AND BREAKFAST

FIRST LOOK STUDIOS. Nov. 2, 2007. (Miles Brandman) Macaulay Culkin, Kuno Becker, Eliza Dushku, Alexis Dziena, Joanna Miles, Eric Lively, Jaime Ray Newman.

SEX AND THE CITY

NEW LINE CINEMA. May 14, 2008. (Michael Patrick King) Sarah Jessica Parker, Kim Cattrall, Kristin Davis, Cynthia Nixon, Chris Noth, Candice Bergen, Jennifer Hudson, David Eigenberg, Evan Handler, Jason Lewis, Mario Cantone, Lynn Cohen, Willie Garson.

SEX DRIVE

SUMMIT ENTERTAINMENT. Sept. 24, 2008. (Sean Anders) Josh Zuckerman, Amanda Crew, Clark Duke, James Marsden, Seth Green, Alice Greczyn, Katrina Bowden.

SEX, HOPE AND LOVE

SONET FILM. May, 2005. Swedish. (Lisa Ohlin) Krister Henriksson, Ing-Marie Carlson, Lennart Jahkel, Mira Eklund, Oliver Lofteen, Else Marie Brandt, Peter Edding, Kristina Radstrom.

SHADOW BOXING

March, 2005. Russian. (Aleksei Sidorov) Denis Nikiforov, Yelena Panova, Andrei Panin, John Amos, Ivan Makarevich, Aleksandr Kyznetsov, Dmitri Shevchenko, Pavel Derevyanko.

SHADOWBOXER

TETON FILMS. July, 2006. (Lee Daniels) Cuba Gooding, Jr., Helen Mirren, Vanessa Ferlito, Macy Gray, Joseph Gordon-Levitt, Mo'Nique, Stephen Dorff.

THE SHADOWLESS

NARSIST FILM. April, 2009. Turkish. (Umit Unal) Selcuk Yontem, Hakan Karahan, Taner Birsel, Onuryay Everentan, Yigit Kusbeygi, Tales Farzan, Arsen Gurzap, Umut Karardag, Bigkem Karavus, Ertan Saban, Fuat Onan, Serkan Senalp, Aydemir Akbas, Zeynep Kumral, Ozay Fecht.

THE SHAGGY DOG

BUENA VISTA. March, 2006. (Brian Robbins) Tim Allen, Robert Downey, Jr., Kristin Davis, Danny Glover, Spencer Breslin, Jane Curtin, Zena Grey, Philip Baker Hall, Shawn Pyfrom, Craig Kilborn.

SHAKE HANDS WITH THE DEVIL

SEVILLE PICTURES. Aug., 2007. Canadian. (Roger Spottiswoode) Roy Dupuis, Owen Lebakeng Sejake, James Gallanders, Odile Katesi Gakire, Michel Mongeau, John Sibi-Okumu, Robert Lalonde, Tom McCamus, Akin Omotoso, Michel Ange Nzojibwami, Jean-Hughes Anglade, Deborah Kara Unger.

SHARKS 3D

3D ENTERTAINMENT. Feb., 2005. (Jean-Jacques Mantello) Geoffrey Bateman. Documentary. IMAX.

SHE'S THE MAN

DREAMWORKS. March, 2006. (Andy Fickman) Amanda Bynes, Channing Tatum, Laura Ramsey, Vinnie Jones, Robert Hoffman, Alex Breckinridge, Julie Hagerty, David Cross, Jonathan Sadowsky, Amanda Crew, Jessica Lucas, Brandon Jay McLaren, Clifton Murray, James Snyder, James Kirk, Emily Perkins.

SHEITAN

MARS DISTRIBUTION. Feb., 2006. French. (Kim Chapiron) Vincent Cassel, Olivier Barthelemy, Roxane Mesquida, Nico Le Phat Tan, Ladj Ly, Leila Bekhti, Francois Levantal, Monica Bellucci, Julie-Marie Parmentier, Gerald Thomassin.

SHOOT 'EM UP

NEW LINE CINEMA. July, 2007. (Michael Davis) Clive Owen, Paul Giamatti, Monica Bellucci, Daniel Pilon, Sidney Mende-Gibson, Lucas Mende-Gibson, Kaylyn Yellowlees, Julian Richings.

SHOOTER

PARAMOUNT. March, 2007. (Antoine Fuqua) Mark Wahlberg, Michael Pena, Danny Glover, Kate Mara, Elias Koteas, Rhona Mitra, Rade Sherbedgia, Levon Helm, Ned Beatty, Tate Donovan, Justin Louis.

SHOOTING SILVIO

CINEDANCE. April, 2007. Italian. (Berardo (cq) Carboni) Federico Rosati, Sofia Vigliar, Melanie Gerren, Alessandro Haber, Antonino Iuorio, Fabrizio Raggi, Giovanni Visentin, Mia Benedetta, Gianni Lillo, Antonella Bavaro, Giovanni Martorana, Marcello Prayer, Isabella Arnaud, Cristina Pavone, Antonio Biondi, Erlend Oye, Marco Travaglio.

SHOPPEN

X VERLEIH. June, 2007. German. (Ralf Westhoff) Sebastian Weber, Anna Boeger, Felix Hellmann, Katharina Schubert, David Baalcke, Julia Koschitz, Martin Butzke, Kathrin von Steinburg, Matthias Bundschuh, Mediha Cetin, Thomas Limpinsel, Lisa Wagner, Oliver Buergin, Julia Heinze, Stephan Zinner, Anja Klawun, Christian Pfeil, Tanja Schleiff, Wilm Roil.

SHORTCUT TO HAPPINESS

YARI FILM GROUP. July, 2007. (Harry Kirkpatrick) Anthony Hopkins, Jennifer Love Hewitt, Alec Baldwin, Dan Aykroyd, Kim Cattrall, Barry Miller, Amy Poehler, Mike Doyle.

SHORTS

WARNER BROS. Aug. 8, 2009. (Robert Rodrigues) Jon Cryer, William H. Macy, Leslie Mann, James Spader, Jimmy Bennett, Kat Dennings, Jake Short, Devon Gearhart, Leo Howard, Trevor Gagnon, Rebel Rodriguez, Jolie Vanier.

SHREK THE THIRD

PARAMOUNT. May, 2007. (Chris Miller) Voices: Mike Myers, Eddie Murphy, Cameron Diaz, Antonio Banderas, Julie Andrews, John Cleese, Rupert Everett, Eric Idle, Justin Timberlake. Animated.

SHUTTER

20TH CENTURY FOX. March 20, 2008. (Banjong Pisanthanakun) Joshua Jackson, Rachael Taylor, Megumi Okina, David Denman, John Hensley, Maya Hazen, James Kyson Lee, Yoshiko Miyazaki, Kei Yamamoto.

THE SILENCE BEFORE BACH

Jan., 2008. Spanish. (Pere Portabella) Christian Brembeck, Alex Brendemuhl, Feodor Atkine, Daniel Ligorio, Georg C. Biller, Georgina Cardona, Franz Schuchart.

THE SILENCE OF THE LARK

REVOLVER. June, 2005. Italian. (David Ballerini) Ivan Franek, Marco Baliani, Flavio Bucci, Anna Maria Gherardi, Pietro Ragusa, Augusto Zucchi.

SILENT HILL

SONY PICTURES ENTERTAINMENT. April, 2006. Canadian-French. (Christophe Gans) Radha Mitchell, Sean Bean, Laurie Holden, Deborah Kara Unger, Kim Coates, Tanya Allen, Alice Krige, Jodelle Ferland.

SIMON KONIANSKI

HAUT ET COURT RELEASE (IN FRANCE) OF A VERSUS PROD., RTBF (BELGIUM)/HAUT ET COURT (FRANCE)/FORUM FILMS (CANADA). July, 2009. Belgian, French, Canadian. (Micha Wald) Jonathan Zaccai, Popeck CQ, Abraham Leber, Irene Herz, Nassim Ben Abdelmoumen, Marta Domingo, Ivan Fox.

THE SIMPSONS MOVIE

20TH TWENTIETH CENTURY FOX. July, 2007. (David Silverman) Voices: Dan Castellaneta, Julie Kavner, Nancy Cartwright, Yeardley Smith, Harry Shearer, Hank Azaria, A. Brooks. Animated.

SIN CITY

DIMENSION FILMS. March, 2005. (Frank Miller, Robert Rodriguez) Bruce Willis, Jessica Alba, Devon Aoki, Alexis Bledel, Powers Boothe, Rosario Dawson, Benicio Del Toro, Michael Clarke Duncan, Carla Gugino, Josh Hartnett, Rutger Hauer, Jaime King, Michael Madsen, Brittany Murphy, Clive Owen, Mickey Rourke, Nick Stahl, Elijah Wood, Marley Shelton.

SIN NOMBRE

FOCUS FEATURES. Jan. 18, 2009. (Cary Joji Fukunaga) Sayra - Paulina Gaitan, Edgar Flores, Kristyan Ferrer, Tenoch Huerta Mejia, Diana Garcia, Luis Fernando Pena, Hector Jimenez.

SINGH IS KINNG

An Indian Films release of an Adlabs presentation of a Hari Om Prods. production, in association with Blockbuster Movie Entertainers. Aug., 2008. Indian. (Anees Bazmee) Akshay Kumar, Katrina Kaif, Om Puri, Sonu Sood, Javed Jaffrey, Kamal Chopra, Manoj Pahwa, Neha Dhupia, Kirron Kher, Ranvir Shorey, Snoop Dogg.

THE SINGING REVOLUTION

ABRAMORAMA. Dec. 17, 2007. (James Tusty) Narrator: Linda Hunt. Documentary.

THE SISTERHOOD OF THE TRAVELING PANTS

WARNER BROS. May, 2005. (Ken Kwapis) Amber Tamblyn, Alexis Bledel, America Ferrera, Blake Lively, Jenna Boyd, Bradley Whitford, Nancy Travis, Rachel Ticotin, Mike Vogel, Michael Rady.

THE SISTERHOOD OF THE TRAVELING PANTS 2

WARNER BROS. July 30, 2008. (Sanaa Hamri) Amber Tamblyn, Alexis Bledel, America Ferrera, Blake Lively, Rachel Nichols, Tom Wisdom, Rachel Ticotin, Leonardo Nam, Michael Rady, Shohreh Aghdashloo, Blythe Danner, Jesse Williams.

SIX DAYS

SEVENTH ART RELEASING. May, 2007, Israeli-Canadian-French. (Ilan Ziv) Narrator: John Tarzwell. Documentary.

SIX SEX SCENES AND A MURDER

EAST MEETS WEST. May 21, 2008. (Julio Rubio) Richard Anthony Crenna, Jr., Kristin Minter, Jasper Watts, Christine Suzanne Gilb,

Gregory Pedemonte, Regina Melzer, Amy Jo Brojan, Kristen Nice, Jordan Westfall, Doug Woodbury, Jeffery Davis, Michelle Chantal, Ricky Saenz, Bruno Kanter, Greg Plitt, Bob Ramos.

SIXTY SIX

UIP (IN THE U.K.) Oct., 2006. British. (Paul Weiland) Gregg Sulkin, Helena Bonham Carter, Eddie Marsan, Catherine Tate, Peter Serafinowicz, Ben Newton, Stephen Rea, Geraldine Somerville, Richard Katz.

SK8 LIFE

Dec., 2006. Canadian. (Wyeth Clarkson) Kris Foley, Kathy Miller, Mark Bajcar, Silas Borsos, Chad Dickson, Alison Metasi, Dustin Montie, Jarvis Nigelsky.

THE SKELETON KEY

UNIVERSAL PICTURES. July, 2005. (Iain Softley) Kate Hudson, Gena Rowlands, John Hurt, Peter Sarsgaard, Joy Bryant, Maxine Barnett, Tom Uskali, Jen Apgar, Forrest Landis, Jamie Lee Redmon, Ronald McCall, Jeryl Prescott Sales, Isaach De Bankole.

THE SKEPTIC

IFC FILMS. March 3, 2009. (Tennyson Bardwell) Tim Daly, Tom Arnold, Zoe Saldana, Andrea Roth, Edward Herrmann, Robert Prosky, Bruce Altman.

SKIN FOR SALE

SOROLLA FILMS PRESENTATION OF A TIEMPOS DIFICILES. July, 2005. Spanish. (Vicente Perez Herrero) Bibian Norai, Nacho Vidal, Anastassia, Maria Bianco, Malena Conde, Narcis Bosch, Jose Maria Ponce, Laura Brent, Roby Blake. Documentary.

SKINWALKERS

LIONSGATE. Aug., 2007. (James Isaac) Jason Behr, Elias Koteas, Rhona Mitra, Kim Coates, Natassia Malthe, Matthew Knight, Sarah Carter, Lyriq Bent, Tom Jackson, Rogue Johnston, Shawn Roberts, Barbara Gordon.

SKY FIGHTERS

PATHE DISTRIBUTION. Sept., 2005. French. (Gerard Pires) Benoit Magimel, Clovis Cornillac, Alice Taglioni, Geraldine Pailhas, Philippe Torreton, Jean-Baptiste Puech, Christophe Reymond, Fiona Curzon, Jean-Michel Tinivelli, Frederic Van Den Driessche, Eric Poulain, Pierre Poirot, Peter Hudson.

SKY HIGH

BUENA VISTA. July, 2005. (Mike Mitchell) Michael Angarano, Kurt Russell, Kelly Preston, Danielle Panabaker, Kevin Heffernan, Lynda Carter, Mary Elizabeth Winstead, Bruce Campbell, Dave Foley, Steven Strait, Dee-Jay Daniels, Nicholas Braun, Kelly Vitz, Jim Rash, Jake Sandvig, Will Harris, Khadijah, Malika, Kevin McDonald, Cloris Leachman.

SLOW BURN

LIONSGATE. April, 2007. (Wayne Beach) Ray Liotta, LL Cool J, Mekhi Phifer, Bruce McGill, Chiwetel Ejiofor, Taye Diggs, Jolene Blalock.

SMILE

B.D. FOX MARKETING AND DISTRIBUTION. March, 2005. (Jeff Kramer) Mika Boorem, Luoyong Wang, Yi Ding, Beau Bridges, Linda Hamilton, Cheri Oteri, Sean Astin, Shuai ChiChi, Jonathon Trent, Erik von Detten, Jia Song, Essie Shure.

SMOKIN' ACES

UNIVERSAL. Jan., 2007. (Joe Carnahan) Ben Affleck, Andy Garcia, Alicia Keys, Ray Liotta, Jeremy Piven, Ryan Reynolds, Peter Berg, Taraji Henson, Chris Pine, Martin Henderson, Justin Bateman, Nestor Carbonell, Common, Joseph Ruskin, Kevin Durand, Maury Sterling, Curtis Armstrong, Tommy Flanagan, Davenia McFadden, Alex Rocco, Joel Edgerton, David Proval, Vladimir Kulich, Wayne Newton.

SMOTHER

VARIANCE FILMS. Sept. 26, 2008. (Vince Di Meglio) Diane Keaton, Dax Shepard, Liv Tyler, Mike White, Ken Howard, Selma Stern, Jerry Lambert, Don Lake.

SNAKES ON A PLANE

NEW LINE CINEMA. Aug., 2006. (David R. Ellis) Samuel L. Jackson, Julianna Margulies, Nathan Phillips, Bobby Cannavale, Flex Alexander, Todd Louiso, Sunny Mabrey, Kenan Thompson, Rachel Blanchard, Lin Shaye, David Koechner, Elsa Pataky, Byron Lawson, Keith Dallas, Tom Butler.

THE SNIPER

MEDIA ASIA FILMS. Aug., 2009. Chinese. (Dante Lam) Richie Jen, Huang Xiaoming, Edison Chen, Bowie Lam, Liu Kai-chi, Jack Kao, Wilfred Lau, Mango Wong, Michelle Ye, Charmaine Fong, Tung Wai.

THE SOLOIST

PARAMOUNT. March 10, 2009. (Joe Wright) Jamie Foxx, Robert Downey, Jr., Catherine Keener, Tom Hollander, Lisagay Hamilton, Nelsan Ellis, Rachael Harris, Stephen Root, Lorraine Toussaint, Marcos De silvas.

SOMETHING NEW

FOCUS FEATURES. Jan., 2006. (Sanaa Hamri) Sanaa Lathan, Simon Baker, Mike Epps, Donald Faison, Blair Underwood, Wendy Raquel Robinson, Alfre Woodard, Golden Brooks, Taraji P. Henson, Earl Billings.

SON OF THE MASK

NEW LINE CINEMA. Feb., 2005. (Lawrence Guterman) Jamie Kennedy, Alan Cumming, Liam Falconer, Ryan Falconer, Traylor Howard, Steven Wright, Bob Hoskins, Bear.

SOPHIE'S REVENGE

PERFECT WORLD, CHINA FILM GROUP (IN CHINA)/CJ ENTERTAINMENT (IN SOUTH KOREA). Oct., 2009. Chinese, South Korean. (Eva Jin) Zhang Ziyi, Fan Bingbing, Peter Ho, Seo Ji-seob, Yao Chen, Ruby Lin, Cheng Qian, Wang Ji, Song Zhuoyuan, Cheng Yi, Zhang Boyue, Yin Xu.

SORORITY ROW

SUMMIT ENTERTAINMENT (IN U.S.)/HOYTS (IN AUSTRALIA). Sept. 4, 2009. (Stewart Hendler) Briana Evigan, Leah Pipes, Rumer Willis, Jamie Chung, Audrina Patridge, Julian Morris, Margo Harshmann, Matt Lanter, Carrie Fisher, Matt O'Leary.

SOUL MATE

IRANIAN FILM SOCIETY. June, 2005. Iranian. (Mehdi Fakhim-Zadeh) Mehdi Fakhim-Zadeh, Roya Nonahali, Nasser Aghaie, Afsaneh Nasseri, Farhad Sharifi, Matin Azizpour.

SOUL MEN

MGM. Oct. 29, 2008. (Malcolm D. Lee) Samuel L. Jackson, Bernie Mac, Sharon Leal, Adam Herschman, Sean Hayes, Affion Crockett, John Legend.

SPACE CHIMPS

20TH CENTURY FOX. July 12, 2008. (Kirk DeMicco) Andy Samberg, Cheryl Hines, Patrick Warburton, Jeff Daniels, Omid Abtahi, Stanley Tucci, Jane Lynch, Zack Shada, Kristin Chenoweth, Kenan Thompson, Carlos Alazraqui.

SPECIAL ESCORT

20TH CENTURY FOX (GERMANY). Nov., 2007. German. (Maggie Peren) Florian Lukas, Sebastian Bezzel, Gustav Peter Woehler, Kostja Ullmann, Herbert Knaup, Lisa Maria Potthoff, Nina Kronjaeger.

SPECIAL NEEDS

TROMA ENTERTAINMENT. Dec. 2, 2007. (Isaak James) Isaak James, Eva James, Michael C. Kricfalusi, Jared Morgenstern, Randall Middleton, Sabina Maschi, Brian Whisenant.

SPEED RACER

WARNER BROS. April 30, 2008. (the Wachowski Brothers) Emile Hirsch, Christina Ricci, John Goodman, Susan Sarandon, Matthew Fox, Roger Allam, Paulie Litt, Benno Furmann, Hiroyuki Sanada, Richard Roundtree, Kick Gurry, John Benfield, Christian Oliver, Moritz Bleibtreu, Ralph Herforth, Ashley Walters, Scott Porter.

SPIDER-MAN 3

SONY PICTURES ENTERTAINMENT. April, 2007. (Sam Raimi) Tobey Maguire, Kirsten Dunst, James Franco, Thomas Haden Church, Topher Grace, Bryce Dallas Howard, Rosemary Harris, J.K. Simmons, James Cromwell, Theresa Russell, Dylan Baker, Bill Nunn, Bruce Campbell, Elizabeth Banks, Ted Raimi, Perla Haney-Jardine, Willem Dafoe, Cliff Robertson.

THE SPIDERWICK CHRONICLES

PARAMOUNT. Feb. 9, 2008. (Mark Waters) Freddie Highmore, Mary-Louise Parker, Nick Nolte, Sarah Bolger, Andrew McCarthy, Joan Plowright, David Strathairn, Seth Rogen, Martin Short.

THE SPIRIT

LIONSGATE. Dec. 17, 2008. (Frank Miller) Gabriel Macht, Eva Mendes, Sarah Paulson, Dan Lauria, Paz Vega, Eric Balfour, Jaime King, Scarlett Johansson, Samuel L. Jackson, Louis Lombardi, Stana Katic, Richard Portnow, Johnny Simmons.

SPLINTER

MAGNET. Oct. 23, 2008. (Toby Wilkins) Jill Wagner, Paulo Costanzo, Shea Whigham, Rachel Kerbs.

SPLINTERHEADS

PALADIN. Oct. 30, 2009. (Brant Sersen) Thomas Middleditch, Rachael Taylor, Christopher McDonald, Lea Thompson, Dean Winters, Frankie Faison, Edmund Lyndeck, Jason Rogel, Pamela Shaw, Jason Mantzoukas.

SPRINGTIME IN PARIS

REZO FILMS. Jan., 2006. French. (Jacques Bral) Eddy Mitchell, Sagamore Stevenin, Pascale Arbillot, Pierre Santini, Jean-Francois Balmer, Gerard Jugnot, Maxime Leroux, Anne Roussel, Geraldine Danon, Florence Darel.

ST. TRINIAN'S

ENTERTAINMENT FILM DISTRIBUTORS. Dec., 2007. British. (Oliver Parker, Barnaby Thompson) Rupert Everett, Colin Firth, Lena Headey, Jodie Whittaker, Russell Brand, Anna Chancellor, Stephen Fry, Celia Imrie, Toby Jones, Caterina Murino, Fenella Woolgar, Talulah Riley, Mischa Barton, Gemma Arterton, Lily Cole, Tamsin Egerton, Amara Khan, Antonia Bernath, Holly Mackie, Lucy Punch.

STALAGS

April, 2008. Israeli. (Ari Libsker) Edi Keider, Ezra Narkis, Na'ama Shik, Sidra Ezrahi, Hanna Yablonska. Documentary.

STAN HELSING: A PARODY

ANCHOR BAY ENTERTAINMENT (IN U.S.). Oct. 23, 2009. (Bo

Zenga) Steve Howey, Diora Baird, Desi Lydic, Kenan Thompson, Leslie Nielsen.

STANLEY KUBRICK'S BOXES

July, 2008. British. (Jon Ronson) Deborah Davis, Bernd Eichhorn, Tony Frewin, Jan Harlan, Manuel Harlan, Anya Kubrick, Christiane Kubrick, Rick Senat, Julian Senior, Vincent Tilsley, Judy Tobey, Leon Vitali.

STAR TREK

PARAMOUNT. April 21, 2009. (J.J. Abrams) Chris Pine, Zachary Quinto, Leonard Nimoy, Eric Bana, Bruce Greenwood, Karl Urban, Zoe Saldana, Simon Pegg, John Cho, Anton Yelchin, Ben Cross, Winona Ryder, Chris Hemsworth, Jennifer Morrison, Rachel Nichols, Robau - Faran Tahir, Clifton Collins, Jr.

STAR WARS: THE CLONE WARS

WARNER BROS. Aug. 7, 2008. (Dave Filoni) Matt Lanter, Ashley Eckstein, James Arnold Taylor, Bradley Baker, Tom Kane, Nika Futterman, Ian Abercrombie, Corey Burton, Catherine Taber, Matthew Wood, Kevin Michael Richardson, David Acord, Samuel L. Jackson, Anthony Daniels, Christopher Lee.

STAR WARS: EPISODE III -- REVENGE OF THE SITH

20TH CENTURY FOX. May, 2005. (George Lucas) Ewan McGregor, Natalie Portman, Hayden Christensen, Ian McDiarmid, Samuel L. Jackson, Christopher Lee, Jimmy Smits, Frank Oz, Peter Mayhew, Ahmed Best, Oliver Ford Davies, Temuera Morrison, Anthony Daniels, Silas Carson, Kenny Baker, Keisha Castle-Hughes, Jay Laga'aia, Bruce Spence, Wayne Pygram, David Bowers.

STARDUST

PARAMOUNT. July, 2007. (Matthew Vaughn) Claire Danes, Michelle Pfeiffer, Robert De Niro, Charlie Cox, Sienna Miller, Ricky Gervais, Jason Flemyng, Rupert Everett, Peter O'Toole, Mark Strong, Kate Magowan.

STATE OF PLAY

UNIVERSAL. (IN U.S.) April 8, 2009. (Kevin Macdonald) Russell Crowe, Ben Affleck, Rachel McAdams, Helen Mirren, Robin Wright Penn, Jason Bateman, Jeff Daniels.

STATE PROPERTY 2

LIONS GATE. April, 2005. (Damon Dash) Beanie Sigel, Victor N.O.R.E. Santiago, Damon Dash, Michael Bentt, Omillio Sparks, Oshino, Freeway, Young Gunz, Mariah Carey, Omahrya.

STATES OF GRACE

MAIN STREET MOVIE CO. Oct., 2005. (Richard Dutcher) Ignacio Serricchio, Lucas Fleischer, Lamont Stephens, Rachel Emmers, Jo-Sei Ikeda, J.J. Boone, Allah Chatman, DeSean Terry, Jeff Kelly, John Pentecost.

STAY

20TH CENTURY FOX. Oct., 2005. (Marc Forster) Ewan McGregor, Naomi Watts, Ryan Gosling, Janeane Garofalo, B.D. Wong, Bob Hoskins, Kate Burton, Michael Gaston, Mark Margolis, Elizabeth Reaser.

STAY ALIVE

BUENA VISTA. March, 2006. (William Brent Bell) Jon Foster, Samaire Armstrong, Frankie Muniz, Jimmi Simpson, Wendell Pierce, Sophia Bush, Adam Goldberg.

STEAL A PENCIL FOR ME

RED ENVELOPE ENTERTAINMENT. Oct 23, 2007. (Michele Ohayon) Jack Polak, Ina Soep, Ellen Ten Damme, Jeroen Krabbe. Documentary.

STEALING AMERICA: VOTE BY VOTE

DIRECT CINEMA LIMITED. July 14, 2008. (Dorothy Fadiman) Bob Hagan, Robert F. Kennedy, Jr., Ion Sancho, Charles Lewis, Bruce O'Dell, Chuck Herrin, Greg Palast, Paul Craig Roberts, John Zogby, John Boyd, Matthew Damschroder, Bob Fitrakis, Jonathan Simon, Chris Hood, Pat Leahan, Dr. Avi Rubin, Charles Traylor, Dr. Jonathan Simon. Narrator: Peter Coyote. Documentary.

STEALTH

SONY PICTURES ENTERTAINMENT. July, 2005. (Rob Cohen) Josh Lucas, Jamie Foxx, Jessica Biel, Sam Shepard, Joe Morton, Ebon Moss-Bachrach, Richard Roxburgh, Wentworth Miller.

STELLA'S WAR

INDEPENDENT FILMS. April, 2009. Dutch. (Diederik van Rooijen) 89Maartje Remmers, Javier Guzman, Keesje Rietvelt, Teun Kuilboer, Thijs Roemer, Micha Hulshof, Anna Drijver. (Alain Tasma) Gaspard Ulliel, Jasmine Trinca, Michel Boujenah, Anna Galiena, Sarah Adler, Hanna Laszlo, Lior Ashkenasi, Meriam Zohar, Tsahi Grad, Adhib Jaasan.

STEP BROTHERS

SONY PICTURES ENTERTAINMENT. July 14, 2008. (Adam McKay) Will Ferrell, John C. Reilly, Mary Steenburgen, Richard Jenkins, Adam Scott, Kathryn Hahn, Andrea Savage.

STEP UP

BUENA VISTA. Aug., 2006. (Anne Fletcher) Channing Tatum, Jenna Dewan, Damaine Radcliff, De'Shawn Washington, Mario, Drew Sidora, Rachel Griffiths, Josh Henderson, Tim Lacatena, Alyson Stoner, Heavy D, Deirdre Lovejoy.

STEP UP 2 THE STREETS

WALT DISNEY STUDIOS. Feb. 11, 2008. (John M. Chu) Briana Evigan, Robert Hoffman, Will Kemp, Sonja Sohn, Adam G. Sevani, Cassie Ventura, Danielle Polanco, Telisha Shaw, Black Thomas, Channing Tatum, Christopher Scott, Mari Koda, Janelle Cambridge, Luis Rosado, Harry Shum, Jr., LaJon Dantzler, Boogie.

THE STEPFATHER

SONY PICTURES ENTERTAINMENT. Oct. 16, 2009. (Nelson McCormick) Dylan Walsh, Sela Ward, Penn Badgley, Amber Heard, Sherry Stringfield, Paige Turco, Jon Tenney.

STEPS

ALTA FILMS. June, 2005. Spanish. (Federico Luppi) Ana Fernandez, Alberto Jimenez, Susana Hornos, Gines Garcia Millan, Eva Cobo, Fabian Vena, Jordi Dauder.

STICK IT

BUENA VISTA. April, 2006. (Jessica Bendinger) Jeff Bridges, Missy Peregrym, Vanessa Lengies, Nikki SooHoo, Maddy Curley, Kellan Lutz, John Patrick Amedori, Mio Dzakula, Svetlana Efremova, Jon Gries, Gia Carides, Tarah Paige, Polly Holliday, Julie Warner, Annie Corley, Bart Conner, Tim Daggett, Elfi Schlegel, John Kapelos.

STOP-LOSS

PARAMOUNT. March 13, 2008. (Kimberly Peirce) Ryan Phillippe, Abbie Cornish, Channing Tatum, Joseph Gordon-Levitt, Ciaran Hinds, Timothy Olyphant, Victor Rasuk, Rob Brown, Mamie Gummer, Josef Sommer, Linda Emond, Alex Frost.

STOLEN CHILDHOODS

BALCONY RELEASING. May, 2005. (Len Morris) Pharis Harvey, Kailash Satyrarthi, Wangari Maathai, Bruce Harris, Inderjit Khurana, Sen. Tom Harkin. Narrator: Meryl Streep.

STOMP THE YARD

SONY PICTURES ENTERTAINMENT. Jan., 2007. (Sylvain White) Columbus Short, Meagan Good, Ne-Yo, Darrin Henson, Brian White, Laz Alonso, Valarie Pettiford, Jermaine Williams, Allan Louis, Harry Lennix, Chris Brown.

THE STONE MERCHANT

MEDUSA. Sept., 2006. Italian-British. (Renzo Martinelli) Harvey Keitel, Jordi Molla, Jane March, F. Murray Abraham.

STORM

SANDREW METRONOME. Nov., 2005. Swedish. (Marlind/Stein) Eric Ericson, Eva Rose, Jonas Karlsson, Lina Englund, Sasha Becker, Adam Lundgren, Karl Norrhall, Peter Engman, Jacqueline Ramel, Mattias Padin Varela, Per Ragnar, Joel Kinnaman, Sofia Hvittfeldt, Oscar Akermo, Christian Hollbrink.

STORMBREAKER

ENTERTAINMENT FILM DISTRIBUTORS (IN U.K.)/THE WEINSTEIN CO. (IN U.S.). July, 2006. British-German. (Geoffrey Sax) Alex Pettyfer, Ewan McGregor, Mickey Rourke, Bill Nighy, Sophie Okonedo, Alicia Silverstone, Missi Pyle, Sarah Bolger, Ashley Walters, Damian Lewis, Robbie Coltrane, Stephen Fry, Andy Serkis, Jimmy Carr.

STRAIGHTHEADS

VERVE PICTURES (IN U.K.)/SONY PICTURES ENTERTAINMENT (IN U.S). April, 2007. British. (Dan Reed) Gillian Anderson, Danny Dyer, Anthony Calf, Ralph Brown, Steven Robertson, Francesca Fowler, Adam Rayner, Anthony Byrne, Gugu Mbatha-Raw, Neil Finnigan.

STRANGE WILDERNESS

PARAMOUNT. Feb. 1, 2008. (Fred Wolf) Steve Zahn, Allen Covert, Jonah Hill, Kevin Heffernan, Ashley Scott, Peter Dante, Harry Hamlin, Robert Patrick, Joe Don Baker, Justin Long, Jeff Garlin, Ernest Borgnine.

THE STRANGERS

ROGUE PICTURES. May 19, 2008. (Bryan Bertino) Liv Tyler, Scott Speedman, Gemma Ward, Kip Weeks, Laura Margolis, Glenn Howerton.

STREET FIGHTER: THE LEGEND OF CHUN-LI

20TH CENTURY FOX. Feb. 27, 2009. (Andrzej Bartkowiak) Kristin Kreuk, Chris Klein, Neal McDonough, Robin Shou, Moon Bloodgood, Josie Ho, Taboo, Michael Clarke Duncan.

STREET KINGS

FOX SEARCHLIGHT. April 1, 2008. (David Ayer) Keanu Reeves, Forest Whitaker, Hugh Laurie, Chris Evans, Cedric "The Entertainer" Kyles, Jay Mohr, Terry Crews, Naomie Harris, Martha Higareda, John Corbett, Amaury Nolasco.

STRENGTH AND HONOR

SLOWHAND RELEASING/MARON PICTURES. Dec. 7, 2007. (Mark Mahon. Michael Madsen, Vinnie Jones, Patrick Bergin, Richard Chamberlain, Michael Rawley, Gail Fitzpatrick, Luke Whelton, Sheridan Mahon, Finbar Furey, Myles Horgan.

SUBDIVISION

BUENA VISTA INTL.. Aug., 2009. Australian. (Sue Brooks) Gary Sweet, Ashley Bradnam, Brooke Satchwell, Steve Bisley, Bruce Spence, Aaron Fa'Aoso, Kathryn Beck, Kris McQuade, Denise Roberts, James Stewart, John Batchelor.

SUDDENLY
SONET FILM. Nov., 2006. Swedish. (Johan Brisinger) Michael Nyqvist, Anastasios Soulis, Moa Gammel, Catherine Hansson, Sten Ljunggren, Anita Wall, Philip Zanden, Carl Ljunggren, Teresia Bjork, Stig Engstrom, Dylan Thomas, Johan Kjellgren.

SUPER CAPERS
ROADSIDE ATTRACTIONS. March 16, 2009. (Ray Griggs) Justin Whalin, Michael Rooker, Ryan McPartlin, Samuel Lloyd, Danielle Harris, Ray Griggs, Christine Lakin, Jon Polito, Adam West, June Lockhart, Doug Jones, Clint Howard, Tom Sizemore.

SUPERHERO MOVIE
METRO-GOLDWYN-MAYER. March 28, 2008. (Craig Mazin) Drake Bell, Sara Paxton, Christopher McDonald, Kevin Hart, Brent Spiner, Jeffrey Tambor, Ryan Hansen, Robert Hays, Marion Ross, Robert Joy, Pamela Anderson, Leslie Nielsen, Dan Castellaneta, Simon Rex, Keith David, Kurt Fuller, Jenica Bergere, Tracy Morgan, Regina Hall, Craig Bierko, Miles Fisher, John Getz, Charlene Tilton, Lil' Kim.

SURROGATES
WALT DISNEY STUDIOS MOTION PICTURES. Sept. 23, 2009. (Jonathan Mostow) Bruce Willis, Radha Mitchell, Rosamund Pike, Boris Kodjoe, James Francis Ginty, James Cromwell, Ving Rhames, Jack Noseworthy, Devin Ratray, Michael Cudlit.

SUENO
DESTINATION FILMS. Sept., 2005. (Renee Chabria) John Leguizamo, Ana Claudia Talancon, Elizabeth Pena, Nestor Serrano, Jose Maria Yazpik, Terri Hoyos, Jose Jose, Jsu Garcia, Rafael Simon, Rick Simon, Kal PennKal Penn, Bernard White, Mel Gorham, Erica Munoz, Michael Pena.

THE SUMMER OF MY FIRST KISS
01 DISTRIBUTION. June, 2006. Italian. (Carlo Virzi) Laura Morante, Gabriela Belisario, Iacopo Petrini, Andrea Renzi, Gigio Alberti, Regina Orioli, Neri Marcore.

SUMMER RAIN
SOGEPAQ. Nov., 2006. British-Spanish. (Antonio Banderas) Alberto Amarilla, Maria Ruiz, Felix Gomez, Raul Arevalo, Fran Perea, Marta Nieto, Mario Casas, Antonio Garrido, Antonio Zafra, Berta de la Dehesa, Victor Perez, Cuca Escribano, Lucio Romero, Juan Diego, Victoria Abril.

SUMMERCAMP!
ARGOT PICTURES. July, 2007. (Bradley Beesley, Sarah Price) Documentary.

SUMMER HOURS
MK2 DIFFUSION. March, 2008. French. (Olivier Assayas) Juliette Binoche, Charles Berling, Jeremie Renier, Edith Scob, Dominique Reymond, Valerie Bonneton, Isabelle Sadoyan, Kyle Eastwood, Alice de Lencquesaing, Emile Berling.

SUNDAY LIGHT
SONY PICTURES RELEASING (SPAIN). Nov., 2007. Spanish. (Jose Luis Garci) Alfredo Landa, Paula Echevarria, Alex Gonzalez, Kiti Manver, Manuel Galiana, Toni Acosta, Carlos Larranaga, Andrea Tenuta, Enrique Villen, Francisco Algora.

SUNNY
SHOWBOX/MEDIAPLEX. July, 2008. South Korean. (Lee Joon-ik) Su Ae, Jeong Jin-yeong, Ju Jin-mo, Eom Tae-woong, Jeong Gyeong-ho, Cheong Gyeong-ho, Shin Hyeon-tak, Park Yun-ho, Lee Ju-shil, Jo Mi-ryeong.

SUNNY SPELLS
REZO FILMS. July, 2008. French. (Diasteme) Bruno Todeschini, Emma de Caunes, Lea Drucker, Olivier Marchal, Linh-Dan Pham, Olivier Py, Jeanne Rosa, Judith el-Zein, Frederic Andrau.

SWEENEY TODD: THE DEMON BARBER OF FLEET STREET
DREAMWORKS-PARAMOUNT. Nov. 29, 2007. (Tim Burton) Johnny Depp, Helena Bonham Carter, Alan Rickman, Timothy Spall, Sacha Baron Cohen, Jayne Wisner, Jamie Campbell Bower, Edward Sanders, Laura Michelle Kelly.

SWING VOTE
WALT DISNEY STUDIOS. July 28, 2008. (Joshua Michael Stern) Kevin Costner, Paula Patton, Kelsey Grammer, Dennis Hopper, Nathan Lane, Stanley Tucci, George Lopez, Madeline Carroll, Charles "Chip" Esten, Richard Petty, Mare Winningham, Mark Moses, Nana Visitor, Richard Petty, Willie Nelson, Tony Blankley, Aaron Brown, Campbell Brown, Tucker Carlson, James Carville, Matt Frei, Mary Hart, Ariana Huffington, Larry King, Anne Kornblut, Bill Maher, Chris Matthews, Lawrence O'Donnell.

TAARE ZAMEEN PAR: EVERY CHILD IS SPECIAL
UTV. Dec., 2007. Indian. (Aamir Khan) Darsheel Safary, Aamir Khan, Tanay Chheda, Sachet Engineer, Tisca Chopra, Vipin Sharma, Lalitha Lajmi.

SUNSHINE
20TH CENTURY FOX (IN U.K.)/FOX SEARCHLIGHT (IN U.S.). March, 2007. British-U.S. (Danny Boyle) Cillian Murphy, Chris Evans, Rose Byrne, Michelle Yeoh, Hiroyuki Sanada, Cliff Curtis, Troy Garity, Benedict Wong, Mark Strong, Chipo Chung, Archie Paloma Baeza, Sylvie Macdonald.

SUPERCROSS: THE MOVIE
20TH CENTURY FOX. Aug., 2005. (Steve Boyum) Steve Howey, Mike Vogel, Cameron Richardson, Sophia Buh, Aaron Cater, Channing Tatum, J.D Pardo, Carolina Garcia, Ryan Locke, Robert Patrick, Robert Carradine.

SUPERBAD
SONY PICTURES ENTERTAINMENT. July, 2007. (Greg Mottola) Jonah Hill, Michael Cera, Christopher Mintz-Plasse, Bill Hader, Seth Rogen, Martha MacIsaac, Emma Stone, Aviva, Joe Lo Truglio, Kevin Corrigan.

SUPERMAN RETURNS
WARNER BROS. June, 2006. (Bryan Singer) Brandon Routh, Kate Bosworth, James Marsden, Frank Langella, Eva Marie Saint, Parker Posey, Kal Penn, Sam Huntington, Kevin Spacey, Tristan Lake Leabu, James Karen, David Fabrizio, Jack Larson, Noel Neill, Marlon Brando.

SURF'S UP
SONY PICTURES ENTERTAINMENT. May, 2007. (Ash Brannon, Chris Buck) Voices: Shia LaBeouf, Jeff Bridges, Zooey Deschanel, Jon Heder, James Woods, Diedrich Bader. Animated.

SYDNEY WHITE
UNIVERSAL. Sept., 2007. (Joe Nussbaum) Amanda Bynes, Matt Long, Sara Paxton, John Schneider, Jack Carpenter, Crystal Hunt, Jeremy Howard.

SYMPATHY
April, 2007. (Andrew Moorman) Steven Pritchard, Aaron Boucher, Marina Shtelen.

SYRIANA
WARNER BROS. Nov., 2005. (Stephen Gaghan) George Clooney, Matt Damon, Jeffrey Wright, Chris Cooper, William Hurt, Mazhar Munir, Tim Blake Nelson, Amanda Peet, Christopher Plummer, Alexander Siddig, Akbar Kurtha, William C. Mitchell, Sonnell Dadral, Max Minghella, David Clennon, Robert Foxworth, Mark Strong.

T

TABLEAU
Feb., 2008. Hungarian-German. (Gabor Dettre) Zoltan Mucsi, Imre Csuja, Peter Scherer, Geza Tordy, Dezso Szegedi.

TAKE A BREAK!
TFM. June, 2005. French. (Bruno Herbulot) Fabrice Luchini, Amira Casar, Elsa Zylberstein, Francois Cluzet, Valerie Bonneton, Coraly Zahonero, Arno Chevrier.

TAKE THE LEAD
NEW LINE CINEMA. March, 2006. (Liz Friedlander) Antonio Banderas, Rob Brown, Yaya DaCosta, Alfre Woodard, Lauren Collins, Brandon D. Andrews.

TAKEN
EUROPACORP (IN FRANCE)/20TH CENTURY FOX (IN U.S.). March, 2008. French. (Pierre Morel) Liam Neeson, Maggie Grace, Famke Janssen, Leland Orser, Jon Gries, David Warshofsky, Holly Valance, Katie Cassidy, Xander Berkeley, Olivier Rabourdin, Gerard Watkins, Arben Bajraktaraj, Nathan Rippy, Camille Japy, Nicolas Giraud, Goran Kostic.

THE TAKING OF PELHAM 1 2 3
SONY PICTURES ENTERTAINMENT. June 2, 2009. (Tony Scott) Denzel Washington, John Travolta, John Turturro, Luis Guzman, Michael Rispoli, James Gandolfini, Frank Wood, John Benjamin Hickey, Gary Basaraba, Ramon Rodriguez, Gbenga Akinnagbe, Katherine Sigismund, Jake Siciliano, Aunjanue Ellis, Alex Kaluzhsky, Tonye Patano, Jason Butler Harner.

TAKING WOODSTOCK
FOCUS FEATURES. May 15, 2009. (Ang Lee) Demetri Martin, Dan Fogler, Henry Goodman, Jonathan Groff, Eugene Levy, Jeffrey Dean Morgan, Imelda Staunton, Emile Hirsch, Liev Schreiber, Skylar Astin, Kevin Chamberlin, Kelli Garner, Paul Dano, Daniel Eric Gold, Mamie Gummer, Edward Hibbert, Steven Kunken, Andy Prosky, Kevin Sussman, Richard Thomas, Darren Pettie.

TALENTO DE BARRIO
MAYA RELEASING (IN U.S.). Oct., 2008. Puerto Rico. (Jose Ivan Santiago, George Rivera) Daddy Yankee, Angel "Maestro" Rodriguez, Cesar "TNT" Farrait, Katiria Soto, Angelica Alcaide, Norma Colon, Norman Santiago, Rafael Acevedo, Eddie Dee.

TALK TO ME
FOCUS FEATURES. May, 2007. (Kasi Lemmons) Don Cheadle, Chiwetel Ejiofor, Cedric the Entertainer, Taraji P. Henson, Mike Epps, Martin Sheen, Vondie Curtis Hall.

TALK TO ME ABOUT LOVE
01 DISTRIBUTION. March, 2008. Italian-Spanish. (Silvio Muccino) Silvio Muccino, Aitana Sanchez-Gijon, Carolina Crescentini, Andrea Renzi, Flavio Parenti, Max Mazzotta, Geraldine Chaplin,

Giorgio Colangeli.

TALLADEGA NIGHTS: THE BALLAD OF RICKY BOBBY
SONY PICTURES ENTERTAINMENT. July, 2006. (Adam McKay) Will Ferrell, John C. Reilly, Sacha Baron Cohen, Gary Cole, Michael Clarke Duncan, Leslie Bibb, Jane Lynch, Amy Adams, Andy Richter, Molly Shannon, Greg Germann, Houston Tumlin, Grayson Russell, David Koechner, John D. King, Pat Hingle, Dale Earnhardt, Jr., Dick Berggren, Mike Joy, Larry McReynolds, Darrell Waltrip, Jamie McMurray, Bob Jenkins, Elvis Costello, Mos Def, Bill Weber, Benny Parsons, Wally Dellenbach.

TAMBOURINE
IRANIAN FILM SOCIETY. Aug., 2008. Iranian. (Parisa Bakhtavar) Baran Kosari, Saber Abbar, Mehran Modiri, Negare Forouzandeh, Omid Rouhani, Gohare Kheirandish, Bahareh Rahnama, Niloufar Khoshkholgh, Nima Shahrokshahi, Mohammad Reza Sharifnia, Akram Mohammadi, Amin Hayai, Hamed Behdad, Melika Sharifinia.

TAPAS
FILMAX. May, 2005. Spanish. (Jose Corbacho, Juan Cruz) Angel de Andres Lopez, Maria Galiana, Elvira Minguez, Ruben Ochandiano, Alberto de Mendoza, Dario Paso, Alberto Jo Lee, Amparo Moreno, Ferran Adria.

TASHAN
YASH RAJ FILMS. April, 2008. Indian. (Vijay Krishna Acharya) Akshay Kumar, Saif Ali Khan, Kareena Kapoor, Anil Kapoor, Yashpal Sharma, Manoj Pahwa, Sanjay Mishra.

TAXI 4
ARP SELECTION. Feb., 2007. French. (Gerard Krawczyk) Samy Naceri, Frederic Diefenthal, Bernard Farcy, Emma Sjoberg-Wyklund, Edouard Montoute, Jean-Christophe Bouvet, Jean-Luc Couchard, Francois Damiens, Mourade Zeguendi, Djibril Cisse.

TAXI NO. 9211
UTV MOTION PICTURES. March, 2006. Indian. (Milan Luthria) Nana Patekar, John Abraham, Sameera Reddy, Sonali Kulkarni, Shivaji Satam, Aakash Khurana, Kurush Deboo, Priyanka Chopra, Sanjay Dutt.

TEAR THIS HEART OUT
20TH CENTURY FOX. Dec., 2008. Mexican-Spanish. (Roberto Sneider) Ana Claudia Talancon, Daniel Gimenez Cacho, Jose Maria de Tavira.

TELL NO ONE
EUROPACORP DISTRIBUTION. Nov., 2006. French. (Guillaume Canet) Francois Cluzet, Andre Dussollier, Marie-Josee Croze, Kristin Scott Thomas, Nathalie Baye, Francois Berleand, Jean Rochefort, Guillaume Canet, Gilles Lellouche, Olivier Marchal, Philippe Lefebvre, Florence Thomassin, Marina Hands, Jalil Lespert, Eric Savin.

THE TEN COMMANDMENTS
PROMENADE PICTURES. Oct. 15, 2007. (Bill Boyce) Christian Slater, Alfred Molina, Elliott Gould, Christopher Gaze, Kathleen Barr, Lee Tockar, Matt Hill. Narrator - Ben Kingsley.

TEN EMPTY
DENDY FILMS. May, 2008. Australian. (Anthony Hayes) Daniel Frederiksen, Geoff Morrell, Lucy Bell, Tom Budge, Brendan Cowell, Blazey Best, Jack Thompson.

TEN 'TIL NOON
RADIO LONDON FILMS. March, 2007. (Scott Storm) Alfonso Freeman, Rayne Guest, Thomas Kopache, Jenya Lano, Rick D. Wasserman, George Williams.

TENACIOUS D IN THE PICK OF DESTINY
NEW LINE CINEMA. Nov., 2006. (Liam Lynch) Jack Black, Kyle Gass, JR Reed, Troy Gentile, Ronnie James Dio, Paul F. Tompkins.

THE TENANTS
Jan., 2005. (Danny Green) Dylan McDermott, Snoop Dogg, Rose Byrne, Seymour Cassel, Niki J. Crawford, Aldis Hodge.

THE TENDER HOOK
Aug., 2008. Australian. (Jonathan Ogilvie). Hugo Weaving, Rose Byrne, Matt Le Nevez, Pia Miranda, Tyler Coppin, John Batchelor.

TENDERNESS
LIONSGATE AUSTRALIA. May, 2009. Australian. (John Polson) Sophie Traub, Jon Foster, Russell Crowe, Laura Dern, Alexis Dziena, Arija Bareikis, Michael Kelly.

TERMINATOR SALVATION
WARNER BROS. May 14, 2009. (McG) Christian Bale, Sam Worthington, Moon Bloodgood, Helena Bonham Carter, Anton Yelchin, Jadagrace.

TETRO
AMERICAN ZOETROPE. April 29, 2009. (Francis Ford Coppola) Vincent Gallo, Alden Ehrenreich, Maribel Verdu, Klaus Maria Brandauer, Carmen Maura, Rodrigo De La Serna, Leticia Bredice, Mike Amigorena, Sofia Castiglione, Erica Rivas.

THE TEXAS CHAINSAW MASSACRE: THE BEGINNING
NEW LINE CINEMA. Oct., 2006. (Jonathan Liebesman) Jordana Brewster, Taylor Handley, Diora Baird, Matt Bomer, R. Lee Ermey, Andrew Bryniarski, Lee Tergesen, Terrence Evans, Kathy Lamkin, Marietta Marich, Leslie Calkins, Tim DeZarn, Allison Marich, Marcus Nelson, Lew Temple, Cyia Batten.

THAT EVENING SUN
DOGWOOD ENTERTAINMENT. March 21, 2009. (Scott Teems) Hal Holbrook, Ray McKinnon, Walton Goggins, Mia Wasikowska, Carrie Preston, Barry Corbin, Dixie Carter.

THEM
MARS DISTRIBUTION. Jan., 2006. French. (David Moreau, Xavier Palud) Olvia Bonamy, Michael Cohen.

THERE WILL BE BLOOD
PARAMOUNT VANTAGE (in U.S.)/MIRIMAX (International). Oct. 25, 2007. (Paul Thomas Anderson) Daniel Day-Lewis, Paul Dano, Kevin J. O'Connor, Ciaran Hinds, Dillon Freasier, Sydney McCallister, David Willis, David Warshofsky, Colton Woodward, Colleen Foy, Russell Harvard.

THE THING ABOUT MY FOLKS
Jan., 2005. (Raymond De Felitta) Peter Falk, Paul Reiser, Olympia Dukakis, Elizabeth Perkins, Mackenzie Connolly, Lydia Jordan, Ann Dowd, Claire Beckman, Mimi Lieber, Catherine Taormina. Voice: Rachel Robinson.

THINGS WE LOST IN THE FIRE
DREAMWORKS-PARAMOUNT. Oct. 4, 2007. (Susanne Bier) Halle Berry, Benicio Del Toro, David Duchovny, Alison Lohman, Omar Benson Miller, John Carroll Lynch, Alexis Llewellyn, Micah Berry, Robin Weigert, Paula Newsome.

THE THIRD PART OF THE WORLD
SHELLAC DISTRIBUTION. June, 2008. French. (Eric Forestier) Clemence Poesy, Eric Ruf, Maya Sansa, Gaspard Ulliel, Momoko Fructus, Jean-Damien Barbin, Jean-Luc Bideau, Scali Delpeyrat.

THIRST
CJ ENTERTAINMENT (SOUTH KOREA)/FOCUS FEATURES INTL. (U.S.).May 14, 2009. South Korean, U.S. (Park Can-wook) Song Kang-ho, Kim Ok-vin, Kim Hae-suk, Shin Ha-gyun, Park In-hwan, Oh Dal-su, Song Yeong-chang, Mercedes Cabral.

THIRTEEN AMONG A THOUSAND
NOTRO FILMS. Nov., 2005. Spanish. (Inaki Arteta) Antonio Llanos Gancedo, Francisco Maranon, Carmen Villar, Pedro Ma. Baglietto, Rosario Zabala, Ma. Victoria Vidaur. Documentary.

THIRTYFIVE SOMETHING
DIAPHANA DISTRIBUTION. Jan., 2005. French-Belgium. (Cecile Telerman) Mathilde Seigner, Anne Parillaud, Judith Godreche, Pascal Elbe, Thierry Neuvic, Mathias Mlekuz, Pierre Cassignard, Pascal Elso, Marc Citti, Bernard Yerles, Riton Liebman, Marina Tome.

THIS CHRISTMAS
SONY PICTURES ENTERTAINMENT. Oct. 24, 2007. (Preston A. Whitmore) Delroy Lindo, Idris Elba, Loretta Devine, Chris Brown, Keith Robinson, Laz Alonso, Columbus Short, Sharon Leal, Lauren London, Mekhi Phifer, Regina King, DeNetria Champ.

THIS NIGHT IS STILL OURS
BUENA VISTA INTL. ITALY. March, 2008. Italian. (Paolo Genovese, Luca Miniero) Nicolas Vaporidis, Valentina Izumi, Massimiliano Bruno, Ilaria Spada, Maurizio Mattioli, Franco Califano, Paola Tiziana Cruciani, Hal Yamanouchi, Taiyo Yamanouchi, Zhang Xu, John Yat Liu, Nishino Massatosi, Shi Yang, Luca Angeletti, Ettore Bassi, Giovanni Floris, Michele La Ginestra, Francesco Pannofino.

THOSE HAPPY DAYS
SND. July, 2006. French. (Eric Toledano, Olivier Nakache) Jean-Paul Rouve, Marilou Berry, Omar Sy, Julie Fournier, Jean Benguigui, Josephine de Meaux, Lannick Gautry, Guillaume Cyr, Jacques Boudet, Catherine Hosmalin, Jean-Michel Lahmi.

THOSE WHO REMAIN
STUDIOCANAL. Sept., 2007. French. (Anne Le Ny) Vincent Lindon, Emmanuelle Devos, Yeelem Jappain, Anne Le Ny, Gregoire Oestermann, Christine Murillo, Ophelia Kolb Kasapoglu.

THREE AND OUT
WORLDWIDE BONUS ENTERTAINMENT. April, 2008. British. (Jonathan Gershfield) Mackenzie Crook, Colm Meaney, Imelda Staunton, Gemma Arterton, Antony Sher.

THREE COUPLES LOOKING FOR TROUBLE
CHALLENGE FILMS. April, 2005. French. (Jacques Otmezguine) Aurelien Recoing, Samuel Labarthe, Claire Nebout, Philippine Leroy-Beaulieu, Laurence Cote, Hippolyte Girardot, Delphine Rollin, Clotilde De Bayser, Steve Suissa.

THREE DOLLARS
DENDY FILMS/FOOTPRINT FILMS. Feb., 2005. Australian. (Robert Connolly) David Wenham, Frances O'Connor, Sarah Wynter, Joanna Hunt-Prokhovnik, Robert Menzies, Nicole Nabout, David Roberts, Christopher Bunworth, John Flaus.

TICKET TO OUTER SPACE
GAUMONT COLUMBIA TRISTAR FILMS. Jan., 2006. French. (Eric Lartigau) Kad, Olivier, Marina Fois, Guillaume Canet, Andre Dussollier, Pierre-Francois Martin-Laval, Frederic Proust, Thierry Fremont, Fred Maranber.

TICKLING LEO

BARN DOOR PICTURES. Aug. 19, 2009. (Jeremy Davidson) Eli Wallach, Lawrence Pressman, Daniel Sauli, Annie Parisse, Ronald Guttman, Victoria Clark.

THE TIGER AND THE SNOW

01 DISTRIBUTION. Oct., 2005. (Roberto Benigni) Roberto Benigni, Nicoletta Braschi, Jean Reno, Emilia Fox, Amid Farid, Giuseppe Battiston, Andrea Renzi, Gianfranco Varetto, Chiara Pirri, Anna Pirri, Abdelhafid Metalsi, Lucia Poli, Tom Waits.

THE TIGER BRIGADES

TFM DISTRIBUTION. April, 2006. French. (Jerome Cornuau) Clovis Cornillac, Diane Kruger, Edouard Baer, Olivier Gourmet, Stefano Accorsi, Jacques Gamblin, Thierry Fremont, Lea Drucker, Didier Flamand, Philippe Duquesne, Alexandre Medvedev, Richard Valls, Andre Marcon, Agnes Soral, Alexandre Arbatt, Mathias Mlekuz, Pierre Berriau, Eric Prat, Gerard Jugnot.

TIM BURTON'S CORPSE BRIDE

WARNER BROS. PICTURES. Sept., 2005. (Mike Johnson, Tim Burton) Voices: Johnny Depp, Helena Bonham Carter, Emily Watson, Tracey Ullman, Paul Whitehouse, Joanna Lumley, Albert Finney, Richard E. Grant, Christopher Lee, Michael Gough, Jane Horrocks, Enn Reitel, Deep Roy, Danny Elfman, Stephen Ballantyne, Lisa Kay.

TIMECRIMES

Dec., 2007. Spanish. (Nacho Vigalondo) Karra Elejalde, Barbara Goenaga, Nacho Vigalondo, Candela Fernandez.

THE TIME TRAVELER'S WIFE

WARNER BROS. Aug. 6, 2009. (Robert Schwentke) Rachel McAdams, Eric Bana, Arliss Howard, Ron Livingston, Stephen Tobolowsky, Michelle Nolden, Jane McLean, Hailey McCann, Tatum McCann, Brooklynn Proulx, Alex Ferris.

TIRANT LO BLANC: THE MAIDENS' CONSPIRACY

DEAPLANETA. April, 2006. Spanish-British. (Vicente Aranda) Caspar Zafer, Esther Nubiola, Leonor Watling, Ingrid Rubio, Charlie Cox, Victoria Abril, Giancarlo Giannini, Jane Asher, Sid Mitchell, Rafael Amargo.

TMNT

WARNER BROS. (IN NORTH AMERICA)/WEINSTEIN CO. (INTERNATIONAL). March, 2007. U.S.-Hong Kong. (Kevin Munroe) Voices: Chris Evans, Sarah Michelle Gellar, Mako, Patrick Stewart, Mitchell Whitfield, James Arnold Taylor, Mikey Kelley, Nolan North, Ziyi Zhang, Kevin Smith, John DiMaggio, Paula Mattioli, Kevin Michael Richardson, Fred Tatasciore. Narrator: Laurence Fishburne. Animated.

TOM-YUM-GOONG

SAHAMONGKOLFILM INTL. (IN THAILAND)/THE WEINSTEIN CO. (IN U.S.). Jan., 2006. Thai. (Prachya Pinkaew) Tony Jaa, Phettkai Wongkamlao, Bongkod Kongmalai, David Asavanond, Jin Xing, Johnny Nguyen, Damian de Montemas, Nathan B. Jones, Jonathan Patrick Foo, Lateef Crowder.

TOO BEAUTIFUL

MEDUSA FILM. April, 2005. Italian. (Ugo Fabrizio Giordani) Costantino Vitagliano, Daniele Interrante, Alessandra Pierelli, Jennifer Poli, Ernesto Mahieux, Massimo Molea, Kiara Tomaselli, Fanny Cadeo, Fausto Sciarappa, Anna Melato, Daniela Danesi, Maurizio Amigoni, Fabio Ferrari, Stefano Antonucci.

TOOTH & NAIL

AFTER DARK FILMS. Nov. 12, 2007. (Mark Young) Rachel Miner, Nicole DuPort, Rider Strong, Michael Kelly, Alexandra Barreto, Emily Catherine Young, Zack Robidas, Kevin E. Scott, Beverly Hynds, Patrick Durham, Jonathan Sachar, Robert Carradine, Vinnie Jones, Michael Madsen.

TORRENTE 3: THE PROTECTOR

UIP. Oct., 2005. Spanish. (Santiago Segura) Santiago Segura, Jose Mota, Javier Gutierrez, Yvonne Scio, Carlos Latre, Tony Leblanc, Fabio Testi, Enrique Villen, Silvia Gambino.

TORTILLA HEAVEN

ARCHANGEL RELEASING. March, 2007. (Judy Hecht Dumontet) Jose Zuniga, Miguel Sandoval, Olivia Hussey, George Lopez, Marcelo Tubert, Irene Bedard, Lupe Ontiveros, Alexis Cruz, Judy Herrera, Del Zamora, Ana Ortiz, Elaine Miles, Elpidia Carrillo, Geno Silva, Rick Gutierrez, Deborah Chavez, Scott Cleverdon, Jonathan Levit, Danny Peck.

TOTAL DENIAL

MK PRODUCTION (IN U.S.). Oct., 2007. Bulgarian. (Milena Kaneva) Ka Hsaw Wa, Katie Redford, Dan Stormer, Daniel Petrocelli. Documentary.

TOUCH THE SKY

ALTA FILMS. Sept., 2007. Spanish-Argentinian. (Marcos Carnevale) Chete Lera, Montse German, Raul Arevalo, Facundo Arana, Veronica Echegui, Betiana Blum, Lidia Catalano, China Zorrilla.

TOWARDS DARKNESS

PEACE ARCH ENTERTAINMENT/NEGRET FILMS. March 3, 2008. (Antonio Negret) A Peace Arch Entertainment/Negret Films release of a Negret Roberto Urbina, David Sutcliffe, Tony Plana, William Atherton, America Ferrera, Cameron Daddo, Alejandra Borrero, Fernando Solorzano.

THE TRAIL

GAUMONT. Jan., 2006. French. (Eric Valli) Julian Sands, Eriq Ebouaney, Camille Summers, Clint Dyer, Siyabonga Shibe.

TRAILER PARK BOYS: THE MOVIE

SCREEN MEDIA FILMS. Jan., 2008. Canadian. (Mike Clattenburg) Robb Wells, John Paul Tremblay, Mike Smith, John Dunsworth, Pat Roach, Lucy Decoutere, Sarah Dunsworth, Cory Bowles, Michael Jackson, Barrie Dunn, Nichole Hiltz.

TRAIN KEEPS A ROLLIN'

Feb., 2008. Hungarian. (Robert Koltai) Tomas Kimmel Szabo, Robert Koltai, Judit Pogany, Karoly Gesztesi, Sandor Gaspar, Katinka Egres.

TRANSFORMERS

PARAMOUNT. June, 2007. (Michael Bay) Shia LaBeouf, Tyrese Gibson, Josh Duhamel, Anthony Anderson, Megan Fox, Rachael Taylor, John Turturro, Jon Voight, Kevin Dunn, Michael O'Neill, Julie White, Amaury Nolasco, Bernie Mac, Johnny Sanchez. Voices: Peter Cullen, Hugo Weaving, Mark Ryan, Jess Harnell, Robert Foxworth, Jimmie Wood, Darius McCrary, Charlie Adler, Reno Wilson.

TRANSFORMERS: REVENGE OF THE FALLEN

PARAMOUNT. June 15, 2009. (Michael Bay) Shia LaBeouf, Megan Fox, Josh Duhamel, Tyrese Gibson, John Turturro, Ramon Rodriguez, Kevin Dunn, Rainn Wilson, Julie White, Hugo Weaving, Peter Cullen, Mark Ryan, Robert Foxworth, Anthony Anderson, Tony Todd.

THE TRANSPORTER 2

EUROPACORP (IN FRANCE)/20TH CENTURY FOX (IN U.S.). Aug., 2005. French. (Louis Leterrier) Jason Statham, Amber Valetta, Alessandro Gassman, Kate Nauta, Hunter Clary, Francois Berleand, Jason Flemyng, Jeff Chase, Keith David.

TRANSPORTER 3

LIONSGATE. (IN U.S.). Nov. 17, 2008. (Olivier Megaton) Jason Statham, Natalya Rudakova, Francois Berleand, Robert Knepper, Jeroen Krabbe.

THE TREATMENT

NEW YORKER FILMS. April, 2006. (Oren Rudavsky) Chris Eigeman, Famke Janssen, Ian Holm, Harris Yulin, Stephanie March, Blair Brown, Roger Rees, Stephen Lang.

TRES BIEN, MERCI

GEMINI FILMS. Jan., 2007. French. (Emmanuelle Cuau) Gilbert Melki, Sandrine Kiberlain, Olivier Cruveiller, Christophe Odent, Nathalie Akoun-Cruveiller, Frederic Pierrot, Camille Japy, Emmanuel Salinger.

TRISTAN & ISOLDE

20TH CENTURY FOX. Jan., 2006. British-German-Czech. (Kevin Reynolds) James Franco, Sophia Myles, Rufus Sewell, David Patrick O'Hara, Mark Strong, Henry Cavill, Bronagh Gallagher, Ronan Vibert, Lucy Russell, JB Blanc, Graham Mullins, Thomas Sangster.

TROPIC THUNDER

DREAMWORKS/PARAMOUNT. July 24, 2008. (Ben Stiller) Ben Stiller, Jack Black, Robert Downey, Jr., Nick Nolte, Steve Coogan, Jay Baruchel, Danny McBride, Brandon T. Jackson, Bill Hader, Brandon Soo Hoo, Reggie Lee, Trieu Tran, Matthew McConaughey, Tom Cruise.

TROUBLE

TFM DISTRIBUTION (IN FRANCE)/FILMS DE L'ELYSEES (BELGIUM). March, 2005. French-Belgium. (Harry Cleven) Benoit Magimel, Natacha Regnier, Olivier Gourmet, Hannah Novak.

TRUFFE

CHRISTAL FILMS. Aug., 2008. Canadian. (Kim Nguyen) Celine Bonnier, Roy Dupuis, Pierre Lebeau, Danielle Proulx, Jean-Nicolas Verreault, Michele Richard, Claude Lemieux, Jean Lapointe.

TRUST THE MAN

20TH CENTURY FOX. Aug., 2006. (Bart Freundlich) David Duchovny, Julianne Moore, Billy Crudup, Maggie Gyllenhaal, Eva Mendes, Ellen Barkin, Garry Shandling, James Le Gros.

THE TRUTH ABOUT LOVE

July, 2005. British. (John Hay) Jennifer Love Hewitt, Dougray Scott, Jimi Mistry, Branka Katic, Kate Miles, Emma Noble, Karl Howman, Simon Webber.

TRY ME

ARP SELECTION. March, 2006. French. (Pierre Francois Martin-Laval) Pierre Francois Martin-Laval, Julie Depardieu, Pierre Richard, Kad Merad, Wladimir Yordanoff, Isabelle Nanty, Jules-Angelo Bigarnet, Frederic Proust, Marina Fois.

TURISTAS

20TH CENTURY FOX. Nov., 2006. (John Stockwell) Josh Duhamel, Melissa George, Olivia Wilde, Desmond Askew, Beau Garrett, Max Brown, Agles Steib, Miguel Lunardi.

TURKISH GAMBIT

March, 2005. Russian. (Dzhanik Fauziev) Yegor Beroyev, Olga Krasko, Dmitri Pevtsov, Daniel Olbrychski, Aleksandr Likov, Marat Basharov, Vladimir Ilyin, Didier Bienaime, Victor Verzhbitsky, Aleksandr Baluyev, Aleksei Guskov.

TWILIGHT

SUMMIT ENTERTAINMENT. Nov. 18, 2008. (Catherine Hardwicke) Kristen Stewart, Robert Pattinson, Billy Burke, Peter Facinelli, Elizabeth Reaser, Cam Gigandet, Ashley Greene, Anna Kendrick, Nikki Reed, Taylor Lautner, Kellan Lutz, Jackson Rathbone, Michael Welch, Gil Birmingham, Justin Chon, Christian Serratos, Jose Zuniga, Rachelle Lefevre, Edi Gathegi, Sarah Clarke, Waylan Forge.

TWO FOR THE MONEY

UNIVERSAL. Oct., 2005. (D.J. Caruso) Al Pacino, Matthew McConaughey, Rene Russo, Armand Assante, Jeremy Piven, Jaime King.

THE TWO SIDES OF THE BED

BUENA VISTA INTL. Jan., 2006. Spanish. (Emilio Martinez-Lazaro) Ernesto Alterio, Guillermo Toledo, Alberto San Juan, Maria Esteve, Pilar Castro, Lucia Jimenez, Secun de la Rosa, Veronica Sanchez.

TWO STEP

01 DISTRIBUTION. Sept., 2005. Italian. (Andrea Barzini) Kledi Kadiu, Laura Chiatti, Genti Kame, Stefania Barca, Monica Vallerini, Nathalie Guetta, Andrea Sartoretti, Paola Carleo, Riccardo Zinna, Riccardo Rossi, Lucio Patane, Augusto Zucchi, Fatos Haxhiraj.

TWO WEEKS

MGM. Nov., 2006. (Steve Stockman) Sally Field, Ben Chaplin, Tom Cavanagh, Julianne Nicholson, Glenn Howerton, James Murtaugh, Clea Duvall.

TYLER PERRY'S THE FAMILY THAT PREYS

LIONSGATE. Aug 18, 2008. (Tyler Perry) Alfre Woodard, Sanaa Lathan, Rockmond Dunbar, Kadee Strickland, Cole Hauser, Taraji P. Henson, Robin Givens, Tyler Perry, Kathy Bates, Sebastian Siegel.

TYLER PERRY'S I CAN DO BAD ALL BY MYSELF

LIONSGATE. Sept. 11, 2009. (Tyler Perry) Tyler Perry, Taraji P. Henson, Adam Rodriguez, Brian White, Hope Olaide Wilson, Kwesi Boakye, Freddy Siglar, Gladys Knight, Mary J. Blige, Marvin L. Winans.

TYLER PERRY'S MADEA GOES TO JAIL

LIONSGATE. Feb. 20, 2009. (Tyler Perry) Tyler Perry, Derek Luke, Keshia Knight Pulliam, David Mann, Tamela Mann, RonReaco Lee, Ion Overman, Vanessa Ferlito, Viola Davis, Sofia Vergara, Dr. Phil McGraw, Rev. Al Sharpton, Whoopi Goldberg, Steve Harvey, Joy Behar, Elisabeth Hasselbeck, Judge Greg Mathis.

TYLER PERRY'S MEET THE BROWNS

LIONSGATE. March 21, 2008. (Tyler Perry) Angela Bassett, Rick Fox, Margaret Avery, Frankie Faison, Jenifer Lewis, Lance Gross, Sofia Vergara, Lamman Rucker, Tamela Mann, David Mann, Irma P. Hall, Tyler Perry.

TYLER PERRY'S WHY DID I GET MARRIED?

LIONSGATE. Oct. 12, 2007. (Tyler Perry) Tyler Perry, Janet Jackson, Jill Scott, Malik Yoba, Richard T. Jones, Michael Jai White, Lamman Rucker, Sharon Leal, Tasha Smith, Denise Boutte.

TYPHOON

CJ ENTERTAINMENT (IN S. KOREA)/PARAMOUNT CLASSICS (IN U.S.). July, 2006. South Korean. (Kwak Kyung-taek) Jang Dong-geon, Lee Jeong-jae, Lee Mi-yeon, Kim Kab-su, David Lee McInnis, Chatthapong Phantana-angkul, Heo Wook, Seon Ho-jin, Shin Seong-il, Park Chan-yeong, Kim Gwan-hun, Min Ji-hwan.

U2 3D

NATIONAL GEOGRAPHIC ENTERTAINMENT. Dec. 18, 2007. (Catherine Owens) Bono, the Edge, Adam Clayton, Larry Mullen, Jr.

UGLY MELANIE

SND. Nov., 2008. French. (Jean-Patrick Benes, Allan Mauduit) Marilou Berry, Frederique Bel, Pierre Francois Martin-Laval, Josephine de Meaux, Thomas Ngijol, Chantal Lauby, Alice Pol, Gil Alma, Liliane Rovere, Charles Meurisse.

THE ULTIMATE GIFT

BIGGER PICTURE. March, 2007. (Michael O. Sajbel) Drew Fuller, James Garner, Ali Hillis, Abigail Breslin, Lee Meriwether, Brian Dennehy, Bill Cobbs.

ULTIMATUM

MARS DISTRIBUTION (IN FRANCE) RELEASE OF A CIPANGO, STUDIO 37, FRANCE 3 CINEMA (FRANCE)/LAMA FILMS (ISRAEL)/FILM KAIROS (ITALY). Oct., 2009. French, Israeli, Italian.

ULTRAVIOLET

SONY PICTURES ENTERTAINMENT. March, 2006. (Kurt Wimmer) Milla Jovovich, Cameron Bright, Nick Chinlund, Sebastien Andrieu, William Fichtner.

UMRAO JAAN

ADLABS. Nov., 2006. Indian. (J.P. Dutta) Aishwarya Rai, Abhishek Bachchan, Shabana Azmi, Suneil Shetty, Divya Dutta, Himani Shivpuri, Kulbhushan Kharbanda, Puru Raj Kumar, Vishwajeet Pradhan, Parikshit Sahni, Ayesha Julka, Maya Alagh.

UN MONDE A NOUS

MARS DISTRIBUTION. July, 2008. French. (Frederic Balekdjian) Edouard Baer, Anton Balekdjian, Nassereba Keita, Philippe Lefebvre, Mariame Gaye, Julien Frison, Morgan Pierrard, Xavier Maly, Veronique Gallet, Alain Chabat.

UNBORN IN THE USA: INSIDE THE WAR ON ABORTION

FIRST RUN FEATURES. June, 2007. (Stephen Fell, Will Thompson) Steve Wagner, David Lee, Peggy Hartshorn, Joe Scheidler, John Brockhoeft, Don Spitz, Frank Pavone, Matt Trewhella. Documentary.

THE UNCERTAIN GUEST

DEAPLANETA. Oct., 2005. Spanish. (Guillem Morales) Andoni Gracia, Monica Lopez, Francesc Garrido, Agustin Villaronga, Minnie Marx, Pablo Derqui, Violeta Llueca.

UNDERCLASSMAN

MIRAMAX FILMS. Aug., 2005. (Marcos Siega) Nick Cannon, Shawn Ashmore, Roselyn Sanchez, Kelly Hu, Ian Gomez, Hugh Bonneville, Cheech Marin.

UNDERDOG

BUENA VISTA. Aug., 2007. (Frederik Du Chau) Jim Belushi, Peter Dinklage, Patrick Warburton, Alex Neuberger, Taylor Momsen, John Slattery. Voices: Brad Garrett, Amy Adams, Jason Lee.

THE UNDERDOG KNIGHT

BEIJING CIWEN FILM & TV PROD. CO. March, 2009. Chinese. (Ding Sheng) Liu Ye, Anthony Wong, You Yong, Sun Honglei, Ma Jingwu, Yu Rongguang, Liu Yang, Ellen Chan, Wang Zhian, Jiang Yi, Zheng Hongtao, Zhao Yaodong.

UNEARTHED

AFTER DARK FILMS. June 14, 2007. (Matthew Leutwyler) Emmanuelle Vaugier, Luke Goss, Beau Garrett, Charlie Murphy, Tonantzin Carmelo, Whitney Able, Tommy Dewey, M.C. Gainey, Russell Means, Miranda Bailey.

UNDERWORLD: EVOLUTION

SONY PICTURES ENTERTAINMENT. Jan., 2006. (Len Wiseman) Kate Beckinsale, Scott Speedman, Tony Curran, Derek Jacobi, Bill Nighy, Steven Mackintosh, Shane Brolly, Brian Steele, Zita Gorog, Scott McElroy, John Mann, Michael Sheen.

UNDISCOVERED

LIONS GATE FILMS. Aug., 2005. (Meiert Avis) Pell James, Steven Strait, Kip Pardue, Shannyn Sossamon, Carrie Fisher, Peter Weller, Fisher Stevens, Stephen Moyer, Ashlee Simpson.

UNIDENTIFIED

FIVE & TWO PICTURES. Oct., 2006. (Rich Christiano) Jonathan Aube, Josh Adamson, Jenna Bailey, Lance Zitron, Rebecca St. James, Michael Blain-Rozgay.

UNDER THE SNOW

CRONOPIA. July, 2008. Spanish. Laura de Pedro, Gabriel Latorre, Asun Aguinaco, Xabi Yarnoz, Aurora Moneo.

UNFINISHED SKY

PALACE FILMS (IN AUSTRALIA)/A-FILM DISTRIBUTION (IN NETHERLANDS). Aug., 2007. Australian-Dutch. (Peter Duncan) William McInnes, Monic Hendrickx, David Field, Bille Brown, Roy Billing, Christopher Sommers.

THE UGLY TRUTH

SONY PICTURES ENTERTAINMENT. July 17, 2009. (Robert Luketic) Katherine Heigl, Gerard Butler, Eric Winter, John Michael Higgins, Bree Turner, Nick Searcy, Kevin Connolly, Cheryl Hines, Bonnie Somerville, Yvette Nicole Brown, Nate Corddry, Noah Matthews.

THE UNBORN

ROGUE PICTURES. Jan. 6, 2009. (David S. Goyer) Odette Yustman, Gary Oldman, Cam Gigandet, Meagan Good, Idris Elba, Jane Alexander, Atticus Shaffer, James Remar, Carla Gugino.

UNDER THE SEA 3D

WARNER BROS. Feb. 3, 2009. (Howard Hall) Narrator: Jim Carrey. Documentary.

UNITED 93

UNIVERSAL. April, 2006. (Paul Greengrass) David Alan Basche, Richard Bekins, Susan Blommaert, Ray Charleson, Christian Clemenson, Khalid Abdalla, Lewis Alsamari, Ben Sliney, Maj. James Fox, Gregg Henry.

UNKNOWN

IFC FIRST TAKE. Oct., 2006. (Simon Brand) Jim Caviezel, Greg Kinnear, Joe Pantoliano, Barry Pepper, Jeremy Sisto, Bridget Moynahan, Peter Stormare, Clayne Crawford.

UNSPOOLED

NECESSARY NOMAD. Oct. 2, 2008. (Keir Moreano) Nicole Vicius, Larry Brustoski, Maurice Singer, Norm Golden, Matthew Santo. Narrators: Keir Moreano, Mario Diaz.

(UNTITLED)

PARKER FILM CO. Jan. 10, 2009. (Jonathan Parker) Adam Goldberg, Marley Shelton, Eion Bailey, Lucy Punch, Vinnie Jones, Zak Orth, Ptolemy Slocum, Michael Panes, Svetlana Efremova, Janet Carroll,

Ben Hammer.

UNTRACEABLE

SONY PICTURES ENTERTAINMENT. Jan. 9, 2008. (Gregory Hoblit) Diane Lane, Billy Burke, Colin Hanks, Joseph Cross, Mary Beth Hurt, Peter Lewis, Tyrone Giordano, Perla Haney-Jardine, Tim De Zarn.

UP

WALT DISNEY PICTURES. May 29, 2009. (Peter Docter, Bob Peterson) Voices: Ed Asner, Christopher Plummer, Jordan Nagai, Bob Peterson, Delroy Lindo, Jerome Ranft, John Ratzenberger, David Kaye, Pete Docter, David Kaye, Elie Docter, Jeremy Leary.

UP IN THE AIR

PARAMOUNT. Sept. 5, 2009. (Jason Reitman) George Clooney, Vera Farmiga, Anna Kendrick, Jason Bateman, Danny McBride, Melanie Lynskey, Amy Morton, Sam Elliott, J.K. Simmons, Zach Galifianakis.

URBANSCAPES

July, 2006. U.S.-Italian. (Lorena Lucinao, Filippo Piscopo) Gen. Gordon Baker, Marion Baker, Mel Rosenthal, Camillo J. Vergara. Documentary.

V.O.S.

ALTA CLASSICS. July, 2009. Spanish. (Cesc Gay) Agata Roca, Vicenta Ndongo, Paul Berrondo, Andres Herrera.

VACANCY

SONY PICTURES ENTERTAINMENT. April, 2007. (Nimrod Antal) Luke Wilson, Kate Beckinsale, Frank Whaley, Ethan Embry.

THE VALET

GAUMONT COLUMBIA TRISTAR FILMS. March, 2006. French. (Francis Veber) Gad Elmaleh, Alice Taglioni, Daniel Auteuil, Kristin Scott Thomas, Richard Berry, Virginie Ledoyen, Dany Boon, Michel Jonasz, Michel Aumont, Patrick Mille, Laurent Gamelon, Michele Garcia, Karl Lagerfeld.

VALIANT

BUENA VISTA. March, 2005. British-U.S. (Gary Chapman) Voices: Ewan McGregor, Ricky Gervais, Tim Curry, Jim Broadbent, Hugh Laurie, Brian Lonsdale, Dan Roberts, John Cleese, John Hurt, Pip Torrens. Animated.

VALKYRIE

MGM. Dec. 9, 2008. U.S.-German. (Bryan Singer) Tom Cruise, Kenneth Branagh, Bill Nighy, Tom Wilkinson, Carice van Houten, Thomas Kretschmann, Terence Stamp, Eddie Izzard, Kevin R. McNally, Christian Berkel, Jamie Parker, David Bamber, Tom Hollander, David Schofield, Kenneth Cranham, Halina Reijn, Werner Daehn, Harvey Friedman, Matthias Schweighofer.

VALLEY OF THE HEART'S DELIGHT

INTERCONTINENTAL DRIFT. Nov. 17, 2007. (Tim Boxell) Gabriel Mann, Bruce McGill, Diana Scarwid, Emily Harrison, Tom Bower, Pete Postlethwaite, Joe Mandragona, Ron Rogge, Joe Orrach, Rod Gnapp, David Barth, Bob Greene, Howard Swain, Pete Quartroli, Val Diamond, Geoff Hoyle, Cully Fredricksen, Michael Sommer, Jeffrey Hillard.

VALLEY OF THE WOLVES: IRAQ

PANA FILM. Feb., 2006. Turkish. (Serdar Akar) Necati Sasmaz, Billy Zane, Ghassan Massoud, Berguzar Korel, Gurkan Uygun, Diego Serrano, Kenan Coban, Erhan Ufak, Gary Busey, Spencer Garrett, Nusret Senay, Tayfun Eraslan, Ismet Hurmuzlu, Jihad Abdou, Yavuz Imsel, Mauro Martino, Egemen Yavuz, Umut Ugur, Ziver Ciftci.

VANTAGE POINT

SONY PICTURES ENTERTAINMENT. Feb. 19, 2008. (Pete Travis) Dennis Quaid, Matthew Fox, Forest Whitaker, Bruce McGill, Edgar Ramirez, Said Taghmaoui, Ayelet Zurer, Zoe Saldana, Sigourney Weaver, William Hurt, James Le Gros, Eduardo Noriega, Richard T. Jones, Holt McCallany, Leonardo Nam.

VAMPIRE PARTY

SND. Aug., 2008. French. (Stephen Cafiero, Vincent Lobelle) Patrick Mille, Frederique Bel, Julie Fournier, Vincent Desagnat, Sam Karmann, Helene de Fougerolles, Antoine Dulery, Gilles Gaston Dreyfus, Jean-Luc Couchard, Tcheky Karyo.

VAN GOGH: BRUSH WITH GENIUS

MACGILLIVRAY FREEMAN (IN U.S.). Sept., 2008. French. (Francois Bertrand) Jacques Gamblin, Helene Seuzaret. Documentary.

THE VENETIAN DILEMMA

March, 2005. (Carole Rifkind, Richard Rifkind) Roberto D'Agostino, Paolo Lanapoppi, Danilo Palmieri, Michela Scibilia. Documentary.

THE VELVETEEN RABBIT

FAMILY 1 FILMS. Feb. 21, 2009. (Michael Landon, Jr.) Matthew Harbour, Una Kay, Kevin Jubinville.Voices: Jane Seymour, Tom Skerritt, Ellen Burstyn, Chandler Wakefield.

VENOM

DIMENSION FILMS. Sept., 2005. (Jim Gillespie) Agnes Bruckner, Jonathan Jackson, Laura Ramsey, D.J. Cotrona, Rick Cramer, Meagan Good, Bijou Phillips, Pawel Szadja, Davetta Sherwood, Stacey Travis, Marcus Brown, James Pickens, Jr., Method Man, Deborah Duke.

VERDICT ON AUSCHWITZ: THE FRANKFURT AUSCHWITZ TRIAL 1963-1965

FIRST RUN FEATURES. Jan., 2007. German. (Rolf Bickel, Dietrich Wagner) Herman Langbein, Joachim Kugler, Dr., Fritz Baueur, many others. Narrator: Edgar M. Boehke. Documentary.

THE VERY BIG APARTMENT

MARS DISTRIBUTION. Jan., 2007. French. (Pascal Thomas) Laetitia Casta, Mathieu Amalric, Pierre Arditi, Noemie Lvovsky, Carmen Durand, Stephanie Pasterkamp, Gisele Casadesus, Valerie Decobert, Mariam N'Diaye, Cheik Doukoure, Jean-Francois Balmer, Pierre Lescure, Hana Gruvman.

THE VERY VERY BIG COMPANY

PATHE. Nov., 2008. French. (Pierre Jolivet) Roschdy Zem, Marie Gillain, Jean-Paul Rouve, Adrien Jolivet, Arlette Thomas, Nicolas Marie, Guilaine Londez, Wilfried Romoli, Anne Loiret, Scali Delpeyrat.

VICE

41 INC. (IN U.S.). May, 2008. Canadian. (Raul Sanchez Inglis) Michael Madsen, Daryl Hannah, Mykelti Williamson, Mark Boone, Jr. Kurupt, John Cassini, Nicholas Lea, Martin Cummins, Aaron Pearl, Emy Aneke, Matthew Robert Kelly, Bette Linde.

VIEW FROM A GRAIN OF SAND

Nov., 2006. U.S.-Afghanistan. (Meena Nanji) Shapiray Hassan, Daoud Hassan, Wajia, Roeena Mohmand. Narrator: Meena Nanji. Documentary.

VISHWATHULASI

Sept., 2005. Indian. (Sumathy Ram) Padmashree Mammootty, Nandita Das, Manoj Kjayan, Mohit, Ambili Devi, Anirudh, Delhi Ganesh.

VOICE

CINEMA SERVICE. July, 2005. South Korean. (Equan Choe) Kim Ok-bin, Seo Ji-hye, Cha Ye-ryeon, Kim Seo-hyeong, Im Hyeon-gyeong.

VOISINS VOISINES

EUROZOOM. July, 2005. (Malik Chabane) Frederic Diefenthal, Anemone, Jackie Berroyer, Mohamed Fellag, Gwendoline Hamon, Insa Sane, Hakim Sahraoui, Candice Berner, Nora Armani, Sarah Maldoror, Nisan Doman, Rajkumar Bhan.

VOLVER

WARNER BROTHER INTL. SPAIN (IN SPAIN)/SONY PICTURES CLASSICS (IN U.S.). March, 2006. Spanish. (Pedro Almodovar) Penelope Cruz, Lola Duenas, Blanca Portillo, Carmen Maura, Yohana Cobo, Chus Lampreave, Antonio de la Torre, Leandro Rivera, Carmen Machi, Yolanda Ramos, Maria Isabel Diaz.

W.

LIONSGATE. Oct. 6, 2008. (Oliver Stone) Josh Brolin, Elizabeth Banks, Ellen Burstyn, James Cromwell, Richard Dreyfuss, Scott Glenn, Toby Jones, Stacy Keach, Bruce McGill, Thandie Newton, Jeffrey Wright, Ioan Gruffudd, Noah Wyle, Dennis Boutsikaris, Michael Gaston, Brent Sexton, Paul Rae, Rob Corddry, Marley Shelton, Colin Hanks, Jason Ritter.

WAIST DEEP

ROGUE PICTURES. June, 2006. (Vondie Curtis Hall) Tyrese Gibson, Meagan Good, Larenz Tate, H. Hunter Hall, Kimora Lee Simmons, The Game.

WAITING...

LIONS GATE FILMS. Sept., 2005. (Rob McKittrick) Ryan Reynolds, Anna Faris, Justin Long, David Koechner, Luis Guzman, Chi McBride, John Francis Daley, Kaitlin Doubleday, Patrick Benedict, Alanna Ubach, Vanessa Lengies, Max Kasch, Andy Milonakis, Dane Cook, Jordan Ladd, Emmanuelle Chriqui, Wendie Malick, Monica Monica, Travis Resor, J.D. Evermore.

WAITING FOR SOMEONE

BAC FILMS. Jan., 2007. French. (Jerome Bonnell) Jean-Pierre Darroussin, Emmanuelle Devos, Eric Caravaca, Florence Loiret-Caille, Sylvain Dieuaide, Sabrina Ouazani.

WAITRESS

FOX SEARCHLIGHT. Jan., 2007. (Adrienne Shelly) Keri Russell, Nathan Fillion, Cheryl Hines, Adrienne Shelly, Lew Temple, Eddie Jemison, Jeremy Sisto, Andy Griffith.

WAKE UP SID

UTV MOTION PICTURES. Oct., 2009. Indian. (Ayan Mukerji) Ranbir Kapoor, Konkona Sen Sharma, Anupam Kher, Supriya Pathak, Namit Das, Shikha Talsania.

WALL-E
WALT DISNEY STUDIOS. June 25, 2008. (Andrew Stanton) Ben Burtt, Elissa Knight, Jeff Garlin, Fred Willard, Ben Burtt, John Ratzenberger, Kathy Najimy, Sigourney Weaver.

WALLACE & GROMIT: THE CURSE OF THE WERE-RABBIT
DREAMWORKS. Sept., 2005. British. (Nick Park, Steve Box) Voices: Peter Sallis, Ralph Fiennes, Helena Bonham Carter, Peter Kay, Nicholas Smith, Liz Smith. Animated.

WAL-MART: THE HIGH COST OF LOW PRICE
Nov., 2005. (Robert Greenwald). Documentary.

WAQT: THE RACE AGAINST TIME
EROS INTERNATIONAL (IN U.K., U.S.). April, 2005. Indian. (Vipul Amrutlal Shah) Amitabh Bachchan, Akshay Kumar, Priyanka Chopra, Shefali Shah, Boman Irani, Rajpal Yadav.

WAR
LIONSGATE. Aug., 2007. (Philip G. Atwell) Jet Li, Jason Statham, John Lone, Devon Aoki, Luis Guzman, Saul Rubinek, Ryo Ishibashi, Sung Kang, Mathew St. Patrick.

WAR MADE EASY: HOW PRESIDENTS AND PUNDITS KEEP SPINNING US TO DEATH
MED. July, 2007. (Loretta Alper, Jeremy Earp) Norman Solomon. Narrator: Sean Penn. Documentary.

WAR OF THE WORLDS
PARAMOUNT. June, 2005. (Steven Spielberg) Tom Cruise, Dakota Fanning, Miranda Otto, Justin Chatwin, Tim Robbins, Rick Gonzalez, Yul Vazquez, Lenny Venito, Lisa Ann Walter, Ann Robinson, Gene Barry. Narrator: Morgan Freeman.

THE WARLORDS
MEDIA ASIA. Jan., 2008. Hong Kong-Chinese. (Peter Chan) Jet Li, Andy Lau, Takeshi Kaneshiro, Xu Jinglei.

WATCHMEN
WARNER BROS. (IN U.S.)/PARAMOUNT (INTERNATIONAL).
Feb. 25, 2009. (Zack Snyder) Malin Akerman, Billy Crudup, Matthew Goode, Carla Gugino, Jackie Earle Haley, Jeffrey Dean Morgan, Patrick Wilson, Matt Frewer, Stephen McHattie, Laura Mennell, Rob LaBelle, Robert Wisden.

THE WATER HORSE
SONY PICTURES ENTERTAINMENT. Nov. 29, 2007. (Jay Russell) Emily Watson, Alex Etel, Ben Chaplin, David Morrissey, Priyanka Xi, Marshall Napier, Joel Tobeck, Erroll Shand, Brian Cox, Craig Hall.

WE ARE MARSHALL
WARNER BROS. Dec., 2006. (McG) Matthew McConaughey, Matthew Fox, Anthony Mackie, David Strathairn, Ian McShane, Kate Mara, January Jones.

WE JAM ECONO: THE STORY OF THE MINUTEMEN
July, 2005. (Tim Irwin) D. Boon, George Hurley, Mike Watt, Gregg Ginn, Henry Rollins, Ian MacKaye, Jello Biafra, Richard Hell, Richard Meltzer, Thurston Moore, Raymond Pettibon, Byron Coley, Colin Newman, John Doe, Flea, J. Mascis. Documentary.

WE LIVE IN PUBLIC
INTERLOPER FILMS. Jan. 19, 2009. (Ondi Timoner) Documentary.

WE WENT TO WONDERLAND
March, 2008. British-Chinese. (Xiaolu Guo) XiuLin, Li Heying. Documentary.

WE WERE JUST DREAMING
FOLKETS BIO. April, 2005. Swedish. (Lena Lucki Stein) Altansukh Khaidav, Timurbataar Khaidav, Gongoryn Khaidav. Documentary.

WEATHER GIRL
SECRET IDENTITY. Jan. 17, 2009. (Blayne Weaver) Tricia O'Kelley, Patrick J. Adams, Ryan Devlin, Kaitlin Olson, Mark Harmon, Alex Kapp Horner, Marin Hinkle, Jon Cryer, Jane Lynch.

THE WEATHER MAN
PARAMOUNT. Oct., 2005. (Gore Verbinski) Nicolas Cage, Michael Caine, Hope Davis, Gemmenne de la Pena, Nicholas Hoult, Michael Rispoli, Gil Bellows, Judith McConnell.

WEDDING CRASHERS
NEW LINE CINEMA. July, 2005. (David Dobkin) Owen Wilson, Vince Vaughn, Christopher Walken, Rachel McAdams, Isla Fisher, Jane Seymour, Ellen Albertini Dow, Keir O'Donnell, Bradley Cooper, Ron Canada, Henry Gibson.

THE WEDDING DATE
UNIVERSAL. Feb., 2005. (Clare Kilner) Debra Messing, Dermot Mulroney, Amy Adams, Jack Davenport, Sarah Parish, Jeremy Sheffield, Peter Egan, Holland Taylor, Jolyon James, C. Gerod Harris, Martin Barrett, Jay Simon, Stephen Lobo.

THE WEDDING DAY
UGC DISTRIBUTION. July, 2005. French. (Didier Caron) Denis Cherer, Valerie Baurens, Stephane Boutet, Patrick Zard, Marie-Helene Lentini, Veronique Barrault, Fred Nony, Valerie Vogt, Pierre-Jean Cherrer, Francoise Lepine, Maaike Jansen, Catherine Ekerle, Jean-Pierre Jacovella, Jean Martiny, Gwenaelle Simon, Renato Ribeiro, Eric Laugerias, Bernard Fructus.

THE WEDDING DIRECTOR
01 DISTRIBUTION. April, 2006. Italian-French. (Marco Bellocchio) Sergio Castellitto, Donatella Finocchiaro, Sami Frey, Gianni Cavina, Bruno Cariello, Maurizio Donadoni, Simona Nobili, Claudia Zanella, Corinne Castelli, Silvia Ajelli, Aurora Peres, Giacomo Guernieri.

WELCOME TO DONGMAKGOL
SHOWBOX/MEDIAPLEX. Sept., 2005. South Korean. (Park Gwang-hyeon) Jeong Jae-yeong, Shin Ha-gyun, Gang Hye-jeong, Im Ha-ryong, Seo Jae-gyeong, Ryu Deok-hyeon, Steve Taschler.

WELCOME HOME ROSCOE JENKINS
UNIVERSAL. Feb. 5, 2008. (Malcolm D. Lee) Martin Lawrence, Margaret Avery, Joy Bryant, Louis C.K., Michael Clarke Duncan, Mike Epps, Mo'Nique, Nicole Ari Parker, Cedric the Entertainer, James Earl Jones, Damani Roberts.

WELCOME TO THE QUIET ROOM
Nov., 2007. Japanese. (Matsuo Suzuki) Yuki Uchida, Kankuro Kudo, Yu Aoi, Ryo, Shinobu Otake, Shinya Tsukamoto, Satoshi Tsumabuko, Mai Takahashi.

THE WESTERN TRUNK LINE
Oct., 2006. Chinese-Japanese. (Li Jixian) Running time: 98 Min. Li Jie, Zhang Dengfeng, Shen Jiani, Zhao Haiyan.

WHAT HAPPENS IN VEGAS
20TH CENTURY FOX. May 3, 2008. (Tom Vaughan) Cameron Diaz, Ashton Kutcher, Rob Corddry, Lake Bell, Jason Sudeikis, Treat Williams, Deirdre O'Connell, Michelle Krusiec, Dennis Farina, Zach Galifianakis, Queen Latifah, Dennis Miller. Documentary.

WHAT IF...?
HAUT & COURT. March, 2008. French. (Lea Fazer) Alice Taglioni, Jocelyn Quivrin, Thierry Lhermitte, Pascale Arbillot, Scali Delpeyrat, Julie Ferrier.

WHAT LOVE IS
BIG SKY MOTION PICTURES. March, 2007. (Mars Callahan) Cuba Gooding, Jr., Matthew Lillard, Mars Callahan, Sean Astin, Andrew Daly, Anne Heche, Gina Gershon, Tamala Jones, Shiri Appleby, Judy Tylor, Victoria Pratt, Gillian Shure.

WHATEVER WORKS
SONY PICTURES CLASSICS (IN U.S.). April 22, 2009. (Woody Allen) Larry David, Evan Rachel Wood, Patricia Clarkson, Ed Begley, Jr., Michael McKean, Henry Cavill, John Gallagher, Jr., Jessica Hecht, Carolyn McCormick, Christopher Evan Welch.

WHAT'S UP SCARLET?
OPEN CITY ENTERTAINMENT. Sept., 2007. (Anthony Caldarella) Susan Priver, Musetta Vander, Sally Kirkland, Jere Burns.

WHEN A STRANGER CALLS
SONY PICTURES ENTERTAINMENT. Feb., 2006. (Simon West) Camilla Belle, Tommy Flanagan, Tessa Thompson, Brian Geraghty, Clark Gregg, Derek de Lint, Kate Jennings Grant, David Denman, Arthur Young, Madeline Carroll, Steve Eastin, Lance Henriksen.

WHEN DARKNESS FALLS
SONET FILM. Oct., 2006. Swedish. (Anders Nilsson) Oldoz Javidi, Lia Boysen, Reuben Sallmander, Per Graffman, Bahar Pars, Mina Azarian, Cesar Sarachu, Peter Engman, Annika Hallin, Nisti Sterk, Anja Lundqvist, Zeljko Santrak, Jonathan Blode, Christopher Wollter, Bibi Andersson, Tobias Aspelin, Magnus Rossman.

WHEN DO WE EAT?
THINKFILM. April, 2006. (Salvator Litvak) Michael Lerner, Lesley Ann Warren, Ben Feldman, Shiri Appleby, Adam Lamberg, Cynda Williams, Jack Klugman, Mili Avital, Meredith Scott Lynn, Mark Ivanir, Max Greenfield.

WHERE THE WILD THINGS ARE
WARNER BROS. Oct. 8, 2009. (Spike Jonze) Max Records, Catherine Keener, Mark Ruffalo, Lauren Ambrose, Chris Cooper, James Gandolfini, Catherine O'Hara, Forest Whitaker, Paul Dano.

WHIP IT
FOX SEARCHLIGHT. PICTURES. Aug. 27, 2009. (Drew Barrymore) Ellen Page, Marcia Gay Harden, Kristen Wiig, Drew Barrymore, Juliette Lewis Daniel Stern, Landon Pigg, Alia Shawkat, Andrew Wilson, Jimmy Fallon, Zoe Bell, Eve, Ari Graynor.

THE WHITE COUNTESS
SONY PICTURES CLASSICS. Nov., 2005. British-U.S.-German-Chineese. (James Ivory) Ralph Fiennes, Natasha Richardson, Vanessa Redgrave, Hiroyuki Sanada, Lynn Redgrave, Allan Corduner, Ying Da, Madeleine Daly, Dan Herzberg.

WHITE ON RICE
TIGER INDUSTRY FILMS. March 17, 2009. (Dave Boyle) Hiroshi Watanabe, Nae, Mio Takada, Lynn Chen, James Kyson Lee, Justin Kwong, Pepe Serna, Joy Osmanski, Cathy Shim, Ron D. Eliot, Bruce Campbell.

THE WHITE RIBBON
SONY PICTURES CLASSICS (IN NORTH AMERICA) RELEASE OF AN X FILME CREATIVE POOL (GERMANY)/LES FILMS DU

LOSANGE (FRANCE)/WEGA FILM (AUSTRIA)/LUCKY RED (ITALY) MAY 20, 2009. German, Austrian, French, Italian. (Michael Haneke) Christian Friedel, Leonie Benesch, Ulrich Tukur, Ursina Lardi, Burghart Klaussner, Steffi Kuhnert, Josef Bierbichler, Gariela Maria Schmeide, Rainer Bock, Susanne Lothar, Maria-Victoria Dragus, Leonard Proxauf, Janina Fautz, Eddy Grahl, Ernst Jacobi.

THE WHITE MASAI

Sept., 2005. German. (Hermine Huntgeburth) Nina Hoss, Jacky Ido, Katja Flint, Nino Prester, Janek Rieke.

WHITE NOISE

UNIVERSAL. Jan., 2005. (Geoffrey Sax) Michael Keaton, Chandra West, Deborah Kara Unger, Ian McNeice, Sarah Strange, Nicholas Elia, Mike Dopud.

THE WHITE PLANET

BAC DISTRIBUTION. Feb., 2006. French-Canadian. (Thierry Ragobert, Thierry Piantanida, Jean Lemire) Narrator: Luis Etienne. Documentary.

WHO DOES SHE THINK SHE IS?

ARTISTIC LICENSE FILMS. Oct. 13, 2008. (Pamela Tanner Boll) Maye Torres, Janis Wunderlich, Mayumi Oda, Camille Musser, Angela Williams.

WHO IS NORMAN LLOYD?

JOURNEYMEN FILMS. Nov. 29, 2007. (Matthew Sussman) Norman Lloyd, Peggy Lloyd, Karl Malden, Ray Bradbury, Cameron Diaz, Arthur Hiller, Pat Hitchcock, Roy Christopher, Tom Fontana.

WHO'S YOUR CADDY?

MGM. July 2007. (Don Michael Paul) Antwan "Big Boi" Andre Patton, Jeffrey Jones, Tamala Jones, Sherri Shepherd, Faizon Love, Finesse Mitchell, Garrett Morris, Tony Cox, Cam Gigandet, Chase Tatum, Jennifer Lewis, Susan Ward, Todd Sherry.

WHY MEN DON'T LISTEN AND WOMEN CAN'T PARK

CONSTANTIN FILM. Dec., 2007. German. (Leander Haussmann) Benno Fuermann, Jessica Schwarz, Matthias Matschke, Annika Kuhl, Uwe Ochsenknecht, Nadja Becker, Sasha Schmitz, Tom Schilling, Lars Rudolph, Florentine Lahme, Katja Flint, Thomas Kretschmann, Peter Lohmeyer.

WICKED LAKE

FEVER DREAMS. July 11, 2008. (Zach Passero) Carlee Baker, Eve Mauro, Michael Esparza, Eryn Joslyn, Robin Sydney, Luke Y. Thompson, Tim Thomerson.

THE WICKER MAN

WARNER BROS. Aug., 2006. (Neil LaBute) Nicolas Cage, Ellen Burstyn, Kate Beahan, Frances Conroy, Molly Parker, Leelee Sobieski, Diane Delano.

WIDE AWAKE

CJ ENTERTAINMENT. Oct., 2007. South Korea. (Lee Gyu-man) Kim Myeong-min, Yu Jun-sang, Kim Tae-woo, Jeong Yu-seok, Kim Yu-mi, Kim Roe-ha, Baek Seung-hwan.

THE WILD

BUENA VISTA. April, 2006. (Steve "Spaz" Williams) Kiefer Sutherland, Jim Belushi, Eddie Izzard, Janeane Garofalo, William Shatner, Richard Kind, Greg Cipes. Animated.

WILD CHILD

UNIVERSAL (IN U.K.) Aug., 2008. British. (Nick Moore) Emma Roberts, Natasha Richardson, Shirley Henderson, Alex Pettyfer, Aiden Quinn, Kimberley Nixon, Georgia King, Juno Temple, Sophie Wu, Linzey Cocker, Daisy Donovan, Nick Frost.

WILD HOGS

BUENA VISTA. Feb., 2007. (Walt Becker) Tim Allen, John Travolta, Martin Lawrence, William H. Macy, Ray Liotta, Marisa Tomei, Kevin Durand, M. C. Gainey, Jill Hennessy, Dominic Janes, Tichina Arnold, Stephen Tobolowsky, Jason Sklar, Randy Sklar, John C. McGinley, Peter Fonda, Ty Pennington.

WILDERNESS

MOMENTUM PICTURES. Aug., 2006. British. (Michael J. Bassett) Sean Pertwee, Alex Reid, Toby Kebbell, Stephen Wight, Luke Neal, Ben McKay, Lenora Crichlow, Karly Greene, Adam Deacon, Richie Campbell, Stephen Don, John Travers.

THE WIND

ALTA CLASSICS. July, 2005. Argentinian-Spanish. (Eduardo Mignogna) Federico Luppi, Antonella Costa, Pablo Cedron, Esteban Meloni, Mariana Brisky, Ricardo Diaz Mourelle.

WIND CHILL

SONY PICTURES ENTERTAINMENT. April, 2007. (Gregory Jacobs) Emily Blunt, Ashton Holmes, Martin Donovan.

WINGED CREATURES

PEACE ARCH ENTERTAINMENT. June 24, 2008. (Rowan Woods) Kate Beckinsale, Dakota Fanning, Guy Pearce, Forest Whitaker, Embeth Davidtz, Troy Garity, Jackie Earle Haley, Jennifer Hudson, Josh Hutcherson, Jeanne Tripplehorn, Robin Weigert, Tim Guinee, Marty Maguire, James LeGros, Julio Oscar Mechoso.

WINTER PASSING

YARI FILM GROUP. Sept., 2005. (Adam Rapp) Ed Harris, Zooey Deschanel, Will Ferrell, Amelia Warner, Amy Madigan, Dallas Roberts, Robert Beitzel, Deirdre O'Connell.

WIRED TO WIN: SURVIVING THE TOUR DE FRANCE

March, 2006. (Bayley Silleck) Baden Cooke, Jimmy Casper. Narrator: Alfred Molina. Documentary. Imax.

WITLESS PROTECTION

LIONSGATE. Feb. 22, 2008. (Charles Robert Carner) Larry the Cable Guy, Ivana Milicevic, Yaphet Kotto, Peter Stormare, Eric Roberts, Joe Mantegna, Jenny McCarthy.

THE WOMEN

PICTUREHOUSE. Sept. 2, 2008. (Diane English) Meg Ryan, Annette Bening, Eva Mendes, Debra Messing, Jada Pinkett Smith, Bette Midler, Candice Bergen, Carrie Fisher, Cloris Leachman, Debi Mazar, India Ennenga, Jill Flint, Ana Gasteyer, Joanna Gleason, Tilly Scott Pedersen.

WOMEN IN THE PARK

ALTA CLASSICS. Jan., 2007. Spanish. (Felipe Vega) Adolfo Fernandez, Blanca Apilanez, Emma Vilarasau, Barbara Lennie, Alberto Ferreiro, Javier Albala.

WOMEN IN TROUBLE

GATO NEGRO FILMS. March 15, 2009. (Sebastian Gutierrez) Carla Gugino, Connie Britton, Adrianne Palicki, Emmanuelle Chriqui, Sarah Clarke, Marley Shelton, Rya Kihlstedt, Cameron Richardson, Josh Brolin, Simon Baker, Joseph Gordon-Levitt, Isabella Gutierrez, Caitlin Keats.

WORLD TRADE CENTER

PARAMOUNT. July, 2006. (Oliver Stone) Nicolas Cage, Michael Pena, Maggie Gyllenhaal, Maria Bello, Stephen Dorff, Jay Hernandez, Michael Shannon.

WORLD'S GREATEST DAD

DARKO ENTERTAINMENT. Jan. 18, 2009. (Bobcat Goldthwait) Robin Williams, Alexie Gilmore, Daryl Sabara, Geoff Pierson, Henry Simmons, Mitzi McCall, Evan Martin, Jermaine Williams, Tony V CQ, Lorraine Nicholson, Zach Sanchez.

X GAMES 3D: THE MOVIE

WALT DISNEY MOTION PICTURES. Aug. 10 2009. (Steve Lawrence) Shaun White, Danny Way, Bob Burnquist, Ricky Carmichael, Travis Pastrana, Kyle Loza. Narrator: Emile Hirsch.

THE X-FILES: I WANT TO BELIEVE

20TH CENTURY FOX. July 23, 2008. (Chris Carter) David Duchovny, Gillian Anderson, Amanda Peet, Billy Connolly, Alvin "Xzibit" Joiner, Callum Keith Rennie.

X-MEN: THE LAST STAND

20TH CENTURY FOX. May, 2006. (Brett Ratner) Hugh Jackman, Halle Berry, Ian McKellen, Famke Janssen, Anna Paquin, Kelsey Grammer, James Marsden, Rebecca Romijn, Shawn Ashmore, Aaron Stanford, Vinnie Jones, Patrick Stewart, Ellen Page, Ben Foster, Dania Ramirez, Michael Murphy, Shohreh Aghdashloo, Josef Sommer, Bill Duke, Daniel Cudmore, Eric Dane.

X-MEN ORIGINS: WOLVERINE

20TH CENTURY FOX. April 28, 2009. (Gavin Hood) Hugh Jackman, Liev Schreiber, Danny Huston, Will.i.am, Lynn Collins, Kevin Durand, Dominic Monaghan, Taylor Kitsch, Daniel Henney, Ryan Reynolds.

XXX: STATE OF THE UNION

SONY PICTURES ENTERTAINMENT. April, 2005. (Lee Tamahori) Ice Cube, Willem Dafoe, Scott Speedman, Peter Strauss, Samuel L. Jackson, Xzibit, Michael Roof, Sunny Mabrey, Nona Gaye, John G. Connolly.

YEAR ONE

SONY PICTURES ENTERTAINMENT. June 12, 2009. (Harold Ramis) Jack Black, Michael Cera, Oliver Platt, David Cross, Christopher Mintz-Plasse, Vinnie Jones, Hank Azaria, Juno Temple, Olivia Wilde, June Diane Raphael, Xander Berkeley, Horatio Sanz, David Pasquesi, Matthew J. Willig, Paul Rudd.

THE YES MEN FIX THE WORLD

SHADOW. Feb. 6, 2009. (Andy Bichlbaum, Mike Bonnano) Andy Bichlbaum, Mike Bonnano.

YIDDISH THEATER: A LOVE STORY

NEW LOVE FILMS. Nov., 2007. Israeli. (Dan Katzir) Zypora Spaisman, David Romeo, Felix Fibich, Shifra Lerer, Seymour Rechzeit, Sally and Jechiel Dobekire, Roni Neuman, Joad Kohn. Documentary.

YONKERS JOE

MAGNOLIA PICTURES. Dec. 4, 2008. (Robert Celestino)

Chazz Palminteri, Christine Lahti, Tom Guiry, Michael Lerner, Linus Roache, Michael Rispoli, Roma Maffia, Frank John Hughes.

YOO-HOO, MRS. GOLDBERG

INTL. FILM CIRCUIT. June 20, 2009. (Aviva Kempner) Ruth Bader Ginsberg, Ed Asner, Norman Lear, Madeline Gilford, Larry Robinson, Arlene McQuade, Viola Harris, Anne Schwartz, David Schwartz, Glen D. Smith, Jr., Susan Stamberg, Judith Abrams.

YOU AND YOUR STUPID MATE

March, 2005. Australian. (Marc Gracie) Nathan Philips, Angus Sampson, Samir Malik, Rachel Hunter, Madeleine West, William McInnes.

YOU DON'T MESS WITH THE ZOHAN

SONY PICTURES ENTERTAINMENT. May 28, 2008. (Dennis Dugan) Adam Sandler, John Turturro, Emmanuelle Chriqui, Nick Swardson, Lainie Kazan, Ido Mosseri, Rob Schneider, Dave Matthews, Michael Buffer.

YOU LOOK SO HANDSOME

GAUMONT COLUMBIA TRISTAR FILMS. Jan., 2006. French. (Isabelle Mergault) Michel Blanc, Medeea Marinescu, Wladimir Yordanoff, Benoit Turjman, Eva Darlan, Veronique Silver, Renee Le Calm, Dora Doll, Liliane Rovere.

YOU MAY LAUGH BUT I'M LEAVING

REZO. Jan., 2005. French. (Philippe Harel) Judith Godreche, Sagamore Stevenin, Ariane Seguillon, Coralie Revel, Wladimir Yordanoff, Patrick Chesnais, Guillaume Gallienne.

YOU MUST BE THE WOLF

MYSELF, PABLO FILM. May, 2005. Italian. (Vittorio Moroni) Ignazio Oliva, Valentina Carnelutti, Valentina Merizzi, Sara D'Amario, Gianluca Gobbi, Amandio Pinheiro, Vera Gondola, Elena Bertalli, Mauro Mannella, Antonia Terrinha.

YOU, ME AND DUPREE

UNIVERSAL. July, 2006. (Anthony Russo, Joe Russo) Owen Wilson, Kate Hudson, Matt Dillon, Seth Rogen, Amanda Detmer, Todd Stashwick, Michael Douglas, Harry Dean Stanton, Lance Armstrong.

YOU'LL MISS ME

UGC DISTRIBUTION. June, 2009. French. (Amanda Sthers) Carole Bouquet, Pierre Arditi, Anne Marivin, Patrick Mille, Fred Testot, Monique Chaumette, Michael Lonsdale, Ariane Seguillon, Melanie Thierry, Cecile Cassel, Melanie Page, Karine Silla, Yves Jacques, Hyacinthe Imayanga.

THE YOUNG VICTORIA

MOMENTUM. Feb. 5, 2009. (Jean-Marc Vallee) Emily Blunt, Rupert Friend, Paul Bettany, Miranda Richardson, Jim Broadbent, homas Kretschmann, Mark Strong, Jesper Christensen, Harriet Walter, Jeanette Hain, Julian Glover, Michael Maloney, Michiel Huisman, Genevieve O'Reilly, Rachael Stirling, Michaela Brooks.

YOUNG@HEART

FOX SEARCHLIGHT. June, 2007. (Stephen Walker) Narrator: Stephen Walker. Documentary.

YOUR LIFE IN 65 MINUTES

ALTA CLASSICS. July, 2006. Spanish. (Maria Ripoll) Javier Pereira, Marc Rodriguez, Oriol Vila, Tamara Arias, Nuria Gago, Irene Montala.

YOURS, MINE & OURS

PARAMOUNT. Nov., 2005. (Raja Gosnell) Dennis Quaid, Rene Russo, Rip Torn, Linda Hunt, Jerry O'Connell, David Koechner, Sean Faris, Katija Pevec, Dean Collins, Tyler Patrick Jones, Haley Ramm, Brecken Palmer, Bridger Palmer, Ty Panitz, Danielle Panabaker, Drake Bell, Miki Ishikawa, Slade Pearce, Lil' JJ, Miranda Cosgrove, Andrew Vo, Jennifer Habib, Jessica Habib, Nicholas Roget-King.

YOUTH

SOROLLA FILMS. Jan., 2005. Spanish. (Ramon Termens, Carles Torras) Roger Coma, Aina Clotet, Pau Roca, Jordi Dauder, Aleix Rengel, Ariadna Cabrol, Mohamed Bouachmir..

YUMENO

Aug., 2005. Japanese. (Yoshitaka Kamada) Nahana, Katsuya Kobayashi, Shikoh Kanai, Yuna Natsuo, Shihemitsu Ogi.

THE ZARTALE WOMEN'S JOURNEY

Jan., 2006. French. (Claude Mourieras) Documentary.

ZATHURA: A SPACE ADVENTURE

SONY PICTURES ENTERTAINMENT. Oct., 2005. (Jon Favreau) Jonah Bobo, Josh Hutcherson, Dax Shepard, Kristen Stewart, Tim Robbins. Voice: Frank Oz.

ZE FILM

EUROPACORP. Feb., 2005. French. (Guy Jacques) Clement Sibony, Dan Herzberg, Micky El Mazroui, Karina Testa, Miki Manojlovic, Lorant Deutsch, Catherine Wilkening, Catherine Zrditi, Francois Morel, Dominique Pinon, Samir Guesmi.

ZEROPHILIA

MICROANGELO ENTERTAINMENT. Nov., 2006. (Martin Curland) Taylor Handley, Dustin Seavey, Alison Folland, Kyle Schmid, Rebecca Mozo, Gina Bellman, Marieh Delfino, Kelly LeBrock, Adam Zolotin, Chris Meyer, Rick Stear.

ZHANG SI DE

Aug., 2005. Chineese. (Yin Li) Wu Jun, Tang Guoqiang, Zou Shuang, Sun Yuncheng, Zheng Hao, Ding Kai, Li Wannian, Wang Zihong, Liu Ying.

ZINDA

Jan., 2006. Indian. (Sanjay Gupta) Sanjay Dutt, John Abraham, Lara Dutta, Mahesh Manjrekar, Celina Jaitley.

ZODIAC

PARAMOUNT (IN N. AMERICA), WARNER BROS. (INTERNATIONAL). Feb., 2007. (David Fincher) Mark Ruffalo, Jake Gyllenhaal, Robert Downey, Jr., Anthony Edwards, Brian Cox, Charles Fleischer, Zack Grenier, Philip Baker Hall, Elias Koteas, John Lacy, Donal Logue, John Carroll Lynch, Dermot Mulroney, Chloe Sevigny, Ed Setrakian, John Getz, John Terry, Candy Clark, Adam Goldberg, James Le Gros.

ZOMBIE STRIPPERS

TRIUMPH FILMS. April 10, 2008. (Jay Lee) Robert Englund, Jenna Jameson, Roxy Saint, Penny Drake, Whitney Anderson, Jennifer Holland, Shamron Moore, Jeannette Sousa, Carmit Levite, Johnny Hawkes, Brad Milne, Zak Kilberg, Jen Alex Gonzalez, Jessica Custodio, Laura Bach, Catero Colbert, Billy Beck, Travis Woods, Calvin Green, Joey Medina.

ZOMBIELAND

SONY PICTURES ENTERTAINMENT. Sept. 23, 2009. (Ruben Fleischer) Woody Harrelson, Jesse Eisenberg, Emma Stone, Abigail Breslin, Amber Heard, Bill Murray, Derek Graf.

ZONAD

ELEMENT PICTURES DISTRIBUTION. July, 2009. Irish. (John Carney) Simon Delaney, David Pearse, Rory Keenan, Janice Byrne, Geoff Minogue, Donna Dent, Kevin Maher, Brian de Salvo, Don Wycherley, David Murray.

ZOOM

SONY PICTURES ENTERTAINMENT. Aug., 2006. (Peter Hewitt) Tim Allen, Courteney Cox, Chevy Chase, Spencer Breslin, Kevin Zegers, Kate Mara, Michael Cassidy, Ryan Newman, Rip Torn.

Production Companies

Histories of the Major Motion Picture Studios

COLUMBIA PICTURES (SONY PICTURES ENTERTAINMENT, INC.)

Columbia Pictures can trace its beginnings to the CBC Films Sales Co., formed in 1920 by Harry Cohn, Jack Cohn and Joe Brandt, all of whom had previously worked together at Universal Studios. CBC was set up to make a series of shorts known as Screen Snapshots, showing the off-screen activities of movie stars to publicize their current pictures. Soon the new company expanded to produce westerns and other comedy shorts and in 1922 produced its first feature, "More To Be Pitied Than Scorned." In 1924, the owners renamed their company Columbia Pictures.

Two years later, Columbia had advanced to the point where it began to open film exchanges of its own instead of selling films outright to theatres for a flat fee and established a studio with two stages and a small office building. Sam Briskin was hired as general manager. In 1929, it produced its first all-talking feature, "The Donovan Affair." This low-budget murder mystery was directed by Frank Capra. By this time, the company had opened a home office in New York where Jack Cohn functioned as vice president and treasurer, while Harry ran the production operation on the West Coast.

In 1931, Brandt sold his interest in Columbia and retired. The next year, Harry Cohn assumed the title of president, while retaining his post as production chief. In 1935, Columbia purchased a 40-acre ranch in Burbank for location filming (later expanded to 80 acres). The company's first big artistic success was in 1934 with Capra's "It Happened One Night," which was not only the top box office draw of 1934, but a winner of five major Academy Awards including Best Picture. Capra followed this with such hits as "Mr. Deeds Goes to Town" (1936), "Lost Horizon" (1937), "You Can't Take It With You" (1938) and "Mr. Smith Goes to Washington" (1939).

Throughout the '40s Columbia prospered and by the end of the decade, it could claim to be one of the industry's major studios. Unlike the other studios, Columbia did not own any theatres and was not affected by the industry's Consent Decrees which forced those studios to divest themselves of their exhibition properties. Commercial hits of the period included "Gilda" (1946), "The Jolson Story" (1946) and "Jolson Sings Again" (1949).

In 1951, Columbia diversified into television by forming Screen Gems, a wholly owned subsidiary set up to make programs and commercials. Founder Harry Cohn died in 1958. The successor management—headed by veterans of the company Abe Schneider and Leo Jaffe—made major investments in British film production and released "Lawrence of Arabia" (1962), "A Man for All Seasons" (1966) and the musical "Oliver!" (1968). Other hits of the '60s were "Guess Who's Coming to Dinner" (1967) and "To Sir With Love" (1967). The success of these and others was attributable to Mike Frankovich, who became production head in 1954 and was succeeded by Stanley Schneider, whose father, Abe, headed the company at the time. Another son of Abe, Bert, and Bob Rafelson co-produced "Easy Rider" in 1969, one of the biggest hits in Columbia's history.

At the beginning of the '70s, Herbert Allen, Jr., a former Wall Street banker, bought control of Columbia and took over as president and CEO. Allen brought in new management headed by Alan Hirschfield and David Begelman, who produced such hits as "Shampoo" (1975) and "Close Encounters of the Third Kind" (1977). Begelman's successor as production chief was Frank Price (who had previously headed Universal Television) and under his regime the company produced such successful films as "Kramer vs. Kramer" (1979), "Tootsie" (1982) and "Ghostbusters" (1984). In 1982, Columbia was purchased by the Coca-Cola Company. Under its aegis Columbia, Home Box Office and CBS, Inc. joined forces to finance a new production company, TriStar Pictures. At the start, it was emphasized that the new company would be separate from Columbia, with TriStar using Columbia's distribution. Price departed in 1985 and in 1986 David Puttnam, an independent British producer, was signed as chairman. Succeeding him was Dawn Steel, who was named president. In 1989, TriStar was made a unit of Columbia Pictures with Jeff Sagansky, president of TriStar, reporting to Ms. Steel.

Columbia Pictures Entertainment was formed in 1987 by Coca-Cola to restructure its entertainment business. CPE consisted of two film-production companies: Columbia Pictures and TriStar Pictures; two television arms: Columbia Pictures Television, Merv Griffin Enterprises, and Loews Theatre Management Corp.

In September 1989, Columbia Pictures Entertainment was purchased by the Sony Corporation of Japan. Sony previously acquired CBS Records in 1987. Producers Jon Peters and Peter Guber were brought in as co-chairmen. In 1991, Peters resigned from his position as co-chairman, the company was renamed Sony Pictures Entertainment, Inc. and Mark Canton left Warner Bros. to become the new chairman of Columbia Pictures. In June, 1994, Fred Bernstein was put in charge of the motion picture units at Columbia Pictures, TriStar Pictures, Sony Pictures Classics and Triumph Releasing Corporation. Later that summer, the marketing and distribution arms of these divisions were consolidated under the direction of Sid Ganis as president. In September 1994, Peter Guber announced his resignation as Sony chairman, with Alan J. Levine named as his successor. Sony was forced to write off $3.2 billion in 1995, but the Japanese parent company vowed to maintain its Hollywood commitment. In September of 1996, Canton was removed as chairman of Columbia Pictures, followed in October of that year by the resignation of Levine, who was replaced by John Calley, formerly of MGM/UA. Mr. Canton's removal was accompanied by that of Lisa Henson and Barry Josephson, Columbia Pictures presidents; Marc Platt was ousted as was his successor Robert Cooper, TriStar Pictures president along with Stacey Snider, Tristar production president, Alan Levine, Sony Pictures chairman, and Fred Bernstein, Columbia TriStar president. This was a rather strange turn of events, as the deposed team was responsible for Sony's record $1.3 billion in domestic box office for 1997, having developed such movies as "Jerry Maguire," "Anaconda," "The Fifth Element" and "My Best Friend's Wedding."

Calley reorganized and restructured Sony Pictures

Entertainment, closing the TriStar Motion Picture Group and bringing the remaining executives over to Columbia Pictures which became Sony Pictures Entertainment's principal production arm. SPE also resurrected a past label, Screen Gems, to make films in the $4-5 million range.

In 1998, Jeff Sagansky left Columbia to join the newest network, Pax TV. Sony Pictures Classics, the art film distributor arm of Sony Corp., despite a profitable 1998, came under criticism for its co-presidents' insistence on earning a profit on each of their releases and failing to take on more commercial fare. Although its revenues of $20 million for the first seven months of 1998 were twice its 1997 grosses, SPC was surpassed in 1995 by Miramax, a younger arthouse, but one that has taken more financial risks. After a two-year legal battle, Sony lost its claim to the movie rights for the lucrative James Bond franchise. In a settlement with MGM, Sony gave up its claim for a meager $5 million, but ended up with the rights to Spiderman.

In early 1999, Sony Pictures Entertainment signed a groundbreaking deal with 30 screenwriters stating that in exchange for one film each over the next four years, each writer would receive up-front fees as well as 2% of gross receipts.

On October 3, 1999, Sony bade a final farewell to its cofounder, Akio Morita who died at the age of 78.

In 2000, Sony continued to struggle, releasing several expensive features that generated little box office interest. "What Planet Are You From?" cost $50 million and grossed only $6.5 million, while "I Dreamed of Africa" cost $40 million and brought in $6.5 million. Even the highly anticipated summer films, "The Patriot" and "Hollow Man" underperformed at the box office, barely breaking even. John Calley did slow the outrageous spending and losses that once plagued the studio, but as of 2000, was still looking for blockbusters to return Sony to its former prominence. Despite Monday-morning box office woes, Sony Pictures Entertainment increased overall sales 55% since Calley took over in 1996 through 2000. In large part sales increases were attributed to its pay-TV, video and TV-content businesses.

In 2000, parent Sony restructured, and Sony Pictures Entertainment was placed under the Sony Broadband Entertainment umbrella. That year the company created a digital entertainment unit, Sony Pictures Digital Entertainment, and restructured its top management in preparation for Chairman and CEO John Calley's planned departure in 2003. In a move geared to meet the targeted programming needs of the upcoming broadband decade, Sony Pictures Entertainment (SPE) consolidated its two domestic television operations into a new division, Columbia TriStar Domestic Television.

Sony's 2000 sales were $6,106 million, showing one year growth of 34.6%.

In 2001, Sony had hits with "The Wedding Planner," "A Knight's Tale," "Ali" and "Not Another Teen Movie" while Sony Pictures Classics continued to enjoy box office and citical success with "Crouching Tiger, Hidden Dragon."

In 2002, Sony sold its stake in exhibitor, Loews Cineplex Entertainment and scored a record breaking year with a number of huge releases, including "Spider-Man," "Men in Black II," and "Stuart Little 2." On Aug. 19, 2002, SPE surpassed $1.27 billion in domestic ticket sales, breaking a respected ent. industry record. Before year-end, SPE planned 12 additional releases starring industry box office stars like Adam Sandler, Eddie Murphy, Jennifer Lopez and Nicolas Cage in films such as "I Spy," "Maid in Manhattan," "Eight Crazy Nights" and award season hopefuls "Punch Drunk Love" and "Adaptation." Going into the holiday season, SPE commanded more than 20 percent of the total box office marketshare.

Anticipating the retirement of longtime studio head John Calley, Sony Corp. of American chairman & CEO, Howard Stringer renewed his contract and promoted Yair Landau (president, Sony Pictures Digital Entertainment), Amy Pascal (Columbia Pictures chair) and Jeff Blake (president, worldwide marketing and distribution for Columbia TriStar Motion Picture Group) to the co-equal posts of vice-chairmen, Sony Pictures Entertainment. They replaced former COO, Mel Harris, who left the company in September.

While not as huge as 2002, Sony had a big year at the box office in 2003. Meanwhile the electronics coglomerate announced a reduction in 20,000 jobs over the next three years, of which 1,700 would be cut from the studio workforce. Sony paid 55% of the budgets for Joe Roth's Revolution Studios and has been very dependent on them for hit films. In 2003 Revolution delivered hits, such as "Anger Management" along with misses like "Gigli." Sony also signed a co-production deal with the very successful Spyglass Productions run by Gary Barber and Roger Birnbaum. The year also marked the exit of John Calley after nearly seven years as chairman. The company brought in Harvard-educated Michael Lynton as its new chmn. & CEO in Jan. 2004. With a finance background in mergers and acquisitions, Lynton entered the entertainment industry in 1987 as president of Disney Publishing and later as pres. of Disney's Hollywood Pictures. Before joining SPE, Lynton also had been president, Time Warner International; president, AOL International, and CEO of AOL Europe.

Lynton's mergers & acquisition background made him ideally suited to lead Sony's next evolution as an entertainment company: the acquisition of Metro-Goldwyn-Mayer. On September 23, 2004, Sony Corporation of America announced a definitive agreement to acquire Metro-Goldwyn-Mayer (MGM). MGM had been courted by other companies, but in a move that took the industry somewhat by surprise, Sony and its equity partners Providence Equity Partners, Texas Pacific Group, Comcast Corporation and DLJ Merchant Banking Partners, put together the winning deal. The investor group would pay $12 in cash per share, plus would assume MGM's approximately $2 billion in debt. Additionally, J.P. Morgan Chase committed to lead a bank syndicate that would provide up to $4.25 billion in senior debt financing together with Credit Suisse First Boston.

Post-acquisition MGM continues as an active producer of film and television projects, and greenlights projects under the MGM and United Artists banners. MGM still operates under the Metro-Goldwyn-Mayer name as a private company headquartered in Los Angeles, CA. SPE's role will be to co-finance and produce new motion pictures with MGM as well as distribute MGM's existing film and television content through Sony Pictures' global distribution channels.

In a strategic move to bring SPE and MGM content to a broad cable viewing base, SPE and the equity partners in the MGM transaction agreed to a broad programming and distribution arrangement that allows for the distribution of Sony Pictures' and MGM content on equity partner Comcast Corporation's video on demand platform, and for the creation of a joint venture, to be managed by Comcast. The venture would establish new cable channels featuring Sony Pictures and MGM content, bringing Sony product to Comcast's more than 21 million cable television customers.

Howard Stringer replaced Noboyuki Idei in June of 2005 as Chairman and CEO of Sony Corp. and became one of the few non-Japanese to run a major Japanese company. The parent consumer electronics manufacturer had been struggling and in 2005 was in the midst of its second restructuring plan in three years. The movie division had some disappointments during the year, including "Stealth" and "Bewitched;" both underperformed and failed to drive positive financial results for Sony, especially if compared to the previous year's blockbuster "Spider-Man 2" and how it bolstered the bottom line.

Sony Pictures Entertainment (SPE) executives enjoyed 2006. More than 50 percent of its releases debuted in the top slot, with 10 number one opening weeks for SPE films. By September, Sony Pictures nabbed first place in the 2006 industry market share race, generating more than $1.15 billion in North American ticket sales and capturing 17.6% off all tickets sold. In Sept., chairman of the studio's Motion Picture Group, Amy Pascal, extended her deal with the studio to 2011 and was elevated to co-chairman of SPE, alongside Michael Lynton, SPE chairman & CEO. Sony Pictures Animation, formed in May 2002, launched its first feature film in September 2006 with the release of "Open Season." Its first forayinto animation delivered respectable box office receipts of $77.1 million in its first 31 days in theatres. Columbia Pictures made it into the Top 20 of all-time largest opening weekends with its release of the controversystirring "The Da Vinci Code," a highly revisionist view of Jesus Christ's life and based on the best-selling novel by Dan Brown. Add the star power of Tom Hanks and direction by Ron Howard to this compelling story, and SPE could predict a public flocking to theatres. And they did. The "Code" raked in $77.1 million during its opening weekend and had a cumulative worldwide total of $747.2 million through early fall. On the lighter side of its 2006 slate, writer-star Will Ferrell delivered comic relief, NASCAR-style, to theatres this summer in "Talladega Nights: The Ballad of Ricky Bobby," with box office receipts of $148.2 million through mid-October.

Sony broke industry records in 2006 with more than $1.6 billion in box office receipts in the U.S., but their share dipped 15% in 2007 to just over $1.0 billion, in spite of the top grossing film worldwide, "Spider-Man 3," which did $890.5 million. Michael Lynton signed a new contract extension to lead the company's film and television units until 2012. Lynton and Amy Pascal, co-chairman of the unit, both report to Howard Stringer, who has been chairman since 2005. The company has made a major push in production and distribution internationally over the last few years both in film and television, often with local partners. Sony Pictures Classics remains the champion of the specialized distributors, winning their seventh Best Foreign Language Oscar for "The Lives of Others."

In 2008 Michael Lynton entered his fourth year as Chairman and CEO and Amy Pascal, Co-Chairman, SPE and Chairman, Sony Motion Pictures Group, finished her 20th year of employment with the company. Total sales for the fiscal year ended March 2008 was $7.6 billion and interestingly, Howard Stringer threw his support behind rival Toshiba's Blu-Ray Disc to make that the de facto standard for high definition recording and playback, at the expense of Sony's HD DVD format. Sony Pictures Releasing grossed considerably more than one billion domestically, with "Hancock" doing $600 million at the boxoffice worldwide.

Amid the financial gloom in late 2008, Sony slashed its profit and sales forcasts for the second time for fiscal 2008 in the last two quarters. For the fiscal year beginning March 2009, Sony expected operating profit to decline 57% from $4.7 billion to $2 billion.

Under chairman-CEO Howard Stringer, Sony moved aggressively to cut costs in 2009, slashing 16,000 jobs and closing eight plants. These efforts have finally started draining the sea of red ink, and Sony now expects its net loss for the fiscal year to total $1.04 billion, down from the previous prediction of $1.32 billion. The picture division reported a 30.4% year-on-year drop in sales — or 20% on a U.S. dollar basis — to $1.52 billion, with both theatrical and home entertainment revenues falling. There was no hit to match "Hancock" from the fiscal second quarter last year, though "District 9," "The Ugly Truth" and "Julie and Julia" recorded solid numbers. Sony Pictures Animation's "Cloudy With a Chance of Meatballs" landed in 2009's domestic gross boxoffice Top 20 with $121mm, coming in at number 17 on the list.

Howard Stringer continued to trim costs in 2010, while overhauling Sony's businesses units to create better synergies between its content and its electronic devices. However, profit has been elusive in Sony's television and video game units. Those businesses are now back on track and should remain strong due to rising consumer interest in 3-D televisions and brisker sales of game consoles.

Sony Pictures Entertainment, which last year cut about 3.5 percent of its workers, executed a new round of job reductions that eliminated 6.5 percent of its global workforce. In a letter to employees, Michael Lynton and Amy Pascal said the cuts would be spread across the studio's divisions, though most would be in its home entertainment and information technology operations. A steady decline in DVD revenue has forced Hollywood studios to cut staff and consolidate operations. Sony's theatrical-market share in 2010 was 13.3% or fifth among the major studios.

RECENT COLUMBIA/SPE/SONY PICTURES ANIMATION RELEASES

2000	The Patriot, Hollow Man, Random Hearts, 28 Days, I Dreamed of Africa, What Planet Are You From?
2001	The Wedding Planner, A Knight's Tale, The Animal, America's Sweethearts, Ali.
2002	Spider-Man, Men in Black II, Stuart Little 2, Swept Away, XXX, I Spy.
2003	Bad Boys II, Anger Management, S.W.A.T., Charlie's Angels: Full Throttle, Once Upon A Time in Mexico.
2004	Spider-Man 2, Secret Window, White Chicks (with Revolution Studios), Little Black Book (with Revolution Studios), 13 Going on 30 (with Revolution Studios), Christmas With the Kranks (with Revolution Studios), Closer, Spanglish,The Forgotten, The Grudge.
2005	Hitch, Are We There Yet, The Exorcism of Emily Rose, Bewitched, The Mask of Zorro, Rent, All the King's Men, Fun With Dick and Jane.
2006	RV, The Da Vinci Code, Click (with Revolution Studios), Monster House, Talladega Nights: The Ballad of Ricky Bobby, The Pink Panther,

	Oliver Twist, Running With Scissors.
2007	Spider-Man 3, Superbad, Ghost Rider, Stomp the Yard, Surf's Up, We Own the Night
2008	Hancock, You Don't Mess with the Zohan, Step Brothers, Pineapple Express, Quantum of Solace.
2009	Angels & Demons, Julie & Julia, This Is It (Michael Jackson documentary), Cloudy With A Chance Of Meatballs.
2010	The Karate Kid, Grown Ups, The Other Guys, Salt, Eat Pray Love, The Bounty Hunter.

RECENT SONY PICTURES CLASSICS RELEASES

1999	Run Lola Run, The Dreamlife of Angels, The Winslow Boy, Sweet and Lowdown.
2000	Crouching Tiger, Hidden Dragon, Bossa Nova, Trixie, Groove, Pollock.
2001	Pauline and Paulette, Secret Ballot, Haiku Tunnel.
2002	Sunshine State, Mad Love, Autofocus, Love Liza, My Wife Is an Actress.
2003	Winged Migration, The Tiplets of Bellville, The Fog of War, The Company.
2004	Riding Giants, The Triplets of Belleville, Carandiru, The Fog of War, Being Julia, Baadasssss!, She Hate Me, Bad Education, Warriors of Heaven and Earth.
2005	Kung Fu Hustle, House of Flying Dragons, The Merchant of Venice, Junebug, Capote, White Countess, Breakfast on Pluto.
2006	Who Killed The Electric Car?, Sketches of Frank Gehry.
2007	The Lives of Others, Volver, Curse of the Golden Flower, Black Book, The Valet, Sleuth.
2008	The Wackness, Baghead, When Did You Last See Your Father, Rachel Getting Married, The Class, I've Loved You So Long.
2009	It Might Get Loud, Coco Before Chanel, The Damned United.
2010	You Will Meet a Tall Dark Stranger, Animal Kingdom, Please Give.

THE WALT DISNEY COMPANY

In 1923, Walt Disney set up an animation studio with his brother Roy. Five years later, he introduced his most famous creation, Mickey Mouse, in a cartoon called "Steamboat Willie." It was an immediate hit and Disney began his series of Silly Symphony cartoons, based on musical themes, the first of which was called "The Skeleton Dance." From 1929 through 1931, Disney distributed his products through Columbia Pictures. In 1932, distribution was through United Artists with about 20 cartoons per year, half of them featuring Mickey Mouse and the others in the Silly Symphony series. Production cost of the cartoons was about $50,000 each. UA paid Disney 60% of rentals received from exhibitors, and his gross income at the time was in the neighborhood of one and a half million dollars per year.

Disney's contract with UA expired in 1937. He switched over to RKO, for whom he produced his first feature-length cartoon, "Snow White and the Seven Dwarfs," followed by "Pinnochio" (1940), "Fantasia" (1940), "Dumbo" (1941), "Bambi" (1942), "Cinderella" (1950) and "Peter Pan" (1953), all released by RKO.

RKO's financial troubles, which led to its demise in 1958, caused Walt Disney Productions to break with it in 1953 and form its own national distribution unit, Buena Vista. Buena Vista's first release was "The Living Desert" (1953), winner of the Academy Award for feature documentary and an outgrowth of the True-Life Adventure shorts started in 1948. Disneyland in Anaheim, California, opened in 1955.

Rising costs in the production of animation films caused Disney to concentrate on live-action features, such as "20,000 Leagues Under the Sea" (1954) which took in over $11 million in domestic rentals, and "Mary Poppins" (1964) which made more than $45 million.

Walt Disney died in 1966. Roy Disney's death in 1971 left no surviving Disney family members at the studio's helm. Walt Disney World in Central Florida (near Orlando) opened in 1971. In 1983, Ron Miller, Walt's son-in-law, was made chief executive and started Touchstone Pictures, a subsidiary designed to make adult-oriented films. In 1984, Touchstone delivered "Splash." In the same year, a drive for new leadership was spearheaded by Roy Disney, son of Walt's brother of the same name. Frank Wells, former vice chairman of Warner Bros. and Michael Eisner, president of Paramount, were hired in 1984 with Eisner as chairman, Wells as president and Disney serving as vice chairman. Early in 1990, the Company announced a massive, ten-year expansion agenda that would add hundreds of new rides and shows to its existing theme parks, and provide for the building of additional attractions in Southern California and Florida. Euro-Disneyland opened near Paris in 1992.

Disney continued to do well in its motion picture division with "Pretty Woman," "Dick Tracy" and new division Hollywood Pictures' "Arachnophobia" and "The Hand That Rocks the Cradle." The 1991 animated feature "Beauty and the Beast" took in over $145 million in the U.S., and became the first animated feature nominated for Best Picture. This success was followed by 1992's "Aladdin" which became the first Disney release to gross more than $200 million in the U.S.

In 1993, Disney purchased the highly successful independent distributor Miramax, which would continue to operate as a separate company.

1994 saw the death of Frank Wells. "The Lion King" became the highest grossing film in Disney history. Jeffrey Katzenberg, crucial to the revitalization of the company's animation department, resigned as chairman to join Steven Spielberg and David Geffen in their own entertainment company, DreamWorks SKG. David Hoberman was named president of Disney's motion picture divisions. However, his departure after eight months threw the weight of responsibilities over to new chairman of the motion picture group, Joe Roth. The year ended with Disney becoming the first distributor to achieve annual box office revenues of over $1 billion.

The big entertainment news of 1995 was the company's $19 billion purchase of Capital Cities/ABC. Michael Eisner named Creative Artists Agency chairman Michael Ovitz as president of the Walt Disney Company. Ovitz was removed as chairman in November of 1996 (with a severance package rumored to be in excess of $90 million, much to the ire of Disney stock-holders).

Three years later, the dispute between Jeffrey Katzenberg, the former Disney animation chairman, and Michael Eisner, was still bubbling. Katzenberg was allegedly promised 2% share of revenues from projects begun while still at Disney. Mr. Eisner disputed the claim. In November of 1997, Disney attorneys admitted that Katzenberg was owed the money under the terms of his employment contract. The pact was thrown out of court, and handed over to a "rent-a-judge." In light of Mr. Ovitz's settlement in 1996, many speculated that Disney would make a preemptive settlement offer rather than risk the rent-a-judge's decision for an amount that would upset Disney stockholders. Mr. Katzenberg's lawsuit was for $500 million.

Miramax's celebrated two good years, with Oscar wins in 1997 for "The English Patient" and for "Good Will Hunting" a year later. Dimension also fared well in 1998, increasing its revenue from $14 million in 1993, to $120 million in 1998. In 1997, Dimension made up 45% of Miramax's total grosses with only three releases: "Scream 2," "Operation Condor," and "Mimic." Despite its success, Miramax lost some of its top executives in 1997, and chairmen Bob and Harvey Weinstein had to entrust their key personnel with additional duties. President Richard Sands was promoted to chairman, making him the only executive to have the title besides the Weinsteins.

Miramax scored again in 1998 with "Shakespeare in Love" which enjoyed both box office and critical success.

In July 1999, Disney agreed to settle the suit brought by its former studio chief, Jeffrey Katzenberg, who claimed over $500 million in damages for bonuses he said he was owed. Leaks about the settlement put the figure paid to Katzenberg between $100 million to close to $250 million.

Other financial woes were plaguing the company. Despite box office gross exceeding $500 million in the summers of 1998 and 1999, Disney as a whole had been in a two-year slump, during which earnings dropped 21% through the fiscal third quarter of 1999 (ending June 30) and shares lost an annual average of 1.3%. Eisner had been struggling ever since company president Frank Wells died in a helicopter crash in 1994. Eisner had yet to choose a second-in-command from the ranks of Disney's talented executives. However, the motion picture division remained one of Disney's most profitable businesses with 1999 box office revenue up by $150 million.

As a result of an overall drop in revenue, Eisner initiated a review of capital spending. In spite of the studio's profitability, cuts were to be widespread. Eisner slashed development deals and offloaded hundreds of millions of dollars in costs, including staff and production overhead at Miramax and Disney.

Personnel changes at Disney in 1999 included Peter Schneider's promotion to President of Walt Disney Pictures and Robert Iger's selection to head up the newly streamlined operations of Buena Vista International.

In 2000, Peter Schneider began to make his presence felt. Schneider was one of the executives responsible for "Mulan," "Tarzan," "The Lion King" and "Beauty & The Beast" and pursued making Disney even more family-friendly with dramas such as "Disney's The Kid" and "Remember the Titans." Schneider was also keen to make the most of Disney's franchises, encouraging synergy among the divisions, as evidenced by the films "Pirates of the Caribbean" and "Country Bears," based on Disneyland rides; "Recess" and "The Tigger Movie" derived from animated series; and the stage production of "The Lion King." Disney continues to produce adult-oriented fare with Jerry Bruckheimer and others, but recognizes that the road to profit is through multiple-division branding and family product.

Also in 2000, Nina Jacobsen became sole president of the Buena Vista Motion Picture Group after Todd Garner left to join Joe Roth and Rob Moore at Revolution Studios.

With theme-park attendance plummeting and several commercial-free days of nonstop news on its ABC television network, investors heard a good deal about the Sept. 11, 2001 effect on Disney's financial health. Travel by American consumers to tourist sites such as Disney's parks declined after the events of September 11th. Disney's two parks account for a large percentage of total income. Disney had a strong summer season at the box office which helped to offset weak attendance at its theme parks and slowing revenue from its broadcast outlets.

After Peter Schneider's abrupt departure from Disney in June, 2001, Michael Eisner finally promoted Richard Cook to the position of chairman, Walt Disney Studios in February 2002. Eisner had tried to woo talent friendly producers such as Brian Grazer and Armyan Bernstein, but his overtures were rejected. Disney continued to be troubled by a downturn in its theme-park revenues in 2002 and a slate of movies that limited its market share. Accordingly, analysts downgraded the company's long-term debt several times in 2002. Ironically, Disney's first animated picture Oscar came for the Japanese anime film, "Spirited Away." Miramax continued its winning ways with Best Picture Oscar-winner "Chicago" surpassing "Good Will Hunting" as its highest grossing film.

2003 set two box office records for Disney with "Finding Nemo," a co-production with Pixar Animation Studios, supplanting "Lion King" as their highest grossing film ever and "The Pirates of the Caribbean: Curse of the Black Pearl," which became the company's highest grossing live action film and the first PG-13 film released through the Walt Disney Pictures label. Changes were looming at Disney in late 2004. On Sept. 9, 2004, CEO Michael Eisner announced he would retire when his contract expired in 2006 and end a more than 20-year run as Disney's top exec. Disney executives were also faced with the distinct likelihood that key suppliers would exit the Disney fold. Executives spent over a year in negotiations to renew Disney's deal with Pixar Animation Studios, but on Sept. 30, 2004, company pres. Bob Iger said it would be "unlikely" that a new distribution deal with Pixar would be struck. In late October, contract talks also stalled with Miramax's Bob and Harvey Weinstein. Disney had until March 2005 to renew their personal contracts.

Inside Disney, Eisner and Iger indicated a new focus to deliver more Disney-branded family movies. Recent Touchstone box office failures like "The Alamo" and "Hidalgo" help Disney make its case to emphasize titles truer to Disney's family-centered history and roots. The refocus would in reality mean a 50-50 split between Walt Disney Pictures and Touchstone, rather than the 70-30 split in favor of Touchstone evident the past few years.

Economically, exits by Pixar and Miramax would hurt the studio in terms of box office and home video. Pixar's "Finding Nemo" accounted for 23% ($340 million) of Disney's total $1.5 billion film grosses in 2003. Two years earlier, "Monsters, Inc." brought in $239 million. Miramax delivered box office revenues of $609 million, $395 million and $695 million, respectively, from 2001 to 2003. By comparison, Buena Vista in those three years earned $887 million, $1.1 billion and $1.5 billion. As a company, The Walt Disney Company reported higher financial results through the end of nine months (ending June 30, 2004). Diluted earnings per share were $0.29, up 21 percent versus the prior year, led by operating income growth at its Media Networks, Parks and Resorts and Consumer Products segments.

After running Disney for 20 years and enduring several contentious years recently, Michael Eisner left the Board of Directors on September 30, 2005. Two elements of Eisner's employment contract, a 2% share on profits in excess of $100mm and options to over 500k shares of Disney stock at the trading price when he took the job, made him one of the 400 wealthiest Americans. Robert Iger became CEO. Ironically, Eisner left the board on the same day that Harvey and Bob Weinsteins' contracts ended and they left the company they founded, Miramax, and parent Disney to start a new company. Iger inherited a company on the upswing with strong studio performance expected in fiscal 2006. Earnings at ABC had improved dramatically due to the strong lineup and ratings, ESPN costs were under control and theme park attendance remained good.

At the studio level, the impact of the Weinsteins' departure at the end of 2005 was lessened by shoring up Disney/Pixar Animation relations. In May 2006 Disney completed the acquisition of Pixar Animation Studios in an all-stock transaction, where 2.3 Disney shares were issued for each Pixar share. Based on Pixar's fully diluted shares outstanding, the transaction was valued at $7.4 billion ($6.3 billion net of Pixar's cash of just over $1 billion). The deal made Pixar Chairman & CEO Steve Jobs Disney's largest shareholder and came with a seat for Jobs on Disney's bd. of directors as a non-independent member. Pixar's credits over the past 15 years, most in production and/or distribution collaboration with Walt Disney Pictures, have included the blockbusters "Toy Story," "A Bug's Life," "Toy Story 2," "Monsters, Inc.," "Finding Nemo," "The Incredibles" and most recently, "Cars." Pixar's core management remains in place, and Pixar continues to produce under the Pixar label. Dr. Ed Catmull, previously Pixar president, now serves as president of the new Disney and Pixar animation studios and reports to Iger and Dick Cook, chairman of The Walt Disney Studios. In addition, John Lasseter, previously Pixar executive v.p., serves as chief creative officer of the animation studios, as well as principal creative advisor at Walt Disney Imagineering.

Amidst the relief of keeping box office gold Pixar part of the Disney fold, Disney chief Iger announced in mid-July a restructuring of studio entertainment operations which would reduce studio workforce by approximately 650 positions as reported in Disney's third quarter 10-Q SEC filing. The corporate push to do more with less to unleash shareholder value continues across the industry.

Disney's "Pirates of the Caribbean: Dead Man's Chest" and the Disney/Pixar "Cars" release accounted for more than $665 million in domestic box office receipts and through the summer were the year's top box office draw. Disney, a Dow 30 company, reports annual revenues topping $30 billion.

When Robert Iger took over for Michael Eisner in 2005, there were questions about his ability to run the company. Shareholders Roy Disney and Stanley Gold even filed a lawsuit to void his election to the board. By 2007, Iger had increased profits for the first half of 2007 by 79% to $2.63 billion and quieted even his most severe critics. The financial results have been due in part to the strong performances of the Motion Picture Studios with films like the "Pirates of the Caribbean" franchise. Dick Cook has run that division since 2002, but has been employed by Disney since 1970 when he started as an amusement ride operator.

Disney bought Pixar in 2006 for $7.4 billion and there was a lot of concern that the two companies would have difficulty merging their corporate cultures. By 2008 it was clear that the integration is working well. "WALL-E" and "Bolt" were two of the biggest hits of the year for the studio theatrically and unleashed a torrent of related retail products across all segments of the company. Although Disney's market share in 2008 slipped from its strong showing in recent years, they ended strongly with "High School Musical 3: Senior Year," "Beverly Hills Chihuahua" and "Bolt."

In late September 2009, Dick Cook, a 38 year veteran of Disney who started as a ride operator and rose to become Chairman of Walt Disney Studios, resigned. Cook was genial, well-liked and a brilliant marketing executive. Rich Ross, a 13-year Disney veteran and president of Disney Channels Worldwide, was named Cook's replacement in early October. Chuck Viane, President of Walt Disney Studios Motion Pictures Distribution, presided over a fair year at the Box office in 2009, leaving Disney in the middle of the studio pack with a 11.3% market share. Pixar's animated "UP" soared with $293mm during the Summer and "The Proposal" and "G-Force" in 3-D did $164mm and $119mm respectively.

The latter part of the year provided the backdrop for Disney's announcement that it would acquire Marvel Entertainment in a transaction valued at approximately $4 billion. Under the deal, Disney acquires ownership of Marvel, including its more than 5,000 Marvel characters. Disney plans to build on Marvel's strong global brand and world-renowned library of characters including Iron Man, Spider-Man, X-Men, Captain America, Fantastic Four and Thor, among others and across multiple platforms.

Disney's distribution subsidiary, Miramax Films, endured a dismal 2009 as parent Disney slashed 70% of Miramax's workforce in October to 20 people, reduced the number of movies it will now release to just three a year and folded much of its key marketing and distribution operations into its own studio. Disney will shut down Miramax's New York headquarters and its Los Angeles office and maintain a small dedicated staff at its Burbank lot. Daniel Battsek, who headed up the Miramax specialty label, was fired after working for the Disney organization for 18 years, mostly in the studio's international operation in London. Early in 2009 Miramax had little success with "Adventureland" and Stephan Frears', "Cheri." In December, Robert DeNiro starred in "Everybody's Fine," along with Drew Barrymore and Kate Beckinsale.

Last September, Disney fired its longtime chairman, Dick Cook and and replaced him with Rich Ross, a children's television executive from within Disney.

Throughout 2010 Ross has made a series of changes in the personnel, culture and business models of Disney to reflect his views about a changing business model where social media and new delivery, distribution and marketing systems are changing the landscape radically. He started experimenting with unconventional advertising campaigns that raised the ire of producers such as Jerry Bruckeheimer and went against industry standards for a DVD release on "Alice in Wonderland" that had Exhibitors up in arms. Executing Robert Iger's mandate to increase synergy among various corporate divisions by building company-wide franchises, Ross asked Pixar Animation to help Disney's live-action filmmaking. He brought in Sean Bailey to run production and M T Carney, who has no film experience, to run marketing.

Other significant changes in 2010 included selling

Miramax and making Touchstone films the distribution brand for Dreamworks projects. Disney was also the first studio to have two billion dollar releases in one year: "Alice in Wonderland" and "Toy Story 3."

RECENT DISNEY RELEASES

2000 Dinosaur, Keeping the Faith Disney's The Kid, Coyote Ugly, Gone in Sixty Seconds, Unbreakable.

2001 Pearl Harbor, The Princess Diaries, The Royal Tenebaums, Atlantis: The Lost Empire.

2002 Tuck Everlasting, The Santa Clause 2, Lilo & Stitch, Signs, The Rookie, Sweet Home Alabama.

2003 Finding Nemo, Pirates of the Caribbean: The Curse of the Black Pearl, Bringing Down the House, Freaky Friday.

2004 Princess Diaries 2, The Incredibles, National Treasure, Ladder 49.

2005 Pacifier, Flight Plan, Herbie: Fully Loaded, Shopgirl, Chicken Little, The Chronicles of Narnia: The Lion, The Witch and the Wardrobe.

2006 Pirates of the Caribbean: Dead Man's Chest, Cars, (with Pixar), Eight Below, Step Up, Shaggy Dog, Invincible, The Guardian, The Santa Clause 3: The Escape Clause, Glory Road.

2007 Pirates of the Caribbean: At the World's End, Wild Hogs, Ratatouille, Meet the Robinsons, Bridge to Terabithia, The Game Plan.

2008 The Chronicles of Narnia: Prince Caspian, WALL-E, Beverly Hills Chihuahua, High School Musical 3: Senior Year, Bolt.

2009 Up, The Proposal, G-Force, Disney's A Christmas Carol, Old Dogs

2010 Alice in Wonderland, Toy Story 3, Secretariat, The Sorcerer's Apprentice, Prince of Persia.

RECENT MIRAMAX RELEASES

1999 An Ideal Husband, Music of the Heart, Princess Mononoke, She's All That, The Faculty, In Too Deep.

2000 Down to You, The Yards, Scary Movie, Scream 3.

2001 Chocolat, Spy Kids, Bridget Jones' Diary, The Others, The Shipping News.

2002 Frida, Spy Kids 2, Ararat, Gangs of New York.

2003 Chicago, Kill Bill: Vol. 1, Scary Movie 3, Spy Kids 3-D: Game Over, Cold Mountain.

2004 Shall We Dance, Kill Bill: Vol. 2, Ella Enchanted, Finding Neverland, Pride and Prejudice.

2005 Sin City, The Brothers Grimm, The Adventures of Sharkboy and Lavagirl in 3-D, Hostage.

2006 Scary Movie 4, Hollywoodland, Venus, The Hoax.

2007 The Queen, Gone-Baby-Gone, Becoming Jane, The Diving Bell and the Butterfly.

2008 No Country for Old Men, Smart People, Brideshead Revisited.

2009 The Boys Are Back, Everybody's Fine, Chéri.

2010 Disney announced the sale of Miramax to Ron Tutor and Filmyard Holding in July 2010, but as of November 2010 the deal had not closed.

DREAMWORKS

DreamWorks SKG was founded in 1994 by director Steven Spielberg, former Disney executive Jeffrey Katzenberg, and record mogul David Geffen. DreamWorks started out with a few dreamy deals including a 10-year, $1 billion HBO licensing agreement with HBO; a $100 million programming partnership with ABC; a $50 million animation studio co-founded with Silicon Graphics; and a $30 million joint venture with Microsoft to produce interactive software. The first release for the infant studio was "The Peacemaker" in September 1997, starring George Clooney. In a surprise move, DreamWorks devised a new distribution paradigm, opting for self-distribution, rather than relying on one of the major studios' distribution arms, and by attempting to book the film theatre-by-theatre in order to optimize grosses.

The fledgling company managed to silence many of its critics, with the success of its movie releases. "Antz," proved the highest grossing non-Disney animation film, and the first post-Disney animation film for Mr. Katzenberg. The summer of 1998 brought "Deep Impact" and "Saving Private Ryan" which were the company's first real blockbusters. The company had more of a problem dealing with the development of their new headquarters at Playa Vista, near L.A. Intl. Airport. The project, announced in December 1995, went stale when DreamWorks began having disagreements with Playa Capital, the owners of the site since 1997. Playa Capital wanted to share some of the proposed studio lot, but DreamWorks opposed the idea. In October 1998, the two reached an agreement in which Playa Capital surrendered its claim for part of the property. However, on July 1, 1999, DreamWorks announced that they were pulling out of the deal and would, continue to work out of their offices in Universal City.

Jeffrey Katzenberg settled his $500 million suit against Disney for an undisclosed amount somewhere between $100 and $250 million.

DreamWorks enjoyed a good year at the box office in 2000, with two films in the Top 10 highest grossing movies of the year. "Gladiator" had an astounding $35 million opening weekend, DreamWorks' strongest to date.

DreamWorks also landed a three-picture distribution deal with Woody Allen who ended his longtime relationship with Jean Doumanian's Sweetland Films.

The studio scored an early summer hit in 2001 with "Shrek," which became that year's highest grossing film with more than $265 million at the box office. Following its release on video, the purchase of 2.5 million "Shrek" DVDs in three days set a record, making it the fastest selling title of the year.

Also in 2001, the company exited its GameWorks venture when the arcades failed to catch on quickly. Burger King formed an ongoing alliance with DreamWorks to promote animated and live-action films, including "Spirit: Stallion of the Cimarron," released Memorial Day weekend. In personnel, Michael De Luca (New Line) became the new president of production at DreamWorks Pictures in 2001.

In 2002, DreamWorks continued to make a strong showing at the box office while signing on new talent like Eddie Murphy and Todd Field to ensure future returns. The studio also secured $1.5 billion in financing to fund production and a third digital animation facility.

DreamWorks continued to produce a reliable slate of a limited number of releases each year. "Catch Me If You Can" did most of its business in 2003, eventually grossing over $100 million in North America. "Old School" also performed well. At year end, DreamWorks announced it was close to a deal to sell its music unit to Vivendi Universal for $100 million. This marked a narrowing of the focus of the company to a core of motion picture production. The company focused on both live action and computer animated films such as "Shrek 2" and "Shark Tale."

The company's narrowed focus proved to be a smart move. DreamWorks' summer 2004 release of "Shrek 2" broke industry box office records, grossing $436 million in the U.S. and $850 million worldwide — making it the biggest animated picture of all time. (The first "Shrek" took in $476 million worldwide.) Its follow-up animated release, "Shark Tale," released in October, also gained box office attention, surpassing $120 million at the box office within the first few weeks of its release. The company's next computer-generated feature, Madagascar, was in the works and scheduled for release in spring 2005.

These box office successes made the ideal backdrop for DreamWorks executives to announce an IPO of DreamWorks Animation. The animation unit's shares sold to the public represented about 27 percent of the new entity, which trades under the stock symbol DWA. Jeffrey Katzenberg is company CEO and controls it with partner David Geffen through super-voting stock. The two did not sell off any of their stake during the IPO. Steven Spielberg does not have an operating role in the company or own super-voting shares. At that time, DreamWorks SKG remained a privately held company.

Also in 2004, DreamWorks extended its home video and foreign theatrical distribution pact with Universal Pictures, keeping DreamWorks product in Universal channels until 2010. The pact covered foreign theatrical distribution rights for live-action and animated features, as well as worldwide home video rights.

Circumstances changed substantially in 2005. After spinning out DreamWorks Animation as a public entity in 2004, DreamWorks SKG found itself in play. Both Paramount and Universal were kicking the tires. DreamWorks Animation would not be included in any transaction but all 59 titles in DreamWorks' library with films such as Academy Award winning Best Picture "American Beauty" would be.

The timing for a DreamWorks acquisition may have been precipitated by the fact both Universal and Paramount were searching for new content to fill their foreign pipelines. The 24-year international distribution alliance through UIP ended in Jan. 2007 and left both organizations scrambling to provide international markets with quality product. While interest in DreamWorks as an acquisition target brewed for the remainder of the year, DreamWorks celebrated two hits in the release of "Madagascar" and "The Ring Two." "The Island" was a major disappointment but "Just Like Heaven" and "Red Eye" did well at the end of summer. "Wallace & Gromit in The Curse of the Were-Rabbit" opened in the fall and was loved by critics and families.

DreamWorks saw an end of an era in 2006 when it signed over its independence to Paramount Pictures in an acquisition transaction valued at $1.6 billion, a deal including cash and assumption of debt. Under the agreement, Steven Spielberg and David Geffen of DreamWorks remain in their respective roles as producer/director and chairman. Additionally, the company entered into an exclusive seven-year agreement to distribute films from DreamWorks Animation, led by Chairman Jeffrey Katzenberg. One of Paramount's first orders of business was to find a buyer for the DreamWorks film library to lessen the financial burden of the transaction. During the spring, Soros Strategic Partners, LP and Dune Entertainment II, LLC, an affiliate of Dune Capital Management, LP, agreed to buy the film library for $900 million. Terms called for Soros and Dune to acquire all 59 DreamWorks live action films released through September 15, 2005. Additionally, Soros entered into an exclusive five-year agreement with Paramount to distribute the library.

In the spring of 2006, DreamWorks welcomed Universal Pictures' top exec Stacey Snider, who had been Universal Pictures chairman and CEO since 1999, as DreamWorks' new co-chairman and CEO. During her tenure at Universal, that studio experienced a remarkable turnaround. Snider has consistently made lists of the most powerful women in entertainment and ranked 59 among Forbes' The Most Powerful Women In 2005.

Among the studio's releases during the year were animated "Over the Hedge," teen flick "She's the Man," the animated "Flushed Away," (co-prod. with the UK's Aardman Animation) and "Dreamgirls."

DreamWorks produced most of the hits for Paramount in 2007 including, "Blades of Glory," "Shrek the Third" and "Transformers" and are expected to contribute the bulk of Paramount's $220 million profit this year on grosses approaching $1.4 billion. However, just two years after Viacom acquired DreamWorks, a serious rift appeared in the relationship. Steven Spielberg and David Geffen reported feeling underappreciated by Viacom and that they were talking to other studios about what happens when their contracts expire. Viacom CEO Phillipe Dauman countered that the departure of the DreamWorks crew would be "immaterial" to the parent company.

Since its $1.6 billion acquisition by Paramount in Dec. 2005 relations between the two companies were acrimonious, and culminated in a separation in October 2008. Co-founder and partner David Geffen negotiated the deal for principal Steven Spielberg and co-chairman and CEO Stacey Snider but did not become part of the newly independent DreamWorks 2.0.

Spielberg and Snider formed the new DreamWorks with $550 million in equity from India's Reliance BIG Entertainment and was assembling at press time another $700 million through J.P. Morgan Chase & Co. DreamWorks and Paramount planned to remain partners on 30-40 projects, while, separately, Spielberg will be involved as producer in another four Paramount projects, including the "Transformers" sequel. The new DreamWorks plans to produce six films annually. It signed a distribution pact in the fall with Universal Studios, calling for DreamWorks to pay Universal an 8% distribution fee, with Universal advancing film marketing costs. Universal would handle worldwide distribution except for India, which RBE will oversee, and any DW/Par co-productions would likely see global distribution shared with Universal.

By February 2009, the distribution deal with Universal collapsed and the Walt Disney Studios stepped in and reached a distribution agreement with DreamWorks Studios, name of the latest incarnation of Spielberg's filmmaking operations. The agreement outlined a five-year, 30 movie distribution deal, with Disney's Touchstone label distributing the films and Disney handling DVD sales and pay-TV distribution on cable's "Starz." DreamWorks will pay Disney a distribution fee of 10 percent of each movie's revenue.

Both DreamWorks Studios and independent

DreamWorks Animation did well at the boxoffice in 2009, with DreamWorks' "Transformers: Revenge of the Fallen" coming in number one at the domestic boxoffice with $402mm as of November 2009 and DreamWorks Animations' "Monsters v. Aliens" coming in at number six with $198mm.

In 2010, Spielberg and Tom Hanks released the 10-part television project, "The Pacific," on HBO. "Real Steel" will be released by Disney in 2011 and "Cowboys and Aliens" will be released by Universal in 2011. Dreamworks and Dreamworks Animation were responsible for a large amount of Paramount's boxoffice in 2010 with hits such as "Dinner for Schmucks," "How to Train Your Dragon" and "Shrek Forever After."

RECENT DREAMWORKS RELEASES (Includes Live-Action and DreamWorks Animation releases)

1999	Prince of Egypt, American Beauty, The Haunting.
2000	Almost Famous, Meet the Parents, Gladiator, What Lies Beneath.
2001	Shrek, Evolution, The Last Castle, The Curse of the Jade Scorpion.
2002	The Ring, The Road to Perdition, Spirit: Stallion of the Cimarron, The Tuxedo, Catch Me If You Can
2003	Old School, Head Of State, Biker Boyz, House of Sand and Fog.
2004	Shrek 2, The Terminal, Anchorman, Surviving Christmas.
2005	Madagascar, The Ring Two, The Island, Just Like Heaven, Red Eye, Wallace & Gromit in the Curse of the Were-Rabbit, Match Point.
2006	Over the Hedge, She's The Man, Flushed Away, Dream Girls.
2007	Transformers, Shrek the Third, Blades of Glory, The Kite Runner, Bee Movie.
2008	Kung Fu Panda, Tropic Thunder, Eagle Eye, Madagascar: Ecape 2 Africa, The Soloist.
2009	Transformers: Revenge of the Fallen, Hotel for Dogs, I Love You Man, The Uninvited, Monsters v. Aliens.
2010	Dinner for Schmucks, She's Out of My League, The Spy Next Door, How to Train Your Dragon, Shrek Forever After.

METRO-GOLDWYN-MAYER / UNITED ARTISTS, INC. (OWNED BY SONY CORP. AND GROUP OF EQUITY PARTNERS)

Metro-Goldwyn-Mayer, Inc. was originally founded by exhibitor Marcus Loew. In 1910, after several years of expansion, Loew organized Loew's Consolidated Enterprises, succeeded the next year by Loew's Theatrical Enterprises. In 1920, Loew's acquired the Metro Pictures Corporation, which later turned out such films as "The Prisoner of Zenda," "Scaramouche" and "The Four Horsemen of the Apocalypse." In 1924, Loew and his associates, Nicholas and Joseph Schenk and Adolph Zukor, acquired the Goldwyn Company (founded in 1917), and Loew's became the owner of the merged Metro-Goldwyn stock. Loew's then acquired Louis B. Mayer Pictures and the services of Mayer, Irving Thalberg and J. Robert Rubin. The company was renamed Metro-Goldwyn-Mayer.

In 1936 and 1937, legal control of the entire production and distribution organization was vested in Loew's, with Metro-Goldwyn-Mayer used merely as a trade name. On February 6, 1952, the consent decree against Loew's, Inc. provided for a divorce between the producing and distributing phases of the corporation and its domestic exhibition activities and interests. Among notable pictures in the company's history have been "Ben Hur" (silent), "The Thin Man," "Mutiny on the Bounty," "Goodbye Mr. Chips," "Mrs. Miniver," "The Wizard of Oz," "Gone With the Wind," "Meet Me in St. Louis," "King Solomon's Mines," "Ben Hur" (sound), "Doctor Zhivago," "2001: A Space Odyssey" and many more.

In 1973, the company ceased its own distribution and licensed domestic distribution to United Artists and foreign distribution to CIC. In June 1980, the motion picture operations of MGM, Inc. were sold to stockholders as Metro-Goldwyn-Mayer Film Co. United Artists was purchased by the Metro-Goldwyn-Mayer Film Co. in 1981, with the former company becoming a wholly owned subsidiary of the latter. In 1983, the name of the parent company was changed to MGM/UA Entertainment Co. In 1986, Turner Broadcasting System purchased MGM/UA and sold the UA portion to Tracinda Corporation along with MGM motion picture and television production, distribution and the home entertainment division. The MGM lot and lab were sold by Turner to Lorimar-Telepictures. Turner retained only the MGM film library. During this period, MGM-UA produced "Moonstruck," "Rain Man" and "A Fish Called Wanda."

Pathe Communications Corporation acquired MGM/UA in November 1990 with Giancarlo Parretti as chairman. The new company was now renamed MGM-Pathe. In 1991, Parretti was removed as chairman with control given to Alan Ladd, Jr., and MGM-Pathe was given a $145 million loan from Credit Lyonnais, allowing them to start film distribution after months of inactivity. Due to loans and transactions totalling $885 million, Pathe was $395 million in debt to Credit Lyonnais. In 1992, Credit Lyonnais bought up 98.5% of MGM, thereby officially disposing of Parretti. Following this move, the company was again renamed Metro-Goldwyn-Mayer, Inc. In July of 1993, Alan Ladd, Jr. was replaced by former Paramount Pictures chairman Frank G. Mancuso. In 1994, the distribution arm was once again bearing the title MGM/UA and the revived studio had a major hit with the science-fiction film "Stargate." 1995 proved that Metro-Goldwyn-Mayer was again a major force with a number of critical and financial successes such as "Get Shorty" and "Leaving Las Vegas." Although "The Birdcage" was a big hit, in early 1996, MGM was the target of yet another bidding war. In late July of 1996 MGM was purchased (again) by Kirk Kerkorian and a consortium of investors, including Australian television magnate Kerry Packer, for $1.3 billion.

In 1997, MGM purchased the movie-related business of John Kluge's Metromedia Group, including Orion Pictures. Less than two years after buying MGM for the third time, Kerkorian put MGM on the auction block again. Faced with a cash crisis, MGM froze television production and made cutbacks in the number of features planned for release.

In October of 1997, MGM, Inc. announced Goldwyn Films, a division specializing in film production that takes on horror pics, oddball comedies and off-beat movies. Not to be confused with Samuel Goldwyn Co., the reincarnation of the company was swallowed up first by Metromedia, then by MGM. MGM continued to struggle, despite the box office success of "Armageddon" and "Tomorrow Never Dies." By the spring of 1999 however, things were beginning to look up. As part of a plan to revitalize the ailing studio, MGM announced a companywide restructuring under the new leadership of Alex Yemenidjian, the new chairman & CEO. Through the Orion and PolyGram acquisitions, MGM had the world's largest film library with over 5,000 titles. MGM also won its legal battle with Sony over the rights to the James Bond franchise, negotiated an early termination of its Home Video contract with Warner and signed a multi-picture deal with Miramax.

In October 1999, MGM posted the results of its first profitable quarter in over three years. A $750 million equity offering was expected to provide funding for new film and television production initiatives while the company turned an eye toward expansion in cable and satellite.

2000 saw the profits continue, with 3rd-quarter results showing improved cash flow and exceeding expectations. Much of the credit went to MGM's film library and aggressive licensing to television and home video and DVD sales though MGM's own distribution channels. MGM also closed several movie-channel deals worldwide for which they can provide current and future content through their film library and new product.

MGM had slated 21 films for 2001 release under new head of production, Alex Gartner and new distribution head, Ian Sutherland. By September of 2001, however, the studio had only released 10 of the 21 films planned, pushing seven releases back to 2002. MGM's biggest successes of the year were "Hannibal," "Bandits" and "Legally Blonde" which helped to offset the disappointing performance of "Original Sin" and "Antitrust."

MGM planned to release a total of 20 films in 2002, mostly at non-peak times in an ongoing effort to pull itself out of the box office doldrums. As it turned out, MGM hit its goal of profitability one quarter earlier than expected. By the third quarter of 2002, in spite of slightly lower than expected box office, the studio was in the black, thanks in part to strong home video performance and TV revenues. The studio continued to emphasize lower-cost filmmaking, with the production budget for 2003 set at $250 million — the same level as in 2002, minus costs on the James Bond picture, "Die Another Day." With successes like "Barbershop," which cost only $12 million, the formula was working.

Charman-CEO Alex Yemenidjian continued to stress this theatrical philosophy in 2003, with modestly budgeted films aimed at target demos, with a mix of sequels and remakes such as "Legally Blonde 2," "Walking Tall" and "Barbershop 2." Meanwhile, MGM's library continued to generate substantial revenue, with both DVD and home video revenue up over 50% compared to 2002. The Lion found itself in play again in 2004. Time Warner had all but sewn up a deal to acquire MGM, when Sony Corporation of America swept in at the last minute with a proposal that was ultimately approved by MGM's board of directors in late September. The $4.9 billion transaction involved Sony and a consortium of equity investors which included: Providence Equity Partners, Texas Pacific Group, Comcast Corporation and DLJ Merchant Banking Partners. The offer shook out to $12 in cash per MGM share plus the assumption of MGM's approximately $2 billion in debt and closed in mid-2005. Shaping the role of consortium investors, defining future product distribution channels and tackling day-to-day studio operation issues made the transaction complex by both Hollywood and Wall Street's standards.

During 2005 MGM co-financed "The Amityville Horror," the much-nominated and awarded "Capote" and "Into the Blue," all of which were distributed by Sony Entertainment or Sony Pictures Classics. Upcoming projects included three storied franschises; the new Bond film, "Casino Royale," the new Rocky film, "Rocky Balboa" and "The Pink Panther" featuring Steve Martin as Inspector Clouseau. MGM post-transaction highlights included: MGM remains a private company owned by the consortium; Comcast, which invested $300 million, will create several cable and video-on-demand channels using the combined MGM & Sony library; JP Morgan Chase also committed to lead a bank syndicate to provide up to $4.25 billion in senior debt financing together with Credit Suisse First Boston; MGM continues as an active producer of film and TV projects, and continues to greenlight projects under the MGM and United Artists banners.

After the transaction, MGM's executive suite was virtually swept out. An interesting development happened in late 2005 when Harry Sloan was named chairman and CEO of MGM and also became a private investor in the company. Sloan, who had just sold SBS Broadcasting, Europe's second largest broadcast company, had previously headed New World Entertainment, Marvel Entertainment Group and Lions Gate. Many thought the deal with Sony would mark the end of MGM, but there was a clause in the Sony deal where MGM could become their own distributor and cease that arrangement.

Operationally, Sloan came with a plan. He had been quoted in the trade press, saying, "The best product is being made outside the studio system" and shared the observation that studios are at their best when they are marketing and distributing films. Reflecting this viewpoint, he quickly assembled a management team adept at film marketing and distribution. In Jan. 2006, Rick Sands, formerly of independent-spirited DreamWorks and Miramax, became COO. A 25-year Paramount Pictures distribution veteran, Clark Woods, joined as MGM president, domestic theatrical distribution. With diminished emphasis on production, MGM made cuts, eliminating 1,000 staff for $200 million in savings. The 400 remaining staffers began working from Sloan's new, straightforward playbook. It read: Produce, but produce selectively, releasing only two to three films a year; and, aggressively market and distribute an annual slate of up to 20 independent films. Yet, in a surprise move that signaled plenty of sizzle left to MGM's production ambitions, MGM announced Nov. 2, 2006, that its United Artists division snagged the production duo of Paula Wagner and Tom Cruise to reignite the artist-friendly label. Wagner signed on as CEO and Cruise is producing and starring in UA films, giving UA an A-lister with proven box office appeal. MGM indicated the label would produce up to four films a year.

MGM Chairman Harry Sloan announced in 2007 that he was putting together funding for the studios' franchise pictures — James Bond, The Pink Panther, The Terminator and The Hobbit and also putting together funding for the films produced by Tom Cruise and Paula Wagner's revitalized UA. Having concluded a distribution deal for the bulk of the product from the Weinstein Company last year, MGM is starting to become a significant distributor again, with 20 titles on next year's release slate. The first of the new UA product to be distributed this year was the $35 million-budgeted, "Lions for Lambs," with Tom Cruise, Meryl Streep and Robert Redford.

2008 saw a shift in strategy for MGM: with the cancellation of the Weinstein distribution deal and other "rent-a - distributor deals," the company starting focusing on ambitious in-house production and financing of their own slate for distribution. To that end, Mary Parent, a former Universal executive, was hired and began buying scripts and books aggressively. However, Paula Wagner, Tom Cruise's long time partner, left UA in August, although she retains an ownership interest. Wagner's departure raised questions about the $500 million revolving fund from Merrill Lynch that was alloted to UA features, particularly when MGM has two J.P. Morgan credit lines for $450 million that will not cover Parent's ambitious production plans. The studio is looking to raise another $500 to $600 million which will be extraordinarily difficult given the state of the capital markets.

Harry Sloan was ousted as MGM CEO in 2009 but remained as non-executive chairman. Management duties were turned over to a trio of executives: Mary Parent, CFO Bedi Singh and turnaround specialist, Stephen Cooper, who was brought in as vice chairman. Providing some stability on the distribution front was veteran Erik Loomis, who is President of Worldwide Theatrical Distribution, Home Entertainment and Acquisitions. There was not much on the release schedule until "Fame" opened in September and MGM's share of the boxoffice was not even in the top twelve among distributors for 2009. "The Cabin in the Woods" was pushed back until February 2010. Films planned for the rest of 2010 included "Hot Tub Machine" on March 19th and Kevin James in "Zookeeper" for October. Re-makes of "Red Dawn" and "Poltergeist" will arrive in the Fall.

2010 was a tumultuous year for MGM as Spyglass Entertainment's Gary Barber and Roger Birnbaum battled Lionsgate, supported by Carl Ichan, for control of the studio. Barber and Birnbaum were in advanced talks to run MGM with a plan to merge their company's assets into MGM and change the $4 billion creditors debt into equity in the merged entity. Late in the year, Ichan and Lionsgate came up with their proposal. Icahn currently owns 33% of Lionsgate. Ironically, Icahn is backing Lionsgate on the MGM bid, but has been fighting with their management for years and still plans to replace the Lionsgate board at their next annual meeting.

He already held a substantial part of MGM's $4 billion debt and offered to buy $963 million more by guaranteeing to debtholders that they will receive at least 45¢ on the dollar as long as they agree to vote against the proposed merger with Spyglass. Production and Distribution at MGM have come to a standstill and in the middle of these negotiations, Mary Parent, Chairman and Co-CEO left the company in mid-October.

RECENT MGM RELEASES

1999	Flawless, The World Is Not Enough, Tea With Mussolini, Stigmata, The Thomas Crown Affair.
2000	Things You Can Tell Just By Looking At Her, Supernova, Original Sin.
2001	Hannibal, Jeepers Creepers, Legally Blonde, Bandits, No Man's Land, Ghost World.
2002	Babershop, Die Another Day, Windtalkers, Bowling for Columbine.
2003	Legally Blonde 2: Bigger, Bolder, Blonder, Agent Cody Banks, Jeepers Creepers II, Out of Time.
2004	De-Lovely, The Dust Factory, The Yes Men (UA release), Hotel Rwanda (UA release), Undertow (UA release).
2005	Beauty Shop, The Amityville Horror.
2006	Casino Royale, Romance & Cigarettes (UA release), National Lampoon's Van Wilder—The Rise of Taj, Harsh Times, Flyboys.
2007	Halloween, 1408, Lions for Lambs, The Mist, The Great Debaters.
2008	Deal, Igor, Vicky Cristina Barcelona, Valkyrie.
2009	Fame.
2010	Hot Tub Time Machine, Red Dawn.

PARAMOUNT PICTURES (A VIACOM COMPANY)

Adolph Zukor formed the Engadine Corporation in 1912, which evolved into Famous Players Film Company. W. W. Hodkinson, from General Film Company, formed Paramount Pictures Corporation in 1914, distributing Zukor products and the products of the Jesse L. Lasky Feature Play Company and others. Famous Players-Lasky Corp. was incorporated in 1916. In 1917, twelve production companies merged with it and the corporation integrated production and distribution by acquiring a national distribution system through a merger with Artcraft Pictures and Paramount Pictures. Famous Players-Lasky began acquiring theatres in 1919 with Southern Enterprises, Inc. (135 theatres); followed in later years by New England Theatres, Inc. (50 theatres), the Butterfield Theatre Circuit (70 theatres) and Balaban & Katz (50 theatres). Theatres in the West and Midwest were acquired later.

Paramount's first great star was Mary Pickford. B.P. Schulberg was named head of production in 1925. In April 1927, the corporate name was changed to Paramount Famous Lasky Corporation, and in April of 1930 it became Paramount Publix Corporation, which declared bankruptcy in 1933. Lasky and Schulberg left the company at this point. In 1935, it was reorganized under the name of Paramount Pictures. During this period, the studio's greatest asset was Mae West, whose outrageous hits, "She Done Him Wrong" and "I'm No Angel," caused much furor among censors.

The company regained its footing in the late 1930s and 1940s with such popular stars as Bing Crosby, Bob Hope, Ray Milland and Dorothy Lamour, as well as high-profile films from notable directors Ernst Lubitsch, Preston Sturges, Billy Wilder and Cecil B. DeMille. The 1940s saw such blockbuster hits as "For Whom the Bell Tolls," "Going My Way" and "Samson and Delilah." In 1949, as a result of the Consent Decree, Paramount split into two companies: Paramount Pictures Corp. for production and distribution, and United Paramount Theatres for theatre operation. After WWII, Paramount introduced a new process called VistaVision to compete with 20th Century Fox's Cinema Scope. The first film in the process was the Bing Crosby-Danny Kaye hit musical "White Christmas," followed by Cecil B. De Mille's 1956 remake of "The Ten Commandments."

Paramount merged with Gulf & Western Industries in 1966, with Paramount as a subsidiary retaining its own management. Robert Evans was brought in as production head under Charles Bludhorn, head of Gulf & Western. Bludhorn expanded theatrical film production and increased the company's investment in TV production (an area Paramount had been slow to develop). Evans had great success with "Love Story" (1970) and two Francis Ford Coppola pictures, "The Godfather" (1972) and "The Godfather, Part II" (1974). With the departure of Evans in 1975, the company moved ahead under Barry Diller as CEO and later under Frank

Mancuso, promoted from vice president of distribution to chairman of Paramount Pictures in 1984. The decade of the 1980s brought the company many successes including the "Star Trek" series, the "Indiana Jones" films, "Fatal Attraction" and "Top Gun." Ned Tanen left Universal Pictures to become president of Paramount. In 1989, Gulf and Western changed its name to Paramount Communications, Inc. and Davis began streamlining Paramount Communications in order to focus on entertainment and publishing.

In 1991, Mancuso was replaced by former NBC head Brandon Tartikoff, who resigned in 1992 to be replaced by Sherry Lansing. In the winter of 1994, Viacom, Inc. purchased the company for $9.75 billion. Viacom head Sumner Redstone appointed Jonathan Dolgen, formerly of Sony, to oversee entertainment at both Paramount and Viacom.

Earlier in 1994, the studio soared at the box office with "Forrest Gump" which became the highest grossing movie in Paramount history.

In 1996, Viacom president and CEO Frank Biondi was dismissed with no replacement. That summer, "Mission: Impossible," a remake of the classic television show, became a smash hit, taking in $75 million over the six-day Memorial Day weekend.

Viacom entered 1997 in a slump and with investor confidence low, for the most part due to the poor fortunes of the Viacom-owned Blockbuster Video chain.

In March 1998, James Cameron's "Titanic" grosses reached a record $1 billion plus, worldwide. Although the revenues of "Titanic" more than covered the $200 million production cost, the hard fact remains that the already phenomenal cost of movie production keeps going up.

Parent company Viacom's fortunes improved dramatically in 1999. Viacom decided to sell a minority stake in the Blockbuster video chain in 1999 with plans to shed the rest over the next year. Viacom agreed to buy TV network CBS in an enormous deal valued at about $35 billion. The acquisition was the biggest media transaction in history and catapulted Viacom to the second-largest entertainment firm in the world (behind Time Warner). Chairman Sumner Redstone, who controls 67% of Viacom's voting stock through his privately held company, National Amusements, remained as chairman and CEO of the combined firm. CBS president Mel Karmazin became president and COO.

Like the other studios, Paramount spent 2000 streamlining its operations, ridding itself of costly production deals and creating synergy between broadcast, cable and motion picture divisions for multi-franchise content. In 2001, Paramount joined MGM, Sony Pictures Entertainment, Universal Studios and Warner Bros. in a joint venture to create an on-demand movie service, the first service to offer a broad selection of theatrically-released motion pictures via digital delivery for broadband Internet users in the United States.

The studio enjoyed box office success with "Zoolander," "Rat Race," "Lara Croft: Tomb Raider" and the highly anticipated "Vanilla Sky."

In 2002, Paramount had a few disappointments at the box office. "K-19: The Widowmaker" and "The Four Feathers" underperformed, but were offset by the success of "The Sum of All Fears."

Under the leadership of Sumner Redstone, Viacom became a huge media conglomerate that in addition to Paramount included: Paramount Television, CBS, MTV, Showtime, Infinity Broadcasting, BET and Blockbuster. Throughout 2003, Mel Karmazin served as president and COO of Viacom Entertainment Group, with Sherry Lansing, chairman of the Motion Picture Group. "The Italian Job" and "How to Lose a Guy in 10 Days" were 2003 hits and "Paycheck" opened at year end.

During 2004, Paramount executives announced a departure from "holding the line on expenses" and pursued a pricier, higher profile production strategy for its future releases. To retain more control over future projects, Paramount acquired between $200 million and $300 million in equity production funding from Merrill Lynch in Aug. 2004. For the past decade, Paramount minimized its risk by seeking co-financing from other studios and would sell off foreign rights to its films. With its new funding, Paramount planned to retain more control over its projects and attract proven box office talent to their titles. Whether Paramount uses its new funding for acquisitions like its 2004 purchase of "Sky Captain and the World of Tomorrow," plan more annual releases than its current 16-18 per year, or spend more than Paramount's current $60-$70 milllion per film remained to be seen.

Paramount's parent, Viacom, spent 2004 shaking up its executive slate. The often-stormy relationship between Chairman Sumner Redstone and President and COO Mel Karmazin culminated in Karmazin's June 2004 resignation. When Redstone's replacement was not Karmazin's number two, Jonathan Dolgen (chairman of Viacom's Entertainment Group), he, too, resigned. Redstone tapped two veteran broadcast and cable executives from among Viacom's management ranks to lead the company. Leslie Moonves and Tom Freston were annointed co-president and co-COOs of Viacom. Moonves was chairman and CEO of CBS, while Freston helmed Viacom's MTV Networks unit, a position he had held since 1987. Redstone indicated he would step down as CEO within three years and the appointments were part of a corporate succession plan to prepare for the next generation of Viacom's senior management.

There were major people changes at Paramount in 2005. Sherry Lansing who ran the studio for a dozen years retired and was replaced by television veteran, Brad Grey. He in turn hired Gail Berman from Fox television to take over the production reins from Donald De Line. Even Paramount Classics received a new chief, talent agent John Lesher. Profits for Paramount surged in 2005, primarily on the strength of higher theatrical revenue, domestic home video and international pay TV.

In 2005 Sumner Redstone split Viacom into two in an effort to unlock shareholder value, separating its high growth cable and film operations from its "value" broadcast and radio business. After the split, Viacom was run by Tom Freston. CBS Corporation, which included CBS, UPN (deceased operating in Sept. 2006), new broadcast network The CW, Simon & Schuster and Infinity Broadcasting, is run by Les Moonves. Redstone controls both companies and also serves as chairman of both. It is interesting that National Amusements, his closely held exhibition company, is the vehicle through which he controls these two huge media entities. Tom Freston was shown the door in 2006 because an underperforming Viacom didn't live up to Redstone's expectations. Redstone brought in two trusted executives, Philippe Dauman and Thomas Dooley to reshape the company. Dauman's history with Redstone goes back 20 years. He served as principal outside counsel to Viacom and represented Redstone in acquiring Viacom in 1987. He then served in several key senior management positions through the years, including Viacom's general counsel and secretary; deputy chairman and exec. v.p. Dauman was also a director on Viacom's bd. from 1987 to 2000. He left Viacom in 2000 and co-founded DND Capital Partners, a private equity firm specializing in media and telecommunication investments. In Sept. 2006, Redstone tapped Dauman to be president and CEO of Viacom. Dooley, Dauman's founding partner of DND Capital Partners, spent the majority of his career also working for Redstone, holding various corporate positions at Viacom from 1980 to 2000. Dooley rejoined Viacom's board in 2006 and in September Redstone created a new post for Dooley, senior executive v.p. & chief administrative officer. One of Dooley's key goals is to improve communication with investors and Wall Street analysts. He reports to Dauman.

Freston was not the only big name to be shown the door in 2006. Paramount did not renew its long-time production deal with C/W Productions, comprised of the duo of actor/producer Tom Cruise and producer Paula Wagner. Since C/W Prods. began in 1993, the company produced films as varied as "War of the Worlds," "The Last Samurai," "The Others" and "Vanilla Sky." It has generated worldwide box office grosses in excess of $2.9 billion.

Eyes will be on Paramount execs to see how they fill the void of losing live-action star Cruise and his box office appeal to another studio. (Cruise and Wagner announced in November 2006 they would be teaming with MGM's United Artists unit and structured a deal that includes them running the studio and taking a "substantial minority financial stake" in UA.)

Because of the cyclical nature of the movie business, investors may be willing to give Paramount more time for its execs to improve studio performance. The true critics to please will be the ones from Wall Street, and their eyes are on Dauman to outline a plan to shore up earnings which lag behind competitors Disney and News Corp. Investors also want to know how Viacom will regain its younger viewers being lured to Internet sites like YouTube and other social networking and entertainment sites. Freston didn't have answers fast enough for Redstone or investors. Dauman knew this going in, so look for Viacom to develop an aggressive strategy for tackling this issue.

Paramount had the largest share of the domestic box office in 2007, powered mostly by films from DreamWorks — "Transformers," "Shrek the Third," "Blades of Glory" and "Norbit," which is ironic because Steven Spielberg and David Geffen stated that they are not particularly happy and have been talking to other studios about moving when their contracts expire in 2009. Philippe Dauman countered that while they were important to Paramount, their leaving would have a negligible impact on Viacom's bottom line. Revenues for Viacom in 2007 rose 24% to $3.27 billion from $2.63 billion last year, mostly attributed performance of film and home video. Sumner Redstone, Viacom Chairman, also got in a very public feud with his daughter, Shari Redstone, over succession and the ultimate disposition of the family theatre circuit, National Amusements.

Dreamworks did separate amicably from Paramount at the end of 2008, once again becoming an independent studio and signed a distribution deal with Universal, returning Steven Spielberg to his roots where he has maintained his production offices even after Dreamworks was acquired by Viacom. DreamWorks and Paramount plan to remain partners on 30-40 projects, while, separately, Spielberg will be involved as producer in another four Paramount projects, including the "Transformers" sequel that will be released next summer. Paramount took the opportunity of Dreamwork's departure to reduce their release schedule to 20 films annually and restructured Paramount Vantage, merging its marketing, distribution and production units with Paramount's.

There was considerable financial turmoil at year end, when Sumner Redstone had to sell $233 million of Viacom and CBS stock to meet loan covenants for parent holding company, National Amusements. Although Redstone did not sell any preferred shares, with Viacom's 53% price drop and CBS down over 70%, control of Viacom may become an issue in 2009.

The distribution deal with the new DreamWorks Studios fell apart in February 2009, but projects remained in the pipeline to help Paramount finish 2009 with a 16.6% market share, number two behind Warner Bros. Jim Tharpe, president of domestic distribution for Paramount, and his team released three extraordinary films during the Summer with "Transformers: Revenge of the Fallen," (with DreamWorks) doing over $400mm, J.J. Abrams' re-imagined "Star Trek" beaming up $260mm and "G.I. Joe: The Rise of the Cobra" delivering $150mm. Christmas brought George Clooney in "Up in the Air" and Peter Jackson's "The Lovely Bones," with Mark Wahlberg, Susan Sarandon and Rachel Weisz. "Shutter Island," based on the Dennis Lehane best selling book, will be the first release of 2010, followed by a Dreamworks Animation 3-D film, "How to Train Your Dragon," in March. In Summer, Paramount will release new installments of "Iron Man" and "Shrek" in 3-D. That will be followed by "The Last Airbender" and "Dinner for Schmucks" starring Steve Carell.

Paramount Chairman and CEO Brad Grey fired Paramount Film Group President John Lesher and Production President Brad Weston in June. After the shakeup, Adam Goodman was upped to president, Paramount Film Group. Grey may be banking on the former DreamWorks executive continuing to muster boxoffice success under the Paramount banner.

In 2010, Paramount Pictures had a terrific year and was the first studio to cross $1 billion for the fourth year in a row. The studio currently holds the top spot in market share, driven by films like "Iron Man 2," "How to Train Your Dragon," "Shrek Forever After," "Jackass" and "Paranormal Activity."

However, Viacom continues to struggle with its Filmed Entertainment businesses, primarily due to a massive drop in DVD sales. In the last quarter, revenue from the Filmed Entertainment segment was down 10% year-over-year and management reduced headcount by 53. Licensing and consumer products will merge into the Motion Picture Promotions unit. The production and development of home entertainment and digital formats will remain under Paramount Digital Entertainment, whereas the Paramount Pictures Worldwide Television Distribution will manage the distribution of movies on digital platforms.

This year the company acquired the global rights to the Teenage Mutant Ninja Turtles and the remaining 51% interest it did not own of the DreamWorks live-action film library.

RECENT PARAMOUNT RELEASES

2000	Wonder Boys, The Next Best Thing, Mission Impossible 2, Shaft, The Original Kings of Comedy, Rules of Engagement.
2001	What Women Want, Zoolander, Rat Race, Along Came a Spider, Lara Croft: Tomb Raider, Vanilla Sky, Jimmy Neutron.
2002	K-19: The Widowmaker, The Sum of All Fears, Serving Sara, Four Feathers, Narc.
2003	The Italian Job, How to Lose a Guy in 10 Days, Lara Croft Tom Raider: The Cradle of Life, The School of Rock, Paycheck.
2004	A Series of Unfortunate Events (with DreamWorks), Alfie, The SpongeBob Squarepants Movie, Sky Captain and the World of Tomorrow, Team America, The Manchurian Candidate.
2005	Sahara, The Longest Yard, The War of the Worlds, Four Brothers, Aeon Flux, Yours, Mine & Ours.
2006	Last Holiday, Failure to Launch, Mission Impossible III, Nacho Libre, Barnyard, World Trade Center, Broken Bridges, Jackass Number Two.
2007	Shrek the Third, Transformers, Bee Movie, Beowulf, Blades of Glory, Disturbia, Norbit.
2008	Iron Man, Indiana Jones and the Kingdom of the Crystal Skull, Kung Fu Panda, Tropic Thunder, Revolutionary Road, The Curious Case of Benjamin Button
2009	Transformers: Revenge of the Fallen, Star Trek, G.I. Joe: The Rise of the Cobra, Up in the Air, The Lovely Bones.
2010	Shutter Island, Iron Man 2, How to Train Your Dragon, Shrek Forever After, Jackass 3-D, Dinner for Schmucks, Paranormal Activity, The Fighter.

TWENTIETH CENTURY FOX (A NEWS CORPORATION COMPANY)

Twentieth Century Fox Film Corporation was started by William Fox, a pioneer in the arcade and nickelodeon business. Fox became a member of the exhibition firm of Fox, Moss and Brill and established the Greater New York Film Rental Company. In 1913, he organized the Box Office Attraction Company, acquiring the services of Winfield Sheehan. On February 1, 1915, the Fox Film Corporation was founded, combining production, exhibition and distribution under one name and with film exchanges in a dozen cities.

In 1917, Fox Films moved into its Sunset Studio in Hollywood. In 1926, Fox introduced Movietone, a sound-on-film process developed by Theodore Case and Earl I. Sponable.

In 1929, Fox began a series of reorganizations and financial deals, principally the purchase by Fox Films of Loew's, Inc. By order of the courts, Fox's ownership of Loew's was later dissolved and various banking interests acquired control of Loew's. During these reorganizations, William Fox's connections with the company were discontinued. Sidney R. Kent became the company's president.

In 1935, The Fox Film Corporation merged with Twentieth Century Pictures, headed by Joseph M. Schenck, and the company assumed its present corporate name. This merger brought Darryl F. Zanuck into the company as vice president in charge of production. Schenck became chairman of the board and continued in that position until his resignation in June 1942, when Wendell L. Wilkie took over the post. Zanuck remained as production head until 1956, when Buddy Adler succeeded him. Upon Adler's death, Robert Goldstein and then Peter G. Levathes took over studio reins. Spyros P. Skouras, a leading theatre operator, became president. On July 25, 1962, Darryl F. Zanuck was elected president and Skouras was named chairman of the board, a position he held until 1969. Richard D. Zanuck was named executive vice president in charge of worldwide production. The Zanucks turned an ailing company into an industry leader. In 1969, Darryl Zanuck was made chairman of the board and CEO and Richard Zanuck was made president.

In 1971, 20th Century Fox Film Corporation weathered a trying proxy fight which had the resounding effect of giving the company added resolve. A new managerial team was elected by the Board of Directors which saw Dennis C. Stanfill succeeding Richard Zanuck as president of the company. Shortly thereafter, Stanfill was elevated to the position of chairman of the board of directors and the studio's CEO. In 1972, Fox's East Coast offices were consolidated with the West Coast offices.

In 1981, Fox merged with a company owned by Marvin Davis. In 1985, Davis sold the company to Rupert Murdoch's News Corporation and Fox, Inc. was formed, consolidating the principal operating units: Twentieth Century Fox Film Corporation, Fox Television Stations, Inc. and Fox Broadcasting Company. In the summer of 1989, revamping signalled a new emphasis on motion pictures. The company appointed Joe Roth, an independent producer and director, as chairman of its major filmmaking unit and renamed it the Fox Film Corporation, marking the first time a film director had run a major studio since Ernst Lubitsch headed Paramount Pictures in 1935. Roth's first picture for Fox, "Die Hard 2," proved to be a hit in the summer of 1990. This was followed by the gigantic success of "Home Alone" which went on to become the second highest grossing film in the studio's history following 1977's "Star Wars." At that time, the science-fiction epic had dethroned the company's previous record-holder, "The Sound of Music."

Roth announced his resignation in December of 1992. His replacement, Peter Chernin, was a Fox television executive. In 1994, Fox released the James Cameron film "True Lies" which reportedly cost in excess of $100 million to produce. In 1996, "Independence Day" became one of the top-grossing films in history. In the Winter of 1996-97, George Lucas' ground-breaking "Star Wars" trilogy was re-released theatrically, with new state-of-the-art special effects footage added, and all three immediately broke box-office records (again). The 1997 release of James Cameron's "Titanic" was delayed from its scheduled July release until the Fall of 1997, ostensibly due to extensive special-effects re-shooting. With this feature Cameron broke the "Waterworld" record by setting a new negative cost record rumored to be in excess of $200 million. Late in the year, Fox threatened Disney's monopoly on animated musicals, with its own mega-budgeted animated feature release, "Anastasia."

In 1998, Fox, Inc. went public. 20th Century Fox and Fox 2000 then operated under the supervision of Bill Mechanic, chairman of Fox Filmed Entertainment.

In late 1999, Fox Filmed Entertainment promoted Tom Rothman to President of 20th Century Fox Film Group, a newly created executive post charged with overseeing production operations for Twentieth Century Fox and Fox 2000. Elizabeth Gabler replaced Laura Ziskin as head of Fox 2000, which despite failing box office, still planned to produce around 15 pictures per year.

After 1998's record year, box office revenue continued to be healthy in 1999, largely driven by the summer release of "Star Wars Episode 1: The Phantom Menace" which, by Labor Day, had grossed $421 million. It was, however, the only superhit of the year.

The year 2000 brought blockbusters "Big Momma's House" and "X-Men," though midsummer's "Me, Myself and Irene" proved to be a disappointment despite Jim Carrey's leading role. Earnings for the quarter ending September 30th were $119 million (EBITDA) versus $62 million for the previous year, showing a nice rebound after the post-Titanic doldrums. Fox continued to reap strong returns from its television product. In 2000, the company was the largest producer of programming for the U.S. market. Fox began 2001 with "Cast Away," its biggest hit of the year. Other successes included "Dr. Dolittle 2," "Planet of the Apes" and "Moulin Rouge," which was re-released at year's end for Oscar consideration. 2002 was a very successful year for Fox Filmed Entertainment with "Minority Report" and "Star Wars: Episode II-Attack of the Clones," two of the top grossing films of the year.

In 2003 profits for the filmed entertainment division of Fox, Inc. grew more than 40% on contributions from "X2," "Daredevil," "Daddy Day Care" and other films. "Master and Commander: The Far Side of the World" was the year end release. The Studio's successful classic division, Fox Searchlight, also added significantly to the bottom line with hits like, "28 Days Later," "Bend It Like Beckham" and "Antwone Fisher."

Fox's Entertainment Group continued delivering double-digit profits during 2004. Its net income increased 31 percent to a record $1.4 billion, upping earnings per share by 23 percent to a record $1.44. The group also completed its acquisition of a 34 percent interest in the DIRECTV Group, saw strong advertising growth at Fox News and FX; and posted record Filmed Entertainment operating income gains from a string of theatrical hits and healthy home entertainment sales of film and television titles. Box office appeal for "The Day After Tomorrow," ($530 million worldwide gross) "Dodgeball" ($110 million domestic gross since June 1) and "I, Robot" (with $144 million domestic gross to date) provided sound results while Fox Searchlight enjoyed critical success with "Sideways" and many other films.

Fox had another extraordinary year in 2005, leading all the studios in market share and posting record earnings for the fourth consecutive year. The last film in George Lucas' epic series, "Star Wars: Episode III — Revenge of the Sith" led the parade and was the highest grossing film, doing over $380 million domestically. By June of this year Fox had released three other mega-hits including, "Mr. & Mrs. Smith" with Angelina Jolie and Brad Pitt, "Fantastic Four," a new franchise property and "Robots." All of these did over $125 million in North America. The fall brought "In Her Shoes" with Cameron Diaz and Shirley MacLaine, "Stay" and the Johnny Cash story, "Walk the Line." Steve Martin reprised his role in "Cheaper By The Dozen 2" at Christmas.

For parent News Corp., 2005 brought record income at the filmed entertainment, cable network programming, newspapers, television, magazines and book publishing. "Chief" Rupert Murdoch announced he would spend $1-$2 billion on Web and internet acquisitions in the next year. John Malone's Liberty Media owns an 18% stake in Fox, and the company voted to extend the "poison pill" plan for two years or until it figured out how to buy back the shares from Malone. Succession became an issue again when Rupert's son, Lachlan, resigned. Murdoch declined to say whether his other son, James, or Peter Chernin were in line as a possible successor.

News Corp. remains on the upswing. In November 2006, investors were poised to hear first-quarter sales of $5.9 billion, up 4 percent from 2005, and earnings of 21 cents a share, an increase of 17 percent.

The Fox studio's 2006 slate of films illuminated a good year at the domestic box office. The shining stars for the studio were: "X-Men: The Last Stand," ($234 million), "Ice Age: The Meltdown," ($195 million), "The Devil Wears Prada," ($125 million), "Big Mommas House 2" ($70 million) and "The Omen," ($55 million).

Although News Corp.'s core businesses remain the mainstay of earnings, investor buzz and concern (and this carries over to all the big media companies) is about the growth taking place in interactive and new media companies. By the end of 2005, News Corp. formed Fox Interactive Media and completed the acquisition of Intermix Media, Inc. for approximately $580 million in cash, or the equivalent of $12 per common share. Both MySpace.com and Intermix's more than 30 sites became part of Fox's new interactive media unit. MySpace.com is the leading lifestyle portal for networking online.

The addition of MySpace, and Intermix's network of sites, helped News Corp. nearly double its U.S. web traffic to more than 45 million unique monthly users, putting the company in the top echelon of most trafficked content sites on the Internet today. Launched less than three years ago, MySpace.com is the fifth ranked web domain in terms of page views according to comScore Media Metrix. Integrating web profiles, blogs, instant messaging, e-mail, music downloads, photo galleries, classified listings, events, groups, chatrooms, and user forums, MySpace.com created a connected community where users put their lives online. As a result of its popularity and use among young consumers, MySpace.com is a favorite with online advertisers.

Although it came with the hefty purchase price of $580 million, News Corp. validated the transaction in Aug. 2006 when it announced a multi-year search technology and services agreement with search giant Google. Google became the exclusive search and keyword targeted advertising sales provider for Fox Interactive Media's growing network of web properties including MySpace.com Under the terms of the agreement, Google will be obligated to make guaranteed minimum revenue share payments to Fox Interactive Media of $900 million based on Fox achieving certain traffic and other commitments. These guaranteed minimum revenue share payments are expected to be made over the period beginning in the first quarter of 2007 and ending in the second quarter of 2010.

Rupert Murdoch's News Corp. announced two major deals in 2007; the acquisition of Dow Jones & Company, the publisher of The Wall Street Journal and the launch of a business channel to compete with GE's CNBC. Full year operating income grew 15% in 2007, to $4.45 billion. Filmed Entertainment contributed $1.2 billion to that growth, driven by record results on a strong theatrical slate and subsequent home entertainment releases. "Fantastic Four: Rise of the Silver Surfer," "Night at the Museum" and "Live Free or Die Hard" contributed $240 million, $570 million and $320 million worldwide respectively.

In August 2008, News Corporation chairman Rupert Murdoch warned, with a good degree of prescience, that the company was entering an "increasingly difficult economic environment" but says its strong balance sheet will help it weather the storm. News Corp. reported a 17% increase in net profit for 2007-08 to $5.61 billion, but anticipated profit growth would slow to between 4% and 6% in 2008-09 as the economy slowed. The News Corp result was boosted by strong contributions from the company's 20th Century Fox film studio, European pay-TV business Sky Italia and international newspaper divisions.

While the distribution division's market share dropped to slightly over 10% through the end of October, the final quarter of 2008 saw strong theatrical results with "Australia," "The Day the Earth Stood Still," "Marley & Me" and from Fox Searchlight, "The Wrestler."

News Corporation's top management changed hands in 2009, with News Corp. President and COO Peter Chernin stepping down mid-year. Chernin, 57, joined News Corporation in 1989 and served as president and COO since October 1996. During his two decades with the Company, Chernin headed both Twentieth Century Fox Filmed Entertainment and, earlier, the Fox Broadcasting Company. News Corp. Chairman and CEO K. Rupert Murdoch tapped another long-time colleague, Chase Carey, as Chernin's replacement. Carey spent 15 years as a senior executive at News Corp. before becoming CEO of The DIRECTV Group in 2003.

The filmed entertainment group garnered 11.3% market share through November 2009. A Summer of successful sequels saw the release of the smash "Ice Age: Dawn of the Dinosaurs," $196mm, "X-Men Origins: Wolverine" at $180mm and the comedy, "Night at the Museum: Battle of the Smithsonian" which grossed $177mm. Year-end brought the much anticipated "Avatar," directed by James Cameron, which played on 2,500 3-D screens and another 2,000 in the regular format and "Alvin and the Chipmunks: The Squeakquel.

Fox had an extraordinary year in 2010 powered by the unprecedented success of "Avatar" which grossed over $760 million domestically and $2.78 billion worldwide, delivering a 14.8% market share among the studios. The rest of the release schedule was fair including titles such as "The Lightning Thief," "Date Night," "Wall Street: Money Never Sleeps," and "Knight and Day" all grossing less than $100 million. The sole exception was "The A-Team" which did $110 million.

Tom Rothman manages all feature film and TV production, marketing and global distribution for Fox with Co-Chairman and CEO Jim Gianopulos. Rothman was the first president of Fox Searchlight, one of the two survivors of the studio "classic" divisions. Fox Searchlight has given us some of the best-films to emerge from studio financiers: "Fantastic Mr Fox," "Cyrus," "Never Let Me Go," "Black Swan" and "Slumdog Millionaire."

RECENT FOX RELEASES

2000	The Beach, Big Momma's House, Me, Myself and Irene, X-Men, Men of Honor, Cast Away.
2001	Moulin Rouge, Dr. Dolittle 2, Joe Somebody, Shallow Hal, Planet of the Apes.
2002	Minority Report, Life or Something Like It, High Crimes, Star Wars: Episode II-Attack of the Clones, Swim Fan.
2003	X2, Daddy Day Care, Daredevil, The League of Extraordinary Gentlemen, Runaway Jury, Master and Commander: The Far Side of the World.
2004	The Day After Tomorrow, Dodgeball, Taxi, Alien vs. Predator, First Daughter, Paparazzi, Flight of the Phoenix, Fat Albert.
2005	Star Wars: Episode III - Revenge of the Sith, Mr. & Mrs. Smith, Fantastic Four, Robots, In Her Shoes, Walk the Line.
2006	The Omen, X-Men: The Last Stand, The Devil Wears Prada, Borat, John Tucker Must Die, A Good Year, A Night at the Museum.
2007	Fantastic Four: Rise of the Silver Surfer, Live Free or Die Hard, The Simpsons Movie.
2008	Horton Hears a Who?, Meet the Spartans, Max Payne, Australia, The Day the Earth Stood Still, Marley & Me.
2009	Avatar, Alvin and the Chipmunks—the Squeakquel, Jennifer's Body, All About Steve, Night At The Museum: Battle of the Smithsonian.
2010	The Lightning Thief, Date Night, Wall Street: Money Never Sleeps, The A-Team, Knight and Day.

RECENT FOX SEARCHLIGHT RELEASES

2004	Johnson Family Vacation, Napoleon Dynamite, The Clearing, I "Heart" Huckabees, Garden State, Sideways.
2005	Roll Bounce, Bee Season, The Ringer, Night Watch.
2006	Little Miss Sunshine, The Hills Have Eyes, Phat Girlz, The Last King of Scotland.
2007	Notes on a Scandal, Waitress, The Savages, The Hills Have Eyes 2, 28 Days Later.
2008	Under the Same Moon, The Secret Life of Bees, Slumdog Millionaire, The Wrestler.
2009	500 Days of Summer, Whip It, Adam, Amelia, Fantastic Mr. Fox, Crazy Heart.
2010	Just Wright, Our Family Wedding, Conviction, 127 Hours, Black Swan.

UNIVERSAL PICTURES (PART OF NBC UNIVERSAL, A GE COMPANY)

Universal Pictures was formed in 1912, when exhibitor Carl Laemmle amalgamated Bison 101, Nestor, Powers and several other organizations, including his own firm. Laemmle had earlier founded Laemmle Film Service and released his first Independent Motion Picture Company feature "Hiawatha" in 1909. Universal launched the star system by hiring Florence Lawrence for $1,000 a week and billing her as "Queen of the Screen." Universal acquired a studio in 1914. In 1915, production was moved to its present site, Universal City. Contracted stars included Wallace Reid, Lon Chaney, Mary Pickford, Rudolph Valentino and Boris Karloff. "Foolish Wives" ("the first million-dollar feature"), "The Hunchback of Notre Dame," "All Quiet On the Western Front" and others were filmed in the decades that followed. On March 16, 1920, Laemmle and R. H. Cochrane assumed complete control of the company.

In 1936, Universal named new management, with J. Cheever Cowdin as chairman of the board and Nate J. Blumberg as president beginning in 1938. Under the new management, Universal embarked upon the policyof developing star values and such stars as Deanna Durbin, Abbott & Costello, Maria Montez, Donald O'Connor and others were put under contract.

In 1946, the company underwent its second transformation, eliminating the production of all so-called "B" pictures, westerns and serials. This followed a merger and acquisition of the assets of International Pictures Corp. of Leo Spitz and William Goetz, who became production heads and the Universal-International trademark emerged. Universal also completed a distribution deal with the J. Arthur Rank organization for the American distribution of British pictures produced by Rank. 1946 also saw the emergence of United World Pictures, a wholly owned Universal subsidiary, to handle the production and distribution of non-theatrical films including the Bell and Howell Film Library and Castle Films.

1950 saw the resignation of Cowdin with Blumberg assuming full command. Alfred E. Daff, who had been foreign sales manager, assumed the top post in the foreign distribution set-up and then became director of world sales. In 1951, Decca Records acquired approximately 28% of Universal's common stock to make it the largest single stockholder in the company. In 1952, Decca Records became the controlling stockholder of Universal. Milton R. Rackmil, president of Decca Records, was made a member of the Universal board and subsequently elected president of Universal in July 1952.

In 1962, MCA consolidated with Decca and made Universal Pictures Company the theatrical film producing division of MCA, Inc. In 1964, the creation of the Universal City Studios image started with the separate motion picture and television arms. That same year, the company began its profitable Universal Studios Tour. In 1966, Universal Pictures became a division of Universal City Studios, Inc., a subsidiary of MCA, Inc. The company entered a successful period of high-profile hits including "Thoroughly Modern Millie," "Airport," "American Graffiti," "The Sting," "Earthquake" and Steven Spielberg's "Jaws," which in 1975 became the highest grossing movie to that date.

In 1982, Universal released Steven Spielberg's "E.T.: The ExtraTerrestrial," which became the top-grossing film of all time, racking up over $228 million in film rentals in the domestic market alone. Other recent successes have included the "Back to the Future" series, "Field of Dreams," "Born on the Fourth of July," and "Fried Green Tomatoes."

1990 saw two major events in the studio's recent history. A fire swept through the back lot in Universal City destroying acres of sets and causing millions of dollars worth of damage.

MCA Inc. was purchased by the Matsushita Electrical Industrial Company for an estimated $6.6 billion, the most expensive sale of an American company to the Japanese in history. In 1993, Spielberg's "Jurassic Park" grossed over $300 million, placing it as the second highest grossing film of all time right behind "E.T." Spielberg was also responsible for "Schindler's List," the first black-and-white Academy Award winner for Best Picture in 33 years. Seagram Co. purchased 80% of MCA Inc. in 1995 for $5.7 billion, with Seagram's president & CEO Edgar Bronfman, Jr. serving as acting chairman of the entertainment company. With this change of ownership, Lew Wasserman stepped down and was named chairman emeritus, and Sid Sheinberg ended his 22-year reign as president. In the summer of 1995, Universal released "Waterworld," which held the dubious distinction of being the most expensive movie ever made, a staggering $175 million, until Paramount's "Titanic" came in with a $200 million production tab in 1997. Unlike Titanic, however, Waterworld experienced critical drubbings and a lackluster domestic box office, but went on to earn money for thecompany in the international market. "The Lost World," Steven Spielberg's sequel to his mega-hit "Jurassic Park," opened Memorial Day weekend to a record-breaking $90.2 million at approximately 6,000 screens (nearly one-quarter of the screens in the United States). Universal also purchased art house distributor October Films in 1997.

The departure of Steven Spielberg and Amblin Entertainment placed the burden on Ron Howard and partner Brian Grazer's Imagine Entertainment as Universal Pictures' major provider. Although the history between Universal and Imagine goes back some 10 years, and although the company has accounted for more than $2.6 billion in grosses, Universal's need for Imagine to put out box office hits has deepened in Mr. Spielberg's absence. To fill the hole left by Spielberg, Universal signed production deals with Will Smith, Penny Marshall, Mike Nichols and Danny Devito. During this time Universal announced a plan to increase its annual output from 12 films in 1997, to somewhere between 20 and 25, by year 2000.

Universal went through some executive cuts in April 1998. Although there were no explanations offered for the restructuring, speculation arose that the changes were the by-product of Edgar Bronfman, Jr.'s, dissatisfaction with Universal's performance in 1997-98.

Universal's lagging sales and string of disappointing films in 1998 (such as "Meet Joe Black" and "Babe: Pig in the City" resulted in Universal posting more than $130 million in losses. Universal's film business, however, turned the corner in 1999 thanks to the success of its releases of "The Mummy," "Notting Hill" and "American Pie." The company's box office grosses for 1999 through October totaled about $775 million compared to 1998's $315 million for the same period. In addition, the studio's market share grew from 2.4 percent in 1998 to 12.9 percent in 1999, without adding extra movies to its roster.

In 2000, merger-mania hit Universal. In a three-way deal worth $34 billion, Seagram (Universal's 92% owner) was acquired by French companies Vivendi and Canal Plus to create a multinational media giant. The merger was approved by the EC, simplifying the process that plagued the AOL-TimeWarner merger. The new company, Vivendi Universal, was chaired by Jean-Marie Messier (Vivendi), Pierre Lescure (Canal Plus) and Edgar Bronfman, Jr. (Seagram) who offered the Studio executives his assurance that film production would be business-as-usual despite the merger. Meanwhile, Brian Grazer and Ron Howard's Imagine Entertainment signed on for another five years with Universal after a brief flirtation with DreamWorks, guaranteeing the box-office health of Universal in the near future.

In 2001 the company bought music download site MP3.com for its music group and textbook publisher Houghton Mifflin for its publishing unit. Also in 2001, Vivendi Universal agreed to buy News Corp.'s 50% stake in Stream (Italian pay-TV operator), which it planned to merge with its Telepiu service, forming a new entity. But the biggest news of the year came when Vivendi Universal announced that it would merge the operations of Universal Studios and French movie company Studio Canal.

Universal's Home Video unit scored with the release of "Shrek" (DreamWorks) which became the fastest selling DVD of the year, setting a record in its first weekend. Box office was also strong with summer blockbusters "Jurassic Park III" and "The Mummy Returns." These and other hits helped parent company Vivendi to show 30% growth in third-quarter sales.

In 2002, the French media company Vivendi Universal bought the entertainment assets of USA Networks (now named USA Interactive) and created Vivendi Universal Entertainment. VUE's primary holdings included Universal Studios and Universal Television Group. Vivendi Universal owned 93% of VUE; Chairman and CEO Barry Diller's USA Interactive, owned 6%.

In July 2002, embattled VUE Chairman Jean-Marie Messier was ousted from the company and later replaced by Jean-Rene Fourtou. While VUE was doing well with its filmed and television entertainment, the parent company VUE faced a debt crisis which foreshadowed the sale of its entertainment unit to General Electric's NBC, which was completed mid-year 2004. Universal had a strong year in 2003 on a comparative basis with releases such as "American Wedding," "Sea Biscuit," and "Bruce Almighty." Interestingly, Nikki Rocco remains the only woman to ever head a major studio's distribution arm.

Although change is imminent for merging organizations, the new NBC Universal has left Universal Pictures pretty much intact to do what it does best: produce a variety of films appealing to a broad audience. Its 2004 slate underscored this "something for everyone" mindset and included the comedic sequels, "Meet the Fockers" and "Bridget Jones: The Edge of Reason" (following "Meet the Parents" and "Bridget Jones' Diary"); the romantic comedy "Wimbledon;" the sports drama "Friday Night Lights" starring Billy Bob Thornton produced with Imagine Films; and the Ray Charles' story, "Ray," which had been generating award buzz long before the film's Oct. 29 theatre release.

Universal Pictures' recent releases earned awards and made money — what more could studio execs ask for in the year after being introduced to new owners? The strategy to let studio execs to their own devices paid off with both blockbusters and beautiful accolades. The critically acclaimed biopic "Ray" (two Oscars — Best Actor and Best Sound Mixing) and "Friday Night Lights" (one of AFI's movies of the year official selections) were beneficiaries of industry accolades while the moviegoing public's thirst for "The Bourne Supremacy" and "Meet the Fockers" (which also brought Barbra Streisand back to the big screen and teamed with Dustin Hoffman) helped those releases earn blockbuster status. "Supremacy" earned more than $176 million in the U.S. and "Meet the Fockers" became the highest grossing live-action comedy of all time with worldwide box-office receipts topping the $400 million mark. Universal suffered disappointment, however, with the Ron Howard directed and Russell Crowe starring, "Cinderella Man." Although this heartwarming film was critically well received and the audiences that saw it, liked it, it grossed far below expectations with $61 million. At one point, AMC, the theatre circuit, offered to refund admission to anyone who did not like the film, to no avail.

Focus Features, the specialty films unit of Universal Pictures which was formed in May 2002, also has been churning out Academy Award winners with Roman Polanski's "The Pianist," Sofia Coppola's "Lost in Translation," Michel Gondry's "Eternal Sunshine of the Spotless Mind," and Walter Salles' "The Motorcycle Diaries." Recent works include Joe Wright's "Pride and Prejudice," starring Keira Knightley; Fernando Meirelles' "The Constant Gardener," starring Ralph Fiennes and Rachel Weisz; and Harold Ramis' "The Ice Harvest," starring John Cusack and Billy Bob Thornton. In the home entertainment arena, Universal Studios Home Entertainment was expected to bring in nearly $400 million to the home entertainment market from 2005 releases of Universal titles such as "Meet the Fockers" and "White Noise."

Early in 2006, Universal Pictures Chairman Stacey Snider announced she was leaving the studio after 10 years on the job to join DreamWorks SKG as its co-chairman and CEO. Universal promoted two of its executives with strong marketing and production experience to fill the void. Marc Shmuger was named chairman and David Linde received a co-chairman nod. Shmuger's association with Universal goes back to May 1998 when he was named president of marketing for Universal Pictures. He became vice chairman in Dec. 2000 and while vice chairman also served as co-chairman of NBC Universal's Marketing Council, which oversees cross-promotion priorities for all film and TV properties owned by NBC Universal. Linde joined Universal Pictures in May 2002 as co-president (with James Schamus) of Universal's newly formed specialty unit, Focus Features. While at Focus, Linde oversaw a diverse and critically acclaimed slate including Roman Polanski's "The Pianist," Sofia Coppola's "Lost in Translation," Fernando Mereilles' "The Constant Gardener" and Ang Lee's "Brokeback Mountain." During that time, the company garnered 53 Academy Award nominations, and 11 Academy Award wins. In addition to responsibilities at Focus Features, in 2004 Linde was named president of Universal's Rogue Pictures label.

In its third quarter earnings call Oct. 13, 2006, parent company GE reported "another tough quarter" for NBC Universal, but it was a quarter in line with GE's expectations and filmed entertainment showed solid gains in revenues. As a company, GE revenues were up 20%, operating profit down 10%. (It explained strong revenue driven by film and DVDs versus 2005). Film revenue was up 48% to a little more than $350 million and the unit had five DVD releases versus one a year ago.

Ron Meyer, CEO of Universal Studios, is currently the longest-serving studio head, having survived three changes in ownership. Formerly, he was one of the founders of Creative Artists Agency. Meyer's responsibilities include film production, theme park and studio operations. During 2007 Universal had three of the top grossing films with "The Bourne Ultimatum," "Knocked Up" and "I Now Pronounce You Chuck and Larry." Universal closed a 7-year worldwide distribution deal with Steven Spielberg's Dreamworks in October 2008, which is expected to begin in 2009 and include approximately 6 films per year. Stacey Snider and Spielberg recently departed Paramount Pictures and found financing for their production slate from India's Reliance Big Entertainment. David Geffen will not be part of the new company and Dreamworks Animation remains at Paramount for the next several years.

Universal Pictures had four films that grossed over $100 million in the first half of 2008 including, "The Incredible Hulk," "Wanted," "Mamma Mia!" and "The Mummy: Tomb of the Dragon Emperor." In June a large fire at a back lot at Universal Studios destroyed the iconic courthouse square from "Back to the Future" and many sets although, fortunately, the motion picture negative vaults were spared. Universal Studios sold one of its two specialty film labels, Rogue Pictures, to Relativity Media, a private production and financing company. Late in the year, Universal Pictures extended a co-financing deal with Relativity that would provide $3 billion to Universal over the next seven years for dozens of big-budget films which is fortunate in light of the difficulty in the financial markets in the last quarter of 2008.

Universal Pictures Distribution has been led by the first female president of distribution, Nikki Rocco, since 1996 and she had pretty good results and a 9.1% market share in 2009. The year started slowly with "Bruno," "Land of the Lost," "Drag Me to Hell," "Duplicity" and "Funny People" delivering below par results. "Fast & Furious" and "Public Enemies" were bright spots but Ron Meyer's disappointment with the film product resulted in Marc Schmuger and David Linde being dismissed. Changes at the corporate level could materialize at NBC Universal in 2010. As of mid-November, Cable giant Comcast was in talks to purchase a 51% controlling stake in NBC Universal with GE retaining 49% ownership in a joint venture arrangement. Advising Comcast on the transaction is former News Corp. executive Peter Chernin.

Comcast's Steve Burke will succeed Jeff Zucker as the new CEO of NBC Universal at the end of 2010, when Comcast takes control of NBC Universal. Comcast Corp. and General Electric Co., which currently own NBC, had telegraphed a change since last December, when Comcast agreed to buy a 51 percent stake in NBC Universal from GE. That deal, worth $13.75 billion, still hasn't cleared regulatory hurdles, but is expected to be completed at year end.

Universal had a mediocre year at the boxoffice. Adam Fogelson, who recently took over as chairman of Universal Pictures stated "on balance this was a pretty good summer for us, but that doesn't change that we've had a rough run. If there was a surprise hit this summer, it was the animated "Despicable Me," which so far has raked in more than $446 million world-wide and over $248 million in the U.S. "Despicable Me" was a major victory for Universal Pictures, which has struggled after releasing a string of box-office disappointments, a legacy of previous production executives.

RECENT UNIVERSAL RELEASES

2000 Meet the Parents, The Nutty Professor II: The Klumps, Erin Brokovich, U-571, Billy Elliot, How the Grinch Stole Christmas, The Family Man, Head Over Heels.

2001 The Fast and the Furious, American Pie 2, Jurassic Park III, The Mummy Returns, Spy Game, A Beautiful Mind.

2002 D-Tox, Dragonfly, The Bourne Identity, Red Dragon, Undercover Brother.

2003 Bruce Almighty, Hulk, Seabiscuit, The Rundown, Dr Seuss' The Cat in the Hat.

2004 Wimbledon, Friday Night Lights, Ray, Bridget Jones: The Edge of Reason, Meet the Fockers.

2005 Cinderella Man, The 40 Year Old Virgin, Prime, Serenity, Two For The Money, Jarhead, Doom, First Descent, The Producers, Munich, King Kong.

2006 Curious George, Inside Man, The Break-Up, United 93, The Fast and the Furious: Tokyo Drift, You-Me-And-Dupree, Miami Vice, The Black Dahlia, Accepted, Man of the Year.

2007 Knocked Up, Even Almighty, I Now Pronounce You Chuck and Larry, Bourne Ultimatum, American Gangster, Charlie Wilson's War.

2008 The Incredible Hulk, Wanted, Mamma Mia!, The Mummy: Tomb of the Dragon Emperor, Changeling, Frost/Nixon.

2009 Bruno, Land of the Lost, Drag Me to Hell, Duplicity, Funny People, Fast & Furious, Public Enemies.

2010 Despicable Me, Couples Retreat, Get Him to the Greek, Devil.

RECENT FOCUS FEATURES/ROGUE PICTURES RELEASES (Rogue Pictures sold to Relativity Media in 2008)

2002 Monsoon Wedding, The Pianist, Far from Heaven.

2003 How to Deal, Lost in Translation, 21 Grams, The Texas Chainsaw Massacre.

2004 The Motorcycle Diaries, Eternal Sunshine of the Spotless Mind, Vanity Fair.

2005 Brokeback Mountain, Assault on Precinct 13, Unleashed, Broken Flowers, The Constant Gardener, Pride and Prejudice, Cry Wolf, Prime.

2006 Catch A Fire, Hollywoodland, Something New, Fearless, Waist Deep, Scoop.

2007 Eastern Promises, Lust, Caution, Atonement, Reservation Road, Burn Before Reading, In Bruges.

2008 Burn After Reading, Miss Pettigrew Lives for a Day, Milk.

2009 The Limits of Control, Thirst, Away We Go, Taking Woodstock.

2010 The American, A Serious Man, The Kids Are Alright, Babies, Somewhere.

WARNER BROS. (A TIME WARNER COMPANY)

Warner Bros. Pictures, Inc. may be said to have its origins in the 90-seat Cascade Theatre set up by Harry Warner and his three brothers, Sam, Albert and Jack in New Castle, PA, in 1905. The brothers soon branched out into distribution, establishing film exchanges in Pennsylvania and Virginia. In 1913, they moved into film production with Warner Features. Warner Features' first production was 1918's "My Four Years in Germany." In 1920-22 they averaged only two or three features per year. Warner Bros. was incorporated in 1923 to produce as well as distribute and release 14 pictures, including the first of the famous Rin-Tin-Tin series. Scripts were written by Darryl F. Zanuck, an ambitious writer who soon worked his way up to become the company's production chief under Jack Warner. Harry was president; Albert, treasurer; and Sam shared production responsibilities with Jack. Zanuck stayed until 1933 and was succeeded by Hall Wallis, who held the post for the next decade. In 1925, Warner acquired Vitagraph, Inc., which operated 34 exchanges in the U.S. and Canada, and two other concerns with foreign exchanges. That same year, the company began its experiments with sound, collaborating with Western Electric to produce a sound-on-disc process (called Vitaphone) for synchronized film sound.

The first Vitaphone program premiered in August 1926, including some musical shorts and the feature "Don Juan" with John Barrymore backed by a full musical and sound-effects track. Owing to this success, the studio released the feature "The Jazz Singer" in October 1927, with dialogue and certain musical numbers in sound and in 1928, "the first 100% all-talking picture—Lights of New York," a one-hour feature that broke box office records. In 1927, Sam Warner died.

The new sound technology brought Warner Bros. to the

forefront of the industry. It further expanded its theatre holdings and studio facilities, acquiring the Stanley Company of America theatre circuit in 1928, First National Pictures which had a 135-acre studio and back lot, along with exchanges and theatres, and a number of music publishing companies. Those acquisitions greatly helped in the production of the Warner Bros. musicals including "Forty-Second Street," the "Gold Diggers" series, "Footlight Parade" and others. Along with the other motion picture companies, Warner Bros. suffered in the early days of the Depression. Sales of some assets and theatres, along with drastic cuts in production costs, enabled the company to recover and to take advantage of the boom in the 1940s.

In 1953, the company completed the reorganization it was forced to undergo by the government's Consent Decree. Stockholders approved a plan to separate the company into two entities: the theatres were sold to Fabian Enterprises, Inc., and the company was renamed Stanley Warner Corporation. The "new" production-distribution company remained Warner Bros. Pictures, Inc. In 1956, Harry and Albert sold their shares in the company to an investment group headed by Serge Semenenko and Charles Allen, Jr. Jack retained his shares, remaining the largest single stockholder and becoming president of the company. The Warner pre-1948 film library of 850 features and 1,000 shorts was sold to United Artists in 1956.

On July 15, 1967, a subsidiary of Seven Arts Productions Limited (a Canadian-based company headed by Eliot Hyman) acquired substantially all the assets and business of Warner Bros. Pictures, Inc. The company subsequently was called Warner Bros.-Seven Arts Limited. In 1969, Warner Bros.-Seven Arts was acquired by Kinney National Service, Inc., headed by Steven J. Ross, and changed its name in 1971 to Warner Communications, Inc. The studio reverted to the original name of Warner Bros. and appointed Ted Ashley as studio chief. The studio's successes during this period included "Superman," "The Exorcist" and "All the President's Men." Robert A. Daly succeeded Ashley as Warner Bros. chairman and CEO in 1980.

In 1989, Warner Communications was acquired by Time, Inc. in an $18 billion merger that created one of the largest communications and entertainment companies in the world. Time-Warner, as the new company was called, consisted of Warner and its subsidiaries, Time Publishing, Home Box Office, Cinemax, HBO Video and American Television & Communications Corp. John Peters and Peter Guber were instrumental in aiding Warner to rebound from a two-year box office slump. In the summer of 1989, Peters and Guber produced "Batman," which brought in domestic rentals of over $150 million, making it the fourth top-grossing film of all time to that date.

In early 1991, the company announced a partnership with several European entertainment companies to produce 20 films. Time-Warner continued to hold a 50% interest in Cinamerica Limited Partnership, a company that included Mann Theatres and Festival Theatres in California, and Trans-Lux Theatres in the East. In October 1991, two Japanese companies, Toshiba Corp. and C. Itoh & Co., paid $500 million each for a combined 12.5% stake in the company. In May 1993, the company created a new division, Warner Bros. Family Entertainment, to release movies aimed at the children's market, including the hit "Free Willy."

In the autumn of 1995, Time-Warner began negotiations for the $7.3 billion purchase of the Turner Broadcasting System. These negotiations were the subject of intense FTC scrutiny in 1996, due to the 20% stake cable giant TCI held in Turner, but were finally approved by Warner Bros. stockholders on October 10, 1996. Although Turner-owned New Line Cinema was originally to be auctioned off, in May of 1997 the company was removed from the sale shelf, with no plans for its future by Time-Warner, but with its release schedule and creative autonomy intact.

After 18 stagnant months, New Line scored big with the release of "The Wedding Singer." The success was due to the new formula of releasing quirky, non-studio material such as, "Wag the Dog" and "Boogie Nights." The company is also concentrating on producing movies with potential ancillary value. New Line's arthouse division, Fine Line Features, went through changes of its own, under the leadership of its new president, Mark Ordesky.

In April 1998, New Line announced the launching of Fine Line's international and distribution division, Fine Line International, headed by Mr. Ordesky and New Line International president, Rolf Mittweg.

In 1998, New Line's domestic ticket sales climbed 42%, and the studio's 8% market share put it ahead of majors like Universal Pictures, DreamWorks, and MGM for a sixth-place finish at the U.S. box office. New Line grossed over $200 million with "Austin Powers: The Spy Who Shagged Me," continuing its boxoffice success. Sara Risher celebrated her 25th year with New Line Cinema by creating a new in-house production company called ChickFlicks.

In July 1999, Robert Daly and Terry Semel stunned the entertainment world by telling Time Warner Chairman Gerald Levin and other directors of the studio's parent company that they would not renew their contracts after their 19-year tenure with the company. Effective October 1999, Barry Meyer, executive vice president and COO of Warner Bros., was promoted to chairman and CEO, and Alan Horn, chairman and CEO of Castle Rock Entertainment, became president and COO. 1999 box office was favorable, with four films surpassing the $100 million domestic box office mark: "You've Got Mail," "Analyze This," "The Matrix" and "Wild Wild West."

In 2000, Time-Warner agreed to an acquisition by AOL. The merger was held up by various regulatory concerns in Washington DC and Brussels. There were many plans for the new entity, AOL Time-Warner, to achieve synergies in bringing Warner's film product to cable and the Internet.

Both Warner and New Line enjoyed box office success in 2000, with the phenomenal grosses of "The Perfect Storm" and the impressive opening of "The Cell." With 2000's "Pokemon: The Movie," "The Powerpuff Girls" and "Harry Potter" in the pipeline, Warner pursued synergy with other Time-Warner-owned units. Offering numerous opportunities for TV and consumer-product merchandising, these types of movie releases allowed Warner to make the most of its distribution channels throughout the AOL-Time-Warner empire.

Warner's slate for 2001 included "AI: Artificial Intelligence," "Training Day," the highly anticipated star-studded "Ocean's Eleven" and the first in the Harry Potter franchise which generated an advance ticket-buying frenzy. Warner's future looked bright with "The Matrix: sequels, a new "Batman," and several Harry Potter projects to come. With so many merchandising tie-ins in the pipeline, Warner created a new position for Brad Ball (McDonalds)—Executive Vice President, Domestic Corporate Marketing.

In 2001, New Line scored with "Rush Hour 2" which grossed over $225 million.

The AOL Time Warner merger was completed in 2001. Following the merger, Warner Bros. transferred its majority interest in the WB Television Network to sister company Turner Broadcasting. It also closed down all of its Warner Bros. Studio Stores citing poor sales and declining interest in movie-related merchandise. Later that year Warner Bros. Pictures released "Harry Potter and the Sorcerer's Stone" which made $93.5 million in domestic box office receipts in its opening weekend, breaking Universal Pictures' $72.1 million record with "Jurassic Park: The Lost World." The film went on to become 2001's top-grossing film in domestic box office receipts.

2002 was a very positive year for Warner, with several high grossing films, and more sequels ("The Matrix," "Harry Potter") in the pipeline.

Symptomatic of the problems plaguing the company for the last several years, Time Warner removed the "AOL" from its corporate moniker in October 2003. The SEC and the Department of Justice had been looking at the corporations accounting practices since at least the summer of 2002 and both Richard Parson and Steve Case had been subpoenaed in the ongoing probe. However, the filmed entertainment division had an extremely strong year driven by such titles as "The Matrix Reloaded," "The Matrix Revolutions" and "Terminator 3: The Rise of the Machines."

New Line continued to scare up big box office numbers in 2003 with "Freddy v. Jason," "Texas Chainsaw Massacre" and the conclusion to the Tolkien trilogy, "The Lord of the Rings: The Return of the King."

In Jan. 2004, Warner Bros. International Cinemas became the first Western cinema investor in history to receive approval from the Chinese Government for majority ownership in a joint venture, holding 51% of a multiplex cinema in Nanjing, which opened April 2004. Warner Bros. Pictures released the third installment in the Harry Potter franchise: "Harry Potter and the Prisoner of Azkaban," and enjoyed a more than $200 million box office take in less than a week of its release. The release of "Troy" with box office draw Brad Pitt enjoyed worldwide success and in June Warner Bros. International crossed the billion-dollar mark for the fourth year in a row and the seventh time overall—in record time for the studio.

The studio anticipated a strong holiday season at the box office, largely fueled by star power: Tom Hanks in the family-friendly "Polar Express," "Ocean's Twelve" with George Clooney and a star-filled ensemble cast including movie favorite Julia Roberts; Leonardo DiCaprio as the lead in "The Aviator," and the release of "Alexander" from film master Oliver Stone.

Warner Bros. Pictures' "Million Dollar Baby" packed a knockout punch at the 2004 Academy Awards: earning Best Picture, Best Actress (Hilary Swank) and Best Supporting Actor (Morgan Freeman) honors. Momentum for "Million Dollar Baby" continued through the year helping it make the top films of 2005 list along with Warner Bros. Pictures' "Charlie and the Chocolate Factory" ($206 million at domestic b.o.), "Batman Begins" ($205 million at domestic b.o.), "The Aviator" (with Miramax, ($103 million domestic b.o.), "The Dukes of Hazard" ($80 million domestic b.o.), "Constantine" ($76 million domestic b.o.), Tim Burton's "Corpse Bride" ($52 million domestic b.o.) and "Racing Stripes" ($49 million domestic b.o.). It released the fourth installment of the phenomenally successful Harry Potter franchise: "Goblet of Fire" November 18, 2005, and banked on the holiday season to bring out the fans who supported the three previous "Potters of Gold" at the box office.

Warner Independent Pictures also had a successful year with its release of "March of the Penguins" ($77 million in domestic b.o.), which remains the second highest grossing documentary (behind "Fahrenheit 9/11" with $119 million) and the sixth highest grossing independent film of all time, as of Oct. 10, 2005. Released late in 2005, Warner Independent created industry buzz with its release of "Good Night and Good Luck," directed by George Clooney. Clooney also wrote the screenplay and starred in the film which follows the broadcasting legend Edward R. Murrow and his producer, Fred Friendly, (played by Clooney) during Murrow's legendary on-air confrontations with Senator Joseph McCarthy that helped bring the infamous politician down. Whether giving the public something visually spectacular a la "Charlie and the Chocolate Factory," or the introspective and thought-provoking fare served up in "Good Night and Good Luck," Time Warner entertainment companies kept compelling films in theatres throughout the year.

Time Warner's New Line Cinema and HBO jointly created Picturehouse in 2005 — a theatrical distribution company to release independent films. Headed by Bob Berney, Picturehouse offered a diverse 2006 release slate including "Fur," starring Nicole Kidman and Robert Downey, Jr.; "Pan's Labyrinth," directed by Guillermo Del Toro; and Robert Altman's "A Prairie Home Companion," with Woody Harrelson, Tommy Lee Jones, Garrison Keillor, Kevin Kline, Lindsay Lohan, Virginia Madsen, John C. Reilly, Maya Rudolph, Meryl Streep and Lily Tomlin.

Recognizing the rapid changes in content delivery outside theatres and a spotlight on digital distribution of content, WB organized its businesses involved in the digital delivery of entertainment content to consumers under Warner Bros. Home Entertainment Group in late 2005.

Warner Bros. started 2006 with "The Lake House" starring Sandra Bullock and Keanu Reeves. The Wachowski brothers, known for their Matrix series, unleashed another futurisic thriller on March 19th with "V For Vendetta," starring Natalie Portman. While Warner Bros.' executives hoped for blockbuster status, the film underperformed expectations, bringing in just $70 million in the U.S. The release of "Poseidon," another film anticipated to draw a huge audience, drew only $60.7 million in its U.S. release. With the absence of a Harry Potter film on its '06 slate, Warner Bros. needed something super to happen at the box office, and it did with the release of "Superman Returns," which brought in $200 million in the U.S. One of Warner Bros.' Fall releases, Martin Scorsese's, "The Departed," had churned out more than $95 million at the domestic box office in its first four weeks of release, which should help the studio end 2006 on a good note. This is important to parent Time Warner, because the filmed entertainment business accounted for 26 percent of the company's total sales in the first quarter and 20 percent of operating profits. By the third quarter, TW's earnings release noted filmed entertainment revenues decreased 10%, or by $260 million, compared to the previous year. (Filmed entertainment is comprised of Warner

Bros. Entertainment & New Line Cinema.) Its filmed entertainment operating income before depreciation and amortization also declined in the third quarter 14% ($33 million) to $210 million. This figure represented lower contributions from theatrical product compared to the year-ago period. Yet, when looking at Time Warner results as a whole, investors should have been pleased. TW share price in the fall was at its highest level since 2002, hitting a 52-week trading high of $20.08.

2007 marked the seventh consecutive year that Warner Bros. did over $1.0 billion in domestic box office, driven by hit films such as "Harry Potter and the Order of the Phoenix," "300," a holdover from 2006, "Happy Feet," and "Ocean's Thirteen." Other film production and distribution subsidiaries — New Line Cinema, Picturehouse and Warner Independent Pictures — all produced films that worked as well. Although, Time Warner chief, Richard Parsons, has had his hands full trying to figure out what to do with AOL seven years after their merger, the filmed entertainment companies continue to deliver top-line growth for the parent.

Box office records were shattered by Warner Bros. in 2008, driven by the spectacular success of the second highest grossing film of all time, "The Dark Knight." Earlier in the year as part of a cost-saving consolidation ordered by CEO Jeff Bewkes, New Line was restructured, a significant number of the 600 staffers and Co-CEOs Bob Shaye and Michael Lynne left the company. New Line became a production label within Warner Bros. Similarly, Warner Bros. Pictures president & COO Alan Horn announced that both Picturehouse and Warner Independent Pictures would be closed in an effort to reduce costs and reduce the flow of product from 25-30 films a year to 18-20.

Dan Fellman, Warner Bros. president of domestic distribution, has presided over 10 consecutive years with over $1 billion in box office receipts. For 2009, Warner Bros. was positioned to break its all-time record of over $2 billion. Warner's market share was almost 20% at year's end. "Harry Potter and the Half-Blood Prince," "The Hangover," "Terminator Salvation" and "Watchmen" were all stand-out performers. "The Box" with Cameron Diaz opened in November as did "The Blind Side" and "Ninja Assassin."

Warner Bros. had a strong 16.5% share of the domestic boxoffice in 2010 with strong performances by "Valentine's Day," "Clash of the Titans 3D," "Sex and the City 2," "Inception" and "Hereafter." The studio canceled its planned 3D release of "Harry Potter and the Deathly Hallows, Part I," saying it ran out of time to properly convert the film into a 3D format, although the second installment of the film next Summer will be in 3D. After "Avatar," became the highest-grossing film of all time, Hollywood studios rushed to produce 3D movies to take advantage of audience enthusiasm for 3D and the higher ticket prices charged for that format. However, this created a debate over the quality of 3D needed to satisfy audiences and not kill the golden goose. Warner Bros. took an interesting position and said quality issues stood at the forefront of canceling its 3D release of "Potter."

RECENT WARNER BROS. RELEASES

2000 The Perfect Storm, Any Given Sunday, The Art of War, Space Cowboys, Pokemon.

2001 AI: Artificial Intelligence, Harry Potter and the Sorcerer's Stone, Training Day, Ocean's Eleven, The Lord of the Rings: The Fellowship of the Ring.

2002 The Adventures of Pluto Nash, Ballistic: Ecks vs. Sever, City by the Sea, The Divine Secrets of the Ya-Ya Sisterhood, Analyze That, Harry Potter and the Chamber of Secrets, Scooby Doo.

2003 The Matrix Reloaded, Terminator 3: Rise of the Machines, Kangaroo Jack, The Matrix Revolutions.

2004 Harry Potter and the Prisoner of Azkaban, Troy, The Polar Express, Ocean's 12, Alexander,The Phantom of the Opera.

2005 Racing Stripes, Constantine, Miss Congeniality 2, Batman Begins, Charlie and the Chocolate Factory, The Dukes of Hazzard, Corpse Bride, Harry Potter and the Goblet of Fire, Rumor Has It.

2006 V for Vendetta, Firewall, Poseidon, The Lake House, Superman Returns, The Departed, The Prestige, Flags of our Fathers.

2007 Harry Potter and the Order of the Phoenix, 300, Ocean's Thirteen, The Bucket List.

2008 The Dark Knight, Get Smart, Journey to the Center of the Earth, Four Christmases, Yes Man, Gran Torino.

2009 Harry Potter and the Half-Blood Prince, The Hangover, Terminator Salvations, Watchmen, The Box, Ninja Assassin.

2010 Valentine's Day, Clash of the Titans 3D, Sex and the City 2, Inception, Hereafter, Due Date, Harry Potter and the Deathly Hallows, Yogi Bear 3D.

RECENT NEW LINE/FINE LINE RELEASES

1999 Austin Powers: The Spy Who Shagged Me, The Bachelor, Magnolia.

2000 Frequency, The Cell, Dancer in the Dark, Saving Grace, State and Main.

2001 Rush Hour 2, The Lord of the Rings: Fellowship of the Ring, Blow, I Am Sam, Life As A House, Hedwig and the Angry Inch, The Anniversary Party.

2002 Austin Powers in Goldmember, Mr. Deeds, All About the Benjamins, About Schmidt.

2003 The Lord of the Rings: The Two Towers, FreddyVs. Jason, Elf, The Lord of the Rings: The Return of the King.

2004 Cellular, Raise Your Voice, Blade: Trinity, Birth, After the Sunset, A Dirty Shame, Maria Full of Grace.

2005 Wedding Crashers, Monster-In-Law, Vera Drake, The Upside of Anger, King's Ransom, The Man, A History Of Violence, Domino, Just Friends, The New World, Running Scared, Take the Lead, Final Destination, The Year of the Yao, The Holy Girl, The Bridge of San Luis Rey, Last Days.

2006 Final Destination 3, Take the Lead, Snakes on a Plane, The Texas Chainsaw Massacre: The Beginning.

2007 Rush Hour 3, Hairspray, Rendition, Martian Child, The Golden Compass.

2008 Semi-Pro, Kit Kittredge: An American Girl, Appaloosa.

2009 The Time Traveler's Wife, The Final Destination 4, My Sister's Keeper, Ghosts of Girlfriends Past, 17 Again, Friday the 13th, He's Just Not That Into You.

2010 Sex and the City 2, Valentine's Day.

MOTION PICTURE PRODUCERS & DISTRIBUTORS

Also see Large Format Producers, Film Distributors in Key Cities, Non-Theatrical Motion Picture Companies.

100% ENTERTAINMENT
(Production company)
201 North Irving Blvd., Los Angeles, CA. 90004.
TEL: (323) 461-6360. FAX: (323) 934-0440.
www.100percentent.com
PRESIDENT & CEO
Stanley Isaacs - sisaacs100@mac.com
EXECUTIVE STORY EDITOR
Cooper Boone

1ST MIRACLE PICTURES
(Distribution company)
3439 W. Cahuenga Blvd., Hollywood, CA 90068.
TEL: (323) 874-6000. FAX: (718) 874-4252.
CEO
Moshe Bibiyan
PRESIDENT
Simon Bibiyan

1492 PICTURES
(No unsolicited material or query letters)
12711 Ventura Blvd., Ste. 350, Studio City, CA 91604.
TEL: (818) 508-2055. FAX: (818) 508-2056.
WRITER, DIRECTOR, PRODUCER & PARTNER
Chris Columbus
PRESIDENT & PRODUCER & PARTNER
Michael Barnathan
SENIOR V.P., PRODUCTION
Jennifer Blum
VICE PRESIDENT
Karen Swallow
DIRECTOR, DEVELOPMENT
Michelle Miller

40 ACRES & A MULE FILMWORKS
75 South Elliot Place, Brooklyn, NY 11217.
TEL: (718) 624-3703. FAX: (718) 624-2008.
CHAIRMAN
Spike Lee

44 BLUE PRODUCTIONS, INC.
(Production company)
4040 Vineland Ave., Ste. 105, Studio City, CA 91604.
TEL: (818) 760-4442. FAX: (818) 760-1509.
email: reception@44blue.com www.44blue.com
CO-OWNER & PRESIDENT
Rasha Drachkovitch
CO-OWNER & EXECUTIVE PRODUCER
Stephanie Drachkovitch
SENIOR V.P., PRODUCTION
Stuart Zwagil
EXECUTIVE IN CHARGE OF PRODUCTION
Sarah Poage
HEAD, CURRENT PROGRAMMING
David Hale
HEAD, DEVELOPMENT
Lisa Knapp

8 STAR ENTERTAINMENT
(Distribution company)
4647 Kingswell Ave., Ste. 129, Los Angeles, CA 90027.
TEL/FAX: (323) 665-4898.
email: info@8starentertainment.com
www.8StarEntertainment.com
CONTACT
Cida Goncalves

360 PICTURES
(Motion picture producer)
301 N. Canon Dr., Ste. 207, Beverly Hills, CA 90210.
TEL: (310) 205-9900. FAX: (310) 205-9909.
PRODUCER & PRESIDENT
Frank Mancuso, Jr.
SENIOR V.P., PRODUCTION
Jennifer Nieves
PRODUCER
Tara L. Craig

ABILENE PICTURES
1201 West 5th St., Ste F-190, Los Angeles, CA 90017.
DIRECTOR
Gregory Hoblit - (310) 587-3331, (323) 850-2485
V.P., DEVELOPMENT
Beverly Graf - (818) 980-1530

ACAPPELLA PICTURES
(Motion picture & TV producer)
5 Suess Path, Quogue, NY 11959 .
TEL: (631) 653-8881. FAX: (631) 653-8884.
PRESIDENT
Charles Evans, Jr.
PRODUCTION & DEVELOPMENT
Charmaine Parcaro

ACE STORYBOARD ON DEMAND
(Storyboards, concepts art)
31455 West St., S. Laguna Beach, CA 92641.
TEL: (949) 499-9964. email: mark@markpacella.com
www.acestoryboards.com
ART DIRECTOR
Mark Pacella

ACTUALITY PRODUCTIONS
20335 Ventura Blvd., Ste. 300, Woodland Hills, CA 91364.
TEL: (818) 444-5000. FAX: (818) 444-5001.
www.actualityproductions.com
PRESIDENT
Bruce L. Paisner
EXECUTIVE V.P.
Jerry Shevick
MANAGER
Aurelia White

ORLY ADELSON PRODUCTIONS
(Motion picture & TV producer)
12304 Santa Monica Blvd., Ste. 115, Los Angeles, CA 90025.
TEL: (310) 442-2012. FAX: (310) 442-2013.
PRESIDENT
Orly Adelson
V.P., DEVELOPMENT
Jonathan Eskenas
DEVELOPMENT ASSISTANT
Alexi Mazareas

AEI-ATCHITY ENTERTAINMENT INTERNATIONAL, INC.
(Production company. Television and motion pictures)
518 S. Fairfax Ave., Los Angeles, CA 90036.
TEL: (323) 932-0407. FAX: (323) 932-0321.
email: jp@aeionline.com www.aeionline.com
www.thewriterslifeline.com
PARTNER & CEO
Ken Atchity
AEI PARTNER, PRESIDENT & COO
Chi-li Wong
V.P., DEVELOPMENT
Brenna Lui
SUBMISSIONS COORDINATOR
Jennifer Pope

MINDY AFFRIME PRODUCTIONS
1429 Avon Park Terrace, Los Angeles, CA 90026.
TEL: (323) 661-4481. FAX: (323) 644-0680.
email: minaffrime@aol.com www.findshivas.com
PRESIDENT & PRODUCER
Mindy Affrime

AGAMEMNON FILMS, INC.
(Production)
650 N. Bronson Ave., Ste. B-225, Los Angeles, CA 90004.
TEL: (323) 960-4066. FAX: (323) 960-4067.
www.agamemnon.com
PRESIDENT, CEO & CO-FOUNDER
Fraser C. Heston
PRODUCER
Alex Butler
DEVELOPMENT
Heather Thomas

AGILITY STUDIOS
(Production company)
3250 Ocean Park Blvd., Ste. 200, Santa Monica, CA 90405.
TEL: (310) 314-1440. FAX: (310) 496-3292.
email: info@agilitystudios.com www.agilitystudios.com
CEO
Scott Erlich
V.P., PRODUCTION
Zev Suissa

ALBUQUERQUE STUDIOS
(Production, Sound Stages)
5650 University Blvd. SE, Albuquerque, NM 87106.
TEL: (505) 227-2000. email: info@abqstudios.com
www.abqstudios.com
EXECUTIVE DIRECTOR
Jeremy Hariton - jeremy_hariton@abqstudios.com

ALCON ENTERTAINMENT, LLC
(Film & TV production)
10390 Santa Monica Blvd., Ste. 250, Los Angeles, CA 90025.
TEL: (310) 789-3040. FAX: (310) 789-3060.
CO-PRESIDENT & CO-FOUNDER
Broderick Johnson
CO-PRESIDENT & CO-FOUNDER
Andrew A. Kosove
COO
Scott Parish
PRESIDENT WORLDWIDE MARKETING
Richard Ingber
ECEUTIVE V.P., DEVELOPMENT
Steven P. Wegner
SENIOR V.P., PYHSICAL PRODUCTION
Yolanda Cochran
SENIOR VP., BUSINESS AFFAIRS
Dave Fierson
V.P., OPERATIONS & ADMINISTRATION
Chris Alexander
V.P,, DEVELOPMENT
Jesse Israel
V.P,, MARKETING & PUBLICITY
Jennifer Petruniak

ALFA-FILM ENTERPRISES, INC.
(Motion picture & TV producer & distributor)
264 S. La Cienega Blvd., #1138, Beverly Hills, CA 90211.
TEL: (310) 858-1005. FAX: (310) 858-1050.
email: sidarfov@earthlink.net
PRESIDENT
Anatoly A. Fradis
V.P., DISTRIBUTION &ACQUISITION
Olga Fradis

ALIVE FILMS
(Motion picture producer)
32801 S. Kihei Rd., Kihei, HI 96753. TEL: (808) 891-0022.
FAX: (808) 879-2734. email: alivewow@maui.net
CHAIRMAN
Shep Gordon

ALPINE PICTURES, INC. / SUMMERTIME ENTERTAINMENT
(Distribution company)
3500 W. Magnolia Blvd., Burbank, CA 91505.
TEL: (818) 333-2600. FAX: (818) 333-2616.
email: michaeld@alpinepix.com www.alpinepix.com
CEO
Ryan J. Carroll
PRESIDENT
Roland Carroll
PRESIDENT, INTERNATIONAL SALES & DISTRIBUTION
Anthony Rene' Torres
EXECUTIVE V.P.
James A. Jones

AMAZING MOVIES
(Motion picture worldwide producer & distributor)
7471 Melrose Ave., Ste. 7, Los Angeles, CA 90046.
TEL: (323) 852-1396. FAX: (323) 658-7265.
email: amazingmov@aol.com www.amazingmovies.biz
PRESIDENT/CEO
Douglas C. Witkins
VICE PRESIDENT
Matt Giedlinski

AMERICAN CINEMA INTERNATIONAL
(Independent entertainment company that creates, produces and distributes filmed entertainment throughout the world)
15363 Victory Blvd., Van Nuys, CA 91406.
TEL: (818) 907-8700. FAX: (818) 907-8719.
email: acimail@aci-americancinema.com
www.aci-americancinema.com
CEO
George Shamieh - george@aci-americancinema.com
PRESIDENT
Chevonne O'Shaughnessy -
chevonne@aci-americancinema.com
MARKETING & SALES
Laura Voros - laura@aci-americancinema.com

THE AMERICAN FILM COMPANY
(Production company)
2415 Main St., Santa Monica, CA 90405. TEL: (310) 664-1999.
www.theamericanfilmco.com
PRODUCER & WRITER
Robert Stone, Webster Stone, Brian Falk

AMERICAN MUTOSCOPE AND BIOGRAPH CO.
(Production company)
269 S. Beverly Drive, Suite #710,Beverly Hills, California 90212. TEL: (310) 288-3400. FAX: (310) 288-6840.
www.biographcompany.com
PRESIDENT/CEO
Thomas R. Bond, II
V.P. & COO
Frank Marks
V.P., COMMERCIAL PRODUCTION
Darrell Mapson - dmapson@biographcompany.com

AMERICAN WORLD PICTURES
16027 Ventura Blvd., Ste. 320, Encino, CA 91436.
TEL: (818) 380-9100. FAX: (818) 380-0050.
email: info@americanworldpictures.com
www.americanworldpictures.com
PRESIDENT & CEO
Mark L. Lester- mark@americanworldpictures.com
PRESIDENT, PRODUCTION
Dana Duborsky - dana@americanworldpictures.com
V.P., WORLDWIDE SALES
Jeffrey Goldman - jeffery@americanworldpictures.com
SERVICING COORDINATOR
Matt Giedlinski - matt@americanworldpictures.com

AMERICAN ZOETROPE
(Motion picture & TV producer)
1641 N. Ivar, Los Angeles, CA 90028. TEL: (323) 460-4420.
FAX: (323) 460-4459. www.zoetrope.com
V.P., PRODUCTION & ACQUISITION
Michael Zakin
LEGAL COUNSEL
Giselle Galper

AM PRODUCTIONS & MANAGEMENT
8899 Beverly Blvd., Ste. 713, Los Angeles, CA 90048.
TEL: (310) 275-9081. FAX: (310) 275-9082.
ACTOR & EXECUTIVE PRODUCER
Ann-Margret
EXECUTIVE PRODUCER
Alan Margulies
EXECUTIVE PRODUCER & WRITER
Roger Smith
EXECUTIVE ADMINISTRATOR
Sasha Nagy

AMSELL ENTERTAINMENT, INC.
(Motion picture, TV & video distributor)
12001 Ventura Pl., Ste. 404, Studio City, CA 91604.
TEL: (818) 766-8500. email: amsellent@sbcglobal.net
PRESIDENT
Alan Solomon

ANCHOR BAY ENTERTAINMENT INC.
(Distribution Company)
PRESIDENT
2401 W. Big Beaver Rd., Ste. 200, Troy, MI 48084.
TEL: (248) 816-0909. FAX: (248) 205-1713.
email: questions@anchorbayent.com
www.anchorbayentertainment.com
PRESIDENT
Bill Clark
EXECUTIVE V.P., WORLDWIDE ACQUISITIONS
Kevin Kasha
EXECUTIVE V.P., WORLDWIDE SALES
Raymond Zinar
EXECUTIVE V.P., WORLDWIDE MARKETING
Gordon Prend
SENIOR V.P., MARKETING
Julie Cartwright
SENIOR V.P., WORLDWIDE BUSINESS OPERATIONS
Brian Daley
SENIOR V.P., OPERATIONS
Erin McGregor
SENIOR V.P., SALES
Sally Seraphim
SENIOR V.P., BUSINESS AFFAIRS
Richard Turner

CRAIG ANDERSON PRODUCTIONS
(Motion picture, independent film & TV producer)
444 N. Larchmont Blvd., Ste. 109, Los Angeles, CA 90004.
TEL: (323) 463-2000. FAX: (323) 463-2022.
email: info@cappix.com www.cappix.com
EXECUTIVE PRODUCERS
Craig Anderson, Peter Karabats
PRODUCER
Chris Ufland
CREATIVE
Nathan Santell
V.P., DEVELOPMENT
David Markus

APATOW PRODUCTIONS
(Production company)
11788 W. Pico Blvd., Los Angeles, CA 90064.
TEL: (310) 943-4400. FAX: (310) 479-0750.
WRITER/DIRECTOR/PRODUCER
Judd Apatow
HEAD, DEVELOPMENT
Nicholas Weinstock
ASSISTANT TO JUDD APATOW
Alyson Buoncristiani, Lisa Yadavia, Chelsea Peters, Stacy Dollar,

No unsolicited submissions accepted.

APOSTLE
(Motion picture, independent film & TV producer)
568 Broadway, Ste. 301, New York, NY 10012.
TEL: (212) 541-4323. FAX: (212) 541-4330.
www.apostlenyc.com
ACTOR/DIRECTOR/PRODUCER
Denis Leary
PRESIDENT/MOTION PICTURES & TV
Jim Serpico
SENIOR V.P., PRODUCTION
Tom Sellitti
DIRECTOR, FILM DEVELOPMENT
Doug Baldinger
V.P., TV DEVELOPMENT
Adrienne O'Riain

APPARITION
2000 Avenue of the Stars, Ste. 620N., Los Angeles, CA 90067.
TEL: (213) 253-4610.
email: contact@apparition.com www.apparition.com
FOUNDING PARTNER
Bill Pohlad

APPLEDOWN FILMS, INC.
(Motion picture, independent film & TV producer)
9687 W. Olympic Blvd., Beverly Hills, CA 90212.
TEL: (310) 552-1833. FAX: (310) 552-1331.
PRODUCER & WRITER
Larry Spiegel
PRODUCER
Judy Goldstein

AQUARIUS RELEASING, INC. / AQUARIUS MEDIA CORP.
(Producer, distributor; exhibition)
P.O. Box 590 Englewood, NJ 07631. TEL: (201) 541-1912.
FAX: (201) 541-2365.
CEO
Terry Levene
SECRETARY & TREASURER
Sarai Berenstein
FOREIGN SALES
Harry Sloan
TV SYNDICATION
Irving Grossbard

ARENAS FILMS
(Specializing in the Hispanic market. Film label that acquires, produces, finances, markets and distributes films tailored to Hispanic audiences)
3375 Barham Blvd., Los Angeles, CA 90068.
TEL: (323) 785-5555. FAX: (323) 785-5560.
email: info@arenasgroup.com www.arenasgroup.com
PRESIDENT& CEO
Santiago Pozo
PRESIDENT, DISTRIBUTION
Larry Gleason
EXECUTIVE V.P., MARKETING
John Butkovich
V.P., MARKETING, PUBLICITY & PROMOTION
Isaac Cuevas

Arenas has a second business unit, Arenas Films, which produces, acquires, markets and ditributes films in all venues including theatrical, DVD and television. A library that includes titles such as: Empire, Nicotina, Imaging Argentina, Culture Clash In America and Three Wise Men.

ARTHOUSE FILMS, INC.
(Distribution company)
Post Factory, 161 Avenue of the Americas, 11th Flr., New York, NY 10013. TEL: (212) 966-1760. FAX: (212) 202-3538.
email: info@arthousefilmsonline.com
www.arthousefilmsonline.com
V.P.
Erin Owens
HEAD, ACQUISITIONS & PRODUCTION
David Koh
PRINCIPAL
Lilly Bright

THE ARTISTS' COLONY
(Motion picture, independent film & TV producer)
256 S. Robertson Blvd., Ste. 1500, Beverly Hills, CA 90211.
TEL: (310) 720-8300. email: theartistscolony@sbcglobal.net
www.theartistscolony.com
PRODUCER
Lloyd A. Silverman
V.P., FINANCE
Mike McMullen
DEVELOPMENT DIRECTORS
Steve Grill, Firoze Salimi
EXECUTIVE ASSISTANT
Dan Borenstein

ASCENT MEDIA GROUP
520 Broadway, 5th Flr., Santa Monica, CA 90401.
TEL: (310) 434-7000. FAX: (310) 434-7001.
CHAIRMAN
William R. Fitzgerald
PRESIDENT, CREATIVE SERVICES
Bob Solomon
COO, NETWORK SERVICES
Scott Davis

ASTRON FILMS CORPORATION
(Writers, producers, directors, independent financiers of films)
360 W. 22nd St., New York, NY 10011. TEL: (212) 989-6089.
FAX: (212) 627-5191.
PRESIDENT & CHAIRMAN
Jack O'Connell
CREATIVE DIRECTOR
Patricia Kay Williams

THE ASYLUM
(Motion picture producer & distributor)
72 E. Palm Ave., Burbank, CA 91502.
TEL: (323) 850-1214. FAX: (818) 260-9811.
email: info@theasylum.cc www.theasylum.cc
PARTNER
Paul Bales
PARTNER, PRODUCTION
David Michael Latt
PARTNER, DOMESTIC SALES & ACQUISITIONS
David Rimawi

ATLAS ENTERTAINMENT
(Motion picture & independent film producer)
9200 Sunset Blvd., 10th Flr., Los Angeles, CA 90069.
TEL: (310) 786-8900. FAX: (310) 777-2185.
PRODUCER & PARTNER
Charles Roven, Alex Gartner
CFO
Ted MacKinney
EXECUTIVE V.P.
Alan Glazer
PRODUCER
Steve Alexander, Richard Suckle
CREATIVE EXECUTIVE
Andy Horwitz

ATMAN ENTERTAINMENT
(Motion picture & TV producer)
c/o Sean Gascoine, United Agents, Ltd., 12-26 Lexington St., London, UK W1F 0LE. TEL: 44-77-6887-4467.
US: (310) 995-7567 www.atmanentertainment.com
PRODUCER
Ross Grayson Bell
CREATIVE EXECUTIVE
Matt Valenti

ATTITUDE FILMS
300 Mercer St., Ste. 26L, New York, NY 10003.
TEL: (212) 995-9008. FAX: (212) 254-5135.
www.attitudefilms.com
SENIOR V.P.
Andrew Chang

AUGUST ENTERTAINMENT
(Motion picture distributor)
269 S. Beverly Drive, Ste. 888, Beverly Hills, CA 90212.
TEL: (310) 739-9904. FAX: (323) 658-7654.
email: augustent@mindspring.com
www.augustentertainment.com
PRESIDENT
Gregory Cascante
CFO
Elizabeth Davis

AURORA PRODUCTIONS
(Motion picture, independent film & TV producer)
8642 Melrose Ave., Ste. 200, Los Angeles, CA 90069.
TEL: (310) 854-6900. FAX: (310) 854-0583.
email: info@aurora-prod.com www.aurora-prod.com
PRESIDENT
William Stuart

AUTOMATIC PICTURES

(Motion picture producer)
5225 Wilshire Blvd., Ste. 525, Los Angeles, CA 90038.
TEL: (323) 935-1800. FAX: (323) 935-8040.
email:automaticpictures@hotmail.com
PRODUCER
Frank Beddor
CREATIVE EXECUTIVE
Liz Cavalier
V.P., NEW MEDIA/CREATIVE EXECUTIVE
Nate Barlow

AVALANCHE! ENTERTAINMENT

(Motion picture, independent film & TV producer)
11041 Santa Monica Blvd., Ste. 511, Los Angeles, CA 90025.
TEL: (310) 477-1464. FAX: (818) 729-0929.
PRESIDENT & PRODUCER
Richard Hull

AVENUE PICTURES

(Motion picture, independent film & TV producer)
1112 Montana Ave., Santa Monica, CA 90403.
TEL: (310) 862-9330. FAX: (310) 744-0002.
email: caryasst@avenuepictures.com
CHAIRMAN & CEO
Cary Brokaw
CFO/CONTROLLER
Judy Geletko

BAD ROBOT PRODUCTIONS

(Production Company)
1221 Olympic Blvd., Santa Monica, CA 90404.
TEL: (310) 664-3456.
EXECUTIVE
J.J. Abrams
TEAM
Bryan Burk, Kathy Lingg, Sherryl Clark, Athena Wickham, Lindsey Paulson, Dave Baronoff
ASSISTANT TO J.J. ABRAMS
Michelle Rejwan
Company produces films and TV series.

THE BADHAM COMPANY

(Motion picture, independent film & TV producer)
16830 Ventura Blvd., Ste. 300, Encino, CA 91436.
TEL: (818) 990-9495. FAX: (818) 981-9163.
www.badhamcompany.com
DIRECTOR & PRODUCER
John Badham
V.P., DEVELOPMENT
Alf Hewitt

BALCONY RELEASING, LTD

(Distribution company)
26 Mill Lane, Ste. 300, Amherst, MA 01002.
TEL: (413) 253-6781. FAX: (413) 253-6782.
www.balconyfilm.com
FOUNDER
Connie White
FOUNDER
Greg Kendall

BALLPARK PRODUCTIONS

(Motion picture, independent film producer)
P.O. Box 508, Venice, CA 90294. TEL: (310) 827-1328.
FAX: (310) 577-9626.
PRODUCER
Michael Schiffer

BALLYHOO, INC.

(Motion picture & TV producer)
6738 Wedgewood Place, Los Angeles, CA 90068.
TEL: (323) 874-3396. email: michaelbesman1@aol.com
PRODUCER
Michael Besman - michaelbesman1@aol.com

ALAN BARNETTE PRODUCTIONS

(Motion picture, independent film & TV producer)
9100 Wilshire Blvd., Ste. 400W, Beverly Hills, CA 90212.
TEL: (818) 954-1766. FAX: (818) 954-1160.
EXECUTIVE PRODUCER
Alan Barnette
DIRECTOR
Aaron Sandler

BARNHOLTZ ENTERTAINMENT

23300 Ventura Blvd., 2nd Flr., Woodland Hills, CA 91364.
TEL: (818) 591-1900. FAX: (818) 591-5960.
email: bbarnholtz@aol.com www.noamp.com
PRESIDENT & CEO
Barry Barnholtz
CFO
Kate Barnholtz
SENIOR V.P., BUSINESS AFFAIRS
Matthew Fladell
DIRECTOR, ACQUISITIONS
Anthony King
DIRECTOR, OPERATIONS
Diane Healey
EXECUTIVE ASSISTANT
Liana Bryer

BARNSTORM FILMS

73 Market St., Venice, CA 90291. TEL: (310) 396-5937.
FAX: (310) 450-4988.
PRODUCER & DIRECTOR
Tony Bill
PRODUCER
Helen Bartlett

BATJAC PRODUCTIONS, INC.

9595 Wilshire Blvd., #610, Beverly Hills, CA 90212-2506.
TEL: (310) 278-9870. FAX: (323) 272-7381.
PRESIDENT
Mrs. Michael A. Wayne

BATTLE PLAN PRODUCTIONS

(Production company. Features & TV Series)
6533 Hollywood Blvd., Ste. 311, Los Angeles, CA 90028.
TEL: (323) 315-9588. FAX: (323) 315-9589.
PRESIDENT/PRODUCER
Marc Frydman
PRESIDENT/PRODUCER/WRITER/DIRECTOR
Rod Lurie
PRODUCER
James Spies
ASSISTANTS
Darius Wadia, Matt Varosky

THE BAUER COMPANY

(Motion picture, independent film & TV producer)
9720 Wilshire Blvd., Mezzanine, Beverly Hills, CA 90212.
TEL: (310) 247-3880. FAX: (310) 247-3881.
PRODUCER
Martin R. Bauer
MANAGER
Joshua Bauer, Lowell Shapiro

CAROL BAUM PRODUCTIONS

(Motion picture producer)
8899 Beverly Blvd., Ste. 721, Los Angeles, CA 90048.
TEL: (310) 550-4575.
PRODUCER
Carol Baum
ASSISTANT
Zach Guglin

BAY FILMS

(Film & TV producer)
631 Colorado Ave., Santa Monica, CA 90401.
TEL: (310) 319-6565. FAX: (310) 319-6570.
DIRECTOR & PRODUCER
Michael Bay
V.P., DEVELOPMENT
Matthew Cohan
EXECUTIVE ASSISTANT TO MICHAEL BAY
Annie Connors
ASSOCIATES
Edward Albolote, Mike Kase

BEACON PICTURES

(Motion picture producer; no unsolicited material)
2900 Olympic Blvd., Santa Monica, CA 90401.
TEL: (310) 260-7000. FAX: (310) 260-7050.
www.beaconpictures.com
CHAIRMAN
Armyan Bernstein

THE BEDFORD FALLS COMPANY

409 Santa Monica Blvd., Penthouse, Santa Monica, CA 90401.
TEL: (310) 394-5022. FAX: (310) 394-5825.
EXECUTIVE PRODUCER & WRITER & DIRECTOR
Marshall Herskovitz
EXECUTIVE PRODUCER & WRITER & DIRECTOR
Edward Zwick (310) 394-2697
PRODUCER
Joshua Gummersall (310) 394-5355

LAWRENCE BENDER PRODUCTIONS

(Production Company)
8530 Wilshire Blvd., Ste. 500, Beverly Hills, CA 90211.
TEL: (323) 951-4600. FAX: (323) 951-4601.
PRODUCER & PARTNER
Lawrence Bender
PRODUCTION
Kevin Brown
PRODUCER
Karen Barber
DEVELOPMENT
Janet Jeffries

BENDERSPINK
(Production Company)
110 S. Fairfax Ave., Ste. 350, Los Angeles, CA 90036.
TEL: (323) 904-1800. FAX: (323) 904-1802.
email: info@benderspink.com www.benderspink.com
EXECUTIVE
Chris Bender, J.C. Spink, Charlie Gogolak, Brian Spink, Jill McElroy, Jake Weiner, Alex Kerr, Langley Perer

BERMANBRAUN
(Production company)
2900 W. Olympic Blvd., 3rd Flr., Santa Monica, CA 90404.
TEL: (310) 255-7272.
PRINCIPAL
Gail Berman, Lloyd Braun
COO/CFO
Mike Weetman
HEAD, FEATURE FILM DEVELOPMENT
Andrew Mittman
HEAD, BUSINESS OPERATIONS
Jerry Longarzo
HEAD, TV
Gene Stein

BIG BEACH
(Production company; No unsolicited submissions)
41 Great Jones St., 5th Flr., New York, NY 10012.
TEL: (212) 473-5800. FAX: (212) 473-5805.
email: info@bigbeachfilms.com www.bigbeachfilms.com
PARTNER
Marc Turtletaub, Peter Saraf

THE BIGGER PICTURE
(Distributor digital content for theatres)
21051 Warner Center Lane, Ste. 250, Woodland Hills, CA 91367. TEL: (818) 587-5424. FAX: (818) 587-4890.
email: info@thebiggerpicture.us www.thebiggerpicture.us
PRESIDENT
Jonathan Dern - idern@the biggerpicture.us

JENNIFER BIRCHFIELD-EICK PRODUCTIONS
(Production company)
15445 Ventura Blvd., Ste. 110, Sherman Oaks, CA 91403.
TEL: (818) 981-8833. FAX: (818) 981-8412.
PRODUCER
Jenny Birchfield-Eick

BLUE TULIP PRODUCTIONS
(Motion picture, independent film & TV producer)
2128 Narcissus Court, Venice, CA 90291.
TEL: (310) 458-2166. FAX: (310) 578-1445.
email: contact@bluetulipprod.com
http://www.bluetulipprod.com/
PRODUCER/DIRECTOR
Jan De Bont
PRODUCER
Christopher Stanley

BOARDWALK ENTERTAINMENT
(Motion picture & TV producer)
210 E. 39th St., New York, NY 10016. TEL: (212) 679-3800.
FAX: (212) 679-3816. email: Boardwalk@infohouse.com
CHAIRMAN
Alan Wagner
PRESIDENT
Susan Wagner

BONA FIDE PRODUCTIONS
(Motion picture producer)
8899 Beverly Blvd., Ste. 804, Los Angeles, CA 90048.
TEL: (310) 273-6782. FAX: (310) 273-7821.
PRODUCER
Albert Berger, Ron Yerxa
DEVELOPMENT
Carlo Martinelli
STORY EDITOR
Ken Furer

BONEYARD ENTERTAINMENT
(Motion picture, TV & Internet producer)
863 Park Ave., Ste. 11E, New York, NY 10021.
TEL: (212) 628-8600. FAX: (212) 628-8615.
email: boneyardentertainment@gmail.com
PRESIDENT & CEO
Daniel J. Victor

BOXING CAT FILMS
11500 Hart St., North Hollywood, CA 91605.
TEL: (818) 765-4870. FAX: (818) 765-4975. www.timallen.com
PRODUCER & ACTOR
Tim Allen
COO/PRODUCER
Brett Gregory
DEVELOPMENT EXECUTIVE
Anastasia Stanecki

BRICKMAN MARKETING
395 Del Monte Ctr., #250, Monterey, CA 93940.
TEL: (831) 633-4444. FAX: (831) 633-4499.
email: brickman@redshift.com www.brickmanmarketing.com
OWNER
Wendy Brickman

BRILLSTEIN ENTERTAINMENT PARTNERS
(Production, distribution and talent management company)
9150 Wilshire Blvd., Ste. 350, Beverly Hills, CA 90212.
TEL: (310) 275-6135. FAX: (310) 275-6180.
CEO
Jonathan Liebman
CFO
David Zwarg
PARTNER
Cynthia Pett-Dante, Marc Gurvitz, Aleen Keshishian
PRESIDENT, TELEVISION
Peter Traugott
SENIOR EXECUTIVE V.P. & PARTNER
Sandy Wernick
EXECUTIVE V.P., TELEVISION
Rachel Kaplan
EXECUTIVE V.P., BUSINESS AFFAIRS
Amy Weiss

BRISTOL BAY PRODUCTIONS
(Production company)
1888 Century Park E., Ste. 1400, Los Angeles, CA 90067.
TEL: (310) 887-1000. FAX: (310) 887-1001.
www.bristolbayproductions.com
CEO, ANSCHUTZ FILM GROUP
David Weil
CEO
Michael Bostick
CFO
Francesca Lindley
EXECUTIVE V.P., PHYSICAL PRODUCTION
Doug Jones
EXECUTIVE V.P., BUSINESS & LEGAL AFFAIRS
Frank Smith
SENIOR V.P., DEVELOPMENT
Amanda Morgan-Palmer
SENIOR V.P., DEVELOPMENT & PRODUCTION
Evan Turner
SENIOR V.P., PHYSICAL PRODUCTION
Mylan Stepanovich
SENIOR V.P., POST PRODUCTION
Jonas Thaler
V.P., FINANCE & STRATEGIC PLANNING
Ryan Jones
V.P., CONTROLLER
Peter Wasek

BROOKLYN FILMS
3815 Hughes Ave., Culver City, CA 90232.
TEL: (310) 841-4300. FAX: (310) 204-3464.
DIRECTOR & PRODUCER
Jon Avnet
PRODUCER
Jake Avnet
EXECUTIVE V.P., FINANCE & ADMINISTRATION
Carol Chacamaty
SENIOR V.P., DEVELOPMENT & PRODUCTION
Marsha Oglesby

BROOKSFILMS LIMITED
(Motion picture producer)
9336 W. Washington Blvd., Culver City, CA 90232.
TEL: (310) 202-3292. FAX: (310) 202-3225.
PRESIDENT
Mel Brooks
ASSISTANT
Shelby Van Vliet

JERRY BRUCKHEIMER FILMS & TELEVISION
(Production company)
1631 10th St., Santa Monica, CA 90404. TEL: (310) 664-6260.
FAX: (310) 664-6261. www.jbfilms.com
PRODUCER/CHAIRMAN/CEO
Jerry Bruckheimer
PRESIDENT
Mike Stenson
PRESIDENT, TV
Jonathan Littman
PRESIDENT, PRODUCTION
Chad Oman
EXECUTIVE V.P., TV
Kristie Anne Reed
SENIOR V.P., PRODUCTION
Melissa Reid
PRODUCER/DIRECTOR, POST PRODUCTION
Pat Sandston

V.P., TV
Mike Azzolino
V.P., PRODUCTION
Michael Milberg
V.P., MARKETING & PUBLICITY
Michael Singer
DIRECTOR, DEVELOPMENT
Charles Vignola
CREATIVE EXECUTIVE
John Campbell

Produces features, reality TV, syndication & TV series.

THE BUBBLE FACTORY

8840 Wilshire Blvd., 3rd Flr., Beverly Hills, CA 90211.
TEL: (310) 358-3000. FAX: (310) 358-3299.
PARTNER
Sid Sheinberg, Bill Sheinberg, Jon Sheinberg
MANAGER, CONTACT ADMINISTRATION
Wendy Brennan
DIRECTOR, ACCOUNTING & ADMINISTRATION
Caryn Santoro
DIRECTOR, OPERATIONS
Jackie Winawer

BUNIM/MURRAY PRODUCTIONS

(Production company)
6007 Sepulveda Blvd., Van Nuys, CA 91411.
TEL: (818) 756-5100. FAX: (818) 756-5140.
www.bunim-murray.com
CHAIRMAN
Jonathan Murray
PRESIDENT
Gil Goldschein
EXECUTIVE IN CHARGE OF PRODUCTION
John Greco
EXECUTIVE V.P., CURRENT PROGRAMMING & DEVELOPMENT
Scott Freeman
EXECUTIVE V.P., ENTERTAINMENT & PROGRAMMING
Jeff Jenkins
SENIOR V.P., BUSINESS & LEGAL AFFAIRS
David Berson
SENIOR V.P., BUSINESS DEVELOPMENT
Fabian Andre
V.P., BMP FILMS & CASTING
Sasha Alpert
V.P., DEVELOPMENT
Erin Cristall
V.P., OPERATIONS
Bart Peele
V.P., POST PRODUCTION
Mark Raudonis
MANAGER, NEW MEDIA
Kesila Childers

Bunim-Murray Productions produces reality TV, syndication, TV series and made-for-TV/cable movies & features.

BURRUD PRODUCTIONS, INC.

(Production company)
Corporate Headquarters and Administration Offices / Business Correspondence Address:
468 N. Camden Dr., 2nd Flr., Beverly Hills, CA 90210.
TEL: (310) 860-5158. FAX: (562) 595-5986.
email: info@burrud.com www.burrud.com
PRESIDENT & CEO
John Burrud
EXECUTIVE V.P., BUSINESS AFFAIRS
Stanley Green
V.P., ADMINISTRATION
Shannon Mead
CO-EXECUTIVE PRODUCER/DIRECTOR
Richard Swindell
CO-EXECUTIVE PRODUCER/SUPERVISING PRODUCER
Ashley Crary

Burrud produces TV series, documentaries & films.

BUTCHERS RUN FILMS

(Motion picture producer)
1041 N. Formosa Ave., Santa Monica Bldg. E. 200, W. Hollywood, CA 90046. TEL: (310) 246-4630.
FAX: (310) 385-9522.
ACTOR & PRODUCER & DIRECTOR
Robert Duvall
PRODUCER
Rob Carliner
DIRECTOR, DEVELOPMENT
Brian Ferrantino

CAMELOT PICTURES

(Film production and finance)
9255 W. Sunset Blvd., Ste 711, West Hollywood, CA 90069.
TEL: (310) 288-3000. FAX: (310) 288-3054.
email: info@camelot-pictures.com www.camelot-pictures.com
PRESIDENT
Gary Gilbert
VICE PRESIDENT
Jordan Horowitz
ASSISTANT
Shauna Bogetz

CAPITOL FILMS

(Production and distribution)
10100 Santa Monica Blvd., Ste. 1250, Los Angeles, CA 90067.
TEL: (310) 286-7200. FAX: (310) 286-7210.
email: films@capitolfilms.com www.capitolfilms.com

Bridge House, 2nd Flr., 63-65 N. Wharf Rd., London W2 1LA United Kingdom. TEL: 44-20-7298-6200.
FAX: 44-20-7298-6201.
CHAIRMAN
David Bergstein
MANAGING DIRECTOR
Peter Naish
GENERAL COUNSEL
Hannah Leader
MARKETING MANAGER
Jemma Setterfield
SALES EXECUTIVE
Jessica Malik

CASTLE HILL PRODUCTIONS

(Distribution company)
245 W. 55th St., 10th Flr., New York, NY 10019.
TEL: (646) 822-9231. FAX: (646) 822-9230.
email: mbalsam@peacearch.com www.peacearch.com
CEO
Mark Balsam
V.P., ADVERTISING
Dale Chrisman

Acquired by Canadian Peace Arch Entertainment Group in Dec. 2006. Distributes motion pictures, independent film & TV content. All genres.

CASTLE ROCK ENTERTAINMENT

(Production company)
335 N. Maple Dr., Ste. 350, Beverly Hills, CA 90210-3867.
TEL: (310) 285-2300. FAX: (310) 285-2345.
email: first.lastname@castle-rock.com www.castle-rock.com
PRODUCER & DIRECTOR
Rob Reiner, Andy Scheinman
CHAIRMAN & CEO, CASTLE ROCK ENTERTAINMENT
Martin Shafer
PRESIDENT, MOTION PICTURES
Liz Glotzer
EXECUTIVE ASSISTANT TO ROB REINER
Pam Jones
EXECUTIVE ASSISTANT TO MARTIN SHAFER
Tricia Owen - Tricia.Owen@castle-rock.com
OFFICE MANAGER
Charlie Nadler

Part of Warner Bros. Entertainment. Produces features and develops/distributes projects for TV.

CAVU PICTURES

(Distribution company)
630 Ninth Ave., Ste. 411, New York, NY 10036.
TEL: (212) 246-6300. FAX: (212) 246-6086.
email: cavupictures@aol.com www.cavupictures.com
PRESIDENT
Michael Sergio
HEAD, DISTRIBUTION & MARKETING
Isil Bagdadi

CBS CORPORATION

(Production & distribution company. See also Broadcast networks for additional information)
51 W. 52nd St., New York, NY 10019. TEL: (212) 975-4321.
www.cbs.com
EXECUTIVE CHAIRMAN AND FOUNDER
Sumner Redstone
PRESIDENT/CEO, CBS CORPORATION
Leslie Moonves
SENIOR ADVISOR TO CEO
Nancy Tellem
EXECUTIVE V.P., HUMAN RESOURCES & ADMINISTRATION, CBS CORPORATION
Anthony Ambrosio
EXECUTIVE V.P./GENERAL COUNSEL
Louis Briskman
EXECUTIVE V.P., PLANNING, POLICY & GOVERNMENT RELATIONS
Martin Franks
EXECUTIVE V.P./CFO
Joseph Ianniello
EXECUTIVE V.P., CHIEF COMMUNICATIONS OFFICER
Gil Schwartz
EXECUTIVE V.P., INVESTOR RELATIONS
Adam Townsend
SENIOR V.P., CONTROLLER & CHIEF ACCOUNTING

OFFICER
Thomas S. Shilen, Jr.
SENIOR V.P., DEPUTY COUNSEL & SECRETARY
Angelina Straka
SENIOR V.P., STRATEGIC DEVELOPMENT
Zander Lurie
SENIOR V.P., CBS COMMUNICATIONS GROUP
Dana McClintock

CBS FILMS

(Production Company)
11800 Wilshire Blvd., Los Angeles, CA 90025.
TEL: (310) 575-7700. www.cbsfilms.com
PRESIDENT/CEO
Amy Baer
COO
Bruce Tobey
CFO
Reid Sullivan
EXECUTIVE V.P., BUSINESS AFFAIRS
Jack Bleck
EXECUTIVE V.P., tHEATRICAL DISTRIBUTION
Steve Friedlander
EXECUTIVE V.P., WORLDWIDE MARKETING
Debbie Miller
EXECUTIVE V.P., PHYSICAL PRODUCTION
David Scott Rubin
EXECUTIVE V.P., POST PRODUCTION
Jack Schuster
EXECUTIVE V.P./GENERAL COUNSEL
Rik Toulon
SENIOR V.P., CREATIVE & CONTENT
Teri Boggess
SENIOR V.P., MEDIA & RESEARCH
Cherie Crane
SENIOR V.P., PRODUCTION FINANCE
Jon Davidson
SENIOR V.P., PRODUCTION
Maria Faillace
SENIOR V.P./GENERAL SALES MANAGER
Bob Kaplowitz
SENIOR V.P., PHYSICALL PRODUCTION
Tracy McGrath
SENIOR V.P., PUBLICITY
Maggie Schmidt
SENIOR V.P., STRATEGIC PLANNING & PROMOTIONS
Mimi Slavin
SENIOR V.P., POST PRODUCTION
Diana Tauder
V.P., LEGAL AFFAIRS
Derek Arteta
V.P., EXHIBITOR RELATIONS
Suzanne Hansen
V.P., FINANCE
Kelvin Kon
V.P., SALES WESTERN
David Magedman
V.P., DISTRIBUTION OPERATIONS
Tim Mason
V.P., CREATIVE ADVERTISING
Eric Mickelson
V.P., COMMUNICATIONS
Grey Munford
V.P., SALES EASTERN
Bruce Placke
V.P., COMMUNICATIONS
Grey Munford
V.P., PRODUCTION
Mark Ross
V.P./CONTROLLER
Glenda Savage

CBS INTERACTIVE

7800 Beverly Blvd., Los Angeles, CA 90036.
TEL: (323) 575-2345. www.cbs.com
CEO, CBS INTERACTIVE
Quincy Smith
PRESIDENT, CBS INTERACTIVE
Neil Ashe
PRESIDENT, CBS INTERACTIVE MUSIC GROUP
David Goodman
EXECUTIVE V.P./CFO, CBS INTERACTIVE
Mary Hentges
EXECUTIVE V.P., GENERAL MANAGER, CBS INTERACTIVE, MOBILE
Jeff Sellinger
SENIOR V.P., GENERAL MANAGER, CBSSPORTS.COM
Jason Kint
SENIOR V.P., OPERATIONS, CBS INTERACTIVE
Sam Parker
SENIOR V.P., GENERAL MANAGER, CBS INTERACTIVE, BUSINESS
Greg Mason
CHIEF CLIENT OFFICER
Dave Morris
SENIOR V.P., GENERAL MANAGER, CBS INTERACTICE, ENTERTAINMENT & LIFESTYLE
Anthony Soohoo
SENIOR V.P., CBS MOBILE
Ron Gelick
V.P., COMMUNICATIONS
Sarah Cain
GENERAL MANAGER, GAMES, MUSIC & LIFESTYLE, CBS INTERACTIVE
Stephen Snyder

CECCHI GORI PICTURES

(Motion picture, independent film & TV producer, developer & acquisitions)
5555 Melrose Ave. Bob Hope 203, Paramount Pictures Studios
Los Angeles, CA 90049. TEL: (323) 956-5954.
FAX: (323) 862 2254. email: info@cgglobalmedia.com
www.cecchigori.com
PRESIDENT
Gianni Nunnari
CFO
Ludy Blasco
V.P., CREATIVE AFFAIRS
Nathalie Peter-Contesse
LEGAL COUNSEL
Claire Ambroshio

CHARTOFF PRODUCTIONS

(Motion picture & film producer)
1250 Sixth St., Ste. 101, Santa Monica, CA 90401.
TEL: (310) 319-1960. FAX: (310) 319-3469.
CEO
Robert Chartoff
PRESIDENT
Lynn Hendee

CINEMA EPOCH

10940 Wilshire Blvd., 16th Flr., Los Angeles, CA 90024.
TEL: (310) 443-4244. email: info@cinemaepoch.com
www.cinemaepoch.com
PRESIDENT
Gregory Hatanaka
EXECUTIVE V.P.
Eunseon Ha
MARKETING & PRODUCTION
Tony Young
MARKETING & ACQUISITIONS
Warren Hong
MARKETING & PRODUCTION
Edwin A. Santos
PRODUCTION EXECUTIVES
Becky Bordo, Tiffany Bowyer

CINE EXCEL ENTERTAINMENT

(Full service production & post production company)
1102 N. Screenland Dr., Burbank, CA 91505.
TEL: (323) 754-5500. FAX: (818) 848-4478.
email: cineexcel@msn.com www.cineexcel.com
PRESIDENT
David Huey
V.P., LEGAL AFFAIRS
Noel Lawrence
V.P., INTERNATIONAL
Yoko Suenaga
V.P., MARKETING & DISTRIBUTION
Ed Tillman

CINEMA CONCEPTS TSC

(Studio & editing services, preview & policy trailers, animation, digital production services-HD post/mastering/film-out, screening rooms)
2030 Powers Ferry Rd., Ste. 214, Atlanta, GA 30339.
TEL: (770) 956-7460, (800) SHOWADS. FAX: (770) 956-8358.
email: info@cinemaconcepts.com www.cinemaconcepts.com
CHAIRMAN/CEO
Stewart Harnell

THE CINEMA GUILD

(Motion picture, independent film & TV distributor)
115 W. 30th St., Ste. 800, New York, NY 10001.
TEL: (212) 685-6242. FAX: (212) 685-4717.
email: info@cinemaguild.com www.cinemaguild.com
PRESIDENT
Philip S. Hobel
CHAIRMAN
Mary Ann Hobel
DIRECTOR, DISTRIBUTION
Ryan Krivoshey
DIRECTOR, EDUCATIONAL
Lindsay Dedo

CINEMANSON MARKETING & DISTRIBUTION CORP.
(Producer Representation; Marketing & distribution consultants)
5 Rivercrest Rd., Riverdale, NY 10471.
TEL/FAX: (718) 796-4918. email: Cinemanson@aol.com
PRESIDENT
Arthur Manson

CINEMA SEVEN PRODUCTIONS
(Motion picture producer)
154 W. 57th St., Ste. 112, New York, NY 10019.
TEL: (212) 315-1060. FAX: (212) 315-1085.
144 S. Beverly Dr., Ste. 407, Beverly Hills, CA 90212.
TEL: (310) 247-1444. FAX: (310) 247-1477.
email: cin7prod@aol.com
HEAD OF PRODUCTION
Pasquale Botta (NY)
Julius Ortiguero (CA)
V.P., BUSINESS AFFAIRS
James Deyarmin

CINERGI PICTURES ENTERTAINMENT, INC.
(Motion picture & independent film producer)
406 Wilshire Blvd., Santa Monica, CA 90401.
TEL: (310) 315-6000. FAX: (310) 828-0443.
CHAIRMAN & CEO
Andrew Vajna
SENIOR V.P., PRODUCTION
James Middleton

CINETEL FILMS, INC.
(Motion picture & TV distributor)
8255 Sunset Blvd., Los Angeles, CA 90046.
TEL: (323) 654-4000. FAX: (323) 650-6400.
email: mrubin@cinetelfilms.com
CEO
Paul Hertzberg
EXECUTIVE V.P
Lisa Hansen
SENIOR V.P., INTERNATIONAL DISTRIBUTION
Marcy Rubin - mrubin@cinetelfilms.com

CINEVILLE/KEYSTONE STUDIOS
3400 Airport Ave., Santa Monica, CA 90405.
TEL: (310) 397-7150. FAX: (310) 397-7155.
email: info@cineville.com www.cineville.com
CO-PRINCIPAL
Carl Colpaert, Christoph Henkel
PARTNER
Lee Caplin, Larry Cohen, Luke Stefano
SENIOR V.P., FINANCE
Gina Carollo
SENIOR V.P., INTERNATIONAL SALES
Rene Leda
SENIOR V.P., PRODUCTION
Dale Winsor Tanguay
SENIOR V.P., HOME VIDEO
Anatol Chavez
V.P., OPERATIONS
Sarah Wachel

CITY ENTERTAINMENT
(Production company)
266-1/2 S. Rexford Dr., Beverly Hills, CA 90212.
TEL: (310) 273-3101. FAX: (310) 273-3676.
PRESIDENT/PRODUCER
Joshua D. Maurer, Alixandre Witlin

CLASSIC MEDIA, INC.
(A division of Entertainment Rights, PLC)
85 Fifth Ave., 6th Flr., New York, NY 10003.
TEL: (212) 659-1959. FAX: (212) 659-1958.
email: info@classicmedia.com www.classicmedia.tv
Royalty House, 3rd Flr., 72-74 Dean St., London W1D 3SG.
TEL: 44 (0) 208-762-6200. FAX: 44 (0) 208-762-6299.
email: UKinfo@classicmedia.tv
EXECUTIVE V.P., SALES AND CO-PRODUCTION
Douglas Schwalbe
SENIOR V.P., GENERAL MANAGER/HOMEVIDEO
Robert Mayo
SENIOR V.P., MARKETING
Nicole Blake

CONCRETE ENTERTAINMENT
468 N. Camden Dr., Ste. 200, Beverly Hills, CA 90210.
TEL: (310) 860-5611. FAX: (310) 860-5600.
email: ck.concrete@gmail.com
ACTRESS & PRODUCER
Alicia Silverstone
MANAGER & PRODUCER
Carolyn Kessler, Michael Packenham

CONNECTICUT FILM CENTER, LLC
76 Progress Dr., Stamford, CT 06902. TEL: (203) 348-2500.
FAX: (203) 348-5200. email: info@ctfilmcenter.com
www.ctfilmcenter.com
PRESIDENT
Kevin Segalla - ksegalla@ctfilmcenter.com
MANAGING DIRECTOR
Bruce Heller
LOCATIONS DEPARTMENT MANAGER
Kodi Smith
OPERATIONS MANAGER
Kristin Sampiere
PROJECT MANAGER
Kelly McInnis

CONSTANTIN FILM DEVELOPMENT, INC. / CONSTANTIN TELEVISION
(European locations; motion picture, independent film & TV producer)
9200 W. Sunset Blvd., Ste. 800, West Hollywood, CA 90069.
TEL: (310) 247-0300. FAX: (310) 247-0305.
Feilitzschstraße 6, D-80802 München. TEL: (49-89 444-460.
FAX: (49-89 44 4-460-666. www.constantin-film.com
CEO
Bernhard Burgener
CFO
Hanns Beese
PRODUCTION DIRECTOR
Martin Moszkowicz
DIRECTOR, HOME ENTERTAINMENT
Franz Woodtli
CA CONTACT
Lisa Kregness, Robert Kulzer, Marsha Metz, Bernd Eichinger

CONUNDRUM ENTERTAINMENT
(Motion picture producer)
325 Wilshire Blvd., Ste. 201, Santa Monica, CA 90401.
TEL: (310) 319-2800. FAX: (310) 319-2808.
PRESIDENT
Bobby Farrelly, Peter Farrelly,
PRODUCER
Bradley Thomas, Mark Charpentier, Clemens Franek, Kevin Barnett, Keis Meyer

CRAVEN FILMS
(Motion picture & TV producer)
5 W. 19th St., New York, NY 10011. TEL: (212) 463-7190.
FAX: (212) 463-7190. email: info@cravenfilms.com
www.cravenfilms.com
PRESIDENT
Michael Craven
VICE PRESIDENT
Ernest Barbieri

CROSSROADS FILMS
(Production company)
136 W. 21st St., 7th Flr., New York, NY 10011.
TEL: (212) 647-1300. FAX: (212) 647-9090.
8630 Pine Tree Place, Los Angeles, CA 90069.
TEL (310) 659-6220. FAX: (310) 659-3105.
www.xroadsfilms.com
PARTNER
Dan Landau, Camille Taylor
COO
Ed Pliner
HEAD, PRODUCTION, FEATURES
Paul Miller
V.P/EXECUTIVE, PRODUCTION & DEVELOPMENT
Eunice Lee (LA) - (310) 659-6220
HEAD, DEVELOPMENT, FEATURES
Claire Pacaha
DIRECTOR, NEW MEDIA
David Title

CROWN INTERNATIONAL PICTURES, INC.
8701 Wilshire Blvd., Beverly Hills, CA 90211.
TEL: (310) 657-6700. FAX: (310) 657-4489.
email: crown@crownintlpictures.com
www.crownintlpictures.com
PRESIDENT & CEO
Mark Tenser
V.P., FINANCE
Willie De Leon
DIRECTOR, PUBLICITY & ADVERTISING
Lisa Agay

CRYSTAL PYRAMID PRODUCTIONS
(Video production, post-production, Animation and mobile editing rental facility)
7323 Rondel Court, San Diego, CA 92119.
TEL: (800) 365-8433, (619) 644-3000, FAX: (619) 644-3001.
email: cpp@newuniquevideos.com www.crystalpyramid.com
CEO & PRESIDENT
Mark Schulze
PRODUCER & V.P.
Patty Mooney

MULTIMEDIA PRODUCER
Luke Junger

CRYSTAL SKY, LLC

10203 Santa Monica Blvd., 5th Flr., Los Angeles, CA 90067.
TEL: (310) 843-0223. FAX: (310) 553-9895.
email: sales@crystalsky.com www.crystalsky.com
CO-CHAIRMAN
Hank Paul, Dorothy Paul
CHAIRMAN/CEO
Steven Paul
PRESIDENT, CRYSTAL SKY PICTURES, LLC
Benedict Carver
PRESIDENT, CRYSTAL SKY WORLDWIDE SALES, LLC
Daniel Diamond

CURB ENTERTAINMENT INTERNATIONAL CORP.

(Motion picture producer & distributor; TV & video distributors)
3907 W. Alameda Ave., Burbank, CA 91505.
TEL: (818) 843-8580. FAX: (818) 566-1719.
email: info@curbentertainment.com
www.curbentertainment.com
CHAIRMAN
Mike Curb
PRESIDENT
Carole Curb Nemoy - ccurb@curb.com
HEAD, WORLDWIDE SERVICES
Eddie Francis
DIRECTOR/HEAD OF DISTRIBUTION & POST SERVICES
Mona Kirton - mkirton@curb.com
ACQUISITIONS
Christy Peterson - cpeterson@curb.com

CHESTNUT RIDGE PRODUCTIONS

(Motion picture production company)
8899 Beverly Blvd., Ste. 800, Los Angeles, CA 90048.
TEL: (310) 285-7011.
PRODUCER/ OWNER
Paula Wagner
CREATIVE EXECUTIVE
Sarah Baker

DF INDIE STUDIOS

(Production and Distribution company)
New York, NY 10001. TEL: (212) 828-7304.
email: info@dfindiestudios.com www.dfindiestudios.com
CEO
Mary E. Dickinson
PRESIDENT/COO
Charlene Fisher
CFO
Rita Chiappetta-Thibault
EXECUTIVE V.P., PRODUCTION
Amy Slotnik
CONSULTING HEAD OF PRODUCTION & FINANCE
John Hadity
CONSULTING HEAD OF DISTRIBUTION
Ira Deutchman

D/F MANAGEMENT

(Management/Production company)
270 Lafayette St., Ste. 402, New York, NY 10012.
TEL: (212) 343-0069, (310) 558-3333
PARTNER
Frank Frattaroli (NY), Steve Dontanville (LA)
ASSOCIATES
Marnie Briskin, Charles Mastropietro
8607 E. Washington Blvd., #7, Culver City, CA 90232.
TEL: (310) 558-3333.
ASSOCIATE
Daniel Pancotto

DM PRODUCTIONS

(Motion picture production company)
10201 W. Pico Blvd., Bldg. 12, Los Angeles, CA 90035.
TEL: (310) 455-5526. FAX: (310) 828-0443.
PRODUCER
David Matalon

THE SEAN DANIEL COMPANY

(Production company)
12429 Ventura Ct., 2nd Flr., Studio City, CA 91604.
TEL: (818) 508-8165. FAX: (310) 806-6951.
PRODUCER
Sean Daniel
DIRECTOR DEVELOPMENT
Jason Brown

DANJAQ, LLC

(Motion picture producer; distribution through Sony)
c/o Yahoo Center, 2400 Broadway St., Ste. 310, Santa Monica, CA 90404. TEL: (310) 449-3185. FAX: (310) 449-3189.
PRESIDENT
Michael Wilson
CEO
David Pope
V.P., PRODUCTION & DEVELOPMENT
Barbara Broccoli

DAVIS ENTERTAINMENT COMPANY

(Motion picture & TV producer)
150 S. Barrington Pl., Los Angeles, CA 90049.
TEL: (310) 556-3550. FAX: (310) 556-3688.
CHAIRMAN, DAVIS ENTERTAINMENT CO.
John A. Davis - (310) 556-3550
PRESIDENT, PRODUCTION
Derek Dauchy - (310) 889-8006
EXECUTIVE V.P.
Brooke Brooks - (310) 556-3550
EXECUTIVE V.P., PRODUCTION
Brian Manis - (310) 889-8012
EXECUTIVE V.P., PRODUCTION
Adam Schroeder - (310) 889-8015
HEAD, DJ CLASSICZ
Dallas Jackson
PRESIDENT, TV
Michael Forman - (310) 889-8017
DIRECTOR, DEVELOPMENT
Ira Napolliello - (310) 889-8004

DI NOVI PICTURES

(Motion picture & TV producer; no unsolicited submissions)
720 Wilshire Blvd., Ste. 300, Santa Monica, CA 90401.
TEL: (310) 458-7200. FAX: (310) 458-7211.
PRODUCER
Denise Di Novi
PRESIDENT
Alison Greenspan

DIGITAL DOMAIN

(Motion picture & TV producer)
300 Rose Ave., Venice, CA 90291. TEL: (310) 314-2800.
FAX: (310) 314-2701. www.digitaldomain.com
CEO
Cliff Plumer
PRESIDENT, FEATURE FILM OPERATIONS
Gloria Borders
CFO
Kevin Weston
PRESIDENT, COMMERCIAL DIVISION & EXECUTIVE PRODUCER
Ed Ulbrich
EXECUTIVE PRODUCER
Mark Miller
HEAD, PRODUCTION
Jody Madden

DINO DE LAURENTIIS COMPANY

(Motion picture producer)
100 Universal City Plaza, Bldg., 5195, Universal City, CA 91608. TEL: (818) 777-2111. FAX: (818) 866-5566.
PRODUCER
Dino De Laurentiis
PRESIDENT & PRODUCER
Martha De Laurentiis
BUSINESS AFFAIRS
Stuart Boros
CORPORATE AFFAIRS
Meryl Pestamo

THE WALT DISNEY COMPANY

(Production and distribution company. The following are Disney units involved in TV, home entertainment & interactive industries)
500 S. Buena Vista St., Burbank, CA 91521. TEL: (818) 560-1000.
FAX: (818) 840-5737. www.thewaltdisneycompany.com
PRESIDENT & CEO
Robert A. Iger
CO-CHAIR, DISNEY MEDIA NETWORKS/PRESIDENT, DISNEY-ABC TELEVISION GROUP
Anne Sweeney
CO-CHAIR, DISNEY MEDIA NETWORKS/PRESIDENT, ESPN, INC. & ABC SPORTS/CHAIRMAN, ESPN BOARD OF DIRECTORS
George Bodenheimer
CHAIRMAN, THE WALT DISNEY STUDIOS
Richard Ross
CHAIRMAN, WALT DISNEY INTERNATIONAL
Andy Bird
CHAIRMAN, DISNEY CONSUMER PRODUCTS
Andrew Mooney
CHAIRMAN, WALT DISNEY PARKS & RESORTS
Thomas O. Staggs
CHIEF CREATIVE OFFICER, WALT DISNEY & PIXAR ANIMATION, PRINCIPAL CREATIVE ADVISOR, WALT DISNEY IMAGINEERING
John Lasseter
PRESIDENT, PIXAR & WALT DISNEY ANIMATION STUDIOS
Ed Catmull

CO-PRESIDENTS, DISNEY INTERACTIVE MEDIA GROUP
James Pitaro, John LPleasants
SENIOR EXECUTIVE V.P., GENERAL COUNSEL, SECRETARY
Alan N. Braverman
SENIOR EXECUTIVE V.P. & CFO
Thomas O. Staggs
EXECUTIVE V.P., CORPORATE COMMUNICATIONS
Zenia Mucha
SENIOR EXECUTIVE V.P./GENERAL COUNSEL/SECRETARY
Alan N. Braverman

WALT DISNEY INTERNATIONAL
500 S. Buena Vista St., Burbank, CA 91521.
TEL: (818) 560-1000.
CHAIRMAN
Andy Bird
PRESIDENT LATIN AMERICA
Diego Lerner
SENIOR V.P. & GENERAL COUNSEL
Jeffrey N. Paule
SENIOR V.P./CFO
Brian Spaulding
MANAGING DIRECTOR, CHINA
Stanley Cheung
MANAGING DIRECTOR, RUSSIA
Marina Jigalova-Ozkan

WALT DISNEY STUDIOS MOTION PICTURES—DISTRIBUTION
500 S. Buena Vista St., Burbank, CA 91521.
TEL: (818) 560-1000. FAX: (818) 972-3905
PRESIDENT
Chuck Viane
EXECUTIVE V.P., GENERAL SALES MANAGER
Chris LeRoy
SENIOR V.P., WORLDWIDE DIGITAL CINEMA & CINEMA PROGRAMMING
Jason Brenek
SENIOR V.P., GENERAL COUNSEL
Bob Cunningham
SENIOR V.P., ADMINISTRATION
Gary Weaver
SENIOR V.P.,/GENERAL MANAGER, WORLDWIDE SPECIAL EVENTS & THE MUPPETS
Lylle Breier
SENIOR V.P., BUSINESS/LEGAL AFFAIRS
Denise Brown
V.P., WORLDWIDE DIGITAL CINEMA OPERATIONS
Paul Holliman
V.P., SPECIAL EVENTS
Paul Baribault, Diane Connors
V.P., SPECIAL EVENTS PRODUCTION
Rick Buche
V.P., SPECIAL EVENTS, SHOW PRODUCTION/TALENT
Kevin Frawley
V.P., SPECIAL EVENTS OPERATIONS
Bob Gault
V.P., PRODUCTION SERVICES
Mike Kern
V.P., EXHIBITOR RELATIONS
Nancy Klueter
V.P., SALES ADMINISTRATON
Marc Laffie
V.P., BUSINESS/LEGAL AFFAIRS
Anne Moebes
V.P., SHOW DIRECTOR, SPECIAL EVENTS
Barnette Ricci
V.P., NATIONAL PRINT CONTROL
Debbie White
EXECUTIVE DIRECTOR, OPERATIONS, EL CAPITAN THEATRE
Ed Collins
EXECUTIVE DIRECTOR, CREATIVE SERVICES
Linda English
EXECUTIVE DIRECTOR, ACCOUNTS RECEIVABLE/CASH
Colleen Gibbons
EXECUTIVE DIRECTOR, EXHIBITOR RELATIONS
Susan Griesi

WALT DISNEY STUDIOS MOTION PICTURES—WESTERN SALES
3800 W. Alameda, 9th Flr., Burbank, CA 91521-6170.
TEL: (818) 840-1984. FAX: (818) 972-9543.
V.P., WEST SALES
Patrick Pade
EXECUTIVE DIRECTORS, SALES
Dean Gordon, Steve Schoenburg
DIRECTOR, SALES
Bill Crane, Steve Getzler, Brian Hicks, Leon Ittel, Jeff Prill, Kerry Silver
SENIOR MANAGER, SALES OPERATIONS
Steve Frintner
SALES MANAGER
Kelly Markle, Kim Thompson

WALT DISNEY STUDIOS MOTION PICTURES—EASTERN SALES
1500 Broadway, New York, NY 10036. TEL: (212) 536-6400. FAX: (212) 536-6409.
V.P., SALES
Ken Caldwell
EXECUTIVE DIRECTOR, SALES
Dennis Meagher, John Molson
DIRECTOR, SALES
Leo Fisch, Matt Kalavsky, Al Webster
SENIOR SALES MANAGER
Chadd Barksdale, Greg Skurow
SALES MANAGER
Carol Toppin, Rose Marie Schulz,
OFFICE MANAGER
Tony Quinn

WALT DISNEY STUDIOS MOTION PICTURES—CANADA SALES OFFICE
Simcoe Place, 200 Front St. West, #3001, Toronto, Ontario, M5V 3L4 Canada. TEL: (416) 964-9275. FAX: (416) 596-3382.
V.P., SALES
Anthony Macina
DIRECTOR, SALES
Tony Schittone, Karen Burke
SUPERVISOR/MANAGER, MARKETING
Antonella Zappone
OFFICE MANAGER
Cecilia Araya

WALT DISNEY STUDIOS MOTION PICTURES NON-THEATRICAL
3800 West Alameda, #971, Burbank, CA 91505.
TEL: (818) 840-1920. FAX: (818) 557-0797.
SENIOR V.P., NON THEATRICAL
Linda Palmer
EXECUTIVE DIRECTOR
Mary Tallungan
DIRECTOR
Melinda Gilmore

WALT DISNEY STUDIOS MOTION PICTURES MARKETING
500 South Buena Vista St., Burbank, CA 91521.
TEL: (818) 560-1000.
PRESIDENT, MARKETING
M.T. Carney
EXECUTIVE V.P., MARKETING
Kevin Campbell
EXECUTIVE V.P., WORLDWIDE RESEARCH
Dana Lombardo
EXECUTIVE V.P., CREATIVE PRINT SERVICES
John Sabel
EXECUTIVE V.P., & CREATIVE DIRECTOR, CREATIVE ADVERTISING & CONTENT
David Singh
SENIOR V.P., MARKETING
Nic Crawley
SENIOR V.P., MEDIA
Kristy Frudenfeld
SENIOR V.P., GLOBAL PUBLICITY
Michelle Sewell
SENIOR V.P., CREATIVE FILM SERVICES
Jeff Schechtman, Joe Tamusaities, Constance Wells
V.P., MEDIA OPERATIONS
Nina Anderson
V.P., MARKETING STRATEGY & COMMUNICATIONS
Asad Ayaz
V.P., BROADCAST MEDIA
George Bloom
V.P., GLOBAL PUBLICITY
Julie Fontaine, Nina Heyn, Oliver Mourox, Ryan Stankevich, Anne Stavola
V.P., GLOBAL PROMOTIONS
Don Gross
V.P., INTEGRATED MARKETING & SYNERGY
Hilary Hartling
V.P., WORLDWIDE RESEARCH
Perry Kim
V.P., CREATIVE FILM SERVICES
Mark Laffontant, Barbara Lange
V.P. MARKETING, CANADA
Greg Mason
V.P., CREATIVE FILM SERVICES
Alyson Jones, Rhona Nici-Parry, Steve Nuchols
V.P., CREATIVE PRINT SERVICES
Kari Miller, Steve Nuchols
V.P., DIGITAL MARKETING
Justin Pertschuk
V.P., MEDIA
Tiffany Pimm
V.P., WORLDWIDE RESEARCH
Ted Skidmore
V.P., EAST COAST PUBLICITY
Anne Stavola

V.P., TV SPECIALS
Cardon Walker
V.P., FINANCE
Ruth Walker

THE WALT DISNEY STUDIOS
CHAIRMAN, THE WALT DISNEY STUDIOS
Rich Ross
PRESIDENT, THE WALT DISNEY STUDIOS
Alan Bergman
PRESIDENT, WALT DISNEY STUDIOS MOTION PICTURE PRODUCTION
Sean Bailey
CHIEF CREATIVE OFFICER, WALT DISNEY & PIXAR ANIMATION STUDIOS/PRINCIPAL CREATIVE ADVISOR
John Lasseter

WALT DISNEY STUDIOS MOTION PICTURE PRODUCTION
(Production Company)
500 S. Buena Vista St., Burbank, CA 91521.
TEL: (818) 560-1000. www.disney.com
PRESIDENT, WALT DISNEY STUDIOS MOTION PICTURE PRODUCTION
Sean Bailey
PRESIDENT, PHYSICAL PRODUCTION, WALT DISNEY STUDIOS MOTION PICTURE PRODUCTION
Bruce Hendricks
EXECUTIVE V.P., PRODUCTION, WALT DISNEY STUDIOS MOTION PICTURE PRODUCTION
Kristin Burr
EXECUTIVE V.P., WALT DISNEY STUDIOS MOTION PICTURE PRODUCTION/GENERAL MANAGER, WALT DISNEY STUDIOS INTERNATIONAL PRODUCTIONS
Jason T. Reed
EXECUTIVE V.P., PRODUCTION
Brigham Taylor
EXECUTIVE V.P., MUSIC BUSINESS & LEGAL AFFAIRS
Scott Holtzman
EXECUTIVE V.P., VISUAL EFFECTS & PRODUCTION
Art Repola
SENIOR V.P., PRODUCTION
Whitney Green
SENIOR V.P., PHYSICAL PRODUCTION
Jerry Ketcham
SENIOR V.P., PRODUCTION FINANCE
Paul Steinke
V.P., PRODUCTION
LouAnne Brickhouse, Tendo Nagenda
V.P., PRODUCTION RESOURCES
Calvin Tindal

WALT DISNEY STUDIOS MOTION PICTURE INTERNATIONAL
500 S. Buena Vista St., Burbank, CA 91521.
TEL: (818) 560-1000.
PRESIDENT, EUROPE, MIDDLE EAST & AFRICA
Diego Lerner
EXECUTIVE V.P., WORLDWIDE PUBLICITY
Teri Meyer
SENIOR V.P., INTL. MARKETING & CREATIVE MARKETING
Nic Crawley
SENIOR V.P., MARKETING/FEATURE ANIMATION
Donald Evans
SENIOR V.P., INTERNATIONAL PUBLICITY
Michelle Sewell
V.P., CREATIVE PRINT SERVICES
Mari Gastineau, Ticole Richards
V.P., INTERNATIONAL PUBLICITY
Nina Heyn, Maggie Todd
SENIOR V.P., SALES & MARKETING, ASIA/PACIFIC
Jeff Forman
V.P./GENERAL MANAGER, AUSTRIA
Ferdinand Morawetz
V.P., MANAGING DIRECTOR, AUSTRALIA & NEW ZEALAND
Alan Finney
GENERAL MANAGER, BELGIUM
Gil Van Laer
GENERAL MANAGER, BRAZIL
Rodrigo Saturnino Braga
EXECUTIVE V.P., GENERAL MANAGER, EUROPE
Daniel Frigo
GENERAL MANAGER, FINLAND
Jussi Makela
EXECUTIVE V.P., FRANCE
Jean De Rivieres
GENERAL MANAGER, GERMANY
Thomas Menne
GENERAL MANAGER, INDONESIA, SINGAPORE & MALAYSIA
Brett Hogg
V.P., GENERAL MANAGER, IRELAND
Trish Long
SENIOR V.P./GENERAL MANGER, ITALY
Paul Zonderland
GENERAL MANAGER, KOREA
Hyuk Jo Kwon
GENERAL MANAGER, MEXICO
Philip Alexander
GENERAL MANAGER, NORWAY
Inger Warendolph
GENERAL MANAGER, PHILLIPINES
Victor Cabrera
SENIOR V.P./GENERAL MANAGER, SPAIN
Javier Vasallo Tome
SENIOR V.P./GENERAL MANAGER, SWEDEN, PAN SCANDANAVIA
Eric Broberg
V.P./MANAGING DIRECTOR, SWITZERLAND
Roger Crotti
GENERAL MANAGER, TAIWAN
Laura Folta
OPERATONS MANAGING DIRECTOR, VENEZUELA
Anibal Codebo

WALT DISNEY STUDIOS WORLDWIDE HOME ENTERTAINMENT
3900 W. Alameda Ave., Burbank, CA 91505.
TEL: (818) 560-1000. www.disney.com
PRESIDENT, DISTRIBUTION, THE WALT DISNEY STUDIOS
Bob Chapek
EXECUTIVE V.P./GENERAL MANAGER, WALT DISNEY STUDIOS HOME ENTERTAINMENT
Lori MacPherson
EXECUTIVE V.P., WORLDWIDE MARKETING & PRODUCT MANAGEMENT
Gordon Ho
GENERAL MANAGER, ASIA PACIFIC, LATIN AMERICA & EMERGING MARKETS
Daniel Solnicki
SENIOR V.P., BRAND MARKETING & PRODUCT MANAGEMENT, NORTH AMERICA
Gabrielle Chamberlin
SENIOR V.P., GLOBAL CREATIVE MARKETING
Chris Connelly
SENIOR V.P., WORLDWIDE SALES
Ken Gastro
SENIOR V.P., SALES & DISTRIBUTION, NORTH AMERICA
Jeanne Hobson
SENIOR V.P., WORLDWIDE BUSINESS & LEGAL AFFAIRS
Kristin McQueen
SENIOR V.P., WORLWIDE CREATIVE SERVICES & DVD PRODUCTION
Andy Siditsky
SENIOR V.P., WORLDWIDE SALES, DISTRIBUTION & TRADE MARKETING
Julie Sneddon
SENIOR V.P./GENERAL MANAGER, EUROPE
Cecilia Tosting
SENIOR V.P., FINANCE, NORTH AMERICA
Tracy Wilson
V.P., WORLDWIDE CONSUMER STRATEGIC INTELLIGENCE
Jim Bowman
V.P., WORLDWIDE PROCESS INTEGRATIONS & INFORMATION TECHNOLOGIES
Steve Dahl
V.P., WORLDWIDE COMMUNICATIONS
Eric Maehara
V.P., WORLDWIDE HUMAN RESOURCES
Richard Ramsey
V.P., WORLWIDE PUBLICITY
Liz West

PIXAR ANIMATION STUDIOS
(A wholly-owned subsidiary of The Walt Disney Company)
1200 Park Ave., Emeryville, CA 94608. TEL: (510) 752-3000.
FAX: (510) 752-3151. www.pixar.com
CHIEF CREATIVE OFFICER
John A. Lasseter
PRESIDENT
Dr. Ed Catmull
GENERAL MANAGER
Jim Morris

DISNEYTOON STUDIOS
500 S. Buena Vista St., Burbank, CA 91521.
TEL: (818) 560-5000.
EXECUTIVE V.P., GENERAL MANAGER
Andrew Millstein
SENIOR V.P., GENERAL MANAGER
Meredith Roberts
V.P., PRODUCTION
Sean Lurie
V.P., FINANCE & OPERATIONS
Daniel Thein
V.P., MUSIC PRODUCTION
Brett Swain
DIRECTOR, HUMAN RESOURCES
Lindsay Nadler

DISNEY INTERACTIVE MEDIA GROUP
CO-PRESIDENT
James Pitaro, John Pleasants
EXECUTIVE V.P/CTO
Bud Albers
EXECUTIVE V.P/GENERAL MANAGER, DISNEY INTERACTIVE STUDIOS
Graham Hopper
EXECUTIVE V.P./GENERAL MANAGER, DISNEY ONLINE STUDIOS
Lane Merrifield
EXECUTIVE V.P., BUSINESS DEVELOPMENT & OPERATIONS
Larry Shapiro
EXECUTIVE V.P./MANAGING DIRECTOR, DISNEY ONLINE
Paul Yanover
SENIOR V.P., HUMAN RESOURCES
Gary Randall
V.P., COMMUNICATIONS
Matthew Kelly
V.P., REAL ESTATE & RESORT DEVELOPMENT
Martin Shumaker
V.P., DEVELOPMENT TDR
John Verity
V.P., CREATIVE
Kathryn Klatt
V.P., EXECUTIVE PRODUCTION DESIGNER
Oscar Lange, Jr.
V.P., EXECUTIVE PRODUCER
Kathryn Mangum, Thomas Morris
V.P., A&FE MANAGEMENT
Craig Russell
V.P., PROJECT MANAGEMENT
David Todd
V.P., PROJECT MANAGEMENT HONG KONG DISNEYLAND
John Verity
V.P. SHOW RIDE ENGINEERING
Michael Withers

DISTANT HORIZON LTD.

(Motion picture distributor, South Africa. A wholly owned subsidiary of Videovision Entertainment)
8282 Sunset Blvd., Ste. A, Los Angeles, CA 90046.
TEL: (323) 848-4140. FAX: (323) 848-4144.
email: la@distant-horizon.com www.distant-horizon.com
CEO
Anant Singh
V.P., DEVELOPMENT & PRODUCTION
Brian Cox
V.P., ACQUISITIONS
Sanjeev Singh

MAUREEN DONLEY PICTURES

914 Westwood Blvd., Ste. 591, Los Angeles, CA 90024.
TEL: (310) 441-0834. FAX: (310) 441-1595.
email: mcd@mdpix.com WWW.MDPIX.COM
PRODUCER
Maureen Donley
VICE PRESIDENT
Lauren Sands

THE DONNERS' COMPANY

(Motion picture, independent film & TV producer)
9465 Wilshire Blvd., Ste. 430, Beverly Hills, CA 90212.
TEL: (310) 777-4600. FAX: (310) 777-4610.
PRODUCER & DIRECTOR
Richard Donner - (310) 777-6730
PRODUCER
Lauren Shuler Donner - (310) 777-6725
PRESIDENT
Jack Leslie

DOTSON-WOOLEY ENTERTAINMENT GROUP

123 Walton Ferry Rd., Hendersonville, TN 37075.
TEL: (615) 824-1947. FAX: (615) 264-0462.
email: dotwool@bellsouth.net
PARTNER
Linda S. Dotson, Sheb Wooley

DOUBLE FEATURE FILMS

(Motion picture, independent film & TV producer)
9320 Wilshire Blvd., Ste. 210, Beverly Hills, CA 90212.
TEL: (310) 887-1100. FAX: (310) 887-1110.
CO-CHAIRMEN
Michael Shamberg, Stacey Sher
EXECUTIVE V.P.
Carla Santos Shamberg
VICE PRESIDENTS, DEVELOPMENT
Taylor Latham, Josh Rothstein
OFFICE MANAGER
Ameet Shukla

JEAN DOUMANIAN PRODUCTIONS

(Motion picture, independent film & TV producer)
595 Madison Ave., Ste. 2200, New York, NY 10022.
TEL: (212) 486-2626. FAX: (212) 688-6236.
PRESIDENT
Jean Doumanian
DIRECTOR, PRODUCTION & DEVELOPMENT
Patrick Daly

DREAMWORKS

(Production company)
100 Universal City Plaza, Universal City, CA 91608.
TEL: (818) 733-7000. www.dreamworks.com
East Coast Office: 650 Madison Ave., 22nd Flr., New York, NY 10022. TEL: (212) 588-6229. FAX: (212) 588-6233.
CO-PRINCIPAL, PRODUCER/DIRECTOR
Steven Spielberg
CO-PRINCIPAL, CHAIRMAN & CEO
Stacey Snider
COO
Jeff Small
CFO
Larry Wasserman
CO-HEAD, THEATRICAL PRODUCTION
Holly Bario, Mark Sourian
HEAD, MARKETING
Christine Birch
HEAD, CASTING
Leslee Feldman
HEAD, PUBLICITY
Chip Sullivan
THEATRICAL PRODUCTION
Chloe Dan, Jonathan Eirich, Kira Goldberg
THEATRICAL PRODUCTION/HEAD, STORY DEPARTMENT
Andrea McCall
THEATRICAL & PHYSICAL PRODUCTION
Steven Molen, Shelly Strong
HEAD BUSINESS AFFAIRS
Chris Floyd
BUSINESS AFFAIRS
Phillip Goore
HEAD, LEGAL AFFAIRS
Grant Gullickson
LEGAL AFFAIRS
Marcia Daley

DreamWorks SKG, part of Viacom's Paramount Pictures since its $1.6 billion acquisition in Dec. 2005, is once again independent after separating from Paramount in Oct. 2008. Co-founder and partner David Geffen negotiated the deal for principal Steven Spielberg and co-chairman and CEO Stacey Snider but did not become part of the newly independent DreamWorks Studios. They signed a distribution deal with The Walt Disney Studios in 2009.

DREAMWORKS ANIMATION SKG, INC.

1000 Flower St., Glendale, CA 91201. TEL: (818) 695-5000.
FAX: (818) 695-9944. www.dreamworksanimation.com
CEO
Jeffrey Katzenberg
CHAIRMAN
Roger A. Enrico
COO
Ann Daly
CO-PRESIDENT, PRODUCTION PRESIDENT, LIVE THEATRICAL
Bill Damaschke
CO-PRESIDENT, PRODUCTION
John Batter
PRESIDENT/CFO
Lew Coleman
CAO
Heather O'Connor
WORLDWIDE HEAD, FRANCHISE STRATEGY & DISTRIBUTION
Kelley Avery
HEAD, DEVELOPMENT
Alex Schwartz
HEAD, WORLDWIDE MARKETING & CONSUMER PRODUCTS
Anne Globe
DEVELOPMENT EXECUTIVE
Damon Ross, Chris Kuser
GENERAL COUNSEL
Andrew Chang
BUSINESS & LEGAL AFFAIRS
Jamie Kershaw, Alison Lima

DREYFUSS/JAMES PRODUCTIONS

(Motion picture & TV producer)
2418 Laurel Pass, Los Angeles, CA 90046.
TEL: (323) 822-0140. FAX: (323) 822-0440.
email: kyle@djprods.com www.djprods.com
OWNER & EXECUTIVE PRODUCER
Richard Dreyfuss
OWNER & EXECUTIVE PRODUCER
Judith James

ASSOCIATE
Kyle Bowe, Erin Condron

DRIVE-BY FILM SHOOTING CO.

(Motion picture & TV producer)
1149 N. Gower St., Los Angeles, CA 90038.
TEL: (323) 785-2100. www.michaeladdis.com
WRITER & DIRECTOR
Michael Addis - ma@michaeladdis.com
DIRECTOR, DEVELOPMENT
Phil Shuster

EARTH LION PRODUCTIONS

18653 Ventura Blvd. # 441, Tarzana, CA 91356.
TEL: (818) 206-0250. FAX: (818) 206-0250.
www.earthlion.com
PRODUCER
Bonnie Rutherford - bonnie@earthlion.com
CREATIVE EXECUTIVE
Sam Franklin

ECHELON STUDIOS

4340 W. Verdugo Ave., Burbank, CA 91505.
TEL: (818) 524-2771. FAX: (818) 500-1644.
email: corporate@echelonstudios.us www.echelonstudios.us
PRESIDENT & CEO
Eric Louzil
V.P., DOMESTIC & INTERNATIONAL SALES
Tim Kelly
V.P., INTERNATIONAL SALES
Sandro Gohoho
V.P., GRAPHIC DESIGN
Eric Robert Louzil
V.P., PUBLIC RELATIONS
Vincent Marinaccio
V.P., ACQUISITIONS
Rosalbina Anchante
ACCOUNTING & CLIENT RELATIONS
Darrion Osby

EDMONDS ENTERTAINMENT

(Motion picture & TV producer)
1635 N. Cahuenga Blvd., 5th Flr., Los Angeles, CA 90028.
TEL: (323) 860-1550. FAX: (323) 860-1537.
PRESIDENT/CEO
Tracey E. Edmonds
SENIOR V.P., TV & FILM
Sheila Ducksworth
EXECUTIVE ASSISTANT TO TRACEY E. EDMONDS
Adris DeBarge

Edmonds Entertainment produces TV series, Reality TV and features.

EL DORADO PICTURES

(Motion picture & TV producer)
725 Arizona Ave., Ste. 404, Santa Monica, CA 90401.
TEL: (818) 888-3700. FAX: (818) 887-1843
www.alecbaldwin.com
PRODUCER
Alec Baldwin
ASSISTANT TO ALEC BALDWIN
Summer Grindle, Monica Hopkins

ELECTRIC ENTERTAINMENT

(Production company)
940 N. Highland Ave., Ste. A, Los Angeles, CA 90038.
TEL: (323) 817-1300. FAX: (323) 467-7155.
www.electric-entertainment.com
PRESIDENT
Dean Devlin
PARTNER
Marc Roskin, Kearie Peak, Rachel Olschan
HEAD, BUSINESS & LEGAL AFFAIRS
Rebecca Rising

ELEMENT FILMS

(Production Company; No unsolicited material)
7966 Beverly Blvd., 3rd. Flr., Los Angeles, CA 90048.
TEL: (323) 330-8000. FAX: (323) 330-8001.
OWNER
Sam Nazarian
PARTNER & PRESIDENT
Adam Rosenfelt
COO
Marc Schaberg
CFO
Clint Kisker
V.P., BUSINESS & LEGAL AFFAIRS
Wendy Heller
EXECUTIVE ASSISTANT
Katie McMillan

EMERGING PICTURES

245 W. 55th St., 4th Flr., New York, NY 10019.
TEL: (212) 245-6767. FAX: (212) 202-4984.
email: info@emergingpictures.com www.emergingpictures.com
CHAIRMAN
Barry Rebo
PRESIDENT
Giovanni Cozzi
CEO
Ira Deutchman
CFO
Tim Wallace
V.P., DISTRIBUTION
Josh Green

EMPIRE PICTURES

(Production company)
1900 Blue Heights Dr., Los Angeles, CA 90069.
TEL: (323) 654-4100. FAX: (323) 887-4800.
PRESIDENT
Michael Birnbaum

ESCAPE ARTISTS II

(Motion picture producer)
10202 W. Washington Blvd., Astaire Bldg., 3rd Flr., Culver City, CA 90232. TEL: (310) 244-8833. FAX: (310) 244-2151.
PARTNER
Todd Black, Jason Blumenthal, Steve Tisch
EXECUTIVE V.P., BUSINESS & LEGAL AFFAIRS
David Bloomfield
V.P., FINANCE & ADMINISTRATION
Kim Skeeters
DIRECTOR, DEVELOPMENT
Lance Johnson

ETERNITY PICTURES, INC.

(Motion picture producer & distributor)
7421 Beverly Blvd., Ste. 9, Los Angeles, CA 90036.
TEL: (323) 932-9939. FAX: (323) 932-9949.
email: production@eternitypictures.com
PRODUCERS
Willi Baer, Carmen M. Miller

THE ROBERT EVANS COMPANY

(Motion picture producer)
5555 Melrose Ave., Lubitsch Bldg. #117, Los Angeles, CA 90038-3197. TEL: (323) 956-8800. FAX: (323) 862-0070.
CHAIRMAN
Robert Evans
PRODUCER
Jennifer Howard, Henri M. Kessler
DIRECTOR, DEVELOPMENT
James Sikura - James_Sikura@Paramount.com

EVOLUTION ENTERTAINMENT

(Production company)
901 N. Highland Ave., Los Angeles, CA 90038.
TEL: (323) 850-3232. FAX: (323) 850-0521.
PARTNER/PRODUCER
Mark Burg, Oren Koules
CREATIVE EXECUTIVE
Erick Salomon
GENERAL MANAGER
Justine Stevenson

FACE PRODUCTIONS/JENNILIND PRODUCTIONS

335 N. Maple Dr., Ste. 175, Beverly Hills, CA 90210.
TEL: (310) 205-2746. FAX: (310) 285-2386.
WRITER, ACTOR, DIRECTOR
Billy Crystal
V.P., DEVELOPMENT, FEATURES
Samantha Sprecher
ASSISTANT TO MR. CRYSTAL
Carol Sidlow

THE FILM DEPARTMENT

(Production company)
8439 Sunset Blvd., 2nd Flr., Los Angeles, CA 90069.
TEL: (323) 785-3700. www.filmdept.com
CEO
Mark Gill
CFO
Bernd Stephan
PRESIDENT & COO
Neil Sacker
PRESIDENT, PRODUCTION
Robert Katz
EXECUTIVE V.P., BUSINESS & LEGAL AFFAIRS
Dan Stutz
V.P., BUSINESS & LEGAL AFFAIRS
Rina Dhaliwal
V.P., PHYSICAL PRODUCTION
Ian Watermeier

FILMS AROUND THE WORLD, INC.

(Motion picture distributor)
The Long Island City Art Center, 44-02 23rd Street - Studio 407, Long Island City, New York 11101, U.S.A.

TEL: (212) 599-9500. FAX: (212) 599-6040.
email: alexjr@pipeline.com www.filmsaroundtheworld.com
PRESIDENT
Alexander W. Kogan, Jr. - alexjr@pipeline.com
V.P.,
Beverly Partridge

FILM MOVEMENT

(Distribution company)
109 W. 27th St., Ste. 9B, New York, NY 10001.
TEL: (212) 941-7744. FAX: (212) 941-7812.
email: info@filmmovement.com www.filmmovement.com
PRESIDENT
Adley Gartenstein
V.P., TECHNOLOGY
Chris Russell
V.P., BUSINESS DEVELOPMENT
Meghan Wurtz
V.P., ACQUISITIONS & DISTRIBUTION
Rebeca Conget
MARKETING & PUBLICITY
Claire Weingarten
NON-THEATRICAL SALES
Cambria Matlow

WENDY FINERMAN PRODUCTIONS

(Production company)
144 S. Beverly Dr., Ste. 304, Beverly Hills, CA 90212.
TEL: (310) 694-8088. FAX: (310) 694-8088.
PRODUCER
Wendy Finerman
VICE PRESIDENT
Lisa Zupan
ASSISTANT
Belinda Rungsea

FIRST INDEPENDENT PICTURES

(Motion picture, independent film & TV distributor)
2999 Overland Ave., Ste. 218, Los Angeles, CA 90064.
TEL: (310) 838-6555. FAX: (310) 838-9972.
email: aan@firstindependentpictures.com
www.firstindependentpictures.com
PRESIDENT
Gary Rubin
MARKETING & ACQUISITIONS MANAGER
Angel An

FIRST LOOK STUDIOS

(Production & distribution company)
2000 Ave. of the Stars, Ste. 410, Los Angeles, CA 90067.
TEL: (424) 202-5000. FAX: (424) 202-5050.
email: info@firstlookstudios.com www.firstlookstudios.com
CEO
Bill Lee
PRESIDENT, INTERNATIONAL SALES & DISTRUBUTION
Christian Mercuri
PRESIDENT, DOMESTIC T.V. & STRATEGIC PLANNING
Dave Sobieraj
EXECUTIVE V.P., THEATRICAL DISTRIBUTION
Andy Gruenberg
EXECUTIVE V.P., WORLDWIDE MARKETING
Brooke Ford
SENIOR V.P., SALES, HOME ENTERTAINMENT
Marie O'Reilly-Thein

FIRST RUN FEATURES

(Motion picture, independent film & TV distributor)
The Film Center Building, 630 Ninth Ave., Ste. 1213, New York, NY 10036. TEL: (212) 243-0600. FAX: (212) 989-7649.
email: info@firstrunfeatures.com www.firstrunfeatures.com
PRESIDENT
Seymour Wishman
VICE PRESIDENT
Marc A. Mauceri
MARKETING DIRECTOR
Judith Mizrachy

FLOWER FILMS, INC.

(Motion picture producer)
7360 Santa Monica Blvd., West Hollywood, CA 90046.
TEL: (323) 876-7400. FAX: (323) 876-7401.
PARTNER
Drew Barrymore, Nancy Juvonen
V.P., PRODUCTION
Chris Miller
V.P., DEVELOPMENT
Ember Truesdell
CREATIVE DIRECTOR
Brent Kyle

FORTIS FILMS

(Motion picture producer)
8581 Santa Monica Blvd., Ste. 1, West Hollywood, CA 90069.
TEL: (310) 659-4533.
ACTOR/PRODUCER
Sandra Bullock
V.P., PRODUCTION
Maggie Biggar
OFFICE MANAGER
Bryan Moore

FORWARD PASS, INC.

(Motion picture producer)
12233 W. Olympic Blvd., Ste. 340, Los Angeles, CA 90064.
TEL: (310) 207-7378.
WRITER & PRODUCER & DIRECTOR
Michael Mann

FOX, INC.

(See News Corporation)

FREESTYLE RELEASING

(Distribution company)
6310 San Vicente Blvd., Ste. 500, Los Angeles, CA 90048.
TEL: (323) 330-9920. FAX: (323) 330-9939.
www.freestylereleasing.com
CO-PRESIDENT
Mark Borde - Mark@freestylereleasing.com
CO-PRESIDENT
Susan Jackson - jacksusan@gmail.com
GENERAL SALES MANAGER
Mike Simon - mike@freestylereleasing.com

FRELAINE

(Production company)
8383 Wilshire Blvd., 5th Flr., Beverly Hills, CA 90211.
TEL: (323) 848-9729. FAX: (323) 848-7219.
email: lindsay@frelaine.com
PRODUCER
Jim Jacks
ASSISTANT
Lindsay Jacks

FRESH PRODUCE FILMS

(Production company)
11684 Ventura Blvd., Ste. 214, Studio City, CA 91604.
TEL: (843) 937-6337. email: mpfp2002@yahoo.com
PRESIDENT & PRODUCER
Marshall Persinger

FURTHUR FILMS

(Motion picture producer & developer)
100 Universal City Plaza, Bldg. 1320/4G, Universal City, CA 91608. TEL: (818) 777-6700. FAX: (818) 866-1278.
825 8th Ave., 30th Flr., New York, NY 10019.
TEL: (212) 333-1421. FAX: (212) 333-8163.
PRODUCER
Michael Douglas
EXECUTIVE V.P.
Robert Mitas
CONTROLLER
Angela Congelose
PUBLICIST
Allen Burry (NY)

GENERATE

(Production and management company)
1545 26th St., Ste. 200, Santa Monica, CA 90404.
TEL: (310) 255-0460. FAX: (310) 255-0461.
www.generatela.com
CEO
Jordan Levin
PRESIDENT, GENERATE STUDIOS
Pete Aronson
CFO
Chris Gwiazda
V.P., DEVELOPMENT
Caitlin McGinty
EXECUTIVE V.P., BUSINESS & LEGAL AFFAIRS
Tim Stephen
HEAD, SALES
Scott Haugenes
HEAD, PRODUCTION
Michael Petok

GIANT SCREEN FILMS

(Distribution company)
500 Davis St., Ste. 1005, Evanston, IL 60201.
TEL: (847) 475-9140. FAX: (847) 475-9145.
email: info@gsfilms.com www.gsfilms.com
CO-FOUNDER
Don Kempf, Steve Kempf
V.P., DEVELOPMENT & OPERATIONS
Andy Wood
DIRECTOR, MARKETING
Tina Ratterman
DIRECTOR, FINANCE
Rob Grzymala

DIRECTOR, DISTRIBUTION & OPERATIONS
Steve Jennings

GK FILMS

(Motion picture & independent production & finance co./foreign distribution)
1411 Fifth St., Ste. 200 Santa Monica, CA 90401.
TEL: (310) 315-1722. FAX: (310) 315-1723.
email: contact@gk-films.com www.gk-films.com
CEO
Graham King
COO
Bahman Naraghi
PRESIDENT, GK FILMS
Peter Schlessel
PRESIDENT, THEATRICAL DISTRIBUTION, FILM DISTRICT
Bob Berney
PRESIDENT, INTL. DISTRIBUTION
Lisa Wilson
EXECUTIVE V.P, BUSINESS & LEGAL AFFAIRS
Julie Roach
EXECUTIVE V.P., PRODUCTION
David Crockett
EXECUTIVE V.P., GK FILMS
Adrian Alperovich
SENIOR V.P., MARKETING & PUBLICITY
Maxine Leonard
SENIOR V.P., DEVELOPMENT
Grey Rembert
SENIOR V.P., FINANCE
Paula Marcus

THE GOATSINGERS

(Motion picture producer)
177 W. Broadway, 2nd Flr., New York, NY 10013.
TEL: (212) 966-3045. FAX: (212) 966-4362.
PRESIDENT
Harvey Keitel
EXECUTIVE ASSISTANT/PRODUCTION OFFICE MANAGER
Leslie Peterson

FREDERIC GOLCHAN PRODUCTIONS

(Motion picture & independent film producer)
c/o Radar Pictures, 10900 Wilshire Blvd., 14th Flr., Los Angeles, CA 90024. TEL: (310) 208-8525, (310) 854-3030. FAX: (310) 208-1764. email: fgfilm@aol.com
PRESIDENT
Frederic A. Golchan
ASSISTANT, DEVELOPMENT
Kami Lemke

GOLDCREST FILMS INTERNATIONAL, INC.

65-66 Dean St., London, W1D 4PL, UK.
TEL: 44-20-7437-8696. FAX: 44-20-7437-4448.
email: info@goldcrestfilms.com www.goldcrestfilms.com
CHAIRMAN
John Quested
PRESIDENT
Stephen Johnson
DIRECTOR
Nick Quested
HEAD OF FILM
Penny Wolf
PRODUCTION & ACQUISITIONS
Susan England
SALES & ACQUISITIONS
Marica Nunes
INTERNATIONAL SALES
Laura Wu, Marcia Nunes
SALES & MARKETING
Sam Lefevre

New York: 799 Washington St., New York, NY 10014.
TEL: (212) 243-4700. www.goldcrestfilms.com
MANAGING DIRECTOR
Tim Spitzer - (212) 897-3967

SAMUEL GOLDWYN FILMS

(Motion picture producer & distributor)
9570 W. Pico Blvd., Ste. 400, Los Angeles, CA 90035.
TEL: (310) 860-3100. FAX: (310) 860-3198.

1133 Broadway, Ste. 926, New York, NY 10010.
TEL: (212) 367-9435. FAX: (212) 367-0853.
email: info@samuelgoldwynfilms.com
www.samuelgoldwynfilms.com
CHAIRMAN
Samuel Goldwyn, Jr.
PRESIDENT
Meyer Gottlieb
SENIOR V.P., PUBLICITY
Liza Burnett Fefferman (NY)
V.P., ACQUISITIONS
Peter Goldwyn
MANAGER, DEVELOPMENT
Tristen Tuckfield

DIRECTOR, CONTRACT ADMINISTRATION
Rorri Feinstein

GOOD NEWS HOLDINGS

(Production company)
15490 Ventura Blvd., Ste. 210, Sherman Oaks, CA 91403.
TEL: (818) 883-1333. FAX: (818) 501-9103.
email: info@goodnewsholdings.com
www.goodnewsholdings.com
CO-FOUNDER & CHAIRMAN
George Barna
PRESIDENT & CEO
Christopher Chisholm
COO
Shawn Carroll
LEGAL & CORPORATE
Joshua S. Wattles

GORDON FILMS, INC.

(Motion picture producer & distributor)
119 W. 57th St., Ste. 319, New York, NY 10019.
TEL: (212) 757-9390. FAX: (212) 757-9392.
PRESIDENT
Richard Gordon

GOTHAM METRO STUDIOS, INC.

(Production, development, finance, film distribution, television and video production)
TEL: (310) 394-9100. email: info@GothamMetro.com
www.GothamMetro.com
CHIEF EXECUTIVE OFFICER, EXECUTIVE PRODUCER
Michael J Lasky - mj@GothamMetro.com
PRODUCTION CONSULTANT
David Craddick - dave@GothamMetro.com
Peter Liapis - peter@Gotham Metro.com
OUTSIDE COUNSEL/BUSINESS & LEGAL AFFAIRS
Howard Behar - howard@GothamMetro.com
FINANCE CONSULTANT
Markus Baettig - markus@GothamMetro.com

GRACIE FILMS

(Motion picture & TV producer)
10202 W. Washington Blvd., Poitier Bldg., Culver City, CA 90232. TEL: (310) 244-4222. FAX: (310) 244-1530.
www.graciefilms.com
PRODUCER & WRITER & DIRECTOR
James L. Brooks
PRESIDENT
Richard Sakai
PRESIDENT, MOTION PICTURES
Julie Ansell
EXECUTIVE V.P.
Denise Sirkot

GRAINY PICTURES

(Producer; No unsolicited submissions)
TEL: (512) 697-9547. www.grainypictures.com
CO-PRESIDENT
Janet Pierson - janet@grainypictures.com
John Pierson

GREENESTREET FILMS, INC.

(Motion picture, independent film & TV producer)
609 Greenwich St., 6th Flr., New York, NY 10014.
TEL: (212) 609-9000. FAX: (212) 609-9099.
email: general@gstreet.com www.greenestreetfilms.com
CO-PRESIDENT/FOUNDING PARTNER
John Penotti
CO-PRESIDENT/HEAD, PRODUCTION
Tim Williams
COO
Mike Hogan
V.P., BUSINESS AFFAIRS
Broan Kornreich
V.P., DEVELOPMENT
Amanda Essick
V.P., FINANCE
Shane Kelly

GREEN HAT FILMS

(Production company)
4000 Warner Blvd., Bldg. 66, Rm. 100, Burbank, CA 91522.
TEL: (818) 954-3210. FAX: (818) 954-3214.
DIRECTOR & PRESIDENT
Todd Phillips
EXECUTIVE V.P., PRODUCTION
Scott Budnick
PRODUCER
Daniel Goldberg
DIRECTOR, DEVELOPMENT
Mark O'Connor
EXECUTIVE ASSISTANTS
Joseph Garner, Anastasia Nairne

GROUNDSWELL PRODUCTIONS

(Production company)
11925 Wilshire Blvd., Ste. 310, Los Angeles, CA 90025.
TEL: (310) 385-7540. FAX: (310) 385-7541.
email: info@groundswellfilms.com www.groundswellfilms.com
CEO
Michael London
PRESIDENT
Jonathan Fischer
SENIOR V.P., PRODUCTION
Jocelyn Hayes-Simpson, Daniel Pipski

HARPO PRODUCTIONS, INC.

(Production company)
110 N. Carpenter St., Chicago, IL 60607.
TEL: (312) 633-1000. FAX: (312) 633-1111, (312) 633-1976.
PRESIDENT, PRODUCTION
Sheri Salata
EXECUTIVE V.P.
Eric Logan
EXECUTIVE V.P., CREATIVE DEVELOPMENT
Valerie Schaer
MEDIA & CORPORATE RELATIONS
Lisa Halliday

Harpo Productions, Inc. produces the award-winning "The Oprah Winfrey Show"; creates and develops original TV programming for primetime, syndication and cable television; and operates Oprah.com (www.oprah.com), a premier lifestyle website.

HARGROVE ENTERTAINMENT, INC.

(Full service entertainment company)
P.O. Box 750338, Forest Hills, NY 11375-0338.
TEL: (718) 657-0542. email: tvsales@HargroveTV.com
www.HargroveTV.com
PRESIDENT
Peter M. Hargrove

HAVOC, INC.

16 West 19th St., 12th Flr., New York, NY 10011.
TEL: (212) 924-1629. email: info@havoc-films.com
PRODUCER & DIRECTOR & WRITER & ACTOR
Tim Robbins

HEARST ENTERTAINMENT, INC.

(Production and distribution company)
300 West 57th St., 15th Flr., New York, NY 10019.
TEL: (212) 969-7553. FAX:(646) 280-1553.
www.hearstent.com
PRESIDENT, HEARST ENTERTAINMENT, INC./EXECUTIVE V.P., HEARST ENTERTAINMENT & SYNDICATION/ V.P., HEARST CORPORATION
Bruce L. Paisner
SENIOR V.P., SALES & MARKETING, HEARST ENTERTAINMENT
Stacey Valenza - svalenza@hearst.com
CONTRACTS & PROMOTIONAL MATERIAL
Nadine Rahiman - nrahiman@hearst.com

THE JIM HENSON COMPANY

(Production company)
Hollywood Headquarters: 1416 N. La Brea Ave., Hollywood, CA 90028. TEL: (323) 802-1500. FAX: (323) 802-1825.
www.henson.com www.puppetup.com

New York: 627 Broadway, 9th Flr., New York, NY 10012.
TEL: (212) 794-2400. FAX: (212) 439-7452.
CHAIRMAN
Brian Henson
CEO
Lisa Henson
PRESIDENT, COO, THE JIM HENSON COMPANY
Peter Schube, Esq.
EXECUTIVE V.P., WORLDWIDE FINANCIAL OPERATIONS
Laurie Don
SENIOR V.P., ADMINISTRATION
Joe Henderson
SENIOR V.P., CHILDREN'S TV
Halle Stanford
SENIOR V.P., FEATURE FILMS
Jason Lust
SENIOR V.P., BUSINESS & LEGAL AFFAIRS
Dan Scharf
SENIOR V.P., GLOBAL CONSUMER PRODUCTS
Melissa Segal
V.P., MARKETING & PR
Nicole Goldman - ngoldman@henson.com
V.P., NEW MEDIA
Allyson Smith

HERE MEDIA, INC.

(distribution company)
10990 Wilshire Blvd., PH, Los Angeles, CA 90024.
TEL: (310) 806-4288. FAX:(310) 806-4268
email: mark.umbach@heremedia.com www.heremedia.com
FOUNDER/CHAIRMAN
Paul Colichman, Stephen P. Jarchow
COO
Andrew Tow
EXECUTIVE V.P.,GENERAL MANAGER
Stephen Macias
EXECUTIVE V.P., DISTRIBUTIONS & ACQUISITIONS
Mark Reinhart
SENIOR V.P., ORIGINAL PROGRAMMING
Meredith Kadlec
SENIOR V.P., INTEGRATED MARKETING & PUBLICITY
Josh Rosenzweig

HOME BOX OFFICE, INC.

(A premium service and subsidiary of Time Warner, Inc.)
1100 Ave. of the Americas, New York, NY 10036.
TEL: (212) 512-1000. FAX: (212) 512-5517.

2500 Broadway, Ste. 400, Santa Monica, CA 90404.
TEL: (310) 382-3000. www.hbo.com
CHAIRMAN & CEO
Bill Nelson
HBO CO-PRESIDENT
Eric Kessler, Richard Plepler
PRESIDENT, HBO PROGRAMMING GROUP & WEST COAST OPERATIONS
Michael Lombardo
PRESIDENT, HBO FILMS
Len Amato
PRESIDENT, HBO MINISERIES
Kary Antholis
PRESIDENT, HBO SPORTS
Ross Greenburg
PRESIDENT, HBO HOME ENTERTAINMENT
Henry McGee
PRESIDENT, PROGRAMMING, DISTRIBUTION & INTERNATIONAL
Simon Sutton
PRESIDENT, DOMESTIC DISTRIBUTION
Scott Carlin
PRESIDENT, HBO ENTERTAINMENT
Sue Naegle
PRESIDENT, HBO DOCUMENTARY FILMS
Sheila Nevins
PRESIDENT, PROGRAMMING SALES
Charles Schreger
EXECUTIVE V.P., PROGRAM PLANNING
Dave Baldwin
EXECUTIVE V.P., AFFILIATE SALES
steve Davidson
EXECUTIVE V.P., TECHNOLOGY & OPERATIONS
Barbara Jaffe
EXECUTIVE V.P./CFO
Robert Roth
EXECUTIVE V.P., AFFILIATE MARKETING
Olivia Smashum
EXECUTIVE V.P., CREATIVE SERVICES
Chris B. Spencer
SENIOR V.P., BUSINESS AFFAIRS/FILM ACQUISITIONS
Royce Battleman
SENIOR V.P., FILM PROGRAMMING
Doris Casap
SENIOR V.P./CONTROLLER
Joseph Tarulli
SENIOR V.P./ASSISTANT CONTROLLER (LA)
Richard Battaglia

HBO FILMS

PRESIDENT HBO FILMS
Len Amato
PRESIDENT HBO MINISERIES
Kary Antholis
EXECUTIVE V.P., BUSINESS AFFAIRS & PRODUCTION
Glenn Whitehead
SENIOR V.P., PRODUCTION
Janet Graham Borba
SENIOR V.P., CREATIVE AFFAIRS
Robert Conte
SENIOR V.P., CASTING, HBO FILMS
Carrie Frazier
SENIOR V.P./CHIEF COUNSEL (West Coast Programming)
Jeffrey Guthrie
SENIOR V.P., PRODUCTION
Jay Roewe
V.P., CASTING
Amy Berman
V.P., BUSINESS AFFAIRS
Susanna Felleman
V.P., POST PRODUCTION
Mark Hoerr
V.P., POST PRODUCTION
Cynthia Davis Kanner
V.P., DEVELOPMENT & PRODUCTION, MINISERIES
John Murchison
V.P., PRODUCTION
Ginny Nugent

V.P., DEVELOPMENT & PRODUCTION, FILMS
Jenni Sherwood
V.P., CHIEF LABOR COUNSEL (WEST COAST PROGRAMMING)
Molly Wilson
V.P., BUSINESS AFFAIRS
Suzanne Young
V.P., POST PRODUCTION
Holly Schiffer Zucker
V.P., DEVELOPMENT & PRODUCTION, FILMS (NY)
Maria Zuckerman

HBO DOCUMENTARY/FAMILY

PRESIDENT
Shiela Nevins
V.P., HBO FAMILY & DOCUMENTARY PROGRAMMING
Dolores Morris
V.P., HBO DOCUMENTARY FILMS
Nancy Abraham, Sara Bernstein
V.P., DOCUMENTARY FILMS
Lisa Heller, John Hoffman, Jackie Glover

PETER HYAMS PRODUCTIONS, INC.

(Motion picture producer)
1453 3rd St. Promenade, Ste. 315, Santa Monica, CA 90401-2397. TEL: (310) 393-1553. FAX: (310) 393-1554.
DIRECTOR & WRITER
Peter Hyams
DIRECTOR, DEVELOPMENT
Ryan Belenzon

HYDE PARK ENTERTAINMENT

(Motion picture producer)
14958 Ventura Blvd., Ste. 100, Sherman Oaks, CA 91403.
TEL: (818) 783-6060. FAX: (818) 783-6319.
CHAIRMAN & CEO
Ashok Amritraj
PRESIDENT, HYDE PARK INTERNATIONAL
Mimi Steinbauer
EXECUTIVE V.P., BUSINESS AFFAIRS
Douglas McClure
EXECUTIVE VP, WORLDWIDE OPERATIONS
Patrick Aiello
V.P., POST PRODUCTION
Joe D'Angelo
V.P., FINANCE
Katie Lavery

ICON PRODUCTIONS, LLC

(Motion picture producer)
808 Wilshire Blvd., 4th Flr., Santa Monica, CA 90401.
TEL: (310) 434-7300. FAX: (310) 434-7377.
CHAIRMAN
Bruce Davey
CEO
Mark Gooder
COO
Vicki Christianson
SENIOR V.P., FEATURES
Stefanie Huie

IDENTITY FEATURES, INC.

(Motion picture producer & distributor)
9201 4th Avenue, 7th Flr., Brooklyn, NY 11209.
TEL: (212) 685-8400, (646) 725-4000.
email: idenittyfeatures@gmail.com www.identityfeatures.com/
PRODUCER/DIRECTOR
James Arcuri
PRODUCER
Lauen Levine, Roger de Anfrasio

IFC FILMS

(Distribution company)
11 Penn Plaza, 18th Flr., New York, NY 10001.
TEL: (646) 273-7200. FAX: (646) 273-7250. www.ifcfilms.com
PRESIDENT
Jonathan Sehring
EXECUTIVE V.P., DISTRIBUTION, OPERATIONS & BUSINESS DEVELOPMENT
Lisa Schwartz
V.P., ACQUISITIONS & PRODUCTION
Arianna Bocco
V.P., SALES & DISTRIBUTION
Mark Boxer
V.P., POST PRODUCTION & DIGITAL ASSETS
Frank Moshier
V.P., FILM BUSINESS OPERATIONS
Judy Silverman
V.P., GENRAL MANAGER, IFC CENTER
John Vanco
V.P., THEATRICAL & HOME ENTERTAINMENT MARKETING
Ryan Werner

IFM WORLD RELEASING, INC.

(Motion picture, independent film & TV producer & distributor)
1328 E. Palmer Ave., Glendale, CA 91205.
TEL: (818) 243-4976. FAX: (818) 550-9728.
email: contact@ifmfilm.com www.ifmfilm.com
PRESIDENT
Antony I. Ginnane
EXECUTIVE V.P.
Ann Lyons
V.P., INTERNATIONAL
Anthony J. Lyons

IM INTERNATIONALMEDIA AG

(International distributor)
Kaulbachstrasse 1, Munich 80539, Germany
TEL: 49-89-9810-7100. FAX: 49-89-9810-7199.
email: info@internationalmedia.de www.internationalmedia.de
CEO
Konstantin Thoeren

IMAGEMOVERS DIGITAL

(Production company)
12641 Beatrice St., Los Angeles, CA 90066.
TEL: (310) 862-9700. www.imagemoversdigital.com
WRITER, DIRECTOR, PRODUCER & PARTNER
Robert Zemeckis
PRODUCER & PARTNER
Steve Starkey, Jack Rapke

IMAGI SERVICES (USA) LIMITED

(Imagi Studios Limited)
19/f, Eight Commercial Tower, 8 Sun Yip St., Chai Wan, Hong Kong. TEL: (852) 3103-6500. email: info@imagi.com.hk
www.imagi.com.hk

Los Angeles Office: Imagi Services (USA) Limited, 15301 Ventura Blvd., Bldg. D., Ste. 210, Sherman Oaks, CA 91403.
TEL: (818) 986-3988. email: sharonthompson@imagius.com
www.imagi.com.hk
FOUNDER, CO-CEO & CHIEF CREATIVE OFFICER
Francis Kao Wai Ho
CO-CEO (HONG KONG)
Douglas E. Glen
HEAD, PRODUCTION
Erin Corbett, Ken Tsumura
COO
Andrew Kopperud
EXECUTIVE V.P., DEVELOPMENT
Paul Wang
V.P., HUMAN RESOURCES
Kathy Dossett

IMAGINE ENTERTAINMENT

(Motion picture, film & TV producer)
9465 Wilshire Blvd., 7th Flr., Beverly Hills, CA 90212.
TEL: (310) 858-2000. FAX: (310) 858-2020.
www.imagine-entertainment.com
PRODUCER/CO-CHAIR
Brian Grazer
DIRECTOR/CO-CHAIR
Ron Howard
CO-CHAIR, IMAGINE FILMS
Karen Kehela Sherwood
PRESIDENT, IMAGINE ENTERTAINMENT
Michael Rosenberg
PRESIDENT, MOTION PICTURE PRODUCTION
Kim Roth
CO-PRESIDENT, PRODUCTION
Erica Huggins
EXECUTIVE V.P., ADMINISTRATION & OPERATIONS
Robin Ruse-Rinehart Barris
EXECUTIVE V.P., MOTION PICTURES
Jeremy Steckler
VICE PRESIDENT, MOTION PICTURES
Sarah Bowen, Anna Culp, Chris Wade
V.P., FINANCE
Christy Sterling
DIRECTOR, DEVELOPMENT
Chris Wade
CREATIVE EXECUTIVE
Leah Estrin, Erin Fredman

IMAGINE TELEVISION

SENIOR EXECUTIVE V.P., DEVELOPMENT
Robin Gurney
EXECUTIVE V.P., BUSINESS AFFAIRS
Skip Chasey
SENIOR V.P., COMEDY DEVELOPMENT, CURRENT PROGRAMMING
Erin Nowocinski

IMPRINT ENTERTAINMENT

(Production Company)
100 Universal City Plaza, Bungalow 7152, Universal City, CA 91608. TEL: (818) 733-5410. FAX: (818) 733-4307.
email: info@imprint-ent.com www.imprint-ent.com
PARTNER
Mark Morgan, Michael Becker

PRODUCER/ MANAGER
Eva Lontschoritsch

THE INDEPENDENT GROUP, LLC

(Talent Management; Film & Television Packaging)
6363 Wilshire Blvd., Ste. 115, Los Angeles, CA 90048.
TEL: (310) 854-2300. FAX: (310) 464-6950.
email:mail@independentgroup.com
www.independentgroup.com
MANAGER/PARTNER
Steven Jensen
MANAGER/PRODUCER/PARTNER
Claudine Vacca

INDEPENDENT DISTRIBUTION PARTNERSHIP

(Distribution company)
1133 Broadway, Ste. 926, New York, NY 10010.
TEL: (212) 367-9435. FAX: (212) 367-0853.
PRESIDENT
Michael Silberman
SENIOR V.P., PUBLICITY
Liza Burnett Fefferman
DIRECTOR, MARKETING
Neil Marks
DIRECTOR, DISTRIBUTION SALES
Heath Shapiro
DIRECTOR, PRINT AND POST SERVICES
Phil Fornabaio
DIRECTOR, FINANCE & ADMINISTRATION
Adam Wallace
DIRECTOR, PUBLICITY
Teresa DiMartino

INDICAN PICTURES

(Distributes feature films, home video, cable/television, VOD)
8424-A Santa Monica Blvd. #752, W. Hollywood, CA 90069.
TEL: (323) 650-0832. FAX: (323) 650-6832.
email: sales@indicanpictures.com www.IndicanPictures.com
PRESIDENT
Shaun Hill
VICE PRESIDENT
Randolph Kret
ACQUISITIONS
Daniel Schneider
PUBLICITY
D. Jarvis
MARKETING
Amit Aggarwal
SALES
David Williams

INDUSTRY ENTERTAINMENT PARTNERS

(Motion picture, independent film & TV producer)
955 S. Carrillo Dr., 3rd Flr., Los Angeles, CA 90048.
TEL: (323) 954-9000. FAX: (323) 954-9009.
FEATURE/TV PRODUCTION
Keith Addis, Sara Bottfeld, Eryn Brown, Bill Butler, Greg Carr, Sandra Chang, Andrew Deane, Dianne Fraser, Helena Heyman, Henry Huang, Tracey Murray, Heather Nunn, Jess Rosenthal, Dan Spilo

IRISH DREAMTIME

(Motion picture producer)
3000 W. Olympic Blvd., Bldg. 3, Ste. 2332, Santa Monica, CA 90404. TEL: (310) 449-4081.
PRODUCER & PARTNER
Pierce Brosnan
PRODUCER & PARTNER
Beau St. Clair

ITALTOONS CORP.

(International distributor of video & film products)
1375 Broadway, 3rd Flr., New York, NY 10018.
TEL: (212) 730-0280. email: info2@italtoons.com
www.italtoons.com
PRESIDENT
Giuliana Nicodemi

JUDGE-BELSHAW ENTERTAINMENT, INC.

411 Clermont St., Ste. 2, Brooklyn, NY 11238.
TEL: (646) 257-5841. FAX: (917) 591-2415.
email: mail@judgebelshaw.com www.judgebelshaw.com
PARTNER
George Belshaw, Jonathan M. Judge

JUNCTION ENTERTAINMENT

(Production company)
500 S. Buena Vista St., Animation 1-B, Burbank, CA 91521-1616. TEL: (818) 560-2800. FAX: (818) 841-3176.
PRODUCER & DIRECTOR
Jon Turtletaub - (818) 560-2070
PRODUCER
Dan Shotz - (818) 560-3670, Karim Zreik

JUNCTION FILMS

(Production company)
9615 Brighton Way, Ste. M110, Beverly Hills, CA 90210.
TEL: (310) 246-9799. FAX: (310) 246-3824.
PRODUCER
Brad Wyman, Donald Kushner, Allwyn Kushner

JUST SINGER ENTERTAINMENT/STEVE WHITE FILMS

(Features, made-for-TV/cable movies, miniseries, TV series)
4146 Vicasa Dr., Calabasas, CA 91302.
TEL: (818) 610-2600. FAX: (818) 222-1121.
email: justsinger@gmail.com
EXECUTIVE PRODUCER/OWNER
Sheri Singer, Steve White

MARTY KATZ PRODUCTIONS

(Motion picture producer)
23852 Pacific Coast Hwy., #297, Malibu, CA 90265.
TEL: (310) 589-1560. FAX: (310) 589-1565.
email: martykatzproductions@earthlink.net
www.martykatzproductions.com
PRODUCER
Marty Katz
DIRECTOR, DEVELOPMENT
Campbell Katz

KELLER ENTERTAINMENT GROUP, INC.

(Producer & distributor)
1093 Broxton Ave., Ste. 246, Los Angeles, CA 90024.
TEL: (310) 443-2226. FAX: (310) 443-2194.
www.kellerentertainment.com
CEO
Max Keller - email: max@kellerentertainment.com
PRESIDENT
Micheline Keller
DIRECTOR, DEVELOPMENT
David Keller
ADMINISTRATOR
Alex King

THE KENNEDY/MARSHALL COMPANY

619 Arizona Ave., Santa Monica, CA 90401.
TEL: (310) 656-8400. FAX: (310) 656-8430.
PRODUCER
Kathleen Kennedy
PRODUCER & DIRECTOR
Frank Marshall
V.P., DEVELOPMENT
Adam Yoelin
ASSISTANTS
Mary Radford, Elyse Klaits

KEY CREATIVES, LLC

(Production company)
1800 N. Highland Ave., Ste. 500, Los Angeles, CA 90028.
TEL: (323) 785-7950. FAX: (323) 785-7901.
CHAIRMAN & CEO
Ken Kamins

KILLER FILMS, INC.

(Independent film producer)
526 W. 26th St., Ste. 715, New York, NY 10001.
TEL: (212) 473-3950. FAX: (212) 473-6152.
www.killerfilms.com
PARTNER/PRODUCER
Christine Vachon, Pamela Koffler
DEVELOPMENT
David Kaplan

SIDNEY KIMMEL ENTERTAINMENT

(Production company)
9460 Wilshire Blvd., Ste. 500, Beverly Hills, CA 90212.
TEL: (310) 777-8818. FAX: (310) 777-8892. www.skefilms.com
CHAIRMAN/CEO
Sidney Kimmel
PRESIDENT
Jim Tauber
CFO
Richard Lewis
SENIOR V.P., BUSINESS & LEGAL AFFAIRS
Nicholas Hanks
SENIOR V.P., PRODUCTION
Dylan Tarason
V.P., FINANCE/CONTROLLER
Monique Jones

KINGSGATE FILMS, INC.

(Motion picture & TV producer)
8954 W. Pico Blvd., 2nd Flr., Los Angeles, CA 90035.
TEL: (310) 281-5880. FAX: (310) 281-2633.
email: KG1@kingsgatefilms.com www.kingsgatefilms.com
ACTOR & PRODUCER
Nick Nolte

PRODUCER
Greg Shapiro

KINO LORBER/ INTERNATIONAL CORP.

(Film distributor)
333 W. 39th St., Ste. 503, New York, NY 10018.
TEL: (800) 562-3330, (212) 629-6880. FAX: (212) 714-0871.
email: contact@kino.com www.kino.com
CO-PRESIDENT
Donald Krim, Richard Lorber
V.P.
Elizabeth Sheldon
DIRECTOR, PUBLICITY
Rodrigo Brandao
DIRECTOR, SALES
Eric Wilkinson

THE KONIGSBERG CO.

7919 Sunset Blvd., 2nd Flr., Los Angeles, CA 90046.
TEL: (323) 845-1000. FAX: (323) 845-1020.
email: fkonigsberg@gmail.com
EXECUTIVE PRODUCER
Frank Konigsberg

KOPELSON ENTERTAINMENT

(Motion picture, independent film & TV producer)
15335 Morrison St., Ste. 375, Sherman Oaks, CA 91403.
TEL: (818) 817-7162. FAX: (310) 550-8911.
PRODUCER & CO-CHAIRMAN
Arnold Kopelson - (818) 817-7175
Anne Kopelson - (818) 817-7170
PRESIDENT PRODUCTION
Ryan Engle - (818) 817-7165
CREATIVE EXECUTIVE
Emily Aaronson
EXECUTIVE ASSISTANT TO ANNE KOPELSON
Tyler Hisel

KRASNOFF FOSTER ENTERTAINMENT

(Production company)
c/o Paramount Pictures, 5555 Melrose Ave., Marx Bros. Bldg.
Room 110, Los Angeles, CA 90038. TEL: (323) 956-3934.
PRODUCER
Gary Foster, Russ Krasnoff
V.P., FEATURE DEVELOPMENT
Heather Petrigala
V.P., FEATURE DEVELOPMENT
Krista Carpenter

FRED KUEHNERT PRODUCTIONS

(Motion picture & independent film producer)
1601 Hilts Ave. #2, Los Angeles, CA 90024.
TEL: (310) 470-3363. email: FKuehnert@roadrunner.com
MANAGING PARTNER & PRODUCER
Fred Kuehnert
PARTNER/PRODUCER
Robert Birmingham, Billy Verkin
EXECUTIVE ASSISTANT
Sandra Chouinard

THE KUSHNER-LOCKE COMPANY

(Motion picture, independent film & TV producer & distributor)
280 S. Beverly Dr., Ste. 205, Beverly Hills, CA 90212.
TEL: (310) 275-7508. FAX: (310) 275-7518.
www.kushnerlocke.com
OFFICER
Alice Neuhauser

THE LADD COMPANY

(Motion picture, independent film & TV producer)
9255 Sunset Blvd., Ste. 620, West Hollywood, CA 90069.
TEL: (310) 777-2060. FAX: (310) 777-2061.
PRESIDENT
Alan Ladd, Jr.
V.P., DEVELOPMENT
Natasha Klibansky - (310) 777-2064

LAKESHORE ENTERTAINMENT GROUP, LLC.

(Motion picture producer & distributor)
9268 W. Third St., Beverly Hills, CA 90210.
TEL: (310) 867-8000. FAX: (310) 300-3015.
email: info@lakeshoreentertainment.com
www.lakeshoreentertainment.com
CHAIRMAN & CEO
Thomas B. Rosenberg
PRESIDENT, LAKESHORE ENTERTAINMENT
Gary Lucchesi
COO
Eric Reid
CFO
Marc Reid
EXECUTIVE V.P. & HEAD, PRODUCTION
Richard Wright
SENIOR V.P., BUSINESS & LEGAL AFFAIRS
Robert Benun
SENIOR V.P., DEVELOPMENT
Robert McMinn
V.P., BUSINESS & LEGAL AFFAIRS
Jennifer Brooks
V.P., PHYSICAL PRODUCTION
Andre Lamal
V.P., FINANCE
Dawn Ryan
DEVELOPMENT EXECUTIVE
Scott Herbst
OFFICE MANAGER
Kjose Elliot

LARGER THAN LIFE PRODUCTIONS

(Motion picture producer)
100 Universal City Plaza, Bldg. 5138, Universal City, CA
91608. TEL: (818) 777-4004. FAX: (818) 866-5677.
PRINCIPAL
Gary Ross
PRODUCER
Allison Thomas
PRODUCTION EXECUTIVE
Robin Bissell
DIRECTOR, DEVELOPMENT
Naketha Mattocks
CREATIVE EXECUTIVE
Casey Crowe

LATHAM ENTERTAINMENT

(Production company)
3200 Northline Ave., Ste. 210, Greensboro, NC 27408.
TEL: (336) 315-1440. FAX: (336) 315-1450.
email: info@lathamentertainment.com
www.lathamentertainment.com
PRESIDENT & PRODUCER
Walter Latham
LIVE EVENTS COORDINATOR
Bill Young
OPERATIONS MANAGER
Yulonda Smith

LAUFER FILM.COM

2340 Bellfield Ave., Cleveland, OH 44106.
TEL: (216) 229-4444. FAX: (216) 229-1214.
www.lauferfilm.com
CHAIRMAN
William C. Laufer
PRESIDENT
Tiffany A. Laufer

LEISURE TIME FEATURES

(Motion picture distributor)
40 Worth St., Rm. 1214, New York, NY 10013.
TEL: (212) 267-4501. FAX: (212) 267-4501.
email bpleisure@aol.com www.leisurefeat.com
PRESIDENT
Bruce Pavlow

THE LEVINSON/FONTANA COMPANY

(Production company)
185 Broome St., New York, NY 10002. TEL: (212) 206-3585.
FAX: (212) 206-3581. www.tomfontana.com
www.levinson.com
EXECUTIVE PRODUCER/DIRECTOR/WRITER
Barry Levinson
EXECUTIVE PRODUCER/WRITER
Tom Fontana
CFO/ BUSINESS AFFAIRS
Amy Solan
DIRECTOR, DEVELOPMENT
Jason Sosnoff

LIGHTHOUSE PRODUCTIONS

(Motion picture, independent films & TV producer)
120 El Camino Dr., Ste. 212, Beverly Hills, CA 90212.
TEL: (310) 859-4923. FAX: (310) 859-7511.
email: lighthouseprods@gmail.com
PRODUCER
Michael Phillips, Juliana Maio
DIRECTOR, DEVELOPMENT
Dianne Bloom

LIGHTMOTIVE, INC.

(Motion picture & TV producer)
10351 Santa Monica Blvd., #402, Los Angeles, CA 90025.
TEL: (310) 282-0660.
email: info@lightmotive.com www.lightmotive.com
PARTNER & CEO
Roland Joffe

LIGHTSTORM ENTERTAINMENT

(Production Company)
919 Santa Monica Blvd., Santa Monica, CA 90401.
TEL: (310) 656-6100. FAX: (310) 656-6102.

CHAIRMAN & CEO
James Cameron
PARTNER/COO
Jon Landau
V.P., PRODUCTION RESOURCES, SERVICES & TECHNOLOGY
Geoff Burdick
COORDINATOR, PRODUCTION RESOURCES, SERVICES & TECHNOLOGY
Joe Hagg, Charlie Palafox

LION ROCK PRODUCTIONS

(Motion picture, independent film & TV producer)
5100 Goldleaf Circle, Ste. 230, Los Angeles, CA 90056.
TEL: (323) 293-8833. FAX: (323) 293-8883.
DIRECTOR & PRODUCER
John Woo
PRODUCER
Terence Chang
SENIOR V.P.,
Lori Tilkin
DIRECTOR, FEATURE DEVELOPMENT
Todd Weinger

LIONSGATE

(Production and distribution company)
2700 Colorado Ave., Santa Monica, CA 90404.
TEL: (310) 449-9200. FAX: (310) 255-3870.
email: general-inquiries@lgf.com www.lionsgate.com
CO-CHAIRMAN & CEO
Jon Feltheimer
VICE CHAIRMAN
Michael Burns
CO-COO & PRESIDENT
Steve Beeks
CO-COO & PRESIDENT, MOTION PICTURE GROUP
Joe Drake
CFO
Jim Keegan
GENERAL COUNSEL & EXECUTIVE V.P., OF BUSINESS
Wayne Levin
CHIEF EXECUTIVE, LIONSGATE, UK
Zygi Kamasa
PRESIDENT, TV PROGRAMMING & PRODUCTION
Kevin Beggs
PRESIDENT, ACQUISITIONS & CO-PRODUCTIONS
Jason Constantine
PRESIDENT, GRINDSTONE
Barry Brooker
PRESIDENT, LIONSGATE MUSIC & PUBLISHING
Jay Faires
PRESIDENT, MOTION PICTURES MANDATE
Nathan Kahane
PRESIDENT, MANDATE INTERNATIONAL
Helen Lee-Kim
PRESIDENT, DIGITAL MEDIA
Curt Marvis
CO-PRESIDENT, DEBMAR-MERCURY
Ira Bernstein, Mort Marcus
CO-PRESIDENT, PRODUCTION
Michael Paseornek, Alli Shearmur
CO-PRESIDENT, FILM MARKETING
Sarah Greenberg, Tim Palen
MANAGING DIRECTOR, INTERNATIONAL TV
Peter Iacone
SENIOR EXECUTIVE V.P., MOTION PICTURE GROUP
Robert McEntegart
EXECUTIVE V.P. & COO, LIONSGATE TV
Sandra Stern
EXECUTIVE V.P., SUPPLY CHAIN & OPERATIONS
Akin Ceylan
EXECUTIVE V.P., HUMAN RESOURCES & ADMINISTRATION
Nancy Coleman
EXECUTIVE V.P., CIO
Leo Collins
EXECUTIVE V.P., PRODUCTION
Lisa Ellzey
EXECUTIVE V.P., TV DISTRIBUTION & DIGITAL SALES
Jon Ferro
EXECUTIVE V.P., BUSINESS & LEGAL AFFAIRS
James Gladstone
EXECUTIVE V.P., CORPORATE DEVELOPMENT
Brian Goldsmith
EXECUTIVE V.P., TV PRODUCTION
Gary Goodman
EXECUTIVE V.P./GENERAL MANAGER, TV GUIDE ONLINE
Paul Greenberg
EXECUTIVE V.P., SALES & DISTRIBUTION, HOME ENTERTAINMENT
Jed Grossman
EXECUTIVE V.P., FINANCE
Wes Guarino
EXECUTIVE V.P., INTERNATIONAL MARKETING
Brent Jack
EXECUTIVE V.P., BUSINESS & LEGAL AFFAIRS, ACQUISITIONS & CO-PRODUCTIONS
Wendy Jaffe
EXECUTIVE V.P., FAMILY ENTERTAINMENT
Ken Katsumoto
EXECUTIVE V.P., STRATEGIC PLANNING & OPERATIONS
Sean Kisker
EXECUTIVE V.P., FINANCIAL PLANNING & ANALYSIS
Ulrik Knap
EXECUTIVE V.P., PHYSICAL PRODUCTION, MANDATE
Kelli Konop
EXECUTIVE V.P., STRUCTURED FINANCE
Mark Manuel
EXECUTIVE V.P., BUSINESS & LEGAL AFFAIRS
Robert Melnik
EXECUTIVE V.P., FAMILY ENTERTAINMENT & MARKETING
Anne Parducci
EXECUTIVE V.P., EXHIBITOR RELATIONS
Mike Polydoros
EXECUTIVE V.P., INTERNATIONAL BUSINESS DEVELOPMENT
Paul Presburger
EXECUTIVE V.P., GENERAL MANAGER, HOME ENTERTAINMENT
Ron Schwartz
EXECUTIVE V.P., PRODUCTION
Donna Sloan
EXECUTIVE V.P., GENERAL MANAGER, DOMESTIC DISTRIBUTION
David Spitz
EXECUTIVE V.P., DOMESTIC TV SALES
Rand Stoll
EXECUTIVE V.P., TV DEVELOPMENT
Barbara Wall
EXECUTIVE V.P., POST PRODUCTION & DELIVERY SERVICES
Bob Wenokur
EXECUTIVE V.P., GENERAL MANAGER, BUSINESS AFFAIRS, LIONSGATE MUSIC & PUBLISHING
Lenny Wohl
SENIOR V.P., DVD PRODUCTION
Miguel Casillas
SENIOR V.P., INTERNATIONAL TV SALES
Craig Cegielski
SENIOR V.P., BUSINESS AFFAIRS TV
Matthew J. Kearns
SENIOR V.P., ACQUISITIONS & CO-PRODUCTIONS
Eda Kowan
SENIOR V.P., TV MARKETING
Priscilla Pesci
SENIOR V.P., DISTRIBUTION SERVICES
Danny St. Pierre
SENIOR V.P., INVESTOR RELATIONS & EXECUTIVE COMMUNICATION
Peter Wilkes - (310) 255-3726
V.P., INTERNATIONAL TV MARKETING
Teri Fleming
V.P., TV
Andy Richley
DIRECTOR, TV SALES
Hana Zidek
EXECUTIVE PRODUCER, DIGITAL MEDIA
Alex Barkaloff
MANAGER, INTERNATIONAL TV
Tori Crotts
MANAGER, TV
Whitney Timmons
COORDINATOR, INTERNATIONAL TV SALES
Max Lucas

Lionsgate acquired independent production and distribution company Mandate Pictures in September 2007. Mandate continues to operate from Beverly Hills under its existing brand.

LITTLE ENGINE PRODUCTIONS

(Production company)
500 S. Buena Vista Ave., Animation 3F-6, Burbank, CA 91521.
TEL: (818) 560-4670.
PARTNER & PRODUCER
Gina Matthews, Grant Scharbo
DIRECTOR, DEVELOPMENT
Mitchell Gutman

LIVE ACTION PICTURES

(Production & post-production video services)
P.O. Box 5155, Beverly Hills, CA 90210. TEL: (800) 470-4602, (310) 276-8196. www.johnlongenecker.com
PRODUCER/DIRECTOR
John Longenecker - John@JLemail.com

LIVEPLANET

(Motion picture & TV producer)
2644 30th St., Santa Monica, CA 90405. TEL: (310) 664-2400. FAX: (310) 664-2401. email: info@liveplanet.com

www.liveplanet.com
FOUNDERS
Ben Affleck, Matt Damon
CEO
Larry Tanz
SENIOR V.P., DEVEOPMENT & PRODUCTION
Marc Joubert, Keith Quinn
V.P., FINANCE & OPERATIONS
Emilie Golub

LONGBOW PRODUCTIONS

(Motion picture, independent film & TV producer)
14716 Burbank Blvd., Sherman Oaks, CA 91411.
TEL: (818) 602-4297. email: mail@longbowfilms.com
PARTNER
Richard Kughn, Ronnie D. Clemmer, Bill Pace
DIRECTOR, INFORMATION
Herman Hong

WARREN LOCKHART PRODUCTIONS, INC.

(Motion picture and TV production company)
P.O. Box 11629, Marina Del Rey, CA 90295.
TEL: (310) 306-4661. FAX: (310) 301-0536.
email: warren@lockhartproductions.com
PRESIDENT
Warren L. Lockhart

LOWSON INTERNATIONAL STUDIOS

(Motion picture, documentary and television production company)
P.O. Box 12766, Marina del Rey, CA 90295.
TEL: (310) 827-6798. email: lowsonintl@aol.com
www.lowsoninternational.com
CEO & COO
Kathleen Lowson

LUCASARTS ENTERTAINMENT COMPANY

(Video game producer & distributor)
P.O. Box 29908, San Francisco, CA 94129-0908,
1110 Gorgas Ave., San Francisco, CA 94129.
TEL: (415) 746-8000, (410) 568-3670. www.lucasarts.com
PRESIDENT
Jerry Bowerman
V.P., PRODUCTION OPERATIONS
Matt Manuel
ASSOCIATE GENERAL COUNSEL
Nell O'Donnell
V.P., FINANCE
Kevin Parker
V.P., GLOBAL PUBLISHING
Mary Bihrx

LUCASFILM, LTD.

(Motion picture producer)
P.O. Box 29901, San Francisco, CA 94129.
TEL: (415) 623-1000. www.lucasfilm.com
CHAIRMAN OF THE BOARD
George W. Lucas, Jr.
PRESIDENT & COO
Micheline Chau
V.P. OF FINANCE & CHIEF ACCOUNTING OFFICER
Steve Condiotti
V.P. & GENERAL MANAGER, LUCASFILM ANIMATION
Gail Currey
PRESIDENT, INDUSTRIAL LIGHT & MAGIC
Chrissie England
CHIEF TECHNOLOGY OFFICER
Richard Kerris
V.P. & GENERAL MANAGER, SKYWALKER SOUND
Glenn Kiser
PRESIDENT, LUCAS LICENSING
Howard Roffman
CHIEF ADMINISTRATIVE OFFICER
Ian van der Voort

MACEDON MEDIA, INC.

(Production company)
4816 Orchard Street, Suite 1000, Dearborn, MI 48126.
TEL: (248) 565 5603. email: spiroff@macedonmedia.com
www.macedonmedia.com
PRESIDENT/CEO/PRODUCER/DIRECTOR
Tom Spiroff

MAD CHANCE

(Motion picture producer)
Warner Bros., 4000 Warner Blvd., Burbank, CA 91522.
TEL: (818) 954-3500. FAX: (818) 954-3586
www.madchance.com
PRODUCER
Andrew Lazar - andrew@madchance.com
V.P., PRODUCTION & DEVELOPMENT
Miri Yoon - miri@madchance.com
VRATIV EXECUTIVE
Alana Mayo

MAGNOLIA PICTURES

(Distribution company)
49 W. 27th St., 7th Flr., New York, NY 10001.
TEL: (212) 924-6701. FAX: (212) 924-6742.
email: info@magpictures.com www.magpictures.com
CEO
Bill Banowksy
PRESIDENT
Eamonn Bowles
SENIOR V.P.
Matt Cowal, Tom Quinn
V.P., ACQUISITIONS
Dori Begley
HEAD, HOME ENTERTAINMENT
Randy Wells
HEAD, INTERNATIONAL SALES
Laird Adamson
HEAD, BUSINESS & LEGAL
Chris Matson

MALIBU BAY FILMS

(Motion picture distributor)
P.O. Box 17244, Beverly Hills, CA 90209-3244.
TEL: (310) 278-5056. www.andysidaris.com

MALPASO PRODUCTIONS

(Motion picture producer)
4000 Warner Blvd., Bldg. 81, Burbank, CA 91522-0811.
TEL: (818) 954-3367. FAX: (818) 954-4803.
PRODUCER & ACTOR & DIRECTOR
Clint Eastwood
PRODUCER
Robert Lorenz
EDITOR
Joel Cox

MANDALAY PICTURES

(Motion picture producer & distributor)
4751 Wilshire Blvd., 3rd Flr., Los Angeles, CA 90010.
TEL: (323) 549-4300. FAX: (323) 549-9832.
www.mandalay.com
CHAIRMAN & CEO
Peter Guber
VICE CHAIRMAN & COO
Paul Schaeffer
PRESIDENT, MANDALAY PICTURES
Cathy Schulman
PRESIDENT, MANDALAY VISION
Celine Rattray
EXECUTIVE V.P., MOTION PICTURE PRODUCTION
David Zelon
EXECUTIVE V.P., CORPORATE OPERATIONS
Shelly Riney
EXECUTIVE V.P.
Peter Strauss
EXECUTIVE V.P., MOTION PICTURE PRODUCTION
David Zelon
SENIOR V.P., BUSINESS AFFAIRS
Michelle Hastings
SENIOR V.P., PRODUCTION & DEVELOPMENT
Scarlett Lacey
V.P., PRODUCTION & DEVELOPMENT
Adam Stone, Hardy Justice (NY)
MANAGER, BUSINESS AFFAIRS ADMINISTRATION
Carmody Herzberg
CREATIVE CONSULTANT
Marcy Drogin
BUSINESS AFFAIRS CONSULTANT
Alan Krieger

MANDATE PICTURES

(Production company. A Lionsgate company)
2700 Colorado Ave., Ste. 501, Santa Monica, CA 90404.
TEL: (310) 360-1441. FAX: (310) 360-1447.
email: info@mandatepictures.com
PRESIDENT
Nathan Kahane - nk@mandatepictures.com
CFO
Matt Bakal - mbakal@mandatepictures.com
EXECUTIVE V.P., PHYSICAL PRODUCTION
Kelli Konop
SENIOR V.P.s, PRODUCTION
Lawrence Grey, Nicole Brown
SENIOR V.P., BUSINESS & LEGAL AFFAIRS
Dan Freedman
V.P., MARKETING & PUBLICITY
Candice Grabois
V.P., BUSINESS & LEGAL AFFAIRS
Craig A. Kessler
DIRECTOR, PHYSICAL PRODUCTION
Jennie Yamaki
DIRECTOR, DEVELOPMENT
Mary Lee

MANDY FILMS

(Motion picture & TV producer)
9201 Wilshire Blvd., #206, Beverly Hills, CA 90210.
TEL: (310) 246-0500. FAX: (310) 246-0350.
PRESIDENT
Leonard Goldberg
V.P., DEVELOPMENT & PRODUCTION
Amanda Goldberg

MANIFEST FILM COMPANY

(Production Company)
1810 14th St., Ste. 201, Santa Monica, CA 90404.
TEL: (310) 450-9339.
email: info@manifestfilms.com
PRODUCER
Janet Yang

LAURENCE MARK PRODUCTIONS

(Motion picture & TV producer)
10202 W. Washington Blvd., Poitier Bldg., Culver City, CA 90232. TEL: (310) 244-5239. FAX: 310-244-0055.
PRESIDENT & PRODUCER
Laurence Mark
SENIOR V.P.
David Blackman
CREATIVE EXECUTIVE
Tamara Chestna
PRODUCTION OFFICE MANAGER
Petra Alexandria

MARVEL STUDIOS, INC.

c/o Raleigh Studios, 1600 Rosecrans Ave., Bldg 7A, Ste. 110
Manhattan Beach, CA 90266.
TEL: (310) 727-2700. FAX: (310) 536-0415. www.marvel.com

Marvel Entertainment, Inc., 417 5th. Ave., New York, NY 10016. TEL: (212) 576-4000.
PRESIDENT, MARVEL STUDIOS
Kevin Feige
CO-PRESIDENT, MARVEL STUDIOS
Louis D'Esposito
PRESIDENT, MARVEL ANIMATION
Eric Rollman
COO
Tim Connors
CCO, MARVEL ENTERTAINMENT
Joe Quesada
EXECUTIVE V.P., VISUAL EFFECTS
Victoria Alonso
EXECUTIVE V.P., INTERNATIONAL MARKETING
Douglas Finberg
EXECUTIVE V.P., OFFICE OF THE CHAIRMAN
Alan Fine, John Turitzin
EXECUTIVE V.P., GLOBAL DIGITAL MEDIA GROUP
Ira Rubenstein
SENIOR V.P., PRODUCTION FINANCE
Mike Revell
SENIOR V.P., RETAIL DEVELOPMENT
Mark Rhodes
SENIOR V.P., LEGAL AFFAIRS
Mike Ross
SENIOR V.P., PLANNING & INVESTOR RELATIONS
Rob Steffens
SENIOR V.P., PRODUCTION & DEVELOPMENT
Craig Kyle
SENIOR V.P., LEGAL AFFAIRS
Elizabeth Lynch
SENIOR V.P., PRODUCTION & DEVELOPMENT
Stephen Broussard
SENIOR V.P., PRODUCTION & DEVELOPMENT, FEATURES
Jeremy Latcham
V.P., PRODUCTION & DEVELOPMENT
Jodi Hildebrand
V.P., ANIMATION DEVELOPMENT
Cort Lane
DIRECTOR, DEVELOPMENT FEATURES
Tom Cohen
DIRECTOR, CREATIVE DEVELOPMENT, ANIMATION
Joshua Fine
DIRECTOR, INFORMATION & STUDIO TECHNOLOGY
Sean Flynn
EXECUTIVE COUNSEL, BUSINESS & LEGAL AFFAIRS
Ryan Potter
MARKETING CONSULTANT
Tom Sherak

Disney announced on August 31, 2009 that it had acquired Marvel Entertainment and its portfolio of over 5,000 characters for approximately $4 billion.

MATRIXX INTERNET DISTRIBUTION

(Home of pay-per-view.com - homevideo.net and independent-production.tv)
223 W. Lancaster Ave., Devon, PA 19333.
TEL: (800) 576-2001, (610) 688-9212.
email: contact@mecfilms.com www.mecfilms.com/mid
PRESIDENT & CEO
James Jaeger
SENIOR V.P., MARKETING
Dan Kingsley
DIRECTOR, PUBLIC RELATIONS
Lorraine Sterling

THE MATTHAU COMPANY, INC.

(Production Company)
4250 Wilshire Blvd., Los Angeles, CA 90010.
TEL: (310) 454-3300. email: creativedirector@matthau.com
www.matthau.com
PRESIDENT
Charles Matthau
HEAD, PRODUCTION
Michael Meltzer
DIRECTORS, CREATIVE AFFAIRS
Lana Morgan, Judd Rubin
DIRECTOR, TECHNOLOGY
Jeff Bullard
BUSINESS AFFAIRS
Jessica Cooper
STORY EDITOR
Reuben Sack

MBST ENTERTAINMENT, INC.

(Production company)
345 N. Maple Dr., Ste. 200, Beverly Hills, CA 90210.
TEL: (310) 385-1820. FAX: (310) 385-1834.
PARTNER
Larry Brezner, David Steinberg, Stephen Tenenbaum
MANAGER
Jonathan Brandstein, Andrew D. Tenenbaum

MEDIA 8 ENTERTAINMENT

(Production company)
15260 Ventura Blvd., Suite 710, Sherman Oaks, CA. 91403.
TEL: (818) 325-8000. FAX: (818) 325 8020.
email: info@media8entertainment.com
www.media8entertainment.com
PRESIDENT
Stewart Hall
CFO
Devin Cutler
V.P., ACQUISITIONS
Audrey Delaney
DIRECTOR, CREATIVE AFFAIRS
Randy Dannenberg

MERCHANT-IVORY

(Motion picture producer & distributor)
P.O. Box 338 - Coooper Station, New York, NY 10276.
TEL: (212) 582-8049. FAX: (201) 222-1448.
email: contact@merchantivory.com www.merchantivory.com
PRESIDENT/DIRECTOR
James Ivory
EXECUTIVE V.P./PRODUCER (EUROPE)
Paul Bradley
EXECUTIVE V.P./PRODUCER (USA)
Pierre Proner
COORDINATOR/ DIRECTOR, DEVELOPMENT (USA)
Neil Jesuele
COORDINATOR
Simon Oxley (EUROPE)

METRO-GOLDWYN-MAYER STUDIOS, INC. (MGM)

(Production & distribution company)
10250 Constellation Blvd., Los Angeles, CA 90067.
TEL: (310)-449-3000. FAX: (310) 449-3100. www.mgm.com

1350 Ave. of the Americas, New York, NY 10019-4870.
TEL: (212) 708-0300. FAX: (212) 708-0337. www.mgm.com
CO-CHAIRMEN/CEOs
Gary Barber, Roger Birnbaum
VICE CHAIRMAN
Stephen Cooper
PRESIDENT, FINANCE & ADMINISTRATION & CFO
Bedi A. Singh
CO-PRESIDENT, WORLDWIDE TV
Gary Marenzi, Jim Packer
SENIOR EXECUTIVE V.P.
Charlie Cohen
PRESIDENT, WORLDWIDE THEATRICAL DISTRIBUTION, HOME ENTERTAINMENT & ACQUISITIONS
Erik Lomis
SENIOR EXECUTIVE V.P., WORLWIDE MOTION PICTURES GROUP
Charlie Cohen
EXECUTIVE V.P., WORLDWIDE TELEVISION & LEGAL AFFAIRS
Gerald Ament
EXECUTIVE V.P., SECRETARY & GENERAL COUNSEL
Scott Packman

EXECUTIVE V.P., THEATRICAL MARKETING MGM, PRESIDENT, MARKETING, UNITED ARTISTS
Michael Vollman
EXECUTIVE V.P., WORLDWIDE DIGITAL MEDIA
Douglas Lee
EXECUTIVE V.P., BUSINESS AFFAIRS
Jonathan Bader
EXECUTIVE V.P., PRODUCTION, WORLDWIDE MOTION PICTURE GROUP
Cale Boyter
EXECUTIVE V.P., WORLDWIDE THEATRICAL PHYSICAL PRODUCTION
Dan Kolsrud
EXECUTIVE VICE PRESIDENTS/GENERAL SALES MANAGER, DOMESTIC THEATRICAL DISTRIBUTION
Jim Orr
EXECUTIVE V.P., WORLDWIDE TV DISTRIBUTION, NORTH AMERICA
Joe Patrick
SENIOR V.P., THEATRICAL MARKETING & NATIONAL PARTNERSHIPS
Christine Batista
SENIOR V.P., NATIONAL PUBLICITY
Kristen Borella
SENIOR V.P., FINANCE
Chris Bosco
SENIOR V.P., THEATRICAL BUSINESS AFFAIRS
Erik Ellner
SENIOR V.P., ADMINISTRATION, DOMESTIC THEATER DISTRIBUTION
Jeff Greenspun
SENIOR V.P., THEATRICAL PRODUCTION
Luke Ryan
SENIOR V.P., THEATRICAL MARKETING
Justin Slobig
V.P., NATIONAL PUBLICITY
Kristin Borella
V.P., BUSINESS AFFAIRS
Stephen Fisch
V.P., DEVELOPMENT, WORLDWIDE MOTION PICTURE GROUP
Becky Sloviter
V.P., EXHIBITOR RELATIONS
Kathy Vlesmas
V.P., DIRECT-TO-VIDEO PRODUCTION
Jason Weiss
DIVISION V.P., DOMESTIC THEATRICAL DISTRIBUTION
Sharon Jaeckel, Lawrence Massey
DIRECTOR, CORPORATE PUBLICITY
Grey Munford
DIRECTOR, DEVELOPMENT
Pam Silverstein

During 2010, Metro-Goldwyn-Mayer Inc., was subject to a fierce takeover battle between Spyglass' Gary Barber and Roger Birnbaum and a Carl Ichan backed Lionsgate. The company went into a pre-packaged bankruptcy, with $4 billion in debt converted into equity, and the creditors finally approved the Spyglass proposal. The company owns a large library of films, comprising approximately 4,100 titles.

MIDNIGHT ENTERTAINMENT

(Production company)
11846 Ventura Blvd., Ste. 208, Studio City, CA 91604.
TEL: (818) 752-0197. FAX: (818) 752-1789.
DIRECTOR & PRODUCER
Wes Craven
PRODUCER
Jonathan Craven
V.P., DEVELOPMENT
Cody Zwieg
CREATIVE EXECUTIVE
Carly Feingold
EXECUTIVE ASSISTANT
Andrew Schwarz

MINDFIRE ENTERTAINMENT

3740 Overland Ave., Ste. E, Los Angeles, CA 90034.
TEL: (310) 204-4481. FAX: (310) 204-5882.
email: info@mindfireentertainment.com
www.mindfireentertainment.com
CHAIRMAN
Mark Gottwald

MIRACLE PICTURES

(Motion picture & TV producer)
1223 Wilshire Blvd., #916, Santa Monica, CA 90403.
TEL: (310) 392-3011. FAX: (310) 392-2021.
email: miraclela@aol.com
PRESIDENT
A. Kitman Ho
ADMINISTRATION & DEVELOPMENT
Robb Earnest

MIRAMAX FILMS

(Production and Distribution company)
161 Ave. of the Americas, New York, NY 10013.
TEL: (917) 606-5500. FAX: (917) 606-5643
www.miramax.com

8439 Sunset Blvd., West Hollywood, CA 90069.
TEL: (323) 822-4100. FAX: (323) 822-4216.

Miramax was sold to Filmyard Holdings in 2010, owned by Ron Tutor and his partners, who bought the Miramax library from Disney for slightly more than $600 million. The deal includes the rights to more than 700 film titles at the company built by Harvey and Bob Weinstein and bought by Disney in the early 1990s.

THE MIRISCH CORPORATION OF CALIFORNIA

(Motion picture, independent film & TV producer)
100 Universal City Plaza, Bldg. 1320 #2C, Universal City, CA 91608-1085. TEL: (818) 777-1271. FAX: (818) 866-1422.
PRODUCER
Walter Mirisch

MISHER FILMS

(Production company)
12233 Olympic Blvd., Ste. 130, Los Angeles, CA 90064.
TEL: (310) 405-7999. FAX: (310) 405-7991.
www.misherfilms.com
PRODUCER/OWNER
Kevin Misher
PRODUCTION EXECUTIVE
Andrew Berman, Kevin Ping Chang
ASSISTANT
Leigh Janiak

MOD3 PRODUCTIONS

(Production company)
10390 Wilshire Blvd., Ste. 1104, Los Angeles, CA 90024.
TEL: (310) 285-8036. www.mod3productions.com
PARTNER
Danny Gold - dgold@mod3productions.com
Matthew Asner - masner@mod3productions.com

MODA ENTERTAINMENT, INC.

590 Madison Ave., 21st Flr., New York, NY 10022.
TEL: (212) 873-3324. FAX: (212) 504-3215.
email: info@modaentertainment.com
www.modaentertainment.com
CEO
Richard Zampella
EXECUTIVE V.P.,
John Mulholland
VICE PRESIDENT
Jack Green
PUBLIC & INVESTOR RELATIONS
Shannon Mulholland

THE MONTECITO PICTURE COMPANY/COLD SPRING PICTURES, LLC

(Motion picture & TV producer)
9465 Wilshire Blvd., Ste. 920, Beverly Hills, CA 90212.
TEL: (310) 247-9880, (805) 565-8590. FAX: (310) 247-9498, (805) 565-1893.
EXECUTIVE
Ivan Reitman, Tom Pollock, Joe Medjuck

MOONSTONE ENTERTAINMENT

(Motion picture producer & distributor)
P.O. Box 7400, Studio City, CA 91614.
www.moonstonefilms.com
TEL: (818) 985-3003. FAX: (818) 985-3009.
CEO
Ernst Stroh
PRESIDENT
Yael Stroh
EXECUTIVE V.P.
Luz Moretti
V.P., FINANCE
Greg Majerus
DIRECTOR, PRODUCTION & MARKETING
Michael Grant, Shahar Stroh

MORGAN CREEK PRODUCTIONS

(Production company)
10351 Santa Monica Blvd., Ste. 200, Los Angeles, CA 90025.
TEL: (310) 432-4848. FAX: (310) 432-4844.
www.morgancreek.com
CHAIRMAN & CEO
James G. Robinson
CHAIRMAN & COO
Rick Nicita
CFO
Gary Stutman
EXECUTIVE V.P., WORLDWIDE MARKETING
Greg Mielcarz
SENIOR V.P., DEVELOPMENT
Larry Katz

SENIOR V.P.
David Robinson
V.P., PHYSICAL & POST PRODUCTION
Andy Fraser
PRESIDENT, INTERNATIONAL SALES
Daniel Diamond
MANAGING DIRECTOR, INTERNATIONAL
Brian Robinson
BUSINESS & LEGAL AFFAIRS
Don Hardison

MOTION CITY FILMS

(Film, video & interactive media producer)
1847 Centinela Ave., Santa Monica, CA 90404.
TEL: (310) 264-4870. FAX: (310) 264-4871.
email: editor@motioncity.com www.motioncity.com
PRODUCING DIRECTOR
G. Michael Witt

MOTION PICTURE CORPORATION OF AMERICA

(Motion picture producer & distributor)
10635 Santa Monica Blvd., Ste. 180, Los Angeles, CA 90025.
TEL: (310) 319-9500. FAX: (310) 319-9501.
www.mpcafilm.com
CHAIRMAN & CEO
Brad Krevoy
EXECUTIVE V.P., PRODUCTION
Brad Jenkel
SENIOR V.P., INTERNATIONAL SALES & MARKETING
Francisco Gonzalez
SENIOR V.P., DEVELOPMENT & PRODUCTION OPERATIONS
Reuben Liber
V.P., DEVELOPMENT & PRODUCTION
Mike Callaghan
DIRECTOR, PRODUCTION
Justin Bursch

MOVING PICTURES, LTD.

(Motion picture & video support; equipment rentals & sales)
812 West Layton Ave., Salt Lake City, UT 84104.
TEL: (801) 973-0632. FAX: (801) 973-0380.
email: mail@movingpics.net www.movingpics.net
CONTACT
Troy Parkinson

MOZARK PRODUCTIONS

(Features & television producer)
4024 Radford Ave., Bldg. 5, #104, Studio City, CA 91604.
TEL: (818) 655-5779. FAX: (818) 655-5129.
email: mozark@mptp.com
EXECUTIVE PRODUCER & WRITER
Linda Bloodworth-Thomason
EXECUTIVE PRODUCER & DIRECTOR
Harry Thomason
PRODUCER
Douglas Jackson

MR. MUDD

(Motion picture, independent film & TV producer)
137 N. Larchmont Blvd., #113, Los Angeles, CA 90036.
TEL: (323) 932-5656. www.mrmudd.com
PRODUCER & DIRECTOR
John Malkovich
PRODUCER
Lianne Halfon, Russ Smith

MUSE PRODUCTIONS, INC.

(Motion picture, independent film & TV producer. No unsolicited submissions)
15 Brooks Ave., Unit B, Venice, CA 90921.
TEL: (310) 450-2576. FAX: (310) 574-2614.
www.musefilm.com
PRESIDENT
Chris Hanley
CO-PRESIDENT
Roberta Hanley
HEAD, PRODUCTION
Bradford L. Schlei
PRODUCTION EXECUTIVE
Jonathan Fong

MUTUAL FILM COMPANY

150 S. Rodeo Dr., Ste. 120, Beverly Hills, CA 90212.
TEL: (310) 855-7355. FAX: (310) 855-7356.
email: inquiries@mutualfilm.com
PRINCIPAL
Gary Levinsohn
V.P., OPERATIONS & ADMINISTRATION
Lesly Gross
V.P., DEVELOPMENT & PRODUCTION
Shelly Clippard

MYRIAD PICTURES

(Production and distribution company)
3015 Main St., Ste. 400, Santa Monica, CA 90405.
TEL: (310) 279-4000. FAX: (310) 279-4001.
www.myriadpictures.com
PRESIDENT & CEO
Kirk D'Amico
CFO
Kevin Forester
EXECUTIVE V.P., MARKETING & PUBLICITY
Pam Rodi
SENIOR V.P., DISTRIBUTION
Jeffrey Engelen
SENIOR V.P., BUSINESS & LEGAL AFFAIRS
David Ducar
V.P., PRODUCTION & DEVELOPMENT
Amanda Blue
V.P., DISTRIBUTION
Lisa Gutberlet
DIRECTOR, SALES & ADMINISTRATION
Romana Samaritani
DIRECTOR, SERVICING
Val Sivkov
MANAGER, ACCOUNTING
Rachel Bozung
MANAGER, MARKETING & PUBLICITY
Amanda Dettrow

NALA FILMS

(Production company)
2016 Broadway, Santa Monica, CA 90404.
TEL: (310) 264-2555. FAX: (310) 828-6146.
email: productionservices@nalafilms.com www.nalafilms.com
CEO
Emilio Diez Barroso
PRESIDENT & COO
Darlene Caamaño-Loquet
SENIOR V.P., FINANCE
Chris Doss
DIRECTOR, DEVELOPMENT
Rudolf Scalese

NATIONAL GEOGRAPHIC FILMS

(Motion picture & TV producer)
9100 Wilshire Blvd., Ste. 401E, Beverly Hills, CA 90212.
TEL: (310) 858-5800. FAX: (310) 858-5801.
www.nationalgeographic.com
PRESIDENT
Daniel Battsek
V.P., ACQUISITIONS & PRODUCTION
Kattie Evans
CREATIVE EXECUTIVE
Kenna Jones

NATIONAL LAMPOON

(Production & Distribution company)
8228 Sunset Blvd., Los Angeles, CA 90046.
TEL: (310) 474-5252. FAX: (310) 474-1219.
email: cora@nationallampoon.com www.nationallampoon.com
PRESIDENT/CEO
Timothy S. Durham
PRESIDENT/WORLDWIDE DISTRIBUTION
Tom Daniels

NBC UNIVERSAL CORPORATE

(Production company)
3000 W. Alameda Ave., Burbank, CA 91523-0001.
TEL: (818) 840-4444, (818) 777-1000. www.nbcuni.com
CHAIRMAN, NBC ENTERTAINMANE & UNIVERSAL MEDIA STUDIOS
Jeff Gaspin
CO-CHAIRMAN, NBC ENTERTAINMENT & UNIVERSAL MEDIA STUDIOS
Marc Graboff
CHAIRMAN, NBC UNIVERSAL SPORTS & OLYMPICS
Dick Ebersol
CHIEF MARKETING OFFICER, NBC UNIVERSAL TELEVISION GROUP
PRESIDENT & CEO, NBC UNIVERSAL ENTERTAINMENT
Jeff Zucker
PRESIDENT & COO, UNIVERSAL STUDIOS
Ron Meyer
PRESIDENT, NBC UNIVERSAL INTERNATIONAL
Peter Smith
PRESIDENT, PRIMETIME ENTERTAINMENT & INTERNATIONAL TV PRODUCTION, NBC ENTERTAINMENT & UNIVERSAL MEDIA STUDIOS
Angela Bromstad
PRESIDENT, NBC NEWS
Steve Capus
PRESIDENT, NBC TV NETWORK & MEDIA WORKS
John Eck

PRESIDENT, INTERNATIONAL TV PRODUCTIONS, NBC UNIVERSAL INTERNATIONAL (LONDON)
Michael Edelstein
PRESIDENT, AD SALES
Marianne Gambelli
PRESIDENT, GLOBAL NETWORKS & DIGITAL INITIATIVES, NBC UNIVERSAL INTERNATIONAL
Roma Khanna
PRESIDENT, BUSINESS OPERATIONS, STRATEGY & DEVELOPMENT
Salil Mehta
PRESIDENT, NBC UNIVERSAL DIGITAL MEDIA SALES
Peter Naylor
PRESIDENT, NBC UNIVERSAL SALES & MARKETING
Mike Pilot
PRESIDENT, NBC LOCAL MEDIA DIVISION
John Wallace
PRESIDENT, RESEARCH & MEDIA DEVELOPMENT, NBC
Alan Wurtzel
EXECUTIVE V.P., HUMAN RESOURCES
Marc Chini
EXECUTIVE V.P. & CFO
Lynn Calpeter
EXECUTIVE V.P. & GENERAL COUNSEL
Rick Cotton
EXECUTIVE V.P., CORPORATE COMMUNICATIONS, NBC UNIVERSAL
Allison Gollust
EXECUTIVE V.P., NBC UNIVERSAL STRATEGIC PARTNERSHIP GROUP
Jay Linden
EXECUTIVE V.P., DIVERSITY
Paula Madison
EXECUTIVE V.P., CABLE AD SALES, NBC UNIVERSAL
Steve Mandala
EXECUTIVE V.P., NBC ENTERTAINMENT & NBC UNIVERSAL CABLE PUBLIC RELATIONS
Rebecca Marks
EXECUTIVE V.P., INTERNATIONAL TV PRODUCTIONS, NBC UNIVERSAL INTERNATIONAL
Deborah Oppenheimer
EXECUTIVE V.P., CIO
H. David Overbeeke
EXECUTIVE V.P., TV PRODUCTION, TECHNOLOGY & OPERATIONS BUSINESS
Dan Renaldo
EXECUTIVE V.P., NEWS, PROMOTION & ORIGINAL CONTENT, NBC UNIVERSAL TELEVISION STATIONS
Phyllis Schwartz
EXECUTIVE V.P., GLOBAL POLICY STRATEGIES & ALLIANCES, NBC UNIVERSAL
Cory Shields
EXECUTIVE V.P./COO, NBC UNIVERSAL AD SALES
Edward Swindler
EXECUTIVE V.P., ALTERNATIVE PROGRAMMING & DEVELOPMENT, NBC ENTERTAINMENT & UNIVERSAL MEDIAL STUDIOS
Paul Teledgy
SENIOR V.P., STRATEGIC INITIATIVE
Michael Bass
SENIOR V.P., STRATEGIC MARKETING
Barbara Blangiardi
SENIOR V.P., TECHNOLOGY & OPERATIONS, NBC UNIVERSAL TELEVISION STATIONS & NETWORK OPERATIONS
Matthew Braatz
SENIOR V.P., LOCAL DIGITAL MEDIA & MULTIPLATFORM, NBC LOCAL MEDIA DIVISION
Brian Buchwald
SENIOR V.P., MOBILE PLATFORM DEVELOPMENT
Salil Dalvi
SENIOR V.P./GENERAL MANAGER, NBC EVERYWHERE
Mark French
SENIOR V.P., INTERNAL COMMUNICATIONS, NBC UNIVERSAL & CORPORATE AFFAIRS UNIVERSAL STUDIOS
Cindy Gardner
SENIOR V.P., CORPORATE COMMUNICATIONS & MEDIA RELATIONS
Kathy Kelly-Brown
SENIOR V.P., PUBLICITY, MARKETING, CORPORATE COMMUNICATIONS, NBC
Curt King
SENIOR V.P., MARKET DEVELOPMENT
Deborah Reichig
SENIOR V.P., COMMERCIAL EXCELLENCE
John Sabino
SENIOR V.P., STRATEGIC GROWTH INITIATIVES, NBC UNIVERSAL TELEVISION STATIONS
Steve Schwaid
SENIOR V.P., ENTERTAINMENT PUBLICITY
Deborah Thomas
V.P., TALENT DEVELOPMENT, NBC UNIVERSAL
Kelly Edwards
V.P., INTERNATIONAL TV PRODUCTION
Mike Beale
V.P., PROGRAMMING & PROMOTIONS, TELEMUNDO CABLE
Yolanda Foster
V.P., PUBLICITY, NBC ENTERTAINMENT
Nate Kirtman
V.P., INCLUSION & BUSINESS DIVERSITY
Debra Langford
GENERAL MANAGER, STRATEGIC VENTURES, NBC UNIVERSAL
Mike Steib

UNIVERSAL STUDIOS

PRESIDENT & COO, UNIVERSAL STUDIOS
Ron Meyer
CHAIRMAN, UNIVERSAL PICTURES
Adam Fogelson
CO-CHAIRMAN, UNIVERSAL PICTURES
Donna Langley
VICE CHAIRMAN, UNIVERSAL PICTURES/ EXECUTIVE V.P., UNIVERSAL STUDIOS
Rick Finkelstein
CO-PRESIDENT, PRODUCTION
Jimmy Horowitz
EXECUTIVE V.P./CFO
Sean Gamble
EXECUTIVE V.P., HUMAN RESOURCES
Kenneth L. Kahrs
EXECUTIVE V.P. & GENERAL COUNSEL
Maren Christensen
CO-PRESIDENT, MARKETING, UNIVERSAL PICTURES
Michael Moses
SENIOR V.P., MEDIA RELATIONS, UNIVERSAL PICTURES
Kori Bernards
SENIOR V.P., LITIGATION
David Burg
SENIOR V.P., INTERNAL COMMUNICATIONS, NBC UNIVERSAL & CORPORATE AFFAIRS, UNIVERSAL STUDIOS
Cindy Gardner
SENIOR V.P., INDUSTRIAL RELATIONS
Keith Gorham
V.P., EMPLOYMENT COUNSEL
Nestor Barrero
V.P., LABOR RELATIONS
Stephanie Caprielian
V.P., HUMAN RESOURCES
Primo Custodio
V.P., ANTI-PIRACY OPERATIONS
Karen Elliott
V.P., SENIOR LABOR COUNSEL
Sheldon Kasdan
V.P., SENIOR TRADEMARK COUNSEL
Anne Nielsen
V.P., GOVERNMENT AFFAIRS
Steve Nissen
V.P., GENERAL TAX COUNSEL
Marc Palotay
V.P., LABOR & LEGAL AFFAIRS
William Phillips, Jr.
V.P., LEGAL
Crystal Wright

Universal Studios is a part of NBC Universal, one of the world's leading media and entertainment companies in the development, production, and marketing of entertainment, news, and information to a global audience.

UNIVERSAL STUDIOS HOME ENTERTAINMENT

10 Universal City Plaza, Universal City, CA 91608.
TEL: (818) 777-1000. www.universalstudios.com
PRESIDENT, UNIVERSAL STUDIOS HOME ENTERTAINMENT & UNIVERSAL PICTURES DIGITAL PLATFORMS
Craig Kornblau
EXECUTIVE V.P./COO
Tom Emrey
EXECUTIVE V.P., MARKETING
Hilary Hoffman
EXECUTIVE V.P., SALES
Dick Longwell
EXECUTIVE V.P., GENERAL MANAGER, UNIVERSAL STUDIOS HOME ENTERTAINMENT FAMILY PRODUCTIONS
Glen Ross
SENIOR V.P., MARKETING SERVICES
Pam Blum
SENIOR V.P., ANIMATION, UNIVERSAL STUDIOS HOME ENTERTAINMENT FAMILY PRODUCTIONS
Ellen Cockrill

SENIOR V.P., LIVE-ACTION PRODUCTION, UNIVERSAL STUDIOS HOME ENTERTAINMENT FAMILY PRODUCTIONS
Patti Jackson
SENIOR V.P., BUSINESS & LEGAL AFFAIRS
Christine Lawton
SENIOR V.P./CFO, PLANNING & FINANCE
John Morici
SENIOR V.P., COMMUNICATIONS & PUBLICITY
Lea Porteneuve
SENIOR V.P., WORLDWIDE HD MARKETING
Robert Read
V.P., TV & CATALOG MARKETING
Jeff Ackermann
V.P., NEW RELEASE BRAND MARKETING
Sandy Choi
V.P., FAMILY MARKETING
Paige Lewis
V.P., DIGITAL MARKETING
Mike Wokosin

UNIVERSAL PICTURES
100 Universal City Plaza, Universal City, CA 91608.
TEL: (818) 777-1000 www.universalstudios.com
CHAIRMAN
Adam Fogelson
CO-CHAIRMAN
Donna Langley
VICE CHAIRMAN, UNIVERSAL PICTURES & EXECUTIVE V.P., UNIVERSAL STUDIOS
Rick Finkelstein
PRESIDENT, UNIVERSAL PICTURES
James M. Horowitz
PRESIDENT, PRODUCTION
Debbie Liebling
PRESIDENT, PHYSICAL PRODUCTION
Andrew Fenady
PRESIDENT, MARKETING
Eddie Egan
PRESIDENT, UNIVERSAL HOME ENTERTAINMENT, UNIVERSAL PICTURES DIGITAL PLATFORMS
Craig Kornblau
PRESIDENT, INTERNATIONAL
David Kosse
PRESIDENT, UNIVERSAL PICTURES INTERNATIONAL ENTERTAINMENT
Eddie Cunningham
PRESIDENT, INTERNATIONAL PRODUCTION & ACQUISITIONS, UNIVERSAL PICTURES INTERNATIONAL
Christian Grass
PRESIDENT, FILM MUSIC & PUBLISHING
Mike Knobloch
PRESIDENT, DISTRIBUTION
Nikki Rocco
PRESIDENT, UNIVERSAL PARTNERSHIPS & LICENSING
Stephanie Sperber
EXECUTIVE V.P., GENERAL MANAGER, DISTRIBUTION
Nicholas Carpou
EXECUTIVE V.P., CREATIVE ADVERTISING
Frank Chiocchi
EXECUTIVE V.P., UNIVERSAL PICTURES INTERNATIONAL
Duncan Clark
EXECUTIVE V.P., MEDIA ADVERTISING
Suzanne Cole
EXECUTIVE V.P., PRODUCTION
Peter Cramer, Tracy Falco
EXECUTIVE V.P., GENERAL MANAGER, DISTRIBUTION
Mark Gaines
EXECUTIVE V.P./CFO, UNIVERSAL STUDIOS
Sean Gamble
EXECUTIVE V.P., MUSIC CREATIVE AFFAIRS
Harry Garfield
EXECUTIVE V.P., NATIONAL PUBLICITY
Alissa Grayson
EXECUTIVE V.P., PHYSICAL PRODUCTION
Bret Johnson
EXECUTIVE V.P., PRODUCTION
Jeffrey Kirschenbaum
EXECUTIVE V.P., SALES & CATEGORY MANAGEMENT, USHE
Richard Longwell
EXECUTIVE V.P., POST PRODUCTION
Greig McRitchie
EXECUTIVE V.P., CREATIVE ADVERTISING
Maria Pekurovskaya
EXECUTIVE V.P./GENERAL MANAGER, FAMILY PRODUCTION, HOME ENTERTAINMENT
Glenn Ross
EXECUTIVE V.P., BUSINESS DEVELOPMENT & STRATEGIC PLANNING
Jessica Schell
EXECUTIVE V.P., UNIVERSAL PARTNERSHIPS & LICENSING
Amy Taylor
EXECUTIVE V.P., INTERNATIONAL PRODUCTION, FOCUS FEATURES INTERNATIONAL (LONDON)
Clare Wise
EXECUTIVE V.P., WORLDWIDE CREATIVE OPERATION
Dan Wolfe
SENIOR V.P., CREATIVE ADVERTISING
Scott Abraham
SENIOR V.P./GENERAL MANAGER, DISTRIBUTION
Eugene Amodeo
SENIOR V.P., BROADCAST ASSETS
Austin Barker
SENIOR V.P., VISUAL EFFECTS PRODUCTION
Jennifer Bell
SENIOR V.P., CREATIVE SERVICES
Julie Berk
SENIOR V.P., MEDIA RELATIONS
Kori Bernards
SENIOR V.P., MARKETING SERVICES
Pam Blum
SENIOR V.P., SPECIAL PROJECTS
Hollace Davids
SENIOR V.P., STORY DEPARTMENT
Romy Dworman
SENIOR V.P./COO, HOME ENTERTAINMENT
Thomas Emrey
SENIOR V.P., MARKET RESEARCH
Charles Gaylord
SENIOR V.P., CREATIVE ADVERTISING
Jackson George
SENIOR V.P., EXHIBITOR RELATIONS
John C. Hall
SENIOR V.P., BRAND MARKETING, USHE
Hilary Hoffman
SENIOR V.P., CASTING
Julie Hutchinson
SENIOR V.P., LIVE ACTION PRODUCTION, USHE
Patti Jackson
SENIOR V.P., PHYSICAL PRODUCTION
Jeff LaPlante
SENIOR V.P., UNIVERSAL PICTURES INTERNATIONAL DISTRIBUTION & MARKETING/ MANAGING DIRECTOR LOS ANGELES
Jack Ledwith, Jr.
SENIOR V.P., UNIVERSAL PICTURES INTERNATIONAL PUBLICITY
Mark Markline
SENIOR V.P., PRODUCTION
Michael McCormick
SENIOR V.P./CFO, USHE FINANCE
John Morici
SENIOR V.P., NEW MEDIA
Doug Neil
SENIOR V.P., STRATEGIC MARKETING
David O'Connor
SENIOR V.P., CREATIVE SERVICES
Pam Postrel
SENIOR V.P., WORLDWIDE HD MARKETING
Rober Read
SENIOR V.P., PRODUCTION, USHE
Tom Ruzicka
SENIOR V.P., DIGITAL PLATFORMS
Adam Rymer
SENIOR V.P., WORLDWIDE DIGITAL ASSET MANAGEMENT
Stanley Scoggins
SENIOR V.P., HUMAN RESOURCES
Kay Straky
SENIOR V.P., FIELD OPERATIONS
Greg Sucherman
SENIOR V.P., CORPORATE ALLIANCES, UNIVERSAL PARTNERSHIPS & LICENSING
Stephanie Testa
SENIOR V.P., EAST COAST PUBLICITY
Amy Thomases
SENIOR V.P., INTERNATIONAL PUBLICITY
Kate Wyhowska
V.P., SPECIAL PROJECTS
Linda Pace Alexander
V.P., DIGITAL PRODUCTION
Matt Apice
V.P., PRODUCTION
Erik Baiers
V.P., CREATIVE SERVICES, USHE
Stacy Barger
V.P., UP DVD PRODUCTION, USHE
Colleen Benn
V.P., OPERATIONS, DISTRIBUTION
Gary Chong
V.P., DISTRIBUTION
Joan Corrado, Mary Costello
V.P., CONSUMER PRODUCTS
Ray De La Rosa

REGIONAL V.P., LATIN AMERICAN MARKETING, UNIVERSAL PICTURES INTERNATIONAL
Mauricio Duran
V.P., STILLS DEPARTMENT
Bette Einbinder
V.P., DOMEATIC MARKET & DISTRIBUTION FINANCE
Gavin Feinberg
V.P., DISTRIBUTION
Lynne Francis, Paul Ginsburg
V.P., DVD OPERATIONS, USHE
Mark Halperin
V.P., NATIONAL PUBLICITY
Teresa Johnson
V.P., PRINT CONTROL
Mark Link
V.P., PRODUCTION
Kristin Lowe
V.P., TECHNOLOGY
Bill Mandel
V.P., MARKET RESEARCH
Peter Marks
V.P., EXHIBITOR RELATIONS
Scott Rieckhoff
V.P., DISTRIBUTION
Gary Rocco, Bruce Thompson
V.P., PUBLICITY
Amanda Scholer
V.P., MANUFACTURING & LOGISTICS, USHE
Heidi Turk
V.P., MARKETING FINANCE
David Yuratich
DIRECTOR, DEVELOPMENT
Meredith Frenkel, Franklin Leonard, Anikah McLaren
CREATIVE EXECUTIVE
Kiska Higgs
MANAGING DIRECTOR, UNIVERSAL PICTURES MEXICO
Jose Ernesto Espinosa
MANAGING DIRECTOR, UNIVERSAL PICTURES UK
Ian Foster
MANAGING DIRECTOR, UNIVERSAL PICTURES INTERNATIONAL, FRANCE
Stephane Huard
MANAGING DIRECTOR, UNIVERSAL PICTURES INTERNATIONAL, UK & IRELAND
Niels Swinkels

FOCUS FEATURES

(A division of Universal Studios)
Los Angeles: 100 Universal City Plz., Universal City, CA 91608. TEL: (818) 777-7373.
New York: 65 Bleecker St., 3rd Flr., New York, NY 10012. TEL: (212) 539-4000. www.roguepictures.com www.focusfeatures.com
CEO/FOCUS FEATURES
James Schamus
PRESIDENT, PRODUCTION D
John Lyons
PRESIDENT, WORLDWIDE MARKETING
David Brooks
PRESIDENT, INTERNATIONAL SALES & DISTRIBUTION (LONDON)
Alison Thompson
PRESIDENT, THEATRICAL DISTRIBUTION
Jack Foley
PRESIDENT, WORLDWIDE PUBLICITY, EXECUTIVE V.P., MARKETING
Adriene Bowles
EXECUTIVE V.P., SALES
Linda Ditrinco
EXECUTIVE V.P., STRAGEIC PLANNING, BUSINESS AFFAIRS & ACQUISITIONS
Avy Eschenasy
EXECUTIVE V.P., PHYSICAL PRODUCTION
Jane Evans
EXECUTIVE V.P., BUSINESS AFFAIRS
Howard Meyers
SENIOR V.P., CREATIVE ADVERTISING, AUDIO VISUAL
Myles Bender
SENIOR V.P., MARKETING
David Bloch
SENIOR V.P., CREATIVE ADVERTISING, PRINT & MEDIA
Blair Green
SENIOR V.P., INTERNATIONAL SALES
Peter Kujawski
SENIOR V.P., EUROPEAN PRODUCTION (LONDON)
Teresa Moneo
SENIOR V.P., INTERNATIONAL MARKETING & PUBLICITY (LONDON)
Heta Paarte
SENIOR V.P., PRODUCTION
Kahli Small
SENIOR V.P., INTERNATIONAL SALES
Tim Spencer
SENIOR V.P., MEDIA RESEARCH
Rob Wilkinson
V.P., OPERATIONS
Gordon Ampel
V.P., FINANCE
Susan Anderson
V.P., NEW MEDIA
Nicole Butte
V.P., PUBLICITY (NY)
V.J. Carbone
V.P., EXHIBITOR MARKETING
Eric Carr
V.P., BUSINESS AFFAIRS
Timothy Collins
V.P., WESTERN DIVISION SALES
Jim Donlon
V.P., PUBLICITY
Harlan Gulko, Deette Kearns, RJ Millard , Kyle Thorpe
V.P., POST PRODUCTION
Jeffrey Roth

UNIVERSAL PICTURES INTERNATIONAL ENTERTAINMENT

(International distributor)
80-110 New Oxford St., Prospect House, 4th Flr., London W1A 1HB UK. TEL: (44-207) 079-6000. FAX: (44-207) 079-6488. www.universalstudios.com
PRESIDENT, UNIVERSAL PICTURES INTERNATIONAL ENTERTAINMENT
Eddie Cunningham
CFO
Rowan Conn
SENIOR V.P., MARKETING, LICENSEES & EMERGING MARKETS
Melanie Nicholas
SENIOR V.P., UNIVERSAL A&R GROUP
Helen Parker
V.P., INTERNATIONAL MARKETING
Darren Linton
V.P., COMMUNICATIONS
Denise Bassett
V.P., STRATEGIC INITIATIVES
Johnny Fewings
REGIONAL MANAGING DIRECTOR, UNIVERSAL PICTURES FRANCE & BENELUX
Pauline Grimaldi
REGIONAL MANAGING DIRECTOR, UNIVERSAL PICTURES, GERMANY, AUSTRIA, SWITZERLAND, IBERIA, RUSSIA & ITALY
Dirk Lisowsky
MANAGING DIRECTOR, UNIVERSAL PICTURES IBERIA
Edgar Adelmund
MANAGING DIRECTOR, UNIVERSAL PICTURES RUSSIA
Egor Borisov
MANAGING DIRECTOR, UNIVERSAL PICTURES MEXICO
Fernando Del Rio
MANAGING DIRECTOR, GANEON UNIVERSAL ENTERTAINMENT, JAPAN
Tim Harada
MANAGING DIRECTOR, UNIVERSAL PICTURES ITALY
David Moscato
MANAGING DIRECTOR, UNIVERSAL PICTURES AUSTRALIA & NEW ZEALAND
Liz Van Hooven
MANAGING DIRECTOR, UNIVERSAL PICTURES NORDIC
Ivor Viljoen
MANAGING DIRECTOR, UNIVERSAL PICTURES BRAZIL
Marcelo Bermudez

MACE NEUFELD PRODUCTIONS

(Motion picture & TV producer)
8730 Wilshire Blvd., Ste. 410, Beverly Hills, CA 90211. TEL: (310) 401-6868. FAX: (310) 401-6866.
PRINCIPAL
Mace Neufeld
DIRECTOR, DEVELOPMENT
Robyn Shwer
CREATIVE EXECUTIVE
Ben Crane

GIL NETTER PRODUCTIONS

(Production company)
1645 Abbott Kinney Blvd., #320, Venice, CA 90291. TEL: (310) 394-21644.
CHAIRMAN/PRODUCER
Gil Netter
DEVELOPMENT EXECUTIVE
Thomas Carstens

NEW CRIME PRODUCTIONS

(Motion picture producer)
1041 N. Formosa Ave., Formosa Bldg., #219, West Hollywood, CA 90046. TEL: (323) 850-2525. email: newcrime@aol.com
WRITER & PRODUCER & ACTOR
John Cusack

PRESIDENT/PRODUCER
Grace Loh
DIRECTOR, OPERATIONS
Kevin Lawn
ASSISTANT TO JOHN CUSACK
Judy Heinzen

NEW GENERATION FILMS, INC.

(Motion picture & film producer & distributor)
304 N. Edinburgh Ave., Los Angeles, CA 90048.
TEL: (323) 655-7705, (323) 655-7702. FAX: (323) 655-7706.
email: ngf@newgenerationfilmsinc.com
www.newgenerationfilmsinc.com
PRESIDENT & CO-CHAIRMAN
Evgeny Afineevsky
EXECUTIVE PRESIDENT, PRODUCER
Svetlana Anufrieva
V.P., LEGAL AFFAIRS
Alexander Walker, III
V.P., PRODUCTION, PRODUCER
Victor Freilich
PRESIDENT DISTRIBUTION & FINANCING/PRODUCER
Mark Saint Juste

NEW HOLLYWOOD MOTION PICTURE & TELEVISION STUDIOS, INC.

(Feature motion picture and feature documentary production and post-production)
1910 St. Joe Ctr. Rd., Ste. 22, Fort Wayne, IN 46825.
TEL: (260) 918-2271, (310) 598-5812.
email: archer@newhollywoodonline.com
www.NewHollywoodOnline.com
CONTACT
Mark Archer

NEW LINE CINEMA

(Production company. Company was absorbed into Warner Bros. in 2008. Currently operates as a production unit within Warner Bros.)
1325 Avenue of the Americas, 30th Flr. New York, NY 10019.
V.P., PRODUCTION AND ACQUISITIONS
Merideth Finn

116 N. Robertson Blvd., Ste. 200., Los Angeles, CA 90048.
TEL: (310) 854-5811. FAX: (310) 967-6465. www.newline.com
PRESIDENT AND COO, NEW LINE PRODUCTIONS, INC.
Toby Emmerich
PRESIDENT, PRODUCTION
Richard Brener
EXECUTIVE V.P., STRATEGY AND OPERATIONS
Carolyn Blackwood
EXECUTIVE V.P., MARKETING
Christina Kounelias
SENIOR V.P./HEAD, BUSINESS AND LEGAL AFFAIRS
Craig Alexander
EXECUTIVE V.P., POST PRODUCTION
Jody A. Levin
EXECUTIVE V.P., MUSIC, WATERTOWER
Jason Linn
SENIOR V.P., PHYSICAL PRODUCTION
Katherine Beyda
SENIOR V.P., PRODUCTION
Walter Hamada, Michele Weiss
V.P., PUBLICITY & CORPORATE COMMUNICATIONS
Candice McDonough
V.P., PRODUCTION
Sam Brown, Michael Disco
V.P., PRODUCTION (NY)
Merideth Finn - (212) 506-4297
V.P., BUSINESS & LEGAL AFFAIRS
Robyn Martin
V.P., SALES & PRODUCT DEVELOPMENT
Genevieve Morris
V.P., MARKETING, MUSIC
Joe Kara
V.P., PROMOTION & DIGITAL DEVELOPMENT, MUSIC
Kevin Kertes
V.P., FINANCE & ROYALTY ACCOUNTING, MUSIC
Peter Axelrad

NEW HORIZONS PICTURE CORP.

(Motion picture & TV producer & distributor)
11600 San Vicente Blvd., Los Angeles, CA 90049.
TEL: (310) 820-6733. FAX: (310) 207-6816.
email: films@newhorizonspictures.com
www.newhorizonspictures.com
PRESIDENT & CEO
Roger Corman
SENIOR EXECUTIVE V.P.
Julie Corman
PRODUCER (NY)
Catherine Corman
EXECUTIVE V.P. &V.P., FINANCE
Tom Krentzin
DIRECTOR, BUSINESS AFFAIRS
Germaine Simiens

VINCENT NEWMAN ENTERTAINMENT

(Production company)
8840 Wilshire Blvd., 3rd Flr., Beverly Hills, CA 90211.
TEL: (310) 358-3050. FAX: (310) 358-3289.
email: general@liveheart-vne.com@aol.com
PRODUCER
Vincent Newman
PRODUCER'S ASSOCIATE
Ryan Breen

NEWMARKET CAPITAL GROUP

(Motion picture & independent film distributor, producer & financier)
Newmarket Films and Newmarket Capital Group, 202 N. Canon Dr., Beverly Hills, CA 90210. TEL: (310) 858-7472. FAX: (310) 858-7473. email: info@newmarketfilms.com
www.newmarketfilms.com
CEO/CO-CHAIRMAN
Nigel Sinclair
CFO
Andy Mayson
ACQUISITIONS/CREATIVE AFFAIRS
Leilani Forby
OFFICE MANAGER
Lauren Morrison

NEWS CORPORATION

(News Corporation Units involved in TV production and distribution)
10201 W. Pico Blvd., Bldg. 100, Los Angeles, CA 90035.
TEL: (310) 369-1000. FAX: (310) 203-1454.

P.O. Box 900, Beverly Hills, CA 90213.

1211 Ave. of the Americas, 3rd Flr., New York, NY 10036.
TEL: (212) 556-2400. www.fox.com
CHAIRMAN & CEO, NEWS CORPORATION
K. Rupert Murdoch
DEPUTY CHAIRMAN, PRESIDENT & COO, NEWS CORPORATION
Chase Carey
CHAIRMAN & CHIEF EXECUTIVE EUROPE & ASIA
James Murdoch
SENIOR EXECUTIVE V.P. & CFO
David DeVoe
CHAIRMAN & CEO, FOX NEWS CHANNEL, FOX BUSINESS NETWORK & CHAIRMAN, FOX TELEVISION STATIONS & TWENTIETH TELEVISION
Roger Ailes
SENIOR EXECUTIVE V.P. & GROUP GENERAL COUNSEL
Lawrence A. Jacobs
EXECUTIVE V.P. & DEPUTY CFO
John Nallen
EXECUTIVE V.P., CHIEF HUMAN RESOURCES OFFICER
Beryl Cook
CHIEF EXECUTIVE EUROPEAN TELEVISION
Tom Mockridge
EXECUTIVE V.P., GOVERNMENT AFFAIRS
Michael Regan
SENIOR V.P., DEPUTY GENERAL COUNSEL & CHIEF COMPLIANCE AND ETHICS OFFICER
Genie Gavenchak
SENIOR V.P., CORPORATE AFFAIRS & COMMUNICATIONS
Teri Everett
SENIOR V.P., INVESTOR RELATIONS
Reed Nolte

TWENTIETH CENTURY FOX, PRODUCTION

10201 W. Pico Blvd., Los Angeles, CA 90035.
TEL: (310) 369-1000. www.fox.com
CO-CHAIRMAN/CEO FOX FILMED ENTERTAINMENT
James Gianopulos
CO-CHAIRMAN/CEO FOX FILMED ENTERTAINMENT
Tom Rothman
PRESIDENT, PRODUCTION, TCF
Emma Watts
PRESIDENT, POST-PRODUCTION
Ted Gagliano
PRESIDENT, PHYSICAL PRODUCTION
Joe Hartwick
PRESIDENT, FOX MUSIC, INC.
Robert Kraft
PRESIDENT, NEW MEDIA & DIGITAL DISTRIBUTION
Peter Levinsohn
EXECUTIVE V.P., PHYSICAL PRODUCTION
Fred Baron
EXECUTIVE V.P., POST PRODUCTION
Fred Chandler
EXECUTIVE V.P., LEGAL AFFAIRS
Bob Cohen
EXECUTIVE V.P., PHYSICAL PRODUCTION
Kimberly Cooper
EXECUTIVE V.P., STUDIO OPERATIONS
J.R. DeLang

EXECUTIVE V.P., STRATEGY & BUSINESS DEVELOPMENT, FOX FILMED ENTERTAINMENT
Marc DiLorenzo
EXECUTIVE V.P., FOX FILMED ENTERTAINMENT
Greg Gelfan
EXECUTIVE V.P., OPERATIONS STRATEGY/CFO, FFE
Dean Hallett
EXECUTIVE V.P., PHYSICAL PRODUCTION
Mike Hendrickson
EXECUTIVE V.P., FEATURE TALENT
Donna Isaacson
EXECUTIVE V.P., PRODUCTION, TCF
Jeremy Kramer
EXECUTIVE V.P., BUSINESS AFFAIRS
Steve Plum, Mark Resnick
EXECUTIVE V.P., LITIGATION
Gary D. Roberts
EXECUTIVE V.P., PRODUCTION FINANCE & BUSINESS AFFAIRS
Victoria Rossellini
EXECUTIVE V.P., ACQUISITIONS
Tony Safford
EXECUTIVE V.P., FINANCE/DEPUTY CFO
Jane Waxman
SENIOR V.P., PRODUCTION, TCF
Steve Asbell
SENIOR V.P., CREATIVE AFFAIRS
Ted Dodd
SENIOR V.P., CHIEF INFORMATION OFFICER
John Herbert
SENIOR V.P., BUSINESS AFFAIRS
Paul Hoffman
SENIOR V.P., PHYSICAL PRODUCTION
Thomas Imperato
SENIOR V.P., PRODUCTION, TCF
Peter Kang
SENIOR V.P., FEATURE CASTING
Christian Kaplan
SENIOR V.P., MEDIA, POST PRODUCTION & TECHNICAL OPERATIONS
Steve Rosenberg
SENIOR V.P., PRODUCTION, FOX HOME ENTERTAINMENT
Tom Siegrist
SENIOR V.P., PHYSICAL PRODUCTION
David Starke
V.P., PRODUCTION, TCF
Drew Crevello, John Fox, Lauren Levy, Steven Puri
V.P., PHYSICAL PRODUCTION
Michael Heard
V.P., ACQUISITIONS
Ray Strache
V.P., PRODUCTION DEVELOPMENT ACCOUNTING
Aaron Williams
V.P., DIGITAL MARKETING
Jake Zim
EXECUTIVE DIRECTOR, FEATURE TALENT
Brehan Fitzgerald

TWENTIETH CENTURY FOX, DISTRIBUTION
PRESIDENT, DOMESTIC DISTRIBUTION
Bruce Snyder
CO-PRESIDENT, INTERNATIONAL THEATRICAL
Paul Hanneman
CO-PRESIDENT, INTERNATIONAL THEATRICAL
Tomas Jegeus
CO-PRESIDENT, DOMESTIC THEATRICAL MARKETING
Pamela Levine
CO-PRESIDENT, DOMESTIC THEATRICAL MARKETING
Tony Sella
COO, INTERNATIONAL THEATRICAL & HOME ENTERTAINMENT
Mary McLaren
PRESIDENT, PRODUCTION, TCF
Emma Watts
PRESIDENT, NEW MEDIA & DIGITAL DISTRIBUTION
Peter Levinson
EXECUTIVE V.P., OPERATIONS, WORLDWIDE HOME ENTERTAINMENT
Paul Chambers
EXECUTIVE V.P., STRATEGY & BUSINESS DEVELOPMENT, FOX FILMED ENTERTAINMENT
Marc Di Lorenzo
EXECUTIVE V.P., MARKETING & DIGITAL CONTENT
Jeffrey Godsick
EXECUTIVE V.P., EUROPEAN THEATRICAL
Paul Higginson
EXECUTIVE V.P., DIGITAL EXHIBITION & NON-THEATRICAL SALES
Julian Levin
EXECUTIVE V.P., MEDIA & MARKETING PLANNING, DOMESTIC THEATRICAL MARKETING
Julie Rieger
EXECUTIVE V.P., PUBLICITY & FIELD MARKETING, TCF
Carol Sewell
SENIOR V.P., DOMESTIC DISTRIBUTION, EASTERN/ NORTHERN FILM SALES
Chris Aronson
SENIOR V.P., MARKETING, INTERNATIONAL THEATRICAL
Kieran Breen
SENIOR V.P., INTERNATIONAL PUBLICITY
Hilary Clark
SENIOR V.P., INTERNATIONAL MARKETING
Franco De Casare
SENIOR V.P., FEATURE FILM PROMOTIONS
Rita Drucker
SENIOR V.P./CIO
John Herbert
SENIOR V.P., EUROPEAN THEATRICAL
Todd Huntley
SENIOR V.P., NORTHERN EUROPE
Steven Leighton
SENIOR V.P., DOMESTIC DISTRIBUTION, WESTERN/ SOUTHERN FILM SALES
Bert Livingston
SENIOR V.P., CORPORATE COMMUNICATIONS
Chris Petrikin
SENIOR V.P., MARKETING, DOMESTIC THEATRICAL MARKETING
Matt Smuckler
SENIOR V.P., CREATIVE ADVERTISING, DOMESTICAL THEATRICAL MARKETING
Mike Southerly
SENIOR V.P., MARKETING & CREATIVE ADVERTISING, DOMESTICAL THEATRICAL MARKETING
Peter Stougaard
V.P., STRATEGIC MARKETING, INTERNATIONAL THEATRICAL
Melanie Bartlett
V.P., CREATIVE ADVERTISING, INTERNATIONAL THEATRICAL
Mark Davis
V.P., SALES & STRATEGIC PLANNING
Craig Dehmel
V.P., CREATIVE CONTENT, INTERNATIONAL THEATRICAL
Martin Gaiss
V.P., STRATEGIC MARKETING, INTERNATIONAL THEATRICAL
Britta Gamper
V.P., PRINT CONTROL OPERATIONS
Rick Griffith
V.P., ASIA PACIFIC, INTERNATIONAL MARKETING
Sunder Kimatrai
V.P., BRANDED ENTERTAINMENT, DIGITAL CONTENT, FOX FILMED ENTERTAINMENT
Roger Mincheff
V.P., CREATIVE ADVERTISING, INTERNATIONAL THEATRICAL
Christi Mykles
V.P., ACQUIRED MARKETING
Jeff Yordy
V.P., DIGITAL MARKETING
Jake Zim

TWENTIETH CENTURY FOX ANIMATION
(Production company)
10201 W. Pico Blvd., Bldg. 58, Los Angeles, CA 90035.
TEL: (310) 369-1000. FAX: (310) 369-3907. www.fox.com
PRESIDENT, TWENTIETH CENTURY FOX ANIMATION
Vanessa Morrison
V.P., PRODUCTION
Peter Gal, Karen Rupert Toliver
EXECUTIVE DIRECTOR, DEVELOPMENT, BLUE SKY STUDIOS
Lisa Fragner
CREATIVE EXECUTIVES
Ralph Millero

FOX 2000
PRESIDENT, PRODUCTION
Elizabeth Gabler
EXECUTIVE V.P., PRODUCTION
Carla Hacken
SENIOR V.P., PRODUCTION
Rodney Ferrell
V.P., PRODUCTION
Erin Siminoff
CREATIVE EXECUTIVE
Marisa Paiva
LITERARY CONSULTANT
Drew Reed (NY) - (212) 556-8140
STORY EDITOR
Chris Goldberg (NY) - (212) 556-8140
LITERARY SCOUT
Riley Kathryn Ellis

FOX SEARCHLIGHT PICTURES, PRODUCTION
10201 W. Pico Blvd., Bldg. 38, Los Angeles, CA 90035.
TEL: (310) 369-1000. www.foxsearchlight.com

CO-PRESIDENT, FOX SEARCHLIGHT PICTURES
Steve Gilula, Nancy Utley-Jacobs
PRESIDENT, PRODUCTION
Claudia Lewis
EXECUTIVE V.P., PHYSICAL PRODUCTION
Liz Sayre
SENIOR V.P., FINANCE & OPERATIONS
Jill Gwen Braginets
SENIOR V.P., PRODUCTION
David Greenbaum, Matthew Greenfield, Zola Mashariki
SENIOR V.P., LEGAL AFFAIRS
Chris Maxwell
SENIOR V.P., MEDIA
Dan Pittman
SENIOR V.P., PRODUCTION
Jeremy Steckler
SENIOR V.P., LEGAL AFFAIRS
Chris Maxwell, Jamie Taylor
V.P., BUSINESS AFFAIRS
Megan C. O'Brien
SENIOR V.P., MEDIA
Dan Pittman
V.P., POST PRODUCTION
Nikki Scalise
CREATIVE EXECUTIVE
DanTram Nguyen

FOX SEARCHLIGHT PICTURES, DISTRIBUTION

CO-PRESIDENT
Stephen Gilula
CO-PRESIDENT
Nancy Utley
EXECUTIVE V.P., MARKETING
Larry Baldauf
EXECUTIVE V.P., MARKETING
Michelle Hooper
EXECUTIVE V.P., ACQUISITIONS
Tony Safford
EXECUTIVE V.P., GENERAL SALES MANAGER
Sheila DeLoach
SENIOR V.P., SALES & MARKETING, SEARCHLIGHT INTERNATIONAL
Rebecca Kearey
SENIOR V.P., NATIONAL PUBLICITY
Diana Loomis (NY)
SENIOR V.P., MEDIA
Dan Pittman
HEAD, SEARCHLIGHT INTERNATIONAL (UK)
Kate Gardiner
V.P., CREATIVE ADVERTISING
Flavia Amon
V.P., SPECIAL EVENTS & PROMOTIONS
Ruth Busenkell
V.Ps., NATIONAL PUBLICITY
Cassandra Butcher, Melissa Holloway, Angela Johnson
V.P., NATIONAL PUBLICITY (NY)
Barry Dale Johnson
V.P., IN-THEATRE MARKETING
Branden Miller
V.P., CORPORATE COMMUNICATIONS
Russell Nelson
V.P., NEW MEDIA
Graham Retzik
V.P., DISTRIBUTION, (WEST COAST)
Richard Shamban
V.P., CREATIVE ADVERTISING
Patrick Starr
V.P., WESTERN FIELD PUBLICITY & PROMOTIONS
Isabelle Sugimoto
V.P., EAST COAST DISTRIBUTION
Derval Whelan

NICKELODEON MOVIES

(Motion picture studio)
5555 Melrose Ave., Modular Bldg. 2nd Flr., Los Angeles, CA 90038. FAX: (323) 862-1386. www.nick.com
PRESIDENT
Scott Aversano
EXECUTIVE V.P.
Chris Salvaterra
VICE PRESIDENT
Dorian Howard
CREATIVE EXECUTIVE
Jain Yu

NORADOR PRODUCTIONS, LTD.

(Motion picture producer & distributor)
101 West 79th St., Ste. 12A, New York, NY 10024.
TEL: (212) 877-6417. FAX: (212) 877-1949.
email: noraspers@aol.com
PRESIDENT
Nora Coblence

NORTHERN ARTS ENTERTAINMENT

(Motion picture producer & distributor)
10866 Wilshire Blvd., Ste. 850, Los Angeles, CA 90024.
TEL: (323) 422-9099. FAX: (310) 480-9099.
www.northernartsentertainment.com
CEO, PARTNER, ACQUISITIONS
John Lawrence Ré
PRESIDENT, PARTNER, DISTRIBUTION
Larry Jackson
PARTNER (LA)
Anthony Masucci
V.P., THEATRICAL ACQUISITIONS (LA/NY)
Ava Lazar

NU IMAGE/MILLENNIUM FILMS

(Production & distribution company)
6423 Wilshire Blvd., Los Angeles, CA 90048.
TEL: (310) 388-6900. FAX: (310) 388-6901.
email: info@nuimage.net www.nuimage.net
CO-CHAIRMAN & CHIEF EXECUTIVE OFFICER
Avi Lerner, Danny Dimbort
CFO
Trevor Short
HEAD, PRODUCTION & CREATIVE AFFAIRS
Boaz Davidson
PRESIDENT, INTERNATIONAL SALES & DISTRIBUTION
Christian Mercuri
PRESIDENT, MILLENNIUM FILMS
John Thompson
PRESIDENT, DOMESTIV T.V. & VIDEO
Dave Sobieraj
GENERAL COUNSEL
Frank DeMartini
EXECUTIVE V.P., DEVELOPMENT
Joe Gatta
EXECUTIVE V.P., BUSINESS AFFAIRS
Lonnie Ramati

LYNDA OBST PRODUCTIONS

(Motion picture, independent film & TV producer)
10202 W. Washington Blvd., Astaire Bldg. Ste.1000, Culver City, CA 90232. TEL: (310) 244-6112. FAX: (310) 244-0092.
www.lyndaobstproductions.com
PRODUCER
Lynda Obst
V.P., PRODUCTION
Rachel Abarbanell

OCCIDENTAL ENTERTAINMENT

(Production company)
1149 N. McCadden Place, Hollywood, CA 90038.
TEL: (323) 282-5184. FAX: (323) 464-0099.
www.OccidentalEntertainment.com
CHAIRMAN
Albert Sweet
EXECUTIVE V.P., COO
Richard Howard
CFO
Richard Glaser
V.P., CONTROLLER
Tanya Rebrova

OFFSPRING ENTERTAINMENT

(Production company)
500 S. Buena Vista St., Burbank, CA 91521.
TEL: (818) 560-5645. FAX: (818) 560-5642.
DIRECTOR/PARTNER
Adam Shankman
PRODUCER/PARTNER
Jennifer Gibgot
EXECUTIVE V.P.
Jim Badstibner
ASSOCIATE PRODUCER
Matt Smith
ASSISTANT TO ADAM SHANKMAN
Sunja Knapp
ASSISTANT TO JENNIFER GIBGOT
Tom Kuljurgis
ASSISTANT TO LAUREN LEVY
Danielle Randall

OMEGA ENTERTAINMENT

(Motion picture & TV producer & distributor)
European Headquarters: 23 Amfitheas Ave., Paleo Faliro, Athens 17564, Greece. TEL: (30210) 948 0055.
FAX: (30210) 948 0069.
Los Angeles Office: 315 South Beverly Dr., Ste. 200, Beverly Hills, CA 90212. TEL: (310) 855-0516. FAX: (310) 553-3814.
email: production@omegapicusa.com www.omegapic.com
PRESIDENT & CEO
Nico Mastorakis
PRESIDENT, OMEGA EUROPE
K. Tsanakali

V.P., TELEVISION
Pete Williams

ON STILTS PRODUCTIONS

(Production Company)
9699 N. Hayden Rd., Ste. 108, PMB 233, Scottsdale, AZ 85258. TEL: (310) 391-6053. email: OSP14@aol.com
PRODUCER
Peter Stelzer

ORIGINAL FILM

(Production Company)
11466 San Vicente Blvd., Los Angeles, CA 90049.
TEL: (310) 575-6950. FAX: (310) 575-6990.
PRODUCER & OWNER
Neal Moritz
PRODUCTION EXECUTIVE
Tania Landau, Toby Jaffe, Elizabeth Buraglio, Amanda Lewis, Ori Marmur, Jeni Mulein
HEAD, TV
Vivian Cannon

OUR STORIES FILMS

(Production company)
1635 N. Cahuenga Blvd., Los Angeles, CA 90028.
TEL: (323) 817-0090. FAX: (323) 817-0091.
www.ourstoriesfilms.com
CHAIRMAN & CEO
Robert L. Johnson
PRESIDENT & COO
Tracey Edmonds
V.P., DEVELOPMENT
Glendon Palmer
DIRECTOR, PRODUCTION ADMINISTRATION
Jeff Willis

OUT OF THE BLUE... ENTERTAINMENT

(Motion picture producer)
10202 W. Washington Blvd., Astaire Bldg., Ste.1200, Culver City, CA 90232-3195. TEL: (310) 244-7811.
FAX: (310) 244-1539. email: info@outoftheblueent.com
www.outoftheblueent.com
CONTACT
Sid Ganis, Nancy Hult Ganis, Carlo Eugster, Toby Conroy, Marta Gene Camp, Carrick Bartle

OUTERBANKS ENTERTAINMENT

(Motion picture, independent film & TV producer)
1149 N. Goweer St., #101, Los Angeles, CA 90038.
TEL: (323) 785-2221. FAX: (323) 785-3926.
email: firstname@outerbanks-ent.com
WRITER & DIRECTOR & PRODUCER
Kevin Williamson
ASSISTANT TO KEVIN WILLIAMSON
Charlie Charbonneau

OUTLAW PRODUCTIONS

(Motion picture producer)
c/o Sony Pictures Entertainment, 10202 W. Washington Blvd., Sidney Poitier Bldg., Ste. 3214, Culver City, CA 90232.
TEL: (310) 244-3445. FAX: (310) 244-1139.
www.outlawfilm.com
PRODUCER
Deb Newmyer
V.P., PRODUCTION & DEVELOPMENT
Michael Glassman

OVERBROOK ENTERTAINMENT

(Production company)
450 N. Roxbury Dr., 4th Flr., Beverly Hills, CA 90210.
TEL: (310) 432-2400. FAX: (310) 432-2401.
PARTNER
Will Smith, James Lassiter, Ken Stovitz
FILM EXECUTIVE
Gary Glushon, Tracey Nyberg, Jeff Sommerville
TELEVISION EXECUTIVE
Heather Courtney
GENERAL MANAGER
Jana Babatunde-Bey

OVERTURE FILMS

(Motion picture studio - see Relativity Media)
Overture Films, the 3-year-old independent film studio, formerly owned by John Malone's Liberty Media, shut down after it failed to find interested buyers. The company will no longer produce movies, and its marketing and distribution operations have been taken over by Relativity Media.

OXYGEN MEDIA, INC.

(Production Company)
75 Ninth Ave., New York, NY 10011. TEL: (212) 651-2000.
FAX: (212) 651-2099. www.oxygen.com

6650 Romaine Ave., Lot D, Bldg. 40, Hollywood, CA 90038.
TEL: (323) 860-3500. FAX: (323) 860-3501.
CO-FOUNDER
Oprah Winfrey, Marcy Carsey, Caryn Mandabach, Tom Warner
PRESIDENT, NBC UNIVERSAL WOMEN & LIFESTYLE ENTERTAINMENT NETWORKS
Lauren Zalaznick
GENERAL MANAGER
Jason Klarman
SENIOR V.P., COMMUNICATIONS
Cameron Blanchard
SENIOR V.P., RESEARCH & STRATEGIC INSIGHTS
Tony Cardinale
SENIOR V.P., ORIGINAL PROGRAMMING & DEVELOPMENT
Amy Introcaso-Davis
SENIOR V.P., AD SALES
Susan Malfa
SENIOR V.P., MARKETING & BRAND STRATEGY
Jane Olson
V.P., CFO
Cynthia Chu
V.P., ADVERTISING SALES
Michael DuPont
V.P., ORIGINAL PROGRAMMING & DEVELOPMENT
Bryan Hale
V.P., CREATIVE DIRECTOR
Gerry Logue
V.P., COMMUNICATIONS
Julie Rothman

PALISADES TARTAN

156 W. 56th St., Ste. 901, New York, NY 10019.
TEL: (212) 265-2323. FAX: (212) 265-2766.
email: info@palisadestpictures.com www.tartanfilmsusa.com
PRESIDENT/CEO
Soumya Sriraman
CHARIMAN
Vin Roberti
V.P., ACQUISITIONS
Elliot Koss
US MARKETING & SALES
Rick Stelow - rstelow@palisadestartan.com
UK MARKETING & SALES
Hugh David - hdavid@palisadespictures.com

In May 2008, Palisades Media Asset Fund acquired Tartan Films US & UK library assets and branded their new division Palisades Tartan.

PALM PICTURES

(Distribution company)
76 Ninth Ave., Ste. 1110, New York, NY 10011.
TEL: (212) 320-3600. FAX: (212) 320-3609.
email: david.koh@palmpictures.com www.palmpictures.com
CHAIRMAN
Chris Blackwell
MANAGING PARTNER
Marina Grasic, Jan Korbelin
GENERAL MANAGER
Lisa Nishimura - Lisa.nishimura@palmpictures.com
HEAD, THEATRICAL DISTRIBUTION & ACQUISITIONS
Ed Arentz
HEAD, ACQUISITIONS & PRODUCTION
David Koh
HEAD, THEATRICAL MARKETING
Andy Robbins
DIRECOTR, OPERATIONS
Cindy Banach

PARADOX PRODUCTIONS, INC.

(Production company)
801 Tarcuto Way, Los Angeles, CA 90077.
TEL: (310) 440-8133. FAX: (310) 472-6467.
email: doubledox@aol.com
PRESIDENT
John Pasquin

PARIAH

(Motion picture & TV production)
9744 Wilshire Blvd., Ste. 205, Beverly Hills, CA 90212.
TEL: (310) 461-3460. FAX: (310) 246-9622.
OWNER
Gavin Polone
V.P., PHYSICAL PRODUCTION
Kathy Landsberg
DIRECTOR, DEVELOPMENT
Lauren Pfeiffer

PARKWAY PRODUCTIONS

(Motion picture producer)
7095 Hollywood Blvd., #1009, Hollywood, CA 90028.
TEL: (323) 874-6207. FAX: (323) 874-3124.
email: parkwayprods@aol.com
DIRECTOR
Penny Marshall
EXECUTIVE ASSISTANT
Kelly Calligan

ASSISTANT
Terry Trahan

PARTICIPANT MEDIA

335 N. Maple Dr., Ste. 245, Beverly Hills, CA 90210.
TEL: (310) 550-5100. FAX: (310) 550-5106.
email: info@participantproductions.com
www.participantmedia.com
FOUNDER
Jeff Skoll
CEO
Jim Berk
PRESIDENT
Ricky Strauss
COO
Jeff Ivers
CFO
Robert Murphy
EXECUTIVE V.P., DOCUMENTARY PRODUCTION
Diane Weyermann
EXECUTIVE V.P., PRODUCTION
Jonathan King
EXECUTIVE V.P., MARKETING
Kathy Jones, Buffy Shutt
EXECUTIVE V.P., SOCIAL ACTION & ADVOCACY
John Schreiber
SENIOR V.P., TELEVISION
John Moser
SENIOR V.P., PRODUCTION
Erin Stam
SENIOR V.P., PUBLISHING
Lynn Hirshfield
SENIOR V.P., SOCIAL ACTION CAMPAIGN DEVELOPMENT
Liana Schwarz
SENIOR V.P., BUSINESS AFFAIRS
Bonnie Stylides
V.P., PUBLICITY
Jeffrey Sakson
SENIOR DIRECTOR, DOCUMENTARIES
Courtney Sexton
CREATIVE EXECUTIVE
Angel Lopez
GENERAL MANAGER, TAKEPART.COM
Chris Gebhardt

PATRIOT PICTURES, LLC.

(Motion picture & independent film producer & distributor)
P.O. Box 46100, West Hollywood, CA 90069.
TEL: (323) 874-8850. FAX: (323) 874-8851.
email: M1.asst1@patriotpictures.com
www.patriotpictures.com www.unionpatriotcapital.com
PRESIDENT & CEO
Michael Mendelsohn
V.P., PRODUCTION
Charles Kienzle

DANIEL L. PAULSON PRODUCTIONS

(Motion picture & TV producer & developer)
9056 Santa Monica Blvd., Ste. 203A, W. Hollywood, CA 90069.
TEL: (310) 278-9747. FAX: (310) 278-9751.
email: dlpprods@sbcglobal.net
PRESIDENT
Daniel L. Paulson
DIRECTOR, ADMINISTRATION
Steve A. Kennedy
DEVELOPMENT ASSOCIATE
Julie Zehnpfennig

PB MANAGEMENT

(Motion picture, independent film & TV producer)
6449 W. 6th St., Los Angeles, CA 90048. TEL: (323) 653-7284.
FAX: (323) 653-5285. email: capnett@hotmail.com
PRESIDENT
Paul Bennett

PCH FILMS

(Production Company)
3380 Motor Ave., Los Angeles, CA 90034.
TEL: (310) 841-5817. FAX: (310) 841-5823.
PRODUCER/DIRECTOR/ACTOR
James Keach
PRODUCER
Trevor Albert
PRODUCER/ACTRESS
Jane Seymour
V.P., PRODUCTION
Nick Hippisley-Coxe
V.P., DEVELOPMENT
Jarrod Murray
PRODUCTION/DEVELOPMENT
Kayla Thornton, Debra Pearl

ZAK PENN'S COMPANY

6260 W. Third St., Ste. 432, Los Angeles, CA 90036.
TEL: (323) 939-1700. FAX: (323) 930-2339.
WRITER & PRODUCER
Zak Penn
V.P., DEVELOPMENT
Mike Chamoy
ASSISTANT
Hannah Rosner

PERMUT PRESENTATIONS

(Motion picture & TV producer)
1801 Ave. of the Stars, Ste. 505, Los Angeles, CA 90067.
TEL: (310) 248-2792. FAX: (310) 248-2797.
PRODUCER & PRESIDENT
David Permut
V.P., PRODUCTION
Steven A. Longi
DEVELOPMENT ASSOCIATE
Chris Mangano

DANIEL PETRIE JR. & COMPANY

(Motion picture & TV producer)
18034 Ventura Blvd., Ste. 445, Encino, CA 91316.
TEL: (818) 708-1602. FAX: (818) 774-0345.
DIRECTOR & WRITER & PRODUCER
Daniel Petrie, Jr.
V.P., PRODUCTION & DEVELOPMENT
Rick Dugdale

STEPHEN PEVNER, INC.

382 Lafayette St., #8, New York, NY 10003.
TEL: (212) 674-8403. FAX: (212) 529-3692.
email: stephen@stephenpevnerinc.com spevner@aol.com
PRODUCER
Stephen Pevner

PFEFFER FILM

(Motion picture producer)
500 S. Buena Vista St., Animation Bldg., 2F-8, Burbank, CA 91521. TEL: (818) 560-3177. FAX: (818) 843-7485.
PRODUCER
Rachel Pfeffer

PHOENIX PICTURES

(Motion picture, independent film & TV producer & distributor)
9415 Culver Blvd, Culver City, CA 90232.
TEL: (424) 298-2788. FAX: (424) 298-2688.
email: dnugent@phoenixpictures.com
www.phoenixpictures.com
CHAIRMAN & CEO
Mike Medavoy - (424) 298-2398
PRESIDENT & COO
Arnold Messer - (424) 298-2401
CO-PRESIDENT, PRODUCTION
Brad Fischer - (424) 298-2598
David Thwaites - (424) 298-2424
EXECUTIVE V.P. & CFO
Christopher Trunkey
BUSINESS AFFAIRS
Jess Wittenberg
EXECUTIVE V.P., BUSINESS AFFAIRS
Rochel Blachman
V.P., CONTRACT ADMINISTRATION
Diane Isaacs
CREATIVE EXECUTIVE
Ed McGurn, Doug McKay
ACCOUNTANT
Deborah Nugent

PICTUREHOUSE

(Closed by Warner Bros. October 3, 2008. See GK Films -Bob Berney - and River Road Entertainment and Apparition - Bill Pohlad)

PLAN B ENTERTAINMENT

(Production company; No unsolicited submissions)
9150 Wilshire Blvd., Ste. 350, Beverly Hills, CA 90212.
TEL: (310) 275-6135. FAX: (310) 275-5234.
PRESIDENT
Dede Gardner
PRODUCER
Jeremy Kleiner

PLATINUM STUDIOS, INC.

(Motion picture & TV producer, comics to film)
2029 S. Westgate Ave, Los Angeles, CA 90025.
TEL: (310) 807-8100. FAX: (310) 887-3943
email: info@platinumstudios.com www.platinumstudios.com
CHAIRMAN/CEO
Scott Mitchell Rosenberg
PRESIDENT & COO
Brian Altounian
V.P., CONTENT DEVELOPMENT
Dan Forcey
CONSULTANT
Randy Greenberg

MARC PLATT PRODUCTIONS
(Motion picture, TV & stage producer)
100 Universal City Plaza, Bung. 5163, Universal City, CA 91608. TEL: (818) 777-8811. FAX: (818) 866-6353.
PRODUCER
Marc Platt
PRESIDENT
Adam Siegal
CONTACT
Joey Levy, Jared LeBoff, Nik Mavinkurve, Tia Maggini, Dana Krupinsky, Nik Mavinkurve, Claire Wihnyk, Conor Welch

PLUM PICTURES
(Production company)
636 Broadway, Ste. 814, New York, NY 10012.
TEL: (212) 529-5820. FAX: (212) 529-5824.
email: plumpic@plumpic.com www.plumpic.com
PRODUCER
Galt Niederhoffer - Galt@plumpic.com
HEAD, DEVELOPMENT
Joy Goodwin
HEAD, POST PRODUCTION
Riva Marker
HEAD, PHYSICAL PRODUCTION
Pam Hirsch

MARTIN POLL FILMS, LTD.
(Motion picture, independent film & TV producer)
945 Fifth Ave., #4G, New York, NY 10021 .
TEL: (212) 396-2589. FAX: (212) 288-2135.
email: mpoll@pollfilms.com
PRESIDENT/PRODUCER
Martin Poll
EXECUTIVE V.P., CREATIVE
Adam Cohen

PORCHLIGHT ENTERTAINMENT
(Motion pictures, animation & worldwide distribution)
11050 Santa Monica Blvd. 3rd Flr., Los Angeles, CA 90025.
TEL: (310) 477-8400. FAX: (310) 477-5555.
email: info@porchlight.com www.porchlight.com
PRESIDENT/CEO
Bruce D. Johnson - bjohnson@porchlight.com
V.P., CHILDREN'S PROGRAMMING
Shea Fontana
DIRECTOR, DISTRIBUTION & SALES
Tracy Morse
MANAGER, HOME ENTERTAINMENT
Herb Dorfman

OTTO PREMINGER FILMS, LTD.
(Motion picture & TV producer & distributor)
3500 W. Olive Ave., Ste. 300, Burbank, CA 91505.
TEL: (818) 766-2689. FAX: (818) 766-1605.
email: info@ottopremingerfilms.com
www.ottopremingerfilms.com
PRESIDENT
Victoria Preminger
VICE PRESIDENT
Hope B. Preminger

EDWARD R. PRESSMAN FILM CORP.
(Film producer)
47 Murray St., New York, NY 10007. TEL: (212) 489-3333, (310) 450-9692. FAX: (212) 489-2103, (310) 450-9705.
email: annie@pressman.com www.pressman.com
CEO/CHAIRMAN
Edward R. Pressman
HEAD, BUSINESS & LEGAL AFFAIRS
Jon Katz
DIRECTOR, DEVELOPMENT
Sarah Ramey

PRETTY PICTURES
(Producer Company)
100 Universal City Plz., Bldg. 2352-A, 3rd Flr., Universal City, CA 91608. TEL: (818) 733-0926. FAX: (818) 866-0847.
PRODUCER
Gail Mutrux
STORY EDITOR
Tore Schmidt

QED INTERNATIONAL
(Production company)
1800 N. Highland Ave., 5th Flr., Los Angeles, CA 90212.
TEL: (323) 785-7900. FAX: (323) 785-7901. www.qedintl.com
CEO
Bill Block
COO
Paul Hanson
GENERAL COUNSEL
Christopher Corabi
DIRECTOR, INTERNATIONAL SALES
John Freidberg

QUALIA CAPITAL
(Distribution company, manages the former Rysher, Gaylord and Pandora libraries)
Carneige Hall Tower, 152 W. 57th St., 21st Flr., New York, NY. 10019. TEL: (212) 672-0090. FAX: (212) 672-0091.
www.qualiacapital.com
MANAGING PRINCIPAL
Amir Malin, Ken Schapiro
MANAGING DIRECTOR
Patrick Gunn - pgun@qualiacapital.com
V.P.
David Cragnotti

RADAR PICTURES
10900 Wilshire Blvd., Ste. 1400, Los Angeles, CA 90024.
TEL: (310) 208-8525. FAX: (310) 208-1764.
CHAIRMAN/CEO
Ted W. Field
COO
David Boyle
V.P., PRODUCTION
Mike Weber
CREATIVE EXECUTIVE
Francesca DeLaurentis

RAINBOW FILM COMPANY/
(Motion picture producer & distributor)
9165 Sunset Blvd., Ste. 300, Los Angeles, CA 90069.
TEL: (310) 271-0202. FAX: (310) 271-2753.
email: lester310@earthlink.net www.rainbowreleasing.com
PRESIDENT
Henry Jaglom
DIRECTOR, DISTRIBUTION
Sharon Lester Kohn - lester310@earthlink.net
DEVELOPMENT
Lauren Beck

RAT ENTERTAINMENT/RAT TV
(Production company)
100 Universal City Plaza, Bungalow 5196, Universal City, CA 91608. TEL: (818) 733-4644. FAX: (818) 733-4612.
DIRECTOR & PRODUCER
Brett Ratner
PRESIDENT, RAT T.V.
Martha Haight
HEAD, FEATURE DEVELOPMENT
John Cheng

RECORDED PICTURE COMPANY
(Motion picture & independent film producer)
24 Hanway St., London W1T 1UH. TEL: (44 207) 636-2251.
FAX: (44-207) 636-2261. email: rpc@recordedpicture.com
www.recordedpicture.com
PRODUCER & CHAIRMAN
Jeremy Thomas
CEO/ BUSINESS AFFAIRS
Peter Watson
COO, FINANCE
Stephan Mallmann
BUSINESS AFFAIRS EXECUTIVE
Richard Mansell
ACQUISITIONS & DEVELOPMENT EXECUTIVE
Matthew Baker
DEVELOPMENT EXECUTIVE
Alainee Kent
COMPANY ACCOUNTANT
Stuart Cook

RED BIRD PRODUCTIONS
(Motion picture, independent film & TV producer)
3623 Hayden Ave., Culver City, CA 90232.
TEL: (310) 202-1711. FAX: (310) 202-7496.
PRESIDENT & ACTOR & DIRECTOR & PRODUCER
Debbie Allen

RED HOUR FILMS
(Motion picture producer)
629 N. La Brea, Los Angeles, CA 90036. TEL: (323) 602-5000.
FAX: (323) 602-5001.
WRITER & DIRECTOR & PRODUCER
Ben Stiller
PRODUCER
Stuart Cornfeld
CREATIVE EXECUTIVE
Kit Giordano
STORY EDITOR
Michael J. Rosenstein
ASSISTANT TO BEN STILLER
Jill Remis
ASSISTANT TO STUART CORNFELD
Noelia Estrada

RED OM FILMS, INC.
(Production company)
3000 Olympic Blvd., Bldg. 3, Ste. 2330, Santa Monica, CA

90404. TEL: (310) 594-3467.
PRODUCER
Julia Roberts, Lisa Gellen, Philip Rose

RED WAGON ENTERTAINMENT

(Motion picture producer)
c/o Sony Pictures Studios, 10202 W. Washington Blvd., Hepburn Bldg. W., Culver City, CA 90232-3195.
TEL: (310) 244-4466. FAX: (310) 244-1480.
PRODUCER
Douglas Z. Wick, Lucy Fisher
EXECUTIVE V.P
Rachel Shane
VICE PRESIDENT
Josh Goldenberg, Alexandra Loewy
CREATIVE EXECUTIVE
Josh Goldberg
STORY EDITOR
Dana Horgan
ASSISTANT
Josh Phillips, Bryan Clavenna, Nicholas DeCell, Benjamin Hasskamp, Matthew Solomon, Mickey Stanley

REGENCY ENTERPRISES

(Motion picture, independent film & TV producer)
10201 W. Pico Blvd., Bldg. 12, Los Angeles, CA 90035.
TEL: (310) 369-8300. FAX: (310) 969-0470.
www.newregency.com
CHAIRMAN
Bob Harper, Hutch Parker
PRODUCER
Arnon Milchan
EXECUTIVE V.P./CFO/COO
Louis Santor
EXECUTIVE V.P., CHIEF MARKETING OFFICER
John Hegeman
EXECUTIVE V.P., BUSINESS & LEGAL AFFAIRS. & GENERAL COUNSEL
William S. Weiner
EXECUTIVE V.P., PRODUCTION
Kara Francis, Amy Israel
EXECUTIVE V.P., PHYSICAL PRODUCTION
Thomas Imperato
EXECUTIVE V.P., BUSINESS AFFAIRS
Eric Roth
SENIOR V.P., FINANCE, CHIEF ACCOUNTING OFFICER
Robert S. Corzo
SENIOR V.P., POST-PRODUCTION
Elissa Loparco
SENIOR V.P., PRODUCTION
Navid McIlhargey
V.P., PRODUCTION
Heidi Sherman Grey
DIRECTOR, FEATURE & LITERARY DEVELOPMENT
Michelle Kroes
CREATIVE EXECUTIVE
Dan Wilson
STORY EDITOR
Justin Lam

REGENT ENTERTAINMENT, INC.

8411 Preston Rd., Ste. 650, Dallas TX 75225.
TEL: (214) 373-3434. FAX: (214) 361-2535.
10990 Wilshire Blvd., Penthouse, Los Angeles CA 90024.
TEL: (310) 806-4288. FAX: (310) 806-4268.
email: info@regententertainment.com
www.regententertainment.com
CHAIRMAN & CEO
Stephen P. Jarchow
PRESIDENT, REGENT RELEASING
John Lambert
CO-PRESIDENT, REGENT WORLDWIDE SALES
Liz Mackiewitz, Adam Wright
CFO
David Gould
SENIOR V.P., ADMINISTRATION
Alice Andrade
SENIOR V.P., BUSINESS & LEGAL AFFAIRS, REGENT WORLDWIDE SALES
Joan Danto
SENIOR V.P., REGENT MEDIA & PACIFIC FILMS
Lowell Dean Cox
SENIOR V.P., MARKETING & CORPORATE COMMUNICATIONS
Stephen Macias
DIRECTOR, PRODUCTION
Richard Carroll

RELATIVITY MEDIA, LLC

(Production and Distribution company)
8899 Beverly Blvd., Ste. 510, West Hollywood, CA 90048.
TEL: (310) 859-1250. FAX: (310) 859-1254.
CEO/MANAGING DIRECTOR
Ryan Kavanaugh
COO
Andrew Marcus
CFO
Bill Sutman
PRESIDENT
Michael Joe
PRESIDENT, WORLDWIDE PRODUCTION
Tucker Tooley
PRESIDENT, MARKETING,DISTRIBUTION & NEW MEDIA
Peter Adee
PRESIDENT, THEATRICAL DISTRIBUTION
Kyle Davies
EXECUTIVE V.P., PRODUCTION
Robbie Brenner
EXECUTIVE V.P., STRUCTURED FINANCE
Ramon Wilson
EXECUTIVE V.P., BUSINESS AFFAIRS
Philip Elway
CONTROLLER
Kenny Lynch
SENOR V.P., PRODUCTION
Shannon Gaulding
DIRECTOR, OPERATONS
Eva Quiroz
PHYSICAL PRODUCTION EXECUTIVE
Physical Production Executive

RENAISSANCE PICTURES

(Motion picture, independent film & TV producer)
315 S. Beverly Dr., Ste. 216, Beverly Hills, CA 90212.
TEL: (310) 785-3900. FAX: (310) 785-9176.
DIRECTOR & EXECUTIVE PRODUCER
Sam Raimi
EXECUTIVE PRODUCER
Robert Tapert
PRODUCER, CREATIVE EXECUTIVE
J.R. Young
PRODUCTION EXECUTIVE
Grant Curtis
ARCHIVING
Ben Ketai
OFFICE MANAGER/ASSISTANT TO MR. TAPERT
David Pollison

RENFIELD PRODUCTIONS

(Production company)
1041 N. Formosa Ave., Writer's Bldg. 321, West Hollywood, CA 90046. TEL: (323) 850-3905. FAX: (323) 850-3907.
email: development@renfieldproductions.com
www.renfieldproductions.com www.trailersfromhell.com
PRODUCER & PRESIDENT
Michael Finnell
DIRECTOR/PRODUCER
Joe Dante
DIRECTOR, DEVELOPMENT
T. L. Kittle
DEVELOPMENT EXECUTIVE
Mark Alan

REVEILLE, LLC

(Production company)
100 Universal City Plaza, Bungalow 5180/5170, Universal City, CA 91608. TEL: (818) 733-1218. FAX: (818) 733-3303.
MANAGING DIRECTOR/HEAD, WORLDWIDE DISTRIBUTION/PRESIDENT, REVEILLE INTERNATIONAL
Christopher Grant
MANAGING DIRECTOR/HEAD, WORLDWIDE BUSINESS & OPERATIONS
Lee Rierson
MANAGING DIRECTOR/CO-HEAD, DOMESTIC TV/HEAD, DIGITAL
Howard Owens
HEAD, NONSCRIPTED ENTERTAINMENT
Robin Ashbrook
HEAD, UNSCRIPTED DEVELOPMENT
Noah Oppenheim
EXECUTIVE V.P., SCRIPTED T.V.
Carolyn Bernstein
EXECUTIVE V.P., INTERNATIONAL DISTRIBUTION & CREATIVE AFFAIRS
John Pollak
SENIOR V.P., BUSINESS & OPERATIONS
Martin Rakusen
V.P., DOMESTIC SCRIPTED T.V.
Todd Cohen
V.P., BRAND DEVELOPMENT & PRODUCTION
Chad Bennett
V.P., BUSINESS & LEGAL AFFAIRS
Jeff Friedman
V.P., INTERNATIONAL DISTRIBUTION & CREATIVE AFFAIRS
Matt Vassallo

REVELATIONS ENTERTAINMENT
(Motion picture & TV producer)
1221 2nd St., 4th Fl., Santa Monica, CA 90401.
TEL: (310) 394-3131. FAX: (310) 394-3133.
email: info@revelationsent.com www.revelationsent.com
ACTOR, DIRECTOR, PRODUCER & PRESIDENT
Morgan Freeman
CEO, PRODUCER
Lori McCreary
CEO, DIGITAL REVELATIONS
Sam Edge
V.P., PRODUCTION
Cory McCrum
V.P., DEVELOPMENT
Tracy Mercer
BUSINESS MANAGER & CONSULTANT
Stuart Hammer
EXECUTIVE ASSISTANT
Mitch del Valle

RIALTO PICTURES
(Distribution company)
45 E. 72nd St., #16A, New York, NY 10021.
TEL: (212) 717-6773. FAX: (212) 288-8543.
email: rialtonyc@aol.com www.rialtopictures.com
CO-PRESIDENT
Bruce Goldstein, Adrienne Halpern
NATIONAL SALES DIRECTOR
Eric Di Bernardo

RIVER ONE FILMS
(Production company)
8 Stuyvesant Oval, Ste. 10C, New York, NY 10009.
TEL: (917) 748-6834. email: Riveronefilms@yahoo.com
PRESIDENT & PRODUCER
Thomas J. Mangan, IV

RIVER ROAD ENTERTAINMENT
(Production company - Also see Apparition)
2000 Avenue of the Stars, Ste. 620N, Los Angeles, CA 90067.
TEL: (213) 253-4610. FAX: (310) 843-9551.
www.riverroadentertainment.com
PRODUCER/CEO
Bill Pohlad
PRESIDENT
Mitch Horwits
HEAD, PHYSICAL PRODUCTION
Frank Hildebrand
HEAD, BUSINESS AFFAIRS
Deborah Zipser
HEAD, CREATIVE AFFAIRS
Sarah Hammer
BUSINESS AFFAIRS
Angie Miller
CREATIVE EXECUTIVE
Tom Skapars

RKO PICTURES
2034 Broadway, Santa Monica, CA 90404.
TEL: (310) 277-0707. FAX: (310) 566-8940.
750 Lexington Ave., Ste. 2200, New York, NY 10022.
TEL: (212) 644-0600. FAX: (212) 644-0384.
email: info@rko.com www.rko.com
CHAIRMAN & CEO
Ted Hartley
VICE CHAIRMAN
Dina Merrill
PRESIDENT
Andrew Matthews
EXECUTIVE V.P., PRODUCTION & DEVELOPMENT
Vanessa Coifman
V.P., PRODUCTION
Kevin Cornish
V.P., PRODUCTION & FINANCE
Rachel Rose
V.P., MARKETING & DISTRIBUTION
Dylan Wiley
CREATIVE EXECUTIVE
Jonathan Reiman

ROADSIDE ATTRACTIONS
(Distribution company)
7920 Sunset Blvd., Ste. 402, Los Angeles, CA 90046.
TEL: (323) 882-8490. FAX: (323) 882-8493
email: info@roadsideattractions.com
www.roadsideattractions.com
CO-PRESIDENT
Howard Cohen, Eric d'Arbeloff
SENIOR V.P., DISTRIBUTION
Gail Blumenthal
V.P., PUBLICITY
David Pollick
PUBLICITY
Meghann Burns
DISTRIBUTION
Eddie Dotson
POST PRODUCTION
Oliver Levey
ACQUISITIONS & BUSINESS AFFAIRS
Dustin Smith
MARKETING CONSULTANT
Dennis O'Connor
EXHIBITOR RELATIONS
Will Preuss

AMY ROBINSON PRODUCTIONS
(Motion picture, independent film & TV producer)
101 Broadway, Ste. 405, Brooklyn, NY 11211.
TEL: (718) 645-599-2202. email: arobinsonprod@gmail.com
PRODUCER
Amy Robinson
DIRECTOR, DEVELOPMENT
Kelly Faircloth

ZVI HOWARD ROSENMAN PRODUCTIONS
635A Westbourne Dr., Los Angeles, CA 90069.
TEL: (310) 659-2100. email: bigzr@mac.com
PRESIDENT
Zvi Howard Rosenman

ROXIE RELEASING
(U.S. theatrical distributor)
3125 16th St., San Francisco, CA 94103. TEL: (415) 431-3611.
FAX: (415) 431-2822.
email: billbanning2@gmail.com www.roxie.com
CEO
Bill Banning
CO-PRESIDENT, DISTRIBUTION
Rick Norris
CFO
Alan Holt

SCOTT RUDIN PRODUCTIONS
(Production company)
c/o Walt Disney Studios, 500 S. Buena Vista St., Old Animation Bldg., Ste. 2H, Burbank, CA 91521-1759.
TEL: (818) 560-4600. FAX: (818) 560-4608.
120 W. 45th St., 10th. Flr., New York, NY 10036.
TEL: (212) 704-4600.
PRODUCER
Scott Rudin
PRESIDENT
David Bernardi
V.P.
Aaron Janus

SAMUELSON PRODUCTIONS LIMITED
(Motion picture, independent film producer)
10401 Wyton Dr., Los Angeles, CA 90024-2527.
TEL: (310) 208-1000. FAX: (323) 315-5188.
13 Manette St., London W1V 5LB. TEL: (44 207) 439-4900.
FAX: (44 207) 439-4901. email: info@samuelson.la
www.samuelson.la
OWNER
Peter Samuelson - Petersam@who.net
CONTROLLER
Saryl Hirsch
ASSISTANT
Brian Casey

GARY SANCHEZ PRODUCTIONS
1710 N. La Brea Ave., Los Angeles, CA 90046.
TEL: (323) 465-4600. FAX: (323) 465-0782.
www.garysanchezprods.com
PRESIDENT
Gary Sanchez
EXECUTIVE
Will Ferrell, Adam McKay, Chris Henchy, Jessica Elbaum, Owen Burke, Kevin Missick

SANDER/MOSES PRODUCTIONS, INC.
500 S. Buena Vista St., Burbank, CA 91521-1657.
TEL: (818) 560-4500. FAX: (818) 560-8777.
email: info@sandermoses.com www.sandermoses.com
EXECUTIVE PRODUCER/WRITER/DIRECTOR
Ian Sander, Kim Moses
V.P., DEVELOPMENT
Nichelle Protho
ASSISTANT
Betsy DeMik, Amanda Toye

SANFORD/PILLSBURY PRODUCTIONS
(Motion picture, independent film & TV producer)
708 Euclid St., Santa Monica, CA 90402.
TEL: (310) 486-9006. FAX: (310) 393-5013
PRODUCER
Sarah Pillsbury, Midge Sanford

SARABANDE PRODUCTIONS
(Motion picture, independent film & TV producer)
715 Broadway, Ste. 210, Santa Monica, CA 90401.

TEL: (310) 395-4842, (310) 264-4294.
PRESIDENT
David Manson
EXECUTIVE V.P.,
Arla Sorkin Manson

SATURN FILMS

(Motion picture producer)
9000 Sunset Blvd., #911, Los Angeles, CA 90069.
TEL: (310) 887-0900. FAX: (310) 248-2965.
www.saturnfilms.com
CEO & PRODUCER
Nicolas Cage
PRESIDENT & PRODUCER
Norm Golightly
V.P., DEVELOPMENT
Matt Summers
ASSISTANT
Rolly Lee, Michael Davison, Kelly Moore

JOEL SCHUMACHER PRODUCTIONS

(Production company)
10960 Wilshire Blvd., Ste. 1900, Los Angeles, CA 90024.
TEL:(310) 472-7602. FAX: (310) 270-4618.
OWNER
Joel Schumacher
CO-PRODUCER
Aaron Cooley
EXECUTIVE ASSISTANT TO JOEL SCHUMACHER
Jeff Feuerstein

SCOTT FREE PRODUCTIONS

(Production company)
614 N. La Peer Dr., West Hollywood, CA 90069.
TEL: (310) 360-2250. FAX: (310) 360-2251.
CO-CHAIRMAN
Ridley Scott, Tony Scott
PRESIDENT, FILM
Michael Costigan
PRESIDENT, TELEVISION
David W. Zucker
COO
Malcolm Reeve
HEAD, UK OPERATIONS
Liza Marshall
SENIOR V.P., FEATURE DEVELOPMENT
Michael Ellenberg
SENIOR V.P, NON-FICTION & BRANDED ENTERTAINMENT
Mary Lisio
DIRECTOR, FILM DEVELOPMENT
Maresa Pullman
DIRECTOR, T.V. DEVELOPMENT
Jordan Sheehan, Blake Smith
ASSISTANT
Amal Baggar, Tom Moran, Laura Martinez, Elizabeth Mosely, Miguel Reyes

SCREEN MEDIA VENTURES, LLC

(Distribution company)
757 Third Ave., 3rd Flr., New York, NY 10017.
TEL: (212) 308-1790. FAX: (212) 308-1791.
email: info@screenmedia.net www.screenmedia.net
PRESIDENT
Joseph E. Kovacs
PRESIDENT, SCREEN MEDIA FILMS
Robert Baruc
EXECUTIVE V.P., SALES & ACQUISITIONS
Suzanne Blech
EXECUTIVE V.P., BUSINESS AFFAIRS & DEVELOPMENT
David Fannon
SENIOR V.P., INTERNATIONAL SALES
Almira Malyshev
SENIOR V.P., SALES
William Northrop
V.P., INTERNATIONAL SALES & ACQUISITIONS
Michael Dwyer
V.P., OPERATIONS
Donna Tracey
DIRECTOR, OPERATIONS, THEATRICAL & VIDEO
Tom Yagielski
MANAGER, THEATRICAL MARKETING & ACQUISITIONS
Caroline Weisberg

SENATOR ENTERTAINMENT COMPANY

(Motion picture producer)
9000 W. Sunset Blvd., 16th Flr., West Hollywood, CA 90069.
TEL: (310) 248-4700. FAX: (310) 248-4720.
email: info@senatorentertainment.com
CEO & PRESIDENT
Marco Weber
EXECUTIVE V.P., PRODUCTION & DEVELOPMENT
Vanessa CoifmanV.P., ACQUISITIONS & DOMESTIC DISTRIBUTION
Orly Ravid
V.P. PRODUCTION & FINANCE
Rachel Rose
STORY EDITOR
Courtney Rabada
ASSISTANT
Marie-Amelie Rechberg

SENATOR ENTERTAINMENT AG

(International distributor))
Schonhauser Allee 53, Berlin 10437, Germany.
TEL: 49-30-8809-1655. FAX: 49-30-8809-1774.
email: info@senator.de www.senator.de
CEO
Helge Sasse
ATTORNEY
Christopher Borgmann
MANAGING DIRECTOR
Peter Heinzemann
HEAD, ACQUISITIONS
Solveig Fina
HEAD, LEGAL
Celia Kakies

SEVEN ARTS PICTURES

(Independent film producer)
6121 Sunset Blvd., Ste. 512, Hollywood, CA 90028.
TEL: (323) 634-0990. FAX: (323) 634-1061.
www.7artspictures.com
CHAIRMAN & FOUNDER
Peter M. Hoffman
COO
Kate Hoffman
PRODUCER & PARTNER
Susan Hoffman
V.P., BUSINESS AFFAIRS
Justin Kelly
V.P., SALES & DISTRIBUTION
Eric Min
V.P., FINANCE
Marcia Matthew
DIRECTOR, FINANCE
David Bailey
DIRECTOR, DEVELOPMENT & MARKETING
Caroline Couret-Delegue
ASSISTANT
Linda Silverthorn

SEVENTH ART RELEASING

(Motion picture, independent film & TV producer & distributor)
1614 N. Fairfax Ave., Los Angeles, CA 90046.
TEL: (323) 845-1455. FAX: (323) 845-4717.
email: seventhart@7thart.com www.7thart.com
PRINCIPAL
Udy Epstein
V.P., ACQUISITIONS, DEVELOPMENT & MARKETING
Shane Griffin
V.P., THEATRICAL DISTRIBUTION & PUBLIC RELATIONS
Oliver Ike
V.P., EDUCATIONAL SALES & OUTREACH
James Eowan

SHADY ACRES ENTERTAINMENT

(Motion picture, independent film & TV producer)
100 Universal City Plaza, Bldg. 6111, Universal City, CA 91608. TEL: (818) 777-4446. FAX: (818) 866-6612.
PRINCIPAL
Tom Shadyac
CONTACT
Michael Bostick, Ginny Durkin, Dagan Handy, Tom Shadyac, Jason Wilson, Jordan Wolfe, Amanda Morgan Palmer, Greta Bramberg, Anderson Hopkins, Lalo Vasquez

SHOWCASE ENTERTAINMENT, INC.

(Distribution company)
Warner Center, 21800 Oxnard St., Ste. 150, Woodland Hills, CA 91367. TEL: (818) 715-7005. FAX: (818) 715-7009.
www.showcaseentertainment.com
PRESIDENT & CEO
David A. Jackson - david@showcaseentertainment.com
EXECUTIVE V.P.
Shauna Shapiro Jackson
shauna@showcaseentertainment.com
CFO
Bruce Livingston - bruce@showcaseentertainment.com
SENIOR V.P., DISTRIBUTION
Teresa Dokey - teresa@showcaseentertainment.com
V.P., WORLDWIDE DISTRIBUTION SERVICES
Leslie Allmon - leslee@showcaseentertainment.com
V.P., ACQUISITIONS
Cara Shapiro - cara@showcaseentertainment.com
DIRECTOR, INTERNATIONAL SALES
Scott Bedno - scott@showcaseentertainment.com
SALES ADMINISTRATION & MARKET COORDINATOR
Linda Paolucci - linda@showcaseentertainment.com

SHOWSCAN ENTERTAINMENT
468 N. Camden Dr., #200, Beverly Hills, CA 90210.
TEL: (310) 858-5589. FAX: (310) 765-6255.
www.showscan.com
SENIOR V.P., SALES & MARKETING
Sue Y. Kim
SENIOR V.P., PRODUCTION
Woody Park
V.P., WORLDWIDE DISTRIBUTION
Marcelo Floriao
Producer & distributor of contents for media based attractions; developer & producer of large-format films, feature animation films, CGI & TV programming.

SHOWTIME NETWORKS INC.
1633 Broadway, New York, NY 10019. TEL: (212) 708-1600.
10880 Wilshire Blvd., Ste. 1600, Los Angeles, CA 90024.
TEL: (310) 234-5200. FAX: (310) 234-5393. www.sho.com
CHAIRMAN/CEO
Matthew C. Blank
PRESIDENT
Robert Greenblatt (LA)
EXECUTIVE V.P., BUSINESS AFFAIRS
Melinda Benedek (LA)
EXECUTIVE V.P., PROGRAM ACQUISITIONS, PLANNING & DISTRIBUTION
Matthew Duda (LA)

SIGNATURE PICTURES
(Motion picture producer; No unsolicited screenplays etc.)
8285 Sunset Blvd., Ste. 7, Los Angeles, CA 90046.
TEL: (310) 848-9005. FAX: (323) 848-9305.
email: james@signaturepictures.com
www.signaturepictures.com
PRODUCER
Illana Diamant
PRESIDENT
Moshe Diamant
PRODUCTION EXECUTIVE
James Portolese - james@signaturepictures.com

SIKELIA PRODUCTIONS
(Motion picture, independent film & TV producer)
110 W. 57th St., 5th Flr., New York, NY 10019.
TEL: (212) 906-8800. FAX: (212) 906-8891.
DIRECTOR
Martin Scorsese
PRODUCER
Barbara De Fina
PRESIDENT, PRODUCTION
Emma Tillinger

SILVERFILM PRODUCTIONS, INC.
510 Park Ave., #9B, New York, NY 10022.
TEL: (646) 282-0312.
PRESIDENT
Raphael Silver
VICE PRESIDENT
Joan Micklin Silver

SILVERLINE ENTERTAINMENT
(Motion picture & TV movies)
21550 Oxnard St., Ste. 300, Woodland Hills, CA 91367.
TEL: (818) 710-8899. FAX: (818) 710-8848.
email: admin@silverlineentertainment.com
www.silverlineentertainment.com
CEO
Leman Cetiner - leman.cetiner@silverlineentertainment.com
V.P., DEVELOPMENT & DISTRIBUTION
Robert Yap - robert.yap@silverlineentertainment.com

SILVER LION FILMS
(Motion picture producer)
701 Santa Monica Blvd., Ste. 240, Santa Monica, CA 90401.
TEL: (310) 393-9177. FAX: (310) 458-9372.
www.silverlionfilms.com
PRODUCER
Lance Hool, Conrad Hool
CASTING
Carla Hool
DIRECTOR, DEVELOPMENT
Darren Brandl, Veronica Hool
ASSISTANT
Justin Vesci

SILVER PICTURES
(Motion picture & TV producer)
4000 Warner Blvd., Bldg. 90, Burbank, CA 91522.
TEL: (818) 954-4490. FAX: (818) 954-3237.
CHAIRMAN
Joel Silver
COO/CO-PRESIDENT, DARK CASTLE
Steve Richards
PRESIDENT/CO-PRESIDENT, DARK CASTLE
Andrew Rona
SENIOR V.P., PRODUCTION
Alex Heineman
V.P. FINANCE
Adam Kuhn
V.P., PRODUCTION
Ethan Erwin
CREATIVE EXECUTIVE, T.V.
Erika Huttas
CREATIVE EXECUTIVE
Sean Finegan
DIRECTOR, DEVELOPMENT
Sarah Meyer

SINGLE CELL PICTURES
(Production company)
1016 N. Palm Ave., West Hollywood, CA 90069.
TEL: (310) 360-7600. FAX: (310) 360-7011.
PRODUCER
Michael Stipe, Sandy Stern
DVELOPMENT
David Rothley

SITTING DUCKS PRODUCTIONS
2578 Verbena Dr., Los Angeles, CA 90068.
TEL: (323) 461-2095. FAX: (323) 461-2106.
email: sittingducks@earthlink.net
EXECUTIVE PRODUCER
Michael Bedard, Elizabeth Daro

SKYLARK ENTERTAINMENT, INC.
12405 Venice Blvd., Ste. 237, Los Angeles, CA 90066.
TEL: (310) 390-2659.
PRESIDENT & PRODUCER
Jacobus Rose

DANIEL SLADEK ENTERTAINMENT CORP.
8306 Wilshire Blvd., #510, Beverly Hills, CA 90211.
TEL: (323) 934-9268. FAX: (323) 934-7362.
email: dansladek@aol.com www.danielsladek.com
CEO & PRODUCER
Daniel Sladek
PRODUCER/DEVELOPMENT
Chris Taaffe
FINANCIAL AFFAIRS
Marian Salas

SMOKEHOUSE PICTURES
(Motion picture, independent film & TV producer)
12001 Ventura Pl., Ste. 200, Studio City, CA 91604.
TEL: (818) 432-0330. FAX: (818) 432-0337.
PARTNER
George Clooney, Grant Heslov
SENIOR V.P.
Nina Wolarsky
CREATIVE EXECUTIVE
Alex Meenehan

SMOKIN GUN PRODUCTIONS
(News Media segment production company; No submissions)
4872 Filly Ln., Riverside, CA 92509. TEL: (951) 685-8237, (818) 939-2534. email: dannohanks@smokin-gun-productions
www.smokin-gun-productions.com
OWNER/PRODUCER/WRITER/PRIVATE INVESTIGATOR TO THE NEWS MEDIA
Dan "Danno" Hanks

SNAPDRAGON FILMS, INC.
23852 Pacific Coast Hwy., Ste. 373, Malibu, CA 90265.
TEL: (310) 456-0101. FAX: (310) 456-7504.
DIRECTOR & PRODUCER & WRITER
Bonnie Palef - bpalef@earthlink.net
PRODUCER ASSITANT
Michael Stellman

SNEAK PREVIEW ENTERTAINMENT, INC.
(Motion picture, independent film & TV producer; talent & literary managers)
6705 Sunset Blvd. 2nd Flr., Hollywood, CA 90028.
TEL: (323) 962-0295. FAX: (323) 962-0372.
email: indiefilm@sneakpreviewentertain.com
www.sneakpreviewentertain.com
MANAGERS/PRODUCERS
Steven J. Wolfe - sjwolfe@sneakpreviewentertain.com
Michael J. Roth - mjroth@sneakpreviewentertain.com
V.P. PRODUCTION & DEVELOPMENT
Scott Hyman
DIRECTOR, FINANCE ADMINISTRATION
Gints Krastins
OFFICE MANAGER
Matt Rubenstein

SOLO ONE PRODUCTIONS
8205 Santa Monica Blvd., Ste. 1279, Los Angeles, CA 90046-5912. TEL: (323) 658-8748. FAX: (323) 658-8749.
email: solo1productions@aol.com

ACTRESS/ PRODUCER
Marlee Matlin
PRODUCER
Jack Jason

SONY PICTURES ENTERTAINMENT, INC.

10202 W. Washington Blvd., Culver City, CA 90232.
TEL: (310) 244-4000. FAX: (310) 244-2626.
CHAIRMAN & CEO, SPE
Michael Lynton
CO-CHAIRMAN, SPE/CHAIRMAN, MOTION PICTURE GROUP, SPE
Amy Pascal
VICE CHAIRMAN, SPE/CHAIRMAN, WORLDWIDE MARKETING & DISTRIBUTION, CTMPG
Jeff Blake
PRESIDENT, WORLDWIDE AFFAIRS
Peter Schlessel
SENIOR E.V.P. & CHIEF FINANCIAL OFFICER, SPE
David Hendler
SENIOR E.V.P. & GENERAL COUNSEL & ASST. SECRETARY, SPE
Leah Weil
EXECUTIVE V.P./CAO CORPORATE FINANCE, SPE
Ron McNair
SENIOR V.P. & CORPORATE TREASURER, SPE
Simon Baker
VICE PRESIDENT, SCA
Karen Halby

COLUMBIA TRISTAR MOTION PICTURE GROUP

(A Sony Pictures Entertainment company)
10202 W. Washington Blvd., Culver City, CA 90232.
TEL: (310) 244-4000. FAX: (310) 244-2626.
CHAIRMAN, MOTION PICTURE GROUP, SPE
Amy Pascal
PRESIDENT, PRODUCTION ADMINISTRATION & SPS OPS
Gary Martin
PRESIDENT, INTERNATIONAL MOTION PICTURE PRODUCTION
Deborah Schindler
PRESIDENT, WORLDWIDE MUSIC
Lia Vollack
EXECUTIVE V.P., MUSIC CREATIVE AFFAIRS
Spring Aspers
EXECUTIVE V.P., BUSINESS AFFAIRS
Brian Burkin, Ronni Coulter
EXECUTIVE V.P., POST PRODUCTION
James Honore
EXECUTIVE V.P., CFO
Stefan Litt
SENIOR V.P., PRODUCTION ADMINISTRATION
Pete Corral, Andy Given
SENIOR V.P., FEATURE PRODUCTION
Lori Furie
SENIOR V.P., POST PRODUCTION
Russ Paris
SENIOR V.P., MARKETING & DISTRIBUTION
Paula Parker
SENIOR V.P., MUSIC ADMINISTRATION
Raul Perez
SENIOR VICE PRESIDENT, INTERNATIONAL POST PRODUCTION
Beverly Starr
SENIOR V.P., BUSINESS AFFAIRS
Mark Wyman
V.P, PRODUCTION ADMINISTRATION
Debra Grieco Bergman
V.P, POST PRODUCTION
Desmond Cannon, Vincent Scotti
V.P, EUROPEAN PRODUCTION, SPAIN
Jordi Gasull
V.P, WORLDWIDE THEATRICAL RESEARCH
Patricia Kendig
V.P, MUSIC LICENSING
Donald Kennedy
V.P, PRODUCTION ADMINISTRATION
Adam Moos
V.P, STORY DEPT.
Karen Moy
V.P, BUSINESS AFFAIRS
Daniel Primozic
V.P, WORLDWIDE THEATRICAL RESEARCH
Abe Recio
V.P, INTERNATIONAL POST PRODUCTION
Paul Stapley-Tovey
V.P, INTERNATIONAL PRODUCTION
Paul Stapley-Tovey
V.P, PRODUCTION, FRANCE
Candice Zaccagnino

COLUMBIA PICTURES

(A Sony Pictures Entertainment Company)
10202 W. Washington Blvd., Culver City, CA 90232.
TEL: (310) 244-4000. FAX: (310) 244-2626.
CHAIRMAN, MOTION PICTURE GROUP, SPE
Amy Pascal
PRESIDENT
Doug Belgrad
PRESIDENT
Matt Tolmach
PRESIDENT, BUSINESS AFFAIRS & ADMINISTRATION
Andrew Gumpert
EXECUTIVE V.P., PRODUCTION
Elizabeth Cantillon, Andrea Giannetti
SENIOR V.P., PRODUCTION
Samuel Dickerman, Jonathan Kadin
SENIOR V.P., EUROPEAN PRODUCTION
Iona Macedo
SENIOR V.P., BUSINESS AFFAIRS
Michael Marshall
V.P., PRODUCTION
Devon Franklin, Adam Milano, Rachel O'Connor

SCREEN GEMS

(A Sony Pictures Entertainment Company)
10202 W. Washington Blvd., Culver City, CA 90232.
TEL: (310) 244-4000.
PRESIDENT
Clinton Culpepper
EXECUTIVE V.P., GENERAL MANAGER
Pam Kunath
EXECUTIVE V.P., MARKETING
Loren Schwartz
SENIOR V.P., PRODUCTION
Gilbert Dumontet
SENIOR V.P., BUSINESS AFFAIRS
Michael Helfand
SENIOR V.P., PUBLICITY
Danielle Misher
SENIOR V.P., PRODUCTION
Peter Nelson, Eric Paquette, Nick Phillips, Scott Strauss

SONY PICTURES CLASSICS

(A Sony Pictures Entertainment Company)
550 Madison Ave., 8th Flr., New York, NY 10022.
TEL: (212) 833-8833. FAX: (212) 833-4190.
www.spe.sony.com/classics
CO-PRESIDENT
Michael Barker, Tom Bernard
EXECUTIVE V.P., ACQUISITIONS
Dylan Leiner
SENIOR V.P., OPERATIONS
Grace Murphy
SENIOR V.P., MARKETING
Carmelo Pirrone
SENIOR V.P., SALES
Tom Prassis
V.P., BUSINESS AFFAIRS
Diane Buck

SONY PICTURES RELEASING

(A Sony Pictures Entertainment Company)
10202 W. Washington Blvd., Culver City, CA 90232.
TEL: (310) 244-4000. FAX: (310) 244-4337.
PRESIDENT, RELEASING
Rory Bruer
PRESIDENT, DISTRIBUTION
Jim Amos
EXECUTIVE V.P. & GENERAL SALES MANAGER
David Garel
SENIOR V.P., SALES
Glenn Abrams
SENIOR V.P., SALES ADMINISTRATION
Craig Bartlet
SENIOR V.P. & GM, CANADA
Michael Brooker
SENIOR V.P., EXHIBITOR RELATIONS
Ann-Elizabeth Crotty
SENIOR V.P., WORLDWIDE PRINT OPERATIONS
Michael Jones
SENIOR V.P., WORLDWIDE NON-THEATRICAL SALES
Rana Matthes
SENIOR V.P., SALES, SOUTHERN DIVISION
Juli Mitchell
SENIOR V.P., DIGITAL CINEMA OPERATIONS
Scott Sherr
SENIOR V.P., WESTERN DIVISION
Adrian Smith
SENIOR V.P., SALES, MIDWESTERN DIVISION
Jim Weiss
V.P., EXHIBITOR RELATIONS
Wendy Armitage
V.P., SALES, EASTERN DIVISION
Adam Bergerman
V.P., SALES, CANADA
Tim Bishop

V.P., WORLDWIDE DISTRIBUTION ANALYSIS
John Cacavas
V.P., SALES, CENTRAL DIVISION
Kristen Calder
V.P., SALES, SOUTHERN DIVISION
Patricia Dougherty
V.P., FINANCIAL ADMINISTRATION
Ellen Mandel
V.P., SALES, WESTERN DIVISION
Ross Merrin
V.P., SALES, SOUTHERN DIVISION
Juli Mitchell
V.P., PRINT OPERATIONS
Rosemarie Ortiz
V.P., REPERTORY SALES & ACQUISITIONS
Michael Schlesinger
V.P., CANADIAN MEDIA & COOP ADVERTISING
Donna Slack
V.P., SALES, EASTERN DIVISION
John Spinello

SONY PICTURES RELEASING INTERNATIONAL
PRESIDENT, DISTRIBUTION
Mark L. Zucker
SENIOR V.P., INTERNATIONAL DISTRIBUTION & OPERATIONS
Ralph Alexander, Jr.
EXECUTIVE V.P., THEATRICAL CREATIVE ADVERTISING
Ignacio Darnaude
EXECUTIVE V.P., MARKETING, ACQUISITIONS & LOCAL LANGUAGES
Sal Ladestro
EXECUTIVE V.P., PUBLICITY AND PROMOTIONS
Susan van der Werff
SENIOR V.P., INTERNATIONAL DISTRIBUTION
Steve Bruno
SENIOR V.P., INTL. MEDIA
Gina Kilberg
SENIOR V.P., INTL. DISTRIBUTION
Steven O'Dell
SENIOR V.P., INTL. OPERATIONS
Jay Sands
SENIOR V.P., FILM DISTRIBUTION, SPE-JAPAN
Noriaki (Dick) Sano
SENIOR V.P., MARKETING, LATIN AMERICA
Vittorio Tamburini
V.P., DISTRIBUTION
Mimi Burri
V.P., GLOBAL PROMOTIONS
Zachary Eller
V.P., PUBLICITY/ACQUISITIONS & LOCAL PRODUCTIONS
Catherine Escandell
V.P., INTERNATIONAL PRINT SERVICES
Stephen Foligno
V.P., FILM DISTRIBUTION MARKETING, SPE-JAPAN
Megumi Fukasawa
V.P., PRINT PRODUCTION
Alexander Kostich

SONY PICTURES HOME ENTERTAINMENT
(A Sony Pictures Entertainment Company)
10202 W. Washington Blvd., Culver City, CA 90232.
TEL: (310) 244-4000. FAX: (310) 244-2626.
PRESIDENT, SPHE WORLDWIDE
David Bishop
SENIOR E.V.P., WORLDWIDE MARKETING
Lexine Wong
EXECUTIVE V.P., NORTH AMERICA & INTERNATIONAL
Matthew Brown
EXECUTIVE V.P., WORLDWIDE OPERATIONS
Aodan Coburn
EXECUTIVE V.P., ADVANCED TECHNOLOGIES
Don Eklund
SENIOR V.P., MOBILE ENTERTAINMENT
Eric Berger
SENIOR V.P., WORLDWIDE MARKETING
Alison Biggers
SENIOR V.P., VENDOR MANAGED INVENTORY
Geri Bluerock
SENIOR V.P., BUSINESS PLANNING & COMMERCIAL STRATEGY
Claude Borna
SENIOR V.P., SPHE, SPE-JAPAN
Kento Doi
SENIOR V.P., PRODUCTION
Gilbert Dumontet
SENIOR V.P., WORLDWIDE PUBLICITY
Fritz Friedman
SENIOR V.P., MARKETING
Tracey Garvin
SENIOR V.P., INTERNATIONAL FINANCE & ACCOUNTING
Tim Jacobson
SENIOR V.P., BUSINESS AFFAIRS
Pam Kunath
SENIOR V.P., SALES OPERATIONS
Michael Landesberg
SENIOR V.P., BUSINESS DEVELOPMENT
Stephen Lyons
SENIOR V.P., INTERNATIONAL
T. Paul Miller
SENIOR V.P., MARKETING, MEDIA & CONSUMER RESEARCH
Jane Mohon
SENIOR V.P., WORLDWIDE CREATIVE ADVERTISING
Kelly Nielsen
SENIOR V.P., STRATEGIC DEVELOPMENT
Jason Spivak
SENIOR V.P. & CFO
Bill Stellman
SENIOR V.P., SALES/RETAIL EXPANSION
Jack Talley
SENIOR V.P., POST PRODUCTION SERVICES
Brad Word
SENIOR V.P., PRODUCTION SERVICES
Robert Ziegler
V.P. & MANAGING DIRECTOR, LATIN AMERICA
Fernando Amieva
V.P., MARKETING
Jennifer Anderson
V.P., OPERATIONS
Steve Belmont
V.P., SALES
David Blair
V.P., EUROPEAN OPERATIONS
Natasha Currie
V.P., RESEARCH
Eric Daly
V.P., PRODUCTION SERVICES
Thomas Dohner
V.P., CANADA
Derrick Forster
V.P., FINANCE
Barbara Franqui-Hevener
V.P., DOMESTIC SALES
Joel Goldman
V.P., INTERNATIONAL
Amy Heller, Tony Ishizuka
V.P., VENDOR MANAGED INVENTORY
Sheela Jairaj
V.P., SALES OPERATIONS
Michael Landesberg
V.P., INTERNATIONAL BUSINESS DEVELOPMENT
Rich Marty
V.P., SUPERCOMM
Matt McIntosh
V.P., WORLDWIDE PROGRAMMING
Michelle Mikesell
V.P., AFFIRM FILMS
Rich Peluso
V.P., CATALOGUE & TV MARKETING
Marc Rashba
V.P., INTERNATIONAL ADMINISTRATION
Joe Reid
V.P., INTERNATIONAL RETAIL OPERATIONS
David Rowlands
V.P., WORLDWIDE CREATIVE ADVERTISING
Gregg Shack
V.P., BUSINESS DEVELOPMENT
Norman Tajudin
V.P., SPE-JAPAN
Yoshiki Terashima
V.P., SUPPLY CHAIN OPERATIONS
Michael Thielen
V.P., INTERNATIONAL DISTRIBUTION
Russell Wood
V.P., PLANNING & CONTROL, SPE-JAPAN
Masayoshi Yamano

SONY PICTURES DIGITAL PRODUCTION
3960 Ince Blvd., Culver City, CA 90232. TEL: (310) 840-8676.
FAX: (310) 840-8390.
PRESIDENT
Bob Osher
SENIOR V.P., MARKETING & COMMUNICATIONS
Don Levy
V.P., MARKETING
Becky Chaires
V.P., DEVELOPMENT
Michael Lachance
V.P., ARTIST RECRUITMENT & IPAX
Ken Maruyama
V.P., STRATEGIC ALLIANCES
Michael Wayne

SONY PICTURES ANIMATION
9050 W. Washington Blvd., Culver City, CA 90232.
TEL: (310) 840-8000. FAX: (310) 840-8100.

PRESIDENT, PRODUCTION
Hannah Minghella
SENIOR V.P., DEVELOPMENT
Nate Hopper
V.P., DEVELOPMENT
Alexa Amin
V.P., DEVELOPMENT
Michael Lachance

SONY PICTURES TECHNOLOGIES
10202 W. Washington Blvd., Culver City, CA 90232.
TEL: (310) 244-4000.
PRESIDENT
Chris Cookson
EXECUTIVE V.P., ADVANCED TECHNOLOGIES
George Joblove
SENIOR V.P., 3D TECHNOLOGY CENTER
Buzz (David) Hays

SONY PICTURES IMAGEWORKS
(A Sony Pictures Entertainment Company)
9050 W. Washington Blvd., Culver City, CA 90232.
TEL: (310) 840-8000. FAX: (310) 840-8100.
EXECUTIVE V.P. & EXEC. PRODUCER, PROD. INFRAS.
Debbie Denise
EXECUTIVE V.P., GENERAL MANAGER
Randy Lake
SENIOR V.P., IMAGEWORKS INTERACTIVE
Emmanuelle Borde
SENIOR V.P., OPERATIONS
Thomas Hershey
SENIOR V.P., DIGITAL PRODUCTION
Stanley Szymanski
V.P., CLIENT SERVICES, IMAGEWORKS INTERACTIVE
J.D. Black
V.P., PRODUCTION & TECHNOLOGY, IMAGEWORKS INTERACTIVE
Scott Nourse
V.P., SYSTEMS ENGINEERING
Alberto Velez
CTO, SONY PICTURES IMAGEWORKS
Rob Bredow

SONY PICTURES WORLDWIDE ACQUISITIONS GROUP
10202 W. Washington Blvd., Ste. 209, Culver City, CA 90232.
TEL: (310) 244-4000. FAX: (310) 244-0635.
PRESIDENT
Steven Bersch
SENIOR E.V.P. & GENERAL MANAGER
Adrian Alperovich
EXECUTIVE V.P., LEGAL
David Steinberg
V.P., ACQUISITIONS
Lia Buman
V.P., ACQUISITIONS
Scott Shooman

SONY PICTURES WORLDWIDE MARKETING & DISTRIBUTION
10202 W. Washington Blvd., Culver City, CA 90232.
TEL: (310) 244-4000. FAX: (310) 244-2626.
www.sonypictures.com
CHAIRMAN, WORLDWIDE MARKETING & DISTRIBUTION
Jeff Blake
PRESIDENT, WORLDWIDE DIGITAL MARKETING
Dwight Caines
PRESIDENT, WORLDWIDE CREATIVE ADVERTISING
Tommy Gagotta
CO-PRESIDENT, WORLDWIDE THEATRICAL MARKETING
Marc Weinstock
PRESIDENT, WORLDWIDE STRATEGIC MARKETING
David Kaminow
SENIOR EXECUTIVE V.P., MARKETING
Nigel Clark
EXECUTIVE V.P., PUBLICITY
Andre Caraco
EXECUTIVE V.P., CREATIVE ADVERTISING
William Loper
EXECUTIVE V.P., MEDIA
Stefanie Napoli
EXECUTIVE V.P., PUBLICITY
Gigi Semone
SENIOR V.P., SPECIAL EVENTS
Alison Bossert
SENIOR V.P., MEDIA RELATIONS
Steve Elzer
SENIOR V.P., PUBLICITY
Wendy Lightbourn, Marisa McGrath
SENIOR V.P., CREATIVE ADVERTISING
Michael Pavlic
SENIOR V.P., WORLDWIDE DIGITAL MEDIA
Elias Plishner
SENIOR V.P., PUBLICITY
Ileen Reich
SENIOR V.P., GLOBAL MARKETING PARTNERSHIPS
Mary Goss Robino
SENIOR V.P., CREATIVE MEDIA
Nancy Tate
V.P., STRATEGIC MARKETING & RESEARCH
Seth Byers
V.P., DIGITAL MARKETING STRATEGY
Amy Conley
V.P., WORLDWIDE TRAFFIC SERVICES
Rick Davidson
V.P., PHOTOGRAPHY DEPARTMENT
Milissa Douponce
V.P., MARKETING
Joseph Epstein
V.P., WORLDWIDE DIGITAL MARKETING STRATEGY
Michael Fisk
V.P., PUBLICITY
Pamela Godwin-Austen
V.P., INTERNATIONAL MEDIA
Sharri Lear
V.P., CREATIVE ADVERTISING
Dianna Mannheim
V.P., CREATIVE CONSUMER MARKETING
Randy Nellis
V.P., MARKETING PRODUCTION
Jim Rodriguez
V.P., INTEGRATED MEDIA PARTNERSHIPS & FIELD PROMOTIONS
Jason Rumminger
V.P., MARKETING
Mike Schlitt
V.P., AUDIO VISUAL
Arthur Shapiro
V.P., BRANDED INTEGRATION
Katherine Talutis
V.P., PRINT ADVERTISING
Mark Walker
V.P., CREATIVE CONTENT
Kristin Withers
V.P., MEDIA
Ann Yoo

CRACKLE
(Online video network. A SONY Pictures Entertainment Company)
9336 W. Washington Blvd., Culver City, CA 90232.
TEL: (310) 845-2626. www.crackle.com
SENIOR V.P., VIDEO NETWORKS
Eric Berger
V.P., NETWORKS & MARKETING
Mark Cregar

2-WAY TRAFFIC
(A Sony Pictures Entertainment company)
Middenweg 1, 1217 HS Hilversum, The Netherlands.
CEO
Kees Abrahams
CFO
Jeroen Tielens
CCO
Taco Katelaar
HEAD, LEGAL
Andrew Moss
HEAD, INTERNATIONAL PRODUCTION
Rod Taylor
HEAD, PRESS & PR
Yvette Dore

SPIRIT DANCE ENTERTAINMENT
(Motion picture, independent film & TV producer)
1023 N. Orange Dr., Los Angeles, CA 90038-2317.
TEL: (323) 512-7988. FAX: (323) 512-7996.
PRESIDENT/PRODUCER/DIRECTOR
Forest Whitaker

SPRING CREEK PRODUCTIONS, INC.
(Production company)
4000 Warner Blvd., Bldg. 144, Ste. 100B, Burbank, CA 91522.
TEL: (818) 954-2100. FAX: (818) 954-2130.
PRODUCER
Paula Weinstein
VICE PRESIDENT
Jeffrey Levine

SPYGLASS ENTERTAINMENT
(Motion picture, independent film & TV producer)
10900 Wilshire Blvd., Los Angeles, CA, 90024.
TEL: (310) 443-5800. FAX: (310) 443-5912.
www.spyglassentertainment.com
CO-CHAIRMAN & CEO
Gary Barber, Roger Birnbaum
PRESIDENT
Jonathan Glickman
EXECUTIVE V.P., CFO
Jose Gutierrez

EXECUTIVE V.P., POST PRODUCTION
Rebekah Rudd
SENIOR V.P., PHYSICAL PRODUCTION
Peter Oillataguerre
SENIOR V.P., PRODUCTION
Adam Rosenberg
SENIOR V.P., BUSINESS & LEGAL AFFAIRS
Scott Sebasty
V.P., PRODUCTION FINANCE
Brian Bruskrud
V.P., PRODUCTION
Cassidy Lange
V.P., LEGAL AFFAIRS
Alison Chavez
V.P., INTERNAITONAL DISTRIBUTION & FINANCE
Myleen Llaurado
V.P., FINANCE
Jared Lindsey
V.P., INFORMATION TECHNOLOGY
Michael Naud
EXECUTIVE DIRECTOR
Kim Buttlar, Marlena Thomas
STORY EDITOR
Matt Dines

During 2010, Metro-Goldwyn-Mayer Inc., was subject to a fierce takeover battle between Spyglass' Gary Barber and Roger Birnbaum and a Carl Ichan backed Lionsgate. MGM went into a pre-packaged bankruptcy, with $4 billion in debt converted into equity, and the creditors finally approved the Spyglass proposal. Gary Barber and Roger Birnbaum will become Co-Chairmen/CEOs of MGM.

STAMPEDE ENTERTAINMENT

(Motion picture, independent film & TV producer)
3000 Olympic Blvd., Ste. #2525, Bldg. #2, Santa Monica, CA 90404. TEL: (310) 264 4229. FAX: (310) 552-7800.
email: info@stampede-entertainment.com
www.stampede-entertainment.com
PARTNER, CO-CHAIRMAN & CEO
Nancy Roberts
PARTNER & CO-CHAIRMAN
S.S. Wilson
PARTNER
Brent Maddock

STARZ LLC

(A production & distribution company)

STARZ ENTERTAINMENT

(Distribution Company)
8900 Liberty Circle, Englewood, CO 80112.
TEL: (720) 852-7700. FAX: (720) 852-8555.
www.starz.com
PRESIDENT/CEO, STARZ, LLC
Chris Albrecht
PRESIDENT /COO
William Myers
PRESIDENT, ANCHOR BAY ENTERTAINMENT
Bill Clark
EXECUTIVE V.P./GENERAL COUNSEL
Steve Beabout
EXECUTIVE VP/CFO
Glenn Curtis
DEPUTY GENERAL COUNSEL/SENIOR V.P., BUSINESS & LEGAL AFFAIRS, PRODUCTION
Marc Barson
EXECUTIVE V.P., WORLDWIDE DISTRIBUTION, STARS MEDIA
Gene George
MANAGING DIRECTOR, ORIGINAL PROGRAMMING
Carmi Zlotnik
EXECUTIVE V.P., AFFILIATE SALES & MARKETING
Edward Huguez
EXECUTIVE V.P., FINANCE & ACCOUNTING
Scott MacDonald
EXECUTIVE V.P., MARKETING
Nancy McGee
EXECUTIVE V.P., STRATEGY & BUSINESS DEVELOPMENT
John Penney
EXECUTIVE V.P., PROGRAMMING & ACQUISITIONS
Stephan Shelanski
SENIOR V.P., HUMAN RESOURCES & ADMINISTRATION
Sheryl Anderson
SENIOR V.P., PROGRAMMING & PUBLICITY
Paul Campbell
SENIOR V.P., AFFILIATE SALES
Christine Carrier
SENIOR V.P., PRODUCT PLANNING & DEVELOPMENT
David Charmatz
SENIOR V.P., DIGITAL MEDIA, BUSINESS DEVELOPMENT
Marc DeBevoise
SENIOR V.P., AFFILIATE SALES
Debbie Egner
SENIOR V.P., CREATIVE SERVICES
Emilio Mata
SENIOR V.P., MARKETING
Ferrell McDonald
SENIOR V.P., PROGRAMMING OPERATIONS & INFORMATION TECHNOLOGY
Ray Milius
SENIOR V.P., AFFILIATE SALES
Andy Nigolian
SENIOR V.P., BUSINESS & LEGAL AFFAIRS, PROGRAMMING
Michelle Parker
SENIOR V.P., MARKETING
Kelly Ruebel-Bumann
SENIOR V.P., PROGRAM PLANNING & SCHEDULING
Jonathan Shair
SENIOR V.P., SALES & AFFILIATE MARKETING
Keno Thomas
SENIOR V.P., BUSINESS AFFAIRS, PROGRAMMING
Richard Turner
SENIOR V.P., BUSINESS AFFAIRS, DISTRIBUTION
Richard Waysdorf
V.P., PROGRAM & PROMOTION PLANNING & SCHEDULING
Debbie Alther
V.P., PRODUCT PLANNING & DEVELOPMENT
Linda Brauns
V.P., PROGRAMMING PUBLICITY
Chelsye Burrows
V.P., AFFILIATE SALES
Tom Gove
V.P., ONLINE MARKETING
Ann Ivancie
V.P., PROGRAMMING OPERATIONS
Amy Kline
V.P., AFFILIATE SALES
Randall McCurdy
V.P., PROGRAMMING ANALYTICS
Suzanne Sell
V.P., PROGRAM ACQUISITIONS
Nancy Silverstone
V.P., BUSINESS AFFAIRS, MARKETING
Tim Sweeney
V.P., PUBLIC RELATIONS, STARZ MEDIA
Jonathan Taylor
EXECUTIVE DIRECTOR, CORPORATE COMMUNICATIONS
Eric Beckers
EXECUTIVE DIRECTOR, MARKETING, SALES & CORPORATE RESEARCH
Neal Massey

Produces animation, documentaries, Internet content, mobile content, specials & TV series.

STARZ

(Production company)
9242 Beverly Blvd., Ste. 200, Beverly Hills, CA 90210.
TEL: (424) 204-4110. FAX: (720) 852-7700.
www.stars.com
PRESIDENT & CEO, STARZ, LLC
Chris Albrecht
PRESIDENT & COO, STARZ MEDIA & STARZ ENTERTAINMENT
Bill Myers
MANAGING DIRECTOR, STARZ MEDIA
Carmi Zlotnik
EXECUTIVE V.P./CFO, STARZ LLC/COO, STARZ ANIMATION
Glenn Curtis
EXECUTIVE V.P., WORLDWIDE DISTRIBUTION
Gene George
EXECUTIVE V.P., STRATEGY * BUSINESS DEVELOPMENT
John Penney
EXECUTIVE V.P., PROGRAMMING, STARZ ENTERTAINMENT
Stephan Shelanski
SENIOR V.P., STRATEGIC MARKETING & PROMOTION (NY)
Paul Campbell
SENIOR V.P., DIGITAL MEDIA, BUSINESS DEVELOPMENT & STRATEGY (NY)
Marc DeBevoise
SENIOR V.P., WORLDWIDE MARKETING, STARZ MEDIA
Ferrell McDonald
SENIOR V.P., NETWORK OPERATIONS
Jonathan Shair
SENIOOR V.P., BUSINESS & LEGAL AFFAIRS, PROGRAMMING
Richard Turner
DEPUTY GENERAL COUNSEL/SENIOR V.P., BUSINESS & LEGAL AFFAIRS
Marc Barson
V.P., PRODUCTIONS, STARZ PRODUCTIONS
Karen Bailey
V.P., DOMESTIC SALES
Alecia Dixon
V.P., STARZ ORIGINALS
Marta Fernandez

V.P., PRODUCTION FINANCE
Richter Hartig
V.P., STARZ ORIGINALS
Robert Markovich
V.P., PUBLICITY, STARZ
Jonathan Taylor
HEAD OF STUDIO, FILM ROMAN
Jay Fukuto
HEAD OF STUDIO, STARZ ANIMATION (TORONTO)
David Steinberg
Produces feature and TV content: animation, direct-to-video/DVD, documentaries, Internet content, made-for-TV/Cable movies, mini-series, reality TV, specials & TV series.

FILM ROMAN, A STARZ COMPANY
(Production company)
2950 N. Hollywood Way, 3rd Flr., Burbank, CA 91505.
TEL: (818) 748-4000. FAX: (818) 748-4613.
www.filmroman.com
COO
Glenn Curtis
HEAD, STUDIO
Jay Fukuto
DEPUTY GENERAL COUNSEL/ ENIOR V.P., BUSINESS & LEGAL AFFAIRS
Marc Barson
EXECUTIVE V.P., WORLDWIDE DISTRIBUTION
Gene George
V.P., BUSINESS DEVELOPMENT, VISUAL EFFECTS
Carin Davis
V.P., PROJECT DEVELOPMENT & SALES
Heather Kenyon
V.P., WORLDWIDE DISTRIBUTION
Alesha Serold
V.P., PUBLICITY
Jonathan Taylor

STATE STREET PICTURES
(Motion picture, independent film & TV producer)
8075 W. Third St., Ste. 306, Los Angeles, CA 90048.
TEL: (323) 556-2240. FAX: (323) 556-2242.
PRODUCER
Robert Teitel
DIRECTOR
George Tillman, Jr.
V.P., PRODUCTION & DEVELOPMENT
Rene Rigal

THE HOWARD STERN PRODUCTION COMPANY
(Motion picture, independent film & TV producer)
10 E. 44th St., New York, NY 10017. TEL: (212) 867-1200.
FAX: (212) 867-2434.
PRESIDENT
Howard Stern
AGENT
Don Buchwald

STRAND RELEASING
(Motion picture, independent film & TV producer & distributor)
6140 W. Washington Blvd., Culver City, CA 90232.
TEL: (310) 836-7500. FAX: (310) 836-7510.
email: strand@strandreleasing.com www.strandreleasing.com
CO-PRESIDENT
Jon Gerrans, Marcus Hu
V.P., SALES & DISTRIBUTION
David Bowlds
V.P., OPERATONS, HOME ENTERTAINMENT
Chantal Chauzy
DIRECTOR, OPERATIONS & PUBLICITY
Samantha Klinger
DIRECTOR, ACQUISITIONS
Brandon Peters

STUART STREET PRODUCTIONS, INC.
(Theater, motion picture & television producer)
Stuart Street Playhouse, 200 Stuart St., Boston, MA 02116.
TEL: (617) 423-1202. email: napssp@gmail.com
www.nickpaleologos.net
PRESIDENT
Nicholas Paleologos

STUDIOCANAL/CANAL + DISTRIBUTION
(Distributor & sales)
1, Place du spectacle, Issy-les Moulineaux 92130, France
TEL: 33-1-7135-1113. FAX: 33-1-7135-1186.
email: pascale.hornus@canal-plus.com www.studiocanal.com
301 N. Canon Drive, Ste. 210, Beverly Hills, CA 90210.
TEL: (310) 247-0994. FAX: (310) 247-0998.
www.studiocanal.com
CEO
Olivier Courson
CFO, FINANCE
Romain Bessi
COO
Camille Trumer
EXECUTIVE V.P., BUSINESS AFFAIRS
Sylvie Arnould
EXECUTIVE V.P., INTERNATIONAL DISTRIBUTION & DEVELOPMENT
Rodolphe Buet
EXECUTIVE V.P., HOME ENTERTAINMENT
Françoise Guyonnet
EXECUTIVE V.P., INTERNATIONAL PRODUCTION & REMAKE DEVELOPMENT
Ron Halpern
U.S. CONTACT
Barbara DiNallo

SUMMIT ENTERTAINMENT
(Motion picture producer & full service domestic distributor)
1630 Stewart St., Ste. 120, Santa Monica, CA 90404.
TEL: (310) 309-8400. FAX: (310) 828-4132.
www.summit-ent.com
CO-CHAIRMAN/CEO
Robert G. Friedman
CO-CHAIRMAN/PRESIDENT
Patrick Wachsberger
COO
Bob Hayward
PRESIDENT, WORLDWIDE MARKETING
Nancy Kirkpatrick
CFO
Ron Hohauser
PRESIDENT, SUMMIT INTERNATIONAL (UK)
David Garrett
PRESIDENT, DOMESTIC THEATRICAL DISTRIBUTION
Richard Fay
PRESIDENT, DOMESTIC TELEVISION DISTRIBUTION
Alex Fragen
PRESIDENT, PRODUCTION & ACQUISITIONS
Erik Feig
PRESIDENT, HOME ENTERTAINMENT
Steve Nickerson
EXECUTIVE V.P., GENERAL COUNSEL
David Friedman
EXECUTIVE V.P., HOME ENTERTAINMENT
Sandy Friedman
EXECUTIVE V.P., GENERAL SALES MANAGER
Bobby Gerber
EXECUTIVE V.P., BUSINESS AFFAIRS
Andrew Matosich
EXECUTIVE V.P., MARKETING
Jack Pan
SENIOR V.P., INTERNATIONAL SALES
Ralpho Borgos
SENIOR V.P., MEDIA
Gail Heaney
SENIOR V.P., HEAD, PHYSICAL PRODUCTION
Andi Isaacs
SENIOR V.P., PUBLICITY
Eric Kops
SENIOR V.P., HEAD, LEGAL AFFAIRS
Patricia Laucella
SENIOR V.P., ACQUISITIONS & CO-PRODUCTIONS
Michael Schaefer
SENIOR V.P., PRODUCTION
Geoff Shaevitz
SENIOR V.P., CREATIVE ADVERTISING
Tim Sommerfeld
GENERAL SALES MANAGER, DOMESTIC DISTRIBUTION
William Lewis
DOMESTIC EASTERN DIVISION MANAGER
Pam Araugo
V.P., PRODUCTION
Meredith Milton, Jean Song
V.P., ACQUISITIONS
Michael Schaefer
CREATIVE EXECUTIVE
Ashley Schlaifer

TAPESTRY FILMS, INC.
9328 Civic Center Dr., Beverly Hills, CA 90210.
TEL: (310) 275-1191. FAX: (310) 275-1266.
email: tapestryfilms@tapestryfilms.com
PRODUCER & PARTNER
Peter Abrams, Robert L. Levy
V.P., PRODUCTION & DEVELOPMENT
Michael Schreiber
BUSINESS AFFAIRS
Alicia Hopkins
CREATIVE EXECUTIVE
Katherine Blasband

TAURUS ENTERTAINMENT COMPANY
(Motion picture, independent film & TV producer & distributor)
c/o Paramount Pictures, 5555 Melrose Ave., Marx Brothers 103/104, Los Angeles, CA 90036.
TEL: (818) 935-5157. FAX: (818) 686-5379.

email: taurusentco@yahoo.com www.taurusec.com
PRESIDENT & CEO
James Dudelson
PRESIDENT & CFO
Robert Dudelson
V.P., PRODUCTION & POST PRODUCTION
Ana Clavell
DIRECTOR, AQUISITIONS
Stephan Gorel
CONTRACT ADMINSITRATOR
Cyndi Stone

TAYLOR MADE FILMS
(Motion picture, independent film & TV producer)
1270 Stone Canyon, Los Angeles, CA 90077.
TEL: (310) 472-1763. FAX: (310) 472-8698.
email: tmadefilms@aol.com www.taylormadefilms.net
PRESIDENT & PRODUCER
Geoffrey Taylor

TEITELBAUM ARTISTS GROUP
(Talent management & production company)
8840 Wilshire Blvd., Beverly Hills, CA 90211.
TEL: (310) 358-3250. FAX: (310) 358-3251.
PRESIDENT
Mark Teitelbaum

TELLING PICTURES, INC.
(Motion picture, independent film & TV producer & distributor)
10 Arkansas St., Ste. F, San Francisco, CA 94107.
TEL: (415) 864-6714. email: info@tellingpictures.com
www.tellingpictures.com
PRODUCER & DIRECTOR
Rob Epstein
PRODUCER & DIRECTOR
Jeffrey Friedman
OFFICE MANAGER
James Chan

TEMPLE HILL PRODUCTIONS
(Production company)
9255 Sunset Blvd., Ste. 801, Los Angeles, CA 90069.
TEL: (310) 270-4383. FAX: (310) 270-4395.
PARTNER
Marty Bowen, Wyck Godfrey
DIRECTOR, DEVELOPMENT
Amanda Countner Brown
CREATIVE DIRECTOR
Matthew Cohen
ASSISTANT
Isaac Klausner, Adam Londy

THINKFILM
(Distribution company)
72 Madison Ave., 6th Flr., New York, NY 10016.
TEL: (212) 444-7900. FAX: (212) 444-7901.
email: info@thinkfilmcompany.com www.thinkfilmcompany.com
CHAIRMAN
David Bergstein
V.P., ACQUISITIONS & DEVELOPMENT
Ben Stambler

THOMPSON/STARR ORGANIZATION
PMB 11236, Beverly Hills, CA 90213-4236. TEL: (818) 998-8126.
FAX: (818) 773-8962. email: tsorg@webtv.net
PRESIDENT
Joey Thompson
SALES
Jen Starr, Georges Alain
ACQUISITIONS
William Thompson
MARKETING
Chaya Finton

THREE STRANGE ANGELS, INC.
(Motion picture producer)
8750 Wilshire Blvd., Ste. 300 E, Beverly Hills, CA 90211.
TEL: (310) 601-2291. FAX: (310) 601-2298.
PRODUCER
Lindsay Doran

TIDEWATER ENTERTAINMENT, INC.
(Production)
3841 Mentone Ave., Ste. 9, Culver City, CA 90232.
TEL: (310) 202-0030. FAX: (310) 855-9110.
PRESIDENT
Bill Unger - william_unger@hotmail.com

TIG PRODUCTIONS, INC.
(Motion picture, independent film & TV producer)
4450 Lakeside Dr., Ste. 225, Burbank, CA 91505.
TEL: (818) 260-8707. FAX: (818) 260-0440.
FOUNDER/CEO
Kevin Costner
CREATIVE EXECUTIVE
Jasa Abreo
ASSISTANT
Austin Gilmore

THE STEVE TISCH COMPANY
(Motion picture producer)
10202 W. Washington Blvd., Astaire Bldg., 3rd Flr., Culver City, CA 90232. TEL: (310) 244-6612. FAX (310) 204-2713.
PRODUCER
Steve Tisch - (310) 244-6612
V.P., ADMINISTRATION FINANCE
Kim Skeeters - (310)244-6619
DIRECTOR, DEVELOPMENT
Lacy Boughn

TOOLEY PRODUCTIONS
(Motion picture, television & independent film producer)
8899 Beverly Blvd., Ste. 510, West Hollywood, CA 90048.
TEL: (310) 859-1250. FAX: (310) 859-1254.
email: tooleyproduction@aol.com
PRODUCER & CO-CHAIRMAN
Tucker Tooley
CREATIVE EXECUTIVE/EXECUTIVE ASSISTANT
Christopher Wilhem

TOTEM PRODUCTIONS
(Motion picture, independent film & TV producer)
614 N. La Peer Drive, West Hollywood, CA 90069.
TEL: (323) 650-4994. FAX: (323) 650-1961.
email: totempro@aol.com
CO-CHAIRMAN
Tony Scott
ASSISTANT
Tom Moran, Steve Robbins

TOWER OF BABBLE ENTERTAINMENT
(Production company)
854 N. Spaulding Ave., Los Angeles, CA 90046.
TEL: (323) 230-6128. FAX: (323) 822-0312.
email: info@towerofb.com www.towerofb.com
PRODUCER/WRITER
Beau Bauman
DIRECTOR/WRITER
Jeff Wadlow

TRIBECA PRODUCTIONS
(Production company)
375 Greenwich St., 8th Flr., New York, NY 10013.
TEL: (212) 941-4000. FAX: (212) 941-4044.
www.tribecafilm.com www.tribecafilmfestival.org
PARTNER
Robert De Niro, Jane Rosenthal
V.P., DEVELOPMENT
Brandon Brito
V.P., PRODUCTION
Meghan Lyvers
CREATIVE EXECUTIVE
Berry Welsh

TRILOGY ENTERTAINMENT GROUP
(Motion picture, independent film & TV producer)
1207 Fourth St., Ste. 400, Santa Monica, CA 90401.
TEL: (310) 656-9733. FAX: (310) 424-5816.
email: mail@trilogyent.com
PARTNER
Pen Densham, John Watson
V.P., PRODUCTION
Alex Daltas
CREATIVE EXECUTIVE
Nevin Densham
CREATIVE CONSULTANT
Howard Han

TROMA ENTERTAINMENT, INC.
(Producer & distributor)
36-40 11th Street, Long Island City, NY 11106.
TEL: (718) 391-0110. FAX: (718) 391-0255.
email: webmaster@troma.com www.troma.com
PRESIDENT
Lloyd Kaufman
VICE PRESIDENT
Michael Herz
DVD & T.V. SALES
Matt Manjourides
PRESS & PUBLIC RELATIONS
Anne Koester

TYPE A FILMS
(Production company)
100 Universal City Plaza, Bldg. 1320, Ste. 2-E, Universal City, CA 91608. TEL: (818) 777-6222. FAX: (818) 866-2866.
PRODUCER
Reese Witherspoon

PRESIDENT
Jennifer Simpson
ASSISTANT
Rachel Bati, Allison Dorenbosch

UFLAND PRODUCTIONS

(Motion picture, independent film & TV producer)
963 Moraga Dr., Los Angeles, CA 90049.
TEL: (310) 476-4520. FAX: (310) 476-4891.
email: ufland.productions@verizon.net
PRODUCER
Harry J. Ufland, Mary Jane Ufland

UGLY BETTY PRODUCTIONS

618 Carroll Street, #2, Brooklyn, NY 11215.
TEL: (718) 399-7544. FAX: (718) 399-7415.
www.uglybetty.com
FOUNDING PARTNER/PRODUCER
Amanda Doss
FOUNDER PARTNER/DIRECTOR
Bo Mehrad

UNDERGROUND FILMS

(Production Company)
447 S. Highland Ave., Los Angeles, CA 90036.
TEL: (323) 930-2588. FAX: (323) 930-2334.
www.undergroundfilms.net
PRODUCERS
Nick Osborne - (323) 930-2650 nick@undergroundfilms.net
Trevor Engelson - (323) 930-2569
EXECUTIVE
Oliver Obst - 323) 930-2085
MANAGERS
Josh McGuire Turner, Evan Silverberg

UNIQUE FEATURES

(Production company)
116 N. Robertson Blvd., 9th Flr., Los Angeles, CA 90048.
TEL: (310) 492-8009. (212) 649-4980.
PRINCIPAL
Michael Lynne (NY), Bob Shaye
EXECUTIVES
NY - Julie Crowne, Christina Delgado, Leah Holzer, Mark Kaufman
LA - Jonna Smith, Adam Paulsen, Anand Shah

UNITED ARTISTS

(Production company)
10250 Constellation Blvd.,11th Flr., Los Angeles, CA 90067.
TEL: (310) 449-3777. FAX: (310) 586-8727.
www.unitedartists.com
COO
Elliott Kleinberg
PRESIDENT, PRODUCTION
Don Granger
HEAD, BUSINESS AFFAIRS
Christa Zofcin

VANGUARD DOCUMENTARIES

P.O. Box 26635, Brooklyn, NY 11202-6624.
TEL: (212) 517-4333. email: charleshobson@yahoo.com
www.vanguarddocumentaries.com
EXECUTIVE PRODUCER
Charles Hobson

VALHALLA MOTION PICTURES

(Motion picture, independent film & TV producer)
3201 Cahuenga Blvd.,West Los Angeles, CA 90068.
TEL: (323) 850-3030. FAX: (323) 323-850-3038.
email: vmp@valhallapix.com
CHAIRMAN & CEO
Gale Anne Hurd
CFO/HEAD OF BUSINESS AFFAIRS
Julie Thomson
EXECUTIVE V.P., PRODUCTION & DEVELOPMENT
Beatrice Springborn
V.P.
Ben Roberts
CREATIVE EXECUTIVE
Kris Henigman

VERDON-CEDRIC PRODUCTIONS

(Motion picture, independent film & TV producer)
P.O. Box 2639, Beverly Hills, CA 90213. TEL: (310) 274-7253.
PRODUCER & DIRECTOR & WRITER & ACTOR
Sidney Poitier

VIACOM, INC.

(A leading global media company, with preeminent positions in broadcast and cable television, radio, outdoor advertising, and online Viacom Entertainment Group)
1515 Broadway, New York, NY 10036. TEL: (212) 258-6000.
FAX: (212) 258-6175, (212) 258-6464. www.viacom.com

5555 Melrose Ave., Los Angeles, CA 90038
TEL: (323) 956-5000.

VIACOM ENTERTAINMENT GROUP

EXECUTIVE CHAIRMAN OF THE BOARD AND FOUNDER
Sumner M. Redstone
PRESIDENT & CEO
Philippe P. Dauman
SENIOR EXECUTIVE V.P., CHIEF ADMINISTRATIVE OFFICER AND CFO
Thomas E. Dooley
EXECUTIVE V.P., CORPORATE COMMUNICATIONS
Carl Folta
EXECUTIVE V.P., GENERAL COUNSEL AND SECRETARY
Michael Fricklas
CFO
James W. Barge
EXECUTIVE V.P., HUMAN RESOURCES & ADMINISTRATION
Denise White
SENIOR V.P./CONTROLLER
Katherine Gill-Charest

Viacom is a leading global entertainment content company, with prominent and respected brands in focused demographics. Offering programming and content for television, motion pictures and digital platforms, Viacom's world-class brands include MTV Networks (MTV, VH1, Nickelodeon, Nick at Nite, Comedy Central, CMT: Country Music Television, Spike TV, TV Land, Logo and more than 130 networks around the world), BET Networks, Paramount Pictures, Paramount Home Entertainment, and Famous Music. More information about Viacom and its businesses is available at www.viacom.com

PARAMOUNT DIGITAL ENTERTAINMENT

5555 Melrose Ave., DeMille 106, Los Angeles, CA 90038-3197. TEL: (323) 956-5000. www.paramount.com
PRESIDENT
Thomas Lesinski
EXECUTIVE V.P., DIGITAL ENTERTAINMENT/GENERAL MANAGER
Alex Carloss
EXECUTIVE V.P., BUSINESS AFFAIRS & LEGAL
Ron Sufrin
SENIOR V.P., DIGITAL DISTRIBUTION, THE AMERICAS
Malik Ducard
SENIOR V.P., VIDEO GAMES
John Kavanagh
SENIOR V.P., BUSINESS AFFAIRS
Mark Lieblein
SENIOR V.P., CREATIVE DEVELOPMENT & PRODUCTION
Keith Quinn
SENIOR V.P., DIGITAL DISTRIBUTION, EUROPE, MIDDLE EAST, AFRICA
John Robson
V.P., PRODUCT DEVELOPMENT
Geremie Camara
V.P., INTERACTIVE GLOBAL MARKETING
Ivo Gerscovich
V.P., MOBILE, THE AMERICAS
Madeline Herdrich
V.P., BUSINESS AFFAIRS
Shane Kao
V.P., INTERACTIVE LICENSING
Luke Letizia
V.P., DIGITAL CONTENT LICENSING
Larry McCallister
V.P., DIGITAL DISTRIBUTION, ASIA PACIFIC
Dennis Miyata
V.P., FINANCE & PLANNING
Michael Pierce

PARAMOUNT PICTURES CORPORATION

CHAIRMAN AND CEO
Brad Grey
VICE CHAIRMAN
Rob Moore
PRESIDENT, PARAMOUNT FILM GROUP
Adam Goodman
CHIEF OPERATING OFFICER
Frederick Huntsberry
EXECUTIVE V.P./CFO
Mark Badagliacca
CO-PRESIDENT, DOMESTIC THEATRICAL MARKETING
Megan Colligan
CO-PRESIDENT, DOMESTIC THEATRICAL MARKETING
Josh Greenstein
PRESIDENT, PARAMOUNT WORLDWIDE HOME ENTERTAINMENT
Dennis Maguire
PRESIDENT, DOMESTIC THEATRICAL DISTRIBUTION
Jim Tharp
PRESIDENT, PARAMOUNT PICTURES INTERNATIONAL
Andrew Cripps
PRESIDENT, PARAMOUNT DIGITAL ENTERTAINMENT
Thomas Lesinski
PRESIDENT, PARAMOUNT WORLDWIDE TELEVISION DISTRIBUTION
Hal Richardson

PRESIDENT, CONSUMER PRODUCTS & RECREATION GROUP
Michael Corcoran
PRESIDENT, PARAMOUNT FAMOUS PRODUCTIONS
Louis Feola
PRESIDENT, PARAMOUNT STUDIO GROUP
Randall Baumberger
GENERAL COUNSEL
Rebecca Prentice
EXECUTIVE V.P., PARAMOUNT PICTURES
Daniel Ferleger
CHIEF INFORMATION OFFICER
Abe Wong
EXECUTIVE V.P., WORLDWIDE HUMAN RESOURCES
Heidi Gonggryp

PARAMOUNT PICTURES DOMESTIC DISTRIBUTION DIVISION, MOTION PICTURE GROUP
PRESIDENT, DOMESTIC THEATRICAL DISTRIBUTION
Jim Tharp
EXECUTIVE V.P., OPERATIONS
Mark Christiansen
EXECUTIVE V.P./GENERAL SALES MANAGER
Don Harris
SENIOR V.P., NON-THEATRICAL SALES
Joan Filippini
SENIOR V.P., IN-THEATRE MARKETING
Patricia Gonzalez
SENIOR V.P., STRATEGY & OPERATIONS
Jeanie Han
SENIOR V.P., FINANCE
Jim Smith
SENIOR V.P., ASSISTANT GENERAL COUNSEL
Paul Springer

PARAMOUNT PICTURES INTERNATIONAL
Building 5, Chiswick Park, 566 Chiswick High Road. London W4 5YF, United Kingdom. TEL: 44 20 3184 2100.
www.paramountpicturesinternational.com
PRESIDENT
Andrew Cripps
EXECUTIVE V.P., INTERNATIONAL DISTRIBUTION & OPERATIONS
Roger Pollock
EXECUTIVE V.P., INTERNATIONAL MARKETING
Ian George
EXECUTIVE V.P., LEGAL & BUSINESS AFFAIRS
Philip Solomons
EXECUTIVE V.P., FINANCE
Lauren Miller
SENIOR V.P., INTERNATIONAL CREATIVE AFFAIRS
Chas Evans
SENIOR V.P., DISTRIBUTION, EMEA
Mark Viane
SENIOR V.P., INTERNATIONAL PUBLICITY
Katherine Willing
V.P., INTERNATIONAL OPERATIONS
Dan Olliff
V.P., INTERNATIONAL PROMOTIONS
Lucy Thomas
V.P., INTERACTIVE MARKETING
Heath Tyldesley
V.P., INTERNATIONAL CREATIVE (LA)
Andrew Williams
SENIOR DIRECTOR, DISTRIBUTION, EMEA
Yit-Ching Lee
DIRECTOR, INTERNATIONAL SALES REPORTING
Jaakko Niemela
SENIOR V.P., DISTRIBUTION, LATIN AMERICA
Jorge Peregrino
V.P./MANAGING DIRECTOR, AUSTRALASIA
Mike Selwyn
MANAGING DIRECTOR, PARAMOUNT PICTURES SPAIN
Pierre Auger
GENERAL MANAGER, PARAMOUNT PICTURES CHINA
Zhe Chen
MANAGING DIRECTOR, PARAMOUNT PICTURES NEW ZEALAND
Peter Garner
V.P., MANAGING DIRECTOR, PARAMOUNT PICTURES UK
Chris Hedges
GENERAL MANAGER, PARAMOUNT PICTURES MEXICO
Michael Horn
MANAGER, PARAMOUNT PICTURES IRELAND
Niamh McCaul
GENERAL MANAGER, PARAMOUNT PICTURES FRANCE
Frederick Moget
PRESIDENT, PARAMOUNT PICTURES JAPAN
Ichiro Okazaki
V.P./MANAGING DIRECTOR, PARAMOUNT PICTURES BRAZIL
Cesar Silva
GENERAL MANAGER, PARAMOUNT PICTURES GERMANY
Sven Sturm

PARAMOUNT PICTURES MOTION PICTURE MARKETING
CO-PRESIDENT, DOMESTIC MARKETING
Josh Greenstein
CO-PRESIDENT, DOMESTIC MARKETING
Megan Colligan
EXECUTIVE V.P., CREATIVE ADVERTISING
Amanda Edwards
EXECUTIVE V.P., PUBLICITY
Katie Martin Kelley
EXECUTIVE V.P., INTERACTIVE MARKETING STRATEGY & FILM PRODUCTION
Amy Powell
EXECUTIVE V.P., WORLDWIDE MARKETING/ADVERTISING
Steve Siskind
EXECUTIVE V.P., WORLDWIDE MARKETING PARTNERSHIPS
Leeanne Stables
SENIOR V.P., MOTION PICTURE MARKETING OPERATIONS
Leslie H. Anderson
SENIOR V.P., PRINT PRODUCTION
John Barry
SENIOR V.P., CREATIVE ADVERTISING
Erik Counter
SENIOR V.P., MARKETING, CANADA
Greg Ferris
SENIOR V.P., MARKET RESEARCH
Jeff Hall
SENIOR V.P., NATIONAL ADVERTISING
Carey Loomis
SENIOR V.P., MARKETING FINANCE & ADMINISTRATION
Ellen Martello
SENIOR V.P., CREATIVE ADVERTISING
Amy Mastriona
SENIOR V.P., INTERACTIVE MARKETING
Amy Powell
SENIOR V.P., NATIONAL PUBLICITY
Jessica Rovins
SENIOR V.P., SPECIAL PROGRAMMING
William Rus
SENIOR V.P., EAST COAST PUBLICITY
Julie Tustin (NY)
SENIOR V.P., NATIONAL PUBLICITY
David Waldman
SENIOR V.P., SPECIAL PROGRAMMING
Joe Whitmore
SENIOR V.P., FIELD PUBLICITY & PROMOTIONS
Alicia Wyld
V.P., NATIONAL PUBLICITY
Michael Agulnek
V.P., WAST COAST PUBLICITY
Nancy Bannister (NY)
V.P., MARKETING PARTNERSHIPS
Chris Cerbo
V.P., BRAND MARKETING
George Clement
V.P., MARKETING POST PRODUCTION
Craig Cox, Shaylee Dunn
V.P., CREATIVE ADVERTISING
Scott Fleisher, Peter Giannascoli
V.P., ANIMATION PUBLICITY
Jeff Hare
V.P., MARKETING PARTNERSHIPS
Brian Miller
V.P., MARKETING SERVICES
Kay Nalbandian
V.P., CREATIVE ADVERTISING
Jordan Peed
V.P., INTERACTIVE MARKETING TECHNOLOGY
Geoffrey Springer
V.P., NATIONAL ADVERTISING
Faye Ugolnik
V.P., INTERACTIVE MARKETING
Megan Wahtera, Bryan Warman, Mickey Worsnup
V.P., REGIONAL PUBLICITY
Aurora Weinstock

PARAMOUNT PICTURES PRODUCTION DIVISION, MOTION PICTURE GROUP
PRESIDENT, PARAMOUNT FILM GROUP
Adam Goodman
PRESIDENT, PRODUCTION
Marc Evans
PRESIDEN., POST-PRODUCTION
Marty Cohen
PRESIDENT, MUSIC
Randy Spendlove
EXECUTIVE V.P., PRODUCTION
David Beaubaire
EXECUTIVE V.P., FEATURE PRODUCTION MANAGEMENT
Lee E. Rosenthal
EXECUTIVE V.P., PRODUCTION FINANCE
Roderick Smith

EXECUTIVE V.P., STORY DEPARTMENT
Mark Miner
SENIOR V.P., PRODUCTION
Greg Mooradian
SENIOR V.P., PRODUCTION
Geoff Stier
V.P., PRODUCTION
Ashley Brucks, Eben Davidson, Elizabeth Raposo
DIRECTOR, CREATIVE EXECUTIVE
Andrew Calof
CREATIVE DIRECTOR
Amanda Brown, Annie Laks, Alison Small
HEAD, CASTING
Terri Taylor
EXECUTIVE DIRECTOR, MARKETING, WORLDWIDE TELEVISION DISTRIBUTION
Michelle VenDange

VIEW ASKEW PRODUCTIONS, INC.

(Motion picture producer)
P.O. Box 93339, Los Angeles, CA 90093. TEL: (323) 969-9423. FAX: (323) 969-9008. email: gailmstanley@aol.com
www.viewaskew.com
PRESIDENT
Kevin Smith
VICE PRESIDENT
Scott Mosier
ASSISTANT TO KEVIN SMITH
Meghan Quinlan

VILLAGE ROADSHOW PICTURES

(Subsidiary of VRL)
100 N. Crescent Dr., Ste. 323, Beverly Hills, CA 90210.
TEL: (310) 385-4300. FAX: (310) 385-4301.
www.villageroadshowpictures.com
CHAIRMAN & CEO
Bruce Berman
CFO
Matthew Velkes
EXECUTIVE V.P., MARKETING & DISTRIBUTION
Melissa Anna
SENIOR V.P., LEGAL & FINANCIAL AFFAIRS
Kevin Berg
V.P., PRODUCTION
Matt Skiena
DIRECTOR, MEDIA & DISTRIBUTION
Linda Cuevas
DIRECTOR, FILM FINANCE
Michael Lee

Film development, production, distribution and marketing advice and services to the production division.

VIVENDI ENTERTAINMENT

(Distribution company)
111 Universal Hollywood Dr., Ste. 400, Universal City, CA 91608. TEL: (310) 274-7253.
email: info@vivendient.com www.vivendient.com
PRESIDENT
Tom O'Malley
EXECUTIVE V.P., GENERAL MANAGER
Mitch Budin
EXECUTIVE V.P., MARKETING
Mark Kristol
SENIOR V.P., BUSINESS DEVELOPMENT
Yolanda Macias
SENIOR V.P., STRATEGIC PLANNING & OPERATIONS
Craig Bergstein
SENIOR V.P., RETAIL STRATEGIES
Lisa Gibson
SENIOR V.P., BRAND MARKETING & PARTNER RELATIONS
Norbert Hudak

JON VOIGHT ENTERTAINMENT

(Motion picture producer)
10203 Santa Monica Blvd., 5th Flr., Los Angeles, CA 90067.
TEL: (310) 843-0223. FAX: (310) 553-9895.
PRESIDENT
Jon Voight

WALDEN MEDIA

(Production company)
1888 Century Park East, 14th Flr., Los Angeles, CA 90067.
TEL: (310) 887-1000. FAX: (310) 887-1001. www.walden.com
CEO
Michael Bostick
CEO, ANSCHUTZ FILM GROUP
David Weil
CO-FOUNDER/PRESIDENT (BOSTON)
Micheal Flaherty
CFO
Francesca Lindley
EXECUTIVE V.P., GENERAL COUNSEL
Frances X. Flaherty
EXECUTIVE V.P., PHYSICAL PRODUCTION
Doug Jones
SENIOR V.P., DEVELOPMENT & PRODUCTION
Amanda Morgan Palmer
SENIOR V.P., MARKETING
Heather Johnson Phillips
SENIOR V.P., PHYSICAL PRODUCTION
Mylan Stepanovich
SENIOR V.P. BUSINESS & LEGAL AFFAIRS
Frank Smith
SENIOR V.P., POST PRODUCTION
Jonas Thaler
SENIOR V.P., DEVELOPMENT & PRODUCTION
Evan Turner
V.P., EDUCATION & PROFESSIONAL DEVELOPMENT (BOSTON)
Randy Testa
V.P., FINANCE & STRATEGIC PLANNING
Ryan Jones
V.P., PUBLISHING (BOSTON)
Debbie Kovacs
V.P., CONTROLLER
Peter Wasek

WARNER BROS. ENTERTAINMENT INC.

(Producer & distributor; A Time Warner Company)
4000 Warner Blvd., Burbank CA 91522. TEL: (818) 954-6000.
www.warnerbros.com
CHAIRMAN & CEO
Barry M. Meyer
PRESIDENT & COO
Alan F. Horn
EXECUTIVE V.P., CORPORATE COMMUNICATIONS & PUBLIC AFFAIRS
Susan Fleishman
EXECUTIVE V.P., INTERNATIONAL
Richard J. Fox
PRESIDENT, DOMESTIC DISTRIBUTION, WARNER BROTHERS PICTURES
Dan Fellman
PRESIDENT, WARNER BROTHERS DIGITAL DISTRIBUTION
Thomas Gewecke
PRESIDENT, WARNER BROTHERS STUDIO FACILITIES
Jon Gilbert
PRESIDENT, WARNER BROTHERS COMSUMER PRODUCTS
Brad Globe
PRESIDENT, WORLDWIDE MARKETING, WARNER BROTHERS PICTURES
Sue Kroll
PRESIDENT, DISTRIBUTION, WARNER BROTHERS PICTURES INTERNATIONAL
Veronika Kwan-Rubinek
PRESIDENT, TELEPICTURES PRODUCTIONS
Hilary Estey McLoughlin
PRESIDENT, DC ENTERTAINMENT
Diane Nelson
PRESIDENT, WARNER BROTHERS INTERNATIONAL CINEMAS
Millard Ochs
PRESIDENT, WORLDWIDE PHYSICAL PRODUCTION, WARNER BROTHERS PICTURES
Steve Papazian
PRESIDENT, WARNER BROTHERS PICTURES GROUP EXECUTIVE V.P. & CFO
Edward A. Romano
PRESIDENT, WARNER BROTHERS TELEVISION GROUP
Bruce Rosenblum
PRESIDENT, WARNER BROTHERS TELEVISION PRODUCTION
Peter Roth
PRESIDENT, WARNER HOME VIDEO
Ronald J. Sanders
PRESIDENT, WARNER BROTHERS INTERNATIONAL TELEVISION
Jeffrey R. Schlesinger
PRESIDENT, WORLDWIDE BUSINESS AFFAIRS, WARNER BROTHERS PICTURES
Steven Spira
PRESIDENT, WARNER BROTHERS INTERACTIVE INTERACTIVE ENTERTAINMENT
Martin Tremblay
PRESIDENT, WARNER BROTHERS DOMESTIC TELEVISION DISTRIBUTION
EXECUTIVE V.P. & GENERAL COUNSEL
John Rogovin
PRESIDENT, HOME ENTERTAINMENT GROUP
Kevin Tsujihara
COO, THE CW
John D. Maatta
EXECUTIVE V.P., WARNER BROTHERS THEATRE VENTURES
Gregg Maday
EXECUTIVE V.P., CHIEF MARKETING OFFICER, WARNER BROTHERS. TELEVISION GROUP
Lisa Gregorian

EXECUTIVE V.P., BUSINESS MANAGEMENT, WARNER BROSTHERS TELEVISION GROUP
Craig Hunegs
SENIOR V.P./CIO
James L. Halsey
SENIOR V.P., CONTROLLER
Reginald Harpur
SENIOR V.P., INTELLECTUAL PROPERTY
Dean Marks
SENIOR V.P., WORLDWIDE CORPORATE COMMUNICATIONS
Paul McGuire
SENIOR V.P., CORPORATE BUSINESS DEVELOPMENT & STRATEGY
Gary Meisel
SENIOR V.P., MARKETING & OPERATIONS, WARNER BROS. WORLDWIDE TELEVISION MARKETING
Sonia Borris
SENIOR V.P./DEPUTY GENERAL COUNSEL
Zazi Pope, Sheldon Presser, Jeremy Williams
SENIOR V.P., PUBLIC AFFAIRS
Lisa Rawlins
SENIOR V.P., CORPORATE COMMUNICATIONS
Scott Rowe
SENIOR V.P., TV FINANCIAL MANAGEMENT
Laura Valan

WARNER BROS. PICTURES PRODUCTION
PRESIDENT, WARNER BROS. PICTURES GROUP
Jeff Robinov
PRESIDENT, WORLDWIDE PHYSICAL PRODUCTION
Steve Papazian
PRESIDENT, MUSIC
Paul Broucek
PRESIDENT, WORLDWIDE BUSINESS AFFAIRS
Steve Spira
EXECUTIVE V.P., BUSINESS AFFAIRS
Patti Connolly
EXECUTIVE V.P., DIGITAL PRODUCTION, ANIMATION & VISUAL EFFECTS
Chris deFaria
EXECUTIVE V.P., PHYSICAL PRODUCTION
Bill Draper, Mark Scoon
EXECUTIVE V.P., PRODUCTION
Jessica Goodman, Lynn Harris, Courtenay Valenti
EXECUTIVE V.P., MUSIC
Darren Higman
EXECUTIVE V.P., CASTING
Lora Kennedy
EXECUTIVE V.P., PRODUCTION & CREATIVE DEVELOPMENT
Greg Silverman
EXECUTIVE V.P., POST PRODUCTION
Marc Solomon
SENIOR V.P., MUSIC
Carter Armstrong
SENIOR V.P., BUSINESS AFFAIRS
Courtney Armstrong, Dan Furie, Jody Levinson, Jun Oh
SENIOR V.P., PRODUCTION
Jonathan Berg, Sarah Schechter
SENIOR V.P., PHYSICAL PRODUCTION
Kate Beyda, Ravi Mehta
SENIOR V.P., PRODUCTION RESOURCES
Musette Buckley
SENIOR V.P., FEATURE CASTING
Kristy Carlson
SENIOR V.P., POST PRODUCTION
William Daly, Jody Levin
SENIOR V.P., BUSINESS & LEGAL AFFAIRS
Susan Essex
SENIOR V.P., PRODUCTION BUDGETING & MANAGEMENT
Vince Heileson
SENIOR V.P./GENERAL COUNSEL
Richard Levin
SENIOR V.P., BUSINESS & LEGAL AFFARIS, MUSIC
Lisa Margolis
SENIOR V.P., CLEARANCE, MUSIC
Roberta Thornburg

WARNER BROS. PICTURES MARKETING
PRESIDENT
Sue Kroll
EXECUTIVE V.P., EUROPEAN MARKETING
Con Gornell
EXECUTIVE V.P., MARKETING
Blair Rich
EXECUTIVE V.P., MARKETING ADMINISTRATION/ OPERATIONS
Fiona Watts
EXECUTIVE V.P., MARKETING, NEW LINE PRODUCTIONS
Christina Kounelias
EXECUTIVE V.P., CREATIVE ADVERTISING
Massey Rafani
EXECUTIVE V.P., WORLDWIDE MEDIA ADVERTISING
Lynn Whitney
EXECUTIVE V.P., INTERNATIONAL MARKETING
Lynne Frank
SENIOR V.P., INTERNATIONAL MARKETING
Samantha Bird
SENIOR V.P., INTERNATIONAL MEDIA & PLANNING
Michael Carlin
SENIOR VICE PRESIDENT, CREATIVE ADVERTISING
Christian Davin, Michael Jones, Keri Moore, John Stanford
SENIOR V.P., PROMOTIONS
Gene Garlock
SENIOR V.P., PUBLICITY
Juli Goodwin
SENIOR V.P., WORLDWIDE MARKET RESEARCH
Lewis Oberlander
SENIOR V.P., MARKETING SERVICES
Susan Steen

DOMESTIC DISTRIBUTION
PRESIDENT, DOMESTIC DISTRIBUTION
Daniel R. Fellman
EXECUTIVE V.P. & GENERAL SALES MANAGER
Jeff Goldstein
SENIOR V.P., DISTRIBUTION SERVICES
Stella Burks
SENIOR V.P., EASTERN DIVISION
Frank Carroll
SENIOR V.P., SOUTHERN & MIDWESTERN DIVISION
Daniel Chinich
SENIOR V.P., NON-THEATRICAL SALES
Jeff Crawford
SENIOR V.P./DISTRICT MANAGER, CANADA
Andy Faux
SENIOR V.P., ASSISTANT GENERAL SALES MANAGER
Scott Forman
SENIOR V.P. & GENERAL COUNSEL
Connie Minnett
SENIOR V.P., EXHIBITOR & MARKETING SERVICES
Kelly O'Connor
SENIOR V.P., SYSTEMS & SALES OPERATIONS
Don Tannenbaum
SENIOR V.P., WESTERN DIVISION & LARGE FORMAT
Mike Viane
SENIOR V.P., ADMINISTRATION
Howard Welinsky

WARNER BROS. PICTURES INTERNATIONAL
PRESIDENT, DISTRIBUTION
Veronika Kwan-Rubinek
EXECUTIVE V.P., DISTRIBUTION
Nancy Carson
EXECUTIVE V.P., EUROPE & LATIN AMERICA DISTRIBUTION
Monique Esclavissat
SENIOR V.P., INTERNATIONAL OPERATIONS
David Brander
SENIOR V.P., DISTRIBUTION
Thomas Molter, Brenda Johns
SENIOR V.P., OPERATIONS
Jack Nguyen
SENIOR V.P., EMEA PRODUCTION & BUSINESS AFFAIRS
Adam Smith
SENIOR V.P., ASIA DISTRIBUTION
Erlina Suharjono
SENIOR V.P., FINANCE
David Williamson

WARNER BROS. THEATRE VENTURES
EXECUTIVE V.P.
Gregg Maday
V.P., BUSINESS & LEGAL AFFAIRS
Raymond Wu

WARNER BROS. ANIMATION, INC.
411 N. Hollywood Way, Burbank, CA 91505.
EXECUTIVE V.P., CREATIVE
Sam Register
SENIOR V.P., BUSINESS & LEGAL AFFAIRS & ADMINISTRATION
Ed Adams
SENIOR V.P., SERIES & ALTERNATIVE ANIMATION
Peter Gerardi
V.P., DIGITAL WEB GROUP
Sam Ades
V.P., SERIES
Jay Bastian
V.P., FINANCE & ADMINISTRATION
Debbie Lindquist
V.P., PRODUCTION
Bobbie Page
V.P., ESTIMATING & PRODUCTION ACCOUNTING
Athena Wingate

Series: Mucha Lucha, Teen Titans, What's New Scooby Doo?, Baby Looney Tunes, Krypto the Superdog, The Batman, Xiaolin Showdown, Justice League Unlimited.

DC ENTERTAINMENT
PRESIDENT, DC ENTERTAINMENT
Diane Nelson
CO-PUBLISHER, DC COMICS
Dan Dido
CO-PUBLISHER, DC COMICS
Jim Lee
CHIEF CREATIVE OFFICER
Geoff Johns
EXECUTIVE V.P, FINANCE & OPERATIONS
Patrick Caldon
EXECUTIVE V.P., SALES, MARKETING & BUSINESS DEVELOPMENT
John Rood
SENIOR V.P. & EXECUTIVE EDITOR, VERTIGO
Karen Berger
SENIOR V.P./EXECUTIVE EDITOR, VERTIGO
Karen Berger
SENIOR V.P., CREATIVE DIRECTOR
Richard Bruning
SENIOR V.P., BUSINESS & LEGAL AFFAIRS
Amy Genkins
SENIOR V.P., CREATIVE AFFAIRS
Gregory Noveck
SENIOR V.P., SALES & MARKETING
Steve Rotterdam
SENIOR V.P., BRAND MANAGEMENT
Cheryl Rubin
EDITOR, MAD MAGAZINE
John Ficarra

WARNER BROS. HOME ENTERTAINMENT GROUP
4000 Warner Blv., Burban, CA 91522. TEL: (818) 954-6000.
PRESIDENT
Kevin Tsujihara
EXECUTIVE V.P., EMERGING TECHNOLOGY
Chuck Dages
EXECUTIVE V.P., WORLDWIDE FINANCE, PLANNING & SYSTEMS
Jim Gewert
SENIOR V.P., WORLDWIDE STRATEGIC PROMOTIONS & COMMUNICATIONS
Jim Noonan

WARNER HOME VIDEO
4000 Warner Blvd., Burbank, CA 91522. TEL: (818) 954-6000.
www.warnerbros.com
PRESIDENT
Ron Sanders
PRESIDENT, THE AMERICAS
Mark Horak
PRESIDENT, INTERNATIONAL WARNER HOME VIDEO & WARNER BROS. DIGITAL DISTRIBUTION
Jim Wuthrich
EXECUTIVE V.P/GENERAL MANAGER, THEATRICAL CATALOG
Jeffrey Baker
EXECUTIVE V.P./GENERAL MANAGER, NON-THEATRICAL FRANCHISE
Jeff Brown
EXECUTIVE V.P., WORLDWIDE SUPPLY CHAIN MANAGEMENT
Daniel Miron
EXECUTIVE V.P./GENERAL MANAGER, NEW RELEASES
Mike Saksa

WARNER BROS. DIGITAL DISTRIBUTION
4000 Warner Blvd., Burbank, CA 91522. TEL: (818) 954-6000.
PRESIDENT
Thomas Gewecke
PRESIDENT, INTERNATIONAL HOME VIDEO & DIGITAL DISTRIBUTION
Jim Wuthrich
EXECUTIVE V.P., INTERNATIONAL, WARNER BROS. DIGITAL DISTRIBUTION & WARNER HOME VIDEO, ASIA PACIFIC
Marc Gareton
SENIOR V.P., VIDEO ON DEMAND
Andrew Mellett
SENIOR V.P., BUSINESS & LEGAL AFFAIRS & GENERAL COUNSEL
Clarissa Weirick
V.P., MARKETING
Michele Edelman
V.P., MOBILE, WARNER BROS. DIGITAL DISTRIBUTION & WARNER BROS. TELEVISION GROUP
Natalie Farsi
V.P., BROADBAND ACCOUNTS
Derek Gray
V.P., STRATEGIC PARTNERSHIPS
Deanne Lewis, Todd Looney
V.P., BUSINESS & LEGAL AFFAIRS (UK)
Nick Macrae
V.P., PLANNING
Christopher Pak
V.P., ECOMMERCE
Jurgen Pauguet
V.P., BUSINESS DEVELOPMENT
Maria Seidman
V.P., FINANCE
Marc Verville
V.P., BUSINESS DEVELOPMENT
Maria Seidman
V.P., BUSINESS & LEGAL AFFAIRS
Carolyn Wessling

WARNER BROS. DIGITAL MEDIA SALES/WARNER BROS. MEDIA SALES
4000 Warner Blvd., Burbank, CA 91522. TEL: (818) 954-6000.
SENIOR V.P., SALES & GENERAL SALES MANAGER
Roseanne Cacciola
SENIOR V.P., SALES PLANNING & OPERATIONS
Helene Sperling
SENIOR V.P./GENERAL SALES MANAGER
Peter Wright
V.P./EAST COAST SALES MANAGER
Jason Hernandez
V.P., MEDIA SALES
John Buckholtz, Joel Lewin, Gina Ciorciari
V.P., SALES
Angela Gaspar
V.P., WESTERN REGION MEDIA SALES
Marisusan Trout
V.P., MEDIA SALES, MIDWEST REGION
Philip Peters

WARNER BROS. INTERACTIVE ENTERTAINMENT
PRESIDENT
Martin Tremblay
SENIOR V.P., WORLDWIDE MARKETING
Russell Arons
SENIOR V.P., OPERATIONS
Debra Baker
SENIOR V.P., ONLINE & DIGITAL GAMES
Jeff Junge
SENIOR V.P., DEVELOPMENT & PRODUCTION
Samantha Ryan
V.P., FINANCE & ADMINISTRATION
Steve Chalk
V.P., BUSINESS DEVELOPMENT & LICENSING
Scott Johnson
V.P., SALES, AMERICAS
Kevin Kebodeaux
DEPUTY GENERAL COUNSEL
Jennifer Stump

WARNER PREMIERE
(Production company, Direct-to-Video/DVD)
4000 Warner Blvd., Burbank, CA 91522-0001.
TEL: (818) 954-6000. www.warnerbros.com
EXECUTIVE V.P./GENERAL MANAGER
Eva Davis
SENIOR V.P., PRODUCTION
Matt Bierman
V.P., BUSINESS CONTINUITY PLANNING
Michael Vinyard
V.P., RISK MANAGEMENT
Richard West
V.P., BUSINESS PLANNING
Patti Byam

WASHINGTON SQUARE FILMS
310 Bowery 2nd Flr., New York, NY 10012.
TEL: (212) 253-0333. FAX: (212) 253-0330. www.wsfilms.com
HEAD, INDEPENDENT FILM SALES
Amy Hobby - amyhobby@wsfilms.com
BOOKING/OFFICE MANAGER
Jamie Askin - jaskin@wsfilms.com

WEED ROAD PICTURES
(Motion picture & TV producer)
4000 Warner Blvd., Bldg. 81, Ste. 115, Burbank, CA 91522.
TEL: (818) 954-3771. FAX: (818) 954-3061.
email: weedroad@earthlink.net
PRODUCER
Akiva Goldsman
PRESIDENT, PRODUCTION
Kerry Foster
EXECUTIVE V.P., PRODUCTION
Emily Cummins
ASSISTANT
Alex Block, Nicki Cortese

THE WEINSTEIN COMPANY
(Producer & distributor)
345 Hudson St., 13th Flr., New York, NY 10014.
TEL: (646) 862-3400. FAX: (917) 368-7000.
5700 Wilshire Blvd. Suite 600., Los Angeles, CA 90036.

TEL: (323) 822-207-3200. www.weinsteinco.com
CO-CHAIRMAN
Bob Weinstein, Harvey Weinstein
PRESIDENT, PRODUCTION
Donna Gigliotti
PRESIDENT, DOMESTIC T.V. DISTRIBUTION
David Spiegelman
PRESIDENT, INTERNATIONAL DISTRIBUTION
David C. Glasser (LA)
PRESIDENT, BUSINESS & LEGAL AFFAIRS
Andrew Kramer
EXECUTIVE V.P., PHYSICAL AND POST PRODUCTION
Tim Clawson (LA)
EXECUTIVE V.P., HOME ENTERTAINMENT
Barry Gordon (LA)
EXECUTIVE V.P, FINANCE/ CFO
Larry Madden (NY)
GENERAL COUNSEL
Peter Hurwitz
EXECUTIVE V.P,, PUBLICITY
Liz Biber (LA)
EXECUTIVE V.P., STRATEGIC INITIATIVES, INVESTMENTS
David Hutkin
EXECUTIVE V.P., BUSINESS & LEGAL AFFAIRS
Laine R. Kline (LA)
EXECUTIVE V.P., ACCOUNTING & FINANCIAL REPORTING
Irwin Reiter
EXECUTIVE V.P., INTERNATIONAL & DISTRIBUTION
Michael Rothstein
EXECUTIVE V.P., PROMOTIONS & INTEGRATED MARKETING
Lance Still
SENIOR V.P., PRODUCTION & CASTING
Kelly Carmichael
SENIOR V.P., INTERNATIONAL SALES & DISTRIBUTION
Jonathan Kier
SENIOR V.P., FINANCE & BUSINESS DEVELOPMENT
Andrew Kim
SENIOR V.P., POST PRODUCTION
Matthew Landon
SENIOR V.P., POST PRODUCTION
Jeff Maynard (LA)
SENIOR V.P., DISTRIBUTION
Laurent Ouaknine
SENIOR V.P., PRODUCTION & DEVELOPMENT
Eric Robinson
SENIOR V.P., BUSINESS & LEGAL AFFAIRS
Eric Sherman (LA)
SENIOR V.P., PRODUCTION, DIMENSION FILMS
Matthew Stein
SENIOR V.P., ACQUISITIONS & LEGAL AFFAIRS
Michal Podell Steinberg
V.P., PRODUCTION & DEVELOPMENT
Abby Ex, Ben Famiglietti
V.P., BUSINESS & LEGAL AFFAIRS
Daniel Helberg (LA)
V.P., PRODUCTION FINANCE
Scott Maziroff (LA)
V.P., TV & FILM PRODUCTION & DEVELOPMENT
Barbara Schneeweiss (LA)
DIRECTOR, PRODUCTION & DEVELOPMENT
Lucas Carter
DIRECTOR, PUBLICITY
Pantea Ghaderi (LA)
DIRECTOR, ACQUISITIONS
Daniel Guando
STRATEGIC INITIATIVES, INVESTMENTS & BANKING
Vivian Tarn
MANGER, BUSINESS & LEGAL AFFAIRS
Steve DeLuca
MANAGER, PUBLICITY
Spencer Peeples

DIMENSION FILMS
PRESIDENT, BUSINESS & LEGAL AFFAIRS
Andrew Kramer (LA)
GENERAL COUNSEL
Peter Hurwitz
EXECUTIVE V.P., BUSINESS & LEGAL AFFAIRS
Laine R. Kline

WEINTRAUB/KUHN PRODUCTIONS
(Production company)
1351 Third St. Promenade, Ste. 200, Santa Monica, CA 90401.
TEL: (310) 458-3300. FAX: (310) 458-3302.
PRODUCER
Fred Weintraub, Tom Kuhn
V.P., DEVELOPMENT
Jackie Weintraub
CREATIVE DIRECTOR
Marlo Ehrlich
BUSINESS AFFAIRS
Maxwell Meltzer

WILDWOOD ENTERPRISES, INC.
(Motion picture & independent film producer)
725 Arizona Ave., Ste. 306, Santa Monica, CA 90401.
TEL: (310) 451-8050.
OWNER
Robert Redford
DEVELOPMENT
Connie Wethington, Bill Holderman

WINKLER FILMS, INC.
(Motion picture, independent film & TV producer)
190 North Canon Drive, Ste. 302, Beverly Hills, CA 90212.
TEL: (310) 858-5780. FAX: (310) 858-5799.
www.winklerfilms.com
CEO, PRODUCER & DIRECTOR
Irwin Winkler
PRESIDENT
Jill Cutler
DIRECTOR/PRODUCER
Charles Winkler

WITT-THOMAS-HARRIS PRODUCTIONS
(Motion picture producer; Does not accept submission requests)
11901 Santa Monica Blvd., Ste. 596, W. Los Angeles, CA 90025. TEL: (310) 472-6004. FAX: (310) 260-7051.
PARTNER
Paul Junger Witt, Susan Harris, Tony Thomas
ASSISTANT
Ellen Benjamin, Marlene Fuentes

THE WOLPER ORGANIZATION
(Motion picture & TV producer)
4000 Warner Blvd., Bldg. 14, Rm. X, Burbank, CA 91522-0001.
TEL: (818) 954-1421. FAX: (818) 954-1593.
PRESIDENT & EXECUTIVE PRODUCER
Mark M. Wolper
EXECUTIVE V.P., DEVELOPMENT
Kevin Nicklaus
PRODUCTION SUPERVISOR
Kathleen Doise
DEVELOPMENT ASSISTANT
Sam Alexander

WONDERLAND SOUND & VISION
(Production company. Produces TV series & features)
8739 Sunset Blvd., West Hollywood, CA 90069.
TEL: (310) 659-4451. FAX: (310) 659-4482.
http://www.wonderlandsoundandvision.com/
PARTNER
McG
PRESIDENT, WONDERLAND TELEVISION
Peter Johnson
V.P., DEVELOPMENT
Jeanne Allgood
V.P., DEVELOPMENT
David Manpearl
ASSISTANT TO McG
Andy Shapiro

WORKING TITLE FILMS
(Motion picture, independent film & TV producer)
9720 Wilshire Blvd., Beverly Hills, CA 90212.
TEL: (310) 777-3100. FAX: (310) 777-5243.
www.workingtitlefilms.com
CHAIRMAN
Tim Bevan, Eric Fellner
PRESIDENT, PRODUCTION
Liza Chasin
PRESIDENT, WORKING TITLE TELEVISION
Shelley McCrory
HEAD, FILM
Debra Hayward
COO
Angela Morrison
HEAD, PHYSICAL PRODUCTION
Michelle Wright
SENIOR V.P., DEVELOPMENT
Evan Hayes
LITERARY AQUISITIONS
Amelia Granger

WORLD FILM SERVICES, INC.
(Motion picture, independent film & TV producer & distributor)
150 E. Fifth Ave., 29th Flr., New York, NY 10155.
TEL: (212) 632-3456. FAX: (212) 632-3457.
CEO
John Heyman
VICE PRESIDENT
Pamela Osowski
V.P., DEVELOPMENT
Mark Montgomery
CANADA
Roy Krost

CREATIVE EXECUTIVE
Dahlia Heyman, Jessica Stickles

YARI FILM GROUP (YFG)

(Production and distribution company)
10850 Wilshire Blvd., 6th Flr., Los Angeles, CA 90024.
TEL: (310) 689-1450. FAX: (310) 234-8975.
email: info@yarifilmgroup.com www.yarifilmgroup.com
PRESIDENT
Bob Yari
COO
Bill Immerman
CFO
Dennis Brown
EXECUTIVE V.P., PRODUCTION
Brad Jenkel
HEAD, T.V.
Jonathan Berry
SENIOR V.P., RESIDULAS & PARTICIPATION
MaryAnn Swinhart
SENIOR V.P/GENERAL COUNSEL
Elizabeth Bell
SENIOR V.P, WORLDWIDE DELIVERY
Liz Antonelli
V.P., BUSINESS & LEGAL AFFAIRS
Gerald Gottesman, C.J. Vranca
PUBLICITY & MEDIA EXECUTIVE
Babak Marjan
CREATIVE EXECUTIVE
Farnaz Fahid, Michelle Reed

THE SAUL ZAENTZ COMPANY

2600 Tenth St., Berkeley, CA 94710.
TEL: (510) 549.1528. FAX: (510) 486-2115.
email: info@zaentz.com www.zaentz.com
PRODUCER
Saul Zaentz

THE ZANUCK COMPANY

(Producer, theatrical motion pictures)
9465 Wilshire Blvd., Ste. 930, Beverly Hills, CA 90212.
TEL: (310) 274-0261. FAX: (310) 273-9217.
email: zanuckco@aol.com
PRODUCER
Richard D. Zanuck, Lili Fini Zanuck
DIRECTOR, DEVELOPMENT
Lily Phillips
ASSISTANT
Brenda Berriford

ZEITGEIST FILMS, LTD.

(Distributor, independent films)
247 Centre St., 2nd Flr., New York, NY 10013.
TEL: (212) 274-1989. FAX: (212) 274-1644.
email: mail@zeitgeistfilms.com
www.zeitgeistfilm.com
CO-PRESIDENT
Emily Russo, Nancy Gerstman
HEAD, THEATRICAL SALES
Clemence Taillandier - clemence@zeitgeistfilms.com
DIRECTOR, HOME MEDIA PRODUCTION
Shannon Attaway - shannon@zeitgeistfilms.com
DIRECTOR, FINANCE & ADMINISTRATION
Cristela Henriquez - cristela@zeitgeistfilms.com
DIRECTOR, HOME MEDIA SALES & MARKETING
Ian Stimler - ian@zeitgeistfilms.com
DIRECTOR, THEATRICAL MARKETING
Nadja Tennstedt - nadja@zeitgeistfilms.com

ZUCKER PRODUCTIONS

1250 6th St., Ste. 201, Santa Monica, CA 90401.
TEL: (310) 656-9202. FAX: (310) 656-9220.
DIRECTOR
Jerry Zucker
PRODUCER
Janet Zucker, Melysa Lovell, Eric Katz

Large Format Producers & Distributors

APERTURE FILMS, LTD.
3534 Hayden Ave., Culver City, CA 90232.
TEL: (310) 202-3939. FAX: (310) 842-9898.
email: info@aperturefilms.com www.aperturefilms.com
PRINCIPALS/MANAGING DIRECTORS
Josh Colover - jcolover@aperturefilms.com
Chris Blum - cblum@aperturefilms.com

ARCLIGHT PRODUCTIONS
732 N. Highland Ave., Hollywood, CA 90038.
TEL: (323) 464-7791. FAX: (323) 464-7406.
email: info@arclightprods.com www.arclightprods.com
CONTACT
Steven Kochones

ARGENTINE PRODUCTIONS
(Feature Avid Adrenaline HD, Avid Express Pro with MOJO)
603 Washington Rd., Ste. 501, Pittsburgh, PA 15228.
TEL: (412) 341-6448. FAX: (412) 341-4410.
email: peter@argentineproductions.com
www.argentineproductions.com
FOUNDER
Peter Argentine

RON ASCHER COMMUNICATIONS
293 Terrace Pl., Buffalo Grove, IL 60089. TEL: (847) 687-5815.
FAX: (847) 537-7929.
FOUNDER
Ron Ascher - rascherprod@sbcglobal.net

ASTORIA FILMS
545 Eighth Ave., Ste. 401, New York, NY 10018.
TEL: (212) 330-0607. email: info@astoriafilms.com
www.astoriafilms.com
CEO
Roy Carlo
PRESIDENT, MOTION PICTURE GROUP
James LaVita
CFA
Errol Horowitz
V.P., TALENT & MEDIA RELATIONS
Tom Kelly - tomkelly@astoriafilms.com

BETTINA PRODUCTIONS, LTD.
624 S. June St., Los Angeles, CA 90005. TEL: (323) 937-2101.
FAX: (323) 937-2103.
PRESIDENT
Walter Doniger

BLUE MOUNTAIN FILM ASSOCIATES INC.
148 Waverly Pl., New York, NY 10014. TEL: (212) 645-0745.
email: Bsilleck@aol.com
PRESIDENT
Bayley Silleck

CHUCK DAVIS/TIDAL FLATS, LTD.
(Director of Photography)
1215 Surf Ave., Pacific Grove, CA 93950. TEL: (831) 649-1086.
FAX: (831) 649-0986. email: cdocean@earthlink.net
www.tidalflatsphoto.com
CONTACT
Chuck Davis

Director of photography on large format, features, commercials and tv documentaries. A specialist in underwater filming, and shooting the marine environment.

DCM PRODUCTIONS, INC.
(Produce large format films and UPM feature films)
1611 19th St., Manhattan Beach, CA 90266.
TEL/FAX: (310) 545-2119. email: dcmprods@aol.com
CONTACT
Doug Merrifield

DENALI PRODUCTIONS, INC.
1070 Detroit St., Denver, CO 80206. TEL: (800) 231-3456,
(303) 394-3456. CELL: (303) 877-3456.
email: dougmill@earthlink.net www.bobcarmichael.com
EXECUTIVE PRODUCER
Doug Millington

DISCOVERY COMMUNICATIONS
One Discovery Pl., Silver Spring, MD 20910.
TEL: (240) 662-0000. www.discovery.com

GIANT SCREEN FILMS
(Distribution Company)
500 Davis St., Ste. 1005, Evanston, IL 60201. TEL: (847) 475-9140.
FAX: (847) 475-9145. email: info@gsfilms.com www.gsfilms.com
CO-FOUNDER
Don Kempf, Steve Kempf
SENIOR. DIRECTOR OF DISTRIBUTION & BUSINESS DEVELOPMENT
Derek Threinen

ROBERT GINTY FILMS
16255 Ventura Blvd., Ste. 625, Encino, CA 91436.
TEL: (310) 890-2686. email: ginty@robertginty.com
www.robertginty.com
CEO
Robert Ginty

GRAPHIC FILMS CORPORATION
3341 Cahuenga Blvd., Hollywood, CA 90068.
TEL: (323) 851-4100. FAX: (323) 851-4103.
email: pnovros@graphicfilms.com www.graphicfilms.com
CONTACT
Paul Novros

KEN GROSS MANAGEMENT
12135 Stanwood Dr., Los Angeles, CA 90066.
TEL: (310) 391-2999. FAX: (310) 391-2990.
email: kgmla@pacbell.net
PRESIDENT
Ken Gross
VICE PRESIDENT
Daryl DePollo

HOWARD HALL PRODUCTIONS
2171 La Amatista Rd., Del Mar, CA 92014-3031.
TEL: (858) 259-8989. FAX: (858) 792-1467.
email: orders@howardhall.com www.howardhall.com
CONTACT
Howard Hall, Michele Hall

IDEAL ENTERTAINMENT, INC.
TEL: (323) 939-3399. email: info@ideal-entertainment.com
PRESIDENT & PRODUCER
Jon Shapiro

IMAGINARY FORCES
6526 W Sunset Blvd., Los Angeles, CA 90028.
TEL: (323) 957-6868. FAX: (323) 957-9577.
email: information@imaginaryforces.com
www.imaginaryforces.com
DIRECTOR, BUSINESS DEVELOPMENT
Danixa Diaz

530 W 25th St., Ste. 501, New York, NY 10001.
TEL: (646) 486-6868. FAX: (646) 486-4700.
CREATIVE DIRECTOR & MANAGING PARTNER
Maribeth Philips

IMAX CORPORATION
(Large-format film producer & distributor)
3003 Exposition Blvd., Santa Monica, CA 90404.
TEL: (310) 255-5500. FAX: (310) 315-1759. www.imax.com
CHAIRMAN & PRESIDENT, FILMED ENTERTAINMENT
Greg Foster
EXECUTIVE V.P., & CHIEF OF OPERATIONS, FILMED ENTERTAINMENT
Margaret E.G. Wilson
SENIOR V.P., FILM DISTRIBUTION & DEVELOPMENT
Phil Groves

INFINITY FILMWORKS
(Motion picture producer of large-format features)
15461 Victory Blvd., Van Nuys, CA 91406.
TEL: (818) 262-9689.
email: mjoseph@infinityvideosolutions.com
www.infinityvideosolutions.com
EXECUTIVE PRODUCER/DIRECTOR
Keith Melton

THE KENNEDY/MARSHALL COMPANY
619 Arizona Ave., Santa Monica, CA 90401.
TEL: (310) 656-8400. FAX: (310) 656-8430.

PRODUCER
Kathleen Kennedy
PRODUCER/DIRECTOR
Frank Marshall
ASSISTANT TO FRANK MARSHALL
Mary Radford

LOBO MEDIA PRODUCTIONS

650 Ward Dr., Ste. I, Santa Barbara, CA 93111-3307.
TEL: (805) 964-2132. FAX: (805) 964-0737.
email: info@Lobofilms.com www.Lobofilms.com
PRESIDENT
Kathleen Wolfe

MACGILLIVRAY FREEMAN FILMS

(Producer & distributor of large-format films)
P.O. Box 205, Laguna Beach, CA 92652. TEL: (949) 494-1055.
FAX: (949) 494-2079. www.macfreefilms.com
PRESIDENT
Greg MacGillivray
COO
Harrison Smith

MELWOOD PICTURES

2617 El Caminito Ave., La Crescenta, CA 91214.
TEL: (818) 248-4040. FAX: (818) 248-4070.
email: info@melwoodpictures.com www.melwoodpictures.com
FOUNDER & CHAIRMAN
Max Howard - mhoward@melwoodpictures.com
FOUNDER & COO
John McKenna
V.P., CREATIVE DEVELOPMENT
Sandra Staggs
DIGITAL PRODUCTION EXECUTIVE
Jay Shindell
STUDIO ADMINISTRATOR
Rosemary Healy

METANOIA PRODUCTIONS

1544 Euclid St., Ste. 1, Santa Monica, CA 90404.
TEL: (310) 293-9194. email: doug@metanoiaproductions.com
CONTACT
Douglas Fahleson

DENNIS EARL MOORE PRODUCTIONS, INC.

137 Atlantic Ave., Brooklyn Heights, NY 11201-5504.
TEL: (718) 875-8024. FAX: (718) 522-4358.
email: demp@dempinc.com www.dempinc.com
CONTACT
Dennis Earl Moore

NATIONAL WILDLIFE PRODUCTIONS

11100 Wildlife Center Dr., Reston, VA 20190-5362.
TEL: (703) 438-6069. FAX: (703) 438-6076.
www.nwf.org/About/TV-Productions.aspx

NELSON MADISON FILMS

4820 San Fernando Rd., Los Angeles, CA 91204.
TEL: (818) 550-6213. www.nelsonmadisonfilms.com
PRODUCERS
Linda Nelson - linda@nelsonmadisonfilms.com
Michael Madison

NWAVE PICTURES SA

(Producer of 3D/4D Ride & Attraction Films, 3D Giant Screen & 3D Feature Films)
Rue des Allies 282, 1190 Brussels, Belgium.
TEL: (322) 347-6319. FAX: (322) 347-2454. www.nwave.com
CHAIRMAN
Eric Dillens - edillens@nwave.com

RAYMOND WAGNER PRODUCTIONS, INC.

9595 Wilshire Blvd., Ste. 1020, Beverly Hills, CA 90212.
TEL: (310) 278-1970. FAX: (310) 274-2662.
PRESIDENT
Raymond Wagner
DIRECTOR, DEVELOPMENT
Christine McBride

SBK PICTURES, INC.

123 Coulter Ave., Ardmore, PA 19003. TEL: (610) 658-5858.
FAX: (610) 658-0809. www.sbkpictures.com

SHOCONCEPTS CREATIVE SERVICES, INC.

5410 Wilshire Blvd., Ste. 910, Los Angeles, CA 90036.
TEL: (818) 521-5624. www.shoconcepts.com
EXECUTIVE PRODUCER
Steve Ryan - steve.ryan@shoconcepts.com

SHOWSCAN ENTERTAINMENT

468 N. Camden Dr. #200, Beverly Hills, CA 90210.
TEL: (310) 858-5589. FAX: (310) 765-6255.
email: sales@showscan.com www.showscan.com
SENIOR V.P., SALES & MARKETING
Sue Y. Kim
V.P., WORLDWIDE DISTRIBUTION
Marcelo Floriao

Producer & distributor of contents for media based attractions; developer & producer of large-format films, feature animation films, CGI & TV programming.

SLINGSHOT ENTERTAINMENT

15030 Ventura Blvd., Ste. 912, Sherman Oaks, CA 91403.
TEL: (818) 755-8888. FAX: (818) 990-2872.
email: info@slingshotent.com www.slingshotent.com
CONTACT
Craig Huxley

SONY PICTURES CLASSICS

(A Sony Pictures Entertainment Company)
550 Madison Ave., 8th Flr., New York, NY 10022.
TEL: (212) 833-8833. FAX: (212) 833-4190.
www.sonyclassics.com
CO-PRESIDENT
Michael Barker, Tom Bernard, Marcie Bloom
EXECUTIVE V.P., ACQUISITIONS
Dylan Leiner
SENIOR V.P., OPERATIONS
Grace Murphy
SENIOR V.P., ADVERTISING & PUBLICITY
Carmelo Pirrone
V.P., BUSINESS AFFAIRS
Diane Buck
S.V.P., SALES
Tom Prassis

WILD CHILD ENTERTAINMENT, INC.

(Large-format motion picture producer, distributor & consultant)
69 Church St., Seymour, CT 06483-2611. TEL: (203) 888-2405.
email: WildChildEnt@compuserve.com
www.wildchildentertainment.com
PRESIDENT
Hans Kummer

NON-THEATRICAL MOTION PICTURE COMPANIES

Following is a list of producers, distributors and film libraries handling educational, entertainment and advertising pictures for non-theatrical distribution to schools, clubs, civic organizations, and teaching groups, as well as television.

THE AHERN GROUP
(Produce videos for corporate and the Federal Government)
3701A Malden Ave., Baltimore, MD 21211. TEL: (410) 367-9660.
FAX: (410) 367-9661. email: don@theaherngroup.com
www.theaherngroup.com
PRESIDENT/TREASURER
Christopher A'Hern

CIFEX CORPORATION
(Foreign films & productions)
20547 Linksview Way, Boca Raton, FL 33434-4262.
TEL: (561) 883-5548. FAX: (561) 883-2712.
email: cifex@prodigy.net
PRESIDENT
Gerald J. Rappoport

CONTINENTAL FILM PRODUCTIONS CORP.
(Film & video producers/audio visual installations)
1466 Riverside Dr., P.O. Box 5126, Chattanooga, TN 37406.
TEL: (423) 622-1193. FAX: (423) 629-0853.
www.continentalfilm.com
PRESIDENT
James L. Webster - jim.webster@continentalfilm.com

CRAVEN FILM CORPORATION
(Documentaries & industrials, commercials & PSAS)
5 W. 19 St., 3rd Flr., New York, NY 10011-4216.
TEL: (212) 463-7190. FAX: (212) 627-4761.
email:info@cravenfilms.com www.cravenfilms.com
PRESIDENT
Michael Craven

WALT DISNEY STUDIOS MOTION PICTURES NON-THEATRICAL
(Film Distributor)
3800 W. Alameda Ave., #971, Burbank, CA 91505.
TEL: (818) 840-1920. FAX: (818) 557-0797.
SENIOR V.P., NON-THEATRICAL
Linda Palmer

FILMS FOR EDUCATORS/FILMS FOR TV
(Cardiac angiogram duplication, digital to film, and pre-post production)
420 E. 55th St., Ste. 6L, New York, NY 10022.
TEL: (646) 456-3328. FAX: (212) 980-9826.
PRESIDENT
Harlan B. DeBell

HARDCASTLE FILMS INC.
(Beta-cam SP production)
7319 Wise Ave., St. Louis, MO 63117. TEL: (314) 647-4200,
(314) 647-4201.
DIRECTOR
Jeff Hardcastle

HUGH & SUZANNE JOHNSTON, INC.
(Educational & documentaries)
16 Valley Rd., Princeton, NJ 08540. TEL: (609) 924-7505.
PRESIDENT
Hugh Johnston
VICE PRESIDENT
Suzanne Johnston

LEE MENDELSON FILM PRODUCTIONS, INC.
(TV productions)
330 Primrose Rd., Ste. 215, Burlingame, CA 94010.
TEL: (650) 342-8284. FAX: (650) 342-6170.
CO-PRESIDENT
Glenn Mendelson, Jason Mendelson

NFL FILMS, INC.
One NFL Plaza, Mt. Laurel, NJ 08054. TEL: (856) 222-3500,
(877) NFL-5675. FAX: (856) 722-6779.
email: comments@films.nfl.com www.nflfilms.com
PRESIDENT
Steve Sabol

PENFIELD PRODUCTIONS, LTD.
(Film & video production; SD & HD production services)
35 Springfield St., Agawam, MA 01001. TEL: (413) 786-4454.
FAX: (413) 789-4240. www.penfieldprod.com
PRESIDENT
John Shanahan

PLAYHOUSE PICTURES
(Specializes in animated tv commercials)
P.O. Box 2089, Hollywood, CA 90078. TEL: (323) 851-2112.
email: playpix@aol.com www.playhousepictures.com
PRESIDENT
Ted Woolery

STEAM
(Commercial Production, Broadcast design)
3021 Airport Ave., Ste. 201, Santa Monica, CA 90405.
TEL: (310) 636-4620. FAX: (310) 636-4621.
email: info@steamshow.com www.steamshow.com
CONTACT
Scott Bryant - scott@steamshow.com

SWAIN FILM & VIDEO
(Industrial and other video productions)
1404 South Tuttle Ave., Sarasota, FL 34239.
TEL: (941) 365-8433. FAX: (941) 365-5359.
www.swainmedia.com
PRESIDENT
Tony Swain - tony@swainmedia.com
VICE PRESIDENT
Mike Swain

SWANK MOTION PICTURES, INC.
(Film & video distributor)
10795 Watson Rd., St. Louis, MO 63127. TEL: (800) 876-5577,
FAX: (314) 984-0590. www.swank.com
CHAIRMAN
Tim Swank

TR PRODUCTIONS, INC.
(Video presentations for corporate communications)
209 W. Central St., Natick, MA 01760. TEL: (800) 472-7449,
(508) 650-3400. email: info@trprod.com www.trprod.com
PRESIDENT
Cary Benjamin

TEL-AIR INTEREST, INC.
(Film producers)
2040 Sherman St., Hollywood, FL 33020. TEL: (954) 924-4949.
FAX: (954) 924-4980. email: telair@aol.com www.telairint.com
PRESIDENT
Grant H. Gravitt, Jr.

Full production services, 35' x 60' sound stage, 15' x 20' insert stage, cyc wall, Avid/Beta SP editing, pro tools audio, TV programming and syndication.

VAN VLIET MEDIA
(Digital transfers video-to-film/computer to film/spots, shorts & features/cardiac angiogram dup. for film, digital & video)
A Film for Educators Company, 420 E. 55th St., Ste. 6L, New York, NY 10022. TEL: (646) 456-3328. FAX: (212) 980-9826.
email: vanvlietmedia@att.net www.vanvlietmedia.com
PRESIDENT
Harlan B. DeBell

WEST GLEN COMMUNICATIONS, INC.
(Film & video producers & distributers specializing in educational; Producers of "The Popcorn Report")
1430 Broadway, 9th Flr., New York, NY 10018.
TEL: (212) 921-2800. FAX: (212) 944-9055.
email: info@westglen.com www.westglen.com
PRESIDENT
Stan Zeitlin
CONTACT
Ed Lamoureaux - elamoureaux@westglen.com

Production Services

ADVERTISING, MARKETING & PUBLICITY

11:24 DESIGN ADVERTISING, INC.
323 Culver Blvd., Ste. 211, Playa del Rey, CA 90293.
TEL: (310) 821-1775. FAX: (310) 821-1972.
email: artsims@1124design.com www.1124design.com
CEO
Art Simms

Focus on creative print, radio and TV advertising campaigns for film, TV and web companies.

30SIXTY ADVERTISING & DESIGN, INC.
800 N. Alameda St., Ste.200. Los Angeles, CA 90012..
TEL: (213) 217-4900. email: creative@30sixtydesign.com
jrigberg@30sixtydesign.com bizdev@30sixtydesign.com
www.30sixtydesign.com
PRESIDENT & FOUNDER
Henry Vizcarra
CONTACT
Jennifer Rigberg

An entertainment advertising and design firm specializing in key art design, DVD and game packaging, consumer products and all forms of theatrical and home entertainment advertising and collateral. In business more than 25 years.

A CREATIVE GROUP
2550 N. Hollywood Way, Ste. 100. Burbank, CA 91505.
TEL: (818) 748-4800. FAX: (818) 847-8625.
www.acreativegroup.com
CHAIRMAN, CREATIVE ENTERTAINMENT
Robert Douglas Woodruff
CEO
Richard P. Storrs
PRESIDENT
Kathryn Findling

A Creative Group consists of two companies: Creative Entertainment Services, Inx. and Creative Television Marketing, specializing in entertainment marketing and inexpensive brand exposure across various media properties through product placement, short-form advertising, promotions, event marketing, advertising and game show prize promotions.

ADPLANET.NET
26 Edwards Dr., Brewster, MA 02631. TEL: (800) 288-7678, (508) 896-5411 ext. 201. FAX: (800) 434-3738, (508) 632-8807.
email: info@adplanet.net www.adplanet.net
PRESIDENT
Jon Liebling

Source for promotional products, trade show giveaways and custom screen-printed or embroidered apparel. Company represents thousands of factories worldwide. Catalogs are available online.

ADMARKETING, INC.
1801 Century Park E, Ste. 2000, Los Angeles, CA 90067.
TEL: (310) 203-8400. FAX: (310) 277-7621.
email: advertising@admarketing.com www.admarketing.com
PRESIDENT
Jack Roth

Full-service agency.

ADVERTISING FOR MEDIA
6520 Platt Ave., Ste. 200, West Hills, CA 91307.
TEL: (818) 999-9366. FAX: (866) 563-6193.
email: info@afmla.com www.afmla.com
CONTACT
Ken Rose - ken@afmla.com
Bill Buck - bill@afmla.com
Elizabeth Ferris - elizabeth@afmla.com
Jeff Bruner - jeff@afmla.com

A full service advertising representation firm specializing in motion picture, television and music production.

ALLIED INTEGRATED MARKETING
(A full service agency for the entertainment industry with 20 offices in the US and Canada)
Boston Headquarters: 545 Boylston St., 11th Flr, Boston, MA 02116.
TEL: (617) 859-4800. www.alliedim.com
CHAIRMAN
Gerry Feldman
PRESIDENT
Clint Kendall

Los Angeles Office: 6908 Hollywood Blvd. 3rd Flr., Hollywood, CA 90028. TEL: (323) 954-7644.
EXEXUTIVE V.P., LOS ANGELES
Kymn Goldstein

New York Office: Five Penn Plaza, 21st Flr., New York, NY 10001. TEL: (212) 944-1990
EXECUTIVE V.P., NEW YORK
Seth Leifer

See website for additional office locations.

AMBERGATE ASSOCIATES/KDM
4367 Hwy. 78, Ste. 116, P.O. Box 2050, Julian, CA 92036.
TEL: (760) 765-2427. FAX: (760) 765-2498.
email: ekalish@ambergate.net www.ambergate.net
CONTACT
Eddie Kalish

Active in all aspects of marketing, distribution & financing. Services include film and DVD/video/TV production, marketing & distribution. Ambergate Associates, LLC, undertakes all supervisory duties connected with the marketing and release of an entertainment project, whether corporate, a television production or a motion picture.

AMERICAN ASSOCIATION OF ADVERTISING AGENCIES, INC. (A.A.A.A.)
Headquarters office: AAAA, 405 Lexington Ave., 18th Flr., New York, NY 10174-1801. TEL: (212) 682-2500.
FAX: (212) 682-8391.
www.aaaa.org
PRESIDENT & CEO
Nancy Hill
EXECUTIVE V.P.
Michael D. Donahue
COO, CFO
Laura J. Bartlett
BOARD SECRETARY
Michele Adams
SENIOR V.P., AGENCY RELATIONS & MEMBERSHIP
Jennifer Seidel

AMERICAN ENTERTAINMENT MARKETING
(Specializes in targeting the Spanish and English speaking US Latino market)
4519 Admiralty Way, Ste. D, Marina Del Rey, CA 90292.
TEL: (310) 574-1300. email: info@aem-la.com
www.aem-la.com
PRESIDENT
Ivette Rodriguez

AMP AGENCY
Boston Headquarters: 77 N. Washington St., Boston, MA 02114. TEL: (617) 723-8929. FAX: (617) 723-2188.
email: info@ampagency.com www.ampagency.com
PRESIDENT
Gary Colen - (617) 723-8929
V.P., STRATEGIC MARKETING GROUP
Steve McCall

Los Angeles: 6300 Wilshire Blvd., Ste. 2150, Los Angeles, CA 90048. TEL: (323) 937-7070. FAX: (323) 937-7891.
email: info@ampagency.com www.ampagency.com

New York: 151 W 26th St., New York, NY 10001.
TEL: (212) 244-4307. FAX: (212) 244-4311.

See website for additional offices and services. AMP Agency is part of Alloy Media + Marketing, a provider of nontraditional media programs reaching targeted consumer segments. Alloy manages a diverse array of assets and services in interactive, display, direct mail, content production and educational programming. Alloy Media + Marketing works with over 1500 companies including half of the Fortune 200.

THE ANGELLOTTI COMPANY
12423 Ventura Ct., Studio City, CA 91604.
TEL: (818) 506-7887. FAX: (818) 506-8822.
email: Tony@Angelcopr.com
PRESIDENT
Tony Angellotti
SENIOR PUBLICIST
Christine Foy, Cari Sanders

THE ANT FARM
(Creates and produces advertisements for feature films, TV programs and video games using a variety of media formats)
110 S. Fairfax Ave., Ste. 200, Los Angeles, CA 90036.
TEL: (323) 850-0700. FAX: (323) 850-0777.
email: info@theantfarm.net www.theantfarm.net
CEO
Rodd Perry
CO-PRESIDENT, CREATIVE DIRECTOR, AUDIO/VISUAL
Amanda Edwards, Andy Solomon

COO & CFO
Melissa Palazzo
PRESIDENT, PRINT DIVISION
Julian Hills

The Ant Farm has been recognized with dozens of Key Art and Golden Trailer Awards for campaigns.

ARENAS

3375 Barham Blvd., Los Angeles, CA 90068.
TEL: (323) 785-5501. FAX: (323) 785-5560.
email: info@arenasgroup.com www.arenasgroup.com
PRESIDENT& CEO
Santiago Pozo
PRESIDENT, DISTRIBUTION
Larry Gleason
EXECUTIVE V.P., MARKETING
John Butkovich - john@arenasgroup.com
CONTROLLER
Martha Rodriguez
V.P., MARKETING MEDIA
Leyla Fletcher
V.P., MARKETING, PUBLICITY & PROMOTIONS
Isaac Cuevas - isaac@arenasgroup.com
V.P. ESPANA
Gonzolo Martin
CONSULTANT, HISPANIC MARKETING, STRATEGIC MEDIA PLANNING & BUYING
Rosy Thompson

Arenas is a diversified entertainment and media company founded in 1988 to market entertainment products to U.S. Latino audiences. Services embrace marketing strategy, creative advertising, media planning, media buying, research, publicity, promotion, production, post-production and distribution. Serves both the Latino and U.S. general market.

ASPECT RATIO

(Produces entertainment advertising for the motion picture, television, and radio industries)
1347 N. Cahuenga Blvd., Hollywood, CA 90028.
TEL: (323) 467-2121. FAX: (323) 467-0901.
email: mark_t@aspectratio.com www.aspectratio.com
CEO
Mark Trugman

The company offers motion picture and campaigns services. Its clients include studios and independents.

JANE AYER PUBLIC RELATIONS, INC.

13400 Riverside Dr., #209, Sherman Oaks, CA 91423.
TEL: (818) 990-8544. email: jane@janeayerpr.com
www.janeayerpr.com

Founded in 1991, Jane Ayer Public Relations (JAPR) is a leading public relations marketing agency that provides successful campaigns for entertainment and interactive companies.

BABLOVE AGENCY, INC.

220 E. Speedway Blvd., Tucson, AZ 85705.
TEL: (520) 322-9060. FAX: (520) 327-9260.
email: paul@brworkgroup.com www.bablove.com
PRESIDENT & CREATIVE DIRECTOR
Paul Bablove
V.P., ACCOUNT SUPERVISOR
David Tomlinson
MEDIA DIRECTOR
Liz Durkin
SENIOR ART DIRECTOR
Lisa Tomlinson

Full-service advertising agency.

BAKER, WINOKUR, RYDER

(Publicity, Public Relations)
California office: 405 S. Beverly Dr., 5th Flr., Beverly Hills, CA 90212. TEL: (310) 550-7776. FAX: (310) 550-1701.
CO-CEO
Paul Baker, Larry Winokur
PRESIDENT
Nanci Ryder
MANAGING DIRECTOR
Cindy Guagenti

New York Office: 250 W. 57th St., Ste. 1317, New York, NY 10107. TEL: (212) 582-0700. FAX: (212) 901-3995.

BARCLAY COMMUNICATIONS

2999 N. 44th St., #300, Phoenix, AZ 85018.
TEL: (602) 277-3550. FAX: (602) 277-1217.
email: maryo@barclaycomm.com
CEO
Mary O'Hanlon
MANAGER, ENTERTAINMENT DIVISION
Alison Frost

Some of Barclay's clients include Walt Disney Pictures, Walt Disney Home Entertainment, Universal Pictures & Universal Home Entertainment.

BBDO WORLDWIDE, NEW YORK

1285 Ave. of the Americas, New York, NY 10019.
TEL: (212) 459-5000. FAX: (212) 459-6645.
email: jennifer.neal@bbdo.com www.bbdo.com

BBDO is part of Omnicom Group Inc. (NYSE: OMC - News; www.omnicomgroup.com). Omnicom is a leading global advertising, marketing and corporate communications company. Omnicom's branded networks and numerous specialty firms provide advertising, strategic media planning and buying, interactive, direct and promotional marketing, public relations and other specialty communications services to over 5,000 clients in more than 100 countries.

BEAR ENTHUSIAST MARKETING GROUP

4520 E. Thousand Oaks Blvd., Ste. 200, Westlake Village, CA 91362. TEL: (805) 371-7950. FAX: (805) 371-7956.
email: info@bearemg.com pr@bearemg.com
www.bearemg.com
PRESIDENT & CEO
Bruce Bear
DIRECTOR, PUBLIC RELATIONS
Amy Brown

BENDER/HELPER IMPACT, INC.

11500 W. Olympic Blvd., Ste. 655, Los Angeles, CA 90064.
TEL: (310) 473-4147. FAX: (310) 473-1408.
www.bhimpact.com
PARTNER, CO-FOUNDER
Dean Bender

Full service communications public relations firm serving the entertainment industry.

BERNSTEIN ENTERTAINMENT

12581 Venice Blvd., Ste. 204, Los Angeles, CA 90066.
TEL: (310)915-0404. email: DBernsteinPR@aol.com
www.bernsteinentertainment.com
PRESIDENT
Daniel Bernstein
V.P., TALENT RELATIONS
Bill McCoy
ENTERTAINMENT PUBLICIST
Jordan Kizwani - JKIZWANI7@GMAIL.COM

A full service public relations company specializing in entertainment, corporate and B2B campaigns.

BLOCK-KORENBROT PUBLIC RELATIONS

The North Market Bldg., 100 S. Fairfax Ave., #310, Los Angeles, CA 90036. TEL: (323) 634-7001. FAX: (323) 634-7030.
OWNER/CONTACT
Melody Korenbrot

BLT & ASSOCIATES, INC.

(DVD Packaging, Interactive, Motion Graphics, Print & Film Trailers)
6430 Sunset Blvd., 8th Flr., Hollywood, CA 90028.
TEL: (323) 860-4000. FAX: (323) 860-0890.
email: blt@bltomato.com www.bltomato.com
CONTACT
Whitney Robinson

BNC (BRAGMAN NYMAN CAFARELLI)

(Merged with PMK. See full listing under PMK-BNC)

BRAMSON & ASSOCIATES

7400 Beverly Blvd., Los Angeles, CA 90036.
TEL: (323) 938-3595. FAX: (323) 938-0852.

BRICKMAN MARKETING

(Documentary, Special Interest, Children's Video & DVD Publicity)
395 Del Monte Ctr., #250, Monterey, CA 93940.
TEL: (831) 633-4444. FAX: (831) 633-4499.
email: brickman@brickmanmarketing.com
www.brickmanmarketing.com
OWNER
Wendy Brickman

THE BROKAW COMPANY

(Established more than 25 years ago, The Brokaw Company represents a variety of musical, theatrical, film, TV, production and literary talents)
9255 Sunset Blvd., #804, Los Angeles, CA 90069.
TEL: (310) 273-2060. FAX: (310) 276-4037.
email: brokawc@aol.com www.brokawcompany.com
PARTNERS
David Brokaw, Sanford Brokaw, Joel Brokaw

LEO BURNETT USA

(Publicity, public relations)
Headquarters: 35 W. Wacker Dr., Chicago, IL 60601.
TEL: (312) 220-5959. FAX: (312) 220-3299.
email: belief@leoburnett.com www.leoburnett.com

New York Office: 170 Varick St., 5th Flr., New York, NY 10013.
TEL: (212) 759-5959. FAX: (212) 752-4065.

See website for worldwide office locations and services.

BURSON-MARSTELLER

(Burson-Marsteller is part of Young & Rubicam brands, a subsidiary of WPP.)
230 Park Ave. S, New York, NY 10003-1528.
TEL: (212) 614-4000. FAX: (212) 614-4084 (Advertising Dept.), (212) 598-5407 (Main Fax). email: ContactUS@BM.com
www.burson-marsteller.com
KEY CONTACT/MANAGING DIRECTOR, NY MARKET
Tony Telloni - (212) 614-4454 - tony.telloni@bm.com

Los Angeles Office: 2425 Olympic Blvd, Ste. 200E, Santa Monica, CA 90404. TEL: (310) 309-6600. FAX: (310) 309-6630.
KEY CONTACT/MARKET CHAIR, SO. CA. MARKET
Fred Muir - Fred.Muir@bm.com

See website for information about executives and additional office locations. Full-service multimedia agency. One of its emerging specialty areas is Digital Media. Burson-Marsteller offers clients: Interactive reputation management; online image shaping & digital business management.

JON BYK ADVERTISING

140 S. Barrington Ave., Los Angeles, CA 90049.
TEL: (310) 476-3012. FAX: (310) 476-3016.
www.bykadvertising.com
PRESIDENT
Tim Byk - tim@bykadvertising.com

A full service agency.

CARAT USA

(Owned by global marketing giant Aegis plc; Carat is a network of more than 4,600 people in 63 countries. U.S. offices in Atlanta, Boston, Chicago, Dallas, Los Angeles, New York & San Francisco)

CARAT ATLANTA

3390 Peachtree Rd. NE, Ste. 700, Atlanta, GA 30326.
TEL: (404) 231-1232. FAX: (404) 239-9755.
email: Stuart.Ketelsen@carat.com

CARAT BOSTON

200 Clarendon St., 23rd Flr., Boston, MA 02116.
TEL: (617) 449-4100. FAX: (617) 449-4200.
email: Michael.Nicholas@carat.com

CARAT CHICAGO

401 N. Michigan Ave., 14th Flr., Chicago, IL 60611.
TEL: (312) 384-4500. FAX: (312) 384-5200.
email: Jennifer.WhiteLee@carat.com

CARAT DALLAS

Dallas 3333 Lee Pkwy., Ste. 400, Dallas, TX 75219.
TEL: (972) 715-1200. FAX: (972) 716-9935.
email: jouette.travis@carat.com

CARAT LOS ANGELES

2450 Colorado Ave., Ste. 300, East Santa Monica, CA 90404.
TEL: (310) 255-1000. FAX: (310) 255-1050.
email: John.cate@carat.com

CARAT NEW YORK

(U.S. Headquarters)
150 E. 42nd St., New York, NY 10017. TEL: (917) 326-7110.
email: Steven.feuling@carat.com

CARAT SAN FRANCISCO

475 Brannan St., Ste. 410, San Francisco, CA 94107.
TEL: (415) 541-2700. FAX: (415) 975-0848.
email: John.cate@carat.com

Company offers media communications planning, integrated solutions, advice and consultancy services.

CHASEN & COMPANY

(Public relations for films, awards campaigns, filmmaker PR, home video, soundtrack strategies and campaigns)
8899 Beverly Blvd., Ste. 405, Los Angeles, CA 90048.
TEL: (310) 274-4400. FAX: (310) 274-4467.
email: firstname@chasenpr.com
OWNER
Ronni Chasen - ronni@chasenpr.com
VICE PRESIDENT
Jeff Sanderson
PUBLICIST
Allie Lee

THE CIMARRON GROUP

(Entertainment marketing)
6855 Santa Monica Blvd., Hollywood, CA 90038.
TEL: (323) 337-0300. FAX: (323) 337-0333.
email: info@cimarrongroup.com www.cimarrongroup.com
CEO
Robert J. Farina
CO-PRESIDENTS, CIMARRON ENTERTAINMENT
Terry Curtin, Damon Wolf
SENIOR V.P., DOMESTIC THEATRICAL AUDIO VISUAL
Geoff Calnan
PRESIDENT, CREATIVE DIRECTOR, CREATIVE SERVICES
George Anderson

Services include key art design & film trailers.

CMG WORLDWIDE

(A leader in intellectual property rights management)
10500 Cross Point Blvd., Indianapolis, IN 46256.
TEL: (317) 570-5000. FAX: (317) 570-5500. www.cmgww.com
CHAIRMAN, CEO & FOUNDER
Mark Roesler
COO
Greg Thompson
GENERAL COUNSEL & INTERNATIONAL LICENSING EXECUTIVE
Jeong-Ho Lee
DIRECTOR, MARKETING & LICENSING
Samira Ali
V.P., CORPORATE COMMUNICATIONS
Stacey Whitmore

Los Angeles Office: 9229 W. Sunset Blvd., Ste. 820, West Hollywood, CA 90069. TEL: (310) 651-2000. FAX: (310) 570-5500.

Services also include: merchandise licensing, advertising/promotional licensing, brand development/extension & sponsorship negotiation.

COMMUNICATIONS PLUS, INC.

102 Madison Ave. S., 7th Flr., New York, NY 10016.
TEL: (212) 686-9570. FAX: (212) 686-9687.

WARREN COWAN & ASSOCIATES

8899 Beverly Blvd, Ste. 919, Los Angeles, CA 90048.
TEL: (310) 275-0777. FAX: (310) 247-0810.
SENIOR V.P.
Richard Hoffman, Kevin Sasaki, Jeff Sanderson
CONTACT
Jazmine Vincenty - jvincenty@wcpr.net

CREATIVE PRODUCTIONS

(Integrated Marketing)
4510 E. Pacific Coast Hwy., Ste. 500, Long Beach, CA 90804.
TEL: (562) 985-1363. FAX: (562) 985-1365.
email: info@creativeproductions.com
www.creativeproductions.com
CONTACT
Robert Peterson, Deborah Castro

CUSHMAN AMBERG COMMUNICATIONS

1 E. Wacker Dr., Ste. 3750, Chicago, IL 60601.
TEL: (312) 263-2500. FAX: (312) 263-1197.
www.cushmanamberg.com
PRESIDENT
Thomas L. Amberg - tamberg@cushmanamberg.com

St. Louis Office: 7777 Bonhomme, Ste. 2200, St. Louis, MO 63105. TEL: (314)-725-6400.
VICE PRESIDENT & GENERAL MANAGER
Robert Amberg - ramberg@cushmanamberg.com

DAVIS ELEN ADVERTISING, INC.

865 S. Figueroa St., 12th Flr., Los Angeles, CA 90017.
TEL: (213) 688-7000. FAX: (213) 688-7190.
www.daviselen.com
CHAIRMAN &CEO
Mark Davis - markdavis@daviselen.com
PRESIDENT
Bob Elen - bobelen@daviselen.com

See website for additional office locations.

DDA PUBLIC RELATIONS, LTD.

DDA Los Angeles: 8981 Sunset Blvd., Ste. 201, Los Angeles, CA 90069. TEL: (310) 205-4868. FAX: (310) 205-4899.
email: info@ddapr.com www.ddapr.com
CHAIRMAN & FOUNDER (LONDON)
Dennis Davidson - dennis.davidson@ddapr.com
CEO
Lawrence Atkinson - lawrence.atkinson@ddapr.com
SENIOR V.P. (LOS ANGELES)
Mariangela Ferrario Hall - mariangela.hall@ddapr.com
Dana Archer - dana.archer@ddapr.com
SENIOR PUBLICIST (LOS ANGELES)
Kimberlie Traceski, Julia Orr
PUBLICIST (LOS ANGELES)
Christelle Dupont, Clifford Ng, Michael Hebler

DDA Public Relations, London: 72 New Cavendish St., London W1G 8AU. TEL: +44 (0) 20 7932 9800. FAX: +44 (0) 20 7932 4950. email: info@ddapr.com

Independent international entertainment public relations co. that provides motion picture publicity and corporate media relations services for the entertainment industry. Offices in London, Sydney and Los Angeles with associates around the world. See website for additional information.

DDB WORLDWIDE, INC.
(206 offices in 96 countries. DDB is part of the Omnicom Group, Inc.)
437 Madison Ave., 20th Flr., New York, NY 10022.
TEL: (212) 415-3075. FAX: (212) 415-3424.
email: pat.sloan@ddb.com www.ddb.com
PRESIDENT & CEO, DDB WORLDWIDE
Chuck Brymer
CHAIRMAN & CHIEF CREATIVE OFFICER, DDB WORLDWIDE
Bob Scarpelli
PRESIDENT, DDB NORTH AMERICA
Dick Rogers
CHIEF COMMUNICATIONS OFFICER
Jeff Swystun - (212) 415-2186 Jeff.Swystun@ddb.com
SENIOR V.P., CORPORATE DIRECTOR OF PUBLIC AFFAIRS
Pat Sloan - (212) 415-2109 pat.sloan@ddb.com

DOREMUS & COMPANY
200 Varick St., 11th Flr., New York, NY 10014.
TEL: (212) 366-3000. FAX: (212) 366-3060.
www.doremus.com
CEO
Carl Anderson
PRESIDENT,
Howard Sherman
MANAGING DIRECTOR, NEW YORK
Allison Womack
MANAGING DIRECTOR SAN FRANCISCO
Garrett Lawrence
MANAGING DIRECTOR LONDON
Alasdair Morrison - alasdair.m@doremus.co.uk
MANAGING DIRECTOR LONDON
Alasdair Morrison - alasdair.m@doremus.co.uk

San Francisco: 555 Market St., 19th Flr., San Francisco, CA 94105. TEL: (415) 273-7800. FAX: (415) 398-0854.
MANAGING DIRECTOR
Garrett Lawrence

London: 10 Regents Wharf, All Saints St., London N19RI United Kingdom. TEL: +44 (0) 20 7360 6700.
FAX: +44 (0) 20 7360 6701.

LARRY DORN ASSOCIATES
(Product placements, world backgrounds-stock footage)
5820 Wilshire Blvd., Ste. 306, Los Angeles, CA 90036.
TEL: (323) 935-6266. FAX: (323) 935-9523.
email: lda_la@msn.com
PRESIDENT
Larry Dorn
CONTACT
Lucy Kohn

DRAFT FCB
(Full marketing communication agency. Part of the Interpublic Group of Companies, Inc.)

Chicago Headquarters: 633 N. St. Clair, Chicago, IL 60611.
TEL: (312) 425-5000. www.draftfcb.com

Chicago: 101 E. Erie St., West Campus, Chicago, IL 60611.
TEL: (312) 425-5000. email: info@draftfcb.com

New York: 100 W. 33rd St. New York, NY 10001.
TEL: (212) 885-3000. FAX: (212) 885-2803.
email: info@draftfcb.com www.draftfcb.com

San Francisco: 1160 Battery St., Ste. 250, San Francisco, CA 94111. TEL: (415) 820-8000. email: info@draftfcb.com

Seattle: 605 Fifth Ave. S, Ste. 900, Seattle, WA 98104.
TEL: (206) 223-6464. email: info@draftfcb.com

Orange County: 17600 Gillette Avenue, Irvine, CA 92614.
TEL: (949) 851-3050. FAX: (949) 567-9465.

EXECUTIVE CHAIRMAN
Howard Draft
CEO & PRESIDENT
Laurence Boschetto
VICE CHAIRMAN, WORLDWIDE CHIEF CREATIVE OFFICER
Jonathan Harries
CFO
Neil Miller
PRESIDENT, NORTH AMERICA
Mark Modesto

EDELMAN PUBLIC RELATIONS WORLDWIDE
Chicago Office: 200 E. Randolph St., 63rd Flr., Chicago, IL 60601. TEL: (312) 240-3000. FAX: (312) 240-2900.

New York Office: 250 Hudson St., 16th Flr., New York, NY 10013. TEL: (212) 768-0550. FAX: (212) 704-0128.
email: new.york@edelman.com www.edelman.com

Los Angeles Office: 5900 Wilshire Blvd., 24th and 25th Flrs., Los Angeles, CA 90036. TEL: (323) 857-9100.
FAX: (323) 857-9117. email: los.angeles@edelman.com

Los Angeles office specialties include digital entertainment, and media training industries. Its anti-piracy programs for the music and film industry have received international coverage and impact.
FOUNDER & CHAIRMAN
Daniel J. Edelman
PRESIDENT & CEO (WORLDWIDE)
Richard Edelman
PRESIDENT & CEO, U.S.
Matthew J. Harrington - matthew.harrington@edelman.com

See website for additional offices and executives located worldwide.

ENTERTAINMENT COMMUNICATIONS NETWORK
Corporate office: 4370 Tujunga Ave., Ste. 210, Studio City, CA 91604. TEL: (818) 752-1400. FAX: (818) 752-1444.
email: sales@ECNMedia.com www.ecnmedia.com

ECN distributes information for the entertainment, media and broadcast arenas. Delivery capabilities: can deliver or collect thousands of simultaneous messages within minutes. ECN maintains media databases exceeding 120,000 contacts.

EURO RSCG WORLDWIDE
350 Hudson St., New York, NY 10014. TEL: (212) 886-2000.
FAX : (212) 886-2016. email: worldwide@eurosscg.com
www.euroscg.com
CEO
David Jones
CHIEF CREATIVE
Jim Schmidt

FELDMAN PUBLIC RELATIONS
13636 Ventura Blvd., #440 Sherman Oaks, CA 91423.
TEL: (310) 859-9062.
CONTACT
Brenda Feldman

FIFTEEN MINUTES
8436 W. Third St., Ste. 650, Los Angeles, CA 90048.
TEL: (323) 556-9700. FAX: (323) 556-9710.
email: info@fifteenminutes.com
FOUNDER & CHAIRMAN
Howard Bragman
PRESIDENT & COO
Bill Harrison

A media and public relations agency for corporate and filmed enterainment, crisis management, celebrity representation, consumer and lifestyle brands, special events.

FIRESTONE PRODUCTIONS
1525 Opechee Way, Glendale, CA 91208.
TEL: (323) 461-7500. FAX: (323) 230-8720.
email: info@firestoneproductions.com
www.firestoneproductions.com
CONTACT
Scott Firestone

Handles variety of projects from quick turnaround sales tapes to high-end film projects. Clients include broadcast networks, film studios and corporations. Scott Firestone's body of work includes writing and directing for Enterainment Tonight, Hard Copy, Extra and American Journal. Long-form programming work includes documentaries and films for various cable networks and studios.

B.D. FOX INDEPENDENT
(Marketing & self-distribution for independent films)
23307 Bocana St., Malibu, CA 90265. TEL: (310) 456-7190.
www.bdfox.com
PRESIDENT & CEO
Brian D. Fox - (310) 456-7190 brianf@bdfox.com
ACQUISITIONS
Karen Roberts - (310) 430-9068 karenr@bdfox.com

GARD AND GERBER
711 S.W. Alder St., 4th Flr., Portland, OR 97205.
TEL: (800) 800-7132, (503) 221-0100. FAX: (503) 221-6928.
www.gardandgerber.com
PRESIDENT & CEO
Brian Gard
SENIOR V.P. CLIENT SERVICES
Scott Sparling

GARIS PR AND MEDIA GROUP
310 S. Twin Oaks Valley Rd., #107-200, San Marcos, CA 92078. TEL: (760) 471-4807.
Hollywood - TEL: (424) 245-5131.
La Costa - TEL: (760) 471-4807.
email: publicity@nationalpublicist.com www.nationalpublicist.com
COORDINATOR
Brittany Scott

GORDON GELFOND ASSOCIATES
P.O. Box 17818, Beverly Hills, CA 90219. TEL: (310) 203-9982.
FAX: (310) 203-9512. email: ggelfond@aol.com
PRESIDENT
Gordon Gelfond

GOLIN HARRIS
111 E. Wacker Dr., Chicago, IL 60601. TEL: (312) 729-4000.
CHAIRMAN (IL)
Al Golin
PRESIDENT & CEO
Fred Cook

Los Angeles: 601 W. 5th St., 4th Flr., Los Angeles, CA 90071. TEL: (213) 623-4200. FAX: (213) 895-4745.
email: info@golinharris.com www.golinharris.com
REGIONAL MANAGING DIRECTOR (CA)
Judy Johnson - jjohnson@golinharris.com

GREY WORLDWIDE
(Advertising)
200 Fifth Ave., New York, NY 10010. TEL: (212) 546-2020. FAX: (212) 546-2001. www.greyglobalgroup.com
CHAIRMAN & CEO
Jim Heekin - jim.heekin@grey.com
VICE CHAIRMAN, CHIEF CREATIVE OFFICER
Tim Mellors
CHIEF COMMUNICATIONS OFFICER
Owen Dougherty - (212) 546-2022 odougherty@grey.com

See website for additional locations and executives.

GS ENTERTAINMENT MARKETING GROUP
522 N. Larchmont Blvd., Los Angeles, CA 90004.
TEL: (323) 860-0270. FAX: (323) 860-0279.
email: stevenzeller@gsemg.com
PRESIDENT & CEO
Steven Zeller

GUTTMAN ASSOCIATES
118 S. Beverly Dr., Ste. 201, Beverly Hills, CA 90212.
TEL: (310) 246-4600. FAX: (310) 246-4601.
PRESIDENT
Dick Guttman
SENIOR V.P.
Beverly Magid, Rona Menashe

HAMMER CREATIVE ADVERTISING
(Publicity company focusing on video games and movies)
6311 Romaine St., 3rd Flr., Hollywood, CA 90038.
TEL: (323) 606-4700. FAX: (323) 463-8130.
email: info@hammercreative.com www.hammercreative.com
CEO
Mark Pierce
CONTACT
Jim Botko

Film/TV productions, Film/TV talent, product placement, promotions, film trailers, key art design and more.

HANSON & SCHWAM PUBLIC RELATIONS
9350 Wilshire Blvd., Ste. 315, Beverly Hills, CA 90212.
TEL: (310) 248-4488. FAX: (310) 248-4499.
email: gerryporter@hspr.net geneschwam@hspr.net
www.hspr.net
PRESIDENT & OWNER
Gene Schwam - geneschwam@hspr.net
CONTACT
Krista Gugliotti - krista@hspr.net

HARRISON & SHRIFTMAN
(Publicity company)
Los Angeles: 8523 Sunset Blvd., Los Angeles, CA 90069.
TEL: (310) 855-1600. FAX: (310) 855-7510.
www.hs-pr.com

New York: 141 W. 36th St., 12th Flr., New York, NY 10018.
TEL: (917) 351-8600. FAX: (917) 351-8601.
www.hs-pr.com

Miami: 1680 Meridian Ave., Miami Beach, FL 33139.
TEL: (305) 534-0008. FAX: (305) 534-0158.
PARTNER
Elizabeth Harrison, Lara Shriftman

A public relations, special events and marketing firm specializing in building brands in the luxury sector, including fashion, lifestyle, travel and hospitality, publishing and entertainment industries.

HAUSER ADVERTISING
309 Bellino Dr., Pacific Palisades, CA 90272.
TEL: (310) 459-5911. FAX: (310) 459-5919.
email: moreinfo@hauser-advertising.com
www.hauser-advertising.com
PRINCIPAL
Cliff Hauser
CONTACT
Krystyne Spence

TV spots and promos; branding and broadcast design; film trailers & key art design.

HAWK3I
(Integrated marketing strategy, process & promotion)
4855 Ward Rd., Ste. 200, Wheat Ridge, CO 80033.
TEL: (303) 432-7700. FAX: (720-274-9688.
email: don@hawk3i.com
PRESIDENT
Don Hawkinson

Hawk3i's production team has won dozens of awards for film and video programs for over 20 years.

BERNARD HODES GROUP
(Recruitment advertising and more for a variety of industries, including the entertainment field)
Los Angeles: 4755 Alla Rd., Ste. 2000, Marina Del Rey, CA 90292. TEL: (310) 482-4301. FAX: (310) 482-4302.
SENIOR V.P., WESTERN REGION
Philip Gentile - pgentile@hodes.com

New York: 220 E. 42nd St., New York, NY 10017.
TEL: (212) 999-9711. FAX: (646) 658-0445.
email: info@hodes.com www.hodes.com
BRANCH MANAGER, NEW YORK
Jo Bredwell - jbredwell@hodes.com

See website for additional offices and contacts.

NATALIE HOFFMAN & ASSOCIATES
429 Santa Monica Blvd., Ste. 620, Santa Monica, CA 90401.
TEL: (310) 656-3430. FAX: (310) 656-3425.

Acquisition of celebrity talent for foreign advertising agencies.

HORIZON MEDIA, INC.
(Publicity company. Film/TV talent)
New York Office: 75 Varick St., New York, NY 10013.
TEL: (212) 220-5000 www.horizonmedia.com
NEW YORK CONTACT
Stephen Hall - shall@horizonmedia.com
Los Angeles: 1940 Century Park E, 3rd Flr., Los Angeles, CA 90067. TEL: (310) 282-0909. FAX: (310) 277-9692, (310) 229-8104.
LOS ANGELES CONTACT
Zachary Rosenberg - zrosenberg@horizonmedia.com
PRESIDENT & CEO
Bill Koenigsberg
EXECUTIVE V.P., MARKETING SERVICES
Carl Kotheimer
EXECUTIVE V.P., BROADCAST
Aaron Cohen

See website for additional offices and contacts.

I/D PUBLIC RELATIONS
Los Angeles: 8409 Santa Monica Blvd., West Hollywood, CA 90069. TEL: (323) 822-4800. FAX: (323) 822-4880.
email: la@id-pr.com

New York: 150 W. 30th St., 19th Flr., New York, NY 10001.
TEL: (212) 334-0333. FAX: (212) 334-8444.
email: info@id-pr.com

London Office: 124-128 Barlby Rd., Unit 27, London W10 6BL.
TEL: +44 (20) 3008 6050. FAX: +44 (20) 3008 6054.
V.P., TALENT & HEAD, LONDON OPERATIONS
Rupert Fowler
CEO
Kelly Bush
COO
Mara Buxbaum
SENIOR EXECUTIVE V.P.
Cari Ross
SENIOR V.P., ENTERTAINMENT
Eric Kops
V.P., COMMUNICATIONS
John Koch
V.P., TALENT
Carrie Byalick, Jodi Gottlieb
V.P., MUSIC & BRANDS
Allison Elbl
V.P., BRAND STRATEGIES
Heather Greenfield
V.P., ENTERTAINMENT & BRAND STRATEGIES
Brooke Lawer
V.P., TALENT & BRANDS
Bebe Lerner
DIRECTOR, FILM
Barry Dale Johnson
DIRECTOR, TALENT
Jillian Fowkes
SENIOR ACCOUNT EXECUTIVE
Lauren Burton Horowitz, Chet Mehta,
ACCOUNT EXECUTIVE
Sheri Goldberg, Shannon Sonnier
DIRECTOR, EMERGING PLATFORMS
Natalie Lent
SENIOR PUBLICIST
Megan Moss, Annick Muller, Jennifer Plante
PUBLICIST
Tamar Cohen, Nisha Darbar, Chris Kanarick, Bryna Rifkin, Rebecca Sides Capellan

IMAGINARY FORCES

Los Angeles: 6526 W. Sunset Blvd., Hollywood, CA 90028.
TEL: (323) 957-6868. FAX: (323) 957-9577.
email: information@imaginaryforces.com
www.imaginaryforces.com

New York: 530 W. 25th St., Ste. 501, New York, NY 10001.
TEL: (646) 486-6868. FAX: (646) 486-4700.
CO-FOUNDERS, CO-MANAGING DIRECTORS
Peter Frankfurt, Chip Houghton
EXECUTIVE PRODUCER/GENERAL MANAGER, NEW YORK
Anita Olan
FILM MARKETING, EXECUTIVE PRODUCER, FILM ADVERTISING
Annabelle Apley - annabelle@imaginaryforces.com
BROADCAST, DIRECTOR, BUSINESS DEVELOPMENT
Danixa Diaz - danixa@imaginaryforces.com
FILM TITLES
Kathy Kelehan - kathy@imaginaryforces.com

INCLUSIVE PR

(Publicity. Unit, festival and film release publicity)
6646 Hollywood Blvd., Ste. 205, Hollywood, CA 90028.
TEL: (323) 460-4111. FAX: (323) 460-4909.
email: micottrell@earthlink.net
FILM PUBLICIST
Mickey Cottrell

INDIE PR

(Independent films and filmmakers)
4370 Tujunga Ave., Ste. 105, Studio City, CA 91604.
TEL: (818) 753-0700. FAX: (818) 753-0709.
email: info@indie-pr.com www.indie-pr.com
OWNER
Linda Brown, Jim Dobson
PUBLICIST
Karen Fried

INFOMERCIAL SOLUTIONS, INC.

30748 Davey Jones Dr., Agoura Hills, CA 91301.
TEL: (818) 879-1140.
email: david@infomercialsolutions.com
www.infomercialsolutions.com
PRESIDENT
David Schwartz

INITIATIVE MEDIA

Worldwide Headquarters: One Dag Hammarskjold Plaza, New York, NY 10017. TEL: (212) 605-7000. www.initiative.com
CEO, WORLDWIDE
Richard Beaven
PRESIDENT, NORTH AMERICA
Tim Spengler
WORLDWIDE DIRECTOR, COMMUNICATION PLANNING
Janet Fitzpatrick-Wilks
PRESIDENT, EUROPE, MIDDLE EAST & AFRICA
Mário Mateus
PRESIDENT, LATIN AMERICA
Annetta Cembrano
SENIOR V.P., DIRECTOR, WORLDWIDE MARKETING & BUSINESS DEVELOPMENT
Erin Flaxman - erin.flaxman@us.initiative.com

Los Angeles: 5700 Wilshire Blvd., Ste. 400, Los Angeles, CA 90036. TEL: (323) 370-8014. FAX: (323) 370-8950.
www.initiative.com

Initiative is a worldwide media strategy, planning and buying organization, operating 91 offices in 70 countries. Initiative brings together for clients media expertise, consumer and trends research, and cutting edge technology to deliver effective media communications solutions for marketers to build brands. It is one of the Interpublic Group of Companies [NYSE:IPG].

THE INK TANK

(Promotions, public relations and event management)
2461 Queen St. E, Toronto, ON M4E 1H8.
TEL: (416) 690-7557. FAX: (416) 690-9236.
email: js@theinktank.com www.theinktank.com
FOUNDER
Jacqueline Spicer
MARKETING & PUBLIC RELATIONS
Katrina White
PUBLIC RELATIONS
Peter Ashworth

INTER/MEDIA ADVERTISING

15760 Ventura Blvd., First Flr., Encino, CA 91436.
TEL: (818) 995-1455. FAX: (818) 995-7115.
www.intermedia-advertising.com
PRESIDENT & COO
Robert B. Yallen
EXECUTIVE V.P.
Lucy St. George
SENIOR V.P. & CFO
Malena Cruz
SENIOR V.P., GROUP ACCOUNT DIRECTOR
Donna Wald
SENIOR V.P., MEDIA DIRECTOR
Richard Pike
PRESIDENT & COO, MEDIA POINT NETWORK
Jay Levin
V.P., CREATIVE DIRECTOR, INTER/MEDIA ADVERTISING, PRESIDENT, INTER/IMAGE PRODUCTIONS, PRESIDENT, INTERPOST PRODUCTIONS-EDITORIAL
Oscar Bassinson

JENSEN COMMUNICATIONS, INC.

709 E. Colorado, Ste. 220, Pasadena, CA 91101.
TEL: (626) 585-9575. FAX: (626) 564-8920.
email: info@jensencom.com www.jensencom.com
CONTACT
Michael Jensen
V.P., PUBLIC RELATIONS
Meghan Helsel
VICE PRESIDENT
Susan Stewart
PUBLICIST
Erin Podbereski

International media, marketing and management firm specializing in public relations serving a diverse range of clients in the entertainment industry, cause-related politics and the arts.

JWT

North American Headquarters: 466 Lexington Ave., New York, NY 10017. TEL: (212) 210-7000. FAX: (212) 210-7299.
www.jwt.com
CHAIRMAN & CEO, JWT WORLDWIDE
Bob Jeffrey
PUBLIC RELATIONS
Kenneth Hein - kenneth.hein@jwt.com
NEW BUSINESS
Lee Davis - lee.davis@jwt.com
Public relations, publicity. See website for offices and contacts worldwide.

MILTON KAHN ASSOCIATES, INC.

(Public relations)
P.O. Box 50353, Santa Barbara, CA 93150.
TEL: (805) 969-8555. FAX: (805) 969-2645.
email: miltonkahnpr@miltonkahnpr.com
www.miltonkahnpr.com
PRESIDENT & CEO
Milton Kahn

KAISER CREATIVE

6304 Allot Ave., Valley Glen, CA 91401. TEL: (818) 267-5130.
FAX: (818) 994-2323. email: info@kaiserCreative.com
www.kaisercomm.com
PRESIDENT
David Kaiser

Services include Entertainment / Theatrical One Sheets, Broadcast & Print Advertising, Home Entertainment/Packaging, Film/Video Direction & Production, Broadcast Design, Web Site (GUI) and Gaming/Package Design.

KAISER MARKETING

11400 W. Olympic Blvd., Ste. 600, Los Angeles, CA 90064.
TEL: (310) 479-8999. FAX: (310) 479-0414.
email: chris@kaisermarketing.com www.kaisermarketing.com
PRESIDENT & CEO
Michael Kaiser

KAPLAN THALER GROUP, LTD.

Worldwide Plaza, 825 Eighth Ave., 34th Flr., New York, NY 10019-7498. TEL: (212) 474-5000. FAX: (212) 474-5702.
email: kaplanthalergroup@kaplanthaler.com
www.kaplanthaler.com
CEO & CHIEF CREATIVE OFFICER
Linda Kaplan Thaler
PRESIDENT
Robin Koval
MANAGING DIRECTOR, CREATIVE SERVICES
Gerry Killeen
MANAGING DIRECTOR, BUSINESS DEVELOPMENT
Matthew Anderson - matthew.anderson@kaplanthaler.com
MANAGING DIRECTOR, CORPORATE COMMUNICATIONS
Tricia Kenney - tricia.kenney@kaplanthaler.com

Kaplan Thaler Group is an independent unit of The Publicis Groupe, one of the world's largest marketing communications holding companies.

DAN KLORES COMMUNICATIONS

(Public relations and integrated marketing)
386 Park Ave. S, 10th Flr., New York, NY 10016.
TEL: (212) 685-4300. FAX: (212) 685-9024.
email: contact@dkcnews.com www.dkcnews.com
CHAIRMAN & CEO
Dan Klores

PRESIDENT
Sean Cassidy
MANAGING DIRECTOR & MANAGING PARTNER
John Marino
MANAGING DIRECTOR, CHIEF OF STAFF
Matthew Traub
MANAGING DIRECTOR
Joe DePlasco, Diane Briskin, William Cunningham, Jeffrey Klein, Joseph Scott Miranda
EXECUTIVE V.P.
Liz Anklow, Bruce Bobbin, Robert Leonard, Susan Novak

Major motion pictures; news releases, integrated marketing.

LBI

(Formerly Special Ops Media)
The Puck Building, 295 Lafayette St., 8th Flr., New York, NY 10012. TEL: (212) 274-0470. email: hellonewyork@lbi.com
www.lbi.com

Atlanta: 1888 Emery St. NW, Ste. 400, Atlanta, GA 30318.
TEL: (404) 267-7616. email: helloatlanta@lbi.com
CEO
Christian Anthony
CO-PRESIDENTS
Judith Carr, Jason Klein
COO
Frank Pedersen
EXECUTIVE CREATIVE DIRECTOR
Cedric Devitt

LBi is a marketing and technology agency with the ability to guide brands digitally. See website for further information and global office listings.

LCO—LEVINE COMMUNICATIONS OFFICE

1180 S. Beverly Dr., #301, Los Angeles, CA 90035.
TEL: (310) 300-0950. FAX: (310) 300-0951.
email: info@LCOonline.com www.lcoonline.com
FOUNDER
Michael Levine - mlevine@LCOonline.com
ACCOUNT MANAGER
Alastair Duncan - aduncan@LCOonline.com

For more than 20 years, award-winning LCO has created innovative and dynamic public relations plans for a host of renowned entertainment and business clients. LCO offers media relations, event/conference work, materials creation, ancillary services and strategic communications.

LEE & ASSOCIATES, INC.

(Public relations and advertising)
145 S. Fairfax Ave., Ste. 301 Los Angeles, CA 90036.
TEL: (323) 938-3300. FAX: (323) 938-3305.
email: leeassociatespr@aol.com www.leeassociates.com
FOUNDER & PRESIDENT
Leo Pearlstein
PRINCIPAL & VICE PRESIDENT
Howard Pearlstein, Frank Pearlstein
MEDIA RELATIONS DIRECTOR
Katherine Griffith

LEVINSON ASSOCIATES

(International marketing support)
1440 Veteran Ave., Ste. 650, Los Angeles, CA 90024.
TEL: (323) 663-6940. FAX: (323) 663-2820.
email: leviinc@aol.com
CONTACT
Jed Leland, Jr.

LIPPIN GROUP, INC.

(Entertainment/media public relations and marketing firm)
Los Angeles: 6100 Wilshire Blvd., #400, Los Angeles, CA 90048. TEL: (323) 965-1990. FAX: (323) 965-1993.
email: losangeles@lippingroup.com
www.lippingroup.com

New York: 369 Lexington Ave., 22nd Flr., New York, NY 10017-6506. TEL: (212) 986-7080. FAX: (212) 986-2354.
email: newyork@lippingroup.com

London: 31 Southampton Row, London, WC1B 5HJ.
TEL: +44 (0) 203-008-5405. FAX: +44 (0) 203-008-6011.
email: london@lippingroup.com
CHAIRMAN & CEO
Dick Lippin

MACY + ASSOCIATES

Los Angeles: 411 Culver Blvd., Los Angeles, CA 90293.
TEL: (310) 821-5300. FAX: (310) 821-8178.
email: kmacy@macyinc.com www.macyinc.com

San Francisco: 1750 Montgomery St., San Francisco, CA 94111. TEL: (415) 954-8550. FAX: (415) 954-8598.

Integrates advertising, public relations, graphic design and electronic communications services for its clients, which include entertainment industry companies.

MARCUS THOMAS, LLC

24865 Emery Rd., Cleveland, OH 44128. TEL: (888) 482-4455. (216) 292-4700. FAX: (216) 378-0396.
email: askus@marcusthomasad.com
CHAIRMAN EMERITUS
Donald M. Marcus
CHAIRMAN
Harvey L. Scholnick

MARKHAM/NOVELL COMMUNICATIONS, LTD.

(Corporate communications, public relations & marketing support)
236 Fifth Ave. 9th Flr., New York, NY 10001.
TEL: (212) 687-1765. FAX: (212) 687-1978.
email: info@markhamnovell.com
www.markhamnovell.com
CONTACT
Arthur Novell

MARLIN ENTERTAINMENT GROUP

1720 Post Rd. E, Westport, CT 06880. TEL: (203) 255-6100 ext. 28. FAX: (203) 255-6103. email: neal@marlinent.com
www.marlinent.com
PRESIDENT
Neal Frank

MCCANN ERICKSON

New York: 622 Third Ave., New York, NY 10017.
TEL: (646) 865-2000. FAX: (646) 487-9610.
email: contact@mccann.com www.mccannworldgroup.com

Los Angeles: 5700 Wilshire Blvd., Ste. 225, Los Angeles, CA 90036. TEL: (323) 900-7100. www.mccannworldgroup.com
COO, MCCANN WORLDGROUP & REGIONAL DIRECTOR, MCCANN ERICKSON, NORTH AMERICA
Eric Keshin

See website for additional office locations.

MEDIALINK

(See Synaptic Digital listing)

MELAMED RILEY ADVERTISING

1468 W. Ninth St., Ste. 440, Cleveland, OH 44113.
TEL: (800) 222-4045, (216) 241-2141. FAX: (216) 479-2437.
www.melamedriley.com
PRESIDENT
Sara Melamed
EXECUTIVE CREATIVE DIRECTOR
Rick Riley

MIGHTY OAK MEDIA

4118 Davana Rd., Sherman Oaks, CA 91423.
TEL: (818) 990-2385. FAX: (818) 990-6085.
email: nedelson@mightyoakmedia.com
www.mightyoakmedia.com
EXECUTIVE PRODUCER, CREATIVE DIRECTOR
Noah Edelson

Mighty Oak Media is a creative agency. Its production capabilities enable it to execute all aspects of on-air promotion, short form and series programming from concept to completion. Services include: Channel image packages, Branding campaigns, Show launches, Feature film trailers & TV spots, Episodic promos, Generic promos, Contest spots, Sizzle reels, Podcasts & more.

DAVID MIRISCH ENTERPRISES

(Celebrity and event coordinators)
2342 Caringa Way, Ste. C, Carlsbad, CA 92009.
TEL: (760) 603-8111. FAX: (760) 603-8334.
email: david@dmirisch.com www.davidmirisch.com

David Mirisch Enterprises produces celebrity fundraising events for nonprofit organizations. More than 6,000 celebrities are in the organization's database.

MOCEAN

(A CMP Entertainment Group company)
2440 S. Sepulveda Blvd., Los Angeles, CA 90064.
TEL: (310) 481-0808. FAX: (310) 481-0807.
email: info@moceanla.com www.moceanla.com
CEO
Craig Murray
PRESIDENT
Michael Milntire
EXECUTIVE V.P. ENTERTAINMENT & MARKETING
Kevin Aratari - kevina@mocean.tv
EXECUTIVE V.P. THEATRICAL
Scott Goldman - scottg@moceania.com

An entertainment, advertising, marketing, branding and production company.

MOROCH

3625 N. Hall St., #1100, Dallas, TX 75219.
TEL: (214) 520-9700. FAX: (214) 520-5611.
www.moroch.com

FOUNDER
Tom Moroch
CHAIRMAN & CEO
Pat Kempf
PRESIDENT & COO
Rob Boswell
SENIOR PARTNER
Brad Ball
EXECUTIVE CREATIVE DIRECTOR
Jim Sykora, Troy Scillian
CHIEF MARKETING OFFICER
Jack Phifer
CORPORATE MEDIA DIRECTOR
Carol Dodson

See website for additional office contact information.

MOTION PICTURE MAGIC

(Entertainment marketing)
3605 W. Pacific Ave., Burbank, CA 91505.
TEL: (818) 953-7494. FAX: (818) 953-7113.
email: MotionPictureMagic@sbcglobal.net
www.motionpicturemagic.com
PRESIDENT
Mark Mills - MarkMills.MPM@sbcglobal.net
DIRECTOR, MARKETING
Tony Wilson - TonyWilson.MPM@sbcglobal.net

Branded integration and placement in film and TV.

MOTION PICTURE PLACEMENT

(Product placement and promotional tie-ins)
10625 Chandler Blvd., N. Hollywood, CA 91601.
TEL: (818) 760-2319. FAX: (818) 760-2904.
email: jh@mppusa.com productions@mppusa.com
sales@mppusa.com www.mppusa.com
PRINCIPAL
Joel Henrie

MPRM PUBLIC RELATIONS

5670 Wilshire Blvd., Ste. 2500, Los Angeles, CA 90036.
TEL: (323) 933-3399. FAX: (323) 939-7211.
email: info@mprm.com www.mprm.com
CO-PRESIDENT
Rachel McCallister, Mark Pogachefsky
EXECUTIVE V.P. & COO
Alan Amman
V.P., ENTERTAINMENT
Bill Horn, Shari Mesulam, Rene Ridinger
EXECUTIVE DIRECTOR, DIGITAL MEDIA & TECHNOLOGY
Susan Yin
SENIOR MANAGER, DIGITAL MARKETING &
PUBLIC RELATIONS, SPREAD SOLUTIONS
Clay Dollarhide

Emerging media, home video/DVD releases, cable networks, directors, special events. mPRm launches networks and creates campaigns for TV series, movies and mini-series. Clients span broadcast, cable and public TV and include first run syndication.

CRAIG MURRAY PRODUCTIONS

(Merged with Mocean. See full listing under Mocean)

JULIAN MYERS PUBLIC RELATIONS AND AMIGO DAY

13900 Panay Way, Ste. R-217, Marina Del Rey, CA 90292.
TEL: (310) 827-9089. FAX: (310) 827-9838.
email: julian@julianmyerspr.com
CEO & OWNER
Julian Myers

NATIONAL CINEMEDIA, LLC

(On-screen advertising, alternative entertainment and events)
Headquarters: 9110 E. Nichols Ave., Ste. 200, Centennial, CO 80112-3405. TEL: (800) 828-2828, (303) 792-3600.
FAX: (303) 792-8800. www.ncm.com

ADVERTISING & PROMOTIONS
TEL: (800) 727-3361. FAX: (303) 792-8606.
email: intheatre@ncm.com www.ncm.com
CHAIRMAIN, PRESIDENT & CEO
Kurt C. Hall
PRESIDENT OF SALES & CHIEF MARKETING OFFICER
Clifford E. Marks
EXECUTIVE V.P. & CFO
Gary W. Ferrera
EXECUTIVE V.P. & OPERATIONS OFFICER
Thomas C. Galley
EXECUTIVE V.P. & GENERAL COUNSEL
Ralph E. Hardy

National CineMedia, Inc. operates the largest digital in-theatre network in North America that allows advertisement, alternative entertainment and events distribution, utilizing its proprietary digital content network.

NEALE ADVERTISING ASSOCIATES

10201 Riverside Dr., Ste. 200, Toluca Lake, CA 91602.
TEL: (818) 508-7003. FAX: (818) 508-3141.
email: TEDN236302@aol.com
PRESIDENT
Ted Neale

NEW WAVE ENTERTAINMENT

2660 W. Olive Ave., Burbank, CA 91505.
TEL: (818) 295-5000. FAX: (818) 295-5001. www.nwe.com

Design and Interactive Offices: 3003 W. Olive Ave., Burbank, CA 91505. TEL: (818) 259-5000.
CEO
Paul Apel
COO
Rick Nowak
PRESIDENT, HOME ENTERTAINMENT
Michael Meadows
PRESIDENT, TALENT MANAGEMENT
Barry Katz

New Wave Entertainment is a full service entertainment agency covering design, interactive, marketing, music production and talent management.

NEXT EXIT CREATIVE

979 N. La Brea Ave., Hollywood, CA 90038.
TEL: (323) 874-5038. FAX: (323) 874-7902.
email: info@nextexitcreative.com sales@nextexitcreative.com
www.nextexitcreative.com

Services include: creative strategy and development, graphic design, interactive design, DVD menu design, web design, advertising, brand development and strategy, photographic retouching and compositing.

OBEDIENT MEDIA, INC.

(Now listed under Michael Pace Interactive)

OCTAGON

Headquarters: 800 Connecticut Ave., 2nd Flr., Norwalk, CT 06854. TEL: (203) 345-7400. FAX: (203) 354-7401.
www.octagon.com www.octagonNA.com (North America)
PRESIDENT & CEO, OCTAGON WORLDWIDE
Rick Dudley
PRESIDENT, OCTAGON MARKETING NORTH AMERICA
Jeff Shifrin

Sports and entertainment company. Engagement marketing; consulting, events, promotions, PR and property representation; athletes and personalities; management and procurement; Television: rights, production, sales, distribution, new media strategies; and music and entertainment: management and production. It is part of Interpublic's Constituent Management Group (CMG). Has alliance with public relations firm Rogers & Cowan. See website for office locations worldwide.

OGILVY & MATHER, INC.

Headquarters: 636 11th Ave, New York, NY 10036.
TEL: (212) 237-4000. FAX: (212) 237-5123.
email: lauren.crampsie@ogilvy.com www.ogilvy.com

California: 3530 Hayden Ave., Culver City, CA 90232.
TEL: (310) 280-2200. FAX: (310) 280-2699.
CHAIRMAN
Shelly Lazarus
GLOBAL CEO, OGILVY & MATHER WORLDWIDE
Miles Young
CFO
Steve Goldstein
WORLDWIDE CREATIVE DIRECTOR
Tham Khai Meng

DALE C. OLSON & ASSOCIATES

292 S. La Cienega Blvd., Beverly Hills, CA 90211.
TEL: (310) 657-6681. email: dolson2000@earthlink.net
PRESIDENT
Dale Olson

ONLINE PROMOTIONS GROUP

c/o Cinnamon Entertainment Group, LLC / 411 E. 70th St., #2F, New York, NY 10021. TEL: (646) 320-5162. FAX: (609) 296-7431.
email: robert@onlinepromotionsgroup.com
www.onlinepromotionsgroup.com
CEO
Rob Salerno
CTO
Martin Weinberger

Online Promotions Group is an interactive agency for marketing entertainment brands in music, TV, film, sports, games, theatre, books, magazines, comedy, performance art and models.

MICHAEL PACE INTERACTIVE

(Formerly Obedient Media, Inc.)
(Multi-media marketing, DVD authoring & creative, audio/video production and more)
628 Vernon Ave., Studio A, Venice Beach, CA 90291.
TEL: (310) 428-7991. email: michaelpace@me.com
www.michael-pace.com

CREATIVE MEDIA PRODUCER & DIRECTOR
Michael Pace

PARROT MEDIA NETWORK
2917 N. Ontario St., Burbank, CA 91504. TEL: (818) 567-4700. FAX: (818) 567-4600. www.parrotmedia.com
PRESIDENT & CEO
Bob Mertz - rwmertz@parrotmedia.com

Parrot remains on the forefront of electronic database, communication, fulfillment and entertainment services.

PASADENA ADVERTISING MARKETING DESIGN
51 W. Dayton St., Ste. 100, Pasadena, CA 91105.
TEL: (626) 584-0011. FAX: (626) 584-0907.
www.pasadenaadv.com
PRESIDENT & CEO
Suzanne Marks
V.P., CREATIVE
J. Anthony Nino

PLA MEDIA
(Public relations and marketing)

1303 16th Ave. S, Nashville, TN 37212.
TEL: (615) 327-0100. FAX: (615) 320-1061.
email: info@plamedia.com pam.lewis@plamedia.com
www.plamedia.com
SENIOR PUBLICIST
Kay Waggoner - kay.waggoner@plamedia.com
PUBLIC RELATIONS & MARKETING ACCOUNT EXECUTIVE
Nicole Zeller - nicole.zeller@plamedia.com

PMK-BNC
(Merger between PMK/HBH and BNC in 2010. Publicity, public relations)
8687 Melrose Ave., 8th Flr., Los Angeles, CA 90069.
TEL: (310) 854-4800. FAX: (310) 854-4848. www.pmkhbh.com

New York: 622 Third Ave., 8th Flr., New York, NY 10017.
TEL: (212) 582-1111. FAX: (212) 582-6666.
CHAIRMAN &CEO
Michael Nyman
VICE CHAIRMAN
Brad Cafarelli
CHAIRMAN & CEO ENTERTAINMENT, MEDIA RELATIONS
Cindi Berger
CEO OPERATION, BRAND MARKETING, PUBLIC RELATIONS
Chris Robichaud

PMK-BNC represents film and TV projects and corporate brands. A unit of Momentum Worldwide, the promotional and marketing arm of Interpublic's McCann Worldgroup.

FREDELL POGODIN & ASSOCIATES
(Indie Film PR)
7223 Beverly Blvd., Ste. 202, Los Angeles, CA 90036.
TEL: (323) 931-7300. FAX: (323) 931-7354.
email: pr@fredellpogodin.com
OWNER
Fredell Pogodin

THE POLLACK PR MARKETING GROUP
1901 Ave. of the Stars, Ste. 1040, Los Angeles, CA 90067.
TEL: (310) 556-4443. FAX: (310) 286-2350.
email: info@ppmgcorp.com www.ppmgcorp.com
CEO
Noemi Pollack
PRESIDENT
Stefan Pollack
VICE PRESIDENT
Will Ostedt

PR NEWSWIRE
(A United Business Media company)
New York Headquarters: 350 Hudson St., Ste. 300, New York, NY 10014. TEL: (800) 776-8090. FAX: (800) 793-9313.
email: media_services@prnewswire.com
www.prnewswire.com

California: 865 S. Figueroa St., Ste. 2500, Los Angeles, CA 90017. TEL: (800) 321-8169, (213) 362-7707.
FAX: (800) 473-5152, (213) 488-1152.
CEO
Ninan Chacko
DIRECTOR, PUBLIC RELATIONS (NY OFFICE)
Rachel Meranus- (201) 360-6776 rachel.meranus@prnewswire.com
MEDIA RELATIONS MANAGER (CA OFFICE)
John Evans - (480) 945-1483

See website for offices worldwide. Company provides electronic distribution, targeting, measurement and broadcast services on behalf of tens of thousands of corporate, government, association, labor, non-profit, and other customers worldwide. Using PR Newswire, these organizations are able to reach a variety of critical audiences including the news media, the investment community, government decision-makers, and the general public with their up-to-the-minute messages in text and multimedia format.

PUBLIC RELATIONS ASSOCIATES
8455 Beverly Blvd., #303, Los Angeles, CA 90048.
TEL: (310) 659-0380. FAX: (310) 659-5270.

THE RALEIGH GROUP
Promote Yourself PR & Seminars, P.O. Box 701, Carefree, AZ 85377. TEL: (480) 488-4840. email: raleigh@promoteyourself.com
www.promoteyourself.com
CONTACT
Raleigh R. Pinskey

REGBERG & ASSOCIATES, INC.
10877 Wilshire Blvd., Ste. 1102, Los Angeles, CA 90024.
TEL: (310) 475-5735. FAX: (310) 470-3101.
email: regberg@aol.com www.regberg.com
PRESIDENT
Scott Regberg

ROGERS & COWAN
Pacific Design Center, 8687 Melrose Ave., 7th Flr., Los Angeles, CA 90069. TEL: (310) 854-8100.
FAX: (310) 854-8106. email: inquiries@rogersandcowan.com
www.rogersandcowan.com
CEO
Tom Tardio - ttardio@rogersandcowan.com

New York: 919 Third Ave., 18th Flr., New York, NY 10022.
TEL: (212) 445-8400. FAX: (212) 445-8290.

London, Product Placement: Fox Court, 14 Gray's Inn Rd., London WC1 X8WS, United Kingdom.
ACCOUNT MANAGER, PRODUCT PLACEMENT
Kate Kelly - TEL: +44 (0) 844 875 1456.
FAX: +44 (0) 844 826-8315.

London, Entertainment PR & Consumer Marketing:
84 Eccleston Sq. London, SWiV 1PX
ACCOUNT DIRECTOR, ENTERTAINMENT PR & CONSUMER MARKETING
Emma McCorkell - TEL: +44 (0) 203 048 0480.
FAX: +44 (0) 203 048 0401.

The agency designs and implements campaigns for entertainment clients, such as film production and distribution companies, cable and network TV programming, record labels, recording artists, celebrities and athletes, videogame publishers and distributors and digital media companies. Rogers & Cowan also creates integrated marketing solutions for consumer and technology brands seeking to build a connection with consumers through entertainment and lifestyle influences.

STAN ROSENFIELD & ASSOCIATES
2029 Century Park E., Ste. 1190, Los Angeles, CA 90067.
TEL: (310) 286-7474. FAX: (310) 286-2255.

Boutique public relations agency which represents A+ talent.

SAATCHI & SAATCHI

Los Angeles: 3501 Sepulveda Blvd., Torrance, CA 90505.
TEL: (310) 214-6000. FAX: (310) 214-6360.
email: first initial + surname@ saatchila.com
www.saatchila.com
CEO
Kurt Ritter
PRESIDENT
Charles Maguy
CFO
Michael Webb
EXECUTIVE CREATIVE OFFICER
Mike McKay
CHIEF STRATEGY OFFICER
Mark Turner

New York: 375 Hudson St., New York, NY 10014-3620.
TEL: (212) 463-2000. FAX: (212) 463-9855. www.saatchiny.com
CEO AND CHAIRMAN & CEO, AMERICAS
Mary Baglivo
CHIEF CREATIVE OFFICER
Con Williamson
EXECUTIVE V.P., DIRECTOR OF FINANCE & OPERATIONS
James Orsini
EXECUTIVE V.P., CHIEF STRATEGY OFFICER
Claudine Cheever
EXECUTIVE V.P., GLOBAL GENERAL MANAGER
Peter Hubbell
NEW BUSINESS CONTACT
Eric Damassa - (212) 463-2937 eric.damassa@saatchiny.com

Saatchi & Saatchi New York is the largest agency in the 153-office Saatchi & Saatchi global network, part of Publicis Groupe, the world's fourth largest communications group.

SCREENVISION CINEMA NETWORK
1411 Broadway, New York, NY 10018. TEL: (800) 724-MOVIE, (212) 497-0423. FAX: (212) 497-0500. www.screenvision.com

California: 429 Santa Monica Blvd., Ste. 340, Santa Monica, CA 90401. TEL: (310) 656-8080.
PRESIDENT & CEO
Matthew Kearney
V.P. WESTERN NATIONAL/REGIONAL SALES
Seeta Zieger - szieger@screenvision.com
V.P. EASTERN NATIONAL/REGIONAL SALES
John Harman - jharmon@screenvision.com

Screenvision is a leading cinema advertising company, providing premium marketing and media solutions for advertisers and comprehensive representation of the cinema advertising interests of its theatrical exhibitor partners. Screenvision provides national and regional advertisers with on-screen advertising, in-lobby promotions and integrated marketing programs, servicing these advertisers through offices in New York City, Chicago, Detroit, Kansas City and Los Angeles. See website for additional office contact information.

NANCY SELTZER & ASSOCIATES

Los Angeles Office: 6220 Del Valle Dr., Los Angeles, CA 90048.
TEL: (323) 938-3562. FAX: (323) 938-0589.
email: nseltzer@nsapr.com
OWNER/PUBLICIST
Nancy Seltzer

New York Office: 1775 Broadway, New York, NY 10019.
TEL: (212) 307-0117. FAX: (212) 307-0182.

SGI MARKETING

18034 Ventura Blvd., Ste. 275, Encino, CA 91316.
TEL: (818) 921-9857. email: bscott4733@aol.com
CONTACT
Brien Scott

SLATE PR

8322 Beverly Blvd., Ste. 201, Los Angeles, CA 90048.
TEL: (323) 556-0580. FAX: (323) 653-5416.
PARTNERS:
Robin Baum, Andy Gelb, Stephen Huvane, Ina Treciokas

New York Office: TEL: (646) 360-1320. FAX: (212) 509-8927.
PUBLICITY
Erica Gray
EVENTS
Shawn Purdy

SMZ PR PARTNERS

(Simons Michelson Zieve, Inc.)
900 Wilshire Dr., Troy, MI 48084-1600. TEL: (248) 362-4242.
FAX: (248) 362-2014. email: info@smz.com www.smz.com
CHAIRMAN
Jim Michelson
PRESIDENT
Jamie Michelson

SPECIAL OPS MEDIA

(Merged with LBI in 2010. See full listing under LBI.)

SPELLING COMMUNICATIONS

865 S. Figueroa St., Ste. 1100, Los Angeles, CA 90017.
TEL: (213) 415-7400. FAX: (213) 415-7405.
email: info@spellcom.com www.spellcom.com
CEO
Daniel Spelling
V.P.
Brian McWilliams

SSA PUBLIC RELATIONS

15260 Ventura Blvd., Ste. 1730, Sherman Oaks, CA 91403.
TEL: (818) 907-5929. email: info@ssapublicrelations.com
www.ssapr.com

New York: 148 Madison Ave., 16th Flr. PH-1, New York, NY 10016. TEL: (212) 679-4750. FAX: (212) 679-4725.
CEO
Steve Syatt
VICE PRESIDENT
Elliott Chang

SSA is a public relations and marketing firm for an impressive roster of U.S. and international television and theatrical film production/distribution companies; home video suppliers; network, cable and syndication companies; and talent.

STUDIO CITY

California: 4705 Laurel Canyon Blvd., Ste. 400, Studio City, CA 91607. TEL: (818) 557-7777. FAX: (818) 557-6777.
email: stu@studiocity.com www.studiocity.com
PRESIDENT & FOUNDER
Stu Weiss

New York: 252 7th Ave., New York, NY 10001.
TEL: (212) 777-5755. www.studiocity.com

SYNAPTIC DIGITAL

(Formerly Medialink)
(Synaptic Digital is a communications company that provides professionally-produced video and audio content on behalf of companies on Web, TV and Radio)

708 Third Ave., New York, NY 10017.
TEL: (800) 843-0677, (212) 682-8300. FAX: (212) 682-5260.
email: learnmore@synapticdigital.com
www.synapticdigital.com

Atlanta: TEL: (770) 622-7011. FAX: (770) 476-2912.

Chicago: 225 N. Michigan Ave., 19th Flr., Chicago, IL 60611.
TEL: (312) 856-8861. FAX: (212) 222-9810.

Los Angeles: (323) 653-8535.

San Francisco Office: One Embarcadero Center, Ste. 500, San Francisco, CA 94111. TEL: (415) 296-8877.
FAX: (415) 296-9929.

Washington D.C.: National Press Bldg., 529 14th St. NW, Ste. 450, Washington, D.C. 20045. TEL: (202) 628-3800.
FAX: 202) 628-2377.
PRESIDENT & CEO
Jim Lonergan
COO
Nick Abramovich
EXECUTIVE V.P., NORTH AMERICAN SALES
Tom Morrisey

See website for complete office listings.

TARGET ENTERPRISES

16501 Ventura Blvd., Ste. 515, Encino, CA 91436.
TEL: (818) 905-0005. FAX: (818) 905-1444.
www.targetenterprises.com

Satellite and video for on location broadcast, flyaway packages, engineering and set-up crews for remotes and remote site management.

T.G.I.F. COMMUNICATIONS

41 Sea Colony Dr., Santa Monica, CA 90405.
TEL: (310) 314-1111. email: bob@tgifcomm.com
infoconnect@tgifcomm.com www.tgifcomm.com
CREATIVE DIRECTOR
Bob Friday

THOMPSON COMMUNICATIONS

580 Haddon Ave., Collingswood, NJ 08108.
TEL: (609) 386-0019. FAX: (609) 386-8579.
email: steve@thomcomm.net www.thomcomm.net
CONTACT
Stephen C. Thompson

Services include film marketing and producer representing the development, financing, production, promotion and distribution of feature films.

TIERNEY COMMUNICATIONS

200 S. Broad St., Philadelphia, PA 19102.
TEL: (215) 790-4100. FAX: (215) 790-4363.
www.tierneyagency.com
PRESIDENT & CEO
Mary Stengel Austen
EXECUTIVE V.P. & GENERAL MANAGER,
PUBLIC RELATIONS
Steve Albertini - salbertini@tierneyagency.com
EXECUTIVE CREATIVE DIRECTOR
Patrick Hardy

TMG ENTERTAINMENT

420 Lincoln Rd., Ste. 446, Miami Beach, FL 33139.
TEL: (866) 533-7617. FAX: (888) 816-9316.
email: paolo@tmg-intl.com
PRESIDENT
Paolo Sadri

TMG Entertainment is an independent, full-service event management and production firm worldwide.

TRACY-LOCKE PARTNERSHIP

1999 Bryan St., Ste. 2800, Dallas, TX 75201.
TEL: (214) 259-3500. FAX: (214) 259-3550.

Los Angeles: 340 Main St., Los Angeles, CA 90291.
TEL: (310) 907-1554. FAX: (310) 907-1655.
www.tracylocke.com

New York: 379 W. Broadway, 3rd Flr., New York, NY 10012.
TEL: (212) 284-1600. FAX: (212) 284-1601.
CEO
Ron Askew
PRESIDENT, CHIEF TALENT OFFICER
Beth Ann Kaminkow
EXECUTIVE CREATIVE DIRECTOR, WEST
Regan Holley
CHIEF MARKETING OFFICER
Jim Sexton

Brand to retail marketing agency. See website for additional office locations.

TRAILER PARK

6922 Hollywood Blvd., 12th Flr., Hollywood, CA 90028.
TEL: (310) 845-3000. FAX: (310) 845-3470.
www.trailerpark.com
CEO
Rick Eiserman
PRESIDENT
Benedict Coulter
PRESIDENT, THEATRICAL & THEATRICAL HOME ENTERTAINMENT
Matt Brubaker
PRESIDENT, TV DIVISION & TV HOME ENTERTAINMENT
Mike Leathers
PRESIDENT, INTERACTIVE
Julianne LaMarche
MANAGING DIRECTOR, INTEGRATED PRODUCTION
Rupert Samuel

Trailer Park offers diverse entertainment marketing services.

UNIQUESCREEN MEDIA, INC.

(A Cinedigm company)
314-10th Ave. S, Ste. 160, Waite Park, MN 56387.
www.uniquescreenmedia.com
SALES AND AGENCY CONTACT
Stacey Sherman - staceys@uniquescreenmedia.com
EXECUTIVE DIRECTOR OF EXHIBITOR RELATIONS
Alison Schroeder - alison@uniquescreenmedia.com

UniqueScreen Media creates the advertisements that play before movies in more than 3,800 screens that reside in over 450 theatres across the U.S.

VISTA GROUP

4561 Colorado Blvd., Los Angeles, CA 90039.
TEL: (818) 551-6789. FAX: (818) 551-6880.
email: edahlquist@mail.vistagroupusa.com
www.vistagroupusa.com
DIRECTOR OF CLIENT SERVICES
Eric C. Dahlquist, Jr.

Vista Group is an entertainment marketing agency in Los Angeles specializing in public relations, marketing, trademark licensing and motion picture and television product placement.

WANG & WILLIAMS

11400 W. Olympic Blvd., 2nd Flr., Los Angeles, CA 90064.
TEL: (310) 312-0061. FAX: (310) 312-0082.
CONTACTS
Ming Wang, Denise Williams

WIDESCREEN MEDIA GROUP

3826 Beresford Road E., West Palm Beach, FL 33417.
TEL: (877) 345-6237. FAX: (877) 374-9912.
email: info@widescreenmedia.com
www.widescreenmedia.com
CEO/PRESIDENT
James Erickson - james@widescreenmedia.com

Produces on-screen digital cinema advertising.

WIDESCREEN CREATIVE SERVICES

5900 N. Australian Ave., Ste. 11, Mangonia Park, FL 33407.
TEL: (877) 345-6237. FAX: (877) 374-9912.
email: design@widescreenmedia.com
www.widescreenmedia.com

WideScreen Creative Services produces high-definition video, 2D and 3D animation, TV and radio ads, and can unify and centralize clients' media efforts. The company also produces marketing and educational DVDs, websites, logos and print material. Widescreen Creative Services is a licensed advertising agency and produces on-screen digital cinema advertising.

WINSTON DAVIS ASSOCIATES

955 S. Carrillo Dr., Ste. 200, Los Angeles, CA 90048.
TEL: (323) 930-8535. www.winstondavis.com
CONTACTS
Robert Solomon - robert@winstondavis.com
Dean Blagg - dean@winstondavis.com

Produces: Trailers, TV spots, home entertainment trailers, home entertainment TV spots, TV to DVD, broadcast TV, sizzle reels, Internet media, radio spots, corporate, tribute reels & motion graphics.

YOUNG & RUBICAM, INC.

285 Madison Ave., New York, NY 10017-6486.
TEL: (212) 210-3000. FAX: (212) 490-9073. www.yr.com
PRESIDENT & CEO, YR NORTH AMERICA
Tom Sebok - tom.sebok@yr.com

YR Irvine: 7535 Irvine Center Dr., Irvine, CA 92618.
TEL: (949) 754-2000

ANIMATION

ANIMATION EQUIPMENT, SOFTWARE

ANIMATION TOOLWORKS, INC.
18484 S.W. Parrett Mountain Rd., Sherwood, OR 97140.
TEL: (877) 625-6438. FAX: (503) 925-0221.
email: info@animationtoolworks.com
www.animationtoolworks.com
CONTACT
Howard Mozeico

CATALINA GRAPHIC FILMS
27001 Agoura Rd., Ste. 100, Calabasas Hills, CA 91301.
TEL: (800) 333-3136, (818) 880-8060. FAX: (800) 333-3136, (818) 880-1144. www.cgf-inc.com
www.catalinagraphicfilms.com

Custom coater of pressure sensitive materials for the digital, off-set, screen, industrial and specialty markets.

CHROMACOLOUR INTERNATIONAL
5, 1410 28th St. NE, Calgary, Alberta T2A 7W6, Canada.
TEL: (800) 665-5829, (403) 250-5880. FAX: (403) 250-7194.
email: info@chromacolour.com www.chromacolour.com

Chromacolour is a leader in the manufacture and sale of supplies, software and equipment for traditional and digital animation. Although primarily associated with top-quality animation paint, available in more than 1,800 colors, company also provides a broad range of industry-specific equipment, furniture, software and supplies.

CHYRON CORP.
Headquarters: 5 Hub Dr., Melville, NY 11747.
TEL: (631) 845-2000. www.chyron.com

A pioneer of graphics as a service for all digital video media, Chyron continues to define and dominate the world of digital and broadcast graphics with Web, Mobile, HD, 3D, and newsroom integration solutions.

ALAN GORDON ENTERPRISES
5625 Melrose Ave., Hollywood, CA 90038.
TEL: (323) 466-3561. FAX: (323) 871-2193.
email: contactus@alangordon.com www.alangordon.com
CONTACT
Grant Loucks

Motion picture and video support equipment, rental and sales facilities. In addition, company manufactures a variety of proprietary products, including the renowned and popular Academy Award-winning Mark Vb Director's Viewfinder, HD Redhead lights, plus motion picture, photogrammetric, and stereo plotting instruments.

PIXEL MAGIC
10635 Riverside Dr., Toluca Lake, CA 91602.
TEL: (818) 760-0862. FAX: (818) 760-4983.
www.pixelmagicfx.com
VFX SUPERVISOR
Ray McIntyre, Jr.
V.P. GENERAL MANAGER
Ray Scalice

Visual effects facility. A div. of OCS/Freeze Frame. Established in 1994, company now creates optical techniques from a full digital platform.

QUANTEL, INC.
Headquarters: Quantel Limited, Turnpike Rd., Newbury, Berkshire RG14 2NX, United Kingdom.
TEL: +44 (0) 1635 48 222. FAX: +44 (0) 1635 815 815.
email: firstname.lastname@quantel.com www.quantel.com

U.S. Head Office: Quantel Inc., 25 West 43rd St., Ste. 1118, New York, NY 10036. TEL: (212) 944 6820. FAX: (212) 944 6813.
www.quantel.com
DISTRICT SALES MANAGER
Lee Turvey - lee.turvey@quantel.com

Los Angeles: 3800 Barham Blvd., Los Angeles, CA 90068.
TEL: (323) 436-7600. FAX: (323) 878-2596.
V.P. SALES
Eric Thorne - eric.thorne@quantel.com

Animation equipment, including digital intermediate-2K or 4K resolution. See website for additional office locations.

T.S. COMPUTERS AND VIDEO
11300 Hartland St., North Hollywood, CA 91605.
TEL: (818) 760-4445. FAX: (818) 505-1811.
email: videosales@vgn.com www.vgn.com
DIRECTOR OF SALES
Brenda Scileppi

Digital Video Editing System Sales & Rentals, Compositing & High-End Paint/Animation Software & Hardware.

OPTICAL EFFECTS & PHOTOGRAPHY, CEL, CLAY AND DIGITAL ANIMATION

11:11 MEDIA WORKS
(Digital)
6611 Valjean Ave., Ste. 1018, Van Nuys, CA 91406.
TEL: (818) 780-4466. FAX: (818) 780-4467.
email: roger@1111mw.com www.1111mediaworks.com
PRESIDENT, CREATIVE DIRECTOR
Roger Nall

3DPAINT & F/X, L.L.C.
412 7th St., Santa Monica, CA 90402. TEL: (310) 458-1916.
email: info@3dpaint.com www.3dpaint.com
PRESIDENT
Tom Polson

2-D & 3-D Animation, Animatics, Compositing, Digital FX & Motion Graphics.

A & S ANIMATION
(Character animation & show development)
8137 Lake Crowell Circle, Orlando, FL 32836.
TEL: (407) 370-2673. FAX: (407) 370-2602.
email: marksimon@storyboards-east.com www.funnytoons.tv
DIRECTOR
Mark Simon

A&S Animation, Inc. develops and produces character animation for TV, commercials, training videos and the web. Over 75 international awards.

AARDMAN ANIMATIONS
Gas Ferry Rd., Bristol, Avon BS1 6UN England.
TEL: (01 17) 984-8485. FAX: (01 17) 984-8486.
email: mail@aardman.com www.aardman.com
CHIEF EXECUTIVE CHAIRMAN
David Sproxton
CREATIVE DIRECTOR
Peter Lord
DIRECTOR
Nick Park

ACE STORYBOARD ON DEMAND
31455 West St., S. Laguna Beach, CA 92677.
TEL: (949) 499-9964. www.markpacella.com
www.acestoryboards.com
ART DIRECTOR
Mark Pacella - mark@markpacella.com

Storyboards, concept art & flesh animation; film credits. Also live-action storyboards.

ACME FILMWORKS
6525 Sunset Blvd., Garden Ste. 10, Hollywood, CA 90028.
TEL: (323) 464-7805. FAX: (323) 464-6614.
email: acmeinfo@acmefilmworks.com
www.acmefilmworks.com
EXECUTIVE PRODUCER
Ron Diamond - rjd@acmefilmworks.com
PUBLICITY
Rebecca Battle - pr@acmefilmworks.com

Stop Motion, Photo Collage, Motion Graphics, 2-D Digital Animation.

ACORN ENTERTAINMENT
(3D/Digital & 2D Animation; Pre-visualization, Storyboard & Design for Theatrical & Broadcast)
5777 W. Century Blvd., 10th Flr., Los Angeles, CA 90045.
TEL: (323) 238-4650. email: info@acornentertainment.com
www.acornentertainment.com
PRESIDENT
Thad Weinlein - thad@acornentertainment.com
DESIGN, BROADCAST GRAPHICS
Bill Hastings - Bill@acornentertainment.com
COMMERCIAL DIVISION
Mary Chis Wall - Mary@acornentertainment.com

AMALGAMATED PIXELS, INC.
(2-D, 3-D digital animation, digital matte printing)
2475 Townsgate Rd., Ste. 220, Westlake Village, CA 91361.
TEL: (818) 865-8423. FAX: (818) 875-9032.
www.apixels.com
PRESIDENT, PRODUCTION
Derry Frost - dfrost@apixels.com

DIRECTOR, BUSINESS DEVELOPMENT
Bonnie Kanner - bkanner@apixels.com

ANIMAL MAKERS
(Animatronic animals)
11991 Discovery Ct. Moorpark, CA 93021.
TEL: (805) 523-1900. FAX: (805) 523-1903.
email: jim@animalmakers.com www.animalmakers.com
CONTACT
Jim Boulden

ANIMATION ENTERTAINMENT
(Computer animation website)
3830 Valley Centre Dr., Ste. 705-833, San Diego, CA 92130.
TEL: (858) 793-1900. FAX: (858) 793-1942.
www.animationtrip.com
CONTACT
Steven Churchill - steven@animationtrip.com

ANIMOTION
501 W. Fayette St., Syracuse, NY 13204. TEL: (315) 471-3533.
email: info@animotioninc.com www.animotioninc.com
CONTACT
David Hicock, Larry Royer

Company also does animation for the web and web design.

ARC SCIENCE SIMULATIONS
1122 N. Denver Ave., Loveland, CO 80537.
TEL: (800) 759-1642, (970) 667-1168. FAX: (970) 667-1105.
email: sales@arcscience.com www.arcscience.com
PRESIDENT
Tom Ligon

ASSOCIATES & YAMASHITA
13600 Marina Pointe Dr., Ste. 1007, Marina Del Rey, CA 90292. TEL: (310) 664- 9500. www.aayamashita.com
PRESIDENT
Allen Yamashita - allen@simexos.com

Computer animation, graphics, digital effects and specialty venue films.

B1 MEDIA
(Digital; Interactive Design & DVD-ROM)
11846 Ventura Blvd., Ste. 300, Studio City, CA 91604.
TEL: (818) 755-8800. FAX: (818) 755-8818.
email: b1@b1media.com www.b1media.com
CEO
Brian Johnson

BAGDASARIAN PRODUCTIONS
1192 E. Mountain Dr., Montecito, CA 93108.
TEL: (805) 969-3349. FAX: (805) 969-7466.
www.chipmunks.com
CHAIRMAN & CEO
Ross Bagdasarian
PRESIDENT
Janice Karman

BIFROST LASERFX
(3D animation and laser animation)
6733 Sale Ave., West Hills, CA 91307. TEL: (818) 704-0423.
email: howie@howiewood.net www.howiewood.net
OWNER
Howard Shore

BLT & ASSOCIATES, INC.
(Entertainment marketing. Print, broadcast, A/V, film trailers, promotional TV trailers)
6430 Sunse Blvd., 8th Flr., Hollywood, CA 90028.
TEL: (323) 860-4000. FAX: (323) 860-0890.
email: blt@bltomato.com www.bltomato.com
CONTACT
Whitney Robinson

BLUE SKY STUDIOS
(See Twentieth Century Fox)

BLUR STUDIO, INC.
589 Venice Blvd., Venice, CA 90291. TEL: (310) 581-8848.
FAX: (310) 581-8850. email: tim@blur.com
PRESIDENT & CREATIVE DIRECTOR
Tim Miller

BROADWAY VIDEO DESIGN
1619 Broadway, 10th Flr., New York, NY 10019.
TEL: (212) 265-7600. email: info@broadwayvideo.com
www.broadwayvideo.com
DIRECTOR, OPERATIONS
Kim Caffiero - kcaffiero@broadwayvideo.com

BUZZCO ASSOCIATES, INC.
(2D animation)
33 Bleecker St., New York, NY 10012. TEL: (212) 473-8800.
FAX: (212) 473-8891. email: info@buzzzco.com
www.buzzzco.com
CONTACT
Candy Kugel

CALABASH ANIMATION
657 W. Ohio St., Chicago, IL 60654. TEL: (312) 243-3433.
FAX: (312) 243-6227. www.calabashanimation.com
EXECUTIVE PRODUCER & CGI DIRECTOR
Sean Henry
LEAD ANIMATION DIRECTOR
Wayne Brejcha
ARTIST
Diane Grider, Priscilla Olson, Gary Whitney, Jackie Smessaert-Brennan, Ben Chow, Charles Ramsey

Produces everything from traditional 2D "cel" character animation to Flash and 3D computer generated ("CG") animation – and also produces animated cartoons and short films.

CHIODO BROS. PRODUCTIONS, INC.
110 W. Providencia Ave., Burbank, CA 91502.
TEL: (818) 842-5656. FAX: (818) 848-0891.
email: klowns@chiodobros.com www.chiodobros.com
PRESIDENT
Stephen Chiodo

CINEMA CONCEPTS TSC
2030 Powers Ferry Rd., Ste. 214, Atlanta, GA 30339.
TEL: (800) 746-9237, (770) 956-7460. FAX: (770) 956-8358.
email: info@cinemaconcepts.com www.cinemaconcepts.com
PRESIDENT
Stewart Harnell

Studio & editing services, preview & policy trailers, animation, digital prod. services-HD poor/mastering/film-out, screening rooms-film & digital, pre-show content-JPEG 2000.

CINESITE, LTD.
Medius House, 2 Sheraton St., London W1F 8BH UK.
TEL: +44 20 7973 4000. FAX: +44 20 7973 4040.
email: filmfx@cinesite.co.uk televisionfx@cinesite.co.uk
www.cinesite.com

Visual effects for the film and television industries.

CLICK 3X
16 W. 22nd St., New York, NY 10010. TEL: (212) 627-1900.
FAX: (212) 627-4472. www.click3X.com
PRESIDENT, PARTNER
Peter Corbett
CREATIVE DIRECTOR, CLICKFIRE MEDIA
Nick Adgerian
CREATIVE DIRECTOR, CLICK3X ENTERTAINMENT
Ders Hallgren
HEAD, SALES
Trevor King - trevor@click3x.com
SENIOR SALES
Jenn Johnson - jennjohnson@click3x.com
Connor Swegle - connor@click3x.com

Click 3X focuses on commercial and feature film, broadcast and web projects.

CREATIVE CHARACTER ENGINEERING
(Full-service animatronic & digital effects; rental silicone babies)
16110 Hart St., Van Nuys, CA 91406. TEL: (818) 901-0507.
FAX: (818) 901-8417. www.creativecharacter.com
CREATIVE DIRECTOR & OWNER
Andrew Clement
SHOP MANAGER
Lancel Reyes

CREST ANIMATION PRODUCTIONS
(2-D and 3-D)
333 N. Glenoaks Blvd., 3rd Flr., Burbank, CA 91502.
TEL: (818) 846-0166. FAX: (818) 846-6074.
email: info@crestcgi.com

CRYSTAL PYRAMID PRODUCTIONS
(Animation, video production, nonlinear editing, crews & stock footage)
7323 Rondel Court, San Diego, CA 92119.
TEL: (800) 365-8433, (619) 644-3000. FAX: (619) 644-3001.
email: crystalp@crystalpyramid.com www.crystalpyramid.com
PRESIDENT
Mark Schulze
PRODUCER & V.P.
Patty Mooney - patty@crystalpyramid.com
MULTIMEDIA PRODUCER
Luke Jungers

NEW & UNIQUE VIDEOS
(Stock footage & distribution)
7323 Rondel Ct., San Diego, CA 92119.
TEL: (619) 644-3000. FAX: (619) 644-3001.
email: video@newuniquevideos.com
www.newuniquevideos.com
PRODUCER & V.P.
Patty Mooney

Quality stock footage at a great price. A subsidiary of Crystal Pyramid Inc.

CURIOUS PICTURES

(Computer animation, cel and stop-motion animation)
440 Lafayette St., 6th Flr., New York, NY 10003.
TEL: (212) 674-1400. FAX: (212) 674-0081.
email:info@curiouspictures.com
animation@curiouspictures.com www.curiouspictures.com
MANAGING PARTNER
Marina Grasic
MANAGING PARTNER
Jan Korbelin
SENIOR V.P., HEAD OF STUDIO
Camille Geier
CREATIVE DIRECTOR
Dominie Mahl
PARTNER, EXECUTIVE PRODUCER
Lewis Kofsky
PARTNER, EXECUTIVE PRODUCER
Leopoldo Gout
MANAGING DIRECTOR, COMMERCIALS
Mary Knox
HEAD OF PRODUCTION
John Cline

Curious directors, designers, artists, technologists, and animators create and produce film, TV, commercials, on-air graphics, toys, and games for audiences worldwide.

CYBER F/X

(3D laser scanning for digitizing marquettes, objects, people)
2940 N. Naomi St., Burbank, CA 91504. TEL: (818) 246-2911.
FAX: (818) 452-9613. email: info@cyberfx.com
www.cyberfx.com
PRESIDENT & FOUNDER
Dick Cavdek

DIGISCOPE DIGITAL VISUAL EFFECTS

(Special effects for motion pictures)
1447 Cloverfield Blvd., Santa Monica, CA 90404.
TEL: (310) 315-6060. FAX: (310) 828-5856.
email: mary@digiscope.com www.digiscope.com
PRESIDENT
Mary Stuart-Welch
VFX PRODUCER
Terron Pratt - terron@digiscope.com
VFX SUPERVISOR
Dion Hatch - dion@digiscope.com

DIGITAL DOMAIN

(Full-service animation company)
300 Rose Ave., Venice, CA 90291. TEL: (310) 314-2800.
FAX: (310) 664-2701. www.digitaldomain.com

Canada: 1618 W. 8th St., Vancouver, BC v6J 1V4.
TEL: (778) 783-6000. FAX: (778) 783-6099.
CEO
Cliff Plumer
PRESIDENT, FEATURE FILM PRODUCTION
Gloria Borders
PRESIDENT, COMMERCIAL PRODUCTION
Ed Ulbrich - commercials@d2.com
HEAD OF PRODUCTION
Jody Madden
EP, SALES & MARKETING
Tanya Cohen

DIGITAL NATION, INC.

(Digital; SCI & Cineon workstations; digital compositing and film restoration)
6311 Grape Pl., Los Angeles, CA 90068. TEL: (323) 957-2600.
email: grodner@gmail.com www.digitalnationinc.com
OWNER/OPERATOR
Scott Grodner

WALT DISNEY STUDIOS

WALT DISNEY ANIMATION STUDIOS

(Part of Walt Disney Studios)
500 S. Buena Vista St., Burbank, CA 91521.
TEL: (818) 560-1000. www.disneyanimation.com
CHAIRMAN, WALT DISNEY STUDIOS
Rich Ross
PRESIDENT, WALT DISNEY STUDIOS
Alan Bergman
EXECUTIVE V.P. & CHIEF TECHNOLOGY OFFICER WALT DISNEY STUDIOS
Greg Brandeau
SENIOR V.P., COMMUNICATIONS, THE WALT DISNEY STUDIOS
Heidi Trotta
CO-FOUNDER, PIXAR ANIMATION STUDIOS, PRESIDENT, WALT DISNEY & PIXAR ANIMATION STUDIOS
Dr. Ed Catmull
CHIEF CREATIVE OFFICER, PIXAR & WALT DISNEY ANIMATION STUDIOS, PRINCIPAL CREATIVE ADVISOR, WALT DISNEY IMAGINEERING
John Lasseter

PIXAR ANIMATION STUDIOS

(Wholly owned subsidiary of The Walt Disney Company since Jan. 2006)
1200 Park Ave., Emeryville, CA 94608. TEL: (510) 922-3000.
FAX: (510) 922-3151.
CO-FOUNDER, PIXAR ANIMATIONS STUDIOS & PRESIDENT, PIXAR & WALT DISNEY ANIMATION STUDIOS
Dr. Ed Catmull

DISNEY/PIXAR ANIMATION STUDIO, VANCOUVER

GENERAL MANAGER
Amir Nasrabadi
CREATIVE DIRECTOR
Dylan Brown
CHIEF TECHNICAL OFFICER
Darwyn Peachey

Formed in May 2009. Focus on nonfeature projects with Disney and Pixar's legacy characters. Short-form quality computer ani mation for theme parks, DVDs, television and theatrical exhibition.

DISNEY CHANNELS WORLDWIDE

3800 W. Alameda Ave., Burbank, CA 91505.
TEL: (818) 569-7500. PRESS FAX: (818) 558-1241.
www.disneychannel.com
PRESIDENT, DISNEY CHANNELS WORLDWIDE
Carolina Lightcap
PRESIDENT, ENTERTAINMENT & CHIEF CREATIVE OFFICER, DISNEY CHANNELS WORLDWIDE
EXECUTIVE V.P., DISNEY MEDIA ADVERTISING SALES & MARKETING GROUP
Tricia Wilber
SENIOR V.P., ORIGINAL SERIES & DISNEY TELEVISION ANIMATION
Eric Coleman
SENIOR V.P., ORIGINAL MOVIES, DISNEY CHANNEL
Michael Healy
SENIOR V.P., PLAYHOUSE DISNEY WORLDWIDE
Nancy Kanter
SENIOR V.P., MARKETING & CREATIVE
Richard Loomis

Walt Disney Television Animation (DTVA) was integrated into Disney Channel Worldwide in Nov. 2005. Animation operations continue as part of Disney Channel operations.

D.L.T. ENTERTAINMENT LIMITED

(Production & distribution company)
U.S. Headquarters: 124 E. 55th St., New York, NY 10022.
TEL: (212) 245-4680. FAX: (212) 315-1132.
email: info@dltentertainment.com www.dltentertainment.com

U.K. Headquarters: 10 Bedford Sq., London, England WC1B 3RA. TEL: +44 (020) 7631-1184. FAX: +44 (020) 7636-4571.
CHAIRMAN
Don Taffner
VICE CHAIRMAN
John Fitzgerald
PRESIDENT
Don Taffner, Jr.
COO & CFO
Jeff Cotugno
DIRECTOR, PUBLIC TELEVISION SALES
Lisa Simon

Distributes animation, children and family programming, comedy, documentary, drama, educational and reality TV.

DNA PRODUCTIONS, INC.

2201 W. Royal Ln., Ste. 275, Irving, TX 75063.
TEL: (214) 352-4694. FAX: (214) 496-9333.
www.dnahelix.com
CONTACT
Keith Alcorn, John Davis

DREAMWORKS ANIMATION SKG, INC.

1000 Flower St., Glendale, CA 91201. TEL: (818) 695-5000, (818) 695-3900 (investor relations). FAX: (818) 695-9944.
www.dreamworksanimation.com
CEO & DIRECTOR
Jeffrey Katzenberg
COO
Ann Daly
PRESIDENT & CFO
Lewis Coleman
CO-PRESIDENT PRODUCTION/PRESIDENT LIVE THEATRICAL
Bill Damaschke
CO-PRESIDENT, PRODUCTION
John Batter
GENERAL COUNSEL & CORPORATE SECRETARY
Andrew Chang
HEAD, WORLDWIDE MARKETING & CONSUMER PRODUCTS
Anne Globe

HEAD OF CORPORATE FINANCE
Rich Sullivan
CHIEF ACCOUNTING OFFICER
Heather O'Connor

DUCK STUDIOS

2205 Stoner Ave., Los Angeles, CA 90064. TEL: (310) 478-0771.
FAX: (310) 478-0773. email: info@duckstudios.com
www.duckstudios.com
EXECUTIVE PRODUCER
Mark Medernach - mark@duckstudios.com

Animation for commercials, film and TV titles, multimedia; 2D and 3D computer animation, cel, character design, digital compositing, digital ink & paint.

ENOKI FILMS U.S.A., INC.

(Japanese animation)
16430 Ventura Blvd., Ste. 308, Encino, CA 91436.
TEL: (818) 907-6503. FAX: (818) 907-6506.
email: info@enokifilmsusa.com www.enokifilmsusa.com

RUSS FARBER

(Blue screen effects, setup, networking & trouble-shooting computers on location)
19324 Oxnard St., Tarzana, CA 91356. TEL: (818) 708-8113.
email: refent@pacbell.net

FILM ROMAN

(A Starz Media company. Independent animation studio)
2950 N. Hollywood Way, Burbank, CA 91505.
TEL: (818) 748-4000. FAX: (818) 748-4613.
www.filmroman.com
CEO
Kent Rice
PRESIDENT, COO
Scott Greenberg
HEAD OF PRODUCTION
Jay Fukuto
SENIOR V.P., PRODUCTION
Mike Wolf
V.P., BUSINESS DEVELOPMENT (ANIMATION, COMMERCIALS & VISUAL EFFECTS)
Carin Davis

A top independent animation company for over 20 years.

FLEISCHER STUDIOS, INC.

10160 Cielo Dr., Beverly Hills, CA 90210. TEL: (310) 276-7503.
FAX: (310) 276-1559. email: stanhandman@yahoo.com
PRESIDENT
Mark Fleischer

FLYING FOTO FACTORY, INC.

P.O. Box 1166, Durham, NC 27702. TEL: (919) 490-1370.
email: kathyb@flyingfoto.com info@flyingfoto.com
www.flyingfoto.com
V.P., SALES & MARKETING
Kathy Bennett

F-STOP, INC.

(Opticals & titles)
120 S. Buena Vista St., Burbank, CA 91505.
TEL: (818) 843-7867. FAX: (818) 842-7706.
CONTACT
Todd Hall

GALAXIE ENTERTAINMENT CO.

(Animation, optical effects, photography & stereoscopic-3D)
P.O. Box 922405, Sylmar, CA 91392. TEL: (818) 362-6005.
FAX: (818) 362-6005.
CONTACT
Dave Gregory

JIM GAMBLE PUPPET PRODUCTIONS

(Puppet show and workshops)
25014 Broadwell Ave., Harbor City, CA 90710.
TEL: (310) 541-1921. FAX: (310) 541-2195.
email: office@jimgamble.com www.jimgamble.com

GRACIE FILMS

(TV animation)
10202 W. Washington Blvd., Sidney Poitier Bldg., 2nd Flr.,
Culver City, CA 90232. TEL: (310) 244-4000.
FAX: (310) 244-1530. www.graciefilms.com
PRODUCER/WRITER/DIRECTOR
James L. Brooks
PRESIDENT
Richard Sakai
PRESIDENT, MOTION PICTURES
Julie Ansell
EXECUTIVE V.P./CFO
Denise Sirkot

HEARST ENTERTAINMENT, INC.

(Distribution for animated series)
300 West 57 St., 15th Fl., New York, NY 10019.
TEL: (212) 969-7574. FAX: (646) 280-1574.
www.hearstent.com
SENIOR V.P., SALES & MARKETING
Stacey Valenza - svalenza@hearst.com
ASSISTANT TO STACEY VALENZA
Nadine Rahiman

See website for animation library.

HEARST ENTERTAINMENT PRODUCTIONS

(Production)
20335 Ventura Blvd., Ste. 300, Woodland Hills, CA 91364.
TEL: (818) 444-5010. FAX: (818) 444-5011. www.hearst.com
EXECUTIVE V.P.
Jerry Schevick
EXECUTIVE DIRECTOR
Jennifer Freeman
DIRECTOR
Aurelia White

Made-for-TV/Cable movies, animation, reality & documentary series & specials.

THE JIM HENSON COMPANY

(Production company)
Hollywood Headquarters: 1416 N. La Brea Ave., Hollywood, CA 90028. TEL: (323) 802-1500. FAX: (323) 802-1829.
www.henson.com www.puppetup.com

New York: 627 Broadway, 9th Flr., New York, NY 10012.
TEL: (212) 794-2400. FAX: (212) 439-7452.
CHAIRMAN
Brian Henson
CEO
Lisa Henson
PRESIDENT, COO
Peter Schube, Esq.
EXECUTIVE V.P., OPERATIONS & FINANCE
Laurie Don
SENIOR V.P., FEATURE FILMS
Jason Lust
SENIOR V.P., ADMINISTRATION
Joe Henderson
SENIOR V.P., BUSINESS & LEGAL AFFAIRS
Dan Scharf
EXECUTIVE V.P., CHILDREN'S ENTERTAINMENT
Halle Stanford
SENIOR V.P., GLOBAL CONSUMER PRODUCTS
Melissa Segal
SENIOR V.P., FEATURE FILMS
Jason Lust
SENIOR V.P., MARKETING & PUBLIC RELATIONS
Nicole Goldman - ngoldman@henson.com
CREATIVE SUPERVISOR
Peter Brooke
GENERAL MANAGER, NY WORKSHOP
Connie Peterson

HYPERION PICTURES

(Live action and TV animation)
6725 Sunset Blvd., Ste. 240, Hollywood, CA 90028.
TEL: (323) 871-0022. FAX: (323) 871-0044.
www.hyperionpictures.com
FOUNDER
Tom Wilhite
HYPERION STAFF
Willard Carroll, Bruce Smith, Chris Young, Rishabh Jain, Christian Mills, Nicholas Kimball

ILLUMINATION ENTERTAINMENT

1805 Colorado Ave., Santa Monica, CA 90404.
TEL: (310) 593-8800.
FOUNDER
Chris Meledandri
CREATIVE DIRECTOR
John Cohen
PRODUCTION
Janet Healy

JAMBALAYA STUDIO

FOUNDER
Bruce Smith

Jambalaya Studio was established specifically to produce ethnically diverse animation projects for television, feature films, DVD, and new media. The company was co-founded by Bruce Smith, one of the animation industry's top designer-directors, and Hyperion Pictures, for 22 years a leading independent producer of youth-oriented live-action and animated entertainment.

ICE TEA PRODUCTIONS

160 E. 38th St., #15B, New York, NY 10016.
TEL: (212) 557-8185. FAX: (212) 687-1299.
email: info@iceteaproductions.com
www.iceteaproductions.com
PRESIDENT
Rich Durkin

Ice Tea Productions represents animation directors. The company built its business on recommending who is right for an animation project...whether it represents them or not.

INDUSTRIAL LIGHT & MAGIC (ILM)
(A Lucasfilm Ltd. Co. Special effects and post-production)
P.O. Box 29909, San Francisco, CA 94129.
TEL: (415) 746-3000. FAX: (415) 746-3015.
www.ilm.com
PRESIDENT& GENERAL MANAGER
Lynwen Brennan
ADVISER (FORMER PRESIDENT)
Chrissie England
EXECUTIVE IN CHARGE OF MARKETING & GLOBAL PRODUCTION
Gretchen Libby
EXECUTIVE IN CHARGE OF PRODUCTION OPERATIONS
Janet Lewin

Company is known for its model making, matte painting, computer-generated imagery, digital animation and a variety of related processes required in the production of visual effects.

JIM KEESHEN PRODUCTIONS
1516 Colby Ave., Apt. 7, Los Angeles, CA 90025.
TEL: (310) 478-7230. email: animatics@aol.com
PRESIDENT
Jim Keeshan

Story doctor, visual development and pre-production; previsualization specialists.

KENIMATION ANIMATION SERVICES
(Titles and computerized moves on photos or artwork to film)
1424 N. Wilcox Ave., Los Angeles, CA 90028.
TEL: (323) 462-2679. email: kenru@comcast.net
CONTACT
Ken Rudolph

GENE KRAFT PRODUCTIONS
2549-B Eastbluff Dr., 222, Newport Beach, CA 92660.
TEL: (949) 721-0609. email: gkraft@ientertainment.ws
OWNER
Gene Kraft

KURTZ & FRIENDS
1023 N. Hollywood Way., Burbank, CA 91505.
TEL: (818) 841-8188. FAX: (818) 841-6263.
email: info@kurtzandfriends.com www.kurtzandfriends.com
DIRECTOR
Bob Kurtz
PRODUCER
Boo Lopez

LAIKA/HOUSE
1400 N.W. 22nd Ave., Portland, OR 97210.
TEL: (503) 225-1130. FAX: (503) 226-3746.
email: ask_us@laika.com www.laika.com/house
PRESIDENT & CEO
Travis Knight
PRESIDENT, EXECUTIVE PRODUCER
Lourri Hammack
CO-EXECUTIVE PRODUCER
Jan Johnson
CREATIVE DIRECTOR
Kirk Kelley

Cel, stop motion, CG, flash, motion graphics for film television, advertising, internet.

LATI2D
714 N. Laurel Ave., Los Angeles, CA 90046.
TEL: (323) 852-1425. email: info@lati2d.com www.lati2d.com
PRESIDENT & CHIEF CREATIVE OFFICER
Water Kerner

Est. 1993. Digital Animation, 2D and 3D Design and Animation, Network Branding, 3D Character Design, Original Content, DVD Menu & Game Creation & Animation, Open Title Sequences, Logo Design, & Website creation, basically anything for Film, TV or Interactive Media in need of exceptional ideas and powerful Motion Graphic Design.

LANDMARK ENTERTAINMENT GROUP
(Independent entertainment design & production company)
3900 W. Alameda Ave., Ste. 100, Burbank, CA 91505.
TEL: (818) 569-4900. FAX: (818) 569-4902.
www.landmarkusa.com
CONTACT
Lydia Christopher

LEPREVOST CORPORATION
6781 Wildlife Rd., Malibu, CA 90265. TEL: (310) 704-3042.
FAX: (310) 457-6142. email: info@leprevost.com
www.leprevost.com
EXECUTIVE PRODUCER
John H. LePrevost

LePrevost is a design and motion branding company that specializes in the TV, film & new media industries.

LINKER SYSTEMS, INC.
13612 Onkayha Circle, Irvine, CA 92620. TEL: (949) 552-1904.
FAX: (949) 552-6985. www.linker.com www.linkersystems.com
www.animationstand.com

2D character animation, 3D, image compositing, film-quality special effects opticals. Win & Mac versions.

LIVE WIRE PRODUCTIONS & VFX
(Visual effects animation & compositing; commercial production)
P.O. Box 245, Palos Verdes, CA 90274. TEL: (310) 831-6227.
www.livewireprod.com
PRODUCER
Kristen Simmons

WARREN LOCKHART PRODUCTIONS, INC.
(Multi dimensional film and TV production company)
4344 Promenade Way, 108p, Marina Del Rey, CA 90292.
TEL: (310) 306-4661.
email: warren@lockhartproductions.com
PRESIDENT
Warren L. Lockhart

LUMENI PRODUCTIONS, INC.
1632 Flower St., Glendale, CA 91201-2357.
TEL: (818) 956-2200. FAX: (818) 956-3298. www.lumeni.com
EXECUTIVE PRODUCER
Marshall "Tony" Valdez - tony@lumeni.com

Services include: DI Color Timing, 2D, 3D & stereo computer graphics, animation, special effects for film, including digital trailers, film finishing & title design. Serving the entertainment industry for 29+ years.

MANGA ENTERTAINMENT
(Japanese animation. A Starz company)
215 W. Superior St., Ste. 600, Chicago, IL 60610.
TEL: (312) 751-0020. FAX: (312) 751-2483.
email: info@manga.com www.manga.com
MANAGING DIRECTOR
Kaoru Mfaume

MAVERICK DIGITAL
(Digital effects)
Maverick Digital NYC: 601 W. 26th St., Ste. 1507, New York, NY 10001. TEL: (212)337-8004. www.maverickdigital.net

Denver: 1750 Gilpin St., 3rd Flr., Denver, CO 80218.
TEL: (720) 941-6415.

Phoenix: 15333 Pima Rd., Ste. 235, Scottsdale, AZ 85260.
TEL: (623) 398-2592.

MEGA ENTERTAINMENT INTERNATIONAL, INC.
252 7th Ave. Apt. 6Z, New York, NY 10001.
TEL: (212) 242-0088. email: mega@megaentertainment.com

LEE MENDELSON FILM PRODUCTIONS, INC.
330 Primrose Rd., Ste. 215, Burlingame, CA 94010.
TEL: (650) 342-8284. FAX: (650) 342-6170.
CO-PRESIDENTS
Glenn Mendelson, Jason Mendelson

METHOD STUDIOS
730 Arizona Ave., Santa Monica, CA 90401.
TEL: (310) 434-6500. www.methodstudios.com
MANAGING DIRECTOR
Alex Frisch
CREATIVE DIRECTOR
Aron Hjartarson
ANIMATION SUPERVISOR
Matt Hackett
SENIOR EXECUTIVE PRODUCER & VICE PRESIDENT
Gabby Gourrier
EXECUTIVE PRODUCER - NEW YORK
Jay Licthman

New York: 545 Fifth Ave. Ste. 2, New York, NY 10017.
TEL: (212) 907-1200. FAX: (212) 907-1201.
WEST COAST REPRESENTATION
Vicky Miller - (323) 646-3151. vickyreps@mac.com
EAST COAST, MIDWEST REPRESENTATION
Gay Guthry - (312) 642-0022

Ascent Media Group announced that beginning January 1, 2009, two of its boutique visual effects studios, Riot and Method, would unite operations under the Method name, to offer clients high-end visual effects for commercials, music videos and feature films. Services include: digital post-production in NTSC and PAL, Telecine HD, Datacine, Inferno, Fire HD, Henry, VYVX capabilities, 3D CGI, scanning and recording, compression & duplication. Recruiting: Send reels to: method-sm-recruiting@methodstudios.com

MORGAN CREEK PRODUCTIONS
(Production company; Also motion picture animation)
10351 Santa Monica Blvd., Ste. 200, Los Angeles, CA 90025.
TEL: (310) 432-4848. FAX: (310) 432-4844.
www.morgancreek.com

CO-CHAIRMAN & CEO
James G. Robinson
CO-CHAIRMAN & COO
Rick Nicita
MANAGING DIRECTOR, INTERNATIONAL
Brian Robinson
SENIOR V.P., DEVELOPMENT
Larry Katz
SENIOR V.P., PRODUCTION
David C. Robinson
V.P., DEVELOPMENT
Larry Katz
SENIOR V.P., MARKETING
Greg Mielcarz

MOTION CITY FILMS

(Film, video & interactive media producer)
1424 4th St., #604, Santa Monica, CA 90401.
TEL: (310) 434-1272. www.motioncity.com
PRODUCING DIRECTOR
G. Michael Witt - witt@motioncity.com

M3D STUDIOS, INC.

(3D)
19528 Ventura Blvd., #444, Tarzana, CA 91356.
TEL: (818) 785-6662. FAX: (818) 785-6810.
email: mail@planetm3d.com www.planetm3d.com
CEO
Marcel Nottea

NELVANA COMMUNICATIONS, INC.

(Production & distribution company. A Corus Entertainment Co.)
U.S. Office (Nelvana Communications)
520 Broadway, Ste. 350, Santa Monica, CA 90401.
TEL: (310) 496-4257. FAX: (310) 496-4491. www.nelvana.com
www.corusent.com
PRESIDENT & CEO, CORUS ENTERTAINMENT
John M. Cassaday
EXECUTIVE V.P. & PRESIDENT, CORUS TELEVISION
Doug Murphy

ADDITIONAL NELVANA OFFICES:
NELVANA LIMITED
42 Pardee Ave., Toronto, ON M6K 1X8 Canada.
TEL: (416) 535-0935. FAX: (416) 530-2832.

NELVANA INTERNATIONAL LIMITED
228-230 Airport House / Shannon Free Zone,
Shannon County Clare Ireland. TEL: (011) 353-61-474-244.
FAX: (011) 353-61-474-233.

NELVANA ENTERPRISES, INC.
55 Rue Bretagne, Paris, France, 75003.
TEL: +33 1-42-71-08-28. FAX: +33 1-42-71-01-44.

Founded in 1971, Nelvana is a leading global children's and family entertainment company composed of an animation studio and divisions that span production and development, worldwide TV sales and distribution, merchandising, home entertainment, music, interactive and publishing. Nelvana is owned by Corus Entertainment, a Canadian media and entertainment company.

NEST FAMILY ENTERTAINMENT

(Animated videos)
1421 S. Beltline Rd., Ste. 300, Coppell, TX 75019.
TEL: (800) 632-0030, (972) 402-7100. FAX: (800) 221-8729.
email: SalesSupport@NestFamily.com
www.nestfamily.com
www.nestlearning.com www.nestentertainment.com
PRESIDENT
Ernie Frausto

NICKELODEON

(A subsidiary of MTV- a Viacom Company)
231 W. Olive Ave., Burbank, CA 91502. TEL: (919) 736-3000.
www.nick.com
PRESIDENT, NICHELODEON, MTVN KIDS & FAMILY GROUP
Cyma Zarghami
PRESIDENT, ANIMATION, NICKELODEON, MTVN KIDS & FAMILY GROUP
Brown Johnson
SENIOR V.P. NICKELODEON, PROGRAMMING PARTNERSHIPS & GENERAL MANAGER, NICKTOONS
Keith Dawkins
EXECUTIVE V.P., TALENT & WEST COAST GENERAL MANAGER, NICKELODEON/MTVN KIDS FAMILY GROUP
Paula Kaplan
SENIOR V.P. & GENERAL MANAGER ANIMATION STUDIOS
Mark Taylor
Santa Monica: 2600 Colorado Ave., 2nd Fl. Santa Monica, CA 10404.

NICKELODEON ANIMATION STUDIO

231 Olive Ave. Burbank, CA 91502. TEL: (818) 736-3000.

OBEDIENT MEDIA, INC.

(See Michael Pace Interactive

OFFHOLLYWOOD DIGITAL

(CGI, HD, Animation & Titles)
580 Broadway, 8th Flr., New York, NY 10012.
TEL: (212) 260-8400. FAX: (212) 260-2437.
email: info@offhollywoodny.com www.offhollywooddigital.com
POST SERVICES CONTACT
Megan Milnes - megan@offhollywoodny.com

OPTICAM, INC.

(Motion picture titles and end crawls, motion control downshooter, photo-rotos animation camera service)
810 Navy St., Santa Monica, CA 90405. TEL: (800) 345-6394, (310) 396-4665. email: opcam@aol.com

ORBIT PRODUCTIONS

915 14th St., Modesto, CA 95354. TEL: (800) 716-7428, (209) 529-4835. FAX: (209) 571-2307.
email: info@orbitproductions.com www.orbitproductions.com
PRODUCER
Kevin Aguirre

OUTPOST 12 STUDIOS

1033 O St., Ste. 12, Lincoln, NE 68508. TEL: (402) 475-7678.
FAX: (402) 475-7701. email: info@outpost12studios.com
www.outpost12studios.com
PRESIDENT
Michael Domgard - mike@outpost12studios.com
V.P. & CREATIVE DIRECTOR
Chad Gleason

Services include: Animation, visual effects, video production and pre-show entertainment and policy trailers.

MICHAEL PACE INTERACTIVE

(Formerly Obedient Media, Inc. Multi-media marketing, DVD authoring & creative, audio/video production and more)
628 Vernon Ave., Studio A, Venice Beach, CA 90291.
TEL: (310) 428-7991. email: michaelpace@michael-pace.com
www.michael-pace.com

New media jack-of-all-trades company that can script, stage, cast, shoot, edit, design and animate in 2D & 3D and finish.

PERENNIAL PICTURES FILM CORP.

(Character animation)
2102 E. 52nd St., Indianapolis, IN 46205. TEL: (317) 253-1519.
email: mail@perennialpictures.com www.perennialpictures.com
PRESIDENT
G. Brian Reynolds - brian.reynolds@perennialpictures.com
SENIOR VICE PRESIDENT
Russ Harris

THE PICTURE MILL

(Cel, Digital & Titles. Animated Logos & Graphics/VFX)
6422 Homewood Ave., Hollywood, CA 90028.
TEL: (323) 465-8800. FAX: (323) 456-8875.
www.picturemill.com
EXECUTIVE DIRECTOR
Rick Probst - rick@picturemill.com
CREATIVE DIRECTOR
William Lebeda

PIXEL LIBERATION FRONT

1285 Electric Ave., Venice, CA 90291. TEL: (310) 396-9854.
FAX: (310) 396-9874. email: plf@thefront.com
www.thefront.com
FOUNDER
Colin Green

PIXEL MAGIC

(2D and 3D)
10635 Riverside Dr., Toluca Lake, CA 91602.
TEL: (818) 760-0862. FAX: (818) 760-4983.
email: sales@pixelmagicfx.com www.pixelmagicfx.com
VFX SUPERVISOR
Ray McIntyre, Jr
V.P. & GENERAL MANAGER
Ray Scalice

PORCHLIGHT ENTERTAINMENT

(Motion pictures, animation & worldwide distribution)
11050 Santa Monica Blvd., 3rd Flr., Los Angeles, CA 90025.
TEL: (310) 477-8400. FAX: (310) 477-5555.
email: info@porchlight.com www.porchlight.com
PRESIDENT & CEO
Bruce D. Johnson - bjohnson@porchlight.com
SENIOR V.P.
Don Mirisch
V.P., CHILDREN'S PROGRAMMING
Shea Fontana

PORCHLIGHT HOME ENTERTAINMENT

(U.S. domestic home entertainment division)
GENERAL MANAGER, PORCHLIGHT HOME ENTERTAINMENT
Herb Dorfman - hdorfman@porchlight.com

Porchlight Home Entertainment focuses on the distribution of kids and family programming, acquired from leading producers worldwide, in addition to the release of the company's new productions and programs from its substantial library.

POSTWORKS

PostWorks/New York, 100 Avenue of the Americas, 10th Flr., New York, NY 10013. TEL: (212) 894-4050.
FAX: (212) 941-0439. email: inquiry@pwny.com
www.pwny.com
EXECUTIVE VICE PRESIDENT, SALES
Joe Caterini

PROTOZOA PICTURES

(Animation, Digital FX & Title Design)
104 N. 7th St., Brooklyn, NY 11211. TEL: (718) 388-5280.
FAX: (718) 388-5425. www.protozoa.com

PUPPET STUDIO

(Puppets)
10903 Chandler Blvd., N. Hollywood, CA 91601.
TEL: (818) 506-7374. email: steve@thepuppetstudio.com
CONTACT
Steve Sherman

RAINMAKER ENTERTAINMENT

(Cel, clay and digital animation)
2025 W. Broadway, Ste. 500, Vancouver, BC Canada V6J 1Z6.
TEL: (604) 714-2600. FAX: (604) 714-2641.
email: info@rainmaker.com
CEO
Warren Franklin
PRESIDENT, EXECUTIVE PRODUCER
Catherine Winder
SENIOR V.P., PRODUCTION & OPERATIONS
Kim Dent Wilder

REALITY CHECK STUDIOS

(Motion Graphics and Design, 3D)
726 S. Flower St. Burbank, CA 91502.
TEL: (323) 465-3900. FAX: (323) 465-3600.
email: info@realityx.com www.realityx.com
PARTNER
Andrew Heimbold - andrew@realityx.com
Steven Heimbold - steven@realityx.com

REMBRANDT FILMS

(Distribution company)
34 Cross Pond Rd., Pound Ridge, NY 10576.
TEL: (914) 763-5817.
email: info@rembrandtfilms.com www.rembrandtfilms.com
PRESIDENT
Adam Snyder

REZN8 PRODUCTIONS, INC.

(Full-service animation company, including motion graphics and interactive/interface design)
6430 Sunset Blvd., Ste. 500, Hollywood, CA 90028.
TEL: (323) 957-2161. FAX: (323) 464-8912.
email: motion@rezn8.com www.rezn8.com
EXECUTIVE CREATIVE DIRECTOR
Paul Sidlo
EXECUTIVE PRODUCER
Julie Warford

RHYTHM & HUES STUDIOS

(Computer animation)
2100 E. Grand Ave., El Segundo, CA 90245.
TEL: (310) 448-7500. FAX: (310) 448-7600.
www.rhythm.com
FILM DIVISION, PRESIDENT
Lee Berger - (310) 448-7727 - lee@rhythm.com
COMMERCIAL STUDIOS DIVISION
EXECUTIVE PRODUCER
Paul Babb - babb@rhythm.com
DESIGN DIVISION, EXECUTIVE PRODUCER
Stacy Burstin - stacy@rhythm.com

RUBY-SPEARS PRODUCTIONS, INC.

(Animation. Family and children's entertainment)
3500 W. Olive Ave., Ste. 300, Burbank, CA 91505.
TEL: (818) 840-1234. email: info@rubyspears.com
www.rubyspears.com
PRESIDENT
Joe Ruby
VICE PRESIDENT
Ken Spears

SCHOLASTIC MEDIA

Scholastic, Inc. Headquarters: 557 Broadway, 5th Flr., New York, NY 10012. TEL: (212) 343-6100. www.scholastic.com
EXECUTIVE V.P. & PRESIDENT, SCHOLASTIC MEDIA
Deborah A. Forte

Leading media and consumer educational products for children.

SOUP2NUTS

(Animation studio)
311 Arsenal St., Watertown, MA 02472. TEL: (617) 600-2222.
FAX: (617) 600-2200. email: jody@soup2nuts.tv

Scholastic Media is comprised of four main groups: Scholastic Productions, Scholastic Marketing & Consumer Products, Scholastic Audio Group and SE Distribution, and also includes two production studios — Soup2Nuts, a cutting edge animation studio, and Weston Woods® Studio — as well as the company's highly successful Interactive Products Group consisting of interactive product development and Click! Interactive Learning Club.

J.J. SEDELMAIER PRODUCTIONS, INC.

(Commercials and animated shorts)
199 Main St., 10th Flr., White Plains, NY 10601.
TEL: (914) 949-7979. FAX: (914) 949-2082.
email: sedelmaier@aol.com www.jjsedelmaier.com
PRESIDENT & DIRECTOR
J.J. Sedelmaier

SINGLE FRAME FILMS

(Cut out & stop motion, drawn animation, training, & consultation)
3940 Avery St., Detroit, MI 48208. TEL: (313) 664-7847.
email: info@singleframefilms.com www.singleframefilms.com
CONTACT
Gary Schwartz

SIX FOOT TWO PRODUCTIONS

(Full-service animation company)
25 Ebbtide Passage, Corte Madera, CA 94925.
TEL: (415) 927-0880. FAX: (415) 927-0550.
email: animate@sixfoottwo.com www.sixfoottwo.com
EXECUTIVE PRODUCER
Suzanne Atherly
DIRECTOR & CREATIVE LEAD
Robbin Atherly

SMITHGROUP COMMUNICATIONS, INC.

(Animation for films, commercials and theatrical trailers)
267 S.E. 33rd Ave., Portland, OR 97214. TEL: (503) 239-4215.
FAX: (503) 239-1570. email: smithgrp@smithgrp.com
www.smithgrp.com
PRESIDENT
Phil Bevans

SONY PICTURES ANIMATION

9050 W. Washington Blvd., Culver City, CA 90232.
TEL: (310) 840-8000. FAX: (310) 840-8100.
PRESIDENT, PRODUCTION
Hannah Minghella
SENIOR V.P., DEVELOPMENT
Nate Hopper
SENIOR V.P., BUSINESS AFFAIRS
Barbara Zipperman
V.P., ANIMATION
Andrea Miloro
V.P., DEVELOPMENT
Alexa Amin

SONY PICTURES IMAGEWORKS

(A Sony Pictures Entertainment Company)
9050 W. Washington Blvd., Culver City, CA 90232.
TEL: (310) 840-8000. FAX: (310) 840-8100.
www.imageworks.com
EXECUTIVE V.P. & GENERAL MANAGER
Randy Lake
EXECUTIVE V.P. PRODUCTION & EXECUTIVE PRODUCER
Debbie Denise
SENIOR V.P., OPERATIONS
Tom Hershey
SENIOR V.P., INTERACTIVE
Emmanuelle Borde
SENIOR V.P., MARKETING & COMMUNICATIONS, SONY PICTURES ANIMATION & SONY PICTURES IMAGEWORKS
Don Levy - donlevy@sonypictures.com
CHIEF TECHNOLOGY OFFICER & VISUAL EFFECTS SUPERVISOR
Rob Bredow
V.P. RECRUITING, ACADEMIC RELATIONS & ANIMATION ARTISTS MANAGEMENT
Ken Maruyama

LEONARD SOUTH PRODUCTIONS

5319 Craner Ave., N. Hollywood, CA 91601.
TEL: (818) 760-8383. FAX: (818) 766-8301.
PRESIDENT
Leonard South

SPECTAK PRODUCTIONS, INC.

(Laser special effects)
222 N. Sepulveda Blvd., Ste. 2000, El Segundo, CA 90245.
TEL: (310) 335-2038. FAX: (310) 335-2048.
email: info@spetak.com www.spectak.com.au

PRESIDENT & CEO
Ric Birch - (310) 666-2050 - ricspectak@cs.com

MICHAEL SPORN ANIMATION, LTD.
35 Bedford St., Lower Level., New York, NY 10012.
TEL: (212) 242-0647.
email: studio@michaelspornanimation.com
www.michaelspornanimation.com
DIRECTOR
Michael Sporn

SPUMCO, INC.
(Full-service animation company)
413 E. Harvard St., Glendale, CA 91205.
TEL: (323) 462-2943.
PRESIDENT
John Kricfalusi

STARGATE STUDIOS
1001 El Centro St., South Pasadena, CA 91030.
TEL: (626) 403-8403. FAX: (626) 403-8444.
www.stargatefilms.com
CEO, FOUNDER & VISUAL EFFECTS SUPERVISOR & DIRECTOR OF PHOTOGRAPHY
Sam Nicholson
PRESIDENT
Darren Frankel
EXECUTIVE V.P., DEVELOPMENT & VISUAL FX SUPERVISOR/PRODUCER
James Riley
CHIEF TECHNOLOGY OFFICER
Joseph Meier, Ph.D.
DIGITAL COMPOSITING SUPERVISOR
Chris Martin

Van Nuys: 6827 Valjean Ave., Van Nuys, CA 91406.
TEL: (818) 778-0851. FAX: (818) 778-0879.

Vancouver: 225 W. 8th Ave., 4th Flr., Vancouver, BC V5Y 1N3 Canada. TEL: (877) 488-1241. FAX: (604) 488-1242.

Services include: previsualization, film & HD production, matte painting, 3D, compositing, The Virtual Backlot, main titles, editorial.

STOKES/KOHNE ASSOCIATES, INC.
(Full-service animation company)
742 Cahuenga Blvd., Hollywood, CA 90038.
TEL: (323) 468-2340. email: dmisk@stokeskohne.com
www.stokeskohne.com
CONTACT
Dan Kohne

THRESHOLD ENTERTAINMENT
(Animation studios)
1649 11th St., Santa Monica, CA 90404. TEL: (310) 452-8899.
FAX: (310) 452-0736. email: sales@thethreshold.com
www.thethreshold.com
CEO
Larry Kasanoff
PRESIDENT
Joshua Wexler

TECHNICOLOR

TECHNICOLOR ANIMATION
250 E. Olive Ave., #300, Burbank, CA 91502.
TEL: (818) 480-5100. FAX: (818) 480-5200.
www.technicolorinteractive.com
CONTACT
Steven Wendland - steven.wendland@technicolor.com

A Thomson company. Thomson is a provider of digital video technologies, systems and services to the media, entertainment & communications industries. Services provided: concept art, in-game animation, in-game art asset creation, in-game cinematics, marketing assets, renders & trailers, pre-rendered cinematics and more.

TECHNICOLOR INTERACTIVE SERVICES
(Part of the newly created Digital Productions division of Technicolor)
1117 Isabel Street, Burbank, CA 91506. TEL: (818) 559-1535.
email: info@technicolorinteractive.com

TLC ENTERTAINMENT/THE MINI-MOVIE STUDIO
CBS Studios, 4024 Radford Ave., Studio City, CA 91604.
TEL: (818) 655-6155. FAX: (818) 655-6254.
email: TLC@TLCEntertainment.com
CONTACT
George Taweel

TMS ENTERTAINMENT, LTD.
(Character and 2-D anime)
15760 Ventura Blvd., Ste. 806, Encino, CA 91436.
TEL: (818) 905-8881. FAX: (818) 905-0815. www.tms-e.com

TOON MAKERS, INC.
17333 Ludlow St., Granada Hills, CA 91344.
TEL: (818) 832-8666. email: info@toonmakers.com
www.toonmakers.com
EXECUTIVE PRODUCER & CEO
Rocky Solotoff - rocky@toonmakers.com

TWENTIETH CENTURY FOX ANIMATION
10201 W. Pico Blvd. Bldg. 58, Los Angeles, CA 90035.
TEL: (310) 369-1000. FAX: (310 369-3907. www.fox.com
PRESIDENT
Vanessa Morrison
V.P. PRODUCTION
Karen Rupert Toliver

BLUE SKY STUDIOS
(A wholly owned subsidiary of Fox Filmed Entertainment, a subsidiary of Twentieth Century Fox)
One American Lane. Greenwich, CT 06831
TEL: (203) 992-6000. FAX: (203) 992-6001.
info@blueskystudios.com
COO & CFO
Brian Keane
HEAD OF DEVELOPMENT
Lisa Fragner
V.P.
Chris Wedge
CREATIVE EXECUTIVE
Christina Witoshkin

VICON / HOUSE OF MOVES
(Motion capture)
5419 McConnell Ave., Los Angeles, CA 90066.
TEL: (310) 306-6131. FAX: (310) 437- 4229.
email: moveme@vicon.com www.moves.com www.vicon.com
V.P., PRODUCTION
Brian Rausch - rausch@moves.com
EXECUTIVE PRODUCER
Scott Gagain - scott.gagain@moves.com

VIDE-U PRODUCTIONS
9976 W. Wanda Dr., Beverly Hills, CA 90210.
TEL: (310) 276-5509. FAX: (310) 276-1183.
CONTACT
Bradly Fridman

VISUAL CONCEPT ENGINEERING
(Digital effects and motion control)
13300 Ralston Ave., Sylmar, CA 91342-7608.
TEL: (360) 828-1459. email: vceinc@aol.com www.vce.com
PRESIDENT
Peter Kuran

VRSET
(Virtual Reality Set Productions)
Los Angeles, CA:
TEL: (818) 881-5050. www.VRset.com
V.P., PRODUCTION
David Victory - David@VRset.com

3D & effects; interactive solutions; virtual reality set productions. Corporate video and commercial producer.

WARNER BROS. ANIMATION
(Animation, Direct-to-DVD/Video, Features & TV Series)
411 N. Hollywood Way, Burbank, CA 91505.
TEL: (818) 977-8700. www.warnerbros.com
PRESIDENT, WARNER BROS. TELEVISION GROUP
Bruce Rosenblum
PRESIDENT, WARNER BROS. TELEVISION
Peter Roth
EXECUTIVE V.P., CREATIVE AFFAIRS
Sam Register
SENIOR V.P., DOMESTIC PRODUCTION
Howard Schwartz
SENIOR V.P. SERIES & ALTERNATIVE ANIMATION
Peter Girardi
V.P. POST PRODUCTION
Tim Iverson
CHARACTER DESIGNER
Andres "Tommy" Tejeda
DIRECTOR, PUBLICITY
Gary Miereanu

W!LD BRAIN ANIMATION STUDIOS
(Full-service animation company. A division of Wild Brain Entertainment)
15000 Ventura Blvd., Sherman Oaks, CA 91403 (919) 290-7080. info@wildbrain.com www.wildbrain.com

New York: 56 W. 22nd St., 9th Flr., New York, NY 10010.
TEL: (917) 305-8600. FAX: (212) 645-3405.
email: info@wildbrain.com www.wildbrain.com
NEW BUSINESS INQUIRIES
Marge Dean - (310) 271-1400
MEDIA CONTACT
Kelly Kimball - (310) 271-1400 - media@wildbrain.com

FRED WOLF FILMS
(Full-service animation company)
4222 W. Burbank Blvd., Burbank, CA 91505.

TEL: (818) 846-0611. FAX: (818) 846-0979.
email: administration@fredwolffilms.com
www.fredwolffilms.com
PRESIDENT
Fred Wolf

MIKE YOUNG PRODUCTIONS

20335 Ventura Blvd., Ste. 225, Woodland Hills, CA 91364.
TEL: (818) 999-0062. FAX: (818) 999-0172.
email: info@mikeyoungproductions.com
www.mikeyoungproductions.com
PRINCIPAL
Mike Young, Liz Young, Bill Schultz

Mike Young Productions is one of the largest independent animation studios in the world. Its producers work round the clock with a state-of-the-art, completely digital production facility in its Los Angeles-based headquarters and an international production studio in Merthyr Mawr, Wales, a 500-year old barn which has been converted into a state-of-the-art studio, boasting the latest advances in animation technology. In partnership with France's MoonScoop Group, the company owns Taffy Entertainment, a leading worldwide distribution, brand management and entertainment company dedicated to the rights management, marketing and sales of MYP's properties, as well as other studios' brands.

CASTING DIRECTORS

ABA PICTURE VEHICLES & CASTING SERVICES
8306 Wilshire Blvd., PMB 900, Beverly Hills, CA 90211.
TEL: (310) 323-9028. FAX: (310) 323-3144.
www.abaaa.com
CEO
Antoinette Meier

ABC ENTERTAINMENT CASTING
500 S. Buena Vista St., Burbank, CA 91521-4651.
TEL: (818) 560-1000. FAX: (818) 460-6903. www.abc.com
EXECUTIVE V.P., CASTING, ABC ENTERTAINMENT
Keli Lee
V.P., CASTING
Ayo Davis, Sandi Logan, Claudia Ramsumair
EXECUTIVE DIRECTOR, CASTING
Randi Chugerman
DIRECTOR, CASTING
John Villacorta
MANAGER, CASTING
Marcello Bellisano, Karen Noble

ABC ENTERTAINMENT CASTING (NEW YORK)
157 Columbus Ave., 2nd Flr., New York, NY 10023.
TEL: (212) 456-3631.
EXECUTIVE DIRECTOR, PRIMETIME CASTING
Marci Phillips
EXECUTIVE DIRECTOR, PRIMETIME CASTING & TALENT RELATIONS
Janet Murphy
MANAGER, PRIMETIME CASTING
Geoffrey Soffer, Victoria Visgilio
COORDINATOR, PRIMETIME CASTING
Justin Borgstahl

AKIMA'S CASTING & MANAGEMENT
(Native American & Latino casting)
P.O. Box 7088, Van Nuys, CA 91409. TEL:(818) 988-9168.
CASTING DIRECTOR
Akima Castaneda

SANDE ALESSI CASTING
13731 Ventura Blvd., 2nd FLr., Sherman Oaks, CA 91423.
TEL: (818) 222-9980 www.sandealessicasting.com
CONTACTS
Sande Alessi, Jennifer Asessi, Kristan Berona

Films: Pirates of the Caribbena 4, Water for Elephants, Michael Jackson's "This Is It," The Case of Benjamin Button. TV: Glee, CSI, Curb Your Enthusiasm.

AL MEDIA MOVERS, INC.
10444 Magnolia Blvd., North Hollywood, CA 91601.
TEL/FAX: (310) 237-6438. email: info@media-movers.com
www.media-movers.com
CONTACT
Lawrence Vishnu

Dubbing (Lip-sync & U.N.Style), Subtitling, Voiceovers, Closed Captioning, Translation & Transcription in all Asian, Indian, European, African & Middle-Eastern languages for all media formats.

AMERICAN INDIANS IN FILM (AMERIND)
(Casting of Native Americans)
65 N. Allen Ave., Ste. 105, Pasadena, CA 91106.
TEL: (626) 578-0344.
CEO
Sonny Skyhawk

AQUILA WOOD CASTING
1680 Vine St., Ste. 806, Los Angeles, CA 90028.
TEL: (323) 460-6292.
CASTING DIRECTORS
Deborah Aquila, Jennifer Smith, Tricia Wood
CASTING ASSOCIATES
Samantha Finkler, Erin Toner, Lisa Zagonia
ASSISTANT
Saraphina Monaco

Recent casting credits: The A Team, Untraceable, The Express, Eagle Eye, Twilight, The Spirit, Formosa Betrayed, The Answer Man, Push, Valentine's Day, Nutcracker: The Untold Story, The Ugly Truth, Fame.

ASG CASTING
4144 Lankership Blvd. Ste. 202, North Hollywood, CA 91606.
TEL: (818) 762-0200. FAX: (818) 753-9322.
email: arlene@asgcasting.com www.asgcasting.com
CASTING DIRECTORS
Arlene Schuster-Goss, Justin Radley

TV, Commercials, Film.

AUTOMATIC SWEAT
5243 W. Washington Blvd., Los Angeles, CA 90016.
TEL: (323) 934-5141.
CASTING DIRECTOR
John Papsidera, Jennifer Cram
ASSISTANT
Dylan Jury

Recent casting projects: Inception, The Girl in the Park, Primeval, Black Christmas, The Prestige, Zoom, My Super Ex-Girlfriend, Ghost Town, The Dark Knight, Love Lies Bleeding, Enchanted, The Informers, 12 Rounds, Zombieland and more.

RISE BARISH CASTING
1216 Fifth St., Santa Monica, CA 90401.
TEL: (310) 457-456-9018. FAX: (310) 457-3117.
email: rbarish@charter.net

TERRY BERLAND CASTING
2329 Purdue Ave., Los Angeles, CA 90064.
TEL: (310) 275-0601, (310) 775-6608.
www.berlandcasting.com
CASTING DIRECTOR
Terry Berland
ASSOCIATE
Karmen Leech

BEAU BONNEAU CASTING
84 First St., San Francisco, CA 94105.
TEL: (Producers) (415) 777-1142. (Actors) (415) 346-2278.
FAX: (415) 777-1994. email: info@beaubonneaucasting.com
www.beaubonneaucasting.com

Casting for film, television, commercials, industrials, print.

BOSTON CASTING
129 Braintree St., Ste. 107 Boston, MA 02134.
TEL: (617) 254-1001. FAX: (617) 254-3003.
www.bostoncasting.com
CASTING DIRECTORS
Angela Peri, Lisa Lobel, Hillary Missan
DIRECTOR OF MARKETING & CASTING DIRECTOR
Julie Arvedon
CASTING DIRECTOR, EXTRAS
Ashley Skomurski

New England's largest casting agency. Recent casting projects: The Fighter, Knight and Day, Edge of Darkness, What Doesn't Kill You, The Proposal, Paul Blart: Mall Cop and Pink Panther 2.

DEEDEE BRADLEY CASTING
6767 Forest Lawn Drive, Ste. 100, Los Angeles, CA 90068.
TEL: 818-977-8956.

2nd Location: Warner Bros., 300 Television Plaza, Burbank, CA 91505. TEL: (818) 954-7841.
CASTING DIRECTOR
Deedee Bradley (CSA)
ASSISTANT
Alison Mize

Casting for TV series Veronica Mars, Rock Me Baby, Smallville, Katie Joplin, Two of a Kind, The Jamie Foxx Show, Party Down, Cupid, 90210 (2009 series).

BROWN/WEST CASTING
7319 Beverly Blvd., Ste. 10, Los Angeles, CA 90036.
TEL: (323) 938-2575. FAX: (323) 938-2755.
CONTACT
Ross Brown, Mary West

BURROWS/BOLAND CASTING
c/o The Firm, 9465 Wilshire Blvd., 6th Flr., Beverly Hills, CA 90212. TEL: (310) 503-4719. FAX: (310) 860-8253.
email: victoriabcasting@gmail.com www.burrowsboland.com
CASTING DIRECTOR
Victoria Burrows, Scot Boland
ASSOCIATE
Tineka Becker

U.S. Casting for Monster House, The Lord of the Rings, King Kong, The Polar Express, Hostage, No Good Deed, The Lord of the Rings: The Two Towers, The Lord of the Rings: The Fellowship of the Ring, Broken, Saving Sarah Cain, Resident Evil: Extinction, The Christmas Cottage, The Lovely Bones, others.

CASTING BROTHERS
Fifth Street Studios, 1216 Fifth St., Santa Monica , CA 90401.
TEL: (818) 763-1361.
email: castingbrothers@gmail.com www.castingbrothers.com
DIRECTORS:
Alan Kaminsky
Joshua Rappaport

THE CASTING COMPANY

12750 Ventura Blvd., Ste. 102, Studio City, CA 91604.
TEL: (818) 487-5600. email: assistant@janeandjanet.com
www.janeandjanet.com
CASTING DIRECTORS
Jane Jenkins, Janet Hirshenson, Michelle Lewitt
V.P., BUSINESS AFFAIRS
Michael Hirshenson

Since 1981, Jane Jenkins and Janet Hirshenson of The Casting Company have cast over 100 feature films. Both are charter members of the Casting Society of America, as well as members of the Academy of Motion Picture Arts and Sciences and The Television Academy.

CASTING SOCIETY OF AMERICA

606 N. Larchmont Blvd., #4B, Los Angeles, CA 90004.
TEL: (323) 463-1925. FAX: (323) 463-5753.
www.castingsociety.com
PRESIDENT
Pam Dixon
VICE PRESIDENT
Jason Wood
SECRETARY
Venus Kanani
V.P., NEW YORK
Bernard Telsey
ARIZONA MEMBERS
Faith Hibbs-Clark, Darlene Wyatt, Helen

CALIFORNIA MEMBERS
Sande Alessi, Alaine Alldaffer,Julie Alter, Nick Anderson, Deborah Aquila, Maureen A. Arata, Carrie Audino Danielle Aufiero.

Patrick Baca,Justine Baddeley, Lyndsey Baldasare, Deborah Barylski, Elizabeth Barnes-Keener, Samantha Barrie, Fran F. Bascom, Lisa Beach, Matthew Jon Beck, Eyde Belasco, Mark Bennett, Amy Berman, Chemin Sylvia Bernard, Juel Bestrop, Sharon Bialy, Tammara Billik, Barbie Block, Susan Bluestein, Sunday Boling, Allyson Bosch, Judith Bouley, Lisa Bourne, DeeDee Bradley, Dylann Brander, Megan Branman, Kate Brinegar, Amy McIntyre Britt, Corbin Bronson, Krisha Bullock, Leah Buono.

Craig Campobasso, J.C. Cantu, Kristy Carlson, Ferne Cassel, Lucy Cavallo, Denise Chamian, Joanna Colbert, Anya Colloff, Ruth Conforte, Stephanie Corsalini, Gretchen Rennell Court, Carmen Cuba, Collin Daniel, Scott David, Eric Dawson, Shawn Dawson, Liz Dean, Trisha Debski, Angela Demo, Joanne DeNaut, Ron Digman, Paul Dinh-McCrillis, Pam Dixon-Mickelson, Michael Donovan, Dorian Dunas.

Susan Edelman, Donna Ekholdt, Felicia Fasano, Sarah Halley Finn, Geralyn Flood, Barbara Fiorentino, Nancy Foy, Dorian Frankel, Carrie Frazier, Dean Fronk, Risa Bramon Garcia, Helen Geier, Cathy Sandrich Gelfond, Lesli Gelles, Scott Genkinger, Brad Gilmore, Shani Ginsberg, Jan Glaser, Susan Glicksman, Suzanne Goddard-Smythe, Gail Goldberg, Peter Golden, Libby Goldstein, Carol Goldwasser, Jeremy Gordon, Jeff Greenberg, Harriet Greenspan, Brett Greenstein, Bonnie Grisan, Elisha Gruer, Pamela Rack Guest, Sheila Guthrie.

Natalie Hart, René Haynes, Nina Henninger, Dawn Hershey, Richard Hicks, Aszur Hill, Randi Hiller, Marc Hirschfeld, Janet Hirshenson, Beverly Holloway, Carla Hool, Michael Hothorn, Vicki Huff, Julie Hutchinson, Donna Isaacson, Sara Isaacson, Sheila Jaffe, Jason James, Jane Jenkins, Joey Paul Jensen, Tara-Anne Johnson, Jenny Jue, Ania Kamieniecki-O'Hare, Venus Kanani, Christian Kaplan, Paula Kaplan, Tracy Kaplan, Christal Karge, Lisa Miller Katz, Sarah Katzman, Jason Kennedy, Lora Kennedy, Peggy Kennedy, Sibby Kirchgessner, Beth Klein, Thom Klohn, Nancy Klopper, Sari Knight, Ronna Kress, Carol Kritzer, Lindsey Hayes Kroeger.

Bob Lambert, Ruth Lambert, Linda Lamontagne, Jason La Padura, Stephanie Laffin, Larry LaFond, Jennifer Lare, Meredith Layne, Keli Lee, Sally Lear, Amy Lieberman, Kelli Lerner, Matthew Lessall, John Levey, Heidi Levitt, Jennifer Levy, Michelle Lewitt, Meg Liberman, Amy Lieberman, Sharon Lieblein, Caroline Liem, Tracy Lilienfield, Dave Linden, Amy Lippens, Robin Lippin, Kara Lipson, Leslie Litt, Sandi Logan, Molly Lopata, June Lowry Johnson, Linda Lowy, Natalie Lyon, Steve Maisel, Francine Maisler, Rebecca Mangieri, Debi Manwiller, Mindy Marin, Cathy Henderson Martin, Liz Marx, Ricki Maslar, Peter Matyas, John McAlary, John McCarthy, Helen McCready, Robert McGee, Howard Meltzer, Jeffrey A. Meshel, Michelle Metzner, Joseph Middleton, Monika Mikkelsen, Kenneth Miller, Rick Millikan, Meg Morman, Donna Morong, Roger Mussenden, Brian Myers.

Nancy Nayor, Bruce H. Newberg, Patricia Noland, Sarah Noonan, Wendy O'Brien, Pauline O'con, Gillian O'Neill, Lori Openden, Greg Orson, Robyn Owen, Marvin Paige, Mark Paladini, John Papsidera, Ellen Parks, Cami Patton, Marshall Peck, Donald Paul Pemrick, Marci Phillips, Linda Phillips Palo, Gayle Pillsbury, Adrianna Porcaro, Susan Putnam, Yesi Ramirez, David Rapaport, Johanna Ray, Robi Reed, Kevin Reher, Cathy Reinking, Barbara Remsen, Damona Resnick, Britney Roberts, Jamie Sparer Roberts, Debby Romano, Veronica Collins Rooney, Julie Rose, Stacey Rosen, Donna Rosenstein, Marcia Ross, Marisa Ross, David Rubin.

Marnie Saitta, Tess Sanchez, Laura Schiff, Jean Scoccimarro, Erika Sellin, Julie Selzer, Pamel Shae, Mandy Sherman, Wendy Siegel, Alyson Silverberg, Becky Silverman, Erica Silverman, Margery Simkin, Sherry Sims, Mary Jo Slater, Eric Souliere, Camille St. Cyr, Sally Stiner, Andrea Stone-Brokaw, Catherine Stroud, Lori Sugar, Judy Taylor, Terri Taylor, Rachel Tenner, Mark Teschner, Sherry Thomas, Mark Tillman, Robert J. Ulrich, Nikki Valko, Bernie Van De Yacht, Gene Vassilaros, Mary Vernieu, Kim Davis Wagner, Dava Waite-Peaslee, Georgianne Walken, Katy Wallin, Karina Walters, Paul Weber, April Webster, Wendy Weidman, Alyssa Weisberg, Judy Blye WilsonJason Wood, Tricia Wood, Barbara Wright, G. Charles Wright, Seth Yanklewitz, Rhonda Young, Bonnie Zane, Debra Zane, Lisa Zarowin, Gary Zuckerbrod.

FLORIDA MEMBERS
Ellen Jacoby, Dee Miller, Mark Mullen, Sori Sheryl Wyman
GEORGIA MEMBERS
Shay Bentley Griffin
IDAHO MEMBERS
Catrini McGregor
ILLINOIS MEMBERS
David O'Connor, Mickie Paskal, Jennifer S. Rudnicke, Claire Simon
LOUISIANA MEMBERS
Elizabeth Coulon
Ryan Glorioso
MARYLAND MEMBERS
Pat Moran, Betsy Royall
MASSACHUSETTS MEMBERS
Angela Peri, Carolyn Pickman
MISSOURI MEMBERS
Kim Marie Swanson
NEW JERSEY MEMBERS
Adam Caldwell, Joan D'Inecco

NEW MEXICO MEMBERS
Jo Edna Boldin, Kathryn Brink, Rody Kent

NEW YORK MEMBERS
Alaine Alldaffer, Eve Battaglia, Rori Bergman, Jay Binder, Mary Clay Boland, Jack Bowdan, Mark Brandon, Nora Brennan, Dale Brown, Craig Burns, James Calleri, Tiffany Little Canfield, William Cantler, David Caparelliotis, Jim Carnahan, Michael Cassara, Ellen Chenoweth, Howie Cherpakov, Kathleen Chopin, Jodi Collins, Jessica Daniels, Findley Davidson, Paul Davis, Anne Davison, Rob Decina, Jack Doulin, Lois Drabkin, Daryl Eisenberg, Jennifer Euston, Bess Fifer, Bonnie Finnegan, Alexa L. Fogel, Janet Foster, Paul Fouquet, Patrick Goodwin, Jill Greenberg-Sands, Judy Henderson, Marc Hirschfeld, Rachel Hoffman, Stephanie Holbrook, Kimberly Hope, Stuart Howard, Justin Huff, Philip Huffman, Steven Jacobs, Rosalie Joseph, Avy Kaufman, Gayle Keller, Stephanie Klapper, Bethany Knox, Lynn Kressel, Megan Larche, Ellen Lewis, Manada Mackey, Jamibeth Margolis, Pat McCorkle, Norman Meranus, Russ Meyerson, Kim Miscia, Kim Moarefi, Melinda Moss, Arnold J. Mungioli, Elissa Myers, Mele Nagler, Marci Phillips, Nancy Piccione, Nina Pratt, Amelia Rasche, Laura Rosenthal, Carrie Rosson, Zoe E. Rotter, Tara Rubin, Jen Rudin, Suzanne Ryan, Mark Saks, Amy Schecter, Laura Schutzel, Susan Shopmaker, Mark Simon, Geoffrey Soffer, Laura Stanczyk, Irene Stockton, Jonathan K. Strauss, Merri Sugarman, Daniel Swee, Bernard Telsey, Todd Thaler, Lina Todd, Cindy Tolan, Julie Tucker, Allison Twardziak, David Vaccari, Nikole Vallins, Michele B. Weiss, Eric Woodall, Liz Woodman, Leslie Zaslower.

NORTH CAROLINA MEMBERS
Jordan Beswick, Craig Fincannon, Lisa Fincannon, Mark Fincannon

OHIO MEMBERS
D. Lynn Meyers

OREGON MEMBERS
Lena Veenker

PENNSYLVANIA MEMBERS
Diane Heery, Donna Belajac, Jason Loftus, Nancy Mosser, Kathy Wickline

SOUTH CAROLINA MEMBERS
Richard Futch

TEXAS MEMBERS
Diana Guthrie, Donise L. Hardy

UTAH MEMBERS
Catrine McGregor

VIRGINIA MEMBERS
Erica Arvold, Lilian Burch, Carlyn Davis

WASHINGTON MEMBERS
Nike Imoru, Patti Kalles, Stephen Salamunovich

INTERNATIONAL MEMBERS
ENGLAND MEMBERS
Carol Dudley, Nancy Bishop

CASTING SOLUTIONS
P.O. Box 20164, New York, NY 10011. TEL: (212) 875-7373.
email: castsolutions@gmail.com www.castingsolutions.com
CASTING DIRECTOR
Liz Ortiz Mackes

THE CASTING STUDIOS
5724 W 3rd St, Los Angeles, CA 90036.
TEL: (323) 954-0007. FAX: (323) 954-0933.

CBS TELEVISION CASTING
c/o CBS Studio Center, 4024 Radford Ave., Studio City, CA 91604-2190. TEL: (818) 655-1500, (212) 975-3851 (NY).
EXECUTIVE V.P., TALENT & CASTING, CBS PARAMOUNT NETWORK TELEVISION ENTERTAINMENT GROUP
Peter Golden
SENIOR V.P., CASTING
Meg Liberman
V.P., CASTING
Lucy Cavallo, Karen Church, Amy Herzig (East Coast), Fern Orenstein
DIRECTOR CASTING (NY)
Katharina Eggman, Alison Rinzel
ASSISTANT TO PETER GOLDEN/SENIOR TALENT COORDINATOR
Marilyn Fischer

CENTER THEATRE GROUP CASTING
601 W. Temple St., Ste. 112, Los Angeles, CA 90012.
TEL: (213) 972-7374. FAX: (213) 972-7645.
www.centertheatregroup.com
CASTING DIRECTOR
Erika Sellin
ASSOCIATE CASTING DIRECTOR
Bonnie Grisan
CASTING ASSISTANT
Jared Pascoe

CENTRAL CASTING
Corporate Office: Entertainment Partners, 2835 N. Naomi St., Burbank, CA 91504. TEL: (818) 955-6000.
www.entertainmentpartners.com

Central Casting Los Angeles: 220 S. Flower St., Burbank, CA 91502. TEL: (818) 562-2700. FAX: (818) 562-2786.

New York: 875 6th Ave., Ste. 2411, New York, NY 10011.
TEL: (646) 205-8244. FAX (212) 947-4859.

CIRCUIT RIDER TALENT & MANAGEMENT
(A division of Dotson-Wooley Entertainment Group: Bookings, casting, career management)
123 Walton Ferry Rd., Hendersonville, TN 37075.
TEL: (800) 420-8568, (615) 824-1947. FAX: (615) 264-0462.
email: dotwool@bellsouth.net
PRESIDENT
Linda Dotson

ANNELISE COLLINS CASTING
3435 Ocean Park Ave., Ste. 107, Santa Monica, CA 90405.
TEL: (310) 586-1936. FAX: (866) 366-8681.
email: annelisecast@yahoo.com www.annelisecast.com

CRICKET FEET CASTING
(Specializing in SAG indie feature films)
P.O. Box 1417, Hollywood, CA 90028. TEL: (310) 395-9540.
CASTING DIRECTOR
Bonnie Gillespie

THE CW CASTING
3300 W. Olive Ave. 3rd Flr. Burbank, CA 91505.
TEL: (818) 977-2500.
EXECUTIVE V.P., TALENT & CASTING
Lori Openden
DIRECTOR, CASTING
Dana Theodoratos

BILL DANCE CASTING
4605 Lankershim Blvd., Ste. 110, N. Hollywood, CA 91602.
TEL: (818) 754-6634. FAX: (818) 754-6643.
www.billdancecasting.com
OWNER/CASTING DIRECTOR
Bill Dance
CASTING DIRECTOR
Terence Harris, Sheri Tucker

Recent film casting credits include: Alice in Wonderland, Angels & Demons, Frost-Nixon, Sea Biscuit, A Beautiful Mind, Spanglish, Monster House, Red Eye, Hollywoodland, Bobby.

DELANCY-CASTRO CASTING
11684 Ventura Blvd., #474, Studio City, CA 91604.
TEL: (818) 760-3110. FAX: (818) 760-1382.
email: rdelancy@mindspring.com
CASTING DIRECTORS
Richard DeLancy
Eric C. Castro

DIPRIMA CASTING
(TV & film, union & non-union)
Hounds Ear Club, 328 Shulls Mill Rd., Boone, NC 28607.
TEL: (305) 672-9232. email: barbara@diprimacasting.com
www.diprimacasting.com
CASTING DIRECTOR
Barbara DiPrima

THE SARAH FINN COMPANY (FINN HILLER)
588 N. Larchmont Blvd., 1st Flr., Los Angeles, CA 90004.
TEL: (323) 460-7040. FAX: (323) 460-2317.
CASTING DIRECTOR
Sarah Halley Finn

Finn's recent casting: Wall Street: Money Never Sleeps, Iron Man 2, Kick-Ass, Fast & Furious, Race to Witch Mountain (2009 version), Hotel for Dogs, W. Iron Man, Never Back Down, Vantage Point, Quid Pro Quo.

MEGAN FOLEY CASTING & CO.
13425 Ventura Blvd., Ste. 200, Sherman Oaks, CA 91423.
TEL: (818) 216-9350. FAX: (909) 336-9109.
email: sendtomegan@charter.net www.meganfoleycasting.com
OWNERS
Megan Foley, Chuck Marra

FOX BROADCASTING COMPANY CASTING
10201 W. Pico Blvd., Bldg. 100, Los Angeles, CA 90035.
TEL: (310) 369-1000, (212) 556-2400 (NY).
EXECUTIVE V.P., CASTING
Marcia Shulman
SENIOR V.P., CASTING, COMEDY
Bob Huber
V.P. CASTING, DRAMA
Kim Williams
V.P., EAST COAST CASTING
Amy Christopher
COORDINATOR, EAST COAST CASTING
Clint Alexander

New York: 1211 Avenue of the Americas, New York, NY 10036.
TEL: (212) 556-2400

JEFF GERRARD/CASTING DIRECTOR
4705 Laurel Canyon Blvd., Ste. 200, Studio City, CA 91607.
TEL: (818) 782-9900. FAX: (818) 782-0030.
email: jeff@jeffgerrard.com www.jeffgerrard.com

LOUIS GOLDSTEIN & ASSOCIATES CASTING
(aka Paradoxe Casting) 7441 Sunset Blvd. Los Angeles, CA 90046. TEL: (818) 817-4371, (805) 746-4650.
email: lgoldcast@aol.com
CASTING DIRECTORS
Louis Goldstein, Diane Silvester

CAROL GRANT CASTING
P.O. Box 5710, Balboa Island, CA 92662. TEL: (818) 237-0282.
FAX: (714) 878-9670. cgcasting@yahoo.com
www.cargrantcasting.com

JEFF GREENBERG CASTING
10201 W. Pico Blvd., Bldg. 226, Room 115, Los Angeles, CA 90035. TEL: (310) 369-8363. FAX: (310) 969-0009.
CASTING DIRECTOR
Jeff Greenberg
CONTACT
Allen Hooper

TV casting includes: Modern Family, Eli Stone, Valentine, Out of Practice, Stacked, Jake In Progress, Frasier, I'm With Her, It's All Relative, According to Jim.

AARON GRIFFITH CASTING
(Casting for features and television)
8440 Santa Monica Blvd., Ste. 200, Los Angeles, CA 90069.
TEL: (323) 654-0033. email: aaron@castingdirector.nu

Recent film cast credits include: The Bondage, Orangelove, Simple Things, Dog Lover's Symphony, Heavens Fall, Dorm Daze 2, Driftwood, The Phobic, Penny Dreadful, The Wizard of Gore, The Take, Scar, Dr. Fugazzi.

JEFF HARDWICK CASTING
3940 Laurel Canyon Blvd., #1158, Studio City CA 91604.
TEL: (818) 752-9898. FAX: (818) 752-9890.
email: jeff@jeffhardwickcasting.com
www.jeffhardwickcasting.com

Film, television.

NANCY HAYES CASTING
400 Treat Ave., #E, San Francisco, CA 94110.
TEL: (415) 558-1675. email: nancy@hayescasting.com
www.hayescasting.com

Casting for films, industrials, commercials.

RICHARD HICKS CASTING/FIREFLY CASTING
(Film & TV)
6333 W. 3rd St., Ste. 915, Los Angeles, CA 90036.
TEL: (323) 857-1699.

CASTING DIRECTORS
Richard Hicks, David Rubin
CASTING ASSISTANT
Rick Messina

HISPANIC TALENT CASTING OF HOLLYWOOD

P.O. Box 46123, Los Angeles, CA 90046. TEL: (323) 934-6465.
email: billhooey@earthlink.net.
CONTACT
Bill Hooey

HOWELL MANAGEMENT

P.O. Box 2540, Merrifield, VA 22116. TEL: (703) 560-1405.
FAX: (703) 560-1406. email: info@howellmanagement.com
www.howellmanagement.com

Books talent for commercials, film, TV, print, fashion, voiceovers, promotional & spokes modeling.

SUSAN JOHNSTON CASTING

P.O. Box 1514, Studio City, CA 91614. TEL: (323) 969-4800.
www.susanjohnstoncasting.com

Casting for film and television.

DEBORAH KURTZ CASTING, INC.

11751 Mississippi Ave., Ste. 140, Los Angeles , CA 90025.
TEL: (310) 477-6555.

ROSS LACY CASTING

200 S. LaBrea, Los Angeles, CA 90036. TEL: (323) 330-1020.
FAX: (323) 954-9391. email: ross@rosslacycasting.com
www.rosslacycasting.com

LEAR CASTING, CSA / MARILEE LEAR CSA

1414 Hollywood Blvd., Las Vegas, NV 89110.
TEL: (702) 438-9111, (702) 235-7876 (Casting).
FAX: (702) 453-6601. email: mlear@learenterprises.com
www.leartalentguide.com
CEO
Marilee Lear
CASTING ASSISTANT
Connie Allison

JOHN LEVEY

4000 Warner Blvd., Bldg. 1, Burbank, CA 91522.
TEL: (818) 954-1687. FAX: (818) 954-3657.
CONTACT
John Levey - (818) 954-4080
ASSISTANT TO JOHN LEVEY
Melanie Burgess - (818) 954-4080

Casting for TV shows. Levey is the senior v.p, casting, for John Wells Productions.

LIEN COWAN CASTING

7461 Beverly Blvd., Ste. 203, Los Angeles, CA 90036.
TEL: (323) 937-0411. FAX: (323) 937-2070.
email: info@broad-cast.tv www.leancow.tv
CASTING DIRECTORS
Michael Lien, Dan Cowan

MEDIA ACCESS OFFICE/EDD

Verugo Jobs Center, 1255 S. Central Ave., Glendale, CA 91204. TEL: (818) 409-0448. FAX: (818) 507-4319.
email: gcastane@edd.ca.gov
PROGRAM DIRECTOR/CASTING LIAISON
Gloria M. Castaneda

Casting liaison office for performers with disabilities.

MIMI WEBB MILLER

321 Santa Monica Blvd., Third Flr., Santa Monica, CA 90401.
TEL: (310) 452-0863. FAX: (310) 581-5277.
email: mwmcasting@yahoo.com

Location casting; real people & SAG.

NATIVE AMERICAN INDIAN TALENT & CASTING COMPANY

116 E. Keetrowah #A, Tahlequah, OK 74464.
TEL: (918) 458-5199. email: naitca@fullnet.net
www.talequah.com

NBC ENTERTAINMENT CASTING

100 Universal Plaza, Bldg. 1320, Ste. 1D, Universal City, CA 91608. TEL: (818) 777-3790. FAX: (818) 866-3050.
SENIOR V.P. CASTING
Grace Wu
SENIOR V.P., CASTING, Los Angeles
Steven O'Neill
V.P., CASTING, Los Angeles
Brian Dorfman
V.P., CASTING (New York)
Jennifer McNamara

NEVADA CASTING GROUP, INC.

5440 Louie Lane, Ste. 108, Reno, NV, 89511.
TEL: (775) 322-8187. FAX: (775) 322-0161.
email:inquiry@nevadacasting.group.com
www.nevadacasting.group.com

OWNER
Zak Gilbert
CONTACT
Juli Green

DAVID O'CONNOR CASTING COMPANY

1017 W. Washington Blvd., Ste. 2A, Chicago, IL 60607.
TEL: (312) 226-9112. FAX: (312) 226-9921.
email: david@oconnorcasting.tv www.oconnorcasting.tv

JEFF OLAN CASTING

14044 Ventura Blvd., Ste. 209, Sherman Oaks, CA 91423.
TEL: (818) 285-5462. FAX: (818) 285-5470.
email: jeffolancasting@yahoo.com www.jeffolancasting.com
OWNER
Jeff Olan

MARVIN PAIGE CASTING

P.O. Box 69434, W. Hollywood, CA 90069.
TEL: (818) 760-3040. FAX: (818) 766-3889.

PRIME CASTING

6430 Sunset Blvd., Ste. 425, Hollywood, CA 90028.
TEL: (323) 962-0377, (323) 962-0378. FAX: (323) 466-4166.
email: info@primecasting.com www.primecasting.com
CASTING DIRECTORS
Peter Alwazzan, Heather Sirota

Extras casting, principal casting, payroll service, casting facility.

REEL SOUTHERN CASTING

(A division of Dotson-Wooley Entertainment Group)
c/o CRTM-123 Walton Ferry Rd., Hendersonville, TN 37075-3616. TEL: (800) 420-8568. FAX: (615) 264-0462.
email: dotwool@bellsouth.net
PRESIDENT
Linda Dotson

Talent & Music Casting/Theatrical, TV & Commercial.

GABRIELLE SCHARY CASTING

2601 Ocean Park Blvd., #120, Santa Monica, CA 90405.
TEL: (310) 450-0833. FAX: (310) 450-7794.
email: gabrielleschary@earthlink.net
www.gabriellescharycasting.com

TINA SEILER CASTING

P.O. Box 2001, Toluca Lake, CA 91610. TEL: (818) 628-1953.
email: tinacasting789@yahoo.com

LILA SELIK CASTING

(Commercials, films, TV, industrials)
1551 S. Robertson Blvd., Ste. 202, Los Angeles, CA 90035.
TEL: (310) 556-2444. FAX: (310) 556-3266.
email: casting@prodigy.net www.castingbylilaselik.com

AVA SHEVITT CASTING

321 Santa Monica Blve. Ste. 300, Santa Monica, CA 90401.
TEL: (310) 656-4600. FAX: (310) 656-4610.

SHOOTING FROM THE HIP CASTING

c/o Zydeco Studios, 11217 Ventura Blvd., Studio City, CA 91604 TEL: (818) 506-0613. FAX: (818) 506-8858.
email: franceneselkirkcasting@gmail.com
www.shootingfromthehipcasting.com
CASTING DIRECTOR
Francene Selkirk-Ackerman

Film, TV and commercials casting.

LYNN STALMASTER

9911 West Pico Boulevard, Los Angeles, CA 90035.
TEL: (310) 552-0983.

One of the casting profession's pioneers, Lynn Stalmaster is credited with helping cast 228 films and 150 TV series and TV movies in his 50+ years as an independent casting director. Stalmaster was one of the founding members of the Casting Society of America and received the Hoyt Bowers Award for Outstanding Contribution to the Casting Profession at the 2003 Artios Ceremony.

STUDIO TALENT GROUP

1328 12th St., Ste. 1 & 3, Santa Monica, CA 90401.
TEL: (310) 393-8004. FAX: (310) 393-2473.
email: phil@studiotalentgroup.com
www.studiotalentgroup.com
PRESIDENT
Phillip L. Brock

Actors and multi-talent.

JULIET TAYLOR CASTING

140 W. 57th St., Ste. 4B, New York, NY 10019.
TEL: (212) 245-4635. FAX: (212) 956-7697.

TIJER LILY CO.

P.O. Box 154437, Riverside, RI 02915.
email: info@tijerlily.com

PRESIDENT, OWNER
Tara J. Ryan

Native American arts and entertainment company includes database for Native American talent.

SUSAN TYLER CASTING

c/o On Your Mark Studios. 13425 Ventura Blvd., Sherman Oaks, CA 91423. TEL: (818) 506-0400. FAX: (818) 762-8449. email: susan@tylercasting.com www.tylercasting.com
CASTING DIRECTOR
Susan Tyler, Sophia Ready

TRILOGY CASTING

13425 Ventura Blvd., 2nd Flr, Sherman Oaks, CA 91423.
TEL: (310) 650-3077, (818) 720-1647. FAX: (919) 985-2313.
www.trilogytalent.com
CASTING DIRECTORS
Susie Mains, Jim Divisek

(Casting for TV, film)

ULRICH/DAWSON/KRITZER CASTING

4705 Laurel Canyon Blvd., Suite 301, Valley Village, CA 91607.
TEL: (818) 623-1818. FAX: (818) 623-1819.
CASTING DIRECTORS
Robert Ulrich, Eric Dawson, Shawn Dawson, Carol Kritzer
Liz Dean
ASSOCIATE
Sibby Kirchgessner

Casting for TV.

VALKO/MILLER CASTING

3500 W. Olive Ave., Suite 780, Burbank, California 91505.
TEL: (818) 953-7743.
CASTING DIRECTORS
Nikki Valko, Ken Miller
ASSOCIATE
Peter Pappas

VOICECASTER

1832 W. Burbank Blvd., Burbank, CA 91506-1348.
TEL: (818) 841-5300. FAX: (818) 841-2085.
email: casting@voicecaster.com www.voicecaster.com
OWNER
Huck Liggett

WEBER & ASSOCIATES CASTING

10250 Constellation Blvd., Ste. 2060, Los Angeles, CA 90067.
TEL: (310) 449-3685. FAX: (310) 449-8749.
CONTACT
Paul Weber

APRIL WEBSTER & ASSOCIATES

800 South Main, #309, Burbank, CA 91506. TEL: (818) 526-4242.
CASTING DIRECTORS
April Webster, Scott David, Sara Isaacson

WILSHIRE CASTING

11684 Ventura Blvd., #118 Studio City, CA 91604.
TEL: (818) 623-9200. FAX: (818) 623-0900.
email: wilshirecasting@aol.com
CONTACT
Catherine Wilshire

PETER WISE ASSOCIATES CASTING

91335 Reseda, CA
TEL: (818) 343-8936. FAX: (818) 345-1792.
email: castwise@aol.com
PRESIDENT
Peter Wise

KEITH WOLFE CASTING

1438 N. Gower, Ste. 39, Hollywood, CA 90028.
TEL:(323) 469-5595. email: silverscreen@adelphia.net
www.keithwolfe.com

LORI WYMAN CASTING

16499 N.E. 19th Ave., Ste. 203, N. Miami Beach, FL 33162.
TEL: (305) 354-3901. FAX: (305) 354-3970.
email: lori@loriwymancasting.com www.loriwymancasting.com

DEBRA ZANE CASTING

9696 Culver Blvd., Ste. 110, Culver City, CA 90232.
TEL: (310) 558-0400. www.debrazanecasting.com
CONTACT
Tannis Vallely

GARY ZUCKERBROD CASTING

6767 Forest Lawn Dr., Ste. 103, Los Angeles, CA 90068.
TEL: (818) 977-4281
OWNER
Gary Zuckerbrod
ASSOCIATE
Becky Silverman

CONSULTANTS & TECHNICAL ADVISORS

ACCOMMODATING IDEAS, INC.
(Sign-language consultants)
3807 W. Sierra Hwy. #6, PMB 4335, Acton, CA 93510.
TEL: (818) 386-6348. FAX: (818) 386-6352.
email: aiterps@ai-ada.com www.ai-ada.com

ACCURATE ENGLISH
(Accent reduction)
13101 Washington Blvd., Ste. 231, Los Angeles, CA 90066.
TEL: (800) 871-1317, (310) 568-0077.
email: info@accurateenglish.com www.accurateenglish.com
HEAD TRAINER
Lisa Mojsin, M.A.

ADVANCED FIRE & RESCUE SERVICES
(Fire Rescue Standby, EMT and Fire Personnel; Fire Trucks: Antique and New)
16205 Lost Canyon Rd., Santa Clarita, CA 91351.
TEL: (818) 837-7336, (661) 299-4801. FAX: (661) 298-3069.
email: Eng12capt@yahoo.com www.advancedfire.com
CONTACT
Craig Sanford

AERIAL FOCUS PRODUCTIONS
(Aerial extreme sports, skydiving, BASE jumping, ultralights, hang gliding, stock library)
P.O. Box 369, Haleiwa, Hawaii 96712. TEL: (805) 455-3142.
email: aerialfcs@aol.com www.aerialfocus.com

AGENDA MEDIA
Agenda Media Services, Inc., 5445 Balboa Blvd., Ste. 112, Encino, CA 91316. TEL: (818) 990-5343. FAX: (818) 990-5344.
email: info@agenda.net www.agenda.net
DIRECTOR OF OPERATIONS & MEDIA CONTACT
Bryant Cameron - 818-990-5343 bryant.cameron@agenda.net

Agenda Media is a leading distributor and software developer of digital asset management solutions and a resource to the media and entertainment industry.

ALEXANDER TECHNIQUE / ACTOR'S MOVEMENT SPECIALIST
(Movement choreography)
P.O. Box 3194, Beverly Hills, CA 90212. TEL: (310) 209-9023.
www.alexandertechworks.com
CONTACTS
Jean-Louis Rodrigue, Kirstof Konrad

Specialize in the Alexander Technique for acting and musical performance. Conducts private instruction, group classes and workshops around the world.

AZRA HISTORICAL RESOURCES
(Leavey Foundation for Historic Preservation, Inc. Historical production resources)
Leavey Foundation, 13763 Granada Dr., Magalia, CA 95954.
TEL: (530) 877-4173 (rings to residence after hours)
email: azrahist@ushist.com www.ushist.com
COORDINATOR
Terrance C. Leavey

BEE PEOPLE UNLIMITED
(Insect handlers, trainers and research services)
P.O. Box 343, Claremont, CA 91711. TEL: (800) 924-3097, (909) 869-7690, (909) 626-2929. FAX: (909) 869-7391.
CONTACTS
Gregg Manston, Debra Copple

BLACKSTONE MAGIK ENTERPRISES, INC.
(Magic technical advisers, consultants)
12800 Puesta Del Sol, Redlands, CA 92373.
TEL: (909) 792-1227. FAX: (909) 794-2737.
email: magik@blackstonemagic.com
www.blackstonemagic.com

BOONE'S ANIMALS FOR HOLLYWOOD, INC.
31550 Oakhorn Ave., Castaic, CA 91384. TEL: (661) 257-0630.
FAX: (661) 257-4274. email: info@boonesanimals.com
www.boonesanimals.com
OWNER & ANIMAL TRAINER
Boone Narr

For over three decades Boone's Animals and its trainers have worked with every major studio on hundreds of films, TV shows, and commercials. Boone's Animals For Hollywood has extensive experience with difficult animal work, stunts, and cutting edge computer enhanced film making technology.

BROADCAST BUSINESS CONSULTANTS, LTD.
(Talent payment and negotiations)
246 N. Franklin Tpke., Ramsey, NJ 07446-1604.
TEL: (212) 687-3525. FAX: (212) 949-8143.
email: info@broadcastbusiness.com
www.broadcastbusiness.com

PAUL BRONSTON, M.D.
(Medical advisor)
1 Jib St., #202, Marina Del Rey, CA 90292. TEL: (310) 301-9426.
FAX: (310) 823-2433. email: drprotec@gmail.com

BUDGETS BY DESIGN
(Schedules & budgets)
428 Spencer St., Glendale, CA 91202.
TEL: (818) 507-4449. FAX: (818) 507-4464.
email: budgets@earthlink.net
CONTACT
Yudi Bennett

CALIFORNIA HISTORICAL GROUP WWII LIVING HISTORY ASSOCIATION
(World War II technical advice)
P.O. Box 1950, Costa Mesa, CA 92628. TEL: (714) 641-3421.
FAX: (714) 546-9035. www.chgww2.com
PRESIDENT & FILM WORK LIAISON
Anthony Ardisone - editor@associatedblast.com

CALIFORNIA SAILING ACADEMY
(Boating advisor and nautical antiques for rent)
14025 Panay Way, Marina Del Rey, CA 90292.
TEL: (310) 821-3433. FAX: (310) 821-4141.
email: rufus@ucla.edu www.californiasailingacademy.com
DIRECTOR
Paul Miller

"CALL THE COPS"
(S.W.A.T. tactics, patrol/homicide procedures)
TEL: (888) 548-0911. email: call-the-cops@sbcglobal.net
CONTACT
Randy Walker

CARAVAN WEST PRODUCTIONS
(Consulting and production rentals)
35660 Jayhawker Rd., Agua Dulce, CA 91390.
TEL: (661) 268-8300. FAX: (661) 268-8301.
email: caravanwest@earthlink.net www.caravanwest.com
CONTACT
Peter Sherayko

Consulting work: gun coaching, technical consulting, stunt coordinating, background casting, historical authenticity and more. Production rentals include: guns 'n gear, saddles 'n all, tipis, Native American and cowboy wardrobes. Sherayko specializes in firearms instruction and Westerns consultation for the era 1860-1910.

THE CHARTER CONNECTION, FILM BOATS, INC.
(Marine coordination & consulting)
5015 Pacific Ave., Marina Del Rey, CA 90292.
TEL: (800) 242-7877, (310) 827-4105. FAX: (310) 827-0381.
email: thecharterconnection@filmboats.com
email: Bertram@filmboats.com www.filmboats.com
CONTACT
Bertram McCann

Office: 3109 Pico Blvd., Santa Monica, CA 90405.
TEL: (310) 827-4105. FAX: (310) 827-0381.

CINEMAAQUATICS
(Nautical film services & coordination)
TEL: (818) 365-7999. info@cinemaaquatics.com

COMBAT CASTING
P.O. Box 46159, Los Angeles, CA 90046. TEL: (818) 618-2527.
FAX: (818) 784-4530. email: Staff@combatcasting.com
www.combatcasting.com
FOUNDER & PRESIDENT
Jody Hart
WRITER, DIRECTOR, MILITARY ADVISOR
Jared Chandler

The first and only Veterans owned and operated production company in Hollywood that specializes in Military projects. Military technical advisors, police technical advisorrs, actors, stunt performers, precision drivers & production company. All of Combat Casting actors have served or are serving honorably in the U.S. Military/Foreign Military and/or Police/SWAT.

CURT DECKERT ASSOCIATES, INC.
(Technical and management consultants, specializing in optical technology R&D)
18061 Darmel Pl., Santa Ana, CA 92705. TEL: (800) 394-0748, (714) 639-0746. FAX: (714) 639-0746.
email: curt@cdeckert.com www.cdeckert.com
www.deckert.net www.eyedesignbook.com
CONTACT
Curt Deckert, CMC, PhD

JOHN DIETSCH/FLYFISHING CONSULTANT
(Flyfishing consultant)
12233 W. Olympic Blvd., Ste. 314, Los Angeles, CA 90064.
TEL: (310) 979-7170. FAX: (310) 979-7173.
email: john@castlecreekproductions.com www.hook.tv
CONTACT
John Dietsch

THE ETIQUETTE COMPANY
P.O. Box 54, Dana Point, CA 92629.
TEL: (949) 493-6700. FAX: (949) 493-6700.
email: enquiries@theetiquettecompany.com
www.theetiquettecompany.com
FOUNDER
Naomi Torre Poulson

EXECUTIVE YACHT MANAGEMENT, INC. FILM SERVICES DIVISION
(Picture and camera boats; also marine prod. consulting)
644 Venice Blvd., Marina Del Rey, CA 90291-4801.
TEL: (877) 295-0161, (310) 306-2555. FAX: (310) 306-1147.
email: info@yacht-management.com
www.yacht-management.com

EXTREME SPORTS FILMING
(Action sports specialist)
3419 Via Lido, #145, Newport Beach, CA 92663.
TEL: (562) 596-7105. email: efilming@sbcglobal.net
CONTACT
Miles Flewitt

Marine, air and land; production facilities, location, equipment, talent, vehicle coordination/trucks & cars, and more.

FILM BUDGET PRO
(Detailed schedule, detailed budget, budget top sheet & budget, schedule and tax incentive consulting)
TEL: (323) 574-9696. FAX: (888) 699-9778.
email: jacob@filmbudgetpro.com www.filmbudgetpro.com
FOUNDER
Jacob Mosler

FROGMEN UNLIMITED
(Professional stunt group with a broad range of "real world" military special operations capabilities)
30041 Garces Ct., Tehachapi, CA 93561.
TEL: (661) 821-1210. email: thefrogmen@aol.com
www.frogmen.com www.STTU.com
CONTACT
Mark V. Lonsdale

Stunts, safety, rigging, aerial & high work, diving & aquatic action, underwater film support, military & law enforcement, technical advisory & training.

JUNGLE EXOTICS
16215 Cajon Blvd., San Bernardino, CA 92407.
TEL: (909) 887-3500. FAX: (909) 887-0953.
email: info@junglexontics.com www.junglexotics.com
OWNERS & TRAINERS
Joe Camp, Tammy Maples

With more than 1,000 credits since 1982, Jungle Exotics provides rentals of domestic and exotic animals to the motion picture, television, print and video industry.

NORMAN KENT PRODUCTIONS
(Skydiving, hang gliding and aerial stunts. More than 25 years experience, with many film and TV credits)
P.O. Box 1749. Flagler Beach, FL 32136. TEL: (386) 446-0505.
email: info@normankent.com www.normankent.com
CONTACT
Norman Kent

LANGUAGE.NET
(Translation services, dialect coaching & interpreting services. From any language to any language)
804 Main St., Venice, CA 90291. TEL: (310) 399-1790.
FAX: (310) 399-1901. email: info@language.net
www.language.net
CONTACT
Melanie Goodman

LIN-DEL ASSOCIATES
(Consultants on period props; primarily vehicles)
13601 Ventura Vlvd., #35, Sherman Oaks, CA 91423.
TEL: (310) 453-0193, (516) 374-0173. FAX: (310) 453-0193.
CONTACT
Alan Linsky

WARREN LOCKHART CREATIVE CONSULTING
(Film & TV production consultants)
P.O. Box 11629, Marina Del Rey, CA 90295.
TEL: (310) 821-1414. FAX: (310) 301-0536.
email: warren@lockhartproductions.com
CONTACT
McKenzie Allen

LOS ANGELES CHINESE LEARNING CENTER
(Chinese culture & translation services)
401 N. Garfield Ave., Ste. 1, Alhambra , CA 91801.
TEL: (626) 487-8909 (626) 282-9186. FAX: (626) 282-9252.
email: abacustranslation@gmail.com
www.chinese-school.netfirms.com/Chinese_translator.html
DIRECTOR
Samuel Chong

LOS ANGELES HELICOPTERS
(Aerial technical advisors)
3501 Lakewood Blvd., Long Beach, CA 90808.
TEL: (800) 976-HELI, (562) 377-0396. FAX: (562) 377-0449.
email: Fly@lahelicopters.com www.lahelicopters.com
CEO
Michael Rogers
DIRECTOR OF OPERATIONS
Andre Hutchings
GENERAL MANAGER
Kim Orahoske

MAGIC SNOW SYSTEMS
(Snow and snow special effects)
8581 Santa Monica Blvd., Ste. 219, Los Angeles, CA 90069.
TEL: (310) 289-9852. FAX: (310) 858-8260.
email: info@magicsnow.com www.magicsnow.com
PRESIDENT
Adam Williams

MARSHALL/PLUMB RESEARCH ASSOCIATES
(Legal research, script clearances)
4150 Riverside Dr., # 209, Burbank, CA 91505.
TEL: (818) 848-7071. FAX: (818) 848-7702.
email: info@marshall-plumb.com www.marshall-plumb.com

East Coast: 83 Wheeler Rd., Marstons Mill, MA 02648-1133.
TEL: (800) 304-1179. TEL: (508) 428-1179.
FAX: (508) 428-1487.

Canada: 65 Heward Ave., Ste. A206, Toronto, ON M4M 2T5.
TEL: (416) 645-8028.

LARRY MOSS SPEECH & DIALECT SERVICES
(Coaching in dialect, diction, acting and accent reduction)
855 3rd St., Ste. 305, Santa Monica, CA 90403. TEL: (310) 392-0815.
email: starcoach@earthlink.net

MOTION PICTURE MARINE
(Complete marine production services company, with more than 23 years of experience)
616 Venice Blvd., Marina del Rey, CA 90291.
TEL: (310) 822-1100. FAX: (310) 822-2679.
email: info@motionpicturemarine.com
www.motionpicturemarine.com

PANPIPES MAGICKAL MARKETPLACE
(Occult technical advisers)
1641 N. Cahuenga Blvd., Hollywood, CA 90028.
TEL: (323) 462-7078. email: info@panpipes.com
panpipes@sbcglobal.net
www.panpipes.com
CONTACT
Vicky Adams

PULSEPOINT GROUP
Communications Management Consulting)
8491 Sunset Blvd., Ste. 2000, Los Angeles, CA 90069.
TEL: (310) 360-0211. FAX: (310) 360-0250.
email: bfeldman@pulsepointgroup.com
www.pulsepointgroup.com
PRINCIPAL
Bob Feldman - bfeldman@pulsepointgroup.com
Jeff Hunt - jhunt@pulsepointgroup.com
Paul Walker - pwalker@pulsepointgroup.com

Focus is on three main areas: organizational optimization, boardroom services and digital transformation. Special expertise with entertainment companies.

SANTA ANITA PARK
(Technical advisors, horse racing)
285 W. Huntington Dr., Arcadia, CA 91007.
TEL: (626) 574-7223. FAX: (626) 446-1456.
email: comments@santaanita.com www.santaanita.com

SCHEDUALL
(A leading global provider of Enterprise Resource Management (ERM) products for the broadcast, satellite/transmission,

media, and entertainment industries)
Headquarters: 2719 Hollywood Blvd., Hollywood, FL 33020.
TEL: (954) 334-5406. FAX: (954) 334-5420.
email: info@scheduall.com www.scheduall.com
CONTACT
Lisette Reed - (954) 334-5406 lreed@scheduall.com

Los Angeles: 6080 Center Dr., 6th Flr., Los Angeles, CA 90045. TEL: (310) 212-5505. FAX: (866) 541-6163.
email: info@scheduall.com

London: Princess House, 50 Eastcastle St., London, UK W1W 8EA. TEL: +44 (0) 20 7636 0707.
FAX: +44 (0) 20743 3555.

ScheduALL is a market leader with a 20-year track record of success and more than 1,200 clients worldwide. ScheduALL's software offers comprehensive workflow and resource management capabilities that enable clients to optimize personnel, resources, and bandwidth utilization in a way that directly translates into increased productivity and ROI. ScheduALL's modular approach and scalable product-sets provide a collaborative platform for users in the broadcast, production, post-production, satellite/network transmission, and newsroom environments.

THE SHINDLER PERSPECTIVE, INC.

(Management consulting on business issues for creative, technology & emerging companies)
16060 Ventura Blvd., #105-#246, Encino, CA 91436.
TEL: (818) 223-8345. FAX: (480) 247-4190.
email: Marty@iShindler.com www.ishindler.com
CONTACT
Marty Shindler

THE SIGN LANGUAGE COMPANY

(Sign Language Consultants, Interpreters & Tutors)
12050 Guerin St., Unit 204, Studio City, CA 91604.
TEL: (818) 763-1215. FAX: (818) 763-3708.
email: scriptla@aol.com www.signlanguageco.com
CONTACT
Bill Pugin

STUNT COORDINATORS, INC.

(Action specialists)
2016 Rayshire St., Thousand Oaks, CA 91362. TEL: (818) 886-5417.
email: info@stuntcoordinatorsinc.com
fletcher-risk@verizon.net www.stuntcoordinatorsinc.com

Bringing feature film caliber stunts to the commercial industry. Coordinators have an understanding of commercial budgets and compressed production schedules. Members have over 125 years of combined experience in stunt coordinating and 2nd unit directing, records of impeccable safety and references from A-list directors and top advertising agencies.

STUNT WINGS

(A complete source of adventure sports talent, pre-production and production equipment)
12623 Gridley St., Sylmar, CA 91342. TEL: (818) 367-2430.
FAX: (818) 367-5363. email: stuntwings@me.com
www.stuntwings.com
CONTACT
John Greblo

Services include: pre-production: bidding, location scouting & permits; talent: aerial sports, cinematography & coordinators; rentals: aerial sports equipment & camera mounts; rigging: hang gliding, paragliding & skydiving; and prop design: custom aircraft models, radio controlled & miniature.

SWORDPLAY FENCING, INC. — TIM WESKE

(Fencing & sword fight choreography. Sword training for film & TV)
64 E. Magnolia Blvd., Burbank, CA 91502.
TEL: (818) 421-2926. FAX: (818) 566-4357.
email: info@timweske.com www.timweske.com
CONTACT
Tim Weske

THRILLSEEKERS UNLIMITED, INC.

(Since 1992, extreme sports for film, TV and S.A.G. stuntpersons)
3172 N. Rainbow Blvd., Ste. 321, Las Vegas, NV 89108.
TEL: (702) 699-5550. FAX: (702) 436-5554.
Hollywood Stunt Office: TEL: (323) 691-8705.
email: info@thrillseekersunlimited.com
www.thrillseekersunlimited.com www.richhopkins.tv
www.bulletprooftalkradio.com
PRESIDENT & CEO
Rich Hopkins

MADEMOISELLE IRENE UJDA (YESTERYEARS DANCERS)

(Period re-enactment & historical consultant, specializing in 18th & 19th century dance)
2546 1/2 Corralitas Dr., Los Angeles, CA 90039.
TEL: (310) 244-8028. email: irene_ujda@spe.sony.com
www.yesteryearsdancers.com

DON WAYNE MAGIC, INC.

(Magic technical consultant and director for TV, film & Broadway.)
10907 Magnolia Blvd., Ste. 467, North Hollywood, CA 91601.
TEL: (818) 763-3192. FAX: (818) 985-4953.
email: info@DonWayneMagic.com www.donwaynemagic.com

MICHAEL WIESE PRODUCTIONS

(One-on-one consulting to assist film & videomakers with packaging, financing, developing, producing, marketing or distribution)
11288 Ventura Blvd., Ste. 621, Studio City, CA 91604.
TEL: (818) 379-8799. FAX: (818) 986-3408.
www.mwp.com
VICE PRESIDENT
Ken Lee - kenlee@mwp.com

THE WING GALLERY

(Since 1975, a source for Wildlife, Western, Folk, Americana, Japanese, Fantasy, Cat Art and Collectibles)
13632 Ventura Blvd., Sherman Oaks, CA 91423.
TEL: (800) 422-9464, (818) 981-9464. FAX: (818) 981-2787.
email: winggallery@winggallery.com www.winggallery.com
OWNER
Mark Dietrich

COSTUMES & PROPS — SALES & RENTALS

20TH CENTURY FOX — FOX PRODUCTION SERVICES: COSTUME
(Contemporary wardrobe, early 1900's, 1960's, 1970's & accessories rental)
10201 W. Pico Blvd., Bldg. 99, Los Angeles, CA 90035.
TEL: (310) 369-1897. FAX: (310) 369-2487.
email: costumes@fox.com
EXECUTIVE DIRECTOR, MARKETING
Shari Schroder

ABC COSTUME SHOP
575 N.W. 24th St., Miami, FL 33127. TEL: (305) 573-5657.
FAX: (305) 573-5658. www.abccostumeshop.com
OWNER
Franco Carretti

ABC STUDIOS
(Costume Department)
545 Circle Seven Dr., Glendale, CA 91201.
TEL: (818) 553-4800. FAX: (818) 545-0468.
www.abcsftp.com
COSTUME DEPARTMENT SUPERVISOR
Janet Jensen

ACADEMY OF THEATRICAL COMBAT
(Swords & weapons. Also swordplay and combat training)
2115 N. Glenoaks Blvd., Burbank, CA 91504.
TEL: (818) 364-8420. email: info@theatricalcombat.com
www.theatricalcombat.com
CONTACT
Dan Speaker

ACE PROPS
Pier 40@Houston St., Ground Flr., New York, NY 10014.
TEL: (212) 727-7969. FAX: (212) 727-7679.
email: acevideo@earthlink.net www.aceprops.com
CONTACT
Tony Cozzi

ACTION UNLIMITED
(Weapons)
6025 Honeysuckle Ln., San Bernardino, CA 92407.
TEL: (909) 823-CINE. email: nick@actionunlimited.net
www.actionunlimited.net
OWNER
Nick Plantico

ADAMM'S STAINED GLASS
1426 4th St., Santa Monica, CA 90401.
TEL: (866) 764-6513, (310) 451-9390. FAX: (310) 451-9386.
email: adamm@adammsgallery.com www.adammsgallery.com
CONTACT
Adam Gritlefeld

Stained and leaded glass; beveled glass; etched & carved glass; Tiffany lamps; custom & restoration repair; hand blown art glass; vases; perfume bottles; sculptures & paper weights.

AERO MOCK-UPS
(Airline cabin interiors)
13126 Saticoy St., North Hollywood, CA 91605.
TEL: (818) 982-7327. FAX: (818) 982-0122.
email: info@aeromockups.com www.aeromockups.com
PRESIDENT
Richard Chan

AGAPE UNIFORM COMPANY
3606 W. Washington Blvd., Los Angeles, CA 90018.
TEL: (323) 731-0621.

AIM PRODUCTIONS, INC.
(Product placement, entertainment promotions)
37-11 35th Ave., Ste. 3B, Astoria, NY 11106.
TEL: (718) 729-9288. FAX: (718) 786-0137.
email: contact@aimproductionsinc.com
www.aimproductionsinc.com
PRESIDENT
Patricia Ganguzza

AIR HOLLYWOOD
(Aircraft mockups, props, set dressing, stock footage)
13240 Weidner St., Pacoima, CA 91331.
TEL: 877-4-MOCKUPS, (818) 890-6801. FAX: (818) 890-7041.
www.airhollywood.com
CEO
Talaat Captan
VICE PRESIDENT
Robert Shalhoub

AIRPOWER AVIATION RESOURCES
(Antique, civilian and military aircraft)
702 Paseo Vista, Thousand Oaks, CA 91360.
TEL: (805) 499-0307. FAX: (805) 498-0357.
email: info@airpower-aviation.com www.airpower-aviation.com
CONTACT
Michael Patlin

ALFONSO'S BREAKAWAY GLASS, INC.
(Breakaway props)
8070 San Fernando Rd., Sun Valley, CA 91352.
TEL: (818) 768-7402, (866) 768-7402. FAX: (818) 767-6969.
email: abgag2@aol.com www.alfonsosbreakawayglass.com
OWNER
Alfonso Guiterrez

ALLAN UNIFORM RENTAL SERVICE, INC.
(dba I.Buss-Allan Uniforms)
121 E. 24th St., 7th Flr., New York, NY 10010.
TEL: (212) 529-4655. FAX: (212) 505-7781.
email: info@ibuss-allan.com www.ibuss-allan.com

ALMOST CHRISTMAS PROPSHOPPE
(Holiday decorations, animated Santas, elves and sleighs. One of the largest Christmas prop houses in L.A. area)
5057 Lankershim Blvd., N. Hollywood, CA 91601.
TEL: (818) 285-9627. FAX: (866) 213-9627.
email: info@almostchristmaspropshoppe.com
www.almostchristmaspropshoppe.com
OWNER
Cathy Christmas

ALTMAN LUGGAGE
135 Orchard St., New York, NY 10002. TEL: (800) 372-3377, (212) 254-7275. FAX: (212) 254-7663.
email: info@altmanluggage.com
www.altmanluggage.com

AMERICAN COSTUME CORP.
(Period wardrobe, 1770-1970; also uniforms 1750 to present)
12980 Raymer St., N. Hollywood, CA 91605.
TEL: (818) 764-2239. FAX: (818) 765-7614.
PRESIDENT
Diana Foster

ANA SPECIAL EFFECTS
(Breakaway glass)
7021 Hayvenhurst Ave., Van Nuys, CA 91406.
TEL: (818) 909-6999. FAX: (818) 782-0635.
email: anaspfx@aol.com www.anaspecialeffects.com
OWNERS
Gladys Nary, Judy Albain

ANATOMORPHEX
(Animatronic animals and aliens, special effects make-up, costumes and miniatures)
8210 Lankershim, Ste. 14, North Hollywood, CA 91605.
TEL: (818) 768-2880. FAX: (818) 768-4808.
email: anatofx@hotmail.com www.anatomorphex.com
CONTACT
Robert Devine

ANTIQUARIAN TRADERS
4851 S. Alameda St., Los Angeles, CA 90058.
TEL: (310) 247-3900. FAX: (310) 247-8864.
email: info@AntiquarianTraders.com
www.AntiquarianTraders.com

AQUAVISION
(Marine props and fabrication)
3708 E. 4th St., Long Beach, CA 90814. TEL: (562) 433-2863.
email: bobanderson@aquavision.net www.aquavision.net
PRESIDENT
Bob Anderson

BARAKAT GALLERY
(Miscellaneous props; Specialty Art, Jewelry & Rare Coins)
405 N. Rodeo Dr., Beverly Hills, CA 90210.
TEL: (310) 859-8408. FAX: (310) 276-1346.
email: barakat@barakatgallery.com www.barakatgallery.com
CONTACT
Fayez Barakat

BEDFELLOWS
(Contemporary furniture)

12250 Ventura Blvd., Studio City, CA 91604.
TEL: (818) 985-0500. FAX: (818) 985-0617.
www.bedfellowsfurniture.com
CONTACT
Barbara Dixon

BRILES WING & HELICOPTER, INC.

16303 Waterman Dr., Van Nuys, CA 91406.
TEL: (818) 994-1445. FAX: (818) 994-1447.
email: info@toflyla.com www.toflyla.com
GENERAL MANAGER
Lance Strumpf

PAT BRYMER CREATIONS

(Custom fantasy walk arounds and puppets)
136 N. Ave. 61, Ste. 102, Los Angeles, CA 90042-4263.
TEL: (323) 259-0400. FAX: (323) 259-0358.
email: characters@pbcreations.com www.pbcreations.com

CALIFORNIA SAILING ACADEMY

(Boating advisor and nautical antiques for rent)
14025 Panay Way, Marina Del Rey, CA 90292.
TEL: (310) 821-3433. FAX: (310) 821-4141.
email: rufus@ucla.edu
DIRECTOR
Paul Miller

CALIFORNIA SURPLUS MART

(Military Surplus; sales only)
6263 Santa Monica Blvd., Hollywood, CA 90038.
TEL: (323) 465-2197. FAX: (323) 465-2418.

CAMERA READY CARS

(A division of Gaffoglio Family Metalcrafters, Inc.)
11161 Slater Ave., Fountain Valley, CA 92708.
TEL: (714) 444-2000 ext. 511. FAX: (714) 444-2444.
email: sales@metalcrafters.com www.metalcrafters.com

CELEBRITY EYEWORKS

c/o Independent Studio Services, 9545 Wentworth St., Sunland, CA 91040. TEL: (818) 951-5600.
FAX: (818) 951-2850. email: starspecs@socal.rr.com
OWNER/CONTACT
Michael Hirsch

CENTRE FIREARMS CO., INC.

10 W. 37th St., Ste. 7, New York, NY 10018. TEL: (212) 244-4040, (212) 244-4044. FAX: (212) 947-1233.

CINEMA VEHICLE SERVICES

(Rentals, all makes and models)
12580 Saticoy St. #A, North Hollywood, CA 91605.
TEL: (818) 780-6272. FAX: (818) 780-1340.
www.cinemavehicles.com
CONTACT
Bob Hartwig - bob@cinemavehicles.com

CINTAS CORPORATION

(Uniforms)
711 Hawaii St., El Segundo, CA 90245. TEL: (310) 725-2850.
www.cintas.com

CLASSIC CAR SUPPLIERS

(Car brokerage firm for the film and TV industry)
See NationwidePictureCars.com

CONTINENTAL SCENERY

(Painting experts for motion pictures, theatrical and photographic backdrops)
7802 Clybourn Ave., Sun Valley, CA 91352. TEL: (818) 768-8075.
FAX: (818) 768-6939. www.continentalscenery.com
OWNER
Frank Pera

COOPER FILM CARS

(Offers photography and special event space)
137 Perry St., New York, NY 10014. TEL: (212) 929-3909.
FAX: (212) 633-6952. www.cooperclassiccars.com
MANAGER
Noah Levinson

COSTUME ARMOUR, INC.

(Costume armour, custom sculpture and props)
2 Mill St., Bldg. 1, Ste. 101, Cornwall, NY 12518.
TEL: (845) 534-9120. FAX: (845) 534-8602.
email: info@www.costumearmour.com
www.customarmour.com
CONTACT
Michelle Truncale

COSTUME RENTALS CO.

11149 Vanowen St., N. Hollywood, CA 91605.
TEL: (800) 400-7444, (818) 753-3700. FAX: (818) 753-3737.
email: crcresearch@hughes.net www.costumerentalscorp.com
CONTACT
Mel B. Sabino

ELIZABETH COURTNEY COSTUMES

4019 Tujunga Ave., Studio City, CA 91604.
TEL: (818) 763-8615. FAX: (818) 506-0772.

CREATIVE FILM CARS

167 Madison Ave, New York, NY 10016. TEL: (212) 864-4060.
FAX: (212) 696-4060. email: info@creativefilmcars.com
www.creativefilmcars.com
PRESIDENT
Donald Almquist
CEO
John Ficarra

Top-notch vehicles for every kind of production. Thousands of vehicles from 1880-2010.

CREATIVE COSTUME CO.

(Sales & rentals to public and the film industry)
242 W. 36th St., 8th Flr., New York, NY 10018.
TEL: (212) 564-5552. FAX: (212) 564-5613.
email: costume@creativecostume.com
www.creativecostume.com
CONTACT
Linda Carcaci, Susan Handler

Alterations included. Available costumes include theatrical, period costumes and holiday costumes.

CUSTOM CHARACTERS

(Character costuming)
621 Thompson Ave., Glendale, CA 91201-2032.
TEL: (818) 507-5940. FAX: (818) 507-1619.
www.customcharacters.com
FOUNDERS
Ryan Rhodes, Dres Herron

DESERT PROPS

42848 150th St. E., Lancaster, CA 93535.
TEL: (661) 946-1515. FAX: (661) 946-0454.
email: clubed@avlocations.com www.avlocations.com

WALT DISNEY STUDIOS PRODUCTION

(Furniture,vehicles, costumes, miscellaneous props)
500 S. Buena Vista St., Property Bldg., Burbank, CA 91521.
TEL: Craft Services - (818) 560-1386.
Costumes - (818) 560-4800. Vehicles - (818) 560-1285.
http://studioservices.go.com/production/backlot_services.html

DR. CHRISTMAS RENTS, INC.

(Custom Christmas props)
800 N. Victory Blvd., Burbank, CA 91502. TEL: (310) 854-0886.
www.drchristmas.com
CONTACT
Bob Pranga, Debi Staron

DOZAR OFFICE FURNITURE

9937 Jefferson Blvd., 1st Flr., Culver City, CA 90232.
TEL: (310) 559-9292. FAX: (310) 559-9009.
www.dozarrents.com
CONTACT
Toni Hoyt

Production offices and sets. Video villages and dressing rooms.

E. C. 2 COSTUMES

4019 Tujunga Ave., Studio City, CA 91604.
TEL: (818) 506-7695. FAX: (818) 506-0772.

EASTERN COSTUME

7243 Coldwater Canyon, N. Hollywood, CA 91605.
TEL: (818) 982-3611. FAX: (818) 982-1905.
email: info@easterncostume.com www.easterncostume.com
OWNERS
James & Pam Livie

ECLECTIC ENCORE PROPERTIES, INC.

620 W. 26th St., 4th Flr., New York, NY 10001.
TEL: (212) 645-8880. FAX: (212) 243-6508.
www.eclecticprops.com
PRESIDENT
Suri Bieler - sbieler@eclecticprops.com

ERA AVIATION

6160 Carl Brady Dr., Anchorage, AK 99502.
TEL: (800) 866-8394, (907) 266-8394. FAX: (907) 266-8391.
email: sales@flyera.com www.flyera.com

EXECUTIVE YACHT MANAGEMENT, INC. FILM SERVICES DIVISION

(Picture and camera boats; also marine prod. consulting)
644 Venice Blvd., Marina Del Rey, CA 90291-4801.
TEL: (877) 295-0161, (310) 306-2555. FAX: (310) 306-1147.
email: info@yacht-management.com
www.yacht-management.com

EVENT SOLUTIONS

(Formerly Des Cartes Catering. Full-service events/catering)
3975 Landmark St., Culver City, CA 90232.
TEL: (877) 231-9267. FAX: (310) 310-4139.
www.eventsolutions.com

EXTREME SPORTS FILMING

(Marine services, production services, picture vehicles)

3419 Via Lido, Ste. 145, Newport Beach, CA 92663.
TEL: (562) 596-7105. FAX: (562) 596-7125.
email: miles@extremesportsfilming.com
www.extremesportsfilming.com
PRESIDENT
Miles Flewitt

EYES ON MAIN
(Custom-made eyeglass frames)
3110 Main St., Ste. A, Santa Monica, CA 90405.
TEL: (888) 287-8177, (310) 399-3302. FAX: (310) 399-7682.

FLORAL PROP RENTAL
(Centerpieces, columns & urns, candeleabras, aisle posts, canopies, arches)
714 Wall St., Los Angeles, CA 90014. TEL: (213) 622-1700.
email: floralproprental@floralproprental.com
www.floralproprental.com

PETER GEYER ACTION PROPS & SETS
(Breakaways, including rubber, razor and barbed wire)
8235 Lankershim Blvd., Ste. G, N. Hollywood, CA 91605.
TEL: (818) 768-0070. www.actionprops.com

GLENDALE COSTUMES
746 W. Doran St., Glendale, CA 91203. TEL: (818) 244-1161.
FAX: (818) 244-8576.
OWNER
Tim Deitlein

GLOBAL EFFECTS, INC.
(Custom manufacture and rental of props, costumes, space-suits, armor, miniatures, sets, creatures)
7115 Laurel Canyon Blvd., N. Hollywood, CA 91605.
TEL: (818) 503-9273. FAX: (818) 503-9459.
email: info@globaleffects.com rent@globaleffects.com
www.globaleffects.com
PRESIDENT
Chris Gilman - chris@globaleffects.com
RENTAL DEPARTMENT MANAGER
Skip Wilder

GREGORY'S TUX SHOP
12051 Magnolia Blvd., N. Hollywood, CA 91607.
TEL: (888) 968-4889 (818) 980-5480. FAX: (818) 980-5084.
email: customerservice@tuxedosonline.com
www.tuxedosonline.com

GROSH SCENIC RENTALS, INC.
(Backdrop & drapery rental)
4114 Sunset Blvd., Hollywood, CA 90029. TEL: (877) 363-7998, (323) 662-1134. FAX: (323) 664-7526.
email: info@grosh.com www.grosh.com
PRESIDENT
Amanda Uhlein - amanda@grosh.com

HAND PROP ROOM, INC.
5700 Venice Blvd., Los Angeles, CA 90019.
TEL: (323) 931-1534. FAX: (323) 931-2145.
email: info@hpr.com www.hpr.com

HOLLYWOOD CINEMA ARTS, INC.
(Over 1 million props, rentals and sales)
(Art Rentals & Sales; Custom Framing, Fake Foods, Luggage, Lamps, Photography & Picture Rentals)
8110 Webb Ave., North Hollywood, CA 91605.
TEL: (818) 504-7333. FAX: (818) 504-6464.
email: hollywoodcinemaarts@gmail.com www.hcarts.com
MANAGER
John Cleveland

HOLLYWOOD GLASS COMPANY
5119 Hollywood Blvd., Los Angeles, CA 90027.
TEL: (323) 661-7774. FAX: (323) 661-7261.

HOLLYWOOD PICTURE VEHICLES & THE BOSEWS COLLECTION
1028 N. LaBrea Ave., Hollywood, CA 90038.
TEL: (323) 466-2277. FAX: (323) 466-6541.
email: execmalibu@earthlink.net
www.hollywoodpicturevehicles.com
CONTACT
Don Thomas

HOLLYWOODTOYSANDCOSTUMES.COM
(Bella Brands, LLC. dba Hollywoodtoysandcostumes.com)
7251 W. Lake Mead Blvd., Ste. 300, Las Vegas, NV 89128.
TEL: (866) 232-1829. email: cs@hollywoodtoysandcostumes.com

HOLLYWOOD TOYS AND COSTUMES (STORE)
6600 Hollywood Blvd., Hollywood, CA 90028.
TEL: (888) 760-3330, (323) 464-4444. FAX: (323) 464-4644.

HOUSE OF PROPS
(Fine arts prop rentals)
1117 N. Gower St., Hollywood, CA 90038.
TEL: (323) 463-3166. FAX: (323) 463-8302.
email: info@houseofpropsinc.com www.houseofpropsinc.com
CONTACT
Phillip Torf

INDEPENDENT STUDIO SERVICES
(Props, weapons, product placement)
9545 Wentworth St., Sunland, CA 91040. TEL: (818) 951-5600.
FAX: (818) 951-2850. email: rentals@issprops.com
weapons@issprops.com www.issprops.com
CONTACT
Paul Rauch

INFLATABLE MARKETPLACE
1810 Gillespie Way, Ste. 202, El Cajon, CA 92020.
TEL: (800) 728-4466, (619) 258-4466. FAX: (619) 258-0732.
email: info@inflatablemarketplace.com
www.inflatablemarketplace.com

INTERNATIONAL COSTUME
(See Platinum Costume)

IT'S A WRAP! PRODUCTION WARDROBE SALES
3315 W. Magnolia Blvd., Burbank, CA 91505.
TEL: (818) 567-7366. FAX: (818) 567-0910.
email: movieclothes@aol.com www.itsawraphollywood.com
West address: 1164 S. Robertson Blvd., Los Angeles, CA 90035. TEL: (310) 246-9727.

IWASAKI IMAGES OF AMERICA
(Food replicas)
16927 S. Main St., Ste. C, Gardena, CA 90248.
TEL: (310) 225-2727. FAX: (310) 225-3737.
email: sales@iwasaki-images.com www.iwasaki-images.com

IZQUIERDO STUDIO
(Custom costumes and props)
118 W. 22nd St., 9th Flr., New York, NY 10011.
TEL: (212) 807-9757. FAX: (212) 366-5249.

JET SETS
6910 Farmdale Ave., North Hollywood, CA 91605.
TEL: (818) 764-5644. FAX: (818) 764-6655.
www.jetsets.com
DIRECTOR OF OPERATIONS
Doug Morris - dougmorris@jetsets.com
Fabrication for TV, commercials, movies, stills, music videos, themed environments & exhibits.

KNIGHT WRITER SCENIC
(Breakaway, custom, furniture, miscellaneous, mock-up)
TEL: (661) 810-9510, (661) 263-0718. FAX: (661) 244-4451.
email: bobknight@knightscenes.com www.knightscenes.com
CONTACT
Bob Knight

KUTTNER PROP RENTALS, INC.
601 W. 26th St., 3rd Flr., New York 10001.
TEL: (212) 242-7969. FAX: (212) 242-1293.
CONTACT
Barbara Genest

L.A. EYEWORKS
7407 Melrose Ave., Los Angeles, CA 90046. TEL: (323) 653-8255.
FAX: (323) 653-8176. email: eyeworksstore@laeyeworks.com
PUBLICITY
Brent Zerger - (323) 938-2161 ext. 125 brentzerger@laeyeworks.com

LEXINGTON
(Custom design & fabrication - sales only - no rentals)
12660 Branford St., Los Angeles, CA 91331.
TEL: (818) 768-5768. FAX: (818) 768-4217.
email: info@lex-usa.com rkessing@lex-usa.com
www.lexingtonscenery.com
PRESIDENT & CEO
Richard Bencivengo

LIBERTY THEATRICAL DECOR
22313 Meekland Ave., Hayward, CA 94541.
TEL: (510) 889-1951. FAX: (510) 889-1602.
email: libertyrig@aol.com
OWNER
Don Nethercott

LUCKY ENTERTAINMENT
(Gaming equipment, carnival equipment, food carts, jukeboxes, video & pinball machines & artificial cake)
10271 Almayo Ave., Ste. 101, Los Angeles, CA 90064.
TEL: (310) 277-9666. FAX: (310) 284-8151.
www.luckyentertainment.com

THE MANNEQUIN GALLERY
12350 Montague St., Unit E, Pacoima, CA 91331.
TEL: (818) 834-5555. FAX: (818) 834-5558.
email: mannequingallery@yahoo.com
www.mannequingallery.com
CONTACT
Shelley Wilkey

MED + RENT, INC.
P.O. Box 10248, Burbank, CA 91510.
Street Address: 435 E. Bethany, Burbank, CA 91504.
TEL: (818) 834-5800. FAX: (818) 834-5900. www.medrent.com

MODERN PROPS
5500 W. Jefferson Blvd., Los Angeles, CA 90016.
TEL: (323) 934-3000. FAX: (323) 934-3155.
email: info@modernprops.com (rentals)
www.modernprops.com
Vancouver: 3773 Still Creek Ave., Burnaby, BC V5C 4E2.
TEL: (604) 415-0115.
CONTACT
Olivier Albin - Olivier@modernprops.com

MOTION PICTURE COSTUME COMPANY
(A Division of Motion Picture Supplies, Inc.)
3811 Valhalla Dr., Burbank, CA 91505. TEL: (818) 557-1247.
FAX: (818) 557-1695. email: costumesMPCC@earthlink.net
PRESIDENT
Michele Archer

Period wardrobe: Modern & period uniforms & prop rentals.

MOTION PICTURE MARINE
616 Venice Blvd., Marina Del Rey, CA 90291. TEL: (310) 822-1100.
FAX: (310) 822-2679. www.motionpicturemarine.com
PRESIDENT
David Grober

MOVIE VEHICLES.COM
(See NationwidePictureCars.com)

MR. SCENERY
(Staging, set construction project management & rentals)
TEL: (818) 753-8200. FAX: (818) 573-8220.
email: mrscenery@sbcglobal.net www.mrscenery.net
CONTACT
Martin Rivera

MUSIC PROP SERVICES
(Musical instruments for film & TV)
7309 Clybourn Ave., #6, Sun Valley, CA 91352.
TEL: (818) 982-4100. email: info@musicprops.com
www.musicprops.com

NATIONAL HELICOPTER SERVICE
16750 Roscoe Blvd., Van Nuys Airport, Van Nuys, CA 91406.
Mailing address: P.O. Box 17150, Encino, CA 91416.
TEL: (818) 345-5222. FAX: (818) 782-0466.
www.nationalhelicopter.com
CONTACT
Richard Hart - rhart@nationalhelicopter.com

NATIONWIDEPICTURECARS.COM
8491 Sunset Blvd. #269, Hollywood, CA 90069.
TEL: (310) 659-1711. email: userhelp@movievehicles.com.
www.movievehicles.com
FOUNDER
Michael J. Kopilec

NBC UNIVERSAL STUDIOS
(Facilities rental)
100 Universal City Plaza, #4250-3, Universal City, CA 91608.
TEL: (818) 777-2784. FAX: (818) 866-1543.
email: beverly.hadley@nbcuni.com
www.filmmakersdestination.com.

NETWORK ART SERVICE
(Graphics & props)
1330 N. Clybourn Ave., Burbank, CA 91505.
TEL: (818) 843-5078. FAX: (818) 843-2528.
CONTACT
Dan Walker

NIGHTS OF NEON
(Prop rental and custom signage)
13815 Saticoy St., Van Nuys, CA 91402. TEL: (818) 756-4791.
FAX: (818) 756-4744. email: lisa@nightsofneon.com
www.nightsofneon.com
PRESIDENT
Lisa Schulte

NORCOSTCO, INC.
3606 W. Magnolia Blvd., Burbank, CA 91505.
TEL: (800) 220-6915, (818) 567-0753. FAX: (818) 567-1961.
email: California@norcostco.com www.norcostco.com
GENERAL MANAGER
Wayne Thornton

Norcostco is a supplier of stage lighting, lamps, dimming systems, automated lighting, costumes, mascots, theatrical makeup, wigs and props. Manufactures: stage drops and draperies, rigging systems, fog machines and atmospheric effects, intercoms, paint and painting supplies, platforms, special effects, and stage hardware. It also has a large rental selection. See website for office locations.

OMEGA/CINEMA PROPS
(Large selection of props)
5857 Santa Monica Blvd., Los Angeles, CA 90038.
TEL: (323) 466-8201.
email: customerservice@omegacinemaprops.com
www.omegacinemaprops.com

OUR SECRET JEWELERS
(Custom cubic zirconia and jewelry rentals)
246 S. Robertson Blvd., Beverly Hills, CA 90211.
TEL: (310) 358-8404. FAX: (310) 358-0179.

PALACE COSTUME & PROP COMPANY
835 N. Fairfax Ave., Los Angeles, CA 90046.
TEL: (323) 651-5458. FAX: (323) 658-7133.
email: rentals@palacecostume.com www.palacecostume.com
CONTACT
Seo Alonzo

PARAMOUNT COSTUME DEPARTMENT
5555 Melrose Ave., Edith Head Bldg., Rm. 200, Hollywood, CA 90038. TEL: (323) 956-5288. FAX: (323) 862-2342.
MANAGER
Anna M. Contrenas

PARAMOUNT PICTURES CABINET & FURNITURE SHOP
(Breakaway — Furniture)
c/o Paramount Pictures Backlot Operations. 5555 Melrose Ave., Freeman Bldg., Hollywood, CA 90038.
TEL: (323) 956-5248. FAX: (323) 862-4455.
www.paramountbacklot.com

PARAMOUNT PICTURES TECHNICAL SERVICES
(Prop monitors, sound gear, vintage microphones & equipment racks)
5555 Melrose Ave., Mae West Bldg., Rm. 205, Hollywood, CA 90038. TEL: (323) 956-1652. FAX: (323) 862-3950.
www.paramountstudios.com

PARAMOUNT PICTURES SPECIAL EFFECTS PROP SHOP
5555 Melrose Ave., Hollywood, CA 90038.
TEL: (323) 956-4488. www.paramountstudios.com

PERIOD PROPS
(General props)
1536 Evergreen St., Burbank, CA 91505. TEL: (818) 848-PROP, (818) 807-6677. email: periodprops@aol.com
CONTACT
David Inskeep

PICTURE CARS EAST, INC.
72 Huntington St., Brooklyn, NY 11231. TEL: (800) 319-3388, (718) 852-2300. FAX: (718) 858-1583.
CONTACT
Gino Lucci

PLATINUM COSTUMES
(Formerly International Costume)
1423 Marcellina Ave., Torrance, CA 90501.
TEL: (888) 904-9944, (310) 320-6392. FAX: (310) 320-3054.
www.platinumcostume.com

PROP SERVICES WEST
(Rents home furnishings for set decoration. A division of Occidental Entertainment Group Holdings)
4625 Crenshaw Blvd., Los Angeles, CA 90043.
TEL: (323) 290-2600. FAX: (323) 461-4571.
www.propserviceswest.com
CONTACT
Gary Lustgarten - gary@propserviceswest.com

PROPS DISPLAYS & INTERIORS, INC.
132 W. 18th St., New York, NY 10011. TEL: (212) 620-3840.
FAX: (212) 620-5472. email: stephen@pdiinc.com
CONTACT
Stephen Sebbane

PROPS FOR TODAY
330 W. 34th St. 12th Flr. New York, NY 10001.
TEL: (212) 244-9600. FAX: (212) 244-1053.
email: info@propsfortoday.com www.propsfortoday.com

THE PROP STORE
(Sales of costumes and props used in film, television)
9035 Eton Ave., Unit A. Canoga Park, CA 91304.
TEL: (818) 727-7829. FAX: (818) 727-7958.
CHIEF OPERATIONS OFFICER, LOS ANGELES
Brandon Alinger - brandon@propstore.com

QUARTERMASTER UNIFORM COMPANY MAIL ORDER
P.O. Box 4147, Cerritos, CA 90703. TEL: (800) 444-8643.
FAX: (562) 304-7335. email: help@qmuniforms.com
www.qmuniforms.com

RETAIL STORE LOCATIONS:
2543 W. 6th Street, Los Angeles, CA 90057.

TEL: (213) 351-9632.

750 Long Beach Blvd., Long Beach, CA 90813.
TEL: (562) 436-6247.

REEL CLOTHES & PROPS

(Miscellaneous props & furniture. Sales only; no rentals)
Box 4482, Sunland, CA 91040. TEL: (818) 951-7692.
email: sales@reelclothes.com www.reelclothes.com
OWNER
Holly Haber

RENEGADE EFFECTS GROUP

11312 Hartland St., North Hollywood, CA 91605.
TEL: (818) 980-8848. FAX: (818) 980-8849.
email: info@renegadeeffects.com www.renegadeeffects.com

Custom props; historic & modern weapons & armor, costumes,miniatures, animatronics, make-up effects. Renegade also has rental department.

ROCK & WATER CREATIONS, INC.

(GFRC reinforced concrete boulders, rock cliff panels)
815 5th St., Filmore, CA 93015. TEL: (805) 524-5600, ext. 10.
FAX: (805) 524-7339. email: info@rock-n-water.com
www.rock-n-water.com
PRESIDENT
Roger Embury

RUBIE'S COSTUME CO., INC.

(Costumes, accessories, rentals, mascots, seasonal)
120-08 Jamaica Ave., Richmond Hill, Queens, NY 11418.
TEL: (718) 846-1008. Customer Service: TEL: (516) 326-1500.
FAX: (718) 846-6174. www.rubies.com

SANTA FE WRECKING CO.

727 E. Washington Blvd., Los Angeles, CA 90021.
TEL: (213) 765-8166. FAX: (213) 765-0374.
email: info@santafewrecking.com www.santafesalvage.net

Miscellaneous props; vintage to present-day residential building materials. The co. buys and sells architectural salvage items and offers a large collection of authentic vintage fixtures.

SHELLY'S DANCE & COSTUME WEAR

(General costumes)
2089 Westwood Blvd., Los Angeles, CA 90025.
TEL: (310) 475-1400. FAX: (310) 470-6125.

SHOWGRITS

(Miscellaneous props; camera-ready prop food; food stylist)
TEL: (818) 567-2405. FAX: (818) 567-0038.
email: jean@showgrits.com www.showgrits.com
CONTACT
Jean Hodges

SNOW BUSINESS, INC.

(Icebergs, icicles, igloos, snowmen, snowballs & ice sculptures)
21318 Hart St., Canoga Park, CA 91303. TEL: (818) 884-3009.
FAX: (818) 884-3110. email: la@snowbusiness.com
www.snowbusiness.com
CONTACT
Roland Hathaway

SOMPER FURS

2270 W. Washington Blvd., Los Angeles, CA 90018.
TEL: (310) 273-5262. FAX: (310) 273-7270.
email: info@somperfurs.com www.somperfurs.com

SPORTS STUDIO

8654 Hayden Pl., Culver City, CA 90232. TEL: (310) 559-3999.
FAX: (310) 559-4767. email: info@sportsstudion.net
www.sportsstudio.net

A full service production agency specializing in sports for the entertainment industry from locating actors and athletes, to designing uniforms, coordinating sports-related scenes and producting full scale sports spectacle sequences.

STICKS & STONES FX

(Specialty props, costume design, custom build only; make-up effects and puppets. Sales only. No rentals)
10535 Tujunga Canyon Blvd., Tujunga, CA 91042.
TEL: (818) 352-9538. FAX: (818) 353-6979.
www.sticksandstonesfx.com
CONTACTS
Rob Burman, Jennifer E. McManus

STUDIO PICTURE VEHICLES

(Transportation: police vehicles, armored trucks, ambulances, taxis and all picture car needs)
7502 Wheatland Ave., Sun Valley, CA 91352.
TEL: (818) 781-4223. FAX: (818) 506-4789.
CONTACT
Kenny Fritz

THE SWORD & THE STONE

(Edged weapons and armour fabrication, rental and sales)
723 N. Victory Blvd., Burbank, CA 91502. TEL: (818) 562-6548.
FAX: (818) 562-6549. email: swatton@dslextreme.com
tony@swordandstone.com www.swordandstone.com
FOUNDER & OWNER
Tony Swatton

TRIANGLE SCENERY, DRAPERY & LIGHTING COMPANY

(Sales, manufacturing, design, installation, repair and rentals of drapery, rigging, scenic and lighting accessories)
1215 Bates Ave., Los Angeles, CA 90029.
TEL: (323) 662-8129. FAX: (323) 662-8120. www.tridrape.com
PRESIDENT/GENERAL MANAGER
Terry Miller - tcmill@aol.com

MIKE TRISTANO & CO.

14431 Ventura Blvd., PMB 185, Sherman Oaks, CA 91423.
TEL: (818) 888-6970. FAX: (818) 888-6447.
email: mtristano@sbcglobal.net

Prop weapons, blank firing weapons, on-set weapons handlers and armorer. Also stocks: police & SWAT gear; western firearms and holsters; pirate weapons & gear; and military props.

UNITED AMERICAN COSTUME CORP.

(Period wardrobe, 1770-1970; also uniforms, 1750 to present)
12980 Raymer St., N. Hollywood, CA 91605.
TEL: (818) 764-2239. FAX: (818) 765-7614.
PRESIDENT
Diana Foster

USHIST HISTORICAL RESOURCES

(Civil War, Indian Wars, weapons, cowboy costumes)
Leavey Foundation/Pair-O-Dice Mercantile, 208 Pearson Rd., Paradise, CA 95969. TEL: (530) 877-4173.
FAX: (530) 876-8241. email: azrahist@ushist.com
www.ushist.com

WARNER BROS. STUDIOS, FACILITIES — WIG RENTALS

4000 Warner Blvd., Burbank, CA 91522.
Costumes: TEL: (818) 954-1297, (818) 954-2151 (wigs).
FAX: (818) 954-3685.

WESTERN COSTUME CO.

11041 Vanowen St., N. Hollywood, CA 91605.
TEL: (818) 760-0900. FAX: (818) 508-2190.
email: wccmail@westerncostume.com
www.westerncostume.com

WONDERWORKS / ACTION SETS & PROPS

7231 Remmet Ave,, Canoga Park, CA 91303.
TEL: (818) 992-8811. FAX: (818) 347-4330.
email: brickprice@aol.com www.wonderworksweb.com
PRESIDENT
Brick Price

WOVEN ACCENTS

(Rents high quality rugs for movies, TV, commericials, still photo shoots)
525 N. La Cienega Blvd., Los Angeles, CA 90048.
TEL: (800) 222-RUGS, (310) 652-6520. FAX: (310) 652-6594.
email: inforug310@wovenonline.com www.wovenonline.com

ENTERTAINMENT LAWYERS

AKIN, GUMP, STRAUSS, HAUER & FELD, LLP
2029 Century Park E., Ste. 2400, Los Angeles, CA 90067.
TEL: (310) 229-1000. FAX: (310) 229-1001.
email: losangelesinfo@akingump.com www.akingump.com

See website for additional office locations.

ARNOLD & PORTER
777 S. Figueroa St., 44th Flr., Los Angeles, CA 90017-2513.
TEL: (213) 243-4000. FAX: (213) 243-4199.
www.arnoldporter.com

Arnold & Porter LLP has extensive experience representing the leading names in the entertainment industry, including U.S. and international companies and individuals involved in film, television, music, cable industries, and publishing. See website for additional office locations. Offices located in Brussels, Denver, London, Los Angeles, New York, Northern Virginia, San Francisco, Washington, DC.

ASHERSON, KLEIN & DARBINIAN
9150 Wilshire Blvd., Ste. 210, Beverly Hills, CA 90212.
TEL: (310) 247-6070. FAX: (310) 278-8454.
GENERAL PARTNER
Neville Asherson, Anna Darbinian

Specializes in all aspects of Immigration Law. Represents international entertainers, athletes and others with extraordinary abilities who wish to work in the U.S.

STEPHEN BARON
1299 Ocean Ave., Ste. 312, Santa Monica, CA 90401.
TEL: (310) 260-6060. FAX: (310) 260-6061.

Specializes in entertainment law working with actors, producers, directors, writers, and musicians.

GREG S. BERNSTEIN
(Law Offices of Greg Bernstein, A Professional Corporation)
9601 Wilshire Blvd., Ste. 240, Beverly Hills, CA 90210-5288.
TEL: (310) 247-2790. FAX: (310) 247-2791.
www.thefilmlaw.com
ATTORNEY
Greg S. Bernstein

Motion picture finance/distribution law, entertainment syndication law.

BINGHAM MCCUTCHEN, LLP
(Firm of nearly 1,000 lawyers throughout the U.S., Europe & Asia)
355 S. Grand Ave., Ste. 4400, Los Angeles, CA 90071-3106.
TEL: (213) 680-6400. FAX: (213) 680-6499.
www.bingham.com
FILM FINANCE ATTORNEY, PARTNER
Rose PeBenito Shiner, Ronald K. Sittler, William F. Abrams, Jonathan M. Albano, Robert C. Bertin, Anthony R. Callobre, Michael A. Conza, Joshua M. Dalton, Rachelle Dubow Debra L. Fischer, Bruce A. Friedman, Sarah K. Gagan, Linda J. Groves, Geoffrey T. Holtz, Neal A. Rosen, Leslie H. Shapiro, Timothy J. Stephens, Richard S. Taffet, Barbara Freedman Wand, Richard J. Welch
TELECOMMUNICATIONS, MEDIA & TECHNOLOGY ATTORNEY/PRACTICE LEADER
Andrew D. Lipman, Catherine Wang

Practice areas include: Entertainment law and film finance.

BLOOM, HERGOTT, DIEMER, ROSENTHALL & LAVIOLETTE, LLP
150 S. Rodeo Dr., 3rd Flr., Beverly Hills, CA 90212.
TEL: (310) 859-6800. FAX: (310) 859-2788.
ATTORNEY
Jacob A. Bloom, Leigh Brecheen, Stephen F. Breimer, Ralph Brescia, Eric M. Brooks, Thomas B. Collier, John Diemer, David B. Feldman, Candice S. Hanson, Alan S. Hergott, Tina J. Kahn, Patricik M. Knapp, John LaViolette, Stuart Rosenthal, Michael Schenkman, Richard D. Thompson

COUNTRYMAN & MCDANIEL
5933 W. Century Blvd., Ste. 1111, Los Angeles, CA 90045.
TEL: (310) 342-6500. FAX: (310) 342-6505.
www.cargolaw.com
ATTORNEY
Byron E. Countryman, Michael S. McDaniel

Customs broker attorneys.

COWAN, DEBAETS, ABRAHAMS & SHEPPARD, LLP
41 Madison Ave., 34th Flr., New York, NY 10010.
TEL: (212) 974-7474. FAX: (212) 974-8474. www.cdas.com
PARTNER
Frederick P. Bimbler, Susan H. Bodine, Andrea F. Cannistraci, Al J. Daniel, Jr., Timothy J. DeBaets, M. Kulburg Reedy, Robert L. Seigel, J. Stephen Sheppart, Marc H. Simon, Kenneth N. Swezey
WEST COAST COUNSEL
Steven M. Weinberg

West Coast Office: 30765 Pacific Coast Hwy. Ste. 411, Malibu, CA 90265. TEL: (310) 457-6100. FAX: (310) 457-9555.

Providing legal services in entertainment law, publishing, art law, copyright, trademark, trusts and estates, commercial/corporate transactions, real estate, digital media & litigation.

DAVIS, WRIGHT, TREMAINE, LLP
865 S. Figueroa St., Ste. 2400, Los Angeles, CA 90017.
TEL: (213) 633-6800. FAX: (213) 633-6899. www.dwt.com
PRACTICE CONTACT
Jill R. Cohen

Entertainment, film television, programming and production, intellectual property litigation.

DEL, SHAW, MOONVES, TANAKA, FINKELSTEIN & LEZCANO
2120 Colorado Ave., Ste. 200, Santa Monica, CA 90404.
TEL: (310) 979-7900. FAX: (310) 979-7999.
CONTACT
Nina L. Shaw

DONALDSON & CALLIF
(An Entertainment Law practice)
400 S. Beverly Dr., Ste. 400, Beverly Hills, CA 90212.
TEL: (310) 277-8394. FAX: (310) 277-4870.
www.donaldsoncallif.com
ATTORNEY
Michael C. Donaldson, Lisa A. Callif

Firm structures deals and negotiates contracts for individuals and corporations involved in the development, production, distribution and exploitation of entertainment products and intellectual property rights in all media. Also works with book authors, screen writers, performers, directors and producers as well as institutions such as studios, networks, guilds and talent agencies.

THE LAW OFFICE OF JUDITH C. DORNSTEIN, INC.
9025 Wilshire Blvd., Fifth Flr., Beverly HIlls, CA 90211.
TEL: (310) 278-5568. FAX: (310) 278-2271.
email: judith@dornsteinlaw.com www.dornsteinlaw.com

ERVIN, COHEN & JESSUP
9401 Wilshire Blvd., 9th Fl., Beverly Hills, CA 90212.
TEL: (310) 273-6333. FAX: (310) 859-2325.
email: info@ecjlaw.com www.ecjlaw.com

Intellectual Property Law.

FELKER, TOCZEK, GELLMAN, SUDDLESON
10880 Willshire Blvd., Ste. 2070, Los Angeles, CA 90024.
TEL: (310) 441-8000. FAX: (310) 441-8010.
ENTERTAINMENT ATTORNEY
Chris Abramson, Patti C. Felker, Bruce Gellman, Derek Kroeger, Eric Suddleson, Tred Toczek

FRANKFURT, KURNIT, KLEIN & SELZ, P.C.
488 Madison Ave., 9th Flr., New York, NY 10022.
TEL: (212) 980-0120. FAX: (212) 593-9175.
www.fkks.com
ENTERTAINMENT PARTNER
Alison Cohen, Victoria Cook, Lisa E. Davis, Michael P. Frankfurt, Richard B. Heller, Richard Hofstetter, Brian G. Murphy, Amy Nickin, Thomas Selz, Michael Williams, Tim Craig, Melissa Georges, Ronald S. Konecky, Stuart Silfen, Bernard C. Topper, Jean Voutsinas, S. Jean Ward, Iddo I. Arad, Hamish R.P. Berry, Christopher R. Chase, Mark A. Merriman, Cameron A. Myler, Tara Pietri, Maggie Pisacane

A full-service law firm with a focus on the media, entertainment, and advertising industries.

FREDRICKS & VON DER HORST
12121 Wilshire Blvd., Ste. 900, Los Angeles, CA 90025.
TEL: (310) 820-3600. FAX: (310) 820-1832.
email: fv@fredrickslaw.com www.fredrickslaw.com
CONTACT
Dennis F. Fredricks, Esq.

Production counsel services for all stages of filmmaking. Literary acquisition, packaging, development, financing and production-agreements; international co-production and co-financing agreements; domestic and international distribution agreements. See website for additional practice areas within Entertainment Law.

FREEDMAN & TAITELMAN, LLP
(Entertainment litigation and consultation)
1901 Ave. of the Stars, Ste. 500, Los Angeles, CA 90067.
TEL: (310) 201-0005. FAX: (310) 201-0045. www.ftllp.com
ATTORNEY
Joshua G. Blum, Bryan Freedman, Jonathan M. Genish, Jesse A. Kaplan, Michael Taitelman, David Marmorstein, Bradley Kreshek, Gerry Greengard, Jacqueline Brown, Brian E. Turnauer, Ronald S. Whitaker, September Rea, Steven B. Stiglitz, Monish Coelho

GANG, TYRE, RAMER & BROWN, INC.
132 S. Rodeo Dr., Beverly Hills, CA 90212.
TEL: (310) 777-4800. FAX: (310) 777-4801.
PARTNER
Bruce M. Ramer, Donald S. Passman, Harold A. Brown, Lawrence D. Rose, Kevin S. Marks, Gregg Harrison, J. Eugene Salomon, Jr., Cheryl M. Snow, Tom R. Camp, Biance J. Levin, Tara Kole

Focus on general transactional representation in the entertainment industries and intellectual property, personal business matters, wealth transfers and real estate.

GARVIN & COMPANY, PC
9401 Wilshire Blvd., Ninth Flr., Beverly Hills, CA 90212.
TEL: (310) 278-7300. FAX: (310) 278-7306.
CONTACT
Thomas Garvin

GENDLER & KELLY
450 N. Roxbury Dr., Penthouse 1000, Beverly Hills, CA 90210.
TEL: (310) 285-6400. FAX: (310) 275-7333.
PARTNER
Michael Gendler, Kevin M. Kelly
ATTORNEY
Marc Golden, Brian Fortman

GERDES LAW
8950 W. Olympic Blvd., Ste. 382, Beverly Hills, CA 90211.
TEL: (310) 746-5745. FAX: (310) 858-6703.
www.gerdeslaw.com
ATTORNEY
Ted Gerdes

GIBSON, DUNN & CRUTCHER, LLP
2029 Century Park E., Ste. 4000, Los Angeles, CA 90067.
TEL: (310) 552-8500. FAX: (310) 551-8741.
ATTORNEY
Lawrence J. Ulman, Ruth Fisher, Scott Edelman, David Hernand

GIPSON, HOFFMAN & PANCIONE
1901 Ave. of the Stars, Ste. 1100, Los Angeles, CA 90067.
TEL: (310) 556-4660. FAX: (310) 556-8945.
ENTERTAINMENT ATTORNEY
Lawrence R. Barnett, B. Raymond Gross

GLASER, WEIL, FINK, JACOBS, HOWARD & SHAPIRO, LLP
10250 Constellation Blvd., 19th Flr., Los Angeles, CA 90067.
TEL: (310) 553-3000. FAX: (310) 556-2920.
email: info@glaserweil.com www.glaserweil.com
ATTORNEY
Patricia Glaser, Robert Shapiro, Jonathan Altschul, John Mason, Jonathan Binderman

Practice covers a broad spectrum of transactions and intellectual property matters, including: Agreements regarding Internet content; domestic and international motion picture and TV production contracts and related litigation; film, TV and recording finance and distribution agreements; purchase, sale and valuation of film libraries; literary property acquisitions; merchandising and licensing agreements and related litigation; trademark and copyright licenses; service contracts for actors, writers, directors and other talent; intellectual property litigation to protect or contest the enforceability of patents, trademarks, trade names and copyrights.

GLICKFELD, FIELDS & JACOBSON
315 S. Beverly Dr., Ste. 145, Beverly Hills, CA 90212.
TEL: (310) 550-7222. FAX: (310) 550-6222.
ATTORNEY
Craig M. Fields, Larry Jacobson

JEFFREY L. GRAUBART
350 West Colorado Blvd., Pasadena, CA 91105.
TEL: (626) 304-2800. FAX: (626) 304-2807.

GREENBERG GLUSKER
1900 Ave. of the Stars, 21st Flr., Los Angeles, CA 90067.
TEL: (310) 553-3610. FAX: (310) 553-0687.
www.greenbergglusker.com
ENTERTAINMENT ATTORNEY
Kenneth Basin, Hillary Bibicoff, Caroline Heindel Burgos, Candace Carlos, Ricardo Cestero, Robert S. Chapman, Bonnie

JACKOWAY, TYERMAN, WERTHEIMER, AUSTEN, MANDELBAUM, MORRIS & KLEIN
1925 Century Park East, Watt Plaza, 22nd Flr., Los Angeles, CA 90067. TEL: (310) 553-0305. FAX: (310) 553-5036.
PARTNER
Karl Austen, Jeffrey Bernstein, Joseph D'Onofrio, Alan Epstein, Andrew Galker, Robert Getman, James Jackoway, Deborah Klein, James Mandlebaum, Nigel McNulty
ATTORNEY
Shadi Azarpour, Paul Bernstein, Kimberly Jaime, Robert Koch, Lisa McArthur

JACOBSON & COLFIN, PC
60 Madison Ave., Ste. 1026, New York, NY 10010.
TEL: (212) 691-5630. FAX: (212) 645-5038.
email: thefirm@thefirm.com www.thefirm.com
ATTORNEY
Bruce E. Colfin, Jeffrey E. Jacobson

JEFFER, MANGELS, BUTLER & MITCHELL, LLP
1900 Ave. of the Stars, 7th Flr., Los Angeles, CA 90067.
TEL: (310) 203-8080. FAX: (310) 203-0567.
www.jmbm.com

Entertainment law services include: Negotiating and documenting project financing; assisting clients with acquiring, licensing and selling film and TV libraries containing thousands of titles and more.

JOHNSON & JOHNSON, LLP
439 Canon Dr., Ste. 200, Beverly Hills, CA 90210.
TEL: (310) 975-1080. FAX: (310) 975-1095.
email: njohnson@jjllplaw.com www.jjllplaw.com
ATTORNEY
Neville L. Johnson, Douglas L. Johnson, Lan P. Vu, Mathias D. Maciejewski, Erin L. Pfaff, James T. Ryan

Entertainment law: Represents actors, producers, directors, screenwriters, authors, personal managers, production companies, musicians, composers, publishers & independent record companies.

KATTEN, MUCHIN, ROSENMAN, LLP
2029 Century Park E, Ste. 2600, Los Angeles, CA 90067.
TEL: (310) 788-4400. FAX: (310) 788-4471.
www.kattenlaw.com
ENTERTAINMENT AND MEDIA (AND MEDIA FINANCE)
Susan A. Grode (practice co-chair)
Michael S. Hobel (practice co-chair)
ATTORNEY
Melissa B. Bloom, Mark A. Conley, Harrison J. Dossick, David Halberstadter, Kristin L. Holland, Joyce S. Jun, Heather McCauley, Efran R. Miron, Kamilah K. Smith, Gail Migdal Title, Roby J. Yadegar

See website for additional office locations.

KATZ, GOLDEN & SULLIVAN, LLP
2001 Wilshire Blvd., Ste. 400, Santa Monica, CA 90403.
TEL: (310) 998-9200. FAX: (310) 998-9177.
email: info@KGSRLAW.COM www.kgs-law.com
ATTORNEY
Steven B. Katz, Diane A. Golden, Mary E. Sullivan, Shep Rosenman, Lee Rosenbaum

KEHR, SCHIFF & CRANE
12400 Wilshire Blvd., Ste. 1300, Los Angeles, CA 90025-1030.
TEL: (310) 820-3455. FAX: (310) 820-4414.
PARTNER
Robert L. Kehr, Joel P. Schiff, Paul N. Crane

KENOFF & MACHTINGER, LLP
1901 Ave. of the Stars, Ste. 1775, Los Angeles, CA 90067.
TEL: (310) 552-0808. FAX: (310) 277-0653.
email: jay@km-entertainmentlaw.com
lsmach@km-entertainmentlaw.com
PARTNERS
Jay S. Kenoff, Leonard S. Machtinger

JEFFREY G. KICHAVEN
(Professional mediation and arbitration)
707 Wilshire Blvd., 47th Flr., Ste. 4750, Los Angeles, CA 90017. TEL: (888) 425-2520. (310) 721-5785 (direct line).
email: jk@jeffkichaven.com www.jeffkichaven.com
CONTACT
Jeffry G. Kichaven - (310) 721-5785

Practice areas include: Entertainment & intellectual property. Mediates disputes involving production & distribution for film, TV and music industries; additionally, mediates disputes between agents and managers.

KING, HOLMES, PATERNO & BERLINER, LLP
1900 Avenue of the Stars, 25th Flr, Los Angeles, CA 90067.
TEL: (310) 282-8989. FAX: (310) 282-8903. www.khpblaw.com
ATTORNEY
Howard King, Keith T. Holmes, Peter T. Paterno, Jill Berliner, Steven J. Plinio, Leslie E. Frank, Seth Miller, Michelle N.

Jubelirer, Charles Lozow, Joseph M. Carlone, Jeffrey P. Lilberman, Danna L. Cook

Represent a boadr range of individuals and companies in all areas of motion picture, television and music industries.

KINSELLA, WEITZMAN, ISER, KUMP & ALDISERT

808 Wilshire Blvd., 3rd Flr., Santa Monica, CA 90401.
TEL: (310) 566-9850. FAX: (310) 566-9850.
www.kwikalaw.com
PARTNER
Gregory J. Aldisert, Chad Fitzgerald, Shawn Chapman Holley, Lawrence Iser, Dale Kinsella, Gregory P. Korn, Michael J. Kump, Alan P. Kossoff, Patricia A. Millet, Kristen L. Spanier
ASSOCIATE
Jennifer J. McGrath, Jeremiah T. Reynolds, Gregory Gabriel, Chad Fitzgerald, Amber B. Holley, Jonathan Steinsapir, Randall C. Whattoff, David W. Swift

JONATHAN KIRSCH

1880 Century Park E, Ste. 515, Los Angeles, CA 90067.
TEL: (310) 785-1200. FAX: (310) 286-9573.
email: jk@jonathankirsch.com www.jonathan-kirsch.com

KIRTLAND & PACKARD, LLP

2361 Rosecrans Ave., 4th Flr., El Segundo, CA 90245.
TEL: (310) 536-1000. FAX: (310) 536-1001.
www.kirtland-packard.com
ENTERTAINMENT ATTORNEY
Michael L. Kelly, James T. La Chance, Robert Churella

KLEINBERG LOPEZ LANGE CUDDY & KLEIN, LLP

2049 Century Park E, Ste. 3180, Los Angeles, CA 90067.
TEL: (310) 286-9696. FAX: (310) 277-7145.
ATTORNEY
Kenneth Kleinberg, Robert M. Lange, Christine S. Cuddy, Philip I. Klein, Stephanie L. Rosenberg, Uri M. Emerson-Fleming, Adrian Lopez

KRAMER & KASLOW

23901 Calabasas Rd., Ste. 2013, Calabasas, CA 91302.
TEL: (818) 224-3900. FAX: (818) 224-3911.
www.kramer-kaslow.com/entertainment
CONTACT
Philip A. Kaslow

Extensive experience in the three major areas of independent film production: finance, production and distribution.

LAVELY & SINGER

2049 Century Park East, Ste. 2400, Los Angeles, CA 90067.
TEL: (310) 556-3501. FAX: (310) 556-3615.
www.lavelysinger.com
ATTORNEY
John H. Lavely, Jr., Martin D. Singer, Brian G. Wolff, Lynda Goldman, Michael D. Holtz, William J. Briggs II, Paul N. Sorrell, Evan N. Spiegel

Represent talent-side clientel including some of Hollywood's most prestigious actors, producers, directors, writers, recording artists and other individuals and entities affiliated with the entertainment industry.

LEONARD, DICKER & SCHREIBER

9430 Olympic Blvd., Ste. 400, Beverly Hills, CA 90212.
TEL: (310) 551-1987. FAX: (310) 277-8050.

LEWIS, BRISBOIS, BISGAARD & SMITH, LLP

221 N. Figueroa, Ste. 1200, Los Angeles, CA 90012.
TEL: (213) 250-1800. FAX: (213) 250-7900. www.lbbslaw.com

See website for additional offices.

LICHTER, GROSSMAN, NICHOLS, ADLER & FELDMAN, INC.

(Dedicated exclusively to Entertainment Law)
9200 Sunset Blvd., Ste. 1200, Los Angeles, CA 90069.
TEL: (310) 205-6999. FAX: (310) 205-6990.
ATTORNEY
Peter Grossman, Linda Lichter, Peter Nichols, Michael I. Adler, James M. Feldman, Stephen P. Clark, Jonathan E. Shikora, Melissa A. Rogal

MARK LITWAK & ASSOCIATES

433 N. Camden Dr., Ste. 1010, Beverly Hills, CA 90210.
TEL:(310) 859-9595. FAX: (310) 859-0806.
email: Law2@marklitwak.com www.marklitwak.com
CONTACT
Mark Litwak, Esq.

LINER, GRODE, STEIN, YANKELEVITZ, SUNSHINE, REGENSTREIF & TAYLOR, LLP

1100 Glendon Ave., 14th Flr., Los Angeles, CA 90024.
TEL: (310) 500-3500. FAX: (310) 500-3501.
email: info@linerlaw.com www.linerlaw.com

LOEB & LOEB, LLP

10100 Santa Monica Blvd., Ste. 2200, Los Angeles, CA 90067.
TEL: (310) 282-2000. FAX: (310) 828-2200.
www.loeb.com

New York Office: 345 Park Ave., New York, NY 10154.
TEL: (212) 407-4000. FAX: (212) 407-4990.
ENTERTAINMENT ATTORNEY, PARTNER
Roger Arar, Curtis W. Bajak, Ivy K. Bierman, Saul D. Brenner, Marc Chamlin, Scott Edel, Craig A. Emanuel, John T. Frankenheimer, Kevin Garlitz, Seth Gelblum, Jeffrey D. Goldman, David Grace, Thomas Guida, Carolyn Hunt, Erik Hyman, Channing D. Johnson, Kenneth L. Kraus, Michael L. Mallow, Michael A. Mayerson, Daniel O'Connell Offner, Nigel Pearson, Stephen Saltzman, Michael Streams, James D. Taylor, Deborah White, Susan Zukerman Williams, Scott Zoike

Firm practices in the following Entertainment Law areas: Advertising Law; Antitrust Law; Entertainment Law; Entertainment Finance; Fashion and Luxury Brands; Intellectual Property Law; International Law; Labor and Employment Law; Mergers and Acquisitions; Real Estate Law; Talent; Tax Law; Tax Exempt Organizations Law; Patent, Trademark, Copyright and Unfair Competition.

MANATT, PHELPS & PHILLIPS, LLP

Trident Center, 11355 W. Olympic Blvd., Los Angeles, CA 90064. TEL: (310) 312-4000. FAX: (310) 312-4224.
www.manatt.com
ATTORNEY
Joseph Horacek, III, Gerald A. Margolis, Laurence M. Marks, L. Peter Parcher, L. Lee Phillips, Jordan Yospe

MAYOR, GLASSMAN & GAINES

11726 San Vicente Blvd., Ste. 400, Los Angeles, CA 90049-5006. TEL: (310) 207-0007. FAX: (310) 207-3578.

MCKUIN, FRANKEL, WHITEHEAD

141 El Camino Dr., Ste. 100 Beverly Hills, CA 90212.
TEL: (310) 786-8777. FAX: (310) 786-8756.
PARTNER
Michael Castrillo, David Colden, Jeff Frankel, Lev Ginsburg, Robert Goldman, Joel McKuin, Jennifer Schaeffer, Scott Whitehead

MILLER, BARONDESS, LLP

1999 Avenue of the Stars, Ste. 1000, Los Angeles, CA 90067.
TEL: (310) 552-4400. FAX: (310) 552-8400.
email: info@millerbarondess.com www.millerbarondess.com
PARTNERS
Louis R. (Skip) Miller, Alexander (Sasha) Frid, Braan A. Procel, Daniel S. Miller

Entertainment litigation

MITCHELL, SILERBERG & KNUPP, LLP

11377 W. Olympic Blvd., Los Angeles, CA 90064.
TEL: (310) 312-2000. FAX: (310) 312-3100.
email: info@msk.com www.msk.com
ENTERTAINMENT PRACTICE CHAIR
Phillip Davis, James F. Guerra, Patty Mayer

Entertainment Practice Areas: Film and television finance; development agreements; acquisition and distribution agreements; commercial tie-ins and product placement; theatre and stage; business planning & strategy; operations; and corporate services; intellectual property law, litigation.

MORRISON & FOERSTER

555 W. Fifth St., Ste. 3500, Los Angeles, CA 90013.
TEL: (213) 892-5200. FAX: (213) 892-5454.
email: info@mofo.com www.mofo.com
MANAGING PARTNER (LOS ANGELES)
Gregory B. Koltun

See website for additional offices.

MORRIS, YORN, BARNES & LEVINE, P.C.

200 Avenue of the Stars, 3rd Flr, North Tower, Los Angeles, CA 90067. TEL: (310) 319-3900. FAX: (310) 319-3999.
www.bmkylaw.com
ATTORNEY
Stephen Barnes, Jeffrey Erdlich, Gregg Gelman, Pamela Hicks, Alex Kohner, Larry Kopeikin, David Krintzman, Uven Le, Jared Levine, Jared E. Levine, Kevin Morris, Todd Rubinstein, Kevin Yorn

MYMAN, ABELL, FINEMAN, GREENSPAN & LIGHT, LLP

11601 Wilshire Blvd., Ste. 2200, Los Angeles, CA 90025.
TEL: (310) 231-0800. FAX: (310) 207-2680.
www.mymangreenspan.com
ENTERTAINMENT ATTORNEY
Leslie B. Abell, Glenn Davis, Tom Fineman, David Fox, Eric Greenspan, Jennifer Grega, Jeffrey Light, Sean Marks, Laurie Megery, Tamara Milagros-Butler, Mobert Minzer, Francois Mobassen, Tod Mumford, Robert M. Myman, Aaron D. Rosenberg, Kim Stenton, Steve Younger

A full service entertainment law firm that specializes in film, television, music, internet and digital industries.

NELSON, DAVIS, WETZSTEIN
233 Wilshire Blvd., Ste. 900, Santa Monica, CA 90401.
TEL: (424) 214-4800
ATTORNEY
Peter Nelson, George Davis, Mark Wetzstein

LOUISE NEMSCHOFF
606 N. Larchmont Blvd., Ste. 309, Los Angeles, CA 90004.
TEL: (323) 461-0200. FAX: (323) 461-0250.

Entertainment, copyright and trademark law & intellectual property.

NOVIAN & NOVIAN, LLP
1801 Century Park E., Ste. 1201, Los Angeles, CA 90067.
TEL: (310) 553-1222. FAX: (310) 553-0222.
www.novianlaw.com
ENTERTAINMENT ATTORNEY
Farhad Novian, Evelyn S. Ginossi, William R. H. Mosher

O'MELVENY & MYERS
1999 Ave. of the Stars, 7th Flr., Los Angeles, CA 90067-6035.
TEL: (310) 553-6700. FAX: (310) 246-6779. www.omm.com
PARTNER
Christopher Brearton, Joseph Calabrese, Matthew Eriamouspe, Robert Haymer, David Marroso, Sean A. Monroe, Christopher Murray, Christopher C. Murray, Daniel Petrocelli, Stephen Scharf, Victor Jih, Matthew Kline, M. Randall Oppenheimer, James Pearl, Marvin Putnam, Robert Schwartz, Linda Smith, Robert Welsh

LAW OFFICES OF ALVARO PASCOTTO
555 W. Fifth St., Ste. 3500, Los Angeles, CA 90013.
TEL: (213) 892-5635. FAX: (213) 892-5637.
ATTORNEY
Alvaro Pascotto

Entertainment law. Of Counsel to Morrison & Foerster, LLP. Languages spoken: English, French, Spanish & Italian.

GERALD F. PHILLIPS
2029 Century Park E., Ste. 1200, Los Angeles, CA 90067.
TEL: (310) 277-7117. FAX: (310) 286-9182.
email: gphillips@plljlaw.com

Mediator, arbitrator, billing expert & entertainment industry lawyer. Known for work in Entertainment Industry, for over 50 years.

PILLSBURY WINTHROP SHAW PITTMAN, LLP
725 S. Figueroa, Ste. 2800, Los Angeles, CA 90017.
TEL: (213) 488-7100. FAX: (213) 629-1033.
www.pillsburylaw.com

PROSKAUER ROSE, LLP
2049 Century Park E, 32nd Flr., Los Angeles, CA 90067-3206.
TEL: (310) 557-2900. FAX: (310) 557-2193.
www.proskauer.com

New York Office: 1585 Broadway, New York, NY 10036.
TEL: (212) 969-3000. FAX: (212) 969-2900.
ENTERTAINMENT GROUP
Jeffrey A. Horwitz - (212) 969-3229 jhorwitz@proskauer.com
Charles B. Ortner - (212) 969-3990 cortner@proskauer.com
Bert H. Deixler - (310) 284-5663 bdeixler@proskauer.com

Entertainment Practice Areas: Motion picture production & distribution; motion picture finance; entertainment labor and employment relations; entertainment contracts; copyright counseling; entertainment litigation; counseling in corporate and secured transactions; intellectual property; trade secret counseling; trademark selection, registration & licensing; copyright office and tribunal practice.

QUINN, EMANUEL
865 S. Figueroa St., 10th Flr., Los Angeles, CA 90017.
TEL: (213) 443-3000. FAX: (213) 443-3100.
www.quinnemanuel.com
ATTORNEY
John Quinn, David Quinto, Kathleen Sullivan, Jeff Conciatori, Bob Raskopf, Claude Stern, Bruce Van Dalsem, Gary Sans

Entertainment and media litigation.

ROBBINS, KAPLAN, MILLER & CIRESI
2049 Century Park E., Ste. 3400, Los Angeles, CA 90017.
TEL: (310) 552-0130. FAX: (310) 229-5800. www.rkmc.com
ENTERTAINMENT ATTORNEY
Michael J. Plonsker, Yakub Hazzard, Mark Passin

Entertainment and media litigation

ROSENFELD, MEYER & SUSMAN, LLP
(Entertainment law, intellectual property, litigatoin & real estate)
9601 Wilshire Blvd., Ste. 710, Beverly Hills, CA 90210-5288.
TEL: (310) 858-7700. FAX: (310) 860-2430. www.rmslaw.com
ATTORNEY
Todd Bonder, William N. Canby, Ron Dolecki, Renee Farrell, Francie R. Gorowitz, Eric Greenfeld, Lawrence Kartiganer, Ryan Lapine, Burt Levitch, Marvin Meyer, Ovvie Miller, Jeffrey Nagin

SEYFARTH, SHAW, LLP
One Century Plaza, Ste. 3500, 2029 Century Park E, Los Angeles, CA 90067-3063. TEL: (310) 277-7200.
FAX: (310) 201-5219. www.seyfarth.com
PARTNER
Kenwood C. Youmans - (310) 201-5218
kyoumans@seyfarth.com

Intellectual property: Advertising, promotions & sweepstakes; copyright; Internet law; patent; privacy & security law; technology; trademark.

SHELDON MAK ROSE & ANDERSON
100 E. Corson St., 3rd Flr., Pasadena, CA 91103-3842.
TEL: (626) 796-4000. FAX: (626) 795-6321.
email: daniel@usip.com www.usip.com
ENTERTAINMENT ATTORNEY
Daniel J. Coplan

Intellectual property law.

SHEPPARD, MULLIN, RICHTER & HAMPTON, LLP
1901 Ave. of the Stars, Ste. 1600, Los Angeles, CA 90067.
TEL: (310) 228-3700. FAX: (310) 228-3701.
www.sheppardmullin.com
ENTERTAINMENT PRACTICE LEADERS
Robert A. Darwell, Martin D. Katz

Entertainment practice: motion picture and television development; finance, production and distribution; advertising/sweepstakes; branded entertainment; games; intellectual property; licensing and merchandising; mergers, corporate finance, acquisitions and other strategic corporate transactions; music; First Amendment convergence; online/technology publishing; & sports. Also litigation over disputes arising from all of the foregoing.

SKADDEN, ARPS, SLATE, MEAGHER & FLOM, LLP & AFFILIATES
300 S. Grand Ave., Ste. 3400, Los Angeles, CA 90071.
TEL: (213) 687-5000. FAX: (213) 687-5600.
email: info@skadden.com www.skadden.com
PARTNER
Jeffrey Cohen, David C. Elsman, Brian J. McCarthy, Harriet S. Posner, Nick P. Saggese

Media and Entertainment Group provides a full range of legal counsel relating to mergers, acquisitions and joint ventures, financings, restructurings, litigation, intellectual property issues, antitrust and other regalatory matters; and develpment, licensing and production negotiations.

SLOANE, OFFER, WEBER & DERN
9601 Willshire Blvd., Beverly Hills, CA 90210
TEL: (310) 248-5100. FAX: (310) 205-9805.
PARTNER
Warren Dean, Harris Hartman, Robert Offer, Jason Sloane, Lindsey Strasberg, David Weber

SLOSS LAW OFFICE
555 W. 25th St., 4th Flr., New York, NY 10001.
TEL: (212) 627-9898. FAX: (212) 627-9498.
email: office@slosslaw.com www.slosslaw.com
ATTORNEY
John Sloss, Paul Brennan, Jerry L. Dasti, Jacqueline Eckhouse, Josh Grier, Bethany Haynes Jaime Herman, Alison Hunter, Karen Segall

Sloss Law Office L.L.P. is a full-service entertainment law firm providing counsel in business transactions for the entertainment, sports and media industries.

STANKEVICH GOCHMAN, LLP
9777 Wilshire Blvd., Ste. 550, Beverly Hills, CA 90212.
TEL: (310) 859-8825. FAX: (310) 859-8830.

STECKBAUER WEINHART, JAFFE, LLP
333 S. Hope St., 36th Flr., Los Angeles, CA 90071-1406.
TEL: (213) 229-2868. FAX: (213) 229-2870. www.swjlaw.com
ATTORNEY
Mark Gochman, Mark Stankevich

STROOCK & STROOCK & LAVAN, LLP
2029 Century Park E, Los Angeles, CA 90067-3086.
TEL: (310) 556-5800. FAX: (310) 556-5959. www.stroock.com
ENTERTAINMENT ATTORNEY
John Gatti (partner) Schuyler M. Moore (partner), Jeffrey L. Schumway (partner), Matthew C. Thompson (partner), Daniel A. Rozansky (partner)
ASSOCIATE
Eric F. Harbert, Sally C. James, Lex Kuo, John J. Lucas, Glen G. Mastroberte, David McGriff, Benjamin T. Potter

Stroock's transactional entertainment attorneys assist financiers, studios, networks, production companies and individuals with financing, production, licensing transactions and general corporate work.

TISDALE & NICHOLSON, LLP
2029 Century Park E., Ste. 900, Los Angeles, CA 90067.

TEL: (310) 286-1260. FAX: (310) 286-2351. www.T-NLaw.com
ENTERTAINMENT ATTORNEY
Jeffrey A. Tisdale, Kevin Hughes, Frank M. Lunn, David Emmanuel Rosen

Firm represents domestic and foreign entities and individuals involved in the entertainment industry, both domestically and internationally, including music, music publishing, theatre, commercial and cable television, and motion pictures. Structures and negotiates contracts relating to personal services of performers and industry executives, licensing, project financing, production, publishing and promotion. The firm also provides representation in respect to entertainment-related litigation and labor matters.

TOBEROFF & ASSOCIATES

2049 Century Park E., Ste. 2720, Los Angeles, CA 90067.
TEL: (310) 246-3333. FAX: (310) 246-3101. www.T-NLaw.com
PARTNER
Marc Toberoff

Intellectual property specialists

HARRIS TULCHIN & ASSOCIATES, LTD.

(Attorneys at Law)
11377 W. Olympic Blvd., Trident Center, 2nd Flr., Los Angeles, CA 90064. TEL: (310) 914-7979. FAX: (310) 914-7927.
email: Entesquire@aol.com www.medialawyer.com
ATTORNEY
Harris Tulchin

Firm recently had published "The Independent Film Producer's Survival Guide: A Business and Legal Sourcebook," by Gunnar Erickson, Harris Tulchin and Mark Halloran. See website for book details.

LAWRENCE J. TURNER

13245 Riverside Dr., Ste. 330, Sherman Oaks, CA 91423.
TEL: (818) 386-9485.

TYRE, KAMINS, KATZ, GRANOF

1880 Century Park E., Ste. 300, Los Angeles, CA 90067.
TEL: (310) 553-6822. FAX: (310) 552-9024.
email: pmenes@tyrekamins.com bmenes@tyrekamins.com
ATTORNEY
Cameron Williams, Alan Jay Cohen, Garrett J. Brown

SUZANNE VAUGHAN, APC

6848 Firmament Ave., Van Nuys, CA 91406.
TEL: (818) 988-5599. FAX: (818) 988-5577.
email: suzy@suzyvaughan.com www.suzyvaughan.com
PRESIDENT & CEO
Suzy Vaughan

Intellectual property, right of publicity, entertainment law, production legal, estate representation.

A. CHANDLER WARREN, JR.

7715 W. Sunset Blvd., Ste. 100, Los Angeles, CA 90046.
TEL: (323) 876-6400. FAX: (323) 876-3170.
email: achandlerwarren@aol.com

WEIL, GOTSHAL & MANGES

767 5th Ave., New York, NY 10053. TEL: (212) 310-8000.
FAX: (212) 310-8007. www.weil.com

Offices around the globe.

WEISSMANN, WOLFF, BERGMAN, COLEMAN, GRODIN & EVALL, LLP

9665 Wilshire Blvd., Ninth Flr., Beverly Hills, CA 90212.
TEL: (310) 858-7888. FAX: (310) 550-7191.
www.weissmannwolff.com
ENTERTAINMENT ATTORNEY
Stan Coleman - scoleman@wwllp.com
Carolyn Conrad - cconrad@wwllp.com
Peter J. Dekom - pdekom@wwlip.com
David G. Stanley - dstanley@wwlip.com
Alan L. Grodin - agrodin@wwllp.com
Wayne Kazan - wkazan@wwllp.com
Todd M. Stern - tstern@wwllp.com
Matthew N. Sugarman - msugarman@wwllp.com
Eric Weissman - eweissmann@wwllp.com

WILDMAN HARROLD, ALLEN & DIXON

9665 Wilshire Blvd., Ste. 200, Beverly Hills, CA 90212.
TEL: (310) 860-8700. FAX: (310) 860-3800. www.wildman.com
PARTNER
Nancy Derwin-Weiss, Alan L. Friel, Justine Young Gottshall, James D. Nguyen, Jamie Rubin, Dominique R. Shelton

Recently expanded media and entertainment practice.

WOLF, RIFKIN, SHAPIRO, SCHULMAN & RABKIN, LLP

11400 W. Olympic Blvd., 9th Flr., Los Angeles, CA 90064.
TEL: (310) 478-4100. FAX: (310) 479-1422.
www.wrslawyers.com

ENTERTAINMENT ATTORNEY
Michael Wolf, Neal K. Tabachnick, Roger Goff, David Hochman, Charles Harder, Jeff Abrams, Raagin Knight, Hany Fangary, Christopher Heck, Joseph Petro, Ryan Stonerock

ROBERT J. YOUNG

11664 National Blvd., Ste. 441, Los Angeles, CA 90064.
TEL: (310) 820-2988. FAX: (310) 820-8466.
email: rjy24@aol.com

Licensing & theatrical financing.

ZIFFREN & ZIFFREN

1801 Century Park E., Ste. 2400, Los Angeles, CA 90067.
TEL: (310) 286-9971.
ATTORNEY
Leo G. Ziffren, Lester Ziffren

ZIFFREN, BRITTENHAM, LLP

1801 Century Park W., Los Angeles, CA 90067.
TEL: (310) 552-3388. FAX: (310) 553-7068.
ATTORNEY
Kenneth Ziffren, John G. Branca, Harry M. Brittenham, Samuel Fischer, Clifford Gilbert-Lurie, Kathleen Hallberg, Dennis Luderer

Founded in 1979, this transactional entertainment law firm represents both talent and corporate clients, in the motion picture, television, music and multimedia areas.

ZUBER & TAILLIEU, LLP

Los Angeles County Office: 10866 Wilshire Blvd., Ste. 300, Los Angeles, CA 90024. TEL: (310) 807-9700.
FAX: (310) 807-9701. www.zuberlaw.com

New York Office: 1325 Ave. of the Americas, 28th Flr., New York, NY 10019. TEL: (212) 763-8610. FAX: (212) 763-8611.

ENTERTAINMENT ATTORNEY

Oliver Taillieu - otallier@ztllp.com

Josh Lawler - jlawler@ztllp.com

Ryan Smith - rsmith@ztllp.com

Firm represents distribution and production companies, motion picture producers, academy award-nominated directors and screenwriters, film stars, regulars on top-rated TV shows, talk show hosts, record companies, musicians, best-selling authors, and other artists. Provides counsel to clients regarding: Film and TV production contracts, movie and TV development contracts, film and video distribution agreements, entertainment representation agreements, music industry agreements, licensing agreements, royalty agreements, business formation, entertainment partnership agreements, business financing agreements, entertainment litigation, arbitration and more.

Film Preservation, Processing, Repair & Storage

ALPHA CINE LABORATORY, INC.

(Processing. Acquired Forde Motion Picture Labs in 2009)
9800 40th Ave. S, Seattle, WA 98118. TEL: (206) 682-8230.
FAX: (206) 682-6649. www.alphacine.com
PRESIDENT
Don Jensen
PRODUCTION MANAGER & SENIOR COLOR TIMER
Bill Scott
DIRECTOR OF DIGITAL FILM SERVICES
Marc Brown
V.P., BUSINESS DEVELOPMENT
Jannat Gargi

ARCHION TECHNOLOGIES

(Networked storage systems for the professional video market & premier alternative non-linear storage for post production)
824 N. Victory Blvd., Burbank, CA 91502.
TEL: (888) 655-8555, (818) 840-0777. FAX: (818) 840-0877.
email: info@archion.com www.archion.com
CEO
Mark Bianchi
COO
Reuben Lima
CHIEF TECHNOLOGY OFFICER
James A. Tucci
EXECUTIVE V.P., SALES
Daniel Stern

ASCENT MEDIA LABORATORY

(Film restoration & preservation; film output, positive film printing, negative development)
3611 N. San Fernando Blvd., Burbank, CA 91505.
TEL: (818) 840-7307. FAX: (818) 840-7802.
www.ascentmedia.com
CEO
William R. Fitzgerald
EXECUTIVE V.P., STRATEGIC SOLUTIONS
Tom Kuehle
SENIOR V.P., ASCENT MEDIA, MANAGING DIRECTOR, COMPANY 3
Stefan Sonnenfeld
SENIOR V.P. ENTERTAINMENT TELEVISION & SALES, CREATIVE SERVICE GROUP
Bill Romeo
SENIOR V.P., CORPORATE DEVELOPMENT
Emily Keeton
SENIOR V.P., BUSINESS DEVELOPMENT
Drake Pruitt

BONDED SERVICES

Los Angeles: 3205 Burton, Burbank, CA 91504.
TEL: (818) 848-9766. FAX: (818) 848-9849.
email: sales@bonded.com www.bonded.com
GENERAL MANAGER
Ramona Casanova

Since the 1930s, providing the entertainment industry with media storage and distribution services. Company's climate-controlled vaults store more than 7,000,000 reels of film, video and audio-related material worldwide. Locations in Los Angeles, London, New York, Toronto, Amsterdam, Hong Kong and Paris.

CALIBAN FILMWORKS

(Film preservation, rejuvenation & repair)
1262 Lago Vista Pl., Beverly Hills, CA 90210.
TEL: (310) 385-9332. FAX: (310) 385-1364.
email: laurie66@aol.com
HEAD OF PRODUCTION
Laurie Shearing

CHACE AUDIO BY DELUXE

(Audio post production & sound restoration; acquired by Deluxe Digital Media July 1, 2009.)
201 S. Victory Blvd., Burbank, CA 91502. TEL: (800) 842-8346, (818) 842-8346. FAX: (818) 842-8353. www.chace.com
V.P. AUDIO, DELUXE DIGITAL MEDIA AND HEAD OF CHACE
Bob Heiber - bobheiber@chace.com
GENERAL MANAGER
James Eccles - jameseccles@chace.com
TECHNICAL OPERATIONS MANAGER
Chris Reynolds - chrisreynolds@chace.com

Services include: audio compression, dubbing, editorial, film inspection & repair, optical sound recording, optical soundtrack negative playback-COSPTM, restoration & revitalization, sound transfers, synchronization/conforms.

CINE MAGNETICS DIGITAL & VIDEO LABORATORIES

100 Business Park Dr., Armonk, NY 10504.
TEL: (914) 273-7500. FAX: (914) 273-7575.
email: sales@cinemagnetics.com www.cinemagnetics.com

West Coast: 3765 Cahuenga Blvd W., Studio City, CA 91604.
TEL: (818) 623-2560. FAX: (818) 623-2565
PRESIDENT
Joseph J. Barber, Jr
V.P. & GENERAL MANAGER
Kenneth Wynne
TECHNICAL DIRECTOR
Tim Willis

DVD authoring & compression, Video-On-Demand (VOD), video streaming, digital asset mgt., DVD & CD replication and duplication (large & small quantities), video duplication (all formats & standards), foreign language subtitling and language replacement, custom design, printing and packaging, 800# inbound order capturing, e-commerce integration, warehousing and distribution & optical media replication.

CINE LAB

(Full-service 16mm motion picture lab)
315 Pleasant St., Ste. 11, Fall River, MA 02721.
TEL: (877) 246-3522. (508) 672-1204. www.cinelab.com

New York Drop: The Standby Program, 123 W. 18th St., 7th Flr., New York, NY 10011. TEL: (212) 206-7858.
CONTACT
Brad Chandler - chandler@cinelab.com

CINEFILM

(Film processing and SD/HD Transfers)
2156 Faulkner Rd. NE, Atlanta, GA 30324.
TEL: (800) 633-1448, (404) 633-1448. FAX: (404) 633-3867.
email: csr@cinefilmlab.com www.cinefilmlab.com
CUSTOMER SERVICE MANAGER
Jim Ogburn
ACCOUNT MANAGER
Joe Huggins

Full-service lab: processing 16 and 35 mm color negative; two lab runs a day and can provide all print needs in 16 / 35mm including answer prints, interpositive, dupe negatives, and release prints. In addition, company provides HD 10bit uncompressed DI correction through digital transfer suites for transfer to 35mm laser film outs. Other services: Final cut, HD conversions, digital intermediate film/out.

CINERIC, INC.

630 Ninth Ave., Ste. 508, New York, NY 10036.
TEL: (212) 586-4822. FAX: (212) 582-3744.
www.cineric.com
PRESIDENT & FOUNDER
Balázs Nyari
DIRECTOR, PRESERVATION & RESTORATION
Tom Heitman

Film post production facility. Primary specialties are visual effects and titles.

CINETECH

27200 Tourney Rd., Ste. 100, Valencia, CA 91355.
TEL: (877) 492-9000. (661) 222-9073 ext. 204.
FAX: (661) 253-3637.
SENIOR V.P. OPERATIONS
Herb Brady
MANAGER, RESTORATION & TECHNICAL SERVICES
Joseph Olivier
TECHNICAL SERVICE
David Osterkamp

Associated with Ascent Media. Specializes in the preservation of and restoration of original negatives, YMC masters, interpositives, internegatives, fine grain masters, dupe negatives, release prints and audio tracks. Services include: Front-end negative, developing & answer printing, film scanning & recording, motion picture digital restoration, digital YCM separation masters, photo-chemical restoration & preservation, positive & negative film mastering, continuous contact & optical liquid-gate printing, & nitrate handling.

CONTINENTAL FILM & DIGITAL LAB, INC.

(Processing, print and transfers)
1998 N.E. 150 St., North Miami, FL 33181.
TEL: (800) 327-8396, (305) 949-4252. FAX: (305) 949-3242.
email: continental FL@aol.com www.cfadl.com

OWNER
Steven H. Krams
VICE PRESIDENT, U.S. SALES
Libby Moyer

CREST DIGITAL

(35mm & 16mm lab services, negative processing and prints, color correction, film, HD video and audio restoration, full DVD services)
Post Services: 1000 N. Highland Ave., Hollywood, CA 90038.
TEL: (323) 860-1300. FAX: (323) 461-8901.
www.crestnational.com

Headquarters: 3845 E. Coronado St., P.O. Box 68057, Anaheim, CA 92807. TEL: (800) 309-3472.

CRUSH CREATIVE

(Custom photo lab; creative retouching)
1919 Empire Ave., Burbank, CA 91504. TEL: (800) 300-3686, (818) 842-1121. email: john.davies@crushcreative.com
www.crushcreative.com
SENIOR V.P., SALES MANAGER
John Davies

DELTA VIDEO PRODUCTIONS

(Video post production)
7525 E. Camelback Rd., #102 Scottsdale, AZ 85251.
TEL: (480) 949-6817. FAX: (480) 949-6823.
email: DeltaProVid@aol.com
OWNER
Teresa Johnson

DELUXE

DELUXE DIGITAL MEDIA

15301 Ventura Blvd., Bldg. B, Ste 200 , Sherman Oaks, CA 91403. (818) 380-8138.
V.P., POST PRODUCTION SERVICES
Kari Gruber - kari.gruber@bydeluxe.com

Digital restoration & distribution; audio layback; aspect ratio manipulation (HD, NTSC, PAL); automated broadcast duplication (data to data, video to data, video to video, data to video); climate-controlled vault for active videotape master storage; DVD specialty authoring & distribution; editorial TV formatting; encoding HD, SD, Hi-resolution; HD upconversions, downconversions, cross conversions; international broadcast distribution; NTSC/PAL standards & format conversions.

DELUXE FILM REJUVENATION WEST

10810 Cantara St., Sun Valley, CA 91406.
TEL: (818) 771-5390. FAX: (818) 771-5395.
www.bydeluxe.com
CONTACT
Syed Ahmed - syed.ahmed@bydeluxe.com

Provides film inspection & editing, elements storage and management & climate control, product manufacturing (35 mm reels, cores & rawstock cans), on-site certified film destruction.

DELUXE ARCHIVE SOLUTIONS

200 S. Flower St., Burbank, CA 91502. TEL: (818) 525-2128.
www.deluxearchivesolutions.com
V.P.
Tyler R. Leshney - tyler.leshney@bydeluxe.com

Deluxe Archive Solutions was created to address the growing needs of archivists and collection managers in the university, museum, government, "not-for-profit" and entertainment communities. Offering a complete suite of physical and digital asset management solutions. Deluxe Archive Solutions has the expertise to enable successful preservation and access strategies for our customers.

DELUXE ENTERTAINMENT SERVICES GROUP

200 S. Flower St., Burbank, CA 91502. TEL: (323) 960-8447.
www.bydeluxe.com
EXECUTIVE V.P., SALES & MARKETING
Maggie MacConnell - maggie.macconnell@bydeluxe.com

Print distribution & logistics; exhibitor services, trailer breakdown, trailer chase, theatrical print distribution; theatrical fulfillment with 29 locations nationwide.

DIGITAL NATION, INC.

(Digital; SCI & Cineon workstations; digital compositing and film restoration)
6311 Grape Pl., Los Angeles, CA 90068. TEL: (323) 957-2600.
email: grodner@gmail.com www.digitalnationinc.com
OWNER/OPERATOR
Scott Grodner

DUART FILM AND VIDEO

(Preservation, processing, repair & storage)
245 W. 55th St., New York, NY 10019. TEL: (800) 523-8278, (212) 757-4580. FAX: (212) 333-7647 (SALES).
info@duart.com www.duart.com

ENCORE HOLLYWOOD

(Post production & visual effects)
6344 Fountain Ave., Hollywood, CA 90028.
TEL: (323) 466-7663. FAX: (323) 466-5539.
www.encorehollywood.com/
SALES
Barbara Marshall - bmarshall@encorehollywood.com
Cliff Dugan - cdugan@encorehollywood.com
Jennifer Tellefsen - jtellefsen@encorehollywood.com
Michael Loljan - mkoljan@encorehollywood.com
Robert Glass - rglass@endcorehollywood.com
VISUAL EFFECTS
Tim Jacobsen - tjacobsen@encorehollywood.com

Encore Hollywood specializes in post production and visual effects for episodic TV and MOWs, commercials, music videos and feature films. It also offers a fully equipped digital intermediat theatre &feature HD dailies.

FILM PRESERVE

(Restoration)
2 Depot Plaza, #202-B, Bedford Hills, NY 10507.
TEL: (914) 242-9838. FAX: (914) 242-9854.
CONTACT
Robert A. Harris

FILM TECHNOLOGY COMPANY, INC.

(Restoration)
726 N. Cole Ave., Hollywood, CA 90038. TEL: (323) 464-3456.
FAX: (323) 464-7439. email: denise@filmtech.com
www.filmtech.com
CONTACT
Alan Stark - alan@filmtech.com

FILMACK STUDIOS

(Film transfers, print duplication and distribution and Scotchgard film protector coaters)
223 W. Erie St., #4NW, Chicago, IL 60605-2574.
TEL: (800) 345-6225. FAX: (312) 427-4866.
email: inquiries@filmack.com www.filmack.com
OWNER
Robbie Mack

FILMCORE DISTRIBUTION

(Vaulting services-short form)
Hollywood: 2130 N. Hollywood Way, Burbank, CA 91505.
TEL: (818) 526-3700. FAX: (818) 526-3701.
email: distribution@filmcore.com www.filmcore.net

San Francisco: 545 Sansome St., 7th Flr., San Francisco, CA 94111. TEL: (415) 397-8400.
email:distributionsf@filmcore.com

New York: 1495 Fifth Ave., 6th Flr., New York, NY 10010.
TEL: (212) 459-0290. email: distributionny@filmcore.com

FILMTREAT INTERNATIONAL CORP.

(Film preservation, restoration and repair)
4224 Orchard St., Long Island City, NY 11101.
TEL: (718) 784-4040. FAX: (718) 784-4766.
CONTACT
Y. W. Mociuk, Sam Borodinsky

FILMWORKERS/ASTRO LABS, INC.

(Processing, transfers & printing)
61 W. Erie St., Chicago, IL 60610. TEL: (312) 280-5500.
FAX: (312) 280-5510.
CONTACT
Manuela Hung

FOTOKEM

(Preservation, processing, repair, storage, transfer)
2801 W. Alameda Ave., Burbank, CA 91505.
TEL: (800) 368-6536, (818) 846-3101. FAX: (818) 841-2130.
email: sales@fotokem.com www.fotokem.com

GRACE & WILD STUDIOS

(Formerly HD Studios--Processing, repair, transfers; leading provider of motion picture services in midwest)
23689 Industrial Park Dr., Farmington Hills, MI 48335.
TEL: (248) 471-6010. FAX: (248) 473-8330.
email: info-hd@gw-hdstudios.com
http://www.gracewild.com/hdstudios
SENIOR V.P. & MANAGING DIRECTOR
Keith Neff
V.P., SALES & PRODUCTION SUPPORT SERVICES
Ginny Hart

Processing, repair, transfers.

HIGHLAND LABORATORIES

(All formats of video duplicating; restoration of old video formats)
Pier 96, Administration Bldg., San Francisco, CA 94124.
TEL: (415) 981-5010. FAX (415)981-5019.
www.highlandlab.com
PRESIDENT
B. Brose

HOLLYWOOD FILM COMPANY

(Motion picture equipment manufacturer & restoration services)
9265 Borden Ave., Sun Valley, CA 91352.
TEL: (818) 683-1130. FAX: (818) 683-1139.
email: sales@HollywoodFilmCo.com
www.hollywoodfilmco.com
CONTACT
Vincent Carabello

HOLLYWOOD VAULTS, INC.

(Film preservation, off-site storage)
Vault: 742 N. Seward St., Hollywood, CA 90038.
TEL: (800) 569-5336, (323) 461-6464. FAX: (323) 461-6479.
email: vault@hollywoodvaults.com www.hollywoodvaults.com
PRESIDENT
David Wexler

INTERMISSION PRODUCTIONS, LTD.

(Subsidiary of Cinedustrial, Inc. Film restoration, DVD release and theatrical)
502 N. 5th Ave., Maywood, IL 60153. TEL: (708) 345-7088.
email: interprod1@aol.com
PRESIDENT
Michael Dawson

IRON MOUNTAIN

(Film inspection & cleaning; film preservation; rejuvenation & repair)
Headquarters: 745 Atlantic Ave., Boston, MA 02111.
TEL: (800) 899-IRON, (617) 535-4766.
www.ironmountain.com

LASER PACIFIC MEDIA CORP.

(A Kodak company. Post production services)
809 N. Cahuenga Blvd., Los Angeles, CA 90038.
TEL: (323) 462-6266. FAX: (323) 960-2192.
email: info@laserpacific.com www.laserpacific.com
GENERAL MANAGER, MASTERING UNIT
Ron Burdett - (323) 960-2141 rburdett@laserpacific.com
VISUAL EFFECTS SERVICES
Mike Pryor - mpryor@laserpacific.com
DIRECTOR, SALES, TV, POST PRODUCTION SERVICES
Ian Kerner - (323) 462-6266 ext 2178
ikerner@laserpacific.com
DIRECTOR, FEATURE FILM SALES
Sheryl Goodhead - (323) 960-2166 sgoodhead@laserpacific.com

LEVEL 3 POST

(Part of Ascent Media, a Liberty Media Co. Scratch & Dirt Repair)
2901 W. Alameda Ave., 3rd Flr., Burbank, CA 91505.
TEL: (818) 840-7200. FAX: (818) 840-7801.
email: sales@level3post.com
V.P., SALES
Michael Kolijan

LIPSNER-SMITH COMPANY

(Film cleaning equipment; film printers, negative and print laboratory equipment and planning services)
4700 Chase, Lincolnwood, IL 60712-1689.
TEL: (800) 323-7520, (847) 677-3000. FAX: (847) 677-1311.
email: sales@lipsner.com www.lipsner.com

European Office: Unit 6, Swan Wharf Business Center, Uxbridge UB8 2RA, England. TEL: +44 (0) 2000-478485.
FAX: 44 (0)1895-274692. email: sales@rtico.com

MAGNO SOUND & VIDEO

(Comprehensive post production facility for film & TV)
729 7th Ave., New York, NY 10019. TEL: (212) 302-2505.
FAX: (212) 819-1282. email: staff@magnosound.com
www.magnosoundandvideo.com
CONTACT
Bob Friedman, David Friedman

MATCHFRAME MEDIA GROUP

(A full service post production facility serving motion picture, television and multimedia clients for over 20 years. Also rentals)
Main Facility: 610 N. Hollywood Way, Ste. 101, Burbank, CA 91505. TEL: (818) 840-6800. FAX: (818) 840-2726.
www.matchframevideo.com

This site offers Avid Offline Suites, Avid Symphony and Symphony Nitrus finishing, Final Cut Pro HD, and a Pro Control Audio Suite. Matchframe has introduced the MTI Correct DRS Film Restoration System to its array of high end digital gear. DRS is the choice for all digital film restoration and film finishing work. Work in HD or SD as well as Digital Intermediate. Remove selectively dirt, blemishes, stains and other film imperfections. Restore film to its original perfection. Company uses Digital Vision's DVNR Film Management and Electronic Noise Reduction System, including High Speed Dust Busting.

MEDIA DISTRIBUTORS

(Supplies film and accessories for Film & TV industries)
Los Angeles Facility: 10960 Ventura Blvd. Studio City, CA 91604. TEL: (888) 889-3130, (818) 980-9916.
FAX: (818) 980-9265. email: la@mediadistributors.com
www.mediadistributors.com
CEO/FOUNDER
Steve Klein
PRESIDENT
Richard Myerson

New York: 645 West 27th St., New York, NY 10001.
TEL: (877) 827-7862, (212) 375-1800. FAX: (212) 564-5540.
email: ny@mediadistributors.com

Northern California: TEL: (888) 504-3676, (415) 321-5939.
FAX: (415) 321-5932. email: sf@mediadistributors.com

San Diego: 43391 Business Pkwy., #C3, Temecula, CA 92590.
TEL: (888) 222-7887, (951) 693-0336. FAX: (951) 296-0999.
email: sd@mediadistributors.com

Miami: 2694 Aviation Ave., 2nd Flr., Miami, FL 33133.
TEL: (305) 441-2258. email: jahret@mediadistributors.com

Since 1998, Media Distributors has become one of the largest independent distributors of professional motion picture stock, videotape, recording, storage and data media in the U.S. Company represents every major manufacturer including Sony, Fuji, Maxell, Panasonic, Rimage, Primera, Archion, Quantum, Imation and HP.

METHOD STUDIOS

(Formerly R!OT)
New York: 218 W. 18th St., 12 Flr., New York, NY 10011.
TEL: (212) 907-1200. FAX: (212) 907-1201.
www.methodstudios.com
CONTACT, NEW YORK
Jay Lichtman - jay@methodstudios.com

California: 730 Arizona Ave., Santa Monica, CA 90401.
TEL: (310) 434-6500. www.methodstudios.com
CONTACT, CALIFORNIA
Gabby Goumier - gabby@methodstudios.com
Robert Owens - robert@methodstudios.com

London: 142 Wardour St., London W1F 8dd UK
TEL: +44 (0)20 7131 6431. FAX: +44 (0)20 7878 7800.

Ascent Media Group announced in 2009, two of its boutique visual effects studios, Riot and Method, would unite operations under the Method name, to offer clients high-end visual effects for commercials, music videos and feature films. Services include: digital postproduction in NTSC and PAL, Telecine HD, Datacine, Inferno, Fire HD, Henry, VYVX capabilities, 3D CGI, scanning and recording, compression & duplication. Recruiting: Send reels to: method-sm-recruiting@methodstudios.com

NEXT GENERATION MEDIA

(Transfers)
350 E. Royal Ln., Bldg. 4, #110, Irving, TX 75039.
TEL: (972) 869-0100. FAX: (972) 869-2117.

NOVASTAR DIGITAL SOUND

(Film preservation, rejuvenation & repair)
6430 Sunset Blvd., Ste. 103, Hollywood, CA 90028.
TEL: (323) 467-5020. FAX: (323) 957-8707.
www.novastarpost.com
CO-FOUNDER, PRESIDENT
Bob Sky
DIRECTOR, OPERATIONS
Nav Singh
RESTORATION ENGINEER
Jeff Kloth, Michael Kalifa, David Bell
PRESERVATION & RESTORATION ENGINEER
Lance Watsky

PACIFIC TITLE ARCHIVES

Los Angeles: 4800 W. San Vicente Blvd., Los Angeles, CA 90019. TEL: (323) 938-3711. FAX: (323) 938-6364.
www.pacifictitlearchives.com

Hollywood: 10717 Vanowen St., North Hollywood, CA 91605.
Outside CA: (800) 968-9111, (818) 760-4223.
FAX: (818) 760-1704. email: david@Pacifictitlearchives.com

Burbank: 3520 Valhalla Dr., Burbank, CA 91505.
TEL: (818) 239-1960. FAX: (818) 239-1965.

Burbank: 2240 Screenland Dr., Burbank, CA 91505.
TEL: (818) 239-1960. FAX: (818) 972-9117.
PRESIDENT & CEO
Peter L. Hubbard
VICE PRESIDENT
Ty Humes
DIRECTOR, CLIENT SERVICES
Ken Smith
DIRECTOR, STRATEGIC ALLIANCES
Jennifer Feiner

PRIME FOCUS

(Formerly Post Logic--Independent post-production and digital intermediate)
1800 N. Vine St., Ste. 100, Hollywood, CA 90028.
TEL: (323) 461-7887. FAX: (323) 461-7790.
email: info@prime focus.com www.primefocus.com

FOUNDER, GLOBAL CEO
Namit Malhotra

Digital intermediate, digital restoration, telecine, audio, editorial.

PRO8MM

2805 W. Magnolia Blvd., Burbank, CA 91505.
TEL: (818) 848-5522. FAX: (818) 848-5956.
email: info@pro8mm.com www.pro8mm.com
CONTACT
Phil Vigeant

Pro8mm specializes in hybrid 8 and 16mm format film products and services. Inventors of Super 8 negative film and the popular MAX-8, 16 x 9 super 8 format. Specialties include crystal sync super 8 and 16mm film cameras, over 24 different negative film stocks, award-winning same day processing & digital mastering. Broadcast quality archival transfers for industry and consumers.

PRODUCERS FILM CENTER

(Storage)
948 N. Sycamore Ave., Hollywood, CA 90038.
TEL: (323) 851-1122. FAX: (323) 850-8271.
email: info@filmstorage.net www.filmstorage.net

PRO-TEK MEDIA PRESERVATION SERVICES

(A Kodak company. Film inspection & cleaning; film preservation, rejuvenation & repair; film storage)
3110 N. San Fernando Blvd., Burbank, CA 91504.
TEL: (323) 468-4450. FAX: (323) 468-4486.
email: protekjh@kodak.com www.motion.kodak.com
V.P. PRESERVATION SERVICES
Rick Utley
MANAGER
Jim Harwood

SEWARD FILM & TAPE VAULTS

(Film storage)
1010 N. Seward St., Hollywood, CA 90038.
TEL: (323) 653-4390. FAX: (818) 508-7958.
email: eliza_t@pacbell.net
OWNER
Eliza Thorne - (818) 209-0516 (cell)

T&T OPTICAL EFFECTS

(Film preservation, rejuvenation & repair; motion picture lab; negative cutting)
1905 S. Victory Blvd., Ste. 5, Glendale, CA 91201.
TEL: (818) 846-6475. email: ttefx@earthlink.net

TECHNICOLOR, INC.

Professional Film Division, 6040 Sunset Blvd., Hollywood, CA 90028. TEL: (323) 817-6287.
FAX: (818) 761-4835. email: diane.upson@technicolor.com
www.technicolor.com
CONTACT
Zak Christian - christian.zak@technicolor.com

New York: 110 Leroy St., New York, NY 10014.
TEL: (212) 886-5200. FAX: (212) 886-5249.
www.technicolor.com
CONTACT
Clark Henderson - clark.henderson@technicolor.com

Film processing, large format and trailer printing, full laboratory services, preservation & restoration. See website for additional locations worldwide.

TRACKWISE AT FULL HOUSE PRODUCTIONS, INC.

(Preservation and repair)
630 9th Ave., New York, NY 10010.
TEL: (212) 645-2228. FAX: (212) 627-02838.
email: trackwise@fullhouseny.com www.fullhouseny.com
PRODUCTION SERVICES
Phil Lee

WARNER BROS. PHOTO LAB

4000 Warner Blvd., Burbank, CA 91522. TEL: (818) 954-7118.
FAX: (818) 954-6732. email: photolab@warnerbros.com
www.wbphotolab.warnerbros.com www.wbsf.com
PRESIDENT
Jon Gilbert
V.P., POST PRODUCTION SERVICES
William Angarola
PHOTO LAB & DIGITAL SERVICES
Greg Dyro - (818) 954-7118

YCM LABORATORIES

(Film preservation, rejuvenation & repair)
3140 Clybourn Ave., Burbank, CA 91505.
TEL: (818) 843-5300. FAX: (818) 842-7006.
CONTACT
Richard Dayton

FILM STOCK

CHRISTY'S EDITORIAL FILM & VIDEO SUPPLY, INC.

(Film stock & videotape supplier)
3625 W. Pacific Ave., Burbank, CA 90505.
TEL: (800) 556-5706, (818) 845-1755. FAX: (818) 845-1756.
email: info@christys.net www.christys.net
CONTACT
Craig Christy
DIGITAL SERVICES
JJ Nigro, Dan Downer
FILM
Sheli Christy, Al Limeres, Jay McLean

For over 35 years, Christy's Editorial has provided a complete line of film supplies, film equipment, digital editing systems, digital storage, professional decks, peripherals, support equipment as well as post production facilities to the motion picture and TV Industry. Also offers 24-hour edit bays with full services for post production professionals. Rents Avids.

EASTMAN KODAK COMPANY

(Film stock & videotape manufacturer/supplier; raw film stock, negative reversal film)
Headquarters: 343 State St., Rochester, NY 14650.
TEL: (800) 621-3456. FAX: (585) 724-1089.
www.motion.kodak.com
http://motion.kodak.com/US/en/motion/Products/Distribution_And_Exhibition/Print_Films/index.htm
MOTION PICTURE FILM & DIGITAL EXECUTIVES
COO, WORLDWIDE OPERATIONS, FILM, PHOTOFINISHING & ENTERTAINMENT GROUP, GENERAL MANAGER, RETAIL PRINTING & V.P.
Brad W. Kruchten
PRESIDENT & GENERAL MANAGER, ENTERTAINMENT IMAGING, FILM, PHOTOFINISHING & ENTERTAINMENT GROUP AND V.P.
Kimberly A. Snyder
GENERAL MANAGER, DIGITAL PRINTING SOLUTIONS AND V.P.
Isidre Rosello

California Sales Office: 6700 Santa Monica Blvd., Los Angeles, CA 90038. TEL: (800) 621-3456, (323) 464-6131.
FAX: (323) 468-1568.

New York Sales Office: 360 W. 31st St., New York, NY 10001.
TEL: (212) 631-3400. FAX: (212) 631-3470.

See website for additional sales contacts throughout U.S.

FILM EMPORIUM

(Kodak, Fuji & Ilford film stock, videotape & cameras & prod. insurance)
New York: 274 Madison Ave., Ste. 404, New York, NY 10016.
TEL: (800) 371-2555, (212) 683-2433. FAX: (212) 683-2740.
email: info@filmemporium.com

Los Angeles: Sunset Gower Studios, 1438 N. Gower St., Box 72, Hollywood, CA 90028. TEL: (866) 611-FILM, (323) 464-5144.
FAX: (323) 646-7348. email: info@filmemporium.com
www.filmemporium.com

FUJIFILM NORTH AMERICA MOTION PICTURE GROUP.

2200 W. Magnolia Blvd., Burbank, CA 91506.
TEL: (888) 424-3854, (323) 857-8900. FAX: (323) 465-8279.
www.fujifilm.com www.fujifilmusa.com

Photographic Film and Paper, Film Cameras, Digital Cameras, Digital Printers, Minilab Systems, Motion Picture Films, Recording Media.

MEDIA DISTRIBUTORS

(Supplies film and accessories for Film & TV industries)
Los Angeles: 10960 Ventura Blvd., Studio City, CA 91604.
TEL: (888) 889-3130, (818) 980-9916. FAX: (818) 980-9265.
email: la@mediadistributors.com www.mediadistributors.com
CEO/FOUNDER
Steve Klein
PRESIDENT
Richard Myerson

New York: 645 West 27th St., New York, NY 10001.
TEL: (877) 827-7862, (212) 375-1800. FAX: (212) 564-5540.
email: ny@mediadistributors.com

Seattle: 8310 154th Ave. NE, Redmond, WA 98052.
TEL: (888) 964-1780, (206) 264-1780. FAX: (206) 264-2531.
email: seattle@mediadistributors.com

San Francisco: 1219 Folsom St., San Francisco, CA 94103.
TEL: (888) 504-3676, (415) 321-5939. FAX: (415) 321-5932.
email: sf@mediadistributors.com

San Diego: 43114 Blackdeer Loop #E, Temecula, CA 92590.
TEL: (888) 222-7887, (951) 693-0336. FAX: (951) 296-0999.
email: sd@mediadistributors.com

Atlanta: TEL: (678) 967-4713. FAX: (404) 862-3058.
email: jahret@mediadistributors.com

Since 1998, Media Distributors has become one of the largest independent distributors of professional motion picture stock, videotape, recording, storage and data media in the U.S. Company represents every major manufacturer including Sony, Fuji, Maxell, Panasonic, Rimage, Primera, Archion, Quantum, Imation and HP.

PLASTIC REEL CORP. (PRC)

(Audiotape supplier, film stock & videotape supplier)
8140 Webb Ave., N. Hollywood, CA 91605.
TEL: (818) 504-0400. FAX: (818) 504-0946.

PRO8MM

(Film stock & videotape supplier)
2805 W. Magnolia Blvd., Burbank, CA 91505.
TEL: (818) 848-5522. FAX: (818) 848-5956.
email: info@pro8mm.com www.pro8mm.com

Pro8mm specializes in hybrid 8 and 16mm format film products and services. Inventors of Super 8 negative film and the popular MAX-8, 16 x 9 super 8 format. Specialties include crystal sync super 8 and 16mm film cameras, over 24 different negative film stocks, award-winning same day processing, digital mastering on the Y front URSA diamond for super8, regular8, 16mm and super 16mm. Broadcast quality archival transfers for industry and consumers.

SPECTRA FILM AND VIDEO

(Specializes in sale of Super 8, Regular 8, 16mm & 35 mm)
5626 Vineland Ave., N. Hollywood, CA 91601.
TEL: (818) 762-4545. FAX: (818) 762-5454.
email: sales@spectrafilmandvideo.com
www.spectrafilmandvideo.com

VIDEOTAPE PLUS

(Film stock & videotape supplier)
12130 Sherman Way, N. Hollywood, CA 91605.
TEL: (818) 764-7420. FAX: (818) 764-6947.

FINANCIAL SERVICES

PROJECT FINANCING

AMBERGATE ASSOCIATES/KDM

(Ambergate seeks out financial availability in countries around the world. Identifies potential partners and brings them together)
4367 Hwy. 78, Ste. 116. P.O. Box 2050, Julian, CA 92036.
TEL: (760) 765-2427. FAX: (760) 765-2498.
email: ekalish@ambergate.net
CONTACT
Eddie Kalish

BANK OF AMERICA NT & SA / COMMERCIAL BANKING ENTERTAINMENT OFFICE

2049 Century Park E., #200, Los Angeles, CA 90067.
TEL: (310) 785-6062. FAX: (310) 785-6100.

BANK OF NEW YORK MELLON CORPORATION

One Wall Street, New York, NY 10286. TEL: (212) 495-1784.
www.bnymellon.com

Media Division consists of 15 professionals based in New York City and London who manage more than 120 relationships. Clients include cable, radio and television broadcasting companies, as well as publishing, multimedia, entertainment, theatre and other media organizations.

BMO CAPITAL MARKETS

3 Times Square, New York, NY 10036. TEL: (212) 702-1111, (671) 960-2355. FAX: (617) 451-1291.
MANAGING DIRECTOR, BUSINESS SERVICES & MEDIA GROUP
Susan Wolford
MANAGING DIRECTOR/DIGITAL ENTERTAINMENT/BROADCASTING/NETWORK PROGRAMING
Lee Westerfield

Group capabilities: M&A advisory services; public equity and debt underwriting; syndicated lending; private placements; risk management and other financial services.

BRITISH COLUMBIA FILM

(Production financing)
2225 W. Broadway, Vancouver, BC, V6K 2E4, Canada.
TEL: (604) 736-7997. FAX: (604) 736-7290.
email: bcf@bcfilm.bc.ca www.bcfilm.bc.ca
PROJECT DEVELOPMENT FUND BUSINESS ANALYST
Janine Bizzocchi Steele - jsteele@bcfilm.bc.ca

BRITISH CONNECTION

11955 Missouri Ave., Ste. 10, Los Angeles, CA 90025.
TEL: (310) 820-7280. FAX: (310) 820-3286.
email: info@britconnection.com www.britconnection.com
EXECUTIVE DIRECTOR
Judy Hevenly

CAPELLA FILMS, INC. & CONNEXION AMERICAN MEDIA

9200 Sunset Blvd., Ste. 315, Los Angeles, CA 90069.
TEL: (310) 247-4700. FAX: (310) 247-4701.
PRESIDENT
Craig Arrington

CITY NATIONAL BANK

Entertainment Division, 400 N. Roxbury Dr., 5th Flr., Beverly Hills, CA 90210. TEL: (310) 888-6200. FAX: (310) 888-6238.
www.cnb.com
EXECUTIVE V.P. & MANAGER ENTERTAINMENT DIVISION
Martha Henderson

Entertainment division includes a team of 150 entertainment banking professionals in Beverly Hills and New York. The div. provides financial services to: business management companies, talent agencies, entertainment law firms, personal management companies and production companies. Services include: talent and holding escrows; cash management services; investment management, asset management & liquidity management services; international services including foreign exchange contracts and foreign drafts; and production financing.

COMERICA BANK, CALIFORNIA

(Entertainment financing)
9777 Wilshire Blvd., 4th Flr., Beverly Hills, CA 90212.
TEL: (800) 292-1300 (EST), (800) 589-1400 (Central, Mountain and Pacific), (310) 281-2400. FAX: (310) 281-2476.
www.comerica.com
PRESIDENT
Morgan Rector - (310) 281-2400

Comerica Entertainment Group's specialties include: financing worldwide contracts and estimates using its extensive international relationship base and proprietary information database; expertise in various international tax benefit programs and territorial co-production financing structures; financing "case by case," working closely with clients to find the most appropriate financial arrangements for each project or company. Comerica's clients include principals, film and television producers, entertainment technology companies, foreign and domestic sales agents, and post-production houses.

CYTRE INVESTMENTS BV

Flexolaan 41A, 1411 KC Naarden, The Netherlands.
TEL: +31 35 6959090. FAX: +31 35 6959044.

Cyrte is a Netherlands-based investment company that has an active interest in media investments. Its most recent acquisition included the financing of the Exclusive Media Group, which now combines Los Angeles-based New Market Films with Spitfire Pictures and London-based Hammer Films.

ENTERTAINMENT PARTNERS

(Entertainment Partners is a leading provider of production management services in the entertainment industry)
UNITED STATES OFFICES:
Los Angeles: 2835 N. Naomi St., Burbank, CA 91504-2024.
TEL: (818) 955-6000, (818) 955-6299 (Marketing).
FAX: (818) 845-6507. www.entertainmentpartners.com
CEO & PRESIDENT
Markham L. Goldstein
EXECUTIVE V.P., MARKETING & SALES
Michael Hill

Central Casting: 220 S. Flower St., Burbank, CA 91502-2101.
TEL: (818) 562-2700. FAX: (818) 562-2786.
www.centralcasting.org

New York: 875 6th Ave., 15th Flr., New York, NY 10001-3507.
TEL: (646) 437-9000. FAX: (212) 947-4787.

Orlando: 2000 Universal Studios Plaza, Ste. 620, Orlando, FL 32819-7606. TEL: (407) 354-5900. FAX: (407) 351-4037.

Offers a full range of integrated products and services designed to increase productivity and decrease costs. Services include budgeting, scheduling & payroll.

FIRST CALIFORNIA FINANCIAL GROUP, INC. / ENTERTAINMENT INDUSTRIES DIVISION

3027 Townsgate Rd., Ste. 300, Westlake Village, CA 91361.
TEL: (805) 322-9655. email: InvestorRelations@FCalGroup.com
www.fcalgroup.com www.fcbank.com

GOTHAM METRO STUDIOS, INC.

(Production, development production finance, film distribution, TV & video production)
Gotham Metro Inc./Corp. Office: TEL: (310) 394-9100.
email: info@GothamMetro.com
www.GothamMetro.com
FOUNDER & GMS REPRESENTATIVE
Michael J Lasky - mj@gothammetro.com
FINANCE CONSULTANT
Markus Baettig - markus@gothammetro.com

ICB ENTERTAINMENT FINANCE

(A division of Imperial Capital Bank)
500 N. Brand Blvd., Ste. 1650, Glendale, CA 91203.
TEL: (818) 254-2242. FAX: (818) 459-7082.
email: info@icbef.com www.icbef.com
VICE PRESIDENT
Charles H. Kim
V.P., OPERATIONS & PORTFOLIO MANAGER
Lisa Thomas-Stoute
DEPUTY MANAGING DIRECTOR
David Hutkin

J.P. MORGAN SECURITIES, INC. ENTERTAINMENT INDUSTRIES GROUP

(Formerly Chase Securities, Inc. / Entertainment Industries Group. Entertainment financing. J.P. Morgan Securities is the nonbank subsidiary of J.P. Morgan Chase)
1999 Ave. of the Stars, 27th Flr., Los Angeles, CA 90067.
TEL: (310) 860-7000. FAX: (310) 860-7260.
MANAGING DIRECTOR & GROUP HEAD
David Shaheen
MANAGING DIRECTOR
Christa Thomas
PRINCIPAL, ENTERTAINMENT ADVISORY UNIT
Alan Levine, Ken Lemberger

Group's role is raising capital through syndicated financings, private placements and stock offerings, helping restructuring businesses, advising on management issues and securing production, distribution and licensing arrangements.

SIDNEY KIMMEL ENTERTAINMENT

(Independent motion picture production and financing company)
9460 Wilshire Blvd., Ste. 500, Beverly Hills, CA 90212.
TEL: (310) 777-8818. FAX: (310) 777-8892. www.skefilms.com
CHAIRMAN & CEO
Sidney Kimmel
PRESIDENT
Jim Tauber
CFO
Richard Lewis
CREATIVE
Mark Mikutowicz
SENIOR V.P. & LEGAL AFFAIRS
Nicholas Hanks

KIMMEL INTERNATIONAL/SIERRA PICTURES

250 Hudson St., 10th Flr., New York, NY 10013.
TEL: (212) 431-5550. FAX: (212) 431-5822.
email: kimmelny@skefilms.com www.skefilms.com
PRESIDENT, KIMMEL INTERNATIONAL
Mark Lindsay - mlindsay@skefilms.com
PRESIDENT, SIERRA PICTURES
Nick Meyer
EXECUTIVE V.P., BUSINESS AFFAIRS
Jill Silfen - jsilfen@skefilms.com

Sidney Kimmel Entertainment is the Beverly Hills/New York based motion picture production and financing company, headed by veteran producer Sidney Kimmel.

KRAMER & KASLOW

23901 Calabasas Rd., Ste. 2013, Calabasas, CA 91302.
TEL: (818)224-3900. FAX: (818) 224-3911.
email: entertainment@kramer-kaslow.com
www.kramer-kaslow.com
ENTERTAINMENT FINANCE
Harmon M. Kaslow

The entertainment law firm has been involved with Negative Pick-Ups, Gap Financing, Private/Equity Financing, and Insurance-Backed Financing.

NATIXIS BLEICHROEDER, INC.

1345 Ave. of the Americas, New York, NY 10105-4300.
TEL: (212) 698-3000. FAX: (212) 299-4444. www.natexisblr.us
EXECUTIVE V.P., U.S. CAPITAL MARKETS
Gregg Schoenberg - gregg.schoenberg@blr.natixis.com

The group raises capital for and provides financing guidance to clients within the Energy, Commodities, Health Care and Media industries. Within these sectors, Capital Markets utilizes its industry knowledge, awareness of the latest market trends and distribution strength to help generate high-quality demand for its clients' offerings.

NEUBERGER & BERMAN

(The 70-year-old company became an employee-owned firm May 4, 2009. Provider of global equity, fixed income and alternative investment solutions)
Headquarters: 605 3rd Ave., New York, NY 10158.
TEL: (800) 223-6448, (212) 476-9000. FAX: (212) 476-9090.
www.nb.com
CHAIRMAN & CEO
George Walker
PRESIDENT
Joseph V. Amato

Los Angeles: 1999 Ave. of the Stars, Ste. 2050, Los Angeles, CA 90067. TEL: (310) 843-4949. www.nb.com
HEAD, SOCAL REGION
Scott Marantz

NEWMARKET CAPITAL GROUP

(Acquired by Cyrte Investments BV. See listing under Cyrte)

NILES CAPITAL GROUP, INC.

(Now offers film and entertainment financing)
9461 Charleville Blvd, Ste. 346, Beverly Hills, CA 90212.
TEL: (310) 413-4431. FAX: (310) 919-3025.
email: brian@nilescapital.com
PRESIDENT
Brian Evans

OCEAN PACIFIC CAPITAL

(Real estate financing for movie theatres)
2 Corporate Park, Ste. 102, Irvine, CA 92606.
TEL: (800) 595-1474, (949) 263-9000. FAX: (949) 263-9999.
email: loanmanager@oceanpacificcapital.com
www.oceanpacificcapital.com
PRESIDENT
Charles A. Elfsten - celfsten@opcstaff.com
SENIOR V.P.
Butch Itakura - bitakura@opcstaff.com
CUSTOMER SERVICE MANAGER
Eric Rivas - erivas@opcstaff.com

OCEANA MEDIA FINANCE, LLC

(Formed in 2007 as a specialty finance company providing asset-backed secured financing for the production & marketing of feature films with production budgets between $2 million and $7 million. As of April 1, 2009, operates as a subsidiary of Core Financial Group: www.corefg.com)
9150 Wilshire Blvd., Ste. 270, Beverly Hills, CA 90212.
TEL: (310) 883-4803. www.oceanamediafinance.com
FOUNDER & CEO
Myles Nestel
DEVELOPMENT & OPERATIONS
Jeff Strebinger - jeff@oceanmediafinance.com
HEAD OF BUSINESS & LEGAL AFFAIRS
Anthony Callie

Offers four types of financing: pre-production bridge loans, mezzanine gap loans, print and advertising financing and equity investments.

OPPENHEIMER & CO.

Headquarters: 125 Broad St., New York, NY 10004.
TEL: (800) 221-5588, (212) 668-8000. email: info@opco.com
www.opco.com

Los Angeles: 10880 Wilshire Blvd., Los Angeles, CA 90024.
TEL: (310) 446-7100. FAX: (310) 446-7411. www.opco.com

THE PULLMAN GROUP, LLC

(The Pullman Group® LLC is a principal investment bank and specialty finance company servicing the entertainment and intellectual property industries)
1370 Ave. of the Americas, 26th Flr., New York, NY 10019.
TEL: (212) 750-0210. FAX: (212) 750-0464.
www.pullmanbonds.com
FOUNDER/CHAIRMAN/CEO
David Pullman - dpullman@pullmanbonds.com

REGENT ENTERTAINMENT PARTNERSHIP, LP

10990 Wilshire Blvd., Penthouse. Los Angeles, CA 90024.
TEL: (310) 806-4288. FAX: (310) 806-4268.
email: info@regententertainment.com
www.regententertainment.com
CHAIRMAN OF THE BOARD
Stephen P. Jarchow
BOARD MEMBER
Paul Colichman, David Kruger
CEO
Mark Reinhart
PRESIDENT, REGENT RELEASING LLC
John Lambert
PRESIDENT, REGENT WORLDWIDE SALES LLC
Adam Wright
SENIOR V.P., FINANCE & OPERATIONS, REGENT WORLDWIDE SALES, LLC
Lowell Dean Cox
SENIOR V.P., BUSINESS & LEGAL AFFAIRS, REGENT WORLDWIDE SALES LLC
Joan Danto
SENIOR V.P., ADMINISTRATION
Alice Andrade
SENIOR V.P., REGENT MEDIA LLC
Stephen Macias

Regent companies include: Regent Studios, Regent Worldwide, Regent Releasing, Regent Theaters, Regent Library, Regent Programming Services. The organization produces, distributes and finances a variety of motion picture and television content.

RELATIVITY MEDIA, LLC

(Relativity Media, LLC is a media and entertainment company which focuses on creating, financing and distributing first class, studio quality entertainment content and intellectual property across multiple platforms)
8899 Beverly Blvd., Ste. 510, West Hollywood, CA 90048.
TEL: (310) 859-1250. FAX: (310) 859-1254.
www.relativitymediallc.com
CEO
Ryan Kavanaugh
PRESIDENT
Michael Joe
COO
Andrew Marcus
PRESIDENT, PRODUCTION
Tucker Tooley
CHIEF FINANCIAL OFFICER
Bill Sutman

Relativity also owns and operates Rogue Pictures, a company that specializes in the production and distribution of lower-budget genre films, as well as the label's entire library of films. Relativity also owns RelativityREAL, a joint venture with veteran TV producer Tom Foreman, which produces reality TV content.

SCREEN AUSTRALIA

Level 4, 150 William St., Woolloomooloo, NSW 2011, Australia
TEL: (61 2) 8113-5800. FAX: (61 2) 9357-3737.

email: info@screenaustralia.gov.au
www.screenaustralia.gov.au
CHAIRMAN
Glen Boreham
DEPUTY CHAIR
Ian Robertson

Screen Australia provides support to Australian film, television, documentary and digital media makers and aims to put the industry on a new growth path. On July 1, 2008, Screen Australia became the Commonwealth Government's new screen agency that replaced the Australian Film Commission, Film Australia and the Film Finance Corporation.

SCREEN CAPITAL INTERNATIONAL

345 N. Maple Dr., Ste. 294, Beverly Hills, CA 90210.
TEL: (310) 205-2490. FAX: (310) 205-2495.
email: info@screencapital.com
FOUNDER
David Molner

In May 2008, Screen Capital International, as a major shareholder, teamed with J.P. Morgan Chase (supplying line of credit), U.K.-based Aramid Entertainment Fund, private investors and William Morris Independent to form Incentive Filmed Entertainment, which will fund up to 50 motion pictures with its $100 million fund.

SMITH BARNEY

(A div. of Citigroup Global Capital Markets, Inc. Entertainment finance)
9665 Wilshire Blvd., 6th & 7th Flrs., Beverly Hills, CA 90212.
TEL: (310) 285-2634. email: lisa.a.detanna@smithbarney.com
www.smithbarney.com
SENIOR V.P.
Lisa Detanna

STONEHENGE CAPITAL COMPANY, LLC

236 Third St., Baton Rouge, LA 70801. TEL: (225) 408-3000.
FAX: (225) 408-3090. www.stonehengecapital.com
PRESIDENT
Thomas J. Adamek
MANAGING DIRECTOR
Michael Kirby, Gordon S. LeBlanc, Jr.,
David Webber, John P. Witten
VICE PRESIDENT
William "Robert" Lay
DIRECTOR & ASSOCIATE GENERAL COUNSEL
William B. Owens, Jr.

Company has closed more than $600 million in tax credit transactions. Services include: film tax credit financing, venture capital and private equity funds; provides equity, mezzaine or debt financing to select entertainment facilities, including: theatres, film & TV production facilities and sports and amusement facilities.

THE TCW GROUP, INC.

Headquarters: 865 S. Figueroa, Ste. 1800, Los Angeles, CA 90017. TEL: (213) 244-0000. FAX: (213) 244-0741.
www.tcw.com
CHAIRMAN AND FOUNDER
Robert A. Day
VICE CHAIRMAN & CEO
Mark I. Stern
EXECUTIVE V.P., HEAD OF INVESTMENT OPERATIONS
Joseph M. Burschinger
EXECUTIVE V.P., GENERAL COUNSEL
Michael E. Cahill

West Los Angeles: 11100 Santa Monica Blvd., Los Angeles, CA 90025. TEL: (310) 235-5900.

New York: 1251 Ave. of the Americas, Ste. 4700, New York, NY 10020. TEL: (212) 771-4000.

Houston: 333 Clay St., Ste. 4150, Houston, TX 77002.
TEL: (713) 615-7400.

TCW offers institutional and individual investors a wide array of US Equities, US Fixed Income, Alternatives and International strategies.

UNION BANK OF CALIFORNIA ENTERTAINMENT GROUP

(Entertainment Financing)
445 S. Figueroa, 16th Flr., Los Angeles, CA 90071.
TEL: (310) 551-8940. www.unionbank.com
SENIOR V.P.
David M. Musicant
ENTERTAINMENT FINANCE V.P. & MANAGER
Bryan J. LaCour
Experience working with studios, independent producers, distributors, and interactive media firms. Bank supports projects by providing working capital and managing foreign exchange and collection accounts. It also provides specialized treasury management services for the industry.

WALDEN VENTURE CAPITAL

(New media financing)
750 Battery St., Ste. 700, San Francisco, CA 94111.
TEL: (415) 391-7225. FAX: (415) 391-7262. www.waldenvc.com
MANAGING DIRECTOR
Art Berliner, Matt Miller, Larry Marcus, George Sarlo

THEATRE REAL ESTATE FINANCING

ENTERTAINMENT PROPERTIES TRUST

(Real estate financing for movie theatres & destination entertainment)
30 W. Pershing Rd., Ste. 201, Kansas City, MO 64108.
TEL: (888) EPR-REIT, (816) 472-1700. FAX: (816) 472-5794.
email: info@eprkc.com www.eprkc.com
PRESIDENT & CEO
David M. Brain
CHIEF INVESTMENT OFFICER
Morgan G. (Jerry) Earnest, II

COMPLETION BONDS & INSURANCE

ABACUS INSURANCE BROKERS, INC.

12300 Wilshire Blvd., Ste. 400, Los Angeles, CA 90025.
TEL: (310) 207-5432. FAX: (310) 207-8526.
email: info@abacus.com www.abacus.net
PRESIDENT
Leon Lewin
V.P., PROGRAM DEVELOPMENT
Darren Lewin, CPCU, CPA CMA
V.P., TECHNOLOGY & CONTACT
Kevin Lewin - kevin.lewin@abacus.net

AIG (AMERICAN INTERNATIONAL GROUP, INC.)

(Entertainment insurance writers)
70 Pine St., New York, NY 10028. TEL: (212) 770-8405.
FAX: (212) 809-1533. www.aig.com
MEDIA CONTACT
Joe Norton - (212) 770-3144

AON / ALBERT G. RUBEN INSURANCE SERVICES, INC.

(Insurance for production)
Global Headquarters: 200 E. Randolph St., Chicago, IL 60601.
TEL: (312) 381-1000.

15303 Ventura Blvd., Ste. 1200, Los Angeles, CA 91403.
TEL: (800) 752-9157, (818) 742-1400. FAX: (818) 953-2480.
email: ruben@aon.com www.albertgruben.com
MANAGING DIRECTOR
Paul Jones

New York Office: 48 W. 25th St., 12th Flr., New York, NY 10010-2703. TEL: (212) 627-7400. FAX: (212) 633-1457.

www.aon.com

AON / RUBEN-WINKLER ENTERTAINMENT INSURANCE BROKERS

20 Bay St., Toronto, ON M5J 2N9, Canada.
TEL: (416) 868-2460. FAX: (416) 868-2469.
email: rebenwinkler@aon.ca www.aon.ca

BERKETT INSURANCE AGENCY

11150 W. Olympic Bld., Ste. 1100, Los Angeles, CA 90064.
TEL: (310) 857-5757. FAX: (310) 857-5750.
www.berkettinsurance.com
CEO
Lloyd S. Berkett
PRESIDENT
Jeff Berkett - jberkett@berkettinsurance.com
MARKETING MANAGER, COMMERCIAL LINES
Carol Gold - cogold@berkettinsurance.com

Independent agents and brokers who represent carriers worldwide, enabling a wide range of coverage options for clients. Placements generally go only to those insurers with an acceptable Best Rating and with reputations to back that financial strength with superior service.

C&S INTERNATIONAL INSURANCE BROKERS, INC.

19 Fulton St., Ste. 308A, New York. NY 10038.
TEL: (212) 406-4499. FAX: (212) 406-7584.
www.csins.com
PRESIDENT
Debra Kozee

CHUBB GROUP INSURANCE

15 Mountain View Rd., Warren, NJ 07054.
TEL: (908) 903-2000. FAX: (908) 903-2027. www.chubb.com
V.P. WORLDWIDE ENTERTAINMENT MANAGER
Gene Williams

For more than 40 years, Chubb has been underwriting film productions. From film to video, analog to digital, and SD to HD, Chubb has provided protection to film producers over the years for myriad risks and exposures. Chubb's Film Producers risk policy provides essential insurance solutions for a wide variety of productions, including: films, TV productions, commercials, documentaries, music videos, educational films, corporate or institutional productions and commercial still photographers.

COLONY WEST FINANCIAL & INSURANCE

(Property, liability & workers compensation)
Corporate Office: 555 Riverdale Dr., #E, Glendale, CA 91204. TEL: (818) 556-6791. FAX: (888) 503-5553. www.colony-west.com

Orange County: 1855 W. Katella Ave., #325, Orange, CA 92867. TEL: (714) 542-4870. FAX: (888) 943-3681.

San Diego: 2020 Camino del Rio N. #400, San Diego, CA 92108. TEL: (800) 485-5554. FAX: (800) 943-3681.

COPANS & ASSOCIATES

(Production & cast insurance, medical & employee benefits)
5638 Briarcliff Rd., Los Angeles, CA 90068.
TEL: (323) 962-2461. FAX: (323) 962-4942.
CONTACT
Jeff Copans

DEWITT STERN GROUP, INC.

(Insurance)
420 Lexington Ave., Ste. 2700, New York, NY 10170.
TEL: (212) 867-3550. FAX: (212) 949-2293.

DeWitt Stern of California Insurance Services: 801 N. Brand Blvd., Ste. 650, Glendale, CA 91203. TEL: (818) 623-5400. FAX: (818) 623-5500. www.dewittstern.com
MANAGING DIRECTOR
A. LeConte Moore - CMoore@dewittstern.com
SENIOR V.P., NEW YORK
Peter Marshall - pmarshall@dewittstern.com
MANAGING DIRECTOR, CALIFORNIA
John Hamby - jhamby@dewittstern.com

DeWitt Stern is a privately held insurance brokerage and risk advisory specializing in commercial, personal, fine art, employee benefits, FinPro, entertainment and professional liability servics for individuals and mid market clients. In entertainment, provides: contingency coverages, entertainment package policies, special production coverage, other required production coverage & wrap-up coverage.

ENTERTAINMENT BROKERS INTERNATIONAL, A ONEBEACON COMPANY

(International production insurance, contract coverage)
Los Angeles: 10940 Wilshire Blvd., 17th Flr., Los Angeles, CA 90024. TEL: (310) 824-0111. FAX: (310) 824-5733.
email: BCody@ebi-ins.com www.ebi-ins.com

Westlake Village: 5655 N. Lincero Canyon Rd., Ste. 521, Westlake Village, CA 91362. TEL: (818) 889-8290.
FAX: (818) 889-1269.

New York: 77 Water St., New York, NY 10005.
TEL: (212) 307-0111. FAX: (212) 307-0598.

FILM FINANCES, INC.

(A leader in completion guarantee services supplying completion bonds to film, television, digital and interactive productions)
9000 Sunset Blvd., Ste. 1400, Los Angeles, CA 90069.
TEL: (310) 275-7323. FAX: (310) 275-1706.
email: ffi@ffi.com www.ffi-web.com
CO-PRESIDENT
Kurt Woolner - kb@ffi.com
Steve Ransohoff, Esq. - bigsteve@ffi.com
SENIOR V.P., PRODUCTION
Susan Muir - smuir@ffi.com
CHIEF TECHNOLOGY OFFICER
Darcy Weber - darce@ffi.com
V.P., BUSINESS & LEGAL AFFAIRS
Gregory Trattner - gregory@ffi.com
V.P., PRODUCTION
Dave Bennett - db@ffi.com
Steve Berman -sberman@ffi.com
Matt Warren - tangent@ffi.com
VICE PRESIDENT
Paula Schmit - paula@ffi.com
OFFICE MANAGER
Dina Brokaw - dina@ffi.com

ADDITIONAL OFFICES:
U.K. Office: Film Finances, Ltd., 15 Conduit St., London, England W1S 2XJ. TEL: (44 207) 629-6557.
FAX: (44 207) 491-7530.

Australia Office: Film Finances, Inc. (c/o Samson Productions) Pty., Ltd. The Entertainment Quarter, 205/122 Lang Rd., Moore Park, NSW 2021, Australia. TEL: (61 2) 8353-2600.
FAX: (61 2) 8353-2601.

Canada Office: Film Finances Canada, Ltd., 2 Berkley St., Ste. 310,, Toronto, ON M5A-4J5. TEL: (416) 778-6397.
FAX: (416) 406-7418. email: info@filmfinancescanada.com
www.filmfinancescanada.com

Denmark: Film Finances Scandinavia ApS, Gammel Strand 34,1202, Copenhagen K, Denmark.
TEL: 45-33-43 1000. FAX: 45-33-43 1009.

Japan: Film Finances Japan Ltd., 602 Yaesu Duplex Rs 2-29-13 Hacchobori Chuo-ku Tokyo 104-0032, Japan.
TEL: +81-(0)3-3523-9465. FAX: +81-(0)3-3523-9466.

South Africa: Film Finances South Africa, Unit F6 Pinewood Square, Pinewood Office Park, 33 Riley Rd., Woodmead, South Africa. TEL: +27 11 807 0087. FAX: +27 11 807 0247.

FIREMAN'S FUND INSURANCE COMPANY, A COMPANY OF ALLIANZ

(Covering the production of some of the world's biggest movies — and stars — since the "Golden Age" of Hollywood)
Corporate Headquarters: 777 San Marin Dr., Novato, CA 94998. TEL: (800) 227-1700, (415) 899-2000.
FAX: (415) 899-3600. www.firemansfund.com
ENTERTAINMENT INSURANCE CONTACT
Wendy Diaz - (818) 487-6111 askentertainment@ffic.com

Coverages include liability and loss coverage, as well as insurance to cover delays, illness or death of a performer, and a host of other situations that can affect a large-scale entertainment project. Fireman's Fund Insurance also offers additional entertainment-related coverages such as: accounts receivable, antique auto, cameras, electronic equipment, excess & surplus lines, film, fine arts, inland related property, leased property, mobile property, musical instruments and theatrical property. The company works exclusively with independent agents who specialize in handling entertainment clients. If you are interested in Fireman's Fund Entertainment insurance products and services, contact Suzy Wozniak.

GALLAGHER ENTERTAINMENT SERVICES

(Insurance broker)
505 N. Burbank Blvd., Ste. 600, Glendale, CA 91203.
TEL: (818) 539-1220. FAX: (818) 539-1520.
email: brian_kingman@ajg.com www.ajg.com/entertainment
MANAGING DIRECTOR
Brian Kingman, Konrad Dowling, Shirley Griffith-Bourke, Diane Yount
NEW YORK CONTACT
Alice Fay Prine - (800) 355-6014

Company has brokered the insurance for 90% of the American Film Institute's Top 100 Films.

GNW-EVERGREEN INSURANCE SERVICES, LLC

(Production, insurance, D.E.C.E. producers & vendors)
The Alomar Bldg., 16030 Ventura Blvd., Ste. 500, Encino, CA 91436. TEL: (818) 257-7500. www.gnw-evergreen.com
OWNER & COO
Andrew Forchelli - (818) 257-7483
ENTERTAINMENT PRODUCER
Peter Tempkins - (615) 630-7625
HUMAN RESOURCES MANAGER
Linda Kahn - (818) 257-7431

Insurance coverage for location and studio shoots for film and television productions as well as major events like the Emmy(R) Awards.

EVELYN HUDSON INSURANCE

(Low budget & independent production liability insurance)
1355 Westwood Blvd., Ste. 12, Los Angeles, CA 90024.
TEL: (310) 477-0568. FAX: (310) 477-0569.
OWNER & BROKER
Evelyn Hudson

INTERNATIONAL FILM GUARANTORS

2828 Donald Douglas Loop N, 2nd Flr., Santa Monica, CA 90405. TEL: (310) 309-5660. FAX: (310) 309-5696.
email: usinfo@ifgbonds.com www.ifgbonds.com

United Kingdom: 19 Margaret St., London W1W 8RR.
TEL: +44 20 7636 8855. FAX: +44 20 7323 9356.
email: ukinfo@ifgbonds.co.uk
CEO
Steven Mangel (California) - smangel@ifgbonds.com
SENIOR V.P., PRODUCTION FINANCE
Pat Mealiffe - pmealiff@ifgbonds.com
SENIOR V.P., PRODUCTION
Frank Isaac - fisaac@ifgbonds.com
Michael Levine - mlevine@ifgbonds.com
SENIOR V.P., POST PRODUCTION
Michael Harker - mharker@ifgbonds.com
SENIOR V.P., BUSINESS AFFAIRS
Steven Leib - sleib@ifgbonds.com
V.P., DISTRIBUTION
Andy Coleman - acoleman@ifgbonds.com
OFFICE MANAGER
Julie Westby - jwestby@ifgbonds.com
MANAGING DIRECTOR, IFG LONDON
Luke Randolph - luke.randolph@ifgbonds.co.uk

Established in 1990, IFG has written more than $11.5 billion in completion guaranties for more than 575 films. In 2007, IFG began providing completion guaranties to the interactive entertainment industry. IFG is a wholly owned subsidiary of Fireman's Fund Insurance Company, the market leading insurer of major

Hollywood film productions. Fireman's Fund is part of Allianz AG, one of the largest, strongest and most respected financial services firms in the world.

LA XCESS INSURANCE BROKERS, INC.

(An affiliate of DeWitt Stern Group)
National Entertainment Wholesalers, 10474 Santa Monica Blvd., Ste. 306, Los Angeles, CA 90025-6931.
TEL: (800) 995-9170, (818) 623-5410. FAX: (818) 623-5510.
email: insurance@laxcess.com www.laxcess.com
PRESIDENT
Richard Rutkin
V.P.
Aaron M. Ma - ama@laxcess.com
ASSISTANT V.P.
Jodi Riggins - jriggins@laxcess.com

Within the entertainment industry L.A.Xcess Insurance Brokers, Inc. specializes in production companies, equipment rental houses, theatrical troupes, musical groups, promoters, venues, shell corporations, post production houses, Internet content providers and website developers. They also offer coverage for "DICE"— Documentaries, Industrial, Commercial and Educational) production companies with film shoots of under 30 days.

ALLEN LAWRENCE & ASSOCIATES, INC.

(Entertainment insurance)
7033 Owensmouth Ave., P.O. Box 7948, Canoga Park, CA 91309-7948. TEL: (800) 995-9170, (818) 704-0700.
FAX: (818) 348-5472. email: information@allenlawrence.com
www.allenlawrence.com
CHAIRMAN & CEO
Allen Lawrence
PRESIDENT & COO
George E. Martini

A leader in commercial insurance, surety, employee benefits and services. Staff provides service in loss control, occupational safety & health engineering, risk and claims management and human resources consulting. Provides competitive traditional insurance options as well as custom-designed, proprietary alternative risk programs including captives and self-insured groups.

MANAGEMENT BROKERS INSURANCE AGENCY

(Group & individual life & disability)
9301 Wilshire Blvd., Ste. 206, Beverly Hills, CA 90210.
TEL: (310) 278-5943. FAX: (310) 278-6285.
PRESIDENT
Richard Horowitz
FINANCE EXECUTIVE
Jean Latimer

MARSH, INC.

(Liability, entertainment property)
777 S. Figueroa St., Ste. 2200, Los Angeles, CA 90017.
TEL: (213) 624-5555. FAX: (213) 346-5928. www.marsh.com
GLOBAL ENTERTAINMENT PRACTICE LEADER
Diane Valencia - diane.g.valencia@marsh.com (213) 346-5055
MEDIA CONTACT
Al Modugno - Alfred.J.Modugno@marsh.com

Risk management services. Works on clients' behalf to negotiate traditional business coverages such as property and liability, errors and omissions and specialty coverage for the entertainment industry, including: cast coverage, negative film/faulty stock, aircraft liability, railroad protective liability insurance, watercraft coverage, animal mortality, weather insurance, event cancellation coverage, prize indemnity and advertising wrap-up.Marsh has 24,000 employees and provides advice and transactional capabilities to clients in over 100 countries. Marsh is a unit of Marsh & McLennan Companies (MMC), a global professional services firm with more than 54,000 employees and annual revenue exceeding $11 billion. See website for global office locations.

MARSHALL ENTERTAINMENT INSURANCE, INC.

(Maroevich, O'Shea & Coghlan Insurance)
2000 Universal Studios Plaza, Ste. 625, Orlando, FL 32819.
TEL: (407) 363-1537. FAX: (407) 352-3308.
email: kpm@marshallentertainment.com
www.marshallentertainment.com
PRESIDENT & CEO
Karen Marshall

Coverages include: General liability, professional liability, third party property damage liability, auto liability, completion bonds, worker's compensation, cast insurance, props-sets-wardrobe, non-owned aircraft liability, watercraft, miscellaneous equipment, faulty film-tape-processing-editing, non-appearance, venue insurance, extra expense, animal mortality, bad weather, guild/union travel accident and negative film/video. Producers packages are available.

MOC INSURANCE SERVICES

(Insurance & risk management to the entertainment industry)
44 Montgomery St., 17th Flr., San Francisco, CA 94104.
TEL: (800) 951-0600. FAX: (415) 957-0577. www.mocins.com
CEO & PRESIDENT
Van Maroevich
SENIOR V.P., ENTERTAINMENT
Steve Elkins - (415) 357-9222 selkins@mocins.com

PETERSEN INTERNATIONAL UNDERWRITERS

23929 Valencia Blvd., Ste. 215, Valencia, CA 91355.
TEL: (800) 345-8816, (661) 254-0006. FAX: (661) 254-0604.
email: piu@piu.org www.piu.org
PRINCIPAL
W. Harold Petersen, Michael Petersen, Mark Petersen, Thomas Petersen

D.R. REIFF & ASSOCIATES

(Insurance brokers to the Entertainment Industry)
320 W. 57th St., New York, NY 10019. TEL: (800) 827-7363, (212) 603-0231. FAX: (212) 247-0739.
www.reiffinsurance.com
CONTACT
Dennis Reiff - reiffd@reiffinsurance.com

REYNOLDS & REYNOLDS, INC.

(Insurance brokers; movie theatre specialists. NATO endorsed agent)
300 Walnut St., Ste. 200, Des Moines, IA 50309-2244.
TEL: (800) 767-1724. FAX: (515) 243-6664.
email: info@reynolds-reynolds.com
V.P.
Sandy Bell - (515) 557-1209
V.P.
Stan W. Reynolds - (515) 557-1234

MAURICE TAYLOR INSURANCE BROKERS, INC.

(Entertainment insurance)
P.O. Box 29127, Los Angeles, CA 90029-0127.
TEL: (323) 662-9110. FAX: (323) 660-0749.
email: mtinsbkr@aol.com
PRESIDENT
Maurice Taylor

TAYLOR & TAYLOR ASSOCIATES, INC.

(Entertainment coverage, film, TV, video & photography)
New York: 16 E. 40th St., 11th Flr., New York, NY 10016.
TEL: (212) 490-8511. FAX: (212) 490-7236.
www.taylorinsurance.com
PRESIDENT
Scott Taylor

California: 15060 Ventura Blvd., Ste. 210, Sherman Oaks, CA 91403. TEL: (818) 981-9700. FAX: (818) 981-9703.

TRAVELERS

Travelers Encore Entertainment, c/o Securities Dept., One Tower Sq., Hartford, CT 06183. TEL: (860) 277-0111.
www.travelers.com/business/nationalprograms/entertainment/index.aspx
REGIONAL V.P., WESTERN REGION
Yvonne Cordova - 818.409.4050 ytcordov@travelers.com
CHIEF UNDERWRITING OFFICER
Kevin Topper - 818.409.4060 kmtopper@travelers.com
MANAGING DIRECTOR, EASTERN REGION
Eric Oxboel - (917) 778-6461 eoxboel@travelers.com
MANAGING DIRECTOR, MIDWESTERN REGION
Frank Lothenbach - (651) 310-2156 flothenb@@travelers.com

INQUIRIES OUTSIDE U.S.:
CANADA:
Travelers. Ste. 200, 20 Queen St. W, P.O. Box 5, Toronto, ON M5H 3R3. TEL: (416) 366-8301.
CONTACT
Lynne Pepper - lpepper@travelers.com

UK:
Travelers Insurance Co., Ltd., 60 Gracechurch St., London EC3V 0HR GBR. TEL: +44 020-7645-4100.
CONTACT
Alex (Jonathan) Clegg - aclegg@travelers.com

IRELAND:
Travelers Insurance Co., Ltd., Block 1, Harcourt Centre, Harcourt St., Dublin 2 IRL. TEL: +00-3531-609-5600.
CONTACT
David J. Bourke - dbourke@travelers.com

Since 1997, Travelers Encore Entertainment has provided all facets of the entertainment industry with highly specialized insurance coverage and service.

UNION BANK OF CALIFORNIA

Entertainment Division, 9460 Wilshire Blvd., Beverly Hills, CA 90212. TEL: (310) 550-6500. FAX: (310) 550-6447.
V.P., MANAGER
Bryan J. LaCour

UNITED AGENCIES, INC.

301 E. Colorado Blvd., Ste. 200, Pasadena, CA 91101.
TEL: (800) 800-5880, (626) 535-8318. FAX: (626) 577-1346.

email: mail@unitedagencies.com www.unitedagencies.com

GENERAL MANAGER
Joan Panasiti - jpanasiti@unitedagencies.com
ENTERTAINMENT DEPARTMENT MANAGER
Nick Latshaw - (818) 295-2268

United Agencies has been providing Entertainment Insurance to clients for over 25 years. Whether insuring a generator, an editing system or a camera package, the agency has the expertise and connections to provide clients with the proper coverage. The agency specializes in serving the insurance needs of: rental houses, post production facilities, documentary and commercial production and vehicle rental companies.

THE WATKINS GROUP & ASSOCIATES, LLC

(Life insurance, retirement, disability, tax deferred, estate planning & annuities)
5120 W. Goldleaf Cir., Ste. 170, Los Angeles, CA 90056.
TEL: (323) 782-8991. FAX: (323) 291-4026.
SENIOR PARTNER
Cedric L. Watkins II, J.D., M.B.A., C.F.P.

WELLS FARGO INSURANCE SERVICES

520 Pike St., Ste. 2000, Seattle, WA 98101.
TEL: (800) 876-0505, (206) 701-5811. FAX: (206) 701-5100.
www.wellsfargo.com
EXECUTIVE V. P. - WEST
H. David Wood -(602) 381-2944
david_wood@wellsfargois.com
REGIONAL MARKETING DIRECTOR, SOUTHERN CALIFORNIA
Sam Elliott - (310) 543-9995

Brokerage professionals who work with clients and insurance underwriters. Wells Fargo Insurance Services professionals insure a wide variety of communications risks, working with the following kinds of organizations: advertising agencies, digital media, entertainment, Internet services, multimedia companies, special events and broadcasting companies.

MARKET RESEARCH & ANALYSIS

ARBITRON INC. (NYSE: ARB)

Headquarters: 142 W. 57th St., New York, NY 10019.
TEL: (212) 887-1300. FAX: (212) 887-1390, (212) 887-1558.
www.arbitron.com
PRESIDENT & CEO
William T. Kerr
EXECUTIVE V.P., U.S. MEDIA SERVICES & CFO
Sean Creamer
EXECUTIVE V.P. & CHIEF LEGAL OFFICER
Tim Smith
EXECUTIVE V.P., CHIEF SALES & MARKETING OFFICER
Carol Hanley
EXECUTIVE V.P. ORGANIZATION EFFECTIVENESS & CORPORATE COMMUNICATIONS
Marilou Legge
SENIOR V.P., ENGINEERING & CHIEF TECHNOLOGY OFFICER
Taymoor Arshi
CHIEF STATISTICAL OFFICER
Al Tupek

Arbitron offers market research for cable TV, the Internet and outdoor advertising.

ROBERT A. BRILLIANT, INC.

(TV, film & promotion research)
13245 Riverside Dr., #530, Sherman Oaks, CA 91423.
TEL: (818) 386-6600. FAX: (818) 990-9007.
email: rabcorp@rab-inc.com
PRESIDENT
Robert A. Brilliant

CERTIFIED REPORTS, INC.

(A Market Force Company)
26 Tech Valley Dr., E. Greenbush, NY 12061.
TEL: (518) 758-6400. FAX: (518) 758-6451.
www.certifiedreports.com
PRESIDENT
Jim Radcliff

Nationwide theatrical checking: trailer, lobby patron counts; promotional materials installations.

CINEMASCORE

8812 Rainbow Ridge Dr., Las Vegas, NV 89117.
TEL: (702) 255-9460.
MANAGER
Harold Mintz

CinemaScore conducts film audience surveys, asking moviegoers to assign a letter grade of A to F to the film they just viewed. It also conducts surveys to determine other audience views and preferences. It conducts a demographic breakdown of its survey results and sells this information to interested film industry companies.

EXHIBITOR RELATIONS CO., INC.

(Box-office tracking)
1262 Westwood Blvd., Los Angeles, California 90024.
TEL: (310) 441-7400. FAX: (310) 475-0316.
email: info@ercboxoffice.com www.ercboxoffice.com

EXPERIAN SIMMONS

(Formerly known as Simmons Market Research Bureau)
29 Broadway, New York, NY 10006. TEL: (212) 863-4500.
FAX: (212) 863-4495. www.smrb.com
GENERAL MANAGER
Ken Wollenberg
SENIOR V.P., ECR BUSINESS DEVELOPMENT
Gary Warech - Gary.Warech@experian.com

Simmons Market Research Bureau and OTX, one of the world's leading online market research companies, introduced Movie BehaviorGraphicsTM. The service creates a link between OTX's "Movie Dailies," an awareness and interest tracker in the motion picture business, and the Simmons National Consumer Study (NCS), which includes everything from products people buy and brands they prefer, to their lifestyles, attitudes and media preferences.

THE GALLUP ORGANIZATION

502 Carnegie Center, Ste. 300, Princeton, NJ 08540.
TEL: (609) 924-9600. FAX: (609) 927-2541. www.gallup.com

World Headquarters: 901 F St., N.W., Washington, D.C. 20004.
TEL: (202) 715-3030. FAX: (202) 715-3045.
CHAIRMAN, PRESIDENT & CEO
James K. Clifton
VICE CHAIRMAN OF RESEARCH & CONSULTING
Gale Muller
WORLDWIDE CONTACT/GALLUP ORGANIZATION
Sarah Van Allen - email: sarah_van_allen@gallup.com

GFK GROUP (GERMAN: GFK)

Marion Eisenblätter, Nordwestring 101, 90319 Nuremberg, Germany. TEL: (49 911) 395-2440. FAX: (49 911) 395-2686.
email: media@gfk.com www.gfk.com/media
MEDIA SECTOR
William R. Wessels

European market research firm, which tracks consumers' tastes in and purchases of grocery and nonfood items, broadcast media, and other merchandise and services worldwide.

HOOVER'S, INC.

(Provides comprehensive company, industry and market intelligence)
5800 Airport Blvd., Austin, TX 78752. TEL: (512) 374-4500.
FAX: (512) 374-4501. www.hoovers.com
PRESIDENT
Hyune Hand
EXECUTIVE V.P., MARKETING
Peter Poulin
EXECUTIVE V.P., SALES
Karen Kennedy
V.P., TECHNOLOGY
Mamie Jones
V.P., ADVERTISING SALES & OPERATIONS
Mark Walters

JOAN PEARCE RESEARCH ASSOCS.

(Errors and omissions clearance; legal services)
8111 Beverly Blvd., #308, Los Angeles, CA 90048.
TEL: (323) 655-5464. FAX: (323) 655-4770.
MANAGER
Callista Card

NEXT REALTY

(Market studies, feasibility reports, film zone analysis for exhibitiors)
2 Northfield Plaza, Ste. 320, Northfield, IL 60093.
TEL: (847) 881-2000. FAX: (847) 881-2070.
email: basb1@aol.com
MANAGING PRINCIPAL
Barry A. Schain, Robert Caplin

NIELSEN

NIELSEN ENTERTAINMENT PRACTICE

(Box office tracking and anaylsis systems)
6255 Sunset Blvd., 19th Flr., Hollywood, CA 90028.
TEL: (323) 860-4600. FAX: (323) 860-4610.
www.nielsenedi.com
PRESIDENT, GLOBAL MEDIA CLIENT SERVICES
Dave Thomas

The Nielsen Entertainment Practice provides consistent, in-depth and up-to-the minute identification and analysis of your entertainment product. Nielsen: measures mobile entertainment sales; tracks music and music-video product sales as well radio-station music plays; monitors in-home entertainment through DVD and video sales; provides research solutions for motion pictures (projects and industry); tests pilots and episodes for television products; collects, monitors and analyzes retail book sales; conducts audience measurement and seeks consumer insights for Console and PC video gaming.

NIELSEN IAG RESEARCH

345 Park Ave. S, 12th Flr., New York, NY 10010.
TEL: (212) 871-5200. FAX: (212) 871-5300. www.iagr.net

Los Angeles: 1801 Century Park West, Los Angeles, CA 90067. TEL: (310) 277-5555. FAX: (310) 277-5010.
EXECUTIVE V.P. & CHIEF RESEARCH OFFICER
Paul Donato

Nielsen IAG collects metrics about every ad, product placement, and program sponsorship occurring across all broadcast and major cable networks during primetime.

NIELSEN MEDIA RESEARCH, INC.

770 Broadway, 15th Flr., New York, NY 10003.
TEL: (646) 654-8300. www.nielsenmedia.com
VICE CHAIRMAN, NIELSEN MEDIA RESEARCH & EXECUTIVE V.P., THE NIELSEN COMPANY
Susan D. Whiting
PRESIDENT, MEDIA PRODUCTS
Stever Hasker
PRESIDENT, MEDIA CLIENT SERVICES
Dave Thomas

A business unit of VNU. Nielsen Media Research – U.S. Nielsen Media Research is the leading provider of TV audience measurement and related services in the United States. Local rating services estimate audiences for each of 210 television markets in the U.S., including electronic metered service in 54 markets. Nielsen Media Research also provides competitive advertising intelligence information through Nielsen Monitor-Plus, and Internet usage and advertising information through Nielsen/NetRatings.

PLUNKETT RESEARCH, LTD.

P.O. Drawer 541737, Houston, TX 77254-1737. TEL: (713) 932-0000.
FAX: (713) 932-7080. email: customersupport@plunkettresearch.com
www.plunkettresearch.com
CEO & PUBLISHER
Jack W. Plunkett

Plunkett Research, Ltd. is a leading provider of industry sector analysis and research, industry trends and industry statistics. Fee-based research reports and online subscription services include Entertainment Industry research & analysis. Plunkett Research, Ltd. was established in 1985.

QUIGLEY PUBLISHING COMPANY

P.O. Box 740, Groton, MA 01450. TEL: (978) 448-0272.
FAX: (978) 448-9325. www.quigleypublishing.com
PUBLISHER
William J. Quigley

A div. of QP Media, Inc. Publishers of The International Motion Picture Almanac and The International Television & Video Almanac. The International Motion Picture Almanac, published annually since 1930, includes thousands of company listings, credits for current films and films released in the prior five years, statistics and awards, and complete coverage of all aspects of the Industry, including production, distribution and exhibition. The International Television & Video Almanac is the companion to The International Motion Picture Almanac and has been published since 1955. Each edition contains over 500 pages of biographies and an additional 600 pages of reference material on television programs, broadcast, cable and satellite, production services, the video industry, statistics and awards. Included are detailed listings for thousands of companies.

RENTRAK CORP.

(Business intelligence for the entertainment industry)
7700 N.E. Ambassador Pl., 3rd Flr., Portland, OR 97220.
TEL: (503) 284-7581. FAX: (503) 331-2734.
email: sales@rentrak.com www.rentrak.com

Rentrak Theatrical Unit/Los Angeles, CA: 15000 Ventura Blvd., Ste. 201, Sherman Oaks, CA 91403. TEL: (818) 728-8880.
CEO
Bill Livek
PRESIDENT & CHIEF STRATEGY OFFICER
Kenneth Papagan
COO & CFO
David Chemerow
EXECUTIVE V.P., INFORMATION TECHNOLOGY & CHIEF INFORMATION OFFICER
Amir Yazdani
PRESIDENT, AMI DIVISION
Cathy Hetzel
EXECUTIVE V.P., THEATRICAL WORLDWIDE
Ron Giambra
SENIOR V.P., HOME ENTERTAINMENT MEDIA & IS
Christopher Roberts
PRESIDENT, PPT DIVISION
Marty Graham
SENIOR V.P., SALES & CUSTOMER RELATIONS
Timothy Erwin

SNL KAGAN

(Research and analysis of entertainment, communications and media industries)
1 Lower Ragsdale, Bldg. 1 - Ste. 130, Monterey, CA 93940.
TEL: (831) 624-1536. FAX: (831) 625-3225.
email: SNLKaganSales@kagan.com www.snl.com/kagan
SENIOR V.P., ENTERTAINMENT & PROGRAMMING
Derek Baine
SENIOR V.P. & MEDIA EXPERT/BROADCAST & CABLE TV
Robin Flynn
ANALYST/TELEVISION PROGRAMMING/VALUATION OF TELEVISION CONTENT LIBRARIES
Deana Myers
SENIOR ANALYST, MEDIA & TELECOM SECTORS
Sharon Armbrust
LEAD CABLE ANALYST
IanI Olgeirson
SENIOR ANALYST, INTERNATIONAL MEDIA MARKETS
Ben Reneker

See website for additional offices.

VMS

(News monitoring, keyword back-searches; integrated media intelligence services)
Corporate Headquarters: 1500 Broadway, New York, NY 10036. TEL: (800) VMS-2002. email: sales@vmsinfo.com
www.vmsinfo.com

California Office: 6430 W. Sunset Blvd., #400, Los Angeles, CA 90028. TEL: (323) 762-2000. FAX: (323) 762-2038.
email: lasales@vmsinfo.com www.vmsinfo.com
CEO
Peter Wengryn
COO
Jonathan Cape
PRESIDENT, PROFESSIONAL SERVICES DIVISION
James Waggoner
SENIOR V.P., NEWS SALES
Roy H. McInnis
SENIOR V.P., ADVERTISING SERVICES SALES
Leslie Stubin
SENIOR V.P., BROADCAST MEDIA & AFFILIATE RELATIONS
Joseph Scotti
CHIEF MARKETING OFFICER
Michael Giovia

See website for additional office locations.

Sound Studios & Services

2B PRODUCTIONS, INC.
(Full-service audio post production facility specializing in sound design and mixing)
1674 Broadway, Ste. 902, New York, NY 10019.
TEL: (212) 765-8202. FAX: (212) 765-8234.
email: kaizad@2binc.com www.2binc.com

AB AUDIO VISUAL ENT., INC.
(Audio post production, sound design, music compostion, editing, non-linear video editing & equipment rentals)
3765 Marwick Ave., Long Beach, CA 90808.
TEL: (562) 429-1042. FAX: (562) 429-2401.
email: arlan@abaudio.com www.abaudio.com
PRESIDENT
Arlan H. Boll

ABSOLUTE POST
2633 N. San Fernando Blvd., Burbank, CA 91504.
TEL: (818) 842-7966. FAX: (818) 842-8815.
www.absolutepost.tv
OWNER
Dave Rosen
SUPERVISING SOUND EDITOR/RE-RECORDING MIXER
Mike Draghi
STUDIO COORDINATOR
Misty Tamburelli
SOUND EDITOR
Kyle Claussen
SOUND EDITING, MIXING AND MUSIC PRODUCTION
Tracy Bartelle

Film sound mixing & rerecording; recording studio; sound editing; sound effects library; sound post facility; sound transfer service; video audio mixing & sweetening.

AL MEDIA MOVERS, INC.
10444 Magnolia Blvd., North Hollywood, CA 91601.
TEL/FAX: (310) 237-6438. email: info@media-movers.com
www.media-movers.com
CONTACT
Lawrence Vishnu

Dubbing (Lip-sync & U.N.Style), Subtitling, Voiceovers, Closed Captioning, Translation & Transcription in all Asian, Indian, European, African & Middle-Eastern languages for all media formats.

ALLIED POST AUDIO
1642 17th St., Santa Monica, CA 90404. TEL: (310) 392-8280.
email: info@alliedpost.com www.alliedpost.com
OWNERS
Woody Woodhall, Wendy Woodhall

Audio post production and recording studio for film,TV, commercials, radio, Internet & multimedia. Services include soundmixing & sweetening; sound editing; sound effects library; ADR; voiceovers; foley & music editing.

AMERAYCAN RECORDING STUDIOS
5719 Lankershim Blvd., N. Hollywood, CA 91601.
TEL: (818) 760-8733. FAX: (818) 760-2524.
www.paramountrecording.com

APM MUSIC
6255 Sunset Blvd., Ste. 820, Hollywood, CA 90028.
TEL: (800) 543-4276, (323) 461-3211. FAX: (323) 461-9102.
www.apmmusic.com
ACCOUNT EXECUTIVES
Bruce Amdur, Lauren Bell, Brian Brasher, Rob Cairns, Deborah Fisher, Bob Frymire, Craig Gruimmarra, Matthew Gulknecht, George Maloian, Adam Kane Norcott, Marsha Still, Tia Sommer, Giselle Vaseonez

THE AUDIO DEPARTMENT
(Audio recording & mixing)
119 W. 57th St., 4th Flr., Ste. 400, New York, NY 10019.
TEL: (212) 586-3503. FAX: (212) 245-1675.
www.theaudiodepartment.com

AUDIO MECHANICS
(Sound restoration and noise reduction)
1200 W. Magnolia Blvd., Burbank, CA 91506.
TEL: (818) 846-5525. email: info@audiomechanics.com
www.audiomechanics.com
CONTACT
John Polito

AUDIOBANKS
(Recording studio; sound editing; sound effects library; video audio mixing & sweetening)
1660 9th St., Santa Monica, CA 90404. TEL: (310) 581-1660.
FAX: (310) 581-1661. email: info@audiobanks.com

AVID TECHNOLOGY, INC.
(Motion picture film editing equipment)
101 S. First St., Ste. 200, Burbank, CA 91502.
TEL: (818) 557-2520. FAX: (818) 557-2558. www.avid.com

New York: 575 Lexington Ave., 14th Flr., New York, NY 10022.
TEL: (212) 983-2424. FAX: (212) 983-8718.

With Mainstream HD Editorial: Media Composer Nitris DX, Media Composer Mojo DX. See website for additional offices.

BELL SOUND STUDIO
(Film sound mixing & rerecording)
916 N. Citrus Ave., Los Angeles, CA 90038.
TEL: (323) 461-3036. FAX: (323) 461-8764.
email: bellsound@bellsound.com www.bellsound.com

CAPITOL STUDIOS & MASTERING
(Recording studio & scoring stage)
1750 N. Vine St., Hollywood, CA 90028. TEL: (323) 871-5001.
FAX: (323) 871-5058.
STUDIO DIRECTOR, RECORDING & MIXING
Paula Salvatore - paula.salvatore@capitolstudios.com
MASTERING
Matt Graber - matt.graber@captiolstudios.com

CHACE AUDIO BY DELUXE
(Audio post production & sound restoration; acquired by Deluxe Digital Media July 1, 2009)
201 S. Victory Blvd., Burbank, CA 91502. TEL: (800) 842-8346, (818) 842-8346. FAX: (818) 842-8353. www.chace.com
V.P. AUDIO, DELUXE DIGITAL MEDIA AND HEAD OF CHACE
Bob Heiber - bobheiber@chace.com
GENERAL MANAGER
James Eccles - jameseccles@chace.com
TECHNICAL OPERATIONS MANAGER
Chris Reynolds - chrisreynolds@chace.com

Services include: audio compression, dubbing, editorial, film inspection & repair, optical sound recording, optical soundtrack negative playback-COSPTM, restoration & revitalization, sound transfers, synchronization/conforms.

CLAY DIGITAL SOUND
(Sound editorial services)
3610 W. Magnolia Blvd., Burbank, CA 91505.
TEL: (323) 876-3477.
CONTACT
Paul Clay - paulbclay@aol.com

CLOUD NINETEEN
3767 Overland Ave., Ste. 104, Los Angeles, CA 90034.
TEL: (310) 839-5400. FAX: (310) 839-5404.
email: info@cloud19.com www.cloud19.com
PRESIDENT
Scott Boutté
TECHNICAL DIRECTOR
Bray Merritt

Film sound mixing & rerecording; recording studio; sound editing; sound post facility. Full post production services.

CREATIVE MEDIA RECORDING
(Audio post production for video)
11105 Knott Ave., Ste. G, Cypress, CA 90630. TEL: (714) 892-9469.
email: timkeenan@creativemediarecording.com
info@creativemediarecording.com
www.creativemediarecording.com
OPERATIONS DIRECTOR
Tim Keenan
PRODUCTION COORDINATOR
Linda Keenan

Services include: Audio sweetening for video, narration recording, ISDN capabilities, sound effects and Foley, location sound clean-up, production music scores, audio for radio and TV spots.

CRESCENDO STUDIOS
(Audio post production & commercial spots)
615 Battery St., Ste. 500, San Francisco, CA 94111.
TEL: (415) 834-0580. FAX: (415) 834-0599.
email: info@crescendostudios.com www.crescendostudios.com
OWNER
Laurence J. Hyman
DIRECTOR OF OPERATIONS
Jason Plunkett
PRODUCER
McKell Smith
SENIOR ENGINEER & TECHNICAL DIRECTOR
Craig Helmholz
SENIOR ENGINEER
Erik Motyl, Matt Wood

CREST DIGITAL
Corporate Headquarters: 3845 E. Coronado St., P.O. Box 68057, Anaheim, CA 92807. TEL: (800) 309-3472. www.crestdigital.com

Post Services: 1000 N. Highland Ave., Hollywood, CA 90038. TEL: (800) 961-TAPE, (323) 860-1300. FAX: (323) 461-8901.
CONTACT
David Cipes, Jon Truckenmiller

Recording studio; sound editing; sound effects library; sound post facility; sound transfer service; video audio mixing & sweetening.

DB SOUND & MUSIC
(Post production for film & TV sound editing)
TEL: (310) 467-5991. email: bondelev@mac.com
PRESIDENT
David J. Bondelevitch

Bondelevitch is an assistant professor, V.P of the Cinema Audio Society and a former president, Motion Picture Sound Editors. He maintains a blog at: http://Bondelev.Blogspot.com/

DELUXE DIGITAL MEDIA
(Post production)
200 S. Flower St., Burbank CA 91502. TEL: (206) 521-9193 (Seattle), (818) 557-0070 (Burbank).
CONTACT
Andy Pratt - andy.pratt@bydeluxe.com

Digital restoration & distribution; audio layback; aspect ratio manipulation (HD, NTSC, PAL); automated broadcast duplication (data to data, video to data, video to video, data to video); climate-controlled vault for active videotape master storage; DVD specialty authoring & distribution; editorial TV formatting; encoding HD, SD, Hi-resolution; HD upconversions, downconversions, cross conversions; international broadcast distribution; NTSC/PAL standards & format conversions.

DEWOLFE MUSIC
25 W. 45th St., Ste. 401,New York, NY 10036.
TEL: (212) 382-0220. FAX: (212) 382-0278.
email: info@dewolfemusic.com www.dewolfemusic.com
CEO
Andrew Jacobs
PRESIDENT
Marcie Jacobs
LICENSING COORDINATOR
Valerie Sene

WALT DISNEY STUDIOS POST PRODUCTION — SOUND
(Sound editing; sound effects library)
500 S. Buena Vista St., Casting Bldg., Burbank, CA 91521.
CONTACT
Sound Editorial - (818) 560-7525
Dubbing - (818) 560-1576
Editorial, Sound - (818) 560-5233
Sound Transfer - (818) 560-1135.
FAX: (818) 562-3262. email: studiooperations@disneyonline.com
http://studioservices.go.com/postproduction/index.html
VICE PRESIDENT
Gil Gagnon
BUENA VISTA SOUND
MANAGER, SOUND SCHEDULING-DUBBING
PJ Aminpour
SENIOR MANAGER, DVD & SOUND TRANSFER
Glenn Ragland
DIRECTOR, ENGINEERING
Steve Boze
PROJECTION SCHEDULING
Sal Valletta
ADR SCHEDULING
Dawn Biro

DOLBY LABORATORIES, INC.
(Dolby Laboratories develops & delivers products & technologies that make the entertainment experience more realistic)
100 Potrero Ave., San Francisco, CA 94103-4886.
TEL: (415) 558-0200. FAX: (415) 863-1373. www.dolby.com
CHAIRMAN & FOUNDER
Ray Dolby
PRESIDENT & CEO
Kevin Yeaman
EXECUTIVE V.P. & GENERAL COUNSEL
Mark Anderson
SENIOR V.P., HUMAN RESOURCES
Andrew Dahlkemper
EXECUTIVE V.P. & CFO
Murray J. Demo
EXECUTIVE V.P., SALES & MARKETING
Ramzi Haidamus
EXECUTIVE V.P., PRODUCTS & TECHNOLOGIES
Michael Rockwell
SENIOR V.P.
Ioan Allen
SENIOR V.P., SALES
J. Stuart Mitchell
SENIOR V.P., MARKETING
Robin Selden
SENIOR V.P., CHIEF TECHNOLOGY OFFICER
Craig Todd

DOLBY PRODUCTION SERVICES GROUP
Dolby Burbank: 3601 W. Alameda Ave., Burbank, CA 91505-5300. TEL: (818) 823-2800.

Dolby New York: 1350 Ave. of the Americas, 28th Flr., New York, NY 10019. TEL: (212) 767-1700.

Dolby Wootton Bassett: Wootton Bassett Wiltshire SN4 8QJ England. TEL: +44 1793 842100.

Production services for motion picture professionals. See website for additional offices.

EDGEWOOD STUDIOS
Howe Center, Unit 12B Ste. 90, Rutland, VT 05701.
TEL: (802) 773-0510. FAX: (802) 773-3481.
email: david@edgewoodstudios.com
www.edgewoodstudios.com
CONTACT
David Giancola

Full-service production facility/equipment rental, production services for hire, music publishers, feature film trailer editing.

FORTITUDE STUDIOS
(Sound editing; sound effects library; video audio mixing & sweetening)
727 N. Victory Blvd., Burbank, CA 91502. TEL: (818) 842-0820.

FOX STUDIOS POST PRODUCTION SERVICES
10201 Pico Blvd., Los Angeles, CA 90035. TEL: (310) 369-7678, Sound Mixing: (310) 369-5665. FAX: (310) 339-4407.
email: foxinfo@fox.com www.foxstudios.com
AUDIO TRANSFER - (310) 369-7678
ADR - (310) 369-5665
FOLEY/SCORING/SOUND EDITORIAL/SOUND MIXING - (310) 369-5655

FULL HOUSE STUDIOS
(Full-service audio recording studio)
630 9th Ave., New York, NY 10036.
TEL: (212) 645-2228. FAX: (212) 627-2838.
www.fullhouseny.com

GLOBUS BROTHERS STUDIOS
44 W. 24th St., New York, NY 10010. TEL: (212) 243-1008.
www.globus.cc

HENSON RECORDING STUDIOS
(Recording studio: four studios & mix room)
1416 N. La Brea Ave., Hollywood, CA 90028.
TEL: (323) 856-6680. FAX: (323) 856-2712.
www.hensonrecording.com
STUDIO MANAGER
Faryal Russell - Faryal@hensonrecording.com

JOHN HILL MUSIC
527 3rd Ave., #261, New York, NY 10016.
TEL: (212) 683-2273. email: jhmusic@mindspring.com

West Coast: 4646 Willis Ave., #110, Sherman Oaks, CA 91403. TEL: (818) 986-7197

I.D.E.A.S.
(Integrated creative content studio, full-service facility with HD)
755 Stage Lane, Lake Buena Vista, FL 32830.
TEL: (407) 601-7878. FAX: (407) 560-2830.
CONTACT
John Lux - ext. 1308

IF/X PRODUCTIONS
(Interactive effects)
1840 Eddy St., San Francisco, CA. TEL: (415) 345-8876.
FAX: (415) 345-8905.
PRESIDENT
George Daugherty

JUICE STUDIOS
(Audio production for advertising and entertainment industries, including radio, TV and film)
1648 10th St., Santa Monica, CA 90404. TEL: (310) 460-7830.
FAX: (310) 460-7845. email: oscar@juicewest.com
www.juicewest.com
OPERATIONS MANAGER
Oscar Morales

LARSON STUDIOS
(Audio post-production)
6520 Sunset Blvd., Los Angeles, CA, 90028.
TEL: (323) 469-3986. FAX: (323) 469-8507. www.larson.com
PRESIDENT & CEO
Rick Larson - rick@larson.com

EXECUTIVE V.P.
Jim Henderson - jim@larson.com
V.P., OPERATIONS
Scott Turner - scott@larson.com
V.P., SALES & MARKETING
Richard D. Ellis - rellis@larson.com

Seward Studio: 823 Seward St., Hollywood, CA 90088.

L.A. STUDIOS, INC.

(Film sound mixing & rerecording; video audio mixing & sweetening)
3453 Cahuenga Blvd. West, Hollywood, CA 90068.
TEL: (323) 851-6351. FAX: (323) 876-5347.
email: janec@lastudios.com www.lastudios.com
GENERAL MANAGER/SCHEDULING
Jane Curry

THE LOT

1041 N. Formosa Ave., W. Hollywood, CA 90046.
TEL: (323) 850-3180. FAX: (323) 850-3190.
email: info@thelotstudios.com www.skyepartners.com

Exclusively managed by Skye Partners, Entertainment Real Estate. Sound stage rentals, Screening Rooms, Telecommunications equipment rental, motorized equipment, Lighting and grip rental and more.

CHRIS MANY MUSIC — SILVERSTORM STUDIOS

(Composing)
9441 Vanalden Ave., Northridge, CA 91324.
TEL: (818) 885-0848. FAX: (818) 885-0488.
PRESIDENT
Chris Many
STUDIO MANAGER
Nancy Many

MARGARITA MIX

(Part of The L.A. Studios, Inc.)
1661 Lincoln Blvd., Santa Monica, CA 90404.
TEL: (310) 396-3333. FAX: (310) 396-9633.
PRODUCER
Whitney Warren - whitney.warren@lastudios.com
OFFICE MANAGER
Michele Millard - michele.millard@lastudios.com

Los Angeles/Margarita Mix Hollywood: 6838 Romaine St., Hollywood, CA 90038. TEL: (323) 962-6565.
FAX: (323) 962-8662.
OPERATIONS MANAGER & SCHEDULING
Veneta Butler - veneta.butler@lastudios.com

MERCURY SOUND STUDIOS

632 Thompson Ave., Glendale, CA 91201.
TEL: (818) 545-8090. FAX: (818) 545-8641.
www.mercurysoundstudios.com
PRESIDENT & RE-RECORDING MIXER
Paul Ratajczak
RERECORDING MIXER & CHIEF ENGINEER
Jason Brennan
MANAGING DIRECTOR, STUDIO OPERATIONS
Marcel Lehrer - marcel@mercurysoundstudios.com

Film sound mixing & re-recording, sound editing, ADR and Foley recording. THX, 35mm, video & total automation.

METHOD STUDIOS

(Formerly R!OT)
New York: 218 W. 18th St., 12 Flr., New York, NY 10011.
TEL: (212) 907-1200. FAX: (212) 907-1201.
www.methodstudios.com
CONTACT, NEW YORK
Jay Lichtman - jay@methodstudios.com

California: 730 Arizona Ave., Santa Monica, CA 90401.
TEL: (310) 434-6500. www.methodstudios.com
CONTACT, CALIFORNIA
Gabby Goumier - gabby@methodstudios.com
Robert Owens - robert@methodstudios.com

London: 142 Wardour St., London W1F 8dd UK.
TEL: +44 (0)20 7131 6431. FAX: +44 (0)20 7878 7800.

Ascent Media Group announced in 2009, two of its boutique visual effects studios, Riot and Method, would unite operations under the Method name, to offer clients high-end visual effects for commercials, music videos and feature films. Services include: digital post-production in NTSC and PAL, Telecine HD, Datacine, Inferno, Fire HD, Henry, VYVX capabilities, 3D CGI, scanning and recording, compression & duplication. Recruiting: Send reels to: method-sm-recruiting@methodstudios.com

MUSIC ROOM PICTURES

(Film production, post production, film & video, sound design for interactive toys and games)
525 S. Francisca Ave., Redondo Beach,CA 90277.
TEL: (310) 316-4551, (310) 503-1198 (cell).
email:mrp@aol.com www.musicroomonline.com
PRESIDENT
John Reed

NAMRAC MUSIC

(Music publishing, recording studio & sound stage)
Sound City Center Stage, 15456 Cabrito Rd., Van Nuys, CA 91406. TEL: (818) 304-0573. FAX: (818) 787-3981.
www.soundcitycenterstage.com
PRESIDENT
Tommy R. Skeeter

NAVESYNC, INC.

(Video screening editing; 24 frame video)
74 Kent St., Brooklyn, NY 11222.
TEL: (212) 244-7177.
PRESIDENT
Joe Trammell

NOVASTAR DIGITAL SOUND

(Post production)
6430 Sunset Blvd., #103, Hollywood, CA 90028.
TEL: (323) 467-5020. FAX: (323) 957-8707.
email: contact@novastarpost.com www.novastarpost.com
PRESIDENT
Bob Sky
DIRECTOR OF OPERATIONS
Nav Singh

NT AUDIO

(Recording and developing optical soundtrack negatives)
1833 Centinela Ave., Santa Monica, CA 90404.
TEL: (310) 828-1098. FAX: (310) 828-9737. www.ntaudio.com
PRESIDENT
Tom McCormick
OPERATIONS MANAGER
Jon Seifert - jon@ntaudio.com
Dave Lomino - dave@ntaudio.com
QC THEATER MANAGER
Steve Levy - steve@ntaudio.com

PARAMOUNT RECORDING STUDIOS

(Analogue-to-digital audio recording & sound mastering, post production)
6245 Santa Monica Blvd., Hollywood, CA 90038.
TEL: (323) 465-4000. FAX: (323) 469-1905.
email: info@paramountrecording.com
www.paramountrecording.com
MASTERING ENGINEER
Mike Lazer

PICTURE HEAD

(Post production finishing facility)
1132 Vine St., Hollywood, CA 90038. TEL: (323) 466-2066.
FAX: (323) 466-2717. www.picturehead.com
PRESIDENT
Ray Cecire - ray@picturehead.com

PIERPAOLO TIANO

(Original music; sound editing; sound effects library)
933 Palm Ave., West Hollywood, CA 90069.
TEL: (323) 578-2443. email: info@ptiano.com
www.soundviewmusic.com
CONTACT
Pierpaolo Tiano

POINT 360

(Post production services)
1133 N. Hollywood Way, Burbank, CA 91505.
TEL:(866)968-4336, (818) 556-5700. FAX: (818) 556-5753.
email: sales-burbank@point360.com www.point360.com

Services include: Audio post, digital intermediate, encoding, duplication, edit, graphics, visual effects, telecine & DVD.

POP SOUND

(An Ascent Media company)
625 Arizona Ave., Santa Monica, CA 90401.
TEL: (310) 587-1200. FAX: (310) 587-1222.
email: scheduling@popsound.com www.popsound.com
MANAGING DIRECTOR
Doug Clark - dclark@popsound.com

PRIMALSCREAM MUSIC

(Music and sound for advertising)
1616 Butler Ave., Los Angeles, CA 90025. TEL: (310) 478-8227.
email: info@primalscreammusic.com
www.primalscreammusic.com
CREATIVE DIRECTOR/EXECUTIVE PRODUCER
Nicole Dionne
PRODUCER/SOUND ENGINEER AND MIXER
Scott Burton
SALES
Jim Runge

PRIVATE ISLAND TRAX

1882 S. Cochran Ave., Los Angeles, CA 90019.
TEL: (323) 856-8729.
email: info@privateislandtrax.com

www.privateislandtrax.com
MUSIC PRODUCER/AUDIO POST SUPERVISOR/ RE-RECORDING MIXER, CHIEF ENGINEER
Michael McDonald

Sound editing, sound effects library, sound post facility, sound transfer service, video audio mixing & sweetening, film sound mixing & rerecording, recording studio.

RALEIGH STUDIOS

5300 Melrose Ave., Hollywood, CA 90038.
SCREENING BOOKINGS TEL:(323) 871-5649.
FAX: (323) 871-5600. www.raleighstudios.com
CEO
Linden Nelson
DIRECTOR, POST PRODUCTION
Mike Donahue - MichaelD@raleighstudios.com
GENERAL MANAGER
Yolanda Montellano - (323) 466-3111

Production services department with stage equipment rentals to transportation to set construction and more. Three theatres seating 36, 38, 160 with 35mm and digital projection; and complete catering, reception and event facilities in studio cafe and stages. Multiple facilities in California, Baton Rouge, LA, Detroit, MI, Atlanta, GA, Budapest Hungary.

SHORELINE STUDIOS

(Audio post-production)
100 Wilshire Blvd., Ste. 150, Santa Monica, CA 90401.
TEL: (310) 394-4932. FAX: (310) 458-7802.
email: info@shorelinestudios.com www.shorelinestudios.com

SKYWALKER SOUND

(A LucasFilm Ltd. Company. Audio post production)
P.O. Box 3000, San Rafael, CA 94912. TEL: (415) 662-1000.
FAX: (415) 662-2429. email: info@skysound.com
www.skysound.com
BUSINESS, ADMINISTRATIVE
Phil Benson
DIRECTOR OF OPERATIONS
Josh Lowden

SONY PICTURES POST PRODUCTION

(Post production facilities)
10202 W. Washington Blvd., Culver City, CA 90232.
TEL: (310) 244-5722. FAX: (310) 244-4152.
www.sonypicturespost.com
EXECUTIVE V.P., SOUND, PROJECTION & VIDEO
Richard Branca - (310) 244-5191
EXECUTIVE V.P., THEATRICAL & TV SOUND EDITORIAL
Tom McCarthy - (310) 244-4365
MOTION PICTURE SOUND MIXER
Deb Adair, Bill W. Benton, Chris Carpenter, David Giammarco, Jeffrey J. Haboush, Tateum Kohut, Andy Koyama, Paul Massey, Greg Orloff, Greg P. Russell
TELEVISION SOUND MIXER
John Boyd, William Freesh, Wayne Heitman, Mark Linden, Derek Marcil, Russell Smith Nello Torri

SOUND FACTORY

6357 Selma Ave., Hollywood, CA 90028. TEL: (323) 469-1186.
FAX: (323) 465-5579. email: mail@sunsetsound.com
CONTACT/BOOKING INFORMATION
Craig Hubler

SOUNDCASTLE INTERACTIVE STUDIOS

(Audio recording since 1970)
1334 3rd St. Promenade, Ste. 208, Santa Monica, CA 90401.
TEL: (310) 394-6014. email: soundcastle@earthlink.net
www.soundcastle.com

Services: advertising, e-commerce, web publishing, interactive design, hi-def AV production, multimedia development.

SOUNDELUX

(An Ascent Media company. Post production sound company)
7080 Hollywood Blvd., Ste. 1100, Hollywood, CA 90028.
TEL: (323) 603-3200. FAX: (323) 603-3233.
www.soundelux.com
FOUNDERS
Lon Bender, Wylie Stateman

SOUNDSCAPE PRODUCTIONS

(Audio division of Dubscape, Inc. Dubbing & audio mixing)
7543 Loma Verde Ave., Canoga Park, CA 91303.
TEL: (818) 456-1051.
email: info@dubscape.com www.dubscape.com
CHIEF ENGINEER
Gregg Hall

STARDUST FILM, INC.

(Production sound for motion pictures and television)
7510 Sunset Blvd., #240, Hollywood, CA 90046.
FAX: (818) 753-0769. email: pvm@stardustfilm.com
www.stardustfilm.com
PRESIDENT
Peter V. Meiselmann, C.A.S. - +43 664 11 200 79 (cell, Austria)

STUDIO M PRODUCTIONS UNLIMITED

4032 Wilshire Blvd., #403, Los Angeles, CA 90010.
TEL: (213) 389-7372.
OWNER
Senator Mike Michaels, C.A.S.

SUNSET SOUND

(Recording studio)
6650 Sunset Blvd., Hollywood, CA 90028. TEL: (323) 469-1186.
FAX: (323) 465-5579. email: mail@sunsetsound.com
www.sunsetsound.com
CONTACT/BOOKING INFORMATION
Craig Hubler

TECHNICOLOR

Technicolor has partnered with content creators since 1915. Today, its divisions are comprised of: Creative Services, Digital Productions, Home Entertainment Services & Digital Content Delivery. It maintains offices around the world. Since 2001, Technicolor has been part of the French-headquartered electronics and media conglomerate Thomson.
HEAD, TECHNICOLOR
Lanny Raimondo
HEAD, CREATIVE SERVICES
Joe Berchtold

TECHNICOLOR SOUND

TECHNICOLOR SOUND CONTACTS/U.S.
1117 Isabel St., Burbank, CA 91506. TEL: (818) 524-1327.
CONTACT
Mark Kaplan - mark.kaplan@technicolor.com

Key capabilities of Technicolor sound facilities include: - ADR and voiceover recording, foley, full DVD sound services, full transfer and layback, mixing stages, music and effects, SAP sound services, sound design and editorial and sound restoration, including digital air. Major studios and leading independent production companies rely on Technicolor for a wide base of formats, including feature film, television, documentary, game, commercial, DVD release, trailers and new media. Technicolor's sound facilities are located in: Los Angeles, Toronto, Montreal, London, Rome and Bangkok.

THX LTD.

(Custom engineered cinemas)
1600 Los Gamos Dr., Ste. 231, San Rafael, CA 94903.
TEL: (415) 492-3900. FAX: (415) 492-3988. www.thx.com
GENERAL MANAGER
David Pierce
V.P., TECHNOLOGY
Richard Dean
V.P., SALES
Robert Hewitt
ACCOUNT EXECUTIVE
Andrew Poulain

THX technologies and certification programs are implemented throughout the production chain—from the set and studio to movie theatres and playback devices. THX offers a complete range of digital mastering, certification and custom-tailored quality control (QC) services that give content providers the means to quickly and cost¬effectively introduce high-quality DVD titles to market.

TODD-AO

(Formerly an Ascent Media company, Todd-AO became part of CSS Studios, LLC, a wholly owned division of Discovery Communications in Sept. 2008. It's sister companies: Soundelux, Sound One, Modern Music, POP Sound and The Hollywood Edge are also part of CSS Studios, LLC.)

TODD-AO BURBANK

(Comprehensive post production facility)
2901 W. Alameda Ave., Burbank CA, 91505.
TEL: (818) 840-7225. FAX: (818) 840-7219. www.toddao.com
ENGINEER/OPERATIONS MANAGER
Steve Bartkowicz - (818) 840-7236 sbartkowicz@toddao.com

TODD-AO HOLLYWOOD

(Comprehensive audio post facility)
900 Seward St., Hollywood, CA 90028. TEL: (323) 962-4000.
FAX: (323) 466-4062. www.toddao.com
DIRECTOR, OPERATIONS
Richard Burnette - (323) 962-4050 rburnette@toddao.com
CHIEF ENGINEER
Pat Stoltz - (310) 315-5047 pstoltz@toddao.com
TRANSFERS/LAYBACKS
Nat Suckley - (323) 962-4110 nsuckley@toddao.com

Services include: ADR, re-recording/mixing, transfer, sound design, sound editorial, sound supervision.

TODD-AO WEST

3000 Olympic Blvd., Bldg. 1, Santa Monica, CA 90404.
TEL: (310) 315-5000. FAX: (310) 315-5099. www.toddao.com

OPERATIONS
Matt Dubin - (310) 315-5000 mdubin@toddao.com
Shelly Hovland - (310) 315-5071 shovland@toddao.com
CHIEF ENGINEER
Gary Simpson- (310) 365-5047 gsimpson@toddao.com

Services include: ADR, Re-recording/mixing, foley and voice over recording for TV and feature films.

UNIVERSAL STUDIOS

UNIVERSAL STUDIOS - SOUND

(Sound mixing & dubbing, special effects, sound recording for major motion pictures)
100 Universal City Plaza, Henry Mancini Bldg. 2315, 2nd Flr., Universal City, CA 91608. TEL: (818) 777-0169.
FAX: (818) 866-1494. www.filmmakersdestination.com
SENIOR V.P., SOUND SERVICES
Chris Jenkins
V.P. ADMINISTRATION, SOUND OPERATIONS
Steven Williams - steve.d.williams@nbcuni.com
V.P., POST PRODUCTION ENGINEERING, SOUND
Doc Goldstein
DIRECTOR, FEATURE SOUND SERVICES
Kirsten Smith
DIRECTOR, TELEVISION SOUND SERVICES
Michael Bertram

UNIVERSAL STUDIOS SOUND EDITORIAL

100 Universal City Plaza, Bldg. 2313B, Universal City, CA 91608. TEL: (800) 892-1979, (818) 777-3636.
FAX: (818) 866-1619. email: studio.operations2@nbcuni.com
www.filmmakersdestination.com
SUPERVISING SOUND EDITOR/DESIGNER & DIRECTOR, SOUND EDITORIAL DEPARTMENT
Scott Hecker - scott.hecker@nbcuni.com
SUPERVISING SOUND EDITOR, DESIGNER, THEATRICAL
Elliott Koretz elliott.koretz@nbcuni.com

UNIVERSAL MASTERING STUDIOS

(Restoration, mastering, CDR duplication, CD enhancing)
UMS Hollywood: 3400 Cahuenga Blvd., Building C, Hollywood, CA 90068. TEL: (818) 286-6233. www.universalmastering.com
CONTACT
Nick Dofflemyer - nick.d@umusic.com

UMS Manhattan: 1755 Broadway, 4th Flr., New York, NY 10019. TEL: (212) 331-2920.
ASSOCIATE DIRECTOR OF STUDIO ADMINISTRATION
Tamara Gallo
CONTACT
Alex Cables - alex.cables@umusic.com

UMS Santa Monica: 2220 Colorado Ave., Santa Monica, CA 90404. TEL: (310) 865-8458.
CONTACT
Nick Dofflemyer - nickd@umusic.com

UMS Monterey Mexico: Av. Santo Domingo, #12, Col. Nicolas Bravo, San Nicolas de Iso Garza, NL C.P. 66430.
TEL: +11 52 81 88 65 79 00.
CONTACT
Miguel Portugal - miguelportugal@disa.com.mx

UMS Internet Mastering
CONTACT
(212) 331-2980 umsinternetmastering@umusic.com

UMS is part of the Universal Music Group family, with studios in New York, Los Angeles and Monterey Mexico.

USL, INC.

(Ultra Stereo Labs, Inc. Cinema sound equipment, including processors, booth monitors, crossovers, ADA devices, exciter lamps, test equipment)
181 Bonetti Dr., San Luis Obispo, CA 93401-7310.
TEL: (805) 549-0161. FAX: (805) 549-0163. www.uslinc.com
PRESIDENT
James A. (Jack) Cashin
VICE PRESIDENT
Felicia Cashin - Felicia@uslinc.com
SALES DIRECTOR
Clint Koch - clint@uslinc.com

WARNER BROS. STUDIO FACILITIES POST PRODUCTION SERVICES — BURBANK

(Scoring, mixing, post production, sound services)
4000 Warner Blvd., Bldg. 4, Rm. 101, Burbank, CA 91522.
TEL: (818) 954-2515. FAX: (818) 954-4138. www.wbsf.com
SENIOR V.P., POST PRODUCTIONS SERVICES
Kim Waugh - kim.waugh@warnerbros.com
V.P., POST PRODUCTION SERVICES
Bill Angarola - bill.angarola@warnerbros.com
DIRECTOR, ENGINEERING
Kevin Collier - kevin.collier@warnerbros.com
DIRECTOR, BUSINESS DEVELOPMENT
Dean Hilborne - dean.hilborne@warnerbros.com
MANAGER, OPERATIONS
Damon Banks - damon.banks@warnerbros.com
SUPERVISOR, DVD AUDIO MASTERING
Tim Hoggatt - tim.hoggatt@warnerbros.com
SUPERVISOR, ARCHIVAL MASTERING
John Yanez - john.yanez@warnerbros.com
SUPERVISOR, AUDIO RESTORATION
Robert Corti - robert.corti@warnerbros.com
SOUND SUPERVISOR, ANCILLARY MARKETS
Tracie Gallo - tracie.gallo@warnerbros.com

Warner Bros. Post Production Services crafts sound for motion pictures, television and emerging media. Sound services include: re-recording, sound superivision and editorial, ADR, foley, scoring, transfer, archival services, restoration services, laydown/layback, DVD audio mastering, engineering, picture editorial rooms, screening rooms and projection services and mobile ADR.

WESTLAKE RECORDING STUDIOS

(Recording studio, audio service & sales)
7265 Santa Monica Blvd., West Hollywood, CA 90046.
TEL: (323) 851-9800. FAX: (323) 851-9386.
email: bookings@thelakestudios.com
OWNER
Steve Burdick, Al Machera
STUDIO MANAGER
Sara Clark

WOODS END RECORDING STUDIO / 100% SOUND

(Full-service audio production studio, sound design, ADR, mix to picture, original music)
114 Catherine St., Saratoga Springs, NY 12866.
TEL: (518-699-4396. www.100percentsound.com
CONTACT
Charlie Eble - charlie@100percentsound.com
Will Severin - willseverin@100percentsound.com

WORKSHIRT MUSIC

(Music composition for film and TV)
7510 Sunset Blvd, #1022 Los Angeles, CA 90046.
TEL: (323) 466-6046. email: chris@workshirtmusic.com
www.workshirtmusic.com
OWNER
Chris Anderson

ZAENTZ MEDIA CENTER

(Now owned by Wareham Development)
2600 Tenth St., Berkeley, CA 94710. TEL: (510) 486-2286.
FAX: (510) 486-2062. www.zaentzmediacenter.com
CONTACT
Anna Stenberg - astenberg@warehamdevelopment.com

Special Effects

11:11 MEDIAWORKS
(Visual effects design & production; wire & rig removal, scratch & negative repair)
6611 Valjean Ave., Ste. 108, Van Nuys, CA 91406.
TEL: (818) 780-4466. FAX: (818) 780-4467.
email: info@1111mw.com www.1111mediaworks.com
CONTACT
Roger Nall

310 STUDIOS
(Post-production, visual effects and motion graphic design)
419 S. Flower St., Burbank, CA 91502. TEL: (818) 566-3083.
FAX: (818) 747-7637. email: info@310studios.com
www.310studios.com
PRESIDENT
Bill Jones - billy@310studios.com

3D BOB PRODUCTIONS
(Character animation, compositing, modeling visual effects)
21601 Devonshire St., Ste. 112, Chatsworth, CA 91311.
TEL: (818) 559-9700. FAX: (818) 559-9768.
email: info@3dbob.com www.3dbob.com
OWNER
Bob Arvin

ACCU-CAST
(Specialty Alginates- dustless formulas for every application- SFX Makeup. Prop Duplication and Life Casting)
64682 Cook Ave., #130, Bend, OR 97701.
TEL: (866) 618-8461. FAX: (541) 388-1971.
email: info@accu-cast.us www.accu-cast.us
CONTACT
Lucinda Baker

ACTION UNLIMITED
(Mechanical effects; pyrotechnic effects)
6025 Honeysuckle Lane, San Bernardino, CA 92407.
TEL: (909) 823-CINE. email: nick@actionunlimited.net
www.actionunlimited.net
OWNER
Nick Plantico

ADVANCED FIRE & RESCUE SERVICES
(Fire rescue standby, EMT and fire personell, fire trucks, antique or new)
16205 Lost Canyon Rd., Santa Clarita, CA 91351.
TEL: (818) 837-7336. FAX: (661) 298-3069.
email: eng12capt@aol.com www.advancedfire.com
CONTACT
Craig Sanford

ALCONE COMPANY
(Make up supply company, beauty, character, gore)
545 49th Ave., Long Island City, NY 11101.
TEL: (800) 466-7446. (718) 361-8373. www.alconeco.com
NYC store: 322 W. 49th St., New York, NY 10019.
TEL: (212) 757-3734.

ALMOST HUMAN
(All aspects of professional makeup effects, prosthetics & animatronics)
3650 Eagle Rock Blvd., Los Angeles, CA 90065.
TEL: (310) 838-6993. FAX: (310) 838-6999.
email: studio@almosthuman.net www.almosthuman.net
OWNER
Robert Hall

AMALGAMATED DYNAMICS
(Special make-up and creature effects design)
20100 Plummer St., Chatsworth, CA 91311.
TEL: (818) 882-8638. FAX: (818) 882-7327.
email: info@studioadi.com www.studioadi.com
OWNERS
Alec Gillis, Tom Woodruff, Jr.

AMALGAMATED PIXELS
(2D & 3D digital animation, compositing for visual effects)
2575 Townsgate Rd., Ste 220, Westlake Village, CA 19161.
TEL: (818) 865-8423. FAX (818) 575-9032.
email: mmorreale@apixels.com www.apixels.com

AMERICAN HI DEFINITION, INC.
(High quality large screen video projection systems for the entertainment industry)
7635 Airport Business Park Way, Van Nuys, CA 91406.
TEL: (818) 222-0022. email: erez@hi-def.com
www.hi-def.com
PRINCIPAL
Ady Gill, Erez Ram

AMERICAN PAPER OPTICS, LLC
(3-D products)
2995 Appling Rd., Ste. 106, Bartlett, TN 38133.
TEL: (901) 381-1515. FAX: (901) 381-1517.
email: sales@3dglassesonline.com
www.3dglassesonline.com
PRESIDENT
John Jerit

ANA SPECIAL EFFECTS
(Breakaway glass, mechanical effects-rain, wind & snow)
7021 Hayvenhurst Ave., Van Nuys, CA 91406.
TEL: (818) 909-6999. FAX: (818) 782-0635.
CONTACT
Gladys Nary

ANATOMORPHEX
(Animatronic animals and aliens, special effects make-up, costumes and miniatures)
8210 Lankershim, Ste. 14, North Hollywood, CA 91605.
TEL: (818) 768-2880. FAX: (818) 768-4808.
email: anatofx@hotmail.com www.anatomorphex.com
CONTACT
Robert Devine

ANGSTROM LIGHTING
(Full service lighting and special effects for the entertainment industry)
837 N. Cahuenga Blvd., Hollywood, CA 90038.
TEL: (866) 275-9211, (323) 462-4246. FAX: (323) 462-8190.
email: info@angstromlighting.com www.angstromlighting.com
PRESIDENT & CEO
Frank Klinkenberg

ANIMAL MAKERS
(Animatronic animals)
775 E. Cochran St., Ste. F, Simi Valley, CA 93065.
TEL: (805) 527-6200. FAX: (805) 527-6210.
email: jim@animalmakers.com www.animalmakers.com
CREATIVE DIRECTOR
Jim Boulden
PRODUCER, HUMAN RESOURCES, CORPORATE SECRETARY
Coral Boulden
ANIMATRONICS SUPERVISOR
Jim Greenall

ANTHEM VISUAL EFFECTS, INC.
(Compositing, visual effects)S
110 Cambie St., Ste. 200, Vancouver, BC V6B 2M8, Canada
TEL: (604) 669-9936. FAX: (604) 669-9926
www.anthemfx.com
PRESIDENT & VISUAL EFFECTS SUPERVISOR
Lee Wilson
CFO & VISUAL EFFECTS PRODUCER
Lisa Sepp-Wilson

ARTEFFEX
(Animatronics, puppets, specialty costumes, miniatures, creatures, models & props)
911 Mayo St., Los Angeles, CA 90042. TEL: (818) 506-5358.
FAX: (323) 255-4599. email: danno@acfxo.com acfx@att.net
www.acfxo.com
CONTACT
Dann O'Quinn

ASYLUM VISUAL EFFECTS
(Compositing, modeling, visual effects)
631 Wilshire Blvd., Ste. 2A, Santa Monica, CA 90401.
TEL: (310) 395-4975. FAX: (310) 395-5625.
www.asylumfx.com
CONTACT
Nathan McGuinness

AVATAR LABS
(Interactive design, front & back end technology, visual effects)
3060 Ventura Blvd., Ste. 102, Encino, CA 91436.
TEL: (818) 784-2200. FAX: (818) 784-2204.
email: info@avatarlabs.com www.avatarlabs.com

DAVE BARCLAY STUDIO
(character design, sculpture, puppetry, animatronics, real-time performance capture)
312 S. Keystone St., Burbank, CA 91506.
TEL: (818) 847-0030. email: dave@davebarclay.com
www.davebarclay.com

BELLFX, LLC
(Precision parts assembly for motion picture production)

1908 First St., San Fernando, CA 91340.
TEL: (818) 365-8470. FAX: (818) 365-8471.
email: bellfx@pacbell.net www.bellfx.com
OWNER
Brent Bell

BFX IMAGEWORKS
(2D & 3D CG animation, compositing, modeling, visual effects, storyboarding, on-set supervision)
14658 Tupper St., North Hills, CA 91402. TEL: (818) 893-5212.
email: info@bfximageworks.com www.bfximageworks.com

BIFROST LASERFX
(3D computer animation & laser visual effects)
6733 Sale Ave., West Hills, CA 91307. TEL: (818) 704-0423.
email: howie@howiewood.net www.howiewood.net
OWNER/CONTACT
Howard Shore

BIG FILM DESIGN
(Visual effects & title sequences for feature films)
594 Broadway, Ste. 1001, New York, NY 10012.
TEL: (212) 627-3430. FAX: (212) 989-6528.
email: info@bigfilmdesign.com www.bigfilmdesign.com
PRESIDENT & CREATIVE DIRECTOR
Randy Balsmeyer
COMPOSITING SUPERVISOR
David Piombino
PRODUCER
Adrienne Winterhalter

BLACKLIGHT FILMS
(Stock film footage)
3371 Cahuenga Blvd. W, Los Angeles, CA 90068.
TEL: (323) 436-7070. FAX: (323) 436-2230.
email: sales@blacklightfilms.com www.blacklightfilms.com
EXECUTIVE PRODUCER, DIRECTOR, PRESIDENT
Louis Schwartzberg

BLACKSTONE MAGIK ENTERPRISES, INC.
(Magic illusions for special effects; producing & consulting)
12800 Puesta Del Sol, Redlands, CA 92373-7408.
TEL: (909) 792-1227. FAX: (909) 794-2737.
email: magik@blackstonemagic.com
www.blackstonemagic.com

JOE BLASCO MAKEUP CENTER HOLLYWOOD / JOE BLASCO COSMETICS
(Makeup effects)
1670 Hillhurst Ave., Los Angeles, CA 90027.
TEL: (800) 634-0008, (323) 467-4949. FAX: (323) 664-1834.
email: hollywood@joeblasco.com www.joeblasco.com

BLUEROOM POST
(Compositing, visual effects)
Mbs Media Campus, 1600 Rosecrans Ave., Bldg. 7, Manhattan Beach, CA 90266. TEL: (310) 727-2600. FAX: (310) 727-2601.
email: john@blueroomfx.com www.blueroomfx.com

Baton Rouge: Celtic Media Center, 10000 Celtic Dr., Baton Rouge, LA 70809. TEL: (225) 330-6900.

New Orleans: FBT Film & Entertainment Office, 909 Poydras St., Ste. 2250, New Orleans, LA 70112. TEL: (504) 584-5888.

BLUESCREEN, LLC
(Production and post-production for film and video bluescreen and greenscreen)
137 N. Larchmont Blvd., Ste. 508, Los Angeles, CA 90004.
TEL: (323) 467-7572. www.bluescreen.com
CONTACT
Bob Kertesz - bob@bluescreen.com

BLUR STUDIO, INC.
(Computer generated effects for games, movies & TV)
589 Venice Blvd., Venice, CA 90291. TEL: (310) 581-8848.
FAX: (310) 581-8850. www.blur.com

BOND
(Editorial, motion graphics, visual effects, 2D & 3D high-end)
665 Broadway, 12th Flr., New York, NY 10012.
TEL: (212) 533-9400. FAX: (212) 533-9443.
www.bondedit.com
FOUNDER/MANAGING DIRECTOR
Jeff Beckerman - jeff_beckerman@bondedit.com

BOOM BOOM EFFECTS
(Mechanical effects; pyrotechnic effects; stunt rigging; atmosphere effects)
11100-8 Sepulveda Blvd., Ste. 339, Mission Hills, CA 91345.
TEL: (818) 772-6699. FAX: (818) 772-6689.
email: boomboomefx@aol.com
CONTACT
Bob Calvert

BRAIN ZOO STUDIOS
(A full-service CGI/Animation & FX studio)
16509 Saticoy St., Van Nuys, CA 91406.
TEL: (818) 785-1124. FAX: (818) 904-1753.
email: info@brainzoostudios.com www.brainzoostudios.com
OWNER
Mohammed Davoudian

BRANAM ENTERPRISES, INC.
(Theatrical rigging & rentals)
310 S. Long Beach Blvd., Compton, CA 90221.
TEL: (310) 637-4727. FAX: (310) 637) 4735.
email: mail@branament.com www.branament.com
PRESIDENT
Joe Branam
DIRECTOR OF SALES & MARKETING
Richard Ocean

BRILLIG PRODUCTIONS, LLC
(Mechnical design for creature effects)
13958 Huston St., Sherman Oaks, CA 91423.
TEL: (818) 995-0271. FAX: (818) 783-9014.
email: brillig@brilligprods.com www.brilligprods.com
CONTACT
Jurgen Heimann

BROADWAY VIDEO
(Compositing and visual effects)
1619 Broadway, 10th Flr., New York, NY 10019.
TEL: (212) 265-7600. FAX: (212) 713-1535.
email: info@broadwayvideo.com www.broadwayvideo.com
PRESIDENT
Christina McGinnis

BROOKLYN MODEL WORKS INC.
(Fabrication of miniature & oversize props & prototypes, architectural models)
60 Washington Ave., Brooklyn, NY 11205.
TEL: (718) 834-1944. FAX: (718) 596-8934.
email: john@brooklynmodelworks.com
www.brooklynmodelworks.com
PRESIDENT
John Kuntzsch

BUF, INC.
(Visual effects)
7720 W. Sunset Blvd., Los Angeles, CA 90046.
TEL: (323) 512-6000. FAX: (323) 512-6075. www.buf.com
PRESIDENT
Pierre Buffin
PRODUCER
Steven Adams - steven.adams@buf.com

BURMAN STUDIO, INC.
(Distributor of products for special effects makup, molds, model making, puppetry and animatronics)
13536 Saticoy St., Van Nuys, CA 91402. TEL: (818) 782-9833.
FAX: (818) 782-2863. email: info@burmanindustries.com
www.burmanindustries.com
OWNER
Barney Burman, Rob Burman

THE BURMAN STUDIO, INC.
(Special make-up effects and prosthetics)
4706 W. Magnolia Blvd., Burbank, CA 91505.
TEL: (818) 980-6587. FAX: (818) 980-6589.
CONTACT
Bari Dreiband-Burman

CAPTAIN DAVE'S MARINE SERVICES, INC.
(Boats, barges, trucks, & submarines for the film industry. Also mechanical shark with complete underwater service)
1438 W. 14th St., Long Beach, CA 90813. TEL: (562) 437-4772.
PAGER: (562) 799-7814. FAX: (562) 354-7103.
email: dave@captaindavesmarine.com
CONTACT
David W.L. Hilchey

THE CHARACTER SHOP, INC.
(Animatronics, Prosthetics, Puppets, Realistic Effects, Scary Effects, Whimsical Effects)
1464 Madera Rd., #N-310, Simi Valley, CA 93065.
TEL: (805) 306-9441. FAX: (805) 306-9444.
email: lazzwaldo@aol.com www.character-shop.com
CONTACT & PRESIDENT
Rick Lazzarini

CHELSEA POST
(Visual effects)
221 W. 26th St., New York, NY 100001. TEL (212) 727-1234.
FAX: (212) 255-6644. www.amvchelsea.com
POST PRODUCTION DIRECTOR
Jeffrey McLaughlin - jmclaughlin@amvchelsea.com

CHIODO BROS. PRODUCTIONS, INC.
110 W. Providencia Ave., Burbank, CA 91502.
TEL: (818) 842-5656. FAX: (818) 848-0891.
email: klowns@chiodobros.com www.chiodobros.com
PRESIDENT
Stephen Chiodo

CHRYON CORP.
(Character generators, graphics for broadcast effects)
5 Hub Dr., Melville, NY 11747. TEL: (631) 845-2000.
FAX: (631) 845-3895. www.chyron.com

CIMMELLI, INC.
(Mechanical effects, model shop, atmospherics)
16 Walter St., Pearl River, NY 10965. TEL: (845) 735-2090.
FAX: (845) 735-1643. email: info@cimmellifx.com
www.cimmellifx.com
OWNER
Hugo Cimmelli

CINEMA ENGINEERING COMPANY
14737 Arminta St., Unit B, Panorama City, CA 91402.
TEL: (818) 780-5404. FAX: (818) 780-5405.
email: cinemaengineering@tcsn.net
www.cinema-engineering.com

Provides the entertainment industry with motion-picture camera repair, modifications and custom designed photographic equipment services. Co. specializes in servicing Mitchell cameras, but all professional 16mm, 35mm, 65mm and Vista Vision cameras are welcome. Clients include major motion-picture studios, TV and commercial production companies, special effects houses and dozens of award-winning Directors of Photography, Special Effects Supervisors and Cameramen.

CINEMA MAKEUP SCHOOL
(Special makeup effects character makeup, beauty, body painting, airbrush makeup, hairstyling, film & TV)
(3780 Wilshire Blvd., 3rd Flr., Los Angeles, CA 90010.
TEL: (213) 368-1234. FAX: (213) 739-0819.
email: info@cinemamakeup.com www.cinemamakeup.com
DIRECTOR OF ADMISSIONS
Lee Joyner

CINESITE, INC.
(A Kodak company. Visual effects/London; digital film mastering, scanning & recording, digital restoration/Hollywood)
Los Angeles: 1017 N. Las Palmas Ave., Los Angeles, CA 90038. TEL: (323) 468-1589. FAX: (323) 468-2180.
www.cinesite.com

London: Medius House, 2 Sheraton St., London, W1F 8BH.
TEL: +44 20 7973 4000. FAX: +44 20 7973 4040.
email: filmfx@cinesite.co.uk televisionfx@cinesite.co.uk
scan-record@cinesite.co.uk miniatures@cinesite.co.uk

CINNABAR CALIFORNIA, INC.
(Creates sets and special effects for feature films, TV shows and commercials)
4571 Electronics Place, Los Angeles, CA 90039.
TEL: (818) 842-8190. FAX: (818) 842-0563. www.cinnabar.com
GENERAL MANAGER
Kip Katz

CIS VSX GROUP
(Visual effects, 2D and 3D digital effects, all-format compositing)
1144 N. Las Palmas Ave., Hollywood, CA 90038.
TEL: (323) 463-8811. FAX: (323) 962-1859.
email: info@cishollywood.com www.cishollywood.com
PRESIDENT & GENERAL MANAGER
Don Fly
EXECUTIVE V.P. & GENERAL MANAGER
Dennis Hoffman

Vancouver: 50 Second St., Vancouver BC Canada
TEL: (604) 874-8700. FAX: (604) 872-2106.
email: info@cis-vancouver.com

CLOUD NINETEEN
3767 Overland Ave., Ste. 104, Los Angeles, CA 90034.
TEL: (310) 839-5400. FAX: (310) 839-5404.
email: info@cloud19.com www.cloud19.com
PRESIDENT
Scott Boutté
TECHNICAL DIRECTOR
Bray Merritt

Film sound mixing & rerecording; recording studio; sound editing; sound post facility, motion graphics and compositing. Full post production services.

CLOUTIER REMIX
(Hair, makeup and wardrobe stylists)
2632 La Cienega Ave., Los Angeles, CA 90034.
TEL: (310) 839-8722. www.cloutierremmix.com
DIRECTOR
Madeline Leonard - madeline@cloutierremix.com

COMPANY 3
(Compositing, otpical special effects, 3D, scanning & film output, visual effects)
1661 Lincoln Blvd., Ste. 400, Santa Monica, CA 90404.
TEL: (310) 255-6600. FAX: (310) 255-6602.
email: info@company3.com www.company3.com
V.P. FEATURE SERVICES (LA & NY)
Jackie Lee

New York: 218 W. 18th St., 12th Flr., New York, NY 10011.
TEL: (212) 687-4000. FAX: (212) 687-2719.

THE COMPANY DIGITAL
(Complete production company with full range of equipment rental & HD post production services)
12210 1/2 Nebraska Ave., West Los Angeles, CA 90025.
TEL: (310) 919-0950. FAX: (310) 857-6664.
email: info@thecompany.tv www.thecompany.tv
DIRECTOR
Cameron Casey, Lamont Edwards, Christopher Gosch, Tom Oesch, Russell Kostner, Warren Oliver

CONTROLLED AIRSTREAMS, INC.
(Wind, snow, rain, atomospheric effects, trailer mounted)
32180 Mulholland Hwy., Malibu, CA 90265.
TEL: (818) 597-1977. FAX: (818) 597-0536.
CONTACT
Gary Cerveny - garycerveny@aol.com

COSTFX VISUAL EFFECTS
(Compositing, photographic special effects, visual effects)
319 W. Alamar Ave., Santa Barbara, CA 93105.
TEL: (805) 682-3972. FAX: (805) 455-7574.
OWNER/VISUAL EFFECTS SUPERVISOR
Lance Wilhoite

CREATIVE CHARACTER ENGINEERING
(Computer graphics, animatronics, silicone babies, character-based visual effects for film & TV)
16110 Hart St., Van Nuys, CA 91406. TEL: (818) 901-0507.
FAX: (818) 901-8417. www.creativecharacter.com
CREATIVE DIRECTOR
Andrew Clement - andyCCE@earthlink.net

THE CREATIVE GROUP
(Post production for TV & cable networks)
1601 Broadway, 10th Flr., New York, NY 10019.
TEL: (212) 935-0145. FAX: (212) 838-0853.
SALES
Mike Buckner - mbuckner@creativegroup.tv
OPERATIONS
Chris Portelli - cportelli@creativegroup.tv

CURIOUS PICTURES
(Produces live-action, special effects, graphics, comedy and animation of all types, maya, flash, cel animation, stop motion, after effects)
440 Lafayette St., 6th Flr., New York, NY 10003.
TEL: (212) 674-1400. FAX: (212) 674-0081.
email: info@curiouspictures.com press@curiouspictures.com
www.curiouspictures.com
MANAGING PARTNER
Marina Grasic - mgrasic@curiouspictures.com
Jan Korbelin - jkorbelin@curiouspictures.com

CUSTOM COLOR CONTACTS
(Custom designed contact lenses for motion picture and TV special effects)
Studio Optix, 55 W. 49 St., New York, NY 10020.
TEL: (800) 598-2020, (212) 765-4444. FAX: (212) 765-4459.
email: info@customcontacts.com www.customcontacts.com
PRINCIPAL
Dr. Mitchell Cassel

DAILY POST
(post production, motion capture)
6701 Center Dr. W. Ste. 1111, Los Angeles, CA 90045.
TEL: (310) 417-4844. FAX: (310) 410-1542.
email: sales@dailypost.tv www.dailypost.tv

DE LA MARE ENGINEERING, INC.
(Electrical apparatus manufacturing for special effects)
1908 First St., San Fernando, CA 91340-2610.
TEL: (818) 365-9208. FAX: (818) 365-8775.

DIGISCOPE
(Visual digital effects)
1447 Cloverfield Blvd., Ste. 100, Santa Monica, CA 90404.
TEL: (310) 315-6060. FAX: (310) 828-5856.
VFX SUPERVISOR
Dion Hatch - Dion@digiscope.com
DIGITAL PRODUCER
Terron Pratt - Terron@digiscope.com

DIGITAL DOMAIN
(Full-service animation company; digital visual effects for film,

TV & commercials)
300 Rose Ave., Venice, CA 90291. TEL: (310) 314-2800.
FAX: (310) 664-2701. www.digitaldomain.com

Vancouver: 1618 W. 8th Ave., Vancouver, BC V6J 1V4.
TEL: (776) 783-6000. FAX: (776) 783-6099
CEO
Cliff Plumer
PRESIDENT, FEATURE FILM PRODUCTION
Gloria Borders
PRESIDENT, COMMERCIAL PRODUCTION
Ed Ulbrich
HEAD OF PRODUCTION
Jody Madden
HEAD OF CG
Thaddeus Beier

DIGITAL JUNGLE

(3D stereoscopic, Editorial, visual effects)
6363 Santa Monica Blvd., Hollywood, CA 90038.
TEL: (323) 962-0867. FAX: (323) 962-9960.
email: info@digijungle.com www.digijungle.com

DIMENSION 3

(Stereoscopic (3D) film & video, 3D glasses)
5240 Medina Rd., Woodland Hills, CA 91364-1913.
TEL: (818) 592-0999. FAX: (818) 592-0987. www.d3.com
PRESIDENT
Daniel Symmes

DUART FILM & VIDEO

(Visual effects, scanning, film output, digital services)
245 W. 55th St., New York, NY 10019.
TEL: (212-757-4580. FAX: (212) 333-7647.
email: info @duart.com www.duart.com
CEO
Charles Darby
PRODUCER
Lisa Ortiz, Tom Werenko

EDEN FX

(3D animation, full motion matte painting, compositing, modeling, blue/green screen)
1438 N. Gower St., Box 19, Bldg. 50, Hollywood, CA 90028.
TEL: (323) 993-7050. FAX: (323) 993-7051.
email: info@edenfx.com www.edenfx.com
CO-FOUNDER/VFX SUPERVISOR
John Gross

THE EFFECTS GROUP

(Mechanical effects: pyrotechnic, rain, wind, snow, flying, stunt rigging)
137 N. Larchmont Blvd., Ste. 224, Los Angeles, CA 90004.
TEL: (323) 876-0992. FAX: (323) 876-0288.
email: thefxgroup@sbcglobal.net www.theeffectsgroup.net

EFFECTS IN MOTION

(A division of Reelistic FX, Inc. Supplies & operates equipment and devices that move sets and props)
21318 Hart St. Canoga Park, CA 91303. TEL: (818) 346-2484.
FAX: (818) 346-2710. email: don8@pacbell.net www.rfx.com
CONTACT
Don Gray

EFILM

(A Deluxe company. Digital film laboratory)
1146 N. Las Palmas Ave., Hollywood, CA 90038.
TEL: (323) 463-7041. FAX: (323) 465-7342.
email: info_1@efilm.com www.efilm.com
CREATIVE DIRECTOR
Steven J. Scott

E.I. SCHOOL OF PROFESSIONAL MAKEUP

(Make-up effects)
1622 N. Highland Ave., Hollywood, CA 90028.
TEL: (323) 871-8318. FAX: (323) 871-8367.
email: admissions@ei.edu www.ei.edu

ENCORE HOLLYWOOD

(Post production & visual effects)
6344 Fountain Ave., Hollywood, CA 90028.
TEL: (323) 466-7663. FAX: (323) 467-5539.
www.encorehollywood.com/
V.P., SALES MANAGER, ETV
Cliff Dugan - cdugan@encorehollywood.com
VFX
Tom Kendall - tkendall@encorehollywood.com
Stephen Fleet - sfleet@encorehollywood.com

Encore Hollywood specializes in post production and visual effects for episodic TV and MOWs, commercials, music videos and feature films. It also offers a fully equipped digital intermediat theatre &feature HD dailies.

ENTITY FX

(3D modeling and animation, stereo 3D imagery, CGI character creation, 2D compositing, onset supervision)
1437 Seventh St., Ste. 300. Santa Monica, CA 90401.
TEL: (310) 899-9779. FAX: (310) 899-3113.
emai: info@entityfx.com www.entityfx.com
PRESIDENT
Mat Beck
GENERAL MANAGER
Ellyn Lewis

EUE / SCREEN GEMS STUDIOS

EUE / SCREEN GEMS STUDIOS NEW YORK

222 E. 44th St., New York, NY 10017. TEL: (212) 450-1600.
FAX: (212) 450-1616. www.screengemsstudios.com/ny
EXECUTIVE VICE PRESIDENT
Mitchell Brill - mbrill@euescreengems.com

EUE/SCREEN GEMS STUDIOS NORTH CAROLINA

1223 N. 23rd St., Wilmington, NC 29405. TEL: (910) 343-3500.
www.screengemsstudios.com/nc
CONTACT
Bill Vassar - vassar@euescreengems.comS

EXTREME SPORTS FILMING

(Action sports specialist)
3419 Via Lido, #145, Newport Beach, CA 92663.
TEL: (562) 596-7105. email: miles@extremesportsfilming.com
www.extremesportsfilming.com
CONTACT
Miles Flewitt

Marine, air and land; production facilities, location, equipment, talent, vehicle coordination/trucks & cars, and more.

FANTASY II FILM EFFECTS, INC.

(Miniatures, digital special effects)
415 S. Flower St., Burbank, CA 91502. TEL: (818) 843-1413.
FAX: (818) 848-2824.
CONTACT
Gene Warren, Jr.

RUSS FARBER

(Blue screen effects, setup, networking & troubleshooting computers on location)
19324 Oxnard St., Tarzana, CA 91356. TEL: (818) 882-8220.
email: refent@pacbell.net

FILM ROMAN VISUAL EFFECTS

(Compositing, visual effects, pre-visualization, 2D & 3D animation, 2D &3D hybrid, flash animation)
2950 N. Hollywood Way, Burbank, CA 91505.
TEL: (818) 748-4000. www.filmroman.com

FILMTRIX, INC.

P.O. Box 809, North Hollywood, CA 91603-0809.
TEL: (818) 980-9001. CELL: (818) 808-9321. FAX: (818) 980-9004.
email: filmtrix@mac.com www.filmtrix.com
CONTACT
Kevin Pike

FLASH FILM WORKS

(Compositing; visual effects)
743 Seward St., Hollywood, CA 90038. TEL: (323) 468-8855.
FAX: (323) 468-8040. email: flash@flashfilmworks.com
www.flashfilmworks.com
PRESIDENT
William Mesa

FOTOKEM

(Full service motion picture, TV and commercial post production services, visual effects)
2801 W. Alameda Ave., Burbank, CA 91505.
TEL: (818) 846-3101. FAX: (818) 841-6030.
email: sales@fotokem.com www.fotokem.com

FULL MENTAL JACKET

(Visual effects, 3D virtual sets, virtual environments)
816 Hyperion Ave., Los Angeles, CA 90029.
TEL: (323) 640-2914. FAX: (509) 693-8875.
email: info@fullmentaljacket.com www.fullmentaljacket.com
DIRECTOR, BUSINESS DEVELOPMENT
Dave Connor

F/X CONCEPTS, INC.

(Mechanical effects; pyrotechnic effects)
11118 Ventura Blvd., Studio City, CA 91604.
TEL/FAX: (818) 508-1094.
CONTACT
Lou Carlucci

GALAXIE ENTERTAINMENT CO.

(Animation, optical effects, photography & stereoscopic-3D)
P.O. Box 922405, Sylmar, CA 91392. TEL: (818) 362-6005.
FAX: (818) 362-6005.
CONTACT
Dave Gregory

Producer of theatrical feature films; ProHD Digital Cinematography and Post-Production; Stereoscopic-3D specialists; and visual & photographic effects, animation: computer & stop motion.

GARDEN OF ALLAH

(Compositing, visual effects)
11684 Ventura Blvd., Ste. 814, Studio City, CA 91604.
TEL: (323) 650-1556. email: efreet@pacbell.net
www.gardenofallah.com
PRINCIPAL
Michael Hoover

GENTLE GIANT STUDIOS, INC.

(Rapid prototyping, digital modeling, sculpting and painting)
7511 N. San Fernando Rd., Burbank, CA 91505.
TEL: (818) 504-3555. FAX: (818) 504-3554.
www.gentlegiantstudios.com
PRESIDENT
Karl Meyer

ROGER GEORGE RENTALS

(Mechanical effects, wind, fire, rain, snow, pyrotechnic)
14525 Bessemer St., Van Nuys, CA 91411.
TEL: (818) 994-3049. FAX: (818) 994-9432.
email: sales@rogergeorge.com www.rogergeorge.com

PETER GEYER ACTION PROPS & SETS

(Breakaways, including rubber, fake razor and barbed wire)
8235 Lankershim Blvd., Ste. G, N. Hollywood, CA 91605.
TEL: (818) 768-0070.

GILDERFLUKE & COMPANY, INC.

(Robotics and sound systems)
205 S. Flower St., Burbank, CA 91502. TEL: (800) 776-5972.
TEL: (818) 840-9484. FAX: (818) 840-9485.
email: info@gilderfluke.com www.gilderfluke.com
SALES
Lisa Franzke - lisaF@gilderfluke.com

East Coast: 7041 Grand National Dr., Ste. 128, Orlando, FL 32819. TEL: (407) 354-5954. FAX: (407) 354-5955.
email: toni@gilderfluke.com

GOLIATH PICTURES

(compositing, visual effects, pre-visuals, storyboards, visual effects supervision)
16313 Clark Ave., Bellflower, CA 90706. TEL: (562) 920-7004.
FAX: (562) 925-8910. email: david@goliathpictures.com
www.goliathpictures.com
PRINCIPAL
David J. Negron, Jr.

GLOBAL EFFECTS, INC.

(Prop rental, makeup effects, mechanical effects)
7115 Laurel Canyon Blvd., North Hollywood, CA 91605.
TEL: (818) 503-9272. FAX: (818) 503-9459.
www.globaleffects.com

GRANT MCCUNE DESIGN, INC.

(Mechanical effects, pyrotechnic, smoke stage)
6836 Valjean Ave., Van Nuys, CA 91406.
TEL: (818) 779-1920. FAX: (818) 781-9108.
email: mike@gmdfx.com www.gmdfx.com
CONTACT
Michael Yost

GRAY MATTER VISUAL EFFECTS

(2D Compositing, photo real 3D effects, 3D set extensions, onsite supervision of motion control, vfx stunt support)
1503 Abbot Kinney Blvd., Venice, CA 90291.
TEL: (310) 581-1555. FAX: (310) 581-1525.
email: contact@gmfx.com www.graymatterfx.com
CEO/CO-OWNER
Margaux MacKay
CREATIVE DIRECTOR/CO-OWNER
Gray Marshall

Vancouver: 3rd Flr., 177 W. 7th Ave., Vancouver BC V5Y IL8.
TEL: (604) 872-3299. FAX: (604) 872-3290.
email: ashley@gmfx.com

HAMMERHEAD PRODUCTIONS

(Visual effects)
13400 Ventura Blvd., Sherman Oaks, CA 91423.
TEL: (818) 986-5335. www.hammerhead.com
PRESIDENT
Jamie Dixon - jamie@hammerhead.com
V. P., EXECUTIVE PRODUCER
Dan Chuba - dan@hammerhead.com
VFX SUPERVISOR
Rebecca Marie - rebecca@hammerhead.com

HBO STUDIO PRODUCTIONS

(Full-service production and post production facility)
120-A E. 23rd St., New York, NY 10010. TEL: (212) 512-7800.
FAX: (212) 512-7788.
DIRECTOR, SALES
Paul Brzozowski

THE JIM HENSON COMPANY

(Production company)
Hollywood Headquarters: 1416 N. La Brea Ave., Hollywood, CA 90028. TEL: (323) 802-1500. FAX: (323) 802-1829.
www.henson.com www.puppetup.com

New York: 627 Broadway, 9th Flr., New York, NY 10012.
TEL: (212) 794-2400. FAX: (212) 439-7452.
CHAIRMAN
Brian Henson
CEO
Lisa Henson
PRESIDENT, COO
Peter Schube, Esq.
EXECUTIVE V.P., OPERATIONS & FINANCE
Laurie Don
SENIOR V.P., FEATURE FILMS
Jason Lust
SENIOR V.P., ADMINISTRATION
Joe Henderson
SENIOR V.P., BUSINESS & LEGAL AFFAIRS
Dan Scharf
EXECUTIVE V.P., CHILDREN'S ENTERTAINMENT
Halle Stanford
SENIOR V.P., GLOBAL CONSUMER PRODUCTS
Melissa Segal
SENIOR V.P., FEATURE FILMS
Jason Lust
SENIOR V.P., MARKETING & PUBLIC RELATIONS
Nicole Goldman - ngoldman@henson.com
CREATIVE SUPERVISOR
Peter Brooke
GENERAL MANAGER, NY WORKSHOP
Connie Peterson

HOLOGRAPHIC STUDIOS

(Holographic images & projections)
240 E. 26th St., New York, NY 10010. TEL: (212) 686-9397.
FAX: (212) 481-8645. email: drlaser@holographer.com
www.holostudios.com
FOUNDER/PRESIDENT
Jason Sapan

HOLLYWOOD BACKDROPS, FLATS & RISERS

(Mac Sennaett Stage)
1215 Bates Ave., Los Angeles, CA 90029.
TEL: (323) 660-8466.
email: sharrisc@sbcglobal.net www.macsennettstage.com

HOUSE OF MOVES MOTION CAPTURE STUDIOS

(Visual effects, motion capture, animation, 2D &3D art. A Vicon Company)
5419 McConnell Ave., Los Angeles, CA 90066.
TEL: (310) 306-6131. www.moves.com

I.D.E.A.S.

(Integrated creative content studio, full-service facility, motion graphics with HD. An Integrity Arts & Technology Company)
64 E. Concord St., Orlando, FL 32801. TEL: (407) 601-7878.
FAX: (407) 412-6990. www.ideasorlando.com
PRESIDENT
John Lux - jlux@ideasorlando.com
SENIOR V.P., BUSINESS DEVELOPMENT
Shirley Decker - sdecker@ideasorlando.com

IMAGE CREATORS, INC.

2712 6th St., Santa Monica, CA 90405. TEL: (310) 392-3583, (310) 202-8286. www.imagecreators.net
OWNER & CEO
Fred Spencer

Animatronics, puppet creatures, costume characters, prosthetic make-up effects, live-action characters.

INDUSTRIAL LIGHT & MAGIC (ILM)

(A Lucasfilm, Ltd. Co. Special effects and post-production)
P.O. Box 29909, San Francisco, CA 94129.
TEL: (415) 746-3000. FAX: (415) 746-3015.
www.ilm.com
PRESIDENT& GENERAL MANAGER
Lynwen Brennan
ADVISOR (FORMER PRESIDENT)
Chrissie England
EXECUTIVE IN CHARGE OF MARKETING & GLOBAL PRODUCTION
Gretchen Libby
EXECUTIVE IN CHARGE OF PRODUCTION OPERATIONS
Janet Lewin

Company is known for its model making, matte painting, computer-generated imagery, digital animation and a variety of related processes required in the production of visual effects.

INTERESTING PRODUCTS
(Liquid nitrogen fog, and LN systems for effects)
328 N. Albany Ave., Chicago, IL 60612.
TEL: (773) 265-0600. FAX: (773) 265-0700.
email: in2fog@attglobal.net www.interesting-products.com
PRESIDENT
Larry Schoeneman

IO FILM
(Visual effects, scanning and film output, optical special effects)
1415 N. Cahuenga Blv., Hollywood, CA 90028.
TEL: (323) 822-4444. FAX: (323) 467-7300. www.iofilm.net
V.P., BUSINESS DEVELOPMENT
Richard Jordan - rjordan@iofilm.net

KA-CHEW!
(A Klasky Csupo Company. Animation & design, compositing, modeling, visual effects)
1238 N. Highland Ave., Hollywood, CA 90038.
TEL: (323) 468-3020. FAX: (323) 468-3021. www.kachew.com
EXECUTIVE PRODUCER
John Andrews

KISMET PICTURES
(Full production services, digital editing, animation, visual effects)
12210 Michigan St., Studio 19, Grand Terrace, CA 92313.
TEL: (909) 783-0493. email: studio@kismetpictures.com
www.kismetpictures.com
PRESIDENT & CEO
Jeffrey Underwood

KNB EFX GROUP, INC.
(Make-up effects, animatronics and puppets)
9300 Eton Ave., Chatsworth, CA 91311.
TEL: (818) 901-6562. FAX: (818) 994-4685.
email: info@knbefxgroup.com www.knbefxgroup.com
OWNER
Greg Nicotero, Howard Berger

GENE KRAFT PRODUCTIONS
29 Calvados, Newport Beach, CA 92657. TEL: (949) 721-0609.
email: gkraft@ientertainment.ws
OWNER
Gene Kraft

LASER PACIFIC MEDIA CORP.
(A Kodak company. Post production services)
809 N. Cahuenga Blvd., Los Angeles, CA 90038.
TEL: (323) 462-6266. FAX: (323) 960-2192.
email: info@laserpacific.com www.laserpacific.com

LaserPacific provides visual effects services for both television and feature films. The VFX department is fully integrated with the TV and feature film pipelines. LaserPacific is also working closely with sister company Cinesite Europe, who provide a full range of VFX capabilities along with award-winning artists.

LEGEND FILMS, INC.
(Colorization and 2D to 3D conversion, color effects for black & white films and tv)
3721 Valley Center Dr., Ste. 500 San Diego, CA92130.
TEL: (858) 793-4420. FAX: (858) 793-4421.
www.legendfilms.com
PRESIDENT/ FOUNDER
Barry B. Sandrew, Ph.D - bsandrew@legendfilms.com

LEGEND 3D
(Conversion from 2D to 3D for film, television, ads)
3721 Valley Center Dr., Ste. 500, San Diego, CA 92130.
TEL: (858) 793-4420. FAX: (858) 783-4421.
www.legend3D.com
CEO
David Martin
CHIEF MARKETING OFFICER & EXECUTIVE V.P., NEW BUSINESS
Geoff Goodman

LIGHTNING STRIKES
(High intensity lighting for motion picture, television, special effects)
6601 Santa Monica Blvd., Los Angeles, CA 90038.
TEL: (323) 461-6361. FAX: (323) 461-3067.
www.luminycorp.com
SALES
David Pringle - dpringle@luminycorp.com
RENTALS
Robert Burdige - rburdige@luminycorp.com

LINKER SYSTEMS, INC.
13612 Onkayha Circle, Irvine, CA 92620. TEL: (949) 552-1904.
FAX: (949) 552-6985. www.linker.com www.linkersystems.com
www.animationstand.com

2D character animation, 3D, image compositing, film-quality special effects opticals. Win & Mac versions.

LIVE WIRE PRODUCTIONS & VFX
(Visual effects animation & compositing, motion tracking, 3D animation, matte painting; commercial production)
P.O. Box 245, Palos Verdes, CA 90274. TEL: (310) 831-6227.
email: info@livewirefilm.com www.livewirefilm.com
PRODUCER
Kristen Simmons

LUMENI PRODUCTIONS, INC.
1632 Flower St., Glendale, CA 91201-2357. TEL: (818) 956-2200.
FAX: (818) 956-3298. www.lumeni.com
EXECUTIVE PRODUCER
Marshall "Tony" Valdez - tony@lumeni.com

Services include: DI color timing; 2D, 3D & stereo computer graphics; animation; special effects for film, including digital trailers, film finishing & title design. Has served the entertainment industry for 29+ years.

MAGIC SNOW SYSTEMS
(Snow and snow special effects)
8581 Santa Monica Blvd., Ste. 219, Los Angeles, CA 90069.
TEL: (310) 289-9852. FAX: (310) 858-8260.
email: info@magicsnow.com www.magicsnow.com
PRESIDENT
Adam Williams

MAKE UP MANIA! OF NEW YORK
(Special effects design, production & implementation)
182 Allen St., New York, NY 10002. TEL: (800) 711-7182, (212) 533-5900. email: info@makeupmania.com
www.makeupmania.com

MAKEUP & EFFECTS LABORATORIES, INC. (M.E.L.)
(Animatronics, props, costumes, special effects make-up)
7110 Laurel Canyon Blvd., Bldg. E, N. Hollywood, CA 91605.
TEL: (818) 982-1483. FAX: (818) 982-5712.
email: info@melefx.com www.melefx.com
CONTACT
Paul Elliott - paul@melefx.com

MAKEUP & MONSTERS
(Creaturessuits, specialty costumes, puppets, hand props, illustration, sculpture, makeup)
21115 Devonshire St., #109, Chatsworth, CA 91311.
TEL: (818) 886-6587. FAX: (818) 709-6587.
email: monstermaker@makeupandmonsters.com
www.makeupandmonsters.com

MAKING UP
(Makeup & hair for film, video, HD, TV, commercials and print. Member of IATSE Local 706)
1630 Crespo Dr., La Jolla, CA 92037. TEL: (858) 459-6063.
Cell: (619) 990-6063. FAX: (858) 459-6035.
email: doris@dorislew.com www.dorislew.com
CONTACT
Doris Lew-Jensen

MASTERSFX, INC.
(Character FX: prosthetic FX, animatronics, & digital FX)
10316 Norris Ave., Unit D, Arleta, CA 91331.
TEL: (818) 834-3000. email: todd@mastefx.com
www.mastersfx.com
PRESIDENT
Todd Masters

MASTERS FX CANADA, INC.
3822 1st Ave., Burnaby BC CANADA V5C 3W1.
TEL: (604) 683-5311. FAX: (604) 299-5399.

MATCHFRAME VIDEO
(visual effects, HD)
610 N. Hollywood Way, Burbank, CA 91505.
TEL: (818) 840-6800. FAX: (818) 840-2726.
email: sales@matchframevideo.com
www.matchframevideo.com
COO
Mark Newton

MATTE WORLD DIGITAL
(Specialists in 2D & 3D environment creations)
24 Digital Dr., Ste. 6, Novato, CA 94949. TEL: (415) 382-1929.
FAX: (415) 382-1999. email: fx@matteworld.com
www.matteworld.com
CONTACT
Ken Rogerson

MATTHEW MUNGLE/W.M. CREATIONS, INC.
(Makeup effects)
5755 Tujunga Ave., North Hollywood, CA 91601.
TEL: (818) 763-6692. FAX: (818) 763-6693.
email: mm@wmmufx.com www.matthewmungle.com

MAVERICK DIGITAL
(Digital effects)
New York: 601 26th St., Ste. 1507, New York, NY 10001.
TEL: (212) 337-8004. email: info@maverickdigital.com
www.maverickdigital.net

Maverick Digital Denver: 1750 Gilpin St., 3rd Flr., Denver, CO 80218. TEL: (720) 941-6415.

Maverick Digital Phoenix: 15333 Pima Rd., Ste. 235, Scottsdale, AZ 85260. TEL: (623) 398-2592.

MEDIA FABRICATORS, INC.
(Video & data projection equipment, special effects)
5067 W. Washington Blvd., Los Angeles, CA 90016.
TEL: (323) 937-3344. FAX: (323) 937-1142.
email: mediafab@mediafab.com www.mediafab.com
PRESIDENT
Barry Fluster

MEDIAMATION, INC.
(Entertainment media integration for hydraulic, pneumatic & electric animatronics)
2213 Border Ave., Torrance, CA 90501. TEL: (310) 320-0696.
FAX: (310) 320-0699. email: sales@mediamat.com
www.mediamat.com
PRESIDENT & CEO
Alison Jamele
V.P. & CTO
Dan Jamele

METHOD STUDIOS
(Formerly R!OT)
New York: 545 Fifth Ave. Ste. 2, New York, NY 10017.
TEL: (212) 907-1200. FAX: (212) 907-1201.
MANAGING DIRECTOR
Alex Frisch
CREATIVE DIRECTOR
Aron Hjartarson
ANIMATION SUPERVISOR
Matt Hackett
SENIOR EXECUTIVE PRODUCER & VICE PRESIDENT
Gabby Gourrier
EXECUTIVE PRODUCER & DIRECTOR OF PRODUCTION
Helen Hughes
CONTACT
Chad Malbon - cmalbon@methodstudios.com

California: 730 Arizona Ave., Santa Monica, CA 90401.
TEL: (310) 434-6500. www.methodstudios.com
MANAGING DIRECTOR
Alex Frisch
HEAD, 3D
Andy Boyd
WEST COAST REPRESENTATION
Brent Novick - brentnovick@sbcglobal.net

Ascent Media Group announced that beginning January 1, 2009, two of its boutique visual effects studios, Riot and Method, would unite operations under the Method name, to offer clients high-end visual effects for commercials, music videos and feature films. Services include: digital post-production in NTSC and PAL, Telecine HD, Datacine, Inferno, Fire HD, Henry, VYVX capabilities, 3D CGI, scanning and recording, compression & duplication. Recruiting: Send reels to: method-sm-recruiting@methodstudios.com

MIGRANT FILM WORKER
(Indep. effects supervisor & designer. More than 25 years experience. Visual effects & animation)
6948 Saint Estaban St., Tujunga, CA 91042.
TEL: (818) 416-8278. email: jv2@migrantfilmworker.com
www.migrantfilmworker.com
CONTACT
John Van Vliet

MILITARY TECH TEMPS, INC.
(Prop master, military technical advisor)
101 N. Victory Blvd., Ste. 1270, Burbank, CA.
TEL: (818) 628-8003.
MILITARY TECHNICAL ADVISOR
Oscar Borrero

MODERN VIDEOFILM
(Compositing, visual effects)
4411 W. Olive Ave., Burbank, CA 91505.
TEL: (818) 840-1700. www.mvfinc.com
EXECUTIVE V.P. SALES
Jon Johnson - jjohnson@mvfinc.com

MOLE-RICHARDSON CO.
(Lighting, mechanical effects, wind machines, fog machines, cobweb making equipment)
937 N. Sycamore Ave., Hollywood, CA 90038.
TEL: (323) 851-0111. email: info@mole.com www.mole.com

MOTION CITY FILMS
(Animation, editorial, digital effects)
1424 Fourth St., #604, Santa Monica, CA 90401.
TEL: (310) 434-1272. www.motioncity.com
CONTACT
G. Michael Witt - witt@motioncity.coms

MOVING PICTURES
(Compositing, visual effects, full production capabilities)
222 E. 44th St., 8th Flr., New York, NY 10017.
TEL: (212) 924-7364. FAX: (212) 450-7910.
email: info@mpny.ty www.mpny.tv
PRODUCER/DIRECTOR
Ron Honsa

NBC UNIVERSAL

NBC UNIVERSAL ARTWORKS
(Visual effects, special effects)
30 Rockefeller Plaza, New York, NY 10112.
TEL: (212) 664-5972. www.nbcartworks.com
V.P
David Steel
EXECUTIVE CREATIVE DIRECTOR
Carlos Asmar
OPERATIONS DIRECTOR
Greg Francis

NBC BURBANK
(Production, post production, staging, costumes)
3000 W. Alameda Ave., Burbank, CA 91523.
TEL: (818) 840-4724. FAX: (818) 840-3472.
www.filmmakersdestination.com
DIRECTOR, PRODUCTION & TECHNICAL SERVICES
Carl Geller - carl.geller@nbcuni.com

NBC UNIVERSAL STUDIOS
(Props, mechanical effects, wind, wave, fog, rain)
100 Universal City Plaza, Bldg. 8166/1, Universal City, CA 91608. TEL: (818) 777-2784. FAX: (818) 866-1543.
www.filmmakersdestination.com
CONTACT
Beverly Hadley - beverly.hadley@nbcuni.com

NETWORK ART SERVICE
(Graphics & props)
1330 N. Clybourn Ave., Burbank, CA 91505.
TEL: (818) 843-5078. FAX: (818) 843-2528.
CONTACT
Dan Walker

NEW DEAL STUDIOS, INC.
(Visual effects, design, miniatures, effects, photography and digital)
4121 Redwood Ave., Los Angeles, CA 90066.
TEL: (310) 578-9929. FAX: (310) 578-7370.
email: info@newdealstudios.com www.newdealstudios.com
CEO
Shannon Blake Gans
DIRECTOR & VFX SUPERVISOR
Ian Hunter, Matthew Gratzner, Ken Locsmandi, Nick Delgado

NOVOCOM
(A Via worldwide co. Corporate branding, broadcast corporate design)
Malibu Studio: 29652 Cuthbert Rd., Malibu, CA 90265.
TEL: (310) 589-2782. FAX: (310) 589-5261.
email: jridgway@novo.com www.novo.com
CEO & CREATIVE DIRECTOR
John Ridgway

OPTIC NERVE STUDIOS
(Make-up, prosthetics, animatronics, specialty props)
9818 Glenoaks Blvd., Sun Valley, CA 91352.
TEL: (818) 771-1007. FAX: (818) 698-0434.
email: info@opticnervefx.com www.OpticNerveFX.com
CEO
Glenn Hetrick

OWEN MAGIC SUPREME
(Creator & manufacturer of magical effects)
734 N. McKeever Ave., Azusa, CA 91702. TEL: (626) 969-4519.
FAX: (626) 969-4614. email: alanz@owenmagic.com
www.owenmagic.com

PARADISE FX CORP.
(Film & video 3D production, large format cinematography)
7011 Hayvenhurst Ave., Van Nuys, CA 91406.
TEL: (818) 785-3100. FAX: (818) 785-3313.
email: info@paradisefx.com www.paradisefx.com
PRESIDENT/CO-FOUNDER
Tim Thomas
CTO/CO-FOUNDER
Max Penner

PARAMOUNT PICTURES
(Props, break-a-ways, mechanical effects, pyrotechnics, rain, wind, fog and snow effects)
Special Effects Department, 555 Melrose Ave., Marathon Mill, Hollywood, CA 90038. TEL: (323) 956-5140.

FAX: (323) 862-2325. www.paramountstudios.com

PERPETUAL MOTION PICTURES

(Digital effects, 2D, 3D animation, motion control, miniatures)
16654 Soledad Canyon Rd., #198, Santa Clarita, CA 91387.
TEL: (661) 294-0788. FAX: (661) 294-0786.
email: info@pmpfx.com www.pmpfx.com
CONTACT
Richard Malzahn

PIXEL LIBERATION FRONT

(Previsualization, post visualization, 3D creation, compositing, motion capture)
1285 Electric Ave., Venice, CA 90291. TEL: (310) 396-9854.
email: plf@thefront.com www.thefront.com
CREATIVE DIRECTOR
Stephen Laws

PIXEL MAGIC

10635 Riverside Dr., Toluca Lake, CA 91602.
TEL: (818) 760-0862. FAX: (818) 760-4983.
email: sales@pixelmagicfx.com www.pixelmagicfx.com
VICE PRESIDENT
Ray McIntyre, Jr.

Visual effects facility. A div. of OCS/Freeze Frame. Compositing, visual effects.

PLAYGROUND

(Special effects, compositing, 3D animations)
1813 Centinela Ave., Santa Monica, CA 90404.
TEL: (310) 315-3800. FAX: (310) 315-3801.
email: info@playgroundla.com www.playgroundla.com

PRIME FOCUS

(Formerly Post Logic Studios, Inc. Visual effects, compositing, scanning & film output)
1800 N. Vine St., Hollywood, CA 90028. TEL: (323) 461-7887.
FAX: (323) 461-7790. www.primefocusworld.com

New York: 435 Hudson St., 7th Flr., New York, NY 10014.
TEL: (212) 520-3150. FAX: (212) 520-3155.

Vancouver: 1255 W. Pender St., Vancouver, BC V6E 2V1.
TEL: (604) 733-7030. FAX: (604) 733-7093.

QUANTEL, INC.

New York: 25 West 43rd St., Ste. 222, New York, NY 10036.
TEL: (212) 944 6820. FAX: (212) 944 6813.
www.quantel.com
CONTACT
Lee Turvey - lee.turvey@quantel.com

Los Angeles: 3800 Barham Blvd., Ste. 315, Los Angeles, CA 90068. TEL: (323) 436-7600. FAX: (323) 878-2596.
CONTACT
Eric Thorne - eric.thorne@quantel.com

Animation equipment, including digital intermediate-2K or 4K resolution. Quantel provides both hardware and software across post production, DI and broadcast for multiple resolution, team-working production environments.

RADIUM

(Visual effects, compositing, motion capture, optical special effects)
2115 Colorado Ave., Santa Monica, CA 90404.
TEL: (310) 656-0156. FAX: (310) 264-6441. www.radium.com
EXECUTIVE PRODUCER
Dan Bryant

RAINMAKER ENTERTAINMENT

(Cel, clay and digital animation, motion capture)

2025 W. Broadway, Ste. 500, Vancouver, BC Canada V6J 1Z6.
TEL: (604) 714-2600. FAX: (604) 714-2641.
email: info@rainmaker.com
CEO
Warren Franklin

RANDO PRODUCTIONS, INC.

(Mechanical special effects, customized; New Ro-Motion RM-36)
11939 Sherman Rd., North Hollywood, CA 91605.
TEL: (818) 982-4300. FAX: (818) 982-4320.
email: joer@randoproductions.com
www.randoproductions.com
CONTACT
Joe Rando

REALITY CHECK SYSTEMS

(Compositing, optical special effects, visual effects for broadcast, animation with 3D)
726 S. Flower St., Burbank, CA 91502. TEL: (323) 465-3900, (323) 465-3900. FAX: (323) 465-3600.
email: info@realityx.com www.realityx.com
PRESIDENT
Andrew Heimbold

REEL EFX

(Mechanical effects; special effects product manufacturer sales and rentals; real-time special effects)
5539 Riverton Ave., N. Hollywood, CA 91601. TEL: (818) 762-1710.
FAX: (818) 762-1734. www.reelefx.com
PRESIDENT
Jim Gill - jim@reelefx.com

REELISTIC FX

(Rentals, pyrotechnics, miniatures, motion controlled gimbals and flying devices)
21318 Hart St., Canoga Park, CA 91303. TEL: (818) 621-2484.
FAX: (818) 346-2710. www.r-fx.com
PRESIDENT
John Gray

RENEGADE EFFECTS GROUP

(Costumes, props, sets, weapons, armour, special effects)
11312 Hartland St., North Hollywood, CA 91605.
TEL: (818) 980-8848. FAX: (818) 980-8849.
email: info@renegadeeffects.com wwwrenegadeeffects.com

REZN8 PRODUCTIONS, INC.

(Compositing, modeling, animation, visual effects)
460 Euclid St., Santa Monica, CA 90405.
TEL: (310) 925-1469. email: sales@resn8.com
www.resn8.com
EXECUTIVE CREATIVE DIRECTOR
Paul Sidlo

RHYTHM & HUES STUDIOS

(Computer animation; special effects animation: CG animation & visual effects)
2100 E. Grand Ave., El Segundo, CA 90245.
TEL: (310) 448-7500. FAX: (310) 448-7600. www.rhythm.com
PRESIDENT, FILM DIVISION
Lee Berger - (310) 448-7727 lee@rhythm.com
V.P., DEVELOPMENT
Pauline Ts'o - tso@rhythm.com
EXECUTIVE PRODUCER, DESIGN DIVISION
Stacey Burstin
HEAD OF PRODUCTION, LIVE ACTION
Kat Dillon - kat@rhythm.com
DIRECTOR OF DEVELOPMENT
Venecia Duran - vduran@rhythm.com

RING OF FIRE STUDIOS

(Compositing & visual effects)
1538 20th St., Santa Monica, CA 90404. TEL: (310) 966-5055.
FAX: (310) 966-5056. email: info@ringoffire.com
www.ringoffire.com
PARTNER
John Myers - jmyers@ringoffire.com
DIRECTOR OF MARKETING
Amy Grgich - amy@ringoffire.com

New York: 118 W. 22nd St., 8th Flr., New York, NY 10011.
TEL: (212) 671-2060.

RSPINC.

(Makeup, effects, animatronics, puppetry, mechanical effects)
7117 Dume Dr., Malibu, CA 90265. TEL: (310) 457-4499.
email: robertshort@robertshort.com www.robertshort.com
PRESIDENT
Robert Short

SET STUFF RENTALS

(Equipment rental for environmental effects, rain, smoke, fog, fire, wind)
1105 N. Sycamore Ave., Hollywood, CA 90038.
TEL: (323) 993-9500. FAX: (323) 993-9506.
email: info@setstuffrentals www.setstuffrentals.com

SFX STUDIO, INC.

(Special effects make up, character design, prosthetics, animatronics)
18-145 Schoolhouse St., Coquitlam, BC V3K 4X8.
TEL: (604) 205-5142. FAX: (604) 618-5177.
www.sfxstudio.com
OWNER/DESIGNER
Joel Echollier - joel@sfxstudio.com

THE SHAPE SHOP

(Model making, prototypes, mold making, pattern making for the entertainment industry)
16708 Gramercy Pl., Unit B, Torrance, CA 90247.
TEL: (800) 379-5756, (310) 532-4391.
email: info@theshapeshop.com www.theshapeshop.com
CONTACT
John Ferrari

SIGHT EFFECTS

(Visual effects for commercials, telecine)

901 Abbot Kinney Blvd., Venice, CA 90291.
TEL: (310) 392-0999. FAX: (310) 399-1334.
www.sighteffects.com
EXECUTIVE PRODUCER
Melissa Davies - melissa@sighteffects.com

SINGLE FRAME FILMS
(Animation)
3940 Avery St., Detroit, MI 48208. TEL: (313) 833-1520.
email: info@singleframefilms.com www.singleframefilms.com
CONTACT
Gary Schwartz

SIX FOOT TWO PRODUCTIONS
(Traditional & digital animation & digital post-production visual effects)
25 Ebbtide Passage, Corte Madera, CA 94925.
TEL: (415) 927-0880. FAX: (415) 927-0550.
email: animate@sixfoottwo.com www.sixfoottwo.com
DIRECTOR, CREATIVE LEAD
Robbin Atherly

SNOW BUSINESS, INC.
(Artificial snow and ice, winter effects)
21318 Hart St., Canoga Park, CA 91303. TEL: (818) 884-3009.
FAX: (818) 884-3110. email: snowbizla@aol.com
www.snowbusinesshollywood.com
CONTACT
Roland Hathaway, John Gray

SONY PICTURES IMAGEWORKS
(A Sony Pictures Entertainment Company)
9050 W. Washington Blvd., Culver City, CA 90232.
TEL: (310) 840-8000. FAX: (310) 840-8100.
www.imageworks.com
EXECUTIVE V.P. & GENERAL MANAGER
Randy Lake
EXECUTIVE V.P. PRODUCTION & EXECUTIVE PRODUCER
Debbie Denise
SENIOR V.P., INTERACTIVE
Emmanuelle Borde
SENIOR V.P., PUBLIC RELATIONS & COMMUNICATIONS, SONY PICTURES ANIMATION & SONY PICTURES IMAGEWORKS
Don Levy - donlevy@sonypictures.com
SENIOR V.P., ANIMATION PRODUCTION
Barry Weiss
CHIEF TECHNOLOGY OFFICER & VISUAL EFFECTS SUPERVISOR
Rob Bredow
SENIOR VISUAL EFFECTS SUPEVISOR
Ken Ralston
ANIMATION DIRECTOR
Spencer Cook, Peter Nash, Troy Saliba, David Schaub
ANIMATION SUPERVISOR
Chris Williams
DIGITAL EFFECTS SUPERVISOR
Rob Engle, Ken Hahn, Daniel Maury, Seth Maury, Peter Nofz, David Smith
VISUAL EFFECTS SUPERVISOR
Jim Berney, Jerome Chen, Richard Hoover, Don Keler, Scott Stokdyk, Pete Travers

CG Animation, visual effects, motion capture 3d stereoscopic and interactive.

SOTA FX
(Monsters for movies)
7338 Valjean Ave., Van Nuys, CA 91406. TEL: (818) 780-1003.
FAX: (818) 780-4315. email: roy@sotaproductions.com
www.sotaproduction.com
CONTACT
Roy Knyrim

SPECIAL EFFECTS UNLIMITED, INC.
(Environmental effects, wind, rain, fog, pyro and fire effects, miniatures, custome made props, flying & rigging equipment)
1005 N. Lillian Way, Hollywood, CA 90038. TEL: (323) 466-3361.
FAX: (323) 466-5712. www.specialeffectsunlimited.com

SPECTAK PRODUCTIONS, INC.
(Laser special effects; major events producer)
222 N. Sepulveda Blvd., Ste. 2000, El Segundo, CA 90245.
TEL: (310) 335-2038. FAX: (310) 335-2048.
email: info@spetak.com www.spectak.com
PRESIDENT & CEO
Ric Birch
CONTACT
Tanya Rountree

See website for international locations.

SPECTRAL MOTION, INC.
(Visual effects including creature, makeup, animatronics)
1849 Dana St., Glendale, CA 91201. TEL: (818) 956-6080.
FAX: (818) 956-6083. email: info@spectralmotion.com
www.spectralmotion.com
FOUNDER
Mike Elizalde

SPECTRUM EFFECTS, INC.
(Mechanical effects, stunt coordination, pyrotechnics)
Santa Clarity, CA. TEL: (661) 510-5633.
email: info@specialeffects.com www.spectrumeffects.com
OWNER
Matt Kutcher - matt.specialeffects@gmail.com

STARGATE FILMS
(Film & HD prduction, matte painting, 3D, compositing & editorial services, virtual locatons)
1001 El Centro St., South Pasadena, CA 90038.
TEL: (626) 403-8403. FAX: (626) 403-8444.
email: info@stargatefilms.com www.stargatefilms.com
FOUNDER/CEO
Sam Nicholson
EXECUTIVE V.P., DEVELOPMENT
James Riley

Vancouver: 1225 W. 8th Ave., 4th Flr., Vancouver BC V5Y IN3 Canada. TEL: (877) 488-1241. FAX: (604) 48812-42.

STEELE STUDIOS
(3D stereoscopic, compositing, visual effects, motion graphics, 2D & 3D animation)
5737 Masmer Ave., Culver City, CA 90230.
TEL: (310) 656-7770. FAX: (310) 656-7771.
email: info@steelevfx.com www.steelvfx.com

STICKS & STONES FX
(Specialty props, costume design, custom build only; make-up effects and puppets. Sales only. No rentals)
10535 Tujunga Canyon Blvd., Tujunga, CA 91042.
TEL: (818) 352-9538. FAX: (818) 353-6979.
email: jemrtb@verizon.net www.sticksandstonesfx.com
CONTACT
Rob Burman, Jennifer E. McManus

STOKES/KOHNE ASSOCIATES, INC.
(Full-service animation company; visual effects, providing specialized cinematography and photography for film, broadcast and print)
742 Cahuenga Blvd., Hollywood, CA 90038.
TEL: (323) 468-2340. email: dmisk@stokeskohne.com
www.stokeskohne.com
CONTACT
Dan Kohne

Services include: graphics, fx design, live action, tabletop, motion control, film stop motion, digital stop motion, macro cinematography, hi-speed cinematography, HD, HD/2K uncompressed editing & post, blue/green screen, organic/abstract fx and stock footage.

SWAY STUDIO
(Visual effects for film, TV & commercials)
3535 Hayden Ave., 4th Flr., Culver City, CA 90232.
TEL: (310) 844-7000. FAX: (310) 844-7050.
www.swaystudio.com
CONTACT
Jason Cohan - jasonc@swaystudio.com

SYNTHESPIAN STUDIOS, INC.
(Design & character animation studio)
5355 Cartwright Ave., #117, North Hollywood, CA 91601.
TEL: (818) 753-1822. www.synthespians.net
EXECUTIVE PRODUCER
Amanda Roth - ar@sythespians.net

MATT SWEENEY SPECIAL EFFECTS
(Special equipment for special effects & stunts)
14201 Bessemer St., Van Nuys, CA 91401.
TEL: (818) 902-9354. FAX: (818) 902-1513.
email: orderdesk@sweeney-special-effects.com
www.sweeney-special-effects.com
CONTACT
Matthew Sweeney, Lucinda Strub

TECHNICOLOR VFX & ANIMATION
(2D compositing & 3D visual effects, animation, optical effects)
2255 N. Ontario, Ste. 360, Burbank, CA 91504.
TEL: (818) 260-2615. www.technicolor.com
CONTACT
Rob Anker - rob.anker@technicolor.com

TIPPETT STUDIO
(Full-service visual effects facility. Specialty: CG character animation)
2741 10th St., Berkeley, CA 94710. TEL: (510) 649-9711.
FAX: (510) 649-9399. email: info@tippett.com
www.tippett.com
FOUNDER
Phil Tippett

TLC CREATIVE PRODUCTIONS
13428 Maxella Ave., #261, Marina Del Rey CA 90292.
TEL: (800) 447-3585, (310) 822-6790. www.TLCiscreative.com
OWNER
Kevin Bilda - kevin@TLCiscreative.com
LOGISTICS & PRODUCTION MANAGER
Jeff Ward - jeff@TLCiscreative.com

Special Effects provider.

TRIBAL SCENERY
(Set design & construction, mechanical effects)
3216 Vanowen St., Burbank, CA 91505. TEL: (818) 558-4045.
FAX: (818) 558-4356. email: tscenery@earthlink.net
www.tribalscenery.com

MIKE TRISTANO WEAPONS & SPECIAL EFFECTS
14431 Ventura Blvd., PMB 185, Sherman Oaks, CA 91423.
TEL: (818) 888-6970. FAX: (818) 888-6447.

Prop weapons, blank firing weapons, on-set weapons handlers and armorer. Also stocks: police & SWAT gear; western firearms and holsters; pirate weapons & gear; and military props.

ULTRA EFFECTS
(Air, waater & land rc vehicles, robotics, CGI modeling)
5011 S. Reino Rd., Newbury Park, CA 91320.
TEL: (805) 499-1506.
CONTACT
Jeff Vasquez - jeffvasquez@verizon.net

ULTIMATE EFFECTS
16805 Sierra Highway, Canyon Country, CA 91351.
TEL: (661) 298-3033. FAX: (661) 298-3028.
email: ultmtfx@aol.com www.ultimateeffects.com
CONTACT
John Hartigan, Beverley Hartigan

Full-service effects company that provides: mechanical effects, pyrotechnics, coordination, all on set practical effects.

VIDEO POST & TRANSFER, INC.
(Film to tape transfer, video online editing, audio, broadcast design, 3D animation, visual effects)
2727 Inwood Rd., Dallas, TX 75235. TEL: (214) 350-2676.
FAX: (214) 352-1427. email: roberth@videopost.com
www.videopost.com
PRESIDENT
Robert Haasz

VIEW POINT CREATIVE
(Creative services)
254 Second Ave., Needham, MA 02494. TEL: (781) 449-5858, (310) 822-3013 (Los Angeles). FAX: (781) 449-7272.
www.viewpointcreative.com
DIRECTOR, BUSINESS DEVELOPMENT
Amy Coblenz - acoblenz@viewpointcreative.com

VIEW STUDIO, INC.
(Digital design & special effects for new media, television & film. Recently launched www.ecology.com)
385 Toro Canyon Rd., Carpinteria, CA 93013.
TEL: (805) 745-8814. email: bob@viewstudio.com
www.viewstudio.com
CONTACT
Bob Engelsiepen

VISUAL CONCEPT ENGINEERING
(Digital effects and motion control)
13300 Ralston Ave., Sylmar, CA 91342-7608.
TEL: (818) 367-9187. email: vce@vce.com www.vce.com
PRESIDENT
Peter Kuran

WARNER BROS. STUDIO FACILITIES
(Special effects/Prop shop)
4000 Warner Blvd., Bldg. 44, Burbank, CA 91522.
TEL: (818) 954-1365. FAX: (818) 954-1424.
email: wbsf@warnerbros.com www.wbsf.com

DON WAYNE MAGIC EFFECTS
(Magic illusions)
10907 Magnolia Dr., Ste. 467, N. Hollywood, CA 91601.
TEL: (818) 763-3192. FAX: (818) 985-4953.
email: info@donwaynemagic.com www.donwaynemagic.com

WEST POST DIGITAL
(Full post production services, visual effects)
1703 Stewart St., Santa Monica, CA 90404.
TEL: (310) 857-5000. FAX: (310) 857-9031.
email: edit@westpostdigital.com www.westpostdigital.com

WILDFIRE, INC. LIGHTING & VISUAL EFFECTS
(Manufacturer of ultraviolet blacklights)
2908 Oregon Ct., Ste. G1, Torrance, CA 90503.
TEL: (800) 937-8065, (310) 755-6780. FAX: (310) 755-6781.
email: sales@wildfirefx.com rentals@wildfirefx.com
www.wildfire.fx.com

WONDERWORKS, INC.
(Models, miniatures, special effects)
7231 Remmet Ave., Canoga Park, CA 91302.
TEL: (818) 992-8811. FAX: (818) 347-4330.
www.wonderworksweb.com
PRESIDENT
Brick Price - brickprice@aol.com

WUNDERFILM, INC.
(Main title design, visual effects, network promos, corporate identity, pilot presentations)
2276 La Grenada, Hollywood, CA 90068-2724.
TEL: (323) 845-4100. FAX: (323) 845-4101.
email: jeff@wunderfilm.com www.wunderfilm.com
OWNER
Jeff Wunderlich

KEVIN YAGHER PRODUCTIONS, INC.
(Special effects make-up and animatronics)
6615 Valjean Ave., Van Nuys, CA 91406. TEL: (818) 374-3210.
FAX: (818) 374-3214. email: info@kevinyagher.com
www.kevinyagher.com

STOCK SHOTS

A LUNA BLUE
(Royalty free stock footage and photographs)
2163 Vista Del Mar Ave., Los Angeles, CA 90068.
TEL: (323) 871-8919. FAX: (323) 464-0502.
email: sales@alunablue.com raymond@alunablue.com
www.alunablue.com
OWNER
Raymond Pettitt

ACADEMY OF MOTION PICTURE ARTS & SCIENCES
(Motion picture stills)
Fairbanks Center of Motion Picture Study / Margaret Herrick Library. 333 S. La Cienega Blvd., Beverly Hills, CA 90211.
TEL: (310) 247-3036, ext. 280. email: photographs@oscars.org
www.oscars.org
CONTACT
Faye Thompson

ALL STOCK FOTO
(Part of the marketing network of: StockPhotoFinder.com, Inc.)
10 E. 23rd St., Ste. 500, New York, NY 10010.
TEL: (212) 929-6965. email: info@StockPhotoFinder.com
www.stockfoto.com

StockPhotoFinder aggregates the largest quantity of professional stock photos in the industry, approximately 30 million images. It makes these images available via its public search engines and via private, customized sites for corporations. StockPhotoFinder makes its unique, time-saving research tools available as "white label" search resources to be branded by major corporations that license photos and footage.

AM STOCK-CAMEO FILM LIBRARY
(35 mm and HD, Aerials, Buildings, Cities, Nature & Skylines; features free research, custom shooting and operates with license fees)
10513 Burbank Blvd., N. Hollywood, 91601. TEL: (818) 762-7865.
FAX: (818) 762-6480. email: researcher@amstockcameo.com
www.amstockcameo.com
LIBRARIAN
Chris Angelich

The library contains more than 2.3 million feet of 35 mm negative and 140,000 different clips.

AMERICAN MUSEUM OF NATURAL HISTORY LIBRARY - SPECIAL COLLECTIONS
Central Park W. at 79th St., New York, NY 10024.
TEL: (212) 769-5420. FAX: (212) 769-5009.
email: speccol@amnh.org
http://library.amnh.org/special/index.html

The museum archives includes the Institutional Archives, the Photographic collection, the Moving Image and Sound Collections, the Art Collection and the Memorabilia Collection. For photographic reproductions: If you have submitted a request for a photograph with an image number or with an attached image belonging to one of the museum's collection, you can expect to hear from the museum's Digital Photographer within two weeks to arrange for the delivery of a scanned image. Photo requests submitted based on a description may take two weeks to identify the image or to verify that the image is in the museum's collection. Requesting permission to use an image requires completion/submission of the museum's request form available on the library web site at http://library.amnh.org/special/permission.pdf Please note the museum staff does not sign other institutions' licensing agreements and invoices for permission to publish or broadcast images are generated solely by the above form. For any other information, including the rates for digital scans and publication fees, please see website at http://library.amnh.org/special/index.html

AMERICAN STOCK PHOTOGRAPHY, INC.
3470 Wilshire Blvd., Ste. 545, Los Angeles, CA 90010.
TEL: (800) 272-4749, (213) 386-4600. FAX: (213) 365-7171.
email: info@americanstockphotos.com
www.americanstockphotos.com

American Stock Photography, Inc. is a rights-controlled (not royalty-free), general subject, stock photo agency. Rates are based on use, media, circulation, extent and length of campaign. License becomes valid upon payment of the invoice. Copyrighted photographs cannot be further utilized, loaned, rented, copied or syndicated without an additional licensing agreement.

AP ARCHIVE
450 W. 33rd St.,14th Flr., New York, NY 10001.
TEL: (212) 621-7400. FAX:(212) 621-7489.
email: northamerica-sales@aparchive.com
www.aparchive.com
SALES COORDINATION MANAGER
Fulvia Cassarino - (212) 621-7494 fcassarino@ap.org

Associated Press archive footage. Can also license footage from ABC News, Sky News and many other partners. See website for locations and contacts worldwide.

CARL BARTH IMAGES
(Representing the Stock House collection and more)
P.O. Box 5325, Santa Barbara, CA 93150-5325.
TEL: (805) 637-0881. email: carlbarthimages@cox.net
www.carlbarthimages.com
CONTACT
Carl Barth

Providing second unit direction and production supervision, title backgrounds, special effects sequences, moving car backgrounds and stock footage for film & TV for close to 30 years.

BBC MOTION GALLERY
(Full selection)
New York: BBC Worldwide Americas, 747 Third Ave., 29th Flr., New York, NY 10017. TEL: (212) 705-9399. FAX: (212) 705-9342.
email: motiongallery.ny@bbc.com www.bbcmotiongallery.com

Los Angeles: BBC Worldwide, 4144 Lankershim Blvd., Ste. 200, N. Hollywood, CA 91602. TEL: (818) 299-9720.
FAX: (818) 299-9763. email: motiongallery.la@bbc.com
www.bbcmotiongallery.com

Access a range of unique, high-quality stock footage, ready to preview, purchase and immediately download. BBC is a gateway to 2.5 million hours of content offline and has expert researchers available to help customers find exactly what they need. See website for addtional offices worldwide.

BEST SHOT, INC.
(Full selection; all formats-Film HD)
4301 W. Cayuga St., Tampa, FL 33614. TEL: (813) 877-2118.
FAX: (813) 874-3655. email: images@bestshotfootage.com
www.bestshotfootage.com
CONTACT
Dan Klein

THE BRIDGEMAN ART LIBRARY INTERNATIONAL
(Full selection)
65 E. 93rd St., New York, NY 10128. TEL: (212) 828-1238.
FAX: (212) 828-1255. email: newyork@bridgemanart.com
www.bridgemanart.com
MARKETING EXECUTIVE, NEW YORK
Kim Tidwell
INTERNATIONAL CONTACTS
London: The Bridgeman Art Library.
TEL: +44 (0)20 7727 4065. london@bridgeman.co.uk

Paris: Bridgeman Giraudon
TEL: +33 (0)1 55 80 79 10. paris@bridgeman.fr

Berlin: Bridgeman Berlin
TEL: +49 (0)30 88 92 02 76. berlin@bridgeman-berlin.de

The Bridgeman Art Library is a leading source of fine art with images from over 8,000 collections and 29,000 artists. Organization represents museums, galleries and artists throughout the world by providing a central source of fine art for image users. In addition to fine art images, the Bridgeman archive includes: Architecture; History & Politics; Travel & Exploration; Decorative Arts & Design; Contemporary Art; Photography; Religion & Philosophy; Science & Medicine; Ancient & World Civilizations; Music, Theatre and Literature; Sport.

BUDGET FILMS STOCK FOOTAGE, INC.
(Vintage and contemporary)
4427 Santa Monica Blvd., Los Angeles, CA 90029.
TEL: (323) 660-0187. FAX: (323) 660-5571.
email: filmclip@aol.com www.budgetfilms.com
MANAGER, STOCK FOOTAGE ARCHIVE
Layne Murphy

CHERTOK ASSOCIATES, INC. (JAZZ ON FILM)
(Musical performances on film; specialty is jazz performances)
18 Old Schoolhouse Rd., New City, NY 10956.
TEL: (845) 461-7986. email: jazzfilm@mail.com
CONTACT/PRESIDENT
Michael Chertok

Footage: Vintage Jazz, African-American Lifestyle, Pop Culture, Tap Dance and more.

DICK CLARK PRODUCTIONS
(Licenses footage for TV broadcast, theatrical release & DVD distribution)
2900 Olympic Blvd., Santa Monica, CA 90404.
TEL: (310) 255-4600. email: jjames@dickclark.com

www.dickclarkproductions.com
CONTACT
Jeff James

Over 10,000 musical performances and over 2,400 hours of TV programming.

CRYSTAL PYRAMID PRODUCTIONS

(Animation, video production, nonlinear editing & stock footage)
7323 Rondel Court, San Diego, CA 92119.
TEL: (800) 365-8433, (619) 644-3000. FAX: (619) 644-3001.
email: cpp@newuniquevideos.com www.crystalpyramid.com
PRESIDENT
Mark Schulze
PRODUCER & V.P.
Patty Mooney - patty@crystalpyramid.com
MULTIMEDIA PRODUCER
Luke Jungers

NEW & UNIQUE VIDEOS

(Stock footage & distribution)
7323 Rondel Ct., San Diego, CA 92119.
TEL: (619) 644-3000. FAX: (619) 644-3001.
email: video@newuniquevideos.com
www.newuniquevideos.com
PRODUCER & V.P.
Patty Mooney

Quality stock footage. Part of Crystal Pyramid Productions.

DOUBLETIME PRODUCTIONS

162 Pond View Dr., Port Washington, NY 11050.
TEL: (866) 226-4474, (516) 869-1170. FAX: (516) 869-1171.
email: info@doubletimeproductions.com
www.doubletimeproductions.com

Footage includes: AMTRAK Official Licensing, Animals, Beaches and Sunsets, Chicago, Cityscapes, Deserts, Florida, Landscapes, Lifestyles, Mountains, New York Panoramic and Rural Scenes, North American Wildlife, Northwest, Rocky Mountain Scenery, Scenics, Southwest, Traffic, Trains, Transportation & Travel.

CLASSIC IMAGES

(1900 to contemporary)
469 S. Bedford Dr., Beverly Hills, CA 90212.
TEL: (800) 949-CLIP, (310) 277-0400. FAX: (310) 277-0412.
email: sales@classicimg.com www.classicimg.com
PRESIDENT
Marcie Alexander

THE CLIP JOINT FOR FILM

833-B N. Hollywood Way, Burbank, CA 91505.
TEL: (818) 842-2525. FAX: (818) 842-2644.
email: clipjoint4film@aol.com

CNN IMAGESOURCE

One CNN Center, 12th Flr., North Tower, Atlanta, GA 30303.
TEL: (866) 462-4350, (404) 827-3326. FAX: (404) 827-1840.
email: cnn.imagesource@turner.com
www.cnnimagesource.com

A video source for accidents/disasters, beauty shots, business, celebrities, crime, environment, politics, terrorism and war/military.

COLLEGIATE IMAGES

13450 Sunsrise Blvd., Ste. 170, Sunrise, FL 33323.
TEL: (954) 343-8000, (818) 625-1606. FAX: (954) 343-8001.
www.collegiateimages.com

Collegiate Images is the centralized licensing and rights clearance agency that manages the ditribution of copyrighted intellectual property content, focusing exclusively on college sports.

CORBIS MOTION

Corbis headquarters: 710 Second Ave., Ste. 200, Seattle, WA 98104. TEL: (800) 260-0444 (North American sales).
email: sales@corbis.com

Chicago: 118 N. Clinton, Ste. 100-11, Chicago, IL 60661-2395.
TEL: (312) 464-1255. FAX: (312) 632-1119.
email: sales.chi@corbis.com www.corbismotion.com

Los Angeles: 6060 Center Dr., Ste. 100, Los Angeles, CA 90045. TEL: (323) 602-5700. FAX: (323) 602-5837.
email: infola@corbismotion.com

New York: 902 Broadway, New York, NY 10010.
TEL: (212) 777-6200. FAX: (212) 533-4034.
email: info@corbismotion.com

Creative resource providing a comprehensive selection of photography, illustration, footage and rights clearance services. Through its partnership with Thought Equity Motion, Corbis Motion provides access to content from leading film and entertainment companies, including: National Geographic, Sony Pictures Entertainment, Smithsonian Channel, Paramount Pictures, MGM Studios and HBO Archives. Content includes HD footage. Free comps and research. See website for additional offices worldwide.

F.I.L.M. ARCHIVES, INC.

(Vintage, contemporary, animation, and news/lifestyles)
35 W. 35th St., Ste 504, New York, NY 10001.
TEL: (212) 696-2616. FAX: (212) 696-0021.
email:info@filmarchivesonline.com
www.filmarchivesonline.com
PRESIDENT & CEO
Mark Trost
V.P., ONLINE OPERATIONS
Karen Doogan
DIRECTOR OF RESEARCH
Kate Wilkinson
DIRECTOR, LIBRARY MANAGEMENT
Emily Drew
ASSOCIATE DIRECTOR OF RESEARCH
Sarah Feuquay

FILM & VIDEO STOCK SHOTS, INC.

10442 Burbank Blvd., N. Hollywood, CA 91601-2217.
TEL: (888) 436-6824, (818) 760-2098. FAX: (818) 760-3294.
email: stockshots@earthlink.net www.stockshots.com
PRESIDENT
Stephanie Siebert

See website for category list and for licensing rates. Ten seconds per shot minimum. Three-tier competitive pricing.

FOOTAGE BANK

1733 Abbot Kinney Blvd., Ste. C, Venice, CA 90291.
TEL: (888) 653-1400, (310) 822-1400. FAX: (310) 822-4100.
email: info@footagebank.com www.footagebank.com

Available footage includes: 35mm and High Def, Aerials, Animals, Archival, Landscapes, Space, Technology, Time-Lapse, Travel, Underwater & Worldwide Locations.

FOOTAGE HOLLYWOOD

(Specialize in hard to get film and TV footage)
10520 Magnolia Blvd., North Hollywood, CA 91601.
TEL: (818) 760-1500. FAX: (818) 760-1532.
email: footagehollylwood@FootageHollywood.com
www.footagehollywood.com
PRESIDENT
Jeanette Pugliese
CONTACT
Troy Szebin - troys@footagehollywood.com

FOOTAGE SEARCH, INC.

(Niche collections of ocean and nature footage)
300 Foam St., Monterey, CA 93940. TEL: (866) 375-2313, (831) 375-2313. FAX: (831) 621-9559.
email: info@footagesearch.com support@footagesearch.com
www.footagesearch.com www.OceanFootage.com
www.NatureFootage.com
CONTACT
Dan Baron - dan@footagesearch.com

FOTOSEARCH

(Publitek, Inc. dba Fotosearch. Photos and stock footage. Royalty-free)
21155 Watertown Rd., Waukesha, WI 53186-1898.
TEL: (800) 827-3920, (262) 717-0740.
FAX: (262) 717-0745. www.fotosearch.com

GETTY IMAGES

Chicago: 122 S. Michigan Ave., Ste. 900, Chicago, IL 60603.
TEL: (800) 462-4379 (sales), (312) 344-4500.
email: sales@gettyimages.com www.gettyimages.com

Los Angeles: 6300 Wilshire Blvd., 16th Flr., Los Angeles, CA 90048. TEL: (800) 462-4379 (sales), (323) 202-4200.
email: sales@gettyimages.com

New York: 75 Varick St., New York, NY 10013.
TEL: (800) 462-4379 (sales), (646) 613-4000.
email: sales@gettyimages.com

Seattle: 601 N. 34th St., Seattle, WA 98103.
TEL: (888) 888-5889 (sales), (206) 925-5000.
email: sales@gettyimages.com

Collections consist of rights-managed footage from AP Archive, ApexStock, Archive Films, Dick Clark Productions, Inc., Discovery FootageSource, Image Bank Film, Universal Studios, Warner Bros. Entertainment, WireImage Video. Royalty-free footage is available from: 3D4Medical.com, A Luna Blue, Artbeats, Artbox, BLOOMimage, Bondstreet Images, Digital Vision, FilmDisc, Flashfilm, Foodcollection Footage, OmniReelLife, Photodisc, Post Holes, Redhot Footage, Reelhouse, Rocketclips, Rubberball, SplashdownDirect.com, Stock Footage World and Triangle Collection.

GLOBAL IMAGEWORKS

65 Beacon St., Haworth, NJ 07641. TEL: (201) 384-7715.
FAX: (201) 501-8971. email: info@globalimageworks.com
www.globalimageworks.com

Global ImageWorks specializes in unique contemporary and historic footage covering a variety of categories including global conflict and military ops, extensive 9/11 archive, aerials and world destinations, music performances, celebrity, interviews, pop culture, lifestyles, nature, time lapse/special effects, home movies, thrills/stunts/extreme sports, extreme weather, Hurricane Katrina, re-enactments, emergency rescue and response, firefighters among others. Footage is available in a variety of formats including HD and 35mm. Additional services: research and clearances.

HBO ARCHIVES

1100 Ave. of the Americas, New York, NY 10036.
TEL: (212) 512-7171. FAX: (212) 512-5225.
email: footage@hboarchives.com www.hboarchives.com

Footage includes: Entertainment news collection, contemporary stock from HBO films, HD, Iconic sports, newsreels & royalty-free wildlife footage.

HOLLYWOOD NEWSREEL SYNDICATE, INC.

(Celebrity)
1622 N. Gower St., Hollywood, CA 90028. TEL: (323) 469-7307.
FAX: (323) 833-5920. www.hollywoodnewsreel.com
CONTACT
Rick Spalla - rickspalla@yahoo.com

INTER VIDEO, INC.

(C.G.W. Enterprises dba Inter Video Computer graphics, news, fake news, public domain & TV shows)
2211 N. Hollywood Way, Burbank, CA 91505.
TEL: (818) 843-3624. FAX: (818) 843-6884.
email: video@intervideo24.com www.intervideo24.com
PRESIDENT
Richard Clark - rclark@intervideo24.com
SALES
Chris Olson - colson@intervideo24.com

IRON ORCHID FILMS

The Villa Professional Center, 400 Hobron Ln., Ste. 405, Honolulu, HI 96815. TEL: (808) 955-1000.
FAX: (808) 949-6948. email: filmhawaii@aol.com
www.filmhawaii.com

A full-service film production company in Hawaii, with stock footage galleries.

ITN SOURCE

116 John St., Ste. 701, New York, NY 10038.
TEL: (888) 385-0080, (212) 385-2077. FAX: (646) 792-4668.
email: nysales@itnsource.com www.itnsource.com
V.P., ITN SOURCE
Ian CheeWah

ITN Source has one of the largest collections of moving image libraries in the world, housing over 800,000 hours of iconic and inspiring footage captured over three centuries. See website for additional offices and contacts worldwide.

JALBERT PRODUCTIONS, INC.

(Summer & winter sports library)
230 New York Ave., Huntington, NY 11743.
TEL: (631) 351-5878. FAX: (631) 351-5875.
email: info@jalbertfilm.com www.jalbertfilm.com
V.P., SYNDICATION SALES
Carol Randel

Archives include more than three million feet of original film ranging from elite competition for every summer and winter sport, to scenics and travel images and to an array of personalities. The past six years have been dedicated to recording HD images. In addition to stock footage, JPI is a leader in sports television and film production and syndication.

JUPITERIMAGES

North America: Jupiterimages Corporation, 6000 N. Forest Park Dr., Peoria, IL 61614. TEL: (800) 764-7427, (309) 687-0187. FAX: (703-770-5349.
email: sales@jupiterimages.com www.jupiterimages.com

United Kingdom: Jupiterimages (UK) Ltd., Unit 5, Finch Dr., Springwood, Braintree, Essex CM7 2SF. TEL: (800) 056-7533, +44 (0) 1376-333-780. FAX: +44 (0) 1376-528-522.
email: sales@jupiterimages.co.uk www.jupiterimages.com

Jupiterimages is a leading images company with over seven million images online serving creative professionals with brands like BananaStock, Botanica, Brand X Pictures, Comstock Images, Creatas Images, FoodPix, Goodshoot, Polka Dot Images, Nonstock, PictureQuest, PR Direct, Thinkstock Images, Thinkstock Footage, AbleStock.com, Clipart.com, liquidlibrary, PhotoObjects.net, Animation Factory, FlashFoundry.com and Photos.com. Jupiterimages offers both Rights-Managed and Royalty-Free stock images via single image download, CD collections or subscriptions from the world's leading photo agencies, many exclusively. See www.jupiterimages.com for additional offices and assistance around the world.

CLAY LACY AVIATION

Corporate Headquarters: 7435 Valjean Ave., Van Nuys, CA 91406. TEL: (800) 432-2904, (818) 989-2900.
FAX: (818) 904-3450. www.flyclaylacy.com

Boeing Field Operations: 8285 Perimeter Rd. S, Seattle, WA 98108. TEL: (800) 768-1101, (206) 762-6000.

Clay Lacy's Astrovision equipped aircraft have filmed over 2,800 projects, including military, general aviation, airlines, television and feature films world-wide.

KESSER IMAGE LIBRARY

(Full selection)
4601 Ponce de Leon Blvd., Ste. 250, Coral Gables, FL 33146.
TEL: (800) STK-FTGE, (305) 663-4443. FAX: (305) 663-4446.
email: research@kesser.com www.kesser.com
CONTACT
Charles Carpenter

Emmy award-winning producer Carl Kesser has traveled the world capturing unique images across broad categories. The library has acquired representation of archival and hard to find images from some of the world's most recognized cinematographers.

LIBRARY OF MOVING IMAGES, INC.

(Rare and classic film clips)
6671 Sunset Blvd., #1581, Hollywood, CA 90028.
TEL: (323) 469-7499. FAX: (323) 469-7559.
email: mylmi@pacbell.net www.libraryofmovingimages.com
OWNER
Michael Peter Yakaitis

Moving images from the early 1870s-present. Library carries newsreels, feature films, documentaries, politics, world events, Hollywood royalty, war footage and more. Library is owner-operated.

LOUIS B. MAYER LIBRARY/AMERICAN FILM INSTITUTE

2021 N. Western Ave., Los Angeles, CA 90027.
TEL: (323) 856-7654, (323) 856-7600. FAX: (323) 467-4578.
www.afi.com/about/library.aspx

The AFI Collection: Film and videotape archive material available for research and reuse, subject to certain restrictions. The American Film Institute (AFI) Collection at the Library of Congress includes over 27,500 titles and consists primarily of theatrical features and shorts. The center is not a custodial archive. While information about the AFI Collection may be obtained directly from the center, information regarding access should be obtained from the Library of Congress, Motion Picture, Broadcasting and Recorded Sound Division and other appropriate archives.

NATIONAL GEOGRAPHIC DIGITAL MOTION

1145 17th St. NW, Washington, DC 20036.
TEL: (866) 523-9097, (866) 523-9097, (720) 212-0820 (UK/Europe).
email:ngsales@thoughtequity.com www.ngdigitalmotion.com

National Geographic Digital Motion (formerly known as National Geographic Film Library) is the digital film library and archive for the Emmy Award-winning film produced by National Geographic Television. Possesses a century's worth of the world's most captivating digital film archive from around the globe, with thousands of hours of clips added each year. The digital archive is filled with unparalleled visuals: not only nature and wildlife, but also people and cultures, history and archaeology, adventure and exploration, and news and current events.

NBC NEWS ARCHIVES

(Complete archives of NBC News)
30 Rockefeller Plaza, Rm. 496-S , New York, NY 10112.
TEL: (212) 664-3797. FAX: (212) 703-8558.
email: footage@nbc.com www.nbcnewsarchives.com
MANAGER
Yuien Chin

Over 75 years of news coverage—a treasure trove of one-on-one interviews, documentaries on religion, World War II, the Vietnam War, and investigative reports, features, social commentary, sports and entertainment testifying to more than half a century of generational changes. Online text database and streaming video of news programs 2000 – present.

PASSPORT INTERNATIONAL PRODUCTIONS

10520 Magnolia Blvd., North Hollywood, CA 91601.
TEL: (818) 760-1500. FAX: (818) 760-1532.
email: licensing@passportentertainment.com
www.passportentertainment.com
SALES
Andrea Miller - ext. 211

Passport maintains one of the largest film archives anywhere, containing thousands of rare newsreels, vintage television programs, exclusive celebrity interviews, and theatrical trailers.

PRODUCERS LIBRARY SERVICE

(Full selection; Hollywood history)
10832 Chandler Blvd., N. Hollywood, CA 91601.
TEL: (800) 944-2135, (818) 752-9097. FAX: (818) 752-9196.
email: research@ producerslibrary.com
www.producerslibrary.com

ROBERTSTOCK / CLASSICSTOCK

4203 Locust St., Philadelphia, PA 19104.
TEL: (800) 786-6300. FAX: (800) 786-1920.
email: info@robertstock.com www.robertstock.com
www.classicstock.com

SONY PICTURES STOCK FOOTAGE

(From Sony Pictures Entertainment)
10202 W. Washington Blvd., Culver City, CA 90232.
TEL: (866) 275-6919, (310) 244-3704.
email: stockfootage@spe.sony.com
www.sonypicturesstockfootage.com

For free research or further assistance, including questions about pricing or licensing, please contact Sony: from within the U.S., toll-free: (866) 275-6919; or outside U.S.: (310) 244-3704. Via email, use: stockfootage@spe.sony.com. Sony Pictures Stock Footage is the stock footage arm of Sony Pictures Entertainment and offers online access to more than 125,000 clips. Originally filmed for Columbia Pictures, TriStar feature films, Screen Gems and Sony Pictures Television, this predominantly 35mm collection is available in HD or any other digital format with competive pricing and quick turnaround times. The library also includes a premium collection of stunts, pyrotechnics and other ultra-highproduction value shots.

THE SOURCE STOCK FOOTAGE LIBRARY, INC.

140 S. Camino Seco, Ste. 308, Tucson, AZ 85710.
TEL: (520) 298-4810. FAX: (520) 290-4376.
email: Requests@sourcefootage.com www.sourcefootage.com
LIBRARY MANAGER
Don French

STOCK MEDIA CORPORATION

1123 Broadway, Ste. 1006, New York, NY 10010.
TEL: (212) 463-8300. FAX: 212) 929-6965.
email: info@stockmedia.net www.stockmedia.net

THOMSON REUTERS

(Media products: newswires, pictures, video, online syndication, news graphics and more)
3 Times Square, 18th Flr., New York, NY 10036.
TEL: (800) 257-5126, (646) 223-4000. FAX: (646) 223-4390.
www.thomsonreuters.com

U.S. Media Office: 311 S. Wacker Dr., 12th Flr., Chicago, IL 60606. TEL: (312) 408-8500.

U.S. Media Office/Washington, D.C.: 1333 H St. NW, Ste. 510, Washington, D.C. 20005. TEL: (202) 898-8300.

From raw news footage with natural sound to ready-to-air packages or live exclusive reports on what's moving the world's financial markets, Reuters extensive network of television journalists and camera crews in more than 80 locations globally deliver fast, quality video coverage.

THOUGHT EQUITY MOTION

Headquarters: 1530 16th St., 6th Flr., Denver, CO 80202.
TEL: (866) 815-6599. FAX: (720) 382-2719.
email: sales@thoughtequity.com www.ThoughtEquity.com

Chicago: 205 N. Michigan Ave., Ste. 1610, Chicago, IL 60601. TEL: (312) 233-2567.

Los Angeles: 4130 Cahuenga Blvd., Ste. 315, Universal City, CA 91602. TEL:(818) 432-4000.

New York: 240 W. 35th St., Ste. 1201, New York, NY 10001. TEL: (917) 267-5460.

Tokyo: 5th FioreSakuragaoka, 11-2 Sakuragaoka, Shibuya-ku, Tokyo 150-0031 Japan. TEL: +81-3-5459-4641.

Sydney: 12 Carlotta St., Artarmon, Sydney, NSW 2064 Australia. TEL: +61 2 9438 1888.

Thought Equity Motion is a world leader in providing access to high quality film, video and music content. The company's forward-thinking approach to digital video has produced an array of products and services to meet the exploding demand of emerging media. Widely recognized for its expertise in licensing rights, Thought Equity Motion is the licensing agent for renowned media companies, including: Paramount Pictures, MGM, NBC News, HBO, National Geographic, SonyPictures, NBC Sports, the NCAA and hundreds of others. With offices located around the world, Thought Equity Motion offers a broad, deep content collection. This vast collection, combined with leading-edge technology, makes Thought Equity Motion a preferred destination for multimedia professionals.

UCLA FILM & TELEVISION ARCHIVE

(Historical)
1015 N. Cahuenga Blvd., Hollywood, CA 90038.
TEL: (323) 466-8559, ext. 10. FAX: (323) 461-6317.
email: footage@ucla.edu www.cinema.ucla.edu
CONTACT
Candace Lewis

Available film footage for direct licensing spans 1896-1981.

UNIVERSAL STUDIOS MEDIA LICENSING

(Archive licensed footage)
100 Universal City Plaza, 1440/15, Universal City, CA 91608.
TEL: (818) 777-1273. FAX: (818) 866-2399.
email: Roni.Lubliner@nbcuni.com.com
www.universalclips.com
CONTACT
Roni Lubliner

VIDEO TAPE LIBRARY, LTD.

(Established in 1984; broad categories of footage available)
1525 N. Crescent Heights Blvd., Ste. 2, Los Angeles, CA 90046. TEL: (323) 656-4330. FAX: (323) 656-8746.
email: vtl@videotapelibrary.com www.videotapelibrary.com
PRESIDENT
Melody St. John

WEST GRAND MEDIA, LLC

(Early motown artists)
933 Cecina Way, Los Angeles, CA 90077.
TEL: (818) 772-4443. FAX: (818) 772-4454.

6255 Sunset Blvd., Ste. 1110, Los Angeles, CA 90028.
TEL: (323) 856-3500. FAX: (323) 465-4471.
www.westgrandmedia.com
CONTACT
Michael Lovesmith - mlovesmith@westgrandmedia.com

WHITE RAIN FILMS

(Production, documentary/non-profit & stock footage)
2009 Dexter Ave. N, Seattle, WA 98109. TEL: (800) 816-5244, (206) 682-5417. FAX: (206) 682-3038.
email: bill@whiterainfilms.com www.whiterainfilms.com
CONTACTS
Brad Bolling, Bill Phillips, Chris Auger

WIREIMAGE

75 Varick St., 5th Flr., New York, NY 10013.
TEL: (800) 462-4379, (212) 686-8900. FAX: (646) 613-3601.
www.wireimage.com

WireImage Los Angeles/Sales: 6300 Wilshire Blvd, 16th Flr., Los Angeles, CA 90048. TEL: (800) 462-4379.
FAX: (323) 202-4204.

WireImage provides up-to-the-minute entertainment footage to leading broadcast and mobile carriers, and online properties worldwide. The footage division specializes in licensing wholly owned and represented entertainment content, in both raw and packaged forms. Wireimage is a division of Getty Images, Inc. Images are captured by professional photographers using state-of-the-art digital equipment and delivered to clients via website, FTP, or physical media. Online service is available 24/7 to search, browse and immediately download JPEG images in both low and high resolutions. All content is encoded with subject, date, venue, location, and caption information. WireImage adds approximately 90 new events 5,500 images) per day. See website for additional sales offices worldwide.

WPA FILM LIBRARY

16101 S. 108th Ave., Orland Park, IL 60467.
TEL: (800) 777-2223, (708) 460-0555. FAX: (708) 460-0187.
email: sales@wpafilmlibrary.com www.wpafilmlibrary.com

Footage available from 1895-21st Century, Americana, classic commercials and industrial films, HD, historic, music, politics and UFO collection. Known for extensive historic footage, but the contemporary HD, film and video collections keep growing. Free expert research, free screeners (up to two hours per project) and a searchable online database are available.

STUDIO & EDITING SERVICES & EQUIPMENT RENTALS

ADDRESS ONE
(Production and post production)
c/o Raleigh Studios, 662 N. Van Ness Ave., Ste. 301,
Los Angeles, CA 90004. TEL: (310) 838-7783.
FAX: (323) 960-4961. www.addressone.tv
CONTACT
Tess Thompson - tess@addressone.tv

AFTERSHOCK DIGITAL
(Post production editing)
8222 Melrose Ave., Ste. 304, Los Angeles, CA 90046.
TEL: (323) 658-5700. FAX: (323) 658-5200.
email: fritzfeick@excite.com www.editkings.com
CONTACT
Fritz Feick

AMERICAN FILM & TAPE, INC.
(Manufacturer of splicing tape, editorial and theatre leaders, laboratory leaders, dark room custom slitting & perforating)
20928 Osborne St., Unit H, Canoga Park, CA 91304.
TEL: (818) 885-6641. FAX: (818) 885-6217.
email: alsfilm@aol.com
MANAGER
Al Lansdale

AMERICAN ZOETROPE
(Production company & post production services)
916 Kearny St., San Francisco, CA 94133. TEL: (415) 788-7500.
FAX: (415) 989-7910. www.zoetrope.com

DVD Lab, transfers & dubs, sound mixing, editing/screening, telecine.

ARCHION TECHNOLOGIES
(Post production. One of the entertainment industry's largest storage solution providers to Avid storage systems)
824 N. Victory Blvd., Burbank, CA 91502. TEL: (888) 655-8555,
(818) 840-0777. FAX: (818) 840-0877.
email: info@archion.com www.archion.com
CEO
Mark E. Bianchi
COO
Reuben Lima
CHIEF TECHNOLOGY OFFICER & CONTACT
James Tucci
EXECUTIVE V.P., SALES
Daniel Stern

AUTHENTIC DESIGN
(Digital imaging, graphic design & still photography)
P.O. Box 310, Malibu, CA 90265. TEL: (818) 707-0007.
email: authentic@earthlink.net
OWNER
Stephen Morales

BIG TIME PICTURE COMPANY
12210-1/2 Nebraska Ave., W. Los Angeles, CA 90025.
TEL: (310) 207-0921. FAX: (310) 826-0071.
www.bigtimepic.com
CONTACT
Susan - Susan@bigtimepic.com

Digital post production; 35mm film & video, all formats. Also an Apple ProVideo reseller. Screening room; 40 office & editorial suites; Avid and Final cut rentals and sales; technical support.

CCI DIGITAL
(Post production services)
2921 W. Alameda Ave., Burbank, CA 91505.
TEL: (818) 562-6300. FAX: (818) 562-8222.
www.ccidigital.com
PRESIDENT
Rick Morris

CHACE AUDIO BY DELUXE
(Audio post production & sound restoration; acquired by Deluxe Digital Media July 1, 2009.)
201 S. Victory Blvd., Burbank, CA 91502. TEL: (800) 842-8346,
(818) 842-8346. FAX: (818) 842-8353. www.chace.com
V.P. AUDIO, DELUXE DIGITAL MEDIA AND HEAD OF CHACE
Bob Heiber - bobheiber@chace.com
GENERAL MANAGER
James Eccles - jameseccles@chace.com
TECHNICAL OPERATIONS MANAGER
Chris Reynolds - chrisreynolds@chace.com

Services include: audio compression, dubbing, editorial, film inspection & repair, optical sound recording, optical soundtrack negative playback-COSPTM, restoration & revitalization, sound transfers, synchronization/conforms.

BOB CHENOWETH RENTALS
1860 E. North Hills Dr., La Habra, CA 90631. TEL: (562) 691-1652.
email: chenowethrg@msn.com

CHRISTY'S EDITORIAL
(Post production equipment, editing & video supplies since 1969)
3625 W. Pacific Ave., Burbank, CA 91505.
TEL: (800) 556-5706, (818) 845-1755. FAX: (818) 845-1756.
email: info@christys.net www.christys.net
GENERAL MANAGER
Craig Christy
DIGITAL SERVICES
JJ Nigro, Dan Downer
FILM
Sheli Christy, Al Limeres, Jay McLean

Also offers 24-hour edit bays with full services for post production professionals. Rents Avids.

CINEMA CONCEPTS TSC.
(Studio & editing services, preview & policy trailers, animation, digital production services-HD poor/mastering/film-out, screening rooms)
2030 Powers Ferry Rd., Ste. 214, Atlanta, GA 30339.
TEL: (800) SHOWADS. TEL: (770) 956-7460.
FAX: (770) 956-8358. email: info@cinemaconcepts.com
www.cinemaconcepts.com
PRESIDENT
Stewart Harnell

CREST DIGITAL
1000 N. Highland Ave., Hollywood, CA 90038. TEL: (800) 961-TAPE,
(323) 860-1300. FAX: (323) 461-8901. www.crestdigital.com

Post production. Provides DVD/CD, post production and digital asset management services to major film studios, software companies, record labels and industrial clients.

DELUXE ENTERTAINMENT SERVICES GROUP
Headquarters: 5433 Fernwood Ave., Hollywood, CA 90027.
TEL: (323) 960-8454. FAX: (323) 960-7016.
V.P., MARKETING
Cathy Main

Deluxe Entertainment Services Group is a leading provider of complete film and digital solutions for production, post production theatrical release, broadcast, video duplication, archiving and asset management in locations strategically located in major markets throughout the world.

DELUXE / EFILM, HOLLYWOOD
EFILM Digital Labs
1144 N. Las Palmas Ave., Hollywood, CA 90038.
TEL: (323) 463-7041. FAX: (323) 465-7342.
www.efilm.com
CONTACT
David Hays - david.hays@efilm.com

Services: 4k / 2k Digital Intermediates, Digital Previews, HD / SD Color Timing, Digital Trailers, 35mm/16mm Scanning & 35mm Recording, Tape-to-Film HD / SD, DI to DCI Digital Cinema Mastering, YCM Black & White, Separation Masters, Colorstream Look Design.

DELUXE LABORATORIES, INC.
1377 North Serrano Ave. (mailing address)
5433 Fernwood Ave. (facility entrance), Hollywood, CA 90027.
TEL: (323) 960-3600. FAX: (323) 960-7016.
www.bydeluxe.com
CONTACT
Steven VanAnda - steven.vananda@bydeluxe.com

35mm processing & film dailies; HD & SD telecine dailies (packaged through Deluxe Digital Media); special processes—ACE, CCE & Cross Process; collaboration with EFILM on Digital Intermediaries; answer printing & intermediates; bulk release printing.

DELUXE POST-PRODUCTION, BURBANK
200 S. Flower St., Burbank, CA 91502. TEL: (818) 525-2100.
FAX: (818) 525-2101. email: tony.ferkranus@bydeluxe.com
www.bydeluxe.com
CONTACT
Jeff Maher - jeff.maher@bydeluxe.com

Services: Audio Layback (includes ProTools services), Aspect Ratio Manipulation (HD, NTSC, PAL), Automated Broadcast Duplication (data to data, video to data, video to video, data to video), Climate Controlled Vault for Active Videotape Master Storage, Digital Restoration & Distribution, DVD Specialty Authoring & Duplication, Editorial Television Formatting, Encoding HD, SD, Hi-Resolution, HD Upconversions, Downconversions, Cross Conversions, International Broadcast Distribution, NTSC/PAL Standards & Format Conversions.

DELUXE TELECINE, SHERMAN OAKS

Deluxe Digital Media, 15301 Ventura Blvd., Bldg. B/Ste. 200, Sherman Oaks, CA 91403. TEL: (818) 380-8138.
FAX: (818) 380-8129. www.bydeluxe.com
CONTACT
Kari Grubin - kari.grubin@bydeluxe.com

Hi definition and standard definition dailies; mastering on Spirit Datacine or tape/data color correction using the daVinci 2K Color Corrector; transfers from Super16, 16mm, 35mm (2-perf, 3-perf, 4-perf and 8-perf Vista Vision) to all HD and SD formats: HD 4:4:4, HD 4:2:2, 1080 @ 23.98PsF, 1080i, 720p, NTSC and PAL. See website for Deluxe services and locations worldwide.

WALT DISNEY STUDIOS POST PRODUCTION SERVICES

500 S. Buena Vista St., Burbank, CA 91521.
TEL: (818) 560-1000. www.stu-ops.disney.com
DEPARTMENTS
NEGATIVE CUTTING - (818) 505-5139
EDITING EQUIPMENT & ROOMS - (818) 560-1291
GRIP EQUIPMENT, RENTAL - (818) 560-5600
LIGHTING EQUIPMENT, RENTAL - (818) 560-5600
TRAILERS/VANS/TRUCKS/VEHICLES/
RENTAL - (818) 560-1285
NON-LINEAR EDITING, PICTURE - (818) 560-1915
SOUND TRANSFER - (818) 560-1135
TELECINE - (818) 560-1135
TIMES SQUARE STUDIOS - (212) 930-7751

EAGLE EYE POST

(Servicing, renting & sale of editing equipment)
10815 Burbank Blvd., N. Hollywood, CA 91601.
TEL: (818) 506-6100. FAX: (818) 506-4313.
www.eagleeyedigital.com

EDGEWOOD STUDIOS

(Studio rental, studio editing and equipment rental and more)
Howe Center, Unit 12B, Ste. 90, Rutland, VT 05701.
TEL: (802) 773-0510. FAX: (802) 773-3481.
email: dave@edgewoodstudios.com
www.edgewoodstudios.com
PRESIDENT
David Giancola

ENCORE HOLLYWOOD

(Post production & visual effects)
6344 Fountain Ave., Hollywood, CA 90028.
TEL: (323) 466-7663. www.encorehollywood.com
MANAGING DIRECTOR
Barbara Marshall - bmarshall@encorehollywood.com
DIRECTOR, VISUAL EFFECTS
Tim Jacobsen - tjacobsen@encorehollywood.com

Encore Hollywood specializes in post production and visual effects for episodic TV and MOWs, commercials, music videos and feature films. It also offers a fully equipped digital intermediat theatre &feature HD dailies.

ELECTRIC PICTURE SOLUTIONS

3753 Cahuenga Blvd. W, Studio City, CA 91604.
TEL: (818) 766-5000. FAX: (818) 623-7547.
www.electricpicturesolutions.com
EDITOR & PRESIDENT
David Pincus - (818) 535-3301(cell) dp@picturesolutions.com

Studio City/Santa Monica/New York City/Baton Rouge. Avid / Lightworks/Final Cut Pro editing system rentals/editing suites; standard DEF / High DEF rentals and online.

ENTERTAINMENT POST

639 S. Glenwood Place, Burbank, CA 91506.
TEL: (818) 846-0411. FAX: (818) 846-1087.

Negative & print telecine dailies; dailies direct to Avid disk; Avid film & media composer rental; on-site & off-site Avid installation; production office space rental; 24-hour technical support.

FPC, INC.

(A Kodak company. Photographic equipment & supplies)
4575 Hwy. 91 N., Mountain City, TN 37683-8003.
TEL: (423) 727-6761. FAX: (423) 727-5161.

HAMMER CREATIVE

6311 Romaine St., 3rd Flr., Los Angeles, CA 90038.
TEL: (323) 606-4700. FAX: (323) 463-8130.
email: info@hammercreative.com www.hammerfilm.com

Post production. Creates campaigns and marketing materials for the theatrical, home entertainment, international, corporate and TV markets. Theatrical trailers, promos, TV and radio spots, corporate and sales reels, key art posters, DVD and VHS box art, Titles, logos, Web design, in-store environments and DVDs.

HOLLYWOOD FILM CO.

(Motion picture equipment manufacturer & restoration services)
9265 Borden Ave., Sun Valley, CA 91352.
TEL: (818) 683-1130. FAX: (818) 683-1139.
email: sales@HollywoodFilmCo.com
www.hollywoodfilmco.com
CONTACT
Vincent Carabello

LASER PACIFIC MEDIA CORP.

(A Kodak company. Post production services)
809 N. Cahuenga Blvd., Los Angeles, CA 90038.
TEL: (323) 462-6266. FAX: (323) 960-2192.
email: info@laserpacific.com www.laserpacific.com
GENERAL MANAGER, MASTERING UNIT
Ron Burdett - (323) 960-2141 rburdett@laserpacific.com
VISUAL EFFECTS SERVICES
Mike Pryor - mpryor@laserpacific.com
DIRECTOR, SALES, TV, POST PRODUCTION SERVICES
Ian Kerner - (323) 462-6266 ext 2178
ikerner@laserpacific.com
DIRECTOR, FEATURE FILM SALES
Sheryl Goodhead - (323) 960-2166 sgoodhead@laserpacific.com

MAGIC FILM & VIDEO WORKS

(Post production Services)
4110 W. Magnolia Blvd., Burbank, CA 91505.
TEL: (818) 845-8781. FAX: (818) 563-1660. www.mfvw.com
CONTACT/FOUNDER
Syd Cole - scole@mfvw.com

HD and SD Telecine & Post Services; Negative Conforming.

MAGNO SOUND & VIDEO

(Comprehensive post production facility for film & TV)
729 7th Ave., New York, NY 10019. TEL: (212) 302-2505.
FAX: (212) 819-1282. email: staff@magnosound.com
www.magnosoundandvideo.com
DIRECTOR
Maria Pon

MATCHFRAME MEDIA GROUP

(A full service post production facility serving motion picture, television and multimedia clients for over 20 years. Also rentals)
Main Facility: 610 N. Hollywood Way, Ste. 101, Burbank, CA 91505. TEL: (818) 840-6800. FAX: (818) 840-2726.
www.matchframevideo.com

Westside Facility: 1545 26th St., Santa Monica, CA 90404.

This site offers Avid Offline Suites, Avid Symphony and Symphony Nitrus finishing, Final Cut Pro HD, and a Pro Control Audio Suite.

METHOD STUDIOS

(Formerly R!OT)
New York Office: 545 Fifth Ave. Ste. 2, New York, NY 10017.
TEL: (212) 907-1200. FAX: (212) 907-1201.
MANAGING DIRECTOR
Alex Frisch
CREATIVE DIRECTOR
Aron Hjartarson
ANIMATION SUPERVISOR
Matt Hackett
SENIOR EXECUTIVE PRODUCER & VICE PRESIDENT
Gabby Gourrier
EXECUTIVE PRODUCER & DIRECTOR OF PRODUCTION
Helen Hughes
CONTACT
Chad Malbon - cmalbon@methodstudios.com

California: 730 Arizona Ave., Santa Monica, CA 90401.
TEL: (310) 434-6500. www.methodstudios.com
MANAGING DIRECTOR
Alex Frisch
HEAD, 3D
Andy Boyd
WEST COAST REPRESENTATION
Brent Novick - brentnovick@sbcglobal.net

Ascent Media Group announced that beginning January 1, 2009, two of its boutique visual effects studios, Riot and Method, would unite operations under the Method name, to offer clients high-end visual effects for commercials, music videos and feature films. Services include: digital post-production in NTSC and PAL, Telecine HD, Datacine, Inferno, Fire HD, Henry, VYVX capabilities, 3D CGI, scanning and recording, compression & duplication. Send reels to: method-sm-recruiting@methodstudios.com

MONTANA EDIT

(Rental facility & education center, post production)
1131 Montana Ave., Santa Monica, CA 90403.
TEL: (310) 454-3332. email: info@montanaedit.com
wolf@montanaedit.com www.montanaedit.com

GENERAL MANAGER
Tony Borton

OTTO NEMENZ INTERNATIONAL INC.

(Camera rentals, Arriflex, Movie Cam, etc.)
870 N. Vine St., Hollywood, CA 90038. TEL: (323) 469-2774.
FAX: (323) 469-1217. www.ottonemenz.com
CONTACT
Fritz Heinzle

NEWEDIT, INC.

(Post production)
8300 Beverly Blvd., Los Angeles, CA 90048. TEL: (323) 653-3575.
FAX: (323) 653-8855. www.newedit.com
CONTACT
Stan Cassio

NITELITE EDITORIAL

(Complete editing services)
3350 N. Studebaker Rd., Long Beach, CA 90808.
TEL: (310) 738-2647. FAX: (310) 496-1527.
email: info@nitelitepictures.com sssnitelite.org
EXECUTIVE PRODUCER
Harry Lowell

Edit bays support AVID, Final Cut and After Effects. All suites offer numerous real-time effects and offer online HD capabilities.

NT PICTURE & SOUND

(Post production, telecine, editorial suites, dubs, Avid DS, 24P syncing)
1400 N. Cahuenga Blvd., Hollywood, CA 90028.
TEL: (323) 957-4200. FAX: (323) 957-4212.
www.ntaudio.com
ACCOUNT REPRESENTATIVE
Edel Adam - edel@ntaudio.com
SALES MANAGER
Gary Galvin - gary@ntvideo.com

PACIFIC TITLE & ART STUDIO

(Optical and digital services. Visual effects, titles, film opticals)
Digital Facilities: 7215 Santa Monica Blvd., Los Angeles, CA 90046. TEL: (323) 436-3850. FAX: (323) 769-3701.
email: sales@pactitle.com www.pactitle.com
CEO
David McCarthy, Jr. - dmccarthy@pactitle.com
SENIOR V.P., BUSINESS DEVELOPMENT
Ladd Lanford - ladd@pactitle.com
CREATIVE DIRECTOR
Bruce Schluter - bschluter@pactitle.com
EXECUTIVE PRODUCER, VISUAL EFFECTS
Crystal Dowd - cdowd@pactitle.com

Provides a full range of stat-of-the-art digital and optical services from 2D image manipulation to multilayer compositing, 3D animation, wire and object removal, motion tracking, negative preparation, rendering, rotoscoping, HD and D1 to film transfers, scanning and laser film recording, film restoration and more.

PASADENA PRODUCTION STUDIOS

(Studio rentals)
39 E. Walnut St., Pasadena, CA 91103. TEL: (626) 584-4090.
FAX: (626) 584-4099.
TRAFFIC MANAGER
Kristen Judge

PELICAN PICTURES

(Full-service TV and film production facility)
614 E. Rutland St., Covington, LA 70433. TEL: (985) 809-3456.
email: joe@pelicanpictures.com www.pelicanpictures.com
DIRECTOR
Joe Sanford
EXECUTIVE PRODUCER
Bobbie Westerfield - bobbie@pelicanpictures.com
PRODUCER/DP
Philip Braun - philip@pelicanpictures.com

PICTURE HEAD

(Post production finishing facility)
1132 Vine St., Hollywood, CA 90038. TEL: (323) 466-2066.
FAX: (323) 466-2717.
PRESIDENT
Darin Kuhlmann

PIVOTAL POST

4142 Lankershim Blvd., North Hollywood, CA 91602-2829.
TEL: (818) 760-6000. FAX: (818) 760-6011.
email: jeff@pivotalpost.com www.pivotalpost.com
PARTNER
Jeff Buchignani

PLANET VIDEO

(Full-service editing, demo reels)
1617 N. El Centro, Ste. 12, Los Angeles, CA 90028.
TEL: (323) 651-3600. email: pv@planet-video.com
www.planet-video.com

CONTACT
D.C. Douglas
OPERATIONS MANAGER
Gerry Sackman
PICTURE EDITOR
Daryl Baskin

POST LOGIC

(Independent post-production and digital intermediate)
1800 N. Vine St., Ste. 100, Hollywood, CA 90028.
TEL: (323) 461-7887. FAX: (323) 461-7790.
www.postlogic.com
CONTACT
Tracey Grimes - (323) 461-7887 ext. 323
sales-inquiries@postlogic.com

Digital intermediate, digital restoration, telecine, audio, editorial.

NewYork: 435 Hudson St., 7th Flr., New York, NY 10014.
TEL: (212) 520-3150. FAX: (212) 520-3155.
CONTACT
Peter Bavaro - pbavaro@postlogic.com

Telecine, editorial EFX, digital restoration, audio, quality control.

PRECISION PRODUCTIONS + POST

10718 McCune Ave., Los Angeles, CA 90034.
TEL: (310) 839-4600. FAX: (310) 839-4601.
email: info@precisionpost.com www.precisionpost.com
CEO/PRESIDENT & CLIENT RELATIONS
Joseph Arnao - Arnao@precisionpost.com
EXECUTIVE PRODUCER
Marie Soto - Marie@precisionpost.com
OPERATIONS/SCHEDULING
Jason Baran - Jason@precisionpost.com

PRIME DIGITAL MEDIA SERVICES

(DVD replication & video duplication services)
28109 Ave. Stanford, Valencia CA 91355. TEL: (661) 964-0220.
FAX: (661) 964-0550. www.primedigital.com

Other services include: High-Def/Standard Definition Editorial, video compression & file conversion, DVD design & authoring & replication, broadcast duplication, QC services, standards conversion, digital restoration/remastering, color correction, format conversion & varispeeding, translation, subtitling & closed captioning.

QUARTERMOON

(Editing: commercials & longform films, trailors & music videos)
12 Morand Ln., Wilton, CT 06897. TEL: (203) 247-5550.
email: info@quartermoon.com www.quartermoon.com
OWNER & EDITOR
Gary Balionis - gb@quartermoon.com

RALEIGH STUDIOS

(Raleigh Studios is an independent studio with multiple locations and services throughout the country)
Raleigh Studios Hollywood: 5300 Melrose Ave., Hollywood, CA 90038. TEL:(323) 960-FILM (for all locations), (323) 871-5649.
FAX: (323) 871-5600, (323) 871-5629.
email: info@raleighstudios.com www.raleighstudios.com
DIRECTOR, STUDIO OPERATIONS
Yolanda Montellano - (323) 466-3111
CONTACT
Mike Donahue - MichaelD@raleighstudios.com

Hollywood services/facilities: 11-acre complex of 12 sound stages, production facilities and support space. It offers: control rooms, offices, cycloramas, hydraulic lifts, post facilities, screening rooms, premiere dressing rooms, mill space, production services and on lot cafe

Raleigh Studios Baton Rouge, LA: 10000 Mayfair Dr., Baton Rouge, LA 70809.

Raleigh Studios Playa Vista: 5600 Campus Center Dr. Playa Vista, CA 90266.

Housing two of the largest sound stages in the country at 75,000 square feet each with a towering 72 feet of clearance. Raleigh Studios Playa Vista is home to large-scale movie production.

Raleigh Studios Manhattan Beach: 1600 Rosecrans Ave., Manhattan Beach, CA 90266-3708. TEL: (310) 727-2700.

Manhattan Beach is the new home and worldwide headquartersfor Marvel Studios. Raleigh and Marvel's facilities consist of a 23-acre complex with 14 sound stages with production support space. Raleigh Studios Manhattan Beach also offers: Complete set lighting dept., modern production offices attached to stages, star dressing rooms, hair and makeup rooms, separate office support space for independent producers and productions, expendable store and commissary.

RED CAR

(Editing for commercials, trailers & promos)
Red Car Los Angeles: 9336 W. Washington Blvd., Bldg. J, 1st Flr., Ste. B, Culver City, CA 90232. www.redcar.com
CONTACT
Jennifer Lederman - (310) 828-7500

Red Car New York: 196 Mercer St., Penthouse, New York, NY 10012. TEL: (212) 982-5555.
MANAGING DIRECTOR
Jennifer Lederman
HEAD OF SALES
Angelina Powers

See website for additional locations.

ROCKBOTTOM RENTALS

(Walkie talkie and phone rentals. See website for complete list)
1310 Westwood Blvd., Los Angeles, CA 90024.
TEL: (310) 315-2600. FAX: (310) 582-1178.
email: khris@rockbottomrentals.com
www.rockbottomrentals.com

ROUNDABOUT ENTERTAINMENT, INC.

(An independent post production facility; audio post production, video post production & stages)
3915 Burbank Blvd., Burbank, CA 91505. TEL: (818) 842-9300.
FAX: (818) 842-9301. email: roundabout@roundabout.com
www.roundabout.com
CONTACT
Craig Clark

Roundabouts competitive HD packages include: online editing, color correction, wide format to 4x3 pan and scan aspect ratio, sound editorial and design, ADR and Foley, re-recording, domestic and international mastering, full QCs and duplication.

RUNWAY, INC.

10575 Virginia Ave., Culver City, CA; 90232-3520.
TEL: (310) 636-2000. FAX: (310) 636-2034.
email: sales@runway.com www.runway.com
PRESIDENT
Howard Brock
ACCOUNT MANAGER
Daniel Bernato, Nancy Jundi

Locations in Burbank, Santa Monica, Hollywood & Culver City. Equipment: Avid—Unity, Meridien, Adrenaline, Nitris HD, media composer software, Mojo; Final cut pro HD; Xsan; editing suites; HD screenings; deck rental; hi-def monitors; workflow development; 24/7 tech support; system integration.

SDI MEDIA

Global Headquarters: 10950 Washington Blvd., Studio B., Culver City, CA 90232. TEL: (310) 388-8800. FAX: (310) 388-8950.
email: usa_los_angeles@sdimediagroup.com
sales@sdimediagroup.com info@sdimediagroup.com
www.sdi-media-usa.com
CEO
Walter Schonfeld
PRESIDENT, SDI MEDIA GROUP
Paul Falzone
EXECUTIVE V.P. & CFO
Mary Ann Fialkowski
CHIEF INFORMATION OFFICER
Josh Arensberg

A leading provider of dubbing and subtitling services, operating in 32 countries spanning Europe, Asia and the Americas. Worldwide, SDI owns and oeprates 89 recording rooms and 28 mixing rooms. Provides language dubbing and subtitling services for theatrical, home video & DVD releases. Company is dedicated to translating & localizing creative content for distribution in all media anywhere in the world.

SONY PICTURES / POST PRODUCTION FACILITIES

(A Sony Pictures Entertainment company. Full-service post production)
10202 W. Washington Blvd., Culver City, CA 90232.
TEL: (310) 244-5722. FAX: (310) 244-2626.
www.sonypicturespost.com
EXECUTIVE V.P., SOUND, VIDEO & PROJECTION
Richard Branca
EXECUTIVE V.P., THEATRICAL & TV SOUND EDITORIAL
Tom McCarthy
EXECUTIVE DIRECTOR, POST SOUND FACILITIES
Greg Jacobs - (310) 244-5749
V.P., OPERATIONS
Julianne McCormack - (310) 244-5714
MANAGER, VIDEO & SOUND OPERATIONS
Robin Haskins - (310) 244-5467
MANAGER, DIGITAL PICTURE EDITORIAL
Eric Rigney - (310) 244-5728
SOUND RECORDING & LIBRARIAN
Greg Abarta - (310) 244-4135
CHIEF PROJECTIONIST, PROJECTION ROOM
Michael McLaren - (310) 244-5721
SUPERVISOR, EDITORIAL SERVICES
Brittany Flores - (310) 244-5739
STAGE MANAGER, POST PRODUCTION FACILITIES
Mike Rizzuto - (310) 244-5226

Editorial suites: 255 editorial suites located throughout eight buildings; suites rage in sizes from small to extra large; can be equipped with DSL and LAN. Traditional editorial equipment rental includes: film benches, power rewinds & coding machines.

LEONARD SOUTH PRODUCTIONS

(Pre- and post production services)
5319 Craner Ave., N. Hollywood, CA 91601.
TEL: (818) 760-8383. FAX: (818) 766-8301.
email: lensouth@sbcglobal.net
PRESIDENT
Leonard South

TOTAL DIGITAL PRODUCTIONS

1500 Flower St., Glendale, CA 91201. TEL: (818) 241-9792.
FAX: (818) 241-9796. email: req4info@total-digital.com
PRESIDENT
Hillard Fitzkee

Full-service production house. Sound stage with control room; editing: online; linear, services.

UNIVERSAL STUDIOS

UNIVERSAL STUDIOS DIGITAL SERVICES

(Full-service post-production facility)
100 Universal City Plaza, Bldg. 3153, Universal City, CA 91608. TEL: (818) 777-1111. FAX: (818) 866-5258.
www.filmmakersdestination.com
CONTACT
Ron Silveira - ron.silveira@nbcuni.com
Kathy Ochse - kathy.ochse@nbcuni.com
Harvey Landy - harvey.landy@nbcuni.com

Universal Studios Digital Services provides 2K, High Definition and Standard Definition film transfers, scanning, tape-to-tape and tapeless (server-based) color correction, pan and scan, editing, digital effects compositing, paintbox, graphics, dirt concealment, restoration, video duplication, conversions, video encoding and other video related services for internal and external customers. Additional services include: Pixel Power HD/SD character generator w/unlimited fonts, video printer, HD & SD quality control with operator video room without operator (any format), film prep and synchronization, video stock purchases, shipping, packaging and prep.

UNIVERSAL STUDIOS EDITORIAL FACILITIES

(Editing equipment and room rentals)
100 Universal City Plaza, Bldg. 2282, Room 154A, Universal City, CA 91608. TEL: (818) 777-4728. FAX: (818) 733-4290.
www.filmmakersdestination.com
CONTACT
Keith Alexander - (818) 777-4728 keith.alexander@nbcuni.com

Universal Studios Editorial Facilities provides cutting-edge editing equipment rentals and customized editorial rooms to internal and third-party clients with highly trained technicians available 24 hours a day, 7 days a week. Facilities offer more than 200 editorial rooms, including small to extra-large suites and rooms available with full Avid Digital Editing System set-up, including: Avid Adrenaline (Mac and PC) Systems, Avid Nitris, DX Systems, Avid Symphony Systems, Avid Media Composer 9000XL Meridiens, Pro Tools, and Fibre Storage and Unity.

VAN LING

Visual Effects Supervisor, DVD Producer, Graphic Designer
5203 Silver Arrow Dr., Rancho Palos Verdes, CA 90275.
TEL: (310) 544-5004. FAX: (310) 265-6631.
email: van@vanlingpro.com www.vanlingpro.com

WARNER BROS. STUDIOS FACILITIES

(Post production)
4000 Warner Blvd., Burbank, CA 91522. TEL: (818) 954-2511.
FAX: (818) 954-2901. email: wbsf@warnerbros.com
wbsfproductionsound@warnerbros.com www.wbsf.com
SENIOR V.P., POST PRODUCTION
Kim Waugh - kim.waugh@warnerbros.com
V.P., POST PRODUCTION SERVICES
Bill Angarola
DIRECTOR OF ENGINEERING
Keving Collier - kevin.collier@warnerbros.com
DIRECTOR, BUSINESS DEVELOPMENT
Dean Hilborne - dean.hilborne@warnerbros.com
BUSINESS DEVELOPMENT
Bob Beresh - bob. beresh@warnerbros.com
MANAGER, OPERATIONS
Damon Banks - damon.banks@warnerbros.com
SUPERVISOR, DVD AUDIO MASTERING
Tim Hoggatt - tim.hoggatt@warnerbros.com
SUPERVISOR, ARCHIVAL MASTERING
John Yanez - john.yanez@warnerbros.com
SUPERVISOR, AUDIO RESTORATION
Robert Corti - robert.corti@warnerbros.com
SOUND SUPERVISOR, ANCILLARY MARKETS
Tracie Gallo - tracie.gallo@warnerbros.com

MANAGER, CLIENT SERVICES
Shannon Rutecki - (818) 954-4817 shannon.rutecki@warnerbros.com

Offers more than 30 rental and services departments. In 2009, Warner Bros. Post Production Services completed construction on two new premier facilities, ADR 2 and Re-Recording Stage 12. ADR 2 is used primarily for automated dialogue replacement on TV projects, while Stage 12 services the feature film community. See website for comprehensive directory of services.

XZACTO DIGITAL DYNAMICS

(Film & video post, motion graphic design, CGI visual effects)
9306 Beatties Ford Rd., Huntersville, NC 28078.
TEL: (704) 398-8888. email: info@xzacto.com
www.xzacto.com

ZAENTZ MEDIA CENTER

2600 Tenth St., Berkeley, CA 94710. TEL: (510) 486-2286.
FAX: (510) 486-2062. www.zaentzmediacenter.com
CONTACT
Anna Stenberg - astenberg@warehamdevelopment.com

Recording studios, Screening rooms, office suites.

SUBTITLES & CAPTIONS

AL MEDIA MOVERS, INC.
10444 Magnolia Blvd., North Hollywood, CA 91601.
TEL/FAX: (310) 237-6438. email: info@media-movers.com
www.media-movers.com
CONTACT
Lawrence Vishnu

Dubbing (Lip-sync & U.N.Style), Subtitling, Voiceovers, Closed Captioning, Translation & Transcription in all Asian, Indian, European, African & Middle-Eastern languages for all media formats.

CAPTIONMAX
(Closed-captioning, encoding, subtitling, webcast captioning, audio description)
World headquarters: 2438 27th Ave. S, Minneapolis, MN 55406. TEL: (800) 822-3566, (612) 341-3566.
FAX: (612) 341-2345. www.captionmax.com
PRESIDENT
Max Duckler

Burbank, CA: 441 N. Varney, Burbank, CA 91502. TEL: (818) 295-2500. FAX: (818) 295-2509.

New York, NY: 159 W. 25th St., Ste. 1009, New York, NY 10001. TEL: (212) 462-0060. FAX: (212) 462-0061.

Washington, DC: 26171 Glasgow Dr., S. Riding, VA 20152. TEL: (703) 347-7735. FAX: (703) 327-7695.

CINETYP, INC.
843 Seward St., Hollywood, CA 90038. TEL: (323) 463-8569.
FAX: (323) 463-4129. email: info@cinetyp.com
www.cinetyp.com
CEO & PRESIDENT
John H. Bell - John.Bell@cinetyp.com
GENERAL MANAGER
Dave Margolis - Dave.Margolis@cinetyp.com

Foreign language and theatrical captions. Services include: Subtitles, captions, digital cinema, closed captioning and/or subtitles for DVD & video, script/list services and translations.

CREST DIGITAL
1000 N. Highland Ave., Hollywood, CA 90038. TEL: (800) 961-TAPE, (323) 860-1300. FAX: (323) 461-8901. www.crestdigital.com

Post production. Provides DVD/CD, post production and digital asset management services to major film studios, software companies, record labels and industrial clients.

CTS LANGUAGE LINK™
Evergreen International Plaza, 911 Main St., Ste. 10, Vancouver, WA 98660. TEL: (800) 208-2620, (360) 693-7100.
FAX: (360) 693-9292. email: info@ctslanguagelink.com
www.ctslanguagelink.com
PRESIDENT & CEO
Jeff Barger
COO
Pam Ballard

Language translation and interpreting services support more than 240 languages and dialects.

DELUXE DIGITAL STUDIOS - SOFTITLER - BURBANK
2400 Empire Ave., Ste. 300, Burbank, CA 91504.
TEL: (818) 565-4400. FAX: (818) 565-4444. www.softitler.com
CONTACT
Jim Ziskin - jim.ziskin@bydeluxe.com

DVD subtitling & localization; theatrical translation services & subtitling; closed captioning. Reaching the world in more than 50 languages.

GLOBAL LANGUAGE SERVICES
2027 Las Lunas St., Pasadena, CA 91107. TEL: (626) 792-0862.
FAX: (626) 792-8793. email: aebi@hss.caltech.edu
globallang@aol.com
CONTACT
Dr. Andreas Aebi

IMAGINARY FORCES
6526 W. Sunset Blvd., Hollywood, CA 90028.
TEL: (323) 957-6868. FAX: (323) 957-9577.
www.imaginaryforces.com
HEAD OF MARKETING
Jonathan Neeley - jonathan@imaginaryforces.com
DIRECTOR, BUSINESS DEVELOPMENT
Danixa Diaz - danixa@imaginaryforces.com
FILM TITLES
Kathy Kelehan - kathy@imaginaryforces.com
New York Office: 530 W. 25th St., New York, NY 10001.
TEL: (646) 486-6868. FAX: (646) 486-4700.

IMAGINARY FORCES (IF) is an entertainment and design company based in Hollywood and New York. Its award-winning work spans the diverse industries of feature film production, entertainment marketing and promotion, corporate branding, architecture, advertising and interactive media.

LUMENI PRODUCTIONS, INC.
1632 Flower St., Glendale, CA 91201-2357. TEL: (818) 956-2200.
FAX: (818) 956-3298. www.lumeni.com
EXECUTIVE PRODUCER
Marshall "Tony" Valdez - tony@lumeni.com

Services include: DI color timing; 2D, 3D & stereo computer graphics; animation; special effects for film, including digital trailers, film finishing & title design. Has served the entertainment industry for 29+ years.

PRIME DIGITAL MEDIA SERVICES
(DVD replication & video duplication services)
28109 Ave. Stanford, Valencia CA 91355. TEL: (661) 964-0220.
FAX: (661) 964-0550. www.primedigital.com

Other services include: High-Def/Standard Definition Editorial, video compression & file conversion, DVD design & authoring & replication, broadcast duplication, QC services, standards conversion, digital restoration/remastering, color correction, format conversion & varispeeding, translation, subtitling & closed captioning.

LVT LASER SUBTITLING, INC.
609 Greenwich St., Ste. 4B, New York, NY 10014.
TEL: (212) 343-1910. FAX: (212) 965-1338.
email: newyork@lvtusa.com www.lvtusa.com www.lvt.fr
INTERNATIONAL COORDINATOR
JH Rudes

MARCLAND INTERNATIONAL COMMUNICATIONS
(Language dubbing; voiceover; translation; subtitles)
P.O. Box 3100, Burbank, CA 91508. TEL: (800) 526-7708,
(818) 557-6677. www.marcland.com
EXECUTIVE DIRECTOR
Alfredo Marco Fulchignoni

MASTERWORDS
1512 11th St., #203, Santa Monica, CA 90401-2907.
TEL: (310) 394-7998. FAX: (310) 394-7954.

MEDIA ACCESS GROUP AT WGBH
(Closed captions, subtitles, video description, mopix)
Boston Office: One Guest St., Boston, MA 02135. TEL: (617) 300-3600.
FAX: (617) 300-1020. email: access@wgbh.org
http://main.wgbh.org/wgbh/pages/mag/about/staff-listing.html
DIRECTOR, MEDIA ACCESS GROUP AT WGBH
Brian Donavan

California: 300 E. Magnolia Blvd., 2nd Flr., Burbank, CA 91502.
TEL: (818) 562-1919. FAX: (818) 562-3388.
email: access@wgbh.org
DIRECTOR, WEST COAST
Linda Idoni

PACIFIC TITLE & ART STUDIO
(Optical and digital services. Visual effects, titles, film opticals)
Digital Facilities: 7215 Santa Monica Blvd., Los Angeles, CA 90046. TEL: (323) 436-3850. FAX: (323) 769-3701.
email: sales@pactitle.com www.pactitle.com
CEO
David McCarthy, Jr. - dmccarthy@pactitle.com
SENIOR V.P., BUSINESS DEVELOPMENT
Ladd Lanford - ladd@pactitle.com
CREATIVE DIRECTOR
Bruce Schluter - bschluter@pactitle.com
EXECUTIVE PRODUCER, VISUAL EFFECTS
Crystal Dowd - cdowd@pactitle.com

Provides a full range of state-of-the-art digital and optical services from 2D image manipulation to multilayer compositing, 3D animation, wire and object removal, motion tracking, negative preparation, rendering, rotoscoping, HD and D1 to film transfers, scanning and laser film recording, film restoration and more.

PEOPLESUPPORT RAPIDTEXT, INC.
(Video/subtitling, titles & closed captions)
1801 Dove St., Newport Beach, CA 92660.
TEL: (949) 399-9200. FAX: (949) 399-9216.
email: tcinfo@peoplesupport.com

Rapidtext, Inc., and its subsidiary, The Transcription Company, specialize in high-value transcription and captioning services for clients in insurance, law enforcement, entertainment, education, and medical. RapidText offers advanced, custom voice-to-text solutions for fast-turnaround transcription, realtime captioning, offline captioning, timecoding, indexing, and translation.

SDI MEDIA

Global Headquarters: 10950 Washington Blvd., Studio B., Culver City, CA 90232. TEL: (310) 388-8800. FAX: (310) 388-8950.
email: usa_los_angeles@sdimediagroup.com
sales@sdimediagroup.com info@sdimediagroup.com
www.sdi-media-usa.com
CEO
Walter Schonfeld
PRESIDENT, SDI MEDIA GROUP
Paul Falzone
EXECUTIVE V.P. & CFO
Mary Ann Fialkowski
CHIEF INFORMATION OFFICER
Josh Arensberg

A leading provider of dubbing and subtitleing services, operating in 32 countries spanning Europe, Asia and the Americas. Worldwide, SDI owns and oeprates 89 recording rooms and 28 mixing rooms. Provides language dubbing and subtitling services for theatrical, home video & DVD releases. Company is dedicated to translating & localizing creative content for distribution in all media anywhere in the world.

SOFTNI CORP.

11400 W. Olympic Blvd., #200, Los Angeles, CA 90064.
TEL: (310) 312-9558. FAX: (310) 312-9557. www.softni.com
PRESIDENT & CEO
José M. Salgado - jmsalgado@softni.com

SoftNI Corporation is a leader in the creation of viewer-oriented subtitling, closed captioning and dubbing solutions for the film, television, DVD and cable/satellite industries. Company's most recent releases: the Subtitler Suite™ and the CaSat Suite™, open-architecture, multi-purpose family of subtitling products, designed to meet all possible subtitling needs, from the translation and subtitling of home videos by independent translators to the demand of multinational cable/satellite services; the Cinema Subtitler™ for traditional and digital theatrical subtitling; the Live Subtitler™ and Live Captioner ™ which allow users to translate and add subtitles, closed captions and Teletext to live transmissions via cable, satellite and webcasting.

TITRA CALIFORNIA, INC.

733 Salem St., Glendale, CA 91203. TEL: (818) 244-3663.
FAX: (818) 244-6205. email: titra@titra.com www.titra.com
MANAGING DIRECTOR
Rob Dekker

Laser subtitles. See website for additional locations.

TWO HEADED MONSTER, INC.

(Video/Subtitling—Titles & Closed Captions)
725 Arizona Ave., Santa Monica, CA 90401.
TEL: (310) 319-5370. FAX: (310) 319-5380.

VITAC

(Closed captioning, subtitling & translation in 40+ languages)
4605 Lankershim Blvd., Ste. 250, N. Hollywood, CA 91602.
TEL: (888) 528-4822, (818) 755-0410. FAX: (818) 755-0411.
email: yelena-m@vitac.com www.vitac.com
PRESIDENT & CEO
Patricia Prozzi
EXECUTIVE V.P., SALES & MARKETING
James Ballard - jim-b@vitac.com
MANAGER, CLIENT SERVICES
Debbie Hammond
DIRECTOR OF OPERATIONS, MULTI-LANGUAGE SUBTITLING
Yelena Makarczyk

Washington, D.C. Office: 1501 Wilson Blvd., Ste. 1003, Arlington, VA 22209. TEL: (703) 807-2766. FAX: (703) 807-2761.
email: Heather-Y@vitac.com
CONTACT
Heather York

Corporate Headquarters: 101 Hillpointe Dr., Canonsburg, PA 15317-9503. TEL: (800) 278-4822, (724) 514-4000.
FAX: (724) 514-4111.
PITTSBURGH SALES
Darryn Cleary - (724) 514-4081 darryn-c@vitac.com

ZAK/PAPERNO

(Post production: Video/Subtitling-Titles & Closed Captions)
7000 Beverly Blvd., Los Angeles, CA 90036.
TEL: (323) 937-2517.
CONTACT
Michael Zak

TRANSCRIPTION, INTERPRETING & TRANSLATION

AUDIO TO GO

(Transcription & translation services)
42 W. 89th St., Apt. E, New York, NY 10024.
TEL: (212) 721-1183. FAX: (212) 721-1273.
email: info@a2g.com www.a2g.com

BLUE 105

2600 W. Olive Ave., 5th Flr., Burbank, CA 91505.
TEL: (818) 563-4335, (818) 563-4223. www.blue105.com

Subtitling: Broadcast, High-Definition Distribution, DVD Distribution, Video Distribution, Airline Distribution, Theatrical Distribution, Corporate, Internet. Captioning services; dubbing services and more.

CAPTIONS, INC.

(Closed-captions, subtitles, translations)
640 S. Glenwood Place, Burbank, CA 91506.
TEL: (818) 260-2700. FAX: (818) 260-2821.
email: captions@captionsinc.com www.captionsinc.com
DIRECTOR, MARKETING & SALES
Ed Premetz - (818) 260-2756 Ed_Premetz@captionsinc.com

CTS LANGUAGE LINK™

Evergreen International Plaza, 911 Main St., Ste. 10, Vancouver, WA 98660. TEL: (800) 208-2620, (360) 693-7100.
FAX: (360) 693-9292. email: info@ctslanguagelink.com
www.ctslanguagelink.com
PRESIDENT & CEO
Jeff Barger
COO
Pam Ballard

Language translation and interpreting services support more than 240 languages and dialects.

DELUXE DIGITAL STUDIOS - SOFTITLER - BURBANK

2400 Empire Ave., Ste. 300, Burbank, CA 91504.
TEL: (818) 565-4400. FAX: (818) 565-4444.
www.softitler.com
CONTACT
Jim Ziskin - jim.ziskin@bydeluxe.com

DVD subtitling & localization; theatrical translation services & subtitling; closed captioning. Reaching the world in more than 50 languages.

IPROBE MULTILINGUAL SOLUTIONS, INC.

(Media creation & localization services in the 6,912 languages of the world)
5 W. 36th St., Ste. 402, New York, NY 10018.
TEL: (212) 489-6035. FAX: (212) 202-4790.
email: info@iProbeSolutions.com www.iProbeSolutions.com
CONTACT
Julie H. Setbon

Services include: Foreign language casting, voice-overs, subtitling, translation, transcription, interpreting, cross-cultural consulting, video production.

ISI

6180 Laurel Canyon Blvd., Ste. 245, N. Hollywood, CA 91606.
TEL: (818) 753-9181. FAX: (818) 753-9617.
email: info@isitrans.com quotes@isitrans.com
www.isitrans.com
CEO & FOUNDER
George Rimalower

LANGUAGE.NET

(Translation services, interpreting services & dialect coaching. From any language to any language)
804 Main St., Venice, CA 90291. TEL: (310) 399-1790.
FAX: (310) 399-1901. email: info@language.net
www.language.net
CONTACT
Melanie Goodman

LINGUATHEQUE

(Translation; Script Adaptation & Timing; Dubbing & Voiceovers; Dialect Coaching & Interpreting)
2219 W. Olive Ave., #261, Burbank, CA 91506.
TEL: (800) 440-5344. FAX: (818) 549-9593.
email: linguatheque@sbcglobal.net lingua@linguatheque.com
www.linguatheque.com
CONTACT
Karen Delaney

Linguatheque has introduced post-production services using professionally trained talents for foreign language voice-overs, dubbing and dialect coaching. In partnership with a state-of-the-art recording and on-line facility the company delivers high-quality master tapes in a variety of formats.

NATIONAL CAPTIONING INSTITUTE

(Closed-captioning, subtitlings & translations)
1900 Gallows Rd., Ste. 3000, Vienna, VA 22182.
TEL: (703) 917-7600. FAX: (703) 917-9853.
email: mail@ncicap.org www.ncicap.org
NATIONAL DIRECTOR, SALES & MARKETING
Juan Mario Agudelo -jagudelo@ncicap.org

California Office: 303 N. Glenoaks Blvd., Ste. 200, Burbank, CA 91502. TEL: (818) 238-0068. FAX: (818) 238-4266.
CONTACT
Elissa Sarna - esarna@ncicap.org

Dallas Office: 7610 N. Stemmons Freeway, Ste. 200, Dallas, TX 75247. TEL: (214) 647-4360. FAX: (214) 647-4386.
CONTACT
Christy Roney - croney@ncicap.org

PRIME DIGITAL MEDIA SERVICES

(DVD replication & video duplication services)
28109 Ave. Stanford, Valencia CA 91355. TEL: (661) 964-0220. FAX: (661) 964-0550. www.primedigital.com

Other services include: High-Def/Standard Definition Editorial, video compression & file conversion, DVD design & authoring & replication, broadcast duplication, QC services, standards conversion, digital restoration/remastering, color correction, format conversion & varispeeding, translation, subtitling & closed captioning.

STS FOREIGN LANGUAGE SERVICES

(A division of STS Media Services, Inc. Foreign language translations, subtitling, voice-overs, studio transcription services)
P.O. Box 10213, Burbank, CA 91510. TEL: (818) 563-3004.
email: info@stsforeignlanguage.com
info@studiotranscription.com www.STSForeignLanguage.com

Talent Agencies

A+ ACTORS OF TEXAS, LLC
(Represents talent in: film, commercial, industrials, promotional, Print Work, and Voice-Over work)
4900 Bissonnet #210, Bellaire, TX 77401. TEL: (713) 349-0000.
FAX: (713) 664-8098. email: aplusactorstx@aol.com
www.aplusactors.com
OWNER/AGENT
Pat Skiles, Gina Pack

ABRAMS ARTISTS AGENCY
(Full-service talent agency)
9200 Sunset Blvd., 11th Flr., Los Angeles, CA 90069.
TEL: (310) 859-0625. FAX: (310) 276-6193.
email: contactLA@abramsartists.com
CHAIRMAN & CEO
Harry Abrams - harry.abrams@abramsart.com
HEAD, BUSINESS AFFAIRS
Brian Cho
BUSINESS AFFAIRS
Sunny Valencia
CO-HEAD, MOTION PICTURES/TV
Joe Rice, Marni Rosenzweig
MOTION PICTURES/TV
Harold Augenstein, Eric Emery, Gregg A. Klein, Sharon Paz, William Pennell
HEAD, HOSTING/EMCEES/REALITY/BROADCAST JOURNALISM & ALTERNATIVE PROGRAMMING, NEW MEDIA
Alec Shankman
HOSTING/MCS/REALITY/BROADCAST JOURNALISM & ALTERNATIVE PROGRAMMING
Joe Rose, Brandon Martinez
HEAD, YOUTH DIVISION/MOTION PICTURES & TV
Wendi Green
YOUTH DIVISION/MOTION PICTURES & TV
Jennifer Millar
HEAD, COMMERCIALS (ON-CAMERA) & VOICE DIVISION
Mark Measures
COMMERCIALS
Valerie Chiovetti, Kristin Nava, Marna Palmer
COMMERCIALS, YOUTH DIVISION
Jeremy Apody
COMMERCIALS, VOICE DIVISION
Mark Measures, Mark Quinn, Adrienne McWhorter, Melanie Thomas, Eric Hurst
HUMAN RESOURCES
Norma Robbins

ABRAMS ARTISTS AGENCY-NEW YORK
275 7th Ave., 26th Flr., New York, NY 10001.
TEL: (646) 486-4600. FAX: (646) 486-0100.
email: theatrical.ny@abramsart.com www.abramsartists.com
CHAIRMAN & CEO
Harry Abrams
CO-MANAGING DIRECTOR, SENIOR V.P., VOICE-OVER
Neal Altman
CO-MANAGING DIRECTOR, V.P., THEATRICAL/MOTION PICTURES/TV
Robert Attermann
CELEBRITIES/HOSTS/MCS/BROADCAST JOURNALISTS/REALITY TV/ALTERNATIVE PROGRAMMING
Mark Turner, Ms. Trey Weiss
V.P., COMMERCIALS
Ms. Tracey Goldblum
CHILDREN, COMMERCIALS
Bonnie Shumofsky
COMMERCIALS
Amy Mazur, Alison Quartin
YOUTH/THEATRICAL/MOTION PICTURES/TV
Rachel Altman, Ellen Gilbert
THEATRICAL/MOTION PICTURES/TV
Danielle Delawder, Richard Fisher, Paul Reisman
CO-HEAD, LITERARY
Sarah Douglas, Chas. Kopelman
LITERARY
Beth Blickers, Ron Gwiazda, Morgan Jenness, Kate Navin, Maura Teitelbaum, Peter Hagan
PRINT
Genine Esposito, Joe Thompson
VOICE-OVER
Jenny Brown, Jessica Felrice, Billy Serow
VOICE-OVER PROMOS
Jonathan Saul
BUSINESS AFFAIRS
Vincent DeVito

ABOVE THE LINE AGENCY
(Literary agents)
468 N. Camden Dr., #200, Beverly Hills, CA 90210.
TEL: (310) 859-6115. FAX: (310) 859-6119.
www.abovethelineagency.com
OWNER
Rima Greer
VICE PRESIDENT
Bruce Bartlett

AGENCY FOR THE PERFORMING ARTS, INC.
405 S. Beverly Dr., Beverly Hills, CA 90212.
TEL: (310) 888-4200. FAX: (310) 888-4242.
www.apa-agency.com
CHAIRMAN EMERITUS
Roger Vorce
PRESIDENT & CEO
Jim Gosnell
SENIOR V.P., TALENT
Jeff Witias
EXECUTIVE V.P., FEATURE LITERARY
David Saunders
EXECUTIVE V.P., TV LITERARY
Lee Dinstman
V.P., TV LITERARY
Matt Ochacher
V.P., FEATURE LITERARY
Steven Fisher
FEATURE LITERARY
David Boxerbaum
TV LITERARY
Robert Gumer
LITERARY
Debbie Deuble-Hill, Lindsay Howard, Jack Leighton, Melissa Orton, Sheryl Petersen, Ryan Saul
HEAD, REALITY/ALTERNATIVE TV
Hayden Meyer
ALTERNATIVE TV
Marc Kamler, Ra Kumar, Josh Levenbrown, Alan Moore
SENIOR V.P., TALENT
Jeff Witjas
V.P., TALENT
Ryan Martin, Barry McPherson, Paul Santana
TALENT
Dan Baron, Jimmy Cundiff, Brian Dow, Todd Eisner, Tyler Grasham, Jonathan Perry, Scott Simpson, Mike Wilson, Everly Lee, Regan Frisby
SENIOR V.P., COMEDY
Danny Robinson
COMEDY
Jackie Miller-Knobbe, Eric Murphy, Tim Scally

New York: 250 W. 57th St., Ste. 1701, New York, NY 10107.
TEL: (212) 687-0092. FAX: (212) 687-0176.
www.apa-agency.com
COMEDY AGENT
Mike Berkowitz, Avi Gilbert, Bryan Raisa
MUSIC/PERFORMING ARTS AGENT
Christine Barkley, Fred Hansen and Nick Trusty

Nashville: 3010 Poston Ave., Nashville, TN 37203.
TEL: (615) 297-0100. FAX: (615) 297-5434.
www.apa-agency.com

AGENTS FOR THE ARTS
(Full-service)
203 W. 23rd St., 3rd Flr., New York, NY 10011.
TEL: (212) 229-2562. FAX: (212) 463-9313.
OWNER
Carole J. Russo

AL MEDIA MOVERS, INC.
10444 Magnolia Blvd., North Hollywood, CA 91601.
TEL/FAX: (310) 237-6438. email: info@media-movers.com
www.media-movers.com
CONTACT
Lawrence Vishnu

Dubbing (Lip-sync & U.N.Style), Subtitling, Voiceovers, Closed Captioning, Translation & Transcription in all Asian, Indian, European, African & Middle-Eastern languages for all media formats.

ALVARADO REY AGENCY
(Represents talented actors from Latin America, Europe and the U.S. theatrically and commercially in Los Angeles)
7906 Santa Monica Blvd., Ste. 205, West Hollywood, CA 90046. TEL: (323) 656-2277. FAX: (323) 656-2299.
email: youth@alvaradorey.com info@alvaradorey.com
www.alvaradorey.com

OWNER/AGENT
Nikkolas Rey
AGENT
Aaron Leider

MICHAEL AMATO AGENCY
(Full-service talent agency)
P.O. Box 15804, Jersey City, NJ 07305.
TEL: (212) 247-4456. FAX: (212) 664-0641, (201) 356-9946.
email: amatotheatricalagency@yahoo.com
PRESIDENT
Michael Amato
TALENT MANAGER
Andrea Dasilva

AMSEL, EISENSTADT & FRAZIER, INC.
(Represents actors, children, comedians, teens/young adults)
5055 Wilshire Blvd., Ste. 865, Los Angeles, CA 90036.
TEL: (323) 939-1188. FAX: (323) 939-0630.
CO-OWNER/THEATRICAL AGENTS
Michael Eisenstadt, John Frazier
THEATRICAL/COMMERCIAL
Gloria Hinojosa
YOUTH THEATRICAL/COMMERCIAL
Nicole Jolley, Milton Perea
THEATRICAL
Ryan Olson
COMMERCIAL
Indra Rose

ANDREADIS TALENT AGENCY, INC.
(Talent & commercial)
119 W. 57th St., Ste. 711, New York, NY 10019.
TEL: (212) 315-0303. FAX: (212) 315-0311.
email: andreadis@verizon.net
OWNER & AGENT
Barbara Andreadis

ARIA TALENT
(Owned by Ford Model Management)
1017 W. Washington Blvd., Ste. 2-C, Chicago, IL 60607.
TEL: (312) 850-9671. FAX: (312) 226-5523.
www.ariatalent.com
DIRECTOR, TV/FILM
Robert Schroeder
TV/FILM
Donna Simon Dunn

Agency represents: actors for commerical, film, TV and theatre, broadcast journalists and newscasters, children, comedians, hosts/emcees, print models, runway models, teens/young adults and musical theatre performers.

ARTIST MANAGEMENT AGENCY
835 5th Ave., Ste. 411, San Diego, CA 92101. TEL: (619) 233-6655.
email: nanci@artistmanagementagency.com
www.artistmanagementagency.com
PRESIDENT
Nanci Washburn

Orange County: 261 Bush St., Santa Ana, CA 92701.
TEL: (714) 558-7373.

Represents actors for episodic TV, feature film, commercials, print, industrials and voice-over.

ARTISTS AGENCY, INC.
(Represents book authors, hosts/MCs, producers & TV writers)
230 W. 55th St., Ste. 29D, New York, NY 10019.
TEL: (212) 245-6960. FAX: (212) 333-7420.
PRESIDENT
Jonathan Russo
TALENT
Nikole Tsabasis, Barry Weiner
ASSISTANT
Erin McLaughlin

By referral only; no unsolicited material.

ASSOCIATED BOOKING CORP. AGENCY
(Musical talent)
501 Madison Ave., #603, New York, NY 10022.
TEL: (212) 874-2400. FAX: (212) 769-3649.
email: musicbiz@mindspring.com info@abcbooking.com
www.abcbooking.com
PRESIDENT
Oscar Cohen
V.P., AGENT
Lisa Cohen

RICHARD ASTOR AGENCY
(Actors and singers)
250 W. 57th St. Ste. 2014, New York, NY 10107.
TEL: (212) 581-1970. FAX: (212) 581-1980.

Photos and résumé accepted by mail only. All types for film, TV, soaps & theatre. No children, models or voice-overs.

BAUMAN REDANTY & SHAUL AGENCY
(Actors)
California: 5757 Wilshire Blvd., Ste. 473, Los Angeles, CA 90036. TEL: (323) 857-6666. FAX: (323) 857-0368.
CONTACT
David Shaul
TALENT REPRESENTATIVE
Adam Lazarus, Evan Miller
ASSISTANT
Jordan Forman, Erin Gallegos

New York: 1650 Broadway, Ste. 1410, New York, NY 10019.
TEL: (212) 757-0098. FAX: (212) 489-8531.
CONTACT
Mark Redanty
TALENT REPRESENTATIVE
Charles Bodner, Tim Marshall
ASSISTANT
Kristin Lavo

No unsolicited submissions.

BRADY, BRANNON & RICH
(Hosting. On-camera and voiceover for commercials & infomercials. Voiceovers for all areas)
5670 Wilshire Blvd., Ste. 820, Los Angeles, CA 90036.
TEL: (323) 852-9559. FAX: (323) 852-9579.

BRASS ARTISTS & ASSOCIATES
(Agency)
9025 Wilshire Blvd., Ste. 400, Beverly Hills, CA 90211.
TEL: (310) 246-3486. FAX: (310) 246-1879.
email: info@thebrassagency.com www.thebrassagency.com
AGENT, COMMERCIAL
Randy Cabrera
AGENT, THEATRICAL
Jack Iannaci, Michael Dragomir
AGENT, YOUTH, COMMERCIAL & THEATRICAL
April Baker
AGENT
Tony Ferrar

Represents actors for film/TV, seniors, teens/young adults & voiceover artists. Submissions by mail only. Referrals are preferred.

BREVARD TALENT GROUP, INC.
(Theatrical)
301 E. Pine St., Ste. 175, Orlando, FL 32801.
TEL: (407) 841-7775. FAX: (407) 841-7716.
email: traci@brevardtalentgroup.com
www.BrevardTalentGroup.com
PRESIDENT
Traci Danielle

DON BUCHWALD & ASSOCIATES, INC.
California Office: 6500 Wilshire Blvd., Ste. 2200, Los Angeles, CA 90048. TEL: (323) 655-7400. FAX: (323) 655-7470.
email: info@buchwald.com www.buchwald.com
PRESIDENT, LOS ANGELES OFFICE
Tim Angle - tim@buchwald.com
SENIOR V.P., AGENT, TALENT
Julia Buchwald
V.P., TALENT
Michael Greenwald
AGENT, TALENT
Neil Bagg, Tracy Christian, Hannah Roth, Spencer Willis
AGENT, BROADCAST
David Swift
AGENT, YOUTH
Kristy Dax, Pamela Fisher
TV, LITERARY
Tim Angle
ADMINISTRATION
Tracy Kamar

New York: 10 E. 44th St., New York, NY 10017. TEL: (212) 867-1200. FAX: (212) 867-2434, (212) 972-3209.

OWNER/FOUNDER/CEO/PRESIDENT
Don Buchwald - don@buchwald.com
EXECUTIVE V.P., LEGAL & ADMINISTRATIVE AFFAIRS
Richard Basch
CFO & V.P.
Stephen Fisher
BUSINESS ADMINISTRATION
Ana Mouradian
TALENT PAYMENT
Ana Mouradian, Joanne DePersia, Lorraine Bray, Bryan Brooks, Noelle Gonzalez, Susan Langford, Steve Perez & Katrina Rosa
DIRECTOR INFORMATION SYSTEMS
Charles Buchwald
EXECUTIVE V.P., BUSINESS AFFAIRS, FILM, TV & THEATRE
Richard Basch
EXECUTIVE V.P., FILM, TV & THEATRE
Ricki Olshan
EXECUTIVE V.P.
Robyn Stecher

DIRECTOR, CELEBRITY ENDORSEMENTS
Lisa Roina
AGENT, BROADCAST
Tony Burton
AGENT, YOUTH
Victoria Kress, Pam Roth
AGENT, COMMERCIALS, ON-CAMERA
David Elliott, Michael Raymen, Robyn Starr
AGENT, FILM, TV & THEATRE
David Lewis, Jonathan Mason, Joanne Nici, Rachel Sheedy, Alan Willig
AGENT, YOUTH COMMERCIAL
Pamela Roth
AGENT, VOICEOVER
Katherine Ryan, Robin Steinfeld

DEPARTMENT CONTACT INFORMATION:
Narration - (212) 867-1070
Broadcast - (212) 634-8380, (323) 655-7400
PA/Comedy - (323) 655-7400
Legit - (212) 867-1200, (323) 655-7400
Literary - (323) 602-2335
Youth - (212) 634-8351, (323) 951-4539

CAA/CREATIVE ARTISTS AGENCY

(Literary & talent)
California: 2000 Ave. of the Stars, Los Angeles, CA 90067. TEL: (424) 288-2000. FAX: (424) 288-2900.
www.caa.com www.caaspeakers.com

Beijing: 10/F Ste. 1001, China View Tower 1, No. 2 Jia, East Gongti Rd., Chaoyang Dist., Beijing, China 100027. TEL: (+86 10) 8587 1320. FAX: (+86 10) 8587 1319.

Calgary: 822-11 Ave. SW, Ste. 204, Calgary, AB T2R 0E5. TEL: (403) 206-3120. FAX: (403) 775-4338.

Nashville: 3310 West End Ave., Ste. 500, Nashville, TN 37203. TEL: (615) 383-8787.

New York: 162 Fifth Ave., 6th Flr., New York, NY 10010. TEL: (212) 277-9000.

London: 2 Queen Caroline St., Hammersmith, London W6 9DX UK. TEL: 020- 8323-8016. FAX: 020-8323-8317.

St. Louis: 222 S. Central Ave., Ste. 1008, St. Louis, MO 63105. TEL: (314) 862-5560. FAX: (314) 862-4754.

Stockholm: Riddargatan 23, 114 57 Stockholm, Sweden. TEL: +46 8 667 4110. FAX: +46 8 663 8254.
PRESIDENT & MANAGING PARTNER
Richard Lovett
MOTION PICTURE TALENT, MANAGING DIRECTOR
Kevin Huvane, Bryan Lourd
MOTION PICTURE LITERARY, MANAGING DIRECTOR
David O'Connor
HEAD OF COMMUNICATIONS
Michael Mand
COMMUNICATIONS
Missy Davy, Beth McClinton
DEPARTMENT CO-HEAD, MOTION PICTURE TALENT
Tracy Brennan, Jimmy Darmody
MOTION PICTURE TALENT
Chris Andrews, Martin Baum, Darren Boghosian, David Bugliari, Matthew DelPiano, Ben Dey, Jaime Feld, Ryan Heck, Jason Heyman, Kimberly Hodgert-Evangelatos, Ara Keshishian, Michael Kives, Rick Kurtzman, Peter Levine, Josh Lieberman, Tony Lipp, Joel Lubin, Thao Nguyen, Michael Nilon, Kelly Tiffan O'Connor, Jeremy Plager, Hylda Queally, Fred Specktor, Jeffery Speich, Nick Styne, Mick Sullivan, Jim Toth, Jack Whigham, Warren Zavala
MOTION PICTURE MARKETING
Megan Crawford, Marissa Garcia
MOTION PICTURE BUSINESS AFFAIRS
Roger Batchelder, Steven Brookman, Jenna Gambaro, Fred Gauthier, Matthew Leaf, Charles Melniker, Glen Meredith, Joanna Mulas, Eileen Rapke, Wendy Schneider-Nogradi, Keith Sears, Sheldon Sroloff, Marc Von Arx
DEPARTMENT CO-HEAD, MOTION PICTURE LITERARY
Todd Feldman, Risa Gertner
MOTION PICTURE LITERARY
Dan Aloni, Rowena Arguelle, Jay Baker, Spencer Baumgarten, John Campisi, Maha Dakhil, J.P. Evans, Craig Gering, Scott Greenberg, Billy Hawkins, Rand Holston, Adam Kanter, Brian Kend, Christopher Lawson, Alex Lerner, Jon Levin, Byrdie Lifson-Pompan, Dianne McGunigle, Gregory McKnight, Dan Rabinow, Carin Sage, Brian Siberell, Martin Spencer, Elizabeth Swofford
MOTION PICTURE LITERARY, BOOKS
Robert Bookman, Richard Green, Simon Green, Shari Smiley, Matthew Snyder, Sally Willcox
DEPARTMENT HEAD, MOTION PICTURE FILM FINANCE
Rick Hess
MOTION PICTURE, FILM FINANCE
Micah Green, Brian Kavanaugh-Jones, Ben Kramer, Dan Steinman (NY), Roeg Sutherland
DEPARTMENT HEAD, TV
Steven Lafferty
TELEVISION
Janine Argiriou, Roy Ashton, Alan Berger, Adam Berkowitz, Glenn Bickel, Rosanna Bilow, Alan Braun, Pierre Brogan, Greg Cavic, Joseph Cohen, Kevin Cooper, Andy Elkin, Nancy Etz, Tony Etz, Jason Fox, Sean Gruman, Chris Harbert, Alix Hartley, Jeffrey Jacobs, Nancy Jones, Frank Jung, Michael Katcher, Rob Kenneally, Grant Kessman, Max Kisbye, Christina Kuo, Renee Kurtz, Rick Lefitz, Martin Lesak, Brett Loncar, Ryan Ly, Sara Malek, Olivia Metzger, Peter Micelli, Andrew Miller, Ted Miller, Elizabeth Newman, Brian Pike, Raj Raghavan, Michael Rosenfeld, Sonya Rosenfeld, Andrea Ross, Chris Simonian, Jaclyn Singer, Steve Smooke, Andy Stabile, Catherine Stellin, Jonathan Swaden, Steve Tellez, Bruce Vinokour, Tiffany Ward, Kathy White, Tom Young, Bill Zotti
TV, BUSINESS AFFAIRS
Teri Eaton, Daniel Grover, Gregory Pulis, Jon Ringquist
CO-HEAD OF CAA MARKETING
Jae Goodman, David Messinger
MARKETING
Andrew Ault, Stephen Baik, Jay Brooker, Jesse Coulter, Will Hobbs, Ben James, Erin James, Sandra Kang, John Kaplan, Michael Matsumoto, Ned McNeilage, Michelle McQuaid, Robin Moraetes (NY), Jack Oh, Haeran Park, Carol Powley, Matt Rotondo, Mark Shambura, Lori Tabb
DEPARTMENT HEAD, BUSINESS DEVELOPMENT
Michael Yanover
BUSINESS DEVELOPMENT
Omid Ashtari, Nathan Coyle, Adam Devejian, Matt Mazzeo, Craig Vaughan, Brian Weinstein
SPEAKERS
Peter Jacobs, Amie Yavor
CHINA
Jessica Chen, Jonah Greenberg, H. Liu, Peter Loehr, Dong Hui Wang

THE CAMPBELL AGENCY

(Founded in 1989. Fashion and commercial print; TV commercials; on-camera and voice actors; hair & makeup artists. Texas Talent Agency License #233)
Two Turtle Creek, 3838 Oak Lawn Ave., Ste. 900, Dallas, TX 75210. TEL: (214) 522-8991. FAX: (214) 522-8997.
www.thecampbellagency.com
PRESIDENT & DIRECTOR OF FASHION & COMMERCIAL PRINT
Nancy Campbell
TALENT DIVISION, FILM AND VOICE OVER AGENT
Nancy Tasker Johnson
TALENT DIVISION, ON CAMERA COMMERCIAL & INDUSTRIAL AGENT
Sharon Hendricks Howell
FASHION AND COMMERCIAL PRINT
Peter John
CO-DIRECTOR, CHILDREN'S DIVISION
Barbara Blanchette, Diana Dyer
NEW FACES/DEVELOPMENT DIRECTOR
Saúl Jimenez
BUSINESS MANAGER
Robin Burns
OFFICE COORDINATOR
Amy Greer

CARSON-ADLER AGENCY, INC.

(Theatre, film, TV & commercials; children & young adults)
250 W. 57th St., Ste. 2030, New York, NY 10107.
TEL: (212) 307-1882. FAX: (212) 541-7008.
www.carsonadler.com
PRESIDENT & OWNER
Nancy Carson
SENIOR AGENT
Bonnie Deroski, Shirley Faison

Carson-Adler Agency is a licensed employment agency by the state and city of New York and a member of the National Association of Talent Representatives.

CAVALERI & ASSOCIATES

(Full-service talent agency)
178 S. Victory Blvd., Ste. 205, Burbank, CA 91502.
TEL: (818) 955-9300. FAX: (818) 955-9399.
email: cavaleri@hotmail.com
OWNER/AGENT
Ray Cavaleri
CHILDREN/YOUNG ADULTS
Cinthia Becks
LITERARY
Al Choi

CELEBRITY SUPPLIERS

(Celebrities, TV and movies)
2756 N. Green Valley Pkwy., #449, Las Vegas, NV 89014.
TEL: (702) 451-8090. email: info@EntertainmentServices.com
www.celebritysuppliers.com
PRESIDENT
A.J. Sagman

AGENT
S. Rosenthal, Deb Manning

THE CHASIN AGENCY

(Theatrical, writers and directors)
8899 Beverly Blvd., Ste. 716, Los Angeles, CA 90048.
TEL: (310) 278-7505. FAX: (310) 275-6685.
OWNER, AGENT ALL AREAS
Tom Chasin
TALENT
Kelly Duncan-Joiner
ASSISTANT
Matt Gogal

CIRCLE TALENT ASSOCIATES

(Actors for commercials)
433 N. Camden Dr., #400, Beverly Hills, CA 90210.
TEL: (310) 285-1585, (310) 279-5155.
email: circletalent@sbcglobal.net
PRINCIPAL/THEATRICAL/COMMERCIAL AGENT
Jennifer Lee Garland
CONTACT
Donna H. Lee

CIRCUIT RIDER TALENT MANAGEMENT

123 Walton Ferry Rd., Hendersonville, TN 37075.
TEL: (615) 824-1947. FAX: (615) 264-0462.
email: dotwool@bellsouth.net
PRESIDENT
Linda S. Dotson

COLLEEN CLER AGENCY

(Represents children, teens & adults for print, commercials, TV and film)
178 S. Victory Blvd., #108, Burbank, CA 91502.
TEL: (818) 841-7943. email: colleen@colleencler.com
agent@colleencler.com www.colleencler.com
CONTACT
Colleen Cler

CLI TALENT AGENCY

(Commercials; on camera and voiceover)
843 N. Sycamore Ave., Los Angeles, CA 90038.
TEL: (323) 461-3971. FAX: (323) 461-1134.
PRESIDENT
Leanna Levy
SENIOR AGENT
Richard Ohanesian

COAST TO COAST TALENT GROUP, INC.

(Talent and literary agency. Actors for film/TV, directors, producers, adult theatrical, adult commercial, print, pro sports and youth division)
3350 Barham Blvd., Los Angeles, CA 90068.
TEL: (323) 845-9200. FAX: (323) 845-9213.
email: info@ctctalent.com www.ctctalent.com
PRINCIPAL, BUSINESS AFFAIRS
Jeremiah Doryon
PRINCIPAL, MOTION PICTURES/TV/ADULT
Elyah Doryon
HEAD, ADULT COMMERICALS/CELEBRITY ATHLETES
Hugh Leon
DIRECTOR, CHILDREN'S DIVISION
Meredith Fine
COMMERCIALS, CHILDREN
Renata Dobrucki, Sydel Lisi
ASSISTANT, ADULT COMMERCIALS
Dawn Goodson
ASSISTANT, CHILDREN
Reagan Wallace

CONTEMPORY ARTISTS, LTD.

(Represents producers, writers and directors for film & TV)
610 Santa Monica Blvd., Ste. 202, Santa Monica, CA 90401.
TEL: (310) 395-1800. FAX: (310) 394-3308.
PRESIDENT
Ronnie Leif

CORALIE, JR. AGENCY

(Actors)
907 S. Victory Blvd. Burbank, CA 91502. TEL: (818)842-5513.
OWNER/AGENT
Coralie, Jr.
AGENT, ACTORS & ACTRESSES
Stuart Edward

CUNNINGHAM, ESCOTT, SLEVIN, DOHERTY TALENT AGENCY

(Adult on camera, voice over and print; full-service for youth)
Los Angeles: 10635 Santa Monica Blvd., Ste. 130, Ste. 135, Ste. 140, Los Angeles, CA 90025-4900.
Commercial/TEL: (310) 475-2111.
FAX: (310) 475-1929.
email: partners@cesdtalent.com info@cesdtalent.com
www.cesdtalent.com www.cesdvoices.com
PRESIDENT, PARTNER
Ken Slevin
CHAIRMAN, PARTNER
T.J. Escott
SECRETARY/TREASURER/PARTNER
Paul Doherty
VOICEOVER COMMERCIAL AGENT, SCALE, ESPANOL AND CELEBRITY CLIENTS
Beau Berdahl
VOICEOVER, ANIMATION & PUPPETRY AGENT, SCALE AND CELEBRITY CLIENTS
Pat Brady
VOICEOVER COMMERCIAL AGENT, SCALE, ESPAÑOL & CELEBRITY CLIENTS
Sumeet Iyengar, Cathey Lizzio
DIRECTOR, ON-CAMERA COMMERCIALS
David Ziff
ON-CAMERA COMMERCIAL AGENT
Adrienne Berg, Dedra Galiher
TV FILM AGENT
Jennifer Patredis
TV FILM AGENT/YOUNG TALENT VOICEOVER AGENT
Melissa Berger, Carol Lynn Sher, Larry Wiedemann
VOICEOVER PROMO-TRAILER-NARRATION
Vincent Biunno
DIRECTOR, VOICEOVER PROMO-TRAILER-NARRATION
Sam Glick

New York: 257 Park Ave. S, Ste. 900, New York, NY 10010.
TEL: (212) 477-1666. FAX: (212) 979-2011.
email: info@cesdtalent.com www.cesdtalent.com
www.cesdvoices.com
DIRECTOR, VOICEOVER/PROMO DIVISION
Donna Mancino
YOUTH ON-CAMERA & VOICEOVER COMMERCIAL, ESPAÑOL & ANIMATION AGENT
Jason Bercy
VOICEOVER COMMERCIAL AGENT, SCALE, ESPAÑOL & CELEBRITY CLIENTS
Tom Celia, Billy Collura, Anita Reilly
ON-CAMERA COMMERCIAL AGENT
Maura Maloney, Kirsten Walther, Lakey Wolff

DIGITAL ARTISTS AGENCY

13323 W. Washingon Blvd., Ste. 304, Los Angeles, CA 90066.
TEL: (310) 788-3918. FAX: (310) 788-3415.
email: info@d-a-a.com www.d-a-a.com
FOUNDER
Bob Coleman - bcoleman@d-a-a.com
EXECUTIVE ASSISTANT
Jennifer Heusser

Representation, career management and development sources for digital visual effects artists; Specializes in feature film, entertainment TV, commercials, music videos.

DIVERSE TALENT GROUP, INC.

(A talent and literary agency)
1925 Century Park E, 8th Flr., Ste. 880, Los Angeles, CA 90067. TEL: (310) 201-6565. FAX: (310) 201-6572.
email: info@diversetalentgroup.com
www.diversetalentgroup.com
PRESIDENT/PARTNER/AGENT, PACKAGING & CONTRACTS (BELOW THE LINE)
Christopher Nassif
PARTNER/AGENT, LITERARY
Susan Sussman
AGENT, LITERARY
Amanda Brammall, Mickey Freiberg
JR. AGENT, LITERARY
Crystal Lewis, Lori Mason
ADULT THEATRICAL HEAD/DIRECTOR
Tom Harrison
AGENT, THEATRICAL
Suzanne Bennett-Harrison
JR. AGENT, THEATRICAL
Kathy Beasly, Rochelle Hartson
AGENT, COMMERCIAL
Wendy Morrison
JR. AGENT, COMMERCIAL
Laura Bowman
AGENT, TALENT
Nicole Cataldo
JR. AGENT, TALENT
Cole Harris
JR. AGENT, PACKAGING
Zachary Solov
AGENT, YOUTH THEATRICAL/COMMERCIAL
Jackie Lewis
ACCOUNTING & HUMAN RESOURCES
Marty Eaden

Representation for: Diverse Models (Lifestyle/Commercial Print), Diverse Youth (Youth), Diverse Theatrical Dance (Choreographer & Triple Threat Division.

DOUGLAS, GORMAN, ROTHACKER & WILHELM, INC.
1501 Broadway, Ste. 703, New York, NY 10036.
TEL: (212) 382-2000. FAX: (212) 719-2878.
OWNER
Jim Wilhelm
AGENT
Joel Carlton, Josh Pultz
JR. AGENT
Nicole Wichinsky

Represents actors for film/TV, choreographers, dancers, directors and musical theatre performers. Submissions by mail only.

EXTREME SPORTS FILMING
(Action sports specialist)
3419 Via Lido, #145, Newport Beach, CA 92663.
TEL: (714) 235-7578. email: efilming@sbcglobal.net
CONTACT
Miles Flewitt

Marine, air and land; production facilities, location, equipment, talent, vehicle coordination/trucks & cars, and more.

THE FIELD CECH AGENCY
(Literary agency; no referrals)
12725 Ventura Blvd., Ste. D, Studio City, CA 91604.
TEL: (818) 980-2001. FAX: (818) 980-0754.
CONTACT
Maggie Field, Judy Cech

FILM ARTISTS ASSOCIATES
(Commercial talent.)
21044 Ventura Blvd., #215, Woodland Hills, CA 91364.
TEL: (818) 883-5008.
CEO & COMMERCIAL AGENT
Cris Dennis

FRONTIER BOOKING INTERNATIONAL, INC.
(Children to young adults)
1560 Broadway, Ste. 1110, New York, NY 10036.
TEL: (212) 221-0220. email: john@frontierbooking.com
www.frontierbooking.com
AGENT
John Shea, Heather Finn, Marion Falk

Represents a variety of successful performers from actors and models to singers, designers, and voiceover artists.

THE GAGE GROUP, INC.
(Theatre, film, literary, TV, commercial)
14724 Ventura Blvd., Ste. 505, Sherman Oaks, CA 91403.
TEL: (818) 905-3800. FAX: (818) 905-3322.
PRINCIPAL, PRESIDENT, TALENT, LITERARY
Martin Gage
COMMERCIALS
Mark Fadness
TALENT
Olivia Bowe, Gerry Koch, Kitty McMillan, Arthur Toretzky
ASSISTANT
Zach Hostetter, Cassandra Johnson

New York: 450 Seventh Ave., Ste. 1809, New York, NY 10123.
TEL: (212) 541-5250. FAX: (212) 956-7466.
AGENT
Philip Adelman, Wendie Adelman, Steven Unger
ASSOCIATE AGENT
Erika Karnell
ASSISTANT
Chris Foster, Tyler Cohn

GARBER TALENT AGENCY
(Theatre, film and TV)
2 Pennsylvania Plaza, Ste. 1910, New York, NY 10121.
TEL: (212) 292-4910.
OWNER
Karen Garber

DALE GARRICK INTERNATIONAL
(Motion pictures, TV, soaps and commercials)
1017 N. La Cienega Blvd., #109, West Hollywood, CA 90069.
TEL: (310) 657-2661.
PRINCIPAL/TALENT/THEATRICAL
Dale Garrick

THE GERLER AGENCY
(Theatrical, motion picture, TV, literary, commercial and print)
3349 Cahuenga Blvd. W, Ste. 1, Los Angeles, CA 90068.
TEL: (323) 850-7386. FAX: (323) 850-7490.
email: act@thegerleragency.com www.thegerleragency.com
OWNER/AGENT
Don Gerler
HEAD, MOTION PICTURE & TELEVISION
Douglas Bennett
AGENT
Daniel Katzman

Open to new talent. Email submissions only; no phone calls or drop offs.

GERSH
(Full-service talent agency)
9465 Wilshire Blvd., 6th Flr., Beverly Hills, CA 90212.
TEL: (310) 274-6611. FAX: (310) 274-3923.
www.gershagency.com www.gershsports.com
www.gershcomedy.com
CO-PRESIDENT
Bob Gersh (Talent), David Gersh (Literary)
SENIOR MANAGING PARTNER, CO-HEAD, TALENT
Leslie Siebert
SENIOR PARTNER, V.P., COMEDY & PERSONAL APPEARANCE
Rick Greenstein
PARTNER
David DeCamillo (Co-Head, Talent), Ken Kaplan (Talent), Abram Nalibotsky (Co-Head, Literary), Frank Wuliger (Literary)
EXECUTIVE V.P., BUSINESS AFFAIRS
Stephen M. Kravit
V.P., CO-HEAD, TV LITERARY
Rob Golenberg
V.P., TALENT
Allison Band
V.P., BELOW-THE-LINE
Barbara Halperin
HEAD, FILM FINANCING & PACKAGING
Jay Cohen
HEAD, TALENT
Alex Yarosh
ALTERNATIVE TV
Melissa Campbell
BELOW-THE-LINE
Erin Searcy
BELOW-THE-LINE, LITERARY
Melanie Ramsayer
COMEDY
TJ Markwalter, Bernie Spektor
COMEDY & PERSONAL APPEARANCE
Douglas Edley, Sara Sheragy
LITERARY
Eric Garfinkel, Lee Keele, David Kopple, Sandra Lucchesi, Greg Pedicin, Sarah Self
MOTION PICTURE LITERARY
Carolyn Sivitz
TALENT
Nick Collins, Jennifer Craig, Melanie Elman, Chris Fioto, Steven Gersh, Carlos Gonzalez, Bradley Lefler, Brett Norensberg, Paul Rosicker, Sarah Shyn, Nate Steadman, Daisy Wu
TV LITERARY
Todd Christopher, Lynn Fimberg, Barry Kotler, Amy Retzinger
TV LITERARY & LITERARY
Sean Barclay

GERSH (NEW YORK)
41 Madison Ave., 33rd Flr., New York, NY 10010.
TEL: (212) 997-1818. FAX: (212) 391-8459.
www.gershagency.com
SENIOR PARTNER, V.P., TALENT
William Butler
PARTNER
John Buzzetti (Literary/Theatrical), Stephen Hirsh (Talent), Rhonda Price (Talent)
ADMINISTRATION, OFFICE MANAGER, HUMAN RESOURCES
Earl Penney
BELOW-THE-LINE
Mira Yong
BELOW-THE-LINE, THEATRICAL & LITERARY
Scott Yoselow
BOOKS
Phyllis Wender
LITERARY, THEATRICAL
Seth Glewen, Joyce Ketay, Carl Mulert
TALENT
Kyetay Beckner, Randi Goldstein, Jason Gutman, Jennifer Konowal, Lindsay Porter, Roland Scahill
TALENT COORDINATOR
Christopher Highland
ASSISTANT
Ebony Amoroso to Kyetay Beckner, Aaron Bergman to Randi Goldstein, Rachel Caris to Jason Gutman, Cortney Chen to Stephen Hirsh, Matt Depaola to William Butler, Adam Draves to Mira Yong, Anne Loder to Lindsay Porter, Alex Reveliotty to Scott Yoselow, Joseph Rosswog to John Buzzetti, Carrie Sansone to Carl Mulert, Jessica Sarbo to Joyce Ketay, Melissa Shapiro to Seth Glewen, Rachel Zeidman to Roland Scahill
OFFICE SERVICES COORDINATORY
Ross Cunningham

Represents: actors for film/TV, book authors, comedians, directors, producers, screenwriters, sports personalities and TV writers.

GRANT, SAVIC, KOPALOFF & ASSOCIATES

(Talent & Literary Agency)
6399 Wilshire Blvd., Ste. 414, Los Angeles, CA 90048.
TEL: (323) 782-1854. FAX: (323) 782-1877.
email: contact@gsktalent.com www.gsktalent.com
CONTACT
Susan Grant, Ivana Savic, Larry Metzger

Represents film professionals both behind and in front of the camera, ranging from cinematographers, production and costume designers, editors and other key below-the-line crew to producers, visual fx people, directors and actors.

GREENE & ASSOCIATES

(Agency, TV and film)
190 N. Canon Dr., Ste. 200, Beverly Hills, CA 90210.
TEL: (310) 550-9333. FAX: (310) 550-9334.
PRESIDENT
Michael Greene - michael@greenetalent.com
AGENT, FILM/TV/COMMERCIALS
Azeem Chiba
AGENT, FILM/TV/COMMERCIALS, YOUTH TALENT
Katie Donahue, Abbie Waters
AGENT, FILM/TV/YOUNG TALENT
Matt Fletcher
AGENT, FILM & LITERARY
Angelo Padilla
ASSISTANT
Jim Lighte to Michael Greene, Sabrina Bolin, Jim Victor

LARRY GROSSMAN & ASSOCIATES

(Literary agency)
2129 Ridge Dr., Los Angeles, CA 90049. TEL: (310) 550-8127. FAX: (310) 550-8129.

BUZZ HALLIDAY & ASSOCIATES

(Actors, directors and choreographers)
144 S. Doheny, Ste. 206, Los Angeles, CA 90048.
TEL: (310) 275-6028. email: buzzagent@earthlink.net
CONTACTS
Buzz Halliday, Gail Honeystein

Submission policy: Do not phone or drop-off. Mail only to: P.O. Box 481275, Los Angeles, CA 90048.

BEVERLY HECHT AGENCY

(Commercials for children; limited theatrical for adults)
3500 W. Olive Ave., Ste. 1180, Burbank, CA 91505.
TEL: (818) 559-5600. FAX: (818) 559-7485.
www.beverlyhecht.com
OWNER & COMMERCIAL & THEATRICAL AGENT
Teresa Valente-Dahlquist
THEATRICAL AGENT
Robert Depp
ASSISTANT
Michelle Reinhart

HENDERSON/HOGAN AGENCY

850 Seventh Ave., Ste. 1003, New York, NY 10019.
TEL: (212) 765-5190. FAX: (212) 586-2855.
email: abutler@hendersonhogan.com
tmilam@hendersonhogan.com

Los Angeles: 8929 Wilshire Blvd., Ste. 312, Los Angeles, CA 90069. TEL: (310) 854-0160. FAX: (310) 854-0794.
PRESIDENT
George Lutsch
AGENT
Alex Butler, David Cash, Ethan Salter
ASSISTANT
Thompson Milam, Jeffrey Levin, Brent Hagata

DANIEL HOFF AGENCY

(Represents all ages for film, TV, commercials & voiceovers)
5455 Wilshire Blvd., Ste. 1100, Los Angeles, CA 90036.
TEL: (323) 932-2500. FAX: (323) 932-2501.
www.danielhoffagency.com
OWNER/COMMERCIAL & PRINT AGENT
Daniel Hoff
HEAD, MOTION PICTURE & MUSICAL THEATRE AGENT
Nancy Abt - abtassistant@danielhoffagency.com
YOUTH AGENT
Ninna Sexsmith - ninna@danielhoffagency.com
TELEVISION/FILM AGENT
Kevin Turner - kevin@danielhoffagency.com
COMMERCIAL & PRINT AGENT
Laura Molina
VOICEOVER DEPARTMENT HEAD
Lynda McCarrell
ASSISTANT
Cynthia Johnson, Anna Leigh Simmons, Dave Secor, Barbara Niles

THE HOFFLUND COMPANY

9465 Wilshire Blvd., Ste. 420, Beverly Hills, CA 90212.
TEL: (310) 859-1971. FAX: (310) 859-7250.
email: lbasst@hofflundco.com
PERSONAL MANAGER & PRODUCER
Judy Hofflund
MANAGER
Laura Berwick, Becca Kovacik
ASSISTANT
Vanessa Joyce, David Schilling, Giovanna Silvestre, Polly Spektor

No unsolicited material.

THE HOUSE OF REPRESENTATIVES

(Represents actors, children, comedians, hosts, seniors, teens& young adults)
11434 Sixth St., Ste. 1, Santa Monica, CA 90401.
TEL: (310) 451-2345. FAX: (310) 451-3451.
email: agents@thehouseofreps.com
AGENT
Pam Braverman, Denny Sevier, Tim Weissman

HOWARD TALENT WEST

(Commercials and theatrical)
10657 Riverside Dr., Toluca Lake, CA 91602.
TEL: (818) 766-5300. FAX: (818) 760-3328.
OWNER & THEATRICAL AGENT
Bonnie Howard
COMMERCIAL AGENT
Lynn Eriks

IFA TALENT AGENCY

(Theatrical, TV and film; Represents actors & directors)
8730 Sunset Blvd., #490, Los Angeles, CA 90069.
TEL: (310) 659-5522. FAX: (310) 659-3344.
AGENTS
Ilene Feldman, David Lillard, Wendy Murphey, Christy Hall, Toni Zimmerman

IMAGE MODEL & TALENT AGENCY

44 West Flagler St., Ste. 2450, Miami, FL 33130.
TEL: (305) 375-0448. FAX: (305) 375-0449.
email: info@imagemodel-talent.com
www.imagemodel-talent.com

INNOVATIVE ARTISTS

(Full-service talent and literary agency)

INNOVATIVE ARTISTS/LOS ANGELES

1505 Tenth St., Santa Monica, CA 90401.
TEL: (310) 656-0400. FAX: (310) 656-0456.
email: talent@iala.com www.innovativeartists.com
OWNER & PRESIDENT
Scott Harris (LA)
EXECUTIVE V.P., TALENT
Nevin Dolcefino
V.P., ALTERNATIVE/NON-SCRIPTED
Kimberly Carver
V.P. & CFO
Harvey Finkel
V.P., BELOW-THE-LINE
Debbie Haeusler
V.P., BUSINESS AFFAIRS
Paul Blechner
V.P., COMMERCIALS & VOICEOVER
Marcia Hurwitz
V.P., TALENT
Jonathan Howard, Craig Shapiro
ALTERNATIVE/NON-SCRIPTED
Barb Frederick
BEAUTY
Kim Byrd, Michele De La Riva
BELOW-THE-LINE
Cecilia Banck, Robbyn Foxx, Heather Griffith, Jeff Mahoney, Craig Mizrahi
COMEDY/PERSONAL APPEARANCE
Stu Golfman
COMMERCIALS
Cher Van Amburg
COMMERCIALS AND VOICE-OVER
Marci Polzin, Luanne Salandy-Regis, Jill Witterschein
LITERARY
Michael Pio, Jim Stein
TALENT
Abby Bluestone, Thomas Cushing, Ryan Daly, Robert Haas, Melissa Hirschenson, Stephen LaManna, David Lederman, Steve Muller, Cori Pembleton, David Rose, Matthey Shaffer, Sommer Smith, Marnie Sparer, Sheila Wenzel

INNOVATIVE ARTISTS/NEW YORK

235 Park Ave. S., 10th Flr., New York, NY 10003.
TEL: (212) 253-6900. FAX: (212) 253-1198.
email: talent@iany.com
V.P. TALENT
Gary Gersh
V.P., BEAUTY
Maury DiMauro
BEAUTY
Ross Haime, Nipa Parikh, Rae Ruff, Aubrey Urban

ON-CAMERA
Marla Haut, Michael Shera, Heather Stewart
VOICE-OVER
Allan G. Duncan, Eileen Schellhorn (and promos), Debra Sherry, Shari Hoffman (and promos)
YOUNG TALENT
Barbara Coleman (and on-camera), Halle Madia, Jaime Misher

INNOVATIVE ARTISTS/CHICAGO

541 N. Fairbanks, Ct. 27th Flr., Chicago, IL 60611.
TEL: (312) 832-1113. FAX: (312) 832-1124.
email: studio@iachicago.com www.iachicago.com
MANAGER
Sue Geraghty
AGENT
Linda Bracilano, Laurie Lambert, Sandy Norman, Sharon Wottrich

Chicago office represents voiceover artists. Send CD with contact information. No walk-ins.

INTERNATIONAL CREATIVE MANAGEMENT, INC. - CA

10250 Consellation Blvd., Los Angeles, CA 90067.
TEL: (310) 550-4000. FAX: (310) 550-4100.
www.icmtalent.com
CHAIRMAN & CEO
Jeffrey Berg
VICE CHAIRMAN
Robert Broder
PRESIDENT
Chris Silbermann
CHIEF BUSINESS DEVELOPMENT OFFICER / GENERAL COUNSEL
Richard B. Levy, Esq.
COO
Dan Donahue
CHIEF INFORMATION OFFICER
Greg Chun
CORPORATE SECRETARY
Robin Weitz
CONTROLLER
Joe Friedman
CONTRACT ADMINISTRATION
Erin Oremland
CORPORATE COMMUNICATIONS
Michelle Suess
HEAD, FINANCE & ACCOUNTING
Greg Arvesen

DEPARTMENTS
HEAD, GLOBAL BRANDED ENTERTAINMENT
Carol Goll
GLOBAL BRANDED ENTERTAINMENT
Jesse Albert, Andrew Francis, Jason Pinyan, Penny Reiss, Karen Sellars, April Tombs
HEAD, INTERNATIONAL & INDEPENDENT FILM
Hal Sadoff
INTERNATIONAL & INDEPENDENT FILM
Bic Tran, Peter Trinh
HEAD, MOTION PICTURE LITERARY
Nicole Clemens
MOTION PICTURE LITERARY
John Burnham, Harley Copen, Emile Gladstone, Todd Harris, Aaron Hart, Todd Hoffman, Sophy Holodnik, Ava Jamshidi, Bruce Kaufman, Doug MacLaren, Shan Ray, Nick Reed, Nathan Ross, David Styne, Lars Theriot, Joanne Wiles
HEAD, MOTION PICTURE PRODUCTION
Paul Hook
MOTION PICTURE PRODUCTION
Dan Baime, Craig Bernstein, Tad Lumpkin, Tom Marquardt, Michael Runnels
EXECUTIVE V.P., MOTION PICTURE TALENT
Jack Gilardi, Eddy Yablans
V.P., MOTION PICTURE TALENT
Joe Funicello
HEAD, MOTION PICTURE TALENT
Toni Howard
MOTION PICTURE TALENT
Lorrie Bartlett, Carol Bodie, Pam Brockie, Carter Cohn, Justin Deanda, Stephen Fisher, Lisa Gallant, Guido Giordano, Hildy Gottlieb, Chris Hart, Chuck James, Andrea Nelson Meigs, Nigel Meiojas, Scott Schacter, Dana Sims, David Unger, Meredith Wechter, Scott Wexler
HEAD, TV
Ted Chervin
HEAD, TV INTERNATIONAL
Greg Lipstone
TV INTERNATIONAL
Steven Grossman, Michael Kagan, Kimberly Oelman, Dana Lee Schuman
HEAD, TV TALENT
Mike Jelline
TV TALENT
Leigh Brillstein, Tom Burke, Andy Cohen, Logan Eisenberg, Iris Grossman, Janet Kaye, Brian Mann, Dar Rollins, John Sacks
CO-HEAD, TV LITERARY
Kevin Crotty, Chris von Goetz
TV LITERARY
Cecelia Andrews, Mickey Berman, Carel Cutler, Hrishi Desai, Sean Freidin, Mark Gordon, Erik Horine, Josh Hornstock, Dan Norton, Janet Carol Norton, Lanny Noveck, Greg Shephard, Paul Alan Smith, Pete Stone, Michael Tenzer
V.P., SENIOR SUBSIDIARY RIGHTS, MOTION PICTURE LITERARY
Ron Bernstein, Adam Weinstein

ICM/NEW YORK

(Full-service agency)
825 Eighth Ave., 26th Flr., New York, NY 10019.
TEL: (212) 556-5600. FAX: (212) 556-5665.
www.icmtalent.com
CO-HEAD, PUBLICATIONS
Esther Newberg, Sloan Harris
EXECUTIVE V.P., PUBLICATIONS
Amanda Urban
PUBLICATIONS
Tina Wexler
AGENT
Boaty Boatwright
GLOBAL BRANDED ENTERTAINMENT
Dee Brathwaite
LITERARY
Lisa Bankoff, Andrea Barzvi, Herb Cheyette, Kristine Dahl, John DeLaney, Elizabeth Farrell, Colin Graham, Jennifer Joel, Kate Lee, Heather Schroder
MOTION PICTURE TALENT
Joshua Pearl, Adam Schweitzer
LECTURES
Betsy Berg

ICM/LONDON

61 Frith St., London W1D 3JL, England.
TEL: +44 207 851 4853.

J E TALENT, LLC

(Full-service agency,film, television, commercial, V/O SAG, AFTRA, AEA)
323 Geary St., Ste. 302, San Francisco, CA 94102.
TEL: (415) 395-9475. FAX: (415) 395-9301.
email: info@jetalent.com www.JETalent.com
OWNER
John J. Erlendson

JORDAN, GILL & DORNBAUM

(Children to early 20's, commercials, TV and film)
1133 Broadway, Ste. 623, New York, NY 10010.
TEL: (212) 463-8455. FAX: (212) 691-6111.
OWNERS/COMMERCIALS
Robin Dornbaum, Jeffrey Gill
COMMERCIALS
David McDermott
THEATRICAL
Jan Jarrett

THE KAPLAN STAHLER AGENCY

(Literary and theatrical agency)
8383 Wilshire Blvd., #923, Beverly Hills, CA 90211.
TEL: (323) 653-4483. FAX: (323) 653-4506.
email: info@kaplanstahler.com www.kaplanstahler.com
TV LITERARY
Mitchell T. Kaplan, Elliot J. Stahler
AGENT, TV LITERARY
Dino Carlaftes, Gordon Hvolka, Zac Simmons, Bradley Stewart Glenn, Sean Zeid

Represents directors, producers & TV writers

KAZARIAN/SPENCER/RUSKIN & ASSOCIATES

(Full-service talent agency)
11969 Ventura Blvd., 3rd Flr., Box 7409, Studio City, CA 91604. TEL: (818) 769-9111. FAX: (818) 769-9840.
www.ksawest.com
PRESIDENT & ON-CAMERA
Cindy Kazarian
V.P., FINANCE
Tory Preston
PARTNER & V.P., ON-CAMERA
Alicia Ruskin
AGENT, CHOREOGRAPHY/DIRECTORS
Victoria Morris
AGENT, ON-CAMERA
Brooke Nuttall, Samantha Weisman
AGENT, FILM & TELEVISION
Mitchell Shankman
AGENT, HOSTING
Cindy Kazarian, Fred Wostbrock, Mitch Shankman
AGENT, YOUNG PEOPLE
Philip Marcus, Bonnie Ventis, Jody Alexander

New York: Media Arts Bldg., 311 W. 43rd St., Ste. 1107, New York, NY 10036. TEL: (212) 582-7572. FAX: (212) 582-7448.

KJAR & ASSOCIATES
(Manages established actors)
10153-1/2 Riverside Dr. Ste. 255, Toluca Lake, CA 91602-2313. TEL: (818) 760-0321.
ADULT/TV/FILM/EQUITY/LITERARY
Brandon Kjar - brandonkjar@earthlink.net
LITERARY
Maria Hanson, Molly Sweet
ASSOCIATE
Victoria Fisher, Paula Singerman

PAUL KOHNER AGENCY
(Talent & literary agency)
9300 Wilshire Blvd., #555, Beverly Hills, CA 90212.
TEL: (310) 550-1060. FAX: (310) 276-1083.
PRESIDENT
Pearl Wexler
HEAD, LITERARY
Stephen Moore
AGENT
Sheree Cohen, Samantha Crisp, Amanda Glazer

THE KRASNY OFFICE, INC.
(Commercials, film, theatre & TV)
1501 Broadway, Ste. 1303, New York, NY 10036.
TEL: (212) 730-8160. FAX: (212) 768-9379.
OWNER
Gary Krasny
AGENT
Norma Eisenbaum, B. Lynne Jebens, Tom Kammer

LALLY TALENT AGENCY (LTA)
630 Ninth Ave., Ste. 800, New York, NY 10036.
TEL: (212) 974-8718.
OWNER
Dale Lally, Stephen Laviska

Actors for TV, theatre and film. No children. Pictures & résumés are accepted by mail only. No phone calls, visits or tapes.

LENHOFF & LENHOFF
830 Palm Avenue, West Hollywood, CA 90069.
TEL: (310) 855-2411. FAX: (310) 855-2412.
www.lenhoff.com
PRESIDENT
S. Charles Lenhoff - charles@lenhoff.com
CFO
Lisa Lenhoff - lisa@lenhoff.com
ASSOCIATE
Tommy Carrigan

Represents TV writers, screenwriters, producers, directors, book authors & cinematographers.

LIONEL LARNER, LTD.
119 W. 57th St., Ste. 1412, New York, NY 10019.
TEL: (212) 246-3105. FAX: (212) 956-2851.

BUDDY LEE ATTRACTIONS, INC.
38 Music Square E, Nashville, TN 37203.
TEL: (615) 244-4336. FAX: (615) 726-0429.
email: tconway@blanash.com www.buddyleeattractions.com
PRESIDENT &CEO
Tony Conway
EXECUTIVE V.P.
Joan Saltel
AGENT
Jon Folk, Bob Kinkead, Gary Kirves, David Kiswiney, Steve Peck

Represents actors, book authors, comedians, composers, hosts, music artists, music editors, music producers, speakers/lecturers & sports personalities.

JACK LENNY ASSOCIATES
(Choreographers, directors and overseas shows)
9454 Wilshire Blvd., Ste. 600, Beverly Hills, CA 90212.
TEL: (310) 271-2174. FAX: (310) 246-9883.

THE LEVIN AGENCY
(Actors, TV, film, commercials, and equity)
8484 Wilshire Blvd., Ste. 750, Beverly Hills, CA 90211.
TEL: (323) 653-7073. FAX: (323) 653-0280.
email: gcrivers@yahoo.com
OWNER
Sid Levin

KEN LINDNER & ASSOCIATES, INC.
(News broadcasters and hosts)
2029 Century Park E, Ste. 1000, Los Angeles, CA 90067.
TEL: (310) 277-9223. FAX: (310) 277-5806.
www.kenlindner.com
CEO
Ken Lindner
ASSISTANT TO CEO
Jill Walter
EXECUTIVE VICE PRESIDENTS/AGENT
Susan Levin, Karen Wang-Lavelle
CHIEF CORPORATE COUNSEL
Kristin Allen
DIRECTOR, OPERATIONS
Tom Ragonnet
DIRECTOR, NEWS & PROGRAMMING
Melissa Van Fleet
TALENT REPRESENTATIVE
C.J. Woods

LOOK TALENT
(Full-service talent agency)
166 Geary St., Ste. 1406, San Francisco, CA 94108.
TEL: (415) 781-2841. FAX: (415) 781-5722.
email: joan@looktalent.com www.looktalent.com
OWNER & AGENT
Joan Spangler (SAG, AFTRA, AEA)
AGENT, COMMERCIAL
Oorala Yamada

JANA LUKER TALENT AGENCY
(Actors for commercials, film and TV)
1923 1/2 Westwood Blvd., Ste. 3, Los Angeles, CA 90025.
TEL: (310) 441-2822. FAX: (310) 441-2820.
PRESIDENT
Jana Luker
SENIOR AGENT
Kathy Keeley

LYNNE & REILLY AGENCY
10725 Vanowen St., Ste. 113, North Hollywood, CA 91605.
TEL: (818) 755-6434.
OWNERS
Teresa Reilly, Julie Lynne

THE MACK AGENCY
5726 Woodman Ave., Ste. 4, Van Nuys, CA 91401.
TEL: (818) 753-6300. FAX: (818) 753-6311.
email: patty@themackagency.net www.themackagency.net
OWNER
Patricia Mack

IATSE; AIC; MVPA; features; TV; commercials; music videos. Represents cinematographers, producers, production designers & interactive game developers.

MARSH, BEST & ASSOCIATES
(Below-the-line talent)
9150 Wilshire Blvd., #220, Beverly Hills, CA 90212.
TEL: (310) 285-0303. FAX: (310) 285-0218.
email: info@marshbest.com www.marshbest.com
CHAIRPERSON & CFO
Sandra Marsh
PRESIDENT & COO
Claire Best
AGENT
Shawn Burns, Rocco Hindman, Rochelle Sharpe, Michael Vasquez
EXECUTIVE ASSISTANT
Lori Di Costanzo, Meg Olsen

MARTIN & DONALDS TALENT AGENCY, INC.
(TV and film)
Miami Office: 2131 Hollywood Blvd., Ste. 308, Hollywood, FL 33020. TEL: (954) 921-2427. FAX: (954) 921-7635.
email: mdtalent@bellsouth.net www.martinanddonalds.com
OWNER & PRESIDENT
Sharon Martin
SAG DEPARTMENT
Sharon Martin
NON UNION DEPARTMENT
Joyce Glusman
PRINT DEPARTMENT
Kristie Martin, Lyn Foley

North Carolina Office: 221 Kanuga Forest Dr., Hendersonville, NC 28739. TEL: (866) 694-1160. FAX: (866) 694-1041.
www.martinanddonalds.com
OWNER & AGENT
Sharon Martin
AGENT, NON-UNION TV & FILM
Joyce Glusman

THE MCCABE GROUP
(Actors)
8285 Sunset, Ste. 1, Los Angeles, CA 90046.
TEL: (323) 650-3738. FAX: (323) 650-6014.
email: bmccabe@atalentagency.com www.atalentagency.com
THEATRICAL
Brian McCabe, Sandy Oroumieh

MEDIA ARTISTS GROUP
(Full-service talent agency)
6300 Wilshire Blvd., Ste. 1470, Los Angeles, CA 90048.
TEL: (323) 658-5050. FAX: (323) 658-7842.

PRINCIPAL & PRESIDENT, THEATRICAL
Raphael Berko
PRINCIPAL & PRESIDENT, MEDIA ARTISTS GROUP
LITERARY
Barbara Alexander

MEDIA TALENT GROUP

9200 Sunset Blvd., Ste. 550, W. Hollywood, CA 90069.
TEL:(310) 275-7900. FAX: (310) 275-7910.
CHAIRMAN & CEO
Geyer Kosinski
MANAGER, LITERARY & DIRECTORS
Chris Davey
TALENT MANAGER
Oren Segal

High-profile clients only.

METROPOLITAN TALENT AGENCY / MTA INTERACTIVE

(Actors, writers and directors)
204 N. Rossmore Ave., Los Angeles, CA 90004.
TEL: (323) 857-4500, (323) 857-4510. FAX: (323) 857-4599, (323) 857-4509. www.mta.com
PRESIDENT/TALENT/LITERARY
Christopher Barrett
TALENT
Sara Schedeen, Tom Markley

MGA TALENT

(Represents actors and actresses for TV, film & commercials)
269 S. Beverly Dr., Ste. 1088, Beverly Hills, CA 90212.
TEL: (818) 763-8400. email: rob@mgatalent.com
www.mgatalent.com
PERSONAL MANAGEMENT, TV & FILM PRODUCTION
Robert Pafundi, Attorney at Law

THE MIRISCH AGENCY

(Specializing in below-the-line talent)
1925 Century Park E, Ste. 1070, Los Angeles, CA 90067.
TEL: (310) 282-9940. FAX: (310) 282-0702.
email: robin@mirisch.com www.mirisch.com
OWNER/PRESIDENT/AGENT
Lawrence A. Mirisch
AGENT
Beth Reiter, Robin Schreer

MONTANA ARTISTS AGENCY, INC.

(Full-service below-the-line talent)
7715 Sunset Blvd., 3rd Flr., Los Angeles, CA 90046.
TEL: (323) 845-4144. FAX: (323) 845-4155.
www.montanartists.com
PRESIDENT & CEO
Jon Furie
V.P., BUSINESS & LEGAL AFFAIRS
Eric Klein
HEAD, FINANCE & OPERATIONS
Julian Savodivker
HEAD, COMMERCIALS DEPARTMENT
Nick Malkin
SENIOR AGENT, FEATURES & TV
Karen Berch
AGENT, FEATURES & TV
Brady Torgeson
TV COORDINATOR
Eric Ernst
AGENT, COMMERCIALS & MUSIC VIDEOS, MAKE-UP ARTISTS & HAIR STYLISTS
Leslie Alyson

THE MORGAN AGENCY

(Full-service talent agency)
1200 N. Doheny Dr., Los Angeles, CA 90069.
TEL: (310) 860-0530. FAX: (310) 388-0761.
www.themorganagency.com
PRESIDENT
Keith Lewis
AGENT, NON-UNION COMMERCIALS & PRINT, ADULT
Rich Smith
ASSISTANT TO PRESIDENT
Lilly Colon
ASSISTANT
Doug Haley

NAKED VOICES, INC.

(Voiceover)
900 N. Franklin Ste., Ste. 709, Chicago, IL 60610 .
TEL: (312) 563-0136. email: info@nakedvoices.com
www.nakedvoices.com
CONTACT
Debby Kotzen

OMNIPOP TALENT GROUP

(Comedic talent and sketch actors)
4605 Lankershim Blvd., Ste. 201, Toluca Lake, CA 91602.
TEL: (818) 980-9267. FAX: (818) 980-9371.
email: omni@omnipop.com www.omnipop.com
PRESIDENT, WEST COAST THEATRICAL DIVISION
Bruce Smith
WEST COAST THEATRICAL ASSISTANT
Jess Knox

OMNIPOP TALENT GROUP — NEW YORK

55 W. Old Country Rd., Hicksville, NY 11801.
TEL: (516) 937-6011. FAX: (516) 937-6209.
PRESIDENT, EAST COAST THEATRICAL DIVISION
Tom Ingegno
V.P., CORPORATE DIVISION
Barbara Klein

ORLANDO MANAGEMENT

(Represents below-the-line talent)
15134 Martha St., Sherman Oaks, CA 91411.
TEL: (818) 781-9233. FAX: (818) 781-9237.
email: kirk@orlandomanagement.com
www.orlandomanagement.com
PRESIDENT & OWNER
Kirk Orlando

OSBRINK TALENT AGENCY

4343 Lankershim Blvd., Ste. 100, Universal City, CA 91602.
TEL: (818) 760-2488. FAX: (818) 760-0991.
email: contact@osbrinkagency.com www.osbrinkagency.com
CONTACT
Cindy Osbrink, Scott Wine
V.P., HEAD, YOUTH COMMERICAL & V.P., OPERATIONS
Angela Strange
AGENT, ADULT COMMERCIAL
Crista Augustynovich
AGENT, ADULT THEATRICAL
Galit Finkelstein
AGENT, VOICE-OVER
Maureen Rose
AGENT, YOUTH THEATRICAL
Emily Urbani

FIFI OSCARD AGENCY

(Full-service talent agency)
110 W. 40th St., 16th Flr., New York, NY 10018.
TEL: (212) 764-1100. FAX: (212) 840-5019.
email: agency@fifioscard.com www.fifioscard.com
MANAGING PARTNER
Peter Sawyer
V.P.
Carmen LaVia
AGENT
Frances Del Duca, Carolyn French (literary), Kevin McShane

OTTO MODEL & TALENT AGENCY

(Full-service model and talent agency)
1460 N. Sweetzer Ave., West Hollywood, CA 90069.
TEL: (323) 650-2200. FAX: (323) 650-1134.
email: ottomodels@aol.com jason@ottomodels.com
tereza@ottomodels.com www.ottomodels.com
OWNER
Jason Otto

PAKULA/KING & ASSOCIATES

(Actors for film and TV)
9229 Sunset Blvd., Ste. 315, Los Angeles, CA 90069.
TEL: (310) 281-4868. FAX: (310) 281-4866.
OWNER
Joel King
AGENT
Hilary Steinberg, Gabe Watkins
ASSISTANT
Jessica Dallow, Jay Soria

DOROTHY PALMER TALENT AGENCY, INC.

(Full-service talent agency.)
235 W. 56th St., Ste. 24K, New York, NY 10019.
TEL: (212) 765-4280. FAX: (212) 977-9801.
email: dptalent@verizon.net
www.dorothypalmertalentagency.com
TALENT & LITERARY AGENT
Dorothy Palmer

Prefers phone calls. Packages independent films. Also runs literary agency; Affiliated with AFTRA, SAG & WGA. Represents: actors, book authors, broadcast/newscasters, children, comedians, dancers, hosts/MCs, Print models, Producers, Runway models, screenwriters, seniors, speakers/lecturers, sports personalities, teens & young adults, TV writers, variety artists, voiceover artists & singers.

PANGEA MANAGEMENT GROUP

(Part of the RDF Media Group)
225 Santa Monica Blvd., 5th Flr., Santa Monica, CA 90401.
TEL: (310) 309-6155. FAX: (310) 309-6152.
email: contactus@rdfusa.com www.pangeamg.tv

CEO
Chris Coelen
PRESIDENT & GENERAL COUNSEL
Kirk Schenck
SENIOR V.P.
Karrie Wolfe
DIRECTOR, SCRIPTED DEVELOPMENT
Brian Lenard
HEAD, DIGITAL MEDIA
Max Benator
MANAGER
Jessica Weiner
HEAD OF PUBLICITY & MARKETING
Brooke Fisher

Management company, focusing on the intellectual property rights of scripted and reality formats through its relationship with the best of British and European producers.

PARADIGM, A TALENT & LITERARY AGENCY

LOS ANGELES:

360 N. Crescent Dr., North Bldg., Beverly Hills, CA 90210.
TEL: (310) 288-8000. FAX: (310) 288-2000.
www.paradigmagency.com
CHAIRMAN
Sam Gores
CFO
Jim Caskey
EXECUTIVE V.P., BUSINESS AFFAIRS
Craig Wagner
EXECUTIVE V.P., BUSINESS DEVELOPMENT
Lawrence Antoine
EXECUTIVE V.P., CORPORATE RELATIONS
Brad Turell
CO-HEAD, MOTION PICTURE TALENT
Michael Lazo, Steve Small
HEAD, MOTION PICTURE TALENT
Andrew Rogers
MOTION PICTURE TALENT
Ryan Bartlett, Jason Carter, Matt Eskander, Jack Kingsrud, Jim Osborne, Sara Ramaker, Stephanie Ramsey, Brad Schenck, Chris Schmidt, Erwin More
TV TALENT
Alisa Adler, Judith Moss
CO-HEAD, TV LITERARY DEPARTMENT
Jeff Benson, Debbee Klein
TV LITERARY
Zadoc Angell. Bill Douglass, Doug Fronk, Jill Gillett, Ian Greenstein, Andy Patman, Michael Van Dyck
HEAD, ARTIST MARKETING
Lori Sale
HEAD, WORLDWIDE ALTERNATIVE PROGRAMMING
Steve Wohl
REALITY
Mitch Kapler
HEAD, MOTION PICTURE FINANCE GROUP
Norman Aladjem
MOTION PICTURE FINANCE GROUP
Andrew Ruf
HEAD, MOTION PICTURE LITERARY
Valarie Phillips
MOTION PICTURE LITERARY
Trevor Astbury, Lee Cohen, Rich Freeman, Marc Helwig, Scott Henderson, Mark Ross, Christopher Smith, Lucy Stille
HEAD, PARADIGM ARTIST MARKETING/BRANDED ENTERTAINMENT
Randy Smith
BRANDED ENTERTAINMENT
Kathlene Trihn, Sam Olsteen, Sean Barth, Jessica Love

NEW YORK:

360 Park Ave. S., 16th Flr., New York, NY 10110.
TEL: (212) 897-6400. FAX: (212) 764-8941.
www.paradigmagency.com
COO
Joel Rudnick
THEATRICAL/MOTION PICTURES/TV
Sarah Fargo, Scott Metzger, Thomas O'Donnell, Rosanne Quezada, Richard Schmenner, Clifford Stevens
LITERARY BOOKS
Lydia Wills, Jason Yarn

MONTEREY:

509 Hartnell St., Monterey, CA 93940. TEL: (831) 375-4889. FAX: (831) 375-2623.

NASHVILLE:

124 12th Ave. S, Ste. 410, Nashville, TN 37203.
TEL: (615) 251-4400. FAX: (615) 251-4401.

Paradigm provides representation to clients across its motion picture, television, music, comedy and personal appearances, theatre, books, new media, commercial and physical production departments.

PHOENIX ARTISTS, INC

(Actors)
321 W. 44th St., Ste. 401, New York, NY 10036.
TEL: (212) 586-9110. FAX: (212) 586-8019.

PLAYERS TALENT AGENCY

16130 Ventura Blvd., Ste. 235, Encino, CA 91436.
TEL: (818) 990-9577. FAX: (323) 297-2877.
email: playerstnt@yahoo.com
OWNER & AGENT
Joe Kolkowitz

Broadcast journalists/newscasters, comedians, hosts/MCs, sports personalities, and Hispanic talent. Also represents athletes and ethnic performers who are ex-athletes.

JIM PREMINGER, AGENCY

(Literary and talent agency)
10866 Wilshire Blvd., 10th Flr., Los Angeles, CA 90024.
TEL: (310) 459-6600. FAX: (310) 496-3004.
email: general@premingeragency.com
www.premingeragency.com
PRINCIPAL/LITERARY
Jim Preminger
LITERARY
Dean A. Schramm
ASSISTANT TO MR. PREMINGER
Christine Work

PROGRESSIVE ARTISTS AGENCY

(Actors and theatrical)
1041 N. Formosa Ave., W. Hollywood, CA 90046.
TEL: (323) 850-2992.
CONTACT
Bernard Carneol, Belle Zwerdling
YOUTH DIVISION, THEATRICAL & COMMERCIAL
Jillana Devine

QUATTRO MEDIA

(Literary, specializing in new media, producers, writers & directors)
171 Pier Ave., #328, Santa Monica, CA 90405.
TEL: (323) 828-2289.
PARTNER
Jim Strader

RELATIVITY MANAGEMENT

8899 Beverly Blvd. Ste. 510 W. Hollywood, CA 90048.
TEL: (310) 859-1296. FAX: (310) 859-1254.
CONTACT
Laina Cohn, Michael Sugar

THE MARION ROSENBERG OFFICE

(Actors, screenwriters, directors and authors)
P.O. Box 69826, Los Angeles, CA 90069. TEL: (323) 822-2793. FAX: (323) 388-5798. email: joey@marionrosenberg.com
AGENT
Marion Rosenberg
ASSISTANT
Joey De Paolo

THE ROTHMAN BRECHER AGENCY

(Literary agency)
9250 Wilshire Blvd., Ste. 840, Beverly Hills, CA 90212.
TEL: (310) 247-9898. FAX: (310) 247-9888.
email: reception@rothmanbrecher.com
PARTNER & TV AGENT
Dan Brecher, Robb Rothman
CFO
Jim Rothman
FEATURE AGENT
Jim Ehrich
TV AGENT
Andrea Kavoosi, Dennis Kim, Vanessa Livingston, Camran Shafii

IRV SCHECHTER & COMPANY

(Animation)
9460 Wilshire Blvd., #300, Beverly Hills, CA 90212.
TEL: (310) 278-8070. FAX: (310) 278-6058.
email: asst@iscagency.com
CONTACT
Irv Schechter

SCHULLER TALENT/NY KIDS

276 Fifth Ave., 10th Flr., New York, NY 10001.
TEL: (212) 532-6005. FAX: (212) 252-1256.
email: margaret@schullertalent.com
PRESIDENT & AGENT
Margaret Matuka

KATHLEEN SCHULTZ ASSOCIATES

(Theatrical, equity, motion picture and TV)
6442 Coldwater Canyon, Ste. 117, Valley Glen, CA 91606.
TEL: (818) 760-3100. FAX: (818) 760-3125.
email: kschultzassoc@aol.com

OWNER
Kathleen Schultz
AGENT, COMMERCIALS/PRINT
Jennifer Trendowski

SEVEN SUMMITS PICTURES & MANAGEMENT

(Full-service agency for film and TV)
8906 W. Olympic Blvd., Garden Level, Beverly Hills, CA 90211.
TEL: (310) 550-6777. FAX: (310) 550-0606.
PARTNER
William Blaylock, Sarah Jackson
TALENT & LITERARY MANAGER
Nicolas Bernheim
LITERARY MANAGER
Paul Canterna
ASSISTANT
Kris Koller

DAVID SHAPIRA & ASSOCIATES, INC. (DSA)

(Actors for film and TV; alternative TV)
193 N. Robertson Blvd., Beverly Hills, CA 90211.
TEL: (310) 967-0480. FAX: (310) 659-4177.
email: mc@dsa-agency.com sf@sda-agency.com
OWNER & CEO
David Shapira
AGENT
Mark Scroggs, Matt Shapira, Susan A. Simons
ASSOCIATE
Susan Fincham, Mike Jaglin
ADMINISTRATIVE ASSISTANT
Monique Calderon

SHELDON PROSNIT AGENCY

(Specializing in below-the-line talent)
800 S. Robertson Blvd., Ste. 6, Los Angeles, CA 90035.
TEL: (310) 652-8778. FAX: (310) 652-8772.
www.lspagency.net
FEATURES/TELEVISION CONTACT
Robin Sheldon, Jane Prosnit, Rebecca Fayyad
COMMERCIALS/MUSIC VIDEOS
Gregg Dallesandro, Shari L. Shankewitz

THE SKOURAS AGENCY

(Represents below-the-line talent, film & TV talent & commercial talent)
1149 Third St., 3rd Flr., Santa Monica, CA 90403.
TEL: (310) 395-9550. FAX: (310) 395-4295.
email: features@skouras.com www.skouras.com
OWNER & AGENT
Spyros Skouras
PARTNER, FEATURES
Lara Polivka Sackett
AGENT, FEATURES
Hillary Corinne Cook
AGENT, COMMERCIALS
Hillary McQuaide, Marie Perry, Holland Murray

MICHAEL SLESSINGER & ASSOCIATES

(Full-service talent agency for actors)
8730 Sunset Blvd., Ste. 220, West Hollywood, CA 90069.
TEL: (310) 657-7113.
VICE PRESIDENT
Michael Slessinger
CONTACTS
Billy Miller, Meegan Kelso

SMS TALENT, INC.

(Adult theatrical)
8730 Sunset Blvd., Ste. 440, Los Angeles, CA 90069.
TEL: (310) 289-0909.
PARTNER
Charles Silver, Donna Massetti, Marilyn Szatmary, Greg Mehlman

SCOTT STANDER & ASSOCIATES, INC.

(Film, TV, commercials, theatre, national tours, concert, variety acts & comedians)
13701 Riverside Dr., Ste. 201, Sherman Oaks, CA 91423.
TEL: (818) 905-7000. FAX: (818) 990-0582.
email: info@scottstander.com www.scottstander.com
PRESIDENT & AGENT
Scott Stander - scott@scottstander.com
AGENT/FILM/TV/COMMERCIALS
Jackie Stander - jackie@scottstander.com

SUITE A MANAGEMENT, TALENT & LITERARY AGENCY

120 El Camino Dr., Ste. 202, Beverly Hills, CA 90212.
TEL: (310) 278-0801. FAX: (310) 278-0807.
email: suite-a@earthlink.net
AGENT PRINCIPAL
Lloyd D. Robinson
ASSISTANT
Kevin Douglas, Letitia Schuartz

Represents writers, producers and directors; specializing in made for TV movies and low- to mid-budget features.

SUTTON, BARTH & VENNARI, INC.

(On camera, commercials and voiceover)
145 S. Fairfax Ave., Ste. 310, Los Angeles, CA 90036.
TEL: (323) 938-6000. FAX: (323) 935-8671.
emal: info@sbvtalent.com www.sbvtalent.com
PRESIDENT
Rita Vennari
AGENTS
Anna Rodriguez, Robin Lamel, Mary Ellen Lord, Pam Sparks

TALENT TREK AGENCY

(Actors for film and TV)
2021 21st Ave. S., Ste. 102, Nashville, TN 37212.
TEL: (615) 279-0010. FAX: (615) 279-0013.
AGENT
Evelyn Foster, Kimberly Frank

TISHERMAN GILBERT MOTLEY DROZDOSKI TALENT AGENCY, INC.

(Actors for voiceovers and on-camera commercials only)
6767 Forest Lawn Dr., Ste. 101, Los Angeles, CA 90068.
TEL: (323) 850-6767. FAX: (323) 850-7340.
email: auditions@tgmdtalent.com www.tgmdtalent.com
AGENT
Vanessa Gilbert, Kevin Motley, Ilko Drozdoski, Sally Kadison, Jennifer York

TWENTIETH CENTURY ARTISTS

19528 Ventura Blvd., Ste. 612, Tarzana, CA 91356.
TEL: (818) 325-3832. FAX: (818) 713-1709.
PRESIDENT
Diane Davis-Olf

Adult theatrical motion picture & TV literary representation

UNITED TALENT AGENCY

(Full-service agency, providing representation in the areas of film, TV, independent film, reality TV, books, music, digital media & entertainment marketing/lifestyle branding & licensing)
9560 Wilshire Blvd., Ste. 500, Beverly Hills, CA 90212.
TEL: (310) 273-6700. FAX: (310) 247-1111.
www.unitedtalentagency.com
CHAIRMAN, BOARD MEMBER, AGENT
James Berkus
BOARD OF DIRECTORS, PARTNER, AGENT
Peter Benedek, Tracey Jacobs (co-head, talent), David Kramer, Jay Sures, Jeremy Zimmer
CFO
Jeff Dalla Betta
CAO
Michael Conway
PARTNER, HEAD, INDEPENDENT FILM GROUP
Richard Klubeck
HEAD, MOTION PICTURE BUSINESS AFFAIRS
Jim Meenaghan
HEAD, TELEVISION BUSINESS AFFAIRS
Rich Shuter
HEAD, TELEVISION, SCRIPTED
Matt Rice
HEAD, TELEVISION, UNSCRIPTED
Michael Camacho
HEAD, CORPORATE COMMUNICATIONS
Chris Day - (310) 860-3723 dayc@unitedtalent.com
BUSINESS AFFAIRS
Thora Leiken, Lauren Menkes, Mike Rubi, Leroy Simmons
PARTNER, AGENT
Jeremy Barber, (motion picture & literary), Blair Belcher, Andrew Cannava, Dan Erlij (TV literary), Wayne Fitterman, David Guillod, Lisa Jacobson, Steve Rabineau (motion picture literary), Larry Salz (TV literary), Howard Sanders (motion picture literary)
AGENT
Robert Arakelian, Tobin Babst, Joel Begleiter, Brinda Bhatt, Adam Biren, Jason Burns, Carlos Carreras, Sarah Clossey, Stephanie Comer, James Degus, Marissa Devins, Barbara Dreyfus, Gueran Ducoty, Kassie Evashevski, Rebecca Ewing, Jacob Fenton, Charlie Ferraro, David Flynn, Peter Franciosa, Paula Friedman, Veronica Gabriel, Jay Gassner, Nancy Gates, Mitchell Gossett, Allan Haldeman, Rio Hernandez, Lee Horvitz, Jon Huddle, Ben Jacobson, Ennis Kamcili, Josh Katz, James Kearney, Keya Khayatian, Rob Kim, Billy Lazarus, Hayley Lozitsky, Jenny Maryasis, Yuli Masinovsky, Leslie Maskin, Lauren Meisels, Lauren Meltzner, John Pantle, Chris Pappas, David Park, Tim Phillips, Rob Prinz, Gina Ramirez, Shani Rosenzweig, Ruthanne Secunda, Jason Shapiro, Bec Smith, Darren Statt, Kevin Stolper, Max Stubblefield, Geoff Suddleson, Julien Thuan, Sarah Victor, Sarah Warda, Nikki Wheeler, Haena Worthing, Jo Yao
AGENT, ALTERNATIVE TV DEPARTMENT
Michael Camacho (head, alternative TV) Brett Hansen, Carlos Carreras, Lee Horvitz, Joe LaBracio, Geoff Suddleson, Jonathan Swaden, Feroz Taj, Michael Camacho

AGENT, UTA ONLINE DEPARTMENT
Jason Nadler, Barrett D. Garese, Ryan Reber, Jon Zimelis

ANNETTE VAN DUREN AGENCY

(Representing writers and animators)
11684 Ventura Blvd., #235, Studio City, CA 91604.
TEL: (818) 752-6000. FAX: (818) 752-6985.
email: avagency@pacbell.net

WARDLOW & ASSOCIATES

(Writers and directors for film and TV)
14000 Palawan Way, Ste. 36, Marina del Rey, CA 90292.
TEL: (310) 452-1292. FAX: (310) 452-9002.
email: warlowaso@aol.com
PARTNER, LITERARY, THEATRICAL
David Wardlow
LITERARY
Jeff Ordway

WILLIAM MORRIS ENDEAVOR ENTERTAINMENT

(New agency formed from combining the William Morris Agency with the Endeavor Agency, LLC. Companies agreed to merge in April 2009)
Los Angeles: 9601 Wilshire Blvd., Beverly Hills, CA 90210.
TEL: (310) 285-9000. www.wma.com

Additional Los Angeles Office: One William Morris Pl., Beverly Hills, CA 90212.
CHAIRMAN OF THE BOARD EMERITUS
Norman Brokaw
CHAIRMAN OF THE BOARD/CEO EMERITUS
Jim Wiatt
CO-CEO
Ariel Emanuel, Patrick Whitesell, David Wirtschafter
COO
Irv Weintraub
CFO
Michael Dates
SENIOR V.P., GENERAL COUNSEL
David Kekst
V.P., CORPORATE COMMUNICATIONS
Christian Muirhead
V.P., TREASURY MANAGEMENT
Michael Page
INTELLECTUAL PROPERTY
Johnny Levin, Cristina Patwa
HEAD, WILLIAM MORRIS CONSULTING
Paul Bricault
WILLIAM MORRIS CONSULTING
Frank Catapano, Gabe Gordon, Greg Johnson, Aaron Lenzini, Kevin Murray, Edward Ryan, Mark Sacks, Tom Sebastian, Jamie Shortill, Bryan Thoensen
DIRECTOR, CHINA OPERATIONS
Grace Chen
CLIENT MARKETING
Sara Newkirk
HEAD, TALENT
Gaby Morgerman
TALENT
Diego Airaldi, Hanley Baxter, Jonathan Bluman, Michelle Bohan, Thor Bradwell, Esther Chang, Julie Colbert, Michael Cooper, Brian DePersia, Sean Elliott, Philip Grenz, Lisa Hallerman, Scott Henderson, Adam Isaacs, Brandt Joel, Brandon Liebman, Bonnie Liedtke, Ed Limato, Douglas Lucterhand, Boomer Malkin, Priyanka Mattoo, Brent Morley, Kami Putnam-Heist, Jennifer Rawlings, Stephanie Ritz, Elyse Scherz , Sharon Sheinwold, Megan Silverman, Brad Slater, Nick Stevens, Phillip Sun, Brian Swardstrom, Jason Trawick, Adam Venit, Kevin Volchok, Andrew Weitz, Troy Zien
CO-HEAD, WORLDWIDE TELEVISION
Mark Itkin
WORLDWIDE HEAD, NONSCRIPTED TV
John Ferriter
TV
Scott Agostoni, Adam Gelvan, Cameron Kadison, Chris Newman, Laurie Pozmantier, Joshua Pyatt, Collin Reno, Tom Repicci, Matthew Saul, Amir Shahkhalili, David Sherman, Suzy Unger, Evan Warner
HEAD, TV LITERARY
Cori Wellins
TV, LITERARY
Zachary Druker, Lindsay Dunn, Hugh Fitzpatrick, Tony Freinberg, Blake Fronstin, Ari Greenburg, Paul Haas, Lisa Harrison, Elise Hartley, Greg Hodes, Nancy Josephson, Erin Junkin, Theresa Kang, Marc Korman, Margaret Mendelson, Melissa Myers, Richard Rosen, Scott Seidel, Matt Solo, David Stone, Julie Weitz, Richard Weitz, Thomas Wellington
ALTERNATIVE TV
Ivo Fischer, Greg Horangic, Lance Klein, Amanda Kogan, Sean Perry
WORLDWIDE HEAD, MOTION PICTURES & INTELLECTUAL PROPERTY
John Fogelman
MOTION PICTURES
Nicole David, George Freeman, Craig Kestel, Mike Simpson, Roya Weiner
HEAD, MOTION PICTURE LITERARY
Danny Greenberg
MOTION PICTURE LITERARY
Adriana Alberghetti, Bryan Besser, Kimberly Bialek, Rob Carlson, Rich Cook, Philip d'Amecourt, Chris Donnelly, Mike Eisner, Michael Esola, Daniel Gabai, Jeff Gorin, Elia Infascelli-Smith, David Karp, Richie Kern, Charles King, Sarah Lemkin, Adam Levine, David Lubliner, Robert Newman, Philip Raskind, Eric Reid, Cliff Roberts, Lisbeth Rowinski, Dawn Saltzman, Jason Spitz, Bill Weinstein
LITERARY
Anna DeRoy, Alicia Gordon, Lauren Heller Whitney
PHYSICAL PRODUCTION
Stacey Karp, Troy Knowles, Devin Mann, Jonathan Silverman
HEAD, WILLIAM MORRIS ENDEAVOR ENTERTAINMENT INDEPENDENT
Graham Taylor
WILLIAM MORRIS ENDEAVOR ENTERTAINMENT INDEPENDENT
Mark Ankner, Liesl Copland, Jerome Duboz, Alexis Garcia, Emily Hirsch
CO-HEAD, COMMERCIALS
Cary Berman, Jessica Thomas
COMMERCIALS
Troy Bailey, Brittany Balbo, Tim Curtis, Todd Jacobs, Katie Krell, Brooke Slavik,
Will Ward
DIGITAL MEDIA GROUP
Jared Lake, Kim Verbonitz
HEAD, SPORTS & ENTERTAINMENT
Jill Smoller
SPORTS & ENTERTAINMENT
Philip Button, Carla Laur, Carrie Wiener
HEAD, VOICEOVER
Erik Seastrand
VOICEOVER
Anna Rodriguez
HEAD, NEW MEDIA & DIGITAL STRATEGY
Chris Jacquemin
GENERAL COUNSEL
Tom McGuire
HEAD, FEATURE BUSINESS AFFAIRS
Ann Du Val
HEAD, MOTION PICTURE BUSINESS AFFAIRS
June Horton
HEAD, TV BUSINESS AFFAIRS
Catherine Sugar
BUSINESS AFFAIRS
Ruth Chen, Ruth Estrada, Robyn Goldman, Mary Harding, Sherry Hines, Vikki Karan, Donica Patel, Angela Petillo, Brian Rabolli, Deb Shuwarger, Stuart Tenzer, Lawrence Thompson, Kelly Weiss, Tybalt Whitney
STAFF ATTORNEY
Lily Conviser

New York Office: 1325 Ave. of the Americas, New York, NY 10019. TEL: (212) 586-5100. FAX: (212) 246-3583. www.wma.com

Second New York office: 152 W. 57th St., 25th Flr., New York, NY 10019. TEL: (646) 278-2900. FAX: (646) 278-2902.

COO, NEW YORK, TV, CABLE & NETWORK PACKAGING
Cara Stein
HEAD, MOTION PICTURE TALENT, EAST COAST
Randi Michel
MOTION PICTURE TALENT
Bonnie Bernstein, Eric Bevans, Jeff Hunter
HEAD, EAST COAST, TV/CABLE PACKAGING
Jonathan Rosen
TV, CABLE PACKAGING
Jason Hodes
TV, LITERARY
Dan Shear
TV, NEWS
Jim Griffin, Jacqueline Harris, Jim Ornstein, Henry Reisch, Ken Slotnick, Scott Wachs
TV
Mark Mullett
LITERARY
Mel Berger, Bill Clegg, Michelle Feehan, Tracy Fisher, Suzanne Gluck, Dorian Karchmar, Eric Lupfer, Erin Malone, Jay Mandel, Andy McNicol, Eric Simonoff, Jennifer Rudolph Walsh
MOTION PICTURE LITERARY
Laura Bonner, Shawn Coyne, Trena Keating, Kirby Kim, Rebecca Oliver
THEATRE
Val Day, David Kalodner, Biff Liff, Jonathan Lomma, Susan Weaving, Derek Zasky
COMMERCIALS
Strand Conover, Jeff Googel, Marc Guss

LECTURES
Bethany Dick, Jeff Lesh
BUSINESS AFFAIRS
Don Aslan, Catherine Bennett, Richard Charnoff, Alicia Everett, Annette Frankel, David Schmerler and Eric Zohn

Agency represents actors for film/TV, book authors, broadcast journalists/newscasters, choreographers, comedians, composers, directors, hosts/MCs, interactive game developers, music artists, musical theatre performers, playwrights, producers, screenwriters, speakers/lecturers, sports personalities, TV writers and voiceover artists.

SHIRLEY WILSON & ASSOCIATES

(Children and adults)
5410 Wilshire Blvd., Ste. 806, Los Angeles, CA 90036.
TEL: (323) 857-6977. FAX: (323) 857-6980.
CONTACT
Shirley Wilson, Harold Gray

WORKING ARTISTS

(IATSE, ACE. Facilitates the introduction of gifted writers, directors and producers to appropriate venues)
9563 Langdon Ave., North Hills, CA 91343.
TEL: (818) 907-1122. FAX: (818) 891-1293.
email: info@workingartists.net www.workingartists.net

WORLD CLASS SPORTS

840 Apollo St., #314, El Segundo, CA 90245.
TEL: (310) 535-9120. FAX: (310) 535-9128.
email: wcsagent@pacbell.net
SENIOR AGENT
Andrew Woolf, Don Franken

Sports talent, college or national level, for commercials and print. Represent sports celebrities for endorsements and appearance

Digital Production, Distribution, Exhibition & Equipment

Digital Production & Mastering Services

CAMERAS, LENSES, LIGHTING & MISC. PRODUCTION GEAR

16X9, INC.
(Production equipment, HD tools)
28314 Constellation Rd., Valencia, CA 91355.
TEL: (661) 295-3313. FAX: (661) 295-3314. www.16X9inc.com
VICE PRESIDENT
Jeff Giordano - jeffg@16x9inc.com
TECHNICAL SUPPORT MANAGER
James Lee - jamesl@16x9inc.com
NATIONAL SALES SPECIALIST
Gregg Hamlin - gregg@16x9inc.com
CREATIVE DIRECTOR/MARKETING
Michael Ibanez - michael@16x9inc.com
SHIPPING/RECEIVING
Tony Garcia - TonyG@16x9inc.com

ABEL CINE TECH
(Equipment dealer, camera rental and film services)
CA: 801 South Main St., Burbank, CA 91506.
TEL: (888) 700-4416, (818) 972-9078. FAX: (818) 972-2673.
DIRECTOR OF OPERATIONS
Ron Ayers - (818)-972-9078 ext. 302

NY: 609 Greenwich Street, New York, NY 10014.
TEL: (888) 223-1599, (212) 462-0100. FAX: (212) 462-0199.
www.abelcine.com
CEO/DIR OF SALES AND MARKETING
Pete Abel - (212) 462-0141
COO/DIRECTOR OF OPERATIONS
Rich Abel - (212) 462-0161
DIRECTOR OF TECHNOLOGY
Jesse Rosen - (212) 462-0186
DIGITAL CINEMA SPECIALIST
Sean Coles - (818) 972-9078 ext. 311 (LA)
Jamie Alac - (212) 462-0191 (NY)

AMERICAN GRIP, INC.
(Camera accessory equipment)
8468 Kewen Ave., Sun Valley, CA 91352. TEL: (800) I GRIP & GO, (818) 768-8922. FAX: (818) 768-0564.
email: sales@americangrip.com www.americangrip.com
CONTACT
Lance Alan Snoke, Philip Garrett

ANTON/BAUER, INC.
(Storage batteries (mfrs.), cameras and lights)
14 Progress Dr., Shelton, CT 06484-6216.
TEL: (800) 422-3473, (203) 929-1100. FAX: (203) 925-4988.
email: websales@antonbauer.com www.antonbauer.com
Europe@antonbauer.com
VICE PRESIDENT
Shin Minowa
CFO
Kurt Dan
SALES EXECUTIVE
Paul Dudeck

ATLAS SPECIALTY LIGHTING
(specialized lighting as well as optical systems and components, DiStar® Lamps and DiStar® Fiberoptic Equipment and more)
Headquarters: 1111 W. 22nd Street, Hialeah, FL 33010.
TEL: (305) 885-8941. www.asltg.com

7304 N. Florida Ave., Tampa, FL 33604. TEL: (813) 238-6481.
FAX: (813) 238-6656. email: sales@asltg.com
MANAGER
Ralph Felten, Jr. - rfelten@asltg2.com
Bob Ray

International Sales: 1111 W. 22nd St., Hialeah, FL 33010.
TEL: (305) 885-8941.

AXSYS TECHNOLOGIES
(Stabilized Camera Systems, a division of General Dynamics Advanced Information Systems)
Headquarters: 175 Capital Blvd., Ste., 103, Rocky Hill, CT 06067. TEL: (860) 257-0200. FAX: (860) 594-5750.

Stabilized Camera Systems: 380 Crown Point Circle, Grass Valley, CA 95945. TEL: (530) 271-2500. FAX: (530) 271-2550.
email: ircamerainfo@axsys.com www.axsys.com
stabilizedcamerainfo@axsys.com
V.P. / GENERAL MANAGER
Bob McGill
V.P. SALES WORLDWIDE
Alex Giuffrida - (818) 203-8871 email:agiuffrida@axsys.com
DIRECTOR U.S. SALES
Pete Greer - (443) 463-3632 email: pgreer@axsys.com

Acquired Cineflex, LLC. Gyro-stabilized aircraft camera and advanced optical systems, HD aerial photography for broadcast and production, government agencies purchase from Axsys and its approved distributors, advanced high-quality thermal imaging cameras and related equipment to support Military, Homeland Security, Dept. of Defense, Law enforcement programs.

B & H FOTO & ELECTRONICS CORP.
(Audio, cameras & photo gear, computers, digital photography, projection & viewing, and more)
420 9th Ave., New York, NY 10001. TEL: (800) 606-6969, (212) 444-6615. (Sales). FAX: (800) 947-7008, (212) 239-7770.
www.bhphotovideo.com

BAND PRO FILM/DIGITAL, INC.
(Film and digital equipment)
California: 3403 W. Pacific Ave., Burbank, CA 91505.
TEL: (818) 841-9655. FAX: (818) 841-7649.

New York: 645 West 27th St., New York, NY 10001.
TEL: (212) 227-8577. FAX: (212) 564-5540. www.bandpro.com
PRESIDENT/CEO
Amnon H. Band - amnon.band@bandpro.com
SALES MANAGER / CINEALTA SPECIALIST
Nir Reches - nir.reches@bandpro.com
V.P. TECHNICAL SERVICES
Jeff Cree, SOC - jeff.cree@bandpro.com

BOGEN IMAGING, INC.
(Division of The Vitec Group, Became Manfrotto Dist. in 2010. Professional support solutions aimed at the photographic, video, lighting and live entertainment markets)
565 E. Crescent Ave., Ramsey, NJ 07446.
TEL: (201) 818-9500. FAX: (201) 818-9177.
email: info@manfrottodistribution.us www.bogenphoto.com

CANON U.S.A., INC.
(HD-EC lenses, a Division of Canon Broadcast & Communications (BCTV)
Broadcast & Communications Div./Headquarters:
65 Challenger Rd., Ridgefield Park, NJ 07660.
TEL: (800) 321-4388 (Sales). FAX: (201) 807-3333.
www.canonbroadcast.com
SALES CONTACTS
Rich Eilers - reilers@cusa.canon.com
Patrick Breheny - pbreheny@cusa.canon.com
John Rose - jrosejr@cusa.canon.com

Los Angeles: 15955 Alton Parkway, Irvine, CA 92618.
TEL: (949) 753-4330 (Sales). FAX: (949) 753-4337.
SALES CONTACTS
Tom Bender - tbender@cusa.canon.com
Joe Patton - jpatton@cusa.canon.com
Stephanie Franz - sfranz@cusa.canon.com

CANON U.S.A.
(XL1s and GL1 DV & HD & digital camcorders)
Video Division: One Canon Plaza, Lake Success, NY 11042.
TEL: (800) 828-4040, (516) 328-5000. FAX: (516) 328-5009.
www.canondv.com
PRESIDENT/CEO
Joe Adachi

CHAPMAN/LEONARD STUDIO EQUIPMENT
(Camera support equipment and accessories)
12950 Raymer St., N. Hollywood, CA 91605.
TEL: (888) 883-6559, (818) 764-6726. FAX: (888) 502-7263.
email: cristine@chapman-leonard.com
www.chapman-leonard.com
PRESIDENT
Leonard T. Chapman
COO/SPECIAL PROJECTS/LEGAL
Charles Huenergardt - chuckh@chapman-leonard.com
CONTROLLER AND ACCOUNTING
Ryan O'Hara

CHIMERA COMPANY
(Designer and manufacturer of quality lighting products for film, video, and still photography)
1812 Valtec Ln., Boulder, CO 80301. TEL: (888) 444-1812, (303) 444-8000. FAX: (303) 444-8303.
email: salesinfo@chimeralighting.com www.chimeralighting.com
MANAGER OF SALES AND BUSINESS DEVELOPMENT
Eileen Healy - ext. 103
SALES, DEALER RELATIONS
Phil Cousins - ext.102

SALES, CUSTOMER CARE REPRESENTATIVE
Laura Plantell - ext. 104

CINEKINETIC

(Camera support gear, engineering software)
2 Avon Ct., Thornlie, W.A. 6108. Australia.
TEL: +1 212 202 0675. FAX: 61 8 9493-2168.

U.S.: 345 W. 85th St., New York, NY 10024.
TEL: (212) 202-0675.
email: info@cinekinetic.com www.cinekinetic.com

COOL-LUX

(Lighting tools for the professional videographer, Digital and HD design and engineering)
1268 Humbracht Circle, Bartlett, IL 60103-1631.
TEL: (800) 223-2589. FAX: (630) 830-2525.
email: sales@cool-lux.com www.cool-lux.com

COPTER VISION, LLC

7625 Havenhurst Ave., Ste., 36, Van Nuys, CA 91406-1705.
TEL: (818) 782-6673. FAX: (818) 782-6636.
email: info@coptervision.com www.coptervision.com

Remote-control camera helicopters with 360 degree 3 axeslight-weight camera systems for film, video, still photography. Other products: Rollvision, Flexvision, manufactures video triggers.

DESISTI LIGHTING/DESMAR CORP.

(Lighting products)
Headquarters: via Cancelliera 10/a, 00040 Albano Laziale, Rome. TEL: +39-06-93499. FAX: +39-06-9343489.
email: desisti@desisti.it www.desisti.it
CONTACT
Fabrizio Bucci - fabrizio_bucci@desisti.it

US: 1011, Hwy. 22 East - Ste. D, Mountainside, NJ 07092.
TEL: (908) 317-1120. FAX: (908) 317-0021.
www.desistilighting.com
CONTACT
Frank Kosuda - (908) 317-8005 frank_kosuda@desistiusa.com

EGRIPMENT USA

(Camera cranes, remote heads, and support gear)
7625 Hayvenhurst Ave., Unit 27, Van Nuys, CA 91406.
TEL: (818) 787-4295. FAX: (818) 787-6195.
email: egripment@socal.rr.com www.egripment.com

EZ FX, INC.

(Camera support equipment/cine & video jibs & accessories)
324 Maguire Rd., Ocoee, FL 34761. TEL: (800) 541-5706.
FAX: (407) 877-6603. email: sales@ezfx.com www.ezfx.com
Tech Support/International: TEL: (407) 877-2335.
PRESIDENT
Steve Bonin

FAST FORWARD VIDEO

(Digital disk recorders for video-assist)
1151 Duryea Ave., Irvine, CA 92614. TEL: (800) 755-8463, (949) 852-8404. FAX: (949) 852-1226.
email; sales@ffv.com www.ffv.com
dIRECTOR/MARKETING
Nicole Hollinger - nhollinger@ffv.com
SALES ADMINISTRATION
Claudette Kay - claudette@ffv.com

MARK FORMAN PRODUCTIONS

(HD production services)
300 West 23rd St., Ste., 14 A/B New York, NY 10011.
TEL: (212) 633-9960, (212) 633-8482. FAX: (212) 807-0121.
email: www.screeningroom.com
www.digitalcinematography.com

Mark Forman is a member of The Society of Motion Picture and Television Engineers and The Society of Camera Operators.

FORMATT FILTERS

(HD specific and glass camera filters and related lens products)
Unit 23, Aberaman Park Industrial Estate, Aberaman, Aberdare, Mid Glamorgan, Wales, CF 44 6DA. UK.
TEL: 00 44 (0)1685 870 979. FAX: 00 44 (0)1685 877 007.
email: info@formatt.co.uk
Sales: cerianne.summerill@formatt.co.uk www.formatt.co.uk
GENERAL MANAGER
Paul Stephen - paul.stephens@formatt.co.uk

FUJI FILM USA, INC.

(Digital recording media, Fujifilm Corporation is a wholly-owned subsidiary of Fujifilm Holdings Corporation)
200 Summit Lake Dr., Valhalla, NY 10595-1356.
TEL: (800) 755-3854, (914) 789-8100. FAX: (914) 789-8490.
www.fujifilm.com

FUJI SALES OFFICES
Northeast: 1100 King George Post Rd., Edison, NJ 08837.
TEL: (800) 659-3854, (732) 857-3000.

Southeast: 250 Scientific Dr., Ste. 300, Norcross, GA 30092.
TEL: (800) 366-3854, (770) 813-5100.

Midwest: 850 Central Ave., Hanover Park, IL 60133.
TEL: (800) 869-8600, (312) 924-5800.

Southwest: 4100 W. Royal Ln., Ste. 175, Irving, TX 75063.
TEL: (800) 927-3854, (972) 862-5500.

West: 6200 Phyllis Dr., Cypress, CA 90630.
TEL: (800) 326-0800, (714) 372-4200.

FUJINON, INC.

(Digital cinema lenses)
Broadcast & Communications Division: 10 High Point Dr., Wayne, NJ 07470. TEL: (973) 633-5600. FAX: (973) 633-5216.
www.fujinon.com

SALES OFFICE:
Los Angeles: West Bay Business Park, 2621-A Manhattan Beach Blvd., Redondo Beach, CA 90278-1604.
TEL: (310) 536-0800. FAX: (310) 536-0022.
WESTERN REGIONAL SALES
Miles Shozuya - miles.s@fujinon.com

Northeast: 10 High Point Dr., Wayne, NJ 07470-7434.
TEL: (973) 686-2417. FAX: (973) 686-2465 .
GENERAL TECHNICAL SUPPORT
Mr. Eddie Lee - edwin.lee@fujinon.com

West: West Bay Business Park, 2621-A Manhattan Beach Blvd., Redondo Beach, CA 90278-1604 . TEL: (310) 536-0800. FAX: (310) 536-0022. email: ca.service@fujinon.com
REGIONAL SERVICE MANAGER
Mr. Joe Nieman

Southeast: 1231 Collier Road, Ste. G, Atlanta, Ga. 30318.
TEL: (404) 351-1470. FAX: (404) 351-7035.
REGIONAL SERICE MANAGER
Wilson Zeferino - wzeferino@fujinon.com

GAM PRODUCTS

(Lighting products for motion picture, photography, TV, theatre, display, amusement parks and other specialty applications)
4975 W. Pico Blvd., Los Angeles, CA 90019.
TEL: (323) 935-4975. FAX: (323) 935-2002.
email: questions@gamonline.com www.gamonline.com
PRESIDENT
Joe Tawil - joetawil@gamonline.com
ADMINISTRATIVE & SALES SUPPORT
Cathy Vera - cathyvera@gamonline.com
REHEARSAL HALL MANAGER
Lynn Smith - lynnsmith@gamonline.com

GAM's wide range of special effects projection devices include the Scene Machine, the SX4, FilmFX and TwinSpin. GAM created the original off-the-shelf stainless-steel pattern (gobo) and the original deep-dyed polyester color filters GAMCOLOR, and available rehearsal hall.

GLIDECAM INDUSTRIES, INC.

23 Joseph St., Kingston, MA 02364. TEL: (800) 600-2011, (800) 949-2089, (781) 585-7900. FAX: (781) 585-7903.
email: sales@glidecam.com www.glidecam.com
PARTNER
Martine Stevens, David Stevens

Offers a wide variety of camera stabilizers (camera stabilization systems) for use with motion picture cameras, video cameras, and video camcorders

HAMLET

(Digital HD-SDI test and measurement equipment)
Corporate Head Office: Hamlet Video International, Ltd. Maple House, 11 Corinium Business Centre, Raans Rd., Amersham Bucks, HP6 6FB, UK. TEL: +44 (0)1494 729728.
FAX: +44 (0)1494 723 237.

UK & INTERNATIONAL SALES
Stephen Rutherford - +44 (0)1494 729728
stever_hamlet.co.uk

Hamlet USA: Sencore, Inc., 3200 Sencore Dr, Sioux Falls, SD 57107. TEL: (800) 736-2673, (605) 339-0100.
FAX: (605) 339-7032.
CONTACT
Tony Oehlerking - (605) 376-2450
tony.oehlerking@sencore.com

HOODMAN

(Monitor and viewfinder hoods, manufactures unique digital camera accessories)
20445 Gramercy Place, Ste. #201, Torrance, CA 90501.
TEL: (800) 818-3946, (310) 222-8608. FAX: (310) 222-8623.
email: sales@hoodmanusa.com www.hoodmanusa.com

IKEGAMI ELECTRONICS

(Digital HD cameras)
37 Brook Ave., Maywood, NJ 07607. TEL: (201) 368-9171.
FAX: (201) 569-1626. email: service@ikegami.com
www.ikegami.com
BROADCAST/PRO VIDEO PRODUCTS
Alan Keil - akeil@ikegami.com

West Coast Office: 2631 Manhattan Beach Blvd., Redondo Beach, CA 90278. TEL: (310) 297-1900. FAX: (310) 536-9550.
CONTACT
Justin Chang - jchang@ikegami.com

Midwest Office: P.O. Box 161, Bloomingdale, IL 60108.
TEL: (630) 372-8777.
CONTACT
Rich Johnson - rjohnson@ikegami.com

Southeast Office: 710 East Hillsboro Blvd., Suite 100, Deerfield Beach, Florida 33441. TEL: (954) 571-7177.
FAX: (954) 571-77607.
CONTACT
Dennis Disinger - ddisinger@ikegami.com

INNOVISION OPTICS

(Specialized lenses, support, and motion-control products for the film and television industries)
1719 21st St., Santa Monica, CA 90404. TEL: (310) 453-4866.
FAX: (310) 453-4677. email: sales@innovision-optics.com
www.innovision-optics.com
CONTACT
Mark Centkowski - mark@innovision-optics.com

INTEGRATED LIGHTING SYSTEMS

9309 South Toledo Ave., Ste. A, Tulsa, OK 74137.
TEL: (877) 325-9400, (918) 523-9400. FAX: (918) 523-9401.
www.integratedlighting.com

Lighting Systems to provide a professional, all-inclusive planning, engineering, installation and aftermarket lighting equipment service to the worldwide television, video, film and stage industries.

ISCO / FILTERFABRIK GMBH & CO., KG

(Manufacturer of cinema projection lenses for all film formats and projectiontypes, anamorphic attachments for 3-chip DLP and for LCD/DLP projectors)
Anna-Vandenhoeck-Ring 5, 37081 Göttingen, Germany.
TEL: +49 (0) 551 5058-3. FAX: +49 (0) 551 505-8410.
email: info@isco.eu www.iscoprecisionoptics.com
CONTACT
Wolfgang Wilhelm - wilhelm@isco.eu

USA: 191 Peachtree St., Ste. 3300, Atlanta, GA 30303.
TEL: (678) 420-3473. www.isco-usa.us
MANAGER SALES & MARKETING-HOME CINEMA PRODUCTS
Brian Ludvigsen - (678) 420-3473
brian.ludvigsen@isco-usa.us

(Representing: Schneider-Kreuznach, Schneider Optics, Inc., and ISCO)

JVC PROFESSIONAL PRODUCTS COMPANY

(CineLine digital cinematography cameras)
JVC Headquarters & East Coast Sales: 1700 Valley Rd., Wayne, NJ 07470. TEL: (800) 247-3608, (973) 317-5000.
FAX: (973) 317-5030. email: proinfo@jvc.com www.jvc.com
PRESIDENT & REPRESENTATIVE DIRECTOR
Kunihiko Sato

JVC Midwest Sales: 705 Enterprise St., Aurora, IL 60504.
TEL: (800) 851-2020.

JVC West Coast Sales: 5665 Corporate Ave., Cypress, CA 90630. TEL: (800) 995-4582, (800) 252-5722.

JVC Professional Worldwide Contacts/JVC International Headquaters: Victor Service & Engineering Co., Ltd.
IPSMD (International Prof. Systems Marketing Division)
1F, Ishizuka Building, 5-11-1 Yahiro, Sumida-ku, Tokyo 131-0041. TEL: 03-6381-8400. FAX: 03-6381-8401.
www.jvc-victor.co.jp

K 5600 LIGHTING

(Innovative lighting instruments and accessories)
10434 Burbank Blvd., N. Hollywood, CA 91601.
TEL: (800) 662-5756, (818) 762-5756. FAX: (818) 762-6629.
email: info@k5600.com www.K5600.com

Florida Office: P.O. Box 292905, Davie, FL 33329-2905.
TEL: (954) 680-9575. FAX: (954) 680-1575.
email: beth@k5600.com

France Office: 475 rue de Flins, 78410 Bouafle, France.
TEL: +33 (0) 1-30-90-5600. FAX: +33 (0) 1-30-95-36-07.
email: info@k5600lighting.com

KINO FLO

(Innovative lighting instruments and accessories)
2840 N. Hollywood Way, Burbank, CA 91505.
TEL: (818) 767-6528. FAX: (Sales) (818) 767-7517,
(Rental) (818) 252-0290. www.kinoflo.com
Sales email: Sales@kinoflo.com
PRESIDENT
Frieder Hochheim - Fhochheim@kinoflo.com
SALES MANAGER
Scott Stueckle - Sstueckle@kinoflo.com
CONTACT/SALES US WEST COAST/CANADA
Tom Jacob - Tjacob@kinoflo.com

LEADER INSTRUMENTS CORP.

(Digital HD test and measurement equipment)
6484 Commerce Dr., Cypress, CA 90630.
TEL: (800) 645-5104, (714) 527-9300. FAX: (714) 527-7490.
email: sales@leaderusa.com www.leaderusa.com
V.P. SALES & MARKETING
George Gonos
DIRECTOR OF WESTERN SALES
Dr. Pete Anderson

LEVITON MFG. COMPANY, INC.

(Gels and lighting accessories)
201 North Service Rd., Melville, NY 11747.
TEL: (800) 323- 8920. FAX: (800) 832-9538.
www.colortran.com www.leviton.com

LOCATION SOUND CORP.

(Location audio equipment)
10639 Riverside Dr., N. Hollywood, CA 91602.
TEL: (800) 228-4429, (818) 980-9891. FAX: (818) 980-9911,
(Rental) (818) 980-7932. email: information@locationsound.com
salesdept@locationsound.com www.locationsound.com
SR. SALES REPRESENTATIVE
Val Asuncion - ext. 353 asuncion@locationsound.com
SALES REPRESENTATIVE
Dave Auslender - ext. 340 auslender@locationsound.com

LONG VALLEY EQUIPMENT

(Camera support gear also handheld support gear)
165 Fairview Ave., Long Valley, NJ 07853-3178.
TEL: (908) 876-1022. FAX: (908) 876-1938.
email: longvalley@embarqmail.com www.longvalleyequip.com

LOWEL-LIGHT MANUFACTURING, INC.

(Lighting instruments and accessories)
90 Oser Ave., Hauppauge, NY 11788. TEL: (800) 645-2522.
FAX: (631) 273-2557. email: info@lowel.com
equipq@lowel.com www.lowel.com

LTM CORP. OF AMERICA

(Lighting instruments and accessories)
7755 Haskell Ave., Van Nuys, CA 91406-1906.
TEL: (818) 780-9828. FAX: (818) 780-9848.
www.ltmlighting.com
WEST COAST CONTACT
Stuart Guerrero - stuart.guerrero@ltmlighting.us
EAST COAST CONTACT
Mike Keppler - mike@kepplerengineers.com

MANFROTTO DISTRIBUTION

(Division of the Vitec Group)
565 E. Crescent Ave., Ramsey, NJ 07446.
TEL: (201) 818-9500. FAX: (201) 818-9177.
email: info@manfrottodistribution.us www.manfrotto.com

MAXELL CORP. OF AMERICA

(Digital recording media, a wholly owned subsidiary of Hitachi Maxell, Ltd. (Hitachi Maxell), based in Osaka, Japan)
US Headquarters: 3 Garret Mountain Plaza, 3rd Flr., Ste 300, Woodland Park, NJ 07424-3352. TEL: (800) 533-2836,
(973) 653-2400. FAX: (201) 796-8790.
email: techsupp@maxell.com www.maxell-usa.com
EXECUTIVE V.P. SALES
Peter Brinkman

MICRODOLLY

(Camera support systems)
3110 W. Burbank Blvd., Burbank, CA 91505-2313.
TEL: (818) 845-8383. FAX: (818) 845-8384.
www.microdolly.com

MILLER FLUID HEADS

(Tripods, pedestals and heads)
30 Hotham Parade, Artarmon, NSW, Sydney, 2064, Australia.
TEL: +61 2 9439-6377. FAX: +61 2 9438-2819.
Sales email: daniel.sissons@miller.com.au www.miller.com.au

Miller Camera Support LLC (USA): 218 Little Falls Rd., Cedar Grove, NJ 07009-1231. TEL: (973)-857-8300.
FAX: (973) 857-8188. Sales email: gus@millertripods.us

MIRANDA TECHNOLOGIES, INC.

(Downconverters for external monitors. Acquired OmniBus Systems 2010)
3499 Douglas - B. Floreani, Montreal, QC, H4S 2C6, Canada.
TEL: (514) 333-1772. FAX: (514) 333-9828. www.miranda.com
CANADIAN SALES MANAGER
Roy Folkman - roy.folkman@miranda.com

CA Office: 125 Crown Point Court, Grass Valley, CA 95945.
TEL: (514) 333-2117. FAX: (514) 333-2112
email: ussales@miranda.com

MOLE-RICHARDSON

(Lighting, grip, camera accessories, support, and heads)
937 N. Sycamore Ave., Hollywood, CA 90038-2384.
TEL: (323) 851-0111. FAX: (323) 851-5593.
email: info@mole.com www.mole.com

MOVIE TECH

(Camera support equipment: cranes, dollies, light systems, remote heads & accessories)

Headquarters: Martin-Kollar-Str. 9, 81829 Munchen, Germany. TEL: 49 (0) 89-43 68 91 3. FAX: 49 (0) 89-43 68 91 55.
email: info@movietech.de www.movietech.de

US: 2150 Northmont Pkwy., Ste. A, Duluth, GA 30096-5835. TEL: (877) 824-5808, (678) 417-6352. FAX: (678) 417-6273.
email: usa@movietech.de

MUSCO
(Giant lighting rigs (also mobile) with services specializing in sports stadiums worldwide)
100 1st. Ave., West, P.O. Box 808, Oskaloosa, IA 52577.
TEL: (800) 825-6030, (641) 673-0411. FAX: (641) 673-4852.
www.musco.com
CEO
Joe Crookham
SALES MANAGER
Mike Shindler - mike.shindler@musco.com

NRG RESEARCH
(Audio, Power & Lighting solutions for TV professionals)
159 Ort Ln., Merlin, OR 97532.
Mailing Address: P.O. Box 390, Merlin, OR 97532.
TEL: (541) 479-9433. FAX: (541) 471-6251.
email: info@nrgresearch.com www.nrgresearch.com

O'CONNER ENGINEERING
Camera Dynamics, Inc., 2701 N. Ontario St., Burbank, CA 91504. TEL: (818) 847-8666. FAX: (818) 847-1205.
email: info@ocon.com www.ocon.com
CONTACT:
Jeannine McQuillan - ext. 500 sales@ocon.com

O'Connor is a division of Sachtler. Manufactures fluid heads, tripods and accessories for the tv industry. Provides camera support solutions.

PANASONIC
(HD cinema cameras, tapeless implementations for cameras, recorders, and related products)
3330 Cahuenga Blvd. W, Los Angeles, CA 90068.
TEL: (323) 436-3500. www.panasonic.com/business
COUNSELOR
Cassius Titus

In 2004, Panasonic introduced its P2 IT News Gathering (ING) System. Leading broadcasters into the tapeless future, Panasonic's solid state memory based P2 products use the same DV compression format embraced by over 700 broadcast operations around the world.

PANAVISION
(HD Cinema cameras, including the Genesis™ Super 35 Digital Cinematography Camera System, recorders and digital services)
Panavision/Panavision Remote Systems, 6219 De Soto Ave., Woodland Hills, CA 91367-2602. TEL: (818) 316-1000.
FAX: (818) 316-1111. www.panavision.com

Panavision California: 6735 Selma Ave., Hollywood, CA 90028. TEL: (323) 464-3800. FAX: (323) 467-0522.
MARKETING CONTACT
Dan Donovan

Panavision Florida: 2000 Universal Studios Plaza, Ste. 900, Orlando, FL. 32819-7606. TEL: (407) 363-0990.
FAX: (407) 363-0180.
MARKETING CONTACT
Mindy Bee

Panavision New York: 150 Varick St., 2nd Fl., New York, NY 10013. TEL: (212) 606-0700. FAX: (212) 244-4457.
www.panavisionnewyork.com

Panavision Dallas: 8000 Jetstar Dr., Irving, TX 75063.
TEL: (800) 260-1846, (972) 929-8585. FAX: (972) 929-8686.
MARKETING CONTACT
John Schrimpf

PANTHER GMBH
Raiffeisenallee 3, D-82041 Oberhaching-Munich, Germany.
TEL: +49 89 6139 00 01. FAX: +49 89 6131 00 0.
email: contact@panther.tv wwwpanther.tv
www.panther-gmbh.de

US: SLx, LLC.: 7358 Radford Ave., N. Hollywood, CA 91605. TEL: (818) 764-1313. FAX: (818) 764-1144.
email: contact@sl-x.us www.sl-x.us

Large camera cranes. Panther recently established a broadcast division to support needs of the HD & broadcast market. US distributor: Abel Cine Tech.

PORTA-BRACE (K&H PRODUCTS)
(Field monitor cases)
940 Water St., North Bennington, VT 05257-9810.
TEL: (802) 442-8171. FAX: (802) 442-9118.
www.info@portabrace.com www.portabrace.com
SALES CONTACT
Ken Barry - ext. 301 ken@portabrace.com

PRODUCTION GEAR, LTD.
(Suppliers of broadcast and production equipment)
Millennium Studios, 5 Elstree Way, Borehamwood, Hertfordshire, WD6 1SF UK. TEL: (0) 20-8236-1212.
FAX: (0) 20-8236-1414. www.optexint.com
email: info@productiongear.co.uk

International: TEL:+44 208 236 1212. FAX: +44 208 236 1414.
CONTACT
Simon Beer - simon@productiongear.co.uk

PROSOURCE/BROADCAST MARKETING, LTD.
(Film and video production equipment)
1515 Black Rock Turnpike, Fairfield, CT 06825.
TEL: (800) 322-7767, (203) 335-2000. FAX: (203) 335-3005.
email: contact@prosourcebmi.com www.prosourcebmi.com

SACHTLER CORP. OF AMERICA
(Tripods, heads, and camera support)
Camera Dynamics, Inc.: 709 Executive Blvd., Valley Cottage, NY 10989. TEL: (845) 268-0100. FAX: (845) 268-0113.
email: info-cd-usa@vitecgroup.com sales@sachtlerusa.com
www.sachtler.com
CONTACT
Bob Carr

SCHNEIDER OPTICS, CENTURY DIVISION
(Video and film lenses, accessories, filters, projection lenses, subsidiary of Schneider Optics, Inc.)
7701 Haskell Ave., Van Nuys, CA 91406. TEL: (800) 228-1254, (818) 766-3715. FAX: (818) 505-9865.
email: projection@schneideroptics.com
www.centuryoptics.com

SCHNEIDER OPTICS, INC.
(Projection lenses, digital lenses, filters)
285 Oser Ave., Hauppauge, NY 11788. TEL: (800) 645-7239, (631) 761-5000. FAX: (631) 761-5090.
email: info@schneideroptics.com www.schneideroptics.com
CEO
Dwight Lindsey
DIRECTOR, CINEMA TECHNICAL SERVICES
Fred Morris
SALES ADMINISTRATOR
Henry W. Greese - hgreese@schneideroptics.com

CA: Schneider Optics, 7701 Haskell Ave., Vany Nuys, CA 91406. TEL: (800) 228-1254, (818) 766-3715. FAX: (818) 505-9865.

SEKONIC DIVISION OF MAMIYA AMERICA
(Light meters. See website for dealer/distributor locations)
Sekonic USA: 8 Westchester Plz., Elmsford, NY 10523.
TEL: (914) 347-3300. FAX: (914) 347-3309.
email: info@sekonic.com www.sekonic.com

SHURE BROTHERS, INC.
5800 W. Touhy Ave., Niles, IL 60714-4608.
TEL: (800) 25-SHURE, (847) 600-2000. FAX: (847) 600-1212.
email: info@shure.com www.shure.com

Microphones and professional audio products. Based in U.S. with regional offices in Europe and Asia. See website for additional locations.

SONY BROADCAST & PROFESSIONAL CO.
(24P HD CineAlta production system. See website for more information about professional broadcast products and service)
Executive Office: Sony Corporation of America: 550 Madison Ave, New York, NY 10022-3211. TEL: (212) 833-6800.

Operating Headquarters: Sony Broadcast and Business Solutions Company: One Sony Drive, Park Ridge, NJ 07656.
TEL: (201) 930-1000. www.sony.com/production
www.sony.com/professional www.sony.com/business
www.sony.com/CineAlta

SPECTRA CINE, INC.
(Portable light meters)
3607 W. Magnolia Blvd., Burbank, CA 91505.
TEL: (818) 954-9222. FAX: (818) 954-0016.
email: info@spectracine.com www.spectracine.com

STRAND LIGHTING, INC.
(Innovative lighting instruments, accessories, control systems and software. A Philips Group Brand)
267 5th Ave., 4th Flr., New York, NY 10016.
TEL: (212) 213-8219. FAX: (212) 532-2843.
www.strandlight.com
NORTHEAST REGIONAL MANAGER
Jack Nettleton - (716) 474-1070 (mobile)
jack.nettleton@philips.com

TEKTRONIX, INC.
(Digital HD test, monitoring, and measurement devices)
14150 S.W. Karl Braun Dr., P.O. Box 500, Beaverton, OR 97077. TEL: (800) 833-9433. FAX: (503) 627-3247.
www.tek.com

THOMSON BROADCAST, INC.
(Products for broadcast/tv/film professionals. LDK-7000 and 6000 digital cinema cameras and more)
Headquarters: 1, rue de l'Hautil, ZA des Boutries BP 150, 78 702 Conflans St. Honorine, France.
TEL: +33 (0)1 34 90 31 00. FAX: +33 (0)1 34 90 30 00.

www.thomson.net www.thomsongrassvalley.com

US Contact: 104 Feedings Hill Road, Southwick, MA 01077. TEL: (786) 226-8866.

All other countries: TEL: (800) 80 80 20 20, +33 1 48 25 20 20.

TIFFEN MANUFACTURING CORP.

(Camera accessories; filters, video, digital HT, DFX software)
90 Oser Ave., Hauppauge, NY 11788-3886.
TEL: (631) 273-2500. FAX: (631) 273-2557. www.tiffen.com

TRANSVIDEO

(Flat-panel camera monitors)
11712 Moorpark St., #112B, N. Hollywood, CA 91604.
TEL: (818) 985-4903. FAX: (818) 985-4921.
email: marianne@transvideointl.com

France: Z.I. BP 526, F 27135 Verneuil sur Avre, France.
TEL: +33 2 3232 2761. FAX: +33 2 3260 1479.
email: info@transvideo.fr www.transvideointl.com

ULTIMATTE CORP.

(Digital HD blue and green screen compositing)
20945 Plummer St., Chatsworth, CA 91311.
TEL: (818) 993-8007. FAX: (818) 993-3762.
email: sales@ultimatte.com www.support@ultimatte.com
www.ultimatte.com

VIDEOTEK, INC.

(Digital HD monitoring products. Subsidiary of Harris Corp.)
243 Shoemaker Rd., Pottstown, PA 19464. TEL: (800) 231-9673, (610) 327-2292. FAX: (610) 327-9295. www.videotek.net
www.broadcast.harris.com

DIGITAL DAILIES

ASCENT MEDIA

520 Broadway, 5th Fl., Santa Monica, CA 90401.
TEL: (310) 434-7000. FAX: (310) 434-7111.
www.ascentmedia.com
V.P., SALES
Bridget Allen - (818) 281-0946 bridgetallen@ascentmedia.com

Offers integrated digital media services including digital asset management, post production, content duplication and distribution.

INTERNET PRO VIDEO (IPV)

(Digital dailies services)
IPV Limited, The Quorum: Barnwell Rd., Cambridge, CB5 8RE. UK. TEL: +44 (0) 1223 413 690. FAX: +44 (0) 1223 413 692.
email: sales@ipv.com www.ipv.com
EVP SALES & MARKETING
Nigel Booth

U.S.: Listec Video Corp., 40 Oser Ave., Unit 3, Hauppauge, NY 11788. TEL:(631) 273-3020. FAX: (631) 382-8182.
sales-usa@ipv.com

LEVEL 3 POST (ASCENT MEDIA/A LIBERTY MEDIA CO.)

(Part of Ascent Media/A Liberty Media Co.)
2901 West Alameda Ave., 3rd Flr., Burbank, CA 91505.
TEL: (818) 840-7200. FAX: (818) 840-7801.
email: info@level3post.com www.level3post.com
VP/OPERATIONS
Darrell Anderson - (323) 988-6632 danderson@ascentmedia.com

Primarily specializing in television shows, Level 3 Post's repertoire includes sit-coms, one-hour dramatic television and reality-based programs. Company offers an extensive suite of both standard and high definition services, including linear and non-linear editing, compositing, titles, graphics, duplication, color correction and dailies transfers.

ONSTREAM MEDIA CORP.

1291 S.W. 29th Ave., Pompano Beach, FL 33069.
TEL: (866) 857-1960, (954) 917-6655. FAX: (954) 917-6660.
email: info@onstreammedia.com www.onstreammedia.com
SENIOR VP/CHIEF MARKETING OFFICER
David Galssman

New York: 221 West 26th St., New York, NY 10001.
TEL: (646) 381-2055. FAX: (646) 807-4777.
email: onsmny@onstreammedia.com

Digital asset management ASP technology provides the necessary tools for webcasting, webconferencing and content publishing services.

TELESTREAM, INC.

(Internet streaming technologies)
848 Gold Flat Rd., Ste. 1, Nevada City, CA 95959.
TEL: (877) 681-2088, (530) 470-1300. FAX: (530) 470-1301.
email: info@telestream.net www.telestream.net
VP/MARKETING
Barb DeHart

GRAPHICS SOFTWARE

ADOBE SYSTEMS

(Mac and Windows software for digital nonlinear editing, effects and typography)
345 Park Ave., San Jose, CA 95110-2704.
TEL: (408) 536-6000. (800) 833-6687 (Cust. Service).
FAX: (408) 537-6000. www.adobe.com

AUTODESK, INC.

(High-end 3D animation software)
111 McInnis Pkwy., San Rafael, CA 94903.
TEL: (415) 507-5000. FAX: (415) 507-5100.
www.autodesk.com

U.S. South: 3780 Mansell Rd., Ste. 200, Alpharetta, GA 30022. TEL: (770) 645-1415. FAX: (770) 645-8380.

U.S. East: 41 100 Commercial St., Manchester, NH 03101. TEL: (603) 621-3100. FAX: (603) 621-3383.

APPLE (PRO DIGITAL PRODUCTION SOFTWARE)

1 Infinite Loop, Cupertino, CA 95014. TEL: (877) 412-7753, Software sales: (800) 692-7753. www.apple.com/software/pro

CAMBRIDGE ANIMATION SYSTEMS

(Digital animation software)
Titan House, Castle Park, Cambridge, CB3 0AY, UK.
TEL: +44 1223 488200. FAX: +44 1223 488201.
email: sales@cambridgeanimation.com
info@cambridgeanimation.com www.cambridgeanimation.com

DISCREET

(A division of Autodesk, Inc.)
Headquarters: 111 McInnis Pkwy., San Rafael, CA 94903.
TEL: (415) 507-5000. FAX: (415) 507-5100.

Canada: 210 King St. E, Toronto, Ont. M5A 1J7, Canada.
TEL: (416) 362-9181. FAX: (416) 369-6140.
www.autodesk.com

Software for digital media creation, mgt. and delivery across all disciplines from film and TV visual effects, color grading and editing to animation, game development, Web and design visualization.

EI TECHNOLOGY GROUP, LLC

(High-end 3D animation software)
435 W. Nakoma, Ste. 101, San Antonio, TX 78216.
TEL: (210) 377-2525. FAX: (210) 579-6668.
sales@eitechnologygroup.com www.electricimage.com
MEDIA RELATIONS
Brad Parscale - brad@eitechnologygroup.com

NEWTEK, INC.

(Lightwave 3D software)
5131 Beckwith Blvd., San Antonio, TX 78249.
TEL: (800) 862-7837 (Cust. Service), (210) 341-8444 (Sales).
FAX: (210) 370-8002 (Sales). SoutheastSales@newtek.com
www.newtek.com

REALVIZ CORP.

(High-end Windows-based image processing software)
350 Townsend St., San Francisco, CA 94107.
TEL: (415) 615-9800. FAX: (415) 615-9805.
wwwinfo@realviz.com www.realviz.usa@realviz.com
CEO
Dominique Pouliquen

Realviz develops and markets image processing software that enables the production of 2D and 3D digital images for the film industry, audio-visual production, multi-media industry, CAD, architecture, video game and digital imaging.

HD POST/MASTERING/FILM-OUT/AUDIO POST/FACILITIES

24FPS PRODUCTIONS

(Digital HD production services)
50 W. 23rd St., 7th Flr., New York, NY 10010.
TEL: (646) 638-0659. FAX: (212) 206-6986.
email: info@24fpsproductions.com
www.24fpsproductions.com

AMERICAN MEDIA GROUP

(Digital HD production and post services, encoding, authoring and duplication)
3350 Scott Blvd., #19, Santa Clara, CA 95054.
TEL: (408) 486-0923. FAX: (408) 486-9826.
email: info@amg.tv www.amg.tv

AMERICAN PRODUCTION SERVICES, LLC

(Digital HD production and post services)
150 Nims Spring Dr., Fort Mill, SC 29715.
TEL: (803) 548-2290. FAX: (803) 548-3406.
email: bmoody@apsvideo.com www.apsvideo.com

CHACE PRODUCTIONS, INC.

(Audio post production & sound restoration; acquired by Deluxe Digital Media, July 1, 2009)
201 S. Victory Blvd., Burbank, CA 91502. TEL: (800) 842-8346, (818) 842-8346. FAX: (818) 842-8353. www.chace.com
VP AUDIO, DDM
Robert Heiber

Services include: audio compression, dubbing, editorial, film inspection & repair, optical sound recording,COSPTM, restoration, revitalization, sound transfers, synchronization/conforms.

CINERIC

(Digital effects, film out, and titles)
630 Ninth Ave., Ste. 508, New York, NY 10036.
TEL: (212) 586-4822. FAX: (212) 582-3744. www.cineric.com

CINEMA CONCEPTS TSC., INC.

2030 Powers Ferry Rd., Ste. 214, Atlanta, GA 30339.
TEL: 800-746-9237, (770) 956-7460. FAX: (770) 956-8358.
email: info@cinemaconcepts.com www.cinemaconcepts.com
CHAIRMAN/CEO
Stewart Harnell

Studio & editing services, preview & policy trailers, CGI & stereoscopic 3D animation, digital production services-HD, post/mastering/film/out/JPEG-2000 encoding, screening rooms-film & digital, pre-show content.

CINESITE, INC. (A KODAK COMPANY)

(Digital production, post-production, digital intermediate, computer graphics, transfer, restoration, and archiving services)
1017 N. Las Palmas Ave., Los Angeles, CA 90038-2400.
TEL: (323) 468-1589. FAX: (323) 468-2180. www.cinesite.com

Digital visual effects, film scanning and recording and digital mastering for the feature film and television industry.

COLOSSALVISION

(Digital HD production services)
26 Broadway, 6th Flr. Ste., #666, New York, NY 10004.
TEL: (212) 269-6333. FAX: (212) 269-4334.
email: info@colossalvision.com www.colossalvision.com

CRAWFORD COMMUNICATIONS, INC.

(Digital HD post and transfer facility, satellite, internet production services)
3845 Pleasantdale Rd., Atlanta, GA 30340.
TEL: (800) 831-8027, (678) 421-6600. FAX: (678) 421-6631.
www.crawford.com
VP DIGITAL MEDIA SERVICES
Vincent Lyons - (323) 344-4529 vlyons@encompass-m.com

CREST DIGITAL

3845 E. Coronado St., Anaheim, CA 92807.
TEL: (800) 309-3472, (714) 666-2266. FAX: (714) 666-8671.
www.crestnational.com

Post Services: 1000 N. Highland Ave., Hollywood, CA 90038.
TEL: (800) 961- TAPE, (323) 860-1300. FAX: (323) 461-8901.

Recording studio, sound editing, sound effect library, sound post facility, sound transfer service, video audio mixing and sweetening. Digital compression for V.O.D., Final cut pro/Avid editing, HD/SD)

DFW (DIGITAL FILM WORKS)

(Full range of services, including digital scanning, blue/green screen compositing, digital paint, matte compositing and more)
3330 Cahuenga Blvd. W., Ste. 300, Los Angeles, CA 90068.
TEL: (323) 874-9981. FAX: (323) 874-3916. www.dfw-la.com
PRESIDENT
Peter W Moyer - peter@dfw-la.com
VICE PRESIDENT
Cosmas Paul Bolger, Jr.

DUART FILM AND VIDEO

(Complete film lab)
245 W. 55th St., New York, NY 10019. TEL: (800) 523-8278, (212) 757-4580. FAX: (212) 333-7647. info@duart.com
www.duart.com
CONTACT
Steve Blakely - sblakely@duart.com

Arri Laser film/tape transfer, DVD Encoding/Authoring, Film/HD Mastering/Restoration, Complete Sound & HD Video Services, EFX, Streaming Video, and Documentary Distribution-National Film Network.

DVS DIGITAL VIDEO, INC.

300 E. Magnolia Blvd., Ste. 102, Burbank, CA 91502.
TEL: (818) 846-3600. FAX: (818) 846-3648.
email: info@dvsus.com www.dvsus.com
PRESIDENT
Peter Spoer

EFILM DIGITAL LABORATORIES

(A Deluxe Co., digital film laboratory)
1146 N. Las Palmas Ave., Hollywood, CA 90038.
TEL: (323) 463-7041. FAX: (323) 465-7342. info_1@efilm.com
www.efilm.com
EXEC V.P./TECHNICAL SERVICES/CLIENT RELATIONS
Beverly Wood

ENCORE HOLLYWOOD

(A subsidiary of Ascent Media Group, LLC. Digital HD post and mastering)
6344 Fountain Ave., Hollywood, CA 90028-8116.
TEL: (323) 466-7663. FAX: (323) 466-5539.
email: info@encorehollywood.com www.encorehollywood.com
V.P. SALES
Michael Koljan

FILMLOOK, INC.

(Digital image-enhancement technology)
2917 W. Olive Ave., Burbank, CA 91505. TEL: (818) 845-9200.
FAX: (818) 845-9238. email: lookinfo@filmlook.com
www.filmlook.com
CLIENT RELATIONS/MARKETING/SALES
Anna Cordova - anna@filmlook.com

FOTOKEM

(Full-service motion picture and video lab)
2801 W. Alameda Ave., Burbank, CA 91505.
TEL: (800) FOTOKEM, (818) 846-3101. FAX: (818) 841-2130.
email: sales@fotokem.com www.fotokem.com

GRACE & WILD, INC.

(Digital HD post and transfer facility)
23689 Industrial Park Dr., Farmington Hills, MI 48335.
TEL: (248) 471-6010. FAX: (248) 473-8330.
email: info-hd@gw-hdstudios.com www.graceeild.com

HD CINEMA

(Digital HD production and post)
12233 W. Olympic Blvd., Ste. 120, Los Angeles, CA 90064.
TEL: (310) 434-9500, Equip. & post services: (310) 689-2470.
www.hdcinema.com

East Coast CT: 1771 Post Rd. East, #220, Westport, CT 06880.
TEL: (203) 221-0233.
CONTACT
Jeff Blauvelt - jeff@hd-cinema.com

IO FILM

(Digital intermediates, film scanning, film recording, HD to film, visual effects)
1415 N. Cahuenga Blvd., Hollywood, CA 90028.
TEL: (323) 822-4444. FAX: (323) 467-7300.
email: websales@postgroup.com www.iofilm.net

IVC (INTERNATIONAL VIDEO CONVERSIONS)

(A Point 360 Company. Digital transfer and mastering services also for the Internet performs MPEG-1, MPEG-4 and Windows Media 9 digital compression)
2777 Ontario St., Burbank, CA 91504. TEL: (818) 569-4949.
FAX: (818) 569-3659. email: sales@ivchd.com
www.ivchd.com

NY: 227 East 45th St., 6th Flr., New York, NY 10017.
TEL: (212) 953-6999. FAX: (312) 937-9528.
email: sales-point360ny@point360.com www.mipost.com

KODAK DIGITAL CINEMA

(Digital cinema mastering, distribution, and projection. Partnered with SRS Labs (www.srslabs.com) to bring SRS Circle Surround Sound into its digital cinema pre-show high definition entertainment systems)
6700 Santa Monica Blvd., Los Angels, CA 90038-1203.
TEL: (323)464-6131. FAX: (323) 468-1568, (323)-468-2124.
www.kodak.com/go/dcinema

New York: 360 West 31st St., New York, NY 10001-2727.
TEL: (212) 631-3400. FAX: (212) 631-3470.

LASER PACIFIC MEDIA CORP.

(Wholly owned subsidiary of Eastman Kodak. Full digital post-production services)
809 N. Cahuenga Blvd., Hollywood, CA 90038.
TEL: (323) 462-6266. FAX: (323) 960-2134.
email: info@laserpacific.com www.laserpacific.com

MOVIOLA

(Sales, rentals, education)
1135 N. Mansfield Ave., Hollywood, CA 90038.
TEL: (800) 468-3107, (323) 467-3108. FAX: (323) 464-1518.
www.moviola.com
V.P.
Michael Mostin - (323) 467-3108, ext. 264. mmostin@moviola.com

New York: 545 W. 45th St., New York, NY 10036. TEL: (323) 467-1116.
FAX: (323) 466-2522.
DIRECTOR, EDUCATION & PRODUCTION
Johnathon Amayo - jamayo@moviola.com

THE ORPHANAGE

(Post services, creates visual effects for film and TV commercials)
39 Mesa St., Ste. 201, San Francisco, CA 94129.
TEL: (415) 561-2570. FAX: (415) 561-2575.
V.P./EXECUTIVE PRODUCER
Paul Grimshaw

6725 Sunset Blvd., Ste. 220, Hollywood, CA 90028.
TEL: (323) 469-6700. FAX: (323) 469-6701.

email: vfx@theorphanage.com www.theorphanage.com
EXECUTIVE PRODUCER
Liz Roewe

THE POST GROUP

(Group of campanies that compliment each other to provide a full range of post services for TV, film and multimedia projects. Digital HD post, intermediate, mastering)
6335 Homewood Ave., Hollywood, CA 90028-8105.
TEL: (323) 462-2300. FAX: (323) 462-0836.
email: info@postgroup.com www.postgroup.com

POST OP MEDIA

(Comprehensive audio and video post-production co-operative)
2020 14th St., N. Ste., 406, Arlington, VA 22204.
TEL: (703) 525-7000. FAX: (703) 525-7001.
email: info@post-opmedia.com www.post-opmedia.com
CONTACT
Brian Cunneff - Audio post production
Henry Holdren - Video post production

POSTWORKS NEW YORK

(HD and SD editing to sound design; color correction to film recording; digital intermediate testing and screening and more)
100 Ave. of the Americas, 10th Fl., New York, NY 10013.
TEL: (212) 894-4000, (212) 894-4050. FAX: (212) 941-0439.
email: inquiry@postworks.com www.pwny.com

222 East 44th St., 11th Flr., New York, NY 10017.
TEL: (212) 500-2700. FAX: (212) 682-5869.
EXECUTIVE V.P.
Domenic Rom

PRIME DIGITAL MEDIA SERVICES

(DVD replication & video duplication services)
28111 Stanford Ave., Valencia, CA 91355.
TEL: (661) 964-0220. FAX: (661) 964-0550.
email: brigitte@primedigital.com www.primedigital.com

PRIME FOCUS

(Digital HD post-production.)
1800 N. Vine, St., Hollywood, CA 90028.
TEL: (323) 461-7887. FAX: (323) 461-7790.
Sales: inquiries@postlogic.com www.postlogic.com
V.P. BUSINESS DEVELOPMENT, FILM, & VFX
Amit Gupta

New York: 435 Hudson St., 7th Flr., New York, NY 10014.
TEL: (212) 520-3150. FAX: (212) 520-3155.
MANAGING DIRECTOR, OPERATIONS, POST PRODUCTION
Anthony Matt

REALITY CHECK STUDIOS

(Digital design and visual effects studio)
6100 Melrose Ave., Los Angeles, CA 90038.
TEL: (323) 465-3900, (323) 908-7000. FAX: (323) 465-3600.
email: info@realityx.com www.realityx.com
PARTNER
Andrew Heimbold - andrew@realityx.com
Kory Jones - kory@realityx.com
Steven Heimbold - steven@realityx.com

SHOOTERS POST & TRANSFER

(Color correction, compositing, computer graphics, Downconversions, file transfers, film to HD/Datacine, non-linear online, tape to tape correction, tiltling/character generation & up-conversions)
The Curtis Center Suite, 1050 Independence Sq. W, Philadelphia, PA 19106. TEL: (215) 861-0100.
FAX: (215) 861-0099.
email: info@shootersinc.com www.shootersinc.com

SWELL, INC.

(Digital HD post and transfer facility)
455 N. Cityfront Plz. Dr., 18th Fl., Chicago, IL 60611.
TEL: (312) 464-8000. FAX: (312) 464 8020. www.swellinc.com
CONTACT
Benjamin Husmann

TECHNICOLOR CREATIVE SERVICES

(Full range of post services)
6087 W. Sunset Blvd., Bldg. 70, Hollywood, CA 90028.
TEL: (323) 467-1244. FAX: (323) 461-2561.
info@technicolor.com www.technicolorcreativeservices.com
PRESIDENT
Mike Doggett

Mastering for digital cinema release:
1631 Gardena Ave., Glendale, CA 91204. TEL: (818) 500-9090.
FAX: (818) 500-4099. email: jordan.jacobs@thomson.net
www.vidfilm.com

HD and SD Dailies Transfer, DVD Dailies, Digital Dailies Preview (HD projection), 6K/4K/2K Film Scanning, Digital Trailers, 4K/2K/HD Picture Conforming, Resolution-Independent Visual Effects Color Correction 4K/2K/HD/SD, 4K/2K/HD titles, Duplication and QC, Digital Mastering, Standards Conversion, Editorial, Telecine, 4K/2K/HD laser film recording.

TECHNIQUE

(Digital mastering services, subsidiary of Thomson's Digital Content Solutions division)
2233 N. Ontario St., Ste. 100, Burbank, CA 91504.
TEL: (818) 260-2652. FAX: (818) 260-4007.
email: technique@technicolor.com www.technicolor.com
CONTACT
Julie Purcell - julie.purcell@thomson.net

TODD AO CORP.

(Part of CSS Studios, LLC, a wholly owned division of Discovery Communications, 2008. Audio post services)
Audio post facility: 900 Seward St., Hollywood, CA 90028.
TEL: (323) 962-4000. FAX: (323) 466-4062. www.toddao.com
DIRECTOR OF OPERATIONS
Richard Burnette - (323) 962-4050
FEATURE STAGES
Kim Jimenez - (323)603-3255
TRANSFER/LAYBACKS
Nat Suckley - (323) 962-4110

Services include: ADR, re-recording/mixing, transfer, sound design, sound editorial, sound supervision.

Post production facility: 2901 W. Alameda Ave., Burbank, CA 91505. TEL: (818) 840-7225. FAX: (818) 840-7219.
ENGINEER/OPERATIONS MANAGER
Steve Bartkowicz- (818) 840-7236
DIRECTOR, TELEVISION SERVICES
Dan Gillett - (818) 840-7173

Todd-AO West: 3000 Olympic Blvd.,Bldg. 1, Santa Monica, CA 90404. TEL: (310) 315-5000. FAX: (310) 315-5099.
OPERATIONS
Matt Dubin - (310) 315-5000
Shelly Hovland - (310) 315-5071

Services include: ADR, re-recording/mixing, foley and voice over recording for TV and feature films.

TOTAL DIGITAL PRODUCTIONS, INC.

(Full service production house)
1500 Flower St., Glendale, CA 91201. TEL: (818) 241-9792.
FAX: (661) 298-1836. email: req4info@total-digital.com
www.total-digital.com
PRESIDENT
Hillard L. Fitzkee - hillard@total-digital.com

VTA, INC.

(Digital HD post and transfer facility)
1575 Sheridan Rd., NE, Atlanta, GA 30324-3233.
TEL: (404) 634-6181. FAX: (404) 320-9704. www.vta.com
THEATRE SYSTEMS SALES
Glenn Martin - glenn.martin@vta.com

HD POST/MASTERING TECHNOLOGY

ABEKAS

(HD digital disk recording; editing systems)
1490 O'Brien Dr., Menlo Park, CA 94025.
TEL: (650) 470-0900. FAX: (650) 470-0913. www.abekas.com
CO-FOUNDER/PRESIDENT/CEO
Junaid Sheikh
CHIEF PRODUCT MANAGER
Douglas Johnson

ADIC (ADVANCED DIGITAL INFORMATION CORP.)

(Merger with Quantum Corp. 2006. Storage area network technology)
1650 Technology Dr., Ste. 700, San Jose, CA 95110-1382.
TEL: (408) 944-4000. FAX: (408) 944-4040 www.quantum.com
EXECUTIVE V.P./COO/CFO
Jon W. Gacek
CTO
Jeffrey Tofano

APPLE COMPUTER, INC.

(Digital editing, DVD authoring, and web streaming hardware and software)
1 Infinite Loop, Cupertino, CA 95014. TEL: (408) 996-1010,
Sales Support: (800) 676-2775. FAX: (408) 974-7740.
www.apple.com

AVICA TECHNOLOGY

(Compressed and uncompressed digital storage for production, has exclusive licensing agreement with DTS)
1201 Olympic Blvd., Santa Monica, CA 90404.
TEL: (800) 706-0077 ext. 145, (310) 450-9090 ext. 145.
FAX: (310) 450-5353. email: contact@avicatech.com
sales@avicatech.com www.avicatech.com

AVID TECHNOLOGY, INC.

(Digital nonlinear editing for all applications. See website for additional offices)
75 Network Drive, Burlington, MA 01803.
TEL: (978) 640-6789. FAX: (978) 640-3366. www.avid.com

Los Angeles: 101 South First St., Ste. 200, Burbank, CA 91502.

TEL: (818) 557 2520. FAX: (818) 557-2558.

New York: 575 Lexington Ave., 14th Flr., New York, NY 10022. TEL: (212) 983-2424. FAX: (212) 983-8718, (212) 983 9770.
CEO / PRESIDENT
Gary G. Greenfield
SENIOR V.P. WORLDWIDE MARKETING
Ronald Greenberg

BOXX TECHNOLOGIES

(Developer of high-end hardware and software. Partnered with DLT Solutions, 2010)
10435 Burnet Rd., Ste. 120, Austin, TX 78758.
TEL: (877) 877-2699, (512) 835-0400. FAX: (512) 835-0434.
www.boxxtech.com
DIRECTOR OF SALES
John Civatte - ext. 324 jcivatte@boxxtech.com

CIPRICO, INC.

(High performance networked storage solution)
7003 W. Lake St., Ste. 400, St. Louis Park, MN 55426.
TEL: (952) 540-2400. FAX: (952) 540-2402.
email: sales@ciprico.com www.ciprico.com
VP Sales/Marketing
Don McDonell - dmcdonell@ciprico.com

DIGITAL VISION, INC. (US)

(Digital intermediate, restoration, image enhancement, conforming systems)
4605 Lankershim Blvd., Ste. 700, North Hollywood, CA 91602.
TEL: (818) 769-8111. FAX: (818) 769-1888.
email: support@digitalvision.se www.digitalvision.se

DOREMI LABS, INC.

(Uncompressed HD and MPEG2 disk recorders and the V1 digital media server)
1020 Chestnut St., Burbank, CA 91506. TEL: (818) 562-1101.
FAX: (818) 562-1109. email: info@doremilabs.com
sales@doremitechno.com www.doremilabs.com

DVS DIGITAL VIDEO, INC.

(High capacity uncompressed HD disk recorder products)
300 E. Magnolia Blvd., Ste. 102, Burbank, CA 91502.
TEL: (818) 846-3600. FAX: (818) 846-3648.
email: info@dvsus.com www.dvsus.com
MANAGING DIRECTOR
Peter Spoer

EMC CORP.

(Digital storage solutions)
176 South St., Hopkinton, MA 01748. TEL: (508) 435-1000,
(866) 438-3622 (sales). FAX: (508) 435-8910. www.emc.com

EVERTZ

(HD keyers, converters, and digital film solutions)
5292 John Lucas Dr., Burlington, Ont., L7L 5Z9, Canada.
TEL: (877) 995-3700, (905) 335-3700. FAX: (905) 335-3573.
email: sales@evertz.com www.evertz.com
DIRECTOR OF SALES (NY & EASTERN USA)
Orest Holyk - ext. 268 orest@evertz.com
V.P. SALES (CENTRAL & WESTERN USA)
Joe Cirincione - (480) 419-2855 joe@evertz.com

GRASS VALLEY, A THOMSON BRAND

(Specter 2K digital intermediate system, D-6 VooDoo data & video recorders. See website for worldwide sales office locations)
2255 N. Ontario St., Ste. 150, Burbank, CA 91504.
TEL: (818) 729-7706. FAX: (818) 729-7777.
email: us.northwest.systems.sales@thomson.net
www.thomsongrassvalley.com
CONTACT
Chris Piscitelli

LEITCH

(HD signal processing design and distribution for the television industry. Post-production)
600 W. 5th Ave., Naperville, IL 60563. TEL: (800) 231-9673,
(630) 605-2410. www.leitch.com
CONTACT
Paul Schwantes - PSCHWANT@harris.com

MATHEMATICAL TECHNOLOGIES, INC. (MTI)

(Automated digital restoration of motion pictures)
209 Angell St., P.O. Box 2476, Providence, RI 02906.
TEL: (401) 831-1315. FAX: (401) 831-1318.
email: film_sales@mtifilm.com www.mtifilm.com
CONTACT
Michael Russell

CA: 1016 N. Sycamore Ave., Hollywood, CA 90038.
TEL: (323) 465-6478. FAX: (323) 465-6487.
DIRECTOR OF WORLDWIDE SALES:
Belinda S. Merritt - ext. 201 belinda.merritt@mtifilm.com

MTI is a leading supplier of software solutions for film and video post production and MTI systems were used for the first ever mastering of a major animated feature for digital cinema release in which the feature was never printed to film.

MATROX ELECTRONIC SYSTEMS

(Digital editing products)
1055 St. Regis Blvd., Dorval, Que., H9P 2T4, Canada.
TEL: (514) 822-6000. FAX: (514) 822-6363. www.matrox.com

Software and hardware solutions in the fields of Graphics, Video editing, Image processing and new business media.

MEDEA CORPORATION

(Acquired by Avid Technology. Digital storage systems)
Avid Technology Park, One Park West, Tewksbury, MA 01876.
TEL: (800) 949-2843, (978) 640-6789. FAX: (978) 640-3366.
email: info@medea.com www.medea.com www.avid.com
CHAIRMAN/PRESIDENT/CEO
Gary Greenfield
V.P., CUSTOMER OPERATIONS
Beth Martinko

ORACLE AMERICA, INC.

(Solaris based visual workstations and servers. Formerly Sun Microsystems, Inc.)
4150 Network Circle, Santa Clara, CA 95054.
TEL: (800) 786-0404, (650) 960-1300. FAX: (408) 276-3804.
www.sun.com/media
CONTACT
Hanifa A. Baporia - hanifa.baporia@sun.com

PINNACLE SYSTEMS

(CineWave Mac based digital nonlinear 24p HD edit system, radial light film scanner, A Division of Avid Technology, Inc.)
European Headquarters: Pinnacle Systems GmbH, Frankfurter Str. 3 c, Braunschweig, D-38122 Germany.
TEL: ++49 89 50206 0.

U.S.: 280 N. Bernardo Ave., Mountain View, CA 94043.
TEL: (650) 526-1600. FAX: (650) 526-1601.
www.pinnaclesys.com

QUANTEL, INC.

(Digital editing, compositing, effects, and graphics systems)
Headquarters: Turnpike Rd., Newbury, Berkshire RG14 2NX United Kingdom. TEL: +44 (0) 1635 48 222.
FAX: +44 (0) 1635 815 815. www.quantel.com

Los Angeles: 3800 Barham Blvd., Ste. 315, Los Angeles, CA 90068. TEL: (323) 436-7600. FAX: (323) 878-2596.
V.P. SALES
Eric Thorne - (323) 436-7608 eric.thorne@quantel.com

New York: 25 West 43rd St., Ste. 1118, New York, NY 10036-7410. TEL: (212) 944-6820. FAX: (212) 944-6813.
DISTRICT SALES MANAGER
Lee Turvey - lee.turvey@quantel.com

SGI

(IRIX OS based visual workstations and servers, data storage)
Headquarters: 46600 Landing Pkwy., Fremont, CA 94538.
TEL: (800) 800-7441 (Sales), (510) 933-8300. www.sgi.com

Production: digital infrastructure, digital publishing, film mastering, content creation. Broadcast: broadcast systems, on-air graphics, digital archive.

SNELL & WILCOX, INC.

(HD 24P production systems)
3519 Pacific Ave., Burbank, CA 91505. TEL: (818) 556-2616.
FAX: (818) 556-2626. email: support.us@snellgroup.com
www.snellwilcox.com

East Coast: 274 Madison Ave., Ste. 1704, New York, NY 10016.
TEL: (212) 481-2416. FAX: (212) 481-2642.
PRESIDENT, AMERICAS
Jonathan Goldstein

Delivering technologies and products that move content seamlessly among analog, digital, high definition and file-based systems and bridges the world's multiplicity of line/field and color standards.

SONY BROADCAST & PROFESSIONAL CO.

123 W. Tryon Ave., Teaneck, NJ 07666. TEL: (201) 833-5300.
FAX: (201)833-5312. TeaneckService@am.sony.com
www.sony.com/production www.sony.com/professional
www.sony.com/business www.sony.com/CineAlta

24P HD CineAlta production system, digital betacam and DVCAM product lines, XPRI nonlinear editing system. See website for professional broadcast products and service.

STEENBECK, INC.

(Digital and film based editing & viewing technologies)
Keizersveld 31, 5803 AM Venray, Nederland.
TEL: +31 (0) 478-630300. FAX: +31 (0) 478-690007.
email: info@steenbeck.com www.steenbeck.com

TERANEX SYSTEMS, INC.

(HD format converters)
2800 Discovery Dr., Ste. 270, Orlando, FL 32826.
TEL: (407) 858-6000. FAX: (407) 858-6001.
email: info@teranex.com www.teranex.com

UNIVERSAL STUDIOS DIGITAL SERVICES

(Full-service post-production facility, color correction, duplication, editing, encoding & telecine)
100 Universal City Plaza, Bldg. 3153, Universal City, CA 91608. TEL: (818) 777-1111. FAX: (818) 866-5258.
www.universalstudios.com/studio
www.filmmakersdestination.com
CONTACT
Ron Silveira - ron.silvera@nbcuni.com

SOUND/AUDIO POST TECHNOLOGY

AMEK, HARMAN INTERNATIONAL INDUSTRIES, LTD

(Manufacturer of digital audio consoles and signal processors.)
Cranborne House, Cranborne Rd., Potters Bar, Herts, EN6, 3JN, UK. TEL: +44 (0) 1707-665-000. FAX: +44 (0) 1707-660-742. email: info@harmanprouk.com www.amek.com
V.P. SALES
Adrian Curtis - adrian.curtis@harmanpro.com

US: Harman Pro North America, 400 Atlantic St., 15th Flr., Stamford, CT 06901. TEL: (203) 920-328-3500 .
FAX: (818) 920-3209. email: soundcraft-usa@harman.com

DIGIDESIGN

(Division of Avid Technology. Digital audio post solutions and systems)
2001 Junipero Serra Blvd., Daly City, CA 94014-3886.
TEL: Support: (650) 731-6100, (650) 731-6300.
FAX: (650) 731-6375. www.digidesign.com
SENIOR V.P. WORLDWIDE MARKETING
Ronald Greenberg

EUPHONIX, INC.

(Digital audio consoles. A division of Avid Technology)
1330 West Middlefield Rd., Mountain View, CA 94043.
TEL: (650) 855-0400. FAX: (650) 969-3510.
Support: www.euphonix.com/artist/support/contact.php
www.euphonix.com

FAIRLIGHTUS, INC.

(Consoles, digital audio workstations)
PO Box 112, West Milford, NJ 07480. TEL: (310) 600-8584.
FAX: (626) 628-3686. accounts@fairlightus.com
www.fairlightus.com

14 Hirth Drive, Newfoundland, NJ 07435.
TEL: (310) 600-8584. FAX: (626) 628-3686.
DIRECTOR OF SALES
Philippe Guichard - (626) 825-0093 philippe@fairlightus.com

FOSTEX CORP. OF AMERICA

(Audio recording equipment for film & video production & post)
9 Mars Court, Boonton, NJ 07005.
TEL: (973) 394-0015. FAX: (973) 394-0800.
email: sales@fostexUSA.com www.fostexUSA.com

HARRISON BY GLW

(Digital audio consoles)
1024 Firestone Pkwy., Nashville, TN 37086-3505.
TEL: (615) 641-7200. FAX: (615) 641-7224.
email: info@harrisonconsoles.com www.glw.com
CONTACT
Gary Thielman, Charley White

OTARI USA SALES, INC.

(Digital audio consoles and multitrack recorders)
21110 Nordhoff St., Ste. G/H, Chatsworth, CA 91311.
TEL: (818) 734-1785. FAX: (818) 734-1786.
email: sales@otari.com www.otari.com

SOLID STATE LOGIC

(Digital post/film audio mixing consoles)
5757 Wilshire Blvd., Bldg. #401, Los Angeles, CA 90036-3628.
TEL: (323) 549-9090. FAX: (323) 549-3488.
email: lasales@solidstatelogic.com www.solidstatelogic.com

SONY BROADCAST & PROFESSIONAL CO.

123 W. Tryon Ave., Teaneck, NJ 07666. TEL: (201) 833-5300.
FAX: (201) 833-5312. www.sony.com/production
www.sony.com/professional www.sony.com/business
www.sony.com/CineAlta

24P HD CineAlta production system. See website for more information about professional broadcast products and service.

SOUNDCRAFT

(Soundboards & consoles for live and recorded sound)
Harman Pro North America: 8500 Balboa Blvd., Northridge, CA 91329. TEL: (818) 920-3212. FAX: (818) 920-3209.
email: soundcraft-usa@harmon.com www.soundcraft.com
V.P. SALES & MARKETING
Ralph Quintero - rquintero@harman.com
NATIONAL SALES MANAGER
Tom Der - tder@harman.com

TEAC AMERICA, INC.

(Audio recording technologies for digital post)
Teac Professional Division, 7733 Telegraph Rd., Montebello, CA 90640. TEL: (323) 726.0303. FAX: (323) 727-7632.
www.teac.com

TELECINE/SCANNERS/COLOR CORRECTION/FILM OUT

ARRI, INC.

(Motion picture cameras and post production equipment)
25 Enterprise Ave North, Secaucus, New Jersey 07094.
TEL: (212) 757-0906. FAX: (212) 713-0075.
www.cameraservice.com
PURCHASING DEPARTMENT MANAGER
Luciana Lenihan

2385 Stirling Rd., Fort Lauderdale, FL 33312.
TEL: (954) 322-4545. FAX: (954) 322-4188.
www.arri.com www.illuminationdynamics.com
GENERAL MANAGER
Ed Stamm

ARRI, Inc. is a wholly owned subsidiary of Arnold & Richter Cine Technik. Complete range of ARRI cameras & lighting products; specially developed products such as the LCC (Laptop Camera Controller, Obie Light, VariCon, ArriSoft Lights & Lighting Kits)

CELCO

(High resolution film out recorders)
8660 Red Oak Ave., Rancho Cucamonga, CA 91730.
TEL: (909) 481-4648. FAX: (909) 481-6899.
email: info@celco.com www.celco.com
CONTACT WORLDWIDE SERVICE MANAGER
Greg Puetz - (951) 543-8263 greg@celco.com

CINTEL, INC.

(Film scanners and image enhancement tools)
Cintel International Ltd., Watton Rd., Ware, Hertfordshire, SG12 OAE, UK. TEL: +44 (0) 1920 463939.
FAX: +44 (0) 1920 460803. email: sales@cintel.co.uk
www.cintel.co.uk
CONTACT
SIMON CLARK

U.S. West Coast: 28910 Ave. Penn, Ste. 202, Valencia, CA 91355-4184. TEL: (661) 294-2310. FAX: (661) 294-1019.
email: sales@cintel.co.uk www.cintel.co.uk
CONTACT
Curtis Christianson - sales@cintel.co.uk

U.S. East Coast: 80 Red Schoolhouse Rd., Ste. 102, Chestnut Ridge, NY, 10977. TEL: (845) 371-7220. FAX: (845) 371-6896.

DA VINCI

4397 N.W. 124 Ave., Coral Springs, FL 33065.
TEL: (954) 688-5600. FAX: (954) 575-5936.
email: info@davsys.com www.davsys.com
GENERAL MANAGER
Bill Robertson
V.P., ENGINEERING
David Johnson

HD and SD color enhancement system, uncompressed digital storage and restoration solutions, an Acterna Corporation company.

GRASS VALLEY, A THOMSON BRAND

(Spirit DataCine, Spectar 2K digital intermediate system)
2255 N. Ontario St., Ste. 150, Burbank, CA 91504.
TEL: (800) 547-8949, (818) 729-7700. FAX: (818) 729-7777.
email: sales-usa@grassvalleygroup.com
www.thomsongrassvalley.com

IMAGICA CORPORATION OF AMERICA

(2K digital film scanners)
1840 Century Park E # 750, Los Angeles, CA 90067-2107.
TEL: (310) 277-1790. FAX: (310) 306-2334.
www.imagica.com
CONTACT
wm-inquiry@web.imagica.co.jp

INNOVATION TK, LTD.

(2K Telecine systems)
Scott House, Hagsdell Rd., Hertford, Hertforshire SG13 8BG. England. TEL: +44 1992 553533. FAX: +44 1992 558979.
email: info@innovation-tk.com www.innovation-tk.com

OXBERRY

(Digital film scanners, software and film out cameras)
180 Broad St., Carlstadt, NJ 07072. TEL: (201) 935-3000.
FAX: (201) 935-0104. email: info@oxberry.com www.oxberry.com

PANDORA INTERNATIONAL

(Pogle color correction technology)
3575 Cahuenga Blvd. W, Ste. 370, Los Angeles, CA 90068.
TEL: (323) 882-1800. FAX: (323) 882-1801.
email: admin@pandora-int.com www.pandora-int.com

PINNACLE SYSTEMS

(Radial light film scanner)
280 N. Bernardo Ave., Mountain View, CA 94043.
TEL: (650) 526-1600. FAX: (650) 526-1601.
www.pinnaclesys.com

SONY BROADCAST & PROFESSIONAL CO.

(Vialta digital telecine)
1 Sony Dr., Park Ridge, NJ 07656. TEL: (800) 686-7669, (201) 930-1000. www.sony.com/production
www.sony.com/professional www.sony.com/business
www.sony.com/CineA

DIGITAL DISTRIBUTION & RESOURCES

DIGITAL CINEMA DISTRIBUTION

CINEDIGM DIGITAL CINEMA CORP.

(Formerly Access Integrated Technologies, Inc. Company announced name change Nov. 2008)
Headquarters: 55 Madison Ave., Ste. 300, Morristown, NJ 07960. TEL: (973) 290-0080. FAX: (973) 290-0081.
email: info@cinedigm.com www.cinedigm.com

Digital Cinema Offices: 6255 Sunset Blvd., Ste. 1025, Hollywood, CA 90028. TEL: (323) 463-2144.
FAX: (323) 463-1319.
CHAIRMAN & CEO
Bud Mayo
PRESIDENT, MEDIA SERVICES GROUP
Chuck Goldwater
PRESIDENT & COO, SOFTWARE DIVISION
Jim Miller
PRESIDENT, COO, DIGITAL MEDIA SERVICES DIVISION
Gerd Jakuszeit
PRESIDENT & COO, UNIQUE SCREEN MEDIA, A CINEDIGM COMPANY
William A. McGlamery
PRESIDENT, PRESIDENT, CINEDIGM ENTERTAIMENT GROUP
Jonathan Dern
DIRECTOR, CORPORATE COMMUNICATIONS
Suzanne Moore - (973) 290-0056 ext. 181
smoore@cinedigm.com

Cinedigm provides digital cinema networked services along with its Library Management Server(R) and Theatre Command Center(R) to enable theatres across the United States to play digital showings of Hollywood features. The company's 24/7 satellite operations delivers feature movies, alternative content advertising, and pre-show entertainment, including live 2-D and 3-D events through its CineLive(R) satellite network, expanding box office sales and developing new ways to attract incremental revenues. Through its alternative content distribution division, the company offers channels of programming including Opera, Kidtoons, Faith-based Concerts, Sports and Anime.

ENTRIQ, INC.

5857 Owens Ave., Ste. 300, Carlsbad, CA 92008.
TEL: (760) 795-2600. FAX: (760) 795-2626. www.irdeto.com
SYSTEMS ADMINISTRATOR
Paul Ragland - (507) 344-3049 paul.ragland@entriq.com

Develops and manages pay media infrastructure, delivers streaming media, provides turn-key solutions to protect it. Merged with sister company Irdeto, May 2009.

GLOBAL CROSSING

(Broadband communications)
100 Ashford Center N., Ste., 460, Atlanta, GA 30338-4865.
TEL: (800) 836-7000. www.globalcrossing.com
CONTACT
Jaimie Munson - jaimie.munson@globalcrossing.com

UK: Chineham Gate, Crockford Lane, Basingstoke, Hampshire, U.K. RG24 8NA. TEL: +44 (0) 800 496-1000 (Sales), +44 (0) 845 000 1000 (General Inquiries).
email: marketing2@globalcrossing.com

HARMONIC DATA SYSTEMS

(Encryption)
549 Baltic Way, Sunnyvale, CA 94089. TEL: (800) 788-1330, Outside U.S.: (408) 542-2500. FAX: (408) 542-2511.
Support: RMA@harmonicinc.com www.harmonicinc.com
CEO
Dr. Patrick J. Harshman, PhD

IRDETO

Northup North Business Park, 2320 130th Ave., NE, Ste. E-200, Bellevue, WA 98005. TEL: (425) 497-2800. FAX: (425) 497-2801.
email: americas@irdeto.com www.irdeto.com

Provides reliable software technologies that protect and monetize digital assets and maximize return on any content sent over any network, to any device. Merged with sister company, Entriq, Inc., May 2009.

OMNEON VIDEO NETWORKS

(Digital networking solutions, storage)
1237 E. Arques Ave., Sunnyvale, CA 94085-3913.
TEL: (408) 585-5000. FAX: (408) 585-5099.
email: sales@omneon.com www.omneon.com
SENIOR V.P. MARKETING & BUSINESS
Geoff Stedman

QUANTUM DIGITAL, LTD.

(Supplier of satellite solutions to UK cinemas)
26 Granville St., Aylesbury, Buckinghamshire, HP20 2JR, UK.
TEL: +44 (0) 7900-813605. email: marc@quantumdigital.co.uk
www.quantumdigital.co.uk

SIGHTSOUND TECHNOLOGIES

311 South Craig St., Ste., 205, Pittsburgh, PA 15213.
TEL: (412) 621-6100. www.sightsound.com
PRESIDENT & CEO
Scott Sander - sander@sightsound.com

WAM!NET, A DIVISION OF SAVVIS

(Outsourcing provider of managed computing and network infrastructure for IT applications)
1 Savvis Pkwy., Town & Country, MO 63017. TEL: (888) 638-6771, (314) 628-7000. email: info@savvis.net www.savvis.net
V.P. & CHIEF INFORMATION OFFICER
Jack MacKay

PRINCIPAL STUDIO CONTACTS

THE WALT DISNEY COMPANY

ABC Television, 500 S. Buena Vista St., Burbank, CA. 91521.
TEL: (818) 460-5284. www.disney.com
www.stu-ops.disney.com
SENIOR V.P., WORLDWIDE NEW TECHNOLOGY AND DEVELOPMENT
Bob Lambert

DREAMWORKS, SKG

100 Universal City Plaza, Bldg. 5121, Universal City, CA 91608. TEL: (818) 733-7000. www.dreamworks.com
OPERATIONS & ADMINISTRATION
Mark Christiansen

MGM

10250 Constellation Blvd., Los Angeles, CA 90067.
TEL: (310) 449-3000. FAX: (310) 449-3024. www.mgm.com
PRESIDENT OF NETWORKS
Bruce Tuchman
EXECUTIVE V.P. WORLDWIDE DIGITAL MEDIA
Douglas A. Lee

NBC UNIVERSAL/UNIVERSAL PICTURES

100 Universal City Plaza, Ste., 2160/8G, Universal City, CA 91608. TEL: (310) 840-8676. FAX: (310) 840-8390.
www.nbcuni.com
V.P. NEW MEDIA, NBC UNIVERSAL CABLE
Michael Bonner
V.P. MARKETING, DIGITAL DISTRIBUTION
Stacy Melle

PARAMOUNT PICTURES

5555 Melrose Ave., Sturgess Bldg., Room 102, Hollywood, CA 90038. TEL: (323) 956-5000. FAX: (323) 862-8738.
www.paramount.com www.nbcuni.com
PRESIDENT, PARAMOUNT DIGITAL ENTERTAINMENT
Thomas Lesinski

SONY PICTURES ENTERTAINMENT, INC.

9050 W., Washington Blvd., Culver City, CA 90232.
TEL: (310) 840-8000. FAX: (310) 840-8100.
www.imageworks.com
PRESIDENT SONY PICTURES DIGITAL PRODUCTIONS
Bob Osher

TWENTIETH CENTURY FOX

10201 West Pico Blvd., Bldg. 100, 3220, Los Angeles, CA 90035. TEL: (310) 277-2211. FAX: (310) 203-1558.
EXECUTIVE V.P., DIGITAL EXHIBITION & SPECIAL PROJECTS
Julian Levin

WARNER BROS. STUDIOS

4000 Warner Blvd., Burbank, CA. 91522-0001.
TEL: (818) 954-6000. www.warnerbros.com

PRESIDENT OF DIGITAL DISTRIBUTION
Thomas Gewecke

RESOURCES

AMERICAN FILM INSTITUTE
(Advancing and preserving the art of the moving image)
2021 N. Western Ave., Los Angeles, CA 90027-1657.
TEL: (323) 856-7600. FAX: (323) 467-4578. www.afi.com
CONTACT
Kelly Dorsey

AMERICAN SOCIETY OF CINEMATOGRAPHERS
1782 N. Orange Dr., Hollywood, CA 90028.
TEL: (800) 448-0145, (323) 969-4333. FAX: (323) 882-6391.
email: office@theasc.com www.theasc.com
PRESIDENT
Michael Goi, ASC
VICE PRESIDENT
Richard Crudo, ASC

CREATIVEPLANET
(Project management software and entertainment information databases)
810 7th Ave., 27th Fl., New York, NY 10019.
TEL: (212) 378-0400. www.creativeplanet.com
EDITORIAL DIRECTOR
Cristina Clapp - (213) 228-0381 cclapp@nbmedia.com

DIGITAL CINEMA CONSORTIUM
(Japanese consortium of leading digital cinema interests)
Pacific Interface, 5351 Hilltop Crescent, Oakland, CA 94618.
TEL: (510) 547-2758. FAX: (510) 547-1726.

DIGITAL CINEMA INITIATIVES, LLC
6834 Hollywood Blvd., Ste. 500, Hollywood, CA 90028.
TEL: (323) 769-2880. FAX: (323) 769-2885.
email: dci.info@dcimovies.com www.dcimovies.com
CONTACT
Don Tannenbaum

Joint venture of Disney, Fox, Paramount, Sony Pictures Entertainment, Universal and Warner Bros. Studios. DCI's primary purpose is to establish and document voluntary specifications for an open architecture for digital cinema that ensures a uniform and high level of technical performance, reliability and quality control.

EASTMAN KODAK
(Filmmaker services)
Entertainment Imaging, 6700 Santa Monica Blvd., Los Angeles, CA 90038-1203. TEL: (323) 464-6131.
FAX: (323) 468-1568, (323) 468-2124.

New York: 360 West 31st St., New York, N Y 10001-2727.
TEL: (212) 631-3400. FAX: (212) 631-3470.
www.kodak.com/go/motion

ENTERTAINMENT TECHNOLOGY CENTER (ETC)
(Digital cinema lab)
509 W. 29th St., Los Angeles, CA 90007. TEL: (213) 743-1600.
FAX: (213) 743-1803. email: info@etcenter.org
www.etcenter.org

Mail: Entertainment Technology Center at USC, 509 West 29th St., Los Angeles, CA 90089-0520
EXECUTIVE DIRECTOR
David Wertheimer - (213) 743-1600

EXPRESSION COLLEGE FOR DIGITAL ARTS
(Education)
6601 Shellmound St., Emeryville, CA 94608.
TEL: (877) 833-8800, (510) 654-2934. FAX: (510) 658-3414.
www.expression.edu/contact_us

FINAL DRAFT, INC.
(Scriptwriting software)
26707 W. Agoura Rd., Ste. 205, Calabasas, CA 91302.
TEL: (888) 320-7555 (US), (818) 906-8930 (Intl).
FAX: (818) 995-4422. email: sales@finaldraft.com
www.finaldraft.com

FRANCE TELECOM
(Digital cinema research facility)
1270 Ave. of the Americas, New York, NY 10020-1700.
TEL: 0 (800) 364-775, (212) 332-2100. FAX: (212) 245-8605.
email: webmaster@ftna.com www.francetelecom.com

ICA CREATIVE
2452 Black Rock Tpke., Ste., 11 Fairfield, CT 06825-2400.
TEL: (800) 835-9292 ext. 2, (203) 372-4443.
FAX: (203) 372-4445. www.ica-online.com
CONTACT
Jon Lewis - Jon@ICACreative.com

Freelance and full-time staffing for broadcast designers, animators, 3D artists, web designers, video editors, FX compositors, camera crews and others.

THE LOS ANGELES FILM SCHOOL
(Digital filmmaking facilities)
6363 W. Sunset Blvd., #500, Los Angeles, CA 90028-7317.
TEL: (877) 952-3456, (323) 860-0789. FAX: (323) 634-0044.
www.lafilm.com

MOTION PICTURE ASSOCIATION OF AMERICA, INC.
(Trade association)
Office of the Chairman and CEO: 1600 Eye St., NW, Washington, DC 20006. TEL: (202) 293-1966.
FAX: (202) 296 7410. www.mpaa.org

CA: 15301 Ventura Blvd., Bldg. E, Sherman Oaks, CA 91403.
TEL: (818) 995-6600. FAX: (818) 285-4403.

NATO (NATIONAL ASSOCIATION OF THEATRE OWNERS)
(Theatre owner's international trade association)
750 First St., NE, Ste. 1130, Washington, DC 20002.
TEL: (202) 962-0054. FAX: (202) 962-0370.
email: nato@natodc.com www.natoonline.org
PRESIDENT & CEO
John Fithian
EXECUTIVE DIRECTOR
Kathy Conroy
DIRECTOR OF MEDIA & RESEARCH AND CALIFORNIA OPERATIONS CHIEF
Patrick Corcoran
INDUSTRY ISSUES LIAISON
Brigitte Buehlman

NIST (NATIONAL INSTITUTE OF STANDARDS & TECHNOLOGY)
(Standards-setting body)
NIST, 100 Bureau Dr., Stop 1070, Gaithersburg, MD 20899-1070. TEL: (301) 975-6478, TTY: (301) 975-8295.
email: inquiries@nist.gov www.nist.gov
CONTACT
Charles Fenimore - fenimore@nist.gov

PRODUCTIONHUB
(Online production guide/search engine)
1809 E. Winter Park Rd., Orlando, FL 32803.
TEL: (877) 629-4122, (407) 629-4122. FAX: (407) 629-8884.
www.productionhub.com
CEO
John Pokorny - jpokorny@productionhub.com

QP MEDIA, INC.
(Digital cinema integration and services)
64 Wintergreen Ln., Groton, MA 01450. TEL: (978) 448-0272.
FAX: (978) 448-9325. email: info@qpmedia.com
www.qpmedia.com
PRESIDENT
William J. Quigley

SMPTE (SOCIETY OF MOTION PICTURE & TELEVISION ENGINEERS)
(International technical society)
3 Barker Ave., 5th Flr., White Plains, NY 10601.
TEL: (914) 761-1100. FAX: (914) 761-3115.
email: smpte@smpte.org www.smpte.org
DIRECTOR OF OPERATIONS
Sally-Ann D'Amato - ext. 4965
DIRECTOR, ENGINEERING & STANDARDS
Peter Symes - ext. 4961

VISIONBOX MEDIA GROUP
(Digital production/consulting)
3272 Motor Ave., Ste. G, Los Angeles, CA 90034.
TEL: (310) 204-4686. FAX: (310) 204-4603.
email: questions@visionboxmedia.com
www.visionboxmedia.com
CEO/PRODUCER
John Bard Manulis
DIRECTOR OPERATIONS AND POST-PRODUCTION
Bill Newcomb

VISUAL EFFECTS SOCIETY
5535 Balboa Blvd., Ste. 205, Encino, CA 91316-1544.
TEL: (818) 981-7861. FAX: (818) 981-0179.
www.visualeffectssociety.com
EXECUTIVE DIRECTOR
Eric Roth
DIRECTOR OF OPERATIONS
Brent Armstrong
DIRECTOR OF DEVELOPMENT
Robert Morgenroth

Digital Cinema Equipment & Services

DIGITAL CINEMA SERVERS

AVICA TECHNOLOGY

(Entered into an exclusive licensing agreement with DTS, 2010)
1201 Olympic Blvd., Santa Monica, CA 90404.
TEL: (800) 706-0077 ext. 145, (310) 450-9090 ext. 145.
FAX: (310) 450-5353. email: contact@avicatech.com
sales@avicatech.com www.avicatech.com

Compressed and uncompressed digital storage for production. Has exclusive licensing agreement with DTS.

AVID TECHNOLOGY, INC.

75 Network Drive, Burlington, MA 01803. TEL: (978) 640-6789. FAX: (978) 640-3366. www.avid.com

Los Angeles: 101 South First St., Ste. 200, Burbank, CA 91502. TEL: (818) 557-2520. FAX: (818) 557-2558.

New York: 575 Lexington Ave., 14th Fl., New York, NY 10022. TEL: (212) 983-2424. FAX: (212) 983-8718, (212) 983 9770.
CHAIRMAN/CEO/PRESIDENT
Gary Greenfield
VP/CUSTOMER SUCCESS
Beth Martinko

Pluto Technologies server. See website for additional offices. Digidesign, M-Audio, Pinnacle Systems, Sibelius, Softimage, and Sundance Digital are trademarks or registered trademarks of Avid Technology, Inc. or its subsidiaries.

DIGITAL VISION

U.S. West Coast: Avid Technology, Inc.: 101 South First St., Ste. 200, Burbank, CA 91502. TEL: (818) 557-2520. FAX: (818) 557-2558.

London: Avid Technology Europe, Ltd.: 3rd Fl., Swan House, 52 Poland Street, London W1F 7NH, UK.
TEL: +44 207-534-2800. FAX: +44 207-534-2801.
email: inf@digitalvision.uk www.digitalvision.uk
CTO
Simon Cuff
V.P. WORLDWIDE SALES
Kelvin Bolah

EVS DIGITAL CINEMA

Belgium: Liege Science Park, 16 Rue Bois Saint-Jean, B-4102 Ougree, Belgium. TEL: +32 4 361 7000.
FAX: +32 4 391 7099. email: marketing@evs.tv
sales@evs.tv support@evs.tv corpcom@evs.tv

U.S. East Coast: 9 Law Dr., Ste. 200, Fairfield, NJ 07004. TEL: (973) 575-7811. FAX: (973) 575-7812. www.usa@evs.tv

U.S. West Coast: 101 South First St., Ste., 404, Burbank, CA 91504. www.usa@evs.tv

GRASS VALLEY GROUP

(A subsidiary of Thomson. MPEG Stream Servers)
Worldwide Headquarters: 400 Providence Mine Road, Nevada City, CA 95959. TEL: (530) 478-3000. FAX: (530) 478-3166.

U.S. West Coast Sales Office: 2255 North Ontario St., Ste. 150, Burbank, CA 91504. TEL: (818) 729-7706.
FAX: (818) 729-7777.
us.northwest.systems.sales@thomson.net
www.thomsongrassvalley.com

U.S. East Coast Sales Office: 535 E. Crescent Ave., Ramsey, NJ 07446. TEL: (201) 390-1778. FAX: (201) 818-4002.
www.thomsongrassvalley.com

KODAK DIGITAL CINEMA

6700 Santa Monica Blvd., Los Angeles, CA 90038-1203.
TEL: (323) 464-6131. FAX: (323) 468-1568, (323) 468-2124.

360 West 31st St., New York, NY 10001-2727.
TEL: (800) 621- 3456, (212) 631-3400. FAX: (212) 631-3470.

NEC CORPORATION OF AMERICA

4111 W. Alameda Ave., Burbank, CA 91505. www.necam.com
TEL: (818) 556-2888, SALES: (818) 557-2500, TECH SUPPORT: (866) 632-6431.
email: digital.cinema@necam.com
email: cinema.support@necam.com
GENERAL MANAGER, DIGITAL CINEMA DIVISION
Lourdes Wojtecki - (214) 262-3722
lourdes.wojtecki@necam.com

Digital cinema and post-house projectors: comprhensive in-theatre and in-lobby advertising solutions; alternative content processors; digital cinema servers.

QUVIS, INC.

(Provider of Hi fidelity high resolution motion imaging technology)
2921 S.W. Wanamaker Dr., Ste. 107, Topeka, KS 66614.
TEL: (800) 554-8116, (785) 272-3656. FAX: (785) 272-3657.
email: support@quvis.com www.quvis.com

Provides servers, recorders, players, encoding, real time mastering, recording of content SD-4K for production, post prod. digital dailies, digital exhibition.

TECHNICOLOR

(A Thomson Company)
2233 N. Ontario St., Ste. 300, Burbank, CA 91504.
TEL: (818) 260-3800. FAX: (818) 260-4007.
email: info@technicolor.com www.technicolor.com

Creative Services: 110 Leroy St., New York, NY 10014.
TEL: 212) 609-9400. FAX: (212) 609-9450.
CHAIRMAN/CEO
Frederic Rose
TECHNOLOGY BUSINESS GROUP
Béatrix de Russé
STRATEGY, TECHNOLOGY & MARKETING
Vince Pizzica
TECHNICOLOR BUSINESS GROUP
Lanny Raimondo
THOMSON CONNECT AND BUSINESS OPERATIONS
Andrew Levido

Company provides full menu of film and digital production services to assist: film production, theatrical services, home entertainment, television broadcasting, out-of-home media, commercials and games. See website for comprehensive list of services and facilities.

DIGITAL EXHIBITORS

AMC ENTERTAINMENT, INC.

AMC Entertainment, Inc., P. O. Box 725489, Atlanta, GA 31139-9923. TEL: (877) 262-4450. www.amctheatres.com

BROADWAY WORLDWIDE, INC.

(Parent of Broadway Television Network)
268 West 44th St., 3rd. Fl., New York, NY 10036.
TEL: (212) 471-6060. FAX: (212) 471-6088.
email: BMB@BroadwayTV.com www.broadwayonline.com
CEO
Bruce Brandwen - BMB@BroadwayTV.com

A leader in the high definition, surround-sound production and worldwide distribution of Broadway musicals captured live-in-performance for digital cinema, pay-per-view (PPV) systems, DVD, Internet video on demand, cable and broadcast television.

EMERGING PICTURES CORPORATION

245 West 55th St., 4th Flr., New York, NY 10019.
TEL: (212) 245-6767. FAX: (212) 202-4984.
www.emergingpictures.com
MANAGING PARTNER
Barry Rebo - brebo@emergingpictures.com
MANAGING PARTNER
Ira Deutchman - ira@emergingpictures.com
EXECUTIVE V.P. CFO
W. Timothy Wallace
V.P. OF DISTRIBUTION
Josh Green

Emerging Pictures Corporation's theatrical exhibition network is called Emerging Cinemas. Company operates digital cinema theatres within performing arts venues.

ENTERPRISE BROADCASTING CORP.

(Special-purpose digital cinema theatres)
5900 Butler Ln., Scotts Valley, CA 95066. TEL: (831) 461-9000.
FAX: (831) 461-5700. email: info@ebc.cc
FOUNDER/CEO
Tom Wade

FORMAN HD SCREENING ROOM

(HD screening room)
300 West 23rd St., New York, NY 10011. TEL: (212) 633-9960.
FAX: (212) 807-0121. www.screeningroom.com
CONTACT
Mark Forman - mark@screeningroom.com

LANDMARK THEATRES

(Theatre circuit with digital cinema locations)
2222 S. Barrington Ave., Los Angeles, CA 90064-1297.

TEL: (310) 473-6701. FAX: (310) 473-8622.
www.landmarktheatres.com

REGAL ENTERTAINMENT GROUP

(Adding digital projectors, high-speed data networking equipment and satellite links to majority of its locations)
7132 Regal Ln., Knoxville, TN 37918. TEL: (865) 922-1123, Customer Relations: (877) 835-5734. FAX: (865) 922-3188.
www.regalcinemas.com

EXHIBITOR PRODUCTS & SERVICES

THE BIGGER PICTURE

21045 Califa, Ste. 101, Woodland Hills, CA 91367.
TEL: (818) 587-4880. FAX: (818) 587-4890.
www.thebiggerpicture.us
FOUNDER/PRESIDENT
Jonathan Dern - jdern@thebiggerpicture.us
CO-CEO/ & CO-PRESIDENT (BP/KTF, LLC)
Greg Rutkowski

An AccessIT Company. Alternative content distribution division offering channels of programming including opera, kidtoons, faith based concerts, sports and anime.

CINEDIGM DIGITAL CINEMA CORP.

(Formerly Access Integrated Technologies, Inc. Company announced name change Nov. 2008)
Headquarters: 55 Madison Ave., Ste. 300, Morristown, NJ 07960. TEL: (973) 290-0080. FAX: (973) 290-0081.
email: info@cinedigm.com www.cinedigm.com

Digital Cinema Offices: 6255 Sunset Blvd., Ste. 1025, Hollywood, CA 90028. TEL: (323) 463-2144.
FAX: (323) 463-1319.
CHAIRMAN & CEO
Bud Mayo
PRESIDENT, MEDIA SERVICES GROUP
Chuck Goldwater
PRESIDENT & COO, SOFTWARE DIVISION
Jim Miller
PRESIDENT, COO, DIGITAL MEDIA SERVICES DIVISION
Gerd Jakuszeit
PRESIDENT & COO, UNIQUE SCREEN MEDIA, A CINEDIGM COMPANY
William A. McGlamery
PRESIDENT, PRESIDENT, CINEDIGM ENTERTAIMENT GROUP
Jonathan Dern
DIRECTOR, CORPORATE COMMUNICATIONS
Suzanne Moore - (973) 290-0056 ext. 181
smoore@cinedigm.com

Cinedigm provides digital cinema networked services along with its Library Management Server(R) and Theatre Command Center(R) to enable theatres across the United States to play digital showings of Hollywood features. The company's 24/7 satellite operations delivers feature movies, alternative content advertising, and pre-show entertainment, including live 2-D and 3-D events through its CineLive(R) satellite network, expanding box office sales and developing new ways to attract incremental revenues. Through its alternative content distribution division, the company offers channels of programming including Opera, Kidtoons, Faith-based Concerts, Sports and Anime.

ELECTRONIC THEATRE CONTROLS (ETC)

3031 Pleasant View Rd., P.O. Box 620979, Middleton, WI 53562-4809. TEL: (800) 688-4116, (608) 831-4116.
FAX: (608) 836-1736. email: mail@etcconnect.com
www.etcconnect.com
CEO
Fred Foster
PRESIDENT
Dick Titus
V.P. PROFESSIONAL SERVICES
Sarah Danke
V. P. WORLDWIDE SALES
Mark Vassallo

Lighting controls, consoles, and fixtures, dimming equipment and power distribution components with worldwide offices. See website for more information.

ENTERTAINMENT SUPPLY & TECHNOLOGIES, LLC.

4971 Van Dyke Rd., Lutz, FL 33558. TEL:(813) 960-1646.
FAX: (813) 961-7209. www.ensutec.com
PRESIDENT/CEO
Barney Bailey
V.P.
Ron Eiben - reiben@ensutec.com

Provides digital projection equipment, 35mm projection equipment, Xenon lamps, sound, seating, aisle lighting, crowd control ropes and posts, poster cases, screens, frames, screen drapes, acoustical panels, concession & ticketing casework, concession equipment, 2-way radios, parts, supplies, janitorial equipment, turn-key project management, installations, defixturing service, design, planning and drafting services.

NATIONAL CINEMEDIA, INC.

(In theatre advertising services)
9110 E. Nichols Ave., Ste. 200, Centennial, CO 80112-3405.
TEL: (800) 828-2828, (303) 792-3600. Advertising & Promotions: (800) 727-3361. FAX: (303) 792-8800.
email: customerservice@ncm.co www.nationalcinemedia.com
CHAIRMAN/PRESIDENT & CEO
Kurt C. Hall
PRESIDENT, SALES & MARKETING
Clifford E. Marks
EXEC. V.P. & CHIEF TECHNOLOGY & OPERATIONS OFFICER (CO)
Tom C. Galley
EXECUTIVE V.P./CFO
Gary W. Ferrera

NY: 122 E. 42nd St., Ste. 511, New York, NY 10168-0599.
TEL: (212) 931-8100. FAX: (212) 931-8135.
SENIOR V.P., EAST COAST SALES
Beth Hoff - (212) 931-8101 beth.hoff@ncm.com

CA: 21700 Oxnard St., Ste.,640, Woodland Hills, CA 91367.
TEL: (818) 227-3720. FAX: (818) 227-3759.
SENIOR V.P., WEST COAST SALES
Doug Gellerman - (818) 227-3737 doug.gellerman@ncm.com

IL: 500 N. Michigan Ave., Ste. 1802, Chicago, IL 60611.
TEL: (312) 755-9773. FAX: (312) 755-9844.
SENIOR V.P. CENTRAL DIVISION SALES
Pam Biederman - (312) 245-5265 pam.biederman@ncm.com

San Francisco: 450 Mission Street, 5th Fl., San Francisco, CA 94105. TEL: (415) 359-2826. FAX: (415) 359-2626.
ACCOUNT DIRECTOR
Paige McBeath - (415) 490-4176 paige.mcbeath@ncm.com

PROJECTION & DISPLAY

AMERICAN CINEMA EQUIPMENT, INC.

(Projection & sound equipment, seats, digital projection)
1927 N. Argyle St., Portland, OR 97217-6752.
TEL: (800) 956-6589, (503) 285-7015. FAX: (503) 285-6765.
email: info@cinequip.com www.cinequip.com
PRESIDENT/CEO
Scott R. Hicks
V.P., SALES & MARKETING
Doug Sabin - doug@cinequip.com

ATLAS SPECIALTY LIGHTING

(Entertainment lighting; Xenon lighting and projection equipment)
Headquarters/Intl. Sales: 1111 W. 22nd St., Hialeah, FL 33010.
TEL: (305) 885-8941. sales@asltg.com www.asltg.com

Domestic Sales: 7304 N. Florida Ave., Tampa, FL 33604-4838.
TEL: (813) 238-6481. FAX: (813) 238-6656.
GENERAL MANAGER
Ralph Felten, Jr. - rfelten@asltg2.com
HEAD OF PROJECTION DESIGN
Bob Ray - sales@asltg.com

Supplies complete projection equipment, digital sound systems, digital cinema equipment.

BARCO PROJECTION SYSTEMS

(Leading manufacturer of digital cinema projection systems)
Headquarters: Barco N.V., Pres. Kennedypark 35, 8500 Kortrijk, Belgium. TEL: +32 56 233211. FAX: +32 56 26 22 62.
CHAIRMAN
Herman Daems
PRESIDENT/CEO
Eric Van Zele
PRESIDENT MEDIA/ENTERTAINMENT & SIMULATION DIVISION
Filip Pintelon

U.S.: 11101-A Trade Center Dr., Rancho Cordova, CA 95670.
TEL: (916) 859-2500. FAX: (916) 859-2515.
Tech Support: (866) 469-8036. www.barco.com
PRESIDENT NORTH AMERICA
Dave Scott

High performance large-screen display systems for theatrical presentations of digital content; screen advertising displays; post production & outdoor display applications.

CHRISTIE DIGITAL SYSTEMS U.S.A., INC.

(DLP® projectors and on-screen advertising solutions)
10550 Camden Dr., Cypress, CA 90630.
TEL: Support: (800) 221-8025, (714) 236-8610.
FAX: (714) 503-3375. www.christiedigital.com
PRESIDENT AND COO
Gerry Remers
V.P., ENTERTAINMENT SOLUTIONS
Craig Sholder

DA-LITE SCREEN CO.

(Projection screens)
3100 N. Detroit St., P.O. Box 137, Warsaw, IN. 46581-0137.

TEL: (800) 622-3737, (574) 267-8101. FAX: (877) 325-4832, (574) 267-7804. email: info@da-lite.com www.da-lite.com
V.P. SALES
Blake Brubaker - bbrubaker@da-lite.com
SALES CONSULTANT
Ken Smith - ksmith@da-lite.com
Andre White - awhite@da-lite.com

DFE TECHNOLOGIES

7536 Tyrone Ave., Unit H, Van Nuys, CA 91405.
TEL: (323) 469-8400. FAX: (323) 469-7500.
email: info@dfetechnologies.com
marketing@dfetechnologies.com
COO
Jeff Hopkins
V.P.
Matthew Wimmers

The DFE Network Port, DFE BackPac and DFE SmartPac units facilitate the distribution of digital content to theatres.

DIGITAL PROJECTION, INC.

(Ultra bright, electronic cinema projection systems for large format video data, or HDTV imagery in large venues)
55 Chastain Rd., NW, Ste. 115, Kennesaw, GA 30144.
TEL: (770) 420-1350. FAX: (770) 420-1360.
www.digitalprojection.com
CUSTOMER SERVICE MANAGER
Michelle Bowles - mbowles@digitalprojection.com

DIGITAL MEDIA SYSTEMS, INC.

248 W. 35th St., Ste., 1203, New York, NY 10001.
TEL: (212) 643-4000. FAX: (212) 643-4100.
email: info@dmediainc.com www.dmediainc.com
OWNER
Gregg V. Paliotta - GreggP@Dmediainc.com

Digital Cinema, 35mm projection, sound, sales, service and rentals, special screenings for the motion picture industry. Advancement of D-Cinema and 3D technologies.

ENTERTAINMENT SUPPLY & TECHNOLOGIES, LLC.

4971 Van Dyke Rd., Lutz, FL 33558. TEL:(813) 960-1646.
FAX: (813) 961-7209. FAX: (813) 961-7209. www.ensutec.com
PRESIDENT/CEO
Barney Bailey
V.P.
Ron Eiben - reiben@ensutec.com

Provides digital projection equipment, 35mm projection equipment, Xenon lamps, sound, seating, aisle lighting, crowd control ropes and posts, poster cases, screens, frames, screen drapes, acoustical panels, concession & ticketing casework, concession equipment, 2-way radios, parts, supplies, janitorial equipment, turn-key project management, installations, defixturing service, design, planning and drafting services.

HARKNESS SCREENS

(All types of screens & frames, including outdoor air-screens)
10 Harkness Blvd., Fredericksburg, VA 22401-7085.
TEL: (540) 370-1590. FAX: (540) 370-1592.
email: infousa@harkness-screens.com
www.harknesshall.com
V.P. SALES & Marketing
Dennis Pacelli

HOLLYWOOD THEATRE EQUIPMENT, INC.

(Dealer for all 35mm & 70mm projection & sound equipment)
1941 N. 66th Ave., Hollywood, FL 33024. TEL: (954) 920-2832.
FAX: (954) 986-6914. email: HWDTHEATRE@aol.com
SALES
Don Gallagher

JVC

(Digital Cinema Projectors)
1700 Valley Rd., Wayne, NJ 07470. TEL: (800) 247-3608, (973) 317-5000. FAX: (973) 317-5030. email: proinfo@jvc.com
www.jvc.com/pro
PRESIDENT/CEO
Kirk Hirota

KODAK DIGITAL CINEMA

(Kodak Digital Cinema uses JVC D-ILM technology)
6700 Santa Monica Blvd., Los Angeles, CA 90038-1203.
TEL: 800-621-3456, (323) 464-6131. FAX: (323) 468-1568, (323) 468-2124. www.kodak.com/go/dcinema

New York: 360 W. 31st. St., NY, New York 10001-2727.
TEL: (212) 631-3400. FAX: (212) 631-3470.

LESNA, INC.

(Projection screens)
8487 8th Ave., Montreal, Quebec H1Z 2X2. Canada.
TEL: (514) 721-6914. FAX: (514) 721-7188.
email: info@lesna.com www.lesna.com
OWNER
Noel Anfousse - noel@lesna.com
PROJECT MANAGER
Valérie Lavoie - support@lesna.com

MARCEL DESROCHERS, INC. (MDI)

(Acquired by Ballantyne of Omaha, Inc. 2009. Specialty "silver" screens required for certain 3-D cinema technologies including the Real D 3-D technology)
1440 Raoul-Charrette, Joliette, Quebec J6E 8S7. Canada.
TEL: (877) 755-3795, (450) 755-3795. FAX: (450) 755-3122.
email: sales@strong-mdicinema.com www.mdicinema.com
EXECUTIVE V.P.
Benoit Mailloux
TECHNICAL SUPPORT
Daniel Conroy

MIRANDA TECHNOLOGIES, INC.

(Image processing for display)
3499 Douglas-B, Floreani, Montreal, Quebec, H4S 2C6, Canada. TEL: (514) 333-2111. FAX: (514) 333-9828.
www.miranda.com
SENIOR V.P. SALES & MARKETING
Spiro Plagakis - spiro.plagakis@miranda.com

U.S.: 125 Crown Point Ct., Grass Valley, CA 95945..
TEL: (973) 379-0089. FAX: (973) 379-1953.
email: ussales@miranda.com
REGIONAL SALES DIRECTOR (WEST)
John McCluskey - (949) 302-2572
john.mccluskey@miranda.com

NEC TECHNOLOGIES, INC.

(HD cinema system)
1250 N. Arlington Heights Rd., Ste. 500, Itasca, IL 60143-1248.
TEL: (800) 632-4636, (630) 775-7900. FAX: (630) 775-7901.
PRESIDENT/CEO
Takayuki Okada
SENIOR VICE PRESIDENT/PRESIDENT, NEC UNIFIED SOLUTIONS
Jeff Kane

PANASONIC

(TI DLP based projectors)
3330 Cahuenga Blvd. W., Los Angeles, CA 90068.
TEL: (800) 528-8601, (323) 436-3500.
www.panasonic.com/hdcinema

PHILIPS, LTI

13700 Live Oaks Ave., Baldwin Park, CA 91706.
TEL: (626) 480-0755. FAX: (626) 480-0855. www.philips.com
GLOBAL SALES MANAGER
Ana Simonian
CINEMA SALES MANAGER NORTH AMERICA
Bob Simminger - bob.simminger@philips.com

Philips LTI is a specialty discharge lamp manufacturer. Products include Xenon lamps for cinema, digital cinema and stage & studio lighting.

SONY BROADCAST & PROFESSIONAL CO.

(4K Digital Cinema)
6080 Center Dr., Los Angeles, CA 90025. TEL: (201) 930-1000.
FAX: (201) 930-4752. www. sony.com/4k
PRESIDENT/BROADCAST AND BUSINESS SOULUTIONS
John Scarcella
V.P. DIGITAL CINEMA
Gary Johns - gary.johns@am.sony.com
GENERAL MANAGER, DIGITAL PRODUCTION SYSTEMS
Andrew Stucker
DIGITAL CINEMA PRODUCT MANAGER
Steve Banaszek

Sony electronics' 4K digital cinema technology offers exhibitors a complete "plug and play" solution. The projector's 4K resolution (approx. 8.8 million pixels) delivers four times the resolutions of today's high-resolution tv's. 4K projectors are manufactured, sold and serviced by Sony.

STEWART FILMSCREEN CORPORATION

(Projection screens)
1161 W. Sepulveda Blvd., Torrance, CA 90502-2737.
TEL: (800) 762-4999, (310) 784-5300. FAX: (310) 326-6870.
email: comments@stewartfilm.com www.stewartfilm.com
EXECUTIVE VICE PRESIDENT
Don Stewart

European Office: Mileparken 29, 2730 Herlev, Denmark.
TEL: +45 3648 2204. FAX: +45 3648 2299.
email: info@stewartfilm-europe.com

STRONG CINEMA PRODUCTS

(A Ballantyne of Omaha Company. Manufacturer of screens and frames)
4350 McKinley St., Omaha, NE 68112. TEL: (402) 453-4444.
FAX: (402) 453-7238.
PRESIDENT/CEO
John P. Wilmers
V.P. LIGHTING
P.L. Wong
V.P. TECHNICAL SERVICES
Pat Moore

Offers 35mm & 70 mm film projection equipment, digital systems solutions, dedicated to design, installation and service of the complete range of film and digital systems. Also lighting products and services that enhance visual experience for audiences worldwide.

TEXAS INSTRUMENTS DLP PRODUCTS

(DLP cinema "black chip" projection technologies)
6550 Chase Oaks Blvd., Plano, TX 75023.
TEL: (214) 567-6839. FAX: (214) 567-3816. www.dlp.com
CHAIRMAN/PRESIDENT/CEO
Rich Templeton

YEM ELETEX, INC.

(Image processing for display. Yem, Inc. merged with Eletex, Inc., 2007)
8-2-56 Nanko Higashi, Suminoe-ku, Osaka-shi, Osaka, 559-0031 Japan. TEL: +81 6 6612 3111. www.yemeletex.co.jp
PRESIDENT/CEO
Shinichiro Nakahara

THEATRE AUDIO SPEAKERS/SYSTEMS

BGW SYSTEMS

(An Amplifier Technologies, Inc. company. Power amplifiers)
1749 Chapin Rd., Montebello, CA 90640. TEL: (323) 278-0001.
FAX: (323) 278-0083. email: info@bgw.com www.bgw.com
DIRECTOR, BGW OPERATIONS
Angie Masincup-Scott - angie@bgw.com

CROWN INTERNATIONAL

(Manufacturer of professional audio power amplifiers. Acquired by Harman International)
1718 W. Mishawaka Rd., Elkhart, IN 46517. P.O. Box 1000, Elkhart, IN 46515. TEL: (800) 342-6939, (219) 294-8200.
FAX: (219) 294-8301.
Customer Service: customerservice@harman.com
Support: support@iqaudiosystems.com www.crownintl.com
SENIOR V.P./R&D
Gerald Stanley

DOLBY LABORATORIES, INC.

(Develops & delivers products & technologies that make the entertainment experience more realistic)
100 Potrero Ave., San Francisco, CA 94103-4886.
TEL: (415) 558-0200. FAX: (415) 863-1373. www.dolby.com

CA: 3601 West Alameda Ave., Burbank, CA 91505-5300.
TEL: (818) 823-2800. FAX: (818) 557-0890.

CA: 100 Potrero Ave., San Francisco, CA 94103-4886.

TEL: (415) 558-0200. FAX: (415) 863-1373.

CA: 999 Brannan St., San Francisco, CA 91403-4938.
TEL: (415) 645-5000. FAX: (415) 645-4000.

CA: 475 Brannen St., Ste. 300, San Francisco, CA 94107-5420.
TEL: (415) 357-7000. FAX: (415) 645-4000.

CA: 3975 Freedom Circle, 4th Fl., Santa Clara, CA 95054.
TEL: (408) 330-3300. FAX: (408) 330-3200.

CA: Office/Factory: 175 S. Hill Dr., Brisbane, CA 94005-1272.
TEL: (415) 715-2500. FAX: (415) 715-2570.

PA: 1040 Stony Hill Rd., Yardley, PA 19067-5509.
TEL: (267) 757-2300. FAX: (267) 757-2301.

NY: 1350 Avenue of the Americas, 20th Fl., New York, NY, 10019-4703. TEL: (212) 767-1700. FAX: (212) 767-1705.

UK: Wootton Bassett, Wiltshire SN4 8QJ, England.
TEL: +44 1793 842100. FAX: +44 1793 842101.

Canada: 2985 Virtual Way, Bldg. 3, Ground Fl., Ste., 150, Vancouver, BC, V5M 4X7, Canada. TEL: (604) 216-0020.
FAX: (604) 215-6900.
CHAIRMAN/FOUNDER
Ray Dolby
PRESIDENT/CEO
Kevin Yeaman
SENIOR V.P., MANAGING DIRECTOR (UK)
David Watts
SENIOR V.P. SALES
J. Stuart Mitchell
SENIOR MARKETING DIRECTOR, DOLBY DIGITAL CINEMA
Page Haun
SENIOR DIRECTOR, PRODUCTION SERVICES
Bill Allen
SENIOR DIRECTOR, CINEMA SALES
Guy Hawley
V.P./STRATEGIC SALES
Tony Spath
V.P. WORLDWIDE PRODUCTION SERVICES
David Gray
EXEC. V.P. PRODUCTS & TECHNOLOGIES
Michael Rockwell

DTS, INC.

(Expert provider of digital entertainment services for content owners and cinema exhibitors worldwide)
Corporate Headquarters: 5220 Las Virgenes Rd., Calabasas, CA 91302. TEL: (818) 436-1000. FAX: Requested Not to be contacted. email: cinemainfo@dtsonline.com
www.dtsonline.com

Canada: DTS Canada ULC: 375 Water St. Ste., 638, Vancouver, BC V6B 5C6. TEL: (866) 466-1525,
(604) 605-1525. FAX: (604) 605-1521.

DTS (Asia) Limited: 2214-2215, Shell Tower, Times Square, Causeway Bay, Hong Kong. TEL: +852 3101-9361.
FAX: +852.3101.9559.

Japan: 4F Excel T.Y. Bldg., 1-16-13, Ebisu Minami, Shibuya-ku Tokyo, 150-0022, Japan. TEL: +81 3 5794 5288.
FAX: +81 3 5794 5266. www.dtstech.co.jp
CHAIRMAN/PRESIDENT & CEO
Jon Kirchner
SENIOR V.P., STRATEGY & BUSINESS DEVELOPMENT
Patrick Watson
EXECUTIVE V. P. FINANCE/CFO
Mel Flanigan
SENIOR V. P., RESEARCH & DEVELOPMENT & ENGINEERING
Rick Beaton
EXECUTIVE V. P. & COO
Brian Towne
CORPORATE VP AND PRESIDENT-JAPAN
Nao Ohtake

EASTERN ACOUSTICS WORKS

(designs to provide dynamic full-range audio throughout a huge venue, enhancing the overall entertainment experience)
1 Main St., Whitinsville, MA 01588. TEL: (800) 992-5013, (508) 234-6158. FAX: (800) 322-8251, (508) 234-8251.
www.eaw.com
FOUNDERS
Ken Berger, Kenton Forsythe

EDWARDS TECHNOLOGIES, INC.

(Founded in 1984, Edwards Technologies, Inc. (ETI) audio visual entertainment technology for theme parks, corporate headquarters, museums, libraries, casinos, restaurants, retail stores and entertainment venues worldwide)
139 Maryland St., El Segundo, CA 90245. TEL: (310) 536-7070.
FAX: (310) 322-1459. email: Support@ETIemail.com
www.edwardstechnologies.com
PRESIDENT & CEO
Brian Edwards - Brian.Edwards@ETIemail.com
PROJECT COORDINATOR
Dana Carsley - Dana.Carsley@ETIemail.com

HIGH PERFORMANCE STEREO

64 Bowen St., Newton, MA 02459-1820. TEL: (617) 244-1737.
FAX: (617) 244-1737. email: info@hps4000.com
www.hps4000.com
FOUNDER & PRESIDENT
John Allen

JBL PROFESSIONAL

8400 Balboa Blvd., Northridge, CA 91329.
TEL: (818) 894-8850. FAX: (818) 830-7801 (Sales).
FAX: (818) 830-7865 (Marketing). www.jblpro.com
PRESIDENT
John Carpanini
DIRECTOR CINEMA MARKETING
Chuck Goodsell - cgoodsell@harmon.com

KLIPSCH AUDIO TECHNOLOGIES

(Theatre sound & listening devices)
3502 Woodview Trace., Ste. 200, Indianapolis, IN 46268.
TEL: (800) 274-5547, (317) 860-8100. FAX: (317) 860-9178.
www.klipsch.com
CEO/CHAIRMAN
Fred Klipsch
VICE CHAIRMAN
Judy Klipsch
PRESIDENT & COO
Paul Jacobs
PRESIDENT, GLOBAL SALES
Dave Kelley
PRESIDENT GLOBAL OPERATIONS & KLIPSCH BRAND
Michael F. Klipsch

KRIX LOUDSPEAKERS PTY, LTD.

(designing and providing premium cinema loudspeaker systems since 1980 and is a major installation consultant and contractor within the Australian cinema industry and supplier of purpose built loudspeaker solutions for cinemas worldwide)
14 Chapman Rd., Hackham, 5163 SA, Australia.
Postal Address: P.O. Box 37, Hackham, 5163, SA, Australia.
TEL: 61 8 8384-3433. FAX: 61 8 8384-3419.
email: krix@krix.com.au www.krix.com.au

MARTIN AUDIO, LTD.

(Theatre sound & listening devices)
P.O. Box 33009, Waterloo, ON., N2T 2MG, Canada.
TEL: (519) 747-5853. FAX: (519) 747-3576.
email: infona@martin-audio.com www.martin-audio.com
DIRECTOR OF US OPERATIONS
Robert Hofkamp - rhofkamp@martin-audio.com

QSC AUDIO PRODUCTS, LLC.

(Amplifier, loudspeaker, networked audio, remote monitor and control manufacturer)
1665 MacArthur Blvd., Costa Mesa, CA 92626.
TEL: (800) 854-4079, (714) 754-6175. FAX: (714) 754-6174.
email: info@qscaudio.com www.qscaudio.com
DIRECTOR OF SALES, CINEMA
Francois Godfrey - FRANCOIS_GODFREY@qscaudio.com

SONY CINEMA PRODUCTS CORP.

(digital film sound format comprised of the SDDS soundtrack, optically printed on both edges of 35mm film, and SDDS playback hardware)
10950 Washington Blvd., Culver City, CA 90232-4026.
TEL: (310) 244-5777. FAX: (858) 942-3857. www.sdds.com
CONTACT
Nicole Ross - (858) 942-2624 nicole.ross@am.sony.com

TAD/PIONEER

(Audio Speakers)
12141 Mariners Way, Garden Grove, CA 92843.
TEL: (800) 897-8373, (714) 554-8520. www.tad-pioneer.com

THX, LTD.

(Custom engineered speakers for cinemas)
1600 Los Gamos Dr., Ste. 130, San Rafael, CA 94903-1806.
TEL: (415) 492-3900. FAX: (415) 492-3930.
email: cinema@thx.com www.thx.com
V.P. SALES
Robert Hewitt
DIRECTOR/CINEMA & STUDIO PROGRAMS
Andrew Poulai

The Exhibition Industry

THEATRE CIRCUITS

Theatre	Address	City	State	Zip	Screens

ALAMO DRAFTHOUSE CINEMA

8 theatres, 49 screens.
13809 Research Blvd., Ste. 735, Austin, TX 78750. TEL: (512) 219-7800. FAX: (512) 532-0820. www.drafthouse.com
CEO
John Martin

THEATRES

Theatre	Address	City	State	Zip	Screens
Alamo at the Ritz	320 E. 6th St.	Austin	TX	78701	2
Alamo Lake Creek	13729 Research Blvd./Lake Creek Shopping Center	Austin	TX	78750	7
Alamo Village	2700 W. Anderson Lane/Village Shopping Center	Austin	TX	78757	4
Alamo South Lamar	1120 S. Lamar	Austin	TX	78704	6
Alamo West Oaks	Westheimer & Hwy. 6/West Oaks Mall	Houston	TX	77082	6
Alamo Mason Park	531 S. Mason Rd.	Katy	TX	77450	7
Alamo Westlakes	1255 S.W. Loop 410/West Lakes Shopping Center	San Antonio	TX	78227	9
Alamo Winchester	181 Kernstown Commons Blvd.	Winchester	VA	22602	8

ALLEN THEATRES, INC.

14 theatres, 95 screens.
133 Wyatt Dr. Suite #3, Las Cruces, NM TEL: (575) 524-7933. FAX: (505) 326-2647. www.allentheaters.com
PRESIDENT/FILM BUYER
Larry F. Allen
VICE PRESIDENT/SECRETARY-TREASURER
Lane E. Allen

THEATRES

Theatre	Address	City	State	Zip	Screens
Fiesta Twin	23 W. Main	Cortez	CO	81321	2
Aviator 10	3199 N. White Sands	Alamogordo	NM	88310	10
Cinema 3	2322 W. Pierce	Carlsbad	NM	88220	3
North Plains	2809 N. Prince	Clovis	NM	88101	7
Allen 8	1819 20th St.	Farmington	NM	87401	8
Animas 10	4601 E. Main, Animas Shopping Mall	Farmington	NM	87402	10
Aztec 5	911 W. Aztec	Gallup	NM	87301	5
Red Rock 6	3711 Church Rock St.	Gallup	NM	87301	6
Eagle 7	1609 Joe Harvey Blvd.	Hobbs	NM	88240	7
Cineport 10	700 Telshor	Las Cruces	NM	88011	10
Telshor Cinemas 12	2811 N. Telshor Blvd.	Las Cruces	NM	88011	12
Video 4	1005 S. El Paseo	Las Cruces	NM	88011	4
Galaxy 8	4501 N. Main	Roswell	NM	88201	8
Sierra Cinema	721-D Mechum	Ruidoso	NM	88345	3

ALLIANCE ENTERTAINMENT/GREAT ESCAPE THEATRES

25 theatres, 291 screens.
300 Professional Court, Ste. 200, New Albany, IN 47150. TEL: (812) 945-4006. FAX: (812) 945-4076. www.greatescapetheatres.com
PRESIDENT & CEO
Anne Ragains
COO
Chance Ragains
CFO
Bill Leonhart
V.P, OPERATIONS
David Poland
V.P. FILM
Web Brainerd
V.P., CONSTRUCTION & DEVELOPMENT
Lee Turberville
DIRECTOR, OPERATIONS, EAST
Frank Mack
DIRECTOR, OPERATIONS, WEST
George Smith
IT DIRECTOR
Jamie Bowles
OPERATIONS ADMIN. MGR.
William Geltmaker

THEATRES

Theatre	Address	City	State	Zip	Screens
Hamilton Mill Great Escape 14	2160 Hamilton Mill Pkwy.	Dacula	GA	30019	14
McDonough Great Escape 16	115 Fosters Dr.	McDonough	GA	30253	16
Moline Great Escape 14	4101 38th St.	Moline	IL	61265	14
Bedford Great Escape 7	2929 Great Escape Dr.	Bedford	IN	47421	7
Madison Great Escape 6	744 Jefferson Ct.	Madison	IN	47250	6
New Albany Great Escape 16	300 Professional Ct., Ste. 100	New Albany	IN	47150	16
Noblesville Great Escape 10	10075 Town & Country Blvd.	Noblesville	IN	46060	10
River Falls Great Escape 12	951 Louis & Clark Pkwy.	Clarksville	IN	47219	12
Seymour Great Escape 8	357 Tanger Blvd., Ste. 401	Seymour	IN	47274	8
Bowling Green Great Escape 12	323 Great Escape Dr.	Bowling Green	KY	42101	12
Bowling Green Great Escape 10	2626 Scottsville Rd.	Bowling Green	KY	42101	10
Shelbyville Great Escape 8	Brighton Circle	Shelbyville	KY	40065	8
LaGrange Great Escape	410 S. First St.	LaGrange	KY	40031	8
Wilder Great Escape 14	103 Crossing Dr.	Wilder	KY	41076	14
O'Fallon Great Escape 14	900 Caledonia Dr.	O'Fallon	MO	63368	14
Gravois Bluffs	754 Gravois Bluffs Blvd.	Fenton	MO	63026	14
Omaha Great Escape 16	7740 Crowne Point Ave.	Omaha	NE	68134	16
Massillon Great Escape 12	175 Cherry St. N.E.	Massillon	OH	44646	12
Oxford Great Escape 4	10 N. Beech St.	Oxford	OH	45056	4

Theatre	Address	City	State	Zip	Screens
Lebanon Valley Great Escape 10	2200 Lebanon Valley Mall	Lebanon	PA	17042	10
Harrisburg Great Escape 14	3501 Paxton St.	Harrisburg	PA	17111	14
Williamsport Great Escape 12	965 Lycoming Mall Circle	Pennsdale	PA	17756	12
Simpsonville 14 IMAX	780 South St	Simpsonville	SC	29681	14
Clarksville Great Escape 16	1810 Tiny Town Rd.	Clarksville	TN	37042	16
Nitro Great Escape 12	12 JW Dr.	Nitro	WV	25143	12

AMC ENTERTAINMENT, INC.

367 US theatres, 5,038 US screens, 47 international theatres, 663 international screens.
Headquarters: 920 Main St., Kansas City, MO 64105. TEL: (816) 221-4000. FAX: (816) 480-4617. www.amctheatres.com
CHAIRMAN, CEO & PRESIDENT, AMC ENTERTAINMENT, INC.
Gerardo Lopez
EXECUTIVE V.P. & CFO, AMC ENTERTAINMENT, INC.
Craig R. Ramsey
EXECUTIVE V.P., NORTH AMERICA OPERATIONS, AMERICAN MULTI-CINEMA, INC.
John D. McDonald
EXECUTIVE V.P., AMC ENTERTAINMENT INTERNATIONAL, INC.
Mark A. McDonald
EXECUTIVE V.P. & CMO, AMC ENTERTAINMENT, INC.
Stephen Colenaro
PRESIDENT, PROGRAMMING
Robert J. Lenihan
PRESIDENT, FILM PROGRAMMING
Sonny Gourley
SENIOR V.P., GENERAL COUNSEL & SECRETARY, AMC ENTERTAINMENT, INC.
Kevin M. Connor
SENIOR V.P., HUMAN RESOURCES, AMC ENTERTAINMENT, INC.
Keith Wiedenkeller
SENIOR V.P., SPECIALTY PROGRAMMING
Debbie Pennie
SENIOR V.P., STRATEGY & STRATEGIC PARTNERSHIPS
Elizabeth Frank
V.P. & CAO, AMC ENTERTAINMENT, INC.
Chris A. Cox
DIRECTOR, PUBLIC RELATIONS, AMC ENTERTAINMENT, INC.
Justin Scott

THEATRES

Theatre	Address	City	State	Zip	Screens
AMC Fiesta Square 16	3033 N. College	Fayetteville	AR	72703	16
AMC Arrowhead 14	7700 W. Arrowhead Towne Ctr., Ste. 1079	Glendale	AZ	85308	14
AMC Westgate 20	9400 W. Hanna Dr.	Glendale	AZ	85031	20
AMC Mesa Grand 24	1645 S. Stapely Dr.	Mesa	AZ	85204	24
AMC Ahwatukee 24	4915 E. Ray Rd.	Phoenix	AZ	85044	24
AMC Arizona Center 24	565 N. 3rd St.	Phoenix	AZ	85004	24
AMC Deer Valley 30 IMAX	3033 W. Agua Fria Freeway	Phoenix	AZ	85027	30
AMC Desert Ridge 18	21001 N. Tatum Blvd., Ste. 32	Phoenix	AZ	85050	18
AMC Esplanade 14	2515 E. Camelback Rd.	Phoenix	AZ	85016	14
AMC Loews Foothills 15	7401 La Cholla Blvd., Ste. 144	Tucson	AZ	85741	15
AMC 12 At Downtown Disney	1565 Disneyland Dr.	Anaheim	CA	92802	12
AMC Deer Valley 16	4204 Lone Tree Way	Antioch	CA	94509	16
AMC Santa Anita 16	400 S. Baldwin Ave., Ste. 940-U	Arcadia	CA	91007	16
AMC Burbank 16	125 Palm Ave.	Burbank	CA	91502	16
AMC Burbank Town Center 6	770 N. 1st St.	Burbank	CA	91501	6
AMC Burbank Town Center 8	201 E. Magnolia Blvd. #345	Burbank	CA	91501	8
AMC Otay Ranch 12	2015 Birch Rd.	Chula Vista	CA	91915	12
AMC Puente Hills 20	1560 S. Azusa Ave.	City of Industry	CA	91748	20
AMC Covina 30	1414 N. Azusa Ave.	Covina	CA	91722	30
AMC Cupertino Square 16	10123 N. Wolfe Rd.	Cupertino	CA	95014	16
AMC Bay Street 16	5614 Bay St., Ste. 220	Emeryville	CA	94608	16
AMC Fullerton 20	1001 S. Lemon St.	Fullerton	CA	92832	20
AMC Glendora 12	1337 E. Gladstone St.	Glendora	CA	91740	12
AMC La Jolla 12	8657 Villa La Jolla Dr.	La Jolla	CA	92037	12
AMC Marina Pacifica 12	6346 E. Pacific Coast Hwy.	Long Beach	CA	90803	12
AMC Pine Square 16	245 Pine Ave., Ste. 100	Long Beach	CA	90802	16
AMC Avco Center 4	10840 Wilshire Blvd.	Los Angeles	CA	90024	4
AMC Century 15	10250 Santa Monica Blvd. #2000	Los Angeles	CA	90067	15
AMC Magic Johnson Crenshaw 15	4020 Marlton Ave.	Los Angeles	CA	90008	15
AMC Manteca 16	848 Lifestyle St.	Manteca	CA	95337	16
AMC Loews Marina 6	13455 Maxella Ave., Store #270	Marina Del Rey	CA	90292	6
AMC Montebello 10	1475 N. Montebello Blvd.	Montebello	CA	90640	10
AMC Atlantic time Square 14	450 N. Atlantic Ave	Monterey Park	CA	91754	14
AMC Plaza Bonita 14	3050 Plaza Bonita Rd.	National City	CA	91590	14
AMC Norwalk 20	12300 E. Civic Center Dr.	Norwalk	CA	90650	20
AMC Ontario 30	4549 Mills Circle	Ontario	CA	91764	30
AMC 30 At The Block	20 City Blvd. W., Ste. 1	Orange	CA	92868	30
AMC Victoria Gardens 12	12600 N. Main St.	Rancho Cucamonga	CA	91739	12
AMC Galleria South Bay 16	1815 Hawthorne Blvd., Ste. 368	Redondo Beach	CA	90278	16
AMC Tyler 16	3775 Tyler Ave.	Riverside	CA	92503	16
AMC Fashion Valley 18	7037 Friars Rd.	San Diego	CA	92108	18
AMC Mission Valley 20	1640 Camino Del Rio N.	San Diego	CA	92108	20
AMC Palm Promenade 24	770 Dennery Rd.	San Diego	CA	92154	24
AMC Loews Metreon 16 IMAX	101 Fourth St.	San Francisco	CA	94103	16
AMC Van Ness 14	1000 Van Ness Ave.	San Francisco	CA	94109	14
AMC Eastridge 15	2190 Eastridge Loop	San Jose	CA	95122	15
AMC Saratoga 14	700 El Paseo De Saratoga	San Jose	CA	95130	14
AMC Mercado 20	3111 Mission College Blvd.	Santa Clara	CA	95054	20
AMC Loews Broadway 4	1441 3rd St. Promenade	Santa Monica	CA	90401	4
AMC Santa Monica 7	1310 3rd St.	Santa Monica	CA	90401	7
AMC Criterion 6	1313 3rd St. Promenade	Santa Monica	CA	90401	6
AMC Del Amo 18	3525 Carson St.	Torrance	CA	90503	18
AMC Rolling Hills 20	2591 Airport Dr.	Torrance	CA	90505	20

Theatre	Address	City	State	Zip	Screens
AMC Tustin 14	2457 Park Ave.	Tustin	CA	92782	14
AMC Loews Citywalk 19	100 Universal City Plaza	Universal City	CA	91608	19
AMC Promenade 16	21801 Oxnard St.	Woodland Hills.	CA	91367	16
AMC Arapahoe 16	6696 S. Parker Rd.	Aurora	CO	80016	16
AMC Southland 16	23995 E. Plaza Ave.	Aurora	CO	80016	16
AMC Brighton 12	320 Pavilions Place	Brighton	CO	80601	12
AMC Flatiron 14	61 W. Flatiron Circle	Broomfield	CO	80021	14
AMC Castle Rock 12	3960 Limelight Ave.	Castle Rock	CO	80109	12
AMC Cherry Creek 8	3000 E. 1st Ave.	Denver	CO	80206	8
AMC Bergen Park 7	1153 BergenPkwy #M358	Evergreen	CO	80439	7
AMC Cinema Saver 6	2525 Worthington Circle	Fort Collins	CO	80526	6
AMC Highlands 24	103 W. Centennial Blvd.	Highlands Ranch	CO	80129	24
AMC Bowles 12	8035 W. Bowles Ave	Littleton	CO	80123	12
AMC Twent M 10	18625 Stage Run Rd.	Parker	CO	80134	10
AMC Orchard 12	14653 Orchard Pkway	Westminster.	CO	80020	12
AMC Westminster Promenade 24	10655 Westminster Blvd.	Westminster.	CO	80020	24
AMC Loews Danbury 16	4 International Dr.	Danbury	CT	06810	16
AMC Loews Plainville 20	220 New Britain Ave.	Plainville	CT	06062	20
AMC Loews Georgetown 14	3111 K St., N.W.	Washington	DC	20007	14
AMC Loews Uptown 1	3426 Connecticut Ave. N.W.	Washington	DC	20008	1
AMC Mazza Gallerie 7	5300 Wisconsin Ave. N.W.	Washington	DC	20015	7
AMC Altamonte 18	433 E. Altamonte Dr.	Altamonte Springs	FL	32701	18
AMC Aventura 24	19501 Biscayne Blvd. #3001	Aventura	FL	33180	24
AMC Regency 20	2496 W. Brandon Blvd.	Brandon	FL	33511	20
AMC Celebration 2	651 Front St.	Celebration	FL	34747	2
AMC Tri City 8	5140 E. Bay Dr.	Clearwater	FL	33764	8
AMC Cocowalk 16	3015 Grand Ave., #322	Coconut Grove	FL	33133	16
AMC Ridge Plaza 8	9200 State Rd. 84	Davie	FL	33324	8
AMC Coral Ridge10	3401 N.E. 26th Ave.	Fort Lauderdale	FL	33306	10
AMC Sheridan 12	4999 Sheridan St.	Hollywood	FL	33021	12
AMC Regency 24	9451 Regency Sq. Blvd.	Jacksonville	FL	32225	24
AMC Pleasure Island 24	1500 Buena Vista Dr., P.O. Box 10000	Lake Buena Vista	FL	32830	24
AMC Lakes Square 12	10401-015 US Hwy. 441 S.	Leesburg	FL	34788	12
AMC Mall Of Americas 14	7795 W. Flager, Spc. 1	Miami	FL	33144	14
AMC Merchants Crossing 16	15201 N. Cleveland Ave.	North Fort Myers	FL	33903	16
AMC West Oaks 14	9415 W. Colonial Dr.	Ocoee	FL	34761	14
AMC Woodland Square 20	3128 Tampa Rd.	Oldsmar	FL	34677	20
AMC Orange Park 24	1910 Wells Rd.	Orange Park	FL	32073	24
AMC Loews Universal Cineplex 20	6000 Universal Blvd., #740	Orlando	FL	32819	20
AMC Tyrone 6	2281 Tyrone Ct.	Saint Petersburg	FL	33710	6
AMC Sarasota 12	8201 S. Tamiami Trail	Sarasota	FL	34238	12
AMC Sunset Place 24	5701 Sunset Dr., Ste. 300	South Miami	FL	33143	24
AMC Tallahassee Mall 20	2415 N. Monroe St.	Tallahassee	FL	32303	20
AMC Veterans 24	9302 Anderson Rd.	Tampa	FL	33634	24
AMC Westshore 14	210 Westshore Plaza	Tampa	FL	33609	14
AMC Indian River 24	6200 20th St., Rm. 600	Vero Beach	FL	32966	24
AMC Mansell 14	7730 N. Point Pkwy.	Alpharetta	GA	30022	14
AMC Fork & Screen Buckhead	3340 Peachtree Rd., N.E.	Atlanta	GA	30326	6
AMC Magic Johnson Greenbriar Mall 12	2841 Greenbriar Pkwy. S.W.	Atlanta	GA	30331	12
AMC Parkway Pointe 15	3101 Cobb Pkwy., Ste. 201	Atlanta	GA	30339	15
AMC Phipps Plaza 14	3500 Peachtree Rd. N.E.	Atlanta	GA	30326	14
AMC Avenue Forsythe	350 Peachtree Parkway	Cumming	GA	30041	12
AMC North Dekalb 16	2042 Lawrenceville Hwy., Ste. F-22	Decatur	GA	30033	6
AMC Barrett Commons 24	2600 Cobb Place Ln. N.W.	Kennesaw	GA	30144	24
AMC Colonial 18	825 Lawrenceville-Suwanee Rd.	Lawrenceville	GA	30043	18
AMC Discover Mills 18	5900 Sugarloaf Pkwy., Ste. 415	Lawrenceville	GA	30043	18
AMC Stonecrest 16	8060 Mall Pkwy.	Lithonia	GA	30038	16
AMC Southlake 24	7065 Mount Zion Circle	Morrow	GA	30260	24
AMC Council Bluffs 17	3220 23rd Ave.	Council Bluffs	IA	51501	17
AMC Dubuque 14	2835 N.W. Arterial	Dubuque	IA	52002	14
AMC Plaza 3	300 Main St.	Keokuk	IA	52632	3
AMC Toler 2	911 W. Washington St.	Benton	IL	62812	2
AMC Carbondale 8	1263 E. Main St.	Carbondale	IL	62901	8
AMC Plaza 5	1047 W. Broadway	Centralia	IL	62801	5
AMC Will Rogers 2	705 Monroe Ave.	Charlestown	IL	61920	2
AMC Ford City 14	7601 S. Cicero Ave.	Chicago	IL	60652	14
AMC 600 North Michigan 9	600 N. Michigan	Chicago	IL	60611	9
AMC Pipers Alley 4	1608 N. Wells	Chicago	IL	60614	4
AMC River East 21	322 E. Illinois St.	Chicago	IL	60611	21
AMC Galewood 14	5530 W. Homer St.	Chicago	IL	60639	14
AMC Chicago Ridge 6	500 Chicago Ridge Mall	Chicago Ridge	IL	60415	6
AMC Cicero 14	4779 W. Cermak Rd.	Cicero	IL	60804	14
AMC Loews Country Club Hills 16	4201 W. 167th St.	Country Club Hills	IL	60478	16
AMC Loews Crestwood 18	13221 Rivercrest Dr.	Crestwood	IL	60445	18
AMC Village M 6	2917 N. Vermillion St.	Danville	IL	61832	6
AMC Eastgate 6	625 Lewis and Clark Blvd,	East Alton	IL	62024	6
AMC Edwardsville 12	6633 Center Grove Rd.	Edwardsville	IL	62025	12
AMC Galesburg 8	1401 W. Carl Sandburg Dr.	Galesburg	IL	61401	8
AMC Harrisburg 4	5 S. Main St.	Harrisburg	IL	62946	4
AMC Lory 2	810 Main Street	Highland	IL	62249	2
AMC Jerseyville 2	117 E. Pearl St.	Jerseeyville	IL	62052	2
AMC Lake Hill 14	311 N. Randall Rd.	Lake In the Hills	IL	60156	12
AMC Quarry 14	9201 63rd St.	Hodgkins	IL	60525	14
AMC Yorktown 17	80 Yorktown Shopping Center	Lombard	IL	60148	17
AMC Yorktown Premium 1	80 Yorktown Shopping Center	Lombard	IL	60148	1
AMC Machesney 14	1860 Anjali Way	Machesney	IL	61115	14
AMC Illinois 8	3107 Civic Circle Blvd.	Marion	IL	62959	8
AMC Mattoon 10	2509 Hurst Dr.	Mattoon	IL	61938	10
AMC Randhurst 16	101 E. Euclid Ave.	Mount Prospect	IL	60056	16
AMC Mount Vernon 8	400 Potomac Blvd.	Mount Vernon	IL	62864	8
AMC Naperville 16	2815 Show Place Dr.	Naperville	IL	60564	16

Theatre	Address	City	State	Zip	Screens
AMC New Lenox 14	1320 W. Mapole St.	New Lenox	IL	60451	14
AMC Niles 12	301 Golf Mill Ctr.	Niles	IL	60714	12
AMC Norridge 10	4520 N. Harlem Ave.	Norridge	IL	60706	14
AMC Northbrook 14	1525 Lake Cook Rd.	Northbrook	IL	60062	14
AMC Paris 2	119 N. Central Ave.	Paris	IL	61944	2
AMC Pekin 14	1124 Edgewater Dr	Pekin	IL	61554	14
AMC Quincy 6	300 N. 33rd St	Quincy	IL	62301	6
AMC Mall 3	3429 Quincy Mall	Quincy	IL	62301	3
AMC Rockford 16	8301 E. State St.	Rockford	IL	61108	16
AMC Woodfield 20	601 N. Martingale Rd. Ste. 105	Schaumburg	IL	60173	20
AMC Village Ceneter 18	7000 Carpenter Rd	Skokie	IL	60077	18
AMC Barrington 30	175 Studio Dr.	South Barrington	IL	60010	30
AMC Parkway Point 8	3025 Lindbergh Blvd.	Springfield	IL	62704	8
AMC Springfield 12	3141 Mercantile Dr.	Springfield	IL	62702	12
AMC Springfield 8	2945 S. Dirksen Pkwy	Springfield	IL	62703	8
AMC Taylorville 2	117 W. Main Cross St.	Taylorville	IL	62568	2
AMC Rivertree Court 8	701 N. Milwaukee Ave	Vernon Hills	IL	60061	8
AMC Vernon Hills 8	555 Lakeview Pkwy.	Vernon Hills	IL	60061	8
AMC Cantera 30	28250 Diehl Rd.	Warrenville	IL	60555	30
AMC Woodridge 18	10000 Woodward Ave.	Woodridge	IL	60517	18
AMC Bloomington 11	1351 S. College Mall Rd.	Bloomington	IN	47404	11
AMC Bloomington 12	2029 W. 3rd St.	Bloomington	IN	47404	12
AMC Columbus 12	555 Creekview Ct.	Columbus	IN	47201	12
AMC Greenwood 14	461 S. Greenwood Park Dr.	Greenwood	IN	46142	14
AMC Evensville 16	5600 Pearl Dr.	Evansville	IN	47712	16
AMC Castleton 14	6020 E. 82nd St.	Indianapolis	IN	46250	14
AMC Clearwater 12	4016 E. 82nd St.	Indianapolis	IN	46250	12
AMC Loews College Park 14	3535 W. 86th St.	Indianapolis	IN	46268	14
AMC Indianapolis 17	4325 S. Meridian St.	Indianapolis	IN	46217	17
AMC Traders 12	5920 W. 86th St	Indianapolis	IN	46278	12
AMC Washington 12	10280 E. Washington St	Indianapolis	IN	46299	12
AMC Kokomo 12	1530 E. Boulevard.	Kokomo	IN	46902	12
AMC Marion 12	713 N Theatre Rd.	Marion	IN	46952	12
AMC Hobart 12	2590 Southlake Mall Dr.	Merrillville	IN	46410	12
AMC Merrillville 10	2360 E. 79th Ave.	Merrillville	IN	46410	10
AMC Michigan City 14	100 Meijer Dr.	Michigan City	IN	46360	14
AMC Muncie 12	860 E. Princeton Ave.	Muncie	IN	47303	12
AMC Muncie 7	3401 W. Community Dr.	Muncie	IN	47304	7
AMC Eastwood 2	663 E. Main St.	Peru	IN	46970	2
AMC Princeton 4	301 Broadway St	Princeton	IN	47670	4
AMC Richmond 10	600 Commerce Rd	Richmond	IN	47374	10
AMC Richmond 11	4713 National Rd. E.	Richmond	IN	47374	11
AMC Schereville 12	1400 Eagle Dr.	Schereville	IN	46375	12
AMC Schereville 16	875 Deer Creek Dr.	Schereville	IN	46375	16
AMC South Bend 16	450 W. Chippewa Ave.	South Bend	IN	46614	16
AMC Honey Creek 8	3131 S 3rd St	Terre Haute	IN	47802	8
AMC Terre Haute 12	3153 S. 3rd Place	Terre Haute	IN	47802	12
AMC Vincennes 8	1496 S. Hart St. Rd	Vincennes	IN	47591	8
AMC Indiana 2	419 E. Main St.	Washington	IN	47501	2
AMC Town Center 20	11701 Nall Ave.	Leawood	KS	66211	20
AMC Studio 28 KC	12075 S. Strang Line Rd.	Olathe	KS	66062	28
AMC Newport Levee 20	One Levy Way, Ste. 4100	Newport	KY	41071	20
AMC Hammond Palace 10	801 C M Fagan Dr.	Hammond	LA	70403	10
AMC Elmwood Palace 20	1200 Elwood Park Blvd.	Harahan	LA	70123	20
AMC Westbank Palace 16	1151 Manhattan Blvd.	Harvey	LA	70058	16
AMC Houma Palace 10	5737 W. Park Ave.	Houma	LA	70364	10
AMC Clearview Palace 12	4486 Veterans Memorial Blvd.	Metairie	LA	70006	12
AMC Boston Common 19	175 Tremont St.	Boston	MA	02111	19
AMC Braintree 10	121 Grandview Rd.	Braintree	MA	02184	10
AMC Burlington 10	20 S. Ave.	Burlington	MA	01804	10
AMC Harvard Square 5	10 Church St.	Cambridge	MA	02138	5
AMC Chestnut Hill 5	27 Boylston St., Ste. B	Chestnut Hill	MA	02467	5
AMC Liberty Tree Mall 20	100 Independence Way	Danvers	MA	01923	20
AMC Framingham Premium 1	22 Flutie Pass	Framingham	MA	01701	1
AMC Framinghm 15	22 Flutie Pass	Framingham	MA	01701	15
AMC Methuen 20	90 Pleasant Valley St.	Methuen	MA	01844	20
AMC North Dartmouth 12	140 N. Dartmouth Mall	North Dartmouth	MA	02747	12
AMC Tyngsboro 12	440 Middlesex Rd.	Tyngsboro	MA	01879	12
AMC White Marsh 16	8141 Honeygo Blvd.	Baltimore	MD	21236	16
AMC Security Square 8	1717 Rolling Rd.	Baltimore	MD	21244	8
AMC Center Park 8	4001 Powder Mill Rd.	Beltsville	MD	20705	8
AMC Columbia 14	10300 Little Patuxent Pkwy.	Columbia	MD	21044	14
AMC Rio Cinemas 18	9811 Washingtonian Center.	Gaithersburg	MD	20878	18
AMC White Flint 5	11301 Rockville Pike	Kensington	MD	20895	5
AMC Magic Johnson Capital Center 12	800 Shoppers Way	Largo	MD	20774	12
AMC Country Club Mall 6	1280 Vocke Rd.	Lavale	MD	21502	6
AMC Lexington Park 6	21882 FDR Blvd.	Lexington Park	MD	20653	6
AMC Owings Mills 17	10100 Mill Run Circle	Owings Mills	MD	21117	17
AMC Towson Commons 8	435 York Rd., Ste. 200	Towson	MD	21204	9
AMC St Charles Town Center 9	11115 Mall Circle	Waldorf	MD	20603	9
AMC Star Great Lakes 25	4300 Baldwin Rd.	Auburn Hills	MI	48326	25
AMC Star Gratiot 21	35705 S. Gratiot Ave.	Clinton Twp.	MI	48035	21
AMC Star Fairlane 21	18900 Michigan Ave.	Dearborn	MI	41826	21
AMC Star Grand Rapids 18	3000 Alpine Ave.	Grand Rapids	MI	49544	18
AMC Star Holland 8	12271 James St.	Holland	MI	49424	8
AMC Livonia 20	19500 Haggerty Rd.	Livonia	MI	48152	20
AMC Star John R 15	32289 John R Rd.	Madison Heights	MI	48071	15
AMC Meridian Mall 6	1999 Central Park Dr.	Okemos	MI	48864	6
AMC Star Southfield 20	25333 W. 12 Mile Rd.	Southfield	MI	48034	20
AMC Forum 30	44681 Mound Rd.	Sterling Heights	MI	48314	30
AMC Coon Rapids 16	10051 Woodcrest Dr. N.W.	Coon Rapids	MN	55433	16

Theatre	Address	City	State	Zip	Screens
AMC Eden Prairie 18	8251 Flying Cloud Dr., Ste. 2400	Eden Prairie	MN	55344	18
AMC Southdale 16	400 S. Dale Center	Edina	MN	55435	16
AMC Inver Grove	5567 Bishop Ave.	Inver Grove Heights	MN	55076	16
AMC Arbor Lakes 16	12575 Elm Creek Blvd. N.	Maple Grove	MN	55369	16
AMC Block E 15	600 Hennepin ave.	Minneapolis	MN	55403	15
AMC Rosedale 14	850 Rosedale Center	Roseville	MN	55113	14
AMC Town Plaza 5	2136 William St. #205	Cape Girardeau	MO	63703	5
AMC Chesterfield 14	3000 Chesterfield Mall	Chesterfield	MO	63017	14
AMC Creve Coeur 12	10465 Olive Blvd	Creve Coeur	MO	63141	12
AMC West Olive 16	12657 Olive St.	Creve Coeur	MO	63141	16
AMC Farmington 4	838 Valley Creek Dr.	Farmington	MO	63640	4
AMC Independence 20	19200 E. 39th St. S	Independence	MO	64057	20
AMC Barrywoods 24	8101 Roanridge Rd.	Kansas City	MO	64151	24
AMC Parkway 14	8600 Ward Pkwy., Ste. 14	Kansas City	MO	64114	14
AMC Mainstreet 6	1400 Main St.	Kansas City	MO	64105	6
AMC Kennett 1	224 1st St.	Kennett	MO	63857	1
AMC Flat River 2	300 W. Main St.	Park Hills	MO	63601	2
AMC Poplar Bluff 8	3525 S. Westwood Blvd.	Poplar Bluff	MO	63901	8
AMC Crestwood Plaza 10	248 Crestwood Plaza	Saint Louis	MO	63126	10
AMC Esquire 7	6706 Clayton Rd.	Saint Louis	MO	63117	7
AMC Carolina 22	9541 S. Boulevard	Charlotte	NC	28273	22
AMC Northlake 14	7325 Northlake Mall Dr.	Charlotte	NC	28216	14
AMC Concord 24	8421 Concord Mills Blvd.	Concord	NC	28027	24
AMC Oakview 24	3555 S. 140th Plaza	Omaha	NE	68144	24
AMC Brick Plaza 10	3 Brick Plaza	Bricktown	NJ	08723	10
AMC Bridgewater 7	400 Commons Way Ste. 380	Bridgewater	NJ	08807	7
AMC Cherry Hill 24	2121 Route 38	Cherry Hill	NJ	08002	24
AMC Clifton Commons 16	405 Route 3 E.	Clifton	NJ	07014	16
AMC Deptford 8	1740 Clements Bridge Rd.	Deptford	NJ	08096	8
AMC Deptford Mall 6	1795 Deptford Center Rd.	Deptford	NJ	08096	6
AMC East Hanover 12	145 Route 10 E.	East Hanover	NJ	07936	12
AMC Monmouth Mall 15	Route 35 & 36	Eatontown	NJ	07724	15
AMC Menlo Park 12	390 Menlo Park Mall	Edison	NJ	08837	12
AMC Jersey Gardens 20	651 Kapkowski Rd.	Elizabeth	NJ	07201	20
AMC Freehold Metroplex 14	101 Trotters Way	Freehold	NJ	07728	14
AMC Hamilton 24	325 Sloan Ave.	Hamilton	NJ	08619	24
AMC Newport Centre 11	30-300 Mall Dr. W.	Jersey City	NJ	07303	11
AMC Aviation Plaza 12	1200 S. Stiles St.	Linden	NJ	07036	12
AMC Marlton 8	800 N. Route 73	Marlton	NJ	08053	8
AMC Mountainside 10	1021 Route 22 E.	Mountainside	NJ	07092	10
AMC Loews New Brunswick 18	17 US Highway #1	New Brunswick	NJ	08901	18
AMC Garden State 16	1 Garden State Plaza (Route 4 & 17)	Paramus	NJ	07652	16
AMC Ridgefield Park 12	75 Challenger Rd.	Ridgefield Park	NJ	07660	12
AMC Rockaway 16	363 Mount Hope Ave.	Rockaway	NJ	07866	16
AMC Seacourt 10	Seacourt Pavilion, 635 Bay Ave.	Toms River	NJ	08753	10
AMC Wayne 14	67 Willowbrook Blvd.	Wayne	NJ	07470	14
AMC Essex Green 9	495 Prospect Ave.	West Orange	NJ	07052	9
AMC Rainbow Plaza 10	2321 North Rainbow Rd.	Las Vegas	NV	89106	10
AMC Maple Ridge 8	4276 Maple Rd., Ste. C	Amherst	NY	14226	8
AMC Bay Terrace 6	211-01 26th Ave.	Bayside	NY	11360	6
AMC Bay Plaza 13	2210 Bartow Ave.	Bronx	NY	10475	13
AMC Fresh Meadows 7	190-02 Horace Harding Blvd.	Fresh Meadows	NY	11365	7
AMC Roosevelt Field 8	Roosevelt Field Mall	Garden City	NY	11530	8
AMC Shore 8	37 Wall St.	Huntington	NY	11743	8
AMC Nassau Metroplex 10	3585 Hempstead Turnpike	Levittown	NY	11756	10
AMC Galleria Metroplex 16	1 Galleria Dr.	Middletown	NY	10940	16
AMC Empire 25	234 W. 42nd St	New York	NY	10036	25
AMC 19th Street East 6	890 Broadway	New York	NY	10003	6
AMC 34th Street 14	312 W. 34th St.	New York	NY	10001	14
AMC 72nd Street 1	1230 Third Ave.	New York	NY	10021	1
AMC 84th Street 6	2310 Broadway	New York	NY	10024	6
AMC Kips Bay 15	570 Second Ave.	New York	NY	10016	15
AMC Lincoln Square 13	1998 Broadway	New York	NY	10023	13
AMC Orpheum 7	1538 Third Ave. (86th St.)	New York	NY	10028	7
AMC Village 7	66 Third Ave. (11th St.)	New York	NY	10003	4
AMC Magic Johnson Harlem 9	2309 Frederick Douglas Blvd.	New York	NY	10027	9
AMC Port Chester 14	40 Westchester Ave.	Port Chester	NY	10573	14
AMC Fantasy 5	18 N. Park Ave.	Rockville Ctr.	NY	11570	5
AMC Stony Brook 17	2196 Nesconset Hwy.	Stony Brook	NY	11790	17
AMC Vestal Towne Square 9	2425 Vestal Pkwy.	Vestal	NY	13850	9
AMC Webster 12	2190 Empire Blvd.	Webster	NY	14580	12
AMC Palisades Center 21	4403 Palisades Ctr. Dr.	West Nyack	NY	10994	21
AMC Raceway 10	1025 Corporate Dr.	Westbury	NY	11590	10
AMC Ridge Park Square 8	4788 Ridge Rd.	Brooklyn	OH	44144	8
AMC Easton Town Center 30 IMAX	275 Easton Town Center	Columbus	OH	43219	30
AMC Lennox 24	777 Kinnear Rd.	Columbus	OH	43212	24
AMC Dublin 18	6700 Village Pkwy.	Dublin	OH	43017	18
AMC Hamilton 10	877 N.W. Washington Blvd.	Hamilton	OH	45013	10
AMC Hamilton 8	1453 Main St,	Hamilton	OH	45013	8
AMC Loews Richmond Town Square 20	631 Richmond Rd.	Richmond Hghts	OH	44143	20
AMC Crossroads 16	1211 E. I-240 Service Rd.	Oklahoma City	OK	73149	16
AMC Quail Springs 24	2501 W. Memorial Rd., Ste. E	Oklahoma City	OK	73134	24
AMC Southroad 20	4923 E. 41st St.	Tulsa	OK	74135	20
AMC Tilghman 8	4608 Broadway	Allentown	PA	18104	8
AMC Neshaminy 24	3900 Rockhill Dr., Neshaminy Mall #660	Bensalem	PA	19020	24
AMC Woodhaven 10	1336 Bristol Pike	Bensalem	PA	19020	10
AMC Colonial Commons 9	5114 Jonestown Rd.	Harrisburg	PA	17112	9
AMC 309 Cinema 9	1210 Bethlehem Pike	North Wales	PA	19454	9
AMC Granite Run 8	1067 W. Baltimore Pike	Media	PA	19063	8
AMC Franklin Mills 14	1149 Franklin Mills Circle	Philadelphia	PA	19154	14
AMC Plymouth Meeting 12	494 Germantown Pike	Plymouth Meeting	PA	19462	12

Theatre	Address	City	State	Zip	Screens
AMC Marple 10	400 S. State Rd.	Springfield	PA	19064	10
AMC Stroud Mall 7	Rte. 611-160 Stroud Mall	Stroudberg	PA	18360	7
AMC Painters 9	112 Wilmington Pike	West Chester	PA	19382	9
AMC Waterfront 22	300 W. Waterfront Dr.	West Homestead	PA	15120	22
AMC Dutch Square 14	800 Bush River Rd.	Columbia	SC	29210	14
AMC Parks At Arlington 18	3861 S. Cooper St.	Arlington	TX	76015	18
AMC Barton Creek 14	2901 Capital of Texas Hwy.	Austin	TX	78746	14
AMC Grand 24	10110 Technology Blvd. E.	Dallas	TX	75220	24
AMC Northpark 15	8687 N. Central Expwy., #3000	Dallas	TX	75225	15
AMC Valley View 16	13331 Preston Rd., #2300	Dallas	TX	75240	16
AMC Palace 9	220 E. Third St.	Fort Worth	TX	76102	9
AMC Sundance 11	304 Houston St.	Fort Worth	TX	76102	11
AMC Stonebriar 24	2601 Preston Rd., Ste. 300	Frisco	TX	75034	24
AMC Firewheel 18	100 Coneflower Dr.	Garland	TX	75040	18
AMC Grapevine 30	3150 Grapevine Mills Pkwy.	Grapevine	TX	76051	30
AMC Highlands 12	4090 Barton Creek	Highland Village	TX	75077	12
AMC Gulf Pointe 30	11801 E. So Sam Houston Pkwy.	Houston	TX	77089	30
AMC Studio 30 Houston	2949 Dunvale	Houston	TX	77063	30
AMC Willowbrook 24	17145 Tomball Pkwy.	Houston	TX	77064	24
AMC Deerbrook 24	20131 Hwy. 59 N	Humble	TX	77338	24
AMC Irving Mall 14	2433 Irving Mall	Irving	TX	75062	14
AMC Katy Mill 20	5000 Katy Mills Circle, #131	Katy	TX	77494	20
AMC Mesquite 30	19919 IH 635	Mesquite	TX	75149	30
AMC Huebner Oaks 24	11075 IH 10 W.	San Antonio	TX	78230	24
AMC Rivercenter 9	849 E. Commerce St., Ste. 800	San Antonio	TX	78205	9
AMC Spring 10	20115 Holzwarth Rd.	Spring	TX	77388	10
AMC Fountains 18	11225 Fountain Lake Dr.	Stafford	TX	77477	18
AMC First Colony 24	3301 Town Centre Blvd. S.	Sugar Land	TX	77479	24
AMC Loews Layton Hills 9	728 W. 1425 N.	Layton Hills	UT	84041	9
AMC Hoffman 22	206 Swamp Fox Rd.	Alexandria	VA	22314	22
AMC Courthouse 8	2150 Clarendon Blvd.	Arlington	VA	22201	8
AMC Loews Shirlington 7	2772 S. Randolph St.	Arlington	VA	22206	7
AMC Hampton 24	1 Town Center Way	Hampton	VA	23666	24
AMC Tysons Corner 16	7850 Tysons Corner Center	McLean	VA	22102	16
AMC Lynnhaven 18	1001 Lynnhaven Mall Loop	Virginia Beach	VA	23452	18
AMC Potomac 18	2700 Potomac Mills Circle, #886-F3	Woodbridge	VA	22192	18
AMC Factoria 8	3505 Factoria Blvd. S.E.	Bellevue	WA	98006	8
AMC Cascade Mall 14	200 Cascade Mall Dr.	Burlington	WA	98233	14
AMC Kent Station 14	426 Ramsay Way	Kent	WA	98032	14
AMC Lakewood Mall 12	5721 Main St. S.W.	Lakewood	WA	98499	12
AMC Alderwood Mall 16	18733-33rd Ave. W.	Lynwood	WA	98037	16
AMC Loews Redmond Town Center 8	16451 N.E. 74th St.	Redmond	WA	98052	8
AMC Renton Village 8	25 S. Grady Way	Renton	WA	98055	8
AMC Oak Tree 6	10006 Aurora Ave. N.	Seattle	WA	98133	6
AMC Uptown 3	511 Queen Ann Ave. N.	Seattle	WA	98109	3
AMC Pacific Place 11	600 Pine St., Ste. 400	Seattle	WA	98101	11
AMC Kitsap 8	10055 Kitsapp Mall Blvd. N.W., P.O. Box 3246	Silverdale	WA	98383	8
AMC River Park Square 20	808 W. Main St., Ste. 334	Spokane	WA	99201	20
AMC Narrows 8	2208 Mildred St.	Tacoma	WA	98466	8
AMC Southcenter 16	633 Southcenter	Tukwila	WA	98188	16
AMC Woodinville 12	17640 Garden Way N.E.	Woodinville	WA	98072	12
AMC Fitchburg 18	6091 McKee Rd.	Fitchburg	WI	53719	18
AMC Johnson Creek 12	420 Village Walk Lane	Johnson Creek	WI	53038	12
AMC Desert South 15	1301 Wiscinsin Dells Pkwy	Lake Delton	WI	53940	15
AMC Mayfair 18	2500 N. Mayfair Rd., Ste. M186	Wauwatosa	WI	53226	18

ARCLIGHT CINEMAS

3 theatres, 45 screens.

(A subsidiary of Pacific Theatres Exhibition Corp)

120 N. Robertson Blvd, Los Angeles, CA 90048. TEL: (310) 657-8420, 594-7034. FAX: (310) 657-6736. www.arclightcinemas.com

THEATRES

Theatre	Address	City	State	Zip	Screens
ArcLight Hollywood & Cinerama Dome	6460 Sunset Blvd.	Los Angeles	CA	90028	15
ArcLight Pasadena	336 E. Colorado Blvd	Pasadena	CA	91101	14
ArcLight Sherman Oaks	15301 Ventura Blvd.	Sherman Oaks	CA	91403	16

ATLAS CINEMAS

4 theatres, 47 screens.

22624 Lakeshore Blvd., Euclid, OH 44123. TEL: (216) 731-1701. FAX: (216) 731-2138. www.atlascinemas.net

PRESIDENT
Albert Saluan

THEATRES

Theatre	Address	City	State	Zip	Screens
Atlas Cinemas Midway Mall 8	2650 Midway Mall	Elyria	OH	44035	8
Atlas Lakeshore 7	22624 Lakeshore Blvd.	Euclid	OH	44123	7
Atlas Cinemas Diamond Ctr. 16	9555 Diamond Center Dr.	Mentor	OH	44060	16
Atlas Great Lakes Stadium 16	7860 Mentor Ave.	Mentor	OH	44060	16

B & B THEATRES

30 theatres, 204 screens.

P.O. Box 171, 114 W. 2nd, Salisbury, MO 65281. TEL: (660) 388-5219. Liberty Office: 2101 W. Kansas, Liberty, MO 64068. TEL: (816) 407-7469.
FAX: (816) 407-9805. www.bbtheatres.com

PRESIDENT & FILM BUYER
Robert Bagby
CHAIRMAN
Elmer Bills
FILM BUYER
Brad Bills

Theatre	Address	City	State	Zip	Screens
THEATRES					
Tavernier Cinema 5	91298 Overseas Hwy	Tavernier	FL	33070	5
Roxy 4	302 E. Main	Chanute	KS	66720	4
The Majestic	229 W. 6th St.	Concordia	KS	66901	4
Dodge City Village 8	Village Square Mall, 2601 Central	Dodge City	KS	67801	8
Eldorado Central Cinema	300 E. Central Ave., P.O. Box 310	El Dorado	KS	67042	6
Independence Cinema	121 Laurel St.	Independence	KS	67301	4
Sterling Six	1802 1/2 E. St., P.O. Box 381	Iola	KS	66749	6
Iola 54 Drive-In	1300 2200 St.	Gas City	KS	66749	1
McPherson Cinema 4	316 N. Main St.	McPherson	KS	67460	4
Cowley Cinema 8	23046 Avery Ave., P.O. Box 840	Winfield	KS	67156	8
Bolivar Cinema 4	800 E. Aldrich Rd., Ste. 10	Boliver	MO	65613	4
Grand 6	2880 N. Grand Dr., P.O. Box 77	Chillicothe	MO	64601	6
Festus Eight	1522 Pkwy. W., P.O. Box 834	Festus	MO	63028	8
Fulton Cinema 8	521 Commons Dr., P.O. Box 825	Fulton	MO	65251	8
Hannibal Cinema 5	#7 Northport Shopping Center	Hannibal	MO	63401	5
B&B Theatres Cineplex	2727 Cantrell Rd., P.O. Box 308	Harrisonville	MO	64701	6
Grand 6	2880 N. Grand Dr., P.O. Box 77	Chillicothe	MO	64601	6
Festus Eight	1522 Pkwy. W., P.O. Box 834	Festus	MO	63028	8
Fulton Cinema 8	521 Commons Dr., P.O. Box 825	Fulton	MO	65251	8
Main Street Cinema 8	100 Main Street	Hannibal	MO	63401	8
Lake West Cinema 5	1651 Hwy. 0, Bldg. C-1	Gravois Mills	MO	65037	5
Ritz 8 Theatre	925 S. Jefferson	Lebanon	MO	65536	7
Cannonball 6	1125 Franklin, P.O. Box 528	Lexington	MO	64067	6
Liberty Cinema 12	2101 W. Kansas, P.O. Box 1247	Liberty	MO	64069	12
Moberly Five & Drive	3000 N. Morley	Moberly	MO	65270	6
Monett Cinema 8	507 Plaza Dr.	Monett	MO	65708	8
Neosho Six	1601 Malcolm Mosby Dr.	Neosho	MO	64850	6
Warrenton Cinema 8	265 Veterans Memorial Pkwy.	Warrenton	MO	63383	8
Waynesville Cinema 8	100 Tre'Mont Centre, P.O. Box 311	Waynesville	MO	65583	8
Wildwood 10 with Marquee Suites	16820 Main Street,	Wildwood	MO	63040	10
Claremore Cinema 8	1407 W. Country Club Rd.	Claremore	OK	74017	8
El Reno Cinema 8	3000 S. Country Club Rd.	El Reno	OK	73036	8
B&B Theatres Windsor 10	4623 A NW 23Rd Street	Oklahoma City	OK	73127	10
Miami Cinema 4	222 N. Main	Miami	OK	74355	4
Sapulpa Cinema 8	1245 New Sapulpa Rd.	Sapulpa	OK	74066	8
BOOKING ACCOUNTS					
4 Theatres, 28 Screens.					
Harrisonville Cinema 6	2727 Cantrell Rd., P.O. Box 308	Harrisonville	MO	64701	6
Downtown Cinema 8	115 N. Elson	Kirksville	MO	63501	8
Sullivan Cinema 6	3001 N. Service Rd., W.	Sullivan	MO	63080	6
Great 8	#5 Prairie Dell Plaza	Union	MO	63084	8

BOSTON CULINARY GROUP

22 theatres, 133 screens.
(each theatre individually owned and operated)
55 Cambridge Pkwy., Cambridge, MA 02142. TEL: (617) 499-2700. FAX: (617) 225-0897.
email: theaters@bcginc.com www.yourneighborhoodtheatre.com
PRESIDENT & CEO
Joseph Armstrong, Jr.
V.P., DEVELOPMENT
Mark Benvenuto
V.P., OPERATIONS
Mark Benvenuto
FILM BUYER
Dan Seddon

Theatre	Address	City	State	Zip	Screens
THEATRES					
Groton Cinemas	Poquonneck Rd.	Groton	CT	06340	6
Seymour Ent. Cinemas	814 Derby Ave.	Seymour	CT	06483	12
East Bridgewater Cinemas	225 Bedford St.	E. Bridgewater	MA	02333	6
Edgartown Ent. Cinemas	65 Maine St.	Edgartown	MA	02539	2
Sharon Cinemas	700 S. Main St.	Sharon	MA	02067	8
Bangor Mall Cinemas	557 Stillwater Ave.	Bangor	ME	04001	10
Maine Coast Mall Cinemas	Maine Coast Mall	Ellsworth	ME	04605	2
Wells Five Star Cinemas	75 Wells Plaza/Box 10	Wells	ME	04090	7
Windham Mall Cinemas	795 Roosevelt Trail	Windham	ME	04062	7
Claremont Cinemas	345 Washington St.	Claremont	NH	03034	6
Gilford Cinemas 8	9 Old Lake Shore Rd.	Gilford	NH	03246	8
MT Valley Mall Theater	32 Mt Valley Blvd.	N. Conway	NH	03860	7
North Conway Twin	P.O. Box 3068	N. Conway	NH	03860	2
Cedar Lane Cinemas	503 Cedar Lane	Teaneck	NJ	07666	4
Hudson Cinemas	701 Route 440	Jersey City	NJ	07304	7
Lafayette Cinema	97 Lafayette Ave.	Suffern	NY	10901	1
Seaford Cinemas	3951 Merrick Rd.	Seaford	NY	11783	8
Island Cinemas	105 Chases Ln.	Middletown	RI	02842	10
Opera House Cinema	19 Tuoro St.	Newport	RI	02840	3
Skingstown Ent. Cinemas	30 Village Square Dr.	Skingstown	RI	02879	8
Rustic Tri View Drive In	Route 146	North Smithfield	RI	02876	3
Kipling Cinemas	770 Putney Rd.	Brattleboro	VT	05301	6

BOW TIE CINEMAS

17 theatres, 143 screens.
641 Danbury Rd., Ridgefield, CT 06877. TEL: (203) 659-2600. FAX: (203) 659-2601. email: jmasher@bowtiecinemas.com www.bowtiecinemas.com
OWNER
Charley Moss, Ben Moss
CHIEF OPERATING OFFICER
Joe Masher
CHIEF FILM OFFICER
Spencer Klein
DIRECTOR, FACILITIES & CONSTRUCTION
Steve Ventor
OPERATIONS MANAGER
Ike Rivera

Theatre	Address	City	State	Zip	Screens

DIRECTOR, IT & MIS
Dan Miller
CONTROLLER
Bob Schmiedel
BOOKER
Denis Foley, Kelly Wasserman

THEATRES

Theatre	Address	City	State	Zip	Screens
Criterion Cinemas at Greenwich Plaza	2 Railroad Ave.	Greenwich	CT	06830	3
Palace 17 & Odyssey Theater	330 New Park Ave.	Hartford	CT	06106	17
The Playhouse	89 Elm St.	New Canaan	CT	06840	2
Criterion Cinemas	86 Temple St.	New Haven	CT	06510	9
Royale 6	542 Westport Ave.	Norwalk	CT	06851	6
Regent 8	64 N. Main St.	South Norwalk	CT	06854	8
Majestic 6	118 Summer St.	Stamford	CT	06901	6
Landmark 9	5 Landmark Sq.	Stamford	CT	06905	9
Marquis 16	100 Quarry Rd.	Trumbull	CT	06611	16
Criterion Cinemas at Blue Back Square	42 S. Main St.	W. Hartford	CT	06107	6
Wilton 4	21 River Rd.	Wilton	CT	06897	4
Movieland 7	218 E. Valley Rd.	Basalt	CO	81623	7
Harbour 9	2474 Solomons Island Rd.	Annapolis	MD	21401	9
Mall 11	1020 Annapolis Mall	Annapolis	MD	21401	11
American Theater	1450 E. Ave.	Bronx	NY	10462	7
Movieland 6	400 State St.	Schenectady	NY	12305	6
Movieland at Boulevard Square	1301 N. Boulevard	Richmond	VA	23230	17

BRENDEN THEATRES

7 theatres, 90 screens.
4321 W. Flamingo Rd., Las Vegas, NV 89103. TEL: (702) 507-1520. www.brendentheatres.com
OWNER, PRESIDENT & CEO
Johnny Brenden
EXECUTIVE V.P. & COO
Bruce Coleman - bcoleman@brendencorp.com
SENIOR V.P. & CFO
Lee Craner
DIRECTOR, FILM
Chris Hatzmichael
SPECIAL EVENTS & MARKETING MANAGER
Brian Epling - bepling@brendencorp.com
EXECUTIVE DIRECTOR, PUBLIC RELATIONS
Jerry Olivarez - jerryo@brendencorp.com

THEATRES

Theatre	Address	City	State	Zip	Screens
Kingman 4	4055 Stockton Hill Road	Kingman	AZ	86409	4
Concord 14	1985 Willow Pass Rd.	Concord	CA	94520	14
Modesto 18	1021 Tenth St.	Modesto	CA	95354	18
Pittsburg 16	4085 Century Blvd.	Pittsburg	CA	94565	16
Vacaville 16	531 Davis St.	Vacaville	CA	95688	16
AVI 8	10000 Aha Macav Pkwy.	Laughlin	NV	89029	8
Las Vegas 14 IMAX	4321 W. Flamingo Rd.	Las Vegas	NV	89103	14

CAMERA CINEMAS

4 theatres, 24 screens.
P.O. Box 720728, San Jose, CA 95172-0728. TEL: (408) 998-3022. FAX: (408) 294-3300. email: cameracinema@aol.com www.cameracinemas.com
OWNER
James Zuur
FILM BUYER
Jack NyBlom
OFFICE & WEBSITE MANAGER
Ron Regalia

THEATRES

Theatre	Address	City	State	Zip	Screens
Camera 7 Pruneyard	1875 S. Bascom Ave.	Campbell	CA	95008	7
Los Gatos	41 N. Santa Cruz Ave.	Los Gatos	CA	95030	2
Camera 3 - ComedySportz - Cafe Too!	288 S. Second St.	San Jose	CA	95113	3
Camera 12	201 S. Second St.	San Jose	CA	95113	12

CARMIKE CINEMAS

247 theatres, 2,285 screens.
1301 First Ave., P.O. Box 391, Columbus, GA 31902-0391. TEL: (706) 576-3400. FAX: (706) 576-3880. www.carmike.com
PRESIDENT & CEO
S. David Passman, III
SENIOR V.P., FINANCE, TREASURER & CFO
Richard Hare
SENIOR V.P., OPERATIONS, COO
Fred Van Noy
SENIOR V.P., GENERAL COUNSEL & SECRETARY
F. Lee Champion
SENIOR V.P., CONCESSIONS & ASSISTANT SECRETARY
H. Madison Shirley
V.P., GENERAL MANAGER, THEATRE OPERATIONS
Gary Krannacker
V.P., FILM
Larry Collins
DIRECTOR, MARKETING
Dale Hurst
DIRECTOR, HUMAN RESOURCES
Sadie Marshall
DIRECTOR, REAL ESTATE DEVELOPMENT
Jim Zehr

Theatre	Address	City	State	Zip	Screens
THEATRES					
Wynnsong	2111 E. University Ave., P.O. Box 3461	Auburn	AL	36831	16
Carmike	3443 Lorna Ridge Rd.	Birmingham	AL	35216	10
Summit	321 Summit Blvd.	Birmingham	AL	35243	16
Wynnsong	500 Commons Dr., Homewood, AL 35219	Birmingham	AL	35209	12
Carmike	1950 Market Platz Center	Cullman	AL	35055	10
Century Cinema	607 Fourteenth St. S.E., P.O. Box 988	Decatur	AL	35602	8
Regency	Cox Creek Hwy., P.O. Box 1017	Florence	AL	35631	12
Carmike	1359 Old Monrovia Rd., P.O. Box 11727	Huntsville	AL	35814	10
Carmike	4900 Government Blvd.	Mobile	AL	36616	14
Wynnsong	785 Schillinger Rd., S.	Mobile	AL	36695	16
Eastdale	1001 Eastern Blvd.	Montgomery	AL	36117	8
Promenade	2399 Cobbs Ford Rd.	Prattville	AL	36066	12
Martin	No. 65220 Hwy. 77, P.O. Box 42	Talladega	AL	35161	3
Oaks	2250 Harrison St.	Batesville	AR	72501	7
Sugar Creek	#10 Sugar Creek Center	Bella Vista	AR	72714	10
Faulkner	3 Faulkner Plaza	Conway	AR	72032	6
Carmike	5716 Townson Ave., P.O. Box 6088	Fort Smith	AR	72906	14
Harrison	617 Hwy. 62 & 65 N.	Harrison	AR	72601	8
Central City	909 Higdon Ferry Rd.	Hot Springs	AR	71901	10
Village	729 E. Hwy. 62	Mountain Home	AR	72653	5
Pines Mall	2901 Pines Mall Dr., #500	Pine Bluff	AR	71601	8
Carmike	1550 Pulsar Drive, P.O. Box 16100	Colorado Springs	CO	80935	10
Chapel Hills	1701 Briargate Blvd.	Colorado Springs	CO	80920	15
Carmike	3636 Manhattan Ave., P.O. Box 272182	Fort Collins	CO	80527	10
Mall	51027 Hwy. 6 & 24, P.O. Box 1399	Glenwood Springs	CO	81601	3
Carmike	590 24 1/2 Rd., P.O. Box 3178	Grand Junction	CO	81502	7
Carmike	2495 W. 29th. St.	Greeley	CO	80634	5
Chief Plaza	813 Lincoln Ave., P.O. Box 775821	Steamboat Springs	CO	80477	4
Carmike	US Route 13; Dover Mall	Dover	DE	19901	14
Royal Palm	2507 53rd Ave. E., P.O. Box 998; Oneco, FL 34264	Bradenton	FL	34203	20
Amelia Island	1132 14th St. S., P.O. Box 258	Fernandina Beach	FL	32035	7
Palm Cinema	4226 Old Hwy. 37	Lakeland	FL	33812	3
Carmike	4049 W. 23rd	Panama City	FL	32405	10
Mall	Hwy. 231 & State Rd., 772218 N. Cove Blvd.	Panama City	FL	32405	4
Carmike	161 E. Nine Mile Rd.	Pensacola	FL	32534	10
Lakeshore	901 US 27 N. #120	Sebring	FL	33870	8
Wynnsong	2823 Nottingham Way, P.O. Box 72346	Albany	GA	31707	16
Cinema	1610-D Vienna Rd., P.O. Box 276	Americus	GA	31709	2
Carmike	1575 Lexington Rd., P.O. Box 80436	Athens	GA	30608	12
Martin	222 Wallace C. Bryan Pkwy., P.O. Box 833	Calhoun	GA	30703	3
Riverstone	5 Reinhardt College Pkwy.	Canton	GA	30114	15
Carmike	1129 N. Tennessee St., P.O. Box 200842	Cartersville	GA	30120	12
Carmike	5555 Whittlesey Blvd.	Columbus	GA	31904	15
Hollywood Conn.	1683 Whittlesey Rd., Columbus, GA 31902	Columbus	GA	31904	10
Peachtree	3131 Manchester Expwy., Columbus, GA 31902	Columbus	GA	31909	8
Conyers Crossing	1536 Dogwood Dr., SE	Conyers	GA	30094	16
Carmike	2150 E. Walnut Ave.	Dalton	GA	30722	9
Carmike	2103 Veterans Blvd, Ste. 25, P.O. Box 5007	Dublin	GA	31040	8
Wynnsong	7290 Ingersoll St., Bldg. 1687, P.O. Box 52618	Fort Benning	GA	31905	10
Batlefield	1099 Battlefield Pkwy.	Fort Oglethorpe	GA	30742	10
Carmike	201 Main St.	LaGrange	GA	30240	10
Carmike	2400 N. Columbia St. #39	Milledgeville	GA	31061	6
Carmike	87 Newnan Station Rd., P.O. Box 71278	Newnan	GA	30271	10
Carmike	511 Stephenson Ave., P.O. Box 14213	Savannah	GA	31416	10
Wynnsong	1150 Shawnee St., P.O. Box 60158	Savannah	GA	31420	11
Carmike	1905 Scenic Hwy., Ste. 6000 (Atlanta, GA) P.O. Box 504	Snellville	GA	30078	12
Cinema	610 Brannen St., P.O. Box 833	Statesboro	GA	30459	12
Cinema	216 N. Virginia Ave.	Tifton	GA	31794	6
Wynnsong	2435 Edgewood Rd. S.W., P.O. Box 10136	Cedar Rapids	IA	52404	12
Cobblestone	8501 Hickman Rd.	Des Moines	IA	50322	9
Southridge	6720 S.E. 14th Ave.	Des Moines	IA	50315	12
Southern Hills	4400 Sergeant Rd.	Sioux City	IA	57703	12
Wynnsong	P.O. Box 3551	Urbandale	IA	50322	16
Carmike	4031 Poleline Rd., P.O. Box 5430	Chubbuck	ID	83202	7
Pine Ridge	4455 Yellowstone, P.O. Box 5430	Chubbuck	ID	83202	10
Palace	415 Detroit Dr.	Bloomington	IL	61704	10
Parkway	2103 N. Veterans, Ste. 300	Bloomington	IL	61704	8
Beverly	910 Meijer Dr.	Champaign	IL	61821	18
Strand	2360 S. Mount Zion Rd.	Decatur	IL	62521	10
Market Square	2160 Sycamore Rd.	Dekalb	IL	60115	10
Hickory Point	Hickory Point Mall	Forsyth	IL	62535	12
Lincoln	215 S. Kickapoo St.	Lincoln	IL	62656	4
Cinema	306 University Dr., P.O. Box 189	Macomb	IL	61455	2
Orpheum	515 W. Gore Rd.	Morris	IL	60450	10
University	1010 S. Main St.	Normal	IL	61761	8
Peru Mall	Peru Mall, Ste. MT, 13940 Rd.	Peru	IL	61354	8
Sauk Valley	4110 E. 30th St.	Sterling	IL	61081	8
Sunnyland	#40 Sunnyland Plaza	Washington	IL	61571	10
Capri	205 Dry Branch Dr.	Crawfordsville	IN	47933	8
Encore Park	2701 Cassopolis St.	Elkhart	IN	46514	14
Carmike	3930 E. Dupont Rd.	Fort Wayne	IN	46825	20
Seth Childs	2610 Farm Bureau Rd.	Manhattan	KS	66502	12
Cinema	Hwy. 421 S., P.O. Box 101; Grays Knob, KY 40829	Harlan	KY	40829	4
Martin	4000 Ft. Campbell Blvd., P.O. Box 530	Hopkinsville	KY	42241	5
Carmike	3151 Mapleleaf Dr., P.O. Box 55248	Lexington	KY	40509	10
Cinema	1579 US Hwy. 68	Maysville	KY	41056	4
Cinema	900 US Hwy. 25 E., Middlesboro Mall Box 28	Middlesboro	KY	40965	4
Carmike	5725 Johnston St., P.O. Box 2319	Lafayette	LA	70503	10
Royal Knight	101 South Second	Alpena	MI	49707	3
State Cinemas	206 N. Second Ave.	Alpena	MI	49707	3
Lakeview Square	5775 Beckley Rd.	Battle Creek	MI	49015	10
Big Rapids Cinema	213 S. Michigan Ave.	Big Rapids	MI	49307	4
Birchwood Cinema	4350 24th Ave. Ste. 15	Fort Gratiot	MI	48059	10
Copper	1703 W. Memorial Dr.	Houghton	MI	49931	5
Plaza Cinemas	1700 N. Wisner St.	Jackson	MI	49202	8
Harbor Cinemas	3857 W. US 10	Ludington	MI	49431	8
Deleft Cinemas	130 W. Main St.	Marquette	MI	49855	5
Royal Cinemas	1351 O'Dovero Dr.	Marquette	MI	49855	10

Theatre	Address	City	State	Zip	Screens
Fashion Square Cinemas	4511 Fashion Square Blvd.	Saginaw	MI	48604	10
Varsity Cinemas	1098 W. 3 Mile Rd.	Sault Ste. Marie	MI	49783	10
Grand Traverse Cinema	3200 S. Airport Rd. W. Unit 15	Traverse City	MI	49684	9
Horizon Cinemas	3587 Market Place Cr.	Traverse City	MI	49684	10
Carmike	15630 Cedar Ave., P.O. Box 240-803	Apple Valley	MN	55124	15
Cinema	220 Stadium Rd., P.O. Box 1299	Mankato	MN	56002	6
Cinema	1 N. German St., P.O. Box 67	New Ulm	MN	56073	3
Oakdale	1188 Helmo Ave., N.	Oakdale	MN	55128	20
Kandi	1605 S. 1st St. S.	Willmar	MN	56201	6
University	727 N. Charles St.	Warrensburg	MO	64093	8
Carmike	2255 Overland Ave., P.O. Box 80245	Billings	MT	59108	7
Wynnsong	2456 Central Ave., P.O. Box 80245	Billings	MT	59101	10
Campus Square	1611 S. 11th Ave.	Bozeman	MT	59715	8
Plaza	3100 Harrison Ave., P.O. Box 3453	Butte	MT	59701	6
Carmike	1601 Marketplace Dr., Ste. 75, P.O. Box 1439	Great Falls	MT	59404	10
Camike	3640 Mullan Rd., Missoula, MT 59808	Missoula	MT	59802	10
Village	3804 S. Reserve St., Missoula, MT 59808	Missoula	MT	59801	6
Carmike	299-I Swannanoa River Rd., P.O. Box 9340	Asheville	NC	28805	10
Cinema	1018 N. Lake Park Blvd., P.O. Box 2047	Carolina Bch.	NC	28428	4
Plaza	Dunn Plaza Shopping Center, P.O. Box 511	Dunn	NC	28334	2
Wynnsong	1807 Martin Luther King Blvd., P.O. Box 52618	Durham	NC	27717	15
Kingsway	220-L West Kings Hwy., P.O. Box 3161	Eden	NC	27288	4
Carmike	Freeway @ Morganton Rd., P.O. Box 40535	Fayetteville	NC	28309	12
Marketfair	1916 Skibo Rd., Ste. 300	Fayetteville	NC	28314	15
Wynnsong	3039 Boone Trail Ext.	Fayetteville	NC	28304	7
Cinema	Tri City Mall, P.O. Box 786	Forest City	NC	28043	4
Carmike	4882 Koger Blvd.	Greensboro	NC	27407	18
Carmike	1685 E. Fire Tower Rd.	Greenville	NC	27834	12
Cinema	500 McCotter Blvd. Hwy. 70, P.O. Box 450	Havelock	NC		6
Carmike	2000 S.E. Catawba Valley Blvd., P.O. Box 147	Hickory	NC	28603	14
Carmike	2705 N. Main St., Ste. 117, P.O. Box 5483	High Point	NC	27262	8
Carmike	350 Western Blvd.	Jacksonville	NC	28541	16
Westgate	Westgate Plz. Shop. Ctr. Blvd., P.O. Box 641	Lenoir	NC	28645	2
Cinema	235 Talbert Blvd., P.O. Box 1106	Lexington	NC	27292	8
Cinema	2220 N. Aspen St., P.O. Box 356	Lincolnton	NC	28092	8
Cinema	3017 Bridges St., P.O. Box 988	Morehead City	NC	28557	3
Park Place	9525 Chapel Hill Rd.	Morrisville	NC	27560	16
Blueridge	600 Blueridge Rd.	Raleigh	NC	27606	14
Carmike	5501 Atlantic Springs Rd.	Raleigh	NC	27658	15
Carmike	2201 - 4 E. Dixson Blvd.	Shelby	NC	28150	10
Cinema	1109 W. 15th St., P.O. Box 3973	Washington	NC	27889	7
Carmike	111 Cinema Dr., P.O. Box 3925	Wilmington	NC	28406	16
Carmike	1501 Ward Blvd.	Wilson	NC	27893	10
Carmike	3640 Reynolda Rd., P.O. Box 11107	Winston-Salem	NC	27106	10
Wynnsong	1501 Hanes Mall Blvd., P.O. Box 24817	Winston-Salem	NC	27103	12
Carmike	2700 State St., P.O. Box 1622	Bismarck	ND	58502	8
Lake	25 Fourth Street S., P.O. Box 758	Devils Lake	ND	58301	3
Cinema	Hwy. 22 & I-94; Prairie Hills Mall 1681 3rd Ave. W.	Dickinson	ND	58601	3
Carmike	2306 32nd Ave. S., P.O. Box 13116	Grand Forks	ND	58208	10
Columbia	3100 32nd Ave. S., P.O. Box 13116	Grand Forks	ND	58208	4
Stadium	2400 10th St. S.W., Ste. 604, Dakota Mall	Minot	ND	58701	9
Carmike	1000 S. Dewey St. Ste. 110	North Platte	NE	69101	6
Monument	2302 Frontage Rd.	Scottsbluff	NE	69361	6
Cinema	418 West Main, P.O. Box 1464	Artesia	NM	88210	2
Carmike	1875 Cinema Dr., Walmart Plaza, P.O. Box 15	Olean	NY	14760	8
Ashtabula Mall	3315 N. Ridge East, Ashtabula Mall, Unit 400	Ashtabula	OH	44004	6
Carmike	906 Interstate Dr.	Findlay	OH	45840	12
Findlay	1800 Tiffin Ave. #E-10	Findlay	OH	45840	6
Ohio Valley Mall	700 Banfield Ave., P.O. Box 8016	Saint Clairsville	OH	43950	11
Plaza	4314 Milan Rd., Unit 700, P.O. Box 2501	Sandusky	OH	44871	8
Cinema	100 Mall Dr.	Steubenville	OH	43952	6
Carmike	2600 W. Broadway, P.O. Box 1207	Ardmore	OK	73402	5
Dunkin Theatre	207 E. Broadway, P.O. Box 947	Cushing	OK	74023	1
Carmike	1501 Plato Rd., P.O. Box 758	Duncan	OK	73533	6
Carmike	7102 N.W. Cache Rd.	Lawton	OK	73507	8
Carmike	2812 W. Shawnee By-Pass, P.O. Box 1307	Muskogee	OK	74401	6
North Park	800 E. Prospect, P.O. Box 68	Ponca City	OK	74601	4
Cinema Center	3031 N. Harrison, P.O. Box 937	Shawnee	OK	74802	8
Hornbeck	125 N. Bell, P.O. Box 937	Shawnee	OK	74802	2
Carmike	1909 N. Perkins Rd., P.O. Box 277	Stillwater	OK	74076	10
Carmike	750 N.E. Circle Blvd.	Corvallis	OR	97330	12
Carmike	1700 Catasauqua, P.O. Box 90175	Allentown	PA	18103	16
Carmike	600 Logan Valley Mall	Altoona	PA	16602	8
Park Hills Plaza	West Plank Rd.	Altoona	PA	16602	7
Plaza	6800 Big Beaver Blvd.	Beaver Falls	PA	15010	6
Cinema	900 Chambersburg Mall (Greentown)	Chambersburg	PA	17201	7
Laura Mall	University Dr., Laurel Mall Shop. Center	Connellsville	PA	15425	4
Cranberry Mall	Route 19 & Freedom Rd.	Cranberry Township	PA	16066	8
Wynnsong	401 Vine St., Hollywood Square, P.O. Box 373	Delmont	PA	15626	12
Cinema	Dubois Mall	Dubois	PA	15801	5
Carmike	Route 30, Westmoreland Mall Annex	Greensburg	PA	15601	15
Cinema	Indiana Mall, 2334 Oaklane Ave. Ste. 4	Indiana	PA	15701	4
Galleria	1500 Washington Rd.	Mount Lebanon	PA	15228	6
Carmike	700 Ft. Couch Rd., S. Hills Village, P.O. Box 113-448	Pittsburgh	PA	15241	10
Southland	629 Clairton Blvd.	Pleasant Hills	PA	15236	9
Coventry	650 W. Schuylkill Rd.	Pottstown	PA	19464	8
Cinema	501 Benner Pike, Route 150	State College	PA	16801	6
Carmike	1372 W. Main St., Uniontown Mall	Uniontown	PA	15401	6
Maxi Saver	2001 Mountain View Dr.	West Mifflin	PA	15142	12
Wymossing	800 Brekshire Blvd.	Wymossing	PA	19610	8
James Island	1743 Central Park Rd.	Charleston	SC	29412	8
Astro	403 College Ave.	Clemson	SC	29631	3
Carmike	122 Afton Court, P.O. Box 2143, Irmo, SC 29063	Columbia	SC	29212	14
Wynnsong	5320 Forest Dr., P.O. Box 6855	Columbia	SC	29206	10
Cinema	118 W. Carolina Ave., P.O. Box 817	Hartsville	SC	29550	2
Broadway	1175 Celebrity Circle, P.O. Box 2836	Myrtle Beach	SC	29578	16
Colonial	10177 N. Kings Hwy.	Myrtle Beach	SC	29572	12
Camelot	2016 Columbia Rd., K-Mart Shop. Ctr., P.O. Box 1801	Orangeburg	SC	29116	4
Cinema	2150 Cherry Rd., P.O. Box 11911	Rock Hill	SC	29731	7
Carmike	1855 E. Main St., Ste. 14-PMB	Spartanburg	SC	29307	7

Theatre	Address	City	State	Zip	Screens
Wynnsong	1640 John B White, Sr. Blvd.	Spartanburg	SC	29301	7
Carmike	3315 6th Ave. S.E., Ste. 4	Aberdeen	SD	57401	9
Carmike	230 Knollwood Dr., P.O. Box 3418	Rapid City	SD	57709	10
Rushmore	350 East Disk Dr., P.O. Box 3418	Rapid City	SD	57709	7
Carmike	3404 Gateway Blvd., P.O. Box 90625	Sioux Falls	SD	51106	7
Yankton Mall	2101 Broadway Ave., Ste. 5	Yankton	SD	57078	5
Bell Forge	5400 Bell Forge Ln. E. (Nashville, TN)	Antioch	TN	37011	10
Hickory	901 Bell Rd. (Nashville, TN)	Antioch	TN	37013	8
Bijou	215 Broad St.	Chattanooga	TN	37402	7
Wynnsong	2210 Gunbarrel Rd., P.O. Box 21585	Chattanooga	TN	37424	10
Governor's Square	2801 Wilma Rudolph Blvd.	Clarksville	TN	37040	10
Highland	1181 S. Jefferson	Cookeville	TN	38503	12
Carmike	710 US Hwy. 51 Bypass WPMB 600	Dyersburg	TN	38024	9
Thoroughbred	633 Frazier Dr., P.O. Box 682261	Franklin	TN	37068	20
Rivergate	800 Rivergate Pkwy., P.O. Box 229	Goodlettesville	TN	37070	8
Capri	11 E. By-Pass, P.O. Box 700	Greenville	TN	37744	2
Northgate	310 Ring Rd.	Hixson	TN	37343	14
Johnson City	1805 N. Roan St.	Johnson City	TN	37601	14
Carmike	5020 Millertown Pike, P.O. Box 27408	Knoxville	TN	37917	10
Movies	175 N. Seven Oaks Dr., Bldg. 300	Knoxville	TN	37922	7
Wynnsong	200 N. Peters Rd.	Knoxville	TN	37923	16
Movies	2108 Jacksboro Pike	Lafollette	TN	37766	2
Wynnsong	721 Myatt Dr.	Madison	TN	37115	10
Foothills	507 Foothills Plaza	Marysville	TN	37801	12
College Square	2250 E. Morris Blvd., P.O. Box 1475	Morristown	TN	37816	9
Wynnsong	2626 Cason Square Blvd.	Murfreesboro	TN	37133	16
Bellevue	120 Belle Forest Circle	Nashville	TN	37221	8
Oneida Cinema	Hwy 27 N., P.O. Box 4668	Oneida	TN	37841	3
Cinema	718 S. Main St.	Springfield	TN	37172	1
Park Central	3234 S. Clack St.	Abilene	TX	79606	6
Carmike	3003 S. Expwy. #281, P.O. Box 3430	Edinburg	TX	78539	20
Carmike	9840 Gateway Blvd. N.	El Paso	TX	79924	16
Carmke	201 Tall Pines Rd.	Longview	TX	75608	10
Cinema	4600 S. Medford, Lufkin Mall, P.O. Box 1408	Lufkin	TX	75901	9
Carmike	3801 N. St, Northview Plz. Shop. Ctr., P.O. Box 630991	Nacogdoches	TX	75961	6
Pines Theatre	340 N. 4th St., P.O. Box 1026	Silsbee	TX	77656	1
Carmike	7415 S. Broadway	Tyler	TX	75703	14
Century City	4105 Maplewood	Wichita Falls	TX	76308	6
Sikes	238 Sikes Center, 3111 Midwestern Pkwy.	Wichita Falls	TX	76308	10
Wynnsong	4925 N. Edgewood Dr.	Provo	UT	84604	12
Carmike	1600 W. Fox Park Dr. (Salt Lake City, UT)	West Jordan	UT	84088	12
HW Connection	3217 S. Decker Lake Dr.	West Valley City	UT	84119	15
Carmike	1005 Garden Blvd.	Charlottesville	VA	22901	6
Carmike	801 Lakeside Dr., P.O. Box 10033	Lynchburg	VA	24506	8
River Ridge	3405 Candlers Mt. Rd., F315 River Ridge Mall	Lynchburg	VA	24502	4
Carmike	1100 Alverser Dr. (Richmond, VA), P.O. Box 1185	Midlothian	VA	23113	10
Carmike	4494 Electric Rd. S.W.	Roanoke	VA	24014	10
Valley	1700 Apperson Dr.	Salem	VA	24153	8
Apple Blossom	1850 Apple Blossom Dr., Apple Blossom Mall	Winchester	VA	22601	6
Cinema Center	601 E. Jubal Early Dr.	Winchester	VA	22601	6
Carmike	1331 Center Park Way, P.O. Box 2835, Pasco, WA 99302	Kennewick	WA	99336	12
Oakwood	4800 Golf Rd. #4	Eau Claire	WI	54701	12
Valley Theatre	4400 Hwy. 16	Lacrosse	WI	54603	6
Pine Tree Mall Cinemas	2727 Cahill Rd.	Marinette	WI	54143	9
Cinema	Mercer Mall, P.O. Box 6394	Bluefield	WV	24701	8
Mall	9540 Mall Rd.	Morgantown	WV	26505	12
Cole Square	517 Cole Square Shop	Cheyenne	WY	28001	3
Frontier	1400 Dell Range Blvd.	Cheyenne	WY	82009	9

CASPER MGMT., DBA THE REEL THEATRE

6 theatres, 31 screens.

4500 W. Overland Rd., Boise, ID. 83705-2813. TEL: (208) 388-3876. www.reeltheatre.com

THEATRES

Theatre	Address	City	State	Zip	Screens
Country Club Plaza Reel	4550 Overland,	Boise	ID		6
Northgate Reel Theatre	6950 W. State St.	Boise	ID		6
Nampa Reel Theatre	2104 Caldwell Blvd.	Nampa	ID		6
The Reel Thetare	310 E. Oak St.,	Pocatello	ID		2
The Reel Theatre 8	477 S.E. 13th Street	Ontario	OR		8
The Huish Reel Theatre	131 N. Main,	Richfield	UT		3

CHAKERES THEATRES

14 theatres, 51 screens.

222 N. Murray St., Box 1200, Springfield, OH 45501. TEL: (937) 323-6447. FAX: (937) 325-1100.
email: info@chakerestheatres.com www.chakerestheatres.com

PRESIDENT & CEO
Philip H. Chakeres
VICE PRESIDENT
Harry N. Chakeres, Valerie C. Baker
DIRECTOR OF ADVERTISING
Paul Ramsey
FILM BUYER
Fred Schweitzer

THEATRES

Theatre	Address	City	State	Zip	Screens
Chakeres Franklin Square 6	161 Franklin Square Shopping Ctr.	Frankfort	KY	40604	6
Chakeres University Cinema	159 E. Main St.	Morehead	KY	40351	1
Chakeres Bellefontaine Cinema 8	888 E. Sandusky St.	Bellefontaine	OH	43311	8
Chakeres Celina 5	116 N. Main St.	Celina	OH	45822	5
Chakeres Lake Drive-In	8477 State Rte. 703	Celina	OH	45822	1
Chakeres Melody 49 Drive-In	State Rte. 49	Dayton	OH	45322	2
Chakeres Skyborn Drive-In	Rte. 235 & Haddix Rd.	Fairborn	OH	45324	1
Chakeres Scioto Breeze Drive-In	State Rte. 23	Lucasville	OH	45648	2
Chakeres Melody Cruise-In	4025 E. National Rd.	Springfield	OH	45505	2
Chakeres Upper Valley 5	1475 Upper Valley Pike	Springfield	OH	45504	5
Chakeres Cinema 10	3115 E. National Rd.	Springfield	OH	45505	10
Chakeres Urbana 1 & 2	216 S. Main St.	Urbana	OH	43078	2

Theatre	Address	City	State	Zip	Screens
Chakeres Wilmington Plaza 5	1276 Romback Ave.	Wilmington	OH	45177	5
Chakeres Wilmington Drive-In	1129 N. Rte. 134	Wilmington	OH	45177	1

CINELUX THEATRES

7 theatres, 35 screens.

P.O. Box 6395, San Jose, CA 95150-6395. TEL: (408) 559-7469. FAX: (408) 559-7466. www.CineLuxTheatres.com

PRESIDENT
Paul D. Gunsky

THEATRES

Theatre	Address	City	State	Zip	Screens
CineLux Plaza Theatres	2501 Winchester Blvd.	Campbell	CA	95008	7
CineLux Almaden Cinema 5	2306 Almaden Rd., #P	San Jose	CA	95125	5
CineLux Chabot Cinema	2853 Castro Valley Blvd.	Castro Valley	CA	94546	1
CineLux Delta Cinema Saver	641 First St.	Brentwood	CA	94513	2
Cinelux 41st Avenue Cinema	1475 41st Avenue	Capitola	CA	95010	3
CineLux Tennant Station Stadium 11	750 Tennant Ave.	Morgan Hill	CA	95037	11
CineLuxe Scotts Valley Cinema	226 Mount Hermon Road	Scotts Valley	CA	95066	6

CINEMA CENTER

6 theatres, 56 screens.

502 S. Market St., Millersburg, PA 17061. TEL: (717) 692-4744. FAX: (717) 692-3073. www.cinemacenter.com

PRESIDENT & OWNER
Marvin R. Troutman
CEO
Gina Troutman DiSanto
EXECUTIVE V.P., DEVELOPMENT
Van Troutman
EXECUTIVE V.P., OPERATIONS
Trudy Withers
FILM BUYER
Al Milgram

THEATRES

Theatre	Address	City	State	Zip	Screens
Cinema Center of Bloomsburg	1879 Columbia Blvd.	Bloomsburg	PA	17815	12
Cinema Center of Camphill	3431 Simpson Ferry Rd.	Camp Hill	PA	17011	12
Cinema Center of Selinsgrove	Susquehanna Valley Mall, Ste. T1	Selinsgrove	PA	17870	12
Cinema Center at Fairgrounds Square	3050 N. Fifth St. Hwy., Ste. A1	Reading	PA	19605	10
Sky-Vu Drive-In	Rte. 25	Gratz	PA	17030	1
Cinema Center of Williamsport	300 W. Fouth St.	Williamsport	PA	17701	9

CINEMA ENTERTAINMENT CORP.

16 theatres, 120 screens.

Box 1126, St. Cloud, MN 56302. TEL: (320) 251-9131. FAX: (320) 251-1003. www.cectheatres.com

PRESIDENT
Robert Ross
VICE PRESIDENT
Tony Tillemans
V.P., FINANCE
Tony Ross
SECRETARY
Dave Ross
DIRECTOR, FILM BUYER & MARKETING
Dwight Gunderson
ASSISTANT FILM BUYER
Kim Carter
OPERATIONS
Greg Carter, Roger Hansen
CONCESSIONS MANAGER
Andy Bergstrom

THEATRES

Theatre	Address	City	State	Zip	Screens
Mall 8	550 S. Gear Ave., Ste. 3	Burlington	IA	52601	8
Clinton 8	2340 Valley W.	Clinton	IA	52732	8
Fort 8	1417 Central Ave.	Ft. Dodge	IA	50501	8
Cinema West 8	4710 4th St. S.W.	Mason City	IA	50401	8
Ottumwa 8	1215 Theatre Dr.	Ottumwa	IA	52501	8
Mall Cinema 7	2510 Bridge Ave.	Albert Lea	MN	56007	7
Bemidji Theatre 9	5284 Theatre Ln.	Bemidji	MN	56601	9
Breckenridge 6	320 Minnesota Ave.	Breckenridge	MN	56520	6
Faribo West Mall Theatre	200 Western Ave.	Faribault	MN	55021	6
Marshall 6 Theatre	230 W. Lyon	Marshall	MN	56258	6
Cinema 6 Theatre	8426 Enterprise Dr.	Mountain Iron	MN	55768	6
Winona 7	70 W. 2nd St.	Virginia	MN	55987	7
Center 7	3100 23rd St.	Columbus	NE	68601	7
Norfolk 7	120 S. 3rd	Norfolk	NE	68701	7
Hudson 12	520 Stage Line Rd.	Hudson	WI	54016	12
Lake 7	1769 County Hwy. S.	Rice Lake	WI	54868	7

CINEMA WEST

12 theatres, 91 screens.

P.O. Box 750595, Petaluma, CA 94975. TEL: (707) 762-0990. FAX: (707) 762-3969. www.cinemawest.com

CONTACT
Beth Beazor

THEATRES

Theatre	Address	City	State	Zip	Screens
Angels 5 Theatre	1228 S. Main St.	Angels Camp	CA	95222	5
Cloverdale 4 Cinemas	121 E. First St	Cloverdale	CA	95425	4
Fairfax 5 Theatres	9 Broadway	Fairfax	CA	94930	5
Palladio 16 Cinemas	240 Palladio Parkway	Folsom	CA	95630	16
Fortuna Theatre	1241 Main St.	Fortuna	CA	95540	6
Livermore Cinemas	2490 First St.	Livermore	CA	94550	13
Contra Costa Cinema	555 Center Ave.	Martinez	CA	94553	8
Boulevard Cinemas	200 'C' St.	Petaluma	CA	94952	13

Theatre	Address	City	State	Zip	Screens
Sebastopol Cinemas	6868 McKinley St.	Sebastopol	CA	95472	9
Sonoma Cinemas	200 Siesta Way	Sonoma	CA	95476	6
Tiburon Playhouse	40 Main St.	Tiburon	CA	94920	3
Noyo Theatre	57 E. Commerical St.	Willits	CA	95490	3

CINEMAGIC THEATRES

9 theatres, 91 screens.
Midwest Theatres Corporation, P.O. Box 1386, Maple Grove, MN 55311. TEL: (763) 746-0228. FAX: (763) 572-8005. www.cinemagictheatres.com
PRESIDENT, CEO
Steven L. Tripp
CFO & BUSINESS DEVELOPMENT
Bryan J. Sieve
V.P., OPERATIONS
Bruce S. Berry
FILM BUYER
Todd Tepley
SPECIAL EVENTS COORDINATOR
Lisa A. Sieve
OFFICE MANAGER
Renee L. Strine

THEATRES

Theatre	Address	City	State	Zip	Screens
Great Lakes Cinema 7	1698 Exchange St.	Okoboji	IA.	51355	7
CineMagic 7 Theatres	1301 18th Ave. N.W.	Austin.	MN.	55912	7
Atlantis 15	14401 Burnhaven Dr.	Burnsville	MN.	55337	15
Century 9 Theatres	766 Century Ave.	Hutchinson	MN.	55350	9
Chateau 14	3450 E. Circle Dr.	Rochester	MN.	55906	14
CineMagic Hollywood Stadium 12	2171 Superior Dr. N.W.	Rochester	MN.	55901	12
Metropolitan 15	4300 O'Day Ave.	St. Michael	MN.	55376	15
CineMagic 5	621 S. Minnesota	St. Peter	MN.	56082	5
CineMagic Stadium 7 Theatres	2521 Hwy. 25 N.	Menomonie	WI	54751	7

CINEMARK USA, INC.

296 U.S. theatres, 3,842 U.S. screens; Foreign holdings: 130 theatres, 1,066 screens; TOTAL: 408 theatres, 4,657 screens.
3900 Dallas Pkwy., Ste. 500, Plano, TX 75093. TEL: (972) 665-1000. FAX: (972) 665-1004. www.cinemark.com
CHAIRMAN
Lee Roy Mitchell
CEO
Alan Stock
PRESIDENT AND COO
Tim Warner
PRESIDENT, CINEMARK INTERNATIONAL
Valmir Fernandes
EXECUTIVE V.P. AND ASSISTANT SECRETARY
Tandy Mitchell
EXECUTIVE V.P./CFO/ASSISTANT SECRETARY
Robert Copple
SENIOR V.P., GENERAL COUNSEL & SECRETARY
Michael Cavalier
SENIOR V.P., FILM LICENSING
Steve Bunnell
SENIOR V.P., REAL ESTATE
Tom Owens
SENIOR V.P., OPERATIONS
Robert Carmony
SENIOR V.P., PURCHASING
Walter Hebert
V.P., CONSTRUCTION
Don Harton
V.P., CINEMARK INTERNATIONAL
Ken Higgins
V.P., THEATRE TECHNOLOGY
Damian Wardle
V.P., HUMAN RESOURCES
Brad Smith
V.P. & DIRECTOR, THEATRE OPERATIONS
Steve Zuehlke
V.P. & ASSISTANT DIRECTOR, THEATRE OPERATIONS
Jeff Stone
V.P., FOOD & BEVERAGE
Bob Shimmin
V.P., REAL ESTATE COUNSEL
Paul Ledbetter
V.P., DEVELOPMENT
Randy Recer
V.P., TAX
Vatoni Ragsdale
V.P. & CHIEF TECHNOLOGY OFFICER
Doug Fay
V.P. & CONTROLLER
Joe Manzi
V.P., PURCHASING
Steve Owen
V.P., FINANCIAL SYSTEMS AND SPECIAL PROJECTS
Greg Muse
V.P., FINANCIAL PLANNING AND ANALYSIS
Richard Stanley
V.P., MARKETING & COMMUNICATIONS
James Meredith

THEATRES

Theatre	Address	City	State	Zip	Screens
Century 16	301 E. 36th Ave.	Anchorage	AK	99503	16

Theatre	Address	City	State	Zip	Screens
Cinemark Tinseltown USA	17314 I-30	Benton	AR	72015	14
Cinema 6	Hwy. 65 at I-40	Conway	AR	72032	6
Cinemark Tandy 10	4188 E. McCain Blvd.	N. Little Rock	AR	72117	10
Cinemark Mesa 16	1051 N. Dobson Rd.	Mesa	AZ	85201	16
Cinemark 10	2175 El Mercado Loop	Sierra Vista	AZ	85635	10
Century El Con 20	3601 E. Broadway	Tucson	AZ	85716	20
Century Gateway 12	770 N. Kolb	Tucson	AZ	85710	12
Century Park 16	1055 W. Grant Rd.	Tucson	AZ	85705	16
789Century Park Place 20	5870 E. Broadway Blvd.	Tucson	AZ	85711	20
Cinemark Movies 10	34491 Date Palm Dr.	Cathedral City	CA	92234	10
Cinemark 14	801 E. Ave.	Chico	CA	95926	14
Cinemark Movies 8	Promenade Shopping Center	Chino	CA	91710	8
Century Cinema	41 Tamal Vista Blvd.	Corte Madera	CA	94925	1
Century 20 Daly City	1901 Junipero Serra Blvd.	Daly City	CA	94015	20
Cinemark Blackhawk Movies 7	4175 Blackhawk Plaza Circle	Danville	CA	94526	7
Imperial Vally Mall 14	3651 S. Dogwood Rd.	El Centro	CA	92243	14
Century Laguna 16	9349 Big Horn Blvd.	Elk Grove	CA	95758	16
Century 14	261 Iron Point Rd.	Folsom	CA	95630	14
Cinedome 8	39153 Farwell Dr.	Fremont	CA	94538	8
Cinemark Movies 8	Hanford Mall	Hanford	CA	93230	8
Huntington Beach	7777 Edinger Ave.	Huntington Beach	CA	92647	20
Cinemark 22	2600 W. Ave.	Lancaster	CA	93534	22
Cinemark Movies 12	44790 Valley Central Way	Lancaster	CA	93534	12
Century Larkspur	500 Larkspur Landing Cr.	Larkspur	CA	94939	4
Cinemark at The Pike	99 S. Pine Ave.	Long Beach	CA	90802	14
Cinéarts Sequoia	25 Throckmorton Ave.	Mill Valley	CA	94941	2
Century 20 Great Mall	1010 Great Mall Dr.	Milpitas	CA	95035	20
Monterey 13	1700 Del Monte Center	Monterrey	CA	93940	13
Century Cinema 16	1500 N. Shoreline Blvd.	Mountain View	CA	94043	16
Cinedome 8	825 Pearl St.	Napa	CA	94559	8
Cinedome 7	6000 New Park Mall	Newark	CA	94560	7
Century 8	12827 Victory Blvd.	North Hollywood	CA	91606	8
Century Rowland Plaza	44 Rowland Way	Novato	CA	94945	8
Century Stadium 25	1701 W. Katella Ave.	Orange	CA	92867	25
Cinemark at Antelope Valley Mall	1475 W. Ave. P	Palmdale	CA	93551	16
Cinéarts @ Palo Alto Square	3000 El Camino Real	Palo Alto	CA	94306	2
Century 16 Downtown P. Hill	125 Crescent Dr.	Pleasant Hill	CA	94523	16
Cinéarts 5 @ Pleasant Hill	2314 Monument Blvd.	Pleasant Hill	CA	94523	5
Century @ The River	71800 Hwy. 111	Rancho Mirage	CA	92270	15
Cinemark Movies 10	980 Old Alturas Rd.	Redding	CA	96003	10
Cinemark Movies 8	359 Park Marina Circle	Redding	CA	96001	8
Century Park 12	557 E. Bayshore Rd.	Redwood City	CA	94063	12
Redwood Downtown 20	825 Middlefield Rd.	Redwood City	CA	94063	20
Century Hilltop 16	3200 Klose Way	Richmond	CA	94806	16
Century Roseville 14	1555 Eureka Rd.	Roseville	CA	95661	14
Century 16 Greenback Lane	6233 Garfield Ave.	Sacramento	CA	95841	16
Downtown Plaza 7	445 Downtown Plaza	Sacramento	CA	95814	7
Northridge 14	350 Northridge Shopping Ctr.	Salinas	CA	93906	14
Century Tanforan 20	The Shops at Tanforan	San Bruno	CA	94066	20
Century 9 San Francisco Centre	835 Market St.	San Francisco	CA	94103	9
Cinéarts at The Empire	85 W. Portal Ave.	San Francisco	CA	94127	3
Century 10 Berryessa	1171 N. Capital Ave.	San Jose	CA	95132	10
Century 24	741 Winchester Blvd.	San Jose	CA	95128	1
Century 25	1694 Saratoga Ave.	San Jose	CA	95129	1
Century Capitol 16	3690 Hillcap Ave.	San Jose	CA	95136	16
Oakridge 20	925 Blossom Hill Rd.	San Jose	CA	95123	20
Century 16 Bayfair Mall	15555 E. 14th St.	San Leandro	CA	94578	16
Century 12 San Mateo	320 E. 2nd Ave.	San Mateo	CA	94401-3906	12
Century Northgate	7000 Northgate Dr.	San Rafael	CA	94903	15
Century Regency	280 Smith Ranch Rd.	San Rafael	CA	94903	6
Cinéarts Marin	101 Caledonia	Sausalito	CA	94965	3
Cinemark Movies 14	W. Valley Mall	Tracy	CA	95376	14
Century 25 Union Landing	32100 Union Landing	Union City	CA	94587	25
Vallejo 14	109 Plaza Dr.	Vallejo	CA	94591	14
Century 10 Downtown	555 E. Main St.	Ventura	CA	93001	10
Century Stadium 16	2875 Elba St.	Ventura	CA	93003	16
Cinemark at The Mall at Victor Valley	14470 Bear Valley Rd.	Victorville	CA	92392	16
Cinemark Movies 10	12353 Mariposa Rd.	Victorville	CA	92392	10
Walnut Creek 14	1201 Locust St.	Walnut Creek	CA	94596	14
Cinemark Movies 5	1579 A E. St.	Woodland	CA	95776	5
Cinemark Movies 8	1410 Whyler Rd.	Yuba City	CA	95993	8
Century Aurora	14300 E. Alameda Ave.	Aurora	CO	80012	16
Century Boulder	1700 29th St.	Boulder	CO	80301	16
Cinemark Carefree Circle	3305 Cinema Point	Colorado Springs	CO	80922	17
Cinemark Tinseltown USA	1545 E. Cheyenne Mountain Blvd.	Colorado Springs	CO	80906	20
Cinemark Fort Collins	4721 S. Timberline Rd.	Fort Collins	CO	80525	16
Cinemark Greeley Mall	2160 Greeley Mall	Greeley	CO	80631	12
Century 16 Bel Mar	440 S. Teller St.	Lakewood	CO	80226	16
Cinemark Tinseltown	Eagleridge Shopping Center	Pueblo	CO	81008	14
Cinemark Movies 10	1796 W. Newport Pike	Wilmington	DE	19804	10
Cinemark Tinseltown	4535 Southside Blvd.	Jacksonville	FL	32216	20
Cinemark 20 at Festival Bay	Festival Bay	Orlando	FL	32819	20
Cinemark Movies 10	157 Banks Station	Fayetteville	GA	30214	10
Cinemark Tinseltown	134 Pavillion Pkwy.	Fayetteville	GA	30214	17
Cinemark Movies 12	1317 Buckeye Ave.	Ames	IA	50010	12
Cinemark North Grand 5	North Grand Mall	Ames	IA	50010	5
Varsity II	2412 Lincoln Way	Ames	IA	50014	2
Jordan Creek 20	101 Jordan Creek Pkwy.	W. Des Moines	IA	50266	20
Century Stratford Square	804 Stratford Square	Bloomingdale	IL	60108	16
Cinemark Movies 10	1600 N. State	Bourbonnais	IL	60914	10
Deer Park 16	21600 W. Field Pkwy.	Deer Park	IL	90010	16
Evanston 18 / Cinéarts 6	1715 Maple Ave.	Evanston	IL	60201	18
Cinemark Movies 10	2601 Plainfield Rd.	Joliet	IL	60435	10
Cinemark Movies 8	3101 Hennepin Dr.	Joliet	IL	60435	8
Cinemark Melrose Park	1001 W.N. Ave.	Melrose Park	IL	60160	10
Cinemark Tinseltown USA	320 S. Lincoln Way	North Aurora	IL	60542	17
Cinemark @ Seven Bridges	6500 Route 53	Woodridge	IL	60517	17
Cinemark Greentree 10	757 E. Lewis & Clark Pkwy.	Clarksville	IN	47129	10
Cinemark Movies 8	1848 E. Stop 13 Rd.	Indianapolis	IN	46227	8
Cinemark Movies 8 Washington Market	Washington Market	Indianapolis	IN	46219	8

Theatre	Address	City	State	Zip	Screens
Cinemark Movies 14	910 W. Edison	Mishawaka	IN	46545	14
Cinemark Movies 6	6424 N. Grape Rd.	Mishawaka	IN	46545	6
Cinemark at Valparaiso	700 Porter's Vale Blvd.	Valparaiso	IN	46383	12
Cinemark 20	5500 Antioch	Merriam	KS	66202	20
Cinemark Movies 10	400 Winchester Ave.	Ashland	KY	41101	10
Cinemark Fayette Mall	3800 Mall Rd.	Lexington	KY	40503	16
Cinemark Lexington Green Movies 8	200 Lexington Green Circle	Lexington	KY	40503	8
Cinemark Woodhill Movies 10	Woodhill Mall	Lexington	KY	40509	10
Cinemark Tinseltown USA	4400 Towne Center Dr.	Louisville	KY	40241	18
Cinemark Paducah	Kentucky Oaks Mall	Paducah	KY	42001	12
Cinemark Richmond Mall Movies 8	Richmond Mall	Richmond	KY	40475	8
Cinemark Baton Rouge	10000 Perkins Rowe	Baton Rouge	LA	70810	16
Cinemark Lake Charles	548 W. Prien Lake Rd.	Lake Charles	LA	70601	14
Cinemark Cinema 10	4700 Milhaven Rd.	Monroe	LA	71203	10
Cinemark Tinseltown	8400 Millicent Way	Shreveport	LA	71105	17
Cinemark Tinseltown 17	220 Blanchard St.	West Monroe	LA	71291	17
Cinemark at Hampshire Mall	367 Russell St.	Hadley	MA	1035	12
Cinemark Movies 16	28600 Dequindre Rd.	Warren	MI	48092	16
Cinemark River Hills Movies 8	River Hills Mall	Mankato	MN	56001	8
Cinemark Palace at The Plaza	500 Nichols Rd.	Kansas City	MO	64112	15
Cinemark 16	15171 Crossroads Pkwy.	Gulfport	MS	39503-3525	16
Cinemark Tinseltown USA	411 Riverwind Dr.	Pearl	MS	39208	17
Cinemark Movies 8	Barnes Crossing Mall	Tupelo	MS	38802	8
Cinemark 8 Helena	750 Great Northern Blvd.	Helena	MT	59601	8
Cinemark Asheboro	400 Randolph Mall	Asheboro	NC	27203	7
Cinemark Brassfield Cinema Ten	2101 New Garden Rd.	Greensboro	NC	27410	10
Cinemark Movies 10	9508 Northeast Court	Matthews	NC	28105	10
Cinemark Tinseltown USA	Innes St. Market	Salisbury	NC	28146	14
Cinemark 16	Lions Head Plaza	Somerdale	NJ	08083	16
Century Rio 24 Plex	4901 Pan American Fwy., N.E.	Albuquerque	NM	87109	24
Century 14 Downtown Albuq.	100 Central Ave. S.W.	Albuquerque	NM	87102	14
Cinemark Movies 8	4591 San Mateo Blvd. N.E.	Albuquerque	NM	87109	8
Cinemark Movies West	9201 Coors Rd. N.W.	Albuquerque	NM	87114	8
Cinedome 12	851 S. Boulder Hwy.	Henderson	NV	89015	12
Century 18 Sam's Town	5111 Boulder Hwy.	Las Vegas	NV	89122	18
Century Orleans	4500 W. Tropicana Blvd.	Las Vegas	NV	89103	18
Century South Point	9777 Las Vegas Blvd. S.	Las Vegas	NV	89123	16
Century Suncoast 16	9090 Alta Dr.	Las Vegas	NV	89144	16
Santa Fe Station	4949 N. Rancho	Las Vegas	NV	89130	16
Century Park Lane 16	210 E. Plumb Ln.	Reno	NV	89502	16
Century Riverside	11 N. Sierra St.	Reno	NV	89501	12
Century Summit Sierra	13965 S. Virgina St.	Reno	NV	89511	16
Century Sparks	1250 Victorian Ave.	Sparks	NV	89431	14
Cinemark Movies 10	2613 W. Henrietta Rd.	Rochester	NY	14623	10
Cinemark Tinseltown USA	2291 Buffalo Rd.	Rochester	NY	14624	18
Cinemark Carnation Cinema 5	2500 W. State St.	Alliance	OH	44601	5
Cinemark Barington Town Center 10	140 Barington Town Square Dr.	Aurora	OH	44202	10
Cinemark Tinseltown	Southern Park Mall	Boardman	OH	44512	7
Cinemark Woodland Mall Cinema 5	1234 N. Mall St.	Bowling Green	OH	43402	5
Cinemark Carriage Place Movies 12	Carriage Place	Columbus	OH	43220	12
Cinemark Stoneridge Plaza Movies 16	Stoneridge Plaza Shopping Center	Gahanna	OH	43230	16
Cinemark at Macedonia	8161 Macedonia Commons	Macedonia	OH	44056	15
Cinemark Springfield Sq. Cinema 10	Springfield Square	Mansfield	OH	44906	10
Cinemark Movies 10	6284 Dressler Rd. N.W.	North Canton	OH	44720	10
Cinemark Tinseltown U.S.A.	4720 Mega St. N.W.	North Canton	OH	44720	15
Cinemark Ontario	2355 Walker Lake Rd.	Ontario	OH	44906	14
Cinemark Miami Valley Cinema 6	Miami Valley Centre Mall	Piqua	OH	45356	6
Cinemark Movies 10	Park Place Shopping Center	Sandusky	OH	44870	10
Cinemark Strongsville	17450 Southpark Center	Strongsville	OH	44136	14
Cinemark Tiffin Mall	870 W. Market St.	Tiffin	OH	44883	8
Cinemark at Valley View	6001 Canal Rd.	Valley View	OH	44125	24
Cinemark Movies 10	The Shops of Willoughby Hills	Willoughby Hills	OH	44092	10
Cinemark Movies 10	4108 Burbank Rd.	Wooster	OH	44691	10
Cinemark Movies 8	469 Boardman/Poland Rd.	Youngstown	OH	44512	8
Cinemark Zanesville	3575 Maple Ave.	Zanesville	OH	43701	12
Cinemark Cinema 6	N. Hills Shopping Center	Ada	OK	74820	6
Cinemark Cinema 8	3812 S. Elm Place	Broken Arrow	OK	74011	8
Cinemark Tinseltown	6001 N. Martin Luther King Blvd.	Oklahoma City	OK	73111	20
Cinemark Cinema 8	1112 E. Charles Page Blvd.	Sand Springs	OK	74063	8
Cinemark Movies 8	6808 S. Memorial	Tulsa	OK	74011	8
Cinemark Tulsa	10802 E. 71 St. S.	Tulsa	OK	74133	18
Century 16 Beaver Hills Crossing	3200 S.W. Hocken Ave.	Beaverton	OR	97005	16
Cinemark Tinseltown USA	651 Medford Center	Medford	OR	97501	15
Century 16 Eastport Plaza	4040 S.E. 82nd Ave.	Portland	OR	97266	16
Century Clackamas Town Center	Clackamas Town Center	Portland	OR	97266	20
Cinemark 17	2900 Gateway	Springfield	OR	97477	17
Cinemark Movies 12	Gateway Mall	Springfield	OR	97477	12
Cinemark Movies 6	7501 Crater Lake Hwy.	White City	OR	97503	6
Cinemark Millcreek Cinema 6	975 Millcreek Mall	Erie	PA	16565	6
Tinseltown USA	1910 Rotunda Dr.	Erie	PA	16509	17
Cinemark Center Township Marketplace	99 Wagner Rd.	Monaca	PA	15061	12
Cinemark 20	40 Glenmaura National Blvd.	Moosic	PA	18507	20
Cinemark 18	Galleria at Pittsburgh Mills	Tarentum	PA	15084	18
Cinemark at Myrtle Beach	2100 Coastal Grand Circle	Myrtle Beach	SC	29577	14
Cinemark Movies 8	4488 Ladson Rd.	Summerville	SC	29485	8
Century Stadium 14	2400 S. Carolyn	Sioux Falls	SD	57106	14
Cinemark Tinseltown USA	755 W. Main St.	Oak Ridge	TN	37830	14
Century 12 Abilene	3818 John Knox Dr.	Abilene	TX	79606	12
Cinemark Allen 16	921 SH 121	Allen	TX	75013	16
Cinemark Hollywood 16	9100 Canyon Dr.	Amarillo	TX	79119	16
Cinemark Tinseltown 9	Six Flags Mall	Arlington	TX	76011	9
Cinemark Cinema 4	218 Wood St.	Athens	TX	75751	4
Cinemark Southpark Meadows	9900 S. IH-35 Service Rd. SB	Austin	TX	78748	14
Cinemark Tinseltown 17	5501 S IH-35 Northbound	Austin	TX	78744	17
Cinemark Tinseltown 15	3855 Interstate 10 S.	Beaumont	TX	77705	15
Cinemark Hill Country Galleria	12800 Hwy. 71 W.	Bee Cave	TX	78738	14
Cinemark Cinema 4	1801 E. FM 700	Big Spring	TX	79720	4
Cinemark Movies 10	3471 Old Hwy. 77	Brownsville	TX	78520	10
Cinemark Sunrise Mall	2370 N. Expwy.	Brownsville	TX	78521	17
Cinemark 14	280 Uptown Blvd.	Cedar Hill	TX	76201	14

Theatre	Address	City	State	Zip	Screens	Digital	DMA
Cinemark Cedar Park	1335 E. Whitestone Blvd	Cedar Park	TX	78613	12		
Cinemark Cinema 6	1643 W. Henderson	Cleburne	TX	76031	6		623
Cinemark Movies 18	1401 Earl Rudder Freeway South	College Station	TX	77845	18		625
Century 16	6685 S. Padre Island Dr.	Corpus Christi	TX	78412	16		600
Cinemark Dollar Cinemas	5858 S. Padre Island Dr.	Corpus Christi	TX	78412	7		600
Cinemark Cinema IV	1803 W. Seventh Ave.	Corsicana	TX	75110	4		623
Cinemark 12 Cypress	25720 Northwest Frwy	Cypress	TX	77429	12		
Cinemark 17	11819 Webb Chapel Rd.	Dallas	TX	75234	17		623
Cinemark Movies 8	Plaza Del Sol Mall	Del Rio	TX	78840	8		641
Cinemark 14	2825 Wind River Ln.	Denton	TX	76210	14		623
Mall De Las Aguilas 7	455 S. Bibb St.	Eagle Pass	TX	78852	7		641
Cielo Vista Mall 14	8401 Gateway W.	El Paso	TX	79925	14		765
Cinemark El Paso	7440 Remcon Circle	El Paso	TX	79912	14		765
Cinemark Tinseltown USA	11855 Gateway Blvd. W.	El Paso	TX	79936	20		765
Cinemark Hollywood USA Movies 15	Movies 15	Garland	TX	75041	15		623
Cinemark Movies 16	220 E. Westchester Pkwy.	Grand Prairie	TX	75052	16		623
Cinemark Tinseltown Grapevine	911 State Hwy. 114 W.	Grapevine	TX	76051	17		623
Cinemark Harker Heights	201 E. Central Texas Expwy.	Harker Heights	TX	76548	16		
Cinemark 16	401 S. Expwy. 83	Harlingen	TX	78550	16		636
Cinemark Movies 10	Sun Valley Mall	Harlingen	TX	78550	10		636
Cinemark Memorial City	310 Memorial City Mall	Houston	TX	77024	16		618
Cinemark Tinseltown	12920 N.W. Freeway	Houston	TX	77040	16		618
Cinemark Tinseltown USA	11450 E. Freeway	Jacinto City	TX	77029	17		618
Cinemark 19	1030 W. Grand Pkwy. N.	Katy	TX	77449	19		618
Cinemark Movies 14	3250 W. Pleasant Run Rd.	Lancaster	TX	75146	14		623
Cinemark Mall Del Norte	5300 San Dario	Laredo	TX	78041	16		749
Cinemark Movies 12	5412 San Bernardo	Laredo	TX	78041	12		749
Cinemark 15 Vista Ridge Mall	Vista Ridge Mall	Lewisville	TX	75067	15		623
Cinemark Movies 8	Vista Ridge Mall	Lewisville	TX	75067	8		623
Cinemark Movies 16	5721 58th St.	Lubbock	TX	79424	16		651
Cinemark Tinseltown Lubbock	2535 82nd St.	Lubbock	TX	79423	17		651
Cinemark Lufkin 12	109 Miles Way	Lufkin	TX	75901	12		709
Cinemark 12 Mansfield	2041 N. Hwy. 287, Ste. 901	Mansfield	TX	76063	12		623
Cinemark Hollywood USA	100 W. Nolana Loop	McAllen	TX	78504	17		636
Cinemark Movies 8	1800 S. 16th	McAllen	TX	78501	6		636
Cinemark Movies 14	1701 S. Central Expwy.	McKinney	TX	75069	14		623
Cinemark Tinseltown USA	2422 E. Expwy. 83	Mission	TX	78572	17		636
Cinemark Movies 8	7560 N.E. Loop 820	N. Richland Hills	TX	76180	8		623
Century 12 Odessa	4221 Preston Smith Rd.	Odessa	TX	79762	12		633
Cinemark Movies 8	1225 N.E. Loop 286	Paris	TX	75460	8		623
Cinemark Hollywood Movies 20	2101 E. Beltway 8	Pasadena	TX	77503	20		618
Cinemark at Pearland	3311 Silver Lake Dr.	Pearland	TX	77581	12		618
Cinemark Tinseltown 20	15436 FM 1825	Pflugerville	TX	78660	20		635
Cinemark Movies 8	El Centro Mall	Pharr	TX	78577	8		636
Cinemark Town Centre 6	1001 I-27 N. Hwy. 70	Plainview	TX	79072	6		651
Cinemark Legacy	7201 Central Expwy. Ste. #100	Plano	TX	75025	24		623
Cinemark Movies 10	Westpark Village	Plano	TX	75075	10		623
Cinemark Tinseltown Plano	3800 Dallas Pkwy.	Plano	TX	75093	20		623
Cinemark 12 Rockwall	2125 Summer Lee	Rockwall	TX	75032	12		623
Cinemark Rosenburg 12	3420 Vista Dr.	Rosenburg	TX	77471	12		618
Cinemark Roundrock	4401 N. IH-35	Round Rock	TX	78664	14		635
Movies 8	2132 N. Mays St.	Round Rock	TX	78664	8		635
Cinemark Tinseltown USA	4425 Sherwood Way	San Angelo	TX	76901	14		661
Cinemark Movies 16	5063 Loop 410 N.W.	San Antonio	TX	78229	16		641
Cinemark Movies 7	2510 Texoma Pkwy.	Sherman	TX	75092	7		657
Cinemark Sherman	3310 Town Center St.	Sherman	TX	75091	12		657
Cinemark Cinema 6	2900 W. Washington	Stephenville	TX	76401	6		623
Cinemark Texarkana 14	4230 St. Michael Dr.	Texarkana	TX	75503	14		612
Cinemark Movies 12	10000 E. F. Lowry Expwy.	Texas City	TX	77591	12		618
Cinemark at Market Street	9595 Six Pines Dr.	The Woodlands	TX	77380	5		618
Cinemark Tinseltown 17	1600 Lake Robbins Dr.	The Woodlands	TX	77380	17		618
Victoria 12	7806 Navarro	Victoria	TX	77904	12		626
Cinemark 18	20915 Gulf Freeway	Webster	TX	77598	18		618
Cinemark Movies 10	2113 W. Expwy. 83	Weslaco	TX	78596	10		636
Cinemark 14 Wichita Falls	2915 Glenwood Ave.	Wichita Falls	TX	76308	14		627
Cinemark American Fork	715 W. 180 N.	American Fork	UT	84003	12		770
Tinseltown USA	Layton Hills Mall	Layton	UT	84041	17		770
Cinemark Tinseltown 14	3651 Wall Ave.	Ogden	UT	84405	14		770
Holiday Village 4	1776 Park Ave. #4	Park City	UT	84060	4		770
Cinemark 16	1200 Town Center Blvd.	Provo	UT	84601	16		770
Cinemark Movies 8	2424 N. University Pkwy.	Provo	UT	84604	8		770
Century 16	125 E. 3300 S.	Salt Lake City	UT	84115	16		770
Cinemark Sugarhouse Movies 10	2227 S. Highland Dr.	Salt Lake City	UT	84106	10		770
Century 16 Union Heights	7670 S. Union Park Ave.	Sandy	UT	84047	16		770
Cinemark Movies 9	9539 S. 7th E. #2	Sandy	UT	84070	9		770
Cinemark 24 Jordan Landing	7301 S. Jordan Landing	West Jordan	UT	84084	24		770
Cinemark Valley Fair 9	3601 S. 2700 W.	West Valley City	UT	84119	9		700
Cinemark Tinseltown USA	3004 Linden Dr.	Bristol	VA	24201	14		531
Cinemark Movies 10	4300 Portsmouth Blvd.	Chesapeake	VA	23321	10		544
Cinemark Movies 10	3700 Candlers Mountain Rd.	Lynchburg	VA	24502	10		573
Cinemark 18	880 N. Military Hwy.	Norfolk	VA	23502	18		544
Century Federal Way	2001 S. Commons	Federal Way	WA	98003	16		819
Century Olympia	625 Black Lake Ln.	Olympia	WA	98512	14		819
Cinemark Tinseltown USA	Southport Plaza	Kenosha	WI	53142	14		617
Cinemark	2399 Meadowbrook Rd.	Bridgeport	WV	26330	10		598
Cinemark Tinseltown	88 W. Pender, 3rd Fl.	Vancouver	BC	V6B6N9	12		

CITY CINEMAS

(See Reading International)

CLARK THEATRES

5 theatres, 12 screens.

P.O. Box 310570, Enterprise, AL 36331-0570. TEL: (334) 347-1129. FAX: (334) 347-8242.

OWNER

Mack Clark, Jr.

GENERAL MANAGER

Walter C. (Charlie) Andrews

Theatre	Address	City	State	Zip	Screens
THEATRES					
Clark Theatre on the Square	Court Square	Andalusia	AL	36420	3
Clark Cinemas I & II	608 Boll Weevil Cir.	Enterprise	AL	36330	2
Clark Cinemas III & IV	621 Boll Weevil Cir.	Enterprise	AL	36330	2
College Cinemas I, II & III	501 Plaza Dr., Ste. 137	Enterprise	AL	36330	3
Clark Twin Cinemas	Hwy. 231 & Andrews Ave.	Ozark	AL	36360	2

CLASSIC CINEMAS

13 theatres, 97 screens.

(A division of Tivoli Enterprises, Inc.) 603 Rogers St., Downers Grove, IL 60515-3773. TEL: (630) 968-1600. FAX: (630) 968-1626.
www.classiccinemas.com

PRESIDENT
Willis Johnson
VICE PRESIDENT
Christopher Johnson
CORPORATE SECRETARY
Shirley Johnson
FILM BUYER
Lou Michael
MARKETING MANAGER
Mark Mazrimas

THEATRES

Theatre	Address	City	State	Zip	Screens
CC Cinema 12 Theatre	100 Besinger Dr.	Carpentersville	IL	60110	12
CC Tivoli Theatre	5021 Highland Ave.	Downers Grove	IL	60515	1
CC Elk Grove Theatre	1050 Town Ctr.	Elk Grove	IL	60007	8
CC York Theatre	150 N. York Rd.	Elmhurst	IL	60126	9
CC Fox Lake Theatre	115 Towne Centre Ln.	Fox Lake	IL	60020	9
CC North Riverside Mall Theatre	7501 West Cermak Road	North Riverside	IL	60546	6
CC Lindo Theatre	115 S. Chicago Ave.	Freeport	IL	61032	9
CC Meadowview Theatre	55 Meadowview Ctr.	Kankakee	IL	60901	3
CC Paramount	213 N. Schuyler Ave.	Kankakee	IL	60901	5
CC Ogden 6 Theatre	1227 E. Ogden Ave.	Naperville	IL	60563	6
CC Lake Theatre	1022 Lake St.	Oak Park	IL	60301	7
CC Charlestowne 18	3740 E. Main St.	St. Charles	IL	60174	18
CC Woodstock Theatre	209 Main St.	Woodstock	IL	60098	4

CLEARVIEW CINEMA CORP.

48 theatres, 258 screens.

97 Main St., Chatham, NJ 07928. TEL: (908) 918-2000. FAX: (973) 377-4303. www.clearviewcinemas.com

SENIOR V.P. & GENERAL MANAGER
Doug Oines
V.P., FACILITIES
Luann Satchell
V.P., FILM
Craig Zeltner
V.P. MARKETING & BUSINESS DEVELOPMENT
Beth Simpson Crimmins
V.P., DIVISIONAL CONTROLLER
Walter Kaufmann

THEATRES

Theatre	Address	City	State	Zip	Screens
Strathmore Cinema 4	1055 Rte. 34	Aberdeen	NJ	07747	4
Bergenfield Cinema 5	58 S. Washington Ave.	Bergenfield	NJ	07621	5
Bernardsville Cinema 3	5 Minebrook Rd., Rte. 202	Bernardsville	NJ	07924	3
Caldwell Cinema 4	317 Bloomfield Ave.	Caldwell	NJ	07006	4
Chester Cinema 6	Chester Springs Shopping Ctr.,169, Rte. 206	Chester	NJ	07930	6
Allwood Cinema 6	96 Market St.	Clifton	NJ	07012	6
Closter Cinema 4	130 Closter Plaza	Closter	NJ	07624	4
Mansfield Cinema 14	1 Mansfield Plaza, 1965 Rte. 57	Hackettstown	NJ	07840	14
Hoboken Cinemas	409-415 14th St.	Hoboken	NJ	07030	6
Kinnelon 11	25 Kinnelon Rd.	Kinnelon	NJ	07405	11
Madison Cinema 4	14 Lincoln Pl.	Madison	NJ	07940	4
Millburn Cinema 4	350 Millburn Ave.	Millburn	NJ	07041	4
Clairidge Cinemas	486 Bloomfield Ave.	Montclair	NJ	07042	6
Headquarters 10 Theatres	72 Headquarters Plaza Mall	Morristown	NJ	07960	10
Middlebrook Galleria Cin.10	1502 Rte. 35 S.	Ocean Township	NJ	07712	10
Parsippany Cinema 12	3165 Rte. 46	Parsippany	NJ	07054	12
Red Bank Art Cinema	36 White St.	Red Bank	NJ	07701	2
Warner Quad	190 E. Ridgewood Ave.	Ridgewood	NJ	07450	4
South Orange 5	1 SOPAC Way	South Orange	NJ	07079	5
Succasunna Cinema 10	P.O. Box 352, 21 Sunset Strip	Succasunna	NJ	07876	10
Beacon Hill 5/Summit	343 Springfield Ave.	Summit	NJ	07901	5
Tenafly Cinema 4	4 1/2 Railroad Ave.	Tenafly	NJ	07670	4
Bellevue Cinema 4	260 Bellevue Ave.	Upper Montclair	NJ	07043	4
Washington Twp. Cinemas	249 Pascack Rd.	Washington Township	NJ	07676	3
Wayne Preakness Cinemas	1220 Hamburg Tpk., Preakness Shopping Ctr.	Wayne	NJ	07470	4
Babylon Cinemas	34 Main St.	Babylon	NY	11702	3
Grand Avenue Cinemas	1849 Grand Ave.	Baldwin	NY	11510	5
Bedford Playhouse	633 Old Post Rd.	Bedford	NY	10506	2
Bronxville Cinemas	84 Kraft Ave., P.O. Box 732	Bronxville	NY	10708	3
Franklin Square Cinemas	989 Hempstead Turnpike	Franklin Square	NY	11010	6
Squire Cinemas	115 Middle Neck Rd.	Great Neck	NY	11021	7
Larchmont Playhouse	1975 Palmer Ave.	Larchmont	NY	10538	3
Mamaroneck Playhouse	243 Mamaroneck Ave.	Mamaroneck	NY	10543	4
Manhasset Cinemas	430 Plandome Rd.	Manhasset	NY	11030	3
Mt. Kisco Cinemas	144 E. Main St.	Mount Kisco	NY	10549	5
New City Cinema 6	202 S. Main St.	New City	NY	10956	6
Herricks Cinema 4	3324 Hillside Ave.	New Hyde Park	NY	11040	4
62nd & Broadway Cinema	1871 Broadway	New York	NY	10023	1
Chelsea Cinemas	260 W. 23rd St.	New York	NY	10011	9
First & 62nd Cinemas	400 E. 62nd St.	New York	NY	10021	6
Ziegfeld Theatre	141 W. 54th St.	New York	NY	10019	1
Port Washington Cinemas	114 Main St.	Port Washington	NY	11050	7
Soundview Cinema	7-9 Soundview Marketplace, Shore Rd.	Port Washington	NY	11050	6
Roslyn Cinemas	20 Tower Place	Roslyn	NY	11576	4

Theatre	Address	City	State	Zip	Screens
Cinema 100	Greenburgh Shopping Ctr., 93 Knollwood Rd.	White Plains	NY	10607	4
Central Plaza Cinema	2630 Central Park Ave.	Yonkers	NY	10710	4
Bala Theatre	157 Bala Ave.	Bala Cynwyd	PA	19004	3
Anthony Wayne Cinema	109 W. Lancaster Ave.	Wayne	PA	19087	5

CLEVELAND CINEMAS

8 theatres, 67 screens.

6200 SOM Center Rd., #C-20, Cleveland, OH 44139. TEL: (440) 349-3306. FAX: (440) 349-0210. www.clevelandcinemas.com

PRESIDENT

Jonathan Forman

THEATRES

Theatre	Address	City	State	Zip	Screens
Apollo Theatre	19 E. College St.	Oberlin	OH	44074	1
Capitol Theatre	1390 W. 65th St.	Cleveland	OH	44102	5
Cedar Lee Theatre	2163 Lee Rd.	Cleveland Heights	OH	44118	6
Shaker Square Cinemas	13116 Shaker Square	Cleveland	OH	44120	6
Tower City Cinemas	230 Huron Rd.	Cleveland	OH	44113	11
Chagrin Cinemas	8200 E. Washington St.	Chagrin Falls	OH	44023	14
Plaza Cinemas at Chapel Hill	500 Howe Ave.	Cuyahoga Falls	OH	44221	8
Solon Cinemas	6185 Enterprise Pkwy.	Solon	OH	44139	16

COBB THEATRES

19 theatres, 234 screens.

2000 B SouthBridge Pkwy., Ste. 100, Birmingham, AL 35209. TEL: (205) 802-7766. FAX: (205) 802-7771. www.cobbtheatres.com

CONTACT

Judy Sanders

THEATRES

Theatre	Address	City	State	Zip	Screens
Pinnacle 14 Cinemas	3780 Gulf Shores Pkwy.	Gulf Shores	AL	36542	14
Movies 4	1007 Hwy., 78 W.	Jasper	AL	35501	4
Hollywood 16 Cinemas	4250 Old Greensboro Rd.	Tuscaloosa	AL	35405	16
CineBistro at Solaris	141 E. Meadow Dr.	Vail	CO	81657	3
Jupiter 18	201 N. US #1, Ste. B-6	Jupiter	FL	33477	18
Lakeside Village 18 Cinemas	1650 Town Center Dr.	Lakeland	FL	33803	18
Merritt Square 16	777 E. Merritt Isl. Causeway	Merritt Island	FL	32952	16
Cinebistro at Dolphin Mall	11471 N.W. 12th St. Ste. 615	Miami	FL	33172	5
Dolphin 19 Cinemas	11471 N.W. 12 St.	Miami	FL	33172	19
Miami Lakes 17 Cinemas	6711 Main St.	Miami Lakes	FL	33014	17
Cobb Grand 18	17355 N.W. 59th Ave.	Miami Lakes	FL	33015	18
Merritt Square 16	777 E. Merritt Island Causeway	Merritt Island	FL	32952	16
Downtown 16 Cinemas	11701 Lake Victoria Gardens Ave., Ste. 1201	Palm Beach Gardens	FL	33410	16
Grove 16 & Cine Bistro	6333 Wesley Grove Blvd	Wesley Chapel	FL	33544	16
Grand 10 Cinemas	920 Spring Lake Square N.W.	Winter Haven	FL	33881	10
CineBistro at Hyde Park Village	1609 West Swann Ave	Tampa	Fl	33909	5
CineBistro at Peninsula Town Ctr.	4401 W. Claiborne Square	Hampton	VA	23666	5
Cobb Village 12 (opens 2011)		Leesburg	VA		12
CineBistro at Stony Point	9200 Stony Point Pkwy	Richmond	VA	23235	5

COMING ATTRACTIONS THEATRES, INC.

20 theatres, 145 screens.

1644 Ashland St., Ashland, OR 97520. TEL: (541) 488-1021. FAX: (541) 482-9290. www.catheatres.com

OWNER & CEO

John C. Schweiger

PRESIDENT

Daryn McLennan

EXECUTIVE V.P.

Larry McLennan

VICE PRESIDENT & THEATRE OPERATIONS

Julie Vogan

THEATRES

Theatre	Address	City	State	Zip	Screens
Minor Theatre	1013 H St	Arcata	CA	95521	3
Crescent City Cinemas	375 "M" St.	Crescent City	CA	95531	8
Broadway Cinema	1223 Broadway St	Eureka	CA	95501	12
Mill Creek Cinema	1575 Betty Court	McKinleyville	CA	95519	8
Mt. Shasta Cinemas	118 Morgan Way	Mt. Shasta	CA	96067	6
Ashland Street Cinemas	1644 Ashland St.	Ashland	OR	97520	6
Varsity Theatre	166 E. Main St.	Ashland	OR	97520	5
Astoria Gateway Cinemas	1875 Marine Dr.	Astoria	OR	97103	7
Movies Six Cinemas	1111 N.E. "D" St.	Grants Pass	OR	97526	6
Southgate Cinemas	1625 S.W. Ringuette St.	Grants Pass	OR	97527	8
Pelican Cinemas	2643 Biehn St.	Klamath Falls	OR	97601	10
McMinnville Cinemas	300 N.E. Norton Ln.	McMinnville	OR	97128	10
Newport Cinemas	5836 N. Coast Hwy.	Newport	OR	97365	3
Pony Village Cinemas	1611 Virginia	North Bend	OR	97459	11
Harvard Cinemas	3161 W. Harvard Ave.	Roseburg	OR	97471	3
Roseburg Cinemas	1750 N.W. Hughwood	Roseburg	OR	97470	8
Seaside Cinema	1026 12th Ave.	Seaside	OR	97138	6
Lincoln City Cinemas	3755 S.E. High School Dr.	Lincoln City	OR	97367	6
SouthShore Mall Cinemas	1017 S. Boone St.	Aberdeen	WA	98520	10
Midway Cinema	181 N.E. Hampe Way	Chehalis	WA	98532	10

CONSOLIDATED THEATRES

(see Reading International)

CONSOLIDATED THEATRES

(see Regal Entertainment Group)

DANBARRY CINEMAS

8 theatres, 82 screens.

105 W. 4th St., Ste. 1000, Cincinnati, OH 45202. TEL: (513) 784-1521. FAX: (513) 784-1554. www.danbarry.com

OWNER

Daniel J. Heilbrunn, Barry A. Kohn

Theatre	Address	City	State	Zip	Screens

GENERAL MANAGER
Aaron Bates
THEATRES

Danbarry Dollar Saver Cinemas	7650 Turfway	Florence	KY	41042	10
Danbarry Dollar Saver Cinemas	5190 Glenncrossing Way	Cincinnati	OH	45238	12
Danbarry Dollar Saver Cinemas	4450 Eastgate Blvd.	Cincinnati	OH	45245	8
Danbarry Dollar Saver Cinemas	601 Cincinnati Mills Dr.	Cincinnati	OH	45240	8
Danbarry Cinemas Chillicothe	119 Pawnee Rd.	Chillicothe	OH	45601	10
Danbarry Dollar Saver Cinemas	8300 Lyons Ridge Dr.	Dayton	OH	45458	12
Danbarry Dollar Saver Cinemas	7650 Waynetowne Blvd.	Huber Heights	OH	45424	12
Danbarry Cinemas Middletown	3479 Dixie Hwy.	Middletown	OH	45005	10

DESTINTA THEATRES

6 theatres, 85 screens.
11 Kipp Ave., Lodi, NJ 07644. TEL: (973) 473-8002. FAX: (973) 473-8808. www.destinta.com
CEO
Thomas J. Rizzo
CFO
Larry Haber
SENIOR V.P., OPERATIONS
John Spare
CONTROLLER
Jim Cioci
DIRECTOR, PROMOTIONS
Sean Crean
OFFICE MANAGER
Sharon Toth

THEATRES

Metro Square 12	49 College St.	Middletown	CT	06457	12
Independence 12	2465 S. Broad St.	Hamilton	NJ	08610	12
New Windsor 12	215 Quassaick Ave..	New Windsor	NY	12553	12
Clarion 7	Clarion Mall, 22631 Rte. 68, Ste. 80	Clarion	PA	16214	7
Chartiers Valley 20	1025 Washington Pike	Bridgeville	PA	15017	20
Plaza East 22	1701 Lincoln Hwy.	N. Versailles	PA	15137	22

DICKINSON THEATRES, INC.

24 theatres, 262 screens.
6801 W. 107th St., Overland Park, KS 66212. TEL: (913) 432-2334. FAX: (913) 432-9507. www.dtmovies.com
PRESIDENT & CEO
John Hartley
EXECUTIVE V.P., FILM & MARKETING
Ron Horton
CFO/CORPORATE SECRETARY
Bruce Wittman

THEATRES

Chenal 9 Digital plus IMAX	17825 Chenal Parkway	Little Rock	AR	72223	9
Gateway 12 IMAX	1935 S. Signal Butte	Mesa	AZ	85209	12
Palm Valley 14 Theatre	1325 N. Litchfield Rd.	Palm Valley	AZ	85338	14
Flinthills 8 Theatre	1614 Industrial Rd.	Emporia	KS	66801	8
Mall 8 Hutchinson Theatre	1500 E. 11th St., P.O. Box 2318	Hutchinson	KS	67504	8
Westside 4	1600 W. 6th St.	Junction City	KS	66441	4
Great Mall 16 Theatre	20060 W. 151st	Olathe	KS	66061	16
Palazzo 16 Theatre	8601 W. 135th St.	Overland Park	KS	66223	16
Westglen 18 Theatre	16301 Midland Dr.	Shawnee	KS	66217	18
Northrock 14 Theatre	3151 Penstemon	Wichita	KS	67226	14
Belton 8 Theatre	1207 E. North Ave. Hwy. 58	Belton	MO	64012	8
Blue Springs 8 Theatre	1901 N. 7 Hwy.	Blue Springs	MO	64015	8
Northglen 14 Theatre	4900 N.E. 80th St.	Kansas City	MO	64119	14
Eastglen 16 Theatre	1451 N.E. Douglas St.	Lee's Summit	MO	64086	16
Smithfield 10 Theatre	175 S. Equity Dr.	Smithfield	NC	27577	10
Imperial 3 Theatre	3207 W. 12th St.	Hastings	NE	68901	3
Arrowhead Mall 10 Theatre	501 N. Main #102	Muskogee	OK	74401	10
Penn Square 10 Theatre	1901 N.W. Expwy., Ste. 2100	Oklahoma City	OK	73118	10
Starworld 20 Theatre	10301 S. Memorial Dr.	Tulsa	OK	74133	20
West End Pointe 8	12825 N.W. 10th	Yukon	OK	73099	8
Easley 8 Theatre	5065 Calhoun Memorial Hwy.	Easley	SC	29640	8
Greenwood 10 Theatre	533 Bypass Hwy. 72 N.W.	Greenwood	SC	29649	10
Seneca 8 Theatre	675 Bypass 123	Seneca	SC	29678	8
Central Mall 10 Theatre	3100 Hwy. 365, Space 25	Port Arthur	TX	77642	10

DIPSON THEATRES, INC.

12 theatres, 57 screens.
388 Evans St., Williamsville, NY 14221. TEL: (716) 626-9613. FAX: (716) 626-9614. email: info@dipsontheatres.com www.dipsontheatres.com
PRESIDENT & CEO
Michael Clement

THEATRES

Batavia Mall 1 & 2	6 Alva Place W.	Batavia	NY	14020	2
Amherst Theatre	3500 Main St.	Buffalo	NY	14226	3
North Park Theatre	1428 Hertel Ave.	Buffalo	NY	14216	1
Market Arcade Film & Arts Cntr.	639 Main St.	Buffalo	NY	14203	8
West River Centre	30170 Grand River Ave	Farmington Hills	NY	48336	8
McKinley 6 Theatres	MaKinley Mall	Hamburg	NY	14219	6
Lakewood Cinema 8	171-3 Fairmount Ave.	Lakewood	NY	14750	8
Chautauqua Mall 2	500 Chautauqua Mall	Lakewood	NY	14750	2
Flix Theatre	4901 Transit Rd	Lancaster	NY	14086	11
Eastern Hills Cinema	4545 Transit Rd.	Williamsville	NY	14221	3
Bradford's Main St. Movie House	123 Main St.	Bradford	PA	16701	2
Warren Mall Cinemas	1666 Market St.	Warren	PA	16365	3

Theatre	Address	City	State	Zip	Screens

DOUGLAS THEATRE CO.

(See Marcus Theatres Corp.)

EMAGINE ENTERTAINMENT, INC.

6 theatres, 76 screens.
44425 W. 12 Mile Road, Novi, MI 48377. TEL: (248) 468-2990. FAX: (248) 920-0806. email: ruthd@emagine-entertainment.com
www.emagine-entertainment.com
EXECUTIVE V.P. SALES & MARKETING
Ruth Daniels
EXECUTIVE V.P. OPERATIONS
Chris Brandt
V.P. TECHNICAL
David Zylstra

THEATRES

Theatre	Address	City	State	Zip	Screens
Emagine Cinema Hollywood	12280 Dixie Highway	Birch Run	MI	48415	10
Emagine Canton	39535 Ford Rd	Canton	MI	48187	18
Emagine Novi	44425 W 12 Mile Rd	Novi	MI	48377	18
Emagine Woodhave	21720 Allen Rd	Woodhaven	MI	48183	10
Emagine Rochester Hills	200 Barclay Circle	Rochester Hills	MI	48307	10
Emagine Royal Oak Theatre	200 Main Street	Royal Oak	MI	48067	10

ENTERTAINMENT CINEMAS

13 theatres, 107 screens.
7 Central St., South Easton, MA 02375. TEL: (508) 230-7600. FAX: (508) 238-1408. www.entertainmentcinemas.com
PRESIDENT
Bill Hanney

THEATRES

Theatre	Address	City	State	Zip	Screens
Ent. Cinemas Seymour 12	814 Derby Ave.	Seymour	CT	06483	12
Ent. Cinemas Fresh Pond	168 Alewife Brook Pkwy	Cambridge	MA	02138	10
Ent. Cinemas Edgartown 2	65 Main St.	Edgartown	MA	02539	2
Ent. Cinemas Falmouth Cinema Pub	28 Tea Ticket Highway	Falmouth	MA	02536	3
Ent. Cinemas Leominster 10	45 Sack Blvd., 100 Searstown Mall	Leominster	MA	01453	10
Ent. Cinemas South Dennis	2-6 Enterprise Rd	South Dennis	MA	02660	12
Ent. Cinemas Springfield Cinemas	1250 St. James Ave	Springfield	MA	01104	14
Ent. Cinemas Windham 7	Route 302	N. Windham	ME	04062	7
Ent. Cinemas Wells 7	Wells Shopping Cntr., Route 1	Wells	ME	04090	7
Ent. Cinemas Concord 6	192 Loudon Rd.	Concord	NH	03301	6
Ent. Cinemas Lebanon 6	Rte. 4 Miracle Mile Plz.	Lebanon	NH	03766	6
Ent. Cinemas N. Conway 10	P.O. Box 3068, Mall Theatre, Rte 16 & 302	N. Conway	NH	03860	10
Ent. Cinemas S. Kingston 8	30 Village Sq. Dr.	S. Kingston	RI	02881	8

EPIC THEATRES

7 theatres, 81 screens.
P.O. Box 2076, Deland, FL 32721. TEL: (386) 736-6830. FAX: (386) 738-2596. email: corporate@epictheatres.com
PRESIDENT
Frank DeMarsh
VICE PRESIDENT
Clint DeMarsh

THEATRES

Theatre	Address	City	State	Zip	Screens
Epic Theatres of Clermont	2405 S. Hwy. 27	Clermont	FL	34711	16
Victoria Square 6	1798 S. Woodland Blvd.	DeLand	FL	32721	6
New Smyrna Beacon Theatres	1401 S. Dixie Fwy.	New Smyrna Bch.	FL	32168	12
Epic Theatres of Palm Coast	1185 Central Ave.	Palm Coast	FL	32164	14
Epic Theatres of St. Ausustine	112 Theatre Dr	St. Augustine	FL	32086	16
Epic Theatres of Hendersonville	200 Thompson St.	Hendersonville	NC	28793	12
Pioneer Drive-In Theatre	1985 N. Main St.	Butler	PA	16003	5

EVERGREEN ENTERTAINMENT COMPANY, LLC

6 theatres, 38 screens.
929 Old Highway 8 NW, Ste. 200, New Brighton, MN 55112. TEL: (651) 636-1417. FAX: (651) 636-1418. www.lakesandriverscinemas.com
PRESIDENT
James H. Payne
VICE PRESIDENT
Steven J. Payne
GENERAL MANAGER
Richard Lepsch
BOOKKEEPER
Beth Firchow
FILM BUYER
Neil O'Leary

THEATRES

Theatre	Address	City	State	Zip	Screens
Northwoods Cinema 10	300 Allan Ave.	Owatonna	MN	55060	10
Washington Square Cinema 5	121 W. Front St.	Detroit Lakes	MN	56501	5
Fairlakes Cinema 5	1201 N. State St.	Fairmont	MN	56031	5
Westridge Cinema 5	2001 W. Lincoln Ave.	Fergus Fails	MN	56537	5
Watertown Cinema 5	1111 14th St. S.E.	Watertown	SD	57201	5
Falls Cinema 8	2179 E. US Hwy. 8	St. Croix Falls	WI	54024	8

EXTREME CINEMAS (LAKE CINEMA, INC.)

4 theatres, 30 screens.
email: information@lakecinema.com www.lakecinema.com

THEATRES

Theatre	Address	City	State	Zip	Screens
Marquis Cinema 10	2828 Richbourg Lane	Crestview	FL	32536	10
The Breeze Cinema 8	1233 Crane Cove Boulevard	Gulf Breeze	FL	32563	8
The Ridge Cinema 8	4915 Highway 90	Pace	FL	32571	8
Lake Cinema 4	1030 Ninth St	Morgan City	LA	70380	4

Theatre	Address	City	State	Zip	Screens

FLAGSHIP CINEMAS

12 theatres, 112 screens.
55 Cambridge Parkway Ste. 200, Cambridge, MA 02142. TEL: (617) 844-1777. FAX: (617) 679-0800.
email: info@flagshipcinemas.com www.flagshipcinemas.com
PRESIDENT
John J. Crowley, Jr.
VICE PRESIDENT
Paul Wenger
FILM BUYER
Pauline Jandrue, Dan Seddon
THEATRES

Theatre	Address	City	State	Zip	Screens
Flagship Cinema Homestead 14	2250 N.E. 8th St., Campbell Dr.	Homestead	FL	33033	14
Flagship Cinema New Bedford	500 Kings Hwy., Fieldstone Marketplace	New Bedford	MA	02745	12
Flagship Cinemas Wareham	39 Doty St.	Wareham	MA	02576	8
Flagship Churchville Flagship	2408 Churchville Rd., Campus Hills Shpg. Cntr.	Bel Air	MD	21015	7
Flagship Cinemas Auburn 10	746 Center St.	Auburn	ME	04210	10
Flagship Cinema Lewiston	855 Lisbon St., Promenade Mall	Lewiston	ME	04240	10
Flagship Cinema Oxford	1570 Main St.	Oxford	ME	04270	7
Flagship Cinema Rockland	9 Moody Dr.	Thomaston	ME	04861	10
Flagship Cinema Derry 12	10 Ashleigh Dr.	Derry	NH	03038	12
Flagship Cinema Waterville 8	247 Kennedy Memorial Dr.	Waterville	ME	04901	8
Flagship Cinema Carrolltown 6	6405 West Hemlock Rd.	Eldersburg	MD	21784	6
Flagship Cinemas Mechanicsburg	4950 Carlisle Pike	Mechanicsburg	PA	17050	8

FOOTHILLS ENTERTAINMENT COMPANY

4 theatres, 15 screens.
P.O. Box 2549, Kilgore, TX 75663-2549. TEL: (903) 758-4749. FAX: (903) 758-0720. email: bmovies@aol.com www.foothillsentertainment.com
PRESIDENT
Byron Berkley

THEATRES

Theatre	Address	City	State	Zip	Screens
Plaza Cinema 3	1301 Lone Star St.	Henderson	TX	75652	3
Jackson Cinema 3	1710 S. Jackson St., Box 2421	Jacksonville	TX	75766	3
4 Star Cinema	1607 Hwy. 259 S.	Kilgore	TX	75663	6
Brazos Cinema 3	2801 Hwy. 180 E.	Mineral Wells	TX	76068	3

FRIDLEY THEATRES, INC.

28 theatres, 101 screens.
1321 Walnut St., Des Moines, IA 50309. TEL: (515) 282-9287. FAX: (515) 282-8310. www.fridleytheatres.com
PRESIDENT
R. L. Fridley
V.P. & FILM BUYER
Brian Fridley

THEATRES

Theatre	Address	City	State	Zip	Screens
State Street Theatre	315 E. State St.	Algona	IA	50511	3
The Springwood 9	2829 S. Ankeny Blvd.	Ankeny	IA	50021	9
Atlantic	28 W. Fifth St.	Atlantic	IA	50022	2
Carroll 5 Theatre	407 N. Main St.	Carroll	IA	51401	5
Cinema 4	1013 N. 18th St.	Centerville	IA	52544	4
American	108 E. Main	Cherokee	IA	51012	3
Strand Theatre	309 W. Adams St.	Creston	IA	50801	1
Viking 3	111 N. Mechanic	Decorah	IA	52101	3
Riviera Theatre	2209 Main	Emmetsburg	IA	50536	1
Grand 3 Theatre	1031 Central Ave.	Estherville	IA	51334	3
Strand Theatre	921 Main St.	Grinnell	IA	50112	3
Humota	515 Sumner Ave.	Humboldt	IA	50548	1
Paramount 3	105 S. 1st St.	Indianola	IA	50125	7
Sierra Theatre	212 E. State St.	Jefferson	IA	50129	1
Village 1 & 2 Theatre	212 E. Robinson	Knoxville	IA	50138	2
Plaza 5 Theatre	2500 S. Center St.	Marshalltown	IA	50158	9
Temple 2	115 N. Main St.	Mt. Pleasant	IA	52641	2
Plaza 4	1903 Park Ave.	Muscatine	IA	52761	4
Paramount Theatre	26 S. Fredrick Ave.	Oelwein	IA	50662	2
Penn Centre Twin	216 2nd Ave.	Oskaloosa	IA	52577	2
Copper Creek 9	1325 Copper Creek Dr.	Pleasant Hill	IA	50317	9
Cinema 5	251 N. Main	Sioux Center	IA	51250	5
Spencer 3	504 Grand Ave.	Spencer	IA	51301	3
Southpark Theatre	901 S.W. 1th	Spencer	IA	51301	7
Vista 3	712 Lake Ave.	Storm Lake	IA	50588	3
State Theatre	123 E. Washington St.	Washington	IA	52353	1
Rivoli 3	528 W. 2nd St.	Hastings	NE	68902	3
Cinema 3	224 W. View Plaza	McCook	NE	69001	3

GALAXY THEATRES, LLC

11 theatres, 116 screens.
15060 Ventura Blvd., Ste. 350, Sherman Oaks, CA 91403. TEL: (818) 986-9000. FAX: (818) 784-0106. www.galaxytheatres.com
CEO
Frank Rimkus
CONTACT
Rafe Cohen

THEATRES

Theatre	Address	City	State	Zip	Screens
Atascadero Colony Square	El Camino Real & Highway 41	Atascadero	CA		10
Porterville 9	631 N. Indiana St.	Porterville	CA	93257	9
Riverbank 12	2525 Patterson Rd.	Riverbank	CA	95367	12
Galaxy 10	1575 Retherford St.	Tulare	CA	93274	10
Galaxy Fandango	4000 S. Curry St.	Carson City	NV	89701	10
Galaxy-Cannery	2121 E. Craig Rd.	N. Las Vegas	NV	89030	14
Galaxy M	222 Via Marnell Way	Las Vegas	NV	89119	11
Galaxy Highland	6700 Middle Fisk Rd.	Austin	TX	78752	10
Galaxy Uptown	4649 Pt Fosdick Dr. N.W.	Gig Harbor	WA	98335	10
Monroe 12	One Galaxy Way	Monroe	WA	98272	12
Galaxy Narrows 8	2208 Mildred St. W	Tacoma	WA	98466	8

Theatre	Address	City	State	Zip	Screens

GEJU THEATRES

5 theatres, 12 screens.

1526 21st St, Mitchell, NE 69357. TEL: (308) 623-3138. www.gejutheatres.com

THEATRES

Theatre	Address	City	State	Zip	Screens
Alliance Theatre	410 Box Butte Ave.	Alliance	NE		5
Sandhills Drive-In	2617 County Rd 57	Alliance	NE		1
Eagle Theatre	244 Main St	Chadron	NE		4
Hot Springs Theatre	241 N river St	Hot Springs	SD		1
Dogie Theatre	11 Main St.	Newcastle	WY		1

GEORGIA THEATRE COMPANY II

30 theatres, 300 screens.

50 Cinema Lane, St. Simons, GA 31522. TEL: (912) 634-5192. FAX: (912) 634-5195. www.GeorgiaTheatreCompany.com

CHAIRMAN & CEO
William J. Stembler
PRESIDENT/COO
Aubrey Stone
V.P., CONSTRUCTION
Scott Bagwell
SECRETARY/TREASURER
Joan Mannheim
V.P., FINANCE
Dennis P. Merton
V.P., OPERATIONS
Jeff Mobley
V.P., FILM
Kip Smiley

THEATRES

Theatre	Address	City	State	Zip	Screens
Beechwood Stadium Cinemas 11	196 Alps Rd.	Athens	GA	30606	11
Georgia Square Value Cinemas 5	3710 Atlanta Hwy.	Athens	GA	30606	5
Masters Value Cinemas 7	2824 Washington Rd.	Augusta	GA	30909	7
Glynn Place Stadium Cinemas 11	551 Mall Blvd.	Brunswick	GA	31525	11
Carrollton Stadium Cinemas 10	1135 Bankhead Hwy.	Carrollton	GA	30116	10
Galleria Mall Stadium Cinemas 15	2980 Watson Blvd	Centerville	GA	31028	15
Commerce Stadium Cinemas 6	340 Banks Crossing Dr	Commerce	GA	30529	6
Dawson 400 Stadium Cinemas 10	189 N. 400 Center Ln.,	Dawsonville	GA	30534	10
Venture Value Cinemas 12	3750 Venture Dr.	Duluth	GA	30096	12
Heart of Georgia Stadium Cinemas 5	1167 Cochran Hwy.	Eastman	GA	31023	5
Evans Stadium Cinemas 14	4365 Towne Ctr. Dr.	Evans	GA	30809	14
Hollywood Stadium Cinemas 15	120 Green Hill Cir. N.W.	Gainesville	GA	30501	15
Griffin Stadium Cinemas 10	1367 N. Expressway	Griffin	GA	30223	10
Liberty Stadium Cinemas 9	565 W. Oglethorpe Hwy.	Hinesville	GA	31313	9
Town Center Value Cinemas 10	700 Gwinnett Dr., Ste 216	Lawrenceville	GA	30045	10
Merchant's Walk Stadium Cinemas 12	1301 Johnson Ferry Rd.	Marietta	GA	30068	12
Park 12 Cobb Stadium Cinemas 12	2925 W. Frank Gordy Pkwy.	Marietta	GA	30066	12
Moultrie Stadium Cinemas 6	495 Hampton Way	Moultrie	GA	31768	6
Kings Bay Stadium Cinemas 9	201 City Smitty Dr.	St Marys	GA	31558	9
Island Cinemas 7	44 Cinema Ln.	St Simons	GA	31522	7
Gateway Cinemas 7	U.S. 19 South	Thomasville	GA	31792	7
Valdosta Stadium Cinemas 16	1680 Baytree Rd..	Valdosta	GA	31602	16
Ashley Value Cinemas 8	2812 N. Ashley St..	Valdosta	GA	31602	8
Parkway Value Cinemas 6	821 Russell Pkwy.	Warner Robins	GA	31088	6
Houston Lakes Stadium Cinemas 10	1121 Highway 96	Warner Robins	GA	31099	10
Mall Stadium Cinemas 7	2260 Brunswick Hwy.	Waycross	GA	31501	7
Cherokee Stadium Cinemas 16	355 Cinema View	Woodstock	GA	30189	16
Beacon Stadium Cinemas 10	12961 Cortez Blvd.	Brooksville	FL	34613	10
Beacon Stadium Cinemas 12	1121 Broad St.	Sumter	SC	29150	12
Danville Stadium Cinemas 12	3601 Riverside Dr.	Danville	VA	24541	12

GOODRICH QUALITY THEATERS, INC.

30 theatres, 277 screens.

4417 Broadmoor S.E., Grand Rapids, MI 49512. TEL: (616) 698-7733. FAX: (616) 698-7220. www.gqti.com

PRESIDENT & SECRETARY
Robert Emmett Goodrich
TREASURER & CFO
Ross Pettinga
FILM BUYER
Wanda J. Holst
COO
Martin S. Betz
ASSISTANT COO
Matthew Johnson
CONCESSIONS MANAGER
Brian Nuffer
DIRECTOR OF BUSINESS TECHNOLOGY
Vance Bowers
CONTROLLER
Sue Howard
MARKETING/CREATIVE DIRECTOR
Kelly Owens

THEATRES

Theatre	Address	City	State	Zip	Screens
Randall 15 IMAX	550 N. Randall Rd.	Batavia	IL	60510	15
Kendall 10	95 5th St.	Oswego	IL	60543	10
Willow Knolls 14	4100 W. Willow Knolls Dr.	Peoria	IL	61615	14
Savoy 16	232 W. Burwash.	Savoy	IL	61874	16
Brownsburg 8	1555 North Green St.	Brownsburg	IN	46112	8
Huntington 7	350 Hauenstein Rd.	Huntington	IN	46750	7
Hamilton 16 IMAX	13825 Norell Rd.	Indianapolis	IN	46060	16
Eastside 9	300 Farabee Dr.	Lafayette	IN	47905	9
Lafayette 7	3525 McCarty Ln.	Lafayette	IN	47904	7

Theatre	Address	City	State	Zip	Screens
Wabash Landing 9	300 E. State St.	Lafayette	IN.	47906	9
Lebanon 7	1600 North Lebanon St.	Lebanon	IN.	46052	7
Portage 16 IMAX	5935 US Route 6.	Portage	IN.	46368	16
Quality 16	3686 Jackson Rd.	Ann Arbor	MI	48103	16
W. Columbia 7	2500 W. Columbia	Battle Creek	MI	49015	7
Bay City 8	4101 Wilder Rd.	Bay City	MI	48706	8
Cadillac 5	202 S. Mitchell St.	Cadillac	MI	49601	5
Canton 7	435 Ford Rd.	Canton	MI	48187	7
Grand Haven 9	17220 Hayes St.	Grand Haven	MI	49417	9
Hastings 4	213 W. State St.	Hastings	MI	49058	4
Holland 7	500 Waverly Rd.	Holland	MI	49423	7
Jackson 10	1501 N. Wisner	Jackson	MI	49202	10
Kalamazoo 10	820 Maple Hill Dr.	Kalamazoo	MI	49009	10
Lansing Mall 6	921 Mall Dr.	Lansing	MI	48917	6
Ada Lowell 5	2175 W. Main St.	Lowell	MI	49331	5
Oxford 7	48 S. Washington	Oxford	MI	48371	7
Krafft 8	2725 Krafft Rd.	Port Huron	MI	48060	8
Saginaw 12	3250 Kabobel	Saginaw	MI	48604	12
Three Rivers 6	120 Enterprise Dr.	Three Rivers	MI	49093	6
Forum 8	1209 Forum Katy Pkwy.	Columbia	MO	65203	8
Capital 8	3550 Country Club Dr.	Jefferson City	MO	65109	8

GREAT EASTERN THEATRES

4 theatres, 11 screens.

3361 Executive Pkwy., Ste 300, Toledo, OH 43606. TEL: (419) 537-8679. FAX: (419) 537-0087. email: wgetco@sbcglobal.net
www.greateasterntheatres.com

THEATRES

Theatre	Address	City	State	Zip	Screens
Maumee Indoor Theatre	601 Conant St	Maumee	OH.	43537	3
Paramount Cinema	301 S Front St	Fremont	OH.	43420	4
Sprinfield Drive-In	1040 Springmill Rd	Mansfield	OH.	44901	2
Sundance Kid Drive-In	4500 Navarre Ave	Oregon	OH.	43616	2

GREATER HUNTINGTON THEATRE CORP.

4 theatres, 33 screens.

P.O. Box 1957, 401 11th St., Ste. 805, Huntington, WV 25720-1957. TEL: (304) 523-0185. FAX: (304) 525-1153. www.ourshowtimes.com

CHAIRMAN
Jack S. Hyman
PRESIDENT
Derek Hyman
VICE PRESIDENT
Greg Pauley

THEATRES

Theatre	Address	City	State	Zip	Screens
Pierce Point Cinema 10	1255 W. Ohio Pike	Cincinnati	OH.	45102	10
Park Place Stadium Cinemas	600 Washington St.	Charleston	WV	25301	11
Cinema Theatre	1021 4th Ave.	Huntington	WV	25701	4
Fountain Place Cinema 8	102 George Kostas Dr.	Logan	WV	25601	8

HARKINS THEATRES

32 theatres, 443 screens.

7511 E. McDonald Dr., Scottsdale, AZ 85250. TEL: (480) 627-7777. FAX: (480) 443-0950. www.harkinstheatres.com

OWNER
Dan Harkins
PRESIDENT
Mike Bowers
CFO
Greta Newell
DIRECTOR, OPERATIONS
Racheal Wilson
DIRECTOR, ENGINEERING
Kirk Griffin
DIRECTOR, HUMAN RESOURCES
Gina Thompson
DIRECTOR, FILM BUYING
Noel Kendall
DIRECTOR, MARKETING
Bryan Laurel
DIRECTOR, CONCESSIONS/BUSINESS DEVELOPMENT
Tyler Cooper
IT DIRECTOR
Aron Barr

THEATRES

Theatre	Address	City	State	Zip	Screens
Gateway Pavilions 18	10250 W. McDowell Rd.	Avondale	AZ	85323	18
Casa Grande 14	1341 N. Promenade Pkwy.	Casa Grande	AZ	85222	14
Chandler Fashion 20	3159 W. Chandler Blvd.	Chandler	AZ	85226	20
Chandler Crossroads 12	2980 E. Germann Rd.	Chandler	AZ	85286	12
Flagstaff 11	1959 S. Woodlands Village Blvd.	Flagstaff	AZ	86001	11
Santan Village 16	2298 E. Williams Field Rd.	Gilbert	AZ	85295	16
Fiesta 5	1520 S. Longmoor	Mesa	AZ	85202	5
Superstition Springs 25	6950 E. Superstition Springs Blvd.	Mesa	AZ	85220	25
Arrowhead 18	16046 N. Arrowhead Fountain Ctr. Dr.	Peoria	AZ	85345	18
Park West 14	9804 W. Northern	Peoria	AZ	85345	14
Arcadia 8	3975 E. Thomas Rd.	Phoenix	AZ	85018	8
Christown 14	1620 W Montebello	Phoenix	AZ	85015	14
Metrocenter 12	9615-A Metro Pkwy. W.	Phoenix	AZ	85051	12
Norterra 14	2550 W. Happy Valley Road	Phoenix	AZ	85085	14
North Valley 16	3420 E. Bell Rd.	Phoenix	AZ	85032	16
Scottsdale 101/Cine Capri	7000 E. Mayo Blvd.	Phoenix	AZ	85054	14
Tucson Spectrum 18	5455 S. Calle Santa Cruz	Tucson	AZ	85706	18
Prescott Valley 14	7202 Pav Way	Prescott Valley	AZ	86314	14
Camelview 5	7001 E. Highland Ave.	Scottsdale	AZ	85251	5
Fashion Square 7	7014 E. Camelback Rd.	Scottsdale	AZ	85253	7

Theatre	Address	City	State	Zip	Screens
Shea 14	7354 E. Shea Blvd.	Scottsdale	AZ	85260	14
Sedona 6	2081 Hwy. 89A	Sedona	AZ	86336	6
Arizona Mills 24	5000 Arizona Mills Cir.	Tempe	AZ	85282	24
Centerpoint 11	730 S. Mill Ave.	Tempe	AZ	85281	11
Tempe Marketplace 16	2000 E. Rio Salado Pkwy.	Tempe	AZ	85281	16
Valley Art Theatre	505 S. Mill Ave.	Tempe	AZ	85821	1
Yuma Palms 14	1321 S. Yuma Palms Pkwy.	Yuma	AZ	85365	14
Chino Hills 18	3100 Chino Ave.	Chino Hills	CA	91709	18
Moreno Valley 16	22350 Town Circle	Moreno Valley	CA	92553	16
Northfield 18/Cine Capri	8300 E. 49th Ave.	Denver	CO	80238	18
Bricktown 16/Cine Capri	150 E. Reno Ave.	Oklahoma City	OK	73104	16
Southlake Center 14/Cine Capri	1450 Plaza Place	Southlake	TX	76092	14

HOLLYWOOD THEATRES

51 theatres, 555 screens.

919 S.W. Taylor St., Ste. 800, Portland, OR 97205. TEL: (503) 221-7090. FAX: (503) 796-0229. www.gohollywood.com

CHAIRMAN, PRESIDENT & CEO
Scott C. Wallace
SENIOR V.P. & COO
Clyde Cornell
SENIOR V.P. & CFO
Chuck Kirk
EXECUTIVE V.P. & HEAD FILM BUYER
Paul Rosenfeld
SENIOR V.P., REAL ESTATE & DEVELOPMENT
Scott Hall
V.P., CONCESSIONS
Doug Hawkins
V.P., MARKETING
Erin Anderson
V.P., CONSTRUCTION & DESIGN
Julie Lane

THEATRES

Theatre	Address	City	State	Zip	Screens
Mobile Stadium 18	1250 Satchell Paige Dr.	Mobile	AL	36606	18
Gilbert Stadium Cinemas	1012 S. Gilbert Rd.	Gilbert	AZ	85296	14
New Barstow Cinema 6	1503 E. Main St.	Barstow	CA	92311	6
New Malibu Theatre	3822 Crosscreek Rd.	Malibu	CA	90265	2
Mainplace Stadium Cinemas	403 W. Main St.	Merced	CA	95341	13
Interquest Stadium 14	11250 Rampart Hill View	Colorado Springs	CO	80920	14
River City Marketplace 14	12884 City Center Blvd.	Jacksonville	FL	32218	14
Prince Kuhio Theatre	111 E. Puainako St.	Hilo	HI	96720	9
Kress Cinema 4	174 Kamehameha Ave.	Hilo	HI	96720	4
Restaurant Row 9	500 Ala Moana Blvd.	Honolulu	HI	96813	9
Maui Mall Megaplex	70 E. Kahnumanu Ave.	Kahalui	HI	96732	12
Makalapua Stadium Cinemas	74-5469 Kamakaeha Ave.	Kailua-Kona	HI	96740	10
Wharf Cinema 3	658 Front St.	Lahaina	HI	96761	3
Front St. Theatre	900 Front St., Bldg. G	Lahaina	HI	96761	4
Village Cinema 3	4805 10th St.	Great Bend	KS	67530	3
Southwind 12	3433 Iowa St.	Lawrence	KS	66046	12
Hollywood Stadium 14	6200 S.W. 6th Ave.	Topeka	KS	66615	14
West Ridge 8	1727 S.W. Wanamaker	Topeka	KS	66604	8
Hollywood Stadium 14	69348 Louisiana State Hwy. 21	Covington	LA	70433	14
Stadium 14	2800 Goodwin Pointe Dr.	Columbia	MO	65201	14
Northstar 14	201 N. Northpark Ln.	Joplin	MO	64801	14
Forum 4	1101 E. 18th St.	Rolla	MO	65401	4
Hollywood Theaters 10	5405 N. Belt Hwy. Bldg. "M"	St. Joseph	MO	64506	10
Gallatin Mall Cinemas	2825 W. Main St.	Bozeman	MT	59718	11
Horizon Stadium 8	50 US Hwy. 50	Stateline	NV	89449	8
Indian Mound 11	771 S. 30th St.	Heath	OH	43056	11
Movies 8	100 Washington Park Mall	Bartlesville	OK	74005	8
Spotlight 14	1100 N. Interstate Dr.	Norman	OK	73072	14
Movies 6	4901 N. Kickapoo	Shawnee	OK	74801	6
Palace 12	4107 S. Yale	Tulsa	OK	74135	12
Crown Center Cinemas	1500 W. Chestnut St.	Washington	PA	15301	14
Star 12	4455 Dowlen Rd.	Beaumont	TX	77706	12
Movies 14	301 W. Rendon-Crowley Rd.	Burleson	TX	76028	14
Heartland Mall Cinemas	300 Early Blvd.	Early	TX	76802	8
MacArthur Marketplace 14	8505 Walton Rd.	Irving	TX	75063	16
Killeen Stadium 14	2501 E. Central Texas Expy.	Killeen	TX	76543	14
Laredo Stadium 14	2401 Jacaman Rd.	Laredo	TX	78041	14
Movies 9	120 US Hwy. 31	Longview	TX	75603	9
Hollywood Stadium 14	3070 N. Eastman Rd.	Longview	TX	75605	14
Tall City 14	4915 W. Loop 250 N.	Midland	TX	79707	14
Permian Palace 11	4101 E. 42nd St.	Odessa	TX	79762	11
Tyler Rose 14	1250 S.W. Loop 323	Tyler	TX	75701	14
Jewel 16	7200 Woodway Dr.	Waco	TX	76712	16
Hollywood Stadium 12	1001 Mountaineer Dr.	Granville	WV	26534	12

INTERNATIONAL THEATRES

Theatre	Address	City	State	Zip	Screens
Nu'uuli Place	128 Nu'uuli Place	Pago Pago	AS	96799	2
Guam Megaplex	235 Pas St.	Tamuning	GUAM	96911	14
Saipan Megaplex	2860 Costco Dr., Box 2109	Chalan Kanoa, Saipan	MP	96950	7
Hollywood Theaters at Camana Bay	55 Market St.	Grand Cayman	CI.	BWI	6

INTERSTATE AMUSEMENTS, INC.

6 theatres, 25 screens.

P.O. Box T, Twin Falls, ID 83301. TEL: (208) 734-2402. FAX: (208) 734-8687.

PRESIDENT
John Love
VICE PRESIDENT
Byron Kluth
SECRETARY & TREASURER
Cathy Roper

Theatre	Address	City	State	Zip	Screens

MANAGING DIRECTOR
Larry Roper

THEATRES

Theatre	Address	City	State	Zip	Screens
Twin Cinema 12	160 Eastland Dr.	Twin Falls	ID.	83301	12
Orpheum Theatre	164 Main Ave.	Twin Falls	ID.	83301	1
Odyssey Theatre	1485 Pole Line Rd.	Twin Falls	ID.	83301	6
Jerome Cinema 4	955 W. Main	Jerome	ID.	83338	4
Motor-Vu Drive In	240 Eastland Dr.	Twin Falls	ID.	83301	1
Grand-Vu Drive In	Grandview Dr.	Twin Falls	ID.	83301	1

IPIC ENTERTAINMENT

1 theatre, 6 screens.
2400 East Commercial Blvd., #711, Ft. Lauderdale, FL. 33308. TEL: (954) 438-5700. FAX: (954) 438-5704. www.ipic.com
PRESIDENT & CEO
Hamid Hashemi - hamid.hashemi@ipic.com
CFO, SENIOR V.P., FINANCE
Jim Beynon - jim.beynon@ipic.com
COO, SENIOR V.P., OPERATIONS
Deane Hashemi - deane.hashemi@ipic.com
V.P., OPERATIONS
Bill Scheidhauer - bill.scheidhauer@ipic.com
V.P., HUMAN RESOURCES
Tim McGriff - tim.mcgriff@ipic.com
V.P., TECHNOLOGY
Darryl Leversuch - darryl.leversuch@ipic.com
V.P., MARKETING
Jim Lee - jim.lee@ipicentertainment.com

THEATRES

Theatre	Address	City	State	Zip	Screens
IPic Entertainment	Bayshore Town Center, 5800 Bayshore Dr.	Glendale	WI	53217	6
IPic Entertainment	Village 121 (Coming Soon)	Plano	TX		

KERASOTES SHOWPLACE THEATRES, LLC

(AMC Entertainment, Inc. acquired substantially all of the assets of Kerasotes during 2010 - 95 locations, 957 screens)
3 theatres, 42 screens.
224 N. DesPlaines, Ste. 200, Chicago, IL 60661-1134. TEL: (312) 775-3160. FAX: (312) 258-9943.
www.showplaceicon.com www.kerasotes.com
CHAIRMAN & CEO
Tony Kerasotes
PRESIDENT & COO
Dean Kerasotes
CFO
Jim DeBruzzi
DIRECTOR, OPERATIONS
Tim Johnson
HEAD FILM BUYER
Pat Rembusch
IT DIRECTOR
Andy Gift
DIRECTOR, REAL ESTATE
Robert Gallivan
TECHNICAL DIRECTOR/EQUIPMENT BUYER
Fred Walraven
DIRECTOR, CONSTRUCTION
Michael Policicchio
HUMAN RESOURCE, MANAGER
Bridget Gerken

THEATRES

Theatre	Address	City	State	Zip	Screens
Showplace ICON at Roosevelt	150 W. Roosevelt Rd	Chicago	IL	60605	14
ShowPlace 14	650 Plaza Dr.	Seacaucus	NJ	07094	14
Showplace ICON at the West End	Park Place Blvd & W 16th St.	St. Louis	MN.	55416	14

KRIKORIAN PREMIERE THEATRES, LLC

8 theatres, 102 screens.
2275 West 190th St., Ste. 201, Torrance, CA 90504. TEL: (310) 856-1270. FAX: (310) 856-1299. www.kptmovies.com
PRESIDENT & CEO
George Krikorian
FILM BUYER
Mike Pade
DIRECTOR, OPERATIONS
Todd Cummings

THEATRES

Theatre	Address	City	State	Zip	Screens
Buena Park Metroplex 18	8290 La Palma Ave.	Buena Park	CA	90620	18
Chino Marketplace Spectrum 12	3750 Grand Ave. (Closed for Remodeling)	Chino	CA	91710	12
Downey Cinmea 10	8200 3rd St.	Downey	CA	90241	10
Monrovia Cinema 12	410 S. Myrtle Ave.	Monrovia	CA	91016	12
Pico Rivera Village Walk 15	8540 Whittier Blvd.	Pico Rivera	CA	90660	15
Redlands Cinema 14	340 N. Eureka St.	Redlands	CA	92373	14
San Clemente Cinema 6	641-B Camino De Los Mares	San Clemente	CA	92673	6
Vista Village 15 Metroplex	25 Main St.	Vista	CA	92083	15

LAEMMLE THEATRES

8 theatres, 37 screens.
11523 Santa Monica Blvd., Los Angeles, CA 90025. TEL: (310) 478-1041. FAX: (310) 478-4452. www.laemmle.com
CHIEF OFFICERS
Gregory Laemmle, Jay Reisbaum, Kevin Gallagher

Theatre	Address	City	State	Zip	Screens

THEATRES

Theatre	Address	City	State	Zip	Screens
Laemmle Music Hall 3	9036 Wilshire Blvd.	Beverly Hills	CA	90211	3
Laemmle's Claremont 5	450 W. 2nd St.	Claremont	CA	91711	5
Laemmle's Town Center 5	17200 Ventura Blvd.	Encino	CA	91316	5
Laemmle Sunset 5	8000 Sunset Blvd.	Los Angeles	CA	90046	5
Laemmle's Royal	11523 Santa Monica Blvd.	Los Angeles	CA	90025	1
Laemmle's Playhouse 7	673 E. Colorado	Pasadena	CA	91103	7
Laemmle's Monica 4	1332 Second St.	Santa Monica	CA	90401	4
Laemmle's Fallbrook 7	6731 Fallbrook Ave.	West Hills	CA	91307	7

LANDMARK THEATRES

55 theatres, 220 screens.

2222 S. Barrington Ave., Los Angeles, CA 90064. TEL: (310) 473-6701. FAX: (310) 312-2364. www.landmarktheatres.com

PRESIDENT
Kevin Parke
COO
Ted Mundorff
V.P., OPERATIONS
Chuck Delagrange

THEATRES

Theatre	Address	City	State	Zip	Screens
Albany Twin	1115 Solano Ave.	Albany	CA	94706	2
Aquarius Theatre	430 Emerson St.	Palo Alto	CA	94301	2
Bridge Theatre	3010 Geary Blvd.	San Francisco	CA	94118	1
California Theatre	2113 Kittredge St.	Berkeley	CA	94704	3
Clay Theatre	2261 Fillmore	San Francisco	CA	94115	1
Embarcadero Center Cinemas	1 Embarcadero Ctr., Promenade Level	San Francisco	CA	94111	5
Guild Theatre	949 El Camino Real	Menlo Park	CA	94025	1
Hillcrest Cinemas	3965 5th Ave.	San Diego	CA	92103	5
Ken Theatre	4061 Adams Ave.	San Diego	CA	92116	1
La Jolla Village Cinemas	8879 Villa La Jolla Dr.	La Jolla	CA	92037	4
Lumiere Theatre	1572 California St.	San Francisco	CA	94109	3
Nuart Theatre	11272 Santa Monica Blvd.	Los Angeles	CA	90025	1
Opera Plaza Cinema	601 Van Ness Ave.	San Francisco	CA	94102	4
Piedmont Theatre	4186 Piedmont Ave.	Oakland	CA	94611	3
Regent Theatre	1045 Broxton Ave.	Los Angeles	CA	90024	1
Shattuck Cinemas	2230 Shattuck Ave.	Berkeley	CA	94704	10
The Landmark - Westside	10850 W. Pico	Los Angeles	CA	90064	12
Chez Artiste	4150 E. Amherst Ave.	Denver	CO	80222	3
Esquire Theatre	590 Downing St.	Denver	CO	80219	2
Greenwood Village	5415 Landmark Place	Greenwood Village	CO	80111	6
Mayan Theatre	110 Broadway	Denver	CO	80203	3
E- Street Cinema	555 11th St. N.W.	Washington	DC	20004	8
Midtown Art Cinema	931 Monroe Dr.	Atlanta	GA	30308	8
Landmark Century Center Cinema	2828 N. Clark St.	Chicago	IL	60657	7
Renaissance Place	1850 2nd St.	Highland Park	IL	60035	5
Keystone Art Cinema	8702 Keystone Crossing, # 201A	Indianapolis	IN	46240	7
Embassy Cinema	16 Pine St.	Waltham	MA	2154	6
Kendall Square Cinema	1 Kendall Square	Cambridge	MA	2139	9
Bethesda Row Cinema	7235 Woodmont Ave.	Bethesda	MD	20814	8
Harbor East	645 President St.	Baltimore	MD	21202	7
Main Art Theatre	118 N. Main St.	Royal Oak	MI	48067	3
Maple 3	4135 W. Maple Rd.	Bloomfield	MI	48301	3
Edina Cinema	3911 W. 50th St.	Edina	MN	55424	4
Lagoon Cinema	1320 Lagoon Ave.	Minneapolis	MN	55408	5
Uptown Theatre	2906 Hennepin Ave.	Minneapolis	MN	55408	1
Plaza Frontenac	210 Plaza Frontenac	St. Louis	MO	63131	6
Tivoli Theatre	6350 Delmar	Universal City	MO	63130	3
Sunshine Cinema	143 E. Houston St.	New York	NY	10002	5
Ritz at the Bourse	400 Ranstead St.	Philadelphia	PA	19106	5
Ritz East	125 S. 2nd St.	Philadelphia	PA	19106	2
Ritz V	214 Walnut St.	Philadelphia	PA	19106	5
Inwood Theatre	5458 W. Lovers Ln.	Dallas	TX	75209	3
Magnolia Theatre	3699 McKinney Ave., Ste. 100	Dallas	TX	75204	5
River Oaks Theatre	2009 W. Gray	Houston	TX	77019	3
Crest Cinema Center	16505 5th Ave., N.E.	Seattle	WA	98155	4
Egyptian Theatre	801 E. Pine	Seattle	WA	98122	1
Guild 45th Theatre	2115 N. 45th	Seattle	WA	98103	2
Harvard Exit Theatre	807 E. Roy	Seattle	WA	98102	2
Metro Cinemas	4500 8th Ave. N.E., #200	Seattle	WA	98105	10
Neptune Theatre	1303 N.E. 45th	Seattle	WA	98105	1
Seven Gables Theatre	911 N.E. 50th St.	Seattle	WA	98105	1
Varsity Theater	4329 University Way N.E.	Seattle	WA	98105	3
Downer Theatre	2689 Downer Ave.	Milwaukee	WI	53211	2
Oriental Theatre	2230 N. Farwell Ave.	Milwaukee	WI	53202	3

LOEKS THEATRES, INC. (CELEBRATION! CINEMA)

11 theatres, 150 screens.

2121 Celebration Dr. NE, Grand Rapids, MI 49525. TEL: (616) 447-4200. FAX: (616) 447-4201. www.celebrationcinema.com

PRESIDENT, CEO
John D. Loeks
COO
JD Loeks
CFO
Nancy Hagan
V.P., PROGRAMMING
Ron VanTimmeren
V.P., FACILITIES
Roger Lubs
V.P., PEOPLE
Steve Forsythe
V.P. & CTO
Kenneth Baas
V.P., OPERATIONS & REVENUE DEVELOPMENT
Kenyon Shane

Theatre	Address	City	State	Zip	Screens

V.P., MARKETING
Steve Van Wagoner

THEATRES

Theatre	Address	City	State	Zip	Screens
Celebration! Cinema	1468 Cinema Way	Benton Harbor	MI	49022	14
Celebration! Cinema/IMAX Theatre N.	2121 Celebration Dr. N.E.	Grand Rapids	MI	49525	18
Celebration! Cinema South	1506 Eastport Dr. S.E.	Grand Rapids	MI	49508	16
Celebration! Cinema Woodland	3195 28th St. S.E.	Grand Rapids	MI	49512	14
Celebration! Cinema Rivertown	3728 Rivertown Pkwy.	Grandville	MI	49418	20
Celebration! Cinema /IMAX Theatre	200 E. Edgewood Blvd.	Lansing	MI	48911	20
Celebration! Cinema	4935 E. Pickard	Mt. Pleasant	MI	48858	11
Getty Drive-In	920 E. Summit	Muskegon	MI	49441	4
Cinema Carousel	4289 Grand Haven Rd.	Muskegon	MI	49441	16
Plaza 1 and 2	3450 Henry St.	Muskegon	MI	49441	2
Celebration! Crossroads	6600 Ring Rd	Portage	MI	49024	15

LOGAN LUXURY THEATRES

4 theatres, 11 screens.
209 N. Lawler St., Mitchell, SD 57301. TEL: (605) 996-9022. FAX: (605) 996-9241. www.loganmovie.com
PRESIDENT
Jeff Logan
VICE PRESIDENT
Linda Logan
BOOKER & FILM BUYER
Jim Wilson

THEATRES

Theatre	Address	City	State	Zip	Screens
Dells Theatre	511 E. 4th St.	Dell Rapids	SD	57022	1
Huron Luxury Cinemas	215 Dakota Ave. S.	Huron	SD	57350	4
Luxury 5 Cinemas	209 N. Lawler St.	Mitchell	SD	57301	5
Starlite Drive-In	N. Hwy. 37	Mitchell	SD	57301	1

MAIN STREET THEATRES

6 theatres, 36 screens.
email: grau@mainstreettheatres.com www.mainstreettheatres.com

THEATRES

Theatre	Address	City	State	Zip	Screens
Main Street 7	Fremont Mall 866 E 23rd St	Fremont	NE	68025	7
Main Street Pioneer 3	110 S 11th St.	Nebraska City	NE	68410	3
Main Street Holland Plaza	717 8th St.	Orange City	IA.	51041	6
Main Street 3	401 9th St	Sheldon	IA.	51201	3
Main Street Legacy 3	712 w Sheridan	Shenandoah	IA.	51601	3
Main Street Promenade 14	924 4th St	Sioux City	IA.	51101	14

MALCO THEATRES, INC.

32 theatres, 320 screens.
5851 Ridgeway Ctr. Pkwy., Memphis, TN 38120. TEL: (901) 761-3480. FAX: (901) 681-2044. www.malco.com
CHAIRMAN
Richard Lightman
PRESIDENT & CEO
Stephen Lightman
SENIOR V.P., MARKETING & CORPORATE DEVELOPMENT
Robert Levy
SENIOR V.P., THEATRE OPERATIONS
James Tashie
V.P, CFO & TREASURER
Bill Blackburn
V.P. & HEAD FILM BUYER
Jeff Kaufman
V.P., TECHNICAL SUPPORT
Mike Thompson
V.P., CONCESSIONS OPERATIONS
Larry Etter
V.P. & DISTRICT MANAGER
James Lloyd
V.P., THEATRE OPERATIONS & CONSTRUCTION
David Tashie
V.P. & DIVISION MANAGER
Don Burchett
V.P., CORPORATE COMMUNICATIONS
Alan Denton
CO-OP ADVERTISING
Jeff Martin
SALES, MARKETING & PROMOTIONS COORDINATOR
Karen Scott
DISTRICT MANAGER
Donald Terry, Ricky Bourgeous, Nathan McDaniel
IT DEPARTMENT
John Tashie

THEATRES

Theatre	Address	City	State	Zip	Screens
Malco Trio Cinema	Hwy. 18 E. At I-55	Blytheville	AR	72315	3
Razorback 12	3956 N. Steele	Fayetteville	AR	72703	12
Fayetteville Mall Twin	4201 N. College	Fayetteville	AR	72701	2
Cinema 12	1200 Waldron Rd., Ste. 140	Fort Smith	AR	72904	12
Mall Trio Theatre	5111 Rogers Ave.	Fort Smith	AR	72903	3
Malco Cinema 13	2001 E. Highland Dr.	Jonesboro	AR	72401	13
Hollywood 12	2407 E. Parker Dr.	Jonesboro	AR	72401	12
Hollywood Cinema 6	120 Dearman Dr.	Monticello	AR	71655	6
Rogers Cinema 12	621 N. 46th St.	Rogers	AR	72756	12
Pinnacle Cinema	3951 S. Perry Rd.	Rogers	AR	72758	12
Malco Springdale 9	2940-G W. Sunset	Springdale	AR	72762	9
Van Buren Cinema	1636 N. 12th Ct.	Van Buren	AR	72956	8

Theatre	Address	City	State	Zip	Screens
Owensboro 12	5333 Frederica St.	Owensboro	KY	42303	12
Malco Trio Cinema	1045 E. Malone	Sikeston	MO	63801	3
Columbus Cinema 8	2320 Hwy. 45 N.	Columbus	MS	39701	8
Corinth Cinema 10	2505 S. Harper Rd.	Corinth	MS	38834	10
Grandview Cinema	221 Grandview Blvd.	Madison	MS	39110	17
Oxford Studio Cinema	1111 Jackson Ave. W.	Oxford	MS	38655	8
DeSoto 16	7130 Malco Blvd.	Southaven	MS	38671	16
Tupelo Commons 10	861 Cliff Gookin Blvd.	Tupelo	MS	38804	10
Bartlett Cinema 10	2809 Bartlett Blvd.	Bartlett	TN	38134	10
Stage Road Cinema	7930 Hwy. 64	Bartlett	TN	38133	13
Towne Cinema 16	380 Market Blvd.	Collierville	TN	38017	16
Cordova Cinema	1080 Germantown Pkwy.	Cordova	TN	38018	16
Forest Hill	3180 Village Shops Dr.	Germantown	TN	38138	8
Paradiso Cinema	584 S. Mendenhall.	Memphis	TN	38117	16
Ridgeway Four	5853 Ridgeway Ctr. Pkwy.	Memphis	TN	38120	4
Raleigh Springs 12	3384 Austin Peay	Memphis	TN	38128	12
Wolfchase Galleria	2766 N. Germantown Pkwy.	Memphis	TN	38133	8
Majestic 20	7051 Malco Crossing	Memphis	TN	38115	20
Studio on the Square	2105 Court St.	Memphis	TN	38104	5
Summer Drive-In	5310 Summer Ave.	Memphis	TN	38122	4

MANN THEATRES OF MINNESOTA

11 theatres, 79 screens.

900 East 80th St., Bloomington, MN 55420. TEL: (952) 767-0102. FAX: (952) 767-0103. www.manntheatresmn.com

PRESIDENT
Stephen Mann
VICE PRESIDENT
Benjie Mann
FILM BUYER & BOOKER
Neil O'Leary

THEATRES

Theatre	Address	City	State	Zip	Screens
Movies 10 in Brainerd	14145 Bqxter Dr	Baxter	MN	56401	10
Champlin Cinema 14	11500 Theatre Dr.	Champlin	MN	55316	14
Cottage View Drive-In	9338 E. Point Douglas Rd.	Cottage Grove	MN	55016	1
Grand Rapids Cinema 8	113 S. 21st St.	Grand Rapids	MN	55744	8
Hibbing Cinema 8	4015 9th Ave. W	Hibbing	MN	55740	8
Hopkins Cinema 6	1118 Main St.	Hopkins	MN	55343	6
Maple Grove Cinema 10	13644 80th Cir.	Maple Grove	MN	55369	10
Plymouth Cinema 12	3400 Vicksburg Ln.	Plymouth	MN	55447	12
St. Louis Park Cinema 6	5400 Excelsior Blvd.	St. Louis Park	MN	55416	6
Grandview 1 & 2 Theatres	1830 Grand Ave.	St. Paul	MN	55105	2
Highland 1 & 2 Theatres	760 S. Cleveland Ave.	St. Paul	MN	55116	2

MARCUS THEATRES CORPORATION

56 theatres, 683 screens.

100 E. Wisconsin Ave., 20th Flr., Ste. 2000, Milwaukee, WI 53202-4122. TEL: (414) 905-1500. FAX: (414) 905-2189. www.marcustheatres.com

CHAIRMAN
Steve Marcus
CEO MARCUS CORPORATION
Greg narcus
PRESIDENT
Bruce J. Olson
SENIOR V.P. & FILM BUYER
Paul Silk
SENIOR V.P., OPERATIONS
Mark Gramz
V.P., MARKETING, CONCESSIONS & PURCHASING
Robert Menefee
V.P., FINANCE, PLANNING & DEVELOPMENT
Jeff Tomachek
V.P., FILM
Rick Neals
FILM BOOKER
Jason Gudex, Anne Sampson, VaLois Bunch
FILM PROMOTIONS MANAGER
VaLois Bunch
DIRECTOR, HUMAN RESOURCES
John Brannan
DIRECTOR, CONCESSIONS & PURCHASING
Bruce Porlier
CHIEF INFORMATION TECHNOLOGY OFFICER
Kim Lueck
DIRECTOR, PROJECTION TECHNOLOGY
Mark Collins
MARKETING & COMMUNICATIONS MANAGER
Carlo Petrick
ADVERTISING MANAGER
Bret Hoffmann
DIRECTOR, SALES
Clint Wisialowski
DIRECTOR FOOD & BEVERAGE
Omar Andrietsch

THEATRES

Theatre	Address	City	State	Zip	Screens
College Square Theatre	1065 College Square Mall	Cedar Falls	IA	50613	12
Coral Ridge Mall	1451 Coral Ridge Ave.	Coralville	IA	52241	10
Sycamore Mall	1602 Sycamore St.	Iowa City	IA	52240	12
Crossroads (Waterloo)	2450 Crossroads Blvd.	Waterloo	IA	50702	12
Marcus Cinema Addison	1555 W. Lake St.	Addison	IL	60101	21
Marcus Cinema Chicago Heights	1301 Hilltop Ave.	Chicago Heights	IL	60411	14
Marcus Cinema Elgin Fox	111 S. Randall Rd.	Elgin	IL	60123	15
Marcus Cinema Gurnee	6144 Grand Ave., Gurnee Mills Mall	Gurnee	IL	60031	20
Marcus Cinema Orland Park	16350 S. LaGrange Rd.	Orland Park	IL	60467	14

Theatre	Address	City	State	Zip	Screens
Duluth Theatre	300 Harbor Dr.	Duluth	MN	55802	10
Marcus Cinema Elk River	Elk River Mall, 570 Freeport Rd.	Elk River	MN	55330	17
Marcus Cinema Hastings	1325 S. Frontage Rd.	Hastings	MN	55033	9
Lakes Theatre	4351 Stebner Rd.	Hermantown	MN	55811	10
Safari	925 30th Ave. S.	Moorhead	MN	56560	7
Marcus Cinema Oakdale	5677 Hadley Ave. N.	Oakdale	MN	55128	17
Marcus Cinema Rosemount	15280 Carrousel Way	Rosemount	MN	55068	8
Marcus Cinema Shakopee	1116 Shakopee Town Square	Shakopee	MN	55379	11
Parkwood	1533 Frontage Rd. N.	Waite Park	MN	56387	18
Twin Creek Cinema	3909 Raynor Pkwy.	Bellevue	NE	68123	16
East Park	220 N. 66th St.	Lincoln	NE	68505	6
Edgewood Cinema - Lincoln	5220 S. 56th St.	Lincoln	NE	68516	6
Lincoln Grand	1101 P St.	Lincoln	NE	68508	14
SouthPointe Cinema - Lincoln	2920 Pine Lake Rd.	Lincoln	NE	68516	6
Marcus Midtown Cinema	3201 Farnam Street	Omaha	NE	68131	5
20 Grand	14304 W. Maple Rd.	Omaha	NE	68164	19
Village Pointe Cinema	304 N. 174th St.	Omaha	NE	68118	16
Century Theatre	3931 9th Ave. S.W.	Fargo	ND	58103	10
West Acres Theatre	4101 17th Ave. S.W.	Fargo	ND	58103	14
Marcus Cinema Crosswoods	200 Hutchinson Ave.	Columbus	OH	43235	17
Marcus Cinema Pickerington	1776 Hill Rd. N.	Pickerington	OH	43147	17
Marcus Cinema Hollywood	513 N. Westhill Blvd.	Appleton	WI	54914	14
Marcus Appleton East	W3091 Van Roy Road	Appleton	WI	54915	16
Marcus Valley Value Cinemas	1401 Valley Fair Mall	Appleton	WI	54915	6
Marcus Cinema Bay Park	755 Willard Dr.	Ashwaubenon	WI	54304	16
Marcus Cinema Hillside	2950 Hillside Dr.	Delafield	WI	53018	14
Marcus Cinema Green Bay	1000 Kepler Dr.	Green Bay	WI	53411	12
Marcus Cinema Eastgate	5202 High Crossing Blvd.	Madison	WI	53718	16
Marcus Cinema Point	7825 Big Sky Dr.	Madison	WI	53719	16
Marcus Cinema Menomonee Falls	W180 N9393 Premier Ln.	Menomonee Falls	WI	53051	16
Marcus Cinema North Shore	11700 N. Port Washington.	Mequon	WI	53092	11
Marcus Cinema Northtown	7440 N. 76th St.	Milwaukee	WI	53223	8
Marcus Cinema Southgate	3330 S. 30th St.	Milwaukee	WI	53215	10
Marcus Cinema Cedar Creek	10101 Market St., Box D20	Mosinee	WI	54455	10
Marcus Cinema Ridge	5200 S. Moorland Rd.	New Berlin	WI	53151	20
Marcus Cinema South Shore	7261 S. 13th St.	Oak Creek	WI	53154	16
Marcus Cinema Value Oak Creek	6912 S. 27th St.	Oak Creek	WI	53154	8
Marcus Cinema Oshkosh	340 S. Koeller Rd.	Oshkosh	WI	54901	12
Marcus Cinema Campus	103 Watson St.	Ripon	WI	54971	1
Marcus Cinema Saukville	350 S. Riverside Dr.	Saukville	WI	53080	12
Marcus Cinema Sheboygan	3226 Kohler Memorial Dr.	Sheboygan	WI	53081	13
Marcus Cinema Sturtevant	10411 Washington Ave.	Sturtevant	WI	53177	13
Superior Theatre	69 N. 28th St.	Superior	WI	54880	7
Marcus Ho-Chunk Cinema	135 Wittig Rd.	Tomah	WI	54660	6
Marcus Majestic Cinema	770 N. Springdale Rd.	Waukesha	WI	53186	16
Marcus Cinema LaCrosse	2032 Ward Ave.	LaCrosse	WI	54601	11

MARQUEE CINEMAS

21 theatres, 202 screens.

552 Ragland Rd., Beckley, WV 25801. TEL: (304) 255-4036. FAX: (304) 252-0526. www.marqueecinemas.com

PRESIDENT & CEO
Curtis E. McCall
EXECUTIVE V.P.
James M. Cox
CFO
Cindy Ramsden
DIRECTOR, OPERATIONS
Harry L. Newman
DIRECTOR, MARKETING
Robin A. Shumate
OPERATIONS
Rob Thompson, Chris Prichard, Dave Sebolt

THEATRES

Theatre	Address	City	State	Zip	Screens
Westbrook 12	314 Flatrock Pl.	Westbrook	CT	06498	12
Coralwood 10 Cinemas	2301 Del Prado Blvd.	Cape Coral	FL	33990	10
Highland Cinemas	2400 Happy Valley Rd.	Glasgow	KY	42142	8
Mimosa 7	101 Green St.	Morganton	NC	28655	7
Statesville 10	Foldgers Dr.	Statesville	NC	28625	10
Wakefield 12	10600 Common Oaks Dr.	Wake Forest	NC	27614	12
Orchard 10	1311 Rte. 37 W.	Toms River	NJ	08755	10
Orchard 14	20 Ellinwood Dr.	New Hartford	NY	13413	14
Steamtown Mall 8	301 Lackawanna Ave.	Scranton	PA	18503	8
Fort Henry Cinemas II	2101 Fort Henry Dr.	Kingsport	TN	37664	11
Southpoint Cinemas	5800 Southpoint Blvd.	Fredericksburg	VA	22407	9
Wytheville Commons 8	187 Dominion St.	Wytheville	VA	24382	8
Galleria 14	200 Galleria Plaza	Beckley	WV	25801	14
Southridge Cinemas 12	331 Southridge Blvd.	Charleston	WV	25309	12
Pullman Square 16	3rd Ave. Pullman Sq.	Huntington	WV	25701	16
Seneca Showcase	Greenbier Valley Mall	Lewisburg	WV	24901	2
Southridge 12	331 Southridge Blvd	South Charleston	WV	25309	12
Crossroads	22 Crossroads Mall	Mt. Hope	WV	25880	6
Nicholas Showplace	300 Merchants Walk Plaza	Summersville	WV	26651	4
Highlands 14	150 Sims Circle	Triadelphia	WV	26059	14
McDowell 3	McDowell St.	Welch	WV	24801	3

MCMENAMINS THEATRE-PUBS

8 theatres, 8 screens.

430 N. Killingsworth, Portland, OR 97217. TEL: (503) 223-0109. FAX: (503) 294-0837. email: generalinfo@mcmenamins.com www.mcmenamins.com

COO - PUBS
Lars Raleigh - Lraleigh@mcmenamins.com

THEATRES

Theatre	Address	City	State	Zip	Screens
Old St. Francis School Theatre	700 NW Bond St	Bend	OR	97701	1
Grand Lodge Compass Room Theatre	3505 Pacific Ave	Forest Grove	OR	97116	1

Theatre	Address	City	State	Zip	Screens
Bagdad Theatre	3702 SE Hawthorne Blvd	Portland	OR	97214	1
Kennedy School Theatre	5736 NE 33rd Ave	Portland	OR	97211	1
Mission Theatre	1624 NW Glisan	Portland	OR	97209	1
St. Johns Theatre	8203 N Ivanhoe	Portland	OR	97203	1
Edgefield Power Station Theatre	2126 SW Halsey St	Troutdale	OR	97060	1
Olympic Club Theatre	112 N Tower Ave	Centralia	WA	98531	1

MEGAPLEX THEATRES

4 theatres, 6 screens.

P.O. Box 477, Jackson Center, OH 45334-0477. www.metheatres.com

THEATRES

Theatre	Address	City	State	Zip	Screens
Megaplex 8	2935 Thanksgiving Way	Lehi	UT		8
Megaplex 12	165 s Rio Grande St	Salt Lake City	UT		12
Megaplex 13					13
Hi-Road Drive-In	8059 State Rte. 68 N.	Kenton	OH	43326	1

M.E. THEATRES

4 theatres, 6 screens.

P.O. Box 477, Jackson Center, OH 45334-0477. www.metheatres.com

THEATRES

Theatre	Address	City	State	Zip	Screens
Ada Theatre	215 S. Main St.	Ada	OH	45810	1
Elder	106 W. Pike St.	Jackson Center	OH	45334	1
Kenton	221 W. Franklin St.	Kenton	OH	43326	3
Hi-Road Drive-In	8059 State Rte. 68 N.	Kenton	OH	43326	1

METROPOLITAN THEATRES CORP.

18 theatres, 89 screens.

8727 W. Third St., Los Angeles CA 90048. TEL: (310) 858-2800. FAX: (310) 858-2860. www.metrotheatres.com

CEO

Bruce C. Corwin

PRESIDENT

David Corwin

SENIOR V.P., OPERATIONS

Dale Davison

V.P., FILM MARKETING & ADVERTISING

Alan Stokes

V.P., OPERATIONS

Tim Spain

DIRECTOR OF CONCESSIONS

Adam Martin

THEATRES

Theatre	Address	City	State	Zip	Screens
Calexico 10 Theatre	2441 Scaroni Rd.	Calexico	CA	92231	10
Fairview Twin	255 N. Fairview	Goleta	CA	93117	3
Camino Real Cinemas	7040 Marketplace Dr.	Goleta	CA	93117	6
Park Theatre	6504 Pacific Blvd.	Huntington Park	CA	90255	2
Teatro Fiesta	305-100 E. 4th St.	Santa Ana	CA	92701	2
Arlington Theatre	1317 State St.	Santa Barbara	CA	93101	1
Fiesta 5 Theatre	916 State St.	Santa Barbara	CA	93101	5
Metro 4 Theatre	618 State St.	Santa Barbara	CA	93101	4
Paseo Nuevo Cinemas	8 W. De La Guerra Pl.	Santa Barbara	CA	93101	4
Plaza De Oro Twin	371 S. Hitchcock Way	Santa Barbara	CA	93105	2
Riviera Theatre	2044 Alameda Padre Serra	Santa Barbara	CA	93103	1
Isis Theatre	406 E. Hopkins	Aspen	CO	81611	4
MetroLux 14 Theatre	1380 N. Denver Ave.	Loveland	CO	80537	14
Wildhorse 6 Stadium Cinemas	655 Marketplace Plaza	Steamboat Springs	CO	80487	6
Bigwood 4 Cinemas	801 N. Main St.	Hailey	ID	83333	4
Redstone 8 Cinema	6030 N. Market St.	Park City	UT	84098	8
Village 8 Cinemas	4295 Blackcomb Way	Whistler	B.C.	VON 1B4	8
Garibaldi 5 Cinemas	40198 Glenalder Place	Squamish	B.C.	VON 3G0	5

MINI THEATRES

57 theatres, 255 screens.

5507 Avenue N, 3rd Flr., Brooklyn, NY 11234. TEL: (347) 587-6700. FAX: (347) 587-6205. www.minitheatresbooking.com

PARTNER

Marty Goldman, Jeff Goldman

BOOKING ACCOUNT THEATRES

Theatre	Address	City	State	Zip	Screens
Movieplex 8	95 Storrs Rd.	Mansfield	CT	06250	8
Village Art	Rte. 27	Mystic	CT	06355	3
Diamond State Drive-In	Rte. Box 13	Felton	DE	19943	1
Harvest Moon Drive-In	1123 S. Sangamon Ave.	Gibson City	IL	60936	2
Didleys		Metamora	IL	61548	1
Onarga	113 N. Pine	Onarga	IL	60955	1
Cinema Pub	137 Teaticket Hwy.	Falmouth	MA	02536	3
Gloucester Cinema	74 Essex Ave.	Gloucester	MA	01930	3
FineArts	17 Summer St.	Maynard	MA	01754	3
Route 1	501 E. Washington St.	N. Attelboro	MA	02760	2
Movieplex 8	80 Rear Main St.	North Adams	MA	01247	8
Island	Circuit Ave.	Oaks Bluff	MA	02557	1
Strand	Oak Bluffs Ave.	Oaks Bluff	MA	02557	1
Cinemagic	6 Merrill St.	Salisbury	MA	01952	9
Capawock	Main St.	Vineyard Haven	MA	02568	1
Tower South Hadley	19 College St.	South Hadley	MA	01075	2
Cinemagic Clarks Pond	333 Clarks Pond Pkwy.	Portland	ME	04106	8
Cinemagic 12	779 Portland Rd.	Saco	ME	04072	12
Cinemagic 16	183 Country Rd.	Westbrook	ME	04092	16
Cinemagic 15	1226 Hooksett Rd.	Hooksett	NH	03106	15
Weirs Drive-In	Rte. 3	Laconia	NH	03246	4
Cinemagic 12	11 Executive Park Dr.	Merrimack	NH	03054	12
Newton Theatre	234 Spring St.	Newton	NJ	07860	2
Delsea Drive-In	2203 S. Delsea Dr.	Vineland	NJ	08360	2
Bay Drive-In	Rte. Box 26	Alexandria Bay	NY	13607	2

Theatre	Address	City	State	Zip	Screens
Hollywood		Au Sable Forks	NY		2
Fingerlakes Drive-In	Clark St. Rd.	Auburn	NY	13021	1
Movieplex	Fingerlakes Mall	Auburn	NY	13021	10
Malta Drive-In	R.R. 9	Ballston Spa	NY	12020	2
American	98 Main St.	Canton	NY	13617	5
Movieplex Carmel	150 Route 52	Carmel	NY	10512	8
Crandell	Main St.	Chatham	NY	12037	1
Park Theater	Main St.	Cobleskill	NY	12043	1
Movieplex	10520 Bennett Rd.	Dunkirk	NY	14048	8
Glen Cove Cinemas	5 School St.	Glen Cove	NY	11542	6
Glen Drive-In	Lake George Rd.	Glens Falls	NY	12801	2
Movieplex Hudson	350 Fairview Ave.	Hudson	NY	12534	8
Lake Theatre	Main St.	Indian Lake	NY	12842	1
Tamarac Cafe	Route Box #28	Inlet	NY	13360	1
Movieplex Johnstown	236 N. Comrie Ave.	Johnstown	NY	12095	9
Palace	26 Main St.	Lake Placid	NY	12946	4
Valley Twin	20 Albany St.	Little Falls	NY	13365	2
Town Hall	Shady Ave.	Lowville	NY	13367	1
Valleybrook Drive-In	337 S. James St.	Lowville	NY	13367	1
56 Auto Drive-In	Andrews St.	Massena	NY	13662	1
Movieplex Massena	Haven Shopping Plaza	Massena	NY	13662	8
Hathaway Drive-In	Route Box #67	N. Hoosick	NY	12133	1
Cinema Twin 2	219 Ford St.	Ogdensburg	NY	13669	2
Strand	Main St.	Old Forge	NY	13420	4
Crystal Cinema	94 Victory Hwy.	Painted Post	NY	14870	8
Roxy	20 Main St.	Potsdam	NY	13676	4
Strand	Main St.	Schroon Lake	NY	12870	1
Unadilla DI	Wellsbridge Rd.	Unadilla	NY	13849	1
Munson	310 Guesee St.	Utica	NY	13502	1
Uptown Theatre	2014 Genesee St.	Utica	NY	13502	3
Mahoning Valley Drive-In	Seneca Rd.	Lehighton	PA	18235	1
Pike Drive-In	5490 Hwy. 15	Montgomery	PA	17752	3
State Theatre	130 W. College Ave.	State College	PA	16801	1
Empire	17 Water St.	Block Island	RI.	02871	1
Pier	3 Beach St.	Narragansett	RI.	02882	1
Plaza	Rutland Plaza	Rutland	VT	05701	9
Palace 9	10 Fayette Rd.	South Burlington	VT	05403	9
Springfield 2	26 Main St.	Springfield	VT	05156	2
Westway	Westway Mall	West Rutland	VT	05777	4

MJR THEATRES, INC. (MOVIES JUST RIGHT)

7 theatres, 116 screens.

13691 W. Eleven Mile Rd., Oak Park, MI 48237. TEL: (248) 548-8282. FAX: (248) 548-4706. www.mjrtheatres.com

PRESIDENT
Michael R. Mihalich
V.P. & FILM BUYER
Candi Mihalich
V.P., OPERATIONS
Dennis Redmer
DIRECTOR, MARKETING
Robin Hansen

THEATRES

Theatre	Address	City	State	Zip	Screens
Adrian Digital Cinema 10	3150 N. Adrian Hwy.	Adrian	MI	49221	10
Brighton Town Square Cinema 20	8200 Murphy Dr.	Brighton	MI	48116	20
Chesterfield Crossing Digital 16	50675 Gratiot Ave.	Chesterfield	MI	48051	16
Partridge Creek Digital Cinema 14	17400 Hall Rd.	Clinton Township	MI	48038	14
Southgate Cinemas	15651 Trenton Rd.	Southgate	MI	48195	20
Market Place Sterling Heights 20	35400 VanDyke	Sterling Heights	MI	48312	20
Waterford Cinema	7501 Highland Rd.	Waterford	MI	48327	16

THE MOVIE EXPERIENCE (SANBORN THEATRES, INC.)

6 theatres, 56 screens.

13 Corporate Plaza, Newport Beach, CA 92660. TEL: (949) 640-2370. www.movieexperience.com

PRESIDENT
Bruce Sanborn
CHIEF FINANCIAL & OPERATIONS OFFICER
Gary Richardson
FILM BUYER
Lisa Kanno

THEATRES

Theatre	Address	City	State	Zip	Screens
Blue Jay Cinema 4 at Lake Arrowhead	27315 N. Bay Rd.	Blue Jay	CA	92317	4
Movie Experience 14 at Gardenwalk	321 W. Katella	Anaheim	CA	92802	14
Movie Experience 17 at CA Oaks	41090 California Oaks Rd.	Murrieta	CA	92562	17
Movie Experience 7 at Downtown Centre	888 Marsh St.	San Luis Obispo	CA	93401	7
Movie Experience 4 at The Fremont	1035 Monterey	San Luis Obispo	CA	93401	4
Movie Experience 10 at Tower Plaza	27531 Ynez Rd.	Temecula	CA	92591	10

MULLER FAMILY THEATRES

8 theatres, 104 screens.

20653 Keokuk Ave., Lakeville, MN 55044. TEL: (952) 469-2883. FAX: (952) 985-5643. www.mullerfamilytheatres.com

DIRECTOR, OPERATIONS
Dale Haider

THEATRES

Theatre	Address	City	State	Zip	Screens
Delano 5 Theatre	4423 US Hwy. 12	Delano	MN	55328	5
East Bethel 10 Theatre	18635 Ulysses N.E.	East Bethel	MN	55005	10
Lakeville 21 Theatre	20653 Keokuk Ave.	Lakeville	MN	55044	21
Monticello 15 Theatre	9375 Deegan Ave.	Monticello	MN	55362	15
WillowCreek 12 Theatre	9900 Shelard Pkwy.	Plymouth	MN	55441	12
Waconia 6 Theatre	101 W. 1st St.	Waconia	MN	55387	6
White Bear Township 17 Theatre	1180 County Rd. J.	White Bear Twnshp.	MN	55110	17
Rogers 18 Theatre	13692 Rogers Dr.	Rogers	MN	55374	18

Theatre	Address	City	State	Zip	Screens

MUVICO THEATERS

9 theatres, 154 screens.
3101 N. Federal Hwy., 6th Fl., Ft. Lauderdale, FL 33306. TEL: (954) 564-6550. FAX: (954) 564-6553. www.muvico.com
PRESIDENT & CEO
Neil F. Bretan
V.P., FINANCE
Alan Rainbeau
FILM BUYER
Hank Lightstone
V.P., OPERATIONS
James Herd, Jr.
V.P. PURCHASING & FACILITIES
David Thollander

THEATRES

Theatre	Address	City	State	Zip	Screens
Muvico Thousand Oaks 14	166 W. Hillcrest Dr.	Thousand Oaks	CA	91360	14
Muvico Hileah 14	780 W. 49th St.	Hialeah	FL	33012	14
Muvico Palm Harbor 10	37912 U.S. Hwy 19N	Palm Harbor	FL	34684	10
Muvico Pompano 18	2315 N. Federal Hwy.	Pompano Beach	FL	33062	18
Muvico Baywalk 20	151 2nd Ave. N.	St. Petersburg	FL	33701	20
Muvico Centro Ybor 20	1600 E. 8th Ave., #A-200	Tampa	FL	33605	20
Muvico Starlight 20	18002 Highwoods Preserve Pkwy.	Tampa	FL	33647	20
Muvico Parisian 20	545 Hibiscus St.	W. Palm Beach	FL	33401	20
Muvico Rosemont 18	9701 Bryn Mawr Ave	Rosemont	IL	60018	18

NATIONAL CINEMEDIA

(See Advertising & Publicity and Digital Cinema Equipment & Services - Exhibitor Products & Services)
9110 E. Nichols Ave., Ste. 200, Centennial, CO 80112. TEL: (800) 828-2828, (303) 792-3600. FAX: (303) 792-8663. www.nationalcinemedia.com
PRESIDENT & CEO
Kurt C. Hall
ASSISTANT
Kathleen Rush
EXECUTIVE V.P., & CFO
Gary Ferrera
EXECUTIVE V.P., CHIEF OPERATIONS & TECHNOLOGY OFFICER
Tom Galley
122 E. 42nd St., Ste. 511, New York, NY 10168. TEL: (212) 931-8100.
PRESIDENT. MARKETING AND SALES
Cliff Marks
EXECUTIVE V.P., MARKETING & SALES
Dave Kupiec

NATIONAL AMUSEMENTS, INC.

34 U.S. theatres, 455 U.S. screens; 21 U.K. theatres, 276 U.K. screens; 22 South American theatres, 229 screens; 3 Russian theatres. Total: 77 theatres, 960 screens, 4 U.S. IMAX, 1 Argentinian IMAX.
Mailing address: P.O. Box 9126, Dedham, MA 02027-9126. Street address: 846 University Avenue, Norwood, MA 02062-2631. TEL: (781) 461-1600. FAX: (781) 326-1306. www.nationalamusements.com
PRESIDENT
Shari E. Redstone
V.P., OPERATIONS
Steve Horton
SENIOR V.P., FILM BOOKING
George Levitt
SENIOR V.P. & GENERAL COUNSEL
Thaddeus Jankowski
V.P., INTERNATIONAL OPERATIONS
Duncan Short
V.P., CONCESSIONS OPERATIONS
Bill LeClair
V.P., REAL ESTATE
William J. Moscarrelli
V.P., MARKETING
Scott Bernstein
V.P. ADVERTISING/PROMOTIONS
Elaine Purdy
SENIOR V.P., FINANCE & ADMINISTRATION
Richard Sherman
V.P., INFORMATION TECHNOLOGY
Joseph Mollo
V.P., CONSTRUCTION
John Townsend
V.P., FILM INTERNATIONAL
Mark Walukevich
ASST. V.P. & DEPUTY GENERAL COUNSEL
Patricia Reeser
ASST. V.P. & DEPUTY GENERAL COUNSEL
Shawn Sullivan
ASST. V.P., CONCESSIONS MARKETING
John Zawalich
ASST. V.P., FINANCE
Mike Kszystyniak
ASST. VP, HUMAN RESOURCES
Maureen Dixon

THEATRES

Theatre	Address	City	State	Zip	Screens
Showcase Bridgeport	286 Canfield St.	Bridgeport	CT	06605	12
Fairfield Cinemas	40 Black Rock Tpk.	Fairfield	CT	06430	9
Showcase Cinema de Lux Legacy Pl.	670 Legacy Place	Dedham	MA	02026	15
Showcase Cinema de Lux Patriot Place	24 Patriot Place	Foxboro	MA	02035	14
Showcase Cinemas Lawrence 7-14	141 Winthrop Ave.	Lawrence	MA	01843	8
Showcase Cinemas Lowell	32 Reiss Avenue	Lowell	MA	01851	14

Theatre	Address	City	State	Zip	Screens
Showcase Cinemas N. Attleboro	640 S. Washington St.	N. Attleboro	MA	02760	12
Showcase Cinemas Randolph	73 Mazzeo Dr.	Randolph	MA	02368	16
Showcase Cinema de Lux Revere	565 Squire Rd.	Revere	MA	02151	20
Showcase Seekonk Route 6	100 Commerce Way	Seekonk	MA	02771	10
Showcase Cinemas Woburn	25 Middlesex Canal Pkwy.	Woburn	MA	01801	14
Blackstone Valley 14: Cinema de Lux	70 Worcester Providence Tpk.	Millbury	MA	01527	14
Showcase Cinemas Worcester North	135 Brooke St.	Worcester	MA	01606	18
Town Center Plaza	319 Rte. 30 N.	East Windsor	NJ	08520	15
Edgewater Multiplex Cinemas	339 River Rd.	Edgewater	NJ	07020	16
City Center 15: Cinema de Lux	19 Mamaroneck Ave.	White Plains	NY	10601	15
Greenburgh Multiplex Cinemas	320 Saw Mill River Rd.	Greenburgh	NY	10523	10
All Westchester Saw Mill Multiplex	151 Saw Mill River Rd.	Hawthorne	NY	10532	10
Cross County Multiplex	Two South Dr.	Yonkers	NY	10704	10
Concourse Plaza Multiplex	214 E. 161st St.	Bronx	NY	10451	10
Whitestone Multiplex	2505 Bruckner Blvd.	Bronx	NY	10465	14
College Point Multiplex	28-55 Ulmer St.	Whitestone	NY	11357	12
Linden Blvd. Multiplex	2784 Linden Blvd.	Brooklyn	NY	11208	14
Commack Multiplex	100 Long Island Expy.	Commack	NY	11725	15
Farmingdale Multiplex	1001 Broad Hollow Rd.	Farmingdale	NY	11735	14
Broadway Multiplex	955 Broadway Mall	Hicksville	NY	11801	12
Island 16: Cinema de Lux	185 Morris Ave.	Holtsville	NY	11742	16
Jamaica Multiplex	159-02 Jamacia Ave.	Jamaica	NY	11432	15
Green Acres Cinemas	610 W. Sunrise Hwy.	Valley Stream	NY	11581	6
Sunrise Multiplex	750 W. Sunrise Hwy.	Valley Stream	NY	11582	14
Springdale 18: Cinema de Lux	12064 Springfield Pike	Cincinnati	OH	45246	18
Providence Place Cinema	10 Providence Place Mall	Providence	RI	02903	16
Showcase Cinemas Warwick	1200 Quaker Ln.	Warwick	RI	02886	15
Showcase Cinemas Warwick Mall	400 Bald Hill Rd.	Warwick	RI	02886	12

NCG (NEIGHBORHOOD CINEMA GROUP)

12 theatres, 113 screens.

314 Comstock, Owosso, MI 48867. TEL: (989) 725-8755. FAX: (989) 723-0359. www.ncgmovies.com

CEO

Gary Geiger, Steve Smith

CFO/FILM BUYER

Shelly Davis

V.P., CORPORATE DEVELOPMENT

Jeff Geiger

COO

Mark Henning

THEATRES

Theatre	Address	City	State	Zip	Screens
NCG Acworth Cinema	4421 Cinema Dr.	Acworth	GA	30101	12
NCG Auburn Cinemas	1111 Smaltzway	Auburn	IN	46706	8
Alma Cinemas	3002 W. Monroe	Alma	MI	48801	6
Clio Cinemas	2151 W. Vienna Rd.	Clio	MI	48420	4
Coldwater Cinemas	414 N. Willowbrook Rd.	Coldwater	MI	49036	7
Trillium NCG Cinemas	8220 Trillium Circle	Grand Blanc	MI	48439	15
Greenville Cinemas	1500 N. Lafayette Rd.	Greenville	MI	48828	7
Lansing Cinemas	2205 Lake Lansing Rd.	Lansing	MI	48912	18
Lapeer Cinemas	1650 DeMille Rd.	Lapeer	MI	48445	8
Midland Cinemas	6540 Cinema Dr.	Midland	MI	48640	11
Owosso Cinemas	314 Comstock	Owosso	MI	48867	7
Gallatin Cinema	1035 Greensboro Dr.	Gallatin	TN	37066	10

NOVA CINETECH, INC.

4 theatres, 33 screens.

4688 E. 29th Rd., Sandwich, IL 60548. TEL: (815) 786-6577. FAX: (815) 786-6337. www.novacinemas.com

PRESIDENT

Albert "Buck" Kolkmeyer

FILM BUYER

Molly Wetzel

SECRETARY/TREASURER

Kara Walker

THEATRES

Theatre	Address	City	State	Zip	Screens
Nova 10 Cinemas	4353 Merle Hay Rd.	Des Moines	IA	50310	11
Nova Cinemas at Sabal Palm	2539 S. Federal Hwy.	Ft. Pierce	FL	34982	6
Nova 6	2018 36th Ave.	Moline	IL	61265	6
Paradise Theatre	2014 Pkwy. Dr.	West Bend	WI	53095	10

PACIFIC THEATRES

12 theatres, 150 screens.

120 N. Robertson Blvd., Los Angeles, CA 90048. TEL: (310) 657-8420. FAX: (310) 657-6736. www.pacifictheatres.com

BOARD CHAIRMAN

Michael R. Forman

CEO

Christopher Forman

COO

Nora Dashwood

EXECUTIVE V.P., HEAD FILM BUYER

Gretchen McCourt

THEATRES

Theatre	Address	City	State	Zip	Screens
Glendale 18	322 Americana Way	Glendale	CA	91210	18
Winnetka 21	9201 Winnetka Ave.	Chatsworth	CA	91311	21
Commerce 14	950 Goodrich Blvd.	City of Commerce	CA	90022	14
Vineland Drive-In	443 N. Vineland Ave.	City of Industry	CA	91746	4
Culver Stadium 12	9500 Culver Blvd.	Culver City	CA	90232	12
Beach Cities 16	831 S. Nash St.	El Segundo	CA	90245	16
Lakewood Center 16	5200 Faculty Ave.	Lakewood	CA	90712	16
The Grove 14	189 The Grove Dr.	Los Angeles	CA	90036	14
Manhattan Village 6	3560 Sepulveda Blvd.	Manhattan Beach	CA	90266	6
Fashion Center 10	9400 N. Shirley Ave.	Northridge	CA	91324	10

Theatre	Address	City	State	Zip	Screens	
Sherman Oaks 5	14424 Milbank St.	Sherman Oaks	CA	91423	5	803
Paseo 14	336 E. Colorado Blvd., Ste. B201B	Pasadena	CA	91101	14	807

PARAGON ENTERTAINMENT

2 theatres, 26 screens.
www.paragon-ent.net
CEO
Michael F. Whalen
COO
Hank Lightstone
V.P., DEVELOPMENT
Michael Wilson

THEATRES

Theatre	Address	City	State	Zip	Screens
Muvico Coco Walk	3015 Grand Ave	Coconut Grove	FL	33133	14
Muvico Village 12	50 Towne Center Blvd	Fredericksburg	VA	22407	12

PATRIOT CINEMAS, INC.

7 theatres, 37 screens.
101 Derby St. Ste 202., Hingham, MA 02043. TEL: (781) 749-8300. FAX: (781) 749-3993. www.patriotcinemas.com
PRESIDENT
Philip J. Scott
VICE PRESIDENT
David A. Kiolbasa, Edith L. Scott
FILM BOOKER & BUYER
David A. Scott

THEATRES

Theatre	Address	City	State	Zip	Screens
Patriot Cinemas, Hanover Mall	1775 Washington St.	Hanover	MA	02339	10
Patriot Cinemas, Loring Hall	65 Main St.	Hingham	MA	02043	1
Patriot Cinemas, Hingham Shipyard	25 Shipyard Dr.	Hingham	MA	02043	6
Patriot Cinemas, The Mill Wharf Plaza	1 Mill Wharf Plaza	Scituate Harbor	MA	02066	2
Patriot Cinemas, Cameo Theatre	14 Columbian St..	S. Weymouth	MA	02190	2
Patriot Cinemas, Nickelodeon 6	One Temple St.	Portland	ME	04101	6
Patriot Cinemas, E. Providence 10	Route 1A	Rumford	RI	02916	10

PHOENIX BIG CINEMAS MANAGEMENT, LLC.

24 theatres, 186 screens.
9111 Cross Park Dr., Ste. E-275, Knoxville, TN 37923. TEL: (865) 692-4061. www.PhoenixTheatres.com
PRESIDENT & CEO
Phil Zacheretti
V.P., OPERATIONS
Fred L. Buffum
HEAD FILM BUYER
Alexander F. Ellis
V.P., FINANCE
Cindy Taylor
V.P., MARKETING & ADVERTISING
Karen J. Lane
DIRECTOR, PURCHASING
Moya Myers
DIRECTOR, FOOD & BEVERAGE
Denise Ferro
DIRECTOR, CAPITAL IMPROVEMENTS
Vince Emmons
DIRECTOR, OPERATIONS
Chris Gehring

THEATRES

Theatre	Address	City	State	Zip	Screens
Phoenix Big Cinemas Dos Lagos 15	2710 Lakeshore Dr.	Corona	CA	92883	15
BIG Cinemas Fremont 7	39160 Paseo Padre Pkwy	Fremont	CA	94538	7
BIG Cinemas Norwalk 8	13917 Pioneer Blvd.	Norwalk	CA	90650	8
BIG Cinemas Towne 3	1433 The Alameda	San Jose	CA	95126	3
Phoenix Theatres Lake Worth 8	5881 Lake Worth Road	Greenacres	FL	33463	8
BIG Cinemas Roxy Cinema Grill	1553 Palm Bay Road NE	Palm Bay	FL	32905	10
Phoenix South DeKalb 12	2801 Candler Rd.	Decatur	GA	30034	12
Phoenix Peachtree 8	6135 Peachtree Pkwy.	Norcross	GA	30092	8
BIG Cinemas Golf Glen 5	9180 West Golf Rd.	Niles	IL	60714	5
Phoenix Legends 14 Theatre	841 Village W. Pkwy.	Kansas City	KS	66111	14
Phoenix Theatres Kyova Mall 10	10699 US Route 60, Ste 103	Ashland	KY	41102	10
BIG Cinemas Capitol 8 Theatres	455 Madison Square Dr.	Madisonville	KY	42431	8
Cherokee Phoenix Theatres	61 Sequoyah Trail	Cherokee	NC	28719	2
BIG Cinemas Movie City 8	1655 Oak Tree Rd. (Edison Cinemas- Pathmark Plaza)	Edison	NJ	08820	8
Phoenix Adlabs - Columbia Park 12	3137 Kennedy Blvd.	North Bergen	NJ	07047	12
BIG Cinemas Bombay Theatre	68-25 Fresh Meadow Ln.	Fresh Meadows	NY	11365	1
BIG Cinemas Manhattan	239 E. 59th St.	New York	NY	10022	1
Phoenix Theatres Eastgate 10	1345 Som Center Rd.	Mayfield Heights	OH	44124	10
Willoughby Hills 10	27613 Chardon Rd.	Willoghby	OH	44092	10
BIG Cinemas Towne Crossing 8	925 W. Andrew Johnson Hwy.	Greeneville	TN	37745	8
BIG Cinemas The Forge Cinemas	2530 Parkway, Ste. 7	Pigeon Forge	TN	37863	8
Phoenix Worldgate 9 Theatres	13025 Worldgate Dr.	Herndon	VA	20170	9
Phoenix Main Gate Movies 10	NEX Mall Complex-Bldg. CD-12, 1500 Mall Dr.	Norfolk	VA	23511	10
Phoenix Adlabs - Loehmann's Twin Cinema	7291 Arlington Blvd..	Falls Church	VA	22042	2

POLSON THEATRES

11 theatres, 26 screens.
P.O. Box 999, Polson, MT 59860. TEL: (406) 883-5603. FAX: (406) 883-5639. www.polsontheatres.com
OWNER
Howard Pickerill, Ayron Pickerill
GENERAL MANAGER
Gary Dupuis

Theatre	Address	City	State	Zip	Screens

HEAD FILM BUYER
Becky Dupuis

THEATRES

Theatre	Address	City	State	Zip	Screens
River Cinemas	526 Main St.	Salmon	ID	83467	2
Glacier Cinemas	111 E. Main	Cutback	MT	59427	2
Big Sky Cinemas	560 N. Montana	Dillon	MT	59725	2
Valley Cinemas	600 2nd Ave. S	Glasgow	MT	59230	2
Havre Cinemas	328 2nd St.	Havre	MT	59501	4
Judith Theatres	219 West Main	Lewiston	MT	59457	2
Showboat Cinemas	416 Main St.	Polson	MT	59860	2
Entertainer Cinema	410 Main St.	Ronan	MT	59864	1
Roxy Cinema	231 Main St.	Shelby	MT	59474	1
Mountain Cinemas	6475 Hwy. 93 S.	Whitefish	MT	59937	4
Prairie Cinemas	314 Main St.	Wolf Point	MT	59201	2

R/C THEATRES MANAGEMENT CORP.

13 theatres, 106 screens.
231 W. Cherry Hill Ct., Box 1056, Reisterstown, MD 21136. TEL: (410) 526-4774. FAX: (410) 526-6871. www.rctheatres.com
CHAIRMAN
J. Wayne Anderson
PRESIDENT & CEO
Scott R. Cohen
EXECUTIVE V.P. & CFO
David G. Phillips
CONTROLLER
Richard A. Hershel
SENIOR FILM BUYER
Jan S. Anderson
DIVISION MANAGERS
David Knight (VA & NC)

THEATRES

Theatre	Address	City	State	Zip	Screens
OceanWalk 10	300 N. Atlantic Ave.	Daytona Beach	FL	32118	10
Frostburg Cinemas 3	10701 New Georges Creek Rd.	Frostburg	MD	21532	3
Reading Movies 11 & IMAX	30 N. 2nd St.	Reading	PA	19601	11
Wilkes-Barres 14	24 E. Northampton	Wilkes-Barre	PA	18701	14
Apple Blossom Movies 16	1850 Apple Blossom Dr.	Winchester	VA	22601	16

MANAGED THEATRES

Theatre	Address	City	State	Zip	Screens
Hollywood Cinemas	5509 Oregon Ave.	Arbutus	MD	21227	4
Hatteras Movies	Hwy. 12	Avon	NC	27915	4
Corolla Movies	815 E. Ocean Trail	Corolla	NC	27927	4
Kill Devil Hills Movies 10	1803 N. Croatan Hwy.	Kill Devil Hills	NC	27948	10
Gateway Movies	20 Presidential Circle	Gettysburg	PA	17325	8
Hanover Movies	380 Eisenhower Dr.	Hanover	PA	17331	16
Covington Movies	139 N. Maple Ave.	Covington	VA	24426	3
State Cinema 3	12 W. Nelson St.	Lexington	VA	24450	3

RAVE MOTION PICTURES

61 theatres, 918 screens.
2101 Cedar Springs Road, Suite 800, Dallas TX 75201. TEL: (972) 692-1700. FAX: (972) 692-1709.
email: information@ravemotionpictures.com www.ravemotionpictures.com
PRESIDENT & CEO
Thomas W. Stephenson, Jr.
EXECUTIVE V.P. & CFO
Arthur Starrs, III
SENIOR V.P., TECHNOLOGY
Bryan A. Rakowski
SENIOR V.P., FILM
Spencer Klein
V.P., MARKETING
Jeremy Devine
V.P., HUMAN RESOURCES
Kira Shropshire
V.P., OPERATIONS
Brad Wardlow

THEATRES

Theatre	Address	City	State	Zip	Screens
RRC Lee Branch 15	801 Doug Baker Blvd.	Birmingham	AL	35242	15
RRC Jubilee Square 12	6898 Hwy. 90	Daphne	AL	36526	12
RRC Hoover 15	4450 Creekside Ave	Hoover	AL	35244	15
RRC Valley Bend 18	1485 Four Mile Rd. S.E.	Huntsville	AL	35802	18
RRC Festival Plaza 16	7925 Vaughn Rd.	Montgomery	AL	36116	16
RRC Wharf 15	23151 Wharf Ln.	Orange Beach	AL	36561	15
RRC Vestavia Hills 10	1911 Kentucky Ave.	Vestavia Hills	AL	35216	10
RC Colonel Glenn 18	18 Colonel Glenn Plaza Dr.	Little Rock	AR	72210	18
RDM Brentwood	2525 Sand Creek Rd.	Brentwood	CA	94513	14
RC Bridge 18	6081 Center Dr.	Los Angeles	CA	90045	18
RC Enfield 12	90 Elm St.	Enfield	CT	06082	12
RC Berlin 12	19 Frontage Road	Kensington	CT	06037	12
RC Buckland Hills 18	99 Redstone Rd	Manchester	CT	06045	18
RC Connecticut Post 14	1201 Boston Post Rd Ste 3000	Milford	CT	06460	14
RC North Haven 12	550 Universal Dr	North Haven	CT	06473	12
RC Southington 12	1821 Meriden Waterbury St	Southington	CT	06489	12
RRC Destin Commons 14	4000 Legendary Dr.	Destin	FL	32541	14
RRC Viera 16	2241 Town Centre Ave.	Melbourne	FL	32940	16
RRC Bayou 15	5149 Bayou Blvd.	Pensacola	FL	32503	15
RRC Pensacola 18	6596 North W. St.	Pensacola	FL	32508	18
RRC Port St. Lucie West 14	1900 N. W. Courtyard	Port St. Lucie	FL	34986	14
RC Davenport 53 18	3601 E 53rd St	Davenport	IA	52807	18
RRC Grand Prairie 18	5311 W. American Prairie Dr.	Peoria	IL	61615	18
RRC Jefferson Pointe 18	4250 W. Jefferson Blvd.	Fort Wayne	IN	46804	18
RRC Metropolis 18	2940 Futura Pkwy.	Plainfield	IN	46168	18
RC Florence 14	7860 Mall Rd	Florence	KY	41042	14

Theatre	Address	City	State	Zip	Screens
RC Preston Crossings 16	9700 Preston Crossing Blvd	Okolona	KY	40229	16
RC Stonybrook 20	2745 S. Hurstbourne Parkway	Louisville	KY	40220	20
RRC Baton Rouge 16	16040 Hatteras Ave.	Baton Rouge	LA	70816	16
RRC Mall of Louisiana	9168T Picardy Ave. Extension	Baton Rouge	LA	70836	15
RC Eastfield 16	1655 Boston Road - Route 20	Springfield	MA	01129	16
RC West Springfield 15	864 Riverdale Road	West Springfield	MA	01089	15
RRC City Place 14	180 Portage Rd.	Kalamazoo	MI	49007	14
RC Ann Arbor 20	4100 Carpenter Road	Ypsilanti	MI	48197	20
RC Flint West 14	1591 South Graham Road	Flint	MI	48532	14
RDM Westroads 14	10000 California Street	Omaha	NE	68114	14
RC Hazlet 12	2821 Highway 35	Hazlet	NJ	07730	12
RC Ritz Center 16	900 Haddonfield-Berlin Rd	Voorhees	NJ	08043	16
RDMTown Square 18	6587 Las Vegas Blvd. S.	Las Vegas	NV	89119	18
RC The Greene 14	4489 Glengarry Drive	Beavercreek	OH	45440	14
RC Western Hills 14	5870 Harrison Avenue	Cincinnati	OH	45248	14
RC Polaris Mall18	1071 Gemini Pl.	Columbus	OH	43240	18
RC Huber Heights 16	7737 Wayne Town Boulevard	Huber Heights	OH	45424	16
RC Fallen Timbers 14	2300 Village Drive West	Maumee	OH	43537	14
RC Kings Island 12	5937 Kings Island Drive	Mason	OH	45040	12
RC Milford 16	500 Rivers Edge Drive	Milford	OH	45150	16
RCLevis Commons 12	2005 Hollenbeck Dr.	Perrysburg	OH	43551	12
RC Franklin Park 16	5001 Monroe Street	Toledo	OH	43623	16
RC Dayton South16	195 Mall Woods Dr	West Carrollton	OH	45449	16
RDM West Chester 18	9415 Civic Center Blvd.	West Chester	OH	45067	18
RMP Promenade 16	2805 Center Valley Pkwy.	Center Valley	PA	18034	16
RC University City 6	230 S 40th St @ Walnut St	Philadelphia	PA	19104	6
RC Pittsburgh North 11	9700 McKnight Road	Pittsburgh	PA	15237	11
RRC East Ridge 18	5080 S. Terrance	Chattanooga	TN	37412	18
RC Ridgmar 13	2300 Green Oaks Rd.	Fort Worth	TX	76116	13
RRC Hickory Creek 16	380 S. Stemmons Frwy.	Hickory Creek	TX	76205	16
RRC Yorktown 15	15900 Yorktown Crossing	Houston	TX	77084	15
RC Northeast Mall 18	1101 Melbourne Rd.	Hurst	TX	76053	18
RC Centreville 12	6201 Multiplex Drive	Centreville	VA	20121	12
RC Fairfax Corner 14	11900 Palace Way	Fairfax	VA	22030	14
RC Reston 13	11940 Market Street	Reston	VA	20190	13

READING INTERNATIONAL, INC.

9 theatres. 56 screens.
500 Citadel Dr., Ste. 300, Commerce, CA 90040. TEL: (213) 235-2240. FAX: (213) 235-2229. www.readingrdi.com
PRESIDENT, DOMESTIC CINEMAS
Robert F. Smerling
COO, DOMESTIC CINEMAS
Ellen M. Cotter
PRESIDENT, LIVE THEATERS
Margaret Cotter
DIRECTOR, DOMESTIC REAL ESTATE
Brett Marsh

THEATRES

Theatre	Address	City	State	Zip	Screens
Manville 12-Plex	180 N. Main St.	Manville	NJ	08835	12
Angelika Film Center & Café - New York	18 W. Houston St.	New York	NY	10012	6
Cinemas 1, 2 & 3	1001 3rd Ave.	New York	NY	10022	3
East 86th Street Cinemas	210 E. 86th St.	New York	NY	10028	4
Village East	181 2nd Ave.	New York	NY	10003	7
Angelika Film Center & Café - Dallas	5321 E. Mockingbird Ln., Ste. 230	Dallas	TX	75206	8
Angelika Film Center & Café - Houston	510 Texas Ave.	Houston	TX	77002	8
Angelika Film Center & Café - Plano	7205 Bishop Dr., Ste. E6	Plano	TX	75024	5
Tower Theatre	2508 Land Park Dr.	Sacramento	CA	95818	3

REGAL ENTERTAINMENT GROUP

543 theatres, 6,739 screens, 16 IMAX in 38 states and the District of Columbia.
7132 Regal Ln., Knoxville, TN 37918. TEL: (865) 922-1123. FAX: (865) 922-3188. www.regalcinemas.com
EXECUTIVE CHAIRMAN
Michael L. Campbell
CEO
Amy E. Miles
PRESIDENT & COO
Gregory W. Dunn
EXECUTIVE V.P. & CFO
David H. Ownby
EXECUTIVE V.P., SECRETARY & GENERAL COUNSEL
Peter B. Brandow
SENIOR V.P., FILM
Ted Cooper
SENIOR V.P., IT & CIO
David King
CHIEF ADMINISTRATIVE OFFICER & COUNSEL
Randy Smith
SENIOR V.P., PURCHASING & CPO
Rob Del Moro
SENIOR V.P., MARKETING & ADVERTISING
Dick Westerling
SENIOR V.P., FINANCE
Corey Coggin
SENIOR V.P., OPERATIONS
Neal Pinsker
SENIOR V.P., REAL ESTATE
Robert Crane
SENIOR V.P., CONSTRUCTION/TECHNICAL SERVICES
Ron Reid
SENIOR V.P., FILM - ALTERNATIVE
Denise Gurin
SENIOR V.P., FILM FINANCE
Bob Engel

Theatre	Address	City	State	Zip	Screens

SENIOR V.P., BUSINESS RELATIONS
Ray Nutt

THEATRES

Theatre	Address	City	State	Zip	Screens
Dimond Center 9 Cinemas	800 E. Dimond Blvd., Ste. 210	Anchorage	AK	99515	9
Totem 8 Theatres	3131 Muldoon Rd.	Anchorage	AK	99504	8
Tikahtnu Stadium 16	1102 N. Muldoon Rd.	Anchorage	AK	99504	16
Goldstream Stadium 16	1855 Airport Rd.	Fairbanks	AK	99701	16
Kambe Theatre 3	215 N. Willow St.	Kenai	AK	99611	3
Trussville Stadium 16	5895 Trussville Crossings Pkwy.	Birmingham	AL	35235	16
River Oaks Cinema 8	2203 Family Security Place SW	Decatur	AL	35603	8
Hollywood Stadium 18	3312 S. Memorial Pkwy.	Huntsville	AL	35802	18
Breckenridge Stadium 12	1200 Breckenridge Dr.	Little Rock	AR	72207	12
Pavilions 11	9090 E. Indian Bend	Scottsdale	AZ	85250	11
Alhambra Renaissance 14	1 E. Main St.	Alhambra	CA	91801	14
Atlantic Palace 10	700 W. Main St.	Alhambra	CA	91801	10
Aliso Viejo Stadium 20	26701 Aliso Creek Rd.	Aliso Viejo	CA	92656	20
Anaheim Hills 14	8032 E. Santa Ana Canyon Rd.	Anaheim Hills	CA	92808	14
Arroyo Grande Stadium 10	1160 W. Branch St.	Arroyo Grande	CA	93420	10
Auburn Stadium 10	500 Nevada St.	Auburn	CA	95603	10
Bakersfield Stadium 14	9000-G Ming Ave.	Bakersfield	CA	93311	14
Berkeley 7	2274 Shattuck Ave.	Berkley	CA	94704	7
Brea Stadium 10 West	155 W. Birch	Brea	CA	92621	10
Brea Stadium 12 East	155 W. Birch St.	Brea	CA	92821	12
Calabasas Stadium 6	4767 Commons Way	Calabasas	CA	91302	6
Camarillo 12	680 Ventura Blvd.	Camarillo	CA	93010	12
Canyon Country Stadium 10	18800 Soledad Canyon Rd.	Canyon Country	CA	91351	10
Cerritos Stadium 10	12761 Towne Center Dr.	Cerritos	CA	90701	10
UA Galaxy @ Los Cerritos 11	435 Los Cerritos Center	Cerritos	CA	90703	11
Rancho Del Rey Stadium 16	1025 Tierra Del Rey	Chula Vista	CA	91910	16
Sunrise 4	5926 Sunrise Mall	Citrus Heights	CA	95610	4
Clovis Movies 8	2301 Villa Ave.	Clovis	CA	93612	8
Corona Crossings Stadium 18	2650 Tuscany St.	Corona	CA	92881	18
Metro Pointe Stadium 12	901 S. Coast Dr.	Costa Mesa	CA	92626	12
Davis Holiday 6	101 F St.	Davis	CA	95616	6
Davis Stadium 5	420 G St.	Davis	CA	95616	5
Hacienda Crossings Stadium 20 + IMAX	5000 Dublin Blvd.	Dublin	CA	94568	21
Parkway Plaza Stadium 18	405 Pkwy. Plaza	El Cajon	CA	92020	18
Rancho San Diego Stadium 15	2951 Jamacha Rd.	El Cajon	CA	92019	15
El Dorado Hills Stadium 14	2101 Vine St.	El Dorado Hills	CA	95762	14
El Monte 8	10661 Valley Blvd.	El Monte	CA	91731	8
Emery Bay Stadium 10	6330 Christie Ave.	Emeryville	CA	94608	10
Escondido Stadium 16	350 W. Valley Pkwy.	Escondido	CA	92025	16
Fairfield Stadium 16	1549 Gateway Blvd.	Fairfield	CA	94533	16
Foothill Towne Center Stadium 22	26602 Towne Center Dr.	Foothill Ranch	CA	92610	22
Broadway Faire 10	3351 W. Shaw Ave.	Fresno	CA	93711	10
Fresno Stadium 21	7750 N. Blackstone Ave.	Fresno	CA	93720	21
Manchester Stadium 16	2055 E. Shields Ave.	Fresno	CA	93726	16
Garden Grove Stadium 16	9741 Chapman Ave.	Garden Grove	CA	92841	16
Hemet Cinema 12	2369 W. Florida Ave.	Hemet	CA	92545	12
Indio Metro 8	81725 Hwy. 111	Indio	CA	92201	8
Irvine Spectrum 21	65 Fortune Dr.	Irvine	CA	92618	21
Market Place Stadium 10	13728 Jamboree Rd.	Irvine	CA	92602	10
University Town Center 6	4245 Campus Dr.	Irvine	CA	92612	6
Westpark 8	3755 Alton Pkwy.	Irvine	CA	92606	8
Jackson Cinema 4	201 Vukovich Way	Jackson	CA	95642	4
La Canada 8	1919 Verdugo Blvd.	La Canada Flintridge	CA	91011	8
La Habra Stadium 16	1351 W. Imperial Hwy.	La Habra	CA	90631	16
La Verne Stadium 12	1950 E. Foothill Blvd.	La Verne	CA	91750	12
Ocean Ranch 7	32401 Golden Lantern St.	Laguna Niguel	CA	92677	7
Long Beach Stadium 26	7501 E. Carson Blvd.	Long Beach	CA	90808	26
UA Long Beach 6	E. 6601 Pacific Coast Hwy.	Long Beach	CA	90803	6
Marina Del Rey 6	4335 Glencoe Ave.	Marina Del Rey	CA	90292	6
Regency 7	635 Fairfield Dr.	Merced	CA	95340	7
Eastvale Stadium 14	12285 Limonite Ave.	Mira Loma	CA	91752	14
Kaleidoscope Stadium 10	27741 Crown Valley Pkwy., Unit 301	Mission Viejo	CA	92691	10
Modesto Stadium 10	3969 McHenry Blvd.	Modesto	CA	95356	10
Island 7	999 Newport Center Dr.	Newport Beach	CA	92660	7
Newport 6	300 Newport Center Dr. E.	Newport Beach	CA	92660	6
Jack London Stadium 9	100 Washington St.	Oakland	CA	94607	9
Oceanside Stadium 16	401 Mission Ave.	Oceanside	CA	92054	16
Ontario Mountain Village Stadium 14	1575 N. Mountain Ave.	Ontario	CA	91762	14
Ontario Palace Stadium 22	4900 E. 4th St.	Ontario	CA	91764	22
Palm Springs Stadium 9	789 E. Tahquitz Canyon Way	Palm Springs	CA	92262	9
Placerville Stadium 8	337 Placerville Dr.	Placerville	CA	95667	8
Rancho Mirage Stadium 16	72-777 Dinah Shore Dr.	Rancho Mirage	CA	92270	16
Rancho Santa Margarita 6	30632 Santa Margarita Pkwy.	Rancho Sta Margarita	CA	92688	6
Jurupa Stadium 14	8032 Limonite Ave.	Riverside	CA	92509	14
Riverside Plaza Stadium 16	3535 Riverside Plaza Dr.	Riverside	CA	92506	16
Promenade 13	550 Deep Valley Dr.	Rolling Hills Estates	CA	90274	13
Olympus Pointe 12	520 N. Sunrise Ave.	Roseville	CA	95661	12
Arden Fair 6	1739 Arden Way	Sacramento	CA	95815	6
Laguna Village 12	8755 Center Pkwy Dr.	Sacramento	CA	95823	12
Natomas Marketplace Stadium 16	3561 Truxel Rd.	Sacramento	CA	95834	16
Horton Plaza 14	475 Horton Plaza	San Diego	CA	92101	14
Mira Mesa Stadium 18	10733 Westview Pkwy.	San Diego	CA	92126	18
Stonestown Twin 2	501 Buckingham Way	San Francisco	CA	94132	2
San Jacinto Metro 12	1599 San Jacinto Ave.	San Jacinto	CA	92583	12
San Marcos Stadium 18	1180 W. San Marcos Blvd.	San Marcos	CA	92069	18
Crow Canyon Stadium 6	2525 San Ramon Valley Blvd.	San Ramon	CA	94583	6
Valencia Stadium 12	24435 Town Center Dr.	Santa Clarita	CA	91355	12
Riverfront Stadium 2	155 S. River St.	Santa Cruz	CA	95060	2
Santa Cruz 9	1405 Pacific Ave.	Santa Cruz	CA	95060	9
Santa Maria 10	1521 S. Bradley Rd.	Santa Maria	CA	93454	10
Civic Center Stadium 16	2751 Tapo Canyon Rd.	Simi Valley	CA	93065	16
Simi Valley Plaza 10	1457 Los Angeles Ave.	Simi Valley	CA	93065	10
Sonora Stadium 10	901 Sanguinetti Rd.	Sonora	CA	95370	10
South Gate Stadium 20	8630 Garfield Ave.	South Gate	CA	90280	20
Stockton City Centre Stadium 16	222 N. El Dorado St.	Stockton	CA	95202	16
Stockton Holiday Cinema 8	6262 N. West Ln.	Stockton	CA	95210	8

Theatre	Address	City	State	Zip	Screens
Temecula Stadium 15	40750 Winchester Rd.	Temecula	CA	92591	15
Turlock Stadium 14	2323 W. Main	Turlock	CA	95380	14
Tustin Marketplace 6	2961 El Camino Real	Tustin	CA	92782	6
Ukiah Stadium 6	612 S. State St.	Ukiah	CA	95482	6
Visalia Sequoia Mall 12	3355 S. Mooney Blvd.	Visalia	CA	93277	12
Visalia Stadium 10	120 S. Bridge St.	Visalia	CA	93279	10
West Covina Stadium 18	265 S. Glendora Ave.	West Covina	CA	91790	18
Westminster 10	6721 Westminster Blvd.	Westminster	CA	92683	10
Colorado Center 9	2000 S. Colorado Blvd.	Denver	CO	80222	9
Continental 6	3635 S. Monaco Blvd.	Denver	CO	80237	6
Denver Pavilions 15	500 16th St. #310	Denver	CO	80202	15
Greenwood Plaza 12	8141 E. Arapahoe Rd.	Englewood	CO	80112	12
West Village Stadium 12	14225 W. Colfax Ave.	Golden	CO	80401	12
Colorado Mills Stadium 16	14500 W. Colfax Ave., Ste. 600	Lakewood	CO	80401	16
Meadows 12	9355 Park Meadows Dr.	Littleton	CO	80124	12
Twin Peaks Mall 10	1250 S. Hover Rd.	Longmont	CO	80501	10
Colony Square 12	1164 W. dilon Rd	Loiusville	CO	80020	12
Canyon View 14	648 Market St.	Grand Junction	CO	81505	14
Branford Stadium 12	325 E. Main St.	Branford	CT	06405	12
Stonington 10	85 Voluntown Rd.	Pawcatuk	CT	06379	10
Stratford Stadium 14	411 Barnum Ave., Route 1	Stratford	CT	06614	14
Brass Mill Stadium 12	495 Union St.	Waterbury	CT	06706	12
Waterford 9	123 Cross Rd., P. O. Box 722	Waterford	CT	06385	9
Gallery Place Stadium 14	701 Seventh St. N.W.	Washington	DC	20001	14
Peoples Plaza Cinema Stadium 17	1100 Peoples Plaza	Newark	DE	19702	17
Brandywine Town Center 16	3300 Brandywine Pkwy.	Wilmington	DE	19803	16
Movies @Wekiva Riverwalk 8	2141 N. Semoran Blvd.	Apopka	FL	32703	8
Shadowood 16	9889 W. Glades Rd.	Boca Raton	FL	33434	16
Bonita Springs Stadium 12	25251 Chamber of Commerce Dr.	Bonita Springs	FL	34135	12
Oakmont 8	4801 Cortez Rd. W.	Bradenton	FL	34210	8
Magnolia Place Stadium 16	9645 Westview Dr.	Coral Springs	FL	33067	16
Crystal River Mall 9	1801 N.W. Hwy. 19	Crystal River	FL	34428	9
Delray Beach 18	1660 S. Federal Hwy.	Del Ray Beach	FL	33483	18
Sun Plaza Stadium 8	427 Mary Esther Blvd.	Fort Walton Beach	FL	32548	8
Belltower 20	13499 Belltower Dr.	Ft Myers	FL	33907	20
Cypress Creek Station Stadium 16	6415 N. Andrews Ave.	Ft. Lauderdale	FL	33334	16
Gulf Coast 16	10028 Gulf Center Dr.	Ft. Myers	FL	33913	16
Gainesville Cinema Stadium 14	Butler Plaza	Gainesville	FL	32608	14
Royal Park Stadium 16	3702 W. University Ave.	Gainesville	FL	32607	16
Oakwood 18	2800 Oakwood Blvd.	Hollywood	FL	33020	18
Citrus Cinemas 6	2635 E. Gulf to Lake Hwy.	Inverness	FL	34453	6
Avenues Stadium 20	9525 Phillips Hwy.	Jacksonville	FL	32256	20
Beach Boulevard Stadium 18	14051 Beach Blvd.	Jacksonville	FL	32250	18
Treasure Coast Mall Stadium 16	3290 N. Federal Hwy.	Jenson Beach	FL	34957	16
Cinema Key West 6	3338 N. Roosevelt Blvd.	Key West	FL	33040	6
The Loop Stadium 16	3232 N. John Young Parkway	Kissimmee	FL	34741	16
Cinema 90 6	Hwy. 90 W.	Lake City	FL	32055	6
Eagle Ridge Mall 12	955 Eagle Ridge Dr. & Hwy. 27	Lake Wales	FL	33853	12
Largo Mall 8	10500 Ulmerton Rd. E.	Largo	FL	33771	8
Santa Rosa 10	300 Mary Esther Blvd.	Mary Esther	FL	32569	10
The Falls 12	9000 S.W. 136th St.	Miami	FL	33176	12
Kendall Village Stadium 16	8595 S.W. 124 Ave.	Miami	FL	33183	16
Palace 18	11865 S.W. 26th St.	Miami	FL	33175	18
South Beach Stadium 18	1120 Lincoln Rd. Mall	Miami Beach	FL	33139	18
Hollywood Stadium 20	6006 Hollywood Dr.	Naples	FL	34109	20
Hollywood Stadium 16	2801 S.W. 27th Ave.	Ocala	FL	34474	16
Marketplace 8	822-4 Saxon Blvd.	Orange City	FL	32763	8
Pointe Orlando 21	7200 US Hwy. 19 N.	Orlando	FL	32819	21
Waterford Lakes Stadium 20	541 N. Alafaya Trail	Orlando	FL	32828	20
Ormond Beach Cinema 12	215 Williamson Blvd.	Ormond Beach	FL	32174	12
Oviedo Marketplace Stadium 22	1500 Oviedo Marketplace Blvd.	Oviedo	FL	32765	22
Regency Stadium 11	1515 W. 23rd St.	Panama City	FL	32406	11
Westfork Stadium 13	15999 Pines Blvd.	Pembroke Pines	FL	33027	13
Park Place Stadium 16	7200 US Hwy. 19 N.	Pinellas Park	FL	33781	16
Town Center Stadium 16	1441 Tamiami Trail, Unit 701	Port Charlotte	FL	33948	16
Port Orange 6	1015 Eagle Lake Trail	Port Orange	FL	32129	6
Hollywood 18, Port Richey	6701 Cinema Dr. (34668)	Port Richey	FL	34668	18
Royal Palm Beach Stadium 18	1003 State Rd. 7	Royal Palm Beach	FL	33411	18
Seminole Towne Center	430 Towne Centre Cir.	Sanford	FL	32771	10
Hollywood Stadium 20	1993 Main St.	Sarasota	FL	34236	20
Mall St Augustine 6	2121 US 1 S, Ponce DeLeon Mall	St Augustine	FL	32086	6
Sawgrass Stadium 23	2600 N.W. 136th Ave.	Sunrise	FL	33323	23
Governor's Square Stadium 12	1501 Governor's Square Blvd.	Tallahassee	FL	32301	12
Miracle 5	1815 Thomasville Rd.	Tallahassee	FL	32303	5
Citrus Park Stadium 20	7999 Citrus Park Town Ctr. Mall	Tampa	FL	33625	20
Searstown Mall 10	3550 S. Washington Ave.	Titusville	FL	32780	10
Winter Park Village Stadium 20	510 N. Orlando Ave.	Winter Park	FL	32789	20
Southland Mall 16	20505 S. Dixie Hwy.	Miami	FL	33189	16
North Point Market 8	6500 N. Point Pkwy.	Alpharetta	GA	30202	8
Atlantic Station Stadium 16	261 19th St., N.W., Ste. 1250	Atlanta	GA	30363	16
Perimeter Pointe 10	1155 Mt. Vernon Hwy.	Atlanta	GA	30338	10
Tara Cinemas 4	2345 Cheshire Bridge Rd., N.E.	Atlanta	GA	30324	4
Augusta Exchange Stadium 20	1144 Agerton Ln.	Augusta	GA	30909	20
Regal Stadium 22 @ Austell	2480 E.W. Connector Rd.	Austell	GA	30106	22
Mall of Georgia Stadium 20 Plus IMAX	3333 A Buford Dr.	Buford	GA	30519	21
Hollywood Stadium 24 @ N. I-85	3265 N.E. Expwy. Access	Chamblee	GA	30341	24
Arbor Place Stadium 18	6600 Douglas Blvd.	Douglasville	GA	30135	18
Medlock Crossing Stadium 18	9700 Medlock Bridge Rd., Ste. 170	Duluth	GA	30097	18
Town Center Stadium 16	2795 Town Center Dr.	Kennesaw	GA	30144	16
Georgian 14	232 Newnan Crossing Bypass	Newnan	GA	30265	14
Eisenhower Square 6	1100 Eisenhower Dr.	Savannah	GA	31406	6
Savannah Stadium 10	1132-34 Shawnee Ave.	Savannah	GA	31419	10
Snellville Oaks Stadium 14	2125 E. Main St.	Snellville	GA	30078	14
Dole Cannery Stadium 18	735 B Iwilei Rd.	Honolulu	HI.	96817	18
Windward Stadium 10	46-056 Kamehameha Hwy. SPC N6	Kaneohe	HI.	96744	10
Keauhou Stadium 7	78-6831 Ali'I Dr. H-24	Keauhou-Kona	HI.	96740	7
Pearl Highlands Stadium 12	1000 Kamehameha Hwy. #231	Pearl City	HI.	96782	12
Grand Teton Stadium 14	2707 S. 25th E.	Ammon	ID.	83406	14
Boise Downtown Stadium 9	760 Broad St.	Boise	ID.	83702	9
Boise Stadium 21	7709 Overland Rd.	Boise	ID.	83709	21

Theatre	Address	City	State	Zip	Screens
Riverstone Stadium 14	2416 Old Mill Loop	Coeur D Alene	ID	83814	14
Nampa Stadium 14	2001 N. Cassia St.	Nampa	ID	83651	14
Bolingbrook Showplace 12	1221 W. Boughton Rd	Bolingbrook	IL	60440	12
City North 14	2600 N. Western Ave.	Chicago	IL	60647	14
Webster Place 11	1471 W. Webster Ave	Chicago	IL	60614	11
Showplace 16	5000 W. Rte. 14	Crystal Lake	IL	60014	16
Lake Zurich 12	755 S. Rand Rd.	Lake Zurich	IL	60047	12
Lincolnshire Stadium 20 Plus IMAX	300 Pkwy. Dr.	Lincolnshire	IL	60069	21
Round Lake Beach Stadium 18	550 E. Rollins Rd.	Round Lake Beach	IL	60073	18
Gardens 1-6	4999 Ol Orchard Center, Ste. N47	Skokie	IL	60077	6
Gardens 7-13	4999 Ol Orchard Center, Ste. A21	Skokie	IL	60077	7
Cantera 30	28250 Diehl Rd	Warrenville	IL	60555	30
Shiloh Crossing Stadium 18	10400 E. US 36, Bldg. #800	Avon	IN	46123	18
Village Park Cinema Stadium 17	2222 E. 146th St.	Carmel	IN	46032	17
Coldwater Crossing 8	211 W. Washington Center Rd.	Fort Wayne	IN	46825	8
Greenwood 14	461 S. Greenwood Park Dr	Greenwood	IN	46142	14
Circle Center 9	49 W. Maryland St.	Indianapolis	IN	46204	9
Eagle Highlands 10	4015 Shore Dr.	Indianapolis	IN	46254	10
Galaxy Stadium 14	8105 E. 96Th Ave.	Indianapolis	IN	46256	14
Hamburg Pavilion Stadium 16	1949 Starshoot Rd.	Lexington	KY	40509	16
Citiplace Stadium 11	2610 Citiplace Dr.	Baton Rouge	LA	70808	11
Bossier Corners Cinema 9	2800 Shed Rd.	Bossier City	LA	71111	9
Louisiana Boardwalk Stadium 14	2 River Colony Dr.	Bossier City	LA	71111	14
Lake Charles 10	3416 Derek Dr.	Lake Charles	LA	70605	10
Lee Hills 6	1350 Boone St.	Leesville	LA	71446	6
Bellingham Stadium 14	259 Hartford Ave.	Bellingham	MA	02019	14
Fenway Stadium 13	401 Park Dr., Ste. #7	Boston	MA	02215	13
Harwich 6	195 Route 137	East Harwich	MA	02645	6
Cape Cod Mall Stadium 12	793 Iyannough Rd.	Hyannis	MA	02601	12
Independence Mall 14	101 Independence Mall Way	Kingston	MA	02364	14
Berkshire Mall 10	Rte. 8 & Old State Rd.	Lanesboro	MA	01237	10
Solomon Pond Stadium 15	591 Donald J. Lynch Blvd.	Marlborough	MA	01752	15
Mashpee Commons 6	38 Nathan Ellis Hwy.	Mashpee	MA	02649	6
Nickelodeon 5	Rt 151 Nathan Ellis Hwy.	North Falmouth	MA	02556	5
Swansea Stadium 12	207 Swansea Mall Dr.	Swansea	MA	02777	12
Silver City Galleria 10	2 Galleria Mall Dr.	Taunton	MA	02780	10
Westborough Stadium 12	231 Turnpike Rd.	Westborough	MA	01581	12
Bel Air Cinema Stadium 14	409 Constant Friendship Blvd.	Abingdon	MD	21009	14
Eastpoint 10	7938 Eastern Blvd.	Baltimore	MD	21224	10
Bethesda 10	7272 Wisconsin Ave.	Bethesda	MD	20814	10
Bowie Stadium 14	15200 Major Lansdale Blvd.	Bowie	MD	20716	14
Snowden Square Stadium 14	9161 Commerce Center Dr.	Columbia	MD	21046	14
Westview Stadium 16	5243 Buckeystown Pike	Frederick	MD	21704	16
Germantown Stadium 14	20000 Century Blvd.	Germantown	MD	20874	14
Marley Station 8	7900 Governor Richie Hwy.	Glen Burnie	MD	21061	8
Valley Mall Stadium 16	17301 Valley Mall Rd.	Hagerstown	MD	21740	16
Hunt Valley Stadium 12	11511 McCormick Rd.	Hunt Valley	MD	21030	12
Royale 14	6505 America Blvd.	Hyattsville	MD	20782	14
Rockville Center Stadium 13	199 E. Montgomery Ave.	Rockville	MD	20850	13
Salisbury Stadium 16	2322 N. Salisbury Rd.	Salisbury	MD	21801	16
Majestic 20	900 Ellsworth Dr.	Silver Spring	MD	20910	20
Westminster 9	400 N. Center St.	Westminster	MD	21157	9
Augusta 10	23 Market Place Dr.	Augusta	ME	04330	10
Brunswick 10	19 Gurnet Rd.	Brunswick	ME	04011	10
Falmouth 10	206 US Route 1	Falmouth	ME	04105	10
Commerce Township Stadium 14	3033 Springvale Dr.	Walled Lake	MI	48390	14
Eagan Stadium 16	2055 Cliff Rd.	Eagan	MN	55122	16
Brooklyn Center Stadium 20	6420 Camden Ave. N.	Minneapolis	MN	55430	20
St. Louis Mills Stadium 18	5555 St. Louis Mills Blvd., Ste. 525	Hazelwood	MO	63042	18
Kansas City Stadium 18 Cinemas	3200 Ameristar Dr.	Kansas City	MO	64161	18
Clinton Center 10	201 Clinton Center	Clinton	MS	39056	10
Parkway Place Stadium 10	1075 Pkwy. Blvd.	Flowood	MS	39208	10
Sawmill Square 5	910 Sawmill Rd.	Laurel	MS	39440	5
Bonita Lakes 9	1680 Bonita Lakes Circle	Meridian	MS	39301	9
Natchez Mall 4	350 John R. Junkin Dr.	Natchez	MS	39120	4
North Park Stadium 14	250 Ring Rd.	Ridgeland	MS	39157	14
Westbrook 4	454 Brookway Blvd.	Brookhaven	MS	39601	4
Beaver Creek 12	1441 Beaver Creek Commons Dr.	Apex	NC	27502	12
Beaucatcher Cinemas 7	321 Haw Creek Ln.	Asheville	NC	28805	7
Cinebarre Biltmore Square 5	800 Brevard Rd	Asheville	NC		5
Hollywood Cinemas 14	1640 Hendersonville Rd.	Asheville	NC	28803	14
Boone Cinema 7	210 New Market St. Centre	Boone	NC	28607	7
Crossroads 20	501 Caitboo Ave.	Cary	NC	27511	20
Timberlyne 6	120 Banks Dr.	Chapel Hill	NC	27515	6
Crownpoint Stadium 12	9630 Monroe Rd.	Charlotte	NC	28270	12
Manor Twin	609 Providence Rd.	Charlotte	NC	28207	2
Arboretum 12	8008 Providence Rd.	Charlotte	NC	28277	12
Park Terrace 6	4289 Park Rd.	Charlotte	NC	28209	6
Phillips Place 10	6911 Phillips Place Ct.	Charlotte	NC	28210	10
Starlight Stadium 14	11240 US Hwy. 29	Charlotte	NC	28262	14
Stonecrest @ Piper Glen Stadium 22	7824 Rea Rd.	Charlotte	NC	28277	22
Towne Square 10	2600 Timber Dr.	Garner	NC	27529	10
White Oak 14	1205 Timber Dr. E.	Garner	NC	27529	14
Franklin Square Stadium 14	3778 E. Franklin Blvd.	Gastonia	NC	28054	14
Greensboro Grande 16	3205 Northline Ave.	Greensboro	NC	27408	16
Greenville Grande 14	750 S.W. Greenville Blvd.	Greenville	NC	27834	14
Palladium 14	5830 Samet Dr.	High Pointe	NC	27265	14
Oak Hollow Mall 7	931 Eastchester Dr.	High Point	NC	27265	7
Birkdale Stadium 16	16950 Birkdale Commons Pkwy.	Huntersville	NC	28078	16
Union Square 8	1911 Dickerson Blvd.	Monroe	NC	28110	8
Raleigh Grande 16	4840 Grove Barton Rd.	Raleigh	NC	27613	16
Brier Creek Stadium 14	8611 Brier Creek Pkwy.	Raleigh	NC	27617	14
North Hills Stadium 14	4150 Main at North Hills St.	Raleigh	NC	27609	14
Mayfaire 16	900 Town Center Dr.	Wilmington	NC	28405	16
Concord 10	282 Louden Rd.	Concord	NH	03301	10
Hooksett 8	100 Technology Dr.	Hooksett	NH	03106	8
Manchester 9	1279 S. Willow St.	Manchester	NH	03103	9
Fox Run 15	45 Gosling Rd.	Newington	NH	03801	12
Portsmouth 5	581 Lafayette Rd.	Portsmouth	NH	03801	5
Burlington Stadium 20	250 Bromley Blvd.	Burlington	NJ	08016	20

Theatre	Address	City	State	Zip	Screens
Manahawkin 10	733 Route 72 E.	Manahawkin	NJ	08050	10
Hamilton Commons Stadium 14	4215 Black Horse Pike	Mays Landing	NJ	08330	14
Moorestown Mall 7	Route 38 & Lenola Rd.	Moorestown	NJ	08057	7
Commerce Center Stadium 18	2399 Route 1 S.	North Brunswick	NJ	08902	18
Pohatcong 12	1246 Hwy. 22 E.	Phillipsburg	NJ	08865	12
Market Fair Stadium 10	3521 US Route 1	Princeton	NJ	08540	10
Washington Township 14	121 Tuckahoe Rd.	Sewell	NJ	08080	14
Hadley Theatre Stadium 16	1000 Corporate Court	South Plainfield	NJ	07080	16
Cross Keys Cinema Stadium 12	151 American Blvd.	Turnersville	NJ	08012	12
504Cumberland Mall Stadium 14	3849 S. Delsea	Vineland	NJ	08360	14
504Cottonwood Theatre Stadium 16	10000 N.W. Coors Blvd.	Albuquerque	NM	87114	16
Four Hills Theatre 10	13120 Central S.E.	Albuquerque	NM	87123	10
High Ridge Theatre 8	12921 Indian School N.E.	Albuquerque	NM	87112	8
Winrock VI	201 Winrock Center	Albuquerque	NM	87110	6
Devargas Mall Cinema 6	562 N. Guadalupe	Santa Fe	NM	87501	6
UA North 6	4250 Cerrillos Rd.	Santa Fe	NM	87505	6
Santa Fe 14	2474 Zafarano Dr.	Santa Fe	NM	87507	14
Fiesta Stations 12	777 W. Lake Mead Pkwy.	Henderson	NV	89015	12
Green Valley Ranch Stadium 10	2300 Paseo Verde	Henderson	NV	89052	10
Sunset Station Stadium 13 Theatre	1301-A W. Sunset Rd.	Henderson	NV	89014	13
Boulder Station 11 Theatre	4111 Boulder Hwy.	Las Vegas	NV	89121	11
Colonnade Stadium 14	8880 S. Eastern Ave.	Las Vegas	NV	89123	14
Red Rock Stadium 16	11011 W. Charleston Blvd.	Las Vegas	NV	89135	16
Showcase Theatre 8	3769 S. Las Vegas Blvd.	Las Vegas	NV	89109	8
Texas Station Stadium 18	2101 N. Texas Star Ln.	Las Vegas	NV	89030	18
Village Square Stadium 18	9400 W. Sahara Ave.	Las Vegas	NV	89117	18
Colonie Center Stadium 13		Albany	NY		13
Crossgates Stadium 18	120 B Washington Ave. Ext.	Albany	NY	12203	18
Binghamton Stadium 12	900 Front St.	Binghamton	NY	13905	12
Court Street Stadium 12	106 Court St.	Brooklyn	NY	11201	12
Sheepshead Bay 14	3907 Shore Pkwy.	Brooklyn	NY	11235	14
Elmwood Regal Center 16 IMAX	2001 Elmwood Ave.	Buffalo	NY	14207	16
Walden Galleria 16	2001 Elmwood Ave.	Buffalo	NY	14207	16
Great Northern Mall 10	Route 481 & 31	Clay	NY	13041	10
Clifton Park Center 8	22 Clifton Country Rd.	Clifton Park	NY	12065	8
Shoppingtown Mall 10	3649 Erie Blvd. E.	DeWitt	NY	13214	10
East Hampton Cinema 6	30 Main St.	East Hampton	NY	11937	6
Farmingdale Stadium 10	20 Michael Ave.	Farmingdale	NY	11735	10
Fishkill 10	Route 9, Hudson Valley Outlet Center	Fishkill	NY	12524	10
Brandon Cinemas 2	70-20 Austin St.	Forest Hills	NY	11375	2
Midway Cinemas Stadium 9	108-22 Queens Blvd.	Forest Hills	NY	11375	9
Atlas Park Stadium 8	80-28 Cooper Ave., Ste. 6216	Glendale	NY	11385	8
Hampton Bays 5	119 W. Montauk Hwy.	Hampton Bays	NY	11946	5
Arnot Mall 10	3300 Chambers Rd.	Horseheads	NY	14845	10
Culver Ridge Plaza 16	2255 Ridge Rd. E.	Irondequoit	NY	14622	16
Ithaca Mall 14	40 Catherwood Rd	Ithaca	NY	14850	14
Hudson Valley Mall 12	1300 Ulster Ave.	Kingston	NY	12401	12
Latham Circle Mall 10	800 New Loudon Rd.	Latham	NY	12110	10
Kaufman Astoria Stadium 14	35-30 38th St.	Long Island City	NY	11101	14
Lynbrook Theatre 6	321 Merrick Rd.	Lynbrook	NY	11563	6
UA Cortlandt Town Center Stadium 11	3131 E. Main St.	Mohegan Lake	NY	10547	11
New Roc City Stadium 18 Plus IMAX	33 Le Count Place	New Rochelle	NY	10801	19
64th And 2nd Ave. 3	1210 Second Ave.	New York	NY	10021	3
Battery Park Stadium 16	102 N. End Ave.	New York	NY	10281	16
East 85th Street 1	1629 First Ave.	New York	NY	10028	1
E-Walk Stadium 13	247 W. 42nd St.	New York	NY	10036	13
Union Square Stadium 14	850 Broadway	New York	NY	10003	14
Niagara Falls Stadium 12	720 Builders Way	Niagara Falls	NY	14304	12
Quaker Crossing Stadium 18	3450 Amelia Dr.	Orchard Park	NY	14127	18
Galleria Mall 16	2001 South Rd.	Poughkeepsie	NY	12601	16
Aviation Mall 7	578 Aviation Rd.	Queensbury	NY	12804	7
E. Greenbush 8	279 Troy Rd.	Rensselaer	NY	12144	8
Greece Ridge Stadium 12	176 Greece Ridge Center Dr.	Rochester	NY	14626	12
Henrietta Cinema Stadium 18	525 Marketplace Dr.	Rochester	NY	14623	18
Ronkonkoma Cinema Stadium 9	565 Portion Rd.	Ronkonkoma	NY	11779	9
Wilton Mall 8	3065 Route 50	Saratogo Springs	NY	12866	8
Southampton 4 Theatres	43 Hill St.	Southampton	NY	11968	4
Hylan Plaza 5	107 Mill Rd.	Staten Island	NY	10306	5
Staten Island Stadium 16	2474 Forest Ave.	Staten Island	NY	10303	16
Carousel Mall 19	9586 Carousel Ctr	Syracuse	NY	13290	19
Eastview Mall 13	70 Eastview Mall Dr.	Victor	NY	14564	13
Westbury Theatre Stadium 12	7000 Brush Hollow Rd.	Westbury	NY	11590	12
Transit Center Stadium 18 Plus IMAX	6707 Transit Rd.	Williamsville	NY	14221	19
Yonkers 6	2548 Central Park Ave.	Yonkers	NY	10710	6
Independence Stadium 10	1210 Independence Ave.	Akron	OH	44310	10
Interstate Park Cinema Stadium 18	1089 Interstate Pkwy.	Akron	OH	44312	18
Montrose Movies Stadium 12	Market Square at Montrose	Akron	OH	44333	12
Fairfield Commons Stadium 20	2651 Fairfield Commons	Beavercreek	OH	45431	20
Middleburg Town Sq. Stadium 16	18348 Bagley Rd.	Cleveland	OH	44130	16
Severance Town Center Stadium 14	3492 Mayfield Rd.	Cleveland Heights	OH	44118	14
Georgesville Square Stadium 16	1800 Georgesville Square Dr.	Columbus	OH	43228	16
Cobblestone Square Stadium 20	5500 Cobblestone Rd.	Elyria	OH	44035	20
Hudson Cinema 10	5339 Darrow Rd.	Hudson	OH	44236	10
River Valley Mall 10	River Valley Mall	Lancaster	OH	43130	10
American Mall Stadium 12	2830 W. Elm St.	Lima	OH	45805	12
Lafayette Center Cinema 7	430 Pike St.	Marietta	OH	45750	7
Southland Cinema 7	1415 Marion-Waldo Rd.	Marion	OH	43302	7
Mayfield Heights 10	1345 SOM Center Rd.	Mayfield Heights	OH	44124	10
Medina Stadium 16	200 W. Reagan Pkwy.	Medina	OH	44256	16
New Towne Cinema 8	400 Mill Ave. S.E., Ste. 703	New Philadelphia	OH	44663	8
Boulevard Centre Stadium 14	24 Blvd. Centre	Niles	OH	44446	14
Crocker Park Stadium 16	30147 Detroit Rd.	Westlake	OH	44145	16
Willoughby Commons Stadium 16	36655 Euclid Ave.	Willoughby	OH	44094	16
Austintown Plaza 10	6020 Mahoning Ave.	Youngstown	OH	44515	10
Cinemasouth Cinema 10	7420 South Ave.	Youngstown	OH	44512	10
Richmond Town Center 20	631 Richmond Rd.	Richmond Heights	OH	44143	20
Deerfield Town Center 16	5500 Deerfield Blvd.	Mason	OH	45040	16
Albany 7 Cinemas	1350 S.E. Waverly Dr.	Albany	OR	97321	7
Old Mill Stadium 16	680 S.W. Powerhouse Dr.	Bend	OR	97702	16
Pilot Butte 6 Theatres	2717 N.E. Hwy. 20	Bend	OR	97702	6

Theatre	Address	City	State	Zip	Screens
Ninth Street 4 Cinemas	1750 N.W. 9th St.	Corvallis	OR	97330	4
Valley River Center 15	500 Valley River Center	Eugene	OR	97401	15
Stark Street Stadium 10	2929 N.E. Kane Dr.	Gresham	OR	97030	10
Evergreen Parkway Stadium 13	2625 N.W. 188th	Hillsboro	OR	97124	13
Movies On TV Stadium 16	S.W. 2929 234th Ave.	Hillsboro	OR	97123	16
Hilltop 9 Cinema	325 Beavercreek Rd.	Oregon City	OR	97045	9
Broadway Metro 4 Theatres	1000 S.W. Broadway	Portland	OR	97205	4
Division Street Stadium 13	16603 S.E. Division St.	Portland	OR	97236	13
Fox Tower Stadium 10	846 S.W. Park Ave.	Portland	OR	97205	10
Lloyd Center Stadium 10 Cinema	1510 N.E. Multnomah Blvd.	Portland	OR	97232	10
Lloyd Mall 8 Cinema	2320 Lloyd Center Mall	Portland	OR	97232	8
Pioneer Place Stadium 6	340 S.W. Morrison St.	Portland	OR	97204	6
Movieland 7	501 Marion St. N.E.	Salem	OR	97301	7
Santiam Stadium 11	365 Lancaster Dr. S.E.	Salem	OR	97301	11
Sherwood Stadium 10	15995 S.W. Tualatin-Sherwood Rd.	Sherwood	OR	97140	10
Bridgeport Village Stadium 18	7329 S.W. Bridgeport Rd.	Tigard	OR	97224	18
Tigard 11 Cinemas	11626 S.W. Pacific Hwy.	Tigard	OR	97223	11
Wilsonville Stadium 9 Cinema	29300 S.W. Town Center Loop	Wilsonville	OR	97070	9
Lancaster Mall 17	831 Lancaster Dr, N.E.	Salem	OR	97301	17
Saucon Valley Stadium 10	3717 Route 378	Bethlehem	PA	18015	10
Moraine Pointe Cinema 10	300 Moraine Pointe Plaza	Butler	PA	16001	10
Carlisle Commons Stadium 8	250 Noble Blvd.	Carlisle	PA	17013	8
Plymouth Meeting 10	1011 W. Ridge Pike	Conshohocken	PA	19428	10
Downingtown Cinema Stadium 16	100 Quarry Rd.	Downingtown	PA	19335	16
Barn Plaza Stadium 14	1745 Easton Rd.	Doylestown	PA	18901	14
East Whiteland Stadium 9	593 W. Lancaster Ave.	East Whiteland	PA	19355	9
Northampton Cinema 14	3720 Easton-Nazareth Hwy.	Easton	PA	18045	14
Schuylkill Mall 4	Schuylkill Mall	Frackville	PA	17931	4
Harrisburg Stadium 14	1500 Caughey Dr.	Harrisburg	PA	17112	14
Hazleton Stadium 10	400 Laurel Mall	Hazleton	PA	18202	10
King Of Prussia Stadium 16	300 Goddard Blvd.	King Of Prussia	PA	19406	16
Manor Stadium 16	1246 Millersville Pike	Lancaster	PA	17603	16
Oxford Valley Theatre Stadium 14	43 Middletown Blvd.	Langhorne	PA	19047	14
Main Street Theatre 6	3720-40 Main St.	Manayunk	PA	19127	6
Edgmont Square 10	4777 W. Chester Pike	Newton Square	PA	19073	10
Oaks Stadium 24	180 Mill Rd.	Oaks	PA	19456	24
Grant Plaza 9	1619 Grant Ave.	Philadelphia	PA	19115	9
Riverview Plaza 17	1400 S. Christopher Columbus Blvd.	Philadelphia	PA	19147	17
Richland Crossing 12	185 N.W. End Blvd.	Quakertown	PA	18951	12
69th Street 9	53 S. 69Th St.	Upper Darby	PA	19082	9
Warrington Crossing Stadium 22	104 Easton Rd., Bldg F	Warrington	PA	18976	22
West Manchester Mall Stadium 13	1800 Loucks Rd.	York	PA	17404	13
Aiken Mall 8	300 E. Gate Dr.	Aiken	SC	29802	8
Starlight Stadium 14	141 Interstate Blvd.	Anderson	SC	29621	14
Columbia Cinema 7	3400 Forest Dr., Ste. 3000	Columbia	SC	29204	7
Columbiana Grande 14	1250 Bower Pkwy.	Columbia	SC	29212	14
Sandhill Cinema 16	450 Town Center Place	Columbia	SC	29229	16
Swamp Fox Stadium 14	3400 Radio Rd.	Florence	SC	29501	14
Hollywood Stadium 20	1025 Woodruff Rd.	Greenville	SC	29607	20
Cherrydale 16	3221 Pleasantburg Dr.	Greenville	SC	29609	16
Pastime Pavilion 8	929 N. Lake Dr.	Lexington	SC	29072	8
Manchester 14	1935 Cinema Dr.	Rock Hill	SC	29730	14
Palmetto Grande 16	Mt. Pleasant Towne Centre, 1319 Theater Dr.	Mt. Pleasant	SC	29464	16
Charles Towne Square Stadium 18	2401 Mall Dr.	North Charleston	SC	29406	18
Spartan 16	855 Spartan Blvd.	Spartanburg	SC	29301	16
Westgate Mall Cinema 8	205 Blackstock Rd.	Spartanburg	SC	29301	8
Azalea Square Stadium 16	215 Azalea Square Blvd.	Summerville	SC	29483	16
Hamilton Place 10-17	2000 Hamilton Place Blvd.	Chattanooga	TN	37421	8
Streets of Indian Lake Cinema 16	120 Indian lake Blvd.	Hendersonville	TN	37075	16
Downtown West Cinema 8	1640 Downtown West Blvd.	Knoxville	TN	37919	8
Knoxville Center Stadium 10	3051 B Knoxville Center Mall	Knoxville	TN	37924	10
Pinnacle Stadium 18	11240 Parkside Dr.	Knoxville	TN	37922	18
Riviera 8	510 S. Gay St.	Knoxville	TN	37902	8
West Town Mall Stadium 9	7600 Kingston Pike	Knoxville	TN	37919	9
Providence 14	401 S. Mt. Juliet Rd., Ste. 490	Mt. Juliet	TN	37122	14
Green Hills Stadium 16	3815 Greenhills Village Dr.	Nashville	TN	37215	16
Hollywood Stadium 27	719 Thompson Ln	Nashville	TN	37204	27
Tullahoma Cinemas 8	2221 N. Jackson St.	Tullahoma	TN	37388	8
Amarillo Star Stadium 14	8275 Amarillo Blvd. W.	Amarillo	TX	79106	14
Arbor Cinema @ Great Hills	9828 Great Hills Trail	Austin	TX	78759	8
Gateway Stadium 16	9700 Stonelake Blvd.	Austin	TX	78759	16
Metropolitan Stadium 14	901 Little Texas Ln.	Austin	TX	78745	14
Westgate Stadium 11 Theatres	4477 S. Lamar Blvd.	Austin	TX	78745	11
Lakeline Mall 9	11200 Lakeline Mall Dr.	Cedar Park	TX	78613	9
635Galaxy Theatre Stadium 10	11801 Mccree Rd.	Dallas	TX	75238	10
Keystone Park 16	13933 N. Central Expwy.	Dallas	TX	75243	16
Fossil Creek Stadium 11	N. 6100 Frwy.	Ft Worth	TX	76137	11
UA Eastchase Market Stadium 9	8301 Ederville	Ft Worth	TX	76120	9
Grand Prairie 10	510 Westchester	Grand Prairie	TX	75052	10
Greenway Grand Palace Stadium 24	3839 Weslayan St.	Houston	TX	77027	24
Houston Marq*E. Stadium 23	7600 Katy Freeway	Houston	TX	77024	23
North Creek 10	7807 San Dario	Laredo	TX	78045	10
Live Oak Stadium 18	7901 Pat Booker Rd.	Liveoak	TX	78233	18
Alamo Quarry Stadium 14	255 E. Basse	San Antonio	TX	78209	14
Cielo Vista Stadium 18	2828 Cinema Ridge	San Antonio	TX	78238	18
Fiesta 16 Stadium Theatres	12631 Vance Jackson	San Antonio	TX	78230	16
Northwoods 14	17640 Henderson Pass	San Antonio	TX	78232	14
Potomac Yard Stadium 16	3575 Jefferson Davis Hwy.	Alexandria	VA	22305	16
Kingstowne 16	5910 Kingstowne Center Dr.	Alexandria	VA	22315	16
Ballston Common Stadium 12	671 N. Glebe Rd.	Arlington	VA	22203	12
Fox 16	22875 Brambleton Plaza	Brambleton	VA	20148	16
Culpeper Stadium 4	210 S. Main St.	Charlottesville	VA	22701	4
Downtown Mall 6	200 W. Main St.	Charlottesville	VA	22902	6
Seminole Square Cinema 4	2306 India Dr.	Charlottesville	VA	22901	4
Greenbrier Cinema 13	600 Jarman Rd.	Chesapeake	VA	23320	13
New River Valley 11	400 New River Rd.	Christiansburg	VA	24073	11
Southpark Cinema 6	374 Southpark Mall	Colonial Heights	VA	23834	6
Fairfax Towne Center 10	4110 W. Ox Rd.	Fairfax	VA	22033	10
Fredericksburg 15	3301 Plank Rd. Rte. 3W	Fredericksburg	VA	22401	15
Virginia Center Stadium 20	10091 Jeb Stuart Pkwy.	Glen Allen	VA	23059	20

Theatre	Address	City	State	Zip	Screens
Harrisonburg Stadium 14	381 University Blvd.	Harrisonburg	VA	22801	14
Manassas Stadium 14	11380 Bulloch Dr.	Manassas	VA	20109	14
Commonwealth 20	5001 Commonwealth Centre Pkwy.	Midlothian	VA	23112	20
Kiln Creek Cinema Stadium 20	100 Regal Way, Victory Center	Newport News	VA	23602	20
Macarthur Center Stadium 18	300 Monticello Ave.	Norfolk	VA	23510	18
Shortpump Stadium 14	11650 W. Broad St.	Richmond	VA	23233	14
West Tower Cinemas 10	8998 W. Broad St.	Richmond	VA	23229	10
Westhampton Cinema 2	5706 Grove Ave.	Richmond	VA	23226	2
Valley View Grande 16	4730 Valley View Blvd.	Roanoke	VA	24012	16
Aquia 10	2850 Jefferson Davis Hwy.	Stafford	VA	22554	10
Staunton Mall Cinema 6	90 Lee Jackson Hwy., Ste. 196	Staunton	VA	24401	6
Countryside Stadium 20	45980 Regal Plaza	Sterling	VA	20165	20
Harbour View Grande 16	5860 Harbour View Blvd.	Suffolk	VA	23435	16
Columbus Stadium 12	104 Constitution Dr.	Virginia Beach	VA	23462	12
Pembroke Cinema 8	4576-76 Virginia Beach Blvd.	Virginia Beach	VA	23462	8
Strawbridge Marketplace Stadium 12	2133 General Booth Blvd.	Virginia Beach	VA	23454	12
New Town 12	4911 Courthouse St.	Williamsburg	VA	23188	12
Auburn Stadium 17 Theatres	1101 Super Mall Way, Ste. 901	Auburn	WA	98001	17
Crossroads 8 Cinema	1200 156th Ave. N.E.	Bellevue	WA	98004	8
Bellis Fair 6 Cinema	#5 Bellis Fair Pkwy.	Bellingham	WA	98226	6
Sehome 3 Cinemas	3300 Fielding Ave.	Bellingham	WA	98225	3
Sunset Square Cinema 6	1135 E. Sunset Dr.	Bellingham	WA	98226	6
Tall Firs 10	20751 State Rte. 410 E.	Bonneylake	WA	98390	10
Everett Stadium 16	1402 Everett Mall Way #133	Everett	WA	98208	16
Issaquah 9 Theatre	1490 N.W. 11th Ave.	Issaquah	WA	98027	9
Three Rivers Mall 5	1301 Grade St.	Kelso	WA	98626	5
Columbia Mall Stadium 8	701 Columbia Center	Kennewick	WA	99336	8
Martin Village Stadium 16	5400 E. Martin Way	Lacey	WA	98516	16
Lakewood Cinema Stadium 15	2410 84th St. S.	Lakewood	WA	98499	15
Triangle Quad Cinemas	1228 Washington Way	Longview	WA	98632	4
Alderwood 7 Theatres	3501 184th St. S.W.	Lynwood	WA	98037	7
Marysville Cinema 14	9811 State Ave.	Marysville	WA	98270	14
Mount Lake 9 Theatre	6009 S.W. 244th St.	Mt Lake Terrace	WA	98043	9
South Sound Cinema 10	1435 Olney Ave. S.E.	Port Orchard	WA	98366	10
Poulsbo Stadium 10	N.W. 750 Edvard St.	Poulsbo	WA	98370	10
Longston Place Stadium 14	13317 Meridian St. E.	Puyallup	WA	98373	14
South Hill Cinema 6	3500 S. Meridian	Puyallup	WA	98373	6
Bella Botega Stadium 11 Cinema	8890 N.E. 161st Ave.	Redmond	WA	98052	11
East Valley Stadium 13 Cinema	3751 E. Rd. Hwy.	Renton	WA	98055	13
Silverdale 4 Theatres	9923 Clear Cr.Rd. N.W.	Silverdale	WA	98383	4
Northtown Mall Stadium 12	4750 N. Division St.	Spokane	WA	99207	12
Spokane Valley Stadium 12	14760 E. Indiana Ave.	Spokane	WA	99216	12
Parkway Plaza Stadium 12	5910 S. 180th St.	Tukwila	WA	98188	12
Cascade Stadium 16 Cinemas	1101 S.E. 160th Ave.	Vancouver	WA	98683	16
Cinema 99 Stadium 11	9010 N.E. Hwy. 99	Vancouver	WA	98665	11
City Center Stadium 12	801 C St.	Vancouver	WA	98660	12
Vancouver Plaza 10 Cinema	7800 N.E. Fourth Plain	Vancouver	WA	98662	10
Meridian 16	1501 7th Ave.	Seattle	WA	98101	16
College Avenue Stadium 16	W3091 Van Roy Rd.	Buchanan	WI	54915	16
Martinsburg Stadium 10	950 Foxcroft Ave.	Martinsburg	WV	25401	10
Grand Central Mall 12	700 Grand Central Mall	Vienna	WV	26105	12

REGENCY THEATRES,INC.

22 theatres, 123 screens.

26901 Agoura Rd., Ste. 260, Calabasas Hills, CA 91301 TEL: (818) 224-3825. www.regencymovies.com

OWNER & PRESIDENT

Lyndon Golin

EXECUTIVE

Jeff Colvin

THEATRES

Theatre	Address	City	State	Zip	Screens
Agoura Hills 8	29045 Agoura Road	Agoura Hills	CA	91301	8
Foothill Cinema 10	854 E Alosta Ave.	Azusa	CA	9170	10
East Hills Mall	3100 Mall View Rd	Bakersfield	CA	93306	10
Paseo Camarillo Cinemas	390 North Lantana Street	Camarillo	CA	93010	3
Granada Hills 9	16830 Devonshire St.	Granada Hills	CA	91344	9
Charter Center Cinemas	7822 Warner Avenue	Huntington Beach	CA	92647	5
Laguna South Coast Cinemas	162 South Coast Highway	Laguna Beach	CA	92651	2
Rancho Niguel 8	25471 Rancho Niguel Road	Laguna Niguel	CA	92677	8
Towngate 8	12625 Frederick Street, Suite L	Moreno Valley	CA	92553	8
Academy Cinemas	1003 E. Colorado Blvd	Pasadena	CA	91106	6
Lido Theatre	3459 Via Lido	Newport Beach	CA	92663	1
Perris 10	1688 N. Perris Blvd.	Perris	CA	92571	10
Rialto Stadium 8	300 West Base Line Road	Rialto	CA	92376	8
Sterling 6	2373 Sterling Ave	San Bernardino	CA	92404	6
San Juan Capistrano	26762 Verdugo Street	San Juan Capistrano	CA	92675	5
South Coast Village	1561 W Sunflower Ave	Santa Ana	CA	92704	3
Santa Paula 7	550 W. Main St	Santa Paula	CA	93060	7
Westlake Village Twin	4711 Lakeview Canyon Road	Westlake Village	CA	91361	2
Bruin Theatre	948 Broxton Avenue	Los Angeles	CA	90024	2
Village Theatre	961 Broxton Avenue	Los Angeles	CA	90024	1
Tamarac Square Cinemas	7777 E. Hampden Avenue	Denver	CO	80231	4
Tropicana Cinemas	3330 East Tropicana	Las Vegas	NV	89121	5

REPUBLIC THEATRE GROUP, LLC.

6 theatres, 61 screens.

1231 Woodland Drive, Elizabethtown, KY 42701. TEL: (270) 769-1501. FAX: (270) 737-6649. www.republictheatres.com

CEO

Isaac M. Boutwell

PRESIDENT

Ernest L. Powell

COO

Mitchell O. Bryson

SECRETARY

Angela Helm

Theatre	Address	City	State	Zip	Screens

THEATRES

Studio 10 Cinemas	1624 E. State Highway 44	Shelbyville	IN.	46167	10
Georgetown 14	3898 Lafayette Rd.	Indianapolis	IN.	46254	14
Movie Palace Cinemas	11231 Woodland Dr.	Elizabethtown	KY	42701	12
Dixie Dozen Cinemas	6801 Dixie Highway	Louisville	KY	40258	12
Showtime Cinemas	31 W. Radcliff Plaza	Radcliff	KY	40160	5
Portsmouth Cinmeas	1623 Chillicothe Street	Portsmouth	OH	45662	8

REYNOLDS THEATRES ENTERTAINMENT INC.

4 theatres, 20 screens.
122 W. Main St., Box 737, Elmwood, IL 61529. TEL: (309) 742-8586. FAX: (309) 742-8587. www.reynoldstheatres.com
PRESIDENT
Vern O. Reynolds - vern@reynoldstheatres.com

THEATRES

Garden Theatre	62 N. Main St.	Canton	IL	61520	2
Palace Theatre Elmwood	122 W. Main St.	Elmwood	IL	61529	1
Morton Cinema 5	2115 S. Main St.	Morton	IL	61550	5
Peoria Cinemas 12	3225 N. Dries Ln.	Peoria	IL	61604	12

ROGERS CINEMA, INC.

9 theatres, 49 screens.
407 S. Maple, P.O. Box 280, Marshfield, WI 54449. TEL: (715) 387-3437. FAX: (715) 387-2165. www.rogerscinema.com
OWNER & PRESIDENT
Paul J. Rogers

THEATRES

Rogers Cinema 5	236 Front St.	Beaver Dam	WI	54493	5
Rogers Cinema 5	510 Shelden Ave.	Houghton	MI	49931	5
Rogers Cinema 8	419 S. Central	Marshfield	WI	54449	8
Rogers Grand Theatre 4	208 Wolf River Plaza	New London	WI	54961	4
Rogers Cinema 6	1010 Maple St.	Sparta	WI	54656	6
Rogers Cinema 4	1601 6th St.	Stevens Point	WI	54481	4
Rogers Cinema 6	2825 S. Church St.	Stevens Point	WI	54481	6
Rogers Rosa Theatre 4	218 S. Main	Waupaca	WI	54981	4
Rogers Cinema 7	220 E. Grand Ave.	Wisconsin Rapids	WI	54494	7

SANTIKOS THEATRES

8 theatres, 114 screens.
18402 US Hwy 281 N. Ste. 229, San Antonio, TX 78259. TEL: (210) 496-1300. FAX: (210) 496-2720. www.santikos.com
OWNER/PRESIDENT
John Santikos
THEATRE OPERATIONS
Art Seago
DIRECTOR, COMMUNICATIONS
Meghan Vincent

THEATRES

Santikos Bijou at Crossroads	4522 Fredericksburg Rd.	San Antonio	TX	78201	6
Santikos Embassy 14	13707 Embassy Row	San Antonio	TX	78216	14
Santikos Rialto Cinema Bistro & Piccolo	2938 N.E. Loop 410	San Antonio	TX	78218	13
Santikos Mayan Palace 14	1918 S.W. Military Dr.	San Antonio	TX	78221	13
Santikos Northwest 14	7600 IH-10 W	San Antonio	TX	78230	14
Santikos Palladium IMAX	17703 IH-10 W	San Antonio	TX	78257	19
Santikos Silverado 16	11505 W. Loop 1604 N.	San Antonio	TX	78250	16
Santikos Silverado 19 IMAX	24720 Tomball Pkwy.	Tomball	TX	77375	19

SCREENLAND THEATRES

4 theatres, 12 screens.
1656 Washington, Kansas City, MO 64108. TEL: (816) 421-9700. www.screenland.com

THEATRES

Screenland Armour	408 Armour Rd.	Kansas City	MO	64116	1
Screenland Theatre at the Crossroads	1656 Washington	Kansas City	MO	64108	1
Screenland Crown Center	2450 Grand Blvd., 3rd Floor	Kansas City	MO	64108	2
Plaza 8 Theatre	2219 N Belt Hwy	Saint Josephy	MO	64506	8

SHOWPLACE CINEMAS

5 theatres, 54 screens.
4200 N. Third Ave., Evansville, IN 47710. TEL: (812) 426-0133. www.showplacecinemas.com

THEATRES

Showplace Cinemas Connersville 8	2235 Park Rd.	Connersville	IN.	47331	8
Showplace Cinemas North 9	4200 N. Third Ave.	Evansville	IN.	47710	9
Showplace Cinemas East 18	1801 Morgan Center Dr.	Evansville	IN.	47710	18
Showplace Cinemas South 7	950 Hebron Dr.	Evansville	IN.	47714	7
Showplace Cinemas Newburgh 12	8099 Bell Oaks Dr.	Newburgh	IN.	47630	12

SHOWPLEX CINEMAS, INC.

10 theatres, 81 screens.
9201 W. 133rd, Ste. A, Overland Park, KS 66213. TEL: (913) 432-2334. FAX: (913) 432-9507. Email: customerservice@showplexcinemas.com
www.showplexcinemas.com

THEATRES

Lakewood 8	2939 Lakewood Village Dr.	North Little Rock	AR	72116	8
Mall Stadium 7	3404 West 13th Street	Grand Island	NE	68803	7
Island Twin 2	2228 N. Webb Rd.	Grand Island	NE	68803	2
Mall 8 Hays	2981 Vine	Hyas	KS	67601	8
Central Mall 10	2259 S. 9 Street	Salina	KS	67401	10
Mall 8 Pittsburg	202 East Centennial Drive	Pittsburg	KS	66762	8
Springfield 8	3200 E. Montclair	Springfield	MO	65806	8
Oakwood Mall 8	4125 W. Owen K Garriott Rd. #72	Enid	OK	73703	8

Theatre	Address	City	State	Zip	Screens
Central Mall 12	40 Central Mall	Lawton	OK	73501	12
Owasso 10	12601 East 86th Street North	Owasso	OK	74055	10

SIGNATURE THEATRES

2 theatres, 15 screens.

135 Hutton Ranch Rd., Ste. 103, Kalispell, MT 59901. TEL: (406) 756-2771. FAX: (406) 756-2777. www.signaturetheatres.com

OWNER, CHAIRMAN & PRESIDENT
Philip Harris, III
OWNERS
Philip Harris, Sr.
Douglas Stephens
FILM BUYER
Bill Herting

THEATRES

Theatre	Address	City	State	Zip	Screens
Signature Midway Drive-In	3115 Hwy. 40 W.	Columbia Falls	MT	59901	1
Signature Stadium 14	185 Hutton Ranch Rd.	Kalispell	MT	59901	14

SOUTHERN THEATRES, LLC (AM STAR THEATERS)

18 locations, 266 screens.

305 Baronne St., Ste. 900, New Orleans, LA 70112. TEL: (504) 297-1133. FAX: (504) 297-1138. www.thegrandtheatre.com

CEO
George Solomon
COO
Tim Spain
CFO
Beth Price
V.P., OPERATIONS
Brian Blatchley
REGIONAL DIRECTOR
Jack Wagner, Eric Kullander

THEATRES

Theatre	Address	City	State	Zip	Screens
AmStar Stadium 14	820 Colonial Promenade Pkwy.	Alabaster	AL	35007	14
AmStar Stadium 12	700 Quintard Dr.	Oxford	AL	36201	12
AmStar Stadium 12	1120 TownPark Ln.	Lake Mary	FL	32746	12
The Grand 16	500 South Pier Park Dr.	Panama City Beach	FL	32413	16
AmStar Stadium 16	5996 Zebulon Rd.	Macon	GA	31210	16
AmStar Stadium 14	150 Langley Dr.	Nicholasville	KY	40356	14
The Grand 14	2039 N. Mall Dr.	Alexandria	LA	71301	14
The Grand 14	2315 Kaliste Saloom Rd.	Lafayette	LA	70508	14
The Grand 16	3141 Johnston St.	Lafayette	LA	70503	16
The Grand 10	1000 Parkview Dr.	New Iberia	LA	70563	10
The Grand 16	1950 Gause Blvd. W.	Slidell	LA	70460	16
The Grand 18	11470 Cinema Dr.	D'Iberville	MS	39540	18
The Grand 18	100 Grand Dr.	Hattiesburg	MS	39401	18
The Grand 16	2700 Vanstory	Greensboro	NC	27407	16
AmStar Stadium 14	206 Norman Station Blvd.	Mooresville	NC	28117	14
The Grand 18	5601 University Pkwy.	Winston-Salem	NC	27105	18
AmStar Stadium 14	193 Civic Center Blvd.	Anderson	SC	29625	14
The Grand 14	4029 I-45 N.	Conroe	TX	77304	14

SR ENTERTAINMENT GROUP

13 theatres, 140 screens.

927 College Ave., Santa Rosa, Ca 95404. TEL: (707) 523-1586. Email: npearlmutter@theatreservices.com www.northamericancinemas.com

PRESIDENT & CEO
Daniel F. Tocchini
SECRETARY/TREAURER
Amy A. Tocchini
V.P. OPERATIONS
Neil Pearlmutter

THEATRES

Theatre	Address	City	State	Zip	Screens
Roxy Stadium 14	85 Santa Rosa Ave.	Santa Rosa	CA	95404	14
Airport Stadium 12	409 Aviation Blvd.	Santa Rosa	CA	95403	12
3rd Street Cinema	620 3rd St.	Santa Rosa	CA	95404	10
Raven Film Center	415 Center St.	Healdsburg	CA	95448	4
Lighthouse 4	525 Lighthouse Ave.	Pacific Grove	CA	93950	4
Plaza Stadium 14	255 W. 5th St.	Oxnard	CA	93030	14
Roxy Stadium 11	5001 Verdugo Way	Camarillo	CA	93012	11
Sierra Vista Cinemas 16	1300 Shaw Ave.	Clovis	CA	93612	16
Lodi Stadium 12	109 N. School St.	Lodi	CA	95240	12
The Metro 4 Cinema	123 East 7th Street	Hanford	CA	93230	4
Mary Pickford Theatre	36-850 Pickfair St.	Cathedral City	CA	92234	14
Blue Oaks Cinema 16	6692 Lone Tree Blvd	Rocklin	CA	95765	16
Stadium 9 Cinemas	1955 S. Casino Drive	Laughlin	NV	89029	9

STARPLEX CINEMAS

22 theatres, 228 screens.

12400 Coit Rd., Ste. 800 Dallas, TX 75251. TEL: (214) 692-6494. FAX: (214) 692-8982. www.starplexcinemas.com

CEO
Steve Holmes
COO
Tod Hanna
FILM BUYER
AJ Roquevert

THEATRES

Theatre	Address	City	State	Zip	Screens
Bakersfield Movies 6	4200 California Ave.	Bakersfield	CA	93309	6
Woodbridge Movies 5	4626 Barranca Pkwy.	Irvine	CA	92604	5
La Mirada 7	La Mirada Theatre Center, 15296 Rosecrans Ave.	La Mirada	CA	90638	7
Normal Stadium 14	201 McKnight	Normal	IL	61761	14
Coventry 13	5495 Coventry Ln.	Fort Wayne	IN	46804	13

Theatre	Address	City	State	Zip	Screens
Wespointe Movies 10	5275 Westpointe Plaza Dr.	Columbus	OH	43228	10
Robinson Crossing 6	1300 N. Interstate Dr.	Norman	OK	73072	6
Crossroads Movies 8	7400 Pole Rd.	Oklahoma City	OK	73149	8
Northpark 7	12100 N. May Ave., Ste. G	Oklahoma City	OK	73120	7
Corpus Stadium 16	5218 Silverberry	Corpus Christi	TX	78417	16
East Pointe Movies 12	8300 Gateway E.	El Paso	TX	79907	12
Forney Stadium 12	600 N. FM 548	Forney	TX	75126	12
Hulen Stadium 10	6330 Hulen Bend Blvd.	Fort Worth	TX	76132	10
Irving Cinema 10	4205 W. Pioneer Dr.	Irving	TX	75061	10
Kingwood Movies 14	350 Northpark Drive	Kingwood	TX	77339	14
Lake Jackson Brazos Stadium 14	100 Hwy. 332 W.	Lake Jackson	TX	77566	14
Mesquite Cinema 10	227 U.S. Hwy. 80 E.	Mesquite	TX	75150	10
Lake Worth Movies 14	6600 NW Loop 820	Lake Worth	TX	76135	14
Rio Grande Stadium 10	4586 E. US Hwy. 83	Rio Grande City	TX	78582	10
Sulphur Springs 6	500 E. Shannon Rd.	Sulphur Springs	TX	75482	6
Waco Galaxy 16	333 S. Valley Mills Dr.	Waco	TX	76710	16
Gateway 8	2501 S. Gateway Center Place	Federal Way	WA	98003	8

STORYTELLER THEATRES CORPORATION (FORMERLY TRANS-LUX)

9 theatres, 68 screens.

2209 Miguel Chauez Rd. #A, Santa Fe, NM 87505. TEL: (505) 989-9300. www.trans-luxtheatres.com

CO-CEO
Matt Brandt, Thomas Brandt
V.P. & GENERAL MANAGER
Thomas Becker
FILM BUYER
Paola De La Cruz
SENIOR DISTRICT MANAGER
Nick Sanchez
DISTRICT MANAGER
Jay Schwartz
DIRECTOR, CONCESSIONS
Ron Lujan
DIRECTOR, ADVERTISING & MARKETING
Renee Parish

THEATRES

Theatre	Address	City	State	Zip	Screens
Desert Sky Cinema	70 W. Duvall Mine Rd.	Sahuarita	AZ	85629	6
Skyline Cinema	312 US Hwy. 6	Dillon	CO	80435	8
Gaslight Twin Cinemas	102 E. Fifth St.	Durango	CO	81301	2
Durango 9 Cinema	900 Translux Dr.	Durango	CO	81301	7
Metrolux 14	6085 Skypond Dr.	Loveland	CO	80538	14
DreamCatcher 10	33771 S. US Hwy. 285	Espanola	NM	87532	10
Starlight Cinema	2226 Sun Ranch Village Loop	Los Lunas	NM	87031	8
Storyteller Cinemas	110 Old Talpa Canon Rd.	Taos	NM	87571	7
Fox Theatre	505 S. 20th St.	Laramie	WY	82070	6

STARLIGHT CINEMAS

5 theatres, 33 screens.

www.starlightcinemas.com

THEATRES

Theatre	Address	City	State	Zip	Screens
Cinema City	5635 E. La Palma Ave.	Anaheim Hills	CA	92807	8
Triangle Square Cinemas	1870 Harbor Blvd	Costa Mesa	CA	92627	7
4 Star Cinemas	12111 Valley View St.	Garden Grove, CA.	CA	92840	4
Whittier Village Stadium Cinemas	7038 Greenleaf Ave.	Whittier	CA	90601	8
Terrace Cinemas	28901 S. Western Ave.	Rancho Palos Verdes	CA	90275	6

SUNRISE CINEMAS

(Know as Dreier Theatres until 1999)
7 theatres, 58 screens.

www.sunrisecinemas.com

THEATRES

Theatre	Address	City	State	Zip	Screens
Deerfield Mall	3984 W. Hillsboro Blvd.	Deerfield Beach	FL	33442	8
Triangle Square Cinemas	1870 Harbor Blvd	Costa Mesa	CA	92627	7
4 Star Cinemas	12111 Valley View St.	Garden Grove, CA.	CA	92840	4
Whittier Village Stadium Cinemas	7038 Greenleaf Ave.	Whittier	CA	90601	8
Terrace Cinemas	28901 S. Western Ave.	Rancho Palos Verdes	CA	90275	6

ST LOUIS CINEMAS

4 theatres, 15 screens.

www.stlouiscinemas.com

THEATRES

Theatre	Address	City	State	Zip	Screens
Granite City	1243 Niedringhaus Ave.	Granite City	IL	62040	3
Chase Park Cinemas	212 N. Kingshighway Blvd.	St Louis	MO	63108	5
Galleria Six Cinemas	30 Saint Louis Galleria	St Louis	MO	63117	6
Moolah Theatre & Lounge	28901 S. Western Ave.	Saint Louis	MO	63108	1

TEXAS CINEMAS, INC.

3 theatres, 15 screens.

1250 Wonderworld Dr.,San Marcos, TX 78666. TEL: (512) 353-7077. FAX: (512) 353-8586. www.texascinema.com

THEATRES

Theatre	Address	City	State	Zip	Screens
MarketPlace	651 Business Loop I-35,Ste. 1010	New Braunfels	TX	78130	10
Starplex	1250 Wonderland Dr.	San Marcos	TX	78666	10
Showplace	321 N. LBJ Dr.	San Marcos	TX	78666	3

TOUCHSTAR

6 theatres, 41 screens.

TEL: (407) 854-5254. www.touchstarcinemas.com

Theatre	Address	City	State	Zip	Screens

THEATRES

Madison Sq. Stadium 1-8	5905 University Dr.	Huntsville	AL	35806	8
Madison Sq. Stadium 9-12	5905 University Dr.	Huntsville	AL	35806	4
Spring Hill 8	2955 Commercial Way	Spring Hill	FL	34606	8
Southchase 7	12441 South Orange Blossom Trail	Orlando	FL	32837	7
Colonial Promenade 6	4672 East Colonial Drive	Orlando	FL	32803	6
Seminole 8	7990 Liberty Lane	Seminole	FL	33772	8

ULTRASTAR CINEMAS

13 theatres, 121 screens.

1060 Joshua Way, Vista, CA 92081. TEL: (760) 597-5777. FAX: (760) 597-5297. www.ultrastarmovies.com

PRESIDENT & CEO
Alan Grossberg
SENIOR V.P. & COO
John Ellison, Jr.
V.P., OPERATIONS
Damon Rubio
V.P., MARKETING & ADVERTISING
Julie Bravo
DIRECTOR, CONCESSIONS & TRAINING
Kevin Stengel

THEATRES

UltraStar Lake Havasu 10	5601 Hwy. 95 Bldg. I	Lake Havasu	AZ	86403	10
UltraStar Surprise Pointe 14	13649 N. Litchfield Rd.	Surprise	AZ	85374	14
UltraStar Scottsdale Pavilions	Freeway Loop 101 and Indian Bend Rd.	Scottsdale	AZ	85250	11
UltraStar Apple Valley 14	22311 Bear Valley Rd., #A	Apple Valley	CA	92308	14
UltraStar Galaxy 6	5256 S. Mission Rd.	Bonsall	CA	92003	6
UltraStar La Costa 6	6941 El Camino Real	Carlsbad	CA	92009	6
UltraStar Chula Vista 10	555 Broadway, #2050	Chula Vista	CA	91910	10
UltraStar Flower Hill Cinema 4	2630 Via De La Valle	Del Mar	CA	92014	4
UltraStar Fontana 8	16741 Valley Blvd.	Fontana	CA	92335	8
UltraStar Mission Marketplace 13	431 College Blvd.	Oceanside	CA	92057	13
UltraStar Poway Creekside Plz. 10	13475 Poway Rd.	Poway	CA	92064	10
UltraStar Del Mar Highlands 8	12905 El Camino Real	San Diego	CA	92130	8
UltraStar Mission Valley 7	7510 Hazard Center Dr.	San Diego	CA	92108	7

UNITED ENTERTAINMENT CORP.

13 theatres, 118 screens.

P.O. Box 1736, St. Cloud, MN 56302. TEL: (320) 203-1003. FAX: (320) 203-1229. www.uecmovies.com

PRESIDENT & CEO
Mike Ross
VICE PRESIDENT of OPERATIONS
John Shorba
CONTROLLER
Carol Bowman
THEATRE OPERATIONS MANAGER
Steve Ross
BUYER
John Zenner
DEVELOPMENT MANAGER
Mike Daniels
IT MANAGER
Dan Hyndman

THEATRES

Premiere Theatre 7	2933 Brock Lane	Bedford	IN	47421	7
Premiere Theatre 7	2125 Larrick Rd.	Cambridge	OH	43725	7
Premiere Theatre 7	2950 West Carlton Rd	Hillsdale	MI	49242	7
Premiere Theatre 7	11535 Upper Gilchrist Rd	Mt Vernon	OH	43050	7
Premiere Theatre 7	1176 Hill Farm Rd	Kinston	NC	28504	7
Premiere Theatre 14	821 Benvenue Rd	Rocky Mount	NC	27804	14
UEC Theatres 14	137 Pleasant Grove Rd SW	Cleveland	TN	37353	14
UEC Theatres 12	125 Premiere Dr	State College	PA	16801	12
Premiere Theatre 12	105 Tenth Place	Goldsboro	NC	27534	12
Premiere Theatre 8	50 Theatre Dr	Norwalk	OH	44857	8
College 9	3031 Carnegie Dr	State College	PA	16803	9
Diamond 8 Cinema	32260 Mission Trail	Lake Elsinore	CA	92530	8
Nelco Cineplex 6	600 Cinema Dr	Greenville	MS	38701	6

WARREN THEATRES, LLC.

4 theatres, 57 screens.

PO Box 782560, Wichita, KS 67268. TEL: (316) 685-3773. www.warrentheatres.com

THEATRES

21st St. Warren	9150 W. 21st St	Wichita	KS	67205	17
13th Avenue Warren	11611 E 13th St	Wichita	KS	67205	20
Old Town Theatre Grille	353 N. Mead	Wichita	KS	67202	6
Moore Warren	1000 Telephone Rd	Moore	OK	73160	14

WEHRENBERG THEATRES, INC.

16 theatres, 224 screens.

12800 Manchester Rd., St. Louis, MO 63131. TEL: (314) 822-4520. FAX: (314) 822-8032. www.wehrenberg.com

CHAIRMAN/CO-CEO
Ronald P. Krueger
PRESIDENT/CO-CEO
James F. Hoffmeister
V.P. & FILM BUYER
Doug Whitford
DIRECTOR, MARKETING
Kelly Hoskins

DIRECTOR, CONCESSIONS
Brett Havlik

THEATRES

Wehrenberg Galaxy 16 Cine	5340 Council St.	Cedar Rapids	IA	62402	16
Wehrenberg Galaxy 14 Cine	1111 Wylie Dr.	Bloomington	IL	61701	14
Wehrenberg St. Clair Cine 10	50 Ludwig Dr.	Fairview Heights	IL	62208	10
Wehrenberg O'Fallon 15 Cine	1320 Central Park Dr.	O'Fallon	IL	62269	15
Wehrenberg Galaxy 14 Cine	4340 Maine Ave. S.E.	Rochester	MN	55904	14
Wehrenberg Cape West 14 Cine	247 Siemers Dr.	Cape Girardeau	MO	63703	14
Wehrenberg Town Square 14	7805 Highway N.	Dardenne Prairie	MO	63368	12
Wehrenberg Jamestown 14 Cine	209 Jamestown Mall	Florissant	MO	63034	14
Wehrenberg Osage Village 5 Cine	Factory Outlet Village	Osage Beach	MO	65065	5
Wehrenberg Ronnies 20 Cine	5320 S. Lindbergh Blvd.	Sappington	MO	63126	20
Wehrenberg Campbell 16 Cine	4005 South Ave.	Springfield	MO	65807	16
Wehrenberg St. Charles 18 Cine	1830 S. 1st Capital Dr. S.	St. Charles	MO	63303	18
Wehrenberg Arnold 14 Cine	1912 Richardson Rd.	St. Louis	MO	63131	14
Wehrenberg Des Peres 14 Cine	12800 Manchester Rd.	St. Louis	MO	63131	14
Wehrenberg Galaxy 14 Cine	450 THF Blvd.	St. Louis	MO	63005	14
Wehrenberg Mid Rivers 14 Cine	I-70 & Midrivers Mall Rd.	St. Louis	MO	63125	14

WESTATES THEATRES

19 theatres, 100 screens.
1111 Brickyard Rd., Ste. 106, Salt Lake City, UT 84106. TEL: (801) 487-6233. FAX: (801) 487-6633. www.movieswest.com

THEATRES

Page Mesa Theatre	42 S. Lake Powell Blvd.	Page	AZ	86040	1
Montpelier Centre Theatre	806 Washington	Montpelier	ID	83254	1
Elko Cinema 4	1145 Connally	Elko	NV	89801	4
Elko Crystal 5	676 Commercial	Elko	NV	89801	5
Mesquite Stadium 6	749 W. Mesquite Blvd.	Mesquite	NV	89027	6
Cedar City Cinema 8	1040 Sage Way, P.O. Box 20893	Cedar City	UT	84720	8
Cedar City Fiddler 6	170 E. Fiddler Canyon Rd.	Cedar City	UT	84720	6
Logan Movies 5	91 E. 2440 N.	Logan	UT	84341	5
University Stadium 6	1225 N. 200 E.	Logan	UT	84341	6
Providence Stadium 8	535 W. 100 N.	Providence	UT	84332	8
Holladay Center Cinema 6	1945 E. Murray-Holladay Rd.	Salt Lake City	UT	84117	6
Pineview Stadium 10	2376 E. Red Cliff Dr.	St. George	UT	84770	10
St. George Cinema 6	905 S. Main St.	St. George	UT	84770	6
St. George Flood Street 4	170 North	St. George	UT	84770	4
St. George Stadium 8	1091 N. Bluff St.	St. George	UT	84770	8
Washington Red Cliff Cinemas	1750 Red Cliffs Dr.	St. George	UT	84790	4
Tooele Cinema 6	1600 N. Pine Canyon Rd.	Tooele	UT	84074	6

LCA ENTERPRISES

Water Gardens Cinema 6	912 W. Gardens Dr.	Pleasant Grove	UT	84062	6

W. F. CINEMA HOLDINGS, L.P. (MANN THEATRES)

11 theatres, 71 screens.
P.O. Box 20077, Encino, CA 91416-0077; 16530 Ventura Blvd., Ste. 500, Encino, CA 91436.
TEL: (818) 784-6266. FAX: (818) 784-8659. www.manntheatres.com
CEO
Peter Dobson
DIRECTOR OF OPERATIONS
Mark Behrang
DIRECTOR, FINANCE
Gaylyn Okimoto
DIRECTOR, FILM & MARKETING
Sandy Rodriguez
DIRECTOR, HUMAN RESOURCES
Jason Hebert
DIRECTOR, CONCESSIONS & PURCHASING
Sally Basada

THEATRES

Mann Glendale Exchange 10	128 N. Maryland Ave.	Glendale	CA	91206	10
Mann Glendale Marketplace 4	144 S. Brand Blvd.	Glendale	CA	91206	4
Mann Granada Hills 9	16830 Devonshire St.	Granada Hills	CA	91344	9
Mann Grauman's Chinese Theatre	6925 Hollywood Blvd.	Hollywood	CA	90028	1
Mann Chinese 6	6801 Hollywood Blvd., Ste. 335	Hollywood	CA	90028	6
Mann Bruin 1	948 Broxton Ave.	Los Angeles	CA	90024	1
Mann Village 1	961 Broxton Ave.	Los Angeles	CA	90024	1
Mann Criterion 6	1313 Third St. Promenade	Santa Monica	CA	90401	6
Mann Janss Marketplace 9	255 N. Moorpark Rd.	Thousand Oaks	CA	91360	9
Mann Plant 16	7876 Van Nuys Blvd.	Van Nuys	CA	91402	16
Mann Village 8	180 Promenade Way	Westlake Village	CA	91362	8

WILDWOOD THEATRES

3 theatres, 29 screens.
557 Cottonwood Ave,. Hartland, WI 53029. TEL: (262) 369-1990. FAX: (262) 369-1650. www.wildwoodtheatres.com
COMPANY OFFICERS
Anthony Groh, Hank Furlong

THEATRES

Luxury 10	2799 Cranston Rd.	Beloit	WI	53511	10
Movies 10	3100 Deerfield Dr.	Janesville	WI	53546	10
Rock Theatres 9	1620 Newport Rd.	Janesville	WI	53546	9

ZURICH CINEMA CORP.

9 theatres, 55 screens.
5181 Brockway Ln., Fayetteville, NY 13066. TEL: (315) 446-9081. FAX: (315) 446-6235.
OWNER, PRESIDENT & FILM BUYER
Conrad Zurich
VICE PRESIDENT
Linda Zurich

DIRECTOR OF OPERATIONS
Jamison Mills

THEATRES

Elmira Drive-In	Route 352	Elmira	NY	14903	2
Geneva Movieplex 8	371 Hamilton St.	Geneva	NY	14456	8
Hollywood Theatre	2221 Brewerton Rd.	Mattydale	NY	13211	1
Glenwood Movieplex 9 of Oneida	Route 5 & 46	Oneida	NY	13421	9
Southside Oneonta Mall	Route 23	Oneonta	NY	13820	9
Oswego Cinema 7	138 W. 2nd St.	Oswego	NY	13126	7
Pittsford Cinema	3349 Monroe Ave.	Rochester	NY	14618	9
Rome Cinemas 8	1122 Erie Blvd. W.	Rome	NY	13440	8
West Rome Drive-In	Route 69	Rome	NY	13440	2

Circuit Theatres in the Top 50 U.S. Markets

Listed are national circuit theatres and major regional circuit theatres in the 50 largest U.S. metropolitan markets. The hierarchy used to sort this list is as follows: Market size then alphabetically by circuit name, state (for markets including cities in more than one state), municipality and theatre name. Smaller regional circuits, independent theatres and major national circuits with only one theatre in a market have been excluded. Market regions are determined by broadcast coverage of major television, radio and cable stations and distribution of major newspapers (designated market areas).

The top 50 U.S. markets, in 2010, in order of decreasing size:

1 New York
2 Los Angeles
3 Chicago
4 Philadelphia
5 Dallas-Ft. Worth
6 San Francisco-Oakland-San Jose
7 Boston, MA (Manchester)
8 Atlanta
9 Washington, DC (Hagerstown)
10 Houston
11 Detroit
12 Phoenix
13 Seattle-Tacoma
14 Tampa-St. Petersburg (Sarasota)
15 Minneapolis-St. Paul
16 Denver
17 Miami-Fort Lauderdale
18 Cleveland-Akron (Canton)
19 Orlando-Daytona Beach-Melbourne
20 Sacramento-Stockton-Modesto
21 St. Louis
22 Portland
23 Pittsburgh
24 Charlotte
25 Indianapolis
26 Raleigh-Durham (Fayetteville)
27 Baltimore
28 San Diego
29 Nashville
30 Hartford & New Haven
31 Salt Lake City
32 Kansas City
33 Cincinnati
34 Columbus
35 Milwaukee
36 Greenville-Spartanburg, Asheville, Anderson
37 San Antonio
38 West Palm Beach-Ft. Pierce
39 Harrisburg-Lancaster-Lebanon-York
40 Birmingham (Anniston and Tuscaloosa)
41 Grand Rapids-Kalamazoo-Battle Creek
42 Las Vegas
43 Norfolk-Portsmouth-Newport News
44 Albuquerque-Santa Fe
45 Oklahoma City
45 Greensboro-High Point-Winston Salem
47 Jacksonville
48 Austin
49 Louisville
50 Memphis

NEW YORK, NY (DMA 501)

AMC ENTERTAINMENT

Theatre	City	State	Screens
AMC Loews Danbury 16	Danbury	CT	16
AMC Loews Brick Plaza 10	Bricktown	NJ	10
AMC Bridgewater 7	Bridgewater	NJ	7
AMC Clifton Commons 16	Clifton	NJ	16
AMC Loews East Hanover 12	East Hanover	NJ	12
AMC Loews Monmouth Mall 15	Eatontown	NJ	15
AMC Loews Menlo Park 12	Edison	NJ	12
AMC Loews Jersey Gardens 20	Elizabeth	NJ	20
AMC Loews Freehold Metroplex 14	Freehold	NJ	14
AMC Loews Newport Centre 11	Jersey City	NJ	11
AMC Aviation Plaza 12	Linden	NJ	12
AMC Loews Mountainside 10	Mountainside	NJ	10
AMC Loews New Brunswick 18	New Brunswick	NJ	18
AMC Garden State 16	Paramus	NJ	16
AMC Loews Ridgefield Park 12	Ridgefield Park	NJ	12
AMC Rockaway 16	Rockaway	NJ	16
AMC Loews Meadow 6	Secaucus	NJ	6
AMC Meadows 8 (Plaza 8)	Secaucus	NJ	8
AMC Loews Seacourt 10	Toms River	NJ	10
AMC Loews Wayne 14	Wayne	NJ	14
AMC Essex Green 9	West Orange	NJ	9
AMC Loews Bay Terrace 6	Bayside	NY	6
AMC Bay Plaza 13	Bronx	NY	13
AMC Loews Kings Plaza 6	Brooklyn	NY	6
AMC Loews Fresh Meadows 7	Fresh Meadows	NY	7
AMC Loews Roosevelt Field 8	Garden City	NY	8
AMC Loews Shore 8	Huntington	NY	8
AMC Loews Nassau Metroplex 10	Levittown	NY	10
AMC Loews Galleria Metroplex 16	Middletown	NY	16
AMC Empire 25	New York	NY	25
AMC Loews 19th Street East 6	New York	NY	6
AMC Loews 34th Street 14	New York	NY	14
AMC Loews 72nd Street 1	New York	NY	1
AMC Loews 84th Street 6	New York	NY	6
AMC Loews Kips Bay 15	New York	NY	15
AMC Loews Lincoln Square 13	New York	NY	13
AMC Loews Lincoln Square Imax	New York	NY	1
AMC Loews Orpheum 7	New York	NY	7
AMC Loews Village 7	New York	NY	4
AMC Magic Johnson Harlem 9	New York	NY	9
AMC Loews Port Chester 14	Port Chester	NY	14
AMC Loews Fantasy 5	Rockville Ctr.	NY	5
AMC Loews Stony Brook 17	Stony Brook	NY	17
AMC Loews Palisades Center 21	West Nyack	NY	21
AMC Loews Raceway 10	Westbury	NY	10

BOSTON CULINARY GROUP

Theatre	City	State	Screens
Cedar Lane Cinemas	Teaneck	NJ	4
Hudson Cinemas	Jersey City	NJ	7
Lafayette Cinema	Suffern	NY	1
Seaford Cinemas	Seaford	NY	8

BOW TIE CINEMAS

Theatre	City	State	Screens
Criterion Cinemas	Greenwich	CT	3
The Playhouse	New Canaan	CT	2
Royale 6	Norwalk	CT	6
Regent 8	South Norwalk	CT	8
Majestic 6	Stamford	CT	6
Landmark 9	Stamford	CT	9
Marquis 16	Trumbull	CT	16
Wilton 4	Wilton	CT	4
American Theater	Bronx	NY	7

CLEARVIEW CINEMAS

Theatre	City	State	Screens
Strathmore Cinema 4	Aberdeen	NJ	4
Bergenfield Cinema 5	Bergenfield	NJ	5
Bernardsville Cinema 3	Bernardsville	NJ	3
Caldwell Cinema 4	Caldwell	NJ	4
Cinema 23/Cedar Grove	Cedar Grove	NJ	5
Chester Cinema 6	Chester	NJ	6
Allwood Cinema 6	Clifton	NJ	6
Closter Cinema 4	Closter	NJ	4
Mansfield Cinema 15	Hackettstown	NJ	14
Kinnelon 11	Kinnelon	NJ	11
Madison Cinema 4	Madison	NJ	4
Millburn Cinema 4	Millburn	NJ	4
Clairidge Cinemas	Montclair	NJ	6
Headquarters 10 Theatres	Morristown	NJ	10
Middlebrook Galleria Cin.10	Ocean Township	NJ	10
Parsippany Cinema 12	Parsippany	NJ	12
Red Bank Art Cinema	Red Bank	NJ	2
Warner Quad	Ridgewood	NJ	4
South Orange 5	South Orange	NJ	5
Succasunna Cinema 10	Succasunna	NJ	10
Beacon Hill 5/Summit	Summit	NJ	5
Tenafly Cinema 4	Tenafly	NJ	4
Bellevue Cinema 4	Upper Montclair	NJ	4
Washington Twp. Cinemas	Washington Township	NJ	3
Wayne Preakness Cinemas	Wayne	NJ	4
Babylon Cinemas	Babylon	NY	3
Grand Avenue Cinemas	Baldwin	NY	5
Bedford Playhouse	Bedford	NY	2
Bronxville Cinemas	Bronxville	NY	3
Franklin Square Cinemas	Franklin Square	NY	6
Squire Cinemas	Great Neck	NY	7
Larchmont Playhouse	Larchmont	NY	3
Mamaroneck Playhouse	Mamaroneck	NY	4
Manhasset Cinemas	Manhasset	NY	3
Mt. Kisco Cinemas	Mount Kisco	NY	5
New City Cinema 6	New City	NY	6
Herricks Cinema 4	New Hyde Park	NY	4
62nd & Broadway Cinema	New York	NY	1
Chelsea Cinemas	New York	NY	9
First & 62nd Cinemas	New York	NY	6
Ziegfeld Theatre	New York	NY	1
Port Washington Cinemas	Port Washington	NY	7
Soundview Cinema	Port Washington	NY	6
Roslyn Cinemas	Roslyn	NY	4
Cinema 100	White Plains	NY	4
Central Plaza Cinema	Yonkers	NY	4

DESTINTA THEATRES

Theatre	City	State	Screens
New Windsor 12	New Windsor	NY	12

ENTERTAINMENT CINEMAS

Theatre	City	State	Screens
Ent. Cinemas Stratford 14	Stratford	CT	14
Ent. Cinemas Seaford 8	Seaford	NY	8

LANDMARK THEATRES

Theatre	City	State	Screens
Sunshine Cinema	New York	NY	5

MARQUEE CINEMAS

Theatre	City	State	Screens
Orchard 10	Toms River	NJ	10

NATIONAL AMUSEMENTS

Theatre	City	State	Screens
Fairfield Cinemas	Fairfield	CT	9
Showcase Bridgeport	Bridgeport	CT	12
Edgewater Multiplex Cinemas	Edgewater	NJ	16
Hazlet Multiplex	Hazlet	NJ	12
Showcase at the Ritz Center	Voorhees	NJ	16
City Center 15: Cinema de Lux	White Plains	NY	15
Greenburgh Multiplex Cinemas	Greenburgh	NY	10
All Westchester Saw Mill Multiplex	Hawthorne	NY	10
Cross County Multiplex	Yonkers	NY	10
Concourse Plaza Multiplex	Bronx	NY	10
Whitestone Multiplex	Bronx	NY	14
College Point Multiplex	Whitestone	NY	12
Linden Blvd. Multiplex	Brooklyn	NY	14
Commack Multiplex	Commack	NY	15
Farmingdale Multiplex	Farmingdale	NY	14
Broadway Multiplex	Hicksville	NY	12
Island 16: Cinema de Lux	Holtsville	NY	16
Jamaica Multiplex	Jamaica	NY	15
Green Acres Cinemas	Valley Stream	NY	6
Sunrise Multiplex	Valley Stream	NY	14

PHOENIX ADLABS THEATRE MANAGEMENT, LLC

Theatre	City	State	Screens
Movie City 8	Edison	NJ	8
Columbia Park 12	North Bergen	NJ	12
Bombay Theatre	Flushing	NY	1
The ImaginAsian Theater	New York	NY	1

READING INTERNATIONAL, INC.

Theatre	City	State	Screens
Manville 12-Plex	Manville	NJ	12
Angelika Film Center & Café	New York	NY	6
Cinemas 1, 2 & 3	New York	NY	3
East 86th Street Cinemas	New York	NY	4
Village East	New York	NY	7

REGAL ENTERTAINMENT GROUP

Theatre	City	State	Screens
Stratford Stadium 14	Stratford	CT	14
Manahawkin 10	Manahawkin	NJ	10
Marlboro Cinema Stadium 8	Morganville	NJ	8
Commerce Center Stadium 18	North Brunswick	NJ	18
Pohatcong 12	Phillipsburg	NJ	12
Hadley Theatre Stadium 16	South Plainfield	NJ	16
Court Street Stadium 12	Brooklyn	NY	12
Sheepshead Bay 14	Brooklyn	NY	14
East Hampton Cinema 6	East Hampton	NY	6
Farmingdale Stadium 10	Farmingdale	NY	10
Fishkill 10	Fishkill	NY	10
Brandon Cinemas 2	Forest Hills	NY	2
Midway Cinemas Stadium 9	Forest Hills	NY	9
Atlas Park Stadium 8	Glendale	NY	8
Hampton Bays 5	Hampton Bays	NY	5
Hudson Valley Mall 12	Kingston	NY	12
Kaufman Astoria Stadium 14	Long Island City	NY	14
Lynbrook Theatre 6	Lynbrook	NY	6
New Roc City Stadium 18 Plus IMAX	New Rochelle	NY	19
64th And 2nd Ave. 3	New York	NY	3
Battery Park Stadium 16	New York	NY	16
East 85th Street 1	New York	NY	1
E-Walk Stadium 13	New York	NY	13
Union Square Stadium 14	New York	NY	14
Galleria Mall 16	Poughkeepsie	NY	16
Ronkonkoma Cinema Stadium 9	Ronkonkoma	NY	9
Southampton 4 Theatres	Southampton	NY	4
Hylan Plaza 5	Staten Island	NY	5
Staten Island Stadium 16	Staten Island	NY	16
Westbury Theatre Stadium 12	Westbury	NY	12
Yonkers 6	Yonkers	NY	6

STARPLEX CINEMAS

Theatre	City	State	Screens
Columbia Park Cinema 12	North Bergen	NJ	12

LOS ANGELES, CA (DMA 803)

AMC ENTERTAINMENT

Theatre	City	State	Screens
AMC 12 At Downtown Disney	Anaheim	CA	12
AMC Santa Anita 16	Arcadia	CA	16
AMC Burbank 16	Burbank	CA	16
AMC Burbank Town Center 6	Burbank	CA	6
AMC Burbank Town Center 8	Burbank	CA	8
AMC Puente Hills 20	City of Industry	CA	20
AMC Covina 30	Covina	CA	30
AMC Fullerton 20	Fullerton	CA	20
AMC Marina Pacifica 12	Long Beach	CA	12
AMC Pine Square 16	Long Beach	CA	16
AMC Avco Center 4	Los Angeles	CA	4
AMC Century 15	Los Angeles	CA	15
AMC Magic Johnson Crenshaw 15	Los Angeles	CA	15
AMC Loews Marina 6	Marina Del Rey	CA	6
AMC Montebello 10	Montebello	CA	10
AMC Plaza Bonita	National City	CA	14
AMC Norwalk 20	Norwalk	CA	20
AMC Ontario 30	Ontario	CA	30
AMC 30 At The Block	Orange	CA	30
AMC Victoria Gardens 12	Rancho Cucamonga	CA	12
AMC Galleria South Bay 16	Redondo Beach	CA	16
AMC Loews Broadway 4	Santa Monica	CA	4
AMC Santa Monica 7	Santa Monica	CA	7
AMC Del Amo 18	Torrance	CA	18
AMC Rolling Hills 20	Torrance	CA	20
AMC Tustin 14	Tustin	CA	14
AMC Loews Citywalk 19	Universal City	CA	19
AMC Promenade 16	Woodland Hills	CA	16

ARCLIGHT CINEMAS

Theatre	City	State	Screens
Hollywood & Cinerama Dome	Los Angeles	CA	15
Sherman Oaks	Sherman Oaks	CA	16

CINEMARK USA

Theatre	City	State	Screens
Cinemark Movies 8	Chino	CA	8
Huntington Beach	Huntington Beach	CA	20
Cinemark 22	Lancaster	CA	22
Cinemark Movies 12	Lancaster	CA	12
Cinemark at The Pike	Long Beach	CA	14
Century 8	North Hollywood	CA	8
Century Stadium 25	Orange	CA	25
Cinemark at Antelope Valley Mall	Palmdale	CA	16
Century 10 Downtown	Ventura	CA	10
Century Stadium 16	Ventura	CA	16
Cinemark at The Mall at Victor Valley	Victorville	CA	16
Cinemark Movies 10	Victorville	CA	10

HARKINS THEATRES

Theatre	City	State	Screens
Chino Hills 18	Chino Hills	CA	18
Moreno Valley 16	Moreno Valley	CA	16

HOLLYWOOD THEATRES

Theatre	City	State	Screens
New Barstow Cinema 6	Barstow	CA	6
New Malibu Theatre	Malibu	CA	2

KRIKORIAN PREMIERE

Theatre	City	State	Screens
Buena Park Metroplex 18	Buena Park	CA	18
Chino Marketplace Spectrum 12	Chino	CA	12
Krikorian theatres 15 at Dos Lagos	Corona	CA	15
Downey	Downey	CA	10
Monrovia Cinema 12	Monrovia	CA	12
Pico Rivera Village Walk 15	Pico Rivera	CA	15
Redlands	Redlands	CA	14
San Clemente	San Clemente	CA	6

LAEMMLE THEATRES

Theatre	City	State	Screens
Laemmle Music Hall	Beverly Hills	CA	3
Laemmle's Claremont 5	Claremont	CA	5
Laemmle's Town Center 5	Encino	CA	5
Laemmle's Grande	Los Angeles	CA	4
Laemmle Sunset 5	Los Angeles	CA	5
Laemmle's Royal	Los Angeles	CA	1
Laemmle's One Colorado	Pasadena	CA	8
Laemmle's Playhouse 7	Pasadena	CA	7
Laemmle's Monica 4	Santa Monica	CA	4
Laemmle's Fallbrook 7	West Hills	CA	7

LANDMARK THEATRES

Theatre	City	State	Screens
Nuart Theatre	Los Angeles	CA	1
Regent Theatre	Los Angeles	CA	1
The Landmark - Westside	Los Angeles	CA	12

METROPOLITAN THEATRES

Theatre	City	State	Screens
Park Theatre	Huntington Park	CA	2
University Village Cinemas	Riverside	CA	10
Teatro Fiesta	Santa Ana	CA	2

THE MOVIE EXPERIENCE

Theatre	City	State	Screens
Blue Jay Cinema 4	Blue Jay	CA	4
Movie Experience 14	Anaheim	CA	14
Movie Experience 17	Murrieta	CA	17
Movie Experience 10	Temecula	CA	10

NATIONAL AMUSEMENTS

Theatre	City	State	Screens
The Bridge: Cinema de Lux	Los Angeles	CA	17
The Bridge IMAX	Los Angeles	CA	1

PACIFIC THEATRES

Theatre	City	State	Screens
Glendale 18	Glendale	CA	18
Winnetka 21	Chatsworth	CA	21
Commerce 14	City of Commerce	CA	14
Vineland Drive-In	City of Industry	CA	4
Culver Stadium 12	Culver City	CA	12
Beach Cities 16	El Segundo	CA	16
Lakewood Center 16	Lakewood	CA	16
The Grove 14	Los Angeles	CA	14
Manhattan Village 6	Manhattan Beach	CA	6
Fashion Center 10	Northridge	CA	10
Sherman Oaks 5	Sherman Oaks	CA	5

PHOENIX ADLABS THEATRE MANAGEMENT, LLC

Theatre	City	State	Screens
Norwalk 8	Norwalk	CA	8

REGAL ENTERTAINMENT GROUP

Theatre	City	State	Screens
Alhambra Renaissance 14	Alhambra	CA	14
Atlantic Palace 10	Alhambra	CA	10
Aliso Viejo Stadium 20	Aliso Viejo	CA	20
Anaheim Hills 14	Anaheim Hills	CA	14
Brea Stadium 10 West	Brea	CA	10
Brea Stadium 12 East	Brea	CA	12
Calabasas Stadium 6	Calabasas	CA	6
Camarillo 12	Camarillo	CA	12
Canyon Country Stadium 10	Canyon Country	CA	10
Cerritos Stadium 10	Cerritos	CA	10
UA Galaxy @ Los Cerritos 11	Cerritos	CA	11
Corona Crossings Stadium 18	Corona	CA	18
Metro Pointe Stadium 12	Costa Mesa	CA	12
Triangle Square 8	Costa Mesa	CA	8
El Monte 8	El Monte	CA	8
Foothill Towne Center Stadium 22	Foothill Ranch	CA	22
Garden Grove Stadium 16	Garden Grove	CA	16
Hemet Cinema 12	Hemet	CA	12
Irvine Spectrum 21	Irvine	CA	21
Market Place Stadium 10	Irvine	CA	10
University Town Center 6	Irvine	CA	6
Westpark 8	Irvine	CA	8
La Canada 8	La Canada Flintridge	CA	8
La Habra Stadium 16	La Habra	CA	16
La Verne Stadium 12	La Verne	CA	12
Ocean Ranch 7	Laguna Niguel	CA	7
Long Beach Stadium 26	Long Beach	CA	26
UA Long Beach 6	Long Beach	CA	6
Marina Del Rey 6	Marina Del Rey	CA	6
Eastvale Stadium 14	Mira Loma	CA	14
Kaleidoscope Stadium 10	Mission Viejo	CA	10
Island 7	Newport Beach	CA	7
Newport 6	Newport Beach	CA	6
Ontario Mountain Village Stadium 14	Ontario	CA	14
Ontario Palace Stadium 22	Ontario	CA	22
Terrace Cinema 6	Rancho Palos Verdes	CA	6
Rancho Santa Margarita 6	Rancho Sta Margarita	CA	6
Jurupa Stadium 14	Riverside	CA	14
Riverside Plaza Stadium 16	Riverside	CA	16
Promenade 13	Rolling Hills Estates	CA	13
San Jacinto Metro 12	San Jacinto	CA	12
Valencia Stadium 12	Santa Clarita	CA	12
Civic Center Stadium 16	Simi Valley	CA	16
Simi Valley Plaza 10	Simi Valley	CA	10
South Gate Stadium 20	South Gate	CA	20
Temecula Stadium 15	Temecula	CA	15
Tustin Marketplace 6	Tustin	CA	6
West Covina Stadium 18	West Covina	CA	18
Westminster 10	Westminster	CA	10

STARPLEX CINEMAS

Theatre	City	State	Screens
Woodbridge Movies 5	Irvine	CA	5
La Mirada 7	La Mirada	CA	7

ULTRASTAR CINEMAS

Theatre	City	State	Screens
UltraStar Fontana 8	Fontana	CA	8

W.F. CINEMA HOLDINGS (MANN THEATRES)

Theatre	City	State	Screens
Mann Agoura Hills 8	Agoura Hills	CA	8
Mann Beverly Center 13	Los Angeles	CA	13
Mann Glendale Exchange 10	Glendale	CA	10
Mann Glendale Marketplace 4	Glendale	CA	4
Mann Granada Hills 9	Granada Hills	CA	9
Mann Grauman's Chinese Theatre	Hollywood	CA	1
Mann Chinese 6	Hollywood	CA	6
Mann Bruin 1	Los Angeles	CA	1
Mann Festival Westwood 1	Los Angeles	CA	1

Mann Village 1 ....Los Angeles...............CA.......1
Mann Criterion 6 ....Santa Monica ....CA.......6
Mann Janss Marketplace 9...........Thousand Oaks ....CA.......9
Mann Plant 16..............................Van Nuys...................CA.....16
Mann Village 8 ....Westlake Village ....CA.......8

CHICAGO, IL (DMA 602)

AMC ENTERTAINMENT

AMC Ford City 14 ....Chicago ....IL.......14
AMC Loews 600 North Michigan 9...Chicago ....IL 9
AMC Loews Pipers Alley 4 ....Chicago ....IL 4
AMC River East 21 ....Chicago ....IL.......21
AMC Chicago Ridge 6.....................Chicago Ridge ....IL 6
AMC Loews Country Club Hills 16 ...Country Club Hills.......IL.......16
AMC Loews Crestwood 18 ....Crestwood ....IL.......18
AMC Loews Quarry 14....................Hodgkins ....IL.......14
AMC Yorktown 17...........................Lombard ....IL.......17
AMC Yorktown Premium 1 ....Lombard ....IL 1
AMC Randhurst 16..........................Mount Prospect ....IL.......16
AMC Loews Norridge 10 ....Norridge ....IL.......14
AMC Northbrook 14 ....Northbrook ....IL.......14
AMC Loews Streets Of Woodfield 20...Schaumburg ....IL.......20
AMC Loews Gardens 1/6 ....Skokie ....IL 6
AMC Loews Gardens 7/13 ....Skokie ....IL 7
AMC Barrington 30 ....South Barrington ....IL.......30
AMC Cantera 30 ....Warrenville ....IL.......30
AMC Loews Woodridge 18............Woodridge ....IL.......18

CARMIKE CINEMAS

Market Square ....Dekalb.........................IL.......10
Orpheum...Morris.........................IL.......10
Peru Mall ....Peru ....IL 8

CINEMARK USA

Century Stratford Square ....Bloomingdale..............IL.......16
Cinemark Movies 10 ....Bourbonnais ....IL.......10
Deer Park 16...................................Deer Park ....IL.......16
Evanston 18 / Cinéarts 6...............Evanston ....IL.......18
Cinemark Movies 10 ....Joliet ....IL.......10
Cinemark Movies 8 ....Joliet ....IL 8
Cinemark Melrose Park.................Melrose Park ....IL.......10
Cinemark Tinseltown USA.............North Aurora..............IL.......17
Cinemark @ Seven Bridges ....Woodridge..................IL.......17
Cinemark at Valparaiso ....Valparaiso ....IN 12

CLASSIC CINEMAS

CC Cinema 12 Theatre ....Carpentersville ....IL.......12
CC Tivoli Theatre ....Downers Grove...........IL 1
CC Elk Grove Theatre ....Elk Grove ....IL 8
CC York Theatre.............................Elmhurst.....................IL 9
CC Fox Lake Theatre ....Fox Lake.....................IL 9
CC Meadowview Theatre..............Kankakee ....IL 3
CC Paramount ....Kankakee ....IL 5
CC Ogden 6 Theatre.....................Naperville ....IL 6
CC Lake Theatre............................Oak Park ....IL 7
CC Charlestowne 18......................St. Charles ....IL.......18
CC Woodstock Theatre.................Woodstock..................IL 4

GOODRICH QUALITY THEATRES

Randall 15 IMAX............................Batavia ....IL.......15
Kendall 10.......................................Oswego ....IL.......10
Portage 16 IMAX............................Portage.......................IN 16

KERASOTES SHOWPLACE THEATRES

ShowPlace 12 ....Bolingbrook ....IL.......12
City North 14 ....Chicago ....IL.......14
ShowPlace 14 ....Chicago ....IL.......14
Webster Place 11 ....Chicago ....IL.......11
ShowPlace 14 ....Cicero..........................IL.......14
Geln 10..Glenview.....................IL.......10
Lake in the Hills 12 ....Lake in the Hills...........IL.......12
ShowPlace 16 ....Naperville ....IL.......16
ShowPlace 14 ....New Lenox ....IL.......14
ShowPlace 12 ....Niles ....IL.......12
Village Crossing 18.........................Skokie ....IL.......18
River Tree Court.............................Vernon Hills ....IL 8
ShowPlace 8....................................Vernon Hills ....IL 8
ShowPlace 12 ....Hobart ....IN 12
LaPorte Cinema ....LaPorte.......................IN 4
Merrillville 10 ....Merrillville ....IN 10
ShowPlace 14 ....Michigan City..............IN 14
ShowPlace 12 ....Schererville ....IN 12
ShowPlace 16 ....Schererville ....IN 16

LANDMARK THEATRES

Landmark Century Cntr Cinema....Chicago ....IL 7
Renaissance Place ....Highland Park.............IL 5

MARCUS THEATRES

Marcus Cinema Addison ....Addison ....IL.......21
Marcus Cinema Chicago Heights ..Chicago Heights ....IL.......14
Marcus Cinema Elgin Fox ....Elgin...........................IL.......15
Marcus Cinema Gurnee ....Gurnee ....IL.......20
Marcus Cinema Orland Park ....Orland Park ....IL.......14

NOVA CINETECH

Nova 8 ....Naperville ....IL 8

REGAL ENTERTAINMENT GROUP

Showplace 16 ....Crystal Lake ....IL.......16
Lake Zurich 12 ....Lake Zurich ....IL.......12
Lincolnshire Stadium 20 Plus IMAX...Lincolnshire ....IL.......21
Round Lake Beach Stadium 18.....Round Lake Beach .....IL.......18

PHILADELPHIA, PA (DMA 504)

AMC ENTERTAINMENT

AMC Loews Cherry Hill 24 ....Cherry Hill ....NJ 24
AMC Deptford 8 ....Deptford ....NJ 8
AMC Deptford Mall 6.....................Deptford ....NJ 6
AMC Hamilton 24 ....Hamilton ....NJ 24
AMC Marlton 8..............................Marlton ....NJ 8
AMC Tilghman 8 ....Allentown....................PA 8
AMC Neshaminy 24 ....Bensalem ....PA 24
AMC Woodhaven 10......................Bensalem ....PA 10
AMC Granite Run 8.......................Media ....PA 8
AMC Franklin Mills 14 ....Philadelphia................PA 14
AMC Plymouth Meeting 12...........Plymouth Meeting.......PA 12
AMC 309 Cinema 9.......................Spring House..............PA 9
AMC Marple 10..............................Springfield ....PA 10
AMC Painters 9.............................West Chester..............PA 9

CARMIKE CINEMAS

Carmike ....Dover..........................DE.....14
Carmike ....Allentown....................PA 16
Coventry ....Pottstown....................PA 8
Wymossing ....Wymossing ....PA 8

CINEMA CENTER

Cinema Center at Fairgrounds Sq .Reading......................PA 10

CINEMARK USA

Cinemark Movies 10 ....Wilmington..................DE.....10
Cinemark 16 ....Somerdale ....NJ 16

CLEARVIEW CINEMA

Bala Theatre ....Bala Cynwyd ....PA 3
Anthony Wayne Cinema ....Wayne ....PA 5

DESTINTA THEATRES

Independence 12 ....Hamilton ....NJ 12

LANDMARK THEATRES

Ritz at the Bourse ....Philadelphia................PA 5
Ritz East ....Philadelphia................PA 2
Ritz V...Philadelphia................PA 5

NATIONAL AMUSEMENTS

Atco Multiplex ....Atco............................NJ 14
Town Center Plaza ....East Windsor ....NJ 15
The Bridge: Cinema de Lux-UPenn ..Philadelphia................PA 6

R/C THEATRES MANAGEMENT CORP.

Reading Movies 11 & IMAX...........Reading.......................PA 11

RAVE MOTION PICTURES

RMP Promenade 16.......................Center Valley ....PA 16

REGAL ENTERTAINMENT GROUP

Peoples Plaza Cinema Stadium 17...Newark.......................DE.....17
Brandywine Town Center 16 ....Wilmington ....DE......16
Burlington Stadium 20.....................Burlington ....NJ 20
Hamilton Commons Stadium 14 ....Mays Landing..............NJ 14
Moorestown Mall 7..........................Moorestown.................NJ 7
Market Fair Stadium 10...................Princeton....................NJ 10
Washington Township 14.................Sewell.........................NJ 14
Cross Keys Cinema Stadium 12 ....Turnersville.................NJ 12
Cumberland Mall Stadium 14............Vineland ....NJ 14
Saucon Valley Stadium 10 ....Bethlehem ....PA 10
Plymouth Meeting 10 ....Conshohocken ....PA 10
Downingtown Cinema Stadium 16....Downingtown...............PA 16
Barn Plaza Stadium 14 ....Doylestown..................PA 14
East Whiteland Stadium 9.................East Whiteland.............PA 9
Northampton Cinema 14 ....Easton ....PA 14
King Of Prussia Stadium 16.............King Of Prussia............PA 16
Oxford Valley Theatre Stadium 14.....Langhorne...................PA 14
Main Street Theatre 6 ....Manayunk.....................PA 6
Edgmont Square 10 ....Newton Square ....PA 10
Oaks Stadium 24..............................Oaks............................PA 24
Grant Plaza 9 ....Philadelphia.................PA 9
Riverview Plaza 17..........................Philadelphia.................PA 17
Richland Crossing 12 ....Quakertown..................PA 12
69th Street 9....................................Upper Darby.................PA 9
Warrington Crossing Stadium 22 ......Warrington...................PA 22

DALLAS/FT. WORTH, TX (DMA 623)

AMC ENTERTAINMENT

AMC Parks At Arlington 18...........Arlington ....TX 18
AMC Grand 24 ....Dallas ....TX 24
AMC Loews Cityplace 14 ....Dallas ....TX 14
AMC Northpark 15 ....Dallas ....TX 15
AMC Valley View 16 ....Dallas ....TX 16

Theatre	City	State	Screens
AMC Palace 9	Fort Worth	TX	9
AMC Sundance 11	Fort Worth	TX	11
AMC Grapevine 30	Grapevine	TX	30
AMC Irving Mall 14	Irving	TX	14
AMC Mesquite 30	Mesquite	TX	30

CINEMARK USA

Theatre	City	State	Screens
Cinemark Tinseltown 9	Arlington	TX	9
Cinemark Cinema 4	Athens	TX	4
Cinemark 14	Cedar Hill	TX	14
Cinemark Cinema 6	Cleburne	TX	6
Cinemark Cinema IV	Corsicana	TX	4
Cinemark 17	Dallas	TX	17
Cinemark 14	Denton	TX	14
Cinemark Hollywood USA Movies 15	Garland	TX	15
Cinemark Movies 16	Grand Prairie	TX	16
Cinemark Tinseltown Grapevine	Grapevine	TX	17
Cinemark Movies 14	Lancaster	TX	14
Cinemark 15 Vista Ridge Mall	Lewisville	TX	15
Cinemark Movies 8	Lewisville	TX	8
Cinemark 12 Mansfield	Mansfield	TX	12
Cinemark Movies 14	McKinney	TX	14
Cinemark Movies 8	N. Richland Hills	TX	8
Cinemark Movies 8	Paris	TX	8
Cinemark Legacy	Plano	TX	24
Cinemark Movies 10	Plano	TX	10
Cinemark Tinseltown Plano	Plano	TX	20
Cinemark 12 Rockwall	Rockwall	TX	12
Cinemark Cinema 6	Stephenville	TX	6

FOOTHILLS ENTERTAINMENT CO.

Theatre	City	State	Screens
4 Star Cinema	Kilgore	TX	6
Plaza Cinema 3	Henderson	TX	3
Brazos Cinema 3	Mineral Wells	TX	3
Jackson Cinema 3	Jacksonville	TX	3

HARKINS THEATRES

Theatre	City	State	Screens
Southlake Center 14/Cine Capri	Southlake	TX	14

HOLLYWOOD THEATRES

Theatre	City	State	Screens
Movies 14	Burleson	TX	14
MacArthur Marketplace 14	Irving	TX	16

LANDMARK THEATRES

Theatre	City	State	Screens
Inwood Theatre	Dallas	TX	3
Magnolia Theatre	Dallas	TX	5

NOVA CINETECH, INC.

Theatre	City	State	Screens
Nova Cinema	Terrell	TX	5

RAVE MOTION PICTURES

Theatre	City	State	Screens
RMP Ridgmar 13	Fort Worth	TX	13
RMP Hickory Creek 16	Hickory Creek	TX	16
RMP Northeast Mall 18	Hurst	TX	18

READING INTERNATIONAL, INC.

Theatre	City	State	Screens
Angelika Film Center & Café	Dallas	TX	8
Angelika Film Center & Café	Plano	TX	5

REGAL ENTERTAINMENT GROUP

Theatre	City	State	Screens
Galaxy Theatre Stadium 10	Dallas	TX	10
Keystone Park 16	Dallas	TX	16
Fossil Creek Stadium 11	Ft Worth	TX	11
UA Eastchase Market Stadium 9	Ft Worth	TX	9
Grand Prairie 10	Grand Prairie	TX	10

STARPLEX CINEMAS

Theatre	City	State	Screens
Forney Stadium 12	Forney	TX	12
Hulen Stadium 10	Fort Worth	TX	10
Irving Cinema 10	Irving	TX	10
Mesquite Cinema 10	Mesquite	TX	10

SAN FRANCISCO-OAKLAND-SAN JOSE, CA (DMA 807)

AMC ENTERTAINMENT

Theatre	City	State	Screens
AMC Bay Street 16	Emeryville	CA	16
AMC Loews Metreon 15 IMAX	San Francisco	CA	15
AMC Van Ness 14	San Francisco	CA	14
AMC Eastridge 15	San Jose	CA	15
AMC Saratoga 14	San Jose	CA	14
AMC Mercado 20	Santa Clara	CA	20

BRENDEN THEATRES

Theatre	City	State	Screens
Concord 14	Concord	CA	14
Pittsburg 16	Pittsburg	CA	16

CAMERA CINEMAS

Theatre	City	State	Screens
Camera 7 Pruneyard	Campbell	CA	7
Los Gatos	Los Gatos	CA	2
Camera 3/ComedySportz/Cafe Too!	San Jose	CA	3
Camera 12	San Jose	CA	12

CINELUX THEATRES

Theatre	City	State	Screens
CineLux Plaza Theatres	Campbell	CA	7
CineLux Almaden Cinema 5	San Jose	CA	5
CineLux Chabot Cinema	Castro Valley	CA	1
CineLux New Delta Cinema	Brentwood	CA	2
CineLux Tennant Station Stadium 11	Morgan Hill	CA	11

CINEMA WEST

Theatre	City	State	Screens
Angels Theatre	Angels Camp	CA	5
Clover Cinemas	Cloverdale	CA	4
Fairfax Theatre	Fairfax	CA	5
Fortuna Theatre	Fortuna	CA	6
Livermore Cinemas	Livermore	CA	13
Los Banos Cinemas	Los Banos	CA	6
Contra Costa Cinema	Martinez	CA	8
Boulevard Cinemas	Petaluma	CA	13
Sebastopol Cinemas	Sebastopol	CA	9
Sonoma Cinemas	Sonoma	CA	6
Tiburon Playhouse	Tiburon	CA	3
Noyo Theatre	Willits	CA	3

CINEMARK USA

Theatre	City	State	Screens
Century Cinema	Corte Madera	CA	1
Century 20 Daly City	Daly City	CA	20
Cinemark Blackhawk Movies 7	Danville	CA	7
Cinedome 8	Fremont	CA	8
Century Larkspur	Larkspur	CA	4
Cinéarts Sequoia	Mill Valley	CA	2
Century Cinema 16	Mountain View	CA	16
Cinedome 8	Napa	CA	8
Cinedome 7	Newark	CA	7
Century Rowland Plaza	Novato	CA	8
Cinéarts @ Palo Alto Square	Palo Alto	CA	2
Century 16 Downtown P. Hill	Pleasant Hill	CA	16
Cinéarts 5 @ Pleasant Hill	Pleasant Hill	CA	5
Century Park 12	Redwood City	CA	12
Redwood Downtown 20	Redwood City	CA	20
Century Hilltop 16	Richmond	CA	16
Century Tanforan 20	San Bruno	CA	20
Century 9 San Francisco Centre	San Francisco	CA	9
Cinéarts at The Empire	San Francisco	CA	3
Century 10 Berryessa	San Jose	CA	10
Century 24	San Jose	CA	1
Century 25	San Jose	CA	1
Century Capitol 16	San Jose	CA	16
Oakridge 20	San Jose	CA	20
Century 16 Bayfair Mall	San Leandro	CA	16
Century 12 San Mateo	San Mateo	CA	12
Century Northgate	San Rafael	CA	15
Century Regency	San Rafael	CA	6
Cinéarts Marin	Sausalito	CA	3
Century 25 Union Landing	Union City	CA	25
Vallejo 14	Vallejo	CA	14
Walnut Creek 14	Walnut Creek	CA	14

LANDMARK THEATRES

Theatre	City	State	Screens
Albany Twin	Albany	CA	2
Aquarius Theatre	Palo Alto	CA	2
Bridge Theatre	San Francisco	CA	1
California Theatre	Berkeley	CA	3
Clay Theatre	San Francisco	CA	1
Embarcadero Center Cinemas	San Francisco	CA	5
Guild Theatre	Menlo Park	CA	1
Lumiere Theatre	San Francisco	CA	3
Opera Plaza Cinema	San Francisco	CA	4
Piedmont Theatre	Oakland	CA	3
Shattuck Cinemas	Berkeley	CA	10

METROPOLITAN THEATRES

Theatre	City	State	Screens
Oaks Theatre	Berkeley	CA	2

PACIFIC THEATRES

Theatre	City	State	Screens
Paseo 14	Pasadena	CA	14

READING INTERNATIONAL, INC.

Theatre	City	State	Screens
Rohnert Park 16	Rohnert Park	CA	16

REGAL ENTERTAINMENT GROUP

Theatre	City	State	Screens
Deer Valley Stadium 16	Antioch	CA	16
UA East Hills 10	Bakersfield	CA	10
Berkeley 7	Berkley	CA	7
Hacienda Crossings Stadium 20/IMAX	Dublin	CA	21
Emery Bay Stadium 10	Emeryville	CA	10
Jack London Stadium 9	Oakland	CA	9
Stonestown Twin 2	San Francisco	CA	2
Crow Canyon Stadium 6	San Ramon	CA	6
Ukiah Stadium 6	Ukiah	CA	6

BOSTON, MA (DMA 506)

AMC ENTERTAINMENT

Theatre	City	State	Screens
AMC Loews Boston Common 19	Boston	MA	19
AMC Braintree 10	Braintree	MA	10
AMC Burlington 10	Burlington	MA	10
AMC Loews Harvard Square 5	Cambridge	MA	5
AMC Chestnut Hill 5	Chestnut Hill	MA	5
AMC Loews Liberty Tree Mall 20	Danvers	MA	20
AMC Framingham Premium 1	Framingham	MA	1
AMC Framinghm 15	Framingham	MA	15
AMC Tyngsboro 12	Tyngsboro	MA	12

BOSTON CULINARY GROUP

Theatre	City	State	Screens
East Bridgewater Cinemas	E. Bridgewater	MA	6
Edgartown Ent. Cinemas	Edgartown	MA	2
Sharon Cinemas	Sharon	MA	8
Gilford Cinemas 8	Gilford	NH	8
Kipling Cinemas	Brattleboro	VT	6

ENTERTAINEMNT CINEMAS

Theatre	City	State	Screens
Ent. Cinemas Edgartown 2	Edgartown	MA	2
Ent. Cinemas Leominster 10	Leominster	MA	10
Ent. Cinemas Stoughton Pub	Stoughton	MA	1
Ent. Cinemas Concord 6	Concord	NH	6
Ent. Cinemas S. Kingston 8	S. Kingston	RI	8
Ent. Cinemas Brattleboro 6	Brattleboro	VT	6
Ent. Cinemas W. Dover 3	W. Dover	VT	3

FLAGSHIP CINEMAS

Theatre	City	State	Screens
Flagship Cinema Derry 12	Derry	NH	12

LANDMARK THEATRES

Theatre	City	State	Screens
Embassy Cinema	Waltham	MA	6
Kendall Square Cinema	Cambridge	MA	9

NATIONAL AMUSEMENTS

Theatre	City	State	Screens
Circle Cinemas	Brookline	MA	7
Showcase Cinemas Dedham	Dedham	MA	12
Showcase Lawrence 1-6	Lawrence	MA	6
Showcase Cinemas Lawrence 7-14	Lawrence	MA	8
Showcase Cinemas Lowell	Lowell	MA	14
Showcase Cinemas Randolph	Randolph	MA	16
Showcase Cinemas Revere	Revere	MA	20
Showcase Cinemas Woburn	Woburn	MA	14
Blackstone Valley 14: Cinema de Lux	Millbury	MA	14
Showcase Cinemas Worcester N.	Worcester	MA	18

PATRIOT CINEMAS

Theatre	City	State	Screens
Patriot Cinemas, Hanover Mall	Hanover	MA	10
Patriot Cinemas, Loring Hall	Hingham	MA	1
Patriot Cinemas, The Mill Wharf Plz.	Scituate Harbor	MA	2
Patriot Cinemas, Cameo Theatre	S. Weymouth	MA	2

REGAL ENTERTAINMENT GROUP

Theatre	City	State	Screens
Bellingham Stadium 14	Bellingham	MA	14
Fenway Stadium 13	Boston	MA	13
Harwich 6	East Harwich	MA	6
Cape Cod Mall Stadium 12	Hyannis	MA	12
Independence Mall 14	Kingston	MA	14
Solomon Pond Stadium 15	Marlborough	MA	15
Mashpee Commons 6	Mashpee	MA	6
Nickelodeon 5	North Falmouth	MA	5
Westborough Stadium 12	Westborough	MA	12
Concord 10	Concord	NH	10
Hooksett 8	Hooksett	NH	8
Manchester 9	Manchester	NH	9
Fox Run 15	Newington	NH	12
Portsmouth 5	Portsmouth	NH	5

SPINELLI CINEMAS

Theatre	City	State	Screens
Barrington Station Cinema 6	Barrington	NH	6
Strand Theatre	Dover	NH	3
Plymouth Theatre	Plymouth	NH	2
Lilac Mall Cinema 4	Rochester	NH	4

ATLANTA, GA (DMA 524)

ALLIANCE ENTERTAINMENT

Theatre	City	State	Screens
McDonough Great Escape 16	McDonough	GA	16

AMC ENTERTAINMENT

Theatre	City	State	Screens
AMC Mansell 14	Alpharetta	GA	14
AMC Fork & Screen Buckhead	Atlanta	GA	6
AMC Magic Johnson Greenbriar Mall 12	Atlanta	GA	12
AMC Parkway Pointe 15	Atlanta	GA	15
AMC Phipps Plaza 14	Atlanta	GA	14
AMC Avenue Forsythe	Cumming	GA	12
AMC North Dekalb 16	Decatur	GA	6
AMC Barrett Commons 24	Kennesaw	GA	24
AMC Colonial 18	Lawrenceville	GA	18
AMC Discover Mills 18	Lawrenceville	GA	18
AMC Stonecrest 16	Lithonia	GA	16
AMC Southlake 24	Morrow	GA	24

CARMIKE CINEMAS

Theatre	City	State	Screens
Carmike	Athens	GA	12
Martin	Calhoun	GA	3
Riverstone	Canton	GA	15
Carmike	Cartersville	GA	12
Conyers Crossing	Conyers	GA	16
Carmike	Newnan	GA	10
Carmike	Snellville	GA	12

CINEMARK USA

Theatre	City	State	Screens
Cinemark Movies 10	Fayetteville	GA	10
Cinemark Tinseltown	Fayetteville	GA	17

GEORGIA THEATRE CO.

Theatre	City	State	Screens
Beechwood Stadium Cinemas 11	Athens	GA	11
Georgia Square Value Cinemas 5	Athens	GA	5
Carrollton Stadium Cinemas 10	Carrollton	GA	10
Dawson 400 Stadium Cinemas 10	Dawsonville	GA	10
Venture Value Cinemas 12	Duluth	GA	12
Hollywood Stadium Cinemas 15	Gainesville	GA	15
Griffin Stadium Cinemas 10	Griffin	GA	10
Town Center Value Cinemas 10	Lawrenceville	GA	10
Merchant's Walk Stadium Cinemas 12	Marietta	GA	12
Park 12 Cobb Stadium Cinemas 12	Marietta	GA	12
Cherokee Stadium Cinemas 16	Woodstock	GA	16

LANDMARK THEATRES

Theatre	City	State	Screens
Midtown Art Cinema	Atlanta	GA	8

NCG (NEIGHBORHOOD CINEMAS GROUP)

Theatre	City	State	Screens
NCG Acworth Cinema	Acworth	GA	12

NOVA CINETECH, INC.

Theatre	City	State	Screens
Nova Cinema	Commerce	GA	6

REGAL ENTERTAINMENT GROUP

Theatre	City	State	Screens
Atlantic Station Stadium 16	Atlanta	GA	16
Perimeter Pointe 10	Atlanta	GA	10
Tara Cinemas 4	Atlanta	GA	4
Regal Stadium 22 @ Austell	Austell	GA	22
Mall of Georgia Stadium 20 Plus IMAX	Buford	GA	21
Hollywood Stadium 24 @ N. I-85	Chamblee	GA	24
Arbor Place Stadium 18	Douglasville	GA	18
Medlock Crossing Stadium 18	Duluth	GA	18
Town Center Stadium 16	Kennesaw	GA	16
Georgian 14	Newnan	GA	14
Snellville Oaks Stadium 14	Snellville	GA	14
Bonita Lakes 9	Meridian	MS	9

WASHINGTON, DC (DMA 511)

AMC ENTERTAINMENT

Theatre	City	State	Screens
AMC Loews Dupont Circle 5	Washington	DC	5
AMC Loews Georgetown 14	Washington	DC	14
AMC Loews Uptown 1	Washington	DC	1
AMC Mazza Gallerie 7	Washington	DC	7
AMC Loews Center Park 8	Beltsville	MD	8
AMC Loews Rio Cinemas 18	Gaithersburg	MD	18
AMC Loews White Flint 5	Kensington	MD	5
AMC Magic Johnson Capital Center 12	Largo	MD	12
AMC Country Club Mall 6	Lavale	MD	6
AMC Loews Lexington Park 6	Lexington Park	MD	6
AMC St Charles Town Center 9	Waldorf	MD	9
AMC Hoffman 22	Alexandria	VA	22
AMC Courthouse 8	Arlington	VA	8
AMC Loews Shirlington 7	Arlington	VA	7
AMC Tysons Corner 16	McLean	VA	16
AMC Springfld 10	Springfield	VA	10
AMC Potomac 18	Woodbridge	VA	18

CARMIKE CINEMAS

Theatre	City	State	Screens
Cinema	Chambersburg	PA	7
Apple Blossom	Winchester	VA	6
Cinema Center	Winchester	VA	6

LANDMARK THEATRES

Theatre	City	State	Screens
E- Street Cinema	Washington	DC	8
Bethesda Row Cinema	Bethesda	MD	8
Harbor East	Baltimore	MD	7

MARQUEE CINEMAS

Theatre	City	State	Screens
Southpoint Cinemas	Fredericksburg	VA	9

NATIONAL AMUSEMENTS

Theatre	City	State	Screens
Fairfax Corner 14: Cinema de Lux	Fairfax	VA	14
Centreville Multiplex	Centerville	VA	12
Lee Highway Multiplex	Merrifield	VA	14
Reston Town Center Multiplex	Reston	VA	13

PHOENIX ADLABS THEATRES MANAGEMENT, LLC

Theatre	City	State	Screens
Union Station 9	Washington	DC	9
Laurel 6 Cinema	Laurel	MD	6
Worldgate 9 Theatres	Herndon	VA	9
Loehmann's Twin Cinema	Falls Church	VA	2

R/C THEATRES

Theatre	City	State	Screens
Frostburg Cinemas 3	Frostburg	MD	3
Apple Blossom Movies 16	Winchester	VA	16

REGAL ENTERTAINMENT GROUP

Theatre	City	State	Screens
Gallery Place Stadium 14	Washington	DC	14
Bowie Stadium 14	Bowie	MD	14
Westview Stadium 16	Frederick	MD	16
Germantown Stadium 14	Germantown	MD	14
Valley Mall Stadium 16	Hagerstown	MD	16
Royale 14	Hyattsville	MD	14
Rockville Center Stadium 13	Rockville	MD	13
Majestic 20	Silver Spring	MD	20

Potomac Yard Stadium 16 ... Alexandria ... VA ... 16
Kingstowne 16 ... Alexandria ... VA ... 16
Ballston Common Stadium 12 ... Arlington ... VA ... 12
Fairfax Towne Center 10 ... Fairfax ... VA ... 10
Fredericksburg 15 ... Fredericksburg ... VA ... 15
Manassas Stadium 14 ... Manassas ... VA ... 14
Aquia 10 ... Stafford ... VA ... 10
Countryside Stadium 20 ... Sterling ... VA ... 20
Martinsburg Stadium 10 ... Martinsburg ... WV ... 10

HOUSTON, TX (DMA 618)

ALAMO DRAFTHOUSE CINEMA
Alamo West Oaks ... Houston ... TX ... 6
Alamo Mason Park ... Katy ... TX ... 7

AMC ENTERTAINMENT
AMC Gulf Pointe 30 ... Houston ... TX ... 30
AMC Studio 30 Ho ... Houston ... TX ... 30
AMC Willowbrook 24 ... Houston ... TX ... 24
AMC Deerbrook 24 ... Humble ... TX ... 24
AMC Katy Mill 20 ... Katy ... TX ... 20
AMC Loews Spring 10 ... Spring ... TX ... 10
AMC Loews Fountains 18 ... Stafford ... TX ... 18
AMC First Colony 24 ... Sugar Land ... TX ... 24

CINEMARK USA
Cinemark Memorial City ... Houston ... TX ... 16
Cinemark Tinseltown ... Houston ... TX ... 16
Cinemark Tinseltown USA ... Jacinto City ... TX ... 17
Cinemark 19 ... Katy ... TX ... 19
Cinemark Hollywood Movies 20 ... Pasadena ... TX ... 20
Cinemark at Pearland ... Pearland ... TX ... 12
Cinemark Rosenburg 12 ... Rosenburg ... TX ... 12
Cinemark Movies 12 ... Texas City ... TX ... 12
Cinemark at Market Street ... The Woodlands ... TX ... 5
Cinemark Tinseltown 17 ... The Woodlands ... TX ... 17
Cinemark 18 ... Webster ... TX ... 18

LANDMARK THEATRES
River Oaks Theatre ... Houston ... TX ... 3

RAVE MOTION PICTURES
RMP Houston 15 ... Houston ... TX ... 15

READING INTERNATIONAL, INC.
Angelika Film Center & Café ... Houston ... TX ... 8

REGAL ENTERTAINMENT GROUP
Greenway Grand Palace Stadium 24 ... Houston ... TX ... 24
Houston Marq*E. Stadium 23 ... Houston ... TX ... 23

SANTIKOS THEATRES
Santikos Silverado 19 IMAX ... Tomball ... TX ... 19

SOUTHERN THEATRES, LLC
The Grand 14 ... Conroe ... TX ... 14

STARPLEX CINEMAS
Brazos Stadium 14 ... Lake Jackson ... TX ... 14

DETROIT, MI (DMA 505)

AMC ENTERTAINMENT
AMC Star Great Lakes 25 ... Auburn Hills ... MI ... 25
AMC Star Gratiot 21 ... Clinton Twp. ... MI ... 21
AMC Star Fairlane 21 ... Dearborn ... MI ... 21
AMC Laurel Park 10 ... Livonia ... MI ... 10
AMC Livonia 20 ... Livonia ... MI ... 20
AMC Star John R 15 ... Madison Heights ... MI ... 15
AMC Star Rochester Hills 10 ... Rochester Hills ... MI ... 10
AMC Star Southfield 20 ... Southfield ... MI ... 20
AMC Forum 30 ... Sterling Heights ... MI ... 30
AMC Star Taylor 10 ... Taylor ... MI ... 10

CARMIKE CINEMAS
Birchwood Cinema ... Fort Gratiot ... MI ... 10

CINEMARK USA
Cinemark Movies 16 ... Warren ... MI ... 16

GOODRICH QUALITY THEATRES
Quality 16 ... Ann Arbor ... MI ... 16
Canton 7 ... Canton ... MI ... 7
Oxford 7 ... Oxford ... MI ... 7
Krafft 8 ... Port Huron ... MI ... 8

LANDMARK THEATRES
Main Art Theatre ... Royal Oak ... MI ... 3
Maple 3 ... Bloomfield ... MI ... 3

MJR THEATRES
Allen Park Cinema ... Allen Park ... MI ... 5
Brighton Town Square Cinema ... Brighton ... MI ... 20
Chesterfield Crossing ... Chesterfield ... MI ... 16
Partridge Creek Cinema 14 ... Clinton Township ... MI ... 14
Southgate Cinemas ... Southgate ... MI ... 20
Market Place Cinemas ... Sterling Heights ... MI ... 20
Waterford Cinema ... Waterford ... MI ... 16

NATIONAL AMUSEMENTS
Showcase Ann Arbor ... Ypsilanti ... MI ... 20

NEIGHBORHOOD CINEMA
Lapeer Cinemas ... Lapeer ... MI ... 8

PHOENIX ADLABS THEATRE MANAGEMENT, INC.
Novi Town Center 8 ... Novi ... MI ... 8

REGAL ENTERTAINMENT GROUP
Commerce Township Stadium 14 ... Walled Lake ... MI ... 14

PHOENIX, AR (DMA 753)

AMC ENTERTAINMENT
AMC Arrowhead 14 ... Glendale ... AZ ... 14
AMC Westgate 20 ... Glendale ... AZ ... 20
AMC Mesa Grand 24 ... Mesa ... AZ ... 24
AMC Ahwatukee 24 ... Phoenix ... AZ ... 24
AMC Arizona Center 24 ... Phoenix ... AZ ... 24
AMC Deer Valley 30 IMAX ... Phoenix ... AZ ... 30
AMC Desert Ridge 18 ... Phoenix ... AZ ... 18
AMC Esplanade 14 ... Phoenix ... AZ ... 14
AMC Cupertino Square 16 ... Cupertino ... CA ... 16

CINEMARK USA
Cinemark Mesa 16 ... Mesa ... AZ ... 16

DICKINSON THEATRES, INC.
Gateway 12 IMAX ... Mesa ... AZ ... 12
Palm Valley 14 Theatre ... Palm Valley ... AZ ... 14

HARKINS THEATRES
Gateway Pavilions 18 ... Avondale ... AZ ... 18
Casa Grande 14 ... Casa Grande ... AZ ... 14
Chandler Fashion 20 ... Chandler ... AZ ... 20
Chandler Crossroads 12 ... Chandler ... AZ ... 12
Flagstaff 11 ... Flagstaff ... AZ ... 11
Santan Village 16 ... Gilbert ... AZ ... 16
Fiesta 5 ... Mesa ... AZ ... 5
Superstition Springs 25 ... Mesa ... AZ ... 25
Arrowhead 18 ... Peoria ... AZ ... 18
Park West 14 ... Peoria ... AZ ... 14
Arcadia 8 ... Phoenix ... AZ ... 8
Christown 14 ... Phoenix ... AZ ... 14
Metrocenter 12 ... Phoenix ... AZ ... 12
Norterra 14 ... Phoenix ... AZ ... 14
North Valley 16 ... Phoenix ... AZ ... 16
Scottsdale 101/Cine Capri ... Phoenix ... AZ ... 14
Tucson Spectrum 18 ... Tucson ... AZ ... 18
Prescott Valley 14 ... Prescott Valley ... AZ ... 14
Camelview 5 ... Scottsdale ... AZ ... 5
Fashion Square 7 ... Scottsdale ... AZ ... 7
Shea 14 ... Scottsdale ... AZ ... 14
Sedona 6 ... Sedona ... AZ ... 6
Arizona Mills 24 ... Tempe ... AZ ... 24
Centerpoint 11 ... Tempe ... AZ ... 11
Tempe Marketplace 16 ... Tempe ... AZ ... 16
Valley Art Theatre ... Tempe ... AZ ... 1

HOLLYWOOD THEATERS
Gilbert Stadium Cinemas ... Gilbert ... AZ ... 14

REGAL ENTERTAINMENT GROUP
Pavilions 11 ... Scottsdale ... AZ ... 11
Sonora Village 10 ... Scottsdale ... AZ ... 10

WESTATES THEATRES
Page Mesa Theatre ... Page ... AZ ... 1

TAMPA-ST. PETERSBURG, FL (DMA 539)

AMC ENTERTAINMENT
AMC Regency 20 ... Brandon ... FL ... 20
AMC Tri City 8 ... Clearwater ... FL ... 8
AMC Woodland Square 20 ... Oldsmar ... FL ... 20
AMC Tyrone 6 ... Saint Petersburg ... FL ... 6
AMC Sarasota 12 ... Sarasota ... FL ... 12
AMC Veterans 24 ... Tampa ... FL ... 24
AMC Westshore 14 ... Tampa ... FL ... 14

CARMIKE CINEMAS
Royal Palm ... Bradenton ... FL ... 20
Palm Cinema ... Lakeland ... FL ... 3
Lakeshore ... Sebring ... FL ... 8

COBB THEATRES
Lakeside Village 18 Cinemas ... Lakeland ... FL ... 18
Merritt Square 16 ... Merritt Island ... FL ... 16
Grand 10 Cinemas ... Winter Haven ... FL ... 10

DICKINSON THEATRES, INC.
Lakeland Sq. 10 Cinemas ... N Lakeland ... FL ... 10

MUVICO THEATRES
Muvico Palm Harbor 10 ... Palm Harbor ... FL ... 10
Muvico Baywalk 20 ... St. Petersburg ... FL ... 20
Muvico Centro Ybor 20 ... Tampa ... FL ... 20
Muvico Starlight 20 ... Tampa ... FL ... 20

REGAL ENTERTAINMENT GROUP

Oakmont 8	Bradenton	FL	8
Crystal River Mall 9	Crystal River	FL	9
Citrus Cinemas 6	Inverness	FL	6
Eagle Ridge Mall 12	Lake Wales	FL	12
Largo Mall 8	Largo	FL	8
Park Place Stadium 16	Pinellas Park	FL	16
Hollywood 18, Port Richey	Port Richey	FL	18
Hollywood Stadium 20	Sarasota	FL	20
Citrus Park Stadium 20	Tampa	FL	20

SEATTLE-TACOMA, WA (DMA 819)

AMC ENTERTAINMENT

AMC Loews Factoria 8	Bellevue	WA	8
AMC Loews Cascade Mall 14	Burlington	WA	14
AMC Kent Station 14	Kent	WA	14
AMC Loews Lakewood Mall 12	Lakewood	WA	12
AMC Loews Alderwood Mall 16	Lynwood	WA	16
AMC Loews Redmond Town Center 8	Redmond	WA	8
AMC Renton Village 8	Renton	WA	8
AMC Cinerama 1	Seattle	WA	1
AMC Loews Oak Tree 6	Seattle	WA	6
AMC Loews Uptown 3	Seattle	WA	3
AMC Pacific Place 11	Seattle	WA	11
AMC Kitsap 8	Silverdale	WA	8
AMC Narrows 8	Tacoma	WA	8
AMC Southcenter	Tukwila	WA	16
AMC Loews Woodinville 12	Woodinville	WA	12

CINEMARK USA, INC.

Century Federal Way	Federal Way	WA	16
Century Olympia	Olympia	WA	14

COMMING ATTRACTIONS

SouthShore Mall Cinemas	Aberdeen	WA	10
Midway Cinema	Chehalis	WA	10

GALAXY THEATRES

Galaxy Uptown	Gig Harbor	WA	10
Monroe 12	Monroe	WA	12
Galaxy 6	Tacoma	WA	6

LANDMARK THEATRES

Crest Cinema Center	Seattle	WA	4
Egyptian Theatre	Seattle	WA	1
Guild 45th Theatre	Seattle	WA	2
Harvard Exit Theatre	Seattle	WA	2
Metro Cinemas	Seattle	WA	10
Neptune Theatre	Seattle	WA	1
Seven Gables Theatre	Seattle	WA	1
Varsity Theater	Seattle	WA	3

REGAL ENTERTAINMENT GROUP

Auburn Stadium 17 Theatres	Auburn	WA	17
Crossroads 8 Cinema	Bellevue	WA	8
Bellis Fair 6 Cinema	Bellingham	WA	6
Sehome 3 Cinemas	Bellingham	WA	3
Sunset Square Cinema 6	Bellingham	WA	6
Tall Firs 10	Bonneylake	WA	10
Everett Stadium 16	Everett	WA	16
Issaquah 9 Theatre	Issaquah	WA	9
Martin Village Stadium 16	Lacey	WA	16
Lakewood Cinema Stadium 15	Lakewood	WA	15
Alderwood 7 Theatres	Lynwood	WA	7
Marysville Cinema 14	Marysville	WA	14
Mount Lake 9 Theatre	Mt Lake Terrace	WA	9
South Sound Cinema 10	Port Orchard	WA	10
Poulsbo Stadium 10	Poulsbo	WA	10
Longston Place Stadium 14	Puyallup	WA	14
South Hill Cinema 6	Puyallup	WA	6
Bella Botega Stadium 11 Cinema	Redmond	WA	11
East Valley Stadium 13 Cinema	Renton	WA	13
Silverdale 4 Theatres	Silverdale	WA	4
Parkway Plaza Stadium 12	Tukwila	WA	12
Meridian 16	Seattle	WA	16

MINNEAPOLIS-ST. PAUL, MN (DMA 613)

AMC ENTERTAINMENT

AMC Mall Of America 14	Bloomington	MN	14
AMC Eden Prairie 18	Eden Prairie	MN	18
AMC Southdale 16	Edina	MN	16
AMC Arbor Lakes 16	Maple Grove	MN	16
AMC Rosedale 14	Roseville	MN	14

CARMIKE CINEMAS

Carmike	Apple Valley	MN	15
Oakdale	Oakdale	MN	20
Kandi	Willmar	MN	6

CINEMA ENTERTAINMENT CORP.

Amigo 9	Bemidji	MN	9
Cinema 6	Faribault	MN	6
Marshall 6	Marshall	MN	6
Hudson 12	Hudson	WI	12
Lake 7	Rice Lake	WI	7

CINEMAGIC THEATRES

Atlantis 15	Burnsville	MN	15
Century 9 Theatres	Hutchinson	MN	9
Metropolitan 15	St. Michael	MN	15
CineMagic 5	St. Peter	MN	5
CineMagic Stadium 7 Theatres	Menomonie	WI	7

EVERGREEN ENTERTAINMENT

Northwoods Cinema 10	Owatonna	MN	10
Evergreen Cinema 8	Red Wing	MN	8
Falls Cinema 8	St. Croix Falls	WI	8

KERASOTES SHOWPLACE THEATRES

ShowPlace 16 Coon Rapids	Coon Rapids	MN	16
ShowPlace 16	Inver Grove Hts.	MN	16
Block E Stadium15	Minneapolis	MN	15

LANDMARK THEATRES

Edina Cinema	Edina	MN	4
Lagoon Cinema	Minneapolis	MN	5
Uptown Theatre	Minneapolis	MN	1

MANN MINNESOTA

Movies 10 at Westgate	Baxter	MN	10
Champlin Cinema 14	Champlin	MN	14
Cottage View Drive-In	Cottage Grove	MN	1
Hopkins Cinema 6	Hopkins	MN	6
Maple Grove Cinema 10	Maple Grove	MN	10
Plymouth Cinema 12	Plymouth	MN	12
St. Louis Park Cinema	St. Louis Park	MN	6
Grandview 1 & 2 Theatres	St. Paul	MN	2
Highland 1 & 2 Theatres	St. Paul	MN	2

MARCUS THEATRES

Marcus Cinema Elk River	Elk River	MN	17
Marcus Cinema Hastings	Hastings	MN	9
Marcus Cinema Oakdale	Oakdale	MN	17
Marcus Cinema Rosemount	Rosemount	MN	8
Marcus Cinema Shakopee	Shakopee	MN	11
Parkwood	Waite Park	MN	18

MULLER FAMILY THEATRES

Delano 5 Theatre	Delano	MN	5
East Bethel 10 Theatre	East Bethel	MN	10
Lakeville 21 Theatre	Lakeville	MN	21
Monticello 15 Theatre	Monticello	MN	15
WillowCreek 12 Theatre	Plymouth	MN	12
Waconia 6 Theatre	Waconia	MN	6
White Bear Township 17 Theatre	White Bear Twnshp.	MN	17
Rogers 18 Theatre	Rogers	MN	18

REGAL ENTERTAINMENT GROUP

Eagan Stadium 16	Eagan	MN	16
Brooklyn Center Stadium 20	Minneapolis	MN	20

MIAMI-FT. LAUDERDALE, FL (DMA 528)

AMC ENTERTAINMENT

AMC Aventura 24	Aventura	FL	24
AMC Cocowalk 16	Coconut Grove	FL	16
AMC Ridge Plaza 8	Davie	FL	8
AMC Coral Ridge10	Fort Lauderdale	FL	10
AMC Sheridan 12	Hollywood	FL	12
AMC Mall Of Americas 14	Miami	FL	14
AMC Sunset Place 24	South Miami	FL	24

COBB THEATRES

Cinebistro at Dolphin Mall	Miami	FL	5
Dolphin 19 Cinemas	Miami	FL	19
Miami Lakes 17 Cinemas	Miami Lakes	FL	17
Hialeah Grand 18	Miami Lakes	FL	18

FLAGSHIP CINEMAS

Flagship Cinema Homestead 14	Homestead	FL	14

MUVICO THEATRES

Muvico Paradise 24	Davie	FL	24
Muvico Hialeah 14	Hialeah	FL	14
Muvico Pompano 18	Pompano Beach	FL	18

REGAL ENTERTAINMENT GROUP

Magnolia Place Stadium 16	Coral Springs	FL	16
Cypress Creek Station Stadium 16	Ft. Lauderdale	FL	16
Oakwood 18	Hollywood	FL	18
Cinema Key West 6	Key West	FL	6
The Falls 12	Miami	FL	12
Kendall Village Stadium 16	Miami	FL	16
Palace 18	Miami	FL	18
South Beach Stadium 18	Miami Beach	FL	18
Westfork Stadium 13	Pembroke Pines	FL	13
Sawgrass Stadium 23	Sunrise	FL	23

CLEVELAND, OH (DMA 510)

ALLIANCE ENTERTAINMENT			
Massillon Great Escape 12	Massillon	OH	12

AMC ENTERTAINMENT			
AMC West Market Plaza 7	Akron	OH	7
AMC Ridge Park Square 8	Brooklyn	OH	8
AMC Plaza Chapel 8	Cuyahoga Falls	OH	8
AMC Magic Johnson Randall Pk Mall 12	North Randall	OH	12
AMC Loews Richmond Town Square 20	Richmond Hghts	OH	20
AMC Westwood 6	Rocky River	OH	6

ATLAS CINEMAS			
Atlas Lakeshore 7	Euclid	OH	7
Atlas Cinemas Diamond Ctr. 16	Mentor	OH	16
Atlas Great Lakes Stadium 16	Mentor	OH	16

CARMIKE CINEMAS			
Ashtabula Mall	Ashtabula	OH	6
Plaza	Sandusky	OH	8

CINEMARK USA			
Cinemark Carnation Cinema 5	Alliance	OH	5
Cinemark Barington Town Center 10	Aurora	OH	10
Cinemark at Macedonia	Macedonia	OH	15
Cinemark Springfield Sq. Cinema 10	Mansfield	OH	10
Cinemark Movies 10	North Canton	OH	10
Cinemark Tinseltown U.S.A.	North Canton	OH	15
Cinemark Ontario	Ontario	OH	14
Cinemark Movies 10	Sandusky	OH	10
Cinemark Strongsville	Strongsville	OH	14
Cinemark at Valley View	Valley View	OH	24
Cinemark Movies 10	Willoughby Hills	OH	10
Cinemark Movies 10	Wooster	OH	10

CLEVELAND CINEMAS			
Cedar Lee Theatre	Cleveland Heights	OH	6
Shaker Square Cinemas	Cleveland	OH	6
Tower City Cinemas	Cleveland	OH	11
Chagrin Cinemas	Chagrin Falls	OH	14
Plaza Cinemas at Chapel Hill	Cuyahoga Falls	OH	8
Solon Cinemas	Solon	OH	16

REGAL ENTERTAINMENT GROUP			
Independence Stadium 10	Akron	OH	10
Interstate Park Cinema Stadium 18	Akron	OH	18
Montrose Movies Stadium 12	Akron	OH	12
Severance Town Center Stadium 14	Cleveland Heights	OH	14
Cobblestone Square Stadium 20	Elyria	OH	20
Hudson Cinema 10	Hudson	OH	10
Mayfield Heights 10	Mayfield Heights	OH	10
Medina Stadium 16	Medina	OH	16
New Towne Cinema 8	New Philadelphia	OH	8
Crocker Park Stadium 16	Westlake	OH	16
Willoughby Commons Stadium 16	Willoughby	OH	16
Richmond Town Center 20	Richmond Heights	OH	20

DENVER, CO (DMA 751)

AMC ENTERTAINMENT			
AMC Flatiron 14	Broomfield	CO	14
AMC Highlands 24	Highlands Ranch	CO	24
AMC Orchard 12	Westminster	CO	12

BOW TIE CINEMAS			
Movieland 7	Basalt	CO	7

CARMIKE CINEMAS			
Carmike	Fort Collins	CO	10
Mall	Glenwood Springs	CO	3
Carmike	Greeley	CO	5
Chief Plaza	Steamboat Springs	CO	4

CINEMARK USA			
Century Aurora	Aurora	CO	16
Century Boulder	Boulder	CO	16
Cinemark Fort Collins	Fort Collins	CO	16
Cinemark Greeley Mall	Greeley	CO	12
Century 16 Bel Mar	Lakewood	CO	16

HARKINS THEATRES			
Northfield 18/Cine Capri	Denver	CO	18

KERASOTES SHOWPLACE THEATRES			
Olde Town 14	Arvada	CO	14
Arapahoe Crossing 16	Aurora	CO	16
Southlands 16	Aurora	CO	16
Brighton Pavalions 12	Brighton	CO	12
Castle Rock Stadium 12	Castle Rock	CO	12
Cherry Creek 8	Denver	CO	8
Bergen Park 7	Evergreen	CO	7
Cinema Saver 6	Ft. Collins	CO	6
Bowles Crossing 12	Littleton	CO	12
Colony Square 12	Louisville	CO	12
20 Mile Village 10	Parker	CO	10

LANDMARK THEATRES			
Chez Artiste	Denver	CO	3
Esquire Theatre	Denver	CO	2
Greenwood Village	Greenwood Village	CO	6
Mayan Theatre	Denver	CO	3

METROPOLITAN THEATRES			
Isis Theatre	Aspen	CO	4
MetroLux 14 Theatre	Loveland	CO	14
Wildhorse 6 Stadium Cinemas	Steamboat Springs	CO	6

REGAL ENTERTAINMENT GROUP			
Colorado Center 9	Denver	CO	9
Continental 6	Denver	CO	6
Denver Pavilions 15	Denver	CO	15
Greenwood Plaza 12	Englewood	CO	12
West Village Stadium 12	Golden	CO	12
Colorado Mills Stadium 16	Lakewood	CO	16
Meadows 12	Littleton	CO	12
Twin Peaks Mall 10	Longmont	CO	10

STARPLEX CINEMAS			
Tiffany Plaza Movies 6	Denver	CO	6

TRANS LUX			
Trans-Lux Skyline Cinema	Dillon	CO	8
Trans-Lux Metrolux 14	Loveland	CO	14
Trans-Lux Fox Theatre	Laramie	WY	6

ORLANDO-DAYTONA BEACH, FL (DMA 534)

AMC ENTERTAINMENT			
AMC Altamonte 18	Altamonte Springs	FL	18
AMC Celebration 2	Celebration	FL	2
AMC Pleasure Island 24	Lake Buena Vista	FL	24
AMC Lakes Square 12	Leesburg	FL	12
AMC West Oaks 14	Ocoee	FL	14
AMC Loews Universal Cineplex 20	Orlando	FL	20

CINEMARK USA			
Cinemark 20 at Festival Bay	Orlando	FL	20

EPIC THEATRES			
Victoria Square 6	DeLand	FL	6
Beacon 12 Theatre	New Smyrna Bch.	FL	12

NOVA CINEMAS			
Nova Cinemas at Palm Bay W.	Palm Bay	FL	10

R/C THEATRES			
OceanWalk 10	Daytona Beach	FL	10

RAVE MOTION PICTURES			
RMP Melbourne 16	Melbourne	FL	16

REGAL ENTERTAINMENT GROUP			
The Loop Stadium 16	Kissimmee	FL	16
Hollywood Stadium 16	Ocala	FL	16
Marketplace 8	Orange City	FL	8
Waterford Lakes Stadium 20	Orlando	FL	20
Ormond Beach Cinema 12	Ormond Beach	FL	12
Oviedo Marketplace Stadium 22	Oviedo	FL	22
Port Orange 6	Port Orange	FL	6
Seminole Towne Center	Sanford	FL	10
Searstown Mall 10	Titusville	FL	10
Winter Park Village Stadium 20	Winter Park	FL	20

SOUTHERN THEATRES, LLC			
AmStar Stadium 12	Lake Mary	FL	12

SACRAMENTO, CA (DMA 862)

BRENDEN THEATRES			
Modesto 18	Modesto	CA	18
Vacaville 16	Vacaville	CA	16

CINEMARK USA			
Century Laguna 16	Elk Grove	CA	16
Century 14	Folsom	CA	14
Century Roseville 14	Roseville	CA	14
Century 16 Greenback Lane	Sacramento	CA	16
Downtown Plaza 7	Sacramento	CA	7
Cinemark Movies 14	Tracy	CA	14
Cinemark Movies 5	Woodland	CA	5
Cinemark Movies 8	Yuba City	CA	8

GALAXY THEATRES, LLC			
Riverbank 12	Riverbank	CA	12

KERASOTES SHOWPLACE THEATRES, LLC			
Showplace 16	Manteca	CA	16

READING INTERNATIONAL, INC.			
Tower Theatre	Sacramento	CA	3

REGAL ENTERTAINMENT GROUP			
Auburn Stadium 10	Auburn	CA	10
Sunrise 4	Citrus Heights	CA	4
Davis Holiday 6	Davis	CA	6

Davis Stadium 5 ... Davis ... CA ... 5
El Dorado Hills Stadium 14 ... El Dorado Hills ... CA ... 14
Fairfield Stadium 16 ... Fairfield ... CA ... 16
Jackson Cinema 4 ... Jackson ... CA ... 4
Modesto Stadium 10 ... Modesto ... CA ... 10
Placerville Stadium 8 ... Placerville ... CA ... 8
Olympus Pointe 12 ... Roseville ... CA ... 12
Arden Fair 6 ... Sacramento ... CA ... 6
Laguna Village 12 ... Sacramento ... CA ... 12
Natomas Marketplace Stadium 16 ... Sacramento ... CA ... 16
Sonora Stadium 10 ... Sonora ... CA ... 10
Stockton City Centre Stadium 16 ... Stockton ... CA ... 16
Stockton Holiday Cinema 8 ... Stockton ... CA ... 8
Turlock Stadium 14 ... Turlock ... CA ... 14

ST. LOUIS, MO (DMA 609)

ALLIANCE ENTERTAINMENT

O'Fallon Great Escape 14 ... O'Fallon ... MO ... 14

AMC ENTERTAINMENT

AMC Chesterfield 14 ... Chesterfield ... MO ... 14
AMC Creve Coeur 12 ... Creve Coeur ... MO ... 12
AMC West Olive 16 ... Creve Coeur ... MO ... 16
AMC Crestwood Plaza 10 ... Saint Louis ... MO ... 10
AMC Esquire 7 ... Saint Louis ... MO ... 7

B & B THEATRES

Festus Eight ... Festus ... MO ... 8
Warrenton Cinema 8 ... Warrenton ... MO ... 8
Downtown Cinema 8 ... Kirksville ... MO ... 8
Sullivan Cinema 6 ... Sullivan ... MO ... 6
Great 8 ... Union ... MO ... 8

KERASOTES SHOWPLACE THEATRES

Plaza ... Centralia ... IL ... 5
Eastgate Cinema ... East Alton ... IL ... 6
ShowPlace 12 ... Edwardsville ... IL ... 12
Lory Theatre ... Highland ... IL ... 2
Stadium Theatre ... Jerseyville ... IL ... 2
ShowPlace 4 ... Farmington ... MO ... 4
Movies ... Park Hills ... MO ... 2

LANDMARK THEATRES

Plaza Frontenac ... St. Louis ... MO ... 6
Tivoli Theatre ... Universal City ... MO ... 3

REGAL ENTERTAINMENT GROUP

St. Louis Mills Stadium 18 ... Hazelwood ... MO ... 18

WEHRENBERG THEATRES

Wehrenberg St. Clair Cine 10 ... Fairview Heights ... IL ... 10
Wehrenberg O'Fallon 15 Cine ... O'Fallon ... IL ... 15
Wehrenberg Jamestown 14 Cine ... Florissant ... MO ... 14
Wehrenberg Ronnies 20 Cine ... Sappington ... MO ... 20
Wehrenberg St. Charles 18 Cine ... St. Charles ... MO ... 18
Wehrenberg Arnold 14 Cine ... St. Louis ... MO ... 14
Wehrenberg Des Peres 14 Cine ... St. Louis ... MO ... 14
Wehrenberg Galaxy 14 Cine ... St. Louis ... MO ... 14
Wehrenberg Mid Rivers 14 Cine ... St. Louis ... MO ... 14

PORTLAND, OR (DMA 820)

CINEMARK USA

Century 16 Beaver Hills Crossing ... Beaverton ... OR ... 16
Century 16 Eastport Plaza ... Portland ... OR ... 16
Century Clackamas Town Center ... Portland ... OR ... 20

COMING ATTRACTIONS

Astoria Gateway Cinemas ... Astoria ... OR ... 7
McMinnville Cinemas ... McMinnville ... OR ... 10
Newport Cinemas ... Newport ... OR ... 3
Seaside Cinema ... Seaside ... OR ... 6
Lincoln City Cinemas ... Lincoln City ... OR ... 6

REGAL ENTERTAINMENT GROUP

Albany 7 Cinemas ... Albany ... OR ... 7
Stark Street Stadium 10 ... Gresham ... OR ... 10
Evergreen Parkway Stadium 13 ... Hillsboro ... OR ... 13
Movies On TV Stadium 16 ... Hillsboro ... OR ... 16
Hilltop 9 Cinema ... Oregon City ... OR ... 9
Broadway Metro 4 Theatres ... Portland ... OR ... 4
Division Street Stadium 13 ... Portland ... OR ... 13
Fox Tower Stadium 10 ... Portland ... OR ... 10
Lloyd Center Stadium 10 Cinema ... Portland ... OR ... 10
Lloyd Mall 8 Cinema ... Portland ... OR ... 8
Pioneer Place Stadium 6 ... Portland ... OR ... 6
Movieland 7 ... Salem ... OR ... 7
Santiam Stadium 11 ... Salem ... OR ... 11
Sherwood Stadium 10 ... Sherwood ... OR ... 10
Bridgeport Village Stadium 18 ... Tigard ... OR ... 18
Tigard 11 Cinemas ... Tigard ... OR ... 11
Wilsonville Stadium 9 Cinema ... Wilsonville ... OR ... 9
Lancaster Mall 17 ... Salem ... OR ... 17
Three Rivers Mall 5 ... Kelso ... WA ... 5
Triangle Quad Cinemas ... Longview ... WA ... 4
Cascade Stadium 16 Cinemas ... Vancouver ... WA ... 16
Cinema 99 Stadium 11 ... Vancouver ... WA ... 11
City Center Stadium 12 ... Vancouver ... WA ... 12
Vancouver Plaza 10 Cinema ... Vancouver ... WA ... 10
Old Mill Stadium 16 ... Bend ... OR ... 16
Pilot Butte 6 Theatres ... Bend ... OR ... 6

PITTSBURGH, PA (DMA 508)

AMC ENTERTAINMENT

AMC Loews Waterfront 22 ... West Homestead ... PA ... 22

CARMIKE CINEMAS

Plaza ... Beaver Falls ... PA ... 6
Laura Mall ... Connellsville ... PA ... 4
Cranberry Mall ... Cranberry Township ... PA ... 8
Wynnsong ... Delmont ... PA ... 12
Carmike ... Greensburg ... PA ... 15
Cinema ... Indiana ... PA ... 4
Galleria ... Mount Lebanon ... PA ... 6
Carmike ... Pittsburgh ... PA ... 10
Southland ... Pleasant Hills ... PA ... 9
Carmike ... Uniontown ... PA ... 6
Maxi Saver ... West Mifflin ... PA ... 12
Mall ... Morgantown ... WV ... 12

CINEMARK USA

Cinemark Center Township Marketplace ... Monaca ... PA ... 12
Cinemark 18 ... Tarentum ... PA ... 18

CLEVELAND CINEMAS

South Side Works Cinema ... Pittsburgh ... PA ... 10

DESTINTA THEATRES

Clarion 7 ... Clarion ... PA ... 7
Chartiers Valley 20 ... Bridgeville ... PA ... 20
Plaza East 22 ... N. Versailles ... PA ... 22

DICKINSON THEATRES

Mall 8 Pittsburg Theatre ... Pittsburg ... KS ... 8

EPIC THEATRES

Pioneer Drive-In Theatre ... Butler ... PA ... 5

HOLLYWOOD THEATRES

Crown Center Cinemas ... Washington ... PA ... 14

NATIONAL AMUSEMENTS

Showcase Cinemas West ... Pittsburgh ... PA ... 12
Showcase Cinemas North ... Pittsburgh ... PA ... 11

REGAL ENTERTAINMENT GROUP

UA Cortlandt Town Center Stadium 11 ... Mohegan Lake ... NY ... 11
Moraine Pointe Cinema 10 ... Butler ... PA ... 10

CHARLOTTE, NC (DMA 517)

AMC ENTERTAINMENT

AMC Carolina 22 ... Charlotte ... NC ... 22
AMC Northlake 14 ... Charlotte ... NC ... 14
AMC Concord 24 ... Concord ... NC ... 24

CARMIKE CINEMAS

Carmike ... Hickory ... NC ... 14
Westgate ... Lenoir ... NC ... 2
Cinema ... Lincolnton ... NC ... 8
Carmike ... Shelby ... NC ... 10
Cinema ... Rock Hill ... SC ... 7

CINEMARK USA

Cinemark Movies 10 ... Matthews ... NC ... 10
Cinemark Tinseltown USA ... Salisbury ... NC ... 14

MARQUEE CINEMAS

Mimosa 7 ... Morganton ... NC ... 7
Statesville 10 ... Statesville ... NC ... 10

REGAL ENTERTAINMENT GROUP

Boone Cinema 7 ... Boone ... NC ... 7
Crownpoint Stadium 12 ... Charlotte ... NC ... 12
Manor Twin ... Charlotte ... NC ... 2
Arboretum 12 ... Charlotte ... NC ... 12
Park Terrace 6 ... Charlotte ... NC ... 6
Phillips Place 10 ... Charlotte ... NC ... 10
Starlight Stadium 14 ... Charlotte ... NC ... 14
Stonecrest @ Piper Glen Stadium 22 ... Charlotte ... NC ... 22
Franklin Square Stadium 14 ... Gastonia ... NC ... 14
Birkdale Stadium 16 ... Huntersville ... NC ... 16
Union Square 8 ... Monroe ... NC ... 8
Manchester 14 ... Rock Hill ... SC ... 14

SOUTHERN THEATRES, LLC

AmStar Stadium 14 ... Mooresville ... NC ... 14

INDIANAPOLIS, IN (DMA 527)

ALLIANCE ENTERTAINMENT

Bedford Great Escape 7 ... Bedford ... IN ... 7
Noblesville Great Escape 10 ... Noblesville ... IN ... 10

AMC ENTERTAINMENT

Theatre	City	State	Screens
AMC Greenwood 14	Greenwood	IN	14
AMC Clearwater 12	Indianapolis	IN	12
AMC Loews College Park 14	Indianapolis	IN	14

CINEMARK USA

Theatre	City	State	Screens
Cinemark Movies 8	Indianapolis	IN	8
Cinemark Movies 8 Washington Market	Indianapolis	IN	8

GOODRICH QUALITY THEATRES

Theatre	City	State	Screens
Hamilton 16 IMAX	Indianapolis	IN	16

KERASOTES SHOWPLACE THEATRES

Theatre	City	State	Screens
ShowPlace 11	Bloomington	IN	11
ShowPlace West 12	Bloomington	IN	12
ShowPlace 12	Columbus	IN	12
ShowPlace 12	Indianapolis	IN	12
ShowPlace 12	Indianapolis	IN	12
ShowPlace 12	Indianapolis	IN	12
ShowPlace 16 & IMAX	Indianapolis	IN	16
ShowPlace 12	Kokomo	IN	12
ShowPlace 12	Marion	IN	12
ShowPlace 7	Muncie	IN	7
ShowPlace 12	Muncie	IN	12
Castle Theatre	New Castle	IN	1
Eastwood Cinema	Peru	IN	2

LANDMARK THEATRES

Theatre	City	State	Screens
Keystone Art Cinema	Indianapolis	IN	7

RAVE MOTION PICTURES

Theatre	City	State	Screens
RMP Metropolis 18	Plainfield	IN	18

REGAL ENTERTAINMENT GROUP

Theatre	City	State	Screens
Shiloh Crossing Stadium 18	Avon	IN	18
Village Park Cinema Stadium 17	Carmel	IN	17
Circle Center 9	Indianapolis	IN	9
Eagle Highlands 10	Indianapolis	IN	10
Galaxy Stadium 14	Indianapolis	IN	14

BALTIMORE, MD (DMA 512)

AMC ENTERTAINMENT

Theatre	City	State	Screens
AMC Loews White Marsh 16	Baltimore	MD	16
AMC Security Square 8	Baltimore	MD	8
AMC Columbia 14	Columbia	MD	14
AMC Loews Valley Center 9	Owings Mills	MD	8
AMC Owings Mills 17	Owings Mills	MD	17
AMC Towson Commons 8	Towson	MD	9

BOW TIE CINEMAS

Theatre	City	State	Screens
Harbour 9	Annapolis	MD	9
Mall 11	Annapolis	MD	11

FLAGSHIP CINEMAS

Theatre	City	State	Screens
Flagship Churchville Flagship	Bel Air	MD	7

MUVICO

Theatre	City	State	Screens
Muvico Egyptian 24	Hanover	MD	24

R/C THEATRES

Theatre	City	State	Screens
Hollywood Cinemas	Arbutus	MD	4

REGAL ENTERTAINMENT GROUP

Theatre	City	State	Screens
Bel Air Cinema Stadium 14	Abingdon	MD	14
Eastpoint 10	Baltimore	MD	10
Bethesda 10	Bethesda	MD	10
Snowden Square Stadium 14	Columbia	MD	14
Marley Station 8	Glen Burnie	MD	8
Hunt Valley Stadium 12	Hunt Valley	MD	12
Westminster 9	Westminster	MD	9

RALEIGH-DURHAM, NC (DMA 560)

CARMIKE CINEMAS

Theatre	City	State	Screens
Plaza	Dunn	NC	2
Wynnsong	Durham	NC	15
Carmike	Fayetteville	NC	12
Marketfair	Fayetteville	NC	15
Wynnsong	Fayetteville	NC	7
Park Place	Morrisville	NC	16
Blueridge	Raleigh	NC	14
Carmike	Raleigh	NC	15
Carmike	Wilson	NC	10

DICKINSON THEATRES, INC.

Theatre	City	State	Screens
Smithfield 10 Theatre	Smithfield	NC	10

REGAL ENTERTAINMENT GROUP

Theatre	City	State	Screens
Beaver Creek 12	Apex	NC	12
Crossroads 20	Cary	NC	20
Timberlyne 6	Chapel Hill	NC	6
Towne Square 10	Garner	NC	10
White Oak 14	Garner	NC	14
Raleigh Grande 16	Raleigh	NC	16
Brier Creek Stadium 14	Raleigh	NC	14
North Hills Stadium 14	Raleigh	NC	14

SAN DIEGO, CA (DMA 825)

AMC ENTERTAINMENT

Theatre	City	State	Screens
AMC La Jolla 12	La Jolla	CA	12
AMC Fashion Valley 18	San Diego	CA	18
AMC Mission Valley 20	San Diego	CA	20
AMC Palm Promenade 24	San Diego	CA	24

KRIKORIAN PREMIERE

Theatre	City	State	Screens
Vista Village 15 Metroplex	Vista	CA	15

LANDMARK THEATRES

Theatre	City	State	Screens
Hillcrest Cinemas	San Diego	CA	5
Ken Theatre	San Diego	CA	1
La Jolla Village Cinemas	La Jolla	CA	4

READING INTERNATIONAL, INC.

Theatre	City	State	Screens
Grossmont Center 10	La Mesa	CA	10
Carmel Mountain 12	San Diego	CA	12
Gaslamp 15	San Diego	CA	15
Town Square 14	San Diego	CA	14

REGAL ENTERTAINMENT GROUP

Theatre	City	State	Screens
Rancho Del Rey Stadium 16	Chula Vista	CA	16
Parkway Plaza Stadium 18	El Cajon	CA	18
Rancho San Diego Stadium 15	El Cajon	CA	15
Escondido Stadium 16	Escondido	CA	16
Oceanside Stadium 16	Oceanside	CA	16
Horton Plaza 14	San Diego	CA	14
Mira Mesa Stadium 18	San Diego	CA	18
San Marcos Stadium 18	San Marcos	CA	18

ULTRASTAR CINEMAS

Theatre	City	State	Screens
UltraStar Lake Havasu 10	Havasu	AZ	10
UltraStar Galaxy 6	Bonsall	CA	6
UltraStar La Costa 6	Carlsbad	CA	6
UltraStar Chula Vista 10	Chula Vista	CA	10
UltraStar Flower Hill Cinema 4	Del Mar	CA	4
UltraStar Mission Marketplace 13	Oceanside	CA	13
UltraStar Poway Creekside Plz. 10	Poway	CA	10
UltraStar Del Mar Highlands 8	San Diego	CA	8
UltraStar Mission Valley 7	San Diego	CA	7

NASHVILLE, TN (DMA 659)

ALLIANCE ENTERTAINMENT

Theatre	City	State	Screens
Clarksville Great Escape 16	Clarksville	TN	16

CARMIKE CINEMAS

Theatre	City	State	Screens
Martin	Hopkinsville	KY	5
Bell Forge	Antioch	TN	10
Hickory	Antioch	TN	8
Governor's Sq.	Clarksville	TN	10
Highland	Cookeville	TN	12
Thoroughbred	Franklin	TN	20
Rivergate	Goodlettesville	TN	8
Wynnsong	Madison	TN	10
Wynnsong	Murfreesboro	TN	16
Bellevue	Nashville	TN	8
Cinema	Springfield	TN	1

NEIGHBORHOOD CINEMA

Theatre	City	State	Screens
Gallatin Cinema	Gallatin	TN	10

REGAL ENTERTAINMENT GROUP

Theatre	City	State	Screens
Streets of Indian Lake Cinema 16	Hendersonville	TN	16
Bellevue Cinema Stadium 12	Nashville	TN	12
Green Hills Stadium 16	Nashville	TN	16
Hollywood Stadium 27	Nashville	TN	27
Opry Mills Stadium 20 Plus IMAX	Nashville	TN	21
Tullahoma Cinemas 8	Tullahoma	TN	8

HARTFORD & NEW HAVEN, CT (DMA 533)

AMC ENTERTAINMENT

Theatre	City	State	Screens
AMC Loews Plainville 20	Plainville	CT	20

BOSTON CULINARY GROUP

Theatre	City	State	Screens
Groton Cinemas	Groton	CT	6
Seymour Ent. Cinemas	Seymour	CT	12

BOW TIE CINEMAS

Theatre	City	State	Screens
Palace 17 & Odyssey Theater	Hartford	CT	17
Cinema City	Hartford	CT	4
Criterion Cinemas	New Haven	CT	9
Criterion Cinemas at Blue Back Sq.	W. Hartford	CT	6

DESTINTA THEATRES

Theatre	City	State	Screens
Metro Square 12	Middletown	CT	12

ENTERTAINMENT CINEMAS

Theatre	City	State	Screens
Ent. Cinemas Bloomfield 8	Bloomfield	CT	8
Ent. Cinemas Seymour 12	Seymour	CT	12

MARQUEE CINEMAS

Westbrook 12 .... Westbrook .... CT 12

NATIONAL AMUSEMENTS

Showcase Berlin .... Berlin .... CT 12
Cinema de Lux: Buckland Hills .... Manchester .... CT 19
Enfield Cinemas .... Enfield .... CT 12
Showcase Southington .... Southington .... CT 12
Showcase North Haven .... N. Haven .... CT 12
Cinema de Lux 14: Connecticut Post .... Milford .... CT 14

REGAL ENTERTAINMENT GROUP

Branford Stadium 12 .... Branford .... CT 12
Stonington 10 .... Pawcatuk .... CT 10
Brass Mill Stadium 12 .... Waterbury .... CT 12
Waterford 9 .... Waterford .... CT 9

KANSAS CITY, MO (DMA 616)

AMC ENTERTAINMENT

AMC Town Center 20 .... Leawood .... KS 20
AMC Studio 30 Kc .... Olathe .... KS 30
AMC Independence 20 .... Independence .... MO 20
AMC Barrywoods 24 .... Kansas City .... MO 24
AMC Parkway 14 .... Kansas City .... MO 14

B & B THEATRES

Grand 6 .... Chillicothe .... MO 6
Cannonball 6 .... Lexington .... MO 6
Liberty Cinema 12 .... Liberty .... MO 12
Marshall Cinema .... Marshall .... MO 3
Harrisonville Cinema 6 .... Harrisonville .... MO 6

CARMIKE CINEMAS

University .... Warrensburg .... MO 8

CINEMARK USA

Cinemark 20 .... Merriam .... KS 20
Cinemark Palace at The Plaza .... Kansas City .... MO 15

DICKINSON THEATRES

Plaza 6 Leavenworth Theatre .... Leavenworth .... KS 6
Great Mall 16 Theatre .... Olathe .... KS 16
Palazzo 16 Theatre .... Overland Park .... KS 16
Westglen 18 Theatre .... Shawnee .... KS 18
Belton 8 Theatre .... Belton .... MO 8
Blue Springs 8 Theatre .... Blue Springs .... MO 8
Northglen 14 Theatre .... Kansas City .... MO 14
Eastglen 16 Theatre .... Lee's Summit .... MO 16

HOLLYWOOD THEATRES

Southwind 12 .... Lawrence .... KS 12

PHOENIX ADLABS THEATRE MANAGEMENT, LLC

Phoenix Legends 14 Theatre .... Kansas City .... KS 14

REGAL ENTERTAINMENT GROUP

Kansas City Stadium 18 Cinemas .... Kansas City .... MO 18

COLUMBUS, OH (DMA 535)

AMC ENTERTAINMENT

AMC Easton Town Center 30 IMAX .... Columbus .... OH 30
AMC Lennox 24 .... Columbus .... OH 24
AMC Dublin 18 .... Dublin .... OH 18

CINEMARK USA

Cinemark Carriage Place Movies 12 .... Columbus .... OH 12
Cinemark Stoneridge Plaza Movies 16 .... Gahanna .... OH 16

DANBARRY CINEMAS

Danbarry Cinemas Chillicothe .... Chillicothe .... OH 10

MARCUS THEATRES

Marcus Cinema Crosswoods .... Columbus .... OH 17
Marcus Cinema Pickerington .... Pickerington .... OH 17

RAVE MOTION PICTURES

RMP Polaris Mall18 .... Columbus .... OH 18

REGAL ENTERTAINMENT GROUP

Middleburg Town Sq. Stadium 16 .... Cleveland .... OH 16
Georgesville Square Stadium 16 .... Columbus .... OH 16
River Valley Mall 10 .... Lancaster .... OH 10
Southland Cinema 7 .... Marion .... OH 7

STARPLEX CINEMAS

Westpointe 10 .... Columbus .... OH 10

SALT LAKE CITY, UT (DMA 770)

AMC ENTERTAINMENT

AMC Loews Layton Hills 9 .... Layton Hills .... UT 9

CARMIKE CINEMAS

Wynnsong .... Provo .... UT 12
Carmike .... West Jordan .... UT 12
HW Connection .... West Valley City .... UT 15

CINEMARK USA

Cinemark American Fork .... American Fork .... UT 12
Tinseltown USA .... Layton .... UT 17
Cinemark Tinseltown 14 .... Ogden .... UT 14
Holiday Village 4 .... Park City .... UT 4
Cinemark 16 .... Provo .... UT 16
Cinemark Movies 8 .... Provo .... UT 8
Century 16 .... Salt Lake City .... UT 16
Cinemark Sugarhouse Movies 10 .... Salt Lake City .... UT 10
Century 16 Union Heights .... Sandy .... UT 16
Cinemark Movies 9 .... Sandy .... UT 9
Cinemark 24 Jordan Landing .... West Jordan .... UT 24

METROPLOITAN THEATRES

Redstone 8 Cinema .... Park City .... UT 8

WESTATES THEATRES

Cedar City Cinema 8 .... Cedar City .... UT 8
Cedar City Fiddler 6 .... Cedar City .... UT 6
Logan Art Cinema .... Logan .... UT 1
Logan Movies 5 .... Logan .... UT 5
University Stadium 6 .... Logan .... UT 6
Providence Stadium 8 .... Providence .... UT 8
Holladay Center Cinema 6 .... Salt Lake City .... UT 6
Pineview Stadium 10 .... St. George .... UT 10
St. George Cinema 6 .... St. George .... UT 6
St. George Flood Street 4 .... St. George .... UT 4
St. George Stadium 8 .... St. George .... UT 8
Washington Red Cliff Cinemas .... St. George .... UT 4

CINCINNATI, OH (DMA 515)

ALLIANCE ENTERTAINMENT

Wilder Great Escape 14 .... Wilder .... KY 14
Oxford Great Escape 4 .... Oxford .... OH 4

CARMIKE CINEMAS

Cinema .... Maysville .... KY 4

CHAKERES

Chakeres Wilmington Plaza 5 .... Wilmington .... OH 5
Chakeres Wilmington Drive-In .... Wilmington .... OH 1

DANBARRY CINEMAS

Danbarry Dollar Saver Cinemas .... Florence .... KY 10
Danbarry Dollar Saver Cinemas .... Cincinnati .... OH 12
Danbarry Dollar Saver Cinemas .... Cincinnati .... OH 8
Danbarry Dollar Saver Cinemas .... Cincinnati .... OH 8
Danbarry Dollar Saver Cinemas .... Dayton .... OH 12
Danbarry Cinemas Middletown .... Middletown .... OH 10

GREATER HUNTINGTON THEATRE CORP.

Pierce Point Cinema 10 .... Cincinnati .... OH 10

KERASOTES SHOWPLACE THEATRES

Cinemas 10 .... Hamilton .... OH 10
ShowPlace 8 .... Hamilton .... OH 8

NATIONAL AMUSEMENTS

Florence Cinemas .... Florence .... KY 9
Showcase Cincinnati Mills .... Cincinnati .... OH 10
Springdale 18: Cinema de Lux .... Cincinnati .... OH 18
Showcase Western Hills .... Cincinnati .... OH 14
Kenwood Towne Centre .... Cincinnati .... OH 5
Showcase Kings Island .... Mason .... OH 12
Showcase Cinemas Milford 16 .... Milford .... OH 16

RAVE MOTION PICTURES

RMP West Chester 18 .... West Chester .... OH 18

REGAL ENTERTAINMENT GROUP

Deerfield Town Center 16 .... Mason .... OH 16

MILWAUKEE, WI (DMA 617)

AMC ENTERTAINMENT

AMC Mayfair 18 .... Wauwatosa .... WI 18

CINEMARK USA

Cinemark Tinseltown USA .... Kenosha .... WI 14

KERASOTES SHOWPLACE THEATRES

Kerasotes Star Cinema 12 .... Johnson Creek .... WI 12

LANDMARK THEATRES

Downer Theatre .... Milwaukee .... WI 2
Oriental Theatre .... Milwaukee .... WI 3

MARCUS THEATRES

Marcus Cinema Hillside .... Delafield .... WI 14
Marcus Cinema Menomonee Falls .... Menomonee Falls .... WI 16
Marcus Cinema North Shore .... Mequon .... WI 11
Marcus Cinema Northtown .... Milwaukee .... WI 8
Marcus Cinema Southgate .... Milwaukee .... WI 10
Marcus Cinema Ridge .... New Berlin .... WI 20
Marcus Cinema South Shore .... Oak Creek .... WI 16
Marcus Cinema Value Oak Creek .... Oak Creek .... WI 8
Marcus Cinema Regency .... Racine .... WI 8
Marcus Cinema Saukville .... Saukville .... WI 12

Marcus Cinema Sheboygan	Sheboygan	WI	13
Marcus Cinema Sturtevant	Sturtevant	WI	13
Marcus Majestic Cinema	Waukesha	WI	16

NOVA CINETECH

Showboat	Lake Geneva	WI	6
Geneva 4 Theatre	Lake Geneva	WI	4
Paradise Theatre	West Bend	WI	10
Cinema Brewhaus	West Bend	WI	3
Hartford Theatre	Hartford	WI	8
Theatres of Whitewater	Whitewater	WI	4

GREENVILLE-SPARTANBURG, SC (DMA 567)

CARMIKE CINEMAS

Carmike	Asheville	NC	10
Cinema	Forest City	NC	4
Astro	Clemson	SC	3
Carmike	Spartanburg	SC	7
Wynnsong	Spartanburg	SC	7

DICKINSON THEATRES, INC.

Easley 8 Theatre	Easley	SC	8
Greenwood 10 Theatre	Greenwood	SC	10
Seneca 8 Theatre	Seneca	SC	8

EPIC THEATRES

Epic Theatres of Hendersonville	Hendersonville	NC	12

PHOENIX ADLABS THEATRE MANAGEMENT, LLC

Cherokee Phoenix Theatres	Cherokee	NC	2

REGAL ENTERTAINMENT GROUP

Beaucatcher Cinemas 7	Asheville	NC	7
Hollywood Cinemas 14	Asheville	NC	14
Starlight Stadium 14	Anderson	SC	14
Hollywood Stadium 20	Greenville	SC	20
Cherrydale 16	Greenville	SC	16
Spartan 16	Spartanburg	SC	16
Westgate Mall Cinema 8	Spartanburg	SC	8

SOUTHERN THEATRES, LLC

AmStar Stadium 14	Anderson	SC	14

SAN ANTONIO, TX (DMA 641)

ALAMO DRAFTHOUSE CINEMA

Alamo Westlakes	San Antonio	TX	9

AMC ENTERTAINMENT

AMC Huebner Oaks 24	San Antonio	TX	24
AMC Rivercenter 9	San Antonio	TX	9

CINEMARK USA

Cinemark Movies 8	Del Rio	TX	8
Mall De Las Aguilas 7	Eagle Pass	TX	7
Cinemark Movies 16	San Antonio	TX	16

REGAL ENTERTAINMENT GROUP

Live Oak Stadium 18	Liveoak	TX	18
Alamo Quarry Stadium 14	San Antonio	TX	14
Cielo Vista Stadium 18	San Antonio	TX	18
Fiesta 16 Stadium Theatres	San Antonio	TX	16
Northwoods 14	San Antonio	TX	14

SANTIKOS THEATRES

Santikos Bijou at Crossroads	San Antonio	TX	6
Santikos Embassy 14	San Antonio	TX	14
Santikos Rialto Cinema Bistro & Piccolo	San Antonio	TX	13
Santikos Mayan Palace 14	San Antonio	TX	13
Santikos Northwest 14	San Antonio	TX	14
Santikos Palladium IMAX	San Antonio	TX	19
Santikos Silverado 16	San Antonio	TX	16

WEST PALM BEACH-FT. PIERCE, FL (DMA 548)

AMC ENTERTAINMENT

AMC Indian River 24	Vero Beach	FL	24

COBB THEATRES

Jupiter 18	Jupiter	FL	18
Downtown 16 Cinemas	Palm Beach Gardens	FL	16

MUVICO THEATRES

Muvico Palace 20	Boca Raton	FL	20
Muvico Boynton Beach 14	Boynton Beach	FL	14
Muvico Parisian 20	W. Palm Beach	FL	20

NOVA CINEMAS

Nova Cinemas at Sabal Palm	Ft. Pierce	FL	6

PHOENIX ADLABS THEATRE MANAGEMENT, LLC

Phoenix Lake Worth Cinema 8	Greenacres	FL	8

RAVE MOTION PICTURES

RMP St. Lucie West 14	Port St. Lucie	FL	14

REGAL ENTERTAINMENT GROUP

Shadowood 16	Boca Raton	FL	16
Delray Beach 18	Del Ray Beach	FL	18
Treasure Coast Mall Stadium 16	Jenson Beach	FL	16
Royal Palm Beach Stadium 18	Royal Palm Beach	FL	18

GRAND RAPIDS, MI (DMA 563)

AMC ENTERTAINMENT

AMC Star Grand Rapids 18	Grand Rapids	MI	18
AMC Star Holland 8	Holland	MI	8

CARMIKE CINEMAS

Lakeview Square	Battle Creek	MI	10

GOODRICH QUALITY THEATRES

West Columbia 7	Battle Creek	MI	7
Grand Haven 9	Grand Haven	MI	9
Hastings 4	Hastings	MI	4
Holland 7	Holland	MI	7
Kalamazoo 10	Kalamazoo	MI	10
Ada Lowell 5	Lowell	MI	5
Three Rivers 6	Three Rivers	MI	6

LOEKS THEATRES

Celebration! Cinema/IMAX Theatre N.	Grand Rapids	MI	18
Celebration! Cinema South	Grand Rapids	MI	16
Studio 28	Grand Rapids	MI	20
Celebration! Cinema Woodland	Grand Rapids	MI	14
Celebration! Cinema Rivertown	Grandville	MI	20
Getty Drive-In	Muskegon	MI	4
Cinema Carousel	Muskegon	MI	16
Plaza 1 and 2	Muskegon	MI	2

NEIGHBORHOOD CINEMA

Coldwater Cinemas	Coldwater	MI	7
Greenville Cinemas	Greenville	MI	7

NOVA CINETECH, INC.

Bohm	Albion	MI	3

RAVE MOTION PICTURES

RMP City Place 14	Kalamazoo	MI	14

BIRMINGHAM, AL (DMA 630)

CARMIKE CINEMAS

Carmike	Birmingham	AL	10
Summit	Birmingham	AL	16
Wynnsong	Birmingham	AL	12
Carmike	Cullman	AL	10
Martin	Talladega	AL	3

COBB THEATRES

Movies 4	Jasper	AL	4

RAVE MOTION PICTURES

RMP Lee Branch 15	Birmingham	AL	15
RMP Patton Creek 15	Hoover	AL	15
RMP Vestavia Hills 10	Vestavia Hills	AL	10

REGAL ENTERTAINMENT GROUP

Trussville Stadium 16	Birmingham	AL	16

SOUTHERN THEATRES, LLC

AmStar Stadium 14	Alabaster	AL	14
AmStar Stadium 12	Oxford	AL	12

HARRISBURG-LANCASTER-LEBANON, PA (DMA 566)

ALLIANCE ENTERTAINMENT

Lebanon Valley Great Escape 10	Lebanon	PA	10
Harrisburg Great Escape 14	Harrisburg	PA	14

AMC ENTERTAINMENT

AMC Colonial Commons 9	Harrisburg	PA	9

CINEMA CENTER

Cinema Center of Camphill	Camp Hill	PA	12
Cinema Center of Palmyra	Palmyra	PA	12
Sky-Vu Drive-In	Gratz	PA	1

R/C THEATRES

Gateway Movies	Gettsburg	PA	8
Hanover Movies	Hanover	PA	16

REGAL ENTERTAINMENT GROUP

Carlisle Commons Stadium 8	Carlisle	PA	8
Harrisburg Stadium 14	Harrisburg	PA	14
Manor Stadium 16	Lancaster	PA	16
West Manchester Mall Stadium 13	York	PA	13

LAS VEGAS, NV (DMA 839)

BRENDEN THEATRES

AVI 8	Laughlin	NV	8
Las Vegas 14 IMAX	Las Vegas	NV	14

CINEMARK USA

Cinedome 12	Henderson	NV	12
Century 18 Sam's Town	Las Vegas	NV	18
Century Orleans	Las Vegas	NV	18
Century South Point	Las Vegas	NV	16
Century Suncoast 16	Las Vegas	NV	16
Santa Fe Station	Las Vegas	NV	16

GALAXY THEATRES

Galaxy Fandango	Carson City	NV	10
Galaxy-Cannery	N. Las Vegas	NV	14
Neonopolis	Las Vegas	NV	11

RAVE MOTION PICTURES

RMP Town Square 18	Las Vegas	NV	18

REGAL ENTERTAINMENT GROUP

Fiesta Stations 12	Henderson	NV	12
Green Valley Ranch Stadium 10	Henderson	NV	10
Sunset Station Stadium 13 Theatre	Henderson	NV	13
Boulder Station 11 Theatre	Las Vegas	NV	11
Colonnade Stadium 14	Las Vegas	NV	14
Rainbow Promenade 10	Las Vegas	NV	10
Red Rock Stadium 16	Las Vegas	NV	16
Showcase Theatre 8	Las Vegas	NV	8
Texas Station Stadium 18	Las Vegas	NV	18
Village Square Stadium 18	Las Vegas	NV	18

WESTATES THEATRES

Virgin River Cinema 4	Mesquite	NV	4
Mesquite Stadium 6	Mesquite	NV	6

NORFOLK-PORTSMOUTH, VA (DMA 544)

AMC ENTERTAINMENT

AMC Hampton 24	Hampton	VA	24
AMC Lynnhaven 18	Virginia Beach	VA	18

CINEMARK USA

Cinemark Movies 10	Chesapeake	VA	10
Cinemark 18	Norfolk	VA	18

PHOENIX ADLABS THEATRE MANAGEMENT, LLC

Phoenix Main Gate Movies 10	Norfolk	VA	10

R/C THEATRES

Hatteras Movies	Avon	NC	4
Corolla Movies	Corolla	NC	4
Kill Devil Hills Movies 10	Kill Devil Hills	NC	10

REGAL ENTERTAINMENT GROUP

Greenbrier Cinema 13	Chesapeake	VA	13
Kiln Creek Cinema Stadium 20	Newport News	VA	20
Macarthur Center Stadium 18	Norfolk	VA	18
Harbour View Grande 16	Suffolk	VA	16
Columbus Stadium 12	Virginia Beach	VA	12
Pembroke Cinema 8	Virginia Beach	VA	8
Strawbridge Marketplace Stadium 12	Virginia Beach	VA	12
New Town 12	Williamsburg	VA	12

ALBUQUERQUE-SANTA FE, NM (DMA 790)

ALLEN THEATRES

Fiesta Twin	Cortez	CO	2
Aviator 10	Alamogordo	NM	10
Cinema 3	Carlsbad	NM	3
Allen 8	Farmington	NM	8
Animas 10	Farmington	NM	10
Centennial Twin	Farmington	NM	2
Aztec 5	Gallup	NM	5
Red Rock 6	Gallup	NM	6
Cinema 7	Hobbs	NM	7
Galaxy 8	Roswell	NM	8
Sierra Cinema	Ruidoso	NM	3

CARMIKE CINEMAS

Cinema	Artesia	NM	2

CINEMARK USA

Century Rio 24 Plex	Albuquerque	NM	24
Century 14 Downtown Albuq.	Albuquerque	NM	14
Cinemark Movies 8	Albuquerque	NM	8
Cinemark Movies West	Albuquerque	NM	8

REGAL ENTERTAINMENT GROUP

Cottonwood Theatre Stadium 16	Albuquerque	NM	16
Four Hills Theatre 10	Albuquerque	NM	10
High Ridge Theatre 8	Albuquerque	NM	8
Winrock VI	Albuquerque	NM	6
Devargas Mall Cinema 6	Santa Fe	NM	6
UA North 6	Santa Fe	NM	6
Santa Fe 14	Santa Fe	NM	14

TRANS LUX

Trans-Lux Gaslight Twin Cinemas	Durango	CO	2
Trans-Lux High Five Cinemas	Durango	CO	7
Trans-Lux DreamCatcher 10	Espanola	NM	10
Trans-Lux Starlight Cinema	Los Lunas	NM	8
Trans-Lux Loma Theatre	Socorro	NM	1
Trans-Lux Storyteller Cinemas	Taos	NM	7

OKLAHOMA CITY (DMA 650)

AMC ENTERTAINMENT

AMC Crossroads 16	Oklahoma City	OK	16
AMC Quail Springs 24	Oklahoma City	OK	24

B & B THEATRES

El Reno Cinema 8	El Reno	OK	8
Ponca Plaza Twin	Ponca City	OK	2

CARMIKE CINEMAS

Dunkin Theatre	Cushing	OK	1
North Park	Ponca City	OK	4
Cinema Center	Shawnee	OK	8
Hornbeck	Shawnee	OK	2
Carmike	Stillwater	OK	10

CINEMARK USA

Cinemark Tinseltown	Oklahoma City	OK	20

DICKINSON THEATRES

Oakwood Mall Theatre	Enid	OK	8
Penn Square 10 Theatre	Oklahoma City	OK	10
West End Pointe 8	Yukon	OK	8

HARKINS THEATRES

Bricktown 16/Cine Capri	Oklahoma City	OK	16

HOLLYWOOD THEATRES

Spotlight 14	Norman	OK	14
Movies 6	Shawnee	OK	6

STAPLEX CINEMAS

Robinson Crossing 6	Norman	OK	6
Crossroads Movies 8	Oklahoma City	OK	8
Northpark 7	Oklahoma City	OK	7

GREENSBORO, NC (DMA 518)

CARMIKE CINEMAS

Kingsway	Eden	NC	4
Carmike	Greensboro	NC	18
Carmike	High Point	NC	8
Cinema	Lexington	NC	8
Carmike	Winston-Salem	NC	10
Wynnsong	Winston-Salem	NC	12

CINEMARK USA

Cinemark Asheboro	Asheboro	NC	7
Cinemark Brassfield Cinema Ten	Greensboro	NC	10

REGAL ENTERTAINMENT GROUP

Greensboro Grande 16	Greensboro	NC	16
Palladium 14	High Pointe	NC	14
Oak Hollow Mall 7	High Point	NC	7

SOUTHERN THEATRES, LLC

The Grand 18	Winston-Salem	NC	18

JACKSONVILLE (DMA 561)

AMC ENTERTAINMENT

AMC Regency 24	Jacksonville	FL	24
AMC Orange Park 24	Orange Park	FL	24

CARMIKE CINEMAS

Amelia Island	Fernandina Beach	FL	7

CINEMARK USA

Cinemark Tinseltown	Jacksonville	FL	20

DICKINSON THEATRES

Palatka Mall Cinemas	Palatka	FL	4

GEORGIA THEATRE COMPANY

Glynn Place Stadium Cinemas 11	Brunswick	GA	11
Kings Bay Stadium Cinemas 9	St Marys	GA	9
Island Cinemas 7	St Simons	GA	7
Mall Stadium Cinemas 7	Waycross	GA	7

HOLLYWOOD THEATRES

River City Marketplace 14	Jacksonville	FL	14

REGAL ENTERTAINMENT GROUP

Theatre	City	State	Screens
Avenues Stadium 20	Jacksonville	FL	20
Beach Boulevard Stadium 18	Jacksonville	FL	18
Cinema 90 6	Lake City	FL	6
Mall St Augustine 6	St Augustine	FL	6
North Point Market 8	Alpharetta	GA	8

MEMPHIS, TN (DMA 640)

CARMIKE CINEMAS

Theatre	City	State	Screens
Carmike	Dyersburg	TN	9

MALCO THEATRES

Theatre	City	State	Screens
Malco Trio Cinema	Blytheville	AR	3
Oxford Studio Cinema	Oxford	MS	8
DeSoto 16	Southaven	MS	16
Bartlett Cinema 10	Bartlett	TN	10
Stage Road Cinema	Bartlett	TN	13
Towne Cinema 16	Collierville	TN	16
Cordova Cinema	Cordova	TN	16
Forest Hill	Germantown	TN	8
Paradiso Cinema	Memphis	TN	16
Ridgeway Four	Memphis	TN	4
Raleigh Springs 12	Memphis	TN	12
Wolfchase Galleria	Memphis	TN	8
Majestic 20	Memphis	TN	20
Studio on the Square	Memphis	TN	5
Summer Drive-In	Memphis	TN	4

MUVICO THEATRES

Theatre	City	State	Screens
Muvico Peabody Place 22	Memphis	TN	22

AUSTIN, TX (DMA 635)

ALAMO DRAFTHOUSE CINEMA

Theatre	City	State	Screens
Alamo at the Ritz	Austin	TX	2
Alamo Lake Creek	Austin	TX	7
Alamo Village	Austin	TX	4
Alamo South Lamar	Austin	TX	6

AMC ENTERTAINMENT

Theatre	City	State	Screens
AMC Barton Creek 14	Austin	TX	14

CINEMARK USA, INC.

Theatre	City	State	Screens
Cinemark Southpark Meadows	Austin	TX	14
Cinemark Tinseltown 17	Austin	TX	17
Cinemark Tinseltown 20	Pflugerville	TX	20
Cinemark Roundrock	Round Rock	TX	14
Movies 8	Round Rock	TX	8

GALAXY THEATRES, LLC

Theatre	City	State	Screens
Galaxy 10	Austin	TX	10

LANDMARK THEATRES

Theatre	City	State	Screens
Dobie Theatre	Austin	TX	4

REGAL ENTERTAINMENT GROUP

Theatre	City	State	Screens
Arbor Cinema @ Great Hills	Austin	TX	8
Gateway Stadium 16	Austin	TX	16
Metropolitan Stadium 14	Austin	TX	14
Westgate Stadium 11 Theatres	Austin	TX	11
Lakeline Mall 9	Cedar Park	TX	9

LOUISVILLE, KY (DMA 529)

ALLIANCE ENTERTAINMENT

Theatre	City	State	Screens
Madison Great Escape 6	Madison	IN	6
New Albany Great Escape 16	New Albany	IN	16
Seymour Great Escape 8	Seymour	IN	8
Shelbyville Great Escape 8	Shelbyville	KY	8
LaGrange Great Escape	LaGrange	KY	8

CINEMARK USA

Theatre	City	State	Screens
Cinemark Greentree 10	Clarksville	IN	10
Cinemark Tinseltown USA	Louisville	KY	18

NATIONAL AMUSEMENTS

Theatre	City	State	Screens
Cinema de Lux 20: Stonybrook	Louisville	KY	20
Kenwood Drive-In	Louisville	KY	1
Showcase 16: Cinema de Lux	Okolona	KY	16

INDEPENDENT THEATRES

The following listing includes U.S. theatres with three or less locations under the same ownership. For exhibitors with four or more theatre locations, please see Circuit Theatres.

ALABAMA

Name	Address	City	State	Zip	Phone	Screens
Playhouse Cinema	1236 Cherokee Rd.	Alexander City	AL	35010	(256) 234-2509	3
Tenn-Tom	210 Broad St.	Aliceville	AL	35442	(205) 373-8751	2
Clark Twin	101 O'Neal Court Sq.	Andalusia	AL	36420	(334) 347-1129	3
Starlite Drive In - Cinemagic	5739 Hwy. 202	Anniston	AL	36202	(256) 741-1411	1
Cinemagic Drive In	1702 South Jefferson St.	Athens	AL	35611	(256) 233-0402	2
Strand Theater	1116 South Main St.	Atmore	AL	36502	(251) 368-2039	1
Alabama Theatre (Summers only)	1817 3rd Ave. N	Birmingham	AL	35203	(205) 252-2262	1
Nova 9	215 S McClesky St. #548	Boaz	AL	35957	(256) 593-8030	9
Sand Mountain Twin Drive In	10480 Hwy. 431	Boaz	AL	35956	(256) 593-5599	2
411 Drive In Theatre	300 County Rd. 265 Center	Centre	AL	35960	(256) 927-2855	1
Marengo Theatre	219 East Washington	Demopolis	AL	36732	(334) 289-0850	1
Davis Cinema 1&2 (Northside 1@2)	209 Executive Park Dr.	Dothan	AL	36303	(334) 792-2151	12
Clark 1-2	621 Bollweville Rd.	Enterprise	AL	36330	(334) 347-3931	4
Clark 3-4	621 Bollweville Rd.	Enterprise	AL	36330	(334) 347-3931	3
College Cinema	501 Plaza Dr. Ste. 137	Enterprise	AL	36330	(334) 347-4911	3
Odyssey Riviera Cinema 12	110 Riviera Blvd.	Foley	AL	36535	(251) 943-3686	12
Hamilton Theatre	2715 Gault Ave. N.	Fort Payne	AL	35967	(256) 845-5518	6
Gadsden Premiere Cinema 16	1001 Rainbow Dr. Ste. 2	Gadsden	AL	35901	(256) 549-0700	16
Blue Moon Drive In	4690 Hwy. 43	Guin	AL	35563	(205) 468-8046	1
Dixie Theater	907 20th St.	Haleyville	AL	35565	(205) 486-8590	2
Dixie Cinema 3	401 Hwy. 17 South	Hamilton	AL	35570	(205) 921-3430	3
Sumter Theater & Pizza	116 Franklin St.	Livingston	AL	35470	(205) 652-4464	1
Our Place	1 Teen Trail	Monroeville	AL	36460	(251) 575-7060	1
Capri Theatre	1045 E Fairview Ave.	Montgomery	AL	36106	(334) 262-4858	1
Continental Drive In	14200 Hwy. 84 W	Newton	AL	36352	(334) 692-3890	4
Clark Twin Cinema	Martindale Plaza	Ozark	AL	36360	(334) 774-4224	2
Piedmont Drive In	1260 Hwy. 278 W	Piedmont	AL	36272	(256) 447-6521	1
King Drive In	1670 Hwy. 60	Russellville	AL	35654	(256) 332-6074	1
Holiday Cinema	1519 E Willow St.	Scottsboro	AL	35768	(256) 259-6246	2
Cahaba Twin Cinema	211 Hwy. 80 East	Selma	AL	36701	(334) 874-6059	2
Plaza Twin	248 E Ft. Williams St.	Sylacauga	AL	35150	(256) 245-4091	2
Thomasville	31 W Front & Nichols	Thomasville	AL	36784	(334) 636-2807	1
Continental Cinema 5	450 US Hwy. 231 N	Troy	AL	36081	(334) 808-8643	5
Drive In	100 Angus St.	Trussville	AL	35173	(205) 467-3434	1
Arts Council	600 Greensboro Ave.	Tuscaloosa	AL	35401	(205) 758-8083	1
Bama Theatre	600 Greensboro Ave.	Tuscaloosa	AL	35403	(205) 758-8083	1

ALASKA

Name	Address	City	State	Zip	Phone	Screens
Bear Tooth Theatre Pub & Grill	1230 West 27th.	Anchorage	AK	99503	(907) 276-4255	1
Valley River	11701 Business Blvd.	Eagle River	AK	99577	(907) 694-5858	6
Blue Loon	2999 Parks Hwy.	Fairbanks	AK	99709	(907) 457-5666	1
Homer Family Theatre	106 W Pioneer Ave.	Homer	AK	99603	(907) 235-6728	1
20th Century #1	222 Front St. Ste. 600	Juneau	AK	99801	(907) 586-3634	2
Glacier Cinemas	9091 Cinema Dr.	Juneau	AK	99801	(907) 789-9191	3
Gold Twin Nikelodeon	510 Kennedy	Juneau	AK	99801	(907) 463-5591	1
Ketchikan Coliseumm	405 Mission St.	Ketchikan	AK	99901	(907) 225-2294	2
Orpheum	102 Center St.	Kodiak	AK	99615	(907) 486-5449	1
Gold Coast Cinema	1 Airport Way	Nome	AK	99762	(907) 443-8200	1
Compass	500 N First St.	Petersburg	AK	99833	(907) 772-7469	1
Liberty Theatre	305 Adams	Seward	AK	99664	(907) 224-5418	1
Coliseum Theatre	310 Marine St.	Sitka	AK	99835	(907) 747-0646	1
Mat-Su Cinemas	2430 Parks Hwy.	Wasilla	AK	99654	(907) 373-7003	3

ARIZONA

Name	Address	City	State	Zip	Phone	Screens
Valley View Cinema Grill 10	2140 N Arizona Ave.	Chandler	AZ	85224	(480) 963-7678	10
Cottonwood Cinema	1389 E Hwy. 89A	Cottonwood	AZ	86326	(928) 649-1111	1
Movies at the Mall	4650 N Hwy. 89 Ste. F2	Flagstaff	AZ	86004	(928) 526-3771	2
Apache Drive In	1 Mile N Hwy. 60	Globe	AZ	85501	(520) 425-4511	1
Roxy Theatre	153 Hopi St.	Holbrook	AZ	86025	(928) 524-6684	1
Black Mesa Theatre	Bashas Shopping Center	Kayenta	AZ	86033	(928) 697-3888	2
Movies-Havasu	180 Swanson Ave.	Lake Havasu City	AZ	86403	(928) 453-0055	10
Lakeside	20 E White Mountain Blvd. Ste. B4	Lakeside	AZ	85929	(928) 367-5157	2
Winchester Theatre	1850 S White Mountain Rd.	Lakeside	AZ	85929	(928) 537-2294	2
WME Village 8	1501 West White Mountain Blvd.	Lakeside	AZ	85929	(928) 368-2005	8
Blue Water Theatres	11300 Resort Dr.	Parker	AZ	85344	(928) 669-5737	4
Sawmill Theatres	201 W Main St. Ste. A	Payson	AZ	85541	(928) 468-7535	6
Cinema Latino de Phoenix	7611 West Thomas Rd.	Phoenix	AZ	85033	(623) 849-3900	6
Frontier Village 10	1771 East Hwy. 69	Prescott	AZ	86301	(928) 445-7515	10
Morenci Theatre	1998B W Thatcher Blvd.	Safford	AZ	85546	(928) 428-5571	1
Sapphire Cineplex	1998B W Thatcher Blvd.	Safford	AZ	85546	(928) 428-5571	6
Victory Discount Theatre	555 Entertainment Ave.	Safford	AZ	85546	(928) 428-1595	1
Desert Sky Cinema	70 W Duval Mine Rd.	Sahuarita	AZ	85629	(520) 393-1212	6
Town Square Cinema	1210 W Cleveland	Saint Johns	AZ	85936	(928) 337-4061	1
Farrelli's Cinema Supper Club	14202 N Scottsdale Rd. #14	Scottsdale	AZ	85254	(480) 905-7200	1
Supervue Theatre	6615 Hwy. 179	Sedona	AZ	86351	(928) 300-2955	1
WME Theatres Show Low 5	1850 S White Mt. Blvd.	Show Low	AZ	85901	(928) 368-2006	5
R & M Cinema	300 E Wilcox	Sierra Vista	AZ	85635	(520) 458-6511	3
Uptown 3 Theatres	4341 S Hwy. 92	Sierra Vista	AZ	85650	(520) 378-0210	3

Name	Address	City	State	Zip	Phone	Screens
El Rio	15 W Main St.	Springerville	AZ	85938	(928) 333-4590	1
Tempe Cinema	1825 E Elliot Rd.	Tempe	AZ	85284	(480) 897-0677	6
De Anza Drive In	1401 S Alvernon Way	Tucson	AZ	85711	(520) 745-2240	4
Grand Cinema Crossroads VI	4811 E Grant Rd. Ste. 150	Tucson	AZ	85712	(520) 327-7067	6
Grand Cinemas Oracle View	4690 N Oracle Rd.	Tucson	AZ	85705	(520) 292-2430	6
The Grand View IV	265 W Valencia	Tucson	AZ	85706	(520) 746-1823	4
The Loft Cinema	3233 E Speedway	Tucson	AZ	85716	(520) 795-0844	2
Saguaro Theatre	176 E Wickenburg Way	Wickenburg	AZ	85390	(928) 684-7189	1
Rex Allen Theatre	150 N Railroad Ave.	Willcox	AZ	85643	(520) 384-4244	2
Winslow Theatre	303 East 2nd St.	Winslow	AZ	86047	(928) 289-4100	1
Main Street Cinema	111 S Main St.	Yuma	AZ	85364	(928) 819-0293	8

ARKANSAS

Name	Address	City	State	Zip	Phone	Screens
Melba Theatre	115 W Main St.	Batesville	AR	72501	(870) 698-9252	1
Main Theatre	207 S Main St.	Berryville	AR	72616	(870) 423-3852	1
Savage Theatre	180 N Broadway	Booneville	AR	72927	(479) 675-3756	1
Silver Screen 4	100 Cinema Blvd.	Cabot	AR	72023	(501) 843-7469	4
Clarksville Cinema	2424 Clark Rd.	Clarksville	AR	72830	(479) 754-4632	4
Gateway Twin Cinema	Hwy. 65 South	Clinton	AR	72031	(501) 745-4474	2
Eldorado Cinema	1936 Northwest Ave.	El Dorado	AR	71730	(870) 862-6362	5
Rialto	113 E Cedar St.	El Dorado	AR	71730	(870) 881-7771	3
Stars Cinema 6	2620 W Hillsboro	El Dorado	AR	71731	(870) 862-1919	6
112 Drive In	3352 Hwy. 112	Fayetteville	AR	72703	(479) 442-4542	1
Broadway Cinema	1101 East Broadway Ave.	Forrest City	AR	72335	(870) 633-5558	4
Hot Springs Mall Cinema	4501 Central Ave.	Hot Sprgs Ntl P	AR	71913	(501) 224-7980	7
Market Street Cinema	1521 Merrill Ste. F 100	Little Rock	AR	72211	(501) 312-8900	5
Riverdale 10	2600 Cantrell Rd.	Little Rock	AR	72202	(501) 296-9468	10
Cameo Theatre	111 N Jackson	Magnolia	AR	71753	(870) 234-1660	3
Ritz Theatre	213 S Main St.	Malvern	AR	72104	(501) 332-2451	2
Kenda Drive In	Hwy. 65 North	Marshall	AR	72650	(870) 448-5400	1
Silver Screen Theatre	1200 S Pine Ave.	Mena	AR	71953	(479) 394-2959	2
North Plaza Cinema	1515 N Business 9	Morrilton	AR	72110	(501) 354-1667	3
Sun Valley 6	704 Cooper Estates	Mountain Home	AR	72653	(870) 425-2095	6
Stone Drive In	Hwy. 87 N 807 Theatre Ln.	Mountain View	AR	72560	(870) 269-3227	1
Paragould Cinema 8	2707 W Kings Hwy.	Paragould	AR	72450	(870) 240-8009	8
Paris Cinema	26 West Walnut	Paris	AR	72855	(479) 963-3476	1
Picwood 11	3800 W Main St.	Russellville	AR	72801	(479) 968-3434	11
Valley Trio 3	3816 E Main St.	Russellville	AR	72801	(479) 968-8161	3
Searcy Cinema 8	2933 E Race St.	Searcy	AR	72143	(501) 279-8179	8
Maxie Theatre	Hwy. 463 South	Trumann	AR	72472	(870) 483-5312	1
Scott Theatre	281 S Main St.	Waldron	AR	72958	(479) 637-3222	1

CALIFORNIA

Name	Address	City	State	Zip	Phone	Screens
Auctions by the Bay Theatre	2700 Saratoga St.	Alameda	CA	94501	(510) 740-0220	1
Alameda Theatre & Cineplex	2317 Central Ave.	Alameda	CA	94501	(510) 769-3456	7
New Niles	127 S Main St.	Alturas	CA	96101	(530) 233-5454	1
Cinema City Theatres	5635 E La Palma Ave.	Anaheim	CA	92807	(714) 970-0865	13
Prime 11 Cinemas Anderson	1816 Highway 273	Anderson	CA	96007	(530) 378-3411	11
Angels 5 Theatres	1228 S Main St.	Angels Camp	CA	95222	(209) 736-6768	5
El Campanil Theatre	602 W 2nd St.	Antioch	CA	94509	(925) 757-9500	1
Aptos Cinema	122 Rancho Del Mar	Aptos	CA	95003	(831) 688-6542	2
Minor Theatre	1013 H St.	Arcata	CA	95521	(707) 822-3456	3
Fair Oaks Theatre	1007 Grand Ave.	Arroyo Grande	CA	93420	(805) 489-2364	1
Century Cinema	6905 El Camino Real	Atascadero	CA	93422	(805) 227-2172	6
Foothill Center 10	854 E Alosta Ave.	Azusa	CA	91702	(626) 334-4997	10
Fox Theatre	2001 H St.	Bakersfield	CA	93301	(661) 324-1369	1
Maya Bakersfield 16	1000 California Ave.	Bakersfield	CA	93304	(661) 636-0484	16
Fox Cineplex	60 W Ramsey St.	Banning	CA	92220	(951) 849-3277	3
Skyline Drive In	31175 Old Hwy. 58	Barstow	CA	92311	(760) 256-4444	2
Playhouse	40 Main St.	Belvedere Tiburon	CA	94920	(415) 435-3585	3
Rialto Cinemas Elmwood	2966 College Ave.	Berkeley	CA	94705	(510) 540-6482	3
Academy Motion Pictures	8949 Wilshire Blvd.	Beverly Hills	CA	90211	(310) 247-3000	2
Aidikoff Theatre	150 S Rodeo Ste. #140	Beverly Hills	CA	90212	(310) 274-0866	1
Creative Artist Agency	9830 Wilshire Blvd.	Beverly Hills	CA	90212	(310) 288-4750	1
Fine Arts	8556 Wilshire Blvd.	Beverly Hills	CA	90211	(310) 701-8925	1
Samuel Goldwyn Theatre	8949 Wilshire Blvd.	Beverly Hills	CA	90211	(310) 247-3000	1
Village North	602 Pine Knot Ave.	Big Bear Lake	CA	92315	(909) 866-5246	3
Village Theatre	40789 Village Dr.	Big Bear Lake	CA	92315	(909) 866-5246	2
Bishop Twin Theatre	237 N Main	Bishop	CA	93514	(760) 873-3575	2
All Star Cinema	691 W Hobson Way	Blythe	CA	92225	(760) 921-3117	3
Cinelux Delta Cinema Saver	641 First St.	Brentwood	CA	94513	(925) 240-7335	2
Parks Plaza	515 McMurray Rd.	Buellton	CA	93427	(805) 688-7434	5
Fall River Theatre	37030 Main St.	Burney	CA	96013	(530) 335-3484	1
Mt. Burney Theatre	37022 Main St.	Burney	CA	96013	(530) 335-2605	1
Paseo Camarillo Cinema	390 N Lantana	Camarillo	CA	93010	(805) 383-2269	3
Roxy Stadium	5001 Verdugo Way	Camarillo	CA	93012	(805) 388-0532 x483	11
Camera 7 Cinemas	1875 South Bascom Ave.	Campbell	CA	95008	(408) 559-6900	3
Plaza 4	2501 Winchester Blvd.	Campbell	CA	95008	(408) 378-2432	4
41st. Avenue Cinema	1475 41st Ave.	Capitola	CA	95010	(831) 479-3504	3
Movie Max Theatre	2385 Marron Rd.	Carlsbad	CA	92008	(760) 729-7148	4
Cinelux Chabot	2853 Castro Valley Blvd.	Castro Valley	CA	94546	(510) 582-2597	10
Mary Pickford Theatre	36850 Pickfair St.	Cathedral City	CA	92234	(760) 328-7444	14
New Pageant Theatre	351 E 6th St.	Chico	CA	95928	(530) 895-1330	1
Clearlake Twin	3380 Washington St.	Clearlake	CA	95422	(707) 994-0589	2
Clover Cinemas	121 E 1st St.	Cloverdale	CA	95425	(707) 894-7920	4
Colusa Cinema	513 Market St.	Colusa	CA	95932	(530) 458-8588	1
Rodgers Theatre	1217 Solano St.	Corning	CA	96021	(530) 824-1773	1
Reds Drive In	395 G St.	Crescent City	CA	95531	(707) 464-1813	1
Reds Showcase Twin	395 G St.	Crescent City	CA	95531	(707) 464-1245	2
Village Theatre	23955 Lake Dr.	Crestline	CA	92325	(909) 338-0068	1
DeMille Theatre	9336 W Washington Blvd.	Culver City	CA	90232	(310) 202-3253	2
Family Twin	9823 Walker St.	Cypress	CA	90630	(714) 828-4161	2

Name	Address	City	State	Zip	Phone	Screens
Platinum Theatres	250 S M St.	Dinuba	CA	93618	(559) 595-9060	1
Dos Palos	1406 Center Ave.	Dos Palos	CA	93620	(209) 392-1010	2
Motor Vu Drive In	385 W Atren Rd.	El Centro	CA	92243	(805) 934-1582	2
Old Town Music	140 Richmond St.	El Segundo	CA	90245	(310) 322-2592	1
La Paloma Theatre	471 South Coast Hwy. 101	Encinitas	CA	92024	(760) 436-5774	1
Broadway Cinema	1223 Broadway Blvd.	Eureka	CA	95501	(707) 441-8467	8
Eureka Concert and Film	612 F St.	Eureka	CA	95501	(707) 442-2970	1
Movies 6	3300 Broadway	Eureka	CA	95501	(707) 443-6899	6
Fairfax	9 Broadway	Fairfax	CA	94930	(415) 453-8505	4
Fillmore Town Theatre	250 Central Ave.	Fillmore	CA	93015	(805) 524-1200	1
Coast Cinema	167 S Franklin St.	Fort Bragg	CA	95437	(707) 964-4540	4
The Fortuna	1241 Main St.	Fortuna	CA	95540	(707) 725-3010	6
Naz Cinema	1763 Acacia Court	Fremont	CA	94536	(510) 745-9340	1
Garberville Theatre	766 Redwood Dr.	Garberville	CA	95542	(707) 923-3580	1
Four Star Cinemas	12111 Valley View	Garden Grove	CA	92845	(714) 898-0284	4
Gardena Cinema	14948 S Crenshaw Blvd.	Gardena	CA	90249	(310) 217-0404	1
Platinum 7	6851 Monterey St.	Gilroy	CA	95020	(408) 846-9722	7
Alex Film	216 N Brand	Glendale	CA	91203	(818) 243-3516	1
Glendale Cinemas	501 N Orange St.	Glendale	CA	91203	(818) 549-9953	5
Del Oro III	165 Mill St.	Grass Valley	CA	95945	(530) 272-1646	3
Nevada	840-C E Main St.	Grass Valley	CA	95945	(530) 477-1100	1
Sierra Cinemas	840-C E Main St.	Grass Valley	CA	95945	(530) 477-1100	4
Sutton Cinema	399 Sutton Way	Grass Valley	CA	95945	(530) 273-0543	2
Hanford Fox Theatre	326 N Irwin St.	Hanford	CA	93230	(559) 584-7823	1
Metro 4	123 E 7th St.	Hanford	CA	93230	(559) 584-2356	4
Raven Theatre	415 Center St.	Healdsburg	CA	95448	(707) 431-1214	5
Granada Theatre	581A McCray St.	Hollister	CA	95023	(831) 638-1688	1
Premiere Cinemas	581A McCray St.	Hollister	CA	95023	(831) 638-1688	6
American Cinematheque	6712 Hollywood Blvd.	Hollywood	CA	90028	(323) 461-2020	1
AMPAS Linwood Dunn Theatre	1313 N Vine	Hollywood	CA	90028	(310) 247-3000	0
Egyptian Theatre 2	6712 Hollywood Blvd.	Hollywood	CA	90028	(323) 467-3475	2
Rustic Theatre	54380 N Circle Dr.	Idyllwild	CA	92549	(951) 659-2747	1
Movies-Imperial	2335 Hwy. 86	Imperial	CA	92251	(760) 353-5572	6
King City Cinema	200 Broadway Ave. Unit B	King City	CA	93930	(831) 385-9137	3
Laguna South Coast Cinema	162 South Coast Hwy.	Laguna Beach	CA	92651	(949) 497-1220	2
Laguna Hills Mall Cinema	24155 Laguna Hills Mall	Laguna Hills	CA	92653	(949) 586-8283	3
Lakeport Five	52 Soda Bay Rd.	Lakeport	CA	95453	(707) 263-0143	5
Lakeport Auto Movie	52 Soda Bay Rd.	Lakeport	CA	95453	(707) 263-0143	1
Lark Theatre	549 Magnolia Ave.	Larkspur	CA	94939	(415) 924-5459	1
Lemoore Stadium Cinemas 10	400 Follett St.	Lemoore	CA	93245	(559) 924-4884	10
Vine 2	1722 West 1st St.	Livermore	CA	94550	(925) 447-2546	2
Lodi Stadium 12	109 N School St.	Lodi	CA	95240	(209) 334-0100	12
Gemini Cinema	1028 North 8th St.	Lompoc	CA	93436	(805) 736-1306	2
The Movies	220 W Barton Ave.	Lompoc	CA	93436	(805) 736-1558	4
Art Theatre	2025 E 4th St.	Long Beach	CA	90814	(562) 438-5435	1
20th Century Fox	10201 W Pico Blvd.	Los Angeles	CA	90035	(310) 369-1000	1
Aero Theatre	1800 N Highland, Ste. 717	Los Angeles	CA	90028	(323) 461-2020	1
Beverly Cinema	7165 Beverly Blvd.	Los Angeles	CA	90036	(323) 938-4038	1
Cinetyp Hollywood	843 Seward St.	Los Angeles	CA	90038	(323) 463-8569	1
El Capitan	6838 Hollywood Blvd.	Los Angeles	CA	90028	(323) 467-7674	1
Harmony Gold Preview House	7655 Sunset Blvd.	Los Angeles	CA	90046	(323) 851-4900	1
Highland Theatre	5604 N Figueroa St.	Los Angeles	CA	90042	(323) 256-5833	3
Iron Mountain	1025 N Highland	Los Angeles	CA	90038	(323) 466-9287	1
Los Feliz 3	1822 N Vermont Ave.	Los Angeles	CA	90027	(323) 664-9623	3
Pickford Theatre	650 N Bronson	Los Angeles	CA	90004	(323) 871-5649	3
Showcase Cinema	614 North La Brea Ave.	Los Angeles	CA	90036	(323) 934-4071	1
Silent Movie	611 N Fairfax Ave.	Los Angeles	CA	90036	(323) 655-2510	1
University Village Theatre	3323 S Hoover	Los Angeles	CA	90007	(213) 748-6321	3
Vista Theatre	4473 Sunset Dr.	Los Angeles	CA	90027	(323) 660-6639	1
Wadsworth Theatre	11301 Wilshire Blvd #226	Los Angeles	CA	90073	(310) 479-3003	1
Los Banos Cinema	923 W Pacheco	Los Banos	CA	93635	(209) 826-7424	6
Premiere Cinemas	245 N Mercy Springs Rd.	Los Banos	CA	93635	(209) 827-9191	6
Los Gatos Cinema	41 N Santacruz	Los Gatos	CA	95030	(408) 395-0203	2
Madera 6	1140 N Gateway Dr.	Madera	CA	93637	(559)673-5381	6
Madera Drive In	1140 N Gateway Dr.	Madera	CA	93637	(559)673-5381	2
Minaret Cinema	437 Meridian Blvd.	Mammoth Lakes	CA	93546	(760)934-3131	2
Marketplace Stadium 10	1321 West Yosemite Ave.	Manteca	CA	95337	(209) 239-8806	10
Contra Costa Cinema	555 Center Ave.	Martinez	CA	94553	(925) 228-9983	5
Mill Creek Cinema 8	1575 Betty Ct.	McKinleyville	CA	95519	(707) 839-2222	8
Cinema 2 Plus	659 West Main	Merced	CA	95340	(209) 722-4042	2
The Merced Theatre	301 W Main St.	Merced	CA	95340	(209) 383-2442	4
State Theatre	1307 J St.	Modesto	CA	95354	(209) 527-4697	1
Mission Drive In 4 Plex	4407 State St.	Montclair	CA	91763	(909) 628-0511	4
The New Osio Cinemas 6	350 Alvarado St.	Monterey	CA	93940	(831) 333-9199	6
Rio Theatre	20396 Bohemian Highway	Monte Rio	CA	95462	(707) 865-0913	1
Mavericks Cinema 3	543 West Los Angeles Ave.	Moorpark	CA	93021	(805) 552-9154	3
Rheem Theatre	350 Park St.	Moraga	CA	94556	(925) 376-0885	4
Cinelux Tennant Station 11	750 Tennant Station Way	Morgan Hill	CA	95037	(408) 778-5900	6
Bay Theatre	464 Morro Bay Blvd.	Morro Bay	CA	93442	(805) 772-2444	1
Magic Theatre	107 Argall Way	Nevada City	CA	95959	(530) 265-8262	1
Regency Lido Theatre	3459 Via Lido	Newport Beach	CA	92663	(949) 673-8351	1
Regency Valley Plaza	6355 Bellingham Ave.	North Hollywood	CA	91606	(818) 760-1963	6
Oakdale Cinemas	832 N Yosemite Blvd.	Oakdale	CA	95361	(209) 848-8993	2
The Met Cinema	40015 Hwy. 49	Oakhurst	CA	93644	(559) 683-1234	5
Paramount	2025 Broadway	Oakland	CA	94612	(510) 893-2300	1
Parkway Theatre @ Lake Merritt	1834 Park Blvd.	Oakland	CA	94606	(510) 834-1506	2
Ojai Playhouse	214 E Ojai Ave.	Ojai	CA	93023	(805) 646-1011	1
Captain Blood's Village Twin	1140 N Tustin Ave.	Orange	CA	92867	(714) 808-0400	2
Feather River Cinemas	2690 Feather River Rd.	Oroville	CA	95965	(530) 534-1992	8
Plaza Stadium 14	255 W 5th St.	Oxnard	CA	93030	(805) 487-8380	14
Lighthouse Cinema	525 Lighthouse Ave.	Pacific Grove	CA	93950	(831) 372-7336	4
Cinemas Palme D'Or	72840 Hwy. 111	Palm Desert	CA	92260	(760) 779-0430	7
Camelot 3	2300 E Baristo Rd.	Palm Springs	CA	92262	(760) 325-6565	3
Stanford	221 University Ave.	Palo Alto	CA	94301	(650) 324-3700	1
Paradise Cinema	6701 Clark Rd.	Paradise	CA	95969	(530) 872-1499	7

Name	Address	City	State	Zip	Phone	Screens
Bianchi Theatres	7770 Rosecrans Ave.	Paramount	CA	90723	(562) 633-6441	11
Pinecrest Theatre	1 Pinecrest Lake Rd.	Pinecrest	CA	95364	(209) 965-3798	1
Arena Theatre	214 Main St.	Point Arena	CA	95468	(707) 882-3272	1
Porter Drive In	155 N Newcomb St.	Porterville	CA	93257	(559) 784-4840	2
Town Hall Theatre	469 W Main St.	Quincy	CA	95971	(530) 283-3402	1
Prime Cinemas Red Bluff	400 S Main St.	Red Bluff	CA	96080	(530) 378-3411	6
Cascade Theatre	1735 Market St.	Redding	CA	96001	(530) 243-8886	1
Ridgecrest Cine	1631 Triangle Dr.	Ridgecrest	CA	93555	(760) 446-6996	5
Galaxy 12	2525 Patterson Rd.	Riverbank	CA	95367	(209) 863-9012	12
Rubidoux Drive In	3770 Opal & Misson Blvd.	Riverside	CA	92509	(951) 683-4478	3
Van Buren Drive In	3035 Van Buren Blvd.	Riverside	CA	92503	(951) 688-2360	3
Crest Theatre	1013 K St.	Sacramento	CA	95814	(916) 442-5189	3
City Tower 3	2508 Land Park Dr.	Sacramento	CA	95818	(916) 442-0985	3
Cameo Cinema	1342 Main St.	Saint Helena	CA	94574	(707) 963-3946	1
Maya Salinas Cinemas	153 Main St.	Salinas	CA	93901	(831) 757-6299	14
Regency Sterling Cinemas	2373 N Sterling Ave.	San Bernardino	CA	92404	(909) 821-9875	6
South Bay Drive In	2170 Coronado Ave.	San Diego	CA	92154	(619) 423-2566	3
Balboa St.	3630 Balboa St.	San Francisco	CA	94121	(415) 221-3117	2
Castro Theatre	429 Castro St.	San Francisco	CA	94114	(415) 621-5288	1
Four Star	2200 Clement	San Francisco	CA	94121	(415) 666-3488	1
Frameline	346 9th St.	San Francisco	CA	94103	(415) 703-8669	1
Letterman Digital Arts Center	1110 Gorgas Ave.	San Francisco	CA	94129	(415) 746-2002	0
Presidio Theatre	2340 Chesnut St.	San Francisco	CA	94123	(415) 776-2988	4
Red Vic Movie House	1727 Haight St.	San Francisco	CA	94117	(415) 668-8999	1
Roxie Cinema	3125 16th St.	San Francisco	CA	94103	(415) 431-3611	1
San Francisco Film Society	39 Mesa St. Ste. 110	San Francisco	CA	94129	(415) 561-5036	1
The Herbst Theatre	401 Van Ness Ave.	San Francisco	CA	94102	(415) 554-6345	1
Victoria Theatre	2961 16th St.	San Francisco	CA	94103	(415) 863-7576	1
Camera 12	201 South 2nd St.	San Jose	CA	95113	(408) 998-3022	12
Bal Theatre	14808 E 14th St.	San Leandro	CA	94578	(510) 895-8300	1
Palm Theatre	817 Palm St.	San Luis Obispo	CA	93401	(805) 547-1106	3
Sunset Drive In	255 Elks Ln.	San Luis Obispo	CA	93401	(805) 544-4592	1
Warner Grand Theatre	478 W Sixth St.	San Pedro	CA	90731	(310) 548-2493	1
Industrial Light & Magic	3160 Kerner Blvd.	San Rafael	CA	94901	(415) 448-2122	1
Rafael Film Center	1118 Fourth St.	San Rafael	CA	94901	(415) 454-5813	3
A Mainplace Theatre 6	2800 N Main St.	Santa Ana	CA	92705	(714) 547-6145	6
Bacara Resort	8301 Hollister Ave.	Santa Barbara	CA	93117	(805) 968-0100	1
Del-Mar	210 Lincoln St.	Santa Cruz	CA	95060	(831) 469-3224	3
Nickelodeon Theatres	210 Lincoln St.	Santa Cruz	CA	95060	(831) 426-7507	4
Skyview Drive In #2	2260 Soquel Dr.	Santa Cruz	CA	95065	(831) 475-3405	2
Sante Fe Springs Drive In	13963 Alondra Blvd.	Santa Fe Springs	CA	90670	(562) 921-4359	1
HiWay Drive In	3170 Santa Maria Way	Santa Maria	CA	93455	(805) 934-1582	1
Airport Cinemas	409 Aviation Way	Santa Rosa	CA	95403	(707) 571-1412	12
Rialto Cinemas Lakeside	551 Summerfield Rd.	Santa Rosa	CA	95405	(707) 539-9771	5
Roxy 14	85 Santa Rosa Ave.	Santa Rosa	CA	95404	(707) 527-7699	14
Roxy on the Square	620 Third St.	Santa Rosa	CA	95404	(707) 525-8909	6
Santee Drive-In	10990 Woodside Ave. N	Santee	CA	92071	(619) 448-4499	2
Scotts Valley Cinema	226 Mt Hermon Rd.	Scotts Valley	CA	95066	(831) 438-5118	6
Bay Theatre	340 Main St.	Seal Beach	CA	90740	(562) 598-9811	1
Sebastopol Cinema 9	6868 McKinley St.	Sebastopol	CA	95472	(707) 829-3921	9
Selma Cinema	2705 Cinema Way	Selma	CA	93662	(559) 891-8636	6
Sebastiani Theatre	476 First St. E.	Sonoma	CA	95476	(707) 996-9756	1
Sonoma Cinemas	200 Siesta Way Ste. 700	Sonoma	CA	95476	(707) 935-1335	4
Heavenly Village Cinema	1021 Heavenly Village Way Ste. 40	S. Lake Tahoe	CA	96150	(530) 544-1684	8
Fox Theatre	242 E Main	Stockton	CA	95202	(209) 464-4369	1
Sierra	501 Main St.	Susanville	CA	96130	(530) 251-1811	2
Uptown	501 Main St.	Susanville	CA	96130	(530) 257-7474	4
Marysville Drive In	6733 Butte Ave.	Sutter	CA	95982	(530) 743-9384	1
Cobblestone	465 N Lake Blvd	Tahoe City	CA	96145	(530) 546-5951	1
Fox Taft	514 Center St.	Taft	CA	93268	(805) 403-7381	3
Hitching Post Theatre	201 S Green St.	Tehachapi	CA	93561	(661) 823-7452	4
Temeku 7	26463 Ynez Rd. #22	Temecula	CA	92591	(951) 296-9310	7
Backlot Theatre	1408 E Thousand Oaks Blvd.	Thousand Oaks	CA	91362	(805) 497-7691	1
Smith's Ranch Drive-In	4584 Adobe Rd.	Twentynine Palms	CA	92277	(760) 361-1531	1
Fox Theatre	15 Maple St.	Watsonville	CA	95076	(831) 724-1209	3
Green Valley Cinema 8	1125 South Green Valley Rd.	Watsonville	CA	95076	(831) 761-8300	6
Prime Cinemas Trinity Theatre	310 Main St.	Weaverville	CA	96093	(530) 378-3411	2
Westwood Crest Theatre	1262 Westwood Blvd.	Westwood	CA	90024	(310) 474-7824	1
Whittier Village Cinema 9	7038 Greenleaf Ave.	Whittier	CA	90602	(562) 945-5271	9
The Opus	236 W Sycamore	Willows	CA	95988	(530) 934-7168	4
Reel Cinema	6742 Wofford Hgts.	Wofford Heights	CA	93285	(760) 376-6910	1
State Theatre	322 Main St.	Woodland	CA	95695	(530) 662-5475	3
Broadway Twin	210 S Broadway	Yreka	CA	96097	(530) 842-6548	2
Cinema 6	56401 29 Palms Hwy.	Yucca Valley	CA	92284	(760) 365-9666	6

COLORADO

Name	Address	City	State	Zip	Phone	Screens
Ski Hi 6	7089 US Hwy. 160	Alamosa	CO	81101	(719) 589-4639	6
Arvada Elvis Cinemas	5157 W 64th Ave.	Arvada	CO	80003	(303) 426-1620	8
Film Society	320 E Hyman Ave.	Aspen	CO	81611	(970) 925-6882	1
Aurora Cinema Grill	13682 E Alameda Ave.	Aurora	CO	80012	(303) 344-5565	3
Buckingham Mall 4	1390 S Havana St.	Aurora	CO	80012	(303) 306-0943	4
Cinema Latino	777 Peoria St.	Aurora	CO	80011	(303) 364-0803	8
Boulder Theatre	2032 14th St.	Boulder	CO	80302	(303) 998-9420	1
Speakeasy Theatre	103 S Harris St.	Breckenridge	CO	80424	(719) 839-1555	1
Sands Theatre	211 Clayton St.	Brush	CO	80723	(970) 842-2466	1
Comanche Drive In	29910 County Rd. 351	Buena Vista	CO	81211	(719) 395-8993	1
Pearl	29910 County Rd. 351	Buena Vista	CO	81211	(719) 395-8993	1
Midway	446 1/2 14th St.	Burlington	CO	80807	(719) 346-7976	1
Skyline	1036 S 12th St.	Canon City	CO	81212	(719) 269-3190	1
Crystal Theatre	251 Euclid	Carbondale	CO	81623	(970) 963-0633	1
Movieland	218 E Valley Rd. Ste. 300	Carbondale	CO	81623	(970) 963-2616	7
Kimball's Peak Three Theatre	115 E Pikes Peak Ave.	Colorado Springs	CO	80903	(719) 447-1947	3
Picture Show	901 N Academy Blvd.	Colorado Springs	CO	80909	(719) 570-7469	8

Name	Address	City	State	Zip	Phone	Screens
88 Drive-In	8780 Rosemary St.	Commerce City	CO	80022	(303) 880-3292	1
Fiesta Twin	23 W Main St.	Cortez	CO	81321	(970) 565-7380	2
West Twin	29 E Victory Way	Craig	CO	81625	(970) 824-2000	2
Egyptian Theatre	452 Main St.	Delta	CO	81416	(970) 874-9770	1
Tru Vu Drive In	1001 Hwy. 92 E.	Delta	CO	81416	(970) 874-9556	1
Elvis Cinemas Tiffany Plaza	7400 E. Hampden Ave.	Denver	CO	80231	(303) 221-1672	6
Starz Filmcenter	900 Auraria Pkwy.	Denver	CO	80204	(303) 893-3456	12
The Historic Oriental Theatre	4335 Forty-Fourth Ave.	Denver	CO	80212	(303) 455-2124	1
Capitol Theatre	1140 Capitol St.	Eagle	CO	81631	(970) 476-3035	4
Riverwalk	34253 Hwy. 6	Edwards	CO	81632	(970) 926-5709	4
Cinderella Twin Drive In	3400 S Platte River Dr.	Englewood	CO	80110	(303) 781-0500	2
Park Theatre	130 Moraine	Estes Park	CO	80517	(970) 586-8904	1
Reel Mountain Theatre	168 Stanley Circle Dr.	Estes Park	CO	80517	(970) 586-6995	3
Holiday Drive In	2206 South Overland Trail	Fort Collins	CO	80521	(970) 221-1244	2
Cover 4 Theatre	314 Main St.	Fort Morgan	CO	80701	(970) 867-2311	4
Valley Drive In	314 Main St.	Fort Morgan	CO	80701	(970) 867-5724	1
Springs Theatre	915 Grand Ave.	Glenwood Springs	CO	81601	(970) 945-6077	1
Cinema at the Avalon	645 Main St.	Grand Junction	CO	81501	(970) 243-7033	1
Peerless Theatre	212 S Interocean Ave.	Holyoke	CO	80734	(970) 854-2453	1
Hippodrome Arts Ctr	215 Cedar St.	Julesburg	CO	80737	(970) 474-3488	1
Mountaineer	269 Hwy. 149 Gunnison	Lake City	CO	81235	(970) 944-2298	1
Lamar Theatre	219 S Main	Lamar	CO	81052	(719) 336-5737	1
Silver City Cinema	115 W 6th St.	Leadville	CO	80461	(719) 486-8107	1
Lincoln Theatre	245 East Ave.	Limon	CO	80828	(719) 775-2114	1
Elvis Cinemas Littleton	6014 S Kipling St.	Littleton	CO	80127	(303) 948-9461	6
Star Drive In	2830 W US Hwy. 160	Monte Vista	CO	81144	(719) 852-2613	1
Vali 3 Theatre	139 Adams St.	Monte Vista	CO	81144	(719) 852-2811	3
Fox Theater	27 South Cascade Ave.	Montrose	CO	81401	(970) 249-8211	3
San Juan	1869 E Main St.	Montrose	CO	81401	(970) 252-9097	2
Star Drive In	600 E Miami Rd.	Montrose	CO	81401	(970) 249-6170	1
Ouray Cinema & Theatre	472 Main St.	Ouray	CO	81427	(970) 325-0144	1
Liberty Theatre	418 Pagosa St.	Pagosa Springs	CO	81147	(970) 264-4578	1
Paradise Theatre	215 Grand Ave.	Paonia	CO	81428	(970) 527-6610	1
Mesa Drive In	2700 Sante Fe Dr.	Pueblo	CO	81006	(719) 542-3345	3
Ute Theatre	408 4th St.	Saguache	CO	81149	(719) 655-2020	1
Storyville Cinema	135 W 1st St.	Salida	CO	81201	(719) 539-7002	2
Capitol Theatre, LLC	148 E 9th Ave.	Springfield	CO	81073	(719) 523-6791	1
Fox 5 Theatre	313 Poplar	Sterling	CO	80751	(970) 522-7744	5
Nugget	207 W Colorado Ave.	Telluride	CO	81435	(970) 728-3030	1
Sheridan Opera House	110 N Oak St.	Telluride	CO	81435	(970) 728-6363	1
Fox Theatre	423 W Main St.	Trinidad	CO	81082	(719) 846-2851	1
Movie Picture Showhouse	3600 E Main	Trinidad	CO	81082	(719) 846-0552	2
Riverwalk Theatre	1st & Main St.	Vail	CO	81657	(970) 476-5661	5
Vail Cascade Resort	1300 Westhaven Dr.	Vail	CO	81657	(970) 333-9689	1
Jones Theater	118 Main St.	Westcliffe	CO	81252	(719) 783-2350	1
Gold Hill Theatres	615 W Midland Ave.	Woodland Park	CO	80863	(719) 687-3555	2
Yuma	307 S Main St.	Yuma	CO	80759	(970) 848-5741	1

CONNECTICUT

Name	Address	City	State	Zip	Phone	Screens
Bantam Cinema	115 Rte. 209	Bantam	CT	06750	(860) 567-0006	2
Bethel Cinema	269 Greenwood Ave.	Bethel	CT	06801	(203) 778-3100	4
Forestville Theatres	815 Pine St.	Bristol	CT	06010	(860) 583-1223	8
Colonial Twin Theatre	27 Railroad St.	Canaan	CT	06018	(860) 824-4488	1
Gallery Cinema	396 Old Hartford Rd.	Colchester	CT	06415	(860) 537-6682	6
Community Theatre Foundation	1424 Post Rd.	Fairfield	CT	06430	(203) 255-6112	2
Cinestudio	300 Summit St.	Hartford	CT	06106	(860) 297-2544	1
Real Art Ways	56 Arbor St.	Hartford	CT	06106	(860) 233-1006	1
Wadsworth Atheunum	25 Prospect St.	Hartford	CT	06103	(860) 278-2670	1
State Theatre Twin	80 W Main St.	Jewett City	CT	06351	(860) 376-6323	2
Oneil Lisbon Landing Cinema 12	162 River Rd.	Lisbon	CT	06351	(860) 376-3965	12
Madison Art	757 Boston Post Rd.	Madison	CT	06443	(203) 245-8449	2
Mansfield Drive In	228 Stafford Rd.	Mansfield Center	CT	06250	(860) 423-4411	3
Holiday Cinema Meriden 10	61 Pomeroy Ave.	Meriden	CT	06450	(203) 265-7069	10
York Square Cinema 1 2 3	55 Broadway	New Haven	CT	06511	(203) 773-3104	3
Garde Art Center	325 State St.	New London	CT	06320	(860) 444-6766	1
Bank Street Theatre	46 Bank St.	New Milford	CT	06776	(860) 354-9911	3
Edmond Town Hall Theatre	45 Main St.	Newtown	CT	06470	(203) 426-0048	1
Niantic Cinema	279 Main St.	Niantic	CT	06357	(860) 739-9995	4
Garden Cinema 1 & 2	26 Isaac St.	Norwalk	CT	06850	(203) 838-2736	3
Ridgefield Playhouse	80 E Ridge St.	Ridgefield	CT	06877	(203) 438-5795	1
Strand	165 Main St.	Seymour	CT	06483	(203) 888-5290	1
Cinema @ Simsbury	530 Bushy Hills Rd.	Simsbury	CT	06070	(860) 658-0187	8
State Art Theatre	990 Hope St.	Springdale	CT	06907	(203) 325-0250	3
Avon Theatre	272 Bedford St.	Stamford	CT	06901	(203) 967-3660	2
State Theatre	990 Hope St.	Stamford	CT	06907	(203) 327-4622	1
Cinerom Torrington	89 Farley Pl.	Torrington	CT	06790	(860) 489-5605	6
Holiday 10	970 N Colony Rd.	Wallingford	CT	06492	(203) 597-0428	0
Holiday 10 Cinema	117 Sharon Rd.	Waterbury	CT	06705	(203) 597-1803	10
Country Cinema	523 Main St.	Watertown	CT	06795	(860) 274-3827	1
Cinerom Winsted	380 New Hartford Rd.	Winsted	CT	06098	(860) 738-6507	9
Gilson Cafe & Cinema	354 Main St.	Winsted	CT	06098	(860) 379-6069	2

DELAWARE

Name	Address	City	State	Zip	Phone	Screens
Clayton Theatre	900 Main St.	Dagsboro	DE	19939	(302) 732-9606	1
Schwartz Center for the Arts	226 S State St.	Dover	DE	19901	(302) 678-3583	1
Everett	45 W Main St.	Middletown	DE	19709	(302) 378-1200	1
Cinema Center 3	401 Newark Shop Ctr.	Newark	DE	19711	(302) 737-3720	3
Movies @ Midway	29 Midway Shop Ctr.	Rehoboth Beach	DE	19971	(302) 645-0200	14
Rehoboth Mall Cinemas	4493 Hwy. 1 Unit 16	Rehoboth Beach	DE	19971	(302) 644-8842	6
Grand Opera House	818 North Market St.	Wilmington	DE	19801	(302) 658-7897	1
Theatre N @ Nemours	1007 Orange St.	Wilmington	DE	19801	(302) 576-2135	1

Name	Address	City	State	Zip	Phone	Screens

DISTRICT ODISTRICT OF COLUMBIA

Name	Address	City	State	Zip	Phone	Screens
Avalon Theatre	5612 Connecticut Ave. NW	Washington	DC	20015	(202) 966-3464	2
Lincoln Theatre	1215 U St. NW	Washington	DC	20009	(202) 328-6000	1
Reel Affirmations	2130 P St. NW Ste. 1011	Washington	DC	20037	(202) 315-1319	1
Visions Cinema	1927 Florida Ave. NW	Washington	DC	20009	(202) 232-5689	2

FLORIDA

Name	Address	City	State	Zip	Phone	Screens
The Picture Show at Altamonte	130 E Altamonte Dr. Ste. 1200	Altamonte Springs	FL	32701	(407) 740-7469	6
Touchstar Cinemas Altamonte 8	303 E Altamonte Dr. #1800	Altamonte Springs	FL	32701	(407) 830-1995	8
Dixie Theatre	100 Market St.	Apalachicola	FL	32320	(850) 653-3200	1
Ruskin Family Drive In Theatre	5011 US Hwy. 41 N	Apollo Beach	FL	33572	(813) 645-1455	1
Arcadia Theatre	1304 E Oak St.	Arcadia	FL	34266	(863) 494-6876	2
Mizner Park 8	301 Plaza Real	Boca Raton	FL	33432	(561) 368-7744	8
Alco Boynton Cinema	9764 S Military Trail	Boynton Beach	FL	33436	(561) 366-7500	8
Desoto Dollar Movies	303 US 301 Blvd. W 911	Bradenton	FL	34205	(941) 744-2950	6
Disney Cruise	405 Atlantis Rd.	Cape Canaveral	FL	32920	(321) 868-2230	1
Vance Theatre	799 Main St.	Chipley	FL	32428	(850) 638-1070	1
Clearwater Cinema Cafe	24095 US Hwy. 19 N.	Clearwater	FL	33763	(727) 797-9808	2
Mann's Clewiston Theatre	100 E Sugarland Hwy.	Clewiston	FL	33440	(863) 983-6494	2
Crestview Cinema 3	789 N Ferdon Blvd.	Crestview	FL	32536	(850) 682-3201	3
Absinthe House Cinematheque	235 Alcazar Ave.	Coral Gables	FL	33134	(305) 446-7144	1
CKM Movie Theatre	439 NE 118th St.	Cross City	FL	32628	(352) 498-4084	1
Joylan Drive In	16414 Hwy. 301 N.	Dade City	FL	33525	(352) 567-5085	1
Deerfield Cinemas 5	2205 W Hillsboro Blvd.	Deerfield Beach	FL	33442	(954) 725-4402	5
Delray Square Cinemas 5	4809 W Atlantic Ave.	Delray Beach	FL	33445	(561) 499-9022	5
Oriole Cinema	7421 W Atlantic Ave.	Delray Beach	FL	33446	(561) 638-0021	5
Cinema Paradiso	503 S E 6th St.	Fort Lauderdale	FL	33301	(954) 760-9898	1
Galleria Cinema 4	2630 E Sunrise Blvd.	Fort Lauderdale	FL	33304	(954) 565-1884	4
Movie Film Service	3780 SW 30th Ave.	Fort Lauderdale	FL	33312	(954) 922-0700	4
Tamarac Showplace Movies, LLC	10036 West McNab Rd.	Fort Lauderdale	FL	33321	(954) 726-7265	5
Swap Shop Drive-In	3291 W Sunrise Blvd.	Fort Lauderdale	FL	33311	(954) 791-7927	13
Weston Cinema 8	1338 SW 160th Ave.	Fort Lauderdale	FL	33326	(954) 385-1950	8
Beach Theatre	6425 Estero Blvd.	Fort Myers Beach	FL	33931	(239) 765-9000	4
Nova Cinemas @ Sabal Palm	2539 S Federal Hwy.	Fort Pierce	FL	34982	(772) 489-8889	6
Cinema Plus	174 Miracle Strip Pkwy.	Ft. Walton Beach	FL	32548	(850) 302-0129	1
Gator Cinemas	6741 W Newberry Rd.	Gainesville	FL	32605	(352) 331-5977	4
Hippodrome State	25 SE 2nd Place	Gainesville	FL	32601	(352) 373-5968	1
Clay Theatre	326 Walnut St.	Green Cove Sprgs	FL	32043	(904) 284-9012	2
Gulf Breeze Cinema 4	1175 Gulf Breeze Pkwy.	Gulf Breeze	FL	32561	(850) 916-9404	4
The Breeze 8	1233 Crain Cove	Gulf Breeze	FL	32561	(850) 934-3315	8
Priest	15 NW First St.	High Springs	FL	32643	(386) 454-2200	1
Flippers Cinema 10	7001 Taft St.	Hollywood	FL	33024	(954) 981-5443	10
Playtime Drive In	6300 Blanding Blvd.	Jacksonville	FL	32244	(561) 436-9583	3
Ritz Theatre & Lavilla Museum	829 N Davis St.	Jacksonville	FL	32202	(904) 632-5555	1
San Marco	1996 San Marco Blvd.	Jacksonville	FL	32207	(904) 396-4845	1
Jacksonville Beach Amphitheatre	11 N Third St.	Jacksonville Beach	FL	32250	(904) 270-1651	1
Ocean Reef	200 Anchor Dr.	Key Largo	FL	33037	(305) 522-1709	1
Lake Worth Drive In	3438 Lakeworth Rd.	Lake Worth	FL	33461	(561) 965-4518	1
Movies of Lake Worth 6	7380 Lake Worth Rd.	Lake Worth	FL	33467	(561) 968-4545	6
Polk Theatre	121 S Florida Ave.	Lakeland	FL	33801	(863) 682-7553	1
Silvermoon Drive In	4100 US 92 West	Lakeland	FL	33815	(407) 682-8227	2
Enzian	1300 S Orlando Ave.	Maitland	FL	32751	(407) 629-1088	1
Marathon Community Theatre	5101 Overseas Hwy.	Marathon	FL	33050	(305) 743-0288	1
Marco Movies	599 S Collier Blvd Ste. 103	Marco Island	FL	34145	(239) 394-3333	4
Cinema World	4345 W New Haven Ave.	Melbourne	FL	32904	(321) 723-4143	16
Premiere Theatres	1800 W Hibiscus Blvd #119	Melbourne	FL	32901	(321) 953-3388	10
Florida Moving Image Archive	101 W Flagler St.	Miami	FL	33130	(305) 375-1505	0
Lejeune Cinema Six	782 NW 42nd Ave.	Miami	FL	33126	(305) 529-8876	6
Valentino	8500 Block of SW 8th St.	Miami	FL	33144	(305) 266-2002	3
IFP Shores Performing Arts Theatre	9806 NE 2nd Ave.	Miami Shores	FL	33150	(305) 458-0280	1
California Club	850 Ives Dairy Rd.	N Miami Beach	FL	33179	(305) 653-3456	6
Naples Drive In Theatre	7700 Davis Blvd.	Naples	FL	34104	(239) 774-2900	2
Pavillion Cinema 6	833 Vanderbilt Beach Rd.	Naples	FL	34108	(239) 596-0062	6
Twin Cities Cinema	1047 E John Sims Pkwy.	Niceville	FL	32578	(850) 678-3815	2
Northside Twin Drive In	2521 N Tamiami Trail	North Fort Myers	FL	33903	(239) 995-2254	2
Intracoastal Cinema	3701 NE 163rd St.	N. Miami Beach	FL	33160	(305) 949-6002	8
West Orange 5	1575 Maguire Rd.	Ocoee	FL	34761	(407) 877-3489	5
Colonial Promenade 6	4672 E Colonial Dr.	Orlando	FL	32803	(407) 888-8224	6
Sand Lake Seven	835 Sand Lake Rd.	Orlando	FL	32809	(407) 888-9956	7
Touchstar Cinemas South Chase 7	12441 S Orange Blossom Trail	Orlando	FL	32837	(407) 888-2027	7
Ridge Cinema 8	4915 Hwy. 90	Pace	FL	32571	(850) 995-1600	8
Hollywood Movie	201 Azalea Plaza Dr.	Palatka	FL	32177	(386) 329-4009	1
Nova Cinema @ Palm Bay	160 Malabar Rd. SW	Palm Bay	FL	32907	(321) 956-8552	10
BMC PGA Cinema	4076 PGA Blvd.	Palm Bch Gardens	FL	33410	(561) 776-4001	6
BMC Promenade East Cinemas	9930 Alt A1A SR 811	Palm Bch Gardens	FL	33410	(561) 624-2669	8
The Picture Show Three	229 St. Joe Plaza Dr.	Palm Coast	FL	32164	(386) 446-6414	3
Pensacola Silver Screen	7280 Plantation	Pensacola	FL	32504	(850) 476-7469	4
Perry 3	118 E Park St.	Perry	FL	32348	(850) 223-6684	3
Fountain Cinema	801 S University Dr. #300	Plantation	FL	33324	(954) 472-5265	8
Mercede Cinema 4	1870 N University Dr.	Plantation	FL	33322	(954) 473-6700	4
Embassy 6	9510 US 19 N.	Port Richey	FL	34668	(727) 264-8978	6
Pot Belly,s Cinema 4	36 Granada St.	Saint Augustine	FL	32084	(904) 797-3721	4
Island Cinema	535 Tarpon Bay Rd.	Sanibel Island	FL	33957	(239) 472-1701	2
Burns Court Cinemas	506 Burns Ln.	Sarasota	FL	34236	(941) 955-3456	3
N&S Fairmount Cinema 6	3750 US 27 North	Sebring	FL	33870	(863) 385-9908	6
Seminole Theatre Company, LLC	7990 Liberty Ln.	Seminole	FL	33772	(727) 320-0757	8
Spring Hill 8	2955 Commercial Way	Spring Hill	FL	34606	(352) 666-6656	8
St Cloud Twin	1110 10th St.	St Cloud	FL	34769	(407) 957-2955	1
Beach Theatre	315 Corey Ave.	St Petersburg	FL	33706	(727) 360-6697	1
Florida Twin Theatre	101 W Call St.	Starke	FL	32091	(904) 964-5451	2
Lyric Theatre	59 SW Flagler Ave.	Stuart	FL	34994	(772) 220-1942	1
Britton 8	3938 S. Dale Mabry Hwy.	Tampa	FL	33611	(813) 839-5400	8

Name	Address	City	State	Zip	Phone	Screens
Channelside Cinemas 10	615 Channelside Dr.	Tampa	FL.	33602	(813) 221-0006	10
Fun-lan Drive In	2302 E Hillsborough Ave.	Tampa	FL.	33610	(813) 237-0886	3
Sunrise Cinemas at Old Park	1609 Swann Ave.	Tampa	FL.	33606	(813) 258-5640	7
Tampa Pitcher Show	14416 N Dale Mabry Hwy.	Tampa	FL.	33618	(813) 963-0578	1
Tampa Theatre	711 Franklin St. Mall	Tampa	FL.	33602	(813) 274-8287	1
B & B Theatres Tavernier Cinema 5	91264 Overseas Hwy.	Tavernier	FL.	33070	(305) 853-7004	2
Old Mill Playhouse	1000 Old Mill Run	The Villages	FL.	32162	(352) 259-1111	8
Rialto 8	1105 Alonzo Ave.	The Villages	FL.	32159	(352) 753-8898	8
Galaxy 12	940 14th Ln.	Vero Beach	FL.	32960	(772) 299-6284	12
The Silver Screen Cafe	12795 W Forest Hill Blvd.	Wellington	FL.	33411	(561) 795-3001	2
Wellington Marketplace	13881 Wellington Trace	Wellington	FL.	33414	(561) 792-4448	8
Metro Cinema Cafe	3020 W New Haven Ave.	West Melbourne	FL.	32904	(321) 727-7819	2
Green Acres River Bridge Cinema 8	6846 Forest Hill Blvd.	West Palm Beach	FL.	33413	(561) 304-0015	8
Aloma Cinema Grill	2155 Aloma Ave.	Winter Park	FL.	32792	(407) 671-4964	1

GEORGIA

Name	Address	City	State	Zip	Phone	Screens
Imagination Theatre	117 Pine Ave. 1st Flr.	Albany	GA	31701	(229) 639-2650	1
Cinevision Screening Room	3300 NE Expy.	Atlanta	GA	30341	(770) 455-8988	1
Fox Theatre	660 Peachtree St. NE	Atlanta	GA	30308	(404) 881-2100	1
Lefont Plaza	1049 Ponce de Leon	Atlanta	GA	30306	(404) 873-1939	2
Lefont Sandy Springs Theatre	5920 Roswell Rd.	Atlanta	GA	30328	(404) 255-0100	8
Starlight Drive In	2000 Moreland Ave. SE	Atlanta	GA	30316	(404) 627-3641	6
Bald Mountain Cinema 3	1650 Backyard Ln.	Blairsville	GA	30512	(706) 745-8227	3
Blue Ridge Twin Cinema	10091 Blue Ridge Rd.	Blue Ridge	GA	30513	(706) 632-7202	2
Swan Drive In	Hwy. 76/Summit St.	Blue Ridge	GA	30513	(706) 632-5235	1
Zebulon Theatre	207 North Broad St.	Cairo	GA	39828	(229) 377-3302	1
West Theatre	112 West Ave.	Cedartown	GA	30125	(770) 748-9062	2
Nova Cinema	340 Tanger Dr.	Commerce	GA	30529	(706) 335-4366	6
Movies 400	415 Atlanta Rd.	Cumming	GA	30040	(678) 947-4473	12
Holly Theatre	69 W Main St.	Dahlonega	GA	30533	(706) 864-3759	1
Wink Theatre	115 W Crawford St.	Dalton	GA	30720	(906) 226-9465	1
Highway 17	2395 Bowman Hwy.	Dewy Rose	GA	30634	(706) 283-3232	2
East Town Twin Cinema	Hwy. 575 Maddox Rd.	Ellijay	GA	30540	(706) 635-5700	2
Grand Theatre	119 S Main St.	Fitzgerald	GA	31750	(229) 426-5090	1
Westside Cinema	403 E Hwy. 80 W	Garden City	GA	31408	(912) 966-9102	2
The Theatre	22 W Jefferson St. Ste. 5	Hazlehurst	GA	31539	(912) 375-5521	1
Fieldstone Cinema 6	1159 Fuller Circle	Hiawassee	GA	30546	(706) 896-3006	4
Movies 278	185 Metromont Rd.	Hiram	GA	30141	(678) 947-4473	15
Jesup Twin Drive-In	3686 Savannah Hwy.	Jesup	GA	31545	(912) 427-7245	2
Strand	169 Cherry St.	Jesup	GA	31545	(912) 427-0077	2
Legacy Covington Square 8	2244 Panola Rd.	Lithonia	GA	30058	(770) 593-8303	8
Pal Theatre	134 West Broad St.	Louisville	GA	30434	(478) 625-9998	1
Douglass Theatre	355 Martin Luther King Blvd.	Macon	GA	31201	(478) 742-2000	1
El Cine Mireles 2	3378 Canton Rd.	Marietta	GA	30066	(678) 290-4126	2
Picture Show Entertainment	4400 Upper Roswell Rd.	Marietta	GA	30062	(770) 321-7818	5
Habersham Hills Cinema 6	2115 Cody Rd.	Mount Airy	GA	30563	(706) 754-3965	6
Galaxy Theatre	4975 Jimmy Carter Blvd.	Norcross	GA	30093	(770) 931-3509	5
Peachtree Cinema 8	6135 Peachtree Pkwy.	Norcross	GA	30092	(770) 448-4792	8
Galazy Cinema Funplex	274 Hwy. 138 South West	Riverdale	GA	30274	(770) 473-1796	14
Movies at Berry Square	2820 Martha Berry Hwy.	Rome	GA	30165	(706) 235-9335	9
Rome 7 Cinemas	2535 Shorter Ave.	Rome	GA	30165	(706) 235-2200	7
Village Theatre	836 Turner McCall Blvd.	Rome	GA	30161	(706) 235-2200	4
Startime Cinema	608 Holcomb Bridge Rd.	Roswell	GA	30076	(770) 993-5411	10
Black Bear Dinner Theatre	32 Dawn Way	Sautee-Nacoochee	GA	30571	(706) 865-0074	1
Trustee Theatre	216 E Broughton St.	Savannah	GA	31401	(912) 525-5040	1
Ritz Theatre	114 South Church St.	Thomaston	GA	30286	(706) 647-7022	1
Thomson Twin Cinema	131 Main St.	Thomson	GA	30824	(706) 595-7317	2
Tiger Drive In	2956 Old US Hwy. 41	Tiger	GA	30576	(706) 782-1611	1
Toccoa Triple Cinema	Hwy.17 South	Toccoa	GA	30577	(706) 886-7346	3
Wilderness Outdoor Movie Theatre	217 Old Hales Gap Rd.	Trenton	GA	30752	(706) 657-8411	1
Sweet Onion Cinema 5	2709 E First St.	Vidalia	GA	30474	(912) 537-0789	5

HAWAII

Name	Address	City	State	Zip	Phone	Screens
Palace Theater	38 Haioi St	Hilo	HI	96720	(808) 934-7010	1
Doris Duke Theatre	900 S. Beretania St.	Honolulu	HI	96819	(808) 532-8700	1
Movie Museum	3566 Harding Avenue	Honolulu	HI	96819	(808) 735-8771	1
Kukui Grove 4 Cinemas	4368 Kukui Grove St.	Lihue	HI	96766	(808) 245-3552	4
Waimea Theater	9691 Kaumualii Hwy.	Kauai	HI	96796	(808) 338-2027	1

IOWA

Name	Address	City	State	Zip	Phone	Screens
Albia Theatre	115 Benton Ave. E	Albia	IA	52531	(641) 932-5511	1
Rose Theatre	318 Broadway St.	Audubon	IA	50025	(712) 563-3259	1
King Theatre	720 12th St.	Belle Plaine	IA	52208	(319) 434-6025	1
Lyric Theatre	431 E Main St.	Belmond	IA	50421	(641) 444-7225	1
Iowa	107 S Washington	Bloomfield	IA	52537	(641) 664-9588	1
Dreamland Theatre	107 Broadway	Carson	IA	51525	(712) 486-2281	1
Sunshine Mine Drive In Theatre	18905 Sunshine Rd.	Centerville	IA	52544	(641) 856-3402	1
Vision II Theatre	327 North Main St.	Chariton	IA	50049	(641) 774-8878	2
Charles Theatre	409 N Main St.	Charles City	IA	50616	(641) 228-3821	1
Brokaw American Theatre	704 Davis Ave.	Corning	IA	50841	(641) 782-3310	1
Moran's Omni 4 Theatres	300 West Broadway Ste. 1	Council Bluffs	IA	51503	(712) 325-6553	4
Star Cinema 16	3220 23rd Ave.	Council Bluffs	IA	51503	(712) 256-7827	16
Cresco	325 2nd Ave. SW	Cresco	IA	52136	(563) 547-4292	1
Crawford County 4	309 Chamberlain Dr.	Denison	IA	51442	(712) 263-8777	4
Fleur Cinema & Cafe	4545 Fleur Dr.	Des Moines	IA	50321	(515) 287-4545	4
Merle Hay Mall Cinema	3800 Merle Hay Mall #700	Des Moines	IA	50310	(515) 252-0804	1
Nova 10 @ Hay Market	4353 Merle Hay Rd.	Des Moines	IA	50310	(515) 270-8221	10
Varsity Theatre	1207 25th St.	Des Moines	IA	50311	(515) 277-0404	1
Elkader Cinema	108 N Main St.	Elkader	IA	52043	(563) 245-2666	1
Co-Ed II	119 W Broadway	Fairfield	IA	52556	(641) 472-3707	2

Name	Address	City	State	Zip	Phone	Screens
Forest Theatre	215 N Clark St.	Forest City	IA	50436	(641) 585-2790	1
Gladbrook Theatre	319 2nd St.	Gladbrook	IA	50635	(641) 473-3456	1
Royal Theatre	414 First St.	Glenwood	IA	51534	(712) 527-1819	1
Grand Theatre	238 Public Sq.	Greenfield	IA	50849	(641) 743-2182	1
Center Theatre	602 7th St.	Grundy Center	IA	50638	(319) 824-6571	1
Colonial Theatre	1120 Main St.	Hamburg	IA	51640	(712) 382-1524	1
Harlan Theatre	621 Court St.	Harlan	IA	51537	(712) 755-2310	3
King Theatre	413 2nd St.	Ida Grove	IA	51445	(712) 364-2829	1
Metropolitan Theatre	515 Washington	Iowa Falls	IA	50126	(641) 648-3605	2
61 Drive In	207 S Main St.	Maquoketa	IA	52060	(563) 674-4367	1
Voy Theatres	208 S Main St.	Maquoketa	IA	52060	(563) 652-2877	3
Pioneer Theatre	905 Okoboji Ave.	Milford	IA	51351	(712) 338-2536	1
Rialto Theatre	405 E Erie St.	Missouri Valley	IA	51555	(712) 642-3826	1
Bijou Theatre	123 2nd St. SW	Mount Vernon	IA	52314	(319) 895-1292	1
Camelot Theatre	1114 6Th St.	Nevada	IA	50201	(515) 382-2281	1
Capri	107 East Market St.	New Sharon	IA	50207	(641) 637-4055	1
Capitol II	116 First St. N.	Newton	IA	50208	(641) 792-1862	2
Great Lakes Cinema 7	1698 Exchange St.	Okoboji	IA	51355	(866) 991-7469	7
Iowa Theatre	910 Iowa Ave.	Onawa	IA	51040	(712) 423-1576	1
Holland Plaza 7	717 8th St. SE	Orange City	IA	51041	(402) 933-0905	7
Watts Theatre	714 Main St.	Osage	IA	50461	(641) 732-4904	1
Lyric Theatre	118 S Fillmore St.	Osceola	IA	50213	(641) 342-3004	1
Wonderland	110 S Main St.	Paullina	IA	51046	(712) 949-2566	1
Pella Cinema	708 Main St.	Pella	IA	50219	(641) 621-0329	3
Rialto	326 N Main	Pocahontas	IA	50574	(712) 335-3434	1
Grand	1507 Broadway St.	Red Oak	IA	51566	(712) 623-3169	1
Main Street 3	401 9th St.	Sheldon	IA	51201	(712) 324-2344	3
Legacy 3	712 W Sheridan	Shendoah	IA	51601	(712) 246-2344	3
Max Theatre	338 Ninth St.	Sibley	IA	51249	(712) 754-2672	2
Promenade Cinema 14	924 4th St.	Sioux City	IA	51101	(712) 277-8310	14
Riviera 4	714 4th St.	Sioux City	IA	51102	(712) 252-2928	2
Story Theatre	511 Broad St.	Story City	IA	50248	(515) 733-4318	1
Sumner Sunset Theatre	111 W 1st St.	Sumner	IA	50674	(563) 578-5307	1
The Wieting Theatre	101 South Church St.	Toledo	IA	52342	(641) 484-4440	1
Palace Theatre	210 W 4th St.	Vinton	IA	52349	(319) 472-9892	1
Main Feature & Pizza Pub	38 W Main St.	Waukon	IA	52172	(563) 568-6134	1
Waverly Palace Theatre	90 E Bremer Ave.	Waverly	IA	50677	(319) 352-1318	3
Billy Joe's Picture Show	1701 25th St.	West Des Moines	IA	50266	(515) 223-9944	1
New Strand Theatre	111 E 3rd St. D	West Liberty	IA	52776	(319) 627-2014	1
Iowa Theatre	119 N John Wayne Dr.	Winterset	IA	50273	(515) 462-2979	1

IDAHO

Name	Address	City	State	Zip	Phone	Screens
Plaza Twin	Riverside Plaza #24	Blackfoot	ID	83221	(208) 785-5554	2
Egyptian Theatre	700 W Main St.	Boise	ID	83702	(208) 387-1273	1
Flicks Movie Theatre	646 Fulton St.	Boise	ID	83702	(208) 342-4288	4
Northgate Reel Cinemas	6950 W State St.	Boise	ID	83703	(208) 377-2620	6
Overland Park Cinema	7051 Overland Rd.	Boise	ID	83709	(208) 377-2431	3
Rex Theatre	7222 Main St.	Bonners Ferry	ID	83805	(208) 267-2682	1
Terrace Drive In	3701 Lake Ave.	Caldwell	ID	83605	(208) 455-1433	3
Roxy	118 S Main St.	Cascade	ID	83611	(208) 382-5560	1
Spud Drive In	231 S State Hwy. 33	Driggs	ID	83422	(208) 354-2727	1
Big Wood 4	801 N Main	Hailey	ID	83333	(208) 578-0971	4
Liberty Theatre	110 N Main St.	Hailey	ID	83333	(208) 788-6195	1
Coeur D'Alene Discount Theatre	300 W. Centa St.	Hayden	ID	83835	(208) 762-7469	6
Centre Theatre	461 Park Ave.	Idaho Falls	ID	83401	(208) 525-3340	2
Motor Vu Drive In	2095 N Yellowstone Hwy.	Idaho Falls	ID	83401	(208) 523-3711	1
Paramount Theatre	2085 Niagara St.	Idaho Falls	ID	83404	(208) 523-1142	3
Sky Vu Drive In	3000 S Yellowstone Hwy	Idaho Falls	ID	83402	(208) 522-3111	1
Magic Lantern	100 2nd St. E, 2nd Flr.	Ketchum	ID	83340	(208) 726-4272	4
Ski Time Cinema	170 1st Ave. North	Ketchum	ID	83340	(208) 726-1039	2
Orchard Cinemas 3	3323 Tenth St.	Lewiston	ID	83501	(208) 746-1022	3
Village Centre Cinemas	2920 Nez Perce Dr.	Lewiston	ID	83501	(208) 798-8080	12
Main Theatre	221 S Main St.	Mackay	ID	83251	(208) 588-2804	1
Frontier	2900 W Stephanie Ct.	Meridian	ID	83642	(208) 898-7690	1
Eastside Cinema	1420 S Blaine St.	Moscow	ID	83843	(208) 882-8078	5
Kenworthy	508 S Main St.	Moscow	ID	83843	(208) 882-4127	1
Take One Cinema	650 W 8th St.	Mountain Home	ID	83647	(208) 587-5338	2
Nampa Reel 6 Cinema	2104 Caldwell Blvd.	Nampa	ID	83651	(208) 377-2620	6
Parma Motor-Vu Drive In	29522 Hwy. 95	Parma	ID	83660	(208) 722-6401	1
Pocatello Reel Theatre	310 E Oak St.	Pocatello	ID	83201	(208) 233-2300	2
Bonner Mall Cinema	300 Bonner Mall Way	Ponderay	ID	83852	(208) 263-7147	6
Post Falls Theatre	1486 West Seltice Way	Post Falls	ID	83854	(208) 773-5064	6
AFEC Rexburg	475 N 2nd East	Rexburg	ID	83440	(208) 359-2600	6
Paramount Twin	38 S Center	Rexburg	ID	83440	(208) 356-7469	2
Teton Vu Drive In	272 S 3rd W	Rexburg	ID	83440	(208) 356-7469	1
Panida Theatre	300 N 1st Ave.	Sandpoint	ID	83864	(208) 255-7801	1
Sandpoint Cinema 4	401 Oak St.	Sandpoint	ID	83864	(208) 263-5811	4
The Shoshone Showhouse	316 S Apple	Shoshone	ID	83352	(208) 886-2636	1
Sun Valley Opera House	1 Sun Valley Rd.	Sun Valley	ID	83353	(208) 622-2244	1
Lamphouse Theatre	223 5th Ave. S	Twin Falls	ID	83301	(208) 736-8600	1
WSC Theatre	375 Ridgeway	Twin Falls	ID	83301	(208) 934-4881	1

ILLINOIS

Name	Address	City	State	Zip	Phone	Screens
Aledo Opera House	1005 N E 5th Ave.	Aledo	IL	61231	(309) 582-0595	1
Arlington Theatre	53 S Evergreen	Arlington Heights	IL	60005	(847) 483-0123	6
Paramount Theatre	8 E Galena Blvd Ste. 230	Aurora	IL	60506	(630) 896-7676	1
Catlow Theatre	116 W Main St.	Barrington	IL	60010	(847) 381-2547	1
Skyview Drive In	5700 North Belt W	Belleville	IL	62223	(618) 233-4400	2
Lincoln Theatre	103 E Main St.	Belleville	IL	62220	(618) 233-0018	3
The Old Red Barn Cinema	305 N Hard Rd.	Benld	IL	62009	(217) 835-6634	2
Bensenville Theatre	9 S Center St.	Bensenville	IL	60106	(630) 860-1404	2
Buffalo Grove Theatre	120 McHenry Rd.	Buffalo Grove	IL	60089	(847) 215-1221	5

Name	Address	City	State	Zip	Phone	Screens
Garden Theatre	62 N Main St.	Canton	IL	61520	(309) 647-0435	2
Carmi Cinemas	105 W Main St.	Carmi	IL	62821	(618) 384-3333	3
The Art Theatre	126 W Church St.	Champaign	IL	61820	(217) 355-0668	1
The Virginia Theatre	203 W Park	Champaign	IL	61820	(217) 356-9053	1
Chicago Audio Works	676 N LaSalle St. 2nd Flr.	Chicago	IL	60610	(312) 337-8282	1
Davis Theatre	4614 N Lincoln Ave.	Chicago	IL	60625	(773) 769-3999	4
Logan Theatre	2646 N Milwaukee Ave.	Chicago	IL	60647	(773) 252-0627	4
Music Box Theatre	3733 N Southport	Chicago	IL	60613	(773) 871-6607	2
Three Penny Theatre	2424 N Lincoln Ave.	Chicago	IL	60614	(773) 525-3449	2
Vic Theatre	3145 Sheffield	Chicago	IL	60657	(773) 472-0449	1
Chillicothe Town Theatre	1029 N 2nd St.	Chillicothe	IL	61523	(309) 274-3545	2
Egyptian Theatre	135 N 2nd St.	De Kalb	IL	60115	(815) 758-1215	1
Avon Theatre	426 N Water St.	Decatur	IL	62523	(217) 422-1776	1
Campus Cinemas	1015 Blackhawk Rd.	Dekalb	IL	60115	(815) 758-8562	4
Midway Drive-In	Old Rte. 2 91 Palmyra Rd.	Dixon	IL	61021	(815) 625-4099	1
Plaza Cinemas	1315 N Galena Ave.	Dixon	IL	61021	(815) 284-4141	4
Grand Theatre	220 E Main St.	Du Quoin	IL	62832	(618) 542-3120	3
34 Drive In Theatre	Old Rte. 34	Earlville	IL	60518	(815) 246-9700	1
Stadium Cinemas	51 Village Square Mall	Effingham	IL	62401	(217) 347-5447	9
Palace Theatre	122 W Main	Elmwood	IL	61529	(309) 742-4211	1
Block Cinema	40 Arts Circle Dr.	Evanston	IL	60208	(847) 491-2448	1
Showtime of Fairfield	130 N Market St.	Fairfield	IL	62837	(618) 842-2777	3
Orpheum	60 South Kellogg	Galesburg	IL	61401	(309) 342-2299	1
The Blue Moonlight Drive In	2875 W Main St.	Galesburg	IL	61401	(309) 341-3121	1
Galva Autovue Drive In	8 James B Young Rd.	Galva	IL	61434	(309) 678-3767	1
Central Theatre	111 N State St.	Geneseo	IL	61254	(309) 944-3603	1
Glen Art Theatre	540 Crescent Blvd.	Glen Ellyn	IL	60137	(630) 415-1976	4
Globe Theatre	105 N 3rd St.	Greenville	IL	62246	(618) 664-4764	3
Lawford Theatre	225 W Main St.	Havana	IL	62644	(309) 543-1225	1
Highland Park Theatre	445 Central Ave.	Highland Park	IL	60035	(847) 432-3322	4
The Orpheum Theatre	316 S Main St.	Hillsboro	IL	62049	(217) 532-6606	2
Lorraine Twin	324 E Main St.	Hoopeston	IL	60942	(217) 283-5311	2
Stadium Cinemas	Main St./Highway 67	Jacksonville	IL	62650	(217) 245-1850	10
Wanee Cinemas	106 S Main St.	Kewanee	IL	61443	(309) 852-2759	2
La Grange Theatre	60 S La Grange Rd.	La Grange	IL	60525	(708) 579-0460	4
Lansing Cinema 8	16621 Torrence Ave.	Lansing	IL	60438	(708) 418-0300	8
Princess Theatre	300 E Center St.	Le Roy	IL	61752	(309) 962-2468	1
Liberty 2 Theatre	708 N Milwaukee Ave.	Libertyville	IL	60048	(847) 362-7989	2
Westside Twin	1305 W Hudson Dr.	Litchfield	IL	62056	(217) 324-2050	3
Arlee Theatre	201 W Elm St.	Mason City	IL	62664	(217) 482-3137	1
McHenry Downtown Theatre	1204 N Green St.	Mc Henry	IL	60050	(815) 344-2004	2
McHenry Drive In	1510 Chapel Hill Lincoln	Mchenry	IL	60050	(815) 385-3990	1
Nova 6	2018-36th Ave.	Moline	IL	61265	(309) 743-1157	6
Reynold's Morton Cinema	2115 S Main St.	Morton	IL	61550	(309) 266-5914	5
State Theatre	153 west Elm St.	Nashville	IL	62263	(618) 327-8714	1
Fairview Drive In	16045 E St. Hwy. 33	Newton	IL	62448	(618) 455-3120	1
Normal Theatre	611 S Linden St.	Normal	IL	61761	(309) 454-9720	1
Arcadia Theatre	238 E Main St.	Olney	IL	62450	(618) 392-3000	3
Harvest Moon Twin Drive In	113 N Pine St.	Onarga	IL	60955	(815) 268-4000	2
Onarga Theatre	101 W. Seminary Ave.	Onarga	IL	60955	(815) 268-9862	1
Roxy 6 Cinemas	827 Lasalle	Ottawa	IL	61350	(815) 433-1816	6
Roseland Theatre	127 S Locust St.	Pana	IL	62557	(217) 562-5141	1
Eagle Theatre of Park Forest	340 Main St.	Park Forest	IL	60466	(708) 283-9098	5
Pickwick Theatre	5 S Prospect Ave.	Park Ridge	IL	60068	(847) 825-5800	4
Nova Landmark 12	3225 N Dries Ln.	Peoria	IL	61604	(309) 682-6350	12
Crescent	307 W Madison St.	Pontiac	IL	61764	(815) 844-6643	2
Apollo Cinemas	455 S Main	Princeton	IL	61356	(815) 875-1707	2
Eagle Theatre	1802 W Main St.	Robinson	IL	62454	(618) 544-5809	1
Hub Theatre	416 Lincoln Hwy.	Rochelle	IL	61068	(815) 562-6328	3
Clark 54 Drive In	19312 US Hwy. 54	Rockport	IL	62370	(217) 285-2805	1
Princess	116 E Lafayette	Rushville	IL	62681	(217) 322-2985	1
Mac's Drive In	2761 S Rte. 37	Salem	IL	62881	(618) 548-5454	1
WOW Cinema 7	101 Duvick Ave.	Sandwich	IL	60548	(815) 786-7777	7
Savanna Times Theatre	222 Main St.	Savanna	IL	61074	(815) 273-2951	2
Boarman Roxy Theatre	124 N Morgan St.	Shelbyville	IL	62565	(217) 774-7699	1
Showtime 6 of Sparta	1325 N Market	Sparta	IL	62286	(618) 443-3343	6
Route 66 Drive In	1700 Recreation Dr.	Springfield	IL	62707	(217) 546-8881	2
Sterling Theatre	402 Locust St.	Sterling	IL	61081	(815) 622-5900	2
Northpoint Cinemas	301 Dannys Dr.	Streator	IL	61364	(815) 672-7759	6
Sycamore Theatres	420 W State St.	Sycamore	IL	60178	(815) 895-2301	3
Liberty Theatre	210 S 4th St.	Vandalia	IL	62471	(618) 283-1953	1
Genimi Cinemas	17 N Main St.	Village Grove	IL	61956	(217) 832-5300	2
RMC Cinemas	113 Plaza Dr.	Waterloo	IL	62298	(618) 939-6630	8
Princess Theatre	213 W Walnut St.	Watseka	IL	60970	(815) 955-2724	1
Cascade Outdoor Theatre	28 W 741 N Ave.	West Chicago	IL	60185	(630) 293-0940	1
Wilmette	1122 Central Ave.	Wilmette	IL	60091	(847) 251-7424	2
S&S Theatrical The MAR Theatre	121 S Main	Wilmington	IL	60481	(815) 712-7978	2
RHYN Dunes #3 Theatre	3398 Sheridan Rd.	Zion	IL	60099	(847) 456-1804	3

INDIANA

Name	Address	City	State	Zip	Phone	Screens
Alex Theatre	407 N Harrison	Alexandria	IN	46001	(765) 724-2292	1
Mounds Mall 10	2109 Scatterfield Rd.	Anderson	IN	46016	(765) 641-8083	10
Paramount Theatre	1124 Meridian Plaza	Anderson	IN	46015	(317) 642-1234	1
Strand Theatre	160 Public Sq.	Angola	IN	46703	(260) 665-7169	1
Attica Devon Theatre	109 W Main St.	Attica	IN	47918	(765) 762-3348	1
Starlite Drive In	7640 S Old State Rd 37	Bloomington	IN	47403	(317) 422-1211	1
Walnut Theatre	24 S Walnut St.	Brazil	IN	47834	(800) 999-8149	1
Bremen Theatre	101 E Plymouth	Bremen	IN	46506	(574) 546-5800	1
Pavilion Cinemas 8	1555 N Green St.	Brownsburg	IN	46112	(317) 852-5925	8
YES Cinema	280 Commons Mall	Columbus	IN	47201	(812) 378-0377	2
Showtime Cinemas	2235 Park Rd.	Connersville	IN	47331	(765) 827-1859	8
Corydon Cinema CTC	Hwy 135 and 337	Corydon	IN	47112	(812) 738-1864	4
Crown Theatre	19 N Court St.	Crown Point	IN	46307	(219) 762-4355	1
Lakeside Cinema	612 Lakeshore Dr.	Culver	IN	46511	(574) 842-2537	1
Rees Cinema	449 Liberty St.	Culver	IN	46511	(574) 842-3674	1

Name	Address	City	State	Zip	Phone	Screens
Royal Theatre	59 S Washington St.	Danville	IN	46122	(317) 745-4899	1
Showplace Cine North 9	4200 N 3rd Ave.	Evansville	IN	47710	(812) 425-1386	13
Showplace East 18	1801 Morgan Center Dr.	Evansville	IN	47715	(812) 479-9732	18
Showplace South	950 S Hebron Ave.	Evansville	IN	47714	(812) 479-8780	9
Embassy Theatre Foundation	125 W Jefferson Blvd.	Fort Wayne	IN	46802	(219) 424-6287	1
Ft Wayne Cinema Center	437 East Berry St.	Fort Wayne	IN	46802	(260) 485-1448	1
Northwood Cinema Grill	6069 Stellhorn	Fort Wayne	IN	46815	(260) 485-1448	2
Fowler	102 E 5th St.	Fowler	IN	47944	(765) 884-1905	1
Frankfort Cinema	1557 E Wabash	Frankfort	IN	46041	(765) 659-2392	2
Mels@Starlight Drive In	1557 E Wabash St.	Frankfort	IN	46041	(765) 325-9131	1
Canary Creek Cinemas & Drive-In	870 Mallory Pkwy	Franklin	IN	46131	(317) 738-1041	8
Artcraft Theatre	57 N Main St.	Franklin	IN	46131	(317) 736-6823	1
Cinema Center Tech	437 E Berry St.	Ft Wayne	IN	46802	(260) 426-3456	1
Garrett Drive In	111 S Randolph	Garrett	IN	46738	(260) 357-3345	1
Slver Screen Cinema	111 S Randolph	Garrett	IN	46738	(260) 357-3345	1
Georgetown Drive In	8200 State Rd 64	Georgetown	IN	47122	(812) 951-2616	1
Linway 11	514 W Lincoln Ave.	Goshen	IN	46526	(574) 534-6132	11
Pickwick	514 W Lincoln Ave.	Goshen	IN	46526	(574) 457-4160	1
Ashley Square	1 E Seminary St.	Greencastle	IN	46135	(765) 653-5374	2
Legacy 6 Cin	2347 W Main St.	Greenfield	IN	46140	(317) 462-6831	6
Gibson Theatre	910 Ann Blvd.	Greensburg	IN	47240	(812) 934-3404	1
Wolf Theatre 6	910 Ann Blvd.	Greensburg	IN	47240	(812) 662-9520	6
Kennedy Theatre	6735 Kennedy Ave.	Hammond	IN	46323	(219) 844-1411	2
Town Theatre	8616 Kennedy Ave.	Highland	IN	46322	(219) 844-8954	1
Art Theatre	230 Main	Hobart	IN	46342	(219) 942-1670	1
Huntington Drive In	1291 Condit St.	Huntington	IN	46750	(260) 356-5445	1
Encore Moviez	9054 Rockville Rd.	Indianapolis	IN	46234	(317) 273-0143	6
Georgetown Cinema 14	3898 Lafayette Rd.	Indianapolis	IN	46254	(317) 536-2422	14
Greenbriar Cinema Grill	1289 W 86th St.	Indianapolis	IN	46260	(317) 254-1995	2
Key Cinemas	4044 S Keystone Ave.	Indianapolis	IN	46227	(317) 784-7454	2
Tibbs Triplex Drive In	480 S Tibbs Ave.	Indianapolis	IN	46241	(317) 243-3810	3
Strand Theatre	221 Main St.	Kendallville	IN	46755	(260) 347-3558	2
Melody Drive In	7055 US 35 S	Knox	IN	46534	(574) 772-2043	2
Pavillion Cinema 7	1600 N Lebanon St.	Lebanon	IN	46052	(765) 483-0522	7
Ohio Theatre	105 E Main St.	Madison	IN	47250	(812) 273-4821	2
Centerbrook Drive-In	6735 State Rd 67 North	Martinsville	IN	46151	(317) 230-8092	1
Crossroads 2 Cinema	6180 Broadway	Merrillville	IN	46410	(219) 980-0589	2
Lake Shore Drive In	100 Rickey Rd.	Monticello	IN	47960	(574) 583-0312	1
Twin Lakes Cinema	107 South Main	Monticello	IN	47960	(219) 253-2246	2
Mooresville Movies	300 S Bridge Crossing	Mooresville	IN	46158	(317) 834-4121	8
Sky Hi Drive In Theatre	1801 S R 28	Muncie	IN	47303	(765) 284-6411	2
Nappanee Theatre	154 N Main	Nappanee	IN	46550	(574) 773-2685	1
Sky-Vue Drive In	5080 S County Rd 500	New Castle	IN	47362	(765) 332-0246	1
Harmonie Haus Cinema	515 S Main St.	New Harmony	IN	47631	(812) 449-6839	2
Showplace Cinema	8099 Bell Oaks Dr.	Newburgh	IN	47630	(812) 853-6843	7
Holiday Drive In	46 E Court St.	Paoli	IN	47454	(812) 849-4992	1
Village West Theatre	119 W Main St.	Plainfield	IN	46168	(317) 839-1191	1
Showland Cinema	7643 Oak Rd	Plymouth	IN	46563	(574) 935-0552	3
Ritz Theatre	200 N Meridian St.	Portland	IN	47371	(260) 726-7489	2
Fountain Stone Theatre	1376 Saint Gaspar Drive	Rensselaer	IN	47978	(219) 866-3804	5
Rochester Times Cinema	618 Main St.	Rochester	IN	46975	(574) 223-2721	2
Ritz Theatre	218 W Ohio St.	Rockville	IN	47872	(765) 569-0628	1
Skyline Drive In	207 South Harrison St.	Shelbyville	IN	46176	(317) 398-9011	1
Strand Theatre	215 S Harrison St.	Shelbyville	IN	46176	(317) 398-9552	1
Kent Theatre	220 S State St.	South Whitley	IN	46787	(260) 248-4153	1
Cinema 67 Drive In	Rte. 2 Box 75	Spencer	IN	47460	(812) 879-4624	1
Tell City Twin	120 Hwy. 66	Tell City	IN	47586	(812) 547-6217	2
Indiana Theatre	683 Ohio St.	Terre Haute	IN	47807	(812) 232-9372	1
Diana Theatre	137 E Jefferson St.	Tipton	IN	46072	(765) 675-4300	1
49er Drive In	675 North Calumet Ave.	Valparaiso	IN	46383	(219) 462-6122	1
North Pointe Cinemas	1060 Mariner Dr.	Warsaw	IN	46580	(574) 268-9214	6
Hoosier Theatre	1335 E 119th St.	Whiting	IN	46394	(219) 473-0711	1
Isis	122 N Monticello St.	Winamac	IN	46996	(574) 946-6966	1
Airline Drive	InState Rd. 32 E	Winchester	IN	47394	(765) 584-2545	1

KANSAS

Name	Address	City	State	Zip	Phone	Screens
Royal Movie Theatre	612 Commercial St.	Atchison	KS	66002	(913) 367-0222	2
Atwood Jayhawk	420 Main St.	Atwood	KS	67730	(785) 626-9462	1
Augusta Historic Theatre	523 State St.	Augusta	KS	67010	(316) 775-2900	1
Solomon Valley Cinema	1124 N Hwy. 14	Beloit	KS	67420	(785) 738-4800	2
IFS Rex	519 Court St.	Clay Center	KS	67432	(314) 918-2714	2
Coffeyville Family Theatre	206 W 10th St.	Coffeyville	KS	67337	(620) 779-1090	2
Colby Cinema & Arcade	1925 S Range Ave.	Colby	KS	67701	(785) 460-9600	2
Derby Plaza Theatre	1300 N Nelson Dr.	Derby	KS	67037	(316) 789-0136	7
Cinema Circle Twin	106 Kincaid	Dodge City	KS	67801	(620) 225-1431	2
South Drive In	106 Kincaid	Dodge City	KS	67801	(316) 225-4301	1
Kanopolis Drive In	208 W 1st St.	Ellsworth	KS	67439	(785) 472-1002	1
Fredonia Cinema	407 N Sixth	Fredonia	KS	66736	(620) 378-4355	2
Sherman Theatre	1203 Main St.	Goodland	KS	67735	(785) 899-6103	1
Twilight Theatre	132 S Main	Greensburg	KS	67054	(620) 723-2445	1
Arrow Theatre	729 Oregon St.	Hiawatha	KS	66434	(785) 742-3706	2
Frontier Stage	305 E Main St.	Hill City	KS	67642	(785) 421-4127	1
Fox Historical Theatre	18 East 1st Ave.	Hutchinson	KS	67501	(620) 663-1981	1
Dickinson Westside 4	1016 W Sixth St.	Junction City	KS	66441	(785) 238-3153	4
Boulevard Drive In	1051 Merriam Ln.	Kansas City	KS	66103	(913) 262-2414	1
Legends 14 Theatre	1841 Village West Pkwy.	Kansas City	KS	66111	(913) 334-0847	14
Kingman Theatre	237 N Main St.	Kingman	KS	67068	(620) 532-3505	1
State Theatre	59 Broadway	Larned	KS	67550	(620) 285-3177	1
Liberty Hall Cinema	644 Massachusetts	Lawrence	KS	66044	(785) 749-1972	2
Landing 4 Theatres	3rd & Delaware	Leavenworth	KS	66048	(913) 651-7887	4
Southgate Cinema 6	1104 S Kansas Ave.	Liberal	KS	67901	(620) 624-0236	4
Finch Theatre	122 E Lincoln Ave.	Lincoln	KS	67455	(785) 524-4169	1
Lucas Area Community Theatre	116 S Main St.	Lucas	KS	67648	(785) 525-6236	1
Astro Theatre	820 Center St.	Marysville	KS	66508	(785) 562-3715	3

Name	Address	City	State	Zip	Phone	Screens
Pageant Drive In	120 E Kansas St.	Medicine Lodge	KS	67104	(620) 886-5358	1
Jarvis Theatre	116 S Pennsylvannia Ave.	Ness City	KS	67560	(785) 798-3300	1
Newton Palace 8	601 SE 36th St. Ste. 112	Newton	KS	67114	(316) 282-0008	8
Midway Drive In Theatre	29591 W 327th St.	Osawatomie	KS	66064	(913) 755-2325	1
Parsons Theatre	210 N 17th	Parsons	KS	67357	(620) 421-4404	5
MajesticTheatre	724 4th St.	Phillipsburg	KS	67661	(785) 543-2724	2
Dream Theatre	639 N Main St.	Russell	KS	67665	(785) 445-1949	1
Cheyenne	209 E Washington	Saint Francis	KS	67756	(785) 332-2747	1
Salina Art Center	242 S Santa Fe	Salina	KS	67401	(785) 827-1431	1
Seneca Theatre	301 Main St.	Seneca	KS	66538	(785) 336-3790	2
Rio Theatre	7204 W 80th	Shawnee Mission	KS	66204	(913) 383-8500	1
The Glenwoods Arts Theatre	9575 Metcalf Ave.	Shawnee Mission	KS	66212	(913) 642-4404	2
Trail Ridge Cinema	7456 Nieman Rd.	Shawnee Mission	KS	66203	(913) 268-0580	3
Ritz Theatre	510 N Main	Stafford	KS	67578	(620) 234-5625	1
The Movies Theatre	200 N Main St.	Ulysses	KS	67880	(620) 356-1732	1
Regent Theatre	114 W Lincoln Ave.	Wellington	KS	67152	(620) 326-8481	1
13th Avenue Warren	11611 E 13th St.	Wichita	KS	67206	(316) 612-0469	12
Movie Machine	4600 W Kellogg #245	Wichita	KS	67209	(316) 945-0024	5
Warren Old Town Theatre Grill	353 N Mead St.	Wichita	KS	67202	(316) 262-7123	5
Palace West	535 S Ridge Rd. Cir.	Wichita	KS	67209	(316) 721-7952	8
Premiere Palace	11010 East Kellogg	Wichita	KS	67207	(316) 685-1315	10
Starlite Drive In	3900 S Hydraulic St.	Wichita	KS	67216	(316) 945-9476	2
Warren 17 Cinemas	9150 W 21 St.	Wichita	KS	67205	(316) 722-7060	17

KENTUCKY

Name	Address	City	State	Zip	Phone	Screens
Keystone Cinema	2725 East John Rowan Blvd.	Bardstown	KY	40004	(502) 350-0128	8
Calvert City Drive In	111 Drive Inn Ln.	Calvert City	KY	42029	(270) 395-4660	1
Green River 6	730 Campbellsville Bypass	Campbellsville	KY	42718	(270) 789-3066	6
Redhound Theatre	1901 Snyder St.	Corbin	KY	40701	(606) 224-1453	1
Tri County Cineplex	1871 Cumberland Falls Hwy.	Corbin	KY	40701	(606) 526-8803	8
Movie Palace	1231 Woodland Dr.	Elizabethtown	KY	42701	(270) 769-1501	12
DanBarry Dollar Saver Turfway	7650 Turfway Rd.	Florence	KY	41042	(859) 647-2838	10
Dan Barry Middletown	3479 Dixie Highway	Franklin	KY	45005	(513) 422-7979	10
Franklin Drive In	6250 Nashville Rd.	Franklin	KY	42134	(270) 586-1905	1
Theatres of Georgetown	401 Outlet Center Dr.	Georgetown	KY	40324	(502) 863-3979	7
Skyline Drive In Theatre	5600 Hodgenville Rd.	Greensburg	KY	42743	(615) 255-5908	1
Countryside Cinema	US Hwy. 60 E	Harned	KY	40144	(270) 756-2883	1
Mall Cinemas	Hwy. 231 North	Hartford	KY	42347	(270) 298-3315	2
Tri City Drive In	Hwy. 231 North	Hartford	KY	42347	(270) 274-3168	1
Fugate's Cinema 3	197 Entertainment Dr. Hwy. 15	Hazard	KY	41701	(606) 439-9930	5
Hillside Theatres	306 Morton Blvd.	Hazard	KY	41701	(606) 436-1171	4
Starlite Drive In	2530 US 60 East	Henderson	KY	42420	(270) 827-5418	2
Kentucky Theatre	214 East Main St.	Lexington	KY	40507	(859) 231-6997	2
Reel Deal Cinemas	163 Canary Rd.	Lexington	KY	40503	(859) 272-4626	6
Regency Cinema 7	1868 Hwy. 192 West	London	KY	40741	(606) 864-6140	7
Baxter Theatres	1250 Bardstown Rd.	Louisville	KY	40204	(502) 459-2288	8
Dixie Dozen Theatres	6801 Dixie Hwy.	Louisville	KY	40258	(502) 935-3790	12
Louisville Palace Theatre	625 South Fourth Ave.	Louisville	KY	40202	(502) 584-7469	1
The Kentucky Theatre	1250 Bardstown Rd.	Louisville	KY	40204	(502) 456-4404	1
Apex Village 8 Cinema	4014 Dutchmens Ln.	Louisville	KY	40207	(502) 894-8697	8
Capitol 8 Theatres	455 Madison Sq. Ave.	Madisonville	KY	42431	(270) 825-3734	8
Tenth Frame Cinemas	930 Camargo Rd.	Mt Sterling	KY	40353	(859) 497-2519	6
Cheri 5	1008 Chestnut St.	Murray	KY	42071	(270) 753-8084	7
Maiden Alley Cinema	112 Maiden Alley	Paducah	KY	42001	(270) 442-7723	1
Sipp Theatre	212 Court St.	Paintsville	KY	41240	(606) 789-9014	1
Bell Theatre	108 West Kentucky Ave.	Pineville	KY	40977	(606) 269-2990	1
Capitol Cinemas	203 West Main St.	Princeton	KY	42445	(270) 365-0200	3
Showtime 4	895 North Dixie Hwy.	Radcliff	KY	40160	(270) 351-6900	4
Key Twin Cinema	2329 Lake Way Dr.	Russell Springs	KY	42642	(270) 866-3070	2
Somerset Stadium 8	100 Mercury Blvd.	Somerset	KY	42503	(606) 451-0067	8
Stanford Drive In	1645 Hustonville Rd.	Stanford	KY	40484	(606) 365-1317	1
Mountain View Drive In	1327 East College Ave.	Stanton	KY	40380	(606) 663-9988	2
Movies 9	40 Winchester Plaza	Winchester	KY	40391	(859) 745-4996	9
Skyvue Twin Drive In	5909 Lexington Rd.	Winchester	KY	40391	(859) 744-6663	2

LOUISIANA

Name	Address	City	State	Zip	Phone	Screens
Lafitte 4 Cinemas	2150 Charity St.	Abbeville	LA	70510	(337) 893-6773	4
Grand 14	2039 North Mall Dr.	Alexandria	LA	71301	(318) 448-7108	14
Amite Cinema IV	809 W Oak St.	Amite	LA	70422	(985) 748-5100	4
Grand Cinema	15365 George O'Neal Rd.	Baton Rouge	LA	70817	(225) 755-3851	8
Magic Cinemas	200 Cumberland	Bogalusa	LA	70427	(985) 730-0300	5
Celebrity Theatre of Broussard	4620 Hwy. 90 East	Broussard	LA	70518	(337) 330-0046	10
Chalmette Movies 9	8700 W Judge Perez Dr.	Chalmette	LA	70043	(504) 277-9738	9
Skyfire Star Theatre	332 North New Hampshire	Covington	LA	70433	(985) 875-7577	1
Queen Cinema 3	231 W Walnut	Eunice	LA	70535	(337) 457-9125	3
Hollywood 9	1401 W Esplanade Ave.	Kenner	LA	70065	(504) 472-6311	9
Grand 16	3141 Johnson St.	Lafayette	LA	70503	(337) 210-1631	16
Fairview Cinema 4	1515 Anthony St.	Morgan City	LA	70380	(985) 399-7460	4
Lake Cinema	1030 9th St.	Morgan City	LA	70380	(985) 384-0280	4
Parkway Cinema 6	1011 Keyser Ave.	Natchitoches	LA	71457	(318) 357-0353	4
Grand of the East	6601 Plaza Dr.	New Orleans	LA	70127	(504) 240-4928	18
Prytania	5339 Prytania St.	New Orleans	LA	70115	(504) 891-2787	1
Saenger Theatre	801 North Rampart St.	New Orleans	LA	70112	(504) 569-1523	1
State Palace	1108 Canal St.	New Orleans	LA	70112	(504) 866-1811	1
St Landry Discount Cinema	1234 Heather Dr.	Opelousas	LA	70570	(337) 942-5100	4
Vista Cinema 4	1234 Heather Dr.	Opelousas	LA	70570	(337) 594-0595	4
Spring Theatre	214 N Main St.	Springhill	LA	71075	(318) 539-6684	1

MAINE

Name	Address	City	State	Zip	Phone	Screens
Auburn Flagship 10	730 Center St.	Auburn	ME	04210	(207) 786-8890	10

Name	Address	City	State	Zip	Phone	Screens
Criterion	35 Cottage St.	Bar Harbor	ME	04609	(207) 288-3441	1
Reel Pizza Cinerama, Inc.	33 Kennebec Place	Bar Harbor	ME	04609	(207) 288-3828	1
Colonial Theatre	163 High St.	Belfast	ME	04915	(207) 338-5087	3
Casablanca	23 Cross St.	Bethel	ME	04217	(207) 824-3248	4
Smitty's Cinema Biddeford	420 Alfred Rd.	Biddeford	ME	04005	(207) 651-5350	8
The Harbor Theatre	185 Townsend Ave.	Boothbay Harbor	ME	04538	(207) 633-0438	1
Bridgton Drive In	Rte. 302	Bridgton	ME	04009	(207) 647-8666	2
Magic Lantern Theatre	69 Main St.	Bridgton	ME	04009	(207) 647-5443	2
Eveningstar Cinema	149 Main St.	Brunswick	ME	04011	(207) 729-6796	1
Alamo Theatre	85 Main St.	Bucksport	ME	04416	(207) 469-0924	1
State Cinemas	12 High St.	Calais	ME	04619	(207) 454-8834	3
Caribou Theatres	66 Sweden St.	Caribou	ME	04736	(207) 492-1243	4
Lincoln	277 Main St.	Damariscotta	ME	04543	(207) 563-3424	1
Grand Auditorium of Hancock	167 Main St.	Ellsworth	ME	04605	(207) 667-9500	1
Narrow Gauge	123 Narrow Gauge	Farmington	ME	04938	(207) 778-2881	7
The Temple Theatre	20 Market Sq.	Houlton	ME	04730	(207) 532-7600	2
Skylite Drive In Fox Theatre	304 Eleventh Ave.	Madawaska	ME	04756	(207) 728-7583	1
Milbridge Theatre	Route 1 Main St.	Milbridge	ME	04658	(207) 546-2038	1
Movies at the Museum	7 Congress St.	Portland	ME	04101	(207) 775-6148	1
Nickelodeon Cinema 6	1 Temple St.	Portland	ME	04101	(207) 772-4022	6
Pride's Corner Drive In.	100 Christy Rd.	Portland	ME	04103	(207) 797-3154	1
Lakeside Theatre	2493 Main St.	Rangeley	ME	04970	(207) 864-5000	1
Strand Theatre	345 Main St.	Rockland	ME	04841	(207) 594-6105	2
Cinemagic 12	779 Portland Rd US Rte. 1	Saco	ME	04072	(207) 282-6234	12
Saco Drive-in	969 Portland Rd	Saco	ME	04072	(207) 284-1016	1
Smitty's Cinema-Sanford	1364 Main St.	Sanford	ME	04073	(207) 490-6677	6
Railroad Square Cinema	17 Railroad Sq.	Waterville	ME	04901	(207) 872-5111	3

MARYLAND

Name	Address	City	State	Zip	Phone	Screens
Bengies Drive In.	3417 Eastern Blvd. East	Baltimore	MD	21220	(410) 686-7400	1
Charles Theatre 5	1711 N Charles St.	Baltimore	MD	21201	(410) 727-3464	5
Rotunda Cinematheque	711 W 40th St.	Baltimore	MD	21211	(410) 235-7595	2
Senator Theatre	5904 York Rd.	Baltimore	MD	21212	(410) 435-9892	1
Cinema Art Bethesda	7235 Woodmont Ave.	Bethesda	MD	20814	(301) 365-3679	1
Indian Head Cinema 5	3047 Bryans Rd.	Bryans Road	MD	20616	(301) 375-9024	5
Cambridge Premier	Rte. 50 2759 Dorchester Sq.	Cambridge	MD	21613	(410) 221-8690	4
Frederick Mall 10	1301 W Patrick St.	Frederick	MD	21702	(301) 682-6404	10
MDL Entertainment Holiday Cinema	100 Baughmans Ln.	Frederick	MD	21702	(301) 662-9392	2
The Palace Theatre	2 E Main St.	Frostburg	MD	21532	(301) 689-5605	1
Hagerstown Cinema 10	20135 Leitersburg Pike Ste. Rte. 60N	Hagerstown	MD	21740	(301) 797-7270	10
Laurel Cinemas 6	371 Armstrong Ave.	Laurel	MD	20707	(301) 604-2886	6
West Nursery 14	1591 W Nursery Rd.	Linthicum Heights	MD	21090	(410) 850-7300	14
Beltway Movies 6	7660 Bel Air Rd.	Parkville	MD	21234	(410) 882-5975	6
Premier Cinemas at Jumpers	8120 Jumpers Hole Rd.	Pasadena	MD	21122	(410) 768-9462	7
APEX Cinemas Calvert Village	200 W Dares Beach Rd.	Prince Frederick	MD	20678	(301) 855-1147	5
Marlow 6	3899 Branch Ave.	Tample Hills	MD	20748	(703) 631-8279	6
Heritage Cineplex	1045 Taylor Ave.	Towson	MD	21286	(410) 832-7686	2

MASSACHUSETTS

Name	Address	City	State	Zip	Phone	Screens
Agawam Family Cinema	866 Suffield St.	Agawam	MA	01001	(413) 786-8900	2
Stage II Cinema Pub	109 R Main St.	Amesbury	MA	01913	(978) 388-2221	1
Capitol Cinema	204 Massachusetts Ave.	Arlington	MA	02474	(781) 648-6022	6
Regent Theatre	7 Medford St.	Arlington	MA	02474	(617) 648-2222	1
Cabot Street Cinema	286 Cabot St.	Beverly	MA	01915	(978) 927-3677	1
Strand Theatre	543 Columbia Rd.	Boston	MA	02125	(617) 799-4094	1
Coolidge Corner	290 Harvard St.	Brookline	MA	02446	(617) 734-2501	2
Brattle Theatre	40 Brattle St.	Cambridge	MA	02138	(617) 876-6838	1
Historic Strand	58 High St.	Clinton	MA	01510	(978) 365-5551	1
Hollywood Hits	7 Hutchinson Dr.	Danvers	MA	01923	(978) 777-8899	7
The Dedham Community Theatre	580 High St.	Dedham	MA	02026	(781) 326-0409	2
Cape Cinema Theatre	35 Hope Lane	Dennis	MA	02638	(508) 385-5644	1
New Harbour Cinemas	374 William S Canning Blvd.	Fall River	MA	02721	(508) 678-5659	8
Cinema World 10	476 John Fitch Hwy.	Fitchburg	MA	01420	(978) 345-1404	10
Orpheum Theatre	1 School St.	Foxboro	MA	02035	(508) 543-4434	3
Gloucester Cinemas 3	74 Essex Ave.	Gloucester	MA	01930	(781) 944-8291	3
Triplex Cinema	70 Railroad St.	Great Barrington	MA	01230	(413) 528-8886	3
Greenfield Garden Cinema	361 Main St.	Greenfield	MA	01301	(413) 773-9260	7
Patriot Cinema	1775 Washington St.	Hanover	MA	02339	(781) 826-4180	6
Chunkys Haverhill Cinema	371 Lowell Ave.	Haverhill	MA	01832	(978) 374-2255	3
Loring Hall Theatre	65 Main St.	Hingham	MA	02043	(781) 749-9825	1
Fine Arts Theatre	19 Summer St.	Maynard	MA	01754	(978) 897-8100	3
Mendon Drive In.	35 Milford St.	Mendon	MA	01756	(508) 473-5840	2
Elm Draught House Cinema	35 Elm St.	Millbury	MA	01527	(508) 865-2838	1
Starlight Theatre & Cafe	1 N Union St.	Nantucket	MA	02554	(508) 228-4479	1
Route 1 Cinema Pub	652 East Washington St.	North Attleboro	MA	02760	(508) 643-4618	2
Pleasant Street Theatre	27 Pleasant St.	Northampton	MA	01060	(413) 586-5828	2
New Art Cinema	237 Commercial St.	Provincetown	MA	02657	(508) 487-9355	3
Little Art Theatre	19 School St.	Rockport	MA	01966	(978) 546-2548	1
Museum Place Cinemas	1 Church St.	Salem	MA	01970	(978) 744-3713	3
Cinema 95	201 Elm St.	Salisbury	MA	01952	(978) 462-3030	6
Heritage Theatre	Heritage Park 280 Rte. 130	Sandwich	MA	02563	(508) 833-7772	6
Patriot Cinemas @ the Wharf	120 Front St. Mill.	Scituate	MA	02066	(781) 545-8501	2
Pothole Pictures	10 Bridge St.	Shelburne Falls	MA	01370	(413) 625-2896	1
Somerville Theatre	55 Davis Sq.	Somerville	MA	02144	(617) 625-4088	5
West Boylston Cinema 1-5	101 W Boylston St.	West Boylston	MA	01583	(508) 835-4861	5
Cameo Twin Theatre	14 Columbian St.	Weymouth	MA	02190	(781) 335-9195	2
Images Cinema	50 Spring St.	Williamstown	MA	01267	(413) 458-1039	1

MICHIGAN

Name	Address	City	State	Zip	Phone	Screens
Alma Cinemas	3002 W Monroe St.	Alma	MI	48801	(989) 463-3895	6

Name	Address	City	State	Zip	Phone	Screens
Michigan Theatre	603 E Liberty St.	Ann Arbor	MI	48104	(734) 668-8397	2
State Theatre	233 S State St.	Ann Arbor	MI	48104	(734) 761-3531	2
Park Theatre	108 E Clinton	Augusta	MI	49012	(269) 731-4952	1
Bad Axe Theatre	309 E Huron Ave.	Bad Axe	MI	48413	(989) 269-7911	2
Cheap Flicks	15375 S Helmer Rd.	Battle Creek	MI	49017	(269) 965-1711	8
State Theatre	913 Washington Ave.	Bay City	MI	48708	(989) 892-2660	1
Beaverton Gem Theatre	120 Ross St.	Beaverton	MI	48612	(989) 435-2434	1
BellAire Theatre	112 N Bridge St.	Bellaire	MI	49615	(231) 533-8469	1
State Theatre	465 E Main St.	Benton Harbor	MI	49022		1
Cinema Hollywood 10	12280 Dixie Hwy.	Birch Run	MI	48415	(989) 624-3461	10
Uptown Palladium 12	250 N Olde Woodward	Birmingham	MI	48009	(248) 723-6240	12
Uptown Birmingham Theatre	211 S Old Woodward Ave.	Birmingham	MI	48009	(248) 723-6230	8
Boyne Cinema	216 S Lake St.	Boyne City	MI	49712	(231) 582-5887	2
Emagine Canton	39535 Ford Rd.	Canton	MI	48187	(734) 721-3456	18
Strand Theatre Caro	1205 E Caro Rd.	Caro	MI	48723	(989) 673-3033	1
Hiway Drive In	2778 E Sanilac	Carsonville	MI	48419	(810) 657-6684	1
Bay Theatre	6750 Main St.	Caseville	MI	48725	(989) 856-2676	1
Cass Theatre	6464 Main St.	Cass City	MI	48726	(989) 872-2252	1
Cinema 3	107 W Antrim St.	Charlevoix	MI	49720	(231) 547-2661	3
Eaton Theatre	235 S Cochran St.	Charlotte	MI	48813	(517) 543-2230	2
Kingston Theatre	406 N Main St.	Cheboygan	MI	49721	(231) 627-5425	5
Ideal Theatre	607 McEwan St.	Clare	MI	48617	(989) 386-9968	1
Clio Theatre	2151 W Vienna Rd.	Clio	MI	48420	(810) 686-6660	4
Capri Drive In	117 W Chicago Rd.	Coldwater	MI	49036	(517) 278-7990	2
Coldwater Cinema	414 N Willowbrook Rd.	Coldwater	MI	49036	(517) 279-9189	7
Loma #3	219 N Paw St.	Coloma	MI	49038	(269) 468-3663	3
Crystal Theatre	114 Main St.	Crystal	MI	48818	(989) 235-5640	1
Ford Wyoming Drive In	10400 Ford Rd.	Dearborn	MI	48126	(313) 846-4372	5
Fox Theatre	2211 Woodward	Detroit	MI	48201	(313) 596-3212	1
Bel Air 10	10100 E 8 Mile Rd.	Detroit	MI	48234	(248) 895-8442	10
Redford	17360 Lahser Rd.	Detroit	MI	48219	(313) 537-1133	1
Ren Cen 4Theatre	Level 2 Tower 200	Detroit	MI	48234	(313) 259-2372	4
5-Mile Drive In	28190 M-152	Dowagiac	MI	49047	(269) 782-7250	1
FamilyTheatre	132 Newman St.	East Tawas	MI	48730	(989) 362-0571	1
Elk Rapids Cinema	205 River St.	Elk Rapids	MI	49629	(231) 264-8622	1
Farmington Civic Theatre	33332 Grand River Ave.	Farmington	MI	48336	(248) 474-5299	2
Phoenix Theatre at Westriver	30170 Grand River	Farmington	MI	48336	(248) 476-0060	9
Fenton Cinema	291 N Alloy Dr.	Fenton	MI	48430	(810) 629-6606	8
Magic Bag	22920 N Woodward Ave.	Ferndale	MI	48220	(248) 544-1991	1
US 23 Drive In #1	5200 Fenton Rd.	Flint	MI	48507	(810) 238-0751	2
Garden Theatre	115 N Michigan Ave.	Frankfort	MI	49635	(231) 352-6628	1
Fremont Theatre	1027 W Main St.	Fremont	MI	49412	(231) 924-5273	2
Gaylord Cinema West	1775 M32 W	Gaylord	MI	49735	(989) 732-3609	6
Sun Theatre	316 Bridge St.	Grand Ledge	MI	48837	(517) 622-5346	1
Celebration Cinema South	1506 E Port Dr. SE	Grand Rapids	MI	49508	(616) 554-9966	16
Wealthy Theatre	1130 Wealthy St. SE	Grand Rapids	MI	49506	(616) 451-8001	1
Rialto Theatre	302 Michigan Ave.	Grayling	MI	49738	(989) 348-5948	1
Greenville Cinema	1500 N Lafayette	Greenville	MI	48838	(616) 754-5171	5
Pic Theatre	426 Quincy St.	Hancock	MI	49930	(847) 215-5505	1
Community Theatre	105 N Huron Ave.	Harbor Beach	MI	48441	(989) 479-9677	1
Sunset Drive In	69017 Red Arrow Hwy.	Hartford	MI	49057	(269) 217-6437	1
Knickerbocker Theatre	86 E 8th St.	Holland	MI	49423	(616) 395-7404	1
Cherry Bowl Drive In	9812 Honor Hwy.	Honor	MI	49640	(231) 325-3414	1
Lode Theatre	510 Sheldon Ave.	Houghton	MI	49931	(847) 215-5505	3
Pines Theatre	4673 W Houghton Lake Dr.	Houghton Lake	MI	48629	(989) 366-9226	1
Howell Theatre	315 East Grand River	Howell	MI	48843	(517) 546-0566	2
Imlay City Cinemas	543 N Cedar St.	Imlay City	MI	48444	(810) 724-6690	3
Ionia Theatre	205 West Main.	Ionia	MI	48846	(616) 527-3860	2
Cloverland Cinemas	932 E Cloverland Dr.	Ironwood	MI	49938	(906) 932-7185	4
Ironwood Theatre	109 East Aurora	Ironwood	MI	49938	(906) 932-0618	1
Country Village Cinema 5	1120 Country Ln.	Ishpeming	MI	49849	(906) 486-7470	5
Michigan Theatre	124 N Mechanic St.	Jackson	MI	49201	(517) 783-0962	1
The Gull Road Cinema 5	5288 Gull Rd.	Kalamazoo	MI	49048	(269) 342-8849	5
Lapeer Cinemas 6	1650 Demille Rd.	Lapeer	MI	48446	(810) 667-7440	8
Pix Arts Council	194 W Nepessing St.	Lapeer	MI	48446	(810) 664-4824	1
American Family Cinema	29584 W 7 Mile Rd.	Livonia	MI	48152	(248) 476-4576	3
Bellaire Theatre-Courtyard Cinemas	248 South Huron	Mackinaw City	MI	49701	(231) 436-7895	5
Riverside Cinema	6746 S River Rd.	Marine City	MI	48039	(810) 765-9405	3
Bogar Theatre	223 E Michigan Ave.	Marshall	MI	49068	(269) 781-2562	2
Midland Cinema 10	6540 Cinema Dr.	Midland	MI	48640	(989) 839-2663	11
Studio M	5221 Bay City Rd.	Midland	MI	48642	(989) 496-2770	3
Milford Cinema Theatre	955 Summit Rd.	Milford	MI	48381	(248) 363-5341	1
Denniston Cinemas	6495 N Monroe St.	Monroe	MI	48162	(734) 241-8700	3
Harbor Theatre	1937 Lakeshore Dr.	Muskegon	MI	49441	(231) 755-1977	2
Premier Lanes & Theatre	33151 23 Mile Rd.	New Baltimore	MI	48047	(586) 725-2228	3
Wonderland Cinemas	402 N Front	Niles	MI	49120	(269) 978-2707	6
Emagine Novi 18	44425 W 12 Mile Rd.	Novi	MI	48377	(248) 468-2990	18
Lake Theatre	117 E Dwight St	Oscoda	MI	48750	(989) 739-2851	1
New Strand	35781 Margurite Lane	Paw Paw	MI	49079	(269) 657-2895	1
Bellaire Petoskey	1540 Anderson St.	Petoskey	MI	49770	(231) 347-0170	8
M-89 Cinema	392 Crossing Oaks Mall	Plainwell	MI	49080	(269) 685-2921	6
Silverdome Drive In	1200 Featherstone	Pontiac	MI	48342	(248) 483-3170	1
McMorran Place Theatre	701 McMorran Blvd.	Port Huron	MI	48060	(810) 985-6166	1
Northstar Cinema	11699 Northland Dr. NE	Rockford	MI	49341	(616) 863-0358	5
Roscommon Cinema	200 N Main	Roscommon	MI	48653	(989) 808-5059	1
Court Street Theatre	1216 Court St.	Saginaw	MI	48602	(989) 249-7469	1
Temple Theatre	203 N Washington St.	Saginaw	MI	48607	(989) 754-7469	1
Firebird Theatre	280 East Sanilac Rd.	Sandusky	MI	48471	(810) 648-2741	3
Michigan Theatre	210 Center St.	South Haven	MI	49090	(269) 637-1662	3
South Lyon Cinema	126 E Lake St.	South Lyon	MI	48178	(248) 437-9000	1
Cinema IV Saint Johns	1043 S US 27	St Johns	MI	48879	(989) 224-9339	4
Tivoli Theatre	307 Railroad St.	Stephenson	MI	49887	(906) 753-9989	1
MJR Market Place Square	35400 Van Dyke	Sterling Heights	MI	48312	(248) 548-8282	20
Strand Theatre	219 W Chicago Rd.	Sturgis	MI	49091	(269) 651-5032	4
Bay Theatre	214 N St. Joseph St.	Suttons Bay	MI	49682	(231) 271-3879	1

Name	Address	City	State	Zip	Phone	Screens
Vickers Theatre	6 N Elm St	Three Oaks	MI	49128	(269) 756-3522	1
Vassar Theatre	140 E Huron St.	Vassar	MI	48768	(989) 823-4000	0
Romeo Theatre	64447 Tipperary	Washington	MI	48095	(586) 752-0897	2
State Wayne Theatre	35310 Michigan Ave. W	Wayne	MI	48184	(734) 326-4602	4
West Branch - Cinema 3	210 W Houghton Ave.	West Branch	MI	48661	(989) 345-7784	2
Northstar	8171 Whitehall Rd.	Whitehall	MI	49461	(231) 893-1547	3
Sun Theatre	150 W Grand River	Williamston	MI	48895	(517) 655-1850	1

MINNESOTA

Name	Address	City	State	Zip	Phone	Screens
Orpheum Theatre	305 W Main St.	Ada	MN	56510	(218) 784-2522	1
Rialto Theatre	220 Minnesota Ave. N.	Aitkin	MN	56431	(218) 927-2824	1
Midway Mall Cinema 7	2910 S Broadway	Alexandria	MN	56308	(320) 763-3669	7
Andover Cinema	1836 Bunker Lake Blvd.	Andover	MN	55304	(651) 982-4747	10
Lido Theatre	309 W Main St.	Arlington	MN	55307	(507) 964-5771	1
Tacora Theatre	320 Main St. North	Aurora	MN	55705	(218) 229-2670	1
CineMagic 7 Theatre	1302 18th Avenue NW	Austin	MN	55912	(507) 433-9191	7
Grand Theatre	215 N Main St.	Baudette	MN	56623	(218) 634-1376	1
Mann Westgate 10	14145 Baxter Dr.	Baxter	MN	56425	(218) 828-6251	10
Buffalo Cinema	100 NE 1st Ave.	Buffalo	MN	55313	(763) 682-4406	7
Canby Theatre	109 Saint Olaf Ave. N	Canby	MN	56220	(507) 223-5873	2
Cass Lake Movie Theatre	417 Maple Ave.	Cass Lake	MN	56633	(218) 335-2568	1
Chanhassen Cinema	570 Market St.	Chanhassen	MN	55317	(952) 974-9796	8
Chaska Cinemas	511 Walnut	Chaska	MN	55318	(952) 361-0049	4
Quarry Cinema 5	111 East Hwy. 23	Cold Spring	MN	56320	(320) 685-4131	5
Comet Theatre	102 South River St.	Cook	MN	55723	(218) 666-5814	1
Grand Theatre	124 E Second St.	Crookston	MN	56716	(218) 281-1820	2
State Theatre	238 E Sheridan St.	Ely	MN	55731	(218) 365-6311	1
Excelsior Dock Cinema	26 Water St.	Excelsior	MN	55331	(952) 474-7419	3
The Fergus Theatre	124 W Lincoln Ave.	Fergus Falls	MN	56537	(218) 736-5453	1
Forest Lake 5 Theatres	1480 S Lake St.	Forest Lake	MN	55025	(651) 464-4222	5
Fosston Theatre	105 First St. W	Fosston	MN	56542	(218) 435-1700	1
Jem Theatre	14 Main St.	Harmony	MN	55939	(507) 886-7469	1
Grand Cinema Hinckley	845 Weber Ave. S	Hinckley	MN	55037	(320) 384-7978	4
Century 9	766 Century Ave.	Hutchinson	MN	55350	(320) 234-6809	7
State III Theatre	35 Washington Ave. E	Hutchinson	MN	55350	(320) 587-0999	3
Cine 5	1319 Third St.	International Falls	MN	56649	(218) 283-2342	5
Historic State Theatre	600 Second St.	Jackson	MN	56143	(507) 847-4360	1
Kasson State Theatre	221 W Main St.	Kasson	MN	55944	(507) 634-7989	1
Kee Theatre	108 N Main St.	Kiester	MN	56051	(507) 294-3410	1
Lesueur	209 S Main	Le Sueur	MN	56058	(507) 665-2434	1
Hollywood Theatre	210 N Sibley Ave.	Litchfield	MN	55355	(320) 693-6131	1
Starlite Drive In	28264 Hwy. 22	Litchfield	MN	55355	(612) 961-8439	5
Falls Cinema	115 1st St. SE	Little Falls	MN	56345	(320) 632-5646	3
Long Drive-In Theatre	24257 Riverside Drive	Long Prairie	MN	56347	(320) 732-3142	1
Palace Theatre	303 E Main St.	Luverne	MN	56156	(507) 283-4463	1
Verne Drive In	1607 S Kniss	Luverne	MN	56156	(507) 283-8042	1
Madelia Theatre	104 W Main St.	Madelia	MN	56062	(507) 642-3211	1
Grand Theatre	623 3rd St. W	Madison	MN	56256	(320) 598-7301	2
Plaza Maplewood Theatre	1847 Larpenteur Ave.	Maplewood	MN	55109	(651) 770-1034	2
Milaca Theatre	160 Central Ave South	Milaca	MN	56353	(320) 266-3033	1
Brookdale 8 Cinemas	5810 Shingle Crk. Pkwy.	Minneapolis	MN	55430	(763) 566-0508	8
Heights Theatre	3951 Central Avenue NE	Minneapolis	MN	55421	(763) 789-4992	1
Oak St. Theatre	309 Oak St. SE	Minneapolis	MN	55414	(612) 331-7563	1
Parkway Theatre	4814 S Chicago Ave.	Minneapolis	MN	55417	(612) 822-2138	1
Riverview Theatre	3800 42nd Ave.	Minneapolis	MN	55406	(612) 729-7360	1
St Anthony Main Theatre	115 Main St. SE	Minneapolis	MN	55414	(612) 331-4724	5
University Film Society	10 Church St.	Minneapolis	MN	55455	(612) 627-4430	1
Walker Art Center	1750 Hennepin Ave.	Minneapolis	MN	55403	(612) 375-7619	1
Yorktown Cinema Grill	3313 Hazelton Rd.	Minneapolis	MN	55435	(952) 841-8418	3
Plaza 3 Theatre	560 1st St.	Montevideo	MN	56265	(320) 269-3135	3
Lake Theatre	318 Elm St.	Moose Lake	MN	55767	(218) 485-8060	1
Paradise	237 S Union	Mora	MN	55051	(320) 679-3964	1
North Branch Cinema	38450 Tanger Dr. Suite 234	North Branch	MN	55056	(612) 202-3891	5
Southgate #3	960 Hwy. 3 S.	Northfield	MN	55057	(507) 663-6185	3
Park Theatre	107 South Main St.	Park Rapids	MN	56470	(218) 732-3461	2
Koronis Cinema	209 Washburne Ave.	Paynesville	MN	56362	(320) 243-3610	2
Comet Theatre	247 First Ave. S	Perham	MN	56573	(218) 346-6225	1
Sunset Cinema	33040 Aspen Wood Dr.	Pequot Lakes	MN	56472	(218) 568-4341	5
Quarry Twin Theatre	204 E Main St.	Pipestone	MN	56164	(507) 825-3522	2
Redwood Falls Twin Theatre	230 E 2nd St.	Redwood Falls	MN	56283	(727) 542-4286	2
Chateau Theatres	971 E Circle Dr. NE	Rochester	MN	55906	(507) 536-7469	14
CineMagic Stadium 12	2170 Superior Dr. NW	Rochester	MN	55901	(507) 280-0309	12
Roso Theatre	310 Main Ave. N	Roseau	MN	56751	(218) 463-2601	1
Princess Theatre	505 1st Ave.	Saint James	MN	56081	(507) 375-4370	1
Mann Highland 1 & 2	760 S Cleveland Ave.	Saint Paul	MN	55116	(651) 698-3085	2
Mounds Theatre	1029 Hudson Rd.	Saint Paul	MN	55106	(651) 772-2253	1
St Peters Cinema 5	621 S Minnesota	Saint Peter	MN	56082	(507) 931-6631	5
Main St.	319 S Main St.	Sauk Centre	MN	56378	(320) 351-7469	5
Sherburn Theatre	116 N Main St.	Sherburn	MN	56171	(507) 764-5121	1
Twin Spin Cinema	151 Progress Circle	Spicer	MN	56288	(320) 796-5500	3
Mann Grandview 2 Theatre	1830 Grand Ave.	St Paul	MN	55105	(651) 698-3344	2
Imation Imax Theatre	12000 Zoo Blvd.	St Paul	MN	55124	(612) 997-9714	1
Staples Theatre	204 NE 4th St.	Staples	MN	56479	(218) 894-3818	1
Galaxy Twin Theatre	15469 Hwy. 59 NE	Thief River Falls	MN	56701	(218) 681-2368	2
Cozy Theatre	223 S Jefferson St.	Wadena	MN	56482	(218) 631-2260	2
Sky Vu Drive In	Hwy. 1	Warren	MN	56762	(218) 745-4027	1
Flame	125 S Broadway	Wells	MN	56097	(507) 553-5158	1
Gopher Theatre	907 Broadway	Wheaton	MN	56296	(320) 563-0315	1
Windom State Theatre	926 4th Ave.	Windom	MN	56101	(507) 831-1641	1
Woodbury 10	1470 Queens Dr.	Woodbury	MN	55125	(651) 731-0782	10
StateTheatre	66 E 4th St.	Zumbrota	MN	55992	(507) 732-5210	1

Name	Address	City	State	Zip	Phone	Screens

MISSISSIPPI

Name	Address	City	State	Zip	Phone	Screens
25 Drive In Theatre	63061 Old Hwy. 25	Amory	MS	38821	(662) 256-8978	1
Amory Twin	Hwy. 6 Glendale Shop Cntr.	Amory	MS	38821	(662) 256-8978	2
New Crescent	211 North Hayden St.	Belzoni	MS	39038	(662) 247-2280	2
Grand 14	11470 Cinema Dr.	Biloxi	MS	39540	(228) 354-9541	14
Imperial Palace 6	850 Bayview	Biloxi	MS	39530	(228) 424-3185	6
Silver Screen Theatre	2650 Beach Blvd Ste. 23	Biloxi	MS	39531	(228) 388-2220	3
Delta Cinemas	11 Third St.	Clarksdale	MS	38614	(662) 345-8482	2
Marion Cinema 2	604 Courthouse Sq.	Columbia	MS	39429	(601) 736-2001	2
Nelco Cinema 6	600 Cinema Dr.	Greenville	MS	38701	(662) 335-5558	6
Guntown Drive In	124 County Rd. 773	Guntown	MS	38849	(662) 869-1091	1
Grand 14	100 Grand Dr.	Hattiesburg	MS	39401	(601) 268-1681	14
Broad Country	601 3rd St. South West	Magee	MS	39111	(601) 849-4676	3
Movie Reel 4	720 Coulter Dr.	New Albany	MS	38652	(662) 534-2287	4
Canal Place Cinema 7	200 Canal Place	Philadelphia	MS	39350	(601) 656-6363	7
Tobie Twin	226 East Main St.	Senatobia	MS	38668	(662) 501-2020	3
Cinema 12	705 12 Hwy. 12 East	Starkville	MS	39759	(662) 323-7222	5
Hollywood Premier Cinema	101 Hollywood Blvd.	Starkville	MS	39759	(662) 320-9139	8

MISSOURI

Name	Address	City	State	Zip	Phone	Screens
Albany Rigney	102 S Smith	Albany	MO	64402	(660) 726-3807	1
Flick Theatre	105 E Main St.	Anderson	MO	64831	(417) 845-6681	1
Princess 3 Theatre	14 W Olive Hwy. 39	Aurora	MO	65605	(417) 693-1245	3
Sunset Drive In	1601 E Church	Aurora	MO	65605	(417) 678-6609	1
Ava Family Theatre	209 S Jefferson	Ava	MO	65608	(417) 683-8558	1
Big Time Cinema	103 S 15th St.	Bethany	MO	64424	(660) 425-7272	1
Ozarks Imax	3562 Shepherd Hills Expwy.	Branson	MO	65616	(417) 335-3533	4
Branson Meadow Cinemas	4740 Gretna Rd.	Branson	MO	65616	(417) 332-0464	11
Cinema II	226 Missouri 181	Cabool	MO	65689	(417) 962-4575	2
Starlite Drive In	15605 N State Hwy. 21	Cadet	MO	63630	(573) 438-4974	2
Crossroads Cinema	1903 N Walnut St.	Cameron	MO	64429	(660) 676-6293	4
Uptown Cinema	202 S Main St.	Carrollton	MO	64633	(660) 542-3432	1
66 Drive In	17231 Old 66 Blvd.	Carthage	MO	64836	(417) 359-5959	1
RagTag Cinemacafe	10 Hitt St.	Columbia	MO	65201	(573) 441-8504	1
19 Drive In	5853 Hwy. 19	Cuba	MO	65453	(573) 885-7752	1
Melba Theatre	300 S Main St.	De Soto	MO	63020	(636) 586-1900	1
B&B Main Street Cinema 8	100 Main St	Hannibal	MO	63401	(573) 248-1966	8
B&B Cinema 6	2727 Cantrell Rd.	Harrisonville	MO	64701	(816) 887-2836	6
Davis Theatre 4	2008 S Main St.	Higginsville	MO	64037	(816) 405-4068	1
Pharaoh Theatre	114 W Maple	Independence	MO	64050	(816) 836-9556	4
Noland Fashion Square 6	13520 E 40 Hwy.	Independence	MO	64055	(816) 478-2223	6
Twin Drive In	1320 291 Hwy.	Independence	MO	64050	(816) 257-2235	2
Truman 4 Theatres	1614 Jefferson St	Jefferson City	MO	65109	(573) 635-8819	4
Crown Center 6	2450 Grand Ave. Ste. 300	Kansas City	MO	64108	(816) 472-6001	6
I-70 Drive In Theatre	8701 E New 40 Hwy.	Kansas City	MO	64129	(816) 456-5191	4
Red Bridge Cinema	11118 Holmes St.	Kansas City	MO	64131	(816) 942-8901	4
Screenland Theatre	1656 Washington St.	Kansas City	MO	64108	(816) 421-2200	1
Tivoli Cinema	4050 Pennsylvania Ste. #200	Kansas City	MO	64111	(816) 914-6970	3
Downtown Cinema 8	115 N Elson	Kirksville	MO	63501	(660) 665-5684	8
Barco Drive In	57 SE 25th Ln.	Lamar	MO	64759	(417) 682-2434	1
Plaza Theatre	1011 A Gulf St.	Lamar	MO	64759	(417) 682-5521	1
Marceline Uptown Theatre	104 N Main St. USA	Marceline	MO	64658	(660) 376-2525	1
Hangar Theatre	1602 S Main	Maryville	MO	64468	(660) 582-7225	5
Memphis	114 W Monroe St.	Memphis	MO	63555	(660) 465-8943	1
Mexico Cinema 3	S Hwy. 54 Teal Lake Mall	Mexico	MO	65265	(573) 581-8383	3
Century 6	E Hwy. K	Nevada	MO	64772	(417) 667-9880	6
Walt Theatre	101 Hickory	New Haven	MO	63068	(573) 237-2411	1
Perryville Park Center	800 City Park Dr.	Perryville	MO	63775	(573) 547-7275	1
Pine Hill Drive In	Hwy. 34 E	Piedmont	MO	63957	(573) 223-2420	1
Farris Theatre	301 W Main St.	Richmond	MO	64085	(816) 776-6684	1
St Andrews Cinema	2025 Golfway Dr.	Saint Charles	MO	63301	(636) 947-1133	3
Trail Theatre	111 N 9th St.	Saint Joseph	MO	64501	(816) 232-6256	1
Chase Park Plaza Theatre	212 N Kings Hwy. Blvd.	Saint Louis	MO	63108	(314) 367-2385	5
Galleria 6 Cinemas	30 St. Louis Galleria	Saint Louis	MO	63117	(314) 725-0856	6
Galaxy Cinema	4104 W Main	Sedalia	MO	65301	(660) 826-4560	6
Owen Drive In	1 Owen Dr.	Seymour	MO	65746	(417) 935-2232	1
Hawkins	516 E Maple	Shelbina	MO	63468	(573) 588-7600	1
Moxie Cinema	408 West Walnut	Springfield	MO	65804	(417) 576-1193	1
The Palace	2220 W Chesterfield Blvd.	Springfield	MO	65807	(417) 881-8191	8
Horseshoe Lake Drive-In	5815 Frederick Ave.	St Joseph	MO	64507	(816) 279-3100	1
Keller Plaza Cinema	4572 Lemay Ferry Rd.	St Louis	MO	63129	(314) 894-0600	8
Moolah Theatre	3821 Lindell Blvd.	St Louis	MO	63108	(314) 446-6869	1
Webster University Theatre	470 E Lockwood Ave.	St Louis	MO	63119	(314) 968-7487	1
Sullivan Six Cinema	3001 N Service Rd. W	Sullivan	MO	63080	(573) 860-4800	6
Plaza Cinema 4	7 Plaza Ste. A	Troy	MO	63379	(573) 581-1613	4
Great Eight Cinema	5 Paririe Dell Plaza	Union	MO	63084	(636) 583-4800	8
21 Drive In	HCR #2 Box 2419 A	Van Buren	MO	63965	(573) 945-2366	1
Vandalia Cinema I & II	1411 W Hwy. 54	Vandalia	MO	63382	(573) 594-3733	2
Belle Starr	112 E Booneslick Rd.	Warrenton	MO	63383	(636) 456-7937	1
Roxy 2	325 Van Buren	Warsaw	MO	65355	(660) 438-6719	2
Cinema 1 Plus	1900 Pheonix Ctr. Dr.	Washington	MO	63090	(636) 239-3670	5
Family Cinema	1221 Independence Dr.	West Plains	MO	65775	(417) 256-3400	2
Glass Sword Cinema 6	101 Lanton Rd.	West Plains	MO	65775	(417) 257-2186	6

MONTANA

Name	Address	City	State	Zip	Phone	Screens
Washoe Theatre	305 Main St.	Anaconda	MT	59711	(406) 563-6161	1
Big Timer Martin Theatre	221 Mcleod St.	Big Timber	MT	59011	(406) 932-4060	1
Amusement Park Drive In	7335 Mossmain Lane	Billings	MT	59101	(406) 245-3212	2
Rialto	116054 S Buxton Rd.	Butte	MT	59750	(406) 846-1880	1
Silver Bow Drive In	6 MI W	Butte	MT	59750	(406) 782-8095	2
Roxy Theatre	25 N Main	Choteau	MT	59422	(406) 466-2194	1

Name	Address	City	State	Zip	Phone	Screens
Redwater Theatre	319 W Main	Circle	MT	59215	(406) 485-2440	1
Orpheum Theatre	7 Fourth Ave. SE	Conrad	MT	59425	(406) 278-9926	1
Madison Theatre	115 Main St.	Ennis	MT	59729	(406) 682-4336	1
Majestic Theatre	215 Dewey Ave.	Eureka	MT	59917	(406) 297-2631	1
Roxy Theatre	188 N 9th Ave.	Forsyth	MT	59327	(406) 346-7699	1
Mountain Rose Theatre	210 Stone St.	Gardiner	MT	59030	(406) 848-9123	1
Rose	215 N Merrill Ave.	Glendive	MT	59330	(406) 377-2828	1
Pharaohplex 4	582 Old Corvallis Rd.	Hamilton	MT	59840	(406) 961-3456	4
Roxy Twin	120 N Second St.	Hamilton	MT	59840	(406) 363-2336	2
Centre Cinema	318 N Center Ave.	Hardin	MT	59034	(406) 665-3628	1
Harlo Theatre	24 N Central Ave.	Harlowton	MT	59036	(406) 632-4324	1
Myrna Loy Center	15 N Ewing	Helena	MT	59601	(406) 443-0287	2
Judith Cinema	219 W Main St.	Lewistown	MT	59457	(406) 538-9509	1
Dome Theatre	602 Mineral	Libby	MT	59923	(406) 293-2703	1
Libby Theatre	1286 US Hwy 2	Libby	MT	59923	(406) 293-2703	1
Empire Twin Theatre	106 North 2nd St.	Livingston	MT	59047	(406) 220-1101	2
Montana	905 Main St.	Miles City	MT	59301	(406) 232-2958	1
Wilma Theatre	131 S Higgins Ste. 200	Missoula	MT	59802	(406) 728-2521	3
Llano Theatre	103 W McGowan St.	Plains	MT	59859	(406) 826-3936	1
Orpheum	119 S Main	Plentywood	MT	59254	(406) 765-1233	1
Sunset Drive In	414 W Boundway	Plentywood	MT	59254	(406) 765-1233	1
Roman Theatre	118 S Broadway	Red Lodge	MT	59068	(406) 446-2233	1
Entertainer Theatre	410 Main St. SW	Ronan	MT	59864	(406) 883-3206	1
HiLine Theatre	1175 Reed St.	Rudyard	MT	59540	(406) 355-4591	1
Cinema Centre	105 First Ave. E	Scobey	MT	59263	(406) 487-2224	1
Centre Theatre	211 S Central	Sidney	MT	59270	(406) 488-1158	1
Strand	105 River St.	Superior	MT	59872	(406) 822-4948	1
Rex Theatre	1033 Main St.	Thompson Falls	MT	59873	(406) 827-4720	1
Lincoln Theatre	211 E Kootenai	Troy	MT	59935	(406) 295-9345	1
Bears Den Cinema	15 Electric St.	West Yellowstone	MT	59758	(406) 646-7777	1
Strand	202 E Main	White Sulphur Spgs	MT	59645	(406) 547-3505	1
Star Theatre	25 W Legion	Whitehall	MT	59759	(406) 287-7909	1

NEBRASKA

Name	Address	City	State	Zip	Phone	Screens
Royal Theatre	126 E Second St.	Ainsworth	NE	69210	(402) 387-1948	1
Gateway Theatre	136 S 4th St.	Albion	NE	68620	(402) 395-3394	1
Geju - Alliance Theatre	410 Box Butte	Alliance	NE	69301	(308) 762-4100	3
Geju - Sandhills Drive In	2617 Country Rt. 57	Alliance	NE	69301	(308) 762-4100	1
Parrot Theatre	603 Main St.	Alma	NE	68920	(308) 928-2695	1
Crystal Theatre	505 Nebraska Ave.	Arapahoe	NE	68922	(308) 962-5341	1
State Theatre	1121 M St.	Auburn	NE	68305	(402) 274-3641	1
12th St. Cinema	1214 12th St.	Aurora	NE	68818	(402) 694-4000	1
Cinema Centre	615 Court St.	Beatrice	NE	68310	(402) 223-5196	2
Holly Theatre	615 Court St.	Beatrice	NE	68310	(402) 223-5196	1
Zorn Theatre	706 Chief	Benkelman	NE	69021	(308) 423-2280	1
Blair 3 Theatres	1645 S Hwy. 30	Blair	NE	68008	(402) 426-4746	3
Tiffany Theatre	317 South 10th	Broken Bow	NE	68822	(308) 872-2393	1
Rodeo Theatre	171 S 8th St.	Burwell	NE	68823	(308) 346-4556	1
State Theatre	706 C Ave.	Central City	NE	68826	(308) 946-2197	2
Geju - Eagle Theatre	224 Main St.	Chadron	NE	69337	(308) 432-2342	4
Isis Theatre	139 W 13th St.	Crete	NE	68333	(402) 826-2422	1
Star Theatre	321 Center Ave N.	Curtis	NE	69025	(308) 367-4350	1
Bonham Theatre	519 E St.	Fairbury	NE	68352	(402) 729-2109	2
River Twin Cinema	1715 Stone St.	Falls City	NE	68355	(785) 742-4387	2
Rosebowl Theatre	611 15th Ave.	Franklin	NE	68939	(308) 425-3313	1
Main Street 7	866 East 23rd	Fremont	NE	68025	(402) 727-8986	7
Rialto Theatre	162 N 9th St	Geneva	NE	68361	(402) 759-3011	2
Gordon Theatre	320 N Main St.	Gordon	NE	69343	(308) 282-0420	2
Sun Theatre	404 10th St.	Gothenburg	NE	69138	(308) 537-3235	1
The Grand Theatre	316 W Third St.	Grand Island	NE	68801	(308) 384-7009	1
Dickinson Imperial Theatre	3207 W 12th St.	Hastings	NE	68901	(402) 463-5757	3
Sun Theatre	421 West Ave.	Holdrege	NE	68949	(308) 237-7275	1
Imperial Theatre	740 Court St.	Imperial	NE	69033	(308) 882-4368	1
Goodhand Theatre	120 S Chestnut St.	Kimball	NE	69145	(308) 235-2449	1
Majestic Theatre	615 N Washington St.	Lexington	NE	68850	(308) 324-2572	1
Joyo Theatre	6118 Havelock Ave.	Lincoln	NE	68507	(402) 466-2441	1
Lynn Theatre	90052 503rd Ave	Lynch	NE	68746	(402) 569-3066	1
Minden Opera House	322 E 5th St.	Minden	NE	68959	(308) 832-0588	1
Nile Theatre	1433 Center Ave.	Mitchell	NE	69357	(308) 623-2727	1
Pioneer Theatres	110 S 11th St.	Nebraska City	NE	68410	(402) 873-4528	3
Prairie Theatre	208 N Spruce St.	Ogallala	NE	69153	(308) 284-2728	2
Dundee Theatre	4952 Dodge St.	Omaha	NE	68132	(402) 681-8601	1
Westwood Plaza	2809 S 125th Ave. #297	Omaha	NE	68144	(402) 697-0552	8
Valley Cinema	129 S 16th St.	Ord	NE	68862	(308) 728-3751	1
Granada Theatre	409 Ogden St.	Oxford	NE	68967	(308) 824-3705	1
Midwest Theatre	1707 Broadway	Scottsbluff	NE	69361	(308) 632-4311	1
Rivoli Theatre	533 Main St.	Seward	NE	68434	(402) 643-6195	1
Fox Theatre	1120 Illinois Ave.	Sidney	NE	69162	(308) 254-5529	2
Carlin Theatre	157 W St. Joseph	Spalding	NE	68665	(308) 497-2341	1
Crest Theatre	106 E 5th St.	Superior	NE	68978	(402) 879-3819	2
Majestic Twin	106 East 5th St.	Superior	NE	68978	(402) 768-6061	2
Jewel II	710 E Hwy. 20	Valentine	NE	69201	(402) 376-2890	2
Chateau Theatre	217 N Tecumseh	Wauneta	NE	69045	(308) 394-5485	1
Sun Theatre	427 Lincoln Ave.	York	NE	68467	(402) 362-1788	3

NEVADA

Name	Address	City	State	Zip	Phone	Screens
BC Cinemas	Hwy. 93	Boulder City	NV	89005	(702) 294-1216	2
Central Theatre	145 W 15 St.	Ely	NV	89301	(775) 289-2202	1
Fallon Theatres	71 S Maine	Fallon	NV	89406	(775) 423-6210	2
Cinedome AKA: Cactus Theatre	6th St & D St.	Hawthorne	NV	89415	(775) 945-2233	1
Incline Village	901 Tahoe Blvd.	Incline Village	NV	89451	(775) 831-2406	1
Luxor Hotel & Casino	3900 Las Vegas Blvd. S	Las Vegas	NV	89119	(702) 262-4565	1

Name	Address	City	State	Zip	Phone	Screens
Tropicana Cinema	3330 E Tropicana Ave.	Las Vegas	NV	89121	(702) 547-9449	6
Horizon Stadium 9	1955 S Casino Dr.	Laughlin	NV	89029	(702) 298-4551	9
Riverside Casino Cinemas	1650 Casino Way	Laughlin	NV	89029	(702) 298-2535	6
Ironwood Stadium Cinema 8	1760 Hwy. 395	Minden	NV	89423		8
Pioneer Theatre	120 South Moapa Valley Blvd.	Overton	NV	89040	(702) 397-2044	1
Carolees Theatre	31900 Las Vegas Blvd. S	Primm	NV	89019	(702) 679-7236	1
Park Cinemas	740 W Winnemucca Blvd.	Winnemucca	NV	89445	(775) 623-3563	2
Casino West Cinema	11 N Main St.	Yerington	NV	89447	(800) 227-4661	1

NEW HAMPSHIRE

Name	Address	City	State	Zip	Phone	Screens
Peterborough Community Theatre	6 School St.	Bennington	NH	03442	(603) 562-5418	1
Royal Cinema	25 Green Sq.	Berlin	NH	03570	(603) 723-8810	2
Colonial Theatre	2050 Main St.	Bethlehem	NH	03574	(603) 869-5603	1
Majestic Cinema	36 Main St.	Conway	NH	03818	(603) 447-6381	1
Nugget Theatre	57 S Main St.	Hanover	NH	03755	(603) 643-7424	4
Park Theatre	19 Main St.	Jaffrey	NH	03452	(603) 532-7711	1
Colonial Theatre	95 Main St.	Keene	NH	03431	(603) 352-2033	1
Keene Cinemas	121 Key Rd.	Keene	NH	03431	(603) 357-5261	6
Northfield Drive-In	Hinsdale Rd, Rt. 63	Keene	NH	03431	(603) 239-4054	1
Rialto Theatre	80 Main St.	Lancaster	NH	03584	(603) 788-4499	1
Lincoln Cinemas 4	100 Main St.	Lincoln	NH	03251	(603) 745-6239	4
O'Neil Apple Tree Cinema 12	16 Orchard View Dr.	Londonderry	NH	03053	(617) 861-9126	12
Premiere 8 Theatres	Route 101 A	Merrimack	NH	03054	(603) 882-9898	8
Chunky Cinema Pub	150 Bridge St.	Pelham	NH	03076	(603) 635-7624	5
The Flying Monkey Movie House	39 S Main St.	Plymouth	NH	03264	(603) 536-2931	2
The Music Hall	28 Chestnut St.	Portsmouth	NH	03801	(603) 436-2400	1
Spinelli Cinemas	23 Lilac Mall Rte. 16	Rochester	NH	03867	(603) 332-3714	4
Spinelli Tri City Cinema 4	20 Tri City Plaza	Somersworth	NH	03878	(603) 749-3572	4
Smitty's Cinema-Tilton	630 W Main St.	Tilton	NH	03276	(603) 286-3275	6
Wilton Town Hall Theatre	40 Main St.	Wilton	NH	03086	(603) 654-9337	2

NEW JERSEY

Name	Address	City	State	Zip	Phone	Screens
Atlantic Cinema 5	82 First Ave.	Atlantic Highlands	NJ	07716	(732) 291-4077	5
Berkeley Cinema	450 Springfield Ave.	Berkeley Heights	NJ	07922	(201) 791-0883	1
Bradley Beach Cinema	110 Main St.	Bradley Beach	NJ	07720	(201) 464-8888	1
Roberts Chatham Cinema	641 Shunpike Hickory SC	Chatham	NJ	07928	(973) 783-4964	1
Cranford Theatre	25 North Ave.	Cranford	NJ	07016	(908) 276-3070	5
Dunellen Theatre	458 North Ave.	Dunellen	NJ	08812	(732) 968-9010	1
Mega Movies	755 State Hwy. Rte. 18 Rues Ln.	East Brunswick	NJ	08816	(732) 613-1117	13
Cinema Plaza 6	240 US Hwy. 202/31	Flemington	NJ	08822	(908) 782-2744	6
Hawthorne Theatre	300 Lafayette Ave.	Hawthorne	NJ	07506	(973) 427-2524	5
Hillsborough Cinemas	111 Raider Blvd.	Hillsborough	NJ	08844	(908) 369-6327	10
Landmark Loew's Jersey	54 Journal Sq.	Jersey City	NJ	07306	(201) 798-6055	1
Lincoln Cinemas	838 Kearney Ave.	Kearny	NJ	07032	(201) 997-9674	6
Reading Manville 12	180 North Main St.	Manville	NJ	08835	(908) 707-4429	12
Maplewood Theatre	155 Maplewood Ave.	Maplewood	NJ	07040	(973) 763-7040	6
Newark Screens	360 Springfield Ave.	Newark	NJ	07103	(973) 642-4708	6
Newton Theatre	234 Spring St.	Newton	NJ	07860	(973) 579-9693	2
Cineplaza	2115 69th St.	North Bergen	NJ	07047	(201) 453-2217	13
Tilton 9 Theatre	331 Tilton Rd.	Northfield	NJ	08225	(609) 645-6835	9
Pennsville Premier Cinema	245 N Broadway	Pennsville	NJ	08070	(856) 678-1667	2
Princeton Garden Theatre	160 Nassau St.	Princeton	NJ	08542	(609) 683-4656	2
Ramsey Cinema	125 East Main St.	Ramsey	NJ	07446	(973) 228-0652	1
Montgomery Cinema	1325 Rte. 206	Rocky Hill	NJ	08553	(609) 924-6283	6
George W. Newman Theatre	1 Williams Plz.	Rutherford	NJ	07070	(201) 939-2907	3
Sparta Theatre	25 Center St.	Sparta	NJ	07871	(973) 729-5745	2
Clearview Cinema 10	21 Sunset Strip	Succasunna	NJ	07876	(973) 584-9508	10
Cedar Lane Cinemas 4	503 Cedar Lane	Teaneck	NJ	07666	(201) 836-3210	4
Destinta Theatre - Independence	2465 South Broad St.	Trenton	NJ	08610	(609) 888-4900	12
Union 7	990 Stuyvesant Ave.	Union	NJ	07083	(908) 686-4374	7
Showcase at the Ritz	900 Berlin Rd.	Voorhees	NJ	08043	(215) 779-1778	16
Abby Cinemas	35 Marshall Hill Rd.	West Milford	NJ	07480	(973) 728-7744	4
Rialto	250 E Broad St.	Westfield	NJ	07090	(908) 232-1481	6
Pascack Quad	182 Center Ave.	Westwood	NJ	07675	(201) 664-3201	6
Movies On The Beach @ Wildwood	4501 Boardwalk	Wildwood	NJ	08260	(925) 413-6200	1
Sea Theatre	4005 Pacific Ave.	Wildwood	NJ	08260	(609) 729-0337	1
The Strand Theatre	3100 Boardwalk	Wildwood	NJ	08260	(609) 729-5589	5

NEW MEXICO

Name	Address	City	State	Zip	Phone	Screens
Guild Cinema	3405 Central Ave. NE	Albuquerque	NM	87106	(505) 255-1848	1
Fiesta Drive In	401 W Fiesta Dr.	Carlsbad	NM	88220	(505) 302-1168	3
Luna Theatre	4 Main St.	Clayton	NM	88415	(505) 374-2712	1
West Theatre	118 West Santa Fe Ave.	Grants	NM	87020	(505) 287-4692	1
Fountain Theatre	1249 El Paseo	Las Cruces	NM	88001	(505) 525-8158	1
Ft Union Drive In	3300 N 7th St.	Las Vegas	NM	87701	(505) 454-1066	1
Kiva Theatre	109 Bridge St.	Las Vegas	NM	87701	(505) 454-0152	1
Reel Deal	2551 Central	Los Alamos	NM	87544	(505) 662-1580	4
Lea	106 E Central	Lovington	NM	88260	(505) 396-5594	1
El Raton Theatre	115 N Second St.	Raton	NM	87740	(505) 445-3721	1
Allen Sierra Cinema 2	721 D Mechem Dr.	Ruidoso	NM	88345	(505) 257-2038	2
Center for Contemporary Arts	1050 Old Pecos Trail	Santa Fe	NM	87505	(505) 982-1338	1
The Screen	1600 St. Michaels Dr.	Santa Fe	NM	87505	(505) 473-6083	3
Pecos Theatre	217 N 4Th St.	Santa Rosa	NM	88435	(505) 472-3098	1
Real West Cinema II	11585 Hwy. 180 East	Silver City	NM	88061	(505) 538-5659	2
Taos Community Auditorium	145 Paseo Del Pueblo Norte	Taos	NM	87571	(505) 758-2052	1
El Cortez Theatre	415 Main St.	Truth or Cons	NM	87901	(505) 894-4901	1
Odeon Theatre	123 S 2nd St.	Tucumcari	NM	88401	(505) 461-0100	1

Name	Address	City	State	Zip	Phone	Screens

NEW YORK

Name	Address	City	State	Zip	Phone	Screens
Spectrum Theatre	290 Delaware Ave.	Albany	NY	12209	(518) 449-8995	7
The Madison	1036 Madison Ave.	Albany	NY	12208	(518) 438-0040	7
Emerald Cinemas	136 Perth Plaza	Amsterdam	NY	12010	(518) 842-1862	10
New Angola Theatre	72 N Main Street	Angola	NY	14047	(716) 549-4866	1
Finger Lakes Drive In	Clark St. Rte. 5 & 20	Auburn	NY	13021	(315) 252-3969	1
Fingerlakes Theatres	1579 Clark St.	Auburn	NY	13022	(585) 249-0270	4
Malta Drive-In	2785 Rte. 9	Ballston Spa	NY	12020	(518) 587-6077	2
Bellmore Playhouse	525 Bedford Ave.	Bellmore	NY	11710	(516) 783-9669	5
Bellmore Movie Theatre	222 Pettit Ave.	Bellmore	NY	11710	(516) 783-3199	1
Empire Cinemas	1620 Rte. 22	Brewster	NY	10509	(845) 278-0031	3
El Rancho Drive In	386 Lakeview Rd.	Broadalbin	NY	12025	(518) 883-3972	1
Ozoner 29 Drive In	386 Lakeview Rd.	Broadalbin	NY	12025	(518) 883-3972	1
Strand Theatre	93 Main St.	Brockport	NY	14420	(585) 637-5632	3
The American Theatre	1450 East Ave.	Bronx	NY	10462	(718) 863-1310	7
BAM Rose Cinema	30 Lafayette Ave.	Brooklyn	NY	11217	(718) 636-4156	4
Cobble Hill Cinema	265 Court St.	Brooklyn	NY	11231	(718) 596-4995	5
The Pavillion Theatre	188 Prospect Park W &14 St.	Brooklyn	NY	11215	(718) 369-0836	8
Eastern Hills Cinema	4545 Transit Rd.	Buffalo	NY	14221	(716) 632-1081	3
Shea's Performing Art Center	646 Main St.	Buffalo	NY	14202	(716) 847-1410	1
Callicoon Theatre	30 Upper Main St.	Callicoon	NY	12723	(845) 887-6020	1
Movietime Canandaigua	Rte. 5 & 20 Wal-Mart Plaza	Canandaigua	NY	14424	(585) 396-0182	10
The Community Theatre	373 Main St.	Catskill	NY	12414	(201) 819-5947	2
Chautauqua Cinema	25 Wythe Ave.	Chautauqua	NY	14722	(716) 484-1873	1
MovieLand 8	200 Thruway Plaza Dr.	Cheektowaga	NY	14225	(716) 895-3662	6
Carol Theatre	6272 St. Rte. 9	Chestertown	NY	12817	(518) 494-0006	1
Plaza 6 Cinemas	255 Tompkins & Glenwood Ave.	Cortland	NY	13045	(607) 756-7057	6
HiWay Drive In	Rte. 9 West	Coxsackie	NY	12051	(518) 731-8672	4
Star Theatre	144 Main St	Dansville	NY	14437	(585) 335-6950	1
Loomis-Delevan Drive In	Rte. 16	Delevan	NY	14042	(716) 496-5660	2
Flix Theatre	4901 Transit Rd.	Depew	NY	14043	(716) 668-1888	10
State Theatre	148 Front St.	Deposit	NY	13754	(607) 467-2727	1
Douglaston Movieworld	242-02 61st Ave.	Douglaston	NY	11362	(718) 423-9203	7
Aurora Theatre	673 Main St. Ste. 4, 2nd Flr.	East Aurora	NY	14052	(716) 652-1660	1
Elwood Cinema	1950 Jericho Turnpike	East Northport	NY	11731	(631) 499-9883	4
Heights Theatre	210 E 14th	Elmira	NY	14903	(607) 733-2533	1
Cinema Saver	19 Madison Ave.	Endicott	NY	13760	(607) 757-2916	5
Fredonia Opera House	9-11 Church St.	Fredonia	NY	14063	(716) 484-1873	1
Geneseo Square Theatres	4180 Lakeville Rd.	Geneseo	NY	14454	(585) 243-4062	6
Smith Opera House	82 Seneca St.	Geneva	NY	14456	(315) 781-5483	1
The Glen Cove Cinemas	5 School St.	Glen Cove	NY	11542	(516) 671-6866	6
Jericho Drive In	Route 9 West Rural Rte. #3	Glenmont	NY	12077	(518) 767-3398	1
Great Neck Arts Ctr	113 Middleneck Rd.	Great Neck	NY	11021	(516) 829-2570	1
Village Cinema Greenport	211 Front St.	Greenport	NY	11944	(631) 477-0346	4
Palace Hamburg	31 Buffalo St.	Hamburg	NY	14075	(716) 649-2295	1
Hamilton Movie Theatre	7 Lebanon St.	Hamilton	NY	13346	(315) 824-8210	3
Capra Cinemas	533 West Front St.	Hancock	NY	13783	(607) 637-2501	2
Bard College	30 Campus Rd.	Hudson	NY	12504	(845) 758-7563	0
Fairview Cinema III	160 Fairview Ste. 101	Hudson	NY	12534	(518) 828-0132	3
Hunter Mountain Drive In	7970 Main St. Rte. 23A	Hunter	NY	12442	(518) 263-4333	1
Hunter Theatre	Main Street	Hunter	NY	12442	(518) 263-4908	1
Hyde Park Drive In	510 Albany Post Rd.	Hyde Park	NY	12538	(845) 229-8959	1
Roosevelt 7	510 Albany Post Rd.	Hyde Park	NY	12538	(845) 229-2007	7
Indian Lake Theatre	Main St.	Indian Lake	NY	12842	(503) 640-6817	1
Tamarack Cafe & Movie House	Rte. 28	Inlet	NY	13360	(315) 357-2001	1
Cinemapolis	171 E State St.	Ithaca	NY	14850	(607) 277-6115	2
Fall Creek Pictures	1201 N Tioga	Ithaca	NY	14850	(607) 272-1256	3
Reg Lenna Civic Center	116 E Third St.	Jamestown	NY	14701	(716) 484-1873	1
Park 60 Drive In 2	1529 Foots Ave.	Jamestown	NY	14701	(716) 484-6065	2
Kew Gardens Cinemas	81-05 Lefferts Blvd.	Kew Gardens	NY	11415	(718) 441-3002	5
Lake Placid Art Center	91 Saranac Ave.	Lake Placid	NY	12946	(518) 523-2512	1
Le Roy Theatre	32 Main St.	Le Roy	NY	14482	(585) 768-4624	1
Hippodrome	1140 St. Rte. 52	Loch Sheldrake	NY	12759	(845) 434-3888	1
Historic Palace Theatre	2 East Ave.	Lockport	NY	14095	(716) 438-1130	1
Transit Drive In	6655 S Transit Rd.	Lockport	NY	14094	(716) 625-8697	4
Long Beach Cinema 4	179 East Park Ave.	Long Beach	NY	11561	(516) 431-7564	4
The Ohmann Theatre	645 William St.	Lyons	NY	14489	(919) 676-8980	1
Valley Brook Drive In	Burdicks Crossing	Lyons Falls	NY	13368	(315) 348-6315	1
West Wayne Theatre	Rte. 31 & W Wayne Plaza	Macedon	NY	14502	(315) 597-4382	1
Emelin Theatre	153 Library Ln.	Mamaroneck	NY	10543	(914) 698-3045	1
Manlius Art Cinema	135 East Seneca St.	Manlius	NY	13104	(315) 682-9817	1
Movieland of Mastic	1708 Montauk Hwy.	Mastic	NY	11950	(631) 281-8571	10
Mattituck Cinemas	10095 Main Rd.	Mattituck	NY	11952	(631) 298-5642	8
Merrick Cinemas	15 Fisher Ave.	Merrick	NY	11566	(516) 623-2330	4
Sunset Drive In	Rte. 31 Telegraph Rd.	Middleport	NY	14105	(716) 735-3099	1
Middletown Discount Cinemas	128 Dolson Ave.	Middletown	NY	10940	(845) 343-3725	5
Moviehouse Triplex	48 Main St.	Millerton	NY	12546	(518) 789-0022	3
Midway Drive In Theatre	2475 N St. Rte. 48	Minetto	NY	13115	(315) 598-2282	1
Montauk Movies	3 Edgemere Rd.	Montauk	NY	11954	(631) 668-1540	1
Monticello Mall Cinema	4412 Rte. 42	Monticello	NY	12701	(845) 794-2601	4
New Paltz Cinema	2 New Paltz Plaza	New Paltz	NY	12561	(845) 255-0464	4
Destinta New Windsor 12	215 Quassaick Ave.	New Windsor	NY	12553	(845) 569-8181	12
Apollo Theatre	253 West 125th St.	New York	NY	10027	(212) 531-5300	1
Cinema Village	22 E 12th St.	New York	NY	10003	(212) 924-3364	3
Directors Guild	110 W 57th St. 6th Flr.	New York	NY	10019	(212) 258-0811	1
Du Art	245 W 55th 8th Flr.	New York	NY	10019	(212) 757-4580	1
Film Forum Triplex	209 W Houston St.	New York	NY	10014	(212) 627-2035	3
Lincoln Plaza 6	1886 Broadway	New York	NY	10023	(212) 757-3458	6
Magno Preview	729 7th Ave. 2nd Flr.	New York	NY	10019	(212) 302-1361	1
New Festival	47 Great Jones St. 6th Flr.	New York	NY	10012	(212) 254-7228	1
NY Film Academy	100 E 17th St. 2nd Flr.	New York	NY	10003	(212) 674-4300	1
Paris Theatre	4 West 58th St.	New York	NY	10019	(212) 593-4872	1
Pioneer Theatre	44 Ave. A	New York	NY	10009	(212) 254-7107	1
Planet Hollywood	1540 Broadway	New York	NY	10036	(212) 333-7822	1

Name	Address	City	State	Zip	Phone	Screens
Quad Cinema	34 West 13th St.	New York	NY	10011	(212) 255-2243	4
Scandinavia House	58 Park Ave.	New York	NY	10016	(212) 879-9779	1
Sound One	1619 Broadway	New York	NY	10019	(212) 603-0500	1
The Kodak Theatre	360 W 31st St. 2nd Flr.	New York	NY	10001	(212) 631-3474	1
Town Hall	123 West 43rd St.	New York	NY	10036	(212) 997-1003	1
Walter Reade Theatre	165 W 65th St.	New York	NY	10023	(212) 875-5638	1
Showplace 6	101 S Main St.	Newark	NY	14513	(315) 331-8007	6
Showtime Cinemas	1124 Union Ave. Rte. 300	Newburgh	NY	12550	(845) 566-6611	10
Four Seasons Cinema 6	2429 Military Rd.	Niagara Falls	NY	14304	(716) 297-0362	6
Riviera Theatre	67 Webster St.	North Tonawanda	NY	14120	(716) 692-2413	1
Colonia Twin	35 S Broad St.	Norwich	NY	13815	(607) 334-2135	2
Ogdensburg Cinemas	219 Ford St.	Ogdensburg	NY	13669	(315) 393-3302	2
Castle Cinema	Rte. 417 W State Hwy.	Olean	NY	14760	(716) 557-8835	2
Oneonta Twin	47 Chestnut St.	Oneonta	NY	13820	(607) 432-8211	2
Tioga Theatre	208 Main St.	Owego	NY	13827	(607) 687-9605	2
Paramount Center for the Arts	1008 Brown St.	Peekskille	NY	10566	(914) 739-2333	1
Pelham Picture House	175 Wolfs Ln.	Pelham	NY	10803	(914) 738-3175	1
Lake St. Plaza Theatres	230A Lake St. Plz.	Penn Yan	NY	14527	(315) 531-8463	3
Silver Lake Drive In	7037 Chapman Rd.	Perry	NY	14530	(585) 237-3372	2
Strand Cinema	25 Brinkerhoff St.	Plattsburgh	NY	12901	(518) 566-7265	2
Jacobs Burns Film Center	364 Manville Rd.	Pleasantville	NY	10570	(914) 769-6070	3
Portville Drive In	East State Rd. Rte. 417	Portville	NY	14770	(716) 373-5838	1
Bardavon Opera House	35 Market St.	Poughkeepsie	NY	12601	(845) 473-5288	1
Overlook Drive In	126 Degarmo Rd.	Poughkeepsie	NY	12601	(845) 452-3912	1
Glen Twin Drive In	963 Rte. 9	Queensbury	NY	12804	(518) 793-0970	2
Lyceum Cinemas	7270 S Broadway St.	Red Hook	NY	12571	(845) 758-3333	7
Upstate Films Rhinebeck	6415 Montgomery St.	Rhinebeck	NY	12572	(845) 876-4546	1
Cinema Theatre	957 S Clinton Ave.	Rochester	NY	14620	(585) 271-1786	1
Little Theatre	240 East Ave.	Rochester	NY	14604	(585) 258-0409	5
Vintage Drive In	1520 West Henrietta Rd.	Rochester	NY	14620	(585) 226-9290	2
Capitol Theatre	220 W Dominic St.	Rome	NY	13440	(315) 337-6277	1
Rosendale Theatre	408 Main St.	Rosendale	NY	12472	(845) 658-8989	1
Reel Meals	86 Congress St.	Saratoga Springs	NY	12866	(518) 583-8883	3
Orpheum Theatre	154 Main St.	Saugerties	NY	12477	(845) 246-6561	3
Sayville Theatres	103 Railroad Ave.	Sayville	NY	11782	(631) 589-0040	4
Fine Arts	365 Central Ave.	Scarsdale	NY	10583	(914) 723-6745	1
Proctors Theatre	432 State St.	Schenectady	NY	12305	(518) 382-3884	1
Scotia Cinema	117 Mohawk Ave.	Schenectady	NY	12302	(518) 346-5440	1
Isaiah's Picture Show	Route 8	Speculator	NY	12164	(518) 548-6199	1
Joylan Theatre	11 W Main St.	Springville	NY	14141	(716) 592-7402	1
Atrium Stadium Cinemas	680 Arthur Kill Rd.	Staten Island	NY	10308	(718) 984-3859	9
Lafayette Theatre	97-99 Lafayette Ave.	Suffern	NY	10901	(845) 369-8180	1
Landmark Theatre	362 S Salina St.	Syracuse	NY	13202	(315) 475-7979	1
Palace Theatre	2384 James St.	Syracuse	NY	13206	(315) 463-9240	1
Westcott Cinema	524 Westcott St.	Syracuse	NY	13210	(315) 479-9911	1
Adirondack State Theatre	100 Park St.	Tupper Lake	NY	12986	(518) 359-3593	1
Stanley Theatre	259 Genesee St.	Utica	NY	13501	(315) 724-5919	1
Uptown Theatre	2014 Genesee St.	Utica	NY	13502	(315) 738-0377	3
Walton Theatre	132 Delaware St. Ste. 3B	Walton	NY	13856	(607) 865-6688	1
Warsaw Cinema	23 S Main St.	Warsaw	NY	14569	(585) 786-3670	1
Glen Theatre	112 North Franklin St.	Watkins Glen	NY	14891	(607) 535-4302	1
The Grand Theatre	144 N Main St.	Wellsville	NY	14895	(585) 593-1466	2
South Bay Cinema, LLC	495 Montauk Hwy. & Rte. 109	West Babylon	NY	11704	(631) 587-7808	5
Westhampton Art Center	76 Main St.	Westhampton Bch	NY	11978	(631) 288-2350	1
Warwick Drive In	5 Warwick Turnpike	Warwick	NY	10990	(845) 986-4400	2
Windham Theatre	11 Vets Rd./SR 23	Windham	NY	12496	(518) 734-6110	1
Palace Theatre	12053 Main St.	Wolcott	NY	14590	(315) 594-2785	1
Tinker Street Cinema	132 Tinker St.	Woodstock	NY	12498	(845) 679-6608	1
Wieting Theatre	168 Main St. Ste. 2	Worcester	NY	12197	(607) 397-9204	1

NORTH CAROLINA

Name	Address	City	State	Zip	Phone	Screens
Earl Cinema 4	127 E Main St.	Ahoskie	NC	27910	(252) 332-5977	4
Badin Road Drive In	2411 Badin Rd.	Albemarie	NC	28001	(336) 314-1985	1
Eastgate Cinemas 5	823 Hwy. 27	Albemarle	NC	28001	(704) 982-8811	5
Andrews Cinema 2	125 Main St.	Andrews	NC	28901	(828) 321-3333	3
Asheville Pizza and Brew	675 Merrimon Ave.	Asheville	NC	28804	(828) 254-1281	1
Fine Arts Theatre	38 Biltmore Ave.	Asheville	NC	28801	(828) 232-0257	1
Atlantic Station 4	Atlantic Station Shop Center	Atlantic Beach	NC	28512	(252) 247-1817	4
Belmont Drive In	314 McAdenville Rd.	Belmont	NC	28012	(704) 825-6044	1
Bessemer City Kings Drive In	1365 Bessemer City-Kings Mt.	Bessemer City	NC	28016	(704) 739-2150	1
The Falls Theatre	101 W Main St.	Brevard	NC	28712	(828) 883-2200	2
Carousel Cinemas	1090 Piper Lane	Burlington	NC	27215	(336) 538-9900	15
Yancey Theater	119 West Main St.	Burnsville	NC	28714	(828) 678-3311	1
Galaxy Cinema	770 Cary Towne Blvd.	Cary	NC	27511	(919) 463-9959	6
Chelsea Cinema	1129 Weaver Dairy Rd.	Chapel Hill	NC	27514	(919) 929-8428	3
Lumina Theatre	700 Market St.	Chapel Hill	NC	27516	(919) 969-8049	5
Varsity Cinemas	123 E Franklin St.	Chapel Hill	NC	27514	(919) 929-8428	2
New Light at the Eastland Mall	5423 Central Ave.	Charlotte	NC	28212	(704) 531-8385	2
Park Terrace	4289 Park Rd.	Charlotte	NC	28209	(704) 523-9771	6
East Park Cinema	122 Southeast Blvd.	Clinton	NC	28328	(910) 592-5004	5
Carolina Mall Cinemas	120 Country Club Dr.	Concord	NC	28025	(704) 788-2404	8
Carolina Theatre	309 W Morgan St.	Durham	NC	27701	(919) 560-3040	1
Eden Drive In	106 Fireman Club Rd.	Eden	NC	27288	(336) 314-1985	1
Rockingham Theatre	205 Gilmer St.	Eden	NC	27288	(336) 623-2174	1
Taylor Twin Cinema	208 S Broad St.	Edenton	NC	27932	(252) 482-3489	2
Carolina Theatre & Grille	115 N Poindexter St.	Elizabeth City	NC	27909	(252) 337-7600	1
Emerald Plantation 4	8700 Emerald Dr.	Emerald Isle	NC	28594	(252) 354-7263	4
Cameo Art House Theatre	225 Hay St.	Fayetteville	NC	28301	(910) 485-7440	1
Ruby Cinemas	2097 Georgia Rd.	Franklin	NC	28734	(828) 369-6876	4
Graham Cinema	119 N Main St.	Graham	NC	27253	(336) 226-1488	1
Carolina Theatre	310 S Greene St.	Greensboro	NC	27401	(336) 333-2600	1
Carousel 15	1305 Battleground Ave.	Greensboro	NC	27408	(336) 230-1732	15
Sedgefield Crossing's Cinema 7	4631 High Point Rd.	Greensboro	NC	27407	(336) 841-9828	7
Market Place Cinemas	907 Beckford Dr.	Henderson	NC	27536	(252) 438-9017	6

Name	Address	City	State	Zip	Phone	Screens
Raleigh Road Outdoor Theatre	PO Box 904	Henderson	NC	27537	(252) 514-6145	1
Skyland Arts Cinemas	538 North Main St.	Hendersonville	NC	28792	(828) 697-2463	1
Carolina Theatres	222 First Ave. Nw	Hickory	NC	28601	(828) 322-7211	2
Westchester Cinema	2200 Westchester Dr. Ste. 116	High Point	NC	27262	(336) 841-9828	2
Starmount Crossing 5	209 Winston Rd.	Jonesville	NC	28642	(336) 526-2287	5
Gem Theatre	111 W First St.	Kannapolis	NC	28081	(704) 932-5126	1
Cinema 2	1500 Atkinson St.	Laurinburg	NC	28352	(910) 291-3155	2
Louisburg Theatre	109 W Nash St.	Louisburg	NC	27549	(919) 496-4770	2
Pioneer Cinema	115 Bu.dleigh St.	Manteo	NC	27954	(252) 473-2175	1
McDowell Twin Cinemas	1240 North Main St.	Marion	NC	28752	(828) 652-8368	2
Marquee Cinemas - Mimosa 7	103 S Green St.	Morganton	NC	28655	(828) 437-8084	7
Downtown Cinema	142 N Main St.	Mount Airy	NC	27030	(336) 786-7998	1
Henn Theatre	38 Tennessee St.	Murphy	NC	28906	(828) 837-2618	1
Neuse Blvd. Cinema	2500 Neuse Blvd.	New Bern	NC	28562	(252) 633-2438	3
Southgate Cinemas	2806 Trent Rd.	New Bern	NC	28562	(252) 635-5301	6
State Theatre	117 N College Ave.	Newton	NC	28658	(828) 464-2171	2
Kleeberg Liberty Theatre	816 Main St.	North Wilkesboro	NC	28659	(336) 838-7273	2
Colony Theatre	5438 Six Forks Rd.	Raleigh	NC	27609	(919) 847-5677	2
Mission Valley Cinema	2109-124 Avent Ferry Rd.	Raleigh	NC	27606	(919) 834-2233	5
Raleighwood Cinema Grill	6609 Falls of Neuse Rd.	Raleigh	NC	27616	(919) 847-0326	7
Rialto Theatre	1620 Glenwood Ave.	Raleigh	NC	27608	(919) 856-8683	1
Six Fork Station Cinema	9500 Forum Dr.	Raleigh	NC	27615	(919) 846-3904	6
Salisbury Mall Cinema	1951 Statesville Blvd.	Salisbury	NC	28147	(704) 797-0255	6
Sunset Drive In	3935 W Dixon Blvd.	Shelby	NC	28152	(704) 434-7782	1
Howell Theatre	141 S Third St.	Smithfield	NC	27577	(919) 938-1201	4
Sunrise Theatre	250 NW Broad St.	Southern Pines	NC	28387	(910) 692-0892	1
Surf Cinemas	4836 Long Beach Rd.	Southport	NC	28461	(910) 457-0420	4
Quinn Theatres	623 East Main St.	Sylva	NC	28779	(828) 586-9716	3
Parkhill 3 Cinemas	1600 Howard	Tarboro	NC	27886	(252) 824-0553	3
Tryon Theatre	45 Trade St.	Tryon	NC	28782	(828) 859-6811	1
Smoky Mountain Cinemas 3	235 Waynesville Plaza	Waynesville	NC	28786	(828) 452-3688	3
Parkway Theatre	171 Greenhill Dr.	West Jefferson	NC	28694	(336) 846-3280	2
Cinema 3 Theatres	627 S Madison St.	Whiteville	NC	28472	(910) 642-4528	3
Thalian Hall	310 Chestnut St.	Wilmington	NC	28401	(910) 343-3663	1
Marketplace Cinemas	2095 Peters Creek Pkwy.	Winston Salem	NC	27127	(336) 725-4616	6

NORTH DAKOTA

Name	Address	City	State	Zip	Phone	Screens
Bijou Show House	82 1 St. SE	Beach	ND	58621	(701) 872-4412	1
Belfield Theatre	Hwy. 85 & Hwy. 10	Belfield	ND	58622	(701) 575-8140	1
Grand Theatre	1486 Interstate Loop	Bismarck	ND	58503	(701) 222-1607	10
Botno Theatre	511 Main St.	Bottineau	ND	58318	(701) 228-2674	1
Bowman Theatre	30 S Main St.	Bowman	ND	58623	(701) 523-3411	1
Audi Theatre	4th Ave & Main St.	Cando	ND	58324	(701) 968-4501	1
Carrington Youth Center Theatre	870 Main St.	Carrington	ND	58421	(701) 652-2159	1
Cavalier Cinema	104 W Main	Cavalier	ND	58220	(701) 265-8902	1
Cooper Theatre	810 Burrel Ave. S W	Cooperstown	ND	58425	(701) 797-2317	1
Dakota Theatre	219 North Main St.	Crosby	ND	58730	(701) 965-6797	1
Fargo Theatre	314 Broadway	Fargo	ND	58102	(701) 239-8385	1
Krieger	307 Main St.	Gackle	ND	58442	(701) 252-2669	1
Kota Theatre	153 N Main St.	Garrison	ND	58540	(701) 463-7356	1
Strand	618 Hill Ave.	Grafton	ND	58237	(701) 352-3513	2
Central Cinema	810 Lincoln Ave.	Harvey	ND	58341	(701) 324-4486	1
Cinema Twin Theatre	500 7th St. NE	Hazen	ND	58545	(701) 748-6101	2
Mayer	501 Main St.	Hebron	ND	58638	(701) 878-4406	1
Hettinger Theatre	113 N Main	Hettinger	ND	58639	(800) 851-2304	1
Bison Twin Theatres	Buffalo Mall	Jamestown	ND	58401	(701) 252-5688	2
Cinema Twin	James Town Mall	Jamestown	ND	58401	(701) 252-9220	2
Kenmare Theatre	9 W Division St.	Kenmare	ND	58746	(701) 385-4263	1
Omega Cinema	Omega City Plaza	Lamoure	ND	58458	(701) 883-5079	1
Roxy Theatre	714 Third St.	Langdon	ND	58249	(701) 256-2199	1
Avalon Theatre	208 Tower Ave.	Larimore	ND	58251	(701) 283-5471	1
Scenic Theatre	419 Main St.	Lisbon	ND	58054	(701) 683-4822	1
Mystic Theatre AKA: Marmarth	51 Main St	Marmarth	ND	58651	(701) 279-6996	1
Delchar Theatre	20 West Main St.	Mayville	ND	58257	(701) 786-2114	1
Oak Park Theatre	1500 4th Ave. NW	Minot	ND	58703	(701) 852-7469	1
Playhouse Theatre	318 Brown Ave.	Mott	ND	58646	(701) 824-2721	1
Rockford Theatre	8 N 8th St.	New Rockford	ND	58356	(701) 947-5963	1
Grand Theatre	115 Second St. S	Oakes	ND	58474	(701) 742-3712	1
Page Theatre	18 Brenton Ave.	Page	ND	58064	(701) 668-2258	1
Lyric Theatre	416 Briggs Ave. S	Park River	ND	58270	(701) 284-7633	1
Rolette Theatre	401 1st Ave. West	Rolette	ND	58366	(701) 246-3267	1
Curt's Theatre	106 Main Ave. E	Rolla	ND	58367	(701) 477-3629	1
Centre Cinema	220 S Main St.	Rugby	ND	58368	(701) 776-2179	1
Regis Theatre	114 S Main St.	Stanley	ND	58784	(701) 628-2689	1
Tioga Theatre	151 First St. NE	Tioga	ND	58852	(701) 664-5888	1
Theatre One & Twos	1315 Main St. W	Valley City	ND	58072	(701) 845-2816	2
Wing Theatre	212 Main St.	Wing	ND	58494	(701) 943-2492	1
Dakota Theatre	12 N 5th St.	Wishek	ND	58495	(701) 452-2150	1

OHIO

Name	Address	City	State	Zip	Phone	Screens
Highland Theatre	824 W Market St.	Akron	OH	44303	(330) 253-0100	1
Linda Theatre	1747 Goodyear Blvd.	Akron	OH	44305	(330) 784-3443	1
Rolling Acres Cinemas	2400 Romig Rd.	Akron	OH	44322	(330) 322-2569	3
Amherst Cinema	260 Church St.	Amherst	OH	44001	(440) 988-7711	1
Pymatuning Lake Drive In	6352 Marvin Rd.	Andover	OH	44003	(412) 225-1503	1
Ashland Square Cinemas	214 Center St.	Ashland	OH	44805	(419) 289-2414	3
Ashtabula Cinema Center	3501 North Ridge Rd. West	Ashtabula	OH	44004	(440) 992-8733	8
Athena Grand	1008 E State St.	Athens	OH	45701	(740) 591-4743	11
Lake Cinema 8	588 W Tuscarawas Ave.	Barberton	OH	44203	(330) 848-2730	8
Magic City Drive In	5602 S Cleveland Masillon	Barberton	OH	44203	(330) 825-4333	2
West Theatre	1017 Wooster Rd. W	Barberton	OH	44203	(330) 825-6912	1
Blanchester Showplace 3	115 E Main St.	Blanchester	OH	45107	(937) 783-2387	3

Name	Address	City	State	Zip	Phone	Screens
Shannon Theatre	119 S Main St.	Bluffton	OH	45817	(419) 358-1141	1
Canton Palace Theatre	605 N Market	Canton	OH	44702	(330) 454-8172	1
Mayfield Drive In	12100 SR 322	Chardon	OH	44024	(330) 289-7412	1
Danbarry Cinemas	119 Pawnee Rd.	Chillicothe	OH	45601	(740) 779-6113	10
Majestic Theatre	45 E 2nd St.	Chillicothe	OH	45601	(740) 772-2041	1
Danbarry Cincinnati Mills	601 Cincinnati Mills Dr.	Cincinnati	OH	45240	(513) 671-1872	8
Danbarry Dollar Saver Eastgate	4450 Eastgate Blvd.	Cincinnati	OH	45245	(513) 947-8222	8
Danbarry Western Hills	5190 Glencrossing Way	Cincinnati	OH	45238	(513) 451-2499	12
Mariemont Theatre	6906 Wooster Pike	Cincinnati	OH	45227	(513) 272-0222	3
Mt. Lookout Cinema Grill	3187 Linwood Ave.	Cincinnati	OH	45208	(513) 321-7999	2
Northgate Cinema	9727 Colerain Way	Cincinnati	OH	45251	(513) 377-2789	7
Parkland Theatre	6550 Parkland Ave.	Cincinnati	OH	45233	(513) 600-7900	1
Clevland Cedar Lee	2163 Lee Rd.	Cleveland	OH	44118		6
Cleveland Cinematheque	11141 East Blvd.	Cleveland	OH	44106	(216) 421-7450	2
Cleveland Film Society	2510 Market Ave.	Cleveland	OH	44113	(216) 623-3456	1
Landerbrook Screening Room	5915 Landerbrook Dr.	Cleveland	OH	44124		1
Memphis Drive In	10543 Memphis Rd.	Cleveland	OH	44144	(216) 941-1598	3
Palace Theatre	1615 Euclid Ave. Ste. 200	Cleveland	OH	44115	(216) 771-4444	1
Playhouse Square Ohio Theatre	1519 Euclid Ave.	Cleveland	OH	44115	(216) 348-5292	1
Tower City 11	230 W Huron Rd.	Cleveland	OH	44113	(216) 564-2031	11
Main Street Theatre	5 North Main St.	Columbiana	OH	44408	(330) 482-9647	1
Cinema City	5737 Scarborough Blvd.	Columbus	OH	43232	(614) 322-5501	8
Drexel Arena Grand Theatre	175 W Nationwide Blvd.	Columbus	OH	43215	(614) 469-5000	8
Drexel East Theatre	2254 East Main St.	Columbus	OH	43209	(614) 231-1050	3
Drexel Gateway	1550 N High St.	Columbus	OH	43201	(614) 222-0947	8
Drexel Grandview Theatre	1247 Grandview Ave.	Columbus	OH	43212	(614) 486-7229	1
Screens at the Continent	6360 Busch Blvd.	Columbus	OH	43229	(614) 318-0551	8
South Drive In	3050 South Hugh St.	Columbus	OH	43212	(614) 491-2583	2
Westland Dollar Cinemas	4265 Shoppers Lane	Columbus	OH	43228	(614) 276-0906	8
Conneaut Plaza Theatre	348 W Main Rd.	Conneaut	OH	44030	(440) 599-8697	2
Hollywood Studios Theatre	460 Downtowner Plaza	Coshocton	OH	43812	(740) 623-8871	2
Danbarry Dollar Saver South Dayton	8300 Lyons Ridge Dr.	Dayton	OH	45458	(937) 291-2680	12
Dixie Twin Drive In	6201 N Dixie Dr.	Dayton	OH	45414	(937) 859-7107	2
Neon Movies	130 E 5th St.	Dayton	OH	45402	(937) 222-8452	1
Page Manor Twin Cinemas	5584 Airway Rd.	Dayton	OH	45431	(937) 253-2444	2
Strand Theatre	28 East Winter St.	Delaware	OH	43015	(740) 362-9023	3
Atlas Cinemas Midway Mall 8	2650 Midway Mall	Elyria	OH	44035	(440) 324-2580	8
Atlas Cinemas Lake Shore 7	22624 Lakeshore Blvd.	Euclid	OH	44123	(216) 731-2138	7
Danbarry Cinemas Middletown	3479 Dixie Hwy.	Franklin	OH	45005	(513) 422-6804	10
Paramount Cinemas	301 S Front St.	Fremont	OH	43420	(419) 332-9160	4
Garretsville Cinema	8009 State St.	Garrettsville	OH	44231	(330) 665-3541	2
Wayne Cinemas	540 S Broadway	Greenville	OH	45331	(937) 548-5511	2
Star Cinemas	2384 Stringtown Rd.	Grove City	OH	43123	(614) 539-3450	8
Holiday Drive In	1816 Old Oxford Hwy.	Hamilton	OH	45013	(513) 929-2999	1
Hayesville Opera House	5 1/2 E Main St.	Hayesville	OH	44838	(419) 368-7100	1
Star Cinemas	211 Harry Sauner Rd.	Hillsboro	OH	45133	(937) 393-6666	6
Danbarry Dollar Saver Huber Heights	7650 Waynetowne Blvd.	Huber Heights	OH	45424	(937) 233-6698	12
University Plaza Theatre	140 Cherry St.	Kent	OH	44240	(330) 673-4451	8
Duncan Theatre	110 N Main St.	Killbuck	OH	44637	(330) 276-7231	1
Orchestra Hall Theatre	236 Walnut Ave.	Lakeside	OH	43440	(419) 798-4461	1
Blue Colony Square Cinemas	726 E Main St.	Lebanon	OH	45036	(513) 932-9499	2
Eastgate Dollar Movies	2100 Harding Hwy.	Lima	OH	45804	(419) 331-3456	4
Lorain Palace Theatre	617 Broadway	Lorain	OH	44052	(440) 245-2323	1
Ohio Theatre	156 N Water St.	Loudonville	OH	44842	(419) 994-1044	1
Springmill Twin Drive In	1040 Springmill Rd.	Mansfield	OH	44906	(419) 747-2156	1
Renaissance Theatre	138 Park Ave. West	Mansfield	OH	44902	(419) 522-2726	2
Sunset Drive In	4018 Rte. 309	Mansfield	OH	44906	(419) 884-8797	1
Palace Marion	276 West Center St.	Marion	OH	43302	(740) 383-2101	1
Marysville Cinemas	121 S Main St.	Marysville	OH	43040	(937) 642-9990	3
Lions Lincoln Theatre	156 LincolnWay East	Massillon	OH	44646	(330) 837-2363	1
Maumee Indoor Theatre	601 Conant St.	Maumee	OH	43537	(419) 897-8902	2
Opera House, Inc	15 West Main St.	Mc Connelsville	OH	43756	(740) 962-3030	1
Atlas Cinemas Diamond Center 16	9555 Diamond Cntr.	Mentor	OH	44060	(440) 352-8846	16
Movies 10	14333 US Rte. 33 South	Nelsonville	OH	45764	(740) 753-3326	10
Lock One Theatre	120 W Monroe St.	New Bremen	OH	45869	(419) 629-2220	1
Quaker Cinema	117 S Broadway	New Philadelphia	OH	44663	(330) 289-1522	2
Midland Theatre	158 W High Ave	Newark	OH	43055	(740) 349-9218	1
USA Cinema	930 Great East Plaza	Niles	OH	44446	(330) 652-8728	6
Virginia Theatre	119 North Main St.	North Baltimore	OH	45872	(419) 257-4900	1
Aut-O-Rama Twin Drive In	33395 Lorain Rd.	North Ridgeville	OH	44039	(440) 327-9595	2
Fox Theatres at Woodville Mall	3725 Williston Rd.	Northwood	OH	43619	(419) 693-8698	4
Premiere Cinemas 8	50 Theatre Dr.	Norwalk	OH	44857	(513) 851-6464	8
Starview Drive In	US Hwy. 20 West	Norwalk	OH	44857	(440) 774-2494	1
Norwalk Theatre (Town & Country)	57 E Main St.	Norwalk	OH	44857	(419) 668-1641	1
Apollo Theatre	19 East College St.	Oberlin	OH	44074	(440) 774-7091	1
Sundance Drive In	4500 Navarre Ave.	Oregon	OH	43616	(419) 691-7055	2
K & L Cinema 20	1469 Mentor Ave.	Painesville	OH	44077	(440) 354-6507	1
Parma Theatre	5826 Ridge Rd.	Parma	OH	44129	(440) 885-0600	3
Portsmouth Cinemas	1623 Chillicothe St.	Portsmouth	OH	45662	(502) 348-7441	8
Midway Drive In	2736 St. Rte. 59	Ravenna	OH	44266	(330) 289-7412	2
Salem Twin Theatre	2350 E State St.	Salem	OH	44460	(330) 332-0797	2
Sandusky State Theatre	107 Columbus Ave.	Sandusky	OH	44870	(419) 626-1950	1
Auto Vue Drive In	1409 4th Ave.	Sidney	OH	45365	(937) 492-5909	1
Winter Drive In	400 Luray Dr.	Steubenville	OH	43952	(740) 266-9092	3
Lynn Auto Drive In	9735 St. Rte. 250 N W	Strasburg	OH	44680	(330) 878-7775	2
Tiffin Drive In	4041 N St. Rte. 53	Tiffin	OH	44883	(419) 443-1889	1
Ohio Theatre	3114 Lagrange St.	Toledo	OH	43608	(419) 241-6785	1
Mayflower 4	9 W Main St.	Troy	OH	45373	(937) 335-9288	4
Sherwood Movies 5	927 N Market	Troy	OH	45373	(937) 335-7466	5
Star Theatre	121 W Wyandot Ave.	Upper Sandusky	OH	43351	(419) 294-1411	1
Blue Sky Drive In	959 Broad St.	Wadsworth	OH	44281	(330) 334-1809	1
Great Oaks Cinema	179 Great Oaks Trail	Wadsworth	OH	44281	(330) 336-4464	2
Wapa Theatre	15 Willipie St.	Wapakoneta	OH	45895	(419) 738-3718	1
Elm Rd. Triple Drive In	1895 Elm Rd. NE	Warren	OH	44483	(330) 372-9732	3
Skye Cinema	455 E Airport Hwy.	Wauseon	OH	43567	(419) 466-1995	6
Hollywood Studio Theatre	5996 Westerville Rd.	Westerville	OH	43081	(614) 901-3911	8

Name	Address	City	State	Zip	Phone	Screens
The Big Picture Cinema	116 E South St.	Wooster	OH	44691	(330) 263-6229	2
Little Art Theatre	247 Xenia Ave. 2nd Flr.	Yellow Springs	OH	45387	(937) 767-7671	1
Oakland Center for Arts	220 W Boardman St.	Youngstown	OH	44501	(330) 746-0404	1

OKLAHOMA

Name	Address	City	State	Zip	Phone	Screens
Heritage Park Theatre	16107 US Highway 83	Altus	OK	73522	(580) 482-3443	7
Rialto Twin Cinemas	516 Flynn St.	Alva	OK	73717	(580) 327-0535	3
Redskin Theatre	221 W Broadway St.	Anadarko	OK	73005	(405) 247-5333	1
The Phoenix Theatre	201 N High St.	Antlers	OK	74523	(580) 298-9820	1
Eastland 4 Theatre	530 Washington Blvd.	Bartlesville	OK	74006	(918) 333-3222	4
Rex II Theatre	129 Buffalo St.	Caddo	OK	74729	(580) 367-2586	1
Liberty	9 W Main	Carnegie	OK	73015	(580) 654-1188	3
H & S Theatre	816 Manvel Ave.	Chandler	OK	74834	(405) 258-0414	1
Heritage Park Theatres	2505 Valley View	Chickasha	OK	73018	(405) 413-6508	6
Broadway Twin	300 S Broadway St.	Cleveland	OK	74020	(918) 356-4321	2
Crown Theatre	1007 W Main St.	Collinsville	OK	74021	(918) 371-2101	1
Washita Theatre	111 S Market	Cordell	OK	73632	(580) 832-4138	1
Palace Theatre	926 W Main St.	Duncan	OK	73533	(580) 255-5588	2
Durant 4 Cinemas	915 W Main St.	Durant	OK	74701	(580) 920-2898	4
Kickingbird Cinemas	1225 E Danforth Rd.	Edmond	OK	73034	(405) 359-6667	8
Flix on 6	2103 S Main	Elk City	OK	73644	(580) 799-0904	4
Royal Theatre	109 N Main St.	Fairview	OK	73737	(580) 227-3511	1
Grove Cinemas	1109 N 3rd St.	Grove	OK	74344	(918) 786-3900	4
Beacon Drive In	2404 S Division St.	Guthrie	OK	73044	(405) 282-6388	1
Mitchell Northridge Cinema 8	1950 Hwy. 64 North	Guymon	OK	73942	(580) 338-8969	8
McCurtain Cinema	Hwy. 70 & Hwy. 259 N.	Idabel	OK	74745	(580) 286-6468	4
89er Cinema	119 E Miles	Kingfisher	OK	73750	(405) 375-3489	1
Vaska Theatre	1902 NW Ferris Ave.	Lawton	OK	73507	(580) 353-5000	1
Cinema 69 Drive In	1116 S George Nigh Hwy.	McAlester	OK	74502	(918) 423-4353	1
Cinema 69 Theatre	1116 S George Nigh Expwy.	Mcalester	OK	74501	(918) 423-4353	4
Coleman Theatre	103 N Main St.	Miami	OK	74354	(918) 540-2425	1
Crystal Theatre	401 W Broadway St.	Okemah	OK	74859	(918) 623-1253	1
Winchester Drive In	6930 S Western Ave.	Oklahoma City	OK	73102	(405) 236-0616	1
Windsor Hills Cinema	4625 NW 23rd St.	Oklahoma City	OK	73127	(866) 327-0049	10
Orpheum Theatre	210 W Seventh St.	Okmulgee	OK	74447	(918) 756-2270	2
Royal Twin	117 E Paul	Pauls Valley	OK	73075	(405) 238-6358	2
Airline Drive In	1900 West Highland	Ponca City	OK	74601	(580) 762-6545	1
Poncan Theatre	104 E Grand Ave.	Ponca City	OK	74601	(580) 765-0943	1
Poteau Twin	2214 N Broadway	Poteau	OK	74953	(918) 647-2900	3
Tower Drive In	2214 N Broadway	Poteau	OK	74953	(918) 647-2900	1
Allred 5 Theatre	225 E Graham	Pryor	OK	74361	(918) 260-6634	5
Strothers Twin Theatre	1110 E Strothers	Seminole	OK	74868	(405) 382-7259	2
Time Theatre	103 E Main St.	Stigler	OK	74462	(918) 967-3187	1
Eagle Theatre	119 W Division St.	Stilwell	OK	74960	(918) 696-2310	1
Green Country Cinema	1100 Heritage Ln.	Tahlequah	OK	74464	(918) 431-1342	6
Admiral Twin Drive In	7355 E Easton St.	Tulsa	OK	74115	(918) 838-3114	2
Circle Cinema	10 S Lewis	Tulsa	OK	74104	(918) 585-3456	1
Eastland Mall Cinema 6	14002 E 21st Ste. B7	Tulsa	OK	74134	(918) 437-6007	6
Super Saver Cinema	5970 A East 31 St.	Tulsa	OK	74135	(918) 665-3330	7
Showest 3	US Hwy. 66	Weatherford	OK	73096	(580) 772-8550	3
Picture Show	119 W Main St.	Wilburton	OK	74578	(918) 465-3081	1
Lakeside Triple	1427 34th St.	Woodward	OK	73801	(580) 256-2182	3
Suburban Cinemas	1425 34th St.	Woodward	OK	73801	(580) 256-2182	3
Yukon 5 Cinema	1219 Garth Brooks Blvd.	Yukon	OK		(405) 354-9132	5

OREGON

Name	Address	City	State	Zip	Phone	Screens
Columbian Theatre	1102 Marine Dr.	Astoria	OR	97103	(503) 325-5505	1
Eltrym Theatre	1809 First St.	Baker City	OR	97814	(541) 523-5439	1
Valley Cinema Pub	9360 SW Beav Hillsdale	Beaverton	OR	97005	(503) 777-0793	3
Old St Francis School Theatre	700 NW Bond St.	Bend	OR	97701	(541) 382-5174	1
Valley Triplex	9360 SW Beav Hillsdale	Beaverton	OR	97415	(541) 469-4632	1
Redwood Theatre	621 Chetco Ave.	Brookings	OR	97415	(541) 412-7575	2
Desert Theatre	68 N Broadway	Burns	OR	97720	(541) 573-4220	1
Cornelius 9 Cinemas	200 North 26th St.	Cornelius	OR	97113	(503) 844-0891	9
Avalon Cinema	160 NW Jackson	Corvallis	OR	97330	(541) 752-4161	1
Dark Side Cinema	215 SW 4th St.	Corvallis	OR	97330	(541) 908-2000	1
Fox Theatre	166 SE Mill St.	Dallas	OR	97338	(503) 623-2578	1
Motor Vu Drive In	315 SE Fir Villa	Dallas	OR	97338	(503) 623-2578	1
OK Enterprise	208 W Main St.	Enterprise	OR	97828	(541) 426-3544	1
Bijou Art Cinema	492 E 13th Ave.	Eugene	OR	97401	(541) 686-2458	2
Florence Cinemas	1930 Hwy. 101	Florence	OR	97439	(541) 997-7127	6
Compass Room Theatre	3505 Pacific Ave.	Forest Grove	OR	97116	(503) 992-9533	1
Forest Theatre	1911 Pacific Ave.	Forest Grove	OR	97116	(503) 359-1105	1
Mt Hood Theatre	401 E Powell Blvd.	Gresham	OR	97030	(503) 661-9909	1
Hermiston Stadium 8	355 W Theatre Ln.	Hermiston	OR	97838	(541) 567-0643	8
Hood River Cinemas	5 Fifth St.	Hood River	OR	97031	(541) 386-5711	5
Skylight Theatre & Pub	107 Oak St.	Hood River	OR	97031	(541) 386-4888	1
La Grande Drive In	404 20th St.	La Grande	OR	97850	(541) 963-3014	1
Granada Theatre	1311 Adams Ave.	La Grande	OR	97850	(541) 963-3014	3
Lake Theatre	106 N State St.	Lake Oswego	OR	97034	(503) 699-4099	2
Showhouse	24 South F St.	Lakeview	OR	97630	(541) 947-3710	1
Kuhn Cinema	668 Main St.	Lebanon	OR	97355	(541) 259-4595	1
Bijou Theatre	1624 NE Hwy. 101	Lincoln City	OR	97367	(541) 994-8255	1
Newport Perf. Arts	1612 NE Hwy. 101	Lincoln City	OR	97367	(541) 994-8255	1
Moonlight Theatre	433 E 3rd St.	Mcminnville	OR	97128	(503) 434-5800	1
Milton - Freewater Drive In	Hwy.11	Milton Freewater	OR	97862	(509) 525-7402	1
99 W Twin	304 East 1st St.	Newberg	OR	97132	(503) 554-0046	2
99 West Drive In	304 East 1st St.	Newberg	OR	97132	(503) 554-0046	1
Cameo	304 E 1st St.	Newberg	OR	97132	(503) 554-0046	1
Reel Theatre 8	477 SE 13th St.	Ontario	OR	97914	(541) 823-0847	8
Pendleton Cinema	415 SW First St.	Pendleton	OR	97801	(541) 278-0482	3
Savoy Theatre	811 Oregon St.	Port Orford	OR	97465	(541) 332-3105	1
Avalon Theatre	3451 SE Belmont St.	Portland	OR	97214	(503) 238-1617	2
Bagdad Theatre	3702 SE Hawthorne	Portland	OR	97214	(503) 236-9234	1
Cinema 21	616 NW 21st Ave.	Portland	OR	97209	(503) 223-4044	1

Name	Address	City	State	Zip	Phone	Screens
Cinemagic	2021 SE Hawthorne	Portland	OR	97214	(503) 231-0071	1
Clinton Street Theatre	2522 SE Clinton St.	Portland	OR	97202	(503) 238-5588	1
Hollywood Theatre	4122 NE Sandy Blvd.	Portland	OR	97212	(503) 493-1128	3
Joy Cinema & Pub	11959 SW Pacific Hwy.	Portland	OR	97223	(503) 639-1482	1
Kennedy School Theatre	5736 NE 33rd Ave.	Portland	OR	97211	(503) 288-2117	1
Laurelhurst Theatre	2735 E Burnside St.	Portland	OR	97214	(503) 238-4088	4
Milwaukee Cinema	11011 SE Main	Portland	OR	97222	(503) 653-2222	3
Mission Theatre & Pub	1624 NW Glisan	Portland	OR	97209	(503) 223-4527	1
Moreland Theatre	6712 SE Milwaukie Ave.	Portland	OR	97202	(503) 236-5257	1
Oak Grove Cinema	16100 SE McLoughlin Blvd.	Portland	OR	97267	(503) 653-3511	8
Roseway Theatre	7229 N E Sandy Blvd.	Portland	OR	97213	(503) 287-8119	1
Saint John's Pub and Theatre	8203 N Ivanhoe	Portland	OR	97203	(503) 283-8609	1
Redmond Theatre	1535 Odem Medo Rd.	Redmond	OR	97756	(541) 548-1244	4
Historic Elsinore Theatre	170 High St. SE	Salem	OR	97301	(503) 375-3574	1
Northern Lights Theatre Pub	3893 Commercial St. SE	Salem	OR	97302	(503) 585-4232	4
Salem Cinema	1127 Broadway NE	Salem	OR	97301	(503) 585-8849	1
Sandy Cinema	16605 Champion Way	Sandy	OR	97055	(503) 826-1208	8
Cannes Cinema Center	1026 12th Ave.	Seaside	OR	97138	(503) 738-0671	5
Palace Theatre	200 North Water St.	Silverton	OR	97381	(503) 873-4181	1
Sisters Movie House	720 Desperado Court	Sisters	OR	97759	(541) 549-8800	4
Star Cinema	350 N Third Ave.	Stayton	OR	97383	(503) 769-3729	1
Rio Theatre	1439 Main St.	Sweet Home	OR	97386	(541) 401-3500	1
Columbia Cinema	2727 West 7th St.	The Dalles	OR	97058	(541) 296-8021	4
Granada Theatre	223 E 2nd St.	The Dalles	OR	97058	(541) 298-4710	1
Coliseum Theatre	310 Main St.	Tillamook	OR	97141	(503) 842-6111	1
Power Station Pub & Theatre	2126 SW Halsey St.	Troutdale	OR	97060	(503) 492-4686	1
Rex Theatre	240 A St. West	Vale	OR	97918	(541) 473-3470	1

PENNSYLVANIA

Name	Address	City	State	Zip	Phone	Screens
19th Street	527 North 19th St.	Allentown	PA	18104	(610) 433-8903	1
Franklin	425-29 Tilghan	Allentown	PA	18102	(610) 433-3640	1
Ambridge Family Theatre	647 Merchant St.	Ambridge	PA	15003	(724) 251-9760	1
Allen Theatre	36 E Main St.	Annville	PA	17003	(717) 867-4766	1
Pitt Theatre	134 E Pitt St.	Bedford	PA	15522	(814) 623-6219	1
Garman Opera House Theatre	116 E High St.	Bellfonte	PA	16823	(814) 353-8803	1
Berwick Theatre	110 E Front St.	Berwick	PA	18603	(570) 752-3633	1
Boyd Theatre	30 West Broad St.	Bethlehem	PA	18018	(610) 866-1521	1
Cinema Center	1879 New Berwick Highway	Bloomsburg	PA	17815	(570) 387-8542	12
State Theatre	61 North Reading Ave.	Boyertown	PA	19512	(610) 367-4737	1
Bradford Main St. Movie House	123 Main St.	Bradford	PA	16701	(814) 363-9388	2
Destinta - Chartiers Valley	1025 Washington Pike	Bridgeville	PA	15017	(412) 914-0998	20
Moonlite Drive In 2	Rd. 4 Rte. 322 W	Brookville	PA	15825	(814) 849-5588	1
Bryn Mawr Film Institute	824 Lancaster Ave.	Bryn Mawr	PA	19010	(215) 348-1878	2
Clearview Mall Cinemas	101 Clearview Circle	Butler	PA	16001	(724) 282-3884	4
Cinema Center Camp Hill	3431 Simpson Ferry Rd.	Camp Hill	PA	17011	(717) 920-9350	12
Rialto Theatre	5 E Main St.	Canton	PA	17724	(570) 673-4444	1
Carlisle Theatre	44 W High St.	Carlisle	PA	17013	(717) 258-0666	1
Skyview Twin Drive In	Rte. 88	Carmichaels	PA	15320	(724) 998-0848	2
Cheswick Theatres	1500 Pittsburg St.	Cheswick	PA	15024	(724) 274-6310	1
Destinta @ Clarion Mall	22631 Rte. 68 Ste. 80	Clarion	PA	16214	(814) 227-2441	7
Ritz Theatre	111 E Market St.	Clearfield	PA	16830	(814) 765-5835	2
Angela III	113 E Phillips St.	Coaldale	PA	18218	(570) 645-7866	3
Mahoning Drive In	Route 433	Coaldale	PA	18218	(570) 645-7866	1
Iris Theatre	157 Adams St.	Cochranton	PA	16314	(814) 425-3786	1
Columbia Drive In	4061 Columbia Ave.	Columbia	PA	17512	(717) 684-7708	1
Corry Drive In	Rte. 6 & 89	Corry	PA	16407	(814) 664-2894	1
Coudersport Theatre	207 North Main St.	Coudersport	PA	16915	(814) 274-8580	1
Point Drive In	Rte. 11	Danville	PA	17821	(570) 275-9926	3
Haar's Drive In	185 Logan Rd.	Dillsburg	PA	17019	(717) 432-3011	1
Ambler Theatre	91 E Court	Doylestown	PA	18901	(215) 345-7855	2
County Theatre	91 E Court St.	Doylestown	PA	18901	(215) 345-7642	2
Comet Drive In	Rd 2 Rte. 119	Dunbar	PA	15431	(724) 628-6160	1
Grand Cinema & Coffee Shop	88 South Courtland St.	East Stroudsburg	PA	18301	(570) 421-5220	3
Poconos Movieplex	400 Foxmoor Dr.	East Stroudsburg	PA	18301	(570) 223-8984	7
Grand Theatre	207 S 2nd Ave.	Elizabeth	PA	15037	(412) 384-0504	1
MoviE-Town	700 North Hanover St.	Elizabethtown	PA	17022	(717) 361-7536	8
Emmaus Theatre	19 S Fourth St.	Emmaus	PA	18049	(610) 967-5489	1
Ephrata Main Theatre	124 East Main St.	Ephrata	PA	17522	(717) 733-9037	2
Majestic Performing Arts & Cinema	25 Carlisle St.	Gettysburg	PA	17325	(717) 337-8237	3
Glen Theatre	37 Manchester St.	Glen Rock	PA	17327	(717) 225-9982	1
Grand Theatre	252 Main St. East	Greenville	PA	18041	(215) 679-4300	1
Guthrie Theatre	232 S Broad St.	Grove City	PA	16127	(724) 458-0900	1
Hamburg Strand	6 South 4th St.	Hamburg	PA	19526	(610) 562-4750	1
Colonial Park 4	Colonial Park Mall	Harrisburg	PA	17109	(717) 652-0307	4
MidTown Cinema	250 Reily St.	Harrisburg	PA	17102	(717) 909-6645	3
Cinema & Drafthouse	31 W Broad St.	Hazleton	PA	18202	(570) 455-0564	1
Laurel Drive In	Route 309	Hazleton	PA	18201	(570) 436-0326	1
Shenango Valley Cinemas	2996 E State St.	Hermitage	PA	16148	(724) 983-1121	12
Cocoaplex Cinemas	1150 Cocoa Ave.	Hershey	PA	17033	(717) 312-1301	7
Cinema 6	1199 Texas Palmyra Hwy. Ste. A	Honesdale	PA	18431	(570) 251-8151	6
Cinema Center Selinsgrove	1 Susquehanna Valley Mall Dr.	Selingsgrove	PA	17870	(570) 374-2049	12
Garden Drive In	Route 11- Rd #2	Hunlock Creek	PA	18621	(570) 735-5933	1
Huntingdon Cinema	717 Washington St.	Huntingdon	PA	16652	(814) 643-2653	5
Hiway Theatre, Inc	212 Old York Rd.	Jenkintown	PA	19046	(215) 886-9802	1
Richland Cinemas	420 Theatre Dr.	Johnstown	PA	15904	(814) 266-3133	10
Silver Drive In	1664 Scalp Ave.	Johnstown	PA	15904	(814) 266-2981	1
Westwood Plaza Theatre & Cafe	1910 Minno Ste. 109	Johnstown	PA	15905	(814) 255-2116	2
Family Drive In	Rte. 6 East of Kane	Kane	PA	16735	(814) 837-9760	1
Strand Twin	32 North White Oak St.	Kutztown	PA	19530	(610) 781-9363	2
Galleria Theatre	Split Rock Lodge	Lake Harmony	PA	18624	(570) 722-9111	1
Zoetropolis Cinema	235 W Lemon	Lancaster	PA	17603	(717) 394-8272	1
HiWay Drive In	Rte. 30 Box 225A	Latrobe	PA	15650	(724) 537-7418	1
Latrobe Family Cinema	315 Latrobe 30 Plaza	Latrobe	PA	15650	(724) 537-5678	2
Mahoning Valley Cinema 8	1241 Blakeslee Blvd. 5 E	Lehighton	PA	18235	(570) 386-4406	8

Name	Address	City	State	Zip	Phone	Screens
Campus Theatre	413 Market St.	Lewisburg	PA	17837	(570) 524-9629	1
Miller 6 Cinema	46 West Market St.	Lewistown	PA	17044	(717) 248-8654	6
Ligonier Theatre	210 W Main St.	Ligonier	PA	15658	(814) 266-4308	1
Port Drive In (Harvest Moon)	Rte. 220 & Rte. 287	Linden	PA	17744	(570) 398-1574	2
Roxy Theatre	220 N Jay St.	Lock Haven	PA	17745	(570) 893-4220	3
Academy Theatre	275 Chestnut St.	Meadville	PA	16335	(814) 337-8211	1
Star Theatre	23 W Seminary St.	Mercersburg	PA	17236	(717) 328-5959	1
Elks Theatre	Emaus & Union St.	Middletown	PA	17057	(717) 533-6600	1
Midway Drive In	Old Rte. 322	Mifflintown	PA	17059	(717) 436-6011	1
Milford Theatre	114 E Catherine St.	Milford	PA	18337	(570) 409-1278	1
Sky Vu Drive In	502 S Market St.	Millersburg	PA	17061	(717) 692-4744	1
Point of View Cinema	121 W Frederick St.	Millersville	PA	17551	(717) 872-4131	1
Pike Drive In	Rte. 15 S.	Montgomery	PA	17752	(570) 547-7232	3
Montrose Theatre	18 Public Ave.	Montrose	PA	18801	(570) 278-3352	1
Casino Theatre	110 Main St. Rte. 611	Mount Pocono	PA	18344	(570) 839-7831	1
Ritz Theatre	9 N Main St.	Muncy	PA	17756	(570) 546-3740	1
Narberth Stadium 2	129 N Narberth Ave.	Narberth	PA	19072	(610) 667-8122	1
Westgate Cinemas	2000 W State St.	New Castle	PA	16101	(724) 652-9072	9
West Shore Theatre	317 Bridge St.	New Cumberland	PA	17070	(717) 774-4266	1
Newtown Theatre	120 North State St.	Newtown	PA	18940	(215) 968-0158	1
Cumberland Drive In	715 Centerville Rd. Rts 11 & 233	Newville	PA	17241	(717) 776-5212	1
Destinta Plaza East	1701 Lincoln Hwy.	North Versailles	PA	15137	(412) 824-9101	22
Roxy Theatre	2004 Main St.	Northampton	PA	18067	(610) 262-7699	1
The Oaks	310 Alleghney River Blvd.	Oakmont	PA	15139	(412) 828-6322	1
Shankweiler's Drive In	Route 309	Orefield	PA	18069	(610) 481-0800	1
Cinema Center 12	2 N Londonderry Sq.	Palmyra	PA	17078	(717) 838-4859	12
International House	3701 Chestnut St.	Philadelphia	PA	19104	(215) 895-6569	1
Prince Music Theatre	1412 Chestnut	Philadelphia	PA	19102	(215) 972-1010	1
Ritz 5 Movies	220 Walnut St.	Philadelphia	PA	19106	(215) 779-1778	5
Ritz At The Bourse	400 Ranstead St.	Philadelphia	PA	19106	(215) 779-1778	5
Ritz East	125 S 2nd St.	Philadelphia	PA	19106	(215) 779-1778	2
Roxy Theatre	2023 Sansom St.	Philadelphia	PA	19103	(215) 923-6699	2
Colonial Theatre	227 Bridge St.	Phoenixville	PA	19460	(610) 917-1228	1
Citadel Cinema	213 S Tulpehocken	Pine Grove	PA	17963	(570) 345-0426	1
Pine Grove Theatre	213 S Tulpehocken	Pine Grove	PA	17963	(570) 345-0426	1
Byham Theatre	101 6th St.	Pittsburgh	PA	15222	(412) 456-1350	1
Harris Theatre	809 Liberty Ave.	Pittsburgh	PA	15222	(412) 471-9702	1
Penn Hills Cinemas	76 Federal Dr.	Pittsburgh	PA	15235	(412) 951-0341	4
SouthSide Works Cinema	425 Cinema Dr.	Pittsburgh	PA	15203	(412) 381-1681	10
Waterworks Cinemas	930 Freeport	Pittsburgh	PA	15238	(412) 784-1217	10
Jackson Theatre	220 N Jefferson St.	Punxsutawney	PA	15767	(814) 938-1008	1
Reading premier Discount Cinemas	3225 5th St. Hwy.	Reading	PA	19605	(610) 929-1015	4
Cinema Center @ Fairground Sq.	3050 N Fifth St.	Reading	PA	19605	(610) 921-5800	5
Diamond Theatre	19 N Michael St.	Saint Marys	PA	15857	(814) 834-7434	2
Sayre Theatre	205 South Elmer Ave.	Sayre	PA	18840	(570) 268-7469	3
Circle Drive In	Carbondale Hwy.	Scranton	PA	18508	(570) 876-1400	1
Endless Mountains Theatre	933 Scranton Carbondale	Scranton	PA	18508	(570) 343-4953	8
Sellersville Theatre	24 West Temple Ave.	Sellersville	PA	18960	(215) 257-5808	1
Broad Theatre	24 W Broad St.	Souderton	PA	18964	(215) 723-3444	1
Keystone Theatre	601 Main St.	Towanda	PA	18848	(570) 268-2787	1
Reynolds Drive In	Route 18	Transfer	PA	16154	(724) 646-2550	1
Dietrich Theatre	60 E Tioga St.	Tunkhannock	PA	18657	(570) 836-0176	2
Riverside Drive In	1114 Lees Lake Lane	Vandergrift	PA	15690	(412) 853-6456	1
Beckys Drive In	4548 Lehigh Dr.	Walnutport	PA	18088	(610) 767-2249	1
Warren Mall Cinemas	1666 Market St.	Warren	PA	16365	(814) 723-6021	3
Struthers Library Theatre	302 W Third Ave.	Warren	PA	16365	(716) 484-1873	2
Mall Cinema	342 Oak Spring Rd.	Washington	PA	15301	(724) 250-7551	8
Sunset Drive In	808 Route 97	Waterford	PA	16441	(814) 796-4883	1
Watson Theatre	131 Main St.	Watsontown	PA	17777	(570) 538-1778	1
Waynesboro Theatre	75 W Main St.	Waynesboro	PA	17268	(717) 762-7879	1
Waynesburg Theatre & Arts Center	41 W High St.	Waynesburg	PA	15370	(724) 627-7407	1
Arcadia Theatre	50 Main St.	Wellsboro	PA	16901	(570) 724-9371	4
Kirby Center	71 Public Sq.	Wilkes Barre	PA	18701	(570) 823-4599	1
Community Arts Cntr.	220 West 4th St.	Williamsport	PA	17701	(570) 327-7655	1
Kendig Square Movies 6	2600 North Willow St. Pike	Willow Street	PA	17584	(717) 464-7565	6
Gap Theatre	47 Broadway	Wind Gap	PA	18091	(610) 863-9828	1
South York Plaza	217 Pauline Dr.	York	PA	17402	(610) 327-6916	4
Strand Capitol	50 N George St.	York	PA	17401	(717) 846-1155	1

RHODE ISLAND

Name	Address	City	State	Zip	Phone	Screens
Empire Theatre	17 Water St.	Block Island	RI	02807		1
Cinema World 16	622 George Washington Way	Lincoln	RI	02865	(321) 288-2637	16
Jane Pickens Theatre	49 Touro St.	Newport	RI	02840	(781) 910-2765	1
Opera House Cinema	19 Touro St.	Newport	RI	02840	(401) 846-0817	3
Avon Cinema	260 Thayer St.	Providence	RI	02906	(401) 421-0020	1
Cable Car Cinema	204 S Main St.	Providence	RI	02903	(401) 272-3970	1
Castle Cinemas Cafe	1039 Chalkstone Ave.	Providence	RI	02908	(401) 270-5199	3
Fienstein Imax	9 Providence Place Ste. R2	Providence	RI	02903	(401) 453-4446	1
Patriot Cinema 10	60 Newport Ave.	Rumford	RI	02916	(401) 438-1757	10
Rustic Drive In Theatre	Rte. 146	N Smithfield	RI	02896	(401) 769-0771	3

SOUTH CAROLINA

Name	Address	City	State	Zip	Phone	Screens
Highway 21 Drive In	Hwy. 21 West	Beaufort	SC	29902	(843) 846-4500	1
Ladys Island Theatre	41 Robert Smalls Pkwy.	Beaufort	SC	29902	(843) 525-0578	3
Plaza Stadium Theatre	41 Robert Smalls Pkwy.	Beaufort	SC	29906	(843) 525-0578	8
Seaturtle Cinema	106 Buckwalter Pkwy.	Bluffton	SC	29910	(843) 686-6969	10
Little Theatre	508 Dekalb St.	Camden	SC	29020	(803) 432-7330	2
American Theatre 2	446 King St.	Charleston	SC	29403	(843) 853-0246	2
South Windmere Cinemas	94 Folly Rd.	Charleston	SC	29407	(843) 571-2346	2
Terrace Theatre	1956 D Maybank Hwy.	Charleston	SC	29412	(843) 762-4247	2
Nickelodeon Theatre	937 Main St.	Columbia	SC	29201	(803) 254-8234	1
Phoenix Columbia Mall Cinema 8	7201 Two Notch Rd.	Columbia	SC	29223	(803) 788-7665	8

Name	Address	City	State	Zip	Phone	Screens
St Andrews Cinema 5	527 St. Andrews Rd.	Columbia	SC	29210	(803) 772-7572	5
Plaza Cinemas	223 Radford Cinemas	Dillon	SC	29536	(843) 774-4405	2
Julia IV	1110 South Irby St.	Florence	SC	29501	(843) 665-8542	4
Capri	302 North Limestone	Gaffney	SC	29340	(864) 489-4691	1
Camelot Cinemas	48 East Antrim Dr.	Greenville	SC	29607	(864) 233-7700	7
Coligny Plaza Theatre	1 North Forest Beach Rd.	Hilton Head Island	SC	29928	(843) 686-3575	1
Northridge Cinema 10	435 William Hilton Pkwy.	Hilton Head Island	SC	29926	(843) 342-3801	10
Park Plaza Cinemas	33 Office Park Rd.	Hilton Head Island	SC	29928	(843) 298-0376	5
Monetta Drive In	5822 Columbia Highway N	Monetta	SC	29063	(803) 685-7949	2
Crenshaw Cinema	359 Whitney Rd.	Spartanburg	SC	29303	(864) 583-6194	7
Union Square	719 N Duncan	Union	SC	29379	(864) 429-5506	6
Ivanhoe Cinema IV	320 Ivanhoe Dr.	Walterboro	SC	29488	(843) 549-6545	4
Sylvia Theatre	27 N Congress St.	York	SC	29745	(803) 684-5590	1

SOUTH DAKOTA

Name	Address	City	State	Zip	Phone	Screens
Lorain Theatre	700 Main St.	Armour	SD	57313	(605) 724-2911	1
Strand	624 Main St.	Britton	SD	57430	(605) 448-2810	1
Showcase Cinema 5	City Plaza	Brookings	SD	57006	(605) 692-8660	5
Bryant Cinema	105 E Main St.	Bryant	SD	57221	(605) 628-2336	1
Voices of the Heartland	12637 Merritt Estes Rd.	Deadwood	SD	57732	(605) 578-3857	1
Dells Theatre	511 E 4th St.	Dell Rapids	SD	57022	(605) 428-3456	1
Lyric Theatre & Bowling Lane	805 G Ave.	Eureka	SD	57437	(605) 284-2261	1
Lyric Theatre	809 Court St.	Faulkton	SD	57438	(605) 598-6573	1
Gregory Cinema	605 Main St.	Gregory	SD	57533	(605) 835-8711	2
Hot Springs	247 N River St.	Hot Springs	SD	57747	(605) 745-4169	1
Huron Cinema 3	215 Dakota Ave. South	Huron	SD	57350	(605) 352-6666	3
Palace Theatre	209 Main St.	Lemmon	SD	57638	(605) 374-3742	1
West Twin Theatre	248 W Hwy. 34	Madison	SD	57042	(605) 256-4981	2
Inland Theatre	303 Ave. C	Martin	SD	57551	(605) 685-1000	1
Schmidti-Mac	220 E Main	Mc Laughlin	SD	57642	(605) 823-4220	1
Midway Drive In	1406 S Broadway	Miller	SD	57362	(605) 853-2703	1
Luxury 5 Cinemas	209 N Lawler St.	Mitchell	SD	57301	(605) 996-5444	5
Starlight Drive In	209 N Lawler St.	Mitchell	SD	57301	(605) 996-9022	1
Mac Theatre	311 N Main St.	Mobridge	SD	57601	(605) 845-2021	1
Pheasant Drive-In	1 Pheasant Estate	Mobridge	SD	57601	(605) 845-2021	1
The Gem Theatre	503 W Pine St.	Philip	SD	57567	(605) 859-3265	1
State I II & III Theatre	123 W Capitol Ave.	Pierre	SD	57501	(605) 224-4568	3
Lyric Theatre	521 Main St.	Platte	SD	57369	(605) 337-2319	1
Elks Theatre	512 Sixth St.	Rapid City	SD	57701	(605) 343-7888	1
Stargate 2	919 East North St.	Rapid City	SD	57701	(605) 718-7683	2
Cinema Theatre	718 S Main St.	Redfield	SD	57469	(605) 472-1999	1
Pheasant Drive In	718 S Main St.	Redfield	SD	57469	(605) 472-1453	1
Sioux Falls Film Society	47704 69th St.	Sioux Falls	SD	57108	(605) 743-5467	1
West Mall 7	2101 W 41st St.	Sioux Falls	SD	57105	(605) 332-7662	7
Siskota Drive In	Hwy. 10 & 81	Sisseton	SD	57262	(605) 881-0808	1
Sisston Theatre	522 Veterans Ave.	Sisseton	SD	57262	(605) 698-7776	1
Northern Hills Cinema 6	1830 N Main St.	Spearfish	SD	57783	(605) 642-4212	6
Idle Hour Theatre	105 S Main	Tripp	SD	57376	(605) 935-6862	1
Pix Theatre	325 Main St.	Winner	SD	57580	(605) 842-3045	1
Winner Drive-In Theatre	East Hwy. 18	Winner	SD	57580	(605) 842-2913	1

TENNESSEE

Name	Address	City	State	Zip	Phone	Screens
Midway Drive In	2131 Highway 30 E.	Athens	TN	37303	(423) 263-2632	1
Tri-Cities Cinemas 7	354 Shadowtown Rd.	Blountville	TN	37617	(423) 279-9708	7
Luez Theatre	219 N Main St.	Bolivar	TN	38008	(731) 658-6005	1
Twin City Drive In	2512 B Volunteer Pkwy.	Bristol	TN	37620	(423) 968-7083	1
Pink Cadillac Drive In	2506 Hwy. 100	Centerville	TN	37033	(931) 729-2386	1
Cleveland Cinema 1 & 2	300 Grove Ave. SW	Cleveland	TN	37311	(423) 476-1362	2
The Ritz	119 N Main St.	Clinton	TN	37716	(865) 457-7451	1
Shady Brook 12	1907 Shady Brook St.	Columbia	TN	38401	(931) 388-8043	12
Bartons Dinner & Movie	210 Rotary Centennial Dr.	Cookeville	TN	38506	(931) 528-2888	1
Palace Theatre	72 S Main St.	Crossville	TN	38555	(931) 484-6133	1
Rocky Top 10 Cinema	1251 Interstate Dr.	Crossville	TN	38555	(931) 456-5677	10
Broadway Drive In	Hwy. 70 East & Buddy Rd.	Dickson	TN	37055	(615) 797-2889	1
Roxy Theatre	646 Hwy. 46 S.	Dickson	TN	37055	(615) 441-8781	8
Dunlap Drive In	347 Rankin Ave.	Dunlap	TN	37327	(423) 949-3759	1
Bonnie Kate Theatres	115 South Sycamore St.	Elizabethton	TN	37643	(423) 543-3310	2
Stateline Drive In	309 Johnson Ave.	Elizabethton	TN	37643	(423) 542-5422	1
Capitol 1 & 2	109 North Main St.	Erwin	TN	37650	(423) 743-4481	2
Montana Drive In	10251 Tullahoma Hwy.	Estill Springs	TN	37330	(931) 967-8500	3
Lincoln Theatre	120 College St. East	Fayetteville	TN	37334	(931) 433-1943	2
Palace Theatre	146 N Water St.	Gallatin	TN	37066	(615) 452-5692	1
Midtown Drive In	2734 Roane St. Hwy.	Harriman	TN	37748	(423) 365-2258	1
Plaza 3 Theatre	1603 Main St.	Humboldt	TN	38343	(731) 784-1086	3
Court Theatre	155 Court Sq.	Huntingdon	TN	38344	(731) 986-5309	1
Castle Cinema	209 Fairgrounds Rd.	Jamestown	TN	38556	(931) 879-9923	2
Real To Reel Cinemas	130 West Springbrook Dr.	Johnson City	TN	37604	(423) 282-3557	5
Halls Cinemas 7	3800 Neal Rd.	Knoxville	TN	37918	(865) 922-9096	7
Tennessee Performing Art Center	604 South Gay St.	Knoxville	TN	37902	(865) 684-1200	1
Lafayette Cinema	204 Coleege St.	Lafayette	TN	37083	(615) 699-5899	1
Macon Drive In	3570 Scottsvillle Rd.	Lafayette	TN	37083	(615) 666-4411	1
Crockett Three Cinemas	2128 North Locust St.	Lawrenceburg	TN	38464	(931) 762-6821	3
Roxy 10	200 Legends Dr.	Lebanon	TN	37087	(615) 444-4664	10
Hiway 50 Drive In	1584 Fayetteville Hwy.	Lewisburg	TN	37091	(931) 270-1591	1
Princess Theatre	72 S Main St.	Lexington	TN	38351	(731) 968-7100	1
Cine 6 Theatres	University Plaza Hwy. 22	Martin	TN	38237	(731) 587-9742	6
Parkway Drive In	2909 East Lamar Alexander Pkwy.	Maryville	TN	37804	(865) 300-8704	1
Three Star Cinemas	1360 Sparta Rd.	Mc Minnville	TN	37110	(931) 473-6339	5
Digiplex Cinema Cafe	3727 Hickory Ridge Mall	Memphis	TN	38115	(901) 794-1451	4
Orpheum Theatre	203 S Main St.	Memphis	TN	38173	(901) 525-7800	1
Paradigm Cinema	2350 East Andrew Johnson Hwy.	Morristown	TN	37814	(423) 585-5361	4
Premiere 6 Theatre	810 North West Broad St.	Murfreesboro	TN	37129	(615) 476-4100	6
Belcourt Theatre	2102 Belcourt Ave.	Nashville	TN	37212	(615) 846-3150	2

Name	Address	City	State	Zip	Phone	Screens
Newport Cinema 4	424 Heritage Blvd. Key	Newport	TN	37821	(423) 625-3429	4
The Martin Movie Theatre	433 W Madison	Pulaski	TN	38478	(931) 363-9865	1
Cinema Four	1287 E Main St.	Rogersville	TN	37857	(423) 921-9369	4
Southgate Cinemas	410 Florence Rd.	Savannah	TN	38372	(731) 925-3954	6
Movies on the Parkway	713 Winfield Dunn Pkwy.	Sevierville	TN	37876	(865) 429-4183	6
Capri Theatre	201 E Depot St.	Shelbyville	TN	37160	(931) 684-7306	2
Sparta Drive In	220 Roberts-Matthews Highway	Sparta	TN	38583	(423) 365-2258	1
AlmaMater Theatre	14399 US 41	Tracy City	TN	37387	(931) 592-8222	1
Stardust Drive In	310 Purple Tiger Dr.	Watertown	TN	37184	(615) 237-0077	1
Oldham Theatre	115 First Ave. North East	Winchester	TN	37398	(931) 967-2516	2
Higgins Moonlite Drive In 2	931 W Main St.	Woodbury	TN	37190	(615) 848-3332	2

TEXAS

Name	Address	City	State	Zip	Phone	Screens
Abilene Community Theatre	801 S Mockingnbird Lane	Abilene	TX	79602	(325) 672-2282	1
Westwood Twin Theatre	3440 N First St.	Abilene	TX	79603	(325) 672-1299	2
Paramount Theatre	352 Cypress	Abilene	TX	79601	(325) 676-9620	1
Premier 10 Abilene	4310 Buffalo Gap Rd.	Abilene	TX	79606	(325) 695-2135	10
Town and Country Drive In	2902 Vogel St.	Abilene	TX	79603	(325) 677-9899	1
Plaza Four	E Hwy. 44	Alice	TX	78332	(361) 664-6687	4
Rangra Theatre	109 E Holland Ave.	Alpine	TX	79830	(432) 837-5111	2
Tascosa Drive In	1999 Dumas Dr.	Amarillo	TX	79110	(806) 359-9485	1
Westgate Mall Cinema 6	7701 I-40 W #638	Amarillo	TX	79121	(806) 352-8910	6
Movie Tavern @ Green Oaks	5727 I-20 West	Arlington	TX	76016	(817) 483-5113	8
Alamo Draft House Village	2700 W Anderson Ln.	Austin	TX	78757	(512) 459-7090	4
Alamo Drafthouse Cinema S. Lamar	1120 S Lamar	Austin	TX	78704	(512) 707-8262	6
Alamo Drafthouse Lake Creek	13729 Research Blvd.	Austin	TX	78750	(512) 219-5408	7
Alamo Drafthouse Ritz	320 E 6th St.	Austin	TX	78701	(512) 474-1320	3
Galaxy Highland 10	6700 Middle Fiskville Rd.	Austin	TX	78752	(512) 467-6165	10
Millenium Youth Entertainment	1156 Hargrave St.	Austin	TX	78702	(512) 472-6932	1
Paramount and State Theatre	713 and 719 Congress Ave.	Austin	TX	78701	(512) 692-0538	2
Chestnut Square Entertainment	1600 Chestnut St.	Bastrop	TX	78602	(512) 581-3500	4
Bay Cinema 4	3408 Avenue F	Bay City	TX	77414	(979) 244-5303	4
Premiere 11	1518 San Jacinto Mall	Baytown	TX	77521	(281) 839-1704	11
Jefferson Theatre	345 Fannin St.	Beaumont	TX	77701	(409) 835-5483	1
Rio 6 Cinema	806 E Houston St.	Beeville	TX	78102	(361) 358-3936	6
Ritz Theatre	1801 E F M St.	Big Spring	TX	79720	(432) 263-7480	3
Morley Cinemas	701 N Main St.	Borger	TX	79007	(806) 435-0845	3
Westwood 3	2100 Hwy. 290 West 6	Brenham	TX	77833	(979) 836-8275	3
Rialto Theatre	408 W Main	Brownfield	TX	79316	(806) 637-7656	1
Palace Theatre	210 Main St.	Canadian	TX	79014	(806) 323-5133	1
Varsity Theatre	2302 Fourth Ave.	Canyon	TX	79015	(806) 655-9529	1
Carthage Twin Theatre	1120 W Panola St.	Carthage	TX	75633	(903) 693-7842	2
Rio Theatre	106 Nacogdoches St.	Center	TX	75935	(936) 598-3864	1
Lone Star 4	1900 Ave. G NW	Childress	TX	79201	(940) 937-6786	4
Sandell Drive In	12 Medical Dr.	Clarendon	TX	79226	(806) 874-2704	1
Texan Theatre	102 E Houston	Cleveland	TX	77327	(281) 592-1533	1
Cliftex Theatres	306 W 5th St.	Clifton	TX	76634	(254) 675-1229	1
Grand 14	4029 I-45 North	Conroe	TX	77304	(936) 856-9949	14
Pine Hollow Cinema 6	2000 I-45 N.	Conroe	TX	77301	(936) 539-6088	6
Cove Theatre	111 W Avenue D	Copperas Cove	TX	76522	(254) 547-2210	1
Five Star Cinema	4147 B Five Points Rd.	Corpus Christi	TX	78410	(210) 381-2610	5
Ritz Theatre	620 E Houston St.	Crockett	TX	75835	(936) 544-7099	1
Guild Theatre	309 W Zavala	Crystal City	TX	78839	(830) 374-5568	1
Morris Theatre	204 N Lamar	Daingerfield	TX	75638	(903) 645-2210	2
Mission Theatre	409 Denrock St.	Dalhart	TX	79022	(806) 244-8702	2
Angelika Film Center Cafe	5321 Mockingbird Ln. Ste. 201	Dallas	TX	75206	(214) 841-4712	8
Lakewood Theatre	1825 Abrams Pkwy.	Dallas	TX	75214	(214) 821-7469	1
Plaza Cinema 3	1510 Hwy. 51 South	Decatur	TX	76234	(940) 627-1162	3
Paul Poag Theatre	746 S Main St.	Del Rio	TX	78840	(830) 774-3277	1
Denton Movie Tavern	916 West University Dr.	Denton	TX	76201	(940) 387-9010	4
Evelyn Twin	705 Bliss St.	Dumas	TX	79029	(806) 935-3621	2
Majestic Theatre	108 N Lamar St.	Eastland	TX	76448	(254) 629-2102	1
Showplace 3 Cinema	820 W Loop Rd.	El Campo	TX	77437	(979) 543-8152	3
Galaxy Drive In	5301 N Interstate 45	Ennis	TX	75119	(972) 875-5505	4
Arcadia Theatre	1417 3rd St.	Floresville	TX	78114	(830) 393-3001	1
Cinema Latino De Fort Worth	4200 S Freeway Ste. 1095	Fort Worth	TX	76115	(817) 926-4594	8
Ridgmar Movie Tavern	6801 Ridgmar Meadow Rd.	Fort Worth	TX	76116	(817) 989-7470	6
Stagecoach Theatre	2254 S US Hwy. 87	Fredericksburg	TX	78624	(830) 456-2835	3
Star Village 8	3980 Boat Club Rd.	Ft Worth	TX	76135	(817) 238-7764	8
Premier Cinemas Eleven	8902 Seawall Blvd.	Galveston	TX	77554	(409) 741-1600	11
Ganado Theatre	120 S Third St.	Ganado	TX	77962	(361) 771-2164	1
Walnut Theatres	3310 W Walnut St.	Garland	TX	75042	(972) 494-0020	2
Cinema-N-Video	2912 S Hwy. 36	Gatesville	TX	76528	(254) 931-0832	1
Last Drive In	2912 S Hwy. 36	Gatesville	TX	76528	(254) 947-0093	2
Georgetown Palace Theatre	810 Austin Ave.	Georgetown	TX	78626	(512) 864-5092	1
Lynn Theatre	510 Saint Paul St.	Gonzales	TX	78629	(361) 449-2957	2
Graham Drive In	1519 E 4th St.	Graham	TX	76450	(940) 549-8960	1
National Theatre	522 Oak St.	Graham	TX	76450	(940) 549-2077	3
Brazos Drive In	1800 W Pearl	Granbury	TX	76048	(817) 559-4473	1
Driftwood Theatre 6	1201 Waters Edge Rd.	Granbury	TX	76048	(817) 573-7318	6
Majestic 12 Theatres	1401 E Joe Ramsey Blvd.	Greenville	TX	75403	(903) 454-7777	12
Cole Theatre	207 East Second St.	Hallettsville	TX	77964	(361) 798-4569	1
Tower Drive In	Highway 6	Haskell	TX	79521	(940) 864-5156	1
Hempstead Theatre	740 12th St.	Hempstead	TX	77445	(979) 826-6406	1
Plaza Cinema 3	1401 Lone Star St.	Henderson	TX	75652	(903) 657-0787	3
Premiere Moovies 6	400 N 25 Mile Rd.	Hereford	TX	79045	(806) 364-0101	6
Regent Highland Park Village	32 Highland Park Village	Highland Park	TX	75205	(214) 526-9668	4
Alamo Drafthouse Cinema	1000 W Oaks Mall #429	Houston	TX	77082	(281) 920-9211	7
Fun Plex	13700 Beechnut St.	Houston	TX	77083	(281) 530-7777	8
NorthOaks Cinema 6	4623 Fm. 1960 W	Houston	TX	77069	(832) 436-0151	6
Sharpstown Center 8 Cinema	7500 BellAir Blvd. Ste. 535	Houston	TX	77036	(713) 995-4333	8
Wind Chimes	13155 Westheimer Rd. Ste. 80	Houston	TX	77077	(281) 920-3546	8
Cinestar of Huntsville	3 Financial Plaza	Huntsville	TX	77340	(936) 291-9044	10
Jackson Cinema 3	1710 S Jackson St.	Jacksonville	TX	75766	(903) 586-2730	3
Jasper Twin Cinema	611 N Fletcher St.	Jasper	TX	75951	(409) 384-8086	2

Name	Address	City	State	Zip	Phone	Screens
Texan Theatre	648 Main St.	Junction	TX	76849	(325) 446-3407	1
Four Star Cinema	1607 N Hwy. 259	Kilgore	TX	75662	(903) 983-1249	4
Killeen Drive In	804 North 10th St.	Killeen	TX	76543	(254) 466-3212	2
Rio 7 Cinema	1601 South Hwy. 77	Kingsville	TX	78363	(361) 516-1355	7
Movieland Theatre	1415 N Dallas Ave.	Lamesa	TX	79331	(806) 201-0144	1
Sky Vue Drive In Theatre	S Big Spring Hwy.	Lamesa	TX	79331	(806) 872-7004	1
Fain Theatre	408 N Jackson	Livingston	TX	77351	(936) 327-4711	1
LanTexTheatre	113 W Main St.	Llano	TX	78643	(325) 247-4158	1
Hometown Cinemas Theatre	120 MLK Industril Blvd. W	Lockhart	TX	78644	(512) 376-5272	2
Showplace 6	6707 S University	Lubbock	TX	79413	(806) 745-3637	6
Stars and Stripes Drive In	5101 Hwy. 84	Lubbock	TX	79416	(972) 233-6957	2
Driftwood Theatre 8	2600 Hwy. 281 N	Marble Falls	TX	78654	(830) 798-9235	8
Marshall Cinema 5	1901 E Travis St.	Marshall	TX	75670	(903) 935-3351	5
Odeon	122 Moody Rd.	Mason	TX	76856	(325) 347-9010	1
Cine El Rey	311 S 17th St.	Mcallen	TX	78502	(956) 971-9829	1
Wes-Mer Drive In	2090 US 83 Business	Mercedes	TX	78570	(956) 514-9292	1
Starplex Mesquite 10	227 US Hwy. 80 East	Mesquite	TX	75150	(972) 329-7553	10
Big Sky Drive In	5906 W Hwy. 80	Midland	TX	79706	(432) 617-4041	2
Lake Country Playhouse	114 N Johnson St.	Mineola	TX	75773	(903) 569-2300	1
Brazos Cin III	2801 Hwy. 180 E #18	Mineral Wells	TX	76067	(940) 325-1931	3
Border Theatre	905 Conway Ave.	Mission	TX	78572	(956) 585-9142	1
Southside Cinema 5	1706 S Jefferson Ave.	Mt Pleasant	TX	75455	(903) 572-6322	5
Miller's Theatre	304 E Washington Ave.	Navasota	TX	77868	(936) 825-3578	1
Marketplace Cinema 12	651 N Business IH 35	New Braunfels	TX	78130	(830) 625-4447	12
Cinema Twin	3330 Bowling Ln.	Orange	TX	77630	(409) 988-0303	2
Dogwood Six	545 E Palestine Ave.	Palestine	TX	75801	(903) 729-7291	6
Cinema Latino De Pasadena	2233 East Southmore Ave.	Pasadena	TX	77502	(713) 477-2888	6
Premiere Pearland Westside Cinema	5050 W Broadway	Pearland	TX	77581	(281) 997-1611	6
Ellis Theatre and Video	217 S Main St.	Perryton	TX	79070	(806) 435-4133	2
Studio Movie Grill	4721 W Park Blvd.	Plano	TX	75093	(214) 361-2966	8
Plestex 3 Theatre	111 E Johnson St.	Pleasanton	TX	78064	(830) 281-3017	3
Twin Dolphin Cinemas	151 Hwy. 35 Bypass	Port Lavaca	TX	77979	(361) 552-8121	2
Cinema 4	2702 Hwy. 35 North	Rockport	TX	78382	(361) 729-5948	4
Alamo Drafthouse Westlake	1255 SW Loop 410	San Antonio	TX	78227	(210) 677-8500	9
IMAX @ River Center	849 East Commerce 483	San Antonio	TX	78205	(210) 247-0230	1
Santikos Rialto Cinema Bistro	2938 NE Loop 410	San Antonio	TX	78218	(210) 656-8261	14
Santikos Rialto Piccolo	2803 Austin Hwy.	San Antonio	TX	78218	(210) 967-7648	4
Santikos Crossroads	4522 Fredericksberg Rd.	San Antonio	TX	78201	(210) 734-4552	6
Santikos Embassy	13707 Embassy Row	San Antonio	TX	78216	(210) 496-4957	14
Santikos Mayan 14	1918 SW Military Dr.	San Antonio	TX	78221	(210) 923-5531	14
Santikos Mission Drive In	3100 Roosevelt Ave.	San Antonio	TX	78214	(210) 532-3259	4
Santikos Northwest	7600 W IH 10 West	San Antonio	TX	78230	(210) 349-6514	14
Santikos Silverado 16	11505 W Loop 1604 N	San Antonio	TX	78250	(210) 695-5279	16
Showplace III	321 N LBJ Dr.	San Marcos	TX	78666	(512) 353-3669	3
Starplex 12	1250 Wonder World Dr.	San Marcos	TX	78666	(512) 805-8005	12
Cozy Theatre	607 Lyons Ave.	Schulenburg	TX	78956	(979) 743-3716	1
King Ranger Theatres	1373 E Walnut	Seguin	TX	78155	(830) 379-8425	5
Main Place Cinema	201 Main Place Blvd.	Seven Points	TX	75143	(903) 432-9019	5
Texas Theatre	217 N Main St.	Shamrock	TX	79079	(806) 256-1212	1
Cross Roads Drive In	216 South Ave. E	Shiner	TX	77984	(361) 594-4510	1
Cinema Snyder	1907 Snyder Shopping Ctr.	Snyder	TX	79549	(325) 574-1559	2
Island Cinema North	4700 Padre Blvd.	S. Padre Island	TX	78597	(956) 761-7839	4
Lyric Cinema	113 Main St.	Spearman	TX	79081	(806) 659-2812	2
Grand theatre	118 E Hamilton	Stamford	TX	79553	(325) 773-3393	1
Texas Theatre	114 East Broadway St.	Sweetwater	TX	79556	(325) 235-8883	2
Howard Theatre	308 N Main St.	Taylor	TX	76574	(512) 352-2995	3
Premiere Temple 16	3111 S 31St St.	Temple	TX	76502	(254) 791-3901	16
Rialto Theatre	406 W Thornton	Three Rivers	TX	78071	(361) 786-2188	2
Premiere Tomball Cinema 6	28497 Tomball Pkwy.	Tomball	TX	77375	(281) 351-6106	6
Midway Drive In	5th & Bell	Turkey	TX	79261	(806) 432-1166	1
Times Square Cinema	5201 S Broadway	Tyler	TX	75703	(903) 581-1818	5
Forum Theatres 6	Highway 90 East	Uvalde	TX	78801	(830) 278-6610	6
Vernon Plaza Theatre	1717 Cumberland	Vernon	TX	76384	(940) 337-3476	2
Buffalo Creek 6	507 North US Hwy. 77	Waxahachie	TX	75165	(972) 923-3361	6
Weatherford Cinema 10	1000 Cinema Dr.	Weatherford	TX	76087	(817) 596-8470	10
Premiere Nasa Dollar 8	20833 Gulf Frwy.	Webster	TX	77598	(281) 332-4679	8
Star Cinema and Grill	1020 Nasa Rd. 1 Ste. 152	Webster	TX	77598	(713) 240-1193	6
Cactus Drive In	1416 S. Bridge	Weslaco	TX	78596	(959) 969-2999	1
Odeum Theatre	118 Grand St.	Whitewright	TX	75491	(903) 821-4791	1
Majestic Theatre	136 W N Commerce	Wills Point	TX	75169	(214) 543-4076	1
Corral Theatre	100 Flite Acre Ranch Rd.	Wimberley	TX	78676	(512) 847-5994	1

UTAH

Name	Address	City	State	Zip	Phone	Screens
Towne Cinemas	120 W Main St.	American Fork	UT	84003	(801) 756-9027	2
Wayne Theatre	11 E Main	Bicknell	UT	84715	(435) 425-3554	1
San Juan Theatre	20 S Main St.	Blanding	UT	84511	(435) 678-2123	1
Capitol Theatre	53 S Main St.	Brigham City	UT	84302	(435) 723-3113	2
Clearfield Job Corps Center	20 W 1700 S	Clearfield	UT	84016	(801) 774-4276	1
Plaza Twin Theatre	420 E Topaz Blvd.	Delta	UT	84624	(435) 864-4551	2
Avalon Theatre	35 N Main St.	Fillmore	UT	84631	(435) 743-6918	1
Star Theatre	163 N Main	Huntington	UT	84528	(435) 687-9026	1
Kamas Theatre	30 N Main	Kamas	UT	84036	(435) 640-5678	1
Kanab Theatre	29 W Center St.	Kanab	UT	84741	(435) 644-2334	1
Kaysville Theatre	21 N Main	Kaysville	UT	84037	(801) 546-3400	3
Megaplex 8 @ Thanksgiving Point	3003 North Thanksgiving Way	Lehi	UT	84043	(801) 768-2700	8
Lewiston Theatre	29 S Main St.	Lewiston	UT	84320	(435) 258-2141	1
Cinefour	2297 North Main St.	Logan	UT	84341	(435) 752-8377	4
Utah Theatre	18 W Center St.	Logan	UT	84321	(435) 752-3072	1
Five Star Cinemas	8325 W 3500 S	Magna	UT	84044	(801) 250-6265	5
Slick Rock 3	580 Kane Creek Blvd.	Moab	UT	84532	(435) 259-5925	3
Walker Cinemas - North Ogden	1610 N Waashington Blvd.	North Ogden	UT	84414	(801) 737-9183	8
Cine Pointe Theatre	151 East 12 St.	Ogden	UT	84404	(801) 392-7474	5
Scera Center for the Arts	745 S State St.	Orem	UT	84058	(801) 225-2569	2
University Mall Cinemas	959 S 700 E	Orem	UT	84097	(801) 226-1985	4
Park City Film Series	1255 Park Ave.	Park City	UT	84060	(435) 615-8291	1

Name	Address	City	State	Zip	Phone	Screens
Redstone 8 Cinemas	6030 N Market	Park City	UT	84098	(435) 575-0220	8
Stadium Cinema	633 S 950 West	Payson	UT	84651	(801) 465-8502	6
Walker Cinemas - Perry	1776 S Highway 89	Perry	UT	84302	(801) 399-1099	5
Crown Theatre	30 W Main St.	Price	UT	84501	(435) 637-1229	1
King Coal theatres	1171 E Main	Price	UT	84501	(435) 637-1229	3
Price Theatre	30 E Main St.	Price	UT	84501	(435) 637-1229	1
Westates Theatres Providence 8	535 W 100 North	Providence	UT	84332	(435) 753-1900	8
Reel Huish	131 North Main St.	Richfield	UT	84701	(435) 896-9119	1
Avalon Theatre	3605 S State St.	Salt Lake City	UT	84117	(801) 278-6368	1
Brewvies Cinema Pub	677 South 200 West	Salt Lake City	UT	84101	(801) 322-3891	2
Broadway Centre Cinemas	111 E Broadway Ste. 99	Salt Lake City	UT	84111	(801) 364-1088	6
Redwood Drive In	3688 S Redwood Rd.	Salt Lake City	UT	84119	(801) 973-7088	6
Showcase Cinema 6	5400 S Redwood Rd.	Salt Lake City	UT	84118	(801) 957-9034	6
Megaplex 12 at the Gateway	165 S Rio Grande St.	Salt Lake City	UT	84101	(801) 325-7522	12
Tower Theatre	876 E 900 S	Salt Lake City	UT	84105	(801) 364-1088	1
Tu Cine Movie	2250 S Redwood Rd. Ste. 4	Salt Lake City	UT	84119	(801) 968-7794	5
Megaplex 17 at Jordan Commons	9335 S State St.	Sandy	UT	84070	(801) 304-4584	17
Spanish 8	790 Expressway Ln.	Spanish Fork	UT	84660	(801) 798-2990	8
Zion Canyon Theatre	145 Zion Park Blvd.	Springdale	UT	84767	(435) 772-2400	1
Motor Vu Drive In	4055 Utah 36	Tooele	UT	84074	(435) 882-9979	1
Ritz Theatres	111 N Main St.	Tooele	UT	84074	(435) 882-9902	2
Sunset Drive In	1620 W Hwy. 40	Vernal	UT	84078	(435) 789-2099	1
Cinemas 5 (Twin & Tri)	1400 W Hwy. 40	Vernal	UT	84078	(435) 789-6999	5
Vernal Theatre	40 E Main St.	Vernal	UT	84078	(435) 789-1167	1
Wendover Cinema	375 Area Blvd.	Wendover	UT	84083	(435) 665-2628	1

VERMONT

Name	Address	City	State	Zip	Phone	Screens
Cinema 7	319 Northside Dr.	Bennington	VT	05201	(802) 442-5572	7
Latchis Cinema	48 Main St.	Brattleboro	VT	05301	(802) 254-6300	3
Ethan Allen 4	1170 N Ave.	Burlington	VT	05401	(802) 863-4200	4
Merrill's Roxy Cinemas	222 College St.	Burlington	VT	05401	(802) 864-4742	6
Sunset Drive In	155 Porter's Point Rd.	Colchester	VT	05446	(802) 863-7948	4
Essex Outlets Cinema	21 Essex Way Bldg. 300	Essex Junction	VT	05452	(802) 878-7231	8
Village Picture Show	263 Depot St.	Manchester Ctr.	VT	05255	(802) 362-2982	2
Marquis Theatre Main	73 Main St.	Middlebury	VT	05753	(802) 388-4841	2
Savoy Theatre	26 Main St.	Montpelier	VT	05602	(802) 229-0598	1
Waterfront Cinemas	137 Waterfront Plaza	Newport	VT	05855	(802) 334-6582	3
Playhouse Movie Theatre	11 S Main St.	Randolph	VT	05060	(802) 728-4012	1
Catamount Film & Arts Ctr.	139 Eastern Ave.	Saint Johnsbury	VT	05819	(802) 748-2600	1
The Palace 9	10 Fayette Rd.	South Burlington	VT	05403	(802) 660-9300	9
Springfield Theatre	26 Main St.	Springfield	VT	05156	(802) 885-3131	2
Star 3 Cinema	18 Eastern Ave.	St Johnsbury	VT	05819	(802) 748-9511	3
Stowe Cinema Threeplex	Rte. 108 & Mountain Rd.	Stowe	VT	05672	(802) 253-8360	3
Mountain Park Cinema	4 Mountain Park Plaza	West Dover	VT	05356	(802) 464-6447	3
Majestic 10	190 Boxwood St.	Williston	VT	05495	(802) 878-5090	10
Woodstock Town Hall Theatre	31 The Green	Woodstock	VT	05091	(802) 457-3981	1

VIRGINIA

Name	Address	City	State	Zip	Phone	Screens
Moonlite Drive In	17555 Lee Hwy.	Abingdon	VA	24210	(276) 628-7881	1
Old Town Theatre	815 1/2 King St.	Alexandria	VA	22314	(703) 683-8486	1
Arlington Cinema-N-Draft	2903 Columbia Pike	Arlington	VA	22204	(703) 486-0345	1
Idlehour	36008 Belle Haven Rd.	Belle Haven	VA	23306	(757) 442-6056	1
Pickett Theatre	2480 W Parade	Blackstone	VA	23824	(434) 292-2613	1
Vinegar Hill Theatre	220 West Market St.	Charlottesville	VA	22902	(434) 977-8458	1
Cinema Cafe	1401 Greenbriar Pkwy. Ste.1112	Chesapeake	VA	23320	(757) 313-8401	4
Island Roxy Theatre	4074 Main St.	Chincoteague Isd	VA	23336	(757) 336-6301	1
Starlite Drive-In Theatre	305 Starlight Dr.	Christiansburg	VA	24073	(540) 382-2202	1
Ballou Park 4	150 Tunstall Rd.	Danville	VA	24541	(434) 792-7377	4
Cinema Arts Theatres	9650 Main St.	Fairfax	VA	22031	(703) 978-6853	6
University Mall Theatre	10659 Braddock Rd.	Fairfax	VA	22032	(703) 273-0876	3
Big Cinemas Loehmanns Cinema	7291 Arlington Blvd.	Falls Church	VA	22042	(703) 573-8593	2
Sunchase Cinema 8	215 Sunchase Blvd.	Farmville	VA	23901	(434) 392-4865	8
Fork Union Drive In	Rte. 15 and 612	Fork Union	VA	23055	(434) 842-3624	1
Royal Cinemas	117 E Main St.	Front Royal	VA	22630	(540) 635-6080	3
Twin County Cinemas III	957 E Stuart Dr.	Galax	VA	24333	(276) 236-7469	3
Hillside Cinema	7321 John Clayton	Gloucester	VA	23061	(804) 693-7766	2
Riverdale Cinema Cafe Premier	1044 Von Shilling Dr.	Hampton	VA	23666	(757) 825-5823	12
Court Square Theatre	61 Graham St.	Harrisonburg	VA	22801	(540) 478-6469	1
York River Crossing	2226 York Crossing Dr.	Hayes	VA	23072	(804) 642-5873	8
Phoenix Theatres Worldgate 9	13025 Worldgate Dr.	Herndon	VA	20170	(703) 318-9315	9
Crossings Twin Cinema	5246 Oaklawn Blvd.	Hopewell	VA	23860	(804) 458-2131	2
Tally Ho Theatre	19 West Market St.	Leesburg	VA	20176	(703) 509-4963	2
Hulls Drive In	2367 N Lee Hwy.	Lexington	VA	24450	(540) 463-2621	1
Page Theatre	33 E Main St.	Luray	VA	22835	(540) 743-9262	5
Manassas Cinemas	8890 Mathis Ave.	Manassas	VA	20110	(703) 368-4132	4
Park Place Drive In	301 Park Blvd.	Marion	VA	24354	(276) 781-2222	1
Hollywood Cinema	6 Hollywood Blvd.	Martinsville	VA	24115	(276) 656-3900	5
Movie Town 5	67 Veterans Rd.	Martinsville	VA	24112	(276) 632-7400	5
Rives Cinema	6 Hollywood Blvd.	Martinsville	VA	24115	(276) 638-2423	2
Phoenix Theatres Main Gate Movies	Bldg. CD-12	Norfolk	VA	23511	(757) 440-5304	10
Naro Expanded Cinema	1507 Colley Ave.	Norfolk	VA	23517	(757) 625-6276	1
Climbing Tree Moviehouse	615 E Riverside Dr.	North Tazewell	VA	24630	(276) 979-1600	3
Roseland Theatre	48 Market St.	Onancock	VA	23417	(757) 787-2209	1
New Millennium Releasing	One New Millennium Dr.	Petersburg	VA	23805	(434) 957-4200	1
Commodore Theatre	421 High St.	Portsmouth	VA	23704	(757) 393-4383	1
Radford Theatre	1065 E Main St.	Radford	VA	24141	(540) 639-0772	1
Byrd Theatre	2916 W Cary St.	Richmond	VA	23221	(804) 937-0388	1
Cinema Cafe	5002 Airport Rd.	Roanoke	VA	24012	(540) 527-1000	2
Grandin Theatre	1310 Grandin Rd SW	Roanoke	VA	24015	(540) 345-6377	5
Eagle Cinema	460 Tanyard Rd.	Rocky Mount	VA	24151	(540) 814-1729	1
Highland Drive In	St. Rte. 11	Rural Retreat	VA	24368	(276) 686-5348	1
Cinema 1 & 2	Hwy 58 E 2030 Bill Tuck Hwy.	South Boston	VA	24592	(434) 572-8792	2

Name	Address	City	State	Zip	Phone	Screens
South Hill Cinemas	833 E Atlantic Ave.	South Hill	VA	23970	(434) 447-8511	2
Cinema Cafe Pembroke Meadow	758 Independence Blvd.	Virginia Beach	VA	23455	(757) 222-4580	8
Cinema Cafe Kemps River 7	1220 Fordham Dr.	Virginia Beach	VA	23464	(757) 747-1396	7
Kimball Theatre	424 W Duke of Gloucester St.	Williamsburg	VA	23185	(757) 565-8670	1
Delco Cinema 2	170-9 Delco Plz.	Winchester	VA	22602	(540) 662-9445	2
Community Theatre	136 N Main St.	Woodstock	VA	22664	(540) 459-2221	3
Family Drive In	136 N Main St.	Woodstock	VA	22664	(540) 459-2221	2

WASHINGTON

Name	Address	City	State	Zip	Phone	Screens
Anacortes Cinema	415 O Ave.	Anacortes	WA	98221	(360) 293-7000	3
Olympic Theatre	107 N Olympic Ave.	Arlington	WA	98223	(360) 435-1856	1
Valley Drive In	401-49th St. NE	Auburn	WA	98002	(253) 852-8239	6
Bainbridge Cinemas	403 Madison Ave.	Bainbridge Island	WA	98110	(206) 855-8173	5
Battleground Cinema	1700 SW 9th Ave.	Battleground	WA	98604	(360) 666-7205	8
Bellevue Galleria Stadium 11	550 106th Ave. NE Ste. 301	Bellevue	WA	98004	(425) 450-1519	11
Lincoln Square Cinemas	700 Bellevue Way NE Ste. 310	Bellevue	WA	98004	(425) 450-9100	16
Pickford Film Center	1416 Cornwall Ave.	Bellingham	WA	98225	(360) 201-3243	1
Admiral Theatre	515 Pacific Ave.	Bellingham	WA	98337	(360) 373-6743	1
Roxy Theatre	270 Fourth St.	Bellingham	WA	98225	(360) 479-0655	1
Olympic Club Hotel & Theatre	116 N Tower Ave.	Centralia	WA	98531	(360) 736-5164	1
Chehalis	558 N Market Blvd.	Chehalis	WA	98532	(360) 269-0380	1
Yardbirds Cinema 3	2100 N National Ave.	Chehalis	WA	98532	(360) 748-1201	3
Alpine Theatre	112 N Main St.	Colville	WA	99114	(509) 684-5595	1
Auto-Vue Drive In	444 Auto View Rd.	Colville	WA	99114	(509) 684-5595	1
Sunset Theatre	102 N Columbia	Connell	WA	99326	(509) 234-7811	1
Village Cinema	515 River Dr.	Coulee Dam	WA	99116	(509) 633-1653	1
Liberty Theatre	344 E Main	Dayton	WA	99328	(509) 382-1380	1
Columbia Cinema Theatre	470 Grant Rd.	East Wenatchee	WA	98802	(509) 884-2454	5
Seaview Theatre	234 A St.	Eastsound	WA	98245	(360) 376-5724	1
Roxy Theatre	109 Washington Ave. North	Eatonville	WA	98328	(360) 832-8390	1
Grand Meridian Cinema	504 Mountain View Ave.	Ellensburg	WA	98926	(425) 743-6269	9
Liberty Theatre	111 E 5th Ave.	Ellensburg	WA	98926	(509) 962-6251	3
Chalet Theatre	1721 Wells St.	Enumclaw	WA	98022	(360) 825-3881	1
Enumclaw Cinema	258 Roosevelt Ave.	Enumclaw	WA	98022	(360) 825-3881	1
Lee Theatre	347 Basin St. NW	Ephrata	WA	98823	(509) 754-4566	3
Everett Theatre	2911 Colby	Everett	WA	98201	(425) 258-6766	1
The Palace	209 Spring St.	Friday Harbor	WA	98250	(360) 370-5666	2
Kirkland Parkplace Cinema	404 Parkplace Center	Kirkland	WA	98033	(425) 827-9131	6
Totem Lake Cinema	12232 NE Totem Lake Way	Kirkland	WA	98034	(206) 280-8880	3
Clyde Theatre	217 First St.	Langley	WA	98260	(360) 221-5525	1
Junction Cinema	565 Hwy. 2	Leavenworth	WA	98826	(509) 548-6684	1
Neptune Theatre	809 Ocean Beach Blvd. S.	Long Beach	WA	98631	(360) 642-8856	2
Clark Fork Theatre	209 E 5th Ave.	Metaline Falls	WA	99153	(509) 446-2584	1
Galaxy 12	One Galaxy Way	Monroe	WA	98272	(360) 863-8665	12
Fairchild Cinema	233 N Block St.	Moses Lake	WA	98837	(509) 764-8214	8
North Bend Theatre	125 Bendigo Blvd.	North Bend	WA	98045	(425) 888-7101	1
Blue Fox Drive In	1403 N Monroe Landing Rd.	Oak Harbor	WA	98277	(360) 675-5667	1
Plaza Cinema 3	1321 SW Barlow St.	Oak Harbor	WA	98277	(360) 279-2226	3
Ocean Shores Cinema 3	631 Point Brown Ave. NW	Ocean Shores	WA	98569	(360) 289-2650	3
Capitol Theatre	416 Washington St. SE #208	Olympia	WA	98501	(360) 790-6337	1
Mirage Omak 3	101 S Main	Omak	WA	98840	(509) 826-1615	3
Omak	101 S Main St.	Omak	WA	98840	(509) 826-5521	1
Reichert's Showhouse	130 North Broadway	Othello	WA	99344	(509) 488-9796	2
Deer Park Cinema	96 Deer Park Dr.	Port Angeles	WA	98362	(360) 452-7186	5
Lincoln Theatre	132 E First St.	Port Angeles	WA	98362	(360) 452-7186	3
Rodeo Triple Drive In	7369 State Hwy. 3 SW	Port Orchard	WA	98367	(360) 674-2026	3
Rose Theatre	235 Taylor St.	Port Townsend	WA	98368	(360) 385-1039	2
Uptown	826 P St.	Port Townsend	WA	98368	(360) 385-0765	1
Wheel In Drive In	210 Theatre Rd.	Port Townsend	WA	98368	(360) 385-0859	1
Audian Theatre	315 E Main St.	Pullman	WA	99163	(509) 334-6683	1
Cordova Theatre	135 N Grand Ave.	Pullman	WA	99163	(509) 334-1002	1
Village Centre Cinemas	1085 SE Bishop Blvd.	Pullman	WA	99163	(509) 334-4662	8
Raymond Theatre	323 Third St.	Raymond	WA	98577	(360) 942-4127	1
Big Picture Redmond	7411 166th Ave. NE, 2nd Level	Redmond	WA	98052	(425) 556-0566	1
New Ritz Theatre	107 E Main St.	Ritzville	WA	99169	(509) 659-1247	1
Roslyn Theatre	101 Dakota St.	Roslyn	WA	98941	(509) 649-3155	1
Admiral Twin	2343 California Ave. SW	Seattle	WA	98116	(206) 938-0360	2
Big Picture El Gaucho	2505 First Ave.	Seattle	WA	98121	(206) 256-0566	1
Columbia City Cinema	4816 Rainier Ave. S	Seattle	WA	98118	(206) 721-3156	1
Des Moines Cinema	22333 Marine View Dr.	Seattle	WA	98198	(206) 878-7987	1
Grand Illusion	1403 NE 50th St.	Seattle	WA	98105	(206) 523-3935	1
Landmark Egyptian	805 Pine St.	Seattle	WA	98122	(206) 781-5755	1
Little Theatre	608 19th Ave. E	Seattle	WA	98112	(206) 329-2629	1
Majestic Bay Theatres	2044 NW Market St.	Seattle	WA	98107	(206) 781-2229	3
Shelton Cinema	517 W Franklin	Shelton	WA	98584	(360) 432-0865	2
Garland Cinema	901 W Garland Ave.	Spokane	WA	99205	(509) 327-2509	1
Metropolitan Theatre	901 West Sprague Ave.	Spokane	WA	99201	(509) 227-7638	1
Stanwood Camano Village Cinema	6996 265th NW	Stanwood	WA	98292	(360) 629-8305	5
Grand Cinemas Yakima Valley	3400 Picard Place	Sunnyside	WA	98944	(509) 837-7182	12
BlueMouse Theatre	2611 N Proctor St.	Tacoma	WA	98407	(253) 752-9500	1
Grand Cinema 3	606 S Fawcett Ave.	Tacoma	WA	98402	(253) 593-4474	3
Galxy Tacoma 6	3102 S 23rd St.	Tacoma	WA	98405	(818) 986-9000	6
Yakama Nation Heritage Theatre	Hwy. 97	Toppenish	WA	98948	(509) 865-2800	1
Alamo Majestic 10	1919 S 14th St.	Union Gap	WA	98903	(509) 248-4155	10
Cinetopia 8	11700 SE 7th St.	Vancouver	WA	98683	(360) 213-2800	8
Kiggins Theatre	1011 Main St.	Vancouver	WA	98660	(360) 608-0632	1
Vashon Theatre	17723 Vashon Hwy. SW	Vashon Island	WA	98070	(206) 463-3232	1
Grand Cinema	1325 W Poplar	Walla Walla	WA	99362	(509) 522-3232	12
Liberty Theatre	111 S Mission St.	Wenatchee	WA	98801	(509) 662-4568	8
Vue Dale Drive In	1546 S Wenatchee Ave.	Wenatchee	WA	98801	(509) 662-4568	2
Uptown Plaza Theatres	202 E Chestnut	Yakima	WA	98901	(509) 575-9501	4
Yakima Cinema	1305 N 16th Ave.	Yakima	WA	98902	(509) 248-0243	10
Yelm Cinemas at PrairiePark	201 Prairie Park St. NE	Yelm	WA	98597	(360) 400-3457	8

Name	Address	City	State	Zip	Phone	Screens

WEST VIRGINIA

Name	Address	City	State	Zip	Phone	Screens
Star Movie Theatre	137 N Washington St.	Berkeley Springs	WV	25411	(304) 258-1404	1
Upshur Cinema 6	Bushy Fork Rd.	Buckhannon	WV	26201	(304) 473-0641	6
Park Place Stadium Cinema	600 Washington St. E	Charleston	WV	25301	(304) 345-6541	11
Elkins Cinema 7	Tygart Valley Mall	Elkins	WV	26241	(304) 636-3762	6
Warner's Drive In	Rte. 220 N Main St.	Franklin	WV	26807	(304) 358-3680	1
Glendale Drive In	W VV Rte. #2	Glen Dale	WV	26038	(304) 845-2064	1
Camelot Theatre	1030 4th Ave.	Huntington	WV	25701	(304) 525-9211	2
Cinema Theatre	1021 4th Ave.	Huntington	WV	25701	(304) 525-9211	4
Lewis Theatre	113 N Court St.	Lewisburg	WV	24901	(304) 645-6038	1
Berkeley Plaza Theatre	Rte. 11N	Martinsburg	WV	25401	(304) 263-5899	7
Meadow Bridge Drive In	Rte. 20	Meadow Bridge	WV	25976	(304) 484-7878	1
South Branch Cinema 6	Hyde St.	Moorefield	WV	26836	(304) 538-8104	6
Warner Theatre	147 High St.	Morgantown	WV	26505	(304) 291-3777	3
Valley Cinema 3	249 North St., Rte. 2	New Martinsville	WV	26155	(304) 455-2581	3
Jungle Drive In Theatre	6600 Old St. Mary's Pike	Parkersburg	WV	26104	(304) 464-4063	1
Shepherdstown Opera House	131 West German St.	Shepherdstown	WV	25443	(304) 876-0674	1
Sunset Drive In	Route 19	Shinnston	WV	26431	(304) 255-0405	1
Robey Theatre	318 Main St.	Spencer	WV	25276	(304) 927-1390	1
Plaza Theatre	400 Penco Rd.	Weirton	WV	26062	(304) 723-4360	1
Towngate Cinema	2118 Market St.	Wheeling	WV	26003	(304) 233-0820	1
The Greenbrier Htl. & Cin.	300 W Main St.	White Sulphur Spgs	WV	24986	(800) 624-6070	1

WISCONSIN

Name	Address	City	State	Zip	Phone	Screens
Abby Theatre	216 N 1st St.	Abbotsford	WI	54405	(715) 223-4376	1
Adams Theatre	157 S Main St.	Adams	WI	53910	(608) 339-3899	1
Amery Theatre	118 N Keller Ave.	Amery	WI	54001	(612) 716-6201	1
Bay Cinemas	420 Main St. W	Ashland	WI	54806	(715) 292-3562	6
Beaver Dam Wisconsin Theatre	236 Front St.	Beaver Dam	WI	53916	(920) 885-6380	4
Beloit Luxury 10	2799 Cranston Rd.	Beloit	WI	53511	(608) 368-1107	10
Falls Cinema I & II	26 S 1st St.	Black River Falls	WI	54615	(715) 284-2716	2
Plaza Theatre	448 Milwaukee Ave.	Burlington	WI	53105	(262) 763-6789	4
Chilton Cinema	26 N Madison St.	Chilton	WI	53014	(920) 371-1585	1
Micon Cinema 8	475 Chippewa Mall Dr.	Chippewa Falls	WI	54729	(715) 720-2291	8
Cornell Theatre	214 Main St.	Cornell	WI	54732	(715) 239-6655	1
De Pere Cinema Cafe	417 George St.	De Pere	WI	54115	(920) 336-4971	1
Durand Theatre	110 East Main St.	Durand	WI	54736	(715) 672-3456	1
Vilas Cinema 5	218 E Wall St.	Eagle River	WI	54521	(715) 479-8967	5
Cameo Budget Theatre	315 S Barstow St	Eau Claire	WI	54701	(715) 832-3355	2
Gemini Drive In	6730 US 12 West	Eau Claire	WI	54701	(715) 874-5101	1
London Square	3109 Mall Dr	Eau Claire	WI	54701	(715) 834-1245	6
Elroy Theatre	122 Main St.	Elroy	WI	53929	(608) 853-0358	1
Fond Du Lac Theatre	1131 W Scott St.	Fond Du Lac.	WI	54937	(920) 922-3430	8
Forest Mall Cinema	755 W Johnson St.	Fond Du Lac.	WI	54935	(920) 921-3010	2
Showtime Cinema	8910 S 102 St.	Franklin	WI	53132	(414) 425-6513	12
Hayward Cinema 4	10270 Lee Rd.	Hayward	WI	54843	(715) 634-9293	4
Park Theatre	15791 US 63.	Hayward	WI	54843	(715) 634-4596	1
Rock Theatres	1620 Newport Ave.	Janesville	WI	53545	(608) 758-2406	9
Wildwood Movies 10	3100 Deerfield Dr.	Janesville	WI	53546	(608) 743-0200	10
Highway 18 Outdoor Theatre	W 6423 Hwy. 18	Jefferson	WI	53549	(920) 674-6700	1
The Field of Scenes Drive In	N3732 Uni Dr.	Kaukauna	WI	54130	(920) 788-1935	1
Keno Drive In	9102 Sheridan Rd.	Kenosha	WI	53143	(262) 694-8710	1
The Rivoli Theatre & Pizzeria	117 N 4th St.	La Crosse	WI	54601	(608) 784-7761	1
Bruce Theatre	116 E Miner Ave.	Ladysmith	WI	54848	(715) 339-2396	1
Miner Theatre	116 E Miner Ave. E	Ladysmith	WI	54848	(715) 762-2293	1
Desert Star Cinema	1301 Wisconsin Dell Pkwy. S	Lake Delton	WI	53940	(608) 253-4728	10
Geneva 4 Theatres	244 Broad St.	Lake Geneva	WI	53147	(262) 248-9208	4
Showboat of Lyons	N2565 Hwy. 120 North	Lake Geneva	WI	53147	(262) 249-9687	6
Majestic Theatre	115 King St.	Madison	WI	53703	(608) 255-8755	1
Orpheum Theatre	216 State St.	Madison	WI	53703	(608) 255-8755	2
University Square Cinema	62 University Sq.	Madison	WI	53715	(608) 796-0400	4
Family Cinema	3651 Dewey St.	Manitowoc	WI	54220	(920) 686-9415	4
Lakeshore Cinema Cafe	1118 Washington St.	Manitowoc	WI	54220	(920) 371-1583	1
Strand 6 Theatres	315 N 8th St.	Manitowoc	WI	54220	(920) 684-9291	6
Mariner Theatre	2000 Ella Ct.	Marinette	WI	54143	(715) 732-6869	2
Rogers Cinema	419 S Central Ave.	Marshfield	WI	54449	(715) 387-2566	7
Broadway Theatre	910 W Broadway Ave.	Medford	WI	54451	(715) 748-5556	2
Stadium 7 Theatre	2521 Hwy. 25 N	Menomonie	WI	54751	(715) 232-8844	7
Cosmo 2 Cinema	813 E Main St.	Merrill	WI	54452	(715) 536-4473	2
Times Cinema	5906 W Vliet St.	Milwaukee	WI	53208	(414) 453-3128	1
Mineral Point Opera House	139 High St.	Mineral Point	WI	53565	(608) 574-7504	1
Goetz Theatre	1704 11th St.	Monroe	WI	53566	(608) 328-8111	3
Sky Vu Drive In	1936 Wisconsin 69	Monroe	WI	53566	(608) 328-8111	1
Montello Theatre	30 E Montello St	Montello	WI	53949	(608) 297-7300	1
Grand Theatre	208 Wolf River Plz.	New London	WI	54961	(920) 982-4920	4
New Richmond Theatre 6	1261 Heritage Drive	New Richmond	WI	54017	(715) 246-4411	6
Park Theatre	199 2nd Ave. N	Park Falls	WI	54552	(715) 762-2293	1
Wildwood Capitol Cinema	1275 Capitol Drive	Pewaukee	WI	53072	(262) 695-2403	12
Cinema North Theatre	205 N Lake Ave.	Phillips	WI	54555	(715) 762-2293	2
Millennium Cinema	151 Millennium Dr.	Platteville	WI	53818	(608) 348-4297	6
Star Cinemas	Hwy. 18 South	Prairie Du Chien	WI	53821	(608) 326-8578	6
Bonham Theatre & Video	564 Water St.	Prairie Du Sac	WI	53578	(608) 643-8504	3
Falls Theatre	105 S Main St.	River Falls	WI	54022	(715) 425-1161	1
Crescent Pitcher Show	220 South Main St.	Shawano	WI	54166		1
Timbers Theatres	24226 1st Ave. N	Siren	WI	54872	(715) 349-8889	4
Stanley Theatre	131 N Broadway	Stanley	WI	54768	(715) 644-5988	1
Campus Cinemas	1601 6th Ave.	Stevens Point	WI	54481	(715) 341-6151	4
Rogers Cinema 6	2725 S Church	Stevens Point	WI	54481	(715) 341-7500	5
Stoughton Cinema 5 Cafe	124 W Main St.	Stoughton	WI	53589	(608) 877-4250	5
Donna Theatre	1820 Alabama	Sturgeon Bay	WI	54235	(920) 746-8371	4
Sturgeon Bay Cinema	1820 Alabama	Sturgeon Bay	WI	54235	(920) 746-8371	6
Tomahawk Cinema	17 W Wisconsin Ave.	Tomahawk	WI	54487	(715) 762-2293	1

Name	Address	City	State	Zip	Phone	Screens
Vernon Square Cinema	1230 N Main St.	Viroqua	WI	54665	(608) 637-0430	3
Town Cinema	308 E Main St.	Watertown	WI	53094	(920) 261-6201	3
Rosa Theatre	218 S Main St.	Waupaca	WI	54981	(715) 258-0500	4
Rosebud Cinema Dafthouse	6823 W North Ave.	Wauwatosa	WI	53213	(414) 607-9446	1
Paradise Theatre	2014 Pkwy. Drive	West Bend	WI	53095	(262) 334-3526	10
West Bend Cinema Brewhaus	125 N Main St.	West Bend	WI	53095	(262) 334-7470	3
Fox Bay Cinema Grill	334 E Silver Spring Dr.	Whitefish Bay	WI	53217	(414) 906-9994	3
Theatres of Whitewater 4	151 S Pearson Ln.	Whitewater	WI	53190	(262) 472-9045	4
Rogers Cinema-Wisconsin Rapids	220 E Grand Ave.	Wisconsin Rapids	WI	54494	(715) 421-3765	7
Lakeland Cinema	1002 2nd Ave.	Woodruff	WI	54568	(715) 358-2586	6

WYOMING

Name	Address	City	State	Zip	Phone	Screens
Ford Theatre	444 Washington	Afton	WY	83110	(307) 886-5684	1
Buffalo Theatre	235 S Main St.	Buffalo	WY	82834	(307) 684-9950	2
America Theatre	119 S Center	Casper	WY	82601	(307) 266-3647	1
Eastridge 4	601 SE Wyoming Blvd.	Casper	WY	82609	(307) 266-3647	4
Fox	230 W Yellowstone	Casper	WY	82601	(307) 266-3647	3
Iris Stadium 8	230 West Yellowstone	Casper	WY	82601	(307) 472-4743	8
Rialto	119 S Center	Casper	WY	82601	(307) 266-3647	1
Capitol City Stadium 12	3410 Concord Rd.	Cheyenne	WY	82001	(307) 638-1595	12
Lincoln Popcorn Palace	1615 Central Ave.	Cheyenne	WY	82001	(307) 638-0774	2
Big Horn Cinemas	2525 Big Horn Ave.	Cody	WY	82414	(307) 587-8009	4
Cody Theatre	1171 Sheridan Ave. Ste. 3	Cody	WY	82414	(307) 587-2712	1
Mesa Theatre AKA: Princess Theatre	104 N 3rd St.	Douglas	WY	82633	(307) 358-6209	1
Valley 4 Cinemas	45 E Aspen Grove	Evanston	WY	82930	(307) 789-0523	4
Foothills Theatres	650 N US 14-16	Gillette	WY	82716	(307) 682-6766	2
Sky Hi Cinema	800 Shoshone Ave	Gillette	WY	82718	(307) 682-7628	2
Star Twin Theatre	699 Uinta Dr.	Green River	WY	82935	(307) 266-3647	2
Jackson Hole Cinema	295 W Pearl	Jackson	WY	83001	(307) 733-2262	2
Movieworks Cinema 4	860 S Hwy. 89	Jackson	WY	83001	(307) 733-2262	4
Teton Thetare	120 N Cache	Jackson	WY	83001	(307) 733-9494	1
Victory Theatre	700 JC Penney Drive	Kemmerer	WY	83101	(307) 877-6685	1
Grand Theatre	250 Main St.	Lander	WY	82520	(307) 332-4437	1
Wyo Theatre	309 S 5th St.	Laramie	WY	82070	(307) 745-8151	1
Hyart Theatre	251 E Main St.	Lovell	WY	82431	(307) 272-9125	1
Valley Theatre	110 E Owen	Lyman	WY	82937	(307) 787-3333	1
Dogie Theatre	111 W Main St.	Newcastle	WY	82701	(307) 746-2187	1
Pinedale Entertainment Center	153 S Entertainment Lane	Pinedale	WY	82941	(307) 367-3056	2
American Dream Drive In	1070 Rd. 9	Powell	WY	82435	(307) 754-5133	1
Vali Cinema	204 N Bent St.	Powell	WY	82435	(307) 754-4211	2
Movies 3	1720 Edinburgh	Rawlins	WY	82301	(307) 324-6624	3
Acme Theatre	312 E Main	Riverton	WY	82501	(307) 856-1303	1
Gem Theatre	119 S 3rd	Riverton	WY	82501	(307) 856-9589	4
Star Stadium 10	2411 Foothill Blvd., Space #7	Rock Springs	WY	82901	(307) 352-3686	8
Centennial Theatre	36 E Alger St.	Sheridan	WY	82801	(307) 672-5797	5
Ritz Theatre	309 Arapahoe	Thermopolis	WY	82443	(307) 864-3118	1
Wyoming 2 Theatre	126 E 20th Ave.	Torrington	WY	82240	(307) 532-2226	2
Cinema West Theatre	609 10th St.	Wheatland	WY	82201	(307) 322-3690	1
Cottonwood Twin Cinemas	101 Pleasant View Dr.	Worland	WY	82401	(307) 347-8414	2

Specialty & Large Format Exhibitors

Specialty exhibitors show non-theatrical films, usually in a proprietary format and occasionally involving mechanical simulations or special viewing devices in conjunction with the film, to non-theatrical audiences (usually museum-goers and amusement park attendees). However, traditional exhibitors are installing limited numbers of specialty screens in multiplexes. For equipment & services, please see the section of this book entitled Specialty Exhibitor Equipment & Services.

IMAX CORPORATION

CORPORATE HEADQUARTERS
2525 Speakman Dr., Sheridan Science and Technology Park, Mississauga, ONT L5K 1B1, Canada. TEL: (905) 403-6500.
FAX: (905) 403-6450. email: info@imax.com www.imax.com
CHAIRMAN
Richard L. Gelfond
CEO
Bradley J. Wechsler
EXECUTIVE V.P., CFO
Joseph Sparaciol
COO
Gary Moss
CHAIRMAN & PRESIDENT, FILMED ENTERTAINMENT
Greg Foster
EXECUTIVE V.P., BUSINESS & LEGAL AFFAIRS & GENERAL COUNSEL
Robert D. Lister
SENIOR V.P. & PRESIDENT DAVID KEIGHLEY PRODUCTIONS 7MM, INC.
David Keighley
EXECUTIVE V.P., TECHNOLOGY
Brian Bonnick
EXECUTIVE V.P., CORPORATE SERVICES & CORPORATE SECRETARY
G. Mary Ruby
EXECUTIVE V.P. THEATRE DEVELOPMENT
Larry T. O'Reilly
EXECUTIVE V.P., CORPORATE & DIGITAL DEVELOPMENT AND THEATRE OPERATIONS
Mark Welton
EXECUTIVE V.P. CORPORATE SERVICES & CORPORATE SECRETARY
G. Mary Ruby
BOARD MEMBER
Bradley J. Wechsler, Richard L. Gelfond, Eric A. Demirian, Neil S. Braun, Kenneth G. Copland, Garth M. Girvan, David W. Lebebron, I. Martin Pompadur, Marc A. Utay

U.S. IMAX THEATRES

(Most IMAX theatres are independently owned and operated. Theatres marked with an asterisk have IMAX 3D capability.)

Theatre	Address	City	State	Phone
McWane Center IMAX Dome Theatre	205 19th Street N	Birmingham	AL	205-714-8300
Spacedome IMAX Theatre, U.S. Space & Rocket Cntr.	1 Tranquility Base	Huntsville	AL	256-837-3400
J.L. Bedsole IMAX Dome, Gulf Coast Exploreum	65 Government Street	Mobile	AL	334-208-6873
AMC IMAX Theatre, AMC Deer Valley 30*	3033 W. Agua Fria Freeway	Phoenix	AZ	602-956-4262
IMAX Theatre Arizona Mills*	5000 Arizona Mills Circle	Tempe	AZ	480-897-4629
Grand Canyon IMAX Theatre	Highway 64 & 180	Tusayan	AZ	520-638-2203
IMAX Theatre Arizona Science Center	600 E. Washington St.	Phoenix	AZ	602-716-2000
Gateway 12 IMAX Theatre	1935 S. Signal Butte	Mesa	AZ	480-354-8030
IMAX Theatre @ Aerospace Education Center	3301 E. Roosevelt Road	Little Rock	AR	501-376-4629
Disney Soarin	Disney's California Adventure	Anaheim	CA	714-781-4565
Desert IMAX Theatre*	68-510 E. Palm Canyon Drive	Cathedral City	CA	760-324-7333
Regal IMAX Theatre, Hacienda Crossing*	5000 Dublin Boulevard	Dublin	CA	925-560-0600
Edwards Irvine Spectrum IMAX Theatre*	Irvine Spectrum	Irvine	CA	949-450-4900
Back To The Future, The Ride	Universal Studios	Los Angeles	CA	818-622-3855
IMAX Theatre, California Science Center*	700 State Drive	Los Angeles	CA	213-744-7400
IMAX Theatre at The Bridge: Cinema de lux*	6081 Center Drive	Los Angeles	CA	310-568-3375
Universal Studios IMAX Theatre*	Citywalk	Los Angeles	CA	818-508-0493
Regal IMAX Theatre, Ontario Palace Stadium 22*	4900 E. 4th Street	Ontario	CA	800-555-8355
Esquire IMAX Theatre*	1211 K Street	Sacramento	CA	916-443-4629
Reuben H. Fleet Science Center	1875 El Prado	San Diego	CA	619-238-1233
Loews IMAX Theatre at Metreon*	101 Fourth Street	San Francisco	CA	415-369-6201
Hackworth IMAX Dome Theatre	201 S. Market Street	San Jose	CA	408-294-8324
Regal IMAX Theatre*	7750 North Blackstone Ave.	Fresno	CA	800-555-8355
Edwards Mira Mesa Stadium 18 & IMAX*	10733 Westview Parkway	San Diego	CA	858-635-7700
Cinemark IMAX Theatre at The Cinemark*	3305 Cinema Point	Colorado Springs	CO	719-596-3212
Lawrence Phipps IMAX Theatre	2001 Colorado Boulevard	Denver	CO	303-322-7009
Regal IMAX Theatre Colorado Center*	2000 S. Colordao Boulevard	Denver	CO	303-757-8665
IMAX Theatre, Showcase Cinemas Buckland Hill*	99 Red Stone Road	Manchester	CT	860-646-4555
IMAX Theatre, The Maritime Centre	10 N. Water Street	Norwalk	CT	203-866-9202
Lockheed Martin IMAX Theater*	6th & Independence Avenue SW	Washington	DC	877-932-4629
Johnson IMAX Theater*	10th & Constitution Avenue NW	Washington	DC	877-932-4629
Pepsi IMAX Theatre*	1801 W. Intl. Speedway Boulevard	Daytona Beach	FL	386-947-6800
Blockbuster IMAX 3D Theatre*	401 S.W. Second Street	Fort Lauderdale	FL	954-463-4629
World Golf Village IMAX Theatre	Golf Hall of Fame	Jacksonville	FL	904-940-4123
IMAX Theatre 1 & 2, Kennedy Space Center*	Mail Code: DNPS	Kennedy Space Cntr	FL	321-452-2121
Woodland Square 20	3128 Tampa Road	Oldsmar	FL	888-262-4386
Back To The Future, The Ride	Universal Studios	Orlando	FL	407-363-8000
IMAX Theatre, National Museum of Naval Aviation	1750 Radford Avenue	Pensacola	FL	888-627-4629
IMAX Theatre, Challenger Learning Center	200 S. Duval Street	Tallahassee	FL	850-645-7796
Channelside Cinemas & IMAX Theatre*	615 Channelside Drive	Tampa	FL	813-221-0700
IMAX Dome at MOSI	4801 E. Fowler Avenue	Tampa	FL	813-987-6100

Regal Pointe Orlando Stadium 20 & IMAX*	9101 International Drive	Orlando	FL	407-248-9228
Muvico Baywalk IMAX*	151 2nd Ave North St.	St. Petersburg	FL	727-502-0965
Muvico Parisian IMAX*	545 Hibiscus St.	West Palm Beach	FL	561-883-0400
Rankin M. Smith, Jr. IMAX Theater, Fernbank Museum	767 Clifton Road NE	Atlanta	GA	404-929-6400
Regal IMAX Theatre, Mall of Georgia*	3333 Buford Drive, Suite 3000	Buford	GA	678-482-5858
IMAX Polynesia	55-370 Kamehameha Highway	Laie	HI	808-293-3280
Regal IMAX Theatre, Boise Stadium 21*	7709 Overland Road	Boise	ID	208-377-9600
Henry Crown MSI OMNIMAX	5700 S. Lake Shore Drive	Chicago	IL	773-684-1414
Navy Pier IMAX Theatre*	600 E. Grand Avenue, Suite 115	Chicago	IL	312-595-5629
Regal IMAX Theatre 20*	300 Parkway Drive	Lincolnshire	IL	847-229-9100
Cinemark IMAX Theatre at Seven Bridges*	6500 Route 53	Woodridge	IL	630-434-2629
IMAX Theatre at Randall 15	550 N. Randall Road	Batavia	IL	630-482-3456
IMAX Theatre, Showplace Cinema East 18*	1801 Morgan Center Drive	Evansville	IN	812-479-9732
IMAX Theatre 3D Theatre, White River State Park*	650 W. Washington Street	Indianapolis	IN	317-634-4567
Portage 16 IMAX	6550 US Highway 6	Portage	IN	219-764-7469
Kerasotes Indianapolis ShowPlace 16 & IMAX*	4325 S. Meridian	Indianapolis	IN	317-784-0989
McLeod/Busse IMAX Dome Theatre	427 First Street	Cedar Rapids	IA	319-363-4629
IMAX Theatre, Putnam Museum*	1717 W. 12th Street	Davenport	IA	563-324-1933
Blank IMAX Dome Theatre, Science Center of Iowa	401 W. Martin Luther King Jr. Pkwy	Des Moines	IA	515-274-4629
IMAX Dome Theatre	1100 N. Plum	Hutchinson	KS	316-662-2305
AMC IMAX Theatre, AMC Studio 30*	12075 S. Strang Line Road	Olathe	KS	816-363-4262
IMAX Theatre, Louisville Science Center IMAX	727 W. Main Street	Louisville	KY	502-561-6100
IMAX Theatre, Showcase Cinemas Stonybrook*	2745 S. Hurstbourne Parkway	Louisville	KY	502-499-6658
Entergy IMAX Theater* New Orleans Aquarium	1 Canal Street	New Orleans	LA	504-565-3020
IMAX Dome Theatre, Sci-Port Discovery Centre	820 Clyde Fant Parkway	Shreveport	LA	318-424-3466
Holiday Square Cinema 12 IMAX	201 North Hwy 190	Covington	LA	504-893-5444
IMAX Maryland Science Center*	601 Light Street	Baltimore	MD	410-685-5225
Mugar Omni Theatre, Museum of Science	1 Science Park	Boston	MA	617-723-2500
Simons IMAX Theatre*	New England Aquarium, Central Wharf	Boston	MA	866-815-4629
Comcast IMAX 3D Theatre at Jordan's Furniture*	1 Underprice Way	Natick	MA	508-424-0088
Comcast IMAX 3D Theatre at Jordan's Furniture*	40 Walkers Brooke Drive	Reading	MA	781-944-9090
IMAX Theatre, Henry Ford Museum*	20900 Oakwood Boulevard	Dearborn	MI	313-271-1570
IMAX Dome Theatre, Detroit Science Center	John Road and Warren	Detroit	MI	313-577-8400
IMAX Theatre Celebration! Village*	2121 Celebration	Grand Rapids	MI	616-474-4231
IMAX Theatre Celebration! Cinema*	200 E. Edgewood Boulevard	Lansing	MI	517-393-7469
AMC IMAX Theatre, AMC Forum 30*	44681 Mound Rd.	Sterling Heights	MI	586-254-5663
Showcase Cinema Ann Arbor	4100 Carpenter Road	Ypsilanti	MI	734-973-8380
NCG Trillium Cinema & IMAX*	8220 Trillium Circle Ave	Grand Blanc	MI	810-695-5000
Duluth OMNIMAX Theatre	301 Harbor Drive	Duluth	MN	218-727-0022
Great Clips Imax Theatre*	12000 Zoo Boulevard	Minneapolis	MN	952-431-4629
Pepsi IMAX Theatre, Valleyfair's Amusement Park	1 Valleyfair Drive	Shakopee	MN	952-445-7600
William L. McKnight-3M, Omnitheatre	120 W. Kellogg Boulevard	St. Paul	MN	651-221-9444
IMAX Theatre Cinemagic Metropolitan	4300 O'Day Avenue	St. Michael	MN	763-746-0229
Ozarks Discovery IMAX Theatre	3562 Shepherd of the Hills Expreesway	Branson	MO	800-419-4832
Sprint IMAX @ Kansas City Zoo	6800 Zoo Drive	Kansas City	MO	816-513-4629
OMNIMAX Theatre, St. Louis Science Center	5050 Oakland Avenue	St. Louis	MO	314-289-4444
IMAX Theatre, Ronnies 20 Cine	5320 S. Lindburgh Boulevard	Sappington	MO	314-822-2463
Yellowstone IMAX Theatre	101 S. Canyon Street	West Yellowstone	MT	406-646-4100
Lozier IMAX Theatre*	3701 10th Street	Omaha	NE	402-738-8401
Hooksett Cinemagic & IMAX*	1226 Hooksett Road	Hooksett	NH	603-644-4629
Brenden IMAX Theatre*	4321 W. Flamingo Road	Las Vegas	NV	702-507-4849
Luxor IMAX Theatre*	3900 Las Vegas Boulevard S.	Las Vegas	NV	702-262-4555
Regal Red Rock Stadium 16 & IMAX*	11011 West Charleston Blvd.	Las Vegas	NV	702-233-6948
IMAX Theatre at Tropicana*	Tropicana Casino and Resort	Atlantic City	NJ	888-505-1435
IMAX Dome Theatre, Liberty Science Center	251 Phillip Street	Jersey City	NJ	201-200-1000
Clyde W. Tombaugh Space Theatre	New Mexico Highway 2001	Alamogordo	NM	505-437-2840
Regal IMAX Theatre*	Transit Centre 18	Buffalo	NY	716-632-4629
IMAX Dome at Leroy R. & Rose W. Grumman	1 Davis Avenue	Garden City	NY	516-572-4111
Regal IMAX Theatre, New Roc City 18*	33 Le Count Place	New Rochelle	NY	914-235-5654
IMAX Theatre, American Museum of Natural History	175-208 Central Parkway	New York	NY	212-769-5100
Loews IMAX Theatre, Lincoln Square*	1998 Broadway	New York	NY	212-336-5000
Cinemark IMAX Theatre at Tinseltown USA*	2291 Buffalo Road	Rochester	NY	585-247-2180
Bristol Omnitheatre	500 S. Franklin Street	Syracuse	NY	315-425-9068
IMAX Theatre at Palisades Center*	4270 Palisades Center Drive	West Nyack	NY	845-358-4629
IMAX Theatre, City Center 15: Cinema de Lux*	19 Mamaroneck Avenue	White Plains	NY	914-747-6000
Observer OMNIMAX Theatre	301 N. Tryon Street	Charlotte	NC	704-372-6261
IMAX Theater Exploris*	201 E. Hargett Street	Raleigh	NC	919-834-4040
Robert D. Lindner Family OMNIMAX	1301 Western Avenue	Cincinnati	OH	513-287-7000
Cleveland Clinic OMNIMAX Theatre	601 Erieside Avenue	Cleveland	OH	216-694-2000
AMC Theatre, AMC Easton 30*	275 Easton Town Center	Columbus	OH	614-428-4300
AMC Lennox Town Center 24 – IMAX	777 Kinnear Rd	Columbus	OH	888-262-4386
IMAX Theatre at the USAF	1100 Spaatz Street	Dayton	OH	937-253-4629
IMAX Theatre, City Center 18: Cinema de Lux*	12064 Springfield Pike	Springdale	OH	513-671-0140
Cinemark IMAX Theatre, The Tulsa*	10802 E. 71st Street S.	Tulsa	OK	918-307-2629
OMNIMAX Theatre at OMSI	1945 S.E. Water Avenue	Portland	OR	503-797-4640
Evergreen Aviation Museum IMAX Theatre*	3850 Three Mile Lane	McMinnville	OR	503-434-4180
Regal Cinemas Bridgeport Village Stadium 18 & IMAX*	7329 SW Bridgeport Road	Tigard	OR	800-326-3264
Select Medical IMAX Theatre*	222 Market Street	Harrisburg	PA	717-221-8201
Regal IMAX Theatre, King of Prussia Stadium 13*	300 Goddard Boulevard	King of Prussia	PA	610-290-1361
Tuttleman IMAX Theatre	222 N. 20th Street	Philadelphia	PA	215-448-1200
Rangos OMNIMAX Theater, Carnegie Science Center	1 Allegheny Avenue	Pittsburgh	PA	412-237-3400
Cinemark IMAX Theatre, Galleria at Pittsburgh Mills	425 Pittsburgh Mills Circle	Tarentum	PA	724-274-0151
Feinstein IMAX Theatre*	9 Providence Place, Suite R2	Providence	RI	401-453-4629
Charleston IMAX Theater*	360 Concord Street	Charleston	SC	843-725-4629
IMAX Discovery Theater, Broadway at the Beach*	1195 Celebrity Circle	Myrtle Beach	SC	843-444-3333
IMAX 3D @ Tennessee Aquarium*	201 Chestnut Street	Chattanooga	TN	423-266-4629
Union Planters IMAX Theatre	3050 Central Avenue	Memphis	TN	901-320-6362
Regal IMAX Theatre, Opry Mills*	570 Opry Mills Drive	Nashville	TN	615-514-4629
Regal Pinnacle Stadium 18 & IMAX*	11240 Parkside Drive	Knoxville	TN	800-326-3264
IMAX Theatre, Bob Bullock Texas State History Museum*	1800 N. Congress Avenue	Austin	TX	512-936-8746

Cinemark IMAX Theatre at Cinemark 17*	11819 Webb Chapel Road	Dallas	TX	972-888-2629
TI Founders IMAX Theatre	1318 Second Avenue	Dallas	TX	214-428-5555
Omni Theatre, Ft. Worth Museum Science & Natural History	1501 Montgomery Street	Fort Worth	TX	888-255-9300
IMAX 3D @ Moody Gardens*	1 Hope Boulevard	Galveston	TX	800-582-4673
Regal IMAX Theatre*	7620 Katy Freeway.	Houston	TX	800-555-8355
Space Center Theatre	1601 NASA Road	Houston	TX	281-244-2100
Wortham IMAX Theatre, Houston Museum Natural Science	1 Hermann Circle Drive	Houston	TX	713-639-4600
San Antonio IMAX Theatre 1 & 2*	217 Alamo Plaza	San Antonio	TX	210-247-4629
Santikos Palladium IMAX	17703 IH 10 West	San Antonio	TX	210-496-2221
Metro Cinema of Colleyville	5655 Colleyville Blvd.	Colleyville	TX	817-503-0724
IMAX Theatre at the Clark Planetarium*	110 S. 40th West	Salt Lake City	UT	801-532-7827
Cricket IMAX Theatre, Megaplex 17 @ Jordan Commons	9400 S. State Street	Sandy	UT	801-304-4577
IMAX Theater, Stephen F. Udvar-Hazy Center	14390 Air & Space Museum Parkway	Chantilly	VA	877-932-4629
IMAX Virginia Air & Space Center*	600 Settlers Landing Road	Hampton	VA	757-727-0900
Ethyl IMAX Dome Theatre	2500 W. Broad Street	Richmond	VA	804-864-1400
ABC Family Channel IMAX 3D Theatre*	717 General Booth Boulevard	Virginia Beach	VA	757-437-4949
Boeing & Eames IMAX Theatres, Pacific Science Center	200 Second Avenue N.	Seattle	WA	206-443-4629
Regal Cinemas Thornton Place Stadium 14 & IMAX	301 NE 103rd St	Seattle	WA	206-517-9943
IMAX Theatre, Riverfront Park	507 N. Howard St.	Spokane	WA	509-625-6686
Star Cinema IMAX	6091 McKee Road	Fitchburg	WI	608-270-1414
Humphrey IMAX Dome Theater	827 N. 7th Center Street	Milwaukee	WI	414-319-4629

INTERNATIONAL LOCATIONS

ARGENTINA

IMAX Theatre Centre Norte	Esteban Echeverria 3750	Buenos Aires	AR	54-11-4762-9600

AUSTRALIA

Coca-Cola IMAX Theatre	Dreamworld Parkway	Coomera	QLD	07-558-81111
IMAX Melbourne*	Rathdowne Street-Carlton Gardens	Melbourne	VIC	03-9663-5454
Panasonic IMAX Theatre*	31 Wheat Road	Sydney	NSW	029-281-3300
North Queensland IMAX Dome Theatre	68 Flinders Street E.	Townsville	QLD	074-750-0800

BULGARIA

Mtel IMAX Theatre	101 Stamboliski Blvd.	Sofia	BG	359-2-929-0055

CANADA

Famous Players IMAX Theatre, Chinook Centre*	6455 MacLeod Trail SW	Calgary	AB	403-212-8098
IMAX Theatre, Edmonton Space & Science Centre	11211-142nd Street	Edmonton	AB	780-451-3344
Famous Players SilverCity IMAX Theatre*	#3030-8882 170 Street	Edmonton	AB	780-444-2400
Famous Players Colossus IMAX Theatre*	20090-91A Avenue	Langley	BC	604-513-8747
Famous Players SilverCity Theatre*	14211 Entertainment Way	Richmond	BC	604-277-5993
Alcan OMNIMAX Theatre	1455 Quebec Street	Vancouver	BC	604-443-7443
CN IMAX Theatre*	201-999 Canada Place	Vancouver	BC	604-682-4629
National Geographic Theatre	675 Belleville Street	Victoria	BC	250-953-4629
IMAX Theate at Portage Place*	Y003-393 Portage Avenue	Winnipeg	MB	204-956-4629
Empire IMAX Theatre*	190 Chain Lake Drive	Halifax	NS	902-876-4800
Famous Players SilverCity IMAX Theatre*	50 Great Lakes	Brampton	ON	905-789-6797
Famous Players Coliseum 10*	309 Rathburn Road W	Mississauga	ON	905-275-3456
Niagara Falls IMAX Theatre	6170 Fallsview Boulevard	Niagara Falls	ON	905-358-3611
Science North IMAX Theatre	100 Ramsey Lake Road	Sudbury	ON	705-522-3700
Cinesphere IMAX Theatre	955 Lakeshore Boulevard W.	Toronto	ON	416-314-9900
Ontario Science Centre OMNIMAX Theatre	770 Don Mills Road	Toronto	ON	416-429-4100
Famous Players Festival Hall IMAX Theatre*	259 Richmond Street W.	Toronto	ON	416-368-5600
Famous Players Colossus 19*	3555 Highway 7 W.	Woodbridge	ON	905-851-4994
SilverCity Gloucester	2385 City Park Drive	Gloucester	ON	613 688 8800
Cineplus IMAX Theatre	Canadian Museum, 100 Laurier Street	Hull	QC	819-776-7010
IMAX Telus Le Vieux-Port de Montreal*	333, de la Commune Street W.	Montreal	QC	514-496-4629
Famous Players Paramount*	977 Rue Street	Montreal	QC	514-878-9100
IMAX Le Theatre	Les Galeries de la Capitale	Quebec City	QC	418-627-8222
Kramer IMAX Theatre	Saskatchewan Science Centre	Regina	SK	306-791-7900

CHINA

IMAX Dome Theatre	No. 2 Yuan Mei Middle Road	Dongguan	CN	86769-228-35268
IMAX Theatre	Harbin 150	Harbin	CN	8645-1881-91198
IMAX Theatre, Nanjing Juvenile	Science & Technology Museum	Nanjing	CN	8625-5244-2551
Hong Kong Space Museum	10 Salisbury Road	Hong Kong	CN	852-2721-0226
IMAX Dome Theatre	2000 Shiji Avenue	Shanghai	CN	862-168-542-000
IMAX Theatre at Peace Cinema*	290 Xizang Zhou Lu	Shanghai	CN	8621-6361-2989
IMAX Theatre China National Film Museum	Nangao Rd, Inner Railway Ring, Cuigezhuan	Beijing	CN	8610-6431-9548
IMAX Theatre Beijing UME	No. 4, Shuag Yu Ke Xue Yuan Nan Lu	Beijing	CN	8610-8211-1601
Studio City Wuhan IMAX Theatre*	4-5F, People's Parade, 608 Zhongshan Dadao Hankou	Wuhan	CN	86-27-8537-9076
Chongqing Children's Palace IMAX Dome Theatre	No. 134, Chongshan 2nd Rd., Yuzhong District	Chongqing	CN	86-23-6362-7108
UA IMAX Theatre	L11, UA MegaBox, 38 Wang Chiu Rd, Kowloon Bay	Hong Kong	CN	852-2757-6155
Suzhou Science and Cultural Arts Center IMAX Theatre*	1 Guanfeng Street	Jiangsu	CN	

CZECH REPUBLIC

Oskar IMAX Theatre*	Palac Flora Vinohradska 149	Prague 3	CZ	42-255-742-021

DENMARK

OMNIMAX Theatre	GL. Kongevej 10	Copenhagen	DK	453-312-1224

ECUADOR

IMAX Theatre Malecon 2000	Fundacion Malecon 2000	Guayaquil	EC	593-425-24529

EGYPT

IMAX Theatre Educational Center*	Future Land	Cairo	EGY	

FRANCE

IMAX Cinema*	Centre Thermal et Touristique	Amneville	FR	089-0780-780
La Geode	26 Avenue Corentin Cariou	Paris	FR	0140-057-999
Gaumont Disney Village IMAX Theatre*	Disney Village	Paris	FR	1-60-43-55-76
L'OMNIMAX*	SEML Parc du Futuroscope RN 10	Poitiers	FR	335-4949-3000
Le IMAX 3D* Futuroscope	SEML Parc du Futuroscope RN 10	Poitiers	FR	3354-949-3000
Le Kinemax	SEML Parc du Futuroscope RN 10	Poitiers	FR	335-4949-3000
Le Solido* Futuroscope	SEML Parc du Futuroscope RN 10	Poitiers	FR	335-4949-3000
IMAX Magic Carpet* Futuroscope	SEML Parc du Futuroscope RN 10	Poitiers	FR	335-4949-3000
Race for Atlantis*	SEML Parc du Futuroscope RN 10	Poitiers	FR	335-4949-3000
Imax Cite de L'Espace, Cite de l'Espace	Avenue Jean Gonord, BP 5855	Toulouse	FR	330-562-715-600

Theatre	Address	City	Country	Phone
GERMANY				
CineStar IMAX Cinema*	Sony Centre at Potsdamer Strasse 4	Berlin	DE	49-302-606-6260
Discovery IMAX Potsdamer Platz*	Marlene-Dietrich-Platz 4	Berlin	DE	493-044-316-131
Galaxy	Berggeistrasse 31-41	Bruhl	DE	49-223-2360
IMAX am Cinecitta Nurnberg*	Gewerbemuseumsplatz 3	Nurnberg	DE	499-112-06667
IMAX 3D Museum Sinsheim*	Obere Au 2	Sinsheim	DE	499-112-06667
IMAX Dome Technik Museum Speyer	Geibstrasse 2	Speyer	DE	496-232-670-880
GREAT BRITAIN				
IMAX Theatre at Millenium Point*		Birmingham	GB	121-202-2222
Sheridan IMAX Cinema*	Pier Aproach	Bournemouth	GB	120-220-0000
IMAX Cinema*	National Museum of Photography	Bradford	GB	870-701-0200
IMAX Theatre At Bristol*		Bristol	GB	845-345-1235
BFI London IMAX Cinema*	1 Charlie Chaplin Walk	London	GB	871-787-2525
Science Museum IMAX Cinema*	Exhibition Road	London	GB	870-870-4868
IMAX Cinema @ The Filmworks*	6-8 Dantzic Street	Manchester	GB	870-588-8999
GUATEMALA				
IMAX Pradera Concepcion	Kilometro 15.5 Carretera a el Salvador	Guatemala City	GT	
INDIA				
Gujarat Science City IMAX 3D Theatre*	Sola Road	Ahmedabad	IN	9179-374-2929
Aeren R IMAX at RAP Adlabs*	Saibabad Industrial Area	Ghaziabad	IN	911-203-012053
Prasad IMAX Theatre*		Hyderbad	IN	9140-2345-3333-36
IMAX Adlabs Theatre	Anik Wadala Link Road	Mumbai	IN	2403-6606
INDONESIA				
Keong Emas IMAX Theatre	Taman Mini Indonesia Indah	Jakarta	ID	622-1840-1021
IRELAND				
Sheridan IMAX Cinema*	Odyssey Pavilion	Belfast	IR	4428-9046-7000
ISRAEL				
IMAX 3D Eilat*	4, Derech Yotam	Eilat	IL	9720-8634-8080
IMAX Theatre	192 Derech Acho Street	Kiryat Biyalik, Haifa	IL	
ITALY				
TIM IMAX Theatre*	viale Ascoli Piceno sn	Riccione	IT	3205-4160-9000
IMAX Theatre Felisia*	Castellaneta Marina	Taranto	IT	0113-909-982-01444
JAPAN				
IMAX Theatre/Cinema Hall	Kanda 61-1, Tashiro, Nakatsugaru-gun	Aomori	JP	8117-285-2810
OMNIMAX Theatre	Nuclear Exhibition Centre	Hamaoka	JP	8153-786-3481
Space Theatre	Municipal Science Hall	Kagoshima	JP	819-925-08511
Mercian Karuizawa IMAX Theatre*		Karuizawa	JP	8126-741-2241
Galaxy Theatre	Space World, Yawatahigashi-ku	Kitakyushu	JP	8193-672-3520
Ocean Theatre	1-3 Mintao-Machi, Minato-ku	Nagoya	JP	815-265-47080
Back to the Future, The Ride	Universal Studios	Osaka	JP	
IMAX 3D Theatre*	5-10, Kaigandori 1-chome, Minato-ku	Osaka	JP	816-657-70004
Science Theatre	4-2-1 Nakanoshima, Kita-ku	Osaka	JP	8166-444-5656
Space Theatre	682-2 Nishikimachi	Saitama	JP	81-468-470-011
Dome Theatre	1055 Kashimae-cho	Sasebo	JP	8195-628-4187
Mercian Shinagawa IMAX Theatre*	4-10-30 Takanawa, Minato-ku	Tokyo	JP	813-542-11114
IMAX Experience Theatre	Tokorozawa Aviation Memorial Park	Tokorozawa	JP	8142-996-2225
KUWAIT				
The Scientific Center IMAX Theatre*	Salmiya	Safat	KW	965-848-8888
MALAYSIA				
DiGi IMAX Theatre*	No.1, Jalan Imbi	Kuala Lumpur	MY	603-2117-3042
MEXICO				
Domo IMAX	Fracc. Jardines del Parque	Aguascalientes	MX	524-499-7803-08
Cinemex IMAX Theatre*	Libramiento Cuern. y Av. Diana	Cuernavaca Morelos	MX	52-77-315-9239
Cinepolis Guadalajara*	Centro Comercial Galerias Guadalajara	Guadalahara Zapopan	MX	52-33-35-40-9090
Explora	Explora Science Centre	Leon, Guanajuato	MX	5247-7711-6711
Cinepolis IMAX Theatre-Perisur*	Anillo Periferico Sur No. 4690	Mexico City	MX	52-55-2122-6060
Megapantalla IMAX Theatre*	Av. Constituyentes 268	Mexico City	MX	525-224-1260
Planetario Alfa	Centro Cultural Alfa	Monterrey	MX	528-303-0002
Cinepolis IMAX Theatre*	Cinepolis Valle Oriente	Monterrey	MX	528-586-0042
IMAX Dome Theatre	Unidad Civicas 5 de Mayo	Puebla	MX	522-235-2099
Cine Planetario	Centro Cultural Tijuana	Tijuana	MX	526-684-1111
Teatro IMAX Acuario de Veracruz*	Blvd. Adolfo Ruiz Cortines	Veracruz	MX	522-299-130-4285
OMNIMAX Theatre	Prolongacion Paseo de Tabasco	Villahermosa	MX	529-312-7997
IMAX Theatre*	Av. Murillo Vidal	Xalapa	MX	11-52-228-813-8510
Sol del Nino IMAX Theatre	Alfonso Esquer Sandez s/n Zona Centro	Mexicali	MX	
Cinepolis IMAX Theatre, Cinepolis Santa Fe	Lateral Autpista Mexico-Toluca	Mexico City	MX	
MegaMax Cinemas IMAX Theatre*	Calz. Jose Vasconcelos 1955	Torreon	MX	
NETHERLANDS				
Pathe Imax*	1101 DS Amsterdam Zuidoost	Amsterdam	NL	09-00-14-58
The Hague, Omniversum	President Kennedylaan 5	Den Haag	NL	317-0354-5454
NEW ZEALAND				
SKYCITY IMAX Theatre	291-297 Queen Street	Auckland	NZ	64-9-302-0002
PHILIPPINES				
San Miguel Coca-Cola IMAX Theatre	SM Mall of Asia	Pasay City	PH	63-2556-4629
POLAND				
Orange IMAX Theatre Katowice*	Gliwicka 44 Street	Katowice	PL	4832-711-5959
Orange IMAX Krakow*	Aleje Pokoju 44 Street	Krakow	PL	4812-2909-090
Orange IMAX Poznan*	ul. K. Druzbickiego 2	Poznan Plaza	PL	662-6262
Orange IMAX Warszawa*	Powsinska 31 Street	Warsaw	PL	4822-550-3333
Orange IMAX Lodz	CH Manufaktura, ul Karskiego 5	Lodz	PL	48-42-664-6446
RUSSIA				
Nescafe IMAX Theatre*	Pravoberezhnaya Street 1	Moscow	RU	7095-77-5 7779
IMAX Theatre Port Cinema	1 Amirkhana St.	Kazan	RU	7843-52-6-5670
Coca-Cola IMAX KinoStar City*	Prospekt Kosmonavtov, 14	St. Petersburg	RU	7812-448-9884
SAUDI ARABIA				
Science Dome	P.O. Box 1941, Cornish Road	Al Khobar	SA	966-3896-7777
SCOTLAND				
IMAX Theatre*	50 Pacific Quay, Glasgow Science	Glasgow	GB	

Theatre	Address	City	Country	Phone
SINGAPORE				
Omni-Theatre	15 Science Centre Road		SG	656-425-2566
Popular IMAX Theatre*	1 Kim Seng Promenade 3	Great World City	SG	1900-912-1234
SLOVAKIA				
Orange IMAX Bratislava*	Ivanska Cesta 18	Bratislava	SK	4212-434-23036
SOUTH AFRICA				
IMAX Theatre	1 Palm Boulevard	Durban	ZA	278-361-93374
IMAX Theatre	Atterbury Road, Menlyn	Pretoria	ZA	271-236-81186
SOUTH KOREA				
CGV IMAX Theatre at CGV Incheon 14*	1130 Kuwol-dong, Namdong-gu	Incheon	KR	823-32-237-1485
63 City IMAX Theatre	60 Yoido-Dong, Youngdungpo-Ku	Seoul	KR	822-789-5505
CGV IMAX Theatre at CGV Yongsan 11*	3-1 Doryongdong	Taejon	KR	82-428-665-164
Imagination Pavilion	Expo Science Park	Taejon	KR	
CGV Seomyon IMAX	Geoplace Bd 5th Floor	Pusan	KR	81-21-544-1122
CGV Ilsan*	867, Ilsan Dong-gu, Janghang-Dong, Western Dom 3F	Goyangsi, Ilsan	KR	823-19-316-600
CGV IMAX Dageu*	15-1 Sail-dong	Daegu	KR	
SPAIN				
IMAX Port Vell*	Calle Moll D'Espanya	Barcelona	ES	349-322-51111
IMAX Madrid*	Calle Meneses	Madrid	ES	349-146-74800
IMAX Yelmo Cineplex Theatre*	Avda. Alfonso Ponce de Leon, 1	Malaga	ES	
IMAX Yelmo Cineplex Theatre*	Fernandez Ladreda	Oviedo-Asturias	ES	11-34-985-11-99-00
L'Hemisferic	Avda. Instituto Obrero de Valencia	Valencia	ES	3496-197-4600
IMAX Yelmo Cineplex Theatre*	Parque Comercial Megapark	Barakaldo-Bizcaia	ES	944-18-1672
SWEDEN				
Cosmonova	Frescativagen 40, P.O. Box 50007	Stockholm	SE	468-519-55130
SWITZERLAND				
IMAX Theatre	Lidostrasse 5	Lucerne	CH	4141-370-4444
TAIWAN				
IMAX 3D Theatre*	720 Chiu-Ju 1st Road 807	Kaohsiung	TW	886-738-00089
Space Theatre	1 Kuan Chien Road	Taichung	TW	8864-2322-6940
IMAX Dome Theatre	363 Kee-Ho Road	Taipei	TW	886-228-314-551
IMAX Theatre	66 Section 2 Chung Shang N. Road	Taipei	TW	8862-259-32211
Samsung IMAX Theatre*	No. 22, Jingye 3st Road	Taipei	TW	886-2-8502-2558
THAILAND				
Krung Thai IMAX Theatre*	1839 Pahnoyothin Road	Bangkok	TH	8866-625-115-555
TURKEY				
Arcelik IMAX Sinemasi	Migros Alieveris Merkezi	Ankara	TR	312-541-1333
IMAX AFM Istinye	Istinye Park AVM	Istanbul	TR	
UNITED ARAB EMIRATES				
IMAX Theatre*	Battuta Shopping Mall, Sheikh Zayed Rd	Dubai	AE	

DESTINATION CINEMA

4155 Harrison Blvd., Ste 201, Ogden, UT 84403. TEL: (801) 392-5881. FAX: (801) 392-2001.
email: infodci@destinationcinema.com www.destinationcinema.com

CEO
Bob Perkins - (310) 802-1138 - bperkins@destinationcinema.com

DIRECTOR OF ACCOUNTING
Paul Nielson

V.P. SALES &MARKETING
Murray Mold - (905) 651-9872 - mmold@destinationcinema.com

DIRECTOR OF BUSINESS DEVELOPMENT
John Markley

Theatre	Address	City	State/Province	Phone
U.S. THEATRES				
Grand Canyon IMAX Theatre	Hwy 64. 118, P.O. Box 3309	Grand Canyon	AZ	(928) 638-2468
Hearst Castle National Geographic Theater	P.O. Box 160, 100 Hearst Castle Road	San Simeon	CA	(805) 927-6811
Myrtle Beach 3D IMAX	1195 Celebrity Circle	Myrtle Beach	SC	(843) 448-4629
Niagara Adventure Theater	P.O. Box 1132, Prospect Park	Niagara Falls	NY	(716) 278-5040
CANADA				
Niagara Falls Theatre	6170 Fallsview Boulevard	Niagara Falls	ON	(905) 358-3611
National Geographic Theatre Victoria	675 Belleville Street	Victoria	BC	(250) 480-4887

MEGASYSTEMS

(Full-service provider of products and services for the large-format film industry)
A Division of Ballantyne/Strong, 4530 McKinley St., Omaha, NE 68112. TEL: (402) 453-4444. FAX: (904) 461-3546.
www.megasystem.com

CONTACT
Ron Lutsock - ron.lutsock@btn-inc.com

U.S. & PUERTO RICO THEATRES

Theatre	City	State
MegaDome at the Chabot Observatory	Oakland	CA
Muvico Pointe 21	Orlando	FL
Douglass Theatre	Macon	GA
Louisiana Arts & Science Center MegaDome	Baton Rouge	LA
MegaDome at Daily Living Science Center	Kenner	LA
Paulucci Space Theater	Hibbing	MN
Russell C. Davis Planetarium MegaSphere	Jackson	MS
Hastings Museum	Hastings	NE
Fleischmann Planetarium	Reno	NV
Strasenburgh Planetarium	Rochester	NY
Muvico Peabody Place 22 Theaters	Memphis	TN
USS Lexington MegaScreen Theatre	Corpus Christi	TX
Cook Center Planetarium	Corsicanna	TX
MegaDome at Central Texas College	Killeen	TX
The Super Screen at Jordan Commons	Sanoy	UT
Science Museum of Western VA MegaDome	Roanoke	VA
Sunrise Science Center & Art Museum	Charleston	WV
Caribbean Cinemas MegaScreen	San Juan	PR

INTERNATIONAL THEATRES

Theatre	City	Country
Movie Wonderland*	Changchun	China
City of Durham Millennium Project	City of Durham	England
Rheged: Upland Kingdom Discovery Center	Cumbria	England
The Palladium 4D Theatre in Thorpe Park*	London	England
Thessalonki Science Center	Thessaloniki	Greece
New Lineo Cinemas Israel	Tel Aviv	Israel
Warner Village Torri Bianche	Vimercate	Italy
LMegaDome at the Japan Science Center	Tokyo	Japan
Kreativum MegaDome Theatre	Karlshamn	Sweden
Akva MegaSphere Theatre	Pitea	Sweden

Specialty & Large Format Exhibitor Services & Equipment

The companies below provide equipment, construction, sound, projectors, etc. for large format and special venue exhibition.

ALCORN MCBRIDE INC.
3300 S. Hiawassee, Bldg. 105, Orlando, FL 32835.
TEL: (407) 296-5800. FAX: (407) 296-5801.
email: info@alcorn.com www.alcorn.com
CONTACT
Grace Warfield
COO
Jeremy Scheinberg

ARC LIGHT EFX
(Lighting, xenon source rental and sales)
9338 San Fernando Rd., Sun Valley, CA 91352.
TEL: (818) 394-6330. FAX: (818) 252-3486. www.arclightefx.com
OWNER & CEO
Greg Smith
CFO
Kary Smith

ARRI/CSC
(Full service film equipment rental company)
Camera Dept: An Arri Group Company, 619 W. 54th St., New York, NY 10019. TEL: (212) 757-0906. FAX: (212) 586-1756.
www.cameraservice.com
COO
Simon Broad - sbroad@cameraservice.com
V.P., OPERATIONS
Hardwrick Johnson - hjohnson@cameraservice.com
CAMERA DEPARTMENT MANAGER
Charles Tammaro - ctammaro@cameraservice.com

Lighting and Grip: 40 Hartz Way, Secaucus, NJ 07094.
LIGHTING DEPARTMENT MANAGER
Glenn Vanderlinden - gvanderlinden@ameraservice.com

BALLANTYNE STRONG INC.
(The source for all cinema and special venue projection applications; Projection equipment, concert spotlights)
4350 McKinley St., Omaha, NE 68112. TEL: (402) 453-4444.
FAX: (402) 453-7238. www.strong-cinema.com
www.ballantyne-omaha.com
PRESIDENT
John Wilmers
SENIOR V.P.
Ray Boegner - ray.boegner@btn-inc.com
SECRETARY TREASURER & CFO
Kevin S. Herrmann
V.P., OPERATIONS
Chris D. Stark

BOSTON LIGHT & SOUND
(Rental & dealer of film & video projectors & sound equipment; service & installation)
290 N. Beacon St., Boston, MA 02135. TEL: (617) 787-3131.
FAX: (617) 787-4257. email: info@blsi.com www.blsi.com
RENTAL MANAGER
Celine Larimer
FILM & VIDEO SYSTEMS MANAGER
Robert Harris

CHRISTIE DIGITAL SYSTEMS U.S.A., INC.
10550 Camden Dr., Cypress, CA 90630. TEL: (714) 236-8610.
FAX: (714) 503-3375. www.christiedigital.com
V.P., ENTERTAINMENT SOLUTIONS
Craig Sholder
SENIOR MANAGER, CINEMA
Keith Watanabe

Manufacturer & distributor of Digital Cinema projectors, film projectors; Xenon consoles, rewinds, bulbs; DLP® projectors & on-screen advertising solutions.

COBALT ENTERTAINMENT TECHNOLOGIES
12565 Strathern St., N. Hollywood, CA 91605.
TEL: (818) 759-5551. FAX: (818) 759-5553.
email: info@cobalt3d.com www.cobalt3d.com
FOUNDER & CEO
Steve Schklair
DIRECTOR, TECHNOLOGY
Bernie Butler-Smith

CREST DIGITAL
3845 E. Coronado St., Anaheim, CA 92807. TEL: (714) 666-2266.
FAX: (714) 666-8671. www.crestnational.com
www.crestdigital.com
CFO/COO
Eric Loong
CONTACT
John Walker

Ultrascan high resolution film to tape scanner for transfer of 65mm, 5, 8, 10, and 15-perf, and 35mm 8-perf Vistavision to HD5, digital and analog. Digital compression for V.O.D. Final cut Pro/Avid editing HD/SD.

DELUXE FILM SERVICES
7620 Airport Business Pkwy., Bldg. 4, Van Nuys, CA 91406.
TEL: (818) 756-2400. FAX: (818) 756-2401.
CONTACT
Debbie Mann - debbie.mann@bydeluxe.com

Print distribution & logistics; exhibitor services, trailer breakdown, trailer chase, theatrical print distribution; theatrical fulfillment with 29 locations nationwide.

DTS, INC.
(Provider of digital entertainment services for content owners and cinema exhibitors worldwide)
Corporate: 5171 Clareton Dr., Agoura Hills, CA 91301.
TEL: (818) 827-2200. FAX: (818) 879-7668.
www.dts.com

DTS Asia Unlimited, 2214-2215, Shell Tower Times Square, Causeway Bay Hong Kong. TEL: (852) 3101-9361, (852) 3101-9362. FAX: (852) 3101-9559.

DTS Canada ULC, 375 Water St., Ste. 638, Vancouver, British Columbia V6B 5C6. TEL: (604) 605-1525. FAX: (604) 605-1521.
CHAIRMAN
Dan Slusser
PRESIDENT & CEO
Jon Kirchner
EXECUTIVE V.P., FINANCE & CFO
Mel Flanigan
EXECUTIVE V.P. AND COO
Brian Towne
EXECUTIVE V.P., LEGAL GENERAL COUNSEL & CORPORATE SECRETARY
Blake Welcher
SENIOR V.P., RESEARCH & DEVELOPMENT & ENGINEERING
Rick Beaton
SENIOR V.P., HUMAN RESOURCES
Sharon Kong Faltemier
SENIOR V.P., STRATEGY & BUSINESS DEVELOPMENT
Patrick Watson

DOLBY LABORATORIES
100 Potrero Ave., San Francisco, CA 94103-4886.
TEL: (415) 558-0200. FAX: (415) 863-1373. www.dolby.com
CHAIRMAN & FOUNDER
Ray Dolby
PRESIDENT & CEO
Kevin Yeaman
SENIOR V.P. HUMAN RESOURCES
Andrew Dahlkemper
SENIOR V.P., CORPORATE DEVELOPMENT
Eric Cohen
EXECUTIVE V.P. AND GENERAL COUNSEL
Mark Anderson
EXECUTIVE V.P. & CFO
Murray Demo
EXECUTIVE V.P., SALES & MARKETING
Ramzi Haidamus
EXECUTIVE V.P., PRODUCTS & TECHNOLOGIES
Michael Rockwell
DIRECTOR MARKETING, MOTION PICTURE
Jim Farney
SENIOR DIRECTOR, CINEMA SALES, AMERICAS
Bobby Pinkston

DOLBY BURBANK
3601 W. Alameda Ave., Burbank, CA 91505-5300.
TEL: (818) 823-2800.
V.P., HOLLYWOOD FILM PRODUCTION
David Gray

DOLBY NEW YORK
1350 Ave. of the Americas, 28th Flr., New York, NY 10019-4703.
TEL: (212) 767-1700. FAX: (212)767-1705.
SENIOR DIRECTOR, PRODUCTION SERVICES
Bill Allen

DOLBY UNITED KINGDOM
Wootton Bassett, Wiltshire SN4 8QJ, England.
TEL: (44 179) 384-2100. FAX: (44 179) 384-2101.
SENIOR V.P., MANAGING DIRECTOR (UK)
David Watts
V.P., INTERNATIONAL SALES
Peter Seagger
V.P., CINEMA
John Iles

ELECTROSONICS
(Special-venue motion-picture projection applications)
3320 N. San Fernando Rd., Burbank, CA 91504.
TEL: (818) 333-3600. FAX: (818) 566-4923.
email: information@electrosonic.com www.electrosonic.com

EVANS & SUTHERLAND
(DIGISTAR 3 digital planetarium projection system, full-dome show production services)
770 Komas Dr., Salt Lake City, UT 84108. TEL: (801) 588-7405, (801) 588-7500. FAX: (801) 588-4520. www.es.com
DIGITAL THEATER SALES
Jeri Panek - jpanek@es.com

HARRAH'S THEATRE EQUIPMENT COMPANY
(Sound, projection, seating, draperies, screens, masking & design services)
25613 Dollar St., Unit #1, Hayward, CA 94544.
TEL: (510) 881-4989. FAX: (510) 881-0448.
CONTACT
Jerry Harrah

ISCO PRECISION OPTICS GMBH
Anna-Vandenhoeck-Ring 5, 37081 Göttingen, Germany.
TEL: (49 551) 505-83. FAX: (49 551) 505-8410.
email: info@iscoprecisionoptics.com
www.iscoprecisionoptics.com
CONTACT
Kathrin Ilse

Manufacturer of cinema projection lenses for all formats and projection types, DLP cinema, HDTV video projection lenses, LCD/DLP projection lenses, anamorphic attachments for 3-chip DLP and for LCD/DLP projectors.

OTTO NEMENZ INTERNATIONAL, INC.
(Camera rentals, Arriflex, Movie Cam, etc.)
870 N. Vine St., Hollywood, CA 90038. TEL: (323) 469-2774.
FAX: (323) 469-1217. www.ottonemenz.com
CONTACT
Fritz Heinzle

PACIFIC TITLE & ART STUDIO
(Optical and digital services)
6350 Santa Monica Blvd., Hollywood, CA 90038.
TEL: (323) 464-0121. FAX: (323) 461-8325.
www.pactitle.com
CEO
David Miller
V.P., SALES/PRODUCER
Rick Sparr

PEACE RIVER STUDIOS
(Equipment design)
9 Montague St., Cambridge, MA 02139. TEL: (888) 884-3686, (617) 491-6262. FAX: (617) 491-6703. www.peaceriverstudios.com
CONTACT
John Borden

Equipment design, motion-controlled camera support systems.

SHOWPERFECT, INC.
(Manufacturer of large format and special venue electronic projectors)
5260-C Bonsai Ave., Moorpark, CA 93021. TEL: (805) 517-1600.
FAX: (805) 241-7405. email: info@showperfect.com
www.showperfect.com
CONTACT
Charles W. Fox

SIMEX-IWERKS
(Specialized theatre manufacturing)
511 King St. W, Ste. 130, Toronto, ON Canada M5V 1K4.
TEL: (416) 597-1585. FAX: (416) 597-0350.
email: info@simex-iwerks.com
www.simex-iwerks.com

4520 Valerio St., Burbank, CA 91505-1046. TEL: (800) 388-8628, (818) 841-7766. FAX: (818) 840-6192.
PRESIDENT & CEO
Michael J. Needham
SENIOR V.P., OPERATIONS
Brian R. Peebles

3D/4D-seat/FX/Simulation/Large Format and Custom Special Venue Attractions, with 250 attractions installed in 30 countries.

SPITZ, INC.
(Supplier of spherical projection domes for use with large format film, planetarium and other multi-media theaters)
700 Brandywine Dr., P.O. Box 198, Chadds Ford, PA 19317.
TEL: (610) 459-5200. FAX: (610) 459-3830.
www.spitzinc.com
PRESIDENT & CEO
Jon Shaw
V.P., OPERATIONS
John Fogleman
DIRECTOR, SALES
Allen Wells
DIRECTOR, MARKETING
Scott Huggins
MEDIA DIRECTOR
Mike Bruno

THORBURN ASSOCIATES, INC.
(Acoustical Consulting and Audio-Visual System engineering and design for commercial, corporate, leisure, public and retail)
P.O. Box 20399, Castro Valley, CA 94546. TEL: (510) 886-7826.
FAX: (510) 886-7828. www.TA-Inc.com
CONTACT
Steve Thorburn

USHIO AMERICA, INC.
(Complete line of specialty and projection lamps)
5440 Cerritos Ave., Cypress, CA 90630. TEL: (714) 236-8600.
FAX: (714) 229-3180. email: customerservice@ushio.com
www.ushio.com
PRESIDENT & CEO
Kenji Hamashima

VISTAMORPH LTD.
35 Whitefield Rd., Govan, Glasgow, G51 2BY
Scotland, United Kingdom.
TEL: (07870) 899469, (0141) 445-6379
email: Vistamorph@aol.com www.vistamorph.com
CONTACT
Chris O'Kane

ACOUSTIC AND NOISE CONTROL WALL COVERINGS

ALPRO ACOUSTICAL SYSTEMS
(A Gordon, Inc. company. Perforated metal ceiling & wall panels and baffles)
5023 Hazel Jones Rd., Bossier City, LA 71111.
TEL: (888) 733-3836, (318) 747-8954. FAX: (800) 877-8746.
email: sales@gordonceilings.com
www.gordonceilings.com
SALES MANAGER
Craig Eychaner

AVL SYSTEMS, INC.
(Acoustical and noise control products for walls and ceilings)
5540 S.W. 6th Place, Ocala, FL 34474. TEL: (800) 228-7842, (352) 854-1170. FAX: (352) 854-1278.
email: info@avlonline.com www.AVLonline.com
PRESIDENT
J. Philip Hale
V.P., SALES
Marianne Mohr

BREJTFUS THEATRICAL INTERIORS
(Manufacturer & supplier of custom artistic sound panels)
410 S. Madison Dr., Tempe, AZ, 85281. TEL: (480) 731-9899.
FAX: (480) 731-9469. email: info@brejtfus.com
550 Front St., San Diego, CA 92101. TEL: (619) 813-6972.
www.brejtfus.com
PRESIDENT
Michael Regan

CLOUD INDUSTRIES, INC.
(Wall & screen drapery, curtains & film handling equipment)
P.O. Box 35, Lawson, MO 64062. TEL: (816) 296-3354.
FAX: (816) 296-7733. www.cloudindustries.com
OWNER, PRESIDENT & CONTROLLER
Mary Shoemaker - mary@cloudindustries.com
V.P., SALES
Chuck Shoemaker - chuck@cloudindustries.com
SALES CONTACT & WEB DESIGNER
Paul Shoemaker

Designer of stage & screen fronts, wall & screen drapery for remodels & new construction; manufacturer of film handling equipment, out of order seat covers & patented stadium seat anchor.

DECOUSTICS CINE-LINE
(Complete cinema acoustic panels for walls and ceilings)
65 Disco Rd., Toronto, ON M9W 1M2, Canada.
TEL: (800) 387-3809, (416) 675-3983. FAX: (416) 675-5546.
www.decoustics.com

U.S. Office:
P.O. Box 615, Getzville, NY 14068-0615.
TEL: (800) 387-3809. FAX: (416) 675-5546.
DIRECTOR OF SALES & MARKETING
Michael Rosenblatt - mrosenblatt@decoustics.com
INTERNATIONAL SALES MANAGER
Carlos Ramirez - cramirez@decoustics.com

DURRA BUILDING SYSTEMS
(Acoustical walls and ceilings)
2747 State Hwy. 160, Whitewright, TX 75491.
TEL: (866) 364-1198, (903) 364-1198. FAX: (903) 364-1108.
email: contact@durra.com www.durra.com
SENIOR V.P.
Bob Brown

ENTERTAINMENT SUPPLY & TECHNOLOGIES, LLC.
4971 Van Dyke Rd., Lutz, FL 33558. TEL: (813) 960-1646.
FAX: (813) 961-7209.
PRESIDENT & CEO
Barney Bailey
VICE PRESIDENT
Ron Eiben - reiben@ensutec.com
VICE PRESIDENT
Barb Cammack - bcammack@ensutec.com
SALES
Gary Wagner - gwagner@ensutec.com

Entertainment Supply & Technologies provides the following: Digital projection equipment, 35mm projection equipment, Xenon lamps, sound equipment, seating, aisle lighting, crowd control ropes & posts, poster cases, screens, frames & screen drapes, acoustical panels, concession & ticketing casework, concession equipment, 2-way radios, parts, supplies, light bulbs, janitorial equipment, turn-key project management, installations defixturing service, design, planning & drafting services.

EOMAC, LTD.
(Acoustic wall and ceiling treatments)
10 Perdue Ct, ON, Canada.
TEL: (866) 925-5797, (905) 970-8059. FAX: (905) 970-8067.
email: eomac@eomac.com www.eomac.com

EOMAC UK LIMITED
Unit 96 Silverbriar, Sunderland Enterprise Park (East), Sunderland, England SR5 2TQ. TEL: 44 (0) 191 5166550.
FAX: 44 (0) 191 5166551. email: eomac@eomac.com
www.eomac.com
CONTACT
Mark Elliott

Manufacture, supply, design and install fabric acoustic wall treatments, ceiling systems, front ends, masking winches and wall carpet.

FAY STUDIOS
(Wall drapery, wall carpeting, sound proofing, seating installations, custom front ends, screen frames and screen installations)
308 S. Linden Ave., Hatboro, PA 19040. TEL: (888) 326-5623, (215) 672-2599. FAX: (215) 689-4607.
email: walter@faystudios.net www.faystudios.net

G&S ACOUSTICS (GOLTERMAN & SABO), INC.
(Acoustical wall panels)
3555 Scarlet Oak Blvd., St. Louis, MO 63122.
TEL: (800) 737-0307, (636) 225-8800. FAX: (636) 225-2966.
email: inquiry@golterman.com www.golterman.com
V.P. & OPERATIONS MANAGER
Ned Golterman - ned@golterman.com

HYTEX INDUSTRIES
(Supplier of accoustical wallcoverings and drapery fabrics)
58 York Ave., Randolph, MA 02368. TEL: (781) 963-4400.
FAX: (781) 986-5956. email: inquiries@hytex.com
www.hytex.com
CONTACT
Rick Rigazio

KINETICS NOISE CONTROL, INC.
(Manufacturer of noise control products for all areas of the entertainment and exhibition industry)
6300 Irelan Place, P.O. Box 655, Dublin, OH 43017-3257.
TEL: (877) 457-2695, (614) 889-0480. FAX: (614) 889-0540.
email: sales@kineticsnoise.com
www.kineticsnoise.com
MARKET MANAGER, THEATRE MARKET
Chris Underwood - cunderwood@kineticsnoise.com

LBI/BOYD
(Acoustical panels & full range of wallcovering)
2275 Auto Centre Dr., Glendora, CA 91740. TEL: (800) 472-7891, (909) 592-1100. FAX: (909) 592-1700. www.lbiboyd.com
PRESIDENT
Mike Lyngle

MBI PRODUCTS
(Manufacturer of acoustical products)
801 Bond St., Elyria, OH 44035-3318. TEL: (440) 322-6500.
FAX: (440) 322-1900. email: sales@mbiproducts.com
www.mbiproducts.com
SALES MANAGER
Charlie Splain

MDC WALLCOVERINGS
(Acoustical wallcoverings)
1200 Arthur Ave., Elk Grove Village, IL 60007.
TEL: (800) 621-4006, (847) 437-4000. FAX: (847) 437-4017.
email: info@mdcwall.com www.mdcwallcoverings.com
EXECUTIVE VICE PRESIDENT
W. Michael Glynn

MELDED FABRICS
(Fabrics for trade shows and display booths)
3 Healey Rd., Dandenong Song, Victoria 3175, Australia.
TEL: 1800 069 539. FAX: (61 3) 9786 4975.

U.S. Distributor, Exhibition & Display:
Lockfast
8481 Duke Blvd., Mason, OH 45040. email: info@lockfast.com

Lockfast
2995 Cobb Intl. Blvd., Kennesaw, GA 30152.
email: sales@lockfast.com

Lockfast
Ste. H, 4724 Mitchell St., N. Las Vegas, NV 89031.
www.lockfast.com

PNC WEST, INC.
(Manufacture, design, install acoustical wall & ceiling panels)

255 N. Pasadena St., #1, Gilbert, AZ 85233.
TEL: (866) 265-4697, (480) 917-1999. FAX: (480) 926-6755.
email: sales@pncwest.com www.pncwest.com
PRESIDENT
Cheryl Van Meter

SOUNDFOLD
(Acoustical wallcoverings, wall carpet, surround speaker brackets, front end screens, frames and hardware)
9200 N. State Rte. 48, Centerville, OH 45458.
TEL: (800) 782-8018. FAX: (937) 885-5115.
email: kpierson@soundfold.com www.soundfold.com
PRESIDENT
Tony Sickels
FIRST V.P.
Thomas Miltner
OFFICE MANAGER
Kelli Pierson

SOUTHERN SCENIC EQUIPMENT CO.
(Theatre & stage drapery; theatre seat refurbishing; retrofit theatres to stadium seating)
1040 Branch Dr., Alpharetta, GA 30004. TEL: (770) 475-0733.
FAX: (770) 475-0910.
PRESIDENT
Ted Yarborough

TECTUM, INC.
(Noise control solution)
P.O. Box 3002, Newark, OH 43058. TEL: (888) 977-9691, (740) 345-9691. FAX (800) 832-8869.
email: wchester@tectum.com www.tectum.com
PRESIDENT
Mike Massaro
SENIOR V.P., SALES & MARKETING, TECHNICAL & CUSTOMER SERVICE
Wayne Chester
MARKETING MANAGER
Steve Udolph
ACCOUNTING / OFFICE MANAGER
Jeannette Clark
CUSTOMER SERVICE
Pam Lonca, Janis Clark

TRIANGLE SCENERY, DRAPERY & LIGHTING COMPANY
(Theatre drapery & rigging; acoustic curtains)
1215 Bates Ave., P.O. Box 29205, Los Angeles, CA 90029.
TEL: (323) 662-8129. FAX: (323) 662-8120.
email: tcmill@aol.com www.tridrape.com
OWNER & PRESIDENT
Terry Miller

TROY ACOUSTICS CORPORATION
(Acoustical materials; acoustical wall & ceiling treatments)
28358 Constellation Rd. #640, Santa Clarita, CA 91355.
TEL: (800) 987-3306, (818) 376-8490. FAX: (818) 376-8495.
email: TroyInfo@TroySoundWalls.com
www.troyacoustics.com
PRESIDENT
Bill Bergiadis
V.P., MARKETING & BUSINESS DEVELOPMENT
Joan Terry Drucker - joan.drucker@troyacoustics.com

WHISPER WALLS
(Acoustic fabric wall systems)
10957 E. Bethany Dr., Aurora, CO 80014. TEL: (800) 527-7817, (303) 671-6696. FAX: (303) 671-0606.
email: sales@WhisperWalls.com www.whisperwalls.com
VICE PRESIDENT
Brad Enter

AISLE, WALL AND MARQUEE LIGHTING

ACTION LIGHTING
(Custom theatre marquee lighting design & production)
310 Ice Pond Rd., Bozeman, MT 59715. TEL: (800) 248-0076, (406) 586-5105. FAX: (406) 585-3078.
email: action@actionlighting.com www.actionlighting.com
SALES
Don Smith

ALL CINEMA SALES & SERVICE
(A Division of East Coast Lamp Sales, Inc. Custom wall, step & aisle lighting sales & installation services, low voltage safety & ecorative lighting design, LED conversions for Cold cathode and neon systems)
120 Laurel Rd., E. Northport, NY 11731. TEL: (800) 628-5788.
FAX: (631) 754-2213. email: mail@allcinemasales.com
www.allcinemasales.com
CONTACT
Jim Kelly - Jim@allcinemasales.com

ATLAS SPECIALTY LIGHTING
(Entertainment lighting, projection equipment, digital sound systems & digital cinema equipment)
1111 West 22nd St., Hialeah, FL 33010. TEL: (305) 885-8941.
FAX: (305) 885-8941. www.asltg.com
MANAGERS
Ralph Felten, Jr. - rfelten@asltg2.com
Bob Ray

CALIFORNIA ACCENT LIGHTING, INC.
(Step, wall and aisle lighting)
2034 E. Lincoln Ave., #431, Anaheim, CA 92806.
TEL: (714) 535-7900. FAX: (714) 535-7902.
email: info@CaliLighting.com sales@CaliLighting.com
www.calilighting.com
NATIONAL SALES MANAGER
Jaime Nunez

CELESTIAL LIGHTING
(Architectural and decorative theatre and casino lighting)
14009 Dinard Ave., Santa Fe Springs, CA 90670.
TEL: (800) 233-3563, (562) 802-8811. FAX: (562) 802-2882.
www.celestiallighting.com
PRESIDENT
Tak Shimada - tak@celestiallighting.com
QUOTATIONS & PROJECT MANAGER
Cecil Powers - cecil@celestiallighting.com
PURCHASING & OPERATIONS MANAGER
Miguel Martinez - miguel@celestiallighting.com
ADMINISTRATIVE ASSISTANT
Stephanie Bouman - stephanie@celestiallighting.com

CINEMA LIGHTING CORPORATION
(Specializing in aisle lighting, wall carpet, floor carpet, VCT, wall paper and ceramic tile installations for the theatre industry)
119 Southeast Pkwy. Ct., Ste. 200, Franklin, TN 37064.
TEL: (615) 599-1266. FAX: (615) 599-1236.
email: steven@cinemalighting.com
CEO
Kirk Campbell
PRESIDENT
Steven C. Strobel

CLACO EQUIPMENT AND SERVICE, INC.
(Drapery systems, theatre chairs, complete digital & film projection, sound, auditorium equipment & service)
1212 S. State St., Salt Lake City, UT 84111. TEL: (801) 355-1250.
FAX: (801) 355-1259. email: sales@clacoequipment.com
www.clacoequipment.com
PRESIDENT
Clayton Stauffer
SALES
Eric Butterworth
SERVICE
Vince Butler

DAVID TYSON LIGHTING, INC.
(Long-life lighting for theatres)
5515 St. Augustine Rd., Jacksonville, FL 32207.
TEL: (800) 385-3148, (904) 730-5119. FAX: (800) 385-3149, (904) 730-5105. www.movietheatrelighting.com
CONTACT
David or Donna Tyson - David@davidtyson.com

EMERGENCY LIGHTING SERVICES, INC.
(Emergency lighting & exit signs, supply & repair; repair, preventive maintenance contracts)
150 Brookside Rd., Waterbury, CT 06708.
TEL: (800) 225-0263. FAX: (203) 596-8991.
email: Ltgservinc@aol.com
SALES
Dave Cordeau - Cordeau@lightingservicesinc.net

ENTERTAINMENT SUPPLY & TECHNOLOGIES, LLC
4971 Van Dyke Rd., Lutz, FL 33558. TEL: (813) 960-1646.
FAX: (813) 961-7209.
PRESIDENT & CEO
Barney Bailey
VICE PRESIDENT
Ron Eiben - reiben@ensutec.com

Entertainment Supply & Technologies provides the following: Digital projection equipment, 35mm projection equipment, Xenon lamps, sound equipment, seating, aisle lighting, crowd control ropes & posts, poster cases, screens, frames & screen drapes, acoustical panels, concession & ticketing casework, concession equipment, 2-way radios, parts, supplies, janitorial equipment, turn-key project management, installations, defixturing service, design, planning & drafting services.

ENTERTAINMENT VENTURES INTERNATIONAL
(Film, TV, music & video production, promotion & packaging, themed entertainment concept design & creation services)
928 N. San Vicente Blvd., Ste. 110, W. Hollywood, CA 90069.
TEL: (310) 278-2800. FAX: (310) 274-0400.
email: entventint@cs.com
DIRECTOR, OPERATIONS
Jim Beatty

V.P., OPERATIONS
Karenbeth Cantrell
FILM & TV PACKAGING
Mark Gregory
PUBLIC RELATIONS
Joyce Miller-Angus

FULL COMPASS SYSTEMS, LTD.

(Audio, video and lighting; sales, repair, and rental services)
9770 Silicon Prairie Pkwy., WI 53593. TEL: (800) 356-5844, (608) 831-7330. FAX: (608) 831-6330.
email: customerservice@fullcompass.com
www.fullcompass.com
NATIONAL SALES MANAGER
Jon Vitale

HIGH END SYSTEMS, INC.

(Automated lighting. See website for U.S. sales reps information)
2105 Gracy Farms Ln., Austin, TX 78758. TEL: (800) 890-8989, (512) 836-2242. FAX: (512) 837-5290. www.highend.com
V.P., WORLDWIDE SALES
Jeff Pelzl - jeff_pelzl@highend.com
SALES & SERVICE OPERATIONS
Betsy Childers - betsy_childers@highend.com

LEHIGH ELECTRIC PRODUCTS

(Manufacturer of lighting and dimming controls)
6265 Hamilton Blvd., Allentown, PA 18106. TEL: (610) 395-3386.
FAX: (610) 395-7735. www.lehighdim.com
PRESIDENT
Lloyd H. Jones
SALES
Demitry Herman - demitry@lehighdim.com
CUSTOMER SUPPORT
April Ziminisky - aprilz@lehighdim.com
WESTERN REGIONAL CONTACT
Roy Frandsen - (801) 465-8338 - rfrandsen@lehighdim.com
EASTERN REGIONAL CONTACT
Damian Delaney - (201) 692-8530 - ddelaney@lehighdim.com

LIGHT BULB DISTRIBUTOR.COM

120 Laurel Rd., E. Northport, NY 11731.
TEL: (631) 754-5655. FAX: (631) 754-2213.
email: mail@lightbulbdistributor.com
www.lightbulbdistributor.com
PRESIDENT
James Kelly
VICE PRESIDENT
Thomas Kelly
SALES
Sean Kelly

Commercial lighting fixture packages designed for end users; Decorative dimmable LED lighting conversions and the latest in energy saving and full spectrum light bulbs. Also sells general purpose and long life light bulbs.

LIGHTING & ELECTRONIC DESIGN, INC. (LED)

141 Cassia Way, Unit C, Henderson, NV 89014.
TEL: (800) 700-5483. FAX: (702) 568-8753.
email: mail@ledlinc.com www.ledlinc.com
PRESIDENT
Janie Lynn - janiel@ledlinc.com
DESIGN ENGINEER
Jerry Laidman

Aisle and step lighting, LED retrofit bulbs, decorative and concession lighting and signage.

MICA LIGHTING COMPANY, INC.

(Fiber optic aisle, step lighting systems; fiber optic ceilings and graphics)
717 S. State College Blvd., Ste. L, Fullerton, CA 92831.
TEL: (877) 761-7777, (714) 738-8448. FAX: (714) 738-7748.
email: info@micalighting.com www.micalighting.com
PRESIDENT
Gayle von Eissler

PASKAL LIGHTING AND GRIP

(Specializes in all types of lighting, grip, packages & trucking for the movie industry)
12685 Van Nuys Blvd., Pacoima, CA 91331.
TEL: (818) 896-5233. FAX: (818) 485-0157.
www.paskal.com

Louisiana Office: Paskal Lighting, 9595 Mansfield Rd., #302, Shreveport, LA 71118. TEL: (318) 682-5660.
FAX: (318) 682-5661.
OWNER & PRESIDENT
Evan Green
OPERATIONS MANAGER
David Miranda - davem@paskal.com
RENTAL MANAGER
Chris Nadal - chris@paskal.com
MARKETING MANAGER
Richard Pilla

PERMLIGHT PRODUCTS

(Decorative lighting, LED aisle lighting, LED wall lighting, LED step lighting)
422 W. Sixth St., Tustin, CA 92780. TEL: (714) 508-0729.
FAX: (714) 508-0920. www.permlight.com
V.P., NORTH AMERICAN SALES
William Hamm

QUALITY INSTALLATIONS

(Installation of aisle, wall and step lighting, seating, wall panels, drapes, wall & floor carpet & screens)
215 E. Orangethorpe, Ste. 327, Fullerton, CA 92832.
TEL: (714) 491-3883. FAX: (714) 491-7514.
email: sales@qualityinstallations.org
www.qualityinstallations.org
CONTACT
David Gutierrez

STRONG CINEMA PRODUCTS

(A Ballantyne of Omaha Co.)
4350 McKinley St., Omaha, NE 68112. TEL: (402) 453-4444.
FAX: (402) 453-7238. www.strong-cinema.com
www.ballantyne-omaha.com
PRESIDENT & CEO
John P. Wilmers
V.P., LIGHTING
Paul Rabinovitz
GENERAL MANAGER, STRONG/MDI Screens, Inc.
Benoit Mailloux
V.P., STRONG TECHNICAL SERVICES, INC.
John Biegel
SALES & MARKETING
Ray Boeener
OPERATIONS
Chris Stark

Strong Cinema Products offer 35mm and 70mm film projection equipment. Strong also helps bring motion picture exhibitors into the 21st Century through Strong Digital Systems, which offers complete solutions for the challenges of the evolving digital world. Strong Technical Services is dedicated to the design, installation, and service of the complete range of film and digital systems. Strong Entertainment Lighting provides lighting products and services that enhance visual experiences for audiences worldwide.

MPO INDUSTRIES

(Manufacturer of low-voltage step, aisle & wall lighting, specializing in movie theatres)
1961 McGaw Ave., Irvine, CA 92614. TEL: (949) 442-1601.
FAX: (949) 442-1609.
email: info@tempoindustries.com www.tempoindustries.com
INSIDE SALES
Jeff Hudgins
SALES MANAGER
John McAllister

TIVOLI, LLC

(Aisle & step lighting; microlamp (LED) linear lighting systems)
15602 Mosher Ave., Tustin, CA 92780.
TEL: (714) 957-6101. FAX: (714) 427-3458.
email: sales@tivolilighting.com www.tivolilighting.com
SALES
Memo Briseno

TUBE LIGHTING PRODUCTS

(Aisle & wall lighting specializing in low-voltage products)
1346 Pioneer Way, El Cajon, CA 92020. TEL: (888) 554-8823, (619) 442-0577. FAX: (619) 442-0578.
www.tubelightingproducts.com
OWNER
Rick Tempkin - rick@tubelightingproducts.com
GENERAL MANAGER
Michelle Royale - michelle@tubelightingproducts.com
NATIONAL SALES MANAGER
Pete Olson - pete@tubelightingproducts.com
OFFICE MANAGER
Eli Tapia - eli@tubelightingproducts.com

VISTA MANUFACTURING, INC.

(Incandescent and LED strip & seat lighting)
52864 Lillian Ave., Elkhart, IN 46514. TEL: (574) 264-0711.
FAX: (574) 264-4174. www.vistamfg.com
CONTACT
Theresa Beasley - theresa@vistamfg.com

WOLF THEATRE SERVICES

(A division of Michael Wolf Interiors, Inc.)
15 Daybreak, Irvine, CA 92614. TEL: (949) 733-8388.
FAX: (949) 733-8389. email: WolfFlow28@cox.net
screencleaner@cox.net www.wolfts.com
PRESIDENT
Michael Wolf
V.P., OPERATIONS
Ilan Wolf

Screen cleaning service; Front end, drapery and speaker installation. Also wall lighting, floor and wall carpet.

WULF INSTALLATIONS, INC.

(Aisle lighting and carpet installations for stadium & sloped-floor theatres)

3908 Seaford Rd., Seaford, VA 23696. TEL: (757) 874-3159.
FAX: (757) 874-3528. email: wulf@wulfinstallations.com
www.wulfinstallations.com
PRESIDENT
Karl Brian Wulf
VICE PRESIDENT
Amy Wulf

ARCHITECTURE, DESIGN AND CONSTRUCTION

AMERICAN CINEMA EQUIPMENT, INC.
(Projection, sound, digital projection & sound, engineering, project management, construction management & seats)
1927 N. Argyle St., Portland, OR 97217.
TEL: (800) 956-6589, (503) 285-7015, (916) 832-9510 (N. CA).
FAX: (503) 285-6765. www.cinequip.com
PRESIDENT
Scott R. Hicks - scott.hicks@cinequip.com
V.P., SALES & MARKETING
Doug Sabin - doug.sabin@cinequip.com

ARROWSTREET, INC.
(Large-scale commercial development projects)
212 Elm St., Somerville, MA 02144. TEL: (617) 623-5555.
FAX: (617) 625-4646. email: info@arrowstreet.com
www.arrowstreet.com
PRESIDENT & CEO
James P. Batchelor
COO
Kathleen E. Chainey
DIRECTOR OF MARKETING
Keri Drake
DIRECTOR, HUMAN RESOURCES
Mary Hickie

BEHR BROWERS ARCHITECTS, INC.
(Large-scale commercial buildings, specializing in motion picture theatres)
340 N. Westlake Blvd., Ste. 250, Westlake Village, CA 91362.
TEL: (805) 496-1101. FAX: (805) 494-1421.
email: bba@behrbrowers.com
www.behrbrowers.com
V.P. & DIRECTOR OF OPERATIONS
Andrew E. Althaus

BENCHMARK DESIGN GROUP
(Furniture for large-scale buildings)
456 Osceola Ave., Jacksonville Beach, FL 32250.
TEL: (904) 246-5060. FAX: (904) 246-9008.
www.benchmarkdesigngroup.com
PRESIDENT
Mark Carroll - mcarroll@benchmarkdesigngroup.com
VICE PRESIDENT
David Lasher - dlasher@benchmarkdesigngroup.com
NATIONAL SALES DIRECTOR
David McAllister - dmcallister@benchmarkdesigngroup.com
DIRECTOR, NEW PRODUCT DEVELOPMENT
Charles Swanson
CUSTOMER SERVICE CONTACTS
Sunny Carden, Jaclyn Ezelle, Alison Doyle, Luzette Gonzalez

BLAIR DESIGN & CONSTRUCTION
(Commercial buildings)
9712 Skillman, Dallas, TX 75243. TEL: (877) 889-0600,
(972) 889-0600. FAX: (972) 889-0660.
email: service@bdcdal.com www.bdcdal.com
VICE PRESIDENT
Richard Nelson - rnelson@bdcdal.com

CINEMA CONSULTANTS & SERVICES INTERNATIONAL, INC.
1250 Brookline Blvd., P.O. Box 9672, Pittsburgh, PA 15226.
TEL: (412) 343-3900. FAX: (412) 343-2992.
email: sales@cinemaconsultantspro.com
www.cinemaconsultantspro.com
PRESIDENT
Ross Falvo

Established in 1990. Specializes in theatre design, theatre consulting, projection & sound design/equipment, concessions design/equipment, interior design & installation of projection, sound seating & acoustic draperies.

CLASSIC ARCHITECTURAL PRODUCTS
(Architectural metal fabrication)
13020 FM 1641, Forney, TX 75126. TEL: (972) 564-2192.
FAX: (972) 564-2190. email: sales@classicusa.com
www.classicusa.com
V.P., BUSINESS DEVELOPMENT
Gary Byrd

COMMERCIAL BLOCK SYSTEMS, INC.
(Insulated concrete forms)
3520 Galaxy Park Place, Ste. A, W. Jordan, UT 84088.
P.O. Box 1477, W. Jordan, UT 84084. TEL: (888) 921-2480,
(801) 280-6607. FAX: (801) 280-5322.
www.commercialblock.com
PRESIDENT
Michael D. Schwab - mike@commercialblock.com
SALES MANAGER
Chris Herschlag - chris@commercialblock.com

CONSTRUCTION SOLUTIONS/STADIUM SEATING
(Large-scale construction, specializing in seating)
6799 Great Oaks Dr., Ste. 207, Memphis, TN 38138.
TEL: (901) 753-4009. FAX: (901) 752-0720.
OWNERS
Scott Reading, Paul Cartwright

DIMENSIONAL INNOVATIONS
(Specialty fabrication, architectual signage & design assist)
3421 Merriam Ln., Overland Park, KS 66203.
TEL: (913) 384-3488. FAX: (913) 384-1074. www.dimin.com
PRESIDENT
Jim Baker - jbaker@dimin.com
VICE PRESIDENT
Tucker Trotter - ttrotter@dimin.com
MARKETING COORDINATOR
Jennifer Corwin - jcorwin@dimin.com

ENTERTAINMENT VENTURES INTERNATIONAL
(Film, TV, music & video production, promotion & packaging; themed entertainment concept design & creation services)
928 N. San Vicente Blvd., Ste. 110, West Hollywood, CA 90069.
TEL: (310) 278-2800. FAX: (310) 274-0400.
email: entventint@cs.com
DIRECTOR, OPERATIONS
Jim Beatty
V.P., OPERATIONS
Karenbeth Cantrell
FILM & TV PACKAGING
Mark Gregory
PUBLIC RELATIONS
Joyce Miller-Angus

FIRST IMPRESSIONS THEME THEATRES
(Design & construction of in-home commercial and condominium theatres, CineLounger custom cinema seating)
12564 N.E. 14th Ave., North Miami, FL 33161.
TEL: (800) 305-7545, (305) 891-6121. FAX: (305) 891-7103.
email: sales@cineloungers.com www.cineloungers.com
PRESIDENT & CEO
Jeffrey W. Smith, C.A.S., A.S.F.D.

GOULD EVANS ASSOCIATES
(Architecture, Interior Design, Planning, Landscape Architecture and Graphic Design)
4041 Mill St., Kansas City, MO 64111. TEL: (800) 297-6655,
(816) 931-6655. FAX: (816) 931-9640.
email: info@gouldevans.com www.gouldevans.com
PRINCIPAL
Scott Stalcup, AIA
VICE PRESIDENT
Carol Martin - carol.martin@gouldevans.com

GRANGER CONSTRUCTION CO., INC.
165 Cedar Pointe Dr., Mooresville, NC 28117.
TEL: (704) 799-0300. FAX: (704) 799-0301.
email: Andrews@grangerconstructioncompany.com
www.grangerconstructioncompany.com
V.P., BUSINESS DEVELOPMENT
Daniel Andrews
BUSINESS DEVELOPMENT MANAGER
Don Kowell

Construction services provided in the Eastern U.S. from company's North Carolina and New York offices.

THE HENRY ARCHITECTS
(Full-service architectural and interior design for multiplex cinemas)
6203 Dayton Ave. N., Seattle, WA 98103. TEL: (206) 784-6964.
FAX: (206) 784-0837. email: henryarchitects@qwest.net
PRESIDENT
Rob Henry

INTERNATIONAL CINEMA EQUIPMENT
(Manufacturer and distributors of professional Motion Picture equipment for cinemas, studios, laboratories and theatres)
A Division of Magna-Tech Electronic Co., Inc.
1998 N.E. 150th St., North Miami, FL 33181-1116.
TEL: (305) 573-7339. FAX: (305) 573-8101.
email: iceco@iceco.com www.iceco.com
PRESIDENT & COO
Steven Krams
VICE PRESIDENT
Dara Reusch
V.P., INTERNATIONAL SALES & MARKETING
Julio Urbay
V.P., TECHNICAL SERVICES
Franscisco Blanco

ARCHITECTURAL DESIGN & DEVELOPMENT
Arturo Quintero

JOHNSON/MCKIBBEN ARCHITECTS
(Large-scale public buildings and movie theatres)
965 Slocum St., Dallas, TX 75207. TEL: (214) 745-7070.
FAX: (214) 745-1515. www.johnsonmckibben.com
PRESIDENT
Michael L. Johnson - michael@johnsonmckibben.com
VICE PRESIDENT
Gary D. McKibben - gm@johnsonmckibben.com

KMD ARCHITECTS
(All types of large-scale building design)
222 Vallejo St., San Francisco, CA 94111.
TEL: (415) 398-5191. FAX: (415) 394-7158.
email: info@kmd-arch.com www.kmdarchitects.com
DIRECTOR, INTERIORS
Juan Diego Perez-Vargas - juandiego@kmd-arch.com

LARGO CONSTRUCTION
(Movie theatre construction)
555 Street Rd., Bensalem, PA 19020. TEL: (800) 272-2432,
(215) 245-0300. FAX: (215) 638-7933.
V.P., THEATRE DIVISION
Jeffrey W. Spence

MARTEK CRS, INC.
(Design, manufacture & installation of custom casework & equipment for concessions, box office & lobby)
8500 Bellman, Shelby Township, MI 48316.
TEL: (586) 630-4100. FAX: (815) 301-8247.
email: info@martek-us.com www.martek-us.com
PRESIDENT
Mike Elliott - (586) 630-4100 - mike@martek-us.com

MESBUR+SMITH ARCHITECTS
(International architectural design consultancy for multiplex cinemas, entertainment complexes and shopping centers)
148 Kenwood Ave.,Ste. 100,Toronto, ON M6C 2S3, Canada.
TEL: (416) 656-5751. FAX: (416) 656-5615.
email: mail@mesbursmith.com www.mesbursmith.com
DESIGN PARTNER
David Mesbur - dmesbur@mesbersmith.com
MANAGING PARTNER
Harold Smith
PROJECT MANAGER
Ramin Moeini - rmoeini@mesbursmith.com

MICHAEL BRADY, INC.
(Architecture, construction management & 3D renderings)
299 N. Weisgarber Rd., Knoxville, TN 37919.
TEL: (865) 584-0999. FAX: (865) 584-5213.
email: mbi@mbiarch.com www.michaelbradyinc.com
CONTACT
Mike Brady

MONTAGUE DESIGN GROUP
(Entertainment interior design solutions)
205 Moss Hill Rd., Irving, TX 75063. TEL: (972) 831-1900.
FAX: (972) 831-8003. email: mdginc@earthlink.net
www.montague-design.com
PRESIDENT
Melissa Montague

OAKVIEW CONSTRUCTION, INC.
(General contractors for all types of large-scale buildings)
1981 G Ave., Box 450, Red Oak, IA 51566. TEL: (712) 623-5561.
FAX: (712) 623-9402. email: oakview@oakviewconst.com
www.oakviewconst.com
CHAIRMAN
Dick Bulkeley
PRESIDENT & CEO
Mike Gawley

PACIFIC CONCESSIONS, INC.
(Concession design; financing for remodeling, acquisitions & construction)
1150 Bayhill Dr., Ste. 220, San Bruno, CA 94066.
TEL: (650) 794-9494. FAX: (650) 794-9490.
email: info@pacificconcessions.com
www.pacificconcessions.com
PRESIDENT
Dan Livak

PARADIGM DESIGN
(Commercial buildings, specializing in movie theatres)
550 3 Mile Rd. NW, Grand Rapids, MI 49544.
TEL: (616) 785-5656. FAX: (616) 785-5657.
email: paradigm@paradigmae.com www.paradigmae.com
VICE PRESIDENT
William H. Brunner - wbrunner@paradigmae.com
MARKETING DIRECTOR
Cassie Ferris

POLLAVISION
1998 N.E. 150th St., North Miami, FL 33181.
TEL: (305) 898-5300. email: Larry@pollavision.com
www.pollavision.com
FOUNDER/PRESIDENT
Larry Polla

POLLAVISION is not an equipment supplier and is not associated with any sales firm. Focuses on designing the most effective technical solution for companies. Works in the areas of: theatre design, engineering & consulting. Provides: engineering drawings, architectural drawings, design room layout, acoustic analysis and design, provides equipment layout and wiring, integration engineering between equipment vendors, system checkout to confirm compliance to specifications, author request for proposals, equipment decisions, system calibration, installation supervision and site surveys.

PROCTOR COMPANIES
(Concession design, fabrication and installation of custom casework and equipment packages)
10497 W. Centennial Rd., Littleton, CO 80127-4218.
TEL: (800) 221-3699, (303) 973-8989. FAX: (303) 973-8884.
email: sales@proctorco.com www.proctorco.com
PRESIDENT
Bruce Proctor

PPR ENTERPRISES, INC.
190 Arovista Circle, Brea, CA 92821. TEL: (714) 529-7863.
FAX: (714) 529-1418. www.pprenterprises.com
VICE PRESIDENT
Pete Rasmussen - ext. 244 - Pete@pprenterprises.com
PROJECT MANAGER
Nicole Potter - ext. 245 - Nicole@pprenterprises.com

RANACK CONSTRUCTORS, INC.
(Design, build & retro-fit construction)
652 S. County Rd. 9E, Ste. 101, Loveland, CO 80537.
TEL: (970) 667-3698. FAX: (970) 667-3694.
email: info@ranack.com www.ranack.com
CONTACT
Doug Shirack - doug_ranack@lpbroadband.net

SIMEX-IWERKS
(Specialized theatre manufacturing)
511 King St. W, Ste. 130, Toronto, ON Canada M5V 1K4.
TEL: (416) 597-1585. FAX: (416) 597-0350.
email: info@simex-iwerks.com www.simex-iwerks.com
PRESIDENT & CEO
Michael J. Needham
EXECUTIVE V.P.
Shiori Sudo
SENIOR V.P., OPERATIONS
Brian R. Peebles

SimEx-Iwerks is a leading creator/developer of 3D/4D-seat/FX/Simulation/Large Format and Custom Special Venue Attractions, with 250 attractions installed in 30 countries. SimEx-Iwerks attractions combine state-of-the-art digital and film technologies with innovative programming.

STADIUM SAVERS, LTD.
(System for stadium construction and retro-fitting)
550 3 Mile Rd. NW, Grand Rapids, MI 49544.
TEL: (616) 785-5598. FAX: (616) 785-5657.
email: stadium@stadiumsavers.com www.stadiumsavers.com
CONTACTS
Dick Murphy, Dwight Huskey, William Brunner

STADIUM SEATING ENTERPRISES, INC.
(Design & manufacture of prefabricated stadium seating systems)
28202 Cabot Rd., Ste. 300, Laguna Niguel, CA 92677.
TEL: (949) 363-7128. FAX: (949) 363-0837.
www.stadiumseating.com
PRESIDENT
Frank B. Moson - frankmoson@stadiumseating.com
VICE PRESIDENT
Carol Lee - clee@stadiumseating.com

THX, LTD.
(Custom engineered cinemas)
1600 Los Gamos Dr., Ste. 231, San Rafael, CA 94903.
TEL: (415) 492-3900. FAX: (415) 492-3988. www.thx.com
V.P., SALES
Mary Crebassa
DIRECTOR, CINEMA STUDIO PROGRAMS
Andrew Poulain
MARKETING
Kristin Klindt
OPERATIONS
Jerry Zernicke

TK ARCHITECTS
(Specializing in entertainment facilities, cinemas & restaurants)
106 W. 11th St., Ste. 1900, Kansas City, MO 64105.
TEL: (816) 842-7552. FAX: (816) 842-1302.
email: tkapo@tkarch.com www.tkarch.com
PRINCIPALS
Tamra Knapp, Mike Cummings, Jack Muffoletto, Ian Wilson
PRESIDENT
Ted Knapp

ASSISTIVE LISTENING SYSTEMS

AUDEX, ASSISTIVE LISTENING SYSTEMS
(Infrared & other types of listening systems)
710 Standard St., Longview, TX 75604. TEL: (800) 237-0716.
www.audex.com
PRESIDENT & CEO
Charles Beatty - cbeatty@audex.com
V.P., SALES & MARKETING
Bill Shepard - bshep@audex.com
MANAGER PRODUCT DEVELOPMENT
Stroud Morton - smort@audex.com
OPERATIONS MANAGER
Brandon Beatty - branbeatty@audex.com
CUSTOMER SERVICES & SALES
Paula Davis - paula@audex.com

BOSTON LIGHT & SOUND
(Rental & dealer of film & video projectors & sound equipment; service & installation)
290 N. Beacon St., Boston, MA 02135. TEL: (617) 787-3131.
FAX: (617) 787-4257. email: info@blsi.com www.blsi.com
RENTAL MANAGER
Celine Larimer
FILM & VIDEO SYSTEMS MANAGER
Robert Harris

NADY SYSTEMS, INC.
(Assistive listening devices. Wireless, microphones, pro-audio)
6701 Shellmound St., Emeryville, CA 94608.
TEL: (510) 652-2411. FAX: (510) 652-5075.
email: ussales@nady.com www.nady.com
CONTACT
Ken Posey - ext. 239 - posey@nady.com

ODYSSEY PRODUCTS, INC.
(Infrared assistive equipment & support services; all types of booth equipment & supplies)
5845 Oakbrook Pkwy., Ste. G, Norcross, GA 30093.
TEL: (770) 825-0243. FAX: (770) 825-0245.
email: info@odyssey-products.com
www.odyssey-products.com
PRESIDENT
Eve Miller
CONTACT
Ken Reeves

PHONIC EAR
2080 Lakeville Hwy., Petaluma, CA 94954. TEL: (800) 227-0735, (707) 769-1110. FAX: (707) 769-9624.
email: customerservice@phonicear.com
www.phonicear.com www.gofrontrow.com

Kongebakken 9, DK-2765 Smørum, Denmark.
TEL: (45) 3917-7101. FAX: (45) 3927-7900.
email: mail@phonicear.com

SENNHEISER ELECTRONIC CORP.
1 Enterprise Dr., Old Lyme, CT 06371. TEL: (860) 434-9190.
FAX: (860) 434-1759. email: sec-media@sennheiserusa.com
www.sennheiserusa.com
PRESIDENT & CEO
John Falcone
V.P., MARKETING
Stefanie Reichert

Solution provider for electro acoustic. Wired and wireless microphone systems, infrared assistive listening systems and headphones.

SOUND ASSOCIATES, INC.
(Distributor of listening systems)
424 W. 45th St., New York, NY 10036. TEL: (888) 772-7686, (212) 757-5679. FAX: (212) 265-1250.
email: info@soundassociates.com www.soundassociates.com
INFRARED, SHOWTRANS & I-CAPTION SYSTEM SALES
Mark Annunziato - ext. 115 - mark@soundassociates.com
Steve Harris - ext. 114 - steveh@soundassociates.com

WILLIAMS SOUND CORP.
(FM and Infrared Hearing Assistance Systems)
10321 W. 70th St., Eden Prairie, MN 55344. TEL: (800) 328-6190, (952) 943-2252. FAX: (952) 943-2174.
email: info@williamssound.com www.williamssound.com
CONTACT
Kathy Callies

ATM MACHINES

ATM LENDERS, LLC
2483 E. Orangethorpe Ave., Fullerton, CA 92831.
TEL: (866) 837-5006. FAX: (714) 525-4576.
email: info@atmlenders.com www.atmlenders.com
ACCOUNT MANAGER
Kathy Perez - kperez@atmlenders.com

ATM ONE
(Div. of Voltage Management Systems)
2552 San Mateo Cir., Palm Springs, CA 92264.
TEL: (800) 489-6025. FAX: (760) 322-1000.
www.atmone.com
CEO
Steve Kirk
PRESIDENT
Eric Keating

GARDA CASH LOGISTICS
Head office: 1390 Barré St., Montreal, Quebec, H3C 1N4.
TEL: (514) 281-2811. FAX: (514) 281-2860.
www.gardacashlogistics.com
PRESIDENT, CASH LOGISTICS, U.S.
Richard Drutman

Provides comprehensive cash management services, including armored transportation, cash vault processing, ATM services, CashLINK cash management and EvenExchange change order services for banking and retail customers.

INNOVUS, INC.
5220 Spring Valley Rd., Ste. 350, Dallas, TX 75254.
TEL: (800) 753-2274, (214) 242-7674. FAX: (214) 242-7670.
www.innovusinc.net
PRESIDENT & CEO
Kevin Reager
CIO & COO
Christopher Schnieper
CFO
Brent Coles
SENIOR V.P., SALES
Dea Lukac

BOX OFFICE, CONCESSION AND ACCOUNTING SYSTEMS

These listings incorporate both hardware and software.

AIR LINK INTERNATIONAL
1189-A, N. Grove St., Anaheim, CA 92806-2110.
TEL: (800) 388-8237, (714) 632-3020. FAX: (714) 632-3621.
email: sales@airlinkint.com www.airlinkint.com
PRESIDENT
Frank "Sonny" Marchette
SALES
Dave Dratwa - ddratwa@airlinkint.com
SERVICE
Rick Blodgett - rblodgett@airlinkint.com

ARMOR SAFE TECHNOLOGIES, LLC
(Cash handling and cash management security systems)
Mailing Address: P.O. Box 560275, The Colony, TX 75056.

5201 S. Colony Blvd., Ste 110, The Colony, TX 75056.
TEL: (800) 835-6011, (972) 624-5734. FAX: (972) 624-5735.
email: service@armorsafe.com sales@armorsafe.com
www.armorsafe.com
REGIONAL SALES MANAGER
Charles Islas - (800) 835-6011 ext. 129 - cislas@armorsafe.com

BOINK SYSTEMS, INC.
3333 N.W., 21st St., Miami, FL 33142. TEL: (800) 462-6465, (305) 636-9993. FAX: (305) 468-6244. email: info@boink.com
www.boink.com
PRESIDENT
William Toro

Products feature The Perfect Attendant™ automated box office ticketing platform. Gives customers the ability to purchase tickets, concessions and watch previews in a simple, self-service environment. Platform handles all forms of payment including: cash, coins, credit, debit, flex passes, coupons and can even serve as an ATM.

CARDLOGIX CORP.
(Manufacturing & sales of Smart Cards; software for automated ticketing)
16 Hughes St., Ste. 100, Irvine, CA 92618. TEL: (949) 380-1312.
FAX: (949) 380-1428. email: sales@cardlogix.com
www.cardlogix.com
PRESIDENT & CEO
Bruce Ross

CINESTAR SOFTWARE
(Offers ticketing and concession software)
Ramon Fernandez, 265, Montevideo 11300, Uruguay.
TEL:(011) 598-2-7104676. FAX: (011) 598-2-7104676.
email: jlopez@cinestarsoftware.com
www.cinestarsoftware.com
INTERNATIONAL SALES MANAGER
Javier Lopez Jaumandreu

CLARITY COMMERCE SOLUTIONS, PLC
317 Inverness Way S., Ste. 140, Englewood, CO 80112.
TEL: (303) 649 9818. FAX: (303) 414-7805.
email: info@claritycommerce.com
www.claritycommerce.com

CEO
Ken Smith
SALES ACCOUNT MANAGER
Steve Bell

Centralized theatre management solutions including ticketing, concessions,hospitality, web, kiosk, handheld, inventory, promotions and much more. Clarity has clients in 19 countries across 5 continents, with multi-language solutions. Clients include: Cineworld/UGC, Crown, EuroPalaces, National Amusements, and Odeon/UCI. Clarity software is installed in 4 of the 5 largest European cinema groups.

Clarity Venue - the company's next generation ticketing and venue management software provides new ways of generating and measuring revenue. Clarity's ticketing and management software optimizes ticketing and concessions sales, lowers overheads, and manages the customer relationship.

GARDA CASH LOGISTICS

Head office: 1390 Barré St., Montreal, Quebec, H3C 1N4.
TEL: (514) 281-2811. FAX: (514) 281-2860.
www.gardacashlogistics.com
PRESIDENT, CASH LOGISTICS, U.S.
Richard Drutman

Provides comprehensive cash management services, including armored transportation, cash vault processing, ATM services, CashLINK cash management and EvenExchange change order services for banking and retail customers.

HOWELL DATA SYSTEMS

(Provide complete theatre solutions for box office, concession, and labor management)
84 Copernicus Blvd., Unit 4, Brantford, ON N3P 1K5, Canada.
TEL: (800) 410-6871. FAX: (416) 703-3627.
www.howelldatasystems.com
CONTACTS
Paul Schafer, Paul Howell

NIELSEN EDI

(Box-office tracking and analysis systems)
6255 Sunset Blvd., 19th Flr., Hollywood, CA 90028.
TEL: (323) 860-4600. FAX: (323) 860-4610.
www.nielsenedi.com
V.P., STRATEGIC RELATIONS
Alan deLemos - alan.delemos@nielsen.com
DIRECTOR, PRODUCT MANAGEMENT
Mike Marcell - mike.marcell@nielsen.com

OMNITERM DATA TECHNOLOGY, LTD.

2785 Skymark Ave., #11, Mississauga, ON L4W 4Y3, Canada.
TEL: (905) 629-4757. FAX:(905) 629-8590.
email: info@omniterm.com www.omniterm.com
PRESIDENT
Ed Coman - ecoman@omniterm.com
V.P., OPERATIONS
Greg Coman - gregcoman@omniterm.com
DIRECTOR, SALES & MARKETING
Darrin Lewis - dlewis@omniterm.com
DIRECTOR, I.T. & PROJECT MANAGEMENT
Mike Richards - mrichards@omniterm.com

Theatre Management Software (TMS) includes automated ticketing, concession point-of-sale (POS), automated box office (ABO) Kiosk, internet ticketing, loyalty, auditorium LCD signage, digital concession menu boards, box office showtime monitor, integrated restaurant, gift card and film settlement applications. Omniterm also has a complete line of hardware solutions for point-of-sale terminals, kiosks and displays. We strive to provide our customers with a "turnkey" solution, addressing all aspects of theatre automation and support.

RADIANT SYSTEMS, INC.

(Theatre management services for box office, back office, consumer-activated kiosk, ticketing, POS)
3925 Brookside Pkwy., Apharetta, GA 30022.
TEL: (877) 794-RADS, (770) 576-6000. FAX: (770) 754-7790.
email: inquiries@radiantsystems.com
www.radiantsystems.com
CEO
John Heyman
COO AND PRESIDENT, RETAIL DIVISION
Andrew S. Heyman
PRESIDENT, RETAIL AND ENTERTAINMENT DIVISION
Chris Lybeer
PRESIDENT, INTERNATIONAL DIVISION
Mark Schoen
PRESIDENT, SPORTS AND ENTERTAINMENT GROUP
Scott Kingsfield
V.P., HUMAN RESOURCES
Keith Hicks

RBS WORLDPAY

600 Morgan Falls Drive, Atlanta, GA 30350.
TEL: (800) 200-5965, (216) 333-1142. FAX: (216) 803-0500.
email: chad.gay@rbsworldpay.us www.rbsworldpay.us
SENIOR ACCOUNT MANAGER
Chad Gay

RBS Worldpay is a full-service provider of electronic payments including credit, debit, gift and loyalty cards.

READY THEATRE SYSTEMS

(Computer box-office ticketing & concessions software)
4 Hartford Blvd., Hartford, MI 49057. TEL: (865) 212-9703.
FAX: (707) 276-7222. email: sales@rts-solutions.com
http://rts-solutions.com

RETRIEVER SOFTWARE, INC.

2525 S. Broadway, Denver, CO 80210. TEL: (888) 988-4470.
FAX: (720) 570-1173. www.venue-pos.com
V.P., SALES
Phil Norrish - pnorrish@venue-pos.com

Touch-screen ticketing & concession systems, integrated theatre & labor management, film booking software, signage software, inventory control & reporting.

SENSIBLE CINEMA SOFTWARE

(Ticketing & concession inventory software; ticketing printers & blank ticket stock)
7216 Sutton Place, Fairview, TN 37062. TEL: (615) 799-6366.
FAX: (615) 799-6367. email: info@sensiblecinema.com
www.sensiblecinema.com
CONTACT
Rusty Gordon

SYSTEM OPERATING SOLUTIONS, INC.

(Sales, service & support of Pacer Ticketing & concession systems)
Shipping Address: 21504 108th St. SE, Snohomish, WA 98290.
Mailing Address: P.O. Box 1076, Monroe, WA 98272.
TEL: (800) 434-3098, (360) 805-1044.
email: sosticketing@comcast.net www.sosticketing.com
SALES
Kim

TICKETINGSYSTEMS.COM

1153 Inspiration Ln., Escondido, CA 92025. TEL: (760) 480-1002.
FAX: (760) 480-6830. email: sales@TicketingSystems.com
www.TicketingSystems.com
PRESIDENT
Bruce L. Hall
CHIEF TECHNICAL OFFICER
Brandon Hall
CHIEF SALES & MARKETING OFFICER
Charles Rock

POS Hardware & Software for "Touch" Ticketing, Concession, Internet Ticketing, Kiosk, Credit Cards, Gift Cards, Loyalty & Rewards Systems.

TICKETPRO SYSTEMS

(Boxoffice ticketing, concessions, LED signs)
205 Pointer Ln., Pearl River, LA 70602. TEL: (888) 627-8776.
FAX: (770) 271-2228. www.ticketpro.org
CEO
Norm Bumbieris norm@ticketpro.org
SALES
Willie Vandenheuvel

TITAN TECHNOLOGY GROUP

(Ticketing and concessions POS solutions provider)
145 W. 45th St., Ste. 603, New York, NY 10036.
TEL: (917) 777-0959. FAX: (917) 777-0961.
email: info@TitanTechGroup.com www.TitanTechGroup.com
BUSINESS DEVELOPMENT
Robert Schofield
MARKETING
Jessica Civitano
OPERATIONS
Christian Cole

TICKETPRO SYSTEMS

(Boxoffice ticketing, concessions, LED signs)
205 Pointer Ln., Pearl River, LA 70602. TEL: (888) 627-8776.
FAX: (770) 271-2228. www.ticketpro.org
CEO
Norm Bumbieris - norm@ticketpro.org
SALES
Willie Vandenheuvel

TITAN TECHNOLOGY GROUP

Ticketing and concessions POS solutions provider)
145 W. 45th St., Ste. 603, New York, NY 10036.
TEL: (917) 777-0959. FAX: (917) 777-0961.
email: info@TitanTechGroup.com www.Titan TechGroup.com
BUSINESS DEVELOPMENT
Robert Schofield

TRANAX TECHNOLOGIES, INC.

(Innovator of self-service technology; self-service ticketing)
30984 Santana St., Hayward, CA 94544.
TEL: (888) 340-2484, (510) 324-2224. FAX: (510) 324-2240.
email: sales@tranax.com www.tranax.com

VISTA ENTERTAINMENT SOLUTIONS

Howard Hughes Center, 6th Fl., 6080 Center Dr., Los Angeles, CA 90045. TEL: (866) US VISTA, (310) 242-6690.
FAX: (310) 242-5201. email: info@vista.co.nz

www.us-vista.com
CONTACT
Murray Holdaway

CARPET AND FLOORING

ARTISANS, INC.
716 River St., P.O. Box 1059, Calhoun, GA 30703.
TEL: (800) 311-8756. FAX: (706) 695-0291.
email: cpierce@marquisind.com www.artisanscarpet.com
CONTACTS
Cheryl Pierce

BONITZ FLOORING GROUP
(Unlimited flooring selection designed to meet your specific needs and goals. See website for additional flooring locations)
Georgia: 1650 Airport Rd., Ste. 110, Kennesaw, GA 30144.
TEL: (770) 952-4093. FAX: (770) 952-4942. www.bonitz.com
Tennessee: 5801 Middlebrook Pike, Knoxville, TN 37921.
TEL: (865) 588-3630. FAX: (865) 584-1452.
email: knoxville@bonitz.com www.bonitz.com
FLOORING SPECIALIST
Becky Roberts

BRINTONS LIMITED
(All types of custom & stock carpeting, commercial & residential, with locations around the world. See website for global contacts)
1000 Cobb Place Boulevard, Bailey Park, Ste. 200, Kennewaw GA 30144. TEL: (877) 332-9013.
email: jdodd@brintonusa.com www.brintonsusa.com

DURKAN CARPET
(Specializes in manufacture of patterned carpets)
405 Virgil Dr., Dalton, GA 30722.
TEL: (800) 241-4580, (706) 278-7037. www.durkan.com
REGIONAL MANAGER
Kerry Galloway
REPRESENTATIVE
Dean Gaffney - (706) 883-7379 dean_gaffney@mohawkind.com

EASTWEST CARPET PLUS, INC.
4406 S. Sepulveda Blvd., Culver City, CA 90230.
TEL: (310) 559-RUGS (7847). FAX: (310) 559-6357.
CONTACT
Larry Sperling

FRANKLIN DESIGNS
208 Industrial Dr., Ridgeland, MS 39157. TEL: (800) 467-0641, (601) 853-9005. FAX: (601) 853-9550.
email: franklindesigns@aol.com www.franklindesigns.com
PRESIDENT
Bobby Franklin
VICE PRESIDENT
Pam Franklin
Manufacturer and installer of custom draperies, cinematic frames, large format and standard screens; seats and wall carpet installation.

MASLAND CARPETS, INC.
(All types of carpeting)
716 Bill Myles Dr., Saraland, AL 36571.
TEL: (800) 633-0468, (251) 675-9080. FAX: (251) 675-6958.
email: gunterw@maslandcarpets.com
www.maslandcontract.com
V.P., NATIONAL ACCOUNTS
Don Dolan
V.P., HOSPITALITY
Paul Breland
MARKETING MANAGER
Wes Gunter

MILLIKEN FLOOR COVERING
(Manufacturer of patterned broadloom carpet & modular carpet)
P.O. Box 2956, LaGrange, GA 30241. TEL: (800) 528-8453, (706) 880-5511. FAX: (706) 880-5888.
www.Millikencarpet.com

OMEGA PATTERN WORKS, INC.
P.O. Box 1308, Chatsworth, Ga. 30705. TEL: (800) 241-4908.
FAX: (866) 375-8633. email: info@omegapatternworks.com
www.omegapatternworks.com
SALES
Kristin Messick - ext. 815 - kmessick@omegapatternworks.com

PROGRESSIVE FLOORING SERVICES, INC.
(Installation of carpet, ceramic, wood and aisle lighting)
100 Heritage Dr., Pataskala, OH 43062.
TEL: (887) 868-9005. FAX: (614) 868-9222.
www.progressive-flooring.com
CEO
Richard A. South
PRESIDENT
Richard J. South
V.P., GM
Nino A. Cervi

WOLF THEATRE SERVICES
(A division of Michael Wolf Interiors, Inc.)
15 Daybreak, Irvine, CA 92614. TEL: (949) 733-8388.
FAX: (949) 733-8389. email: WolfFlow28@cox.net
screencleaner@cox.net
www.wolfts.com
PRESIDENT
Michael Wolf
V.P., OPERATIONS
Ilan Wolf
Screen cleaning service; Front end, drapery and speaker installation. Also wall lighting, floor and wall carpet services.

CONCESSION EQUIPMENT

ALL-STAR CARTS AND VEHICLES, INC.
(Manufacturer of concession carts, kiosks, trailers & trucks)
1565 Fifth Industrial Ct., Bayshore, NY 11706.
TEL: (800) 831-3166. FAX: (631) 666-1319.
email: info@allstarcarts.com www.allstarcarts.com
VICE PRESIDENT
Bob Kronrad

AMERICAN CONCESSION SUPPLY, INC.
(Full line of concession equipment & supplies. Founded in 1987)
2450 Airport Blvd., Unit F, Aurora, CO 80011.
TEL: (800) 783-9337, (303) 361-9337. FAX: (303) 361-9531.
www.americanconcessionsupply.com
CONTACT
David Strum - dstrum@americanconcessionsupply.com

AUTOFRY
(Ventless, fully enclosed and automated deep-frying systems)
Sales: 10 Forbes Rd., Northborough, MA 01532.
TEL: (800) 348-2976. FAX: (508) 393-5750.
www.autofry.com www.mtiproducts.com

AUTOMATIC BAR CONTROLS/WUNDER-BAR
(Food dispensing systems)
790 Eubanks Rd., Vacaville, CA 95688. TEL: (707) 448-5151.
FAX: (707) 448-1521. email: sales@ wunderbar.com
www.wunderbar.com
PRESIDENT & CEO
Rick Martindale - rick@wunderbar.com
V.P., U.S. SALES
Ken Carlson - ken@wunderbar.com
V.P., CORPORATE SALES
Peter Costigan - petec@wunderbar.com

BAER AND ASSOCIATES
(Complete food service packaging)
TEL: (800) 444-8619.
CONCESSION SALES
Mike Ware - mike.ware@baerandassociatesinc.com

BEAVER MACHINE CORP.
(Bulk vending machines)
1341 Kerrisdale Blvd., Newmarket, ON L3Y 8Z8, Canada.
TEL: (800) 265-6772 (USA), (905) 836-4700 (Canada & Intl.).
FAX: (905) 836-4737. email: sales@beavervending.com
www.beavervending.com
MARKETING MANAGER
Heidi Schwarzli

BERRY PLASTICS
(Promotional plastic souvenir cups & other vessels)
101 Oakley St., Evansville, IN 47710.
P.O. Box 959, Evansville, IN 47706-0959.
TEL: (812) 424-2904. FAX: (812) 424-0128.
www.berryplastics.com
CHAIRMAN & CEO
Ira G. Boots

BRASS SMITH, INC.
(Fully adjustable food shield system. See website for sales contacts)
3880 Holly St., Denver, CO 80207. TEL: (800) 662-9595.
FAX: (303) 331-8444. email: sales@brasssmith.com
www.brasssmith.com
DIRECTOR OF MARKETING
Wayne Sirmons - wsirmons@brassmith.com

C. CRETORS & COMPANY
(Popcorn machines, peanut roasters, cotton candy)
3243 N. California Ave., Chicago, IL 60618.
TEL: (800) 228-1885, (773) 588-1690. FAX: (773) 588-2171.
email: Marketing@Cretors.com www.cretors.com
V.P., SALES & MARKETING
Shelly Olesen
MARKETING DIRECTOR
Beth Cretors

CHARITABLE VENDING, INC.
(Snack & drink machines)

8040 University Blvd., Clive, IA 50325.
TEL: (800) 454-2454. FAX: (515) 274-0390.
SALES
Bill Fankell - bfankell@wittern.com

CHART INDUSTRIES/MVE

Distribution & Storage Segment Headquarters: 1300 Airport Dr., Ball Ground, GA 30107. TEL: (770) 479-6531.
TEL: (888) 877-3093 (Cryogenic systems), (800) 247-4446 (Restaurant products customer service).
FAX: (952) 758-8293 (Cryogenic systems), (952) 758-8275 (Restaurant products customer service fax).
www.chart-ind.com

New Prague, MN, Office: Chart, Inc. 407 7th St. NW, New Prague, MN 56071-1000. TEL: (800) 428-3777, (952) 758-4484. FAX: (952) 758-8293.
CHAIRMAN
Samuel F. Thomas
PRESIDENT, DISTRIBUTION & STORAGE
Tom Carey

Chart/MVE beverage and bar equipment includes bulk CO_2 systems, nitrogen beer generators, bulk syrup systems, and CO_2 Monitoring systems. Chart's Carbo-Draught & Carbo-Series products are the preferred dispensing solutions.

CINEMA SUPPLY CO.

(Theatre equipment company)
502 S. Market St., Millersburg, PA 17061. TEL: (800) 437-5505. FAX: (717) 692-3073. www.cinemasupply.com
SALES
Robey Allman

CONCORDIA COFFEE SYSTEMS

(Manufacturer of Acorto brand espresso machine)
1287 120th Ave. NE, Bellevue, WA 98005. TEL: (800) 995-9019, (425) 453-2800. FAX: (425) 453-2167.
email: contactus@concordiacoffee.com
www.concordiacoffee.com
PRESIDENT
David Isett
V.P., SALES & MARKETING
Bill Dixon
V.P., SERVICE
Ray Ross
V.P., OPERATIONS
Wayne Stearns

ENTERTAINMENT SUPPLY & TECHNOLOGIES, LLC

4971 Van Dyke Rd., Lutz, FL 33558. TEL: (813) 960-1646. FAX: (813) 961-7209.
PRESIDENT & CEO
Barney Bailey
VICE PRESIDENT
Ron Eiben - reiben@ensutec.com

Entertainment Supply & Technologies provides the following: Digital projection equipment, 35mm projection equipment, Xenon lamps, sound equipment, seating, aisle lighting, crowd control ropes & posts, poster cases, screens, frames & screen drapes, acoustical panels, concession & ticketing casework, concession equipment, 2-way radios, parts, supplies, janitorial equipment, turn-key project management, installations, defixturing service, design, planning & drafting services.

FIRST VENDING PARTNERS

(Upscale candy displays)
1869 Best Dr., Walled Lake, MI 48390. TEL: (248) 960-0400. FAX: (248) 960-0003. www.firstvending.com
DIRECTOR, NATIONAL SALES
Robert Fidler - rfidler@firstvending.com

GOLD MEDAL PRODUCTS

(Concession equipment & supplies)
10700 Medallion Dr., Cincinnati, OH 45241-4807.
TEL: (800) 543-0862, (513) 769-7676. FAX: (800) 542-1496, (513) 769-8500. email: info@gmpopcorn www.gmpopcorn.com
SENIOR V.P.
John Evans, Jr. - johnevans@gmpopcorn.com
SALES MANAGER
Chris Petroff - cpetroff@gmpopcorn.com
INTERNATIONAL SALES MANAGER
David Garretson - djgarretson@gmpopcorn.com
V.P. SALES & MARKETING
Rob Tieman - rtieman@gmpopcorn.com

GOLDEN LINK, INC.

23 Horton Rd., Washingtonville, NY 10992.
TEL: (845) 497-7067. FAX: (845) 497-7167.
email:jwaaland@goldenlinkinc.com www.goldenlinkinc.com
PRESIDENT
Jeff Waaland
GLOBAL LOGISTICS MANAGER
Rob Rubin

INTERNATIONAL OFFICES:
Golden Link Europe, Ltd. / Tarnok St. 12, Budapest, Hungary 1014. TEL: +36 12253638 .
MANAGING DIRECTOR EUROPE
Alex Pekker - alex.pekker@goldenlink.eu

Golden Link Australia Pty Limited / Level 1, Bldg. 17, 122 Lang Rd. Entertainment Quarter, Moore Park, NSW Australia 2021.
TEL: +61 283541244 .
MANAGING DIRECTOR, AUSTRALIA/NEW ZEALAND
Kathy Hogan - khogan@goldenlinkinc.com.au

Golden Link Asia / 14, Kaki Bukit View, Kaki Bukit Techpark II, Singapore 415950. TEL: +65 9029 7346.
SALES MANAGER, SOUTHEAST ASIA
Georgina Soh - gsoh@goldenlinkinc.com

Global distributor of full line of concession equipment, supplies and packaging. Worldwide leader of licensed in-theatre film-related concessions promotions and originator of the famous Cup Toppers. Represents: C. Cretors and Co., ConAgra Food, LouAna Foods, Ricos Products, J&J Snack Foods.

HOSHIZAKI AMERICA, INC.

(Ice machines, refrigerators/freezers)
618 Hwy. 74 S. Peachtree City, GA 30269.
TEL: (800) 438-6087, (770) 487-2331.
email: marketing@hoshizaki.com www.hoshizakiamerica.com
SENIOR MARKETING MANAGER
Julie Hausmann
MARKETING REPRESENTATIVE
Michele LeBlanc

IMI CORNELIUS, INC.

(Manufacturer of beverage & ice-maker dispensers & slush machines)
101 Broadway St. W., Osseo, MN 55369. TEL: (800) 238-3600, (763) 488-8200. FAX: (763) 488-4298.
email: publications@cornelius.com www.cornelius.com
CONTACT
Tim Hubbard

INTEGRITY ENTERTAINMENT SYSTEMS

3010 Troy-Schenectady Rd., Niskayuna, NY 12309.
TEL: (518) 220-5002. FAX: (518) 220-5003.
PRESIDENT
Gary H. Engvold
CUSTOMER SERVICE REPRESENTATIVE
Tim Dolan

JARCO INDUSTRIES

(Concession equipment and crowd control; Online e-commerce store with over 10,000 items)
200 13th Ave., Unit 16B3, Ronkonkoma, NY 11799.
TEL: (800) 458-7578, (631) 738-1000.
www.concessionstands.com
PRESIDENT & CEO
Justin Stein

LANCER CORP., INC.

(Manufacturer of beverage & ice dispensers)
6655 Lancer Blvd., San Antonio, TX 78219.
TEL: (800) 729-1500, (210) 310-7000. FAX: (210) 310-7242.
www.lancercorp.com
V.P. NORTH AMERICAN SALES
Dan Hunt - danhunt@lancercorp.com
V.P., NATIONAL ACCOUNTS
Vince Giblin - vgiblin@lancercorp.com
MANAGER, NATIONAL ACCOUNTS
Shane Colburn - scolburn@lancercorp.com

MAINSTREET MENU SYSTEMS

(Part of The Howard Company, Inc. Custom menu boards)
1375 N. Barker Rd., Brookfield, WI 53045. TEL: (800) 782-6222, (262) 782-6000. FAX: (877) 782-6515, (262) 782-6515.
email: info@mainstreetmenus.com www.mainstreetmenus.com
MARKETING MANAGER
Dawn Pankow

MANITOWOC FOODSERVICE

(Manufacturer of beverage dispensers, soda & beer systems)
2100 Future Dr., Sellersburg, IN 47172. TEL: (800) 367-4233, (812) 246-7000. FAX: (812) 246-7024.
www.multiplex-beverage.com
V.P., MARKETING
Dean Landeche

MARTEK CRS, INC.

(Design, manufacture & installation of custom casework & equipment for concessions, box office & lobby)
8500 Bellman, Shelby Township, MI 48316.
TEL: (586) 630-4100. FAX: (815) 301-8247.
email: info@martek-us.com www.martek-us.com
PRESIDENT
Mike Elliott - (586) 630-4100 - mike@martek-us.com

MICHAELO ESPRESSO, INC.

(Espresso machines & grinders; sales & service)
3801 Stone Way N, Seattle, WA 98103-8005.
TEL: (800) 545-2883, (206) 695-4950. FAX: (206) 695-4951.
email: mei@michaelo.com www.michaelo.com

DISTRICT SALES MANAGER
Bob Cappelletti

MIDDLEBY CORPORATION
(Fast-cook, nonvented ovens, including the TurboChef brand)
1400 Toastmaster Drive, Elgin, IL 60120. TEL: (847) 741-3300.
FAX: (847) 741-1689, (847) 741-0015.
www.middleby.com

NATIONAL MENUBOARD
(Lighted and magnetic menu boards)
4302 B St. NW, Ste. D, Auburn, WA 98001. TEL: (800) 800-5237,
(253) 859-6068. FAX: (253) 859-8412.
email: lorrie@nationalmenuboard.com
www.nationalmenuboard.com
MANAGER
Lorrie Gallagher

PACIFIC CONCESSIONS, INC.
(Concession design; financing for remodeling, acquisitions & construction)
1150 Bayhill Dr., Ste. 220, San Bruno, CA 94066.
TEL: (650) 794-9494. FAX: (650) 794-9490.
email: info@pacificconcessions.com
www.pacificconcessions.com
PRESIDENT
Dan Livak

PACKAGING CONCEPTS, INC.
(Concession packaging)
9832 Evergreen Industrial Dr., St. Louis, MO 63123.
TEL: (314) 329-9700. FAX: (314) 487-2666.
email: info@packagingconceptsinc.com
www.packagingconceptsinc.com
CEO
John J. Irace - jji@packagingconceptsinc.com
V.P. SALES
Tony Irace

Manufacturers of leak-proof popcorn bags, kid packs, and concession packaging. Exclusive representatives of Solo Cup Company to the theatre industry.

PROCTOR COMPANIES
(Concession design, fabrication and installation of custom casework and equipment packages)
10497 W. Centennial Rd., Littleton, CO 80127-4218.
TEL: (800) 221-3699, (303) 973-8989. FAX: (303) 973-8884.
email: sales@proctorco.com www.proctorco.com
PRESIDENT
Bruce Proctor

ROBINSON/KIRSHBAUM INDUSTRIES, INC.
(Manufacturer of beverage-dispensing equipment; water filtration)
261 E. 157th St., Gardena, CA 90248. TEL: (310) 354-9948.
FAX: (310) 354-9921.
email: support@rki-inc.com www.rki-inc.com
EXECUTIVE V.P.
Bruce Kirshbaum

ROUNDUP FOOD EQUIPMENT
(Antunes Foodservice Equipment, div. of Antunes & Co.
Manufacturer of commercial food equipment; gas pressure switches, pizza grills)
180 Kehoe Blvd., Carol Stream, IL 60188. TEL: (800) 253-2991,
(630) 784-1000. FAX: (630) 784-1650.
email: customerservice@roundupfoodequip.com
www.ajantunes.com
MARKETING
Tom Krisch

SANI-SERV
(Ice cream & beverage dispensers; see website for sales contacts)
P.O. Box 1089 / 451 E. County Line Rd., Mooresville, IN 46158.
TEL: (317) 831-7030. FAX: (317) 831-7036.
www.saniserv.com
PRESIDENT
Bob McAfee
MARKETING MANAGER
Kim Waggoner

SERVER PRODUCTS, INC.
(Restaurant & fast-food equipment)
P.O. Box 98, Richfield, WI 53076. TEL: (800) 558-8722,
(262) 628-5600. FAX: (262) 628-5110.
email: spsales@server-products.com
www.serverproducts.com
V.P., SALES & MARKETING
Ron Ripple - (262) 628-5639

STAR MANUFACTURING INTERNATIONAL, INC.
(Restaurant & concession equipment; hot-dog cookers, popcorn/nacho equipment)
P.O. Box 430129, 10 Sunnen Dr., St. Louis, MO 63143.
TEL: (800) 264-7827, (314) 781-2777. FAX: (800) 264-6666,
(314) 781-4344. email: info@star-mfg.com www.star-mfg.com
PRESIDENT & CEO
Frank Ricchio
V.P., SALES & MARKETING
Tim Gaskill

STEIN INDUSTRIES
(Candy display cases, concession stands, box offices, popcorn poppers & merchandisers, popcorn, nacho warmers, food court and liquor bars)
22 Sprague Ave., Amityville, NY 11701. TEL: (631) 789-2222.
FAX: (631) 789-8888. email: steininc1@aol.com
www.concessionbuilders.com
PRESIDENT
Andrew Stein
SERVICE
Andy Jinks

Stein Industries is the leading designer/manufacturer of concession stands theatre lobby fixtures and food service equipment throughout the world. Stein Industries will also custom fabricate, concession stands, popcorn poppers, popcorn warmers, box office and any related theatre lobby fixtures.

TAYLOR COMPANY
(A div. of Carrier Commercial Refrigeration, Inc.)
750 N. Blackhawk Blvd., Rockton, IL 61072.
TEL: (800) 255-0626, (815) 624-8333. FAX: (815) 624-8000.
email: info@taylor-company.com www.taylor-company.com
MARKETING
Tricia Bennett

Manufacturer of a complete line of frozen dessert, frozen beverage, and cooking equipment supported by a worldwide distributor organization.

VIVIAN OF ST. LOUIS
(Supplies concession stands & related equipment)
1529 Ocello Dr., Fenton, MO 63026. TEL: (800) 325-9517,
(636) 343-1220. FAX: (636) 326-2811.
email: info@viviancompany.com sales@viviancompany.com
service@viviancompany.com www.viviancompany.com
CUSTOMER SERVICE MANAGER
Bill Caruso - bcaruso@viviancompany.com

WESNIC
(All furnishings, interior and exterior)
6000 Bowdendale Ave., Jacksonville, FL 32216.
TEL: (800) 874-8558, (904) 733-8444. FAX: (904) 733-3736.
www.wesnic.com
DIRECTOR OF MARKETING
Bill Gilbert
WESTERN REGION CONTACT
Garrett Holick - (214) 515-9370 - gholick@wesnic.com
SOUTHEASTERN REGION CONTACT
Granger Marchman - (404) 231-4088 - gmarchman@wesnic.com
NORTHEASTERN REGION CONTACT
Sean Sherman - (800) 593-7642 - ssherman@wesnic.com

CROWD CONTROL

ALVARADO MANUFACTURING
(Quick Queue Retractable Belt Stanchions)
12660 Colony St., Chino, CA 91710. TEL: (800) 423-4143,
(909) 591-8431. FAX: (909) 628-1403.
email: information@alvaradomfg.com
www.alvaradomfg.com
NATIONAL SALES MANAGER
David Pierini

BOOTH SUPPLY WAREHOUSE, INC.
P.O. Box 93, Murfreesboro, TN 37133. TEL: (866) 403-6712.
FAX: (866) 856-4116.
SALES REPRESENTATIVE
Ron Purtee - ron@boothsupplywarehouse.com

Projection booth supplies; splicing tape & splicers; mylar leader, film cleaners, miniature lamps, xenon bulbs, Projection ports, Drive-In FM Transmitters, Crowd control-retractable belt systems.

BSI-CROWD CONTROL, LLC
(BSI-Crowd Control, beltway, retractable belt stanchion, traditional lobby-style post and rope)
4965 Jackson St., Denver, CO 80216. TEL: (877) 842-4184,
(303) 565-1670. FAX: (303) 565-1674.
www.bsi-crowdcontrol.com
SALES MANAGER
Tom Albyn - tom.albyn@bsi-crowdcontrol.com

CROWDCONTROLEXPERTS.COM
(Discount Crowd Control Stanchions)
Twin Discovery Systems, 169 Commack Rd., Ste. 370,
Commack, NY 11725. TEL: (631) 367-2005.
FAX (631) 980-4095. email: sales@crowdcontrolexperts.com

CROWN INDUSTRIES, INC.
(Ropes and stanchions for crowd control)
155 N. Park St., East Orange, NJ 07017. TEL: (800) 255-5678,
(973) 672-2277. FAX: (866) 200-5546.
email: help@gocrown.com www.gocrown.com
PRESIDENT
Hugh Loebner

Stanchions and ropes for crowd control, pipe & drape, brass

rails and brass fittings, aluminum easels, brass easels, pedestal tables and folding table legs.

ENTERTAINMENT SUPPLY & TECHNOLOGIES, LLC
4971 Van Dyke Rd., Lutz, FL 33558. TEL: (813) 960-1646.
FAX: (813) 961-7209.
PRESIDENT & CEO
Barney Bailey
VICE PRESIDENT
Ron Eiben - reiben@ensutec.com

Entertainment Supply & Technologies provides the following: Digital projection equipment, 35mm projection equipment, Xenon lamps, sound equipment, seating, aisle lighting, crowd control ropes & posts, poster cases, screens, frames & screen drapes, acoustical panels, concession & ticketing casework, concession equipment, 2-way radios, parts, supplies, janitorial equipment, turn-key project management, installations, defixturing service, design, planning & drafting services.

JARCO INDUSTRIES
(Concession equipment and crowd control; Online e-commerce store with over 10,000 items)
200 13th Ave., Unit 16B3, Ronkonkoma, NY 11799.
TEL: (800) 458-7578. www.concessionstands.com
PRESIDENT & CEO
Justin Stein

LAVI INDUSTRIES
Corporate headquarters: 27810 Avenue Hopkins, Valencia, CA 91355-3409. TEL: (888) 285-8605, (661) 257-7800.
FAX: (661) 257-4938. email: sales@lavi.com www.lavi.com
SALES EXECUTIVE
Scott Wigton

New York: 2 Geneva Rd., Brewster, NY 10509.
TEL: (888) 285-8605, (845) 278-1766. FAX: (845) 278-1765.
email: sales@lavi.com

Public guidance systems for entertainment establishments. Design and build architectural products that withstand heavy public use, while adding an aesthetic value.

LAWRENCE METAL PRODUCTS, INC.
(A Tensator Group Company. Guidance system products including portable posts, ropes, railings, turnstiles & gates)
P.O. Box 400, Bay Shore, NY 11706. TEL: (800) 441-0019,
(631) 666-0300. FAX: (631) 666-0336.
email: sales@lawrencemetal.com www.lawrencemetal.com
PRESIDENT
Michael Vogel
EXECUTIVE V.P., COMMERCIAL OPERATIONS
Richard Prigg
V.P., SALES & BUSINESS DEVELOPMENT
Nick Byrne

CURTAINS AND DRAPERY

AUTOMATIC DEVICES COMPANY
(Drapery controls and curtain tracks)
2121 S. 12th St. Allentown, PA 18103. TEL: (800) 360-2321,
(610) 797-6000. FAX: (610) 797-4088.
email: info@automaticdevices.com www.automaticdevices.com
PRESIDENT
John Samuels

CINEMA CONSULTANTS & SERVICES INTERNATIONAL, INC.
1250 Brookline Blvd., P.O. Box 9672, Pittsburgh, PA 15226.
TEL: (412) 343-3900. FAX: (412) 343-2992.
email: sales@cinemaconsultantspro.com
www.cinemaconsultantspro.com
PRESIDENT
Ross Falvo

Established in 1990. Specializes in theatre design, theater consulting, projection & sound design/equipment, concessions design/equipment, interior design & installation of projection, sound seating & acoustic draperies.

CLACO EQUIPMENT AND SERVICE, INC.
(Drapery systems, theatre chairs; complete digital & film projection, sound, auditorium equipment & service)
1212 S. State St., Salt Lake City, UT 84111. TEL: (801) 355-1250.
FAX: (801) 355-1259. email: sales@clacoequipment.com
www.clacoequipment.com
PRESIDENT
Clayton Stauffer
SALES
Eric Butterworth
SERVICE
Vince Butler

CLOUD INDUSTRIES, INC.
(Wall & screen drapery, curtains & film handling equipment)
P.O. Box 35, Lawson, MO 64062. TEL: (816) 296-3354.
FAX: (816) 296-7733. www.cloudindustries.com
OWNER, PRESIDENT & CONTROLLER
Mary Shoemaker - mary@cloudindustries.com
V.P., SALES
Chuck Shoemaker - chuck@cloudindustries.com
SALES CONTACT & WEB DESIGNER
Paul Shoemaker

Designer of stage & screen fronts, wall & screen drapery for remodels & new construction; manufacturer of film handling equipment, out of order seat covers & patented stadium seat anchor.

ENTERTAINMENT VENTURES INTERNATIONAL
(Film, TV, music & video production, promotion & packaging; themed entertainment concept design & creation services)
928 N. San Vicente Blvd., Ste. 110, West Hollywood, CA 90069.
TEL: (310) 278-2800. FAX: (310) 274-0400.
email: entventint@cs.com
DIRECTOR, OPERATIONS
Jim Beatty
V.P., OPERATIONS
Karenbeth Cantrell
FILM & TV PACKAGING
Mark Gregory
PUBLIC RELATIONS
Joyce Miller-Angus

FRANKLIN DESIGNS
208 Industrial Dr., Ridgeland, MS 39157. TEL: (800) 467-0641,
(601) 853-9005. FAX: (601) 853-9550.
email: franklindesigns@aol.com
www.franklindesigns.com
PRESIDENT
Bobby Franklin
VICE PRESIDENT
Pam Franklin

Manufacturer and installer of custom draperies, cinematic frames, large format and standard screens; seats and wall carpet installation.

S & K THEATRICAL DRAPERIES
(Draperies for large-scale public buildings)
7313 Varna Ave., N. Hollywood, CA 91605. TEL: (818) 503-0596.
FAX: (818) 503-0599. email: info@SKTheatricalDraperies.com
www.sktheatricaldraperies.com

Las Vegas: 2216 Armacost Dr., Henderson, NV 89074.
TEL: (702) 220-9301. FAX: (702) 220-9302.
PRESIDENT
Carmella Skogman - carmella@sktheatricaldraperies.com
SALES MANAGER
Damian Schmidt

TRIANGLE SCENERY, DRAPERY & LIGHTING COMPANY
(Theatre drapery & rigging; acoustic curtains)
1215 Bates Ave., P.O. Box 29205, Los Angeles, CA 90029.
TEL: (323) 662-8129. FAX: (323) 662-8120.
email: tcmill@aol.com www.tridrape.com
OWNER & PRESIDENT
Terry Miller

DIGITAL SOUND SYSTEMS

AMERICAN CINEMA EQUIPMENT, INC.
(Projection, sound, digital projection & sound, engineering, project management, construction management & seats)
1927 N. Argyle St., Portland, OR 97217.
TEL: (800) 956-6589, (503) 285-7015, (916) 832-9510 (N. CA).
FAX: (503) 285-6765. www.cinequip.com
PRESIDENT
Scott R. Hicks - scott.hicks@cinequip.com
V.P., SALES & MARKETING
Doug Sabin - doug.sabin@cinequip.com

BOSTON LIGHT & SOUND
(Rental & dealer of film & video projectors & sound equipment; service & installation)
290 N. Beacon St., Boston, MA 02135. TEL: (617) 787-3131.
FAX: (617) 787-4257. email: info@blsi.com www.blsi.com
RENTAL MANAGER
Celine Larimer
FILM & VIDEO SYSTEMS MANAGER
Robert Harris

CARDINAL SOUND & MOTION PICTURE SYSTEMS, INC.
(Digital sound systems; 16mm, 35mm, & 70mm film and digital projection equipment)
6330 Howard Ln., Elkridge, MD 21075. TEL: (410) 796-5300.
FAX: (410) 796-7995. email: cardinal@cardinalsound.com
www.cardinalsound.com
OFFICE MANAGER
Catherine Rockman

DOLBY LABORATORIES
(Dolby Laboratories develops & delivers products & technologies that make the entertainment experience more realistic)
100 Potrero Ave., San Francisco, CA 94103-4886.
TEL: (415) 558-0200. FAX: (415) 863-1373.
www.dolby.com
PRESIDENT & CEO
Kevin Yeaman

EXECUTIVE V.P., PRODUCTS AND TECHNOLOGIES
Michael Rockwell
SENIOR V.P., HUMAN RESOURCES
Andrew Dahlkemper
SENIOR V.P., SALES
J. Stuart Mitchell
SENIOR MARKETING DIRECTOR, DOLBY DIGITAL CINEMA
Page Haun

LOCATIONS:
999 Brannan St., San Francisco, CA 94103-4938.
TEL: (415) 645-5000. FAX: (415) 645-4000.

Dolby Laboratories, Inc.
475 Brannan Street, Ste. 300, San Francisco, CA 94107-5420.
TEL: (415) 357-7000. FAX: (415) 645-4000.

Dolby Laboratories, Inc. 3975 Freedom Circle, 4th Flr., Santa Clara, CA 95054. TEL: (408) 330-3300. FAX: (408) 330-3200.

Los Angeles Office / Dolby Laboratories, Inc.
3601 W. Alameda Ave., Burbank, CA 91505-5300.
TEL: (818) 823-2800. FAX: (818) 557-0890.
V.P., WORLDWIDE PRODUCTION SERVICES
David Gray

Pennsylvania Office / Dolby Laboratories, Inc.
1040 Stony Hill Rd. Yardley, PA 19067-5509.
TEL: (267) 757-2300. FAX: (267) 757-2301.

Brisbane Office and Factory / Dolby Laboratories, Inc.
175 S. Hill Drive, Brisbane, CA 94005-1272.
TEL: (415) 715-2500. FAX: (415) 715-2570.

New York Office / Dolby Laboratories, Inc.
1350 Avenue of the Americas, 20th Flr., New York, NY 10019-4703. TEL: (212) 767-1700. FAX: (212) 767-1705.
SENIOR DIRECTOR, PRODUCTION SERVICES
Bill Allen

Dolby Canada Corporation / 2985 Virtual Way, Bldg. 3, Ground Flr., Ste. 150, Vancouver, BC V5M 4X7 Canada.
TEL: (604) 216-0020. FAX: (604) 215-6900.

Dolby Laboratories, Inc. / United Kingdom / Wootton Bassett, Wiltshire SN4 8QJ, England. TEL: +44 1793 842100.
FAX: +44 1793 842101.
SENIOR V.P., MANAGING DIRECTOR (UK)
David Watts
SENIOR DIRECTOR, CINEMA SALES
Guy Hawley
V.P., STRATEGIC SALES
Tony Spath

See website for additional international locations.

DTS DIGITAL CINEMA, INC.
(A subsidiary of Beafort California, Inc., a company owned by U.K.-based Beaufort International Group)
9631 Topanga Canyon Place, Chatsworth, CA 91311.
TEL: (818) 401-4300. FAX: (818) 401-4329.
email: cinemainfo@dtsdcinema.com
www.dtsdcinema.com
DIRECTOR, BUSINESS DEVELOPMENT
Jason Vreeman
DIRECTOR, PRODUCT MANAGEMENT
J. Sperling Reich - sperling.reich@dtsdcinema.com
SOUND LICENSING AND CONTENT MANAGEMENT
post-production@dtsdcinema.com
THEATRE SYSTEMS AND INTEGRATION,
CINEMA EQUIPMENT INFORMATION
cinemainfo@dtsdcinema.com

Expert provider of digital entertainment services for content owners and cinema exhibitors worldwide. Digital cinema solutions, pre-show and lobby advertising systems, content prep and delivery services, digital booking systems, network management services.

THX, LTD.
(Custom engineered cinemas)
1600 Los Gamos Dr., Ste. 231, San Rafael, CA 94903.
TEL: (415) 492-3900. FAX: (415) 492-3988. www.thx.com
V.P., SALES
Mary Crebassa
DIRECTOR, CINEMA STUDIO PROGRAMS
Andrew Poulain
MARKETING
Kristin Klindt
OPERATIONS
Jerry Zernicke

EXHIBITOR SERVICES

1 BETTER, LLC
(Premiere full-motion, digital cinema on-screen advertising sales and production agency)
124 Osseo Ave. N, St. Cloud, MN 56303. TEL: (877) 723-8837, (320) 230-9140. FAX: (320) 255-8915. email: sales@1better.net
www.1better.net
PRESIDENT
John Engel - john@1better.net
CONTACT
Carol Engel - carol@1better.net

CENTRAL MOTION PICTURE SERVICE, INC.
4688 E. 29th Rd., Sandwich, IL 60548. TEL: (815) 786-6577.
FAX: (815) 786-6337.
PRESIDENT
Albert "Buck" Kolkmeyer

DATA QUEST, LTD.
(Theatre checkers, headcounts, mystery shopping, employment screenings, undercover operatives, investigations)
896 Beacon St., Boston, MA 02215. TEL: (800) 292-9797, (617) 437-0030. FAX: (877) 362-7272, (617) 437-0034.
email: info@dataquestonline.com www.dataquestonline.com
PRESIDENT
Russ Bubas
SENIOR V.P.
Tracey Turgeon - tturgeon@dataquestonline.com

FILMACK STUDIOS
(On-screen trailers & advertising)
223 W. Erie St., Chigago, IL 60654. TEL: (800) 345-6225.
FAX: (312) 427-4866. WWW.FILMACK.COM
PRODUCTION MANAGER
Robbie Mack - robbie@filmack.com

MOC INSURANCE SERVICES
(Insurance)
44 Montgomery St., 17th Flr., San Francisco, CA 94104.
TEL: (800) 951-0600, (415) 957-0600. FAX: (415) 957-0577.
www.mocins.com
PRESIDENT & CEO
Van Maroevich - (415) 357-9221
SENIOR V.P.
Steve Elkins - (415) 357-9222

NATIONAL CINEMEDIA
(On-screen advertising, alternative entertainment and events)
Headquarters: 9110 E. Nichols Ave., Ste. 200, Centennial, CO 80112-3405. TEL: (800) 828-2828, (303) 792-3600.
FAX: (303) 792-8800. www.ncm.com
ADVERTISING & PROMOTIONS:
TEL: (800) 727-3361. FAX: (303) 792-8800.
email: intheatre@ncm.com customerservice@ncm.com
www.ncm.com
CHAIRMAIN, PRESIDENT & CEO
Kurt C. Hall
PRESIDENT OF SALES & CHIEF MARKETING OFFICER
Clifford E. Marks
EXECUTIVE V.P. & CFO
Gary W. Ferrera
EXECUTIVE V.P. & CHIEF TECHNOLOGY & OPERATIONS OFFICER
Thomas C. Galley
EXECUTIVE V.P. & GENERAL COUNSEL
Ralph E. Hardy

National CineMedia, Inc. operates the largest digital in-theatre network in North America that allows advertisement, alternative entertainment and events distribution, utilizing its proprietary digital content network.

BRANCHES:
500 N. Michigan Ave., Ste. 1802, Chicago, IL 60611.
TEL: (312) 755-9773. FAX: (312) 755-9844.
SENIOR V.P. CENTRAL DIVISION SALES
Pam Biederman - (312) 245-5265 - pam.biederman@ncm.com

21700 Oxnard St., Ste. 640, Woodland Hills, CA 91367.
TEL: (818) 227-3720. FAX: (818) 227-3759.
SENIOR V.P., WEST COAST SALES
Doug Gellerman - (818) 227-3737 - doug.gellerman@ncm.com

450 Mission St., 5th Flr., San Francisco, CA 94105.
TEL: (415) 359-2826. FAX: (415) 359-2626.
CONTACT
Paige McBeath - paige.mcbeath@ncm.com

122 E. 42nd St., Ste. 511, New York, NY 10168.
TEL: (212) 931-8100. FAX: (212) 931-8135.
SENIOR V.P., EAST COAST SALES
Beth Hoff - (212) 931-8101 - beth.hoff@ncm.com

TECHNICOLOR CINEMA DISTRIBUTION
(Freight management, large format distribution & logistics)
3418 State Rte. 73 S, Wilmington, OH 45177.
TEL: (973) 383-6014. www.technicolor.com
CONTACT
Tony Butcher - tony.butcher@thomson.net

5491 E. Philadelphia St., Ontario, CA 91761.
TEL: (909) 974-2231.
CONTACT
Mary Nakagawa-Marti - mary.nakagawa@thomson.net

Provides marketing services, print management & other print services at the above locations.

MARQUEES, SIGNS AND DISPLAYS

ADAPTIVE MICRO SYSTEMS, LLC
7840 N. 86th St., Milwaukee, WI 53224.
TEL: (800) 558-4187, (414) 357-2020. FAX: (414) 357-2029.
www.adaptivedisplays.com
V.P., SALES
Bob Radder
CONTACT
Ben Sewell

Manufacturer of LED customer information display systems, used in a variety of Theatre applications including: Box Office, Lobbies, Auditoriums, & outdoor marquees. Call for a price quote.

BARCO, INC.
11135 Trade Center Dr., Rancho Cordova, CA 95670.
TEL: (916) 859-2500. FAX: (916) 471-6924.
email: Service.media.us@barco.com www.barco.com
V.P., DIGITAL CINEMA
Wim Buyens
V.P., DIGITAL CINEMA, NORTH AMERICA
Todd Hiddick
V.P., PROJECT MANAGEMENT
Carl Rijsbrack

High-performance large-screen display systems for theatrical presentations of digital content; screen advertising displays; post-production & outdoor display applications.

BASS INDUSTRIES
(All types of signage; marquees, lightboxes & boxoffice signs; display cases; cinema home accessories & novelties)
355 N.E. 71st St., Miami, FL 33138-6024. TEL: (800) 346-8575, (305) 751-2716. FAX: (305) 756-6165.
email: sales@bassind.com www.bassind.com
OWNER
Robert Baron
VICE PRESIDENT
Anne Baron
SALES
Sharon Stewart
MARKETING
Chris Vlaun
OPERATIONS
David Baron

BUX-MONT SIGNS, INC.
(Established in 1946. Fabrication & design, marquee letters at discounts; flags and flag poles)
221 Horsham Rd., Horsham, PA 19044. TEL: (866) 675-1040, (215) 675-1040. FAX: (215) 675-4443.
email: buxmontsigns@comcast.net www.buxmontsigns.com
OWNER
Michael Meritz

CUSTOM COLOR CORP.
(Graphic solutions for signage)
2650 N. Burlington, Ave., Kansas City, MO 64116.
TEL: (800) 821-5623, (816) 595-6800. FAX: (816) 595-6801.
www.customcolor.com
CONTACT
Brian Bailey

DAKTRONICS, INC.
(Computer-programmable LED information & video displays, LCD)
201 Daktronics Dr., P.O. Box 5128, Brookings, SD 57006.
TEL: (800) 843-5843, (605) 697-4000. FAX: (605) 697-4700.
email: sales@daktronics.com www.daktronics.com
CEO
Jim Morgan

DATA DISPLAY U.S.A
(LED signs)
5004 Veteran's Memorial Hwy., Holbrook, NY 11741.
TEL: (888) 352-7452, (631) 218-2130. FAX: (631) 218-2140.
email: salesinfo@ddusa.com www.datadisplayusa.com
CEO
Michael Welsh
CONTACT
Staci Shannon

ELECTRONIC CREATIONS, INC.
1153 Inspiration Ln., Escondido, CA 92025. TEL: (760) 480-1002.
FAX: (760) 480-6830. email: sales@TicketingSystems.com
www.TicketingSystems.com
PRESIDENT
Bruce L. Hall
CHIEF TECHNICAL OFFICER
Brandon Hall
CHIEF SALES & MARKETING OFFICER
Charles Rock

POS Hardware & Software for "Touch" Ticketing, Concession, Internet Ticketing, Kiosk, Credit Cards, Gift Cards, Loyalty & Rewards Systems.

ENTERTAINMENT VENTURES INTERNATIONAL
(Film, TV, music & video production, promotion & packaging; themed entertainment concept design & creation services)
Sunset Gower Studios, 1438 N. Gower St., Box 12, Hollywood, CA 90028. TEL: (310) 278-2800. FAX: (310) 274-0400.
email: entventint@cs.com
DIRECTOR, OPERATIONS
Jim Beatty
V.P., OPERATIONS
Karenbeth Cantrell
FILM & TV PACKAGING
Raya Markson
PUBLIC RELATIONS
Joyce Miller-Angus

FAST-AD, INC.
(Marquee letters for signage)
220 S. Center St., Santa Ana, CA 92703. TEL: (800) 451-1907, (714) 835-9353. FAX: (714) 835-4805.
www.fastadletters.com email: fastad@aol.com
PRESIDENT
Guy Barnes
SALES
Bridgette Barnes

GAMMA TECHNOLOGIES
(LED Displays)
20725 N.E. 16 Ave., # A-33, Miami, FL 33179.
TEL: (305) 650-8999. FAX: (305) 650-8812.
email: mail@gamma-tech.com www.gamma-tech.com
PRESIDENT
Shai Dinari

GEMINI, INC.
(Marquee lettering; Gemini Products are only sold through sign professionals & graphics resellers)
103 Mensing Way, Cannon Falls, MN 55009.
TEL: (800) 538-8377, (800) LETTERS. FAX: (800) 421-1256, (507) 263-4887. email: sales@signletters.com
www.signletters.com
ADVERTISING COORDINATOR
Patty Zimmerman

ILIGHT TECHNOLOGIES, INC.
(Offers unique non-alternative LED lighting solutions in a variety of options from straights, curves, to signs)
118 S. Clinton, Ste.370, Chicago, IL 60661.
TEL: (312) 876-8630. FAX: (312) 876-8631.
email: info@ilight-tech.com www.ilight-tech.com

IMAGE NATIONAL
(Electronic sign manufacturer)
16265 Star Rd., Nampa, ID 83687. TEL: (800) 592-8058, (208) 345-4020. FAX: (208) 336-9886.
www.imagenational.com
GENERAL MANAGER
Doug Bender

MAINSTREET MENU SYSTEMS
(Custom menu boards)
1375 N. Barker Rd., Brookfield, WI 53045. TEL: (800) 782-6222, (262) 782-6000. FAX: (262) 782-6515.
email: info@mainstreetmenus.com www.mainstreetmenus.com
MARKETING MANAGER
Dawn Pankow

MOVIEAD CORP.
(Supplier of title art, concession mylars, interior signs & displays; also custom printing and digital graphics)
3500 N. Andrews Ave., Pompano Beach, FL 33064.
TEL: (800) 329-4989, (954) 784-6767.
email: info@moviead.com www.moviead.com
CONTACT
E J Noah - ejnoah@moviead.com

MPO VIDEOTRONICS
(Videowalls; LED displays; electronic signage; digital menu boards)
Corporate: 5069 Maureen Ln., Moorpark, CA 93021.
TEL: (805) 499-8513. FAX: (805) 499-8206.
email: sales@mpo-video.com www.mpo-video.com
SALES
Rick Ayeroff

New York: 1623 Third Ave., Ste. 202, New York, NY 10128.
TEL: (212) 369-2400. FAX: (212) 369-5078.

Portland: 6400 S.E. Lake Rd., Ste. 211, Portland, OR 97222.
TEL: (503) 659-9868. FAX: (503) 659-9727.

MULTIMEDIA LED, INC.
(Electronic message displays)
1450 Hughes Rd., Ste. 200, Grapevine, TX 75254.
TEL: (817) 488-3180. FAX: (817) 488-3485.
www.multimedialed.com
CONTACT
Bob Sawler - bsawler@multimedialed.com

11370 Sunrise Park Dr., Rancho Cordova, CA 95742.
TEL: (888) 98-MMLED. FAX: (916) 852-8325.
email: webquotes@multimedialed.com

DIRECTOR OF MARKETING & INSIDE SALES
Daniel Wheeler - dwheeler@multimedialed.com

NATIONAL MENUBOARD

(Lighted and magnetic menu boards)
4302 B St. NW, Ste. D, Auburn, WA 98001. TEL: (800) 800-5237, (253) 859-6068. FAX: (253) 859-8412.
email: lorrie@nationalmenuboard.com
www.nationalmenuboard.com
MANAGER
Lorrie Gallagher

POBLOCKI SIGN COMPANY, LLC

(Marquees, signs, custom theatre cases and directories)
922 S. 70th St., West Allis, WI 53214. TEL: (414) 453-4010.
FAX:(414) 453-3070. www.poblocki.com
PRESIDENT
David Drury
VICE PRESIDENT
Mark Poblocki
GENERAL MANAGER OF SPECIALTY DISPLAYS
Marcus Higgins - mah@poblocki.com

SCHULT INDUSTRIES, LLC

(Manufacturer of all types of signs & displays)
c/o Schult Design and Display, 900 N.W. Hunter Dr., Blue Springs, MO 64015. TEL: (800) 783-8998, (816) 874-4600.
FAX: (816) 874-4607. email: info@schult.com www.schult.com
SALES
Robert Schult, Jeffrey Schult, Carol Harrison, Keith Schult

SUNNYWELL DISPLAY SYSTEMS

(Manufacturer of LED electronic signs)
3214 Producer Way, Unit B, Pomona, CA 91768.
TEL: (800) 322-0938. FAX: (208) 263-8834.
email: sunnywell@sandpoint.com www.sunnywell.com
HEAD, SALES
James Huang

The SunnyVision "Full Color Display!" This state-of-the-art display system produces color that jumps out to grab your potential customer's attention, and it holds it with crystal clear clarity.

TEXAS DIGITAL SYSTEMS

(Box office, lobby & auditorium LED signs; digital concession menu boards & box office/auditorium LCD's with POS interface)
400 Technology Pkwy., College Station, TX 77845.
TEL: (979) 693-9378. FAX: (979) 764-8650.
email: cinemasales@txdigital.com www.txdigital.com
CINEMA SALES MANAGER
Shawn Medlin - smedlin@txdigital.com

TICKETINGSYSTEMS.COM

1153 Inspiration Ln., Escondido, CA 92025. TEL: (760) 480-1002.
FAX: (760) 480-6830. email: sales@TicketingSystems.com
www.TicketingSystems.com
PRESIDENT
Bruce L. Hall
CHIEF TECHNICAL OFFICER
Brandon Hall
CHIEF SALES & MARKETING OFFICER
Charles Rock

POS Hardware & Software for "Touch" Ticketing, Concession, Internet Ticketing, Kiosk, Credit Cards, Gift Cards, Loyalty & Rewards Systems.

TRANS-LUX CORP.

(LED displays; indoor/outdoor programmable signs. See website for complete list of offices and contacts)
26 Pearl St., Norwalk, CT 06850. TEL: (888) 485-9669 (sales), (800) 243-5662 (human resources), (203) 853-4321.
FAX: (203) 229-0691. email: sales@trans-lux.com
www.trans-lux.com
PRESIDENT & CEO
Michael R. Mulcahy
SENIOR V.P., SALES
Thomas Mahoney
V.P., CORPORATE SALES
Gene Coyne

TRIMOTION

(Trimotion, internally lit three-sided rotating poster cases)
528 Palisades Dr., #118, Pacific Palisades, CA 90272.
TEL: (310) 230-8417. FAX: (310) 230-8418.
email: info@trimotion.com www.trimotion.com
CONTACT
Rick Clemens

WAGNER ZIP-CHANGE, INC.

(Manufacturer of letters for signage)
3100 Hirsch St., Melrose Park, IL 60160. TEL: (800) 323-0744, (708) 681-4100. FAX: (800) 243-4924.
email: sales@wagnerzip.com www.wagnerzip.com
VICE PRESIDENT
Gary Delaquila
NATIONAL SALES MANAGER
Jim Leone
MAJOR ACCOUNT EXECUTIVE
Bob Stanis

MISCELLANEOUS EQUIPMENT & SERVICES

BAY AREA CINEMA PRODUCTS

1025 Pine Meadows Ct, Martinez, CA 94533.
TEL: (925) 372-7603. FAX: (925) 372-7658.
email: bacp2000@aol.com www.bacpinc.com
PRESIDENT
Sam Chavez

Bay Area Cinema Products is both a manufacturer of cinema products and accessories and a full-line Sound and Projection equipment dealer, specializing in equipping industry screening rooms.

BOOTH SUPPLY WAREHOUSE, INC.

P.O. Box 93, Murfreesboro, TN 37133. TEL: (866) 403-6712.
FAX: (866) 856-4116.
SALES REPRESENTATIVE
Ron Purtee - ron@boothsupplywarehouse.com

Projection booth supplies; splicing tape & splicers; mylar leader, film cleaners, miniature lamps, xenon bulbs, Projection ports, Drive-In FM Transmitters, Crowd control-retractable belt systems.

BRADLEY FIXTURES CORP.

(Bathroom fixtures & accessories)
W142 N9101 Fountain Blvd., Menomonee Falls, WI 53051.
TEL: (800) 272-3539, (262) 251-6000. FAX: (262) 251-5817, (262) 251-0128. email: uscanadasales@bradleycorp.com
www.bradleycorp.com
MARKETING MANAGER
Jan Jewell

CAWLEY COMPANY

(Name badges)
1544 N. 8th St., Manitowoc, WI 54220. TEL: (800) 822-9539.
FAX: (920) 686-7080. www.thecawleyco.com
SALES REPRESENTATIVE
Ric Prucha - ricp@thecawleyco.com
SALES ASSOCIATE
Kristin Kiel - kristink@thecawleyco.com
TRADESHOW COORDINATOR
Heather Brey - heatherb@thecawleyco.com

CINEDIGM DIGITAL CINEMA CORP.

(Formerly Access Integrated Technologies, Inc. Company announced name change Nov. 2008)
Headquarters: 55 Madison Ave., Ste. 300, Morristown, NJ 07960. TEL: (973) 290-0080. FAX: (973) 290-0081.
email: info@cinedigm.com www.cinedigm.com

Digital Cinema Offices: 6255 Sunset Blvd., Ste. 1025, Hollywood, CA 90028. TEL: (323) 463-2144.
FAX: (323) 463-1319.
CHAIRMAN & CEO
Bud Mayo
PRESIDENT, MEDIA SERVICES GROUP
Chuck Goldwater
PRESIDENT & COO, SOFTWARE DIVISION
Jim Miller
PRESIDENT, COO, DIGITAL MEDIA SERVICES DIVISION
Gerd Jakuszeit
PRESIDENT & COO, UNIQUE SCREEN MEDIA, A CINEDIGM COMPANY
William A. McGlamery
PRESIDENT, PRESIDENT, CINEDIGM ENTERTAIMENT GROUP
Jonathan Dern
DIRECTOR, CORPORATE COMMUNICATIONS
Suzanne Moore - (973) 290-0056 ext. 181
smoore@cinedigm.com

Cinedigm provides digital cinema networked services along with its Library Management Server(R) and Theatre Command Center(R) to enable theatres across the United States to play digital showings of Hollywood features. The company's 24/7 satellite operations delivers feature movies, alternative content advertising, and pre-show entertainment, including live 2-D and 3-D events through its CineLive(R) satellite network, expanding box office sales and developing new ways to attract incremental revenues. Through its alternative content distribution division, the company offers channels of programming including Opera, Kidtoons, Faith-based Concerts, Sports and Anime.

CINEMA CONSULTANTS & SERVICES INTERNATIONAL, INC.

1250 Brookline Blvd., P.O. Box 9672, Pittsburgh, PA 15226.
TEL: (412) 343-3900. FAX: (412) 343-2992.
email: sales@cinemaconsultantspro.com
www.cinemaconsultantspro.com
PRESIDENT
Ross Falvo

Established in 1990. Specializes in theatre design, theater consulting, projection & sound design/equipment, concessions design/equipment, interior design & installation of projection, sound seating & acoustic draperies.

CINEMA EQUIPMENT & SUPPLIES, INC.
12457 S.W. 130th St., Miami, FL 33186. TEL: (800) 759-5905, (305) 232-8182. FAX: (800) 759-5914, (305) 232-6049.
email: sales@cinemaequip.com www.cinemaequip.com
CONTACT
Guillermo Younger

CON-KOR THEATRE EQUIPMENT, INC.
21 W. 748 Bemis Rd., Glen Ellyn, IL 60137. TEL: (847) 357-8598. FAX: (847) 357-8583. (Night phone) (630) 790-4050.
email: cakorose@aol.com
OWNER
Constantine "Connie" Korose

DANDY AMUSEMENTS INTERNATIONAL, INC.
2265 Ward Ave., Ste. C, Simi Valley, CA 93065.
TEL: (800) 860-7469. FAX: (805) 578-9370.

DURAFORM
(Waste & recycling receptacles, ash urns, benches)
1435 S. Santa Fe Ave., Compton, CA 90221.
TEL: (800) 823-1121, (310) 761-1640. FAX: (310) 761-1646.
email: website@centuryplasticsla.com www.duraformcpi.com
CUSTOMER SERVICES MANAGER
Rick Fingerhut

FANTASY ENTERTAINMENT
(Self-service photo kiosks)
8A Industrial Way, Salem, NH 03079-2837.
TEL: (800) 933-2682 ext. 162, (603) 324-3240.
FAX: (603) 879-9200. email: salesinfo@fantasyent.com
www.fantasyent.com
SALES
Stephen White
INTERNATIONAL SALES DIRECTOR
Keith Whitestone - kwhitestone@efotobooth.com

GENERAL THEATRICAL SUPPLY
(Complete theatrical & cinema equipment & supplies)
2181 W. California Ave. Ste. 250, Salt Lake City, UT 84104.
TEL: (877) 587-6742, (801) 485-5012. FAX: (801) 485-4365.
www.gtsmarketplace.com
SALES
Charlie Johnson - charlie@gtsmarketplace.com

GLASSFORM, A DIVISION OF VANTAGE
(Manufacturer of lobby trash receptacles, benches, ash urns, planters & recycling containers. Interior/Exterior use)
900 Civic Center Dr., National City, CA 91950.
TEL: (800) 995-8322, (800) 842-1121. FAX: (619) 477-2225.
email: info@glassformonline.com www.glassformonline.com
CONTACT
Angela Alpinieri

GOLDBERG BROTHERS, INC.
(Manufacturer of film shipping, booth & lobby equipment; also bowling machine replacement parts. Film-related memorabilia products including reel tables, reel clocks, reel wine racks, reel light fixtures and much more)
8000 E. 40th Ave., Denver, CO 80207. P.O. Box 17048, Denver, CO 80217. TEL: (303) 321-1099. FAX: (303) 388-0749.
email: golbroinc@aol.com www.goldbergbrothers.com
EXECUTIVE V.P.
Randall Urlik

GREAT WESTERN PRODUCTS CO.
(Manufacturer, processor, & distributor of high quality theatre supplies & equipment)
30290 U.S. Hwy. 72, Hollywood, AL 35752. TEL: (800) 239-2143, (256) 259-3578. FAX: (256) 574-2116.
email: info@gwproducts.com www.mycinemastore.com
PRESIDENT
Ralph Ferber - RalphF@gwproducts.com
NATIONAL SALES MANAGER
Mark Hamilton - MarkH@gwproducts.com

KOALA KARE PRODUCTS
(Child care products)
A Division of Bobrick, 6982 S. Wheeling Crt., Centennial, CO 80112. TEL: (888) 733-3456. FAX: (303) 539-8399.
email: info@koalabear.com www.koalabear.com
V.P. & GENERAL MANAGER
Brendan Cherry

LENNOX INDUSTRIES
(Air-conditioning. See website for contacts and office locations)
2100 Lake Park Blvd., Richardson, TX 75080.
TEL: (800) 953-6669, (972) 497-5000. FAX: (972) 497-5112.
www.lennox.com

MANUTECH MANUFACTURING AND DISTRIBUTING
(Manufactures high performance vacuums & blowers. Distributors of quality brand-name theatre cleaning equipment)
P.O. Box. 51295, 2080 Sunset Dr., Pacific Grove, CA 93950.
TEL: (800) 676-2569, (831) 655-8794. FAX: (831) 655-8967.
email: info@manutech.com www.manutech.com
PRESIDENT
Angelo Villucci

MIRACLE RECREATION EQUIPMENT COMPANY
(Specializes in outdoor playground equipment)
P.O. Box 420, 878 Hwy. 60, Monett, MO 65708-0420.
TEL: (800) 523-4202, (417) 235-6917. FAX: (417) 235-6816.
email: pete.babb@miraclerec.com
www.miracle-recreation.com

MODULAR HARDWARE
(Restroom & toilet partition equipment)
Mailing Address: P.O. Box 1889, Cortaro, AZ 85652.
6765 W. Ina Rd., Tucson, AZ 85743.
TEL: (800) 533-0042. FAX: (800) 533-7942.
email: sales@modularhardware.com
www.modularhardware.com
PRESIDENT
Robert Hotch

NAMCO AMERICA, INC.
(Amusement equipment, including video & coin-operated games, prize and ticket redemption and novelties)
951 Cambridge Dr., Elk Grove Village, IL 60007.
TEL: (847) 264-5610. FAX: (847) 264-5611.
www.namcoamerica.com
SALES
Tom Siemieniec - tsiemieniec@namcoamerica.com
Anita Friedl - afriedl@namcoamerica.com
SERVICE
parts@namcoamerica.com

NATION GLASS & GATE SERVICES, INC.
(Emergency repairs & security renovations)
263 Jenckes Hill Rd., Lincoln, RI 02865. TEL: (800) 556-6484, (866) 556 6484. FAX: (401) 333-6696, (401) 333-2779.
www.nationalglass.com
PRESIDENT
Charles J. Vachon
CHIEF OF OPERATIONS
Alan P. Riendeau

NORCON COMMUNICATIONS, INC.
(Amplified window intercom systems)
510 Burnside Ave., Inwood, NY 11096. TEL: (516) 239-0300.
FAX: (516) 239-8915. email: info@talk-thru.com
www.norcon.org
SALES MANAGER
Ishwar Hariprashad

NOVAR CONTROLS CORP.
(Energy management systems)
6060 Rockside Woods Blvd. Ste. 400, Cleveland, OH 44131.
TEL: (800) 348-1235, (216) 682-1600. FAX: (216) 682-1614.
email: info-request@novar.com www.novar.com
VICE PRESIDENT
Dean Lindstrom

R.S. ENGINEERING & MFG.
(Online cinema equipment)
20617 Santa Lucia St., Ste. G, Tehachapi, CA 93561.
TEL: (661) 822-1488. FAX: (661) 822-1205.
email: sales@rsem.com www.rsem.com
www.cinemaparts.com
PRESIDENT
Robert Schultz - rob@rsem.com

RAXXESS
(Commercial and residential audio racks enclosures, media furniture and related accessories)
261 Buffalo Ave., Paterson, NJ 07503. TEL: (800) 398-7299.
FAX: (877) 894-6918. email: info@raxxess.com
www.raxxess.com
PRESIDENT
Hyman Peller

SMART PRODUCTS, INC.
(Manufacturer of check valves, pumps, and related components for applications which include beverage dispensing)
675 Jarvis Dr., Morgan Hill, CA 95037. TEL: (800) 338-0404, (408) 776-3035. FAX: (408) 776-3186.
email: sales@smartproducts.com www.smartproducts.com

TRANE CO.
(Commercial Div. Air-conditioning & chilling systems)
Headquarters: One Centennial Ave., Piscataway, NJ 08902.
TEL: (732) 980-3022. www.trane.com

Commercial Div. Air-conditioning & chilling systems office:
2300 Citygate Dr., Ste. 100, Columbus, OH 43219.
TEL: (614) 473-3500. FAX: (614) 473-3501. www.trane.com
DISTRICT MANAGER
Al Fullerton - alfullerton@trane.com

Trane provides heating ventilation and air conditioning (HVAC) systems and services that enhance the quality and comfort of the air in homes and buildings around the world.

TRI STATE THEATRE SUPPLY CO.
(Complete theatre & concession supply; sales, service & installation; buyer of used & surplus equipment)
3157 Norbrook Dr., Memphis TN 38116. TEL: (800) 733-8249.
FAX: (775) 254-6607. email: info@tristatetheatre.com
www.tristatetheatre.com
CONTACT
Fred Blank

UNIVERSAL CINEMA SERVICES
(Distributors of all types of theatre equipment & supplies)
1010 W. Euless Blvd., Ste. 240, Euless, TX 76040.
TEL: (888) 600-6775, (817) 633-2180. FAX: (817) 633-2190.
email: CustomerService@universalcinema.com
www.universalcinema.com
CHAIRMAN & CEO
Jack Panzeca
PRESIDENT & COO
Stan Lamb
V.P., PURCHASING
Jim Kappus

VEND TREND
(Complete theatre equipment)
Mailing Address: P.O. Box 1056, Reistertown, MD 21136.
TEL: (410) 526-4774. FAX: (410) 526-6871.
email: jwarc1@aol.com
CONTACT
David Phillips

WESNIC
(All furnishings, interior and exterior)
6000 Bowdendale Ave., Jacksonville, FL 32216.
TEL: (800) 874-8558, (904) 733-8444. FAX: (904) 733-3736.
www.wesnic.com
DIRECTOR OF MARKETING
Bill Gilbert
WESTERN REGION CONTACT
Garrett Holick - (214) 515-9370 - gholick@wesnic.com
SOUTHEASTERN REGION CONTACT
Granger Marchman - (404) 231-4088 - gmarchman@wesnic.com
NORTHEASTERN REGION CONTACT
Sean Sherman - (800) 593-7642 - ssherman@wesnic.com

WING ENTERPRISES/LITTLE GIANT LADDERS
(Ladder manufacturer; janitorial supplies)
1198 N. Spring Creek Place, Springville, UT 84663.
TEL: (800) 453-1192, (801) 489-3684. FAX: (801) 489-3685.
www.littlegiantladders.com
DIRECTOR OF CORPORATE SALES
Hugh DeHart - hugh@ladders.com

WOLF THEATRE SERVICES
(A division of Michael Wolf Interiors, Inc.)
15 Daybreak, Irvine, CA 92614. TEL: (949) 733-8388.
FAX: (949) 733-8389. email: WolfFlow28@cox.net
screencleaner@cox.net www.wolfts.com
PRESIDENT
Michael Wolf
V.P., OPERATIONS
Ilan Wolf

Screen cleaning service; Front end, drapery and speaker installation. Also wall lighting, floor and wall carpet services.

WOLFE MERCHANDISING
(Customized point-of purchase displays & menu-board layouts)
587 Hanlan Rd., Woodbridge, ON L4L 4R8, Canada.
TEL: (888) 809-6533, (905) 266-1010. FAX: (905) 266-1015.
email: info@wolfeworks.ca
www.wolfeworks.ca
ACCOUNTS EXECUTIVE
Kathleen Panos

EDWARD H. WOLK, INC.
(All types of theatre equipment and precision parts)
606 E. Brook Dr., Arlington Hts., IL 60005. TEL: (800) 621-4424, (847) 357-8080. FAX: (800) 770-1467.
email: sales@edwolk.com www.edwolk.com
OWNER
Don Markus

PROJECTION ROOM AND FILM HANDLING EQUIPMENT

BIG SKY INDUSTRIES
(Manufacturer and distributor of projection booth equipment; booth supplies)
1475 Park Ave., Alpha, NJ 08865. TEL: (908) 454-6344.
FAX: (908) 454-6373. www.bigskyindustries.net
PRESIDENT/FOUNDER
Mark Smith - mark@bigskyindustries.net
SALES & MARKETING
Mike Avallone - mikea@bigskyindustries.net

BOOTH SUPPLY WAREHOUSE, INC.
Mailing Address: P.O. Box 93, Murfreesboro, TN 37133.
TEL: (866) 403-6712. FAX: (866) 856-4116.
SALES REPRESENTATIVE
Ron Purtee - ron@boothsupplywarehouse.com

Projection booth supplies; splicing tape & splicers; mylar leader, film cleaners, miniature lamps, xenon bulbs, Projection ports, Drive-In FM Transmitters, Crowd control-retractable belt systems.

BOSTON LIGHT & SOUND
(Rental & dealer of film & video projectors & sound equipment; service & installation)
290 N. Beacon St., Boston, MA 02135. TEL: (617) 787-3131.
FAX: (617) 787-4257. email: info@blsi.com www.blsi.com
RENTAL MANAGER
Celine Larimer
FILM & VIDEO SYSTEMS MANAGER
Robert Harris

CINELITE CORPORATION
P.O. Box 549, 99 Limestone Rd., Ridgefield, CT 06877.
TEL: (203) 438-3405. FAX: (203) 438-1419.
SENIOR V.P.
Walter Beatty, Jr. - WalterBeatty@sbcglobal.net

Manufacturer of patented Technalight Technology improving brightness and clarity in cinema film presentation. Technalight Technology xenon console and conversion kits available for all makes and models of other manufactured xenon equipment.

CINEMA CONSULTANTS & SERVICES INTERNATIONAL, INC.
1250 Brookline Blvd., P.O. Box 9672, Pittsburgh, PA 15226.
TEL: (412) 343-3900. FAX: (412) 343-2992.
email: sales@cinamaconsultantspro.com
www.cinemaconsultantspro.com
PRESIDENT
Ross Falvo

Established in 1990. Specializes in theatre design, theater consulting, projection & sound design/equipment, concessions design/equipment, interior design & installation of projection, sound seating & acoustic draperies.

CINEMA EQUIPMENT SALES OF CA, INC.
(Cinema & screening room projection, sound equipment, parts, seating and furnishings)
23011 Moulton Pkwy., #I-5, Laguna Hills, CA 92653.
TEL: (949) 470-0298. FAX: (949) 470-0835.
email: service@cinemadealer.com www.cinema-equip.com
SALES
Carl Williams - carl@cinemadealer.com
Mike Smith

CLACO EQUIPMENT AND SERVICE, INC.
(Drapery systems, theatre chairs; complete digital & film projection, sound, auditorium equipment & service)
1212 S. State St., Salt Lake City, UT 84111. TEL: (801) 355-1250.
FAX: (801) 355-1259. email: sales@clacoequipment.com
www.clacoequipment.com
PRESIDENT
Clayton Stauffer
SALES
Eric Butterworth
SERVICE
Vince Butler

CLOUD INDUSTRIES, INC.
(Wall & screen drapery, curtains & film handling equipment)
Mailing Address: P.O. Box 35, Lawson, MO 64062.
TEL: (816) 296-3354. FAX: (816) 296-7733.
www.cloudindustries.com
OWNER, PRESIDENT & CONTROLLER
Mary Shoemaker - mary@cloudindustries.com
V.P., SALES
Chuck Shoemaker - chuck@cloudindustries.com
SALES CONTACT & WEB DESIGNER
Paul Shoemaker

Designer of stage & screen fronts, wall & screen drapery for remodels & new construction; manufacturer of film handling equipment, out of order seat covers & patented stadium seat anchor.

DIGITAL PROJECTION
(Ultra-bright, electronic cinema projection systems for large format video, data, or HDTV imagery in large venues)
55 Chastain Rd., Ste.115, Kennesaw, GA 30144.
TEL: (770) 420-1350. FAX: (770) 420-1360.
www.digitalprojection.com
SENIOR MARKET DEVELOPMENT MANAGER
Chuck Collins - ccollins@digitalprojection.com
MARKETING COMMUNICATIONS MANAGER
Richard G. Hill

EPRAD, INC.
(Manufacturer automations, lighting controls, fail-safe devices)
6979 Wales Rd., Northwood, OH 43619. TEL: (419) 666-3266.
FAX: (419) 666-8109. www.eprad.com
OWNER & MANAGER
Ted Stechschulte

CONTACT
Tom Lewandowski

GOLDBERG BROTHERS, INC.
(Manufacturer of film shipping, booth & lobby equipment; also bowling machine replacement parts)
8000 E. 40th Ave., Denver, CO 80207, P.O. Box 17048, Denver, CO 80217. TEL: (303) 321-1099. FAX: (303) 388-0749.
email: golbroinc@aol.com www.goldbergbrothers.bizhosting.com
EXECUTIVE V.P.
Randall Urlik

INTERNATIONAL CINEMA EQUIPMENT
(Manufacturer and distributors of professional Motion Picture equipment for cinemas, studios, laboratories and theatres)
A Division of Magna-Tech Electronic Co. Inc., 1998 N.E. 150th St., North Miami, FL 33181-1116. TEL: (305) 573-7339.
FAX: (305) 573-8101. email: iceco@iceco.com
www.iceco.com
PRESIDENT & COO
Steven Krams
VICE PRESIDENT
Dara Reusch
V.P., INTERNATIONAL SALES & MARKETING
Julio Urbay
V.P., TECHNICAL SERVICES
Franscisco Blanco
ARCHITECTURAL DESIGN & DEVELOPMENT
Arturo Quintero

KELMAR SYSTEMS, INC.
(All types of film-handling equipment)
284 Broadway, Huntington Station, NY 11746-1497.
TEL: (631) 421-1230. FAX: (631) 421-1274.
email: kelmarsystems@optonline.net
www.kelmarsystems.com
PRESIDENT
Andrew Marglin

KINETRONICS CORP.
(Manufactures machines, brushes, anti-static cloths & glass cleaner for dust & static removal)
1459 Tallevast Rd., Sarasota, FL 34243. TEL: (800) 624-3204, (941) 951-2432. FAX: (941) 955-5992.
email: order@kinetronics.com www.kinetronics.com
PRESIDENT
Mike Murdock
CUSTOMER SERVICE
Sali Robbins

LAVEZZI PRECISION, INC.
(Manufacturer of high quality precision replacement parts for motion picture projectors)
999 Regency Dr., Glendale Heights, IL 60139.
TEL: (630) 582-1230. FAX: (630) 582-1238.
email: lpi@lavezzifilm.com www.lavezzifilm.com
SALES & MARKETING MANAGER
Stephanie LaVezzi

LEN-D ENTERPRISES
(Distributor & manufacturer of all types of film-handling equipment; splicing tape & splicers, port glass & projection lenses)
6080 Okeechobee Blvd., West Palm Beach, FL 33417.
TEL: (561) 682-3500. FAX: (561) 682-3777.
PRESIDENT
Lenny Dickstein

LIGHTING IMAGES TECHNOLOGY, INC.
(Manufacturer of new motion picture equipment in both 35mm & 70mm formats; custom film related equipment; refurbish used equipment)
2111 Iowa Ave., Ste. E, Riverside, CA 92507.
TEL: (951) 786-9999. FAX: (951) 786-9926.
www.lightingimages.com
SALES
Dick Niccum - dick.niccum@lightingimages.com

LUTRON ELECTRONICS
(Visual & environmental controls)
7200 Suter Rd., Coopersburg, PA 18036. TEL: (610) 282-3800.
FAX: (610) 282-6437. email: intsales@lutron.com
www.lutron.com
CONTACT
David Eisenhauer

See website for additional locations worldwide.

MOVING IMAGE TECHNOLOGIES
(Manufacturer and integrator of cinema digital & film projection equipment)
17760 New Hope St., Ste. B, Fountain Valley, CA 92708.
TEL: (714) 751-7998. FAX: (714) 429-7717.
email: sales@movingimagetech.com
www.movingimagetech.com
EXECUTIVE V.P., SALES & MARKETING
Joe Delgado
V.P., SALES & CUSTOMER SERVICE
Thomas Lipiec

NEUMADE PRODUCTS CORP./XETRON DIVISION
(Motion picture theatre projection equipment)
30-40 Pecks Ln., Newtown, CT 06470. TEL: (203) 270-1100.
FAX: (203) 270-7778. email: gjones@neumade.com
www.Neumade.com
PRESIDENT
Gregg Jones

NORCON COMMUNICATIONS, INC.
(Amplified window intercom systems)
510 Burnside Ave., Inwood, NY 11096. TEL: (516) 239-0300.
FAX: (516) 239-8915. email: info@talk-thru.com
www.norcon.org
SALES MANAGER
Ishwar Hariprashad

ODYSSEY PRODUCTS, INC.
(Infrared assistive equipment & support services; all types of booth equipment & supplies)
5845 Oakbrook Pkwy., Ste. G, Norcross, GA 30093.
TEL: (770) 825-0243. FAX: (770) 825-0245.
email: info@odyssey-products.com www.odyssey-products.com
PRESIDENT
Eve Miller
CONTACT
Ken Reeves

JACK ROE USA, INC.
501 Metroplex Dr.,Ste. 315, Nashville,TN 37211.
TEL: (800) 213-9956. FAX: (615) 331-9370.
email: sales@jackroeusa.com www.jackroeusa.com
CEO
Alan Roe
SALES MANAGER
Ron Lutsock
CUSTOMER SERVICE MANAGER
Chad Pardue
CUSTOMER SERVICE
Charlotte Shepard, Cortez Gilchrist

Splicing tape, cue tape, 35mm film leader and spacing booth editing supplies, platter accessories, cleaning and film cleaning projector oils and lubricants, cinema carbons, exciter and indicator lamps, CIR film splicer and parts, Neutaper/Neumade film splicer and parts, marble film splicer and parts, economy splicer and parts, 35 mm test film, IR units for hearing impaired cinema booster seats and more. See website for full spectrum of cinema products and supplies.

SPECTRA CINE, INC.
(Light-measuring equipment; screen brightness measurement)
3607 W. Magnolia Blvd., Burbank, CA 91505.
TEL: (818) 954-9222. FAX: (818) 954-0016.
email: info@spectracine.com www.spectracine.com
PRESIDENT
Nasir J. Zaidi
V.P., SALES & MARKETING
Bernadette Perez

STRONG CINEMA PRODUCTS
(A Ballantyne of Omaha Co.)
4350 McKinley St., Omaha, NE 68112. TEL: (402) 453-4444.
FAX: (402) 453-7238. www.strong-cinema.com
www.strong-cinema.com www.ballantyne-omaha.com
PRESIDENT & CEO
John P. Wilmers
V.P., LIGHTING
Paul Rabinovitz
GENERAL MANAGER, STRONG/MDI Screens, Inc.
Benoit Mailloux
V.P., STRONG TECHNICAL SERVICES, INC.
John Biegel
SALES & MARKETING
Ray Boeener
OPERATIONS
Chris Stark

Strong Cinema Products offer 35mm and 70mm film projection equipment. Strong also helps bring motion picture exhibitors into the 21st Century through Strong Digital Systems, which offers complete solutions for the challenges of the evolving digital world. Strong Technical Services is dedicated to the design, installation, and service of the complete range of film and digital systems. Strong Entertainment Lighting provides lighting products and services that enhance visual experiences for audiences worldwide.

THE TAPE COMPANY
(Manufactures plastic reels, boxes & film cores)
845 N. Church St., Elmhurst, IL 60126. TEL: (630) 834-3113.
FAX: (630) 758-0930. www.thetapecompany.com
SALES
Frank Sacco - fsacco@thetapecompany.com

TECHNOLOGY INTERNATIONAL
(CE Marking for European film markets)
11311 Business Center Dr., Ste. A, Richmond, VA 23236.
TEL: (800) 810-9000, (804) 794-4144. FAX: (804) 794-4166.
email: ti-sales@techintl.com www.techintl.com

DIRECTOR
Robert Morgan

The Group is a specialized engineering consulting organization whose primary focus is the provision of safety compliance and approval support services to product manufacturers and designers worldwide. Technology International is an expert in both European safety compliance (CE Marking) and Semiconductor machine safety (SEMI S-Guidelines), with a proven track record of providing comprehensive and cost effective services to its clients.

PROJECTOR LAMPS AND LENSES

ADVANCED SPECIALTY LIGHTING
(Wholly owned subsidiary of Advanced Strobe Products, Inc. Manufactures precision optical products for the entertainment, industrial and scientific markets. See website for intl. contacts)
7227 W. Wilson Ave., Harwood Heights, IL 60706.
TEL: (708) 867-3140. FAX: (708) 867-1066.
email: info@aslamps.com www.aslamps.com
DIRECTOR, GLOBAL SALES & MARKETING
Stefanie Farnsworth

ORC xenon short arc cinema lamps manufacturer.

Advanced Strobe:
7227 W. Wilson Ave., Harwood Heights, IL 60706.
TEL: (708) 867-3100. FAX: (708) 867-1103.
email: asp@strobelamps.com www.strobelamps.com

AMERICAN CINEMA EQUIPMENT, INC.
(Projection, sound, digital projection & sound, engineering, project management, construction management & seats)
1927 N. Argyle St., Portland, OR 97217.
TEL: (800) 956-6589, (503) 285-7015, (916) 832-9510 (N. CA).
FAX: (503) 285-6765. www.cinequip.com
PRESIDENT
Scott R. Hicks - scott.hicks@cinequip.com
V.P., SALES & MARKETING
Doug Sabin - doug.sabin@cinequip.com

ATLAS SPECIALTY LIGHTING
(Entertainment lighting, projection equipment, digital sound systems & digital cinema equipment)
7304 N. Florida Ave., Tampa, FL 33604. TEL: (813) 238-6481.
FAX: (813) 238-6656. www.asltg.com
MANAGERS
Ralph Felten, Jr. - rfelten@asltg2.com
Bob Ray

BOSTON LIGHT & SOUND
(Rental & dealer of film & video projectors & sound equipment; service & installation)
290 N. Beacon St., Boston, MA 02135. TEL: (617) 787-3131.
FAX: (617) 787-4257. email: info@blsi.com www.blsi.com
RENTAL MANAGER
Celine Larimer
FILM & VIDEO SYSTEMS MANAGER
Robert Harris

BRIGHT STAR SYSTEMS CORP.
(Full service dealer/installer of projection & sound equipment)
7600 W. 27th St., Ste. 223, Minneapolis, MN 55426.
TEL: (952) 926-2009. FAX: (952) 926-6023.
email: sales@BSSCinema.com www.bsscinema.com

Massachusetts office: 41 Brigham St., Unit 11, Marlborough, MA 01752. TEL: (508) 481-9300. FAX: (508) 481-9700.

CINEMA CONSULTANTS & SERVICES INTERNATIONAL, INC.
1250 Brookline Blvd., P.O. Box 9672, Pittsburgh, PA 15226.
TEL: (412) 343-3900. FAX: (412) 343-2992.
email: sales@cinemaconsultantspro.com
www.cinemaconsultantspro.com
PRESIDENT
Ross Falvo

Established in 1990. Specializes in theatre design, theater consulting, projection & sound design/equipment, concessions design/equipment, interior design & installation of projection, sound seating & acoustic draperies.

CINEMA XENON INTERNATIONAL, INC.
(Distributor of digital and film projector lamps; specializes in large venue Xenon)
261 Valley Vista Dr., Camarillo, CA 93010. TEL: (888) 669-7271, (805) 383-5548. FAX: (805) 389-9611.
email: info@cxilamps.com www.cxilamps.com
PRESIDENT
Dick Stockton

GOLDBERG BROTHERS, INC.
(Manufacturer of film shipping, booth & lobby equipment; also bowling machine replacement parts)
8000 E. 40th Ave., Denver, CO 80207, P.O. Box 17048, Denver, CO 80217. TEL: (303) 321-1099. FAX: (303) 388-0749.
email: golbroinc@aol.com
www.goldbergbrothers.bizhosting.com
EXECUTIVE V.P.
Randall Urlik

ISCO/ B+W FILTERFABRIK GMBH & CO. KG.
Anna-Vandenhoeck-Ring5, 37081Göttingen, Germany.
TEL: (49 551) 505-83. FAX:(49 551) 505-8410.
email: info@isco-usa.us info@isco.eu marketing@isco.eu
www.isco.eu
CONTACT
Kathrin Ilse
U.S.CONTACT
Brian Ludvigsen - (770) 241-8810 - brian.ludvigsen@isco-usa.us

Manufactures cinema projection lenses for all film formats and projectiontypes, anamorphic attachments for 3-chip DLP and for LCD/DLP projectors.

BERN LEVY ASSOCIATES
(Lens cleaning)
21 Whippoorwill Ln., Palmyra, VA 22963. TEL: (434) 589-2171.
FAX: (434) 589-2172.
CONTACT
Bern Levy

L.P. ASSOCIATES, INC.
(Manufacturer of lamp houses, power supply & searchlights; distributor of xenon lamps)
4110 Vanowen Pl., Burbank, CA 91505. TEL: (818) 565-5950.
FAX: (818) 565-5951. email: leonard_lpa@pacbell.net
www.lpassociates.net
CORPORATE OFFICER
Leonard Pincus

NAVITAR, INC.
(MFG projection optics)
200 Commerce Dr., Rochester, NY 14623. TEL: (800) 828-6778, (585) 359-4000. FAX: (585) 359-4999. email: info@navitar.com
www.navitar.com
MANAGER AV SALES
Joseph Pintavalle

OSRAM SYLVANIA
(Osram Xenon lamps)
100 Endicott St., Danvers MA 01923. TEL: (978) 777-1900.
FAX: (978) 750-1247 (display optics division), (978) 750-2152.
email: display-optic@osram.info www.osram.com
www.sylvania.com
V.P. & GENERAL MANAGER, DISPLAY OPTIC
Wayne Steinhoff
CINEMA BUSINESS UNIT MANAGER
Steve Henry

Canada: OSRAM Sylvania Ltd./LTEE. 2001 Drew Rd, Mississauga, ON Canada L5S 1S4.
TEL: (905) 673-6171. FAX: (905) 671-5584.

PERKIN ELMER OPTOELECTRONICS
(Complete line of Cermax Xenonprojection lamps)
44370 Christy St., Fremont, CA 94538-3180.
TEL: (800) 775-67886, (510) 979-6500. FAX: (510) 687-1140.
email: Xenon.lighting@perkinelmer.com www.perkinelmer.com
SALES MANAGER
Brian Hermes - brian.hermes@perkinelmer.com
CONTACT
Joanne Bakerville - ext. 6610

PHILIPS LTI
13700 Live Oaks Ave., Baldwin Park, CA 91706.
TEL: (626) 480-0755. FAX: (626) 480-0855.
email: bob.simminger@philips.com www.ltilamps.com
GLOBAL SALES MANAGER
Ana Simonian
CINEMA SALES MANAGER
Bob Simminger

Philips LTI is a specialty discharge lamp manufacturer. Products include Xenon lamps for cinema, digital cinema and stage & studio lighting.

SCHNEIDER OPTICS, INC.
(Projection lenses; digital lenses and filters)
285 Oser Ave., Hauppauge, NY 11788. TEL: (800) 645-7239, (631) 761-5000. FAX: (631) 761-5090.
email: info@schneideroptics.com www.schneideroptics.com
CEO
Dwight Lindsey
DIRECTOR, CINEMA TECHNICAL SERVICES
Fred Morris
SALES ADMINISTRATOR
Henry W. Greese - hgreese@schneideroptics.com

West Coast Office: Schneider Optics. 7701 Haskell Ave., Van Nuys, CA 91406. TEL: (800) 228-1254, (818) 766-3715.
FAX: (818) 505-9865.

SUPERIOR QUARTZ PRODUCTS, INC.
(Projection lamps. See website for additional contacts)
2701 Baglyos Circle, Bethlehem, PA 18020. TEL: (610) 317-3450.

FAX: (610) 317-3451. email: superior@sqpuv.com www.sqpuv.com
PRESIDENT/CEO
Dennis A. Losco
CFO/DIRECTOR, SALES
Dennis J. Losco
NATIONAL SALES MANAGER
Ernest E. Estrada - (949) 443-0239 - ernie@sqpuv.com

VANTAGE LIGHTING, INC.
(Distributors of projection booth & studio lamps & lenses)
175 Paul Dr., San Rafael, CA 94903-2041. TEL: (800) 445-2677, (415) 507-0402. FAX: (415) 507-0502. email: light@vanltg.com www.vanltg.com
GENERAL MANAGER
Peter Allsman

XENONBULBS.COM
(All types of projector bulbs & lamps)
A subsidiary of R.S. Engineering, 20617 Santa Lucia St., Ste. G, Tehachapi, CA 93561 TEL: (661) 822-1488. FAX: (661) 822-1205. email: staff@xenonbulbs.com
www.XenonBulbs.com
GENERAL MANAGER
Robert Schultz

PROJECTORS

AMERICAN CINEMA EQUIPMENT, INC.
(Projection, sound, digital projection & sound, engineering, project management, construction management & seats)
1927 N. Argyle St., Portland, OR 97217.
TEL: (800) 956-6589, (503) 285-7015,
(916) 832-9510 (N. CA). FAX: (503) 285-6765.
www.cinequip.com
PRESIDENT
Scott R. Hicks - scott.hicks@cinequip.com
V.P., SALES & MARKETING
Doug Sabin - doug.sabin@cinequip.com

ATLAS SPECIALTY LIGHTING
(Entertainment lighting, projection equipment, digital sound systems & digital cinema equipment)
7304 N. Florida Ave., Tampa, FL 33604.
TEL: (813) 238-6481. FAX: (813) 238-6656. www.asltg.com
MANAGERS
Ralph Felten, Jr. - rfelten@asltg2.com
Bob Ray

AUDIO SERVICE COMPANY, INC.
(Projection & sound equipment; service & installation)
P.O. Box 50, Yakima, WA 98907. TEL: (509) 248-7041.
FAX: (509) 453-3074.
CONTACT
Darrell Hoff

AVICA TECHNOLOGY CORP.
(Digital cinema players & equipment)
1201 Olympic Blvd., Santa Monica, CA 90404.
TEL: (800) 706-0077, (310) 450-9090.
email: sales@avicatech.com www.avicatech.com
SALES
Scott Strempel

BARCO, INC.
11135 Trade Center Dr., Rancho Cordova, CA 95670.
TEL: (916) 859-2500. FAX: (916) 471-6924.
email: Service.media.us@barco.com www.barco.com
V.P., DIGITAL CINEMA
Wim Buyens
V.P., DIGITAL CINEMA, NORTH AMERICA
Todd Hiddick
V.P., PROJECT MANAGEMENT
Carl Rijsbrack

High-performance large-screen display systems for theatrical presentations of digital content; screen advertising displays; post-production & outdoor display applications.

BOSTON LIGHT & SOUND
(Rental & dealer of film & video projectors & sound equipment; service & installation)
290 N. Beacon St., Boston, MA 02135. TEL: (617) 787-3131.
FAX: (617) 787-4257. email: info@blsi.com www.blsi.com
RENTAL MANAGER
Celine Larimer
FILM & VIDEO SYSTEMS MANAGER
Robert Harris

CARDINAL SOUND & MOTION PICTURE SYSTEMS, INC.
(Digital sound systems; 16mm, 35mm, & 70mm film and digital projection equipment)
6330 Howard Ln., Elkridge, MD 21075. TEL: (410) 796-5300.
FAX: (410) 796-7995. email: cardinal@cardinalsound.com
www.cardinalsound.com
OFFICE MANAGER
Catherine Rockman

CHRISTIE DIGITAL SYSTEMS U.S.A., INC.
10550 Camden Dr., Cypress, CA 90630. TEL: (714) 236-8610. FAX: (714) 503-3375. www.christiedigital.com
V.P., ENTERTAINMENT SOLUTIONS
Craig Sholder
SENIOR MANAGER, CINEMA
Keith Watanabe

Manufacturer & distributor of Digital Cinema projectors, film projectors; Xenon consoles, rewinds, bulbs; digital projectors, DLP projectors, DLP Cinema projectors & on-screen advertising solutions.

DIGITAL MEDIA SYSTEMS, INC.
(Digital Cinema, 35mm projection, sound, sales, service & rentals)
248 West 35th St., Ste. 1203, New York, NY 10001.
www.dmediainc.com
OWNER
Gregg V. Paliotta - GreggP@Dmediainc.com

DLP CINEMA
(A Texas Instruments company. Cinema projection technology for use in digital cinema applications)
Texas Instruments, 12500 TI Blvd., Dallas, TX 75243-4136.
TEL: (800) 336-5236. FAX: (972) 927-6377. www.dlp.com

ENTERTAINMENT SUPPLY & TECHNOLOGIES, LLC
4971 Van Dyke Rd., Lutz, FL 33558. TEL: (813) 960-1646.
FAX: (813) 961-7209.
PRESIDENT & CEO
Barney Bailey
VICE PRESIDENT
Ron Eiben - reiben@ensutec.com

Entertainment Supply & Technologies provides the following: Digital projection equipment, 35mm projection equipment, Xenon lamps, sound equipment, seating, aisle lighting, crowd control ropes & posts, poster cases, screens, frames & screen drapes, acoustical panels, concession & ticketing casework, concession equipment, 2-way radios, parts, supplies, janitorial equipment, turn-key project management, installations, defixturing service, design, planning & drafting services.

ERNEMANN CINETEC U.S.A.
(Cinema projectors & platters)
430 W. 34th St., #4C, New York, NY 10001.
TEL: (212) 695-0012. FAX: (212) 695-0014.
www.ernemann.com
CONTACT
Roney Weis - roneyintl@aol.com

HOLLYWOOD THEATRE EQUIPMENT, INC.
(Dealer for all 35mm & digital projection & sound equipment)
1941 N. 66 Ave., Hollywood, FL 33024.
TEL: (954) 920-2832. FAX: (954) 986-6914.
email: HWDTHEATRE@aol.com
SALES
Don Gallagher
Don R. Gallagher, Jr. - gahwdtheatre@aol.com

HURLEY SCREEN CORP.
(Custom projection screens and frames)
110 Industry Ln., Forest Hill, MD 21050.
TEL: (877) 487-4912. FAX: (410) 838-8079.
email: information@hurleyscreen.com www.hurleyscreen.com
PRESIDENT
Gregory White
CEO
Gorman W. White, III

JVC PROFESSIONAL PRODUCTS COMPANY
(Digital cinema projectors)
1700 Valley Rd., Wayne, NJ 07470. TEL: (800) 582-5825, (973) 317-5000. FAX: (973) 317-5030. email: proinfo@jvc.com
http://pro.jvc.com
PRESIDENT
Kirk Hirota

JVC Americas Corp. is a wholly owned subsidiary of Victor Company of Japan, Limited. JVC is one of the world's leading developers and manufacturers of sophisticated audio, video and related software products. JVC Professional Products Company distributes a complete line of broadcast portable and studio cameras, recorders and switchers, closed circuit TV equipment, including analog and network (IP) cameras, network video recorders, D-ILA Reference Series projectors, CRT and Flat Panel monitors.

KINOTON AMERICA, INC.
(Manufactures & distributes film projectors, digital cinema projectors and sound equipment)
33 Jacksonville Rd., Unit #1, Towaco, NJ 07082.
TEL: (973) 331-9200. FAX: (973) 331-9203.
www.kinotonamerica.com
SALES
Ernie Tracey
V.P. OPERATIONS
John Gallucci - johng@kinotonamerica.com

KNEISLEY MANUFACTURING COMPANY
(Manufacturer of 35mm Lamphouses and Power Supply)
900 West Miller Rd., P.O. Box 667, Iola, KS 66749.
TEL: (620) 365-6628. FAX: (620) 365-2753.
email: sales@kneisley.com www.kneisley.com
MANAGER
Sarah Noah

NEC CORPORATION OF AMERICA
(Digital cinema and post-house projectors; comprehensive in-theatre and in-lobby advertising solutions; alternative content processors; digital cinema servers)
4111 W. Alameda Ave., Burbank, CA 91505.
TEL: (818) 557-2500 (sales), (866) 632-6431 (technical support).
email: digital.cinema@necam.com cinema.support@necam.com
www.necam.com
GENERAL MANAGER, DIGITAL CINEMA DIVISION
Jim Reisteter - (818) 557-2500 - jim.reisteter@necam.com
MARKETING CONTACT, NEC CORPORATION OF AMERICA
Julia Sullivan - (909) 396-6276 - Julia.sullivan@necam.com

PANASONIC PROJECTOR SYSTEMS COMPANY
Three Panasonic Way, 2-E7, Secaucus, NJ 07094.
TEL: (888) 411-1996 (Projector sales).
www.panasonic.com/projectors
MARKETING MANAGER
Anne Gattoni - (201) 392-6364 - gattonia@us.panasonic.com

Panasonic Projector Systems Company is a supplier of projectors and presenations systems in the U.S. It is a unit of Panasonic Corporation of North America, the principal North American subsidiary of Matsushita Electric Industrial Co., Ltd. of Japan and the hub of its U.S. marketing, sales and service and R&D operations. For more information on Panasonic projectors, visit the company's website: www.panasonic.com/projectors.

PHILIPS LTI
13700 Live Oaks Ave., Baldwin Park, CA 91706.
TEL: (626) 480-0755. FAX: (626) 480-0855.
email: bob.simminger@philips.com
GLOBAL SALES MANAGER
Ana Simonian
CINEMA SALES MANAGER
Bob Simminger

Philips LTI is a specialty discharge lamp manufacturer. Products include Xenon lamps for cinema, digital cinema and stage & studio lighting.

SIMEX-IWERKS
(Specialized theatre manufacturing)
511 King St. W, Ste. 130, Toronto, ON Canada M5V 1K4.
TEL: (416) 597-1585. FAX: (416) 597-0350.
email: info@simex-iwerks.com www.simex-iwerks.com
PRESIDENT & CEO
Michael J. Needham
EXECUTIVE V.P.
Shiori Sudo
SENIOR V.P., OPERATIONS
Brian R. Peebles

SimEx-Iwerks is a leading creator/developer of 3D/4D-seat/FX/Simulation/Large Format and Custom Special Venue Attractions, with 250 attractions installed in 30 countries. SimEx-Iwerks attractions combine state-of-the-art digital and film technologies with innovative programming.

STRONG CINEMA PRODUCTS
(A Ballantyne of Omaha Co.)
4350 McKinley St., Omaha, NE 68112. TEL: (402) 453-4444.
FAX: (402) 453-7238. www.strong-cinema.com
www.strong-cinema.com www.ballantyne-omaha.com
PRESIDENT & CEO
John P. Wilmers
V.P., LIGHTING
Paul Rabinovitz
GENERAL MANAGER, STRONG/MDI Screens, Inc.
Benoit Mailloux
V.P., STRONG TECHNICAL SERVICES, INC.
John Biegel
SALES & MARKETING
Ray Boeener
OPERATIONS
Chris Stark

Strong Cinema Products offer 35mm and 70mm film projection equipment. Strong also helps bring motion picture exhibitors into the 21st Century through Strong Digital Systems, which offers complete solutions for the challenges of the evolving digital world. Strong Technical Services is dedicated to the design, installation, and service of the complete range of film and digital systems. Strong Entertainment Lighting provides lighting products and services that enhance visual experiences for audiences worldwide.

SCREENS AND FRAMES

A&B COMPANY
(Screen, seat, upholstery cleaning, nightly janitorial, carpet & floor cleaning; pressure wash; fire-protectant application)
6536 Fulton Ave., Van Nuys, CA 91401. TEL: (818) 985-7768.
FAX: (818) 763-7914. email: service@AandBCompany.com
www.aandbcompany.com
CONTACT
Mike Fuss

BOSTON LIGHT & SOUND
(Rental & dealer of film & video projectors & sound equipment; service & installation)
290 N. Beacon St., Boston, MA 02135. TEL: (617) 787-3131.
FAX: (617) 787-4257. email: info@blsi.com www.blsi.com
RENTAL MANAGER
Celine Larimer
FILM & VIDEO SYSTEMS MANAGER
Robert Harris

CINEMA TECHNOLOGY SERVICES, LLC
P.O. Box D-400, Pomona, NY 10970-0484. TEL: (845) 354-6563.
FAX: (845) 354-9146. www.ctsnyc.com
PRINCIPAL
Roger Getzoff
OFFICE MANAGER
Leslie Gonzalez

All aspects of theatre installation, renovation and technical services for equipment repair & installation; picture screenings & special shows including video shows.

CLACO EQUIPMENT AND SERVICE, INC.
(Drapery systems, theatre chairs; complete digital & film projection, sound, auditorium equipment & service)
1212 S. State St., Salt Lake City, UT 84111. TEL: (801) 355-1250.
FAX: (801) 355-1259. email: sales@clacoequipment.com
www.clacoequipment.com
PRESIDENT
Clayton Stauffer
SALES
Eric Butterworth
SERVICE
Vince Butler

CLOUD INDUSTRIES, INC.
(Wall & screen drapery, curtains & film handling equipment)
P.O. Box 35, Lawson, MO 64062. TEL: (816) 296-3354.
FAX: (816) 296-7733. www.cloudindustries.com
OWNER, PRESIDENT & CONTROLLER
Mary Shoemaker - mary@cloudindustries.com
V.P., SALES
Chuck Shoemaker - chuck@cloudindustries.com
SALES CONTACT & WEB DESIGNER
Paul Shoemaker

Designer of stage & screen fronts, wall & screen drapery for remodels & new construction; manufacturer of film handling equipment, out of order seat covers & patented stadium seat anchor.

ENTERTAINMENT SUPPLY & TECHNOLOGIES, LLC
4971 Van Dyke Rd., Lutz, FL 33558. TEL: (813) 960-1646.
FAX: (813) 961-7209.
PRESIDENT & CEO
Barney Bailey
VICE PRESIDENT
Ron Eiben - reiben@ensutec.com

Entertainment Supply & Technologies provides the following: Digital projection equipment, 35mm projection equipment, Xenon lamps, sound equipment, seating, aisle lighting, crowd control ropes & posts, poster cases, screens, frames & screen drapes, acoustical panels, concession & ticketing casework, concession equipment, 2-way radios, parts, supplies, janitorial equipment, turn-key project management, installations, defixturing service, design, planning & drafting services.

FRANKLIN DESIGNS
208 Industrial Dr., Ridgeland, MS 39157. TEL: (800) 467-0641, (601) 853-9005. FAX: (601) 853-9550.
email: franklindesigns@aol.com www.franklindesigns.com
PRESIDENT
Bobby Franklin
VICE PRESIDENT
Pam Franklin

Manufacturer and installer of custom draperies, cinematic frames, large format and standard screens; seats and wall carpet installation.

HARKNESS SCREENS
(All types of screens & frames, including outdoor air-screens. See website for additional office and contact information)
10 Harkness Blvd., Fredericksburg VA 22401.
TEL: (540) 370-1590. FAX: (540) 370-1592.
email: infousa@harkness-screens.com
www.harkness-screens.com
V.P., SALES & MARKETING
Dennis Pacelli - D.Pacelli@harkness-screens.com

HURLEY SCREEN CORP.
(A subsidiary of CEMCORP. Custom projection screens and

frames)
110 Industry Ln., P.O. Box 296, Forest Hill, MD 21050.
TEL: (877) 487-4912, (410) 879-3022. FAX: (410) 838-8079.
email: information@hurleyscreen.com www.hurleyscreen.com
PRESIDENT
Gregory White
CEO
Gorman W. White, III

INTERNATIONAL CINEMA EQUIPMENT
(Manufacturer and distributors of professional Motion Picture equipment for cinemas, studios, laboratories and theatres)
A Division of Magna-Tech Electronic Co. Inc., 1998 N.E. 150th St., North Miami, FL 33181-1116. TEL: (305) 573-7339.
FAX: (305) 573-8101. email: iceco@iceco.com
www.iceco.com
PRESIDENT & COO
Steven Krams
VICE PRESIDENT
Dara Reusch
V.P., INTERNATIONAL SALES & MARKETING
Julio Urbay
V.P., TECHNICAL SERVICES
Franscisco Blanco
ARCHITECTURAL DESIGN & DEVELOPMENT
Arturo Quintero

MPO VIDEOTRONICS
(Videowalls; LED displays; electronic signage; digital menu boards)
Corporate: 5069 Maureen Ln., Moorpark, CA 93021.
TEL: (805) 499-8513. FAX: (805) 499-8206.
email: sales@mpo-video.com www.mpo-video.com
SALES
Rick Ayeroff

New York: 1623 Third Ave., Ste. 202, New York, NY 10128.
TEL: (212) 369-2400. FAX: (212) 369-5078.

Portland: 6400 S.E. Lake Rd., Ste. 211, Portland, OR 97222.
TEL: (503) 659-9868. FAX: (503) 659-9727.

NICK MULONE & SON, INC.
(Manufacturer of screen frames for movie theatres & public auditoriums; masking hardware & motors)
100 Highland Ave., Cheswick, PA 15024. TEL: (724) 274-3221.
FAX: (724) 274-4808. email: nick@nickmuloneandson.com
www.nickmuloneandson.com

STAR MAXX, LLC
(Soundfold/drapery cleaning, screen cleaning, seat cleaning)
90 Fern Creek Ln., Union, MO 63084. TEL: (636) 485-1653, (314) 210-7401. FAX: (636) 583-1103.
PRESIDENT, SALES
Leonard J. Waldman
V.P., SALES
Don Waldman
V.P., OPERATIONS
Lee Waldman
SECRETARY
Darlene Waldman

STEWART FILMSCREEN CORP.
(Manufacturer of projections screens for movie theatres. See website for additional offices and contacts)
1161 W. Sepulveda Blvd., Torrance, CA 90502.
TEL: (800) 762-4999, (310) 784-5300. FAX: (310) 326-6870.
email: comments@stewartfilm.com www.stewartfilm.com
VICE PRESIDENT
Don Stewart

STRONG CINEMA PRODUCTS
(A Ballantyne of Omaha Co.)
4350 McKinley St., Omaha, NE 68112. TEL: (402) 453-4444.
FAX: (402) 453-7238. www.strong-cinema.com
www.strong-cinema.com www.ballantyne-omaha.com
PRESIDENT & CEO
John P. Wilmers
V.P., LIGHTING
Paul Rabinovitz
GENERAL MANAGER, STRONG/MDI Screens, Inc.
Benoit Mailloux
V.P., STRONG TECHNICAL SERVICES, INC.
John Biegel
SALES & MARKETING
Ray Boeener
OPERATIONS
Chris Stark

Strong Cinema Products offer 35mm and 70mm film projection equipment. Strong also helps bring motion picture exhibitors into the 21st Century through Strong Digital Systems, which offers complete solutions for the challenges of the evolving digital world. Strong Technical Services is dedicated to the design, installation, and service of the complete range of film and digital systems. Strong Entertainment Lighting provides lighting products and services that enhance visual experiences for audiences worldwide.

STRONG/MDI SCREEN SYSTEMS
(A Ballantyne of Omaha Co.)
1440 Raoul-Charrette, Joliette, Quebec, Canada J6E 8S7
TEL: (877) 755-3795. (450) 755-3795. FAX: (450) 755-3122.
email: sales@mdicinema.com www.mdicinema.com
CEO, STRONG/MDI SCREEN SYSTEMS
Benoit Mailloux
OPERATIONS MANAGER
Francois Barrette
SALES & CUSTOMER SERVICE
Gisele Hounjet
ADMINISTRATIVE DIRECTOR
Suzanne Thouin

Manufacturer of screens and frames.

TECHNI-BRITE, INC.
(Screen cleaning, licensee of TSII)
1302 La Fiesta, Grand Prairie, TX 75052.
TEL: (972) 264-4989. FAX: (866) 223-0124.
email: info@techni-brite.com www.techni-brite.com
PRESIDENT
John Atchley
VICE PRESIDENT
Keri Atchley
V.P., SALES/MARKETING
Dave Woolery

T SCREEN COMPANY
(A division of Big Sky Industries. Manufacturer of screens for motion picture theatres)
1475 Park Ave. Jamison, PA 18929. TEL: (908) 454-0421.
FAX: (908) 454-6373. email: Info@tscreenco.com
www.tscreenco.com
CEO
Mark Smith
SENIOR V.P., SALES
Mitch Schwam
V.P., MANUFACTURING
Mike Avallone

WOLF THEATRE SERVICES
(A division of Michael Wolf Interiors, Inc.)
15 Daybreak, Irvine, CA 92614. TEL: (949) 733-8388.
FAX: (949) 733-8389. email: WolfFlow28@cox.net
screencleaner@cox.net www.wolfts.com
PRESIDENT
Michael Wolf
V.P., OPERATIONS
Ilan Wolf

Screen cleaning service; Front end, drapery and speaker installation. Also wall lighting, floor and wall carpet services.

SEATING AND RE-UPHOLSTERY

A&B COMPANY
(Screen, seat, upholstery cleaning; nightly janitorial; carpet & floor cleaning; pressure wash; fire-protectant application)
6536 Fulton Ave., Van Nuys, CA 91401. TEL: (818) 985-7768.
FAX: (818) 763-7914. email: service@AandBCompany.com
www.aandbcompany.com
CONTACT
Mike Fuss

ABSECON MILLS, INC.
(Supplier of contract upholstery fabrics)
P.O. Box 672, Vienna & Aloe Avenues, Cologne, NJ 08213-0672. TEL: (609) 965-5373. FAX: (609) 965-7474.
email: info@absecon.com www.absecon.com
PRESIDENT & CEO
Randolph Taylor - rtaylor@absecon.com
EXECUTIVE V.P.
David Adair - dadair@absecon.com
V.P., DESIGN & MARKETING
Linda Taylor - ltaylor@absecon.com
DIRECTOR OF COMMUNICATIONS
Gaily Von Schlichting - gvons@absecon.com
EXPORT MANAGER
Margie Cochran - mcochran@absecon.com
DIRECTOR OF COMMUNICATIONS
Gaily Von Schlichting - gvons@absecon.com

AMERICAN SEATING COMPANY
(Theatres, auditoriums, PAC's & stadium seating)
401 American Seating Central NW, Grand Rapids, MI 49504.
TEL: (800) 748-0268, (616) 732-6600. FAX: (616) 732-6502.
email: info@americanseating.com www.americanseating.com
SALES MANAGER
Michael Hoffman

ASSIGNED SEATING & MANUFACTURING GROUP, INC.
(All types of large-facility seating)
P.O. Box 3206, 10854 Central Ave., S. El Monte, CA 91733.
TEL: (626) 454-4599. FAX: (626) 454-4590.
email: seatman1@pacbell.net

PRESIDENT
Chuck Kaplan

CALIFORNIA SEATING & REPAIR COMPANY, INC.
(New & used theatre seating; repairs & refurbishing)
12455 Branford St., Unit 2 & 3, Arleta, CA 91331.
TEL: (818) 890-7328. FAX: (805) 581-0226.
email: deltatyme@aol.com www.californiaseating.com
CONTACT
Tim McMahan

CINEMA CONSULTANTS & SERVICES INTERNATIONAL, INC.
1250 Brookline Blvd., P.O. Box 9672, Pittsburgh, PA 15226.
TEL: (412) 343-3900. FAX: (412) 343-2992.
email: info@cinemaequipment.com
www.cinemaconsultantsinternational.com
PRESIDENT
Ross Falvo

Established in 1990. Specializes in theatre design, theatre consulting, projection & sound design/equipment, concessions design/equipment, interior design & installation of projection, sound seating & acoustic draperies.

CINEMA EQUIPMENT SALES OF CA, INC.
(Cinema & screening room projection, sound equipment, parts, seating and furnishings)
23011 Moulton Pkwy., #I-5, Laguna Hills, CA 92653.
TEL: (949) 470-0298. FAX: (949) 470-0835.
email: service@cinemadealer.com www.cinema-equip.com
SALES
Carl Williams - carl@cinemadealer.com
Mike Smith

CLACO EQUIPMENT AND SERVICE, INC.
(Drapery systems, theatre chairs; complete digital & film projection, sound, auditorium equipment & service)
1212 S. State St., Salt Lake City, UT 84111.
TEL: (801) 355-1250. FAX: (801) 355-1259.
email: sales@clacoequipment.com www.clacoequipment.com
PRESIDENT
Clayton Stauffer
SALES
Eric Butterworth
SERVICE
Vince Butler

CLOUD INDUSTRIES, INC.
(Wall & screen drapery, curtains & film handling equipment)
P.O. Box 35, Lawson, MO 64062. TEL: (816) 296-3354.
FAX: (816) 296-7733. www.cloudindustries.com
OWNER, PRESIDENT & CONTROLLER
Mary Shoemaker - mary@cloudindustries.com
V.P., SALES
Chuck Shoemaker - chuck@cloudindustries.com
SALES CONTACT & WEB DESIGNER
Paul Shoemaker

Designer of stage & screen fronts, wall & screen drapery for remodels & new construction; manufacturer of film handling equipment, out of order seat covers & patented stadium seat anchor.

DOLPHIN SEATING CONNECTION
(World class construction, design, comfort & long warranty)
313 Remuda, Clovis, NM 88101. TEL: (575) 762-6468.
FAX: (575) 763-0440. email: info@dolphinseating.com
www.dolphinseating.com
CONTACT
Sam Snell - sam@dolphinseating.com

ENTERTAINMENT SUPPLY & TECHNOLOGIES, LLC
4971 Van Dyke Rd., Lutz, FL 33558. TEL: (813) 960-1646.
FAX: (813) 961-7209.
PRESIDENT & CEO
Barney Bailey
VICE PRESIDENT
Ron Eiben - reiben@ensutec.com

Entertainment Supply & Technologies provides the following: Digital projection equipment, 35mm projection equipment, Xenon lamps, sound equipment, seating, aisle lighting, crowd control ropes & posts, poster cases, screens, frames & screen drapes, acoustical panels, concession & ticketing casework, concession equipment, 2-way radios, parts, supplies, janitorial equipment, turn-key project management, installations, defixturing service, design, planning & drafting services.

GREYSTONE INTERNATIONAL, INC.
(U.S. manufacturer of high quality theatre chairs, educational auditorium chairs, worship chairs and luxury home theatre chairs)
870 74th St. SW, Grand Rapids, MI 49315.
TEL: (866) 748-4373, (616) 878-5636. FAX: (616) 878-7189.
email: GStanton@greystoneintl.com
seating-sales@greystoneintl.com
www.greystoneintl.com
PRESIDENT
Gaylord Stanton

HUSSEY SEATING COMPANY
(Spectator seating for theatres, auditoriums and arena stadiums)
38 Dyer St. Ext., North Berwick, ME 03906.
TEL: (800) 341-0401, (207) 676-2271. FAX: (207) 676-2222.
email: info@husseyseating.com www.husseyseating.com
MARKETING MANAGER
Ron Bilodeau - rbilodeau@husseyseating.com

IRWIN SEATING COMPANY
(Auditorium seating. See website for additional offices and contacts)
3251 Fruit Ridge NW, Grand Rapids, MI 49544.
TEL: (616) 574-7400. FAX: (616) 574-7411.
email: sales@irwinseating.com www.irwinseating.com
PRESIDENT & CEO
Earle S. Irwin
V.P., SALES
Bruce Cohen
CONTACT
Anne Durell

MANKO SEATING CO.
(Replacement seat covers and backs using original fabrics from our extensive inventory)
50 W. 36th St., New York, NY 10018-8002. TEL: (212) 695-7470.
FAX: (212) 563-0840.
CONTACT
Norman Manko - normanko@aol.com

RANACK CONSTRUCTORS, INC.
(Design, build & retro-fit construction)
652 S. County Rd. 9E, Ste. 101, Loveland, CO 80537.
TEL: (970) 667-3698. FAX: (970) 667-3694.
email: info@ranack.com www.ranack.com
CONTACT
Doug Shirack - doug_ranack@lpbroadband.net

SEATING CONCEPTS
(Seating Concepts, LLC is a world-leading manufacturer of seating for cinemas, public auditoriums, performing arts centers, education facilities and houses of worship)
2225 Hancock St., San Diego, CA 92110.
TEL: (619) 491-3159. FAX: (619) 491-3172.
www.seatingconcepts.com
CINEMA SALES MANAGER
John Fennell - jfennell@seatingconcepts.com

SOUTHERN SCENIC EQUIPMENT CO.
(Theatre seat refurbishing; retrofit theatres to stadium seating; theatre & stage drapery)
1040 Branch Dr., Alpharetta, GA 30004. TEL: (770) 475-0733.
FAX: (770) 475-0910.
PRESIDENT
Ted Yarborough

STADIUM SAVERS, LTD.
(System for stadium construction and retro-fitting)
550 3 Mile Rd. NW, Grand Rapids, MI 49544.
TEL: (616) 785-5598. FAX: (616) 785-5657.
email: stadium@stadiumsavers.com www.stadiumsavers.com
CONTACTS
Dick Murphy, Dwight Huskey, William Brunner

STADIUM SEATING ENTERPRISES, INC.
(Design & manufacture of prefabricated stadium seating systems)
28202 Cabot Rd., Ste. 300, Laguna Niguel, CA 92677.
TEL: (949) 363-7128. FAX: (949) 363-0837.
www.stadiumseating.com
PRESIDENT
Frank B. Moson - frankmoson@stadiumseating.com
VICE PRESIDENT
Carol Lee - clee@stadiumseating.com

TRACK CORPORATION
Track Seating, A division of Track Corporation, 17204 Taft Rd., Spring Lake, MI 49456. TEL: (877) 479-7005, (616) 844-2471.
FAX: (616) 844-2476. email: sales@trackcorp.com
www.trackcorp.com
MIDWEST REGIONAL SALES MANAGER
Jake Wisner - (616) 850-9442 - jawisner@trackseating.com
NORTH EAST REGIONAL SALES MANAGER
Bruce Dahlman - (616) 850-9434 - bdahlman@trackseating.com
SOUTHERN REGIONAL SALES MANAGER
Bob Sprouse - (423) 326-1008 - SprousB@trackcorp.com
WESTERN REGIONAL SALES MANAGER
Ben Stanton - (720) 887-6962 - bstanton@trackseating.com
THEATRE PRODUCTS SPECIALIST
Tom O'Hara - tohara@trackcorp.com

VIP CINEMA SEATING
589 N. Coley Rd., Tupelo, MS 38801. TEL: (662) 841-5866.
FAX: (662) 840-2390. email: steve@vipcinemaseating.com
CONTACTS
Steve Simons, Eddie Powell

Designs, develops and manufactures VIP cinema seating.

CY YOUNG INDUSTRIES, INC.
(On-site seat renovation; replacement seatcovers.

Manufacturer of molded cushions, cupholder armrests, concession trays, booster seats)
16201 W. 110th St., Lenexa, KS 66219. TEL: (800) 729-2610, (913) 438-1776. FAX: (913) 888-1774. www.cyyoungind.com
PRESIDENT & CEO
J.R. Young (Rick)
EXECUTIVE V.P.
Carrie E. Young

SECURITY SERVICES

ADVANCED SURVEILLANCE TECHNOLOGIES, INC.
(Sales and installation of digital recording surveillance camera management systems)
100 Canal Pointe Blvd. Princeton, NJ 08540.
TEL: (877) 393-0999, (609) 921-7721. FAX: (609) 921-9226.
email: sales@surveillancetechnologies.com
www.surveillancetechnologies.com
REGIONAL SALES MANAGER
Chris Bell

ALCOPS
(Blind theatre checkings; background screening)
A Division of Orion Specialists, LLC./5750 W. 95th St., Ste. 320, Overland Park, KS 66207. TEL: (800) 345-7347, (913) 362-0104. FAX: (800) 252-4060. www.alcops.com
OPERATIONS MANAGER
Patti Rentrop

GARDA
Head office: 1390 Barré St., Montreal, Quebec, H3C 1N4.
TEL: (514) 281-2811. FAX: (514) 281-2860.
www.gardaglobal.com.com

Garda is a global security firm. When it comes to physical security, Garda provides a wide array of highly specialized services, which include uniformed protection, in-store loss prevention, airport preboard screening services, executive and asset protection, patrols and alarm response, consulting as well as strike security.

WORLDWIDE SAFE & VAULT, INC.
(Cash-handling safes, access-controlled electronic safe locks, all aspects of physical security hardware)
3660 N.W. 115th Ave., Miami, FL 33178. TEL: (800) 932-2278, (305) 477-9266. FAX: (305) 477-9744.
email: sales@worldwidesafe.com www.worldwidesafe.com
OWNER & PRESIDENT
Scott Hirsch

SOUND EQUIPMENT

ACE COMMUNICATIONS
(Audio-visual equipment rental & sound systems)
625 Locust St., Garden City, NY 11530. TEL: (800) 468-7667.
FAX: (516) 872-8156. email: info@aceav.com www.aceav.com
VICE PRESIDENT
Joe Melfa
MARKETING MANAGER
Amy Fulton

AMERICAN CINEMA EQUIPMENT, INC.
(Projection, sound, digital projection & sound, engineering, project management, construction management & seats)
1927 N. Argyle St., Portland, OR 97217.
TEL: (800) 956-6589, (503) 285-7015, (916) 832-9510 (N. CA).
FAX: (503) 285-6765. www.cinequip.com
PRESIDENT
Scott R. Hicks - scott.hicks@cinequip.com
V.P., SALES & MARKETING
Doug Sabin - doug.sabin@cinequip.com

ATLAS SPECIALTY LIGHTING
(Entertainment lighting, projection equipment, digital sound systems & digital cinema equipment)
7304 N. Florida Ave., Tampa, FL 33604. TEL: (813) 238-6481.
FAX: (813) 238-6656. www.asltg.com
MANAGERS
Ralph Felten, Jr. - rfelten@asltg2.com
Bob Ray

AUDIO SERVICE COMPANY, INC.
(Projection & sound equipment; service & installation)
P.O. Box 50, Yakima, WA 98907. TEL: (509) 248-7041.
FAX: (509) 453-3074.
CONTACT
Darrell Hoff

BGW SYSTEMS
(An Amplifier Technologies Inc. company. Power amplifiers)
1749 Chapin Rd., Montebello, CA 90640. TEL: (323) 278-0001.
FAX: (323) 278-0083. email: info@bgw.com www.bgw.com
SALES
Angie Masincup-Scott - angie@bgw.com

BOSTON LIGHT & SOUND
(Rental & dealer of film & video projectors & sound equipment; service & installation)
290 N. Beacon St., Boston, MA 02135. TEL: (617) 787-3131.
FAX: (617) 787-4257. email: info@blsi.com www.blsi.com
RENTAL MANAGER
Celine Larimer
FILM & VIDEO SYSTEMS MANAGER
Robert Harris

CARDINAL SOUND & MOTION PICTURE SYSTEMS, INC.
(Digital sound systems; 16mm, 35mm, & 70mm film and digital projection equipment)
6330 Howard Ln., Elkridge, MD 21075. TEL: (410) 796-5300.
FAX: (410) 796-7995. email: cardinal@cardinalsound.com
www.cardinalsound.com
OFFICE MANAGER
Catherine Rockman

CINEMA EQUIPMENT SALES OF CA, INC.
(Cinema & screening room projection, sound equipment, parts, seating and furnishings)
23011 Moulton Pkwy., #I-5, Laguna Hills, CA 92653.
TEL: (949) 470-0298. FAX: (949) 470-0835.
email: service@cinemadealer.com www.cinema-equip.com
SALES
Carl Williams - carl@cinemadealer.com
Mike Smith

COMPONENT ENGINEERING
(Manufacturer of LED sound readers, sound system accessories, automation equipment and cue detectors)
4554 9th Ave. NE, #110, Seattle, WA 98105-4711.
TEL: (206) 284-9171. FAX: (206) 286-4462.
email: cs@componentengineering.com
www.componentengineering.com

CROWN AUDIO, INC.
(Crown is a unit of Harman International Industries, Inc. Produces amplifiers, microphones & systems control)
1718 W. Mishawaka Rd., Elkhart, IN 46517. TEL: (800) 342-6939, (574) 294-8200. FAX: (574) 294-8250.
email: audioinfo@crownintl.com www.crownaudio.com
V.P., MARKETING
Marc Kellom
DIRECTOR, MARKETING
Stephen Morris
DIRECTOR OF SALES, INTERCONTINENTAL
Jaime Albors - jalbors@crownintl.com
DIRECTOR OF SALES, EUROPE, MIDDLE EAST & AFRICA
Dave Budge - dbudge@crownintl.com
DIRECTOR OF SALES, ASIA/PACIFIC
Thomas Marcher - tmarcher@crownintl.com

HIGH PERFORMANCE STEREO
(Motion picture sound systems; HPS-4000 systems)
64 Bowen St., Newton, MA 02459-1820. TEL: (617) 244-1737.
email: info@hps4000.com www.hps4000.com
FOUNDER & PRESIDENT
John Allen - jfa@hps4000.com

HOLLYWOOD THEATRE EQUIPMENT, INC.
(Dealer for all 35mm & digital projection & sound equipment)
1941 N. 66 Ave., Hollywood, FL 33024.
TEL: (954) 920-2832. FAX: (954) 986-6914.
email: HWDTHEATRE@aol.com
SALES
Don Gallagher
Don R. Gallagher, Jr. - gahwetheatre@aol.com

INTERNATIONAL ELECTRICAL WIRE/CABLE
(Manufacturer of electronic wire, audio & video cable, LAN & computer cable, coax & fiber optics)
P.O. Box 958184, Hoffman Estates, IL 60195.
TEL: (800) 323-0210, (630) 289-2210. FAX: (630) 860-0305.
email: wiresales@iewcinc.com
SALES MANAGER
Kevin McClure

KINOTON AMERICA, INC.
(Manufactures & distributes film projectors, digital cinema projectors and sound equipment)
33 Jacksonville Rd., Unit #1, Towaco, NJ 07082.
TEL: (973) 331-9200. FAX: (973) 331-9203.
www.kinotonamerica.com
SALES
Ernie Tracey
V.P. OPERATIONS
John Gallucci - johng@kinotonamerica.com

KLIPSCH AUDIO TECHNOLOGIES
(Theatre sound & listening devices)
3502 Woodview Trace, Ste.200, Indianapolis, IN 46268.
TEL: (800) 274-5547, (317) 860-8100.
FAX: (317) 860-9178 (sales and marketing).
email: support@klipsch.com (customerservice)
www.klipsch.com

CEO
Fred S. Klipsch
VICE CHAIRMAN
Judy Klipsch
PRESIDENT & COO
Paul Jacobs
PRESIDENT, GLOBAL SALES
Dave Kelley
PRESIDENT, GLOBAL OPERATIONS & KLIPSCH BRAND
Michael F. Klipsch
PRESS CONTACT
Sarah Knight - (317) 860-8737 sarah.knight@klipsch.com

LOWELL MANUFACTURING CO.
(Racks, power & audio)
100 Integram Dr., Pacific, MO 63069. TEL: (636) 257-3400. FAX: (636) 257-6606. email: sales@lowellmfg.com
www.lowellmfg.com
PRESIDENT
John J. Lowell

MARTIN AUDIO, LTD.
(Theatre sound & listening devices)
P.O. Box 33009, 450 Erb St. W, Waterloo, ON N2N), OA2, Canada. TEL: (519) 747-5853. FAX: (519) 747-3576.
email: infona@martin-audio.com www.martin-audio.com
NATIONAL SALES MANAGER
Rob Hofkamp - rhofkamp@martin-audio.com
SALES ADMINISTRATION MANAGER
Joanne Gaudet

MONSTER CABLE PRODUCTS, INC.
(Since 1979. Cabling)
455 Valley Dr., Brisbane, CA 94005. TEL: (415) 840-2000. FAX: (415) 468-0311, (415) 468-4311.
www.monstercable.com
CONTACT
Daniel Graham - (415) 840-2024 dgraham@monstercable.com

PANASTEREO, INC.
(Premium sound products & panalogic devices)
101 Hollywood Hills Rd., Clarkesville, GA 30523.
TEL: (706) 839-1528. FAX: (678) 349-0672.
www.panastereo.com
PRESIDENT
Norman Schneider

PROJECTED SOUND, INC.
(Replacement parts for drive-in-theatre speakers)
469 Avon Ave., Plainfield, IN 46168-1001. TEL: (317) 839-4111. FAX: (317) 839-2476. email: projectedsnd469@aol.com
VICE PRESIDENT
Dick Hilligoss
SALES
J. Hilligoss

QSC AUDIO PRODUCTS, LLC
(Amplifier, loudspeaker, networked audio, remote monitor and control manufacturer)
1675 MacArthur Blvd., Costa Mesa, CA 92626.
TEL: (800) 854-4079, (714) 754-6175. FAX: (714) 754-6174.
email: info@qscaudio.com www.qscaudio.com
DIRECTOR OF SALES, CINEMA
Francois Godfrey - francois_godfrey@qscaudio.com

STAGE ACCOMPANY USA
(Speakers using Ribbon Compact drivers, amplifiers, other professional sound equipment)
8917 Shore Ct., Brooklyn, NY 11209. TEL: (800) 955-7474.
email: info@stageaccompany.com www.StageAccompany.com
CEO
Paul Silas - paulsilas@stageaccompany.com
MANAGING DIRECTOR
Abraham Son - a.son@stageaccompany.com

THX, LTD.
(Custom engineered cinemas)
1600 Los Gamos Dr., Ste. 231, San Rafael, CA 94903.
TEL: (415) 492-3900. FAX: (415) 492-3930. www.thx.com
V.P., SALES
Mary Crebassa
DIRECTOR, CINEMA STUDIO PROGRAMS
Andrew Poulain
MARKETING
Kristin Klindt
OPERATIONS
Jerry Zernicke

USL, INC.
(Ultra Stereo Labs, Inc. Cinema sound equipment, including processors, booth monitors, crossovers, ADA devices, exciter lamps, test equipment)
181 Bonetti Dr., San Luis Obispo, CA 93401-7310.
TEL: (805) 549-0161. FAX: (805) 549-0163. www.uslinc.com
VICE PRESIDENT
Felicia Cashin - Felicia@uslinc.com
SALES DIRECTOR
Clint Koch - clint@uslinc.com

YAMAHA CORPORATION OF AMERICA, COMMERCIAL AUDIO SYSTEMS DIVISION
(Sound equipment; electronic components & instruments)
P.O. Box 6600, Buena Park, CA 90622. TEL: (714) 522-9011.
email infostation@yamaha.com.
www.yamahacommercialaudiosystems.com
ADVERTISING SALES PROMOTIONAL MANAGER
Doan Hoff
MARKETING MANAGER
Marc Lopez

SOUND REINFORCEMENT

ARCHITECTURAL ACOUSTICS
(Electronics manufacturer; architectural acoustics)
A division of Peavey Electronics Corp., 5022 Hartley Peavey Dr., Meridian, MS 39305. TEL: (601) 483-5365. FAX: (601) 486-1278.
email: aatechsupport@peavey.com marketing@peavey.com
www.peavey.com
SALES
Darry Clark

ASHLY AUDIO, INC.
847 Holt Rd., Webster, NY 14580-9103. TEL: (800) 828-6308, (585) 872-0010. FAX: (585) 872-0739.
email: sales@ashly.com www.ashly.com
MARKETING LITERATURE, PRICING, PRODUCT AVAILABILITY
Margo McAvaney - margo@ashly.com

BGW SYSTEMS
(An Amplifier Technologies Inc. company. Power amplifiers)
1749 Chapin Rd., Montebello, CA 90640. TEL: (323) 278-0001. FAX: (323) 278-0083. email: info@bgw.com www.bgw.com
SALES
Angie Masincup-Scott - angie@bgw.com

CREST AUDIO, INC.
(Amplifiers, consoles, speakers)
5022 Hwy. 493, Meridian, MS 39305. TEL: (866) 812-7378. FAX: (601) 486-1380. email: webmaster@crestaudio.com
www.crestaudio.com

See website for international locations and technical support contacts.

CROWN AUDIO, INC.
(Crown is a unit of Harman International Industries, Inc. Produces amplifiers, microphones & systems control)
1718 W. Mishawaka Rd., Elkhart, IN 46517. TEL: (800) 342-6939, (574) 294-8200. FAX: (574) 294-8250.
email: audioinfo@crownintl.com www.crownaudio.com
V.P., MARKETING
Marc Kellom
DIRECTOR, MARKETING
Stephen Morris
DIRECTOR OF SALES, INTERCONTINENTAL
Jaime Albors - jalbors@crownintl.com
DIRECTOR OF SALES, EUROPE, MIDDLE EAST & AFRICA
Dave Budge - dbudge@crownintl.com
DIRECTOR OF SALES, ASIA/PACIFIC
Thomas Marcher - tmarcher@crownintl.com

JBL PROFESSIONAL
(JBL Professional is a unit of Harman International Industries, Incorporated — www.harman.com — Loudspeaker systems)
8500 Balboa Blvd., Northridge, CA 91329. TEL: (818) 894-8850. FAX: (818) 830-7801 (Sales), (818) 830-7865 (Marketing).
www.jblpro.com
PRESIDENT
John Carpanini
SENIOR DIRECTOR, COMMERCIAL INSTALLED SOUND
Rick Kamlet
DIRECTOR, CINEMA
Chuck Goodsell - charles.goodsel@harmon.com

QSC AUDIO PRODUCTS, LLC
(Amplifier, loudspeaker, networked audio, remote monitor and control manufacturer)
1665 MacArthur Blvd., Costa Mesa, CA 92626.
TEL: (800) 854-4079, (714) 754-6175. FAX: (714) 754-6174.
email: info@qscaudio.com www.qscaudio.com
DIRECTOR OF SALES, CINEMA
Francois Godfrey - francois_godfrey@qscaudio.com

SOUNDCRAFT
(Soundboards & consoles for live and recorded sound)
Harman Pro North America, 8500 Balboa Blvd., Northridge, CA 91329. TEL: (818) 920-3212. FAX: (818) 920-3209.
email: soundcraft-USA@harman.com www.soundcraft.com
V.P., SALES
Nick Owen
NATIONAL SALES MANAGER
Tom Der - tder@harman.com

SPEAKERS

ALLEN PRODUCTS CO., INC.
(Division of Adaptive Technologies Group. Mounting & rigging solutions for speakers and video equipment)
Adaptive Technologies Group-West Coast, 1635 E. Burnett St., Signal Hill, CA 90755. TEL: (562) 424-1100.
FAX: (562) 424-3520. email: info@adattechgroup.com
www.allenproducts.com
PRESIDENT
Paul Allen - pallen@allenproducts.com

ARCHITECTURAL ACOUSTICS
(Electronics manufacturer; architectural acoustics)
A division of Peavey Electronics Corp./5022 Hartley Peavey Dr., Meridian, MS 39305. TEL: (601) 483-5365. FAX: (601) 486-1278.
email: aatechsupport@peavey.com www.peavey.com
SALES
Darry Clark

BOSTON LIGHT & SOUND
(Rental & dealer of film & video projectors & sound equipment; service & installation)
290 N. Beacon St., Boston, MA 02135. TEL: (617) 787-3131.
FAX: (617) 787-4257. email: info@blsi.com www.blsi.com
RENTAL MANAGER
Celine Larimer
FILM & VIDEO SYSTEMS MANAGER
Robert Harris

CERWIN-VEGA, INC.
(Division of the Stanton Group. Professional audio products. See website for additional contacts and offices)
772 S. Military Trail, Deerfield Beach, FL 33442.
TEL: (954) 949-9600. FAX: (954) 949-9590.
email: Info@Cerwin-Vega.com www.cerwin-vega.com
MEDIA RELATIONS
Dan Bruck - (954) 949-9590 - dbruck@cerwin-vega.com

COMMUNITY PROFESSIONAL LOUDSPEAKERS
(Manufacturer of loudspeakers and horns for cinema and theatrical applications, indoor and outdoor venues, both large and small; custom designs available)
333 E. Fifth St., Chester, PA 19013. TEL: (610) 876-3400.
FAX: (610) 874-0190. www.communitypro.com
V.P., NEW BUSINESS DEVELOPMENT
John Wiggins
DIRECTOR, SALES & MARKETING
Julia Lee - sales@communitypro.com
MARKETING COMMUNICATIONS MANAGER
Grace Paoli - ext. 106 - gpaoli@communitypro.com

EASTERN ACOUSTIC WORKS (EAW)
(Manufacturer of loudspeaker systems for cinemas)
A subsidiary of Mackie Designs, Inc., One Main St., Whitinsville, MA 01588. TEL: (800) 992-5013, (508) 234-6158.
FAX: (800) 322-8251, (508) 234-8251. email: info@eaw.com
www.eaw.com
EXECUTIVE V.P., STRATEGIC PRODUCT DEVELOPMENT
Kenton Forsythe
SALES ADMIN
Janet Yacino

ELECTRO-VOICE
Bosch Communications Systems/Telex Communications, Inc., 12000 Portland Ave. S., Burnsville, MN 55337.
TEL: (800) 392-3497, (952) 884-4051. FAX: (952) 884-0043, (952) 736-4582 (public relations fax).
email: buv.orders@us.bosch.com www.electrovoice.com
DISTRICT MANAGER - EASTERN REGION
Harry Klane - Harry.klane@us.bosch.com
DISTRICT MANAGER - CENTRAL REGION
Mike Linden - Mike.linden@us.bosch.com
DISTRICT MANAGER - WESTERN REGION
Mark Storm - Mark.storm@us.bosch.com

Electro-Voice® has provided cinema loudspeaker systems and amplifiers for over 30 years to major theatres around the globe. EV® has brought engineering innovations to cinema sound during this time with Constant Directivity™ horns, at the forefront of neodymium component technology & design, and was the first to offer low-profile 3-way systems like the Variplex™.

FRAZIER LOUDSPEAKER
3030 Canton St., Dallas, TX 75226. TEL: (214) 741-7136.
FAX: (214) 939-0328.
CONTACT
J. E. Mitchell

FULL COMPASS SYSTEMS, LTD.
(Audio, video and lighting; sales, repair, and rental services)
8001 Terrace Ave. Middleton, WI 53562. TEL: (800) 356-5844, (608) 831-7330. FAX: (608) 831-6330.
email: customerservice@fullcompass.com
www.fullcompass.com
NATIONAL SALES MANAGER
Jon Vitale

IRA TEC/PRO AUDIO REPAIR
(Professional audio repair)
12315 S.W. 40th St., Yukon, OK 73099. TEL: (405) 324-5311.
FAX: (405) 324-5355. email: RiraTec@aol.com
www.iratec.50megs.com
OWNER
Ira Rastampour

JBL PROFESSIONAL
(JBL Professional is a unit of Harman International Industries, Incorporated — www.harman.com — Loudspeaker systems)
8500 Balboa Blvd., Northridge, CA 91329. TEL: (818) 894-8850. (Sales), (818) 830-7865 (Marketing). www.jblpro.com
PRESIDENT
John Carpanini
SENIOR DIRECTOR, COMMERCIAL INSTALLED SOUND
Rick Kamlet
DIRECTOR, CINEMA
Chuck Goodsell - charles.goodsell@harmon.com

KLIPSCH AUDIO TECHNOLOGIES
(Theatre sound & listening devices)
3502 Woodview Trace, Ste.200, Indianapolis,IN 46268.
TEL: (800) 274-5547, (317) 860-8100.
FAX: (317) 860-9178 (sales and marketing).
email: support@klipsch.com (customerservice)
www.klipsch.com
CEO
Fred S. Klipsch
VICE CHAIRMAN
Judy Klipsch
PRESIDENT & COO
Paul Jacobs
PRESIDENT, GLOBAL SALES
Dave Kelley
PRESIDENT, GLOBAL OPERATIONS & KLIPSCH BRAND
Michael F. Klipsch
PRESS CONTACT
Sarah Knight - (317) 860-8737 - sarah.knight@klipsch.com

LOUD TECHNOLOGIES, INC.
16220 Wood-Red Rd. NE, Woodinville, WA 98072.
TEL: (866) 858-5832, (425) 892-6500. FAX: (425) 487-4337.
www.loudtechinc.com www.eaw.com
CONTACT
Kyle Fletcher - (425) 402-6224

MILLER & KREISEL SOUND CORP.
9207 Eton Ave., Chatsworth CA 91311. TEL: (818) 701-7010.
FAX: (818) 701-0369, (818) 718-1171.
email: kkmksound@aol.com
DIRECTOR, M&K PROFESSIONAL
Chris Minto

MISCO/MINNEAPOLIS SPEAKER CO., INC.
(Manufacturer of 2"-12" speakers)
2637 32nd Ave. S, Minneapolis, MN 55406. TEL: (800) 276-9955, (612) 825-1010. FAX: (612) 825-7010.
email: info@miscospeakers.com www.miscospeakers.com
CONTACT
Dan Digre

SLS AUDIO
1650 W. Jackson St., Ozark, MO 65721. TEL: (417) 883-4549.
FAX: (417) 883-2723. www.slsaudio.com
CHAIRMAN & CEO
John Glott - jgott@slsaudio.com
DIRECTOR OF ENGINEERING
Tom Harrison - tharrison@slsaudio.com
INTERNATIONAL DIRECTOR/PRO MARKET DEVELOPMENT
R Bob Adams - rbob.adams@slsaudio.com
DIRECTOR OF SALES AND MARKETING - PROFESSIONAL PRODUCTS
Jeff Lowry - marketing@slsaudio.com

STAGE DESIGN

CALIFORNIA STAGE & LIGHTING
(Stage lighting equipment & supplies)
3601 W. Garry Ave., Santa Ana, CA 92704-6424.
TEL: (714) 966-1852. FAX: (714) 966-0104.
email: sales@calstage.com www.calstage.com
PRESIDENT
Jimmy Ray Hutton
RENTAL & SALES CONSULTANTS
Kris Kelley, Bob Mumm
TECHNICAL OPERATIONS MANAGER
Fran Shaw

GROSH SCENIC RENTALS, INC.
(Backdrop & drapery rental)
4114 Sunset Blvd., Hollywood, CA 90029. TEL: (877) 363-7998, (323) 662-1134. FAX: (323) 664-7526. email: info@grosh.com
www.grosh.com
MANAGER OF SALES AND NEW MEDIA
Lindsay Fultz - lindsay@grosh.com

LIBERTY THEATRICAL DECOR
22313 Meekland Av., Hayward, CA 94541. TEL: (510) 889-1951.
FAX: (510) 889-1602. email: libertyrig@aol.com
OWNER
Don Nethercott

THEATRE CLEANING AND MAINTENANCE

A&B COMPANY
(Screen, seat, upholstery cleaning; nightly janitorial; carpet & floor cleaning; pressure wash; fire-protectant application)
6536 Fulton Ave., Van Nuys, CA 91401. TEL: (818) 985-7768.
FAX: (818) 763-7914. email: service@AandBCompany.com
www.aandbcompany.com
CONTACT
Mike Fuss

ACS ENTERPRISES, INC.
(Janitorial services, carpet & screen cleaning and floor care)
P.O. Box 810, Walnut, CA 91788. TEL: (888) 227-5610,
(909) 595-3484. FAX: (909) 595-3447. www.acs-ent.com
CEO
Jose G. Alvarado
V.P., SALES & MARKETING
Patrick Artiaga - ext. 710 - partiaga@acs-ent.com
DIRECTOR, OPERATIONS
Raul Alvarado - ext. 705 - ralvarado@acs-ent.com
DIRECTOR, FACILITY DEVELOPMENT
Wayne Kochanek - ext. 706
CUSTOMER RELATIONS REPRESENTATIVE
Francisco Peratta - ext. 714

APTER INDUSTRIES, INC.
(Manufacturer of cleaning chemicals)
P.O. Box 456, McKeesport, PA 15134-0456.
TEL: (800) 441-7146, (412) 672-9628. FAX: (412) 672-3343.
email: info@apterindustries.com www.apterindustries.com

ATLANTIC THEATRE CLEANING
P.O. Box 39, Pleasant Valley, CT 06063. TEL: (866) 379-6880.
www.atlantictc.net
OWNER, PRESIDENT
Jesus Cachaya - (336) 340-6378 - cachaya.j@atlantictc.net
V.P., SALES & OPERATIONS
Charles Hyatt - (866) 379-6880 - hyatt.ca@atlantictc.net
OPERATIONS MANAGER
Diana Cachaya - (954) 817-1167
cachaya.diana@atlantictc.net

BONUS BUILDING CARE
P.O. Box 300, Indianola, OK 74442. TEL: (918) 823-4990.
FAX: (918) 823-4994. email: franchises@bonusbuildingcare.com
PRESIDENT
Perry White - pwhite@bonusbuildingcare.com

BRAUN BRUSH COMPANY
(Screen cleaning, all types of brushes, environmentally safe cleaning chemicals, popcorn squeegies)
43 Albertson Ave., Albertson, NY 11507. TEL: (800) 645-4111.
FAX: (516) 741-6299. email: Sales@brush.com
www.brush.com
PRESIDENT
Lance Cheney - marketing@brush.com
CUSTOMER SERVICE
Jerilyn Leis

CINCOM–THE MEGAPLEX CINEMA SPECIALISTS
(Movie theatre cleaning)
P.O. Box 2533, Salem, NH 03079. TEL: (800) 992-4403,
(603) 434-0514. FAX: (888) 322-1667.
email: info@Cincom.net sales@cincom.net www.cincom.net
PRESIDENT & CEO
Matthew W. Sinopoli
DIRECTOR, CORPORATE OPERATIONS
Maria Carroca

CINEMA CONSULTANTS & SERVICES INTERNATIONAL, INC.
1250 Brookline Blvd., P.O. Box 9672, Pittsburgh, PA 15226.
TEL: (412) 343-3900. FAX: (412) 343-2992.
email: info@cinemaequipment.com
www.cinemaconsultantsinternational.com
PRESIDENT
Ross Falvo

Established in 1990. Specializes in theatre design, theatre consulting, projection & sound design/equipment, concessions design/equipment, interior design & installation of projection, sound seating & acoustic draperies.

CLEANING SERVICES GROUP
(Daily janitorial, carpet and hard floor care)
230 North St., Danvers, MA 01923. TEL: (800) 683-6572.
FAX: (800) 789-5440. www.cleaningservicesgroup.com
PRESIDENT
Dennis O'Brien
V.P., SALES
Rick Sturgis

CLEANNET USA
9861 Broken Land Pkwy., #208, Columbia, MD 21046.
TEL: (800) 735-8838, (410) 720-6444. FAX: (410) 720-5307.
www.cleannetusa.com

CLEANPAK PRODUCTS, LLC
(Industrial chemical & cleaning products)
5408 N. 59th St., Ste. A, Tampa, FL 33610.
TEL: (800) 790-3090, (813) 740-8611. FAX: (813) 740-8218.
email: sales@cleanpakproducts.com
www.cleanpakproducts.com
PRESIDENT
George Brydon - gtbrydon@cleanpakproducts.com

CREST-TALMADGE
(Janitorial supplies)
1590 Rollins Rd., Burlingame, CA 94010. TEL: (650) 692-7378.
FAX: (650) 692-8059. email: crestsls@aol.com
VICE PRESIDENT
Mark Talmadge

JANI-KING INTERNATIONAL, INC.
16885 Dallas Pkwy., Addison, TX 75001. TEL: (800) JANIKING,
(972) 991-0900. www.janiking.com

KIMBERLY-CLARK PROFESSIONAL
(Towels, tissue, napkins and dispensers)
Headquarters: P.O. Box 619100, Dallas, TX 75261-9100.
TEL: (972) 281-1481. FAX: (972) 281-1490.
email: kcpinfo@kcc.com www.kcprofessional.com
PRESIDENT
Jan B. Spencer
SENIOR V.P. & CHIEF MARKETING OFFICER
Anthony J. Palmer
DIRECTOR, CORPORATE COMMUNICATIONS
Dave Dickson - ddickson@kcc.com

MANUTECH MANUFACTURING AND DISTRIBUTING
(Manufactures high performance vacuums & blowers. Distributors of quality brand-name theatre cleaning equipment)
P.O. Box. 51295, 2080 Sunset Dr., Pacific Grove, CA 93950.
TEL: (800) 676-2569, (831) 655-8794. FAX: (831) 655-8967.
email: info@manutech.com www.manutech.com
PRESIDENT
Angelo Villucci

ONE-STOP BUSINESS
(Theatre cleaning nationwide)
9555 Lebanon Bldg. 1, Ste. 101, Frisco, TX 75035.
TEL: (877) 518-7867 ext. 25. FAX: (866) 991-7867.
www.onestopbiz.net
MARKETING DIRECTOR
Micah Jones - micah@onestopbiz.net

PROSTAR INDUSTRIES
(Janitorial and sanitary supplies & equipment)
1590-A N. Harvey Mitchell Pkwy., Bryan, TX 77803.
TEL: (800) 262-7104, (979) 779-9399. FAX: (800) 423-6254,
(979) 779-7616. email: info@prostarind.com
service@prostarind.com www.prostarindustries.com

PROTOCOL, LLC
(Your personal product vending specialists)
2108 Cheshire Way, Ste. A, Greensboro, NC 27405.
TEL: (800) 227-5336. FAX: (336) 553-0756.
www.protocolvending.com
PRESIDENT
Doug Lang - DougL@protocolvending.com
SALES
Chris Marshall - sales@protocolvending.com

STAR MAXX, LLC
(Soundfold/drapery cleaning, screen cleaning, seat cleaning)
90 Fern Creek Ln., Union, MO 63084. TEL: (636) 485-1653,
(314) 210-7401. FAX: (636) 583-1103.
PRESIDENT, SALES
Leonard J. Waldman
V.P., SALES
Don Waldman
V.P., OPERATIONS
Lee Waldman
SECRETARY
Darlene Waldman

THEATRE SPECIALTY COMPANY, INC.
(Carpet, seat & floor cleaning)
P.O. Box 2126, Loveland, CO 80538. TEL: (877) 701-5271,
(970) 669-5407. FAX: (970) 669-1829.
email: tsc1121@netzero.com
SALES MANAGER
Dave Sizemore

UNITED RECEPTACLE
(Theatre cleaning)
P.O. Box 870, Pottsville, PA 17901. 1400 Laurel Blvd.,
Pottsville, PA 17901-1427. TEL: (800) 233-0314,

(570) 622-7715. FAX: (800) 847-8551, (570) 622-3817.
email: united@unitedrecept.com www.unitedrecept.com
CONTACT
Sheryl Beltz

Leading manufacturer of quality commercial waste receptacles, smokers' urns, recycling containers, planters and accessories from steel, fiberglass, aluminum, marble, wood and concrete in over 1,000 styles and finishes.

WINTERS JANITORIAL
(Cleaning equipment & janitorial supplies)
P.O Box 6408, Lee's Summit, MO 64064. TEL: (888) 483-2945, (816) 777-0609. FAX: (816) 777-0615.
www.theatrecleaning.com www.wintersjanitorial.com
CEO
Rob Winters
V.P., SALES & MARKETING
Doug Schlueter - douglass@wintersjanitorial.com

ZAPATA JANITORIAL BUILDING AND GENERAL SERVICES, INC.
(Janitorial services)
10190 Old Katy Rd., Ste. 510, Houston, TX 77043.
TEL: (877) 492-7282, (713) 827-0205. FAX: (713) 827-1215.
email: zapatajan@sbcglobal.net www.zapatajanitorial.com
PRESIDENT
Alfonso H. Zapata
VICE PRESIDENT
Len Westenberg - lwestenberg@zapatajanitorial.com
SALES
Romeo Palacios

THEATRE EQUIPMENT DEALERS

AMERICAN CINEMA EQUIPMENT, INC.
(Projection, sound, digital projection & sound, engineering, project management, construction management & seats)
1927 N. Argyle St., Portland, OR 97217.
TEL: (800) 956-6589, (503) 285-7015, (916) 832-9510 (N. CA).
FAX: (503) 285-6765. www.cinequip.com
PRESIDENT
Scott R. Hicks - scott.hicks@cinequip.com
V.P., SALES & MARKETING
Doug Sabin - doug.sabin@cinequip.com

ATLAS SPECIALTY LIGHTING
(Entertainment lighting, projection equipment, digital sound systems & digital cinema equipment)
7304 N. Florida Ave., Tampa, FL 33604. TEL: (813) 238-6481.
FAX: (813) 238-6656. www.asltg.com
MANAGERS
Ralph Felten, Jr. - rfelten@asltg2.com
Bob Ray

BIG SKY INDUSTRIES
(Manufacturer and distributor of projection booth equipment; booth supplies)
1475 Park Ave., Alpha, NJ 08865. TEL: (908) 454-6344.
FAX: (908) 454-6373. www.bigskyindustries.net
PRESIDENT/FOUNDER
Mark Smith - mark@bigskyindustries.net
SALES & MARKETING
Mike Avallone - mikea@bigskyindustries.net

BOSTON LIGHT & SOUND
(Rental & dealer of film & video projectors & sound equipment; service & installation)
290 N. Beacon St., Boston, MA 02135. TEL: (617) 787-3131.
FAX: (617) 787-4257. email: info@blsi.com www.blsi.com
RENTAL MANAGER
Celine Larimer
FILM & VIDEO SYSTEMS MANAGER
Robert Harris

CARDINAL SOUND & MOTION PICTURE SYSTEMS, INC.
(Digital sound systems; 16mm, 35mm, & 70mm film and digital projection equipment)
6330 Howard Ln., Elkridge, MD 21075. TEL: (410) 796-5300.
FAX: (410) 796-7995. email: cardinal@cardinalsound.com
www.cardinalsound.com
OFFICE MANAGER
Catherine Rockman

CINEMA EQUIPMENT & SUPPLIES, INC.
12457 S.W. 130th St., Miami, FL 33186. TEL: (800) 759-5905, (305) 232-8182. FAX: (800) 759-5914, (305) 232-6049, (305) 232-8172. email: sales@cinemaequip.com
www.cinemaequip.com
CONTACT
Guillermo Younger

ENTERTAINMENT SUPPLY & TECHNOLOGIES, LLC
4971 Van Dyke Rd., Lutz, FL 33558. TEL: (813) 960-1646.
FAX: (813) 961-7209.
PRESIDENT & CEO
Barney Bailey
VICE PRESIDENT
Ron Eiben - reiben@ensutec.com

Entertainment Supply & Technologies provides the following: Digital projection equipment, 35mm projection equipment, Xenon lamps, sound equipment, seating, aisle lighting, crowd control ropes & posts, poster cases, screens, frames & screen drapes, acoustical panels, concession & ticketing casework, concession equipment, 2-way radios, parts, supplies, janitorial equipment, turn-key project management, installations, defixturing service, design, planning & drafting services.

ERNEMANN CINETEC U.S.A.
(Cinema projectors & platters)
430 W. 34th St., #4C, New York, NY 10001.
TEL: (212) 695-0012. FAX: (212) 695-0014.
www.ernemann.com
CONTACT
Roney Weis - roneyintl@aol.com

HARRAH'S THEATRE EQUIPMENT COMPANY
(All types of theatre equipment)
25613 Dollar St., Unit 1, Hayward, CA 94544-2535.
TEL: (510) 881-4989. FAX: (510) 881-0448.
OWNER
Jerry Harrah

UNIVERSAL CINEMA SERVICES
(Distributors of all types of theatre equipment & supplies)
1010 W. Euless Blvd., Ste. 240, Euless, TX 76040.
TEL: (888) 600-6775, (817) 633-2180. FAX: (817) 633-2190.
email: CustomerService@universalcinema.com
www.universalcinema.com
CHAIRMAN & CEO
Jack Panzeca
PRESIDENT & COO
Stan Lamb
V.P., PURCHASING
Jim Kappus

WORLDWIDE SAFE & VAULT
(Cash-handling safes, access-controlled electronic locks, all aspects of physical security hardware)
3660 N.W. 115th Ave., Miami, FL 33178. TEL: (800) 932-2278, (305) 477-9266. FAX: (305) 477-9744.
email: sales@worldwidesafe.com www.worldwidesafe.com
OWNER & PRESIDENT
Scott Hirsch

TICKETS AND TICKET STOCK

ADMIT ONE PRODUCTS
(Complete source for all your admission needs)
1451 Edinger Ave., Ste. D, Tustin, CA 92780.
TEL: (866) 236-4817, (714) 442-3888. FAX: (714) 442-3889.
www.admitoneproducts.com
SALES DIRECTOR
Richard Simmons
ACCOUNT EXECUTIVE
Kathy Orozco

AMLON TICKET
(Ticket manufacturer)
254 Helicopter Circle, Corona, CA 92880. TEL: (800) 544-2131, (951) 278-8888. FAX: (951) 278-8891.
email: info@amlontickets.com www.amlonticket.com
SALES
Jason Rogers - jason@amlonticket.com

BOCASYSTEMS
(Solutions for the ticketing industry)
1065 S. Rogers Circle, Boca Raton, FL 33487.
TEL: (561) 998-9600. FAX: (561) 998-9609.
email: boca@bocasystems.com (customer service)
www.bocasystems.com
VICE PRESIDENT
Robert Kohn

CINEDIGM DIGITAL CINEMA CORP.
(Formerly Access Integrated Technologies, Inc. Company announced name change Nov. 2008)
Headquarters: 55 Madison Ave., Ste. 300, Morristown, NJ 07960. TEL: (973) 290-0080. FAX: (973) 290-0081.
email: info@cinedigm.com www.cinedigm.com

Digital Cinema Offices: 6255 Sunset Blvd., Ste. 1025, Hollywood, CA 90028. TEL: (323) 463-2144.
FAX: (323) 463-1319.
CHAIRMAN & CEO
Bud Mayo
PRESIDENT, MEDIA SERVICES GROUP
Chuck Goldwater
PRESIDENT & COO, SOFTWARE DIVISION
Jim Miller
PRESIDENT, COO, DIGITAL MEDIA SERVICES DIVISION
Gerd Jakuszeit

PRESIDENT & COO, UNIQUE SCREEN MEDIA, A CINEDIGM COMPANY
William A. McGlamery
PRESIDENT, CINEDIGN ENTERTAIMENT GROUP
Jonathan Dern
DIRECTOR, CORPORATE COMMUNICATIONS
Suzanne Moore - (973) 290-0056 ext. 181.
smoore@cinedigm.com

Cinedigm provides digital cinema networked services along with its Library Management Server(R) and Theatre Command Center(R) to enable theatres across the United States to play digital showings of Hollywood features. The company's 24/7 satellite operations delivers feature movies, alternative content advertising, and pre-show entertainment, including live 2-D and 3-D events through its CineLive(R) satellite network, expanding box office sales and developing new ways to attract incremental revenues. Through its alternative content distribution division, the company offers channels of programming including Opera, Kidtoons, Faith-based Concerts, Sports and Anime.

CINESTAR SOFTWARE

Ramon Fernandez, 265, Montevideo 11300, Uruguay.
TEL:(011) 598-2-7104676. FAX: (011) 598-2-7104676.
email: jlopez@cinestarsoftware.com
www.cinestarsoftware.com
INTERNATIONAL SALES MANAGER
Javier Lopez Jaumandreu

Offers ticketing and concession software.

DILLINGHAM TICKET COMPANY

(Coupon books, thermal ticketbook, passes & wristbands, admission & reserved-seat tickets)
781 Ceres Ave., Los Angeles, CA 90021. TEL: (800) 345-8587, (213) 627-6916. FAX: (213) 623-2758.
email: sales@dillinghamticket.com www.dillinghamticket.com
SALES REPRESENTATIVE
Steve Howson - ext. 404.

ELECTRONIC CREATIONS, INC.

1153 Inspiration Ln., Escondido, CA 92025. TEL: (760) 480-1002.
FAX: (760) 480-6830. email: sales@TicketingSystems.com
www.TicketingSystems.com
PRESIDENT
Bruce L. Hall
CHIEF TECHNICAL OFFICER
Brandon Hall
CHIEF SALES & MARKETING OFFICER
Charles Rock

POS Hardware & Software for "Touch" Ticketing, Concession, Internet Ticketing, Kiosk, Credit Cards, Gift Cards, Loyalty & Rewards Systems.

FANDANGO

(Internet ticketing)
12200 W. Olympic Blvd., Ste. 150, Los Angeles, CA 90064.
TEL: (800) 326-3264, (310) 451-7690. FAX: (310) 451-7861.
email: partnering@fandango.com www.fandango.com
CEO
Chuck Davis
SENIOR V.P. & COO
Rick Butler
CFO
Daniel Murray
V.P., BUSINESS DEVELOPMENT
Christopher Cunningham
V.P., HUMAN RESOURCES
Bethany Ellis
V.P., MARKETING
Ted Hong
V.P., SALES
Dan Mohler

Fandango sells tickets to more than 15,000 screens. Fandango entertains and informs consumers with exclusive film clips, trailers, celebrity interviews, fan reviews and news, while offering them the ability to quickly select a film and conveniently buy tickets in advance.In April 2007, Fandango was acquired by Comcast Interactive Media (CIM), a division of Comcast Corporation (NASDAQ: CMCSA).Comcast Interactive Media develops and operates Internet businesses focused on entertainment, information and communication.

GLOBE TICKET & LABEL CO.

(Custom printed tickets)
1800 Greenleaf, Elk Grove Village, IL 60007.
TEL: (800) 523-5968, (847) 258-1000. FAX: (847) 258-1006.
www.globeticket.com
MIDWEST SALES REPRESENTATIVE
Robert Smith - Bsmith@globeticket.com

HOWELL DATA SYSTEMS

(Provide complete theatre solutions for box office, concession, and labor management)
84 Copernicus Blvd., Unit 4, Brantford, ON N3P 1K5, Canada.
TEL: (800) 410-6871, (888) 737-3282.
email: paul.howell@dexit.com www.howelldatasystems.com
V.P., SALES & MARKETING
Brad De Poorter
CONTACTS
Paul Schafer, Paul Howell

MOVIEFONE

(Part of AOL)
AOL Moviefone/1414 K St., Sacramento, CA 95814.
TEL: (916) 444-3456. www.movies.aol.com

MOVIETICKETS.COM

(Tickets for movies via the Internet and wireless devices)
2255 Glades Rd., Ste. 221A, Boca Raton, FL 33431.
TEL: (561) 886-5500, (561) 998-8000. FAX: (561) 998-2974.
email: marketing@movietickets.com
www.movietickets.com
SENIOR V.P., SALES & MARKETING
Walt Borchers
EXECUTIVE V.P. & GENERAL MANAGER
Joel Cohen

MOVIE CASH (THE PROPERTIES GROUP)

(Reward programs. Universally accepted movie ticket, good for any movie almost anytime)
111 John St., 27th Flr., New York, NY 10038.
TEL: (212) 907-7101. FAX: (212) 907-7125.
www.thepropertiesgroup.com
CEO & PRESIDENT
John Galinos - jgalinos@tpgny.com

Los Angeles: TPG Rewards, Inc.
13323 Washington Blvd., Ste. 306, Los Angeles, CA 90066.
TEL: (310) 279-5005. FAX: (310) 279-5009.
SENIOR V.P., PARTNER
Kim Krefetz

NASHUA CORPORATION

(Point-of-sale tickets/Point-of-sale papers)
915 Rittenhouse Rd., Bldg. 1, Jefferson City, TN 37760.
TEL: (800) 206-0129 ext. 1846, (865) 471-1845.
FAX: (865) 475-6973. www.nashua.com
BUSINESS DEVELOPMENT MANAGER
Cheryl Roach - croach@nashua.com

NATIONAL TICKET COMPANY

P.O. Box 547, Shamokin, PA 17872. TEL: (800) 829-0829, (570) 672-2900. FAX: (800) 829-0888, (570) 672-2999.
email: ticket@nationalticket.com (Customer Service Dept.)
www.nationalticket.com

Custom-printed gift certificates, coupon books, gift cards, thermal point-of-sale ticket stock and more

OMNITERMDATA TECHNOLOGY, LTD.

2785 Skymark Ave., #11, Mississauga, ON L4W 4Y3, Canada.
TEL: (905) 629-4757. FAX:(905) 629-8590.
email: info@omniterm.com www.omniterm.com
PRESIDENT
Ed Coman - ecoman@omniterm.com
V.P., OPERATIONS
Greg Coman - gregcoman@omniterm.com
DIRECTOR, SALES & MARKETING
Darrin Lewis - dlewis@omniterm.com
DIRECTOR, I.T. & PROJECT MANAGEMENT
Mike Richards - mrichards@omniterm.com

Theatre Management Software (TMS) includes automated ticketing, concession point-of-sale (POS), automated box office (ABO) Kiosk, internet ticketing, loyalty, auditorium LCD signage, digital concession menu boards, box office showtime monitor, integrated restaurant, gift card and film settlement applications. Omniterm also has a complete line of hardware solutions for point-of-sale terminals, kiosks and displays. We strive to provide our customers with a "turnkey" solution, addressing all aspects of theatre automation and support.

PRACTICAL AUTOMATION, INC.

(Manufacturer of high-speed printers for computerized ticketing systems and unattended self-service kiosks)
45 Woodmont Rd., Milford CT 06460. TEL: (203) 882-5640.
FAX: (203) 882-5648. email: sales@practicalautomation.com
www.practicalautomation.com
MARKETING & SALES
Bob Donofrio

PREMIER SOUTHERN TICKET COMPANY

(Thermal ticket stock; anti-counterfeiting devices for tickets; e-ticket system, scratch-off tickets for prizes and more)
7911 School Rd., Cincinnati, OH 45249. TEL: (800) 331-2283.
FAX: (513) 489-6867. email: sales@premiersouthern.com
www.premiersouthern.com

PRINTTIXUSA™, INC.

P.O. Box 572585, Salt Lake City, UT 84157.
TEL: (866) 323-5411. FAX: (801) 305-1032.
www.printtixusa.com

PRESIDENT
Terry Schmidt - tschmidt@printtixusa.com

RADIANT SYSTEMS, INC.

(Theatre management services for box office, back office, consumer-activated kiosk, ticketing, POS)
3925 Brookside Pkwy., Apharetta, GA 30022.
TEL: (877) 794-RADS, (770) 576-6000. FAX: (770) 754-7790.
email: inquiries@radiantsystems.com
www.radiantsystems.com
CEO
John Heyman
COO AND PRESIDENT, RETAIL DIVISION
Andrew S. Heyman
PRESIDENT, RETAIL AND ENTERTAINMENT DIVISION
Chris Lybeer
PRESIDENT, INTERNATIONAL DIVISION
Mark Schoen
PRESIDENT, SPORTS AND ENTERTAINMENT GROUP
Scott Kingsfield
V.P., HUMAN RESOURCES
Keith Hicks

RETRIEVER SOFTWARE, INC.

2525 S. Broadway, Denver, CO 80210. TEL: (888) 988-4470.
FAX: (720) 570-1173. www.venue-pos.com
V.P., SALES
Phil Norrish - pnorrish@venue-pos.com

Touch-screen ticketing & concession systems, integrated theatre & labor management, film booking software, signage software, inventory control & reporting.

SENSIBLE CINEMA SOFTWARE

(Ticketing & concession inventory software; ticketing printers & blank ticket stock since 1993)
7216 Sutton Place, Fairview, TN 37062. TEL: (615) 799-6366.
FAX: (615) 799-6367. email: info@sensiblecinema.com
www.sensiblecinema.com
CONTACT
Rusty Gordon

SPLYCE, INC.

(Live ticketing systems and real-time Internet ticketing for cinema, stage, and stadium events)
5775 Soundview Dr., Bldg. E, Gig Harbor, WA 98335.
TEL: (888) 477-5923, (253) 857-6411. FAX: (253) 857-6461.
email: sales@splyce.com www.splyce.com
CONTACT
Dean Burke

THEATRE SUPPORT SYSTEMS

(A full featured box-office program for motion picture theatres)
28732 Persimmon Tree Rd., Anderson, AL 35610-3400.
TEL: (256) 233-6137 (office). email: TSS@TheatreSupport.com
www.theatresupport.com
CONTACT
Jerry Chase

TICKETPRO SYSTEMS

(Boxoffice ticketing, concessions, LED signs)
205 Pointer Ln., Pearl River, LA 70602. TEL: (888) 627-8776.
FAX: (770) 271-2228. www.ticketpro.org
CEO
Norm Bumbieris - norm@ticketpro.org
SALES
Willie Vandenheuvel

TICKETINGSYSTEMS.COM

1153 Inspiration Ln., Escondido, CA 92025. TEL: (760) 480-1002.
FAX: (760) 480-6830. email: sales@TicketingSystems.com
www.TicketingSystems.com
PRESIDENT
Bruce L. Hall
CHIEF TECHNICAL OFFICER
Brandon Hall
CHIEF SALES & MARKETING OFFICER
Charles Rock

POS Hardware & Software for "Touch" Ticketing, Concession, Internet Ticketing, Kiosk, Credit Cards, Gift Cards, Loyalty & Rewards Systems.

TITAN TECHNOLOGY GROUP

Ticketing and concessions POS solutions provider)
145 W. 45th St., Ste. 603, New York, NY 10036.
TEL: (917) 777-0959. FAX: (917) 777-0961.
email: info@TitanTechGroup.com
www.Titan TechGroup.com
BUSINESS DEVELOPMENT
Robert Schofield

VISTA ENTERTAINMENT SOLUTIONS

U.S. Corporate Office: Howard Hughes Center, 6th Flr., 6080 Center Dr., Los Angeles, CA 90045. TEL: (310) 242-6690.
FAX: (310) 242-5201. email: info@vista.co.nz www.us-vista.com
CONTACT
Murray Holdaway - murray.holdaway@vista.co.nz

Vista's offerings include Point of Sale, Combined Ticket and Concession Sales, Ticketing Management, Reporting and a number of optional modules such as Web Connection, and Signage. See website for additional product offerings, solutions and locations worldwide.

WELDON, WILLIAMS & LICK, INC.

(Ticket printing, gift certificate, passes, 30mil gift/loyal cards, discount and readmit coupons)
P.O. Box 168, Fort Smith, AR 72902-0168. TEL: (800) 643-2598, (479) 783-4113. FAX: (479) 783-7050.
www.wwlinc.com
PRESIDENT
Jim Walcott
V.P., SALES
Andy Hendricks
CONTACT
Kasey Aldridge - kaldridge@wwlinc.com

UNIFORMS

AMBASSADOR UNIFORM/STAFF APPAREL SPECIALISTS

300 Craig Rd., Manalapan, NJ 07726.
TEL: (800) 711-5885. FAX: (732) 866-6652.
email: ambassunif@aol.com www.ambassadoruniform.com

ARAMARK UNIFORM & CAREER APPAREL, LLC

(Subsidiary of ARAMARK. Number 2 rental uniform co. in U.S.)
115 N. 1st St., Burbank, CA 91502. TEL: (781) 871-4100 (For International orders), (800) 388-3300 (Customer Service), (800) 677-6060 (Business Sales), (800) 888-2900 (National Accounts). FAX: (800) 436-3132 (Customer Service).
PRESIDENT
Tom Vozzo
SENIOR V.P. & CIO
Patrick Piccininno

CINTAS

(Uniforms)
6800 Cintas Blvd., Cincinnati, OH 45256. TEL: (800) 246-8271, (513) 459-1200. FAX: (513) 573-4130.
CEO
Scott D. Farmer
PRESIDENT AND COO
J. Phillip Holloman

Company designs, manufactures and implements corporate identity uniform programs, provide entrance mats, restroom supplies, promotional products, document management, fire protection, and first aid and safety services for more than 800,000 businesses.

HANOVER UNIFORM COMPANY

(International distributor of all types of uniforms)
529 W. 29th St., Baltimore, MD 21211-2988.
TEL: (800) 541-9709, (410) 235-8338. FAX: (410) 235-6071.
email: info@hanoveruniform.com
www.hanoveruniform.com
CONTACT
Steve Odoherty - (800) 541-9709
sodoherty@hanoveruniform.com

PRIORITY MANUFACTURING

(Hospitality industry uniforms)
571 N.W. 29th St., Miami, FL 33127. TEL: (800) 835-5528, (305) 576-3000. FAX: (305) 576-2672.
www.customuniforms.com
CONTACT
Richard Levy - richard@customuniforms.com

SUPERIOR UNIFORM GROUP

(All types of uniforms)
10055 Seminole Blvd., Seminole, FL 33772. TEL: (727) 397-9611.
FAX: (727) 803-2658. email: info@superioruniformgroup.com
www.superioruniformgroup.com
SALES
David Schechter

UNIFIRST CORPORATION

(Uniforms for a variety of industries)
68 Jonspin Rd., Wilmington, MA 01887. TEL: (800) 225-3364.
email: ufirst@unifirst.com www.unifirst.com

UniFirst is one of North America's largest workwear and textile services companies. The company rents, leases, and sells uniforms, protective clothing, custom corporate workwear, floorcare, and other facility services products to all kinds of businesses.

CONCESSION SUPPLIERS

BEVERAGES

BOYD COFFEE COMPANY
19730 N.E. Sandy Blvd., Portland, OR 97230.
TEL: (503) 666-4545. FAX: (503) 669-2223.
www.boyds.com email: info@boyds.com
V.P., SALES & MARKETING
Daniel Williams

BRAD BARRY CO./CAFFE D'VITA CAPPUCCINO
14020 Central Ave. #580, Chino, CA 91710-5564.
TEL: (909) 591-9493. FAX: (909) 627-3747.
www.caffedvita.com

BREWED AWAKENING
1807 Euclid Ave., Berkeley, CA 94709.
TEL: (510) 540-8865. FAX: (510) 540-8090.
www.1807brewedawakening.com email: brwdawaker@aol.com
CONTACT
Sam Nassar

CADBURY SCHWEPPES
5301 Legacy Dr., Plano, TX 75024.
TEL: (972) 673-6637. FAX: (972) 673-7783.
www.cadburyschweppes.com
CHAIRMAN & CEO
Irene Rosenfeld
COORDINATOR, CORPORATE EVENTS & EXHIBITIONS
Michele Mora

CHINA MIST TEA COMPANY
7435 E. Tierra Buena Ln., Scottsdale, AZ 85260.
TEL: (800) 242-8807, (480) 998-8807. FAX: (480) 596-0811.
email: fsales@chinamist.com www.chinamist.com
CO-FOUNDER, CO-CHAIRMAN & CO-CHIEF EXECUTIVE
Dan Schweiker, John S. Martinson
PRESIDENT & COO
Rommie K. Flammer

THE COCA-COLA COMPANY
One Coca-Cola Plaza, Atlanta, GA 30313.
TEL: (404) 676-2121. FAX: (404) 598-2333.
THEATRE CHANNEL MANAGER
Kristin Wilson - krwilson@na.ko.com

GEHL FOODS, INC.
N116 W15970 Main St., Germantown, WI 53022.
TEL: (262) 251-8570. FAX: (262) 251-9597.
www.gehls.com
NATIONAL SALES MANAGER
Tracy M. Propst

THE ICEE COMPANY
4701 Airport Dr., Ontario, CA 91761.
TEL: (800) 423-3872, (909) 390-4233. FAX: (909) 390-4262.
www.icee.com
V.P., MARKETING
Susan Swisher Woods

JUICY WHIP, INC.
1668 Curtiss Ct., LaVerne, CA 91750.
TEL: (800) 501-4558, (909) 392-7500, (714) 904-7574.
FAX: (909) 392-7507.
email: info@juicywhip.com www.juicywhip.com
PRESIDENT
Gus Stratton

PARROT-ICE DRINK PRODUCTS OF AMERICA, LTD.
13738 FM 529, Houston, TX 77041.
TEL: (800) 777-8676, (713) 896-8798. FAX: (713) 896-6676.
email: sales@parrot-ice.com www.parrot-ice.com
SALES
Bill Robinson

PEPSI-COLA COMPANY
700 Anderson Hill Rd., Purchase, NY 10589.
TEL: (914) 253-2000, (914) 253-3065. FAX: (914) 249-8224.
www.pepsi.com
CONTACT
Clarissa Milano - clarissa.milano@pepsi.com

RIO SYRUP COMPANY, INC.
2311 Chestnut St., St. Louis, MO 63103-2298.
TEL: (800) 325-7666. FAX: (314) 436-7707.
email: flavors@riosyrup.com www.riosyrup.com
PRESIDENT
Phil Tomber

VICTOR PRODUCTS CO.
328 N. 18th St., Richmond, VA 23223.
TEL: (800) 456-5261, (804) 643-9091. FAX: (804) 648-3601.
868 Oklahoma Dr., Chesapeake, VA 23323.
TEL: (757) 485-4063. FAX: (757) 487-5106
email: moreinfo@victorproducts.com www.victorproducts.com

CANDY & CONFECTIONS

ADAMS & BROOKS
1915 S. Hoover St., P.O. Box 7303, Los Angeles, CA 90007.
TEL: (213) 749-3226. FAX: (213) 746-7614.
email: info@adams-brooks.com www.adams-brooks.com
PRESIDENT
John Brooks, Sr.
VICE PRESIDENT
John Brooks, Jr.

AMERICAN INTERNATIONAL CONCESSION PRODUCTS CORP.
62 Bethpage Rd., Hicksville, NY 11801.
TEL: (800) 401-2427, (516) 681-1537. FAX: (516) 681-3362.
email: info@aicpcorp.com www.aicpcorp.com
V.P., SALES
Stephen Sciortino

AMERICAN LICORICE COMPANY
607 Susana Ave., Redondo Beach, CA 90277.
TEL: (310) 316-8689. FAX: (310) 540-7282.
email: ganmando@earthlink.net www.americanlicorice.com
www.redvines.com www.sourpunch.com
BUSINESS MANAGER, SPECIAL MARKETS
Tom Ganley

DIPPIN' DOTS
5101 Charter Oak Dr., Paducah, KY 42001.
TEL: (270) 443-8994. FAX: (270) 443-8997.
www.dippindots.com
FOUNDER & CHAIRMAN
Curt Jones
V.P., SALES
Michael Barrette micbar@dippindots.com

EURO-AMERICAN BRANDS, LLC
95 Route 17 South, Paramus NJ 07652.
TEL: (201) 368-2624. FAX: (201) 368-2512.
www.euroamericanbrands.com
V.P., MARKETING
Greg Smauley
DIRECTOR, MARKETING
Beth Forman

FOLZ VENDING COMPANY
3401 Lawson Blvd., Oceanside, NY 11572.
TEL: (800) 699-8108, (516) 678-6005. FAX: (800) 884-7117.
www.folzvending.com
COO
Robert Allen

THE FOREIGN CANDY COMPANY, INC.
One Foreign Candy Dr., Hull, IA 51239.
TEL: (800) 767-4575. www.foreign-candy.com

GHIRARDELLI CHOCOLATE COMPANY
1111 139th Ave., San Leandro, CA 94578-2631.
TEL: (800) 877-9338. www.ghirardelli.com

HARIBO OF AMERICA, INC.
(Gummy candy)
1825 Woodlawn Dr., Ste. 204, Baltimore, MD 21207.
TEL: (410) 265-8890. FAX: (410) 265-8898. www.haribo.com
CONTACT
Christian Jegen

HERSHEY FOODS CORPORATION
P.O. Box 810, 100 Crystal A Dr., Hershey, PA 17033.
TEL: (800) 468-1714. FAX: (717) 534-8718.
www.hersheys.com

IMPACT CONFECTIONS, INC.
888 Garden of the Gods Rd., Colorado Springs, CO 80907.
TEL: (719) 268-6100. FAX: (719) 268-6197.
email: info@impactconfections.com
www.impactconfections.com
FOUNDER & PRESIDENT
Brad Baker

JELLY BELLY CANDY COMPANY
One Jelly Belly Ln., Fairfield, CA 94533.
TEL: (800) 522-3267, (707) 428-2800. FAX: (707) 428-0819.
www.jellybelly.com
PRESIDENT
Robert M. Simpson
V.P., SPECIALTY SALES
John Pola

JOHNSON CONCESSION SUPPLY
P.O. Box 98, Shawnee, OK 74802.
TEL: (866) 273-1090. FAX: (866) 288-1085.
www.johnsonconcession.com
CONTACT
Roger Johnson

JUDSON-ATKINSON CANDY CO.
4266 Dividend, San Antonio, TX 78219. P.O. Box 200669, San Antonio, TX 78220-0669.
TEL: (800) 962-3984, (210) 359-8380.
FAX: (210) 359-8392. www.judsonatkinsoncandies.com
V.P., SALES & MARKETING
Doyle Huntsman - (866) 872-2263
EASTERN REGIONAL SALES MANAGER
Ken Deecken - (866) 890-5836

JUST BORN, INC.
1300 Stefko Blvd., Bethlehem, PA 18017.
TEL: (800) 445-5787.
email: mdeluca@justborn.com www.justborn.com
CONTACT
Milena DeLuca

JUST BORN, INC. PEANUT CHEWS PLANT
7701 State Rd., Philadelphia, PA 19136.
TEL: (215) 335-4500. FAX: (215) 335-4510.
email: mdeluca@justborn.com www.justborn.com
CONTACT
Milena DeLuca

MARS SNACKFOOD
(M&M's, Skittles, Snickers, Starburst, Milky Way)
800 High St., Hackettstown, NJ 07840.
TEL: (908) 852-1000. FAX: (908) 850-2870. www.mars.com
NATIONAL ACCOUNT MANAGER
Jim Rahilly

MCLANE COMPANY
4747 McLane Pkwy., Temple, TX 76504.
TEL: (254) 771-7500. FAX: (254) 771-7244.
email: contact@mclaneco.com www.mclaneco.com
SALES
Steve Brady - (254) 771-7064

NESTLE USA
2471 Martes, La Verne, CA 91750.
TEL: (909) 593-6556. FAX: (480) 379-3783.
www.nestleusa.com
DIRECTOR SPECIALTY MARKETS
Mike Mosher - mike.mosher@us.nestle.com

NEW ENGLAND CONFECTIONERY
135 American Legion Hwy., Revere, MA 02151.
TEL: (781) 485-4500. FAX: (781) 485-4519.
www.necco.com
CONTACT
Charles Blood

PEZ CANDY, INC.
35 Prindle Hill Rd., Orange, CT 06477.
TEL: (404) 320-3503. FAX: (404) 393-9620.
www.pez.com brandt@pezcandyinc.com
MANAGER, SPECIAL MARKETS USA
Allyn Brandt

THE PROMOTION IN MOTION CO., INC.
P.O. Box 558, 3 Reuten Dr., Closter, NJ 07624.
TEL: (800) 369-7391, (201) 784-5800. FAX: (201) 784-1010.
www.promotioninmotion.com
PRESIDENT
Michael Rosenberg
V.P., SPECIAL MARKETS
Jeff Scudillo - jscudillo@promotioninmotion.com

PUCKER POWDER
(Candy product line which includes dispensing machines, candy, tubes and tops, party packs, and other creative candy products)
1500 Georgia Rd., Bldg. A, Irondale, AL 35210.
TEL: (888) 460-4623, (205) 838-0570. FAX: (205) 838-0999.
email: sales@puckerpowder.com www.puckerpowder.com
NATIONAL SALES REP.
Bruce Goldstein

SARNOW FOOD GROUP
1001 S. Oyster Bay Rd., Bethpage, NY 11714.
TEL: (516) 576-9800 ext. 115. FAX: (516) 576-0730.
www.sarnowfoodgroup.com
V.P., SALES & OPERATIONS
Bill Smith - bsmith@sarnowfoodgroup.com

SHOWTIME CONCESSION
200 S.E. 19th St., Moore, OK 73160.
TEL: (405) 895-9902.
CONTACT
Dave Brennan

TOOTSIE ROLL INDUSTRIES, INC.
7401 S. Cicero Ave., Chicago, IL 60629.
TEL: (800) 877-7655, (773) 838-3400. FAX: (773) 838-3569, (773) 838-3569. email: cbarko@tootsieroll.com
www.tootsie.com
MARKETING ANALYST
Cheryl L. Barko
REGIONAL SALES MANAGER
Mike Romano
SALES MANAGERS
Mike Romano, John Malone

DISTRIBUTORS

CONTINENTAL CONCESSION SUPPLIES, INC.
(Full line theater concession distributor)
250 Fulton Ave., New Hyde Park, NY 11040.
TEL: (800) 516-0090, (516) 739-8777. FAX: (516) 739-8750.
email: info@ccsicandy.com www.ccsicandy.com
V.P., SALES
Adam Gottlieb - adam@ccsicandy.com

PIRYLIS DISTRIBUTORS
(Full service concession wholesale supplier)
221 Sussex Ave., Newark, NJ 07103.
TEL: (973) 482-9326. FAX: (973) 482-0602 www.pirylis.com
SALES CONTACT
Mike - mike@pirylis.com

ICE CREAM & FROZEN DAIRY PRODUCTS

BEN & JERRY'S HOMEMADE
30 Community Dr., S. Burlington, VT 05403-6828.
TEL: (802) 846-1500. FAX: (802) 846-1536. www.benjerry.com
SALES CONTACT
Jeannie Satink

DREYER'S GRAND ICE CREAM
5929 College Ave., Oakland, CA 94618.
TEL: (510) 652-8187. FAX: (510) 601-4473. www.dreyers.com
V.P., SALES
Tony Sarsam

GOOD HUMOR
P.O. Box 19007, Green Bay, WI 54307. 909 Packerland Dr., Green Bay, WI 54303.
TEL: (920) 499-5151. FAX: (920) 496-2099.
www.goodhumor.com

HÄAGEN-DAZS ICE CREAM
Häagen-Dazs Consumer Relations, 5929 College Ave., Oakland, CA 94618.
TEL: (800) 767-0120. www.haagen-dazs.com
PRESIDENT, HAAGEN-DAZS SHOPPE COMPANY (U.S.)
Darin Perry

NESTLE ICE CREAM
Consumer Relations, 5929 College Avenue, Oakland, CA 94618.
TEL: (800) 441-2525. www.nestle-icecream.com
V.P., SALES
Tony Sarsam

MEAT PRODUCTS

EISENBERG GOURMET BEEF FRANKS
3531 N. Elston Ave., Chicago, IL 60618.
TEL: (800) 624-5617, (773) 588-2882. FAX: (773) 588-0810.
www.kellyeisenberg.com
CONTACT
Ed Weinshenker - edw@kellyeisenberg.com
Cliff Eisenberg - cliff@kellyeisenberg.com

HORMEL FOODS CORPORATION
1 Hormel Pl., Austin, MN 55912-3680.
TEL: (800) 523-4635, (507) 437-5611. FAX: (507) 437-5146.
www.hormel.com
V. P., FOODSERVICE SALES
Deanna Brady

KRAFT FOODS/OSCAR MAYER
3 Lakes Dr., Northfield, IL 60093.
TEL: (847) 646-3845 www.kraft.com
EXECUTIVE V.P. & CMO
Mary Beth West

SARA LEE CORPORATION
3500 Lacey Rd., Downers Grove, IL 60515.
TEL: (630) 598-6000. FAX: (630) 598-8220. www.saralee.com

SQUARE H BRANDS, INC./HOFFY HOT DOGS
2731 S. Soto St., Los Angeles, CA 90023.
TEL: (323) 267-4600. FAX: (323) 261-7350.
www.squarehbrands.com
PRESIDENT & CEO
Henry Haskell

VIENNA BEEF
(Hot dogs, chili, deli meat, soups and pickles)
2501 N. Damen Ave., Chicago, IL 60647.
TEL: (773) 278-7800. FAX: (773) 278-4759.
www.viennabeef.com
DIRECTOR, MARKETING
Tom McGlade

PAPER & PLASTIC GOODS

AFFLINK
(Food service and paper distributors and suppliers)
1400 Afflink Pl.,Tuscaloosa, AL 35406. TEL: (800) 222-5521, (205) 345-4180. FAX: (205) 345-0064. www.afflink.com
S.V.P., SUPPLIER DEVELOPMENT
Vince June - vjune@afflink.com

ALTIVITY PACKAGING
(Popcorn containers, theatre trays)
Formerly Field Container Co., LP.
1501 Industrial Park Dr., Tuscaloosa, AL 35401.
TEL: (205) 333-0333. FAX: (205) 333-9862. www.altivity.com

BAGCRAFT PAPERCON
(Paper bags & wraps)
3900 W. 43rd St., Chicago, IL 60632.
TEL: (800) 621-8468, (773) 254-8000. FAX: (773) 254-1641.
email: marketing@pkdy.com www.bagcraft.com
www.pkdy.com
CEO & DIRECTOR
Roger M. Prevot
V.P. AND GENERAL MANAGER
Gene Gentili, Gene Gentili
MANAGER, MARKETING COMMUNICATIONS
Terri Mazur tmazur@pkdy.com

CADDY PRODUCTS, INC.
(Cupholders, concession trays, accessory products and LED lighting technology)
73850 Dinah Shore Dr., Unit 115, Palm Desert, CA 92211.
TEL: (800) 845-0591, (760) 770-1299. FAX: (760) 770-1799.
email: info@caddyproducts.com www.caddyproducts.com
V.P., SALES & MARKETING
Jim Winebarger - jim@caddyproducts.com

CINEMA SCENE MARKETING
(Promotional and stock concession products)
9200 Indian Creek Pkwy., Ste. 200, Overland Park, KS 66210.
TEL: (913) 825-0574. FAX: (913) 825-0591.
www.cinemascenemarketing.com
V.P., WORLDWIDE SALES
Neely Sims - nsims@cinemascenemarketing.com

DART CONTAINER CORPORATION
(Manufacturing quality single-use food service products)
500 Hogsback Rd., Mason, MI 48854.
TEL: (800) 248-5960. FAX: (517) 676-3883. www.dart.biz
CONTACT
Dan McCartin - Dan_McCartin@dart.biz

INTERNATIONAL PAPER FOODSERVICE
6400 Poplar Ave., Tower 1- 6:018, Memphis, TN 38197.
TEL: (800) 537-4141. FAX: (866) 889-7227.
www.ipfoodservice.com
MARKETING MANAGER
Beth McKeithen

MCLANE COMPANY
4747 McLane Pkwy., Temple, TX 76504.
TEL: (254) 771-7500. FAX: (254) 771-7566.
email: contact@mclaneco.com www.mclaneco.com
SALES
Steve Brady - (254) 771-7064

PACKAGING CONCEPTS, INC.
(Concession packaging)
9832 Evergreen Industrial Dr., St. Louis, MO 63123.
TEL: (314) 329-9700. FAX: (314) 487-2666.
email: info@packagingconceptsinc.com
www.packagingconceptsinc.com
CEO
John J. Irace - jji@packagingconceptsinc.com
COO
Tony Irace

Manufacturers of leak proof popcorn bags, kid packs, and concession packaging.

PROMOTIONAL MANAGEMENT GROUP, INC.
(Movie themed theatre concession packaging)
1656 Washington, Ste. 150, Kansas City, MO 64108.
TEL: (816) 221-3833. FAX: (816) 221-6166.
www.pmg-online.com
V.P., SALES & MARKETING
James C. McGinness
SALES & MARKETING MANAGER
Whitney Armstrong

ROCK-TENN COMPANY/WINCHESTER CARTON
P.O. Box 4098, Norcross, GA 30091.
TEL: (770) 448-2193. FAX: (678) 291-7666.
email: stockboxes@rocktenn.com www.rocktenn.com
EXECUTIVE V.P. & GENERAL MANAGER PAPERBOARD
David E. Dreibelbis
EXECUTIVE V.P. & GENERAL MANAGER FOLDING CARTON
Michael E. Kiepura

ROYAL PAPER CORP.

15050 Shoemaker Ave., Santa Fe Springs, CA 90670.
TEL: (562) 903-9030. FAX: (562) 944-6000.
email: info@royal-paper.com www.royal-paper.com
CONTACT
Marianne Abi Aad

SHOWTIME CONCESSION
200 S.E. 19th St., Moore, OK 73160.
TEL: (405) 895-9902.
CONTACT
Dave Brennan

SOLO CUP COMPANY
10100 Reisterstown Rd., Owings Mills, MD 21117.
TEL: (800) 800-0300, (410) 363-1111. www.solocup.com
PRESIDENT/CEO
Robert Korzenski
SENIOR V.P., FOODSERVICE SALES & MARKETING
Malcolm Simmonds

W.N.A./WADDINGTON NORTH AMERICA
(Reuasable & disposable souvenir cups)
2155 W. Longhorn Dr., Lancaster, TX 75134.
TEL: (800) 334-CUPS. FAX: (972) 228-6313.
www.wna-inc.com
SALES
Matthew Materne

ZENITH SPECIALTY BAG COMPANY, INC.
17625 E. Railroad St., City of Industry, CA 91748.
TEL: (800) 962-2247. FAX: (800) 284-8493. www.zsb.com

POPCORN & POPPING OILS

BUNGE NORTH AMERICA, INC.
11720 Borman Dr., St. Louis, MO 63146.
TEL: (314) 292-2000. FAX: (314) 292-2110.
www.bungenorthamerica.com
PRESIDENT & CEO, BUNGE NORTH AMERICA
Carl Hausmann

CARGILL
P.O. Box 9300, Minneapolis, MN 55440-9300.
TEL: 800-CARGILL, (952) 742-7575. www.cargill.com
EXECUTIVE V.P.
David M. Larson

CONAGRA FOODS (SNACK FOODS)
7700 France Ave. S, Ste. 200, Edina, MN 55435.
TEL: (800) 328-6286, (952) 835-6900. FAX: (952) 896-5656.
www.conagrafoods.com
CEO
Gary Rodkin
NATIONAL SALES MANAGER
Mike Donahoe - (952) 896-5668

DALE & THOMAS POPCORN
One Cedar Ln., Englewood, NJ 07631. TEL: (800) POPCORN.
FAX: (201) 645-4848. www.daleandthomaspopcorn.com
VICE PRESIDENT
Brian Stuckelman - brian@daleandthomas.com

ELLIS POPCORN COMPANY, INC.
101 E. Poplar St., Murray, KY 42071. TEL: (800) 654-3358, (270) 753-5451. FAX: (270) 753-7002.
email: dave@ellispopcorn.com www.ellispopcorn.com
SALES MANAGER
Dave Roberts

GREAT WESTERN PRODUCTS CO.
(Manufacturer, processor, & distributor of high quality theatre supplies & equipment)
30290 U.S. Hwy. 72, Hollywood, AL 35752.
TEL: (800) 239-2143, (256) 259-3578. FAX: (256) 574-2116.
email: info@gwproducts.com www.gwproducts.com

www.mycinemastore.com
PRESIDENT
Ralph Ferber - RalphF@gwproducts.com
NATIONAL SALES MANAGER
Mark Hamilton - MarkH@gwproducts.com

JOLLY TIME POP CORN
P.O. Box 178, Sioux City, IA 51102. TEL: (712) 239-1232.
FAX: (712) 239-1268. www.jollytime.com
SALES
Troy Peters - troyp@jollytime.com

KERNEL SEASONS, LLC
(Shake on popcorn seasoning)
2401 E. Devon Ave., Elk Grove Village, IL 60007.
TEL: (866) 328-7672. FAX: (773) 326-0869.
www.nomorenakedpopcorn.com
CONTACT
Krystal LaReese-Gaule - krystal@kernelseasons.com

MCLANE COMPANY
4747 McLane Pkwy., Temple, TX 76504. TEL: (254) 771-7500.
FAX: (254) 771-7566. email: contact@mclaneco.com
www.mclaneco.com
SALES
Steve Brady - (254) 771-7064

MORRISON FARMS POPCORN
Nebraska Popcorn, Inc., 85824 519th Ave., Clearwater, NE
68726. TEL: (402) 887-5335. FAX: (402) 887-4709.
email: michele@morrisonfarms.com
www.nebraskapopcorn.com
PRESIDENT
Frank Morrison
CONTACT
Michele Steskal

MOVIE FOODS
(A subsidiary of Great Western Products Co.)
30290 U.S. Highway 72, Hollywood, AL 35752.
TEL: (800) 633-5091. FAX: (256) 259-2939.
CONTACT
Mr. Shannon Tankersley

ODELL'S
8543 White Fir St. #D-1, Reno, NV 89523.
TEL: (800) 635-0436, (775) 323-8688. FAX: (775) 323-6532.
email: odells@popntop.com www.popntop.com
www.ilovebutter.com
PRESIDENT
Arthur Anderson
DIRECTOR OF CONCESSION SALES
Jo Burgoon

POPCORNOPOLIS
(Gourmet popcorns, handmade using natural ingredients)
224 Oregon St., El Segundo, CA 90245.
TEL: (800) POP-CITY, (310) 414-6700.
www.popcornopolis.com
CEO
Wally Arnold
PRESIDENT
Kathy Arnold

PREFERRED POPCORN, LLC
1132 9th Rd., Chapman, NE 68827.
TEL: (308) 986-2526. FAX: (308) 986-2626.
email: info@preferredpopcorn.com www.preferredpopcorn.com
CEO
Norm Krug

SHOWTIME CONCESSION
200 S.E. 19th St., Moore, OK 73160.
TEL: (405) 895-9902.
CONTACT
Dave Brennan

VENTURA FOODS LLC, LOU ANA DIVISION
P.O. Box 591, Opelousas, LA 70571.
TEL: (800) 551-9080, (337) 948-6561. FAX: (337) 942-3773.
email: mbates@venturafoods.com www.venturafoods.com
DIRECTOR, CONCESSION SALES
Mike Bates

WEAVER POPCORN COMPANY, INC.
9850 W. Point Dr., Ste. 100, Indianapolis, IN 46256.
TEL: (765) 934-2101. FAX: (603) 590-6343.
www.popweaver.com
V.P., SALES CONCESSION
Jim Labas - jim.labas@popweaver.com
CONTACT
Scarlett Kruse - (317) 915-4012

WRIGHT POPCORN & NUT CO.
150 Potrero Ave., San Francisco, CA 94103.
TEL: (415) 861-0912. FAX: (415) 861-6745.
www.wrightpopcorn.com

SNACK FOODS

BAY VALLEY FOODS
(Pickles and cheese sauce)
857-897 School Pl., Green Bay, WI 54307.
TEL: (920) 497-7131. www.bayvalleyfoods.com

BRICKLYN PIZZERIA, LLC
(Quick food pizzas)
12200 N. Stemmons Freeway, Ste. 315, Dallas, TX 75234.
TEL: (214) 761-6250. FAX: (214) 761-6251.
PRESIDENT
Ed Stockley

CONAGRA FOODS (SNACK FOODS)
7700 France Ave. S, Ste. 200, Edina, MN 55435.
TEL: (800) 328-6286, (952) 835-6900. FAX: (952) 896-5656.
www.conagrafoods.com
NATIONAL SALES MANAGER
Mike Donahoe - (952) 896-5668

FUNACHO
(Nacho cheese sauces and related items)
1253 W. Seventh St., Cincinnati, OH 45203.
TEL: (800) 386-2246, (513) 241-9300. FAX: (513) 352-5122.
www.funacho.com
PRESIDENT
Mike Grause
V.P., SALES
Brian Biehn

GEHL FOODS, INC.
N116 W15970 Main St., Germantown, WI 53022.
TEL: (262) 251-8570. FAX: (262) 251-9597. www.gehls.com
NATIONAL SALES MANAGER
Tracy M. Propst

GOLD MEDAL PRODUCTS
(Concession equipment, popcorn poppers and supplies)
10700 Medallion Dr., Cincinnati, OH 45241-4807.
TEL: (800) 543-0862, (513) 769-7676. FAX: (513) 769-8500.
email: info@gmpopcorn.com www.gmpopcorn.com
PRESIDENT
Dan Kroeger - dkroeger@gmpopcorn.com
SENIOR V.P.
John Evans, Jr. - johnevans@gmpopcorn.com
V.P., SALES
Rob Tieman
INTERNATIONAL SALES MANAGER
David Garretson - djgarretson@gmpopcorn.com

HOT COOKIES PRODUCTIONS
(Scoop fresh bite size chocolate chip cookies from our heated display case without the hassle of refrigeration, preparation, baking or waste)
5924 S.W. 68th St., South Miami, FL 33143.
TEL: (305) 667-5577. FAX: (305) 666-5335. www.hotcookies.com
CONTACT
Larry Berrin - larry@hotcookies.com

J & J SNACKS
6000 Central Hwy., Pennsauken, NJ 08109.
TEL: (800) 486-9533, (856) 665-9534. FAX: (856) 910-0462.
www.jjsnack.com
V.P., SALES
Steve Taylor
DIRECTOR, MARKETING
Stacey Inglis-Baron

MICHAEL'S BAKERY PRODUCTS, LLC
(Gourmet frozen and baked cookie dough)
10635 Scripps Ranch Blvd., Ste. D, San Diego, CA 92131.
TEL: (800) 822-5384, (858) 578-0888. FAX: (858) 578-0836.
email: info@michaelscookies.com www.michaelscookies.com
CFO
Scott Summeril
COO
Pedro Escareno

THE NUTTY BAVARIAN
305 Hickman Dr., Sanford, FL 32771.
TEL: (800) 382-4788, (407) 444-6322. FAX: (407) 444-6335.
email: bruno@nuttyb.com www.nuttyb.com
OWNER
David Brent

PIZZAS OF EIGHT
1915 Cherokee St., St. Louis, MO 63118-3218.
TEL: (800) 422-2901, (314) 865-1460. FAX: (314) 865-2449.
email: adrake@pizzasofeight.com www.pizzasofeight.com
CONTACT
Chuck McMillen

RICOS PRODUCTS CO., INC.
621 S. Flores, San Antonio, TX 78204.
TEL: (210) 222-1415. FAX: (210) 226-6453.
email: info@ricos.com www.ricos.com

SALES
Charlie Gomez

SQUARE H BRANDS, INC./HOFFY HOT DOGS
2731 S. Soto St., Los Angeles, CA 90023.
TEL: (323) 267-4600. FAX: (323) 261-7350.
www.squarehbrands.com
PRESIDENT & CEO
Henry Haskell

SUMMIT FOOD ENTERPRISES, INC.
P.O. Box 141, Dedham, MA 02027.
TEL: (508) 787-3435. FAX: (508) 787-3439.
CONTACT
Paul Bonfiglio

VISTAR
12650 E. Arapahoe Rd., Bldg. D, Centennial, CO 80112.
TEL: (303) 662-7175. FAX: (303) 662-7550.
email: info@vistarvsa.com www.vistarvsa.com
PRESIDENT & CEO
George Holm

Vistar of Denver: 6721 York St., Denver, CO 80229.
TEL: (303) 289-8801.
GENERAL MANAGER
Matt McEnerny
SALES MANAGER
Mark McGaughey

WYANDOT, INC.
135 Wyandot Ave., Marion, OH 43302.
TEL: (740) 383-4031. FAX: (740) 387-9751.
www.wyandotsnacks.com
PRESIDENT
Nick Chilton

VENDING MACHINES

FIRST VENDING PARTNERS
(First Vending Partners is the nation's leading provider of custom, high-quality vending displays)
1869 Best Dr., Walled Lake, MI 48390.
TEL: (248) 960-0400. FAX: (248) 960-0003.
www.firstvending.com
PRESIDENT
Howard Rubin - hrubin@firstvending.com

First Vending Partners creates additional revenue stream programs for thousands of high traffic venues. Our upscale and elegant candy displays can be found in malls, movie theatres, grocery stores, mass retailers and a variety of other locations.

PHOTO-ME USA
(Photo booth and vending; medal master kiddy rides)
7211 Patterson Dr., Garden Grove, CA 926841.
TEL: (714) 898-5800. FAX: (714) 898-5877.
www.photo-me.com
CONTACT
Sonny Pham (Western US)
Mike McHale (North Central)
Patrick Garder (North East)

TOMY YUJIN CORPORATION
(Sells bulk toy vending machines)
1601 Dove St., Ste. 115, Newport Beach, CA 92660.
TEL: (949) 476-6580. FAX: (949) 476-6590.
www.gachausa.com
CONTACT
Amanda Newhard

SCREENING ROOMS

All major studios, producers and distributors have screening rooms for their own use. Major circuits also lease theatres as screening rooms.

ACADEMY OF MOTION PICTURE ARTS AND SCIENCES
(Theatres are available for film related events only)
8949 Wilshire Blvd., Beverly Hills, CA 90211.
TEL: (310) 247-3000. FAX: (310) 859-9619. www.oscars.org
THEATRE OPERATIONS
Moray Greenfield

THE CHARLES AIDIKOFF SCREENING ROOM
150 S. Rodeo Dr., #140, Beverly Hills, CA 90212.
TEL: (310) 274-0866. FAX: (310) 550-1794. www.aidikoff.tv
CO-OWNER
Charles Aidikoff
Gregg Aidikoff

AMERICAN FILM INSTITUTE
2021 N. Western Ave., Los Angeles, CA 90027.
TEL: (323) 856-7600. FAX: (323) 467-4578. www.afi.com
CONTACT
Kelly Dorsey

BIG TIME PICTURE COMPANY, INC.
(Digital post production; Avid and Final cut rentals and sales; 35mm/digital/video screening room. Apple ProVideo Reseller)
12210-1/2 Nebraska Ave., W. Los Angeles, CA 90025.
TEL: (310) 207-0921. FAX: (310) 826-0071.
email: susan@bigtimepic.com www.bigtimepic.com

BROADWAY SCREENING ROOM
1619 Broadway, 5th Flr., New York, NY 10019.
TEL: (212) 307-0990. FAX: (212) 307-5727.
email: Broadway@mybsr.com www.mybsr.com

CHICAGO FILMMAKERS
5243 N. Clark, 2nd Flr., Chicago, IL 60640.
TEL: (773) 293-1447. FAX: (773) 293-0575.
email: programming@chicagofilmmakers.org
www.chicagofilmmakers.org
EXECUTIVE DIRECTOR
Brenda Webb

CINEMA CONCEPTS TSC
2030 Powers Ferry Rd., Ste. 214, Atlanta, GA 30339.
TEL: (800) SHOWADS, (770) 956,7460. FAX: (770) 956-8358.
email: info@cinemaconcepts.com www.cinemaconcepts.com
CHAIRMAN/CEO
Stewart Harnell
EXECUTIVE ASSISTANT
Jackie Flood

THE CLIP JOINT FOR FILM
833-B N. Hollywood Way, Burbank, CA 91505.
TEL: (818) 842-2525. FAX: (818) 842-2644.

DIRECTORS GUILD OF AMERICA
7920 W. Sunset Blvd., Los Angeles, CA 90046.
TEL: (310) 289-2023. FAX: (310) 289-5398. www.dga.org
THEATER OPERATIONS MANAGER
Tim Webber

EXPLORATORIUM, MCBEAN THEATER
(125 seats)
3601 Lyon St., San Francisco, CA 94123. TEL: (415) 561-0311.
FAX: (415) 561-0307. www.exploratorium.edu/rentals
CONTACT
Amy Adkins

FILMWORKERS/ASTRO LABS, INC.
61 W. Erie St., Chicago, IL 60610. TEL: (312) 280-5500.
FAX: (312) 280-5510.

LEONARD H. GOLDENSON THEATRE AT ACADEMY OF TELEVISION ARTS & SCIENCES
5230 Lankershim Blvd., N. Hollywood, CA 91601-3109.
TEL: (818) 754-2825. FAX: (818) 761-8524.
email: theatre@emmys.org
THEATRE MANAGER
Vicky Campobasso
DIRECTOR, THEATRE OPERATIONS
Bob Gould

HARMONY GOLD PREVIEW HOUSE
7655 Sunset Blvd., Los Angeles, CA 90046.
TEL: (323) 851-4900. FAX: (323) 851-5599.
www.harmonygold.com
MANAGER, THEATER OPERATIONS
Kathryn Davolio - (323) 436-7204

LOS ANGELES COUNTY MUSEUM OF ART
(Bing Theater is a 600 seat screening room. Brown Auditorium shows rear video for up to 116 people; both fee for usage)
5905 Wilshire Blvd., Los Angeles, CA 90036.
TEL: (323) 857-6039. FAX: (323) 857-6021.
email: events@lacma.org www.lacma.org

MAGNO SOUND & VIDEO
729 Seventh Ave., New York, NY 10019. TEL: (212) 302-2505.
FAX: (212) 819-1282. email: screenings@magnosound.com
www.magnosoundandvideo.com
MAGNO REVIEW 1&2
TEL: (212) 302-2505, ext 3. FAX: (212) 764-1679.
DIRECTOR
Maria Pon - maria@magnosound.com

OCEAN SCREENING ROOM
1401 Ocean Ave., Ste. 110., Santa Monica, CA 90401.
TEL: (310) 576-1831. FAX: (310) 319-9501.
www.oceanscreening.com
CONTACT
Chris Sutton

PACIFIC FILM ARCHIVE
2625 Durant Ave., Berkeley, CA 94720-2250.
TEL: (510) 642-1412. FAX: (510) 642-4889.
email: bampfa@berkeley.edu www.bampfa.berkeley.edu
THEATER OPERATIONS MANAGER
Becky Mertens - bmertens@berkeley.edu

RALEIGH STUDIOS
5300 Melrose Ave., Hollywood, CA 90038. Screening bookings:
TEL: (323) 871-5649. FAX: (323) 871-5600.
www.raleighstudios.com
DIRECTOR POST PRODUCTION
Mike Donahue
GENERAL MANAGER
Yolando Montellno - (323) 466-3111

3 theaters seating 36, 38, 160, with 35mm and digital projection, and complete catering, reception & event facilities in our studio cafe and stages.

TECHNICOLOR
(A Thomson company)
110 Leroy St., New York, NY 10014. TEL: (212) 609-9400.
FAX: (212) 886-5299. www.technicolor.com
CONTACT
Charles Herzfeld - charles.herzfeld@thomson.net

TRIBECA FILM CENTER/TRIBECA SCREENING ROOM
375 Greenwich St., New York, NY 10013-2338.
TEL: (212) 941-2000, (212) 941-2091. FAX: (212) 941-2012.
www.tribecafilmcenter.com
MARKETING & SALES ASSISTANT
Jennifer Piterman

WARNER BROS. POST PRODUCTION SERVICES
4000 Warner Blvd., Burbank, CA 91522. TEL: (818) 954-2515.
FAX: (818) 954-4138. www.wbsf.com
SENIOR V.P.
Kim Waugh - (818) 954-1625

Sound Supervision, Sound Design, Mixing, Scoring, ADR, Foley and Sound Editorial. Picture Editorial Suites, Screening Rooms, DVD Mastering and Sound Restoration.

WILSHIRE SCREENING ROOM
8670 Wilshire Blvd., Ste. 112, Beverly Hills, CA 90211.
TEL: (310) 659-3875. FAX: (310) 861-9005.
THE WESTWOOD CREST THEATRE
1262 Westwood Blvd., Los Angeles, CA 90024.
TEL: (310) 701-8925. FAX: (310) 861-9005.
www.studioscreenings.com
PRESIDENT
Michael S. Hall

WRITERS GUILD THEATER
135 S. Doheny Dr., Beverly Hills, CA 90211.
TEL: (323) 782-4525. FAX: (323) 782-4830.
THEATER MANAGER
Emal Nessary

SAUL ZAENTZ MEDIA CENTER
(Now owned by Wareham Development)
2600 Tenth St., Berkeley, CA 94710. TEL: (510) 486-2286.
FAX: (510) 486-2115. www.zaentzmediacenter.co

PREVIEW & POLICY TRAILERS

ALKEMI ENTERTAINMENT
706 N. Citrus Ave., Los Angeles, CA 90038-3402.
TEL: (323) 525-1155. FAX: (323) 525-1150.
email: info@alkemient.com www.alkemient.com

THE ANT FARM
110 S. Fairfax Ave., Ste. 200, Los Angeles, CA 90036.
TEL: (323) 850-0700. FAX: (323) 850-0777.
email: info@theantfarm.net www.theantfarm.net
CEO
Rodd Perry
COO/CFO
Melissa Palazzo
CO-PRESIDENTS
Andy Solomon, Amanda Edwards
PRESIDENT, PRINT DIVISION
Julian Hills
EXECUTIVE CREATIVE DIRECTOR
Cindy Hauser

ASPECT RATIO
(Film trailers)
1347 N. Cahuenga Blvd., Hollywood, CA 90028.
TEL: (323) 467-2121. FAX: (323) 467-0901.
email: mark_t@aspectratio.com www.aspectratio.com
CEO
Mark Trugman

BIG PICTURE ENTERTAINMENT
3524 Hayden Ave., Culver City, CA 90232. TEL: (310) 836-8888.
FAX: (310) 836-8833. email: info@bigpic1.com
www.bigpic1.com
CONTACTS
Ryan Hegenberger, Barton Diffee

BIG SCIENCE FILM, INC.
2898 Rowena Ave., Ste. 105, Los Angeles, CA 90039.
TEL: (323) 661-4510. FAX: (323) 661-4511.
www.bigsciencefilm.com
CONTACTS
Stuart Robertson, Marti Mattox

BLOOMFILM
P.O. Box 461802, Los Angeles, CA 90046. TEL: (323) 850-5575.
PRESIDENT
Jon Bloom

BLT & ASSOCIATES, INC.
6430 Sunset Blvd., 8th Flr., Hollywood, CA 90028.
TEL: (323) 860-4000. FAX: (323) 860-0890. www.bltomato.com
CONTACT
Whitney Robinson

BRAIN ZOO STUDIOS
16509 Saticoy St., Van Nuys, CA 91406. TEL: (818) 785-1124.
FAX: (818) 904-1753. email: info@brainzoostudios.com
www.brainzoostudios.com
CONTACT
Lori Gloede

THE CIMARRON GROUP
6855 Santa Monica Blvd., Hollywood, CA 90038.
TEL: (323) 337-0300. FAX: (323) 337-0333.
email: info@cimarrongroup.com www.cimarrongroup.com
CONTACT
Lynn Peck

CINEMA CONCEPTS TSC, INC.
2030 Powers Ferry Rd., Ste. 214, Atlanta, GA 30339.
TEL: (800) SHOWADS, (770) 956-7460. FAX: (770) 956-8358.
email: info@cinemaconcepts.com www.cinemaconcepts.com
CHAIRMAN/CEO
Stewart Harnell

Studio & editing services, preview & policy trailers, CGI & Stereoscopic 3D animation, digital production services-HD, post/mastering/film-out/JPEG-2000 encoding, screening rooms-film & digital, Pre-show content.

CREATIVE PARTNERSHIP
6565 Sunset Blvd., Ste. 502, Los Angeles, CA 90028.
TEL: (323) 469-6565. FAX: (323) 469-6525.
email: info@creativepartnershipla.com
www.creativepartnership.co.uk
CONTACT
Karen A. Swann - (323) 469-6565

CRUSE & COMPANY, INC.
7000 Romaine St., Hollywood, CA 90038. TEL: (323) 851-8814.

DELUXE FILM SERVICES
7620 Airport Business Pkwy., Bldg. 4, Van Nuys, CA 91406.
TEL: (818) 756-2400. FAX: (818) 756-2401.
CONTACT
Debbie Mann - debbie.mann@bydeluxe.com

Print distribution & logistics; exhibitor services, trailer breakdown, trailer chase, theatrical print distribution; theatrical fulfillment with 29 locations nationwide.

EMPIRE DESIGN
204 Elizabeth St., New York, NY 10012. TEL: (212) 334-0100.
29 Queen Anne St., London W1G 9HU England.
TEL: (44 207) 7436-2202. www.empiredesign.com
CONTACT (UK & NY)
Sally Milner - Sally@empiredesign.com

FILM POLICE!
4310 N. Mozart St., Chicago, IL 60618. TEL: (773) 463-4010.
FAX:(773) 463-4019. email: info@filmpolice.com
www.filmpolice.com
PRESIDENT
Phillip Koch

FILMACK STUDIOS
223 West Erie St., Chicago, IL 60654. TEL: (800) 345-6225,
(800) FILMACK. FAX: (312) 427-4866.
email: robbie@filmack.com www.filmack.com
PRODUCTION MANAGER
Robbie Mack

FISHBOWL
9191 Thrasher Ave., Los Angeles, CA 90069.
TEL: (310) 550-1111. www.fishbowlfilms.net
CONTACT
Jim Hale - jim@fishbowlfilms.net

GAS STATION ZEBRA
4217 Coldwater Canyon Ave., Studio City, CA 91604.
TEL: (818) 762-2150. FAX: (818) 762-2110.
www.gasstationzebra.com
CONTACT
Michael Johnson, Devin Hawker, Jason Levine

GIARONOMO PRODUCTIONS
665 Broadway, Ste. 1000, New York, NY 10012.
TEL: (212) 995-5200. www.giaronomo.com
CO-PRESIDENT/PRODUCER
Ron Auerbach - ron@giaronomo.com
CO-PRESIDENT/PRODUCER
Giacomo Vieste - giacomo@giaronomo.com
VICE PRESIDENT/SENIOR EDITOR
Philip R. Daccord - phil@giaronomo.com
VICE-PRESIDENT/SENIOR EDITOR
Paul Vincent
PRODUCER
Joe Graceffo

GOODSPOT
2932 Nebraska Ave., Santa Monica, CA 90404.
TEL: (310) 453-5550. FAX: (310) 453-5580. www.goodspot.com
CEO
Richard Kaufman - richard@goodspot.com
PRODUCER
Ramina Garber - romina@goodspot.com

HAMMER CREATIVE
6311 Romaine St., Ste. 7316, Los Angeles, CA 90038.
TEL: (323) 606-4700, (323) 463-9156. FAX: (323) 463-8130.
email: info@Hammer-Creative.com www.hammer-creative.com
OWNER & PRESIDENT
Mark Pierce
CONTACT
Jim Botko

IGNITION CREATIVE
3211 Olympic Blvd., Santa Monica, CA 90404.
TEL: (310) 315-6300. FAX: (310) 315-6399.
www.ignitionla.com

IMAGINARY FORCES
6526 W Sunset Blvd., Los Angeles, CA 90028.
TEL: (323) 957-6868. FAX: (323) 957-9577.
email: information@imaginaryforces.com
www.imaginaryforces.com
DIRECTOR, BUSINESS DEVELOPMENT
Danixa Diaz
530 W 25th St., Ste. 501, New York, NY 10001.
TEL: (646) 486-6868. FAX: (646) 486-4700.
CREATIVE DIRECTOR & MANAGING PARTNER
Anita Olan

IN SYNC ADVERTISING
(Motion picture advertising)
6135 Wilshire Blvd., Los Angeles, CA 90048.
TEL: (323) 965-4810. FAX: (323) 965-8155.
www.insyncad.com
PRESIDENT
Smitty

INTRALINK
155 N. LaPeer Dr., Los Angeles, CA 90048.
TEL: (310) 859-7001. FAX: (310) 859-0738.
www.intralinkfilm.com
FOUNDER/PRESIDENT
Anthony Goldschmidt
CEO/CREATIVE DIRECTOR
Terry Curtin

IRON IMAGE
2510 G. Las Posas Rd., Ste. 410, Camarillo, CA 93010.
TEL: (805) 386-0366. FAX: (805) 293-8514.
email: info@ironimage.com www.ironimage.com
CONTACT
Michelle Griffith

KANDOO FILMS, INC.
4515 Van Nuys Blvd., Ste. 100, Sherman Oaks, CA 91403.
TEL: (818) 789-6777. FAX: (818) 789-2299.
www.kandoofilms.com
FOUNDER & PRESIDENT
Howard Barish - hbarish@kandoofilms.com
V.P., SALES & MARKETING
Rhonda Weddle-Kinosian - rhonda@kandoofilms.com

KINETIC TRAILERS
150 West 22nd St., 3rd Flr., New York, NY 10010.
TEL: (212) 358-4029. www.kinetictrailers.com
CO-PRESIDENT, CREATIVE DIRECTOR & EDITOR
Christy Wilson - c.wilson@kinetictrailers.com
Stephen Garrett - s.garrett@kinetictrailers.com

KO CREATIVE
9300 Wilshire Blvd., Ste. 400, Beverly Hills, CA 90212.
TEL: (310) 288-3820. FAX: (310) 285-2095.
email: info@ko-creative.com www.ko-creative.com
CONTACT
Kristi Kilday

LUMENI PRODUCTIONS, INC.
1632 Flower St., Glendale, CA 91201-2357.
TEL: (818) 956-2200. FAX: (818) 956-3298. www.lumeni.com
EXECUTIVE PRODUCER
Marshall "Tony" Valdez tony@lumeni.com

Services include: DI Color Timing, 2D, 3D & Stereo Computer Graphics, Animation, Special Effects for Film, including Digital Trailers, Film Finishing & Title Design.

MAX-Q
3211 Cahuenga Blvd. W., Ste. 202, Los Angeles, CA 90068.
TEL: (323) 512-7300. www.max-qtrailers.com
CEO
Gene Gamache
PRESIDENT
Craig O'Donnelly

MIGHTY PICTURES, INC.
20 W. 22nd St., Ste 812, New York, NY 10010.
TEL: (212) 206-6557. FAX: (212) 206-3832.
email: info@mightypics.tv www.mightypics.tv
PRESIDENT
Charlie Sadoff
COO
Mary Matyas

MOCEAN
2440 S. Sepulveda Blvd., Ste. 150, Los Angeles, CA 90064.
TEL: (310) 481-0808. FAX: (310) 481-0807.
email: info@moceanla.com www.moceanla.com
PRESIDENT
Michael McIntyre
HEAD OF THEATRICAL DIVISION
Richard Redfield
MANAGING DIRECTOR, BROADCAST DIVISION
Kevin Aratari

O'NEIL & ASSOCIATES, INC.
725 N. Western Ave., Ste. 109, Los Angeles, CA 90029.
TEL: (323) 464-2995.
DIRECTOR
James O'Neil

PALE EDITORIAL
567 Fort Washington Ave., Ste. 3H, New York, NY 10033.
TEL: (718) 312-9746. www.johnpale.com
CONTACT
John Pale - pale.edit@mac.com

PELICAN PRODUCTIONS, INC.
(Products, Printing & Programs to Increase Theatre Profits)
4262 Grand Haven Rd., Muskegon, MI 49441.
TEL: (800) 861-7675, (231) 799-1133. FAX: (231) 799-1144.
email: pelicansales@comcast.net
PRESIDENT
Joe Edick

THE PICTURE MILL
6422 Homewood Ave., Los Angeles, CA 90028.
TEL: (323) 465-8800. FAX: (323) 465-8875.
email: rick@picturemill.com www.picturemill.com
EXECUTIVE DIRECTOR
Rick Probst

PICTURE PRODUCTION COMPANY
710 Seward St., Los Angeles, CA 90038. TEL: (323) 785-2580.
www.theppc.com
CONTACT
Dane McMaster - dane@theppci.com

19/20 Poland St., London W1F 8QF England.
TEL: (44 207) 439-4944.
CONTACT
Steve O'Pray - steve@theppc.com

PIKE PRODUCTIONS, INC.
11 Clarke St., Box 300, Newport, RI 02840.
TEL: (401) 846-8890. FAX: (401) 847-0070.
email: info@pikefilmtrailers.com www.pikeproductionsinc.com
OWNER
James A. Pike

PONGO PRODUCTIONS
3301 Barham Blvd., Ste. 401, Los Angeles, CA 90068.
TEL: (323) 850-3333. FAX: (323) 850-3334.
email: pongo@gopongo.com www.gopongo.com
CEO, SENIOR CREATIVE DIRECTOR
Thomas McGough - tom@gopongo.com

PRESHOW PRODUCTIONS
15811 Wolf Creek, San Antonio, TX 78232.
TEL: (210) 577-2463.
e-mail: preshow@preshowproductions.com
www.preshowproductions.com
CONTACT
Doug Willming

QUARTERMOON
12 Morand Ln., Wilton, CT 06897. TEL: (203) 247-5550.
email: info@quartermoon.com www.quartermoon.com
OWNER & EDITOR
Gary Balionis - gb@quartermoon.com

RANDALL CREATIVE
3729 Ventura Canyon, Sherman Oaks, CA 91423.
TEL: (818) 981-8948. www.randallcreative.com
CO-PRESIDENTS
David Randall - david@randallcreative.com
Mary Zakrasek - mary@randallcreative.com

RED HOTS ENTERTAINMENT
67885 Foothill Rd., Cathedral Canyon Cove, Cathedral City, CA 92234-2436. TEL: (760) 992-7047. FAX: (760) 324-9424.
email: pogmothon@earthlink.net

Warner Brothers Studios, Burbank, CA 91505-4219.
TEL: (818) 795-4235. email: pogmothon@dc.rr.com
DIRECTOR/PRODUCER/SCREENWRITER
Chip Miller
V.P., OPERATIONS
Kit Gleason
V.P., DEVELOPMENT
Daniel Pomeroy
DIRECTOR, POST-PRODUCTION/EDITOR
Sue Travis Miller
PRODUCTION MANAGER
Mark Shelton
PUBLIC RELATIONS
Eileen Sellaro
BUSINESS AFFAIRS
Jo Patsy Hall

SEISMIC PRODUCTIONS
7010 Santa Monica Blvd., Hollywood, CA 90038.
TEL: (323) 957-3350. FAX: (323) 957-3355.
email: info@seismicproductions.com
www.seismicproductions.com

SILVER LINING PRODUCTIONS, INC.
149 S. Barrington Ave., Ste. 770, Los Angeles, CA 90049.
TEL: (310) 289-6650. FAX: (310) 289-6658.
email: bozena@silverliningp.com www.silverliningp.com
EXECUTIVE PRODUCER & DIRECTOR
Bozena Armstrong

SMITHGROUP COMMUNICATIONS, INC.
267 SE 33rd Ave., Portland, OR 97214. TEL: (503) 239-4215.
FAX: (503) 239-1570. email: smithgrp@smithgrp.com
www.smithgrp.com
PRESIDENT
Phil Bevans

SSI ADVANCED POST SERVICES
7165 Sunset Blvd., Hollywood, CA 90046. TEL: (323) 969-9333.
FAX: (323) 969-8333. www.ssi-post.com
CONTACT
Stuart Bartell

LEONARD SOUTH PRODUCTIONS
5319 Craner Ave., N. Hollywood, CA 91601. TEL: (818) 760-8383.
FAX: (818) 766-8301.
PRESIDENT
Leonard South

THE SPARK FACTORY
10 E. Colorado Blvd., Pasadena, CA 91105. TEL: (626) 397-2719.
FAX: (626) 397-2732. www.sparkfactory.com
PRESIDENT
Tim Street - tim@sparkfactory.com

TRAILER PARK
(Entertainment marketing company)
1741 N. Ivar Ave., Hollywood, CA 90028. TEL: (323) 461-4232.
FAX: (323) 461-2632. www.trailerpark.com

6922 Hollywood Blvd., 6th-7th Flr., Hollywood, CA 90028.
TEL: 310-845-3400. FAX: (310) 845-3470.
PRESIDENT
Benedict Coulter
COO
Joel Johnston
CEO
Rick Eiserman
EXECUTIVE V.P. & CREATIVE DIRECTOR
Neal Spector

UNION ENTERTAINMENT DIV
12200 W. Olympic Blvd., Ste. 140, Los Angeles, CA 90064.
TEL: (310) 481-2200. FAX: (310) 481-2248.
www.unioneditorial.com
PRESIDENT, ENTERTAINMENT DIVISION
Jijo Reed - jijo@unioneditorial.com

WEST GLEN COMMUNICATIONS, INC.
(Film & video producers & distributers specializing in educational; Producers of "The Popcorn Report")
1430 Broadway, 9th Flr, New York, NY 10018.
TEL: (212) 921-2800. FAX: (212) 944-9055.
email: info@westglen.com www.westglen.com
PRESIDENT
Stan Zeitlin

WHEELHOUSE CREATIVE
114 W. 17th St. 3rd Flr., New York, NY 10011.
TEL: (323) 207-6756.
www.wheelhousenyc.com
CONTACTS
Rob Lyons

WINSTON DAVIS ASSOCIATES
955 South Carrillo Dr., Ste. 200, Los Angeles, CA 90048.
TEL: (323) 930-8535. www.winstondavis.com
CONTACTS
Robert Solomon - Robert@winstondavis.com
Dean Blagg - Dean@winstondavis.com

MARK WOOLLEN & ASSOCIATES
207 Ashland Ave. Santa Monica, CA 90405. TEL: (310) 399-2690.
FAX: (310) 399-2670.
email: info@markwoollen.net www.markwoollen.com
PRODUCERS
Scott Mitsui - scott@markwoollen.net
Sohini Sengupta - sohini@markwoollen.net

BUYING AND BOOKING SERVICES

21ST CENTURY CINEMAS, INC.
(Booking services representing all the major film companies)
9760 S.W. 99th St., Miami, FL 33176. TEL: (305) 274-6529.
FAX: (305) 595-7602. email: barneyadrianne@aol.com
PRESIDENT
Steven Krams
VICE PRESIDENT
Barnet L. Kaufman

ASHURST AGENCY
210 Turnberry Circle, Fayetteville, GA 30215.
TEL: (770) 461-9851. FAX: (770) 719-1565.
email: ashuragent@aol.com
OWNER
Annette Ashurst

ASSOCIATED BOOKING CORPORATION (ABC)
501 Madison Ave., Ste. 501, New York, NY 10022
TEL: (212) 874-2400. FAX: (212) 769-3649.
email: musicbiz@mindspring.com www.abcbooking.com
PRESIDENT
Oscar Cohen
VICE PRESIDENT
Lisa Cohen

BRAND BOOKING
5807 Andover Dr., Allen, TX 75002. TEL: (972) 202-1637,
(972) 202-1638. FAX: (972) 202-1639.
OWNER & HEAD FILM BUYER
Jerry Brand
FILM BUYERS
Stephanie Bowers
Beth Teal

CALIFORNIA BOOKING
P.O. Box 11, Agoura, CA 91376. TEL: (818) 991-8593.
FAX: (818) 991-8898. email: calbkg2@sbcglobal.net
OWNER
Carol Combs

CENTRAL TALENT BOOKING
105 Mulberry St., 5th Flr., New York, NY 10013
TEL: (212) 765-5777. FAX: (212) 765-9799.
FOUNDER/CEO
Joanna Jordan
CHIEF OF STAFF
Lesley Cahill-Roy

CINEMA BOOKING SERVICE OF NEW ENGLAND
P.O. Box 920827, Needham, MA 02492.
TEL: (781) 444-1174. FAX: (781) 444 7477.
PRESIDENT
Stanton Davis - stadav1@verizon.net

CINEMA FILM BUYING
1245 Hancock St., Ste. 11, Quincy, MA 02169.
TEL: (617) 479-0138. FAX: (617) 479-4287.
OWNER
Martin Zides - mzides@cinemafilmbuying.com

CINEMA SERVICE
9400 N. Central Expwy., #320, Dallas, TX 75231.
TEL: (214) 692-7555. FAX: (214) 692-7559.
email: tim.csc@flexcomp.com
PRESIDENTS
Tim Patton, Rick Slaughter

COMPLETE BOOKING SERVICE
1819 Sabrina Ct., Charlotte, NC 28210. TEL: (704) 643-1522.
FAX: (704) 554-0570.
OWNER
Gary Vanderhorst

CONTINENTAL FILM SERVICES, INC.
13206 Tierra Hts. Rd., Redding, CA 96003. TEL: (530) 275-8881.
FAX: (530) 275-8889.
OWNERS
Richard Gambogi - rgambogi0936@charter.net
Jeanette Gambogi

CO-OPERATIVE THEATRES, INC.
1413 Golden Gate Blvd., Ste. 205, Mayfield Heights, OH
44124. TEL: (440) 461-2700. FAX: (440) 461-0659.
www.cooptheatres.com
PRESIDENT
John Knepp - Knepp89@aol.com
BOOKERS
Frances Volan - FVolan@aol.com
Kurt Miller - Kurtcoop@aol.com

EDDY G. ERICKSON BOOKING SERVICE
3405 Jubilee Trail, Dallas, TX 75229.
TEL: (214) 352-3821.
OWNER
Eddy G. Erickson

FILM SERVICE THEATRE GROUP
Ivy Place II, 4700 South 900 East, Ste. 41-D, Salt Lake City,
UT 84117-4938. TEL: (801) 281-9694. FAX: (801) 281-9764.
PRESIDENT
David Sharp

FLORIN-CREATIVE FILM SERVICES
125 N. Main St., Port Chester, NY 10573.
TEL: (914) 937-1603. FAX: (914) 937-8496.
email: sflorin33@aol.com
PRESIDENT
Steven Florin

FRONTIER BOOKING INTERNATIONAL, INC.
1560 Broadway, Ste. 1110, New York, NY 10036.
TEL: (212) 221-0220. www.frontierbooking.com
DEPARTMENT HEAD
John Shea

INDEPENDENT FILM SERVICES
8900 State Line Rd., Ste. 405, Leawood, KS 66206.
TEL: (913) 381-5555. FAX: (913) 381-5552.
email: indepfilm@earthlink.net
OWNER
Brad Bills

INDEPENDENT THEATRE BOOKING
4523 Park Rd., #A-105, Charlotte, NC 28209.
TEL: (704) 529-1200. FAX: (704) 529-1201.
PRESIDENT & FILM BUYER
Steve Smith
MANAGER, OPERATIONS
Bryan Smith - bryansmithitbs@carolina.rr.com

LESSER THEATRE SERVICE
166 Levinberg Lane, Wayne, NJ 07470. TEL: (973) 872-7000.
FAX: (973) 872-7055.
PRESIDENT
Rob Lawinski - rob@lessertheatreservice.com

MJR THEATRE SERVICE, INC.
13691 W. Eleven Mile Rd., Oak Park, MI 48237.
TEL: (248) 548-8282. FAX: (248) 548-4706.
www.mjrtheatres.com
PRESIDENT
Michael R. Mihalich

MARCUS THEATRES CORPORATION
100 E. Wisconsin Ave., Ste. 2000, Milwaukee, WI 53202-4122.
TEL: (414) 905-1500. FAX: (414) 905-2882.
PRESIDENT
Bruce J. Olson

MESCOP, INC.
P.O. Box 303, Sussex, WI 53089. TEL: (262) 251-6808.
FAX: (262) 251-9033. email: Mescopinc@yahoo.com
PRESIDENT & BUYER
James Florence
BOOKER & OFFICE MANAGER
Carol Brown

MOTION PICTURE COUNSELING
301 Mt. Shasta Dr., San Rafael, CA 94903-1029.
TEL: (415) 491-1234.
OWNER
Ronald Litvin

NORRIS BOOKING AGENCY
1917 Holly Oaks Lake Rd. E., Jacksonville, FL 32225.
TEL: (904) 641-0019.
OWNER
Rex Norris

NORTHWEST DIVERSIFIED ENTERTAINMENT
915 5th Ave. W, Seattle, WA 98119. TEL: (206) 352-4004.
FAX: (206) 352-4008.
OWNER
Benjamin L. Hannah
FILM BUYER
Victoria Hawker - vhawker@mindspring.com
Bruce Goodnow - bgoodnow@mindspring.com

R/C THEATRES BOOKING SERVICE
231 W. Cherry Hill Ct., Box 1056, Reisterstown, MD 21136.
TEL: (410) 526-4774. FAX: (410) 526-6871.

CHAIRMAN
J. Wayne Anderson
PRESIDENT & CEO
Scott R. Cohen
EXECUTIVE V.P. & CFO
David G. Phillips
V.P., FILM
Jan S. Anderson
CONTROLLER
Richard A. Hershel
DIVISION MANAGER
David Knight

ROXY MANAGEMENT COMPANY, INC.

2004 Main St., Northampton, PA 18067-5514.
TEL: (610) 262-7699. email: Roxy1933@aol.com
www.roxytheaternorthampton.com
PRESIDENT
Richard C. Wolfe
VICE PRESIDENT
Todd Lindenmoyer

SARASOTA FILM SOCIETY

10715 Rodeo Dr. #8, Bradenton, FL 34202.
TEL: (941) 364-8662 ext. 2008. FAX: (941) 364-8478.
www.filmsociety.org
EXECUTIVE DIRECTOR
Jerry Kovar - Jerry@filmsociety.org

THEATRE SERVICE NETWORK

105 Oxford Ct., Oswego, IL 60543. TEL: (630) 340-5877.
FAX: (630) 340-5898.
PRESIDENT & FILM BUYER
Steve Felperin
FILM BUYERS
Debra Kovacs, Sarah Felperin
CASHIER
Kimberly Good

TRI-STATE THEATRE SERVICE, INC.

Film Arts Building, 636 Northland Blvd., Cincinnati, OH 45240-3221. TEL: (513) 851-5700. FAX: (513) 851-5708.
email: tristatetheatre@cs.com
FILM BUYERS
Florence Groner, Steve Zeiser

UNITED THEATRE SERVICE

P.O. Box 13153, Mill Creek, WA 98082. TEL: (425) 743-6269.
FAX: (425) 743-2246. email: happymoviequeen@yahoo.com
www.unitedtheatreservice.com
BOOKER/OWNER
Dorothea Maye

Regional Distributors

BOSTON

CINEMA BOOKING SERVICE OF NEW ENGLAND

P.O. Box 920827, Needham, MA 02492.
TEL: (781) 444-1174. FAX: (781) 444-7477.
email: stadav1@verizon.net
PRESIDENT
Stanton Davis

UNIVERSAL PICTURES

One Beacon St., 4th Fl., Boston, MA 02108.
TEL: (617) 378-6508. FAX: (617) 378-6598.
BRANCH MANAGER, BOSTON/NEW HAVEN
Joan Corrado
BRANCH MANAGER, ALBANY/BUFFALO/CINCINNATI
Joe Crimi
SALES MANAGER
David O'Hara
EXHIBITOR RELATIONS
Peter Wright

ZIPPORAH FILMS

1 Richdale Ave. #4, Cambridge, MA 02140. TEL: (617) 576-3603.
FAX: (617) 864-8006. email: info@zipporah.com
www.zipporah.com
DIRECTOR, DISTRIBUTION
Karen Konicek

BUFFALO

FRONTIER AMUSEMENT

100 Broad St., Ste. 4, Tonawanda, NY 14150.
TEL: (716) 695-2382. FAX: (716) 695-2385.
PRESIDENT
Ike Ehrlichmann
VICE PRESIDENT
Mary Beth Lawton
OFFICE MANAGER
Cindy Crossley

CHICAGO

INDEPENDENT FEATURE PROJECT/CHICAGO

1104 S. Wabash #403, Chicago, IL 60605. TEL: (312) 235-0161.
FAX: (312) 235-0162. email: chicago@ifp.org www.ifp.org
EXECUTIVE DIRECTOR
Elizabeth Donius - edonius@ifp.org

UNITED LEARNING

(A division of Discovery Communications)
(Health, education and prevention)
1560 Sherman Ave., #100, Evanston, IL 60201.
TEL: (888) 892-3484, (847) 328-6700. FAX: (847) 328-6706.
email: info@unitedlearning.com www.unitedlearning.com
CEO
Joel Altschul
PRESIDENT
Ron Reed
V.P., MARKETING
Coni Rechner

DALLAS

CLARK/MCCRARY FILM

501 Little John Dr., Irving, TX 75061. TEL: (972) 313-1738.
BRANCH MANAGER
J.C. McCrary

SONY PICTURES RELEASING

MIDWEST DIVISION OF SONY PICTURES RELEASING
1300 E. Lookout Dr., Ste. 340A, Richardson, TX 75082-4106.
TEL: (972) 638-1300. FAX: (972) 638-1323.
SENIOR V.P., MIDWEST DIVISION
Sherman E. Wood
V.P., MIDWEST DIVISION
James Weiss
DISTRICT MANAGER, MIDWEST DIVISION
Karen Calder, Glenn Abrams

SOUTHERN DIVISION OF SONY PICTURES RELEASING
1300 E. Lookout Dr., Ste. 340B, Richardson, TX 75082-4106.
TEL: (972) 638-1350. FAX: (972) 638-1351.
SENIOR V.P., SOUTHERN DIVISION
Juli Mitchell
V.P., SOUTHERN DIVISION
Patricia Dougherty
DISTRICT MANAGER, SOUTHERN DIVISION
Jeff Wayne, Dale Edmondson

UNIVERSAL PICTURES

7502 Greenville Ave., Ste 200, Dallas, TX 75231.
TEL: (214) 360-0022. FAX: (818) 866-6837.
V.P./BRANCH MANAGER, DALLAS/OKLAHOMA CITY/DES MOINES
Bruce Thompson
BRANCH MANAGER, ATLANTA/CHARLOTTE/JACKSONVILLE
James Dixon
BRANCH MANAGER, KANSAS CITY/MEMPHIS/NEW ORLEANS/ST. LOUIS
Dana Poindexter
BRANCH MANAGER,CHICAGO/INDIANAPOLIS/MILWAUKEE/MINNEAPOLIS
Jim Agliata
SALES MANAGER
Dorrine Kaczmarek, Sharla Van Doorn, Lynne Craft
EXHIBITOR RELATIONS, REP. SOUTHERN DIVISION
Elvira Golden

LOS ANGELES

CROWN INTERNATIONAL PICTURES, INC.

8701 Wilshire Blvd., Beverly Hills, CA 90211.
TEL: (310) 657-6700. FAX: (310) 657-4489.
www.crownintlpictures.com
PRESIDENT & CEO
Mark Tenser
SENIOR V.P.
Scott E. Schwimer
V.P., FINANCE
Willie De Leon
DIRECTOR, PUBLICITY & ADVERTISING
Lisa Agay
EXECUTIVE PRODUCER/PRODUCER
Marilyn J. Tenser

WALT DISNEY STUDIOS MOTION PICTURES

3800 W. Alameda, 9th Fl., Burbank, CA 91521-6170.
TEL: (818) 840-1984. FAX: (818) 972-9543.
V.P., WEST SALES
Patrick Pade
EXECUTIVE DIRECTOR, SALES
Dean Gordon, Steve Schoenburg
DIRECTOR, SALES
Bill Crane, Steve Getzler, Brian Hicks, Leon Ittel, Jeff Prill, Kerry Silver
MANAGER, SALES
Kelly Markle
SALES REPRESENTATIVE
Kim Thompson

LIONS GATE FILMS CORP.

2700 Colorado Blvd., Santa Monica, CA 90404.
TEL: (310) 449-9200. FAX: (310) 255-3870.
PRESIDENT, DOMESTIC THEATRICAL DISTRIBUTION
Steve Rothenberg
V.P., HOME ENTERTAINMENT MARKETING
Michael Rathauser

MIRAMAX

3800 W. Alameda Ave., Burbank, CA 91505.
TEL: (818) 569-4800. FAX: (818) 569-5919.
SENIOR V.P./GENERAL SALES MANAGER
Elliot Slutzky - Elliot.Slutzky@Miramax.com

NEW LINE CINEMA DISTRIBUTION, INC.

9000 Sunset Blvd., Ste. 1200, Los Angeles, CA 90069.
TEL: (310) 248-6000. FAX: (310) 248-2960.
SENIOR V.P., WESTERN DIVISION
Larry Levy
DISTRICT MANAGER, SAN FRANCISCO/DENVER
Mark Johnstone
DISTRICT MANAGER, LOS ANGELES
Alex Purcell

PARAMOUNT PICTURES ENTERTAINMENT

5555 Melrose Ave, Hollywood, CA 90038. TEL: (323) 956-5000.
PRESIDENT OF MOTION PICTURE DISTRIBUTION
James Tharp
EXECUTIVE V.P., SALES, MOTION PICTURE DISTRIBUTION
Donald Harris
EXECUTIVE V.P., OPERATIONS, MOTION PICTURE DISTRIBUTION
Mark Christiansen
SENIOR V.P., NON-THEATRICAL SALES
Joan Filippini
SENIOR V.P., IN-THEATRE MARKETING, MOTION PICTURE DISTRIBUTION
Patricia Gonzalez

PARAMOUNT PICTURES SALES DIVISION
15260 Ventura Blvd., #1140, Sherman Oaks, CA 91403.
TEL: (818) 380-7800.
SENIOR V.P., CENTRAL DIVISION
Joseph Saladino
SENIOR V.P., SOUTHERN DIVISION
Emmet Nicaud
SENIOR V.P., WESTERN DIVISION
Jerry Pokorski

SONY PICTURES RELEASING
10202 W. Washington Blvd., Culver City, CA 90232.
TEL: (310) 244-8700.
SENIOR V.P.
Adrian Smith
V.P./MANAGING DIRECTOR
Ross Merrin
DISTRICT MANAGERS
Patricia Dougherty, Kerrilee Wong, Carla Jones

TOHO COMPANY, LTD.
2029 Century Park E., Ste. 1150, Los Angeles, CA 90067.
TEL: (310) 277-1081. FAX: (310) 277-6351.

TROMA ENTERTAINMENT, INC.
(Producer & distributor)
36-40 11th St., Long Island City, NY 11106.
TEL: (718) 391-0110. www.troma.com
PRESIDENT
Lloyd Kaufman
VICE PRESIDENT
Michael Herz
SALES MANAGER
Jeremy Howell

TWENTIETH CENTURY FOX FILM CORP.
23975 Park Sorrento Dr., Ste. 300, Calabasas, CA 91302.
TEL: (818) 876-7200.
V.P., WESTERN DIVISION MANAGER
Corey Ballaban
V.P., SOUTHERN DIVISION MANAGER
R.B. Gautier, II
BRANCH MANAGER, LOS ANGELES
Brett Resnick
SALES MANAGER, LOS ANGELES
Dax Mark
BRANCH MANAGER, DENVER/SAN FRANCISCO
Janet Jackson
BRANCH MANAGER, SEATTLE/PORTLAND/SALT LAKE CITY
Michele Johnson
BRANCH MANAGER, DALLAS/OKLAHOMA
Gavin Smith
BRANCH MANAGER, JACKSONVILLE
Steve Saphos
BRANCH MANAGER, CHARLOTTE/MEMPHIS
LaMont Shedrick
BRANCH MANAGER, ATLANTA/NEW ORLEANS
Michael Parent

UNIVERSAL PICTURES
100 Universal City Plaza, Bldg. 2160, Ste. 7N, Universal City, CA 91608. TEL: (818) 777-0002. FAX: (818) 866-3477.
V.P./LOS ANGELES BRANCH MANAGER
Lynne Francis
BRANCH MANAGER, DENVER/SAN FRANCISCO
Robert Taylor
BRANCH MANAGER, PORTLAND/SEATTLE/SALT LAKE CITY
Marji McCormick
SALES MANAGER
Rose Crockett
SENIOR COORDINATOR, WESTERN REGION
Cynthia Orellana - (818) 777-0096
Rebecca Jansson - (818) 777-0011

WARNER BROS. DISTRIBUTING INC.
15821 Ventura Blvd., Ste. 575, Encino, CA 91436.
TEL: (818) 977-1850. FAX: (818) 986-7559.
SENIOR V.P., ASSISTANT GENERAL SALES MANAGER
Scott Forman - (818) 977-1810
SENIOR V.P., SOUTHERN & MIDWESTERN DIVISIONS
Danny Chinich - (818) 977-1813
V.P., SOUTHERN DIVISION & DALLAS BRANCH
Ron MacPhee - (818) 977-1817
V.P., MIDWESTERN DIVISION & CHICAGO BRANCH
Allison Fields - (818) 977-1840
V.P., WESTERN DIVISION & IMAX
Michael Viane - (818) 977-1851
DIRECTOR OF ADMINISTRATION, WESTERN, MIDWESTERN & SOUTHERN DIVISIONS
Kim Dimarco - (818) 977-1890
BRANCH MANAGER, SEATTLE/MINNIAPOLIS
Ralph Albi - (818) 977-1830
BRANCH MANAGER, SAN FRANCISCO/PORTLAND/IMAX
Cary Silvera - (818) 977-1804
BRANCH MANAGER, KANSAS CITY/ST. LOUIS/INDIANAPOLIS/OKLAHOMA CITY
Darla Pierce - (818) 977-1821
REGIONAL MANAGER, LOS ANGELES/ARIZONA
Gigi Lestak - (818) 977-1811
SALES MANAGER, CHARLOTTE/MEMPHIS
Joe Fasulo - (818) 977-1864
BRANCH MANAGER, DENVER/SALT LAKE CITY/CLASSICS
Linda Evans-Smith - (818) 977-1814
BRANCH MANAGER, JACKSONVILLE/DES MOINES/OMAHA
David Ogden - (818) 977-1844
BRANCH MANAGER, LOS ANGELES/ARIZONA
Bob Devries - (818) 977-1815
BRANCH MANAGER, ATLANTA/NEW ORLEANS
John Lamont - (818) 977-1819

MINNESOTA

IFP MINNESOTA CENTER FOR MEDIA ARTS
2446 University Ave. W., Ste. 100, Saint Paul, MN 55114.
TEL: (651) 644-1912. FAX: (651) 644-5708. www.ifp.org
EXECUTIVE DIRECTOR
Jane Minton - jminton@ifpmn.org

NEW YORK

THE CINEMA GUILD
(Motion picture, independent film & TV distributor)
115 W. 30th St., Ste. 800, New York, NY 10001.
TEL: (212) 685-6242. FAX: (212) 685-4717.
email: info@cinemaguild.com www.cinemaguild.com
CHAIRMAN
Philip S. Hobel
CO-CHAIRMAN
Mary Ann Hobel
DIRECTOR, NON-THEATRICAL & FEATURE FILM DISTRIBUTION
Ryan Krivoshey
OFFICE MANAGER
David Kempski

CORINTH FILMS, INC.
3117 Bursonville Rd., Riegelsville, PA 18077.
TEL: (610) 346-7446. FAX: (610) 346-6345.
email: sales@corinthfilms.com www.corinthfilms.com

WALT DISNEY STUDIOS MOTION PICTURES
1500 Broadway, New York, NY 10036.
TEL: (212) 536-6400. FAX: (212) 536-6409.
V.P., SALES
Ken Caldwell
DIRECTOR, SALES
Matt Kalavsky, Leo Fisch, Al Webster
SALES MANAGER
Carol Toppin, RoseMarie Schulz, Greg Skurow, Chad Barksdale
SALES REPRESENTATIVE
Kristina Crusey
EXECUTIVE DIRECTORS, SALES
Dennis Meagher, John Molson

FIRST RUN FEATURES
(Motion picture, independent film & TV distributor)
The Film Center Building, 630 Ninth Ave., Ste. 1213, New York, NY 10036. TEL: (212) 243-0600. FAX: (212) 989-7649.
email: info@firstrunfeatures.com www.firstrunfeatures.com
PRESIDENT
Seymour Wishman
VICE PRESIDENT
Marc A. Mauceri
MARKETING DIRECTOR
Judith Mizrachy

FOCUS FEATURES
Los Angeles: 100 Universal City Plz., Universal City, CA 91608. TEL: (818) 777-7373.

New York: 65 Bleecker St., 3rd Fl., New York, NY 10012.
TEL: (212) 539-4000. www.roguepictures.com
www.focusfeatures.com

CEO/FOCUS FEATURES
James Schamus
PRESIDENT, FOCUS FEATURES
Andrew Karpen
PRESIDENT, THEATRICAL DISTRIBUTION
Jack Foley
PRESIDENT, PRODUCTION/FOCUS FEATURES
John Lyons
PRESIDENT, WORLDWIDE PUBLICITY, EXECUTIVE V.P., MARKETING
Adriene Bowles
PRESIDENT, MARKETING
David Brooks
PRESIDENT, INTERNATIONAL SALES & DISTRIBUTION
Alison Thompson
EXECUTIVE V.P. OF THEATRICAL DISTRIBUTION & SALES
Linda Ditrinco
EXECUTIVE V.P., STRATEGIC PLANNING, BUSINESS AFFAIRS AND ACQUISITIONS
Avy Eschenasy

FOX SEARCHLIGHT PICTURES
1211 6th Ave., 16th Fl., New York, NY 10036.
TEL: (212) 556-8600, (212) 556-8596. FAX: (212) 840-2557.
REGIONAL SALES COORDINATOR
Anna Osso

INDEPENDENT FEATURE PROJECT
104 W. 29th St., 12th Fl., New York, NY 10001.
TEL: (212) 465-8200. FAX: (212) 465-8525. www.ifp.org
EXECUTIVE DIRECTOR
Michelle Byrd - mbyrd@ifp.org

JACOBS ENTERTAINMENT, INC.
(Key film distributors and key film buyers)
26 Allendale Dr., Rye, NY 10580. TEL: (914) 925-0099.
FAX: (914) 925-9737. email: jacobsfilm@aol.com
www.jacobsentertainment.com
PRESIDENT
Jeffrey Jacobs

KINO INTERNATIONAL CORP.
333 W. 39th St., Ste. 503, New York, NY 10018.
TEL: (800) 562-3330, (212) 629-6880. FAX: (212) 714-0871.
email: contact@kino.com www.kino.com
PRESIDENT
Donald Krim
THEATRICAL SALES DIRECTOR
Gary Palmucci
HOME VIDEO SALES DIRECTOR
Frank Tarzi

MIRAMAX FILMS
161 Ave. of the Americas, New York, NY 10013.
TEL: (917) 606-5660.
SENIOR V.P., INTL. DISTRIBUTION & OPERATIONS
Colleen Seldin

MUSEUM OF MODERN ART FILM LIBRARY
11 W. 53rd St., New York, NY 10019. TEL: (212) 708-9433.
email: info@moma.org www.moma.org
DIRECTOR
Glenn D. Lowry

NEW LINE CINEMA
888 Seventh Ave,. New York, NY 10106. TEL: (212) 649-4890.
FAX: (212) 956-1944.
SENIOR V.P. & EASTERN DIVISION MANAGER, DISTRIBUTION
Jonathan Beal
V.P. & DISTRICT MANAGER, NY/PHILADELPHIA/BUFFALO
Richard Bonanno
V.P. & DISTRICT MANAGER, BOSTON/NEW HAVEN/
PITTSBURGH/D.C.
Mary Navarra
DISTRICT MANAGER/JACKSONVILLE/CINCINNATI
Bruce Placke

NEW YORKER FILMS
21 West 38th St, 14th Fl., New York, NY 10018.
TEL: (212) 645-4600. FAX: (212) 645-3030.
email: info@newyorkerfilms.com www.newyorkerfilms.com
PRESIDENT
Daniel Talbot
V.P. & DIRECTOR, HOME VIDEO
Jose Lopez

PARAMOUNT PICTURES
1633 Broadway, New York, NY 10019. TEL: (212) 654-7000.
SENIOR V.P., EAST COAST SALES DIVISION
Joe Sabatino

SONY PICTURES RELEASING
550 Madison Ave., 7th Fl., New York, NY 10022.
TEL: (212) 833-7623. FAX: (212) 833-6495.
SENIOR V.P.
Jim Amos
VICE PRESIDENT
John Spinello
DISTRICT MANAGER
Adam Bergerman, Janet Murray

TOHO CO., LTD.
1501 Broadway, Ste. 2005, New York, NY 10036.
TEL: (212) 391-9058. FAX: (212) 840-2823. www.toho.co.jp

TROMA ENTERTAINMENT, INC.
(Producer & distributor)
733 Ninth Ave., New York, NY 10019. TEL: (212) 757-4555.
FAX: (212) 399-9885, (212) 957-4497. www.troma.com
PRESIDENT
Lloyd Kaufman

VICE PRESIDENT
Michael Herz
DIRECTOR, INTERNATIONAL SALES
Lisa Borhoum
SALES MANAGER
Jeremy Howell

TWENTIETH CENTURY FOX FILM CORP.
1211 Ave. of the Americas, 16th Fl., New York, NY 10036.
TEL: (212) 556-8600. FAX: (212) 556-8606.
V.P. & EASTERN DIVISION MANAGER
Ron Polon
BRANCH MANAGER, ALBANY/NEW YORK
Lawrence Piller
BRANCH MANAGER, PHILADELPHIA/PITTSBURGH
Joe Reid
V.P. & MID-WEST DIVISION MANAGER
Henri Frankfurter
BRANCH MANAGER, BOSTON/NEW HAVEN
Dan Eckes
BRANCH MANAGER, CINCINNATI/CLEVELAND/INDIANAPOLIS
Ralph Farnham
BRANCH MANAGER, BUFFALO, NY/WASHINGTON DC
Shaunda Lumpkin
BRANCH MANAGER, DETROIT/MINNEAPOLIS/OMAHA
Dave Hansen
BRANCH MANAGER, CHICAGO/MILWAUKEE/DES MOINES
Jackie Santiago
BRANCH MANAGER, KANSAS CITY/ST. LOUIS
Lauren Black

UNIVERSAL PICTURES
825 8th Ave., 30th Fl., New York, NY 10019.
TEL: (212) 445-3819. FAX: (212) 445-3809.
V.P., NY METROPOLITAN MANAGER
Gary Rocco
BRANCH MANAGER, WASHINGTON, D.C.
Steve Turner
BRANCH MANAGER, PHILADELPHIA/PITTSBURGH
Charles Sampayo
SALES MANAGER
Richard Tabin
EXHIBITOR RELATIONS, FIELD REP. EASTERN REGION
Paul Francis

WARNER BROS.
1325 Ave. of the Americas, 29th Fl., New York, NY 10019.
TEL: (212) 636-5000. FAX: (212) 636-5237.
SENIOR V.P., EASTERN DIVISION MANAGER
Frank Carroll - (212) 636-5220
V.P., EASTERN DIVISION, ALBANY, BUFFALO BRANCH MANAGER
Theresa Craven - (212) 636-5830
DISTRICT MANAGER, WASHINGTON, DC
Charles Barcellona - (212) 636-5203
BRANCH MANAGER, DETROIT/PHILADELPHIA
Bruce Blatt - (212) 636-5252
BRANCH MANAGER, NY
Roberta Peterson - (212) 636-5240
BRANCH MANAGER, CINCINNATI, CLEVELAND, PITTSBURGH
Andrew Silverman - (212) 636-5296
MANAGER EXHIBITOR SERVICES EASTERN DIVISION
Millie Gautier - (212) 636-5211
BOSTON BRANCH MANAGER
Andy Strulson - (212) 636-5252

PUERTO RICO

COLUMBIA TRISTAR FILMS OF PUERTO RICO
Metro Square Bldg., Ste. G-2, Metro Office Park, Guaynabo, PR 00968. TEL: (787) 793-1500. FAX: (787) 793-2859.
www.columbiapr.com
SENIOR V.P., SOUTHERN DIVISION
Terry Tharpe
MARKETING MANAGER
Annette Monserrate

UNIVERSAL PICTURES COMPANY OF PUERTO RICO, LLP
P.O. Box 11308, San Juan, Puerto Rico 00910-2408.
TEL: (787) 625-2376, (787) 625-2377. FAX: (787) 625-2378.
BRANCH MANAGER
Wilfred Morneau

SEATTLE

INDEPENDENT FEATURE PROJECT/SEATTLE

1001 Lenora St., Seattle, WA 98121. TEL: (206) 860-8490.
email: seattleinfo@ifp.org www.ifp.org
DEVELOPMENT & ADMINISTRATION
Kristen Parsons

INTERNATIONAL DISTRIBUTORS

CANADA

BUENA VISTA PICTURES DISTRIBUTION CANADA, INC.

Simcoe Place, 200 Front St. West, #3001, Toronto, Ontario, M5V 3L4 Canada. TEL: (416) 964-9275. FAX: (416) 596-3382.
V.P., SALES
Anthony Macina
DIRECTOR, SALES
Tony Schittone

PARAMOUNT PICTURES ENTERTAINMENT

40 University Ave., #900, Toronto, ONT M5J 1T1.
TEL: (416) 969-7000.
SENIOR V.P., CANADA SALES DIVISION
Don Popow

LONDON

UNITED INTERNATIONAL PICTURES (UIP)

Building 5, Third Fl., Chiswick Park, 566 Chiswick High Rd., London W4 5YF. TEL: (44 20) 3184 2500. FAX: (44 20) 3184 2501.
www.uipcorp.com
MANAGING DIRECTOR
John Horgan

EXHIBITOR ORGANIZATIONS

GIANT SCREEN CINEMA ASSOCIATION
750 Meadow Cliff Dr., St. Charles, MO 63303.
TEL: (636) 244-0947. FAX: (636) 244-1380.
www.giantscreencinema.com
PRESIDENT
Gretchen Jaspering - GretchenJaspering@GiantScreenCinema.com
DIRECTOR OF CONFERENCES AND MEMEBERSHIP
Tammy Seldon
BOARD MEMBERS
Therese Andrade, Jonathan Barker, Mark Bretherton, Diane Carlson, Kim Cavendish, Laurent Dondey, Rick Gordon, Mark Katz, Patricia Keighley, Don Kempf, Doug King, Jeffrey Kirsch, Tim Knapp, Mike Lutz, Greg MacGillivray, Toby Mensforth, Andrew Oran, Gil Perez, Gordon Stalans, Phil Streather, Dick Vaughan, Andy Wood

INTERNATIONAL CINEMA TECHNOLOGY ASSOCIATION
770 Broadway, 7th Flr., New York, NY 10003-9595.
TEL: (646) 654-7680. FAX: (646) 654-7694.
email: Edith.Malijan@nielsen.com www.icta-web.com
PRESIDENT
Barry Ferrell
EXECUTIVE DIRECTOR
Robert H. Sunshine
VICE PRESIDENT
Jack Panzeca, Anders Uggelberg
TREASURER
Joe DeMeo
SECRETARY
Sarah Fuller
HONORARY DIRECTOR
Ioan Allen
DIRECTORS
Mike Archer, Steve Bergman, Sam Chavez, Bernard Collard, Bobby Franklin, Chuck Goodsell, Jerry Harrah, Harry Mathias, Bill Mead, Pat Moore, Nick Mulone, Alan Roe, Doug Sabin

NATIONAL ASSOCIATION OF CONCESSIONAIRES
35 E. Wacker Dr., Ste. 1816, Chicago, IL 60601.
TEL: (312) 236-3858. FAX: (312) 236-7809.
email: info@NAConline.org www.naconline.org
EXECUTIVE DIRECTOR
Charles A. Winans - cwinans@NAConline.org
DIRECTOR, COMMUNICATIONS
Susan Cross - scross@NAConline.org
MANAGER, MEMBERSHIP SERVICES
Barbara Aslan - baslan@NAConline.org
CHAIRMAN
Maria Angles, ECM
PRESIDENT
Ron Krueger, II
PRESIDENT ELECT
John Evans, Jr.
TREASURER
Andrew Cretors
VICE PRESIDENT
Terry Conlon, ECM; Jeff Scudillo, Jr., Mike Nast
CONCESSION OPERATOR
Robert Perkins, III, John Bluck, Charlie Neary, Michael J. Ritta, Gary Wattie
DIRECTOR
Rick Abramson, Fred Blank, Phillip R. Couch, Tim Farha, Adam Gottlieb, Krystal LaReese-Gaule, Chris Miller, Bruce Taffet, Mike Ware
REGIONAL VICE PRESIDENT
Arthur Anderson, Brian Biehn, Mark Hamilton, Brian McMillin, Charlie Gomez, Tony Irace, Gina Troutman DiSanto, Arlindo Gomes, Martin Olesen, Ramon Estevez, Alexander Gelshteyn
PAST PRESIDENT
Andrew S. Berwick, Jr., Chris Bigelow, Norman R. Chesler, Larry Etter, CCM, Malco Theatres, Shelley Feldman, Gary Horvath, Doug Larson, Julian Lefkowitz, Jack Leonard, Philip M. Lowe, Vince Pantuso, Bill Rector, Edward S. Redstone, Vernon B. Ryles, Jr., David Scoco, Skip Stefansen
LIFETIME HONORARY MEMBER, BOARD OF DIRECTORS
Frank Liberto, Sydney Spiegel, Van Myers

NATIONAL ASSOCIATION OF THEATRE OWNERS, INC.
P.O. Box 77318, Washington D.C. 20013-7318.
750 First St., NE, Ste. 1130, Washington DC 20002.
TEL: (202) 962-0054. FAX: (202) 962-0370. www.natoonline.org
PRESIDENT & CEO
John Fithian
CHAIRMAN
Tony Kerasotes
VICE CHAIRMAN
Aubrey Stone
VICE PRESIDENT & GENERAL COUNSEL
Gary Klein
SECRETARY
Mark O'Meara
TREASURER
Amy Miles
EXECUTIVE DIRECTOR
Kathy Conroy
NORTH HOLLYWOOD
4605 Lankershim Blvd. #180, North Hollywood, CA 91602.
TEL: (818) 506-1778. FAX: (818) 506-0269.
DIRECTOR OF MEDIA & RESEARCH, CALIFORNIA OPERATIONS CHIEF
Patrick Corcoran
INDUSTRY LIAISON
Brigitte Buehlman
EXECUTIVE COMMITTEE
J. Wayne Anderson (Reisterstown, MD), Peter Brown (Kansas City, MO), Michael Campbell (Knoxville, TN), Nora Dashwood (Los Angeles, CA), Gregory Dunn (Knoxville, TN), Jerome Forman (Los Angeles, CA), Robynn Gabel (Lander, WY), Robert Goodrich (Grand Rapids, MI), Dan Harkins (Scottsdale, AZ), Philip Harris (Kalispell, MT), Ellis Jacob (Toronto, ON), Tony Kerasotes (Chicago, IL), Jerome Magner (Dedham, MA), Stephen Marcus (Milwaukee, WI), LeeRoy Mitchell (Plano, TX), Mark O'Meara (Fairfax, VA), Raffaele Papalia (Lachenaie, QC), Michael Patrick (Columbus, GA), Shari Redstone (Dedham, MA), William Stembler (St. Simons Island, GA), Alan Stock (Plano, TX), Herman Stone (Charlotte, NC)
BOARD OF DIRECTORS
Leslie Aberson (Louisville, KY), Mark T. Adam (Manchester, NH), Bill Adamany, Jr. (Prairie du Chien, WI), Bill Adamany, Sr. (Prairie du Chien, WI), J. Wayne Anderson (Reisterstown, MD), Jeffrey Benson (Dallas, TX), Byron Berkley (Kilgore, TX), Joost Bert (Belgium), Marty Betz (Grand Rapids, MI), Michael Bowers (Scottsdale, AZ), Peter Brown (Kansas City, MO), Michael Campbell (Knoxville, TN), Bill Campbell (Sheridan, WY), Michael Cavalier (Plano, TX), Rick Cohen (Amherst, NY), Scott Cohen (Reisterstown, MD), Jason Cole (Kansas City, MO), David Corwin (Los Angeles, CA), Bruce Corwin (Los Angeles, CA), Nora Dashwood (Los Angeles, CA), Rob Del Moro (Knoxville, TN), Gregory Dunn (Knoxville, TN), Munir Falah (Miami, FL), Tom Fermanian (Saint Adele, QC), Jerome Forman (Los Angeles, CA), Richard Fox (Boca Raton, FL), Donald Fox (New York, NY), A. Alan Friedberg (Boston, MA), Darrell Gabel (Lander, WY), Robert Goodrich (Grand Rapids, MI), Malcolm Green (Boston, MA), J. Syd Hall (Beeville, TX), Dan Harkins (Scottsdale, AZ), Philip Harris (Kalispell, MT), Don Harton (Plano, TX), Salah Hassanein (Solana Beach, CA), Ellis Jacob (Toronto, ON), Willis Johnson (Downers Grove, IL), Bess Joyner (Warsaw, IN), William Kartozian (Danville, CA), Tony Kerasotes (Chicago, IL), Dean Kerasotes (Chicago, IL), Dan Klusmann (Bozeman, MT), Wayne Kullander (Scottsdale, AZ), Rob Kurrus (Melbourne, FL), George Lefont (Atlanta, GA), John Loeks (Grand Rapids, MI), Jeff Logan (Mitchell, SD), Scott Lotter (Paradise, CA), Jerome Magner (Dedham, MA), Stephen Marcus (Milwaukee, WI), LeeRoy Mitchell (Plano, TX), James Murray (Norfolk, MA), Millard Ochs (Burbank, CA), Doug Oines (Chatham, NJ), Bruce J. Olson (Milwaukee, WI), Mark O'Meara (Fairfax, VA), Richard Orear (Kansas City, MO), Joseph Paletta (Peachtree, GA), Raffaele Papalia (Lachenaie, QC), Michael Patrick (Columbus, GA), Ted Pedas (Washington, D.C.), Phil Pennington (Kansas City, MO), Howard Pickerill (Polson, MT), Ayron Pickerill (Polson, MT), Neal Pinsker (Knoxville, TN), Shari Redstone (Dedham, MA), Sumner Redstone (New York, NY), Ron Reid (Knoxville, TN), Michael J. Rembusch (Franklin, IN), Joel Resnick (Plano, TX), Paul Rogers (Marshfield, WI), A. Bruce Sanborn (Newport Beach, CA), John Scaletta (Palatine, IL), David Shesgreen (Plano, TX), Raymond Smith (Knoxville, TN), George Solomon (New Orleans, LA), T.G. Solomon (New Orleans, LA), William Stembler (St. Simons Island, GA), Alan Stock (Plano, TX), Herman Stone (Charlotte, NC), Aubrey Stone (St. Simons Island, GA), Joseph Syufy (San Rafael, CA), Raymond Syufy (San Rafael, CA), Rand Thornsley (Anchorage, AK), William Towey (Dedham, MA), Jan van Dommelen (The Netherlands), Fred Van Noy (Columbus, GA), John Vincent, Jr. (South Wellfleet, MA), Tim Warner (Plano, TX), Richard Westerling (Knoxville, TN), Roy White (Naples, FL), David Wright (Goshen, IN)

NATO OF ALASKA
12040 98th Ave. NE, Ste. 101, Kirkland, WA 98034.
TEL: (425) 823-9456.
EXECUTIVE DIRECTOR
Bruce Gardiner - bruce@gardinerlaw.com

ARIZONA THEATRE OWNERS ASSOCIATION
TEL: (602) 550-9000.
PRESIDENT
Wayne Kullander - wckullander@yahoo.com

NATO OF ARKANSAS
P.O. Box 200815, Arlington, TX 76006-0815. TEL: (817) 226-1690. FAX: (817) 633-2190. email: scnato@earthlink.net
PRESIDENT
Don Burchett
EXECUTIVE DIRECTOR
Rein Rabakukk

NATIONAL ASSOCIATION OF THEATRE OWNERS OF CALIFORNIA/NEVADA (NATO CA/NEV)
11661 San Vicente Blvd., Ste. 830, Los Angeles, CA 90049. TEL: (310) 460-2900. FAX: (310) 460-2901. email: office@natocalnev.org www.natocalnev.org
PRESIDENT & CEO
Milton Moritz
DIRECTOR, MEMBERSHIP SERVICES
Charlene Sievers

NATO OF COLORADO AND WYOMING
P.O. Box 471, Sterling, CO 80751. TEL: (970) 580-7744. http://rockymtnnato.org
ACTING EXECUTIVE DIRECTOR
Belinda Judson - bvj@natodc.com

CONNECTICUT ASSOCIATION OF THEATRE OWNERS
864 Race Brook Rd., Orange, CT 06477. TEL: (203) 795-3883. FAX: (203) 795-6155.
PRESIDENT
Nikki Perakos - nperakos@earthlink.net

NATO OF DISTRICT OF COLUMBIA
PO Box 1150, Brooklandville, MD 21022. TEL: (410) 252-5010.
PRESIDENT
Ted Pedas
EXECUTIVE DIRECTOR
Doug Murdoch

NATO OF FLORIDA
P.O. Box 2076, Deland, FL 32721-2076. TEL: (386) 736-6830.
PRESIDENT
Rob Kurrus
EXECUTIVE DIRECTOR
Belinda Judson

NATO OF GEORGIA
c/o Aubrey Stone, Georgia Theatre Company, 50 Cinema Ln., St. Simons Island, GA 31522. TEL: (912) 634-5192. www.natoofga.com
PRESIDENT
Aubrey Stone
EXECUTIVE DIRECTOR
Belinda Judson

NATO OF IDAHO
P.O. Box 370, Grangeville, ID 82520. TEL: (208) 983-1370.
PRESIDENT, IATO
Jeff Bowen
VICE PRESIDENT, IATO
Chris Wagner
SECRETARY/TREASURER
Karen Cornwell - kjcornwell@citilink.net

NATO OF ILLINOIS
603 Rogers St., Downers Grove, IL 60515. TEL: (630) 968-1600 ext. 4702. FAX: (630) 968-1626. www.natoillinois.com
PRESIDENT
Willis Johnson
VICE PRESIDENT
Tony Kerasotes
EXECUTIVE DIRECTOR
Mary Ann Frank

THEATRE OWNERS OF INDIANA
3982 Powell Rd., #202, Powell, OH 43065. TEL: (317) 357-3660. FAX: (740) 881-5390. email: theatreownersofindiana@yahoo.com
GENERAL MANAGER
Belinda Judson

NATO OF KENTUCKY
3982 Powell Rd., #202, Powell, OH 43065. TEL: (614) 783-5541. FAX: (740) 881-5390. email: midstatesnato@yahoo.com
EXECUTIVE DIRECTOR
Belinda Judson
PRESIDENT
Les Aberson

LOUISIANA ASSOCIATION OF THEATRE OPERATORS (LATO)
P.O. Box 200815, Arlington, TX 76006-0815. TEL: (817) 226-1690. FAX: (817) 633-2190. email: scnato@earthlink.net
PRESIDENT
Shane Morrison
EXECUTIVE DIRECTOR
Rein Rabakukk

NATO OF MICHIGAN
121 W. Allegan, Lansing, MI 48933. TEL: (517) 482-9806. FAX: (517) 482-9934. www.natoofmi.org
PRESIDENT
Charlie Murray
VICE PRESIDENT
Rusty Belcher
EXECUTIVE DIRECTOR
Jack Schick - jschick@karoubassociates.com

MID-ATLANTIC NATO
(Maryland, Virginia, Washington, D.C.)
P O Box 1150, Brooklandville, MD 21022-1150. TEL: (301) 340-8967.
PRESIDENT
Ted Pedas
VICE PRESIDENT
Mark O'Meara
SECRETARY
John Walker
TREASURER
Rick Novak
EXECUTIVE DIRECTOR
Doug Murdoch
BOARD OF DIRECTORS
Ted Pedas, Mark O'Meara, John Walker, Rick Novak, Dan Herrle, Steve Bochan, Pete Gotthold, Elvis Waterman, Paul Sanchez, Roy Tompkins, Wayne Anderson, Keith Spitzer, Sean South, Dave Phillips, Bob Jones

MID-STATES NATO
(Kentucky, Ohio, Tennessee, West Virginia)
3982 Powell Rd., #202, Powell, OH 43065. TEL: (614) 783-5541. FAX: (740) 881-5390. email: midstatesnato@yahoo.com
EXECUTIVE DIRECTOR
Belinda Judson

MONTANA ASSOCIATION OF THEATRE OWNERS (MATO)
P.O. Box 999, Polson, MT 59860. TEL: (406) 883-5603. FAX: (406) 883-5639.
PRESIDENT, MATO
Gary Dupuis - gdupis@centurytel.net
VICE PRESIDENT, MATO
Bill Emerson

MOTION PICTURE EXHIBITORS OF WASHINGTON, ALASKA & OREGON
12040 98th Ave. NE, Ste. 101, Kirkland, WA 98034. TEL: (425) 823-9456. FAX: (425) 823-9040.
PRESIDENT
Bruce Humphrey
EXECUTIVE DIRECTOR
D. Bruce Gardiner

THEATRE OWNERS OF NEW ENGLAND
(MA, ME, NH, RI, VT)
180 Lincoln St., 5th Flr., Boston, MA 02111. TEL: (617) 424-TONE.
EXECUTIVE DIRECTOR
Carl Goldman - jeff@loganmovie.com

NATO OF NEW JERSEY
P.O. Box 19, Belle Mead, NJ 08502. TEL: (908) 369-6327. FAX: (908) 904-4802.
PRESIDENT
Bob Piechota

NEW MEXICO ASSOCIATION OF THEATRE OWNERS
P.O. Drawer 2279, Los Crusa, NM 88004. TEL: (505) 524-7933. FAX: (505) 527-0068. email: allentheatres@zianet.com
PRESIDENT, NMATO
Heather Allen
VICE PRESIDENT, NMATO
Tom Becker

NATO OF NEW YORK STATE
770 Broadway, 7th Flr., New York, NY 10003. TEL: (646) 654-7680. FAX: (646) 654-7694.
EXECUTIVE DIRECTOR
Robert Sunshine - robert.sunshine@nielsen.com
PRESIDENT
Doug Oines

NORTH CENTRAL STATES NATO
(Minnesota, N. Dakota, S. Dakota, Iowa & Nebraska)
209 N. Lawler St., Mitchell, SD 57301. TEL: (605) 996-9022. FAX: (605) 996-9241. email: jeff@loganmovie.com
PRESIDENT
Jeff Logan
VICE PRESIDENT
Davin Anderson

NATO OF OHIO
3982 Powell Rd., #202, Powell, OH 43065. TEL: (614) 783-5541. FAX: (740) 881-5390. email: midstatesnato@yahoo.com

PRESIDENT
Skip Yassenoff
EXECUTIVE DIRECTOR
Belinda Judson

NATO OF OKLAHOMA

P.O. Box 200815, Arlington, TX 76006-0815. TEL: (817) 226-1690.
FAX: (817) 633-2190. email: scnato@earthlink.net
PRESIDENT
Steve Schoaps
EXECUTIVE DIRECTOR
Rein Rabakukk

NATO OF PENNSYLVANIA

P.O. Box 349, Hilltown, PA 18927. TEL: (215) 238-0633.
email: office@natoofpa.com www.NATOOFPA.com
PRESIDENT & CO EXECUTIVE DIRECTOR
Charles Fogel
CO EXECUTIVE DIRECTOR & SECRETARY
Gina Troutman DiSanto

SOUTH CENTRAL STATES NATO

(Arkansas, Louisiana, Oklahoma, Texas)
P.O. Box 200815, Arlington, TX 76006-0815. TEL: (817) 226-1690.
FAX: (817) 633-2190. email: scnato@earthlink.net
EXECUTIVE DIRECTOR
Rein Rabakukk

SOUTHEAST NATO

(Alabama, Florida, Georgia, North Carolina, South Carolina)
3982 Powell Rd., #202, Powell, OH 43065. TEL: (614) 783-5541.
FAX: (740) 881-5390. email: southeastnato@yahoo.com
www.southeastnato.com
PRESIDENT
Marie McClaflin
EXECUTIVE DIRECTOR
Belinda Judson
NATO OF ALABAMA
Rufus Davis
NATO OF FLORIDA, PRESIDENT
Rob Kurrus
NATO OF GEORGIA, PRESIDENT
Norm Shindler
NATO OF NORTH & SOUTH CAROLINA, PRESIDENT
Marie McClaflin

NATO OF TENNESSEE

3982 Powell Rd., #202, Powell, OH 43065. TEL: (614) 783-5541.
email: midstatesnato@yahoo.com
EXECUTIVE DIRECTOR
Belinda Judson

NATO OF TEXAS

P.O. Box 200815, Arlington, TX 76006-0815. TEL: (817) 226-1690.
FAX: (817) 633-2190. email: scnato@earthlink.net
CHAIRMAN
Byron Berkley
PRESIDENT
Syd Hall
EXECUTIVE DIRECTOR
Rein Rabakukk

UTAH ASSOCIATION OF THEATRE OWNERS

35 E. 9270 S., Sandy, UT 84070. TEL: (801) 325-7510.
FAX: (801) 325-7509.
PRESIDENT, UATO
Dick Cornell
VICE PRESIDENT, UATO
Brent Shiner

NATO OF WEST VIRGINIA

3982 Powell Rd., #202, Powell, OH 43065. TEL: (614) 783-5541.
email: midstatesnato@yahoo.com
PRESIDENT
Curtis McCall
EXECUTIVE DIRECTOR
Belinda Judson

NATO OF WISCONSIN & UPPER MICHIGAN

W168 N8936 Appleton Ave., Menomonee Falls, WI 53051.
TEL: (262) 532-0017. FAX: (262) 532-0021.
PRESIDENT & EXECUTIVE DIRECTOR
Paul J. Rogers

UMPA (UNITED MOTION PICTURE ASSOCIATION) (MISSOURI & KANSAS)

8900 State Line Rd., Ste. 405, Leawood, KS 66206.
TEL: (913) 381-5555. FAX: (913) 381-5552.
PRESIDENT
Darryl Smith
EXECUTIVE SECRETARY
Brad Bills

Professional and Government Organizations

MOTION PICTURE ORGANIZATIONS

9900 CLUB
9900 S. Santa Monica Blvd., Beverly Hills, CA 90212.
TEL: (310) 553-0850, (310) 550-8444. FAX: (310) 286-7906.
www.TheFriarsBH.com
CEO
Darren Schaeffer - Darren@9900club.com
CONTROLLER
Sherry Hitt - sherry@9900club.com
EVENT COORDINATOR
Jessica Jimenez - jessica@9900club.com

ACADEMY OF MOTION PICTURE ARTS AND SCIENCES
(Organized June 1927. Membership: approx. 6,500)
8949 Wilshire Blvd., Beverly Hills, CA 90211-1972.
TEL: (310) 247-3000. FAX: (310) 859-9351, (310) 859-9619.

Margaret Herrick Library: 333 S. La Cienega Blvd., Beverly Hills, CA 90211. TEL: (310) 247-3020. www.oscars.org

Pickford Center for Motion Picture Study: 1313 Vine St., Hollywood, CA 90028. email: ampas@oscars.org
PRESIDENT
Tom Sherak
FIRST VICE PRESIDENT
Sid Ganis
VICE PRESIDENT
James L. Brooks
VICE PRESIDENT
Phil Robinson
TREASURER
Hawk Koch
SECRETARY
Annette Bening
EXECUTIVE DIRECTOR
Bruce Davis

BOARD OF DIRECTORS
John Bailey, Craig Barron, Ed Begley Jr., Curt Behlmer, Annette Bening, Kathryn Bigelow, Jim Bissell, Jon Bloom, Rosemary Bradenburg, James L. Brooks, Bruce Broughton, Donn Cambern, Anne Coates, Martha Coolidge, Caleb Deschanel, Richard Edlund, Leonard Engelman, Rob Epstein, Charles Fox, Robert G. Friedman, Sid Ganis, Jim Gianopulos, Mark Goldblatt, Don Hall, Arthur Hamilton, Tom Hanks, Mark Johnson, Kathleen Kennedy, Hawk Koch, Bill Kroyer, Jeffrey Kurland, John Lasseter, Marvin Levy, Lynne Littman, Michael Moore, Kevin O'Connell, Frank Pierson, Robert Rehme, Phil Robinson, Owen Roizman, Tom Sherak, Bill Taylor, Edward Zwick

ALLIANCE OF MOTION PICTURE AND TELEVISION PRODUCERS
(Membership: Major studios, independent production companies and film processing laboratories)
15503 Ventura Blvd., Encino, CA 91436-3140.
TEL: (818) 995-3600. www.amptp.org
PRESIDENT
Carol Lombardini

AMERICAN CINEMATHEQUE
(Organized 1981. Celebrates the moving picture in all its forms through public film and video exhibition)
6712 Hollywood Blvd., Los Angeles, CA 90028.
TEL: (323) 461-2020. FAX: (323) 461-9737.
Program Information: (323) 466-FILM.
email: info@americancinematheque.com
www.americancinematheque.com
CHAIRMAN
Rick Nicita
PRESIDENT
Henry Shields, Jr.
EXECUTIVE DIRECTOR
Barbara Zicka Smith
TREASURER
James G. Robinson
PUBLICITY, MARKETING, ADVERTISING, PROMOTIONS
Margot Gerber - publicity@americancinematheque.com
CHAIRMAN EMERITUS
Peter J. Dekom, Kenneth Kleinberg, Mike Medavoy

BOARD OF DIRECTORS
Peter Bart, Paul Bloch, Bill Block, Colin Callender, Sanford R. Climan, Michael De Luca, Lorenzo di Bonaventura, Wendi L. Doyle, Toby Emmerich, Rick Finkelstein, William Friedkin, Jerry Giaquinta, John Goldwyn, Brian Grazer, Dean Hallett, Thomas Hansen, Godfrey Isaac, Jonathan D. Kaufelt, Anne Keshen, Warren N. Lieberfarb, Edward F. Limato, Robert Mayson, Chris McGurk, Mark Ordesky, Sanford P. Paris, Elisabeth Pollon, Peter Rice, James G. Robinson, Thomas O. Staggs, Steve Tisch, Susan Tolson, Paula Wagner

THE AMERICAN FILM INSTITUTE
(AFI is a national institute providing leadership in screen education and the recognition and celebration of excellence in the art of film, television and digital media)
2021 N. Western Ave., Los Angeles, CA 90027.
TEL: (323) 856-7600. FAX: (323) 467-4578. www.afi.com
BOARD OF TRUSTEES CHAIR
Sir Howard Stringer
BOARD OF DIRECTORS CHAIR
Robert A. Daly
VICE-CHAIRMAN
Jon Avnet, Richard Frank, Marshall Herskovitz, Tom Pollock, Ed Zwick
FOUNDING DIRECTOR
George Stevens, Jr.
PRESIDENT EMERITA
Jean Picker Firstenbert
HONORARY TRUSTEE
Warren Beatty
PRESIDENT & CEO
Bob Gazzale

CHAIRS EMERITI
Gregory Peck, Roger L. Stevens, Charlton Heston, Richard Brandt, Bonita Granville Wrather, Gene F. Jankowski, Frederick S. Pierce, Tom Pollock

BOARD MEMBERS
Gil Amelio, Jon Avnet, Gary Birkenbeuel, Richard Brandt, Mark Canton, John F. Cooke, Roger Enrico, Lawrence Herbert, Marshall Herskovitz, Alan Horn, Gene F. Jankowski, Fay Kanin, Warren N. Lieberfarb, Frederick S. Pierce, Tom Pollock, Robert G. Rehme, Todd Wagner, Edward Zwick

AMERICAN HUMANE ASSOCIATION
(Organized 1877)

NATIONAL HEADQUARTERS:
63 Inverness Dr. E., Englewood, CO 80112. TEL: (800) 227-4645, (303) 792-9900. FAX: (303) 792-5333.

FILM AND TELEVISION UNIT:
15366 Dickens St., Sherman Oaks, CA 91403.
TEL: (818) 501-0123. FAX: (818) 501-8725.
Hotline: (800) 677-3420. www.americanhumane.org/film
PRESIDENT & CEO
Marie Belew Wheatley
COO
Dale Austin
VICE PRESIDENT, CFO
Connie Kindle
VICE PRESIDENT
Sonia Velazquez, Debrah Schnackenberg, Marie McCabe, Michael Blimes, Randy Blauvelt, Karen Rosa, Allie Phillips
V.P., MARKETING & COMMUNICATIONS
Randy Blauvelt

Liaison with the television and motion picture industry as supervisors of animal action in television and motion picture production.

AMERICAN SOCIETY OF COMPOSERS, AUTHORS AND PUBLISHERS (ASCAP)
(Organized February 13, 1914. Membership: over 300,000 songwriters and publishers)

New York: One Lincoln Plaza, New York, NY 10023.
TEL: (212) 621-6000. FAX: (212) 724-9064. www.ascap.com

Los Angeles: 7920 Sunset Blvd., 3rd Flr., Los Angeles, CA 90046. TEL: (323) 883-1000. FAX: (323) 883-1049.

Nashville: Two Music Square W., Nashville, TN 37203.
TEL: (615) 742-5000. FAX: (615) 742-5020.

Atlanta: 950 Joseph E. Lowery Blvd., Ste. 23, Atlanta, GA 30318. TEL: (404) 685-8699. FAX: (404) 685-8701.

Chicago: 1608 N. Milwaukee, Ste. 1007, Chicago, IL 60647.
TEL: (773) 394-4286. FAX: (773) 394-5639.

Miami: 420 Lincoln Rd., Ste. 385, Miami Beach, FL 33139.
TEL: (305) 673-3446. FAX: (305) 673-2446.

London: 8 Cork St., London, W1S3LJ, England.
TEL: (44 207) 439-0909. FAX: (44 207) 434-0073.

Puerto Rico: Ave. Martinez Nadal c/Hill Side 623, San Juan, PR 00920. TEL: (787) 707-0782. FAX: (787) 707-0783.
PRESIDENT & CHAIRMAN
Paul Williams
CEO
John A. LoFrumento
WRITER VICE CHAIRMAN
Jimmy Webb
PUBLISHER VICE CHAIRMAN
Irwin Robinson
TREASURER
James M. Kendrick
SECRETARY
Kathy Spanberger

EXECUTIVE V.P., MARKETING
Philip Crosland
SENIOR V.P., INTERNATIONAL AND UK MEMBERSHIP
Roger Greenaway
SENIOR V.P., MARKETING
Lauren Iossa
V.P., INTERNATIONAL RELATIONS
David Safir
SENIOR V.P., HUMAN RESOURCES
Carolyn Jensen
SENIOR V.P., LEGAL SERVICES
Richard Reimer
A.V.P., SPECIAL PROJECTS/COMMUNICATIONS
Jim Steinblatt
SENIOR V.P., GENERAL COUNSEL
Joan McGivern
COUNSEL TO THE BOARD
Fred Koenigsberg

WRITER BOARD MEMBER
Paul Williams, Richard Bellis, Marilyn Bergman, Bruce Broughton, Hal David, Dan Foliart, Wayland Holyfield, Johnny Mandel, Stephen Paulus, Valerie Simpson, Jimmy Webb, Doub Wood

PUBLISHER BOARD MEMBER
Martin Bandier, Caroline Bienstock, Barry Coburn, John L. Eastman, Roger Faxon, David H. Johnson, Dean Kay, James M. Kendrick, Leeds Levy, David Renzer, Irwin Robinson, Kathy Spanberger

THE ASSOCIATION FOR WOMEN IN COMMUNICATIONS

3337 Duke St., Alexandria, VA 22314. TEL: (703) 370-7436. FAX: (703) 370-7437. email: info@womcom.org www.womcom.org
AWC, COMMUNICATIONS MANAGER
Susan Pinta - spinta@womcom.org
AWC, EXECUTIVE DIRECTOR
Pamela Valenzuela, CAE

ASSOCIATION OF FILM COMMISSIONERS INTERNATIONAL

(Organized 1975)
109 E. 17th St., Ste. 18, Cheyenne, WY 82001.
TEL: (307) 637-4422. FAX: (413) 375-2903.
email: info@afci.org www.afci.org
CEO
Larry Brownell
COMMUNICATIONS MANAGER
Kevin Clark
OPERATIONS MANAGER
Cheryl Cole
DIRECTOR, DEVELOPMENT & EVENTS
Laurie Lehmann

Acts as a liaison between the visual communications industry and local governments or organizations to facilitate on-location production, to stimulate economic benefit for member governments.

BMI (BROADCAST MUSIC, INC.)

NY: 320 W. 57 St., New York, NY 10019. TEL: (212) 586-2000. FAX: (212) 245-8986. email: newyork@bmi.com www.bmi.com

CA: 8730 Sunset Blvd., Third Flr. W., Los Angeles, CA 90069. TEL: (310) 659-9109. FAX: (310) 657-6947. email: losangeles@bmi.com

TN: 10 Music Square E., Nashville, TN 37203. TEL: (615) 401-2000. FAX: (615) 401-2707. email: nashville@bmi.com

FL: 1691 Michigan Ave., Ste. 350, Miami Beach, FL 33139. TEL: (305) 673-5148. email: miami@bmi.com

GA: 3340 Peachtree Rd., NE, Ste. 570, Atlanta, GA 30326. TEL: (404) 261-5151.

PR: MCS Plaza, 255 Ponce de León Ave., Ste. 208, San Juan, PR 00917. TEL: (787) 754-6490. FAX: (787) 753-6765.

UK: 84 Harley House, Marylebone Rd., London NW1 5HN, England. TEL: (44 207) 486-2036. email: london@bmi.com
PRESIDENT & CEO
Del Bryant
EXECUTIVE V.P. & COO
John E. Cody
SENIOR V.P., LICENSING
Michael O'Neill

THE CENTER FOR ASIAN AMERICAN MEDIA

(A nonprofit media arts organization)
145 Ninth St., Ste. 350, San Francisco, CA 94103.
TEL: (415) 863-0814. FAX: (415) 863-7428.
www.asianamericanmedia.org
EXECUTIVE DIRECTOR
Stephen Gong
ADMINISTRATIVE DIRECTOR
Kar Yin Tham
DEVELOPMENT DIRECTOR
Rina Mehta
EXHIBITION & FESTIVAL DIRECTOR
Chi-hui Yang
DIRECTOR OF PROGRAMS
Donald Young

BOARD OF DIRECTORS
Glenn Osaka, Dipti Ghosh, Johnnie D. Giles, John Chung, Gaurav Dhillon, Lisa Hsia, Philomena King, Roger Kuo, Bill Imada, David Lei, Susie Jin Pak, Parmila Ramchandani, Ann Snug-Ruckstuhl, Jean Tsien, France Viana, Mona Lisa Yuchengco

COUNCIL ON INTERNATIONAL NON-THEATRICAL EVENTS (C.I.N.E.)

(Organized 1957)
1112 16th St. NW, Ste. 510, Washington, DC 20036.
TEL: (202) 785-1136. FAX: (202) 785-4114.
email: info@cine.org www.cine.org
EXECUTIVE DIRECTOR
Wendy Revel
DIRECTOR OF COMPETITIONS
Elizabeth (Betsy) Walters

CINE's mission is to serve emerging and established film, video, and new media professionals as their primary career-advancing peer group. CINE conducts the CINE Golden Eagle Film & Video competition twice annually.

ENTERTAINMENT INDUSTRIES FOUNDATION

1201 W. 5th St., Ste. T-700, Los Angeles, CA 90017.
TEL: (213) 240-3900. www.eifoundation.org
PRESIDENT & CEO
Lisa Paulsen
SENIOR V.P & CFO
Merrily Newton
SENIOR V.P., PROGRAMS
Michael Balaoing
V.P., COMMUNICATIONS
Judi Ketcik

FILM SOCIETY OF LINCOLN CENTER

(Organized 1969)
70 Lincoln Center Plaza, 4th Flr. New York, NY 10023-6595.
TEL: (212) 875-5610. FAX: (212) 875-5636. www.filmlinc.com
CHAIRMAN
Ann Tenenbaum
PRESIDENT
Daniel H. Stern
EXECUTIVE DIRECTOR
Mara Manus
PROGRAM DIRECTOR
Richard Pena
DIRECTOR, PRESS AND MARKETING
Jeanne Berney

Presents The New York Film Festival and New Directors/New Films Festival, publishes Film Comment magazine, and runs the Walter Reade Theater.

FILM/VIDEO ARTS, INC.

(Founded 1968)
270 West 96th St., New York, NY 10025. TEL: (212) 222-1770.
www.fva.com
EXECUTIVE DIRECTOR
Andre Gray - andregray@fva.com

Provides independents with training, mentoring and fiscal sponsoring. Also producing film, video and audio works. Young Filmakers Festival.

FRIARS CLUB

57 E. 55th St., New York, NY 10022. TEL: (212) 751-7272.
FAX: (212) 355-0217. www.friarsclub.com
ABBOT
Jerry Lewis
DEAN
Freddie Roman
PRIOR
Stewie Stone
SCRIBE
Stu Cantor
TREASURER
Fred C. Klein
EXECUTIVE DIRECTOR
Michael L. Gyure - michael.gyure@friarsclub.com
EXECUTIVE DIRECTOR EMERITUS
Jean-Pierre L. Trebot

HONORARY OFFICERS
SQUIRE
Steve Lawrence, Jerry Stiller
SCRIBE EMERITUS
Frank Military
GRAND JESTRESS
Joy Behar
BARD
Tony Martin
PROCTOR
Billy Crystal

JESTER
Sid Caesar, Richard Belzer
HERALD
Paul Anka
MONITOR
Richard Lewis
MONK
Robert Klein
TROUBADOUR
Tony Bennett
SAMARITAN
Norman King
KNIGHT
Dennis Farina, Danny Aiello, Tom Jones, Cy Leslie
BISHOP
Leo Greenland

THE HARRY FOX AGENCY, INC.
(HFA is the leading mechanical rights organization in the U.S. and represents almost 36,000 music publishers)
601 West 26th St. Ste. 500, New York, NY 10001.
TEL: (212) 370-5330. FAX: (646) 487-6779. www.harryfox.com
PRESIDENT & CEO
Gary Churgin
SENIOR V.P. AND CFO
Alfred Pedecine
SENIOR V.P. AND CIO
Louis Trebino
SENIOR V.P. BUSINESS AFFAIRS, GENERAL COUNSEL AND CHIEF STRATEGIC OFFICER
Michael Simon
SENIOR V.P., PUBLISHER SERVICES
Edward Hunt
SENIOR V.P., HUMAN RESOURCES AND ADMINISTRATION
Michele Olton

HOLLYWOOD RADIO & TELEVISION SOCIETY
(Chartered in 1947 as a non-profit corporation of the State of California)
13701 Riverside Dr., Ste. 205, Sherman Oaks, CA 91423.
TEL: (818) 789-1182. FAX: (818) 789-1210.
email: info@hrts.org www.hrts.org
PRESIDENT
Kevin Beggs
VICE PRESIDENT
Sarah Timberman
SECRETARY
Sean Perry
TREASURER
Martha Henderson

BOARD OF DIRECTORS
Dick Askin, Jeff Bader, Adam Berkowitz, Jason Burns, Scott Carlin, Stephen Davis, Bob DeBitetto, Craig Erwich, Andy Friendly, Cecile Frot-Coutaz, Leonard Goldstein, Kelly Goode, Ted Harbert, Doug Herzog, Reginald Hudlin, Aaron Kaplan, Tracy Katsky, Tony Knight, Russ Krasnoff, Paul Lee, Jordan Levin, Bob Levinson, Peter Liquori, Gregory Lipstone, Gary Marenzi, Gary Newman, Christina Norman, Ryan O'Hara, Dawn Ostroff, Sear Perry, Matt Rice, Ken Richman, Esq., Robin Schwartz, Stephen Shelanski, TimSpengler, David Stapf, Eric Tannenbaum, Nina Tassler, Sarah Timberman, Jeff Wachtel, Andrea Wong

THE INDEPENDENT FEATURE PROJECT/NEW YORK
(Organized 1979)
104 W. 29th St., 12th Flr., New York, NY 10001-5310.
TEL: (212) 465-8200. FAX: (212) 465-8525.
email: ifpny@ifp.org www.ifp.org
EXECUTIVE DIRECTOR
Michelle Byrd - mbyrd@ifp.org
OFFICE MANAGER
Rupert Chiarella - rchiarella@ifp.org

Non-profit organization that provides information and support services to independent filmmakers. Produces the IFP Market and the IFP Gotham Awards. Co-publishes *Filmmaker: The Magazine of Independent Film* with IFP/West.

INDEPENDENT FEATURE PROJECT/CHICAGO
1104 S. Wabash, Ste. 403, Chicago, IL 60605.
TEL: (312) 235-0161. FAX: (312) 235-0162.
email: chicago@ifp.org www.ifp.org
PRESIDENT
Claire Connelly
EXECUTIVE DIRECTOR
Elizabeth Donius - edonius@ifp.org
ASSISTANT DIRECTOR
Lynn Steadman - lsteadman@ifp.org

INDEPENDENT FEATURE PROJECT/MINNESOTA CENTER FOR MEDIA ARTS
2446 University Ave. W, Ste. 100, Saint Paul, MN 55114.
TEL: (651) 644-1912. FAX: (651) 644-5708.
email: word@ifpmn.org www.ifpmn.org
EXECUTIVE DIRECTOR
Jane Minton - jminton@ifpmn.org
PRESIDENT
Christie Healey
VICE PRESIDENT
Rick Dublin

INDEPENDENT FEATURE PROJECT/PHOENIX
Phoenix Film Foundation, 1700 N 7th Ave., Ste. #250, Phoenix, AZ 85007. TEL: (602) 955-6444. FAX: (602) 955-0966.
email: info@ifpphx.org
EXECUTIVE DIRECTOR
Amanda Melby - amelby@ifpphx.org
OPERATIONS MANAGER
Kristin Rodin - krodin@ifpphx.org
MARKETING DIRECTOR
Aimee Sturdevant-Thelander - athelander@ifpphx.org

INDEPENDENT FILM & TELEVISION ALLIANCE (IFTA)
(Organized 1980)
10850 Wilshire Blvd., 9th Flr., Los Angeles, CA 90024.
TEL: (310) 446-1000. FAX: (310) 446-1600.
email: info@ifta-online.org www.ifta-online.org
PRESIDENT & CEO
Jean M. Prewitt
EXECUTIVE V.P./IFTA & MANAGING DIRECTOR/AFM
Jonathan Wolf
CHAIRPERSON
Lloyd Kaufman
VICE CHAIRPERSON
Richard Guardian
VICE CHAIRPERSON, SECRETARY
Brad Kembel
VICE CHAIRPERSON, FINANCE
Avi Lerner
VICE CHAIRPERSON
Mark Lindsay
CHAIRPERSON, EXPORT ALLIANCE
Elisabeth Costa de Beauregard Rose

BOARD OF DIRECTORS
Steve Bickel, Nicolas Chartier, Mark Damon, Clay Epstein, Kim Fox, Paul Hertzberg, Tatyana Joffe, Jay Joyce, Tony Kandah, Nicole Mackey, Almira Malyshev, Bobby Meyers, Charlotte Mickie, Barbara Mudge, Brian O'Shea, Wendy Reeds, Michael Ryan, Mimi Steinbauer, Lisa Wilson, Adam Wright (Alternates: Kirk D'Amico, Brad Krevoy)

Membership: 175 companies engaged in the production and sale of independently produced films and TV programs to the international market. Produces the American Film Market every November.

INTERNATIONAL DOCUMENTARY ASSOCIATION
(Organized 1982)
1201 West Fifth St., Ste. M270, Los Angeles, CA 90017.
TEL: (213) 534-3600. FAX: (213) 534-3610.
email: info@documentary.org www.documentary.org
EXECUTIVE DIRECTOR
Michael Lumpkin - michael@documentary.org
PROGRAMS & EVENTS MANAGER
Peggy Ellithorpe - peggy@documentary.org
PRESIDENT
Eddie Schmidt
VICE PRESIDENT
Nancy Willen
SECRETARY
Sara Hutchison
CFO/TREASURER
Bob Niemack

BOARD MEMBERS
Beth Bird, Brian Gerber, Lynne Littman, Thomas G. Miller, Elise Pearlstein, Steven Reich, Thomas Rigler, David S. Tenzer, Moises Velez, Sue West

JAPAN SOCIETY/FILM CENTER
(Organized 1907. Promotes Japanese culture by exhibiting Japanese films and films on Japan)
333 E. 47th St., New York, NY 10017. TEL: (212) 832-1155.
FAX: (212) 715-1262. www.japansociety.org
PRESIDENT
Richard J. Wood
SENIOR V.P. & DIRECTOR OF EXTERNAL RELATIONS
Kendall Hubert
PRESS OFFICER
Ayako Akeura
V.P. & DIRECTOR OF CORPORATE & POLICY PROGRAMS
Daniel A. Rosenblum

MOTION PICTURE & TELEVISION FUND
(Service organization providing for the well-being of California's entertainment community, including health, child, and retirement care)
23388 Mulholland Dr., Woodland Hills, CA 91364.

TEL: (818) 876-1888. www.mptvfund.org
Bob Hope Health Center, 335 N. La Brea Ave., Los Angeles, CA 90036. TEL: (323) 634-3850.

Santa Clarita Health Center, 25751 McBean Pkwy., #210, Valencia, CA 91355. TEL: (661) 284-3100.

Toluca Lake Health Center, 4323 Riverside Dr., Burbank, CA 91505. TEL: (818) 556-2700.

Westside Health Center, 1950 Sawtelle Blvd., Ste. 130, Los Angeles, CA 90025. TEL: (310) 996-9355.

Jack H. Skirball Health Center, 23388 Mulholland Dr., Woodland Hills, CA 91364. TEL: (818) 876-1050.

North Valley Health Center, 11550 Indian Hills Rd., #200, Mission Hills, CA 91345. TEL: (818) 876-4770.

Samuel Goldwyn Foundation Children's Center, 2114 Pontius Ave., Los Angeles, CA 90025. TEL: (310) 445-8993.
PRESIDENT & CEO
David B. Tillman, M.D.
CHAIRMAN
A. Robert Pisano

MPTF CORP. BOARD
Robert Beitcher, Darcie A. Denkert, Mark Fleischer, Jim Gianopulos, Michael Karlin, Jeffrey Katzenberg, Hawk Koch, Matthew Loeb, Frank G. Mancuso, Roger L. Mayer, Diane Nelson, A. Robert Pisano, Patrick B. Purcell, Jay D. Roth, Casey Wasserman

MOTION PICTURE ASSOCIATION OF AMERICA, INC.

WASHINGTON, DC:
1600 Eye St. NW, Washington, DC 20006. TEL: (202) 293-1966. FAX: (202) 293-7674. www.mpaa.org
PRESIDENT & INTERIM CEO
Robert Pisano
EXECUTIVE V.P., SPECIAL POLICY ADVISOR
Fritz Attaway
EXECUTIVE V.P., WORLDWIDE GOVERNMENT POLICY
Greg Frazier
SENIOR V.P. & CHIEF COUNSEL, FEDERAL AFFAIRS AND POLICY
Michael O'Leary
SENIOR V.P., STATE & GOVERNMENT AFFAIRS
Vans Stevensonv
V.P., INTERNATIONAL AFFAIRS & TRADE POLICY
Anissa Whitten
V.P. & SENIOR COUNSEL, FEDERAL AFFAIRS & POLICY
Todd Flournoy
V.P. & SENIOR COUNSEL, FEDERAL AFFAIRS & POLICY
Daphna Peled
V.P., CORPORATE COMMUNICATIONS
Angela Martinez

SHERMAN OAKS:
15301 Ventura Blvd., Building E, Sherman Oaks, CA 91403. TEL: (818) 995-6600. FAX: (818) 285-4402. Anti-Piracy Hot Line: 1-800-NO-COPYS.
EXECUTIVE V.P. FINANCE AND ADMINISTRATION & CFO
Lisa Pierozzi
EXECUTIVE V.P. & CHIEF STRATEGY OFFICER
Dean Garfield
SENIOR V.P. & CHIEF TECHNOLOGY OFFICER
Jim C. Williams
EXECUTIVE V.P. & DIRECTOR, WORLDWIDE ANTI-PIRACY
John G. Malcolm
EXECUTIVE V.P. & CHIEF COMMUNICATIONS OFFICER
Seth Oster
V.P., CORPORATE COMMUNICATIONS
Elizabeth Kaltman Barondess

NEW YORK:
200 White Plains Rd., Tarrytown, NY 10591.
TEL: (914) 333-8892. FAX: (914) 333-7541.
DEPUTY DIRECTOR, USAPO, NY, ANTI-PIRACY
Bill Shannon

EUROPE, MIDDLE EAST & AFRICA:
8th and 9th Flrs., Ave. des Arts 46, 1000 Brussels, Belgium.
TEL: (011 322) 778-2711. FAX: (011 322) 778-2700.
PRESIDENT AND MANAGING DIRECTOR, EMEA
Chris Marcich

ASIA/PACIFIC:
No. 1 Magazine Rd., Central Mall #04-07, Singapore 059571.
TEL: (65) 6253-1033. FAX: (65) 6255-1838.
PRESIDENT AND MANAGING DIRECTOR, ASIA-PACIFIC
Michael Ellis

LATIN AMERICA:
Rua Sergipe 475, 10th Flr., Higienopolis, Sao Paulo, SP 01243-001, Brazil. TEL: (55 11) 3667-2080.
FAX: (55 11) 3825-5544.

CANADIAN MOTION PICTURE DISTRIBUTORS ASSOCIATION:
22 St. Clair Ave. E, #1603, Toronto, ON, Canada M4T-2S4.
TEL: (416) 961-1888. FAX: (416) 968-1016.
EXECUTIVE DIRECTOR
Wendy Noss

CMPDA FILM AND VIDEO SECURITY OFFICE:
7900 Taschereau Blvd., Ste. C-210, Brossard, Quebec Canada J4X 1C2. TEL: (450) 672-1990. FAX: (450) 672-1660.

MUSEUM OF MODERN ART, DEPT. OF FILM & MEDIA

(Organized May, 1935)
11 W. 53th St., New York, NY 10019. TEL: (212) 708-9400. FAX: (212) 333-1145. www.moma.org
HONORARY CHAIRMAN
David Rockefeller
HONORARY CHAIRMAN
Ronald S. Lauder
CHAIRMAN EMERITUS
Robert B. Menschel
PRESIDENT EMERITA
Agnes Gund
PRESIDENT EMERITUS
Donald B. Marron
CHAIRMAN
Jerry I. Speyer
PRESIDENT
Marie-Josée Kravis
VICE CHAIRMAN
Sid R. Bass, Leon D. Black, Kathleen Fuld, Mimi Haas, Richard E. Salomon
DIRECTOR
Glenn D. Lowry
TREASURER
Richard E. Salomon
SECRETARY
Patty Lipshutz

NATIONAL ALLIANCE FOR MEDIA ARTS & CULTURE

(A national service organization with membership from the media and arts profession)
145 Ninth St., Ste. 250, San Francisco, CA 94103.
TEL: (415) 431-1391. FAX: (415) 431-1392.
email: namac@namac.org www.namac.org
PRESIDENT
Will K. Wilkins
VICE PRESIDENT
Nettrice R. Gaskins
TREASURER
Katy Chevigny
SECRETARY
Andrea Grover
EXECUTIVE DIRECTOR
Jack Walsh
SENIOR MANAGER, LEADERSHIP PROGRAMS
Daniel "Dewey" Schott
MEMBERSHIP AND PROGRAM MANAGER
Amanda Ault

NATIONAL ASSOCIATION OF THEATRE OWNERS, INC.

P.O. Box 77318, Washington D.C. 20013-7318.
750 First St., NE, Ste. 1130, Washington DC 20002.
TEL: (202) 962-0054. FAX: (202) 962-0370. www.natoonline.org
PRESIDENT & CEO
John Fithian
CHAIRMAN
Tony Kerasotes
VICE CHAIRMAN
Aubrey Stone
SECRETARY
Mark O'Meara
TREASURER
Amy Miles
V.P., GENERAL COUNSEL & DIRECTOR OF GOVT. AFFAIRS
G. Kendrick Macdowell
EXECUTIVE DIRECTOR
Kathy Conroy - (202) 962-0054

NATIONAL COUNCIL OF CHURCHES

Communications Department, 475 Riverside Dr., Ste. 880, New York, NY 10115. TEL: (212) 870-2228.
FAX: (212) 870-2030. www.ncccusa.org
PRESIDENT
Archbishop Vicken Aykazian
GENERAL SECRETARY
Rev. Dr. Michael Kinnamon - mkinnamon@ncccusa.org
PRESIDENT ELECT
Rev. Peg Chemberlin
FIRST VICE PRESIDENT
Rev. Dr. Cheryl H. Wade
VICE PRESIDENT
Rt. Rev. Johncy Itty
VICE PRESIDENTS AT LARGE
Mr. Stan Noffsinger, Rev. Dr. Raymon Hunt
SECRETARY
Rev. José Luis Casal
IMMEDIATE PAST PRESIDENT
Rev. Michael E. Livingston

NATIONAL FILM PRESERVATION FOUNDATION

(Organized 1997)
870 Market St., Ste. 1113, San Francisco, CA 94102.

TEL: (415) 392-7291. FAX: (415) 392-7293.
email: info@filmpreservation.org www.filmpreservation.org
DIRECTOR
Annette Melville
ASSISTANT DIRECTOR
Jeff Lambert
PROGRAMS MANAGER
David Wells
OFFICE MANAGER
Rebecca Payne Collins
PROGRAMS ASSISTANT
Ihsan Amanatullah

BOARD OF DIRECTORS
Roger L. Mayer (Chairman), Charles Benton, Leonard Maltin, Cecilia deMille Presley, John Ptak, Robert G. Rehme, Eric J. Schwartz, Martin Scorsese, The Honorable Fred Thompson, Paula Wagner, Alfre Woodard, James H. Billington (ex officio, The Librarian of Congress)

NATIONAL MUSIC PUBLISHERS' ASSOCIATION, INC.
(Founded in 1917)
101 Constitution Ave. NW, Ste. 705 E., Washington DC, 20001. TEL: (202) 742-4375. FAX: (202) 742-4377.
email: members@nmpa.org www.nmpa.org
PRESIDENT & CEO
David Israelite
CONTACT
Jamie Marotta

BOARD MEMBERS
Martin N. Bandier, Caroline Bienstock, Helene Blue, Lionel Conway, Bob Doyle, John Eastman, Roger Faxon, Neil Gillis, Dave Johnson, Dean Kay, Maxyne Lang, Leeds Levy, Evan Medow, Ralph Peer II, Peter Primont, David Renzer, Irwin Z. Robinson, John Rudolph

The National Music Publishers' Association (NMPA) is a trade association representing over 600 American music publishers, who in turn administrate the catalogs of over 27,000 publishers.

NEW YORK FOUNDATION FOR THE ARTS, INC.
(Promotes freedom to develop and create art and provides opportunities for individual artists)
155 Ave. of the Americas, 6th Flr., New York, NY 10013.
TEL: (212) 366-6900. FAX: (212) 366-1778. www.nyfa.org
EXECUTIVE DIRECTOR
Michael L. Royce - mroyce@nyfa.org
DIRECTOR, FINANCE
JoAnne M. Brockway - jbrockway@nyfa.org
DIRECTOR, DEVELOPMENT
Mark Rossier - mrossier@nyfa.org
EXECUTIVE ASSISTANT
Maria Villafranca - mariav@nyfa.org
OPERATIONS ASSISTANT
Carmen Cuevas-Gomez - cuevas@nyfa.org

NEW YORK STATE COUNCIL ON THE ARTS (NYSCA)
(Funds New York State non-profit art organizations)
175 Varick St, 3rd Flr., New York, NY 10014.
TEL: (212) 627-4455. FAX: (212) 620-5911. www.nysca.org
CHAIR
Danny Simmons
VICE-CHAIR
Dr. Barbaralee Diamonstein-Spielvogel
VICE-CHAIR
Jeff Soref
EXECUTIVE DIRECTOR
Heather Hitchens - hhitchens@nysca.org

NEW YORK WOMEN IN FILM & TELEVISION
(Founded in 1977)
6 E. 39th St., Ste. 1200, New York, NY 10016-0112.
TEL: (212) 679-0870. FAX: (212) 679-0899.
email: info@nywift.org www.nywift.org
PRESIDENT
Alexandra Levi
V.P., COMMUNICATIONS
Esmée
V.P., DEVELOPMENT
Alexis Alexanian
V.P., MEMBERSHIP
Anna Gerb
V.P., PROGRAMMING
Iri Greco
V.P., SPECIAL EVENTS
Janet Stilson
LEGAL COUNSEL
Marsha S. Brooks, Esq.
EXECUTIVE DIRECTOR
Terry Lawler
MEMBERSHIP COORDINATOR
Josefa Jaime

ADVISORY BOARD
Laverne Berry, Jeanne Betancourt, Grace Blake, Mirra Bank Brockman, Michelle Byrd, Karen Cooper, L. Marilyn Crawford, Jean Doumanian, Alice Elliott, Harlene Freezer, Ellen C. Geiger, Carey Graeber, Linda Kahn, Marjorie Kalins, Pat Swinney Kaufman, Wendy Keys, Susan Margolin, Eileen Newman, Joy Pereths, Muriel Peters, Terrie Pologianis, Ruth Pomerance, Marquita Pool-Eckert, Diane Robina, Wendy Sax, Marcie L. Setlow, Joan Micklin Silver, Diane Sokolow, Patrizia Von Brandenstein, Ellen Zalk

Dedicated to helping and promoting equity for women in reaching the highest levels of achievement in film, television and other moving-image media.

SESAC, INC.
(A performing rights organization)
55 Music Square E, Nashville, TN 37203. TEL: (800) 826-9996, (615) 320-0055. FAX: (615) 329-9627. www.sesac.com

NY: 152 West 57th St., 57th Flr., New York, NY 10019.
TEL: (212) 586-3450. FAX: (212) 489-5699.

CA: 501 Santa Monica Blvd., Ste. 450, Santa Monica, CA 90401-2430. TEL: (310) 393-9671. FAX: (310) 393-6497.

GA: 981 Joseph E. Lowery Blvd., NW, Ste. 111, Atlanta, GA 30318. TEL: (404) 897-1330. FAX: (404) 867-1306.

FL: 420 Lincoln Rd, Ste. 502, Miami, FL 33139.
TEL: (305) 534-7500. FAX: (305) 534-7578.
EXECUTIVE V.P., BUSINESS AFFAIRS
Dennis Lord - mevans@sesac.com
SENIOR V.P., WEST COAST OPERATIONS, LATINA, FILM & TV
Pat Rogers - progers@sesac.com
ASSOCIATE V.P., ADVERTISING/CORPORATE RELATIONS
Ellen Bligh Jones - ejones@sesac.com
COORDINATOR, ADVERTISING/CORPORATE RELATIONS
Jocelyn Harms - jharms@sesac.com
MANAGER, NEW MEDIA
Shawn Williams - swilliams@sesac.com

SOCIETY OF COMPOSERS & LYRICISTS
(The non-profit and primary membership organization for professional film, television and multi-media composers, songwriters and lyricists)
8447 Wilshire Blvd., Ste. 401, Beverly Hills, CA 90211.
TEL: (310) 281-2812. FAX: (310) 284-4861.
email: ExecDir@TheSCL.com www.TheSCL.com
PRESIDENT
Dan Foliart
VICE PRESIDENT
Arthur Hamilton, Mark Adler
CFO
Christopher Farrell
EXECUTIVE DIRECTOR
Laura Dunn

ADVISORY BOARD
Alan Bergman, Marilyn Bergman, John Cacavas, Bill Conti, Charles Fox, James Newton Howard, Quincy Jones, Alan Menken, Thomas Newman, Lalo Schifrin, Marc Shaiman, Howard Shore, Alan Silvestri, Patrick Williams, Hans Zimmer

SOCIETY OF MOTION PICTURE AND TELEVISION ENGINEERS
(Organized 1916)
3 Barker Ave., White Plains, NY 10601. TEL: (914) 761-1100.
FAX: (914) 761-3115. www.smpte.org
PRESIDENT
Kenneth C. Fuller
EXECUTIVE V.P.
Peter Lude
DIRECTOR, OPERATIONS
Sally-Ann D'Amato
DIRECTOR, PROFESSIONAL DEVELOPMENT
Joel Welch
MANAGING EDITOR
Dianne Ross Purrier
EXECUTIVE DIRECTOR
Kimberly Maki

UNIFRANCE FILM INTERNATIONAL/FRENCH FILM OFFICE
(Promoting French cinema worldwide)
972 Fifth Ave., New York, NY 10075. TEL: (212) 832-8860.
FAX: (212) 755-0629. email: info@frenchfilm.org
www.unifrance.org
EXECUTIVE DIRECTOR FOR THE U.S.
John Kochman - jkochman@unifrance-usa.org

UNITED STATES CONFERENCE OF CATHOLIC BISHOPS, DEPARTMENT OF COMMUNICATION—OFFICE FOR FILM & BROADCASTING
(Produces movie and television reviews with the goal of providing information about the moral and artistic values)
1011 First Ave., 13th Flr., New York, NY 10022.
TEL: (212) 644-1880. FAX: (212) 644-1886.
email: ofb@email.msn.com www.usccb.org

DIRECTOR, OFFICE FOR FILM & BROADCASTING
Harry Forbes
MEDIA REVIEWER
John Mulderig

VARIETY INTERNATIONAL- THE CHILDREN'S CHARITY
(Organized October 10, 1927. Membership: 15,000)
8455 Beverly Blvd., Ste. 501, Los Angeles, CA 90048.
TEL: (323) 655-1547. FAX: (323) 658-8789.
www.varietychildrenscharity.org
INTERNATIONAL PRESIDENT
Julia Morley
CHAIRMAN OF THE BOARD
Grahame Mapp, AM
INTERNATIONAL CHAIRMAN
Monty Hall, O.C.
MEDICAL ADVISOR
Michael LaCorte, M.D.
TREASURER
Fredrick M. Friedman
DIRECTOR OF DEVELOPMENT & COMMUNICATION
Michael P. Huffman - mhuffman@varietychildrenscharity.org

PAST PRESIDENT
Michael Forman, Jarvis Astaire, Peter J. Barnett, Monty Hall, O.C., Robert R. Hall, Q.C., Salah M. Hassanein, Tony Hatch, John Ratcliff, Michael J. Reilly, Stanley J. Reynolds, Jody Reynolds, Joseph Sinay, Ory Slonim

VICE PRESIDENT
Maureen Arthur-Ruben, Lloyd Barr, FCA, Jack Cannons, AM, Penny Docherty, Tom Fenno, Richard Freeman, Rosalie Gallagher, Tony Hasham, AM, Randall Hester, Nancy Klueter, Peter Legge, OBC, Ken V. Loughnan, AO, Pauline McFetridge, Neil Sinclair, Pamela Sinclair, Bob Stewart, Clark Woods

PRESIDENT'S COUNCIL
Marsha Rae Ratcliff, Wayne Adsett, Fran Blechman, C. Kenneth Greidinger, Gordon Josie, James Murray, Muriel Myerson, George Pitman, Barbara Stewart, Bob Thorpe, OAM, Louis Trepel

AMBASSADOR
Amnon Angel, John Blyth, Doug Christie, J. Douglas Clark, Laurence Davis, Alan Davy, Jeff Goldstein, Marilyn Hall, Norman Kaphan, Sue Mapp, Penelope Mapp, Nicolas Moore, Mary Nakagawa-Marti, Ronnie Nathan, Christine Ostermann, OAM, Sandra Pape, Susan Sullivan, Jill Valenti

CELEBRITY AMBASSADOR
Dame Shirley Bassey, Harry Belafonte, Bob Brown, Lance Burton, Sir Michael Caine, Sir Sean Connery, Rodger Davis, Nick Faldo, Ilene Graff, Paul Hogan, Kamahl, Warren Kermond, Dame Vera Lynn, George Miller, Sir Roger Moore, Bruce Morrow, Jim Nabors, Kim Olson, Peter Reveen, Emma Samms, Chaim Topol, Stuart Wagstaf

VARIETY INTL.-THE CHILDREN'S CHARITY TENTS

TENT 1: Variety of Pittsburgh, Three Penn Center W. One, Ste. 229, Pittsburgh, PA 15276. TEL: (412) 747-2680.
FAX: (412) 747-2681. www.varietypittsburgh.org
EXECUTIVE DIRECTOR
Celia A. Hindes, CFRE - celia@varietytent1.org

TENT 4: Variety of St. Louis, 2200 Westport Plaza Dr., St. Louis, MO 63146. TEL: (314) 453-0453.
FAX: (314) 453-0488.
www.varietystl.org
EXECUTIVE DIRECTOR
Jan Albus - jan@varietystl.org

TENT 5: Variety of Detroit, 30161 Southfield Rd., Ste. 301, Southfield, MI 48076. TEL: (248) 258-5511. FAX: (248) 258-5575.
email: VarietyDetroit@USVariety.org www.variety-detroit.com
EXECUTIVE DIRECTOR
Jennie Cascio

TENT 7: Variety of Buffalo, 195 Delaware Ave., Buffalo, NY 14202. TEL: (716) 854-7577. FAX: (716) 854-2939.
email: VarietyBuffalo@USVariety.org www.variety.buffnet.net
EXECUTIVE DIRECTOR
Richard Goldstein

TENT 8: Variety of Greater Kansas City, 17 Anchor Dr., Lake Tapawingo, MO 64015. TEL: (816) 220-2068. FAX: (816) 224-3734.
email: Variety KansasCity@USVariety.org www.varietykc.org
EXECUTIVE DIRECTOR
Nadine Mummaw

TENT 13: Variety of Philadelphia, 1520 Locust St., 2nd Flr., Philadelphia, PA 19102. TEL: (215) 735-0803.
FAX: (215) 735-2450. www.varietyphila.org
EXECUTIVE DIRECTOR
Andrew Pack - andrewpack@varietyphila.org

TENT 14: Variety of Wisconsin, 999 N. 92nd St., Ste C-120, Wauwatosa, WI 53226. TEL: (414) 266-3812. FAX: (414) 266-2671.
email: WIVariety@chw.org www.varietyofwisconsin.org

TENT 15: Variety of Iowa, 505 5th Ave., Ste. 310, Des Moines, IA 50309. TEL: (515) 243-4660. FAX: (515) 243-5873.
www.varietyofiowa.org
EXECUTIVE DIRECTOR
Sheri McMichael - sheri@varietyiowa.com

TENT 17: Variety of North Texas, 3102 Oak Lawn, Ste. 700, Dallas, TX 75219. TEL: (214) 560-2263. FAX: (214) 210-2902.
www.varietynorthtexas.org
EXECUTIVE DIRECTOR
Lance Hood

TENT 20: Variety of Memphis, 1648 Sycamore View Rd., Memphis, TN 38134. TEL: (901) 373-5369. FAX: (901) 373-5370.
email: VarietyMemphis@USVariety.org
OFFICE MANAGER
Tanna Wolfe

TENT 21: Variety of Georgia, 9800 Medlock Bridge Rd., Ste. 1, Johns Creek, GA 30097. TEL: (678) 994-4210.
www.varietyofgeorgia.org
EXECUTIVE DIRECTOR
Mike Simonds - mike@varietyofgeorgia.org

TENT 23: Variety of New England, 200 Elm St., Dedham, MA 02324. TEL: (781) 461-1600 ext. 462. FAX: (781) 329-0218.

TENT 25: Variety of Southern California, 8455 Beverly Blvd., Ste. 501, Los Angeles, CA 90048. TEL: (323) 655-1547.
FAX: (323) 658-8789. www.varietysocal.org
EXECUTIVE DIRECTOR
Elizabeth O'Neil - Elizabeth@varietysocal.org

TENT 26: Variety of Illinois, AON Center 200 E. Randolph St. Ste. 2200, Chicago, IL 60601. TEL: (312) 822-0660.
FAX: (312) 822-0661. www.varietyclub26.org
EXECUTIVE DIRECTOR
Vince Pagone - vpagone@varietyclub26.org

TENT 27: Variety of Western Michigan, 4165 Spartan Ind. Dr., Grandville, MI 49418. TEL: (616) 531-8600. FAX: (775) 531-7555.
www.variety4kids.org
CHIEF BARKER
Susan Hascall - VarietyWestMich@USVariety.org

TENT 32: Variety of Northern California, 582 Market St., Ste. 907, San Francisco, CA 94104. TEL: (415) 781-3894.
FAX: (415) 781-4226. www.varietync.org
EXECUTIVE DIRECTOR
Ellen Goodman - ellen@varietync.org

TENT 35: Variety of New York, 505 Eighth Ave., Ste. 1800, New York, NY 10018. TEL: (212) 760-2777. FAX: (212) 760-2779.
www.varietyny.org
EXECUTIVE DIRECTOR
Katie Goodspeed - kgoodspeed@varietyny.org

TENT 37: Variety of Colorado, 10497 Centennial Rd., Littleton, CO 80120. TEL: (303) 973-1142. FAX: (303) 973-8884.
email: info@varietycolorado.org www.varietycolorado.org
EXECUTIVE DIRECTOR
Shirley Patenaude - VarietyColorado@USVariety.org

TENT 39: Variety of Southern Nevada, 3401 Sirius Ave., Ste. 1, Las Vegas, NV 89102. TEL: (702) 383-8466. FAX: (702) 383-1196.
email: VarietySoNevada@USVariety.org

TENT 50: Variety of Hawaii, P.O. Box 1180, Kaneohe, HI 96744. TEL: (808) 955-5106. FAX: (808) 235-5574.

TENT 60: Variety of Utah, 2500 Emigration Canyon Rd., Salt Lake City, UT 84108. TEL: (801) 582-0700. FAX: (801) 583-5176.
email: VarietyUtah@USVariety.org

TENT 66: Variety of The Desert, 1729 E. Palm Canyon Dr., Ste. 103. Palm Springs, CA 92264. TEL: (760) 320-1177.
FAX: (760) 327-2971. email: VarietyDesert@USVariety.org
EXECUTIVE ASSISTANT
Amy Bohrmann

TENT 70: Variety of Orlando, 3315 Maggie Blvd., Ste. 100, Orlando, FL 32811. TEL: (407) 422-KIDS.
FAX: (407) 386-3139. www.varietyorlando.org
EXECUTIVE DIRECTOR
Jolie Sester - jolie@varietyorlando.org

TENT 81: Variety of Eastern Tennessee, 7132 Regal Ln., Knoxville, TN 37918. TEL: (865) 925-9539. FAX: (865) 521-8343.
email: VarietyEastTenn@USVariety.org
EXECUTIVE DIRECTOR
Dena Pinsker

CANADA:

TENT 28: Variety of Ontario, 3701 Danforth Ave., Toronto, ON M1N 2G2 Canada. TEL: (416) 367-2828. FAX: (416) 367-0028.
www.varietyontario.com
EXECUTIVE DIRECTOR
Lynne Wallace - lwallace@varietyontario.ca

TENT 47: Variety of British Columbia, 4300 Still Creek Dr., Burnaby, B.C. V5C 6C3 Canada. TEL: (604) 320-0505.
FAX: (604) 320-0535. email: info@variety.bc.ca
www.variety.bc.ca
EXECUTIVE DIRECTOR
Barbie Hislop - Barbie.hislop@variety.bc.ca

TENT 58: Variety of Manitoba, 611 Wellington Crescent, Winnipeg, Manitoba R3M 0A7 Canada. TEL: (204) 982-1058.
FAX: (204) 475-3198. email: varietyclub@mts.net

www.varietyclubofmanitoba.ca
EXECUTIVE DIRECTOR
Wayne Rogers

TENT 61: Variety of Southern Alberta, 201, 3740B - 11A St. NE, Calgary, AB T2E 6M6. TEL: (403) 228-6168. FAX: (403) 245-9282. email: variety@varietyclub61.ab.ca www.varietyclub61.ab.ca

MEXICO:

TENT 29: Variety of Mexico, General Anaya #198, Col. San Diego Churubusco, Mexico, D.F. 04120 Mexico. TEL: (52 56) 05 52 88. FAX: (52 56) 05 69 80. www.varietyclubcom.mx

LONDON:

TENT 36: Variety of Great Britain, Variety Club House, 93 Bayham St., London NW1 0AG, U.K. TEL: (44 207) 428-8100. FAX: (44 207) 428-8111. email: info@varietyclub.org.uk www.varietyclub.org.uk

IRELAND:

TENT 41: Variety of Ireland, Astor House, 29 Lower George's St., Dun Laoghaire, Dublin, Republic of Ireland. TEL: (3531) 236-6670. FAX: (3531) 236-6658.

ISRAEL:

TENT 51: Variety of Israel, 3, Tvu'ot Ha'arets St., Tel Aviv, 69546, Israel. TEL: (972 3) 644-7201. FAX: (972 3) 644-7203. email: variety@bezeqint.net www.variety-israel.co.il
EXECUTIVE DIRECTOR
Riki Ariel

UNITED KINGDOM:

TENT 52: Variety of Jersey, Maufant Variety Youth Centre, Grande Route de St. Martin, St. Saviour JE2 6GT, Jersey, Channel Islands, U.K. TEL: (44 1534) 856 937. FAX: (44 1534) 857 097. www.varietyclub52.org.uk

FRANCE:

TENT 54: Variety of France, "Soleil d'enfance", 7, Blvd., Exelmans, Paris 75016 France. TEL: (33 1464) 72097. FAX: (33 1452) 50737.
EXECUTIVE DIRECTORS
Guillaume Pires
Stephen Boyd - Stephen@varietysa.org.au

BARBADOS:

TENT 73: Variety of The Caribbean (Barbados), The Plantation Complex, Harmony Hall Christ Church, Barbardos. TEL: (246) 266-9258. FAX: (246) 437-3838. email: varietybarbados@caribsurf.com
EXECUTIVE DIRECTOR
Sharron Chandra Cumberbatch

NEW ZEALAND:

TENT 68: Variety of New Zealand, P.O. Box 17276, Greenlane Auckland 1005, New Zealand. TEL: (64 9) 520 4111. FAX: (64 9) 520 1122. www.varietyclub.org.nz
EXECUTIVE DIRECTOR
Lorraine Taylor - lorraine@variety.org.nz

JAPAN:

TENT 83: Variety of Japan, 1-16-11-1110 Senzoku, Taito-ku, Tokyo, Japan 111-0031. TEL: (813) 3871-3608. FAX: (813) 3871-3225. email: tent83@variety-club-japan.jp www.variety-club-japan.jp
EXECUTIVE DIRECTOR
Shizuya Yamada

AUSTRALIA:

VARIETY AUSTRALIA, INC.
Ste. 3, 670 Darling St, Rozelle NSW 2039.
TEL: (61) 2 9555 7577. FAX: (61) 2 9555 7554.
email: anita@varietyaustralia.org.au
www.varietyaustralia.org.au
NATIONAL GENERAL MANAGER
John S. Verco
NATIONAL ADMINISTRATION MANAGER
Anita Spring

TENT 56: Variety of New South Wales, 707 Darling St., Rozelle, NSW 2039, Australia. TEL: (61 2) 9555-1688. FAX: (61 2) 9555 1424. www.varietyaustralia.org.au
CHIEF EXECUTIVE OFFICER
Chris McMillan - chris.mcmillan@varietynsw.org.au

TENT 74: Variety of Western Australia, Ste. 3/63 Shepperton Rd., Victoria Park, WA 6100, Australia. TEL: (61 8) 9355-3655. FAX: (61 8) 9355-5122. www.varietyaustralia.org.au
CHIEF EXECUTIVE OFFICER
Michael Pailthorpe - michael@varietywa.org.au

TENT 76: Variety of Queensland, P.O. Box 2071, Milton Qld 4064, Gold Coast, QLD 9726, Australia. TEL: (61 7) 3368-3321. FAX: (61 7) 3368-3328. email: lesriley@varietyqld.org www.varietyaustralia.org.au

TENT 77: Variety of Victoria, 71/63-85 Turner St. Port Melboourne, Victoria 3205, Australia. TEL: (61 3) 8698.3900. FAX: (61 3) 8698.3933. www.varietyaustralia.org.au
CHIEF EXECUTIVE OFFICER
Norm Hutton - normhutton@varietyvic.org.au

TENT 78: Variety of Tasmania, P.O. Box 893, Sandy Bay, Tasmania, Australia 7005. TEL: (61 3) 6223-1886. FAX: (61 3) 6224-0333. www.varietyaustralia.org.au
CHIEF EXECUTIVE OFFICER
Julie Kent - Juliekent.varietytasmania@bigpond.com

TENT 82: Variety of Northern Territory, GPO Box 4224, Darwin, Northern Territory 0801, Australia. TEL: (618) 8941-3353. FAX: (618) 8941-2171. www.varietyaustralia.org.au
EXECUTIVE DIRECTOR
Jenny Hilyard - jenny@varietynt.org.au

SOUTH AUSTRALIA

TENT 75: Variety of South Australia, P.O. Box 1235, Marleston, Adelaide, South Australia 5033, Australia. TEL: (61 8) 8293-8744. FAX: (61 8) 8293-8725. www.varietyaustralia.org.au
CHIEF EXECUTIVE OFFICER
Stephen Boyd - Stephen@varietysa.org.au

WILL ROGERS MOTION PICTURE PIONEERS FOUNDATION
10045 Riverside Dr., 3rd Flr., Toluca Lake, CA 91602.
TEL: (888) 994-3863, (818) 755-2300. FAX: (818) 508-9816.
www.wrinstitute.org www.wrpioneers.org
CHAIRMAN
Bruce Snyder
PRESIDENT
Jeffrey Goldstein
VICE PRESIDENT
Ted, Sheila DeLoach, Richard M. Fay, David Garel, Chris S. Leroy, John A. Lundin, Nikki Rocco.
TREASURER
Clark Woods
SECRETARY
Chris Aronson
EXECUTIVE DIRECTOR
Todd Vradenburg
EXECUTIVE COMMITTEE
Rory Bruer, Greg Dunn, Daniel R. Fellman, Jerome A. Forman, Sonny Gourley, Erik Lomis, Steve Rapaport, Tom Sherak, Charles Viane. John Lundin
HONORARY CHAIRMEN
Erik Lomis, Salah M. Hassanein, Frank G. Mancuso, Burton Stone, Sumner Redstone, Travis Reid.
MEDICAL ADVISOR
Edward Crandall, Ph.D., M.D.

GUILDS AND UNIONS

ACTORS' EQUITY ASSOCIATION (AAAA AFL CIO CLC)
(Organized May 26, 1913. Membership more than 45,000)
NY: 165 W. 46th St. 15th Flr., New York, NY 10036.
TEL: (212) 869-8530. FAX: (212) 719-9815.

IL: 125 S. Clark St., Ste. 1500, Chicago, IL 60603.
TEL: (312) 641-0393. FAX: (312) 641-6365.

CA: 6755 Hollywood Blvd., 5th Flr., Hollywood, CA 90028.
TEL: (323) 978-8080. FAX: (323) 978-8081.

CA: 350 Sansom St., Ste. 900, San Francisco, CA 94104.
TEL: (415) 391-3838. FAX: (415) 391-0102.

FL: 10319 Orangewood Blvd., Orlando, FL 32821.
TEL: (407) 345-8600. FAX (407) 345-1522.
www.actorsequity.org
PRESIDENT
Nick Wyman
EXECUTIVE DIRECTOR
Mary McColl
NATIONAL DIRECTOR, ORGANIZING & SPECIAL PROJECTS
Flora Stamatiades
CENTRAL REGIONAL DIRECTOR
Kathryn V. Lamkey
EASTERN REGIONAL DIRECTOR
Rick Berg
WESTERN REGIONAL DIRECTOR
Mary Lou Westerfield
NATIONAL DIRECTOR, COMMUNICATIONS
David Lotz
NATIONAL DIRECTOR, FINANCE & ADMINISTRATION
Steve DiPaola

AMERICAN CINEMA EDITORS
(Organized November 28, 1950. Membership: 500)
100 Universal City Plaza, Universal City, CA 91608.
TEL: (818) 777-2900. FAX: (818) 733-5023.
email: amercinema@earthlink.net www.ace-filmeditors.org
PRESIDENT
Randy Roberts
VICE PRESIDENT
Alan Heim
SECRETARY
Lillian Bennson
TREASURER
Ed Abroms

BOARD OF DIRECTORS
Kate Amend, Diane Adler, Anita Brandt-Burgoyne, Edgar Burcksen, Tina Hirsch, Maysie Hoy, Bonnie Koehler, Stephen Lovejoy, Harry B. Miller III, Eric Sears

AMERICAN FEDERATION OF MUSICIANS OF THE UNITED STATES AND CANADA (AFL-CIO)
(Organized October, 1896. Membership: 88,146)
1501 Broadway, New York, NY 10036. TEL: (212) 869-1330.
FAX: (212) 764-6134. www.aflcio.org
INTERNATIONAL PRESIDENT
Thomas F. Lee (NY)
INTERNATIONAL SECRETARY-TREASURER
Sam Folio (NY)
INTERNATIONAL EXECUTIVE BOARD
Joe Parente, Bob McGrew, Erwin Price, Ray Hair, Billy Linneman
INTERNATIONAL VICE PRESIDENT
Harold Bradley, 11 Music Circle, Nashville, TN 37212.
VICE PRESIDENT, CANADA
Bill Skolnik, 75 The Donway West, Ste. 1010, Don Mills, ONT, Canada M3C 2E9.

AMERICAN GUILD OF MUSICAL ARTISTS, INC. (AAAA AFL CIO)
(Organized 1936. Membership: 5,500)
1430 Broadway, 14th Flr., New York, NY 10018.
TEL: (212) 265-3687. FAX: (212) 262-9088.
email: AGMA@MusicalArtists.org www.musicalartists.org
PRESIDENT
Jimmy Odom
VICE PRESIDENT
Gerald Otte, John Coleman, Colby Roberts, Sara Stewart Schumann, Gregory Stapp, LeRoy Lehr
TREASURER
Ray Menard
SECRETARY
Louis Perry
NATIONAL EXECUTIVE DIRECTOR
Alan S. Gordon - (917) 685-6830
DIRECTOR OF OPERATIONS
Gerry Angel - (212) 265-3687 GAngel@MusicalArtists.org
EASTERN COUNSEL
Deborah J. Allton - (646) 345-8696 Deborah@MusicalArtists.org
NEW YORK AREA DANCE EXECUTIVE
James Fayette - (212) 265-3687 James@MusicalArtists.org
AREA REPRESENTATIVES
NATIONAL DANCE EXECUTIVE
Nora Heiber - (415) 552-2800 Nheiber@earthlink.net
WESTERN COUNSEL
John Russum - (310) 215-9554 AGMALA@ca.rr.com
MID-ATLANTIC
Eleni Kallas - (301) 869-8266 AGMADC@comcast.net
MIDWEST
Barbara Hillman - (312) 236-7800 bhillman@cornfieldandfeldman.com

AMERICAN GUILD OF VARIETY ARTISTS (AAAA AFL-CIO)
(Organized July 14, 1939. Registered Membership: 78,000)
NY: 363 7th Ave., 17th Flr., New York, NY 10001.
TEL: (212) 675-1003. FAX: (212) 633-0097.
email: AGVA@agvausa.com agvany@aol.com.
www.agvausa.com

CA: 4741 Laurel Canyon Blvd., #208, Valley Village, CA 91607.
TEL: (818) 508-9984. FAX: (818) 508-3029.
email: agvawest@earthlink.net
PRESIDENT
Rod McKuen
EXECUTIVE SECRETARY-TREASURER
Susanne Doris
EXECUTIVE V.P.
Judy Little
HONORARY PRESIDENT
Phyllis Diller
HONORARY FIRST V.P.
Rip Taylor
REGIONAL VICE PRESIDENT
Emelise Aleandri, Harriet Blake, Mary Capellas, David Cullen, Mary Lynn Cullen, Larry Dorn, John Eaden, Elaine Jacovini, Lesley Jennings, Deirdre Kane, Victoria Reed, Jack Ross, Cody Smith, Dorothy Stratton, Eileen Woods, Dorothy Zuckerman

AMERICAN SOCIETY OF CINEMATOGRAPHERS
1782 N. Orange Dr., Hollywood, CA 90028. TEL: (800) 448-0145, (323) 969-4333. FAX: (323) 882-6391.

P.O. Box 2230, Hollywood, CA 90078. www.theasc.com
PRESIDENT
Michael Goi
VICE PRESIDENT
Richard Crudo, Owen Roizman
TREASURER
Matthew F. Leonetti
SECRETARY
Rodney Taylor
SERGENT AT ARMS
John C. Flinn

BOARD MEMEBER
John Bailey, Stephen Burum, Cutris Clark, George Spiro Dibie, Richard Edlund, John C. Flinn, III, Michael Goi, Stephen Lighthill, Isidore Mankofsky, Daryn Okada, Robert Primes, Nancy Schreiber, Kees Van Oostrum, Haskell Wesler, Vilmos Zsigmond

ASSOCIATED ACTORS AND ARTISTES OF AMERICA (AAAA-AFL-CIO)
(Organized July 18, 1919. Membership: 93,000)
165 W. 46th St., 16th Flr., New York, NY 10036.
TEL: (212) 869-0358. FAX: (212) 869-1746. www.aflcio.org
PRESIDENT
Richard L. Trumka
EXECUCTIVE VICE PRESIDENT
Arlene Holt Baker
EXECUTIVE SECRETARY
Liz Shuler

ASSOCIATED MUSICIANS OF GREATER NEW YORK LOCAL 802 AFM (NEW YORK)
(Organized August 27, 1921. Membership: 9,000)
322 W. 48th St., New York, NY 10036. TEL: (212) 245-4802.
FAX: (212) 489-6030. www.local802afm.org
PRESIDENT
Mary Landolfi - mlandolfi@local802afm.org
FINANCIAL V.P.
Jay Blumenthal
RECORDING V.P.
John O'Conner

ASSOCIATION OF TALENT AGENTS
(Organized April, 1937. Official organization of Hollywood talent agents)
9255 Sunset Blvd., Ste. 930, Los Angeles, CA 90069.

TEL: (310) 274-0628. www.agentassociation.com
www.actorsagentsearch.com
PRESIDENT
Sandy Bresler
VICE PRESIDENT
Sheldon Sroloff, Marilyn Szatmary
TREASURER
Jim Gosnell
SECRETARY
Cindy Kazarian

BOARD OF DIRECTORS
Robert Broder, Paul Doherty, Martin Gage, Harry Gold, Andrew Thau, Steve Kravit, Richard Lawrence, Tom McGuire, Richard Reiner, Denny Sevier, Rita Vennari

THE AUTHORS GUILD, INC.

31 East 32nd St., 7th Flr., New York, NY 10016.
TEL: (212) 563-5904. FAX: (212) 564-8363.
email: staff@authorsguild.org www.authorsguild.org
PRESIDENT
Scott Turow
VICE PRESIDENT
Judy Blume
SECRETARY
Pat Cummings
TREASURER
Peter Petre
EXECUTIVE DIRECTOR
Paul Aiken

BOARD MEMBERS
Barbara Taylor Bradford, Meg Cabot, Susan Cheever, Mary Higgins Clark, James Duffy, Jennifer Egan, Clarissa Pinkola Estes, Peter Gethers, James Gleick, Oscar Hijuelos, Daniel Hoffman, Nicholas Lemann, John r. MacArthur, Stephen Manes, Michele Mitchell, Victor S. Navasky, Douglas Preston, Michelle Richmond, Roxana Robinson, James Shapiro, T.J. Stiles, Jean Strouse, Peg Tyre, Rachel Vail, Sarah Vowell, Nicholas Weinstock, Meg Wolitzer

DIRECTORS GUILD OF AMERICA, INC. (DGA)

(Members: 13,400)
7920 Sunset Blvd., Los Angeles, CA 90046.
TEL: (800) 421-4173, (310) 289-2000. FAX: (310) 289-2029.

NY: 110 W. 57th St., New York, NY 10019. TEL: (800) 356-3754, (212) 581-0370. FAX: (212) 581-1441.

IL: 400 N. Michigan Ave., Ste. 307, Chicago, IL 60611.
TEL: (888) 600-6975, (312) 644-5050. FAX: (312) 644-5776.
www.dga.org
NATIONAL EXECUTIVE DIRECTOR
Jay D. Roth
PRESIDENT
Taylor Hackford
NATIONAL VICE PRESIDENT
Steven Soderbergh
SECRETARY/TREASURER
Gilbert Cates
ASSISTANT SECRETARY/TREASURER
Scott Berger
VICE PRESIDENT
Paris Barclay

BOARD MEMBERS
Herb Adelman, Michael Apted, Stephen Glanzrock, Lesli Linka Glatter, Victoria Hochberg, Cleve Landsberg, Michael Mann, Donald Petrie, Scott L. Rindenow, Ed Sherin, Jesus Trevino

THE DRAMATISTS GUILD OF AMERICA, INC.

1501 Broadway, Ste. 701, New York, NY 10036.
TEL: (212) 398-9366. FAX: (212) 944-0420.
email: info@dramatistsguild.com www.dramatistsguild.com
PRESIDENT
John Weidman
VICE PRESIDENT
Marsha Norman
SECRETARY
David Ives
TREASURER
Jonathan Reynolds
EXECUTIVE DIRECTOR, BUSINESS AFFAIRS
Ralph Sevush - rsevush@dramatistsguild.com
EXECUTIVE DIRECTOR, CREATIVE AFFAIRS
Gary Garrison - ggarrison@dramatistsguild.com

EPISCOPAL ACTORS' GUILD OF AMERICA, INC.

(Organized 1923. Members: 600)
1 E. 29th St., New York, NY 10016. TEL: (212) 685-2927.
FAX: (212) 685-8793. email: actors_guild@msn.com
www.actorsguild.org
EXECUTIVE DIRECTOR
Karen Lehman
PRESIDENT
Elowyn Castle
WARDEN
The Rt. Rev. Andrew R. St. John
TREASURER
Scott Glascock
EMERITA
Florence James
VICE PRESIDENT
Louis Rachow, John M. Flood, Peter Von Berg

INTERNATIONAL BROTHERHOOD OF ELECTRICAL WORKERS (AFL-CIO, CFL)

(Organized Nov. 28, 1891. Membership: 775,000)
900 Seventh St. NW, Washington, DC 20001.
TEL: (202) 833-7000. FAX: (202) 728-7664. www.ibew.org
INTERNATIONAL PRESIDENT
Edwin D. Hill
INTERNATIONAL SECRETARY & TREASURER
Jon F. Walters
DISTRICT OFFICES
AL: Joe S. Davis, 100 Concourse Pkwy., Ste. 300, Brimingham, AL 35244. TEL: (205) 444-9977. FAX: (205) 444-0306.

CA: Michael Mowrey, 2500 Venture Oaks Way, Ste. 250, Sacramento, CA 95833-4221. TEL: (916) 567-0381.

CANADA: Philip Flemming, 1450 Meyerside Dr., Ste. 300, Mississuga, ON L5T 2N5. Canada. TEL: (905) 564-5441.

ID: Ted C. Jensen, 2225 W. Broadway, Ste. H, Idaho Falls, ID 83402. TEL: (208) 529-6555.

IL: Joseph F. Lohman, 8174 Cass Ave., Darien, IL 60561. TEL: (630) 434-1683.

MA: Frank J. Carroll, 4 Armstrong Rd., 2nd Flr., Shelton, CT 06484. TEL: (203) 402-0490.

MO: Curtis E. Henke, 6601 Winchester Ave., Ste. 150, Kansas City, MO 64133. TEL: (816) 358-4632. FAX: (816) 358-5642.

OH: Salvatore J. Chilia, Corporate Plaza 1, 6450 Rockside Woods Blvd S., Ste. 150, Independence, OH 44131. TEL: (216) 328-0004. FAX: (216) 328-0444.

OK: Jonathan B. Gardner, 320 Westway Pl., Ste. 531, Arlington, TX 76018. TEL: (817) 557-1611.

PA: Donald C. Siegel, 500 Cherrington Pkwy., Ste. 325, Coraopolis, PA 15108. TEL: (412) 269-4963.

TN: Robert P. Klein, 5726 Marlin Rd., Ste. 500, Chattanooga, TN 37411-4043. TEL: (423) 894-9095.

IBEW, LOCAL 349 (FILM)

1657 N.W. 17th Ave., Miami, FL 33125. TEL: (305) 325-1330.
FAX: (305) 325-1521. www.ibewlu349.com
BUSINESS MANAGER
Bill Riley
PRESIDENT
David Karcher

IBEW, LOCAL 40 (FILM)

5643 Vineland Ave., North Hollywood, CA 91601.
TEL: (818) 762-4239. FAX: (818) 762-4379.
www.ibewlocal40.com
BUSINESS MANAGER
Bill Brinkmeyer

IBEW, LOCAL 1212 (RADIO AND TELEVISION BROADCAST ENGINEERS)

225 W. 34th St., Ste. 1120, New York, NY 10122.
TEL: (212) 354-6770. FAX: (212) 819-9517.
www.ibew1212.org
PRESIDENT
Frank Viskup
VICE PRESIDENT
Michael Fosso
BUSINESS MANAGER/FINANCIAL SECRETARY
Ralph Avigliano

INTERNATIONAL ALLIANCE OF THEATRICAL STAGE EMPLOYEES & MOVING PICTURE TECHNICIANS, ARTISTS AND ALLIED CRAFTS OF THE U.S., ITS TERRITORIES, AND CANADA (AFL-CIO, CLC)

(Organized nationally, July 17, 1893; internationally, October 1, 1902. The Alliance comprises approximately 500 local unions covering the United States, its territories and Canada)
1430 Broadway, 20th Flr., New York, NY 10018.
TEL: (212) 730-1770. FAX: (212) 921-7699. www.iatse-intl.org
INTERNATIONAL PRESIDENT
Matthew D. Loeb
INTERNATIONAL PRESIDENT EMERITUS
Thomas C. Short
GENERAL SECRETARY & TREASURER
James Wood
GENERAL SECRETARY-TREASURER EMERITUS
Michael W. Proscia
INTERNATIONAL V.P., EMERITUS
Edward C. Powell
VICE PRESIDENT
Timothy Magee, Michael J. Barnes, J. Walter Cahill, Thom Davis, Anthony DePaulo, Damian Petti, Brian J. Lawlor, Michael F. Miller, Jr., John T. Beckman, Jr., Daniel DiTolla, John Ford, John M. Lewis, Craig Carlson

IATSE PRODUCTION

AFFILIATED PROPERTY CRAFTSMEN LOCAL 44 (IATSE-AFL-CIO), HOLLYWOOD
12021 Riverside Dr., N. Hollywood, CA 91607.
TEL: (818) 769-2500. FAX: (818) 769-1739.
email: EBoard@local44.org www.local44.org
PRESIDENT
Erin Hennessey
VICE PRESIDENT
Michael Diersing
SECRETARY/TREASURER
Anthony Pawluc

THE ANIMATION GUILD, LOCAL 839 (IATSE)
1105 N. Hollywood Way. Burbank, CA 91505.
TEL: (818) 845-7500. FAX: (818) 843-0300.
www.animationguild.org
PRESIDENT
Kevin Koch
BUSINESS REPRESENTATIVE
Steve Hulett
VICE PRESIDENT
Earl Kress
SERGEANT AT ARMS
Jan Browning
EXECUTIVE BOARD
Bronwen Barry, Russell Calabrese, John Cataldi, Nicole Dubuc, Bob Foster, Janette Hulett, Karen Carnegie Johnson, Cathy Jones, Karen Nugent, Matt Wayne, Stephan Zupkas

ART DIRECTORS GUILD AND SCENIC, TITLE & GRAPHIC ARTISTS LOCAL 800 (IATSE)
11969 Ventura Blvd., #2nd Flr., Studio City, CA 91604.
TEL: (818) 762-9995. FAX: (818) 762-9997.
www.artdirectors.org
EXECUTIVE DIRECTOR
Scott Roth
ASSOCIATE EXECUTIVE DIRECTOR
John Moffitt

COSTUME DESIGNERS GUILD LOCAL 892
(Founded 1953, Membership: 750)
11969 Ventura Blvd., 1st Flr., Studio City, CA 91604.
TEL: (818) 752-2400. FAX: (818) 752-2402.
email: cdgia@costumedesignersguild.com
www.costumedesignersguild.com
PRESIDENT
Mary Rose - mrose@costumedesignersguild.com
VICE PRESIDENT
Van Broughton Ramsey
vramsey@costumedesignersguild.com
SECRETARY
Ann Major - asomersmajor@costumedesignersguild.com
TREASURER
Marilyn Matthews - mmatthews@costumedesignersguild.com
INTERIM EXECUTIVE DIRECTOR
Rachael M. Stanley
rstanley@costumedesignersguild.com

FIRST AID EMPLOYEES, LOCAL 767 (IATSE), LOS ANGELES
P.O. Box 6309, Burbank, CA 91510-6309. TEL: (818) 606-0005.
FAX: (818) 982-3364. email: sectreasurer@iatse767.org
www.iatse767.org
PRESIDENT
Howard Keys
BUSINESS AGENT
Rana Platz Petersen - (310) 352-1485.

INTERNATIONAL CINEMATOGRAPHERS GUILD, IATSE LOCAL 600, NATIONAL OFFICE - WESTERN REGION HOLLYWOOD
7755 Sunset Blvd., Hollywood, CA 90046.
TEL: (323) 876-0160. FAX: (323) 876-6383.
email: admin@cameraguild.com www.cameraguild.com
NATIONAL PRESIDENT
Steven Poster, ASC
NATIONAL VICE PRESIDENT
Lewis Rothenberg
FIRST VICE PRESIDENT
Rusty Burrell
SECOND VICE-PRESIDENT
John Toll
SECRETARY-TREASURER
Alan M. Gitlin
NATIONAL ASSISTANT SECRETARY TREASURER
Bruce MacCallum
NATIONAL SERGEANT AT ARMS
Michael St. Hilaire

INTERNATIONAL CINEMATOGRAPHERS GUILD, IATSE LOCAL 600, EASTERN REGION NEW YORK
80 Eighth Ave., 14th Flr., New York, NY 10011.
TEL: (212) 647-7300. FAX: (212) 647-7317.
www.cameraguild.com
VICE PRESIDENT
Deborah M. Lipman
RECORDING SECRETARY
Chris Silano
SERGEANT AT ARMS
Angelo Digiacomo
BUSINESS REPS
John Amman, David Blake, Vincent Galindez

INTERNATIONAL CINEMATOGRAPHERS GUILD, IATSE LOCAL 600, CENTRAL REGION FLORIDA
690 Lincoln Rd., Ste. 203, Miami Beach, FL 33139.
TEL: (305) 538-9226. FAX: (305) 538-9259.

INTERNATIONAL CINEMATOGRAPHERS GUILD ILLINOIS
1411 Peterson Ave. Ste. 102, Park Ridge, IL 60068.
TEL: (847) 692-9900. FAX: (847)692-560.
www.cameraguild.com
FIRST VICE-PRESIDENT
Rusty Burrell
SERGEANT AT ARMS
Michael St. Hilaire
CENTRAL REGION DIRECTOR
John Hilsman

MOTION PICTURE COSTUMERS, LOCAL 705 (IATSE), HOLLYWOOD
4731 Laurel Canyon Blvd., Ste. 201, Valley Village, CA 91607-3911. TEL: (818) 487-5655. FAX: (818) 487-5663.
email: mpc705@aol.com www.motionpicturecostumers.org
SECRETARY
Paul DeLucca
BUSINESS REPRESENTIVE
Buffy Snyder

MOTION PICTURE STUDIO GRIPS & MOTION PICTURE STUDIO CRAFTS SERVICE LOCAL 80 (IATSE)
2520 W. Olive Ave., Ste. 200, Burbank, CA 91505.
TEL: (818) 526-0700. www.iatselocal80.org
BUSINESS REPRESENTATIVE
Thom Davis
CORRESPONDING SECRETARY
Rick Schunke

MOTION PICTURE EDITORS GUILD, LOCAL 700 (IATSE), LOS ANGELES
7715 Sunset Blvd., Ste. 200, Hollywood, CA 90046.
TEL: (323) 876-4770. FAX: (323) 876-0861.
www.editorsguild.com
EXECUTIVE DIRECTOR
Ronald G. Kutak - rkutak@editorsguild.com

MOTION PICTURE EDITORS GUILD, LOCAL 700 (IATSE), NEW YORK
145 Hudson St., Ste. 201, New York, NY 10013.
TEL: (212) 302-0700. FAX: (212) 302-1091.
www.editorsguild.com
ASSISTANT EXECUTIVE DIRECTOR
Paul Moore - pmoore@editorsguild.com
OFFICE MANAGER
Sandy Fong-Ging - sfong-ging@editorsguild.com

MOTION PICTURE SCRIPT SUPERVISORS, PRODUCTION OFFICE COORDINATORS AND PRODUCTION ACCOUNTANTS, LOCAL 161
630 9th Ave., #1103, New York, NY 10036.
TEL: (212) 977-9655. FAX: (212) 977-9609.
BUSINESS AGENT
Lynne Twentyman

MOTION PICTURE SET PAINTERS, LOCAL 729 (IATSE), HOLLYWOOD
1811 W. Burbank Blvd., Burbank, CA 91506-1314.
TEL: (818) 842-7729. FAX: (818) 846-3729.
email: ialocal729@earthlink.net www.ialocal729.com
PRESIDENT
Kirk Hansen
VICE PRESIDENT
Greg Smith
BUSINESS REPRESENTATIVE & SECRETARY TREASURER
George A. Palazzo

MOTION PICTURE STUDIO ELECTRICAL LIGHTING TECHNICIANS, LOCAL 728 (IATSE)
11500 Burbank Blvd., Anorth Hollywood, CA 91601.
TEL: (818) 891-0728. FAX: (818) 891-5288.
BUSINESS REPRESENTATIVE SECRETARY
Patric J. Abaravich

MOTION PICTURE STUDIO ART CRAFTSMEN, (ILLUSTRATORS AND MATTE ARTISTS) LOCAL 790 (IATSE), HOLLYWOOD
13245 Riverside Dr., Ste. 300-A, Sherman Oaks, CA 91423.
TEL: (818) 784-6555. FAX: (818) 784-2004.
BUSINESS AGENT
Marjo Bernay

MOTION PICTURE STUDIO MECHANICS, LOCAL 476 (IATSE), CHICAGO
6309 N. Northwest Hwy., Chicago, IL 60631.
TEL: (773) 775-5300. FAX: (773) 775-2477.
www.iatselocal476.org
BUSINESS MANAGER/SECRETARY TREASURER
Mark A. Hogan - markh@iatse476.org

SCRIPT SUPERVISORS/CONTINUITY, COORDINATORS, ACCOUNTANTS & ALLIED PRODUCTION SPECIALISTS GUILD, LOCAL 871 (IATSE)
11519 Chandler Blvd., N. Hollywood, CA 91601.
TEL: (818) 509-7871. FAX: (818) 506-1555.
email: office@ialocal871.org www.ialocal871.org

SET DESIGNERS AND MODEL MAKERS, LOCAL 847 (IATSE), HOLLYWOOD
13245 Riverside Dr., Ste. 300-A, Sherman Oaks, CA 91423.
TEL: (818) 784-6555. FAX: (818) 784-2004.
CORRESPONDING SECRETARY
Suzanne Feller-Otto

STUDIO MECHANICS, LOCAL 479 (IATSE), ATLANTA
1000 Iris Dr., Ste. F, Conyers, GA 30094. TEL: (770) 483-0400.
FAX: (770) 483-0999. email: office@iatse479.com
www.iatse479.com
SECRETARY
Freddy Chancellor
BUSINESS AGENT
Michael Akins

STUDIO MECHANICS, LOCAL 812 (IATSE), DETROIT
20017 Van Dyke St., Detroit, MI 48234. TEL: (313) 368-0825.
FAX: (313) 368-1151. www.iatse812.org
PRESIDENT & BUSINESS AGENT
Timothy Magee

STUDIO MECHANICS, LOCAL 52 (IATSE), NEW YORK
326 W. 48th St., New York, NY 10036. TEL: (212) 399-0980.
FAX: (212) 315-1073. www.iatselocal52.org
SECRETARY/TREASURER
William McGavin

STUDIO MECHANICS, LOCAL 477 (IATSE), FLORIDA
10705 N.W. 33th St., Ste. 110, Miami, FL 33172.
TEL: (305) 594-8585. FAX: (305) 597-9278.
SECRETARY
George Cerchiai
BUSINESS AGENT
Fred Moqse

STUDIO MECHANICS, LOCAL 209 (IATSE), OHIO
1468 W. 9th St., Western Reserve Bldg., Ste. 200, Cleveland, OH 44113. TEL: (216) 621-9537. FAX: (216) 621-3518.
BUSINESS AGENT
Kenneth McCahan
CORRESPONDING SECRETARY
Jonathan Andrews

THEATRICAL WARDROBE UNION, LOCAL 764 (IATSE)
545 W. 45th St., 2nd Flr., New York, NY 10036.
TEL: (212) 957-3500. FAX: (212) 957-3232. www.ia764.org
SECRETARY/TREASURER
Jenna Krempel - jkrempel@ia764.org
BUSINESS REPRESENTATIVE, TELEVISION & FILM
James Hurley - jhurley@ia764.org

EXHIBITION

EXHIBITION EMPLOYEES, LOCAL 829 (IATSE), NEW YORK
386 Park Ave., S., 13th Flr., New York, NY 10016.
TEL: (212) 679-1164. FAX: (212) 679-1421.
www.usa829.org
PRESIDENT/SECRETARY/TREASURER
John V. McNamee, Jr.

MOTION PICTURE PROJECTIONISTS, AUDIO VISUAL ENGINEERS & COMPUTER TECHNICIANS, LOCAL 110 (IATSE), CHICAGO
230 W. Monroe St., Ste. 2511, Chicago, IL 60606.
TEL: (312) 443-1011. FAX: (312) 443-1012.
BUSINESS MANAGER
Steve Altman

MOTION PICTURE PROJECTIONISTS, VIDEO TECHNICIANS, THEATRICAL EMPLOYEES & ALLIED CRAFTS, LOCAL 306 (IATSE), NEW YORK
545 W. 45th St., 2nd Flr., New York, NY 10036.
TEL: (212) 956-1306. FAX: (212) 956-9306. www.local306.org
SECRETARY
Hugo F. Capra
BUSINESS REPRESENTATIVES
Barry Garfman
Miriam L. (Mim) Pollock

PROJECTIONISTS LOCAL 150
P.O. Box 5143, Culver City, CA 90231-5143.
TEL: (818) 557-1677.
BUSINESS REPRESENTATIVE
Carl Belfor

STAGE EMPLOYEES, LOCAL 4 (IATSE), BROOKLYN
2917 Glenwood Rd., Brooklyn, NY 11210.
TEL: (718) 252-8777. FAX: (718) 421-5605.
www.iatselocal4.org
PRESIDENT
Joseph Holler
RECORDING SECRETARY
Terence Ryan - tkryan@iatselocal4.org
BUSINESS MANAGER
Lewis Resnick

STAGE EMPLOYEES, LOCAL 2 (IATSE), CHICAGO
216 S. Jefferson, Ste. 400, Chicago, IL 60661.
TEL: (312) 705-2020. FAX: (312) 705-2011.
www.iatselocal2.com
BUSINESS MANAGER
Craig Carlson

STAGE EMPLOYEES, LOCAL 33 (IATSE), LOS ANGELES
1720 W. Magnolia Blvd., Burbank, CA 91506-1871.
TEL: (818) 841-9233. FAX: (818) 567-1138. www.ia33.org
CORRESPONDING SECRETARY
Jane E. Leslie

THEATRICAL STAGE EMPLOYEES, LOCAL 1 (IATSE), NEW YORK
320 W. 46th St., New York, NY 10036. TEL: (212) 333-2500.
FAX: (212) 586-2437. www.iatselocalone.org
RECORDING-CORRESPONDING SECRETARY
Robert Score

THEATRE EMPLOYEES, LOCAL B-46 (IATSE), CHICAGO
230 W. Monroe St., Ste. 2511, Chicago, IL 60606.
TEL: (312) 443-1011. FAX: (312) 443-1012.
SECRETARY/TREASURER
Steve Altman

TREASURERS AND TICKET SELLERS, LOCAL 750 (IATSE), CHICAGO
446 N. Edgewood, LaGrange Park, IL 60526.
TEL: (708) 579-4305. FAX: (708) 579-4313.
CORRESPONDING SECRETARY
Michael Keenan

TREASURERS AND TICKET SELLERS, LOCAL 857 (IATSE), LOS ANGELES
13245 Riverside Dr., Ste. 300C, Sherman Oaks, CA 91423.
TEL: (818) 990-7107. FAX: (818) 990-8287.
email: info@local857.com
BUSINESS AGENT
Sergio Medina

TREASURERS AND TICKET SELLERS, LOCAL 751 (IATSE), NEW YORK
1430 Broadway, 8th Flr., New York, NY 10018.
TEL: (212) 302-7300. FAX: (212) 944-8687.
PRESIDENT
Gene McElwain

PRODUCER-WRITERS GUILD OF AMERICA PENSION PLAN
1015 N. Hollywood Way, Burbank, CA 91505. TEL: (800) 227-7863, (818) 846-1015. FAX: (818) 566-8445. www.wgaplans.org

PRODUCERS GUILD OF AMERICA
(Founded 1950. Membership: 3,950)
8530 Wilshire Blvd., Ste. 450, Beverly Hills, CA 90211.
TEL: (310) 358-9020. FAX: (310) 358-9520.
email: info@producersguild.org www.producersguild.org
CO-PRESIDENT
Mark Gordon, Hawk Koch
VICE PRESIDENT, MOTION PICTURES
Gary Lucchesi
V.P., TELEVISION
Hayma Washington
TREASURER
Lauren Shuler Donner
EXECUTIVE DIRECTOR
Vance Van Petten

PROFESSIONAL MUSICIANS, LOCAL 47, (AFM, AFL-CIO/CLC)
(Organized October 30, 1894. Membership: 10,000)
817 Vine St., Hollywood, CA 90038. TEL: (323) 462-2161.
FAX: (323) 466-1289. www.promusic47.org
PRESIDENT
Vince Trombetta
SECRETARY/TREASURER
Leslie Lashinksky

SCREEN ACTORS GUILD (AAAA-AFL-CIO)
(Organized July 1933. Membership: 120,000)

National Headquarters: 5757 Wilshire Blvd., Los Angeles, CA 90036-3600. TEL: (800) SAG-0767, (323) 954-1600.
FAX: (323) 549-6603. www.sag.org
PRESIDENT
Ken Howard
SECRETARY-TREASURER
Connie Stevens
NATIONAL EXECUTIVE DIRECTOR
David White
DEPUTY NATIONAL EXECUTIVE DIRECTOR
Pamm Fair
DEPUTY NATIONAL EXECUTIVE DIRECTOR, GENERAL COUNSEL
Duncan Crabtree-Ireland
DEPUTY NATIONAL EXECUTIVE DIRECTOR, CONTRACTS
Ray Rodriguez
SENIOR ADVISOR
John McGuire
COMMUNICATIONS EXECUTIVE DIRECTOR
Pamela Greenwalt
CFO
Arianna Ozzanto
CHIEF INFORMATION OFFICER
Erin Griffin

CA: 5757 Wilshire Blvd., 7th Flr., Los Angeles, CA 90036.
TEL: (323) 549-6459. FAX: (323) 549 6445.
HOLLYWOOD DIVISION EXECUTIVE DIRECTOR
Ilyanne Morden Kichaven

NY: 360 Madison Ave., 12th Flr., New York, NY 10017.
TEL: (212) 944-1030. FAX: (212) 944-6774.
NEW YORK DIVISION EXECUTIVE DIRECTOR
Jae Je Simmons

TX: 15950 N. Dallas Pkwy., Ste. 400, Dallas, TX 75248.
TEL: (972) 361-8185. FAX: (972) 361-8186.
REGIONAL BRANCH DIVISION EXECUTIVE DIRECTOR
Linda Dowell

NATIONAL BOARD OF DIRECTORS HOLLYWOOD DIVISION
Michelle Allsopp, Adam Arkin, Ed Asner, Scott Bakula, Bonnie Barlett, Joseph Bologna, Amy Brenneman, L. Scott Caldwell, Keith Carradine, Gabrielle Carteris, Bernie Casey, Ellen Crawford, Joe d'Angerio, Patrick Fabian, Morgan Fairchild, Frances Fisher, Joely Fisher, Jason George, Elliott Gould, Clark Gregg, Hill Harper, Valerie Harper, Ed Harris, Sumi Haru, Robert Hays, Dule Hill, Anne-Marie Johnson, Lainie Kazan, Clyde Kusatsu, Diane Ladd, John Carroll Lynch, William Mapother, Kent McCord, D.W. Moffett, Esai Morales, Jenny O'Hara, Michael O'Keefe, Pamala Reed, Alan Rosenberg, Doug Savant, Martin Sheen, Nancy Sinatra, Bill Smitrovich, Mandy Steckelberg, Connie Stevens, Renee Taylor, Nancy Travis, Stacey Travis, Marcia Wallace, Kate Walsh, Angela Watson, JoBeth Williams, Jenny Worman

NATIONAL BOARD OF DIRECTORS NEW YORK DIVSISION
Sam Freed, Marc Blum, Paul Christie, Rebecca Damon, Maureen Donnelly, Nancy Giles, Traci Godfrey, Mike Hodge, Richard Masur, Sue-Anne Morrow, Sam Robards, Matt Servitto, Sharon Washington, Liz Zazzi

REGIONAL BRANCH OFFICES:

ARIZONA: Mark DeMichele , 3131 E. Camelback Rd., Ste. 200, Phoenix, AZ 85016. TEL: (800) 724-0767, (602) 383-3780. FAX: (602) 838-3781.

BOSTON: Dona Sommers, 20 Park Plaza, Ste. 822, Boston, MA 02116. TEL: (800) 724-0767, (617) 262-8001. FAX: (617) 262-3006.

CHICAGO: Eric W. Chaudron, One E. Erie St., Ste. 650, Chicago, IL 60611. TEL: (800) 724-0767, (312) 573-8081. FAX: (312) 573-0318.

COLORADO: John Singer, Market Sq. Center, 1400 16th St., Ste. 400, Denver, CO 80202. TEL: (800) 724-0767, (720) 932-8193. FAX: (720) 932-8194.

DALLAS: Brent Anderson, 15950 N. Dallas Pkwy., Ste. 400, Dallas, TX 75248. TEL: (800) 724-0767, (972) 361-8185. FAX: (972) 361-8186.

DETROIT: Peter Tocco, 2000 Town Center, Ste. 1900, Southfield, MI 48075. TEL: (800) 724-0767, (248) 351-2678. FAX: (248) 351-2679.

FLORIDA: Steve Gladstone, 7300 N. Kendall Dr., Ste. 620, Miami, FL 33156. TEL: (800) 724-0767, (305) 670-7677. FAX: (305) 670-1813.

HAWAII: Brenda Ching, 949 Kapiolani Blvd., Ste. 105, Honolulu, HI 96814. TEL: (800) 724-0767, (808) 596-0388. FAX: (808) 593-2636.

HOLLYWOOD: Ilyanne Morden-Kichaven, 5757 Wilshire Blvd., Los Angeles, CA 90036. TEL: (323) 954-1600. FAX: (323) 549-6603.

HOUSTON: Robert Nelson, 15950 N. Dallas Pkwy., Ste. 400, Dallas, TX 75248. TEL: (800) 724-0767, (972) 361-8185. FAX: (800) 311-3216.

LOUISIANA: Jason Tomlinson, 1100 Poydras St., Ste. 2900, New Orleans, LA 70163. TEL: (800) 724-0767, (504) 585-7324. FAX: (504) 585-7326.

NASHVILLE: Mike Montgomery, 7300 N. Kendall Dr., Ste. 620, Miami, FL 33156. TEL: (800) 724-0767, (305) 670-7677. FAX: (800) 844-5439.

NEVADA: c/o 5757 Wilshire Blvd., Los Angeles, CA 90036. TEL: (800) 724-0767, (323) 549-6440. FAX: (323) 549-6460.

NEW MEXICO: c/o Julie Crane, Market Sq. Center, 1400 16th St., Ste. 400, Denver, CO 80202. TEL: (800) 724-0767, (720) 932-8193. FAX: (800) 595-4256.

NEW YORK: Jae Je Simmons, 360 Madison Ave. 12th Flr., New York, NY 10017. TEL: (212) 944-1030. FAX: (212) 944-6774.

NORTH CAROLINA: Jerry Winsett, 7300 N. Kendall Dr., Ste. 620, Miami, FL 33156. TEL: (800) 724-0767, (305) 670-7677. FAX: (800) 844-5439.

ORLANDO: David A. Fazekas, 522 Hunt Club Blvd., Ste. 410, Apopka, FL 32703. TEL: (800) 724-0767, (407) 788-3020. FAX: 407-788-3080.

PHILADELPHIA: John Wooten, 2000 Town Center, Ste. 1900, Southfield, MI 48075. TEL: (800) 724-0767, (248) 351-2678. FAX: (248) 351-2679.

PORTLAND: Robert Blanche, 800 Fifth Ave., Ste. 4100, Seattle, WA 98104. TEL: (800) 724-0767, (206) 224-5696. FAX: (800) 278-6741.

SAN DIEGO: Marty Alvillar, 5757 Wilshire Blvd., Los Angeles, CA 90036. TEL: (800) 724-0767, (323) 954-6440. FAX: (323) 549-6460.

SAN FRANCISCO: Kathryn Howell, 350 Sansome St., Ste. 900, San Francisco, CA 94104. TEL: (800) 724-0767, (415) 391-7510. FAX: (415) 391-1108.

SEATTLE: John Patrick Lowrie, 800 Fifth Ave., Ste. 4100, Seattle, WA 98104. TEL: (800) 724-0767, (206) 224-5696. FAX: (206) 224-5695.

UTAH: Paul Mulder, 3131 E. Camelback Rd., Ste. 200, Phoenix, AZ 85016. TEL: (800) 724-0767, (602) 383-3780. FAX: (800) 859-2964.

WASHINGTON, DC/BALTIMORE: John Badila. 7735 Old Georgetown Rd., Ste. 950, Bethesda, MD 20814. TEL: (800) 724-0767, (301) 657-2560. FAX: (301) 656-3615, (800) 253-9730.

THE SONGWRITERS GUILD OF AMERICA

209 10th Ave. S, Ste. 321, Nashville, TN 37203.
TEL: (615) 742-9945. FAX: (615) 742-9948.
email: corporate@songwritersguild.com
www.songwritersguild.com
PRESIDENT
Rick Carnes
DIRECTOR OF OPERATIONS
Joe Whitt

NY: 1560 Broadway, Ste. 408, New York, NY 10036.
TEL: (212) 768-7902. email: ny@songwritersguild.com
www.songwritersguild.com
EAST COAST PROJECT MANAGER
Mark Saxon

TN: 209 10th Ave. S, Ste. 321, Nashville, TN 37203.
TEL: (615) 742-9945. FAX: (615) 742-9948.
email: nash@songwritersguild.com
www.songwritersguild.com
CENTRAL REGION PROJECT MANAGER
Kimberly Maiers Shaw

Los Angeles office currently in the process of relocation.
email: la@songwritersguild.com

STUNTMEN'S ASSOCIATION

(Organized 1961)
10660 Riverside Dr., 2nd Flr., Ste. E, Toluca Lake, CA 91602.
TEL: (818) 766-4334. FAX: (818) 766-5943.
email: info@stuntmen.com www.stuntmen.com
PRESIDENT
J. Mark Donaldson
VICE PRESIDENT
Conrad Palmisano
2ND VICE PRESIDENT
Jeff Wolfe
3RD VICE PRESIDENT
John Moio
SECRETARY
Chris Doyle
TREASURER
Hugh O'Brien

BOARD MEMBER - board@stuntment.com
Diamond Farnsworth, Norbert Phillips, Alex Daniels
performers)

THEATRE AUTHORITY, INC.

(Organized May 21, 1934. Charitable organization for theatrical
729 Seventh Ave., 11th Flr., New York, NY 10019.
TEL: (212) 764-0156.

WRITERS GUILD OF AMERICA, EAST, INC.

555 W. 57th St., Ste. 1230, New York, NY 10019.
TEL: (212) 767-7800. FAX: (212) 582-1909. www.wgaeast.org
PRESIDENT
Michael Winship - mwinship@wgaeast.org
VICE PRESIDENT
Bob Schneider - bschneider@wgaeast.org
SECRETARY/TREASURER
Gail Lee
EXECUTIVE DIRECTOR
Lowell Peterson - lpeterson@wgaeast.org
ASSISTANT EXECUTIVE DIRECTOR
Ruth Gallo - rgallo@wgaeast.org
Marsha Seeman - mseeman@wgaeast.org
INFORMATION CONTACT
Sherry Goldman - (718) 224-4133 - sherry@goldmanpr.net

WRITERS GUILD OF AMERICA, WEST, INC.

7000 W. Third St., Los Angeles, CA 90048.
TEL: (323) 951-4000. FAX: (323) 782-4800. www.wga.org
PRESIDENT
John Wells
VICE PRESIDENT
Tom Schulman
SECRETARY/TREASURER
David N. Weiss
EXECUTIVE DIRECTOR
David Young
BOARD OF DIRECTORS
John F. Bowman, Linda Burstyn, Ian Deitchman, Carleton Eastlake, Katherine Fugate, David A. Goodman, Howard Michael Gould, Mark Gunn, Karen Harris, Chip Johannessen, Kathy Kiernan, Aaron Mendelsohn, Billy Ray, Howard A. Rodman, Steven Schwartz, Patric M. Verrone, Dan Wilco

STATE & CITY FILM COMMISSIONS

ALABAMA

ALABAMA FILM OFFICE

Alabama Center For Commerce
401 Adams Ave., Ste. 640, Montgomery, AL 36104.
TEL: (334) 242-4195. FAX: (334) 242-2077.
www.shootinalabama.com
DIRECTOR
Eva Golson
LIAISON SPECIALIST
Courtney Murphy - courtney.murphy@tourism.alabama.gov
LOCATION COORDINATOR
Tommy Fell - tommy.fell@tourism.alabama.gov
FILM OFFICE COORDINATOR
Brenda Hobbie - brenda.hobbie@tourism.alabama.gov

MOBILE FILM OFFICE

164 Saint Emanuel St., Mobile, AL 36602. TEL: (251) 438-7100.
FAX: (251) 438-7104. email: golson@cityofmobile.org
DIRECTOR
Eva Golson

BIRMINGHAM/JEFFERSON FILM OFFICE

505 North 20th Street, Ste. 200, Birmingham, AL 35203.
TEL: (205) 241-8125. CEL: (205) 613-3010
FAX: (205) 324-2847.
email: mstricklin@birminghambusinessalliance.com
www.filmbirmingham.org
EXECUTIVE DIRECTOR
Mark L. Stricklin

ALASKA

THE ALASKA FILM GROUP

P.O. Box 92008, Anchorage, AK 99509-2008.
TEL/FAX: (907) 561-6445.
email: afg@alaskafilmgroup.org
www.alaskafilmgroup.org
PRESIDENT
Carolyn Muegge-Vaughan
ALASKA FILM GROUP MANAGER
Robert Arrington

ARIZONA

APACHE JUNCTION CHAMBER OF COMMERCE/ VISITOR'S CENTER

P.O. Box 1747, Apache Junction, AZ 85117.
Street Address: 567 W. Apache Trail, Apache Junction, AZ 85120.
TEL: (480) 982-3141. FAX: (480) 982-3234.
email: AJchamber@qwestoffice.net
www.apachejunctioncoc.com
OFFICE MANAGER
Jan Long

ARIZONA FILM OFFICE

1700 W. Washington, Ste. 220, Phoenix, AZ 85007.
TEL: (800) 523-6695, (602) 771-1193. FAX: (602) 771-1211.
www.azcommerce.com/film
DIRECTOR
Harry Tate
PROGRAM MANAGER
Ken Chapa

CITY OF PHOENIX FILM OFFICE

200 W. Washington, 19th Flr., Phoenix, AZ 85003.
TEL: (602) 262-4850, (602) 534-3456 (film line recording).
FAX: (602) 534-2295. email: filmphx@phoenix.gov
www.filmphoenix.com
PROGRAM MANAGER
Phil Bradstock - philip.bradstock@phoenix.gov
PROGRAM COORDINATOR
Debbie Knoblauch - debbie.knoblauch@phoenix.gov

CITY OF PRESCOTT

P.O. Box 2059, Prescott, AZ 86302. TEL: (928) 777-1204.
FAX: (928) 777-1255. www.cityofprescott.net
FILM COMMISSIONER
Wendy Bridges – wendy.bridges@prescott-az.gov

CITY OF SCOTTSDALE

One Stop Shop, 7447 E. Indian School Rd., # 100, Scottsdale, AZ 85251. TEL: (480) 312-3100. FAX: (480) 312-2888.
www.scottsdaleaz.gov
MEDIA RELATIONS MANAGER
Mike Phillips - (480) 312-7825
SPECIAL EVENTS LIAISON
Nicole Curtis - (480) 312-7673 ncurtis@scottsdaleaz.com

FLAGSTAFF FILM COMMISSION

Flagstaff Convention and Visitors Bureau, 211 W. Aspen Ave., Flagstaff, AZ 86001. TEL: (800) 217-2367, (928) 779-7645.
FAX: (928) 556-1305. www.filmflagstaff.com
CONTACT
Heather Ainardi - hainardi@flagstaffaz.gov

GLOBE MIAMI FILM COMMISSION

1360 N. Broad St., Globe, AZ 85501. PO Box 2539, Globe AZ 85502. TEL: (800) 804-5623, (928) 425-4495.
FAX: (928) 425-3410.
email: sheldon@cybertrails.com
www.globemiamichamber.com
TOURISM DIRECTOR
Ellen Kretsch

LAKE HAVASU AREA FILM COMMISSION

314 London Bridge Rd., Lake Havasu City, AZ 86403.
TEL: (800) 242-8278, (928) 453-3444. FAX: (928) 453-3344.
email: info@golakehavasu.com
www.golakehavasu.com
FILM COMMISSIONER & V.P., CVB
Jarrod Lyman - jarrod@golakehavasu.com
PROJECT MANAGER
Jessica Dietrich - jessica@golakehavasu.com

PAGE/LAKE POWELL FILM COMMISSION

c/o ARAMARK, P.O. Box 1597, Page, AZ 86040.
TEL: (928) 645-1001. FAX: (928) 645-5175.
FILM COMMISSIONER
Steve Ward - Ward-Steve@ARAMARK.com

SAFFORD/GRAHAM COUNTY REGIONAL FILM OFFICE

1111 Thatcher Blvd., Safford, AZ 85546. TEL: (888) 837-1841, (928) 428-2511. FAX: (928) 428-0744.
DIRECTOR
Sheldon Miller

SEDONA FILM OFFICE

P.O. Box 478, Sedona, AZ 86339. TEL: (928) 204-1123. FAX: (928) 204-1064.
email: info@sedonafilmoffice.com www.sedonafilmoffice.com
DIRECTOR
Lori Reinhart

SIERRA VISTA FILM OFFICE

1011 N. Coronado Dr., Sierra Vista, AZ 85635.
TEL: (800) 288-3861, (520) 417-6960. FAX: (520) 417-4890.
www.visitsierravista.com
CONTACT
Erika Breckel - erika@visitsierravista.com

TUCSON FILM OFFICE

Metropolitan Tucson Convention & Visitors Bureau, 100 S. Church Ave., Tucson, AZ 85701. TEL: (877) 311-2489, (520) 770-2151. FAX: (520) 884-629-0160.
www.filmtucson.com
DIRECTOR
Shelli Hall - shall@visitTucson.org
PRODUCTION COORDINATOR
Peter Catalanotte - pcatalanotte@visitTucson.org

WICKENBURG FILM COMMISSION

216 N. Frontier St., Wickenburg, AZ 85390. TEL: (928) 684-5479.
FAX: (928) 684-5470. email: info@wickenburgchamber.com
www.wickenburgchamber.com
EXECUTIVE DIRECTOR
Julie Brooks

YUMA FILM COMMISSION

P.O. Box 172, Yuma, AZ 85366. TEL: (928) 314-9247.
FAX: (928) 341-1616. www.filmyuma.com
PRESIDENT
Bonny Rhodes

ARKANSAS

ARKANSAS FILM COMMISSION

One State Capitol Mall, 4B-505, Little Rock, AR 72201.
TEL: (501) 682-7676. FAX: (501) 682-7394.
www.arkansasedc.com
FILM COMMISSIONER
Christopher Crane - ccrane@arkansasedc.com

EUREKA SPRINGS CITY ADVERTISING AND PROMOTION COMMISSION

121 E. Van Buren, Ste. 3B, Eureka Springs, AR 72632.
TEL. (479) 253-7333. FAX (479) 363-9380.
www.eurekasprings.org
PUBLIC RELATIONS AND PUBLICITY COORDINATOR
Ken Rundel - ken@eurekasprings.org

OZARK-FRANKLIN COUNTY FILM COMMISSION

300 W. Commercial, Ozark, AR 72949. TEL: (479) 667-5337.
FAX: 479-667-0248. email: mainstreetozark@centurytel.net
www.mainstreetozark.com
EXECUTIVE DIRECTOR, MAIN STREET OZARK
Sandy Key

CALIFORNIA

ANTELOPE VALLEY FILM OFFICE
44933 N. Fern Ave., Lancaster, CA 93534. TEL: (661) 723-6090.
FAX: (661) 723-5914. email: peast@cityoflancasterca.org
www.avfilm.com
FILM LIAISON
Pauline East

BERKELEY FILM OFFICE
2030 Addison St., #102, Berkeley, CA 94704-1204.
TEL: (800) 847-4823, (570) 549-7040. FAX: (570) 644-2052.
email: film@visitberkeley.com www.filmberkeley.com
FILM COMMISSIONER
Barbara Hillman

BIG BEAR LAKE FILM OFFICE
39707 Big Bear Blvd., P.O. Box 10000, Big Bear Lake, CA 92315. TEL: (951) 779-6700 ext. 231. FAX: (951) 779-0294.
email: bblfilm@citybigbearlake.com
www.cityofbigbearlake.com
DIRECTOR
Sheri Davis

CALAVERAS COUNTY FILM COMMISSION
P.O. Box 637, Angels Camp, CA 95222. TEL: (800) 225-3764.
FAX: (209) 736-9124. www.filmcalaveras.org
FILM COMMISSIONER
Lisa Mayo - lisa@gocalaveras.com

CALIFORNIA FILM COMMISSION
7080 Hollywood Blvd., Ste. 900, Hollywood, CA 90028.
TEL: (800) 858-4PIX. FAX: (323) 860-2972.
email: filmca@film.ca.gov www.film.ca.gov
DIRECTOR
Amy Lemisch

CATALINA ISLAND FILM COMMISSION
Catalina Island Chamber of Commerce, #1 Green Pier,
P.O. Box 217, Avalon, CA 90704. TEL: (310) 510-7649.
FAX: (310) 510-7607. email: dharris@CatalinaChamber.com
www.catalinachamber.com/media
MARKETING MANAGER & FILM LIAISON
Donna Harris

CHICO CHAMBER/BUTTE COUNTY FILM COMMISSION
c/o Chico Chamber of Commerce, 300 Salem St., Chico, CA 95926. TEL: (530) 891-5556 ext. 315. FAX: (530) 891-3613.
email: info@chicochamber.com www.chicochamber.com
COMMUNICATIONS & MARKETING MANAGER
Alice Patterson - alice@chicochamber.com

CITY OF MALIBU FILM COMMISSION
23815 Stuart Ranch Rd., Malibu, CA 90265. TEL: (310) 456-2489.
FAX: (310) 456-3356. www.ci.malibu.ca.us
FILM COMMISSIONER
Kimberly Nilsson - kim@sws-inc.com
PERMIT COORDINATOR
David Nixon - david@sws-inc.com

CITY OF WEST HOLLYWOOD
8300 Santa Monica Blvd., West Hollywood, CA 90069-4314.
TEL: (323) 848-6489. FAX: (323) 848-6561.
email: wehofilm@weho.org www.weho.org
FILM LIAISON
Terry S. House

EL DORADO, LAKE TAHOE FILM & MEDIA OFFICE
A Division of the El Dorado County Chamber of Commerce,
542 Main St., Placerville, CA 95667. TEL: (800) 457-6279,
(530) 626-4400. FAX: (530) 642-1624.
email: film@eldoradocounty.org www.filmtahoe.com
EXECUTIVE DIRECTOR
Kathleen Dodge

FILLMORE FILM COMMISSION
c/o Fillmore City Hall, 250 Central Ave., Fillmore, CA 93015.
TEL: (805) 524-1500 ext. 214. FAX: (805) 524-5707.
www.fillmoreca.com/film
FILM CONTACT
Angela Mumme - amumme@ci.fillmore.ca.us

FILML.A., INC.
1201 W. 5th St., Ste. T-800, Los Angeles, CA 90017.
TEL: (213) 977-8600. FAX: (213) 977-8610.
email: info@FilmLA.com www.FilmLA.com

FRESNO COUNTY FILM COMMISSION
2220 Tulare St., 8th Flr., Fresno, CA 93721. TEL: (559) 262-4271.
FAX: (559) 442-6969. www.filmfresno.com
FILM COMMISSIONER
Gigi Gibbs - ggibbs@co.fresno.ca.us

HUMBOLDT COUNTY FILM & DIGITAL MEDIA COMMISSION
520 E St., Eureka, CA 95501. TEL: (800) 338-7352,
(707) 444-6633. FAX: (707) 445-9652.
email: filmcom@filmhumboldt.org www.filmhumboldt.org
FILM & DIGITAL MEDIA COMMISSIONER
Mary Cruse

IMPERIAL COUNTY FILM COMMISSION
P.O. Box 1467, El Centro, CA 92244. TEL: (760) 337-4155.
FAX: (760) 337.4144. email: filmhere@sbcglobal.net
www.filmimperialcounty.com
FILM LIAISON
Charla Teeters

THE INLAND EMPIRE FILM COMMISSION
1201 Research Park Dr., Ste. 100, Riverside, CA 92507.
TEL: (951) 779-6700. FAX: (951) 779-0294.
email: info@filminlandempire.com www.filminlandempire.com
DIRECTOR
Sheri Davis - sheridavis@filminlandempire.com

KERN COUNTY FILM COMMISSION
2101 Oak St., Bakersfield, CA 93301. TEL: (800) 500-5376,
(661) 868-5376. FAX: (661) 861-2017.
email: kerninfo@co.kern.ca.us www.filmkern.com
EXECUTIVE DIRECTOR/FILM COMMISSIONER
Rick Davis
ASSISTANT FILM COMMISSIONER
Dave Hook
FILM LIAISON
Kathy Lunstrum

LAKE COUNTY MARKETING PROGRAM
255 N. Forbes St., Lakeport, CA 95453. TEL: (800) 525-3743,
(707) 263-2580. FAX: (707) 263-1012.
email: info@lakecounty.com www.lakecounty.com
DEPUTY CAO FOR ECONOMIC DEVELOPMENT
Debra Sommerfield

LONG BEACH OFFICE OF SPECIAL EVENTS & FILMING
1 World Trade Center, Ste. 300, Long Beach, CA 90831.
TEL: (562) 570-5333. FAX: (562) 570-5335.
www.filmlongbeach.com
FILM COMMISSIONER
Tasha Day - Tasha_Day@longbeach.gov
FILM COORDINATOR
Andy Witherspoon
FILM COORDINATOR
Emily Scott

MENDOCINO COUNTY FILM OFFICE
P.O. Box 1141, Fort Bragg, CA 95437. TEL: (800) 726-2780,
(707) 961-6302. FAX: (707) 964-2056.
www.filmmendocino.com
CHIEF EXECUTIVE OFFICER/FILM LIAISON
Debra De Graw - debra@filmmendocino.com

MODESTO CONVENTION & VISITORS BUREAU
1150 Ninth St., Ste. C, Modesto, CA 95354. TEL: (888) 640-8467,
(209) 526-5588. FAX: (209) 526-5586.
email: info@visitmodesto.com www.visitmodesto.com
CEO/EXECUTIVE DIRECTOR
Jennifer Mullen - jennifer@visitmodesto.com

MONTEREY COUNTY
Monterey County Film Commission, 801 Lighthouse Ave., Ste. 104, Monterey, CA 93940. TEL: (831) 646-0910.
FAX: (831) 655-9250. email: info@filmmonterey.org
www.filmmonterey.org
DIRECTOR, MARKETING & FILM PRODUCTION
Karen Nordstrand - Karen@filmmonterey.org

OAKLAND FILM OFFICE
1 Frank H. Ogawa Plaza, 9th Flr., Oakland, CA 94612.
TEL: (510) 238-4734. FAX: (510) 238-6149.
email: filmoakland@filmoakland.com www.filmoakland.com
FILM COORDINATOR
Ami Zins
ASSISTANT FILM COORDINATOR
Janet Austin

ORANGE COUNTY FILM COMMISSION
California State University, P.O. Box 6850, Fullerton, CA 92834-6850. TEL: (714) 278-7569. FAX: (714) 278-7521.
www.filmorangecounty.org
FILM COMMISSIONER
Janice Arrington - jarrington@fullerton.edu

PALM SPRINGS FILM OFFICE
500 S. Palm Canyon Dr., #222, Palm Springs, CA 92264.
TEL: (760) 864-1313. FAX: (760) 864-1319.
email: info@filminlandempire.com www.filminlandempire.com
DIRECTOR
Sheri Davis - sheridavis@filminlandempire.com
CONTACT
Colleen Gross

PASADENA FILM OFFICE
100 N. Garfield Ave., Ste. 116, Pasadena, CA 91109.
TEL: (626) 744-3964. FAX: (626)-744-4785.
www.filmpasadena.com
FILMING AND SPECIAL EVENTS MANAGER
Ariel Penn - apenn@cityofpasadena.net

FILMING COORDINATOR
Tacey Tague - ttague@cityofpasadena.net
Kristin Dewey - kdewey@cityofpasadena.net

PLACER-LAKE TAHOE FILM OFFICE
175 Fulweiler Ave., Auburn, CA 95603-4543. TEL: (877) 228-3456, (530) 889-4091. FAX: (530) 889-4095. www.placer.ca.gov/films
DIRECTOR
Beverly Lewis - blewis@placer.ca.gov

RIDGECREST REGIONAL FILM COMMISSION
139 Balsam St., Ste. 1700, Ridgecrest, CA 93555.
TEL: (800)-847-4830, (760) 375-8202. FAX: (760) 375-9850.
email: racvb@filmdeserts.com www.filmdeserts.com
FILM COMMISSIONER
Douglas Lueck

SACRAMENTO FILM COMMISSION
1608 I St., Sacramento, CA 95814. TEL: (916) 808-7777.
FAX: (916) 808-7788. www.filmsacramento.com
FILM COMMISSIONER
Lucy Steffens - lsteffens@cityofsacramento.org

SAN BENITO FILM COUNCIL
c/o John Chadwell, 1301 Hickory Court, Hollister, CA 95023.
TEL: (831) 638-1201. FAX: (831) 630-0710.
email: info1@sanbenitocountychamber.com
www.sanbenitocountychamber.com
COORDINATOR
John Chadwell - jechadwell@sbcglobal.net

SAN DIEGO FILM COMMISSION
1010 Second Ave., #1500, San Diego, CA 92101-4912.
TEL: (619) 234-3456. FAX: (619) 234-4631. www.sdfilm.com
FILM COMMISSIONER
Cathy Anderson

SAN FRANCISCO FILM COMMISSION
1 Dr. Carlton B. Goodlett Place, Rm. #473, San Francisco, CA 94102. TEL: (415) 554-6241. FAX: (415) 554-6503.
email: film@sfgov.org www.filmsf.org
CONTACT
Laurel Barsotti, Christine Munday

SAN JOSE FILM & VIDEO COMMISSION
408 Almaden Blvd., San Jose, CA 95110. TEL: (800) 726-5673, (408) 295-9600. FAX: (408) 295-3937
http://sanjose.org/film/
FILM & VIDEO REPRESENTATIVE
Michael Mulhern - (408) 792-4170 mmulhern@sanjose.org

SAN LUIS OBISPO COUNTY FILM COMMISSION
811 El Capitan Way, Ste. 200, San Luis Obispo, CA 93401.
TEL: (800) 634-1414, (805) 781-6375. FAX: (805) 543-9498.
www.sanluisobispocounty.com
ACTING EXECUTIVE DIRECTOR / FILM & TECHNOLOGY MANAGER
Dave Kastner - davek@SanLuisObispoCounty.com

SAN MATEO COUNTY FILM COMMISSION
San Mateo County Convention & Visitors Bureau, 111 Anza Blvd., Ste. 410, Burlingame, CA 94010. TEL: (800) 288-4748, (650) 348-7600. FAX: (650) 348-7687.
www.filmsanmateocounty.com
FILM COMMISSIONER
Brena Bailey - brena@smccvb.com

SANTA BARBARA COUNTY FILM COMMISSION
1601 Anacapa St., Santa Barbara, CA 93101.
TEL: (805) 966-9222 ext. 110. FAX: (805) 966-1728.
email: martine@filmsantabarbara.com
www.filmsantabarbara.com
FILM COMMISSIONER
Geoff Alexander

SANTA CLARITA VALLEY FILM OFFICE
23920 Valencia Blvd., Ste. 100, Santa Clarita, CA 91355.
TEL: (661) 284-1425. FAX: (661) 286-4001.
email: film@santa-clarita.com www.filmsantaclarita.com
FILM ASSOCIATE
Jessica Freude
FILM PERMIT SPECIALIST
Jennifer Jzyk

SANTA CRUZ COUNTY FILM COMMISSION
1211 Ocean St., Santa Cruz, CA 95060. TEL: (800) 833-3494, (831) 425-1234. FAX: (831) 425-1260.
www.santacruzfilm.org
FILM COMMISSIONER
Christina Glynn - cglynn@santacruz.org

SANTA MONICA MOUNTAINS NRA
401 W. Hillcrest Dr., Thousand Oaks, CA 91360.
TEL: (805) 370-2308. FAX: (805) 370-1851.

SHASTA COUNTY FILM COMMISSION
777 Auditorium Dr., Redding, CA 96001. TEL: (800) 874-7562, (530)-225-4105. FAX: (530) 225-4354.
www.visitredding.org
FILM COMMISSIONER
Sherry Ferguson

SIMI VALLEY FILM OFFICE
40 W. Cochran St. Ste 100. Simi Valley, CA 93065. TEL: (805) 526-6234. FAX: (805) 526-6480. email: info@simichamber.org
www.simivalleychamber.org/community/film.aspx
DIRECTOR
Janet Waitkus - janet@simivalleychamber.org

SONOMA COUNTY FILM OFFICE
Economic Development Board, 401 College Ave., Ste. D, Santa Rosa, CA 95401. TEL: (707) 565-7170. FAX: (707) 565-7231.
email: film@sonoma-county.org www.sonomacountyfilm.com

STOCKTON & SAN JOAQUIN FILM COMMISSION
445 W. Weber Ave., Ste. 220, Stockton, CA 95203.
TEL: (877) 778-6258, (209) 547-2770. FAX: (209) 466-5271.
www.visitstockton.org
FILM LIAISON
Wes Rhea wes@stocktonchamber.org

TULARE COUNTY FILM COMMISSION
5961 S. Mooney Blvd., Visalia, CA, 93277.
TEL: (559) 733-6291. FAX: (559) 730-2591.
email: lfeldste@co.tulare.ca.us
FILM COMMISSIONER
Loretta Feldstein - (559) 733-6653 ext. 4308

TUOLUMNE COUNTY FILM COMMISSION
P.O. Box 4020, Sonora, CA 95370. TEL: (800) 446-1333, (209) 533-5663. FAX: (209) 533-2502. www.tcfilm.org
EXECUTIVE DIRECTOR
Jerry Day

VALLEJO/SOLANO COUNTY FILM OFFICE
289 Mare Island Way, Vallejo, CA 94590. TEL: (800) 4-VALLEJO, (707) 642-3653. FAX: (707) 644-2206.
email: film@visitvallejo.com www.visitvallejo.com/film-office
DIRECTOR
Jim Reikowsky

VENTURA COUNTY FILM COMMISSION
1601 Carmen Dr., #215, Camarillo, CA 93010.
TEL: (805) 384-1800. FAX: (805) 384-1805.
PRESIDENT
Bruce Stenslie
OFFICE MANAGER
Kelly Noble - kelly.noble@edc-vc.com

YOSEMITE/MADERA COUNTY FILM COMMISSION
41969 Hwy., 41, Oakhurst, CA 93644. TEL: (559) 760-1143.
FAX: (559) 683-5697. www.maderafilm.com
www.yosemitefilm.com
FILM COMMISSIONER
Dave Wolin - davewolin@earthlink.net

COLORADO

BOULDER COUNTY FILM COMMISSION
2440 Pearl St., Boulder, CO 80302. TEL: (303) 938-2066.
FAX: (303) 938-2098. www.bouldercoloradousa.com
FILM COMMISSIONER, PR & PROJECTS MANAGER
Kim Farin - kim.farin@bouldercvb.com

BRECKENRIDGE FILM COMMISSION
P.O. Box 1535, Breckenridge, CO 80424. TEL: (970) 453-2265.
email: filmbreckenridge@gmail.com
www.filmbreckenridge.com
CONTACT
Ann Lukacs

CLEAR CREEK COUNTY FILM COMMISSION
P. O. Box 100, Idaho Springs, CO 80452. TEL: (866) 674-9237, (303) 567-4660. FAX: (303) 569-6296.
email: info@clearcreekcounty.org www.clearcreekcounty.org

COLORADO FILM COMMISSION
241 S. Cherokee St., Ste. E, Denver, CO 80223.
TEL: (303) 592-4065. FAX: (303) 722-1158.
email: info@coloradofilm.org www.coloradofilm.org
CONTACT
Kevin Shand - kevin.shand@coloradofilm.org

COLORADO SPRINGS FILM COMMISSION
515 S. Cascade Ave., Colorado Springs, CO 80903.
TEL: (719) 685-7635. FAX: (719) 635-4968.
www.filmcoloradosprings.com
FILM LIAISON
Ms. Floy Kennedy - floy@visitcos.com

FORT COLLINS CONVENTION AND VISITORS BUREAU
19 Old Town Square, Ste. 137, Fort Collins, CO 80524.
TEL: (970) 232-3840. FAX: (970) 232-3841.
email: information@ftcollins.com
www.visitftcollins.com
PRESIDENT & CEO
Jim Clark - jclark@ftcollins.com

GLENWOOD SPRINGS FILM COMMISSION
1102 Grand Ave., Glenwood Springs, CO 81601.
TEL: (970) 945-6589. FAX: (970) 945-1531.
www.glenwoodfilmcommission.com
REPRESENTATIVE
Marianne Virgili - marianne@glenwoodchamber.com

GREELEY/WELD COUNTY FILM COMMISSION
902 7th Ave., Greeley, CO 80631. TEL: (800) 449-3866, (970) 352-3566. FAX: (970) 352-3572. www.greeleycvb.com
CONFERENCE & TOURISM DIRECTOR
Kim Parker

SOUTHWEST COLORADO FILM COMMISSION
P.O. Box HH, Cortez, CO 81321-4059. TEL: (970) 565-8227. FAX: (970) 565-1155. email: info@swcolotravel.org
www. swcolotravel.org
CONTACT
Lynn Dyer - lynnd@mesaverdecountry.com

STEAMBOAT SPRINGS/YAMPA VALLEY FILM BOARD, INC. & NORTHWEST COLORADO FILM COMMISSION
Steamboat Springs Chamber Resort Association, P.O. Box 774408, Steamboat Springs, CO 80477. TEL: (970) 879-0880 ext 207. FAX: (970) 879-2543.
email: media@steamboatchamber.com
www.steamboatchamber.com
SPECIAL EVENTS & SPONSORSHIP DIRECTOR
Kara Givnish - (970) 875-7002

TRINIDAD/LAS ANIMAS COUNTY FILM COMMISSION
TEL: (719) 846-7324. FAX: (719) 846-4550.
www.tlac.net
FILM COMMISSIONER
Joe Tarabino - ed@tlac.net

CONNECTICUT

CONNECTICUT FILM DIVISION
One Constitution Plaza, 2nd Flr., Hartford, CT 06103.
TEL: (860) 256-2800. FAX: (860) 256-2811.
email: filminfo@ct.gov www.CTfilm.com
FILM DIVISION DIRECTOR
George Norfleet - george.norfleet@ct.gov
LOCATIONS MANAGER
Mark Dixon - mark.dixon@ct.gov
PRODUCTION SERVICES
Ellen Woolf - ellen.woolf@ct.gov

NEW MILFORD FILM COMMISSION
Town Hall, 10 Main St., New Milford, CT 06776.
TEL: (860) 210-2099. FAX: (860) 210-2623.
www.filmnewmilfordct.org
CHAIRPERSON
Keli Solomon

DELAWARE

DELAWARE FILM OFFICE
Delaware Tourism Office, 99 Kings Hwy., Dover, DE 19901.
TEL: (302) 672-6802. FAX: (302) 739-5749.
http://dedo.delaware.gov/Film.shtml
LIAISON
Linda Parkowski - linda.parkowski@state.de.us

DISTRICT OF COLUMBIA

OFFICE OF MOTION PICTURE & TELEVISION DEVELOPMENT
Government of the District of Columbia, One Judiciary Sq., 441 4th St. NW, Ste. 760, Washington, DC 20001.
TEL: (202) 727-6608. FAX: (202) 727-3246. www.film.dc.gov
DIRECTOR
Crystal Palmer - crystal.palmer@dc.gov

FLORIDA

CHARLOTTE COUNTY FLORIDA FILM OFFICE
18501 Murdock Circle, Ste. 502, Port Charlotte, FL 33948.
TEL: (941) 743-1900. FAX: (941) 743-2245.
email: Visit@charlotteharbortravel.com
www.CharlotteHarborFilm.com
FILM COMMISSIONER
Lindsey Barfield - Lindsey.Barfield@Charlottefl.com

CITY OF FORT LAUDERDALE ECONOMIC DEVELOPMENT DEPARTMENT
100 N. Andrews Ave., Fort Lauderdale, FL 33301.
TEL: (954) 828-6359. FAX: (954) 828-5599.
LIAISON
Karen Reese - Kreese@fortlauderdale.gov

COLLIER COUNTY FILM COMMISSION
755 8th Ave. S., Naples, FL 34102. TEL: (239) 659-3456.
email: collierfilm@aol.com
FILM COMMISSIONER
Maggie McCarty

DAYTONA BEACH AREA FILM OFFICE
126 E. Orange Ave., Daytona Beach, FL 32114.
TEL: (386) 255-0415 ext. 117. FAX: (386) 255-5478.
email: info@FilmDaytonaBeach.com
www.FilmDaytonaBeach.com
FILM COMMISSIONER
Janet Kersey

EMERALD COAST FILM COMMISSION
P.O. Box 609, Ft. Walton Beach, FL 32549-0609.
TEL: (800) 322-3319, (850) 651-7644. FAX: (850) 651-7149.
email: EmeraldFilm@co.okaloosa.fl.us
www.destin-fwb.com/film

FLORIDA GOVERNOR'S OFFICE OF FILM & ENTERTAINMENT
The Capitol, Ste. 2001, Tallahassee, FL 32399-0001.
TEL: (877) 352-3456, (850) 410-4765. FAX: (850) 410-4770.
www.filminflorida.com
STATE FILM COMMISSIONER
Lucia.Fishburne@MyFlorida.com
L.A. LIAISON
Susan Simms - filmflorida@earthlink.net
Los Angeles Office: (818) 508-7772.

FLORIDA KEYS & KEY WEST FILM COMMISSION
1201 White St., Ste. 102, Key West, FL 33040.
TEL: (800) FILM KEYS, (305) 293-1800. FAX: (305) 296-0788.
email: ritabrow@aol.com www.filmkeys.com
DIRECTOR
Rita Brown

FORT LAUDERDALE AREA/BROWARD COUNTY
Film & Television Commission, Broward Alliance, 110 E. Broward Blvd., Ste. 1909, Fort Lauderdale, FL 33301.
TEL: (800) 741-1420, (954) 627-0128. FAX: (954) 524-3167.
www.filmbroward.org
DIRECTOR
Elizabeth Wentworth - ewentworth@browardalliance.org

JACKSONVILLE FILM & TV OFFICE
One West Adams St., Ste. 200, Jacksonville, FL 32202.
TEL: (904) 630-2522. FAX: (904) 630-2919. www.FilmJAX.com
FILM COMMISSIONER
Todd Roobin - troobin@coj.net

LEE COUNTY FILM OFFICE
12800 University Dr., #550, Fort Myers, FL 33907-5337.
TEL: (800) 237-64444, (239) 338-3500, (239) 338-3189.
FAX: (239) 334-1106. email: VCB@leegov.com
www.FortMyersSanibel.com/film
DIRECTOR
Nancy Hamilton

MARTIN COUNTY FILM & TELEVISION COMMISSION
2401 S.E. Monterey Rd., Stuart, FL 34996. TEL: (772) 221-2352.
FAX: (772) 288-5432. email: info@film.martin.fl.us
FILM COMMISSIONER
David Graham

METRO ORLANDO FILM & ENTERTAINMENT COMMISSION
301 E. Pine St., Ste. 900, Orlando, FL 32801.
TEL: (407) 422-7159. FAX: (407) 841-9069. www.filmorlando.com
DIRECTOR
Jennifer Pennypacker
VICE PRESIDENT
Suzy Spang
COORDINATOR
Sheena Carlisle

MIAMI-DADE COUNTY
Miami-Dade Office of Film and Entertainment, 111 N.W. 1st St., Ste. 2200, Miami, FL 33128. TEL: (305) 375-3288.
FAX: (305) 375-3266.
www.filmiami.org
DIRECTOR
Jeff Peel

OCALA/MARION COUNTY FILM COMMISSION
1914 Clatterbridge Rd., Ocala, FL 34471. TEL: (352) 817-3345.
www.Ocalafilm.com
FILM COMMISSIONER
Jude Hagin - Heyjude@ocalafilm.com

OFFICE OF FILM AND EVENT PRODUCTION MANAGEMENT
1700 Convention Center Dr., Miami Beach, FL 33139.
TEL: (305) 673-7070. FAX: (305) 673-7063.
www.filmiamibeach.com
FILM & EVENT PRODUCTION MANAGER
Graham Winick - grahamwinick@miamibeachfl.gov

PALM BEACH COUNTY FILM & TV COMMISSION
1555 Palm Beach Lakes Blvd., Ste. 900, West Palm Beach, FL 33401. TEL: (800) 745-FILM, (561) 233-1000.

FAX: (561) 233-3113. www.pbfilm.com
FILM COMMISSIONER
Chuck Elderd

SARASOTA COUNTY FILM & ENTERTAINMENT OFFICE
2601 Cattlemen Rd., Ste. 201, Sarasota, FL 34232.
TEL: (888) 765-5777, (941) 309-1200 ext. 111.
FAX: (941) 309-1209. www.filmsarasota.com
DIRECTOR
Jeanne D. Corcoran - Jeanne@filmsarasota.com

ST. PETERSBURG-CLEARWATER FILM COMMISSION
13805 58th St. N, Ste. 2-200, Clearwater, FL 33760.
TEL: (727) 464-7241. www.floridasbeachfilm.com
FILM COMMISSIONER
Jennifer Parramore - jp@floridasbeachfilm.com

SPACE COAST FILM COMMISSION
430 Brevard Ave., Cocoa Village, FL 32922. TEL: (877) 572-3224.
(321) 433-4470. FAX: (321) 433-4476.
www.space-coast.com
FILM COMMISSIONER
Bonnie King - bkingfilm@aol.com

TAMPA BAY FILM COMMISSION
401 E. Jackson St., Ste. 2100, Tampa, FL 33602.
TEL: (813) 342-4058. FAX: (813) 223-0083.
www.FilmTampaBay.com
FILM COMMISSION MANAGER
Lindsey Norris - Lnorris@visittampabay.com

GEORGIA

GEORGIA FILM, MUSIC & DIGITAL ENTERTAINMENT OFFICE
75 Fifth St. NW, Ste. 1200, Atlanta, GA 30308.
TEL: (404) 962-4052. FAX: (404) 962-4053.
email: film@georgia.org www.georgia.org
DEPUTY COMMISSIONER
Bill Thompson - bthompson@georgia.org
PROJECT MANAGER
Alison Fibben - afibben@georgia.org
FILM LOCATION SPECIALIST
Lee Thomas - lthomas@georgia.org
Craig Dominey - cdominey@georgia.org

SAVANNAH FILM COMMISSION
P.O. Box 1027, Savannah, GA 31402. TEL: (912) 651-3696.
FAX: (912) 651-0982. www.savannahfilm.org
DIRECTOR, TOURISM & FILM SERVICES
Jay Self - Jay_Self@savannahga.gov
LOCATION SPECIALIST
Ryan Watterson - Ryan_Watterson@savannahga.gov

HAWAII

BIG ISLAND FILM OFFICE
County of Hawaii Department of Research and Development,
25 Aupuni St., Rm. 109, Hilo, HI 96720. Hilo: (808) 961-8366.
FAX: (808) 935-1205. Kona: (808) 327-3663.
email: film@bigisland.com www.filmbigisland.com
FILM COMMISSIONER
John Mason

HAWAII FILM OFFICE
P.O. Box 2359, Honolulu, HI 96804. TEL: (808) 586-2570.
FAX: (808) 586-2572. email: info@hawaiifilmoffice.com
www.hawaiifilmoffice.com
STATE FILM COMMISSIONER
Donne Dawson

HONOLULU FILM OFFICE
530 S. King St., Ste. 306, Honolulu, HI 96813.
TEL: (808) 768-6100. FAX: (808) 768-6102.
email: info@filmhonolulu.com www.filmhonolulu.com
FILM COMMISSIONER
Walea L. Constantinau

KAUAI FILM COMMISSION
4444 Rice St., #200, Lihue, HI 96766. TEL: (808) 241-4948.
FAX: (808) 241-6399. email: info@filmkauai.com
www.filmkauai.com
FILM COMMISSIONER
Art Umezu

MAUI FILM OFFICE
2200 Main St., Ste. 305, Wailuku, HI 96793. TEL: (808) 270-7415.
FAX: (808) 270-7995. email: info@filmmaui.com
www.filmmaui.com
FILM COMMISSIONER
Benita Brazier

IDAHO

IDAHO FILM OFFICE
700 W. State St., Box 83720, Boise, ID 83720-0093.
TEL: (800) 942-8338, (208) 334-2470. FAX: (208) 334-2631.
www.filmidaho.com
DIRECTOR
Peg Owens - peg.owens@tourism.idaho.gov
FILM SPECIALIST
Kat Haase - kat.haase@filmoffice.idaho.gov

ILLINOIS

CHICAGO FILM OFFICE
121 N. LaSalle, Rm. 806, Chicago, IL 60602. TEL: (312) 744-6415.
FAX: (312) 744-1378. email: filmoffice@cityofchicago.org
www.chicagofilmoffice.us
DIRECTOR
Richard M. Moskal - rmoskal@cityofchicago.org
PROJECT COORDINATOR
Kathleen Byrne - (312) 744-2758

ILLINOIS FILM OFFICE
100 W. Randolph, Ste. 3-400, Chicago, IL 60601.
TEL: (312) 814-3600. FAX: (312) 814-8874. www.illinoisfilm.biz
DIRECTOR
Betsy Steinberg

INDIANA

FILM INDIANA
Indiana Economic Development Corporation, One North
Capitol Ave., Ste. 700, Indianapolis, IN 46204-2288.
TEL: (317) 234-2087. FAX: (317) 232-4146.
email: filminfo@iedc.in.gov www.filmindiana.com
DIRECTOR, FILM DEVELOPMENT
Erin Newell

IOWA

CEDAR RAPIDS AREA FILM OFFICE
119 First Ave. SE, Cedar Rapids, IA 52401-5339.
TEL: (800) 735-5557, (319) 398-5009 ext 127.
FAX: (319) 398-5089. www.cedar-rapids.com
PRESIDENT
Tim Boyle - tim@cedar-rapids.com

IOWA FILM OFFICE
200 E. Grand Ave., Des Moines, IA 50309. TEL: (515) 242-4726.
FAX: (515) 242-4795. email: film@iowalifechanging.com
www.traveliowa.com/film
MANAGER
Tom Wheeler

KANSAS

KANSAS FILM COMMISSION
1000 S.W. Jackson St., Ste. 100, Topeka, KS 66612-1354.
TEL: (785) 296-2178. FAX: (785) 296-3490. www.filmkansas.com
DIRECTOR
Peter Jasso - pjasso@kansascommerce.com

WICHITA FILM COMMISSION
515 S. Main, Ste. 115, Wichita, KS 67202. TEL: (800) 288-9424,
(316) 265-2800. FAX: (316) 265-0162. www.VisitWichita.com
VICE PRESIDENT
Olivia Simmons - osimmons@VisitWichita.com
ASSISTANT TO DIRECTOR/WICHITA FILM COMMISSION
Marylin Brooks - mbrooks@gowichita.com

KENTUCKY

KENTUCKY FILM OFFICE
500 Mero St., 2400 Capital Plaza Tower, Frankfort, KY 40601.
TEL: (800) 345-6591, (502) 564-3456.
FAX: (502) 564-7588. www.kyfilmoffice.com
DIRECTOR
Todd Cassidy - Todd.Cassidy@ky.gov

LOUISIANA

CITY OF NEW ORLEANS MAYOR'S OFFICE OF FILM & VIDEO
1340 Poydras, Ste., 1000, New Orleans, LA 70112.
TEL: (504) 658-0923. FAX: (504) 658-4238.
www.filmneworleans.org
DIRECTOR
Jennifer Day - (504) 658-0923 - jjday@cityofno.com
PROJECT MANAGER
Katie Gunnell - (504) 658-4341 - kagunnell@cityofno.com
CONTACT
Carroll Morton - (504) 658-4315 - cgmorton@cityofno.com

OFFICE OF ENTERTAINMENT INDUSTRY DEVELOPMENT
1051 N. 3rd St., Ste. 173, Baton Rouge, LA 70802. P.O. Box
94185, Baton Rouge, LA 70804-9185. TEL: (225) 342-5403.
FAX: (225) 342-5554, (225) 342-5926.
email: led-entertainment@la.gov
www.ledlouisiana.com/opportunities/key-industries/entertainment.aspx
www.LouisianaEntertainment.gov

EXECUTIVE DIRECTOR, ENTERTAINMENT
Sherri McConnell - sherri.mcconnell@la.gov smcconnell@la.gov
DIRECTOR, FILM & TELEVISION
Christopher J. Stelly - chris.stelly@la.gov cstelly@la.gov

SHREVEPORT-BOSSIER FILM COMMISSION
City of Bossier City, 620 Benton Rd., P.O. Box 5337, Bossier City, LA 71171-5337. TEL: (318) 741-8503.
www.shreveport-bossierfilm.com
FILM CONTACT:
Pam Glorioso - gloriosop@bossiercity.org
City of Shreveport, 505 Travis St., Shreveport, LA 71101-3027. TEL: (318) 673-7515.
FILM CONTACT:
Arlena Acree - Arlena.Acree@shreveportla.gov

MAINE

MAINE FILM OFFICE
59 State House Station, Augusta, ME 04333.
TEL: (207) 624-7631. FAX: (207) 287-8070.
www.filminmaine.com
DIRECTOR
Lea Girardin - lea.girardin@maine.gov

MARYLAND

BALTIMORE FILM OFFICE
7 E. Redwood St., Ste. 500, Baltimore, MD 21202.
TEL: (410) 752-8632. FAX: (410) 385-0361.
www.baltimorefilm.com
DIRECTOR
Debbie Donaldson Dorsey - ddorsey@promotionandarts.com

MARYLAND FILM OFFICE
401 E. Pratt St., 14th Fl., Baltimore, MD 21202.
TEL: (800) 333-6632, (410) 767-6340. FAX: (410) 333-0044.
email: filminfo@marylandfilm.org www.marylandfilm.org
DIRECTOR
Jack Gerbes

MASSACHUSETTS

MASS FILM OFFICE
31 St. James Ave., Ste. 260, Boston, MA 02116.
TEL: (617) 254-6101. FAX: (617) 254-6108
www.mafilm.org
EXECUTIVE DIRECTOR
Nicholas Paleologos - nick@mafilm.org
DIRECTOR OF OPERATIONS
Mary Chiochios - mary@mafilm.org

MICHIGAN

MICHIGAN FILM OFFICE
300 N. Washington Square, 4th Flr., Lansing, MI 48913.
TEL: (800) 477-3456, (517) 373-3456. FAX: (517) 241-0867.
www.michiganfilmoffice.org
DIRECTOR
Janet Lockwood - info@michigan.org

MINNESOTA

MINNESOTA FILM & TV BOARD
401 N. 3rd St., Ste. 440, Minneapolis, MN 55401.
TEL: (612) 767-0095. FAX: (612) 767-2425.
email: info@mnfilmtv.org www.mnfilmtv.org
EXECUTIVE DIRECTOR
Lucinda Winter - lucinda@mnfilmtv.org
MARKETING & COMMUNICATIONS COORDINATOR
Rebecca Collins - Rebecca@mnfilmtv.org

SAINT PAUL FILM OFFICE
390 City Hall, 15 W. Kellogg Blvd., Saint Paul, MN 55102.
TEL: (651) 266-8524. FAX: (651) 266-8513.
FILM AND TV LIAISON
Joe Spencer - joe.spencer@ci.stpaul.mn.us

MISSISSIPPI

CANTON FILM OFFICE
P.O. Box 53, Canton, MS 39046. TEL: (800) 844-3369, (601) 859-1307. FAX: (601) 859-0346.
email: canton@cantontourism.com
www.cantontourism.com
EXECUTIVE DIRECTOR
Jo Ann Gordon - jgordon@cantontourism.com

COLUMBUS FILM COMMISSION
P.O. Box 789, 318 B 7th St., North Columbus, MS 39703.
TEL: (800) 327-2686, (662) 329-1191. FAX: (662) 329-8969.
email: ccvb@columbus-ms.org
www.columbus-ms.org
DIRECTOR
James Tsismanakis - james@columbus-ms.org

GREENWOOD CONVENTION & VISITORS BUREAU
P.O. Drawer 739, Greenwood, MS 38935. TEL: (800) 748-9064, (662) 453-9197. FAX: (662) 453-5526. email: info@gcvb.com
www.greenwoodms.org
DIRECTOR
Paige Hunt

MISSISSIPPI FILM OFFICE
Street Address: Woolfolk State Office Building, 501 N. West St., 5th Flr., Jackson, MS 39201. Mailing: P.O. Box 849, Jackson, MS 39205. TEL: (601) 359-3297.
FAX: (601) 359-5048. www.filmMississippi.org
DIRECTOR
Ward Emling - wemling@mississippi.org
ASSOCIATE MANAGER
Nina Parikh - nparikh@mississippi.org
OFFICE MANAGER
Betty Black - bblack@mississippi.org

NATCHEZ FILM COMMISSION
640 S. Canal St., Box G, Natchez, MS 39120.
TEL: (800) 647-6724, (601) 446-6345. FAX: (601) 442-0814.
www.visitnatchez.org
CONTACT
Sally Durkin - sdurkin@visitnatchez.org
Connie Taunton - ctaunton@visitnatchez.org

TUPELO FILM COMMISSION
399 E. Main St., P.O. Drawer 47, Tupelo, MS 38802.
TEL: (800) 533-0611, (662) 841-6599. FAX: (662) 841-6558.
www.tupelo.net www.visitmississippi.org/film
FILM COMMISSIONER
Pat Rasberry - prasberry@tupelo.net

VICKSBURG FILM COMMISSION
P.O. Box 110, Vicksburg, MS 39181. TEL: (800) 221-3536, (601) 636-9421. FAX: (601) 636-9475.
www.visitvicksburg.com
EXECUTIVE DIRECTOR
Bill Seratt - bill@vicksburgcvb.org

MISSOURI

FILM COMMISSION OF GREATER KANSAS CITY
1906 Wyandotte, Kansas City, MO 64108.
TEL: (816) 471-2215. FAX: (816) 471-6500.
email: film@visitkc.com
FILM COMMISSION CHAIR
Teri Rogers - contact@kcfilm.com

MISSOURI FILM COMMISSION
Missouri Film Office, 301 W. High St., #720, Jefferson City, MO 65101. TEL: (573) 522-1288.
email: mofilm@missouri.edu www.mofilm.org
DIRECTOR
Jerry Jones
ASSISTANT DIRECTOR
Andrea Sporcic

MONTANA

BILLINGS CHAMBER CVB FILM LIAISON OFFICE
P.O. Box 31177, Billings, MT 59107. TEL: (800) 711-2630, (406) 245-4111. FAX: (406) 245-7333.
email: info@billingschamber.com
www.billingscvb.visitmt.com
DIRECTOR
Joan E. Kronebusch

CITY OF BUTTE FILM LIAISON OFFICE
1000 George St., Butte, MT 59701. TEL: (800) 735-6814, (406) 723-3177. FAX: (406) 723-1215.
email: chamber@buttecvb.com
www.buttecvb.com
FILM LIAISON TO STATE COMMISSIONER
Connie Kenney
DIRECTOR
Marko Lucich

GREAT FALLS REGION FILM LIAISON
City of Great Falls, P.O. Box 5021, 2 Park Dr. S, Great Falls, MT 59401. TEL: (406) 455-8450. FAX: (406) 727-0005.
FILM LIAISON
Joyce Thares - jthares@greatfallsmt.net

MONTANA FILM OFFICE
301 S. Park Ave., Helena, MT 59620. TEL: (800) 553-4563, (406) 841-2876. FAX: (406) 841-2877.
email: montanafilm@mt.gov www.montanafilm.com
DIRECTOR
Sten Iversen
LOCATION COORDINATOR
John Ansotegui
MULTIMEDIA AND PROJECT COORDINATOR
Sage DuBois

NEBRASKA

NEBRASKA FILM OFFICE
P.O. Box 98907, Lincoln, NE 68509. TEL: (800) 228-4307, (402) 471-3746. FAX: (402) 471-3778.
email: info@filmnebraska.org www.filmnebraska.org
FILM OFFICER
Laurie J. Richards - lrichards@neb.rr.com

OMAHA FILM COMMISSION
1001 Farnam St., Ste. 200, Omaha, NE 68102.
TEL: (866) 937-6624, (402) 444-4660. FAX: (402) 444-4511.
www.visitomaha.com
DIRECTOR
Kathy Rocco - Krocco@visitomaha.com

NEVADA

NEVADA FILM OFFICE-LAS VEGAS
555 E. Washington Ave., Ste. 5400, Las Vegas, NV 89101-1078. TEL: (877) 638-3456, (702) 486-2711. FAX: (702) 486-2712.
email: lvnfo@nevadafilm.com www.nevadafilm.com
DIRECTOR
Charles Geocaris

NEVADA FILM OFFICE RENO/TAHOE
108 E. Proctor St., Carson City, NV 89701. TEL: (800) 336-1600, (775) 687-1814. FAX: (775) 687-4450.
email: ccnfo@bizopp.state.nv.us www.nevadafilm.com

NEW HAMPSHIRE

NEW HAMPSHIRE FILM & TELEVISION OFFICE
20 Park St., Concord, NH 03301. TEL: (603) 271-2220.
FAX: (603) 271-3163. email: film@nh.gov www.nh.gov/film
DIRECTOR
Matthew W. Newton

NEW JERSEY

FILM OFFICE OF THE ATLANTIC CITY CONVENTION & VISITORS AUTHORITY
2314 Pacific Ave., Atlantic City, NJ 08401. TEL: (609) 449-7151.
FAX: (609) 345- 2200. www.atlanticcitynj.com
DIRECTOR, TOURISM
Heather Colache - hcolache@accva.com

NEW JERSEY MOTION PICTURE & TV COMMISSION
P.O. Box 47023, 153 Halsey St., 5th Flr., Newark, NJ 07101.
TEL: (973) 648-6279. FAX: (973) 648-7350.
email: njfilm@njfilm.org www.njfilm.org
DIRECTOR
Steven Gorelick

NEW MEXICO

CITY OF ALBUQUERQUE FILM OFFICE
Economic Development Department, P.O. Box 1293, Albuquerque, NM 87103. TEL: (505) 768-3283.
FAX: (505) 768-3280. www.filmabq.com/
FILM LIAISON
Ann Lerner - alerner@cabq.gov

LAS CRUCES FILM COMMISSION
P.O. Box 20000, Las Cruces, NM 88004. TEL: (575) 202-5604.
www.las-cruces-film.org
FILM LIAISON
Bill McCamey - (575) 202-5604 bmccamey@las-cruces.org
Office Address: Las Cruces Convention & Visitors Bureau
211 N. Water St. Las Cruces, NM 88001. TEL: (575) 541-2444.
FAX: (575) 541-2164. email: cvb@lascrucescvb.org
OFFICE MANAGER
Anna Maya - amaya@las-cruces.org

NEW MEXICO FILM OFFICE
c/o The Jean Cocteau, 418 Montezuma Ave., Santa Fe, NM 87501. TEL: (800) 545-9871, (505) 476-5600.
FAX: (505) 476-5601. email: info@nmfilm.com
www.nmfilm.com
DIRECTOR
Lisa Strout
DEPUTY DIRECTOR
Jennifer Schwalenberg
NM FILMMAKERS PROGRAM
Trish Lopez

OTERO COUNTY FILM OFFICE
1301 N. White Sands Blvd., Alamogordo, NM, 88310.
TEL: (575) 439-4353. FAX: (575) 437-7139.
www.filmotero.com
FILM LIAISON
K. Jan Wafful - jan@filmotero.com

SANTA FE FILM OFFICE
P.O. Box 909, Santa Fe, NM 87504-0909.
TEL: (800) 777-2489, (505) 955-6200.
FAX: (505) 955-6222.
email: scenter@santafe.org www.santafe.org

TAOS COUNTY FILM COMMISSION
121 N. Taos Plaza, Taos, NM 87571. TEL: (505) 751-3646.
FAX: (505) 751-3518. email: info@filmtaos.com
www.filmtaos.com
FILM COMMISSIONER
Jonathan Slator

NEW YORK

BUFFALO NIAGARA FILM COMMISSION
617 Main St., Ste. 200, Buffalo, NY 14203. TEL: (888) 228-3369 ext. 227, (716) 852-0511 ext. 227. FAX: (716) 675-3307.
www.filmbuffaloniagara.com
FILM COMMISSIONER
Tim Clark - clark@buffalocvb.org

CAPITAL-SARATOGA FILM COMMISSION
25 Quackenbush Sq., Albany, NY 12207. TEL: (800) 258-3582, (518) 434-1217 ext. 100. FAX: (518) 434-0887.
email: info@capital-saratogafilm.com
www.capital-saratogafilm.com
DIRECTOR
Deborah A. Goedeke

CITY OF NEW YORK, MAYOR'S OFFICE OF FILM, THEATRE & BROADCASTING
1697 Broadway, Ste. 602, New York, NY 10019.
TEL: (212) 489-6710. FAX: (212)307-6237
www.nyc.gov/film
COMMISSIONER
Katherine Oliver

HUDSON VALLEY FILM COMMISSION
P.O. Box 1406, 86 Mill Hill Rd., Woodstock, NY 12498.
TEL: (845) 679-4265. FAX: (509) 479-5414.
email: info@hudsonvalleyfilmcommission.org
www.hudsonvalleyfilmcommission.org
FILM COMMISSIONER
Laurent Rejto

NASSAU COUNTY FILM OFFICE
One West St., Mineola, NY 11501. TEL: (516) 571-3168.
FAX: (516) 571-6195.
www.nassaucountyny.gov/agencies/filmcom/index.html
DIRECTOR
Debra Markowitz

NEW YORK STATE GOVERNOR'S OFFICE FOR MOTION PICTURE & TELEVISION DEVELOPMENT
633 Third Ave., 33rd Flr., New York, NY 10017.
TEL: (212) 803-2330. FAX: (212) 803-2339.
email: NYFILM@empire.state.ny.us www.nylovesfilm.com
EXECUTIVE DIRECTOR
Pat Swinney Kaufman

ROCHESTER/FINGER LAKES FILM & VIDEO OFFICE
45 East Ave., Ste. 400, Rochester, NY 14604.
TEL: (585) 279-8308. FAX: (585) 232-4822.
www.filmrochester.org
EXECUTIVE DIRECTOR
June Foster
DEPUTY DIRECTOR
Nora Brown - nbrown@visitrochester.com

SUFFOLK COUNTY FILM COMMISSION
H. Lee Dennison Bldg., 2nd Fl., 100 Veterans Memorial Hwy., Hauppauge, NY 11788. TEL: (631) 853-4747. FAX: (631) 853-4888.
www.suffolkcountyfilmcommission.com
DIRECTOR
Michelle Isabelle-Stark

WESTCHESTER COUNTY OFFICE OF FILM & TELEVISION
Michaelian Office Bldg., 148 Martine Ave., Rm. 107, White Plains, NY 10601. TEL: (914) 995-2917. FAX: (914) 995-2948.
www.westchestergov.com/filmoffice
DIRECTOR
Iris G. Stevens - iis3@westchestergov.com

YONKERS FILM OFFICE
Mayor's Office of Film and Television, 87 Nepperhan Ave., Rm. 308, Yonkers, NY 10701. TEL: (914) 377-6549.
FAX: (914) 377-6953.
www.cityofyonkers.com www.yonkersny.gov
DIRECTOR OF FILM AND TELEVISION DEVELOPMENT
DeForest L. Raphael - deforest.raphael@yonkersny.gov

NORTH CAROLINA

CHARLOTTE REGIONAL FILM COMMISSION
1001 Morehead Square Dr., Ste. 200, Charlotte, NC 28203.
TEL: (800) 554-4373, (704) 347-8942. FAX: (704) 347-8981.

www.charlotteusa.com
DIRECTOR
Beth Petty - bpetty@charlotteusa.com

DURHAM CONVENTION & VISITORS BUREAU
101 E. Morgan St., Durham, NC 27701. TEL: (800) 446-8604, (919) 680-8313. FAX: (919) 680-8353.
www.durham-nc.com
DIRECTOR VISITOR SERVICES
Carolyn Carney - carolyn@durham-cvb.com

NORTH CAROLINA FILM OFFICE
4324 Mail Service Center, Raleigh, NC 27699-4324. Physical Address: 301. N. Wilmington St., Raleigh, NC 27601.
TEL: (866) 468-2273, (919) 733-9900. FAX: (919) 715-0151.
www.ncfilm.com
DIRECTOR
Aaron Syrett - asyrett@nccommerce.com aaron@ncfilm.com

PIEDMONT TRIAD FILM COMMISSION
7025 Albert Pick Rd., Ste. 303, Greensboro, NC 27409.
TEL: (336) 393-0001. FAX: (336) 668-3749.
email: info@piedmontfilm.com www.piedmontfilm.com
DIRECTOR
Rebecca Clark

WESTERN NORTH CAROLINA FILM COMMISSION & CREATIVE COMMERCE COMMISSION
134 Wright Brothers Way, Fletcher, NC 28732.
TEL: (828) 687-7234. FAX: (828) 687-7552. www.wncfilm.com
FILM COMMISSIONER
Amanda Baranski - abaranski@awnc.org

WILMINGTON REGIONAL FILM COMMISSION
1223 North 23rd St., Wilmington, NC 28405.
TEL: (910) 343-3456. FAX: (910) 343-3457.
email: commish@wilmingtonfilm.com www.wilmingtonfilm.com
DIRECTOR
Johnny Griffin

NORTH DAKOTA

NORTH DAKOTA FILM COMMISSION
Century Center, 1600 E. Century Ave., Ste. 2, P.O. Box 2057, Bismarck, ND, 58502-2057. TEL: (800) 435-5663, (701) 328-2525. FAX: (701) 328-4878. www.ndtourism.com
FILM COMMISSIONER
Sara Otte Coleman - socoleman@nd.gov
OUTDOORS PROMOTION/FILM COMMISSION
Mark Zimmerman

OHIO

GREATER CINCINNATI & NORTHERN KENTUCKY FILM COMMISSION
602 Main St., Ste. 712, Cincinnati, OH 45202.
TEL: (513) 784-1744. FAX: (513) 768-8963.
email: info@film-cincinnati.org www.filmcincinnati.com
EXECUTIVE DIRECTOR
Kristen Erwin - kje@film-cincinnati.org

GREATER CLEVELAND FILM COMMISSION
1301 East 9th St., Ste. 120, Cleveland, OH 44114-1817.
TEL: (888) 746-FILM, (216) 623-3910. FAX: (216) 623-0876.
www.clevelandfilm.com
EXECUTIVE DIRECTOR
Ivan Schwarz
PRODUCTION COORDINATOR
Sara Dering - SDering@clevelandfilm.com
DIRECTOR OF DEVELOPMENT
Jeanne Romanoff
OFFICE MANAGER
Kammeron Hughes

OKLAHOMA

OKLAHOMA FILM AND MUSIC OFFICE
120 N. Robinson, Ste. 600, Oklahoma City, OK 73102.
TEL: (800) 766-3456, (405) 230-8440. FAX: (405) 230-8640.
www.oklahomafilm.org
DIRECTOR
Jill Simpson - jill@oklahomafilm.org

OREGON

OREGON GOVERNOR'S OFFICE OF FILM & TELEVISION
One World Trade Center, 121 S.W. Salmon St., Ste. 1205, Portland, OR 97204. TEL: (503) 229-5832. FAX: (503) 229-6869.
email: shoot@oregonfilm.org www.oregonfilm.org
EXECUTIVE DIRECTOR
Vince Porter - vince@oregonfilm.org
SENIOR PROJECT MANAGER
Bob Schmaling - bob@oregonfilm.org

PENNSYLVANIA

GREATER PHILADELPHIA FILM OFFICE
Land Title Bldg., 100 S. Broad St., Ste. 600, Philadelphia, PA 19110. TEL: (215) 686-2668. FAX: (215) 686-3659.
email: mail@film.org www.film.org
EXECUTIVE DIRECTOR
Sharon Pinkenson - sharon@film.org

PENNSYLVANIA FILM OFFICE
Department of Community and Economic Development, Commonwealth Keystone Bldg., 400 North St., 4th Flr., Harrisburg, PA 17120-0225. TEL: (717) 783-3456.
FAX: (717) 787-0687. www.filminpa.com
DIRECTOR
Jane Saul - jsaul@state.pa.us

PITTSBURGH FILM OFFICE
The Century Building, 130 7th St., Ste. 202, Pittsburgh, PA 15222. TEL: (888) 744-3456, (412) 261-2744.
FAX: (412) 471-7317. email: info@pghfilm.org
www.pghfilm.org
DIRECTOR
Dawn Keezer
ASSISTANT DIRECTOR
Jessica Conner

RHODE ISLAND

RHODE ISLAND FILM & TV OFFICE
Division of the Rhode Island State Council on the Arts
One Capitol Hill, 3rd Flr., Providence, RI 02908.
Hotline: (401) 222-6666. TEL: (401) 222-3456.
FAX: (401) 222-3018.
www.film.ri.gov
EXECUTIVE DIRECTOR
Steven Feinberg - steven@arts.ri.gov
ASSISTANT TO THE EXECUTIVE DIRECTOR
Carol Conley - CConley@arts.ri.gov

SOUTH CAROLINA

SOUTH CAROLINA FILM COMMISSION
1205 Pendleton St., Rm. 529, Columbia, SC 29201.
TEL: (803) 737-0490. FAX: (803) 737-3104.
email: filmsc@scprt.com www.filmsc.com
COMMISSIONER
Jeff Monks
SENIOR PROJECTS MANAGER
Dan Rogers - danrogers@scprt.com

SOUTH DAKOTA

SOUTH DAKOTA FILM OFFICE
711 E. Wells Ave., Pierre, SD 57501. TEL: (605) 773-3301.
FAX: (605) 773-3256. www.FilmSD.com
FILM & MEDIA RELATIONS REPRESENTATIVE
Emily Currey - FilmSD@state.sd.us

TENNESSEE

EAST TENNESSEE TELEVISION AND FILM COMMISSION
17 Market Sq., #201, Knoxville, TN 37902. TEL: (865) 246-2629.
FAX: (865) 523-2071. www.ettfc.com
FILM COMMISSIONER
Michael D. Barnes - mbarnes@knoxvillechamber.com
PROJECT COORDINATOR
Thomas Duncan - tduncan@knoxvillechamber.com

FILMNASHVILLE
Nashville Convention & Visitors Bureau, One Nashville Pl., 150 4th Ave. N, Ste. G-250, Nashville, TN 37219. TEL: (615) 573-5238.
email: Tessa.Atkins@nashville.gov
www.FilmNashville.org
PRESIDENT
Ken Goddard

MEMPHIS & SHELBY COUNTY FILM AND TELEVISION COMMISSION
50 Peabody Pl., Ste. 250, Memphis, TN 38103.
TEL: (901) 527-8300. FAX: (901) 527-8326.
www.filmmemphis.org
FILM COMMISSIONER
Linn Sitler
DEPUTY FILM COMMISSIONER
Sharon Fox O'Guin

NASHVILLE FILM OFFICE
Mayor's Office of Economic and Community Development, Metropolitan Courthouse, One Public Square, Ste. 102, Nashville, TN 37201. TEL: (615) 862-6024. FAX: (615) 862-6025.
DIRECTOR OF FILM
Marilyn Edwards - marilyn.edwards@nashville.gov

TENNESSEE FILM, ENTERTAINMENT & MUSIC COMMISSION
312 8th Ave. N, Tenn. Tower, 9th Flr., Nashville, TN 37243.
TEL: (877) 818-3456, (615) 741-3456. FAX: (615) 741-5554.
email: tn.film@tn.gov www.tn.gov/film
EXECUTIVE DIRECTOR
Perry Gibson
ASSISTANT TO DIRECTOR
Gisela Moore
PROJECT MANAGER & LOCATION COORDINATOR
Bob Raines
MUSIC & MEDIA COORDINATOR
Nathan Lux

TEXAS

AMARILLO FILM COMMISSION
1000 S. Polk St., Amarillo, TX 79101. TEL: (800) 692-1338, (806) 342-2012. FAX: (806) 373-3909. www.visitamarillotx.com
DIRECTOR, TOURISM AND FILM
Jutta Matalka, CTP - jutta@visitamarillotx.com

AUSTIN FILM OFFICE
301 Congress Ave., Ste. 200, Austin, TX 78701.
TEL: (800) 926-ACVB, (512) 583-7229.
www.austinfilmcommission.com
DIRECTOR
Gary Bond - gbond@austintexas.org

BROWNSVILLE BORDER FILM COMMISSION
P.O. Box 911, City Hall, Brownsville, TX 78520.
TEL: (956) 548-6176. FAX: (956) 542-7803.
www.filmbrownsville.com
FILM COMMISSIONER
Peter Goodman - peter@cob.us

DALLAS FILM COMMISSION
325 N. St. Paul, Ste. 700, Dallas, TX 75201. TEL: (214) 571-1050.
FAX: (214) 665-2907. email: info@filmdfw.com www.filmdfw.com
DIRECTOR
Janis Burklund
ASSISTANT DIRECTOR
Meg Gould
LOCATION COORDINATOR
Jan Thomas

EL PASO FILM COMMISSION
One Civic Center Plaza, El Paso, TX 79901.
TEL: (915) 534-0698, (800) 351-6024. FAX: (915) 532-2963.
www.elpasocvb.com/film
FILM COMMISSIONER
Susie Gaines - sgaines@elpasocvb.com
FILM COMMISSION COORDINATOR
Leah Ramirez - leahramirez@elpasocub.com

HOUSTON FILM COMMISSION
901 Bagby, Ste. 100, Houston, TX 77002. TEL: (800) 365-7575, (713) 437-5251. FAX: (713) 223-3816.
www.houstonfilmcommission.com
EXECUTIVE DIRECTOR
Rick Ferguson - rferguson@ghcvb.org
DEPUTY DIRECTOR
Alfred Cervantes - acervantes@ghcvb.org

SAN ANTONIO FILM COMMISSION
203 S. St. Mary's St., 2nd Flr., San Antonio, TX 78205.
TEL: (210) 207-6730. FAX: (210) 207-6843.
email: filmsa@filmsanantonio.com www.filmsanantonio.com
DIRECTOR
Drew Mayer-Oakes - drew@filmsanantonio.com
LOCATION COORDINATOR
Janet Vasquez - (210) 207-6777 janetv@filmsanantonio.com

SOUTH PADRE ISLAND FILM COMMISSION
7355 Padre Blvd., South Padre Island, TX 78597.
TEL: (800) 657-2373, (956) 761-3005 ext. 108.
www.sopadre.com/film
FILM COMMISSION
Mary K. Hancock - maryk@sopadre.com

TEXAS ASSOCIATION OF FILM/TAPE PROFESSIONALS
2727 Inwood Rd., Dallas, TX 75235. TEL: (877) 256-9298, (214) 561-7330. FAX: (214) 561-7332. email: info@taftp.com
www.taftp.com
OFFICE MANAGER
Sabra Young

TEXAS FILM COMMISSION
P.O. Box 13246, Austin, TX 78711. TEL: (512) 463-9200.
FAX: (512) 463-4114. email: film@governor.state.tx.us
www.texasfilmcommission.com
DIRECTOR
Bob Hudgins
DEPUTY DIRECTOR, FILM FRIENDLY TEXAS PROGRAM MANAGER
Carol Pirie

UTAH

KANAB/KANE COUNTY FILM COMMISSION
78 S. 100 E., Kanab, UT 84741. TEL: (800) SEE-KANE, (435) 644-5033. FAX: (435) 644-5923. www.kaneutah.com
DIRECTOR
Kay Giles

MOAB TO MONUMENT VALLEY FILM COMMISSION
217 East Center St., Moab, UT 84532. TEL: (435) 259-4341.
FAX: (435) 259-4135. email: tara@moabcity.org
www.moabcity.org/filmcommission
FILM COMMISSION DIRECTOR
Tara Campbell

PARK CITY FILM COMMISSION
P.O. Box 1630, Park City, UT 84060. TEL: (800) 453-1360.
FAX: (435) 649-4132. www.parkcityinfo.com
COMMISSIONER
Sue Kapis

UTAH FILM COMMISSION
300 N. State St., Salt Lake City, UT 84114. TEL: (800) 453-8824, (801) 538-8740. FAX: (801) 538-1397. email: film@utah.gov
DIRECTOR
Marshall D. Moore - mdmoore@utah.gov
MARKETING & CREATIVE EXECUTIVE
Ricardo Flores - rcflores@utah.gov

UTAH VALLEY FILM COMMISSION
111 South University Ave., Provo, UT 84601.
TEL: (800) 222-8824, (801) 851-2110. FAX: (801) 851-2109.
www.filmutahvalley.com
SALES MANAGER, FILM COMMISSION
Melissa Nielson - melissan@utahvalley.org

VERMONT

VERMONT FILM COMMISSION
10 Baldwin St., Montpelier, VT 05633-2001.
TEL: (802) 828-3618. FAX: (802) 828-0607.
email: vermontfilm@vermontfilm.com www.vermontfilm.com
EXECUTIVE DIRECTOR
Joe Bookchin
DEPUTY DIRECTOR
Perry Schafer

VIRGINIA

CENTRAL VIRGINIA FILM INSTITUTE
c/o New Millennium Studios, One New Millennium Dr., Petersburg, VA 23805. TEL: (804) 898-2496.
FAX: (804) 862-1200. email: info@cvafilm.org
www.cvafilm.org
EXECUTIVE DIRECTOR
Kay Ingram - kay.ingram@cvafilm.org

CITY OF VIRGINIA BEACH - RESORT MANAGEMENT & SPECIAL EVENTS OFFICE
2101 Parks Ave., Ste. 502, Virginia Beach, VA 23451.
TEL: (757) 385-4800. FAX: (757) 422-3666.
email: vbresort@vbgov.com www.vbgov.com
CONTACT
Heather Bryan, Bill Kelly

VIRGINIA FILM OFFICE
901 E. Byrd St., Richmond, VA 23219. TEL: (800) 854-6233, (804) 545-5530. FAX: (804) 545-5531.
email: vafilm@virginia.org www.film.virginia.org
DIRECTOR
Rita McClenny - rmcclenny@virginia.org
MARKETING MANAGER
Rebecca Beckstoffer - bbeckstoffer@virginia.org
LOCATION MANAGER
Andrew Edmunds - aedmunds@virginia.org

WASHINGTON STATE

CITY OF SEATTLE
Mayor's Office of Film & Music, 700 Fifth Ave., Ste. 5752, P.O. Box 94708, Seattle, WA 98124-4708. TEL: (206) 684-0903.
FAX: (206) 684-0379. www.seattle.gov/filmandmusic
DIRECTOR
James Keblas - james.keblas@seattle.gov

WASHINGTONFILMWORKS
1218 Third Ave., Ste. 1515, Seattle, WA 98101.
TEL: (206) 264-0667. FAX: (206) 382-4343.
email: info@washingtonfilmworks.org
www.washingtonfilmworks.org
EXECUTIVE DIRECTOR
Amy Lillard Dee

WEST VIRGINIA

WEST VIRGINIA FILM OFFICE
c/o WV Division of Tourism, 90 MacCorkle Ave. SW, South

Charleston, WV 25303. TEL: (866) 6WV-FILM, (304) 558-2200.
FAX: (304) 558-1662. www.wvfilm.com
DIRECTOR
Pam Haynes - phaynes@wvfilm.com

WISCONSIN

VISIT MILWAUKEE
648 N. Plankinton, Ste. 425, Milwaukee, WI 53203-2501.
TEL: (800) 554-1448, (414) 273-7222. FAX: (414) 273-5596.
email: info@milwaudkee.org www.visitmilwaukee.org
V.P., PUBLIC RELATIONS
David A. Fantle - DFantle@milwaukee.org

FILM WISCONSIN, INC.
648 N. Plankinton Ave., Ste. 425, Milwaukee, WI 53203.
TEL: (414) 287-4251. FAX: (414) 273-5596.
email: ScottRobbe@gmail.com email: FilmWisconsin@gmail.com
www.filmwisconsin.net
EXECUTIVE DIRECTOR
Scott Robbe

WYOMING

CHEYENNE AREA FILM OFFICE
One Depot Sq., 121 W. 15th St., Ste. 202, Cheyenne, WY
82001. TEL: (800) 426-5009, (307) 778-3133.
FAX: (307) 778-3190. www.cheyenne.org
DIRECTOR
Darren Rudloff - darren@cheyenne.org

JACKSON HOLE CHAMBER OF COMMERCE
P.O. Box 550, Jackson, WY 83001. TEL: (307) 733-3316.
FAX: (307) 733-5585. www.jacksonholechamber.com
TOURISM MANAGER
Heather Falk - heather@jacksonholechamber.com

WYOMING FILM OFFICE
1520 Etchepare Circle, Cheyenne, WY 82007.
TEL: (800) 458-6657, (307) 777-3400.
FAX: (307) 777-2877.
email: info@filmwyoming.com www.filmwyoming.com
www.filmwyoming.blogspot.com
COMMISSIONER
Michell Howard

U.S. TERRITORIES & PROTECTORATES

PUERTO RICO FILM COMMISSION
355 FD Roosevelt Ave., Ste. 106, Hato Rey, PR 00918.
TEL: (787) 758-4747 ext. 2250. FAX: (787) 756-5706.
www.puertoricofilm.com
EXECUTIVE DIRECTOR
Mariella Perez Serrano, Ph.D. - mperez@puertoricofilm.com

U.S. VIRGIN ISLANDS FILM PROMOTION OFFICE
P.O. Box 6400, St. Thomas, U.S.V.I. 00804.
TEL: (800) 372-USVI, (340) 774-8784. FAX: (340) 774-4390.
www.filmusvi.com
FILM COMMISSIONER
Lawrence T. Boschulte - (340) 771-1735 (cell)

FEDERAL GOVERNMENT OFFICES AND FILM & MEDIA SERVICES

DEPARTMENT OF AGRICULTURE

BROADCAST MEDIA & TECHNOLOGY CENTER
1400 Independence Ave., 1614 South Bldg., USDA, Washington, DC 20250-1300. TEL: (202) 720-6072, (202) 720-3068. FAX: (202) 720-5773. www.usda.gov
DIRECTOR
David Black - david.black@usda.gov

DEPARTMENT OF COMMERCE

OFFICE OF PUBLIC AFFAIRS—MEDIA SECTION
Office of the Secretary, 1401 Constitution Ave., N.W., Washington, DC 20230. TEL: (202) 482-4883. FAX: (202) 482-5168. www.commerce.gov
CONTACT
Kevin Griffis - kgriffis@doc.gov

INTERNATIONAL TRADE ADMINISTRATION—OFFICE OF SERVICE INDUSTRIES
Information Industries Division—International Trade in Film & Recorded Music, 1401 Constitution Ave., Rm. H-1124, Washington, DC 20230. TEL: (202) 482-4705. FAX: (202) 482-2669.
INTERNATIONAL TRADE SPECIALIST
David F. Long

NATIONAL TELECOMMUNICATIONS AND INFORMATION ADMINISTRATION
Herbert C. Hoover Bldg., U.S. Department of Commerce/NTIA, 1401 Constitution Ave., NW, Washington, D.C. 20230. TEL: (202) 482-7002. FAX: (202) 219-2077. www.ntia.doc.gov
COMMUNICATIONS DIRECTOR
Todd Sedmak - tsedmak@ntia.doc.gov

NATIONAL TECHNICAL INFORMATION SERVICE
National Audiovisual Center, 5285 Port Royal Rd., Springfield, VA 22161. Customer Contact Center: 800-553-NTIS (6847). www.ntis.gov
CONTACT
Steve Needle - sneedle@ntis.gov

DEPARTMENT OF DEFENSE

ENTERTAINMENT MEDIA
Office of the Assistant Secretary of Defense (Public Affairs), Rm. 2E592, The Pentagon, Washington, DC 20301-1400. TEL: (703) 695-2936. FAX: (703) 695-1149.
SPECIAL ASSISTANT FOR ENTERTAINMENT MEDIA DEPARTMENT OF DEFENSE
Philip M. Strub

DOCUMENTARY FILMS
Office of the Assistant Secretary of Defense (Public Affairs), Rm. 2E565, The Pentagon, Washington, DC 20301. TEL: (703) 695-0169. FAX: (703) 692-5026.
CHIEF, AUDIOVISUAL DIVISION
Terry Mitchell

U.S. ARMY, CHIEF OF PUBLIC AFFAIRS
10880 Wilshire Blvd., Ste. 1250, Los Angeles, CA 90024-4101. TEL: (310) 235-7621. FAX: (310) 235-6075.
DIRECTOR, PUBLIC AFFAIRS & MILITARY TECHNICAL ADVISOR
Lt. Col. Joseph Todd Breasseale - joseph.breasseale@us.army.mil

MARINE CORPS PUBLIC AFFAIRS
10880 Wilshire Blvd., Ste. 1230, Los Angeles, CA 90024. TEL: (310) 235-7272. FAX: (310) 235-7274. email: lapao@covad.net
DIRECTOR
Colonel Bryan Salas

U.S. AIR FORCE, MOTION PICTURE AND TELEVISION LIAISON OFFICE
10880 Wilshire Blvd., Ste. 1240, Los Angeles, CA 90024. TEL: (310) 235-7522. FAX: (310) 235-7500.
CHIEF, ENTERTAINMENT LIAISON
Charles E. Davis

NAVY PUBLIC AFFAIRS, MOTION PICTURE AND TELEVISION OFFICE
Navy Office of Information West, 10880 Wilshire Blvd., Ste. 1220. Los Angeles, CA 90024. TEL: (310) 235-7481. FAX: (310) 235-7856.

MILITARY SERVICES

OFFICE OF THE CHIEF OF ARMY PUBLIC AFFAIRS
Media Relations Division, 1500 Army Pentagon, Rm. 1E475, Washington, DC 20310-1500. TEL: (703) 692-2000. FAX: (703) 697-2159. www.army.mil/institution/armypublicaffairs
CHIEF OF PUBLIC AFFAIRS
Major General Stephen Lanza

DEPARTMENT OF THE NAVY
Chief of Information, 1200 Navy Pentagon, Rm. 4B463, Washington, DC 20350. TEL: (703) 697-7391. FAX: (703) 697-8921. www.navy.mil
ACTING CHIEF INFORMATION OFFICER
Ms. Barbara Hoffman

HEADQUARTERS, U.S. MARINE CORPS.
Department of the Navy, Headquarters, U.S. Marine Corps., 3000 Marine Corps. Pentagon, Rm. 4B548, Washington, DC 20350-3000. TEL: (703) 614-1492. FAX: (703) 697-5362. www.marines.mil
DIRECTOR, MARINE CORPS PUBLIC AFFAIRS
Colonel Bryan Salas

DEPARTMENT OF EDUCATION

OFFICE OF COMMUNICATIONS AND OUTREACH
400 Maryland Ave. SW, Rm. 5W116, Washington, DC 20202. TEL: (202) 401-0762. FAX: (202) 260-8946. www.ed.gov
DIRECTOR, EDITORIAL POLICY, PUBLICATIONS, PRINTING AND AUDIOVISUAL SERVICES
Jacquelyn Zimmermann - jacquelyn.zimmermann@ed.gov

DEPARTMENT OF HEALTH & HUMAN SERVICES

OFFICE OF ASSISTANT SECRETARY PUBLIC AFFAIRS
200 Independence Ave. SW, Room 647-D, Washington, DC 20201. TEL: (202) 690-7850. FAX: (202) 690-6247. www.hhs.gov
ACTING ASSISTANT SECRETARY FOR PUBLIC AFFAIRS
Jenny Backus

ADMINISTRATION FOR CHILDREN & FAMILIES
370 L'Enfant Promenade SW, 2nd Flr., Washington, DC 20447. TEL: (202) 401-9215. FAX: (202) 205-9688.
DIRECTOR, OFFICE OF PUBLIC AFFAIRS
Jeffrey S. Kelley
MEDIA CONTACT
Kenneth J. Wolfe - kenneth.wolfe@acf.hhs.gov

SOCIAL SECURITY ADMIN. OFFICE OF COMMUNICATIONS
440 Altmeyer Building, 6401 Security Blvd., Baltimore, MD 21235. TEL: (410) 965-8904. FAX: (410) 966-9973. www.ssa.gov/pressoffice
PRESS OFFICER
Mark Lassiter

DEPARTMENT OF HOUSING AND URBAN DEV.

OFFICE OF PUBLIC AFFAIRS
HUD Bldg., 451 7th St. SW, Rm. 10130, Washington, DC 20410. TEL: (202) 708-0980. FAX: (202) 619-8153. www.hud.gov
GENERAL DEPUTY ASSISTANT SECRETARY
Neill McG. Coleman

DEPARTMENT OF THE INTERIOR

OFFICE OF COMMUNICATIONS, INTERIOR DEPARTMENT AUDIO NEWS SERVICE
1849 C St. NW, mailstop 6013, Washington, DC 20240. TEL: (202) 208-5089. FAX: (202) 208-3231. www.doi.gov
PUBLIC AFFAIRS SPECIALIST
Ron Tull

DEPARTMENT OF JUSTICE

MULTIMEDIA SECTION
950 Pennsylvania Ave. NW, Washington, DC 20530-0001. TEL: (202) 514-4694. www.justice.gov
DEPUTY ASSISTANT DIRECTOR
Paula Scholz - paula.a.scholz@usdoj.gov

DEPARTMENT OF LABOR

OFFICE OF PUBLIC AFFAIRS
U.S. Department of Labor, 200 Constitution Ave. NW, Room S-1032, Washington, DC 20210. TEL: (202) 693-4650. www.dol.gov
ASSISTANT SECRETARY FOR POLICY
William E. Spriggs

DEPARTMENT OF STATE

INTERNATIONAL COMM. AND INFORMATION POLICY
Department of State, Rm. 6333, 2201 C St. NW, Washington, DC 20520. TEL: (202) 647-5212. FAX: (202) 647-5957. www.state.gov

COORDINATOR
Ambassador Philip L. Verveer

DIRECTORATE OF DEFENSE TRADE CONTROLS
Compliance & Registration Division, 2401 E St. NW, SA-1, Rm. H1200, Washington, DC 20037. TEL: (202) 663-2980.
FAX: (202) 261-8199. email: DDTCResponseTeam@state.gov
www.pmddtc.state.gov
MANAGING DIRECTOR OF DEFENSE TRADE CONTROLS
Robert S. Kovac - (202) 663-2861

OFFICE OF PRESS RELATIONS
Department of State, 2201 C St. NW, Rm. 2109, Washington, DC 20520. TEL: (202) 647-2492. FAX: (202) 647-0244.
www.state.gov
DIRECTOR
Tom Casey
CHIEF PRESS RELATIONS SERV.
Julie Reside

BUREAU OF EDUCATIONAL & CULTURAL AFFAIRS
301 4th St. S.W., Rm. 800, Washington, DC 20547.
TEL: (202) 203-5118. FAX: (202) 203-5115. www.state.gov
ASSISTANT SECRETARY
Ann Stock

INTERNATIONAL BROADCASTING BUREAU OF FEDERAL GOVERNMENT
Public Affairs, Voice of America, 330 Independence Ave., SW, Rm. 3131, Washington, DC 20237. TEL: (202) 203-4959.
FAX: (202) 203-4960. email: pubaff@ibb.gov
PUBLIC AFFAIRS DIRECTOR
Letitia King

DEPARTMENT OF TRANSPORTATION

FEDERAL HIGHWAY ADMINISTRATION
1200 New Jersey Ave., SE, Washington, DC 20590.
TEL: (202) 366-0660. www.dot.gov
ADMINISTRATOR, FEDERAL HIGHWAY ADMINISTRATION
Victor Mendez

NATIONAL HIGHWAY AND TRAFFIC SAFETY ADMINISTRATION
1200 New Jersey Avenue, SE, West Building, Washington, DC 20590. TEL: (888) 327-4236.
ADMINISTRATOR, NATIONAL HIGHWAY TRAFFIC SAFETY ADMINISTRATION
David L. Strickland

DEPARTMENT OF TREASURY

OFFICE OF PUBLIC AFFAIRS
1500 Pennsylvania Ave. NW, Rm. 3442, Washington, DC 20220. TEL: (202) 622-2960. www.ustreas.gov
DEPUTY ASSISTANT SECRETARY, PUBLIC AFFAIRS
Brookly McLaughlin
MEDIA COORDINATOR
Courtney Forsell

EXECUTIVE AGENCIES

BROADCASTING BOARD OF GOVERNORS

330 Independence Ave., SW, Washington, DC 20237.
TEL: (202) 203-4545. FAX: (202) 203-4585. www.bbg.gov
EXECUTIVE DIRECTOR
Jeffrey N. Trimble

ENVIRONMENTAL PROTECTION AGENCY

OFFICE OF MEDIA RELATIONS
1200 Pennsylvania Ave., NW, Mailcode: 1702A, Washington, D.C. 20460. TEL: (202) 564-4355. www.epa.gov

FEDERAL COMMUNICATIONS COMMISSION

445 12th St. SW, Washington, DC 20554. TEL: (888) 225-5322.
FAX: (202) 418-0232. email: fccinfo@fcc.gov www.fcc.gov

OFFICE OF THE CHAIRMAN
445 12th St. SW, Rm. 8-B201, Washington, DC 20554.
TEL: (202) 418-1000.
CHAIRMAN
Julius Genachowski - julius.genachowski@fcc.gov
CONFIDENTIAL ASSISTANT
Maria Gaglio
CHIEF OF STAFF
Edward P. Lazarus
CHIEF COUNSEL AND SENIOR LEGAL ADVISOR
Rick Kaplan

COMMISSIONERS
Michael J. Copps - (202) 418-2000 Michael.Copps@fcc.gov
Robert M. McDowell - (202) 418-2200 Robert.McDowell@fcc.gov
Mignon Clyburn
Meredith Attwell Baker

FEDERAL TRADE COMMISSION

Press Office, 600 Pennsylvania Ave. NW, Washington, DC 20580. TEL: (202) 326-2222. www.ftc.gov
CHAIRMAN
William E. Kovacic
COMMISSIONERS
Pamela Jones Harbour
Jon Leibowitz
J. Thomas Rosch

LIBRARY OF CONGRESS

U.S. COPYRIGHT OFFICE
101 Independence Ave., LM403, Washington, DC 20559-6000.
TEL: (202) 707-8350, (877) 476-0778. FAX: (202) 707-8366.
REGISTER OF COPYRIGHTS
Marybeth Peters

CATALOGING AND ACQUISITIONS DEPARTMENT
101 Independence Ave. SE, LM513, Washington, DC 20540.
TEL: (202) 707-8040.
DIRECTOR
Beacher Wiggins - TEL: (202) 707-5325 bwig@loc.gov

MOTION PICTURE, BROADCASTING AND RECORDED SOUND DIVISION
Madison Bldg., Rm. 338, Washington, DC 20540-4690.
TEL: (202) 707-5840. FAX: (202) 707-2371.
CHIEF OF DIVISION
Gregory Lukow

NATIONAL AERONAUTICS & SPACE ADMINISTRATION

NASA MEDIA RESOURCE CENTER
NASA LBJ Space Center, 2101 NASA Pkwy., Bldg. 423/AP32, Houston, TX 77058-3696. TEL: (281) 483-4231.
FAX: (281) 483-2848. www.nasa.gov/centers/johnson

NATIONAL ARCHIVES AND RECORDS ADMINISTRATION

MOTION PICTURE, SOUND AND VIDEO BRANCH
8601 Adelphi Rd., College Park, MD 20740.
TEL: (301) 837-1649. FAX: (301) 837-3620.
email: mopix@nara.gov www.archives.gov
AUDIOVISUAL REFERENCE LIBRARIAN
Charles De Arman - (301) 837-1649

NATIONAL ENDOWMENT FOR THE ARTS

MEDIA ARTS PROGRAM
1100 Pennsylvania Ave. NW, Rm. 729, Washington, DC 20506.
TEL: (202) 682-5400. FAX: (202) 682-5721.
www.arts.gov
MEDIA ARTS DIRECTOR
Ted Libbey

NATIONAL ENDOWMENT FOR THE HUMANITIES

AMERICA'S MEDIA MAKERS—DIVISION OF PUBLIC PROGRAMS
1100 Pennsylvania Ave. NW, Rm. 426, Washington, DC 20506.
TEL: (202) 606-8269. FAX: (202) 606-8557.
DIRECTOR, DIVISION OF PUBLIC PROGRAMS
Thomas Phelps

SMITHSONIAN INSTITUTION

FILM ARCHIVES
Archives Division, Rm. 3100, MRC 322, National Air and Space Museum, Smithsonian Institution, P.O. Box 37012, Washington, DC 20013-7012. TEL: (202) 633-2337.
FAX: (202) 786-2835.
FILM ARCHIVIST
Mark Taylor

U.S. INTERNATIONAL TRADE COMMISSION

OFFICE OF THE SECRETARY
500 E St. SW, Rm. 112-AA, Washington, DC 20436.
TEL: (202) 205-2000. FAX: (202) 205-2104.
www.usitc.gov
SECRETARY TO THE COMMISSION
Marilyn R. Abbott - (202) 205-2799

TRADE PUBLICATIONS

THE AD AGE GROUP
(Weekly) 711 Third Ave., New York, NY 10017-4036.
TEL: (212) 210-0100, (212) 210-0281. FAX: (212) 210-0200.
www.adage.com
EDITOR-IN-CHIEF
Rance Crain - rcrain@crain.com
PUBLISHING AND EDITORIAL DIRECTOR
David Klein - dklein@crain.com
V.P., PUBLISHER
Allison Arden - aarden@adage.com
EXECUTIVE EDITOR
Abbey Klaassen - aklaassen@adage.com
EDITOR
Jonah Bloom - jbloom@adage.com
MANAGING DIRECTOR, SALES
Jackie Ghedine
ASSOCIATE PUBLISHER
Chris Crain - ccrain@adage.com
CIRCULATION DIRECTOR
John LaMarca - jlamarca@crain.com
EXECUTIVE PRODUCER
Hoag Levins - hlevins@adage.com

THE AMERICAN CINEMATOGRAPHER
(Monthly) Published by American Society of Cinematographers, Inc., P.O. Box 2230, Hollywood, CA 90078.
TEL: (800) 448-0145, (323) 969-4333. FAX: (323) 876-4973.
www.theasc.com
PUBLISHER
Martha Winterhalter
EXECUTIVE EDITOR
Stephen Pizzello

BILLBOARD
(Weekly) 770 Broadway, New York, NY 10003.
TEL: (646) 654-4400. FAX: (646) 654-4681.

5055 Wilshire Blvd., Los Angeles, CA 90036-4396.
TEL: (323) 525-2299. FAX: (323) 525-2394.

49 Music Sq. W., Nashville, TN 37203. TEL: (615) 321-4290. FAX: (615) 320-0454.

Endeavor House, 189 Shaftesbury, London WC2H 8TJ.
TEL: (44 207) 420-6003. FAX: (44 207) 420-6014.
www.billboard.com & www.billboard.biz
SENIOR EDITOR
Jonathan Cohen
BILLBOARD GROUP EDITORIAL DIRECTOR
Tamara Conniff

BOXOFFICE
(Published by Boxoffice Media)
Editorial Offices: 8981 Sunset Blvd., Ste. 309, West Hollywood, CA 90069. TEL: (310) 858-4500. FAX: (310) 858-4503.

Corporate Headquarters: 230 Park Ave. Ste. 1000, New York, NY 10169. TEL: (212) 627-7000. FAX: (212) 627-7007.
email: subscription@boxoffice.com www.boxoffice.com
PUBLISHER
Peter Cane
EDITOR
Chad Greene
CREATIVE DIRECTOR
Kenneth James Bacon
NATIONAL SALES MANAGER
Erick Pinnick
DIRECTOR OF ADVERTISING
Ben Rosenstein - TEL: (212) 627-7000. FAX: (847) 266-1778.

BROADCASTING & CABLE—THE NEWS WEEKLY OF TELEVISION AND RADIO
(Weekly) 360 Park Ave. South, New York, NY 10010.
TEL: (646) 746-6400. FAX: (646) 746-7028.

1701 K St. NW, Ste. 510, Washington, DC 20006.
TEL: (202) 659-3852. FAX: (202) 659-2235.

5700 Wilshire Blvd., #120, Los Angeles, CA 90036.
TEL: (323) 549-4100. FAX: (323) 965-5327.
www.broadcastingcable.com
EDITOR-IN-CHIEF
Ben Grossman - ben.grossman@reedbusiness.com
EXECUTIVE EDITORS
Melissa Grego (Los Angeles)
P.J. Bednarski - pbednarski@reedbusiness.com (New York)
V.P., GROUP PUBLISHER
Larry Dunn - ldunn@nbmedia.com
ASSOCIATE PUBLISHER
Louis Hillelson - lhilleson@nbmedia.com
REGIONAL SALES MANAGER, NEW YORK
Cheryl Mahon - cmahon@reedbusiness.com
Jason Greenblatt - jason.greenblatt@reedbusiness.com
REGIONAL SALES MANAGER, LOS ANGELES
Katie Rosa - katie.rosa@reedbusiness.com
DIRECTOR, SPECIAL PROJECTS
Sandy Friedman - safriedman@reedbusiness.com
GROUP DIRECTOR, CIRCULATION
Denise Robbins - drobbins@nbmedia.com

BROADCASTING & CABLE YEARBOOK
(Annual. Published by ProQuest)
Editorial Office: 630 Central Ave., New Providence, NJ 07974.
TEL: (888) 269-5372. FAX: (908) 219-0182.

Headquarters: 789 E. Eisenhower Pkwy., Ann Arbor, MI 48106.
TEL: (800) 521-0600.
CEO
Marty Kahn
MANAGING EDITOR
Valerie Mahon - (908) 219-0291

CABLE & TV STATION COVERAGE ATLAS
(See Warren Communications News, Inc.)

CELEBRITY SERVICE INTERNATIONAL
Publisher of Celebrity Bulletin (daily) and Celebrity Datebook (bi-monthly) 14 East 44th St., 3rd. Flr., New York, NY 10017.
TEL: (212) 757-7979. FAX: (212) 582-7701.
www.celebrityservice.com
CEO
soroush@celebrityservice.com
PRESIDENT
nancy@celebrityservice.com
COO
Nicole Bagley - nicole@celebrityservice.com
MANAGING DIRECTOR (NY)
Mark Kerrigan - mark@celebrityservice.com
EDITOR, CELEBRITY BULLETIN (NY)
Bill Murray
EDITOR, CELEBRITY DATEBOOK (NY)
Mark Kerrigan

1680 Vine St., Ste. 904, Los Angeles, CA 90028.
TEL: (323) 957-0508. FAX: (323) 957-0559.
MANAGING DIRECTOR (LA)
Karen Abouab - karen@celebrityservice.com
EDITOR, CELEBRITY BULLETIN (LA)
Courtney Kirkpatrick
EDITOR, CELEBRITY DATEBOOK (LA)
Robert Dean

CINEFEX
(Quarterly) P.O. Box 20027, Riverside, CA 92516.
TEL: (800) 434-3339, (951) 781-1917. FAX: (951) 788-1793.
email: circulation@cinefex.com editorial@cinefex.com
www.cinefex.com
PUBLISHER
Don Shay
EDITOR
Jody Duncan

COMMUNICATIONS DAILY
(See Warren Communications News, Inc.)

CONSUMER ELECTRONICS DAILY
(See Warren Communications News, Inc.)

COSTUME DESIGNERS GUILD DIRECTORY
(Online) Costume Designers Guild Local #892, 11969 Ventura Blvd., 1st Flr., Studio City, CA 91604.
TEL: (818) 752-2400. FAX: (818) 752-2402.
email: cdgia@costumedesignersguild.com
www.costumedesignersguild.com
PRESIDENT
Mary Rose - mrose@costumedesignersguild.com
VICE PRESIDENT
Hope Hanafin - hhanafin@costumedesignersguild.com
EXECUTIVE DIRECTOR
Cheryl Downey - cdowney@costumedesignersguild.com

DIGITAL CONTENT PRODUCER
(Monthly)
Penton Media, Inc., 9800 Metcalf Ave., Overland Park, KS 66212-2215. TEL: (913) 341-1300. FAX: (913) 967-1898.
www.digitalcontentproducer.com
MANAGING EDITOR
Lucy Sutton - lucy.sutton@penton.com
EDITORIAL DIRECTOR
Cynthia Wisehart - Cynthia.Wisehart@penton.com
SENIOR EDITOR
Michael Goldman - Michael.Goldman@penton.com

DOCUMENTARY MAGAZINE
1201 W. 5th St., Ste. M320, Los Angeles, CA 90017-2015.
TEL: (213) 534-3600. FAX: (213) 534-3610.
email: info@documentary.org www.documentary.org
EDITOR, DOCUMENTARY MAGAZINE
Thomas White - tom@documentary.org
EXECUTIVE DIRECTOR & PUBLISHER, INTERNATIONAL DOCUMENTARY ASSOCIATION
Michael Lumpkin
PROGRAMS & EVENTS MANAGER, INTERNATIONAL DOCUMENTARY ASSOCIATION
Peggy Ellithorpe - events@documentary.org

FILM & VIDEO MAGAZINE
(Monthly) Organized 1983. 110 William St., 11th Flr., New York, NY 10038. TEL: (212) 621-4900. FAX: (212) 621-4635.
www.filmandvideomagazine.com
ONLINE PUBLISHER, STUDIO & CABLE GROUPS
Alison Johns - ajohns@accessintel.com
EDITOR-IN-CHIEF
Bryant Frazer - bfrazer@accessintel.com
WEST COAST EDITOR
Debra Kaufman - dkaufman@accessintel.com

FILM JOURNAL INTERNATIONAL
(Monthly)
770 Broadway, 7th Flr., New York, NY 10003.
TEL: (646) 654-7680. FAX: (646) 654-7694.
www.filmjournal.com
PUBLISHER & EDITOR
Robert H. Sunshine - robert.sunshine@nielsen.com
EXECUTIVE EDITOR
Kevin Lally - kevin.lally@nielsen.com
ADVERTISING DIRECTOR
Robin Klamfoth - filmjournal_rk@bellsouth.net
ASSOCIATE EDITOR/GRAPHIC DESIGNER
Rex Roberts - rex.roberts@nielsen.com
ADVERTISING DIRECTOR/SHOW DIRECTOR
Andrew Sunshine - andrew.sunsine@nielsen.com

HOLLYWOOD CREATIVE DIRECTORY
5055 Wilshire Blvd., Los Angeles, CA 90036. TEL: (800) 815-0503, Sales: (323) 525-2369, Research: (323) 525-2348.
Sales FAX: (323) 525-2398, Research FAX: (323) 525-2393.
www.hcdonline.com hcdcustomerservice@hcdonline.com
PUBLISHING DIRECTOR
Valencia McKinley

Publishers of Hollywood Creative Directory, Hollywood Representation Directory, Hollywood Distribution Directory, Hollywood Music Industry Directory.

THE HOLLYWOOD REPORTER
(Daily) Corporate: 5055 Wilshire Blvd., Los Angeles, CA 90036. TEL: (323) 525-2000. FAX: (323) 525-2377. Advertising: FAX: (323) 525-2372. Special Issues: FAX: (323) 525-2390.
www.hollywoodreporter.com

New York: 770 Broadway, New York, NY 10003.
TEL: (646) 654-5634. FAX: (646) 654-5637.
BUSINESS EDITOR, NY
Georg Szala - gszalai@hollywoodreporter.com

Washington D.C.: 910 17th St., NW, Ste. 215, Washington, DC 20006. TEL: (202) 833-8845. FAX: (202) 833-8672.
NATIONAL CORRESPONDENT (D.C.)
Brooks Boliek - bboliek@hollywoodreporter.com

London: Endeavour House, 189 Shaftesbury Ave., London WC2H 8TJ. TEL: (44-20 7) 420-6004. FAX: (44-20 7) 420-6054.
BUREAU CHIEF, UK
Stuart Kemp - skemp@eu.hollywoodreporter.com

V.P. AND PUBLISHER
Eric Mika
EDITOR
Elizabeth Guider (LA)
V.P., EXECUTIVE EDITOR
Paula Parisi
EDITOR - DIGITAL MEDIA
Andrew Wallenstein
DEPUTY EDITOR
David Morgan, Carl DiOrio
EXECUTIVE EDITOR, FEATURES
Stephen Galloway
ART DIRECTOR
Deeann J. Hoff
MANAGING EDITORS
Mike Barns, Todd Cunningham
FILM EDITOR
Gregg Kilday
INTERNATIONAL EDITOR
Steve Brennan
TV EDITOR
Nellie Andreeva
BUSINESS EDITOR
Georg Szalai
NEWS EDITOR
Erik Pedersen
V.P., GENERAL MANAGER
P. Andrew Bilbao
FINANCE & OPERATIONS DIRECTOR
Rebecca Eacret
PRODUCTION DIRECTOR
Kelly Jones
AUDIENCE MARKETING DIRECTOR
Katie Fillingame
DIRECTOR, SPECIALS DEVELOPMENT
Kelly McAuliffe
DIRECTOR, MARKETING AND BUSINESS DEVELOPMENT
Vicki Robles

HOME MEDIA MAGAZINE
(Weekly)
201 E. Sandpointe Ave., Ste. 500, Santa Ana, CA 92707.
TEL: (800) 371-6897, (714) 338-6751.
FAX: (714) 338-6711. www.homemediamagazine.com
PUBLISHER
Thomas K. Arnold - Tkarnold@aol.com
EDITOR-IN-CHIEF
Stephanie Prange - sprange@questex.com
ADVERTISING SALES REPRESENTATIVE
John Boezinger - jboezinger@questex.com
MARKETING DIRECTOR
Kristina Kronenberg - kkronenberg@questex.com
ONLINE MANAGER
Renee' Rosado - rrosado@questex.com

I.A.T.S.E. OFFICIAL BULLETIN
(Quarterly) 1430 Broadway, 20th Flr., New York, NY 10018.
TEL: (212) 730-1770. FAX: (212) 921-7699.
email: bulletin@iatse-intl.org www.iatse-intl.org
INTERNATIONAL PRESIDENT
Matthew D. Loeb
GENERAL SECRETARY-TREASURER
James B. Wood

INSIDE FILM MAGAZINE
(Online) 8421 Wilshire Blvd., Ste. 200, Beverly Hills, CA 90211.
TEL: (323) 852-0434. email: editor@insidefilm.com
www.insidefilm.com
EDITOR-IN-CHIEF
Susan Royal
ASSISTANT EDITOR
Alyssa Boyle

ICG MAGAZINE
Published by The International Cinematographers Guild
(Monthly) 7755 Sunset Blvd., Hollywood, CA 90046.
TEL: (323) 876-0160. FAX: (323) 878-1180.
email: info@icgmagazine.com www.cameraguild.com
NATIONAL PRESIDENT, ICG
Steven Poster
EXECUTIVE EDITOR
Neil Mastumoto - neil@icgmagazine.com

INTERNATIONAL MOTION PICTURE ALMANAC
(Annual. Quigley Publishing Company, a division of QP Media, Inc.)
Corporate: P.O. Box 740, Groton, MA 01450.
TEL: (800) 231-8239 (editorial & sales), (978) 448-0272.
FAX: (978) 448-9325. www.quigleypublishing.com
PRESIDENT & PUBLISHER
William J. Quigley - bquigley@quigleypublishing.com
EDITOR
Jayme Kulesz - jkulesz@charter.net
ASSOCIATE EDITOR
Dee Quigley - dquigley@quigleypublishing.com
ASSOCIATE EDITOR & OPERATIONS MANAGER
Michael J. Quigley - mikequigley@quigleypublishing.com

INTERNATIONAL TELEVISION & VIDEO ALMANAC
(Annual. Quigley Publishing Company, a division of QP Media, Inc.)
Corporate: P.O. Box 740, Groton, MA 01450.
TEL: (800) 231-8239 (editorial & sales), (978) 448-0272.
FAX: (978) 448-9325. www.quigleypublishing.com
PRESIDENT & PUBLISHER
William J. Quigley - bquigley@quigleypublishing.com
EDITOR
Jayme Kulesz - jkulesz@charter.net
ASSOCIATE EDITOR
Dee Quigley - dquigley@quigleypublishing.com
ASSOCIATE EDITOR & OPERATIONS MANAGER
Michael J. Quigley - mikequigley@quigleypublishing.com

MARKEE—REGIONAL AMERICA'S MAGAZINE FOR FILM AND VIDEO PRODUCTION
(Monthly) HJK Publications, Inc., 366 E. Graves Ave., Ste. D., Orange City, FL 32763. TEL: (386) 774-8881. FAX: (386) 774-8908.
email: markee@markeemag.com www.markeemag.com
PUBLISHER
Janet Karcher

ASSOCIATE PUBLISHER/EDITOR-IN-CHIEF
Jon Hutchinson
ASSOCIATE EDITOR
Christine Bunish

MEDIA WEEK
(Weekly)
770 Broadway, 7th Flr., New York, NY 10003.
TEL: (800) 641-2030, (646) 654-7601. FAX: (646) 654-5351.
email: info@mediaweek.com www.mediaweek.com
PUBLISHER
Geri FitzGerald - gfitzgerald@mediaweek.com
EDITOR
Michael Bürgi - mburgi@mediaweek.com
EXECUTIVE EDITOR
Jim Cooper - jcooper@mediaweek.com
SENIOR EDITOR
Katy Bachman - kbachman@mac.com
EDITOR, SPECIAL REPORTS
Tony Case - tcase@adweek.com

MILLIMETER MAGAZINE
(Bi-Monthly) Penton Media, Inc., 249 W. 17th St., 3rd Flr., New York, NY 10011. TEL: (877) 652-5295. www.millimeter.com
MANAGING EDITOR
Lucy Sutton - lucy.sutton@penton.com
GROUP PUBLISHER
Wayne Madden - (312) 840-8408
PUBLISHER
Shahla Hebets - (510) 985-3235
EDITORIAL DIRECTOR
Cynthia Wisehart - Cynthia.Wisehart@penton.com
SENIOR EDITOR
Michael Goldman - Michael.Goldman@penton.com

MULTICHANNEL NEWS
360 Park Ave. South, New York, NY 10010.
TEL: (646) 746-6400. Editorial: FAX: (646) 746-6700,
Advertsing: FAX: (646) 746-6703.
www.multichannel.com
V.P./GENERAL MANAGER/PUBLISHER
Larry Dunn - ldunn@reedbusiness.com
EDITOR-IN-CHIEF
Tom Steinert-Threlkeld - tom.steinertthrelkeld@reedbusiness.com
EXECUTIVE EDITOR, CONTENT
Kent Gibbons - kgibbons@reedbusiness.com
ONLINE NEWS EDITOR
Mike Reynolds - mreynolds@reedbusiness.com

PLAYERS DIRECTORY
(Semi-Annual)
2210 W. Olive Ave., Ste. 320, Burbank, CA 91506.
TEL: (310) 247-3058. FAX: (310) 601-4445.
www.playersdirectory.com
EDITOR
Keith W. Gonzales

PRODUCERS MASTERGUIDE
60 E. 8th St., 34th Flr., New York, NY 10003.
TEL: (212) 777-4002. FAX: (212) 777-4101.
www.producers.masterguide.com
PUBLISHER
Shmuel Bension

QUIGLEY PUBLISHING CO., A DIVISION OF QP MEDIA, INC.
(Annual. Publishers of The International Motion Picture Almanac and The International Television and Video Almanac)
Corporate: P.O. Box 740, Groton, MA 01450.
TEL: (800) 231-8239 (editorial & sales), (978) 448-0272.
FAX: (978) 448-9325. www.quigleypublishing.com
CHAIRMAN EMERITUS
Martin S. Quigley
PRESIDENT & PUBLISHER
William J. Quigley - bquigley@quigleypublishing.com
EDITOR
Jayme Kulesz - jkulesz@charter.net
ASSOCIATE EDITOR
Dee Quigley - dquigley@quigleypublishing.com
ASSOCIATE EDITOR & OPERATIONS MANAGER
Michael J. Quigley - mikequigley@quigleypublishing.com

THE REEL DIRECTORY
(Annual) P.O. Box 1910, Boyes Hot Springs, CA 95416.
TEL: (415) 531-9760. FAX: (707) 581-1725.
email: IVISUAL@aol.com www.reeldirectory.com
CONTACT
Lynetta Freeman

SATELLITE WEEK
(See Warren Communications News, Inc.)

SMPTE JOURNAL (SOCIETY OF MOTION PICTURE AND TELEVISION ENGINEERS)
(Monthly)
3 Barker Ave., White Plains, NY 10601.
TEL: (914) 761-1100. FAX: (914) 761-3115. www.smpte.org
PRESIDENT SMPTE
Kenneth C. Fuller
EXECUTIVE VICE PRESIDENT
Peter Lude
EXECUTIVE DIRECTOR
Kimberly Maki
DIRECTOR, OPERATIONS
Sally-Ann D'Amato
MANAGING EDITOR
Dianne Ross Purrier - dpurrier@smpte.org
EDITORIAL DIRECTORS
Tom Scott, Dave Bancroft

SCREEN ACTOR MAGAZINE
(Quarterly)
5757 Wilshire Blvd., 7th Flr., Los Angeles, CA 90036.
TEL: (800) SAG-0767. FAX: (323) 549-6656.
email: screenactor@sag.org www.sag.org
EDITOR-IN-CHIEF
Seth Oster

SHOOT
(The Leading Publication for Commercial, Interactive & Branded Content Production)
(Twice-monthly print issues, Weekly HTML publications The SHOOT edition & iSPOT and website)
21 Charles St., Ste. 203, Westport, CT 06880.
TEL: (203) 227-1699. email: info@shootonline.com
www.shootonline.com
PUBLISHER
Roberta Griefer - rgriefer@shootonline.com
EDITOR
Bob Goldrich - rgoldrich@shootonline.com

TELEVISION & CABLE FACTBOOK
(See Warren Communications News, Inc.)

TELEVISION QUARTERLY
(Quarterly)
National Academy of Television Arts & Sciences, 111 W. 57th St., Ste. 600, New York, NY 10019. TEL: (212) 586-8424.
FAX: (212) 246-8129. www.tvquarterly.net
EDITOR
Fritz Jacobi

TELEVISIONWEEK
(Weekly)
6500 Wilshire Blvd., Ste. 2300, Los Angeles, CA 90048.
TEL: (323) 370-2400. FAX: (323) 653-4425.
PRESIDENT & EDITOR IN CHIEF (NY)
Rance Crain
MANAGING DIRECTOR (LA)
Chuck Ross - chkross@tvweek.com
EDITOR
Greg Baumann - (323) 370-2427 - gbaumann@tvweek.com
EXECUTIVE EDITOR
Tom Gilbert - (323) 370-2420 - tgilbert@tvweek.com
DEPUTY EDITOR
Chris Pursell - (323) 370-2419 - cpursell@tvweek.com

TOUR GUIDE JOURNAL
(Monthly)
Anvil Productions, Inc., 750 Cowan St., Nashville, TN 37207.
TEL: (615) 256-7006. FAX: (615) 256-7004.
email: info@tourguidemag.com www.TourGuideMag.com
PUBLISHER
Larry Smith

TV GUIDE
(Weekly)
Macrovision Solutions, Inc., 11 W 42nd St., 17th Flr., New York, NY 10036. TEL: (212) 852-7500. www.tvguide.com
CEO
Jack Kliger
EDITOR-IN-CHIEF, TV GUIDE ONLINE
Christy Tanner

VARIETY
(Daily and Weekly)
5700 Wilshire Blvd., Ste. 120, Los Angeles, CA 90036.
TEL: (323) 857-6600, (323) 617-9100. FAX: (323) 857-0494.
email: news@variety.com advertising@variety.com
www.variety.com
PRESIDENT
Neil Stiles
V.P., EDITOR-IN-CHIEF
Peter Bart - pbart@reedbusiness.com
EDITOR
Timothy M. Gray - tim.gray@variety.com
EXECUTIVE EDITOR, NEWS
Michael Speier - michael.speier@variety.com
EXECUTIVE EDITOR, FEATURES
Steven Gaydos - steven.gaydos@variety.com
MANAGING EDITOR
Ted Johnson - ted.johnson@variety.com

PUBLISHER
Brian Gott
DIRECTOR OF MARKETING
Kimberly Gebbett

WARREN COMMUNICATIONS NEWS, INC.

(Daily)
Warren Communications News, Inc., 2115 Ward Ct. N.W., Washington, DC 20037. TEL: (202) 872-9200.
FAX: (202) 318-8350. www.warren-news.com
CHAIRMAN, EDITOR & PUBLISHER
Paul Warren
PRESIDENT & EDITOR
Daniel Warren
ASSOCIATE MANAGING EDITOR, COMMUNICATIONS DAILY
Edie Herman
MANAGING EDITOR & ASSISTANT PUB., DIRECTORIES, TELEVISION & CABLE FACTBOOK
Michael C. Taliaferro
ASSOCIATE MANAGING EDITOR, TELEVISION & CABLE FACTBOOK
Gaye Nail
SALES DIRECTOR
William r. Benton

Newsletters: Communications Daily, Communications Business Daily, Washington Internet Daily, Consumer Electronics Daily, Washington Telecom NewsWire, Telecom A.M., Television A.M., The State Telephone Regulation Report and Satellite Week, among others. Warren also publishes numerous reference works, such as the industry-standard 5,000-page Television & Cable Factbook.

GREAT BRITAIN

BROADCAST

(Weekly)
EMAP Media Ltd., Greater London House, Hampstead Rd., London NW1 7EJ. TEL: (44 207) 728 5542.
email: admin@broadcastnow.co.uk
www.broadcastnow.co.uk
EDITOR
Lisa Campbell - lisa.campbell@emap.com - (020 7728 5527)
DEPUTY EDITOR
Emily Booth - emily.booth@emap.com
NEWS EDITOR
Chris Curtis - chris.curtis@emap.com
WEB EDITOR
Michael Rosser - michael.rosser@emap.com

KEMPS FILM, TV & VIDEO HANDBOOK

(Annual)
Reed Business Information, Windsor Court, East Grinstead House, E. Grinstead, West Sussex, RH19 1XA.
TEL: (44 134) 233-2073. email: kemps.mktg@reedinfo.co.uk
www.kftv.com
MARKETING/SALES
Vicky Howlett - kemps.mktg@rbi.co.uk
Jennifer Knight - kemps.mktg@reedinfo.co.uk
US, CARIBBEAN & CANADA
Nicki Webber-Self - nickikemps@aol.com

SCREEN INTERNATIONAL

(Weekly)
Screen International, 33-39 Bowling Green Lane, London EC1R 0DA, England. TEL: (44 207) 505-8080.

Los Angeles: 8271 Melrose Ave., Ste. 204, Los Angeles, CA 90046. TEL: (323) 655-6087. www.screendaily.com
EDITOR-IN-CHIEF
Colin Brown - colinbrown1@earthlink.net
EDITOR
Michael Gubbins - michael.gubbins@emap.com
US EDITOR
Mike Goodridge - (323) 655-6087 - mikegood@earthlink.net

TELEVISUAL

(Monthly)
Televisual Media UK Limited, 48 Charlotte St., London W1T 2NS, England. TEL: (44) 20 3008 5775, (44) 20 3008 5784.
www.televisual.com
MANAGING DIRECTOR
James Bennett - james@televisual.com
EDITOR
Tim Dams - tim@televisual.com
DEPUTY EDITOR
Jon Creamer - jon@televisual.co

The World Market:

Canada

PRODUCTION COMPANIES

ALBERTA

ADVANCE MEDIA
1521 - 29 Ave. SW, Calgary AB T2T 1M4. TEL: (403) 249-0601.
FAX: (403) 249-0204. email: info@advancemedia.ca
www.advancemedia.ca
PRESIDENT
Paul Toth
SENIOR V.P.
Joseph Magyar
PRODUCTION COORDINATOR
Jennifer Rayner

AGITPROP FILMS INC.
58 River Rock Green SE, Calgary, AB T2C 4C2.
TEL: (403) 720-2811. FAX: (403) 279-2519.
email: agitprop@telus.net
PRODUCER
David Christensen

Develops, finances and produces film and television projects for both the domestic and international markets.

ALBERTA CO-PRODUCTIONS INC.
(Subsidiary of Marano Productions, Inc.)
345 – 703 6th Ave. SW, Calgary, AB T2P 0T9.
TEL: (403) 263-2092. FAX: (403) 263-2094.
email: maranoproductions@shaw.ca
PRODUCER
Nancy Marano

From development to financing (nationally and internationally), production, post-production, etc. Interested in co-producing television, theatrical film and television series.

ALBERTA FILMWORKS, INC.
1310 11th St. SW, Calgary, AB T2R 1G6. TEL: (403) 777-9900.
FAX: (403) 777-9914. email: mail@albertafilmworks.com
www.albertafilmworks.com
EXECUTIVE PRODUCER
Doug MacLeod, Tom Cox, Randy Bradshaw, Jordy Randall

ALLIANCE ATLANTIS
(Production company)
121 Bloor St. E., Ste. 1500, Toronto, ON M4W 3M5, Canada.
TEL: (416) 967-1174. FAX: (416) 960-0971
www.allianceatlantis.com

Los Angeles: 1543-7th St., 3rd Flr., Santa Monica, CA 90401.
TEL: (310) 899-8000. FAX: (310) 899-8100.

New York: 1120 Avenue of the Americas, Ste., 1502, New York, NY 10036. TEL: (212) 626-6536. FAX: (212) 626-6537.

Dublin: 40 Westland Row, Dublin 2, Ireland.
TEL: 353-1-449-8400. FAX: 353-1-449-8470.

London: 12/22 Warwick St., 3rd Flr., United Kingdom W1B 5NE.
TEL: +44 20 7287 6800. FAX: +44 20 7287 6880.

Sydney: 401 Darling St., Ste 2, Balmain, Australia, NSW 2041.
TEL: 612-9810-8933. FAX: 612-9810-8966.
CHAIRMAN
Derek H. Burney.
BUSINESS CONSULTANT AND CORPORATE DIRECTOR
David J. Drybrough
PRESIDENT
Thomas C. Strike
CFO
John E. Maguire
SENIOR V.P. & GENERAL COUNSEL
Richard M. Leipsic

Television: CSI: Crime Scene Investigation, CSI: Miami, CSI: New York, Dragon Booster, Lunar Jim

ANAID PRODUCTIONS, INC.
208 – 3132 Parsons Rd., Edmonton, AB T6N 1L6.
TEL: (780) 413-9285. FAX: (780) 465-0580.
email: anaid@anaid.com www.anaid.com
CONTACT
Margaret Mardirossian
GENERAL MANAGER
Laurie McInnes
DIRECTOR, BUSINESS AFFAIRS
Helen Schmidt, CMA
PRODUCER
Deb Proc
PRODUCTION SUPERVISOR
Erin Berube

TV / drama / documentary / MOWs.

BLACK MEDIA WORKS
534 21st Ave. SW, Calgary, AB T2S 0H1. TEL: (403) 802-0010.
FAX: (403) 802-0012. email: info@blackmediaworks.com
www.blackmediaworks.com
DIRECTOR
Darold Black, DGC

Script to screen production services.

BOGART PRODUCTIONS
13 – 9353 50th St., Edmonton, AB T6N 2L5. TEL: (780) 461-9465.
FAX: (780) 461-0657. email: pati.olson@telusplanet.net
CONTACT
Pati Olson

Specializing in the development and production of lifestyle/arts documentaries and non-violent children's programming in the English, French and Aboriginal languages.

BURNING BRIDGE ENTERTAINMENT, INC.
P.O. Box 32108, Calgary, AB T2T 5X6. TEL: (403) 668-9964,
(416) 619-4941. email: office@burningbridge.ca
www.doublevision.ca
CONTACTS
Devon Bolton, Kristen Bolton

Feature films.

CANADIAN WILDERNESS VIDEOS & PRODUCTIONS, INC.
1010 Larch Place, Canmore, AB T1W 1S7. TEL: (403) 678-3795.
email: crvideo@telus.net
PRODUCER/DIRECTOR/CAMERA
Eric Langshaw
RESEARCHER/CAMERA
Rosemary Power

CHAOS A FILM COMPANY, INC.
215 11A St. NW, Calgary, AB T2N 1X9. TEL: (403) 283-2090.
FAX: (403) 283-2092. email: info@chaosafilmcompany.com
www.chaosafilmcompany.com
PRESIDENT
Carolyn McMaster

Feature films.

DB ENTERTAINMENT
3419 Utah Cres NW, Calgary, AB T2N 4A9. TEL: (403) 295-8390.
FAX: (403) 295-8790. email: bix@dbentertainment.com
www.dbentertainment.com
PRESIDENT
Douglas Berquist

Specializing in international co-productions.

DINOSAUR SOUP PRODUCTIONS, INC.
45 Gillian Cres, St. Albert, AB T8N 0V9. TEL: (780) 459-4676.
FAX: (780) 460-8109. email: dinosaursoup@telusplanet.net
CONTACT
Steve Moore

Family programming: animation / drama / lifestyle / documentaries.

EARTH TO SKY PICTURES
476 Berkley Cres NW, Calgary, AB T3K 1A8.
TEL: (403) 274-8261. FAX: (403) 274-9251.
email: mail@earthtoskypictures.com
www.earthtoskypictures.com
PRODUCER
Nancy Laing, Christina Willings
DIRECTOR, DEVELOPMENT
Neil Fleming

FRAME 30 PRODUCTIONS, LTD.
202 – 10816A 82nd Ave., Edmonton, AB T6E 2B3.
TEL: (780) 439-5322. FAX: (780) 431-1905.
email: frame30@frame30.com
www.frame30.com
PRESIDENT/PRODUCER
Michael Hamm

Commercial, corporate and television.

FULL THROTTLE FILMS, INC.
20 – 882 Ryan Pl., Edmonton, AB T6R 2K9.
TEL: (780) 721-6931. FAX: (780) 434-9607.
email: neilthomas@shaw.ca
DIRECTOR/WRITER/PRODUCER
Neil Thomas

Documentaries, doc series, reality & lifestyle. National Geographic Int'l, Discovery Channel (Canada, U.S.A., Asia), PBS, CBC, Global, ABC, CNN, Channel 4 UK, Paramount.

GALLANT PRODUCTIONS, INC.
228 12th St., C North, Lethbridge, AB T1H 2M7.
TEL: (403) 380-4439. FAX: (403) 380-4489.
email: george@gallantproductions.com
www.gallantproductions.com
CONTACT
George Gallant

Educational and documentary programming.

GEEK SHOW PRODUCTIONS, INC.
207 Wahstao Rd., Edmonton, AB T5T 2X8.
TEL: (780) 707-2337. FAX: (780) 484-2180.
email: neilgrahn@shaw.ca www.thegeekshow.com
CONTACT
Neil Grahn

Documentary – educational / performing arts – variety / TV series – comedy.

THE IDEA FACTORY!
18520 Stony Plain Rd., Edmonton, AB T5S 1A8.
TEL: (780) 439-3985. FAX: (780) 439-4051.
email: info@ideafactory.ca www.ideafactory.com
PRESIDENT
Lindsay Speer

ILLUSIONS ENTERTAINMENT CORP.
67 Edgeridge Ct. NW, Calgary, AB T3A 4N9.
TEL: (403) 215-5544, (403) 818-1930. FAX: (403) 215-5545.
email: illusionsentertainment@shaw.ca
PRODUCER
Bruce Harvey

Produces & co-produces with France, Germany, Italy, Spain, UK and USA. Award-winning theatrical films, MOWs and TV series.

IMAGINATION FILM & TELEVISION PRODUCTIONS, INC.
The Griffith Block, 10318 82nd Ave., 3rd Flr., Edmonton, AB T6E 1Z8. TEL: (780) 439-8755. FAX: (780) 430-1871.
email: jordan@imaginationfilm.tv

Primary focus is the creation, development and production of dramatic long-form television, theatrical movies and unique socio-political documentaries.

JOE MEDIA GROUP
200 – 1235 26th Ave. SE, Calgary, AB T2G 0W2.
TEL: (403) 264-5400. FAX: (403) 228-9304.
email: info@joemedia.tv www.joemedia.tv
PRESIDENT/CEO
Joe Novack

Television, commercials and corporate videos.

KARVONEN FILMS, LTD.
2001 91st Ave., Edmonton, AB T6P 1L1
TEL: (780) 467-7167. FAX: (780) 467-7162.
email: films@karvonenfilms.com www.karvonenfilms.com
PRESIDENT
Albert Karvonen
VICE PRESIDENT
Pirkko Karvonen
BUSINESS AFFAIRS
Elise Holm

Specializing in natural history and wildlife films / extensive 16mm and super 16mm stock footage, stills and sound library collected over 30 years of production.

KING MOTION PICTURE CORPORATION
Bell Tower, 1702 – 10104 103rd Ave., Edmonton, AB T5J 0H8.
TEL: (780) 424-2950. FAX: (780) 420-0518.
email: king@thislivingworld.com
PRESIDENT
Douglas Hutton

Creates, develops, produces and distributes quality programs for prime time television.

MYTH MERCHANT FILMS
29 – 26516 Township Rd. 514, Spruce Grove, AB T7Y 1E9.
TEL: (780) 974-9889. FAX: (780) 967-2976.
email: info@mythmerchantfilms.com
www.mythmerchantfilms.com
PRODUCER/DIRECTOR/WRITER
Michael Jorgensen
PRODUCER/WRITER
Carrie Gour

Feature films / factual and dramatic television.

NOMADIC PICTURES
3911 Trasimene Cr. SW, Calgary, AB T3E 7J6.
TEL: (403) 240-0444. FAX: (403) 246-0247.
email: mfrislev@nomadicpictures.com
www.nomadicpictures.com
PRODUCERS
Mike Frislev, Chad Oakes

TV series — drama, MOWs.

PANACEA ENTERTAINMENT
9876A 33rd Ave., 2nd Flr., Edmonton, AB T6N 1C6.
TEL: (780) 490-1220. FAX: (780) 490-5255.
email: info@panaceaentertainment.com
www.panaceaentertainment.com
PRESIDENT
Josh Miller

TV series / features.

POLAR BEAR ENTERTAINMENT
4144 Ramsay Rd., Edmonton, AB T6H 5R2.
TEL: (780) 988-6397. FAX: (780) 438-4054.
email: info@polarbear.ca www.polarbear.ca
CONTACT
Rick Bremness

Television production and production services. Independently owned and operated. Producers of the series Top Dogs.

PYRAMID PRODUCTIONS
2875 107 Ave. SE, Calgary, AB T2Z 3R7. TEL: (403) 234-8566.
FAX: (403) 234-8418. email: office@pyramidproductions.tv
www.pyramidproductions.tv
PRESIDENT
Kirstie McLellan Day

Television – series and shows.

REEL GIRLS MEDIA, INC.
9860A 33rd Ave., Edmonton, AB T6N 1C6.
TEL: (780) 488-0440. FAX: (780) 452-4980.
email: info@reelgirlsmedia.com www.reelgirlsmedia.com
PRESIDENT/PRODUCER
Ava Karvonen

REGAN PRODUCTIONS, LTD.
210 – 605 11th Ave. SW, Calgary, AB T2R 0E1.
TEL: (877) 661-9017, (403) 244-9017. FAX: (403) 244-6216.
email: lregan@reganproductions.com
www.reganproductions.com
CONTACT
Heather Bishop

Video productions / co-productions.

SIX FIGURES PRODUCTIONS
58 River Rock Green SE, Calgary, AB T2C 4C2.
TEL: (403) 720-2811. FAX: (403) 279-2519.
email: agitprop@telus.net
PRODUCER
David Christensen

TV series — drama, MOWs.

SOULEADO ENTERTAINMENT
9353 50th St., Unit 14, Edmonton, AB T6B 2L5.
TEL: (780) 490-4506. email: souleado@compusmart.ab.ca
www.souleado.com

Producing high-quality, intelligent television programming.

TOMALI PICTURES, LTD.
AF44 – 4321 Quesnay Wood Dr. SW, Calgary, AB T3E 7K5.
TEL: (403) 262-8422. FAX: (403) 262-8421.
email: aejackso@tomali.com www.tomali.com
PRESIDENT
Tom Jackson

Documentary / educational / live events.

VOICE PICTURES, INC.
111 – 2526 Battleford Ave., SW, Calgary, AB T3E 7J4.
TEL: (403) 283-9993. FAX: (403) 283-3223.
email: info@voicepictures.com www.voicepictures.com
PRESIDENT
Wendy Hill-Tout

Produces and finances features and MOWs. Co-production experience with the United Kingdom, the United States and Germany.

WHITE IRON PRODUCTIONS, INC.
533 – 1201 5th St. SW, Calgary, AB T2R 0Y6.
TEL: (403) 298-4700. FAX: (403) 233-0528.
email: jwatson@whiteiron.tv www.whiteiron.tv
PRESIDENT/CEO
Lance Meuller
CONTACT
jmerriman@whiteiron.tv

Full-service film and video production; commercial, corporate and long form.

WINNING, DAVID
(Groundstar Entertainment Corp.)
4001 – 918 16th Ave. NW, Calgary, AB T2M 0K3.
TEL: (403) 284-2889, (604) 944-8407.
Toronto: (416) 524-3210. FAX: (403) 282-7797.
email: info@davidwinning.com
www.davidwinning.com

Director / producer / writer — features / episodic: Represented in British Columbia by Anna Archer/Richard Lucas (Lucas Talent Inc.) and in Ontario by Charles Northcote (The Core Group Talent Inc.).

ZOOM COMMUNICATIONS
1918 9th Ave. SW, Calgary, AB T2G 0V2. TEL: (403) 229-2511. FAX: (403) 229-4211. email: info@zoomcom.ca
www.zoomcom.ca
PRESIDENT
Jeff Bradshaw

BRITISH COLUMBIA

THE ACE FILM COMPANY, INC.
400 – 1152 Mainland St., Vancouver, BC V6B 4X2.
TEL: (604) 682-0001. FAX: (604) 682-7346.
email: acefilm@acefilm.com www.acefilm.com
EXECUTIVE PRODUCER
Keli Westgate
DIRECTOR/ CINEMATOGRAPHER
Allen G. Jones

AKA CARTOON
200 – 211 Columbia St., Vancouver, BC V6A 2R5.
TEL: (604) 682-6652. FAX: (604) 682-6259.
email: borroz@akacartoon.com
EXECUTIVE PRODUCER/DIRECTOR
Danny Antonucci
PRODUCER
Dan Sioui

AM PRODUCTIONS, INC.
48 E. 6th Ave., Vancouver, BC V5T 1J4. TEL: (604) 875-9927. FAX: (604) 875-9971. email: tomk@amproductions.com
www.amproductions.com
EXECUTIVE PRODUCER
Tom Konyves

Educational / promotional / corporate / multimedia / production & distribution.

ANAGRAM PICTURES
291 E. 2nd Ave., 3rd Flr., Vancouver, BC V5T 1B8.
TEL: (604) 730-9021. FAX: (604) 730-9042.
email: anagram@anagrampictures.ca
www.anagrampictures.ca
CONTACT
Andrew Currie, Blake Corbet, Trent Carlson, Kevin Eastwood, Mary Anne Waterhouse, Ki Wight

Feature films.

ANNE WHEELER, INC.
13677 Marine Dr., White Rock, BC V4B 1A3.
TEL: (604) 538-3993. FAX: (604) 538-6886.
email: info@annewheeler.com www.annewheeler.com
PRESIDENT
Anne Wheeler

ART YOUNG VIDEO PRODUCTIONS
8387 – 13th Ave., Burnaby, BC V3N 2G8. TEL: (604) 526-8897. FAX: (604) 526-8814. email: artyoung@telus.net
CONTACT
Art Young

Broadcast / corporate / special events / location sound.

ARTHUR HOLBROOK PRODUCTIONS, INC.
1108 Bewdley Ave., Victoria, BC V9A 5M8.
TEL: (250) 477-5057. FAX: (250) 477-5447.
email: aholbrook@shaw.ca
CONTACT
Arthur Holbrook

Film / video.

ARTSY FARTSY PICTURES, INC.
1996 W. 12th Ave., Vancouver, BC V6J 2E9.
TEL: (604) 609-0350. FAX: (604) 648-9797.
email: e.sanchez@artsyfartsypictures.com
www.artsyfartsypictures.com
PRINCIPAL/WRITER/PRODUCER
Elizabeth Sanchez
PRINCIPAL/WRITER/PRODUCER/DIRECTOR
Paul Ziller

Feature films and TV programming.

ASTERISK PRODUCTIONS, LTD.
977 Hampshire Rd., Victoria, BC V8S 4S3.
TEL: (250) 480-5256. FAX: (250) 598-1299.
email: asterisk@islandnet.com www.asterisk.bc.ca
CONTACT
David Springbett, Heather MacAndrew

ATOMIC CARTOONS, INC.
250 – 1125 Howe St., Vancouver, BC V6Z 2K8.
TEL: (604) 734-2866. FAX: (604) 734-2869.
email: paddy@atomiccartoons.com www.atomiccartoons.com
CONTACT
Paddy Gillen

AUDIENCE WRITES, INC.
1996 West 12th Ave., Vancouver, BC V6J 2E9.
TEL: (604) 609-0350. FAX: (604) 648-9797.
email: e.sanchez@artsyfartsypictures.com
PRINCIPAL
Elizabeth Sanchez, Paul Ziller

New media.

AVRIO FILMWORKS, INC.
5865 Marine Dr. W, Vancouver, BC V7W 2S1.
TEL: (604) 218-4757, (702) 768-1918.
email: MDerbas@AvrioFilmworks.com
www.avriofilmworks.com
PRESIDENT/PRODUCER
Michael Derbas

BARDEL ENTERTAINMENT, INC.
548 Beatty St., Vancouver, BC V6B 2L3. TEL: (604) 669-5589. FAX: (604) 669-9079. email: info@bardel.ca www.bardel.ca
CEO
Delna Bhesania
PRESIDENT
Barry Ward

BIG RED BARN ENTERTAINMENT
6556 60th Ave., Delta, BC V4K 4E2. TEL: (604) 946-6329. FAX: (604) 946-2604. email: ken@brbmg.com
www.brbmg.com
CONTACT
Ken Malenstyn

BLT PRODUCTIONS, LTD.
2412 Columbia St., 2nd Fl., Vancouver, BC V5Y 3E6.
TEL: (604) 873-6559. FAX: (604) 873-0122.
email: blt@intergate.ca www.bltproductions.ca
PRESIDENT
Josanne B. Lovick

Film & television production company that develops and produces both live-action and animated productions.

BLUE SKY PRODUCTIONS, INC.
1619 Hampshire Rd., Victoria, BC V8R 5T4.
TEL: (250) 598-4563. email: cellulloyd@shaw.ca
CONTACT
Lloyd Chesley, James Fry

Film & video dramas / documentaries / theatre / television.

BRIGHTLIGHT PICTURES, INC.
c/o The Bridge Studios, 2400 Boundary Rd., Burnaby, BC V5M 3Z3. TEL: (604) 628-3000. FAX: (604) 628-3002.
email: info@brightlightpictures.com
www.brightlightpictures.com
PRODUCTION PARTNERS
Shawn Williamson, Steven Hegyes
SENIOR V.P., PRODUCTION
Brad Van Arragon
V.P., BUSINESS & LEGAL AFFAIRS
Karyn Edwards
V.P., POST-PRODUCTION & DISTRIBUTION
Jonathan Shore
DIRECTOR, DEVELOPMENT
Mary Quinn
DIRECTOR, POST-PRODUCTION
Iasla Webster

Develops, finances and produces independent features and television projects.

CARSON STREET PRODUCTIONS, LTD.
5510 Carson St., Burnaby, BC V5J 2Z2. TEL: (604) 451-1746.
CONTACT
Elaine Gans

Television, documentary, educational.

CHEAP AND DIRTY PRODUCTIONS, INC.
1874 Grant St., Vancouver, BC V5L 2Y8. TEL: (604) 872-7006. FAX: (604) 872-7086. email: cheapanddirty@telus.net
www.cheapanddirty.ca
PRODUCERS
Carolyn Allain, David Ray

Drama, documentary, feature, series.

CINEMAX FILMS, INC.
402 – 1490 Pennyfarthing Dr., Vancouver, BC V6J 4Z3.
TEL: (604) 266-9690.
PRODUCER/PRODUCTION MANAGER
Don McLean

Development & production.

CIRCLE PRODUCTIONS
1620 W. 5th Ave., Vancouver, BC V6J 1N8.
TEL: (604) 714-4288. FAX: (604) 733-1142.

email: info@circleprod.com www.circleprod.com
EXECUTIVE PRODUCER
Chris Bowell, Tom Murray

Commercials and music video production services. See also Ontario.

CLEARWATER FILMS
1 – 2033 Beach Ave., Vancouver, BC V6G 1Z3.
TEL: (604) 897-4445. email: lili@clearwaterfilms.com
www.clearwaterfilms.com
PRODUCER
Jeffrey Cahn
DIRECTOR
Lili Schad

High-quality feature film and documentary production within reasonable budgets.

COMING HOME FILMS, INC.
402 Georgina Point Rd., Mayne Island, BC V0N 2J0.
TEL: (250) 539-5094. email: cominghome@gulfislands.com
www.cominghomefilms.com

COYOTE FILMS, LTD.
400 – 601 W. Broadway, Vancouver, BC V5Z 4C2.
TEL: (604) 685-1417. email: coyote@axion.net
PRESIDENT
Ken Kuramoto

Film and television.

CRESCENT ENTERTAINMENT
304 - 343 Railway St., Vancouver, BC V6A 1A4.
TEL: (604) 357-3606. FAX: (604) 357-3605.
email: crescent@crescent.ca
CONTACT
Jayme Pfahl, Harold Tichenor, Gordon Mark
MANAGING DIRECTOR
Nathan Tichenor

Development / independent production / production services.

CRONE FILMS, LTD.
8175 Pasco Rd. W, Vancouver, BC V7W 2T5.
TEL: (604) 921-6500, (604) 921-6554. email: dcrone@shaw.ca
CONTACT
Robert Crone, CSC, David Crone

EMMERSON DENNEY FILMS
101 – 131 Water St., Vancouver, BC V6B 4M3.
TEL: (604) 742-3456. www.emmerson.ca

Production of feature films and television.

EQMEDIA
309 – 2170 W. 3rd Ave., Vancouver, BC V6K 1L1.
TEL: (604) 629-8657. email: mbrodie@eqmedia.net
www.eqmedia.net
PRESIDENT
Matt Brodie
VICE PRESIDENT
Michael Brown

THE EYES PROJECT DEVELOPMENT CORP.
(A Peace Arch Entertainment company)
200 – 1710 Columbia St., Vancouver, BC V5Y 4A1.
TEL: (888) 588-3608, (604) 688-3937. FAX: (604) 688-3977.
email: sales@theeyes.ca www.theeyes.ca

Lifestyle and documentary programming.

FAST PRODUCTIONS, LTD.
1404 – 1055 Homer St., Vancouver, BC V6B 1G3.
TEL: (778) 786-1628, (604) 341-8354. FAX: (778) 786-1585.
email: fast-productions@shaw.ca
PRODUCER
Cheryl-Lee Fast

Documentary-educational / feature film / television series. Serving producers, writers and directors to get their product and financing scenarios (with Canadian tax credit incentives) production ready.

FLOURISH MEDIA, INC.
501 – 525 Seymour St., Vancouver, BC V6B 3H7.
TEL: (604) 221-2632. email: kolsson@flourishmedia.com
www.flourishmedia.com

Vancouver-based multimedia production company specializing in the development and production of original content for film, television and new media.

FORCE FOUR ENTERTAINMENT
202 – 221 E. 10th Ave., Vancouver, BC V5T 4V1.
TEL: (604) 669-4424. FAX: (604) 669-4535.
email: tv@forcefour.com www.forcefour.com
CEO/EXECUTIVE PRODUCER
Rob Bromley
V.P., BUSINESS AFFAIRS
Gillian Lowery
EXECUTIVE PRODUCER
John Ritchie
PRODUCER
Sharon McNamara

FORWARD FOCUS PRODUCTIONS, LTD.
31 – 784 Thurlow St., Vancouver, BC V6E 1V9.
TEL: (604) 681-4677.
email: mmcewen@sfu.ca
PRESIDENT
Mary Anne McEwen

FRONT STREET PICTURES
202 – 2339 Columbia St., Vancouver, BC V5Y 3Y3.
TEL: (604) 257-4720. FAX: (604) 257-4739.
email: info@frontstreetpictures.com
www.frontstreetpictures.com
PRODUCER
Harvey Kahn, Jaye Gazeley

Television and feature films.

GENESIS COMMUNICATIONS CORP.
P.O. Box 888, Gibsons Landing, BC V0N 1V0.
TEL: (604) 886-3639. email: devadas@telus.net
PRESIDENT/PRODUCER
Robert Nichol

Educational / TV / entertainment programming.

GILDAY, LEN CSC
RR 1 B-46, Bowen Island, BC V0N 1G0. TEL: (604) 947-2388.
FAX: (604) 947-2389. email: bowenfilm@telus.net

Director / documentaries / cinematographer.

GRACE GILROY PRODUCTIONS
210B – 555 Brooksbank Ave., Bldg. 9, Vancouver, BC V7J 3S5. TEL: (604) 983-5111. FAX: (604) 983-5112.
email: gracegilroy@aol.com
PRESIDENT
Grace Gilroy

GRYPHON PRODUCTIONS, LTD.
P.O. Box 93009, 5331 Headland Dr. W, Vancouver, BC V7W 3C0. TEL: (604) 921-7627. FAX: (604) 921-7626.
email: peter@gryphonproductions.com
www.gryphonproductions.com
CONTACT
Peter Von Puttkamer

GYNORMOUS PICTURES, INC.
2687 McBain Ave., Vancouver, BC V6L 2C7.
TEL: (604) 899-4115. email: gynormous2000@yahoo.com
PRESIDENT/PRODUCER
Rosanne Milliken

H3O FILMED ENTERTAINMENT
705 – 1075 Barclay St., Vancouver, BC V6E 1G5.
TEL: (604) 662-3345. FAX: (604) 662-7720.
email: production@h3ofilm.com www.h3ofilm.com
PRESIDENT/CEO
John Curtis - jcurtis@h3ofilm.com
DIRECTOR
David Mackenzie

HADDOCK ENTERTAINMENT, INC.
810 – 207 W. Hastings St., Vancouver, BC V6B 1H7.
TEL: (604) 681-1516. FAX: (604) 684-3530.
email: office@haddockentertainment.com
www.haddockentertainment.com
PRESIDENT
Chris Haddock

Film and television production.

HOLIDAY PICTURES, LTD.
226 – 3495 Cambie St., Vancouver, BC V5Z 4R3.
TEL: (604) 879-6613. email: info@holidaypictures.ca
www.holidaypictures.ca
PRODUCER
Michael Parker, Shan Tam. An independent production company whose focus is on developing and producing original feature films, television programs and documentaries. The principals have established relationships with China, Hong Kong, Taiwan and Japan.

HOWE SOUND FILMS, INC.
4314 W. 13th Ave., Vancouver, BC V6R 2T9. TEL: (604) 224-0091.
FAX: (604) 224-0093. email: info@howesoundfilms.com
www.howesoundfilms.com
PRESIDENT/CEO/EXECUTIVE PRODUCER
Brian McKeown
COO/PRODUCER
Susan Baek

Creative house developing and producing television drama, documentaries and feature films.

INFINITY FEATURES
319 Main St., Vancouver, BC V6A 2S9. TEL: (604) 899-1077.
FAX: (604) 899-1027. email: info@infinityfeatures.net
www.infinityfeatures.net

PRODUCER
Robert Merilees, William Vince, Dave Valleau, Karl Mann, Amy Thillian, Scott Watson
DEVELOPMENT
Pete Valleau, Anna Galvin, Erin Haskett, Rebecca Fisher

INFINITY FILMED ENTERTAINMENT GROUP, LTD.
100 – 873 Beatty St., Vancouver, BC V6B 2M6.
TEL: (604) 681-5650. FAX: (604) 681-5664.
email: production@infinityfilms.ca www.infinityfilms.ca
PRESIDENT/CEO
Shel Piercy
DEVELOPMENT COORDINATOR
Ken Craw
TV series — drama, MOWs / feature films and co-productions.

INSIGHT FILM STUDIOS
112 W. 6th Ave., Vancouver, BC V5Y 1K6.
TEL: (604) 623-3369. FAX: (604) 623-3448.
email: info@insightfilm.com www.insightfilm.com
PRESIDENT/PRODUCER
Kirk Shaw
DIRECTOR/WRITER/CREATIVE CONSULTANT
Maryvonne Micale
V.P., DEVELOPMENT
Brad McAfee
Documentaries for TV, feature films, television commercials & series.

INTERNATIONAL DOCUMENTARY TELEVISION CORP.
73 Alexander St., Vancouver, BC V6A 1B2. TEL: (604) 664-0450.
FAX: (604) 664-0451. email: duncan@doctv.com
www.doctv.com
PRESIDENT
Robert Duncan

INTERNATIONAL KEYSTONE ENTERTAINMENT
300 – 2339 Columbia St., Vancouver, BC V5Y 3Y3.
TEL: (604) 873-9739. FAX: (604) 873-5919.
email: films@keypics.com www.keypics.com
www.westernpost.com
CEO
Robert Vince
PRESIDENT/CFO
Michael Strange
PRESIDENT, PRODUCTION & DEVELOPMENT
Anna McRoberts
V.P., BUSINESS AFFAIRS
Gail Schacht
V.P., WORLDWIDE SALES & DISTRIBUTION
Tim Brown
Integrated filmed entertainment company. Development, production, post-production, sales and distribution of live-action feature films.
USA: E9 – 23410 Civic Centre Way, Malibu, CA 90265.
TEL: (310) 317-4883. FAX: (310) 317-4903.

INTREPID FILMS, INC. / PETER LHOTKA
315 W. 24th St. N, Vancouver, BC V7M 2C7.
TEL: (604) 987-5581. email: lhotka@telus.net
PRODUCER
Peter Lhotka
TV / series / features / MOWs.

IRREVERENT MEDIA, LTD.
237 – 1271 Howe St., Vancouver, BC V6Z 1R3.
TEL: (604) 662-4330. FAX: (604) 608-4778.
email: info@irreverentmedia.com www.irreverentmedia.com
PRODUCER
Tom O'Brien, Harry Sutherland
DISTRIBUTION & MARKETING CONSULTANT
Caroline Stern
Development and production of feature films and TV properties.

JIM HAMM PRODUCTIONS
2555 Trinity St., Vancouver, BC V5K 1E3.
TEL: (604) 874-1110. FAX: (604) 874-1124.
PRESIDENT
Jim Hamm

KEATLEY ENTERTAINMENT
718 – 510 W. Hastings St., Vancouver, BC V6B 1L8.
TEL: (604) 291-9789. FAX: (604) 291-9759.
email: laura@keatleyentertainment.com
PRESIDENT
Julia Keatley

L' ETRANGER FILM PRODUCTIONS, LTD.
647 E. 21st Ave., Vancouver, BC V5V 1R8.
TEL: (604) 707-0677. FAX: (604) 872-1570.
email: etrangerfilmproductions@hotmail.com
PRODUCER
Kimberley Wakefield
Documentary – educational / feature film / television series.

LEGACY FILMWORKS
100 – 2257 Fulton Ave. W, Vancouver, BC V7V 1T7.
TEL: (604) 904-6772. FAX: (604) 904-6774.
email: legacy@legacyfilmworks.com
www.legacyfilmworks.com
PRESIDENT/CEO
Deborah Gabler
V.P., PRODUCTION
Tara Cowell-Plain
Full service production company — feature films and telelvision.

LES STANCHUK VIDEO PRODUCTION
1131 Columbia Ave., Trail, BC V1R 1J1. TEL: (250) 368-9964.
FAX: (250) 368-9965. email: lsvp@bigfoot.com
Industrial / commercial video / photographic services.

LONG TALE ENTERTAINMENT
107 – 1273 Howe St., Vancouver, BC V6Z 1R3.
TEL: (604) 218-3104. FAX: (604) 608-4933.
email: harry@longtale.ca www.longtale.ca
PRESIDENT
Harry Sutherland
PRODUCER
Marc Borja
Educational documentary

M.S.I. ENTERTAINMENT
107 – 1857 W. 4th Ave., Vancouver, BC V6J 1M4.
TEL: (604) 736-3001. FAX: (604) 738-4558.
email: rs@msifilms.com www.msifilms.com
PRESIDENT
Robert Spicer
Television series, drama, MOWs.

MASSEY PRODUCTIONS
249 E. St. James Rd. N., Vancouver, BC V7N 1L3.
TEL: (604) 739-8825. FAX: (604) 739-8835.
email: raymond@networkentertainment.ca
www.networkentertainment.ca
PRODUCER
Raymond Massey

THE MAY STREET GROUP
4412 Wilkinson Rd., Victoria, BC V8Z 5B7.
TEL: (250) 380-6656. FAX: (250) 380-6670.
email: maystreet@maystreet.ca www.maystreet.ca
PRESIDENT
Hilary Pryor
Full creative services from concept to release.

MEDIAWERKZ PRODUCTIONS, LTD.
611 E. Kings Rd. N., Vancouver, BC V7N 1J4.
TEL: (604) 987-1625. email: zinc@telus.net
Documentary / series / new media.

MERCER FILMS
Pier 32 Granville Island, 100 – 1333 Johnston St., Vancouver, BC V6H 3R9. TEL: (604) 689-0880.
FAX: (604) 689-3036. email: patricia@mercerad.com
WRITER/PRODUCER
Terry Mercer
PRODUCER
Paxton Robertson

MVP ENTERTAINMENT, INC.
400 – 1450 Creekside Dr., Vancouver, BC V6J 5B3.
TEL: (604) 731-9194. FAX: (604) 731-7174.
email: info@mvpfilm.com www.mvpfilm.com
PRESIDENT/CEO
Robert Frederick
CREATIVE EXECUTIVE
Bannister Bergen
Production, financing and development of children's / documentaries / feature films / television series.

NERD CORPS ENTERTAINMENT
1256 E. 6th Ave., 3rd Flr., Vancouver, BC V5T 1E7.
TEL: (604) 484-0266. FAX: (604) 484-0267.
email: info@nerdcorps.com www.nerdcorps.com
PRESIDENT
Ken Faier
CEO
Asaph Fipke
SENIOR V.P., PRODUCTION
Chuck Johnson
Full-service film & television development / animation studio.

NETWORK ENTERTAINMENT, INC.
400 – 1168 Hamilton St., Vancouver, BC V6B 2S2.
TEL: (604) 739-8825. FAX: (604) 739-8835.

email: raymond@networkentertainment.ca
www.networkentertainment.ca
PRODUCER
Raymond Massey

Specializing in dramatic sports, entertainment broadcasting and event properties.

NEW CITY PICTURES
1005 Cypress St., Vancouver, BC V6J 3K6.
TEL: (604) 732-7677. FAX: (604) 732-7693.
email: david@newcityfilms.com www.newcityfilms.com

NOVALIS ENTERTAINMENT, LTD.
P.O. Box 71040, 3552 W. 41st Ave., Vancouver, BC V6N 1W0.
TEL: (604) 266-1617. email: info@novalisentertainment.com
www.novalisentertainment.com
PRESIDENT/CEO
Charles K. Pitts

Production & co-productions. Novalis specializes in TV development.

O'MARA & RYAN
4077 Marine Dr. W, Vancouver, BC V7V 1N7.
TEL: (604) 926-9155. email: info@onthebackroads.com
www.onthebackroads.com www.omararyan.com
CONTACT
James O'Mara, Kate Ryan

Photography / directing / writing / producing.

OMNI FILM PRODUCTIONS LIMITED / WATER STREET PICTURES, LTD.
204 – 111 Water St., Vancouver, BC V6B 1A7.
TEL: (604) 681-6543. FAX: (604) 688-1425.
email: info@omnifilm.com www.omnifilm.com
PRESIDENT/EXECUTIVE PRODUCER
Michael Chechik
CONTACT
Michelle McMahon - ext. 112

Award-winning documentaries, factual and lifestyle series, dramas and comedies since 1979.

ORCA PRODUCTIONS, INC.
3425 W. 2nd Ave., Vancouver, BC V6R 1J3. TEL: (604) 732-9387.
FAX: (604) 732-3587. email: info@orcaproductions.com
www.orcaproductions.com

PAN PRODUCTIONS
1770 Brymea Ln., Victoria, BC V8N 6B7. TEL: (250) 389-6781.
FAX: (250) 383-6514. email: jim@panproductions.com
www.panproductions.com
CONTACT
Jim Eidt

Full-service creative / Betacam and HD production / full HD post facility & closed-captioning.

PAPERNY FILMS
2043 Quebec St., 2nd Flr., Vancouver, BC V5T 2Z6.
TEL: (604) 228-1960. FAX: (604) 228-1911.
email: info@papernyfilms.com www.papernyfilms.com
PRESIDENT/EXECUTIVE PRODUCER
David Paperny
PRODUCER/DIRECTOR
Audrey Mehler mercerfilms.com

PETERSEN PRODUCTIONS, INC.
1303 – 289 Drake St., Vancouver, BC V6B 5Z5.
TEL: (604) 669-8890. FAX: (604) 662-8013.
PRESIDENT
Curtis Petersen

USA: 106 Entrada Dr., Unit 8, Santa Monica, CA 90402.
TEL: (310) 230-8616.

PITCAIRN PICTURES, INC.
P.O. Box 497, Lions Bay, BC V0N 2E0. TEL: (604) 921-8899.
FAX: (604) 921-8904. email: jo@pitpix.com
CONTACT
Jo Kirkpatrick

POINT GREY PICTURES, INC.
2043 Quebec St., 2nd Flr., Vancouver, BC V5T 2Z7.
TEL: (604) 221-4426. FAX: (604) 742-9957.
email: info@pointgreypictures.com www.pointgreypictures.com
PRODUCER
Terence McKeown
DIRECTOR/EXECUTIVE PRODUCER
John Zaritsky

Creating documentaries for television and theatrical release,

POINT OF VIEW FILM, INC.
3216 W. 2nd Ave., Vancouver, BC V6K 1K8.
TEL: (604) 734-5035. FAX: (604) 737-0123.
email: michellebjornson@excite.com
PRESIDENT
Michelle Bjornson

Drama & documentary: development / production / release.

PUDDLE DUCK PRODUCTIONS, LTD.
2329 W. 14th Ave., Vancouverc BC V6K 2W2.
TEL: (604) 734-1103. FAX: (604) 734-1150.
email: puddlesbri@aol.com
PRESIDENT
Brian Schecter

QUIXOTE FILMS, INC.
300 – 238 E. 2nd Ave., Vancouver, BC V5T 1B7.
TEL: (604) 707-0636. FAX: (604) 707-0638.
email: gm@quixotefilms.com www.quixotefilms.com
EXECUTIVE PRODUCER
Goff Martin

Complete production services across Canada specializing in foreign commercial production.

RADKE FILM GROUP / STEAM FILMS
330 – 948 Homer St., Vancouver, BC V6B 2W7.
TEL: (604) 682-2507. FAX: (604) 682-2975.
email: infovancouver@radke.tv www.radke.tv
SALES
Michael Haldane, Scott Smith

Commercials and complete productions services across Canada. See also Ontario.

RAVE FILMS
103 – 1815 Pine St., Vancouver, BC V6J 3C8.
TEL: (604) 408-1693. FAX: (604) 408-1670.
email: ravefilm@telus.net
PRODUCER
Sharon McGowan
PRODUCER/WRITER
Peggy Thompson

Film & television development & production.

RAVEN WEST FILMS
701 – 207 W. Hastings St., Vancouver, BC V6B 1H7.
TEL: (604) 681-7121. FAX: (604) 681-7173.
email: info@ravenwestfilms.com www.ravenwestfilms.com
PRODUCER/DIRECTOR
Carl Bessai
ASSOCIATE PRODUCER
Emily Alden

RED LETTER FILMS
202 – 4620 Yew St., Vancouver, BC V6L 2J6.
TEL: (604) 737-3657. FAX: (604) 872-0367.
email: info@redletterfilms.com www.redletterfilms.com
PRESIDENT
Sylvie Peltier

RED STORM PRODUCTIONS
610 – 207 W. Hastings St., Vancouver, BC V6B 1H7.
TEL: (604) 254-1346. FAX: (604) 331-9979.
email: info@redstorm.ca www.redstorm.ca
CONTACT
Arlene Nova Ami

Film and television.

REUNION PICTURES, INC.
20 Brooksbank Ave. N, Vancouver, BC V7J 2B8.
TEL: (604) 904-5615. FAX: (604) 904-5627.
email: info@reunionpictures.ca www.reunionpictures.ca
PRODUCER
Matthew O'Connor, Lisa Richardson, Tom Rowe

Development, financing and production of feature films, MOW's, mini-series and series.

RIVER OF STONE PRODUCTIONS
929 Richards St., Vancouver, BC V6B 3B6. TEL: (604) 685-2045.
FAX: (866) 286-1464. email: mary@riverofstone.com
www.riverofstone.com
PRESIDENT
Mary Sparacio

SAJO PRODUCTIONS, INC.
P.O. Box 888, Gibsons Landing, BC V0N 1V0.
TEL: (604) 886-3639. email: devadas@telus.net
PRESIDENT/PRODUCER
Robert Nichol

Features.

SAVI MEDIA, INC.
3516 W. 13th Ave., Vancouver, BC V6R 2S3.
TEL: (604) 734-1550. FAX: (604) 734-1414.
email: mail@savi-media.com www.savi-media.com
PRESIDENT
Alexandra Raffé
DIRECTOR, CREATIVE AFFAIRS
Tara Twigg

Television drama / feature films / children's series, animation. See also Ontario.

SCINTILLA ENTERTAINMENT, INC.
7593 Whitespray Dr., Vancouver, BC V5X 4T3.
email: info@quadriproperties.com www.ScintillaEnt.com
CONTACT
Pindar Azad

Television production.

SCREEN SIREN PICTURES, INC.
300 – 291 E. 2nd Ave., Vancouver, BC V5T 1B8.
TEL: (604) 687-7591. FAX: (604) 687-4937.
email: info@screensiren.ca www.screensiren.ca
PRESIDENT/PRODUCER
Trish Dolman
PRODUCER
Leah Mallen

Film and television production company that focuses on creating high-quality, innovative documentary and feature films.

SEA TO SKY ENTERTAINMENT
P.O. Box 3640, Garibaldi Highlands, BC V0N 1T0.
TEL: (604) 898-5930. email: apolo@shaw.ca
DIRECTOR
Adriane Polo, Mark McConchie, Kathy Daniels

Film and video.

SELWYN ENTERPRISES, INC.
2917 W. 35th Ave., Vancouver, BC V6N 2M5.
TEL: (604) 731-5257. email: selwyn_jacob@telus.net
EXECUTIVE PRODUCER
Joan Jacob

Film and television.

SEPIA FILMS
1 Strachan Point Rd. W, Vancouver, BC V7W 1C1.
TEL: (604) 921-8790. FAX: (604) 215-0030.
email: sepia@telus.net
PRESIDENT
Vic Sarin
PRODUCER
Tina Pehme, Kim Roberts

Feature films.

SHAVICK ENTERTAINMENT
62 W. 8th Ave., 4th Flr., Vancouver, BC V5Y 1M7.
TEL: (604) 874-4300. FAX: (604) 874-4305.
email: info@shavickentertainment.com
www.shavickentertainment.com
PRESIDENT
James Shavick

SOAPBOX PRODUCTIONS, INC.
106 – 1260 Lynn Valley Rd. N, Vancouver, BC V7J 2A3.
TEL: (604) 983-2555. FAX: (604) 983-2558.
email: nick@soapboxproductions.ca
www.soapboxproductions.ca
EXECUTIVE PRODUCER
Nick Orchard

Children's / documentary – educational / feature film / TV series.

SOMA FILM, VIDEO & TELEVISION, LTD.
RR 1 Box X-26, Bowen Island, BC V0N 1G0.
TEL: (604) 947-0048. email: deepak@somatv.com
PRESIDENT
Deepak Sahasrabudhe
VICE PRESIDENT
Susan Millar

STARVISION ENTERTAINMENT
2933 Oriole Cres, Abbotsford, BC V2T 4C9.
TEL: (604) 619-3677. FAX: (604) 850-9241.
email: starvision@shaw.ca
http://members.shaw.ca/starvision/index.html
CONTACT
Kenneth W. Meisenbacher

Documentaries, corporate, music, educational and training videos. Location scouting services.

STERLING PICTURES, LTD.
17 – 1201 Lamey's Mill Rd., Vancouver, BC V6H 3S8.
TEL: (604) 732-1491. FAX: (604) 732-1426.
email: gboyd@telus.net
PRINCIPAL
Gigi Boyd

STUDIO B PRODUCTIONS
190 Alexander St., 6th Fl., Vancouver, BC V6A 1B5.
TEL: (604) 684-2363. FAX: (604) 602-0208.
email: reception@studiobproductions.com
www.studiobproductions.com
CONTACT
Blair Peters, Chris Bartleman

THREE WAVES STUDIO, INC.
311 – 73 Gorge Rd. W, Victoria, BC V9A 1L9.
TEL: (250) 995-2106. email: 3waves@telus.net
www.threewavesstudio.com
PRODUCER
Peg Ainsley

TRIAD COMMUNICATIONS, LTD.
2751 Oxford St., Vancouver, BC V5K 1N5.
TEL: (800) 600-9762, (604) 253-3990. FAX: (604) 253-0770.
email: triadc@comwave.com www.triadcommunications.ca
CONTACT
Gay Ludlow

TROIKA PRODUCTIONS, INC.
404 – 999 Canada Pl., Vancouver, BC V6C 3E2.
TEL: (604) 990-9020. FAX: (604) 990-9021.
email: troika@axion.net
PRESIDENT/PRODUCER
Walter Daroshin

TRUE WEST FILMS, LTD.
201 – 2050 Scotia St., Vancouver, BC V5T 4T1.
TEL: (604) 879-4590. FAX: (604) 879-4540.
email: inquiry@truewestfilms.com www.truewestfilms.com
PRESIDENT
Elizabeth Yake
DEVELOPMENT DIRECTOR
Gosia Kamela

Films, TV series and documentaries.

VOICEBOX PRODUCTIONS, INC.
825 Powell St., Vancouver, BC V6A 1H7. TEL: (604) 708-5150.
FAX: (604) 708-5171. email: info@voiceboxproductions.com
www.voiceboxproductions.com

YALETOWN ENTERTAINMENT CORP.
4908 Pine Cres, Vancouver, BC V3M 3P6.
TEL: (604) 669-3543. FAX: (604) 669-3543.
email: mcollier@yaletownentertainment.com
www.yaletownentertainment.com
PRESIDENT
Mike Collier

Feature film / television production.

MANITOBA

BUFFALO GAL PICTURES, INC.
777 – 70 Arthur St., Winnipeg, MB R3B 1G7.
TEL: (204) 956-2777. FAX: (204) 956-7999.
email: info@buffalogalpictures.com
www.buffalogalpictures.com
PRESIDENT
Phyllis Laing

EAGLE VISION & CENTURY STREET DISTRIBUTION
509 Century St., Winnipeg, MB R3H 0L8. TEL: (800) 772-0368,
(204) 772-0368. FAX: (204) 772-0360.
info@centurystreet.ca www.centurystreet.ca
CO-PRESIDENT
Wayne Sheldon, Lisa Meeches
V.P., PRODUCTION
Kyle Irving

Children's, documentary, feature film, television.

FARPOINT FILMS
202 – 1335 Erin St., Winnipeg, MB R3E 2S7.
TEL: (204) 222-3755. FAX: (204) 772-0045.
email: info@farpointfilms.com www.farpointfilms.com
PRODUCER/PRINCIPAL
Kyle Bornais
DIRECTOR/PRINCIPAL
John Barnard
WRITER
Chris Charney

FRANTIC FILMS
300 – 70 Arthur St., Winnipeg, MB R3B 1G7.
TEL: (204) 949-0070. FAX: (204) 949-0050.
email: info@franticfilms.com www.franticfilms.com
PRESIDENT/CREATIVE DIRECTOR
Christopher Bond
V.P./PRODUCER
Ken Zorniak
CEO/EXECUTIVE PRODUCER
Jamie Brown

Feature film, TV and multimedia.

JULIJETTE, INC.
1232 Chevrier Blvd., Winnipeg, MB R3T 1Y3.
TEL: (204) 415-3883. FAX: (204) 415-3889.
email: julijetteinc@gmail.com www.julijette.com
CONTACT
Juliette Hagopian

Feature film and television.

KIZUK PRODUCTIONS
78 Stoneham Cres, Winnipeg, MB R2G 3L8.
TEL: (204) 667-6339. email: kizukvideo@shaw.ca
PRESIDENT
Rick Kizuk
SENIOR PRODUCER
Hugh McColl

KONO FILMS, LTD.
81 Claremont Ave., Winnipeg, MB R2H 1W1.
TEL: (204) 237-5649. email: konosite@shaw.ca
PRESIDENT
Charles Konowal

MEMORIA MOTION PICTURE PRODUCTIONS
200 – 690 St Joseph St., Winnipeg, MB R2H 3E2.
TEL: (204) 233-1189. FAX: (204) 233-0811.
email: info@memoriaworldevents.com
www.memoriaworldevents.com
CONTACT
Romeo Jacobucci

Documentary films: Power of the Music, 1938 World Events, Grand Jury Prize winner; World Goes Mad, Again, Historical Documentary

MERIT MOTION PICTURES, INC.
248 Princess St., Winnipeg, MB R3B 1M2.
TEL: (204) 775-4092. FAX: (204) 783-2311.
email: info@meritmotionpictures.com
www.meritmotionpictures.com
PRESIDENT
Merit Jensen-Carr

MIDCANADA ENTERTAINMENT
509 Century St., Winnipeg, MB R3H 0L8.
TEL: (800) 722-0368, (204) 772-0368.
FAX: (204) 772-0360. email: kevin@midcan.com
www.midcanadaentertainment.com
PRESIDENT
Wayne Sheldon
EXECUTIVE PRODUCER
Kevin Dunn

ORIGINAL PICTURES, INC.
602 – 191 Lombard Ave., Winnipeg, MB R3B 0X1.
TEL: (204) 940-3310. FAX: (204) 943-5502.
email: jessicak@originalpicturesinc.com
PRESIDENT/PRODUCER
Kim Todd
CEO
Nicholas Hirst

Feature films and television.

THE SHARING CIRCLE
509 Century St., Winnipeg, MB R3H 0L8.
TEL: (204) 786-1655. FAX: (204) 772-0360.
email: sharingcircle@midcan.com www.thesharingcircle.com
PRESIDENT
Lisa Meeches
VICE PRESIDENT

KYLE IRVING
VONNIE VON HELMOLT FILM
225 Symington Rd., Winnipeg, MB R2C 5J7.
TEL: (204) 229-9879. FAX: (204) 224-9513.
email: vonnievh@shaw.ca
PRESIDENT/PRODUCER
Vonnie Von Helmolt

Features, TV movies, series, documentaries and performing arts specials. Company develops and produces unusual projects based on or featuring the performing arts, literature or comedy.

NEW BRUNSWICK

ATLANTIC MEDIAWORKS
469 King St., Fredericton, N.B. E3B 1E5.
TEL: (506) 458-8806. FAX: (506) 452-2700.
email: bob.miller@atlanticmediaworks.com
www.atlanticmediaworks.com
CONTACT
Bob Miller, Daphne Curtis

Video & film production for TV / corporate.

BEAR PAW PRODUCTIONS
17 Union St., Big Cove, NB E4W 2Z5. TEL: (506) 523-4116, (506) 523-3754. email: bpaw@nb.sympatico.ca
CONTACT
Brian Francis

Documentaries.

BELLEFEUILLE PRODUCTION, LTÉE
35 Toombs St., Moncton, NB E1A 3A4.
TEL: (506) 857-1090. FAX: (506) 857-0352.
email: telvision@nb.aibn.com www.bellefeuilleproduction.ca
PRESIDENT
Jean-Claude Bellefeuille

Documentaries.

CINIMAGE PRODUCTIONS
39 Bromley Ave., Moncton, NB E1C 5T8.
TEL: (506) 386-1616. FAX: (506) 855-7025.
email: cinimage@rogers.com
CONTACT
Monique LeBlanc

Documentaries.

CONNECTIONS PRODUCTIONS
1111 Main Street, suite 203, Moncton, N. B. E1C 1H3 .
TEL: (506) 382-3984. FAX: (506) 382-3980.
email: info@cptv.ca www.cptv.ca
CONTACT
François Savoie, Michael Savoie

Documentaries and varieties. Development / production & direction.

DREAM STREET PICTURES, INC.
75 Archibald St., Moncton, NB E1C 5J2.
TEL: (506) 854-1057. FAX: (506) 382-4144.
email: info@dreamstreetpictures.com
www.dreamstreetpictures.com
PRESIDENT/PRODUCER
Timothy M. Hogan
V.P./PRODUCER
Rick LeGuerrier - rick@dreamstreetpictures.com

TV & feature films / service productions.

FORESIGHT ANIMATION STUDIO
P.O. Box 788, 100 Cameron St., Moncton, NB E1C 8N6.
TEL: (506) 853-3033. FAX: (506) 859-1319.
email: info@foresightanimation.com
www.foresightanimation.com
PRESIDENT
Bob Sissons
VICE PRESIDENT
Janet Spinney, Tony Sissons
EXECUTIVE PRODUCER
Jack Coreau

INNOVATIVE VIDEO SOLUTIONS, LTD.
76 Princess St., Saint John, NB E2L 1K4.
TEL: (506) 693-4487. email: darrell@videosolutions.ca
www.videosolutions.ca
CONTACT
Darrell Bainbridge
Mike Burchill - mike@videosolutions.ca

Documentary, corporate, event and E.N.G. Betacam SP / DVcam production, concept to completion. Meerkat 10' jib with remote head.

LOOGAROO
385 Pleasant St., Miramichi, NB E1V 1X4.
TEL: (506) 622-3333. FAX: (506) 622-3383.
email: gfowler@loogaroo.com www.loogaroo.com
CONTACT
Gene Fowler, Andrew Dunn

Animation production & post-production.

MAX MEDIA, LTD.
849 Barker St., Fredericton, NB E3A 3K4. TEL: (506) 474-0006.
FAX: (506) 472-1496. email: maxmedia@nbnet.nb.ca
CONTACT
Kevin Matthews

Documentaries.

MOLTO ITALIANO FILM PRODUCTIONS, INC. / ZE GROYDS FILMS, INC.
P.O. Box 431, Fredericton, NB E3B 4Z9. TEL: (506) 459-2599.
FAX: (506) 454-9593. email: lloyd_salomone@hotmail.com
CONTACT
Lloyd Salomone

Documentaries / features.

MOZUS PRODUCTIONS
45 Norwood Ave., Moncton, NB E1C 6L8. TEL: (506) 382-1116, (506) 382-1116. FAX: (506) 870-1900.
email: mozus@nb.sympatico.ca
CONTACT
Suzette Lagacé, Maurice Aubin

Documentaries.

PEDERSEN PRODUCTIONS, INC.
12 Rte. 695, Jemseg, NB E4C 3M6. TEL: (506) 657-3300.
FAX: (506) 657-3401. email: mark@pedersenproductions.com

CONTACT
Mark Pedersen

Documentaries / Canadian Antiques Roadshow.

PHANTOM PRODUCTIONS, INC.
1010 Tamarack Dr., Bathurst, NB E2A 4H4.
TEL: (506) 547-8984. FAX: (506) 546-7448.
http://phantomprod.com
DIRECTOR
Tony Larder

PRODUCTIONS APPALACHES
39, rue Brydges Street, Moncton, NB E1C 2E7.
TEL: (506) 382-5511. FAX: (506) 382-5513.
email: rodolphe@nbnet.nb.ca
CONTACT
Rodolphe Caron, France Gallant

Documentaries.

LES PRODUCTIONS GRANA PRODUCTIONS, INC.
261, rue Lutz Street, Moncton, NB E1C 5G4.
TEL: (506) 877-2252. FAX: (506) 877-2255.
email: info@grana.ca
CONTACT
Sam Grana

All genres.

PRODUCTIONS PHARE-EST, INC.
20 – 140 rue Botsford, Moncton, NB E1C 8L9.
TEL: (506) 857-9941. FAX: (506) 857-1806.
email: glosier@nbnet.nb.ca
CONTACT
Cécile Chevrier, Gilles Losier

Documentaries and fictions.

SHORE ROAD PICTURES, INC.
175 Surrey Cres, Fredericton, NB E3B 4L4.
TEL: (506) 455-8959. email: tony.whalen@shoreroadpictures.com
www.shoreroadpictures.com
PRESIDENT/DIRECTOR
Gia Milani
V.P./PRODUCER
Tony Whalen

NEWFOUNDLAND & LABRADOR

2M INNOVATIVE, INC.
683 Water St., 2nd Flr., St. John's, NL A1E 1B5.
TEL: (709) 739-9055. FAX: (709) 739-9065.
email: msexton@nfld.com
WRITER/DIRECTOR
Mary Walsh
PRODUCER
Mary Sexton, Mary Walsh

FIRE CROWN FILMS
348 Mount Scio Rd., St. John's, NL A1B 4L6.
TEL: (709) 753-6542. FAX: (709) 753-0607.
email: firecrown@nl.rogers.com
www.geocities.com/mfwhite@nl.rogers.com
PRODUCER
Marian Frances White

KICKHAM EAST PRODUCTIONS, INC.
127 - 38 Pearson St., St. John's, NL A1A 3R1.
TEL: (709) 738-6474. FAX: (709) 738-6475.
email: jripley@nfld.com
PRODUCER
Jennice Ripley

MORAG LOVES COMPANY, LTD.
P.O. Box 52, Stn. C, St. John's, NL A1C 5H5.
TEL: (709) 739-0447. FAX: (709) 739-0467.
email: info@morag.ca www.morag.ca
PRODUCER/DIRECTOR
Barbara Doran
PRODUCER
Lynne Wilson

Film and television.

PIPERSTOCK PRODUCTIONS, LTD.
24 Quarry Rd., Torbay, NL A1K 1A3. TEL:(709) 437-1753.
email: dermot24@nl.rogers.com
CONTACT
Dermot O'Reilly

Documentaries.

POPE PRODUCTIONS, LTD.
PO Box 5278, St. John's, NL A1C 5W1. TEL: (709) 722-7673.
FAX: (709) 738-7285. email: info@popeproductions.com
www.popeproductions.com
CONTACT
Paul Pope

Feature film / documentary / TV programming.

VIDCRAFT PRODUCTIONS, LIMITED
425 Curling St., Cornerbrook, NL A2H 3K4.
TEL: (709) 785-1157. email: info@vidcraft.com
www.vidcraft.com
CONTACT
Ron O'Connell

Broadcast video / multimedia / documentaries / commercials.

WAVELIGHT PRODUCTIONS
P.O. Box 13305, Stn. A, 42 O'Leary Ave., St. John's, NL A1B 4B7. TEL: (866) 753-2219. FAX: (709) 754-3990.
email: nicky@wavelight.ca www.wavelight.ca
CONTACT
Nicky Despres

TV commercials / corporate videos.

NORTHWEST TERRITORIES

ELLISON, BOB
254 Fairchild Cres, Yellowknife, NT X1A 2A6.
TEL: (867) 766-2355. email: ellison_bob@hotmail.com

40 years of experience in broadcast television.

INUVIALUIT COMMUNICATION SOCIETY
P.O. Box 1704, Inuvik, NT X0E 0T0. TEL: (867) 777-2320.
FAX: (867) 777-2744. email: ics@northwestel.net
CONTACT
Topsy Cockney

Providing programming for APTN.

LONE WOOLF FILM AND TELEVISION PRODUCTION SERVICES
P.O. Box 1536, Yellowknife, NT X1A 2P2. TEL: (867) 873-4588.
FAX: (867) 873-5497. email: terry@lonewoolf.com
www.lonewoolf.com
DP/PRODUCER
Terry Woolf

25 years of award-winning production experience. Cold weather, remote, cross-cultural experience. Gemini Award. Gabriel Award. AFVF Red Ribbon.

TRIVANGARD PICTURES
54 Morrison Dr., Yellowknife, NT X1A 1Z2. TEL: (867) 873-5176.
FAX: (867) 873-4758. email: trivan@theedge.ca
CONTACT
Alex Czarnicki

Writing and development of feature motion pictures.

WESTERN ARCTIC MOTION PICTURES (WAMP)
P.O. Box 2487, Yellowknife, NT X1A 2P8. TEL: (867) 766-2586.
email: wamp@wamp.ca www.wamp.ca
CONTACT
Diane Boudreau

A non-profit video society involved in making artistic-driven films. Non-linear editing, 16mm camera, DV camera package and workshops.

YELLOWKNIFE FILMS, LTD.
P.O. Box 2562, 5021 53rd St., Yellowknife, NT X1A 2P9.
TEL: (867) 873-8610. FAX: (867) 873-9405.
email: ykf@theedge.ca
CONTACT
Alan Booth

Documentaries / film / video. Produced The Northern Lights, the National Film Board of Canada best-seller.

NOVA SCOTIA

AFTERDARK PRODUCTIONS, INC.
303 – 1668 Barrington St., Halifax, NS B3J 2A2.
TEL: (902) 423-3497. FAX: (902) 484-6880.
email: info@afterdarktv.com www.afterdarktv.com
PRODUCER
Chris Cuthbertson, Drew Hagen

Film, TV and documentary production / editing services.

ARCADIA ENTERTAINMENT, INC.
301 - 6454 Quinpool Rd., Halifax, NS B3L 1A9.
TEL: (902) 446-3414. FAX: (902) 446-3416.
email: info@arcadiatv.com www.arcadiatv.com
CONTACT
John Wesley Chisholm

Develops and produces Maritime-related programs which raise interest in oceans and waters.

BIG MOTION PICTURES, LIMITED
P.O. Box 202, 5 Pleasant St., 2nd Flr., Chester, NS B0J 1J0.

TEL: (902) 275-1350. FAX: (902) 275-1353.
email: contact@bigmotionpictures.com
www.bigmotionpictures.com
CONTACTS
Wayne Grigsby, David MacLeod

Develops and produces top-rated TV programs for national and international markets.

BLACK DOG FILMS – THE MONSTER PRODUCTIONS, INC.
10 Stonehaven Rd., Halifax, NS B3N 1G1.
TEL: (902) 431-8448. email: mail@jaydahl.com
CONTACT
Jay Dahl

BLACK RIVER PRODUCTIONS, LIMITED
P.O. Box 55, Mabou, NS B0E 1X0. TEL: (902) 258-3354.
FAX: (902) 258-3244. email: neall@ns.sympatico.ca
www.blackriver.ns.ca
CONTACT
Neal Livingston

Thirty productions since 1968. Bilingual.

CENEX, INC.
202 – 3600 Kempt Rd., Halifax, NS B3K 4X8.
TEL: (902) 446-3775. FAX: (902) 431-4065.
email: scott@cenex.ca www.cenex.ca
CONTACT
Scott Westerlaken

Television commercials and video production services.

CHRONICLE PICTURES
532 – 1657 Barrington St., Halifax, NS B3J 2A1.
TEL: (902) 425-4885. FAX: (902) 425-4851.
email: info@chronicle-pictures.com
www.chronicle-pictures.com
PARTNER
Craig Cameron, Evangelo Kioussis

COLLIDEASCOPE DIGITAL PRODUCTIONS, INC.
5212 Sackville St., 4th Flr., Halifax, NS B3J 1K6.
TEL: (902) 429-8949. FAX: (902) 429-0265.
email: info@collideascope.com www.collideascope.com
CONTACT
Michael-Andreas Kuttner, Steven J.P. Comeau

Producer of TV and interactive media for the children's, youth and young adult markets. Seek national and intl. co-production opportunities to partner on TV projects and/or new media components.

CREATIVE ATLANTIC COMMUNICATIONS, LIMITED
2087 Gottingen Street, Halifax, NS B3K 3B2.
TEL: (902) 423-1989. FAX: (902) 423-3711.
email: info@creativeatlantic.ca www.creativeatlantic.ca
CONTACT
Janice Evans, Greg Jones

TV comedy / drama / documentaries.

CURVE PRODUCTIONS, INC.
5212 Sackville Street, Suite 200, Halifax, NS B3J 1K6.
TEL: (902) 423-0271. email: lara@curveproductions.ca
www.curveproductionsinc.com
CONTACT
Lara Cassidy, Steve Richard

Documentary / corporate / music video / short film / television.

EMOTION PICTURES INCORPORATED
5182 Bishop St., Halifax, NS B3J 1C9. TEL: (902) 422-7604.
FAX: (902) 422-5372. email: contact@emotionpictures.ca
www.emotionpictures.ca
CONTACT
Thom Fitzgerald

3 Needles, The Event, The Wild Dogs, Beefcake, The Hanging Garden.

ENVISION PRODUCTIONS, LIMITED
2103 Bauer St., Halifax, NS B3K 3W4. TEL: (902) 422-1337.
FAX: (902) 446-3944. email: info@envisionproductions.ca
www.envisionproductions.ca
CONTACT
Chuck Lapp

Documentary production.

EYE OF THE STORM MEDIA PRODUCTION, LTD.
6 Plymouth St., Halifax, NS B3M 2S2. TEL: (902) 445-5739.
FAX: (902) 445-0639. email: eyestorm@ns.sympatico.ca
www3.ns.sympatico.ca/jpiccolo
CONTACT
John Piccolo

Specializing in television journalism and factual programs.

FOLKUS ATLANTIC, INC.
67 Hospital St., Sydney, NS B1P 2H9. TEL: (902) 577-3363.
FAX: (902) 562-5106. email: folkus@auracom.com
www.folkus.com
CONTACT
Joan Weeks

Documentary and industrial production for broadcast, promotional and educational videos and CD-ROMs.

HALIFAX FILM
1478 Queen St., 2nd Flr., Halifax, NS B3J 2H7.
TEL: (902) 423-0260. FAX: (902) 422-0752.
email: info@halifaxfilm.com www.halifaxfilm.com
CONTACT
Michael Donovan, Charles Bishop

Original film and television content.

HUMAN SCALE PRODUCTIONS
430 Fracklyn St., Halifax, NS B3H 1A9. TEL: (902) 429-9962.
email: doug@humanscaleproductions.com
www.humanscaleproductions.com
CONTACT
Doug Karr

Specializing in independent film and video for TV and theatrical release.

IDLEWILD FILMS, LIMITED
2370 MacDonald St., Halifax, NS B3L 3G4.
TEL: (902) 454-7866. FAX: (902) 454-7021.
email: niven@ns.sympatico.ca
PRODUCER
Bill Niven

IMX COMMUNICATIONS, INC.
1556 Queen St., Halifax, NS B3J 2H8. TEL: (902) 422-4000.
FAX: (902) 422-4427. email: imx@imx.ca www.imxcommunications.com
PRESIDENT/PRODUCER
Chris Zimmer
DIRECTOR, OPERATIONS & DEVELOPMENT
Ann Bernier
PROJECT COORDINATOR
Robert Hagen

Co-production relationships, both nationally and internationally, with countries including Britain, Spain, Venezuela, France, Belgium, Germany and the U.S.

JOHN WALKER PRODUCTIONS, LTD.
5675 Inglis St., Halifax, NS B3H 1K2. TEL: (902) 423-3436.
FAX: (902) 423-9199. email: walkerfilm@ns.sympatico.ca
www.thefairyfaith.com

LOWENBE HOLDINGS, LTD.
680 Indian Point Rd., Glen Haven, NS B3Z 2T7.
TEL: (902) 823-1409, (902) 823-1404. FAX: (902) 820-2056.
email: jmiller@lowenbe.ca www.lowenbe.ca
PRESIDENT
Jan Miller
CEO
Geoff Leboutillier

Producers (documentary), consultants (co-productions).

LYNK INC PRODUCTIONS
42A Shore Rd., Dartmouth, NS B3A 1A2. TEL: (902) 471-8269.
email: marylynk@ns.sympatico.ca
CONTACT
Mary Lynk

MARITIME TELEVISION & PRODUCTION SERVICES
P.O. Box 518, Lunenburg, NS B0J 2C0. TEL: (902) 634-4815.
FAX: (902) 634-1955. email: mps@ns.sympatico.ca
CONTACT
Robert Bongard, Yvonne Mosley

Develops and produces variety and documentary for television. Equipment and personnel resources for television and commercial productions.

MENTOR PICTURES, LTD.
6A Erskine St., Dartmouth, NS B2Y 1P3. TEL: (902) 466-0978.
FAX: (902) 466-1030. email: a.macvicar@ns.sympatico.ca
www.mentorpictures.com
CONTACT
Andrew MacVicar, Sherry Devanney-MacVicar

Features, commercials & corporate videos.

NEW SCOTLAND PICTURES, INC.
200 – 5212 Sackville St., Halifax, NS B3J 1K6.
TEL: (902) 429-1080. FAX: (902) 429-1190.
email: info@newscotlandpictures.ca
www.newscotlandpictures.ca
CONTACT
Charlie Cahill

Arts and music film and video products for TV, music specials and documentaries for CMT, Vision, Bravo!, CBC, PBS. Production management for music videos shooting in Nova Scotia.

OCEAN ENTERTAINMENT, LIMITED
404 – 1657 Barrington St., Halifax, NS B3J 2A1.
TEL: (902) 423-9056. FAX: (902) 423-9058.
email: ocean@ocean.ca www.ocean.ca
PRESIDENT
Johanna Eliot

Production company specializing primarily in television series and documentaries.

PALPABLE PRODUCTIONS, INC.
P.O. Box 628, 59 Pleasant St., Mahone Bay, NS B0J 2E0.
TEL: (902) 624-1979. email: camelia@palpable.ca
CONTACT
Camelia Frieberg

Wilby Wonderful, Past Perfect, The Five Senses, The Sweet Hereafter, Exotica, Eclipse.

PICTURE PLANT, LTD.
232 Lincoln St Ste A, Lunenburg NS B0J 2C0.
TEL: (902) 640-0174 . FAX: (902) 640-0175.
email: wmacgillivray@pictureplant.com
tgreenlaw@pictureplant.com www.pictureplant.com
PRESIDENT
William MacGillivray
VICE PRESIDENT
Terry Greenlaw

Film and television production.

REDSTAR FILMS, LTD.
533 – 1657 Barrington St., Halifax, NS B3J 2A1.
TEL: (902) 429-5254. FAX: (902) 429-5256.
email: redstarfilm@aol.com
PRESIDENT
Paul Kimball

Producers of film and television.

TELL TALE PRODUCTIONS, INC.
1657 Barrington St., Halifax, NS B3J 2A1.
TEL: (902) 482-6506. FAX: (902) 444-9919.
email: edward@telltale.tv www.telltale.tv
CONTACT
Edward Peill

Documentaries / commercials / EPKs / multimedia.

TOPSAIL PRODUCTIONS
5240 Blowers St., Upper Level, Halifax, NS B3J 1J7.
TEL: (902) 422-0680. FAX: (902) 422-0410.
email: michael.volpe@topsailentertainment.com
www.topsailentertainment.com
CONTACT
Michael Volpe

TRAILER PARK PRODUCTIONS, LIMITED
5240 Blowers St. Upper Level, Halifax, NS B3J 1J7.
TEL: (902) 422-0680. FAX: (902) 422-0410.
email: bdunn@trailerparkproductions.tv
www.trailerparkboys.com
CONTACT
Barrie Dunn, Mike Clattenburg

TV production (Trailer Park Boys).

TRIAD FILM PRODUCTIONS, LTD.
1657 Barrington St #431,Halifax NS, B3J 2A1.
TEL: (902) 422-7174. FAX: (902) 422-8945.
email: triadfilms@eastlink.ca www.triadfilms.ns.ca
CONTACT
Peter d'Entremont

Documentaries and television.

URSA MAJOR FILMS
7770 Hwy 221 RR 2, Centreville, NS B0P 1J0.
TEL: (902) 678 3748.
email: pegasusproductions@compuserve.com
CONTACT
Marke Slipp

ZIJI FILM & TELEVISION PRODUCTIONS, LTD.
The Roy Bldg., 422 – 1657 Barrington St., Halifax, NS B3J 2A1. TEL: (902) 425-5001. FAX: (902) 429-0077.
email: lapatten@ziji.ca www.ziji.ca
PRODUCER/MANAGER, BUSINESS AFFAIRS
Angela De Nicola
WRITER/DIRECTOR
Lesley Ann Patten

Documentaries, features and television. Co-production partnerships.

ONTARIO

100 PERCENT FILM & TELEVISION
701 – 116 Spadina Ave., Toronto, ON M5V 2K6.
TEL: (416) 304-5225. FAX: (416) 304-1222.
email: info@onehundredpercent.ca
www.onehundredpercent.ca
EXECUTIVE PRODUCER
Jan Peter Meyboom, Ken Finkleman

2KNINE CREATIVE LAB
371 Hester St., Thunder Bay, ON P7B 2K9.
TEL: (807) 345-2434. email: info@2knine.com
www.2knine.com
PRODUCER/DIRECTOR
Lee Chambers

9 STORY ENTERTAINMENT
G09 – 33 Fraser Ave., Toronto, ON M6K 3J9.
TEL: (416) 530-9900. FAX: (416) 530-9935.
email: stevej@9story.com vincec@9story.com
www.9story.com
PARTNER
Steve Jarosz, Vince Commisso

Animation content producer.

90TH PARALLEL FILM & TELEVISION PRODUCTIONS, LTD.
203 Gerrard St. E, Toronto, ON M5A 2E7. TEL: (416) 364-9090.
FAX: (416) 364-0580. email: info@90thparallel.ca
www.90thparallel.ca
PRESIDENT/PRODUCER
Gordon S. Henderson

ABUNDANT WATERS PRODUCTIONS, INC.
77 The Westway, Toronto, ON M9P 2B4. TEL: (416) 999-3662.
FAX: (416) 614-3535. email: abundantwaters@rogers.com
PRESIDENT/PRODUCER/DIRECTOR
Robert Parro

Feature films / television / documentaries / music production.

ACME PICTURES
5 – 535 Queen St. E, Toronto, ON M5A 1V1.
TEL: (416) 366-2263. FAX: (416) 366-6355.
email: kelly@acmepictures.com www.acmepictures.com
CREATIVE PRINCIPAL
Ric Randmaa, Bob Barrett

Director, Business Development: Sandie Orlando

AFFINITY PRODUCTIONS
2740B Queensview Dr., Ottawa, ON K2B 2A2.
TEL: (613) 820-4660. FAX: (613) 820-5020.
email: rg@affinityproductions.tv www.affinityproductions.tv
PRESIDENT
Ron Gallant

AIR FARCE PRODUCTIONS, INC.
9B300 – 250 Front St. W, Toronto, ON M5V 3G5.
TEL: (416) 205-3800. FAX: (416) 205-3832.
email: mail@airfarce.com www.airfarce.com
PRODUCER
Roger Abbott, Don Ferguson

AIRCRAFT PICTURES, LIMITED
147 Liberty St., Toronto, ON M6K 3G3. TEL: (416) 558-9179.
FAX: (416) 536-9178. email: info@aircraftpictures.com
www.aircraftpictures.com
PRODUCER
Andrew Rosen, Anthony Leo

ALCHEMIST ENTERTAINMENT
181 Queen St. E, Toronto, ON M5A 1S2. TEL: (416) 203-2996.
FAX: (416) 203-2998.
PRESIDENT/CEO
Damian Lee
CREATIVE EXECUTIVE
Sam Hershoran

ALCINA PICTURES, LTD.
100 – 1 Atlantic Ave., Toronto, ON M6K 3E7.
TEL: (416) 364-3777. FAX: (416) 364-7123.
email: info@alcinapictures.com www.alcinapictures.com

ALLAN KING ASSOCIATES, LIMITED
313 Queen Street West, suite 203, Toronto, ON M5V 2A4.
TEL: (416) 964-7284. FAX: (416) 964-7997.
email: mail@allankingfilms.com www.allankingfilms.com
PRESIDENT
Allan King
VICE PRESIDENT
Colleen Murphy

AMAZE FILM & TELEVISION
101 – 6 Pardee Ave., Toronto, ON M6K 3H5.
TEL: (416) 588-7839. FAX: (416) 588-7276.
email: info@amazefilm.tv www.amazefilm.tv
PRODUCER
Michael Souther, Teza Lawrence
DEVELOPMENT EXECUTIVE
Kirsta Teague

AMBERWOOD ENTERTAINMENT
987 Wellington St., 2nd Flr., Ottawa, ON K1Y 2Y1.
TEL: (613) 238-4567. FAX: (613) 233-3857.
email: info@amberwoodanimation.com
www.amberwoodanimation.com
PRESIDENT/CEO
Sheldon S. Wiseman
PRODUCER
Chantal Ling
SERIES CREATOR
Gerald Tripp

AMÉRIMAGE-SPECTRA
(A division of L'Equipe Spectra)
300 – 500 Queen St. E, Toronto, ON M5A 1V2.
TEL: (416) 777-2500. FAX: (416) 777-2831.
email: patricia.phillips@equipespectra.ca
SENIOR PRODUCER
Patricia Phillips

Documentaries. See also Québec.

ANDRÉ BENNETT PRODUCTIONS
60 Browning Ave., Toronto, ON M4K 1V9.
TEL: (416) 462-1573, (416) 418-8474.
email: andre.m.bennett@sympatico.ca
PRODUCER
André Bennett

ANIMETTE CANADA
210 Romfield Circuit, Thornhill, ON L3T 3J1.
TEL: (905) 881-2099. FAX: (905) 881-4582
CONTACT
Alice Kubik, Milo Kubik

Classical 3D animation / children's puppet films.

ANNE TAIT PRODUCTIONS
304 – 20 Avoca Ave., Toronto, ON M4T 2B8.
email: atait@canadafilm.com
PRESIDENT
Anne Tait

ARLECCHINA PRODUCTIONS, INC.
705 - 253 Merton St., Toronto, ON M4S 3H2.
TEL: (416) 489-9414. FAX: (416) 489-1838.
email: info@arlecchina.com www.arlecchina.com
CONTACT
Magie Matulic

Focuses on women-driven projects.

ARMEDIA COMMUNICATIONS
307 – 3219 Yonge St., Toronto, ON M4N 2L3.
TEL: (905) 889-0076. FAX: (905) 889-0078.
email: maz@armediacommunications.com
www.armediacommunications.com
CONTACT
David Mazmanian

Audio / video production.

ARTCORE PRODUCTIONS, LTD.
2024 Glenada Cres, Oakville, ON L6H 4M6. TEL: (905) 338-3642.
email: artcoreproductions@sympatico.ca
CONTACT
Vlad Kabelik

Film / TV documentary & educational programming.

ASSOCIATED PRODUCERS, LTD.
1001 – 110 Spadina Ave., Toronto, ON M5V 2K4.
TEL: (416) 504-6662. FAX: (416) 504-6667.
email: general@apltd.ca www.associatedproducers.com
PRESIDENT
Simcha Jacobovici
V.P., PRODUCTION
Ric Esther Bienstock
PRODUCER
Felix Golubev

Documentaries, lifestyle and dramatic programming.

AUDACINE, INC.
68 Hamilton St., Toronto, ON M4M 2C8. TEL: (416) 778-4562.
PRESIDENT
Mary Jane Gomes

Director, documentary & feature films.

AVALANCHE FILMS
10 Morrow Ave., Studio G2, Toronto, ON M0R 2J1.
TEL: (416) 516-6410. email: anita@avalanchefilms.com
www.avalanchefilms.com
DIRECTOR
Anita Doron

AVARD
584 Grays Road, Hamilton, ON L8E 2Z6.
TEL: (905) 561-0975. FAX: (905) 561-0975.
email: info@avard.com www.avard.com
PRESIDENT
Bill Moffatt
CREATIVE DIRECTOR
David King
ARTISTIC DIRECTOR
Paul Watson

Non-linear video / 3D animation / edit & effects / WS Betacam SP / DVcam camera crew / website design / print graphics / multimedia design.

AVION FILM PRODUCTIONS
100 – 517 Wellington St. W, Toronto, ON M5V 1G1.
TEL: (416) 598-2232. FAX: (416) 598-0220.
email: andrea@avionfilms.com www.avionfilms.com
EXECUTIVE PRODUCER
Michael Schwartz, Paola Lazzeri
SALES
Andrea Minott

Commercial production services.

AVP
541 Brant Street, suite 8, Bulrington, ON L7R 2G6.
TEL: (800) 275-4287, (905) 206-1304. FAX: (905) 206-1170.
email: avp@avpinc.ca www.avpinc.ca
PRESIDENT
Ron Baker

Television, commercial, video & live event production – specializing in automotive products.

BACK ALLEY FILM PRODUCTIONS, LTD.
15 York View Dr., Toronto, ON M8Z 2G1.TEL: (416) 259-4852.
email: bkalley@sympactico.ca www.backalleyfilms.net
PRODUCER
Janis Lundman
PRODUCER/DIRECTOR
Adrienne Mitchell

BAJAJ FILMS
421 – 680 Queens Quay W, Toronto, ON M5V 2Y9.
TEL: (416) 420-4543. email: jay_bajaj@hotmail.com
www.bajajfilms.com
PRESIDENT
Jay Bajaj

BAMOVA, INC.
122 Edenbridge Dr., Toronto, ON M9A 3G4.
TEL: (647) 401-5505. FAX: (416) 233-8440.
email: nessa@bamovafilms.com
CONTACT
Vanessa Chiara

BAR HARBOUR FILMS, INC.
62 Hazelwood Ave., Toronto, ON M4J 1K5. TEL: (416) 778-4491.
FAX: (416) 778-4144. email: barharbour@sympatico.ca
PRODUCER/WRITER/DIRECTOR
Martin Harbury

Documentaries / drama / film / TV.

BEAR TRACK PRODUCTIONS
74 St Andrews St., Cambridge ON N1S 1M4.
TEL: (519) 464-2585. FAX: (519) 620-8074.
email: brianfilm@gmail.com www.beartrackproductions.com
DIRECTOR/EDITOR
Brian Wayne White

BEEVISION PRODUCTIONS, INC.
75 Highcroft Road, Toronto, ON M4L 3G4.
TEL: (416) 868-1700. FAX: 416-868-9512
email: info@beevision.com www.beevision.com
PRODUCER
Nina Beveridge
DIRECTOR
Paul Hart

BERYT PRODUCTIONS, INC.
1503 – 8111 Yonge St., Thornhill, ON L3T 4V9.
TEL: (905) 764-6872. email: beryt@sympatico.ca
PRESIDENT/PRODUCER
Eliza Haddad

Features / television / documentary.

BIG COAT PRODUCTIONS
107 – 145 Front St. E, Toronto, ON M5A 1E3.
TEL: (416) 507-9829. FAX: (416) 507-9846.
email: info@bigcoatproductions.com
www.bigcoatproductions.com
EXECUTIVE PRODUCER
Catherine Fogarty

THE BIG FILM COMPANY
431 Richmond St. E, Toronto, ON M5A 1R1.
TEL: (416) 360-3739. FAX: (416) 360-0750.
email: dave@bigfilm.ca www.bigfilm.ca
CONTACT
Dave Greenham

Commercials.

BIG FISH PRODUCTIONS

456 Grove St E. Barrie, Ontario, L4M-5W2.
TEL: (705) 719-9065. FAX: (705) 812-9639.
email: peter@bigfishvideo.com www.bigfishvideo.com
PRODUCER/DIRECTOR
Peter Olmstead

Marketing / Audio Productions: Chris Tomack

BIG SOUL PRODUCTIONS, INC.

B102 - 401 Richmond St. W, Toronto, ON M5V 3A8.
TEL: (866) 767-6076, (416) 598-7762. FAX: (416) 598-5392.
email: comments@bigsoul.net www.bigsoul.net
PRESIDENT
Laura Miliken

TV series — drama, MOWs.

BITS & PIECES PICTURE COMPANY

241 Brunswick Ave., Toronto, ON M5S 2M6. TEL: (416) 835-0324.
Head Office Los Angeles: (310) 581-1512.
email: bitsandpiecespicture@canada.com
PARTNER/PRODUCER
Rajiv Maikhuri

BIZNETWORX

300 – 1200 Bay St., Toronto, ON M5R 2A5.
TEL: (416) 972-1230. FAX: (416) 922-1640.
email: brian@ccte.com
CREATIVE DIRECTOR
Brian Couch

Videos / commercials / TV programs for North American business, industry and government. New media development, including online language learning games.

BLACK WALK

99 Sudbury St., Unit 201, Toronto, ON M6J 3S7.
TEL: (416) 533-5864. FAX: (416) 533-2016.
email: info@blackwalk.com www.blackwalk.com
PRESIDENT
Mihkel Harilaid

Feature film and TV.

BLOKLAND PICTURES CORPORATION

4 Webb Ave., Toronto, ON M6P 1M5. TEL: (416) 763-2373.
email: jim@blokland.com www.blokland.com
DIRECTOR
Jim Blokland

Feature films.

BLOMELEY COMMUNICATIONS, INC.

262 – 39 Robertson Rd., Ottawa, ON K2H 8R2.
TEL: (613) 596-9935. FAX: (613) 596-4565.
email: info@blomeley.com www.blomeley.com
CONTACT
Edward A. Blomeley

Founded in 1988, Blomeley Communications Inc. provides communications services, productions and products that meet the needs of its customers.

BLUEMOON PRODUCTIONS, INC.

400 – 2 Berkeley St., Toronto, ON M5A 2W3.
TEL: (416) 955-1855. FAX: (416) 955-0989.
email: contact@bluemoonproductions.com
www.bluemoonproductions.com
EXECUTIVE PRODUCER
John Crampton

TV / video / radio / web — corporate & commercials.

BOOMSTONE ENTERTAINMENT, INC.

205 – 1 Cleopatra Dr., Ottawa, ON K2G 3M9.
TEL: (613) 725-3843. FAX: (613) 725-9327.
email: info@boomstone.com www.boomstone.com
PRESIDENT
Lee Williams

BRAND PRESENCE MEDIA

16 Albert St., Guelph, ON NIG 1C6. TEL: (519) 731-3129.
email: lawrie@brandpresencemedia.com
www.brandpresencemedia.com
CONTACT
Lawrie Rotenberg

Producing branded entertainment.

BREAKTHROUGH FILMS

35 McCaul St, Suite 300, Toronto, ON M5T 1V7.
TEL: (416) 766-6588. FAX: (416) 769-1436.
email: business@breakthroughfilms.com
www.breakthroughfilms.com
CHAIRMAN/EXECUTIVE PRODUCER
Ira Levy
PRESIDENT/EXECUTIVE PRODUCER
Peter Williamson

Documentary / drama / lifestyle.

BROWN ENTERTAINMENT

49 Niagara St., 2nd Flr., Toronto, ON M5V 1C2.
TEL: (416) 362-7696. FAX: (416) 362-6662.
email: chilo@brown25.com www.brown25.com
EXECUTIVE PRODUCER
William Cranor, David Cranor
PRODUCTION
Erik Wilson
HEAD OF SALES
Janie Phair
SALES
Chilo Fletcher

TV series.

BTV COMMUNICATIONS, INC.

300 – 89 Bloor St. W, Toronto, ON M5S 1M1.
TEL: (416) 966-1316. FAX: (416) 966-1310.
email: chris@btv.com www.btv.com
CONTACT
Chris Simpson

Full-service production company specializing in the development, financing, production and distribution of television series and specials for Canadian and international markets.

BUCK PRODUCTIONS, INC.

201 – 543 Richmond St. W, Toronto, ON M5V 1Y6.
TEL: (416) 362-3330. FAX: (416) 362-3336.
email: barbara@buckproductions.com
www.buckproductions.com
EXECUTIVE PRODUCER
Sean Buckley, Emily Pengelly

Film & television, commercial production, corporate video.

C.O.R.E. DIGITAL PICTURES

461 King St. W, Toronto, ON M5V 1K7. TEL: (416) 977-3939.
FAX: (416) 977-0498. email: sales@coredp.com
www.coredp.com
CONTACT
Candice Day

Film & television production.

CALIBRE ENTERTAINMENT

22 Redwood Ave., Toronto, ON M4L 2S6.
TEL: (416) 526-2738. FAX: (416) 465-0626.
email: calum@calibreentertainment.com
www.calibreentertainment.com
PRESIDENT
Calum deHartog
EXECUTIVE ASSISTANT
John Shark

CANADIAN ACCENTS, INC.

26 Yarmouth Rd., Toronto, ON M4K 1V3. TEL: (416) 653-0702.
FAX: (416) 658-3176. email: kaj@canadianaccents.ca
www.canadianaccents.ca
PRESIDENT
Kathy Avrich-Johnson
VICE PRESIDENT
Deborah Day

Feature film / performing arts, variety TV series.

CANAMEDIA FILM PRODUCTIONS, INC.

200 – 381 Richmond St. E, Toronto, ON M5A 1P6.
TEL: (416) 483-7446. FAX: (416) 483-7529.
email: canamed@canamedia.com www.canamedia.com
PRESIDENT/PRODUCER
Les Harris
SECRETARY/TREASURER
Jane Harris
NORTH AMERICAN SALES & ACQUISITIONS
Lee Harris
INTERNATIONAL SALES & ACQUISITIONS
Andrea Stokes
ITN SOURCE SALES & ADMINISTRATION
Céline Senis

CAPRI FILMS, INC.

259 Lakeshore Blvd. E, 2nd Flr., Toronto, ON M5A 3T7.
TEL: (416) 535-1870. FAX: (416) 535-3414.
email: info@caprifilms.com www.caprifilms.com
PRESIDENT
Gabriella Martinelli
GENERAL MANAGER
Robin Crumley - rcrumley@caprifilms.com

Feature films & high-concept television / mini-series.

CCI ENTERTAINMENT

18 Dupont St., Toronto, ON M5R 1V2. TEL: (416) 964-8750.
FAX: (416) 964-1980. email: info@ccientertainment.com
www.ccientertainment.com
CEO/PRESIDENT
Arnie Zipursky
CFO
Gord McIlquham

COO
Annette Frymer
EXECUTIVE V.P., PRODUCTION
Jim Corston

CFC FEATURE FILM PROJECT

2489 Bayview Ave., Toronto, ON M2L 1A8.
TEL: (416) 445-1446 ext. 268. FAX: (416) 445-3158.
email: ffp@cfccreates.com www.cfccreates.com
DIRECTOR/EXECUTIVE PRODUCER
Justine Whyte
PROGRAM/DEVELOPMENT MANAGER
Erin Burke
PROGRAM/ADMINISTRATIVE COORDINATOR
Alan Bacchus

CHADWICK BROTHERS FILM COMPANY, LTD.

332 – 366 Adelaide St. E, Toronto, ON M5A 3X9.
TEL: (416) 363-4600, (416) 823-0444. FAX: (416) 363-8810.
email: jeff@chadwickbrothers.com
holden@chadwickbrothers.com
www.chadwickbrothers.com
CONTACT
Jeff Chadwick, Holden Chadwick

CHESLER / PERLMUTTER PRODUCTIONS, INC.

200 – 129 Yorkville Ave., Toronto, ON M5R 1C4.
TEL: (416) 927-0016. FAX: (416) 960-8447.
email: DMP@chesperl.com
CO-CHAIRMAN
David M. Perlmutter
EXECUTIVE ADMINISTRATOR
Roberta Harron

Feature film / TV / series.

CHINA SYNDROME PRODUCTIONS

80 Citizen Ct., Unit 15, Markham, ON L6G 1A7.
TEL: (905) 513-6373 ext. 22. FAX: (905) 513-0258.
email: paulyee@chinasyndrome.com
www.chinasyndrome.com
CONTACT
Paul Yee

Commercials. Corporate. Ethnic talent and casting. Provides translation, voice & on-screen talent in many Asian languages.

CIN-O-MATIC FILMS

032 - 67 Mowat Ave., Toronto, ON M6C 3E3.
TEL: (905) 883-5561. FAX: (905) 787-1240.
email: tom@cinomaticfilms.com www.cinomaticfilms.com
CONTACT
Tom Strnad, Sean Cisterna

Feature film production company specializing in genre films.

CINEFLIX, INC.

304 – 366 Adelaide St. W, Toronto, ON M5V 1R9.
TEL: (416) 504-7317. FAX: (416) 504-6622.
email: info@cineflix.com www.cineflix.com
CO-CEO
Glen Salzman, Katherine Buck

Producer and distributor of non-fiction programming with offices in Montréal, Toronto, London and Dublin. See also Québec.

CINENOVA PRODUCTIONS, INC.

Production Office: 345 Sorauren Ave. Unit 6, Toronto, ON M6R 2G5. TEL: (416) 363-2600. FAX: (416) 363-2609.
email: info@cinenova.net www.cinenova.net

Corporate Office: 13 Admiral Rd., Toronto, ON M5R 2L4.
TEL: (416) 920-2784. FAX: (416) 920-0578.

Stratford Office: 77 John St. N, Stratford, ON N5A 6K8.
TEL: (519) 273-9150.
CHAIRMAN/CEO
David Lint
PRESIDENT/CO-CEO
Jane Armstrong

Film / TV / large format series & specials.

CIRCLE PRODUCTIONS

490 Adelaide St. W, Toronto, ON M5V 1T2. TEL: (416) 922-9900.
FAX: (416) 922-0548. email: toronto@circleprod.com
www.circleprod.com
EXECUTIVE PRODUCER
Karen Tameanko, Michel Korchinsky

Commercial and music video production services.
See also British Columbia.

CLARE PRODUCTIONS, INC.

299 Queen St. W, Toronto, ON M5V 2Z5.
TEL: (416) 591-7400 ext. 3191. FAX: (416) 351-9241.
email: tiinas@clareproductions.com
PRESIDENT
Tina Soomet

CLEARWATER FILMS, LIMITED

100 – 1255 Yonge St., Toronto, ON M4T 1W6.
TEL: (416) 929-7232. FAX: (416) 929-7225.
email: clearwater@gcadams.on.ca
PRESIDENT
G. Chalmers Adams

CLOUD TEN PICTURES, INC.

11 Export Avenue, St. Catharines ON L2M 5V8.
TEL: (905) 684-5561. FAX: (905) 684-7946.
email: brian.bouchard@cloudtenpictures.com
www.cloudtenpictures.com
CO-CEO
Peter Lalonde, Paul Lalonde
V.P., FILM
André van Heerden

Christian, faith-based film and television production, including Left Behind: The Movie, and television series.

CLOUDLIFE MEDIA

705 - 126 Charlton Ave. W. Hamilton, ON L8P 2C6.
TEL: (905) 777-9196. email: info@cloudlifemedia.com
www.cloudlifemedia.com
PRODUCER
Robert Bruce
PROJECT DEVELOPMENT
Nancy Winlove-Smith

Specializing in ambient, background music, art videos, unique music/video productions for young children.

COMEDYLAB ENTERTAINMENT, INC.

2649 Bloor St. W, Unit B6, Toronto, ON MX8 1A3.
TEL: (416) 236-2085. email: guyincharge@comedylab.tv
www.comedylab.tv
PRESIDENT/EXECUTIVE PRODUCER
Matthew Robillard
SENIOR V.P., PRODUCTION
Andrew Robillard

COMWEB GROUP, INC.

130 Bloor St. W, 5th Flr., Toronto, ON M5S 1N5.
TEL: (416) 920-7050. FAX: (416) 920-4424.
www.comwebgroup.com
CHAIRMAN/CEO
Paul Bronfman - paul@comwebmail.com
CFO
Robert Bruce - rbruce@whites.com

Production, equipment, manufacturing and studio services to the film and television industry.

CONQUERING LION PICTURES

18 Gloucester Ln., 4th Flr., Toronto, ON M4Y 1L5.
TEL: (416) 967-1055. FAX: (416) 923-8580.
email: conquering@bellnet.ca
PRESIDENT
Clement Virgo
VICE PRESIDENT
Damon D'Oliveira

COOKIE JAR ENTERTAINMENT, INC.

266 King St. W, 2nd Flr., Toronto, ON M5V 1H8.
TEL: (416) 977-3238. email: info@thecookiejarcompany.com
www.thecookiejarcompany.com
See also Québec.

COPPERHEART ENTERTAINMENT

1 – 121 John St., Toronto, ON M5V 2E2. TEL: (416) 516-4950.
FAX: (416) 516-1712. email: info@copperheart.ca
www.copperheart.ca
PRODUCER/OWNER
Steve Hoban
PROJECT MANAGER
Mark Smith
BUSINESS AFFAIRS
Karyn Nolan

COPTOR PRODUCTIONS, INC.

419 - 215 Spadina Ave., Toronto, ON M5T 2C7.
TEL: (416) 408-3978. email: info@coptor.com
www.coptor.com
VICE PRESIDENT
Jeremy Edwardes

Television and film production and post-production facility. We do online / off-line animation / motion graphics / music / sound design / line production.

CRAWLEY FILMS, LIMITED

P.O. Box 11069, Stn. H, Nepean, ON K2H 7T8.
TEL: (613) 825-2479. FAX: (613) 825-9300.
email: bstevens@crawleyfilms.ca www.crawleyfilms.ca
CONTACT
Bill Stevens, Jr.

THE CREATIVE ALLIANCE NETWORK

1804 – 65 High Park Ave., Toronto, ON M6P 2R7.
TEL: (416) 885-5263, Los Angeles: (323) 284-5399.
email: bob@soupcan.ca www.soupcan.ca

SENIOR PARTNER
Bob Kane
MANAGING PARTNER
George Colwell
HEAD WRITER
Tom McGee
PRODUCER
Michael Taylor

CRITICAL MASS ENTERTAINMENT
103 – 360 Dufferin St., Toronto, ON M6K 1Z8.
TEL: (416) 934-9343. FAX: (416) 538-3367.
email: christian@movieseals.biz www.cmass.ca
PRESIDENT
Christian Viel

Feature film / TV production.

CROSSROADS CHRISTIAN COMMUNICATIONS, INC.
P.O. Box 5100, 1295 N. Service Rd., Burlington, ON L7R 4M2.
TEL: (905) 332-6400. FAX: (905) 332-6655.
email: davidmainse@crossroads.ca www.crossroads.ca
PRESIDENT
David Mainse

VIDEO PRODUCTION/CROSSROADS TELEVISION SYSTEM
P.O. Box 5321, 1295 N. Service Rd., Burlington, ON L7R 4X5.
TEL: (905) 331-7333. FAX: (905) 332-6005 www.ctstv.com
PRESIDENT
Richard Gray
SALES & MARKETING
Glenn Stewart

CRYPT CLUB PRODUCTIONS, INC.
30 Harcourt Ave., Toronto, ON M4J 1J2.
TEL: (416) 462-0979. FAX: (416) 462-0977.
email: info@thecryptclub.com www.thecryptclub.com
PRODUCER/DIRECTOR
Miguel Gallego

Independent production/distribution company.

CURLCOM PRODUCTIONS, LTD.
365 Colonsay Ct., Oshawa, ON L1J 6H3. TEL: (905) 723-1144.
FAX: (905) 723-5938. email: hobby@thehobbyshow.com
PRESIDENT
Ted Curl

DA DA KAMERA PICTURES
385 – 401 Richmond St. W, Toronto, ON M5A 3A8.
TEL: (416) 586-1503. FAX: (416) 586-1504.
email: ddkpictures@ca.inter.net www.dadakamera.com
PRODUCER
Sherrie Johnson

DANTE ENTERTAINMENT GROUP
344 Dupont Street, Suite 202, Toronto, ON M5R 1V9 CANADA.
TEL: (416) 534-6728. FAX: (416) 534-4792.
email: admin@dante-ent.com www.dante-ent.com

Film, television, web and interactive media production.

DARIUS FILMS, INC.
326 Carlaw Ave., Suite 105, Toronto ON M4M 3N8.
TEL: (416) 922-0007. FAX: (416) 406-0034.
email: info@dariusfilms.com www.dariusfilms. com
PRESIDENT/PRODUCER
Nicholas D. Tabarrok
CFO/VICE PRESIDENT
Jennifer L. Stivala

DAVID BRADY PRODUCTIONS
7942 Loyalist Parkway, Sandhurst, Bath, ON K0H 1G0.
TEL: (613) 352-3377. FAX: (613) 352-9961.
email: mwheeler@davidbradyproductions.com
www.davidbradyproductions.com
PRESIDENT/PRODUCER
David Brady

A production house with feature film and television productions, producing factual and fictional television series.

DECADENCE FILMS
88 Edith Dr., Toronto, ON M4R 1Z2. TEL: (416) 238-9577.
FAX: (416) 352-5026. email: info@decadencefilms.com
www.decadencefilms.com
EXECUTIVE PRODUCER
Alec Kinnear

DECODE ENTERTAINMENT, INC.
235 Carlaw Ave., 5th Flr., Toronto, ON M4M 2S1.
TEL: (416) 363-8034. FAX: (416) 363-8919.
email: decode@decode-ent.com www.decode.tv
CONTACT
Steven DeNure, Neil Court, Beth Stevenson

Family & children's programming.

DEVINE ENTERTAINMENT CORPORATION
504 – 2 Berkeley St., Toronto, ON M5A 2W3.
TEL: (416) 364-2282. FAX: (416) 364-1440.
email: info@devine-ent.com www.devine-ent.com
CONTACT
David Devine, Richard Mozer

Family feature film and television programming.

DEW, SIMON CHRISTOPHER
35 Spruce St., Toronto, ON M5A 2H8. TEL: (416) 923-3432, (416) 931-2280. FAX: (416) 923-6007.
email: cdew@sympatico.ca

DLT PRODUCTIONS, LTD.
1006 – 1230 Marlborough Ct., Oakville, ON L6H 3K6.
TEL: (905) 842-0060. email: dltucker@ca.inter.net
www.dltproductions.com
CONTACT
David Tucker

Production company specializing in documentary film & television, long-form.

DON CARMODY PRODUCTIONS
100 – 30 Booth Ave., Toronto, ON M4M 2M2.
TEL: (416) 406-4000. FAX: (416) 406-4164.
email: don@doncarmody.com www.doncarmody.com
PRESIDENT
Don Carmody

Feature films / made-for-televison movies.

DOUGAL & CO., INC.
146 Millicent St., Toronto, ON M6H 1W4. TEL: (416) 645-0295.
FAX: (416) 645-593. email: info@dougalco.com
www.dougalco.com
CONTACT
Dougal Bichan

Award-winning producer of video, multimedia, live events and integrated communication projects.

DREAMSCAPE VIDEO PRODUCTIONS
2 – 544 Bathurst St., Toronto, ON M5S 2P9.
TEL: (416) 534-7464. email: bsp@interlog.com
CONTACT
Brock Fricker

Audio engineer / producer / SFX editor / video editor / music composer. Thousands of productions, everything from CBC to House Music Production.

E1 TELEVISION
175 Bloor Street East, Suite 1400 - North Tower, Toronto, ON M4W 3R8. TEL: (416) 646-2400. FAX: (416) 979-9255.
email: info@bap.ca www.bap.ca
PRESIDENT
Laszlo Barna

TV series / MOWs / documentaries.

ECAREY PRODUCTIONS
P.O. Box 5822, Stn. A, Toronto, ON M5W 1P2.
TEL: (416) 910-4776. email: erin__carey@hotmail.com (double underscore) www.ecareyproductions.com
MEDIA PRODUCER
Erin Carey

Producing series, documentaries, museum exhibits, infomercials.

EGO FILM ARTS
80 Niagara St., Toronto, ON M5V 1C5. TEL: (416) 703-2137.
FAX: (416) 504-7161. email: questions@egofilmarts.com
www.egofilmarts.com
CONTACT
Atom Egoyan, Marcy Gerstein

ELLIS VISION INCORPORATED
(An Ellis Entertainment Company)
300 – 1300 Yonge St., Toronto, ON M4T 1X3.
TEL: (416) 924-2186. FAX: (416) 924-6115.
email: vision@ellisent.com www.ellisent.com
CHAIRMAN
Ralph C. Ellis
PRESIDENT
Stephen Ellis
DEVELOPMENT DIRECTOR
Sean Connolly

Prime time factual entertainment in all genres, including wildlife, science, history, reality, health, lifestyle and children's.

EMMERSON DENNEY FILMS
121 Portland St., 2nd Flr., Toronto, ON M5V 2N4.
TEL: (416) 504-3456. www.emmerson.ca

Production of feature films and television.

EPITOME PICTURES, INC.
220 Bartley Dr., North York, ON M4A 1G1. TEL: (416) 752-7627.
FAX: (416) 752-7837. email: info@epitomepictures.com
www.epitomepictures.com
CEO/EXECUTIVE PRODUCER
Linda Schuyler

PRESIDENT/EXECUTIVE PRODUCER
Stephen Stohn

TV production.

EXPLORATION PRODUCTION
9 Channel Nine Ct., Toronto, ON M1S 4B5. TEL: (416) 332-4451.
FAX: (416) 332-4208. email: tleadman@ctv.ca
www.exploration.ca
DIRECTOR
Andrew Burnstein
HEAD OF WORLDWIDE PROGRAM DISTRIBUTION
Tony Leadman
HEAD, BUSINESS MANAGEMENT
Deborah James

FACTORY FILMS, INC.
50 Givins St., Toronto, ON M6J 2X8. TEL: (416) 530-4328.
email: tinfish@aol.ca
PRESIDENT
Sari Friedland

FAUST FILMS, INC.
438 Markham St., Toronto, ON M6G 2L2. TEL: (416) 531-5372.
FAX: (416) 531-0929. email: ian@faustfilms.com
www.faustfilms.com
PRODUCER/DIRECTOR/WRITER
Ian Thompson

Focusing on long-form drama.

FEVER FILMS NORTH AMERICA
517 Wellington St. W, Toronto, ON M5V 1G1.
TEL: (416) 591-8652. FAX: (416) 596-8299.
email: ask@feverfilms.ca www.feverfilms.ca
CONTACT
Danielle Schwartz

Providing the highest quality of commercial production while emphasizing production value.

FIELDVIEW ENTERTAINMENT, INC.
200-200 – 131 Bloor St. W, Toronto, ON M5S 1R8.
TEL: (416) 920-7979. email: david@fieldview.com
www.fieldview.com
PRESIDENT/PRODUCER
David Craig Collard

THE FILM WORKS, LTD.
6256 – 2100 Bloor St. W, Toronto, ON M6S 5A5.
TEL: (416) 985-2139. FAX: (416) 928-1052.
www.thefilmworks.ca
CONTACT
Eric Jordan - eric@thefilmworks.ca
Paul Stephens - paul@thefilmworks.ca

Features, television movies and series.

FILMBAY
312 – 2155 Burnamthorpe Rd., Mississauga, ON L5L 5P4.
TEL: (905) 820-7916. email: info@filmbay.com
www.filmbay.com
CEO
John P. Trutnau
CFO
Ryan Branson
MARKETING
Stella Gould
MANAGING DIRECTOR
Bob Walton

FILMBLANC
1901 – 1121 Bay St., Toronto, ON M5S 3L9.
TEL: (416) 214-0300. FAX: (416) 214-0446.
email: noemi@filmblanc.com www.filmblanc.com
PRESIDENT/EXECUTIVE PRODUCER
Noemi Weis

FISHTALES PRODUCTIONS
277 Palmerston Ave., Toronto, ON M6J 2J3.
TEL: (416) 964-0003. email: hfisher@sympatico.ca
DIRECTOR/WRITER
Honey Fisher

Video / filmmaker — documentary / corporate / feature / TV.

FIVE STRANGERS FILMS, LTD.
2300 Yonge Street, P.O. Box 67001, Toronto, ON M4P 3C8.
TEL: (416) 738-8255. FAX: (416) 545-1510.
email: info@fivestrangers.com
www.fivestrangers.com
CONTACT
Marc Morgenstern

Features / television / music videos / commercials / industrials.

FOREVERGREEN TELEVISION & FILM PRODUCTIONS
230 – 181 Carlaw Ave., Toronto, ON M4M 2S1.
TEL: (905) 778-9944. FAX: (905) 628-1769.
email: foreverg@primus.ca
PRESIDENT
Alan Aylward

Creative TV / marketing production.

FRAME FIRST CORP.
7 Jackes Ave., Unit 706, Toronto, ON M4T 1E3.
TEL: (416) 543-0946. FAX: (416) 924-7997.
email: info@framefirst.com www.framefirst.com
CEO/EXECUTIVE PRODUCER
Sean Karimi
PRODUCER
Marc Cohen

Range of production services such as pre-production, production, post-production and concept development.

GAPC ENTERTAINMENT, INC.
180 – 14 Colonnade Rd., Ottawa, ON K2E 7M6.
TEL: (613) 723-3316. FAX: (613) 723-8583.
email: kstewart@gapc.com www.gapc.com
CONTACT
Ken Stewart, Hoda Elatawi

GENERATOR FILM PRODUCTION
504 Wellington St. W, Toronto, ON M5V 1E3.
TEL: (416) 596-8810. FAX: (416) 596-8299.
email: tamara@generatorfilms.com www.generatorfilms.com
EXECUTIVE PRODUCER
Tamara Marcus

Digital / video production — corporate television / commercials.

GENUINE PICTURES
RR 4 11 Links Dr. S, Ashton, ON K0A 1B0. TEL: (613) 253-2296.
FAX: (613) 253-3229. email: office@genuinepictures.com
www.genuinepictures.com
PRESIDENT
Donna Leon

GOLDI PRODUCTIONS, LTD.
1409 Malibou Terr., Mississauga, ON L5J 4B9.
TEL: (905) 855-1510. email: info@goldiproductions.com
www.goldiproductions.com
CONTACT
John Goldi, CSC, Joan Goldi

TV specials, series.

GORDFILM, INC.
68 Standish Ave., Toronto, ON M4W 3B1.
TEL: (416) 967-4777. FAX: (416) 967-3908.
email: kgordfilm@aol.com
CONTACT
Ken Gord

GORICA PRODUCTIONS
295 Silverbirch Ave., Toronto, ON M4E 3L6.
TEL: (416) 324-1332. FAX: (416) 324-9594.
email: gorica@interlog.com www.goricaproductions.com
PRESIDENT
Felice Gorica

HENRY LESS PRODUCTIONS, INC.
12C – 219 Dufferin St., Toronto, ON M6K 3J1.
TEL: (416) 849-4880. FAX: (416) 913-9818.
email: henry@henryless.com www.henryless.com
CONTACT
Angela Donald, Henry Less

Original drama, reality, comedy. Made to Order, food show in 120 plus countries; The Wilkinsons, comedy for CMT; 11 Cameras, drama for CBC; Full Ride, docudrama for ESPN.

HEROIC FILM COMPANY
301 – 12 Camden St., Toronto, ON M5V 1V1.
TEL: (866) 544-3448, (416) 922-4303. FAX: (416) 922-9967.
email: info@heroicfilmcompany.com
EXECUTIVE PRODUCER
Karen Lee Hall, John May, Suzanne Bolch

HOFFERT COMMUNICATIONS CORP.
116 Regina Ave., Toronto, ON M6A 1R7. TEL: (416) 781-4191.
FAX: (416) 787-2202. email: brenda@hoffert.ca
CONTACT
Brenda Hoffert

Film producers / music composers / lyricists / production / contracting / publishing / music licensing.

HUNGRY EYES FILM & TELEVISION, INC.
3 Conrad Ave., Toronto, ON M6G 3G4. TEL: (416) 654-6222.
FAX: (416) 654-1551. email: hungryeyes@sympatico.ca
www.hungryeyes.ca
PRODUCER
Jennifer Holness

Features / television series / documentaries.

IMPORTED ARTISTS FILM CO.
171 East Liberty St, Toronto, ON M6K 3P6.
TEL: (416) 971-5915. FAX: (416) 971-7925.

email: info@importedartists.com www.importedartists.com
CONTACT
Christina Ford, Tom Symes

Film and television / commercial production services.

INDEPENDENT PICTURES, INC.

64 Duncannon Dr., Toronto, ON M5P 2M2. TEL: (416) 488-9228.
email: p-obrian@rogers.com
PRESIDENT
Peter O'Brian

INDIVISUAL PRODUCTIONS

28 Lennox St., Toronto, ON M6G 1J4. TEL: (416) 533-9900.
FAX: (416) 533-5226. email: info@indivisual.tv
www.indivisual.tv
EXECUTIVE PRODUCER/PRESIDENT
Allan Novak

INDUSTRY FILMS

200 – 260 King St. E, Toronto, ON M5A 4L5.
TEL: (416) 815-1717. FAX: (416) 815-0147.
email: shoot@industryfilms.com www.industryfilms.com
HEAD, PRODUCTION
Sophia Peckan
HEAD, SALES
Marni Luftspring
PRESIDENT
Tina Petridis

Commercials.

INNER CITY FILMS, INC. (ICF)

260 Spadina Ave, Suite 400, Toronto, ON M5V 1P1.
TEL: (866) 621-3488, (416) 368-3339. FAX: (416) 368-5234.
email: info@innercityfilms.ca
www.innercityfilms.ca
PRODUCER/DIRECTOR
Alfons Adetuyi
PRODUCER/WRITER
Amos Adetuyi

An award-winning production company producing film and TV programs in a wide range of genres.

INQUISITION PRODUCTIONS, INC.

310 – 446 Spadina Rd., Toronto, ON M5P 3M2.
TEL: (416) 848-8908. FAX: (416) 351-0410.
email: mercedesyaeger@gmail.com
www.inquisitionproductions.com
EXECUTIVE PRODUCER
David Rabinovitch

Documentary – educational.

INSIGHT PRODUCTION COMPANY, LTD.

401 – 489 King St. W, Toronto, ON M5V 1K4.
TEL: (416) 596-8118. FAX: (416) 596-8270.
email: insight@insighttv.com www.insighttv.com
EXECUTIVE PRODUCER
John M. Brunton, Barbara Bowlby

Drama, comedy, variety, documentary, lifestyle & reality programming.

INTERCOM FILMS, LIMITED

1650 Yonge St., Toronto, ON M5P 2B9. TEL: (416) 483-3862.
FAX: (416) 483-1106. email: giltaylor@rogers.com
PRESIDENT
Gilbert W. Taylor

JAMES BRODIE PRODUCTIONS, INC.

10 Dancers Dr., Unionville, ON L6C 2C4. TEL: (905) 887-5534.
FAX: (905) 887-2312. email: jim@jimbrodie.com
www.jimbrodie.com
PRODUCER
Jim Brodie

JAMS PRODUCTIONS, INC.

2206 Holt Rd., Production Trailer 1, Bowmanville, ON L1C 3K7.
TEL: (647) 273-4844, (905) 623-2895. FAX: (905) 623-2895.
email: alan@jamsproductions.ca www.jamsproductions.ca
www.jamsproductions.com
CONTACT
Alan J. Schwarz

TV production / series.

JOHN M. ECKERT PRODUCTIONS, LIMITED

75 Poplar Plains Rd., Toronto, ON M4V 2N1.
TEL: (416) 960-4961.
CONTACT
John M. Eckert

JONSWORTH PRODUCTIONS, INC.

955 Queen St. W, Toronto, ON M6J 3X5.
TEL: (416) 361-9855. FAX: (416) 361-9162.
email: jonsworth@attglobal.net
PRESIDENT
Robert Wertheimer

TV series — drama, MOWs.

JUMPPOINT ENTERTAINMENT

1552 Thurlow St., Orleans, ON K4A 2K9. TEL: (613) 255-2325.
FAX: (613) 837-1029. email: alex@jumppoint.org
www.jumppoint.org
SENIOR PRODUCER/CEO
Alexander Pappas
SENIOR EDITOR
Mike Carss - mike@jumppoint.org
OFFICE ADMINISTRATOR
Naya Maekawa - naya@jumppoint.org

Motion picture and television production company.

JUTUL FILMS, INC

47 Amiens Rd., West Hill, ON M1E 3S7. TEL: (416) 282-4304.
email: jutul@sympatico.ca
CONTACT
Per-Inge Schei

IMAX / 35 / 16mm / DoP / director, fluent in Norwegian.

KALEIDOSCOPE ENTERTAINMENT, INC.

201 – 23 Lesmill Rd., Toronto, ON M3B 3P6.
TEL: (416) 443-9200. FAX: (416) 443-8685.
email: paul@kalent.com
V.P., PRODUCTION
Paul McConvey

TV / film production — drama / children's / documentary.

KEEP IT IN THE FAMILY PRODUCTIONS

23 Stafford St., Toronto, ON M5V 2S2.
TEL: (416) 539-9989. FAX: (416) 539-9969.
email: claude@keepitinthefamilyproductions.com
www.keepitinthefamilyproductions.com
EXECUTIVE PRODUCER
Claude Barnes
PRODUCER
Karyn Koski

KENSINGTON COMMUNICATIONS, INC.

451 Adelaide St. W, Toronto, ON M5V 1T1. TEL: (416) 504-9822.
FAX: (416) 504-3608. email: info@kensingtontv.com
www.kensingtontv.com
PRESIDENT/PRODUCER
Robert Lang

TV series & documentaries / multimedia.

KINETIC PICTURES, INC.

214 Rusholme Rd., Toronto, ON M6H 2Y8.
TEL: (416) 537-2641. email: ian.mcdougall@pathcom.com
PRESIDENT
Ian McDougall

Features / TV drama.

KNIGHT ENTERPRISES

307 – 99 Fifth Ave., Ottawa, ON K1S 5P5. TEL: (613) 730-1728.
FAX: (613) 730-0182. email: info@knight-tv.com
www.knight-tv.com
PRESIDENT
Chris Knight
SENIOR PRODUCER
Kathy Doherty
HEAD, BUSINESS AFFAIRS
Sheldon Spears

TV programming — food, lifestyle, reality.

KNIGHTSCOVE MEDIA CORP.

1121 Leslie St., Suite 2, Toronto, ON M4L 1H9.
TEL: (416) 444-7900. FAX: (416) 444-2473.
email: info@queenstreetentertainment.com
www.knightscove.com/
PRESIDENT/CEO
Leif Bristow

Finances, produces and distributes moderately budgeted ($5 million to $15 million), family-oriented feature-length commercial films on an acquisition production or co-production basis.

KUBLACOM PICTURES, INC.

435 – 325 Dalhousie St., Ottawa, ON K1N 7G2.
TEL: (613) 244-2104. FAX: (613) 244-2105.
email: tv@kublacom.ca www.kublacom.ca
PRESIDENT/PRODUCER
Ed Kucerak

Television production — lifestyle / factual / documentaries.

KUPER PRODUCTIONS, LTD.

301 Forest Hill Rd., Toronto, ON M5P 2N7.
TEL: (416) 782-4553. FAX: (416) 782-4425.
email: kupers@kupers.com
CREATIVE DIRECTOR
Jack Kuper
CONTACT
Terrye Lee

KYBELE FILMS

424 Glenholme Ave., Toronto, ON M6E 3E7.

TEL: (416) 651-2296. email: info@kybelefilms.com
www.kybelefilms.com
PRODUCER/DIRECTOR
Sibel Guvenc

Independent entertainment company; produces, markets and distributes theatrical feature films and TV series.

LAWRENCE MARSHALL PRODUCTIONS
3348 Bayview Ave., Unit A, Toronto, ON M2M 3R9.
TEL: (416) 590-0315. FAX: (416) 590-0317.
email: lmp@sympatico.ca
PRESIDENT
Lawrence Marshall

LIFESTYLE MEDIA
1 – 67A Portland St., Toronto, ON M5V 2M9.
TEL: (416) 977-5575. FAX: (416) 977-5365.
email: email@LifeStyleMedia.ca www.LifeStyleMedia.ca
SENIOR PRODUCERS/PARTNER
Shay Schwartzman, Evan Trestan

LIGHTBOX STUDIOS, INC.
422 Dundas St. E, Toronto, ON M5A 2A8.
TEL: (416) 929-1948. email: lightbox@idirect.com
PRODUCER
Mary Young
ANIMATION DIRECTOR
Greg Duffell

LIVELY MEDIA
828 Richmond Street West, Toronto, ON M5V 2K6.
TEL: (416) 644-1792. FAX: (416) 929-6200.
email: contact@livelymedia.ca www.livelymedia.ca
EXECUTIVE PRODUCER
Leanna Crouch

Factual programming and dramas.

LOCKWOOD FILMS, (LONDON) INC.
12569 Boston Dr., RR 41, London, ON N6H 5L2.
TEL: (519) 657-3994. email: nancycjohnson@hotmail.com
PRESIDENT/PRODUCER
Nancy Johnson
DIRECTOR/PRODUCER
Mark McCurdy

LONE EAGLE ENTERTAINMENT, LTD.
72 Stafford Street. Suite 400, Toronto, ON M6J 2R9.
TEL: (416) 351-9111. FAX: (416) 351-9666.
email: info@loneagle.tv www.loneeagle.tv
PRESIDENT
Mike Geddes
VICE PRESIDENT
Christopher Geddes

TV production, reality programming and distribution.

LOON FILM, INC.
12 – 1254 McIntyre St. W, North Bay, ON P1B 8S1.
TEL: (705) 840-0165. FAX: (705) 497-8736.
email: williamp@nipissingu.ca www.nipissingu.ca
CONTACT
Bill Plumstead

Feature film. TV series That Beautiful Somewhere, www.thatbeautifulsomewhere.com TV series.

LOOPMEDIA, INC.
243 – 401 Richmond St. W, Toronto, ON M5V 3A8.
TEL: (416) 595-6496. FAX: (416) 595-0306.
email: jan@loopmedia.com www.loopmedia.com
DIRECTOR, CLIENT SERVICES
Jan King

A broadcast design, animation and commercial production company providing branding solutions for film, television, advertising and new media industries.

LOTEN MEDIA, INC.
2050 Amherst Heights Dr., Burlington, ON L7P 4M6.
TEL: (416) 598-4699. email: lotenmedia@sympatico.ca
CONTACT
Wendy Loten

TV series production.

LTB FILMS, INC.
401 – 227 Front St., Toronto, ON M5A 1E8 .
TEL: (416) 360-0053. FAX: (416) 360-1253.
email: wayne@ltbfilms.com www.ltbfilms.com
EXECUTIVE PRODUCER
Wayne Fenske
SALES ASSISTANT
Greg Woods - greg@ltbfilms.com
Laura Mendes - laura@ltbfilms.com

Commercials / infomercials / corporate videos.

LUMANITY PRODUCTIONS, INC.
28 Blong Ave., Toronto, ON M4M 1P2.
TEL: (416) 823-6650. FAX: (416) 946-1854.
email: rbudreau@lumanity.com www.lumanity.com
CONTACT
Robert Budreau

Film and television production.

LUSH ART & ENTERTAINMENT
101 – 15 Elm St., Toronto, ON M5G 1H1.
TEL: (416) 575-5521. email: info@lushentertainment.ca
www.lushentertainment.ca
PRODUCER
Michael LeClair, Barbara Cooper

LYNX IMAGES PRODUCTIONS
P.O. Box 5961, Stn. A, Toronto, ON M5W 1P4.
TEL: (416) 925-8422. FAX: (416) 925-8352.
email: info@lynximages.com www.lynximages.com
CONTACT
Russell N. Floren, Andrea Gutsche, Barbara Chisholm

Educational / documentary / TV / book publishing..

MAD FILMS, INC.
300 – 171 East Liberty St., Toronto, ON M6K 3P6.
TEL: (416) 598-1331. FAX: (416) 598-5141.
email: e.mail@madfilmsinc.com www.madfilmsinc.com
EXECUTIVE PRODUCER
Mark Bisson

Commercials.

MAGNETIC STUDIO
184 Napa Valley Ave., Woodbridge, ON L4H 1L1.
TEL: (905) 893-1513. email: peter@magneticstudio.com
www.magneticstudio.com
CONTACT
Peter Lacalamita

Small business dedicated to creating digital illustration and animation for broadcast, print and new media.

MAKIN' MOVIES, INC.
128 Albany Ave., Toronto, ON M5R 3C4. TEL: (416) 516-1833.
email: info@makinmovies.tv www.makinmovies.tv
CONTACT
Maureen Judge

MARBLEMEDIA
200 – 74 Fraser Ave., Toronto, ON M6K 3E1.
TEL: (416) 646-2711. FAX: (416) 646-2717.
email: connect@marblemedia.com www.marblemedia.com
PRODUCER
Mark Bishop, Matt Hornburg

MARCH ENTERTAINMENT
301 – 276 King St. W, Toronto, ON M5V 1J2.
TEL: (416) 604-9000. FAX: (416) 977-1485.
email: info@marchentertainment.com
www.marchentertainment.com
PRESIDENT
Daniel Hawes

MARKHAM STREET FILMS
487 Adelaide St. West, Suite 201, Toronto, ON M5V 1T4 .
TEL: (416) 536-1390. FAX: (416) 536-7986.
email: info@markhamstreet.com
www.markhamstreetfilms.com
CONTACT
Michael McNamara, Judy Holm

Producers / directors / writers of documentaries and feature films.

MARQUIS ENTERTAINMENT, INC.
312 - 73 Richmond Street West, Toronto, ON M5H 4E8.
TEL: (416) 960-9123. FAX: (416) 960-9535.
email: info@marquisent.ca www.marquisent.ca
PRODUCER
Robert Richardson
ASSOCIATE PRODUCER
Colin Rivers

TV series.

MAXX PRODUCTIONS
44 Russell Hill Road, Toronto, ON M4V 2T2.
TEL: (416) 585-9900. FAX: (416) 585-2199.
email: maxx@maxxfilms.com www.maxxfilms.com
CONTACT
Harve Sherman, Ron Grittani

Commercials.

MEDIA HEADQUARTERS FILM & TELEVISION, INC.
760 Bathurst St., Studio 2, Toronto, ON M5S 2R6.
TEL: (416) 537-8384. FAX: (416) 537-8602.
email: contact@mediahqs.net www.mediahqs.net
PRODUCER
Robert Cohen, Shari Cohen

Animation / documentary – educational / performing arts – variety / TV series. Prime-time programming for Canadian and international markets.

MEDIATIQUE

675 King St. W, Toronto, ON M5V 1M9. TEL: (416) 367-8464.
FAX: (416) 367-8466. email: mediatique@mediatique.ca
www.mediatique.ca
PRESIDENT
Daniele Caloz

MERCURY FILMS, INC.

645A Dupont St., Toronto, ON M6G 1Z4. TEL: (416) 516-2661.
FAX: (416) 516-2605. email: mercfilm@istar.ca
www.mercuryfilms.ca
PRODUCER
Nicholas de Pencier
PRODUCER/DIRETOR
Jennifer Baichwal

Documentaries.

MICROTAINMENT PLUS PRODUCTIONS, INC.

59 Mutual St, Toronto, ON M5B 2A9.
TEL: (416) 537-5004. FAX: (416) 537-8984.
email: mail@microtainment.com www.microtainment.com
CHAIRMAN
Garry Blye

Full-service film & TV production.

MONTE-BROOKS PRODUCTIONS

(A division of Monte Media Management)
111 Berkley St., Toronto, ON M5H 2W8. TEL: (519) 896-5219.
FAX: (519) 896-5250. email: info@montemedia.tv
www.montemedia.tv
PRESIDENT
Tino Monte

Brand spots and Infomercials.

MUSE ENTERTAINMENT ENTERPRISES, INC.

940 Lansdowne Ave. Bldg. 15, 4th Flr., Toronto, ON M6H 3Z4.
TEL: (416) 921-2391. email: tweekes@muse.ca
www.muse.ca
CONTACT
Jane Mowbray

Features / TV movies & series. See also Québec.

THE NIGHTINGALE CO.

588 Richmond St. W, Toronto, ON M5V 1Y9.
TEL: (416) 628-1355. FAX: (416) 628-1505.
email: info@dnightingale.com www.dnightingale.com
PRESIDENT
Debbie Nightingale

Boutique production house — features / TV series / documentaries / children's programming.

NORFLICKS PRODUCTIONS

124 Dupont St., Toronto, ON M5R 1V2. TEL: (416) 351-7558.
FAX: (416) 351-8165. email: mail@norflicks.com
www.norflicks.com
PRESIDENT
Richard Nielsen

NORSTAR FILMED ENTERTAINMENT, INC.

301 - 131 Hazelton Avenue, Toronto, ON M5R 2E4.
TEL: (416) 961-6278. FAX: (416) 961-5608.
email: info@norstarfilms.com www.norstarfilms.com
PRESIDENT
Ilana Frank
DIRECTOR, SALES & MARKETING
Kathy Johnson
EXECUTIVE ASSISTANT
Tina Toffoli

NORTH BEND FILM COMPANY

117 Borden St., Toronto, ON M5S 2N2. TEL: (416) 964-6219.
email: nbfilm@rogers.com
PRODUCER
Steve Lucas

NORTHLAND PICTURES

P.O. Box 549, Stn. Adelaide, Toronto, ON M5C 2J6.
TEL: (416) 526-3456. email: streamliner@sympatico.ca
CONTACT
Colin Strayer

Drama / documentary / corporate communication / music video / television commercial production since 1980.

NOVA MOTION PICTURES, LTD.

129 Blantyre Ave., Main Flr., Toronto, ON M1N 2R6.
TEL: (416) 690-1516. FAX: (416) 694-5574.
email: hrosen@novapix.com www.novapix.com
CEO & EXECUTIVE PRODUCER
Howard Rosen

OCNUS PRODUCTIONS

66 Muriel Street, Ottawa, ON K1S 4E1.
TEL: (613) 829-7656. FAX: (613) 820-5020.
email: greg@ocnusproductions.com
www.ocnusproductions.com
PRESIDENT
Greg Lawrence
BUSINESS AFFAIRS
Andrea Wilson - andreaw@ocnusproductions.com

OMNI MEDIA PRODUCTIONS, LIMITED

6 – 235 Martindale Rd., St. Catharines, ON L2W 1A5.
TEL: (800) 561-6664, (905) 684-9455. FAX: (905) 684-4291.
email: tv@omnimedia.com www.omnimedia.com
PRESIDENT
Peter Murray

Production.

OMNI TELEVISION

(Rogers Media Television)
545 Lakeshore Blvd. W, Toronto, ON M5V 1A3. TEL: (416) 260-0047.
FAX: (416) 260-3621. email: info@omnitv.ca www.omnitv.ca
CEO, TELEVISION
Leslie Sole
V.P., STATION MANAGER
Madeline Ziniak
NATIONAL & RETAIL SALES
Jacquie Hood
MANAGER, COMMERCIAL PRODUCTION
Pacifica Virzi

Multilingual commercial prod. expertise / translations / voice-overs.

OZ MEDIA

103 – 6 Pardee Ave., Toronto, ON M6K 3H5.
TEL: (416) 537-0687. FAX: (416) 537-7116.
email: trisha@ozmediagroup.com www.ozmediagroup.com
EXECUTIVE PRODUCER
Trisha Emerson

Commercials.

THE PARTNERS FILM COMPANY, LIMITED

53 Ontario St., Toronto, ON M5A 2V1. TEL: (416) 869-3500.
FAX: (416) 869-3365. email: jms@partnersfilm.com
www.partnersfilm.com
EXECUTIVE PRODUCER
Gigi Realini, Aerin Barnes, Sally Leggett

Commercials.

PEACE ARCH MOTION PICTURES, INC.

(A Peace Arch Entertainment Group Company)
650 - 1867 Yonge St., Toronto, ON M4S 1Y5.
TEL: (416) 777-1177. FAX: (416) 777-1178.
email: Info@PeaceArch.com www.peacearch.com
CEO
Gary Howsam
PRESIDENT
Lewin Webb
PRODUCTION EXECUTIVE
Kate Harrison

Feature film projects. Handles all fulfillment aspects of the film industry including packaging, financing, production and distribution.

PEACE POINT ENTERTAINMENT GROUP

78 Berkeley St., Toronto, ON M5A 2W7. TEL: (416) 365-7734.
FAX: (416) 365-7739. email: info@peacepoint.tv
www.peacepoint.tv
PRESIDENT & EXECUTIVE PRODUCER
Les Tomlin
V.P., HEAD, DEVELOPMENT
Vallery Hyduk

Television / reality programming.

PETER ROWE PRODUCTIONS, INC.

180 Pinewood Trail, Mississauga, ON L5G 2L1.
TEL: (905) 891-9498, (416) 550-4511. FAX: (905) 891-9952.
email: prowe@interlog.com

Producer / director / writer.

PETERSEN PRODUCTIONS, INC.

12 Lewis St., Toronto, ON M4M 2H3. TEL: (416) 461-4660.
FAX: (416) 461-7471.

U.S. Office: 106 Entrada Dr., Unit 8, Santa Monica, CA 90402.
TEL: (310) 230-8616.
PRESIDENT
Curtis Petersen

See also British Columbia.

PHALANX FILMWORKS, INC.

2 Moberly Ave., Toronto, ON M4C 4A8. TEL: (416) 690-9981.
email: phalanx@istar.ca
ASSISTANT DIRECTOR
Michael Bowman

PLUM COMMUNICATIONS INCORPORATED

122 – 1054 Centre St., Thornhill, ON L4J 8E5.
TEL: (905) 695-0123. email: bcole@plumcom.ca
www.plumcom.ca

CONTACT
Bruce Cole

Multimedia production / web design / imaging.

PORTFOLIO ENTERTAINMENT, INC.

602 – 110 Eglinton Ave. E, Toronto, ON M4P 2Y1.
TEL: (416) 483-9773. FAX: (416) 483-6537.
email: portfolio@portfolio-ent.com
www.portfolioentertainment.com/
FOUNDER & PRESIDENT
Lisa Olfman, Joy Rosen
HEAD OF SALES & ACQUISITIONS
Annmarie Lesiuk
DEVELOPMENT MANAGER
Aron Dunn

TV programming: high-quality children's, animation, prime time TV movies, lifestyle, travel, sports, documentary and specials.

POSTMODERN PRODUCTIONS

6 – 80 Carlton St., Toronto, ON M5B 1L6.
TEL: (416) 587-2349. FAX: (416) 413-1620.
email: postmod@total.net
EXECUTIVE PRODUCER
Susan Papp

PRIMITIVE ENTERTAINMENT

300 – 585 Bloor St. W, Toronto, ON M6G 1K5.
TEL: (416) 531-3087. FAX: (416) 531-4961.
email: info@primitive.net www.primitive.net

Documentaries.

PRISMA LIGHT, LTD.

762 Queen St. W, Toronto, ON M6J 1E9. TEL: (416) 504-4321.
FAX: (416) 504-7325. email: info@prismalight.com
www.prismalight.com

Broadcast division creates and produces documentary and drama programming. Media production company specializes in videos, DVDs and CD-ROMs.

PRODIGY PICTURES, INC.

1413 - 85 Bloor St. East, Toronto, ON M4W 3Y1.
TEL: (416) 977-3473. FAX: (416) 977-4549.
email: www.jayfirestone.com www.prodigypictures.com
CONTACT
Jay Firestone, Karen Wookey, Ken Gord

PROPER TELEVISION

201 – 409 King St. W, Toronto, ON M5V 1K1.
TEL: (416) 598-2500. FAX: (416) 598-2550.
email: info@propertelevision.com www.propertelevision.com
EXECUTIVE PRODUCER
Guy O'Sullivan

Factual entertainment & documentary production.

PROTOCOL ENTERTAINMENT, INC.

405 – 80 Spadina Ave., Toronto, ON M5V 2J4.
TEL: (416) 966-2711. FAX: (416) 599-6100.
email: steve@protocolmail.com www.protocolent.com
PRESIDENT & CEO
Steve Levitan

Development, financing, production — television series, movies, mini-series & feature films.

PRYCELESS PRODUCTIONS, LTD.

59 Pine Cres, Toronto, ON M4E 1L3. TEL: (416) 699-6322.
FAX: (416) 699-6168.
PRODUCER
Craig Pryce

PTV PRODUCTIONS

67 Portland St., Toronto, ON M5V 2M9.
TEL: (416) 531-0100. FAX: (416) 537-2145.
email: info@ptvproductions.ca www.ptvproductions.ca
PRESIDENT
Andrea Nemtin

Documentary, lifestyle and children's animation.

QUICKBEAM FILMS NORTH

8 Tunis Ave., Ottawa, ON K1Z 7R5. TEL: (613) 695-6133.
email: quickbeamfilms@gmail.com www.quickbeamfilms.com
PRODUCER
Paul Gordon

Final Cut Pro 3.0 non-linear editing, 16mm photography, camera operator (film and video).

RADICAL SHEEP PRODUCTIONS, INC.

104 – 80 Fraser Ave., Toronto, ON M6K 3E1.
TEL: (416) 539-0363. FAX: (416) 539-0496.
email: contact@radsheep.com www.radsheep.com
CONTACT
John Leitch

TV / film.

RADKE FILM GROUP / STEAM FILMS

125 George St., Toronto, ON M5A 2N4. TEL: (416) 366-9036.
FAX: (416) 366-0006. email: info@radke.tv www.radke.tv

Commercials and complete productions services across Canada. See also British Columbia.

REAL TO REEL PRODUCTIONS

3023 Dundas St. W, Toronto, ON M6P 1Z4. TEL: (416) 763-0001.
FAX: (416) 763-1496. email: info@r2r.ca www.r2r.ca
V.P., EXECUTIVE PRODUCER
Anne Pick

RED APPLE ENTERTAINMENT CORP.

503 – 1 St Clair Ave. W, Toronto, ON M4V 1K7.
TEL: (416) 324-8537. FAX: (416) 324-0942.
email: info@redapple.com www.redapple.com
CONTACT
Rachel Low

Specializing in documentary entertainment.

RED ROVER

345 Adelaide St. W, 5th Flr., Toronto, ON M5V 1R5.
TEL: (416) 591-6500. FAX: (416) 591-6501.
email: pamela@redrover.net www.redrover.net
EXECUTIVE PRODUCER
Danielle Araiche
SALES REPRESENTATIVE
Pamela Cordeiro

Commercials.

REVOLVER FILM COMPANY

101 – 260 King St. E, Toronto, ON M5A 4L5.
TEL: (416) 367-9696. FAX: (416) 367-8992.
email: info@revolverfilms.com www.revolverfilms.com
CONTACT
Jannie McInnes, Niva Chow

RHOMBUS MEDIA, INC.

600 – 99 Spadina Ave., Toronto, ON M5V 3P8.
TEL: (416) 971-7856. FAX: (416) 971-9647.
email: rhombus@rhombusmedia.com
www.rhombusmedia.com
CONTACT
Niv Fichman, Sheena Macdonald, Barbara Willis Sweete, Larry Weinstein

RICOCHET FILM PRODUCTION, LTD.

101 – 200 Tiffield Rd., Toronto, ON M1V 5J1.
TEL: (416) 449-9400. FAX: (416) 449-9498.
email: info@octapixx.com
PRODUCER & CEO
J. Gary Gladman

TV programming / documentaries / co-productions.

ROGERS PROMOTIONS

333 Bloor St. E, 4th Fl., Toronto, ON M4W 1G9.
TEL: (416) 935-6666. FAX: (416) 935-7680.
email: info@rogerspromotions.ca www.rogerspromotions.ca
CONTACT
Christa Dickenson - (416) 935-4704

Full-service film and video production house / post-production services and creative concepts / 2D & 3D animation.

ROSEFIRE FILM, INC.

812 – 77 Huntley St., Toronto, ON M4Y 2P3.
TEL: (416) 925-6258. email: sobleman@web.net
WRITER/PRODUCER/DIRECTOR
David Sobelman

Feature films / documentaries / TV.

S&S PRODUCTIONS, INC.

Dufferin Liberty Centre, 100A – 219 Dufferin St., Toronto, ON M6K 3J1. TEL: (416) 260-0538. FAX: (416) 260-1628.
email: yashie@ssp.ca www.ssp.ca
V.P. & EXECUTIVE PRODUCER
David Smith
DIRECTOR OF OPERATIONS
Hope Lee
BUSINESS AFFAIRS & PLANNING
Yashie Kowlessar

TV comedy & magazine series.

SAILOR JONES MEDIA

232 Scarborough Rd., Toronto, ON M4E 3M6.
TEL: (416) 376-3939. FAX: (416) 946-1889.
email: info@sailorjones.com www.sailorjones.com
PRESIDENT & EXECUTIVE PRODUCER
Barbara Jones

SARRAZIN COUTURE ENTERTAINMENT

C102 – 629 Eastern Ave., Toronto, ON M4M 1E4.
TEL: (416) 461-2030. FAX: (416) 461-3905.
email: talk2@sc-ent.ca www.sc-ent.ca

CONTACT
Pierre Sarrazin, Suzette Couture, Alison Humphrey

SAVI MEDIA, INC.

158 Roxton Rd., 3rd Flr., Toronto, ON M6J 2Y5.
TEL: (416) 597-8484. FAX: (416) 597-9596.
email: mail@savi-media.com www.savi-media.com
PRESIDENT
Alexandra Raffé
DIRECTOR, CREATIVE AFFAIRS
Tara Twigg

TV drama / feature films / children's series, animation. See also British Columbia.

SCREEN DOOR, INC.

18 Gloucester Lane, 3rd Flr., Toronto, ON M4Y 1L5.
TEL: (416) 535-7402. FAX: (416) 535-1839.
email: screendoor@screendoor.org www.screendoor.org
PRODUCER
Mary Young Leckie, Heather Haldane

Formed in 1999 by producers Heather Haldane and Mary Young Leckie.

SERENDIPITY POINT FILMS

9 Price St., Toronto, ON M4W 1Z1. TEL: (416) 960-0300.
FAX: (416) 960-8656. www.serendipitypoint.com
CHARMAN, CEO, & PRODUCER
Robert Lantos
HEAD, BUSINESS & LEGAL AFFAIRS
Mark Musselman
PUBLICITY, MARKETING
Wendy Saffer

SEVENTH MAN FILMS, INC.

159 Sheldrake Blvd., Toronto, ON M4P 2B1.
TEL: (416) 483-3200, (416) 523-9685.
email: bomfog@sympatico.ca
CONTACT
Nicholas Gray

Children's / drama.

SEVENTH::SENSE::STUDIOS::INC

115 Arcola Private, Ottawa, ON K1K 4W9. TEL: (613) 314-1525, (613) 234-3441. FAX: (613) 842-9938.
email: samantha@seventhsensestudios.com
kenneth@seventhsensestudios.com
www.seventhsensestudios.com
PRODUCER
Kenneth McGrath, Samantha Kaine

TV series, dramas, MOWs, independent (feature) films, shorts, commercials, educational, documentary, comedy and web (viral) videos.

SFA PRODUCTIONS, INC.

300 – 55 Adelaide St. E, Toronto, ON M5C 1K6.
TEL: (416) 214-9900. FAX: (416) 214-9300.
email: inquire@sfaproductions.com
www.sfaproductions.com
PRESIDENT & CEO
Sandra Faire
SENIOR V.P. & COO
Trisa Dayot
V.P., TALENT & BUSINESS AFFAIRS
Millan Curry-Sharples
V.P., POST-PRODUCTION
Bronwyn Warren

Feature film & TV — comedy / music / drama / documentary.

SHADOW SHOWS, INC.

18 Gloucester Ln., 4th Flr., Toronto, ON M4Y 1L5.
TEL: (416) 929-9004. FAX: (416) 929-0028.
email: bruce@shadowshows.com
DIRECTOR
Bruce McDonald

SHAFTESBURY FILMS

100 – 163 Queen St. E, Toronto, ON M5A 1S1.
TEL: (416) 363-1411. FAX: (416) 363-1428.
email: mailbox@shaftesbury.org www.shaftesbury.org
CHAIRMAN
Christina Jennings
PRESIDENT
Jonathan Barker
VICE PRESIDENT
Laura Harbin, Scott Garvie

Film & TV.

SHEBANDOWAN FILMS

25 High St. North, Thunder Bay, ON P7B 2W4.
TEL: (807) 345-0221.
email: shebafilms@shaw.ca www.shebafilms.com
PRESIDENT
Kelly Saxberg
VICE PRESIDENT
Ronald Harpelle

SHOES FULL OF FEET

246 Duview Ave., Toronto, ON M2N 4J2.
TEL: (416) 512-0084. FAX: (416) 512-0084.
email: info@shoesfulloffeet.com www.shoesfulloffeet.com
PRESIDENT
Kris Booth
CEO
Bryce Mitchell
COO
Raj Panikkar

Feature and short film production.

SHOOTERS INTERNATIONAL, INC.

63 Berkeley St., Toronto, ON M5A 2W5. TEL: (416) 862-1959.
FAX: (416) 862-7189. email: pbenson@shootersfilm.com,
pmcnamara@shootersfilm.com www.shootersfilm.com
EXECUTIVE PRODUCER
Peter Benson, Pamela McNamara

TV production / commercials / corporate videos / multimedia.

THE SHOOTING EYE CORPORATION

P.O. Box 32022, Stone Church Post Office, Hamilton, ON L8W 3L3. TEL: (905) 387-6099. email: info@shootingeye.com
www.shootingeye.com
PRESIDENT
Jeremy Major

SIENNA FILMS

183 Harbord Street, Toronto, M5S 1H5.
TEL: (416) 703-1126. FAX: (416) 703-8825.
email: siennainfo@siennafilms.com
www.siennafilms.com
PRODUCER
Julia Sereny, Jennifer Kawaja

Award-winning film and TV production company.

SINKING SHIP ENTERTAINMENT

445 – 67 Mowat Ave., Toronto, ON M6K 3E3.
TEL: (416) 533-8172. FAX: (416) 533-3878
email: info@sinkingship.ca www.sinkingship.ca
PRODUCER
Blair Powers, J.J. Johnson, Matt Bishop, Liz Haines

SLANTED WHEEL ENTERTAINMENT, INC.

C303 – 629 Eastern Ave., Toronto, ON M4M 1E4.
TEL: (416) 405-8460. FAX: (416) 405-8218.
email: info@slantedwheel.ca
PRESIDENT
Jon Slan
DIRECTOR, DEVELOPMENT
Rachel Rafelman

Feature films / TV series.

SMILEY GUY STUDIOS

444 Bathurst St., Studio 2, Toronto, ON M5T 2S6.
TEL: (416) 979-8800. FAX: (416) 979-2227.
email: info@smileyguy.com www.smileyguy.com
BUSINESS DEVELOPMENT
Jonas Diamond

Animation.

SOARING HEART PICTURES, INC.

246 – 2025 Guelph Line, Burlington, ON L7P 4X4.
TEL: (416) 992-6750. FAX: (905) 331-1344.
email: byronmckim@soaringheartpictures.com
www.soaringheartpictures.com
PRESIDENT
Byron McKim

Feature film / performing arts – variety.

SOFT CITIZEN

125 George St., Toronto, ON M5A 2NA. TEL: (416) 366-9849.
FAX: (416) 366-6936. email: info@softcitizen.com
www.softcitizen.com
EXECUTIVE PRODUCER & MANAGING DIRECTOR
Eva Preger
SALES & MARKETING
Jacqui Wilkinson

Commercial and music video production.

SOLSTICE ENTERTAINMENT

864 – 313 Richmond St. E, Toronto, ON M5A 4S7.
TEL: (416) 504-7557. FAX: (416) 504-7518.
email: dbalcon@rogers.com
EXECUTIVE PRODUCER
David Balcon

Development, production and distribution of documentary one-offs and series.

SOUND VENTURE INTERNATIONAL

219 – 126 York St., Ottawa, ON K1N 5T5. TEL: (613) 241-5111.

ext. 248. FAX: (613) 241-5010. email: info@soundventure.com
www.soundventure.com
V.P., SENIOR PRODUCER
Tim Joyce

Specializing in documentary, arts and children's programs.

SPARKS PRODUCTIONS, INC.

5 Church St., Toronto, ON M5E 1M2. TEL: (416) 862-2000.
FAX: (416) 862-8364. email: eldon@sparksproductions.com
www.sparksproductions.com
EXECUTIVE PRODUCER
Andy Crosbie
SALES & MARKETING
Eldon Mascoll

Commercials.

SPECTRUM FILMS

79 Lippincott St., Toronto, ON M5S 2P2. TEL: (416) 515-1077, (416) 972-7668. email: spectrum@the-wire.com
www.spectrumtoronto.com
CONTACT
Holly Dale, Janis Cole

SPHINX PRODUCTIONS

24 Mercer St., Toronto, ON M5V 1H3. TEL: (416) 971-9131.
FAX: (416) 971-6014. email: mann@sphinxproductions.com
www.sphinxproductions.com
CONTACT
Ron Mann

SPY ENTERTAINMENT

49C Spadina Ave., Toronto, ON M5V 2J1. TEL: (416) 979-7797.
FAX: (416) 979-3090. email: carlo@spyfilms.com
www.spyfilms.com
EXECUTIVE PRODUCER
Carlo Trulli

Music videos and production services.

STARDUST PICTURES

1010 – 1930 Yonge St., Toronto, ON M4S 1Z4.
TEL: (866) 961-8989, (416) 961-8989. FAX: (416) 961-2423.
email: info@stardustpictures.com www.stardustpictures.com
EXECUTIVE PRODUCER
Justin L. Levine

STORNOWAY PRODUCTIONS, INC.

304 – 1200 Bay St., Toronto, ON M5R 2A5.
TEL: (416) 923-1104. FAX: (416) 923-1122.
email: info@stornoway.com www.stornoway.com

Documentaries / drama.

STORYBOOK FILMS

279 Henry St., Stirling, ON K0K 3E0. TEL: (416) 738-3569.
email: info@storybookfilms.ca www.storybookfilms.ca
PRODUCER/DIRECTOR
Dave Luetjen
WRITER/EDITOR
Kellie Dearman

STORYLINE ENTERTAINMENT

115 Palmerston Ave., Toronto, ON M6J 2J2. TEL: (416) 603-8333.
FAX: (416) 603-6318. email: lisa@storylineentertainment.ca
www.storylineentertainment.com
PRODUCER
Ed Barreveld

STRADA FILMS

788 King Street West, 2nd Flr., Toronto, ON M4W 1Z1.
TEL: (416) 642-2005. FAX: (416) 642-1970.
email: info@stradafilms.ca www.stradafilms.ca
PRODUCER
Sandra Cunningham

Feature film.

SULLIVAN ENTERTAINMENT, INC.

110 Davenport Road, Toronto, ON M5R 3R3.
email: inquire@sullivan-ent.com www.sullivanmovies.com
PRESIDENT
Kevin Sullivan

SUMMER PICTURES

91 Beresford Drive, Richmond Hill, ON M5R 3R3.
TEL: (905) 883-5561. FAX: (905)787-1240.
email: tom@summerpictures.biz www.summerpictures.biz
EXECUTIVE PRODUCER
Tom Strnad, Boris Mojsovski

Full-service production company specializing in feature film development, production and post-production.

SUMMERHILL ENTERTAINMENT

56 Shaftesbury Ave., Toronto, ON M4T 1A3.
TEL: (416) 967-6503. FAX: (416) 967-1292.
email: jbryant@summerhill.tv www.summerhill.tv
PARTNER
Ronald Lillie, Bill Johnston

EXECUTIVE PRODUCER
Lee Herberman
HEAD OF DEVELOPMENT
Patricia Bush
HEAD OF DISTRIBUTION
Adam Block

SUNDOG FILMS

530 Richmond St. W, Rear Bldg., Toronto, ON M5V 1Y4.
TEL: (416) 504-2555. FAX: (416) 504-4545.
email: info@sundogfilms.ca www.sundogfilms.ca
PRESIDENT
Wayne Trickett
VICE PRESIDENT
Robin Trickett

Feature films / commercial production / special effects.

SUSSEX PRODUCTIONS, LTD.

213-56 The Esplanade, Toronto, ON M5S 1J6.
TEL: (416) 368-4039. FAX: (416) 977-5264.
email: jb5@rogers.com
CONTACT
John Board

TERRA ROSSA PICTURES, INC.

9599 Concession 6, Uxbridge, ON L9P 1R2. TEL: (905) 852-1343.
FAX: (905) 852-4031. email: info@terrarossapictures.com
www.terrarossapictures.com
PRESIDENT
Barbara Samuels

Genres: drama series, television movies and mini-series.

TILT CINEMA

1811 – 7 King St. E, Toronto, ON M5C 3C5. TEL: (416) 367-8024.
FAX: (416) 531-0929. email: karen@tiltcinema.com
ian@tiltcinema.com www.tiltcinema.com
CO-FOUNDER
Karen Hanson, Ian Thompson

Film and television production, specializing in documentaries.

TITLECRAFT, LTD.

P.O. Box 11069, Stn. H, Ottawa, ON K2H 7T8.
TEL: (613) 825-2479. FAX: (613) 223-0271.
email: cstevens@titlecraft.com www.titlecraft.com
CONTACT
Caroline Stevens

TORONTO FILMS / 12 TRIBES PRODUCTIONS

10 Bay St, Toronto ON, M5J 2R8.
TEL: (426) 362-6627.
email: torontofilms@sprint.ca
CONTACT
Leonard Pearl

Toronto-based film production company — produces documentaries / lifestyles / series / feature films.

TORSTAR MEDIA GROUP TELEVISION

1 Yonge St. 9th Fl., Toronto, ON M5E 1E6. TEL: (416) 869-4700.
FAX: (416) 869-4566.
email: production@tmgtv.ca www.tmgtv.ca
V.P. & GENERAL MANAGER
Mark Goodale
EXECUTIVE PRODUCER
Cindy MacDougall

Award-winning, full-service video production facility which includes a 3D virtual set studio, digital cameras, AVID edit suites.

TRANSVISION FILMS

9 Veery Ln., Ottawa, ON K1J 8X4. TEL: (613) 741-9292.
FAX: (613) 744-3548. email: rashmi@transvisionfilms.com
www.transvisionfilms.com
CONTACT
Rashmi Rekha

Feature films, documentaries, short films, corporate videos / projects completed in Russia, India, U.S.A. and Canada.

TRAPEZE

250 The Esplanade, Toronto, ON M5A 1J2. TEL: (416) 601-1999.
FAX: (416) 601-1997. email: info@trapeze.com
www.trapeze.com

TREEHOUSE NORTH PRODUCTIONS, INC.

1124 Queen Street East, Toronto, ON M4M 2T1.
TEL:(416) 861-1204, (604) 669-8733. FAX: (416) 861-0220.
email: silver@treenorth.com www.treenorth.com
PRESIDENT & EXECUTIVE PRODUCER
Karen Silver - silver@treenorth.com

A production service company.

TRICON FILMS & TELEVISION

200 – 372 Richmond St. W, Toronto, ON M5V 1X6.
TEL: (416) 341-9926. FAX: (416) 341-0173.
email: info@triconfilms.com www.triconfilms.com
OWNER
Andrea Gorfolova

DIRECTOR, DISTRIBUTION & DEVELOPMENT
Carrie Hall

TRICORD PICTURES

141 Drakefield Rd., Markham, ON L3P 1G9.
TEL: (905) 472-0445. FAX: (905) 472-0448.
email: karen@tricordpictures.com
CONTACT
Karen Pascal

Film & TV development / production.

TRIPTYCH MEDIA, INC.

788 King St. W, 2nd Flr., Toronto, ON M5V 1N6.
TEL: (416) 703-8866. FAX: (416) 703-8867.
email: info@triptychmedia.ca www.triptychmedia.ca
PRODUCER
Robin Cass, Anna Stratton

TRIUNE PRODUCTIONS, INC.

111 Wildwood Cres, Toronto, ON M4L 2K9. TEL: (416) 686-0467.
FAX: (416) 686-0468. email: triune@triune.ca www.triune.ca
CREATIVE PRODUCER/DIRECTOR
Michael Witta
PRODUCER
John Barclay

Drama / educational programs.

TWIN DRAGON FILM PRODUCTIONS, LTD.

6347 Yonge St., North York, ON M2M 3X7.
TEL: (416) 229-1280. FAX: (416) 229-2425.
email: info@twin-dragon.com www.twin-dragon.com
PRESIDENT
Michael McNamara
VICE PRESIDENT
Martin McNamara

Features.

TV2GO

402 – 250 Ferrand Dr., Toronto, ON M3C 3G8.
TEL: (800) 305-2999, (416) 696-9633. FAX: (416) 696-9640.
email: christi@tv2go.com
CONTACT
Carol Patterson, Lawrence Partington

UNTITLED

300 - 272 Richmond Street East, Toronto, ON M5A 1P4.
TEL: (416) 597-1611. FAX: (416) 597-1116.
email: info@untitledfilms.ca www.untitledfilms.ca
MANAGING DIRECTOR
James Davis
EXECUTIVE PRODUCER
Peter Davis
PRODUCER
Tom Evelyn

Commercials.

UP FRONT ENTERTAINMENT, INC. / TAKE 3 PRODUCTIONS, INC.

302 – 49 Spadina Ave., Toronto, ON M5V 2J1.
TEL: (416) 595-5850. FAX: (416) 595-5851.
email: bbarde@upfront.ca www.upfront.ca
PRESIDENT & EXECUTIVE PRODUCER
Barbara Barde
PRODUCER/DIRECTOR OF BUSINESS AFFAIRS
Linda Stregger

TV and film production companies specializing in documentaries, drama, lifestyle series and current affairs and information programs.

VILLAGERS MEDIA PRODUCTIONS

110 Cottingham St., Toronto, ON M4V 1C1.
TEL: (416) 323-3228. FAX: (416) 323-1201.
email: ddeme@villagersmedia.com www.villagersmedia.com
CONTACT
Dawn Deme, Steven Deme

TV drama / documentaries / corporate.

VISION TV INTERNATIONAL INC.

300 – 1300 Yonge St., Toronto, ON M4T 1X3.
TEL: (416) 924-2186. FAX: (416) 924-6115.
email: info@vtvi.com www.vtvi.com
CHAIRMAN
William D. Roberts
PRESIDENT
Stephen Ellis
HEAD OF PRODUCTION
Kip Spidell
DIRECTOR OF DEVELOPMENT
Jessica Schmiedchen

WAXWORKS CREATIVE

100 Conestoga College Blvd., Kitchener, ON N2P 2N6.
TEL: (800) 281-9333, (519) 895-2008. FAX: (519) 895-0542.
email: jime@waxworks.com www.waxworks.com

Corporate / multimedia.

WESTWIND PICTURES

203 – 2 Pardee Ave., Toronto, ON M6K 3H5. TEL: (416) 516-4414.
FAX: (416) 538-0026.
email: clarkdonnelly@westwindpictures.com
www.westwindpictures.com
EXECUTIVE PRODUCER
Clark Donnelly

See also Saskatchewan.

WHITE PINE PICTURES / MAGNOLIA PICTURES

(A division of Investigative Productions, Inc.)
301 – 822 Richmond St. W, Toronto, ON M6J 1C9.
TEL: (416) 703-5580. FAX: (416) 703-1691.
email: info@whitepinepictures.com www.whitepinepictures.com
CONTACT
Peter Raymont

Film / video production.

WHIZBANG FILMS, INC.

24 Ryerson Ave., 4th Flr., Toronto, ON M5T 2P3.
TEL: (416) 516-5899. FAX: (416) 516-9550.
email: info@whizbangfilms.com www.whizbangfilms.com
PRODUCER
Frank Siracusa
VICE PRESIDENT
Paul Gross
ASSOCIATE PRODUCER
Penny McDonald

TV series — drama, MOWs.

WINDBORNE PRODUCTIONS

141 Drakefield Rd., Markham, ON L3P 1G9.
TEL: (905) 472-0445. FAX: (905) 472-0448.
email: karen@windborneproductions.com
www.windborneproductions.com
CONTACT
Karen Pascal

TV & film production.

WINDSWEPT PRODUCTIONS

22 Edgehill Rd., Belleville, ON K8N 2L1. TEL: (613) 962-7045.
FAX: (613) 966-6500. email: wind@cogeco.ca
www.windsweptproductions.ca
CONTACT
Doug Knutson

Documentary, educational and promotional video (DVCProHD) & DVD production / freelance camera & editing.

XENOPHILE MEDIA, INC.

207 Augusta Ave., Toronto, ON M5T 2L6. TEL: (416) 366-2118.
FAX: (416) 946-1189. email: contact@xenophile.ca
www.xenophile.ca
PRODUCER/DIRECTOR/WRITER
Thomas Wallner, Patrick Crowe

Documentaries / games / interactive TV.

YORKTOWN PRODUCTIONS, LTD.

18 Gloucester Ln., 5th Flr., Toronto, ON M4Y 1L5.
TEL: (416) 923-2787. FAX: (416) 923-8580.
email: kimbriggs@yorktownfilms.com
CONTACT
Kim Briggs

ZAMARIA PRODUCTIONS

43 Ashwood Dr., Orangeville, ON L9W 4A5.
TEL: (519) 942-9988. FAX: (519) 942-9913.
email: zamaria@sympatico.ca
PRESIDENT
Charles Zamaria
VICE PRESIDENT
Daria Magas-Zamaria

TV series — drama, MOWs.

PRINCE EDWARD ISLAND

CELLAR DOOR PRODUCTIONS

126 Richmond St., Charlottetown, PE C1A 1H9.
TEL: (902) 628-3880. FAX: (902) 628-2088.
email: productions@cellardoor.tv www.cellardoor.tv
PRESIDENT
Gretha Rose

ISLAND IMAGES

RR 1, 274 Salutation Cove Rd., Bedeque, PE C0B 1C0.
TEL: (902) 887-3620. FAX: (902) 887-3102.
email: islandimages@auracom.com
www.island-images.ca
PRESIDENT
Bill Kendrick

SEAHORSE ENTERTAINMENT, INC.
P.O. Box 894, Charlottetown, PE C1A 7L9.
TEL: (902) 621-0960. FAX: (902) 621-0961.
email: larry@seahorse.tv www.seahorse.tv
PRESIDENT
Larry LeClair
DIRECTOR, PRODUCTION SERVICES
Sean Yeomans

QUÉBEC

AETIOS PRODUCTIONS
C.P. 187, Succursale C, Montréal, QC H2L 4K1 .
TEL: (514) 985-4477. FAX: (514) 985-4482.
email: info@aetiosproductions.com
www.aetiosproductions.com
CONTACT
Marie Routhier - marie@marie-routhier.com

ALLIANCE VIVAFILM
455 Rue Saint-Antoine Ouest, Montréal, QC H2Z 1J1.
TEL: (514) 878-2282. FAX: (514) 878-2419
email: info.vivafilm@alliancefilms.co www.vivafilm.com
PRESIDENT
Guy Gagnon

AMÉRIMAGE-SPECTRA
(A division of L'Equipe Spectra)
400, boul. de Maisonneuve West,9th Flr., Montréal, QC
H3A 1L4. TEL: (514) 525-7833. FAX: (514) 525-8033.
email: pierre.touchette@equipespectra.ca
www.amerimage-spectra.com
PRODUCER
Luc Châtelain - luc.chatelain@equipespectra.ca

See also Ontario.

AMERIQUE FILM
507 – 3575 St-Laurent., Montréal, QC H2X 2T7.
TEL: (514) 844-0302. FAX: (514) 844-5184.
email: amerigo@ameriquefilm.com
VICE PRESIDENT
Martin Paul-Hus

AQUILON FILM, INC.
1253 rue Sainte-Elisabeth, Montréal, QC H2X 3C3.
TEL: (514) 985-2597. email: info@aquilonfilm.com
PRESIDENT
Werner Volkmer

Documentary / educational.

ARTS ET IMAGES PRODUCTIONS
370 Short St., Sherbrooke, QC J1H 2E2. TEL: (819) 822-4131.
FAX: (819) 822-4132. email: aipi@videotron.ca
EXECUTIVE PRODUCER/DIRECTOR
Mario Desmarais

ATOPIA
200 – 3981 Saint-Laurent, Montréal, QC H2W 1Y5.
TEL: (514) 985-0873. FAX: (514) 985-5876.
email: info@atopia.com www.atopia.com
PRESIDENT
Pascal Maeder
WRITER/DIRECTOR
Federico Hidalgo, Simon Sauvé, Shuibo Wang
WRITER
Paulina Robles
DIRECTOR
Daniel Cross

Collaborates with Canadian filmmakers to develop, produce and release independent films.

AVANTI CINE VIDEO
100 – 225 rue Roy est, Montréal, QC H2W 1M5.
TEL: (514) 288-7000. FAX: (514) 288-1675.
email: productions@avanticinevideo.com
www.avanticinevideo.com
CONTACT
Luc Wiseman

BACK ALLEY FILM PRODUCTIONS, LTD.
721 Querbes Ave., Montreal, QCH2V 3W8.
TEL: (514) 866-6873, ext. 302.
email: backkalley@sympatico.ca www.backalleyfilms.ca
PRODUCER
Janis Lundman
PRODUCER/DIRECTOR
Adrienne Mitchell
Also, see Toronto

BBR PRODUCTIONS, INC.
400 de Maisonneuve Blvd. W, 8th Flr., Montréal, QC H3A 1L4.
TEL: (514) 286-2500. FAX: (514) 525-8033.
email: bbr@equipespectra.ca www.bbrproductions.com
PRESIDENT & PRODUCER
Luc Chatelaine
LINE PRODUCER
José Lacelle
ASSISTANT PRODUCER/CONTACT
Natasha Paris

BLUE STORM TÉLÉ
204 – 225 rue Roy E, Montréal, QC H2W 1M5.
TEL: (514) 842-0039. FAX: (514) 842-2276.
email: info@bstorm.ca www.bluestorm.ca
PRESIDENT
Alain Girard
VICE PRESIDENT
Marc St-Onge

CAPITAL J. FILMS
1703-1200 St-Jacques, Montreal, QC H3C 0E9.
TEL: (514) 630-6331. email: jj@capitaljfilms.com
www.capitaljfilms.com
CO-FOUNDER
Jedrzej Jonasz, Ryan J. Noth

CHRISTAL FILMS PRODUCTIONS, INC.
1217, rue Notre-Dame Est, Montréal, QC H2L 2R3.
TEL: (514) 336-9696. FAX: (514) 336-0607.
email: dakerblom@christalfilms.com www.christalfilms.com
PRESIDENT
Christian Larouche

CINAK, LTÉE
1313 Chemin Guthrie, Saint-Armand, QC J0J 1T0.
TEL: (450) 248-3295. email: cinak@bellnet.ca
PRESIDENT
Jean-Pierre Lefebvre

CINÉ QUA NON FILMS INTERNATIONAL
445 St Pierre Street, Office 402,Montreal QC H2Y 2M8.
TEL: (514) 271-4000. FAX: (514) 271-4331.
email: production@cqne.ca
PRODUCER
Renée Claude Riendeau
DIRECTOR/PRODUCER
Bernar Hébert

CINÉ TÉLÉ-ACTION, INC.
1306 rue Ste-Catherine est, Montréal, QC H2L 2H5.
TEL: (514) 524-1118. FAX: (514) 524-2041.
email: info@cineteleaction.com www.cineteleaction.com
PRODUCER
Claudio Luca

Television production / English and French service production.

CINEFLIX, INC.
3510 St. Laurent Blvd., Suite 202, Montreal, QC H2X 2V2.
TEL: (514) 278-3140. FAX: (514) 270-3165.
email: info@cineflix.com www.cineflix.com
CEO
Glen Salzman, Katherine Buck

Producer and distributor of factual programming with offices in Montréal, Toronto, London and Dublin. Building on a strong foundation in fiction filmmaking and one-hour and feature-length documentaries. See also Ontario.

CINEGRAPHE PRODUCTIONS
820 rue De Rougemont, Quebec, QC G1X 2M5.
TEL: (418) 652-3345. FAX: (418) 652-3353.
email: cinegraf@videotron.ca www.cinegraphe.ne
CONTACT
Nicholas Kinsey, Andrée Tousignant

CINÉGROUPE, INC.
1151 Alexandre-DeSève, Montréal, QC H2L 2T7.
TEL: (514) 524-7567. FAX: (514) 849-9846.
email: info@cinegroupe.ca www.cinegroupe.ca
PRESIDENT & CEO
Jacques Pettigrew
SALES/CLIENT SERVICES COORDINATOR
Elaine Bigras

Feature film / animation / TV programming.

CINELANDE & ASSOCIATES, INC.
420 St-Martin, Montréal, QC H3J 1W2. TEL: (514) 931-0066.
FAX: (514) 931-6465. email: info@cinelande.com
www.cinelande.com
PRESIDENT
Alex Sliman
EXECUTIVE PRODUCER
Sylvie Dubé

Commercials and production services.

CINEMAGINAIRE INTERNATIONAL
5144 boul St-Laurent, Montréal, QC H2T 1R8.
TEL: (514) 272-5505. FAX: (514) 272-9841.
email: info@cinemaginaire.com

PRESIDENT
Denise Robert
V.P., PRODUCER
Daniel Louis

CIRRUS COMMUNICATIONS, INC.

1211, St-Mathieu St., Montréal, QC H3H 2P7.
TEL: (514) 270-1918. FAX: (514) 270-1825.
email: cirrus@cirruscom.ca www.cirruscom.ca
PRESIDENT/PRODUCER
Josée Vallée - jvallee@cirruscom.ca
PRODUCER, TELEVISION
André Béraud - aberaud@cirruscom.ca
PRODUCER, FEATURE FILMS
Pierre Even - peven@cirruscom.ca
PRODUCER, BUSINESS DEVELOPMENT
Jacques Blain - jblain@cirruscom.ca

CITE AMERIQUE, INC.

5800 boul St-Laurent, 2nd Flr., Montréal, QC H2T 1T3.
TEL: (514) 278-8080. FAX: (514) 278-4000.
email: info@cite-amerique.com www.cite-amerique.com
PRESIDENT & PRODUCER
Lorraine Richard
V.P., FINANCE
Vivianne Morin
PRODUCERS
Louis Laverdière, Greg Dummett, Luc Martineau, Orlando Arriagada

COMMUNICATIONS CLAUDE HÉROUX PLUS, INC.

4984 Place De La Savane, Montreal, QC. H4P 1Z6.
TEL: (514) 738-3737. FAX: (514) 738-3290.
email: cheroux@cchplus.com
PRESIDENT
Caroline Héroux
EXECUTIVE OFFICER
Stéphanie Héroux

Drama / documentaries / feature films.

COPIE ZERO TELEVISION AND MEDIA

400 – 19 Cours Le Royer O, Montréal, QC H2Y 1W4.
TEL: (514) 284-6565. FAX: (514) 284-0132.
www.copiezero.com
PRESIDENT & EXECUTIVE PRODUCER
Matt Zimbel - matt@copiezero.com
EXECUTIVE PRODUCER
Campbell Webster
ASSOCIATE PRODUCER
David Malahoff

DLI PRODUCTIONS

4301 av. de l'Esplanade, Montreal, QC H2W 1T1.
TEL: (514) 574-7273. FAX: (514) 844-2992.
email: info@dliproductions.ca www.dliproductions.ca
PRESIDENT
Abbey Neidik
PRODUCTION COORDINATOR
Mary Fowles
CHAIRWOMAN
Irene Angelico

DOMINO PRODUCTION, LTD.

4002 Grey Ave., Montréal, QC H4A 3P1. TEL: (514) 484-0446.
FAX: (514) 484-0468. email: jritter@dominofilm.ca
www.dominofilm.ca
PRESIDENT
Jeanne Ritter

EGM PRODUCTIONS

294 Square St-Louis, Montréal, QC H2X 1A4.
TEL: (514) 982-9862. FAX: (514) 982-9666.
email: information@egmfilms.com www.egmfilms.com
PRESIDENT
Brigitte Germain
V.P., DEVELOPMENT
Nardo Castillo

Feature films, television programming.

EQUINOXE PRODUCTIONS, INC.

5000 rue d'Iberville, Suite 224, Montréal QC H2H 2S6.
TEL: (514) 521-9991. FAX: (514) 521-5098.
www.production-equinoxe.com
PRESIDENT
Lyse Lafontaine
SENIOR V.P. & COO
Michael Mosca
HEAD OF DEVELOPMENT & LITERARY ACQUISITION
Francesca Visconti

EYE STEEL FILM, INC.

202 – 4475 boul St-Laurent, Montréal, QC H2W 1Z8.
TEL: (514) 937-4893. FAX: (514) 313-7383.
email: info@eyesteelfilm.com www.eyesteelfilm.com
www.homelessnation.org
PRESIDENT
Daniel Cross

A socially focused independent documentary.

LA FABRIQUE D'IMAGES, LTÉE.

318 rue Sherbrooke est, Montréal, QC H2X 1E6.
TEL: (514) 282-1505. FAX: (514) 282-8784.
email: sraymond@fabimages.com clandry@fabimages.com
www.fabimages.com
CONTACT
Denis Martel, Stéphane Raymond, Claude Landry

Commercial production.

FACTEUR 7

202 – 599 Wellington, Montréal, QC H3C 5T2.
TEL: (514) 975-7788, (514) 971-7650. FAX: (514) 526-2007.
email: production@facteur7.com www.facteur7.com
PRODUCER
Antonello Cozzolino

Producer / Director, Post-Production: Annie Normandin

FILMO BANDITO PRODUCTIONS, INC.

3745 Rue Saint-Jacques #204, Montreal, QC H4C 1H3.
TEL: (514) 937-5091.
email: eagimber@total.net
PRODUCER
Elisabeth-Ann Gimber, Geoff S. Patenaude

FILMS TRAFFIK

395 – 4000 rue St-Ambroise, Montréal, QC H4C 2C7.
TEL: (514) 843-5155. FAX: (514) 843-5514.
email: info@filmstraffik.com www.filmstraffik.com
PRESIDENT & EXECUTIVE PRODUCER
Michel David

Commercials and production services.

LES FILMS VISION 4, INC.

4446 boul St-Laurent 7th Fl., Montréal, QC H2W 1Z5.
TEL: (514) 499-0972. FAX: (514) 844-5498.
email: information@telefiction.com www.telefiction.com
PRODUCER
Claude Veillet, Jacques Bonin
ASSOCIATE PRODUCER
Lucie Veillet

Documentaries / educational / children's / features / TV / new media.

FORUM FILMS, INC.

807 - 400 Atlantic Ave., Montréal, QC H2V 1A5.
TEL: (514) 733-5053. FAX: (514) 733-0095.
email: richard@forumfilms.ca www.forumfilms.ca
PRESIDENT/PRODUCER
Richard Lalonde

GALAFILM PRODUCTIONS, INC.

300 – 5643 rue Clark, Montréal, QC H2T 2V5.
TEL: (514) 273-4252. FAX: (514) 273-8689.
email: info@galafilm.com www.galafilm.com
PRESIDENT
Arnie Gelbart
PRODUCER
Ian Whitehead, Sylvia Wilson, Mike Kronish, Isabelle Riva

GLACIALIS PRODUCTIONS, INC.

280 chemin Boudreau, Cap-Aux-Meules, QC G4T 1H2.
TEL: (418) 986-5960. email: jlemire@glacialis.tv
www.sedna.tv
PRODUCER
Jean Lemire

Specializes in the production of films, television programs and documentary series. Environment, ocean sciences.

GO FILMS

400 av Atlantic, 10th Flr., Outremont, QC H2V 1A5.
TEL: (514) 844-0271. FAX: (514) 844-9127.
email: info@gofilms.qc.ca
PRESIDENT/PRODUCER
Nicole Robert
VICE PRESIDENT/PRODUCER/DIRECTOR
Gabriel Pelletier

GREEN LION PRODUCTIONS

20223 Lakeshore Rd., Baie d'Urfe, QC H9X 1P9.
TEL: (514) 457-5555. FAX: (514) 457-3255.
email: cmullins@greenlionfilms.com
www.greenlionproduction.com
PRODUCER
Catherine Mullins

Independent / documentary films.

GROUP VÉLOCITÉ

(Divisions: Vélocité Productions, Vélocité International)
203 – 895 boul Charest ouest, Québec, QC G1N 2C9.
TEL: (418) 622-4002. FAX: (418) 622-5363.
email: info@velocite.qc.ca www.velocite.qc.ca

PRESIDENT/PRODUCER
Valérie Bissonnette

Documentaries / educational / features / TV.

GROUPE BUZZ IMAGE, INC.

312 Sherbrooke St. E, Montréal, QC H2X 1E6.
TEL: (800) 567-0200, (514) 848-0579. FAX: (514) 848-6371.
email: info@buzzimage.com www.buzzimage.com
PRESIDENT
Richard Cormier
COMMERCIALS & MOTION DESIGN
Eric Bolduc
SALES, TORONTO
Hesty Leibtag

Commercial productions.

GROUPE ECP

200 – 1280 av Bernard, Outremont, QC H2V 1V9.
TEL: (514) 273-4458. FAX: (514) 273-9790.
email: groupe@groupeecp.ca www.ecptelevision.com
PRODUCER
Jean-Yves de Banville, Jean Huppé

Documentaries, variety programs and children's programs.

GROUPE VIA LE MONDE

301 – 1222 rue Mackay, Montréal, QC H3G 2H4.
TEL: (514) 285-1658. FAX: (514) 285-1970.
email: daniel.bertolino@vialemonde.qc.ca
www.vialemonde.com
PRESIDENT/PRODUCER
Daniel Bertolino
VICE PRESIDENT/PRODUCER
Catherine Viau, Christian Charpenel

Programming for television, educational and Internet markets.

HALOGEN FILM SHOP

120 – 4700 St-Ambroise, Montréal, QC H4C 2C7.
TEL: (514) 938-1246. FAX: (514) 938-4827.
email: info@halogenstudio.ca www.halogenstudio.ca
EXECUTIVE PRODUCER
Luc Harvey
LINE PRODUCER
Nicolas Martel

Commercial production, 12,000 sq. ft. studio, edit facilities, visual effects & 3D animation.

HANDEL PRODUCTIONS, INC.

110 – 424 rue Guy, Montréal, QC H3J 1S6. TEL: (514) 487-1881.
FAX: (514) 487-7796. email: info@handelproductions.ca
www.handelproductions.ca
PRESIDENT
Alan Handel
CORPORATE ADMINISTRATOR
Irene Carter

Leading producer of factual TV programs and documentaries.

I CINÉMA TÉLÉVISION

2270 Bennett Ave., Montréal, QC H1V 2T5. TEL: (514) 253-4266.
FAX: (514) 253-0807. email: info@ictv.ca www.ictv.ca
PRESIDENT/EXECUTIVE PRODUCER
Guy Bonnier
EXECUTIVE PRODUCER
Remi St. Gelais

Documentaries.

IDEACOM INTERNATIONAL, INC.

300 – 1000 Amherst St., Montréal, QC H2L 3K5.
TEL: (514) 849-6966. FAX: (514) 849-0776.
email: ideacom@bellnet.ca
CONTACT
Jacques Nadeau, Josette D. Normandeau

IMAGE ENTERTAINMENT CORP., INC.

600 – 417 St-Pierre St., Montréal, QC H2Y 2M4.
TEL: (514) 844-1244. FAX: (514) 844-0554.
email: info@image-cie.com www.image-cie.com
PRESIDENT/PRODUCER
Sylvain Viau
PRODUCTION MANAGER
Guylaine Robidoux, Susane Belec

Specializes in the production and development of audio-visual and cinematographic projects.

INCENDO PRODUCTIONS, INC.

850 – 1 Westmount Sq., Montréal, QC H3Z 2P9.
TEL: (514) 937-3333. FAX: (514) 937-2338.
www.incendomedia.com
CONTACT
Steven Greenberg - sgreenberg@incendomedia.com
Jean Bureau - jbureau@incendomedia.com
MARKETING & PUBLICITY
Anna Sue Greenberg - asgreenberg@incendomedia.com
DREAMWORKS/QUÉBEC THEATRICAL RELEASES
Cécile Morin - cmorin@incendomedia.com

Television programming — movies, series and documentaries.

INDO CANADIAN FILMS INTERNATIONAL

21 – 4500 boul de Maisonneuve ouest, Montréal, QC H3Z 1L7.
TEL: (514) 935-6888. FAX: (514) 935-8588.
email: indocdn.films@attglobal.net
PRESIDENT
Gotham Hooja

INFORMACTION FILMS, INC.

927 – 460 Sainte-Catherine ouest, Montréal, QC H3B 1A7.
TEL: (514) 284-0441 ext. 201. FAX: (514) 284-0772.
email: info@informactionfilms.com www.informactionfilms.com
CONTACT
Nathalie Barton

Documentary films / series.

INFRAME PRODUCTIONS, INC.

1744 Rue William, Montreal QC, H3J 1R4.
TEL: (514) 935-7025. FAX: (514) 935-9238
email: info@InframeOnline.com www.InframeOnline.com
CONTACT
Nick Locporcaro

Documentary / corporates / shorts / DVD / CD.

JET FILMS

1215 rue St-Mathieu, Montréal, QC H3H 2P7.
TEL: (514) 844-1636. FAX: (514) 844-7625.
email: jethro@jetfilms.com www.jetfilms.com
PRESIDENT & EXECUTIVE PRODUCER
Michel Fortin
EXECUTIVE PRODUCER
Michel Boily
MONTRÉAL DIRECTOR
Alain DesRochers, Alexis Durand-Brault (+DOP), Louis-Philippe Eno, Alexandre Franchi, Maxime Giroux, Herman Weeb, Dominique Skoltz, François Péloquin, Patrice Sauvé, Charles-Éric Savard, Yves-Christian Fournier

TORONTO/LA/PARIS DIRECTOR
Jonathan Bensimon (+DOP), Louis-Pascal Couvelaire, Wayne Craig, Robert Logevall, Curtis Wehrfritz

Commercial production company where talent, ideas, resources, and solutions support creativity. Jet Films counts 25 people and a roster of 15 local and international directors.

JPL PRODUCTION, INC.

A408 – 1600 de Maisonneuve Blvd. E, Montréal, QC H2L 4P2.
TEL: (514) 526-2881. FAX: (514) 598-6024.
EXECUTIVE PRODUCER
Real Germaim

TV production.

JVJ PRODUCTIONS, LTD.

300 – 376 Victoria Ave., Westmount, QC H3Z 1C3.
TEL: (514) 336-9696. FAX: (514) 336-6606.
email: jdunning@jvjproductions.com
PRESIDENT
John Dunning

Development of scripts for feature film and TV. Seeking co-production partners.

KERRIGAN PRODUCTIONS, INC.

3877 av Draper, Montréal, QC H4A 2N9. TEL: (514) 486-8456, (514) 238-9775. email: bill@kerrigan.ca www.kerrigan.ca
PRODUCER/DIRECTOR
Bill Kerrigan
WRITER
Louise Roy

LOCOMOTION FILMS

330 Sherbrooke St. E, Montréal, QC H2X 1E6.
TEL: (514) 840-8486. FAX: (514) 840-8844.
email: infoloco@locomotionfilms.com
www.locomotionfilms.com
CONTACT
Christiane Ciupka, Christiane Hamelin

LORENZO ORZARI PRODUCTIONS

6 Libersan, Montréal, QC H9A 2B5. TEL: (514) 685-6170.
email: lorenzo.orzari@sympatico.ca
www3.sympatico.ca/lorenzo.orzari
WRITER/PRODUCER/DIRECTOR
Lorenzo Orzari

Providing properties, adaptations and script solutions for film, TV and new media companies from developement to post.

MACUMBA INTERNATIONAL, INC.

3862 av Parc Lafontaine, Montréal, QC H2L 3M6.
TEL: (514) 521-8303. FAX: (514) 521-0260.
email: macumba@macumbainternational.com
www.macumbainternational.com
PRODUCER
Robert Cornellier, Patricio Henriquez, Raymonde Provencher

Films / documentaries.

MAX FILMS / MAX FILMS INTERNATIONAL
2.102 – 1751 Richardson St., Montréal, QC H3K 1G6.
TEL: (514) 282-8444. FAX: (514) 282-9222.
email: info@maxfilms.ca www.maxfilms.ca
PRESIDENT/PRODUCER
Roger Frappier
PRODUCER
Luc Vandal
DIRECTOR, INTERNATIONAL SALES & MARKETING
Alexandra Wermester

MEDIA PRINCIPIA
Complexe Ex-Centris, 3530 St-Laurent Blvd., Montreal QC.
TEL: (514) 847-3536. FAX: (514) 847-9318.
email: info@mediaprincipia.com www.mediaprincipia.com
CONTACT
Bob Krupinski

Specializing in the use of new technologies in new media.

MELENNY PRODUCTIONS, INC.
300 – 154 Laurier W, Montréal, QC H2T 2N7.
TEL: (514) 270-6170. FAX: (514) 270-6988.
email: melenny@videotron.ca
CONTACT
Richard Goudreau

Producers of feature length films in English and French.

MICRO_SCOPE, INC.
802 – 55 Mont Royal Ave. W, Montréal, QC H2T 2S6.
TEL: (514) 844-4554. FAX: (514) 844-4112.
email: info@micro-scope.ca www.micro-scope.ca
PRODUCER
Luc Derry, Kim McCraw

MILAGRO FILMS
2500 - 75, Rue Queen, Montréal, QC H3C 2N6.
TEL: (514) 939-9969. FAX: (514) 985-2563.
email: info@milagrofilms.ca www.milagrofilms.ca
PRESIDENT
Jean-Marc Felio
OFFICE & DEVELOPMENT MANAGER
Flavie Langlois

MOSKITO FILMS, INC.
206 – 3863 boul Saint-Laurent, Montréal, QC H2W 1Y1.
TEL: (514) 866-3669. FAX: (514) 866-3683.
EXECUTIVE PRODUCER
Richard Ostiguy
PRODUCER
Visant Le Guennec

Commercial production.

MUSE ENTERTAINMENT ENTERPRISES, INC.
3451 St-Jacques, Montréal, QC H4C 1H1.
TEL: (514) 866-6873. FAX: (514) 876-3911.
email: tweekes@muse.ca www.muse.ca
PRESIDENT
Michael Prupas
DIRECTOR, COMMUNICATIONS
Betty Palik
PRESIDENT, PRODUCTION, MONTRÉAL
Irene Litinsky
DIRECTOR, DEVELOPMENT
Jesse Prupas

Ontario Facility: 940 Lansdowne Ave., Bldg. 15, 3rd Flr., Toronto, ON M6H 3Z4. TEL: (416) 921-2391.
CONTACT
Jane Mowbray

Features / TV movies & series.

NOVEM TELEVISION
900 – 4446 boul St-Laurent, Montréal, QC H2W 1Z5.
TEL: (514) 849-3999. FAX: (514) 849-8298.
email: info@novem.biz www.novem.biz
PRESIDENT
Véronique Cloutier

Production / distribution / format rights / world markets.

PARK EX PICTURES, INC.
B2-37 – 1001 rue Lenoir, Montréal, QC H4C 2Z6.
TEL: (514) 933-4133. FAX: (514) 933-3199.
email: info@parkexpictures.ca
PRESIDENT
Kevin Tierney

Feature films / TV series.

PICTURE THIS PRODUCTIONS
202 – 5890 Monkland Ave., Montréal, QC H4A 1G2.
TEL: (514) 484-1145. FAX: (514) 484-3777.
email: info@picturethis.ca www.picturethis.ca
CONTACT
Maureen Marovitch, David Finch, Andrea Feder, Charlene Vacon

PIXCOM INTERNATIONAL
1720 Canal Rd., Montréal, QC H3K 3E6.
TEL: (514) 931-1188. FAX: (514) 931-2126.
email: info@picturethis.ca www.pixcom.com
PRESIDENT
Jacquelin Bouchard
HEAD OF INTL. TELEVISION
Nicola Merola

PMA PRODUCTIONS
1617 Selkirk Ave., Montréal, QC H3H 1C7.
TEL: (514) 939-2509. FAX: (514) 939-2518.
email: info@pmaproductions.com www.pmaproductions.com
PRESIDENT & EXECUTIVE PRODUCER
Kenneth Hirsch

POP6
400 – 777 Commune Rd. W, Montréal, QC H3C 1Y1.
TEL: (514) 288-8877. FAX: (514) 845-8906.
email: pop@pop6.net www.pop6.net
EXECUTIVE PRODUCER
Dominic Saint-Louis, Roddy McManus

PRB MEDIA
107 rue Champêtre, Gatineau, QC J9H 6W4.
TEL: (819) 770-6500. FAX: (819) 770-7551.
www.prb.ca
PRESIDENT & EXECUTIVE PRODUCER
Luc Sauvé - luc@prb.ca
PRODUCER
Mark Collings - mark@prb.ca

Television / new media / service productions.

LES PRODUCTIONS DE L'OEIL, ENR.
860 Gohier, St-Laurent, QC H4L 3J2. TEL: (514) 744-1944.
email: mario-b@sympatico.ca
CONTACT
Mario Bonenfant

PRODUCTIONS ET ÉDITIONS 10E AVE, INC.
209 Jean-Juneau, St. Augustin de Desmaures, QC G3A 2W1.
TEL: (418) 877-0101. email: nsavard@10ave.ca
www.10ave.ca
PRESIDENT & GENERAL MANAGER
Nancy Savard

Production / Business Relations: Natalie Bédard

PRODUCTIONS GRAND NORD QUEBEC, INC.
La Maison Premier Plan, 393 – 1600 av de Lorimier, Montréal, QC H2K 3W5. TEL: (514) 521-7433.
FAX: (514) 522-3013. email: imclaren@grandnord.ca
CONTACT
Ian McLaren

PRODUCTIONS LA FÊTE, INC.
225 Roy street East, Suite 200, Montreal QC H2W 1M5 .
TEL: (514) 848-0417. FAX: (514) 848-0064.
email: info@lafete.com www.lafete.com
PRESIDENT
Rock Demers

Private company that develops and produces feature-length drama and fiction television series in English and French. Non-violent children's feature films.

LES PRODUCTIONS MAG 2, INC.
210 Dominion St., Montréal, QC H3J 2X1. TEL: (514) 937-7999.
FAX: (514) 937-5062. email: info@mag2.ca www.mag2.ca
PRESIDENT & DIRECTOR
Michel Beaudet
V.P., BUSINESS DEVELOPMENT
Yves Coulombe

Documentaries / "making of" productions / commercials / multimedia.

LES PRODUCTIONS POINT DE MIRE
302 – 154 Laurier Ave. W, Montréal, QC H2T 2N7.
TEL: (514) 278-8922. FAX: (514) 278-8925.
email: info@pdemire.com
PRESIDENT & EXECUTIVE PRODUCER, DRAMA
Jean-François Mercier
V.P., EXECUTIVE PRODUCER, NON-FICTION
Raymond Gauthier
PRODUCER, DRAMA & DEVELOPMENT
André Monette

Documentaries & drama for TV / variety / magazines.

LES PRODUCTIONS SOVIMAGE, INC.
201 avenue Laurier Est, bureau 670, Montréal QC H2T 3E6.
TEL: (514) 277-6123. FAX: (514) 277-1139.
email: productions@sovimage.qc.ca www.sovimage.qc.ca
PRESIDENT & PRODUCER
Vincent Garbriele
PRODUCER
Sophie Deschênes

LES PRODUCTIONS VIC PELLETIER
296 rue St-Pierre, Matane, QC G4W 2B9. TEL: (418) 566-2040. FAX: (418) 562-4643. email: info@pvp.ca www.pvp.ca
PRODUCER
Vic Pelletier
V.P., DEVELOPMENT
Robert Tremblay

Documentaries.

LES PRODUCTIONS VIDEOFILMS LIMITEE
414, rue McGill, bur. 202, Montreal, QC H2Y 2G1.
TEL: (514) 844-8611. FAX: (514) 844-4034.
email: videofilms@ca.inter.net
CONTACT
Robert Ménard

Features / TV series.

LES PRODUCTIONS VIRAGE, INC.
605 – 6300 av du Parc, Montréal, QC H2V 4H8.
TEL: (514) 276-9556. FAX: (514) 276-2262.
email: info@virage.ca www.virage.ca
PRODUCERS
Monique Simard, Marcel Simard, Claude Cartier

Documentaries.

REMSTAR CORP.
300 – 85 St. Paul W, Montréal, QC H2Y 3V4.
TEL: (514) 847-1136. FAX: (514) 847-1163.
email: info@remstarcorp.com www.remstarcorp.com
PRESIDENT & CEO
Maxime Rémillard
SENIOR V.P. & COO
Tony Porrello
V.P., PRODUCTION
André Rouleau

Production / distribution / financing.

ROONEY PRODUCTIONS
95 Montée Drouin, Lac-des-Loups, QC J0X 3K0.
TEL: (819) 456-3522. email: info@rooneyproductions.com
www.rooneyproductions.com
PRODUCER/DIRECTOR
Robert Rooney
PRODUCER
Brenda Rooney

Documentaries.

ROSE FILMS, INC.
(Head Office & Production Office)
CP 40, Saint-Paul d'Abbotsford, QC J0E 1A0.
TEL: (450) 379-5304. FAX: (450) 379-5742.
email: production@rosefilms.ca
CONTACT
Claude Fournier, Marie-José Raymond

ROZON — JUST FOR LAUGHS
2101 boul St-Laurent, Montréal, QC H2X 2T5.
TEL: (514) 845-3155. FAX: (514) 845-4140.
www.justforlaughs.ca
PRESIDENT
Gilbert Rozon - grozon@hahaha.com
CEO
Bruce Hills - bhills@hahaha.com
DIRECTOR, TELEVISION
Pierre Girard - pgirard@hahaha.com
DIRECTOR, INTERNATIONAL TELEVISION
Nathalie Bourdon - nbourdon@hahaha.com
INTERNATIONAL SALES
Cristos Sorligas - csorlig@hahaha.com

SPHÈRE MÉDIA PLUS
257 rue St-Jean, Longueuil, QC J4H 2X4.
TEL: (450) 674-3434. FAX: (450) 674-4732.
email: info@spheremedia.ca
www.spheremedia.ca
PRESIDENT & EXECUTIVE PRODUCER
Jocelyn Deschênes
PRODUCERS
Sophie Pellerin, Mélanie Lamothe

TV series.

STONEHAVEN PRODUCTIONS
1331 Greene Ave., Westmount, QC H3Z 2A5.
TEL: (514) 527-2131. FAX: (514) 522-8599.
email: m.taylor@stonehaven.ca
PRESIDENT
Michael C. Taylor - m.taylor@stonehaven.ca
EXECUTIVE V.P.
Karen Coshof - k.coshof@stonehaven.ca

TÉLÉ-VISION, INC.
555 rue Montfort, bureau 200, Montreal, QC H3C 4J3.
TEL: (514) 866-3020. FAX: (514) 866-1696.
email: info@tele-vision.tv www.tele-vision.tv
PRESIDENT
Jean Rémillard
EXECUTIVE V.P.
Daniel Cormier

TV programming in all fields. Documentaries.

TELEFICTION, INC.
4446 boul St-Laurent, 7th Fl., Montréal, QC H2W 1Z5.
TEL: (514) 499-0972. FAX: (514) 844-5498.
email: info@telefiction.com www.telefiction.com
PRESIDENT & CEO
Claude Veillet
EXECUTIVE V.P.
Lucie Veillet

Documentaries / educational / children's / features / television / new media.

TRINÔME, INC.
1157 Sainte-Catherine est, Montréal, QC H2L 2G8.
TEL: (877) 527-9070, (514) 527-9070. FAX: (514) 597-1571.
email: courrier@trinome.com www.trinome.com
PRESIDENT
Pierre Blais
V.P., PRODUCTION
Jocelyne Allard

Animation / children's / documentary / educational / interactive media / TV series — drama, MOWs.

VENDÔME TÉLÉVISION, INC.
5.105 – 1751 rue Richardson, Montréal, QC H3K 1G6.
TEL: (514) 369-4834. FAX: (514) 369-4015.
email: productions@vendometelevision.ca
CONTACT
Ghislaine Mailhot, André Dubois

TV programming — drama / comedy / documentaries.

VENT D'EST FILMS, INC.
1750 rue St-André Rm. 3028, Montréal, QC H2L 3T8.
TEL: (514) 523-3163. FAX: (514) 523-4424.
email: ventdest@videotron.ca
PRODUCTEUR
Bernard Lalonde, Louis Goyer, Nicole Chaput, Stéphane Doyon

VERSEAU INTERNATIONAL, INC.
200 – 225 rue Roy est, Montréal, QC H2W 1M5.
TEL: (514) 848-9814. FAX: (514) 848-9908.
email: info@verseau-international.com
www.verseau-international.com
PRESIDENT & PRODUCER
Aimee Danis
PRODUCER
Eric Fournier

VIDEOGRAPHE PRODUCTION
4550 rue Garnier, Montréal, QC H2J 3S7.
TEL:(514) 521-2116 ext. 15. FAX: (514) 521-1676.
email: martin@videographe.qc.ca www.videographe.qc.ca
CONTACT
Martin Meunier, Martin Renaud

Multimedia and video production centre for independent artists / digital cameras and editing suites.

VIVAVISION GROUP, INC.
1973 Falardeau St., Montréal, QC H2K 2L9.
TEL: (514) 527-9700. FAX: (514) 527-9625.
email: vivavision@vivavision.ca
www.vivavision.ca
PRESIDENT & CEO
Jean-Pierre Morin
V.P., FINANCE
Rita Lamah
V.P., ADMINISTRATION
Frédéric Morin

Live-action youth series, animation series, documentaries, variety programs, as well as feature films. Divisions: Vivatoon (animation); Vivastudio (feature films); Vivalogik (post-production facilities); Vivamondo (distribution).

VIVAVISION GROUP
1973 Falardeau St., Montréal, QC H2K 2L9.
TEL: (514) 527-9700. FAX: 514-527-9625.
email: vivavision@vivavision.ca
PRESIDENT/GENERAL MANAGER/PRODUCER
Jean-Pierre Morin

Variety and magazine shows / documentaries / dramatic series and mini-series for television.

WHALLEY-ABBEY MEDIA HOLDINGS, INC.
300 – 1303 Greene Ave., Westmount, QC H3Z 2A7.
TEL: (514) 846-1940. FAX: (514) 846-1550.
email: hansr@painted-house.com
CONTACT
H. Rosenstein

Award-winning specialists in lifestyle programs and documentaries.

ZGA FILMS & TELEVISION CORP.

4216 St. Hubert, Montréal, QC H2J 2W7. TEL: (514) 525-3066. FAX: (514) 525-1762. email: michel_zgarka@yahoo.ca
PRESIDENT
Michel Zgarka

ZONE3, INC.

300 – 1055 René Lévesque Blvd. E, Montréal, QC H2L 4S5. TEL: (514) 284-5555. FAX: (514) 985-4458. email: mjoseph@zone3.ca www.zone3.ca
CONTACT
Michel Bissonnette, Vincent Leduc, Paul Dupont-Hébert, André Larin

TV and film production — documentaries / children's / arts and variety.

ZULÙ FILMS

454 de la Gauchetiere St. West, Montréal, QC H2Z 1E3. TEL: (514) 844-1222. FAX: (514) 844-6667. email: info@zulufilms.com www.zulufilms.com
ASSOCIATE PRODUCER
François Forgues

Commercials.

SASKATCHEWAN

ANGEL ENTERTAINMENT

2710 Millar Ave., Saskatoon, SK S7K 4J4. TEL: (306) 244-8691. FAX: (306) 933-3183. email: bob@angelentertainment.ca www.angelentertainment.ca
CONTACT
Bob Crowe, Wally Start

BIRDSONG COMMUNICATIONS

806 Victoria Ave, Regina SK, S4N 0R6. TEL: (306) 359-3070. FAX: (306) 525-1204. email: birdsong.ltd@sasktel.net
PRESIDENT/PRODUCER
Don List

Motion picture production services.

CINEPOST FILMS

269B 3rd Ave. S, Saskatoon, SK S7K 1M3. TEL: (306) 244-7788. FAX: (306) 244-7799. email: info@cinepostfilms.com www.cinepostfilms.com
CONTACT
Bill Stampe, June Morgan

Full-service film and video production company specializing in commercial and corporate communication.

CKCK-TV CREATIVE SERVICES

P.O. Box 2000, Hwy. 1 E, Regina, SK S4P 3E5. TEL: (306) 569-2000. FAX: (306) 569-6413. email: ckcknews@ctv.ca www.ctv.ca
DIRECTOR, CREATIVE SERVICES
Geoff Bradley

COOPER ROCK PICTURES, INC.

70 Charles Cres, Regina, SK S4T 5X4. TEL: (306) 790-5690. FAX: (306) 790-5699. email: lkuffner@cooperrock.com
PRESIDENT
Lori Kuffner

FOUR SQUARE PRODUCTIONS

220 – 1808 Smith St., Regina, SK S4P 2N4. TEL: (306) 525-9888. FAX: (306) 525-8588. email: 4square@4square.ca www.4square.ca
PRESIDENT
Gerald B. Sperling
V.P., CREATIVE
Maggie Siggins
PRODUCER, CHINA OFFICE
Bill Siggins

MINDS EYE ENTERTAINMENT

Head Office: 480 Henderson Dr., Regina, SK S4N 6E3. TEL: (306) 359-7618. FAX: (306) 359-3466. email: mindseye@mindseyepictures.com www.mindseyepictures.com
PRESIDENT & CEO
Kevin DeWalt

Main company comprises six departments: Development, Production, Business Affairs, Finance, Administration and New Media.

ONDA, STEPHEN

3035 21st Ave., Regina, SK S4S 0T5. TEL: (306) 525-6921. FAX: (306) 525-5727. email: onda@sasktel.net

Producer / writer / feature / TV / documentary.

PARTNERS IN MOTION

2704 10th Ave., Regina, SK S4T 1E9. TEL: (306) 545-2228. FAX: (306) 569-9616. email: jstecyk@partnersinmotion.com www.partnersinmotion.com
PRESIDENT
Chris Triffo
CEO
Ron Goetz
CFO
Linda Goetz
V.P., BUSINESS AFFAIRS
Jeff Stecyk

PATRICK WOLFE CAMERA OBSCURA

P.O. Box 274, Prince Albert, SK S6V 5R5. TEL: (306) 749-2578.
PRESIDENT
Patrick Wolfe

Educational media production — film / television /radio.

THOMEGA ENTERTAINMENT, INC.

P.O. Box 25104, RPO River Heights, Saskatoon, SK S7K 8B7. TEL: (306) 373-3765. FAX: (306) 244-5504. email: thomega@sasktel.net www.thomega.com
CONTACT
Anthony Towstego

Feature films / TV series/ documentaries.

VÉRITÉ FILMS

1831 College Ave., Regina, SK S4P 4V5. TEL: (306) 585-1737. FAX: (306) 585-7837. email: verite@veritefilms.ca www.veritefilms.ca
PARTNER
Virginia Thompson, Robert de Lint

Producers of Corner Gas, renegadepress.com and Incredible Story Studio.

WESTWIND PICTURES

402 – 2206 Dewdney Ave., Regina, SK S4R 1H3. TEL: (306) 777-0160. FAX: (306) 352-8558. email: michaelsnook@westwindpictures.com www.westwindpictures.com
EXECUTIVE PRODUCER
Michael Snook

See also Ontario.

DISTRIBUTION

THEATRICAL

ATOPIA
#200 - 3981 Saint-Laurent, Montréal, QC H2W 1Y5.
TEL: (514) 985-0873. FAX: (514) 985-5876.
email: info@atopia.com www.atopia.com
PRESIDENT
Pascal Maeder
DOMESTIC & INTERNATIONAL SALES
Joëlle Medina

Develops produce and release independent films. Integrated company, handling projects from development through world sales and theatrical distribution in North America.

BBC WORLDWIDE CANADA, LTD.
#401 - 130 Spadina Ave., Toronto, ON M5V 2L4.
TEL: (416) 362-3223. FAX: (416) 362-3553.
bbcworldwidetv.com
CEO CANADA
Hilary Read
V.P., PROGRAM SALES & CO-PRODUCTIONS
Gwen Jones McCauley

BUENA VISTA PICTURES DISTRIBUTION CANADA, INC.
Sales, Simcoe Place, #3001 - 200 Front St. W, Toronto, ON M5V 3L4. TEL: (800) 263-2853, (416) 964-9275.
FAX: (416) 596-3382. email: tesslin.robinson@disney.com
V.P., SALES
Anthony Macina
DIRECTOR, SALES
Tony Schittone, Karen Burke
MARKETING MANAGER
Antonella Zappone

Distributors of Walt Disney Pictures, ABC Studios and Hollywood Pictures.

PUBLICITY & PROMOTIONS (ALLIED ADVERTISING)
#1410 - 21 St. Clair Ave. E, Toronto, ON M4T 1L9.
TEL: (416) 413-0557. FAX: (416) 416-7958.
www.alliedadv.com
MANAGER PUBLICITY/PROMOTIONS
Robyn Mogil

CAPRI RELEASING
259 Lakeshore Blvd., E., 2nd Flr., Toronto, ON M5A 3T7.
TEL: (416) 535-1870. FAX: (416) 535-3414.
www.caprifilms.com
PRESIDENT & CEO
Gabriella Martinelli
V.P. Capri Vision (division of Capri Films)
Robin Crumley - rcrumley@caprifilms.com

Third-party acquisitions, in-house productions.

CHRISTAL FILMS DISTRIBUTION, INC.
1217 rue Notre Dame, Montréal, QC H2L 2R3.
TEL: (514) 336-9696. FAX: (514) 336-0607.
email: info@christalfilms.com www.christalfilms.com

Ontario: #300 - 550 Queen St. E, Toronto, ON M5A 1V2.
TEL: (416) 777-2500 ext. 222. FAX: (416) 777-2831.
DIRECTOR, ACQUISITIONS & DEVELOPMENT
Tony Wosk - twosk@christalfilms.com
V.P., THEATRICAL DISTRIBUTION
Joanne Senecal - jsenecal@christalfilms.com
DIRECTOR, PROGRAMMING
Sébastien Létourneau - sletourneau@christalfilms.com
DIRECTOR, COMMUNICATIONS
Julie Armstrong-Boileau - jboileau@christalfilms.com

CINÉMA ESPERANÇA INTERNATIONAL, INC.
1106 - 60 Browning Ave., Toronto, ON M4K 1V9.
TEL: (416) 462-1573, (416) 418-8474.
email: andre.m.bennett@sympatico.ca
PRESIDENT & CEO
André Bennett

CINEMAVAULT RELEASING INTERNATIONAL, INC.
#1011 - 175 Bloor St. E, South Tower, Toronto, ON M4W 3R8.
TEL: (416) 363-6060. FAX: (416) 363-2305.
email: admin@cinemavault.com www.cinemavault.com
CEO
Nick Stiliadis
V.P., GENERAL MANAGER
Gerry MoraitisV.P., ACQUISITIONS
Michael Paszt
V.P., INTERNATIONAL DISTRIBUTION
Caroline Stern
DIRECTOR OF ACQUISITIONS
Craig Morrow

CLOUD TEN PICTURES, INC.
11 Export Ave., St. Catharines, ON L2M 5V8.
TEL: (888) 684-5561, (905) 684-5561. FAX: (905) 684-7946.
www.cloudtenpictures.com
CHAIRMAN/OWNER
Paul Lalonde
CEO/PRODUCER/DIRECTOR
André van Heerden

Christian, faith-based film and television production, including Left Behind: The Movie, and television series.

COMET ENTERTAINMENT, INC.
1235 Bay St. 10th Fl., Toronto, ON M5R 3K4.
TEL: (416) 421-4229. FAX: (416) 425-5931.
email: info@cometentertainment.com
www.cometentertainment.com
CEO
Raquel Benitez
COO
Carmen Llanos

Domestic and international distribution of Canadian and international motion picture films and TV programming.

DOMINO FILM AND TELEVISION INTERNATIONAL, LTD.
4002 Grey Ave., Montréal, QC H4A 3P1. TEL: (514) 484-0446.
FAX: (514) 484-0468. www.dominofilm.ca
PRESIDENT
Jeanne Ritter

Domestic & international distribution of Canadian motion pictures, TV programming and DVDs.

EQUINOXE FILMS, INC.
(A division of La Compagnie France Film, Inc.)
#2401 - 505 Rue Sherbrooke St. E, Montréal, QC H2L 4N3.
TEL: (514) 844-0680. FAX: (514) 499-9899.
www.equinox-films.com
PRESIDENT & CEO
Pierre René

FILMS TRANSIT INTERNATIONAL, INC.
252 Gouin Blvd. E, Montréal, QC H3L 1A8.
TEL: (514) 844-3358. FAX: (514) 844-7298.
email: info@filmstransit.com www.filmstransit.com
PRESIDENT & CEO
Jan Rofekamp - janrofekamp@filmstransit.com
OFFICE MANAGER
John Nadai - johnnadai@filmstransit.com

Documentaries / international worldwide sales.

FUNFILM DISTRIBUTION
5146 boul St.-Laurent, Montréal, QC H2T 1R8.
TEL: (514) 272-4956. FAX: (514) 272-9841.
email: funfilm@cinemaginaire.com

IMAX CORPORATION
2525 Speakman Dr., Sheridan Park, Mississauga, ON L5K 1B1. TEL: (905) 403-6500. FAX: (905) 403-6450.
email: info@imax.com www.imax.com
Co-Chairman/Co-CEO
Richard L. Gelfond

U.S.A.: 3003 Exposition Blvd., Santa Monica, CA 90404.
TEL: (310) 255-5500. FAX: (310) 255-5501.
email: - pkeighley@IMAX.com

IMAX Corporate Offices: 110 E. 59th St., New York, NY 10022.
TEL: (212) 821-0100.

Distributing the largest available library of 15/70 films in the industry, including entertainment, space, science and natural history films.

INCENDO MEDIA, INC.
#850 - 1 Westmount Sq., Montréal, QC H3Z 2P9.
TEL: (514) 937-3333. FAX: (514) 937-2338.
www.incendomedia.com
CREATIVE EXECUTIVE
Anna-Sue Greenberg - asgreenberg@incendo.ca
INTERNATIONAL SALES & CO-PRODUCTIONS
Gavin Reardon - greardon@incendo.ca

Distributes television and theatrical programming in English and French in Canada. Incendo represents Paramount Vantage for theatrical distribution both the English and French languages, in Quèbec. Paramount Vantage is the specialty film division of Paramount Pictures – labels include Paramount Pictures, Paramount Vantage, Paramount Classics, DreamWorks Pictures, MTV Films and Nickelodeon Movies.

INDO CANADIAN FILMS INTERNATIONAL

21 – 4500 boul de Maisonneuve ouest, Montréal, ON H3Z 1L7.
TEL: (514) 935-6888. FAX: (514) 935-8588.
email: indocdn.films@attglobal.net
PRESIDENT
Gotham Hooja

INTERNATIONAL KEYSTONE ENTERTAINMENT

#300 - 2339 Columbia St., Vancouver, BC V5Y 3Y3.
TEL: (604) 873-9739. FAX: (604) 873-5919.
email: films@keypics.com www.keypics.com
CEO
Robert Vince
PRESIDENT OF PRODUCTION
Anna McRoberts

IRREVERENT MEDIA, LTD.

South Granville Post, Ste., 29112, Vancouver, BC V6J 0A6.
TEL: (604) 662-4330. FAX: (604) 608-4778.
email: info@irreverentmedia.com www.irreverentmedia.com
PRODUCERS
Tom O'Brien - t.obrien@irreverentmedia.com

Development and production of feature films and television properties.

K FILMS AMERIQUE

P.O. Box 189, Succ DeLorimier, Montréal, QC H2H 2N6.
TEL: (514) 277-2613. FAX: (514) 277-3598.
email: ldussault@filmisle.com www.kfilmsamerique.com
PRESIDENT
Louis Dussault - ldussault@filmisle.com

35mm / home video.

KYBELE FILMS

424 Glenholme Ave., Toronto, ON M6E 3E7.
TEL: (416) 651-2296. email: info@kybelefilms.com
www.kybelefilms.com
PRODUCER & DIRECTOR
Sibel Guvenc

Independent entertainment company engaged in the production, marketing and distribution of theatrical feature films and TV series.

LES FILMS SEVILLE PICTURES / SEVILLE PICTURES

400 De Maisonneuve Blvd., 11th Flr., Montréal, QC H3A 1L4.
TEL: (514) 841-1910. FAX: (514) 841-8030.
email: info@sevillepictures.com www.sevillepictures.com
CO-PRESIDENT, DISTRIBUTION
David Reckziegel - davidr@sevillepictures.com
EXECUTIVE V.P., MARKETING, ACQUISITION & DISTRIBUTION
Pierre Brosseau - pierreb@sevillepictures.com
DIRECTOR, PROGRAMMING, BOOKINGS
Natalie Bélanger - mariepierrec@sevillepictures.com
V.P., MARKETING
Victor Rego - victor@sevillepictures.com
DIRECTOR, MARKETING
Marie-Pier Guy - mariepierg@sevillepictures.com

Distribution of feature films / documentaries / TV programs.

MAPLE PICTURES CORP.

#1001 - 2 Bloor St. W, Toronto, ON M4W 3E2.
TEL: (416) 944-0104. FAX: (416) 944-2212.
info@maplepictures.com www.maplepictures.com
CO-PRESIDENT
Laurie May, Brad Pelman
SENIOR V.P., THEATRICAL DISTRIBUTION
John Bain - jbain@maplepictures.com
DIRECTOR, PUBLICITY & PROMOTION
Angie Burns - aburns@maplepictures.com
DIRECTOR, THEATRICAL DISTRIBUTION
Sarah Necoloff - snecoloff@maplepictures.com

MÉTROPOLE FILMS DISTRIBUTION

5266 boul St.-Laurent, Montréal, QC H2T 1S1.
TEL: (514) 223-5511. FAX: (514) 227-1231.
email: info@metropolefilms.com www.metropolefilms.com
MANAGING DIRECTOR
Charles Tremblay

MGM DISTRIBUTION COMPANY

#1601 - 22 St. Clair Ave. E, Toronto, ON M4T 2S3.
TEL: (416) 644-6241. FAX: (416) 644-6224.
V.P., CANADIAN DIVISION MANAGER
Kevin Pasquino - kpasquino@mgm.com
SALES MANAGER
Tim Smy - tsmy@mgm.com

MONGREL MEDIA, INC.

1028 Queen St. W, Toronto, ON M6J 1H6.
TEL: (416) 516-9775. FAX: (416) 516-0651.
email: info@mongrelmedia.com www.mongrelmedia.com
PRESIDENT
Hussain Amarshi - hussain@mongrelmedia.com
DIRECTOR, THEATRICAL SALES & MARKETING
Tom Alexander - tom@mongrelmedia.com

Theatrical / home video / TV markets / educational.

MOTION PICTURES DISTRIBUTION, LP

(EdgeStone Capital Partners)
#300 - 455 rue St.-Antoine, Montréal, QC H2Z 1J1.
TEL: (514) 878-2282. FAX: (514) 878-2419.

NORSTAR FILMED ENTERTAINMENT, INC.

131 Hazelton Ave., Ste. 301, Toronto, ON M5R 2E4.
TEL: (416) 961-6278. FAX: (416) 961-5608.
email: info@norstarfilms.com www.norstarfilms.com
PRESIDENT
Ilana Frank - ext 248
DIRECTOR OF DEVELOPMENT
Noelle Carbone - ext. 229

Production / financing / distribution / co-productions — theatrical & television.

OASIS INTERNATIONAL

175 Bloor St., E., Ste. 1400, North Tower., Toronto, ON M4W 3R8.
TEL: (416) 646-2400. FAX: (416) 646-2588.
email: info@oasisinternational.com
www.oasisinternational.com
PRESIDENT
Peter Emerson - ext 224 peter@oasisinternational.com
EXECUTIVE V.P.
Valerie Cabrera - (310) 260-2548 valerie@oasisinternational.com
DIRECTOR, INTERNATIONAL SALES
Prentiss Holman - ext 228 prentiss@oasisinternational.com

Film / TV distribution.

OASIS SHAFTESBURY RELEASING

163 Queen St. E, Ste. 100, Toronto, ON M5A 1S1.
TEL: (416) 363-1411. FAX: (416) 363-1428.
email: mailbox@shaftesbury.org www.shaftesbury.org
CHAIRMAN, FOUNDER & CEO
Christina Jennings - cjennings@shaftesbury.org
V.P. SALES/MARKETING & DIGITAL MEDIA
Shane Kinnear - skinnear@shaftesbury.ca

ODEON FILMS, INC.

(EdgeStone Capital Partners)
1500 – 121 Bloor St. E, Toronto, ON M4W 3M5.
TEL: (800) 465-4179, (416) 967-1174. FAX: (416) 934-6999.
www.odeonfilms.com
PRESIDENT
Bryan Gliserman
V.P., DISTRIBUTION, SALES
Darlene Hotton
DIRECTOR, DISTRIBUTION, SALES
Paul Rotz
BOOKER, SALES REPRESENTATIVE
Allan Sullivan
DISTRIBUTION, SALES CLERK
Sharon Foster

PARAMOUNT PICTURES ENTERTAINMENT CANADA, INC.

#900 - 40 University Ave., Toronto, ON M5J 1T1.
TEL: (800) 387-1490, (416) 969-9901. FAX: (416) 922-9931.
www.paramount.com
CANADIAN SALES MANAGER, PARAMOUNT VANTAGE
Tayna Mason
DIRECTOR, IN-THEATRE MARKETING
Harriet Bernstein

Québec Sales: 354-A 7E Ave., Deux-Montagnes, QC J7R 3H8.
TEL: (450) 974-0674. FAX: (450) 974-2770.
MANAGER, QUÉBEC
Robert Montplaisir

Motion Picture Group: Theatrical 35mm (English & French)

OUAT MEDIA

#100 - 488 Wellington St. W, Toronto, ON M5V 1E3.
TEL: (416) 979-7380. FAX: (416) 492-9539.
www.quatmedia.com
MANAGER DISTRIBUTION OPERATIONS
Kristine Estorninos
INTERNATIONAL ACQUISITIONS MANAGER
Miguel Ortega

Owned by Channel Zero Inc., a Canadian-based company specializing in the worldwide distribution of short films.

REMSTAR DISTRIBUTION

85 St.-Paul St. W, Montréal, ON H2Y 3V4.
TEL: (514) 847-1136. FAX: (514) 847-0019.
email: info@remstarcorp.com www.remstarcorp.com

Theatrical — domestic & foreign.

SLIDE SCREEN ENTERTAINMENT, INC.

#135A - 1315 Bishop St., Cambridge, ON N1R 6Z2.
TEL: (519) 740-1266, (519) 658-6920. FAX: (519) 740-6374.
email: ibtsl@bellnet.ca www.independentbooking.net
PRESIDENT
Eric Ball
V.P., SECRETARY & TREASURER
Barbara Ball

North American distributor of Hindi, Farsi, Arabic and other foreign films.

SONY PICTURES RELEASING CANADA

(A division of Columbia Pictures Industries, Inc.)
#100 - 1303 Yonge St., Toronto, ON M4T 1W6.
TEL: (416) 922-5740. www.sonypictures.com

Sales:
SENIOR V.P. & GENERAL MANAGER, CANADA
Michael Brooker - michael_brooker@spe.sony.com

Advertising:
V.P., MEDIA
Donna Slack - (416) 922-5740 donna_slack@spe.sony.com

Québec:
c/o Alliance Atlantis Vivafilm, #300 - 455 rue St. Antoine St., W, Montréal, QC H2Z 1J1. TEL: (514) 878-2282.
FAX: (514) 392-0938. www.allianceatlantisvivafilm.com

THINKFILM

#906 - 2300 Yonge St., Toronto, ON M4P 1E4.
TEL: (416) 488-0037. FAX: (416) 488-0031.
www.thinkfilmcompany.com
PRESIDENT & COO
Jeff Sackman - jsackman@thinkfilmcompany.com
THEATRICAL SALES & MARKETING
Meghan Parnell - mparnell@thinkfilmcompany.com

TVA FILMS

1600 boul. de Maisonneuve 8th Flr., Montréal, QC H2L 4P2.
TEL: (514) 284-2525. FAX: (514) 985-4461.
www.tvafilms.com
PRESIDENT
Yves Dion - yves.dion@tvafilms.com
GENERAL MANAGER OF DISTRIBUTION
Sophie Aird - theatrical@tvafilms.com
DIRECTOR, PROGRAMMING
Sylvain Brabant - sylvain.brabant@tvafilms.com
DIRECTOR OF COMMUNICATIONS & DEVELOPMENT
Marie-Claude Morazain - mcmorazain@tvafilms.com

Ontario: 25 Ontario St., Toronto, ON M5A 4L6.
TEL: (416) 968-0002. FAX: (416) 944-1741.
EXECUTIVE DIRECTOR, DISTRIBUTION
John Fulton - jfulton@tvafilms.com
DIRECTOR, MARKETING
Brian Ware - bware@tvafilms.com

TWENTIETH CENTURY FOX FILM CORPORATION

1106 – 33 Bloor St. E, Toronto, ON M4W 3H1.
TEL: (800) 668-9927. Sales: (416) 921-0001.
Publicity: (416) 515-3365. Advertising: (416) 484-5300.
FAX: (416) 921-9062. www.foxmovies.com
V.P. & GENERAL MANAGER
Barry Newstead
BRANCH MANAGER
Damian O'Regan
PUBLICITY & PROMOTION (CANADA)
Wendy Merry

ADVERTISING NEWSPAPER, FRENCH:
Groupe Popcorn
TEL: (514) 448-5656. FAX: (514) 448-5868.
QUÉBEC DISTRIBUTION REP
Louise Trottier

ADVERTISING NEWSPAPER, ENGLISH:
Allied Advertising
TEL: (416) 413-0557 ext. 226.
FOX PRINT ACCOUNT DIRECTOR
Lisa DeLine

UNIVERSAL FILMS CANADA

2450 Victoria Park Ave., Toronto, ON M2J 4A2.
TEL: (416) 491-3000. FAX: (416) 502-0323.
FAX Publicity: (416) 494-3587. FAX Advertising: (416) 491-5180.
SENIOR V.P., & GENERAL MANAGER
Eugene Amodeo
ADMINISTRATIVE, DISTRIBUTION MANAGER
Sharon Irwin
DIRECTOR, PUBLICITY & PROMOTION
Janice Luke

Québec:
300 – 555 Dr. Frederik-Philips Blvd., St.-Laurent QC H4M 2X4. TEL: (514) 215-2673. FAX: (514) 215-2676.
DIRECTOR
Louise Chartrand Palmos - louise.palmos@nbcuni.com

WARNER BROS. CANADA, INC.

4576 Yonge St., 2nd Flr., North York, ON M2N 6P1.
TEL: (800) 263-2876. FAX: (416) 250-7403.
SENIOR V.P., CANADIAN DIVISION MANAGER
Florent Boulet
V.P., CANADIAN DIVISION THEATRICAL SALES
Andrew Faux
SENIOR V.P., MARKETING
Dianne Schwalm

For Québec 35mm bookings, please refer to Montréal office:
205 – 9900 Cavendish, Ville St. Laurent, QC H4M 2V2.
TEL: (514) 333-6400. FAX: (514) 333-1460.
BRANCH MANAGER
Susan Karam - susan.karam@warnerbros.com

For Ontario 35mm bookings, please refer to Donna Grant (Branch Manager) in Toronto office.

For Maritimes 35mm bookings, please refer to

Margaret Ramsay in Toronto office.

For Alberta / BC 35mm bookings, please refer to

Michelle DeCarle in Toronto office.

For Manitoba / Saskatchewan 35mm bookings, please refer to Glenn Poliah in Toronto office.

For Landmark theatre and in-theatre advertising / promotions (Exhibitor Services), please refer to Brian Ware (Manager, Canadian Exhibitor Services) in Toronto office.

Exhibitors And Exhibition Services

EXHIBITION & CIRCUITS

A THEATRE NEAR YOU (CANADA), INC.

c/o Dolphin Cinema II, 4555 E. Hastings St.,
N. Burnaby. BC V5C 2K3. TEL: (604) 293-0332.

Also operating Hollywood 3 (Surrey, B.C.) and New Westminster 3 (New Westminster, B.C.).

U.S.A. Head Office: P.O. Box 3309, 3813 168th St. NE, Arlington, WA 98223. TEL: (360) 653-9899. FAX: (360) 653-1720.
CHAIRMAN
Al Dabestani

AMC ENTERTAINMENT INTERNATIONAL, INC.

75 Consumers Rd., Canadian Operations Office,
Whitby, ON L1N 9S2. TEL: (905) 665-8410, (905) 665-7210.
FAX: (905) 665-9003. www.amctheatres.com
ACCOUNTING (CANADA)
Pauline Pawson - ext. 136

U.S.A.: 920 Main St., Kansas City, MO 64105.
TEL: (816) 221-4000.

EXECUTIVE V.P., INTERNATIONAL OPERATIONS
Mark A. McDonald
FILM BUYER (CANADA)
Sonny Gourley - (816) 221-4895
HEAD BOOKER
Lucy Aadnesen - (816) 221-4825

AMC Entertainment International, Inc. is a subsidiary of AMC Entertainment Inc. It operates seven Canadian cinemas.

BOULEVARD CINEMAS 2000

113 Richmond Blvd., Napanee, ON K7R 3Z8.
TEL: (613) 354-2597. FAX: (613) 373-9877.
CONTACT
Paul Peterson

Also operating Boulevard Cinemas 2000 Gananoque, Picton Mustang Drive-In.

BROADWAY CINEMAS

518 Broadway St., Tillsonburg, ON N4G 3S7.
TEL: (519) 688-0923. www.broadwaycinemas.ca
PRESIDENT
Len Walker

CARNIVAL CINEMAS

5402 47 St., Red Deer, AB T4N 6Z4. TEL: (403) 341-6565.
FAX: (403) 341-4355. email: carnivl2@telusplanet.net
www.carnivalcinemas.net
CEO
Bill Ramji

CINEMA CITY

(Cinema City is now part of Cineplex Entertainment)

CINEMAS GUZZO

1055 Chemin de Coteau, 2 ème étage, Terrebonne, QC J6W 5Y8. TEL: (450) 961-2945. FAX: (450) 961-9349.
email: promotionsdept@cinemasguzzo.com
www.cinemasguzzo.com
PRESIDENT & CEO
Angelo Guzzo
EXECUTIVE V.P.
Vincenzo Guzzo
ASSISTANT TO THE EXECUTIVE V.P.
Vito Franco
V.P., BUSINESS & CORPORATE LAW
Nathalie Gagnon
DIRECTOR OF ACCOUNTING
José Bruzzese
COMMUNICATIONS, PROMOTIONS
James Dambreville
DIRECTEUR DES OPERATIONS
Mario Quattrociocche
OFFICE DIRECTOR
Ginette Noiseux
TECHNICAL DIRECTOR
Danny Benfeito

Cinémas Guzzo is a regional chain of movie theaters located in the Canadian province of Quebec. There are currently 8 Mega-Plex locations and 4 Cinema locations, all within the greater Montreal area.

CINEMA PARALLELE

3530 boul St.-Laurent, Montréal, QC H2X 2V1.
TEL: (514) 847-9272, (514) 847-2206. FAX: (514) 847-0732.
www.cinemaparallele.ca
DIRECTOR
Caroline Masse

Founded in 1967. A non-profit organization dedicated to the promotion of independent cinema and video in Québec and across Canada. A 90-seat film and video theatre.

LES CINEMAS CINE-ENTERPRISE, INC. SIÈGE SOCIAL

1100 rue Yzes Blais, Lacheine, QC J6V 1P7.
TEL: (888) 581-5757, (450) 581-5757. FAX: (450) 581-0594.
email: reception@cineentreprise.ca www.cineentreprise.ca
PRESIDENT
Raffaele Papalia

CINÉMAS FORTUNE, INC.

Head Office, 300 Chemin Dunlop, Chelsea, QC J9B 2N3.
TEL: (819) 827-1717. email: nstgelais@cinemasfortune.ca
mzampino@cinemasfortune.ca www.cinemasfortune.ca
PRESIDENT
Robert A. Sudermann - suderman@istar.ca
VICE PRESIDENT
Peter Sudermann - suderman@campfortune.com

1255 DeRouen St., Boucherville, QC J4B 7T7.
TEL: (450) 449-5442. FAX: (450) 449-7104.
V.P., BOOKING
Nathalie Fecteau - n.fecteau@videotron.ca

CINEPLEX ENTERTAINMENT

1303 Yonge St., Toronto, ON M4T 2Y9.
TEL: (416) 323-6600. FAX: (416) 323-6683.
www.cineplex.com
KEY EXECUTIVES
PRESIDENT & CEO
Ellis Jacob
CFO
Gord Nelson
SENIOR V.P., GENERAL COUNSEL
Anne Fitzgerald
EXECUTIVE V.P.
Dan McGrath
EXECUTIVE V.P., FILMED ENTERTAINMENT
Michael Kennedy
PRESIDENT, CINEPLEX MEDIA
Sala Bachir
EXECUTIVE V.P., FILM PROGRAMMING
Michael McCartney
SENIOR V.P., HUMAN RESOURCES
Heather Briant
V.P., ALTERNATIVE PROGRAMMING
Brad LaDouceur
V.P., SALES
John Tsirlis
V.P., FILM
Jason Fulsom

Cineplex Entertainment LP owns, leases or has a joint-venture interest in 130 theatres with 1,338 screens serving more than 63.5 million guests annually. Headquartered in Toronto, Canada, Cineplex Entertainment operates theatres from British Columbia to Quebec.

CONSKY THEATRES / OAKBURN INVESTMENTS

425 Walmer Rd., Unit 6A, Toronto, ON M5P 2X9.
TEL: (416) 515-8506. FAX: (416) 515-8507.
CONTACT
Lou Consky

DYNASTY THEATRES

P.O. Box 1596, Melfort, SK S0E 1A0. TEL: (306) 752-5523, (306) 752-5499. www.dynastytheatres.ca
CONTACT
Ken Pyrema

Operating theatres in North Battleford, Melfort & Meadow Lake, SK.

EMPIRE THEATRES, LIMITED
Head Office, 610 E. River Rd., New Glasgow, NS B2H 3S8.
TEL: (902) 755-7620. FAX: (902) 755-7640.
email: empire@empiretheatres.com www.empiretheatres.com
PRESIDENT & CEO
Stuart G. Fraser
EXECUTIVE V.P., OPERATIONS
Kevin J. MacLeod
V.P., OPERATIONS
Brian MacLeod
COMPTROLLER
Jean Reddick

Regional Offices:
190 Chain Lake Dr., Halifax, NS B3S 1C5.
TEL: (902) 876-4848. FAX: (902) 876-4849.
V.P., MARKETING & MEDIA
Dean Leland
BOOKER/BUYER
Greg MacNeil
ADVERTISING
Robert Goguen
IMAX SALES MANAGER
Dean S. Leland

5095 Yonge St., Toronto, ON M2N 6Z4. TEL: (416) 225-6825.
FAX: (416) 225-0737.
V.P., FILM PROGRAMMING
Robert Wales

FESTIVAL CINEMAS
200 – 1788 W. 5th Ave., Vancouver, BC V6J 1P2.
TEL: (604) 734-8700. FAX: (604) 734-7489.
email: info@festivalcinemas.ca www.festivalcinemas.ca
PRESIDENT
Leonard Schein - leonard.schein@festivalcinemas.ca

FESTIVAL CINEMAS:
2236 Queen St. E, Toronto, ON M4E 1G2.
TEL: (416) 690-0667 ext. 1. FAX: (416) 690-0755.
email: jszczur@sympatico.ca www.foxbeach.ca
CONTACT
Jerry Szczur

Festival Cinemas started with the Ridge Theatre in 1978 and has operated the Vancouver East Cinema, Varsity Theatre, Starlight Cinema, Park Theatre, and Fifth Avenue Cinemas. Leonard Schein (the president of Festival Cinemas) also started the Vancouver International Film Festival at the Ridge. Now, Festival Cinemas operates the Fifth Avenue Cinemas, the Park Theatre The Ridge Theatre.

FILM.CA, INC.
171 Speers Rd., Unit 25, Oakville, ON L6K 3W8.
TEL: (905) 338-0494. FAX: (905) 338-6284.
email: info@film.ca www.film.ca
CEO
Jeff Knoll - jknoll@film.ca

Operator – Encore Cinemas (Burlington ON), Central Parkway (Mississauga ON) and Oakville Mews (Oakville ON).

THE FLICKS CINEMA
P.O. Box 154, Stonewall, MB R0C 2Z0. TEL: (204) 467-8401.
CONTACT
Don Smith

FREDERICK TWIN CINEMAS, INC.
385 Frederick St., Kitchener, ON N2H 2P2.
TEL: (519) 747-4342, (519) 896-3500. FAX: (519) 747-4342.
www.fredericktwin.com
CONTACT
Kelly MacLeod - kmacleod@fredericktwin.com

GALLERY CINEMAS (WOODSTOCK), INC.
4351 Morgan Cres, W. Vancouver, BC V7V 2P1.
TEL: (604) 922-3765. FAX: (604) 922-3725.
email: info@gallerycinemas.com www.gallerycinemas.com
PRESIDENT
Chris Van Snellenberg
FILM BOOKER
Eric Ball

GOLDEN THEATRES, LTD.
2800 John St., Unit 16, Markham, ON L3R 0E2.
TEL: (905) 940-3994. FAX: (905) 940-3997.
CONTACT
Eddie Dehmoubed

HIGHLANDS CINEMAS
P.O. Box 85, 4131 Hwy. 121, Kinmount, ON K0M 2A0.
TEL: (705) 488-2107, (705) 488-2199. FAX: (705) 488-9942.
www.highlandscinemas.com
CONTACT
Keith Stata - keithstata@highlandscinemas.com

Five screens.

LANDMARK CINEMAS OF CANADA, LTD.
Head Office – All Departments, 522 11th Ave. SW, 4th Flr., Calgary, AB T2R 0C8. TEL: (403) 262-4255.
FAX: (403) 266-1529 email: info@landmarkcinemas.ca
www.landmarkcinemas.com
PRESIDENT
Brian F. McIntosh
MANAGER, FILM BUYING & BOOKING
Kevin Norman
ADMINISTRATION MANAGER
Sherry Chappell
MANAGER, ADVERTISING & CREATIVE SERV ICES
Donald D. Langkaas
ACCOUNTING MANAGER
Ian Harwood

MAGIC LANTERN THEATRES / RAINBOW CINEMAS
11729 105 Ave., Edmonton, AB T2H 0L9. TEL: (780) 482-1611.
FAX: (780) 482-3520. email: mlt@magiclanterntheatres.ca
mlt@powersurfr.com www.magiclanterntheatres.ca
PRESIDENT
Tom Hutchinson
SECRETARY
Bill Booth

Magic Lantern Theatres currently operates 16 cinema locations with 78 screens across Canada, including 8 cinemas under the Rainbow Cinemas banner.

MAY THEATRES (1984), INC.
4905 50th Ave., Lloydminster, SK S9V 0P7.
TEL: (306) 825-3884. FAX: (306) 825-6172.
CONTACT
Mike May

Operating seven theatres in BC, AB, SK and ON.

THE MOVIE MILL, INC.
1710 Mayor Magrath Dr. S, Lethbridge, AB T1K 2R6.
TEL: (403) 381-1251. FAX: (403) 381-1256.
email: len@moviemill.com www.moviemill.com
PRESIDENT
Leonard Binning

Seven screens. Serving southern Alberta since 1994.

ONTARIO CINEMAS, INC.
745 Mt. Pleasant Rd., Toronto, ON M4S 2N4.
TEL: (416) 481-1186. FAX: (416) 481-5244.
PRESIDENT
Norman Stern
EXECUTIVE ASSISTANT TO MR. STERN
D. Doody

ONTARIO PLACE CORPORATION
955 Lakeshore Blvd. W, Toronto, ON M6K 3B9.
TEL: (416) 314-9758. FAX: (416) 314-9993.

IMAX theatre.

PLAZA THEATRE
1133 Kensington Rd. NW, Calgary AB T2N 3P4.
TEL: (403) 283-2222. FAX: (403) 568-9166.
email: pete@theplaza.ca www.theplaza.ca
CONTACT
Mike Brar

PREMIER OPERATING CORPORATION LIMITED
92 – 1262 Don Mills Rd., Don Mills, ON M3B 2W7.
TEL: (416) 443-1645. FAX: (416) 443-1760.
email: premieroperating@on.aibn.com
PRESIDENT
Madge Allen
V.P., SECRETARY
Brian Allen

THE PRINCESS CINEMA, INC.
6 Princess St. W, Waterloo, ON N2L 2X8. TEL:(519) 885-2950.
FAX: (519) 885-1048. email: john@princesscinemas.com
www.princesscinemas.com
CONTACT
John Tutt

Operating the Princess Cinema and the Princess Twin.

RPL FILM THEATRE
2311 12th Ave., Central Library, Lower Level,
Regina, SK S4P 3Z5. TEL: (306) 777-6104.
FAX: (306) 777-6104. www.reginalibrary.ca
PROGRAMMER
Belinda New

STINSON THEATRES, LTD.
P.O. Box 142, Barrie, ON L4M 4S9. TEL: (705) 726-8190.
FAX: (705) 721-9579. www.stinsontheatres.ca
PRESIDENT
Robert Stinson

BOOKER & BUYER
Cathy Watson

VANCITY THEATRE

1811 Seymour St., Vancouver, BC V6B 3M7.
TEL: (604) 685-0260. FAX: (604) 688-8221.
email: viff@viff.org www.vifc.org
CONTACT
Alan Franey

A luxurious, state-of-the-art 175 seat theatre run by the Vancouver International Film Festival showing festival-type films year-round. Also available for private booking.

FILM BOOKING

ATLANTIC THEATRE SERVICES, LTD.

P.O. Box 2419, 114 Dresden Ave., Saint John, NB E2L 3V9.
TEL: (506) 696-6618. FAX: (506) 696-4472.
CONTACT
Don McKelvie

CATHY WATSON BOOKING SERVICES

100 Idlewood Dr., Midhurst, ON L0L 1X1. TEL: (705) 727-4007.
FAX: (705) 727-7907. email: booker.cathy@rogers.com
CONTACT
Cathy Watson

FILM CIRCUIT

(A div. of the Toronto International Film Festival Group, TIFFG)
1600 – 2 Carlton St., Toronto, ON M5B 1J3.
TEL: (416) 967-7371. FAX: (416) 967-9477.
email: tiffg@torfilmfest.ca www.filmcircuit.ca
DIRECTOR, CANADIAN INITIATIVES
Karen Black - (416) 934-3274 ext. 6
SENIOR MANAGER, FILM CIRCUIT
Robin Rhodes - (416) 934-3245
MANAGER, FILM CIRCUIT RELATIONS
Cindy Morris - (416) 934-3256
MANAGER, FILM CIRCUIT PROGRAMMING/FOR BRITISH COLUMBIA & ALBERTA
Tammy Stone - (416) 934-3205 ext. 9
PROGRAMMING COORDINATOR/ONTARIO (W. OF PORT HOPE), MANITOBA AND SASKATCHEWAN GROUPS
Wendy Blushke - (416) 934-3251 ext. 1
PROGRAMMING COORDINATOR
Matt MacKinnon - (416) 967-7371 ext. 2263

Division of the Toronto International Film Festival Group. Canadian and international films. Consists of 160 active communities throughout Canada.

INDEPENDENT BOOKING & THEATRE SERVICES, LTD.

135A – 1315 Bishop St., Cambridge, ON N1R 6Z2.
TEL: (519) 740-1266. FAX: (519) 740-6374.
email: ibtsl@bellnet.ca www.independentbooking.net
PRESIDENT
Eric Ball
VICE PRESIDENT
Barbara Ball
OFFICE MANAGER, FILM BUYER
Susan Johnson
FILM BUYER
Dawn Rybicki - dawn-ibtsl@bellnet.ca

Booking services for cinemas in Canada and the U.S.A.

KINOSMITH, INC.

223 Humberside Ave., Toronto, ON Canada M6P 1K9.
TEL: (416) 992-2060. FAX: (416) 461-3762.
email: info@kinosmith.com www.kinosmith.com

SATOK CINEMA SERVICES

16 Granite St., Toronto, ON M3H 3K2. TEL: (416) 638-3616.
FAX: (416) 638-3622. email: marksatok@rogers.com
CONTACT
Mark Satok

Booking services for independent theatres and sales of theatre equipment.

SERVICES DE PROGRAMMATION DENHUR KARALEX MULTIMÉDIA, INC.

101 – 17660 Charles, Mirabel, QC J7J 1L8.
TEL: (450) 437-0078. FAX: (450) 437-4656.
CONTACTS
Denis Hurtubise - denis@denhur.qc.ca
Karen Hansen - karen@denhur.qc.ca
Louise Lefebvre - louise@denhur.qc.ca
Catherine Dornier - catherine@denhur.qc.ca

THEATRE AGENCIES / WESTCOAST THEATRE SERVICES

PRAIRIE ALLIED BOOKING, 301 – 522 11th Ave. SW, Calgary, AB T2R 0C8. TEL: (800) 661-8332, (403) 264-4660.
FAX: (403) 264-6571. www.theatreagencies.com
CONTACT
Neil H. Campbell - ncampbell@landmarkcinemas.ca
Syd Sniderman - ssniderman@theatreagencies.ca
Ellen Smeltzer - esmeltzer@theatreagencies.ca
Edith Becker - ebecker@theatreagencies.ca
Ouida Gerat -ogerat@theatreagencies.ca

CONSULTING SERVICES

CINE SOUND & PROJECTION, INC.

258 Raleigh Ave., Toronto, ON M1K 1A8.
TEL: (800) 811-3611, (416) 269-1066. FAX: (416) 269-7991.
email: salestoronto@cinesound.ca www.cinesound.ca
PRESIDENT
Doug Mahaney - dmahaney@cinesound.ca
CONSULTANT, TECHNICIAN
Chuck Nascimento, Ryan Mahaney, Dave Macaulay

Alberta:
4723 101st St., Edmonton, AB T6E 5L6. TEL: (780) 488-4478, (877) 454-1575. FAX: (780) 488-4144.
email: kbell@cinesound.ca
CONTACT
Kevin Bell

CINEAC

2684 Beaubien est, Montréal, QC H1Y 1G7.
TEL: (514) 279-1616. FAX: (514) 279-9492.
email: info@cineac.ca www.cineac.ca
PRESIDENT
Simon Beaudry - simon.beaudry@cineac.ca

Provides services such as Québec's box office statistics, screen tests and marketing research.

KING CINEMA SERVICES

11507 120th St., Edmonton, AB T5G 2Y4.
TEL: (800) 561-3581 (Canada), (780) 455-1622.
FAX: (780) 455-0663. email: info@kingcinemaservices.com
www.kingcinemaservices.com
COO
Neil H. Campbell
SERVICE MANAGER
Eldon Wilson
CUSTOMER SERVICE
Cindy Hopfauf

THE LIGHTNING GROUP

15 Coldwater Rd., Toronto, ON M3B 1Y8. TEL: (416) 227-2324.
FAX: (416) 227-2326. email: hlichtman1@aol.com
PRESIDENT
Howard Lichtman

Marketing consultancy practice. Publisher of The State of the Moviegoing Industry Report.

PLANET 3 COMMUNICATIONS, LTD.

90A Isabella St., 2nd Flr., Toronto, ON M4Y 1N4.
TEL: (416) 922-4459. FAX: (416) 924-0101.
email: joanne@planet3com.net
CONTACT
Joanne Smale

Specializing in consultation and public relations services in the area of entertainment.

SLIDE SCREEN ENTERTAINMENT, INC.

135A – 1315 Bishop St., Cambridge, ON N1R 6Z2.
TEL: (519) 658-6920. FAX: (519) 740-6374.
email: ibtsl@bellnet.ca
PRESIDENT
Eric Ball
V.P., SECRETARY-TREASURER
Barbara Ball

Management services for independent theatres.

THEATRE AGENCIES

301 – 522 11th Ave. SW, Calgary, AB T2R 0C8.
TEL: (800) 661-8332, (403) 264-4660. FAX: (403) 264-6571.
www.theatreagencies.com
COO
Neil H. Campbell - ncampbell@landmarkcinemas.ca,
GENERAL MANAGER
Edith Becker - ebecker@theatreagencies.ca
BOOKING AGENT
Trevor Endo - tendo@theatreagencies.ca
Ouida Gerat - ogerat@theatreagencies.ca

Theatre consulting / film buying & booking.

PRINT DELIVERY

DELUXE FILM SERVICES, LTD.
20 Railside Rd., Toronto, ON M3A 1A3. TEL: (416) 441-1261.
FAX: (416) 441-6341. email: patriciabriffett@bydeluxe.com
CONTACT
Patricia Briffett

Operating 32 depots across North America.

TECHNICOLOR CINEMA DISTRIBUTION
40 Lesmill Rd., Don Mills, ON M3B 2T5. TEL: (416) 449-8597.
GENERAL MANAGER
Karen Davis

Alberta: 3904 1st St. NE, Calgary, AB T2E 3E3.
TEL: (403) 276-6696.
MANAGER
Stephane Monette

British Columbia: 1644 W. 75th Ave., Vancouver, BC V6P 6G2.
TEL: (604) 263-2551.
MANAGER
Suzanne Wallace

Manitoba: 2315 Logan Ave., Winnipeg, MB R2R 2S7.
TEL: (204) 633-1203.
MANAGER
Les David

New Brunswick: 55 Bentley St., St. John, NB E2K 1B2.
TEL: (506) 634-1018.
MANAGER
Tim Boyce

Québec: 2555 Avenue Dollard, LaSalle, QC H8N 3A9.
TEL: (514) 931-6212.
MANAGER
Marie-Claude Boudreau

TICKETING SYSTEMS

INTERALIA, INC.
4110 79th St. NW, Calgary, AB T3B 5C2.
TEL: (403) 288-2706 ext. 106. FAX: (403) 288-5935.
email: info@interalia.com www.interalia.com
CEO
Robert Cormack - rcormack@interalia.com
HEAD OF MARKETING & PRODUCT MANAGEMENT
Steve Hashman - shashman@interalia.com
SALES DIRECTOR
John Tatton - jtatton@interalia.com

Solutions for interactive cinema and theatre messaging.

OMNITERM DATA TECHNOLOGY, LTD.
2785 Skymark Ave., Unit 11, Mississauga, ON L4W 4Y3.
TEL: (905) 629-4757. FAX: (905) 629-8590.
email: info@omniterm.com www.omniterm.com
PRESIDENT
E.S. (Ed) Coman
SALES
George Jankowski, Richard Humber

Box office / concessions P.O.S. systems, including self-serve kiosks, loyalty, stated value, high-speed bank and internet interfaces.

UTILITRAN CORP.
250 – 6815 8th Ave. NE, Calgary, AB T2E 7H7.
TEL: (403) 301-4500, (403) 371-3713. FAX: (403) 301-3716.
email: info@utilitran.com www.utilitran.com
CONTACT
David Branco - david.branco@utilitran.com

Supply chain software solutions.

VCS TIMELESS / VISTA ENTERTAINMENT
702 – 230 Richmond St. W, Toronto, ON M5V 3E5.
TEL: (416) 599-8366. FAX: (416) 599-8367.
email: enquiries@vcstimeless.ca www.vcstimeless.com
V.P., OPERATIONS
David Wiltshire ext 26

Box office & web ticketing / concessions / kiosks & ATMs / PDAs & handhelds / voucher & coupon management / telebooking (IVR) / signage control / air conditioning control / web-based loyalty / film management / staff scheduling / call centre / cash office control / central management reporting / head office systems.

ON-SCREEN ADVERTISING

ADFILMS
22 Wilson St., Hamilton, ON L8R 1C5.
TEL: (905) 522-5695, (866) ADFILMS. FAX: (905) 522-4327.
email: cinema@adfilms.com www.adfilms.com
PRESIDENT
Keith Stinson - keith@adfilms.com
SALES
Robert JeBailey - robert@adfilms.com

Specializing in the placement of advertising on independent movie screens throughout Canada, including Canada's only drive-in theatre network.

CINEPLEX GALAXY, LP
1303 Yonge St., Toronto, ON M4T 2Y9. TEL: (416) 323-6659.
FAX: (416) 323-6677. email: cegesz@cineplexgalaxy.com
www.cineplex.com
PROGRAM MANAGER, CINEMA MARKETING SERVICES
Charlene Egesz

FAMOUS PLAYERS MEDIA
100 – 102 Atlantic Ave., Toronto, ON M6K 1X9.
TEL: (416) 539-8800 ext. 232. FAX: (416) 539-8511.
GENERAL MANAGER
Robert Brown

THEATRE ASSOCIATIONS

ASSOCIATION DES PROPRIETAIRES DE CINEMA ET CINE-PARC DU QUEBEC, INC.
P.O. Box 976 - Station Desjardins, Montreal, QC H5B 1C1.
TEL: (450) 562-7826. FAX: (450) 562-1042.
email: info@apccq.com www.apccq.com
PRESIDENT
Didier Farré
VICE PRESIDENT
Martin Patry
SECRETARY
Mario Fortin
TREASURER
Daniel Seguin
COORDINATOR
Nathalie Albert

ATLANTIC INDEPENDENT THEATRE EXHIBITORS ASSOCIATION
P.O. Box 2419, St. John, NB E2L 3V9.
TEL: (506) 696-6618.
PRESIDENT
Don McKelvie

ATLANTIC MOTION PICTURE EXHIBITORS ASSOCIATION
190 Chain Lake Dr., c/o Empire Theatres Limited,
Halifax, NS B3S 1C5. TEL: (902) 876-4848.
email: leland@empiretheatres.com
PRESIDENT
Wayne Harper
TREASURER
Dean Leland

MOTION PICTURE THEATRE ASSOCIATION OF ALBERTA
c/o The Movie Mill, 1710 Mayor Magrath Dr. S, Lethbridge, AB
T1K 2R6. TEL: (403) 381-1251. FAX: (403) 381-1256
email: len@moviemill.com
CONTACT
Leonard Binning

MOTION PICTURE THEATRE ASSOCIATION OF BC
c/o Paramount Vancouver, 900 Burrard St., Vancouver, BC V6Z 3G5. TEL: (604) 630-1415. email: 1422gm@cineplex.com
PRESIDENT
Ken Mont

MOTION PICTURE THEATRE ASSOCIATION OF MANITOBA
c/o Silver City St. Vital 2402, 160 – 1225 St. Mary's Rd.,
Winnipeg, MB R2M 5E5. TEL: (204) 256-5542.
FAX: (204) 257-5404. email: 2402gm@cineplex.com
PRESIDENT
Andrew Wilson

MOTION PICTURE THEATRE ASSOCIATION OF SASKATCHEWAN
c/o Rainbow Theatres, 3806 Albert St., Golden Mile Centre,
Regina, SK S4S 3R2. TEL: (306) 359-6353.
FAX: (306) 359-6362. www.mptac.ca
PRESIDENT
Wilf Runge

MOTION PICTURE THEATRE ASSOCIATIONS OF CANADA
304 – 1240 Bay St., Toronto, ON M5R 2A7. TEL: (416) 969-7057.
FAX: (416) 922-5667. email: mptac.ca@ca.inter.net
www.mptac.ca
EXECUTIVE DIRECTOR

Adina Lebo
CHAIRMAN
Raffaele Papalia
SECRETARY
Dean Leland
TREASURER
Dan McGrath

MOTION PICTURE THEATRES ASSOCIATION OF ONTARIO
304 – 1240 Bay St., Toronto, ON M5R 2A7.
TEL: (416) 969-7057. FAX: (416) 922-5667.
PRESIDENT
Norman Stern
EXECUTIVE DIRECTOR
Adina Leb

INDOOR THEATRES

Theatres are listed by province, then by the cities within each province. Listings include the theatre name, the licensee/owner, the city's population, and the screen count.

Theatre Name	Licensee/Owner	Population	Screens
ALBERTA			
AIRDRIE			
Roxy	Landmark Cinemas	29,822	3
BANFF			
Cinema Lux Centre	Landmark Cinemas	8,352	5
BROOKS			
Oasis	Landmark Cinemas	13,000	1
CALGARY			
Canyon Meadows	G. Hunter	1,328,000	10
Centennial Planetarium	City of Calgary		6
Crowfoot Crossing	Cineples		12
Empire Studio 10	Empire Theatres, Ltd.		10
Eau Claire Market Theatre			6
Globe Cinema	Landmark Cinemas		2
Moviedome	Al Dadani		9
Paramount Chinook	Cineplex Entertainment, LP		17
Plaza	M. Brar		1
Empire Studio Country Hills	Empire Theatres, Ltd.		16
Sunridge Spectrum	Cineplex Entertainment, LP.		14
Uptown Stage & Screen	The Uptown Group		2
Westhills	Cineplex Entertainment, LP		10
CAMROSE			
Duggan Cinemas	Magic Lantern Theatres	15,686	5
COCHRANE			
Movie House		15,424	3
DRUMHELLER			
Napier		6,277	1
EDMONTON			
Cinema City 12	Cinema City / Cineplex	1,034,945	12
City Centre	Empire Theatres, Ltd.		9
Clareview	Empire Theatres, Ltd.		10
Garneau	Magic Lantern Theatres		1
Gateway	Empire Theatres, Ltd.		8
Metro	Cinema Society		
North Edmonton	Cineplex Entertainment, LP		14
Princess Twin	Magic Lantern Theatres		2
Scotia Bank West Edm. Mall	Cineplex Entertainment, LP		13
Odyssium IMAX	Cineplex Entertainment, LP		1
South Edmonton	Cineplex Entertainment, LP.		16
U of A - Myer Horowitz Theatre	University of Alberta		1
West Mall 8	Cineplex Entertainment, LP.		8
Westmount Centre	Empire Theatres, Ltd.		4
EDSON			
Nova Theatre	Landmark Cinemas	8,098	1
FORT MACLEOD			
Empress	Film Society	3,072	1
FORT MCMURRAY			
Cinema 6	Landmark Cinemas		6
FORT SASKATCHEWAN			
Gemini	Jai Lee	14,957	3
GRANDE PRAIRIE			
Grand Prairie	Cineplex Entertainment, LP.	47,076	10
Jan Cinema	Landmark Cinemas		3
Lyric	Landmark Cinemas		3
HIGH PRAIRIE			
Park	M. & J. Kachnic	2,750	1
HINTON			
Roxy Theatre	Landmark Cinemas	9,738	1
INNISHFAIL			
Century Theatre		7,883	1
JASPER			
Chaba	Dwain Wacko	4,700	2
LAC LA BICHE			
Aurora	B&H Taha	2,758	1
LACOMBE			
Reel to Reel	M Visscher	10,742	2
LEDUC			
Leduc Cinemas	Mohammed Fares	16,967	4
LETHBRIDGE			
Galaxy Cinema Lethbridge	Cineplex Entertainment, LP.	86,659	10
Movie Mill 7	Movie Mill		7
MANNING			
Aurora	Leslie & Paul Snyder	1,493	1
MEDICINE HAT			
Galaxy Cinema	Cineplex Entertainment, LP.	56,997	10
Monarch Theatre			1
OKOTOKS			
Okotoks	Owen Lloyd	17,145	2
OLDS			
Mayfair			1
PEACE RIVER			
Cinema '72 Twin	Magic Lantern Theatres	6,315	2
PINCHER CREEK			
Fox	Edith Becker	3,625	2
PONOKA			
Capitol		6,576	2
PROVOST			
Provost	Reel Entertainment	6,576	2
RED DEER			
Carnival Cinemas	Carnival Cinemas	82,772	8
Park Plaza	Cineplex Entertainment, LP		6
Uptown Cinema Centre	Landmark Cinemas		4
ST. ALBERT			
Grandin	Grandin Theatres	57,719	5
St. Albert			3
ST. PAUL			
Elite	Magic Lantern Theatres	5,106	3
SHERWOOD PARK			
Sherwood Park	Cineplex Entertainment, LP		10
SLAVE LAKE			
Rex	Roy. Evans		1
SPRUCE GROVE			
Magic Lantern Parkland 7	Magic Lantern		7
STETTLER			
Jewel Theatre	Landmark Cinemas	5,418	1
STRATHMORE			
Joyland	Bill & Sheila Crispin	10,225	1
WAINWRIGHT			
Alma	May Theatres (1984), Inc	5,426	3
WETASKIWIN			
Cinema	Mohammed Fare	11,673	3
WHITECOURT			
Vista	Magic Lantern Theatres	8,971	1
BRITISH COLUMBIA			
100 MILE HOUSE			
South Cariboo Theatre		2,000	1

Theatre Name	Licensee/Owner	Population	Screens
ABBOTSFORD			
Towne Cinema Centre	Landmark Cinemas	123,864	9
BURNABY			
Dolphin Cinema	A Theatre Near You, Inc.	202,799	2
SilverCity Metropolis	Famous Players		10
Station Square	Famous Players		7
CAMPBELL RIVER			
Galaxy Theatre	Landmark Cinemas	29,572	4
Showcase	Landmark Cinemas		5
CASTLEGAR			
Kootenay Centre	May Theatres, Inc. (1984)	7,259	5
Castlegar Theatres			1
CHILLIWACK			
Cottonwood 4	Harris Road Ent. Group, Ltd.	69,217	4
Galaxy Cinemas	Galaxy		8
Paramount	Landmark Cinemas		2
COQUITLAM			
SilverCity	Famous Players	114,565	20
COURTENAY			
Rialto Theatre	Landmark Cinemas	21,940	4
CRANBROOK			
Columbia	Landmark Cinemas	18,267	5
CRESTON			
New Tivoli	Robert Geddes	4,826	1
DAWSON CREEK			
Center Cinema	Landmark Cinemas	10,994	1
DUNCAN			
Criterion Twin	Criterion Theatres	4,986	2
FERNIE			
Vogue		5.168	2
FORT NELSON			
Phoenix	Doug Roper	4,514	
FORT ST. JAMES			
Lido	Kirk Nelson	1,355	1
FORT ST. JOHN			
Aurora Cinema Centre	Landmark Cinemas	17,402	5
GIBSONS			
Gibsons Cinema		4,000	1
GOLDEN			
Golden	R & M Coulter	3,811	1
GRAND FORKS			
Gem	Marius Paquet	4,036	1
HAZELTON			
Tri-Town	R. Beertema	293	1
HOPE			
Hope Cinema	Jeff Larson	6,185	1
INVERMERE			
Toby	R.W. Peters	3,002	1
KAMLOOPS			
Aberdeen Mall	Cineplex Entertainment, LP	80,376	10
Paramount	Landmark Cinemas		2
KELOWNA			
Grand 10 Cinema	Landmark Cinemas	106,707	10
Orchard Plaza	Cineplex Entertainment, LP		5
Paramount	Landmark Cinemas		3
KIMBERLEY			
Werner	Karen Franz	6,139	1
LADYSMITH			
Island Cinema	Rahim Manji	7,538	1
LANGFORD			
Criterion Triple	Criterion Theatres	22,459	3
LANGLEY			
Colossus	Famous Players	23,606	18
Colossus / IMAX	Famous Players		1
MISSION			
Silver City	Famouos Players	34,505	12
NAKUSP			
Arrow Lakes	Bill White	1,524	
NANAIMO			
Avalon Cinema Centre	Landmark Cinemas	78,692	8
Galaxy Nanaimo	Cineplex Entertainment, LP		8

Theatre Name	Licensee/Owner	Population	Screens
NELSON			
Civic	Karen Franz	9,258	
N. VANCOUVER			
Esplanade	Empire Theatres, Ltd.	85,562	6
Park & Tilford	Cineplex Entertainment, LP		6
OLIVER			
Oliver	David Lesmeister	4,370	1
PENTICTON			
Pen-Mar Cinema Centre	Landmark Cinemas	31,909	4
PITT MEADOWS			
Meadowtown Centre	Cineplex Entertainment, LP	15,623	10
PORT ALBERNI			
Paramount Theatre	Landmark Cinemas	17,548	1
POWELL RIVER			
Patricia	Ann Nelson		1
PRINCE GEORGE			
FP 6	Cineplex Entertainment, LP	70,981	6
Magic Shadows	Magic Shadows Theatre, Ltd.		1
PRINCE RUPERT			
Prince Rupert	Cineplex Entertainment, LP	12,815	3
QUESNEL			
Carib Twin	D. Hothi	9,326	2
REVELSTOKE			
Roxy	Carl Rankin	7,230	1
RICHMOND			
Richmond Centre	Cineplex Entertainment, LP	174,461	6
Silver City Riverport	Cineplex Entertainment, LP		19
SALMON ARM			
Salmar Classic	Salmon Arm Community Assoc.	16,012	4
Salmar Grand	Salmon Arm Community Assoc.		4
SECHELT			
Ravens Cry Theatre	D. Proby	8,454	1
SIDNEY			
Star	S. Oliver	11,315	2
SMITHERS			
Roi	A. Buchanan	5,217	2
SQUAMISH			
Garbaldi	Resort Cinemas of Whistler	14,949	5
SURREY			
Clova		394,976	1
Hollywood	A Theatre Near You		3
Strawberry Hill	Cineplex Entertainment, LP		12
Studio 12 Guildford	Empire Theatres, Ltd.		12
TERRACE			
Tillicum Twin	W. Young	11,320	2
TRAIL			
Royal	George Mah	7,237	1
VANCOUVER			
Broadway	Raja Cinema	2,116,581	1
CN IMAX	Starboard Theatres		1
Commercial	Raja Cinema		1
Denman	NewGen Entertainment		1
Dunbar	Ken Charko		1
Fifth Avenue	Festival Cinemas		5
Granville	Empire Theatres, Ltd.		7
Hollywood	D. Fairleigh		1
Oakridge	Empire Theatres, Ltd.		3
Park	Festival Cinemas		1
Pacific	Pacific Cinematheque		
Rio	Mike Goyal		
Ridge	Festival Cinemas		1
Science World Omnimax	Science World		1
Scotia Bank Vancouver	Cineplex Entertainment, LP		9
Tinseltown	Cinemark		12
Vancity			3
VanEast	J. Shin		1
Vogue			1
VANDERHOOF			
Grand Reo	K. Niesen	4,064	1
VERNON			
Famous Palyers 7	Famous Players	35,944	7
Towne Theatre			3
VICTORIA			
Capitol	Empire Theatres, Ltd.	78,057	6
Cinecenta	U of Vic Student Union		1
National Geographic IMAX	Royal B.C. Museum		1

Theatre Name	Licensee/Owner	Population	Screens
Roxy Cinegog	Howie Siegel		1
Silver City Victoria	Cineplex Entertainment, LP		10
University	Empire Theatres, Ltd.		4
Vic Theatre	Landmark Clnemas		1
WESTBANK			
Capitol	Landmark Cinemas		5
WHISTLER			
Rainbow	D. Mathieson	9,248	
Village	Resort Cinemas of Whistler		8
Rialto Twin	Criterion Theatres	18,755	2
Criterion	Criterion Theatres		4
WILLIAMS LAKE			
Paradise	D. Hothi	10,744	4

MANITOBA

Theatre Name	Licensee/Owner	Population	Screens
BEAUSEJOUR			
Lyric	M. Baxter	2,823	1
BOISSEVAIN			
Boissevain	Community Theatre	1,497	1
BRANDON			
Capitol Theatre	Sask/Man JV, Ltd.	41,511	9
Univ. of Brandon	Brandon Film Festival		1
DAUPHIN			
Park (Seasonal)	J & B Gowler		1
DELORAINE			
Deloraine	Peggy Saunders	977	1
FLIN FLON			
Big Island Theatre	B. Liefe	5,594	1
GIMLI			
Gimli	Larry Minarik	5,797	1
GLENBORO			
Gaiety	Don Foster	633	1
HARTNEY			
Elks	Keith Evans	400	1
MELITA			
Strand	B. Holden	1,051	1
NEEPAWA			
Roxy	Town of Neepawa	3,298	1
PILOT MOUND			
Tivoli		676	1
PORTAGE LA PRAIRIE			
Cinema Center 3		7,156	3
RESTON			
Memorial	Candy Wanless		1
ROBLIN			
Roblin	Gordon Andrews	1,672	1
SELKIRK			
Garry Theatre	Landmark Cinemas	9,515	1
SOMERSET			
Lorne	R & E Raine	432	1
SOURIS			
Avalon	Town of Souris	1,772	1
STEINBACH			
Keystone	B. Wiebe	11,066	1
STONEWALL			
Flicks	Don J. Smith	4,376	1
ST.-PIERRE-JOLYS			
Cinema Jolys	Lou & Bertell Croteau	839	1
SWAN RIVER			
Star	Brent Scales	3,859	1
THE PAS			
Lido	G. Rivalin	5,589	1
THOMPSON			
Strand	H & G Tsitsos	13,446	1
WINKLER			
Southland	Empire	9,106	5
WINNIPEG			
Cinema City Northgate	Cinema City/Cineplex	694,668	8
Garden City	Famoos Players		2
Globe Cinema	Landmark Cinemas		3

Theatre Name	Licensee/Owner	Population	Screens
Grant Park	Empire Theatres, Ltd.		8
IMAX/Portage Place	Manitou Theatre Management, Ltd.		1
Kildonan Place	Famous Players		6
McGillivray	Cinema City/Cineplex		12
Silver City Polo Park	Famous Players		14
Silver City St. Vital	Famous Players		10
Towne	Landmark Cinemas		8

NEW BRUNSWICK

Theatre Name	Licensee/Owner	Population	Screens
BATHURST			
Apollo	Fred Rudet	12,714	5
CAMPBELLTON			
Paramount	M. Lord	7,384	1
CARAQUET			
Cine Centre 3		4,156	3
DIEPPE			
Crystal Palace	Empire Theatres, Ltd.	18,565	8
EDMUNDSTON			
Cine V	Gallant Enterprises	16,643	3
FREDERICTON			
Empire	Empire Theatres, Ltd.	50,535	10
GRAND FALLS			
Grand 3		5,650	10
MIRAMICHI			
Studio	Empire Theatres, Ltd.	18,129	5
MONCTON			
Empire 8 Trinity	Empire Theatres, Ltd.	64,128	8
ROTHESAY			
Empire	Empire Theatres, Ltd.	11,637	4
SACKVILLE			
Vogue		5,411	1
SAINT JOHN			
Studio	Empire Theatres, Ltd.	68,043	7
TRACADIE-SHIELA			
Cinema Peninsule	Cinema Peninsule, Ltee.	4,474	3
WOODSTOCK			
Atlantic	Dwight Fraser	5,113	3

NEWFOUNDLAND & LABRADOR

Theatre Name	Licensee/Owner	Population	Screens
BURIN			
Burin Theatres	Winston Marshall	2,483	1
CLARENVILLE			
Twin	Clarence Russell	5,274	2
CORNER BROOK			
Majestic	N. Kean	20,083	1
Millbrook	Empire Theatres, Ltd.		2
LABRADOR CITY			
Royal		7,240	
MOUNT PEARL			
Mount Pearl	Empire Theatres, Ltd.	24,671	7
PORT AUX BASQUES			
Grandview	Max Keeping		1
Springdale			
Twilite	Neil Whitehorn	2,764	1
ST. JOHN'S			
Studio	Empire Theatres, Ltd.	100,646	12
STEPHENVILLE			
Harmon	Tony MacDonald	6,588	1

NORTHWEST TERRITORIES

Theatre Name	Licensee/Owner	Population	Screens
FORT SMITH			
Park	Janine Daniels	2,364	1
HAY RIVER			
Riverview Cineplex	Donna Borchuk	3,648	2
YELLOWKNIFE			
Capitol	Premier Operating Corp.	18,700	3

Theatre Name	Licensee/Owner	Population	Screens
NOVA SCOTIA			
AMHERST			
Paramount	Empire Theatres, Ltd.	9,505	3
ANTIGONISH			
Empire Capitol Theatre	Empire Theatres, Ltd.	4,236	
BRIDGEWATER			
Studio	Empire Theatres, Ltd.	7,944	7
DARTMOUTH			
Dartmoutn Crossing	Empire Theatres, Ltd.	70,000	12
Dartmouth	Empire Theatres, Ltd.		6
GREENWOOD			
Zedex Theatre	J. Alexander		1
HALIFAX			
Bayers Lake	Empire Theatres, Ltd.	372,858	17
Bayers Lake - IMAX	Empire Theatres, Ltd.		1
Dartmouth Crossing	Empire Theatres, Ltd.		12
Empire	Empire Theatres, Ltd.		6
Oxford	Empire Theatres, Ltd.		1
Park Lane	Empire Theatres, Ltd.		8
LIVERPOOL			
Astor	Astor Theatre Society		1
LOWER SACKVILLE			
Studio	Empire Theatres, Ltd.		7
NEW GLASGOW			
Studio	Empire Theatres, Ltd.	9,455	7
NEW MINAS			
Empire	Empire Theatres, Ltd.		7
SHELBURNE			
Capitol	Mary Dyokis	4,828	8
SYDNEY			
Studio	Empire Theatres, Ltd.		10
TRURO			
Studio	Empire Theatres, Ltd.	11,765	7
YARMOUTH			
Studio	Empire Theatres, Ltd.	10,304	5
ONTARIO			
AGINCOURT			
Woodside Cinemas		9,440	3
AJAX			
Ajax	Cineplex Entertainment, LP	90,167	10
ALLISTON			
Circle	L&S MacDonald Theatre, Ltd.	17,000	1
ANCASTER			
Silver City	Famous Players	1,681	10
ARNPRIOR			
O'Brien Theatre	Kevin D. Marshall	7,158	2
ANTIKOKEN			
Friendship	Atikoken Native Centre	3,293	1
AURORA			
Cineplex Odeon Aurora 10	Cineplex Entertainment, LP	47,629	10
BARRHAVEN			
Barrhaven	Cineplex Entertainment, LP		7
BARRIE			
Bayfield 7	Golden Theatres, Ltd.	128,430	7
Galaxy	Cineplex Entertainment, LP		12
Imperial	Stinson Theatres, Ltd.		8
BEAVERTON			
Strand	Vernon King Flaherty		1
BELLEVILLE			
Belleville	Mark Rashotte	48,821	1
Belleville 8	Famous Players		8
BOLTON			
Empire	Empire Theatres		7
BOWMANVILLE			
Clarington Place	Cineplex Odeon	69,834	11
BRACEBRIDGE			
Norwood	Muskoka Cinemas 3	15,652	3

Theatre Name	Licensee/Owner	Population	Screens
BRAMPTON			
Gateway	Famous Players	433,806	6
Orion Gate	Cineplex Entertainment, LP		10
Silver City	Famous Players		16
BRANTFORD			
Galaxy	Cineplex Entertainment, LP	90,192	6
BROCKVILLE			
Galaxy Cinemas	Cineplex Odeon	21,957	6
BURK'S FALLS			
Towne	Corp./Burk's Falls	893	1
BURLINGTON			
Encore Cinemas	Film.ca, Inc.	164,415	6
Showcase	Empire Theatres, Ltd.		6
Silver City	Cineplex Entertainment, LP		12
CALEDON			
Empire 7	Empire Theatres	57,050	7
CAMBRIDGE			
Galaxy Cambridge	Cineplex Entertainment, LP	120,371	10
CAMPBELLFORD			
Aron	Aron Cinema, Ltd.		1
CARLETON PLACE			
Carleton Place	Malik Zekry	9,453	2
CHATHAM-KENT			
Chatham Cinema	Stinson Theatres, Ltd.	108,177	6
CLARINGTON			
Clarington Place	Cineplex Entertainment, LP	77,820	11
COBOURG			
Northumberland Mall	Northumberland Mall Theatres	18,210	3
COCHRANE			
Empire	493251 Ontario, Inc.	5,487	1
COLLINGWOOD			
Gayety		17,290	1
Galaxy 7	Cineplex Entertainment, LP		7
CONCORD			
AMC Interchange 30	AMC	8,255	30
CORNWALL			
Galaxy Cornwall	Cineplex Entertainment, LP	45,965	7
DRYDEN			
Cinema 86	Z. Tavares	8,195	1
E. GWILLIMBURY			
Silvercity Newmarket	Famous Players	21,069	16
ELLIOT LAKE			
Lake	L Nice / 705841 Ont, Inc.	11,549	2
ELORA			
Gorge	The Gorge Cinema, Inc.		1
ERIN			
Centre 2000	Town of Erin	11,148	1
ETOBICOKE			
Queensway	Cineplex Odeon	35,000	18
GANANOQUE			
1000 Islands Cinema	Boulevard Cinema, Ltd.	5,285	2
GEORGETOWN			
Georgetown Cinemas		36,690	3
GLOUCESTER			
Silver City	Famous Players	36,690	16
GODERICH			
Park	J.D. Lyons Corp	7,563	1
GUELPH			
Bookshelf	Bookshelf	114,943	1
Galaxy Cinemas	Galaxy		10
HALIBURTON			
Moulou	Consky Theatres		1
HAMILTON			
Jackson Square	Empire Theatres, Ltd.	504,559	6
Movie Palace	Movie Palace		2
Upper James	Cineplex Entertainment, LP		7
Westdale	Peter Sorok		1
HANOVER			
Paramount	J.D. Lyons Corp.	7,147	1
HEARST			
Cartier	Daniel La Rochelle	5,620	1

Theatre Name	Licensee/Owner	Population	Screens
HUNTSVILLE			
Capitol	Stinson Theatres, Ltd.	18,280	2
KANATA			
Kanata 24	AMC	100,200	24
KAPUSKASING			
Royal	A&M. Lebel	8,509	1
KENORA			
Century 1	Len Rattal	15,177	3
KESWICK			
Gem	R.J. Gorman		4
KINCARDINE			
Aztec	Mark Lalonde	11,173	1
KINGSTON			
Capitol	Empire Theatres, Ltd.	117,207	7
Gardiner's Rd.	Cineplex Entertainment, LP		10
ASUS Movie Theatre			1
The Screening Room	Terry Laffier		2
KINMOUNT			
Highlands Cinemas	Keith Stata	3,838	5
KIRKLAND LAKE			
La Salle	W. Sadoquis	8,248	1
KITCHENER			
Fairway Centre	Cineplex Entertainment, LP	204,668	7
Frederick Twin	Frederick Twins Cinema, Ltd.		2
Studio	Empire Theatres, Ltd.		12
LAKESHORE			
Lakeshore Cinemas		33,245	10
LEAMINGTON			
Star	Babcock Theatres	28,833	3
LINDSAY			
Century	Ontario Cinemas		3
LONDON			
Huron Market Place	Cineplex Entertainment, LP	352,395	6
Hyland	Hyland Cinemas, Inc.		3
Rainbow Galleria	Magic Lantern Theatres		7
Silver City	Cineplex Entertainment, LP		12
Wellington	Empire Theatres, Ltd.		8
Western / McKellar Theatre	Univ. Student Council		1
Westmount	Cineplex Entertainment, LP		8
MARATHON			
Marathon	Aaron Schelp	3,863	1
MARKHAM			
First Markham Place	Cineplex Entertainment, LP	261,573	10
MIDLAND			
Galaxy Midland	Cineplex Entertainment, LP	16,300	7
MILTON			
Galaxy Milton	Cineplex Entertainment, LP	53,939	8
MINDEN			
Beaver	Conskey Theatres		1
MISSISSAUGA			
Cine-Starz		668,549	4
Coliseum	Cineplex Entertainment, LP		12
Coliseum / IMAX	Cineplex Entertainment, LP		1
Courtenay Park	AMC Theatres Canada, Inc.		16
Silver City	Cineplex Entertainment, LP		10
Square One	Empire Theatres, Ltd.		10
NAPANEE			
Boulevard	Boulevard Cinema, Ltd.		3
NEW LISKEARD			
Empire	David B. Dymond		2
NEWMARKET			
Silver City	Cineplex Entertainment, LP	74,295	16
NIAGARA FALLS			
IMAX Theatre	Niagara Falls Theatre Venture	82,184	1
Niagara Square	Cineplex Entertainment, LP		10
NORTH BAY			
Galaxy North Bay	Cineplex Entertainment, LP	53,966	7
Capitol	City of North Bay		1
OAKVILLE			
Oakville Mews	Film.ca, Inc.	165,613	5
Silver City	Famous Players		12
Winston Churchill	AMC Theatres of Canada		24
ORANGEVILLE			
Galaxy Orangeville	Cineplex Entertainment, LP	26,925	7
ORILLIA			
Galaxy Orillia	Cineplex Entertainment, LP	30,259	6
OSHAWA			
Oshawa Centre	Cineplex Entertainment, LP		8
OTTAWA			
Bytowne	C.W. Towne Cinema, Inc.	812,129	1
Coliseum	Cineplex Entertainment, LP		12
Empire	Empire Theatres		7
Kanata	AMC Theatres of Canada		24
Mayfair	D. Holford		1
Orleans Town Centre	Empire Theatres, Ltd.		6
Ottawa Family Cinema	Notre Dame Auditorium		1
Silver City Gloucester	Cineplex Entertainment, LP		16
South Keys	Cineplex Entertainment, LP		12
Rainbow St. Laurent	Magic Lantern Theatres		5
Rideau Centre	Empire Theatres, Ltd.		3
OWEN SOUND			
Galaxy Owen Sound	Cineplex Entertainment, LP	21,753	7
PALMERTON			
Norgan			1
PARRY SOUND			
Strand	Gregory Hobson	5,818	2
PEMBROKE			
Algonquin	Peter Sorok	13,930	4
PETAWAWA			
Troyes Theatre	Jeanne Simard	14,651	1
PETERBOROUGH			
Galaxy Peterborough	Cineplex Entertainment, LP		11
PICKERING			
Pickering Mall	Cineplex Entertainment, LP	87,838	8
PICTON			
Regent	The Regent Theatre		1
PORT ELGIN			
Port Elgin	Tom Wright		3
PORT HOPE			
Capitol		16,390	1
RENFREW			
O'Brien	Murray W. Adolph	7,846	2
RICHMOND HILL			
Elgin Mills	Empire Theatres, Ltd.	162,704	10
Silver City	Cineplex Entertainment, LP		14
SARNIA			
Lambton	Cineplex Entertainment, LP	71,419	9
SAULT STE. MARIE			
Galaxy Sault Ste Marie	Cineplex Entertainment, LP	74,948	12
SCARBOROUGH			
Colesium	Famous Players.	602,575	12
Commons	AMC		20
401 & Morningside	Cineplex Odeon		11
Town Centre	Cineplex Odeon		16
SIMCOE			
Premier Cinemas	Strand Theatre, Inc.		2
SIOUX LOOKOUT			
Mayfair	572604 Ontario, Inc.	5,183	1
SMITHS FALLS			
Premier	Premier Operating Corp., Ltd.	8,777	2
ST. CATHARINES			
Studio	Empire Theatres, Ltd.	131,989	8
Town Discount			2
ST. THOMAS			
Galaxy	.	36,110	6
STONEY CREEK			
Silver City Hamilton Mt.	Famous Players	60,000	10
STRATFORD			
Stratford Cinemas	Stratford Amusement, Inc.	30,461	5
SUDBURY			
Science North IMAX Theatre	Science North		1
Silver City	Cineplex Entertainment, LP		12
Rainbow	Magic Lantern Theatres		5
THORNHILL			
Rainbow Promenade	Magic Lantern Theatres		6
THUNDER BAY			
Cumberland	May Theatres (1984), Inc	109,140	5

Theatre Name	Licensee/Owner	Population	Screens
Northland			8
Silver City 1	Cineplex Entertainment, LP		12
TILLSONBURG			
Broadway Cinemas	Tillsonburg Broadway Cinemas, Inc.	14,822	3
TIMMINS			
Cinema Six	Stinson Theatres, Ltd.	42,997	6
TORONTO			
Albion Cinemas	Golden Theatres, Ltd.	5,113,149	6
Beach Cinemas	Alliance Cinemas		6
Bloor	P. Bordonaro		1
Canada Square	Cineplex Entertainment, LP		8
Carlton	Cineplex Entertainment, LP		9
Coliseum Scarborough	Cineplex Entertainment, LP		12
Cumberland	Cineplex Entertainment, LP		4
Eglinton Town Centre	Cineplex Entertainment, LP		16
Empire Empress Walk	Empire Theatres, Ltd.		10
Fairview Mall	Famous Players		6
Fox	Festival Cinemas		1
Grande @ Sheppard	Cineplex Entertainment, LP		10
Harbourfront Studio	Harbourfront Corp.		1
Interchange	AMC Theatres Canada, Inc.		30
Kennedy Commons	AMC Theatres Canada, Inc.		20
Market Square	Rainbow Cinemas		6
Morningside	Cineplex Entertainment, LP		11
Mt. Pleasant	P. Sorok & P. Stasiuk		1
Ontario Place IMAX	Ontario Place		1
Ontario Science Centre IMAX	Ontario Science Centre		1
Queensway	Cineplex Entertainment, LP		18
Rainbow Fairview	Magic Lantern Theatres		6
Rainbow Market Square	Magic Lantern Theatres		6
Rainbow Woodbine	Magic Lantern Theatres		8
Regent	Festival Cinemas		1
Royal Cinema			2
Scotia Bank Theatre	Cineplex Entertainment, LP		13
Scotia Bank Theatre IMAX 1 2D	Cineplex Entertainment, LP		1
Scotia Bank Theatre IMAX 2	Cineplex Entertainment, LP		
Sheppard Grande	Cineplex Odeon		10
Silver City Yonge & Eglinton	Cineplex Entertainment, LP		9
Silver City Yorkdale	Cineplex Entertainment, LP		10
Trenton Centre	Fratelli Theatres, Inc.		3
Varsity	Cineplex Entertainment, LP		12
Woodbine	Rainbow Cinemas		8
Woodside	Golden Theatres, Ltd.		3
Yonge & Dundas	AMC		24
Yonge-Eglinton Centre	Famous Players		9
Yorkdale	Famous Players		10
UXBRIDGE			
Roxy	Alecait Holdings, Inc.	19,169	2
VAUGHAN			
Colossus Woodbridge 1	Famous Players	238,866	17
Colossus Woodbridge IMAX	Cineplex Entertainment, LP		1
WATERLOO			
Galaxy Waterloo	Cineplex Entertainment, LP	97,475	10
Princess	The Princess Cinema, Inc.		1
Princess Twin	The Princess Cinema, Inc		3
WELLAND			
Seaway	Cineplex Entertainment, LP	50,331	7
WHITBY			
Whitby	AMC Theatres Canada, Inc.	111,184	24
WINDSOR			
Devonshire Mall	Cineplex odeon	216,473	12
Silver City	Famous Players		12
Forest Glade	Forest Glade Cinemas		3
Palace	.		4
Silver City	Cineplex Entertainment, LP		12
WINGHAM			
Lyceum	Dale Edger		1
WOODSTOCK			
Gallery	Gallery Cinemas (Woodstock), Inc.	35,480	7

PRINCE EDWARD ISLAND

Theatre Name	Licensee/Owner	Population	Screens
CHARLOTTETOWN			
City Cinema	Derek Martin	32,174	1
Studio	Empire Theatres, Ltd.		8
SUMMERSIDE			
Studio	Empire Theatres, Ltd.	14,500	5

QUÉBEC

Theatre Name	Licensee/Owner	Population	Screens
ALMA			
Complexe Alma	Ghislain Dubois	29,998	4
AMOS			
Cinéma Amos	Denis Bédard	12,584	3
AMQUI			
Cinéma Figaro	Richard Paradis	6,261	3
BAIE-COMEAU			
Cine Centre		22,554	4
BELOEIL			
Cinema Beloeil		20,000	10
BOUCHERVILLE			
Boucherville	Jean Colbert/Cinéplex Div., LP	39,062	10
Cine Parc Odeon	Cineplex Odeon		2
BROSSARD			
Cinéma Brossard	Cinéplex Odeon	71,154	16
CAP-AUX-MEULES			
Cinema Cyrco	Bernard Cyr	2,078	3
CAP-DE MADELINE			
Cinema du Cap		33,022	3
CHANDLER			
Paradiso	Louis Roy	7,914	3
CHÂTEAUGUAY			
Carnaval	Shiraz Tajdin	42,786	6
Chateauguay Encore	Cinéplex Divertissement, LP		5
CHICOUTIMI			
Odyssee		59,764	8
CÔTE-SAINT-LUC			
Cavendish	Cinémas Fortune	31,395	8
COWANSVILLE			
Princesse	Réjean Daigle	12,182	1
DELSON			
Delson	Cinéplex Divertissement, LP	7,322	7
Deux-Montages	Cinémas Guzzo		14
DOLLARD-DES ORMEAUX			
Des Sources 10	Cinémas Guzzo	48,930	10
DORIAN			
Carrefour Dorion	Cinéplex Divertissement, LP		8
DRUMMONDVILLE			
Capitol	Marcel Venne	67,392	8
Cinéma RGFM	Marcel Venne		6
GASPÉ			
Cinéma Baker	Pascal Dennis	14,819	1
GATINEAU			
Cinéma 9 Gatineau	Didier Farré	242,124	9
Cine-Starz			4
Galeries Aylmer	Denis Bedard		6
StarCité	Cinémas Fortune		16
Theatre IMAX	Canadian Museum		1
GRANBY			
Cinéma Elysée	Ciné-Enterprise	59,385	8
GRENVILLE			
Cinema Mega Plex		2,172	18
Laurentien	Yvon Myner		2
JOLIETTE			
Carrefour Joliette	Marcel Venne	19,044	10
KIRKLAND			
Colisée	Famous Players	20,491	12
LACHENAIE			
Triomphe	Ciné-Entreprise		10
LAC-MÉGANTIC			
Mégantic	Bernard Fortier	5,967	2
LA MALBAIE			
La Malbaie	Ciné-Quilles D.L., Inc.	8,959	1
LA POCATIÈRE			
Le Scénario	Marie Josée D'Anjou	4,575	4
LA SARRE			
Cinema La Sarre	Dénis Bedard	7,336	1
LA TUQUE			
Complexe culturel Felix-Leclerc	La Tuque Arts Corp.	11,821	1

Theatre Name	Licensee/Owner	Population	Screens
LAVAL			
Cinema Tops	Antonio Accurso	368,709	8
Colossus	Cinéplex Odeon		18
Mega-plex Pont-Viau	Cinémas Guzzo		16
Parc Laval	Cineplex Odeon		6
LÉVIS			
Cinema des Chutes	André Gilbert	130,006	8
Lido	André Gilbert		9
LONGUEUIL			
Mega-Plex Jacques-Cartier	Cinémas Guzzo	229,330	14
LOUISEVILLE			
Pixel	Robert Binette	7,433	3
MACAMIC			
Cinemak	Dénis Bedard	2,726	1
MAGOG			
Magog	Ginette Pradella	23,880	3
MANIWAKI			
Merlin	Anne Jolivette	4,102	1
MATANE			
Gaiété	Jacques Desjardins	14,742	2
MISTASSINI			
Chaplin II		4,000	4
MONT-LAURIER			
Laurier	Nicolas Lefebvre	13,405	2
MONT-TREMBLANT			
Pine	Tom Fermanian	8,892	2
MONTMAGNY			
Lafontaine	Guy Couillard	11,353	1
MONTRÉAL			
Carrefour Angrigon	Cinémas Fortune	3,635,571	10
Cinéma Banque Scotia			13
Cinéma Beaubien	Corp. de développement le Dauphin		3
Cinéma Impérial	Centre Cinéma Impérial		1
Cinéma ONF	National Film Board		1
Côte de Neiges	Cinémas Fortune		7
Dollar Cinema	Bernie Guregerg		2
Du Parc	Roland Smith		3
Ex-Centris	Daniel Langlois		3
Langelier	Cinémas Guzzo		6
Le Forum	AMC Entertainment, Inc.		22
La Salle			12
Mega-Plex Lacordaire	Cinémas Guzzo		16
Mega-Plex Marché Central	Cinémas Guzzo		18
Mega-Plex Spheretech	Cinémas Guzzo		14
Paradis	Cinémas Guzzo		3
Paramount	Cinéplex Divertissement, LP		12
Paramount IMAX	Cinéplex Divertissement, LP		1
Parallele			4
Place Lasalle	Cinéplex Divertissement, LP		12
Quartier Latin	Cinéplex Divertissement, LP		17
St-Leonard	Dominic Piccolo		4
Star Cité	Cinéplex Divertissement, LP		17
Terrebonne 14			14
NEW CARLISLE			
Royal	Louis Roy	1,370	1
ORFORD			
Ciné-Orford		2,979	2
QUÉBEC CITY			
Beauport	Cinéplex Divertissement, LP	491,142	16
Cinéma Cartier	Martin Brandl		1
Galeries de la Capitale	Cinémas Fortune		12
Place Charest	Cinéplex Divertissement, LP		8
Sainte-Foy	Cinéplex Divertissement, LP		14
REPENTIGNY			
Plaza Repentigny	Ciné-Entreprise	76,237	6
RIMOUSKI			
Lido	Aldéric Racine	42,240	8
RIVIÈRE-DU-LOUP			
Princesse	Guy Simard	18,586	2
ROBERVAL			
Chaplin	Hugues Morin	10,544	3
ROCK FOREST			
Sherbrooke	Galaxy Cinemas	20,693	12
ROUYN-NORANDA			
Paramount	Pierre Gaudreault	39,924	6

Theatre Name	Licensee/Owner	Population	Screens
SAGUENAY			
Jonquière	Ciné Entreprise	143,692	8
SAINT-ANDRÉ-AVELLIN			
Quatre Soeurs	Yvan Tanguay	3,435	4
SAINT-BRUNO DE-MONTARVILLE			
Saint-Bruno 1	Cinéplex Divertissement, LP	24,388	11
SAINT-EUSTACHE			
Cine-Parc		42,062	5
Saint-Eustache	Brigitte Mathers		15
SAINT-FÉLCIEN			
Zoo Sauvage	Guy Bolduc	10,477	2
SAINT-GEORGES-DE-BEAUCE			
Centre-Ville	Michel Busque	29,616	6
SAINT HYACINTHE			
Galeries Saint-Hyacinthe	Jean Colbert	51,616	8
SAINT-JEAN-SUR-RICHELIEU			
BFC Saint-Jean	Denyse Dumont	87,492	1
Le Capitol	Cinéplex Divertissement, LP		6
SAINT-JÉRÔME			
Carrefour du Nord	Guy Gagnon	63,729	8
SAINT-PÂCOME¶			
Louise	Alain Chamberland	2,704	2
SAINT RAYMOND			
Alouette	Nady Moisan	9,273	2
SAINTE-ADÈLE			
Cinéma Pine	Tom Fermanian	10,634	8
SAINTE-ANNE-DES-MONTS			
Haute Gaspésie	Jean-Paul Gaumond	6,772	1
SAINTE-MARIE -DE-BEAUCE			
Lumiere	Michel Busque	11,584	5
SAINTE-THÉRÈSE			
Plaza Sainte-Thérèse	Cinémas Guzzo	25,224	8
SALABERRY DE-VALLEYFIELD			
Le Paris	Jacques Patry	39,672	8
SEPT-ILES			
Ciné-Centre Vidéo	Réjean Guy	25,514	3
SHAWINIGAN			
Biermans	Claude Bellerive	51,904	8
SHERBROOKE			
La Maison du cinema	Jacques Foisy	147,427	10
SOREL-TRACY			
Saint-Laurent	Marcel Venne	34,076	7
TERREBONNE			
Megaplex Terrebonne	Cinémas Guzzo	94,703	14
THETFORD MINES			
Pigalle	Julie Bernier	25,704	3
TROIS-PISTOLES			
CinéPlus	Jacquelin Théberge	3,500	1
TROIS-RIVIÈRES			
Fleur de Lys	Cinéplex Divertissement, LP	126,323	9
VAL D'OR			
Capitol	Louiselle Blais	31,123	5
VICTORIAVILLE			
Galaxy Victoriaville	Cinéplex Divertissement, LP	40,486	7
Laurier	Robert Carrier		4
VILLE-MARIE			
Ville-Marie	Denis Bédard	2,696	1

SASKATCHEWAN

Theatre Name	Licensee/Owner	Population	Screens
ARCOLA			
MacMurray Theatre	Danny Showers	504	1
ASSINIBOIA			
Olympia		2,305	1
BIGGAR			
Majestic	Town of Biggar	2,305	1
CARLYLE			
Cornerstone	Community Theatre Assoc.	1,257	1
CUT KNIFE			
Elks Theatre	Community Theatre Assoc.	532	1

Theatre Name	Licensee/Owner	Population	Screens
ESTERHAZY			
Maple Leaf	Kevin Jones	2,336	1
ESTEVAN			
Orpheum	J. Dougherty	10,084	1
GRAVELBOURG			
Gaiety	W. Laberge	1,089	1
HUDSON BAY			
Community Theatre	Town of Hudson Bay	1,646	1
INDIAN HEAD			
Nitehawk	G & H Stewart Holdings	1,634	1
KINDERSLEY			
Capitol	Magic Lantern Theatres	4,412	1
LLOYDMINSTER			
May Cinema Centre	May Theatres, Inc. (1984)	24,028	6
MAPLE CREEK			
Cypress		2,198	
MEADOW LAKE			
Dynasty Twin	Dynasty Theatres	4,771	2
MELFORT			
Dynasty Twin	Dynasty Theatres	5,192	2
MELVILLE			
Melville Theatre	F. Cox	4,149	1
MOOSE JAW			
Capitol 3		32,132	3
Galaxy Moosejaw	Cineplex Entertainment, LP		6
MOOSOMIN			
Community Theatre	B. Fisch	2,257	1
NIPAWIN			
Roxy	D. McGirr	4,061	1
NORTH BATTLEFORD			
Capitol	Dynasty Theatres	13,190	1
Frontier Twin Cinema	Dynasty Theatres		2
PORCUPINE PLAIN			
Community Theatre	Town of Porcupine Plains	783	1
PRINCE ALBERT			
Galaxy Prince Albert	Cineplex Entertainment, LP	34,138	6
REGINA			
Galaxy Regina	Cineplex Entertainment, LP	179,246	10
Golden Mile			9
IMAX	Saskatchewan Science Centre		1
Rainbow	Magic Lantern Theatres		8
RPL Film Theatre	Regina Public Library		1
Paradise			2
Sask. Centre of the Arts	Sask. Centre of the Arts Bd.		
Southland Mall	Cineplex Entertainment, LP		10
ROCKGLEN			
Dreamland	T. Pyle	366	1
SASKATOON			
Broadway	Friends of the Broadway	202,340	1
Capitol	Empire Theatre, Ltd.		4
Galaxy Cinemas	Cineplex Entertainment, LP		12
Odeon Centre	Cineplex Entertainment, LP		7
Rainbow 8	Magic Lantern Theatres		8
Roxy	Magic Lantern Theatres		2
SHAUNAVON			
Plaza Theatre	H. Goldstein	1,691	
SWIFT CURRENT			
Cinemas 1 & 2	Kathy Pratt	14,946	2
TISDALE			
Falkon	D. Falkner	2,981	1
VAL MARIE			
Palais Royale	Town of Val Marie	137	
WASKESIU			
Twin Pine (Seasonal)	M. Weinrauch		2
WATSON			
Towne	M. Weinrauch	719	
WEYBURN			
Soo Theatre	Landmark Cinemas	9,433	1
YORKTON			
Tower Theatre	Landmark Cinemas	15,038	1

YUKON

Theatre Name	Licensee/Owner	Population	Screens
WHITEHORSE			
Glacier Cinemas		20,461	5
Qwanlin Centre	Landmark Cinemas		2
Yukon Cinema Centre	Landmark Cinemas		2

Drive-In Cinemas

Drive-ins are listed by province, then by the cities within each province. Listings include the drive-in name, the licensee/owner, the city's population, and the capacity.

Theatre Name	Licensee/Owner	Population	Cars
ALBERTA			
EDMONTON			
Stardust Twin		730,372	
REDLIFF			
Gemini		5,096	
BRITISH COLUMBIA			
CRESTON			
Valley	Gerald Chugg	4,826	323
ENDERBY			
Starlite		2,828	
KAMLOOPS			
Kamloops		86,376	
PRINCE GEORGE			
Park		83,349	
SURREY			
Hillcrest		470,000	
MANITOBA			
FLIN FLON			
Big Island	B. & M. Liefe	5,594	250
KILLARNEY			
Shamrock		3,299	996
MORDEN			
Stardust		6,571	200
WINNIPEG			
Cineplex Odeon	Cineplex Odeon	633,451	996
NEW BRUNSWICK			
BERESFORD			
Bayview	J.C. Mourant	12,924	400
BOIS-BLANC			
Satellite	Paul Marcel Albert	1,785	400
HAUT LAMEQUE			
Cineparc Venus	Paul Marcel Albert	1,580	300
SHEDIAC			
Neptune	Sheila LeBlanc	4,292	400
SUSSEX			
Sussex	Sussex Drive In Theatre, Ltd.	2,560	300
NOVA SCOTIA			
CAMBRIDGE STATION			
Cape Breton		656	300
SYDNEY			
Cape Breton	J. Sifnakis	76,575	300
WESTVILLE			
Empire	Empire Theatres, Ltd.	3,879	504
ONTARIO			
BARRIE			
Barrie Triple 1	Stinson Theatres, Ltd.	128,430	475
Barrie Triple 2	Stinson Theatres, Ltd.		340
Barrie Triple 3	Stinson Theatres, Ltd.		300
ELMVALE			
Elmvale		8,195	250
FONTHILL			
Can-View		16,155	

Theatre Name	Licensee/Owner	Population	Cars
GRAND BEND			
Starlite	766280 Ontario, Ltd.	2,000	
GRAVENHURST			
Muskoka D.I.	Muskoka D.I. Theatres, Ltd.		300
GUELPH			
Mustang	John Dadetta	114,943	
HAMILTON			
Starlite 1-2-3	Premier Operating Corp., Ltd.	504,559	
HANOVER			
Hanover	J.D. Lyons Corp.	7,147	300
KINGSTON			
Family Fun World (3 screens)	Dan Wanemacher	117,207	600
LINDSAY			
Lindsay Twin (2 screens)	Larry Baxter	67,926	
LONDON			
Mustang 1	Premier Operating Corp., Ltd.	352,395	
Mustang 2	Premier Operating Corp., Ltd.		806
MIDLAND			
Midland	Port Bolster Drive-In Theatres	16,300	400
OAKVILLE			
Five Twin 1	Premier Operating Corp., Ltd.	165,613	
Five Twin 2	Premier Operating Corp., Ltd.		
Five Twin 3	Premier Operating Corp., Ltd.		943
OWEN SOUND			
Twin 1	Stinson Theatres, Ltd.	21,753	416
Twin 2	Stinson Theatres, Ltd.		300
PEMBROKE			
Skylight	Matt McLaughlin Motors	13,930	200
PETERBOROUGH			
Mustang	Geraldo Parente	74,898	
PORT HOPE			
Port Hope D.I.	Century Theatre Services	16,390	346
SHARON			
North York (3 screens)	N. York DI Theatre, Ltd.	20,555	900
THOROLD			
Can-View 1	Babcock Theatres		420
Can-View 2	Babcock Theatres		595
Can-View 3	Babcock Theatres		574
Can-View 4	Babcock Theatres		462
TORONTO			
The Docks	Docks Entertainment	5,113,149	408
WOODSTOCK			
Oxford	Dave Babcock	35,480	200
PRINCE EDWARD ISLAND			
ALBERTON			
Princess Pat	Anna White	1,115	500
CHARLOTTETOWN			
Brackley Beach	Linda & George Boyle	32,174	500
QUÉBEC			
BOUCHERVILLE			
Odeon 1	Cinéplex Divertissement, LP	39,062	988
Odeon 2	Cinéplex Divertissement, LP		990
DRUMMONDVILLE			
Drummond 1	Marcel Venne	67,392	480
Drummond 2	Marcel Venne		450
GRANDE-RIVIÈRE			
René François	Louis Roy	3,409	325
JOLIETTE			
Joliette 1	Marcel Venne	19,044	530
Joliette 2	Marcel Venne		405

Theatre Name	Licensee/Owner	Population	Seats
Joliette 3	Marcel Venne		287
LÉVIS			
Ciné-Parc Saint-Nicholas 1	Cinéplex Odeon	130,006	698
Ciné-Parc Saint-Nicholas 2	Cinéplex Odeon		550
MASSON-ANGERS			
Templeton 1	Paul Touchet	11,066	230
Templeton 2	Paul Touchet		300
ORFORD			
Orford 1	André Monette	1,153	560
Orford 2	André Monette		500
RIMOUSKI			
Rimouski 1	Claude Pearson	42,240	400
Rimouski 2	Claude Pearson		225
RIVIÈRE-AU RENAUD			
Cartier	Guy & Yves Côté		390
SAINT-EUSTACHE			
Saint-Eustache 1	Brigitte Mathers	42,062	1,050
Saint-Eustache 2	Brigitte Mathers		850
Saint-Eustache 3	Brigitte Mathers		350
Saint-Eustache 4	Brigitte Mathers		550
Saint-Eustache 5	Brigitte Mathers		500
SAINT-GEORGES -DE-BEAUCE			
Saint-Georges 1	Richard Busque	29,616	250
Saint-Georges 2	Richard Busque		175
SAINT-HILAIRE			
Saint-Hilaire 1	André Monette		750
Saint-Hilaire 2	André Monette		550
SEPT-ILES			
Des Iles	Yvan Beaulieu	25,514	800
TROIS-RIVIÈRES			
Trois Rivières 1	Ciné-Entreprise	126,323	750
Trois Rivières 2	Ciné-Entreprise		650

SASKATCHEWAN

Theatre Name	Licensee/Owner	Population	Seats
CARLYLE			
Prairie Dog Park	Ray Boutin	1,257	
KYLE			
Clear Water	Ken Kelk		304
PRINCE ALBERT			
Pine	Wm. Mahon	34,138	
SASKATOON			
Sundown 1 & 2	D. Besenski	202,340	
WATROUS			
Jubilee	B. Crawford	1,808	200
WOLSLEY			
Twilight			20

STUDIOS

ALBERTA

CFB STUDIO CENTRE
136 – 2950 Hochwald Ave. SW, Calgary, AB T3E 7H5.
TEL: (403) 246-6476. FAX: (403) 246-4641.
CONTACT
Peggy Telfer - ptelfer@arcturusrealty.com

50,000 sq. ft. studio / former military base on more than 200 acres / office space / construction area / pool.

FILM ALBERTA STUDIOS
5305 Allard Way, Edmonton, AB T6H 5X8.
TEL: (780) 431-8925. FAX: (780) 438-8535.
www.filmalberta.com
CONTACT
Sam Osman - (780) 777-7777

15,000 sq. ft. sound stage / support facilities.

BRITISH COLUMBIA

AJA TAN STUDIOS
1600 E. Railway St., N. Vancouver, BC V7J 1B5.
TEL: (604) 980-8363. email: ajatan@axion.net
www.ajatan.com
CONTACT
Randy Tan

Two stages — Soundstage 1: 6,000 sq. ft.; Soundstage 2: 5,000 sq. ft. / 75,000 sq. ft. New York street backlot / standing loft residence set / standing restaurant set / construction & support facilities / 8,000 sq. ft. furnished office space.

THE BRIDGE STUDIOS
2400 Boundary Rd., Burnaby, BC V5M 3Z3.
TEL: (604) 482-2000. FAX: (604) 482-2007.
email: info@bridgestudios.com www.bridgestudios.com
CONTACT
Ron Hrynuik

Effects stage over an acre in size / six soundstages on 15 acres / production offices / wardrobe / props / mill & workshop.

CANADIAN MOTION PICTURE PARK STUDIOS
8085 Glenwood Dr., Burnaby, BC V3N 5C8. TEL: (604) 435-2000.
FAX: (604) 433-1405. www.cmppstudios.com
CONTACT
Wolf Isachsen - wolfisachsen@hotmail.com

State-of-the-art purpose-built motion picture park facility offering four stages.

Stage 1: 21,200 sq. ft. Stage 2: 17,000 sq. ft. Stage 3: 17,000 sq. ft. Stage 4: 9,000 sq. ft. with 41 ft. trusses, 17,000 sq. ft. offices and amenities.

CANADIAN MOTION PICTURE PARK 2:
State-of-the-art purpose-built stages.
Stage 5: 22,000 sq. ft. Stage 6: 22,750 sq. ft. with 41 ft. trusses. Special effects stage: 5,000 & 6,000 sq. ft.
Office / wardrobe / amenities / 3 floors, 40,000 sq. ft.

CBC STUDIOS
700 Hamilton St., Vancouver, BC V6B 4A2.
TEL: (604) 662-6274. FAX: (604) 662-6414.
www.cbc.ca/tvfacilities/van
CONTACT
John Baxter - john_baxter@cbc.ca

Studio 40 — 5,700 sq. ft. with 45' clear span with flying grid system / Studio 41 — 4,000 sq. ft. / Studio 44 — 1,300 sq. ft. / green rooms / dressing rooms / makeup / production office space / downtown location.

EAGLE CREEK STUDIOS
4210 Phillips Ave., Unit 8, Burnaby, BC V5A 2X2.
TEL: (604) 788-2229. FAX: (604) 291-0785.
email: info@eaglecreekstudios.com
www.eaglecreekstudios.com
CONTACT
John Lee

58,000 sq. ft. studio / clear span areas with 41' ceilings / 3,000 sq. ft. office space / 5-acre site.

FIRST LIGHT FILM STUDIO
3738 Keith St., Burnaby, BC V5J 5B5.
TEL: (604) 438-9312. FAX: (604) 438-9320.
email: firstlightstudios@telus.net www.firstlightstudios.ca
CONTACT
Lisa Ploss

Soundproof 13,660 sq. ft. sound stage / production office / locking set dec / props storage area / security systems / loading docks / parking / wireless & ethernet ports.

MAMMOTH STUDIOS
c/o North Shore Studios, 555 Brooksbank Ave, N. Vancouver, BC V7J 3S5. TEL: (604) 983-5555. FAX: (604) 983-5554.
www.mammothstudios.ca
CONTACT
Peter Leitch - peterl@nsstudios.ca
Paul Clausen - paulc@nsstudios.ca

Stage 1 — 91,957 sq. ft., 40' clear span / Stage 2 — 123,883 sq. ft., 40' clear span / Stage 3 — 36,487 sq. ft., 25' clear span / 43,000 sq. ft. office space / 36,753 sq. ft. storage space / ample parking.

MJA STUDIO
4961 Byrne Rd., Burnaby, BC V5J 3H6. TEL: (604) 433-1400.
www.mjastudios.com
CONTACT
Wolf Isachsen - wolfisachsen@hotmail.com

Purpose-built acoustically designed 17,000 sq. ft. sound stage has laser level floors / air exchange system / 7,500 sq. ft. of office / commercial kitchen / talent rooms.

NORTH SHORE STUDIOS
555 Brooksbank Ave., N. Vancouver, BC V7J 3S5.
TEL: (604) 983-5555. FAX: (604) 983-5554.
www.nsstudios.ca
CONTACT
Peter Leitch - peterl@nsstudios.ca
Paul Clausen - paulc@nsstudios.ca

Eight sound stages / long-term & temporary offices / mills & support services.

PACIFIC NATIONAL EXHIBITION (PNE)
2901 E. Hastings St., Vancouver, BC V5K 5J1.
TEL: (604) 252-3534. FAX: (604) 251-7761.
email: filming@pne.ca www.pne.ca
CONTACT
Stephanie Lee

Forum building: 44,579 sq. ft., 40 ft. ceiling (60 ft. peak) / Rollerland building: multipurpose / 19,800 sq. ft., 20 ft. ceiling (27 ft. peak) / rooms available for departments, crews, lunchrooms, lockups / construction facilties on-site / variety of exterior architecture / high-speed wireless Internet / daily, weekly and monthly rates / full package quotes available / on-site parking.

PACIFIC STUDIOS
8165 Glenwood Dr., Burnaby, BC V3N 5C8.
TEL: (604) 433-1400. FAX: (604) 433-1405.
email: wolfisachsen@hotmail.com
CONTACT
Wolf Isachsen

Three-acre back lot next to Canadian Motion Picture Park.

THOMAS STUDIOS
140 Riverside Dr., N. Vancouver, BC V7H 1T9.
TEL: (604) 929-5455, (877) 929-5455.
FAX: (604) 929-6653.
www.thomasfx.com
CONTACT
Betty Thomas - bettythomas@thomasfx.com

5,000 sq. ft. sound stage — acoustic and seismic insulation / 20' x 90' blue and green screens / 20' x 75' corner cove white cyc wall / 1,750 sq. ft. furnished production offices / permanent lighting and flying grid / high-speed Internet / phones / fax / parking / production supply sales & equipment rentals on-site.

VANCOUVER FILM STUDIOS
3500 Cornett Rd., Vancouver, BC V5N 2H5.
TEL: (604) 453-5000. FAX: (604) 453-5045.
email: info@vancouverfilmstudios.com
www.vancouverfilmstudios.com
CONTACT
Kim Alexander, Pete Mitchell

13 sound stages with 40' ceilings / leading-edge technology / mill space / office space / full complement of production support and services / 737 aircraft set / helipad / parking.

MANITOBA

MANITOBA PRODUCTION CENTRE
Winnipeg, MB
TEL: (204) 783-6800. FAX: (204) 944-1390.
email: inquiries@mbccc.ca www.manitobaproductioncentre.ca
CONTACTS
Dennis Perko, Catriona Macfarlane-Davies

15,000 sq. ft, 35' clear-span soundstage / 38,000 sq. ft. building and studio / full airconditioned, furnished production suites air, make-up, dressing rooms / wardrobe / high-speed Internet / 5,000 sq. ft. workshop / 4-plus loading docks / 5-acre fenced compound / ample parking / monitored security.

NEW DAY MINISTRIES, INC.

1111 Chevrier Blvd., Winnipeg, MB R3T 1Y2.
TEL: (204) 949-3333. FAX: (204) 949-3334.
www.newday.org

Two studios available for rent. The smaller studio is 1200 sq. ft. with floor to ceiling blue screen and a 12 ft. high overhead grid. The larger studio is just over 8000 sq. ft. with a 40 ft. x 40 ft. white wall and floor and an 18 ft. power grid. Additional space available for green room, audio room, meeting rooms, lunch room and office space. A commercial kitchen, wireless internet and a sky jack are also available. Parking for 150 vehicles and trailers.

NOVA SCOTIA

ELECTROPOLIS MOTION PICTURE STUDIOS, INC.

5091 Terminal Rd., Halifax NS B3J 3Y1.
TEL: (902) 429-1971. FAX: (902) 429-1471.
www.electropolis-studios.com
CONTACT
Greg MacInnes - greg@electropolis-studios.com

Four Halifax-waterfront studios (2,320 sq. ft. – 11,600 sq. ft.) / Stages 1 & 2 have 60'-plus ceilings / Studio 1 has an 80'x40' green screen / production offices / art department / make-up / wardrobe rooms / actor suites / extra rooms / green room / air conditioning.

TOUR TECH EAST SOUND STAGES

170 Thornhill Dr., Dartmouth, NS B3B 1S3.
TEL: (902) 468-2800. FAX: (902) 468-8833.
www.tourtecheast.com
CONTACT
Lori Laderoute - loril@tourtecheast.com

Studio A — 9,375 sq. ft. / Studio B — 3,750 sq. ft. / open-web steel girders ceiling / hardwall cyc / indoor tractor tailer dock / production offices / full audio & lighting services / support facilities / fenced in backlot for parking.

ONTARIO

BERKELEY STUDIO

3250 Bloor St. W, Toronto, ON M8X 2Y4. TEL: (416) 232-6024.
FAX: (416) 232-3103. www.berkeleystudio.org
STUDIO ADMINISTRATOR
Alison Sutherland - asuther@united-church.ca

Full-service facility / 1,500 sq. ft. studio / green screen.

CBC TORONTO PRODUCTION CENTRE

205 Wellington St. W, Toronto, ON M5V 3G7.
TEL: (416) 205-7580. FAX: (416) 205-2496.
www.cbc.ca/tvfacilities/tor
CONTACT
Michael Leclair - michael_leclair@cbc.ca

Studio 40 — 13,000 sq. ft. / Studio 41 — 11,000 sq. ft. / Studio 42 — 11,000 sq. ft. / Studio 43 — 4,400 sq. ft. / Studio 65 — 4,400 sq. ft. / Studios 40, 42 & 43 (HD) control rooms, digital and HD mobile / full slate of graphic design / video and audio post-production facilities / design office to assist and coordinate design services / project management support.

CENTENNIAL COLLEGE @WALLACE STUDIOS

100 – 258 Wallace Ave., Toronto, ON M6P 3M9.
TEL: (416) 537-3471. FAX: (416) 532-3132.
www.wallacestudios.com
CONTACT
Lillyann Goldstein

Three sound studios — green studio — film / television / video / photography. Car ramps. Inside loading docks — truck & ground level loading, free parking, dressing & make-up rooms, kitchen, portable fridges, cafeteria & conference room. Services include casting facilities, production offices, lighting & grip equipment rentals, set construction, service production, sound recording, catering and more. Location shooting / production offices at 3585 & 3595 St. Clair Ave E and 80 Ward St.

CINESPACE FILM STUDIOS

100 – 30 Booth Ave., Toronto, ON M4M 2M2.
TEL: (416) 406-4000. FAX: (416) 406-4164.
email: mail@cinespace.com www.cinespace.com
CONTACT
Jim Mirkopoulos, Steve Mirkopoulos

Facilities include: 30 Booth Ave: three studios / office suites / art department / wardrobe / set storage / production support facilities.

Kleinberg Studios: two studios — standing "White House" interior sets; Great Hall & Oval Office / offices / support facilities / wooded backlot.

Carlaw Production Centre: two office buildings — production offices / casting / editing suites wardrobe / props storage.

DOWNSVIEW PARK FILM STUDIOS

1 – 35 Carl Hall Rd., Downsview, ON M3K 2B6.
TEL: (416) 952-2160. FAX: (416) 952-2225.
www.downsviewpark.ca
CONTACT
Carol Doerr - cdoerr@pdp.ca

Approximately 600 acres, 30 buildings, seven studios (from 57,503 to 14,091 sq. ft.), most with support space / drive-in door / loading docks / 9-acre fenced tarmac area / 20,000 sq. ft. office space in different locations / air conditioned.

DUFFERIN GATE PRODUCTIONS, INC.

20 Butterick Rd., Toronto, ON M8W 3Z8. TEL: (416) 255-2260.
FAX: (416) 255-7488. email: info@dufferingate.com
www.dufferingate.com
PRESIDENT
Mara Di Pasquale - mdisapasquale@dufferingate.com

EPITOME PICTURES, INC.

220 Bartley Dr., Toronto, ON M4A 1G1. TEL: (416) 752-7627.
FAX: (416) 752-7837. www.epitomepictures.com
CONTACT
Stephanie Cohen - scohen@epitomepictures.com

Studio A — 17,920 sq. ft. / Studio B — 12,352 sq. ft. / Studio C — 20,769 sq. ft. / Studio D (2nd Floor) — 20,769 sq. ft. / 4 interior studios / 1 exterior backlot (urban, residential street) / offices / tutoring room / cast greenroom / extras holding / hair, makeup, dressing rooms / 50-plus parking / truck access / loading dock.

FAREWELL STUDIOS

2869 Thornton Rd., Oshawa, ON L1H 7K4. TEL: (905) 655-3849.
email: film@farewellstudios.com www.farewellstudios.com
CONTACT
Barb Chupa

Studio 1 — 54,000 sq. ft. x 85' high clear span / Studio 2 — 42,000 sq. ft. x 65' high clear span / Studio 3 — 32,000 sq. ft. / Studio 4 — 6,000 sq. ft. 22' high / 6,400 sq. ft. support/office space / 25 acres available for temporary or permanent backlots / security gatehouse / 2 extra large SPFX silos / 3 ponds.

GLOBAL TELEVISION NETWORK

Toronto, ON
TEL: (416) 446-5470. FAX: (416) 446-5372.
CONTACT
Michelle Rich - mrich@globaltv.ca

Studio 1 — 3,500 sq. ft. / Studio 2 — 2,400 sq. ft. / makeup, dressing rooms / craft kitchen / full set construction / carpentry shop / blue and green oleos in Studio 2.

THE MASONIC TEMPLE / AGINCOURT PRODUCTIONS

(CTV, Inc.)
888 Yonge St., Toronto, ON M4W 2J2. TEL: (416) 355-3955.
CONTACT
April McCullough

PYMAN STUDIOS

2196 Dunwin Dr. Mississauga, ON Canada L5L 1C7.
TEL: (905) 828-7171. FAX: (905) 828-7660. www.pyman.com
CONTACT
Paul Siemms - paul@pyman.com

Studio 1 — 6,900 sq. ft. / Studio 2 — 1,000 sq. ft. 16' ceilings; 90' hard cyc; three standing sets; two control rooms; makeup/hair/dressing rooms; 34' digital broadcast mobile.

SHOWLINE LIMITED

915 Lakeshore Blvd. E, Toronto, ON M4M 3L5.
TEL: (416) 778-7379. FAX: (416) 778-7380.
email: showline1@bellnet.ca www.showlinestudios.com
CONTACT
Peter Lukas, Richard Lukas

Film / TV sound studios & production offices.

Showline Harbourside Studios: three studios / fully sounded / ample production & support offices.

Showline Trinity Studios: two stages / support facilities / hard-wall cyc.

STUDIO CITY LIBERTY VILLAGE

1 Pardee Ave., Toronto, ON M6K 3H1. TEL: (416) 532-5100,
(866) 221-5300. FAX: (416) 964-1701.
www.studiocitytoronto.com
CONTACT
Wilf Copeland - wilf@studiocitytoronto.com

Studio 1 — 6,000 sq. ft. / Studio 2 — 2,000 sq. ft. / Studio 3 — 1,000 sq. ft. / wired with phone, Internet in all rooms / fully equipped with power grid / camera lockup / sync sound / air conditioning / make-up, hair, dressing rooms / indoor parking.

SULLIVAN STUDIOS

110 Davenport Rd., Toronto, ON M5R 3R3.
TEL: (416) 921-7177 ext 238. FAX: (416) 750-1985, (416) 921-7538.
PRODUCTION MANAGER
Dan Matthews - dmatthews@sullivan-ent.com

Studio A — 8,160 sq. ft. / Studio B — 2,720 sq. ft. / Studio C — 9,600 sq. ft. / Studio D — 11,000 sq. ft. / backlot with period main street / production offices / wardrobe / art department.

TORONTO FILM STUDIOS

629 Eastern Ave., Toronto, ON M4M 1E4.
TEL: (888) 607-1116, (416) 406-1235. FAX: (416) 406-6964.
www.torontofilmstudios.com
CONTACT
Michael Tough - michael@tfstudios.ca

17 film / TV stages (2,200–40,000 sq. ft.) on a 20-acre lot / Stage 3 standing sets — brownstone and corporate/private jet / Stage 7 standing set — 7-series widebody airplane / six production offices / high-speed Internet / support areas including wardrobe, post-production, set decoration, storage and carpentry shops / stages with air conditioning / cyc walls / lighting grids.

Heward Property Specs: Studio 1 — 10,000 sq. ft. / Studio 2 — 10,000 sq. ft. / 30,000 sq. ft. office space / 30,000 sq. ft. studio support space / broadcast studios / post-production facilities. Studio 2 is occupied by Alliance Atlantis for its specialty channels including HGTV and The Food Network.

TORSTAR MEDIA GROUP TELEVISION

1 Yonge St. 9th Flr., Toronto, ON M5E 1E6.
TEL: (416) 869-4700. FAX: (416) 869-4566.
email: info@tmgtv.ca www.tmgtv.ca
V.P. & GENERAL MANAGER
Mark Goodale
EXECUTIVE PRODUCER
Cindy MacDougall

Full-service video production facility which includes a 3D virtual set studio, digital cameras, AVID edit suites.

QUÉBEC

MEL'S CITÉ DU CINÉMA LOCATIONS MICHEL TRUDEL

1777 Carrie-Derick Technoparc, Montréal, QC H3C 6G2.
TEL: (514) 866-2170. FAX: (514) 866-0909.
www.citeducinema.com
CONTACT
Michel Trudel - michel@micheltrudel.tv
Martin Fontaine - martinf@micheltrudel.tv
Sébastien Moïse - sebastien@micheltrudel.tv

12 stages (1,200 sq. ft. – 36,500 sq. ft.) / all stages are soundproofed / air conditioned / grip and electric equipment / cranes, dolly, generators / backlot / offices, workshops & support.

Melrose Studios (Locations Michel Trudel, St.-Hubert, QC): 6 stages (7,680 sq. ft. – 18,468 sq. ft.) / access to former military location with jail cells, hospital, vintage airplanes and airport control tower / access to adjacent airport runways / SFX services (animatronics, miniatures, pyrotechnics) / paint / carpentry / set construction.

PMT VIDEO

201 – 2600 William Tremblay St., Montréal, QC H1Y 3J2.
TEL: (514) 522-5553. FAX: (514) 522-5971. www.pmt.ca
CONTACT
Isabelle Gratton - isabelle@pmt.ca

One stage (5,000 sq. ft.) / live broadcast facility / edit suite.

SOCIÉTÉ RADIO-CANADA

1400 boul Rene-Levesque, Montréal, QC H2L 2M2.
TEL: (514) 597-6323. FAX: (514) 597-7237.
email: pe_services@radio-canada.ca
www.radio-canada.ca/location

7 studios (4,200 sq. ft - 6,880 sq. ft.) / Studios 42, 44, 48 fully digital / Studio 46 fully HD / Studio 42 over 600 seats / rehearsal studios / production services / set design / prosthetic make-up (special effects).

STUDIOS SAINT-MARTIN

300 – 433 Rue St Martin, Montréal QC H2N 2J4.
TEL: (514) 849-1351. FAX: (514) 849-3350.
CONTACT
Albert Ezerzer - albert@groupedayan.com

Studio A — 8,060 sq. ft. / Studio B — 7,038 sq. ft.

SASKATCHEWAN

CANADA SASKATCHEWAN PRODUCTION STUDIOS

1831 College Ave., Regina, SK S4P 4V5. TEL: (306) 798-9800, (306) 798-3456. FAX: (306) 798-7768. www.saskfilm.com
FINANCE OFFICER, STUDIO OPERATIONS
Joel Barton - joel@saskfilm.com

Specs: (clear-span areas)
Soundstage 1 - 4,080 sq. ft.
Soundstage 2 - 7,000 sq. ft.
Soundstage 3 - 8,640 sq. ft.
Soundstage 4 - 14,850 sq. ft.

Special features: Soundstage 1 — 20' to bottom of grid with wraparound curtains / Soundstages 2, 3, 4 — 40' clear-span ceiling height / state-of-the-art, purpose-built in 2002 / dropped floor in Soundstage 4 (32' x 30' x 9' ft. deep — 67,000-gallon capacity) / fully furnished production offices / carpentry shop with paint booth / art department / set storage area / wardrobes and breakdown room / make-up & hair-dressing rooms / green rooms / camera lockup / lunch room and restaurant / on-site support vendors, including grip, lighting, post-production, etc. / production studio sits within a 2,300-acre lakeside park.
Range: Features, MOWs, TV series, commercials.

Major projects: Tideland, Just Friends, Corner Gas, Tommy Douglas

TÉLÉFILM CANADA

TÉLÉFILM CANADA/HEAD OFFICE / SIÈGE SOCIAL

500 – 360 St. Jacques St., Montréal, QC H2Y 1P5.
TEL: (800) 567-0890, (514) 283-6363. FAX: (514) 283-8212.
www.telefilm.gc.ca

OFFICES IN CANADA / BUREAUX AU CANADA

TORONTO
100 – 474 Bathurst St., Toronto, ON M5T 2S6.
TEL: (800) 463-4607, (416) 973-6436. FAX: (416) 973-8606.

HALIFAX
300 – 1717 Barrington St., Halifax, NS B3J 2A4.
TEL: (800) 565-1773, (902) 426-8425. FAX: (902) 426-4445.

VANCOUVER
410 – 609 Granville St., Vancouver, BC V7Y 1G5.
TEL: (800) 663-7771, (604) 666-1566. FAX: (604) 666-7754.

BOARD OF DIRECTORS / CONSEIL D'ADMINISTRATION

CHAIR OF THE BOARD
Michel Roy (Quebec)
CHAIR OF THE AUDIT AND FINANCE COMMITTEE
Yvon Bélanger (Quebec)
CHAIR OF NOMINATING,EVALUATION & GOVERNANCE
G. Grant Machum (Nova Scotia)
CHAIR OF STRATEGIC PLANNING & COMMUNICATION
Marlie Oden (British Columbia)
VICE CHAIR OF THE BOARD
MEMBER / MEMBRE
Ram Krishna Raju (Ontario) (Ex-officio member)
Tom Perlmutter (Ex-officio member / Membre d'office and Government Film Commissioner / Commissaire du gouvernement à la cinématographie, Montréal)

MANAGEMENT / DIRECTION

EXECUTIVE DIRECTOR
Carolle Brabant
DIRECTOR, COMMUNICATIONS
Denise Arab
DIRECTOR, BUSINESS AFFAIRS & CERTIFICATION
Dave Forget
DIRECTOR, NATIONAL & INTERNATIONAL DEVELOPMENT
Sheila de La Varende
DIRECTOR, PUBLIC AND GOVERNMENT AFFAIRS
Jean-Claude Mahé
DIRECTOR, LEGAL SERVICES & CORPORATE SECRETARY
Stéphane Odesse
INTERIM DIRECTOR, ADMINISTRATION & CORPORATE SERVICES
Denis Pion
DIRECTOR, PROJECTS FINANCING
Michel Pradier
DIRECTOR, QUÉBEC OFFICE
Michel Pradier
DIRECTOR, ATLANTIC REGION OFFICE
Gordon Whittaker
DIRECTOR, WESTERN REGION OFFICE
Earl Hong Tai
DIRECTOR, Ontario and Nunavut Regions
Ralph Holt

ABOUT TELEFILM CANADA

Created in 1967 and reporting to the Department of Canadian Heritage, Telefilm Canada is a federal cultural agency dedicated to the development and promotion of the Canadian audiovisual industry. Telefilm provides financial support to the private sector to create distinctively Canadian productions that appeal to domestic and international audiences.

In 2006-2007, Telefilm managed nearly $400 million in financial resources; $261 million was administered on behalf of the Canadian Television Fund. The resources managed by Telefilm are committed through the Canada Feature Film Fund and the Canada New Media Fund enabling Telefilm to act as key financing, strategic and promotional partner on both the international and national scenes.

Consult the website for additional information concerning regional offices, funds and programs, co-production certification, festivals and markets, catalogs and current developments.

INTERNATIONAL COPRODUCTIONS

International coproductions are a key component of Canadian film and television production. They are a favored method of penetrating new markets and facilitating project financing.

Canadians are quite active in the international coproduction area. They promote quality and demonstrate remarkable energy and understanding of markets, making them sought-after partners.

On behalf of the Canadian government, Telefilm administers official international coproduction agreements. These partnerships enable Canadian producers and their foreign counterparts to pool their creative, artistic, technical and financial resources to coproduce films and television programs that enjoy the status of national productions in each of the countries concerned.

At present, Canadian producers may create joint works with their counterparts in more than 50 countries.

Telefilm Canada is a federal cultural agency dedicated to the development and promotion of the Canadian audiovisual industry. With the objective of building larger audiences for Canadian cultural products, the Corporation acts as a partner to the private sector through investments in diverse productions that speak to Canadians and that resonate with audiences around the world. From screenwriting to international markets, Telefilm provides support for all industry activities.

The Corporation oversees a number of funds and programs, including the Canada Feature Film Fund and the Canada New Media Fund. Telefilm is also the administrator of the Canadian Television Fund.

From promoting Canadian films at major festivals and markets to stimulating new international coproduction partnerships, Telefilm Canada is also an innovative and entrepreneurial player on the worldwide market.

Brigitte Monneau
Director, International Coproductions/Telefilm Canada
360, St-Jacques St., Ste. 500, Montréal, QC H2Y 1P5.
TEL: (514) 283-6363. FAX: (514) 283-8212.
email: infocopro@telefilm.gc.ca www.telefilm.gc.ca

OFFICIAL INTERNATIONAL AUDIO-VISUAL CO-PRODUCTION AGREEMENTS SIGNED WITH CANADA

COUNTRY	MIN. PART	CATEGORIES	TWINNING	DATE OF SIGNATURE
ALGERIA	30%*	Cinema, Television	N/A	Revised 1987.06.19
ARGENTINA	20%	Cinema, Television	N/A	1988.09.22
AUSTRALIA	30%	Cinema, Television	N/A	1990.07.23
AUSTRIA	20%	Cinema, Television	Cinema, Television	1999.06.29
BELGIUM	30%*	Cinema	N/A	1984.02.24
BOSNIA-HERZOGOVINA (see Yugoslavia)	20%	Cinema, Television	N/A	1988.02.11
BULGERIA	20%	Cinema, Television	Cinema, Television	2002.04.25
BRAZIL	20%	Cinema, Television	N/A	1995.01.27
CHILE	20%	Cinema, Television	N/A	1994.09.02
**CHINA	15%	Cinema	N/A	1987.02.23
COLOMBIA	20%	Cinema, Television	Cinema, Television	2002.07.10
CROATIA (see Yugoslavia)	20%	Cinema, Television	N/A	1988.11.20
CUBA	20%	Cinema, Television	N/A	1998.04.27
CZECH REPUBLIC	20%	Cinema, Television	N/A	1987.03.25
DENMARK	20%	Cinema, Television	Cinema, Television	1997.12.15
ESTONIA	20%	Cinema, Television	Cinema, Television	2002.05.27
FINLAND	20%	Cinema, Television	Cinema, Television	1998.03.31
FRANCE	20%*	Cinema	N/A	Revised 1992.09.08
	20%	Television	Television	Revised 1989.02.08
	20%	Cinema mini-treaty	N/A	1983.07.11
	20%	Animation mini-treaty	N/A	1985.01.10
	20%	Television development mini-treaty	N/A	1990.03.14
GERMANY	20%	Cinema, Television	N/A	2004.06.22
GREECE	20%	Cinema, Television	Cinema, Television	1997.12.15
HONG KONG	20%	Cinema, Television	N/A	Revised 2001.02.16
HUNGARY	20%	Cinema, Television	N/A	1987.05.07
ICELAND	20%*	Cinema, Television	Cinema, television	Revised 2003.03.28
IRELAND	20%	Cinema, Television	N/A	1989.04.04
ISRAEL	20%	Cinema	N/A	1985.03.18
ITALY	20%*	Cinema, Television, New Media		Revised 1997.11.13
JAPAN	20%	Cinema, Television	N/A	1994.07.20
LATVIA	20%	Cinema, Television	N/A	2003.10.15
LUXEMBOURG	20%	Cinema, Television	Cinema, Television	1996.03.04
MACEDONIA (see Yugoslavia)	20%	Cinema, Television	N/A	1998.11.02
MALTA	20%	Cinema, Television	N/A	1997.09.23
MEXICO	20%	Cinema, Television	N/A	1991.04.08
MOROCCO	20%	Cinema, Television	N/A	1987.05.04
NETHERLANDS	20%	Cinema, Television	Cinema, Television	1989.10.18
NEW ZEALAND	20%	Cinema, Television	Cinema, Television	Revised 1993.06.17
NORWAY	20%	Cinema, Television	Cinema, Television	1998.04.02
PHILIPPINES	20%	Cinema, Television	Cinema, Television	1998.10.16
POLAND	20%	Cinema, Television	N/A	1996.05.27
** ROMANIA	20%	Cinema, Television	N/A	1992.01.23
RUSSIA (Federation)	20%	Cinema, Television	N/A	1995.10.05
SENEGAL	20%	Cinema, Television	Cinema, Television	2000.09.27
SINGAPORE	20%	Cinema, Television	Cinema, Television	1998.11.13
SLOVAKIA	20%	Cinema, Television	Cinema, Television	Revised 2002.06.05
SLOVENIA (see Yugoslavia)	20%	Cinema, Television	N/A	1988.02.11
SPAIN	20%	Cinema, Television	Cinema, Television	2006.10.10
SOUTH AFRICA	20%*	Cinema, Television	Cinema, Television	1997.11.05
SOUTH KOREA	30%*	Television	Television	1995.04.25
SWEDEN	20%	Cinema, Television	Cinema, Television	1994.10.17
SWITZERLAND	20%	Cinema, Television	N/A	1987.10.22
UNITED KINGDOM AND NORTHERN IRELAND	20%	Cinema, Television	Cinema, Television	Revised 1991.07.05
URUGUAY	20%	Cinema, Television	Cinema, Television	2002.09.10
VENEZUELA	20%	Cinema, Television	Cinema, Television	1996.02.15
FORMER YUGOSLAVIA (including Serbia and Montenegro)	20%	Cinema, Television	N/A	1988.02.11

Further information about agreements, consult: www.telefilm.gc.ca Last update, February 20, 2007.

CANADIAN FUNDING SOURCES

ALBERTA FOUNDATION FOR THE ARTS

10708 105th Ave., Edmonton, AB T5H 0A1.
TEL: (780) 427-9968. www.affta.ab.ca

ALBERTA MULTIMEDIA DEVELOPMENT FUND

Alberta Film, 140 Whitemud Crossing, Edmonton. AB T6J 6L7.
TEL: (888) (780) 422-8584, FAX: (780) 422-8582.
email: connie.armstrong@gov.ab.ca
culture.alberta.ca/filmdevelopment
FILM AND TV INFORMATION OFFICER
Connie Armstrong

ASTRAL MEDIA THE HAROLD GREENBERG FUND / LE FONDS HAROLD GREENBERG

English-Language Program / BCE Place, P.O. Box 787,
100 – 181 Bay St., Toronto, ON M5J 2T3.
TEL: (416) 956-5431. FAX: (416) 956-2018.
email: hgfund@tv.astral.com www.astralmedia.com
PRESIDENT
John Galway
MANAGER, SCRIPT DEVELOPMENT & COMMUNICATIONS
Lila Karim
COORDINATOR, ADMINISTRATION & PROGRAMS SUPPORT
Andrea Langford

FRENCH-LANGUAGE PROGRAM

1000 – 2100 rue Ste-Catherine ouest, Montréal, QC H3H 2T3.
TEL: (514) 939-5094. FAX: (514) 939-6585.
email: info@lefonds.astral.com www.astralmedia.com
PRÉSIDENT DIRECTRICE GÉNERALE
Odile Méthot
COORDONNATRICE, ADMINISTRATION ET PROGRAMME DE FINANCEMENT
Isabelle Touchette

BELL BROADCAST AND NEW MEDIA FUND (BELL FUND) / FONDS DE LA RADIODIFFUSION ET DES NOUVEAUX MEDIAS DE BELL

1709 – 2 Carlton St., Toronto, ON M5B 1J3.
TEL: (416) 977-8154. FAX: (416) 977-0694.
email: bellfund@ipf.ca www.bellfund.ca
EXECUTIVE DIRECTOR
Andra Sheffer

QUÉBEC
503 – 4200 boul St-Laurent, Montréal, QC H2W 2R2.
TEL: (514) 845-4418. FAX: (514) 845-5498.
email: fondsbell@ipf.ca
ASSOCIATE DIRECTOR
Claire Dion

BOARD OF DIRECTORS
Paul Hoffert (Chair), Chris Frank (Vice-Chair and Treasurer), Suzanne Guévremont, Veronica Holmes, Jacques Labelle, Jean Lanoix, Ken Murphy, Catherine Warren, Bart Yabsley

BOOK PUBLISHERS ASSOCIATION OF ALBERTA

10523-100 Avenue, Edmonton, AB T5J 0A8.
TEL: (780) 424-5060. FAX: (780) 424-7943
www.bookpublishers.ab.ca/cigf
EXECUTIVE DIRECTOR
Kieran Leblanc

BRAVO!FACT

(Foundation to Assist Canadian Talent)
299 Queen St. W, Toronto, ON M5V 2Z5. TEL: (416) 384-2738.
FAX: (416) 384-2191. email: bravofact@bravo.ca
www.bravofact.com
EXECUTIVE DIRECTOR
Judy Gladstone

BRITISH COLUMBIA ARTS COUNCIL

P.O. Box 9819 Stn. Prov. Govt., Victoria, BC V8W 9W3.
TEL: (250) 356-1718. FAX: (250) 387-4099.
email: sue.donaldson@gov.bc.ca www.bcartscouncil.ca
COORDINATOR, MUSEUMS, VISUAL ARTS & MEDIA ARTS PROGRAMS
Sue Donaldson - (250) 356-1729

BRITISH COLUMBIA FILM

2225 W. Broadway, Vancouver, BC V6K 2E4.
TEL: (604) 736-7997. FAX: (604) 736-7290.
email: bcf@bcfilm.bc.ca www.bcfilm.bc.ca
EXECUTIVE DIRECTOR
Richard Brownsey
DIRECTOR, TAX CREDIT PROGRAM
Robert Wong - ext 104, bwong@bcfilm.bc.ca
DIRECTOR, DEVELOPMENT INITIATIVES & PARTNERSHIPS
Lodi Butler - ext 119, lbutler@bcfilm.bc.ca

CANADA COUNCIL FOR THE ARTS

Media Arts Section, P.O. Box 1047, 350 Albert St., Ottawa, ON K1P 5V8. TEL: (800) 263-5588, (613) 566-4414,
TTY: (613) 565-5194. FAX: (613) 566-4409.
www.canadacouncil.ca

DIRECTOR & CEO

Robert Sirman

CONTACT
Marie-France Thérien ext 5253

CANADIAN AUDIO-VISUAL CERTIFICATION OFFICE (CAVCO)

Department of Canadian Heritage, 25 Eddy St. 9th Flr. (25-09-0), Gatineau, QC K1A 0M5. TEL: (819) 997-0055.
FAX: (888) 811-0055.
email: info@pch.gc.ca www.canadianheritage.gc.ca/cavco/

CANADIAN FILM CENTRE – FEATURE FILM PROJECT

2489 Bayview Ave., Toronto, ON M2L 1A8.
TEL: (416) 445-1446 ext 268. FAX: (416) 445-9481.
email: ffp@cfccreates.com www.cfccreates.com
DIRECTOR/EXECUTIVE PRODUCER
Slawko Klymkiw
MANAGER
Gillian Stanton
DIRECTOR, SPECIAL PROJECTS
Jane Angel

TELUS INNOVATION FUND

TEL: (416) 445-1446 ext 555. email: telus@cfccreates.com
FUND MANAGER
Gillian Stanton

CANADIAN INDEPENDENT FILM AND VIDEO FUND (CIFVF)

203 – 666 Kirkwood Ave., Ottawa, ON K1Z 5X9.
TEL: (888) 386-5555, (613) 729-1900. FAX: (613) 729-4610.
email: info@cifvf.ca www.cifvf.ca
EXECUTIVE DIRECTOR
Robin Jackson

CANADIAN INTERNATIONAL DEVELOPMENT AGENCY (CIDA)

Mass Media Initiative, 200 Promenade du Portage, Gatineau, QC K1A 0G4. TEL: (800) 230-6349, (819) 997-5456.
FAX: (819) 953-6088. email: mmi_imm@acdi-cida.gc.ca
www.acdi-cida.gc.ca/home
CONTACT
Patricia Dupuis - (819) 953-2922, patricia_dupuis@acdi-cida.gc.ca

CANADIAN TELEVISION FUND

50 Wellington St. E., 4th Flr., Toronto, ON M5E 1C8.
TEL: (877) 975-0766, (416) 214-4400. FAX: (416) 214-4420.
email: ctf@canadiantelevisionfund.ca
www.canadiantelevisionfund.ca
PRESIDENT
Valerie Creighton
DIRECTOR, PROGRAM MANAGEMENT
Nathalie Clermont
DIRECTOR, TELEVISION BUSINESS UNIT, TELEFILM CANADA
Dave Forget

COGECO PROGRAM DEVELOPMENT FUND / FONDS COGECO DE DÉVELOPMENT D'EMISSIONS

(administered by the Independent Production Fund)
1709 – 2 Carlton St., Toronto, ON M5B 1J3.
TEL: (416) 977-8966. FAX: (416) 977-0694.
email: info@ipf.ca www.ipf.ca
EXECUTIVE DIRECTOR
Andra Sheffer
BOARD OF DIRECTORS
Peter Mortimer, Robert Roy

Québec
503 – 4200 boul St-Laurent, Montréal, QC H2W 2R2.
TEL: (514) 845-4334. FAX: (514) 845-5498.
email: fipinfo@ipf.ca
ASSOCIATE DIRECTOR
Claire Dion

CORUS ENTERTAINMENT

(Corus Made With Pay Development Fund)
Movie Central, 640 E. Queens Rd. N., Vancouver, BC V7N 1H3. TEL: (604) 988-1602. FAX: (604) 988-1651.
email: shelley.gillen@corusent.com www.corusent.com/

HEAD, CREATIVE & BUSINESS AFFAIRS, MOVIE CENTRAL
Shelley Gillen

CTV NORTHERN ONTARIO SCRIPT DEVELOPMENT FUND

699 Frood Rd., Sudbury, ON P3C 5A3.
TEL: (705) 674-8301. FAX: (705) 674-2706.
email: mjohnson@ctv.ca
CONTACT
Monique Johnson

CTV OTTAWA SCRIPT DEVELOPMENT FUND

P.O. Box 5813, Merivale Depot, Nepean, ON K2C 3G6.
TEL: (613) 274-4414. FAX: (613) 274-4215.
email: mker@ctv.ca, ctvottawa@ctv.ca
CHAIR
Keith Campbell
ADMINISTRATOR
Maggie Ker

CTV SASKATCHEWAN PROGRAM DEVELOPMENT FUND

216 1st Ave. N., Saskatoon, SK S7K 3W3.
TEL: (306) 665-9291. FAX: (306) 665-0450.
email: dgilbertson@ctv.ca
OPERATIONS MANAGER
Denis Gilbertson

CTV SOUTHWESTERN ONTARIO TELEVISION SCRIPT / PROGRAM DEVELOPMENT FUND

P.O. Box 91026, Stn. C, Kitchener, ON N2G 4E9.
TEL: (800) 265-8950, (519) 578-1313. FAX: (519) 743-8857.
email: dwatson@ctv.ca
V.P., GENERAL MANAGER
Dennis Watson

Script development grants.

DIRECTOR ADVISOR PROGRAM

(Administered by COGECO Program Development Fund)
1709 – 2 Carlton St., Toronto, ON M5B 1J3.
TEL: (416) 977-8966. FAX: (416) 977-0694.
email: info@ipf.ca www.ipf.ca (see Guidelines & Applications)
EXECUTIVE DIRECTOR
Andra Sheffer

FONDS D'INVESTISSEMENT DE LA COULTURE ET DES COMMUNICATIONS (FICC)

900 – 485 rue McGill, Montréal, QC H2Y 2H4.
TEL: (514) 394-0700. FAX: (514) 394-0708.
email: infoweb@ficc.qc.ca www.ficc.qc.ca
CEO
Maurice Prud'homme
INVESTMENT MANAGER
Suzanne Laurencelle, Germain Breton, Gysel Poitras

FOREIGN AFFAIRS CANADA

International Cultural Relations Division, 125 Sussex Dr., Ottawa, ON K1A 0G2. TEL: (613) 992-5359.
email: ernest.labreque@international.gc.ca
www.international.gc.ca/arts
FILM & TELEVISION OFFICER
Ernest Labrèque

PEMD-A — PROGRAM FOR EXPORT MARKET DEVELOPMENT

TEL: (613) 996-1408, (613) 996-7156. FAX: (613) 992-3004.
email: pemd-ta@dfait-maeci.gc.ca
www.dfait-maeci.gc.ca/pemd

INDEPENDENT PRODUCTION FUND / FONDS INDEPENDANTDE PRODUCTION

1709 – 2 Carlton St., Toronto, ON M5B 1J3.
TEL: (416) 977-8966. FAX: (416) 977-0694.
email: info@ipf.ca www.ipf.ca
EXECUTIVE DIRECTOR
Andra Sheffer

Québec
503 – 4200 boul St-Laurent, Montréal, QC H2W 2R2.
TEL: (514) 845-4418. FAX: (514) 845-5498.
email: fipinfo@ipf.ca www.ipf.ca
ASSOCIATE DIRECTOR
Claire Dion

The Board of Directors is composed of seven members representing the industry: Charles Ohayon (President), Roman Melnyk (Vice President), Paul Gratton, Heather McGillivray, Peter Mortimer, Denise Robert, Robert Roy

KICK START

Directors Guild of Canada B.C. District Council
430 – 1152 Mainland St., Vancouver, BC V6B 4X2.
TEL: (604) 688-2976. FAX: (604) 688-2610.
email: communications@dgcbc.com www.dgcbc.com
CONTACT
Sorrel Geddes

LA FINANCIERE DES ENTREPRISES CULTURELLES (FIDEC) / QUÉBEC ENTERTAINMENT INVESTMENT, LP

800 – 215 rue Saint-Jacques, Montréal, QC H2Y 1M6.
TEL: (877) 613-3312, (514) 940-2200. FAX: (514) 940-1528.
email: pleblanc@fidecinvest.com www.fidecinvest.com
GENERAL MANAGER
Pierre Leblanc
FINANCIAL ANALYST
Johanne Meunier - jmeunier@fidecinvest.com

MANITOBA ARTS COUNCIL

525 - 93 Lombard Ave., Winnipeg, MB R3B 3B1.
TEL: (866) 994-2787, (204) 945-2237. FAX: (204)945-5925.
email: info@artscouncil.mb.ca www.artscouncil.mb.ca
(see Visual Arts)
PROGRAM CONSULTANT, VISUAL ARTS/FILM/VIDEO
Marian Butler - (204) 945-0399 mbutler@artscouncil.mb.ca

MANITOBA FILM & SOUND RECORDING DEVELOPMENT CORPORATION

410 – 93 Lombard Ave., Winnipeg, MB R3B 3B1.
TEL: (204) 947-2040. FAX: (204) 956-5261.
email: sebastien@mbfilmsound.mb.ca
www.mbfilmsound.mb.ca
SENIOR ANALYST, FILM, TV & TAX CREDITS
Sebastien Nasse

NEW BRUNSWICK FILM / FILM NOUVEAU-BRUNSWICK

Assumption Place, P.O. Box 5001, 770 Main St., 16th Flr., Moncton, NB E1C 8R3. TEL: (506) 869-6868.
FAX: (506) 869-6840. email: nbfilm@gnb.ca www.nbfilm.com
EXECUTIVE DIRECTOR
Roger Y. Cyr
FINANCIAL SERVICES
Ghislain Labbé
ADMINISTRATIVE ASSISTANT
Bernice LeBlanc
LOCATIONS & MARKETING
Margo Flewelling
TRAINING & DEVELOPMENT
Raynald Couturier
DISTRIBUTION
Antoinette Basque-Doiron
MARKETING
Lori Armstrong

NEWFOUNDLAND AND LABRADOR FILM DEVELOPMENT CORPORATION

12 King's Bridge Rd., St. John's, NL A1C 3K3.
TEL: (877) 738-3456, (709) 738-3456. FAX: (709) 739-1680.
email: info@nlfdc.ca www.nlfdc.ca
EXECUTIVE DIRECTOR
Chris Bonnell - chris@nlfdc.ca
MANAGER OF PROGRAMS
Doug Engbrecht - doug@nlfdc.ca
BUSINESS ANALYST
Catherine Bailey - catherine@nlfdc.ca
PROFESSIONAL DEVELOPMENT ADMINISTRATOR
Dorian Rowe - dorian@nlfdc.ca

NOVA SCOTIA FILM DEVELOPMENT CORPORATION

1724 Granville St., Halifax, NS B3J 1X5. TEL: (902) 424-7177.
FAX: (902) 424-0617. email: novascotia.film@ns.sympatico.ca
www.film.ns.ca
PROGRAM ADMINISTRATOR
Linda Wood - (902) 424-7181
TAX CREDITS
John T. Smith - (902) 424-7177 smithjti@gov.ns.ca

NSI DRAMA PRIZE

National Screen Institute, 400 - 141 Bannatyne Ave., Winnipeg, MB R3B 0R3. TEL: (800) 952-9307, (204) 957-8480.
FAX: (204) 966-5811. email: dramaprize@nsi-canada.ca
www.nsi-canada.ca/dramaprize
PROGRAM MANAGER
Joy Loewen

OMNI TELEVISION FUNDS

545 Lakeshore Blvd. W, Toronto, ON M5V 1A3.
TEL: (888) 260-0047, (416) 260-0047.
www.omnibc.ca/info/funds/
CONTACT
Vicki Giannace

ONTARIO ARTS COUNCIL

151 Bloor St. W. 5th Flr., Toronto, ON M5S 1T6.
TEL: (800) 387-0058, (416) 961-1660. FAX: (416) 961-7796.
email: info@arts.on.ca www.arts.on.ca
ACTING MEDIA & VISUAL ARTS OFFICER
Natalie De Vito - (416) 969-7453 ndevito@arts.on.ca

ONTARIO MEDIA DEVELOPMENT CORPORATION (OMDC)
501 – 175 Bloor St. E. South Tower, Toronto, ON M4W 3R8.
TEL: (416) 314-6858. FAX: (416) 314-6876.
email: mail@omdc.on.ca www.omdc.on.ca
CHAIR
Kevin Shea
CEO
(A): Kristine Murphy
COMMUNICATIONS MANAGER & CORPORATE SECRETARY
George McNeillie
DIRECTOR, TAX CREDITS
Jennifer Blitz
DIRECTOR, INDUSTRY DEVELOPMENT (A) & MANAGER, FILM
Donna Zuchlinski
MANAGER, INDUSTRY INITIATIVES
James Weyman
DIRECTOR, BUSINESS AFFAIRS & RESEARCH (A)
Cherith Muir
MANAGER, RESEARCH & STRATEGIC PLANNING
Raina Wells
COMMUNICATIONS OFFICER
Sharon Wilson - (416) 642-6616 swilson@omdc.on.ca

An agency of the Ministry of Culture. Chief Executive Office: Oversees OMDC's activities and supports and works with the agency's Board of Directors to fulfill the agency's mandate.

QUEBECOR FUND / FONDS QUEBECOR
503 – 1030 rue Cherrier, Montréal, QC H2L 1H9.
TEL: (514) 842-2497. FAX: (514) 524-9192.
email: info@fondsquebecor.ca www.quebecorfund.ca
CONTACT
Serge Thibaudeau, Julie Guénette

Deadlines are April 1 and October 1, annually. Guidelines & applications on the website.

ROGERS CABLE NETWORK FUND
333 Bloor St. E. 9th Flr., Toronto, ON M4W 1G9.
TEL: (416) 935-2526. FAX: (416) 935-2527.
www.rogers.com/english
EXECUTIVE DIRECTOR
Robin Mirsky

ROGERS DOCUMENTARY FUND
333 Bloor St. E 9th Fl., Toronto, ON M4W 1G9.
TEL: (416) 935-2526. FAX: (416) 935-2527.
www.rogers.com/english
EXECUTIVE DIRECTOR
Robin Mirsky

ROGERS TELEFUND
333 Bloor St. E. 9th Fl., Toronto, ON M4W 1G9.
TEL: (416) 935-2526. FAX: (416) 935-2527.
www.rogers.com/english/
EXECUTIVE DIRECTOR
Robin Mirsky

SASKATCHEWAN ARTS BOARD
Saskatoon Office, 417 24th St. E, Saskatoon, SK S7K 0K7.
TEL: (800) 667-7526, (306) 964-1155. FAX: (306) 964-1167.
email: doug@artsboard.sk.ca www.artsboard.sk.ca
VISUAL AND MEDIA ARTS CONSULTANT
Doug Townsend - (306) 964-1163

SASKATCHEWAN FILM AND VIDEO DEVELOPMENT CORPORATION (SASKFILM)
1831 College Ave., Regina, SK S4P 4V5.
TEL: (306) 798-9800. FAX: (306) 798-7768.
email: general@saskfilm.com www.saskfilm.com
CEO/Film Commissioner
Suzanne Bell - bell@saskfilm.com
PROGRAM OFFICER
Karen Henders - kphenders@saskfilm.com
LOCATIONS COORDINATOR
David Gane - locations@saskfilm.com

SHAW ROCKET FUND
900 – 630 3rd Ave., SW, Calgary, AB T2P 4L4.
TEL: (403) 750-4517. FAX: (403) 750-4635.
email: agnes@rocketfund.ca www.rocketfund.ca
EXECUTIVE DIRECTOR
Agnes Augustin

SOCIETE DE DEVELOPPEMENT DES ENTREPRISES CULTURELLES (SODEC)
800 – 215 rue Saint-Jacques, Montréal, QC H2Y 1M6.
TEL: (800) 363-0401, (514) 841-2200. FAX: (514) 841-8606.
email: info@sodec.gouv.qc.ca www.sodec.gouv.qc.ca
GENERAL MANAGER, TAX CREDIT PROGRAMS
Jean-Philippe Normandeau
SUPPORT PROGRAMS
Alain Rondeau

SUN TV FUNDS
25 Ontario St., Toronto, ON M5A 4L6. TEL: (416) 601-0010.
email: derek.luis@suntv.canoe.ca www.suntv.canoe.ca/
EXECUTIVE DIRECTOR, INDEPENDENT PRODUCTION
Derek Luis

TECHNOLOGY PEI
Business Investment – Film, Television and New Media
P.O. Box 340, 94 Euston St., 2nd Flr., Charlottetown, PE C1A 7K7. TEL: (902) 368-5336. FAX: (902) 368-6255, (800) 563-3734. email: ndroberts@gov.pe.ca
www.techpei.com
PROGRAM ANALYST
Nancy Roberts

WOMEN IN MEDIA FOUNDATION, INC. (WIMF)
300 – 136 Market Ave., Winnipeg, MB R3B 0P4.
TEL: (204) 984-7995. FAX: (204) 983-0742.
email: rchahal@wimf.org www.wimf.org
EXECUTIVE DIRECTOR
Rita Chahal

YUKON FILM & SOUND COMMISSION
P.O. Box 2703, Whitehorse, YT Y1A 2C6. TEL: (867) 667-5400.
FAX: (867) 393-7040. email: info@reelyukon.com
www.reelyukon.com
FILM COMMISSIONER
Iris Merritt - iris.merritt@gov.yk.ca

PROFESSIONAL SERVICES

COMPLETION GUARANTORS

FILM FINANCES CANADA, (1998) LTD.
Ste. 310,.2 Berkeley Street, Toronto, ON M5A 4J5.
TEL: (416) 778-6397. FAX: (416) 406-7418.
email: info@filmfinancescanada.com
www.filmfinancescanada.com
PRESIDENT
Jim Sternberg
V.P. POST PRODUCTION
Jill Franklin
V.P. PRODUCTION
Moira Holmes
DIRECTOR, BUSINESS AFFAIRS
Antonietta Presta

Provides completion guarantees and bonds for feature films / television / documentaries / animation / multimedia.

GLOBALEX
600 – 2001 McGill College Ave., Montréal, QC H3A 1G1.
TEL: (514) 382-6674. FAX: (514) 382-1642.
email: info@globalex.com www.globalex.com
OFFICE MANAGER
Jacques L. Brouillette

HKMB INTERNATIONAL INSURANCE BROKERS
International Insurance Brokers/900 – 595 Bay St., Toronto, ON M5G 2E3. TEL: (800) 232-2024, (416) 597-0008.
FAX: (416) 597-2313. email: hkmb@hkmb.com
www.hkmb.com
ACCOUNT MANAGER
Alan Hollingsworth - (416) 597-4628 alan.hollingsworth@hkmb.com

EXECUTIVE RECRUITMENT

SEARCHLIGHT RECRUITMENT, INC.
800 – 2 St. Clair Ave. W, Toronto, ON M4T 2T5.
TEL: (416) 645-3776. FAX: (416) 513-0348.
email: phil@searchlight.com www.searchlightcanada.com
MANAGING PARTNER
Daniel Weinzweig
PRINCIPAL
Philippe Frappier

FINANCIAL SERVICES

BACCHUS ENTERTAINMENT, LTD.
Suite 2000, (c/o Mueller Law Firm), Vancouver, BC V6E 3X2.
TEL: (604) 733 7762. FAX: (604) 677 5724.
film@bacchus-entertainment.com
PRESIDENT
Penny O. Green

Financing of entertainment companies and films.

CANADA FILM CAPITAL
130 Bloor St. W, 5th Flr. Toronto, ON M5S 1N5.
TEL: (416) 923-9255. FAX: (416) 920-9134.
email: dcarter@canadafilmcapital.com
www.canadafilmcapital.com
PRESIDENT
David Carter
CORPORATE COUNSEL
Jennifer Liscio
V.P., OPERATIONS
Sante Cardinale

Administration of the Production Services Tax Credit. Also corporate and legal services, certifications, accounting and tax filings.

CIBC WORLD MARKETS
Commercial Banking, 400 Burrard St., 7th Flr., Vancouver, BC V6C 3A6. TEL: (604) 665-1313. FAX: (604) 482-4657.
email: benjamin.rappaport@cibc.com www.cibc.com
SENIOR MANAGER, ENTERTAINMENT FINANCING
Benjamin Rappaport

Corporate and commercial banking services, interim financing of tax credits, funding program commitments, broadcast licenses and distribution guarantees.

COOKSON WALKER, LLP
Chartered Accountants / 200 University Ave., 14th Flr., Toronto, ON M5H 3C6. TEL: (416) 368-7990. FAX: (416) 368-0886.
email: bcookson@cooksonwalker.on.ca
www.cooksonwalker.com
CONTACT
Eric Walker

Tax credit consulting, finance structuring advice, corporate tax planning and compliance for production companies.

CUSTOM HOUSE
International Trade Centre / 517 Fort St., Victoria, BC V8W 1E7. TEL: (604) 805-4836. email: bclackson@customhouse.com
www.customhouse.com
CONTACT
Brent Clackson

Foreign exchange services (deals in more than 100 currencies); international fund transfers allowing clients to control the impact of exchange rate fluctuations.

DEL M PRODUCTIONS, INC.
315 High Park Ave., Toronto, ON M6P 2S8. TEL: (416) 767-0859.
FAX: (416) 766-3675. email: 315hipk@interlog.com
PRESIDENT
Del Mehes

Filing federal & provincial tax credits & other funding applications.

DGC ENTERTAINMENT VENTURES CORPORATION
600 – 110 Yonge St., Toronto, ON M5C 1T6.
TEL: (416) 365-8002. FAX: (416) 365-8037.
www.dgc.ca
CONTACT
Robert Goodwin

EXPORT DEVELOPMENT CANADA (EDC)
151 O'Connor St., Ottawa, ON K1A 1K3.
TEL: (613) 598-2500, (866) 574-0451. FAX: (613) 237-2690.
email: export@edc.ca www.edc.ca

GLOBAL INCENTIVES INC.
400 - 119 Spadina Ave., Toronto, ON M5V 2L1.
TEL: (416) 595-6300. FAX: (416) 595-7300.
www.globalincentivesinc.com
CONTACT
Laura Polley

GROSVENOR PARK PRODUCTIONS, LTD.
P.O. Box 11, 606 – 1090 Don Mills Rd., Toronto, ON M3C 3R6.
TEL: (416) 926-1815. FAX: (416) 926-9594.
email: copro@grosvenorpark.com www.grosvenorpark.com
Head Office: 1310 Montana Ave., 2nd Flr., Santa Monica, CA 90403. TEL: (310) 752-5450. FAX: (310) 393 7679.
CONTACT
Donald Starr

INDEPENDENT FILM FINANCING, INC.
(Division of Axium Entertainment Services)
The Balfour Building / 304 – 119 Spadina Ave., Toronto, ON M5V 2L1. TEL: (416) 598-3270. FAX: (416) 598-5045.
email: film@iff.ca www.iff.ca
VICE PRESIDENT
Len Pendergast

Gap and interim production financing; co-production consulting; tax credit administration services. The exclusive representative, in Canada, of Comerica Entertainment Group.

KAY & WARBURTON
Chartered Accountants /403 – 225 Richmond St. W, Toronto, ON M5V 1W2. TEL: (416) 977-2416. FAX: (416) 977-8549.
email: richard@kwca.com andrew@kwca.com www.kwca.com
CONTACT
Richard Warburton, Andrew Kay

Specializing in the film industry. Tax credit consulting and filing, corporate and personal tax preparation, planning & production audits.

NATIONAL BANK OF CANADA / BANQUE NATIONALE DU CANADA
TV & Motion Picture Group
Montreal: TEL: (514) 394-5000 ext 5224, (866) 827-3456.
Toronto: TEL: (416) 864-7795, (866) 532-3456.
Vancouver: TEL: (604) 661-5542, (866) 866-7866.
www.nbc.ca/filmandtv

Specializing in the financing of film projects and television series, offering a complete range of made-to-measure banking products and services to the film/television production and distribution industry. In addition to producers and distributors, clientele includes post-production, special effects and equipment leasing companies, as well as studios. Flexible, customized loan and service programs: lines of credit, financing of tax credits and national and international presales, gap financing (with FIDEC support), support for productions destined for international distribution (with FIDEC support).

PAUL SIMMONS MANAGEMENT
174 Bedford Rd., Lower Level, Toronto, ON M5R 2K9.
TEL: (416) 920-1500. FAX: (416) 920-7814.

email: paulsimmons@rogers.com
Business management.

PROTOCOL ENTERTAINMENT, INC.

405 – 80 Spadina Ave., Toronto, ON M5V 2J4.
TEL: (416) 966-2711. FAX: (416) 966.2711.
email: steve@protocolmail.com www.protocolent.com
PRESIDENT & CEO
Steve Levitan

Development, financing, production — television series, movies, mini-series & feature films.

RBC ROYAL BANK

Media & Entertainment Group
TEL: (800) 769-2520
www.rbcroyalbank.com/kbi/me.html (English)
www.rbcbanqueroyal.com/ist/me.html (French).

Halifax
Nan MacDonald - (902) 421-8853 nan.macdonald@rbc.com

Montréal
Annie Baribeau - (514) 874-2552 annie.baribeau@rbc.com

Regina
Lawrence Swann - (306) 780-2503 lawrence.swann@rbc.com

Toronto
Dan McMullen - (416) 974-4680 daniel.mcmullen@rbc.com

Vancouver

John Genzel - (604) 684-5706 john.genzel@rbc.com

Financial services for film, television and digital media producers, distributors, broadcasters, music and industry-related companies. Production, operating and equipment loans; payment and deposit products designed for the entertainment industry. Advice is provided on management of foreign exchange risk arising from foreign presales and co-productions, as well as letters of credit.

RBC CAPITAL MARKETS

Communications, Media & Technology
MANAGING DIRECTOR
Dan Coholan - (416) 842-7544

Private placement of equity and debt, public equity and debt, bank credit and strategic and financial advice.

MOSES FINANCIAL

101 – 40 Holly St., Toronto, ON M4S 3C3.
TEL: (416) 487-6004. FAX: (416) 487-6005.
email: moses@istar.ca
CHARTERED ACCOUNTANT & CERTIFIED FINANCIAL PLANNER
Robert Moses

Strategic financial planning; comprehensive accounting and tax services.

SOBERMAN, LLP

Media Services Group / 1100 – 2 St. Clair Ave. E, Toronto, ON M4T 2T5. TEL: (416) 964-7633. FAX: (416) 964-6454.
email: jkulbak@soberman.com www.soberman.com
CONTACT
Jeff Kulbak - (416) 963 7232
Assists small and mid-sized producers, both domestic and foreign, by leveraging relationships with Canadian government certification and taxation authorities, funding authorities, interim financiers and leading industry professionals.

INSURANCE

AON / RUBEN-WINKLER ENTERTAINMENT INSURANCE BROKERS
20 Bay St., Toronto, ON M5J 2N9. TEL: (416) 868-2460.
FAX: (416) 868-2469. email: darlene.milley@aon.ca www.aon.ca
CONTACT
Darlene Milley - darlene.milley@aon.ca
Susan Wallis - susan.wallis@aon.ca
Leanne Savoie - leanne.savoie@aon.ca

ASSURANCES JOE ANGELONE
201 – 7811 boul Louis-H Lafontaine, Anjou, Montréal, QC
H1K 4E4. TEL: (800) 801-0429, (514) 353-1331.
FAX: (514) 353-5652. email: info@assurancesangelone.com
www.assurancesangelone.com
CONTACT
Anthony Angelone

B.F. LORENZETTI & ASSOCIATES, INC.
1605 – 181 University Ave., Toronto, ON M5H 3M7.
TEL: (800) 668-5901, (416) 599-5530. FAX: (416) 599-5458.
email: films@bflcanada.ca www.bflcanada.ca
CONTACT
David Goldsmith

BFL CANADA INSURANCE SERVICES, INC.
British Columbia Office: 200 – 1177 West Hastings St.,
Vancouver, BC V6E 2K3. TEL: (866) 669-9602,
(604) 669-9600. FAX: (604) 683-9316.
CONTACT
Brenda Mendieta, Mark Skeans

BFL CANADA INSURANCE SERVICES, INC.
Québec Office: 2200 – 2001 av McGill College,
Montréal, QC H3A 1G1. TEL: (800) 465-2842, (514) 843-3632.
FAX: (514) 843-4946.
CONTACT
Joanne Camacho, Guylaine D. Boucher

BELL AND GRANT LIMITED
6380 Lady Hammond Rd., Halifax, NS B3K 2S3.
TEL: (902) 429-4150. FAX: (902) 420-1787.
email: info@bellandgrant.com www.bellandgrant.com
CONTACT
Julie Wamboldt

Comprehensive coverage for the film industry at competitive rates.

CG&B GROUP
120 S. Town Centre Blvd., Markham, ON L6G 1C3.
TEL: (800) 615-4746, (905) 615-8641. FAX: (905) 754-3005.
email: bruce.douglas@cgbgroup.com www.cgbgroup.com
MEDIA
Bruce Douglas - (905) 305-5944

Insurance packages for film & video production companies, post-production services, sound studios, lighting technicians, independent cameramen, still photographers and most other business that provides services to the entertainment industry.

CHUBB INSURANCE COMPANY OF CANADA
One Financial Place, 1 Adelaide St. E, Toronto, ON M5C 2V9.
TEL: (416) 863-0550. FAX: (416) 863-5170.
email: smaceachern@chubb.com
MANAGER, FILM DEPARTMENT
Susan MacEachern

CREIGHTON & COMPANY ENTERTAINMENT INSURANCE SERVICES
315 Matheson Blvd. E, Mississauga, ON L4Z 1X8.
TEL: (905) 890-0090. email: steve@creightoninsurance.com
www.creightoninsurance.com
ENTERTAINMENT RISK CONSULTANT
Steve Beatty

EXPORT DEVELOPMENT CANADA (EDC)
151 O'Connor St., Ottawa, ON K1A 1K3. TEL: (613) 598-2500,
(866) 574-0451. FAX: (613) 237-2690. email: export@edc.ca
www.edc.ca

Export, financing and insurance services for film & TV cos.

FOCUS ENTERTAINMENT INSURANCE BROKERS
604 – 1200 Burrard St., Vancouver, BC V6Z 2C7.
TEL: (866) 690-3456, (604) 684-3456. FAX: (604) 684-3437.
email: david@focusinsurance.ca www.focusinsurance.ca
CONTACT
David W. Hamilton

FRASER & HOYT GROUP
107 – 1505 Barrington St., Halifax, NS B3J 3K5.
TEL: (800) 565-8747, (902) 421-1113. FAX: (902) 422-2040.
www.fraserhoyt.com
CONTACT
Don Sinclair - dsinclair@fraserhoyt.com
Kim Livingston - klivingston@fraserhoyt.com

Complete insurance services to the film and video production industry. Entertainment packages, producer's errors and omissions liability, commercial general liability, D.I.C.E. policies, automobile insurance, completion bonds. Access to worldwide insurance markets.

GLOBALEX
600 – 2001 McGill College Ave., Montréal, QC H3A 1G1.
TEL: (514) 382-6674. FAX: (514) 382-1642.
email: info@globalex.com www.globalex.com
ENTERTAINMENT V.P.
Linda Dubuc - (514) 382-9625 ext 275 ldubuc@globalex.com

More than 25 years of experience insuring the production of motion picture and television productions.

HKMB INTERNATIONAL INSURANCE BROKERS
International Insurance Brokers, 900 – 595 Bay St., Toronto,
ON M5G 2E3. TEL: (800) 232-2024, (416) 597-0008.
FAX: (416) 597-2313. email: hkmb@hkmb.com
www.hkmb.com
ACCOUNT MANAGER
Alan Hollingsworth - (416) 597-4628, alan.hollingsworth@hkmb.com

Full range of services from producer's errors & omissions to traditional insurance to completion bonds.

HOLMAN INSURANCE BROKERS, LTD.
400 – 7050 Woodbine Ave., Markham, ON L3R 4G8.
TEL: (800) 567-1279, (905) 886-5630.
email: service@homanins.com
www.holmanins.com
CONTACT
Paul Holman

Entertainment / production insurance.

THE HULL GROUP
BCE Place Bay Wellington Tower, 4200 – 181 Bay St., Toronto,
ON M5J 2T3. TEL: (416) 865-0131. FAX: (416) 865-0896.
email: diane_beckon@thehullgroup.com
www.thehullgroup.com
CONTACT
Diane Beckon

Insurance packages for film & entertainment, broadcasters & communications companies.

JONES BROWN, INC.
1100 – 480 University Ave., Toronto, ON M5G 1V2.
TEL: (416) 408-1920. FAX: (416) 408-4517.
email: tor@jonesbrown.com www.jonesbrown.com

Alberta:
800 – 639 5th Ave. SW, Calgary, AB T2P 0M9.
TEL: (403) 265-1920. FAX: (403) 265-1922.
email: cal@jonesbrown.com

British Columbia:
530 – 999 Canada Place, Vancouver, BC V6C 3E1.
TEL: (604) 608-6323. FAX: (604) 608-1174.
email: van@jonesbrown.com

Complete range of entertainment, sports & special event insurance services.

PREMIERE INSURANCE UNDERWRITING SERVICES, INC.
602– 130 Bloor St. W, Toronto, ON M5S 1N5.
TEL: (416) 487-3900. FAX: (416) 487-0311.
email: mteitelbaum@premiereins.com www.premiereins.com
CONTACT
Mark Teitelbaum

A specialty insurance provider and one of the leading insurers of the Canadian film industry. We are experts in covering all aspects of feature films, documentaries, TV series and many other types of productions, from cast coverage to protecting negatives and equipment, as well as specialized errors and omissions coverage.

PRIME INSURANCE AGENCY, INC.
3600 Kempt Rd., Halifax, NS B3K 4X8. TEL: (902) 484-2223.
FAX: (902) 484-2221. email: paul@primeinsuranceagency.ca
CONTACT
Paul Lipkus, Anne Dunfor

BAKER, J.A. (TONY)
Barrister & Solicitor, 500 Danforth Ave., Toronto, ON M4K 1P6.
TEL: (416) 463-4411. FAX: (416) 463-4562.
email: tbaker1952@aol.com www.tonybakerlaw.com

BEARD WINTER, LLP
701 – 130 Adelaide St. W, Toronto, ON M5H 2K4.
TEL: (416) 593-5555. FAX: (416) 593-7760.
email: jholmes@beardwinter.com www.beardwinter.com
DIRECTOR, FINANCE & ADMINISTRATION
Julie Holmes (416) 306-1811

All matters relating to film production, intellectual property and other contractual matters.

BÉLANGER SAUVÉ SENCRL
1700 – 1 Place Ville Marie, Montréal, QC H3B 2C1.
TEL: (514) 878-3081. FAX: (514) 878-3053.
email: ddicaire@belangersauve.com
www.belangersauve.com
LAWYER
Danielle Dicaire

BLAKE, CASSELS & GRAYDON, LLP
2800 – 199 Bay St., Toronto, ON M5L 1A9. TEL: (416) 863-2279.
email: mark.hayes@blakes.com www.blakes.com
CONTACT
Mark Hayes

British Columbia:
P.O. Box 49314, 2600 – Three Bentall Centre, 595 Burrard St., Vancouver, BC V7X 1L3. TEL: (604) 631-3304.
email: bill.kaplan@blakes.com
CONTACT
Bill Kaplan

BLANEY MCMURTRY, LLP
Maritime Life Tower, 1500 – 2 Queen St. E, Toronto, ON M5C 3G5. TEL: (416) 593-1221. FAX: (416) 593-5437.
email: fhemmings@blaney.com www.blaney.com

BORDEN LADNER GERVAIS, LLP
Scotia Plaza, 40 King St. W, Toronto, ON M5H 3Y4.
TEL: (416) 367-6000. FAX: (416) 367-6749.
email: mllewis@blgcanada.com www.blgcanada.com
CONTACT
Jonathon Dyck - (416) 367-6124 jdyck@blgcanada.com

Québec
900 – 1000 de la Gauchetière W, Montréal, QC H3B 5H4.
TEL: (514) 879-1212. FAX: (514) 954-1905.
email: scoppola@blgcanada.com
CONTACT
Sam Coppola - (514) 954-3110

CASSELS BROCK & BLACKWELL, LLP
2100 Scotia Plaza, 40 King St. W, Toronto, ON M5H 3C2.
TEL: (877) 869-5300, (416) 869-5300. FAX: (416) 360-8877.
www.casselsbrock.com
CONTACT
Leonard Glickman
(416) 869-5993 lglickman@casselsbrock.com
Peter Steinmetz, QC
(416) 869-5725 psteinmetz@casselsbrock.com
Daniel Bourque
(416) 869-5777 dbourque@casselsbrock.com
Stephen I. Selznick
(416) 860-6883 sselznick@casselsbrock.com
Casey Chisick
(416) 869-5403 cchisick@casselsbrock.com
Carol Anne O'Brien
(416) 869-5466 cobrien@casselsbrock.com

DAN JOHNSON ENTERTAINMENT LAW
26 Yarmouth Rd., Toronto, ON M6G 1W6. TEL: (416) 658-2929.
FAX: (416) 658-3176. email: dan.johnson@humewood.ca
www.danjohnsonentertainmentlaw.ca
PRESIDENT
Dan Johnson, BFA, LLB, MBA

Legal services to production and distribution companies, broadcasters, individual producers, associations and guilds. Founder of Dan Johnson Mediation ADR, which provides mediation and negotiation services, and President of Humewood Communications, which provides consulting services to private business and public agencies in the film and TV industries.

DUARTE, TONY B.A., LL.B.
402 – 1670 Bayview Ave., Toronto, ON M4G 3C2.
TEL: (416) 486-1688. FAX: (416) 486-2274.
email: tduarte@duartelaw.com www.duartelaw.com

Entertainment law specialist.

DUNCAN MORIN
Barristers & Solicitors / 701 – 130 Spadina Ave., Toronto, ON M5V 2L4. TEL: (416) 593-2513. FAX: (416) 593-2514.
email: info@duncanmorin.com www.duncanmorin.com
CONTACT
John D. Duncan, Gigi Morin, Jill Fraser

ENTERTAINMENT MEDIA COMMUNICATIONS
88 rue William-Paul, Île-des-Soeurs, Montréal, QC H3E 1R6.
TEL: (514) 769-3059. FAX: (514) 769-9069.
email: ydupras@videotron.ca
LAWYER
Yves Dupras

FASKEN MARTINEAU
The Stock Exchange Tower / P.O. Box 242, 800 Square Victoria, 34th Flr., Montréal, QC H4Z 1E9. TEL: (514) 397-7400.
FAX: (514) 397-7600. www.fasken.com
CONTACT
Chloé Archambault, Stéphane Gilker, Jan-Fryderyk Pleszczynski

FERSTMAN LAW OFFICE
1500 – 2 St. Clair Ave. E, Toronto, ON M4T 2R1.
TEL: (416) 922-0305. FAX: (416) 927-0305.
email: brian@ferstmanlaw.com www.ferstmanlaw.com
CONTACT
Brian Ferstman

Serving film and TV clients for over 20 years.

FRASER – ENTERTAINMENT LAW
415 - 980 Yonge St., Toronto, ON M4W 3V8.
TEL: (416) 967-0080. email: info@fraser-elaw.com
www.fraser-elaw.com
CONTACT
Stephen Fraser

Serving the needs of clients in the film, television and Internet industries in Canada and the U.S.

FRASER MILNER CASGRAIN, LLP
1 First Canadian Place, 100 King St. W, 39th Flr., Toronto, ON M5X 1B2. TEL: (416) 863-4511. FAX: (416) 863-4592.
email: chris.pinnington@fmc-law.com www.fmc-law.com
MANAGING PARTNER
Chris Pinnington

Financing / productions & co-productions / writers' agreements / copyright and intellectual property.

G. CHALMERS ADAMS
Barrister & Solicitor / 100 – 1255 Yonge St., Toronto, ON M4T 1W6. TEL: (416) 929-7232. FAX: (416) 929-7225.
email: info@gcadams.on.ca

GARDINER ROBERTS, LLP
Scotia Plaza, 3100 – 40 King St. W, Toronto, ON M5H 3Y2.
TEL: (416) 865-6600. FAX: (416) 865-6636.
email: gr@gardiner-roberts.com
CONTACT
Brian D. Wynn - (416) 865-6674
Carla D. Crozier - (416) 865-8252

Entertainment law.

GASCON & ASSOCIATES, LLP
Windsor Station / 280 – 1100 de la Gauchetière W, Montréal, QC H3B 2S2. TEL: (514) 879-5606, (416) 250-6505.
FAX: (514) 879-4659. email: shgibson@gaslaw.ca
CONTACT
Sander H. Gibson

Emphasis on secured international financing and commercial transactions; IFTA – Arbitrator; ADR Institute of Canada, Inc. – Chartered Arbitrator; Mediator-Arbitrator; Dispute Resolution Services; L.P. – Toronto.

GOODMANS, LLP
2400 – 250 Yonge St., Toronto, ON M5B 2M6.
TEL: (416) 979-2211. FAX: (416) 979-1234.
email: smitchell@goodmans.ca www.goodmans.ca
PARTNER
Michael A. Levine - (416) 597-4132 mlevine@goodmans.ca
David Zitzerman - (416) 597-4172 dzitzerman@goodmans.ca
Carolyn P. Stamegna - (416) 597-6250 cstamegna@goodmans.ca

ASSOCIATE
Tara Parker - (416) 597-4181 tparker@goodmans.ca
Hilary Goldstein - (416) 597-6290 hgoldstein@goodmans.ca
Samantha Traub - (416) 597-5493 straub@goodmans.ca

British Columbia:
1900 – 355 Burrard St, Vancouver, BC V6C 2G8.
TEL: (604) 682-7737. FAX: (604) 682-7131.

HALL WEBBER, LLP
Entertainment & New Media Law / 400 – 1200 Bay St., Toronto, ON M5R 2A5. TEL: (416) 920-3849. FAX: (416) 920-8373. email: mail@ent-law.com www.ent-law.com
CONTACT
Lon J. Hall lon@ent-law.com
Danny Webber danny@ent-law.com
Kara Russell kara@ent-law.com

Associated with Jordon Jacobs, Barrister & Solicitor, jordan@jordonjacobslaw.com

HEENAN BLAIKIE, LLP
Entertainment Law / P.O. Box 185, 2600 – 200 Bay St., South Tower Royal Bank Plaza, Toronto, ON M5J 2J4. TEL: (416) 360-6336. FAX: (416) 360-8425. email: dbourget@heenan.ca www.heenanblaikie.com
CONTACT
Norman Bacal, Christina Buchli, Lorri Charnetski, Ken Dhaliwal, Allen Garson, Jennifer Good, Jim Russell, David Steinberg, Bob Tarantino, Stephen Zolf

British Columbia:
2200 – 1055 West Hastings St., Vancouver, BC V6E 2E9. TEL: (604) 669-0011. FAX: (604) 669-5101.
CONTACT
Arthur Evrensel, Eva Schmieg, Carol Horn

Québec:
2500 – 1250 René-Lévesque Blvd. W, Montréal, QC H3B 4Y1. TEL: (514) 846-1212. FAX: (514) 846-3427.
CONTACT
Sam Berliner, Dean Chenoy

Comprehensive legal services.

LANG MICHENER, LLP
BCE Place Bay Wellington Tower, P.O. Box 747, 2500 – 181 Bay St., Toronto, ON M5J 2T7. TEL: (416) 360-8600. FAX: (416) 365-1719. www.langmichener.ca
CONTACT
Howard M. Drabinsky

British Columbia:
Royal Centre / P.O. Box 11117, 1500 – 1055 W. Georgia St., Vancouver, BC V6E 4N7. TEL: (604) 689-9111.
CONTACT
Stephen D. Wortley

Development of film, television and theatrical projects for Canada, U.S. and international marketplaces. Financing, syndication and securing of international production and distribution rights. Creation, registration and use of trademarks, titles, merchandising and licensing.

LAVERY, DE BILLY
4000 – 1 Place Ville Marie, Montréal, QC H3B 4M4. TEL: (514) 871-1522. FAX: (514) 871-8977. email: irose@lavery.qc.ca www.laverydebilly.com
CONTACT
Ian Rose

Full range of legal services for clients in the entertainment, media and communications industries.

LEGAULT, JOLY, THIFFAULT
7100 – 380 rue St-Antoine ouest, Montréal, QC H2Y 3X7. TEL: (514) 842-8891. FAX: (514) 842-6202. email: mparent@ljt.ca www.ljt.ca
ATTORNEY
Michel Parent, Lyne Robichaud

(ERIC F.) LEMIEUX, LAWYER
4 – 5656 rue Sherbrooke ouest, Montréal, QC H4A 1W7. TEL: (514) 483-3742. FAX: (514) 484-7621. email: eflemieux@videotron.ca
LAWYER
Eric F. Lemieux

LUSSIER & KHOUZAM, INC.
201 – 825 Querbes Ave., Outremont, QC H2V 3X1. TEL: (514) 271-2731. FAX: (514) 276-5730. email: info@lussierkhouzam.com www.lussierkhouzam.com
CONTACT
Zénaïde Lussier, Rémy Khouzam, Claire Kusy

Entertainment law.

MANCINELLI PROFESSIONAL CORPORATION
Barristers & Solicitors / 901 – 3700 Steeles Ave. W, Vaughan, ON L4L 8K8. TEL: (416) 293-1362. FAX: (416) 293-3503. email: emancinelli@mancinelli.ca www.mancinelli.ca
CONTACT
Edward Mancinelli

Media and entertainment services include: applications for errors and omissions insurance, agency and artist agreements, agency and artist agreements, Canadian work permits and visas, clearances and licensing, music, film, television, multimedia and new media production.

MCCARTHY, TÉTRAULT
4700 – TD Bank Tower, Toronto, ON M5K 1E6. TEL: (416) 362-1812. FAX: (416) 868-0673. email: bgray@mccarthy.ca
CONTACT
Brian Gray

Legal services / strategic planning.

MCMILLAN BINCH MENDELSOHN
BCE Place Bay Wellington Tower, 4400 – 181 Bay St., Toronto, ON M5J 2T3. TEL: (888) 622-4624, (416) 865-7000. FAX: (416) 865-7048. email: info@mcmbm.com www.mcmillanbinch.com
PARTNER
Douglas Barrett

MILLER THOMSON POULIOT SENCRL
1155 boul René-Lévesque ouest, 31st Flr., Montréal, QC H3B 3S6. TEL: (514) 875-5210. FAX: (514) 875-4308. email: djohnston@millerthomsonpouliot.com www.millerthomson.com
PARTNER
David Johnston

PAUL POPESKI LAW OFFICE
656 Oak St., Winnipeg, MB R3M 3R7. TEL: (204) 229-4200. FAX: (204) 489-3969. email: paul@paulpopeskilawoffice.com www.paulpopeskilawoffice.com
CONTACT
Paul Popeski

Specializing in providing legal services to the entertainment industries for over 20 years.

RESONANCE ENTERTAINMENT CORPORATION
439 Castlefield Ave., Toronto, ON M5N 1L4. TEL: (416) 488-5671. FAX: (416) 488-2167. email: jrobinson@resonance-ent.com www.resonance-ent.com
PRESIDENT
John Robinson

Business affairs consulting and legal services to the film and television industry.

RGR, LLP
530 Queen St. E, Toronto, ON M5A 1V2. TEL: (416) 504-5600. FAX: (416) 504-5606. email: info@entlawyers.com www.rgrllp.com
CONTACT
Eboué Hemingway Reinbergs, Sonya Roberts, Stefan Guttensohn

Full-service firm formed to provide Canada's diverse film and television, music and new media communities with legal services tailored to their special needs.

ROBINSON SHEPPARD SHAPIRO
4600 – 800 Place Victoria, Montréal, QC H4Z 1H6. TEL: (514) 878-2631. FAX: (514) 878-1865. email: info@rsslex.com www.rsslex.com
CONTACT
Herbert Z. Pinchuk

SHIBLEY RIGHTON, LLP
700 – 250 University Ave., Toronto, ON M5H 3E5. TEL: (877) 214-5200, (416) 214-5200. FAX: (416) 214-5400. email: jeminns@shibleyrighton.com www.shibleyrighton.com
CONTACT
James E. Minns

Services for production, financing, intellectual property.

STEWART MCKELVEY STIRLING SCALES
P.O. Box 997, Purdy's Wharf Tower One, 900 – 1959 Upper Water St., Halifax, NS B3J 2X2. TEL: (902) 420-3200. FAX: (902) 420-1417. email: halifax@smss.com www.smss.com
CONTACT
Robert J. Aske - (902) 420-3310 raske@smss.com

Media and entertainment law.

STOHN HAY CAFAZZO DEMBROSKI RICHMOND, LLP
133 King St. E, 2nd Flr., Toronto, ON M5C 1G6. TEL: (416) 961-2020. FAX: (416) 961-2021. email: info@stohnhay.com www.stohnhay.com
CONTACTS
Stephen Stohn, Diana Cafazzo, Ron Hay, David Dembroski, Sandra Richmond, Ian Cooper

Entertainment, media and copyright law.

TAYLOR, MCCAFFREY, LLP
400 St. Mary Ave., 9th Fl., Winnipeg, MB R3C 4K5. TEL: (204) 988-0360. FAX: (204) 953-7237. email: dtowers@tmlawyers.com
CONTACT
Devan Towers

Entertainment law / intellectual property.

TOLOMIZENKO (ANDREW) LAW OFFICES

509 – 56 The Esplanade, Toronto, ON M5E 1A7.
TEL: (416) 504-4600. FAX: (416) 504-4008.
email: info@entertainmentlaw.tv www.entertainmentlaw.tv
CONTACT
Andrew Tolomizenko, Valve Leemet

Providing legal services to clients in all areas of the entertainment industry. The majority of our clients seek advice for their film, television and new media projects. Private corporations law is a necessary adjunct to the firm's entertainment industry practice as many clients are production companies. This area of practice involves advising clients on the most appropriate business model for their ventures and managing the majority of a corporation's legal affairs.

WORTON HUNTER & CALLAGHAN

Barristers & Solicitors / 1270 – 555 Calgary Trail NW,
Edmonton, AB T6H 5P9. TEL: (780) 436-8554.
FAX: (780) 436-8566. email: ltc@wortonhunter.com
CONTACT
Linda T. Callaghan

PAYROLL SERVICES, RESEARCH & CLEARANCES, ROYALTIES & COPYRIGHT

PAYROLL SERVICES

CAST & CREW ENTERTAINMENT SERVICES, INC.

202 – 65 Heward Ave., Bldg. A, Toronto, ON M4M 2T5.
TEL: (416) 406-2768. FAX: (416) 406-2722.
email: info_toronto@castandcrew.com www.castandcrew.com

British Columbia:
250 – 4259 Canada Way, Burnaby, BC V5G 1H1.
TEL: (604) 437-6363. FAX: (604) 437-6362.
email: info_vancouver@castandcrew.com

U.S.A. Head Office:
100 E. Tujunga Ave., 2nd Flr., Burbank, CA 91502.
TEL: (818) 848-6022. email: info_accounting@castandcrew.com

Payroll and production accounting software services.

EP CANADA, L.P.

351 Bewicke Ave., N Vancouver, BC V7M 3E9.
TEL: (604) 987-2292. FAX: (604) 987-2399.

500 130 Bloor Street West,Toronto, ON M5S 1N5.
TEL: (416) 923-9255. FAX: (416) 920-9134.
email: jharmer@epcanada.com www.epcanada.com
PRESIDENT
Cheryl Nex - cnex@epcanada.com
V.P.
Sante Cardinale
MANAGER, MARKETING & CLIENT RELATIONS
Andy Micallef

RESEARCH AND CLEARANCES

EASTERN SCRIPT, INC.

9 Wellington St., Kingston, ON K7L 3B7. TEL: (613) 542-3999.
FAX: (613) 542-6971. email: amm@easternscript.com
www.easternscript.com
CONTACT
Anne Marie Murphy

Comprehensive clearance reports for U.S.A., Canada & Europe / title searches / research.

KINESEARCH

201 – 825 Querbes Ave., Outremont, QC H2V 3X1.
TEL: (514) 271-3355. FAX: (514) 276-5730.
email: info@kinesearch.com
CONTACT
Hosanna Ettien

Research services (title search and reports) for producers.

MAYALL, ANN

4638 Leo Lake Rd., Kingston, ON K0H 2N0.
TEL: (613) 387-2323. FAX: (416) 239-4469.
email: ann@mayall.ca
CONTACT
Ann Mayall

For all copyright clearance — music, footage, photos, plays, likenesses, text.

PERMISSION, INC.

230 – 6750 Ave. de l'Esplanade, Montréal, QC J4K 5J3,.
TEL: (514) 341-3330. FAX: (514) 341-6602.
email: l.bourgouin@permission-inc.com
CONTACT
Lucie Bourgouin

THE RIGHTS COMPANY

186 Columbia Rd., Barrie, ON L4N 8E2. TEL: (416) 766-0467.
FAX: (416) 766-1973. email: amy@therightscompany.com
www.therightscompany.com
CONTACT
Amy Lennie

Researches and clears all rights — footage and visuals / underlying rights for talent, music, choreography, etc. / photos, artwork, etc.

ROYALTIES & COPYRIGHTS

CANADIAN RETRANSMISSION COLLECTIVE (CRC) / SOCIETE COLLECTIVE DE RETRANSMISSION DU CANADA (SRC)

74 The Esplanade, Toronto, ON M5E 1A9.
TEL: (416) 304-0290. FAX: (416) 304-0496.
email: info@crc-scrc.ca www.crc-scrc.ca
PRESIDENT & CEO
Carol J. Cooper
MANAGER, AFFILIATE RELATIONS
Patricia A. Turner

CANADIAN SCREENWRITERS COLLECTION SOCIETY

401 – 366 Adelaide St. W, Toronto, ON M5V 1R9.
TEL: (416) 979-7907. FAX: (416) 979- 9273.
email: d.tay@wgc.ca www.wgc.ca
EXECUTIVE DIRECTOR
Maureen Parker
DIRECTOR, MEMBERSHIP & INFORMATION SERVICES
Terry Mark

COPYRIGHT BOARD OF CANADA

899 – 56 Sparks St. Ottawa, ON K1A 0C9.
TEL: (613) 952-8621. FAX: (613) 952-8630.
email: secretariat@cb-cda.gc.ca www.cb-cda.gc.ca
ACTING SECRETARY GENERAL
Gilles Mcdougall
GENERAL COUNSEL
Mario Bouchard

PRODUCERS AUDIOVISUAL COLLECTIVE OF CANADA (PACC) / CIÉTÉ CANADIENNE DE GESTION DES DROITS DES PRODUCTEURS DE MATÉRIEL AUDIO-VISUEL

74 The Esplanade, Toronto, ON M5E 1A9.
TEL: (416) 304-0290. FAX: (416) 304-0496.
email: info@pacc.ca www.pacc.ca
PRESIDENT & CEO
Carol J. Cooper
AFFILIATE RELATIONS
Vanda M. Macura

SOCAN / SOCIETY OF COMPOSERS, AUTHORS AND MUSIC PUBLISHERS OF CANADA / SOCIETE CANADIENNE DES AUTEURS, COMPOSITEURS ET EDITEURS DE MUSIQUE

41 Valleybrook Dr., Toronto, ON M3B 2S6.
TEL: (800) 55-SOCAN, (416) 445-8700.
FAX: (416) 445-7108. email: socan@socan.ca
www.socan.ca
CEO
André LeBel
EXECUTIVE V.P. & COO
Joel Grad
CFO
David Wood
V.P., LEGAL SERVICES & GENERAL COUNSEL
C. Paul Spurgeon
V.P., INDUSTRY RELATIONS & STRATEGIC INTELLIGENCE
Christian Sarrazin
V.P., INFORMATION TECHNOLOGY
Marian Wilson
V.P., HUMAN RESOURCES
Randy Wark
V.P., MEMBER SERVICES
Jeff King
V.P., LICENSING & GENERAL MANAGER QUÉBEC & ATLANTIC DIVISION
France Lafleur
V.P., MEMBER RELATIONS & GENERAL MANAGER, WEST COAST DIVISION
Kent Sturgeon
DIRECTOR, LICENSING, CENTRAL CANADA & NATIONAL POLICIES
Gina Pollock
DIRECTOR, MEMBER RELATIONS
Lynne Foster
DIRECTOR, BUSINESS CHANGE
Dan Greenwood

Edmonton Division:
1045 Weber Centre, 5555 Calgary Trail, Edmonton, AB T6H 5P9. TEL: (800) 51-SOCAN, (780) 439-9049.

FAX: (780) 432-1555.

West Coast Division:
400 – 1201 W. Pender St., Vancouver, BC V6E 2V2.
TEL: (800) 93-SOCAN, (604) 669-5569.
FAX: (604) 688-1142.

Atlantic Division:
802 – 45 Alderney Dr., Queen Sq., Dartmouth, NS B2Y 2N6.
TEL: (800) 70-SOCAN, (902) 464-7000.
FAX: (902) 464-9696.

Québec Division:
500 – 600 boul de Maisonneuve ouest, Montréal, QC H3A 3J2. TEL: (800) 79-SOCAN,
FAX: (514) 849-8446.

Script Services, Translation & Storyboards

JARP
3878 av du Parc-La Fontaine, Montréal, QC H2L 3M6.
TEL: (514) 525-9578. FAX: (514) 525-4255.
email: jarp@aei.ca www.jarp.ca
PRESIDENT
Robert Paquin, PhD

Translation / adaptation / subtitling / dubbing / scriptwriting — TV series / documentaries / features.

LORENZO ORZARI PRODUCTIONS
6 Libersan, Montréal, QC H9A 2B5.
TEL: (514) 685-6170. email: lorenzo.orzari@sympatico.ca
www3.sympatico.ca/lorenzo.orzari/
WRITER/PRODUCER/DIRECTOR
Lorenzo Orzari

Providing properties, adaptations and script solutions for film, TV and new media companies from developement to post.

MAD ACTS ENTERTAINMENT
8775 Crest Dr., Burnaby, BC V3N 4A1.
TEL: (604) 522-9961. email: madacts@hotmail.com
www.madacts.com
CONTACT
Geoff Wong

Storyboards / illustrations / graphic designs: High-quality and affordable artwork for film, TV, commercials, music videos, advertising, character designs, posters, logos, concept art and layouts.

MCALLISTER, WENDY GORDON
3578 Quesnel Dr., Vancouver, BC V6L 2W6.
TEL: (604) 738-4492.

Storyboards — film / TV / commercials.

SEPP STUDIO
21 Foxden Rd., Toronto, ON M3C 2B1.
TEL: (416) 823-9212. FAX: (416) 916-0570.
email: sepp@interlog.com www.sepp.ca
CONTACT
Peter Sepp

Storyboard art services for film and commercials since 1994.

SPLIT EGG, INC.
1020 Graham Rd., Severn Bridge, ON P0E 1N0.
TEL: (705) 689-1883. email: todd@splitegg.com
www.splitegg.com
CONTACT
Todd Sullivan, Troy Sullivan
Storyboards, 2D – 3D design / directing.

Government

CANADIAN HERITAGE / LES TERRASSES DE LA CHAUDIÈRE

Cultural Industries Branch / 15 Eddy St. 6th Flr., Gatineau, QC K1A 0M5. TEL: (866) 811-0055, (866) 811-0055.
email: info@pch.gc.ca www.canadianheritage.gc.ca
DIRECTOR GENERAL
Jean-François Bernier
ASSOCIATE DIRECTOR GENERAL
Annette Gibbons
DIRECTOR, FILM & VIDEO POLICY AND PROGRAMS
Pierre Lalonde
MANAGER
Christine Duplessis, Pierre Carpentier, Christine Renaud, Marcel Morin,
DIRECTOR, MUSIC POLICY & PROGRAMS
Pierre Lalonde

The Cultural Industries Branch provides advice and assistance to the Minister of Canadian Heritage in the formulation and development of policies and programs for the achievement of cultural objectives in the area of film, video and sound recording and publishing.

A guide to financial support programs can be found at: www.canadianheritage.gc.ca/pc-ch/pubs/2007/tdm_e.cfm

CANADIAN RADIO-TELEVISION AND TELECOMMUNICATIONS COMMISSION / CONSEIL DE LA RADIODIFFUSION ET DES TELECOMMUNICATIONS CANADIENNES (CRTC)

General mailing address: CRTC/ Ottawa, ON K1A 0N2.

Central Office:
1 Promenade du Portage, Gatineau, QC J8X 4B1.
TEL: (819) 997-0313, (877) 249-2782. www.crtc.gc.ca

Key Contact Information:
www.crtc.gc.ca/eng/about/whoweare.htm

Complete Address / Telephone list:
www.crtc.gc.ca/eng/contactus.htm

The CRTC is vested with the authority to regulate and supervise all aspects of the Canadian broadcasting system, as well as to regulate telecommunications common carriers and service providers that fall under federal jurisdiction. The CRTC reports to Parliament through the Minister of Canadian Heritage.

LIBRARY & ARCHIVES OF CANADA / ARCHIVES NATIONALES DU CANADA

Audio-Visual Sector / Secteur audio-visuel / 395 Wellington St., Ottawa, ON K1A 0N4. www.collectionscanada.ca
CHIEF, AV ACQUISITION
Richard Lochead - (819) 934-7261. FAX: (819) 934-6808.
CHIEF, FILM PRESERVATION
Dennis Waugh
CHIEF, VIDEO & SOUND PRESERVATION
Brian MacDonald
PUBLIC SERVICE REQUESTS
Micheline Robert - (613) 996-7802

Reference Service: (613) 992-3884

A division of National Archives of Canada with authority to aquire, describe and provide specialized reference services to archivally significant Canadian film, TV and sound documents produced both publicly and privately. Initiated as a project of the Public Archives of Canada in 1969, The Audio-Visual Sector was formally established by Cabinet in January 1976 with a mandate to acquire all film, video and sound collections of national significance. At present, the Audio-Visual Sector holds over 300,000 hours of moving image and sound recordings.

STATISTICS CANADA / STATISTIQUE CANADA

(Culture Statistics Program)
Main Building Rm 2001A, Tunney's Pasture Driveway, Ottawa, ON K1A 0T6. TEL: (800) 263-1136 (Main), (613) 951-8116. FAX: (613) 951-0581.
email: infostats@statcan.ca www.statcan.ca

Culture, Tourism & the Centre for Education Statistics:
DIRECTOR
François Nault
ASSISTANT DIRECTOR
Trish Horricks
CHIEF, ANALYSIS & INTEGRATION
Marla Waltman Daschko - (613) 951-3028
MANAGER, RADIO (LISTENING) & TV (VIEWING)
Lofti Chahdi - (613) 951-3136
MANAGER, FILM & VIDEO (PRODUCTION & DISTRIBUTION) AND HERITAGE INSTITUTIONS
Fidel Ifedi - (613) 951-1569

Established in 1972 within the Institutional Statistics Program of Statistics Canada, the Culture Statistics Program has the mandate to collect, analyze and publish statistical information on the state of culture in Canada and the cultural activities of Canadians. The CSP includes ten major project areas: Book Publishing, Periodicals, Film (four surveys), Radio and Television, Sound Recording, Performing Arts, Heritage Institutions, Cultural Labour Force, Participation of Canadians in Cultural Activities, and Government Expenditures in Culture.

Results of surveys are presented in annual publications and in a quarterly newsletter "Focus on Culture." Customized tabulations are also available for specific research purposes.

UNIONS, GUILDS & PROFESSIONAL ORGANIZATIONS

ACADEMY OF CANADIAN CINEMA & TELEVISION / ACADÉMIE CANADIENNE DU CINÉMA ET DE LA TÉLÉVISION – GENIE, GEMINI & GÉMEAUX AWARDS

National Office:
49 Ontario St., Suite 501, Toronto, ON M5A 2V1.
TEL: (800) 644-5194, (416) 366-2227. FAX: (416) 366-8454.
email: info@academy.ca www.academy.ca
CEO
Sara Morton smorton@academy.ca
DIRECTOR, FINANCE & DEVELOPMENT
Judy Watt jwatt@academy.ca
COMMUNICATIONS MANAGER
Dianna Klisanin dianna@academy.ca
DIRECTOR, DEVELOPMENT, MARKETING & COMMUNICATIONS
Dianna Klisanin dianna@academy.ca
Western Office:
1385 Homer St., Vancouver, BC V6B 5M9. TEL: (604) 684-4528.
FAX: (604) 684-4574. email: info@academy.ca
MANAGER
Clare Contini - ccontini@academy.ca
Québec Office:
106 – 225 rue Roy est, Montréal, QC H2W 1M5.
TEL: (514) 849-7448. FAX: (514) 849-5069.
email: academie@acct.ca
DIRECTOR
Patrice Lachance plachance@acct.ca
AWARDS COORDINATOR
Elaine Ethier
ADMINISTRATION & SPECIAL PROJECTS
Danièle Gauthier

Hosts of the annual Genie Awards for Canadian film, and the annual Gemini and Gémeaux Awards for Canadian television. Year-round providers of educational and professional development programs as well as promotional services. For more information on the awards and programs, contact the local Academy Office.

ACFC WEST, LOCAL 2020 CEP

108 – 3993 Henning Dr., Burnaby, BC V5C 6P7.
TEL: (604) 299-2232 (ACFC). FAX: (604) 299-2243.
email: info@acfcwest.com www.acfcwest.com
BUSINESS MANAGER
Greg Chambers

ACFC West — The Association of Canadian Film Craftspeople, Local 2020 Communications, Energy & Paperworkers Union of Canada — is a technical film union representing craftspeople in 23 departments from Accounting to Transportation.

THE ACTORS' FUND OF CANADA

301 - 1000 Yonge St., Toronto, ON M4W 2K2.
TEL: (877) 399-8392, (416) 975-0304. FAX: (416) 975-0306.
email: contact@actorsfund.ca www.actorsfund.ca
PRESIDENT
Barry Flatman
VICE PRESIDENT
Maria Topalovich
SECRETARY
Pam Winter
TREASURER
Brian Borts, CA
DIRECTOR
Hon. Sarmite Bulte, P.C., Christopher Dean, Hans Engel, Deborah Essery, Deborah Grover, Martin Harbury, Bonnie Kim, Tom McCamus, Colin Mochrie, Donald Mowat, A. Frank Ruffo

Charitable organization providing emergency financial assistance for entertainment industry professionals who are in crisis.

ACTRA (ALLIANCE OF CANADIAN CINEMA, TELEVISION & RADIO ARTISTS)

National Office:
300 – 625 Church St., Toronto, ON M4Y 2G1.
TEL: (800) 387-3516, (416) 489-1311. FAX: (416) 489-8076.
email: national@actra.ca www.actra.ca
NATIONAL PRESIDENT
Ferne Downey
NATIONAL EXECUTIVE DIRECTOR
Stephen Waddell
DIRECTOR, FINANCE & ADMINISTRATION
Anna Falsetta
DIRECTOR, PUBLIC POLICY & COMMUNICATIONS
Ken Thompson
DIRECTOR, RESEARCH
Marit Stiles

UNION OF B.C. PERFORMERS/ACTRA

400 – 1155 West Pender Street, Vancouver, BC V6E 2P4.
TEL: (604) 689-0727. FAX: (604) 689-1145.
email: info@ubcp.com www.ubcp.com

ACTRA ALBERTA

602 – 7015 MacLeod Trail SW , Calgary, AB T2H 2K6.
TEL: (403) 228-3123. FAX: (403) 228-3299.
www.actracalgary.com
BRANCH REPRESENTATIVE
Tina Alford jblaney@actra.ca

ACTRA CALGARY

304 – 1300 8th St. SW, Calgary, AB T2R 1B2.
TEL: (403) 228-3123. FAX: (403) 228-3299.
www.actracalgary.com
BRANCH REPRESENTATIVE
Jennifer Blaney talford@actra.ca

ACTRA EDMONTON

302 – 10324 82nd Ave., Edmonton, AB T6E 1Z8.
TEL: (780) 433-4090. FAX: (780) 433-4099.
www.actraedmonton.com
BRANCH REPRESENTATIVE
Sharon Killey skilley@actra.ca

ACTRA SASKATCHEWAN

212 – 1808 Smith St., Regina, SK S4P 2N4.
TEL: (306) 757-0885. FAX: (306) 359-0044.
www1.actra.ca/sask
BRANCH REPRESENTATIVE
Mike Burns mburns@actra.ca

ACTRA MANITOBA

203 – 245 McDermot Ave., Winnipeg, MB R3B 0S6.
TEL: (204) 339-9750. FAX: (204) 947-5664.
email: manitoba@actra.ca www1.actra.ca/winnipeg
BRANCH REPRESENTATIVE
Rob Macklin

ACTRA MARITIMES

103 – 1660 Hollis St., Halifax, NS B3J 1V7.
TEL: (902) 420-1404. FAX: (902) 422-0589.
email: maritimes@actra.ca www.actramaritimes.ca
BRANCH REPRESENTATIVE
Gary Vermier

ACTRA MONTRÉAL

530 – 1450 City Councillors St., Montréal, QC H3A 2E6.
TEL: (514) 844-3318. FAX: (514) 844-2068.
email: montreal@actra.ca www.actramontreal.ca
REGIONAL EXECUTIVE DIRECTOR
Raymond Guardia

ACTRA OTTAWA

The Arts Court, 170 – 2 Daly Ave., Ottawa, ON K1N 6E2.
TEL: (613) 565-2168. FAX: (613) 565-4367.
email: ottawa@actra.ca www.actraottawa.ca
BRANCH REPRESENTATIVE
Chris Cornish

ACTRA TORONTO PERFORMERS

200 – 625 Church St., Toronto, ON M4Y 2G1.
TEL: (416) 928-2278. FAX: (416) 928-2852.
email: jbarefoot@actratoronto.com www.actratoronto.com
MANAGER
Judy Barefoot

ACTRA NEWFOUNDLAND/LABRADOR

P.O. Box 575, 685 Water St., St. John's, NL A1C 5K8.
TEL: (709) 722-0430. FAX: (709) 722-2113.
email: newfoundland@actra.ca www1.actra.ca/stjohns

ALBERTA MOTION PICTURE INDUSTRIES ASSOCIATION

318 – 8944 182nd St. NW, Edmonton, AB T5T 2E3.
TEL (780) 944-0707. FAX: (780) 426-3057.
email: abrooks@ampia.org www.ampia.org
INTERIM EXECUTIVE DIRECTOR
Jane Bisbee jbisbee@ampia.org

The Alberta Motion Picture Industries Association (AMPIA) is a non-profit professional service association serving the independent motion picture production community in the province of Alberta. AMPIA was founded in 1973 with the single aim of furthering the independent motion picture industry as a viable economic and cultural force within the province.

Historically, AMPIA has been recognized and called upon to serve as a voice for the Alberta film and video industries. In

1994 the Association strengthened this voice by expanding its membership to include a broader base of industry professionals within its voting membership. Likewise, the organization expanded the size and scope of the AMPIA Board of Directors to reflect the various sectors of this dynamic industry.

A monthly newsletter, Keep It Rolling, goes out to more than 500 people in the industry, both members and non-members of AMPIA.

ALBERTA MUSIC INDUSTRY ASSOCIATION

Suite 102, Western Supplies Building, 10722 – 103 Avenue
Edmonton, AB T5J 5G7. TEL: (800) 465-3117, (780) 428-3372.
FAX: (780) 426-0188. email: info@amia.ca www.amia.ca
EXECUTIVE DIRECTOR
Kennedy Jenson
ADMINISTRATIVE MANAGER
Tanya Corbin

The 400-member professional association conducts workshops and seminars. Provincial music industry association comprises studios, record labels, distributors, musicians, songwriters and other music industry professionals.

ALLIANCE FOR CHILDREN & TELEVISION (ACT)

708 – 1400 boul René Levesque est, Montréal, QC H2L 2M2.
TEL: (514) 597-5417. FAX: (514) 597-5205.
www.act-aet.tv
EXECUTIVE DIRECTOR
Caroline Fortier cfortier@act-aet.tv
EVENT & PROJECT COORDINATOR
Sylvie Lamy alliance@act-aet.tv

A national, non-profit organization dedicated to enhancing the television experience of Canadian children. Projects and services include workshops, awards of excellence, a specialized resource library, publications and Prime Time Parent (a media workshop kit).

ALLIANCE QUÉBÉCOISE DES TECHNICIENS DE L'IMAGE ET DU SON (AQTIS)

300 – 533 Ontario St. E, Montréal, QC H2L 1N8.
TEL: (888) 647-0681, (514) 844-2113.
FAX: (514) 844-3540.
www.aqtis.qc.ca
PRESIDENT
Richard Saint-Pierre
DIRECTOR, LABOR RELATIONS
Mathieu Lequin - (514) 985-9797 mathieulequin@aqtis.qc.ca

Represents more than 2,900 Quebec artists and technicians, who work in more than a hundred different trades and professions such as set design, make-up, hairstyling, camera, sound, editing, studio control rooms, production assistance, postproduction, technical effects and support, TV control rooms and TV production.

AMERICAN FEDERATION OF MUSICIANS OF THE UNITED STATES & CANADA (AFM)

1010 – 75 The Donway West, Don Mills, ON M3C 2E9.
TEL: (416) 391-5161. FAX: (416) 391-5165.
email: afmcan@afm.org www.afm.org
V.P., CANADA
Bobby Herriot
EXECUTIVE DIRECTOR
Len Lytwyn

ASSOCIATION DES PRODUCTEURS DE FILMS ET DE TELEVISION DU QUÉBEC (APFTQ)

1030 – 1450 City Councillors St., Montréal, QC H3A 2E6.
TEL: (514) 397-8600. FAX: (514) 392-0232.
email: info@apftq.qc.ca

Represents independent Québec producers, negotiates all collective agreements with artists associations and technicians unions. Also offers consulting services on industrial relations, copyright, financing and taxation to members.

ASSOCIATION DES REALISATEURS ET REALISATRICES DU QUEBEC (ARRQ)

3480 rue Saint-Denis, Montréal, QC H2X 3L3.
TEL: (514) 842-7373. FAX: (514) 842-6789.
email: realiser@arrq.qc.ca www.arrq.qc.ca
PRESIDENT
Jean Pierre Lefebvre
DIRECTRICE-GÉNÉRALE
Lise Lachapelle

Represents over 500 film and television directors in Québec.

THE CALGARY SOCIETY OF INDEPENDENT FILMMAKERS (CSIF)

Building J2, 2711 Battleford Ave. SW, Calgary, AB T3E 7L4.
TEL: (403) 205-4747, (403) 205-4748. FAX: (403) 237-5838.
email: info@csif.org www.csif.org
COORDINATOR, OPERATIONS
Bobbie Todd
PROGRAMMING COORDINATOR
Melanie Wilmink
COORDINATOR, PRODUCTION
David Jones

CANADIAN ACADEMY OF RECORDING ARTS AND SCIENCE (CARAS)

345 Adelaide St. W, Toronto, ON M5V 1R5.
TEL: (416) 485-3135. FAX: (416) 485-4978.
email: info@carasonline.ca www.carasonline.ca
PRESIDENT & CEO
Melanie Berry
V.P., SPECIAL EVENTS & PROGRAMMING
Chris Topping

A not-for-profit organization created to preserve and enhance the Canadian music and recording industries and to contribute to higher artistic and industry standards. The main focus of CARAS is the exploration and development of opportunities to showcase and promote Canadian artists and music through television vehicles such as the JUNO Awards. For more information on the JUNO Awards visit the website.

CANADIAN ACTORS' EQUITY ASSOCIATION

44 Victoria St. 12th Flr., Toronto, ON M5C 3C4.
TEL: (416) 867-9165. FAX: (416) 867-9246.
email: info@caea.com membership@caea.com
www.caea.com
EXECUTIVE DIRECTOR
Arden R. Ryshpan
BUSINESS REPRESENTATIVES
Gwen Bartleman, Dennis Lepsi
MEMBERSHIP ADMINISTRATOR
Shanon Button

Western Office:
510 – 736 Granville St., Vanvouver, BC V6Z 1G3.
TEL: (604) 682-6173. FAX: (604) 682-6174.

CANADIAN ASSOCIATION OF BROADCASTERS (CAB)

Mailing Address:
P.O. Box 627 Stn. B, Ottawa, ON K1P 5S2.

Street Address:
700-45 O'Connor St., Ottawa, ON K1P 1A4.
TEL: (613) 233-4035. FAX: (613) 233-6961.
email: cab@cab-acr.ca www.cab-acr.ca
V.P., FINANCE & ADMINISTRATION
Sylvie Bissonnette

Over 80 years as the national voice of Canada's private broadcasters, representing the vast majority of Canadian programming services, including private radio and television stations, networks, specialty, pay and pay-per-view services.

CANADIAN ASSOCIATION OF FILM DISTRIBUTORS AND EXPORTERS / L'ASSOCIATION CANADIENNE DES DISTRIBUTEURS ET EXPORTATEURS DE FILMS

1001 – 2 Bloor St. W, Toronto, ON M4W 3E2.
TEL: (416) 415-7217. FAX: (416) 944-2212.
email: teast@cafde.ca
CHAIRMAN
Victor Loewy
VICE CHAIRMAN
Patrick Roy
PRESIDENT & CEO
Ted East teast@cafde.ca
TREASURER
Brad Pelman

CANADIAN BROADCAST STANDARDS COUNCIL (CBSC)

P.O. Box 3265 Stn. D, Ottawa, ON K1P 6H8.
TEL: (613) 233-4607. FAX: (613) 233-4826.
email: info@cbsc.ca www.cbsc.ca
NATIONAL CHAIR
Ron Cohen
EXECUTIVE DIRECTOR
John MacNab jmacnab@cbsc.ca

THE CANADIAN CONFERENCE OF THE ARTS

804 – 130 Albert St., Ottawa, ON K1P 5G4.
TEL: (613) 238-3561. FAX: (613) 238-4849.
email: info@ccarts.ca www.ccarts.ca
NATIONAL DIRECTOR
Alain Pineau

The CCA is Canada's oldest and largest arts advocacy organization and artists network. A national, non-governmental, nonprofit association, it endeavours to strengthen public and private support to the arts and enhance the awareness of the role and value of the arts through communication, information, research, promotion and consultation activities. As part of its information program, the CCA publishes various bilingual policy papers and reports on the arts, as well as a handbook — The Directory of the Arts — a selective guide to federal and provincial departments, agencies and people with responsibility for arts and culture and a guide to more than 150 national associations, service organizations and unions in the fields of broadcasting, copyright, crafts, dance, education, film, heritage, music, publishing, recording, theatre, visual arts and writing. The Directory, which is updated bi-annually, also features a listing of provincial arts associations across Canada. The CCA also publishes BLIZZART, a quarterly newsletter on current arts issues.

CANADIAN FILM AND TELEVISION PRODUCTION ASSOCIATION (CFTPA) / ASSOCIATION CANADIENNE DE PRODUCTION DE FILM ET DE TELEVISION (ACPFT)

902 – 151 Slater St., Ottawa, ON K1P 5H3.
TEL: (800) 656-7440, (613) 233-1444. FAX: (613) 233-0073.
email: ottawa@cftpa.ca
PRESIDENT & CEO
Norm Bolen
CFTPA CHAIR
Tom Cox
COO & CHIEF LEGAL OFFICER
John Barrack

British Columbia:
301 – 1140 Homer St., Vancouver, BC V6B 2X6.
TEL: (866) 390-7639, (604) 682-8619. FAX: (604) 684-9294.
email: vancouver@cftpa.ca
V.P., B.C. BRANCH
Neil Haggquist
DIRECTOR, INDUSTRIAL AND EXTERNAL RELATION
Tracey Wood

Ontario:
160 John St., 5th Flr., Toronto, ON M5V 2E5.
TEL: (800) 267-8208, (416) 304-0280. FAX: (416) 304-0499.
email: toronto@cftpa.ca
NATIONAL EXECUTIVE V.P. & COUNSEL
John Barrack
NATIONAL DIRECTOR, INDUSTRIAL RELATIONS
Paula Pettit
NATIONAL INDUSTRIAL RELATIONS MANAGER
Jayson Mosek

A non-profit association promoting the general interest of the independent Canadian film, television and new media industry by lobbying government on policy matters, negotiating labor agreements on behalf of independent producers, offering mentorship programs, seminars, an annual conference and industry publications such as The Guide.

CANADIAN INDEPENDENT MUSIC ASSOCIATION (CIMA)

30 Patrick St., 2nd Flr., Toronto, ON M5T 3A3.
TEL: (416) 485-3152. FAX: (416) 485-4373.
email: admin@cirpa.ca www.cirpa.ca
PRESIDENT
Duncan McKie - 416-485-3152 ext. 232
V.P. OPERATONS
Donna Murphy - 416-485-3152 ext. 225

CANADIAN MEDIA GUILD

300 – 144 Front St. W, Toronto, ON M5J 2L7.
TEL: (416) 591-5333. FAX: (416) 591-7278.
email: info@cmg.ca www.cmg.ca
PRESIDENT
Lise Lareau
VICE PRESIDENT
Scott Edmonds
SENIOR STAFF REPRESENTATIVE
Dan Oldfield
STAFF REPRESENTATIVES
Kathy Viner, Bruce May, Glenn Gray, Keith Maskell, Terri Monture

Atlantic Office:
133 – 1657 Barrington St., Halifax, NS B3J 2A1.
TEL: (902) 471-6070. FAX: (902) 423-6153.
STAFF REPRESENTATIVE
Gerald Whelan

Western Office:
405 – 825 Granville St., Vancouver, BC V6Z 1K9.
TEL: (604) 642-2554.
CONTACT
Rick Warren

CANADIAN MOTION PICTURE DISTRIBUTORS ASSOCIATION (CMPDA)

1603 – 22 St. Clair Ave. E, Toronto, ON M4T 2S4.
TEL: (416) 961-1888. FAX: (416) 968-1016.
email: info@cmpda.org www.cmpda.org
PRESIDENT
Hon. D.C. Frith, P.C.
VICE PRESIDENT
Susan Peacock

One of the country's senior film industry trade associations. It is the Canadian affiliate of the Motion Picture Association Inc. (MPA) and serves as the voice and advocate of the major U.S. studios whose distribution divisions market feature films, prime-time programming for TV, Pay-TV and pre-recorded videos and DVDs in Canada.

CANADIAN MUSICAL REPRODUCTION RIGHTS AGENCY LTD. (CMRRA)

320 – 56 Wellesley St. W, Toronto ON M5S 2S3.
TEL: (416) 926-1966. FAX: (416) 926-7521.
email: inquiries@cmrra.ca www.cmrra.ca
CONTACT
Denise Bennett

CMRRA is Canada's largest music licensing agency.

CANADIAN PICTURE PIONEERS

1762 – 250 The East Mall, Toronto, ON M9B 6L3.
TEL: (416) 368-1139. email: cdnpicturepioneers@rogers.com
www.candianpicturepioneers.com

Formed in 1940 as an organization dedicated to the welfare of all men and women of the motion picture industry. It has grown to its present-day strength of over 900 members in five branches across Canada. Original membership requirements called for 25 years of service in the industry. This period of service has now been reduced to 5 years. Everyone involved in industry, theatrical or home entertainment qualifies for membership; no matter what their job title; doorman, cashier, caretaker, manager, projectionist, booker, corporate employee, industry supplier etc.

The Canadian Picture Pioneers Trust Fund helps any members of the film industry in need by, for example, frequently paying additional medical and special treatment costs, providing wheelchairs and general living expenses. In 1983 the Trust Fund began to provide scholarships to post-secondary students in the industry or have parents working as part of the industry.

CANADIAN SOCIETY OF CINEMATOGRAPHERS (CSC)

131 – 3007 Kingston Rd., Toronto, ON M1M 1P1.
TEL: (416) 266-0591. FAX: (416) 266-3996.
email: admin@csc.ca www.csc.ca
PRESIDENT
Joan Hutton, CSC
VICE PRESIDENT
George Willis , CSC
SECRETARY
Antonin Lhotsky
TREASURER
Joseph Sunday, PhD
MEMBERSHIP
Philip Earnshaw, CSC
EDUCATION
Ernie Kestler
PUBLIC RELATIONS
Nikos Evdemon, CSC

Promotes the art and craft of cinematography. The CSC publishes an annual directory listing its members and their credits. The Society also publishes a newsletter 10 times a year. Subscriptions are available for non-members for $75/year in Canada; $95 outside of Canada.

CANADIAN WOMEN IN COMMUNICATIONS (CWC) / ASSOCIATION CANADIENNE DES FEMMES EN COMMUNICATIONS (AFC)

804 – 67 Yonge St., Toronto, ON M5E 1J8.
TEL: (800) 361-2978, (416) 363-1880. FAX: (416) 363-1882.
email: cwcafc@cwc-afc.com www.cwc-afc.com
PRESIDENT
Stephanie MacKendrick
DIRECTOR OF OPERATIONS
Simone Bowen
MANAGER, REGIONS & PROGRAM DEVELOPMENT
Wendy Jacinto

CWC raises the profile of women working in the communications field through a number of benefits, services, awards and internships, a national mentoring program, local and national events, professional development, high-profile initiatives like the Women on Boards program and through strong partnerships with government agencies, industry corporations and other associations.

COMMERCIAL PRODUCTION ASSOCIATION OF TORONTO (CPAT)

P.O. Box 1204 Stn. A, Toronto, ON M5W 1G6.
TEL: (416) 729-3265. FAX: (416) 729-0019.
email: info@cpat.ca www.cpat.ca
CONTACT
Geoff Cornish, Scott Mackenzie

COMMERCIAL PRODUCTION ASSOCIATION OF WESTERN CANADA

330 – 948 Homer St., Vancouver, BC V6B 2W7.
TEL: (604) 682-2507. FAX: (604) 682-2975.
email: info@cpawc.com www.cpawc.com
CHAIRMAN
Garin Josey

Promotes the ongoing health and success of the commercial

production industry in Western Canada by maintaining a productive and competitive environment. Actively markets the region both nationally and internationally. Membership comprises experienced producers, production managers, production companies, production service companies, suppliers and crew personnel and represents a large portion of the commercial community in British Columbia, Alberta and the Yukon.

COMMUNICATIONS, ENERGY AND PAPERWORKERS UNION (CEP)

301 Laurier Ave. W, Ottawa, ON K1P 6M6.
TEL: (613) 230-5200. FAX: (613) 230-5801.
email: info@cep.ca www.cep.ca
COMMUNICATIONS DIRECTOR
Michelle Walsh

Atlantic Regional Office:
440 – 1077 St. George Blvd., Moncton, NB E1E 4C9.
TEL: (506) 857-8647. FAX: (506) 858-8313.

Ontario Regional Office:
510 – 5915 Airport Rd., Mississauga, ON L4V 1T1.
TEL: (905) 678-0800. FAX: (905) 678-7868.

Québec Regional Office:
9100 – 565 boul Crémazie est, Montréal, QC H2M 2V6.
TEL: (514) 384-9000. FAX: (514) 384-9988.

Western Regional Office:
540 – 1199 W Pender St., Vancouver, BC V6E 2R1.
TEL: (604) 682-6501. FAX: (604) 685-5078.

DIRECTORS GUILD OF CANADA / LA GUILDE CANADIENNE DES REALISATEURS

National Office:
402 – 111 Peter St., Toronto, ON M5V 2H1.
TEL: (888) 972-0098, (416) 482-6640. FAX: (416) 486-6639.
email: mail@dgc.ca www.dgc.ca
PRESIDENT
Alan Goluboff
EXECUTIVE DIRECTOR & CEO
Pamela Brand
MEDIA RELATIONS COORDINATOR
Lisa Mahal

Alberta District Council:
133 - 2526 Battleford Ave. SW, Bldg. B8, Currie Barracks, Calgary, AB T3E 7J4. TEL: (403) 217-8672.
FAX: (403) 217-8678. email: dgc@dgcalberta.ca
www.dgcalberta.ca

Atlantic Region District Council:
333 - 1657 Barrington St., Halifax, NS B3J 2A1.
TEL: (888) 342-6151, (902) 492-3424. FAX: (902) 492-2678.
email: inquiries@dgcatlantic.ca www.dgcatlantic.ca

British Columbia District Council:
430 - 1152 Mainland St., Vancouver, BC V6B 4X2.
TEL: (604) 688-2976. FAX: (604) 688-2610.
email: info@dgcbc.com www.dgcbc.com

Manitoba District Council:
The Union Centre, 202B - 275 Broadway, Winnipeg, MB R3C 4M6. TEL: (204) 940-4300. FAX: (204) 942-2610.
email: dgcmdc@shawcable.com www.dgcmanitoba.ca

Ontario District Council:
15 Toronto St., 9th Flr., Toronto, ON M5C 2E3.
TEL: (416) 925-8200. FAX: (416) 925-8400.
email: odc@dgcodc.ca www.dgcodc.ca

Québec District Council:
200 - 4067 boul St-Laurent, Montréal, QC H2W 1Y7.
TEL: (514) 844-4084. FAX: (514) 844-1067.
email: cqgcr@cam.org

Saskatchewan District Council:
W213B - 2440 Broad St., Regina, SK S4P 4A1.
TEL: (306) 757-8000. FAX: (306) 757-8001.
email: sk.dgc@sasktel.net www.dgcsask.com

DOCUMENTARY ORGANIZATION OF CANADA / DOCUMENTARISTES DU CANADA (DOC)

National Office / Toronto Chapter:
126 – 215 Spadina Ave., Toronto, ON M5T 2C7.
TEL: (877) 467-4485, (416) 599-3844.
www.docorg.ca
CHAIR
John Christou
CO-VICE CHAIR
Michaelin McDermott, Katie McKenna
TORONTO REPRESENTATIVE
Michael McNamara
Alberta Chapter
CONTACT
Brandy Yanchyk

Atlantic / Maritimes Chapter:
CONTACT
Teresa MacInnes

British Columbia Chapter:
email: docbc@docbc.org www.docbc.org

Newfoundland Chapter:
CONTACT
Nigel Markham nmarkham@nfdld.com

Ottawa-Gatineau Chapter:
CONTACT
Jacques Ménard

Québec Chapter:
email: info@docquebec.ca www.docquebec.ca
COORDINATOR
Pepita Ferrarir

Winnipeg Chapter:
CONTACT
Jean du Toit

DOC is a national not-for-profit professional and advocacy organization dedicated to supporting the art of independent documentary filmmaking and filmmakers in Canada. Representing over 650 directors, producers and craftspeople in seven regional chapters, DOC is the national voice of the independent documentary filmmaker. DOC also publishes POV Magazine (quarterly): Individual, $18/year; Institution, $24/year. Contact website for more details.

FEMA – FILM & ELECTRONIC MEDIA ASSOCIATION

P.O. Box 308, London, ON N6P 1P9. TEL: (519) 850-3000, (519) 652-9960. FAX: (519) 652-1541. email: info@fema.on.ca www.fema.on.ca

Co-operative of individuals and companies involved with film and electronic media production in SW Ontario. Call for locations, crews and resources. Contact us for resource guide.

THE GUILD OF CANADIAN FILM COMPOSERS / LA GUILDE DES COMPOSITEURS CANADIENS DE MUSIQUE DE FILM

P.O. Box 22059, 45 Overlea Blvd., Toronto, ON M4H 1N9.
TEL: (866) 657-1117, (416) 410-5076. FAX: (416) 410-4516.
email: gcfc@gcfc.ca www.gcfc.ca
EXECUTIVE DIRECTOR
Maria Topalovich mtopalovich @ rogers.com
ADMINISTRATIVE ASSISTANT
Nicholas Stirling nstirling @ goodmedia.com
MEMBER SERVICES
Penny Seymour penny@gcfc.ca

The Guild of Canadian Film Composers is a national association of professional music composers and producers for film, television and new media. Promoting the music, status and rights of film, television and media composers in Canada.

IATSE — INTERNATIONAL ALLIANCE OF THEATRICAL STAGE EMPLOYEES, MOVING PICTURE TECHNICIANS, ARTISTS AND ALLIED CRAFTS OF THE UNITED STATES, ITS TERRITORIES AND CANADA

Canadian Office:
22 St. Joseph St., Toronto, ON M4Y 1J9.
TEL: (416) 362-3569. FAX: (416) 362-3483.
www.iatse-intl.org
DIRECTOR, CANADIAN AFFAIRS
John M. Lewis

IATSE District 11:
Provinces of Ontario, Quebec, New Brunswick, Nova Scotia, Prince Edward Island, and Newfoundland.

54 Baycroft Ln., Aurora, ON L4G 4R2.
TEL: (905) 726-8668. FAX: (905) 713-1496.
email: iatsedistrict11@sympatico.ca
DISTRICT SECRETARY
Cheryl Batulis

IATSE District 12:
Provinces of Manitoba, Saskatchewan, Alberta and British Columbia.

202 – 128 James Ave., Winnipeg, MB R3B 0N8.
TEL: (204) 943-4634. FAX: (204) 943-8394.
email: i.a.D12@allstream.net www.iad12.com
DISTRICT SECRETARY
Barny Haines

IATSE Local 63:
Stage & Projectionist.

P.O. Box 394, Winnipeg, MB R3C 2H6. TEL: (204) 944-0511.
FAX: (204) 944-0528. email: info@iatse63.org
www.iatse63.com
BUSINESS AGENT
John Gallagher

IATSE Local 173:
Motion Picture Projectionists.

13 Carr Dr., Ajax, ON L1T 3E1. TEL: (416) 697-0330.
FAX: (905) 428-0763.
BUSINESS AGENT
Rob McPherson

IATSE Local 210:
Motion Picture & Stage Technicians.

10428 123rd St., Edmonton, AB T5N 1N7. TEL: (780) 423-1863. FAX: (780) 426-0307. email: iatse210@iatse210.com www.iatse210.com
BUSINESS AGENT
Malcolm Kerr

IATSE Local 212:
Stage and Film.

Bldg. B8 Currie Barracks, 141-2526 Battleford Ave. SW, Calgary, AB T3E 7J4. TEL: (403) 250-2199. FAX: (403) 250-9769. email: ia212@cadvision.com www.iatse212.com
BUSINESS AGENT (FILM)
Tom MacRae

IATSE Local 262:

3173-B rue St-Jacques, Montréal, QC H4C 1G7. TEL: (514) 937-6855. FAX: (514) 846-0165. email: aiestlocal@qc.aira.com www.iatselocal262.com
BUSINESS AGENT, GENERAL
Stéphane Ross

IATSE Local 295:
Motion Picture, Projection & Stage Technicians.

201 – 1808 Smith St., Regina, SK S4P 2N4. TEL: (306) 545-6733. FAX: (306) 545-8440. email: iatse295@sasktel.net
BUSINESS AGENT FILM
Rob Parrell

IATSE Local 300:
Motion Picture, Projection & Stage Technicians.

P.O. Box 1361, Saskatoon, SK S7K 3N9. TEL: (306) 343-8900. FAX: (306) 343-8423.
BUSINESS AGENT (FILM)
Greg McKinnon

IATSE Local 411:
Production Coordinators, Craftservice Providers & Honeywagon Operators.

300 – 629 Eastern Ave. Bldg. C, Toronto, ON M4M 1E4. TEL: (416) 645-8025. FAX: (416) 645-8026. www.iatse411.ca
BUSINESS AGENT
Robert F. Shea

IATSE Local 514:
Motion Picture Technicians.

201 – 705 Bourget St., Montreal, QC H4C 2M6. TEL: (514) 937-7668. FAX: (514) 937-3592. email: info@iatse514.com www.iatse514.com
BUSINESS AGENT
Michel Charron

IATSE Local 667:
International Cinematographers Guild.

9 Gloucester St., Toronto, ON M4Y 1L8. TEL: (416) 368-0072. FAX: (416) 368-6932. www.iatse667.com
BUSINESS REPRESENTATIVE
Rick Perotto

IATSE Local 669:
Camerapersons.

6/210 555 Brooksbank Ave., North Vancouver, BC V7J 3S5. TEL: (604) 983-5580. FAX: (604) 983-5579. email: camera@ia669.com www.ia669.com
BUSINESS AGENT
Don Ramsden

IATSE Local 828:

P.O. Box 22562, 300 Coxwell Ave., Toronto, ON M4L 2A0. TEL: (416) 438-3388. FAX: (416) 462-1695. www.iatse828.com
BUSINESS AGENT
Katherine Lilley

IATSE Local 849:
Motion Picture Technicians.

15 McQuade Lake Cres 2nd Flr., Halifax, NS B3S 1C4. TEL: (902) 425-2739. FAX: (902) 425-7696. www.iatse849.com
BUSINESS AGENT
Charlotte Shurko

IATSE Newfoundland & Labrador Office:

405 - 155 Water St., St. John's, NL A1C 1B3. TEL: (709) 738-7011. FAX: (709) 738-7012.

IATSE Local 856:
Motion Picture Studio Production Technicians.

454 Edmonton St., Winnipeg, MB R3B 2M3. TEL: (204) 953-1100. FAX: (204) 953-1109. email: info@iatse856.com www.iatse856.com
BUSINESS AGENT
Joe Laurin

IATSE Local 873:
Motion Picture Technicians.
104 – 1315 Lawrence Ave. E, Toronto, ON M3A 3R3. TEL: (416) 368-1873. FAX: (416) 368-8457. www.iatse873.com
BUSINESS AGENT
Mimi Wolch

IATSE Local 891:
Motion Picture Technicians.

1640 Boundary Rd., Burnaby, BC V5K 4V4. TEL: (604) 664-8910.

FAX: (604) 298-3456. email: info@iatse.com www.iatse.com
BUSINESS AGENT
Kathleen Higgins

INDEPENDENT MEDIA ARTS ALLIANCE / ALLIANCE DES ARTS MÉDIATIQUES INDÉPENDANTS

304 6560, avenue de l'Esplanade, Montréal, QC H2V 4L5. TEL: (514) 522-8240. FAX: (514) 987-1862. email: info@imaa.ca www.imaa.ca

National network of independent film, video and electronic media producers, distributors and exhibitors from all parts of Canada working to promote the improvement of means and access for independents at every stage of funding, production, distribution and exhibition. IMAA currently represents 84 organizations and more than 12,000 artists and cultural workers.

INSTITUTE OF COMMUNICATIONS AGENCIES

P.O. Box 2350, 500 – 2300 Yonge St., Toronto, ON M4P 1E4. TEL: (800) 567-7422, (416) 482-1396. FAX: (416) 482-1856. email: ica@ica-ad.com

Represents advertising agencies in a wide variety of beneficial activities. The diversity of ICA member agencies is impressive and, when combined, they account for over 90% of national media billings in Canada.

LES RENDEZ-VOUS DU CINÉMA QUÉBÉCOIS

A.111 – 1000 rue Fullum, Montréal, QC H2K 3L7. TEL: (514) 526-9635. FAX: (514) 526-1955.

The Rendez-vous du cinéma québécois offers a yearly review of Québec audio-visual production: all film production as well as a selection of videos and documentaries intended for television. The event, which gathers filmgoers, Québec professionals and foreign partners, ensures the promotion of Québec production.

MANITOBA MOTION PICTURE INDUSTRY ASSOCIATION

376 Donald St., Main Flr., Winnipeg, MB R3B 2J2. TEL: (204) 949-8869. FAX: (204) 947-9290. email: info@mmpia.ca www.mmpia.ca
EXECUTIVE DIRECTOR
Tara Walker
FILM PROGRAMS MANAGER
Jennifer Dupas

MMPIA represents the interests of motion picture professionals in Manitoba. Through its programs and initiatives, MMPIA creates opportunities for the production, promotion and appreciation of film and video in Manitoba.

MEDIA AWARENESS NETWORK

120 - 950 Gladstone Avenue, Ottawa, ON K1Y 3E6. TEL: (613) 224-7221. FAX: (613) 224-1958. email: info@media-awareness.ca www.media-awareness.ca

Media and Internet education resources for teachers and parents.

MOTION PICTURE THEATRE ASSOCIATIONS OF CANADA

304 – 1240 Bay St., Toronto, ON M5R 2A7. TEL: (416) 969-7057. FAX: (416) 922-5667. email: mptac.ca@ca.inter.net www.mptac.ca
CHAIRMAN
Raffaele Papalia
EXECUTIVE DIRECTOR
Adina Lebo
SECRETARY
Dean Leland
TREASURER
Dan McGrath

A national non-profit association for theatre owners whose purpose is to:

a) maintain a national trade association of motion picture theatre exhibitors, consisting of owners, operators, executives and managers

b) forward and promote the general welfare and prosperity of motion picture exhibitors

c) gather, receive and disseminate such information as may seem helpful to members and associated organizations; to interchange ideas in rendering mutual assistance and to provide helpful vocational advice and guidance, and in general to act as a group representing national interests.

The Association's head office is in Toronto, and each province has its own organization.

SHOWCANADA

The Association's annual convention and trade show is held at a different location in Canada each year, and member provinces take turns hosting the three-day event. Four hundred delegates participate in the seminars and social activities, which include screenings of new products.

In 2010 the convention will be held in Vancouver. Please contact Adina Lebo (416) 969-7075 or www.showcanada.ca for details

SHOWCANADA SHOWMANSHIP AWARDS

The Showmanship Awards, presented at a ceremony during each convention, were devised to encourage managers to create promotions around film product and special showings. The current five categories for theatre-level personnel are:

- The Blockbuster Film Award – for studio-initiated films with massive merchandising and promotional components.
- Showmanship Award – for a film-specific campaign which has been developed by a theatre manager or circuit.
- Audience Development Award – for programs focusing on community service and audience development.
- Concessions Award – for the best snack promotion.
- Promotions of Canadian Film, French and English.

MUSIC INDUSTRY ASSOCIATION OF NEWFOUNDLAND AND LABRADOR (MUSICNL)

102 – 155 Water St., St. John's, NL A1C 1B3.
TEL: (709) 754-2574. FAX: (709) 754-5758.
email: info@mianl.ca www.musicnl.ca
PRESIDENT
Janeatt Hogan
V.P.
Donna Roberts
TREASURER
Janet Cull,

Full music industry information.

MUSIC INDUSTRY ASSOCIATION OF NOVA SCOTIA (MIANS)

302 - 5516 Spring Garden RD., Halifax, NS B3J 1G6.
TEL: (902) 423-6271.FAX: (902) 423-8841.
email: info@musicnovascotia.ca www.musicnovascotia.ca
EXECUTIVE DIRECTOR
Scott Long

An association of musicians and industry professionals and amateurs intent on creating a healthier music industry through providing educational activities, initiating programs, lobbying regulatory bodies, advising government, and maintaining information on various organizations, programs and projects that relate to the industry.

NABET LOCAL 700 CEP

203 – 100 Lombard St., Toronto, ON M5C 1M3.
TEL: (416) 536-4827. FAX: (416) 536-0859.
email: info@nabet700.com www.nabet700.com
PRESIDENT
Jonathon Ahee
BUSINESS AGENT
David Hardy

NEW BRUNSWICK PRODUCERS' ASSOCIATION (APNBPA)

c/o Connections Productions, Inc.
306 – 111 Main St., Moncton, NB E1C 5T8.
TEL: (506) 382-3984 ext. 104. FAX: (506) 382-3980.
email: mike@cptv.ca
PRESIDENT
Michel Savoie
VICE PRESIDENT
Tim Hogan

A professional organization of film producers in the province of New Brunswick.

NORTH AMERICAN BROADCASTERS ASSOCIATION (NABA)

P.O. Box 500 Stn. A, Toronto, ON M5W 1E6.
TEL: (416) 598-9877. FAX: (416) 598-9774.
email: contact@nabanet.com www.nabanet.com
SECRETARY GENERAL
John Harding
DIRECTOR, ADMINISTRATION
Anh Ngo

PIONNIERS DU CINEMA DU QUÉBEC / QUÉBEC PICTURE PIONEERS

2396 Beaubien E., Montréal, QC H2G 1N2.
TEL: (514) 722-6682. FAX: (514) 721-6684.
email: info@pionniersducinema.qc.ca
www.pionniersducinema.qc.ca
PRESIDENT
Michael Mosca
GENERAL MANAGER
Mario Fortin

QUICKDRAW ANIMATION SOCIETY

201 – 351 11th Ave. SW, Calgary, AB T2R 0C7.
TEL: (403) 261-5767. FAX: (403) 261-5644.
email: qas@shaw.ca http://qas.awn.com/

A nonprofit artist-run society dedicated to the art of independent animation. QAS supports and encourages the production of innovative independent animation and develops the appreciation of all types of animation as a viable artistic medium.

SASKATCHEWAN MOTION PICTURE ASSOCIATION (SMPIA)

W304 – 2440 Broad St., Regina, SK S4P 4A1.
TEL: (306) 525-9899. FAX: (306) 569-1818.
email: smpia@smpia.sk.ca www.smpia.sk.ca
CEO/EXECUTIVE DIRECTOR (ACTING)
Vanessa Book

SOCIÉTÉ DES AUTEURS DE RADIO, TÉLÉVISION ET CINEMA (SARTEC)

1229 rue Panet, Montréal, QC H2L 2Y6. TEL: (514) 526-9196.
FAX: (514) 526-4124. www.sartec.qc.ca
PRESIDENT
Marc Grégoire

Professional association representing French writers for radio, television and film in Canada.

TEAMSTERS LOCAL 155

490 E. Broadway, Vancouver, BC V5T 1X3.
TEL: (604) 876-8898. FAX: (604) 873-1595.
email: team155@teamsters155.org www.teamsters155.org
PRESIDENT, BUSINESS REPRESENTATIVE
Lorrie Ward

TELEVISION BUREAU OF CANADA

1005 – 160 Bloor St. E, Toronto, ON M4W 1B9.
TEL: (416) 923-8813. FAX: (416) 413-3879.
email: tvb@tvb.ca www.tvb.ca
PRESIDENT
Jim Patterson
MANAGER, RESOURCE CENTRE
Duncan Robertson
RESEARCH ANALYSTS
Adam Miller, Mike Ryan, Jessica Zimbalatti
MANAGER, TELECASTER SERVICES
Rhonda-Lynn Bagnall

Québec:
980 – 550 rue Sherbrooke ouest, Montréal, QC H3A 1B9.
TEL: (514) 284-0425. FAX: (514) 284-0698.
email: tvb@bellnet.ca
TVB SENIOR COORDINATOR
Lyse Groleau

A resource centre for members — television stations, networks and their sales representatives. TVB markets the benefits, values and effectiveness of television as an advertising medium to advertisers and agencies.

TORONTO FILM CRITICS ASSOCIATION

c/o Angela Baldassarre
133 Northcliffe Blvd., Toronto, ON M6E 3K5.
www.torontofilmcritics.com
TEL: (416) 652-2696. FAX: (416) 652-3454.
PRESIDENT
Brian D. Johnson,
VICE PRESIDENT
Norman Wilner
TREASURER
Marc Glassman
FOUNDING MEMBER
Cameron Bailey, Angela Baldassarre, Liz Braun, Marc Glassman, Peter Howell, Brian D. Johnson, Bruce Kirkland, Liam Lacey, Ingrid Randoja, Denis Seguin

Formed in 1997 to promote excellence in both filmmaking and in the criticism of film. At the end of each year the TFCA hosts an award ceremony honoring the best films released in Toronto that year, including awards for Best Film, Best Actor – male & female, Best Director and Best Canadian Film.

UNION DES ARTISTES (UDA)

Siége Social:
400 – 1441 boul Rene-Lévesque ouest, Montréal, QC H3G 1T7. TEL: (514) 288-6682. FAX: (514) 285-6776.
email: endirect@uniondesartistes.com
www.uniondesartistes.com
PRESIDENT
Gaston L'Henreux
PREMIER V.P.
Raymond Legault
DEUXIÈME V.P.
Vincent Champoux

SECRÉTAIRE GÉNÉRALE
Catherine Jalbert
TRÉSORIÈRE
Katerine Mousseau

Section de Québec City:
350 – 580 av Grande-Allée E, Québec, QC G1R 2K2.
TEL: (418) 523-4241. FAX: (418) 523-0168.
CONTACT
Jacques Verret

Section de Toronto:
103 – 625 Church St., Toronto, ON M4Y 2G1.
TEL: (416) 485-7670. FAX: (416) 485-9063.
CONTACT
Marco Defour

VIDEO SOFTWARE DEALERS ASSOCIATION

(A division of Retail Council of Canada)
800 – 1255 Bay St., Toronto, ON M5R 2A9.
TEL: (416) 922-6678. FAX: (416) 922-8011.
www.retailcouncil.org
SENIOR MANAGER, MEMBERSHIP SERVICES
Jodi White - jwhite@retailcouncil.org

The trade organization that represents the home video entertainment industry — includes the home video divisions of all major and independent motion picture studios, major distributors and other related businesses.

WOMEN IN FILM AND TELEVISION – TORONTO (WIFT-T)

601 - 110 Eginton Ave., Toronto, ON M4P 2Y1.
TEL: (416) 322-3430 ext. 221. FAX: (416) 322-3703.
email: wift@wift.com www.wift.com
EXECUTIVE DIRECTOR
Sadia Zaman
PROGRAMMING & BUSINESS AFFAIRS MANGER
Renée Robinson

A leading internationally affiliated professional organization dedicated to the advancement of women and underrepresented groups in screen-based media. WIFT-T offers year-round training and business skills development through its Centre for Media Professionals, networking events and industry awards, providing the tools to succeed in Canada's global entertainment industry. WIFT-T serves more than 3,000 women and men in Canadian screen-based media, connecting them to close to 10,000 leading film, television and new media professionals worldwide.

Membership fees:
Full: $185.50; Associate $132.50.
Friend: $180.20; Students & Seniors $53.00.
Fees include a one-time administration fee and GST.

WOMEN IN FILM & VIDEO / VANCOUVER

1815 Pine St., Unit 102, Vancouver, BC V6J 3C8.
TEL: (604) 685-1152. FAX: (604) 685-1124.
email: info@womeninfilm.ca www.womeninfilm.ca
PRESIDENT
Robyn Wiener
VICE PRESIDENT
Mary Bissell
SECRETARY
Carolyn Combs

A non-profit organization of professional women founded to support, advance, promote and celebrate the professional development and achievements of women involved in the B.C. film, video, TV and multimedia industry through education, training, networking and advocacy.

Full membership: open to all women working in the creative, technical, administrative and service fields. Associate, Friends of WIFVV (men and women), Geographically Distant, Seniors and Student Memberships are available.

Activities: workshops, speakers, screenings, industry initiatives, breakfast club, networking events and mentorship programs.

Publications: Producers Workbook III; Newsletter, Weekly Member E-News.

Membership fees:
Full: New $160.50; Renewal $133.75.
Associate: New $133.75; Renewal $107.00.
Friend: New $133.75; Renewal $107.00.
Students, Seniors & Geographically Distant: New: $80.25.
Renewal: $53.50.

WRITERS GUILD OF CANADA (WGC)

401 – 366 Adelaide St. W, Toronto, ON M5V 1R9.
TEL: (800) 567-9974, (416) 979-7907. FAX: (416) 979-9273.
email: info@wgc.ca www.wgc.ca
EXECUTIVE DIRECTOR
Maureen Parker - ext 5223 m.parker@wgc.ca
DIRECTOR, MEMBERSHIP & INFORMATION SERVICES
Terry Mark
MANAGER, OPERATIONS
Marisa King

Represents more than 1,800 professional screenwriters working in film, television, radio and digital media production. As a guild, the WGC helps further the professional, creative and economic rights of Canadian screenswriters by negotiating and enforcing collective agreements, and works with government agencies to increase Canadian content on movie and television screens.

ALBERTA

CASTING DIRECTORS

THE CASTING LINE CANADA, INC.
P.O. Box 71082 SSPO, Calgary, AB T3B 5K2.
TEL: (604) 676-3172. FAX: (403) 547-7324.
email: thecastingline@shaw.ca
CASTING DIRECTOR
Louise Mackiewicz

Commercial casting services.

CLASSIC CASTING
300 - 8120 Beddington Blvd. NW, P.O. Box 345, Calgary, AB T3K 2A8 TEL: (403) 948-4563. FAX: (403) 948-6771.
email: alysonlockwood@shaw.ca
CONTACT
Alyson Lockwood

DEB GREEN CASTING
16 Midlake Blvd. SE, P.O. Box 232, Calgary, AB T2X 2X7.
TEL: (403) 931-3181. FAX: (403) 931-3979.
email: dgmgreen@canadafilm.com
CONTACT
Deborah Green, CDC

PUBLICISTS

INTERACT PUBLIC RELATIONS, INC.
2101 – 18A St. SW, Calgary, AB T2T 4W3.
TEL: (403) 262-9700. FAX: (403) 262-9701.
email: mark@interactpr.com www.interactpr.com
CONTACTS
Mark Niziol, Phil Parks

Full-service boutique public relations and publicity agency located in Vancouver, BC and Calgary, AB. Western Canada specialists in film and television publicity and promotions, unit publicity, junkets, PA tours, special events, public relations and marketing. See also British Columbia.

TALENT REPS

DAGAZ TALENT
105 – 2526 Battleford Ave., SW, Calgary, AB T3E 7J4.
TEL: (403) 230-3220. FAX: (403) 230-3520.
email: dagaz@dagaztalent.com www.dagaztalent.com
OWNER/AGENT
Roxanne Ellison

ACTRA recognized, roster on website; film / TV / theatre / voice work.

EMPIRE TALENT, INC.
2905 Lindstrom Dr. SW, Calgary, AB T3E 6E5.
TEL: (403) 301-0085. FAX: (403) 301-0086.
email: empireagent@canadafilm.com
CONTACT
Glenda Philipchuk

BRITISH COLUMBIA

CASTING DIRECTORS

AIKINS / COSSEY CASTING
403 – 1755 Broadway W, Vancouver, BC V6J 4S5.
TEL: (604) 739-4612. FAX: (604) 739-4613.
email: saikins@canadafilm.com
CONTACT
Stuart Aikins, Sean Cossey

BETTE CHADWICK CASTING
24 – 2190 W. Broadway, Vancouver, BC V6K 4W3.
TEL: (604) 669-1977.
CASTING DIRECTOR
Bette Chadwick bchadwick@canadafilm.com

CAROLE TARLINGTON CASTING
610 – 525 Seymour St., Vancouver, BC V6B 3H7.
TEL: (604) 254-6316. FAX: (604) 254-6311.
CASTING DIRECTOR
Carole Tarlington tarlington@canadafilm.com

Principal casting for film and television.

CLARK & PAGE CASTING
613 – 744 W. Hastings St., Vancouver, BC V6C 1A5.
TEL: (604) 669-8240. FAX: (604) 669-8249.
email: clark&page@telus.net
CONTACT
Corinne Clark, Jennifer Page

ILLUSIONS PRODUCTION SERVICES, LTD.
12694 18th Ave., South Surrey, BC V4A 1V7.
TEL: (604) 535-4844. FAX: (604) 538-5496.
CONTACT
Susanne (McLellan) de Pencier sdepencier@canadafilm.com

Casting director for commercial, TV series and film for over 20 years.

POWERHOUSE CASTING WEST
13 – 1255 E. 15th Ave., Vancouver, BC V5T 2S7.
TEL: (604) 876-9772. FAX: (604) 876-9770.
email: drew@telmnop.com www.powerhousecasting.com
CONTACT
Drew Walker

CREATIVE REPS

DEBORAH HARRY TALENT
408 – 1917 W. 4th Ave., Vancouver, BC V6J 1M7.
TEL: (604) 739-6565. FAX: (604) 628-7794.
email: dharry@canadafilm.com www.deborahharrytalent.com

Representing principal actors, writers & directors.

LUCAS TALENT, INC.
100 W Pender St., 7th Flr., Vancouver, BC V6B 1R8.
TEL: (604) 685-0345. FAX: (604) 685-0341.
email: info@lucastalent.com www.lucastalent.com
CONTACT
Richard Lucas, Deb Dillistone, Elena Kirschner, Debbie Mahood
LITERARY AGENT
Anna Archer, Doreen Holmes

LOCAL COLOUR (EXTRAS DIVISION)
CONTACT
Ralph Streich - (604) 685-0315

PUBLICISTS

INTERACT PUBLIC RELATIONS, INC.
2628 W. 6th Ave., Vancouver BC V6K 1W7.
TEL: (604) 730-4860. FAX: (604) 730-4861.
email: phil@interactpr.com www.interactpr.com
CONTACT
Phil Parks, Mark Niziol

Full-service boutique public relations and publicity agency located in Vancouver, BC and Calgary, AB. Western Canada specialists in film and television publicity and promotions, unit publicity, junkets, PA tours, special events, public relations and marketing. See also Alberta.

TALENT REPS

COULTISH MANAGEMENT
101A – 2526 Government St., Victoria, BC V8T 4P7.
TEL: (250) 382-2670. FAX: (250) 382-2691.
email: bcoultish@telus.net www.barbaracoultish.ca

CHARACTERS WEST
200 – 1505 W. 2nd Ave., Vancouver, BC V6H 3Y4.
TEL: (604) 733-9800. FAX: (604) 733-6000.
email: characters.office@canadafilm.com www.slfa.com
PRESIDENT
Leonard Bonnell
VICE PRESIDENT
Tyman Stewart
FILM & TV
Murray Gibson, Laila Burton
COMMERCIALS/VOICEOVERS
Gail Murphy
PRODUCTION TALENT
Barbara Bird

DEBORAH HARRY TALENT
408 – 1917 W. 4th Ave., Vancouver, BC V6J 1M7.
TEL: (604) 739-6565. FAX: (604) 628-7794.
email: dharry@canadafilm.com www.deborahharrytalent.com

Representing principal actors, writers & directors.

ECHELON TALENT MANAGEMENT
3674 Oxford St., Vancouver, BC V5K 1P3.
TEL: (604) 689-3639. FAX: (604) 689-0638.

email: echelon@direct.ca
CONTACT
Andrew Ooi, Kate Forrester

Specializing in Asian talent.

EMMERSON DENNEY PERSONAL MANAGEMENT
101 – 131 Water St., Vancouver, BC V6B 4M3.
TEL: (604) 742-FILM (3456). www.emmerson.ca
BOOKING
Joshua Denney

HODGSON MANAGEMENT GROUP, INC.
405 – 1688 Cypress St., Vancouver, BC V6J 5J1.
TEL: (604) 687-7676. FAX: (604) 687-7677.
CONTACT
Elizabeth Hodgson

KING TALENT, INC.
303 – 228 E. 4th Ave., Vancouver, BC V5T 1G5.
TEL: (604) 713-6980. FAX: (604) 713-6981.
email: kingtalent@canadafilm.com www.kingtalent.com
CONTACT
Lisa King, Dylan Collingwood, Liz Coughlin

LLOYD TALENT
106 – 14914 104th Ave., Surrey, BC V3R 1M7.
TEL: (604) 589-7559. FAX: (604) 608-3158.
email: lissa@lloydtalent.com www.lloydtalent.com
CONTACT
Lissa Lloyd, Tom Gusway

LUCAS TALENT, INC.
100 W Pender St. 7th Flr., Vancouver, BC V6B 1R8.
TEL: (604) 685-0345. FAX: (604) 685-0341.
email: info@lucastalent.com www.lucastalent.com
CONTACT
Richard Lucas, Deb Dillistone, Elena Kirschner, Debbie Mahood
LITERARY AGENT
Anna Archer, Doreen Holmes
LOCAL COLOUR (EXTRAS DIVISION)
Ralph Streich - (604) 685-0315

REAL 2 REEL TALENT AGENCY
6 – 20475 Lougheed Hwy., Maple Ridge, BC V2X 9B6.
TEL: (604) 465-8146. FAX: (604) 465-7720.
email: real2reeltalent@canadafilm.com
CONTACT
Garry Derksen

Adults / teens / commercial / film / TV.

REEL KIDS TALENT AGENCY
6 – 20475 Lougheed Hwy., Maple Ridge, BC V2X 9B6.
TEL: (604) 465-8144. FAX: (604) 465-7720.
email: reelkids@canadafilm.com
CONTACT
Garry Derksen

Credited youngsters / commercial / film / TV.

VAN GOGH TALENT
1736 W. 2nd Ave., Vancouver, BC V6J 1H6.
TEL: (604) 924-9195. FAX: (604) 924-9196.
email: vangogh@canadafilm.com
CONTACT
Nancy Van Gogh

VANCOUVER TALENT MANAGEMENT
150 – 220 Cambie St., Vancouver, BC V6B 2M9.
TEL: (604) 688-3667. FAX: (604) 688-9365, (604) 688-4229.
www.vancouvertalent.com
CONTACT
James Falconer, Tea Buechner

MANITOBA

CASTING DIRECTORS

NEXT! CASTING
P.O. Box 69010 Tuxedo Postal Outlet, Winnipeg, MB R3P 2G9.
TEL: (204) 284-6820. FAX: (204) 452-0883.
email: nextcasting@shaw.ca www.nextcasting.ca
EXTRAS & CASTING DIRECTOR
Lori Stefaniuk
EXTRAS CASTING ASSISTANT
Trish Kress

Providing productions with casting, extras casting, doubles and stand-ins. Our hard working team finds directors exactly what they want. Member of MMPIA.

ORIGINAL TALENT CASTING
P.O. Box 68012, Osborne Village Post Office,
Winnipeg, MB R3L 2V9. TEL: (204) 477-0120.
FAX: (204) 477-4666. email: driscoll@mts.net
CONTACT
Kathleen Driscoll

PUBLICISTS

RAS CREATIVE
P.O. Box 47056, 123 Marion St., Winnipeg, MB R2H 0T3.
TEL: (204) 783-7600. FAX: (204) 783-7601.
email: rascreative@yahoo.ca www.ras-creative.com
PRESIDENT
RoseAnna Schick

NOVA SCOTIA

CASTING DIRECTORS

FILMWORKS PRODUCTION SERVICES
1060 Barrington St., Halifax, NS B3H 2R1.
TEL: (902) 423-7375. FAX: (902) 423-3290.
email: info@filmworks.ns.ca www.filmworks.ns.ca
CONTACT
Sheila Lane

Casting principals and extras.

TALENT REPS

THE CASSIDY GROUP TALENT AGENCY
200 – 5212 Sackville St., Halifax, NS B3J 1K6.
TEL: (902) 492-4410. FAX: (902) 492-4411.
email: thecassidygroup@hotmail.com
www.thecassidygroup.com
CONTACT
Bab Dingwall, Brindle Peralta

FOCUS AGENCY, INC.
P.O. Box 2413 DEPS, Dartmouth, NS B2W 4A5.
TEL: (902) 434-8461. FAX: (902) 435-7584.
email: eileen.b@ns.sympatico.ca
www.focusagencyinc.com
CONTACT
Eileen Beck

Principals and extras for TV, commercials, film / voices for videos, documentaries, narration, etc.

ONTARIO

CASTING DIRECTORS

CBC TALENT RESOURCE CENTRE
205 Wellington St. W, Rm. 7F400, Toronto, ON M5V 3G7.
Mail: P.O. Box 500, Stn. A, Toronto, ON M5W 1E6.
TEL: (416) 205-7202. FAX: (416) 205-2489.
email: talent_resource@cbc.ca
CONTACT
Darlene Hebert

CHESLEY, MARSHA
672 Euclid Ave., Toronto, ON M6G 2T7.
TEL: (416) 531-9906. FAX: (416) 531-7026.
CONTACT
Marsha Chesley mchesley@canadafilm.com

CLARE WALKER CASTING
220 – 11 St. Joseph St., Toronto, ON M4Y 3G4.
TEL: (416) 929-0541. FAX: (416) 929-0974.
CONTACT
Clare Walker cwalker@canadafilm.com

CRAIG ALEXANDER CASTING INC., CDC
605 – 10 Mary St, Toronto, ON M4Y 1P9.
TEL: (416) 961-0811. FAX: (416) 961-7095.
CONTACT
Craig Alexander calexander@canadafilm.com

CRYSTAL CASTING, CRYSTAL OLSEN
802 – 110 The Esplanade, Toronto, ON M5E 1X9.
TEL: (416) 803-6576. email: crystalcasting@yahoo.ca
CONTACT
Crystal Olsen

THE DOWNTOWN CASTING FACILITY
93 Berkeley St., Toronto, ON M5A 2W8.
TEL: (416) 777-0033. FAX: (416) 777-9288.
email: ardith@powerhousecasting.com
www.powerhousecasting.com
STUDIO MANAGER
David West Pernica

DUPERE CASTING, INC.
2410 - 85 Thorncliffe Park Dr., Toronto, ON M4H 1L6.
TEL: (416) 778-0774. FAX: (416) 778-5010.
CONTACT
Donna Dupere ddupere@rogers.com
ASSISTANT
Aaron Unrau

FADE TO BLACK CASTING, INC.
847 Adelaide St. W, Toronto, ON M6J 3X1.
TEL: (416) 203-3880. FAX: (416) 203-3885.
email: michael@fadetoblack.tv www.fadetoblack.tv
CONTACT
Michael Stevenson, CDC, Caroline Malette, Trevor Roberts

FILM EXTRAS
P.O. Box 85537, Nortown Postal Outlet, Toronto, ON M5V 0A2.
TEL: (416) 787-4305.
CONTACT
Eleanor Lavendar
Background casting.

FORREST & FORREST CASTING
403 Glencairn Ave., Toronto, ON M5N 1V2.
TEL: (416) 789-0228. FAX: (416) 782-5995.
CONTACT
Susan Forrest, CDC, Sharon Forrest, CDC

GAIL CARR CASTING
64 Marion St., Toronto, ON M6R 1E7. TEL: (416) 537-5989.
FAX: (416) 539-8573.
CONTACT
Gail Carr gailcarrcasting@sympatico.ca

JEFF MARSHALL AND ASSOCIATES CASTING
301A – 3 Charles St. W, Toronto, ON M4Y 1R4.
TEL: (416) 925-8580. FAX: (416) 925-2821.
CONTACT
Jeff Marshall jmarshall@canadafilm.com

JIGSAW CASTING, LTD
60 Sumach St., 2nd Flr., Toronto, ON M5A 3J7.
TEL: (416) 360-0336. FAX: (416) 360-0465.
CONTACT
Shasta Lutz, CDC shasta@jigsawcasting.com
Melissa Cassin, CDC
Larissa Mair, CDC
Union commercials / corporate videos / print / feature films / short films / musical theatre / music videos.

JULI-ANN KAY CASTING
430 – 10 St. Mary St., Toronto, ON M4Y 1P9.
TEL: (416) 929-7121. FAX: (416) 929-7699.
CONTACT
Juli-Ann Kay, CSA, CDC jkay@canadafilm.com

KAREN HAZZARD CASTING
1811 – 140 Carlton St., Toronto, ON M5A 3W7.
TEL: (416) 923-6225.
CONTACT
Karen Hazzard khazzard@canadafilm.com

KIM HURDON CASTING (CDC)
33 Britain St. 2nd Fl., Toronto, ON M5A 1R7.
TEL: (416) 203-6118. FAX: (416) 203-6119.
email: kim@kcasting.com

LEWIS KAY CASTING
201 – 10 St. Mary St., Toronto, ON M4Y 1P9.
TEL: (416) 545-0027. FAX: (416) 849-0117.
email: jlcasting@canadafilm.com
CONTACT
Jenny Lewis, Sarah Kay

LINDA GREARSON CASTING
c/o CBC Radio-Broadcast Centre
P.O. Box 500, Stn. A, Toronto, ON M5W 1E6.
TEL: (416) 205-6011. FAX: (416) 205-5731.
email: linda_grearson@cbc.ca

LISA PARASYN CASTING
373 Front St. E, Toronto, ON M5A 1G4.
TEL: (416) 367-5225. FAX: (416) 368-7052.
CONTACT
Lisa Parasyn lisaparasyn@canadafilm.com

MANN CASTING, INC.
93 Berkeley St., Toronto, ON M5A 2W8.
TEL: (416) 368-1988. FAX: (416) 368-1959.
CONTACT
Gloria Mann gloria@manncasting.com
Steven Mann steven@manncasting.com

MARISSA RICHMOND CASTING (CDC)
244 Briar Hill Ave., Toronto, ON M4R 1J2.
TEL: (416) 480-1663. FAX: (416) 486-3909.
email: mrcasting@canadafilm.com

MARJORIE LECKER CASTING (CDC)
103 – 678 Broadview Ave., Toronto, ON M4K 2P2.
TEL: (416) 778-6046. email: mlecker@sympatico.ca

MASALA BLUE CASTING
11 – 36 Rosecliffe Ave., Toronto, ON M6E 1K9.
TEL: (416) 533-6368. email: masalablue@rogers.com
CONTACT
Paul Jackson

NELLEKE PRIVETT CASTING (CDC)
2 Bleecker St., Toronto, ON M4X 1L8.
TEL: (416) 920-6573. FAX: (416) 920-0402.
CONTACT
Nelleke Privett nprivett@canadafilm.com

POWERHOUSE CASTING
93 Berkeley St., Toronto, ON M5A 2W8.
TEL: (416) 777-0033. FAX: (416) 777-9288.
www.powerhousecasting.com
CASTING DIRECTOR
Kim Everest, CDC kim@powerhousecasting.com
ASSOCIATE CASTING DIRECTOR
Jonathan Payne jonathan@powerhousecasting.com

RDC CASTING
1004 Bathurst St., Toronto, ON M5R 3G7.
TEL: (416) 929-6880. FAX: (416) 929-4624.
CASTING DIRECTOR
Robin D. Cook, CDC rcook@canadafilm.com

ROSS CLYDESDALE CASTING
10 Boulton Ave., Toronto, ON M4M 2J3.
TEL: (416) 972-6397. FAX: (416) 972-9036.
CONTACT
Ross Clydesdale, CDC rclydesdale@canadafilm.com
John Rait

STEPHANIE GORIN CASTING, INC.
62 Ellerbeck St., Lower Level, Toronto, ON M4K 2V1.
TEL: (416) 778-6916. FAX: (416) 778-7717.
email: sgorin@canadafilm.com

SUSAN HART CASTING
43 Yarmouth Gardens, Toronto, ON M6G 1W3.
TEL: (416) 536-8985.
CONTACT
Susan Hart shart@canadafilm.com
Animation, film and television.

TINA GERUSSI CASTING (CDC)
119 Oakwood Ave., Toronto, ON M6H 2W1.
TEL: (416) 658-8455. FAX: (416) 658-8572.
CONTACT
Tina Gerussi tgerussi@canadafilm.com

CREATIVE REPS

CHRISTOPHER BANKS & ASSOCIATES, INC.
410 – 6 Adelaide St. E, Toronto, ON M5C 1H6.
TEL: (416) 214-1155. FAX: (416) 214-1150.
email: info@chrisbanks.com www.chrisbanks.com
CONTACT
Christopher Banks

THE CORE GROUP TALENT AGENCY, INC.
300 – 89 Bloor St. W, Toronto, ON M5S 1M1.
TEL: (416) 955-0819. FAX: (416) 955-0825.
email: info@coregroupta.com
Talent and literary agency.

CREATIVE TECHNIQUE, INC.
483 Euclid Ave., Toronto, ON M6G 2T1.
TEL: (416) 944-0475. FAX: (416) 924-3229.
OWNER
Suzanne DePoe suzanne@ctiam.ca
Represents directors, writers and below the line.

FILMBLANC
1901 – 1121 Bay St., Toronto, ON M5S 3L9.
TEL: (416) 214-0300. FAX: (416) 214-0446.
www.filmblanc.com
PRESIDENT & EXECUTIVE PRODUCER
Noemi Weis noemi@filmblanc.com
Representing directors from around the world.

GREAT NORTH ARTISTS MANAGEMENT, INC.
350 Dupont St., Toronto, ON M5R 1V9. TEL: (416) 925-2051.
FAX: (416) 925-3904. email: gnaminc@gnaminc.com
CONTACT
Ralph Zimmerman, Shain Jaffe, Rena Zimmerman

GREEN LIGHT ARTIST MANAGEMENT, INC.
804 - 1240 Bay St., Toronto, ON M5R 2A7.
TEL: (416) 920-5110. FAX: (416) 920-4113.
email: info@glam.on.ca www.glam.on.ca

CONTACT
Charlotte Rose, Lara Bryant

THE JENNIFER HOLLYER AGENCY, INC.
403 – 119 Spadina Ave., Toronto, ON M5V 2L1.
TEL: (416) 928-1425. FAX: (416) 928-5936.
email: jennifer@jenniferhollyeragency.com
Representing writers and directors exclusively.

MCGUIN & ASSOCIATES, INC.
116 - 20 Shallmar Blvd., Toronto, ON M5N 1J5.
TEL: (416) 920-6884. FAX: (416) 920-8543.
email: mcguin@canadafilm.com
CONTACT
Debi McGuin
Representing children and adult actors in film, television, commercials, print, voice and theatre. Also represent selective directors and writers. Hard copy submissions by mail only.

OSCARS ABRAMS ZIMEL AND ASSOCIATES, INC.
Talent & Literary Agency / 438 Queen St. E, Toronto, ON M5A 1T4. TEL: (416) 860-1790. FAX: (416) 860-0236.
email: info@oazinc.com
CONTACT
Michael Oscars, Gayle Abrams, Perry Zimel

SESLER & COMPANY
200 – 862 Richmond St. W, Toronto, ON M6J 1C9.
TEL: (416) 504-1223, (310) 966-4005 (U.S.).
FAX: (416) 504-3345. email: info@seslercompany.com
www.seslercompany.com
CONTACT
Dora Sesler, Jacqueline Harrington
Michael Pepper (L.A. Office)
Agents for directors of photography / commercials / features / TV

PUBLICISTS

ALLIED ADVERTISING, PUBLIC RELATIONS CANADA
1410 – 21 St. Clair Ave. E, Toronto, ON M4T 1L9.
TEL: (416) 413-0557. FAX: (416) 413-7958.
email: allied@alliedadvpub.com
V.P., ADVERTISING
Jason Wright
ADVERTISING MANAGER
Anna Abramian

EDYE ROME COMMUNICATION SERVICES
7 Darwin Rd., Toronto, ON M5N 2N9.
TEL: (416) 785-6213. FAX: (416) 785-6060.
CONTACT
Edye Rome edyerome@sympatico.ca

HOLMES CREATIVE COMMUNICATIONS
403 – 19 Duncan St., Toronto, ON M5H 3H1.
TEL: (416) 408-2800. FAX: (416) 408-4080.
email: holmes@hccink.com
CONTACT
Beth Sulman
Full-service strategic marketing, unit & launch publicity, press material writing, special events, promotions and media partnerships.

LINDA SHAPIRO PUBLIC RELATIONS, INC.
408 – 12 Rockford Rd., Toronto, ON M2R 3A2.
TEL: (416) 667-1531. FAX: (416) 663-7875.
email: lindashapiro@rogers.com

THE NEXTMEDIA COMPANY, LTD.
59 Strathcona Ave., Toronto, ON M4J 1G9.
TEL: (416) 971-9973. FAX: (416) 971-4828.
email: info@nextmediacompany.com
www.nextmediacompany.com
CEO
Nancy Smith
COMMUNICATIONS
Cara McCutcheon
Advertising, public relations and consulting.

PIDGURSKI, KAREN
265 Rosedale Heights Dr., Toronto, ON M4T 1C7.
TEL: (416) 480-0227.
Unit publicist / feature films.

PLANET 3 COMMUNICATIONS, LTD.
90A Isabella St., 2nd Flr., Toronto, ON M4Y 1N4.
TEL: (416) 922-4459. FAX: (416) 924-0101.
CONTACT
Joanne Smale joanne@planet3com.net
Special events / consultation / public relations.

PREVIEW MARKETING
(a division of Basstoy International Corporation)
71 Barber Greene Rd., Toronto, ON M3C 2A2.
TEL: (416) 445-0544. FAX: (416) 445-2894.
PRESIDENT
Brian A. Stewart - bstewart@tribute.ca
Film & entertainment marketing, promotions, licensing, events, media innovation & publishing.

STAR PR
2209 – 140 Erskine Ave., Toronto, ON M4P 1Z2.
TEL: (416) 488-4436. FAX: (416) 488-8438.
email: starpr@sympatico.ca
CONTACT
Bonne Smith
Film publicity.

VK & ASSOCIATES, INC.
107 – 326 Carlaw Ave., Toronto, ON M4M 3N8.
TEL: (416) 466-9799. FAX: (416) 469-5198.
email: info@vkpr.ca
CONTACT
Virginia Kelly, Nancy Yu
Film / TV marketing.

WAFWOT COMMUNICATIONS CORPORATION
2206 Holt Rd., Production Trailer #1, Bowmanville, ON L1C 3K7. TEL: (647) 273-4844, (905) 623-2895. FAX: (905) 623-2895.
email: alan@jamsproductions.ca www.jamsproductions.ca
CONTACT
Alan J. Schwarz

TALENT REPS

THE ARC, INC.
1147 South Island Rd. RR1, Demorestville, ON K0K 1W0.
TEL: (416) 920-0117. FAX: (613) 476-9038.
CONTACT
MaryJane MacCallum mj@the-arc.ca
Film & television.

BUTLER RUSTON BELL TALENT ASSOCIATES, INC.
310 – 10 St. Mary St., Toronto, ON M4Y 1P9.
TEL: (416) 964-6660. FAX: (416) 960-8979.
email: brb@canadafilm.com
CONTACT
Linda Butler, Estella Ruston, Sam Woodruff, Shelley Black

CALDWELL / JEFFERY
943 Queen St. E, Toronto, ON M4M 1J6.
TEL: (416) 465-6168.
CONTACT
Shari Caldwell, Alicia Jeffery
Boutique agency of well-established actors, directors and writers.

THE CHARACTERS TALENT AGENCY, LTD.
8 Elm St., Toronto, ON M5G 1G7.
TEL: (416) 964-8522. FAX: (416) 964-8206.
TALENT DEPARTMENT
Larry Goldhar, Ron Barry, Ronda Cooper, Gerry Lomberg, Jennifer Gossack, Bryan Misener
HEAD OF LITERARY DEPARTMENT
Carl Liberman
HEAD OF COMMERCIAL & VOICEOVER DEPARTMENT
Donna Trimble
LITERARY AGENT
Brent Sherman

CHINA SYNDROME PRODUCTIONS
80 Citizen Ct., Unit 15, Markham, ON L6G 1A7.
TEL: (905) 513-6373 ext. 22. FAX: (905) 513-0258.
www.chinasyndrome.com
CONTACT
Paul Yee paulyee@chinasyndrome.com
Ethnic talent and casting. Provides translation, voice & on-screen talent in many Asian languages. Commercials. Corporate.

CHRISTOPHER BANKS & ASSOCIATES, INC.
410 – 6 Adelaide St. E, Toronto, ON M5C 1H6.
TEL: (416) 214-1155. FAX: (416) 214-1150.
email: info@chrisbanks.com www.chrisbanks.com
CONTACT
Christopher Banks, Angela Argento

THE CORE GROUP TALENT AGENCY, INC.
300 – 89 Bloor St. W, Toronto, ON M5S 1M1.
TEL: (416) 955-0819. FAX: (416) 955-0825.
email: info@coregroupta.com
Talent and literary agency.

CREATIVE DRIVE ARTISTS
20 Carlton St., Unit 123, Toronto, ON M5B 2H5.
TEL: (416) 530-0550. FAX: (416) 535-5713.
CONTACT
Dani De Lio danidelio@canadafilm.com
Jack Frizelle jfrizelle@canadafilm.com

THE EDWARD G. AGENCY, LTD.
19 Isabella St., Toronto, ON M4Y 1M7.
TEL: (416) 960-8683 ext. 23. FAX: (416) 960-6015.
email: edwardgagency@canadafilm.com
PRESIDENT
Sandie Newton

ETM, LTD.
318 Dundas St. W, Toronto, ON M5T 1G5.
TEL: (416) 413-7800. FAX: (416) 413-7804.
email: edna@etmltd.com www.etmltd.com
VOICEOVER
Edna Khubyar, Paul Smith
ON-CAMERA
Paul Hemrend, Angela Wright

FOUNTAINHEAD TALENT
131 Davenport Rd., Toronto, ON M5R 1H8.
TEL: (416) 538-6888. FAX: (416) 538-2223.
email: info@fountainheadtalent.com
CONTACT
Julie Lafontaine, Kevin Jensen, Faith Halman

FUSION ARTISTS, INC.
300 – 10 St. Mary St., Toronto, ON M4Y 1P9.
TEL: (416) 408-3304. FAX: (416) 408-4867.
www.fusionartistsinc.com
CONTACT
Sandi Sloan sloan@fusionartistsinc.com
Jude Foster foster@fusionartistsinc.com

Exclusive to voiceover talent.

GARY GODDARD AGENCY
305 – 10 St. Mary St., Toronto, ON M4Y 1P9.
TEL: (416) 928-0299. FAX: (416) 924-9593.
email: goddard@canadafilm.com
CONTACT
Celia Chassels, Pam Winter, Kish Iqbal

GLICKMAN TALENT MANAGEMENT
208 – 204 St. George St., Toronto, ON M5R 2N6.
TEL: (416) 960-0565. FAX: (416) 960-3265.
email: aglickman@canadafilm.com
CONTACT
Arleen Glickman, Liz Hampton

GREAT NORTH ARTISTS MANAGEMENT, INC.
350 Dupont St., Toronto, ON M5R 1V9.
TEL: (416) 925-2051. FAX: (416) 925-3904.
email: gnaminc@gnaminc.com
CONTACT
Ralph Zimmerman, Drew Mackenzie, Corina MacLean

HARRISON ARTIST MANAGEMENT, INC.
303A – 489 College St., Toronto, ON M6G 1A5.
TEL: (416) 922-1736. FAX: (416) 922-0701.
email: general@harrisonartistmgmt.ca
CONTACT
Lesley A. Harrison, Elina Levina

HOLLYWOOD NORTH, INC.
18 Thurston Rd., Toronto, ON M4S 2V7.
TEL: (416) 481-1000.
CONTACT
A. Kristin Scythes

Principals agency. Non-union and union.

JORDAN & ASSOCIATES TALENT MANAGEMENT LIMITED
401 – 615 Yonge St., Toronto, ON M4Y 1Z5.
TEL: (416) 515-2028. FAX: (416) 515-1763.
email: jordan@canadafilm.com
CONTACT
Gerry Jordan, Esther Buffery, Stewart Horsley

KG TALENT MANAGEMENT, INC.
55A Sumach St., Toronto, ON M5A 3J6.
TEL: (416) 368-4866. FAX: (416) 368-2492.
email: kgtalent@canadafilm.com
CONTACT
Kathy Gaitt, Monica Brdar, Layla Weinzweig

Agent / manager.

LORRAINE WELLS & COMPANY TALENT MANAGEMENT, INC.
320 – 10 St. Mary St., Toronto, ON M4Y 1P9.
TEL: (416) 413-1676. FAX: (416) 413-1680.
email: lorwells@canadafilm.com
CONTACT
Lorraine Wells

MARGO LANE TALENT
615 – 131 Bloor St. W, Toronto, ON M5S 1S3.
TEL: (416) 964-8982. FAX: (416) 964-5581.
email: margolane@canadafilm.com

MCGUIN & ASSOCIATES, INC.
116 - 20 Shallmar Blvd., Toronto, ON M5N 1J5.
TEL: (416) 920-6884. FAX: (416) 920-8543.
CONTACT
Debi McGuin mcguin@canadafilm.com

Represents children and adult actors in film, TV, commercials, print, voice and theatre. Also represents selective directors and writers. Hard copy submissions by mail only.

THE MESSINGER AGENCY, INC.
501 – 10 St. Mary St., Toronto, ON M4Y 1P9.
TEL: (416) 960-1000. FAX: (416) 960-1001.
email: messenger@bellnet.ca
CONTACT
Fran Messinger

NEWTON LANDRY MANAGEMENT, INC.
19 Isabella St., Toronto, ON M4Y 1M7.
TEL: (416) 960-8683. FAX: (416) 960-6015.
email: reception@newtonlaundry.com
CONTACT
Sandie Newton, Yanick Landry

THE NOBLE CAPLAN AGENCY
1260 Yonge St. 2nd Flr., Toronto, ON M4T 1W6.
TEL: (416) 920-5385.
TALENT DEPARTMENT
Penny Noble, Rich Caplan, Rachel Neville-Fox, Norbert Abrams
COMMERCIALS & FRENCH ON-CAMERA
Kate Eisner
VOICEOVER/FRENCH VOICEOVER
Caroline Young

OSCARS ABRAMS ZIMEL AND ASSOCIATES, INC.
438 Queen St. E, Toronto, ON M5A 1T4.
TEL: (416) 860-1790. FAX: (416) 860-0236.
email: info@oazinc.com
CONTACT
Michael Oscars, Gayle Abrams, Perry Zimel

Talent & literary agency.

PARENT MANAGEMENT, INC.
530 Queen St. E, Toronto, ON M5A 1V2.
TEL: (416) 977-5445. FAX: (416) 977-2441.
email: parent@canadafilm.com
CONTACT
Louise Parent, Barb Godfrey

PHOENIX ARTISTS MANAGEMENT, LTD.
152 Golfdale Rd., Toronto, ON M4N 2B9.
TEL: (416) 964-6464. FAX: (416) 969-9924.
email: phoenix@canadafilm.com
CONTACT
Kathy Kernohan

PREMIER ARTISTS MANAGEMENT, LTD.
300 – 40 Holly St., Toronto, ON M4S 3C3. TEL: (416) 461-6868.
FAX: (416) 461-7677. email: premier@canadafilm.com
CONTACT
Rod Maxwell, Sandra Gillis

SHERRIDA PERSONAL MANAGEMENT, INC.
110 Scollard St., Toronto, ON M5R 1G2.
TEL: (416) 928-2323. FAX: (416) 928-0767.
email: mgmt@sherrida.com www.sherrida.com
CONTACT
Sherrida Rawlings

THE TALENT HOUSE, INC.
204A St George St., Toronto, ON M5R 2N5.
TEL: (416) 960-9686. FAX: (416) 960-2314.
email: info@talenthouse.ca
CONTACT
Bruce Dean, Perrin Lyons, Beth Russell, Kevin Hicks

VOX TALENT
1000 – 1235 Bay St., Toronto, ON M5R 3K4.
TEL: (416) 410-4700, (877) 410-4700, (604) 719-4700 (Vancouver). email: info@voxtalent.com www.voxtalent.com
CONTACT
Dan Sandor, John Levy, Linda Campbell, Christine Grant

Voice-over talent / non-union.

QUÉBEC

CASTING DIRECTORS

AGENCE WHITEROCK
CP 148, Saint-Sauveur, QC J0R 1R0.
TEL: (514) 984-0714. FAX: (514) 227-5416.
email: whiterock@canadafilm.com

CONTACT
Lise White

ANDREA KENYON & ASSOCIATES CASTING

7535 St.-Denis, Montréal, QC H2R 2E7.
TEL: (514) 948-2000. FAX: (514) 948-1604.
email: kenyoncasting@canadafilm.com
CONTACT
Andrea Kenyon, Randi Wells

ELITE CASTING

310 – 3981 boul St.-Laurent, Montréal, QC H2W 1Y5.
TEL: (514) 282-1631. FAX: (514) 844-8223.
email: rbucci@canadafilm.com
CONTACT
Nadia Rona, Vera Miller, Rosina Bucci

Casting services.

CREATIVE REPS

DUCHESNE ARTISTS AGENCY

6031 ave du Parc, Montréal, QC H2V 4H.
TEL: (514) 274-4607. FAX: (514) 274-0591.
email: artistes@goodwin.agent.ca www.agencegoodwin.com
PRESIDENT
Natalie Duchesne

Actors, writers/screenwriters, composers, directors.

PUBLICISTS

CHANTAL DUFRESNE COMMUNICATIONS

4401 rue Garnier, Montréal, QC H2J 3S3.
TEL: (514) 844-9554. FAX: (514) 844-9828.
email: commdufresne@videotron.ca
CONTACT
Chantal Dufresne

COMMUNICATIONS LUCIE CHARLAND

300 – 2266 Parthenais, Montréal, QC H2K 3T5.
TEL: (514) 501-6996. FAX: (514) 521-0484.
email: agence@luciecharland.com www.luciecharland.com

KELLER COMMUNICATIONS

4740 McMahon Ave., Montréal, QC H4B 2B4.
TEL: (514) 489-5263. FAX: (514) 482-3935.
email: kellcomm@videotron.ca
CONTACT
Peter Keller

Publicist.

MAYA COMMUNICATIONS

4475 Andre Laurendeau St., Unit 2, Montréal, QC H1Y 3R6.
TEL: (514) 528-6362. FAX: (514) 528-9177.
email: leeja@maya-communications.com
www.maya-communications.com
PRESIDENT
Leeja Murphy

Unit publicist.

NOVEK COMMUNICATIONS

1002 – 6635 Mackle Rd., Cote St. Luc, QC H4W 2Z7.
TEL: (514) 219-3031. email: movietvpr@aol.com
CONTACT
David Novek

TALENT REPS

AGENCE GINETTE ACHIM, INC.

1053 Laurier Ave. W, Outremont, QC H2V 2L2.
TEL: (514) 271-3737. FAX: (514) 271-8774.
email: aga@ginetteachim.com
CONTACT
Ginette Achim (Tamac member)

AGENCE GOODWIN

200 – 839 Sherbrooke St. E, Montréal, QC H2L 1K6.
TEL: (514) 598-5252. FAX: (514) 598-1878.
email: artistes@goodwin.agent.ca
CONTACT
Camille Goodwin, Marie-Claude Goodwin, Nathalie Goodwin

Actors, writers, music composers, film directors & screenwriters.

AGENCE REISLER TALENT

CP 55067 CSP Fairmont, Outremont, QC H2T 3E2.
TEL: (514) 843-4551. FAX: (866) 906-6106.
email: info@reisler.ca www.reisler.ca
CONTACT
Mollye Reisler, Tania Giampetrone

AVIEL TALENT MANAGEMENT, INC.

718 – 117 St. Catherine St. W, Montréal, QC H3B 1H9.
TEL: (514) 288-8885. FAX: (514) 288-0768.
CONTACT
Shimon Aviel aviel@canadafilm.com
Tova Aviel

DUCHESNE ARTISTS AGENCY

6031 ave du Parc, Montréal, QC H2V 4H.
TEL: (514) 274-4607. FAX: (514) 274-0591.
email: artistes@goodwin.agent.ca www.agencegoodwin.com
PRESIDENT
Natalie Duchesne

Actors, writers/screenwriters, composers, directors.

ERIKA KLUSCH PRODUCTIONS

5677 Hutchison Ave., Montréal, QC H2V 4B5.
TEL: (514) 277-0992. FAX: (514) 270-2544.
CONTACT
Erika Klusch

GLENN TALENT MANAGEMENT

11 St. Joseph Blvd. W, Montréal, QC H2T 2P2.
TEL: (514) 499-3485. FAX: (514) 499-3491.
email: info@glenntalent.ca www.glenntalent.ca
CONTACT
Susan Glenn, Chelsea McIsaac

JEAN-JACQUES DESJARDINS AGENT

201 – 25 1260 rue Crescent, Montréal, QC H3G 2A9.
TEL: (514) 982-1718. FAX: (514) 982-1767.
email: agent@desja.qc.ca www.jjdagent.com
CONTACT
Jean-Jacques Desjardins

LAMPLIGHT AGENCY

923 Poirier, McMasterville, QC J3G 1K2. TEL: (450) 536-0755.
FAX: (450) 714-3707. email: frankie@lamplight-agency.com
www.lamplight-agency.com
CONTACT
Francine Millaire

Represents union, as well as non-union, actors, extras, singers and models. UDA ACTRA welcome as well as extras with skills.

PREMIER ROLE AGENCY

3449 ave de l'Hotel de Ville, Montréal, QC H2X 3B5.
TEL: (514) 844-7653. FAX: (514) 848-9636.
email: info@premierrole.com www.premierrole.com
CONTACT
Helene Mailloux

EDUCATION & TRAINING

ALBERTA

THE BANFF CENTRE
P.O. Box 1020, Banff, AB T1L 1H5. TEL: (403) 762-6100. FAX: (403) 762-6444. email: arts_info@banffcentre.ca www.banffcentre.ca
PRESIDENT & CEO
Mary E. Hofstetter

GRANT MACEWAN COLLEGE
School of Communications /Centre for the Arts Campus P.O. Box 1796, Edmonton, AB T5J 2P2. www.macewan.ca
PROGRAM INFORMATION
Kathleen Byrne - (780) 497-4754. FAX: (780) 497-4506.

RED DEER COLLEGE
Motion Picture Applied Arts Degree / P.O. Box 5005, Red Deer, AB T4N 5H5. TEL: (403) 342-3400 (Administration & Registrar). FAX: (403) 340-8940. www.rdc.ab.ca
HEAD, PERFORMANCE
Larry Reese larry.reese@rdc.ab.ca
HEAD, PRODUCTION
Don Armstrong don.armstrong@rdc.ab.ca

SAIT POLYTECHNIC
1301 – 16th Ave. NW, Calgary, AB T2M 0L4. TEL: (403) 284-8470. FAX: (403) 284-7238. email: media.info@sait.ca www.sait.ca
COORDINATOR
Richard Bourne

UNIVERSITY OF ALBERTA
Film & Media Studies / Department of English and Film Studies. 3-5 Humanities Centre, Edmonton, AB T6G 2E5. TEL: (780) 492-3258. FAX: (780) 492-8142. email: william.beard@ualberta.ca www.humanities.ualberta.ca/
CONTACT
Bill Beard - (780) 492-4886

BRITISH COLUMBIA

THE ART INSTITUTE OF VANCOUVER
3264 Beta Ave., Burnaby, BC V5G 4K4. TEL: (800) 661-1885, (604) 29878-5400. FAX: (604) 298-5403. email: tomlinsd@aii.edu www.aiv.aii.edu
CONTACT
Dawne Tomlinson

CAMOSUN COLLEGE – APPLIED COMMUNICATION PROGRAM
Lansdowne Campus, 3100 Foul Bay Rd., Victoria, BC V8P 5J2. TEL: (250) 370-3397. FAX: (250) 370-3679. email: fernyhol@camosun.bc.ca www.camosun.bc.ca
CONTACT
Lois Fernyhough

CAPILANO COLLEGE FILM CENTRE
2055 Purcell Way Film P Bldg., N Vancouver, BC V7J 3H5. TEL: (604) 990-7868. FAX: (604) 990-7867. www.capcollege.bc.ca

COLUMBIA ACADEMY
1295 W. Broadway Ave., Vancouver, BC V6H 3X8. TEL: (800) 665-9283, (604) 736-3316. FAX: (604) 731-5458. email: info@columbia-academy.com www.columbia-academy.com

CREATIVE WOMEN WORKSHOPS ASSOCIATION
1243 Duchess Ave., W. Vancouver, BC V7T 1H3. TEL: (604) 913-0747. FAX: (604) 913-0747. email: carol@creativewomenworkshops.com www.creativewomenworkshops.com
CONTACT
Carol Whiteman

EMILY CARR INSTITUTE
Art + Design + Media / 1399 Johnston St., Vancouver, BC V6H 3R9. TEL: (800) 832-7788, (604) 844-3820. FAX: (604) 844-3089. email: admissions@eciad.bc.ca www.eciad.bc.ca/

THE GULF ISLANDS FILM & TELEVISION SCHOOL
S-43 C-12 RR2, Galiano Island, BC V0N 1P0. TEL: (800) 813-9993, (250) 539-5729. FAX: (250) 539-3290. email: gifts@gulfislands.com www.giftsfilms.com
SCHOOL DIRECTOR
George Harris
REGISTRAR
Betsy Fairbrother

See website for course calendar.

PACIFIC AUDIO VISUAL INSTITUTE
34 W. 8th Ave., Vancouver, BC V5Y 1M7. TEL: (800) 601-7284. FAX: (604) 873-4295. email: info@pacificav.com www.pacificav.com

PRAXIS CENTRE FOR SCREENWRITERS
3120 – 515 W. Hastings St., Vancouver, BC V6B 5K3. TEL: (604) 268-7880. FAX: (604) 268-7882. email: praxis@sfu.ca www.praxisfilm.com
DIRECTOR
Patricia Gruben

SIMON FRASER UNIVERSITY
School for the Contemporary Arts
8888 University Dr., Burnaby, BC V5A 1S6. TEL: (604) 291-3363. FAX: (604) 291-5907. email: ca@sfu.ca www.sfu.ca/sca
DIRECTOR
Martin Gotfrit
INSTRUCTOR
Colin Browne, Rob Groeneboer, Patricia Gruben, Jacqueline Levitin, Chris Welsby

TARLINGTON TRAINING, INC.
609 – 525 Seymour St., Vancouver, BC V6B 3H7. TEL: (604) 664-0315. FAX: (604) 664-0316. email: ttraining@canadafilm.com www.tarlingtontraining.com

Training actors for film and television. Offering children, youth and adult workshops.

UNIVERSITY OF BRITISH COLUMBIA
Film Program / Department of Theatre, Film and Creative Writing, Brock Hall Annex 2354A – 1874 East Mall, Vancouver, BC V6T 1Z1. TEL: (604) 822-6037. FAX: (604) 822-0508. email: film@interchange.ubc.ca www.filmubc.ca
FILM PROGRAM COORDINATOR
Kate Castelo

Continuing Studies
800 Robson St., Vancouver, BC V6Z 3B7. TEL: (604) 822-1420. FAX: (604) 822-1499. email: film@tech.ubc.ca www.tech.ubc.ca/film

UBC Certificate in Entertainment Administration

VANCOUVER FILM SCHOOL
200 – 198 West Hastings St., Vancouver, BC V6B 1H2. TEL:(800) 661-4101 (North America), (604) 685-5808. FAX: (604) 685-5830. www.vfs.com

VICTORIA MOTION PICTURE SCHOOL, LTD.
751 Discovery St
Victoria BC V8T 1H1.
(250) 381-3032 / (250) 744-8664 / (888) 522-3456.
email: vmps@vicfilm.com www.vicfilm.com

MANITOBA

ACTORS TRAINING CENTRE OF MANITOBA (ATCMB)
502 - 62 Albert St., Winnipeg, MB R3B 1E9. TEL: (204) 957-0061. email: info@actorstrainingcentre.com www.actorstrainingcentre.com

FILM TRAINING MANITOBA
100 – 62 Albert St., Winnipeg, MB R3B 1E9. TEL: (204) 989-9669. FAX: (204) 989-9660. email: info@filmtraining.mb.ca www.filmtraining.mb.ca

NATIONAL SCREEN INSTITUTE – CANADA (NSI)
206 – 70 Arthur St., Winnipeg, MB R3B 1G7. TEL: (800) 952-9307, (204) 956-7800. FAX: (204) 956-5811. email: info@nsi-canada.ca www.nsi-canada.ca

UNIVERSITY OF MANITOBA
Film Studies Program / 364 University College, Winnipeg, MB R3T 2M8. TEL: (204) 474-9581. FAX: (204) 474-7684. email: filmstudies@umanitoba.ca www.umanitoba.ca/faculties/arts/english/film/
PROGRAM CHAIR
George Toles toles@cc.umanitoba.ca

NEW BRUNSWICK

UNIVERSITY OF NEW BRUNSWICK
P.O. Box 4400, Department of English, Carleton Hall 247, Fredericton, NB E3B 5A3. TEL: (506) 453-4676.
FAX: (506) 453-5069. email: temenuga@unb.ca
www.unb.ca/web/finearts/film
DIRECTOR OF FILM STUDIES
Dr. Temenuga Trifonova

Minor in Film Studies

NOVA SCOTIA

NOVA SCOTIA COMMUNITY COLLEGE (NSCC)
NSCC Admissions / P.O. Box 220, Halifax, NS B3J 2M4.
TEL: (902) 491-4911, (866) 679-6722. FAX: (902) 491-3514.
email: admissions@nscc.ca www.nscc.ca

NSCAD UNIVERSITY
5163 Duke St., Halifax, NS B3J 3J6. TEL: (902) 444-9600.
FAX: (902) 425-2420. email: admissions@nscad.ca
www.nscad.ca

ONTARIO

ALGONQUIN COLLEGE
1385 Woodroffe Ave., Nepean, ON K2G 1V8.
TEL: (613) 727-4723. FAX: (613) 727-7707.
www.algonquincollege.com

Broadcast Television

BROCK UNIVERSITY
Scotia Bank Hall 308 / 500 Glenridge Ave.,
St. Catharines, ON L2S 3A1. TEL: (905) 688-5550.
www.brocku.ca/cpcf
ADMINISTRATIVE ASSISTANT
Bridget Cahill ext. 4290

CANADIAN FILM AND TELEVISION PRODUCTION ASSOCIATION
National Mentorship Program
902 – 151 Slater St., Ottawa, ON K1P 5H3.
TEL: (800) 656-7440, (613) 233-1444 ext 238.
FAX: (613) 233-0073. email: nmp@cftpa.ca www.cftpa.ca

CANADIAN SCREEN TRAINING CENTRE / RESEAU D'ATELIERS CINEMATOGRAPHIQUES CANADIENS
61A York St., Ottawa, ON K1N 5T2. TEL: (800) 742-6016,
(613) 789-4720. FAX: (613) 789-4724. email: info@cstc.ca
www.cstc.ca

CARLETON UNIVERSITY
School for Studies in Art & Culture: Film Studies
423 St. Patrick's Bldg., Ottawa, ON K1S 5B6.
TEL: (613) 520-5606. FAX: (613) 520-3575.
email: info@carleton.ca www.carleton.ca
CONTACT
Sue Philips

CENTENNIAL COLLEGE
The Centre for Creative Communication
951 Carlaw Ave., Toronto, ON M4K 3M2. TEL: (416) 289-5100.
FAX: (416) 289-5106. www.thecentre.centennialcollege.ca
CONTACT
Kala Ramachandran

Digital Animation Program
CONTACT
Tara Donovan ext. 8627 tdonovan@centennialcollege.ca

Broadcasting & Film Program
CONTACT
Sheldon Reisler - (416) 289-5000 ext. 8806
sreisler@centennialcollege.ca

CONFEDERATION COLLEGE
Centre for Media Production / P.O. Box 398,
Thunder Bay, ON P7C 4W1.
email: bafoster@confederation.on.ca

Film Production
PROGRAM COORDINATOR
Dennis Austin
TEL: (807) 473-3817. email: daustin@confederationc.on.ca
www.confederationc.on.ca

DIRECTING, ACTING AND WRITING FOR CAMERA WORKSHOP (DAWC)
1407 – 50 Prince Arthur Ave., Toronto, ON M5R 1B5.
TEL: (416) 922-5378.

DURHAM COLLEGE
2000 Simcoe St. N, Oshawa, ON L1H 7K4.
TEL: (905) 721-2000. www.durhamcollege.ca

Animation — Computer Arts

HUMBER COLLEGE SCHOOL OF MEDIA STUDIES
205 Humber College Blvd., Etobicoke, ON M9W 5L7.
TEL: (416) 675-6622 ext. 4111. FAX: (416) 675-9730.
www.humber.ca
PROGRAM COORDINATOR, FILM & TV PRODUCTION:
Michael Glassbourg ext 4489
Donna O'Brien-Sokic ext. 4450
ANIMATION & MULTIMEDIA
Terry Postumus ext. 4942

MCMASTER UNIVERSITY
School of the Arts (SOTA), Togo Salmon Hall 303
1280 Main St. W, Hamilton, ON L8S 4M2.
TEL: (905) 525-9140 ext 27671. FAX: (905) 527-6793.
www.mcmaster.ca
ASSISTANT PROFESSOR
Peter Cockett cockett@mcmaster.ca

See website for a complete list of courses and programs.

NIAGARA COLLEGE (CANADA) SCHOOL OF MEDIA & DESIGN
300 Woodlawn Rd., Welland, ON L3C 7L3. TEL: (905) 735-2211.
FAX: (905) 736-6002.

ONTARIO COLLEGE OF ART & DESIGN
100 McCaul St., Toronto, ON M5T 1W1.
TEL: (416) 977-6000. FAX: (416) 977-6006.
www.ocad.ca
FACULTY OF ART ADMINISTRATIVE ASSISTANT
Winston Tulloch - ext 321 wtulloch@ocad.on.ca

QUEEN'S UNIVERSITY
160 Stuart St., Kingston, ON K7L 3N6. TEL: (613) 533-2178.
email: film@post.queensu.ca www.film.queensu.ca

RYERSON UNIVERSITY
350 Victoria St., Toronto, ON M5B 2K3. TEL: (416) 979-5167.
www.imagearts.ryerson.ca

After a first year of study, you'll specialize in either Film Studies, Still Photography or the New Media.

SENECA COLLEGE
School of Communication Arts / 88 The Pond Rd., Seneca @ York, Toronto, ON M3J 3M6. TEL: (416) 491-5050 ext. 3419.
FAX: (416) 739-1856. email: scainfo@seneca.on.ca
http://scaweb@seneca.on.ca

SHERIDAN COLLEGE
Trafalgar Road Campus / 1430 Trafalgar Rd., Oakville, ON L6H 2L1. TEL: (905) 845-9430. www.sheridanc.on.ca

Skills Training Centre / 407 Iroquois Shore Rd.,
Oakville, ON L6H 1M3. TEL: (905) 845-9430.

Davis Campus:
P.O. Box 7500, 7899 McLaughlin Rd., Brampton, ON L6V 1G6.
TEL: (905) 459-7533.

See website for a complete list of courses and programs available.

TORONTO FILM COLLEGE
36 Eglinton Ave. W, 7/F, Toronto, ON M4R 1A1.
TEL: (800) 568-8090. (416) 484-1577. FAX: (416) 484-1567.
email: tfc@torontofilmcollege.ca

Diplomas: film arts & production / dramatic arts / film promotion & distribution / scriptwriting / digital post-production.

Certificates: filming / acting / scriptwriting / editing.

TORONTO FILM SCHOOL
International Academy of Design & Technology
39 John St., Toronto, ON M5V 3G6. TEL: (800) 361-6664,
(416) 922-3666. FAX: (416) 922-7483.
email: admissions@torontofilmschool.ca
www.torontofilmschool.ca / www.iadt.com

Full-time diploma programs: Acting for Film, Television & Theatre; Computer Animation; Digital Film & Television Production; Digital Video Editing & Design; Entertainment Business Management; Sound Technology (Recording Arts).

TREBAS INSTITUTE
149 College St., Toronto, ON M5T 1P5. TEL: (416) 966-3066.
FAX: (416) 966-0030. email: trebas@trebas.com
www.trebas.com

Career training, since 1979, with programs in film/television production, sound design, studio recording and live sound.

UNIVERSITY OF TORONTO
Cinema Studies / Innis College Rm. 226, 2 Sussex Ave.,
Toronto, ON M5S 1J5. TEL: (416) 978-5809. FAX: (416) 946-0168.
email: cinema.studies@utoronto.ca www.utoronto.ca/cinema

UNIVERSITY OF WATERLOO
Waterloo, ON N2L 3G1. TEL: (519) 885-1211 ext. 3709 or 6923. FAX: (519) 746-4982.
www.arts.uwaterloo.ca/FINE/filmcourse_info.html

UNIVERSITY OF WESTERN ONTARIO
2 – 1151 Richmond St., London, ON N6A 5B8.
TEL: (519) 661-2111. www.uwo.ca/film

UNIVERSITY OF WINDSOR
401 Sunset Ave., Windsor, ON N9B 3P4.
TEL: (519) 253-3000 ext. 2896. www.uwindsor.ca

Communication Studies: Bachelor of Arts, Honors Communication Studies.

WILFRID LAURIER UNIVERSITY
75 University Ave. W, Waterloo, ON N2L 3C5.
TEL: (519) 884-1970 ext. 2476. FAX: (519) 884-8307.
email: pgates@wlu.ca www.wlu.ca/arts/filmstudies
FILM STUDIES COORDINATOR
Dr. Philippa Gates

YORK UNIVERSITY
Department of Film & Video / 224 Centre for Film and Theatre
4700 Keele St., Toronto, ON M3J 1P3. TEL: (416) 736-5149.
FAX: (416) 736-5710. email: filmvideo@yorku.ca
www.yorku.ca/finearts/fv/
ASSOCIATE PROFESSOR, PRODUCTION & CHAIR, DEPARTMENT OF FILM & VIDEO
Brenda Longfellow

QUÉBEC

CENTRE NATIONAL D'ANIMATION ET DE DESIGN
335 boul de Maisonneuve est 3e étage, Montréal, QC H2X 1K1. TEL: (514) 288-3447. FAX: (514) 288-5799.
email: albanef@centrenad.com www.centrenad.com

Training in film and television post-production and animation.

COLLEGE DE BOIS-DE-BOULOGNE
10555 ave de Bois-de-Boulogne, Montréal, QC H4N 1L4.
TEL: (514) 332-3000 ext. 7501. email: admission@bdeb.qc.ca
www.bdeb.qc.ca

Training in animation.

CONCORDIA UNIVERSITY
Faculty of Fine Arts / The Mel Hoppenheim School of Cinema
1455 de Maisonneuve Blvd. W, Montréal, QC H3G 1M8.
TEL: (514) 848-2424 ext. 4666. FAX: (514) 848-4255.
email: cinema@concordia.ca www.cinema.concordia.ca

INSTITUT NATIONAL DE L'IMAGE ET DU SON (INIS)
Centre de Formation Professionelle en Cinéma, Télévision et Medias Interactifs
301 boul de Maisonneuve E, Montréal, QC H2X 1K1.
TEL: (514) 285-1840. FAX: (514) 285-1953.
email: info@inis.qc.ca www.inis.qc.ca

PARLIMAGE CCF
30 – 222 rue Dominion, Montréal, QC H3J 2X1.
TEL: (514) 288-1400. FAX: (514) 288-2989.
email: audiov@parlimageccf.qc.ca
comm.@parlimageccf.qc.ca http://pages.infinit.net/parlimage

Film & television training – producing, acting, directing, technical.

TREBAS INSTITUTE
600 – 550 Sherbrooke St W, Montréal QC H3A 1B9.
TEL: (514) 845-4141. FAX: (514) 845-2581.
email: infomtl@trebas.com www.trebas.com

Career training, since 1979, with programs in film/television production, sound design, studio recording and live sound.

UNIVERSITÉ DU QUÉBEC A MONTRÉAL
Unité de Programmation
CP 8888 Succ Centre-Ville, Montréal QC H3C 3P8.
TEL: (514) 987-3000 ext. 4132. FAX: (514) 987-4650.
www.uqam.ca

SASKATCHEWAN

NEW MEDIA CAMPUS
Saskatoon Campus / 1223 Idylwyld Dr. N, Saskatoon, SK S7L 1A1. TEL: (306) 955-4412, (866) 755-5551.
FAX: (306) 955-5337. email: info@newmediacampus.com
www.newmediacampus.com

UNIVERSITY OF REGINA
Faculty of Fine Arts Department of Media Production & Studies
3737 Wascana Pkwy., Regina, SK S4S 0A2. TEL: (306) 585-4796.
FAX: (306) 585-4439. www.uregina.ca

CINÉMATHÈQUES

CANADIAN FILM INSTITUTE/ INSTITUT CANADIEN DU FILM

(a Division of Cinémathèque Canada)
2 Daly Ave., Ottawa, ON K1N 6E2. TEL: (613) 232-6727.
FAX: (613) 232-6315. email: cfi-icf@magma.ca
www.cfi-icf.ca
EXECUTIVE DIRECTOR
Tom McSorley

CINÉMATHÈQUE ONTARIO

(Division of the Toronto International Film Festival Group)
1600 – 2 Carlton St., Toronto, ON M5B 1J3.
TEL: (416) 967-7371.

Box Office / Membership Info:
TEL: (416) 968-3456. FAX: (416) 967-9477.
email: tiffg@tcinematheque.ca www.cinemathequeontario.ca
DIRECTOR, FESTIVAL CENTRE PROGRAMMING
Jim Hamilton

CONSERVATOIRE D'ART CINÉMATOGRAPHIQUE DE MONTRÉAL

(a Division of Cinémathèque Canada)
1432 de Bleury, Montréal, QC H3A 2J1. TEL: (514) 848-3883.
FAX: (514) 848-3886. email: info@ffm-montreal.org
DIRECTOR GENERAL
Nicolas Desjardins
VICE PRESIDENT
Danièle Cauchard

THE FILM REFERENCE LIBRARY

(division of the Toronto International Film Festival Group)
2 Carlton St., E Mezzanine, Toronto, ON M5B 1J3.
TEL: (416) 967-1517. FAX: (416) 967-0628.
email: libraryservices@tiffg.ca www.filmreferencelibrary.ca
LIBRARY DIRECTOR
Sylvia Frank
SENIOR LIBRARY MANAGER
Eve Goldin
LIBRARY MANAGER
Rosanne Pavicic

LA CINÉMATHÈQUE QUÉBÉCOISE

335 est boul de Maisonneuve ouest, Montréal, QC H2X 1K1.
TEL: (514) 842-9763. FAX: (514) 842-1816.
email: info@cinemateque.qc.ca www.cinematheque.qc.ca
DIRECTEUR GÉNÉRAL
Yolande Root
DIRECTEUR DE LA PROGRAMMATION ET DE LA CONSERVATION
Pierre Jutras
DIRECTRICE DES COMMUNICATIONS
Lyne Richer
CONSERVATEUR DES COLLECTIONS AFFÉRENTES AU FILM:
Pierre Véronneau
DOCUMENTATION
René Beauclair
CONSERVATEUR DU CINÉMA D'AMIMATION
Marco de Blois
CONSERVATEUR TÉLÉVISION ET VIDÉO
Dominique Dugas
COORDONNATEUR DES EXPOSITIONS
Alain Gauthier
COLLECTION DE FILMS
Carmelle Gaudet

PACIFIC CINEMATHEQUE PACIFIQUE

200 – 1131 Howe St., Vancouver, BC V6Z 2L7.
TEL: (604) 688-8202. FAX: (604) 688-8204.
email: info@cinematheque.bc.ca www. cinematheque.bc.ca
EXECUTIVE DIRECTOR
Jim Sinclair

CANADA:
NATIONAL FILM BOARD

NATIONAL FILM BOARD OF CANADA

Mailing Address: P.O. Box 6100. Stn. Centre-ville
Montréal, QC H3C 3H5.

HEAD OFFICE:

Constitution Sq.
1560 – 360 Albert St., Ottawa ON K1A 0M9.
TEL: (613) 992-3615, Sales: (800) 267-7710, (514) 283-9000.
www.nfb.ca

OPERATIONAL HEADQUARTERS:

Norman-McLaren Bldg., 3155 Cote-de-Liesse Rd.,
Montréal, QC H4N 2N4. TEL: (514) 283-9000.

NFB DIRECTORS:

GOVERNMENT FILM COMMISSIONER & NFB CHAIRPERSON
Tom Perlmutter (514) 283-9245
ASSISTANT COMMISSIONER & CORPORATE SERVICES
Claude Joli-Cœur (514) 283-2905
DIRECTOR GENERAL, ENGLISH PROGRAM
Cindy Witten (514) 283-9501
DIRECTOR , FRENCH PROGRAM
Monique Simard (514) 283-9285
DIRECTOR GENERAL, ACCESSIBILITY & DIGITAL ENTERPRISES
Deborah Drisdell (514) 283-3242
DIRECTOR GENERAL, FINANCE, OPERATIONS & TECHNOLOGY
Luisa Frate (514) 283-9050

Produces and distributes social issue documentaries, animation and digital content. Over 12,000 productions.

PRODUCTION CENTRES/STUDIOS

ENGLISH PROGRAM:

Animation Studio:
3155 Côte de Liesse Rd., Montréal, QC H4N 2N4.
TEL: (514) 283-9571. FAX: (514) 283-3211.
email: animation@nfb.ca
EXECUTIVE PRODUCER
David Verrall
PRODUCER
Michael Fukushima, Marcy Page

PACIFIC & YUKON CENTRE:

200 – 1385 W. 8th Ave., Vancouver, BC V6H 3V9.
TEL: (604) 666-3838. FAX: (604) 666-1569.
email: pacific@nfb.ca
EXECUTIVE PRODUCER
Tracey Friesen
PRODUCER
Selwyn Jacob, Martin Rose, Yves Ma

NORTH WEST CENTRE:

100 – 10815 104th Ave., Edmonton, AB T5J 4N6.
TEL: (780) 495-3013. FAX: (780) 495-6412.
email: northwest@nfb.ca
EXECUTIVE PRODUCER
David Christensen
PRODUCER
Bonnie Thompson

PRAIRIE CENTRE:

300 – 136 Market Ave., Winnipeg, MB R3B 0P4.
TEL: (204) 983-3160. FAX: (204) 983-0742.
email: prairie@nfb.ca
EXECUTIVE PRODUCER
David Christensen

ONTARIO CENTRE:

150 John St., Toronto, ON M5V 3C3.
TEL: (416) 973-0904. FAX: (416) 973-9640.
email: ontarioinfo@nfb.ca
EXECUTIVE PRODUCER
Jacques Turgeon
PRODUCER
Anne-Marie Rocher

QUÉBEC CENTRE:

3155 Côte de Liesse Rd., Montréal, QC H4N 2N4.
TEL: (514) 496-2216. FAX: (514) 283-5487.
email: quebeccentre@nfb.ca
EXECUTIVE PRODUCER
Ravida Din
PRODUCER
Kat Baulu

ATLANTIC CENTRE:

Cornwallis House, 201 – 5475 Spring Garden Rd., Halifax NS B3J 3T2. TEL: (902) 426-6000. FAX: (902) 426-8901.
email: atlantic@nfb.ca
EXECUTIVE PRODUCER
Ravida Din
PRODUCER
Paul McNeill

FRENCH PROGRAM:

Animation/Youth Studio, 3155 Côte de Liesse Rd., Montréal, QC H4N 2N4. TEL: (514) 283-9332. FAX: (514) 496-4443.
email: animationjeunesse@nfb.ca
EXECUTIVE PRODUCER
René Chénier
PRODUCER
Marc Bertrand, Julie Roy

QUÉBEC STUDIO:

3155 Cote-de-Liesse Rd., Montréal, QC H4N 2N4.
TEL: (514) 496-1171. FAX: (514) 283-7914.
email: doc.quebec@onf.ca
EXECUTIVE PRODUCER
Jacques Turgeon
PRODUCER
Johanne Bergeron

ACADIA STUDIO:

100 – 95 Foundry St., Heritage Ct., Moncton, NB E1C 5H7.
TEL: (506) 851-6104. FAX: (506) 851-2246.
email: doc.acadie@onf.ca
EXECUTIVE PRODUCER
Jacques Turgeon
PRODUCER
Murielle Rioux-Poirier

ONTARIO & WEST STUDIO:

150 John St., Toronto, ON M5V 3C3. TEL: (866) 663-7668, (416) 973-5382. FAX: (416) 973-2594.
email: doc.ontarioouest@onf.ca
EXECUTIVE PRODUCER
Jacques Turgeon
PRODUCER
Anne-Marie Rocher

ASSISTANCE FOR INDEPENDENT FILMMAKERS

To receive filmmaker assistance program guidelines or to receive an application form, contact the NFB office nearest you.

QUÉBEC:

if you live in Québec, contact:
PRODUCER, ACIC-FAP
Pierre Lapointe - (514) 283-9628. email: p.lapointe@nfb.ca

SALES & CUSTOMER SERVICE IN CANADA (D-10):

P.O. Box 6100, Stn. Centre-ville, Montréal, QC H3C 3H5.
TEL: (800) 267-7710, (514) 283-9000. (Montréal)
Mon. through Fri. from 9 a.m. to 7 p.m. EST.
FAX: (514) 283-7564.

UNITED STATES:

307 – 1123 Broadway, New York, NY 10010.
TEL: (212) 629-8890. FAX: (212) 629-8502.

FRANCE / EUROPE / AFRICA:

5 rue de Constantine, 75007 Paris, France.
TEL: 01-44-18-35-40. FAX: 47-05-75-89.

ALBERTA

ALBERTA FILM COMMISSION

140 Whitemud Crossing, 4211 – 106 Street, Edmonton, AB T6J 6L7 T5J 4L6. TEL: (888) 813-1738, (780) 422-8584.
FAX: (780) 422-8582. email: dan.chugg@gov.ab.ca
www.albertafilm.ca
COMMISSIONER
Jeff Brinton - Jeff.brinton@gov.ab.ca

2ND LOCATION:

Standard Life Building, 639 5th Ave. SW, 3rd Flr., Calgary, AB T2P 0M9. TEL: (403) 297-6241. FAX: (403) 297-6168.

FILM COMMISSIONS

BRITISH COLUMBIA

BRITISH COLUMBIA FILM COMMISSION
Ministry of Small Business and Economic Development
201 – 865 Hornby St., Vancouver, BC V6Z 2G3.
TEL: (604) 660-2732. FAX: (604) 660-4790.
email: info@bcfilm.gov.bc.ca www.bcfilmcommission.com
FILM COMMISSIONER
Susan Croome
MANAGER, PRODUCTION SERVICES
Julie Bernard
MANAGER, COMMUNITY AFFAIRS
Gordon Hardwick

COLUMBIA SHUSWAP FILM COMMISSION
P.O. Box 978, 781 Marine Park Dr. NE, Salmon Arm, BC V1E 4P1. TEL: (250) 832-8194. FAX: (250) 832-3375.
email: abender@csrd.bc.ca www.filmcolumbiashuswap.com
www.csrd.bc.ca www.shuswap.bc.ca
FILM COMMISSIONER
Robyn Cyr - rcyr@csrd.bc.ca

GREATER VICTORIA FILM COMMISSION
P.O. Box 34, 794 Fort St., Victoria, BC V8W 1H2.
TEL: (888) 537-3456, (250) 386-3976. FAX: (250) 386-3967.
email: admin@filmvictoria.com www.filmvictoria.com
FILM COMMISSIONER
Ron Hardy

NANAIMO FILM OFFICE
455 Wallace St., Nanaimo, BC V9R 5J6. TEL: (250) 755-4465.
FAX: (250) 755-4404. www.filmnanaimo.com
CONTACT
Amrit Manhas (250) 755-4465

NORTHERN BRITISH COLUMBIA FILM COMMISSION
201 – 1300 First Ave., Prince George, BC V2L 2Y3.
TEL: (250) 649-3207. FAX: (250) 649-3200.
email: cameron@initiativespg.com www.northernbcfilm.com
CONTACT
Karen Cameron

OKANAGAN FILM COMMISSION
1450 KLO Rd., Kelowna, BC V1W 3Z4. TEL: (250) 717-0087.
FAX: (250) 868-0512. email: info@okanaganfilm.com
www.okanaganfilm.com
FILM COMMISSIONER
Jon Summerland

REGIONAL FILM COMMISSIONS ASSOCIATION OF BC
203 – 871 Island Hwy., Campbell River, BC V9W 2C3.
TEL: (250) 287-2772. email: film.commission@infilm.ca
www.filmbcregions.com
PRESIDENT
Joan Miller
VICE PRESIDENT
Vicci Weller

THOMPSON-NICOLA FILM COMMISSION
300 – 465 Victoria St., Kamloops, BC V2C 2A9.
TEL: (250) 377-8673. BC: (877) 377-8673.
FAX: (250) 372-5048. email: vweller@tnrd.bc.ca
www.tnrdfilm.com
EXECUTIVE DIRECTOR OF FILM
Victoria Weller

VANCOUVER ISLAND NORTH FILM COMMISSION
900 Alder St., Campbell River, BC V9W 2P6.
TEL: (250) 287-2772. email: film.commission@infilm.ca
www.infilm.ca
FILM COMMISSIONER
Joan Miller

MANITOBA

CITY OF WINNIPEG
CAO Secretariat, 510 Main St., 3rd Flr., Winnipeg, MB R3B 1B9. TEL: (204) 986-3058. FAX: (204) 986-7673.
email: kboyce@winnipeg.ca www.winnipeg.com
MANAGER, FILM & CULTURAL AFFAIRS
Kenny Boyce
FILM LIAISON
Kevin Uddenberg - (204) 986-2138.

MANITOBA FILM & SOUND RECORDING DEVELOPMENT CORPORATION
410 – 93 Lombard Ave., Winnipeg, MB R3B 3B1.
TEL: (204) 947-2040. FAX: (204) 956-5261.
email: explore@mbfilmsound.mb.ca www.mbfilmsound.mb.ca
CEO / FILM COMMISSIONER
Carole Vivier
MANAGER, FILM PRODUCTION
Louise O'Brien-Moran

NEW BRUNSWICK

NEW BRUNSWICK FILM / FILM NOUVEAU-BRUNSWICK
Film Place 2000, 250 King St, 4th Flr., Fredericton, NB E3B 9M9. TEL: (506) 453-2555. FAX: (506) 453-2416.
email: nbfilm@gnb.ca www.nbfilm.cA
FINANCIAL SERVICES
Ghislain Labbé
PROJECT EXECUTIVE
Antoinette Basque-Doiron

NEWFOUNDLAND AND LABRADOR

NEWFOUNDLAND AND LABRADOR FILM DEVELOPMENT CORPORATION
12 King's Bridge Rd., St. John's, NL A1C 3K3.
TEL: (709) 738-3456, (877) 738-3456. FAX: (709) 739-1680.
email: info@nlfdc.ca www.nlfdc.ca
EXECUTIVE DIRECTOR
Chris Bonnell - chris@nlfdc.ca
MANAGER, PROGRAMS
Dorian Rowe - dorian@nlfdc.ca
BUSINESS ANALYST
Nancy Benoit - nancy@nlfdc.ca
INDUSTRY ANALYST
Laura Churchill - laura@nlfdc.ca

NORTHWEST TERRITORIES

NWT FILM COMMISSION
Government of the Northwest Territories Dept. of Industry, Tourism & Investment.
P.O. Box 1320, Yellowknife, NT X1A 2L9. TEL: (867) 920-8793.
FAX: (867) 873-0101. email: nwtfilm@gov.nt.ca
www.iti.gov.nt.ca/artscrafts/filmcommission.shtml
FILM COMMISSIONER
Carla Wallis

Location scouting assistance / liaison services with industry, community, production companies & government.

NOVA SCOTIA

NOVA SCOTIA FILM DEVELOPMENT CORPORATION
P.O. Box 34104, Scotia Square, RPO, Halifax, NS B3J 3S1.
TEL: (902) 424-7177. FAX: (902) 424-0617.
email: novascotia.film@ns.sympatico.ca www.film.ns.ca
PRESIDENT & CEO
Ann MacKenzie mackenam@gov.ns.ca

Promotes the province as a film location in the global market-place and provides initial production support to producers who are guests in the province. The Department fulfills a community liaison role for the industry and general public and coordinates the Corporation's communication activities.

NUNAVUT

NUNAVUT FILM
P.O. Box 2398, 8 Storey Astrohill, Unit 107, Iqaluit, NU X0A 0H0. TEL: (867) 979-3012. FAX: (867) 979-3013.
email: info@nunavutfilm.ca www.nunavutfilm.ca
CEO
Cheryl Ashton cheryl@nunavutfilm.ca

ONTARIO

BRAMPTON ECONOMIC DEVELOPMENT OFFICE
33 Queen St. W, Brampton, ON L6Y 1L9.
TEL: (905) 874-2657. FAX: (905) 874-2670.
CONTACT
Norine Richardson - norine.richardson@city.brampton.on.ca

CITY OF MISSISSAUGA – MISSISSAUGA FILM OFFICE
4141 Living Arts Dr., Mississauga, ON L5B 4B8.
TEL: (905) 306-6150. FAX: (905) 306-6101.
email: carmen.ford@mississauga.ca
FILM LIAISON
Carmen Ford

CITY OF TORONTO
Toronto Film and Television Office, Toronto City Hall, North Rotunda, 100 Queen St. W, Toronto, ON M5H 2N2.
TEL: (416) 338-3456. FAX: (416) 392-0675.
email: filmtoronto@toronto.ca www.toronto.ca/tfto
FILM COMMISSIONER
Peter Finestone
MANAGER
Eric Jensen

A free service for location assistance and permits.

THE CORPORATION OF THE TOWN OF HUNTSVILLE
37 Main St. E., Huntsville, ON P1H 1A1. TEL: (705) 789-1751, ext. 2229. FAX: (705) 789-1762.
CONTACT
John M. Finley

DURHAM REGION – FILM LOCATIONS OFFICE
P.O. Box 623, 605 Rossland Rd. E., 5th Flr., Whitby, ON L1N 6A3. TEL: (800) 706-9857, (905) 668-7711.
email: jennifer.taiariol@region.durham.on.ca
CONTACT
Jennifer Taiariol

HAMILTON FILM & TELEVISION OFFICE
1 James St. S., 8th Fl., Hamilton, ON L8P 4R5.
TEL: (905) 546-4233. FAX: (905) 546-4107.
email: film@hamilton.ca www.hamilton.ca/film
MANAGER
Jacqueline Norton

NIAGARA ECONOMIC AND TOURISM CORPORATION
P.O. Box 1042, 2201 St. David's Rd., Thorold, ON L2V 4T7.
TEL: (800) 263-2988, (905) 685-1308. FAX: (905) 688-5907.
email: dbishun@niagaracanada.com www.filmniagara.com
ECONOMIC DEVELOPMENT OFFICER
Daniel Bishun

ONTARIO MEDIA DEVELOPMENT CORPORATION (OMDC)
501 – 175 Bloor St. E., South Tower, Toronto, ON M4W 3R8.
TEL: (416) 314-6858. FAX: (416) 314-6876.
email: mail@omdc.on.ca www.omdc.on.ca
CEO
Karen Thorne-Stone
COMMUNICATIONS MANAGER & CORPORATE SECRETARY
George McNeillie
DIRECTOR, TAX CREDITS
Jennifer Blitz
DIRECTOR, INDUSTRY DEVELOPMENT (A) & MANAGER, FILM
Donna Zuchlinski
MANAGER, INDUSTRY INITIATIVES
James Weyman
DIRECTOR, BUSINESS AFFAIRS & RESEARCH
Cherith Muir
MANAGER, RESEARCH & STRATEGIC PLANNING
Raina Wells
COMMUNICATIONS OFFICER
Sharon Wilson - (416) 642-6616 email: swilson@omdc.on.ca

An agency of the Ministry of Culture. Location services, digital library

OTTAWA-GATINEAU FILM & TV DEVELOPMENT CORP.
138 - 245 Centrum Boulevard, Ottowa, ON K1A 0A1
TEL: (613) 580-2745. FAX: (613) 580-2746.
email: info@ogft.com www.ogft.com
GENERAL MANAGER
Roch Brunette

RICHMOND HILL – OFFICE OF ECONOMIC DEVELOPMENT
225 E. Beaver Creek Rd., Richmond Hill, ON L4B 3P4.
TEL: (800) 780-7831, (905) 771-2523. FAX: (905) 771-2406.
www.richmondhillonline.com
DIRECTOR OF STRATEGIC INITIATIVES
Gwen Manderson gmanderson@richmondhill.ca

Film services - local government liaison, location assistance and free copies of the local film guide.

PRINCE EDWARD ISLAND

TECHNOLOGY PEI
Business Investment – Film, Television and New Media.
P.O. Box 340, 94 Euston St., 2nd Flr., Charlottetown, PE C1A 7K7. TEL: (902) 368-5336. FAX: (902) 368-6255.
email: ndroberts@gov.pe.ca www.techpei.com
PROGRAM ANALYST
Nancy Roberts

Locations Services: provides location and liaison information.

QUÉBEC

ARGENTEUIL-LAURENTIANS FILM & TELEVISION COMMISSION
430 rue Grace, Lachute, QC J8H 1M6. TEL: (450) 562-2446.
FAX: (450) 562-1911. email: info@filmlaurentides.ca
www.filmlaurentides.ca
FILM COMMISSIONERS
Dany Brassard - ext. 253
Marie-Josée Pilon - ext. 256

MONTRÉAL FILM AND TV COMMISSION
801 Brennan St., 5th Flr., Duke Pavillion, Montréal, QC H3C 0G4. TEL: (514) 872-2883. FAX: (514) 872-3409.
email: film_tv@ville.montreal.qc.ca www.montrealfilm.com
FILM COMMISSIONER
Daniel Bissonnette (514) 872-2883
LIAISON
Yan Éthier (514) 872-1503

QUÉBEC CITY FILM & TV COMMISSION
310 – 43 rue de Buade St., Québec, QC G1R 4A2.
TEL: (418) 641-6766. FAX: (418) 691-5777.
email: cctq@ville.quebec.qc.ca www.filmquebec.com
FILM COMMISSIONER
Lorraine Boily
ASSISTANT COMMISSIONER
Karine Latulippe
LIAISON OFFICER
Geneviève Doré

Provides assistance and technical support for your next production.

QUÉBEC FILM & TELEVISON COUNCIL
500 – 204 Saint-Sacrement St., Montréal, QC H2Y 1W8.
TEL: (866) 320-3456, (514) 499-7070. FAX: (514) 499-7018.
email: info@qftc.ca www.qftc.ca
FILM COMMISSIONER
Hans Fraikin
INDUSTRY DEVELOPMENT OFFICER
Christian Beauchesne

SASKATCHEWAN

SASKATCHEWAN FILM AND VIDEO DEVELOPMENT CORPORATION (SASKFILM)
1831 College Ave., Regina, SK S4P 4V5.
TEL: (306) 798-9800. FAX: (306) 798-7768.
email: general@saskfilm.com www.saskfilm.com
CEO/FILM COMMISSIONER
Suzanne Bell - bell@saskfilm.com
PROGRAM OFFICER
Erin Dean - erin@saskfilm.com
LOCATIONS COORDINATOR
David Gane - locations@saskfilm.com

YUKON

YUKON FILM & SOUND COMMISSION
P.O. Box 2703, Whitehorse, YT Y1A 2C6. TEL: (867) 667-5400.
FAX: (867) 393-7040. email: reel.yukon@gov.yk.ca
www.reelyukon.com
FILM COMMISSIONER
Iris Merritt - iris.merritt@gov.yk.ca

$100 FILM FESTIVAL

Bldg. J2, 2711 Battleford Ave. SW,
Calgary, AB T3E 7L4. TEL: (403) 205-4747.
FAX: (403) 237-5838. email: www.festival@csif.org
www.csif.org
PROGRAMMING COORDINATOR
Melanie Wilmink
COMMUNICATIONS COORDINATOR
Farrah Alladin

Presented by the Calgary Society of Independent Filmmakers in mid-March, this festival of short films celebrates the spirit of low budget. Features cash prizes.

2880 FILM BLITZ

5725 Ave de l'Esplanade, Montréal, QC H2T 2Z9.
TEL: (514) 586-6769. email: info@2880.ca www.2880.ca
EXECUTIVE DIRECTOR
Dan Emery

48-hour filmmaking contest. The event celebrates its 6th year in June 2008. Past and present partners the NFB, CBC, Audio Post-Production SPR, La Boite Numerique, SETTE, Le Reservoir, Mainfilm, Montréal Mirror/ICI and Playback Magazine.

ACADEMY OF CANADIAN CINEMA & TELEVISION / ACADÉMIE CANADIENNE DU CINÉMA ET DE LA TÉLÉVISION – GENIE, GEMINI & GÉMEAUX AWARDS

National Office: 49 Ontario St., Ste., 501, Toronto, ON M5A 2V1. TEL: (800) 644-5194, (416) 366-2227.
FAX: (416) 366-8454. email: info@academy.ca
www.academy.ca
CEO
Sara Morton - ext. 240 smorton@academy.ca
DEVELOPMENT AND MARKETING MANAGER
Liz Stanwyck - ext. 242 liz@academy.ca
DIRECTOR OF FINANCE & DEVELOPMENT
Judy Watt - ext. 237 jwatt@academy.ca
AWARDS DIRECTOR
Alex Lalonde - ext. 228 alalonde@academy.ca
GEMINI AWARDS MANAGER
Tiffany Cox - ext. 230 tiffany@academy.ca
GENIE AWARDS MANAGER
Louis Calabro - ext. 234 louis@academy.ca
MEMBERSHIP & ADMINISTRATION MANAGER
Francis Domingue - ext. 245 fdomingue@academy.ca
DIRECTOR OF DEVELOPMENT, MARKETING AND COMMUNICATIONS
Dianna Klisanin - ext. 231 dianna@academy.ca
COMMUNICATIONS MANAGER
Judy Lung - ext. 238 judy@academy.ca
PUBLICATIONS & ARCHIVE COORDINATOR
Genevieve D'Iorio - ext. 227 gdiorio@academy.ca

Hosts of the annual Genie Awards for Canadian film, and the annual Gemini and Gémeaux Awards for Canadian television. Year-round providers of educational and professional development programs as well as promotional services.

Western Office:
Unit 212-2223 West Broadway, Vancouver, BC V6K 2E4.
TEL: (604) 684-4528. FAX: (604) 684-4574.
email: info@academy.ca www.academy.ca/western/
MANAGER, WESTERN DIVISION
Clare Contini - ccontini@academy.ca

Québec Office:
225, rue Roy Est Bureau 106, Montréal, QC H2W 1M5.
TEL: (514) 849-7448. FAX: (514) 849-5069.
email: academie@acct.ca www.acct.ca/
DIRECTOR
Patrice Lachance - plachance@acct.ca
AWARDS ASSISTANT
Samuel Bélisle - gemeaux@acct.ca
ADMINISTRATION & SPECIAL PROJECTS
Danièle Gauthier - dgauthier@acct.ca

ALBERTA FILM AND TELEVISION AWARDS

Alberta Motion Picture Industries Association: #318, 8944 182nd St. NW, Edmonton, AB T5T 2E3.
TEL: (800) 814-7779, (780) 944-0707. FAX: (780) 426-3057.
email: info@ampia.org www.ampia.org
INTERIM EXECUTIVE DIRECTOR
Jane Bisbee - jbisbee@ampia.org
ALBERTA FILM AND TELEVISION AWARDS PRODUCER/EXECUTIVE PRODUCER
Pauline Lancaster - plancaster@ampia.org

Hosted by The Alberta Motion Picture Industries Association (AMPIA).

ANTIMATTER UNDERGROUND FILM FESTIVAL

636 Yates St., Victoria, BC V8W 1L3. TEL: (250) 385-3327.
email: info@antimatter.ws www.antimatter.ws
DIRECTOR
Todd Eacrett
CURATOR
Deborah de Boer

A curated festival of international experimental film and video held annually in September or October.

THE ATLANTIC FILM FESTIVAL ASSOCIATION

Mailing Address: P.O. Box 36139, 220, Halifax, NS B3J 3S9.

Courier Address: 1601 South Park St., Halifax, NS B3J 3S9.
TEL: (902) 422-3456. FAX: (902) 422-4006.
email: festival@atlanticfilm.com
www.atlanticfilm.com
EXECUTIVE DIRECTOR
Gregor Ash
FESTIVAL DIRECTOR
Lia Rinaldo
DIRECTOR, OPERATIONS
Andrea Dawson Gosine

A 10-day celebration of film and video from the Atlantic Provinces, Canada and around the world. The festival also operates Viewfinders Film Festival for youth, Al Fresco Film Festival, an outdoor summer festival and Strategic Partners, an internation co-production conference.

AWARDS OF EXCELLENCE / PRIX D'EXCELLENCE

The Alliance for Children and Television.
1400 René-Lévesque Blvd. East, STE., 708, Montréal, QC H2L 2M2. TEL: (514) 597-5417. FAX: (514) 597-5205.
email: alliance@act-aet.tv www.act-aet.tv
EXECUTIVE DIRECTOR
Caroline Fortier - cfortier@act-aet.tv

Television for Canadian kids.

BANFF MOUNTAIN FILM FESTIVAL

Mailing Address: The Banff Centre, P.O. Box 1020, Banff, AB T1L 1H5.

Courier Address: The Banff Centre, 107 Tunnel Mountain Dr., Banff, AB T1L 1H5. TEL: (800) 884-7574, (403) 762-6100.
FAX: (403) 762-6444. email: press@banffcentre.ca
www.banffmountainfestivals.ca
PRESIDENT & CEO
Mary E. Hofstetter

International film and video competition Festival held in the Fall: Late October or early November.

BANFF WORLD TELEVISION FESTIVAL

102 Boudler Crescent, Ste., 202, Canmore, AB T1W 1L2.
TEL: (403) 678-1216. FAX: (403) 678-3357.
email: info@achillesmedia.com www.banff2006.com

Sales Address: Achilles Media, Ltd., 21 St. Clair Ave., East, Ste., 1420 Toronto, ON M4T 1L9. TEL: (416) 921-3171.
FAX: (416) 921-9878.

Held each June at the Fairmont Banff Springs, is owned by the Banff Telelvision Festival Foundation and produced by Achilles Media Ltd. in conjunction with the Foundation's Board of Directors and Board of Governors.

CALGARY INTERNATIONAL FILM FESTIVAL

1320 - 15 Ave., SW, Calgary, AB T3C 0X7.
TEL: (403) 283-1490. FAX: (403) 457-3784.
email: info@calgaryfilm.com www.calgaryfilm.com

Showcases the best of national and international film to Calgary audiences. The Festival has brought numerous Canadian film premieres and world caliber filmmakers to the city.

CANADIAN FILM CENTRE'S WORLDWIDE SHORT FILM FESTIVAL

2489 Bayview Ave., Toronto, ON M2L 1A8. TEL: (416) 445-1446 ext. 312. FAX: (416) 445-9481. email: shortfilmfest@cfccreates.com
www.worldwideshortfilmfest.com
FESTIVAL DIRECTOR
Eileen Arandiga
PROGRAMMING MANAGER
Tania Reilly

Short film in North America. Top WSFF winners are eligible for both Academy Award and Genie Award consideration.

CANADIAN FILMMAKERS FESTIVAL

229 Palmerston Ave., Toronto, ON M6J 2J3.
TEL: (416) 846-3378. www.canfilmfest.ca

www.myspace.com/canfilmfest
DIRECTOR
Bern Euler - berneuler@canfilmfest.ca

In association with Film Circuit (a division of the Toronto Film Festival Group). Exclusively featuring Canadian films.

CANADIAN INTERNATIONAL ANNUAL FILM FESTIVAL

P.O. Box 60554, Mountain Plaza Mail Outlet, Hamilton, ON L9C 7N7. TEL: (905) 388-5840. FAX: (905) 388-5840.
email: Director@ciaff.info www.ciaff.org
FESTIVAL DIRECTOR
Jon Soyka

Entry deadline: June 30 every year. Open to independent, student & amateur productions. International competitive festival. Check website for rules, entry form and fees.

CANADIAN SOCIETY OF CINEMATOGRAPHERS AWARDS

3007 Kingston Rd., STE., 131, Toronto, ON M1M 1P1.
TEL: (416) 266-0591. FAX: (416) 266-3996.
email: admin@csc.ca www.csc.ca
EXECUTIVE DIRECTOR & AWARDS
Susan Saranchuk

The Awards are presented in March or April each year to members in the following categories: theatrical films / dramatic shorts / TV drama / TV series / documentaries / commercials / music videos / docudrama.

Awards open to members and non-members include: Roy Tash News Film Award – for outstanding cinematography in spot news, by a Canadian cameraman.

Stan Clinton News Essay Award – for cinematographic excellence in a news essay.

Student Films – open to Canadian students attending a college or university during the previous calendar year.

CANADIAN STUDENT FILM FESTIVAL / FESTIVAL DU FILM ETUDIANT CANADIEN

1432 rue Bleury, Montréal, QC H3A 2J1. TEL: (514) 848-7186.
FAX: (514) 848-3886. email: info@ffm-montreal.org
COORDINATOR
Danièle Cauchard

Held during the Montréal World Film Festival. Competitive Festival.

CINÉFEST: SUDBURY INTERNATIONAL FILM FESTIVAL

45 Durham St., Sudbury, ON P3E 3M2.
TEL: (877) 212-3222, (705) 688-1234. FAX: (705) 688-1351.
email: cinefest@cinefest.com www.cinefest.com
FESTIVAL DIRECTOR
Tammy Frick

International films, animations, shorts, documentaries and children's films.

DAWSON CITY INTERNATIONAL SHORT FILM FESTIVAL

Klondike Institute of Art & Culture, Bag 8000, Dawson, YT Y0B 1G0. TEL: (867) 993-5005. FAX: (867) 993-5838.
email: kiac at kiac.ca www.kiac.org
CONTACT
Dan Sokolowski

Over 60 screenings from around the world as well as film workshops, guest speakers and panel discussions.

EDGES FILM FESTIVAL

c/o Media Net, Media Art Resource Centre, #106 – 2750 Quadra St., Victoria, BC V8T 4E8.
TEL: (250) 381-4428. email: director@media-net.bc.ca
www.edgesfestival.com
CONTACT
Peter Sandmark - Peter SandmarkDiviX COdeck

Canadian short film and video works, held each year in the spring.

EDMONTON INTERNATIONAL FILM FESTIVAL

201 – 10816A 82 Ave., Edmonton, AB T6E 2B3.
TEL: (780) 423-0844. FAX: (780) 447-5242.
email: info@edmontonfilmfest.com www.edmontonfilmfest.com

Feature films for all ages, for all tastes.

FESTIVAL DE CINÉMA DES 3 AMÉRIQUES

226 Rue Saint-Joseph Est., Québec, QC G1K 3A9.
TEL: (418) 647-1234. FAX: (418) 647-1112.
email: festival@fc3a.com www.fc3a.com

Cinema from the Americas or with an American thematic.

FESTIVAL DU CINÉMA INTERNATIONAL EN ABITIBI-TEMISCAMINGUE

215 ave., Mercier, Rouyn-Noranda, QC J9X 5W8.
TEL: (819) 762-6212. FAX: (819) 762-6762.
email: info@festivalcinema.ca www.festivalcinema.ca

Three prizes are awarded during the Festival:

Le Grand Prix Hydro-Québec – the public's choice of its preferred full-length feature.

Le Prix Télébec – jury award to the best short- or medium-length feature.

Le Prix Animé – the public's choice of its most loved animation feature.

FESTIVAL INTERNATIONAL DU FILM SUR L'ART / INTERNATIONAL FESTIVAL OF FILMS ON ART

4428, Saint-Laurent Blvd., Ste., 500, Montréal, QC H2W 1Z5.
TEL: (514) 874-1637. FAX: (514) 874-9929.
email: info@artfifa.com www.artfifa.com
GENERAL DIRECTOR & FOUNDER
René Rozon

Check website for festival dates.

FESTIVAL NOUVEAU CINÉMA

3805 Blvd. Saint-Laurent, Montréal, QC H2W 1X9.
TEL: (514) 282-0004, (Info) (514) 844-2172.
FAX: (514) 282-6664. email: info@nouveaucinema.ca
www.nouveaucinema.ca
GENERAL DIRECTOR
Nicolas Girard Deltruc
PROGRAMMING DIRECTOR
Claude Chamberlain

Particularly in cinéma d'auteur and digital creation.

FLICKS INTERNATIONAL FILM FESTIVAL FOR YOUNG PEOPLE

#707 – 601 Spadina Crescent East, 7th Flr., Dleta Bessborough Hotel, SK S7K 3G8. TEL: (306) 956-FILM (3456).
FAX: (306) 664-2344. email: flicksfilmfestival@sasktel.net
www.flicksfilmfest.org
FESTIVAL PRODUCER
Renée Penney

Annually presents a three-day festival with films from across Canada and around the world. Also conducts workshops for children and youth, the Flicks Film Forum.

THE GOVERNOR GENERAL'S PERFORMING ARTS AWARD FOUNDATION

406 - 130 Slater St., Ottawa, ON K1P 6E2.
TEL: (613) 241-5297. FAX: (613) 238-4849.
email: awards@ggpaaf.com www.bce.ca/ggawards
CEO
Jayne Watson - (613) 947-7000 ext. 331 jwatson@nac-cna.ca

Created in 1992, the Awards six performing artists each year for their lifetime body of work and their contribution to the cultural enrichment of Canada. The Foundation also administers the Ramon John Hnatyshyn Award for Voluntarism in the Performing Arts, which recognizes outstanding service to the performing arts by an individual or group. The nomination process is open to the general public for these Awards. Nomination forms and information regarding the process are available on the foundation website.

HOT DOCS

110 Spadina Ave., Ste., 333, Toronto, ON M5V 2K4.
TEL: (416) 203-2155. FAX: (416) 203-0446.
email: info@hotdocs.ca www.hotdocs.ca
EXECUTIVE DIRECTOR
Chris MacDonald
MANAGING DIRECTOR
Brett Hendrie
DIRECTOR, PROGRAMMING
Sean Farnel
DIRECTOR, TORONTO DOCUMENTARY FORUM
Elizabeth Radshaw
DIRECTOR, DEVELOPMENT
Rose Bellosillo
DEVELOPMENT MANAGER, SPONSORSHIP MARKETING
Jennifer Hobbs

Canadian and International documentaries.

IMAGINENATIVE FILM + MEDIA ARTS FESTIVAL

401 Richmond St. W, Ste. 349, Toronto, ON M5V 3A8.
TEL: (416) 585-2333. FAX: (416) 585-2313.
email: info@imaginenative.org www.imaginenative.org
CHAIRMAN
Jason Ryle
VICE CHAIRWOMAN
Gisèle Gordon

Aboriginal film, video, radio and new media.

IMAGES FESTIVAL

401 Richmond St. W, sTE. 448, Toronto, ON M5V 3A8.
TEL: (416) 971-8405. FAX: (416) 971-7412.
email: images@imagesfestival.com www.imagesfestival.com
EXECUTIVE DIRECTOR
Scott Miller Berry

KINGSTON CANADIAN FILM FESTIVAL

www.kingcanfilmfest.com
FESTIVAL DIRECTOR
Alison Migneault - alison@kingcanfilmfest.com

20-25 feature length films, as well as numerous locally produced short films in various venues.

LEO AWARDS

700 – 1155 W. Pender St., Vancouver, BC V6E 2P4.
TEL: (604) 688-4875. FAX: (604) 669-2288.
email: info@leoawards.com www.leoawards.com
PRESIDENT
Walter Daroshin - walter@leoawards.com
PRODUCER
Sonny Wong - sonny@leoawards.com
EVENT MANAGER
Donna Yee - donna@events-one.com

Competitive awards celebrating excellence in British Columbia film & television, with Statuettes for winners and Certificates for nominees. A project of the Motion Picture Arts & Sciences Foundation of British Columbia. Produced by Troika Productions and Events One. See website for Festival dates.

THE LINDA JOY MEDIA ARTS SOCIETY

CBC Radio Building, Ste. 222F, 5600 Sackville St., Halifax, NS B3J 1L2. TEL: (902) 420-4522. FAX: (902) 420-4579.
email: info@lindajoy.com www.lindajoy.com
EXECUTIVE COORDINATOR
Will Roberts
PROGRAMS COORDINATOR
Hillary Titley - programs@lindajoy.com

A non-profit charitable organization that encourages the development of media artists by awarding grants of cash and services. Media arts encompass film, video and other time-based media such as computer-generated works. The annual awards are presented at the Atlantic Film Festival in September. Application forms are available in June.

MONTRÉAL WORLD FILM FESTIVAL

1432 rue Bleury, Montréal, QC H3A 2J1. TEL: (514) 848-3883.
FAX: (514) 848-3886. email: info@ffm-montreal.org
www.ffm-montreal.org
PRESIDENT
Serge Losique

(Montreal International Film Festival)

NIAGARA INDIE FILMFEST

Brock University, 500 Glenridge Ave., St. Catharines, ON L2S 3A1. TEL: (905) 688-5550 ext. 3998.
www.niagaraindiefilmfest.org
MEDIA CONTACT
Deborah Cartmer - (905) 685-8336

Short film and video festival held at Brock University in St. Catharines.

NICKEL INDEPENDENT FILM FESTIVAL

P.O. Box 1644, St. John's, NL A1C 5P3. TEL: (709) 576-3378.
email: nickelfestival@gmail.com www.nickelfestival.com

An independent film and video festival that was created by filmmakers for filmmakers.

NSI FILMEXCHANGE CANADIAN FILM FESTIVAL

National Screen Institute – Canada (NSI)
400-141 Bannatyne Ave., Winnipeg, MB R3B 0R3.
TEL: (800) 952-9307, (204) 956-7800. FAX: (204) 956-5811.
email: info@nsi-canada.com www.nsi-canada.com

March, Winnipeg. Canadian short and feature films.

OTTAWA INTERNATIONAL ANIMATION FESTIVAL

2 Daly Ave., Ste., 120, Ottawa, ON K1N 6E2. TEL: (613) 232-8769.
FAX: (613) 232-6315. email: info@animationfestival.ca
www.animationfestival.ca
MANAGING DIRECTOR
Kelly Neall

September. Competition for independent and commercial animation. Television Animation Conference, workshops, parties and the Animarket.

REELWORLD FILM FESTIVAL

438 Parliament St., Ste. 300, Toronto, ON M5A 3A2.
TEL: (416) 598-7933. FAX: (416) 585-2524.
email: info@reelworld.ca www.reelworld.ca
FESTIVAL FOUNDER & PRESIDENT
Tonya Lee Williams
FINANCE MANAGER
Rodrigo Diaz Varela - rodrigo@reelworld.ca

Not-for-profit film festival and charitable foundation. Festival held annually in April.

SILVER WAVE FILM FESTIVAL

c/o New Brunswick Filmmakers' Co-operative.
732 Charlotte St., Fredericton, NB E3B 1M5.
TEL: (506) 455-1632. FAX: (506) 457-2006.
email: info@nbfilmcoop.com www.swfilmfest.com
EXECUTIVE DIRECTOR
Tony Merzetti
PROGRAMMING/EVENTS & FINANCE
Cathie LeBlanc

SPROCKETS

(Toronto International Film Festival for Children / A division of The Toronto International Film Festival Group)
2 Carlton St., Ste. 1600, Toronto, ON M5B 1J3.
TEL: (416) 967-7371. Box Office: (416) 968-FILM.
FAX: (416) 967-9477. email: sprockets@tiff.ca
www.sprockets.ca
DIRECTOR, YOUTH EDUCATION & SPROCKETS
Jane Schoettle

The festival screens family-oriented live action features, feature-length animation, and both animated and live-action shorts. Curatorial preference is given to films that have been neither broadcast nor theatrically released in Canada before. Sprockets takes place in April of each year.

THE ST. JOHN'S INTERNATIONAL WOMEN'S FILM FESTIVAL / FESTIVAL INTERNATIONAL DES FILMS RÉALISÉS PAR DES FEMMES

Mailing Address: P.O. Box 984, Station C, St. John's, NL A1C 5M3.

Courier Address: 155 Water St., Ste. 301, St. John's, NL A1C 1B3. TEL: (709) 754-3141. FAX: (709) 579-2386.
email: info@womensfilmfestival.com
www.womensfilmfestival.com
EXECUTIVE DIRECTOR
Kelly Davis

Women filmmakers.

THE TORONTO JEWISH FILM FESTIVAL

19 Madison Ave, Toronto, ON M5R 2S2. TEL: (416) 324-9121.
FAX: (416) 324-9415. email: tjff@tjff.ca www.tjff.com
EXECUTIVE DIRECTOR
Helen Zukerman
PROGRAMMING COORDINATOR
Larry Anklewicz

Films of Jewish interest. Canadian filmmakers, as well as hosting filmmakers from around the world.

TORONTO FILM CRITICS ASSOCIATION ANNUAL AWARDS

133 Northcliffe Blvd., Toronto, ON M6E 3K5.
TEL: (416) 652-2696. FAX: (416) 652-3454.
email: angie@3roots.com torontofilmcritics.com
PRESIDENT
Brian D. Johnson
VICE PRESIDENT/SECRETARY
Norman Wilner
TREASURER
Marc Glassman
The TFCA Awards are announced in December each year.

TORONTO INTERNATIONAL FILM FESTIVAL

(A division of The Toronto International Film Festival Group)
2 Carlton St., Ste., 1600, Toronto, ON M5B 1J3.
TEL: (416) 967-7371, (877) 968-3456.
FAX: (416) 967-9477. email: tiffg@tiffg.ca
www.torontointernationalfilmfestival.ca
DIRECTOR & CEO
Piers Handling
MANAGING DIRECTOR
Michèle Maheux
CO-DIRECTOR
Noah Cowan
ASSOCIATE MANAGING DIRECTOR
Allison Bain
SENIOR DIRECTOR, DEVELOPMENT & MARKETING
Lori Willcox
DIRECTOR, COMMUNICATIONS
Andréa Grau
DIRECTOR, FESTIVAL CENTRE PROGRAMMING
Jim Hamilton
DIRECTOR, DEVELOPMENT RELATIONS
David Vella
HEAD OF SALES & INDUSTRY OFFICE
Giulia Filippelli
DIRECTOR, INDUSTRY INITIATIVES
Kelley Alexander
DIRECTOR, SALES & MARKETING
Heather Sinclair
DIRECTOR, PUBLIC AFFAIRS
Maxine Bailey

10-day Festiva. Recent Canadian and international cinema.

THE VANCOUVER INTERNATIONAL FILM FESTIVAL

1181 Seymour St., Vancouver, BC V6B 3M7.
TEL: (604) 683-3456. FAX: (604) 688-8221.

email: viff@viff.org www.viff.org
FESTIVAL DIRECTOR
Alan Franey

VICTORIA INDEPENDENT FILM AND VIDEO FESTIVAL

1215 Blanshard St., Victoria, BC V8W 3J4.
TEL: (250) 389-0444. FAX: (250) 389-0406.
email: festival@victoriafilmfestival.com www.vifvf.com
FESTIVAL DIRECTOR
Kathy Kay - director@victoriafilmfestival.com
OPERATIONS MANAGER
Mike Vardy - operations@victoriafilmfestival.com

Ten-day film celebration with 140 films, a must-attend co-production conference, unique film events and the home of boutique schmooze. Entry deadline October 1st.

WHISTLER FILM FESTIVAL

Mailing Address:
#1004 – 106 4368 Main St., Whistler, BC V0N 1B4.
Office Address: #213-1200 Alpha Lake Rd., Whistler BC V0N 1B1. TEL: (604) 935-8035. FAX: (604) 938-3209.
email: info@whistlerfilmfestival.com
www.whistlerfilmfestival.com
EXECUTIVE DIRECTOR
Shauna Hardy Mishaw
PROGRAM COORDINATOR
Leea Thorne - program@whistlerfilmfestival.com

A charitable, not for profit cultural and educational organization committed to promoting, developing and celebrating a strong film industry in Western Canada.

YORKTON SHORT FILM & VIDEO FESTIVAL, INC.

49 Smith St. E, Yorkton, SK S3N 0H4. TEL: (306) 782-7077.
FAX: (306) 782-1550. email: media@yorktonshortfilm.org
www.yorktonshortfilm.org
EXECUTIVE DIRECTOR
Randy Goulden - director@goldensheafawards.com

Since 1950. See website for schedules and workshops.

YOUNG CUTS FILM FESTIVAL

Young Cuts Inc.: 1010 Sherbrooke St. W, Ste., 1220, Montréal, QC H3A 2R7.
TEL: (514) 285-4591. FAX: (514) 227-5158.
email: info@youngcuts.com www.youngcuts.com
FESTIVAL DIRECTOR
Mike Ryan - mike @ youngcuts.com

Films produced by young adults aged 25 years old and under.

The World Market: Great Britain

EXHIBITION CIRCUITS

ABC CINEMAS, LTD.
(Owned by Odeon Cinemas)
Clarence St., Staines, London TW18 4SP. TEL: (020) 7321 0404.
www.odeon.co.uk

AMC CINEMAS
12 Broadway Plaza, 220 Ladywood Middleway Birmingham
B16 8LP. TEL: (0121) 50 6800. FAX: (0121) 50 6850.
email: ddrabble@amctheatres.com www.amccinemas.co.uk

APOLLO LEISURE (UK), LTD. - CINEMA DIVISION
60 Hamilton St., Saltcoats, Ayrshire, KA21 5DS.
TEL: (01294) 472 772. FAX: (01294) 467 930.
CONTACT
Celina Grahm - (01294) 471 777

ARTIFICIAL EYE FILM COMPANY (FILM DISTRIBUTORS)
14 King St., London WC2E 8HR. TEL: (0207) 240 5353.
FAX: (0207) 240 5252. email: info@artificial-eye.com

BELLEVUE CINEMA
General Enquires, Northfield Ave., London, W13 9RH.
TEL: (020) 8830 0822.

CALEDONIAN CINEMA
6 Murray St., Perth PH1 5PJ. TEL: (0173) 862 3126.
FAX: (0173) 862 180. email: perth@cairstar.co.uk
www.caledoniancinemas.co.uk

CARLTON CLUBS
(Formerly Caledonian Cinemas)
18 Huntley St., Inverness, Scotland 1VI 1LA.
TEL: (01463) 231 1400. FAX: (01463) 225 571.
OPERATIONS DIRECTOR
Brian King - bking@carltonclubs.com

CINEWORLD CINEMAS, LTD.
Cineworld Cinemas PLC
(Merger of Cine-UK and UGC UK)
Power Road Studios, Power Rd., Chiswick, London W4 5PY.
TEL: (0208) 987 5000. FAX: (0208) 742 2998.
email: corporate@cineworld.co.uk www.cineworld.co.uk
CEO
Steve Wiener
CFO
Richard Jones
V.P., OPERATIONS
Matthew Eyre

CIRCLE CINEMAS
Thornbury House, Thornbury Close, Rhiwbina, Cardiff, South
Glamorgan CF14 1UT. TEL: (029) 2052 2606.
www.circlecinemas.co.uk

CITY SCREEN/PICTUREHOUSE CINEMAS
Hardy House, 16-18 Beak St., London W1F 9RD.
TEL: (0207) 734 4342. FAX: (0207) 734 4027.
email: enquiries@picturehouses.co.uk www.picturehouses.co.uk
CONTACT
Tony Jones

COLUMBIA PICTURES CORPORATION, LTD.
25 Golden Square, London W1F 9LU, United Kingdom.
email: Digital_marketing_UK@spe.sony.com

CORONET CINEMAS
103 Notting Hill Gate, London W11 3LB.
Box Office: (0207) 727 6705. Admin. Office: (0207) 221 0123.
www.coronet.org
GENERAL MANAGER
Syed Mohammed

CURZON CINEMAS
Wingate House, 93-107, Shaftsbury Ave., London W1D 5DA.
TEL: (0207) 734 9209. FAX: (0207) 734 1977.
www.curzoncinemas.com
CONTACT
Rob Kenny - (0207) 292 1699 rob.kenny@curzoncinemas.com
Verena Von Stackelberg - verena.stackelberg@curzoncinemas.com

DOMINION CINEMA
18 Newbattle Terrace, Edinburgh, Midlothian EH10 4RT.
TEL: (0131) 447 4771. email: info@dominionproperties.co.uk
www.dominioncinemas.net
CONTACT
Mike Cameron

GENESIS CINEMA
93-95 Mile End Rd., White Chapel, London E1 UJ.
TEL: (0207) 780 2000. email: info@genesis-cinema.co.uk
www.genesis-cinema.co.uk

IMAX THEATRES (UK AND IRELAND)
Belfast: Sheridan IMAX Cinema, Odyssey Pavilion, 2 Queens
Quay, Belfast BT3 9QQ. TEL: (028) 9046 7000.
FAX: (028) 9046 7001. email: info@belfastimax.com
www.belfastimax.com

Birmingham: IMAX Cinema, Thinktank at Millennium Point
Curzon St., Birmingham B4 7XG. TEL: (0121) 202 2222.
email: findout@imax.ac www.imax.ac

Bournemouth: Sheridan IMAX Cinema, Bournemouth BH2 5AA.
TEL: (0120) 220 0000. www.imax.com

Bradford: National Museum of Photography, Film & Television
Bradford, West Yorkshire BD1 1NQ. TEL: (0870) 701 0200.
FAX: (01274) 723 155. email: talk.nmpft@nmsi.ac.uk
www.nmpft.org.uk

Bristol: IMAX Theatre At-Bristol, Bristol 5S1 5DB.
TEL: (0845) 345 1235. www.at-bristol.org.uk

Glasgow: IMAX Cinema, Glasgow Science Centre, 50 Pacific
Quay, Glasgow G51 1EA. TEL: (0141) 420 5000.
FAX: (0141) 420 5011. email: admin@glasgowsciencecentre.org
www.glasgowsciencecentre.org

London: British Film Institute (BFI) London IMAX Cinema,
1 Charlie Chaplin Walk, South Bank, Waterloo, London SE1
8XR. TEL: (0870) 787 2525. email: imax.cinema@bfi.org.uk
www.bfi.org.uk

London: Science Museum IMAX, Exhibition Rd., South
Kensington, London SW7 2DD. TEL: (0870) 870 4868.
email: scimax@nmsi.ac.uk www.sciencemuseum.org.uk

Manchester: UCI Filmworks Manchester, 6-8 Dantzic St.

Manchester M4 2AD. TEL: (0870) 588 8999.
www.thefilmworks.co.uk

IRISH MULTIPLEX CINEMAS (IMC)
(A division of Ward Anderson Group)
Astor House 29 Lower Georges St., Dun Laoghaire Dublin,
Ireland. TEL: (353) 1236 6664. FAX: (353) 1236 6658.
www.imccinemagroup.com
MANAGING DIRECTOR
Leo Ward
CONTACT
Francis Murray - francis.murray@imccinemagroup.com

IRISH FILM INSTITUTE (IFI)
Irish Film Centre, 6 Eustace St., Temple Bar, Dublin, 2 Republic
of Ireland. TEL: (353 1) 679 5744. FAX: (353 1) 677 8755.
email: info@irishfilms.ie www.irishfilm.ie
DIRECTOR
Mark Mulqueen - email: mmulqueen@irishfilms.ie

MAINLINE PICTURES/BLOOM THEATRES
37 Museum St., London WC1A 1LP. TEL: (0207) 242 5523.
FAX: (0207) 430 0170. email: mainline.pictures@BTinternet.com
CONTACT
Maria Nordqvist

THE METRO CINEMA
35-36 Queen St., Derby, Derbyshire DE1 1SA. Box Office:
(01332) 347 765. Administrative Office: (01332) 340 170.
email: metro.cinema@virgin.net
CONTACT
Andrew McIntyre

TARTAN FILMS DISTRIBUTION, LTD.
Royalty House 2, Dean St., London WD 3SG.
TEL: (0207) 494 1400. FAX: (0207) 4391922.
CONTACT
Camilla Summers

MOVIE HOUSE CINEMAS
Yorkgate Leisure Complex, 100-150 York St., Belfast BT15
1WA. TEL: (028) 9035 5717. FAX: (028) 9074 1360.
email: enquiries@moviehouse.co.uk www.moviehouse.co.uk

NATIONAL AMUSEMENTS SHOWCASE CINEMAS
Redfield Way, Lenton, Nottingham NG7 2UW.
TEL: (0115) 986 6766. www.showcasecinemas.co.uk

Main Office USA: 200 Elms St., Dedham, MA 02026.
TEL: (001) 781 461 1600. UK: (01159) 862 508.
FAX: (001) 781 329 4831.
email: pressinquiries@national-amusements.com
www.nationalamusements.com

ODEON CINEMAS, LTD.
54 Whitcomb St., London WC2H 7DN. TEL: (020) 7321 0404.
www.odeon.co.uk
CEO
Rupert Gavin

CONTACT
Debbie Mitchell - (0207) 321 6221

OMNIPLEX HOLDINGS

(A division of Ward Anderson Group)
Film House, 35 Upper Abbey St., Dublin, 1, Ireland.
TEL: (353 1) 236 6664. FAX: (353 1) 236 6668.
www.filminfo.net
MANAGING DIRECTOR
Leo Ward, Kevin Anderson
CONTACT
Chris Daly - (353 1) 236 6661 chris.daly@imccinemagroup.com

PICTUREHOUSE CINEMAS/CITY SCREEN

Hardy House, 16-18 Beak St., London W1F 9RD.
TEL: (0207) 734 4342. FAX: (0207) 734 4027.
email: enquiries@picturehouses.co.uk
www.picturehouses.co.uk
CONTACT
Tony Jones

PRINCE CHARLES CINEMA

7 Leicester Place, London, WC2H 7BY. TEL: (0207) 222 1234.
email: web@princecharlescinema.com
www.princecharlescinema.com

REELTIME CINEMAS

Townhall Buildings, St. Mildred's Rd., Westgate on Sea, Kent CT8 8RE. TEL: (01843) 834 609.
email: enquiries@reeltimecinemas.co.uk
www.reeltime-cinemas.co.uk

SCOTT CINEMAS

Market St., Newton Abbot, Devon, TQ12 2RB.
TEL: (01626) 335 432. FAX: (01626) 335 432.
email: enquiries@scottcinemas.fsnet.co.uk
CONTACT
Peter Hoare

STER CENTURY

(Owned by Aurora Holdings)
10 Chiswick Park, 566 Chiswick High Rd., London W4 5XS.
TEL: (0208) 396 0100. FAX: (0208) 396 0199.
email: customerservices@vuemail.com www.myvue.com
CEO
J. Timothy Richards
COO
Steve Knibbs
MARKETING DIRECTOR
Mark De Quervain

TYNESIDE FILM CINEMA

10 Pilgrim St., Newcastle-Upon-Tyne NE1 6QG.
TEL: (0191) 232 8289. FAX: (0191) 221 0535.
email: boxoffice@tynecine.org www.tynecine.org

Temporary Location: Old Town Hall, West St., Gateshead NE8 1HE. TEL: (0191) 232 8289.

UCI-UNITED CINEMAS INTERNATIONAL UK

(Now pending merger with Odeon)
52 Whitcomb St., London, ENG WC2H 7DN, United Kingdom.
TEL: (0161) 455 4000, (44) 20 7321 0404.
FAX: (0161) 455 4076. www.uci.co.uk
CEO
Rupert Gavin
COO
Roger Harris
SENIOR V.P., CONTINENTAL EUROPE
Jose Batle
MANAGING DIRECTOR
Roger Harris
PERSONAL ASSISTANT TO MANAGING DIRECTOR
Alexis Carol

VUE ENTERTAINMENT, LTD.

(Formerly Warner Village)
10 Chiswick Park, 566 Chiswick High Rd., London W4 5XS.
TEL: (0208) 396 0100. FAX: (0208) 396 0199.
email: customerservices@vuemail.com
www.myvue.com
CEO
J. Timothy Richards
COO
Steve Knibbs
CFO
Alan McNair
MARKETING DIRECTOR
Mark De Quervain

WARD-ANDERSON CINEMA GROUP

Number of Theatres: 36. Number of Screens: 220
(Divisions include Abbey Films, Dublin Cinema Group, IMC Cinema Group and Omniplex Holdings)
Film House, 35 Upper Abbey St., Dublin 1, Ireland.
TEL: (353 1) 236 6664. FAX: (353 1) 236 6668.
www.filminfo.net
CONTACT
Leo Ward, Kevin Anderson

CIRCUIT MULTIPLEXES

Theatre Name	City	Circuit	Screens
ABC	Bath, Avon	Odeon	3
ABC	Bournemouth, Dorset	Odeon	8
ABC	Plymouth	Odeon	3
Apollo	Blackburn	Apollo	5
Apollo	Barrow, Cumbria	Apollo	6
Apollo	Burnley	Apollo	9
Apollo	Fareham	Apollo	5
Apollo	Paignton, Torbay	Apollo	9
Apollo	Leamington Spa	Apollo	6
Apollo	Morecombe	Apollo	4
Apollo	Port Talbot	Apollo	6
Apollo	Redditch	Apollo	7
Apollo	Rhyl	Apollo	5
Apollo	Stafford	Apollo	3
Apollo	Stroud	Apollo	9
Apollo	West End	Apollo	5
Cineworld	Aberdeen	Cineworld	9
Cineworld	Ashford	Cineworld	12
Cineworld	Ashton Under Lyne	Cineworld	14
Cineworld	Bedford	Cineworld	6
Cineworld	Bexleyheath	Cineworld	9
Cineworld	Broad Street, Birmingham	Cineworld	12
Cineworld	Rubery, Birmingham	Cineworld	13
Cineworld	Bishop's Strotford	Cineworld	6
Cineworld	Boldon	Cineworld	11
Cineworld	Bolton	Cineworld	15
Cineworld	Bradford	Cineworld	16
Cineworld	Braintree	Cineworld	12
Cineworld	Bristol	Cineworld	14
Cineworld	Burton on Trent	Cineworld	8
Cineworld	Cambridge	Cineworld	9
Cineworld	Cardiff	Cineworld	15
Cineworld	Castleford	Cineworld	14
Cineworld	Chester	Cineworld	6
Cineworld	Chesterfield	Cineworld	10
Cineworld	Chichester	Cineworld	10
Cineworld	Crawley	Cineworld	15
Cineworld	Didsbury, Greater Manchester	Cineworld	11
Cineworld	Dublin, Republic of Ireland	Cineworld	17
Cineworld	Dundee	Cineworld	9
Cineworld	Eastbourne	Cineworld	6
Cineworld	Edinburgh	Cineworld	13
Cineworld	Falkirk	Cineworld	12
Cineworld	Feltham	Cineworld	14
Cineworld	Renfrew Street, Glasgow	Cineworld	18
Cineworld	Parkhead, Glasgow	Cineworld	7
Cineworld	Gloucester	Cineworld	6
Cineworld	Harlow	Cineworld	6
Cineworld	Hull	Cineworld	9
Cineworld	Huntingdon	Cineworld	10
Cineworld	Ilford	Cineworld	11
Cineworld	Ipswich	Cineworld	11
Cineworld	Isle of Wight	Cineworld	11
Cineworld	St. Helier, Jersey	Cineworld	10
Cineworld	Liverpool	Cineworld	8
Cineworld	Llandudno Junction	Cineworld	9
Cineworld	Chelsea, London	Cineworld	4
Cineworld	Ealing, London	Cineworld	3
Cineworld	Enfield, London	Cineworld	15
Cineworld	Fulham, London	Cineworld	6
Cineworld	Hammersmith, London	Cineworld	4
Cineworld	Haymarket, London	Cineworld	3
Cineworld	Shaftesbury, London	Cineworld	7
Cineworld	Staples Corner, London	Cineworld	6
Cineworld	West India Quay, London	Cineworld	10
Cineworld	Luton	Cineworld	11
Cineworld	Middlesbrough	Cineworld	11
Cineworld	Milton Keynes	Cineworld	16
Cineworld	Newport	Cineworld	13
Cineworld	Northhampton	Cineworld	9
Cineworld	Nottingham	Cineworld	14
Cineworld	Rochester	Cineworld	9
Cineworld	Rugby	Cineworld	9
Cineworld	Runcorn	Cineworld	9
Cineworld	Sheffield	Cineworld	20
Cineworld	Shrewsbury	Cineworld	8
Cineworld	Slough	Cineworld	10
Cineworld	Solihull	Cineworld	9
Cineworld	Southhampton	Cineworld	5
Cineworld	Stockport	Cineworld	10
Cineworld	St. Helens	Cineworld	11
Cineworld	Stevenage	Cineworld	16
Cineworld	Sunderland	Cineworld	12
Cineworld	Swindon	Cineworld	7

Theatre Name	City	Circuit	Screens
Cineworld	Wakefield	Cineworld	12
Cineworld	Wandsworth	Cineworld	14
Cineworld	Weymouth	Cineworld	9
Cineworld	Wigan	Cineworld	11
Cineworld	Wolverhampton	Cineworld	14
Cineworld	Wood Green	Cineworld	12
Cineworld	Yeovil	Cineworld	10
Movie House	Dublin Road, Belfast	Movie House	10
Movie House	Yorkgate, Belfast	Movie House	14
Movie House	Maghera	Movie House	3
Movie House	Glengormley	Movie House	6
Odeon	Aberdeen	Odeon	3
Odeon	Accrington	Odeon	4
Odeon	Allerton	Odeon	1
Odeon	Ayr, Strathclyde	Odeon	4
Odeon	Aylesbury	Odeon	6
Odeon	Banbury	Odeon	2
Odeon	Barnet	Odeon	5
Odeon	Barnsley	Odeon	2
Odeon	Bath	Odeon	1
Odeon	Beckenham	Odeon	6
Odeon	Birmingham	Odeon	8
Odeon	Blackpool	Odeon	10
Odeon	Westover Road, Bournemouth	Odeon	6
Odeon	27 Westover Road, Bournemouth	Odeon	3
Odeon	Bridgend	Odeon	9
Odeon	Brighton	Odeon	8
Odeon	Bristol	Odeon	1
Odeon	Bromborough	Odeon	11
Odeon	Bromley	Odeon	4
Odeon	Bury St Edmunds	Odeon	2
Odeon	Canterbury	Odeon	2
Odeon	Chelmsford	Odeon	8
Odeon	Cheltenham	Odeon	7
Odeon	Chester	Odeon	5
Odeon	Colchester	Odeon	8
Odeon	Coventry	Odeon	9
Odeon	Darlington	Odeon	3
Odeon	Doncaster	Odeon	3
Odeon	Dumfries	Odeon	1
Odeon	Dundee	Odeon	10
Odeon	Dunfermline	Odeon	10
Odeon	Lothian Road, Edinburgh	Odeon	4
Odeon	Wester Hailes, Edinburgh	Odeon	8
Odeon	Epsom	Odeon	8
Odeon	Esher	Odeon	4
Odeon	Exeter	Odeon	4
Odeon	Gerrards Cross	Odeon	2
Odeon	Renfield Street, Glasgow	Odeon	9
Odeon	Springfield Quay, Glasgow	Odeon	12
Odeon	Grimsby	Odeon	3
Odeon	Guildford	Odeon	9
Odeon	Harlow	Odeon	3
Odeon	Harrogate	Odeon	5
Odeon	Hastings	Odeon	4
Odeon	Hemel Hempstead	Odeon	8
Odeon	Hereford	Odeon	1
Odeon	Hull	Odeon	10
Odeon	Ipswich	Odeon	5
Odeon	St.Helier Jersey	Odeon	4
Odeon	Kettering	Odeon	8
Odeon	Kilmarnock	Odeon	8
Odeon	Kingston Upon Thames	Odeon	14
Odeon	Leicester	Odeon	12
Odeon	Lincoln	Odeon	9
Odeon	Leeds Bradford	Odeon	13
Odeon	Liverpool	Odeon	12
Odeon	Camden Town, London	Odeon	5
Odeon	Covent Garden, London	Odeon	4
Odeon	Greenwich, London	Odeon	5
Odeon	Holloway, London	Odeon	8
Odeon	Kensington, London	Odeon	6
Odeon	Leicester Square, London	Odeon	6
Odeon	Marble Arch, London	Odeon	5
Odeon	Muswell Hill, London	Odeon	3
Odeon	Panton Street, London	Odeon	4
Odeon	Putney, London	Odeon	3
Odeon	Streatham, London	Odeon	8
Odeon	Swiss Cottage, London	Odeon	6
Odeon	Wardour Street, London	Odeon	4
Odeon	West End, London	Odeon	2
Odeon	Wimbledon, London	Odeon	12
Odeon	London Road, Liverpool	Odeon	10
Odeon	Switch Island, Liverpool	Odeon	12
Odeon	Maidstone	Odeon	8
Odeon	Manchester	Odeon	14
Odeon	Mansfield	Odeon	8
Odeon	Newcastle Upon Tyne	Odeon	12
Odeon	Nuneaton	Odeon	8
Odeon	George Street, Oxford	Odeon	6
Odeon	Magdalene Street, Oxford	Odeon	2
Odeon	Porstmouth	Odeon	4

Theatre Name	City	Circuit	Screens
Odeon	Plymouth	Odeon	3
Odeon	Quinton	Odeon	4
Odeon	Rochadale	Odeon	9
Odeon	Salisbury	Odeon	5
Odeon	Sheffield	Odeon	10
Odeon	Southampton	Odeon	13
Odeon	Southend	Odeon	8
Odeon	Stoke on Trent	Odeon	10
Odeon	Sutton Cold Field	Odeon	4
Odeon	Richmond, Surrey	Odeon	3
Odeon	Taunton	Odeon	5
Odeon	Tunbridge Wells	Odeon	9
Odeon	Uxbridge	Odeon	9
Odeon	Weston-Super-Mare	Odeon	4
Odeon	South Woodford	Odeon	7
Odeon	Worcester	Odeon	7
Odeon	Wexham	Odeon	7
Odeon	York	Odeon	3
Picturehouse Cinemas	Aberdeen	City Screen	3
Picturehouse Cinemas	Bath	City Screen	2
Picturehouse Cinemas	Brighton	City Screen	1
Picturehouse Cinemas	Cambridge	City Screen	3
Picturehouse Cinemas	East Grinstead	City Screen	2
Picturehouse Cinemas	Edinburgh	City Screen	3
Picturehouse Cinemas	Exeter	City Screen	2
Picturehouse Cinemas	Liverpool	City Screen	3
Picturehouse Cinemas/Clapham	London	City Screen	4
Picturehouse Cinemas/Gate Cinema	London	City Screen	1
Picturehouse Cinemas/Greenwich	London	City Screen	5
Picturehouse Cinemas/Ritzy	London	City Screen	5
Picturehouse Cinemas/Stratford	London	City Screen	4
Picturehouse Cinemas	Oxford	City Screen	2
Picturehouse Cinemas	Southampton	City Screen	2
Picturehouse Cinemas	Stratford-Upon-Avon	City Screen	2
Picturehouse Cinemas	York	City Screen	3
Reeltime/Theatre RoyalBarry, South Wales		Reeltime Cinemas	2
ReeltimePicturedrome Cinema	West Sussex	Reeltime Cinemas	2
Reeltime/Orpheus Cinema	Bristol, Avon	Reeltime Cinemas	3
Reeltime/Plaza Cinema	Dorchester, Dorset	Reeltime Cinemas	2
Reeltime/Kavanagh Cinema	Herne Bay, Kent	Reeltime Cinemas	2
Reeltime/Dreamland Cinema	Margate, Kent	Reeltime Cinemas	2
Reeltime/Commodore Cinema	Ryde, Isle of Wight	Reeltime Cinemas	3
Reeltime/New Century Cinemas	Sittingbourne, Kent	Reeltime Cinemas	2
Reeltime/Carlton Cinema	Westgate on Sea, Kent	Reeltime Cinemas	3
Showcase	Birmingham	National Amusements	12
Showcase	Bluewater/Greenhithe	National Amusements	13
Showcase	Bristol	National Amusements	14
Showcase	Glasgow East Coatbridge	National Amusements	14
Showcase	Coventry	National Amusements	12
Showcase	Derby	National Amusements	11
Showcase	Dudley	National Amusements	14
Showcase	Leeds	National Amusements	16
Showcase	Liverpool	National Amusements	12
Showcase	Wood Green, London	National Amusements	6
Showcase	Manchester	National Amusements	14
Showcase	Nantgarw	National Amusements	12
Showcase	Newham	National Amusements	14
Showcase	Nottingham	National Amusements	13
Showcase	Phoenix Retail Park, Paisley	National Amusements	14
Showcase	Peterborough	National Amusements	13
Showcase	Reading	National Amusements	12
Showcase	Stockton on Teeside	National Amusements	14
Showcase	Walsall	National Amusements	12
UCI	Basildon	UCI	12
UCI	Blanchardstown	UCI	9
UCI	Bracknell	UCI	10
UCI	Brierley Hill,Dudley	UCI	10
UCI	Cardiff	UCI	12
UCI	Warrington, Cheshire	UCI	10
UCI	Clydebank	UCI	12
UCI	Coolock	UCI	12
UCI	Meteor Centre, Derby	UCI	10
UCI	East Kilbride	UCI	9
UCI	Kinnaird Park , Edinburgh	UCI	12
UCI	Hatfield	UCI	10
UCI	High Wycombe	UCI	6
UCI	Huddersfield	UCI	9
UCI	Hull	UCI	8
UCI	Lee Valley	UCI	12
UCI	Whiteleys, London	UCI	8
UCI	Greenwich, London	UCI	14
UCI	Empire Cinema Leicester Square, London	UCI	3
UCI	Surrey Quays, London	UCI	9
UCI	Dantzic Street, Machester	UCI	20
UCI	Trafford Centre, Manchester	UCI	20
UCI	Maidenhead	UCI	8
UCI	North Shields	UCI	9
UCI	Northampton	UCI	10

Theatre Name	City	Circuit	Screens
UCI	Norwich	UCI	14
UCI	Poole	UCI	10
UCI	Port Solent Portsmouth	UCI	6
UCI	Preston	UCI	10
UCI	Scunthorpe	UCI	7
UCI	Sheffield	UCI	10
UCI	Silverlink	UCI	10
UCI	Solihull	UCI	8
UCI	Sutton, Surrey	UCI	6
UCI	Swansea	UCI	10
UCI	Tallaght	UCI	10
UCI	Tamworth	UCI	10
UCI	Telford	UCI	10
UCI	Metro Centre, Gateshead,Tyne and Wear	UCI	11
UCI	Warrington	UCI	10
UCI	West Thurrock	UCI	10
Vue	Bury	Vue Entertainment	12
Vue	Basingstoke	Vue Entertainment	10
Vue	Belfast	Vue Entertainment	12
Vue	Birkenhead	Vue Entertainment	7
Vue	Birmingham	Vue Entertainment	30
Vue	Bolton	Vue Entertainment	12
Vue	Cribbs, Bristol	Vue Entertainment	12
Vue	Longwell, Bristol	Vue Entertainment	10
Vue	Cambridge	Vue Entertainment	8
Vue	Cardiff	Vue Entertainment	14
Vue	Carlisle	Vue Entertainment	7
Vue	Cheshire Oaks	Vue Entertainment	11
Vue	Oaks, Croydon	Vue Entertainment	8
Vue	Grants, Croydon	Vue Entertainment	10
Vue	Dagenham	Vue Entertainment	9
Vue	Doncaster	Vue Entertainment	7
Vue	Edinburgh	Vue Entertainment	12
Vue	Harrow	Vue Entertainment	9
Vue	Hartlepool	Vue Entertainment	7
Vue	Inverness	Vue Entertainment	7
Vue	Islington	Vue Entertainment	9
Vue	Leeds	Vue Entertainment	13
Vue	Leiceste	Vue Entertainment	9
Vue	Finchley Road, London	Vue Entertainment	8
Vue	Lido. Finchley Road, London	Vue Entertainment	8
Vue	Acton, London	Vue Entertainment	9
Vue	Fulham, London	Vue Entertainment	9
Vue	Shepherds Bush, London	Vue Entertainment	12
Vue	West End, London	Vue Entertainment	9
Vue	Newcastle-Under-Lyme	Vue Entertainment	8
Vue	Newcastle Upon Tyne	Vue Entertainment	9
Vue	Norwich	Vue Entertainment	8
Vue	Nottingham	Vue Entertainment	12
Vue	Plymouth	Vue Entertainment	15
Vue	Portsmouth	Vue Entertainment	11
Vue	Preston	Vue Entertainment	7
Vue	Reading	Vue Entertainment	10
Vue	Romford	Vue Entertainment	16
Vue	Salford Quays	Vue Entertainment	7
Vue	Scunsthorpe	Vue Entertainment	7
Vue	Sheffield	Vue Entertainment	11
Vue	Staines	Vue Entertainment	10
Vue	Thurrock	Vue Entertainment	7
Warner Village	Watford	Vue Entertainment	8
Warner Village	Worcester	Vue Entertainment	6
Warner Village	York	Vue Entertainment	12

PRODUCERS & DISTRIBUTORS

1A PRODUCTIONS
Langshot Farm, Acre Valley Rd, Glasgow, Lanarkshire, G64 4DL. TEL/FAX: (01360) 620 855.
email: office@1aproductions.co.uk www.1aproductions.co.uk
MANAGING DIRECTOR
Norman Stone

AARDMAN ANIMATIONS
7 Gasferry Rd., Bristol, BS1 6UN. TEL: (0117) 984 8485.
FAX: (0117) 984 8486. www.aardman.com
DIRECTOR & FOUNDER
Peter Lord, David Sproxton

ABBEY FILMS LIMITED
Astor House, 29 Lower Georges St., Dun Laoire, Dublin.
TEL: (353 1) 236 6686. FAX: (353 1) 236 6658.
www.filminfo.net

ABSOLUTELY PRODUCTIONS, LTD.
77 Beak St., London, W1F 9DB. TEL: (0207) 644 5575.
www.absolutely.biz

ADDICTIVE TELEVISION, LTD.
The Old House, 39A, North Rd., London, N7 9DP.
TEL: (0207) 700 0333. email: mail@addictive.com
www.addictive.com
PRODUCER
Nick Clarke, Graham Daniels

ADVENTURE PICTURES
6 Blackbird Yard, Ravenscroft St., London, E2 7RP.
TEL: (0207) 613 2233. FAX: (0207) 256 0842.
email: mail@adventurepictures.co.uk
www.adventurepictures.co.uk
CEO
Christopher Sheppard

AGFA-GEVAERT (MOTION PICTURE DIVISION)
27 Great West Rd., Brentford, Middlesex, TW8 9AX.
TEL: (0208) 231 4301. FAX: (0208) 231 4315.
email: agfauk@agfa.com www.agfa.co.uk
HEAD OF DIVISION
Philip Hill

AITKEN PRODUCTIONS (APL)
Oddfellows Hall, London Rd., Chipping Norton, OX7 5AR.
TEL: (01608) 641779. FAX: (01608) 641969.
email: help@aitkenproductions.co.uk
www.aitkenproductions.co.uk
MANAGING DIRECTOR
Paul Aitken

ALIBI COMMUNICATIONS PLC.
35 Long Acre, London, WC2E 9JT. TEL: (0207) 845 0400.
FAX: (0207) 379 7035. www.alibifilms.co.uk
CEO
Roger Holmes - rogerholmes@alibifilms.co.uk
PERSONAL ASSISTANT TO CEO
Rebekah Deboo - rebekahdeboo@alibifilms.co.uk
FINANCIAL DIRECTOR
David Glennon - davidglennon@alibifilms.co.uk

ALIVE PRODUCTIONS, LTD.
(A division of Churchill Television)
37 Harwood Rd, London, SW6 4QP. TEL: (0207) 384 2243.
FAX: (0207) 384 2026. email: animation@alivetelevision.com
www.alivetelevision.com
MANAGING DIRECTOR
Gail Screene

ALL FILMS
21, Little Portland St., London, W1W 8BT. TEL: (020) 7612 0190.
FAX: (020) 7612 0199. email: webenquiries@allfilms.co.uk
www.allfilms.co.uk
EXECUTIVE PRODUCER, MANAGING DIRECTOR
Ron Redel - ron.redel@allfilms.co.uk
DIRECTOR
Kasper Barfoed, Tom Geens, Martin Aamund, Alain Duplantier, Michael Feuter, Olivia Lichtenstein, David Smith, Josh Raskin, Bertrand Mandico, Tim Pope

AMARANTH FILM PARTNERS, LTD.
P.O. Box 44636, London, N16 5WP. TEL: (0208) 211 1888.
FAX: (0208) 211 0222. www.amaranthfilms.com
CONTACT
Paul Hill, Rosa Romera

AMY INTERNATIONAL PRODUCTIONS
P.O. Box 55, Minehead, Somerset, TA24 7WA.
TEL: (01398) 371 270. FAX: (01398) 371 428.
DIRECTOR
Susan George

ANGLO-FORTUNATO FILMS
170 Popes Ln., London, W5 4NJ. TEL: (0208) 932 7676.
FAX: (0208) 932 7491. email: anglofortunato@aol.com
MANAGER
Luciano Celentino

ANTELOPE PRODUCTIONS
29B Montague St. London, WC1B 5BW. TEL: (207)209 0099.
FAX: (207)209 0098. email: antelope@antelope.co.uk
www.antelope.co.uk
CONTACT
Mick Csaky - mick.csaky@antelope.co.uk

ANVIL POST PRODUCTION, LTD.
Denham Studios, North Orbital Rd., Denham, Uxbridge Middlesex, UB9 5HL. TEL: (0189)583 3522.
FAX: (0189) 583 5006. email: reception@anvil-post.com
www.anvil-post.com
MANAGING DIRECTOR
Roger Beck

ANGEL EYE MEDIA
9 Rudolf Place, Miles St., London, SW8 1RP.
TEL: (845) 230 0062. FAX: (0)845 230 9562.
53 Bothwell St., Ste. 7, 4th Flr., Glasgow, G2 6TS.
TEL: (845) 230 0062. FAX: (845) 230 9562.
email: info@angeleye.co.uk www.angeleye.co.uk

APEX TELEVISION PRODUCTION & FACILITIES, LTD.
The Vision Centre, Eastern Way, Bury St., Edmunds, Suffolk, IP32 7AB. TEL: (01284) 724 900. FAX: (01284) 700 004.
email: sales@apextv.co.uk www.apextv.co.uk
HEAD OF PRODUCTION
Peter Creswell

APT FILMS
Ealing Studios, Ealing Green, London, W5 5EP.
TEL: (0208) 280 9125. FAX: (0208) 280 9111.
email: admin@aptfilms.com www.aptfilms.com
MANAGING DIRECTOR
Jonny Persey - jonny@aptfilms.com

ARDMORE STUDIOS, LTD.
Herbert Rd., Bray, Co. Wicklow, Ireland.
TEL: (353 1) 286 2971. FAX: (353 1) 286 1894.
email: film@ardmore.ie www.ardmore.ie
MANAGING DIRECTOR
Kevin Moriarty - kevin@ardmore.ie

ARTIFICIAL EYE FILM COMPANY, LTD.
20-22 Stukeley Str., London, WC2B 5LR.
TEL: (0207) 240 5353, FAX: (0207) 240 5242.
email: info@artificial-eye.com www.artificial-eye.com

ARROW FILMS
Orchard Villa Porters Park Drive, Shenley Radlett Herts, WD 9DS. TEL: (01923) 858 306. FAX: (1923) 859 673.
www.arrow.co.uk

ATTICUS DESIGN & MEDIA, LTD.
Pinewood Studios Pinewood Rd., Iver Heath, Buckinghamshire, SL0 0NH. TEL: (0175) 365 0123.
FAX: (0175) 365 0111. www.atticusmedia.net

AUTOCUE, LTD.
265 Merton Rd., London, SW18 5JS. TEL: (0208) 870 0104.
FAX: (0208) 874 3726. email: info@autocue.co.uk
www.autocue.com
CONTACT
Helen Masson

AVS ROTHMAR
The Studio, Common Farm, Milton Common, Thames, Oxfordshire, OX9 2NU. TEL: (01844) 27 9291.
FAX: (01844) 27 9192. email: enquire@avsrothmar.co.uk
www.avsrothmar.co.uk
CONTACT
Alan Fenimore

AXIOM FILMS
2nd Flr. (above The Gate Cinema), 87 Notting Hill Gate, London, W11 3JZ. TEL: (0207) 243 3111. FAX: (0207) 243 315
email: mail@axiomfilms.co.uk www.axiomfilms.co.uk
CONTACT
Lisa Cullen

JANE BALFOUR SERVICES, LTD.
Flat 2, Cresecent Mansions, 122 Elgin Crescent, London, W1 2JN. TEL: (0207) 727 1528. FAX: (0207) 221 9007.

BBC FILMS
Grafton House, 379 Euston Rd., London, NW1 3AU.
TEL: (0207) 765 0091. FAX: (0207) 765 0278.
www.bbc.co.uk/bbcfilms
HEAD OF BBC FILMS
David Thompson

BENTLEY PRODUCTIONS, LTD.
Pinewood Studios, Pinewood Rd, Iver, Buckinghamsire, SLO ONH. TEL: (01753) 656 594. FAX: (01753) 652 638.
www.all3media.com
MANAGING DIRECTOR
Brian True-May

BERMUDA SHORTS
Fifth Fl., Circus House. TEL: (0207) 437 7335.
FAX: (0207) 437 7334. email: info@bermudashorts.com
CEO
Trevor Murphy - trevor@bermudashorts.com

BLACK DOG FILMS
(A division of RSA Films)
42-44 Beak St., London, W1F 9RH. TEL: (0207) 437 7426.
FAX: (0207) 734 4978. www.blackdogfilms.com
MANAGING DIRECTOR
Kai-Lu Hsiung
EXECUTIVE PRODUCER
John Payne - jrpayne@rsafilms.co.uk

BLAST FILMS
Unit C, Imperial Works, Perren St., London, NW5 3E.
TEL: (020) 7267 4260. FAX: (020) 7485 2340.
email: blast@blastfilms.co.uk

BIG TALK PRODUCTIONS, LTD.
83 Great Titchfield St., London, W1P 7FP. TEL: (0207) 255 1131.
FAX: (0207) 436 9347. email: info@bigtalkproductions.com
www.bigtalkproductions.com www.blastfilm.co.uk
EXECUTIVE PRODUCER
Nira Park

THE JON BLAIR FILM COMPANY, LTD.
27 Devonshire Place, London, W1G 6JF. TEL: (0207) 486 6680.
MANAGING DIRECTOR
Jon Blair - jon@jbfc.demon.co.uk

BLUE DOLPHIN FILM DISTRIBUTORS, LTD.
40 Langham St., London, W1W 7AS. TEL: (0207) 255 2494.
FAX: (0207) 580 7670. email: info@bluebdolphinfilms.com
www.bluedolphinfilms.com

BLUE STAR MOVIES
175 - 185 Gray's Inn Rd., London, WC1X 8UE.
TEL: (207) 812 0700. FAX: (207) 812 0650.
email: office@bluestarmovies.com
CHAIRMAN
Pete Maggi
EXECUTIVE PRODUCER
Roberto Almagia

BRAINWAVE MEDIA, LTD.
Yew House, High St., Newport Saffron Walden, Essex, CB11 3QY.
TEL: (01799) 542 620. email: duction@brainwavemedia.com
www.brainwavemedia.com
SENIOR CREATIVE PRODUCER
Brian House
ADMINISTRATION/MARKETING
Andrea Chance - andrea@brainwavemedia.co.uk

BRIGHTER PICTURES, LTD.
10th Flr., Blue Star House, 23-2 Stockwell Rd., London, SW9 9SP. TEL: (0207) 733 7333. FAX: (0207) 733 6333.
email: info@brighter.co.uk www.brighter.co.uk
MANAGING DIRECTOR
Gavin Hay

BRITISH CERMONIAL ARTS (BCA), LTD.
26 Rose St., Wockingham, Berkshire, RG40 1XU.
TEL: (0118) 977 6800. FAX: (0118) 977 6400.
email: info@bcafilm.co.ukm www.bcafilm.co.uk

BRITISH FILM INSTITUTE
21 Stephen St., London, W1T 1LN. TEL: (0207) 255 1444.
FAX: (0207) 436 7950. www.bfi.org.uk
DIRECTOR
Amanda Nevill
PERSONAL ASSISTANT TO DIRECTOR
Brenda Whitehead

BRITISH LION
(Working from Los Angeles Office)
5302 Ethel Ave., Sherman Oaks, CA 91401.
TEL: (818) 789 9112. FAX: (818) 789 2901.
www.britishlionfilms.com
CHAIRMAN/CEO
Peter R.E. Snell

BRITISH SKY BROADCASTING
Grant Way, Isleworth, Middlesex, TW7 5QD.
TEL: (0207) 705 3000. FAX: (0207) 705 3030.
email: viewerr@bskyb.com www.sky.com

BRITISH UNIVERSITIES FILM & VIDEO COUNCIL
77 Wells St., London, W1T 3QJ. TEL: (0207) 393 1500.
FAX: (0207) 393 1555. email: ask@bufvc.ac.uk
www.bufvc.ac.uk
DIRECTOR
Murray Weston

BUENA VISTA PRODUCTIONS LIMITED
3 Queen Caroline St., Hammersmith, London, W6 9PE.
TEL: (0208) 222 1000. FAX: (0208) 222 2827.
www.disney.com
CONTACT
M. Stewart Salter

CALLISTER COMMUNICATIONS, LTD.
88 Causeway End Rd., Lisburn, Co, Antrim, BT28 3ED.
TEL: (028) 9267 3717. www.callister.tv
MANAGING DIRECTOR
John Callister

CAN COMMUNICATE, LTD.
Stable Yard, 52 Worple Way, Richmond Upon Thames S. Urrey, TW10 6DF. TEL: (0870) 241 6350. FAX: (02870) 241 6550.
email: cancommunicate@blueyonder.co.uk

CAPITAL FX, LTD.
2nd Flr., 20 Dering St., London, W1S 1AJ.
TEL: (0207) 493 9998. email: info@capital-fx.co.uk
www.capital-fx.co.uk
CONTACT
Liz Clarke - lizclarke@capital-fx.co.uk

CAPITOL FILMS, LTD.
Bridge House, 2nd Flr., 63-65 Brth Wharf Rd., London, W21 LA. TEL: (0207) 298 6200. FAX: (0207) 298 6201.
email: films@capitolfilms.com www.capitolfilms.co.uk

CAPRICORN PROGRAMMES, LTD.
Hithercroft Court, Wallingford, Oxon OX10 9BT.
TEL: (01491) 838 888. FAX: (01491) 833 333.
email: admin@capricornprogs.co.uk www.capricornprogs.co.uk

CARNABY FILMS
New London House, 172 Drury Lane, London, WC2B 5QR.
TEL: (08704) 586 281. FAX: (08704) 586 282.
email: info@carnabyentertainment.com www.carnabyfilms.com

CARNIVAL FILMS, LTD.
12 Raddington Rd, Ladbroke Grove, London, W10 5TG.
TEL: (0208) 968 0968. FAX: (0208) 968 0177.
email: info@carnival-films.co.uk www.carnival-films.co.uk
FOUNDER & CHAIRMAN
Brian Eastman - brian.eastman@carnival-films.co.uk
MANAGING DIRECTOR
Gareth Neame - gareth.neame@carnival-films.co.uk
PERSONAL ASSISTANT TO FOUNDER & CHAIRMAN
Jessica Hughes - jessica.hughes@carnival-films.co.uk

CATALYST TV
Brook Green Studios, 220 Shepherds Bush Rd, London, W6 7RG. TEL: (0207) 603 7030. FAX: (0207) 603 9518.
MANAGING DIRECTOR
Tony Lareyo

CELTIC FILMS
Lodge House , 69 Beafort St., London, SW3 5AH.
TEL: (0207) 351 0909. FAX: (0207) 351 139.
www.celtiffilms.co.uk

CHAMELEON TELEVISION
Greatminster House, Listerhill, Leeds, West Yorkshire, LS18 5DL. TEL: (0113) 205 0040. FAX: (0113) 281 9454.
email: name@chameleontv.com www.chameleontv.com

CHATSWORTH TELEVISION
62 Shaftsbury Ave., London, W1D 6LT. TEL: (0207) 734 4302.
FAX: (0207) 437 3301. email: info@chatsworth-tv.co.uk
www.chatsworth-tv.co.uk
MANAGING DIRECTOR
Malcolm Heyworth

CHEERFUL SCOUT PRODUCTIONS
25-27 Riding House St., London, W1W 7DU.
TEL: (0207) 291 0444. FAX: (0207) 291 0445.
email: info@cheerfulscout.com www.cheerfulscout.com
MANAGING DIRECTOR
Gary Fitzpatrick, Peter Litten

CHIMERA FILMS AND COMMUNICATION, LTD.
(Japanese Production Company)
Unit 10, Apolllo House, 18 All Saints Rd., London, W11 1HH.
TEL: (0208) 871 5127. FAX: (0208) 871 5128.
email: pro@chimerafilms.co.uk www.chimerafilms.co.uk
CONTACT
Yoshi Tezuka - yoshi@chimerafilms.co.uk

CHRYSALIS VISUAL ENTERTAINMENT
The Chrysalis Bldg., 13 Bramley Rd., London, W10 6SP.
TEL: (0207) 221 2213. email: enquiries@chrysalis.co.uk
www.chrysalis.co.uk

GROUP CHIEF EXECUTIVE (GCE)
Richard Huntingford - ceos.office@chrysalis.co.uk

CINEFILE, LTD.
12 Sunbury Place Edinburgh, EH4 3BY TEL: (0131) 225 6191.
FAX: (0131) 225 6971. email: info@cinefile.co.uk
www.cinefile.co.uk
CONTACT
Ilona Morison

CINECONTACT PRODUCTIONS, LTD.
27 Newman St., London, W1T 1AR. TEL: (0207) 323 1690.
FAX: (0207) 323 1215. email: info@cinecontact.co.uk
www.cinecontact.co.uk
DIRECTOR
Ron Orders, Trevor Boden

CINEMA VERITY PRODUCTIONS, LTD.
11 Addison Ave., London, W11 4QS. TEL: (0207) 460 2777.
FAX: (0207) 371 3329.
PRODUCER
Verity Lambert

CINEWORLD
(Merger of Cine UK and UGC UK)
Power Road Studios, Power Rd., Chiswick, London, W4 5PY.
TEL: (0208) 987 5000. FAX: (0208) 987 2301.
email: corporate@ugccinemas.co.uk www.ugccinemas.co.uk
CONTACT
Sarah Sharp - sarahsharp@ugccinemas.co.uk

CINTEL INTERNATIONAL, LTD.
Watton Rd., Ware, Hertfordshire, SG12 OAE.
TEL: (01920) 463 939. FAX: (01920) 460 803.
email: sales@cintel.co.uk www.cintel.co.uk
CONTACT
Simon Carter

CLARENDON FILM PRODUCTIONS, LTD.
7 Trinity Crescent, London, SW17 7AG. TEL: (0208) 488 9208.
FAX: (0208) 488 3959.

CLASSIC PICTURES, LTD.
Shepperton Studios, Studios Rd., Shepperton, Middlesex,
TW17 0QD. TEL: (01932) 572 016. FAX: (01932) 572 046.
email: info@classicpictures.co.uk www.classicpictures.co.uk
CEO
Robert Garofalo - robert.garofalo@classicpictures.co.uk
HEAD OF ACQUISITIONS/PRODUCER
Lyn Beardsall - lyn.beardsall@classicpictures.co.uk

BRIAN CLEMENS ENTERPRISES, LTD.
Park Farm Cottage, Ampthill, Beds. TEL: (01525) 402 215.
FAX: (01525) 402 954.
MANAGING DIRECTOR
Brian Clemens

COLLINGWOOD O'HARE ENTERTAINMENT, LTD.
10-14 Crown St., London, W3 8SB. TEL: (0208) 993 3666.
FAX: (0208) 993 9595. email: info@crownstreet.co.uk
www.collingwoodohare.com
MANAGING DIRECTOR & PRODUCER
Christopher O'Hare
DIRECTOR
Tony Collingwood

COMPANY PICTURES
Suffolk House, 1-8 Whitfield Place, London, W1T 5JU.
TEL: (0207) 380 3900. FAX: (0207) 380 1166.
email: enquiries@companypictures.co.uk
www.companypictures.co.uk
MANAGING DIRECTOR
George Faber, Charles Pattinson

CONTEMPORARY FILMS
24 Southwood Lawn Rd., Highgate, London, N6 5SF.
TEL: (0208) 340 5715. FAX: (0208) 348 1238.
email: enquiries@contemporaryfilms.com
www.contemporaryfilms.com
CONTACT
Eric Likmaitzky - eric@contemporaryfilms.com

CONTENDER ENTERTAINMENT GROUP
120 New Cavendish St., London, W1W 8SE.
TEL: (0207) 907 3773. FAX: (0207) 907 3777.
email: enquiries@contendergroup.com
www.contendergroup.com
MANAGING DIRECTOR
Richard Bridgwood

CONTENT FILM
19 Heddon St., London, W1R 7LP. TEL: (0807) 851 6500.
FAX: (0207) 851 6505. www.contentfilm.com

COURTYARD PRODUCTIONS - MAIDSTONE
Hollingbourne House, Hollingbourne Kent, ME17 1QJ.
TEL: (0162) 288 0990. www.courtyardstudios.co.uk

CREATIVE FILM PRODUCTIONS
68 Conway Rd, London, N14 7BE. TEL: (0208) 447 8187.
FAX: (0208) 886 3054. www.creativefilm.co.uk
CONTACT
Mark Collins

CROSSROADS MEDIA
(Formerly Cowboy Films, LTD.)
2nd Flr., 87 Notting Hill Gate, London, W11 3JZ.
TEL: (0207) 792 5400. FAX: (0207) 792 0592.
www.crossroadsfilms.com

CURZON FILM DISTRIBUTORS, LTD.
Wingate House, 93-107, Shaftsbury Ave., London, W1D 5DA.
TEL: (020) 7734 9209. FAX: (020) 7734 1977.
CONTACT
Rob Kenny - rob.kenny@curzoncinemas.com
Nicki Tucker - nicki.tucker@curzoncinemas.com

DAN FILMS, LTD.
32 Maple St., London, W1P 5GD. TEL: (0207) 916 4771.
FAX: (0207) 916 4773. email: enquiries@danfilms.com
www.danfilms.com
CONTACT
Sara Sutton

DARLOW SMITHSON PRODUCTIONS
Highgate Business Centre, 33 Greenwood Place, London,
NW5 1LB. TEL: (0207) 482 7027. FAX: (0207) 482 7039.
email: mail@darlowsmithson.com www.darlowsmithson.com
EXECUTIVE CHAIRMAN AND CREATIVE DIRECTOR
John Smithson
MANAGING DIRECTOR
Iain Pelling

DAWKINS ASSOCIATES, LTD.
P.O. Box 615, Boughton Monchelsea, Maidstone, Kent, ME17
4RN. TEL: (01622) 741 900. email: da@ccland.demon.co.uk
MANAGING DIRECTOR
Hilary Dawkins

DAZZLE FILM AGENCY
388 Old St., London, EC1V 9LT. TEL: (0207) 739 7716.
FAX: (0207) 613 85. email: studio@dazzlefilms.co.uk
www.dazzlefilms.co.uk
CONTACT
Dawn Sharpless

DE LANE LEA SOUND CENTRE
75 Dean St., London, W1D 3PU. TEL: (0207) 432 3800.
FAX: (0207) 432 3838. www.delanelea.com
COO
Huw Penallt-Jones - huw@delanelea.com

DELUXE LABORATORIES LIMITED
Denham Media Park, North Orbital Rd., Denham, Uxbridge,
Middlesex, UB9 5HQ. TEL: (01895) 832 323.
FAX: (01895) 832 446. www.bydeluxe.com
CONTACT
Terry Landsbury - terrylandsbury@bydeluxe.com
Simon Valley - simonvalley@bydeluxe.com

DESTINY FILMS, LTD.
Sands Film Studios, 119 Rotherhithe St., London, SE16 4NF.
TEL: (0207) 231 2209. FAX: (0207) 231 2119.
email: info@destinyfilms.co.uk www.destinyfilms.com

DE WARRENNE PICTURES, LTD.
3 Diadem Court, London, W1D 3EF. TEL: (0787) 658 7679.
email: info@dewarrenne.com www.dewarrenne.com
PRODUCER/DIRECTOR
Tom Waller, Michael Pritchett

DIGITAL FILM LAB LONDON, LTD.
6 Berner Mews, Third Flr., London, W1T 3AJ.
TEL: (0845) 658 5726.

Aarhusgade 120, 2100 Copenhagen, Denmark.
TEL: (053) 925 2030. FAX: (053) 925 2031.
email: cph@digitalfilmlab.com www.digitalfilmlab.com

DIME GOCH
Unit 2, Cibyn, Caemarfon, Gwynedd, LL55 2BD.
TEL: (01286) 678 592. FAX: (01286) 678 594.
www.dimegoch.co.uk

DIPLOMAT FILMS, LTD.
Oakdene House, Parkfield Rd., Altrincham, Cheshire WA14
2BT. TEL: (0161) 929 1603. FAX: (0161) 929 1604.
email: mail@diplomatfilms.com www.diplomatfilms.com

WALT DISNEY COMPANY, LTD.
3, Queen Caroline St., Hammersmith, London, W6 9PE.
TEL: (0208) 222 1000. FAX: (0208) 222 2116.
www.disney.co.uk www.thefilmfactor.co.uk

DISTANT HORIZON, LTD.
28 Vernon Dr., Stanmore, Middlesex, HAT7 2BT.
TEL: (0208) 861 5500. FAX: (0208) 861 4411.
email: london@distant-horizon.com www.distant-horizon.com

DLT ENTERTAINMENT/UK, LTD.
10 Bedford Square, London, WC1B 3RA. TEL: (0207) 631 1184.
FAX: (0207) 636 4571. www.dltentertainment.com

EXECUTIVE PRODUCER
John Reynolds

DNA FILMS, LTD.
First Fl., 15 Greek St., London, W1D 4DP. TEL: (0207) 292 8700.
FAX: (0207) 292 870. www.dnafilms.com

DOGWOOF
Studio 311, Panther House, 38 Mount Pleasant
London, WC1X 0AN. TEL: (44) 020 7833 3599.
FAX: (44) 202 7900 3270.
email: info@dogwoof.com www.dogwoof.com.
CHAIRMAN
Andy Whittaker
CEO
Anna Godas
HEAD OF DISTRIBUTION
Oli Harbottle

DOGWOOF PICTURES
2nd Fl., 19 Shorts Garden, London, WC2 H9AT.
TEL: (0207) 395 1217. FAX: (0207) 900 3270.
www.dogwoofpictures.com

DOLBY LABORATORIES, INC.
Interface Park, Wootton Bassett, Wiltshire, SN4 8QJ.
TEL: (01793) 842100. FAX: (01793) 842101.
email: info@dolby.com www.dolby.com
MANAGING DIRECTOR UK
David Watts
MARKETING DIRECTOR
Tony Spathe
MARKET DEVELOPMENT MANAGER
Jason Power

DORSET FILM AND TELEVISION PRODUCTIONS
Belmont Villas, The Nothe, Weymouth, Dorset, DT4 8UW.
TEL: (01305) 777 834. email: dftv_prods@compuserv.com

DRAW PICTURES, LTD.
8A Delancey Passage, London, NW1 7NN. TEL: (0207) 419 4655.
FAX: (0207) 419 4660. email: production@drawpictures.co.uk
www.drawpictures.co.uk
COMPANY DIRECTOR
Patrick Holkamp - patrick@drawpictures.co.uk

DUCK LANE FILM PRODUCTIONS, LTD.
8 Duck Ln., London, W1V 0HZ. TEL: (0207) 439 3912.
FAX: (0207) 437 2260.

E1 ENTERTAINMENT
120 New Cavendish St., London, W1W 6XX.
TEL: (44) 207 907 3773. FAX: (44) 207 907 3777.
www.e1entertainmentuk.com
CONTACT
Genny Rowson - growson@e1ent.com
MANAGING DIRECTOR
Richard Dridgewood
FINANCE DIRECTOR/OPERATIONS DIRECTOR
Charles Ogilvie

EAGLE & EAGLE PRODUCTIONS, LTD.
15 Marlborough Rd., London, W4 4EU. TEL: (0208) 995 1884.
FAX: (0208) 995 5648. email: producer@eagletv.co.uk
www.eagletv.co.uk
PRODUCER & DIRECTOR
Robert Eagle

EATON FILMS
10 Holbein Mews, Lower Sloane St., London, SW1W 8NN.
TEL: (0207) 823 6173. FAX: (0207) 823 6017.
email: eaton.films@talk21.com
DIRECTOR
Judith Bland Gordon
PERSONAL ASSISTANT TO DIRECTOR
Carol Sinclair

ECOSSE FILMS
Brigade House, 8 Parsons Green, London, SW6 4TN.
TEL: (0207) 371 0290. FAX: (0207) 736 3436.
email: webmail@ecossefilms.com www.ecossefilms.com
MANAGING DIRECTOR/EXECUTIVE PRODUCER
Douglas Rae

EDUCATIONAL AND TELEVISIONAL FILMS, LTD.
c/o The British Film Institute, 21 Stephen St., London, W1T
1LN. TEL: (0207) 255 1444. www.bfi.org.uk

ELITE TELEVISION
248 Meanwood Rd., Leeds, West Yorkshire, LS7 2HZ.
TEL: (0113) 262 3342. FAX: (0113) 262 3798.
email: info@elitetv.co.uk www.elitetv.co.uk

ENTERTAINMENT FILM DISTRIBUTORS, LTD.
Eagle House, Jermyn St., London, SW1Y 6HB.
TEL: (0207) 930 7744. FAX: (0207) 930 9399.
www.entertainmentfilms.co.uk
DIRECTOR
Trevor H. Green, Nigel G. Green

EQUATOR FILMS
6 Heddon St., London, W1B BT. TEL: (0207) 025 7000.
FAX: (0207) 930 9399. www.equatorfilms.co.uk
CONTACT
Steve Turney - steve.turney@equatorfilms.co.uk

EROS INTERNATIONAL
Unit 26 23 Sovereign Park, Britannia Way, London, NW10 7PR.
TEL: (0208) 963 870. FAX: (0208) 963 81.
email: UK-business@erosintl.co.uk
www.erosentertainment.com
PRESIDENT
Arjan Lulla

ESPRESSO TV, LTD.
9 York Villas, Brighton, BN1 3TS. TEL: (1273) 730929.
FAX: (1273) 299 403. email: info@espressotv.co.uk

EYE FILM AND TELEVISION, LTD.
Chamberlain House, 2 Dove St., Norwich, Norfolk, NR2 1DE.
TEL: (01603) 762 551. FAX: (01603) 762 420.
email: production@eyefilmandtv.co.uk www.eyefilmandtv.co.uk

EYELINE PRODUCTIONS
10 Park View, Swillington, Leeds, West Yorkshire, LS26 8UJ.
TEL: (07834) 190 030. email: nick@eyelineproductions.co.uk
www.eyelineproductions.co.uk

FAIRLINE PRODUCTIONS, LTD.
15 Royal Terrace, Glasgow, Lanarkshire, G3 7NY.
TEL: (0141) 331 0077. FAX: (0141) 331 0066.
email: team@fairlineproductions.com
www.fairlineproductions.com

FELGATE MEDIA, LTD.
15 Canfield Place, London, NW6 3BT. TEL: (0207) 624 1525.
FAX: (0207) 624 1148.
MANAGER
Mr. P. Elwen

FESTIVAL FILM AND TELEVISION, LTD.
Festival House, Tranquil Passage, Blackheath Village, London,
SE3 0BJ. TEL: (0208) 297 9999. FAX: (0208) 297 1155.
email: info@festivalfilm.com www.festivalfilm.com
MANAGING DIRECTOR
Ray Marshall
PRODUCER
Matt Marshall

FILMBANK DISTRIBUTORS
(Filmbank Distributors Limited is a joint venture between
Warner Bros. Entertainment and Columbia Tristar and has
been operating for 20 years)
92 New Cavendish St., London, W1M 7FA.
TEL: (0207) 98 5959. FAX: (0207) 98 5951.
www.filmbank.co.uk

FILM AND GENERAL PRODUCTIONS, LTD.
4 Bradbrook House, Studio Place, London, SW1X 8EL.
TEL: (0207) 235 4495. FAX: (0207) 245 9853.
CONTACT
Clive Parsons - cparsons@filmgen.co.uk

FILM FINANCES, LTD.
14-15 Conduit St., London, W1R 9TG. TEL: (0207) 629 6557.
FAX: (0207) 491 7530. www.ffi.com
CONTACT
Graham Easton - geaston@filmfinances.co.uk

FILMARKETEERS, LTD.
Lower Ground, 13 Holland Pk, Kensington, W11 3TH.
TEL: (0207) 792 5531. FAX: (0207) 229 2524.
email: filmtwt@aol.com

FIRST FRAME FILMS
6 Glemore Close, Thatcham, Berkshire, RG19 3XR.
TEL: (01635) 865 059. FAX: (01635) 869 010.
email: info@firstframefilms.co.uk www.firstframefilms.co.uk
PRODUCER
Tanya Steel

FIRST INDEPENDENT FILMS, LTD.
Registered Offices: The London Television Centre, Upper
Ground, London, SE1 9LT. TEL: (0207) 528 7767.

FLECHETTE, LTD.
(Formerly Posh Pictures, LTD.)
29 Hyndland Rd., West End Glasgow, G12 9UZ Scotland.
TEL: (0141) 416 0626. FAX: (202) 502 9501.
email: mail@flechette.net www.flechette.net

FOCUS FILM PRODUCTIONS, LTD.
The Rotunda Studios, Rear of 116-118 Finchley Rd., London,
NW3 5HT. TEL: (0207) 435 9004. FAX: (0207) 431 3562.
email: focus@focusfilms.co.uk www.focusfilms.co.uk
CHIEF EXECUTIVE
David Pupkewitz
EXECUTIVE DIRECTOR
Marsha Levin - marsha@focusfilms.co.uk

HEAD OF DEVELOPMENT
Malcolm Kohll - malcolm@focusfilms.co.uk

FORGED FILMS
Third Flr., 8 West Newington Place, Edinburgh, EH9 1QT.
TEL: (0131) 667 0230. FAX: (0131) 667 0230.
email: forgedfilm@blueyonder.co.uk
CONTACT
Nigel R. Smith

MARK FORSTATER PRODUCTIONS, LTD.
27 Lonsdale Rd, London, NW6 6RA. TEL: (0207) 624 1123.
FAX: (0207) 624 1124.
DIRECTOR
Mark Forstater

FOUR STAR FILMS, LTD.
52 Queen Anne St., London, W1M 9LA. TEL: (0207) 935 1186.
FAX: (0207) 487 2900.
DIRECTOR
N. Butt, D.H Malyon

FREEDOM PICTURES
10 Rylett Crescent, Shepherd's Bush, London, W12 9RL.
TEL: (0208) 743 5330. www.freedompictures.co.uk
CONTACT
Tim White - timwhite@freedompictures.co.uk

FREEWAY FILMS, LTD.
33A Pembroke Square, London, W8 6PD. TEL: (0207) 937 9114.
FAX: (0207) 937 3938. email: 100012.3206@compuserve.com
DIRECTOR
John McGrath

FREMANTLEMEDIA, LTD.
1 Stephen St., London, W1T 1AL. TEL: (0207) 691 6000.
FAX: (0207) 691 6100. www.fremantlemedia.com
CEO
Tony Cohen

JANE FULLER ASSOCIATES
10 Golden Square, London, 3AF 9JA. TEL: (0207) 949 2067.
FAX: (0207) 734 9147. email: jane@janefullerassoc.co.uk
CONTACT
Jane Fuller

FUTURE FILMS LIMITED
4-6 Soho Square, London, W1D 3QA. TEL: (0207) 434 6600.
FAX: (0207) 434 6633. www.futurefilmgroup.com
CHIEF EXECUTIVE
Tim Levy - tim@futurefilmgroup.com
MANAGING DIRECTOR
Stephen Margolis - stephen@futurefilmgroup.com

GFD COMMUNICATIONS, LTD.
Unit 15A, Parkmore Industrial Estate, Long Mile Rd., Dublin,
12, Ireland. TEL: (353 1) 456 9500. FAX: (353 1) 456 9342.
email: info@gfd.ie www.gfd.ie
DIRECTOR
Conor M. Anderson - conor@gfd.ie
John Anderson - john@gfd.ie

GALA PRODUCTIONS, LTD.
25 Stamford Brook Rd., London, W6 OXJ. TEL: (0208) 741 4200.
FAX: (0208)741 2323.
CONTACT
David Lindsay - david@galaproductions.co.uk

GANNET FILMS, LTD.
Hookland Farm Cottage, Midhurst, West Sussex, GU29 OQF.
TEL: (01428) 741227. email: info@gannetfilms.co.uk
www.gannetfilms.co.uk
DIRECTOR
Ben Kellett

NOEL GAY ENTERTAINMENT GROUP, LTD.
Shepperton Studios, Studios Rd., Shepperton, Middlesex,
TW17 0QD. TEL: (01932) 592 485. FAX: (01932) 592 172.
email: starbug@attglobal.net
PRODUCER
Christopher Figg

GLOBAL ENTERTAINMENT MANAGEMENT, LTD.
22 Wadsworth Rd., Perivale, Middlesex, UB6 7JD.
TEL: (0208) 991 5015. FAX: (0208) 998 3521.
email: info@hotel-tv.co.uk
MANAGING DIRECTOR
Pransukh Kotak

GOLDCREST FILM AND TELEVISION, LTD.
1 Lexington St., London, W1F 9TB. TEL: (0207) 437 7972.
FAX: (0207) 437 5402. email: info@goldcrest-post.com
www.goldcrestpost.com
CHIEF EXECUTIVE
John Quested
BOOKINGS MANAGER
Fay Stevens

ROBERT GOLDEN PICTURES
3 Chimneys, Pymore Lane, Dottery Bridport, Dorset, DT6 5PS
TEL/FAX: (01308) 421 325. email: rgoldenpics@aol.com
CONTACT
Robert Golden

GRANADA GROUP, PLC.
London Television Centre, Upper Ground, London, SE1 9LT.
TEL: (0207) 620 1620. FAX: (0207) 451 3008.

GRANADA INTERNATIONAL
(A division of ITV Entertainment)
48 Leicester Square, London, WC2H 7FB.
TEL: (0207) 491 1441. FAX: (0207) 493 7677.
email: int.info@granadamedia.com
www.granadamedia.com/international
MANAGING DIRECTOR
Nadine Nohr - (0207) 389 8700 nadine.nohr@granadamedia.com
DIRECTOR OF OPERATIONS & FINANCE
David Johnson - (0207) 389 8692 david.johnson@granadamedia.com
MARKETING DIRECTOR
Paul Raven - (0207) 389 8710 paul.raven@granadamedia.com
SENIOR V.P. SALES, EUROPE
Tim Mutimer - (0207) 389 8659 tim.mutimer@granadamedia.com
DIRECTOR, ACQUISITIONS AND CO-PRODUCTIONS
Emmanuelle Namiech - (207) 389 8645
emmanuelle.namiech@grandamedia.com

GRANITE PRODUCTIONS
5 Hanover Yard, Noel Rd., Islington, London, N1 8BE.
TEL: (0207) 354 3232. FAX: (0207) 354 0205.
MANAGING DIRECTOR
Simon Welfare

GREEN UMBRELLA, LTD.
59 Cotham Hill Cotham, Bristol, BS6 6JR.
TEL: (0117) 906 4336. email: postmaster@umbrella.co.uk
www.umbrella.co.uk
OFFICE MANAGER
Gina Shepherd
MANAGING DIRECTOR
Nigel Ashcroft

GREENPOINT FILMS, LTD.
7 Denmark St., London, WC2H 8LZ. TEL: (0207) 240 7066.
FAX: (0207) 240 7088. email: info@greenpointfilms.com
www.greenpointfilms.co.uk
DIRECTOR
Patrick Cassavetti, Simon Relph, Ann Scott, Ann Sinclair

GRUBER FILMS
Office No. 2, Sheraton St., London, W1F 8BH.
TEL: (08703) 669 313. www.gruberfilms.com
CONTACT
Richard Holmes - richard.holmes@gruberfilms.com
Stephan Schwartz

HAMMER FILM PRODUCTIONS, LTD./BRIDGE MEDIA
92 New Cavendish St., London, W1W 6XN.
TEL: (0207) 637 2322. www.hammerfilms.com

HAMMERWOOD FILM PRODUCERS AND DISTRIBUTORS
306 Portland Rd. Hove, Sussex, BN3 1LP.
TEL: (01273) 277 333. FAX: (01273) 705 451.
CONTACT
Ralph Harvey

HARBOUR PICTURES, LTD.
11 Langton St., London, SW10 0JL. TEL: (0207) 351 7070.
FAX: (0207) 352 3528. email: info@harbourpictures.com
JOINT CHIEF EXECUTIVE
Nick Barton

HARKNESS HALL, LTD.
Unit A, Norton Rd., Stevenage, Herts, SG1 2BB.
TEL: (01438) 725 200. FAX: (01438) 344 400.
email: info@harknesshall.com www.harknesshall.com
MANAGING DIRECTOR
Andrew Robinson
PERSONAL ASSISTANT TO MANAGING DIRECTOR
June Knepper

HARTSWOOD FILMS
Twickenham Studios, The Barons, St. Margarets, Twickenham
Middlesex, TW1 2AW. TEL: (0208) 607 8736.
FAX: (0208) 607 8744. email: films.tv@hartswoodfilms.co.uk
www.hartswoodfilms.co.uk
PRODUCER & CHAIRMAN
Beryl Vertue

HAT TRICK PRODUCTIONS, LTD./TWELVE YARD
10 Livonia St., London, W1F 8AF. TEL: (0207) 434 2451.
FAX: (0207) 287 9791. email: info@hattrick.com
www.hattrick.com
MANAGING DIRECTOR
Jimmy Mulville

HELIFILMS, LTD.
Chalk Pit Farm Studios, Theale, Reading, Berkshire, RG7 5EE
TEL: (01189) 305 408. FAX: (01189) 303 936.

email: info@helifilms.com www.helifilms.homestead.com
PRODUCER
Sara Hine - sara@helifilms.com

JIM HENSON PRODUCTIONS
30 Oval Rd., Campden, London, NW1 7DE.
TEL: (0207) 428 4000. FAX: (0207) 428 4001.
email: info@henson.com www.henson.com
CO-CEO
Brian Henson, Lisa Henson

HIGH POINT FILMS AND TELEVISION, LTD.
25 Elizabeth Mews, London, NW3 4UH. TEL: (0207) 586 3686.
FAX: (0207) 586 3117. email: info@highpointfilms.co.uk
www.highpointfilms.co.uk
CEO
Ronald C.H. de Neef
MANAGING DIRECTOR
Carey Fitzgerald - carey@highpointfilms.co.uk
DIRECTOR
Julie Murphy-Delaney

HIT AND RUN PRODUCTIONS
14 Limekiln Rd., Terenure, Dublin, 12. TEL: (353 1) 450 8642.
FAX: (353 1) 450 8642. www.hitandrunfilms.com
PRUDUCER & DIRECTOR
Barry Dignam - barry@hitandrunfilms.com

HIT ENTERTAINMENT, PLC.
5th Flr., Maple House, 149 Tottenham Court Rd., London, W1T 7NF. TEL: (020) 7554 2500. FAX: (020) 7388 9321.
email: contactus@hitentertainment.com
www.hitentertainment.co.uk

HOLLYWOOD CLASSICS
Linton House, 39151 Highgate Rd., London, NW5 1RS.
TEL: (0207) 424 7280. FAX: (0207) 428 8936.
email: info@hollywoodclassics.com
www.hollywoodclassics.com
DIRECTOR
Joe Dreier, John Flynn (USA)

HOT PROPERTY FILMS
27 Newman St., London, W1T 1PP. TEL: (0207) 291 3755.
FAX: (0207) 323 9467. email: janine@hotpropertyfilms.com
www.hotpropertyfilms.com

HOURGLASS PRODUCTIONS
27 Princes Rd., Wimbledon, London, SE19 1ED.
TEL: (0208) 840 8786. FAX: (0208) 544 0787.
email: productions@hourglass.co.uk www.hourglass.co.uk
DIRECTOR
Martin Chilcott
HEAD OF PRODUCTION
Jacqueline Chilcott

HUDSON FILM, LTD.
24 St. Leonards Terrace, London, SW3 4QG. TEL: (0207) 730 0002.
FAX: (0207) 730 8033. email: hudsonfilm@aol.com
DIRECTOR
Hugh Hudson

ILLUMINATIONS
19-20 Rhiedol Mews, Rhiedol Terrace, London, N1 8NU.
TEL: (0207) 228 8400. FAX: (0207) 359 1151.
email: illuminations@illumin.co.uk www.illumin.co.uk
CHAIRMAN
John Wyver
MANAGING DIRECTOR
Linda Zuck

ILLUSTRA TELEVISION
14 Bateman St., Central Studio, London, W1V 6EB.
TEL: (0207) 437 9611. FAX: (0207) 734 7143.
CONTACT
Douglas Kentish

IMAGICIANS TELEVISION
34 Fouberts Place, London, W1F 7PX. TEL: (0208) 374 4429.
FAX: (0208) 374 4436. email: imagicians@blueyonder.co.uk
www.imagicians.tv
MANAGING DIRECTOR
Alan Scales

IMAGO PUBLISHING, LTD.
Albury Court, Albury Thame Oxforshire, OX9 2LP.
TEL: (0184) 433 7000. FAX: (0184) 339 433 9935.
email: sales@imago.co.uk

INDEPENDENT IMAGE, LTD.
Overhills, Old Coach House, Northdown Rd., Woldingham, Surrey, CR3 7BB. TEL: (01883) 654 867. FAX: (01883) 653 290.
email: info@indimage.com www.indimage.com

INTERNATIONAL BROADCASTING TRUST
143-145 Farringson Rd. London, EC1R 3AB.
TEL: (0207) 239 1441. FAX: (0207) 833 8347.
email: mail@ibt.org.uk www.ibt.org.uk
DIRECTOR
Mark Galloway

INVINCIBLE FILMS, LTD.
Riverside Studios, Crisp Rd, Hammersmith, London, W6 9RL.
TEL: (0208) 237 1150. FAX: (0208) 237 1151.
email: info@infilms.co.uk www.infilms.co.uk
MANAGING DIRECTOR
Hugh Mason

IPSO FACTO FILMS
1 Pink Ln., Newcastle Upon Tyne, NE1 5DW.
TEL: (0191) 230 2585. FAX: (0191) 261 7481.
email: info@ipsofactofilms.com www.ipsofactofilms.com

ITV NETWORK CENTRE
The London Television Centre, Upper Ground, London, SE1 9LT. Registered Office: 200 Grays Inn Rd., London, WC1 V8HF.
TEL: (0207) 020 1620, (0207) 843 8000. FAX: (0207) 843 8158.
www.itvple.com

IWC MEDIA
(Formerly Ideal World Productions)
St. George's Studio, 93-97 St. George's Cross, Glasgow, G3 6JA. TEL: (0141) 353 3222. FAX: (0141) 353 3221.
email: mailglasgow@iwcmedia.co.uk www.iwcmedia.co.uk

London Office: 3-6 Kenrick Place, London, W1U 6HD.
TEL: (0207) 317 2230. FAX: (0207) 317 2231.
email: maillondon@iwcmedia.co.uk
MANAGING DIRECTOR
Sue Oriel - sue.oriel@iwcmedia.co.uk

BRIAN JACKSON FILMS AND TELEVISION, LTD.
39-41 Hanover Steps, St. Georges Fields, Albion St., London, W2 2YG. TEL: (0207) 402 7543. FAX: (0207) 262 5736.
MANAGING DIRECTOR
Brian Jackson

JM CREATIVE
74-78 Park Rd., Cardiff, CF14 7BR. TEL: (02920) 529 925.
FAX: (02920) 529 998.

6 D'Arblay St., London, W1F 8DN. TEL: (020) 7499 3174.
email: enquiries@jmcreative.tv www.jmcreative.tv
MANAGING DIRECTOR
John Morgan

KEMISTRY
43 Charlotte Rd., Shoreditch, London, EC2A 3PD.
TEL: (0207) 729 3636. FAX: (0207) 749 2760.
email: info@kemistry.co.uk www.kemistry.co.uk
PRODUCER
Richard Churchill
PROJECT MANAGER
Helen Barrett

KENILWORTH FILM PRODUCTIONS, LTD.
Newhouse, Mersham, Ashford, Kent, TN25 6NQ.
TEL: (01233) 503 636. FAX: (01233) 502 244.
DIRECTOR
Lord Brabourne, Richard Goodwin

KEO FILMS
101 John St., London, EC1 M4AS. TEL: (0207) 490 3580.
FAX: (0207) 490 8419. email: keo@keofilms.com
www.keofilms.com
DIRECTOR AND PRODUCER
Andrew Palmer

KINEXUS, LTD.
265 Burlington Rd., New Maiden, Surrey, KT3 4NE.
TEL: (0208) 286 5170. FAX: (0208) 286 5175.
MANAGING DIRECTOR
Ben Gooder

LAGAN PICTURES, LTD.
7 Rugby Court Agincourt Avenue, Belfast. TEL: (0289) 032 6125.
FAX: (0289) 032 6125.

LIKE MINDS, LTD.
98 Handsworth Wood Rd., Handsworth Wood, Birmingham, B20 2TN. TEL: (0121) 515 2921. FAX: (0121) 515 3989.
www.like-minds.co.uk
SENIOR PRODUCER
Paul Martin - paulmartin@like-minds.co.uk

LIONSGATE FILMS
Ariel House, 74A Charlotte St., London, W1T 4QJ.
TEL: (0207) 636 3935. FAX: (0207) 323 0961.
www.lionsgate.co.uk

LITTLE BIRD COMPANY, LTD.
Dublin Office: 13 Merrion Square, Dublin, 2.
TEL: (0353 1) 613 1710. FAX: (0353 1) 662 4647.

London Office: 9 Grafton Mews, London, W1T 5HZ.
TEL: (0207) 380 3980. FAX: (0207) 380 3981.
email: info@littlebird.ie www.littlebird.ie
CHAIRMEN
Jonathan Cavendish, James Mitchell

LUX
18 Shacklewell Lane, London, E8 2EZ. TEL: (0207) 503 3980.

FAX: (0207) 503 1606. www.luxonline.org.uk
DIRECTOR
Benjamin Cook

MAINLINE PICTURES/BLOOM THEATRES
37 Museum St., London, WC1A 1LP.
TEL: (0207) 242 5523. FAX: (0207) 430 0170.
email: mainline.pictures@BTinternet.com
CONTACT
Maria Nordqvist

MALONE GILL PRODUCTIONS, LTD.
9-15 Neal St., London, WC2H 9PU. TEL: (0207) 460 4683.
FAX: (0207) 460 4679. email: ikonic@compuserve.com
MANAGING DIRECTOR
Georgina Denison

MARCH HARE PRODUCTIONS, LTD.
Crosslands House, Ash Thomas, Tiverton, Devon, EX16 4NU.
TEL: (01884) 820 877. FAX: (01884) 821 328.

MAYA VISION INTERNATIONAL, LTD.
3rd Flr. 6, Kinghorn St., London, EC1A 7HW.
TEL: (0207) 796 4842. FAX: (0207) 796 4580.
email: info@mayavisionint.com www.mayavisionint.com
PRODUCER/DIRECTOR
Rebecca Dobbs

MCKINNON FILMS
17 Norfolk Rd., London, NW8 6HG. TEL: (0207) 449 0329.
FAX: (0207) 748 2319. email: mckinnonfilms@dial.pipex.com
www.mckinnonfilms.com
CONTACT
Michael McKinnon

THE MEDIA MERCHANTS TELEVISION CO, LTD.
(A Hit Entertainment Company)
Maidstone Studios, Vinters Park, Maidstone, Kent, ME14 5NZ.
TEL: (01622) 684 622. FAX: (01622) 684 627.
www.hitentertainment.com
MANAGING DIRECTOR
Tim Edmunds

MENDOZA FILM PRODUCTIONS
3-5 Barrett St., London, W1U 1AY. TEL: (0207) 935 4674.
FAX: (0207) 935 4417. www.mendozafilms.com

MENTORN BARRACLOUGH CAREY
43 Whitfield St., London, W1T 4HA. TEL: (0207) 258 6888.
FAX: (0207) 258 6800. email: mentorn@mentorn.co.uk
www.mentorn.co.uk
MANAGING DIRECTOR
Charles Thompson

MENTORN OXFORD
35a Great Clarendon St., Oxford, OX2 6AT.
TEL: (0186) 5318450. FAX: (0186) 531 8451.

MENTORN GLASGOW
2nd Fl, 16 Woodside Crescent, Glagow, G3 7UT.
TEL: (0141) 204 6600. FAX: (0141) 204 6666.

MERCHANT IVORY PRODUCTIONS
46 Lexington St., London, W1R 3LH. TEL: (0207) 437 1200.
FAX: (0207) 734 1579. email: contact@merchantivory.co.uk
www.merchantivory.com
PRODUCER
Paul Bradley, James Ivory
PERSONAL ASSISTANT TO PRODUCER
Simon Oxley - simon@merchantivory.com

MERSHAM PRODUCTIONS, LTD.
39 Montpelier Walk, London, SW7 1JH. TEL: (020) 7589 8829.
FAX: (01233) 502 244.
DIRECTOR
Lord Brabourne, Michael John Knatchbull, Richard Goodwin

METRODOME DISTRIBUTION
3rd Flr., Royalty House, 72-74 Dean St., London, W1D 3SG.
TEL: (0207) 534 2060. FAX: (0207) 534 2062.
email: info@metrodomegroup.com www.metrodomegroup.com
CEO
Peter Urie
FINANCE DIRECTOR
Steve Winetroube
GENERAL MANAGER
Sara Frain

MGM UK
10 Stephen Mews, London, W1P 1PP. TEL: (0207) 333 8877.
FAX: (0207) 333 8878. www.mgmuk.com

MIDDLEMARCH FILMS, LTD.
7 Redan St., London, W14 OAB. TEL: (0207) 371 4596.
FAX: (0207) 371 6143. email: films@middlemarch.co.uk
PRODUCTION MANAGER
Ceri Barnes

MILLS MEDIA, LIMITED
2 Morpeth Wharf Twelve Quays, Wirral, CH41 1LF.
TEL: (0151) 649 3600. FAX: (0151) 649 3700.
www.milssmediagroup.com
MANAGING DIRECTOR
Andrew Mills
SALES AND MARKETING DIRECTOR
Norman Seddon

MIRACLE COMMUNICATIONS, LTD.
38 Broadhurst Ave., Edgware, Middlesex, HA8 8TS.
TEL: (0208) 958 8512. FAX: (0208) 958 5112.
CONTACT
Martin Myers - martin@miracle63.freeserve.co.uk

MIRACLES PRODUCTIONS
154 Upper Newtownards Rd., County Antrim, Belfast, BT4 3ET.
TEL: (028) 9047 3838. FAX: (028) 9047 3839.
email: info@miraaclesproduction.com
www.miraclesproduction.com

MIRAMAX FILMS (UK)
Elsley House, 24-30 Great Titchfield St., London, W1W 8BF.
TEL: (0207) 535 8300. FAX: (0207) 535 8334.
www.miramax.com
PUBLICITY DIRECTOR
Bethan Dixon

MOMENTUM PRODUCTIONS
32 Newman St., West End, London, W1T 1PU.
TEL: (0207) 631 0666. FAX: (0207) 631 0676.
email: production@momentum.co.uk
publicity@momentumpictures.co.uk www.momentum.co.uk

ALAN MORE FILMS
Pinewood Studios, Pinewood Rd, Iver, Buckinghamshire, SLO ONH. TEL: (01753) 656789. FAX: (01753) 650988.
email: almorefilm@aol.com
PRODUCER
Alan More

MOVE ON UP, LTD.
Laurel House, High St, Cromarty, Rossshire, IV11 8YR.
TEL: (01381) 600 777. FAX: (01381) 600 778.
email: office@moveonup.tv

MOVIE VENTURES, LTD.
Hill House 1 Little New St. London, EC4 3TR.
TEL: (0207) 493 7920. FAX: (0207) 493 8088.
email: info@movieventures.com www.movieventures.com
CONTACT
M. Katz

MOVING PICTURE COMPANY, LTD.
127 Wardour St., London, W1F 0NL. TEL: (0207) 434 3100.
FAX: (0207) 287 5187. email: producers@moving-picture.com
www.moving-picture.co.uk
CONTACT
Stephanie Bryan

MTV NETWORK EUROPE
Hawley Crescent, London, NW1 8TT. TEL: (0207) 284 7777.
FAX: (0207) 284 7788. email: info@mtve.com www.mtve.com
CEO
Simon Guild

MUSIC ON EARTH/ETV PRODUCTIONS
Brook View, 5 Osbourne Close Oakley Vale Northamptonshire.
TEL: (0153) 674 4070. email: info@musiconearth.co.uk
www.musiconearth.co.uk
PRODUCER
Paul Balmer

NATIONAL FILM AND TELEVISION SCHOOL
Beaconsfield Studios Station Rd., Beaconsfield, HP9 1LG.
TEL: (0149) 467 123. FAX: (0149) 467 4042.

NEBRASKA PRODUCTIONS, LTD.
12 Grove Ave., London, N10 2AR. TEL: (0208) 444 5317.
FAX: (0208) 444 2113.
PRODUCER
Brian Harding

NELSON FILMS
48 Woodsford Sq., London, W14 8DP. TEL: (0207) 603 8987.
FAX: (0207) 603 7665. email: nelsfilm@dircon.co.uk
PRODUCER
David Harrington

N.F.H., LTD.
37 Ovington Sq., London, SW3 1LJ. TEL: (0207) 584 7561.
FAX: (0207) 589 1863.
CONTACT
Ashling Fox, Ciara Martin

NORTHLIGHT EDUCATION
7 Redbourne Ave., London, N3 2BP. TEL: (0208) 343 3161.
FAX: (0208) 343 3161.

ODEON CINEMAS, LTD.
The Broadway, Wimbledon, London, SW19 1QG.

TEL: (0208) 540 9978. FAX: (0208) 543 9125.
www.odeon.co.uk

ONEDOTZERO
Unit 212c, Curtain House, 134-146 Curtain Rd., London, EC2A 3AR. FAX: (207) 729 0057. email: info@onedotzero.com
www.onedotzero.com

OPEN EYE PRODUCTIONS
4th Flr., 47 Dean St., London, W1D 5BE.
TEL: (0207) 287 1998. FAX: (0207) 734 5660.
email: film@openeye.co.uk www.openeye.co.uk

OPEN ROAD FILMS
(Formerly Holmes Associates, Ltd.)
37 Redington Rd., London, NW3 7QY. TEL: (0207) 813 4333.
FAX: (0207) 813 4334, (0207) 916 9172.
email: info@openroadfilms.co.uk www.ashesandsand.com
PRODUCER
Andrew Holmes

OPTIMUM RELEASING
50 Marshall Street., London, W1F 9BQ.
TEL: 020 7534 2700. FAX: 202 7534 2701.
email: info@optimumreleasing.com
www.optimumreleasing.com

ORLANDO TELECISION PRODUCTIONS, LTD. (ORLANDO MEDIA)
Up the Steps Little Tew Chipping Norton Oxfordshire, OX7 4 JB. TEL: (01608) 683 3218. FAX: (01608) 683 364.
www.orlandodigital.co.uk
DIRECTOR
Mike Tomilson

OXFORD SCIENTIFIC FILMS (OSF)
Ground Flr., Network House, Station Yard, Thames, OX9 3UH.
TEL: (01844) 262 370. FAX: (01844) 262 380.
email: uksales@osf.co.uk www.osf.co.uk
SALES DIRECTOR
James Cape
CONTACT
Vicky Turner - vturner@osf.co.uk

DAVID PARADINE PRODUCTIONS, LTD.
First Flr., 5 St. Mary Abbots Place, Kensington, London, W8 6LS. TEL: (0207) 371 3111. FAX: (0207) 602 0411.
email: mail@paradine-productions.com

PARADISE PICTURES, LTD.
44 Westland Row, Dublin, 2. TEL: (353 1) 661 0234.
FAX : (353 1) 661 0108. email: info@paradisepictures.ie
www.paradisepictures.ie
PRODUCER
Colin Cowman - colin@paradisepictures.ie
Liz Kinsella - liz@paradisepictures.ie

PARADOGS, LTD.
206 Panther House, 38 Mount Pleasant, London, WC1X 0AP.
TEL: (0207) 833 1009. FAX: (0207) 486 7397.

PARALLAX INDEPENDENT, LTD.
7 Denmark St., London, WC2H 8L2. TEL: (0207) 836 1478.
FAX: (0207) 497 8062. www.parallaxindependent.co.uk
DIRECTOR
Sally Hibbin

PARAMOUNT PICTURES (UK), LTD.
UIP House, 45 Beadon Rd., Hammersmith, London, W6 0EG.
TEL: (0208) 741 9041. FAX: (0208) 563 4266.
www.paramountpictures.co.uk/

PARK CIRCUS, LTD.
1 Park Terrace., Glasgow, G3 6BY., United Kingdom.
TEL: 44 (0) 141 332 2175. FAX: 44 (0) 141 332 2133.
email: info@parkcircus.com www.parkcircus.com

PARK ENTERTAINMENT, LTD.
4th Flr., 50-51 Conduit St., London, W1S 2YT.
TEL: (0207) 434 4176. FAX: (0207) 434 4179.
email: mail@parkentertainment.com
www.parkentertainment.com
CEO
Jim Howell
HEAD OF FILM ACQUISITION
Simon Barnes

PATHE DISTRIBUTION
Kent House, 14-17 Market Place, Great Titchfield, London, W1N 8AR. TEL: (0207) 323 5151. FAX: (0207) 631 3568.
email: pathe@pathe-uk.com www.pathe.co.uk
DEPUTY MANAGING DIRECTOR
Cameron McCracken

PECCADILLO PICTURES, LTD.
Unit 117, Panther House, 38 Mount Pleasant, London, WC1X 0AN. TEL: (020) 7012 1770. FAX: (020) 7012 1771.
www.parasolpeccadillo.com

PBF MOTION PICTURES
Portsmouth Rd., Ripley, Surrey, GU23 6ER.
TEL: (01483) 225 179. FAX: (0870) 751 5089.
CELL: (0771) 288 1101. email: image@pbf.co.uk
www.pbf.co.uk
DIRECTOR
Peter B. Fairbrass

PEARL & DEAN CINEMAS, LTD.
3 Waterhouse Square, 138-142 Holborn, London, EC1N 2NY.
TEL: (0207) 882 1100. FAX: (0207) 882 1111.
www.pearlanddean.com
CHIEF EXECUTIVE
Kathyrn Jacob - kathryn.jacob@pearlanddean.com
DIRECTOR
Howard Warren - howard.warren@pearlanddean.com

PHANTOM PICTURES
Bagley's Studios, York Way, London, N1 0UZ.
TEL: (0207) 278 7555. FAX: (0207) 278 7567.
email: contact@phantom-pictures.com
www.phantom-pictures.com
PRODUCER
Andreas Bajohra, Bob Portal

PHOENIX FILM AND TELEVISION PRODUCTIONS, LTD.
Three Mile Film Studio, Unit D2, Sugar House Yard, Sugar Hoiuse Lane, London, E15 2QS. TEL: (0208) 536 3690.
FAX: (0208) 536 3699. email: sales@phoenixmedia.co.uk
www.phoenixmedia.co.uk

R J PHILLIPS & CO
12 Newburgh St, London, W1V 1LG. TEL: (0207) 287 3040.
FAX: (0207) 437 2319. email: rjphill@dircon.co.uk

PICTURE PALACE PRODUCTIONS
13 Egbert St., London, NW1 8LJ. TEL: (0207) 586 8763.
FAX: (0207) 586 9048. email: info@picturepalace.com
www.picturepalace.com
PRODUCER & CEO
Malcolm Carddock

PILOT FILM & TELEVISION PRODUCTION, LTD.
The Old Studio, 18 Middle Row, London, W10 5AT.
TEL: (0208) 960 2771. FAX: (0208) 960 2721.
email: info@pilot.co.uk www.pilot.co.uk
EXECUTIVE PRODUCER
Ian Cross

PINEWOOD SHEPPERTON STUDIOS, LTD.
Pinewood Rd., Iver Heath, Buckinghamshire, SL0 0NH.
TEL: (01753) 651 700. FAX: (01753) 656 844.
Shepperton Studios - Studios Rd., Shepperton, Middlesex, TW17 0QD. TEL: (01753) 651 700. FAX: (01753) 656 844.
email: info@pinewoodshepperton.com
www.pinewoodshepperton.com
MANAGING DIRECTOR
Nick Smith - (01753) 656 392
STUDIO MANAGER
Peter Hicks/Pinewood - (01753) 656 457
Kristian Jaggs/Shepperton - (01932) 592 555

THE PINK FILM COMPANY, LTD.
8-18 Smith's Court, London, W1D 7DN. TEL: (0207) 287 5502.
FAX: (0207) 287 5503. www.pinkfilm.com
MANAGING DIRECTOR
Karen Cunningham - karen@pinkfilm.com

PIRATE PRODUCTIONS, LTD.
1 Portobello High St., Edinburgh, EH15 1DW.
TEL: (131) 669 9432. FAX: (560) 116 0471.
email: info@pirateproductions.co.uk
www.pirateproductions.co.uk

POWER HOUSE FILM & TV PRODUCTIONS
No 3 Bedfordbury, Covent Garden, London, WC2N 4BP.
TEL: (0207) 240 2828. FAX: (0207) 240 2282.
email: enquiries@powerhousetv.co.uk
www.powerhouse-tv.co.uk

POZZITIVE TV, LTD.
5th Flr., Paramount House, 162-170 Wardour St., London, W1V 4AB. TEL: (0207) 734 3258. FAX: (0207) 437 3130.
PRODUCER
David Tyler

THE PRODUCERS LIMITED
2 Stonehill Stukeley Meadows Huntington Cambridgeshire, PE29 6ED. TEL: (0845) 234 2444. FAX: (0148) 037 7481.
email: solutions@theproducers.co.uk www.theproducers.co.uk
MANAGING DIRECTOR
Mike Jensen - mick.jensen@theproducers.co.uk
Jenny Edwards
HEAD OF DEVELOPMENT
Tamzin Cary

PROMINENT FEATURES, LTD.
34 Tavistock St., London, WC2E 7PB. TEL: (0207) 497 1100.
FAX: (0207) 497 1133.
DIRECTOR
Steve Abbott, Terry Gilliam, Anne James, Terry Jones, Michael Palin

PTV, LIMITED
The Studios, Hornton Place, Kensington, London, W8 4LZ.
TEL: (0207) 937 9819. FAX: (0207) 937 4326.
email: production@ptvltd.com www.ptvltd.co.uk
MANAGING DIRECTOR
Trevor Rogers, Nigel Schermuly

PYTHON (MONTY) PICTURES, LTD.
Bar Chambers, 40 North Bar Within Beverley, East Yorkshire, HU17 8DL. TEL: (01482) 887 155. FAX: (01482) 869 903.
DIRECTOR
John Cleese, Terry Gilliam, Eric Idle, Terry Jones, Michael Palin
BUSINESS MANAGER
Roger Saunders - rsaund1234@aol.com

QUAD PRODUCTIONS, LTD.
Studio 206, Westbourne Studios, 242 Acklam Rd., London, W10 5JJ. TEL: (0207) 494 9191. FAX: (0207) 494 9192.
www.quadprod.com
EXECUTIVE PRODUCER
Ben Mann - ben@quadprod.com

RANDOM FACTOR PRODUCTIONS, LTD.
Westview, Monk Hills Smarden, Ashford, Kent, TN27 8QH.
TEL: (01233) 770 433. FAX: (01233) 770 433.
email: adam@randomfacto.co.uk

M. RANK BRIMAR, LTD.
(A division of Rank Group)
Greenside Way, Middleton, Manchester, M24 1SN.
TEL: (0161) 681 7072. FAX: (0161) 682 3818.
MANAGING DIRECTOR
Dr. Richard Fenby

RANK FILM SERVICES, LTD.
(A division of Rank Group)
6 Connaught Place, London, W2 2EZ. TEL: (0207) 706 1111.
FAX: (0207) 706 1092. www.rank.com
NON-EXECUTIVE CHAIRMAN
Alun Cathcart
PRESIDENT
Cyril Drabinsky
COMPANY SECRETARY
Charles Cormick

RATPACK FILMS
10 Wiltshire Gardens, Twickenham Middlesex, TW26ND.
TEL: (0208) 296 0555. FAX: (0208) 296 0556.

RDF MEDIA
The Gloucester Bldg., Kensington Village, Avonmore Rd., London, W14 8RF. TEL: (0207) 013 4000. FAX: (0207) 013 4001.
email: contactus@rdfmedia.com www.rdfmedia.com
EXECUTIVE PRODUCER
Jenny Crowther

RECORDED PICTURE COMPANY, LTD.
24 Hanway St., London, W1T 1UH. TEL: (0207) 636 2251.
FAX: (0207) 636 2261. email: rpc@recordedpicture.com
www.recordedpicture.com
CONTACT
Matthew Baker

REDLIGHT PRODUCTION
45 Hydland Rd., Glasgow, Lanarkshire, G12 9UX.
TEL: (0141) 337 3269. FAX: (0141) 357 5486.
CONTACT
Malcolm Wilson - malcolmwilson@hotmail.co.uk

RENAISSANCE FILMS
34-35 Berwick St., London, W1F 8RP. TEL: (0207) 287 5190.
FAX: (0207) 287 5191. email: info@renaissance-films.com
www.renaissance-films.com

RENEGADE FILMS, LTD.
92-93 Great Russell St., London, WC1B 3PS. TEL: (0207) 637 0957.
FAX: (0207) 637 0959. email: renprism@dircon.co.uk
PRODUCER & DIRECTOR
Robert Buckler

REPLAY, LTD.
Museum House, 25 Museum St., London, WC1A 1JT.
TEL: (0207) 637 0473. FAX: (0207) 287 5348.
email: solutions@replayfilms.co.uk www.replayfilms.co.uk
PRODUCER & DIRECTOR
David Young
COMMUNICATIONS DIRECTOR
Howard Brown

REVOLVER ENTERTAINMENT
10 Lambton Place, London, W11 2SH.
TEL: (0207) 243 4300. FAX: (0207) 243 4302.
email: usa@revolvergroup.com www.revolvergroup.com

REUTERS UK VIDEO NEWS/FILM ARCHIVES
85 Fleet St., London, EC4P 4AJ. TEL: (0207) 430 4283.

PETER ROGERS PRODUCTIONS, LTD.
Pinewood Studios, Iver Heath, Bucks, SL0 0NH.
TEL: (01753) 651 700. FAX: (01753) 656 844.
email: carryonoffice@aol.com
DIRECTOR
Peter Rogers, D. E. Malyon

ROMULUS COMPUTER AND VIDEO SYSTEMS
84 Temple Chambers, Temple Ave., London, EC4Y 0HP.
TEL: (0145) 528 5000. FAX: (0207) 352 7457.

ROMULUS FILMS, LTD.
Wessex House, 1 Chesham St., London, SW1X 8ND.
TEL: (0207) 201-3100. FAX: (0207) 201-3131.
email: jcw@romulusfilms@btclick.com

ROUGHNECK MULTIMEDIA
35 The Balcony, Castle Arcade, Cardiff, Borough of Cardiff, CF1 2BW. TEL: (02920) 387 917. FAX: (02920) 667 767.
MANAGING DIRECTOR
Mr. Davies-Llewllyn

RSA FILMS, LTD.
42-44 Beak St., London, W1F 9RH. TEL: (0207) 437 7426.
FAX: (0207) 734 4978. email: twilde@rsafilms.co.uk
www.rsafilms.com
MANAGING DIRECTOR
Kai-Lu Hsiung
DEPUTY MANAGING DIRECTOR
Debbie Garvey

SAFIR FILMS, LTD.
49 Littleton Rd., Harrow, Middlesex, HA1 3SY.
TEL: (0208) 423 0763. FAX: (0208) 423 7963.
CONTACT
Lawrence Safir

SALAMANDER FILM PRODUCTIONS, LTD.
Seven Pines, Lake Rd., Virginia Water, Surrey, GU25 4QP.
TEL: (0134) 484 2349. FAX: (01344) 845 174.
DIRECTOR
Bryan Forbes, Nanette Newman

SANDS FILMS STUDIO
Grices Wharf, 119 Rotherhithe St., London, SE16 4NF.
TEL: (0207) 231 2209. FAX: (0207) 231 2119.
email: info@sandsfilms.co.uk www.sandsfilms.co.uk

SCIMITAR FILMS, LTD.
219 Kensington High St., London, W8 6BD.
TEL: (0207) 734 8385. FAX: (0207) 602 9217.
DIRECTOR
Michael Winner M.A. (Cantab) - winner@ftech.co.uk

SCION FILMS
18 Soho Square, London, W1D 3QL. TEL: (0207) 025 8003.
FAX: (0207) 025 8133. email: info@scionfilms.com
www.scionfilms.com
DIRECTOR
Jeff Abberley, Julia Blackman

SEPTEMBER FILMS, LTD.
Glen House, Glenthorne Rd., London, W6 0NG.
TEL: (0208) 563 9393. FAX: (0208) 741 7214.
email: september@septemberfilms.com
www.septemberfilms.com
CEO
Sammy Nourmand
DIRECTOR, PRODUCTION
Elaine Day

SETON PRODUCTION
Chestnut Coppice Furzefield Chase East Grinsteadx, West Sussex, RH19 2LU. TEL: (01903) 883 720.
email: gawith@compuserve.com

SEVENTH HEAVEN PRODUCTIONS, LTD.
18 Upper Grosvenor St., London, W1X 9PB.
TEL: (0208) 994 4722.

HASAN SHAH FILMS, LTD.
Flat 153, Burnham Towers, Adelaide Rd., London, NW3 3JN.
TEL: (0207) 722 2419. FAX: (0207) 483 0662.
PRODUCER AND DIRECTOR
Hasan Shah

SHART BROS., LTD.
52 Lancaster Rd., London, N4 4PR. TEL: (0207) 263 4435.
FAX: (0207) 436 9233.
PRODUCER
Patrick Shart

SHINE, LIMITED
140 Kensington Church St., Notting Hill, London, W8 4BN.
TEL: (0207) 985 7000. FAX: (0207) 985 7001.
www.shinelimited.com
CHAIRMAN AND CEO
Elisabeth Murdoch

SHORT CIRCUIT FILMS
The Workstation, 15 Paternoster Row, Sheffield, S12 BX.
TEL: (0114) 221 0569. FAX: (0114) 249 2293.

www.shortcircuitfilms.com

SHORTS INTERNATIONAL
25 Beak St., London, W1F 9RT. TEL: (020) 7734 2277.
FAX: (020) 7734 2242. www.britshorts.com

SILVER LIGHT (SCI-FI), LTD.
72 Staunton Rd., Oxford, Oxfordshire, OX3 7TP.
TEL: (01865) 744 451. FAX: (01865) 741 352.
email: mail@silverlightmedia.com www.silverlightonscreen.com

SILVER PRODUCTION (LONDON), LTD.
Bridge Farm, Lower Rd., Britford Salisbury, SP5 4DY.
TEL: (01722) 336 221. FAX: (01722) 336 227.
email: info@silver.co.uk www.silver-productions.co.uk

SKYLINE PRODUCTIONS, LTD.
10 Scotland St., Edinburgh, Midlothian, EH3 6PS.
TEL: (0131) 557 4580. FAX: (0131) 556 4377.
email: admin@skyline.uk.com www.skyline.uk.com
PRODUCER
Trevor Davies
DIRECTOR
Leslie Hills

SILVERFISH PRODUCTIONS LTD.
17-21 Emerald St., London, WC1 3QN.
TEL: (0207) 404 7154. email:Rachelb@silverfish.tv
www.silverfish.tv
DIRECTOR
Mark Lucas

SLATE FILMS
91 Berwick St., London, W1F 0NE. TEL: (0207) 292 7388.
FAX: (0207) 292 6473. email: info@slatefilms.com
www.slatefilms.com
EXECUTIVE PRODUCER
Andrea Calderwood
SCRIPT WRITER
Vicki Patterson

SLEEPING GIANT FILMS
53-58 Clerkenwell Rd., London, EC1M 5PX.
TEL: (0207) 490 5060. FAX: (0207) 490 5060.
DIRECTOR & PRODUCER
Harriet Pacaud

SLICKS INTERNATIONAL
1st Flr., 787 High Rd., London, E11 4QS. TEL: (0208) 539 6529.
FAX: (0208) 558 9891. email: info@slicksinternational.com

SMART EGG PICTURE SERVICES
11-12, Barnard Mews, Barnard Rd., London, SW11 1QU.
TEL: (0207) 350 4550. FAX: (0207) 924 5650.
email: sepsvs@compuserve.com

SODA PICTURES
11-13 Broad Court, London, WC2B 5PY.
TEL: (020) 7240 6060. FAX: (020) 7240 6160.
email: info@sodapictures.com www.sodapictures.com

SOHO COMMUNICATIONS, LTD.
2 Percy St., London, W1P 9FA. TEL: (0207) 637 5825.
FAX: (0207) 436 9740.
MANAGING DIRECTOR
Jon Staton - jstaton@dircon.co.uk

SONY PICTURES EUROPE
(A division of Sony Pictures Entertainment)
Europe House, 25 Golden Square, London, W1F 9LU.
TEL: (0207) 533 1000. FAX: (0207) 533 1015.
www.spe.sony.com
CHAIRMAN AND CEO
Michael Lynton
CO-CHAIRMAN
Amy Pascal

Ireland Office: Seagrave House, 20, Earlsfort Terrace, Dublin 2, Ireland. TEL: (353 1) 616 3200. FAX: (353 1) 616 3210.
MANAGING DIRECTOR
Jerry Flynn
CONTACT
Miriam Andersson - miriam_andersson@spe.sony.com

SPECIFIC FILMS
25 Rathbone St., London, W1T 1NG. TEL: (0207) 580 7476.
FAX: (0207) 434 2676. email: info@specificfilms.com
PRODUCER
Michael Hamlyn, Christian Routh

SPELLCASTER PRODUCTIONS
The Old Mill House, Mendlesham Green, Stowmarket, Suffolk, IP14 5RW. TEL: (01449) 767 315. FAX: (01449) 767 315.
www.spellcaster.freeserve.co.uk
CONTACT
Bob Harvey - bob@spellcaster.freeserve.co.uk

STERLING PICTURES, LTD.
7 Denmark St., London, WC2H 8LZ. TEL: (0207) 240 7241.
FAX: (0207) 240 7088. email: admin@sterlingpictures.com
www.sterlingpictures.com
CONTACT
Michael Riley

SUNSET + VINE PRODUCTION, LTD.
30 Sackville St., London, W1S 3DY. TEL: (0207) 478 7400.
FAX: (0207) 478 7412. email: international@sunsetvine.co.uk
www.sunsetvine.co.uk

SWIPE FILMS
79 Wardour St., London, W1D 6QB. TEL: (020) 7851 8602.
www.swipefilms.com
CONTACT
Frank Mannion - frankswipefilms.com

TALISMAN FILMS, LTD.
5 Addison Place, London, W11 4RJ. TEL: (0207) 603 7474.
FAX: (0207) 602 7422. email: email@talismanfilms.com
PRODUCERS
Richard Jackson, Andrew Lawton

TALKBACK THAMES TELEVISION, LTD.
(A division of Freemantle Media, Ltd.)
20-21 Newman St., London, W1T 1PG.
TEL: (0207) 7861 8000. FAX: (0207) 7861 8001.
www.talkbackthames.tv

1 Stephen St., London, W1T 1AL. TEL: (020) 7691 6000.
CEO
Lorraine Heggessey

TARGET INTERNATIONAL, LTD.
A 29 Barwell Business Pk., Leatherhead Rd., Chessington Castle, Surrey, KT9 2NY. TEL: (0208) 974 1021.
FAX: (0208) 974 2674.
CHAIRMAN
Terry Shand
MANAGING DIRECTOR
Geoffrey Kerpin

TARTAN FILMS DISTRIBUTION, LTD.
Ground Flr., 72 Dean St., London, W1D 3SG.
TEL: (0207) 494 1400. FAX: (0207) 439 1922.
email: info@tartanvideo.com www.tartanvideo.com
MANAGING DIRECTOR
Laura De Casto

TARTAN VIDEO, LTD.
27-28 Poland St., London, W1F 8QW. TEL: (0207) 292 0520.
FAX: (0207) 292 0525. www.tartanvideo.com
MANAGING DIRECTOR
Alan Parkington

DAVID TAYLOR ASSOCIATES
1 Lostock Ave., Poynton Stockport, Cheshire, SK12 1DR.
TEL/FAX: (01625) 850 887. email: dtaylor@clara.net
www.dtaylor.clara.net
MANAGING DIRECTOR
David Taylor

TECHNICOLOR, LTD.
(A division of Thomson Multimedia)
Bath Rd., West Drayton, Middlesex, UB7 0DB.
TEL: (0208) 759 5432. FAX: (0208) 759 6270.
www.technicolor.com
SALES AND CLIENT SERVICES MANAGER
Nigel Dennis - nigel.dennis@thomson.net

TECHNICOLOR, LTD.
(Formerly Metrocolor London, Ltd.)
91 95 Gillespie Rd., Highbury, London, N5 1LS.
TEL: (0207) 326 4422. FAX: (0207)359 2353.

TELESGOP TELEVISION
Unit 6, Technium SA1, King's Rd., The Docks, Swansea, SA1 8PH. TEL: (01792) 485 548. FAX: (01792) 485 550.
email: telesgop@telesgop.co.uk www.telesgoptv.co.uk
MANAGING DIRECTOR
Elin Rhys

TELESCOPE PICTURES
Twichenham Stuios, St. Magaret's, Middlesex, TW1 2AW.
TEL: (0208) 607 8875. FAX: (0208) 607 8879.
PRODUCER
Simon Bosanquet - simonbosanquet@saqnet.co.uk

TELEVIRTUAL
(Formerly Broadsword)
Park House, 31 Cattlemarket St., Norwich, Norfolk, NR1 3DY.
TEL: (01603) 762 211. FAX: (01603) 764 946. www.televirtual.com
FOUNDER & MANAGING DIRECTOR
Tim Child - tim@televirtual.com

THE 39 PRODUCTION COMPANY, LTD.
The Estate Offices, Knebworth House, Knebworth, Hertfordshire SG3 6PY. TEL: (01438) 814 150. FAX: (01438) 816 909.
email: henry.cobbold@btinternet.com www.the39.com

TIGER ASPECT PRODUCTIONS, LTD.
7 Soho St., London W1D 3DQ. TEL: (0207) 4346700.
FAX: (0207) 434 1798. email: general@tigeraspect.co.uk
www.tigeraspect.co.uk
CHAIRMAN
Peter Bennett-Jones
MANAGING DIRECTOR
Andrew Zein

TIGRESS PRODUCTIONS
2 St. Paul's Rd., Clifton, Bristol, Co Bristol BS8 1LT.
TEL: (0117) 933 5600. FAX: (0117) 933 5666.
email: general@tigressbristol.co.uk www.tigressproductions.co.uk
MANAGINFG DIRECTOR
Andrew Jackson

TKO COMMUNICATIONS, LTD.
P.O. Box 130, Hove, East Sussex, BN3 6QU.
TEL: (01273) 550 088. FAX: (01273) 540 969.
email: management@tkogroup.com www.tkogroup.com

TOTEM PRODUCTIONS
Habergham Mill, Coal Clough Ln., Burnley, Lancashire BB11 5BS. TEL: (01282) 457 912. email: info@totem.u-net.com
www.totemproductions.com

TVF PRODUCTIONS
375 City Rd., London EC1V 1NB. TEL: (0207) 837 3000.
FAX: (0207) 833 2185. email: info@tvf.co.uk www.tvf.co.uk

TWENTIETH CENTURY FOX PRODUCTIONS, LTD.
20th Century House, 31-32 Soho Square, London, W1D 3AP.
TEL: (0207) 437 7766. FAX: (0207) 434 2170. www.fox.co.uk

TWICKENHAM FILM STUDIOS, LTD.
The Barons, St. Margaret's, Twickenham, Middlesex, TW1 2AW. TEL: (0208) 607 8888. FAX: (0208) 607 8889.
email: enquiries@twickenhamstudios.com
www.twickenhamstudios.com
CONTACT
G. Humphreys, C. Tipple (Production)

UNITED ARTISTS
(Owned by MGM)
10 Stephen Mews, London W1P 1PP. TEL: (0207) 333 8877.
FAX: (0207) 333 8878. www.mgmuk.com

UNITED CINEMAS INTERNATIONAL (UCI) UK
Lee House, 90 Great Bridgewater St., Manchester M1 5JW.
TEL: (0161) 455 4000. FAX: (0161) 455 4076.
www.uci-cinemas.co.uk
MANAGER
Christopher Hedges
MANAGING DIRECTOR
Roger Harris

UNITED INTERNATIONAL PICTURES (UIP)
UIP House, 45 Beadon Rd., London W6 0EG.
TEL: (0208) 741 9041. FAX: (0208) 748 8990.
email: enquiries@uip.com www.uip.com

Marketing/Promotions: 12 Golden Square, London W1F 9JA
TEL: (0207) 534 5200. FAX: (0207)534 5201.
CHAIRMAN & CEO
Stewart Till
PRESIDENT & COO
Andrew Cripps

UNITED VISUAL ARTIST, LTD.
1 Chapel Ct., London SE1 1HH. TEL: (0207) 378 0303.
FAX: (0207) 378 0304. email: mail@uva.co.uk
www.uva.co.uk

UNITY PICTURES
7A Newburgh St., London W1F 7RH. TEL: (0207) 734 2888.
FAX: (0207) 734 2999. email: admin@unitypictures.co.uk
www.unitypictures.co.uk
DIRECTOR
Hylton Tannenbaum, Alon Ziv, Ravi Swami
PRODUCER
Hilary Davis, David Chiverton

UNIVERSAL PICTURES INTERNATIONAL
76 Oxford St., London, W1D 1BS. TEL: (0207) 307 1300.
FAX: (0207) 307 1301. www.universalpictures.com,
www.universalpictures.co.uk/
PRESIDENT
Pete Smith

UNIVERSAL PICTURES VISUAL PROGRAMMING (UPVP)
(A division of Universal Pictures International)
1 Sussex Place, Hammersmith, London, W6 9EA.
TEL: (0208) 910 5000. FAX: (0208) 742 5579.
www.universalpictures.com
PRESIDENT
Hugh Rees-Parnall

VERA PRODUCTIONS
3rd Flr., 66/68 Margaret St., London W1W 8SR.
TEL: (0207) 436 6116. FAX: (0207) 436 6117.
email: cree@vera.co.uk

VERVE PICTURES
3rd Flr., Kenilworth House, 79-80 Margaret St., London W1W 8TA. TEL: (020) 7436 8001. FAX: (020) 7436 8002.
www.vervepics.com

VIRGIN CINEMAS, LTD.
(Owned by UGC)
Power Road Studios, Power Rd., Chiswick, London W4 5RY.
TEL: (0208) 987 5000. FAX: (0208) 742 2998.

VISIBLE INK TELEVISION, LTD.
Nine Mile Burn, Penicuik, Midlothian EH26 9LX.
TEL: (01968) 661 291. FAX: (01968) 661 291.
email: contact@visibleink.co.uk www.visibleink.co.uk

VIVA FILMS LIMITED
46 Cascade Ave., London N10 3PU. TEL: (0208) 444 5064.
FAX: (0208) 444 1074. www.vivafilms.co.uk
CONTACT
John Goldshmidt - john@vivafilms.co.uk

WALL TO WALL TELEVISION, LTD.
8-9 Spring Place, Kentish Town, London NW5 3ER.
TEL: (0207) 485 7424. FAX: (0207) 267 5292.
email: mail@walltowall.co.uk www.walltowall.co.uk
CEO
Alex Graham

WALPORT INTERNATIONAL, LTD.
15 Park Rd., London NW1 6XN. TEL: (0207) 258 3477.
FAX: (0207) 753 9568.

WARNER BROS. DISTRIBUTORS, LTD.
98 Theobald's Rd., Holborn, London, WC1X 8WB.
TEL: (0207) 984 5000. FAX: (0207) 984 5201.
www.warnerbros.co.uk
DIRECTOR
R. Fox, C. Young, E. Savat

WARNER BROS. OPERATIONAL DIVISION (TELEVISION & VIDEO)
Warner Suite, Leavesden Studios, Watford WD25 7LT.
TEL: (01923) 685 222. FAX: (01923) 685 221.
www.warnerbros.co.uk

WARNER BROS. PRODUCTION, LTD.
Warner Suite, Pinewood Studios, Iver Heath, Bucks SL0 0NH.
TEL: (01753) 654 545. FAX: (01753) 55703.
MANAGING DIRECTOR
R. D. Button
DIRECTOR
E. H. Senat, A. R. Parsons

WARNER SISTERS FILM AND TV, LTD.
The Cottage, Pall Mall Deposit, 124 Barlby Rd., London W10 6BL. TEL: (0208) 876 6911.

WELBECK FILM DISTRIBUTORS, LTD.
52 Queen Anne St., London, W1G 9LA. TEL: (0207) 935 1186.
FAX: (0207) 487 2900.
DIRECTOR
Mrs. J.E. Thomas

THE WORKS UK
4th Fl., Portland House, 4 Great Portland St., London W1W 8QJ. TEL: (020) 7612 0090. FAX: (020) 7612 0091.
MANAGING DIRECTOR
Carl Clifton
CEO
Norman Humphrey
CHAIRMAN
Costa Theo
NON-EXECUTIVE DIRECTOR
James Atherton, Domenico Procacci
HEAD OF BUSINESS AFFAIRS
Andy Ordonez

WORKING TITLE FILMS, LTD.
Oxford House, 76 Oxford St., London, W1B 1DS.
TEL: (0207) 307 3000. FAX: (0207) 307 3001.
www.workingtitlefilms.com
DIRECTOR
Tim Bevan, Eric Fellner

WORLD PRODUCTIONS
16 Dufours Place, London, W1F 7SP. TEL: (0207) 734 3536.
FAX: (0207) 758 7000. email: ellen@world-productions.com
www.world-productions.com
EXECUTIVE PRODUCER
Tony Garnett
DEVELOPMENT PRODUCER
Tim Baker

WORLD WIDE GROUP, LTD.
21-25 St. Anne's Ct., London W1F 0BJ. TEL: (0207) 434 1121.
FAX: (0207) 734 0619. email: pics@worldwidegroup.ltd.uk
CONTACT
R. King, R. Townsend, C. Courtenay Taylor

YASH RAJ FILMS INTERNATIONAL, LTD. (UK)
Wembley Point, 1 Harrow Rd., Wembley, Middlesex HA9 6DE.
TEL: (870) 739 7345. FAX: (870) 739 7346.

email: ukoffice@yashrajfilms.com
CONTACT
Mr. Avtar Panesar

YOUNG FILMS, LTD.
Isle of Skye, Scotland IV44 8RQ. TEL: (01471) 844 444.
FAX: (01471) 844 292. email: info@youngfilms.co.uk
www.youngfilms.co.uk

ZENITH ENTERTAINMENT, LTD.
43-45 Dorset St., London W1U 7NA. TEL: (0207) 224 2440.
FAX: (0207) 224 1027. email: general@zenith-entertainment.co.uk
www.zenith-entertainement.co.uk
CHIEF EXECUTIVE
Steve Matthews

ZEPHYR FILMS LIMITED
33 Percy St., London W1T 2DF. TEL: (0207) 255 3555.
FAX: (0207) 255 3777. email: info@zephyrfilms.co.uk
www.zephyrfilms.co.uk
MANAGING DIRECTOR
Philip Robertson, Chris Curling

ANIMATION

3D IMAGING
The Coach House, Duck Street., Clitheroe, Ribble Valley, BB7 1LP, UK. TEL: 44 844 567 2964, 44 1200 443739. email: contact2@3d-imaging.co.uk www.3d-imaging.co.uk
FOUNDER
Geoff Hodbod

A FOR ANIMATION, LTD.
Unit 3A, The Old Malthouse, Little Ann St., Bristol, BS2 9EB. TEL: (0117) 955 0611. FAX: (0117) 955 0600.
DIRECTOR
Michael Rose

AARDMAN ANIMATIONS
7 Gasferry Rd., Bristol, BS1 6UN. TEL: (0117) 984 8485. FAX: (0117) 984 8486. email: info@aardman.com www.aardman.com
DIRECTOR
Michael Rose
CONTACT
David Sproxton

THE ANIMATION PARTNERSHIP, LTD.
13-14 Golden Square, London, W1F 9JF. TEL: (0207) 636 3300. FAX: (0207) 580 9153. www.animationpartnership.co.uk
CONTACT
Carl Gover - carl@animationpartnership.co.uk

THE ANIMATION PEOPLE, LTD.
22 Great Queen St., Covent Gardens, London, WC2B 5BH. TEL: (0207) 242 7231, 44 202 7836 0411. www.animationpeople.co.uk
CONTACT
Brian Larkin

ANTICS WORKSHOP
42 Champion Hill, Camberwell, London, SE5 8BS. TEL/FAX: (0128) 370 1441. FAX: (870) 052 4258. email: info@antics1.demon.co.uk www.antics1.demon.co.uk
CONTACT
Eva Gloss, Alan Kitching

BARKING MAD PRODUCTIONS
35 Bedforbury, Covent Garden, London, WC2N 4DU. TEL: (44) 020 7836 0411, (44) 01229 823 796. www.animationpeople.co.uk

BERMUDA SHORTS, LTD.
Fifth Fl., Circus Housoe, 21 Titchfield St., London, W1W 8BA. TEL: (0207) 437 7335. FAX: (0207) 437 7334. email: info@bermudashorts.com www.bermudashorts.com
CEO
Trevor Murphy - trevor@bermudashorts.com
PRODUCER
Julie Pye - julie@bermudashorts.com
Lisa Hill - lisa@bermudashorts.com

BLUE-ZOO PRODCUTIONS, LTD.
385 Euston Rd, London, NW1 3AU. TEL: 202 7434 4111. email: info@blue-zoo.co.uk

BOLEXBROTHERS, LTD.
6 Brunel Lock Development, Smeaton Rd., Cumberland Basin, Bristol, BS1 6SE. TEL: (0117) 985 8000. FAX: (0117) 985 8899. email: mail@bolexbrothers.co.uk www.bolexbrothers.co.uk
CONTACT
Andy Leighton

CAMBRIDGE ANIMATION SYSTEMS
Wellington House, East Rd., Cambridge, CB1 1BH. TEL: (01223) 451 048. FAX: (01223) 451 145. email: sales@cambridgeanimation.com www.cambridgeanimation.com

THE CANNING FACTORY
11B Albert Place, London, W8 5PD. TEL: (0207) 937 1136. FAX: (0207) 938 1896. email: all@canningfactory.com www.canningfactory.com
CHAIRMAN
Patrick Moores
MANAGING DIRECTOR
Kate Canning

CAPRICORN DIGITAL
41B Montaug Rd., London, NW4 3ER. TEL: 44 (0) 020 8202 9594. FAX: 44 (0) 870 762 3203. email: info@capricorn-digital.com www.capricorn-digital.com

CARTWN CYMRU
32 Wordsworth Ave., Roath, Cardiff, South Glamorgan, CF24 3FR. TEL: (0129) 2057 5999. FAX: (0129) 2057 5919. email: production@cartwyncymru

CONCEPT MEDIA, LTD.
Orwell Place, 172 Tunbridge Rd., Wateringbury Kent, ME18 5NS. TEL: (0870) 626 1010. FAX: (0870) 165 7428. email: info@concept-media.co.uk www.concept-online.co.uk
MANAGING DIRECTOR
Jeff Weaver

TONY CUTHBERT PRODUCTIONS
7A Langley St., London, WC2H 9JA. TEL: (0207) 437 8884. FAX: (0207) 734 6579. email: info@tonycuthbert.com www.tonycuthbert.com
MANAGING DIRECTOR
Tony Cuthbert

WALT DISNEY PRODUCTIONS, LTD.
3 Queen Caroline St., Hammersmith, London, W6 9PE. TEL: (020) 8222 1000. FAX: (020) 8222 2795. www.disneychannel.co.uk

EALING ANIMATION
90 Brandon St., Southwark, London, SE17 1AL. TEL: (0207) 358 4820. FAX: (0207) 358 4821. email: admin@ealinganimation.co.uk
CONTACT
Richard Randolf

EAST ANGLIAN PRODUCTIONS
Studio House, 21-23 Walton Rd., Frinton-on-Sea, Essex, CO13 0A. TEL: (01255) 676 252. FAX: (01255) 850 528. email: eap@compuserve.com www.eastanglianproductions.co.uk

EDITPOINT VIDEO SERVICES
142 Medway Enterprise Centre Close, Rochester, Kent, ME2 4SV. TEL: (01634) 720 321. email: video@editpoint.co.uk www.editpoint.co.uk

ENTERTAINMENT RIGHTS, PLC.
Colet Court, 100 Hammersmith Rd., London, W6 7JP. TEL: (0208) 762 6200. FAX: (0208) 762 6299. email: info@entertainmentrights.com www.entertainmentrights.com
CEO
Mike Heap

ESPRESSO ANIMATION
100 Oxford St., 5th Flr., London, W1D 1LN. TEL: (0207) 637 9090. FAX: (0207) 637 9339. email: info@espressoanimation.com
DIRECTOR
Philip Vallentin

FAIRWATER FILMS, LTD.
68 Vista Rise, Cardiff, South Glamorgan, CF5 2SD. TEL: (02920) 578 488.

FLICKS FILMS, LTD.
101 Wardour St., London, W1F OUG. TEL: (0207) 734 4892. FAX: (0207) 287 2307. www.flicksfilms.com
CONTACT
Terry Ward

FRAME STORE CFC
9 Noel St., London, W1F 8GH. TEL: (0207) 208 2600. FAX: (0207) 208 2626. email: info@framestore.com www.framestore-cfc.com
MANAGING DIRECTOR
William Sargent

GRIFFILMS, LTD.
Gronant, Penrallt, Isaf Caernarfon, Gwynedd, LL55 1NS. TEL: (01286) 676 678. FAX: (01286) 676 577. email: mail@griffilms.com www.griffilms.com
MANAGING DIRECTOR
Hywel Griffith

HELLZAPOPPIN PICTURES, LTD.
2 Eaton Crescent, Clifton, Bristol, Co Bristol, BS8 2EJ. TEL: (0117) 923 7581. FAX: (0117) 923 7810.

HIBBERT RALPH ANIMATION, LTD.
10 D'Arblay St., London, W1F 8DS. TEL: (0207) 494 3011. FAX: (0207) 494 0383. email: info@hra-online.com www.hra-online.co.uk
CONTACT
Jerry Hibbert

HONEYCOMB ANIMATION STUDIOS
Berkeley House, 27 High St., Cullompton, Devon EX15 1AB. TEL: (01884) 839 202. FAX: (01884) 839 212. email: studio@honeycombanimation.co.uk www.honeycombanimation.co.uk

ICE PICS
111A Wardour St., London, W1V 3DT. TEL: (0207) 437 3505. FAX: (0207) 287 0393. www.icepics.co.uk

CONTACT
Mike Davis - mike@icepics.co.uk

KINGBEE ANIMATION
28 Malden Road., Borehamwood, Herts, WD6 1BW.
TEL: (44) (0) 845 601 6424. email: info@kingbee.co.uk
www.kingbee.co.uk

KING ROLLO FILMS
Dolphin Court, High St., Honiton Devon, EX14 1HT.
TEL: (01404) 45218. FAX: (01404) 45328.
www.kingrollofilms.co.uk
MANAGING DIRECTOR
Leo Nielsen - leo@kingrollofilms.co.uk

KLACTO ANIMATIONS
11 Gordon Rd, London, W5, 2AD. TEL/FAX: (0208) 991 6978.
email: klacto@klacto.com www.klacto.com
CONTACT
Oscar Grillo, Ted Rockley

LEEDS ANIMATION WORKSHOP
45 Bayswater Row, Leeds, LS8 5LF. TEL: (0113) 248 4997.
FAX: (0113) 248 4997. www.leedsanimation.org.uk
CONTACT
Jane Bradshaw

LIQUID TV
1-2 Portland Mews, Soho, London, W1F 8JE.
TEL: (0207) 437 2623. FAX: (0207) 437 2618.
email: info@liquid.co.uk www.liquid.co.uk

MELENDEZ FILMS
Julia House, 44 Newman St., London, W1T 1QD.
TEL: (0207) 323 5273. FAX: (0207) 323 5373.
www.billmelendez.tv
CONTACT
Steven Melendez

THE MILL
(Formerly TJFX Department)
40-41 Great Marlborough St., Soho, London, W1F 7JQ.
TEL: (0207) 287 4041. FAX: (0207) 287 8393.
email: mill.com www.the-mill.com
CEO
Robin Shenfield
MANAGING DIRECTOR
Andy Barmer

RAY MOORE ANIMATION, LTD.
Animation Centre, 113 Humber Rd., London, SE3 7LW.
TEL: (0208) 853 1164. FAX: (0208) 853 3043.
CONTACT
Ray Moore

NISSELL, LTD.
Maxted Close, Hemel Hempstead, Herts, HP2 7BS.
TEL: (01422) 69101.

OSCAR GRILLO & TED ROCKLEY ANIMATIONS
11 Gordon Rd., London, W5, 2AD. TEL/FAX: (0208) 991 6978.
email: klacto@klacto.com www.klacto.com
CONTACT
Oscar Grillo, Ted Rockley

PASSION PICTURES, LTD.
County House, 33-34 Rathbone Place, London, W1T 1JN.
TEL: (0207) 323 9933. FAX: (0207) 323 9030.
email: info@passion-pictures.com www.passion-pictures.com
MANAGING DIRECTOR
Andrew Ruhemann

PICASSO PICTURES, LTD.
9-11 Broadwick St., London, W1F 0DB. TEL: (0207) 437 9888.
FAX: (0207) 437 9040. email: info@picassopictures.com
www.picassopictures.com
CONTACT
Jane Bolton

PUPPET VISUALS
60 Catton Chase, Old Catton, Norwich, Norfolk, NR6 7AS.
TEL: (01603) 482 513.
CONTACT
Jan King

RAGDOLL, LTD.
Timothy's Bridge Rd., Stratford-Upon-Avon, CV37 9NQ.
TEL: (01789) 404 100. FAX: (01789) 404 136.
email: info@ragdoll.co.uk www.ragdoll.co.uk
CONTACT
Suzanne Migliazza
LICENSING
Rosie Neale - rosien@ragdoll.co.uk
PUBLIC RELATIONS
Mary Hagger - maryh@ragdoll.co.uk

HIBBERT RALPH ANIMATION
10 D'Arblay St., London, W1V 3FP. TEL: (0207) 494 3011.
FAX: (0207) 494 0383. email: info@hra-online.com

RED VISION
Cambos House, 3 Canal St., Manchester, M1 3HE.
TEL: (0161) 907 3764. FAX: (0161) 907 3762.
London Office: 32 Fitzroy Square., London, W1T 4QD.
TEL: (0207) 419 2010. FAX: (0207) 419 2011.
email: info@redvision.co.uk www.redvision.co.uk

ROCKY ROAD PRODUCTIONS, LTD.
9 Wellington Rd., Wimbledon Park, London, SW19 8EQ.
TEL: (0208) 947 2404. FAX: (0208) 947 2404.

ROD LORD
(Formerly Pearce Studios, Ltd.)
Old Lodge Farm, Coningsby Lane, Fifield, Maidenhead, Berks,
SL6 2PF. TEL: (01628) 627 032. FAX: (01628) 777 343.
www.rodlord.com
CONTACT
Rod Lord - rod@rodlord.com

SKYLINE IMAGING
The Forum, 277 London Rd., Burgess Hill West Sussex, RH15
9QU. TEL: (0182) 572 1147. email: info@skylineimaging.co.uk
www.skylineimaging.co.uk

SIMONETTI PRODUCTIONS, LTD.
18 Leighton Crescent, Kentish Town London, NW5 2QY.
TEL: (0207) 284 1164. FAX: (0207) 284 1392.
email: ssimonetti@aol.com
MANAGER
Gina Heffler

SIRIOL PRODUCTIONS
3 Mount Stuart Square, Butetown, Cardiff, CF10 5EE.
TEL: (029) 2048 8400. FAX: (029) 2048 5962.
email: enquiries@siriol.co.uk www.siriol-productions.com
MANAGING DIRECTOR
Robin Lyons

SLICED BREAD ANIMATIONS
15 King St., Covent Garden, London, WC2 E 8HN.
TEL: (0207) 379 7873. email: mail@thebestthingsince.com

STARDUST PICTURES, LIMITED
3rd Flr., 25 Newman St., London, W1T 1PN. TEL: (0207) 580 3044.
FAX: (0207) 580 4445. email: mail@stardust-pics.com
www.stardust-pics.com
CHAIRMAN & MANAGING DIRECTOR
Dino Athanassiou

BRIAN STEVENS ANIMATED FILMS, LTD.
11 Charlotte Mews, London, W1P 1LN. TEL: (0207) 637 0535.
FAX: (0207) 323 3892.
CONTACT
Brian Stevens

STIK ANIMATION
22 Kings Acre Downswood Maidstone, Maidstone, ME15 8UP.
TEL: (0162) 286 2634. www.stikanimation.co.uk

STUDIO AKA
30 Berwick St., London, W1F 8RH. TEL: (0207) 434 3581.
FAX: (0207) 437 2309. email: info@studioaka.co.uk
www.studioaka.co.uk
CONTACT
Sue Goffe

RICHARD TAYLOR CARTOON FILMS
Riverview, Waterloo Drive, Clun Shropshire, SY7 8JD.
TEL: (0158) 864 0073. FAX: (0158) 864 0074.
CONTACT
Richard Taylor

TELEVIRTUAL
Thorpe House, 79 Thorpe Rd., Norwich, NR1 1UA.
TEL: (01603) 767 493. FAX: (01603) 764 946.
www.televirtual.com
FOUNDER & MANAGING DIRECTOR
Tim Child - tim@televirtual.com

TRIFFIC FILMS
6 St. Pauls Court St., Stony Stratford, Bucks, MK11 1LJ.
TEL: (01908) 261 234. FAX: (01908) 263 050.
email: info@triffic.co.uk www.triffic.co.uk
DIRECTOR
Tim Searle

TRUNK ANIMATION
3rd Floor, 63 Charterhouse St, London, EC1M 6HJ.
TEL: 44 (0) 207 193 6131. email: info@trunk.me.uk
PRODUCER
Richard Barnett - richard@trunk.me.uk

COSTUME SUPPLIERS

ACADEMY COSTUMES
50 Rushworth St., London, SE1 ORB. TEL: (0207) 620 0771.
FAX: (0207) 928 6287. www.academycostumes.com
email: info@academycostumes.com
DIRECTOR
Adrian Gwillym

ANGELS THE COSTUMIERS
1 Garrick Rd., London, NW9 6AA. TEL: (0208) 202 2244.
FAX: (0208) 202 1820. email: fun@fancydress.com
www.fancydress.com
Head Office: 1 Garrick Rd., London, NW9 6AA.
TEL: (0208) 202 2244. FAX: (0208) 202 1820.
email: info@angels.uk.com www.angels.uk.co
CONTACT
Tim Angel, Jonathan Lipman, Richard Green
MEDIA CONTACT
Benjamin Webb - 44 (0) 7930 408224

THE ANTIQUE CLOTHING SHOP
282 Portobello Rd., London, W10 5TE. TEL: (0208) 964 4830.
FAX: (0208) 992 7996.
CONTACT
Sandy Stagg

ARMS & ARCHERY
The Coach House, London, Rd., Ware, Herts, SG12 9QU.
TEL: (01920) 460 335. FAX: (01920) 461 044.
email: armsandarchery@btconnect.com
www.armsandarchery.co.uk
CONTACT
Terry Goulden - terry@armsandarchery.co.uk

BBC COSTUME + WIGS
172-178 Victoria Rd., London, W3 6UL. TEL: (0208) 576 1761.
FAX: (0208) 993 7040. email: costume@bbc.co.uk
wigs@bbc.co.uk www.bbcresources.com/costumewig
COSTUME CONTACT
Hilary Swift
WIG CONTACT
Philippa Devon

BRYAN PHILIP DAVIES COSTUMES
68 Court Rd., Lewes, East Sussex. BN7 2SA.
TEL/FAX: (01273) 481004.
email: bryan@bpdcostumes.force9.co.uk
www.bpdcostumes.co.uk
OWNER
Byan Philip Davies

CARLO MANZI RENTALS
32 33 Liddell Rd., London, NW6 2EW. TEL: (0207) 625 6391.
FAX: (0207) 625 5386.
CONTACT
Carlo Manzi

COSPROP, LTD.
469-475 Holloway Rd., London, N7 6LE. TEL: (0207) 561 7300.
FAX: (0207) 561 7310. email: enquires@cospop.co.uk
www.cosprop.com
CONTACT
Christine McSweeney

THE COSTUME STUDIO, LTD.
Montgomery House, 159-161 Balls Pond Rd., Islington, N1
4BG. TEL: (0207) 275 9614 / 7388 4481.
FAX: (0207) 837 6576.
email: costume.studio@btconnect.com
www.costumestudio.co.uk
DIRECTOR
RA Griffiths
SECRETARY
P.D. Griffiths
MANAGER
Peter Evans
DIRECTOR
R.A. Griffiths
SECRETARY
P.D. Griffiths

ESCAPADE
150 camden High St., London, NW1 8XD.
TEL: (0207) 485 7384. email:contact@escapade.co.uk
www.escapade.co.uk

FLAME TORBAY COSTUME HIRE
31-35 Market St., Torquay, Devon, TQ1 3AW.
TEL: (01803) 211 930. FAX: (01803) 293 554.
CONTACT
Lionel Digby

M.B.A. COSTUMES
5th Flr., Good Year House, 52-56 Osnaburgh St., London, NW1
3ND. TEL: (0207) 388 4994. FAX: (0207) 383 2038.
www.handembroidery.com
CONTACT
Alistair McCloed, Pearce McCloed

PULLONS PM PRODUCTIONS
St. Georges Studio, Wood End Lane, Coventry West Midlands,
CV7 8DF. TEL/FAX: (01676) 541 390.
www.pm-productions.co.uk
CONTACT
June Pullon

ROBERT ALLSOPP & ASSOCIATES
4 Woodside Ave., Woodside, London, SE25 5DJ.
TEL: (208) 654 4391. FAX: (208) 654 4391.
email: info@raprops.com www.raprops.com

ROYAL NATIONAL THEATRE COSTUME & FURNITURE HIRE
1-3 Brixton Rd., London, SW9 6DE.
TEL: (0207) 735 4774. FAX: (0207) 582 8233.
email: costume_hire@nationaltheatre.org.uk
www.nationaltheatre.org.uk/costumeandfurniturehire

ROYAL NATIONAL THEATRE PROPS HIRE
Salisbury House, Kennington Park Estate, London, SW9 6DE.
TEL: (0207) 820 1358. FAX: (0207) 820 9324.
email: props_hire@nationaltheatre.org.uk
www.nationaltheatre.org.uk/propshire
www.nationaltheatre.org.uk/

ROYAL SHAKESPEARE COMPANY (RSC COSTUME HIRE)
Royal Shakespeare Theatre, Waterside, Sratford Upon Avon
Warwickshire CV37 6BB. TEL: (01789) 403 444.
FAX: (01789) 262 341. email: info@rsc.org.uk
www.rsc.org.uk
HEAD OF COSTUME
Alistair McArthur

EDITING SERVICES

124 FACILITIES
124-126, Horseferry Rd., London, SW1P 2TX.
TEL: (0207) 306 8040. FAX: (0207) 306 8041.
email: 124facilities@channel4.co.uk
CONTACT
Tony Chamberlain - tchamberlain@channel4.co.uk

ASCENT-MEDIA - MEDIA MANAGEMENT SERVICES
Film House, Wardour St., London, W1F 8DD.
TEL: (0207) 878 0000. FAX: (0207) 878 7800.
www.ascentmedia.com
CEO
Jose Royo
EXECUTIVE V.P., CFO
George Platisa
EXECUTIVE V.P., OPERATIONS
Douglas Parrish
CONTACT
Paul Kind - paul.kind@ascentmedia.co.uk

BBC RESOURCES SCOTLAND
Broadcasting House, Glasgow, G12 8DG.
TEL: (08700) 100 222/100 123. www.bbc.co.uk/scotland

BLUE POST PRODUCTION
58 Old Compton St., London, W1D 4UF. TEL: (0207) 437 2626.
FAX: (0207) 439 2477. email: info@bluepp.co.uk
www.bluepp.co.uk
MANAGINFG DIRECTOR
Danny Whybrow
CONTACT
Racheal Dudley - rachael.dudley@bluepp.co.uk

CAPITAL FX, LTD.
2nd Flr., 20 Dering St., London, W1S 1AJ.
TEL: (0207) 493 9998. FAX: (207) 493 9997.
email: info@capital-fx.co.uk www.capital-fx.co.uk
OPERATIONS DIRECTOR
Ian Buckton

CAPITAL STUDIOS
13 Wandsworth Plain, London, SW18 1ET.
TEL: (0208) 874 0131. FAX: (0208) 877 0234.
email: info@capitalstudios.com www.capitalstudios.com
STUDIO MANAGER
Bobbi Johnstone

CLEAR CUT PICTURES
Cranford Studios, 1 Springvale Terrace, Brook Green, London, W14 0AE. TEL: (207) 605 1700. FAX: (207) 603 6883.
email: bookings@clearcutpictures.com
www.clearcutpictures.com
CONTACT
Jo Beighton - jo.beighton@clearcutpictures.com

CLIPPER PICTURES
5 The Island, Wey Meadows, Weybridge, Surrey, KT13 8GJ.
TEL: (0207) 228 2657. email: info@clipperpictures.co.uk
www.clipperpictures.co.uk
CONTACT
Mike Ray

CLOCKHOUSE
34 Hanway St., London, W1T 1UW. TEL: (0207) 436 7702.
FAX: (0207) 436 7679. email: edit@clockhouse.co.uk
www.clockhouse.co.uk
CONTACT
Graham Hobbs, Tony Fox

CUT & RUN, LTD.
Cinema House, 93 Wardour St., London, W1F OUD.
TEL: (0207) 432 9696. FAX: (0207) 432 9697.
email: info@ cutandrun.co.uk www.cutandrun.co.uk
MANAGER/PRODUCER
Angela Hart - angela@cutandrun.tv

EDIT HIRE POST PRODUCTION SERVICES
25 Noel St., Soho,. London, W1F 8GX. TEL: (0207) 434 6606.
FAX: (0207) 434 7157. email: admin@edit-hire.com
www.edit-hire.com

EDV PRODUCTIONS
Canalot Studios, 222 Kensal Rd., London, W10 5BN.
TEL: (0208) 968 7000. FAX: (0208) 968 8696.
email: adam@edv.uk.com www.edv.uk.com

FILM MEDIA SERVICES, LTD.
Unit 2&3, Spacewaye, North Feltham Trading Est., Feltham Middlesex, TW14 0TH. TEL: (0208) 751 7200.
FAX: (0208) 751 7222. email: group@ids-fms.co.uk
www.ids-fms.co.uk
GROUP CHAIRMAN
David De Wilde

FINAL CUT, LTD.
55-57 Great Marlbourough St., London, W1F 7JX.
TEL: (0207) 556 6300. FAX: (0207) 287 2824.
www.finalcut-edit.com
CONTACT
Rick Russell

FLIPSIDE EDITING
15 Southdown Ave., Hanwell London, SW10 9QW.
TEL: (0208) 810 1962. email: james@flipside-editing.com
www.flipside-editing.com
CONTACT
James Dancer
Ian Lancaster - lank@flipside-editing.com
Lee Tyler - lee@flipside-editing.com

FOUNTAIN STUDIOS
128 Wembley Park Dr., Wembley, Middlesex, HA9 8HQ.
TEL: (0208) 900 5800. www.ftv.co.uk

400 COMPANY
Unit B3, Askew Crescent Workshops, 2A Askew Crescent Shepherd's Bush, London, W12 9DP. TEL: (0208) 746 1400.
FAX: (0208) 746 0847. email: leanne@the400.co.uk
www.the400.co.uk

FRONTIER POST
66-67 Wells St., London, W1T 3PY. TEL: (0207) 291 9191.
FAX: (0207) 291 9199. email: info@frontierpost.co.uk
www.frontierpost.co.uk
MANAGING DIRECTOR
Neil Hatton - neilhatton@frontierpost.co.uk

GOLDCREST POST PRODUCTION FACILITIES, LTD.
1 Lexington St., London, W1F 9TB. TEL: (0207) 437 7972.
FAX: (0207) 437 5402. email: mail@goldcrestpost.co.uk
www.goldcrestfilms.com
BOOKINGS MANAGER
Carolyn Wright

HOLLOWAY FILM & TELEVISION, LTD.
21-25 St. Annes Ct., London, W1F 0BJ. TEL: (0207) 494 0777.
FAX: (0207) 494 0309. www.hollowayfilm.co.uk
CEO
David Holloway - david@hollowayfilm.co.uk
BUSINESS MANAGER
Matt Stoddart - matt@hollowayfilm.co.uk

LONDON POST (CONCRETE DESIGN)
34-35 Dean St., London, W1D 4PR. TEL: (0207) 439 9080.
FAX: (0207) 434 0714. email: verity@londonpost.co.uk
info@concretedesign.co.uk www.lconcretedesign.co.uk
CONTACT
Andy Wright

THE LONDON STUDIOS
The London Television Centre, Upper Ground, London, SE1 9LT. TEL: (0207) 261 3473. FAX: (0207) 261 3815.
CONTACT
Debbie Hills

THE MILL
40-41 Great Marlborough St., Soho, London, W1F 7JQ.
TEL: (0207) 287 4041. FAX: (0207) 287 8393.
email: info@the-mill.com www.the-mill.com
MANAGING DIRECTOR
Andy Barmer
PRODUCER
Yvonne Chalkley

MOLINARE
34 Fouberts Place, London, W1F 7PX. TEL: (0207) 478 7000.
FAX: (0207) 478 7299. email: bookings@molinare.co.uk
www.molinare.co.uk
SALES AND MARKETING DIRECTOR
Mark Foligno - (0207) 478 7205 markf@molinare.co.uk

NATS POST PRODUCTION
10 Soho Square, London, W1D 3NT. TEL: (0207) 287 9900.
FAX: (0207) 287 8636. email: bookings@nasts.tv
CONTACT
Louise Thomas

PARALLAX INDEPENDENT, LTD.
7 Denmark St., London, WC2H 8LS. TEL: (0207) 836 1478.
FAX: (0207) 497 8062. www.parallaxindependent.co.uk

PINEWOOD SHEPPERTON STUDIOS, LTD.
Pinewood Rd., Iver Heath, Buckinghamshire, SL0 0NH.
TEL: (01753) 651 700. FAX: (01753) 656 844.

Shepperton Studios: Studios Rd., Shepperton, Middlesex, TW17 0QD. TEL: (01753) 651 700. FAX: (01753) 656 844.
email: info@pinewoodshepperton.com
www.pinewoodshepperton.com

MANAGING DIRECTOR
Steve Jaggs - (01753) 656 732
CONTACT
Matt Richardson - matt.richardson@pinewoodgroup.com

QUANTEL, LTD.
31 Turnpike Rd., Newbury, Berks, RG14 2NX.
TEL: (01635) 482 22. FAX: (01635) 815 815. www.quantel.com
CONTACT
Roger Thornton

THE QUARRY
26-28 Brewer St., London, W1F OSP. TEL: (0207) 437 4961.
FAX: (0207) 437 1491. email: info@the-quarry.co.uk
www.the-quarry.co.uk
EXECUTIVE PRODUCER
Tor Adams - tor@thequarry.co.uk

SATELLITE BROADCAST FACILITIES, LTD.
Unit 20 Commercial Way, Park Royal, London, NW10 7XF.
TEL: (8707) 777 888. FAX: (8707) 777 800.
email: sales@sat-facilities.com www.sbfpost.com

SHEARS POST PRODUCTION SERVICES
Warwick House, Chapone Pl., Dean St., London, W1D 3VS.
TEL: (0207) 437 8182. FAX: (027) 437 8183. www.xpression.tv
CONTACTS
Richard Meadowcroft, Simon Adams

SNG BROADCAST SERVICES
Unit 6, Union Court, 20-22 Union Rd., London, SW4 6JP.
TEL: (0207) 819 2800. FAX: (0207) 819 2801.
email: info@sng.co.uk www.sng.co.uk

TANGRAM POST PRODUCTION
1 Charlotte St., London, W1T 1RB. TEL: (020) 7637 2727.
email: tangrampp@onetel.com
www.tangrampostproduction.co.uk
EDITOR
Simon Rose, Laurence Williamson

THE WHITEHOUSE POST PRODUCTION
21 - 23 Meard Street, London, W1F 0EY.
TEL: (0207) 432 4300. FAX: (0207) 432 4301.
www.whitehousepost.com

UK POST
47 Beak St., London, W1F 9SE. TEL: (207) 734 6060.
FAX: (207) 287 2727.
CONTACT
Kerry Kirkpatrick - kerry.kirkpatrick@ukpost.org.uk

FILM & VIDEO LABORATORIES

BUCKS LABORATORIES, LTD.
714 Banbury Ave., Slough, Berks., SL1 4LR. TEL: (01753) 501 500.
FAX: (01753) 691 762. www.bucks.co.uk
MANAGING DIRECTOR
David Buck
SALES DIRECTOR
Dave Pitwell
PRODUCTION MANAGER
Mick Barham

COLOUR FILM SERVICES, LTD.
26 Berwick St., London, W1F 8RG. TEL: (0207) 734 4543.
10 Wadsworth Rd., Perivale, Greenford, Middlesex, UB6 7JX.
TEL: (0208) 998 2731. FAX: (0208) 997 8738.
email: info@colourfilmservices.co.uk www.colourservices.co.uk
CONTACT
John Ward

COLOUR VIDEO SERVICES, LTD.
10 Wadsworth Rd., Perivale, Greenford, Middlesex, UB6 7JX.
TEL: (0208) 998 2731. FAX: (0208) 997 8738.
www.colourfilmservices.co.uk/
CONTACT
Jess Morgan

DELUXE LABORATORIES LIMITED
North Orbital Rd., Denham, Uxbridge, Middlesex, UB9 5HQ.
TEL: (01895) 832 323. FAX: (01895) 832 446.
www.bydeluxe.com
MANAGING DIRECTOR
Ken Biggins
DIRECTOR OF SALES
Terry Lansbury

FILM & PHOTO, LTD.
13 Colville Rd, London, W3 8BL. TEL: (0208) 992 0037.
FAX: (0208) 993 2409. email: info@film-photo.co.uk
www.film-photo.co.uk

HALLIFORD STUDIOS
Manygate Lane, Shepperton, Middlesex, TW17 9EG.
TEL: (01932) 226 341. FAX: (01932) 246 336.
email: sales@hallifordstudios.com
www.hallifordfilmstudios.co.uk
CONTACT
Charlotte Goddard

METROCOLOR LONDON, LTD.
(Pending Merger with Technicolor)
91/95 Gillespie Rd., Highbury, London, N5 1LS.
TEL: (0207) 226 4422. FAX: (0207) 359 2353.

RANK FILM SERVICES, LTD.
(A division of Rank Group)
6 Connaught Place, London, W2 2EZ. TEL: (0207) 706 1111.
FAX: (0207) 706 1092. www.rank.com
CHAIRMAN
Peter Johnson
CEO
Ian Burke
FINANCE DIRECTOR
Paddy Gallagher

SOHO IMAGING
8-1 Meard St., London, W1V 3HR. TEL: (0207) 437 0831.
FAX: (0207) 734 9471. email: len.thornton@sohoimages.com
www.sohoimages.com

THE STUDIO
21 Cabul Rd., London, SW11 2PR. TEL: (207) 228 522.
FAX: (207) 228 9975. email: thestudio@filmed.com
www.thestudio.co.uk

TECHNICOLOR, LTD.
(Pending merger with metrocolor)
Bath Rd., West Drayton, Middlesex, UB7 0DB.
TEL: (0208) 759 5432. FAX: (0208) 759 6270.
www.technicolor.com
CONTACT
Nigel Dennis (Film)
Simon Wilkinson (Creative Services)

TWICKENHAM FILM STUDIOS, LTD.
The Barons, St. Margaret's, Twickenham, Middlesex, TW1 2AW.
TEL: (0208) 607 8888. FAX: (0208) 607 8889.
email: enquiries@twickenhamstudios.com
www.twickenhamstudios.com
CONTACT
G. Humphreys, C. Tipple (Production)

WORLD WIDE GROUP
21-25 St. Anne's Ct., London, W1F 0BJ. TEL: (0207) 434 1121.
FAX: (0207) 734 0619. email: info@worldwidepictures.tv.
www.worldwidegroup.ltd.uk
CONTACT
Hannah Cookson - hannahc@worldwidegroup.ltd.uk
MANAGING DIRECTOR
Chris Courtney Taylor

FINANCIAL SERVICES

AON/ALBERT G RUBEN
Pinewood Studios, Pinewood Rd., Iver Buckinghamshire, SLO ONH. TEL: (0175) 365 1700. FAX: (0175) 365 3152.
www.aon.co.uk
CONTACT
Liz Yuille

AUDIO VISUAL ASSET MANAGEMENT
Little Orchard House, Bears Den, Kingswood, Surrey, KT20 6PL. TEL: (01737) 830 084. FAX: (01737) 830 063.
www.atst.co.uk
CONTACT
Andy Finny

BAIN HOGG GROUP, LTD.
(See AON)

BRITISH SCREEN FINANCE, LTD.
14-17 Wells Mews, London, W1P 3FL. TEL: (0207) 323 9080.
FAX: (0208) 323 0092. email: info@britishscreen.co.uk
www.filmcouncil.co.uk
CEO
Simon Perry

ENTERTAINMENT INSURANCE BROKERS
Thomson House, 20 Curtain Rd., London, EC2A 3NF.
TEL: (0207) 247 7457. FAX: (0207) 247 5870.

FILM FINANCES, LTD.
14-15 Conduit St., London, W1R 9TG. TEL: (0207) 629 6557.
FAX: (0207) 491 7530. www.ffi.com
CONTACT
Graham Easton - geaston@filmfinances.co.uk
MANAGING DIRECTOR
Phillip Davies

FINELINE MEDIA FINANCE
Heron House, 5 Heron Square, Richmond Upon Thames Surrey, TW9 1EL. TEL: (0208) 334 2100. FAX: (0208) 334 2101.
email: info@fineline.co.uk www.finelinemediafinance.com
CONTACT
Gareth Wilding - garethwilding@fineline.co.uk

GENERAL ENTERTAINMENT INVESTMENTS
Market House, Church St., Harleston, Norfolk, IP20 9BB.
TEL: (01603) 723 711. FAX: (0207) 792 9005.
FOUNDER
John F. Oakley

GUINNESS MAHON & CO., LTD.
2 Gresham St., London, EC2V 7QP. TEL: (0207) 597 4000.
FAX: (0207) 528 0985. email: info@investec.com
www.investec.com
CONTACT
Malcolm Clements

HSBC HOLDINGS, PLC.
8 Canada Square, London, E14 5HQ. TEL: (0207) 991 8888.
FAX: (0207) 992 4880. www.hsbc.com

INTERNATIONAL FILM GUARANTORS INC., LP
19 Margaret St., London, W1W 8RR. TEL: (0207) 636 8855.
FAX: (0207) 323 9356. email: ukinfo@ifgbonds.com
www.ifgbonds.com
CEO
Steven Mangel - smangel@ifgbonds.com

KPMG
8, Salisbury Square, London, EC4Y 8BB. TEL: (020) 7311 1000.
FAX: (0207)311 3311. www.kpmg.co.uk
CHAIRMAN
John Griffith Jones

MEDIA ADVISORY GROUP
5 Elstree Gate, Elstree Way, Borehamwood, Hertfordshire WD6 1JD. TEL: (0208) 207 0602. FAX: (0208) 207 6758.

MOVING IMAGE DEVELOPMENT AGENCY (MIDA)
109 Mount Pleasant, Liverpool, Merseyside L3 5TF.
TEL: (0151) 708 9858. FAX: (0151) 708 9859.
email: enquire@mida.demon.co.uk

OPTIMUM RELEASING
22 Newman St., London, W1T 1PH. TEL: (207) 637 5403.
FAX: (207) 637 5408. email: info@optimumreleasing.com
www.optimumreleasing.com

THE PROJECTOR HIRE COMPANY
Delegate House, 95 Queen St., Maidenhead, Berkshire SL6 1LR. TEL: (8700) 635 939. FAX: (1753) 855 599.
email: sales@video-projector-hire.co.uk
www.video-projector-hire.co.uk

ROLLINS BURDICK HUNTER (INTERNATIONAL), LTD.
(Acquired by AON)
Braintree House, Braintree Rd., Ruislip, Middx., HA4 0YA.
TEL: (0208) 841 4461. FAX: (0208) 842 2124. www.aon.com

RUBEN SEDGWICK INSURANCE SERVICES
(Now AON)

SARGENT-DISC, LTD.
Pinewood Studios, Pinewood Rd., Iver, Bucks. SLO ONH.
TEL: (01753) 630 300. FAX: (01753) 655 881.
email: marketing@sargent-disc.com www.sargent-disc.com

SCOTTISH SCREEN
2nd Flr., 249 West George St., Glasgow, Lanarkshire G2 4QE.
TEL: (0141) 302 1700. FAX: (0141) 302 1714.
email: info@ scottishscreen.com www.scottishscreen.com

SKYLINE FILMS
P.O. Box 8210, London W4 1WH. TEL: (0836) 275 584.
FAX: (0208) 995 2117.

UK FILM COUNCIL, FUNDING
10 Little Portland St., London W1W 7JG. TEL: (0207) 861 7861.
FAX: (0207) 861 7862. email: info@ukfilmcouncil.org.uk
www.ukfilmcouncil.org.uk/funding

UNITED MEDIA ENTERTAINMENT PARTNERS, LTD.
67-69 Whitfield St., London. TEL: (0207) 462 7720.
FAX: (0207) 462 7663. email: info@umepartners.net
www.umegroup.net

WILLIS GROUP LIMITED
10, Trinity Square, London, EC3P 3AX. TEL: (0207)488 8111.
FAX: (0207) 488 8223. www.willis.com
CHAIRMAN AND CEO
Joseph J. Plumeri
PRESIDENT
Grahame J. Millwater

PRODUCTION EQUIPMENT & SUPPLIES

ADVENT COMMUNICATIONS
Nashleigh Hill, Chesham, Buckinghamshire, HP5 3HE.
TEL: (01494) 774 400. FAX: (01494) 791 127.
email: sales@adventcomms.com
www.adventcomms.com
CHIEF EXECUTIVE
Duncan Lewis
MARKETING MANAGER
Gina Melville

AGFA-GEVAERT
(Motion Picture Division)
27 Great West Rd., Brentford, Middlesex, TW8 9AX.
TEL: (0208) 231 4985. FAX: (0208) 231 4915.
www.agfa.co.uk

ALTERED IMAGES
Unit 4 Shepperton Business Park, Govett Avenue, London
Shepperton, TW17 8BA. TEL: 01932 255666.
FAX: 01932 260646. email: sales@alteredimagesltd.com
www.alteredimagesltd.com

AMPEX GREAT BRITAIN
Ampex House, Beechwood, Chineham Business Park
Basingstoke, Hampshire, RG24 8WA. TEL: (01256) 814 410.
FAX: (01256) 814 474. email: sales@ampexgb.co.uk
www.ampexdata.com
CONTACT
Keith Russ - 44 (0) 1256 707 517

AMSTRAD PLC.
Brentwood House, 169 Kings Rd., Brentwood, Essex, CM14
4EF. TEL: (01277) 228 888. FAX: (01277) 211 350.
email: info@amstrad.com www.amstrad.co.uk
CHAIRMAN AND CEO
Sir Alan Sugar

ASTRIS, LTD.
The Cottage, The Strait Mile, Shurlock Row, Reading,
Berkshire, RG10 0QN. TEL: 0118 932 0551.
FAX: 0118 932 0553. email: tony_nowak@compuserve.com
www.astris.tv
MANAGING DIRECTOR
Tony Nowak

AUTOCUE, LTD.
Autocue House, 265 Merton Rd., London, SW18 5JS.
TEL: (0208) 870 0104. FAX: (0208) 874 3726.
email: info@autocue.co.uk www.autocue.co.uk
CONTACT
Lee Spurway - lee.spurway@autocue.co.uk

AWFULLY NICE VIDEO COMPANY, LIMITED
30 Long Lane, Ickenham London, UB10 8TA.
TEL: (1895) 678 477. FAX: (1895) 621 162.
email: nicevideo@aol.com www.awfullynicevideo.com
CONTACT
Graham Maunder, Keith Darbyshire, Debbie Crook

BETTER SOUND, LTD.
31 Cathcart St., London, NW5 3BJ. TEL: (0207) 482 0177.
FAX: (0207) 482 2677. email: admin@bettersound.co.uk
www.bettersound.co.uk

CAMERON VIDEO SYSTEMS, LTD.
Burnfield Rd., Glasgow G46 7TH, Scotland.
TEL: (0141) 637 0368. FAX: (0141) 637 3559.
email: dup@cameronpres.co.uk www.cameronpres.co.uk

CAMERON COMMUNICATIONS, LTD.
Caledonia House, Thornliebank Industrial Estate, Glasgow,
G46 8JT. TEL: (141) 270 8000. FAX: (141) 270 8001.
email: sales@camcomms.com www.camcomms.com

CANON (UK), LTD.
Woodhatch, Reigate, Surrey, RH2 8BF. TEL: (01737) 220 000.
FAX: (01737) 220 022. www.canon.co.uk

CHARTER BROADCAST (UK-LONDON), LTD.
Unit 4, Elstree Distribution Park, Elstree Way, Borehamwood
Herts, WD6 1RU. TEL: (0208) 905 1213. FAX: (0208) 905 1424.
email: enquiries@charter.co.uk www.charter.co.uk
CEO
Michael Breen

CINTEL INTERNATIONAL, LTD.
Watton Rd., Ware, Hertfordshire, SG12 OAE.
TEL: (01920) 463 939. FAX: (01920) 460 803.
email: sales@cintel.co.uk www.cintel.co.uk
MANAGING DIRECTOR
Adam Welsh - awelsh@cintel.co.uk
CONTACT
Simon Clark

COOKE OPTICS, LTD.
(Formerly Taylor Hobson, Ltd.)
Cooke Close, Thurmaston, Leicester, LE4 8PT.
TEL: (0116) 264 0700. FAX: (0116) 264 0707.
email: lenses@cookeoptics.com www.cookeoptics.com

DESISTI LIGHTING (UK), LTD.
15 Old Market St., Thetford, Norfolk, IP24 2EQ.
TEL: (01842) 752 909. FAX: (01842) 753 247.
email: info@desisti.co.uk www.desisti.co.uk

DIGI BROADCAST, LTD.
Link House 140 Tolworth Broadway, Surbiton, London,
KT6 7HT. TEL:+44 (0) 208 339 6047. FAX: +44 (0) 208 339 6072.
email: info@digibroadcast.com www.digibroadcast.com

DOLBY LABORATORIES, INC.
Interface Park, Wootton Bassett, Wiltshire, SN4 8QJ.
TEL: (01793) 842 100. FAX: (01793) 842 101.
London: Hammersmith House, 4th Flr., 5-8 Warwick St.,
London, W1B 5LX. email: info@dolby.com www.dolby.com
SENIOR V.P., MANAGING DIRECTOR (UK)
David Watts

JOE DUNTON CAMERAS, LTD.
Elstree Film Studios, Shenley Rd., Borehamwood, Hertfordshire,
WD6 1JG. TEL: (0208) 324 2311. FAX: (0208) 324 2336.
email: info@joedunton.com www.joedunton.com
CONTACT
Joe Dunton

EDRIC AUDIO VISUAL, LTD.
34-36 Oak End Way, Gerrards Cross, Buckinghamshire, SL9
8BR. TEL: (01753) 481 400. FAX: (01753) 887 163.
email: robin@edric-av.co.uk www.edric-av.co.uk

ELECTRA FILM & TV, LTD.
Wharf House, Brentwaters Business Park, The Ham, Brentford
Middlesex, TW8 8HQ. TEL: (0208) 232 8899.
FAX: (0208) 232 8877. email: mail@electra-tv.com
www.electra-tv.com
CONTACT
Steve Albins

E2V TECHNOLOGIES
106 Waterhouse Ln., Chelmsford, Essex, CM1 2QU.
TEL: (01245) 493 493. FAX: (01245) 492 492.
email: enquiries@e2vtechnologies.com
www.e2vtechnologies.com
PRESIDENT
Mark Hobbs

EXTREME FACILITIES
15-17 Este Rd., London, SW11 2TL. TEL: (0207) 801 9111.
FAX: (0207) 801 9222. email: extreme@global.net.co.uk
www.extremefacilities.com

FUJI PHOTO FILM (UK), LTD.
Unit 10A, St. Martins Business Centre, St Martins Way
Bedfordshire, MK42 0LF. TEL: (1234) 217 724.
FAX: (1234) 572 652. www.fujifilm.co.uk

GE LIGHTING, LTD.
153 Lincoln Rd., Enfield, Middlesex, EN1 1SB.
TEL: (0800) 169 8290. FAX: (0800) 169 8284.
www.gelighting.com

HARKNESS HALL, LTD.
Unit A, Norton Rd., Stevenage, Herts, SG1 2BB.
TEL: (01438) 725 200. FAX: (01438) 344 400.
email: info@harknesshall.com www.harknesshall.com
MANAGING DIRECTOR
Andrew Robinson
PERSONAL ASSISTANT TO MANAGING DIRECTOR
June Knepper

HAYDEN LABORATORIES, LTD.
Hayden House, Chiltem Hill, Chalfont St. Peter, Gerrards
Cross, Bucks, SL9 9UG. TEL: (01753) 888 447.
FAX: (01753) 880 109.

HITACHI DENSHI (UK), LTD.
Hitachi Kokusai Electric UK, Ltd., Windsorhouse, Queensgate, Britannia Rd., Waltham Cross, Hertfordshire, EN8 7NX.
TEL: (845) 121 2177. FAX: (845) 121 2180.
CONTACT
Carol Jackson - carol@hitachi-ke-eu.com

I.C.E. FILM EQUIPMENT, LTD.
Unit 1 Bridge Wharf, 156 Caledonian Rd., London, N1 9UU.
TEL: (0207) 278 0908. FAX: (0207) 278 4552.
email: sales@icefilm.com www.icefilm.com
CONTACT
Peter Bryant, Steve Saltwell

ITN ARCHIVE, LTD./REUTERS TV
Beatrice Okoro, Solomon Wood, 200 Gray's Inn Rd., London, WC1X 8XZ. TEL: (0207) 430 4480. FAX: (0207) 430 4453.
email: sales@itnarchive.com www.itnarchive.com
CONTACT
Michale Keene

JVC PROFESSIONAL EUROPE, LTD.
1st Fl., JVC House 2, Priestley Way, London, NW2 7BA.
TEL: (0208) 208 6200. FAX: (0208) 208 6260.
email: marketing@jvcpro.co.uk www.jvcproeurope.com
ASSISTANT TO MANAGEMENT TEAM
Margaret Scott

KODAK ENTERTAINMENT IMAGING UK
P.O. Box 66, Kodak House, Station Rd., Hemel Hempstead Herts, HP1 1JU. TEL: (01442) 845 945. FAX: (01442) 844 458.
www.kodak.com/UK/en/motion/
DIRECTOR AND GENERAL MANAGER
Brian Kercher

LEE FILTERS, LTD.
Central Way, Walworth Industrial Estate, Andover, Hampshire, SP10 5AN. TEL: (01264) 366 245. FAX: (01264) 355 058.
email: sales@leefilters.com www.leefilters.com

LEE LIGHTING
Wycombe Rd., Wembley, Middlesex, HA0 1QD. TEL: (0208) 900 2900.
FAX: (0208) 902 5500. email: info@lee.co.uk www.lee.co.uk
CONTACT
Patrick McEnallay, Jackie Rowden

LEITCH EUROPE, LTD. CORPORATION
Leitch Europe, Eskdale Rd., Winnersh, Wokingham, Berkshire, RG41 5TS. TEL: (0118) 964 8000. FAX: (0118) 964 8054.
CONTACT
Angela Happle

MGB FACILITIES
Capital House, Sheepscar Court, Meanwood Rd., Leeds, West Yorkshire, LS7 2BB. TEL: (0113) 243 6868. FAX: (0113) 243 8886.
email: contact@mgbtv.co.uk www.mgbtv.co.uk

THE MINIATURE CAMERA COMPANY
7 Portland Mews, London, W1V 3FL. TEL: (0207) 734 7776.
FAX: (0207) 734 1360. email: martin@skarda.net www.skarda.net
CONTACT
Martin Davidson

MOVING PICTURE FILM
56 Poland St., Soho, London, W1F 7NN.
TEL: (203) 040 0400. FAX: (207) 483 1419.

OSRAM, LTD.
Bold Industrial Park, Niells Rd., St. Helens, Merseyside, WA9 4XG. TEL: (01744) 812 221. FAX: (01744) 831 900.
email: csc@osram.co.uk www.osram.co.uk

PANASONIC BROADCAST EUROPE
Willoughby Rd., Brachnell, Berkshire, SL4 5RJ.
TEL: (0118) 902 9200. FAX: (0118) 902 9348.
email: john.joicey@panasonic.pbe.co.uk
www.panasonic-broadcast.com

PANAVISION (UK)
The Metropolitan Centre, Bristol Rd., Greenford, Middex, UB6 8GD. TEL: (0208) 839 7333. FAX: (0208) 578 1536.
www.panavision.co.uk

PHILIPS LIGHTING, LTD.
The Philips Centre, Guildford Business Park, Guilford Surrey, GU2 8XH. TEL: (129) 377 6774. FAX: (148) 357 5534.
email: support@lighting.philips.com www.lighting.philips.com

PHOENIX VIDEO, LTD.
Global House, Denham Media Park, North Orbital Rd. Uxbridge, Middlesex UB9 5HL. TEL: (01895) 837 000.
FAX: (01895) 833 085. email: sales@phoenix-video.co.uk
www.phoenix-video.co.uk

PHOTOMEC (LONDON), LTD.
Valley Rd. Industrial Estate 16, Porters Wood, St. Albans Herts, AL3 6NU. TEL: (01727) 850 0711. FAX: (01727) 843 991.
email: photomec@photomec.co.uk www.photomec.co.uk

CHAIRMAN
David Wright

PHILIP RIGBY & SONS, LTD.
32 Whyteleafe Road Caterham, Surrey, CR3 5EF. TEL: (01883) 332 513.
FAX: (01883) 332 514. www.philiprigby.co.uk
MANAGING DIRECTOR
Phillip Rigby

RONFORD-BAKER
Oxhey Lane, Oxhey, Watford, Herts., WD19 5RJ.
TEL: (0208) 428 5941. FAX: (0208) 428 4743.
email: ronfordbaker@btconnect.com www.ronfordbaker.co.uk

MICHAEL SAMUELSON LIGHTING, LTD.
Pinewood Studios, Iver Heath, Bucks., SL0 0NH.
TEL: (01753) 631 133. FAX: (01753) 630 485.

SHURE ELECTRONICS, LTD.
167-171 Willoughby Ln., London, N17 OSB.
TEL: (0208) 808 2222. FAX: (0208) 808 5599.
email: info@shuredistribution.co.uk www.shure.com

S & H TECHNICAL SUPPORT, LTD.
Unit A, The Old Laundry, Chambercombe Rd., Ilfracombe Devon, EX34 9PH. TEL: (01271) 866 832. FAX: (01271) 865 423.
email: enquiries@starcloth.co.uk www.starcloth.com
CONTACT
Terry Murtha

SHURE DISTRIBUTION UK
167-171 Willoughby Lane, London, N17 0SB.
TEL: (0208) 808 2222. FAX: (0208) 808 5599.
email: info@shuredistribution.co.uk
Marketing email: paulc@shuredistribution.co.uk
www.shuresitribution.co.uk

SIGMA FILMS
Film City Glasgow, Summertown Rd., Glasgow, G51 2LY.
TEL: (01141) 445 0400. FAX: (01141) 445 6900.
www.sigmafilms.com
CONTACT
David Mackenzie, Alastair Mackenzie

SOHO IMAGES GROUP, LTD.
8-14 Meard St., London, W1f 0EQ. TEL: (0207) 437 0831.
FAX: (0207) 734 9471. www.sohoimages.com

SONY BROADCAST & COMMUNICATIONS, LTD.
Jay Close, Viables, Basingstoke, Hants, RG22 4SB.
TEL: (01256) 828 828. FAX: (07092) 380 584.
email: tsg.helpdesk@eu.sony.com

STRAND LIGHTING LIMITED
Unit 3, Hammersmith Studios, Yeldham Rd., Hammersmith London, W6 8JF. TEL: (0208) 735 9790. FAX: (0208) 735 9799.
email: sales@stranduk.com www.strandlight.com

SVT VIDEO SYSTEMS
SVT Building, Holloway Road, Maldon, Essex, CM9 4LR
TEL: 01621 850656. FAX: 01621 859994.
gsteele@svtvideo.com www.svtvideo.com
DIRECTOR
Geoff Steele

TECHNOVISION UK, LTD.
Metropolitan Centre, Bristol Rd., Greenford, Middlesex, UB6 8GD. TEL: (0208) 839 7314. FAX: (0208) 813 2113.
email: info@technovision-london.com
www.technovision-london.com
CONATACT
Paul Jackson

TELENT, PLC.
(Formerly Siemens GEC)
New Century Park, P.O. Box 53, Coventry, CV3 1HJ.
TEL: (0247) 656 2000. www.telent.co.uk

TVE HIRE
TVE House, Milton House, Milton Business Center, Wick Drive, New Milton Hampshire, BH2 5RH. TEL: (0142) 562 5020.
FAX: (0142) 562 5021. email: equiries@tvehire.com
www.tvehire.com

VINTEN RADAMEC
William Vinten Building, Western Way, Bury St. Edmunds Suffolk IP33 3TB. TEL: (0128) 4 752 121. FAX: (0128) 4 750 560.
Sales Fax: (1284) 757 929. email: info@vintenradamec.com
www.vintenradamec.com
CONTACT
David Monkhouse, Mark Osborn¶

VORTEX COMMS
75 The Grove, Ealing, London, England, W5 5LL.
Telephone +44(0)20-8579-2743. FAX: +44(0)20-8840-0018
email: info@vtx.co.uk www.vtx.co.uk

PRODUCTION FACILITIES & SERVICES

ACORN FILM & VIDEO
13 Fitzwilliam Street., Belfast, Northern Ireland, BT9 6AW.
TEL: 028 90240977. FAX: 028 90222309.
roger@acorntv.com www.acorntv.com
MD
Roger Fitzpatrick - roger@acorntv.com
MANAGER
Steve Hillen - steve@acorntv.com

BBC RESOURCES POST PRODUCTION
BBC Television Centre, Wood Lane, London, W12 7RJ.
TEL: (8700) 100 883. FAX: (8700) 100 884.
email: bbcresources@bbcresources.co.uk
www.bbcresources.co.uk

CAPITAL STUDIOS
13 Wandsworth Plain, London, SW18 1ET. TEL: (0208) 874 0131.
FAX: (0208) 871 9737. www.capitalstudios.co.uk.
CONTACT
Clare Phillips - clare.phillips@capitalstudios.co.uk

CHARTER BROADCAST (UK-LONDON), LTD.
Unit 4, Elstree Distribution Park, Elstree Way, Borehamwood
Hertfordshire, WD6 1RU. TEL: (0208) 905 1213.
FAX: (0208) 905 1424. www.charterbroadcast.com
CEO
Michael Breen

CINEBUILD, LTD.
34 Rita Rd., Vauxhall, London, SW8 1JU.
TEL: (0207) 582 8750. FAX: (0207) 793 0467.
email: cinebuild@btclick.com www.cinebuild.com
DIRECTOR
Tony Neale, Patrick Neale

CITY SCREEN PICTUREHOUSE THEATRES
16-18 Beak St., London, W1F 9RD. TEL: (0207) 734 4342.
FAX: (0207) 734 4027.
CONTACT
Tony Jones - (012) 2332 8383

DIGITAL FILM LAB LONDON, LTD.
6 Berners Mews London, W1T 3AJ. TEL: (0845) 658 5726.
email: london@digitalfilmlab.com www.digitalfilmlab.com
CEO
Kris Kolodziejski
CONTACT
Carrie-Anne Hall - petitefilms@onetel.com

DOGHOUSE POST PRODUCTION, LTD.
11 Belgrave Rd., Clifton, Bristol, BS8 2AA.
TEL: (117) 973 5588. email: info@doghousepost.tv
www.doghousepost.tv
MD & SENIOR EDITOR
Jules

FOUNTAIN TELEVISION
128 Wembley Park Dr., Wembley, Middlesex, HA9 8HQ.
TEL: (0208) 900 5800. FAX: (0208) 900 5802. www.ftv.co.uk
STUDIO MANAGER
Tony Edwards

CHARLES H. FOX, LTD.
22 Tavistock St., Covent Garden, London, WC2E 7PY.
TEL: (0207) 240 3111. FAX: (0207) 379 3410.
email: sales@charlesfox.co.uk www.charlelsfox.co.uk

THE CLUB
(Formerly Frontline Television Services)
35 Bedfordbury Covenant Garden, London, WC2 N4DU.
TEL: (0207) 836 04211. FAX: (0207) 379 5210.
email: production@frontlinetv.com www.frontline-tv.co.uk
MANAGING DIRECTOR
Bill Cullen - bill.cullen@frontline-tv.co.uk

FREMANTLEMEDIA, LTD.
(Formerly Thames Television Limited)
1 Stephen St., London, W1T 1AL. TEL: (0207) 691 6000.
FAX: (0207) 691 6100. www.fremantlemedia.com

HAMMERHEAD TV
Unit 19, Liongate Enterprise Park, 80 Morden Rd., Mitcham,
Surrey, CR4 4NY. TEL: (208) 646 5511. FAX: (208) 646 6163.
email: london@hammerheadtv.com www.hammerheadtv.com
OPERATIONS MANAGER
Alex Trezies

INPUT VIDEO GROUP
191a Askew Road, London, England. W12 9AX.
TEL: 020 8740 5222. FAX: 020 8746 0811.
dw@input-video.co.uk www.input-video.co.uk
CONTACT
David Wood

INTERNATIONAL BROADCAST FACILITIES (IBF)
15 Monmouth St., Covent Garden, London, WC2H 9DP.
TEL: (207) 497 1515. FAX: (207) 379 8562.
email: terrys@ibf.co.uk www.ibf.co.uk
FACILITIES MANAGER
Gordon Crabb

ITV
(Formerly Carlton Television Birmingham)
Gas St., Birmingham, B1 JT. TEL: (0121) 643 9898.
FAX: (0121) 633 4473. www.calton.com

THE LEEDS STUDIOS
The Television Centre, Kirkstall Rd., Leeds, LS3 1JS.
TEL: (113) 222 7807. FAX: (113) 222 8282.
www.the-leeds-studios.tv
CONTACT
Lance Tattersall

LONDON STUDIOS/LONDON TELEVISION CENTRE
(Formerly LWT Production Facilities)
Upper Ground, London, SE1 9LT. TEL: (207) 737 8888.
FAX: (207) 928 8405. www.londonstudios.co.uk
MANAGING DIRECTOR
Debbie Hills

MET FILM POST
Ealing Studios, Ealin Green, London, UK. W5 5EP.
TEL: 020 8280 9120. email: jonathan@metfilm-tv.co.uk
www.metfilmpost.co.uk
CONTACT
Jonathan Peake

MOLINARE
34 Fouberts Place, London, W1F 7PX. TEL: (0207) 478 7000.
FAX: (0207) 478 7299. email: bookings@molinare.co.uk
www.molinare.co.uk

Molinare D'Arblay St., 16 D'Arblay St., London, W1F 8EA.
TEL: (207) 758 0500. FAX: (207) 758 0501.
CONTACT
Sam Estensen - same@molinare.co.uk

ONE POST TV
71 Dean St., London, W1D 3SF. TEL: (0207) 439 2730.
FAX: (0207) 434 3331. www.onepost.tv
CONTACT
Matt Adams - matt.adams@onepost.tv

PEERLESS CAMERA CO.
Unit A, 32, Bedfordbury, London, WC2N 4DU.
TEL: (0207) 836 3367. FAX: (0207) 240 2143.
email: info@peerless.co.uk www.peerless.co.uk
CONTACT
Marianne Speight

PRATER AUDIO VISUAL, LTD.
35 Coleraine Rd., Blackheath, London, SE3 7PF.
TEL: (0208) 269 0609. FAX: (0208) 269 0622.
email: info@PraterAV.co.uk www.praterav.co.uk
DIRECTOR
Robin Prater

RUSHES POSTPRODUCTION, LTD.
Old Compton St., London, W1D 4UH. TEL: (0207) 437 8676.
FAX: (0207) 734 2519. www.rushes.co.uk
MANAGING DIRECTOR
Joce Capper - joce@rushes.co.uk

SUITE, LIMITED
28 Newman St., London, W1T 1PR. TEL: (0207) 636 4488.
FAX: (0207) 636 0444. www.suitetv.co.uk
HEAD OF SALES
Shelley Fox - shelley@suitetv.com

THREE MILLS STUDIO
Three Mill Lane, London E3 3DU. TEL: (207) 363 3336.
FAX: (870) 8912 360. email: info@3mills.com
www.threemils.com

TWICKEHAM FILM STUDIOS, LTD.

St. Margaret Rd., Twickenham, Middlesex TW1 2AW.
TEL: (0208) 607 8888. FAX: (208) 607 8889.
email: enquiries@twickenhamstudios.com
www.twickenhamstudios.com

VIDEO EUROPE

20-22 Union Rd., London SW4 6JP. TEL: (0207) 627 9000.
FAX: (0207) 627 9001. email: hire@videoeurope.co.uk
www.videoeurope.co.uk
MANAGING DIRECTOR
Steve Green

VINE POST PRODUCTION, LTD.

3rd Flr., 16-18 Beak Street, London, England. W1F 9RD.
TEL: +44 (0) 20 7434 3500 FAX: .+44 (0) 7973 661153.
info@vine-post.tv www.vine-post.tv
CONTACT
Michael Illingworth

PUBLICITY & MARKETING

AVALON PUBLIC RELATIONS LIMITED
4A Exmoor St., London, W10 6BD. TEL: (020) 7598 7222.
FAX: (020) 7598 7223. email: publicrelations@avalonuk.com
www.avalonuk.com
DIRECTOR OF PRESS AND PUBLICITY
Dan Lloyd
HEAD OF MARKETING
Mark Jackson

THE ASSOCIATES
Monticello House, 45 Russell Square, London, WC1B 4JP.
TEL: (207) 907 4770. FAX: (207) 907 4771.
email: info@the-associates.co.uk www.the-associates.co.uk
MANAGING DIRECTOR
Richard Larcombe - richard@the-associates.co.uk

BLUE DOLPHIN FILMS
40 Langham St., London, W1W 7AS. TEL: (020) 7255 2494.
FAX: (020) 7580 7670. www.bluedolphinfilms.com
CONTACT
Julian Ryan - julianryan@bluedolphinfilms.com

BYRON ADVERTISING, LTD./BYRON PUBLICITY
Byron House, Wallingford Rd., Uxbridge, Middlesex, UB8 2RW.
TEL: (01895) 252131. FAX: (01895) 252 137.
email: enquiries@byronadvertising.co.uk
www.byronadvertising.com
CONTACT
Jeremy Silverstone

BUBBLE & SQUEAK
80 Berwick St., London, W1F 8TU. TEL: (207) 287 4262.
www.bubblesqueak.co.uk
MANAGING DIRECTOR
Sadie Groom
CONTACT
Sadie Paris - sadie@bubblesqueak.co.uk

MAX CLIFFORD ASSOCIATES
Moss House, 15-16 Brooks Mew Mayfair, London, W1K 4DS.
TEL: (020) 7408 2350. FAX: (020) 7409 2294.
www.maxclifford.com
CONTACT
Max Clifford - max@mcapr.co.uk

CHERISH PR
The Swan Centre, Fishers Lane, London, WF1 RX.
TEL: (0208) 996 9543. FAX: (0208) 996 9596.
email: info@cherishpr.com www.cherishpr.com

THE CREATIVE PARTNERSHIP
13 Bateman St., London, W1D 3AH. TEL: (020) 7439 7762.
FAX: (020) 7437 1467. www.creativepartnership.co.uk
MANAGING DIRECTOR
Jim Sturgeon
CONTACT
Nic Ost - nic.ost@thecreativepartnership.co.uk

DENNIS DAVIDSON ASSOCIATES, LTD. (DDA LONDON)
192-198 Vauxhill Bridge Rd., London SW1 1DX.
TEL: (020) 7932 9800. FAX: (020) 7932 4950.
www.ddapr.com
CHAIRMAN & FOUNDER
Dennis Davidson - dennis.davidson@ddapr.com

EDELMAN PUBLIC RELATIONS
Haymarket House, 28-29 Haymarket, London, SW1 4SP.
TEL: (020) 7344 1200. FAX (020) 7344 1222.
email: london@edelman.com www.edelman.com
CEO
Robert Phillips - robert.phillips@elderman.com

FEREF ASSOCIATES, LTD.
17-18 Great Pulteney St., London, W1F 9NE.
TEL: (020) 7 292 6300. FAX: (020) 7292 6301. www.feref.co.uk

LEO BURNETT, LTD.
Warwick Bldg., Kensington Village, Avonmore Rd., London,
W14 8HQ. TEL: (0207) 591 1111, (0207) 071 1296.
FAX: (0207) 591 9126. www.leoburnettemea.com
PRESIDENT
Richard Pinder - richard.pinder@leoburnettemea.com
CORPORATE COMMUNICATIONS DIRECTOR
Trudi Harris - (0207) 071 1354 trudi.harris@leoburnettemea.com
BUSINESS DEVELOPMENT DIRECTOR
Carter Murray - (0207) 071 1218 carter.murray@leoburnettemea.com

FRANKS PR
2nd Flr., The Forum 74-80 Camden St., London, NW1 0EG.
TEL: (020) 7693 6999. FAX: (020)7693 6998.
email: contact@frankpr.it www.frankpr.it

PREMIER PR INC.
(Formerly McDonald And Rutter)
34 Bloomsbury St., London, WC1B 3QJ.
TEL: (207) 637 2600. email: info@mcdonaldrutter.com
CONTACT
Charles McDonald, Jonathan Rutter

ROGERS & COWAN INTERNATIONAL
14 Gray's Inn Rd., London, WC1X 8WS.
TEL: (0870) 990 5422. FAX: (0870) 990 5465.
email: inquires@rogersandcowan.com
www.rogersandcowan.com
ACCOUNT DIRECTOR
Emma McCorkell

TOWN HOUSE PUBLICITY
45 Islington Park St., London, N1 1QB. TEL: (020) 7226 7450.
FAX: (020) 7359 6026.

TRT
The Studio, Gateway Business Centre, Leeds Rd., Sheffield,
S9 3TY. TEL: (114) 242 4383. FAX: (114) 242 4341.
email: info@t-r-t.co.uk www.t-r-t.co.uk

VISICOM DIGITAL MEDIA
Caxton House, 140 High St., Uckfield, East Sussex TN22 1QR.
TEL: (182) 576 7222. FAX: (182) 576 9177.
email: johnm@visicomdigital.com www.visicomdigital.com
CONTACT
John Meakin

SOUND SERVICES

ABBEY ROAD STUDIOS
3 Abbey Rd., St. John's Wood, London, NW8 9AY.
TEL: (0207) 266 7000. FAX: (0207) 266 7250.
email: info@abbeyroad.com www.abbeyroad.co.uk
CONTACT
Colette Barber, Lucy Launder - bookings@abbeyroad.com

APS, LTD.
The Old Town Hall, Lapwing Lane, West Didsbury, Manchester, M20 2WR. TEL: (0161) 448 9990. FAX: (0161) 448 2023.
www.aps-av.com
CONTACT
Julie Kelson - julie@thinkaps.com
DIRECTOR
Ray Buckley, Mark Butcher, Martin Mackenzie, Julie Kelson, Chris Teague

ARDMORE SOUND
Herbert Rd., Bray, County Wicklow, Ireland.
TEL: (3531) 286 5868. FAX: (3531) 286 5871.
email: info@ardmoresound.ie www.ardmoresound.ie
CONTACT
Paul Ardmore

ASCENT-MEDIA - MEDIA MANAGEMENT SERVICES
Film House, Wardour St., London, W1F 8DD.
TEL: (0207) 878 0000. FAX: (0207) 878 7800.
www.ascentmedia.co.uk
DIRECTOR OF SALES
Rachel Joseph

THE AUDIO SUITE
Soho Studios, 8 Allcock St., Birmingham, B9 4TV.
TEL: (121) 224 8234. FAX: (121) 224 8235.
email: info@theaudiosuite.com
CONTACT
Neil Hillman, MPSE

BACKYARD RECORDING STUDIOS
West Pen-y-llan Churchstoke, Montgomery Powys, SY15 6HT.
TEL: (01588) 620 0129. www.backyardstudios.co.uk
MANAGER
Dave Owen - dave@backyardstudios.co.uk

CTS STUDIOS, LTD.
Ste. 1A, Lansdowne House, Lansdowne Rd., London, W11 3LP. TEL: (0207) 467 0099. FAX: (0207) 467 0098.
email: info@landsowne.co.uk www.cts-lansdowne.co.uk
MANAGING DIRECTOR
Adrian Kerridge

D B POST PRODUCTIONS, LTD.
1-8 Batemans Bdlgs., South Soho Square, London, W1D 3EN.
TEL: (0207) 434 0097. FAX: (0207) 287 9143.

DE LANE LEA
75 Dean St., London, W1D 3PU. TEL: (0207) 432 3800.
FAX: (0207) 432 3838. www.delanelea.com

THE DIGITAL AUDIO COMPANY
3 Carleton Business Park, Carleton New Rd., Skipton, North Yorkshire, BD23 2AA. TEL: (01756) 797 100. FAX: (01756) 797 101.
email: info@the-digital-audio.co.uk www.the-digital-audio.co.uk

FOUNTAIN TELEVISION, LTD.
128 Wembley Park Dr., Wembley, Middlesex, HA9 8HQ.
TEL: (0208) 900 5800. www.ftv.co.uk

GRAND CENTRAL SOUND STUDIOS
5-53 Great Marlborough St., London, W1F 7ST.
TEL: (0207) 306 5600. FAX: (0207) 306 5616.
email: info@grand-central-studios.com
www.grand-central-studios.com
MANAGING DIRECTOR
Carole Humphrey

HASKETH MEDIA
2 The Barns, Shrewsbury, SY5 8NW, West Midlands, U.K.
TEL: 44 01743 247082.
MANAGER
Chris Hesketh

HULABALOO STUDIOS
8 Albany Rd., Manchester, Lancashire, M21 0AW.
TEL: (0161) 882 0007. FAX: (0161) 882 0774.
email: admin@hullabaloo-studios.com
www.hullabaloo-studios.com

IBF
15 Monmouth St., London, WC2H 9DA. TEL: (0207) 497 1515.
FAX: (0207) 379 8562. email: post@ibf.co.uk www.ibf.co.uk
Martin Reekie - martinr@ibf.co.uk

INHOUSE PRODUCTIONS, LTD.
Buildin 14 Shepperton Studios Middlesex, TW17 QD.
TEL: (01932) 592 455. FAX: (01932) 592 195.
email: contact@ihpp.co.uk www.ihpp.co.uk

JAI YEN MUSIC
35 Hormead Road, London, W93NQ. TEL: 07790 566648.
MANAGER
Kevin Mills

L.A.L.
Studio 59, Canalot Studios 222 Kensal Rd., Ladbroke Grove, Kensington, W10 5BN, Greater London.
TEL:020 85670961.
MANAGER
David Cohen

LANDSDOWNE MUSIC PUBLISHING, LTD.
Lansdowne House, Lansdowne Rd., London, W11 3LP.
TEL: (0207) 727 0041. FAX: (0207) 792 8904.
www.cts-lansdowne.co.uk
MANAGING DIRECTOR
Adrian Kerridge

MATINEE SOUND & VISION
132-134 Oxford Rd., Reading, Berks, RG1 7NL.
TEL: (0118) 958 4934. FAX: (0118) 959 4936.
email: info@matinee.co.uk www.matinee.co.uk
MANAGING DIRECTOR
Jackie Stuart

MAYFAIR RECORDING STUDIOS
11A Sharpeshall St., London, NW1 8YN. TEL: (020) 7586 7746.
FAX: (020)7586 9721. email: bookings@mayfair-studios.co.uk
www.mayfair-studios.co.uk
CONTACT
Dan Mills

NINTH WAVE AUDIO
Potton Hall, Westleton, Suffolk, IP17 3EF. TEL: (0121) 442 2276.
FAX: (0121) 689 1902. email: info@ninthwaveaudio.com
www.ninthwaveaudio.com

RED BUS RECORDING & VIDEO STUDIOS, LTD.
34 Salisbury St., London, NW8 8QE. TEL: (0207) 402 9111.
FAX: (0207) 723 3064.

SONICA STUDIOS
Welmar Mews, 154 Clapham Park Rd., London, SW4 7DE.
TEL: (207) 498 2990. email: info@sonicamusic.co.uk
www.sonicamusic.co.uk
CONTACT
Mat Clark

THE SOUND COMPANY, LTD.
23 Gosfield St., London, W1W 6HG. TEL: (207) 580 5880.
FAX: (207) 580 6454. email: info@sound.co.uk
www.sound.co.uk
MANAGING DIRECTOR
Geoff Oliver

THE SOUNDHOUSE, LTD.
Unit 11, Goldhawk Industrial Estate, Vinery Way, Brackenbury Rd., Shepherds Bush, London, W6 0BA.
TEL: (0208) 743 2677. FAX: (0208) 740 9122.
email: info@thesoundhousestudios.co.uk
www.thesoundhousestudios.co.uk
DIRECTOR
Paul Deeley

SOUNDS IN MOTION, LTD.
The Media Centre, Culverhouse Cross, Cardiff, CF5 6XJ.
TEL: (292) 059 0521. FAX: (292) 059 0471.
email: enquiries@simpost.co.uk www.simpost.co.uk

ST. ANNE'S POST
20 St. Anne's Ct., London, W1F 0BH. TEL: (207) 155 1500.
FAX: (207) 155 1501. email: info@saintannespost.co.uk
www.saintannespost.co.uk
MANAGING DIRECTOR
Keith Williams - md@saintannespost.co.uk

TRIANGLE POST PRODUCTION
81 Whitfield St., London, W1T 4HG. TEL: (0207) 255 5222.
FAX: (0207) 255 5216. www.triangletelevision.co.uk
MANAGING DIRECTOR
Nicola Warman Johnston

TRIDENT SOUND STUDIO, LTD.
17 St. Annes Ct., London, W1F 0BQ. TEL: (0207) 734 6198.
FAX: (0207) 439 3813. email: info@tridentsoundstudios.co.uk
www.tridentsoundstudios.co.uk

CONTACT
Peter Hughes, Stephen O'Toole

UNIVERSAL SOUND

Old Farm Ln., London Rd., East, Amersham, Bucks, HP7 9DH.
TEL: (01494) 723 400. FAX: (01494) 723 500.
email: foley@UniversalSound.co.uk www.universalsound.co.uk

VIDEOLONDON SOUNDSTUDIOS

16-18 Ramillies St., London W1V 1DL. TEL: (0207) 734 4811.
FAX: (020) 7494 2553. www.videolondon.co.uk

VIDEOSONICS, LTD.

13 Hawley Crescent, Camden Town, London, NW1 8NP.
TEL: (0207) 209 0209. FAX: (0207) 419 4460.
www.videosonics.com
SOUND EDITOR
Stuart Bagshaw
CONTACT
Dennis Weinreich, Peter Hoskins

WARWICK SOUND STUDIOS

Tylers Ct., 111 A Wardour St., London W1F 0UJ.
TEL: (0207) 437 5532. FAX: (0207) 439 0372.
email: info@warwicksound.com www.warwicksound.com

WHITE LIGHTENING GROUP OPERATING AS SILK SOUND

13 Berwick St., Soho, London W1F PW.
TEL: (207) 434 7633. email: info@silk.co.uk www.silk.co.uk

WILD TRACKS AUDIO STUDIOS, LTD.

2nd Flr., 55 Greek St., London W1D 3DX. TEL: (0207) 734 6331.
FAX: (0207) 734 6195. email: bookings@wildtracks.co.uk
www.wildtracks.co.uk
CHAIRMAN
Paul Headland
MANAGING DIRECTOR
Graham Pickford

SPECIAL EFFECTS

AARDMAN ANIMATIONS
7 Gasferry Rd., Bristol, BS1 6UN. TEL: (0117) 984 8485.
FAX: (0117) 984 8486. www.aardman.com
DIRECTOR & FOUNDER
Peter Lord, David Sproxton

ALBATROSS MODELS, SETS, EFFECTS
The Coach House, St Paul's Waldenbury, St Paul's Walden, Hitchin, Herts, SG4 8BP. TEL: (1438) 871 1688.
FAX: (1438) 887 1874. email: enquiries@albatrossmodels.co.uk
www.albatrossmodels.co.uk

ANIMATED EXTRAS
Shepperton Film Studios, Studios Rd., Shepperton, Middlesex, TW17 0QD. TEL: (01932) 572 342.
email: info@animatedextras.com

ARTEM SPECIAL EFFECTS
Perivale Park, Horsenden Lane, South Perivale, Middlesex, UB6 7RH. TEL: (0208) 997 7771. FAX: (0208) 997 1503.
email: info@artem.com www.artem.com
MANAGING DIRECTOR
Mike Kelt

CAPITAL FX, LTD.
2nd Fl., 20 Dering St., London, W1S 1AJ. TEL: (0207) 493 9998.
email: simon.dowling@capital-fx.co.uk www.capital-fx.xo.uk
CONTACT
Simon Dowling

CINE IMAGE FILM OPTICALS
7A Langley St., Covent Garden, London, WC2H 9JA.
TEL: (0207) 240 6222. FAX: (0207) 240 6242.
email: info@cineimage.co.uk www.cineimage.co.uk
CONTACT
Kerrie Grant

CINESITE EUROPE, LTD.
(A Kodak Company)
Medius House, 2 Sheraton St., London, W1F 8BH.
TEL: (0207) 973 4000. FAX: (0207) 973 4040.
email: filmfx@cinesite.co.uk www.cinesite.co.uk
BUSINESS DEVELOPMENT MANAGER
Gillian Roberts

CRAWLEY CREATURES, LTD.
Unit 22-23, Rabans Close, Aylesbury, Buckinghamshire, HP19 8RS. TEL: (01296) 336 315. FAX: (01296) 339 590.
email: j.gibsonharris@btconnect.com
www.crawley-creatures.com
DIRECTOR
Jez Gibson Harris

THE DEFINITIVE SPECIAL PROJECTS, LTD.
P.O. Box 169 Wood End Ardeley, Stevenage, Hertfordshire, SG2 7SG. TEL: (01438) 869 005. FAX: (01438) 869 006.
email: info@laserlightshows.co.uk
www.definitivespecialprojects.co.uk
CONTACT
Steve Hitchins

EFFECTS ASSOCIATES, LTD.
(A Division of Cine Site Europe, Ltd.)
Pinewood Studios, Pinewood Rd., Iver Heath, Bucks, SL0 0NH. TEL: (01753) 652 007. FAX: (01753) 630 127.
email: info@effectsassociates.co.uk
www.effectsassociates.co.uk
PRODUCTION MANAGER
Jess Lewington

THE EFFECTS COMPANY
Ladycross Business Park, Hollow Lane, Dormansland, Surry, RH7 6PB, U.K. TEL: 44 (0) 1342 870111.
FAX: 44 (0) 1342 870999. email: martin@effectsco.com
www.effectsco.com

ELEMENTS SPECIAL EFFECTS, LTD.
Unit 4 Acton Business Centre, School Rd., England, NW10 6TD. TEL: (208) 961 4244. email: info@elementsfx.co.uk
www.elementsfx.co.uk
CONTACT
Nick Rideout

ENTERPRISES UNLIMITED SPECIAL EFFECTS
Unit 10, Glen Industrial Estate Essendine, Stamford Lincolnshire, PE9 4LE. TEL: (178) 075 2166.
FAX: (178) 075 2167. email: website@snowboy.co.uk
www.snowboy.co.uk¶

HALCYON DESIGNS
25 Cortayne Rd., London, SW6 3QA. TEL: (0207) 736 8744.
FAX: (0207) 736 8407. email: fleroux@btclick.com
CONTACT
Fabrice Le Roux

LASER CREATIONS INTERNATIONAL, LTD.
55 Merthyr Terrace, Barnes, London, SW13 8DL.
TEL: (0208) 741 5747. FAX: (0208) 748 9879.
email: contact@lci-uk.com www.lci-uk.com

LIQUID IMAGE STORES
4A, Sheet, Stroes Industrial Estate, Long Eaton, Nottingham Nottinghamshire, NG10 1AU. TEL: (0115) 946 1555.
FAX: (0115) 946 3555. email: office@liquidimage.co.uk
www.liquidimage.co.uk

MILL FILM SHEPPERTON
Shepperton Studios, Studios Rd., Shepperton, Middlesex, TW17 0QD. TEL: (01932) 572 424. FAX: (01932) 568 944.
www.millfilms.co.uk

MILLS MEDIA
(Formerly John Mills Films And Television)
2 Morpeth Wharf, Twelve Quays, Wirral, CH4 1 LF.
TEL: (0151) 649 3600. FAX: (0151) 649 3700.
email: sales@millsmediagroup.com www.milssmediafroup.com
MANAGING DIRECTOR
Andrew Mills

MTFX
Velt House, Elmore, Glouster, GL2 3NY. TEL: (145) 272 9904.
FAX: (145) 272 9904. ww.mtfx.com

OTTER EFFECTS
Kingsway House, 123 Goldsworth Rd. Woking, Surrey, GU21 6LR. TEL: (01932) 846 332. email: email@otterfx.com
www.otterfx.com
CONTACT
Terry Reed

OXFORD SCIENTIFIC (OSF), LTD.
Ground Fl., Network House, Station Yard, Thames, OX9 3UH.
TEL: (01844) 262 370. FAX: (01844) 262 380.
email: enquiries@osf.uk.com www.osf.co.uk
CONTACT
Vicky Turner - vturner@osf.co.uk

PINEWOOD STUDIOS
(Formerly Perdix Firearms, Ltd.
P.O. Box 1670 Salisbury, SP4 6QL. TEL: (01722) 782 402.
FAX: (01722) 782 790. email perdix@eclipse.co.uk
www.perdix.co.uk

QUANTEL, LTD.
31 Turnpike Rd., Newbury, Berkshire, RG14 2NX.
TEL: (01635) 482 22. FAX: (01635) 815 815.
www.quantel.com

SNOW BUSINESS INTERNATIONAL LTD.
The Snow Mill, Bridge Rd., Ebley, Stroud, Gloucestershire, GL5 4TR. TEL/FAX: (1453) 840 077. email: snow@snowbusiness.com
www.snowbusiness.com
CONTACT
Jenni Parsons - jenni@snowbusiness.com

SPECIAL EFFECTS UK, LTD.
Shed 14 Pinewood Studios, Iver Heath Bucks, SL0 0NH.
TEL: (0175) 365 0658. FAX: (0175) 365 0659.
email: info@specialeffectsuk.com www.specialeffectsuk.com
CONTACT
Paul Dunn

TELOS PRODUCTIONS
11 D'Arblay Street, London, W1F 8DT, Scotland.
TEL: 44 20 7479 4170. www.telos.me.uk
MANAGER
Stephen Elson

STUDIO FACILITIES

ARDMORE STUDIOS, LTD.
Herbert Rd., Bray, Co. Wicklow, Ireland. TEL: (353 1) 286 2971.
FAX: (353 1) 286 1894. email: film@ardmore.ie
www.ardmore.ie
MANAGING DIRECTOR
Kevin Moriarty - kevin@ardmore.ie

BLACK ISLAND STUDIOS
Alliance Rd., London, W3 ORA. TEL: (208) 956 5600.
FAX: (208) 956 5604. email: info@islandstudios.net
www.islandstudios.net

CAMBERWELL STUDIOS
Block A, Chartwell Business Park, 61-65 Paulet Road, London,
SE5 9HW. TEL: 0207 737 0007.
Del Wilson - del.wilson@camberwellstrudios.co.uk
SALES DIRECTOR
Andy Woodruff - andy.woodruff@camberwellstudios.co.uk

CAPITAL STUDIOS
13 Wandsworth Plain, London, SW18 1ET.
TEL: (208) 877 1234. FAX: (208) 877 0234.
email: info@capitalstudios.com
www.capitalstudios.com
GENERAL MANAGER
Bobbi Johnstone - bobbi.johnstone@capitalstudios.co.uk

EALING STUDIOS
Ealing Green, Ealing, London, W5 5EP. TEL: (0208) 567 6655.
FAX: (0208) 758 8658. email: info@ealingstudios.com
www.ealingstudios.com
MANAGING DIRECTOR
Sean Hinton

CASTING STUDIOS INTERNATIONAL, LTD.
Ramillies House, 1/2 Ramilles St., London, W1F 7LN.
TEL: (207) 437 2070. FAX: (207) 437 2080.
email: info@castingstudios.com
CHIEF EXECUTIVE
Colin Sweeney

ELSTREE FILM STUDIOS
Shenley Rd., Borehamwood, Hertfordshire, WD6 1JG.
TEL: (208) 953 1600. email: info@elstreefilmstudios.co.uk

FINISHING POST CREATIVE, LTD.
Giltbrook Studios, 10, Giltway, Giltbrook, Nottingham, NG16
2GN. TEL: (115) 945 8800. FAX: (115) 945 8801.
email: mark@finishing-post.co.uk www.finishing-post.co.uk
CONTACT
Mark Harwood

FOUNTAIN TELEVISION
128 Wembley Park Dr., Wembley, Middlesex, HA9 8HQ.
TEL: (0208) 900 5800. www.ftv.co.uk

FRAMESTORE CFC
9 Noel St., London, W1F 8GH. TEL: (207) 208 2600.
FAX: (207) 208 2626.
CONTACT
Jane White - jane.white@framestore-cfc.com

GUERILLA FILMS
35 Thornbury Rd., Isleworth, TW7 4LQ. TEL: (0208) 758 1716.
FAX: (0208) 758 9364. email: info@guerilla-films.com
www.guerilla-films.co.uk
MANAGER
John Bowling

BRIAN JACKSON FILMS AND TELEVISION, LTD.
39 41 Hanover Steps, St. Georges Fields, London, W2 2YG.
TEL: (0207) 402 7543. FAX: (0207) 262 5736.
CONTACT
Brian Jackson

IMAGIST STUDIOS
Units 8 & 9, Second Way, Avonmouth, Bristol, BS11 8DF.
TEL: 0117 938 2000. FAX: 0560 076 9261.
email: emma.vai@imagiststudios.com
www.imagiststudios.com

LEAVESDEN STUDIOS
Hill Farm Ave., Leavesden, Watford, Hertfordshire, WD25 7LT.
TEL: (01923) 685 060. FAX (01923) 685 061.

THE LONDON TELEVISION CENTRE
Upper Ground, London SE1 9LT. TEL: (207) 737 8888.
FAX: (207) 928 8405. www.londonstudios.co.uk

MOLINARE
34 Fouberts Place, London W1V 2BH. TEL: (207) 478 7000.
FAX: (207) 478 7299.
CONTACT
Richard Jones - richardj@molinare.co.uk

PINEWOOD SHEPPERTON STUDIOS, LTD.
Pinewood Rd., Iver Heath, Buckinghamshire, SL0 0NH.
TEL: (01753) 651 700. FAX: (01753) 656 844.
Shepperton Studios: Studios Rd., Shepperton, Middlesex,
TW17 0QD. TEL: (01932) 592 006. FAX: (01932) 568 989.
email: info@pinewoodshepperton.com
www.pinewoodshepperton.com
MANAGING DIRECTOR
Nick Smith - (01753) 656 732
STUDIO MANAGER
Peter Hicks/Pinewood - (01753) 656 457
Kristian Jaggs/Shepperton - (01932) 592 555

RUSHES POST PRODUCTION
66 Old Compton St., London, W1V 5PA.
TEL: (207) 437 8676. FAX: (207) 734 2519.
email: joce@rushes.co.uk www.rushes.co.uk

STUDIO ALBA
54A Seaforth Rd., Stornoway, Isle of Lewis Scotland, HS1
2SD. TEL: (1851) 701 200, (1851) 701 125.
FAX: (1851) 701 094. email: info@studioalba.com
www.studioalba.com

TEDDINGTON STUDIOS
(A Division of Pinewood Shepperton Studios)
Broom Rd., Teddington Lock, Middex, TW11 9NT.
TEL: (0208) 977 3252. FAX: (0208) 943 4050.
email: sales@teddington.tv www.teddington.tv

THREE MILLS STUDIOS
Three Mill Lane, London, E3 3DU. TEL: (207) 363 3336.
FAX: (8708) 912 360. email: info@3mills.com
www.themills.com
STUDIO EXECUTIVE
Derek Watts
OPERATIONS MANAGER
Jason Taylor

TWICKENHAM FILM STUDIOS, LTD.
The Barons, St. Margaret's, Twickenham, Middlesex, TW1
2AW. TEL: (0208) 607 8888. FAX: (0208) 607 8889.
email: enquiries@twickenhamstudios.com
www.twickenhamstudios.com
CONTACT
G. Humphreys, C. Tipple (Production)

WORLD WIDE GROUP, LTD.
21-25 St. Anne's Ct., London W1F 0BJ. TEL: (0207) 434 1121.
FAX: (0207) 734 0619. email: pics@worldwidegroup.ltd.uk
PRODUCER/MANAGING DIRECTOR
C. Courtenay Taylor
PRODUCER
Ray Townsend
CONTACT
Hannah Cookson

BRITISH TRADE ORGANIZATIONS & GOVERNMENT UNITS

ASSOCIATIONS, GUILDS & UNIONS

ADVERTISING ASSOCIATION
7th Fl., 11-19 Artillery Row, London, SW1P 1RT.
TEL: (0207) 340 1100. FAX: (0207) 222 1504.
email: ic@adassoc.org.uk www.adassoc.org.uk
CEO
Tim Lefroy
PRESIDENT
Penny Hughes
CHAIRMAN
Andre McGuinness
VICE CHAIRMAN
Dave Lewis, Rupert Howell
DIRECTOR OF PUBLIC AFFAIRS
Sue Eustace - sue.eustace@adassoc.org.uk

ADVERTISING STANDARDS AUTHORITY
Mid City Place, 71 High Holborn, London, WC1V 6QT.
TEL: (207) 492 2222, (207) 242 8159. FAX: (207) 242 3696.
email: enquiries@asca.org.uk www.asa.org.uk

AGENTS ASSOCIATION
54 Keys House, Dolphin Square, London, SW1V 3NA.
TEL: (0207) 834 0515. FAX: (0207) 821 0261.
email: association@agent-uk.com www.agents-uk.com
PRESIDENT
Michael Vine

AMICUS
(Formerly Amalgamated Engineering & Electrical Union AMICUS/AEEU)
33-37 Moreland St., London, EC1V 8HA.
TEL: (0208) 596 9798. FAX: (0208) 596 9557.
www.amicustheunion.org
REGIONAL SECRETARY
Jennie Brenner

ASSOCIATION OF INDEPENDENT FILM EXHIBITORS
Cornerhouse, 70 Oxford St., Manchester, M1 5NH.
TEL: (161) 200 1510.
CONTACT
David Moultrey

ASSOCIATION OF MOTION PICTURE SOUND (AMPS)
28 Knox St., London, W1H 1FS. TEL/FAX: (0207) 723 6727.
email: admin@amps.net www.amps.net
ADMIN SECRETARY
Brian Hickin

ASSOCIATION OF PROFESSIONAL RECORDING SERVICES, LTD. (APRS)
P.O. Box 22, Totnes, Devon, TQ9 7YZ. TEL: (01803) 868 600.
FAX: (01803) 868 444. www.aprs.co.uk
CHIEF EXECUTIVE
Peter Filleul

BKSTS - THE MOVING IMAGE SOCIETY
Pinewood Studios, Iver Heath, Bucks, SL0 0NH.
TEL: (01753) 656 656. FAX: (01753) 657 016.
email: info@bksts.com www.bksts.com
PRESIDENT
Ted Taylor

BRITISH ACADEMY OF COMPOSERS & SONGWRITERS
British Music House, 25-27, Berners St., London, W1T 3LR.
TEL: (0207) 636 2929. FAX: (0207) 636 2212.
email: info@britishacademy.com www.britishacademy.com
CEO
Chris Green

BRITISH ACADEMY OF FILM AND TELEVISION ARTS
195 Piccadilly, London, W1J 9LN. TEL: (0207) 734 0022.
FAX: (0207) 734 1792. email: web@bafta.org www.bafta.org
PRESIDENT
HRH Prince William of Wales
VICE PRESIDENT
Michael Grade
CHAIRMAN
Duncan Kenworthy
CHIEF EXECUTIVE
Amanda Berry

BRITISH ACTORS' EQUITY ASSOCIATION
Guild House, Upper St. Martin's Lane, London, WC2 9EG.
TEL: (0207) 379 6000. FAX: (0207) 379 7001.
www.equity.org.uk
CONTACT
Andy Prodger

BRITISH BOARD OF FILM CLASSIFICATION
3 Soho Square, London, W1D 3HD. TEL: (0207) 440 1570.
FAX: (0207) 287 0141. www.bbfc.co.uk

BRITISH CINEMA AND TELEVISION VETERANS
22 Golden Square, London, W1F 9AD.
TEL/FAX: (0207) 287 2976.
email: bctv.veterans@btopenworld.com

BRITISH FEDERATION OF FILM SOCIETIES (BFFS)
The Ritz Building Mount Pleasant Campus, Swansea, West Glamorgan, SA1 6ED. TEL: (01792) 481 170.
FAX: (01792) 462 219. email: bffs-admin@sihe.ac.uk
www.bffs.org.uk

BRITISH FILM COMMISSION
10 Little Portland St., London, W1W 7JG.
TEL: (0207) 861 7861. FAX: (0207) 861 7862.
email: info@ukfilmcouncil.org.uk www.ukfilmcouncil.org.uk
CEO
John Woodward
CHAIRMAN
Stewart Till

BRITISH FILM DESIGNERS GUILD
Flat G, 344 Finchley Rd., London, NW8 0NA.
TEL/FAX: (0207) 722 0754. email: enquiries@filmdesigners.co.uk
www.filmdesigners.co.uk
CHAIRMAN
Kevin Phipps
VICE CHAIRMAN
Terry Ackland-Snow
SECRETARY
Susan Whitaker

BRITISH MUSIC INFORMATION CENTRE
(Reference library of works by 20th Century British Composers)
1st Flr., Lincoln House, 75 Westminster Bridge Rd., London, SE1 7HS. TEL: (0207) 928 1902. FAX: (0207) 928 2957.
email: info@bmic.co.uk www.bmic.co.uk
DIRECTOR
Matthew Greenall

BRITISH SOCIETY OF CINEMATOGRAPHERS, LTD.
P.O. Box 2587, Gerrards Cross, Bucks, SL9 7WZ.
TEL: (01753) 888 052. FAX: (01753) 891 486.
email: bscine@btconnect.com www.bscine.com
PRESIDENT
Gavin Finney
SECRETARY
Frances Russell

BRITISH VIDEO ASSOCIATION, LTD. (BVA)
167 Great Portland St., London, W1W 5PE.
TEL: (0207) 436 0041. FAX: (0207) 436 0043.
email: general@bva.org.uk www.bva.uk
DIRECTOR GENERAL
Mrs. Lavinia Carey

BROADCASTING ENTERTAINMENT CINEMATOGRAPH AND THEATRE UNION
373-377 Clapham Rd., London, SW9 9BT.
TEL: (0207) 346 0900. FAX: (0207) 346 0901.
email: info@bectu.org.uk www.bectu.org.uk
GENERAL SECREATRY
Roger Bolton - rbolton@bectu.org.uk
PRESIDENT
Tony Lennon - tony.lennon@mcr1.poptel.org.uk

CASTING DIRECTORS' GUILD
P.O. Box 34403, London W6 0YG. TEL/FAX: (0208) 741 1951.
www.tcdg.co.uk

CINEMA EXHIBITORS' ASSOCIATION
22 Golden Square, London, W1F 9JW. TEL: (0207)734 9551.
FAX: (0207) 734 6147. www.cinemauk.org.uk
CHIEF EXECUTIVE
John Wilkinson
CHAIRMAN
Barry Jenkins

CRITICS' CIRCLE
51 Vartry Rd., London, N15 6PS.
email: info@criticscircle.org.uk www.criticscircle.org.uk
PRESIDENT
Charles Spencer
VICE PRESIDENT
Tom Sutcliffe
HONORARY SECRETARY
Peter Cargin

THE CINEMA AND TELEVISION BENEVOLENT FUND
22 Golden Square London W1F 9AD. TEL: (207) 437 6567.
FAX: (207) 437 7186. email: info@ctbf.co.uk

DIRECTORS GUILD OF GREAT BRITAIN
4 Windmill St., London W1T 2HZ. TEL: (207) 580 9131.
FAX: (207) 580 9132. email: guild@dggb.org www.dggb.org

FEDERATION AGAINST COPYRIGHT THEFT (FACT)
7 Victory Business Centre, Worton Rd., Isleworth, Middlesex, TW7 6DB. TEL: (0208) 568 6646. FAX: (0208) 560 6364.
email: contact@fact-uk.org.uk www.fact-uk.org.uk
DIRECTOR GENERAL
Brian Conlon

FILM DISTRIBUTORS' ASSOCIATION
22 Golden Square, London, W1F 9JW. TEL: (0207) 437 4383.
FAX: (0207) 734 0912. www.launchingfilms.com
CHIEF EXECUTIVE
Mark Batey

FILM EDUCATION
21-22 Poland St., London, W1F 8QQ. TEL: (207) 851 9450.
FAX: (207) 439 3218. www.filmeducation.co.org.uk

FILM LONDON
Suite 6.10, The Tea Building, 56 Shoreditch High St., London, E1 6JJ. TEL: (207) 613 7676. FAX: (207) 613 7677.
email: info@filmlondon.org.uk www.filmlondon.org.uk
CEO
Adrian Wootton
FILM COMMISSIONER
Sue Hayes
EXECUTIVE ASSISTANT
Jane Shaw

GUILD OF BRITISH CAMERA TECHNICIANS
c/o Panavision UK, Metropolitan Centre, Bristol Rd. Greenford, Middex, UB6 8GD. TEL: (0208) 813 1999.
email: admin@gbct.org www.gbct.org
CHAIRMAN
Trevor Coop

GUILD OF BRITISH FILM EDITORS
2 Pembroke Rd., London, W86 NX. TEL: (0207) 602 8319.
email: info@filmeditorsguild.com www.filmeditorsguild.com

INTERNATIONAL VISUAL COMMUNICATION ASSOCIATION (IVCA)
IVCA Business Communication Centre, 19 Pepper St. Glengall Bridge, London, E14 9RP. TEL: (0207) 512 0571.
FAX: (0207) 512 0591. email: ceo@ivca.org
www.ivca.org
CEO
Wayne A. Drew

IRISH ACTORS EQUITY GROUP
Liberty Hall, 9th Fl., Dublin 1, Republic of Ireland.
TEL: (353 1) 858 6401. email: equity@siptu.ie
www.irishactorsequity.ie

IRISH FILM & TELEVISION ACADEMY
First Fl., Palmerstown Centre, Kennelsfort Road, Palmerstown, Dublin 20, Ireland. TEL: 353 1 620 0812.
FAX: 353 1 620 0810. email: info@ifta.ie www.ifta.ie
CEO
Aine Moriarty
COO
Deirdre Hopkins

IRISH FILM INSTITUTE (IFI)
Irish Film Centre, 6 Eustace St., Temple Bar, Dublin, Republic of Ireland. TEL: (353 1) 679 5744. FAX: (353 1) 677 8755.
email: info@irishfilms.ie www.irishfilm.ie
DIRECTOR
Mark Mulqueen - mmulqueen@irishfilms.ie

MECHANICAL COPYRIGHT PROTECTION SOCIETY, LTD.
Copyright House, 29-33 Berners St., London, W1T 3AB.
TEL: (0207) 580 5544. FAX: (0207) 306 4350.
www.mcps.co.uk

MUSICIANS' UNION
60-62 Clapham Rd., London, SW9 0JJ.
TEL: (0207) 582 5566. FAX: (0207) 582 9805.
email: info@musiciansunion.org.uk
www.musiciansunion.org.uk
REGIONAL ORGANIZER
Bob Bennett
GENERAL SECRETARY
John F. Smith

PACT, LTD.
(Producers Alliance for Cinema and Television)
The Eye, 2nd Flr., 1 Proctor St., Holburn, London, WC1V 6DW.
TEL: (0207) 067 4367. FAX: (0207) 067 4377.
249 West George St., Glasgow, G2 4QE.
TEL: (0141) 222 4800. FAX: (0141) 111 4881.
www.pact.co.uk
CHIEF EXECUTIVE
John McVay - john@pact.co.uk

THE PERFORMING RIGHT SOCIETY, LTD. (PRS)
Copyright House, 29-33 Berners St., London, W1T 3AB.
TEL: (0207) 580 5544. FAX: (0207) 306 4350.
www.mcps.co.uk

THE PRODUCTION GUILD OF GREAT BRITAIN
(Formerly the Guild of Film Production Accountants And Financial Administrators)
Pinewood Studios, Iver Heath, Buckinghamshire, SL0 0NH.
TEL: (1753) 651 767. FAX: (1753) 652 803.
email: admin@productionguild.com
www.productionguild.com
CHIEF EXECUTIVE
David Martin
HONORARY PRESIDENT/CHAIRMAN
Kevin Trehy
TREASURER
Bobbie Johnson
Michael O'Sullivan
GENERAL MANAGER
Lynne Hames
ADMIN OFFICER
Patrick Barry - patrick@productionguild.com

VARIETY CLUB OF GREAT BRITAIN
93 Bayham St., London, NW1 0AG. TEL: (0207) 428 8100.
FAX: (0207) 428 8123. www.varietyclub.org.uk

UK FILM COUNCIL
10 Little Portland Street, London, W1W 7JG.
TEL: 44 (0) 20 7861 7861. FAX: 44 (0) 20 7861 7862.
www.ukfilmcouncil.org.uk

WOMEN IN FILM AND TELEVISION
6 Langley St., London, WC2H 9JA. TEL: (0207) 240 4875.
FAX: (0207) 379 1625. email: info@wftv.org.uk
www.wftv.org.uk
CHIEF EXECUTIVE
Jane Cussons - jane@wftv.org.uk

THE WRITERS' GUILD OF GREAT BRITAIN
15 Britannia St., London, WC1X 9JN. TEL: (0207) 833 0777.
FAX: (0207) 833 4777. email: admin@writersguild.org.uk
www.writersguild.org.uk
GENERAL SECRETARY
Bernie Corbett - Corbett@writersguild.org.uk

GOVERNMENT DIVISIONS ON FILM & TELEVISION AFFAIRS

BRITISH COUNCIL
Film and Literature Department, 10 Spring Gardens, London, SW1A 2BN. TEL: (0207) 389 3051. FAX: (0207) 389 3175.
email: film.department@britishcouncil.org www.britfilms.com
CONTACT
Satwant Gill - satwant.gill@britishcouncil.org

THE BRITISH DEFENCE FILM LIBRARY
Chalfont Grove, Chalfont St. Peter, Gerrards Cross, Bucks, SL9 8TN. TEL: (01494) 874 461. FAX: (01494) 872 982.
www.ssvc.co.uk
CONTACT
Robert Dungate - robert.dungate@ssvc.com

BRITISH FILM COMMISSION
10 Little Portland St., London, W1W 7JG. TEL: (0207) 861 7861.
FAX: (0207) 861 7862. email: info@ukfilmcouncil.org.uk
www.ukfilmcouncil.org.uk
CEO
John Woodward
CHAIRMAN
Stewart Till

BRITISH FILM INSTITUTE (BFI)
21 Stephen St., London, W1T 1LN. TEL: (0207) 255 1444.
FAX: (0207) 436 7950. www.bfi.org.uk
DIRECTOR
Amanda Nevill
PERSONAL ASSISTANT TO DIRECTOR
Brenda Whitehead

BRITISH SCREEN ADVISORY COUNCIL
13 Manette St., London, W1D 4AW. TEL: (0207) 287 1111.
FAX: (0207) 287 1123. email: bsac@bsacouncil.co.uk
www.bsac.uk.com
CHAIRMAN
Adam Singer
HONORARY PRESIDENT
Lord Attenborogh of Richmond Upon Thames
DIRECTOR
Fiona Clark-Hackston

CENTRAL OFFICE OF INFORMATION
(COI Ccommunications)
Hercules House, Hercules Rd., London, SE1 7DU.
TEL: (0207) 928 2345. FAX: (0207) 928 5037. www.coi.gov.uk

DEPARTMENT FOR CULTURE, MEDIA & SPORT
2-4 Cockspur St., London, SWIY 5DH. TEL: (0207) 211 6200.
FAX: (0207) 211 6460. email: enquires@culture.gov.uk
www.culture.gov.uk

FILM LONDON
20 Euston Centre, Regent's Place, London, NW1 3JH.
TEL: (0207) 387 8787. FAX. (0207) 387 8788.
email: info@filmlondon.org.uk www.filmlondon.org.uk
CEO
Adrian Wootton - adrian.wooton@filmlondon.org.uk
FILM COMMISSIONER
Sue Hayes
HEAD OF STRATEGY & RESOURCES
Daniela Kirchner

NATIONAL FILM AND TELEVISION SCHOOL
Beaconsfield Studios, Station Rd., Beaconsfield, Bucks HP9 1LG. TEL: (01494) 671 234. FAX: (01494) 674 042.
email: admin@nftsfilm-tv.ac.uk www.nftsfilm-tv.ac.uk
DIRECTOR
Nik Powell

THE SERVICES SOUND & VISION CORPORATION
Chalfont Grove, Chalfont St. Peter, Gerrards Cross, Bucks, SL9 8TN. TEL: (01494) 874 461. FAX: (01494) 872 982.
www.ssvc.co.uk

THE UK FILM COUNCIL
10 Little Portland St., London, W1W 7JG.
TEL: (0207) 861 7861. FAX: (0207) 861 7862.
email: info@ukfilmcouncil.org.uk www.ukfilmcouncil.org.uk
CEO
John Woodward
CHAIRMAN
Tim Beva

The World Market: Europe, Latin America, Asia & The Pacific

Exhibitors

Production Companies

Distribution Companies

Associations

Industry Organizations

ALBANIA

Capital: Tirana
Population: 2,986,952 (July 2010 est.)
Area: 28,748 sq. km.
Source: CIA World Factbook
Country Code: al

DISTRIBUTORS AND PRODUCERS

IDA
Rr. "Thanas Ziko" P. 98- Sh 1- Apt 2, Tirana.
TEL/FAX: (355) 422 7103.

EXHIBITORS

CINEMA PARIS
'Ish Pallati Kultures "All Kelmendi", Tirana, Albania.

ASSOCIATIONS AND ORGANIZATIONS

ALBANIA FILM COMMISSION
Torre Drin, Shoping Center, Nr. 27 Rr. A. Toptani, Tirana, Albania. TEL: (355) 382 026 703. FAX: (355) 425 0840.
email: info@albaniaartinstitute.org
www.albaniafilmcommission.com
CHAIRMAN
Ilir Butka
CHIEF EXECUTIVE
Knidi Bashari
FILM COMMISSIONER
Mihal Rama

ARGENTINA

Capital: Buenos Aires
Population: 41,343,201 (July 2010 est.)
Area: 2,766,890 sq. km.
Source: CIA World Factbook
Country Code: ar

DISTRIBUTORS AND PRODUCERS

AEROPLANO CINE
Mansilla 3895, La Lucila, Buenos Aires 1636.
TEL: 54 11 4792 0010. FAX: 54 11 4792 0010.
email: info@aeroplanocine.com www.aeroplanocine.com

AGUIRRE FILMS
El Salvador 5635, C1414BQE Buenos Aires.
TEL: (54 11) 4777 5213, 4778 0149.
email: info@aguirrefilms.com.ar www.aguirrefilms.com.ar
DIRECTOR
Hernan Kessleman

ALFA FILMS
Av. Corrientes 2025, 2 Piso A, 1045 Buenos Aires.
TEL: (54 11) 4957 9901. email: alfafilms@ssdnet.com.ar

ARTISTAS ARGENTINOS ASOCIADOS
Lavalle 1943 PB B, 1051 Buenos Aires.
TEL: (54 11) 4371 3862, 4374 3610.
email: artasoc@infovia.com.ar

ARTISTAS ARGENTINOS ASOCIADOS
Lavalle 1943 PB B, 1051 Buenos Aires.
TEL: (54 11) 4371 3862, 4374 3610.
email: artasoc@infovia.com.ar

BALDER PRODUCCIONES S.R.L.
Castillo 1357, Piso 1, 1414 Buenos Aires. TEL: (54 11) 4775 7091.
email: info@balder.net www.balder.net

BD CINE
Alvarez Thomas 198, Piso 2, 1427 Buenos Aires.
TEL: (54 11) 4554 5182. email: info@bdcine.net
www.bdcine.com

BS. AS. PRODUCCIONES
Cabello 3791, Piso 3, 1425 Buenos Aires.
TEL/FAX: (54 11) 4802 7444. email: bsasprod@ciudad.com.ar

BUENA VISTA INTERNATIONAL (LATIN AMERICA)
Avenue Santa Fe 1821, 7th Flr., Buenos Aires 1123, Argentina.
TEL: (54 11) 4811 0833. FAX: (54 11) 4811 7977.
PRESIDENT, LA & CARIBBEAN
Diego Lerner

CENTAURO PRODUCCIONES
Paraguay 4645 PB 5, 1425BSQ Buenos Aires.
TEL: (54 11) 4777 4084.
email:info@centauroprod@comar www.centauroprod.com.ar

CINEMA GROUP S.R.L.
Av. Corrientes 2025 6B, 1045 Buenos Aires.
TEL: (54 11) 4954 5129, 4952 2528.
email: ementasti@velocom.com.ar

COLUMBIA TRISTAR FILMS OF ARGENTINA, INC.
Ayacucho 537, 1026 Buenos Aires.
TEL: (54 11) 4375 3815. FAX: (54 11) 4375 0133.
email: columbia_argentina@columbiapictures.com.ar
www.columbiapictures.com.ar
GENERAL MANAGER
Oscar Scarinci

DISTRIBUTION COMPANY S.A.
Ayacucho 595, 1026 Buenos Aires. TEL: (54 11) 4372 9945.
email: info@distribution-company.com
www.distribution-company.com

DIVA PRODUCCIONES
Alcaraz 4271, 1407 Buenos Aires. TEL: (54 11) 4568 9012.
email: info@ divaproducciones.com.ar
www.divaproducciones.com.ar

DISTRIFILMS S.A.
TLavalle 1860, 1051 Capital Federal. Buenos Aires.
TEL: 541-371-3438. FAX: 541-374-9250.
PRESIDENT
Luis Alberto Scalella
VICE PRESIDENT
Manuel Pablo Venacio
SALES MANAGER
Raul Castro

EL CUERVO PRODUCCIONES
Güemes 4032 PB, 1425 Buenos Aires. TEL: (54 11) 4833 6978.
FAX: (54 11) 4831 0269.
email: info@elcuervoproducciones.com
www.elcuervoproducciones.com

EUROCINE
Tucuman 1980, PB, 1050 Buenos Aires.
TEL: (54 11) 4371 3631. FAX: (54 11) 4373 0547.
email: eurocine@navigo.com.ar

FILM SUEZ S.A.
Florida 681, 2 Piso, 1375 Buenos Aires.
FAX: (54 11) 4314 1900. email: informes@filmsuez.com.ar
www.filmsuez.com.ar

LAMPONI CINE
Lavalle 2033, 1015 Buenos Aires. TEL: (54 11) 4375 0647.
email: lamponi@speedy.com.ar

LEDA FILMS S.A.
Virrey Olaguer y Feliú 2462, Piso 3, 1426 Buenos Aires.
TEL: (54 11) 4788 2515. FAX: (54 11) 4788 5220.
email: info@ledafilms.com www.ledafilms.com

LIDER FILMS
Lavalle 2086, 1051 Buenos Aires. TEL/FAX: (54 11) 4953 0924.
email: liderfilm@advancedsl.com.ar

OSCOAR KRAMER PRODUCCIONES
Figueroa Alcorta 3351, Piso 1, Officina 104, 1425 Buenos Aires. FAX: (54 11) 4807 3254. email: okfilms@arnet.com.ar

PRIMER PLANO FILM GROUP S.A.
Riobamba 477, 1025 Buenos Aires.
TEL: (54 11) 4374 8401/8435. FAX: (54 11) 4374 0648.
email: primerplano@primerplano.com.ar
www.primerplanofilms.com.ar

UNITED INTERNATIONAL PICTURES
Ayacucho 520, 1026 Buenos Aires. TEL: 54-11-4373-0261, 54-11-4373-0264. FAX: (54 11) 4373 5098.
MANAGER
Juan Manuel Fascetto

THE WALT DISNEY STUDIO
Malaver 550, 1636, Buenos Aires. TEL: (54 11) 4814 8500.
www.disneylatino.com
CONTACT
Hector Bas - cv.la.@disney.com

WARNER BROS.
Tucuman 1938, 1050 Buenos Aires. TEL: (54 11) 4372 6094.
FAX: (54 11) 4372 6097. email: maicat@ssdnet.com.ar
www.foxlatina.com
GENERAL MANAGER
Anibal Codebo

EXHIBITORS

CINEMARK ARGENTINA S. A.
Beruti 3399, Piso 5,, Capital Federal, CP C1425BBQ Buenos Aires. TEL: (54 11) 5199 9000. FAX: (54 11) 5199 9001. www.cinemark.com.ar
GENERAL MANAGER
Martin Alvarez

Number of Theatres: 8
Number of Screens: 73

HOYTS ARGENTINA
S. Ortiz, 3333 Buenos Aires. TEL: (54 11) 4319 9999. www.hgcc.com.ar

Number of Theatres: 10
Number of Screens: 95

VILLAGE ROADSHOW, LTD.
(For complete listing see Australian branch)
206 Bourke St., Melbourne, VIC 3000, Australia.
TEL: (613) 96 67 66 66. FAX: (613) 96 39 15 40.

Number of Theatres: 6
Number of Screens: 69

ASSOCIATIONS AND ORGANIZATIONS

ARGENTINE COMMISSION OF FILMMAKERS
Lima 319, Piso 10, C1073AGG Buenos Aires.
TEL: (54 11) 4379 0977. FAX: (54 11) 5383 90911.
email: caf.info@incaa.gov.ar www.caf.gov.ar

ARGENTINE CHAMBER FOR THE FILM INDUSTRY (C.A.I.C.)
Av. Callao 157, Piso 8, 1022 Buenos Aires.
TEL: (54 11) 4371 1378. FAX: (54 11) 4372 4148.
email: cine@jcraffo.com.ar

ARGENTINE FOUNDATION FOR CINEMATOGRAPHY EXHIBITORS
Ayacucho 457, Piso 1, Of. 13, 1026 Buenos Aires.
TEL/FAX: (54 11) 4953 1234. email: empcinemato@infovia.com.ar www.fadec.org.ar

ASSOCIATION OF PRODUCERS AND INDEPENDENT PRODUCERS
Rivadavia 1367, Piso 10, 1033 Buenos Aires.
TEL/FAX: (54 11) 4384 8100, 4384 8200.

INCAA (INSTITUTO NACIONAL DE CINE Y ARTES AUDIOVISUALES)
Lima 319, 1073 Buenos Aires. FAX: (54 11) 4383 0029.
email: info@incaa.gov.ar www.incaa.gov.ar

AUSTRALIA

Capital: Canberra
Population: 21,515,754 (July 2010 est.)
Area: 7,686,850 sq. km.
Source: CIA World Factbook
Country Code: au

DISTRIBUTORS AND PRODUCERS

21ST CENTURY PICTURES
41-43 Higginbotham Rd. Unit 4. Gladesville , NSW 2111.
TEL: (610) 2 88 78 88 07. FAX: (610) 2 98 07 71 20.
email: martin@21stcenturypictures.com.au www2.spin.net.au/

ABC FILMS
GPO Box 9994, Sydney, NSW 2001.
TEL: (612) 9950 3977. FAX: (612) 9950 3967.
CONTACT
Vanessa Ware

ALCHEMY FILMS
4/19 Oxlade Dr., New Farm, Brisbane, QLD 4005.
TEL: (617) 3254 2338. FAX: (617) 3254 2338.

ALFRED ROAD FILMS
25a Billyard Ave., Elizabeth Bay, NSW 2011.
TEL: (612) 9356 3344. FAX: (612) 9358 1613.

ALMOST MANAGING CO., P/L
192 Elgin St., Carlton, VIC 3053. TEL: (613) 9347 1800.
FAX: (613) 9347 0235.

APPALOOSA FILMS PTY., LTD.
P.O. Box 2000, South Melbourne, VIC 3205. TEL: (613) 9569 3640.
email: info@appaloosafilms.tv www.appaloosafilms.tv
CONTACT
Steve Thompson

ARANDA FILM PRODUCTIONS PTY., LTD.
75 Edward Rd., Wandin, VIC 3139. TEL/FAX: (613) 5964 4066.
email: bruce@arandafilm.com.au www.arandafilm.com.au

ARCLIGHT FILMS
1201/39 McLaren St., North Sydney 2060.
TEL: (612) 9955 8825. FAX: (612) 9955 8828.
email: info@arclightfilms.com www.arclightfilms.com
CHAIRMAN
Victor Syrms - victor@archlightfilms.com
MANAGING DIRECTOR
Gary Hamilton - gary@archlightfilms.com
GENERAL MANAGER
Ian Gibbons- ian@archlightfilms.com

ARENAFILM
270 Devonshire St,. Surry Hills, NSW 2010.
TEL: (612) 9319 7011. FAX: (612) 9319 6906.
www.arenafilm.com.au
CONTACTS
Robert Connolly, John Maynard

ARTIST SERVICES
33 Nott St., Port Melbourne, VIC 3207. TEL: (613) 9646 3388.
FAX: (613) 9646 7644.
CONTACT
Andrew Knight, Steve Vizzard

AUSTRALIAN FILM INSTITUTE
236 Dorcas St., South Melbourne, VIC 3205.
TEL: (613) 9696 1844. FAX: (613) 9696 7972.
email: info@afi.org.au www.afi.org.au
CEO
James Hewison
EXECUTIVE ASSISTANT TO CEO
Emily Johnston-Gurr - ejohnston-gurr@afi.org.au

AUSTRAL VISION
52 Victoria St., North Sydney, NSW 2060.
TEL: (612) 9922 4311. FAX: (612) 9922 6956.

AVALON FILMS CORPORATION
25 Attunga Rd., Newport, NSW 2106. TEL: (612) 9918 5808.
FAX: (612) 9918 5808. www.avalonfilms.com

BAZMARK
P.O. Box 430, Kings Cross, NSW 1340. TEL: (612) 9361 6668.
FAX: (612) 9361 6667. email: justine@bazmark.com
www.bazmark.com
PRESIDENT
Baz Luhrmann

BBC ENTERPRISES
11th Fl., 50 Berry St., North Sydney, NSW 2060.
TEL: (612) 9957 3777. FAX: (612) 9957 6448.
MANAGING DIRECTOR ASIA PACIFIC
David Vine
MARKETING DIRECTOR ASIA PACIFIC
Jill Bryant
HEAD OF FINANCE & ADMINISTRATION
Cathy Service
HEAD OF PROGRAMME SALES AUSTRALIA/ASIA
Julie Dowding

BEBCO GROUP, LTD
Trafalar Way Camberley, GU146JF Surrey. TEL: (0125)251 7551.
MANAGING DIRECTOR
J. Bence

BECKER ENTERTAINMENT GROUP
(Parent company to Dendy Films and Globe Film Company)
Level 1, 11 Waltham St., Artarmon, NSW 2064.
TEL: (612) 9298 7700. FAX: (612) 9439 1827.
email: info@beckers.com.au www.beckerentertainment.com.au
FILM DISTRIBUTION
Jason Hernandez
FILM PRODUCTION
Nina Therapou

BEYOND DISTRIBUTION
53-55 Brisbane Street, Surry Hills NSW 2010, Australia.
TEL: (612) 9281 1266.
Gary Hamilton

RICHARD BENCE PRODUCTIONS
299 Moray St., South Melbourne, VIC 3205.
TEL: (613) 9690 9922. FAX: (613) 9699 1288.

BENDIGO STREET PRODUCTIONS
22 Bendigo St., Richmond, VIC 3121. TEL: (613) 9420 3377.
FAX: (613) 9420 3654.

BEYOND INTERNATIONAL, LTD.
109 Reserve Rd., Artarmon, NSW 2064.
TEL: (612) 9437 2000. FAX: (612) 9437 2181.
email: investor_relations@beyond.com.au www.beyond.com.au
CEO & MANAGING DIRECTOR
Mikael Borglund

BINNABURA FILM CO. PTY., LTD.
P.O. Box 2124, Clovelly, NSW 2031. TEL: (612) 9665 6135.
FAX: (612) 9665 4378. email: glenysmerle@one.act.au
CONTACT
Glenys Rowe

BLUE-TONGUE FILMS
PO Box 873. Darlinghurst, Sydney, NSW 1300.
TEL: (612) 9356 8478. FAX: (612) 9356 8479
email: info@bluetonguefilms.com www.bluetonguefilms.com

RICHARD BRADLEY PRODUCTIONS
Ste. 8 / 1st Fl., Sydney Theatrical Centre, 2-8 Ennis Rd., Milsons Point, NSW 2061. TEL: (612) 9959 3588.
FAX: (612) 9955 3808. email: rbproductions@bigpond.com
MANAGING DIRECTOR
Richard Bradley

BRAY & HAYES
1/1 Ridge St., North Sydney, NSW 2060.
TEL: (612) 9957 1559. FAX: (612) 9922 1931.

BRILLIANT FILMS
11/39 Rockley Rd., South Yarra, VIC 3141.
TEL: (613) 9826 9682. FAX: (613) 9827 7419.

ROBERT BRUNING
P.O. Box 105, Cremorne Junction, NSW 2090.
TEL: (612) 9906 6144, (612) 9953 5867.
FAX: (612) 9906 5402, (612) 9953 3184.

BUCKINGHAM PICTURE PRODUCTIONS PTY., LTD.
98 Queens Parade, Newport Beach, NSW 2106.
TEL: (612) 9979 9977. FAX: (612) 9979 9279, (612) 9973 1341.
CONTACT
Roger Buckingham

BURROWES FILM GROUP
1st Fl., 407 Coventry St., South Melbourne, VIC 3205.
TEL: (613) 9690 0388. FAX: (613) 9696 1543.

CASCADE FILMS & MELBOURNE FILM STUDIOS
117 Rouse St,. Port Melbourne, VIC 3207.
TEL: (613) 9646 4022. FAX: (613) 9646 6336.
email: info@cascadefilms.com.au www.cascadefilms.com.au
CONTACT
David Parker, Nadia Tass

CBS PARAMOUNT TELEVISION
Ste. 3501, Level 35s Tower, North Point, 100 Miller St., North Sydney, NSW 2060. TEL: (612) 9922 2322. FAX: (612) 9955 6808.

CENTAUR ENTERPRISES PTY., LTD.
15 Heath St., Mona Vale, NSW 2103. TEL: (612) 9999 0656.
CONTACT
John Meagher

CHRISTIAN TELEVISION AUSTRALIA, LTD. (CTA)
National Head Office: GPO Box 3316, Brisbane, QLD 4001.
TEL: (617) 3377 9992. FAX: (617) 3871 0061.
email: admin@cta.asn.au www.cta.asn.au

CINEMATIC SERVICES PTY., LTD.
(A div. of the OSSCCA Film Group; film & TV production services)
P.O. Box 6104, Kangaroo Valley, NSW 2577.
TEL: (614) 1271 4631. email: mail@osscca.com
www.users.bigpond.com/ossccagroup

CINEVEST
(A div. of OSSCCA Film Group; investment and financial services)
P.O. Box 6104, Kangaroo Valley, NSW 2577.
TEL: (614) 1271 4631. email: mail@osscca.com
www.users.bigpond.com/ossccagroup

CIRCA FILMS
Level 1/21 William St. Balaclava, Victoria, 3183.
TEL:(613)-9525 8486. FAX:(613)-9525 8416.

COLOSIMO FILM PRODUCTIONS
22 Hanover St., Fitzroy, VIC 3065. TEL: (613) 9417 1241.
FAX: (613) 9416 1779.

CONTINENTAL MOUNTS AUSTRALIA
3/18-20 Cliff St., Manly, Sydney, NSW 2095.
TEL: (614) 1251 6612. FAX: (612) 9977 0556.
email: info@continentalmounts.com www.continentalmounts.com

DENDY FILMS
19 Martin Place Sydney, NSW 2000.
TEL: (612) 92333 8558. FAX: (612) 9232 3841.
email: info@dendy.com.au www.dendy.com.au
GENERAL MANAGER
Mark Sarfaty

DIGITAL ARTS FILM & TELEVISION
1 Ledger Rd., Beverly, SA 5009. TEL: (618) 8347 4691.
FAX: (618) 8347 4692.

DIGITAL PICTURES
111-114 Chandos St., Crows Nest, NSW 2065.
TEL: (612) 9439 5044. FAX: (612) 9438 2647.
www.digitalpictures.com.au

DIGITAL PICTURES NETWORK
P.O. Box 1418, Crows Nest, NSW 2065. TEL: (612) 9467 3400.
email: realise@digitalpictures.com.au
www.digitalpictures.com.au
Melbourne Office: TEL: (613) 9251 1600.
email: digitalpictures@aav.com.au
GENERAL MANAGER
Pamela Hammond

DISCOVERY INTERNATIONAL
P.O. Box 550, Malvern 3144, VIC. TEL: (613) 563 9344.
FAX: (613) 563 9885.

EASTWAY COMMUNICATIONS
Ste. 202/24 Falcon St., Crows Nest, NSW 2065.
TEL: (612) 9906 1999. FAX: (612) 9439 4387.
CONTACT
John Eastway

EDGECLIFF FILMS
25 Suffolk St., Paddington, NSW 2021. TEL: (612) 9331 6277.
FAX: (612) 9331 2588.

EMPRESS ROAD PRODUCTIONS PTY., LTD.
1-126 Brighton Rd., Bondi, NSW 2026. TEL: (612) 9365 4073.
FAX: (612) 9365 4713.

EN CUE PRODUCTIONS PTY., LTD.
P.O. Box 5291, West End, QLD 4101. TEL: (617) 3844 6242.
FAX: (617) 3844 6285.

ENTERTAINMENT MEDIA PTY., LTD.
159 Eastern Rd., South Melbourne, VIC 3205.
TEL: (613) 9699 9722. FAX: (613) 9699 1764.
email: emedia@bigpond.com
CONTACT
Graeme Preston

FANDANGO AUSTRALIA
PO Box A2372. Sydney South, NSW 1235.
TEL: (612) 9238 0586. FAX: (612) 9238 0586.
email: suemurray@infolearn.com.au

FAST FORWARD PTY., LTD.
Innovation Hse., Technology Park, The Levels, SA 5095.
TEL/FAX: (618) 8260 8139.

FILM AND TELEVISION INSTITUTE, (WA) INC.
92 Adelaide St., Fremantle, WA 6160. TEL: (619) 335 1055.
FAX: (619) 335 1283.

FILM CENTRE AUSTRALIA
E270 The Esplanade, Swan Point, TAS 7275.
TEL/FAX: (613) 6399 4903.

FILM FINANCE
Level 12, 130 Elizabeth St., GPO Box 3886, Sydney, NSW 2000. TEL: (612) 9268 2555. FAX: (612) 9264 8551.
email: ffc@ffc.gov.au www.ffc.gov.au

FILM PARTNERSHIP & ASSOCIATES
12 Fifth St., Black Rock, VIC 3193. TEL: (613) 9589 3622.
FAX: (613) 9534 3502.

FILM VICTORIA
189 Finders Ln. Level 7, Melbourne, Vic 3000.
TEL: (613) 9660 3200. FAX: (613) 9660 3201.
email: contact@film.vic.gov.au www.film.vic.gov.au

FIRST CLASS FILMS
40 Osgathorpe Rd., Gladesville, NSW 2111.
TEL: (612) 9816 1813. email: firstcla@tpgi.com.au
MANAGING DIRECTOR
Robert Marchand

FONTANA FILMS PTY., LTD.
360 Pacific Highway, Crows Nest, NSW 2068.
TEL: (612) 9906 2188. FAX: (612 9906 2337.

FOX STUDIOS AUSTRALIA
Building 16, Driver Ave., Moore Park, NSW 1363.
TEL: (612) 9383 4100. FAX: (612) 9383 4007.
email: enquiries@foxaus.com www.foxstudiosaustralia.com
PRODUCTIONS & MARKETING LIAISON
James Bramley - (612) 9383 4135

FRONTIER FILMS
P.O. Box 294, Harbord, NSW 2096.
TEL: (612) 9938 5762. FAX: (612) 9938 5688.
CONTACT
Frank Shields

FUNNY FARM
3 Lefevre St., Spotswood, Melbourne, VIC 3015.
TEL/FAX: (613) 9399 2900.

GENESIS PRODUCTIONS
60 Boston Rd., Belmont, QLD 4153, P.O. Box 906 Bulimba, QLD 4171. TEL: (617) 3390 5955. FAX: (617) 3390 5822.
email: info@genesisproductions.com.au
www.genesisproductions.com.au

GLOBE FILM CO.
(Div. of Becker Entertainment Group; sister company to Dendy Films)

Level 1, 11 Waltham St., Artarmon, NSW 2064.
TEL: (612) 9466 9611. FAX: (612) 9439 7560.
email: info@dendyfilms.com.au www.dendyfilms.com.au
JOINT GENERAL MANAGERS
Richard Payten - richard@globefilm.com.au
Andrew Mackie - andrew@globefilm.com.au

GOLDEN DOLPHIN PRODUCTIONS
P.O. Box 566, Collaroy, NSW 2097. TEL: (612) 9971 1783.
FAX: (612) 9971 2261.

GREAT FILMS
FORMERLY GREAT SOUTHERN FILMS
53 Park St., South Melbourne, VIC 3205. TEL: (613) 9699 6466.
FAX: (613) 9699 6400. email: team@gsf.com.au
www.greatfilms.com.au
PRODUCER
Helene Nicol - helenen@gsf.com.au
Leanne Tonkes - leannet@gsf.com.au

GREATER UNION ORGANISATION
Level 7, 49 Market St. Sydney, NSW 2000.
TEL: (612) 93 73 66 00. FAX: (612) 93 73 65 46.
email: info@greaterunion.com.au www.greaterunion.com.au
States of Operation: Australia, Germany, UAE, Netherlands.
MANAGING DIRECTOR
Daveid Sargeant
GENERAL MANAGER
Peter Cody

DAVID HANNAY PRODUCTIONS
c/o Vitascope Filmed Entertainment, Glenray Park, 61 Porters Lane Yetholme, NSW 2795. TEL: (612) 9590 7666.
FAX: (612) 6337 5239.

THE HAYDEN ORPHEUM PICTURE PALACE
380 Military Rd., Cremorne, NSW 2090. TEL: (612) 9908 4344.
FAX: (612) 9953 8863. www.orpheum.com.au

HOPSCOTCH FILMS
(A division of New Vision Film Distributors)
Ste. 101, 4-14 Buckingham St., Surry Hills, NSW 2010.
TEL: (612) 9319 0233. FAX: (612) 9690 1433.
email: katwalter@hopscotchfilms.com.au
www.hopscotchfilms.com.au
FOUNDER AND EXECUTIVE PRODUCER
Frank Cox
MANAGING DIRECTOR AND DISTRIBUTOR
Troy Lum, Sandi Don
BOOKINGS MANAGER
Chris Carr - (612) 9319 0233 chris@hopscotchfilms.com.au

HOUSE AND MOORHOUSE FILMS, PTY.
P.O. Box 93, Bondi Road, PO Bondi, NSW 2026.
TEL: (612) 9389 9805. FAX: (612) 9389 9802.
CONTACT
Lynda House

HOYTS CINEMAS PTY, LTD
(Total Theaters: 55. Total Screens: 430)
Level 20, 66-68 Goulburn St. Sydney, NSW 2000.
TEL: (612) 8282 8000. FAX: (612) 8275 6120.
www.hoyts.com.au
CEO
Delfin Fernandez
CFO
Vincent Lloyd

ICON FILM DISTRIBUTION
467 Elizabeth St. Surry Hills, Sydney, NSW 2010.
TEL: (612) 8332 3920. FAX: (612) 9318 1434.
http://www.iconmovies.com.au/

ILLUMINATION FILMS
1 Victoria Ave., Albert Park, VIC 3206. TEL: (613) 9690 5266.
FAX: (613) 9696 5625.

INLAND FILMS PTY., LTD.
27 Surfside Ave., Clovelly, NSW 2031. TEL: (612) 9665 2977.
FAX: (612) 9665 7773.

I-VIEW GROUP
Level 1, 100 Collins St., Melbourne, VIC 3000.
TEL: (6139) 662 3333. FAX: (6139) 662 4518.
email: info@i-view.com.au
CEO
Rino Simonelli

JD PRODUCTIONS
116 Crescent Rd., Newport, NSW 2106. TEL: (612) 9997 1601.
FAX: (612) 9979 5083.

J'ELLY BALLANTYNE PRODUCTIONS
2/40 Marine Parade, St Kilda, VIC 3182. TEL: (613) 9525 4590.
FAX: (613) 9525 3768.
CONTACT
Jane Ballantyne

JNP FILMS
87 Alexander St., Crows Nest, NSW 2065.
TEL: (612) 9439 5855. FAX: (613) 9436 0583.

KALEIDOSCOPE PRODUCTIONS
22 Hewlett St., Waverley, NSW 2024. TEL: (612) 9387 7117.
FAX: (612) 9387 7156.

KAVANAGH PRODUCTIONS PTY., LTD.
7/15 South Terrace, Clifton Hill, VIC 3068.
TEL: (613) 9481 4312. FAX: (613) 9481 4695.

KENNEDY MILLER
Metro Theatre, 30 Orwell St., Kings Cross, NSW 2011.
TEL: (612) 9357 2322. FAX: (612) 9356 3162.

KESTREL VISUAL COMMUNICATIONS
Level 1, 367 Bridge Rd., Richmond, VIC 3121.
TEL: (613) 9429 1688. FAX: (613) 9428 6202.
email: kestrel@kestrel.net.au www.kestrel.net.au

KOJO PICTURES
31 Fullarton Rd, Kent Town, S. Australia 5067.
TEL: (618) 8363 8300. FAX: (618) 8632 8502.
www.kojopictures.com.au

KOOKABURRA PRODUCTIONS PTY., LTD.
101 Eaton Rd., Lindfield, NSW 2070. TEL: (612) 9415 6633.
FAX: (612) 9415 6688.

LATENT IMAGE PRODUCTIONS PTY., LTD.
82 Glenmore Rd., Paddingfton, NSW 2021. TEL: (612) 9331 4155.
FAX: (612) 9331 4135. email: latent@latentimage.com.au
www.latentimage.com.au
WRITER, DIRECTOR AND CEO
Rebel Penfold-Russell
PRODUCER
Vicki Watson

LEA FILMS
P.O. Box 93, North Carlton, VIC 3084. TEL: (613) 9646 9455.
FAX: (613) 9646 0220.

LIONSGATE AUSTRALIA
Lev 29, Chifley Tower, 2 Chifley Square, Sydney, NSW 2000.
TEL: (610) 2 9375 2425. FAX: (610) 2 9375 2121.

LOOK PRODUCTIONS
83 Willoughby Rd., Crows Nest, Sydney, NSW 2065.
TEL: (612) 9436 1647. FAX: (612) 9438 3660.
email: look@lookfilm.com.au www.lookfilm.com.au
EXECUTIVE DIRECTOR
Will Davies

LORI DALE PRODUCTIONS PTY., LTD.
120 Bridport St., Albert Park, VIC 3206. TEL: (613) 9699 8400.
FAX: (613) 9699 3048.

LOVELL FILMS
P.O. Box 701, Avalon Beach, NSW 2107. TEL: (612) 9918 2999.
FAX: (612) 9918 0883. email: patlove@optusnet.com.au

NEW HOLLAND PICTURES
57 Southgate Ave, Cannon Hill, QLD 4170.
TEL: (617) 3399 2799. FAX: (617) 3399 2788.
email: cathy@newhollandpictures.com.au
www.newhollandpictures.com.au

PETER LUCK PRODUCTIONS
19 Edward St., East Balmain, Sydney, NSW 2041.
TEL: (612) 9810 2458. FAX: (612) 9818 5325.
email: plp@pip.com.au www.peterluck.com.au

LUCKY COUNTRY PRODUCTIONS
Tagallant House, Scotland Island, NSW 2105.
TEL: (612) 9977 3405. FAX: (612) 9977 8953.

LYONS-SINCLAIR PRODUCTIONS
P.O. Box 83, Toorak, VIC 3142. TEL/FAX: (613) 9827 4641.
CONTACT
Clayton Sinclair

MACAU LIGHT CORPORATION, LTD.
10/38 Wunulla Rd., Point Piper, NSW 2027.
TEL: (612) 9362 3580. FAX: (612) 9327 8853.
CONTACT
Pauline Rosenberg

MACGOWAN FILMS
402 Bourke St. Surrey Hills, NSW 2010.
TEL: (612) 9357 7366. FAX: (612) 9357 1566.
www.macgowanfilms.com

MADMAN ENTERTAINMENT
1-35 Wellington St, Collingwood, Melbourne, 3066.
TEl: (613)-9419-5444. FAX: (613)-9418-7388.
email: info@madman.com.au www.madman.com.au/

MARLO AUDIO VISUAL
P.O. Box 50, Belgian Gardens, Townsville, QLD 4810.
TEL: (61018) 777 709. FAX: (61018) 180 927.

MASON PICTURE COMPANY
Ste. 3/239 Pacific Hwy., North Sydney, NSW 2060.
TEL: (612) 9959 3500. FAX: (612) 9959 3679.
email: kilner@masonpicturecompany.com
www.masonpicturecompany.com

MAX STUDIOS
19-25 Birmingham St., Alexandria, NSW 2015.
TEL: (612) 9317 2999. FAX: (612) 9667 4528.

MCA (MUSEUM OF CONTEMPORARY ART)
140 George St., The Rocks, NSW 2000. Artistic/Exhibition Programs - TEL: (612) 9245 2437.
Postal Address: P.O. Box R1286, Royal Exchange, NSW 1223.
TEL: (612) 9245 2400. FAX: (612) 9252 4361.
email: mail@mca.com.au programs@mca.com.au
www.mca.com.au
DIRECTOR
Elizabeth Ann Macgregor

M. C. STUART AND ASSOCIATES
2/34 Power St., Balwyn, VIC 3103. TEL: (613) 9888 5830.
FAX: (613) 9888 5831. email: maxstuart@ecomtel.com.au
CONTACT
Max Stuart

MEDIACAST PTY., LTD.
P.O. Box 67, Round Corner, Dural, NSW 2158.
TEL: (612) 9651 4219. FAX: (612) 9482 1298.

METRO SCREEN
Corner of Oxford Rd. and Oatley Rd., Paddington, NSW 2021.
TEL: (612) 9361 5318, (612) 9361 3048. FAX: (612) 9361 5320.
email: metro@metroscreen.org.au www.metroscreen.org.au

MGM
Level 19/111 Pacific Highway, North Sydney, NSW 2060.
TEL: (612) 9492 2000. FAX: (612) 9492 2020.
www.mgm.com/au
MANAGING DIRECTOR, AUSTRALIA
Don Hunton

HARRY M. MILLER AND COMPANY MANAGEMENT PTY., LTD.
174 Cathedral St., Woolloomooloo, NSW 2011.
TEL: (612) 9357 3077. FAX: (612) 9356 2880.

MILTON INGERSON PRODUCTIONS
2a Torrens St., Linden Park, SA 5065. TEL: (618) 8338 1666.
FAX: (618) 8338 2510.

MODERN TIMES PTY., LTD.
P.O. Box 908, Bondi Junction, NSW 2022.
TEL: (612) 9365 2416. FAX: (612) 9365 2454.

MOONLIGHT PROJECTS AND CINEMAS
(A division of Becker Entertainment Group)
Level 2, 2 Darling St., South Yarna, VIC 3141. TEL: (613) 9869 8222.
email: frontdoor@moonprojects.com www.moonlight.com.au
PUBLICITY DIRECTOR
Jillian Bowen

MUSHROOM PICTURES
135 Forbes St. Woolloomooloo, Sydney, NSW 2011.
TEL: (612) 9360 6255. FAX: (612) 9360 7307.
email: info@mushroompictures.com.au
www.mushroompictures.com.au/

N.S.W. FILM & TELEVISION
GPO Box 1744, Sydney, NSW 2000. TEL: (612) 9380 5599.
FAX: (612) 9360 1090.

OPEN EYE
(A div. of OSSCCA Film Group; marketing and dist. of films)
P.O. Box 6104, Kangaroo Valley, NSW 2577.
TEL: (614) 1271 4631. email: mail@osscca.com

ORACLE PICTURES
St. Dugham St., Level 12, 15/19 Boundary St., Rushcutters Bay, NSW 2011. TEL: (612) 9358 3788. FAX: (612) 9357 1723.

ORANA FILMS
12 Tarrant Ave., Bellevue Hill, NSW 2023. TEL: (612) 9326 1915.
FAX: (612) 9327 5517. email: reception@oranafilms.com
www.oranafilms.com
FOUNDER
Richard Dennison
DIRECTORS/PRODUCERS
David Skinner, Mark Norris, Michael Balson

OSSCCA FILM GROUP
(Includes four divsions: Cinematic Services, CineVest, Open Eye and Spectrum Films)
P.O. Box 6104, Kangaroo Valley, NSW 2577.
TEL: (614) 1271 4631. email: mail@osscca.com

OXFORD FILM SERVICES
Ste. 1, 372 Anzac Parade, Kingsford, NSW 2032.
TEL: (612) 9662 8842. FAX: (612) 9662 7663.

PACIFIC LINK COMMUNICATIONS
2A Eltham St., Gladesville 2111, NSW. TEL: (612) 817 5055.
FAX: (612) 879 7297.

PALACE FILMS AND CINEMAS
2/3 Oxford St., Paddington, NSW 2021. TEL: (612) 9360 8366.
FAX: (612) 9360 8599. email: palace@palace.net.au
www.palacefilms.com.au

PARAMOUNT PICTURES
208 Clarence St Sydney, Sydney, NSW 2000.
TEL: (02) 9264 744. FAX: (02) 9264 2953.

DAMIEN PARER PRODUCTIONS
5 Longfellow St., Norman Park, QLD 4170.
TEL: (317) 3899 1555. FAX: (317) 3899 1936.

PAVILLION FILM PTY., LTD.
P.O. Box 701, Avalon Beach, NSW 2107.
TEL: (312) 9918 2999. FAX: (312) 9918 0883.

PEACOCK FILMS PTY., LTD
P.O. Box 7832. Gold Coast MC, Queensland, 4217.
TEL: (6175) 531 6470. FAX: (6175) 531 6432.
email: peacockfilms@winshop.com.au
MANAGING DIRECTOR
Lyn Shannon

POLYGRAM FILMED ENTERTAINMENT
3 Munn Reserve, Sydney 2000. TEL: (612) 207 0500.
FAX: (612) 241 1497.
CONTACT
Richard Sheffield MacClure

POTENTIAL FILMS
P.O. Box 569, North Melbourne, VIC 3051.
TEL: (613) 9328 5000. FAX: (613) 9328 5040.
email: potfilms@ozemail.com.au www.potentialfilms.com
DIRECTOR
Mark Spratt

PRAIRIE DOG FILMS
322 West St. Cammeray, NSW 2062.
TEL: (612) 9959 5303. FAX: (612) 9959 3803.
email: wyoung@bigpond.net.au

PREMIUM FILMS
92 Bay St., Port Melbourne, 3207, Victoria.
TEL: (613) 645 1612. FAX: (613) 645 1591.

QUEST FILMS
4 Marshall Ave., St. Leonards, NSW 2065.
TEL: (612) 9436 1970. CELL: (18) 967 336.
FAX: (612) 9560 0551.
CONTACT
David Perry

REEPRODUCTIONS PTY., LTD.
56 Gipps St., Birchgrove, NSW 2041. TEL: (612) 9818 4908.
FAX: (612) 9810 3086.

R I P PRODUCTIONS
293 Princes St., Port Melbourne, VIC 3207.
TEL: (613) 9646 2055. FAX: (613) 9646 2077.

RKA THE ANIMATION STUDIO
42 Clovelly Rd., Randwick, NSW 2031. TEL: (612) 9326 3388.
FAX: (612) 9326 4192. www.rka-animation.com.au
ANIMATION DIRECTOR
John Kratovil
PRODUCER
Fee MacGregor

RISING SUN PICTURES
Suite 15, 16 Charles Street, Redfern, NSW 2016.
TEL: (612) 9338 6400. FAX: (612) 9338 6401.
email: info@rsp.com.aur www.rsp.com.au/

ROADSHOW COOTE AND CARROLL, PTY.
1st Flr., 608 Harris St., Ultimo, NSW 2009.
TEL: (612) 9211 2211. FAX: (612) 9211 2144.

RONIN FILMS
P.O. Box 1005, Civic Square, Canberra, ACT 2608.
TEL: (612) 6248 0851. FAX: (612) 6249 1640.
www.roninfilms.com.au
MANAGING DIRECTOR
Andrew Pike

SAMSON PRODUCTIONS
FSA#205 Driver Ave., Fox Studios Australia, Moore Park, NSW 1363. TEL: (612) 8353 2600. FAX: (612) 8353 2601.
CONTACT
Sue Milliken

SCREEN AUSTRALIA
(An Australian Government-owned company)
101 Eaton Rd., Linfield, NSW 2070. TEL: (612) 9413 8777.
FAX: (612) 9416 5672. email: info@screenaustralia.gov.au
www.screenaustralia.gov.au

BOARD & MANAGEMENT
Glen Boreham (Chair), Ian Robertson (Deputy Chair), Cherrie Bottger, Robert Connolly, Ross Entwistle, Matthew Liebmann, Rachel Perkins, Greg Smith, Deanne Weir

SEA FILMS PTY., LTD.
3 Heron Way, Hallett Cove, South Australia, 5158.
TEL: (618) 8322 3127. FAX: (618) 8322 4083.
email: enquiries@seafilms.com.au www.seafilms.com.au

SEACAM
(Formerly Helicam)
100 The Entrance Rd., The Entrance, NSW 2261.
TEL: (612) 4333 9990. FAX: (612) 4333 9628.
email: seacam@bigpond.com www.seacam.com.au
EXECUTIVE PRODUCER
Richard Swansborough

SERIOUS ENTERTAINMENT
P.O. Box 600, North Sydney, NSW 2060.
TEL: (612) 9957 5375. FAX: (612) 9955 8600.
CONTACT
Warwick Ross

SEVEN DIMENSIONS PTY., LTD.
8B Surrey Road, South Yarra, VIC 3141. TEL: (613) 9826 2277.
FAX: (613) 9826 4477. email: info7d@7dimensions.com.au
www.7dimensions.com.au

SHARMILL FILMS
Ste. 4, 200 Toorak Rd., South Yarra, VIC 3141.
TEL: (613) 9826 9077. FAX: (613) 9826 1935.
email: nmiller@sharmillfilms.com.au www.sharmillfilms.com.au
EXECUTIVE DIRECTOR
Natalie Miller - nmiller@sharmillfilm.com.au

SHOT PRODUCTIONS
P.O. Box 305, Darlinghurst, NSW 2010. TEL: (612) 9360 5733.
FAX: (612) 9360 5535.

SIDE BY SIDE
(Formerly Great Southern Films)
Ste. 1/171, Domain Rd., South Yarra, VIC 3141.
TEL: (613) 9820 8366. www.sbscom.com.au
DIRECTOR
John Lyons - johnl@sbscom.com.au
PRODUCER
Simone Adamson - simonea@sbscom.com.au

SMILEY FILMS
33 Riley St., Woolloomooloo, NSW 2011.
TEL: (612) 9361 4164. FAX: (612) 9692 8387.

SPIRITED FILMS PTY., LTD.
6 David St., Forest Lodge, NSW 2037. TEL: (612) 9552 2634.
FAX: (612) 9692 8387.

SOKOL FILM PRODUCTIONS
P.O. Box Q755 Queen Victoria Building, Sydney, NSW 1230.
TEL: (612) 9518 8999. FAX: (612) 9518 8388.
CONTACT
Irene Sokol

SONY PICTURES RELEASING PTY., LTD.
(A Sony Pictures Entertainment company)
Level 30, 1 Market St., Sydney, NSW 2000.
TEL: (612) 9272 2900. FAX: (612) 9272 2999.
email: contactus_australia@spe.sony.com
www.columbiafilms.com.au

SORENA
P.O. Box 215, French Forest, NSW 2086.
TEL: (612) 9417 8112, (612) 9417 8138.

SOUTHERN CROSS TELEVISION
1-3 Bowen Rd., Moonah, TAS 7009. TEL: (613) 6344 0202.
FAX: (613) 6343 0340.

SOUTHERN STAR ENTERTAINMENT
10th Fl., 8 West St., North Sydney, NSW 2060.
TEL: (612) 9202 8555. FAX: (612) 9955 8302.
email: general@sstar.com.au www.southernstargroup.com

SPECTRUM FILMS
(A division of the OSSCCA Film Group; post-production services)
Building 53, Fox Studios Australia, Driver Avenue, Moore Park, NSW 1363. TEL: (612) 9383 4455. FAX: (612) 9383 4433.
email: admin@spectrumfilms.com.au mail@osscca.com
www.spectrumfilms.com.au
BUSINESS MANAGER
Josh Pomeranz - jpomeranz@spectrumfilms.com.au

SPOTZ CASTING AGENCIES
10/a 31-37 Thompson St., Bowen Hill, QLD 4006.
TEL: (617) 3854 1949. FAX: (617) 3252 7237.

SPROWLES FILMS INTERNATIONAL PTY., LTD.
8-14 Nelson St., Annandale, Sydney, NSW 2038.
TEL: (612) 9550 5599. FAX: (612) 9550 5742.
email: office@sprowlesfilms.com.au
www.sprowlesfilms.com.au
CONTACT
Peter Sprowles

STRAUSS PRODUCTIONS PTY., LTD.
P.O. Box 167, Round Corner, NSW 2158.
TEL: (612) 9899 1691. CELL: (018) 222 886.
FAX: (612) 9680 2871. email: grant@strauss.com.au
www.strauss.com.au

TAFFNER RAMSEY PRODUCTIONS
Ste. 303, 156 Pacific Hwy., Greenwich, NSW 2065.
TEL: (612) 9437 5433. FAX: (612) 9437 4501.

THOMAS SHERIDAN MEDIA
10 Carlton Rd., Camden Park, SA 5038. TEL: (618) 8294 4468.
FAX: (618) 8294 9434. email: btp@bigpond.com
DIRECTOR
Bill Thomas

TMS DISTRIBUTION
Level 1, 50 King St., Sydney, NSW 2000.
TEL: (612) 9299 5788. FAX: (612) 9299 5704.

TROUT FILMS PTY., LTD.
189 St. Georges Rd., North Fitzroy, VIC 3068.
TEL: (613) 9489 3127. FAX: (612) 9486 3618.
email: troutfilms@ibm.net
DIRECTOR
Chris Warner

ULLADULLA PICTURE COMPANY
Ste. 5, 600 Military Rd., Mosman, NSW 2088.
TEL: (612) 9969 7599. FAX: (612) 9969 5011.

UMBRELLA ENTERTAINMENT
51 Wellington St., Colingwood, VIC 3066.
TEL: (613) 8415 0877. FAX: (613) 8415 1955.
email: info@umbrellaent.com.au www.umbrellaent.com.au
MANAGING DIRECTOR
Jeff Harrison

UNITED INTERNATIONAL PICTURES, PTY
GPO Box 4040, Sydney, NSW 2001.
TEL: 61-2-9264 7444. FAX: 61-2-9264 2499.
MANAGER
Michael Selwyn

VALKYRIE FILMS
68 Bridge Road, Glebe, NSW 2037. TEL: (612) 552 2456.
FAX: (612) 552 2457.

VICTORIAN COUNCIL FOR CHILDREN'S FILM & TV
41 St. Andrews Place, East Melbourne, VIC 3002.
TEL: (613) 9651 1919. FAX: (613) 9651 1238.

VICTORIAN INTERNATIONAL PICTURES
Melbourne Film Studios, 117 Rouse St., Port Melbourne, VIC 3207. TEL: (613) 9646 4777. FAX: (613) 9646 4946.

VILLAGE ROADSHOW LIMITED
206 Bourke St., Melbourne, VIC 3000. TEL: (613) 9667 6666.
FAX: (613) 9639 1540. email: investors@roadshow.com.au
www.villageroadshow.com.au
CHAIRMAN
Robert Kirby
COO
John Iozzi

VISIONLINK & CULT PRODUCTIONS
44 Sailors Bay Rd., Northbridge, NSW 2063.
TEL: (612) 9958 2077. FAX: (612) 9958 2974.
www.visionlink.com.au
PARTNER & DIRECTOR
Steve Griffiths - steve@visionlink.com.au

WALKER CLANCY
Unit 16, 2 Greenkowne Ave., Potts Point, NSW 2021.
TEL: (612) 9358 1163. FAX: (612) 9368 1064.

THE WALT DISNEY COMPANY
149 Castlereagh St., Sydney 2000, NSW. TEL: (612) 268 942.
FAX: (612) 264 1289.

WARNER BROTHERS AUSTRALIA
Pacific Highway, Oxenford, QLD 4210. TEL: (617) 5585 9666.
FAX: (617) 5573 3698. www.movieworldstudios.com.au
V.P., STUDIO OPERATIONS
Lynne Benzie - benzie@movieworldstudios.com.au

WESTBRIDGE PRODUCTIONS PTY., LTD.
P.O. Box 219, Port Douglas, QLD 4871. TEL: (6170) 985 577.
FAX: (6170) 994 295.

WILD VISUALS PTY., LTD.
133 Dowling St., Woolloomooloo, NSW 2011.
TEL: (612) 9331 0877. FAX: (612) 9357 4126.
email: info@wildvisuals.com.au

WORLD VISION ENTERPRISES
2nd Flr., 5-13 Northcliff St., Milsons Point 2061, NSW.
TEL: (612) 922 4722. FAX: (612) 955 8207.

ZAP PRODUCTIONS SERVICES, LTD.
1-2 Bromley Place, London, W1T 6DA, UK.
TEL: (0207) 436 5577. FAX: (0207) 691 7282.
email: mail@zap-productions.co.uk
www.zap-productions.co.uk
CONTACT
Mark Parsons

ZERO 1 ZERO
7 McCabe Place, Willoughby, NSW 2068.
TEL: (612) 9417 5700. FAX: (612) 9417 5879.
email: info@zero1zero.com.au www.zero1zero.com.au

THEATRE EQUIPMENT

AUS-WIDE CINEMA & THEATRE SUPPLY
P.O. Box 205, Geebung, QLD 4030. TEL: (617) 3216 2566.
FAX: (617) 3216 2588.
CONTACT
John Coleman

CAMATIC SEATING
93 Lewis Rd., Wantirna South, VIC 3152.
TEL: (613) 9837 7777. FAX: (613) 9887 3485.

COMPUTONICS
P.O. Box 276, Rockdal, NSW 2216. TEL: (612) 9559 4555.
FAX: (612) 9559 4455.

ENTERTAINMENT SERVICES
Unit 7, 24 Deakin St., Drendale, QLD 4500.
TEL: (617) 3881 3233. FAX: (617) 3881 3122.
CONTACT
Margaret Robbins

FERCO SEATING
No. 7m Jalan Sungau Besar 26/27, Section 2G, Shah Alam
Selangor, Malaysia 40400. TEL: (603) 511 3233.
FAX: (603) 512 9303.
CONTACT
Nadia Gourievidis

GOLD MEDAL
P.O. Box 2274, Mansfield, QLD 4122. TEL: (617) 3829 6228.
FAX: (617) 3343 2998.
CONTACT
Adrian Laugher

ICON SOFTWARE
Ste. 3, 271 Alfred St. N., North Sydney, NSW 2060.
TEL: (612) 9922 1400. FAX: (612) 9957 2459.
CONTACT
Matthew Ezra

IP FOODSERVICE
P.O. Box 81, Kingston, QLD 4114. TEL: (617) 9922 1400.
FAX: (617) 3808 3133.
CONTACT
Andrew Fletcher

KODAK ENTERTAINMENT IMAGING
P.O. Box 90, Coburg, VIC 3058. TEL: (613) 9353 3784.
FAX: (613) 9353 2962.
CONTACT
Karen Eastmure

MARS CONFECTIONARY OF AUSTRALIA
P.O. Box 633, Ballarat, VIC 3055. TEL: (613) 5337 7092.
FAX: (613) 5337 7096.
CONTACT
Steve Porter

NESTLE AUSTRALIA & DISTRIBUTORS
P.O. Box 4320, Sydney, NSW 2000. TEL: (612) 9931 2628.
FAX: (612) 9931 2926.
CONTACT
Brenton Cornell, Nick Johnson

SUPERPOP
P.O. Box 153, Mt. Waverly, VIC 3149. TEL: (613) 9558 8000.
FAX: (613) 9558 8288.
CONTACT
Janis Kondarovkis

TASCOT TEMPLETON CARPETS
119 Church St., Richmond, VIC 3121. TEL: (613) 9428 4925.
FAX: (613) 9429 6234.
CONTACT
Anna M. Pulvirenti

TICKET SYSTEMS
26/380 Eastern Valley Way, Chatswood, NSW 2067.
TEL: (612) 9417 6644. FAX: (612) 9417 6488.
CONTACT
Rowan Morrison

VAL MORGAN CINEMA ADVERTISING
P.O. Box 538, North Sydney, NSW 2095.
TEL: (612) 9929 0388. FAX: (612) 9929 7297.
CONTACT
Angela Grozos

EXHIBITORS

ACE CINEMAS
(Affiliated with Grand Cinemas, Grand Theatre Company)
P.O. Box 2137, Warwick, WA 6024. TEL: (618) 9448 3188.
FAX: (618) 9246 1755. email: grandcin@wanet.com.au
www.moviemasters.com.au
CHAIRMAN
Colin Stiles
MANAGING DIRECTOR
Alan Stiles

Number of Theatres: 4
Number of Screens: 17

ANDERSON MULTIPLEX CINEMAS
P.O. Box 277 Ballarat VIC 3353. TEL:(61) 3 5331 1339.
FAX: (61) 3 5333 4368. email: regent@amcm.com.au
www.andersoncinemas.com.au
MANAGING DIRECTOR
Stephen Anderson
OPERATIONS MANAGER
Andrew Taylor

Number of Theatres: 4
Number of Screens: 35

AUSTRALIAN MULTIPLEX CINEMAS (AMC)
P.O. Box 2152, Brookside Centre, QLD 4520.
TEL: (617) 3355 3353. FAX: (617) 3354 4700.
email: amc@powerup.com.au www.a-m-c.com.au.
CHAIRMAN
James C. Sourris
CEO
Michael Hawkins

Number of Theatres: 6
Number of Screens: 39

BIRCH CARROLL & COYLE CINEMAS
(A div. of Greater Union Organisation, owned by Amalgamated
Holdings Limited; includes Greater Union Cinemas)
State Theatre Building, Level 10, 49 Market St., Sydney, NSW
2000. TEL: (612) 9373 6600. FAX: (617) 9373 6534.
email: info@ahl.com.au www.birch.com.au www.ahl.com.au
MANAGING DIRECTOR, AHL ENTERTAINMENT
Jim Collier

Number of Theatres: 28
Number of Screens: 195

DENDY CINEMAS
(A division of Dendy Films, Becker Entertainment Group)
19 Martin Place, Sydney, NSW 2000.
TEL: (612) 9233 8558. FAX: (612) 9232 3841.
email: dendy@dendy.com.au www.dendy.com.au
HEAD OF DENDY CINEMAS
Mark Sarfaty

Number of Theatres: 6
Number of Screens: 11

ELDORADO 8 AND REGAL TWIN CINEMAS
(Formerly Westside Cinemas)
141 Coonan St., P.O. Box 77, Indooroopilly, QLD 4068.
TEL: (617) 3378 1566. FAX: (617) 3378 1504.
email: manager@eldorado8.com www.eldorado8.com

Regal Twin Cinemas: 381 Honour Ave., Graceville, QLD 4075.
P.O. Box 77, Indooroopilly, QLD 4068. TEL: (617) 3378 1566.
FAX: (617) 3378 1504. email: manager@eldorado8.com
www.eldorado8.com
EXECUTIVE
Ray Roobottom, Judy Roobottom, Paul Roobottom

Number of Theatres: 2
Number of Screens: 10

THE GRAND THEATRE COMPANY
P.O. Box 2137, Warwick, WA 6024. TEL: (618) 9448 3188.
FAX: (618) 9246 1755. email: grandcin@wanet.com.au
www.moviemasters.com.au
CHAIRMAN
Colin Stiles
MANAGING DIRECTOR
Alan Stiles

Number of Theatres: 3
Number of Screens: 19

GREATER UNION CINEMAS
(A div. of Greater Union Organisation, owned by Amalgamated
Holdings Limited; includes Birch Carroll & Coyle Cinemas)
State Theatre Bldg., Level 10, 49 Market St., Sydney, NSW
2000. TEL: (612) 9373 6600. FAX: (617) 9267 5277.

email: info@ahl.com.au www.greaterunion.com.au
www.ahl.com.au
MANAGING DIRECTOR
Richard Parton

Number of Theatres (Australia): 26
Number of Screens (Australia): 202

HAYDEN ORPHEUM PICTURE PALACE
380 Military Rd., Cremorne, NSW 2090. TEL: (612) 9908 4344.
FAX: (612) 9953 8863. www.orpheum.com.au
CHAIRMAN
Mike Walsh
GENERAL MANAGER
Paul Dravet

Number of Theatres: 1
Number of Screens: 6

HOYTS CINEMAS LIMITED
Hoyts Center, 505-523 George St., GPO Box 110, Sydney,
NSW 2000. TEL: (612) 9273 7373. FAX: (612) 9273 7399.
www.hoyts.com.au
EXECUTIVE CHAIRMAN
Paul Johnson
CFO
Wilfred Steiner
GENERAL MANAGER, OPERATIONS
Noel Collier

Number of Theatres: 44
Number of Screens: 338

NOVA CINEMAS
Lygon Court Shopping Centre, 380 Lygon St., Carlton, VIC.
TEL: (613) 9347 5331. FAX: (613) 9347 2695.
EXECUTIVE
Natalie Miller, Barry Peake
OWNER
Natalie Miller, Barry Peake

Number of Theatres: 2
Number of Screens: 15

PACIFIC CINEMAS
P.O. Box 3018, Loganholme, QLD 4129. TEL: (617) 3801 1883.
FAX: (617) 3801 3986. email: eatont@tq.com.au
CHAIRMAN
Terri Jackman
GENERAL MANAGER
Kirrily Nichols

Number of Theatres: 5
Number of Screens: 56

PALACE FILMS AND CINEMAS
233 Whitehorse Rd., P.O. Box 191, Balwyn, VIC 3103.
TEL: (613) 9817 6421. FAX: (613) 9817 6950.
email: palace@palacecinemas.com.au
www.palacecinemas.com.au
MANAGING DIRECTOR
Antonio Zeccola
DIRECTOR
Benjamin M. Zeccola
GENERAL MANAGER
Sam Di Pietro
NATIONAL PROGRAMMING MANAGER
Kim Petalas
NATIONAL MARKETING MANAGER
Gordon Johnston

Number of Screens: 55

READING ENTERTAINMENT AUSTRALIA
98 York Street. South Melbourne, Victoria, 3205.
TEL: (613) 9685 0900. FAX: (613) 9685 0999.
www.readingrdi.com
CHAIRMAN
James J. Cotter
MANAGING DIRECTOR
Wayne Smith
CFO
Andrzej Matyczynski

Number of Theatres: 46
Number of Screens: 293

RONIN FILMS - ELECTRIC SHADOWS CINEMA
(Primarily a distribution company with one arthouse cinema,
Electric Shadows Cinema)
P.O. Box 1005, Civic Square, Canberra, ACT 2608.
TEL: (612) 6248 0851. FAX: (612) 6249 1640.
www.roninfilms.com.au
MANAGING DIRECTOR
Andrew Pike

Number of Theatres: 1
Number of Screens: 3

ROSEVILLE TWIN CINEMAS
112 Pacific Hwy., Roseville, NSW 2069. TEL: (612) 9416-8555.
FAX: (612) 9416 3473. email: katrina@rosevillecinemas.com.au
www.rosevillecinemas.com.au
MANAGER, DIRECTOR & OWNER
Emma van Pinxteren

VILLAGE ANDERSON MANAGEMENT
P.O. Box 277, Ballarat, VIC 3353. TEL: (613) 53 31 13 39.
FAX: (613) 53 33 43 68. email: glabc@vam.com.au
DIRECTOR
Marie Anderson
GENERAL MANAGER
Chris Glab

Number of Theatres: 2
Number of Screen: 17

VILLAGE ROADSHOW LIMITED
206 Bourke St., Melbourne, VIC 3000. TEL: (613) 9667 6666.
FAX: (613) 9639 1540. email: investors@roadshow.com.au
www.villageroadshow.com.au
CHAIRMAN & EXECUTIVE DIRECTOR
Robert G. Kirby
DEPUTY CHAIRMAN, MANAGING DIRECTOR
John R. Kirby
MANAGING DIRECTOR
Graham W. Burke
FINANCE DIRECTOR
Peter Foo
EXECUTIVE DIRECTOR
Peter M. Harvie

Number of Theatres (Australia): 70
Number of Screens (Australia): 582
Number of Theatres Internationally (outside Australia): 56
Number of Screens Internationally (outside Australia): 495
Number of Theatres Worldwide: 126
Number of Screens Worldwide: 1077

Worldwide locations: Austria, Argentina, Czech Republic, Fiji, Greece, Italy, New Zealand, Singapore, Taiwan, UK.

WALLIS THEATRES
139 Richmond Rd., Richmond, SA 5033.
TEL: (618) 8352 1377. FAX: (618) 8352 1865.
email: wallis@wallis.com.au www.wallis.com.au
CHAIRMAN
Bob Wallis
PROGRAM MANAGER
Bob Parr

Number of Theatres: 5

WARNER BROS. INTERNATIONAL THEATRES
4000 Warner Blvd., Bldg. 160, 2nd Fl., Burbank, CA 91522.
TEL: (818) 977 5216. FAX: (818) 977-6655.
PRESIDENT
Millard L. Ochs
V.P., OPERATIONAL FINANCE, INFORMATION SERVICES & ADMINISTRATION
David Bent
SENIOR V.P., WORLDWIDE OPERATIONS
Dave Pearson
V.P., FINANCE
Paul Miller
V.P., BUSINESS AFFAIRS & GENERAL COUNSEL
James Birch
V.P., INTERNATIONAL FILM RELATIONS
Peter Dobson
SENIOR V.P., ARCHITECTURE & CONSTRUCTION
Ira Stiegler

Number of Theatres (Australia): 30
Number of Screens (Australia): 318

ASSOCIATIONS AND ORGANIZATIONS

AUSTRALIAN CINEMATOGRAPHERS SOCIETY
42 Sawyer Lane, Artarmon NSW 2064, P.O. Box 207,
Cammeray, NSW 2062. FAX: (612) 8572 5370.
email: info@cinematographer.org.au
www.cinematographer.org.au
PRESIDENT
Ted Rayment
VICE PRESIDENT
Milton Ingerson

AUSTRALIAN FILM INSTITUTE
49 Eastern Rd. South, Melbourne 3205, Victoria.
TEL: (613) 9696 1844. FAX: (613) 9696 7972.
email: info@afi.org.au www.afi.org.au
CHAIRMAN
Denny Lawrence

AUSTRALIAN FILM, TELEVISION & RADIO SCHOOL
P.O. Box 126, North Ryde, NSW 2113. TEL: (612) 9805 6611.
FAX: (612) 9805 1275. email: info_nsw@aftrs.edu.au
www.aftrs.edu.au
DIRECTOR
Malcolm Long - malcolml@aftrs.edu.au
HEAD OF CINEMATOGRAPHY
Jan Kenny - jank@aftrs.edu.au

HEAD OF PRODUCING
Marian Macgowan
HEAD OF MARKETING
Andrea Hammond - andreah@aftrs.edu.au
SALES & DISTIBUTION MANAGER
Ruth Saunders

AUSTRALIAN SCREEN DIRECTORS ASSOCIATION (ASDA)
P.O. Box 211, Rozelle, NSW 2039. TEL: (612) 9555 7045.
FAX: (612) 9555 7086. www.asdafilm.org.au
EXECUTIVE DIRECTOR
Richard Harris
GENERAL MANAGER
Helen Martin - asda_admin@asdafilm.org.au
PRESIDENT
Donald Crombie

FILM & TELEVISION INSTITUTE, WA, INC (FTI)
92 Adelaide St., Fremantle WA 6160. TEL: (618) 9431 6700.
FAX: (618) 9335 1283. email: fti@fti.asn.au www.fti.asn.au
CEO
Graeme Sward - graemes@fti.asn.au
GENERAL MANAGER
Murray Reynish - murrayr@fti.asn.au
CHAIRPERSON
Lisa Bradock

FILM AUSTRALIA
101 Eton Rd., Lindfield, NSW 2070, Level 12.
TEL: (612) 9413 8777. FAX: (612) 9416 5672.
www.filmaust.com.au
CHAIRMAN
Robert Fisher
CEO
Daryl Karp

NEW SOUTH WALES FILM & TELEVISION OFFICE)
Level 13, 227 Elizabeth St. Sydney, NSW 2000.
TEL: (612) 9264 6400. FAX: (612) 9264 4388.
email: fto@fto.nsw.gov.au www.fto.nsw.gov.au/

MEDIA ENTERTAINMENT AND ARTS ALLIANCE (MEAA)
(Union for those in the media, entertainment and arts industries)
245 Chalmers St., Redfern, NSW 2016. TEL: (612) 9333 0999.
FAX: (612) 9333 0933. www.alliance.org.au

METRO SCREEN
(Centre for independent screen production, training and exhibition)
Sydney Film Centre - Paddington Town Hall, Corner of Oatley Road and Oxford St, P.O. Box 299, Paddington, Sydney. NSW 2021. TEL: (612) 9361 5318. FAX: (612) 9361 5320.
email: metro@metroscreen.org.au www.metroscreen.com.au

NEW SOUTH WALES FILM & TV OFFICE
Level 7, 157 Liverpool St., Sydney, NSW 2000.
TEL: (612) 9264 6400. FAX: (612) 9264 4388.
email: fto@fto.nsw.gov.au www.ftosyd.nsw.gov.au
CHAIRMAN
Shane Simpson
CEO
Jane SMith

PACIFIC FILM & TELEVISION COMMISSION
Level 16, 111 George St., Brisbane, QLD 4000.
TEL: (617) 3224 4114. FAX: (617) 9264 6717.
www.pftc.com.au

SCREEN PRODUCERS ASSOCIATION OF AUSTRALIA (SPAA)
(Industry association of the Australian independent film, TV and commercials production industry) www.spaa.org.au
EXECUTIVE DIRECTOR
Geoff Brown

SCREEN WEST
Western Australian Film & TV, Level 7, Law Chambers, 573 Hay St. Perth, WA 6000. TEL: (618) 9224 7340.
FAX: (618) 9224 7341. email: info@screenwest.com.au
www.screenwest.com.au
CEO
Tania Chambers
COMMUNICATIONS OFFICER
Jody Nunn
CHAIRPERSON
Debra Shorter

THE SOUTH AUSTRALIAN FILM CORPORATION
3 Butler Dr. Hendon Common, Hendon, SA 5014.
TEL: (618)-8348-9300. FAX: (618)-8347-0385.
email: safilm@safilm.com.au www.safilm.com.au/

VILLAGE ROADSHOW
206 Bourke St. Melbourne, VIC 3000. TEL: (613) 96 67 66 66.
FAX: (613) 96 39 15 40. www.villageroadshow.com.au

AUSTRIA

Capital: Vienna
Population: 8,214,160 (July 2010 est.)
Area: 83,858 sq.km.
Source: CIA World Factbook
Country Code: at

DISTRIBUTORS AND PRODUCERS

ABC FILMS
P.O. Box 457, Friedrichgasse 24, A-8010 Graz.
TEL: (43 676) 414 44 11. FAX: (43 316) 82 11 86 11.
email: ngri@eunet.at
CONTACT
Nikos Grigoriadis

AICHHOLZER FILM PRODUCTION
Mariahilfer Straße 58, A-1070 Vienna. TEL: (43 1) 523 40 81.
FAX: (43 1) 526 34 58. email: office@aifilm.at www.aifilm.com
CONTACT
Josef Aichholzer

ALLEGRO FILM
Krummgasse 1A, Wien A-1030. TEL: (431) 712 5036.
FAX: (431) 712 5036 20. email: office@allegrofilm.at
www.allegrofilm.at

AMF ADI MAYER'S FILM
Lindengasse 65, Wien A-1070. TEL: (431) 523 4788.
FAX: (431) 523 4788 40. email: office@amf.at www.amf.at
CONTACT
Philip Morawietz

AMOUR FOU FILM
Lindengasse 32, Wien A-1070. TEL: (431) 994 99110.
FAX: (431) 994 99 11 20. www.amourfou.at

AUSTRIA FILMMAKERS CO-OPERATIVE
Wahringer Strasse 59, Vienna A-1090. TEL: (431) 408 7627.
FAX: (431) 408 3871.

BUENA VISTA INTERNATIONAL (BVI)
Hermannagasse 18, Vienna A-1071. TEL: (431) 526 9467.
FAX: (431) 526 9468.
CONTACT
M. Ferdinand Morawitz

CENTFOX FILM GMBH
Neubaugasse 35, Vienna A-1070. TEL: (431) 932 2629.
FAX: (431) 526 7297.

CINE CARTOON
Schottenfeldgasse 14, Wien A-1070. TEL: (431) 524 0655.
FAX: (431) 524 9310 20. email: office@cinecartoon.com
www.cinecartoon.com

CINECOOP FILM
Mariahilferstr. 1b, Wien A-1060. TEL: (431) 587 9138.
FAX: (431) 587 6735 20. email: office@cinecoop.at
www.cinecoop.at

CINECRAFT FILM, TV & VIDEOPRODUKTION GESMBH
Endresstrasse 18, Vienna A-1230. TEL: (431) 889 0799.
FAX: (431) 889 0799 10. email: office@cinecraft.at
www.cinecraft.at
CONTACT
Felix R. Giuliani

CINEDOC
Hauslabgasse 6-10/1, Wien A-1050. TEL: (431) 545 4645.
FAX: (431) 545 4645 90. email: office@cinedoc.at
www.cinedoc.at

CINE-MERCURY FILM
Ameisgasse 49-51/1A, Wien A-1140. TEL: (431) 924 2420.
FAX: (431) 912 3060. email: cine-mercury@chello.at

CINESTAR
Opernring 19, Vienna A-1010. TEL: (431) 587 8406.
FAX: (431) 587 5711.

COLUMBIA TRISTAR
Laxenburgerstrasse 254, Vienna A-1230. TEL: (431) 597 1515.
FAX: (431) 597 1516. www.columbiatristar.at

CONSTANTIN FILM
Siebensterngasse 37, Vienna A-1070. TEL: (431) 521 2850.
FAX: (431) 521 2860.

CULT-FILM
Spittelberggasse 3/7, Wien A-1070. TEL: (431) 526 0006.
FAX: (431) 526 0006. email: office@cultfilm.at
www.cultfilm.com

CZERNY FILM
Lorgasse 17, Vienna A-1150. TEL: (431) 982 0249.
FAX: (431) 982 4081.

DEGU FILM
Konstanze Webergasse 3, Salzburg A-5020.
TEL: (43662) 831 992. FAX: (43662) 822 688.
email: office@degufilm.at
MANAGING DIRECTOR
Guuter Degu

DOR FILM PRODUCTION
Bergsteiggasse 36, Wien A-1170. TEL: (431) 427 1011.
FAX: (431) 427 1050. email: office@dor-film.at
www.dor-film.at

EINHORN FILM
Unterfeld Strasse 29, P.O. Box 158, Bludenz A-6700.
TEL: (4355) 526 7034. FAX: (4355) 526 36746.
email: info@einhorn-film.at www.einhorn-film.at

EPO FILM PRODUCTIONS
Edelsinn Strasse 58, Vienna A-1120. TEL: (431) 812 3718.
FAX: (431) 812 3718.

EXTRA FILM
Grosse Neugasse 44/24, Vienna A-1040. TEL: (431) 581 7896.
FAX: (431) 587 2743. email: extrafilm@chello.at
www.extrafilm.at

FILMHAUS STOBERGASSE
Stobergasse 11-15, Vienna A-1050. TEL: (431) 545 3244.
FAX: (431) 545 3244.

FILMLADEN
Mariahilferstrasse 58, Vienna A-1070. TEL: (431) 523 4362.
FAX: (431) 526 4749. email: office@filmladen.at
www.filmladen.at

FISCHER FILM
Neustiftgasse 32-34, A-1070 Vienna.
TEL: (43 1) 524 74 25. FAX: (43 1) 524 74 25-3.
email: info@fischerfilm.com www.fischerfilm.com
CONTACT
Markus Fischer

FLEUR FILM
Stadlgasse 2, Enns A-4470. TEL: (431) 7223 2670.
FAX: (431) 7223 2406.
CONTACT
Horst Röber

GOLDEN GIRLS FILM PRODUCTION
Fockygasse 33/1, A-1120 Vienna. TEL: (43 1) 81 05 636.
FAX: (43 1) 81 05 949. email: office@goldengirls.at
www.goldengirls.at

INTERSPOT FILM GES.M.B.H.
Walter-Jurmann-Gasse 4, Wien A-1230. TEL: (431) 80 120.
FAX: (431) 801 20 222. email: headoffice@interspot.at
www.interspot.at
OWNER/MANAGER
Rudolf Klingohr

JUPITER FILM
Hauptplatz 64, A-3040 Neulengbach. TEL: (43 2772) 54001.
FAX: (43 2772) 540014. email: office@jupiter-film.at
www.jupiter-film.at

LISA-FILM
Seilerstatte 13. ViennaA-1010. TEL: (430)1/513 11 15.
FAX: (430)1/513 07 35. email: produktion@lisafilm.at
http://www.lisafilm.at/

LOTUS FILM
A-1150 Wien, Johnstrasse 83, Wien A-1150. TEL: (431) 786 3387.
FAX: (431) 786 3387 11. email: office@lotus-film.co.at
www.lotus-film.co.at
PRODUCER
Erich Lackner

MEDIA EUROPA
Alser Straße 30/1/66, A-1090 Vienna. TEL/FAX: (43 1) 581 61 67.
email: baker@chello.at www.mediaeuropa.com

MISCHIEF FILMS
Goethegasse 1, A-1010 Vienna. TEL: (43 1) 585 23 24 23.
FAX: (43 1) 585 23 24 22. email: office@mischief-film.com
www.mischief-films.com

MUNGO FILM
Larochegasse 13, Wien A-1130. TEL: (431) 876 3600.
FAX: (431) 876 3646. email: mungo-film@utanet.at

NANOOK FILM
Kleine Neugasse 4/1, A-1040 Vienna. TEL/FAX: (43 1) 961 82 60.
email: mail@nanookfilm.com www.nanookfilm.com

NAVIGATOR FILM
Schottenfeldgasse 14, A-1070 Vienna. TEL: (43 1) 524 97 77.
FAX: (43 1) 524 97 77-20. email: office@navigatorfilm.at
www.navigatorfilm.at

NOVOTNY & NOVOTNY PRODUCTION
Weimarerstrasse 22, Wien A-1180. TEL/FAX: (431) 478 7170 20.
email: office@novotnyfilm.at www.novotnyfilm.at
CONTACT
Franz Novotny

PAMMER FILM
Lerchenfelderstrasse 136, Vienna A-1080. TEL: (431) 408 16 300.
FAX: (431) 408 9243. email: tvesely@ppmfilm.com
www.ppmfilm.com

POLYFILM VERLEIH
Margaretenstrasse 78, Vienna A-1050. TEL: (431) 581 3900 20.
FAX: (431) 581 3900 39. email: polyfilm@polyfilm.at
www.polyfilm.at
CONTACT
Hans Koenig

SATEL FILM
A-1040 Wien, Wiedner Hauptstrasse 68, Wien A-1040.
TEL: (431) 558 72 100. FAX: (431) 588 72 106.
email: office@satel.at www.satel.at
CEO
Michael von Wolkenstein
EXECUTIVE DIRECTOR
Dr. Sonja Hofmann

SIXPACK FILM
Neubaugasse 45/13 PO Box 197 ViennaA-1071.
TEL: (431).526.09.90.0. FAX: (431).526.09.92.
email: office@sixpackfilm.com www.sixpackfilm.com

SK FILM
Salzachstrasse 15A, Salzburg A-5026. TEL: (43662) 625 969.
FAX: (43662) 625 969 22. email: sk.film@aon.at

STADKINO FILMVERLEIH
Spittelberggasse 3, Vienna A-1070. TEL: (431) 522 4814.
FAX: (431) 522 4815. email: stadkino@nextra.at
DIRECTOR
Franz Schwartz

STAR FILM GMBH
Strasswalchen, Irrsdorf 123, Wien A-5204. TEL: (43) 6215 6463 60.
FAX: (43) 6215 6463 4. email: mail@star-film.com
www.star-film.com
PRESIDENT
Reinhard Schwabenitzky

STUDIO WEST
Franz-Josef-Straße 20, A-5020 Salzburg.
TEL: (43 662) 876 450. FAX: (43 662) 876 4504.
email: contact@studio-west.net www.studio-west.net
CONTACT
Karin Helml

TERRA FILM
Lienfeldergasse 39, A-1160 Vienna. TEL: (43 1) 484 11 010.
FAX: (43 1) 484 11 0127. email: office@terrafilm.at
www.terrafilm.at
CONTACT
Norbert Blecha

TEAM FILM PRODUCTION
Waaggasse 5, Vienna A-1040. TEL: (431) 587 2542 0.
FAX: (431) 587 2542 27. email: office@teamfilm.at

TOP FILM
Mariahilferstrasse 115, Wien 1060. TEL: (431) 595 3295.
FAX: (431) 595 3295 95.

TTV FILM
Haus 71, Lans. A-6072. TEL: (43 512) 37 74 78.
FAX: (43 512) 37 74 784. email: ttv.film@christianberger.at
www.christianberger.at

VENTO FILM
Leitermayergasse 33/20, A-1180 Vienna.
TEL/FAX: (43 1) 406 03 92. email: contact@ventofilm.com
www.ventofilm.com

UNITED INTERNATIONAL PICTURES
Gesellschaft m.b.H., Neubaugasse 1, Postfach 280,
Vienna A-1071. TEL: 43-1-523 4631. FAX: 43-1-526 7548.
MANAGER
Mark Taylor

WARNER BROS.
Zieglergasse 10, Vienna A-1072. TEL: (431) 523 8626.
FAX: (431) 523 8626 31.

WEGA FILM
Hagelingasse 13, Vienna A-1140. TEL: (431) 982 5742.
email: wegafilm@aon.at www.wegafilm.com

EXHIBITORS

VILLAGE ROADSHOW, LTD.

(For complete listing see Australian branch)
206 Bourke St., Melbourne, VIC, 3000. TEL: (613) 9667 6666.
FAX: (613) 9639 1540.

Number of Theatres: 2
Number of Screens: 18

UNITED CINEMAS INTERNATIONAL

UCI KINOWELT Millennium City, Am Handelskai, Wien 1200.
TEL: (431) 33 760 200. FAX: (431) 33 760 100.
email: Sibral.U@uci-kinowelt.de www.uci-kinowelt.at

Number of Theatres (Austria): 3
Number of Screens (Austria): 38

ASSOCIATIONS & ORGANIZATIONS

ASIFA-AUSTRIA (INTERNATIONAL ANIMATED FILM ASSOCIATION)

Dapontegasse 9/a, Vienna A-1030. TEL/FAX: (431) 714 4082.
email: austria@asifa.net www.asifa.net/austria
CONTACT
Thomas Renoldner

ASSOCIATION OF AUSTRIAN ACTORS

Spittelberggasse 3, Vienna A-1070. TEL/FAX: (431) 522 32 34.
email: contact@austrian-actors.com www.austrian-actors.com
CONTACTS
Fritz von Friedl, Konstanze Breitebner

ASSOCIATION OF AUSTRIAN FILM DIRECTORS

c/o Checkpointmedia Multimediaproduktionen AG, Im Haus der Musik, Seilerstätte 30, Vienna A-1010. TEL: (431) 5130 0000.
FAX: (431) 5130 000 11.
CONTACT
Virgil Widrich

ASSOCIATION OF AUSTRIAN FILM PRODUCERS (AAFP)

Filmstadt Wien, Speisingerstrasse 121, Wien A-1230.
TEL: (431) 888 9622. FAX: (431) 879 339.
email: aafp@austrian-film.com www.austrian-film.com
PRESIDENT
Prof. Dkfm. Peter Mayer
VICE PRESIDENT
Andreas Ebhart

ASSOCIATION OF DISTRIBUTORS

Wiener Hauptstrasse 63, P.O. Box 327, Vienna A-1045.
TEL: (431) 50105 3011. FAX: (431) 50206 376.

AUSTRIAN AMERICAN FILM ASSOCIATION (AAFA)

TEL: (1 719) 26 23 562. FAX: (1 719) 26 23 146. (USA)
email: belvederefilm@yahoo.com web.uccs.edu/aafa/aafa.htm

AUSTRIAN ASSOCIATION OF CINEMATOGRAPHERS

Spittelberggasse 3, Vienna A-1070. TEL: (431) 869 4936.
FAX: (431) 869 5824. email: office@aacamera.org
www.aacamera.org
CONTACT
Kurt Brazda

AUSTRIAN FILM DESIGNERS ASSOCIATION

Stiftgasse 6, 1070 Vienna. TEL/FAX: (43 1) 526 97 41.
email: office@austrianfilm-designers.com
www.austrianfilm-designers.com
CONTACT
Verband österreichischer Filmausstatter (VÖF)

AUSTRIAN DIRECTORS' ASSOCIATION (ADA)

Bösendorferstrasse 4, Vienna A-1010. TEL: (431) 802 7628.
FAX: (431) 803 4956. email: office@directors.at
www.directors.at

ASSOCIATION OF INDEPENDENT CINEMA OPERATORS

Panoramagasse 16, Grax A-8010. TEL: (431) 637 4282.
email: kino@aon.at www.film.co.at

AUSTRIAN FILM COMMISSION (AFC)

Stiftgasse 6, Wien A-1070. TEL: (431) 526 33 230.
FAX: (431) 526 68 01. email: office@afc.at www.afc.at
MANAGING DIRECTOR
Martin Schweighofer - ms@afc.at
DIRECTOR OF INFORMATION
Maria Erler

AUSTRIAN FILM CRITICS' GUILD

Observer-Haus, Lessinggasse 21, Vienna A-1020.
TEL: (431) 213 220. FAX: (431) 213 22 200.
email: kontakt@afcg.at www.afcg.at
CONTACT
Christoph Huber, Sonia Laszlo

AUSTRIAN FILM DESIGNERS ASSOCIATION

Spittelberggasse 3, Vienna 1070. TEL/FAX: (431) 526 9741.
email: austrianfilmdesigners@hotmail.com
www.austrianfilm-designers.com

MANAGER
Florian Reichmann

AUSTRIAN SOCIETY OF SOUND ENGINEERS

Natterergasse 4, Laxenburg A-2361. TEL/FAX: (43) 2236 71 307.
email: mail@oetmv.at www.oetmv.at
CONTACT
Prof. Ing. Hellmut Gottwald

FEDERATION OF FILM TRADE ASSOCIATIONS

Spittelberggasse 3, Vienna A-1070. TEL/FAX: (431) 526 9741.
email: dachverbandfilm@aon.at www.filmschaffende.at
PRESIDENT
Andreas Gruber

NATIONAL TOURIST OFFICE

Margaretenstrasse 1, Vienna A-1040. TEL: (431) 588 660.
FAX: (431) 588 660.

SCREENWRITERS' GUILD AUSTRIA

Stiftgasse 6, A-1070 Vienna. TEL: (43 1) 526 85 03 1.
FAX: (43 1) 526 85 03 550. email: verband@drehbuchforum.at
www.drehbuchforum.at

BAHAMAS

Capital: Nassau
Population: 310,426 (July 2010 est.)
Area: 13,940 sq. km.
Source: CIA World Factbook
Country Code: bs

EXHIBITORS

GALAXY PRODUCTIONS

4 Ketch Close, P.O. Box 40952 Freeport. TEL: (242) 373 4756.

RND CINEMAS LIMITED

P.O. Box EE-17203, Nassau, Bahamas. TEL: (242) 394 6456.
FAX: (242) 394 6457.
PRESIDENT
A. Brent Dean
VICE PRESIDENT
Jerome K. Fitzgerald

ASSOCIATIONS AND ORGANIZATIONS

BAHAMAS FILM COMMISSION

P.O. Box N-3701 Nassau, Bahamas. TEL: (242) 322 4374.
FAX: (242) 356 5904. email: aarcher@bahamas.com
www.bahamasfilm.com

BELGIUM

Capital: Brussels
Population: 10,423,493 (July 2010 est.)
Area: 30,510 sq. km.
Source: CIA World Factbook
Country Code: be

DISTRIBUTORS AND PRODUCERS

ABC DISTRIBUTION

Kaasstraat 4, Antwerpen 2000. TEL: (323) 231 0931.
FAX: (323) 231 0934.
CONTACT
M. Werner Lanneau

ALCYON FILMS

89 Rue de Lorrian, Brussels B-1210. TEL: (322) 426 7981.
FAX: (322) 426 7981.

ALTERNATIVE FILMS

Colignonplein, 10, Brussels 1030. TEL: 32-2-242-1930.
FAX: 32-2-242-0180.
DIRECTOR
Michael Luel

ARIZONA

Grand Rue au Bois, 120, Brussels 1030. TEL: (322) 245.0014.
FAX: (322) 245.5523. email@arizona.be

ATREMIS PRODUCTIONS

60 Rue Gallait. Bruxelles1060. TEL: (322) 216 23 24.
FAX: (322) 216 20 13. email: info@artemisproductions.com
http://www.artemisproductions.com

BE-FILMS

363 av. Louise. BrusselsB-1050.
TEL: (322) 649 66 00. FAX: (322) 649 47 44.
email: info@be-films.com http://www.be-films.com

BEECK TURTLE

Felix Vandenboschstraat 27, Lennik B-1750.
TEL: (322) 582 8318. FAX: (322) 582 8318.

BENELUX FILM DISTRIBUTION
Handelsdokcenter. Stapelplein 70, B302 GentB - 9000.
TEL: (320) 9 235 40 30. FAX: (320) 9 235 40 29.
email: belgie@bfdfilm www.bfdfilm.com

BELGA FILMS
1 Ave. Ariane, Brussels 1200. TEL: (322) 778 6590.
FAX: (322) 778 6743.

BRUSSELS AVE
Rue des Vistandines 1/48, Brussels B-1000.
TEL: (322) 511 9156. FAX: (322) 511 8139.
www.brussels-ave.com
CEO
Jochen Girsch

BUENA VISTA INTERNATIONAL
Chausee Romaine, 468 Romeinsesteenweg, 1853
Grimbergen, Brussels. TEL: (322) 263 1700.
FAX: (322) 263 1797.

CINEART - CINELIBRE
Chaussee de Haecht 270 Bruxelles 1030. TEL: (322) 245 8700.
FAX: (322) 216 2575. www.cineart.be
CONTACT
Elaine DuBois

COLUMBIA TRISTAR
10 rue de Genève, Evere 1140. TEL: (322) 702 3511.
FAX: (322) 702 3515.

ELIZA FILMS
Rue Galterie Saint-Jean 18, Tournai 7500.
TEL: (326) 984 3838. FAX: (326) 984 2433.

FLANDERS IMAGE
Handelskaai 18 Bus. 2, Brussels 1000. TEL: (322) 226 0630.
FAX: (322) 219 1936. email: info@flanders-image.com
www.flanders-image.com

INDEPENDENT FILM DISTRIBUTION
Generaal de Wittelaan 17, Mechelen 2800.
TEL: (321) 521 7253. FAX: (321) 529 4859.

I-SCREEN
Rue Léon Cuissez, 19, Brussels 1050. TEL: (322) 639.8500.
FAX: (322) 639.8510. email: i-screen@brutele.be
www.i-screen.be
CONTACT
Francis de Laveleye

KEY LINE
Ave. Sleeckx, 28/32, Brussels 1030. TEL: (322) 245.6450.
FAX: (322) 245.6740. email: christine@keylinefilm.be
www.keylinefilm.be
CONTACT
Christine Mathieu

KINEPOLIS FILM DISTRIBUTION
9 Blvd. du Centenaire, B 1020 Brussels. TEL: (322) 474 2731.
FAX: (322) 474 2736. www.kinepolis.com

LES FILMS DE L'ELYCEE
7 Rue de Pracelere B-1050 Bruxelles. TEL: (322) 644 0008.
FAX: (322) 644 3897.

LOVO FILMS
Rue Général Tombeur 71, Brussels 1040. TEL: (322) 735 2026.
FAX: (322) 735 1640. email: eric@lovo.be www.lovo.be
CONTACTS
Eric Stinglehanber, François Mercier

NORD FILMS
Ruelle de la Grande Garde B-7500 Tournai. TEL: (326) 984 3838.

NWAVE PICTURES
Rue des Alliés, 282, Brussels 1190, Belgium.
TEL: (322) 347 6319. FAX: (322) 347 2454.
www.nwave.com/

PARADISO ENTERTAINMENT
Poverstraat 82, Relegem-Asse 1731. TEL: (332) 461 0555.
FAX: (332) 461 0822. email: info@paradiso.be
www.paradiso.de

POLYGRAM-INDEPENDENT
Doornveld, bus 42, Zellik 1731. TEL: (322) 463 1130.
FAX: (322) 466 9460.
CONTACT
Marc Punt

PAULINE PICTURES
Rue Berkendael 159 Brussells. TEL: (322) 347 5710.
FAX: (322) 347 2462.

PROGRES FILMS
243 Rue Royale, Brussels B-1210. TEL: (322) 218 0960.
FAX: (322) 218 4354. email: progresfilm@club.innet.be

UNITED INTERNATIONAL PICTURES
288 Rue Royale, Brussels B-1210. TEL: (322) 218 5206.
FAX: (322) 218 7933.

WARNER BROS. BELGIUM
42 Blvd. Brand Whitlock, Brussels B-1200. TEL: (322) 735 4242.
FAX: (322) 735 4919.

ZABRISKIE FILMS
Ave. Général de Gaulle 40, Brussels 1000. TEL: (322) 647 5100.
FAX: (322) 640 0241. www.zabriskiefilms.com
DIRECTOR
Michel Perin - michel@zabriskiefilms.com

EXHIBITORS

FED DES CINEMAS DE BELGIQUE
Av. L. Mommaertslaan 10-12, B-1140, Brussels.
TEL: (322) 218 1455. FAX: (322) 217 2372.
PRESIDENT
Mrs. Claeys-Vereecke
SECRETARY/GENERAL
Guy Morlion

KINEPOLIS GROUP H.V.
Eeuwfeestlaan 20 Brussels 1020. TEL: (32) 2 47 4 26 00.
FAX: (32) 2 47 2 26 06. www.kinepolis.com
CEO
Florent Gijbels
MANAGING DIRECTOR
L. Baelen

UGC BELGIQUE
Av. De La Toison D'or 8, Brussels, B-1050. TEL: (322) 289 7100.
FAX: (322) 289 7101.
GENERAL MANAGER
Andre Harvie

Number of Theatres: 4
Number of Screens: 56

UNITED INTERNATIONAL PICTURES & CO. S.N.C
Rue Royale 288, Brussels B1210.
TEL: 32-2-218 5206. FAX: 32-2-218 7933.
MANAGER
Jean-Paul Bertin

UTOPOLIS BELGIUM NV
Spuibeekstraat 5, Mechelen 2080. TEL: (321) 555 7733.
FAX: (321) 555 8182. email: belgium@utopolis.com
www.utopolis.be
OPERATIONS MANAGER
Stijn Vanspauwen
MARKETING MANAGER
Tanja Piessens

Number of Theatres: 4

ASSOCIATIONS & ORGANIZATIONS

APEC
Association for the Promotion of Belgian Cinema in Education,
73 Ave. de Coccinelles, Brussels B-1170. TEL: (322) 672 9459.

ASSOCIATION OF DIRECTORS AND PRODUCERS
109 Rue du Fort, Brussels B-1060. TEL: (322) 534 3152.
FAX: (322) 534 7637.

ASSOCIATION OF FILM DISTRIBUTORS
18 Chaussée de Wavre, Brussels, 1050. TEL: (322) 513 9442.
FAX: (322) 513 4738.

BELGIAN SOCIETY OF CINEMATOGRAPHERS (SBC)
c/o M. Houssiau, 134, Ave. Van Becelaere, Brussels 1170.
TEL: (322) 673 9003. FAX: (322) 675 2477.

ROYALE FILM ARCHIVE
23 Rue Ravenstein, Brussels B-1000. TEL: (322) 507 8370.
FAX: (322) 513 1272. email:filmarchive@ledonx.be

FEDERATION DES CINEMAS DE BELGIQUE
Rue Royale 241, Brussels B-1210. TEL: (322) 218 1455.
FAX: (322) 217 2372. email: fcb@euronet.be
fcb2@euronet.be
PRESIDENT
Mrs. Claeys-Vereecke
SECRETARY GENERAL
Guy Morlion

BERMUDA

Capital: Hamilton
Population: 68,265 (July 2010 est.)
Area: 53 sq.km.
Source: CIA World Factbook
Country Code: bm

EXHIBITORS

THE LIBERTY THEATRE
49 Union Square, Hamilton, HM 12, Bermuda.
TEL: (809) 292 7296. FAX: (809) 295 5667.
www.libertytheatre.bm
OWNER
Bermuda Industrial Union
CHAIRMAN & PRESIDENT
Derrick Burgess
GENERAL SECRETARY
Helena Burgess
TREASURER
Cecil Durham
MANAGER & FILM BUYER
Nelda L. Simons

BOLIVIA

Capital: Sucre
Population: 9,947,418 (July 2010 est.)
Area: 1,098,580 sq.km.
Source: CIA World Factbook
Country Code: bo

DISTRIBUTORS

MANFER FILMS S.R.L.
Ave. Montes 768, 4th Flr., Box 4709, La Paz.
TEL: (5912) 237 6834. FAX: (5912) 811 2922.
GENERAL MANAGER
Licnio Manay

WAZA FILMS
(Agent for UIP), Edificio Caraas-2do. piso, Avenida 16 de Julio No. 1456, Casilla 2613, La Paz.
TEL: (5912) 354 635. FAX: (5912) 333 805.
DIRECTOR
Walter A. Zalles Viana
MANAGER
Luis F. Zalles Arrieta

BRAZIL

Capital: Brasilia
Population: 201,103,330
Area: 8,511,965 sq. km.
Source: CIA World Factbook
Country Code: br

DISTRIBUTORS & PRODUCERS

C.E.F. REPRESENTACOES
(Agent for Columbia Tristar)
Rua Aarao Reis 538, S/206 Centro, 3012000-000 Belo Horizonte, Mias Gerais. TEL: (5531) 273 2093.

COLUMBIA TRISTAR
Av. Rio Branco, 277-Sobrejola 101-Centro, 20040-009 Rio de Janeiro. TEL: (5521) 524 0023. FAX: (5521) 262 1562.
BRANCH MANAGER
Jorge Correa

DISTRIBUIDORA DE FILMES WERMAR
Av. Farrapos, 146-2nd Fl. Room 21, Porto Alegre, Rio Grande do Sul. TEL: (5551) 226 5579. FAX: (5551) 228 6275.

EUROPA FILMES
Alameda Itapecuru, 320. Barueri. Sãa Paulo06454-080.
TEL: (5511)-4191-1777. FAX: (5511)-4195-2418.
email: mam@centroin.com.br http://www.europafilmes.com.br

FOX/WARNER BROS. FILM DO BRASIL
Calcada dos Cravos 141, Centro Commercial Alphaville, 06453-000 Barueri, Sao Paulo. TEL: (5511) 7296 1400.
FAX: (5511) 7295 1143.

GRUPO NOVO DE CINEMA E TV
Rue Capitao Salomao, 42 -Humaita, Rio de Janiero 22271-040. TEL: (5521) 2539 1538. FAX: (5521) 2266 3637.
email: international@gnctv.com.br www.braziliancinema.com
GENERAL DIRECTOR
Tarcisio Vidigal

GRUPO NOVO DE CINEMA E TV
Rue Capitao Salomao, 42 -Humaita, Rio de Janiero 22271-040. TEL: (5521) 2539 1538. FAX: (5521) 2266 3637.

SETIMA ARTE SERVICOS
Av. Barbosa Lima, 149 S/102, Centro, 50030-330. Recife-Pernambuco. TEL: (5581) 224 3732.

UNITED INTERNATIONAL PICTURES
Caixa Postal 179 ZC-00, Rio de Janeiro. TEL: (5511) 210 2400.
FAX: (5511) 220 9491.
GENERAL MANAGER
Cesar Silva

WARNER BROS. (SOUTH)
Rua Senador Dantas 19-10 Andar, 20031-200 Rio de Janiero.
TEL: (5521) 282 1322. FAX: (5521) 262 0195.
BRANCH MANAGER
Cesar Barata

EXHIBITORS

CINEMARK
Av. Dr. Chucri Zaidan, 920, Flr. 2 - Torre II, 04583-110, Sao Paulo. TEL: (5511) 3048 7048. FAX: (5511) 3048 7047.
www.cinemark.com.br
GENERAL MANAGER
Martin Alvarez

Number of Theatres: 19
Number of Screens: 180

PLAYARTE CINEMAS
Avenida Republica do Libano, 2155-04501-003, Sao Paulo.
TEL: (5511) 575 6996. www.playarte.com.br

UCI BRAZIL
Rua Araujo Porto Alegre, 71 4o, Andar, Rio de Janeiro 20030-010. TEL: (5521) 532 3291.
MANAGING DIRECTOR
Jose Carlos Oliveira

Number of Theatres: 9
Number of Screens: 99

CHILE

Capital: Santiago
Population: 16,746,491 (July 2010 est.)
Area: 756,950 sq.km.
Source: CIA World Factbook
Country Code: cl

DISTRIBUTORS AND PRODUCERS

SILVIO CAIOZZI PRODUCTIONS
Federico Froebel 1755, Santiago. TEL: (562) 209 9031.
FAX: (562) 204 8988.
PRESIDENT
Silvio Caiozzi

BAZUCA FILMS
Av. Ossa 655 Piso 4. La Reina, Santiago 753-0258.
TEL: (562)-756-0425. FAX: (562)-756-0427
email: chansen@bfdistribution.cl http://www.bfdistribution.cl

CHILE INC./WARNER BROS., (SOUTH) INC.
(Columbia Pictures, Tri-Star, Hollywood Pictures, Touchstone Pictures, Orion)
Chilefilms, La Capitania 1200, Las Condes, Santiago.
TEL: (562) 220 3086.

CHILEFILMS S.A.
Manquehue Sur 1165, Las Condes. TEL: (562) 212 8729.
FAX: (562) 212 5766. www.chilefilms.cl
CONTACT
Gonzalo Marambio - gmarambio@chilefilms.cl

CINE CHILE S. A.
(Umbrella organization of the Association of Producers)
Huerfanos 878, Ste. 918, Santiago. TEL: (562) 633 3948.
FAX: (562) 632 5342.

CONATE
Ave. Manquehue Sur 1165, Las Condes, Santiago.
TEL: (562) 220 3086. FAX: (562) 211 9826. www.conate.net
PUBLIC RELATIONS DIRECTOR
Darvelio Méndez - dmendez@conate.net

CUTTER FILMS S.A.
Avenida Chile-España 717, Ñuñoa. TEL: (562) 209 0373.
FAX: (562) 223 1886. email: post@cutterfilms.cl
www.cutterfilms.cl
CONTACT
Manuel Yáñez

ARTHUR EHRLICH
(Rep. for Twentieth Century Fox)
Huerfanos 786, Ste. 210, Santiago. TEL: (562) 633 2503.
FAX: (562) 639 7921.

FILMOCENTRO
Gerona 3450, Santiago. TEL: (562) 225 2203.
FAX: (562) 209 1671.
PRODUCER
Eduardo Larrain

JIRAFA PRODUCCIONES
Pérez Rosales 787 Oficina A, Valdivia. TEL: (56 63) 21 35 56.
FAX: (56 63) 21 35 56. email: bruno@jirafa.cl www.jirafa.cl

KAOS PRODUCCIONES R.M.
Málaga 888, of. 31, Las Condes. TEL: (562) 228 0824.

FAX: (562) 952 5261. email: info@kaosproducciones.cl
www.kaosproducciones.cl
CONTACT
Gilberto Villarroel

PROCINE
Av. Kennedy 5118, Piso 5, Las Condes. TEL: (562) 247 8500.
FAX: (562) 247 8500. email: andres@procine.cl
www.procine.cl
CONTACT
Andrés Silva

ROOS FILM S.A.
Ricardo Matte Pérez 0216, Providencia, Santiago.
TEL: (562) 341 1188. FAX: (562) 341 1199.
email: info@roosfilm.com www.roosfilm.com

TPO - THE PRODUCTION OFFICE / H&B PRODUCTIONS, LTDA
Los Talaveras 30, Nunoa, Santiago. TEL: (562) 341 1702.
FAX: (562) 341 4854. email: office@tpochile.com
www.tpochile.com
PRODUCER
Juan Esteban Harrington - juan@tpochile.com

TWIST FILMS
Arrayan 2724, Providencia, Santiago. TEL: (562) 470 9210.
FAX: (562) 470 9167. www.twistfilms.net

UNITED INTERNATIONAL PICTURES
Huerfanos 786, Office 808, Casilla 3462, Santiago.
TEL: (562) 633 0172. FAX: (562) 633 0562.
MANAGER
Rodrigo Kostner

EXHIBITORS

CINEMARK
Av. Kennedy 9001, Local 3092, Las Condes, Santiago.
TEL: (562) 299 3000. FAX: (562) 299 3001.
email: contactochile@cinemark.com www.cinemark.cl

Number of Theatres: 12
Number of Screens: 95

CONATE
La Capitania 1200, Santiago. TEL: (562) 220 3086.
FAX: (562) 211 9826. www.conate.net
PUBLIC RELATIONS DIRECTOR
Darvelio Méndez - dmendez@conate.net

Number of Screens: 39

HOYTS CHILE
(See Australia listing for further details)
505-523 George St., GPO Box 110, Sydney, NSW 2001.
TEL: (612) 9273 7373. FAX: (612) 9273 7336.
www.hoyts.com.au

Roger de Flores #2736, Piso 6, Las Condes, Santiago.
www.cinehoyts.cl
CEO
Paul Johnson

Number of Theatres: 6

ASSOCIATIONS AND ORGANIZATIONS

ASSOC DE PRODUCTORES DE CINE Y TELEVISION
Federico Froebel 1755, Providencia, Santiago.
TEL/FAX: (562) 209 9031.

SIDARTE, SINDICATO DE ACTORES
Ernesto Pinto Lagarrigue 129, Recoleta, Santiago.
TEL: (562) 735 3761. FAX: (562) 735 3761.

CHINA

(Please see Hong Kong in a separate section below)
Capital: Beijing
Population: 1,330,141,295 (July 2010 est.)
Area: 9,596,960 sq. km.
Source: CIA World Factbook
Country Code: cn

DISTRIBUTORS AND PRODUCERS

CHINA FILM GROUP CORP
31 Xin De Jie, Xi Cheng District 100088 Beijing.
TEL: (86 10) 6226 8023. FAX: (86 10) 6203 4305.
email office@moviechina.com.cn
www.moviechina.com.cn
CONTACT
Yanping Liu

GINGER FILMS
505 Maolian Bldg., 1040 North Suzhou Creek Rd., Shanghai 200085. TEL: (86 21) 6309 0276. FAX: (86 21) 6324 8349.
www.gingerfilms.tv
EXECUTIVE PRODUCER
Xie Deping

GUNG-HO FILMS
25 Sha Jing Hutong, Dongcheng District, Beijing 100009.
TEL: (86 10) 6402 5974. FAX: (86 10) 6406 0596.
email: beijing@gunghofilms.com www.gunghofilms.com
FOUNDER - EXECUTIVE PRODUCER
Michael McDermott

INTERNATIONAL SERVICES B.V.
Suite E1, 22nd Flr., Jiu Shi Fu Xing Mansion, 918 Huai Hai Road Shanghai 200020. TEL: 86-21-6415-8157.
FAX: 86-21-6415-8157.
REPRESENTATIVE
Zhe Chen

MEDIA ASIA GROUP
24/F Cuaseway Bay Plaza 463-483 Lockart Rd., Hong Kong.
TEL: (852) 2314 4288. www.mediaasia.com

SONY PICTURES ENTERTAINMENT BEIJING
Ste. 1819, Beijing Asia Jinjiang Hotel, 8 Xinzhong Xi Je, Gongti Bei Lu, Beijing 100027. TEL: (861) 508 9869.
FAX: (861) 500 7335.

TRIBAL PRODUCTIONS ASIA
Beijing Office: TEL: (86 10) 6532 3672. FAX:(86 10) 853 22865.

Shanghai Office: TEL: (86 21) 2890 3183.
FAX: (86 10) 6101 0220. email: info@tribalproductionsasia.tv
www.tribalproductionsasia.tv

UIP INTERNATIONAL SERVICES B.V.
Suite E1, 22nd Flr., Jiu Shi Fu Xing Mansion, 918 Huai Hai Road, Shanghai 200020, China.
TEL: 86-21-6415-8818 ext 72229 or 72230.
FAX: 86-21-6415-8157.
REPRESENTATIVE
Zhe Chen

EXHIBITORS

BROADWAY CIRCUIT
(State of Operation: Hong Kong, China)
1212 Tower 2, Admiralty Centre, 18 Harcourt Rd., Hong Kong.
TEL: (85) 2 25 29 3898. FAX: (85) 2 25 29 5277.
email: info@cinema.com.hk www.cinema.com.hk
EXECUTIVE DIRECTOR
Lau Siu Man Tessa
PERSONNELL
Audrey Lee

CHINA FILM CINEMA INVESTMENT CO.
25 Xin Jie Kou Wai Du Jie, Hai Dan District, Beijing 100082.
TEL: (8610) 6225 4488 3901. FAX: (8610) 6225 8444.
GENERAL MANAGER
Xing Huibin

SHANGHAI UNITED CINEMA CIRCUIT
No. 322, Anfu Rd., Shanghai 200031.
TEL: 0086 21 64718068. FAX: 0086 21 64312958.
PRESIDENT
Ren Zhonglum
GENERAL MANAGER
Xu Xiaoping

GOLDEN HARVEST ENTERTAINMENT
16/F Peninsula Office Tower, 18 Middle Rd., Kowloon, Hong Kong. TEL: (852) 2352 8222. FAX: (852) 2353 5989.
www.goldenharvest.com
EXECUTIVE DIRECTOR
Fiona Chow
GENERAL MANAGER
Belinda Tang

Number of Theatres (China): 8
Number of Screens (China): 58

CHINA FILM STELLA CINE CIRCUIT
19/F Tower B, Eagle Plaza, No. 26 Xiaoyun Road, Chaoyang District 100016. TEL: 0086 10 84580055.
FAX: 0086 10 84580555.
CONTACT
Wang Hongyu

ASSOCIATIONS & ORGANIZATIONS

BEIJING NEW ALLIANCES CINEMA CO.
67 Beichizi Street, East District, Beijing 100006.
TEL: 0086 10 65598201. FAX: 0086 10 65276354.
www.beijingfilm.net
GENERAL MANAGER
Huang Qunfei
CONTACT
Han Chuanzheng

CHINA ASSIST
B705 International Apartment, No 26 Xibahe Xili Chaoyang District, Beijing 100028. TEL: (86 10) 6201 0110.
FAX: (86 10) 6204 6336. www.chinafilmassist.com
GENERAL MANAGER
Ms. Geng Ling - ling@chinafilmassist.com

CHINA FILM GROUP
31 Xin De Jie, Xi Cheng District, Beijing 100088.
TEL: (86 10) 6203 5305. FAX: (86 10) 6203 4205.
email: office@moviechina.com.cn www.moviechina.com.cn

CHINESE FILM ASSOCIATION
No. 22 East Beisanhaun Ring Rd., Beijing 100018.
TEL: (86 10) 6421 9977. FAX: (86 10) 6421 1870.

CHINA FILM EXPORT & IMPORT CORPORATION
25 Xin Wai St., Beijing 100088. TEL: (861) 225 4488.
FAX: (861) 225 1044.

CHINA FILMMAKERS' ASSOCIATION
22 Beisanhuan Donglu, Beijing 100013. TEL: (861) 421-9977.
FAX: (861) 421 1870.

SHANGHAI UNITED CINEMA CIRCUIT
No. 322, Anfu Rd., Shanghai 200031.
TEL: 0086 21 64718068. FAX: 0086 21 64312958.
CONTACT
Xu Xiaoping

STATE ADMINISTRATION OF RADIO, FILM & TELEVISION (SARFT)
No. 2 Fuxingmenwai St., Xicheng District, Beijing 100866.
TEL: (86 10) 6609 3114. www.sarft.gov.cn
DIRECTOR
Xu Guangchun

WARNER BROS. CONSULTING SERVICES
The Center, F6, No. 989, Chang Le Rd., Shanghai 200031.
TEL: (86 21) 6140 1100. FAX: (86 21) 6140 2795.

XINHUA MEDIA ENTERTAINMENT
6A JianWai Ave., Rm. 2201, 22/F, Tower D, Central International Trade Center, ChaoYang District,
Beijing 100022.
MANAGING DIRECTOR
David U. Lee

COLOMBIA

Capital: Bogota
Population: 44,205,293 (July 2010 est.)
Area: 1,138,910 sq. km.
Source: CIA - World Factbook
Country Code: co

DISTRIBUTORS AND PRODUCERS

CINEMA FILMS
Carerra 17, 91-33, Bogota. TEL: (571) 611 1097.
email: contacto@cinemafilms.com.co
www.cinemafilms.com.co
CONTACT
Juan Carlos Villalobos, Mauricio Pardo

COLUMBIA TRISTAR FILMS OF COLOMBIA
Edificio Teleport, Business Park, Calle 114 No. 9-01, Torre a of 1101, Bogota. TEL: (571) 629 2148. FAX: (571) 629 2249.
www.columbia.com.co

L.D. FILMS
Calle 23 No. 5-85 Interior 201, Bogota. TEL: (571) 341 7285.
FAX: (571) 286 5960.

TWENTIETH CENTURY FOX INTERNATIONAL
Cine Columbia, Carrera 13 #38-85, Bogota. TEL: (571) 285 8431.
FAX: (571) 285 4854.

UNITED INTERNATIONAL PICTURES
Carrera 14 No. 94-65 Piso 2, Bogota. TEL: (571) 635 2530.
FAX: (571) 635 2787.
MANAGER
Maitland Pritchett

EXHIBITORS

CINE COLUMBIA S.A.
Carrera 13, No. 38-85, Santa Fe De Bogota. TEL: (571) 285 8431.
FAX: (571) 287 5160. www.cinecolombia.com.co
OWNER
Mayaguez Organization
CHAIRMAN
Alvaro Correa Holguin
CEO & FILM BUYER
Munir Falah
MANAGER, DISTRIBUTION
Maria Jose Iragorri
V.P., ADMINISTRATION
Alvaro Beltran
V.P., OPERATIONS
Gilberto Gallego
V.P., FINANCE
Eduardo Medrano

CINEMARK COLOMBIA S.A.
Transversal 48, #94-97, Local 2717 Mezzanine, CAFAM La Floresta, Bogota. TEL: (571) 600 0375. FAX: (571) 603 0045.
www.cinemark.com.co
GENERAL MANAGER
Pablo Umana

Number of Theatres: 5

CROATIA

Capital: Zagreb
Population: 4,486,881 (July 2010 est.)
Area: 56,542 sq. km.
Source: CIA World Factbook
Country Code: hr

DISTRIBUTORS AND PRODUCERS

BLITZ FILM & VIDEO
Kamenarka A 1, 10 010 Zagreb. TEL: (385 1) 66 59 500.
FAX: (385 1) 66 59 511. email: blitz@zg.tel.hr
www.blitz-film.com

CONTINENTAL FILM
Zavrtnica 17, 10000 Zagreb Hrvatska. TEL: (385 1) 6194 660.
FAX: (385 1) 6194 663. email: cf-info@continental-film.hr
www.continental-film.hr
VICE PRESIDENT
Vladimir Sobat
MANAGING DIRECTOR
Ivor Šiber

CROATIA FILM D.O.O.
Katanciceva 3, 10 000 Zagreb. TEL: (385 1) 48 13 711.
FAX: (385 1) 48 22 568. email: croatia-film@zg.tel.hr
www.croatia-film.hr

JADRAN FILM DD
Oporovecka 12, 10000 Zagreb. TEL: (385 1) 285 3881.
FAX: (385 1) 285 1394. email: info@jadran-film.com
www.jadran-film.com
PRESIDENT OF THE MANAGING BOARD
Igor Krpan

KINEMATOGRAFI
p.p. 423, Trg Petra Preradovica 4, 10001 Zagreb.
TEL: (385 1) 483 4900. FAX: (385 1) 483 4969.
www.kinematografi.hr
PRESIDENT
Alan Cartlidge

TWENTIETH CENTURY FOX INTERNATIONAL
(See listing of Continental Film)

UIP INTERNATIONAL - VTI
Harambasiceva 19/1, 10000 Zagreb.
TEL: (385) 1 23 95 484. FAX: (308) 1 23 95 8484.
AGENT
Zdravko Karanovic

ZAUDER FILM
Jablanicka 1, 10040 Zagreb. TEL: (3851) 245 724.
FAX: (3851) 245 973. www.zauderfilm.hr

CZECH REPUBLIC

Capital: Prague
Population: 10,201,707 (July 2010 est.)
Area: 78,866 sq. km.
Source: Czech Statistical Office
Country Code: cz

DISTRIBUTORS AND PRODUCERS

ALFA FILM
Dolnomecholupská 209/17 (Film Studio Gatteo), 102 00 Prague 10. TEL: (420) 272 706 450. FAX: (420) 272 705 755.
email: office@alfafilm.net www.alfafilm.net
PRODUCER
Dana Synková, Roman Synek

ANIMATION PEOPLE S.R.O.
Na Doubkové 8, 150 00 Prgue 5. TEL: (420) 602 378 362.
FAX: (420) 251 565 203. www.animation.cz
CONTACT
Michal Podhradský

ARMADA FILMS S.R.O.
Na Zderaze 15, 120 00 Prague 2. TEL: (420) 221 904 444.
FAX: (420) 221 904 300. email: info@armadafilms.cz
www.armadafilms.cz

BELTFILM S.R.O.
Sekaninova 52, 128 00 Prague 2. TEL: (420) 224 936 887.
FAX: (420) 224 936 860. email: info@beltfilm.cz
www.beltfilm.cz
CONTACT
Miloš Remen

BIOSCOP, A.S.
Kunetická 2, 120 00 Prague 2. TEL: (420) 222 25 44 61.
FAX: (420) 222 25 44 62. email: info@bioscop.cz
www.bioscop.cz

BISTRO FILMS
Jánský vršek 325/9 Praha 1 118 00. TEL: (420) 224 818 617.
FAX: (420) 224 818 620. email: menu@bistrofilms.com
www.bistrofilms.com

BONTONFILM
Narodni Trida 28, Prague 1 111 21. TEL 42-02-211 05 280.
FAX: 42-02-242-27931. www.bonton-film.cz
CONTACT
Milica Pechankova

CINEMART
Národní tr. 28, 111 21 Prague 1. TEL: (420) 224 94 91 10.
FAX: (420) 221 10 52 20. email: info@cinemart.cz
www.cinemart.cz

CZECH ANGLO PRODUCTIONS
Krí eneckého nám. 5/322 Praha 5. TEL: (420) 251 815 259.
FAX: (420) 251 814 875. email: czang.prod@mbox.vol.cz

DAWSON PRODUCTION S.R.O.
Pštrossova 21, 110 00 Prague 1. TEL: (420) 224 999 911.
FAX: (420) 224 999 923. email: dawson@dawson.cz
www.dawsonproduction.cz

ENDOR FILMS
Prímetická 1187/4 Praha 4 140 00. TEL: (420) 602 358 373.
FAX: (420) 267 914 169. email: endorfilm@quick.cz
www.endorfilm.cz

ETIC FILMS
Krí eneckého nám. 322, 52 53 Praha 5. TEL: (420) 267 073 171.
FAX: (420) 267 073 181. email: etic@etic.cz www.etic.cz
MANAGING DIRECTOR
Petr Moravec - petr.moravec@etic.cz

FALCON FILM
U Nikolajky 5/833, 150 00 Prague 5. TEL: (420) 224 422 244.
FAX: (420) 224 422 240. email: falcon@falcon.cz
www.falcon.cz

FILM DISTRIBUTION ARTCAM
Rašínovo nábr. 6, 120 00 Prague 2. TEL: (420) 224 918 833.
FAX: (420) 224 919 969. email: artcam@artcam.cz
www.artcam.cz

FILMSERVICE PRODUCTIONS S.R.O.
Ostrovní 30, 110 00 Prague 1. TEL: (420) 221 969 111.
FAX: (420) 221 969 100. email: mail@filmservice.cz
www.filmservice.cz
CONTACT
Daniel Sirotek, Jakub Kolín

HOLLYWOOD CLASSIC ENTERTAINMENT
Psohlavcu 8 147 01 Prague 4. TEL: (420) 244 464 135.
FAX: (420) 244 464 395. www.hce.cz

HAPPY CELULOID S.R.O.
Hellichova 20, 118 00 Prague 1. TEL: (420) 257 320 790.
FAX: (420) 257 315 087. email: celluloid@bon.cz
www.celluloid.cz
CONTACT
Milan Cieslar

JAKUBISKO FILM
Palác Lucerna, Vodickova 36, 116 02 Prague 1.
TEL: (420) 296 236 383. FAX: (420) 296 236 353.
email: info@jakubiskofilm.com www.jakubiskofilm.com

LAJKA FILM
U starého hrbitova 3, 110 00 Prague 1. TEL: (420) 777 867 077.
email: info@lajka-film.cz www.lajka-film.cz

MILK & HONEY FILMS
Josefská 6, 118 00 Prague 1. TEL: (420) 255 707 070.
FAX: (420) 255 707 055. email: info@milkandhoneyfilms.cz
www.milkandhoneyfilms.com

PARTNERSHIP PICTURES S.R.O
Krí eneckého nám. 5/322, 152 00 Prague 5.
TEL: (420) 267 072 117. FAX: (420) 251 814 757.
email: office@partnershippictures.com
www.partnershippictures.com

ROTOR PRODUCTIONS
Kremencova 8/177, 110 00 Prague 1. TEL: (420) 224 934 220.
FAX: (420) 224 930 843. email: rotor@rotor.tv www.rotor.tv
CONTACT
Daniel Heyna Vetrovský

SPACE FILM
Prokopská 8, 118 00 Prague 1. TEL: (420) 257 535 108.
FAX: (420) 257 535 108. email: spacefilms@attglobal.net

SPIN FILM
U Zvonarky 14, 120 00 Prague 2. TEL: (420) 222 521 179.
FAX: (420) 222 521 179. email: spinfilm@spinfilm.cz
www.spinfilm.cz

STARLIGHT PRODUCTIONS
Barrandov Film Studios, Krizeneckeho nam. 322, Blok A4 #208,
152 00 Prague 5. TEL: (420) 267 072 288.
FAX: (420) 267 072 299. email: office@starlite.cz
www.starlite.cz

STILLKING FILMS
Krizneckeho Nam 322 Prague 5152 53.
TEL: (420) 2 6707 3741. FAX: (420) 2 6707 3742.
email: info@stillking.com www.stillking.com

TARGET PICTURES
Masarykovo náb. 1/250, 110 00 Prague 1.
TEL: (420) 224 932 000. FAX: (420) 224 932 004.
email: production@target.cz www.target.cz
CONTACT
Daniel Netušil

VERTIGO FILM
Františka Krí ka 1 / 362, 170 00 Prague 7. TEL: (420) 220 412 250.
FAX: (420) 220 412 251. email: info@.vertigofilm.com
www.vertigofilm.com

VITAL PRODUCTIONS
Národní obrany 49, 160 00 Prague 6. TEL: (420) 233 337 671.
FAX: (420) 233 337 617. email: mail@vital-productions.com

WARNER BROS.
Na porící 30, 110 00 Prague 1. TEL: (420) 221 732 401.
FAX: (420) 221 732 501. email: marketing@warnerbros.cz
www.warner.cz

WILMA FILM
Struharovská 9, 14100 Praha 4. TEL: (420) 272 019 222.
FAX: (420) 272 765 977. email: wilmafilm@volny.cz
www.wilmafilm.cz

UIP INTERNATIONAL - BONTON FILM A.S.
Narodni Trida 28, Prague 1 111 21, Czech Republic.
TEL: 42-02-211 05 280. FAX: 42-02-242-27931.
CONTACT
Milica Pechankova

EXHIBITORS

INTERSONIC TAUNUS PROD., LTD.
Stare Grunty 36, 842 25 Bratislava, Slovakia. TEL: (421) 772 2070.
FAX: (421) 772 1017. www.intersonic.cz

VILLAGE ROADSHOW, LTD.
(For complete listing see Australian branch)
206 Bourke St., Melbourne, VIC, 3000, Australia.
TEL: (613) 9667 6666. FAX: (613) 9639 1540.

Number of Theatres (Czech Republic): 2
Number of Screens (Czech Republic): 22

ASSOCIATIONS & ORGANIZATIONS

ASSOCIATION OF ANIMATED FILM-MAKERS (APD)
Na Doubkové 8, 150 00 Prague 5. TEL: (420) 2515 63200.
FAX: (420) 2515 65203. email: apd@animation.cz.
www.animation.cz
CONTACT
Ivan Vít

ASSOCIATION OF AUDIOVISUAL PRODUCERS (APA)
Národní 28, 110 00 Praha 1. TEL: (420) 2211 05302.
FAX: (420) 2211 05303. email: apa@iol.cz www.apa.iol.cz
CHAIRMAN
Pavel Strnad
GENERAL SECRETARY
Barbora Golatová

CINEMA EXHIBITORS ASSOCIATION
Národní 28, 110 00 Prague 1. TEL: (420) 2211 05301.
FAX: (420) 2211 05303. email: prokopova@cinemart.cz
www.kinari.cz
CHAIRMAN
Miloš Navrátil
GENERAL SECRETARY
Irena Prokopová

CZECH FILM AND TELEVISON ACADEMY
Na ertvách 40, 180 00 Prague 8. TEL: (420) 2848 23442.
FAX: (420) 2848 23444. email: info@cfta.cz www.cfta.cz
PRESIDENT
Karel Kachyna
DIRECTOR
Petr Vachler

CZECH FILM CHAMBER
Národní 28, 110 00 Prague 1. TEL: (420) 2211 05210.
FAX: (420) 2211 05303. email: kucmasova@mediadesk.cz
CHAIRPERSON
Helena Uldrichová
DIRECTOR
Daniela Kucmášová

FILM COMMISSION
Národní 28, 110 00 Prague 1. TEL: (420) 2211 05254.
FAX: (420) 2211 05303. email: info@filmcommission.cz
www.filmcommission.cz

FILM DISTRIBUTORS UNION
U Rajské zahrady 14, 130 00 Prague 3. TEL: (420) 2227 13001.
FAX: (420) 2227 13001. email: ufd@nivelco.cz www.ufd.cz
GENERAL SECRETARY
Anna Cerna

MINISTRY OF CULTURE
M. Horákové 139, 160 41 Prague 6. TEL: (420) 2570 85315.
FAX: (420) 2243 22558. www.mkcr.cz

NATIONAL FILM ARCHIVES
Malešická 12, 130 00 Prague 3. TEL: (420) 2717 70500.
FAX: (420) 2717 70501. email: nfapraha@anet.cz www.nfa.cz

STATE FUND FOR THE SUPPORT AND DEVELOPMENT OF CZECH CINEMATOGRAPHY
M. Horákové 139, 160 41 Prague 6. TEL: (420) 2570 85247.
FAX: (420) 2243 21053. www.mkcr.cz
CONTACT
Ing. Hana Tomášková - hana.tomaskova@mkcr.cz

DENMARK

Capital: Copenhagen
Population: 5,515,575 (July 2010 est.)
Area: 43,094 sq. km.
Source: CIA World Factbook

DISTRIBUTORS AND PRODUCERS

ALL RIGHT FILM DISTRIBUTION
Indiakaj 12, Copenhagen 2100. TEL: (45 3) 543 4000.
FAX: (45 3) 543 4008. email: allright@allright-film.dk
CONTACT
Jesper Smith

ANGEL FILMS
Stockholmsgade 43, Copenhagen 2100. TEL: (45 3) 525 3600.
FAX: (45 3) 525 3610. www.angelfilms.dk
CONTACT
Mogens Glad

BUENA VISTA INTERNATIONAL
Ostergade 26A, 3rd Fl., Copenhagen K DK-1100.
TEL: (45 3) 312 0800. FAX: (45 3) 312 4332.
www.buenavista.dk
CONTACT
Eric Hamre

CAMERA FILM
Mikkel Bryggergade 8, Copenhagen K DK-1460.
TEL: (45 3) 313 6112. FAX: (45 3) 315 0882.
email: mail@camerafilm.dk www.camerafilm.dk

CONSTANTIN APS
Halmtorvet 29, Copenhagen V 1700. TEL: (45 3) 326 6868.
FAX: (45 3) 326 6859.

COSMO FILM A/S
Ryesgade 106A 4 DK-2100, Copenhagen.
TEL: (45) 3538 7200. FAX: (45) 3538 7299. www.cosmo.dk

DANSK REKLAME FILM A/S
Store Kongensgade, 110C, Copenhagen DK 1264.
TEL: (45 3) 339 30988. FAX: (45 3) 39 30989.
email: dansk@tehnefilm.dk
CONTACT
Jannik Hastrup

EDGMONT AUDIO VISUAL
Skelbaekgade 1, DK-1717, Copenhagen V.
TEL: (45) 332 54000. FAX: (45) 312 30488.

FOX FILM
Skelbaekgade 1, 3, Copenhagen V DK-1717. TEL: (45 3) 325 4000.
FAX: (45 3) 123 0488.

GENIUS LOCI
Strandvejen 614, Klampenborg 2930. TEL: (45 2) 190 2980.
www.genius-loci-filmproduction.com
CONTACT
Jacob Jørgensen - jacob@genius-loci-filmproduction.co

GLORIA FILM
Vesterbrogade 149, Copenhagen 1620. TEL: (45 3) 312 8232.
FAX: (45 3) 327 0099.

HUSETS BIOGRAF
Huset, Radhusstraede 13, 2nd Flr., Copenhagen K-1466.
TEL: (45 3) 315 2002. FAX: (45 3) 332 5077.

MINERVA FILM A/S
Baldersgade 6, 2200 København N. TEL: 45 35 82 11 33.
FAX: 45 35 82 13 33. email: info@minervafilm.dk
PRODUCER/CEO
Mikael Windelin - mikael@minervafilm.dk

MOONLIGHT FILMPRODUCTION
Indiakaj 12 DK-2100 Copenhagen. TEL: (45 3) 544 111.
FAX: (45 3) 544 4015. www.moonlight.film.dk

NORDSIK FILM A/S
Mosedalvej 14 2500 Valby. TEL: (45 3) 618 8200.
FAX: (45 3) 618 9300. www.nordiskfilm.com
MANAGING DIRECTOR
Michael Ritto

NORDISK FILM BIOGRAF DISTRIBUTION
NHalmtorvet 29 1700 København V. TEL: (45) 3123 2488.
FAX: (45) 3123 2184.
MANAGING DIRECTOR
Michael Ritto

REGNER GRASTEN FILMPRODUCTION APS
Lykkevei 6 DK-2920 Charlottenlund. TEL: (45 3) 963 4424.
FAX: (45 3) 963 4192. email: grasten@image.dk

SANDREW METRONOME DENMARK
Sondermarksvej 16 DK 2500 Valby. TEL: (45 3) 646 7755.
FAX: (45 3) 644 0969.
email: filmdistribution@sandrewmetronome.dk
CONTACT
Pia Schluntz

SCALA FILM
Centrumpladsen, P.O. Box 215, Svendborg DK-5700.
TEL: (45 6) 221 8866. FAX: (45 6) 221 0821.

SCANBOX ENTERTAINMENT
Vermundsgage 40 A -4 sal 2100 Copenhagen.
TEL: (45 3) 7022 6202. FAX: (45 3) 7022 6201.
www.scanbox.com
CONTACT
Jorgen Kristiansen

SIRIUS FILM
Gammel Kongevej 10, Copenhagen, 2200. TEL: (45 3) 311 7060.
FAX: (45 3) 314 2888. www.siriusfilm.dk
CONTACT
Steen Iversen

SMILE ENTERTAINMENT APS
Indiakaj 12, Copenhagen 2100. TEL: (45 3) 544 1105.
FAX: (45 3) 543 4008. email: timo@smile.dk www.smile.dk
PRESIDENT/CEO
Timo Lahtinen

SFINX FILM/TV APS
Sølvgade 92, baghuset, Copenhagen 1307. TEL: (45 3) 332 3253.
FAX: (45 3) 391 4490. email: info@sfinx-film.dk
www.sfinx-film.dk

SVENSK FILMINDUSTRI DENMARK
Forbindelsesvej 3, 2100 Copenhagen. TEL: (45 7) 026 7626.
FAX: (45 37) 026 7627. email: info@sf-film.dk www.sf-film.dk

TRUST FILM SALES
Filmbyen 12, Hvidovre 2650. TEL: (45 3) 686 8788.
FAX: (45 3) 3677 4448. email: post@trust-film.dk
www.trust-film.dk
CEO
Annakarin Strom

UNITED INTERNATIONAL PICTURES
Haunchvej 13, Frederiksberg C DK-1825. TEL: (45 3) 131 2330.
FAX: (45 3) 123 3420.
GENERAL MANAGER
Michael Berg

WARNER & METRONOME FILM
Sondermarksvej 16, Copenhagen, Valby DK-2500.
TEL: (45 3) 615 94 00. FAX: (45 3) 615 9410.

ZEITGEIST
Avedøre Tværvej 10, Hvidovre DK-2650.
TEL: 45 3686 8747. FAX: 45 3678 8878.
email: zeitgeist@zeitgeist.dk www.zeitgeist.dk

ZENTROPA PRODUCTION
Filmbyen 22 2650 Hvidovre. TEL: (45) 36 78 00 55.
FAX: (45) 36 78 00 77. email: zentrop@zentropa-film.com
www.zentropa.dk
MANAGING DIRECTOR
Peter Aalbæk Jensen, Lars von Trier

EXHIBITORS

NORDISK FILM BIOGRAFER A / S
Axeltorv 9, Copenhagen 1609. TEL: (45 3) 314 7606.
FAX: (45 3) 332 7505.
email: nordisk-film-biografer@nordiskfilm.com
www.nordiskfilm.dk
MANAGING DIRECTOR
Kenneth D. Plummer
GENERAL MANAGER, CINEMAS
John A. Tønnes

MARKETING DIRECTOR
Mikkel Berg
Number of Theatres: 14

ASSOCIATIONS & ORGANIZATIONS

DANISH FILM DISTRIBUTORS ASSOCIATION
Bulowsvej 50A, Fredericksberg DK-1870. TEL: (45) 3536 5616. FAX: (45) 3135 5758.
DIRECTOR
Anne-Grete Wezelenburg

DANISH FILM INSTITUTE
55 Gothersgade, Copenhagen K 1123. TEL: (45 3) 374 3400. FAX: (45 3) 374 3401. email: dfi@dfi.dk www.dfi.dk
CEO
Henning Camre

DANISH FILM MUSEUM AND CINEMATIQUE
55 Gothersgade, 1123 Copenhagen. TEL: (45 3) 374 3400. FAX: (45 3) 374 3599.

DANISH FILM WORKSHOP
55 Gothersgade, 1123 Copenhagen. TEL: (45 3) 374 3480. FAX: (45 3) 374 3490. email: filmworkshop@dfi.dk

DANISH FILM PRODUCERS' ASSOCIATION
Bernhard Bangs Allé 25, Frederiksberg 2000. TEL: (45 3) 386 2880. FAX: (45 3) 386 2888. email: info@pro-f.dk www.pro-f.dk
CONTACT
Klaus Hansen

FILM KONTAKT NORD (FKN)
Vognmagerade 10, 1st Flr. 1120 Copenhagen. TEL: (45 3) 311 5152. FAX: (45 3) 331 2152. www.filmkontact.com
DIRECTOR
Karoline Lidin

NORDIC FILM/TV SOCIETY
c/o MGM Nordisk Film Biografer, Axeltorv 9, Copenhagen DK-1609. TEL: (45) 3314 76906. FAX: (45) 3314 7979. www.nordiskfilm.dk

DOMINICAN REPUBLIC

Capital: Santo Domingo
Population: 9,823,821 (July 2010 est.)
Area: 48,730 sq. km.
Source: CIA World Factbook

EXHIBITORS

REGENCY CARIBBEAN ENTERPRISES, INC.
(d.b.a. Caribbean Cinemas)
Cinema Centro, Avenida George Washington, Santo Domingo. TEL: (809) 688 8710. FAX: (809) 686 2642.
PRESIDENT
Victor Carrady

CARIBBEAN CINEMAS OF THE VIRGIN ISLANDS, INC.
Centro del Cibao SA, Estrella Sadala No. 20, Santiago. TEL: (809) 686 2642. FAX: (809) 971 5991.
ADMINISTRATOR
Amado Perez

ECUADOR

Capital: Quito
Population: 14,790,608 (July 2010 est.)
Area: 283,560 sq.km.
Source: CIA World Factbook

DISTRIBUTORS AND PRODUCERS

CINE LOCACIONES CIA. LTDA.
Whimper 777 y 6 de Diciembre, Quito. TEL: (593 2) 250 2025. email: info@cinelocaciones.com www.filmecuador.com

CONSORCIO FILMCO M.A.
Suecia 277 Avidelos Shyris, Casilla 1717-634, Quito. TEL: (593 2) 701 787. FAX: (593 2) 430 848.
GENERAL MANAGER
Marco Aguas

PELICULAS MEXICANAS DEL ECUADOR S.A.
9 de Octubre 823, Guayaquil. TEL: (593 4) 327 108. FAX: (593 4) 325 289.

PRODUCTORA FILMICA NACIONAL DEL ECUADOR C. LTDA.
Cordova #1015 y 9 de Octubre, P.O. Box 3445, Guayaquil. TEL: (593 4) 564 455. FAX: (593 4) 561 877. email: profilm@impsat.net.ec

TWENTIETH CENTURY FOX INTERNATIONAL
Av. Al Parque y Alonso Torres, Edificio Centrum El Bosque, Oficina 206, Quito. TEL: (593 2) 445 205, 445 206. FAX: (593 2) 445 207.
GENERAL MANAGER
Jose Miguel Barra

EXHIBITORS

CINEMARK
Av. America y Naciones Unidas, Quito. TEL: (593 2) 226 0304. FAX: (593 2) 226 0302. www.cinemark.com.ec
GENERAL MANAGER
Steve Wright
Number of Theatres: 2
Number of Screens: 16

MULTICINES
San Ignacio E12-182 y González Suárez, Quito. TEL: (593 2) 255 5616. FAX: (593 2) 256 0881. www.multicines.com.ec

EGYPT

Capital: Cairo
Population: 80,471,869 (July 2010 est.)
Area: 1,001,450 sq. km.
Source: CIA World Factbook

DISTRIBUTORS AND PRODUCERS

AFLAM FARID SHAWKI
Farid Shawki 36, Sherif St., Cairo.

ALAMIA T. V. & CINEMA
Hussein Kalla-41, Guizira Elwosta, Zamalek, Cairo.

AFLAM MISR ALAMIA
Yousef Shahin 35, Champion St., Cairo.

ARTIST UNITY
Farid Shawki 16, Adly St., Cairo.

BADIE SOBHI
Badie Sobhi 12, Soliman Elhalabi St., Cairo.

CENTRAL FILM
Nagib Spiro, 85, Ramses St., Cairo.

EL-LEITHY FILMS
Ihab El-Leithy 37, Kasr El-Nil St., Cairo.

GAMAL EL-LEITHY
Gamal El-Leithy 11, Saray El-Azbakia St., Cairo.

HANY FILM
Zaki Guirges 4, Soliman Elhalabi St., Cairo.

KASR EL-NIL INTERNATIONAL AHMED SAMI
(Ahmed Sami & Co.) 4, Hussein Almimar St., Kasr El Nil, Cairo. TEL: (202) 574 5416. FAX: (202) 291 8059.

MANAR FILM
Atef Ibrahim, 11, Saray El-Azbakia St., Cairo.

MASR EL-GUIDIDA
Salah Kharma, 36, Orabi St., Cairo.

METRO FILMS OF EGYPT
20 Haroun St., Dokki Giza. TEL: 20-2-748-5199. FAX: 20-2-748-6253.
MANAGER
Amr Osman

MISR EL-ARABIA
Wasef Faiez 12, Soliman Elhalabi St., Cairo.

NASR FILM
Mohamed Hassan 33, Orabi St., Cairo.

OSIRIS FILM
Omran Ali 87, Ramses St., Cairo.

SOAT EL-FANN
D. Abdel Wahab 16, Adly St., Cairo.

TAMIDO FILM
Medhat Sherif 4, Zaki St., Orabi, Cairo.

EXHIBITORS

MGM
35 Talaat Harb St., Cairo. TEL: (202) 393 3897. FAX: (202) 392 7998.
MANAGER
Fouad Nader

TWENTIETH CENTURY FOX IMPORT CORP.
11 Saray el Ezbekieh, Box 693, Cairo. TEL: (202) 591 2477. FAX: (202) 591 2829.
MANAGER
Zagloul Gad El Karim Salama

UNITED MOTION PICTURES
(Licensee for Warner Bros. and Twentieth Century Fox)
7 26th of July St., P.O. Box 923, Cairo. TEL: (202) 591 2477. FAX: (202) 591 2829.
email: cherine@link.net

CHAIRMAN
Antoine Zeind

FIJI

Capital: Suva
Population: 875,983 (July 2010 est.)
Language: English, Fijian, Hindi
Area: 18,270 sq.km.
Source: CIA World Factbook

EXHIBITORS

VILLAGE ROADSHOW, LTD.
(For complete listing see Australian branch)
206 Bourke St., Melbourne, VIC, 3000, Australia.
TEL: (613) 9667 6666. FAX: (613) 9639 1540.

Number of Theatres: 2
Number of Screens: 10

ASSOCIATIONS AND ORGANIZATIONS

THE BRITISH CENTER
Part of the British Embassy, Cairo.
Both the American and British Centers have film libraries.

THE CATHOLIC FILM CENTER
9, Adly St., Cairo.

CENTER CULTURAL FRANCE
One at Al Mounira, Cairo, and at Hiliopolice.

FIJI AUDIO-VISUAL COMMISSION
Ground Flr., Civic House, Victoria Parade.
Suva. GPO Box 18080.
TEL: (679)-330 6662. FAX:(679)-331 4662
email: bolea@fijiaudiovisual.org.fj www.fijiaudiovisual.org.fj

FINLAND

Capital: Helsinki
Population: 5,255,068 (July 2010 est.)
Area: 337,030 sq.km.
Source: CIA World Factbook

DISTRIBUTORS AND PRODUCERS

AL-FILMI OY / MAINSTREAM PICTURES
Ruukintie 10 E, Ruotsinpyhtää 07970. TEL: (358) 500 704 316.
email: arto.lehkamo@mainstream.inet.fi www.mainstream.fi

ALFA PANORAMA FILM & VIDEO
Laipattie 5, Helsinki 00880. TEL: (3589) 759 2600.
FAX: (3589) 755 5460.

ART FILMS PRODUCTION AFP OY
Viides linja 3 A 35, Helsinki 00530. TEL: (358) 40 5006 602.
FAX: (3589) 735 413. email: arto@artfilms.inet.fi
www.artfilmsartohalonen.fi

ARTISTA FILMI OY
PL 69 28401 Ulvila. TEL: (3589) 647 7441.
FAX: (3589) 647 7551. email: timo.koivusalo@artistafilmi.fi

BITAR FILMS OY
Hakunilantie 84 01260 Vantaa. TEL: (358) 9 8767 258.
FAX: (358) 9 8766 068. email: bitar@saunalahti.fi

BLIND SPOT PICTURES OY
Kalliolanrinne 4, Helsinki 00510. TEL: (3589) 7742 8360.
FAX: (3589) 7742 8350. email: spot@blindspot.fi
www.blindspot.fi

BUENA VISTA INTERNATIONAL. FINLAND
Kaisaniemenkatu 2 B, Helsinki 00100. TEL: (3589) 8562 9500.
FAX: (3589) 8562 9550.

CINEMA MONDO
Unioninkatu 10, Helsinki 00130. TEL: (3589) 201 555 804.
FAX: (3589) 201 555 805. www.cinemamondo.fi

CINEPARADISO
Hermannin rantatie 20 00580 Helsinki. TEL: (3589) 582 8634.
email: pvlehtinen@kolumbus.fi www.kolumbus.fi/cineparadiso

COLUMBIA TRISTAR NORDISK FILM
Kaisaniemenkatu 3 B 26, Helsinki 00100.
TEL: (3589) 7420 4400. FAX: (3589) 7420 4420.

DADA-FILMI
Kolmas Linja 5, Helsinki 00530. TEL: (3589) 737 788.
FAX: (3589) 730 734. email: rile@dada.pp.fi

DO FILMS OY
Mechelininkatu 40, Helsinki 00520. TEL: (3589) 6874 4980.
FAX: (3589) 6874 4981. email: info@dofilms.fi www.dofilms.fi

DREAM CATCHER PRODUCTIONS
Kulmavuorenkatu 2, Helsinki 00500. TEL: (3589) 777 2006.
FAX: (3589) 777 2005. www.dreamcatcher.fi
OWNER
Alexis Kourosis - alexis.kouros@dreamcatcher.fi

EDITH FILM OY
Tehtaankatu 5 C 21 00140 Helsinki. TEL: (358) 40 5050 015.
FAX: (358) 9 6227 0026. email: liisa@edithfilm.fi

EUROPA VISION
Koivuvaarankuja 2, Vantaa 01641. TEL: (3589) 852 711.
FAX: (3589) 853 2183.

FANTASIAFILMI OY
Tallberginkatu 1 A 141, Helsinki 00180. TEL: (3589) 400 508 179.
FAX: (3589) 540 78530.
email: nina.koljonen@fantasiafilm.com
www.fantasiafilm.com

FENNADA FILMI OY
Kolmas linja 5 00530 Helsinki. TEL: (358) 9 774 4780.
FAX: (358) 9 730 734. email: kari.sara@fennada-filmi.fi

FILKAS OY
Rukatunturintie 3 K Helsinki 00970. TEL: (358) 40 540 9995.
email: filkas.oy@kolumbus.fi www.kolumbus.fi/filkas.oy

FILMI-FAKTA OY
Rikalantie 8, Helsinki 00970. TEL: (3589) 306 563.
email: ilkka.ilkare@filmifakta.fi www.filmifakta.fi

FILMIKONTTORI OY
Pursimiehenkatu 29-31 A 3.krs, Helsinki 00150.
TEL: (3589) 251 3061. FAX: (3589) 251 30 62.
email: filmikonttori@filmikonttori.com www.filmikonttori.com

FINNKINO OY
Koivuvaarankuja 2, Vantaa 01641. TEL: (3589) 131 191.
FAX: (3589) 1311 9300.
CONTACT
Timo Manty

FLMS BROS & CO
Laivurinkatu 33 C, Ste. 54, Helsinki 00150.
TEL: (358) 40 555 3763. email: juha@flms.fi www.flms.fi

FRESH PRODUCTIONS
Vilhovuorenkuja 16 A 4, Helsinki 00500.
TEL: (358) 45 652 1565. email: mikko.vartiainen@meizo.com
www.fresh.intranetit.net

GATEWAY FILMS OY
Sammatintie 8 H 67, Helsinki 00550. TEL: (358) 50 536 7009.
FAX: (358) 9 738 137. email: lasse.keso@pp.inet.fi

GUERILLAFILMS, LTD.
Kiuastie 7 B 02770 Espoo. TEL:(358) 9 8813 224.
FAX: (358) 358 40 506 2675. email: guerillafilms@elefantti.info

HAKALAX PRODUCTIONS OY
Topeliuksekatu 3b 9A, Helsinki 00260.
TEL: (358) 400 423 364.
email: hakalax@hakalaxproductions.com

HELSINGIN ÄÄNIRAITA OY
Rohdinkuja 8 A, Helsinki 00950. TEL:(3589) 540 6690.
email: studio@aaniraita.fi www.aaniraita.fi

HELSINKI-FILMI OY
Vanha Talvitie 11 A, Helsinki 00580. TEL: (3589) 7740 300.
FAX: (3589) 7740 3060. www.helsinkifilmi.fi
MANAGING DIRECTOR, PRODUCER, WRITER
Aleksi Bardy - aleksi.bardy@helsinkifilmi.fi
CFO
Jorma Reinilä - jorma.reinilä@helsinkifilmi.fi
MARKETING MANAGER
Atte Laurila - atte.laurila@helsinkifilmi.fi

ILLUME LTD. OY
Palkkatilankatu 7. Helsinki 00240. TEL: (3589) 148 1489.
FAX: (3589) 148 1489. email: Illume@illume.fi www.illume.fi

INDIE FILMS OY
Malminkatu 22 C 55, Helsinki 00100. TEL: (3589) 40 563 4603.
email: indiefilms@indiefilms.fi www.indiefilms.fi

JACKPOT FILMSOY
Valumallinpolku 11 33100 Tampere. TEL: (358) 3 2234 210.
FAX: (358) 3 2234 256. email: timo.kahilainen@saunalahti.fi

JUNIPER FILMS OY
Työpajakatu 7, Helsinki 00240. TEL: (3589) 7740 660.
FAX: (3589) 7740 6640. email: outi.limnell@juniperfilms.fi
www.juniperfilms.fi

KINOFINLANDIA
Pyhtaantie 5, Helsinki 00600. TEL: (3589) 278 1783.
FAX: (3589) 278 1763. email: kinofinlandia@kinofinlandia.fi

KINOPRODUCTION OY
Pasilan vanhat veturitallit, Helsinki 00520. TEL: (3589) 685 0460.
FAX: (3589) 685 046 10.

email: kinoproduction@kinoproduction.fi www.kinoproduction.fi

KINOSCREEN
Pohjoisranta 20 B, Helsinki 00170. TEL: (3589) 589 38861.
FAX: (3589) 589 38860.

KINOTAR OY
Vuorikatu 16 A 9, Helsinki 00100. TEL: (3589) 135 1864.
FAX: (3589) 135 7864. email: kinotar@kinotar.com
www.kinotar.com

KOSMOFILMI
Steinbackinkatu 8A, Helsinki 00250. TEL: (3589) 477 3587.
FAX: (3589) 477 3583.

KRISTALLISILMÄ OY / CRYSTAL EYE, LTD.
Tallberginkatu 1/44, Helsinki 00180. TEL: (3589) 694 2308.
FAX: (3589) 694 7224. email: mail@crystaleye.fi
www.crystaleye.fi

KROMA PRODUCTIONS OY
Magnusborg Studios, Porvoo 06100. TEL: (358) 19 534 80 15.
FAX: (358) 19 534 80 16. email: kroma@magnusborg.fi
www.kromaproductions.net

LUMIFILM OY
Sörnäisten rantatie 27 C 5, Helsinki 00500.
TEL: (3589) 622 5882. FAX: (3589) 622 5886.
email: lumifilm@lumifilm.fi www.lumifilm.fi

MAINSTREAM PICTURES
Ruukintie 10 E, Ruotsinpyhtää 07970. TEL: (358) 500 704 31.
email: arto.lehkamo@mainstream.inet.fi
www.mainstream.fi

MANDART PRODUCTION
Kalevankatu 28 A 3, Helsinki 00100. TEL: (3589) 694 3142.
FAX: (3589) 684 3136. email: mandart@mandart.com
www.mandart.com

MILLENNIUM FILM OY
Koskikartanontie 12, Nurmes 77530. TEL: (358) 1351 10 100.
FAX: (358) 135 110 111. email: millennium@millenniumfilm.fi
www.millenniumfilm.fi

MOKUL FILMI OY
Singontie 3 B 7, Marinkainen 68210. TEL: (358) 50 559 3864.
email: kossi.heikki@kolumbus.fi

MRP MATILA RÖHR PRODUCTIONS OY
Tallberginkatu 1 A/141, Helsinki 00180. TEL: (3589) 540 7820.
FAX: (3589) 5407 8210. email: mrp@matilarohr.com
www.matilarohr.com

NAVY BLUE BIRD
Hämeentie 153 B, Helsinki 00560. TEL: (358) 40 566 0374.
email: info@navybluebird.com www.navybluebird.com

NORDISK FILM
Tehtaankatu 27-29 D, 3. krs., Helsinki 00150. TEL: (3589) 6689 990.
FAX: (3589) 6689 9996. email: petri.uitto@nordiskfilm.com
www.nordiskfilmtv.fi

OCTOBER FILM OY
Sampsantie 40 i 34, Helsinki 00610. TEL: (358) 40 709 3331.
email: joonas@octoberfilm.com

OY RABBIT FILMS, LTD
Kiviaidankatu 2 H, Helsinki 00210. TEL: (358) 50 330 5283.
FAX: (358) 9 7319 3211. email: info@rabbitfilms.com
www.rabbitfilms.com

PERFECTO-FILMS OY
Vallilantie 21, Helsinki 00510. TEL: (3589) 7269 5850.
FAX: (3589) 7269 5851. www.perfectofilms.com

PRODUCTION HOUSE
Höyläämöntie 18 A, Helsinki 00380. TEL: (358) 9 229 3260.
FAX: (358) 9 229 32 665.

SILVA MYSTERIUM OY
Pulttitie 16, Helsinki 00880. TEL: (358) 9 7594 720.
FAX: (358) 9 7594 7240.
email: etunimi.sukunimi@silvamysterium.fi
www.silvamysterium.fi

SNAPPER FILMS OY
Pitkänmäentie 52 C, Helsinki 00670. TEL: (3589) 7571 620.
FAX: (3589) 7248 712. www.snapperfilms.com

SOLAR FILMS OY
Veneentekijäntie 20, Helsinki 00210. TEL: (3589) 4174 4700.
FAX: (3589) 4174 4744. www.solarfilms.com

SUNSET PICTURES OY
Hämeentie 153 B, Helsinki 00560. TEL: (358) 440 736 464.

TALENT HOUSE
Tallberginkatu 1 A, loc. 141, Helsinki 00180.
TEL: (358) 0685 2227. FAX: (3589) 685 2229.

TALKING HEADS OY
Lemuntie 4 D, Helsinki 00510. TEL: (358) 9 774 32 00.
FAX: (358) 9 774 32 015. email: talking@talkingheads.fi

UNITED INTERNATIONAL PICTURES OY
Kaisaniemenkatu 1C 98, Helsinki 00100. TEL: 358-9-6841 007.
FAX: 358-9-6841 0010.
MANAGER
Markku Koistinen

URANIA FILM
Hiidentie 1 A 7, Oulu 90550. TEL: (358) 81881 1291.
FAX: (358) 81881 1290.

WALHALLA
Pb 1134, Helsingfors 00101. TEL: (3589) 6220 0044.
FAX: (3589) 6220 0045. email: toimisto@walhalla.fi
www.walhalla.fi

WARNER BROTHERS FINLAND OY
Kaisaniemenkatu 1B A 69, Helsinki 00100.
TEL: (358) 0638 953. FAX: (358) 0638 161.

WIDE MIND PRODUCTIONS OY
Läntinen Brahenkatu 12, Helsinki 00510. TEL: (358) 405 622 044.
FAX: (358) 969 45 194. www.framex.info

YLEISRADIO (YLE)
Radiokatu 5, Helsinki. TEL: (358) 914 801.
email: etusivu.toimitus@yle.fi www.yle.fi

EXHIBITORS

SANREW NETRONOME FILM AB
Kaisaniemenkatu 2B, Helsinki 00100. TEL: (3589) 616 651.
FAX: (3589) 6166 5655.
MANAGING DIRECTOR
Maija Kuusi

ASSOCIATIONS & ORGANIZATIONS

ASSOCIATION OF FINNISH FILM DIRECTORS
Suomen Elokuva Ohjaajaliitto SELO, Pl 116, Helsinki 00171.
TEL: (3589) 50 539 0951. www.selo.fi
EXECUTIVE DIRECTOR
Tommi Saarikivi

ASSOCIATION OF FINNISH FILM WORKERS
Meritullinkatu 33 A, Helsinki 00170. TEL: (3589) 2511 2143.
FAX: (3589) 2511 2191. email: set@teme.fi www.teme.fi/set

ASSOCIATION OF INDEPENDENT PRODUCERS
Fabianinkatu 4 B 14, Helsinki 00130. TEL: (3589) 684 0610.
FAX: (3589) 622 1860. email: marit.hohtokari@satu.fi
www.satu.fi

AVEK—THE PROMOTION CENTRE FOR AUDIOVISUAL CULTURE IN FINLAND
Hietaniemenkatu 2, Helsinki 00100. TEL: (3589) 446 411.
FAX: (3589) 446 414.

CENTRAL ORGANISATION OF FINNISH FILM PRODUCERS
Kaisaniemenkatu 3 B 29, Helsinki 00100. TEL: (3589) 636 305.
FAX: (3589) 176 689.

THE FINNISH FILM ARCHIVE
Pursimiehenkatu 29-31 A, Helsinki 00150. TEL: (3589) 615 400.
FAX: (3589) 6154 0242. email: sea@sea.fi www.sea.fi

THE FINNISH BROADCASTING COMPANY (YLE)
P.O. Box 19633101 Tampere. TEL: (358) 3 345 6111.
FAX: (358) 3 344 2280. www.yle.fi

THE FINNISH CINEMA EXHIBITORS ASSOCIATION (FILMIKAMARI)
Kaisaniemenkatu 3 B 29, Helsinki 00100. TEL: (3589) 6877 2311.
FAX: (3589) 6877 2320. email: filmikamari@filmikamari.fi
www.filmikamari.fi

FINNISH FILM FOUNDATION
Kanavakatu 12, Helsinki 00160. TEL: (3589) 622 0300.
FAX: (3589) 6220 3050. email: keskus@ses.fi www.ses.fi/en
MANAGING DIRECTOR
Jouni Mykkänen

THE FINNISH FILM DISTRIBUTORS´ASSOCIATION
Kaisaniemenkatu 3 B 29, Helsinki 00170.
TEL: (3589) 6877 2311. FAX: (3589) 6877 2320.
email: filmikamari@filmikamari.fi www.filmikamari.fi

FRANCE

Capital: Paris
Population: 64,768,389 64,420,073
Area: 547,030 sq. km.
Source: CIA World Factbook

DISTRIBUTORS AND PRODUCERS

AGENCE DU COURT METRAGE
2 Rue de Toqueville, Paris 75017. TEL: (331) 4469 2660.
FAX: (331) 4469 2669. email: acmpg@noos.fr
www.agencecm.com
GENERAL MANAGER
Philippe Germain

AMLF
21 Rue François 1er, Paris 75008. TEL: (331) 7172 3000.
FAX: (331) 7172 3100. email: pathe@pathe.com
www.pathe.com

ARCHEO PICTURES
9 Rue René Boulanger, Paris 75010. TEL: (331) 4240 4899.
FAX: (331) 4239 9413.

ARP
75 Ave. Des Champs Elysees, Paris 75008.
TEL: (331) 5669 2600. FAX: (331) 4563 8337.
email: arp@arpselection.com www.arpselection.com

ARTEDIS CINEMA ARTS ENTERTAINMENT
12, Rue Raynouard, Paris 75016. TEL: (331) 5392 2929.
FAX: (331) 5392 2920. email: artedisf@aol.com

BAC FILMS
88 rue de la Folie Méricourt, Paris 75011.
TEL: (331) 5353 5252. FAX: (331) 5353 5253.
email: ptribal@bacfilms.com www.bacfilms.com
CONTACT
M. Jean Labadie

CELLULOID DREAMS
2 Rue Turgot, Paris 75009. TEL: (331) 4970 0370.
FAX: (331) 4970 0371. email: info@celluloid-dreams.com
www.celluloid-dreams.com

CIBY DISTRIBUTION
90 Ave. des Champs Elysées, Paris 75008.
TEL: (331) 4421 6417. FAX: (331) 4421 6435.

COLUMBIA TRISTAR FILMS
131 Ave. de Wagram, Paris 75017. TEL: (331) 4440 6000.
FAX: (331) 4440 6201. www.columbiatristar.fr

CONNAISSANCE DU CINEMA
122, Rue La Boétie, Paris 75008. TEL: (331) 4359 0101.
FAX: (331) 4359 6441.

DAVIS FILMS
29, rue Galillée, Paris 75016.
TEL: +33 1 56 59 23 20. FAX: +33 1 56 59 23 10.

DIAPHANA DISTRIBUTION
155 Rue du Faubourg Saint Antoine Paris 75011.
TEL: (331) 534 66666. www.diaphana.fr
CONTACT
Michael Saint-Jean

EUROPA CORP
137 rue du Faubourg, Saint-Honoré, Paris 75008.
TEL: +33 1 53 83 03 03. FAX: +33 1 53 83 03 04.
email: contact@europacorp.com www.europacorp.com

EUROPALACES
21 Rue Francois 1 er, Paris 75008.
TEL: (33) 49 24 40 03. FAX: (33) 49 24 45 10.
CHAIRMAN
Eduardo Malone

FARIANE FILMS
15 Rue de Colonel Pierre Avia, Paris 75015.
TEL: (331) 4662 1777. FAX: (331) 4662 1797.

FILMS SANS FRONTIERES
70 Blvd. de Sebastopol, Paris 75003. TEL: (331) 4277 2184.
FAX: (331) 4277 4266. email: info@films-sans-frontieres.fr
www.films-sans-frontieres.fr
GENERAL MANAGER
Galeshka Moravioff

FRANCE 2
7, esplanade Henri de France, Cedex 15, Paris 75907.
TEL: 01 56 22 60 00. www.france2.fr/

FUTURIKON
12, rue de Turenne, Paris 75004.
TEL: +33 1 44 61 94 61. FAX: +33 1 44 61 94 60.
email: info@futurikon.fr www.futurikon.com

GAUMONT
30 Ave. Charles de Gaulle, Neuilly-sur-Seine 92200.
TEL: (331) 4643 2000. FAX: (331) 4643 2033.
www.gaumont.com
PRESIDENT, WORLDWIDE MARKETING
Frank Chorot

GAUMONT/BUENA VISTA INTERNATIONAL
5 Rue du Colisée, Paris 75008. TEL: (331) 4643 2453.
FAX: (331) 46 43 2051.

GEMINI FILMS
34, Blvd. Sebastopol, Paris 75004. TEL: (331) 4454 1721.
FAX: (331) 4454 1725. email: gemini@easnet.films
www.gemini-films.com
DIRECTOR
Paul Branco

HAUT ET COURT
38, Rue des Martyrs, Paris 75009. TEL: (331) 5531 2727.
FAX: (331) 5531 2728. email: info@hautetcourt.com
www.hautetcourt.com

JECK FILM
5 Rue Rene Boulanger, Paris 75010. TEL: (331) 4240 7800.
FAX: (331) 4803 0264. email: jeckfilm@wanadoo.fr

K—FILMS
7, Rue Commines, Paris 75003. TEL: (331) 4274 7014.
FAX: (331) 4274 7024. email: kfilms@noos.fr www.k-films.fr

K FILMS MULTIMEDIA
33 Blvd. Anatole France, Alès 30100. TEL: (334) 6656 5989.
FAX: (334) 6656 5989. email: malened@wanadoo.fr

K PRODUCTION
8, Impasse Moulive, Toulouse 31400. TEL: (335) 3431 5550.
FAX: (335) 3431 5186.

LES FILMS DU LOSANGE
26 Ave. Pierre 1er de Serfie, Paris 75116.
TEL: (331) 4720 5412, (331) 4443, 8715.
FAX: (331) 4952 0640.
email: info@filmsdulosange.fr www.filmsdulosange.fr

LES FILMS SINGULIER
20 Rue Michelet, Montreuil 93100.
TEL: (331) 4287 5908, (331) 4287, 0202.
FAX: (331) 4287 0189. email: singfilms@yahoo.fr
MANAGING DIRECTOR
Michel Poirier - micpoirier@yahoo.fr

LE STUDIO—CANAL PLUS
17 Rue Dumont D'urville, Paris 75116. TEL: (331) 4443 9800.
COO
Brahin Chioua
HEAD OF INTERNATIONAL SALES
Daniel Marquet

MARATHON INTERNATIONAL
74, Rue Bonaparte, Paris 75006. TEL: (331) 5310 9100.
FAX: (331) 44325 0466. www.marathon.fr
CEO
Olivier Bremond

MERCURE DISTRIBUTION
27, Rue de la Butte auc Cailles, Paris 75013.
TEL: (331) 4416 8844. FAX: (331) 4565 0747.
email: infos@mercure-distribution.fr
www.mercure-distribution.fr
MANAGER
Jacques Le Glou

METROPOLITAN FILMEXPORT
29 Rue Galilée, Paris 75016. TEL: (331) 5659 2300.
FAX: (331) 5357 8401. www.metrofilm.com

MK2
55 Rue Traversiere, Paris 75012. TEL: (331) 4467 3000.
FAX: (331) 4341 3230. email: sales@mk2.com
www.mk2.com

MOMENTO
38 rue de la Chine, Paris 75020. TEL: +33 1 43 66 25 24.
FAX: +33 1 43 66 86 00.
email: infos@momento-production.com
www.momento-production.com

OUTSIDER DIFFUSION
63 Rue Pascal, Paris 75013. TEL: (331) 4335 8174.
FAX: (331) 4707 1049.

PATHE INTERNATIONAL - FRANCE
10, Rue Lincoln, Paris 75008. TEL: (331) 4076 9438.
FAX: (331) 4076 9123. email: sales@patheinternational.fr
www.patheinternational.fr
SALES DIRECTOR
Pascal Diot, Christine Hayet

POINT DU JOUR
38 Rue Croix des Petits Champs, Paris 75001.
TEL: (331) 4703 4000. FAX: (331) 4703 3948.
CONTACT
Jean-Louis Saporito

PRESIDENT FILMS
Immueble le barjac, 1 Blvd. Victor, Paris 75015.
TEL: (331) 4425 0101. FAX: (331) 4425 0195.
PRESIDENT
Hugo Bergson-Vuillaume

PRETTY PICTURES
42, rue Edouard-Vaillant, Montreuil 93100.
TEL: (331) 4851 1612. FAX: (331) 4851 1610.

PYRAMIDE FILMS
5 Rue du Chevalier de Saint-George, Paris 75008.
TEL: (331) 4296 0101. FAX: (331) 4020 0221.
www.pyramidefilms.com
MANAGING DIRECTOR
Josse Pascale

QUINTA COMMUNICATIONS
16 Ave. Hoche, Paris 75008. TEL: (331) 4076 0454.
FAX: (331) 4256 6921. email: office@quintacommunication.com
www.quintacommunication.com

REVCOM INTERNATIONAL/LES FILMS ARIANE
15 Rue du Colonel Pierre Avia, Paris 75015.
TEL: (331) 4662 1777. FAX: (331) 4662 1797.

REZO FILMS
29, Rue du Faubourg-Poissonnière, Paris 75009.
TEL: (331) 411 05014. FAX: (331) 411 05024.
email: infosrezo@rezofilms.com www.rezofilms.com

ROISSY FILMS
58, Rue Pierre Charron, Paris 75008. TEL: (331) 5353 5050.
FAX: (331) 4289 2693. email: contact@roissyfilms.com
www.roissyfilms.com
CEO
Raphael Berdugo

STUDIO CANAL
1 Place du spectacle, Issy-les Moulineaux 92130.
TEL: +33 1 71 35 35 35. FAX: +33 1 71 35 11 98.
email: webmaster@studiocanal.com www.studiocanal.com

TWENTIETH CENTURY FOX
21 Bis Rue Lord Byron Paris 75008. TEL: (331) 539 39398.

U.F.D.
13 rue Madeleine Michelis, Neuilly sur Seine cedex 92522.
TEL: (331) 5524 4600. FAX: (331) 5524 4646.

UNITED INTERNATIONAL PICTURES
1 Rue Meyerbeer, Paris 75009. TEL: (331) 4007 3838.
FAX: (331) 4007 3839. www.uip.com
MANAGER
Jean-Paul Rougier

WARNER BROS.
115-123, Avenue Charles de Gaulle, Neuilly sur Seine 9252.
TEL: (331) 7225 0000. FAX: (331) 4763 4515.
www.warnerbros.fr

EXHIBITORS

CGR CINEMAS
8 rue Blaise Pascal Périgny, La Rochelle Cedex 17039, France
TEL: 05 46 44 85 51. www.cgrcinemas.fr
DIRECTOR GENERAL
Jocelyn Bouyssey
CONTACT
Roger Marc Le Coq

CINE-ALPES
8 rue Blaise Pascal Périgny, La Rochelle Cedex 17039.
www.cgrcinemas.fr
CONTACT
Roger Marc Le Coq

CINE-ALPES
150, rue Haute Tarentaise, 73700 Bourg Saint Maurice.
TEL: (334) 7907 6140. FAX: (334) 7907 6141.
www.cinealpes.fr
PRESIDENT
Gerard Davoine

Number of Theatres: 53
Number of Screens: 110

CINEMA LES ECRANS
9-11, place Denis Dussoubs, 87000 Limoges.
TEL: (335) 5577 4079. FAX: (335) 5579 4991.
PRESIDENT
Michel Fridemann

Number of Screens: 30

CINEMAS 14 JUILLET, NOW OPERATING AS MK2
55, Rue Traversiere, 75012, Paris. TEL: (334) 467 3000.
FAX: (334) 341 3230. www.mk2.fr
PRESIDENT
Marin Karmitz

Number of Theatres: 9
Number of Screens: 44

CIRCUIT GEORGES RAYMOND (CCGR)
8, Rue Blaise Pascal, Z.I. de Perigny, 17039 La Rochelle
Cedex. TEL: (335) 4644 0176. FAX: (335) 4644 5585.
PRESIDENT
Georges Raymond
GENERAL DIRECTOR
Roger-Marc Lecoq

Number of Screens: 330

EUROPA CINEMAS
54, Rue Beaubourg, Pairs F-75003. TEL: (331) 4271 5370.
FAX: (331) 4271 4755. email: europacinema@magic.fr
www.europa-cinemas.org
GENERAL DIRECTOR
Claude-Eric Poiroux

Number of Theatres: 66
Number of Screens: 188

EUROPALACES
2 rue Lamennais, Paris 75008.
TEL: (33) 171 72 30 90. FAX: (33) 171 72 30 82.
www.cinemasgaumont.com
CHAIRMAN
Eduardo Malone

GAUMONT CINEMAS
30, Av. Charles de Gaulle, Neuilly, Sur Seine 92200.
TEL: (331) 4643 2000. FAX: (331) 4643 2428. www.gaumont.fr
CHAIRMAN, CEO, & PRESIDENT
Nicolas Seydoux
EXECUTIVE V.P. & COO
Patrice Ledoux
V.P., EXHIBITION
Jean-Louis Renoux
DIRECTOR OF DEVELOPMENT
Jean-Yves Rabet

Number of Theatres: 41

LES IMAGES MEGARAMA
62. Rue Grande Rue, 25000 Besancon. TEL: (334) 500 0122.
FAX: (334) 500 0199.
GENERAL DIRECTOR
Jean-Pierre Lemoine

Number of Screens: 54

M.K.2
55, Rue Traversiere, 75012 Paris. TEL: (33) 4467 3000.
FAX: (33) 4341 32 30. www.mk2.fr
PRESIDENT
Nathanael Karmitz

Number of Theatres: 10
Number of Screens: 47

PATHE
21 Rue Francois 1er, 75008 Paris. TEL: (33) 4924 4003.
FAX: (33) 4924 4510.
PRESIDENT, PATHE GROUP
Jerome Seydoux
GENERAL DIRECTOR, CINEMAGRAPHIC EXHIBITION
Thierry Marques

Number of Theatres: 42
Number of Screens: 300

SOREDIC
3E, rue de Paris - BP GT339, 35513 Cesson-Sevigne Cedex.
TEL: (332) 9983 7800. FAX: (332) 9983 2937.
email: soredic@soredic.fr www.soredic.fr
PRESIDENT
Philippe Paumelle

Number of Theatres: 30
Number of Screens: 75

UNITED INTERNATIONAL PICTURES SARL
1 Rue Meyerbeer, 75009 Paris. TEL: 33-1-4007 3838.
FAX: 33-1-4742-0822.
MANAGER
Jean-Paul Rougier

UGC FRANCE
24 ave Charles de Gaulle, 92522 Nuyilly-sur-Seine Cedex.
TEL: (33) 1 46 40 44 0. FAX: (33) 1 46 24 37 28. www.ugc.fr
CEO
Guy Verrechia

Number of Theatres: 40
Number of Screens: 365

ASSOCIATIONS & ORGANIZATIONS

AGENCE DU CINÉMA INDÉPENDANT POUR SA DIFFUSION (ACID)
14, Rue Alexandre Parodi, Paris 75010. TEL: (331) 4489 9999.
FAX: (331) 4489 9960. email: acid@lacid.org www.lacid.org

ASSOCIATION DES EXPORTATEURS DE FILMS (ADEF)
11 Rue de Chateaubriand, Paris 75008. TEL: (331) 5376 2630.
FAX: (331) 4563 3735. email: contact@adef.fr
www.adef.fr

ASSOCIATION DES PRODUCTEURS INDÉPENDANTS (API)
15, Rue de Berri, Paris 75008. TEL: (331) 4289 3150.
FAX: (331) 4289 3140.

ASSOCIATION FRANÇAISE DE CINÉMA D'ANIMATION (AFCA)
53 Bis, Rue Rodier, Paris 75009. TEL: (331) 4023 0813.
FAX: (331) 4023 0917. email: contact@afca.asso.fr
www.afca.asso.fr

ASSOCIATION FRANÇAISE DES DIRECTEURS DE LA PHOTOGRAPHIE CINÉMA (AFC)
8, Rue Francoeur, Paris 75018. TEL: (331) 4264 4141.
FAX: (331) 4264 4252. www.afc.fr.st

ASSOCIATION FRANÇAISE DES PRODUCTEURS DE FILMS ET DE PROGRAMMES AUDIOVISUELS (A.F.P.F.)
50 rue de la Justice, Paris 75020. TEL: (331) 4032 4500.
FAX: (331) 4287 0189. email: afpf@free.fr
GENERAL MANAGER
Gerard Depouy

ATELIERS DU CINEMA EUROPEEN (ACE)
29, Rue du Faubourg Poissonnière, Paris 75009.
TEL: (331) 4246 6424. FAX: (331) 4246 6422.
email: info@ace-producers.com www.ace-producers.com

AUXITEC (SOCIETE AUXILIAIRE POUR LE CINEMA ET LA TV)
Ibis Ave. du Roi Albert, Cannes 06400. TEL: (3393) 940 777.
FAX: (339) 3438 8895.

BUREAU DE LIAISON DES INDUSTRIES CINÉMATOGRAPHIQUES (BLIC)
74, Avenue Kléber, Paris 75016. TEL: (331) 5690 3300.
FAX: (331) 5690 3301. email: blic@fndf.org

CENTRE FRANCAIS DU COMMERCE EXTERIEUR
10 Ave. d'Iena, Paris Cedex 16 75783. TEL: (331) 4073 3000.
FAX: (331) 4073 3979. www.cfce.fr

CENTRE NATIONAL DE LA CINEMATOGRAPHIE
12 Rue Lubeck, Paris 75016. TEL: (331) 4434 3440.
FAX: (331) 4434 3473. www.cnc.fr

CHAMBRE SYNDICALE DES PRODUCTEURS & EXPORTATEURS DE FILMS FRANCAIS
5 Rue de Cirque, Paris 75008. TEL: (331) 5389 0130.
FAX: (331) 4225 9427.

CINÉMATHÈQUE FRANÇAISE
4 Rue Longchamp, Paris 75116. TEL: (331) 5365 7474.
FAX: (331) 5365 7465. email: contact@cinemathequefrancaise.com
www.cinemathequefrancaise.com

CICCE
(European Committee Film Industries Commission)
5 Rue du Cirque, Paris 75008. TEL: (331) 4225 7063.
FAX: (331) 4225 9427.

CONSEIL SUPERIEUR DE L'AUDIOVISUEL (CSA)
39-43 Quai Andre-Citroen, Paris Cedex 15 75015.
TEL: (331) 4058 3800. FAX: (331) 4579 0006.

EUROPA CINEMAS
54 Rue Beaubourg. Paris 3 75003. TEL: (331) 4271 5370.
FAX: (331) 4271 4755. email: contact@europa-cinemas.org
www.europa-cinemas.org

FEDERATION INTERNATIONALE DES ASSOCIATIONS DE DISTRIBUTEURS DE FILMS (FIADF)
9 Rue de l'Echelle, 75001 Paris. TEL: (331) 4477 9750.
FAX: (331) 4477 9755.

FEDERATION NATIONALE DES CINEMAS FRANCAIS (FNCF)
15 Rue de Berri, Paris 75008. TEL: (331) 5393 7676.
FAX: (331) 4563 2976. www.fncf.org
PRESIDENT
Jean Labe

FEDERATION NATIONALE DES DISTRIBUTEURS DE FILMS (FNDF)
74 Avenue Kléber, Paris 75016. TEL: (331) 5690 3300.
FAX: (331) 5690 3301. email: films.fndf@fndf.org

FEDERATION OF THEATRE, CINEMA & AUDIOVISUAL UNIONS(FICAM)
14-16 Rue des Lilias, Paris 75015. TEL: (331) 4240 1495.
FAX: (331) 4240 9020. email: info@ficam.fr www.ficam.fr

NATIONAL FILM COMMISSION
33 Rue des Jeûneurs, Paris 75002. TEL: (331) 5383 9898.
FAX: (331) 5383 9899. email: film@filmfrance.net
www.filmfrance.com

FRENCH FEDERATION OF ENTERTAINMENT UNIONS (CGT)
14-16 rue des Lilas, Paris 75019. TEL: (331) 4803 8760.
FAX: (331) 4240 9020. email: fnsac@fnsac-cgt.com
www.fnsac-cgt.com

INSTITUT NATIONAL DE L'AUDIOVISUEL
4 Ave. de l'Europe, Bry-Sur-Marne 94366. TEL: (331) 4983 3160.
FAX: (331) 4983 3216. www.ina.fr

INSTITUT POUR LE FINANCEMENT DU CINÉMA ET DES INDUSTRIES CULTURELLES (IFCIC)
46 Avenue Victor Hugo, Paris 75116. TEL: (331) 5364 5555.
FAX: (331) 5364 5566.

MINISTERE DES AFFAIRES ETRANGERES
244 Blvd. St. Germaine, Paris 75007. TEL: (331) 4317 6699.
FAX: (331) 4317 8538. www.diplomatie.fr

SESAM
16 Place de la Fontaine, Aux Lions, Paris 19 75920.
TEL: (331) 4715 4905. FAX: (331) 4715 8379.

SOCIETE DES REALISATEURS DE FILMS (SRF)
215 Rue de Faubourg-Honoré, Paris 75008.
TEL: (331) 4563 9630. FAX: (331) 4074 0796.

UNIFRANCE FILM INTERNATIONAL
4 Villa Bosquet, Paris 75007. TEL: (331) 4753 9580.
FAX: (331) 4705 9655. email: contact@unifrance.org
www.unifrance.org
PRESIDENT
Margaret Menegoz
GENERAL MANAGER
Véronique Bouffard
HEAD OF PRODUCTION
Laurence Le Roy

UNION DES PRODUCTEURS DE FILMS
1 Place des Deux Ecus, Paris 75001. TEL: (331) 4028 0138.
FAX: (331) 4221 1700.

GERMANY

Capital: Berlin
Population: 82,282,988 (July 2010 est.)
Area: 357,021 sq.km.
Source: CIA World Factbook

DISTRIBUTORS AND PRODUCERS

ALAMODE & CELLULOID DREAMS
Nymphenburgerstr 36-80 strasse 36 Munchen 80335.
TEL: (4989) 1799 9211. FAX: (4989) 1799 9213.
email: info@alamodefilm.de www.alamodefilm.de

ARD/DEGETO FILM GMBH
Am Steinernen Stock 1, Frankfurt 60320. TEL: (4969) 1509 349.
FAX: (4969) 1509 339. email: degato@degato.de
MANAGING DIRECTOR
Hans-Wolfgang Jurgan

ARSENAL FILMVERLEIH STEFAN PAUL KG
PF 21 05 63, Hintere Grabenstr. 20D, Tübingen 72070.
TEL: (4970) 7192 960. FAX: (4970) 7192 961.
email: info@arsenalfilm.de www.arsenal-film.de

ASKARIAN FILM
Niebuhrstrasse 69, Berlin, Prenzlauer Berg D 10435.
TEL/FAX: (4930) 3246 023. email: askarianfilm@web.de
www.don-askarian.am
CONTACT
Don Askaarian

ATLAS FILM UND AV GMBH & CO. KG
Ludgeristrasse 14-16, Duisburg 47057. TEL: (4920) 3378 622.
FAX: (4920) 3362 482.

ATLAS INTERMEDIA FILM
Eduard Rosenthal - Str 30 Weimar 99423. TEL: (4936) 4341 5333.
FAX: (4936) 4341 4343. www.atlas-film.de

ATLAS INTERNATIONAL
Candidplatz 11, Munich Germany 81543. TEL: (4989) 210 9750.
FAX: (4989) 224 332. www.atlasfilm.com
PRESIDENT/CEO
Dieter Menz

BASIS FILM- UND PRODUKTION GMBH
Sudensstr 12, Berlin D 12169. TEL: (4930) 7935 16171.
FAX: (4930) 7911 551. email: info@basisfilm.de
www.basisfilm.de

BAUER FILMVERLEIH-KINO UND GASTRONOMIE
Schmiedingstrasse 19, Postfach 100329, Dortmund 4600.
TEL: (49231) 148 078.

BAVARIA FILM GMBH
Bavariafilmplatz 7, Geiselgasteig, Munich D-82031.
TEL: (4989) 6499 2686. FAX: (4989) 6499 3720.
email: bavaria.international@bavaria-film.de
www.bavaria-film-international.de
MANAGING DIRECTOR
Michael Weber

BAYERISCHER RUNDFUNK (BR)
Bayerischer Rundfunk Rundfunkplatz, Munich, Bavaria 1 D-80300. TEL: 49 089 59 00 01. email: info@br-online.de www.br-online.de

BEAUFILM
Hauptstr 155/V Berlin 10827. TEL: (4930) 7871 9743. FAX: (4930) 7871 9744.

BEATE UHSE FILMVERLEIH
Gutenbergstrasse 12, Flensburg 24941. TEL: (49461) 996 6221.

BETA CINEMA
Robert Burkle Str., 3, Ismaning 85737. TEL: (4989) 9956 2719. FAX: (4989) 9956 2703. email: arothbauer@betacinema.com www.betacinema.com
DIRECTOR
Dirk Schurhoff

BOJE BUCK PRODS./DELPHI FILM
Kantstrasse 12a, Berlin 10623. TEL: (4930) 313 2200. FAX: (4930) 312 9996.

BOLL KINO BETEILIGUNGS GMBH & CO. KG
Wormser Strasse 173, Mainz 55130. TEL: +49 1805 443 110. FAX: +49 1805 443 111. info@boll-kg.de www.boll-kg.de

BUENA VISTA INTERNATIONAL
Kronstadterstr. 9, Munich 81677. TEL: (4989) 9934 0270. FAX: (4989) 9934 0139. www.movie.de
CONTACT
Peter Sundarp

CENTRAL FILMVERTRIEB
Kleiststrasse 9-12, Berlin 10787. TEL: (4930) 214 920. FAX: (4930) 2149 2215.

CINE INTERNATIONAL
Leopoldstrasse 18, Munich D-80802. TEL: (4989) 391 025. FAX: (4989) 331 089. email: email@cine-international.de www.cine-international.de
PRESIDENT
Lilli Tyc-Holm

CINEMA FILMVERLEIH
Braystrasse 20, Munich D-811677. TEL: (4989) 472 061. FAX: (4989) 474 736.

CINEPOOL
Sonnenstrasse 21, Munich D-80331. TEL: (4989) 5587 6188. FAX: (4989) 5587 6188.

CINEVOX
Bavariafilmplatz 7, Gruenwald 82031. TEL: (4989) 641 8000. FAX: (4989) 649 3288.

COLUMBIA TRISTAR FILM (NOW PART OF SONY)
Kemperplatz 1, Berlin 10785. TEL: (4930) 2575 5800. FAX: (4930) 2575 5809. email: info@columbiatristar.de www.columbiatristar.de
GENERAL MANAGER
Martin Bachmann

CONCORDE—CASTLE ROCK/TURNER FILMVERLEIH
Rosenheimer Strasse 143b, Munich 81671. TEL: (4989) 450 6100. FAX: (4989) 4506 1010. email: verkauf@concorde-film.de www.concorde-film.de

CONNEXION FILM VETRIEBS & PRODUKTIONS GMBH
Harvesterhuder Weg 45, Hamburg 20149. TEL: (4940) 419 970. FAX: (4940) 419 9799.

CONSTANTIN FILM
Kaiserstrasse 39, Munich 80801. TEL: (4989) 386 090. FAX: (4989) 3860 9242. www.constantinfilm.de
MANAGER
Thomas Peter Friedl

CONTACT FILMVERLEIH
Huttenstrasse 40, Dusseldorf 40215. TEL: (49211) 374 024. FAX: (49211) 374 025.

DAZU FILM BONN
c/o Daniel Zuta Filmproduktion, Kaiserstrasse 39, Frankfurt Am Main D-60329. TEL: (4869) 253 735. FAX: (4989) 239 058.

DELPHI FILMVERLEIH GMBH
Kurfürstendamm 225, Berlin D 10719. TEL: (4930) 8859 740. FAX: (4930) 8859 7415. email: info@bojebuck.de www.delphi-film.de

ENDFILM
Am Vogelherd 4, Bach 93090. TEL: (4994) 823 377. FAX: (4994) 823 378.

EXCELL AGENTUR GMBH
Keltenring 17, Oberhaching 82041. TEL: (4989) 6790 4833. FAX: (4989) 6790 4642. email: info@efp-online.com www.efp-online.com

MANAGING DIRECTOR
Renate Rose

FILMWELT—PROKINO VERLEIHGEMEINSCHAFT
Ismaninger Strasse 51, Munich D-81675. TEL: (4989) 418 0010. FAX: (4989) 4180 0143.

FASSBINDER FOUNDATION
Kurfürstenstrasse 17, Berlin D 10785. TEL: (4930) 2618 484. FAX: (4930) 2650 214. email: info@fassbinderfoundation.de www.fassbinderfoundation.de

FOX - TWENTIETH CENTURY FOX OF GERMANY
Hainer Web 37-53, Frankfurt Am Main 60599. TEL: (4969) 609 020. FAX: (4969) 627 715. www.fox.com

FUTURA/FILMVERLAG DER AUTOREN
Rambergstrasse 5, Munich 80799. TEL: (4989) 3817 0030. FAX: (4989) 3817 0020.

GMFILMS
Varziner Strasse 3, Berlin D 12159. TEL: (4930) 8519 861. FAX: (4930) 8593 423. email: gmfilms@gmfilms.de www.gmfilms.de

INTERFILM BERLIN - DER KURZFILM VERLEIH
Tempelhofer Ufer 1a, Berlin Kreuzberg. D 10961. TEL: (4930) 2594 2904. FAX: (4930) 2594 2904. email: distribution@interfilm.de www.interfilm.de

JUGENDFILM VERLEIH GMBH
Nuene Schoenhauserstr 20, Berlin 10178. TEL: (4930) 300 6970. FAX: (4930) 3006 9711.

KERYX NOA & PRACELET MULTIMEDIA
Immenried 97, Kisslegg D-88353. TEL: (497563) 8372 8147. FAX: (497563) 8372 8217.

KINOWELT FILMVERLEIH
Postfach 10 12 55, Leipzig D-04012. TEL: (49341) 355960. FAX: (49341) 3559 6999. email: info@kinowelt.de www.kinowelt.de
MANAGERS
Ralph Koch, Bertil le Claire

KIRCH GROUP
Robert-Burklestrasse 2, Ismaning Munich 85737. TEL: (4989) 9956 2155. FAX: (4989) 9956 2751.

KLASING
Siekerwall 21, Bielefeld 33602. TEL: (49521) 5590. FAX: (49521) 559 113.

KUCHENREUTHER FILM GMBH
Sonnen Str. 22, Munich 80807. TEL: (4989) 596 717. FAX: (4989) 596 286.

MAGMAFILM GMBH
AnnastraßE 35-39, Essen 45130. TEL: +49 201 8727260. FAX: +49 201 775668. hbartelt@magmafilm.de www.magma.de

MEDIA LUNA ENTERTAINMENT
Hochstadenstrasse 1-3, Cologne 50674. TEL: (49221) 139 2222. FAX: (49221) 139 2224. email: info@medialuna-entertainment.de www.medialuna-entertainment.de
MANAGING DIRECTOR
Ida Martins

MERCATOR FILMVERLEIH
Werther Str. 73, Bielefeld 33615. TEL: (49521) 124 061. FAX: (49521) 131 010.

MULTI-MEDIA-VERLAG (MMV)
Kaddenbusch 5-7, Dägeling 25578. TEL: +49 4821 890418. FAX: +49 4821 8904818. info@mmv-gmbh.de www.mmv.tv

MUSKATFILM
Ebersstrasse 27 II, Berlin, Schöneberg D 10827. TEL: (4930) 851 1320. FAX: (4930) 8511 320. email: muskatfilm@gmx.de www.muskatfilm.de

NEUE CONSTANTIN FILM
Kaiserstrasse 39, Munich 80801. TEL: (4989) 386 090. FAX: (4989) 3860 9242.

NEUE VISIONEN FILM VERLEIH
Schliemannstr. 5, Berlin, Prenzlauer Berg D 10437. TEL: (4930) 4400 8844. FAX: (4930) 4400 8845. email: neuevisionen@gmx.de www.neuevisionen.de

NIGHTHAWKS PICTURES GMBH & CO. KG
Mangerstrasse 24/25, Potsdam D 14467. TEL: (49331) 2337 982. FAX: (49331) 337 961. email: info@nighthawks-pictures.com www.nighthawks-pictures.com

PANDORA FILM
Hamburger Allee 45, Frankfurt 60486. TEL: (4969) 779 094. FAX: (4969) 707 4033. www.pandorafilm.de

PROGRESS FILMVERLEIH
Immanuelkirchstrasse 14, Berlin 10415. TEL: (4930) 2400 3400.
FAX: (4930) 2400 3499. www.progress-film.de
CONTACT
Angela Henkel - a.henkel@progress-film.de
Sigrid Geerdts - s.geerdts@progress-film.de

SALZGEBER & CO. MEDIEN GMBH
Friedrichstraße 122, Berlin - Mitte D 10117. TEL: (4930) 2852 9090.
FAX: (4930) 2852 9099. email: info@salzgeber.de
www.salzgeber.de

SELLENG FILMAGENTUR
Lietzenburgerstrasse 51, Berlin 1000. TEL: (4930) 213 6788.
FAX: (4930) 213 8187.

SENATOR FILM VERLEIH GMBH
Kurfürstendamm 65, Berlin - Wilmersdorf D 10707 B.
TEL: (4930) 8809 1700. FAX: (4930) 8809 1787.
email: info@senator.de www.senator.de

STARDUST FILMVERLEIH GMBH
Zielstattstr. 42 81379 München. TEL: (4989) 749 47615.
FAX: (4989) 749 47 11. www.stardust-filmverleih.de

TIME MEDIENVERTRIEBS
Nymphenburgerstrasse 158, Munich D-80634.
TEL: (4989) 160 923. FAX: (4989) 162 056.
DISTRIBUTION
Annette Niehues

TOBIS FILMKUNST GMBH & CO.
Pacelliallee 47, Berlin 14195. TEL: (4930) 839 0070.
FAX: (4930) 8390 0765. email: info@tobis.de www.tobis.de

UNITED INTERNATIONAL PICTURES GMBH
Postfach 71 08 48, 60498, Frankfurt Am Main.
TEL: 49-69-669 8190. FAX: 49-69-666 6509.
MANAGER
Paul Steinschulte

UNIVERSUM FILM (UFA)
Neumarkter Str. 28, Munich, Bavaria 81673.
TEL: +49 (0)89 41369600. FAX: +49 (0)89 41369871.
info@universumfilm.de www.universumfilm.de/

VENTURA FILM GMBH
Boxhagener Straße 18, Berlin - Friedrichshain 10245.
TEL: (4930) 2836 530. FAX: (4930) 2836 533.
email: ventura.film@snafu.de www.ventura-film.de

WARNER BROS. FILM
Hans-Henny-Jahn-Weg 35, Hamburg D-22085.
TEL: (4940) 226 500. FAX: (4940) 2265 0109.
email: info@warnerbros.de www.warnerbros.de

ZWEITES DEUTSCHES FERNSEHEN (ZDF)
Lise-Meitner-Str. 9, Mainz 55100.
TEL: +49 (0) 6131 70-1. FAX: +49 (0) 6131 70-2157.
info@zdf.de www.zdf.de/

EXHIBITORS

BROADWAY ENTERTAINMENT GMBH
Merkurstr 9-11, 66849, Landstuhl. TEL: (4963) 7193 7000.
FAX: (4963) 7193 7111.
MANAGING DIRECTORS
Renate Goldhammer, Ernst Pletsch

Number of Screens: 7

BROADWAY FILMTHEATER, GMBH
Im Feld 53, 51427 Bergisch-Gladbach. TEL: (49) 22 04 65 595.
FAX: (49) 22 04 62 450.
MANAGING DIRECTORS
Helmut Brunotte, Claudia Hebbel

BROADWAY FTB GMBH
Paulinstr. 18, 54292 Trier. TEL: (49) 6512 4605.
FAX: (49) 6512 6111.
MANAGING DIRECTOR
Dirk Ziesenhenne

Number of Theatres: 1
Number of Screens: 5

BROADWAY KINO
Ehrenstrasse 11, Cologne 50672. TEL: (49221) 925 6570.
FAX: (49221) 9257 5714. www.broadwaykino.com

CADILLAC
Rosenkavalierplatz 12, Munich 81925. TEL: (4989) 912 000.
FAX: (4989) 916 390.

CASABLANCA GASTST, KULTUR & KINO GMBH
Johannisstr. 17, 26121 Oldenburg. TEL: (49) 441 88 4757.
FAX: (49) 441 88 8072.
MANAGING DIRECTOR
Dr. Detlef Rossman

CINECITTA
Gewerbemuseumsplatz 3, Nurnberg 90403.
TEL: 49 (0) 911206660. FAX: 49 (0) 9112066612.
www.cinecitta.de
OWNER
Wolfram Weber

CINEMAXX H.J. FLEBBE FILMTHEATERBETRIEBE
Friedrich-Ebot-Damm IM, Hamburg 22047.
TEL: (49) 40450 680. FAX: (49) 40 450 68201.
email: info@cinemaxx.de www.cinemaxx.com
PRESIDENT & GENERAL MANAGER
Hans-Joachim Flebbe
GENERAL MANAGER & CFO
H. Scheunemann

Number of Theatres: 43
Germany (40), Denmark (3)

CINESTAR
Muehlenbruecke 9-11, 23552 Luebeck. TEL: (49) 451 7030 200.
FAX: (49) 451 7030 299. www.cinestar.de
MANAGING DIRECTOR
Marlis Kieft, Heiner Kieft
MANAGER
Oliver Fock
CFO
Richard Stotz
HEAD OF COMMUNICATION & ADVERTISING
Lars Kuhne, Saber Romdhani

Number of Theatres: 60
Number of Screens: 380

CITY KINO
Schwanthalerstrasse 7, Munich 80331. TEL: (4989) 598 749.
FAX: (4989) 550 2171.

COLM ENTERTAINMENT AG
Alte Poststr 3, 701 73 Stuggart. TEL: (49) 711 292 245.
FAX: (49) 711 226 3411.
MANAGING DIRECTOR
Roman Colm

COLM FILMTHEATERBETRIEBE
Alte Poststrasse 3, Stuttgart 70197. TEL: (49) 711 650 400.
FAX: (49) 711 657 2530.

DELPHI FILMVERLEIH GMBH
Kurfürstendamm 225, Berlin D 10719. TEL: (4930) 8859 740.
FAX: (4930) 8859 7415. email: info@bojebuck.de
www.delphi-film.de

ECKART AND WOLFRAM WEBER-FTB
Gewerbemuseumpsl 3, 90403 Nurnberg. TEL: (49) 11 20 66 60.
FAX: (49) 11 20 66 612.

ERASMUS KINOVERWALTUNG
Grimmstrasse 30A, Stuttgart 70197. TEL: (49711) 650 400.
FAX: (49711) 657 2530.

FILMTHEATERBETRIEBE BERLIN
Schuchardtweg 9B, Berlin 14109. TEL: (4930) 805 4829.
FAX: (4930) 805 5258.

FILMTHEATERBETRIEBE GEORGE REISS
Sophienstrasse 1, Munich 803333. TEL: (4989) 552 1650.
FAX: (4989) 5521 6525.

FILMTHEATER-VERWVLTUNG REHS
44787 Bochum, Viktoriastr. 29. TEL: (49) 34 96 1710.
FAX: (49) 34 96 17199.

FREYMUTH SCHULTZ VEREINGTE LICHTSPIELE
Jann-Berghaus-Str. 9, 26757 Borkum. TEL: (49) 22 91 810.
FAX: (49) 22 91 8141.

FTB ADRIAN KUTTER
88400 Biberach. TEL: (49) 7351 7 23 31. FAX: (49) 7351 1 37 64.

FTB BERLIN
Schuchardtweg 9, 14109 Berlin. TEL: (49) 30 805 48 29.
FAX: (49) 30 805 52 58.
MANAGING DIRECTOR
Peter H. Vollman

FTB W. BURTH
88212 Marienpl. 4, Ravensurg. TEL: (49) 7 51 36 14 436.
FAX: (49) 7 51 36 14 459.
MANAGING DIRECTOR
Axel Burth

FTB DR. HERIBERT SCHLINKER
34414 Warburg, Johanaistorstr 35. TEL: (49) 56 41 23 63.
FAX: (49) 56 41 54 40.

FTB GEORG REISS GMBH
Sophienstr. 1, Munchen 80333. TEL: (49) 89 55 21 650.
FAX: (49) 89 55 21 6525.

FTB HANS-GEORGE SAWATZKI
55543 Bad Kreuznach, Kreuzstr. 57-63. TEL: (49) 06 71 28883.

FUTURA KINOBETRIEBS GMBH
80799 Munchen, Rambergstr. 5. TEL: (49) 89 38 17 000.
FAX: (49) 8938 17 0020.

FWU FILM INSTITUTE
Bavaria Film Platz 3, Gruenwald 82131. TEL: (4989) 64970.
FAX: (4989) 649 7360.

GILDE DEUTSCHES FILMKUNSTTHEATER
Waldseerstrasse 3, Biberach/Riss 884000.
TEL: (4973) 517 2331. FAX: (4973) 511 3764.

THE GREATER UNION ORGANISATION
(including Birch Carroll & Coyle)
49 Market St., Sydney, NSW 2000, Australia.
TEL: (612) 93 73 66 00. FAX: (612) 93 73 65 32.
MANAGING DIRECTOR
Robert Manson

Number of Theatres: 30 (Germany)
Number of Screens: 246 (Germany)

HANSEATER FILMTHEATERBETRIEBE
Kurfuerstendamm 33, Berlin 10719. TEL: (4930) 883 6086.
FAX: (4930) 883 6520.

HERMANN-CLOSMANN ERBEN D.G. FTB
Biegenstr. 8, 35037 Marburg. TEL: (49) 64 21 17 300.
FAX: (49) 64 21 17 30 40.
MANAGING DIRECTOR
Gerhard Closmann

WALTER H. JANN WERBE & FILMBETR. GMBH
Hauptstr. 16, 82319 Starnberg. TEL: (49) 81 51 1 37 92.
FAX: (49) 81 51 2 83 20.

KIEFT & KIEFT FILMTHEATER GMBH
(Now operating as Cinestar)
Muehlenbruecke 9-11, 23552 Luebeck. TEL: (49) 451 7030 200.
FAX: (49) 451 7030 299. www.cinestar.de
MANAGING DIRECTOR
Marlis Kieft, Heiner Kieft
MANAGER
Oliver Frock

Number of Theatres: 60
Number of Screens: 380

KINEMATOGRAPH FILM GMBH
Biedersteiner Str. 11, 80802 Munchen. TEL: (49) 89 55 71 60.
FAX: (49) 89 59 45 59.
PRESIDENT & OWNER
Dr. Dieter Buchwald
EXECUTIVE V.P.
Klans Ungerer

KINOCENTER OTTOBRUNN
Ottostrasse 72, Ottobrunn 85521. TEL: (4989) 609 4141.
FAX: (4989) 609 9696.

KINOPOLIS MAIN–TAUNUS GMBH & CO.
Main-Taunus-Zentrum, Sulzbach/Hossen, 65843.
TEL: (49) 6 39 14 03 80. FAX: (49) 6 93 14 03 899.
MANAGING DIRECTOR
Wolfgang Theile

KUCHENREUTHER FILM
Sonnenstrasse 22, Munich 80331.
TEL: (4989) 596 717. FAX: (4989) 596 286.

LISELOTTE JAEGER FILMTHEATERBETRIEBE
Holzgraben 26, Frankfurt 60313. TEL: (4969) 285 205.
FAX: (4969) 281 957.

Zeil 125, Frankfurt 60313. TEL: (49) 69 28 52 05.
FAX: (49) 69 28 19 57.

LUDWIG SCHEER & CO. KG-FTB
Juliuspromenade 68, 97070 Wurzburg. TEL: (49) 93 15 31 31.
FAX: (49) 93 15 51 01.

MEGA EXTREM CINEMA GMBH
August-Horch-Str. 2a, 56070 Koblenz. TEL: (49) 2 61 8 09 05 15.
FAX: (49) 2 61 8 09 05 30.
MANAGING DIRECTOR
Dieter Tobolik

MUENSTERSCHE FILMTHEATER
Bahnhofstr. 20-22, 48143 Muenster. TEL: (49) 2 515 60 07.
FAX: (49) 2 515 60 08.

NEUE CONSTANTIN KINOBETRIEBE
Kaiserstrasse 39, Munich 80801.
TEL: (4989) 386 090. FAX: (4989) 3860 9166.

OLYMPIC/HEINZ RIECH & SON
Graf Adolfstrasse 96, Dusseldorf 40210. TEL: (49211) 169 060.
FAX: (49211) 169 0633.

OMNIPLEX FILMTHEATERBETRIEBE
30159 Hannover. Luisenstr. 10-11. FAX: (49) 51 132 27 11.

PALAST/SCHMID & THEILE
Lautenschlagerstrasse 3, Stuttgart 70173. TEL: (49711) 225 750.
FAX: (49711) 225 7599.

PEP FILMTHEATER GMBH
35757 Driedorf, P.O. Box 1221. TEL: (49) 27 75 95 05 03.
FAX: (49) 27 75 95 05 04. email: Plass@gloria.dill.de
MANAGING DIRECTOR
Peter Plass

GERD POLITT FILMTHEATERBETRIEBE
Konigswall 4, 45657 Recklinghausen. TEL: (49) 23 61 93 350.
FAX: (49) 23 61 22 287.

POTSDAM FILM MUSEUM
Martsall, Potsdam 14467. TEL: (49331) 271 810.
FAX: (49331) 271 8126.

ROLF THEILE FILMTHEATERBETRIEBE
Holdgestrasse 12, Darmstadt 6100. TEL: (49615) 129 780.
FAX: (49615) 129 7832.

ROSSLENBROICH-FTB GMBH
Dusseldorfer Str. 2, 40822 Mettman. TEL: (49) 21 04 7 43 66.
FAX: (49) 21 04 7 46 34.
MANAGING DIRECTOR
M. Papenhoff, G. Rosslenbroich

ROYAL PALAST
Goetheplatz 2, Munich 80337. TEL: (4989) 533 956.
FAX: (4989) 530 9618.

SCALA: FTB GMBH
78462 Konstanz Rosgartenstr, 9. TEL: (75) 31 2 45 22.
FAX: (75) 31 1 63 23.
MANAGING DIRECTOR
Kurt Rabe

UFA THEATER AG
Graf-Adolf-Strasse 96, 40210 Dusseldorf. TEL: (49) 211 169 060.
FAX: (49) 211 169 0633.
CEO
Volker Riech

Number of Screens: 500

UNION KG KRUGMANN & WEISCHER
Hamburger St., 152, 22083 Hamburg. TEL: (49) 40 2 07 05.
FAX: (49) 40 29 90 71 77.

UNITED CINEMAS INTERNATIONAL MULTIPLEX GMBH
Oskar-Hoffman-Strasse 156, 44789 Bochum.
TEL: (49) 234 937 190. FAX: (49) 234 937 1913.
www.uci-kinowelt.de

Number of Theatres: 22
Number of Screens: 209

VEREINIGTE LICHTSPIELE
72016 Pf. 2609 Tubingen. TEL: (49) 70 71 2 36 61.
FAX: (49) 70 71 2 14 21.

WETTLAUFER KINOBETRIEBS-GESELLSCHAFT MBJ
82456 Garmisch- Partenkirchen, Postfach. 1624.
TEL: (49) 8821 2370. FAX: (49) 8821 9501 44.
EXECUTIVE
Georg Wettlaufer, Nora Wettlaufer

YORK–KINO GMBH-FTB
Rankestrasse 31, Berlin 10789. TEL: (49) 30 2 12 98 00.
FAX: (49) 30 21 29 80 99. email: yorck@yorck.de
www.yorck.de

Number of Theatres: 15

ASSOCIATIONS & ORGANIZATIONS

BERLIN-BRANDENBURG FILM BOARD
August-Bebel-Strasse 26-53, Potsdam-Babelsberg 14482.
TEL: (49331) 743 870. FAX: (49331) 743 8799.
email: info@medienboard.de www.bbfc.de

GERMAN FILM SERVICE & MARKETING GMBH
Sonnenstr. 21, Munich D-80331. TEL: (4989) 599 7870.
FAX: (4989) 5997 8730. www.german-cinema.de
CHAIRMAN
Alfred Huermer
MANAGING DIRECTOR
Christian Dorsch
DIRECTOR, PUBLIC RELATIONS
Mariette Rissenbeek

FREIWILLIGE SELBSTKONTROLLE DER FILMWIRTSCHAFT GMBH (FSK)
Kreuzberger Ring 56, Wiesbaden 65205. TEL: (49611) 778910.
FAX: (49611) 7789139. email: fsk@spio-fsk.de www.spio.de

GERMAN FEDERAL FILM BOARD
Grosse Präsidentenstrasse 9, Berlin 10178. TEL: (4930) 275770.
FAX: (4930) 27577 111. email: presse@ffa.de www.ffa.de

GERMAN INSTITUTE FOR FILM INFORMATION
Schaumainkai 41, Frankfurt Am Main 60596.
TEL: (4969) 617 045. FAX: (4969) 620 060.

GERMAN INSTITUTE FOR FILM INFORMATION/FILM ARCHIVE
Potsdamer Strasse 2, Berlin 10785. TEL: (4930) 300 9030.
FAX: (4930) 300 90313. email: info@filmmuseum-berlin.de
www.filmmuseum-berlin.de

INSTITUTE FOR FILM AND THE VISUAL ARTS IN EDUCATION
Bavariafilmplatz 3, Geiselgasteig 82031. TEL: (4989) 64971.
FAX: (4989) 649 7300. email: info@fwu.de www.fwu.de
MANAGING DIRECTOR
Dr. Uwe L. Haass

SPITZENORGANISATION DER FILMWIRTSCHAFT E.V.
Kreuzberger Ring 56, Wiesbaden 65205. TEL: (49611) 778910.
FAX: (49611) 7789139. email: spio@spio-fsk.de www.spio.de
CONTACT
Christiane von Wahlert

STATE MINISTER FOR CULTURE AND MEDIA (BKM)
Graurheindorfer Strasse, 198, 53117 Bonn.
TEL: (49) 01888/681 0. FAX: (49) 01888/681 3885.
www.bundesregierung.de
CONTACT
Dr. Hermann Scharnhoop

GREECE

Capital: Athens
Population: 10,749,943 (July 2010 est.)
Area: 131,940 sq. km.
Source: CIA World Factbook

DISTRIBUTORS AND PRODUCERS

AMA FILMS (GEORGE STERGIAKIS & CO)
54 Themistokleous St., Athens 10681. TEL: (30 210) 383 3119, 381 2640. FAX: (30 210) 384 2559.
email: amafilms@amafilms.gr amafilms@otenet.gr
www.amafilms.gr
MANAGING DIRECTOR & PRESIDENT
George Stergiakis
VICE PRESIDENT
Jimmy Stergiakis

HELLINIKI KINIMSTROGRAFIKI ENOSSI (ELKE)
(Distributes films of Warner Bros, Goldcrest, Carolco, Lorimar, Globe, Rank, Thames International, etc.)
96-98 Academias St., Athens 10677. TEL: (30 210) 382 3801.
FAX: (30 210) 380 301.
GENERAL MANAGER
George V. Michaelides

ODEON FILMS (ELKE)
275 Messsogion Ave Athens. TEL: (930 210) 678 6601.
FAX: (30 210) 674 0073. email: odeon@huh.com.gr
www.odeon.gr

OVO FILMS
27 Themistokleous St., Athens 10677. TEL: (30 210) 330 4521.
FAX: (30 210) 330 4523.

PROOPTIKI S. A.
(Distributes films of Columbia Pictures, Orion, Touchstone, Walt Disney, Tri Star, Cannon)
40-42 Koleti St., Athens 10682. TEL: (30 210) 383 3541.
FAX: (30 210) 381 3762. email: info@prooptiki.gr
www.prooptiki.gr
GENERAL MANAGER
Pantelis Metropoulos

ROSEBUD MOTION PICTURES ENTERPRISES
(Distributes independent American, European & Int'l. films)
96-98 Academias St., Athens 10677. TEL: (30 210) 678 6001.
FAX: (30 210) 672 8927.
GENERAL MANAGER
Mairilisa Totomi

SPENTZOS FILMS S. A.
(Distributes films of Twentieth Century Fox, New Line Cinema, independent and European films)
9-13 Gravias St., Athens 10678. TEL: (30 210) 380 9314.
FAX: (30 210) 382 1438.
GENERAL MANAGER
George Spentzos

UNITED INTERNATIONAL PICTURES (UIP)
(Distributes MGM, Paramount, Universal & United Artists films)
4 Gamvetta St., Athens 10678. TEL: (30 210) 3800 240.
FAX: (30 210) 3835 396. email: uip_greece@uip.com
GENERAL MANAGER
Thanos Revis

EXHIBITORS

AMA FILMS (GEORGE STERGIAKIS & CO)
54 Themistokleous St., Athens 10681. TEL: (30 210) 383 3119, 381 2640. FAX: (30 210) 384 2559.
email: amafilms@amafilms.gr amafilms@otenet.gr
www.amafilms.gr
MANAGING DIRECTOR & PRESIDENT
George Stergiakis
VICE PRESIDENT
Jimmy Stergiakis
Number of Theatres: 5

APOSTOLOS FOUKIS
Messoguion St., Athens 11522.
Theatres: Galaxias, Metropolitan

ATTICA CINEPLEX
12 Messoguion St., Athens 16231.
Theatres: Opera I, Opera

K. GEORGOPOULOS S.A.
109 Kifissias St., Athens 11524.
Theatre: Danos

HOME VIDEO HELLAS
325 Messoguion St., Athens 15231.
Theatres: Opera I, Opera II, Radio City, Assos Odcon I, Assos Odcon II, Tropical, Havana, Anessis, Assos Odeon Maroussi, Olympion I and Olympion II, Assos Odeon

IONAIDES FILMS EPE
12 Nikiforou Lytra St., Athens 11474.
Theatre: Astron

STAVROS ISAAKIDES
26 Velvendous St., Athens 11364.
Theatre: Ilyssia

KAPSIS HEIRS
14 Kifissias St., Athens.
Theatre: Anessis

CHRISTOS KARAVIAS & COMPANY
12 Alexandras Ave., Athens.
Theatre: Nirvana

A KARAVOYKYROS – K. FRANTZIS, S.A.
122 Patrission St., Athens 11257.
Theatre: Athena

KONTOULIS
152 EL. Venizelos St., Callithea, Athens.
Theatre: Etoile

FOTIS KOSMIDES
Korae St., Athens 10566.
Theatres: Asty, Hellinis

VICTOR MICHAELIDES
Theatre Palac, 4 Voukoutestiou St., Athens 10565.

PANAYOTOPOULOS
3 Patriarchou Ioakem, Athens 1-673.
Theatre: Embassy

D.P. SKOURAS FILMS
19 Stadium St., Athens 10561.
Theatres: Attikon, Apollon

SPENTZOS FILMS S. A.
9-13 Gravias St., Athens 10678. TEL: (301) 382 0957.
FAX: (301) 382 1438.
Theatres: Ideal, Aliki, ABC, Oscar, Ideal Maroussi

STERIAKIS BROTHERS/AMA FILMS
122 Patrission St., Athens 11257.
Theatre: Athena

VILLAGE ROADSHOW, GREECE
(For complete listing see Australian branch)
11 Mistral St., Neo Psyhiko, Athens 15451.
TEL: (30 210) 685 6833. FAX: (30 210) 685 6830.
Number of Theatres: 4 (Greece)
Number of Screens: 44 (Greece)

ASSOCIATIONS & ORGANIZATIONS

ASSOCIATION OF TECHINICIANS (ETEKT)
25 Veltetsiou St., Athens 106 80. TEL: (301) 360 2379.
FAX: (301) 361 6442.

GREEK ACTORS GUILD
33 Kaningos St., Athens 10677. TEL: (30 210) 381 7369.
FAX: (30 210) 380 8651. email: sei@sei.gr www.sei.gr

GREEK ASSOCIATION OF FILM CRITICS
42-46, Ioulianou str., Athens 104 34, Greece.
TEL: (30210) 882 3920.

GREEK FEDERATION OF FILM SOCIETIES
12, Klisovis str., Athens 10677. TEL: (30 210) 384 7393.
FAX: (30 210) 384 7393. email: okle@filmfiles.gr
www.filmfiles.gr/ff.html

GREEK FILM & TV PRODUCERS UNION (PACT)
K. Palaiologou 73, 152 32 Halandri, Athens.
TEL: (30 210) 682 6743. FAX: (30 210) 684 4078.
email: dharatsi@otenet.gr
PRESIDENT
Vasilis Kolovos
SECRETARY GENERAL
Akindinos Gikas
PUBLIC RELATIONS DIRECTOR
Lila Kafantari

GREEK FILM CENTER
19 Paneoistimiou St., Athens 10671. TEL: (30 210) 3631733.
FAX: (30 210) 361 4336. email: info@gfc.gr www.gfc.gr
PRESIDENT
Diagoras Chronopoulos
VICE PRESIDENT
Demetri Sofianopoulos

GREEK FILM DIRECTORS UNION
Office:11, Tositsa Str., Athens 10683. TEL: (30 210) 822 8936.
FAX: (30 210) 821 1390. email: ees@ath.forhtnet.gr

HELLENIC AUDIOVISUAL INSTITUTE
Vas. Sofias 14, Athens 106 74. TEL: (30 210) 725 8910.
FAX: (30 210) 725 8911.

HELLENIC MINISTRY OF CULTURE
20-22 Bouboulinas St., 106 82 Athens.
TEL: (30 210) 820 1100. www.culture.gr

TANIOTHIKI TIS ELLADOS/GREEK FILM ARCHIVE
1 Kanari St., Athens GR-10671. TEL: (30 210) 361 2046.
FAX: (30 210) 362 8468. email: tain@otenet.gr www.tte.gr
DIRECTOR
Theodoros Adamopoulos
VICE DIRECTOR
Dimitris Hatzis
HEAD OF PROGRAMMING
Maria Komninou
HEAD OF DOCUMENTATION
Emilia Mathes

THESSALONIKI INTERNATIONAL FILM FESTIVAL
9, Alexandras Ave., 11473 Athens, Greece.
TEL: (30 210) 87 06 000. FAX: (30 210) 64 48 143.
email: info@filmfestival.gr www.filmfestival.gr
DIRECTOR
Despina Mouzaki

HONG KONG

Population: 7,089,705 (July 2010 est.)
Area: 425.8 sq mi
Source: CIA World Factbook

FILM DISTRIBUTORS AND PRODUCERS

BOJON FILMS CO., LTD
Unit 3 19/F Billion Trade Ctr. 31 Hung To Road Kwun Tong
Kowloon. TEL: (852) 2336 6169. FAX: (852) 2338 5659.

BUENA VISTA INTERNATIONAL (HONG KONG)
20/F Shell Tower Times Square, 1 Matheson St. Causeway Bay
Hong Kong. TEL: (852) 2203 2000. FAX: (852) 2203 1192.

CELESTIAL PICTURES, LTD
Shaw Administration Bldg., Lot 220 Clearwater Bay Rd., Sai
Kung, Kowloon. TEL: (852) 2927 1111. FAX: (852) 2243 0008.
email: enquiry@celestialpictures.com www.celestialpictures.com

CINE-CENTURY CO
Unit F 20/F Infotech Ctr., 21 Hung To Rd., Kwun Tong, Kowloon.
TEL: (852) 2345 2983. FAX: (852) 2345 0740.
email: cinecentury@on-nets.com www.cinecentury.com.hk

CITY ENTERTAINMENT
Unit B2 17/F Fortune Fty Bldg., 40 Lee Chung St., Chai Wan.
TEL: (852) 2892 0155. FAX: (852) 2838 4930.
www.cityentertainment.com.hk

CHINA STAR ENTERTAINMENT, LTD.
Unit 503/C, Miramar Tower, 1-23 Kimberley Rd., TST, Kowloon.
TEL: (852) 2323 1888. FAX: (852) 2191 9888.
email: movie@chinastar.com.hk www.chinastar.com.hk

CONTINENTAL FILM DISTRIBUTORS
Unit 1922, Star House, 3 Salisbury Rd., Tsimshatsui, Kowloon.
TEL: (852) 730 4373. FAX: (852) 730 2977.

DELON INTERNATIONAL FILM
7B Astoria Bldg., 34 Ashley Rd., Tsimshatsui, Kowloon.
TEL: (852) 376 1168. FAX: (852) 376 2569.

DELTAMAC (HK) CO, LTD
Unit 1002 Nanyang Plaza, 57 Hung To Rd., Kwun Tong,
Kowloon. TEL: (852) 2787 0678. FAX: (852) 2398 1744.
email: sales@deltamac.com.hk www.deltamac.com

DISCOVER CHINA PRODUCTIONS, LTD
26/F Asia Orient Tower 33 Lo9ckart Road Wan Chai.
TEL: (852) 2295 3830. FAX: (852) 2342 9808.
CONTACT
Steven Hon

EMPEROR MULTIMEDIA GROUP
28/F Emperor Group Ctr., 288 Hennessy Rd., Wan Chai.
TEL: (852) 2835 6688. FAX: (852) 2893 4309.
email: albertlee@emg.com.hk www.emg.com.hk

ERA FILMS
Unit 1008-1018 Trans Asia Ctr., 18 Kin Hong St., Kwai Chung
NT. TEL: (852) 2787 3612. FAX: (852) 2787 4367.
email: ceciliayau@erahk.com www.erahk.com

FAR SUN FILM CO, LTD
9/F Tin On Sing Comm Bldg. 41-43 Graham St. Central Hong
Kong. TEL: (852) 2546 2128. FAX: (852) 2548 1706.
www.yofan.com

FOCUS FILM
18/F Futura Plaza, 111-113 How Ming St. Kwun Tong Kowloon.
TEL: (852) 3120 3361. FAX: (852) 2343 3243.
email: daniel@focusfilm.cc www.focusfilm.cc

FOX COLUMBIA TRISTAR/KENTAC INVESTMENTS, LTD.
(Hong Kong sub-distributor for Twentieth Century Fox Film)
Rm. 1218 Tower 2 Admiralty Ctr., 18 Harcourt Rd., Admiralty.
TEL: (852) 2876 3939. FAX: (852) 2866 3985.

GALA FILM
16/F The Penisula Office Tower, 18 Middle Rd. Tsim Sha Tsui
Kowloon. TEL: (852) 2352 8222. FAX: (852) 2351 1683.
CONTACT
Belinda Tang

GOLDEN HARVEST ENTERTAINMENT CO., LTD.
16/F The Peninsula Office Tower, 18 Middle Rd., Tsim Sha
Tsui, Kowloon. TEL: (852) 2352 8222. FAX: (852) 2351 1683.
email: teerachai_t@goldenharvest.com
www.goldenharvest.com

GOLDEN NETWORK ASIA LIMITED
Unit 2205, Futura Plaza, 111-113 How Ming St., Kwun Tong,
Kowloon. TEL: (852) 2751 1886. FAX: (852) 2750 4862.
email: goldnet@netvigator.com
MANAGING DIRECTOR
Connie Wong

GOLDEN PRINCESS AMUSEMENT
23/F Pioneer Ctr., 750 Nathan Rd., Kowloon.
TEL: (852) 2399 6295. FAX: (852) 2626 1910.
email: andrewau@kdc.com.hk

GOLDEN SCENE CO, LTD.
15B Astoria Bldg., 34 Ashley Rd., Tsim Sha Tsui, Kowloon.
TEL: (852) 2265 9999. FAX: (852) 2302 0938.
email: winnie@goldenscene.com www.goldenscene.com

GOLDEN SUN FILM COMPANY
11/F Hing Lok House, 477 Nathan Rd., Kowloon.
TEL: (852) 2385 5939. FAX: (852) 2368 3873.
www.goldenson.film.com
PRESIDENT
Lan Tien Hong

GRAND HYATT FILMS, LTD.
Rm. 901 Hart Ave., Plaza 5-9. Tsim Sha Tsui Kowloon.
TEL: (852) 2710 9377. FAX: (852) 2710 8337.
email: zp2688@sina.com

HUNG'S COMMUNICATIONS, LTD.
1/F, 373A Prince Edward Rd., Kowloon. TEL: (852) 2777 2351.
FAX: (852) 2713 0454. email: hlk@netvigator.com
www.hungscomm.com

IFD FILMS AND ARTS, LTD.
Flat 4 3/F Blk B Vigor Ind Bldg., 14-20 Cheung Tat Rd., Tsing
Yi NT. TEL: (852) 2730 0048. FAX: (852) 2730 8756.
email: sales@ifd.com.hk www.ifd.com.hk

IMAGI STUDIOS LIMITED
19/f, Eight Commercial Tower, 8 Sun Yip St., Chai Wan, Hong
Kong. TEL (852) 3103 6500. email info@imagi.com.hk
www.imagi.com.hk
FOUNDER/CEO
Francis Kao Wai Ho
CO-CEO
Douglas E. Glen

PRESIDENT & CFO
Terry Tse Chi Man
V.P. PRODUCTION
Brett Feeney
CREATIVE DIRECTOR
Felix Ip Wai Ching
V.P. ANIMATION
Tim Cheung

IN-GEAR FILM DISTRIBUTION INTERNATIONAL
Rm. 1612, 113 Argyle St., Kowloon. TEL: (852) 2380 5216. FAX: (852) 2397 1452.

INTERCONTINENTAL GROUP HOLDINGS, LTD.
27/F Wyler Centre, Phase 2, 200 Tai Lin Pai Rd., Kwai Chung, New Territories. TEL: (852) 2481 6693. FAX: (852) 2481 6377. email: ifdl@ intercontinental.com.hk

Subsidiaries: Intercontinental Film Distributors, Mini Cinema Ltd., Intercontinental Video, Jesu International Entertainment, Lauro Films, Intercontinental Communications and Perfect Advertising & Production Co.

JET TONE PRODUCTIONS
21/F Park Commercial Centre. No. 180 Tung Lo Wan Rd., Hong Kong. TEL: (852)-2336-1102. FAX: (852)-2337-9849. email: jettone@netvigator.com http://www.jettone.net/

JOY SALES FILM & VIDEO DISTRIBUTORS
Unit 3101-3104, New Trend Ctr., 704 Prince Edward Rd E, San Po Kong, Kowloon. TEL: (852) 2718 6168. FAX: (852) 2718 6295.

KENTAC INVESTMENTS, LTD (SUBDISTRIBUTOR FOR TWENTIETH CENTURY FOX)
Rm. 1218 Tower 2, Admiralty Ctr., 18 Harcourt Rd. Admirality Hong Kong. TEL: (852) 2876 3939. FAX: (852) 2866 398.

MANDARIN FILMS DISTRIBUTION CO, LTD.
27/F Chinachem Century Tower, 178 Goucster Rd. Wan Chai Hong Kong. TEL: (852) 2579 1718. email: mfdcl@netvigator.com

MEI AH ENTERTAINMENT GROUP, LTD.
Mei Ah Ctr., 28 Chun Choi St., Tseung Kwan O Ind Est NT. TEL: (852) 2751 3388. FAX: (852) 2799 3643. email: meiah@meiah.com www.meiah.com

NEWPORT ENTERTAINMENT
19/F, Southland Bldg., 47 Connaught Rd., Central. TEL: (852) 543 6973. FAX: (852) 544 9574.

PANASIA FILS LIMITED (GOLDEN HARVEST)
16/F The Peninsula Office Tower, 18 Middle Rd., Tsim Sha Tsui, Kowloon Hong Kong. TEL: 852-2352-8222. FAX: 852-2353-5989.
MANAGER
Teerachia Triwongwaranat

PANORAMA DISTRIBUTIONS CO, LTD.
Unit A & B 7/F Union Bldg., 112 How Ming St., Kwun Tong, Kowloon. TEL: (852) 2366 9559. FAX: (852) 2369 0856. email: mail@panorama.com.hk www.panorama.com.hk

SALON FILMS, LTD.
6 Devon Rd., Kowloon Tong, Kowloon. TEL: (852) 2338 0505. FAX: (852) 2338 2539. email: salonhq@salonmedia.com www.salonmedia.com

SAMEWAY PRODUCTIONS, LTD.
Rm. 24 4/F Cosmopolitan Ctr., 760 Nathan Rd. Kowloon TEL: (852) 2787 1317. FAX: (852) 2787 1975. email: sameway@net-yan.com www.sameway.hoops.ne.jp

SOUTHERN FILM
1902 Dominion Centre, 43-59 Queens Rd. East, Wanchai. TEL: (852) 527 7284. FAX: (852) 865 1449.

TIMES PRODUCTION, LTD.
Rm. 1501-1503 Grand Business Plaza, 153 Wai Yip St. Kwun Tong Kowloon. TEL: (852) 2172 4318. FAX: (852) 2172 4418. email: times@i-cable.com

UIP INTERNATIONAL SERVICES
16/F The Peninsula Office Tower, 18 Middle Rd., Tsim Sha Tsui, Kowloon. TEL: (852) 2352 8222. FAX: (852) 2351 1683.
FILM DISTRIBUTION MANAGER
Teerachia Triwongwaranat

THE WALT DISNEY STUDIOS HONG KONG
15th Fl., Citibank Tower, Citibank Plaza, 3 Garden Rd., Central. FAX: (852) 2536 2453.

WARNER BROS. (FAR EAST)
34/F Oxford Hse Taikoo Place, 979 King's Rd., Quarry Bay. TEL: (852) 3128 1200. FAX: (852) 3128 1210.

EXHIBITORS

EDKO FILMS LIMITED/BROADWAY CIRCUIT
1212 Tower II, Admiralty Centre, 18 Harcourt Rd., Hong Kong. TEL: (852) 2529 3898. FAX: (852) 2529 5277.
email: info@cinema.com.hk www.cinema.com.hk
EXECUTIVE DIRECTOR
Lau Siu Man Tessa
THEATRE OPERATIONS
Karen Lam
DISTRIBUTION DEPT.
Audrey Lee
CORPORATE DEVELOPMENT
Tessa Lau
Number of Theatres: 13
Number of Screens: 63

GOLDEN HARVEST ENTERTAINMENT CO., LTD.
(For additional listings see Hong Kong, Thailand & Malaysia) 16/F Peninsula Office Tower, 18 Middle Road, Kowloon. TEL: (852) 2352 8222. FAX: (852) 2353 5989. www.goldenharvest.com
CHAIRMAN
Raymond Chow
MANAGING DIRECTOR
C.K. Phoon
EXECUTIVE DIRECTOR
Stephen Chu
DIRECTOR, FILM DISTRIBUTION
Ada Foo York Ching

Number of Theatres (Hong Kong): 2
Number of Screens (Hong Kong): 26

GOLDEN VILLAGE ENTERTAINMENT
68 Orchard Rd. #07-10/14 Plaza Singapura, Singapore 238839. TEL: (65) 6334 3766. FAX: (65) 6334 8397. email: webmaster@goldenvillage.com.sg www.gv.com.sg
GENERAL MANAGER DISTRIBUTION
Maria Lorenzo

LARK INTERNATIONAL MULTIMEDIA, LTD.
The Gateway, Tower 1, 7th Flr., 25 Canton Rd. Kowloon. TEL: (852) 3104-1789. email: vallone@uacc.com.hk www.uacc.com.hk
DEPUTY CHAIRMAN
David Tso

MULTIPLEX CINEMA LTD.
Unit 1, 27/F Wyler Centre, Phase 2, 200 Tai Lin Pai Rd., Kwai Chung, Hong Kong. TEL: 2481 6693. FAX: 2481 6377. email: mcl@intercontinental.com.hk www.mclcinema.com
CEO
Terri Lai
MANAGING DIRECTOR
Rigo Jesu

Number of Theatres: 6
Number of Screens: 30

STUDIO CITY CINEMA HOLDINGS, LTD.
Rm. 409-411, 4/F, World Commerce Centre, 11 Canton Rd., Kowloon. TEL: (852) 735 4633. FAX: (852) 375 8869.
GENERAL MANAGER
Bob Vallone, Maureen Koh, Ben Keung
EXECUTIVE DIRECTOR
James Kralik, Hamilton Tang
CHAIRMAN
Ira D. Kaye

UNITED ARTISTS CINEMA CIRCUIT, LTD.
Rm. 409-410/F, World Commerce Centre, 11 Canton Rd., Kowloon. TEL: (852) 2736 4633.

VILLAGE ROADSHOW, LTD.
(For complete listing see Australian branch) 206 Bourke St., Melbourne, VIC, 3000, Australia. TEL: (613) 9667 6666. FAX: (613) 9639 1540.

Number of Theatres: 8
Number of Screens: 29

ASSOCIATIONS & ORGANIZATIONS

FEDERATION OF HONG KONG FILM WORKERS
2/F, 35 Ho Man Tin St., Ho Man Tin, Kowloon. TEL: (852) 2194 6955. FAX: (852) 2194 6255. email: mail@hkfilmworkers.com

THE FEDERATION OF MOTION FILM PRODUCERS OF HONG KONG
13/F, Tung Wui Commercial Building, 27 Prat Ave., Tsim Sha Tsui, Kowloon. TEL: (852) 2311 2692. FAX: (852) 2311 1178.

FILM SERVICES OFFICE
(Television and Entertainment Licensing Authority) 40/F, Revenue Tower, 5 Gloucester Rd., Wan Chai. TEL: (852) 2594 5745. FAX: (852) 2824 0595. email: info@fso-tela.gov.hk www.fso-tela.gov.hk

HONG KONG FILM ACADEMY
Rm. 906, Sunbearm Commercial Building, 469-471 Nathan Rd., Kowloon. TEL: (852) 2786 9349. FAX: (852) 2742 7017. email: info@ filmacademy.com.hk www.filmacademy.com.hk

HONG KONG FILM ARCHIVE
(Leisure and Cultural Services Department)
4/F, Hong Kong Film Archive, 50 Lei King Road, Sai Wan Ho.
TEL: (852) 2119 7380. FAX: (852) 2311 5229.
email: hkfa@lcsd.gov.hk www.filmarchive.gov.hk

HONG KONG FILM ARTS ASSOCIATION
Flat A, 5/F, Champagne Court, 16 Kimberley Rd., Tsim Sha Tsui, Kowloon. TEL: (852) 2367 4887, 9343 2026.
FAX: (852) 2369 3484.

HONG KONG FILM CRITICS' ASSOCIATION
4G Hoi To Court, 275 Gloucester Rd., Causeway Bay.
TEL: (852) 2573 7498. FAX: (852) 2574 6726.
email: info@hkfca.org www.hkfca.org

HONG KONG FILM CRITICS SOCIETY
Unit 104, Corn Yan Centre, 3 Jupiter St., Tin Hau.
TEL: (852) 2575 5149. FAX: (852) 2891 2048.
email: hkfilmcs@hknet.com www.filmcritics.org.hk

HONG KONG FILM DIRECTORS GUILD
2/F, 35 Ho Man Tin St., Ho Man Tin, Kowloon.
TEL: (852) 2760 0331. FAX: (852) 2713 2373.
email: hkfdg@netvigator.com

KOWLOON & NEW TERRITORIES MOTION PICTURE INDUSTRY ASSOCIATION
13/F, Tung Wui Commercial Bldg., 27 Prat Ave., Tsim Sha Tsui, Kowloon. TEL: (852) 2311 2692, (852) 2311 2678.
FAX: (852) 2311 1178. email: info@mpia.org.hk
www.mpia.org.hk

HONG KONG MOVIE PRODUCTION EXECUTIVES ASSOCIATION
P.O. Box 1332, Sha Tin, N.T. TEL: (852) 9484 4322.
FAX: (852) 3017 6938. email: mail@hkmpea.com
www.hkmpea.com

HONG KONG THEATRES ASSOCIATION
21/F, Hong Kong Chinese Bank, Causeway Bay Centre, 42-44 Yee Wo Street, Causeway Bay.
TEL: (852) 2576 3833. FAX: (852) 2576 1833.

SOCIETY OF CINEMATOGRAPHERS (HK)
Flat B, 19/F, Block A, Wylie Court, 23 Wylie Path, Ho Man Tin, Kowloon. TEL: (852) 9021 5449. FAX: (852) 2358 3990.

HUNGARY

Capital: Budapest
Population: 9,992,339 (July 2010 est.)
Area: 93,030 sq. km.
Source: CIA World Factbook

DISTRIBUTORS AND PRODUCERS

ANDRÉ SZOTS PRODUCTIONS
(ASP Audióvizuális Szolgáltatások Kft.)
Verecke út 81, Budapest H-1025.
TEL: (361) 325 6564. FAX: (361) 325 6884.
email: aspfilm@interware.hu www.asp.hu

BUDAPEST FILM
Batori u 10, Budapest H-1054. TEL: (361) 111 6650.
FAX: (361) 131 5946.

C47 FILMS
Stollár Béla utca 22, Budapest 1055. TEL: (361) 473 3112.
FAX: (361) 473 3111. email: alex.nemetz@c47films.com
www.c47films.com
EXECUTIVE DIRECTOR
Alex Nemetz

CINEMAGYAR KFT (HUNGAROFILM EX)
Batori u 10, Budapest H-1054. TEL: (361) 111 4614.
FAX: (361) 153 1317.

DUNA/UIP DANUBE
5th Bldg. 2nd Fl., Huvosvolgyi u.54 Budapest 1021.
TEL: 36-1-274-2180. FAX: 36-1-274-2177.
email balint@uipduna.hu www.uipduna.hu
MANAGER
Peter Balint

EUROFILM STUDIO
Rona u 174, Budapest H-1145. TEL: (361) 252 5069.
FAX: (361) 251 3986. email: eurofilm@alexero.hu
MANAGING DIRECTOR & PRODUCER
Peter Miskolczi
PRODUCER
Gabor Varadi

FILM POSITIVE PRODUCTIONS
Videgradl u 9, 11/1, Budapest H-1132. TEL: (361) 238 0200.
FAX: (361) 238 0322. email: info@filmpositive.hu
www.filmpositive.hu
DIRECTOR
Péter Fazakas, Sándor Bisztray, Csaba Fazekas

FLAMEX
Labanc u 22B, Budapest H-1021. TEL: (361) 176 1543.
FAX: (361) 176 0596.

HUNNIA FILMSTUDIO
Rona u 174, Budapest H-1145. TEL: (361) 252 3170.
FAX: (361) 251 6269.

I'M FILM
Hajógyári sziget 132. ép., H-1033 Budapest.
TEL: (361) 250 1473. FAX: (361) 250 0009.
email: imfilm@mail.datanet.hu www.datanet.hu/imfilm

INTERCOM
Bácskai u. 28-36, H-1145 Budapest. TEL: (361) 467 1400.
FAX: (361) 467 4242. email: intercom@intercom.hu
www.intercom.hu
PRESIDENT
Andrew G. Vajna
CEO
Dr. Lajos Csepi

MEGAFILM
Ulászló u. 24, Budapest H-1114. TEL: (361) 365 1750.
FAX: (361) 365 1755. www.megafilm.hu

MOKEP
Bathori u 10, Budapest H-1054. TEL: (361) 111 2097.
FAX: (361) 153 1613. email: film@mokep.hu www.mokep.hu
CEO
Gyorgy Horvath

SKYFILM STUDIO, LTD.
Hûvösvölgyi út 35, Budapest H-1026. TEL: (361) 275 3066.
FAX: (361) 275 3069. email: skyfilm@skyfilm.com
www.skyfilm.hu

STRAWBERRY FILMS
Bimbó u 141/b, Budapest H-1026. TEL: (361) 200 4040.
FAX: (361) 200 6060. email: strawberry@strawberryfilm.hu
www.strawberryfilms.hu

TIVOLI FILM
(Formerly Focus Film, Ltd.)
Huvosvolgyi ut 141, Budapest H-1021. TEL: (361) 275 2320.
FAX: (361) 200 6858. email: mail@tivolifilm.hu
www.tivolifilm.hu
MANAGING DIRECTOR
Denes Skeres

UIP—DANUBE INTERNATIONAL PICTURES
Tarogato u 2-4/2nd Flr., Budapest H-1021. TEL: (361) 176 7291.
FAX: (361) 274 2177.
MANAGER
Peter Balint

EXHIBITORS

BUDAPEST FILM
Bathori u 10, Budapest H-1054. TEL: (361) 111 2494.
FAX: (361) 111 2687.

CORVIN BUDAPEST FILMPALACE
Corvin koz 12, Budapest H-1082. TEL: (361) 303 1500.
FAX: (361) 303 2526.

CINEPLEX ODEON INTERNATIONAL MOZI
Polus Centre, Szentmihalyi ut 131, Budapest 1153.
TEL: (361) 419 4223. FAX: (361) 419 4228.
CONTACT
Ana LeRoux

Number of Theatres: 1
Number of Screens: 6

ASSOCIATIONS & ORGANIZATIONS

ASSOCIATION OF CINEMAS OF HUNGARY
Maria u 19, Szolnok H-5000. TEL: (3656) 420 612.

GUILD OF HUNGARY
Varosligeti Fasor 38, Budapest H-1068. TEL: (361) 342 4760.
FAX: (361) 342 4760.

HUNGARIAN FILM INSTITUTE & ARCHIVE
Budakeszi u 51B, Budapest H-1021. TEL: (361) 176 1322.
FAX: (361) 200 8739. www.filmintezet.hu

MOTION PICTURE FOUNDATION OF HUNGARY
Szalaiu 10, Budapest H-1054. TEL: (361) 1126417.

NATIONAL CULTURAL FUND
Bajza u. 32, Budapest H-1062. TEL: (361) 352 7230.
FAX: (361) 352 7230. email: elnok@nka.hu www.nka.hu
PRESIDENT
László Harsányi, dr.
DIRECTOR
Pál Perlik

ICELAND

Capital: Reykjavik
Population: 308,910 (July 2010 est.)
Area: 103,000 sq. km.
Source: CIA World Factbook

DISTRIBUTORS AND PRODUCERS

BLUE EYES PRODUCTIONS / SÖGN EHF.
Skálholtsstíg 7, Reykjavík 101. TEL: (354) 511 7060.
FAX: (354) 511 7061. email: blueeyes@blueeyes.is
www.blueeyes.is
CONTACT
Agnes Johansen

FILMUS PRODUCTIONS
Grettisgata 87, Reykjavík S-105. TEL: (354) 580 0300.
FAX: (354) 580 0301. email: filmus@filmus.is www.filmus.is
CONTACT
Addi Knútsson

GOOD TIMES DISTRIBUTION
Armuli 40, Reykjavik 108. TEL: (354) 568 5600.
FAX: (354) 568 5601. email: fridbert@goodtimes.is
CONTACT
Fridbert Palsson

GREEN LIGHT DISTRIBUTION
Hverfisgötu 46, Reykjavik 101.
TEL: (354) 551 2260. FAX: (354) 552 5154.
email: amk@icecorp.is www.icecorp.is

HASKOLABIO UNIVERSITY CINEMA
Hagatorg, Reykjavik 107. TEL: (354) 530 1900.
FAX: (354) 530 1901. email: info@haskolabio.is
www.haskolabio.is
MANAGING DIRECTOR
Einar Valdemarsson

ICELANDIC FILM COMPANY
Bankastræti 11, Reykjavik 101. TEL: (354) 562 4615.
FAX: (354) 562 4615. www.kisi.is
CONTACT
Julius Kemp

LAUGARASBIO
Laugaras, Reykjavik 104. TEL: (354) 563 8150. FAX: (354) 568 0910.

MYNDFORM
Tronuhraun 1, 220 Hafnarfjordur. TEL: (354) 534 0400.
FAX: (354) 565 0188. www.myndform.is
CEO
Gunnar Gunnarsson

PEGASUS - PANARCTICA
Sóltún 24, Reykjavík 105. TEL: (354) 511 4590.
FAX: (354) 511 4595. email: info@pegasus.is www.pegasus.is
DIRECTOR
Ágúst Baldursson

SAGAFILM
Laugavegur 176, Reykjavik 105. TEL: (354) 515 4600.
FAX: (354)515 4601. email: sagafilm@sagafilm.is
www.sagafilm.is
DIRECTOR
Jon Thor Hannesson
MANAGING DIRECTOR
Runar Hreinsson

SAM FILM
Alfabakka 8, Reykjavík 109. TEL: (354) 575 8900.
FAX: (354) 587 8910. email: samfilm@samfilm.is
www.sambioin.is
CONTACT
Thorvaldur Arnason

SKIFAN
Lynghäls 5, Reykjavík 108. TEL: (354) 525 5000.
FAX: (354) 525 5001. email: bjossi@skifan.is www.skifan.is/

TRUE NORTH PRODUCTIONS
Klapparstigur 16, Reykjavik 101. TEL: (354) 511 1510.
FAX: (354) 511 1513. email: info@truenorth.is www.truenorth.is
PRODUCER
Leifur B. Dagfinnsson

EXHIBITORS

BORGARBIO
Akuyeri. TEL: (354) 462 3500. FAX: (354) 461 2796.

HASKOLABIO-UNIVERSITY CINEMA
Hagatorg, Reykjavik 107. TEL: (354) 561 1212.
FAX: (354) 562 7135. email: cinema@centrum.is
DIRECTOR
Fridbert Palsson

LAUGARASBIO
Laugaras, Reykjavik 104. TEL: (354) 563 8150. FAX: (354) 568 0910.

REGNBOGINN
Hverfisgata 54, Reykjavik 101. TEL: (354) 462 3500.
FAX: (354) 461 2796.

SAM FILM
Alfabakka 8, Reykjavik 109. TEL: (354) 587 8900.
FAX: (354) 587 8930.

STJOERNUBIO
Laugavegi 94, Reykjavik 101. TEL: (354) 551 6500.
FAX: (354) 554 4630.

ASSOCIATIONS & ORGANIZATIONS

ASSOCIATION OF CINEMA OWNERS
Alfabakka 8. Reykjavík 109. TEL: (354) 575 8900.
FAX: (354) 587 8910. email: samfilm@samfilm.is
www.sambioin.is
CONTACT
Thorvaldur Arnason

ASSOCIATION OF FILM DISTRIBUTORS IN ICELAND
Stjornubio, Laugaveg 94, Reykjavik 101. TEL: (354) 551 6500.
FAX: (354) 554 4630.

ASSOCIATION OF ICELANDIC FILM DIRECTORS
Hverfisgata 46, Reykjavik 121. TEL: (354) 562 1850.
FAX: (354) 552 5154. email: f.thor@icecorp.is www.logs.is

ASSOCIATION OF ICELANDIC FILM PRODUCERS
Tungötu 14, P.O. Box 5367, Reykjavik 125. TEL: (354) 863 3057.
FAX: (354) 555 3065. email: sik@producers.is
www.producers.is
CHAIRMAN
Ari Kristinsson
VICE CHAIRMAN
Jón Thor Hannesson

DIRECTORS GUILD OF ICELAND
Hverfisgata 46, Reykjavij 101. TEL: (354) 551 2260.
FAX: (354) 552 5154.

ICELANDIC FILM CENTRE
Túngata 14, Reykjavik 101. TEL: (354) 863 3057.
FAX: (354) 555 3065. email: info@icelandicfilmcentre.is
www.icelandfilmcentre.ir

ICELANDIC FILMMAKERS ASSOCIATION
Laugavegur 24, P.O. Box 320, Reykjavik 101.
TEL: (354) 562 3225. FAX: (354) 562 7171.

MINISTRY OF CULTURE & EDUCATION
Solvholsgotu 4, Reykjavik 105. TEL: (354) 560 9500.
FAX: (354) 562 3068.

INDIA

Capital: New Delhi
Population: 1,173,108,018 (July 2010 est.)
Area: 3,287,590 sq. km.
Source: CIA World Factbook

PRINCIPAL EXPORTERS

ANAND EXPORTS
730 Chandra Niwas, Annex Shop 2, 11th Rd., Khar, Bombay 400052. TEL: (9122) 646 2755.

CITIZEN INTERNATIONAL
B/6 3rd Flr., Everest, Tardeo Road, Bombay 400034.
TEL: (9122) 495 1688.

FAIRDEAL EXPORTS, LTD.
10 Kashi Kunj, 2nd Flr., Waterfield Road, Bandra, Bombay 400050. FAX: (9122) 604 2429.

NATIONAL FILM DEVELOPMENT CORP., LTD.
Nehru Centre, Dr. A. Besant Road, Worli, Bombay 400018.
TEL: (9122) 495 2662.

NEPTUNE ENTERPRISES
C 8/9 Everest, 4th Flr., Tardeo Rd., Bombay 400034.
FAX: (9122) 492 0890.

PARAMOUNT FILMS OF INDIA, LTD.
Hague Building, Ballard Estate, P.O. Box 623 Mumbai 400 038.
TEL: 91-22-266-6146/6145. FAX: 91-22-261 2856.
GENERAL MANAGER
Sarabjit Singh

RAJSHRI PRODUCTIONS LTD.,-BHAVNA
1st Fl., Opp Kismat Cinema, Prabhadevi, Bombay 400025.
FAX: (9122) 422 9181.

TRIMURTI EXPORTS
B/11 Commerce Centre, Tardeo Road, Bombay 400034.
FAX: (9122) 811 667.

PRINCIPAL IMPORTERS

COLUMBIA TRISTAR FILMS OF INDIA, LTD.
Metro House, 1st Flr., M. G. Rd., Bombay 400020.
TEL: (9122) 201 4264. FAX: (9122) 201 4321.

METRO-GOLDYN-MAYER FILMS OF INDIA, LTD.
Metro House, M. G. Road, Bombay 400020.

PARAMOUNT FILMS OF INDIA, LTD.
(Also representing Universal)
Hague Bldg., Sprott Rd., Bombay 400020. TEL: (9122) 261 3877.
FAX: (9122) 261 2856.
MANAGER
Sarabjit Singh

SATHYAM THEATRE
No. 8 Thiru-vi-ka Road, Chennai. TEL: 044 2852 4875.
FAX: 044 2852 1972.
CONTACT
Kiran Reddy

TWENTIETH CENTURY FOX CORP., (INDIA) LTD.
Metro House, 3rd Flr., M. G. Rd., Bombay 400020.
TEL: (9122) 205 4290. FAX: (9122) 208 9388.
Calcutta: TEL: (9133) 249 5623.
New Delhi: TEL: (9111) 332 0351.
Madras: TEL: (9144) 852 0078.
GENERAL MANAGER
Sunder Kimatrai

UNITED ARTISTS CORP.
Metro House, M. G. Road, Bombay 400020.

UNIVERSAL PICTURES INDIA P, LTD.
Hague Bldg., Sprott Rd., Bombay 400020. TEL: (9122) 266 6146.
FAX: (9122) 261 2856.

WARNER BROS. (F. D.) INDIA
Eros Theatre Bldg., 42 M. Karve Rd., Bombay 400020.
TEL: (9122) 285 6557. FAX: (9122) 285 0984.

Leslie House, 19A Jawarharlal Nehru Rd., Calcutta 700087.
TEL: (9133) 249 5613.

Dinroze Estate, 69 Mount Rd., Madras 600002.
TEL: (9144) 852 5964.

Plaza Thatre Bldg., Connaught Circus, New Delhi 110001.
TEL: (9111) 332 1544.
MANAGING DIRECTOR
J. Fernandes

EXHIBITORS

ADLABS CINEMAS
Bhakti Park, Anik Wadala Link Rd, Wadala Mumbai 400 037.
TEL: (91) 22 2842 3333. FAX: (91) 22 2842 2211.
email: tushar.dhingar@adlabsfilms.com
www.adlabscinemas.com
CHIEF OPERATING OFFICER
Tushar Dhingra

THE BALJI GROUP
8 Thiru-V-Ka Rd., Chennai 600014. TEL: (91) 44 85 24 875,
(91) 44 852 3813. FAX: (91) 44 85 21 972.
CONTACT
KR Subramaniam
MANAGING PARTNER
Mr. Vijaykumar

BIG CINEMAS
2nd and 3rd Flrs., Meadows, Sahar Plaza Complex, Andheri
East, Mumbai 400 059, India. TEL: 91 22 30978888.
email: tushar.dhingra@adlabsfilms.com
Web: www.BIGcinemas.com
COO
Tushar Dhingra

CHAPHALKAR GROUP OF CINEMAS
Mangala Cinema, 111 Shivajinagar, Pune 411005.
TEL: (91) 21 2 323468, 323519. FAX: (91) 21 2 323973.
MANAGING DIRECTOR
Ajay Bijlee
CONTACT
D.D. Prakash Chaphalkar

FAME INDIA LIMITED
Citimall, 2nd Fl., Oshiwara--Andheri Link Road, Andheri
(West), Mumbai 400 053, India. TEL: 91 (22) 6640-3636.
FAX: 91 (22) 6640 3638. email: shravan@fame.co.in
www.famecinemas.com
CEO
Shavran Shroff

INOX LEISURE, LTD.
5th Fl., Viraj Towers, Western Express Highway, Andheri (east),
Mumbai 400 069, India. TEL: 91 (22) 4062 6900.
FAX: 91 (22) 4062 6950. email: alok@inox.co.in
www.inoxmovies.com
COO
Alok Tandon

Total Theaters: 27
Total Screens: 94

MODI U.A.T.C. (PVT), LTD.
4 Lands End, 54 Byramji Jeetibhoy Rd., Bandra, Bombay
400050. TEL: (9122) 645 0000. FAX: (9122) 645 8282.
CHIEF EXECUTIVE
Rajiv Sahai

PRIYA VILLAGE ROADSHOW LIMITED
Priya Cinema and Anupam Cineplex, 50 W. Regal Bldg.,
Connaught Pl., New Delhi 110001.
TEL: (91) 11 37 32 089, 334 0605. FAX: (91) 11 374 71 39.

PVR CINEMAS
Block 2A, 2nd Flr., DLF Corporate Park, Mehraudi-Gurgaon
Road, Gurgaon 122-002. TEL: 0124 56 3271.
FAX: 0124 254 9309. www.pvrcinemas.com
PRESIDENT & CEO
Pramod Arora
CONTACT
Ajjay Bijlee

RAJSHRI PICTURES
42 Virsavarkar Rd., P.O. 9103, Prabha Devi, Bombay 400025,
India. TEL: (912) 422 7705, 430 7688. FAX: (912) 242 9181.

SHRINGAR CINEMAS PVT., LTD.
B-103, Kailash, Juhu Church Rd., Juhu, Mumbai, 400 049,
Maharashtra State. TEL: (91) 22 625 5900.
FAX: (91) 22 625 5272. email: Shrigar001@vsnl.com
www.famecinemas.com
CEO
Shavran Shroff
VP, OPERATIONS
Rishi Negi

SATHYAM CINEMAS
#25 Mamtha Complex, Whites Road, Chennai 600 0014.
TEL: (910) 444 292 0200. FAX: (910) 444 392 0334.
supriya@sathyamcinemas.com www.sathyacinemas.com
COO
Tan Ngaronga
MANAGING DIRECTOR
Kiran Reddy

Number of Theatres (India): 1
Number of Screens (India): 6

VILLAGE ROADSHOW, LTD.
(For complete listing see Australian branch)
206 Bourke St., Melbourne, VIC, 3000, Australia.
TEL: (613) 96 67 66 66. FAX: (613) 96 39 15 40.

Number of Theatres (India): 2
Number of Screens (India): 5

WESTERN INDIA THEATRES LIMITED
Liberty Bldg., 41-42 New Marine Lines, Bombay 400020.
TEL: (91) 22 20 1 42 17, (91) 22 20 1 43 18.
FAX: (91) 22 20 57 939.
CONTACT
Roosi K. Modi, Kamal Barjatiya

INDONESIA

Capital: Jakarta
Population: 242,968,342 (July 2010 est.)
Area: 1,919,440 sq. km.
Source: CIA World Factbook

DISTRIBUTORS

RAPI FILMS
Cikini II, No. 7, Jakarta. TEL: (6221) 314 2860.
FAX: (6221) 310 3005. email: rapifilm@rad.net.id
PRESIDENT & CEO
Gope Samtani

UNITED INTERNATIONAL PICTURES (UIP)
c/o PT Camila Internuse Film, Subentra Bank Building, Ste.
716, Jl Jend, Gatot Subroto Kaz 21, Jakarta 12930, Indonesia.
TEL: (6221) 522 0063. FAX: (6221) 522 0064.
REPRESENTATIVE
Douglas Lee
CONTACT
Nelly Panigoro

EXHIBITORS

CINEMA 21
JL K.H. Wahid Hasyim, No. 96A, Jakarta 10340.
TEL: 62 21 3190 2277. FAX: 62 21 3190 0055.
email: harris@21cineplex.com
www.21cineplex.com
CEO
Harris Lasmana
PRESIDENT
Suryo Suherman
VICE PRESIDENT
Sacheen Lasmana

Number of Theaters: 85
Number of Screens: 368

SUBENTRA GROUP

Subentra Bank Bldg., 21 Jl. Send, Gatot Subroto, Jakarta 12930. TEL: (6221) 522 0122. FAX: (6221) 522 0078.
MANAGING DIRECTOR, EXHIBITION & DISTRIBUTION
Harris Lasmana

Number of Screens: 500

ASSOCIATIONS & ORGANIZATIONS

CINEMATOGRAPH EXHIBITOR'S ASSOCIATION OF INDIA

Flat 22/23B, 1st Flr., Vellard View, Tardeo Rd., Bombay 400034.

EASTERN INDIA MOTION PICTURE ASSOCIATION

98E Chowringhee Square, Calcutta.

FILM FEDERATION OF INDIA

91 Walkeshwar Rd, Bombay 400006.

INDIAN DOCUMENTARY PRODUCERS ASSOCIATION

305 Famous Cine Bldg., Mahalaxmi, Bombay 400018.

INDIAN FILM EXPORTERS ASSOCIATION

305 Famous Cine Bldg., Mahalaxmi, Bombay 400018.

THE INDIAN MOTION PICTURE DISTRIBUTORS ASSOCIATION

33 Vijay Chamber, Tribhuvan Rd., Bombay 400004.

INDIAN MOTION PICTURE PRODUCERS' ASSOCIATION

Dr. Ambedkar Road, Bandra (W), Bombay 400050.

PT CAMILA INTERNUSA FILM

Jl K.H. Wahid Hasyim No. 96A, Building B, 1st Flr., Jakarta, 10340. TEL: 62-21-3190-2277.
FAX: 62-21-3190-0055.
CONTACT
Nelly Panigoro

SOUTH INDIA'S FILM CHAMBER OF COMMERCE

122 Mount Rd., Madras 60002.

ISRAEL

Capital: Jerusalem
Population: 7,233,701 (July 2010 est.)
Area: 20,770 sq. km.
Source: CIA World Factbook

DISTRIBUTORS AND PRODUCERS

ALBERT D. MATALON & CO.

(Agency for Columbia TriStar & Twentieth Century Fox)
13 Yona Hanavi St., Tel Aviv 63302. TEL: (9723) 516 2020.
FAX: (9723) 516 1888.
CONTACT
Amnon Matalon

BIANCA FILM

via fedele lampertico, Roma, Italy 00100.
TEL: +39063296791. http://biancafilm@flashnet.it

FORUM FILM, LTD.

P.O. Box 12598, Herzlia Pituah, Industrial Zone 46766.
TEL: (9729) 562 111. FAX: (9729) 561 581.

GIL PRODUCTIONS

136 Rothschild Blvd., Tel Aviv 65272. TEL: (9723) 686 9797.
FAX: (9723) 686 9898. email: gilprod@actcom.co.il
MANAGING DIRECTOR
Assaf Gil

NACHSHON FILMS

22 Harakeuel St., Tel Aviv 66183. TEL: (9723) 356 40015.
FAX: (9723) 350 05112.

NOAH FILMS/UNITED INTERNATIONAL PICTURES (UIP)

10 Glickson St., Tel Aviv 63567. TEL: (9723) 526 6351.
FAX: (9723) 526 8658. email: alona.wb@globusgroup.co.il
PRESIDENT
Yorum Globus
MANAGER
Sandra Taub

SHAPIRA FILMS

34 Allenby Rd., P.O. Box 4842, Tel Aviv 63325.
TEL: (9723) 510 2530. FAX: (9723) 510 1370.
PRESIDENT
David Shapira

SHOVAL-FILM PRODUCTION

32 Allenby Rd., Tel Aviv. TEL: (9723) 659 288. FAX: (9723) 659 289.

TAMUZ FILMS

5 Pinsker St., Tel Aviv. TEL: (9723) 201 512.
FAX: (9723) 528 1564.

EXHIBITORS

CINEMA CITY INTERNATIONAL

91 Medinat Ha-Yehudim St., Herzlia Pituah 46766.
TEL: 972 9952 6262. FAX: 972 9956 1581. www.cinemacity.nl

Total Theaters: 58 Total Screens: 446

TAMUZ FILMS

5 Pinsker St., Tel Aviv. TEL: (9723) 201 512. FAX: (9723) 528 1564.

STUDIOS

G. G. ISRAEL STUDIOS

Communications Centre, Neve Ilan, D. N. Harei, Yehuda 90850.
TEL: (9722) 349 111. FAX: (9722) 349 9000.

JERUSALEM CAPITAL STUDIOS

P.O. Box 13172, 206 Jaffa Rd., Jerusalem 91131.
TEL: (9722) 701 711. FAX: (9722) 381 658.

ORION FILMS

4 Shamgar St., Jerusalem 90058. TEL: (9722) 238 0221.
FAX: (9722) 238 0925.

TEL AD JERUSALEM STUDIOS

20 Marcus St., P.O. Box 4111, Jerusalem Theatre Bldg., Jerusalem 91040. TEL: (9722) 619 988. FAX: (9722) 611 451.

ASSOCIATIONS & ORGANIZATIONS

ISRAEL FILM CENTRE

Ministry of Industry & Trade, 30 Gershon Agron St., P.O. Box 299, Jerusalem 94190. TEL: (9722) 750 433. FAX: (9722) 245 110.

ISRAEL FILM SERVICE

Ministry of Education & Culture, P.O. Box 13240, Hakirya Romema, Jerusalem 91130. TEL: (9722) 512 248.
FAX: (9722) 526 818.

ITALY

Capital: Rome
Population: 58,090,681 (July 2010 est.)
Area: 301,230 sq. km.
Source: CIA World Factbook

DISTRIBUTORS AND PRODUCERS

AB FILM DISTRIBUTORS

Viale delle Milizie, 2 Rome 00192. TEL: (39 06) 321 9554, 3600 0744. FAX: (39 06) 361 3641. email: abfilm@tiscalinet.it
www.abfilm.it
PRESIDENT
Angelo Bassi

ACADEMY PICTURES

Via Fratelli Ruspoli, 8, Rome. TEL: (39 06) 8840 424.
FAX: (39 06) 8417 043.

ADRIANA CHIESA ENTERPRISES

Via Barnaba Oriani 24A, Rome 00197. TEL: (39 06) 808 6052.
FAX: (39 06) 8068 7855.
email: info@adrianachiesaenterprises.com
www.adrianachiesaenterprises.com

ARTISTI ASSOCIATI INTERNAZIONALE

Via del Santuario, 160, Pescara 65125.
TEL: (39 085) 4154361. FAX: (39 085) 417 3747.
email: staff@artistiassociati.it www.artistiassociati.it

BIM DISTRIBUZIONE

Via Marianna Dionigi, 57, Rome 00191. TEL: (39 06) 323 1057.
FAX: (39 06) 321 1984. www.bimfilm.com
PRESIDENT
M. Valerio De Paolis - aforte@bimfilm.com

BUENA VISTA INTERNATIONAL ITALIA

Via Cantalupo in Sabina 29 (Ingresso C), Rome 0019.
TEL: (39 06) 330 831. FAX: (39 06) 3308 3270.
www.buenavista.it

BUSKIN FILMS

Via P.L. Cattolica 3, Rome 00195. TEL: (39 06) 3903 0435.
FAX: (39 06) 3903 8231. email: info@buskinfilm.com
www.buskinfilm.com
CEO
Antonio Guadalupi
PRESIDENT
Roberto Bessi

CATTLEYA

Via Della Frezza 59, Rome 00186. TEL: (39 06) 367 201.
FAX: (39 06) 367 2050. email: info@cattleya.it www.cattleya.it
CEO
Giovanni Stabilini

CDI (COMPAGNIA DISTRIBUZIONE INTERNAZIONALE)

Via Saleria 292, Rome 00199. TEL: (39 06) 854 8821.

FAX: (39 06) 854 1691. www.cecchigori.com

CECCHI GORI GROUP
Via Valadier 42, Rome 00193. TEL: (39 06) 324 721.
FAX: (39 06) 3247 23 72. www.cecchigori.com

CHANCE FILM
Via G. Mercalli 19, Rome 00197. TEL: (39 06) 808 5041.
FAX: (39 06) 807 0506.

CINECITTA
Via Tuscolana, 1055, Rome 00173.
TEL: +39 06 7229 31. FAX: +39 06 7229 3517.
email: marketing@cinecittastudios.it www.cinecittastudios.it

CIDIF
Via Vicenza 5a, Rome 00185. TEL: (39 06) 446 9636.
FAX: (39 06) 446 9636.

CLEMI CINEMATOGRAFICA
Dott. Giovanni Di Clemente - Amministratore Unico via Salaria, 292, Rome 00199. TEL: (39 06) 854 0542. FAX: (39 06) 841 9749.

COLUMBIA TRISTAR FILMS ITALIA (A DIVISION OF SONY)
Via Cantalupo in Sabina, 29, Rome 00191. TEL: (39 06) 330 8416.
FAX: (39 06) 3308 4251. www.columbiatristar.it

DELTA
Via Elenora Duse 37, Rome 00197. TEL: (39 06) 808 4458.
FAX: (39 06) 807 9331.

EAGLE PICTURES
Via Cesare Beccaria, 23, Rome 00196. TEL: (39 06) 3269 101.
FAX: (39 06) 3207 366. email: info@eaglepictures.com
www.eaglepictures.com
CONTACT
M. Luigi Sala

EUPHON TECHNICOLOUR
Via Po 13-15, San Giuliano, Milanes 20098.
TEL: (39 02) 9828 0406. FAX: (39 02) 9828 0384.

FILMAURO
Via XXIV Maggio, 14, Rome 00187. TEL: (39 06) 699 581.
FAX: (39 06) 6995 8410. www.filmauro.it

FULVIA FILM
Via Bruno Nuozzi 36, Rome 00197. TEL: (39 06) 808 1575.
FAX: (39 06) 808 1510.

GRANATO PRESS
Via Marconi 47, Bologna 40122. TEL: (39 051) 237 737.

GRUNDY PRODUCTIONS
Piazza Udine, Milano 20100. TEL: +39-02281871.
www.grundy.it

GRUPPO BEMA
Via N. Martelli 3, Rome 00197. TEL: (39 06) 808 8551.
FAX: (39 06) 807 5454.

IMPERIAL BULLDOG PRODUCTIONS
Via Michele Amari 24, Rome 00179. TEL: (39 06) 7802394.
FAX: (39 06) 780 6589. www.imperialbulldog.com

INTERNATIONAL MOVIE COMPANY
Lungotevere Flaminio 66, Rome 00196. TEL: (39 06) 361 0344.
FAX: (39 06) 361 2676. email: info@tipota.it

ISTITUTO LUCE
Via Tuscolana 1055, Rome 00173. TEL: (39 06) 729 921.
FAX: (39 06) 722 1127. email: luce@luce.it www.luce.it

ITALIAN INTERNATIONAL FILM
Via Gian Domenico Romagnosi 20, Rome 00196.
TEL: (39 06) 361 1377. FAX: (39 06) 322 5965.
email: ufficio.stampa@iif-online.it www.iif-online.it.

KINA
Piazza Duomo 16, Milan 20122. TEL: (39 02) 8646 4102.
FAX: (39 02) 7200 1817.

LIFE INTERNATIONAL
Via cardinal De Lucca, 1, Rome. TEL: (39 06) 321 5972.
FAX: (39 06) 361 0036.

LUCKY RED
Via Antonio Chinotto, 16, Rome 00195.
TEL: (39 06) 3735 2296. FAX: (39 06) 373 50415.

MEDUSA FILM
Via Aurelia Antica 422-424, Rome 00165.
TEL: (39 06) 663 901. FAX: (39 06) 663 90567.
email: infofilm@medusa.it www.medusa.it

MELAMPO CINEMATOGRAFICA
Via Ludovisi, 35, Rome IT-00187. TEL: +39 06 42014647.
FAX: +39 06 42014671.

MIKADO FILM
Via Vittor Pisani 12, Milan 20124. TEL: (39 02) 670 706 65/85.
FAX: (39 02) 6671 1488.
CONTACT
M. Luigi Musini

MIMA FILMS
Largo V. Alpini 12, Milan 20145. TEL: (39 02) 349 2860.

MORGAN FILM DISTRIBUZIONE
Via Gerolamo Belloni 88, Rome. TEL: (39 06) 3629 8256.
FAX: (39 06) 3629 9651.

MOVIETIME
Via Nicola Ricciotti 11, Rome 00195. TEL: (39 06) 322 6709.
FAX: (39 06) 3600 0950.

MULTIMEDIA FILM DISTRIBUTION
Via L. Ximenes 21, Florence 50125. TEL: (39 055) 225 622.
FAX: (39 055) 233 6726.
CONTACT
Maria Serena, Giancarlo Lastrucci

NEMO DISTRIBUZIONE CINEMATOGRAFICA
Via Livigno 50, Rome 00188. TEL: (39 06) 331 851.
FAX: (39 06) 3367 9491.

OFFICINE UBU
Via Imbonati 4, Milan 20159.
TEL: 39 02 69311631. FAX: 39 02 60730784.
roi@officineubu.com http://www.officineubu.com

PEGASO INTER-COMMUNICATION
L. Gen. Gonzaga del Vodice 4, Rome 00195.
TEL: (39 06) 360 0830. FAX: (39 06) 3611 13251.

PENTA DISTRIBUZIONE
Via Aurelia Antica 422, Rome 00165. TEL: (39 06) 663 901.
FAX: (39 06) 663 9040.

RAI TRADE
Via Novar0, 18, Rome 00195. TEL: (39 06) 3749 8469.
FAX: (39 06) 3751 6222. email: info@raitrade.it
www.raitrade.rai.it
PRESIDENT
Robert Di Russo

SACIS (NOW OPERATING AS RAI CINEMA AND STUDIO CANAL DISTRIBUTION)
Piazza 12 0-0193, Roma. TEL: (39 06) 668 4701.
FAX: (39 06) 687 2141. www.raicinema.it.

SIRIO FILM
Viale Parioli 28 Int. 1, Rome 00197. TEL: (39 06) 808 2144.
FAX: (39 06) 808 8748.

STAR EDIZIONI CINEMATOGRAFICHE
Via Giovanni Da Castel Bolognese 81, Rome 00153.
TEL: +39 06 58317700. FAX: +39 06 58317327.
starcinetv@set.it www.star-group.it/

SURF FILM
Via Padre Filippini 130, Rome 00144. TEL: (39 06) 526 2101.
FAX: (39 06) 529 3816. email: surf@surffilm.com
www.surffilm.com
PRESIDENT
Massimo Vigliar

TWENTIETH CENTURY FOX
Largo Amilcare Ponchielli 6, Rome 00198.
TEL: (39 06) 8530 1060. FAX: (39 06) 8530 0971.
MANAGING DIRECTOR
Osvaldo De Santis

UNITED INTERNATIONAL PICTURES SRL
Via Bissolati 20, Rome 00187. TEL: 39-06-478 941.
FAX: 39-06-4201 1773. www.uip.it
MANAGER
Richard Borg

UNIVERSAL PICTURES
Viale Giulio Cesare, 2, Rome. TEL: (39 06) 367101.
FAX: (39 06) 3671 0240.

VITAGRAPH
Via Schiavonia 1, Bologna 40121. TEL: (39 051) 267 150.
FAX: (39 051) 267 310. email: vitagraph@libero.it
www.vitagraph.it
MANAGING DIRECTOR
Filippo D'Angelo

WARNER BROS. ITALIA
Via Varesse 16B, Rome 00185. TEL: (39 06) 448 891.
FAX: (39 06) 446 2981. www.warnerbros.it

ZENITH DISTRIBUZIONE
Via Soperga 36, Milan 20127. TEL: (39 02) 261 3207.
FAX: (39 02) 261 0768.

EXHIBITORS

CECCHI GORI GROUP
Via Valadier 42, Rome 00193. TEL: (39 06) 324 721.

FAX: (39 06) 3247 23 72. www.cecchigori.com
Number of Screens: 61

CINEMA 5
Via Aurelia Antica 422, Rome 00165. TEL: (39 06) 663 901.
FAX: (39 06) 6639 0440.

ERNESTO DI SARRO
Via Soperga 36, Milan 20127. TEL: (39 02) 260 3207.

ISTITUTO LUCE
Via Tuscolana 1055, Rome 00173. TEL: (39 06) 729 921.
FAX: (39 06) 722 1127. email: luce@luce.it www.luce.it
PRESIDENT
Flavio DeLuca

DAVID QUILLERI
Via Ville Patrizi 10, Rome. TEL: (39 06) 884 4731.

I.T. INTERNATIONAL/FORUM FILM
91 Medinat Ha-Yehudim Street, Herzlia Pituah 46766.
TEL: (972) 9952-6262. FAX: (972) 9956-1581.
www.iti-theatres.com
States of Operation: Israel, Hungary, Poland, Czech Republic
CEO
Mooky Greidinger

RAFFAELE GAUDAGNO
Cinema President, Largo Augusto 1, Milan 20122.
TEL: (39 02) 7602 1410. FAX: (39 02) 7602 2223.

UCI ITALIA SRL
Via Giarezzo No. 4, Milan 20145. TEL: (39 02) 4855 9029.
FAX: (39 02) 469 4998. www.ucicinemas.it
DIRECTOR
Donna Roberts
Number of Theatres: 8

UGC CINÉ CITÉ ITALIA SPA
Via Andrea Solari, 19, 20144, Milan. TEL: (39 02) 8942 3176.
FAX: (39 02) 8320 2240. email: segreteria@ugcitalia.com
www.ugccinemas.co.uk
Number of Theatres: 1
Number of Screens: 12

VILLAGE ROADSHOW, LTD.
(For complete listing see Australian branch)
206 Bourke St., Melbourne, VIC, 3000, Australia.
TEL: (613) 9667 6666. FAX: (613) 9639 1540.
www.villageroadshow.com.au
Number of Theatres: 14 (Italy)
Number of Screens: 146 (Italy)

WARNER VILLAGE CINEMAS
Piazza Augusto Imperatore, 3, Scala C, 2 Piano
Rome 00186. TEL: 3906-688-111. FAX: 3906-6880-8578.

ASSOCIATIONS & ORGANIZATIONS

ASSOCIAZIONE NAZIONALE INDUSTRIE CINEMATOGRAFICHE AUDIOVISIVE E MULTIMEDIALI (ANICA)
Viale Regina Margherita 286, Rome 00198.
TEL: (396) 4423 1480. FAX: (396) 440 4128.
email:anica@anica.it www.anica.it

CINECITTA HOLDING SPA
Via Tuscolana 1055, Rome 00173. TEL: (39 06) 722 861.
FAX: (39 06) 722 1883. www.cinecitta.com
PRESIDENT
Carlo Fuscagni
CEO
Ubaldo Livolsi
MANAGING DIRECTOR
Alessandro Usai
MARKETING AND COMMUNICATION DIRECTOR
Fabio Fabbi

ITALIAN FILM COMMISSION
Via Liszt 21, Rome 00144. TEL: (39 06) 659 921.
email: ice@ice.it www.ice.gov.it

1801 Ave. of the Stars, Ste. 700, Los Angeles, CA 90067. USA.
TEL: (323) 879 0950. FAX: (310) 203 8335.
email: italcomm@itc-ice-la.com www.filminginitaly.com

ITALIAN MINISTRY OF CULTURE
Via del Collegio Romano, 27 Rome 00186. TEL: (39 06) 67231.
www.beniculturali.it
CONTACT
Francesco Ventura, Maria Tresa Fortunato, Nerea Colonnelli,
Via Della Ferracella in Laterano 51, Rome 00184.

JAPAN

Capital: Tokyo
Population: 126,804,433 (July 2010 est.)
Area: 377,835 sq. km.
Source: Source: CIA World Factbook

DISTRIBUTORS AND PRODUCERS

ALCINE TERRAN
c/o Epcott Company, 2F Tokiwa Bldg., 4-5-6 Shibuya, Shibuya-Ku,
Tokyo 150-0002. TEL: (813) 5467 3730. FAX: (813) 5467 3731.
email: minori-i@epcott.com.jp www.alcine-terran.com
PRESIDENT
Akio Horie

ALTAMIRA PICTURES, INC.
#1203 New-Shibuya Bldg.12-3 Udagawa-cho, Shibuya-ku,
Tokyo 150-0042. TEL: (813) 5456 8581. FAX: (813) 3464 2265.
email: altamira@altamira.jp www.altamira.co.jp

ARGO PICTURES
201 Yahata Bldg. 4-10-21 Akasaka, Minato-ku, Tokyo 107-0052. TEL: (813) 3584 6237. FAX: (813) 3584 6238.

ASMIK ENTERTAINMENT
6-1-24-3F Roppongi, Minato-Ku, Tokyo 106-8553.
TEL: (813) 5413 4352. FAX: (813) 5413 2843.
email: webmaster@asmik-ace.co.jp www.asmik-ace.co.jp/

AVEX ENTERTAINMENT
3-1-30, Minami-Aoyama, Minato-ku, Tokyo 107-8577.
TEL: (813) 5413 8993. FAX: (813) 5413 8879.
email: www.avexnet.jp

BUENA VISTA INTERNATIONAL JAPAN
Roppongi DK Bldg., 7-18-23 Roppongi 106, Minato-ku.
TEL: (813) 3746 5009. FAX: (813) 3746 0009.
www.movies.co.jp

CHANNEL COMMUNICATIONS, INC.
303 Mitsuai Bldg., Take-Kanta, Minato-Ku, Tokyo 108.
TEL: (813) 3280 0971. FAX: (813) 3280 0555.

CINE QUA NON FILMS
7F, 33-7 Udagawa-cho, Shibuya-Ku, Tokyo 150 0042.
TEL: (813) 5458 6576. FAX: (813) 5458 6572.
http://cqn.co.jp

COMMUNICA FILM CORP.
401, 5-1-25 Minami-Aoyama, Minato-Ku, Tokyo 107.
TEL: (813) 3409 0431. FAX: (813) 3498 1086.

COMSTOCK
2-12-24-6F, Shibuya, Tokyo 150-0002.
TEL: 03-5464-0526. FAX: 03-5464-0640.
www.cubical.jp

CREATIVE ENTERPRISE INTERNATIONAL, INC. (TOKYO)
Villa Bianca 205, 33-12-2 Cho-Me, Jingu-Mae, Shibuya-Ku,
Tokyo 150. TEL: (813) 3403 4893. FAX: (813) 3404 3766.

DELA CORPORATION
Rozan Bldg. 813, 7-15-13, Roppongi, Minato-ku, 106, Tokyo.
TEL: (813) 479 0591. FAX: (813) 479 0602.

FILM FACE CO., LTD.
#602 13-10 Sakuragaoka-cho, Shibuya-ku, Tokyo 150-0031.
TEL: (813) 3780 4311. FAX: (813) 3780 4316.
email: info@filmface.co.jp www.filmface.jp

FELLAH PICTURES
8-12-8-1F Nishi-Shinjuku, Shinjuku, Tokyo 160-0023.
TEL: 03-5348-7464. FAX: 03-5330-1108.

GAGA COMMUNICATIONS
East Roppongi Bldg., 16-35 Roppongi 3-chome, Minato-ku,
Tokyo 106-0032. TEL: (813) 3589 1026. FAX: (813) 3589 1043.
email: intl@gaga.co.jp www.gaga.co.jp

HAPPINET PICTURES
Komagata Ca Bldg,.2-4-5 Komagata Taito-Ku, Tokyo 111 0043.
TEL: (813) 5828 3940. FAX: (813) 5828 1654.
www.hap-net.com

KADOKAWA PICTURES
3-6 9F Kioicho, Chiyoda,Tokyo 1028302.
TEL: (813) 5213 0693. FAX: (813) 3556 4322.
email: seki@kadokawa-pictures.co.jp
http://kadokawa-pictures.co.jp

IMJ ENTERTAINMENT
7-1-1 Nishi-Gotanda, Shinagawa-ku, Tokyo 141-0031.
TEL: (813) 5759 0167. FAX: (813) 5759 0862.
email: eizou@imjp.co.jp www.imjp.co.jp

KAJIMAVISION PRODUCTION CO., LTD.
6-5-13 Akasaka, Minato-Ku, Tokyo 107.
TEL: (813) 3582 6661. FAX: (813) 3588 0883.

KIROKU EIGASHA PRODUCTIONS, INC.
2-12-1 Yoyogi, Shibuya-Ku, Tokyo 151. TEL: (813) 3370 3386.
FAX: (813) 3370 3469.

KOBUSHI PRODUCTION, INC.
#103 YKB-Daikyocho 12-9 Daikyocho, Shinjuku-ku, Tokyo 160-0015. TEL: (813) 3357 5608. FAX: (813) 3357 5609.

KOUWA INTERNATIONAL CO., LTD.
1-7 Daikanyama, Shibuya-ku, Tokyo 150-0034.
TEL: (813) 3496 6908. FAX: (813) 3496 8225.

LEGEND PICTURES CO., LTD.
c/o Tohokushinsha Film Corp, 4-17-7 Akasaka, Minato-ku, Tokyo 107-8460. TEL: (813) 3582 0211. FAX: (813) 3584 2824.

MADHOUSE
167-0051Suginami Ku 4-30-16 Tokyo.
TEL: (810) 3-5347-2515. email: webmaster@madhouse.co.jp
http://www.madhouse.co.jp/

MAGICA ENTERTAINMENT, INC
2-9-15 Higashigotanda, Shinagawa-ku, Tokyo 141-0022.
TEL: (813) 3280 1688. FAX: (813) 3280 7581.
email: contact@ent.imagica.co.jp

MARS PRODUCTION CO., LTD.
2-14-9 Yakumodai, Chofu-shi, Tokyo 182-0015.
TEL: (814) 2480 4512. FAX: (814) 2480 4513.
email: mars-pro@rio.odn.ne.jp

MICOTT, INC.
3F 31-10 Sakuragaoka-cho, Shibuya-ku, Tokyo 150-0031.
TEL: (813) 6415 6090. FAX: (813) 3496 8445.
email: intl@micott.jp www.micott.jp

MONKEY TOWN PRODUCTION CO., LTD.
#301 Legend Minamidai 5-30-11 Minamidai, Nakano-ku, Tokyo 164-0014. TEL: (813) 3381 7872. FAX: (813) 3381 7872.
email: sarumachi@aol.com

MOVIE-EYE ENTERTAINMENT
6-2-1-4F Ginza, Chuo, Tokyo 104-0061.
TEL: (810) 3-5537-0151. FAX: (810)3-5537-0152.
email: me-tokyo@movie-eye.co.jp www.movie-eye.co.jp

MEDIA INTERNATIONAL CORPORATION
2-14-5 Akasaka, Minato-ku, Tokyo 107.
TEL: (813) 5561 9571. FAX: (813) 5561 9550/49.

MITSUBISHI CORPORATION
3-1, Marunouchi 2-Chome, Chiyoda-ku, Tokyo 100-86.
TEL: (813) 3210 7795. FAX: (813) 3210 7397.

MONSTER FILMS, INC.
4-2-14 Roppongi, Minato-ku, Tokyo 106-0032.
TEL: (813) 6229 1611. FAX: (813) 6229 1622.
www.monsterfilms.jp

MUSHI - PRODUCTION CO., LTD.
2-30-5 Fujimidai, Nerima-ku, Tokyo 177-0034.
TEL: (813) 3990 4153. FAX: (813) 3990 4151.
email: mushipro@interlink.or.jp www.mushi-pro.co.jp

NEXUS (JAPAN), LTD.
47 Poland St., London W1V 3DF. TEL: (0171) 434 9243.
FAX: (0171) 437 3720.

NHK INTERNATIONAL, INC.
Daini Kyodo Bldg., 7-13 Udagawacho, Shibuya-Ku, Tokyo 150.
TEL: (813) 3464 1823. FAX: (813) 3770 1829.
www.nhk.or.jp

NIKKATSU
3-28-12 Hongo. Bunkyo-ku. Tokyo113-0033.
TEL: (813) 56 89 10 18. FAX: (813) 56 89 10 44.
www.nikkatsu.com/

ORIENT FILM ASSOCIATES, INC.
Naoki Bldg., 2-11-14 Minami Aoyama, Minato-Ku, Tokyo 107.
TEL: (813) 334 792 340. FAX: (813) 334 792 319.

PONY CANYON, INC.
5-10 Toranomon 2-chome, Minato-ku, Tokyo 105-8487.
TEL: (813) 5521 8024. FAX: (813) 5521.8122.
email: intl@ponycanyon.co.jp www.ponycanyon.co.jp

PRODUCTION I.G.
3-22-31 Minami-cho, Kokubunji, Tokyo 185-0021.
TEL: 81-42-323-3569. FAX: 81-42-323-9400.
email: info@production-ig.co.jp www.productionig.com

RUMBLE FISH
8-20-33 Ginza, Chuo, Tokyo104-0061.
TEL: 03-3524-7222. FAX: 03-3524-7223.
www.rfish.co.jp

SHOCHIKU COMPANY
Togeki Bldg.1-1 Tsukiji 4-chome, Chuo-ku, Tokyo 104-8422.
TEL: (813) 5550 1623. FAX: (813) 5550 1654.
email: ibd@shochiku.co.jp www.shochiku.co.jp
PRESIDENT & CEO
Junichi (Jay) Sakomoto
EXECUTIVE MANAGING DIRECTOR
Suketsugo Noda

SONY PICTURES ENTERTAINMENT, JAPAN
Sr. Luke's Tower 36F, 8-1 Akashi-cho, Chuo-ku, Tokyo 104-8530. TEL: (813) 5551 0823. FAX: (813) 5551 0837.
www.spe.co.jp

STUDIO GHIBLI
1-4-25 Kajino-cho, Koganei-shi, Tokyo 184-0002.
TEL: 81 422 50 2511. FAX: 81 422 50 2489.
post@ghibli.co.jp www.ghibli.jp

SUNRISE, INC.
44-10 Kami-Igusa 2-chome, Suginami-ku, Tokyo 167-0023.
TEL: (813) 3397 6776. FAX: (813) 3395 6240.

TATSUNOKO PRODUCTIONS COMPANY
3-22-12 Minami-cho, Kokubunji-shi, Tokyo.
TEL: (814) 2-323-9111. www.tatsunoko.co.jp/

TELECOM JAPAN INTERNATIONAL, INC.
80 St. Marks Place, New York, NY 10003.
TEL: (212) 254 2845. FAX: (212) 254 7845.

TKK ASSOCIATES, INC.
2-17-3 Takanawa, Minato-Ku, Tokyo 108-0074.
TEL: (813) 3447 5241. FAX: (813) 3441 7826.
email: tkk@tkkassociates.jp www.tkkassociates.jp
CONTACT
Tak Shibata

TOEI COMPANY
2-17, 3-Chome, GinzaJapan, Chuo-ku 104, Tokyo.
TEL: (813) 535 7621. FAX: (813) 535 7622.
CHAIRMAN & CEO
Shigeru Okada
PRESIDENT & COO
Tan Takaiwa
MANAGING DIRECTOR
Naoshi Yoda

TOHO CO., LTD.
1-2-2 Yurakucho, Chiyoda-ku, Tokyo 100-8415.
TEL: (813) 3591 3530. FAX: (813) 3591 6610.
email: tohointl@toho.co.jp www.toho.co.jp
PRESIDENT
Ilsao Matsuoka
MANAGING DIRECTOR
Satoru Terada

TOHO SEISAKU CO., LTD.
7-7-4 Akasaka, Minato-ku, Tokyo 107. TEL: (813) 3505 7350.
FAX: (813) 3505 7357.

TOHO TOWA COMPANY
Kawakita Memorial Bldg., 18 Ichiban-cho, Chiyoda-ku, Tokyo 102-8537. TEL: (813) 3556 0335. FAX: (813) 3556 0317.
email: intl-dept@tohotowa.co.jp www.toho.co.jp/towa/english.html
PRESIDENT
Hisanori Hiranuma
MANAGING DIRECTOR
Hiro Matsuoka

TOHOKUSHINSHA FILM CORPORATION
4-8-10 Akasaka, Minato-ku, Tokyo 107-8460.
TEL: (813) 5414 0332. FAX: (813) 5414 0430.
email: kokusai@tfc.co.jp www.tfc-movie.net

TV MAN UNION, INC.
30-13 Motoyoyogi-Cho, Shibuya-ku, Tokyo. TEL: (813) 5478 1611.
FAX: (813) 5478 8141.

TWENTIETH CENTURY FOX (FAR EAST)
Fukide Bldg. 4-1-13 Toranomon, Minato-ku, Tokyo.
TEL: (813) 3436 3421. FAX: (813) 3433 5322.

UNITED INTERNATIONAL PICTURES (FAR EAST)
P.O. Box 514 Central, Tokyo 100-8692.
TEL: 81-3-3248 1780. FAX: 81-3-3248 6276.
PRESIDENT & COO
Kiri Inomata

WARNER BROS. THEATRICAL DISTRIBUTION JAPAN
1-2-4 Hamamatsu-Cho, Minato-ku 105, Tokyo.
TEL: (813) 5472 8000. FAX: (813) 5472 8029.
www.warnerbros.co.jp

XANADU
1-56-1 Brocade Building, 2nd Fl., Nerima Ku Asahi Hill, Tokyo 176-0005. TEL: (810) 3 5982 1013.
FAX: (810) 3 5982 1015. www.xanadujapan.co.jp

EXHIBITORS

AMERICAN MULTI-CINEMA (AMC)
920 Main St., Kansas City, MO, U.S. 64105. TEL: (816) 221 4000.
FAX: (816) 480 4617. email: amc@amc.pt www.amc.pt
CHAIRMAN & CEO
Peter Brown
PRESIDENT & COO
Philip M. Singleton
Number of Theatres (Japan): 5

Number of Screens (Japan): 79

SHOCHIKU COMPANY
Togeki Bldg.1-1 Tsukiji 4-chome, Chuo-ku, Tokyo 104-8422.
TEL: (813) 5550 1623. FAX: (813) 5550 1654.
email: ibd@shochiku.co.jp www.shochiku.co.jp
PRESIDENT & CEO
Junichi Sakomoto
MANAGING DIRECTOR
Suketsugo Noda
EXECUTIVE ROSTER
Ikuko Saegusa

TOEI COMPANY
2-17, 3-Chome, Ginza Japan, Chuo-ku 104, Tokyo.
TEL: (813) 535 7621. FAX: (813) 535 7622.
www.toei.co.jp
CHAIRMAN & CEO
Shigeru Okada
PRESIDENT & COO
Tan Takaiwa
MANAGING DIRECTOR
Naoshi Yoda

TOHO CINEMAS, LTD.
Daini Marutaka Bldg., 7th Fl., 7-13-8 Ginza, Chuo-ku, Tokyo 104-8148. TEL: (813) 3549 3549. FAX: (813) 3549 1041.
email: www.tohocinemas.co.jp www.tohotheater.jp
PRESIDENT
Ilsao Matsuoka
MANAGING DIRECTOR
Satoru Terada

TOHO TOWA COMPANY
Kawakita Memorial Bldg., 18 Ichiban-cho, Chiyoda-ku, Tokyo 102-8537. TEL: (813) 3556 0335. FAX: (813) 3556 0317.
email: intl-dept@tohotowa.co.jp www.toho.co.jp/towa/english.html
PRESIDENT
Hisanori Hiranuma
MANAGING DIRECTOR
Hiro Matsuoka

UCI JAPAN KK
4F Izumi Akasaka Bldg., 2-22-24 Akasak, Minato-ku, Tokyo 107. TEL: (813) 3224 3200. FAX: (813) 3224 3212.
www.unitedcinemas.jp

UNITED CINEMAS
Izumi Akasaka Bldg., 4th Flr., 2-22-24, Akasaka, Minato-ku Tokyo 107-0052. TEL (813) 3224 3200.
FAX: 813 3224 3212. www.unitedcinemas.jp
PRESIDENT
Masanori Miyata
MANAGING DIRECTORS
Makoto Sekimoto, Shinya Naiki

Number of Theatres: 20
Number of Screens: 209

WARNER MYCAL CORP.
Izumikan Sanban-cho, Bldg. 3-8, Sanban-cho, Chiyoda-ku, Tokyo 102-0075. TEL: (813) 3262 0201. FAX: (813) 5210 2552.
www.warnermycal.co
CHAIRMAN
Tsutomu Kajita
PRESIDENT
Millard L. Ochs
MANAGER OF PUBLIC RELATIONS
Hiromi Kuse

Number of Theatres: 44
Number of Screens: 338

Akashi (7), Chigasaki (60, Ebetsu (8), Ebina (7), Fukuoka Lucle (9), Fukushima (7), Higahikishiwada (8), Hirosaki (6), Hiroshima (7), Hofu (7), Ibaraki (10), Ichikawamyoden (9), Ishinomaki (7), Itabashi (12), Kakogwa (8), Kamimine (7), Kanazawa (8), Kenoh (7), Kitakami (7), Kitami (7), Kumagaya (8), Kushiro (8), Kuwana (8), Minatomirai (8), Niigata (9), Nishiyamato (7), Ohi (7), Ohnojo (8), Okyouzuka (8), Omihachiman (8), Omiya (8), Otaru (7), Sanda Woodytown (7), Shinyurigaoka (9), Suzuka Bellcity (8), Takamatsu (7), Takaoka (6), Tobata (8), Toyokawa (7), Tsu (7), Tsukimino (9), Utazu (7), Yonezawa (7), Yukarigaoka (8)

ASSOCIATIONS & ORGANIZATIONS

AGENCY FOR CULTURAL AFFAIRS
3-2-2 Kasumigaseki, Chiyoda-ku, Tokyo 100-8959.
TEL: (813) 5253 4111. www.bunka.go.jp/

ALL NIPPON PRODUCERS ASSOCIATION (ANPA)
5F 41-8 Udagawa-Cho, Shibuya-ku, Tokyo 150-0042.
TEL: (813) 3477 7355. FAX: (813) 3477.7340.
email: anpa@pro.email.ne.jp www.producer.or.jp

ASSOCIATION OF JAPANESE ANIMATIONS (AJA)
#304 1-29-7 Takadanobaba, Shinjuku-ku, Tokyo 169-0075.
TEL: (813) 5287 2050/2051. FAX: (813) 5287 2052.
email: office@aja.gr.jp www.aja.gr.jp

DISTRIBUTORS ASSOCIATION OF JAPAN
3F 2-15-2 Ginza, Chuo-ku, Tokyo 104-0061.
TEL: (813) 3524 4114. FAX: (813) 3524 4113.

FEDERATION OF JAPANESE FILMS INDUSTRY, INC.
Tokyu Ginza Bldg. 3F, 2-15-2 Ginza, Chuo-ku, Tokyo 104-0061.
TEL: (813) 3547 1855. FAX: (813) 3547 1854.
email: info@eidanren.com www.eidanren.com

JAPAN ASSOCIATION OF AUDIOVISUAL PRODUCERS, INC.
Shichokaku Bldg., 17-1 Toranomon 1-chome, Minato-ku, Tokyo 105-0001. TEL: (813) 3501 0236. FAX: (813) 3501 0238.
email: inquiry@eibunren.or.jp www.eibunren.or.jp

JAPAN ASSOCIATION OF THEATRE OWNERS
Seieikaikan Bldg., 6-8-2 Shinbashi, Minato-ku, Tokyo 104-0061. TEL: (813) 5408 5446. FAX: (813) 5408 5447.
email: info@zenkoren.or.jp www.zenkoren.or.jp

JAPANESE SOCIETY OF CINEMATOGRAPHERS (JSC)
5F 2-15-14 Shinjuku, Shinjuku-ku, Tokyo 160-0022.
TEL: (813) 3356 7896. FAX: (813) 3356 7897.
email: info@jsc.or.jp www.jsc.or.jp
VICE CHAIRMAN OF THE BOARD
Fujiro Morita
MANAGING DIRECTOR
Masaharu Itoh
DIRECTOR
Youzou Inagaki

JFCPC JAPAN FILM COMMISSION PROMOTION COUNCIL
National Film Center 5F, 3-7-6, Kyobashi, Chuo-ku, Tokyo 104-0031. FAX: (813) 3563 2526. email: info@film-com.jp
www.film-com.jp

JAPAN FILMMAKERS ASSOCIATION
6F Scenario Bldg., 5-4-16 Akasaka, Minato-ku, Tokyo 107-0052. TEL: (813) 3582 2654. FAX: (813) 3582 0368.

JAPAN FOUNDATION
21F 1-12-32 Akasaka, Minato-ku, Tokyo 107-6021.
TEL: (813) 5562 3535. www.jpf.go.jp
PRESIDENT
Kazuo Ogoura

MOTION PICTURE PRODUCERS ASSOCIATION OF JAPAN
Tokyu Ginza Bldg.3F, 2-15-2 Ginza, Chuo-ku, Tokyo 104-0061.
TEL: (813) 3547 1800. FAX: (813) 3547 0909.
email: eiren@mc.neweb.ne.jp www.eiren.org

NATIONAL FILM CENTER, NATIONAL MUSEUM OF MODERN ART, TOKYO (NFC)
3-7-6 Kyobashi, Chuo-ku, Tokyo 104-0031.
TEL: (813) 3561 0823. FAX: (813) 3561 0830.
email: webstaff@momat.go.jp www.momat.go.jp/fc.html

UNI JAPAN FILM (ASSOCIATION FOR THE DIFFUSION OF JAPANESE FILMS ABROAD)
2-11-6, Takeda Bldg, #505, Ginza, Chuo-ku, Tokyo 104-0061.
TEL: (813) 5565 7511. FAX: (813) 5565 7531.
email: office@unijapan.org www.unijapan.org/english

LUXEMBOURG

Capital: Luxembourg
Population: 497,538 (July 2010 est.)
Area: 2,586 sq. km.
Source: CIA World Factbook

DISTRIBUTORS AND PRODUCERS

CLT-UFA INTERNATIONAL
45, bd. Pierre Frieden, L-1543 Luxembourg/Kirchberg.
TEL: (352) 42 142 3925. FAX: (352) 42142 3929.
email: contact@clt-ufa-international.com.
www.clt-ufa-international.com
MARKETING MANAGER
Rebecca Lucas

IRIS PRODUCTIONS S.A.
45 Blvd. Pierre Freidan Batiment KB 2 Bureau 29 LU-1543 Luxembourg. TEL: (352) 260 217. FAX: (352) 4470 7046.
email: info@irisproductions.lu www.irisproductions.lu

LUX FILM DISTRIBUTION
18 Val Sainte-Croix L-1370 Luxembourg.
TEL: (352) 250 393. FAX: (352) 250 394.

EXHIBITORS

UTOPIA S.A.
16, Ave. de Faiencerie, L-1510 Luxembourg.
TEL: (352) 24611. FAX: (352) 224612.
email: utopia@utopia.lu www.utopolis.lu

45 Blvd. J.F. Kennedy L-1855 Luxembourg.
TEL: (352) 429 5111.FAX: (352) 429 5191.
CHAIRMAN & MANAGER
Nico Simon
MANAGER
Luc Nothum
FINANCES
Didier Briere

Number of Theatres: 5
Number of Seats: 720

MALAYSIA

Capital: Kuala Lumpur
Population: 28,274,729 (July 2010 est.)
Area: 329,750 sq. km.
Source: CIA World Factbook

EXHIBITORS & DISTRIBUTORS

(Local addresses and telephone numbers are listed where available, otherwise please contact the corporate headquarters below)

ASIA PACIFIC FILM SERVICES
P.O. Box 1183, Kuching, Sarawak, Borneo, East Malaysia.
TEL: (608) 225 1915. FAX: (608) 225 6839.
MANAGING DIRECTOR
Nigel Goldstk
CONTACT
Tim Hatch

CATHAY ORGANISATION (M) SDN BHD
(A branch of Plantations Berhad, 17th Flr., Wisma Jerneh, 38 Jalan Sultan Ismail, 50250 Kuala Lumpur, Malaysia)
1 Jalan SS22/19 Damansara Jaya, 47400 Petaling Jaya, Selangor, Malaysia 47400. TEL: (603) 71 95 666.
FAX: (603) 71 92 179.
email: corporate_services@cathay.com.sg www.cathay.com.sg
CHAIRMAN
Jen (R) Tan Sri Dato Mohd Ghazali Seth
CHIEF EXECUTIVE
Ong Te Cheong
EXECUTIVE DIRECTOR
Meileen Choo

Number of Theatres: 34
Number of Screens: 47

GOLDEN SCREEN CINEMAS
1 Jalan SS 22/19, Damansara Jaya, Petaling Jaya, Selangor 47400. TEL (603) 7729 5566.
FAX: (603) 7722-1655. email: marketing@gsc.com.my
www.gsc.com.my
GENERAL MANAGER
Irving Chee
SENIOR MANAGER
Liew Aing Suan

SUNNY FILM CORPORATION
Wisma Sunny, 17, Jln. Mewah 2/2A, Taman Subang Mewah, Subang Jaya, Selangor 47500. TEL/FAX: (603) 8023 148.
email: sfc@sunnyfilm.net www.sunnyfilm.com
PRESIDENT
Sunny PH Lim

TANJONG GOLDEN VILLAGE
Level 1, Bukit Raja Shopping Centre, Persiaran Bukit Raja 2, Bandar Baru Klang, 41150 Klang, Malaysia.
TEL: (603) 344 1688. FAX: (603) 2381-3139.
www.tgv.com.my
CONTACT
Chung Shyh Kwong

Number of Screens: 47

TANJONG, PLC
17th Fl., Menara Boustead, Jln Raja Chulan, 50200 Kuala Lumpur. TEL: (603) 244 3388. FAX: (603) 244 3388.

TGV CINEMAS
Level 26, Menara Maxis, Kuala Lumpur City Centre
Kuala Lumpur 50088. TEL: (603) 2381 3140.
FAX: 603 2381 3139. email: shkyhkwong_chung@tgv.com.my
www.tgv.com.my
DIRECTOR
Gerard Nathan
GENERAL MANAGER
Chung Shyh Kwong

Number of Theatres: 12
Number of Screens: 85

TWENTIETH CENTURY FOX FILM
Sendirian Berhad, 22 Jalan Padang Walter Grenier off Jalan Imbi, 55100 Kuala Lumpur. TEL: (603) 242 4396.
FAX: (603) 248 3129.

UNITED INTERNATIONAL PICTURES
No. 22 Jalan SS26/6, Taman Mayang Jaya, 47301 Petaling Jaya, Selangor, Malaysia. TEL: (603) 704 4899.
FAX: (603) 703 7833.
MANAGER
Nicholas Yong

VILLAGE ROADSHOW, LTD.
(For complete listing see Australian branch)
206 Bourke St., Melbourne, VIC, 3000, Australia.
TEL: (613) 9667 6666. FAX: (613) 9639 1540.

Number of Theatres (Malaysia): 40
Number of Screens (Malaysia): 145

WARNER BROS.
24 Jalan Padang Walter Grenier off Jalan Imbi, 55100 Kuala Lumpur. TEL: (603) 242 3669. FAX: (603) 248 9670.

ASSOCIATIONS AND ORGANIZATIONS

DIRECTORS' ASSOCIATION OF MALAYSIA (FDAM)
38 SS 20/10, Damansara Kim, 47400 Petaling Jaya, Selangor [illegible]arul Ehsan. TEL: (603) 7728 2427.

[illegible]ERATION OF FILM PROFESSIONAL SOCIETIES OF [illegible]YSIA
Stu[illegible] 68000[illegible]nca Delima, Lot 1045, Batu 7, Jalan Hulu Klang, [illegible]ang, Selangor Darul Ehsan. TEL: (603) 407 8981.
FAX: (60[illegible]8 1552.

MALAYSIAN [illegible]M PRODUCERS ASSOCIATION
Kompleks Studio [illegible]erdeka, Lot 1662, Batu 8, Hulu Klang, 68000, Ampang, Se[illegible]ggor D.E. TEL: (603) 4108 8660.
FAX: (603) 4107 2291. [illegible]mail: info@fpamal.com
www.fpamal.com
PRESIDENT
YBhg Tan Sri Kamarul Ariffin Mohamed Yassin
VICE PRESIDENT
YBhg Datuk Yusof Haslam

MALAYSIAN MINISTRY OF INFORMATION
Angkasapuri, 50610 Kuala Lumpur. TEL: (603) 282 5333.
FAX: (603) 282 1255.

MINISTRY OF INTERNATIONAL TRADE & INDUSTRY
Block 10, Government Offices Complex, Jalan Duta 50622, Kuala Lumpur. TEL: (603) 254 0033. FAX: (603) 255 0827.

NATIONAL FILM DEVELOPMENT CORPORATION OF MALAYSIA
Kompleks Studio Merdeka, Jalan Hulu Klang, 68000 Ampang, Selangor Darul Ehsan. TEL: (603) 408 5722.
FAX: (603) 407 5216.

MEXICO

Capital: Mexico
Population: 112,468,855 (July 2010 est.)
Area: 1,972,550 sq. km.
Source: CIA World Factbook

DISTRIBUTORS AND PRODUCERS

ALAMEDA FILMS
Avenida Presidente Mazaryk 490 111560 Delegacion Miquel Hidalgo. TEL: (5255) 1055 2333. email: info@alamedafilm.com
www.alamedafilm.com

BUENA VISTA COLUMBIA TRISTAR FILMS
Prol. Paseo de la Reforma No. 600 331 Sante Fe Pena Blanco.
www.columbiapictures.mx

CAMALEON FILMS
Séneca 413 - 1, Col. Polanco, 11560 México, D. F.
TEL: (52 55) 5280 1094. FAX: (52 55) 5280 1094.
CONTACTS
Luis Carreola, Ignacio Carreola

CANANA FILMS
Jose Maria Tornel #14, Colonia San Miguel Chapultepec Mexico City 11850. TEL: (52 55) 4777 7935.
FAX: (52 55) 5272 3553. email: geminiano@canana.net

CENTRAL FILMS
Anatole France 349 Col. Polanco, 11550 Mexico.
TEL: (525) 5262 8740.

CIBERFILMS
Amsterdam 121 - B, Col. Hipódromo Condesa, 06100 México. D. F. TEL: (52 55) 5286 1960. FAX: (52 55) 5286 0903.
CONTACT
Javier Gutiérrez

CINEMATRONICS
Los Andres 210 Col. Lomas de Chapultepec 11000 Mexico.
TEL: (5255) 5249 4480. FAX: (5255) 5540 5191.

COLUMBIA TRISTAR FILMS DE MEXICO
Av. Ejercito Nacional, 343-3er Piso, Col. Granada, Delegacion Miguel Hidalgo, 11520 Mexico D.F.. TEL: (52 55) 531 1428.
FAX: (52 55) 545 1986.

CUCAMONGA FILMS
Belisario Domínguez 128, Col. Del Carmen Coyoacán, 04100 México, D. F. TEL: (52 55) 5658 1348. FAX: (52 55) 5658 5397.
CONTACT
Jorge Chávez

DISTRITO FILMS
Lago Tangañica 23, Col. Granada, 11520 México, D. F.
TEL: (52 55) 8503 4518. FAX: (52 55) 3003 2152.
CONTACT
Héctor Ibarra

FILMACIONES GENESIS
7 Col. San Angel, 01000 México, D. F. TEL: (52 55) 5550 3233.
FAX: (52 55) 5616 2280.

FILM CORE FILMS
Col. Condesa 06140 Mexico. TEL: (5255) 5211 3429.
FAX: (5255) 5553 9434.

LEMON MEDIA
Francisco Petrarca 223-7-4 Col. Chapultepec Morales -
Mexico. TEL: (5255) 5250 8204. FAX: (5255) 5250 8
email: info@lemonfilms.com www.lemonfilms.com

MANTARRAYA PRODUCCIONES
Sultepec 47. Hipodromo Condesa, Mexico Ci Distrito Federal
06170. TEL: (5255) 52730230.
email: jaime@mantarraya.com http://ww mantarraya.com/

METRO PRODUCCIONES
La-Fontaine 69, Col. Polanco, 11560 México. D. F.
TEL: (52 55) 5282 0235. FAX: (52 55) 5282 0897.
CONTACT
Pedro Avila

N.V.G. PRODUCCIONES
Av. Gómez Marín 350 Ed. Movie Star, Col. Valle del campestre,
66265 Garza García, N. L. TEL: (52 867) 8368 2453.
FAX: (52 867) 8368 2425.
CONTACT
Adrián Ochoa Quintana

OMNI PRODUCCIONES
Colorado 51, Col. Nápoles, 03810 México, D. F.
TEL: (52 55) 5687 7962. FAX: (52 55) 5687 9554.

QUADRUM PRODUCCIONES
Tenancingo 15 - A, Col. Condesa, 06140 México, D. F.
TEL: (52 55) 5211 3157. FAX: (52 55) 5211 3157.

TITRA PRODUCCIONES
Taine 152, Col. Chapultepec Morales, 11570 México, D. F.
TEL: (52 55) 5545 1273. FAX: (52 55) 5203 1641.
CONTACT
Mauricio Kuri, Michel Kuri

TRIBU FILMS
Av. México 197, Col. Hipódromo Condesa, 06170 México, D. F.
TEL: (52 55) 5584 2282. FAX: (52 55) 5584 2686.
CONTACT
Alfredo Garza

ULTRA FILMS
Pedernal 511, Col. Jardines del Pedregal, 01900 México, D. F.
TEL: (52 55) 5568 3156. FAX: (52 55) 5568 2011.

UNITED INTERNATIONAL PICTURES S. DE R.L.
Fuente de Trevi No. 23 5. Piso, Lomas de Tecamachalco
Naucalpan de Juarez, Mexico, Edo de.
TEL: 525-589-5727. FAX: 525-589-7022. www.uip.com.mx
MANAGER
Michael Horn

EXHIBITORS

CINEMASTAR LUXURY THEATRES, INC.
1949 Avenida del Oro, Ste. 100, Oceanside, CA, 92056.
TEL: (760) 945 2500. FAX: (760) 945 2510.
www.cinemastar.com

Calz. Tecnológico #2100-64, Mesa de Otay, C.P. 22390,
Tijuana, B.C. TEL: (52 664) 624 3495. FAX: (52 664) 624 3389.
email: informacion@cinemastar.net
CHAIRMAN & CEO
Jack Crosby
PRESIDENT & COO
Frank Moreno
CFO
Norman Dowling
EXECUTIVE V.P.
Neal Austrian, Jr.
PRESIDENT, MEXICO
John D. Prock - jprock@cinemastar.net
DIRECTOR OF OPERATIONS, MEXICO
Lic. Joel A. Díaz - jdiaz@cinemastar.net

Number of Theatres (Mexico): 1
Number of Screens (Mexico): 10

CINEMARK USA, INC.
3900 Dallas Pkwy., Ste. 500, Plano, TX 75093.
TEL: (972) 665 1000. FAX: (972) 665 1004.

Calderon de la Barca 89-3, Col. Polanco, 11560 Mexico D. F.
TEL: (52 55) 5290 1847, 5280 1878. FAX: (52 55) 281 1240.
...co.asp
www.cinemark
CHAIRMAN
Lee Roy M
EXECU T& COO
Tandy
PRE ENT, CINEMARK INTERNATIONAL
Al arner
...ERAL MANAGER, MEXICO
...oberto Jenkins
Number of Theatres: 20
Number of Screens: 192

CINEMEX/CADENA MEXICANA DE EXHIBICION S.A. DE C.V. CINEMEX
Blvd. Manuel Avila Camacho No. 40 Piso 16, Col. Lomas de Chapultepec, Mexico 11000 DF. TEL: (525) 201 5800.
FAX: (525) 201 5813.
CO-DIRECTOR GENERAL
Matthew Heyman
CO-DIRECTOR GENERAL
Adolfo Fastlicht
CO-DIRECTOR GENERAL
Miguel Angel Davila Guzman

CINEPOLIS
(States of Operation: Mexico, Panama, Costa Rica, Guatemala, El Salvador)
Av. Lic. Enrique Ramirez 701-BIS. Morelia, Michoacan 58270.
TEL: (52) 443 3220505. FAX: (52) 443 322 0511.
www.cinepolis.com.mx
CEO
Alejandro Ramirez Magana
COO
Miguel Mier Esparza
Total Theaters: 164, Total Screens: 1389

COMPANIA OPERADORA DE TEATROS S.A. DE C.V. COTSA
Insurgentes Sur 453, Col. Condesa, 06140 Mexico D.F.C.P.
TEL: (525) 264 6010.
GENERAL DIRECTOR
Pablo Hernandez
Number of Theatres: 13
Number of Screens: 64
Mexico City (9), Colima (1), Cordova, Veracruz (1), Jalapa, Vercruz (1), Orizaba, Veracruz (1)

GRUPO CINEMEX
Blvd. Manuel Avila Camacho No. 40 Piso 16, Torre Esmerelda, Lomas de Chapultepec, 11000 Mexico City.
TEL: (52 55) 5201-5800.

MMCINEMAS
Eugenio Garza Sada 135 Sur. Col Roma
Monterrey, Nuevo Leon. TEL: 81 8128 7700.
www.mmcinemas.com
CEO
Rene Martinez
CFO
Javier Vedoya
Number of Theatres: 87
Number of Screens: 808

ORGANIZACION RAMIREZ S.A. DE C.V. MULTICINEMAS & CINEPOLIS
Avenida Enrique Ramirez Miguel #701, Fraccionamiento Las Americas, Morelia, Michoacan 58270. TEL: (524) 3220 526 229, (524) 3220 505. FAX: (524) 3220 511.
PRESIDENT
Enrique Ramirez Villalon
Number of Screens: 670

ASSOCIATIONS AND ORGANIZATIONS

MEXICAN ASSOCIATION OF FILMAKERS (AMFI)
General Anaya 198, Col. San Diego Churubusco, C.P.04120 México D.F. TEL: (52 55) 5605 0055. FAX: (52 55) 5605 9876.
email: amfi@webmedia.com.mx www.amfi.com.mx
GENERAL MANAGER
Carmen Garza

MEXICAN ASSOCIATION OF INDEPENDENT PRODUCERS
Atletas 2, Edificio Luis Buñuel B-201, Col. Country Club, C.P. 04220 México D.F. TEL: (52 55) 5549 3060.
email: ampiac@internet.com.mx

MEXICAN ASSOCIATION OF FILM PRODUCERS & DISTRIBUTORS
División del Norte 3462 Piso Col. Portales, C.P. 03300 México D.F. TEL: (52 55) 5688 7251, 5680 5268, 5688 8705.

MMCINEMAS
Eugenio Garza Sada 135 Sur. Col Roma. Monterrey, Nuevo Leon. TEL: 81 8128 7700. www.mmcinemas.com

CEO
Rene Martinez

Total Theaters: 70, Total Screens: 633

NATIONAL CHAMBER FOR CINEMATOGRAPHY & VIDEOGRAPHY
Av. General Anaya No. 198, Col. San Diego Churubusco, C.P 04120 México, D.F. TEL: (52 55) 5688 0442, 5688 3258. FAX: (52 55) 5604 3202, 5688 8810. www.canacine.org.mx

NATIONAL FILM COMMISSION (CONAFILM)
Av. División del Norte # 2462 5to. piso Col. Portales, C.P. 03300 México D.F. TEL: (52 55) 5688 7813, 5688 0970. email: conafilm@conafilm.org.mx conafilm@prodigy.net.mx www.conafilm.org.mx
PRESIDENT & NATIONAL FILM COMMISSIONER
Sergio A. R. Molina

NATIONAL FOUNDATION FOR CULTURE AND THE ARTS
Av. México Coyoacán No. 371, Col. Xoco México, D.F. TEL: (52 55) 5605 6139. FAX: (52 55) 5605 5533. email: fonca@conaculta.gob.mx www.conaculta.gob.mx

MEXICAN INSTITUTE OF CINEMATOGRAPHY
Insurgentes sur 674, Col. del Valle México, D.F. TEL: (52 55) 5448 5300, 5448 5399. email: imcine@conaculta.gob.mx www.imcine.gob.mx

NETHERLANDS

Capital: Amsterdam
Population: 16,783,092 (July 2010 est.)
Area: 41,526 sq. km.
Source: CIA World Factbook

DISTRIBUTORS AND PRODUCERS

A-FILM DISTRIBUTION
Meeuwenlaan 98-100, P.O. Box 37743 1030 BG Asterdam 2021. TEL: (31 20) 344 5144. FAX: (31 20) 344 5145. email: pim@a-film.nl www.a-film.nl

ADDED ENTERTAINMENT (NOW OPERATING AS PVTV)
Sumatralaan 45/ES.2, Hilversum1217 GP. TEL: (31 35) 677 4776. FAX: (31 35) 677 4562. email: added@pvtv.nl www.pvtv.nl

ANIMATIONWORLD B.V.
P.O. Box 16851, Amsterdam 1001 RJ. TEL: (31 20) 625 8907. FAX: (31 20) 623 4355. email: aniworld@worldonline.nl www.animationworld.com

ARGUS FILM
P.O. Box 18269, Amsterdam 1001 ZD. TEL: (31 20) 625 4585. FAX: (31 20) 622 1418. email: argusfilm@xs4all.nl

BIOSCOOP EXPLOITATIE MINERVA BV
P.O. Box 7220, Amsterdam 1007 JE. TEL: (31 20) 644 6823. FAX: (31 20) 644 8946.

BUENA VISTA INTERNATIONAL (NETHERLANDS)
P.O. Box 349, Badhoevedorp 1170 AH. TEL: (31 20) 658 0300. FAX: (31 20) 659 3349. www.bvimovies.com www.disney.nl

CINEMA INTERNATIONAL
P.O. Box 9228, Amsterdam 1006 AE. TEL: (31 20) 617 7575. FAX: (31 20) 617 7434.

CINEMIEN FILM AND VIDEO DISTRIBUTORS
Amsteldljklo 1074 Amsterdam. TEL: (020) 577 6010. FAX:(020) 577 6029. www.cinemien.nl
CONTACT
Phil van der Linden

CNR FILM RELEASING
Amstellandlaan 78, Weesp 1382 CH. TEL: (31 29) 346 2070. FAX: (3120) 346 2061.

COLUMBIA TRISTAR FILMS
Postbus 533, Amsterdam 1000 AM. TEL: (31 20) 346 2060. FAX: (31 20) 346 2061.

CONCORDE FILM BENELUX
Lange Voorhout 35, Den Haag 2514 EC. TEL: (31 70) 360 5810. FAX: (31 70) 360 4925.

CONTACT FILM CINEMATHEEK
P.O. Box 3100, Amsterdam 6802 DC. TEL: (31 26) 443 4949. FAX: (31 26) 351 1316. email: contactfilm@planet.nl

FILMMUSEUM
P.O. Box 74782, Amsterdam 1070 BT, Vandelpark 3. TEL: (31 20) 589 1400. FAX: (31 20) 683 3401. email: info@filmmuseum.nl www.filmmuseum.nl

FORTISSIMO FILM SALES
Veemarkt 77-79, Amsterdam 1019. TEL: (31 20) 627 3215. FAX: (31 20) 627 1155. email: ffsales@globalxs.nl www.fortissimo.nl

CHAIRMAN
Wouter Barendrecht, Michael Werner

HUNGRY EYE PICTURES
Duivendrechtsekade 82, Amsterdam 1096. TEL: (31 20) 668 6126. FAX: (31 20) 694 1018. email: info@hungryeye.nl www.hungryeye.nl

IL LUSTER PRODUCTIONS
Rijken Hoogt4 3512 GW Utrecht. TEL: (31 30) 240 0768. email: distribution@illuster.nl www.illuster.nl

INDEPENDENT FILMS NEDERLAND B.V.
Hagendornplein 2 1031 BV Amsterdam. TEL: (31 20) 571 1090. FAX: (31 20) 571 1095. email: niels@independentfilms.nl www.independentfilms.nl

INDIES FILM DISTRIBUTION
Regentesselaan 20-26, Hilversum 1217 EG. TEL: (31 35) 538 5300. FAX: (31 35) 538 5301.

KINEPOLIS GROUP
20 Blvd. du Centenaire, Brussels, B 1020. TEL: (322) 474 2600. FAX: (322) 472 2606. www.kinepolis.com
DIRECTOR OPERATIONS, NETHERLANDS
Boudewijn Muts

LAVA FILM DISTRIBUTION & SALES
Korte Leidsedwarsstr. 12 # 512, Amsterdam 1017 RC. TEL: (31 20) 625 5442. FAX: (31 20) 620 2426. email: info@jurafilm.nl www.jurafilm.nl

MELIOR FILMS
Steynlaan 8, Hilversum 1217 JS. TEL: (31 35) 624 5542. FAX: (31 35) 623 5906.

METEOR/POLYGRAM FILM
P.O. Box 432, Hilversum 1217 JS. TEL: (31 35) 626 1500. FAX: (31 35) 624 8418.

MOONLIGHT FILMS
Stationsstraat 4, Helmond 5701 MK. TEL: (31) 492 565 377. FAX: (31) 492 565 710. email: info@moonlightfilms.com www.moonlightfilms.com

MULHOLLAND PICTURES BV
Keizersgracht 649, Amsterdam 1017 DT. TEL: (31 20) 627 4339. FAX: (31 20) 624 9697. email: webmaster@mulhollandpictures.com www.mulhollandpictures.com

NIS FILM DISTRIBUTION HOLLAND
Abba Paulownastraat 76, The Hague 2518 BJ. TEL: (31 70) 356 4208. FAX: (31 70) 356 4681.

PARADISO ENTERTAINMENT NEDERLAND
Anthony Fokkerweg 1, Amsterdam 1059 CM. TEL: (31 20) 615 9222. FAX: (31 20) 614 2027.
CONTACT
Carolijn van Liefland

POLYGRAM FILMED ENTERTAINMENT
P.O. Box 432, Hilversum 1200 AK. TEL: (31 35) 626 1700. FAX: (31 35) 624 8564.

RCV FILM DISTRIBUTION
P.O. Box 142, 1200 AC Jilversum. TEL: (31 35) 625 1230. FAX: (31 35) 625 1288. www.rcv.nl

SHOOTING STAR FILM COMPANY
Prinsengracht 546, Amsterdam 1017 KK. TEL: (31 20) 624 7272. FAX: (31 20) 626 8533. email: info@shootingstar.nl www.shootingstar.nl
CONTACT
Jan Kouwenhoven - jan.kouwenhoven@rcv.nl

STICHTING STEMRA
Prof. E. M. Meijerslaan 3, 1183 AV Amstelveen. TEL: (31 20) 540 7911. FAX: (31 20) 540 7496.

THREE LINES PICTURES
P.O. Box 4007, Hilversum 1200 LA. TEL: (31 35) 623 0555. FAX: (31 35) 623 9966.

TWENTIETH CENTURY FOX
Mozartlaan 27, Hilversum 1217 CM. TEL: (31 35) 622 2111. FAX: (31 35) 623 9966. email: info@fox.nl www.foxfilm.nl

TWIN FILM
Sarphatistraat 183, Amsterdam 1018 GG. TEL: (31 20) 622 8206. FAX: (31 20) 6248729.

UNITED DUTCH FILM COMPANY
Jan Luykenstraat 5-7, Amsterdam 1071 CJ. TEL: (31 20) 675 7774. FAX: (31 20) 675 7754.

UNITED INTERNATIONAL PICTURES
P.O. Box 9255, Amsterdam 1006 AG. TEL: (31 20) 617 7575. FAX: (31 20) 662 3240. www.uip.nl

GENERAL MANAGER
Max van Praag

UPSTREAM PICTURES BV
le Constantijn Huygensstr 20, P.O. Box 59705 1040 LE Amsterdam. TEL: (31 20) 626 2892. FAX: (31 20) 5050 5887. email: info@upstreampictures.nl www.upstreampictures.nl

VERONICA
Postbus 18179. Amsterdam 1001 ZB.
TEL: (310) 20 800 7000. FAX: (310) 20 800 7001.
email: veronicatv@publieksservice.sbs.nl www.veronica.nl

WARNER BROS.
P.O. Box 71857, Amsterdam 1008 EB. TEL: (31 20) 680 2376. FAX: (31 20) 680 2309. www.warnerbros.com

EXHIBITORS

ACTUEEL BIOSCOOPEXPLOITATIE B.V.
Potterstraat 30 - 4611 NJ Bergen, op Zoom, Netherlands.
TEL: (31) 16 42 54 886.
Number of Screens: 5

A.E.M.M. KOOPAL-WASKOWSKY
P.O. Box 1194 - 4801 BD Breda.
Number of Screens: 5

ALHAMBRA THEATRES
Ingang Bolwerkstroat Corresp. Postbus 207 7500 CB Enschede. TEL: (31 53) 431 2525. FAX: (3153) 432 3562. email: office@alhambra.nl www.alhambra.nl
Number of Screens: 7

ASSOCIATION OF DUTCH FILM THEATRES
ANF Filmtheaters, Jan Luijkenstraat 2, Amsterdam 1071 CM. TEL: (31 20) 578 8455. FAX: (31 20) 570 7689.
email: info@filmtheaters.nl www.filmtheaters.nl

A.TH. ABELN
P.O. Box 82 -7890 AB, Klazienaveen. TEL: (31) 59 13 12798. FAX: (31) 59 13 18426.
Number of Screens: 5

B.V. UTRECHTSE FILMONDERNEMING UFIO
Postbus 777 - 3500 AT Utrecht. TEL: (31 30) 232 1312. FAX: (31 30) 231 5227. email: info@bioswolff.nl
www.bioswolff.nl
CEO
Dr. Ir. Ph. Wolff
Number of Screens: 37

CINE CENTER
Lijnbaansgracht 236, Amsterdam 1017 PH.
TEL: (31 20) 623 6615. FAX: (31 20) 625 9983.
email: Cinecenter@cinecenter.nl www.cinecenter.nl
Number of Screens: 4

HET KETELHUIS
Haarlemmerweg 8-10, P.O. Box 58365, Amsterdam 1040 HJ. TEL: (31 20) 684 0112. FAX: (31 20) 684 0098.
email: info@ketelhuis.nl www.ketelhuis.nl

JOGCHEM'S THEATERS BV
Veenestraat 31, 3751 GE Bunschoten, P.O. Box 127, 3750 GC Bunschoten. TEL: (31 33) 298 4884. FAX: (31 33) 298 4908. www.jtbioscopen.nl
MANAGING DIRECTOR & OWNER
W. Van Dommelen
MANAGER
B.J. de Wilde, B. Hulst
Number of Theatres: 13
Number of Screens: 58
Alphen a/d Rijn, Amerefoort, Apeldoorn, Arnhem, Dordrecht, Eindhove, Hilversum, Hertogenbosch, Nijmegen, Doetinchem

KRITERION
Roetersstraat 170, Amsterdam 1018 WE. TEL: (31 20) 623 1708. FAX: (31 20) 625 1479. www.kriterion.nl
Number of Screens: 2

MINERVA BIOSCOPEN
Kromme Mijdrechtstraat 10, P.O. Box 7220, Amsterdam 1007 JE. TEL: (31 20) 644 6823. FAX: (31 20) 644 8946.
email: info@minervabioscopen.nl www.minervabioscopen.nl

THE MOVIES
Haarlemmerdijk 161, Amsterdam 1013 KH.
TEL: (31 20) 624 5790. FAX: (31 20) 620 6758.
email: info@themovies.nl www.themovies.nl

PATHE CINEMAS
P.O. Box 75948, 1070 AX, Amsterdam. TEL: (31 20) 575 1751. FAX: (31 20) 575 1777. www.pathe.nl
MANAGING DIRECTOR
Lauge Nielsen - l.neisen@pathe.nl
Number of Theatres: 12
Number of Screens: 100
Amsterdam (4), Eindhoven (1), Groningen (1), Rotterdam (2), The Hague (2), Utrecht (1), Helmond (1)

STICHTING THEATER LANTAREN/VENSTER
Gouvernestraat 133, P.O. Box 25278, Rotterdam 3001 HG.
TEL: (31 10) 277 2266. FAX: (31 10) 277 2286.
email: mail@lantaren-venster.nl www.lantaren-venster.nl

TAXON BIOSCOOPEXPLOITATIE BV
P.O. Box 2034, Ede 6710 CA. TEL: (31 318) 648 811.
FAX: (31 318) 648 810. email: taxon@bos.nl www.cinemec.nl

UNITED DUTCH FILM COMPANY
Jan Luykenstraat 5-7, Amsterdam 1071 CJ.
TEL: (31 20) 675 7774. FAX: (31 20) 675 7754.

UTOPIA NEDERLAND BV
Dukaatpassage 33, Lelystad 8232 GC. TEL: (31 320) 246506. FAX: (31 320) 280488. email: nederland@utopolis.com
www.utopolis.nl
Number of Screens: 8

WOLFF CINEMA GROUP
Postbus 777 - 3500 AT Utrecht. TEL: (31 30) 232 1312.
FAX: (31 30) 231 5227. email: info@bioswolff.nl
www.bioswolff.nl
CEO
Dr. Ir. Ph. Wolff
Number of Screens: 37

ASSOCIATIONS & ORGANIZATIONS

AMSTERDAMSE ARTS COUNCIL
Kloveniersburgwal 47, Amsterdam 1011 JX.
TEL: (31 20) 626 4315. FAX: (31 20) 626 7584.

AMSTERDAM FUND FOR THE ARTS
Keizerstraat 223, Amsterdam 1016 DV. TEL: (31 20) 624 2443. FAX: (31 20) 624 6053.

ASSOCIATION FOR FILM & TELEVISION PROGRAMME MAKERS (NBF)
Rokin 91, Amsterdam 1012 KL. TEL: (3120) 664 6588.
FAX: (3120) 664 3707. email: nbf@nbf.nl www.nbf.nl

ASSOCIATION OF DUTCH FILM THEATRES
ANF Filmtheaters, Jan Luijkenstraat 2, Amsterdam 1071 CM. TEL: (31 20) 578 8455. FAX: (31 20) 570 7689.
email: info@filmtheaters.nl www.filmtheaters.nl

ASSOCIATION OF NEW FILM AND TELEVISION MAKERS (NFTVM)
P.O. Box 3877, Amsterdam 1001. TEL: (31 20) 622 6931.
email: secretariaat@nftvm.nl www.nftvm.nl

CIRCLE OF DUTCH FILM CRITICS (KNF)
P.O. Box 10650, Amsterdam 1001 ER. TEL: (31 6) 2550 0668. FAX: (31 20) 627 5923. email: info@filmjournalisten.nl

COMMISSARIAAT VOOR DE MEDIA
Emmastraat 51-53, P.O. Box 1426, Hilversum 1200 BK.
TEL: (31 35) 672 1721. FAX: (31 35) 672 1722.

DUTCH ARTS COUNCIL
RJ Schimmelpennincklaan 3, The Hague 2517 JN.
TEL: (31 70) 346 9619. FAX: (31 70) 361 4727.

DUTCH CULTURAL BROADCASTING PROMOTION FUND
Korte Leidsedwarsstraat 12, Amsterdam 1017 RC.
TEL: (31 20) 623 3901. FAX: (31 20) 625 7456.

DUTCH DIRECTORS GUILD (DDG)
Van der Hoopstraat 84 hs, Amsterdam 1051 VL.
TEL: (31 20) 684 2807. FAX: (31 20) 688 5299.
email: info@directorsguild.nl www.directorsguild.nl
CONTACT
Jan Erik Oegema

DUTCH FEDERATION FOR CINEMATOGRAPHY (NFC)
P.O. Box 143, Amstelveen 1180 AC. TEL: (31 20) 426 6100. FAX: (31 20) 426 6110. www.nfc.org
CHAIRMAN
Drs. W.C.W. Wolfers

DUTCH FILM DISTRIBUTORS' ASSOCIATION (NVF)
Teleport Blvd., 110, Amsterdam 1043 EJ. TEL: (31 20) 386 8630. FAX: (31 20) 386 8631. email: info@filmdistributeurs.nl
www.filmdistributeurs.nl
DIRECTOR
Michael C.Lambrechtsen

DUTCH SCREENWRITERS GUILD (NETWERK SCENARIOSCHRIJVERS)
De Lairessestraat 125, Amsterdam 1075 HH.
TEL: (31 20) 624 0803. FAX: (31 20) 624 7755.
email: scenario@vsenv.nl www.netwerkscenario.nl
CONTACT
Willemiek Seligmann

HOLLAND ANIMATION ASSOCIATION
Hoogt 4, Utrecht 3512 GW.
TEL: (31 30) 240 0768. FAX: (31 30) 240 0768.
email: info@holland-animation.nl www.holland-animation.nl

HOLLAND FILM PROMOTION
Jan Luykenstraat 2, Amsterdam 1071 CM.
TEL: (31 20) 570 7575. FAX: (31 20) 570 7570.
email: hf@hollandfilm.nl www.hollandfilm.nl
MANAGING DIRECTOR
Claudia Landsberger
PROJECT COORDINATOR
Marlies Baltus

MINISTRY OF CULTURE AND THE ARTS
P.O. Box 16375, 2500 BJ Den Haag. TEL: (31 70) 412 3456.
FAX: (31 70) 412 3450. email: info@minocw.nl
www.minocw.nl

NETHERLANDS ASSOCIATION OF FEATURE FILM PRODUCERS (NVS)
Rokin 91, Amsterdam 1012 KL. TEL: (31 20) 627 0061.
FAX: (31 20) 627 2040. email: info@speelfilmproducenten.nl
www.speelfilmproducenten.nl

NETHERLANDS FEDERATION FOR CINEMTOGRAPHY
Jan Luykenstraat 2, P.O. Box 75048, Amsterdam 1070 AA.
TEL: (31 20) 679 9261. FAX: (31 20) 675 0398.

THE NETHERLANDS FEDERATION OF FILM PROFESSIONALS (FEDERATIE FILMBELANGEN)
Rokin 91, Amsterdam 1012 KL. TEL: (31 20) 400 4306.
FAX: (31 20) 664 3707. email: info@filmbelangen.nl
www.filmbelangen.nl

NETHERLANDS FILM AND TELEVISION ACADEMY (NFTA)
Markenplein 1, Amsterdam 1011 MV. TEL: (31 20) 527 7333.
FAX: (31 20) 527 7344. email: info@nfta.ahk.nl
www.nfta.ahk.nl

NETHERLANDS INSTITUTE FOR AUDIOVISUAL MEDIA
Neuyskade 94, P.O. Box 97734, The Hague 2509 GC.
TEL: (31 70) 356 4107. FAX: (31 70) 364 7756.

NETHERLANDS INSTITUE FOR FILM EDUCATION
P.O. Box 805, Utrecht 3500 AV. TEL: (31 30) 236 1212.
www.filmeducatie.nl

SCREEN ACTORS GUILD
Rokin 9, Amsterdam 1012 KL. TEL: (31 20) 489 1129.
FAX: (31 20) 664 3707. email: info@actorsguild.nl
www.actorsguild.nl

NEW ZEALAND

Capital: Wellington
Population: 4,252,277 (July 2010 est.)
Area: 268,680 sq. km
Source: CIA World Factbook

DISTRIBUTORS AND PRODUCERS

ARKLES ENTERTAINMENT
5B Rosedale Office Park, 331 Rosedale Rd, Auckland 1311.
TEL: 64 9 526 9225. email: john@arklesentertainment.com
http://www.arklesentertainment.com

BIG PICTURES COMPANY LIMITED
35 Virginia Ave., Eden Terrace, Auckland.
TEL: (649) 377 5352. FAX: (649) 377 5353.
email: info@bigpictures.co.nz www.bigpictures.co.nz

THE WALT DISNEY COMPANY/BUENA VISTA INTERNATIONAL
Top Flr., The Strand, 125 The Strand Parnell, Auckland.
TEL: (649) 302 7567. FAX: (649) 302 7561.
GENERAL MANAGER
Robert Crockett

COLUMBIA TRISTAR NZ LIMITED
Level 1, 19 Hargreaves St., College Hill, Ponsonby, Auckland.
TEL: (649) 366 9499. FAX: (649) 366 9488.
GENERAL MANAGER
Andrew Cornwell

EVERARD FILMS
P.O. Box 3664, Auckland 1. TEL: (649) 302 1193.
FAX: (649) 302 1192.

EYEWORKS TOUCHTONE
5 Graham St, Auckland1301. TEL: 64 9 379 7867.
FAX: 64 9 379 7868. email: tv@touchdowntv.com
http://www.touchdowntv.com

THE FILM UNIT LIMITED
P.O. Box 30465, Fairway Dr., Lower Hutt. TEL: (644) 920 5500.
FAX: (644) 920 5531. email: tfu@filmunit.co.nz
www.filmunit.co.nz
CEO
Sue Thompson
DIRECTOR, POST PRODUCTION
Brian Scadden

FLYING FISH
P.O. Box 6443, Te Aro, 118 Breaker Bay Road, Seatoun, Wellington. TEL: (644) 384 6159. FAX: (644) 385 2165.
www.flyingfish.co.nz

FOOTPRINT FILMS
P.O. Box 1852, Auckland. TEL: (649) 309 8388.
FAX:(649) 373 4722.

THE GIBSON GROUP
119 Taranaki St., Te Aro, Wellington. TEL: (644) 384 7789.
FAX: (644) 384 4727. email: info@gibson.co.nz
www.gibson.co.nz
PRODUCER & MANAGING DIRECTOR
Dave Gibson
DIRECTOR
Yvonne Mackay

NEW ZEALAND FILM COMMISSION
Level 2, The Film Centre, 119 Jervois Quay, PO Box 11 546
Wellington. TEL: +64 4382 7680. FAX: +64 4384 9719.
email: info@nzfilm.co.nz www.nzfilm.co.nz

PICTURE TALK PRODUCTIONS
Top Fl., 4 Waiama St., P.O. Box 56154 Grey Lynn, Auckland.
TEL: (649) 360 0879. FAX: (649) 360 0286.
email: picturetalk@xtra.co.nz www.picturetalk.co.nz
DIRECTOR
Graham Elliott

ROADSHOW FILM DISTRIBUTORS (NZ), LTD.
Level 8, 82 Symonds St., Auckland. TEL: (649) 377 9669.
FAX: (649) 377 9449.
GENERAL MANAGER
Lisa Hubbard

SILVERSCREEN FILMS
Wakefield St., P.O. Box 6284, Te Aro, Wellington.
TEL: (644) 384 9805. email: gdixon@silverscreenfilms.com
www.silverscreenfilms.com
CONTACT
Geoff Dixon

SOUTH PACIFIC PICTURES
8 Tolich Place, Henderson, Auckland. TEL: (649) 839 0999.
FAX: (649) 839 0990. www.southpacificpictures.com
MANAGING DIRECTOR
John Barnett
COO
Andrew Shaw

TWENTIETH CENTURY FOX FILM DISTRIBUTION
Level 7, 82 Symonds St., Auckland. TEL: (649) 309 0955.
FAX: (649) 309 0967.
CEO & MANAGING DIRECTOR
Joyce Moodabe

UNITED INTERNATIONAL PICTURES
P.O. Box 105263, Auckland. TEL: (649) 379 6269.
FAX: (649) 379 6271.
MANAGER
Timothy Ord

WARNER BROS. (NZ)
P.O. Box 8687, Mt. Eden, Auckland. TEL: (649) 377 5223.
FAX: (649) 309 2795.

WINGNUT FILMS
PO Box 15 208, Miramar, Wellington, 6003.
TEL: +64-4-388-9939. FAX: +64-4-388-9449.
email: reception@wingnutfilms.co.nz

EXHIBITORS

EVERARD FILMS
P.O. Box 3664, Auckland 1. TEL: (649) 302 1193.
FAX: (649) 302 1192.

HOYTS CINEMAS
(For additional listings, please see Australia, Chile & Belgium)
Level 4, 120 Mayord Drive, Auckland. TEL: (649) 303 2739.
FAX: (649) 307 0011. email: hoyts@hoyts.co.nz
www.hoyts.co.nz
GENERAL MANAGER
Stuart McInness

Number of Theatres: 7
Number of Screens: 42

VILLAGE ROADSHOW, LTD.
(For complete listing see Australian branch)
206 Bourke St., Melbourne, VIC, 3000, Australia.
TEL: (613) 9667 6666. FAX: (613) 9639 1540.

Number of Theatres (New Zealand): 13
Number of Screens (New Zealand): 84

VILLAGE SKYCITY CINEMAS
82 Symonds St., Auckland. TEL: (649) 309 9137.
FAX: (649) 307 2522. email: jmoodabe@villageskycity.co.nz
www.villageskycity.co.nz
CEO
Joe Moodabe
COO
Joanne Watt
CFO
Jane Carr
MARKETING MANAGER
Lisa Chambers
Number of Theatres: 13
Number of Screens: 85

ASSOCIATIONS AND ORGANIZATIONS

MOVING IMAGE CENTER (MIC)
P.O. BOX 78 172, Grey Lynn, Auckland. TEL: (649) 379 9922.
FAX: (649) 379 9925. email: hello@mic.org.nz
www.mic.org.nz
DIRECTOR
Deborah Lawler-Dormer

NEW ZEALAND FEDERATION OF FILM SOCIETIES, INC.
P.O. Box 9544, Te Aro, Wellington. TEL: (644) 385 0162.
FAX: (644) 801 7304.

NEW ZEALAND FILM AND VIDEO TECHNICIANS GUILD
The Production Village, 27 Napier St., Freeman's Bay,
Auckland. TEL: (649) 360 6032. FAX: (649) 360 6056.
email: info@nztecho.com www.nztechno.com
EXECUTIVE OFFICER
Janet Cervin
PRESIDENT
Alun Bollinger - albol@netaccess.co.nz
VICE PRESIDENT
Murray Milne

NEW ZEALAND FILM ARCHIVE
Te Anakura Whitiahua, 84 Taranaki Street, P.O. Box 11 449,
Wellington. TEL: (644) 384 7647. FAX: (644) 382 9595.
email: info@nzfa.org.nz www.filmarchive.org.nz
CEO
Frank Stark
MARKETING DIRECTOR
Monika Ahuriri

NEW ZEALAND FILM COMMISSION
2nd. Fl., Film Centre, Corner Cable St. and Jervois Quay,
Wellington. TEL: (644) 4382 7680. FAX: (644) 384 9719.
email: info@nzfilm.co.nz www.nzfilm.co.nz
EXECUTIVE MANAGER
Tansy Cuff
DEPUTY CHIEF EXECUTIVE
Mladen Ivancic

SCREEN DIRECTORS GUILD OF NEW ZEALAND (SDGNZ)
5 Blake St, Ponsonby, Auckland. TEL: (649) 360 2102.
FAX: (649) 360 2107. email: office@sdgnz.co.nz
www.sdgnz.co.nz
EXECUTIVE DIRECTOR
Morgan Read
COMMUNICATIONS DIRECTOR
Shonagh Lindsay

SCREEN PRODUCTION AND DEVELOPMENT ASSOCIATION
Ste. 206, The Production Village, 26 Wright St., P.O. Box 9567,
Mt. Cook, Wellington. TEL: (644) 939 6934. FAX: (644) 939 6935.
email: info@spada.co.nz www.spada.co.nz
CHIEF EXECUTIVE
Penelope Borland

NORWAY

Capital: Oslo
Population: 4,676,305 (July 2010 est.)
Area: 324,220 sq. km.
Source: CIA World Factbook

DISTRIBUTORS AND PRODUCERS

ARTHAUS
Filmens hus, Dronningensgate 16, Oslo 0152.
TEL: (47) 2247 4685. FAX: (47) 2247 4692.
MANAGING DIRECTOR
Svend B. Jensen

BUENA VISTA INTERNATIONAL NORWAY
Sjolyst Plass 4, P.O. Box 456 Skoyen N-0213 Oslo.
TEL:(47) 22 47 11 73 50. FAX: (47) 24 11 73 51.
email: inger.warendorph@disney.com
CONTACT
Inger Warendorph

BV-FILM INTERNATIONAL
Kvalavaagsveien 156, Box 17 N-4299, Avaldsnes, N-4262.
TEL: (47) 5284 6460. FAX: (47) 5284 6461.
PRESIDENT
Bjorg Veland - bjorg@bvfilm.com

COLUMBIA TRISTAR NORDISK FILMS DISTRIBUTION AS
Sorkedalsvn 10 D, P.O. Box 17, N-4299 Avaldnes.
TEL: (47) 52 84 64 70. FAX: (47) 52 84 64 71.
email: bjorn_hoenvoll@spe.sony.com

EUROPAFILM
Stortingsgt 30, Oslo N-0161. TEL: (47) 2283 4290.
FAX: (47) 2283 4151.

FIDALGO
Henrik Wergelandsgt 52, P.O. Box 2054 Posebyen, Kristiansand
N-4602. TEL: (47) 3802 4004. FAX: (47) 3802 2354.

KOMMUNENES FILM-CENTRAL
Nedre Voligt 9, Oslo N-0158. TEL: (47) 2236 9530.
FAX: (47) 2242 1469.

NORSK FILM DISTRIBUTION
Stortingsgt 12, Oslo N-0161. TEL: (47) 2242 3600.
FAX: (47) 2242 2313.

SCANDINAVIAN ENTERTAINMENT GROUP
President Harbitzgt 22 A, Oslo 0259. TEL: (47) 2256 2100.
FAX: (47) 2255 1540.
CONTACT
Tore Erlandsen

SF NORGE
P.O. Box 6868 St. Olavs Plass, Grensen 3, Oslo N-0130.
TEL: (47) 2200 7800. FAX: (47) 2200 7801.

UNITED INTERNATIONAL PICTURES
Hegdehaugsvn 27, P.O. Box 7134, Homansbyen, Oslo N-0307.
TEL: 47-22 85 37 37. FAX: 47-22 85 37 38. www.uip.no
MANAGER
Liv Jacobsen Borg

WARNER BROS (NORWAY)
Oscarsgt 55, P.O. Box 7053, Homansbyen, Oslo N-0258.
TEL: (47) 2243 1800. FAX: (47) 2255 4683.

EXHIBITORS

FREDRIKSTAD KINEMATOGRAFER
P.O. Box 1406, Fredrikstad N-1602. TEL: (47) 6930 6070.
FAX: (47) 6930 6074. email: kino@fredrikstad.kommune.no
www.fredrikstadkino.no
CONTACT
Jorgen Soderberg Jansen

KRISTIANSAND KINO
Boks 356, Kristiansand 4601. FAX: (47) 3802 0390.
Number of Theatres: 6

OSLO KINEMATOGRAPHER
P.O. Box 1584, Stortingsgt 16, 0161, Oslo N-0118.
TEL: (47) 2242 7154. FAX: (47) 2282 4368.
email: oslokino@oslokino.no www.oslokino.no
Number of Theatres: 10

SANDNES KINEMATOGRAFER
Boks 14, Sandnes 4301. FAX: (47) 5566 8872.
Number of Theatres: 3

SANDREW METRONOME FILM AB
P.O. Box 1178, Oslo N-0107. TEL: (47) 2282 7000.
FAX: (47) 2282 7810.

TROMSO KINO
Boks 285, Tromso 9001. FAX: (47) 7768 3570.
email: post@tromsokino.no www.tromsokino.no

TRONDHEIM KINO
Prinsensgt. 2B, Trondheim N-7013.
TEL: (47) 7380 8800. FAX: (47) 7380 8801.
email: kino@trondheimkino.no www.trondheimkino.no
Number of Theatres: 13

ASSOCIATIONS & ORGANIZATIONS

NATIONAL ASSOCIATION OF MUNICIPAL CINEMAS
(Now operating as FILM&KINO)
Filmens Hus, Dronningensgate 16, Postboks 446 Sentrum,
Oslo 0104. TEL: (47) 2247 4500. FAX: (47) 2247 4699.
www.filmweb.no
DIRECTOR GENERAL
Lene Loeken
INFORMATION CONSULTANT
Ove Watne - ove@kino.no

NORDIC FILM AND TV FUND
Skovveienz 2, Oslo 0257. TEL: (47) 2328 3939.

FAX: (47) 2256 1223. email: nftf@nftf.net www.nftf.net

MANAGING DIRECTOR
Svend Abrahamsen

NORSK FILMKRITIKERLAG

(Norwegian Society of Film Critics)
Filmens hus, Dronningens gt. 16, Oslo 0152.
TEL: (47) 2311 9321. email: post@filmkritikk.filmenshus.no
www.filmkritikerlaget.no

NORWEGIAN FILM INSTITUTE (NFI)

Boks 482 Sentrum 105 Oslo TEL: (47) 22 47 45 00.
FAX: (47) 22 47 45 99. email: post@nfi.no www.nfi.no

NORWEGIAN FEDERATION OF FILM SOCIETIES

Dronningens Gate 16, OSLO 0152. TEL: (47) 2247 4680.
FAX: (47) 2247 4692. email: nfk@filmclubb.no
www.filmklubb.no

NORWEGIAN FILM AND TV PRODUCERS' ASSOCIATION

Filmens Hus, Dronningensgt 16, Oslo 0152. TEL: (47) 2311 9311.
FAX: (47) 2311 9316.
email: produsentforeningen@produsentforeningen.no
www.produsentforeningen.no
CHAIRMAN
Aage Aaberge

NORWEGIAN FILM DISTRIBUTORS ASSOCIATION

Ovre Slottsgt, 12 N-0157 Oslo. TEL: (47) 22 42 48 44.
FAX: (47) 22 42 30 93. email: no-film@online.no
CONTACT
Kristin Hoenvoll

NORWEGIAN FILM COMMISSION

Georgernes Verft 12, Bergen 5011. TEL: (47) 5556 4343.
FAX: (47) 5556 4348. email: post@norwegianfilm.com
www.norwegianfilm.com
MANAGING DIRECTOR
Truls Kontny

NORWEGIAN FILM FUND

Filmens Hus, Dronninningens Gate 16, Oslo 0152.
TEL: (47) 2247 8040. FAX: (47) 2247 8041.
email: mail@filmfondet.no www.filmfondet.no
DIRECTOR GENERAL
Stein Slyngstad
HEAD OF INFORMATION
Marit Saetre
HEAD OF PRODUCTION
Elin Erichsen

PAKISTAN

Capital: Islamabad
Population: 184,404,791 (July 2010 est.)
Area: 803,940 sq.km.
Source: CIA World Factbook

IMPORTERS

AJRAK ENTERTAINMENT

357 Hotel Metropole, Abdullah Haroon Rd., Karachi, Sindh
75520. TEL: (9221) 565 4214, 565 4215. FAX: (9221) 567 0313.
email: ajrak@ khi.wol.net.pk
PUBLICITY MANAGER
Atiq Ahmed

AL HAVIZ CORPORATION

Al Hafiz Mansion, 11 Royal Park, Lahore. TEL: (9242) 636 3484.

CARRY-ON FILMS

Moon Bldg., 4 Royal Park, Lahore. TEL: (9242) 722 2543.

CLASSIC PICTURES

Ismail Bldg., 5 Royal Park, Lahore. TEL: (9242) 637 3018.

CONTINENTAL TRADERS

Ex-Rally Bros. Bldg., Talpur Rd., Karachi. TEL: (9221) 241 3254.
FAX: (9221) 243 7451.

EVERLAST PICTURES

Haroon Mansion, Royal Park, Lahore. TEL: (9242) 636 3148.

GOLDEN BIRD PICTURES

1, Abbot Rd., Lahore. TEL: (9242) 722 2138.

GOLDEN EAGLE PICTURES

Shaikh Bldg., Royal Park, Lahore. TEL: (9242) 722 2279.

HEENA FILMS

Dar Chambers, Royal Park, Lahore. TEL: (9242) 631 1964.

JAVED PICTURES

Gaba Bldg., Royal Park, Lahore. TEL: (9242) 722 3051.

MANDVIWALLA ENTERTAINMENT, LTD

Nishat Cinema Bldg., M.A. Jinnah Rd., Karachi.
TEL: (9221) 721 9505, 722-3535, 722 3536.
FAX: (9221) 722 7259. email: nishat@gerrys.net
MANAGING DIRECTOR
Nadeem H. Mandviwalla - nadeem_mandviwalla@mandviwalla.com
DIRECTOR
Rehmat K. Fazli - rehmati@yahoo.com
GENERAL MANAGER
Nawab Huzurul Hassan

PAKISTAN INTERNATIONAL CORPORATION

Lyric Cinema Bldg., Garden Rd., Karachi. TEL: (9221) 772 7273.

PARAMOUNT COMMUNICATIONS

Marston Road, Karachi. TEL: (9221) 777 8165.
FAX: (9221) 568 0981.

PULSE GLOBAL COMMUNICATION

Plot 12, Block 7 & 8, Tipu Sultan Rd., Karachi.
TEL: (9221) 453 5001.

STERLING INTERNATIONAL

Paradise Bldg., Near Passport Office, Saddar, Karachi.
TEL: (9221) 566-1412, 526 280.

TEE JEES ENTERPRISES

367 Hotel Metropole, Karachi. TEL: (9221) 522 540.

ZEE RAY ENTERPRISES

209 Hotel Metropole, Karachi. TEL: (9221) 414 089.

EXHIBITORS

AFSHAN CINEMA

Marston Rd., Karachi. TEL: (9221) 772 4344.

ALFALAH CINEMA

Alfalah Bldg., The Mall, Lahore. TEL: (9242) 630 1551.

ANMOL CINEMA

2 Civil Center, Town Ship, Lahore. TEL: (242) 511 0615.

BAMBINO CINEMA

Garden Rd., Karachi. TEL: (9221) 772 9656.

CAPRI CINEMA

M.A. Jinnah Rd., Karachi. TEL: (9221) 721 9904.

GULISTAN CINEMA

Abbot Rd., Lahore. TEL: (9242) 631 3110.

LYRIC CINEMA

Garden Rd., Karachi. TEL: (9221) 772 7274.

MUBARAK CINEMA

34 Abbot Rd., Lahore. TEL: (9242) 630 2308.

NAGINA CINEMA

Lahore. TEL: (9242) 722 6220.

NISHAT CINEMA

M.A. Jinnah Rd., Karachi. TEL: (9221) 721 9505.

PLAZA CINEMA

Queens Rd., Lahore. TEL: (9242) 630 3122.

RATTAN CINEMA

McLeod Rd., Lahore. TEL: (9242) 724 3383.

REGAL CINEMA

65 The Mall, Lahore. TEL: (9242) 724 9477.

SANGEET CINEMA

Shadra, Lahore. TEL: (9242) 274 4290.

SHABISTAN CINEMA

Lahore. TEL: (9242) 636 0731.

SHABISTAN CINEMA

Muree Rd., Rawalpindi. TEL:(92) 70 625.

STAR CINEMA

Garden Rd., Karachi. TEL: (9221) 772 8787.

ASSOCIATIONS & ORGANIZATIONS

THE CENTRAL BOARD OF FILM CENSORS

St. No. 55, F-6/4, Islamabad. TEL: (9251) 920 4163.
FAX: (9251) 920 4338. email: info@cbfc.gov.pk
VICE CHAIRMAN
Zaka-ul-Haq Asghar

THE NATIONAL FILM DEVELOPMENT CORPORATION, LTD.

NAFDEC Complex, Blue Area, Islamabad. TEL: (9251) 821 154.
FAX: (9251) 221 863.

PAKISTAN FILM DISTRIBUTORS' ASSOCIATION

Geeta Bhawan, Lakshmi Chowk, Lahore. TEL: (9242) 58785.

PAKISTAN FILM EXHIBITORS' ASSOCIATION

National Auto Plaza, C Block, 3rd Flr., Marston Rd., Karachi.
TEL: (9221) 772 7764.

PAKISTAN FILM PRODUCERS' ASSOCIATION

Regal Cinema Bldg., The Mall, Lahore. TEL: (9242) 322 904.

PANAMA

Capital: Panama
Population: 3,410,676 (July 2010 est.)
Area: 78,200 sq. km.
Source: CIA World Factbook

DISTRIBUTORS AND PRODUCERS

APERTURA FILMS

P.O. Box 550405. Panama. TEL: (507) 613 6488.
FAX: (507) 233 0495. email: abnerbenaim@yahoo.com
www.aperturafilms.com

KEYLIGHT PRODUCTIONS

P.O. Box 87-2211, Zone 7, Panama City. TEL: (507) 270 0093.
FAX: (507) 226 7923.

UNITED INTERNATIONAL PICTURES OF PANAMA, INC.

PO Box 5252, Panama 5. TEL: 507-214-8449.
FAX: 507-269-4288.
MANAGER
Jose Victoria

VERITE PRODUCCIONES

Avenida "A" Nº25 Costa Del Este, P.O. Box 0832-2237 WTC,
Panama. TEL: (507) 271 4467. FAX: (507) 271 4471.
email: ricky@ veriteproducciones.com
www.veriteproducciones.com
CONTACT
Ricardo Barria

EXHIBITORS

SAVOY LANE FILMS, INC.

Via Espana, Edificio Domino, 1er Piso, Oficina 26, P.O. Box 6-4911, Zona 6, Panama. TEL: (507) 262 6585.
FAX: (507) 264 1805.
DIRECTOR
Enrique Martin
GENERAL MANAGER
Lucio Marcon
MANAGER (PANAMA)
Victor Chizmar

PHILIPPINES

Capital: Manila
Population: 99,900,177 (July 2010 est.)
Area: 300,000 sq. km.
Source: CIA World Factbook

DISTRIBUTORS & PRODUCERS

COLUMBIA PICTURES INDUSTRIES, INC.

Rooms 306-308, Philippine President Lines Bldg., 1000 United Nations Ave., Ermita, Metro Manila 1000. TEL: (632) 521 1381.
FAX: (632) 521 3684.
MANAGER
Victor R. Cabrera

REGAL FILMS

38 Valencia St. Quezon City. TEL: (63-2) 410 649195.
FAX: (63-2) 732 69742. www.regalfilms.com/

UNITED INTERNATIONAL PICTURES

Room 310, Philippine Presidential Lines Bldg., 1000 United Nations Ave., Ermita Metro Manila 1000. TEL: (632) 509304.
FAX: (632) 521 6133.
MANAGER
Tristan Leveriza
REPRESENTATIVE
Christopher Sy

VIVA FILMS

7th Fl., East Tower, Philippine Stock Exchange Ctr.
Exchange Rd., Ortigas Ctr. Pasig City1605.
TEL: (632) 687 1810. email: feedback@viva.com.ph
www.viva.com.ph

WARNER BROS.

Room 311, Philippine Presidential Lines Bldg., 1000 United Nations Ave., Ermita Metro Manila 1000. TEL: (632) 596 991.
FAX: (632) 521 2673.
MANAGER
Lucas Pasiliao

EXHIBITORS

AYALA THEATERS

Greenbelt 1 Mall, Ayala Center, Makati.
TEL: (632) 752 7869. FAX: (632) 752 7879.
www.ayalaland.com.ph
CONTACT
Raffy Prats

MEDEIA FILMES

Rua Tomas Ribeiro 8-20, 1150 Lisboa, Portugal.
TEL: (351) 1317 2029.

Number of Screens: 37

MEDEIA FILMES

Bldg. B SM Corporate Offices, Sm Central Business Park, 1000 Bay Boulevard Bay City Pasay City 1300.
TEL: 632 8335088. FAX: 632 8335087.
email: rdc@smsupermalls.com www.smcinema.com
CEO
Henry Sy, Sr.
PRESIDENT
Hans T. Sy

Number of Theatres: 28
Number of Screens: 178

WARNER LUSOMUNDO

Rua Luciano Cordeiro 113, 1150 Lisboa, Portugal.
TEL: (351) 1315 0860.

Number of Screens: 80

WEST AVENUE THEATER CORPORATION

The SM City, North Ave. cor. EDSA, Quezon City.
TEL: (632) 975 452. FAX: (632) 924 4274.
EXECUTIVE V.P.
Engr. Hans T. Sy
OPERATIONS MANAGER
Ricardo B. David

Number of Screens: 56

ASSOCIATIONS AND ORGANIZATIONS

NATIONAL COMMISSION FOR CULTURE AND THE ARTS

633 NCCA Building, General Luna Street, Intramuros, Manila.
TEL: (632) 527 2192. FAX: (632) 527 2191.
email: info@ncca.gov.ph www.ncca.gov.ph
CHAIRMAN
Ambeth R. Ocampo - oc@ncca.gov.ph
EXECUTIVE DIRECTOR
Cecile Guidote-Alvarez - oed@ncca.gov.ph
DEPUTY EXECUTIVE DIRECTOR
Emilie V. Tiongco - ded@ncca.gov.ph

POLAND

Capital: Warsaw
Population: 38,463,689 (July 2010 est.)
Area: 312,685 sq. km.
Source: CIA World Factbook

DISTRIBUTORS AND PRODUCERS

ANWA FILM INTERNATIONAL

Str. Smolensk 27/3, Krakow 31-12. TEL: (4812) 215 634.

APERTO FILMS

Chocimska 35 / 1. Warsaw. TEL: (504) 200 850.
email: apertofilms@apertofilms.com www.apertofilms.com

BEST FILM

Ul. Twarda 16a, Warsaw 00105. TEL: (4822) 220 1201.
FAX: (4822) 220 1201.

BLACK CAT

Magnoliowa 2, Lublin. TEL: (4881) 774 654.
FAX: (4881) 774 654.

EUROKADR

Potocka Str. 14, Warsaw 01639. TEL: (4822) 233 2491.
FAX: (4822) 233 2491.

FILM ART FOUNDATION

Krakowskie Przedmiescie 21/23, Warsaw 00071.
TEL: (4822) 261 409. FAX: (4822) 635 2001.

FILM DISTRIBUTION AGENCY

Trebacka 3, Warsaw 00074. TEL: (4822) 635 2038.
FAX: (4822) 635 1543.

FILM STUDIO HELIOS

Przybyszewskiego 167, Lodz 93120. TEL: (4842) 812 196.
FAX: (4842) 812 481.

GRAFFITI

Ul, Kolobrzeska 12, 02-923, Warsaw. TEL: (4822) 858 7488.
FAX: (4822) 858 7490. www.graffitifilm.com.pl

IMP

Ul. Hoza 66, Warsaw 00950. TEL: (4822) 628 7081.
FAX: (4822) 628 7691.

ITI CINEMA POLAND

Marszalkowska 138, Warsaw 00004. TEL: (4822) 640 4447.
FAX: (4822) 642 5001.

Wernyhory 14, Warsaw 02727. TEL: (4822) 243 3488.

FAX: (4822) 243 4532.

KRAKATAU
Ul, Kaminskiego 29/12, Lodz. TEL: (4842) 788 536.

NEPTUN FILM
Piwna 22, Gdansk 80831. TEL: (4858) 314 876.
FAX: (4858) 313 744.

NEPTUN VIDEO CENTRE
Grzybowska Str. 6-10, Warsaw 00131. TEL: (4822) 224 0395.
FAX: (4822) 224 5969.

STARCUT FILM-POLAND
6 Wybickiego St, Rumia 84230. TEL: (4858) 219 769.

SYRENA ENTERTAINMENT GROUP
Marsz al kowska 115, Warsaw 00102. TEL: (4822) 827 3500.
FAX: (4822) 827 5204.
PRESIDENT
Jerzy Jednorowski
MANAGING DIRECTOR
Levis Minford

UNITED INTERNATIONAL PICTURES SP. Z.O.O.
ul Domaniewska 41, "Orion" Building 6th Flr.,
Warsaw 02-672. TEL: 48-22-606-0176.
FAX: 48-22-606-0174.
MANAGER
Urszula Malska

VISION
Rydygiera 7, Warsaw 01793. TEL: (4822) 239 0753.
FAX: (4822) 239 2575.

WARNER BROS. POLAND
Ul. Palawska 37/39, Warsaw 02508. TEL: (4822) 249 5959.
FAX: (4822) 249 3598.

EXHIBITORS

APOLLO-FILM STATE FILM DISTRIBUTOR
Pychowicka 7, Krakow 30960. TEL: (4812) 671 355.
FAX: (4812) 671 552.

FILM STUDIO HELIOS
Przybyszewskiego 167, Lodz 93120. TEL: (4842) 812 196.
FAX: (4842) 812 481.

THE GREATER UNION ORGANISATION
(Including Birch, Carroll & Coyle)
49 Market St., Sydney, NSW 2000, Australia. TEL: (612) 9373 6600.
FAX: (612) 9373 6532.
MANAGING DIRECTOR
Robert Manson

Number of Theatres (Poland): 1
Number of Screens (Poland): 4

IFDF MAX
Jagiellonska Str. 26, Warsaw 03719. TEL: (4822) 219 0481.
FAX: (4822) 218 1783.

ITI CINEMA POLAND
Marszalkowska 138, Warsaw 00004. TEL: (4822) 640 4447.
FAX: (4822) 642 5001.

MULTIKINO
(A joint venture of ITI and United Cinemas International)
TEL: (4822) 640 4416. FAX: (4822) 640 4413.
MANAGING DIRECTOR
Aldona Szostakowska

SILVER SCREEN/PORTICO DEVELOPMENT
TEL: (4822) 630 7076. FAX: (4822) 630 7077.
MANAGING DIRECTOR
Frank Stork

UCI JOINT VENTURE CO., POLAND
Multiurino Spa, Powsinska 4, Warsaw 02910.
TEL: (4822) 2640 4416. FAX: (4822) 2640 4413.
DIRECTOR
Aldona Szostakowsk

ASSOCIATIONS & ORGANIZATIONS

ASSOCIATION OF POLISH FILM PRODUCERS AND PRODUCTION MANAGERS
Pulawska 61, Warsaw 02595. TEL: (4822) 245 5586.

ASSOCIATION OF POLISH FILMMAKERS
Krakowskie Przedmiescie, Warsaw 00071. TEL: (4822) 227 6785.
FAX: (4822) 263 51927.

COMMITTEE OF CINEMATOGRAPHY
TEL: (4822) 263 449. FAX: (4822) 276 233.
PRESIDENT
Tadeusz Sciborylski

FEDERATION OF FILM TRADE GUILDS
Pulawska 61, Warsaw 02595. TEL: (4822) 628 4855.
FAX: (4822) 245 5586.

FEDERATION OF NON-PROFESSIONAL FILM CLUBS
Pulawska 61, Warsaw 02595. TEL: (4822) 245 5382.

FILM ART FOUNDATION
Krakowskie Przedmiescie 21/23, Warsaw 00071.
TEL: (4822) 226 1409. FAX: (4822) 635 2001.

POLISH FEDERATION OF FILM SOCIETIES
Plocka 16/34, Warsaw 01138. TEL: (4822) 232 1187.

POLISH FILM AND TV DIRECTOR'S GUILD
Pulawska 67, Warsaw 02595. TEL: (4822) 245 5316.
FAX: (4822) 245 5316.

POLISH SCREENWRITERS GUILD
Al. Jerozolimskie 49m 41, Warsaw 00697. TEL: (4822) 262 81158.

PRIVATE FILM PRODUCERS CLUB
Walbrzyska 14/11, Warsaw 02738. TEL: (4822) 243 2861.

PORTUGAL

Capital: Lisbon
Population: 10,735,765 (July 2010 est.)
Area: 92,391 sq. km.
Source: CIA World Factbook

DISTRIBUTORS AND PRODUCERS

CINEMA NOVO CRL
Rua Aníbal Cunha, 84 - sala 1.6, 4050 - 048 Porto.
TEL: (351) 2220 76050. FAX: (351) 2220 76059.
email: info@fantasporto.online.pt www.fantasporto.online.pt

COLUMBIA TRISTAR & WARNER FILMES DE PORTUGAL
Av. Duque De Loule 90 3 Esq., Lisbon 1000.
TEL: (351) 21572 007. FAX: (351) 21315 5389.
www.warnerlusomundo.pt

COSTA DO CASTELO FILMES SA
Av. Engenheiro Arantes e Oliveira, nº 11A - 1º, 1900-221
Lisbon. TEL: (351) 2184 38020. FAX: (351) 2184 38029.
email: info@costacastelo.pt

FILMES CASTELLO LOPES
R. D. Francisco Manel de Mello, 1, 1º ESQ, 1070-085 Lisbon.
TEL: (351) 213 833 630. FAX: (351) 213 838 637.
email: geral@castelopes.pt

FILMES LUSOMUNDO S.A.
Av. da Liberdade, 266, 1250-149 Lisbon. TEL: (351) 213 187 300.
FAX: (351) 213 187 379. email: geral@lusomundo.pt
www.lusomundo.pt
MANAGING DIRECTOR
Luis Bordallo Silva

FILMES DE TEJO
Av. da Liberdade, nº85, 3º, 1250-140 Lisbon.
TEL: (351) 2132 34 400, 2132 34 401. FAX (351) 2134 71087.
email: efilmesdotejo@filmesdotejo.pt www.filmesdotejo.pt

MEDIAFASHION
Rua mq. sa da Bandeira, 311-1 Gaia 4400-217.
TEL: (351) 2237 07270. FAX: (351) 22370 07276.
www.mediafashion.com
CEO
Fransisco Pinho - fransisco.pinho@mediafashion.com

UNITED INTERNATIONAL PICTURES - LUSOMUNDO AUDIOVISUALS, S.A.
Av. da Liberdade, 266, 1250-149 Lisbon.
TEL: (351) 213 187 300. FAX: (351) 213 187 379.
email: geral@lusomundo.pt www.lusomundo.pt
MANAGING DIRECTOR
Luis Bordallo Silva

ZEPPELIN FILMES, LDA.
Av. de Portugal, 66 - 1º Dto. 2795-554 Carnaxide.
TEL: (351) 214 251 980. FAX: (351) 214 251 989.
email: info@zeppelin-filmes.pt www.zeppelin-filmes.pt

EXHIBITORS

AMERICAN MULTI-CINEMA (AMC)
920 Main St., Kansas City, MO, U.S. 64105. TEL: (816) 221 4000.
FAX: (816) 480 4617. email: amc@amc.pt www.amc.pt
CHAIRMAN & CEO
Peter Brown
PRESIDENT & COO
Philip M. Singleton

Number of Theatres (Porto: Arrabida): 1
Number of Screens: 20

LUSOMUNDO S.A.
Av. da Liberdade, 266, 1250-149 Lisbon. TEL: (351) 213 187 300.
FAX: (351) 213 187 379. email: geral@lusomundo.pt
www.lusomundo.pt

MEDEIA FILMES
Rua da Palmeira, n.º 6, 1200 - 313 Lisbon.
TEL: (351) 21 325 5800. FAX: (351) 21 342 8740.
email: medeiafilmes@mail.telepac.pt www.medeiafilmes.pt

WARNER LUSOMUNDO CINEMAS
(Time Warner Co. and Lusomundo Audiovisuals S.A.)
Rua Luciano Cordeiro 113, 10 Lisbon 1150.
TEL: (351) 21 315 0860. FAX: (351) 21 355 7784.
www.warnerlusomundo.pt

400 Warner Blvd., Bldg. 160, Ste. 250, Burbank, CA, 91522.

U.S. TEL: (1 818) 977 6278. FAX: (1 818) 977 6040.
PRESIDENT
Millard Ochs
VICE PRESIDENT
David Bent
V.P., WORLD OPERATIONS
Dave Pearson

Number of Theatres: 4
Number of Screens: 30
Cascais (7); Colombo (10); Gaia (9); Olivais (4).

ASSOCIATIONS & ORGANIZATIONS

CINEMA AND TELEVISION IMAGE PROFESSIONALS ASSOCIATION
Travessa de Paulo Martins, 24 A, 1300-499 Lisbon.
TEL: (351) 2136 29696. FAX: (351) 9177 76693.
email: aictp@aipcinema.com www.aipcinema.com

INSTITUTE FOR CINEMA, AUDIOVISUALS AND MULTIMEDIA
Rua S. Pedro de Alcântara 45, 1st Flr., 1269-138 Lisbon.
TEL: (351) 21323 0800. FAX: (351) 342 8717.
email: mail@icam.pt

MEDIA DESK PORTUGAL
R. S. Pedro de Alcântara, 45-S/L, 1269-138 Lisbon.
TEL: (351) 2134 78644. FAX: (351) 2134 78643.
email: mediadesk@icam.pt www.mediadesk.icam.pt
COORDINATOR
Amelia Sousa Tavares

PORTUGUESE FILM ARCHIVE AND MUSEUM
Rua Barata Salgueiro, 39, 1269-059 Lisbon.
TEL: (351) 2135 96200. FAX: (351) 2135 23180.
email: cinemateca@cinemateca.pt www.cinemateca.pt
DIRECTOR
João Bénard da Costa
DEPUTY DIRECTOR
José Manuel Costa, Rui Santana Brito

PORTUGAL FILM COMMISSION (ICAM)
Rua S. Pedro de Alcântara 45, 1st Flr., 1269-138 Lisbon.
TEL: (351) 21323 0800. FAX: (351) 343 1952.
email: filmcom@icam.pt www.icam.pt
CHAIRMAN
Elisio Cabralde Oliveira

RUSSIAN FEDERATION

Capital: Moscow
Population: 139,390,205 (July 2010 est.)
Area: 17,075,200 sq. km.
Source: CIA World Factbook

DISTRIBUTORS AND PRODUCERS

ARGUS INTERNATIONAL
6/4, ul. Radio, Moscow, 107005. TEL: (7095) 261 8897.
FAX: (7095) 261 8730. email: argusint@aha.ru
www.argusinternational.ru
GENERAL DIRECTOR
Vladimir Repin
HEAD OF DISTRIBUTION
Natalia Val
DIRECTOR, PRODUCTION
Kirill Polikarpov
MARKETING DIRECTOR & PUBLIC AFFAIRS OFFICER
Sergei Karinsky

ASG VIDEOFILM
Rusakovskaya 2/1-84, Moscow. TEL: (7095) 264 9055.
FAX: (7095) 264 1575.

EAST WEST CREATIVE ASSOCIATES/UIP
9 Voznesensky Pereulok, Moscow, 103009.
TEL: (7095) 229 7100. FAX: (7095) 200 4249.
email: ewca@ewca.ru www.ewca.ru
DIRECTOR GENERAL
Eugene Beginin

BEZELEVS PRODUCTION
119285 Moscow, Pudovkina Street, h. 6 bld 1.
TEL: +7 095 514 04 00. FAX: +7 095 143 17 23.
email: film@bazelevs.ru www.bazelevs.ru
DIRECTOR
Timour Bekmambetov, Leo Gabriadze

BIRD
Mosfilm Studio, 1 Mosfilmovskaia Str. Ste. 408, Moscow
119958. TEL: (7095) 143 9285. FAX: (7095) 232 2720.

CARMEN PREMIER FILM COMPANY
15 Druzhinnikovskaya St., Moscow 123242.
TEL: (7095) 255 9 89. FAX: (7095) 255 0841.
CONTACT
Marina Troubina - rozanova@carmen-film.ru

CENTER SCIP FILM
Volkhonka Str. 5/6 Bldg. 9, Moscow 121019.
TEL: (7095) 203 0360. FAX: (7095) 290 4828.

CENTRAL PARTNERSHIP
1 Zachatievsky Per 15, Moscow. TEL: (7095) 777 49 52.
FAX: (7095) 799 56 70. email: main@centpart.ru

DREAM CO.
14/1 Energeticheskaya Str., Moscow. TEL: (7095) 362 7668.
FAX: (7095) 362 7007.

48 HOURS
7, Rue Kantemirovskaia, Saint-Petersbourg 194100.
TEL: (7812) 248 8747. FAX: (7812) 245 4276.

GEMINI FILM
Bldg. 6, Myansnitskaya St. 40, Moscow 101000.
TEL: (7095) 921 0854. FAX: (7095) 921 2394.
www.geminifilm.ru
PRESIDENT
Michael Schlicht
GENERAL DIRECTOR
Hans-Bodo Mueller

GORKY FILM STUDIOS
8 Eizenshtein St., Moscow 129226. TEL: (7095) 181 0183.
FAX: (7095) 188 0187. email: www.gorkyfilm.ru
www.gorkyfilm.ru

INTERCINEMA
15 Druzhninnikovskaya Str., Moscow 123242.
TEL: (7095) 255 9082. FAX: (7095) 255 9052.
email: post@intercin.ru
CONTACT
Raissa Fomina

KINOCENTRE
15 Druzhinnikovskaya Str. Moscow. TEL: (7095) 255 9082.
FAX: (7095) 973 20 29.
CONYTACT
Ludmila Jvalevskaya

KINOTON
Okruzhnoy Proyezd 16, Moscow 105058.
TEL: (7095) 290 3412. FAX: (7095) 200 5612.

MASTERTAPE
3 Malyi Kislovskyi Pereulok, Moscow 103009.
TEL: (7095) 202 7768. FAX: (7095) 202 9418.

MOST MEDIA
Maly Gnezdnikovsky 7, Moscow 103877.
TEL/FAX: (7095) 956 6885.

PARADISE LTD. AGENCY
12A Christoprudny Blvd., Ste. 601, Moscow 101000.
TEL: (7095) 916 9220. FAX: (7095) 924 1331.

PARK VI PRODUCTION
4 Zubovsky Bulvar, Moscow 119021. TEL: (7095) 201 3180.
FAX: (7095) 201 7787. email: park@parkcinema.ru
www.parkviproduction.ru

SKIP CENTRE
2 Flievskaya St. 7/19, Moscow 121096. TEL: (7095) 145 2459.
FAX: (7095) 145 3355.

SOVENTURE
5 Nizhni Sousalnyi Pereulok, Moscow 109172.
TEL: (7095) 912 3065. FAX: (7095) 911 0665.

SOVEXPORTFILM
14 Kalashny Pereulok, Moscow 103869. TEL: (7095) 290 5009.
FAX: (7095) 200 1256.

TOPLINE PRODUCTION
Schmooze Ekatrina Krasnova, 8 Blvd., 2nd Donskoy, Moscow
117071. TEL: (7095) 952 8677. www.tip.ru

UNITED INTERNATIONAL PICTURES
9 Voznesensky Pereulok, Moscow 103009.
TEL: (7095) 229 7100. FAX: (7095) 200 4249.
email: ewca@ewca.ru www.ewca.ru
DIRECTOR GENERAL
Eugene Beginin

EXHIBITORS

CINEMAPARK

Moscow 125009. TEL: (7095) 933 2841. FAX: (7095) 933 2845.
www.cinemapark.ru

FORMULA KINO MANAGEMENT

(Joint project with Imperia Kino and Karo Film)
Ul. Zemlyanoy Val, 33, Moscow. TEL: (7095) 795 3795.
email: info@formulakino.ru www.formulakino.ru

Number of Theatres: 20
Number of Screens: 51

INVEST KINO PROJECT

1, Maly Tolmachevsky pereulok, Moscow 119017.
TEL: (7095) 777 1100. email: info@ikp.ru www.ikp.ru
GENERAL DIRECTOR
Timofeyev Alexander Ivanovich - atimofeev@ikp.ru
DEPUTY GENERAL DIRECTOR
Murov Vladimir Leonidovich
MARKETING DIRECTOR
Korovina Yulia Borisovna

IMPERIJA KINO

(Joint project with Formula Kino and Karo Film)
Ul. Zemlyanoy Val, 33, Moscow. TEL: (7095) 795 3795.
email: info@formulakino.ru www.formulakino.ru

Number of Theatres: 27
Number of Screens: 70

KARO FILM

(Joint project with Imperia Kino and Formula Kino)
Ul. Zemlyanoy Val, 33, Moscow. TEL: (7095) 795 3795.
email: info@formulakino.ru www.formulakino.ru
CHAIRMAN
Leonid Ogorodnikov
GENERAL MANAGER
Igor Ilchuk

Number of Theatres: 27
Number of Screens: 70

KINOMAX

12 Potter's St., Moscow 109240. TEL: (7095) 915 3600.
FAX: (7095) 915 3601. www.kinomax.ru

KINOSTAR

c/o National Amusements Inc., 200 Elm St. Dedham, MA
02026. U.S. TEL: (1 781) 461 1600. FAX: (1 781) 407 0052.
www.kinostardelux.ru

KRONVERK CINEMA

67/2 Zanewvsky Ave. St. Petersburg.
TEL: 7 (812) 528-66-88. www.eposcinema.com
GENERAL DIRECTOR
Eduard Pichugin

RISING STAR MEDIA

Mkad 41, Moscow 142704. TEL: 7495-755-4488.
FAX: 7495-783-9338. www.kinostardelux.ru
PRESIDENT
IPaul Heth

Number of Theatres: 3
Number of Screens: 37

ASSOCIATIONS & ORGANIZATIONS

COMMITTEE OF CINEMATOGRAPHY OF THE RUSSIAN FEDERATION

7 Mal Gnezdnikovsky Ln., Moscow 103877.
TEL: (7095) 925 1727, 940 0284. FAX: (7095) 925 1928,
940 0284. email: wsis@ifap.ru www.conifap.cpic.ru
CHAIRMAN
Alexander S. Sokolov

FEDERATION OF FILMMAKERS UNIONS

123056, Moscow Vasilyevskaya St.13, Moscow.
TEL: 7 (495) 254 22 72, 251 34 46. FAX: 7 (495) 251 53 70.
CONTACT
Elena Tavrog

FILMMAKERS UNION OF REPUBLIC OF BELARUS

5 Karl Marx St., Minsk, Belarus 220050. TEL: (70172) 271 002.
FAX: (70172) 271 451.

FILM PRODUCERS GUILD OF RUSSIA

Mosfilmmovskaya ul. 1, Moscow 119858.
TEL: (7095) 143 9028. FAX: (7095) 143 9909.
email: waterloo@mosfilm.ru

GOSFILMOFOND OF RUSSIA

(National film archive)
M. Gnezdikovsky Str. 7, Moscow 103877. TEL: (7095) 229 5207.
FAX: (7095) 234 1861. email: filmfond@aha.ru www.aha.ru

KAZAKHINO

Abylai Khana St. 93/95, Alma-Ata 480091, Kazakhstan.
TEL: (7327) 269 2418.

MINISTRY OF CULTURE

Kitaygorodsky Proezd 7, Moscow 103693. TEL: (7095) 925 0608.
FAX: (7095) 925 5198.
DEPUTY HEAD, STATE COMMITTEE OF CINEMATOGRAPHY
Natalia V. Popesku

MOSFILM

1, Mosfilmovskaya Str., 119858, Moscow. TEL: (7095) 143 9225.
email: ikc@mosfilm.ru www.mosfilm.ru
PRESIDENT
Karen Georgievich Shakhnazarov

RUSSIAN CINEMA COUNCIL

Leningradskoe sh., 58 - bldt. 10, 4th Flr., Moscow.
TEL: (7095) 107 5700, 107 5720. FAX: (7095) 788 1096.
www.ruscico.com
DIRECTOR
Elena Koutsenko

STATE FILM CONCERN GRUZIA-FILM

Akhmedeli St. 10A, Tbilisi 308059, Georgia. TEL: (99532) 510 627.
FAX: (99532) 510 010.

STATE FILM CONCERN MOLDOVA FILM

Enunesku St. 10, Kishinev 277012, Moldova.
TEL: (3732) 234 405. FAX: (3732) 234 405.

ST. PETERSBURG CULTURE FUND

Nevsky Prosp. 31, St. Petersburg 191011. TEL: (7812) 311 8349.
FAX: (7812) 315 1701.

SINGAPORE

Capital: Singapore
Population: 4,701,069 (July 2010 est.)
Area: 693 sq. km.
Source: CIA World Factbook

DISTRIBUTORS AND PRODUCERS

ABACUS POST

808 French Rd. #02-165, 200808. TEL: (65) 6288 8500.
FAX: (65) 6288 8100. email: abacusart@pacific.net.sg
MANAGING DIRECTOR
Edwin Lee

ACADEMY VIDEO PRODUCTIONS

133 New Bridge Rd., #04-32/33 Chinatown Point, 059413.
TEL: (65) 6535 9664. FAX: (65) 6532 6534.
email: academyvideo@pacific.net.sg
www.academyvideo.com.sg
DIRECTOR
Michael Poh

AJNA FILMS

476-A Serangoon Rd., 218146. TEL: (65) 6296 6450.
FAX: (65) 6398 1820. email: ajnadat@hotmail.com
CONTACT
Siti Nafisah Bee, Abdul Nizam Khan

ALLSTAR FILM

6001 Beach Rd., #04-00 Golden Mile Tower, 199589.
TEL: (65) 6474 5555, 6471 3333. FAX: (65) 6474 2676.
email: allstar@sing.net.com
MANAGER
Tay Kim Koon

APOSTROPHE FILMS

204 Telok Ayer St., 068640. TEL: (65) 6423 9142.
FAX: (65) 6423 9134. email: dafs@apostrophefilms.com
www.apostrophefilms.com
EXECUTIVE PRODUCER
Kenneth Pon

AQUAFIRE PRODUCTIONS

10A Townshend Rd., 207608. TEL: (65) 6292 4439.
FAX: (65) 6292 4310. email: tania@aquafire.tv
www.aquafire.tv
CREATIVE DIRECTOR
Tania Sng

BECKER ENTERTAINMENT

23A Amoy St., 069858. TEL: (65) 6372 2455.
FAX: (65) 6372 1220. email: fred@becker.com.sg
CONTACT
Richard Dutton

BUENA VISTA COLUMBIA TRISTAR FILMS

30 Merchant Rd., #04-21/23 Riverside Point, 058282.
TEL: (65) 6438 5595. FAX: (65) 6438 4133.
email: brett.hogg@disney.com
GENERAL MANAGER
Brett Hogg

CATHEY-KERIS FILMS PTE, LTD

(Formerly Cathay Asia Films)
11 Unity Rd., #02-01 Robertson Walk, 237995.
TEL: (65) 6337 8181. FAX: (65) 6732 2587.
email: michael_sim@cathay.com.sg www.cathay.com.sg

MANAGER
Violet Kwan

DREAM FOREST PRODUCTIONS
56 Prinsep Street #01-01, 188685. TEL: (65) 6837 2345.
FAX: (65) 6837 0341. www.dreamforest.com.sg

ENG WAH FILM
400 Orchard Rd., 16-16 Orchard Towers, 0923.
TEL: (65) 734 0028. FAX: (65) 65 6235 4897.
email: mail@engwah.com.sg

ENCORE FILMS
42 Toh Tuck Rd., #04-03 Singapore 536718.
TEL: (65) 6464 9402. FAX: (65) 6464 7362.
email: info@encorefilms.com www.encorefilms.com
MANAGING DIRECTOR
Joyce Lee

FAIRMOUNT INTERNATIONAL

200 JALAN SULTAN, 08-02 TEXTILE CENTRE, 0719.
TEL: (65) 296 5904. FAX: (65) 293 4742.
email: fairmont@singnet.com

FILM FORMATIONS PTE, LTD
72B Tras St., 079011. 03-09 Technopreneur Centre.
TEL: (65) 6324 8300. FAX: (65) 6324 8200.
email: enquire@formations.com.sg www.formations.com.sg

FESTIVE FILMS
16 Mohamed Sultan Rd., # 04-02 238965.
TEL: (65) 6238 2120. FAX: (65) 6227 6733.
email: info@festivefilms.com www.festivefilms.com

FILM FORUM
9 Raffles Blvd. #01-06 Milliena Walk 228575.
TEL: (65) 6581 1993. FAX: (65) 6581 7563.
email: doplee@singnet.com.sg
DIRECTOR
David Lee

FOCUS FILMS
23 Jalan Tua Kong, 457222. TEL: (65) 9633 4166.
email: mcfocus@singnet.com.sg
CONTACT
Craig Mcleod

FREEMANTLE PRODUCTIONS ASIA PTE
101B Tanjong Pagar Rd., Singapore 088522.
TEL: (65) 6223 8771. FAX: (65) 6225 1272.
www.fremantlemedia.com
MANAGING DIRECTOR
Susan Carol Adams - sue.adams@fremantlemedia.com

GATEWAY ENTERTAINMENT
Blk 203B Henderson Rd., #03-07/#04-06, 159548.
TEL: (65) 6481 1620. FAX: (65) 6483 4505.
www.gatewa-e.com
CONTACT
Jesse Tan

HAI RUN(S) FILM INDUSTRIES PTE
300 Beach Rd., #12-05 The Concourse, 199555.
TEL: (65) 6292 5780. FAX: (65) 6292 5760.
email: hrfilm@singnet.com.sg
MANAGING DIRECTOR
Au Yuk Sing

HAN PRODUCTIONS
50 Playfair Rd., Noel Bldg. #06-014, 637995.
TEL: (65) 6382 7646. FAX: (65) 6382 7812.
email: hanvideo@pacific.net.sg
EXECUTIVE PRODUCER
Pamela Kuah

LIVE ART INTERNATIONAL PTE, LTD
541 Orchard Rd., #19-03 Liat Towers Singapore 238881.
TEL: (65) 6323 3231. FAX: (65) 6323 3909.
CONTACT
Robert Andrews

LIGHTHOUSE PICTURES
18 Ghim Moh Rd., # 01-1239 Singapore 270019.
TEL: (65) 9858 7365. FAX: (65) 6466 7301.
MANAGING DIRECTOR
Thomas Chai

MEDIACORP RAINTREE PICTURES
(Formerly Raintree Pictures)
Caldecott Broadcast Centre, Andrew Rd., 299939.
TEL: (65) 6350 3119. FAX: (65) 6251 1916.
email: info_rain@raintree.com.sg www.raintree.com.sg
CEO
Daniel Yun

MEGAMEDIA PTE, LTD.
750 Victoria St. Singapore 188662. TEL: (65) 6531 3525.
FAX: (65) 6295 5802. email: emma@megamedia.com.sg
www.megamedia.com.sg
MANAGING DIRECTOR
Emma Neubronner

OAK 3 FILMS
7 Bukit Pasoh Rd., 089821. TEL: (65) 6226 2338.
FAX: (65) 6226 2339. email: oak3films@pacific.net.sg
www.oak3films.com
CONTACT
Lai Jason

PYRAMIDE AV INTERNATIONAL
83 Genting Ln., #06-02 Genting Bldg., 349568.
TEL: (65) 6841 7140. FAX: (65) 6841 7150.
email: info@pyramidav.com.sg www.pyramidav.com.sg
DIRECTOR
J.S. Bajaj

SITTING PICTURES
58 Tras St. #03-01 Singapore 078997. TEL: (65) 6220 8281.
FAX: (65) 6226 2082. email: mail@sittinginpictures.com
www.sittinginpictures.com
EXECUTIVE PRODUCER
Tan Chih Chong

TWENTIETH CENTURY FOX FILM (EAST)
112 Middle Rd., #04-02 Midland House, 188970.
TEL: (65) 6336 3323, 6336 0478. FAX: (65) 6334 4336.
www.foxmovies.com

UNITED INTERNATIONAL PICTURES
1 Scotts Rd., #15-05 Shaw Centre, 228208.
TEL: (65) 6737 2484. FAX: (65) 6235 3667. www.uip.com.sg
MANAGER
Nicholas Yong

WARNER BROS. SINGAPORE
112 Middle Rd., #04-02 Midland House, 188970.
TEL: (65) 6336 3323, 6336 0478. FAX: (65) 6334 4336.
www.warnerbros.com
MARKETING MANAGER
Vereen Foo - vereen.foo@warnerbros.com

YELLOWSTONE PRODUCTIONS
35 Kismis Ave., Singapore 598212. TEL: (65) 6227 0687.
FAX: (65) 6227 3762. www.yellowstoneproductions.com
MANAGING DIRECTOR
Choo Lian Liang

EXHIBITORS

CATHAY THEATRE MANAGEMENT PTE, LTD.
11 Unity St., #02-01 Robertson Walk, 237995.
TEL: (65) 6337 8181. FAX: (65) 6732 1944.
GENERAL MANAGER
Suhaimi Rafdi - suhaimi-rfdi@cathay.com.sg

Number of Theatres: 6
Number of Screens: 24

GOLDEN HARVEST ENTERTAINMENT CO., LTD.
(For additional listings see Hong Kong, Thailand & Malaysia)
16/F Peninsula Office Tower, 18 Middle Rd., Kowloon.
TEL: (852) 2352 8222. FAX: (852) 2353 5989.
CHAIRMAN
Raymond Chow
MANAGING DIRECTOR
C.K. Phoon
EXECUTIVE DIRECTOR
Stephen Chu
DIRECTOR, FILM DISTRIBUTION
Teerachai Triwongwaranat

GOLDEN VILLAGE ENTERTAINMENT
68 Orchard Rd. #07-10/14 Plaza Singapura, 238839.
TEL: (65) 334 3766. FAX: (65) 6334 8397.
email: webmaster@goldenvillage.com.sg www.gv.com.sg
GENERAL MANAGER DISTRIBUTION
Maria Lorenzo
MANAGING DIRECTOR
Kenneth Tan

Number of Theatres: 8
Number of Screens: 64

SHAW ORGANISATION GROUP OF COMPANIES
Shaw Centre, 13th & 14th Storeys, 1 Scotts Rd., 228208.
TEL: (65) 235 2077. FAX: (65) 235 2860. www.shaw.com.sg
SENIOR MANAGER
Chris Shaw - shaw@shaw.com.sg

Number of Theatres: 8
Number of Screens: 41

VILLAGE ROADSHOW, LTD.
(For complete listing see Australian branch)
206 Bourke St., Melbourne, VIC, 3000, Australia.
TEL: (613) 9667 6666. FAX: (613) 9639 1540.

Number of Theatres (Singapore): 8
Number of Screens (Singapore): 58

ASSOCIATIONS AND ORGANIZATIONS

CINEMATOGRAPHY FILM EXHIBITORS ASSOCIATION (CFEA)

1 Scotts Rd., 13th & 14th Storeys Shaw Centre Singapore 228208. TEL: (65) 6235 2077. FAX: (65) 6235 2860. email: bsyap@shaw.com.sg

ENG WAH ORGANIZATION

400 Orchard Road, 16-06 Orchard Towers, Singapore.
TEL: (65) 67340028 FAX: (65) 623 54897
www.ewcinemas.com.sg
EXECUTIVE DIRECTOR
Cynthia Goh

MINISTRY OF INFORMATION & THE ARTS

140 Hill St., #02-02 MICA Bldg., Singapore 179369.
TEL: (65) 6837 9666. FAX: (65) 6338 3093.
email: mica@mica.gov.sg www.mica.gov.sg

MOTION PICTURE ASSOCIATION INTERNATIONAL

101 Thompson Rd., #08-06 United Square Singapore 307591.
TEL: (65) 6253 1033. FAX: (65) 6255 1838.
email: mpassia@mpa.org.sg www.mpaa.org

SINGAPORE FILM SOCIETY

5A Raffles Ave., #05-01 Marina Leisureplex Singapore 039801.
TEL: (65) 9017 0160. FAX:(65) 6250 6167, (65) 6336 1170.
email: sfc@sfc.org.sg www.sfc.org.sg
CHAIRMAN
Kenneth Tan
MANAGING DIRECTOR
Harold Shaw
DIRECTOR
Seto Lok Yin

SOUTH AFRICA

Capital: Pretoria
Population: 49,109,107 (July 2010 est.)
Area: 1,219,912 sq. km.
Source: CIA World Factbook

DISTRIBUTORS AND PRODUCERS

ATOMIC PRODUCTIONS SA (PTY), LTD.

South African Registration: 992426 57 Brommersvlei Rd., Constantia 7806 Cape Town South Africa.
TEL: (2721) 794 2286. FAX: (2721) 794 9960.
email: info@atomic-productions.com
www.atomic-productions.com

ATLAS STUDIOS

P.O. Box 1046 Melville Johannesburg South Africa.
TEL: (2711) 482 7111. FAX: (2711) 726 5960.
email: info@atlasstudios.co.za www.atlasstudios.co.za
CONTACT
Rachel Laureles

CINEWORKS

P.O. Box 12630 Mill St., Cape Town 8010. TEL: (2721) 425 9747.
FAX: (27 21) 425 9748. www.cineworks.co.za

CONCORD FILMS

P.O. Box 8112, Johannesburg 2000. TEL: (2711) 337 5581.
FAX: (2711) 337 3913. email: concorde@icon.co.za
www.impactvideo.co.za

CYCLONE FILMS

302 Lowry Studios, 95 Sir Lowry Rd. Woodstock, Cape Town.
TEL: (27 21) 461 5744. FAX: (27 21) 465 2131.
www.cyclonefilms.co.za

DANCING LIGHT PRODUCTIONS

17 Kloof St., P.O. Box 16561, Seapoint Capetown 8018.
TEL: (27 21) 433 2055. FAX: (27 21) 433 2040.
www.dancinglight.co.za

EMS

24 Napier Rd., Richmond, Johannesburg. TEL: (2711) 482 4470.
FAX: (2711) 482 2552.

DO FILM PRODUCTIONS

2 Plattekloof Rd., Table Mountain Picture Studios Milnerton, 7441 Cape Town, South Africa. TEL: (2721) 552 2233.
FAX: (2721) 552 2263. www.doproductions.com

FILM AFRICA

2 Avalon, 2nd Flr., 123 Hope St., Gardens, Cape Town, 8001 South Africa. TEL: (27 21) 461 7950. FAX: (27 21) 461 7951.
email: info@filmafrika.com www.filmafrika.com

FILM FARE INTERNATIONAL

P.O. Box 24, Crawford 7770. TEL: (2721) 637 8028.
FAX: (2721) 637 3138.

MOONLIGHTING FILMS

9 Lancaster Ave., Craighall Park Johannesburg 2196.
P.O. Box 3189, Parklands 2121. TEL: (27 11) 787 8681.
FAX: (27 11) 787 9906.
PRODUCER
Genevieve Hofmeyr
EXECUTIVE PRODUCER
Philip Key

REELEYES FILM COMPANY

6 Dorman St. Gardens, Cape Town, South Africa, P.O. Box 26709, Hout Bay 7872. TEL: (27 21) 426 2234.
FAX: (27 21) 426 2299. email: info@reeleyesfilm.com
www.reeleyesfilm.com

SAVAGE EYE FILMWORKS

6A Glade Rd., Rondebosch, Cape Town 7700.
TEL: (2721) 686 3858. FAX: (2721) 244 313.

STER-KINEKOR (PTY.) LIMITED

Interleisure Park, 185 Katherine St., Eastgate, Sandton.
TEL: (2711) 4457 7300. FAX: (2711) 444 1003.
www.sterkinekor.co.za
CEO
Ferdi Gazendam
COO
Fiaz Mahomed

UNITAL FILMS INTERNATIONAL

P.O. Box 52737, Saxonwold 2132, Johannesburg, South Africa.
TEL: (2711) 7281422. www.unitalfilms.com

UNITED INTERNATIONAL PICTURES

P.O. Box 651210, Benmore, Johannesburg 2010.
TEL: 27-11-883 3710. FAX: 27-11-883 2023.
MANAGER
Roger Le Comber

EXHIBITORS

STER KINEKOR THEATRES

P.O. Box 5200, Horizon 1730. TEL: (2711) 475 4220.
FAX: (2711) 475 5333. www.sterkinekor.com
CEO
Ferdi Gazendam
COO
Fiaz Mahomed

STUDIOS

FRAMEWORK TELEVISION

PO Box 76461, Wendywood Johannesburg 2144.
TEL: (27) 11-4457700. FAX: (27) 11-2623039.
www.sterkinekor.com
CEO
Ferdi Fazendam
COO
Fiaz Mahomed

SONNEBLOM FILM PRODUCTIONS

P.O. Box 3940, Honeydew 2040. TEL: (2711) 794 2100.
FAX: (2711) 794 2061.

SONOVISION STUDIOS

P.O. Box 783133, Sandton 2146. TEL: (2711) 783 1100.
FAX: (2711) 883 3834.

ASSOCIATIONS & ORGANIZATIONS

AFRICAN FILM AND TELEVISION COLLECTIVE

P.O. Box 42723, Fordsbury 2033. TEL: (2711) 804 5186.
FAX: (2711) 838 3034.

CINEMA THEATRE AND VIDEO UNION

P.O. Box 81338, Parkhurst 2120. TEL: (2711) 782 4273.
FAX: (2711) 492 1221.

DEPARTMENT OF HOME AFFAIRS-FILM DEPARTMENT

Private Bag X114, Pretoria 0001. TEL: (2712) 314 3328.

FILM RESOURCE UNIT

P.O. Box 11065, Johannesburg 2000 South Africa.
TEL: (2711) 838 4280. FAX: (27 11) 838 4451.
email: publicity@fru.co.za www.fru.co.za

GAUTENG FILM OFFICE

GEDA House, 1st Flr., 88 Fox St., Johannesburg South Africa.
TEL: (2711) 833 8750. FAX: (27 11) 833 2137.
email: gfo@geda.co.za www.gfo.co.za

NATIONAL FILM VIDEO AND SOUND ARCHIVES

Private Bag X236, Pretoria 001, South Africa.
TEL: (27 12) 343 9767. FAX: (27 11) 447 2111.
email: motion@pic.pixie.co.za

NATIONAL FILM AND VIDEO FOUNDATION

No. 87 Central St., Houghton, Johannesburg, Gauteng, South Africa 2116. TEL: (27 11) 789 6387. FAX: (27 11) 886 2465.
email: info@nfvf.co.za www.nfvf.co.za

SOUTH AFRICAN SOCIETY OF CINEMATOGRAPHERS (SASC)

P.O. Box 812151 Parkhurst 2120 South Africa.

TEL: (2711) 788 0802. FAX: (27 11) 788 0802.
email: sasc@mweb.co.za

SOUTH AFRICAN FILM AND TELEVISION INSTITUTE
P.O. Box 3512, Halfway House 1685. TEL: (2711) 315 0140.
FAX: (2711) 315 0146.

SOUTH KOREA

Capital: Seoul
Population: 48,636,068 (July 2010 est.)
Area: 98,480 sq. km.
Source: CIA World Factbook

DISTRIBUTORS

BUENA VISTA INTERNATIONAL KOREA
3rd Flr., Sambu Bldg., 676 Seoul Yeoksam-dong Gangnam-gu Seoul. TEL: (822) 527 0260. FAX: (822) 527 0399.

CJ ENTERTAINMENT
Star Tower Bldg., 26th Flr., Yoksam 1-Dong, Seoul.
TEL: (822) 2112-6503. FAX: (822) 2112-6657.
CEO
Dong Ho Park
COO
Pyung Ho Choi

COLUMBIA TRISTAR FILMS OF KOREA
8F Kyoungam Bldg., 157-27 Samseong-dong Gangnam-gu Seoul. TEL: (822) 563 4000. FAX: (822) 593 1221.

I PICTURES
2nd Fl., Pocos Bldg., 725-25 Yeoksam-dong Gangnam-gu Seoul.
TEL: (822) 538 4007. FAX: (822) 539 7005.
email: frankie@ipictures.co.kr

LJ FILM
#201 Donga Bldg., 585-1 Sinsa-dong Gangnam-gu Seoul.
TEL: (822) 3444 2466. FAX: (822) 3444 6858.

MIRO VISION
1-151 Sinmunno 2(i)-ga Jongno-gu Seoul.
TEL: (822) 737 1185. FAX: (822) 737 1184.

TRAIN PICTURES
4th Flr. Chungdam Bldg. 100-14 Cheongdam-dong Gangnam-gu Seoul. TEL: (822) 544 4058. FAX: (822) 544 5939.
email: trainp@trainpictures.co.kr www. trainpictures.co.kr

TUBE ENTERTAINMENT
664-21 Sinsa-dong Gangnam-gu Seoul. TEL: (822) 547 8105.
FAX: (822) 547 8691. email: nana@tube-entertainment.com
www.tube-entertainment.com

TWENTIETH CENTURY FOX KOREA
8F Asea Tower Bldg., 726 Yeoksam-dong Gangnam-gu Seoul.
TEL: (822) 3452 5981. FAX: (822) 3452 7224.

VIDEOVISION ENTERTAINMENT
Block B Sasani Strudios 2 Johansesburg Rd., Highlands North 2192. TEL: (27 11) 440 8485. FAX: (2711) 440 2207.
email: info@ videovisions.co.za www.videovision.co.za

UIP—CIC FILM & VIDEO DISTRIBUTION
3rd Flr., Asea Bldg., 407-11 Sindang-dong Jung-gu.
TEL: (822) 2233 6600. FAX: (822) 2254 1117.

UNITED INTERNATIONAL PICTURES (SDN)
C.P.O. Box 41, Seoul South Korea.
TEL: 82-2-736-6250. FAX: 82-2-736-6251.
MANAGER
Douglas Lee

WALT DISNEY KOREA
4th Flr., Samboo Bldg., 676 Yeok Sam-dong, Kangam-ku, Seoul. TEL: (822) 527 0400. FAX: (822) 527 0399.

WARNER BROS. KOREA
6th Flr., MB Bldg., 221-5 Nonhyeon-dong Gangnam-gu Seoul.
TEL: (822) 547 0181. FAX: (822) 547 8396.

EXHIBITORS

CJ CGV
Shin Sa Dong 602, 4th Flr., Gangnam-Gu, Seoul 100 095.
TEL: 822 2017 1275. www.cgv.co.kr
CEO
Illchun Kim
ASSISTANT MANAGING DIRECTOR
King Jong Hyun, Kim Hong Suhng

CJ ENTERTAINMENT
Star Tower Bldg., 26th Flr., Yoksam 1-Dong, Seoul. South Korea. TEL: (822) 2112-6503. FAX: (822) 2112-6657.
CEO
Dae Joong Ha
COO
Pyung Ho Choi
CFO
Mark Soh

LOTTE CINEMA
Seognjin Blvd 1556-4, Sedcho 3-dong, Seocho-gu, Seoul 138-240. TEL: 822 3470 3596. FAX: (82) 2-419-5541.
www.lottecinema.co.kr
CEO
Kwang-seop Kim
MANAGING DIRECTOR, DISTRIBUTION
Yong Choi Geon
Total Theaters: 43
Total Screens: 33

MEGABOX CINEPLEX
7F Cinehouse B/D, 91-6 Non Hyon Dong
Kang Nam Hu, Seoul. TEL: 822-3218-5500.
COO
Jeong Hun Ryu

VILLAGE ROADSHOW, LTD.
206 Bourke St., Melbourne, VIC, 3000, Australia.
TEL: (613) 9667 6666. FAX: (613) 9639 1540.
Number of Theatres (Korea): 2
Number of Screens (Korea): 25

ASSOCIATIONS AND ORGANIZATIONS

KOREAN FILM ARCHIVE
700 Seocho-Dong, Seocho-Gu, Seoul 137-718.
TEL: (822) 521 3147. FAX: (822) 582 6213.
www.koreafilm.or.kr
PRESIDENT
Lee Hyo-Yin

KOREA FILM INVEST DEVELOPMENT
3rd Fl., Ilsin Bldg., 15-15 Yeouido-dong Yeongdeungpo-gu Seoul.
TEL: (822) 783 3673. FAX: (822) 783 3683.
email: bikin@iic.co.kr

MOTION PICTURE PRODUCERS ASSOCIATION OF KOREA
Sam Yeong Bldg., 3F 70, 4GA, Dong Sun-Dong, Sung Buk-ku, 136-054 Seoul. TEL: (822) 921 0903. FAX: (822) 921 0906.
CHAIRMAN
Kang Dai-jin

SEOUL FILM COMMISSION
1-28 #202, Jeong-dong, Jung-gu, Seoul 100-120.
TEL: (822) 777 7092. FAX: (822) 777 7097.
email: seoulfc@seoulfc.or.kr www.seoulfc.or.kr

SPAIN

Capital: Madrid
Population: 46,505,963 (July 2010 est.)
Area: 504,782 sq. km.
Source: CIA World Factbook

DISTRIBUTORS AND PRODUCERS

ALAS FILMS
Maestro Guerrero 4, Madrid 28015. TEL: (34 91) 547 6664.
FAX: (34 91) 542 7887.

ACRACIA MOTION PICTURES
Ciutat Granada 45, Barcelona08005.
TEL: +34 93 309 50 31. FAX: +34 93 300 52 11.
email: info@arcadiamotionpictures.com

AVALON PRODUCTIONS
Plaza del Cordon, 2. Bajo, Madrid 28005.
TEL: +34 91 366 4364. FAX: +34 91 365 9301.
email: info@avalonproductions.es
http://www.avalonproductions.es

JOSE ESTEBAN ALENDA
Trujillos 7, Madrid 28013. TEL: (34 91) 541 1838.
FAX: (34 91) 548 3791.

ALTA FILMS
Cuesta de San Vicente, 4, Madrid 28008. TEL: (34 91) 542 2702.
FAX: (34 91) 542 8777.

ARABA FILMS
Avda. Doctor Arce, 13, Madrid 28002. TEL: (34 91) 564 9498.
FAX: (34 91) 564 5738. email: araba@arabafilms.com
www.arabafilms.com
CHAIRMAN
T. Nunez

AURUM
Avda. de Burgos 12, 10a ESP 28036 Madrid.
TEL: (34 91) 768 4800. FAX: (34 91) 302 5764.
email: mochaaguilar@aurum.es www.aurum.es

BARTON FILMS S.I.
Iturribide 68, Lonja, Bolbao. TEL: (34 94) 433 7103.

FAX: (34 94) 433 5086.

BAUSAN FILMS
Muntaner 244, 2º 4ª, Barcelona08021.
TEL: +34 93 241 15 11. FAX: +34 93 414 17 97.
email: comercial@bausanfilms.com www.bausanfilms.com

BRB INTERNATIONAL
Autovia Fuencarral Alcobendas, Km. 12 220 Edificio Auge 1, Madrid 28049. TEL: (34 91) 771 1400. FAX: (34 91) 358 9818.
email: brb@ brb.es www.brb.es http://www.brb.es

BUENA VISTA INTERNATIONAL SPAIN
C. Jose Bardasano Baos 9-11, Edificio Gorbea 3, Madrid 28016. TEL: (34 91) 384 9461. FAX: (34 91) 766 9241.

CASTELAO PRODUCCIONES S.A.
Filmax Entertainment c/ Miguel Hernández, 81-87
Distrito Económico de l'Hospitalet
Barcelona, L'Hospitalet de Llobregat 08908.
TEL: +34 93 336 85 55. FAX: +34 93 263 47 78.
www.filmaxentertainment.com

CHROMOSOMA TV PRODUCCIONES S.A.
Peru 174 E-08020 Barcelona. TEL: (34 93) 266 4266.
FAX:(34 93) 266 4014.

CINE COMPANY
Zurbano 74, Madrid 28010. TEL: (34 91) 442 2944.
FAX: (34 91) 441 0098.

COLUMBIA TRI-STAR FILMS DE ESPANA
Hernandez de Tejada 3, Madrid 28027. TEL: (34 91) 377 7100.
FAX: (34 91) 377 7128.
CONTACT
Ernesto Victoria Barcelo

DE PALACIO FILMS
Calle Gibraltar 27, Bajo, Valencia 46006.
TEL: +34-96-380-0256. FAX: +34-96-380-4857.
email: info@depalacio.com www.depalacio.com

DISTRIBUIDORA COQUILLAT
Denia 43, Valencia 46006. TEL: (34 96) 341 7000.
FAX: (34 96) 380 4270.

EL DESEO S.A.
Francisco Navacerrada 24, Madrid 28028.
TEL: +34 91 723 81 99. FAX: +34 91 355 74 67.
email: eldeseo@eldeseo.eshttp www.eldeseo.es/

ESICMA
Maestro Lasalle 15, 28016 Madrid. TEL: (34 91) 345 8708.
FAX: (34 91) 355 7991.

FILMAX GROUP
Miguel Hernández 81-87, Districte Econòmic de l'Hospitalet, L'Hospitalet de Llobregat, Barcelona 08908.
TEL: (34 93) 336 8555. FAX: (34 93) 263 2944. www.filmax.com
CONTACT
Julio Fernandez

FILMAYER INTERNATIONAL
Av. de Burgos, 8-A Planta 10-1, Madrid 28036.
TEL: (34 91) 383 1572. FAX: (34 91) 383 0845. www.filmayer.es

GOLEM DISTRIBUCION
C. Corazon de Maria 56-9B, Madrid 28002.
TEL: (34 91) 519 1737. FAX: (34 91) 416 3626.
email: sugiere@golem.es www.golem.es

HISPANO FOXFILM S.A.E.
Avenida de Bourgos 8-A, Planta 11, Madrid 28036.
TEL: (34 91) 343 4640. FAX: (34 91) 343 4655.

IBEROAMERICANA FILMS INTERNACIONAL
Velazquez 12, 7 & 8, Madrid 28001. TEL: (34 91) 4314246.
FAX: (34 91) 435 5994.
CONTACT
Andres Vicente Gomez

IMPALA MONTILLA
Manuel Motilla 1, Madrid 28016. TEL: (34 91) 350 6200.
FAX: (34 91) 345 1948.
CONTACT
Jose Antonio Sainz de Vicuna

KALEKIA
Comino del Obispo 25, Mostoles, Madrid 28935.
TEL: (34 91) 616 3710. FAX: (34 91) 616 3710.

KANZAMAN S.A.
C/ Alto de las Cabañas 5, Las Rozas de Madrid28231.
TEL: +34 91 640 60 86. FAX: +34 91 710 35 93.
email: kanzaman@kanzaman.es www.kanzaman.es

LATIDO FILMS
C/ Veneras 9 - 6º , Madrid 28013.
TEL: +34 91 548 8877. FAX: +34 91 548 8878.
email: latido@latidofilms.com www.latidofilms.com

LAUREN FILM
Balmes, 87, Bajos, Barcelona 08008. TEL: (34 93) 496 3800.
FAX: (34 93) 323 61 55.

LECAS FILM DISTRIBUCION
Galileo 82, Madrid 28015. TEL: (34 91) 447 4657.
FAX: (34 91) 448 8978.

LIDER FILMS
Isla de Fuenteventura No, 21-10, San Sebastian de los Reyes, Madrid 28700. TEL: (34 91) 663 9000. FAX: (34 91) 663 9320.

LOLAFILMS
C/ General Pardias 9 1D, Madrid 28001
TEL: +34 914 367 400. FAX: +34 914 355 994.
email: international@lolafilms.com www.lolafilms.com

MANGA FILMS
Balmes 243, Barcelona 08006. TEL: +34 93 238 40 30.
FAX: +34 93 238 40 31. email: manga@mangafilms.es
www.mangafilms.es

MEDIAPRO
Gaspar Fabregas, 81, 08950 Esplugeues de Llobregat
Barcelona. TEL: +34 93 476 15 51.
FAX: +34 93 476 15 52. www.mediapro.es

MORENA FILMS
Fernando VI, 17 28004 Madrid. TEL: +34 917002780.
FAX: +34 913194432. email: morenafilms@morenafilms.com

MOVIERECORD
Martires de Alcala 4, Madrid 28015. TEL: (34 91) 559 9205.
FAX: (34 91) 547 5985.
CONTACT
Jesus Martin Sanz

MULTIVIDEO
La Luna 15, Madrid 28004. TEL: (34 91) 522 9347.
FAX: (34 91) 532 8695.

MUSIDORA FILMS
C.Quintana 1, Madrid 28008. TEL: (34 91) 542 0036.
FAX: (34 91) 559 9069.

NEPTUNO FILMS
Cardaire 36-38, Terassa, Barcelona 08221. TEL: (34 91) 784 1622.
FAX: (34 91) 784 2938.

NEW WORLD FILMS INTERNACIONAL
Berlin N4 - Portal 3-Oficina 4, Madrid 28223.
TEL: +34 917 152 010. FAX: +34 917 151 752.
email: info@newworldfilms.net www.newworldfilms.net

NOTRO FILMS
c/ Balmes 243 Atico, Barcelona 08006.
TEL: +34 932 384 030. FAX: +34 932 384 031.
email: marisa@notrofilms.com www.notrofilms.com

PMM MULTIMEDIA
Brezo 4, Los Robles E-28250, Torrelodones Madrid.
TEL: (34 91) 859 0932.
CONTACT
Paco Rodriguez

POLYGRAM FILM ESPANA
Manuel Montilla 1, Madrid 28016. TEL: (34 91) 350 6200.
FAX: (34 91) 350 1371.

PRIME FILMS
C. Agastia, 60, 1°, Madrid 28043. TEL: (34 91) 519 0181.
FAX: (34 91) 413 0772.

REX FILMS
Provenza 197-199, Barcelona 08008. TEL: (34 93) 451 3315.
FAX: (34 93) 453 5391.

SOGEPAQ DISTRIBUCION
C. Gran Via, 32, 1°, Madrid 28013. TEL: (34 91) 524 7220.
FAX: (34 91) 521 0875. email: sogepaqint@sogecable.com
www.soqecine-soqepaq.com
PRESIDENT
Jose Vicuna

SOLIDDA - SOLIEDAD LIMITADA DIFERENCIAS
San Bernardo, 74 2C ESP-28015, Madrid. TEL: (34 91) 524 00 94.
FAX: (34 91) 523 41 13. www.tts.es

SUCESORES DES JESUS RODRIGUEZ DORESTA
Triana 68-1, Las Palmas de Gran Canaria 35002.
TEL: (34 928) 371 560. FAX: (34 928) 371 560.

SUPER FILMS S.A.
Provenza 197/199, Barcelona 08008. TEL: (34 93) 451 3315.
FAX: (34 93) 453 5391.

SURF FILMS
Zurbano 74, Madrid 28010. TEL: (34 91) 442 2944.
FAX: (34 91) 0441 0098.

TELECINCO CINEMA
Crta. de Fuencarral a Alcobendas, 4, Madrid 28049.
TEL: +34 912 014 200. FAX: +34 912 014 303.
www.telecinco.es

TORNASOL FILMS
C/ Veneras, 9, 7th Flr., Madrid 28013.
TEL: +34-915-429-564. FAX: +34 9 1 5428 710.
email: tornasol@tornasolfilms.com
www.tornasol-films.com/home.html

TRIPICTURES
Doce De Octubre 28, Madrid 28009. TEL: (34 91) 574 9008.
FAX: (34 91) 574 9005. www.tripictures.com

U FILMS/UNION FILMS
Maestro Guerrero 4, Madrid 28015. TEL: (34 91) 547 6585.
FAX: (34 91) 542 7887.

UNITED INTERNATIONAL PICTURES
Plaza del Callao 4-6, Madrid 28013. TEL: (34 91) 522 7261.
FAX: (34 91) 532 2384.
MANAGER
Gaulberto Bana

UNIVERSAL PICTURES
Cardenal Marcelo Espinola 8, 6°, Madrid 28016.
TEL: (34 91) 768 8800. FAX: (34 91) 768 8822.

VERTIGO FILMS
Silva 2, 4 E-28013, Madrid. TEL: (34 91) 542 2225.
FAX: (34 91) 541 6985.

VICTORY FILMS
Santa Feliciana, 6, Madrid 28010. TEL: (34 91) 541 8734.
FAX: (34 91) 541 4612. email: victory@teleline.es
MANAGING DIRECTOR
Sergio Lieman

WANDA FILMS
Avenida de Europa 9, Pozuelo, Madrid 28224.
TEL: (34 91) 352 8376. FAX: (34 91) 345 1948.

WARNER ESPANOLA
Manual Montilla 1, Madrid 28016. TEL: (34 91) 350 6200.
FAX: (34 91) 345 1948.

ZEBRA PRODUCCIONES
Avd De Manoteras 18, Edificio Elipse 1, Oficina 3
Madrid28050. TEL: +34 91 383 40 25.
FAX: +34 91 383 36 91.
email: zebra@zebraprod.es www.zebraproducciones.com

EXHIBITORS

ALPHAVILLE
Martin de Los Heros 14, Madrid 28008. TEL: (34 91) 559 3836.
FAX: (34 91) 541 5482.

ALTA FILMS S.A.
Cuesta de San Vicente 4, Martin de los Heros, 12, Madrid
28008. TEL: (34 91) 542 2702. FAX: (34 91) 542 8777.
Number of Screens: 108

AREA CATALANA D'EXHIBICIO CINEMATOGRAFICA, S.A.
221 Mallorca St., 6th Flr., Barcelona 08008. TEL: (3493) 323 6426.
FAX: (3493) 323 7223.
PRESIDENT
Jaime Tarrazon Badia
VICE PRESIDENT
Jaume Camprecios
MANAGER
Francisco Garcia Bascunana
Number of Screens: 300

CINESA
Floridablanca 135 Barcelona 08011. TEL: (34) 93 228 96 00.
FAX: (34) 93 424 38 05. www.cinesa.es
CHIEF OPERATING OFFICER
Jose Battle
MANAGING DIRECTOR
Javier Fernandez
DIRECTOR OF MARKETING & PUBLIC RELATIONS
Raul Cabrera
Total Theaters: 90
Total Screens: 596. www.cinesa.es

CINES GOLEM
Plaza Yamaguchi ES-31008 Pamplona. TEL: (34 94) 8 25 19 03.
FAX: (34 94) 8 17 10 58.
Screens: 5

COLISEO ALBIA
Alameda de Urquijo 13, Bilbao 48008. TEL: (34 94) 423 2148.
FAX: (34 94) 423 1001.

COMPANIA DE INICIATIVAS Y ESPECTACULOS
Floridablanca 135, 08011 Barcelona. TEL: (34 99) 3423 2455.
Number of Screens: 149

DIFUSORA BURGOS - CINES VAN GOLEM
Avda. Arlanzon, 36 ES-09004 Burgos. TEL: (34 94)7 277 971.
FAX: (34 94) 7 256 444.
Screens: 6

DIFUSORA LOGRONO
Cines Golem, Parque de San Adrian s/n, Logrono 26006.
TEL: (34 948) 174 141. FAX: (34 948) 171 058.

EMPRESA BALANA
Provenza 266, 5, Barcelona 08008. TEL: (34 93) 215 9570.
FAX: (34 93) 215 6740.

FRANCISCO HERAS - CINES VAN DYCK
Van Dyke Cinema, Van Dyke 59-61, Salamanca 37005.
TEL: (34 923) 243 538. FAX:(34 923) 24 35 38.
Screens: 10

GRUPO ÁBACO
Juan de la Cierva y Codorniú 12, Parque Tecnológico, Paterna,
Valencia. TEL: (34 96) 136 6111. FAX: (34 96) 136 6240.
email: marketing@grupoabaco.net www.cinesabaco.com
Number of Theatres: 16
Number of Screens: 153

INEPOLIS GROUP
Ciudad de la Imagen Ctra. Madrid a Boadilla, Madrid. 28223.
TEL: (34 91) 512 7014. FAX: (34 91) 474 2606. www.kinepolis.com

LAUREN FILM
Balmes, 87, Bajos, Barcelona 08008. TEL: (34 93) 496 3800.
FAX: (34 93) 323 61 55.

PALAFOX CINEMA
Luchana 15, Madrid 28010. TEL: (34 91) 446 1887.
FAX: (34 91) 447 3441.

PEDRO BALANA
Provenza 266, Barcelona 08008. TEL: (34 93) 215 9570.
FAX: (34 93) 215 6740.

REAL CINEMA
Plaza de Isabel II 7, Madrid 28013. TEL: (34 91) 547 4577.
FAX: (34 91) 547 4650.
Screens: 3

TABEXSA CINE - ALBATROS
Albatros Minicines, Plaza Fray Luis Colomer 4, Valencia
46021. TEL: (34 96) 369 4530. FAX: (34 96) 360 1469.
Screens: 4

UGC SPAIN
Power Road Studios, Power Rd., Chiswick, London, W4 5PY.
TEL: (44 020) 8987 5000.
MANAGING DIRECTOR
Margaret Taylor
Lisa Hynes (PA)
Number of Theatres (Spain): 4
Number of Screens (Spain): 72

UNION CINE CIUDAD
Alameda Multicines, Alameda de Hercules 9-10, Seville 41002.
TEL: (34) 91 5437 5900. FAX: (34) 91 701 0146.
www.cineciudad.com

VERDI PARK
Torrijos 47 ES-08012 Barcelona. TEL: (34 93) 238 78 00.
FAX: (34 93) 238 78 08.
Screens: 4

UNION CINE CIUDAD
Alameda de Hercules 9Y 10, Edifico Alameda Multicines,
41002 Sevilla, Spain. TEL: (34 91) 5437 5900.
FAX: (34 91) 701 0146. email: cineciudad@cineciudad.com
www.cineciudad.com
Number of Theatres: 28
Number of Screens: 206

WARNER LUSOMUNDO CINES DE ESPANA, S.A.
(Warner Bros. International Theatres in partnership with
Lusomundo SGPS, S.A.)
Miniparc, 1 c/Azalea, No.1, Edificip B, Primera planta, El Soto
de la Moraleja Alcobendas, Madrid 28109.
TEL: (34 91) 658 5358. FAX: (34 91) 658 5356.
www.warnerlusomundo.es
EXECUTIVE DIRECTOR
Millard Ochs, Luis Silva, Ele Juarez
MANAGING DIRECTOR
Tomas Naranjo
Number of Theatres: 11
Number of Screens: 123

YELMO CINEPLEX DE ESPANA
Princesa 31, 3rd Flr., Madrid 28008. TEL: (34 91) 1758 9600.

FAX: (34 91) 548 2940. email: yelmo@yelmocpx.com
www.yelmocineplex.es
PRESIDENT & CEO
Ricardo Evole
DIRECTOR
Fernando Evole
CFO
Jaime Gerboles

Number of Theatres: 31
Number of Screens: 297

ASSOCIATIONS & ORGANIZATIONS

ASOCIACIÓN DE DIRECTORES DE PRODUCCIÓN CINEMATOGRÁFICA DE ESPAÑA (ADPCE)
Avenida de Filipinas 26, 1st Flr., Madrid 28003.
TEL: (34 91) 534 7098. FAX: (34 91) 534 7112.
email: adpce@asoc-adpce.es www.asoc-adpce.es
PRESIDENT
Emilio A. Pina

ASSOCIATION OF ANIMATION PRODUCERS (AEPA)
CL Mayor, 28, 2nd Flr., Madrid 28013. TEL: (34 91) 222 8265.
FAX: (34 91) 2228 266. email: aepa@aepa-animation.com
www.aepa-animation.com
PRESIDENT
Enrique Uviedo

ASSOCIATION OF INDEPENDENT PRODUCERS
CL Gaztambide, 11. 2nd Flr. Izda, Madrid 20815.
TEL: (34 91) 543 1941. FAX: (34 91) 543 1941.
PRESIDENT
Tomás Cimadevilla

ASSOCIATION OF SPANISH PRODUCERS
CL Luis Buñuel, 2- 2º Izda., Pozuelo de Alarcon, Madrid 28223.
TEL: (34 91) 512 1660. FAX: (34 91) 512 0148.

FEDERACION ESPANOLA DE PRODUCTORAS DE CINE PUBLICITARIO Y CORTOMETRAJE
Sanchez Pacheco 64 Entreplanta, Madrid 28002.
TEL: (34 91) 413 2454. FAX: (34 91) 519 2019.
email: appe@appe.org www.appe.org

INSTITUTO DE LA CINEMATOGRAFÍA Y DE LAS ARTES AUDIOVISUALES (ICAA)
Plaza del Rey, 1, 3A, Madrid 28004. TEL: (34 91) 701 7258.
FAX: (34 91) 532 3940. email: pilar.torre@icaa.mcu.es
GENERAL DIRECTOR
José María Otero
PROMOTIONS & INTERNATIONAL RELATIONS
Pilar Torre

MINISTRY OF CULTURE
Plaza del Rey 1, Madrid 28071. TEL: (34 91) 532 0093.
FAX: (34 91) 522 9377.

SPANISH FEDERATION OF AUDIOVISUAL PRODUCERS
C. Luis Buñuel, 2, 2º Izq. Ciudad de la Imagen Pozuelo de Alarcón, Madrid 28223. TEL: (34 91) 512 1660.
FAX: (34 91) 512 0148.
PRESIDENT
Pedro Pérez
GENERAL MANAGER
Fabia Buenaventura

UNIÓN DE PRODUCTORES DE CINE Y TELEVISIÓN (UPCT)
CL Costa Rica, 11, Madrid 28016. TEL/FAX: (34 91) 345 2073.
PRESIDENT
Juan Ruiz de Gauna

SWEDEN

Capital: Stockholm
Population: 9,074,055 (July 2010 est.)
Area: 449,964 sq. km.
Source: CIA World Factbook

DISTRIBUTORS AND PRODUCERS

ACNE FILM
Majorsgatan 11, Stockholm 114 47. TEL: (468) 555 799 00.
FAX: (468) 555 799 99. www.acnefilm.com
CONTACT
David Olsson - david@acnefilm.se

ARMSTRONG FILM
Jungfrugatan 6 B, Stockholm 114 44. TEL: (468) 663 95 95.
FAX: (468) 667 45 15. email: soren@armstrongfilm.com
www.armstrongfilm.com
CONTACT
Sören Fernholm

BUENA VISTA INTERNATIONAL
Box 5631, Stockholm S-114 86. TEL: (468) 679 1550.
FAX: (468) 678 01728.
GENERAL MANAGER
Eric Broberg

CAPITOL FILM DISTRIBUTION
Sodravagen 12, Kalmar S-392 33. TEL: (46480) 12215.
FAX: (46480) 24085.

CAPRICORN FILM & TV
Tysta Gatan 9, Box 10204 Srockholm 100 55.
TEL: (468) 662 3620. FAX: (468) 663 1282.
www.capricornfilm.com

CINEMA SWEDEN
P.O. Box 20105, Bromma S-161 02. TEL: (468) 280 738.
FAX: (468) 299 091.

COLUMBIA TRISTAR FILMS (SWEDEN)
Hornsbruksgatan 19, 1 Tr, P.O. Box 9501, Stockholm S-102 74.
TEL: (468) 658 1140. FAX: (468) 841 204. www.filmnytt.com
GENERAL MANAGER
Peter Jansson

DOCKHOUSE FILM & TV PRODUKTION AB
Sjöportsgatan 4, Göteborg 417 64. TEL: (46) 3165 1600.
FAX: (46) 3165 1601. www.dockhouse.se
CONTACT
Hans Ekelund

DRAKFILM
Skånegatan 61, Box 4713, Stockholm 116 92.
TEL: (468) 644 9035. FAX: (468) 644 6185.
email: office@drakfilm.se www.drakfilm.se
CONTACT
Leif Löf

EFTI
Norrlandsgatan 18, Stockholm 111 43. TEL: (468) 678 1210.
FAX: (468) 678 1211. www.efti.se
CONTACT
Carl Molinder

EGMONT FILM
P.O. Box 507, Taby S-183 25. TEL: (468) 5101 0050.
FAX: (468) 5101 2046.

FILMLANCE INTERNATIONAL
Magasin 5, Stockholm Frihamn, Box 271 56 Stockholm 102 52.
TEL: (468) 459 7380. FAX: (468) 459 7389. www.filmlance.se

FOLKETS BIO
P.O. Box 2068, Stockholm S-103 12. TEL: (468) 402 0820.
FAX: (468) 402 0827.

FORSBERG & CO
Skeppargatan 41, Sthlm 114 52. TEL: (468) 5552 3500.
FAX: (468) 5552 3501. email: info@forsberg.se
www.forsberg.se
CONTACT
Patrik Forsberg

FOX FILM
Box 9501, Stockholm S-102 74. TEL: (468) 658 1140.
FAX: (468) 841 204.

Radstugatan 7 Lulea 972 38. TEL: (469) 202 2190.
FAX: (469) 202 2014. www.giraff-film.com
CONTACT
John Olson

JAROWSKIJ
Magasin 1, Frihamnen, Box 27 034, Stockholm 102 51.
TEL: (468) 5030 7700. FAX: (468) 5030 7701.
www.jarowskij.se

ILLUSION FILM AND TV
Tredje Langgatan 413 03 Goteborg. TEL: (463) 1775 2850.
FAX: (463) 1775 2880. email: info@illusiojnfilm.se
www.illusionfilm.se

MEKANO FILM & TV
Magasin 5, Frihamnen, Box 27837, Stockholm 115 93.
TEL: (468) 459 7300. FAX: (468) 459 7399. www.mekano.se

MEMPHIS FILM
Kornhamnstorg 6. Stockholm S-111 27.
TEL: (468) 33 55 76. email: memfis@memfis.se
www.memfis.se/

NORDISK FILM
Karlsrovägen 2 D, Box 49M Danderyd 182 11.
TEL: (468) 587 822 00. FAX: (468) 587 822 03.
www.nordiskfilm.se
MANAGING DIRECTOR
Kenneth D. Plummer
CFO
Carsten Møller
MARKETING DIRECTOR
Mikkel Berg

NORDISK FILM TV AB
Box 53 (Ryssviksvägen 2A), Nacka 131 36.
TEL: (468) 601 32 00. FAX: (468) 601 32 10.
www.nordiskfilm.se

GENERAL MANAGER, FILM DISTRIBUTION
Michael Juncker
GENERAL MANAGER, TV PRODUCTION
Lars Mandal, Stein-Roger Bull

PILOT FILM

Box 4091, TUlkeammaren 904 3 Umea. TEL: (469) 014 6390.
FAX: (469) 014 6340. email: info@pilotfilm.se www.pilotfilm.se

PINGUIN FILM

Östgötagatn 14, Stockholm 116 25. TEL: (468) 640 0350.
FAX: (468) 640 0359. www.pinguin.se

PLANBORG FILM

Granhallsvagen 23, Stocksund S-182 75. TEL: (468) 655 80 70.
FAX: (468) 655 03 40.

POGOFILM AB

Sturegatan 64, Stockholm 114 36. TEL: (468) 545 699 20.
FAX: (468) 663 6750. www.pogofilm.se
CONTACT
Mats Wolgers

SANDREW FILM & TEATR

P.O. Box 5612, Stockholm S-114 86. TEL: (468) 234 700.
FAX: (468) 103 850.

SCANDVISION FILM

Hjulhamnsgatan 3, Malmö 211 34. TEL: (4640) 665 5000.
FAX: (4640) 665 5080. www.scandvision.se

SONET FILM

Tappvagen 24, P.O. Box 20105, Bromma S-161 02.
TEL: (468) 799 6900. FAX: (468) 285 834.
email: lotta@sonetfilm.se www.sonetfilm.se

STOCKHOLM-KÖPENHAVN PRODUKTION AB

Sandhamnsgatan 80, Stockholm 115 28. TEL: (468) 459 1380.
FAX: (468) 459 1395. www.sto-cph.se

SVENSK FILMINDUSTRI

Greta Garbos väg 13 SE, Solna 169 36. TEL: (468) 680 3500.
FAX: (468) 710 4422. email: international@sf.se
www.sfsales.net
SENIOR V.P., INTERNATIONAL DIVISION
Ann-Kristin Westerberg

SVENSKA FILMINSTITUTET

Filmhuset, Borgvagen 1-5, P.O. Box 27126, Stockholm S-102 52.
TEL: (468) 665 1100. FAX: (468) 680 3704.

UNITED INTERNATIONAL PICTURES (SWEDEN)

P.O. Box 9502, Stockholm S-102 74. TEL: (468) 616 7400.
FAX: (468) 843 870.
MANAGER
John Mirisch

WARNER BROS. SWEDEN

Hornsbruksgatan 19, 4th Flr., Stockholm S-117 34.
TEL: (468) 658 1050. FAX: (468) 658 6482.

EXHIBITORS

FOLKETS BIO

Stora Nygatan 21, P.O. Box 2068, Stockholm S-103 12.
TEL: (468) 545 275 20. FAX: (468) 545 275 27.
email: info@folketsbio.se www.folketsbio.se

SANDREW METRONOME FILM AB

P.O. Box 5612, Stockholm S-114 86. TEL: (468) 762 1700.
FAX: (468) 103 850. www.sandrewmetronome.se
PRESIDENT & CEO
Frida Ohrvik
EXECUTIVE V.P.
Eivor Zimmerman

Number of Theatres: 31
Number of Screens: 109

SF BIO AB

SE-169 86, Stockholm. 2783. TEL: (468) 680 3500.
FAX: (468) 680 3748. www.sfe.se
PRESIDENT/CEO
Jan Bernhardsson
V.P., PROGRAMMING
Sture Johansson
V.P., OPERATIONS
Steve Södergren
V.P., MARKETING
Helena Eklund
V.P., BUILDING & DEVELOPMENT
Mats Kullander

Number of Theatres: 33
Number of Screens: 209

SVENSK FILMINDUSTRI

Greta Garbos väg 13 SE, Solna 169 36. TEL: (468) 680 3500.
FAX: (468) 710 4422. email: international@sf.se www.sfe.se
SENIOR V.P. OF INTERNATIONAL DIVISION
Ann-Kristin Westerberg

ASSOCIATIONS & ORGANIZATIONS

SWEDISH DISTRIBUTORS ASSOCIATION

P.O. Box 49084, Stockholm S-100 28. TEL: (468) 785 0400.
FAX: (468) 730 2560.

SWEDISH FILM INSTITUTE

Box 271 26, Filmhuset, Borgvägen 1-5, Stockholm 102 52.
TEL: (468) 665 1100, (468) 665 1113. FAX: (468) 666 3760.
email: info@ sfi.se www.sfi.se
CHAIRMAN
Lisa Söderberg
VICE CHAIRMAN
Torsten Larsson
GENERAL DIRECTOR
Åse Kleveland

SWEDISH FILM PRODUCERS ASSOCIATION

Borgvagen 1, Box 27183, Stockholm. TEL: (468) 665 1100.
FAX: (468) 666 3748. www.swedishfilmproducers.com

THE SWEDISH FILM INSTITUTE

Box 271 26, SE-102 52 Stockholm, Sweden.
Visting address: Filmhuset, Borgvägen 1-5.
TEL: (468) 665 11 00. FAX: (468) 666 37 60.
email: registrator@sfi.se

UNITED INTERNATIONAL PICTURES AB

P.O. Box 9502, Stockholm S-102 74 Sweden.
TEL: 46-8-55 60 65 70. FAX: 46-8-55 60 65 89.
MANAGER
John Mirisch

SWITZERLAND

Capital: Bern
Population: 7,623,438 (July 2010 est.)
Area: 41,290 sq.km.
Source: CIA World Factbook

DISTRIBUTORS AND PRODUCERS

ALEXANDER FILM

Lagernstrasse 6, CH-8037 Zurich. TEL: (411) 362 8443.
FAX: (411) 361 1603.

ALPHA FILMS S. A.

4 Place du Cirque, Case Postale 5311, CH-1211 Geneve 11.
TEL: (4122) 328 0204. FAX: (4122) 781 0676.

ANDROMEDA FILM AG

Neugasse 10, 8005 Zürich. TEL: (4143) 366 8181.
FAX: (4143) 366 8425. email: info@andromedafilm.ch

ASCOT ELITE ENTERTAINMENT

Molkenstrasse 21, Postfach 8026 Zürich.
TEL: (411) 298 81 81. FAX: (411) 298 81 89.
email: info@ascot-elite.ch www.ascot-elite.ch

BERNARD LANG AG

Dorf Strasse 14D, Freienstein, CH-8427 Zurich.
TEL: (411) 865 6627. FAX: (411) 865 6629.

BUENA VISTA INTERNATIONAL, (SWITZERLAND) LTD.

Am Schanzengraben 27, CH-8002 Zurich. TEL: (411) 201 6655.
FAX: (411) 201 7770.

CARAC FILM AG

Zinggstrasse 16, 3007 Bern. TEL: (4131) 372 0040.
FAX: (4131) 372 0481. email: info@carac.ch www.carac.ch
CONTACT
Theres Scherer-Kollbrunner

C-FILMS AG

Hallenstrasse 10, Postfach, 8032 Zürich. TEL: (441) 253 6555.
FAX: (441) 251 5253. email: c-films@c-films.ch
www.c-films.ch
CONTACT
Peter-Christian Fueter

COLUMBUS FILM AG

Steinstrasse 21, CH-8036 Zurich. TEL: (411) 462 7366.
FAX: (411) 462 0112. email: info@columbusfilm.ch
www.columbusfilm.ch

COBRA FILM AG

Carmenstrasse 25 8032 Zürich. TEL: (411) 252 0552.
FAX: (411) 252 0552. email: cobra.film@swissonline.ch
CONTACT
Valerie Fischer

CONDOR FILMS

Restelbergstrasse 107, CH-8044 Zurich. TEL: (411) 361 9612.

DELTA FILM AG

Eierbrechtstrasse 35 8053 Zürich. TEL: (411) 381 33 35.
FAX: (411) 381 33 36.

DSCHOINT VENTSCHR AG
Zentralstrasse 156 8003 Zürich. TEL: (411) 456 3020.
FAX: (411) 456 3025. email: dvfilm@dschointventschr.ch
www.dschointventschr.ch

FAMA-FILM AG
Engelstrasse 52, Postfach, 8004 Zürich. TEL: (411) 245 8660.
FAX: (411) 245 8666. email: info@famafilm.ch www.famafilm.ch

FILMCOOPERATIVE ZURICH
Heinrichstrasse 11, 8005 Zürich. TEL: (411) 448 4425.
FAX: (411) 448 4428. email:wbl@filmcoopi.ch www.filmcoopi.ch
CONTACT
Wolfgang Blosche

FILMFABRIK AG
Widdermoos 15, 9466 Sennwald. TEL: (4181) 740 4282.
FAX: (4181) 740 4283. email: info@filmfabrik.tv www.filmfabrik.tv

HESSEGREUTERT FILM
Badenerstrasse 129, 8004 Zürich. TEL: (4143) 322 1822.
FAX: (4143) 322 1820. email: contact@hessegreutert.ch
www.hessegreutert.ch

KINEPOLIS GROUP
89 Blvd. du Centenaire, B 1020 Brussels. TEL: (322) 474 2600.
FAX: (322) 474 2606. www.kinepolis.com

IMPERIAL FILMS S. A.
Ave. de la Gare 17, CH-1002 Lausanne. TEL: (4121) 732 1830.
FAX: (4121) 738 7882.

INSERT FILM AG
Untere Steingrubenstrasse 19, Postfach 106, 4504 Solothurn.
TEL: (4132) 625 7000. FAX: (4132) 623 6410.
email: info@insertfilm.ch www.insertfilm.ch

LANGFILM, BERNARD LANG AG
Dorfstrasse 14 C 8427 Freienstein. TEL: (4144) 865 66 27.
FAX: (4144) 865 6629. email: info@langfilm.ch
www.langfilm.ch

MOVING IMAGE GMBH
Bruderholzrain 38, 4102 Binningen. TEL: (4179) 444 8168.
email: info@movingimage.ch www.movingimage.ch

POINT PROD' SA
6, rue David Dufour, 1205 Genève. TEL: (4122) 328 4848.
FAX: (4122) 328 4959. email: info@pointprod.ch
www.pointprod.ch

R-FILM GMBH
Räffelstr. 11, 8045 Zürich. TEL: (411) 461 1575.
FAX: (411) 461 1577. email: info@r-film.ch www.r-film.ch

REGINA FILM S. A.
4 Rue de Rive, CH-1204 Geneve. TEL: (4122) 310 8136.
FAX: (4122) 310 9476.

RIALTO FILM AG
Neugasse 6, CH-8021 Zurich. TEL: (411) 444 2277.
FAX: (411) 444 2280. email: info@rialto.ch www.rialto.ch
MANAGING DIRECTOR
Christian Gerig - cgerig@rialto.ch
PUBLICITY DIRECTOR
Tamara Araimi - taraimi@rialto.ch
MARKETING DIRECTOR
Anita Schlegel

SPIEGEL FILM AG
Ebelstrasse 25, Postfach 179, CH-8030 Zurich.
TEL: (411) 252 7406. FAX: (411) 251 1354.

STAMM-FILM AG
Lowenstrasse 20, CH-8023 Zurich. TEL: (411) 211 6615.

STRATIS SA
Rue du Pré-Jérôme 15, 1205 Genève. TEL: (4122) 708 1130.
FAX: (4122) 708 1140. email: info@stratis.net www.stratis.net

TWENTIETH CENTURY-FOX FILM CORPORATION
Baslerstrasse 52, CH-8048 Zürich. TEL: (411) 495 7777.
FAX: (411) 715 7795. email: info@fox.ch www.fox.ch
MANAGER
Peter Danner

UNITED INTERNATIONAL PICTURES (SCHWEIZ)
Signaustrasse 6, CH-8032 Zurich. TEL: (411) 383 8550.
FAX: (411) 383 6112. www.uipfilm.ch
MANAGER
Max Dietiker

VARIO FILM SA
Production Office: Via Clemente Mariani 9, 6900 Lugano.
TEL: (4191) 921 0149. FAX: (4191) 921 0148.
email: pelo@variofilm.com

Administrative Office: Via Burgh 2, C.P. 68, 6944 Cureglia.
TEL: (41 91) 967 1333. FAX: (41 91) 967 3448.
email: contact@variofilm.com www.variofilm.com

VENTURA FILM SA
Casella postale, 6866 Meride. TEL: (4191) 646 2021.
FAX: (4191) 646 0386. email:ventura@venturafilm.ch
www.venturafilm.ch

WARNER BROS. (TRANSATLANTIC)
Baslerstrasse 52, CH-8048 Zürich. TEL: (411) 495 7777.
FAX: (411) 495 7795. www.warnerbros.ch
MANAGING DIRECTOR
Leo Baumgartner

ZODIAC PICTURES INTERNATIONAL, LTD.
Pilatusstrasse 24, 6003 Luzern. TEL: (4141) 211 2202.
FAX: (4141) 211 2203. email: contact@zodiacpictures.com
www.zodiacpictures.com

EXHIBITORS

CINEDOME
Bildstrasse 1 Abtwil, 9030 Switzerland. TEL: (4171) 314 2040.
www.cinedome.ch

CINEMAX MULTIPLEX CINEMA AG
Heinrichstrasse 267 Zurich, 8005 Switzerland.
TEL: (411) 273 22 22. FAX: (41) 1 273 33 54.

CINEMOBIL OPEN AIR CINEMA
Dorfstrasse 77, CH-8105 Regensdorf. TEL: (411) 840 5342.

CINETYP
Obergrundstrasse 101, CH-6005 Lucerne. TEL: (4141) 422 257.
FAX: (4141) 422 746.

EUROPLEX CINEMAS
Rue de la Confederation 8 Geneva, 1204 Switzerland.
TEL: (4121) 614 3333. FAX: (4121) 614 3399.
email: info@europlexcinemas.ch www.europlexcinemas.ch

FILMCOOPERATIVE ZURICH
Fabrikstrasse 21, Postfach 172, CH-8031 Zurich.
TEL: (411) 271 8800. FAX: (411) 271 8038.

KITAG KINO THEATER AG
Laupenstrasse 8, 3008 Bern. TEL: (413) 1390-110.
Number of Screens: 29

LIAG CAPITOL
Bergstrasse 42, CH-8032 Zurich. TEL: (411) 251 5228.
FAX: (411) 251 4444.

QUINNIE CINEMA FILMS, LTD.
Seilestrasse 4, 3011 Bern (Schweiz), Switzerland.
TEL: (413) 1381 1721. FAX: (413) 1398 1272.
OWNER
Roland Probst

V ESPOSITO
4 Rue de Reve, CH-1204 Geneva. TEL: (4122) 782 1417.
FAX: (4122) 310 9476.

WALCH KINOBETRIEBS
Steinentorstrasse 8, CH-4051 Basel. TEL: (4161) 281 0908.
FAX: (4161) 281 6564.

ASSOCIATIONS AND ORGANIZATIONS

CINELIBRE
Swiss Associations of Film Societies and Non-Commercial
Screening Organisations, Postfach 534, CH-3000 Bern 14.
TEL: (4131) 371 61. email: cinelibre@gmx.ch
www.cinelibre.ch

FEDERAL DEPARTMENT OF FOREIGN AFFAIRS
Bundeshaus West, CH-3003 Berne. TEL: (4131) 322 3153.
FAX: (4131) 324 9047. email: info@eda.admin.ch
www.eda.admin.ch

FEDERAL OFFICE OF CULTURE
Sektion Film, Hallwylstrasse 15, CH-3003 Bern.
TEL: (4131) 322 9271. FAX: (4131) 322 9273.

FONCTION CINEMA
Rue du Général Dufour 16, Case Postale 5305 CH, 1211
Geneva 11. TEL: (4122) 328 8554. FAX: (4122) 329 6802.
email: contact@ fonction-cinema.ch www.fonction-cinema.ch

PROCINEMA
(Association of Distributors and Exhibitors)
Postfach 399, 3000 Bern 14, Schwarztorstrasse 56, 3007 Bern.
TEL: (4131) 387 3700. FAX: (4131) 387 3707.
email: info@ProCinema.ch www.procinema.ch

SWISS FILM AND VIDEOPRODUCERS ASSOCIATION (SFVP)
c/o Condor Film, Kreuzstrasse 2, CH-8044 Zürich.
TEL: (441) 256 1515. FAX: (441) 256 1516.
email: m.fueter@condor-communications.com
www.filmproducers.ch
CONTACT
Martin Fueter

SWISS FILM COMMISSION
Place de la Gare 3, 1800 Vevey. TEL: (4121) 648 0380.
FAX: (4121) 648 0381. email: info@filmlocation.ch
www.filmlocation.ch
FILM COMMISSIONER
Cyril Jost

SWISS FILM DISTRIBUTORS ASSOCIATION
Schwarztorstrasse 56, 3007 Bern. TEL: (4131) 387 3702.
FAX: (4131) 387 3714. email: info@filmdistribution.ch
www.filmdistribution.ch

SWISS FILM PRODUCERS' ASSOCIATION
Zinggstrasse 16, CH-3007 Bern. TEL: (4131) 370 1060.
FAX: (4131) 372 4053. email: info@swissfilmproducers.ch
www. swissfilmproducers.ch
PRESIDENT
Willi Egloff
VICE PRESIDENT
Rolf Schmid

SWISS FILMS
Neugasse 6, P.O. Box, CH-8031 Zurich. TEL: (4143) 211 4050.
FAX: (4143) 211 4060. email: info@swissfilms.ch
www.swissfilms.ch

Antenne Romande, 48 Ave. de la Praille, CH-1227 Carouge GE.
TEL: (4122) 308 1240. FAX: (4122) 308 1241.
email: geneva@swissfilms.ch
COMMUNICATION DIRECTOR
Ursula Hartenstein

SWISS FILM THEATRES ASSOCIATION
Effingerstrasse 11, P.O. Box 8175. CH-3001 Bern.
TEL: (4131) 381 5077. FAX: (4131) 382 0373.

TAIWAN

Capital: Taipei
Population: 23,024,956 (July 2010 est.)
Area: 35,980 sq. km.
Source: CIA World Factbook

DISTRIBUTORS

BUENA VISTA FILM CO., LTD.
4th Flr., No. 1, Hsiang Yang Rd., Taipei. TEL: (8862) 383 6309.
FAX: (8862) 382 5348.

COLUMBIA TRISTAR FILMS OF CHINA, LTD.
City Hero Plaza, 8F-A No. 59, Chung-hua Rd., Section 1,
Taipei 100. TEL: (8862) 331 9456. FAX: (8862) 381 4492.

PARAMOUNT FILMS OF CHINA, INC.
(Also MGM of China, Inc., United Artists of China, Inc,
Universal Picture Corp of China, Inc.)
2nd Flr., 18 Kwei Yang St., Section 2, Taipei.
TEL: 886-2-2550-7755. FAX: 886-2-2550-1172.
MANAGER
Eugene Yang

TWENTIETH CENTURY FOX
City Hero Plaza, 8F-A No. 59, Chung-hwa Rd., Section 1,
Taipei 100. TEL: (8862) 315 3773. FAX: (8862) 381 4492.

WARNER BROS. VILLAGE CINEMAS
(Warner Bros. International Theatres in association with Village
Roadshow International)
P.O. Box 167, Taipei 100. TEL: (8862) 389 0159.
FAX: (8862) 311 8526.

4000 Warner Blvd., Bridge Bldg. South, 5th Flr., Burbank, Calif.,
U.S. 91522. TEL: (1 818) 954 6014. FAX: (1 818) 954 6655.
PRESIDENT
Millard Ochs

EXHIBITORS

AMBASSADOR THEATRES
4F, No. 23, Sec. 1, Changan E. Road Taipei 104.
TEL: (8862) 2536 8986. FAX: (8862) 2536 8967.
email: joechang@ambassador.com.tw
www.ambassador.com.tw
CEO
Joe Chang
PRESIDENT
John Chang
CFO
Angel Ko
COO
Sabrina Dai

CINEMARK CORE PACIFIC
B1F, No. 138, Sec. 4 Bade Road, Songshan District
Taipei City 105. TEL: 886 2 3762 1666.
CONTACT
Jack Cheng

STUDIO CITY CINEMA HOLDINGS, LTD.
No. 226-1 Cheng Kung, 1st Rd., B1 B2 Flrs., Kaohslung, Taiwan.
CONTACT
Ben Leung

VILLAGE ROADSHOW, LTD.
206 Bourke St., Melbourne, VIC, 3000, Australia.
TEL: (613) 9667 6666. FAX: (613) 9639 1540.

Number of Theatres (Taiwan): 1
Number of Screens (Taiwan): 17

THAILAND

Capital: Bangkok
Population: 67,089,500 (July 2010 est.)
Area: 514,000 sq. km.
Source: CIA World Factbook

DISTRIBUTORS AND PRODUCERS

THE 6TH ELEMENT
516/96 Soi Ramkamhaeng 39 (tepleela 1). Wangtonglang
District, Bangkok 10310. TEL: (660) 2530 9260-3.
FAX: (660) 2530 9264. email: orr@the6element.com
http://www.the6element.com

APEX INTERNATIONAL CORP.
215 1 6 Rama 1 Rd., Slam Sq., Pathumwa, Bangkok 10500.
TEL: (662) 251 8476. FAX: (662) 255 3131.

CINEAD GROUP
40 19 Sol Amonphannivas 4, Vipavadee Rangsit Rd., Bangkok
10900. TEL: (662) 561 1965. FAX: (662) 561 1887.

CO BROTHERS ORGANISATION
117/2 Phayathai Rd., Rajthevi, Bangkok 10400.
TEL: (662) 251 7163. FAX: (662) 254 7714.

CVD INTERNATIONAL CO., LTD.
61/34 Soi Vipavadee 42, Vipavadeerangsit Rd., Ladyao,
Jatuchack, Bangkok 10900. TEL: (662) 941 9274 87.
FAX: (662) 561 1887. www.cvdgroup.com
CHAIRMAN
Prasarn Maleenon
MANAGING DIRECTOR
Padet Hongfa
DIRECTOR, MARKETING
Brian Arnold Estus

FIVE STARS
31 345 Petchburi Rd., Phayathai, Bangkok 10400.
TEL: (662) 215 0704.

GOLDEN TOWN FILM
69/55 Phayathai Atehn Theater Rd., Bangkok 10400.
TEL: (662) 251 9168. FAX: (662) 259 3117.

HOLLYWOOD FILM DISTRIBUTION
420 Petchburi Rd., Phayathai, Bangkog 10400.
TEL: (662) 251 5211.

MOVIELINK
40/19 Soi Amorn Pannives 4, Vipavadee-Rangsit Rd., Bangkok
TEL: (662) 561 1915.

NONTANUND ENTERTAINMENT
113/10 Suriwong Centre, Suriwong Rd., Bangkok 10500.
TEL: (662) 236 7504. FAX: (662) 253 4830.

PYRAMID ENTERTAINMENT
216/1-6 Rama Rd., Siam Square, Bangkok 10500.
TEL: (662) 252 7416.

SAHA MONGKOL FILM
1081/5 Phaholyothin Rd., Bangkok 10400. TEL: (662) 279 8456.

TWENTIETH CENTURY FOX/WARNER BROS.
Rm. 603, South East Insurance Bldg., 315 Silom Rd., Bangkok
10500. TEL: (662) 233 0920. FAX: (662) 236 4384.

UNITED INTERNATIONAL PICTURES (UIP)
Suite 1109, 11th Flr., Abdulahim Place, 990 Rama IV Road
Silom, Bangrak Bangkok 10500. TEL: 66-2-636-2438.
FAX: 66-2-636-2439.
MANAGER
Silit Switachata

EXHIBITORS

ENTERTAIN GOLDEN VILLAGE
110 Moo 9 Petchkasem Rd., Bang Wa, Pasricharowen,
Bangkok 10160. TEL: (662) 455 0150.

Number of Screens: 73

GOLDEN HARVEST ENTERTAINMENT CO., LTD.
(For additional listings, see Hong Kong, Singapore & Malaysia)
8 King Tung St., Hammer Hill Rd., Kowloon.
TEL: (852) 2352 8222. FAX: (852) 2351 1683.

EXECUTIVES
Raymond Chow, Leonard Ho, Anthony Chow, Peter Chung, S.Y. Ho

Number of Theatres: 13
Number of Screens: 75

MAJOR CINEPLEX
1839 Phaholyothin Road, Ladyao Jatuchak, Bangkok 10900. TEL: (662) 511-5539. FAX: (662) 511-5255. email: brian@majorcineplex.com. www.majorcineplex.com
CHAIRMAN
Vicha Poolvaraluck
PRESIDENT
Panithan Sethabutra

Number of Theatres: 35
Number of Screens: 310

SF CINEMA CITY CO. LTD.
7th Fl. Mah Boonkrong Center, 444 Phayathai Rd., Phatumwan, Bangkok 10330. TEL: (662)-611-7111. FAX: (662)-611-7138. email: management@sfcinemacity.com www.sfcinemacity.com
PRESIDENT
Suwat Thongrompo
DEPUTY MANAGING DIRECTOR
Suvannee Chinchewchan

Number of Theatres: 18
Number of Screens: 129

ASSOCIATIONS & ORGANIZATIONS

AMERICAN MOTION PICTURE ASSOCIATION
Rm. 602, Akane Bldg., 315 Silom Rd., Bangkok 10500. TEL: (662) 234 0240.

MOTION PICTURE EXHIBITORS ASSOC. OF THAILAND
352 Siam Theatre, Tama 1 Rd., Pathumwan, Bangkok 10500.

THAILAND FILM PROMOTION CENTRE
599 Bumrung Muang Rd., Bangkok 10100. TEL: (662) 223 4690. FAX: (662) 253 1817.

THAI MOTION PICTURES PRODUCERS ASSOCIATION
15/79 Soi Chokchairuammit, Viphavadee-Rangsit Rd., Bangkhen, Bangkok 10900. TEL: (662) 275 8833. FAX: (662) 281 8460.

TURKEY

Capital: Ankara
Population: 77,804,122 (July 2010 est.)
Area: 780,580 sq. km.
Source: CIA Worldfactbook

DISTRIBUTORS AND PRODUCERS

BARLIK FILM
Ahududu Cad 32/3, Beyoglu, Istanbul 80060. TEL: (90216) 244 1542. FAX: (90216) 251 0386.

KILIC FILM
Yesilcam SK 26/2, Beyoglu, Istanbul 80070. TEL: (90216) 249 5804. FAX: (90216) 244 1612.

UNITED INTERNATIONAL PICTURES
Filmcilik ve Ticaret Ltd. Sti, Spor Cad. Acisu Sok. 1/7-8, Macka, Istanbul 80200. TEL: (90216) 227 8205. FAX: (90216) 227 8207.
MANAGER
Mehmet Ozduygu

WARNER BROS. A.S. TURKEY
Bronz Sokak, Bronz Apt. 3/6, Macka, Istanbul 80200. TEL: (90216) 231 2569. FAX: (90216) 231 7070. email: haluk.kaplanoglu@warnerbros.com

EXHIBITORS

AFM CINEMA GROUP
Istiklal Caddesi No:24/26 Beyoglu, Istanbul. TEL: (90212) 292 1111. FAX: (90212) 252 9869. www.afm.com.tr
CEO
Fatos Kiziltas
PRESIDENT
Sedat Akdemir
VICE PRESIDENT
Adnan Akdemir
CHAIRMAN
Yalcin Selgur
GENERAL MANAGER
Agah Tansev
GENERAL COORDINATOR
Gediz Tetik
V.P., FINANCE
Berent Akdemir

Number of Theatres: 18
Number of Screens: 78

CINEMAXX H.J. FLEBBE FILMTHEATERBETRIEBE
Mittelweg 176, 20148 Hanburg. TEL: (49) 40450 680. FAX: (49) 40 450 68201.
PRESIDENT & GENERAL MANAGER
Hans-Joachim Flebbe
GENERAL MANAGER & CFO
Michael Pawlowski
DIRECTOR, MARKETING
Jens Thomsen

Number of Theatres (Turkey): 1
Number of Screens (Turkey): 5

ASSOCIATIONS & ORGANIZATIONS

ISTANBUL FOUNDATION FOR CULTURE & ARTS
Besiktas, Istanbul 80700. TEL: (90216) 259 1738. FAX: (90216) 261 8823.

SOCIETY OF IMPORTERS AND DISTRIBUTORS
Yesilcam Sok 7/1, Beyoglu, Istanbul. TEL: (90216) 249 0986.

UNITED ARAB EMERATES (UAE)

Capital: Abu Dhabi
Population: 4,975,593 (July 2010 est.)
Area: 82,880 sq. km.
Source: CIA World Factbook

DISTRIBUTORS AND PRODUCERS

ABU DHABI MEDIA COMPANY
(Oversees the Abu Dhabi/Warner fund)
4th St., Sector 18 Zone 1, Abu Dhabi. TEL: +971 2 4144000. FAX: +971 2 4144001. www.admedia.ae
CHAIRMAN
His Excellency Mohamed Khalaf Al Mazrouei
CEO
Ed Borgerding

Created in 2007 as a public joint stock company from the assets of Emirates Media Incorporated. Abu Dhabi Media Company owns and operates Abu Dhabi Television, Abu Dhabi Sports Channel, Emirates Television Channel, Abu Dhabi Radio, Emarat FM Radio, Holy Quran Radio, Sawt Al Musiqa Radio, Al Ittihad newspaper, Zahrat Al Khaleej magazine, Super magazine and Majid magazine as well as other businesses including United Printing Press. The company is headquartered in Abu Dhabi with offices in Cairo, Dubai and Washington D.C.

GLOBAL ARTS AGENCY
P.O. Box 2696, Abu Dhabi. TEL: (971 2) 793 666. FAX: (971 2) 795 077.

PREMIERE ENTERTAINMENT
P.O. Box 541, Dubai. TEL: (971 4) 366 673. FAX: (971 4) 376 718.

SAHER ART PRODUCTION
P.O. Box 8884, Dubai. TEL: (971 4) 524 278. FAX: (971 4) 527 691.

SHARJAH NATIONAL THEATRE
P.O. Box 5373, Sharjah. TEL: (971 6) 524 4011. FAX: (971 6) 376 338.

STALLIONS HOME VIDEO, LLC
P.O. Box 26566, Dubai. TEL: (971 4) 282 2988. FAX: (971 4) 282 7808.

UAE FILM CO, LLC
P.O. Box 1988, Dubai. TEL: (971 4) 446 665. FAX: (971 4) 446 907.

UAE FILM DISTRIBUTORS, EST
P.O. Box 4152, Abu Dhabi. TEL: (971 2) 345 600. FAX: (971 2) 346 323.

EXHIBITORS

THE GREATER UNION ORGANISATION
(Including BIRCH CARROLL & COYLE)
49 Market St., Sydney, NSW 2000, Australia. TEL: (612) 9373 6600. FAX: (612) 9373 6532.
MANAGING DIRECTOR
Robert Manson

Number of Theatres (UAE): 1
Number of Screens (UAE): 6

U.S. TERRITORIES

PUERTO RICO

Capital: San Juan
Population: 3,978,702 (July 2010 est.)
Area: 9,104 sq. km.

Source: CIA Worldfactbook

EXHIBITORS

CARIBBEAN CINEMAS

1512 Fernandez Juncos San Juan, PR 00909.
TEL: (787) 727-7137. FAX: (787) 728-2274.
(Puerto Rico, Dominican Republic, U.S. Virgin Islands, St. Maarten, Trinidad)
www.caribbeancinemas.com
PRESIDENT & CEO
Victor Carrady

REGENCY CARIBBEAN ENTERPRISES, INC.

(d.b.a. Caribbean Cinemas)
1512 Fernandez Juncos, Stop 22-1/2, Santurce.
TEL: (809) 727 7137. FAX: (809) 728 2274.

U.S. VIRGIN ISLANDS

Capital: Charlotte Amalie
Population: 109,750 (July 2010 est.)
Area: 352 sq. km.
Source: CIA World Factbook

EXHIBITORS

CARIBBEAN CINEMAS OF THE VIRGIN ISLANDS, INC.

P.O. Box 9700, St. Thomas 00801. TEL: (809) 775 2244.
FAX: (809) 724 2274.
ADMINISTRATOR
Jeff McLaughlin
PRESIDENT, CEO & CFO
Victor Carrady
V.P., COO & FILM BUYER
Robert Carrady
THEATRE OPERATIONS
Joe Ramos
Alfredo Morales
EQUIPMENT BUYER
Joel Matos

ALPHABETICAL INDEX OF SUBJECTS

This index lists selected companies, agencies and organizations from major sections of the book. If the company you are looking for is not in the index, please find the company in alphabetical order within the relevant section.

#

A

B

C

D

E

F

G

H

I

J

K

L

M

N

O

P

Q

R

S

T

U

V

W

X, Y, Z